S0-ADM-977

AWARDS 2008

→ DISTINCTIONS 2008

→ DISTINZIONI 2008

→ AUSZEICHNUNGEN 2008

→ DISTINCIONES 2008

→ 2008 年度の評価

FURTHER INFORMATION

→ POUR EN SAVOIR PLUS

→ PER SAPERNE DI PIÙ

→ GUT ZU WISSEN

→ PARA SABER MÁS

→ より詳しく知るには

REGIONAL MAP OF LISTED TOWNS

How to use this guide

TOURIST INFORMATION

Distances from the main towns, tourist offices, local tourist attractions, means of transport, golf courses and leisure activities...

LODGING

From 🏨🏨🏨🏨🏨 to 🏨, ⌂:
categories of comfort.
In red 🏨🏨🏨🏨🏨 ... 🏨, ⌂:
the most pleasant.

GOOD FOOD AND ACCOMMODATION AT MODERATE PRICES

Bib Gourmand.
Bib Hotel.

RESTAURANTS

From XXXXX to X:
categories of comfort.
In red XXXXX ... X:
the most pleasant.

STARS

✿✿✿ Worth a special journey.
✿✿ Worth a detour.
✿ A very good restaurant.

ABBAYE DE FONTFROIDE - 03 Aude - **344** J4 - **rattaché à**
ABBAYE DE SAINT-WANDRILLE – 18 Cher – **323** K6
Montrond
ABBEVILLE - 80 Somme - 24 567 h. - alt.8 - ✉ **80100** - 3
Nord Pas-de-Calais Picardie
Paris 186 - Amiens 51 - Boulogne-sur-Mer 79 -
d'Avignon - ✆ 04 90 81 51 51, par N3 et N7 : 8 k
Office de tourisme, 1 place de l'Amiral Cour
risme.abbeville@wanadoo.fr - Fax 03 22 31
d'Abbeville, Route du Val par rte St-Valéry
- Fax 03 22 24 49 61 - ✉ 80132
Vitraux contemporains★★ de l'église du
légiale St-Vulfran AE **D** - Musée Bouche
Vallée de la Somme★ - Château de Bac

Les Jardins du Château
rte du Port – ✆ 04 79 00 00 46
- welcome@hotelmandjaro.com – Fax
15 ch (1/2 P seult) – 17 suites 250/440
Rest Le Cœur d'Or – ✆ 04 79 01 46
Rest Terrasses du Cœur d'Or – (fe
◆ Lauze, pierre et bois "vieilli" comp
Superbes chambres savoyardes, é
Décor tout bois et coins "cosy" a
Terrasses.

Le Relais de la Poste
rte de Lion, D 541 : 1 km – ✆ 0
– Fermé 31 oct.-18 nov., 1
42 ch – 40/60 € 60/65
◆ Sur la route de la grotte
cadre actuel ou sous les f

Atelier des Saveu
10 bd Croisette – ✆ 04
– Fax 04 93 38 97 90 -
Rest – (dîner seult)
Spéc. Bocal de fo
Mad" tiède à la v
◆ Élégante verriè
joli cadre

OTHER MICHELIN PUBLICATIONS

References for the MICHELIN map and Green Guide which cover the area.

LOCATING THE TOWN

Locate the town on the map at the end of the guide (map number and coordinates).

LOCATING THE ESTABLISHMENT

Located on the town plan (coordinates and letters giving the location).

DESCRIPTION OF THE ESTABLISHMENT

Atmosphere, style, character and specialities.

QUIET HOTELS

quiet hotel.

very quiet hotel.

FACILITIES AND SERVICES

PRICES

nne

aché à St-Amand-

22 **C4**

06

3 22 24 27 92 - Office.tou-

me : 4 km - ✆ 03 22 24 98 58

lcre AM **B** - Façade★ de la col-

hes★ BY **M**

donjon

ch 35 à 70

46 40 – Fermé mi-déc.-mi-avril

AX **b**

lex 300 €

seult) 70/125 €

i) 25 € Enf. 16 €

s luxueux chalets regroupés en hameau.

high-tech et toutes dotées d'une loggia.

Or. Cuisine du terroir et plats simples aux

09 – *info@labastide.com* – *Fax 04 75 46 10 62*

merc. soir et lundi

– **Rest** 16 € (déj. en sem.) 22/52 €

Sévigné, une cuisine traditionnelle servie dans un

s de la terrasse. En hiver, spécialités de truffes.

ch,

0 – *ateliersdessaveurs@luciedurand.com*

nov.-30 déc., dim.

t carte 100/140 €

canard. Canon d'agneau rôti au thym-citron. "Traou

s Côtes de Provence

t sur le ciel azuréen et sobre décor d'inspiration Napoléon

ne cuisine unissant saveurs du Sud-Ouest et de Provence.

îles de Lérins rest,

voir plan d'Antibes AU **d**

00 00 – *bellevue@free.fr* – *Fax 04 93 67 81 78*

e étendue de sable fin des Alpes-Maritimes.

marin.

de Lérins

Commitments

"This volume was created at the turn of the century and will last at least as long".

This foreword to the very first edition of the MICHELIN guide, written in 1900, has become famous over the years and the guide has lived up to the prediction. It is read across the world and the key to its popularity is the consistency of its commitment to its readers, which is based on the following promises.

The MICHELIN guide's commitments:

Anonymous inspections: our inspectors make regular and anonymous visits to hotels and restaurants to gauge the quality of products and services offered to an ordinary customer. They settle their own bill and may then introduce themselves and ask for more information about the establishment. Our readers' comments are also a valuable source of information, which we can then follow up with another visit of our own.

Independence: Our choice of establishments is a completely independent one, made for the benefit of our readers alone. The decisions to be taken are discussed around the table by the inspectors and the editor. The most important awards are decided at a European level. Inclusion in the guide is completely free of charge.

Selection and choice: The guide offers a selection of the best hotels and restaurants in every category of comfort and price. This is only possible because all the inspectors rigorously apply the same methods.

Annual updates: All the practical information, the classifications and awards are revised and updated every single year to give the most reliable information possible.

Consistency: The criteria for the classifications are the same in every country covered by the MICHELIN guide.

... and our aim: to do everything possible to make travel, holidays and eating out a pleasure, as part of MICHELIN's ongoing commitment to improving travel and mobility.

Dear reader,

We are delighted to introduce the 99th edition of The MICHELIN guide France. This selection of the best hotels and restaurants in every price category is chosen by a team of full-time inspectors with a professional background in the industry. They cover every corner of the country, visiting new establishments and testing the quality and consistency of the hotels and restaurants already listed in the guide. Every year we pick out the best restaurants by awarding them from ✿ to ✿✿✿. Michelin stars are awarded to establishments serving cuisine, of whatever style, which is of the highest quality, taking into consideration the quality of ingredients, the flair and skill in their preparation, the combination of flavours, the value for money and the consistency of culinary standards.

Newly promoted restaurants which, over the last year, have raised the quality of their cooking to a new level, whether they have gained a first star, risen from one to two stars, or moved from two to three, are marked with an '**N**' next to their entry to signal their new status in 2008.

We have also picked out a selection of "*Rising Stars*". These establishments, listed in red, are the best in their present category. They have the potential to rise further, and already have an element of superior quality; as soon as they produce this quality consistently, and in all aspects of their cuisine, they will be hot tips for a higher award. We've highlighted these promising restaurants so you can try them for yourselves; we think they offer a foretaste of the gastronomy of the future.

We're very interested to hear what you think of our selection, particularly the "*Rising Stars*", so please continue to send us your comments. Your opinions and suggestions help to shape your guide, and help us to keep improving it, year after year.

Thank you for your support. We hope you enjoy travelling with the MICHELIN guide 2008.

Consult the Michelin Guide at **www.ViaMichelin.com**
and write to us at: **leguidemichelin-france@fr.michelin.com**

Classification & awards

CATEGORIES OF COMFORT

The MICHELIN guide selection lists the best hotels and restaurants in each category of comfort and price. The establishments we choose are classified according to their levels of comfort and, within each category, are listed in order of preference.

🏨🏨🏨🏨🏨	XXXXX	**Luxury in the traditional style**
🏨🏨🏨🏨	XXXX	**Top class comfort**
🏨🏨🏨	XXX	**Very comfortable**
🏨🏨	XX	**Comfortable**
🏨	X	**Quite comfortable**
⌂		**Guesthouse**
sans rest		**This hotel has no restaurant**
avec ch		**This restaurant also offers accommodation**

THE AWARDS

To help you make the best choice, some exceptional establishments have been given an award in this year's guide.
For those awarded a star or a Bib Gourmand, the mention "**Rest**" appears in red in the description of the establishment.
For those awarded a Bib Hotel, the mention "**ch**" appears in blue in the description of the establishment.

THE STARS: THE BEST CUISINE

MICHELIN stars are awarded to establishments serving cuisine, of whatever style, which is of the highest quality. The cuisine is judged on the quality of ingredients, the flair and skill in their preparation, the combination of flavours, the value for money and the consistency of culinary standards.

✿✿✿	**Exceptional cuisine, worth a special journey**
26	One always eats extremely well here, sometimes superbly.
✿✿	**Excellent cooking, worth a detour**
68	
✿	**A very good restaurant in its category**
435	

THE BIB : GOOD FOOD AND ACCOMMODATION AT MODERATE PRICES

510 **Bib Gourmand**
Establishment offering good quality cuisine at a maximum price of 28 € or 35 € in the Paris region (price of a meal not including drinks). Outside the Paris region, these establishments generally specialise in regional cooking.

297 **Bib Hotel**
Establishment offering good levels of comfort and service, with most rooms priced at a maximum price of 72 € or under 88 € in the main cities and popular tourist resorts (price of a room for 2 people not including breakfast).

PLEASANT HOTELS AND RESTAURANTS

Symbols shown in red indicate particularly pleasant or restful establishments: the character of the building, its décor, the setting, the welcome and services offered may all contribute to this special appeal.

to **Pleasant hotels**

Pleasant guesthouses

to **Pleasant restaurants**

OTHER SPECIAL FEATURES

As well as the categories and awards given to the establishment, MICHELIN inspectors also make special note of other criteria which can be important when choosing an establishment.

LOCATION

If you are looking for a particularly restful establishment, or one with a special view, look out for the following symbols:

Quiet hotel

Very quiet hotel

Interesting view

Exceptional view

WINE LIST

If you are looking for an establishment with a particularly interesting wine list, look out for the following symbol:

Particularly interesting wine list
This symbol might cover the list presented by a sommelier in a luxury restaurant or that of a simple inn where the owner has a passion for wine. The two lists will offer something exceptional but very different, so beware of comparing them by each other's standards.

Facilities & services

30 ch	Number of rooms
	Garden – Park – Beach with bathing facilities
	Meals served in garden or on terrace
	Swimming pool: outdoor or indoor
Spa	An extensive facility for relaxation and well-being
	Exercise room – Tennis court
	Lift – Establishment at least partly accessible to those of restricted mobility
A/C	Air conditioning
	Rooms for non-smokers available
	High speed Internet access
	Private dining rooms
	Equipped conference room
	Restaurant offering valet parking (tipping customary)
P P	Car park / Enclosed car park for customers only
	Garage (additional charge in most cases)
	No dogs allowed
M	Nearest metro station
Open / Closed May-October	Dates when open or closed, as indicated by the hotelier.

Prices

Prices quoted in this guide are for autumn 2007. They are subject to alteration if goods and service costs are revised.

By supplying the information, hotels and restaurants have undertaken to maintain these rates for our readers.

In some towns, when commercial, cultural or sporting events are taking place the hotel rates are likely to be considerably higher.

Out of season, certain establishments offer special rates. Ask when booking.

RESERVATION AND DEPOSITS

Some establishments will ask you to confirm your reservation by giving your credit card number or require a deposit which confirms the commitment of both the customer and the establishment. Ask the hotelier to provide you with all the terms and conditions applicable to your reservation in their written confirmation.

CREDIT CARDS

VISA MC AE DC	Credit cards accepted by the establishment: Visa – MasterCard – American Express – Diners Club

ROOMS

ch – 🚹 50/80 €	Lowest price / highest price for a single room
ch – 🚹🚹 60/100 €	Lowest price / highest price for a double or a twin room
☕ 9 €	Price of breakfast
ch ☕	Breakfast included

HALF BOARD

½ P 50/70 €	Lowest and highest prices for half board (room, breakfast and a meal) per person. These prices are valid for a double room occupied by two people for a minimum stay of three nights. If a single person occupies a double room a supplement may apply. Most of the hotels also offer full board terms on request.

RESTAURANT

(13 €)	2 course meal, on weekday lunchtimes
🪙	Menu for less than 18 €
Menu 15 € (déj.)	Set menu served only at lunchtime
Menu 17 € (sem.)	Set menu served only on weekdays
Menu 16/38 €	Cheapest set meal / Most expensive set menu
Carte 24/48 €	**A la carte meal**, drinks not included. The first figure is for a simple meal and includes first course, main dish of the day and dessert. The second price is for a fuller meal (with speciality) including starter, main course, cheese and dessert.
bi	House wine included

Towns

GENERAL INFORMATION

63300	Local postal number *the first two numbers are the same as the département number*
✉ 57130 Ars	Postal number and the name of the postal area
P SP	Prefecture – Sub-prefecture
337 E5	Number of the appropriate sheet and grid square reference of the Michelin road map in the "DEPARTEMENTS France" MICHELIN series
Jura	See the MICHELIN Green Guide Jura
1057 h.	Population (source: www.insee.fr)
alt. 75	Altitude (in metres)
Sta. therm.	Spa
1200/1900	Altitude of resort and highest point reached by lifts
2	Number of cable-cars
14	Number of ski and chair-lifts
	Cross-country skiing
BY **b**	Letters giving the location of a place on a town plan
9	Golf course and number of holes
	Panoramic view, viewpoint
	Airport – Places with motorail pick-up point. *Further information from phone number listed*
	Shipping line – Passenger transport only
i	Tourist information

TOURIST INFORMATION

STAR-RATING

★★★	Highly recommended
★★	Recommended
★	Interesting *Museums and art galleries are generally closed on Tuesday*

LOCATION

	Sights in town
	On the outskirts
N, S, E, O	The sight lies north, south, east or west of the town
② ④	Signs ② or ④ on the town plan show the road leading to a place of interest and correspond to the same signs on MICHELIN road maps.
6 km	Distance in kilometres

Town plans

Hotels

Restaurants

SIGHTS

Place of interest

Interesting place of worship:

- Catholic – Protestant

ROAD

Motorway, dual carriageway

Numbered junctions : complete, limited

Major thoroughfare

One-way street – Unsuitable for traffic or street subject to restrictions

Pedestrian street – Tramway

R. Pasteur Shopping street – Car park – Park and Ride

Gateway – Street passing under arch – Tunnel

Station and railway – Motorail

Funicular – Cable-car

Lever bridge – Car ferry

VARIOUS SIGNS

Tourist Information Centre

Mosque – Synagogue

Tower – Ruins – Windmill – Water tower

Garden, park, wood – Cemetery – Cross

Stadium – Golf course – Racecourse – Skating rink

Outdoor or indoor swimming pool

View – Panorama – Viewing table

Monument – Fountain – Factory

Shopping centre – Multiplex Cinema

Pleasure boat harbour – Lighthouse – Communications tower

Airport – Underground station – Coach station

Ferry services : passengers and cars, passengers only

Reference number common to town plans

Main post office with poste restante and telephone

Hospital – Covered market – Barracks

Public buildings located by letter :

A C - Chamber of Agriculture – Chamber of Commerce

G H J - Gendarmerie – Town Hall – Law Courts

M P T - Museum – Prefecture or sub-prefecture – Theatre

U - University, College

POL. - Police (in large towns police headquarters)

18T Low headroom (15 ft. max.) – Load limit (under 19 t)

Please note: the *route nationale* and *route départementale* road numbers ar currently being changed in France.

Mode d'emploi

INFORMATIONS TOURISTIQUES

Distances depuis les villes principales, offices de tourisme, sites touristiques locaux, moyens de transports, golfs et loisirs...

L'HÉBERGEMENT

De 🏠🏠🏠🏠 à 🏠, ⌂ : catégories de confort.
En rouge 🏠🏠🏠🏠 ... 🏠, ⌂ : les plus agréables.

LES MEILLEURES ADRESSES À PETITS PRIX

Bib Gourmand.
Bib Hôtel.

LES RESTAURANTS

De XXXXX à X : catégories de confort. En rouge XXXXX... X : les plus agréables.

LES TABLES ÉTOILÉES

✿✿✿ Vaut le voyage.
✿✿ Mérite un détour.
✿ Très bonne cuisine.

ABBAYE DE FONTFROIDE - 03 Aude - **344** I4 - ratta

ABBAYE DE SAINT-WANDRILLE – 18 Cher – 32
Montrond

ABBEVILLE - 80 Somme - 24 567 h. - alt. 8 - ✉ 8010
Nord Pas-de-Calais Picardie
Paris 186 - Amiens 51 - Boulogne-sur-Mer 7
d'Avignon - ☎ 04 90 81 51 51, par N3 et N7
Office de tourisme, 1 place de l'Amiral C
risme.abbeville@wanadoo.fr - Fax 03 22
d'Abbeville, Route du Val par rte St-Val
- Fax 03 22 24 49 61 - ✉ 80132
Vitraux contemporains★★ de l'église c
légiale St-Vulfran AE **D** - Musée Bouch
Vallée de la Somme★ - Château de B

Les Jardins du Château
rte du Port – ☎ 04 79 00 00 46
- welcome@hotelmandjaro.com – Fa
15 ch (1/2 P seult) – 17 suites 250/440
Rest Le Cœur d'Or – ☎ 04 79 01 46
Rest Terrasses du Cœur d'Or – (fe
◆ Lauze, pierre et bois "vieilli" comp
Superbes chambres savoyardes, é
Décor tout bois et coins "cosy" au
Terrasses.

Le Relais de la Poste
rte de Lion, D 541 : 1 km – ☎ 04 7
– Fermé 31 oct.-18 nov., 19-
42 ch – 🚹40/60 € 🚹🚹60/65 €
◆ Sur la route de la grotte de N
cadre actuel ou sous les fron

Atelier des Saveurs
10 bd Croisette – ☎ 04 92 9
– Fax 04 93 38 97 90 – Fer
Rest – (dîner seult) 75/1
Spéc. Bocal de foie gr
Mad" tiède à la vanille
◆ Élégante verrière ou
Un joli cadre pour

AUTRES PUBLICATIONS MICHELIN

Références de la carte MICHELIN et du Guide Vert où vous retrouverez la localité.

LOCALISER LA VILLE

Repérage de la localité sur la carte régionale en fin de guide (n° de la carte et coordonnées).

LOCALISER L'ÉTABLISSEMENT

Localisation sur le plan de ville (coordonnées et indice).

DESCRIPTION DE L'ÉTABLISSEMENT

Atmosphère, style, caractère et spécialités.

LES HÔTELS TRANQUILLES

hôtel tranquille.
hôtel très tranquille.

ÉQUIPEMENTS ET SERVICES

PRIX

. Narbonne
– rattaché à St-Amand-
22 **C4**
1 E7
uen 106
t ✆ 03 22 24 27 92 - Office.tou-
26
Somme : 4 km - ✆ 03 22 24 98 58
épulcre AM **B** - Façade★ de la col-
Perthes★ BY **M**
e★
donjon
ch 35 à 70
– Fermé mi-déc.-mi-avril
01 46 40
AX **b**
uplex 300 €
er seult) 70/125 €
ndi) 25 € Enf. 16 €
es luxueux chalets regroupés en hameau.
s high-tech et toutes dotées d'une loggia.
d'Or. Cuisine du terroir et plats simples aux
09 – info@labastide.com – Fax 04 75 46 10 62
merc. soir et lundi
– **Rest** 16 € (déj. en sem.) 22/52 €
évigné, une cuisine traditionnelle servie dans un
de la terrasse. En hiver, spécialités de truffes.
ch,
– ateliersdessaveurs@luciedurand.com
ov.-30 déc., dim.
arte 100/140 €
nard. Canon d'agneau rôti au thym-citron. "Traou
ôtes de Provence
r le ciel azuréen et sobre décor d'inspiration Napoléon
cuisine unissant saveurs du Sud-Ouest et de Provence.
îles de Lérins
rest,
– bellevue@free.fr – Fax 04 93 67 81 78
voir plan d'Antibes AU **d**
de sable fin des Alpes-Maritimes.

Engagements

« Ce guide est né avec le siècle et il durera autant que lui. »

Cet avant-propos de la première édition du guide MICHELIN 1900 est devenu célèbre au fil des années et s'est révélé prémonitoire. Si le guide est aujourd'hui autant lu à travers le monde, c'est notamment grâce à la constance de son engagement vis-à-vis de ses lecteurs. Nous voulons ici le réaffirmer.

Les engagements du guide MICHELIN :

La visite anonyme : les inspecteurs testent de façon anonyme et régulière les tables et les chambres afin d'apprécier le niveau des prestations offertes à tout client. Ils paient leurs additions et peuvent se présenter pour obtenir des renseignements supplémentaires sur les établissements. Le courrier des lecteurs nous fournit par ailleurs une information précieuse pour orienter nos visites.

L'indépendance : la sélection des établissements s'effectue en toute indépendance, dans le seul intérêt du lecteur. Les décisions sont discutées collégialement par les inspecteurs et le rédacteur en chef. Les plus hautes distinctions sont décidées à un niveau européen. L'inscription des établissements dans le guide est totalement gratuite.

La sélection : le guide offre une sélection des meilleurs hôtels et restaurants dans toutes les catégories de confort et de prix. Celle-ci résulte de l'application rigoureuse d'une même méthode par tous les inspecteurs.

La mise à jour annuelle : chaque année toutes les informations pratiques, les classements et les distinctions sont revus et mis à jour afin d'offrir l'information la plus fiable.

L'homogénéité de la sélection : les critères de classification sont identiques pour tous les pays couverts par le guide MICHELIN.

... et un seul objectif : tout mettre en œuvre pour aider le lecteur à faire de chaque déplacement et de chaque sortie un moment de plaisir, conformément à la mission que s'est donnée MICHELIN : contribuer à une meilleure mobilité.

Édito

Cher lecteur,

Nous avons le plaisir de vous proposer notre 99e édition du guide MICHELIN France. Cette sélection des meilleurs hôtels et restaurants dans chaque catégorie de prix est effectuée par une équipe d'inspecteurs professionnels, de formation hôtelière. Tous les ans, ils sillonnent le pays pour visiter de nouveaux établissements et vérifier le niveau des prestations de ceux déjà cités dans le guide. Au sein de la sélection, nous reconnaissons également chaque année les meilleures tables en leur décernant de ✿ à ✿✿✿. Les étoiles distinguent les établissements qui proposent la meilleure qualité culinaire, dans tous les styles, en tenant compte du choix des produits, de la personnalité de la cuisine, de la maîtrise des cuissons et des saveurs, du rapport qualité-prix ainsi que de la régularité. Cette année encore, de nombreuses tables ont été remarquées pour l'évolution de leur cuisine. Un « **N** » accompagne les nouveaux promus de ce millésime 2008, annonçant leur arrivée parmi les établissements ayant une, deux ou trois étoiles.

De plus, nous souhaitons indiquer les établissements « ***espoirs*** » pour la catégorie supérieure. Ces établissements, repérés en rouge dans notre liste et dans nos pages, sont les meilleurs de leur catégorie. Ils pourront accéder à la distinction supérieure dès lors que la régularité de leurs prestations, dans le temps et sur l'ensemble de la carte, aura progressé. Par cette mention spéciale, nous entendons vous faire connaître les tables qui constituent, à nos yeux, les espoirs de la gastronomie de demain.

Votre avis nous intéresse, en particulier sur ces « *espoirs* » ; n'hésitez pas à nous écrire. Votre participation est importante pour orienter nos visites et améliorer sans cesse votre guide.

Merci encore de votre fidélité. Nous vous souhaitons de bons voyages avec le guide MICHELIN 2008.

Consultez le guide MICHELIN sur **www.ViaMichelin.com**
et écrivez-nous à : **leguidemichelin-france@fr.michelin.com**

Classement & distinctions

LES CATÉGORIES DE CONFORT

Le guide MICHELIN retient dans sa sélection les meilleures adresses dans chaque catégorie de confort et de prix. Les établissements sélectionnés sont classés selon leur confort et cités par ordre de préférence dans chaque catégorie.

⌂⌂⌂⌂⌂	XXXXX	**Grand luxe et tradition**
⌂⌂⌂⌂	XXXX	**Grand confort**
⌂⌂⌂	XXX	**Très confortable**
⌂⌂	XX	**De bon confort**
⌂	X	**Assez confortable**
⌂		**Maison d'hôtes**
sans rest		**L'hôtel n'a pas de restaurant**
avec ch		**Le restaurant possède des chambres**

LES DISTINCTIONS

Pour vous aider à faire le meilleur choix, certaines adresses particulièrement remarquables ont reçu cette année une distinction.

Pour les adresses distinguées par une étoile ou un Bib Gourmand, la mention « **Rest** » apparaît en rouge dans le descriptif de l'établissement.

Pour les adresses distinguées par un Bib Hôtel, la mention « **ch** » apparaît en bleu dans le descriptif de l'établissement.

LES ÉTOILES : LES MEILLEURES TABLES

Les étoiles distinguent les établissements, tous styles de cuisine confondus, qui proposent la meilleure qualité de cuisine. Les critères retenus sont : le choix des produits, la personnalité de la cuisine, la maîtrise des cuissons et des saveurs, le rapport qualité-prix ainsi que la régularité.

✿✿✿	**Cuisine remarquable, cette table vaut le voyage**
26	On y mange toujours très bien, parfois merveilleusement.
✿✿	**Cuisine excellente, cette table mérite un détour**
68	
✿	**Une très bonne cuisine dans sa catégorie**
435	

LES BIBS : LES MEILLEURES ADRESSES À PETIT PRIX

☺	**Bib Gourmand**
510	Établissement proposant une cuisine de qualité au prix maximum de 28 € en province et 35 € à Paris (prix d'un repas hors boisson). En province, il s'agit le plus souvent d'une cuisine de type régional.

Bib Hôtel

297 Établissement offrant une prestation de qualité avec une majorité de chambres au prix maximum de 72 € en province et 88 € dans les grandes villes et stations touristiques importantes (prix pour 2 personnes, hors petit-déjeuner).

LES ADRESSES LES PLUS AGRÉABLES

Le rouge signale les établissements particulièrement agréables. Cela peut tenir au caractère de l'édifice, à l'originalité du décor, au site, à l'accueil ou aux services proposés.

- à **Hôtels agréables**
- **Maisons d'hôtes agréables**
- à **Restaurants agréables**

LES MENTIONS PARTICULIÈRES

En dehors des distinctions décernées aux établissements, les inspecteurs MICHELIN apprécient d'autres critères souvent importants dans le choix d'un établissement.

SITUATION

Vous cherchez un établissement tranquille ou offrant une vue attractive ?
Suivez les symboles suivants :

- **Hôtel tranquille**
- **Hôtel très tranquille**
- **Vue intéressante**
- **Vue exceptionnelle**

CARTE DES VINS

Vous cherchez un restaurant dont la carte des vins offre un choix particulièrement intéressant ?
Suivez le symbole suivant :

Carte des vins particulièrement attractive

Toutefois, ne comparez pas la carte présentée par le sommelier d'un grand restaurant avec celle d'une auberge dont le patron se passionne pour les vins de sa région.

Équipements & services

30 ch Nombre de chambres

Jardin de repos – Parc – Plage aménagée

Repas servi au jardin ou en terrasse

Piscine de plein air / couverte

Bel espace de bien-être et de relaxation

Salle de remise en forme – Court de tennis

Ascenseur – Aménagements pour personnes à mobilité réduite

Air conditionné

Chambres non-fumeurs disponibles

Connexion internet haut débit

Salons pour repas privés

Salles de conférences

Restaurant proposant un service voiturier (pourboire d'usage)

Parking / parking clos réservé à la clientèle

Garage (généralement payant)

Accès interdit aux chiens

Station de métro la plus proche

Open / Closed May-October Période d'ouverture ou de fermeture, communiquée par l'hôtelier

Prix

Les prix indiqués dans ce guide ont été établis à l'automne 2007. Ils sont susceptibles de modifications, notamment en cas de variation des prix des biens et des services. Ils s'entendent taxes et service compris. Aucune majoration ne doit figurer sur votre note sauf éventuellement la taxe de séjour. Les hôteliers et restaurateurs se sont engagés, sous leur propre responsabilité, à appliquer ces prix aux clients. À l'occasion de certaines manifestations : congrès, foires, salons, festivals, événements sportifs…, les prix demandés par les hôteliers peuvent être sensiblement majorés. Par ailleurs, renseignez-vous pour connaître les éventuelles conditions avantageuses accordées par les hôteliers.

RÉSERVATION ET ARRHES

Pour la confirmation de la réservation certains établissements demandent le numéro de carte de paiement ou un versement d'arrhes. Il s'agit d'un dépôt-garantie qui engage l'établissement comme le client. Bien demander à l'hôtelier de vous fournir dans sa lettre d'accord toutes précisions utiles sur la réservation et les conditions de séjour.

CARTES DE PAIEMENT

	Cartes de paiement acceptées :
VISA MC AE DC	Visa – MasterCard – American Express – Diners Club

CHAMBRES

ch – 50/80 €	Prix des chambres minimum / maximum pour 1 personne
ch – 60/100 €	Prix des chambres minimum / maximum pour 2 personnes
9 €	Prix du petit-déjeuner
ch	Petit-déjeuner compris

DEMI-PENSION

½ P 50/70 €	Prix de la demi-pension mini / maxi (chambre, petit-déjeuner et un repas) par personne. Ces prix s'entendent pour une chambre double occupée par deux personnes pour un séjour de trois jours minimum. Une personne seule occupant une chambre double se voit souvent appliquer une majoration. La plupart des hôtels de séjour pratiquent également la pension complète.

RESTAURANT

(13 €)	Formule entrée-plat ou plat-dessert au déjeuner en semaine
	Menu à moins de 18 €
Menu 15 € (déj.)	Menu uniquement servi au déjeuner
Menu 17 € (sem.)	Menu uniquement servi en semaine
Menu 16/38 €	Menu le moins cher / le plus cher
Carte 24/48 €	**Repas à la carte hors boisson** Le premier prix correspond à un repas simple comprenant une entrée, un plat et un dessert. Le deuxième prix concerne un repas plus complet (avec spécialité) comprenant deux plats, fromage et dessert.
bi	Boisson comprise

Villes

GÉNÉRALITÉS

63300	Numéro de code postal de la localité *les deux premiers chiffres correspondent au numéro de département*
✉ 57130 Ars	Numéro de code postal et nom de la commune de destination
P SP	Préfecture – Sous-préfecture
337 E5	Numéro de la carte « DEPARTEMENTS France » MICHELIN et coordonnées permettant de se repérer sur la carte
Jura	Voir le Guide Vert MICHELIN Jura
1057 h.	Nombre d'habitants (source : www.insee.fr)
alt. 75	Altitude de la localité
Sta. therm.	Station thermale
1200/1900	Altitude de la station et altitude maximum atteinte par les remontées mécaniques
2	Nombre de téléphériques ou télécabines
14	Nombre de remonte-pentes et télésièges
	Ski de fond
BY **b**	Lettres repérant un emplacement sur le plan de ville
9	Golf et nombre de trous
	Panorama, point de vue
	Aéroport – Localité desservie par train-auto *Renseignements au numéro de téléphone indiqué*
	Transports maritimes
	Transports maritimes pour passagers seulement
i	Information touristique

INFORMATIONS TOURISTIQUES

INTÉRÊT TOURISTIQUE

★★★	Vaut le voyage
★★	Mérite un détour
★	Intéressant

Les musées sont généralement fermés le mardi

SITUATION DU SITE

	A voir dans la ville
	A voir aux environs de la ville
N, S, E, O	La curiosité est située : au Nord, au Sud, à l'Est, à l'Ouest
② ④	On s'y rend par la sortie ② ou ④ repérée par le même signe sur le plan du guide
6 km	Distance en kilomètres

Hôtels

Restaurants

CURIOSITÉS

Bâtiment intéressant

Édifice religieux intéressant :

- Catholique – Protestant

VOIRIE

Autoroute, double chaussée de type autoroutier

Échangeurs numérotés : complet, partiels

Grande voie de circulation

Sens unique – Rue réglementée ou impraticable

Rue piétonne – Tramway

R. Pasteur Rue commerçante – Parking – Parking Relais

Porte – Passage sous voûte – Tunnel

Gare et voie ferrée – Auto-Train

Funiculaire – Téléphérique, télécabine

Pont mobile – Bac pour autos

SIGNES DIVERS

Information touristique

Mosquée – Synagogue

Tour – Ruines – Moulin à vent – Château d'eau

Jardin, parc, bois – Cimetière – Calvaire

Stade – Golf – Hippodrome – Patinoire

Piscine de plein air, couverte

Vue – Panorama – Table d'orientation

Monument – Fontaine – Usine

Centre commercial – Cinéma Multiplex

Port de plaisance – Phare – Tour de télécommunications

Aéroport – Station de métro – Gare routière

Transport par bateau : passagers et voitures, passagers seulement

Pastille de sortie de ville

Bureau principal de poste restante et Téléphone

Hôpital – Marché couvert – Caserne

Bâtiment public repéré par une lettre :

A C - Chambre d'agriculture – Chambre de commerce

G H J - Gendarmerie – Hôtel de ville – Palais de justice

M P T - Musée – Préfecture, sous-préfecture – Théâtre

U - Université, grande école

POL. - Police (commissariat central)

Passage bas (inf. à 4 m 50) – Charge limitée (inf. à 19 t)

Attention : en France, nouvelle numérotation en cours des routes nationales et départementales.

Come leggere la guida

INFORMAZIONI TURISTICHE

Distanza dalle città di riferimento, uffici turismo, siti turistici locali, mezzi di trasporto, golfs e tempo libero...

L'ALLOGGIO

Da 🏨🏨🏨🏨🏨 a 🏨, ⌂:
categorie di confort.
In rosso 🏨🏨🏨🏨🏨 ... 🏨, ⌂:
I più ameni.

I MIGLIORI ESERCIZI A PREZZI CONTENUTI

- Bib Gourmand.
- Bib Hotel.

I RISTORANTI

Da XXXXX a X:
categorie di confort.
In rosso XXXXX ... X:
i più ameni.

LE TAVOLE STELLATE

- ✿✿✿ Vale il viaggio.
- ✿✿ Merita una deviazione.
- ✿ Ottima cucina.

ABBAYE DE FONTFROIDE - 03 Aude - 344 I4 - rattaché à
ABBAYE DE SAINT-WANDRILLE – 18 Cher – 323 K6
Montrond
ABBEVILLE - 80 Somme - 24 567 h. - alt.8 - ✉ 80100 - 3
Nord Pas-de-Calais Picardie
Paris 186 - Amiens 51 - Boulogne-sur-Mer 79 -
d'Avignon - ☎ 04 90 81 51 51, par N3 et N7 : 8 k
Office de tourisme, 1 place de l'Amiral Cour
risme.abbeville@wanadoo.fr - Fax 03 22 31
d'Abbeville, Route du Val par rte St-Valéry
- Fax 03 22 24 49 61 - ✉ 80132
Vitraux contemporains★★ de l'église du
légiale St-Vulfran AE **D** - Musée Boucher
Vallée de la Somme★ - Château de Bag

Les Jardins du Château
rte du Port – ☎ 04 79 00 00 46
– welcome@hotelmandjaro.com – Fax
15 ch (1/2 P seult) – 17 suites 250/440
Rest Le Cœur d'Or – ☎ 04 79 01 46
Rest Terrasses du Cœur d'Or – (fer
• Lauze, pierre et bois "vieilli" comp
Superbes chambres savoyardes, é
Décor tout bois et coins "cosy" au
Terrasses.

Le Relais de la Poste
rte de Lion, D 541 : 1 km – ☎ 04
– Fermé 31 oct.-18 nov., 19
42 ch – 40/60 € 60/65
• Sur la route de la grotte d
cadre actuel ou sous les fr

Atelier des Saveur
10 bd Croisette – ☎ 04 9
– Fax 04 93 38 97 90 –
Rest – (dîner seult) 7
Spéc. Bocal de foie
Mad" tiède à la var
• Élégante verrièr

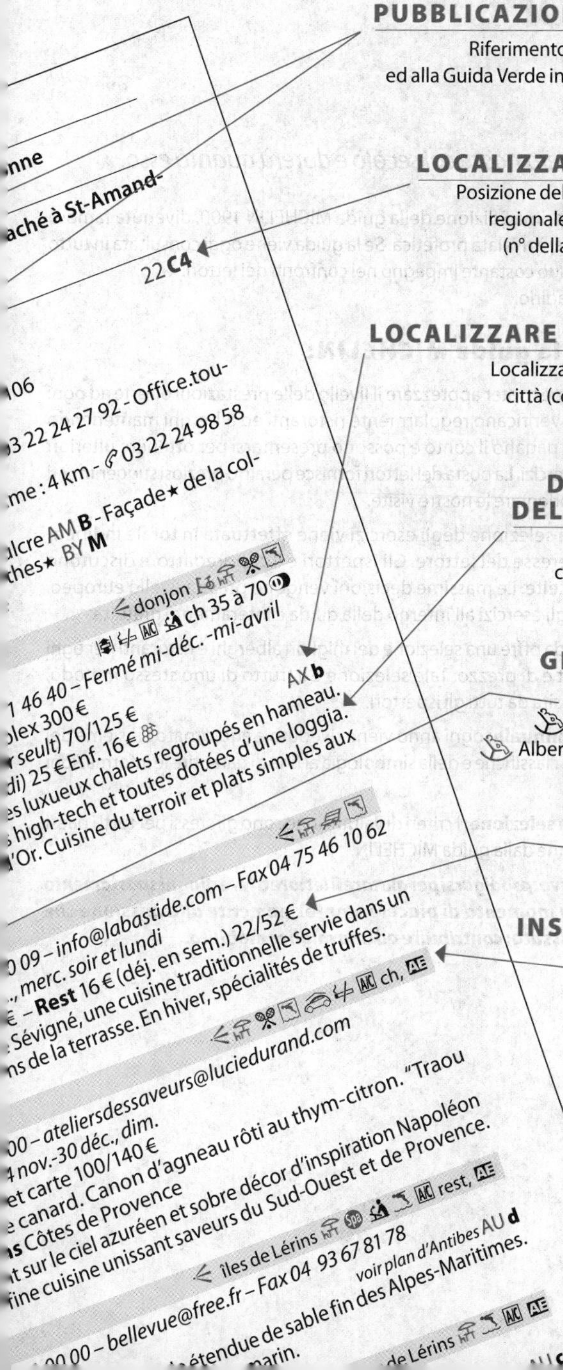

ALTRE PUBBLICAZIONI MICHELIN

Riferimento alla carta MICHELIN ed alla Guida Verde in cui figura la località.

LOCALIZZARE LA CITTÀ

Posizione della località sulla carta regionale alla fine della guida (n° della carta e coordinate).

LOCALIZZARE L'ESERCIZIO

Localizzazione sulla pianta di città (coordinate ed indice).

DESCRIZIONE DELL'ESERCIZIO

Atmosfera, stile, carattere e specialità.

GLI ALBERGHI TRANQUILLI

Albergo tranquillo.
Albergo molto tranquillo.

PREZZI

INSTALLAZIONI E SERVIZI

Principi

« Quest'opera nasce col secolo e durerà quanto esso. »

La prefazione della prima Edizione della guida MICHELIN 1900, divenuta famosa nel corso degli anni, si è rivelata profetica. Se la guida viene oggi consultata in tutto il mondo è grazie al suo costante impegno nei confronti dei lettori.
Desideriamo qui ribadirlo.

I principi della guida MICHELIN:

La visita anonima: per poter apprezzare il livello delle prestazioni offerte ad ogni cliente, gli ispettori verificano regolarmente ristoranti ed alberghi mantenendo l'anonimato. Questi pagano il conto e possono presentarsi per ottenere ulteriori informazioni sugli esercizi. La posta dei lettori fornisce peraltro preziosi suggerimenti che permettono di orientare le nostre visite.

L'indipendenza: la selezione degli esercizi viene effettuata in totale indipendenza, nel solo interesse del lettore. Gli ispettori e il caporedattore discutono collegialmente le scelte. Le massime decisioni vengono prese a livello europeo. La segnalazione degli esercizi all'interno della guida è interamente gratuita.

La selezione: la guida offre una selezione dei migliori alberghi e ristoranti per ogni categoria di confort e di prezzo. Tale selezione è il frutto di uno stesso metodo, applicato con rigorosità da tutti gli ispettori.

L'aggiornamento annuale: ogni anno viene riveduto e aggiornato l'insieme dei consigli pratici, delle classifiche e della simbologia al fine di garantire le informazioni più attendibili.

L'omogeneità della selezione: i criteri di valutazione sono gli stessi per tutti i paesi presi in considerazione dalla guida MICHELIN.

... e un unico obiettivo: prodigarsi per aiutare il lettore a fare di ogni spostamento e di ogni uscita un momento di piacere, conformemente alla missione che MICHELIN si è prefissata: contribuire ad una miglior mobilità.

Caro lettore,

Abbiamo il piacere di presentarle la nostra 99a edizione della guida MICHELIN Francia. Questa selezione, che comprende i migliori alberghi e ristoranti per ogni categoria di prezzo, viene effettuata da un'équipe di ispettori professionisti del settore. Ogni anno, percorrono l'intero paese per visitare nuovi esercizi e verificare il livello delle prestazioni di quelli già inseriti nella guida. All'interno della selezione, vengono inoltre assegnate ogni anno da ✿ a ✿✿✿ alle migliori tavole. Le stelle sono attribuite agli esercizi che propongono la migliore qualità culinaria, in ogni tipo di stile, tenendo conto della scelta dei prodotti, della personalità della cucina, della padronanza delle tecniche di cottura e dei sapori, del rapporto qualità/prezzo, nonché della regolarità. Anche quest'anno, numerose tavole sono state notate per l'evoluzione della loro cucina. Una « **N** » accanto ad ogni esercizio prescelto dell'annata 2008, ne indica l'inserimento fra gli esercizi con una, due o tre stelle.

Desideriamo inoltre segnalare le « ***promesse*** » per la categoria superiore. Questi esercizi, evidenziati in rosso nella nostra lista e nelle nostre pagine, sono i migliori della loro categoria e potranno accedere alla categoria superiore non appena le loro prestazioni avranno raggiunto un livello costante nel tempo, e nelle proposte della carta. Con questa segnalazione speciale, è nostra intenzione farvi conoscere le tavole che costituiscono, dal nostro punto di vista, le principali promesse della gastronomia di domani.

Il vostro parere ci interessa, specialmente riguardo a queste « *promesse* ». Non esitate quindi a scriverci, la vostra partecipazione è importante per orientare le nostre visite e migliorare costantemente la vostra guida.

Grazie ancora per la vostra fedeltà e vi auguriamo buon viaggio con la guida MICHELIN 2008.

Consultate la guida MICHELIN su **www. ViaMichelin.com**
e scriveteci a : **leguidemichelin-france@fr.michelin.com**

Categorie & simboli distintivi

LE CATEGORIE DI CONFORT

Nella selezione della guida MICHELIN vengono segnalati i migliori indirizzi per ogni categoria di confort e di prezzo.Gli esercizi selezionati sono classificati in base al confort che offrono e vengono citati in ordine di preferenza per ogni categoria.

🏨🏨🏨🏨🏨	XXXXX	**Gran lusso e tradizione**
🏨🏨🏨🏨	XXXX	**Gran confort**
🏨🏨🏨	XXX	**Molto confortevole**
🏨🏨	XX	**Di buon confort**
🏨	X	**Abbastanza confortevole**
⌂		**Locande, affittacamere**
sans rest		**L'albergo non ha ristorante**
avec ch		**Il ristorante dispone di camere**

I SIMBOLI DISTINTIVI

Per aiutarvi ad effettuare la scelta migliore, segnaliamo gli esercizi che si distinguono in modo particolare.

Per gli indirizzi che si distinguono con una stella o un Bib Gourmand, la menzione "**Rest**" appare in rosso nella descrizione dell'esercizio

Per gli indirizzi che si distinguono con il Bib Hotel, la menzione "**ch**" appare in blu nella descrizione dell'esercizio.

LE MIGLIORI TAVOLE

Le stelle distinguono gli esercizi che propongono la miglior qualità in campo gastronomico, indipendentemente dagli stili di cucina. I criteri presi in considerazione sono: la scelta dei prodotti, la personalità della cucina, la padronanza delle tecniche di cottura e dei sapori, il rapporto qualità/prezzo, nonché la regolarità.

✿✿✿	**Una delle migliori cucine, questa tavola vale il viaggio**
26	Vi si mangia sempre molto bene, a volte meravigliosamente.
✿✿	**Cucina eccellente, questa tavola merita una deviazione**
68	
✿	**Un'ottima cucina nella sua categoria**
435	

I MIGLIORI ESERCIZI A PREZZI CONTENUTI

Bib Gourmand

510 Esercizio che offre una cucina di qualità, spesso a carattere tipicamente regionale, al prezzo massimo di 28 € (35 € nelle città capoluogo e turistiche importanti).
Prezzo di un pasto, bevanda esclusa.

Bib Hotel

297 Esercizio che offre un soggiorno di qualità al prezzo massimo di 72 € (88 € nelle città e località turistiche importanti) per la maggior parte delle camere. Prezzi per 2 persone, prima colazione esclusa.

GLI ESERCIZI AMENI

Il rosso indica gli esercizi particolarmente ameni. Questo per le caratteristiche dell'edificio, le decorazioni non comuni, la sua posizione ed il servizio offerto.

a **Alberghi ameni**

Locande e affittacamere ameni

a **Ristoranti ameni**

LE SEGNALAZIONI PARTICOLARI

Oltre alle distinzioni conferite agli esercizi, gli ispettori MICHELIN apprezzano altri criteri spesso importanti nella scelta di un esericizio.

POSIZIONE

Cercate un esercizio tranquillo o che offre una vista piacevole?
Seguite i simboli seguenti :

Albergo tranquillo

Albergo molto tranquillo

Vista interessante

Vista eccezionale

CARTA DEI VINI

Cercate un ristorante la cui carta dei vini offra una scelta particolarmente interessante?
Seguite il simbolo seguente:

Carta dei vini particolarmente interessante

Attenzione a non confrontare la carta presentata da un sommelier in un grande ristorante con quella di una trattoria dove il proprietario ha una grande passione per i vini della regione.

Installazioni & servizi

30 ch	Numero di camere
	Giardino – Parco – Spiaggia attrezzata
	Pasti serviti in giardino o in terrazza
	Piscina: all'aperto, coperta
Spa	Centro attrezzato per il benessere ed il relax
	Palestra – Campo di tennis
	Ascensore – Esercizio accessibile in parte alle persone con difficoltà motorie
A/C	Aria condizionata
	Camere disponibili per i non fumatori
	Connessione internet ad alta velocità
	Saloni particolari
	Sale per conferenze
	Ristorante con servizio di posteggiatore (è consuetudine lasciare una mancia)
P P	Parcheggio / Parcheggio chiuso riservato alla clientela
	Garage nell'albergo (generalmente a pagamento)
	Accesso vietato ai cani
M	Stazione della metropolitana più vicina
Open / Closed May-October	Periodo di apertura o chiusura, comunicato dal proprietario

Prezzi

I prezzi che indichiamo in questa guida sono stati stabiliti nell'autunno 2007. Potranno subire delle variazioni in relazione ai cambiamenti dei prezzi di beni e servizi. Essi s'intendono comprensivi di tasse e servizio. Sul conto da pagare non deve figurare alcuna maggiorazione, ad eccezione dell'eventuale tassa di soggiorno. Gli albergatori e i ristoratori si sono impegnati, sotto la propria responsabilità, a praticare questi prezzi ai clienti. In occasione di alcune manifestazioni (congressi, fiere, saloni, festival, eventi sportivi...) i prezzi richiesti dagli albergatori potrebbero subire un sensibile aumento. Per eventuali promozioni offerte, non esitate a chiederle direttamente all'albergatore.

PRENOTAZIONE E CAPARRA

Come conferma della prenotazione alcuni esercizi chiedono il numero di una carta di credito o il versamento di una caparra. Si tratta di un deposito-garanzia che impegna sia l'albergatore che il cliente. Chiedete una lettera di conferma su ogni dettaglio della prenotazione e sulle condizioni di soggiorno.

CARTE DI CREDITO

	Carte di credito accettate :
VISA MC AE DC	Visa – MasterCard –American Express –Diners Club

CAMERE

ch – 🚹 50/80 €	Prezzo minimo / massimo per camera singola
ch – 🚹🚹 60/100 €	Prezzo minimo / massimo per camera doppia.
☕ 9 €	Prezzo per la prima colazione.
ch ☕	Prima colazione compresa

MEZZA PENSIONE

½ P 50/70 €	Prezzo minimo/massimo della mezza pensione (camera, prima colazione ed un pasto) per persona. Questi prezzi sono validi per la camera doppia occupata da due persone, per un soggiorno minimo di tre giorni; la persona singola potrà talvolta vedersi applicata una maggiorazione. La maggior parte degli alberghi pratica anche la pensione completa.

RISTORANTE

(13 €)	Pasto composto dal piatto del giorno, da un antipasto o dessert, a mezzogiorno in settimana
🪙	Pasto per meno di 18 €
Menu 15 € (déj.)	Menu servito solo a mezzogiorno
Menu 17 € (sem.)	Menu servito solo nei giorni feriali
Menu 16/38 €	Menu: il meno caro / il più caro
Carte 24/48	Pasto alla carta bevanda esclusa. Il primo prezzo corrisponde ad un pasto semplice comprendente: antipasto, piatto del giorno e dessert. Il secondo prezzo corrisponde ad un pasto più completo (con specialità) comprendente: due piatti, formaggio e dessert.
bi	Bevanda compresa

Città

GENERALITÀ

63300	Codice di avviamento postale *le prime due cifre corrispondono al numero del dipartimento*
✉ 57130 Ars	Numero di codice e sede dell'Uffico Postale
P SP	Prefettura – Sottoprefettura
337 E5	Numero della carta "DEPARTEMENTS France" MICHELIN e coordinate riferite alla quadrettatura
Jura	Vedere la Guida Verde MICHELIN Jura
1057 h.	Popolazione residente (funte: www.insee.fr)
alt. 75	Altitudine
Sta. therm.	Stazione termale
1200/1900	Altitudine della località e altitudine massima raggiungibile con gli impianti di risalita
2	Numero di funivie o cabinovie
14	Numero di sciovie e seggiovie
	Sci di fondo
BY **b**	Lettere indicanti l'ubicazione sulla pianta
9	Golf e numero di buche
	Panorama, vista
	Aeroporto
	Località con servizio auto su treno *Informarsi al numero di telefono indicato*
	Trasporti marittimi
	Trasporti marittimi (solo passeggeri)
	Informazioni turistiche

INFORMAZIONI TURISTICHE

INTERESSE TURISTICO

★★★	Vale il viaggio
★★	Merita una deviazione
★	Interessante

I musei sono generalmente chiusi il martedì

UBICAZIONE

	Nella città
	Nei dintorni della città
N, S, E, O	Il luogo si trova a Nord, a Sud, a Est, a Ovest della località
② ④	Ci si va dalla uscita ② o ④ indicata con lo stesso segno sulla pianta
6 km	Distanza chilometrica

Piante

Alberghi
Ristoranti

CURIOSITÀ

Edificio interessante
Costruzione religiosa interessante:
- Cattolica – Protestante

VIABILITÀ

Autostrada, doppia carreggiata tipo autostrada
Svincoli numerati: completo, parziale
Grande via di circolazione
Senso unico – Via regolamentata o impraticabile
Via pedonale – Tranvia
R. Pasteur Via commerciale – Parcheggio – Parcheggio Ristoro
Porta – Sottopassaggio – Galleria
Stazione e ferrovia – Auto/Treno
Funicolare – Funivia, Cabinovia
Ponte mobile – Traghetto per auto

SIMBOLI VARI

Ufficio informazioni turistiche
Moschea – Sinagoga
Torre – Ruderi – Mulino a vento – Torre idrica
Giardino, parco, bosco – Cimitero – Via Crucis
Stadio – Golf – Ippodromo – Pista di pattinaggio
Piscina: all'aperto, coperta
Vista – Panorama – Tavola d'orientamento
Monumento – Fontana – Fabbrica
Centro commerciale – Cinema Multisala
Porto turistico – Faro – Torre per telecomunicazioni
S.N.C.F. Aeroporto – Stazione della Metropolitana – Autostazione
Trasporto con traghetto:
- passeggeri ed autovetture, solo passeggeri
(3) Simbolo di riferimento comune alle piante particolareggiate
Ufficio centrale di fermo posta e telefono
Ospedale – Mercato coperto – Caserma
Edificio pubblico indicato con lettera:
A C Camera di Agricoltura – Camera di Commercio
G H J - Gendarmeria – Municipio – Palazzo di Giustizia
M P T - Museo – Prefettura, Sottoprefettura – Teatro
U - Università, grande scuola
POL. - Polizia (Questura, nelle grandi città)
4m4 18T (18) Sottopassaggio (altezza inferiore a m 4,50) – Portata limitata (inf. a 19 t)

Attenzione: in Francia, nuova numerazione per le strade nazionali regionali in corso.

Hinweise zur Benutzung

TOURISTISCHE INFORMATIONEN

Entfernungen zu größeren Städten, Informationsstellen, Sehenswürdigkeiten, Verkehrsmittel, Golfplätze und lokale Veranstaltungen...

DIE UNTERBRINGUNG

Von 🏨🏨 bis 🏨, 🏠:
Komfortkategorien.
In rot 🏨🏨 ... 🏨, 🏠:
Besonders angenehme Häuser.

DIE BESTEN PREISWERTEN ADRESSEN

Bib Gourmand.
Bib Hotel.

DIE RESTAURANTS

Von XXXXX bis X:
Komfortkategorien.
In rot XXXXX ... X: Besonders angenehme Häuser.

DIE STERNE-RESTAURANTS

✿✿✿ Eine Reise wert.
✿✿ Verdient einen Umweg.
✿ Eine sehr gute Küche.

ABBAYE DE FONTFROIDE - 03 Aude - 344 I4 - ratta
ABBAYE DE SAINT-WANDRILLE - 18 Cher - 32
Montrond
ABBEVILLE - 80 Somme - 24 567 h. - alt. 8 - ✉ 801
Nord Pas-de-Calais Picardie
Paris 186 - Amiens 51 - Boulogne-sur-Mer
d'Avignon - ☎ 04 90 81 51 51, par N3 et N
Office de tourisme, 1 place de l'Amiral
risme.abbeville@wanadoo.fr - Fax 03 2
d'Abbeville, Route du Val par rte St-Va
- Fax 03 22 24 49 61 - ✉ 80132
Vitraux contemporains★★ de l'église
légiale St-Vulfran AE D - Musée Bou
Vallée de la Somme★ - Château de

Les Jardins du Château
rte du Port – ☎ 04 79 00 00 46
- welcome@hotelmandjaro.com – F
15 ch (1/2 P seult) – 17 suites 250/4
Rest Le Cœur d'Or – ☎ 04 79 01 4
Rest Terrasses du Cœur d'Or –
• Lauze, pierre et bois "vieilli" co
Superbes chambres savoyardes
Décor tout bois et coins "cosy"
Terrasses.

Le Relais de la Poste
rte de Lion, D 541 : 1 km – ☎ 0
– Fermé 31 oct.-18 nov., 1
42 ch – 🛉40/60 € 🛉🛉60/65
• Sur la route de la grotte d
cadre actuel ou sous les fr

Atelier des Saveu
10 bd Croisette – ☎ 04 9
– Fax 04 93 38 97 90 –
Rest – (dîner seult) 7
Spéc. Bocal de foie
Mad" tiède à la van
• Élégante verrière
Un joli cadre po

ANDERE MICHELIN-PUBLIKATIONEN

Angabe der MICHELIN-Karte und des Grünen MICHELIN-Reiseführers, wo der Ort zu finden ist.

LAGE DER STADT

Markierung des Ortes auf der Regionalkarte am Ende des Buchs (Nr. der Karte und Koordinaten).

LAGE DES HAUSES

Markierung auf dem Stadtplan (Planquadrat und Koordinate).

BESCHREIBUNG DES HAUSES

Atmosphäre, Stil, Charakter und Spezialitäten.

RUHIGE HOTELS

ruhiges Hotel.
sehr ruhiges Hotel.

EINRICHTUNG UND SERVICE

PREISE

Grundsätze

„Dieses Werk hat zugleich mit dem Jahrhundert das Licht der Welt erblickt, und es wird ihm ein ebenso langes Leben beschieden sein."

Das Vorwort der ersten Ausgabe des MICHELIN-Führers von 1900 wurde im Laufe der Jahre berühmt und hat sich inzwischen durch den Erfolg dieses Ratgebers bestätigt. Der MICHELIN-Führer wird heute auf der ganzen Welt gelesen. Den Erfolg verdankt er seiner konstanten Qualität, die einzig den Lesern verpflichtet ist und auf festen Grundsätzen beruht.

Die Grundsätze des MICHELIN-Führers:

Anonymer Besuch: Die Inspektoren testen regelmäßig und anonym die Restaurants und Hotels, um deren Leistungsniveau zu beurteilen. Sie bezahlen alle in Anspruch genommenen Leistungen und geben sich nur zu erkennen, um ergänzende Auskünfte zu den Häusern zu erhalten. Für die Reiseplanung der Inspektoren sind die Briefe der Leser im Übrigen eine wertvolle Hilfe.

Unabhängigkeit: Die Auswahl der Häuser erfolgt völlig unabhängig und ist einzig am Nutzen für den Leser orientiert. Die Entscheidungen werden von den Inspektoren und dem Chefredakteur gemeinsam getroffen. Über die höchsten Auszeichnungen wird sogar auf europäischer Ebene entschieden. Die Empfehlung der Häuser im MICHELIN-Führer ist völlig kostenlos.

Objektivität der Auswahl: Der MICHELIN-Führer bietet eine Auswahl der besten Hotels und Restaurants in allen Komfort- und Preiskategorien. Diese Auswahl erfolgt unter strikter Anwendung eines an objektiven Maßstäben ausgerichteten Bewertungssystems durch alle Inspektoren.

Einheitlichkeit der Auswahl: Die Klassifizierungskriterien sind für alle vom MICHELIN-Führer abgedeckten Länder identisch.

Jährliche Aktualisierung: Jedes Jahr werden alle praktischen Hinweise, Klassifizierungen und Auszeichnungen überprüft und aktualisiert, um ein Höchstmaß an Zuverlässigkeit zu gewährleisten.

... und sein einziges Ziel – dem Leser bestmöglich behilflich zu sein, damit jede Reise und jeder Restaurantbesuch zu einem Vergnügen werden, entsprechend der Aufgabe, die sich MICHELIN gesetzt hat: die Mobilität in den Vordergrund zu stellen.

Lieber Leser

Lieber Leser,

Wir freuen uns, Ihnen die 99. Ausgabe des MICHELIN-Führers Frankreich vorstellen zu dürfen. Diese Auswahl der besten Hotels und Restaurants in allen Preiskategorien wird von einem Team von Inspektoren mit Ausbildung in der Hotellerie erstellt. Sie bereisen das ganze Jahr hindurch das Land. Ihre Aufgabe ist es, die Qualität und Leistung der bereits empfohlenen und der neu hinzu kommenden Hotels und Restaurants kritisch zu prüfen. In unserer Auswahl weisen wir jedes Jahr auf die besten Restaurants hin, die wir mit ✿ bis ✿✿✿ kennzeichnen. Die Häuser, die die beste Qualität bezüglich ihrer Küche bieten, wurden mit Sternen ausgezeichnet. Dabei wird nicht zwischen den einzelnen Stilrichtungen unterschieden, entscheidend waren vielmehr die Auswahl der Produkte, die persönlichen Akzente der Küche, das Knowhow bei der Zubereitung und im Geschmack, das Preis-Leistungs-Verhältnis sowie die immer gleich bleibende Qualität. Dieses Jahr werden ferner zahlreiche Restaurants für die Weiterentwicklung ihrer Küche hervorgehoben. Um die neu hinzugekommenen Häuser des Jahrgangs 2008 mit einem, zwei oder drei Sternen zu präsentieren, haben wir diese mit einem „**N**" gekennzeichnet.

Außerdem möchten wir die *"Hoffnungsträger"* für die nächsthöheren Kategorien hervorheben. Diese Häuser, sind in der Liste und auf unseren Seiten in Rot aufgeführt. Sie sind die besten ihrer Kategorie und könnten in Zukunft aufsteigen, wenn sich die Qualität ihrer Leistungen dauerhaft und auf die gesamte Karte bezogen bestätigt hat. Mit dieser besonderen Kennzeichnung möchten wir Ihnen die Restaurants aufzeigen, die in unseren Augen die Hoffnung für die Gastronomie von morgen sind. Ihre Meinung interessiert uns!

Bitte teilen Sie uns diese mit, insbesondere hinsichtlich dieser *"Hoffnungs-träger"*. Ihre Mitarbeit ist für die Planung unserer Besuche und für die ständige Verbesserung des MICHELIN-Führers von großer Bedeutung.

Wir danken Ihnen für Ihre Treue und wünschen Ihnen angenehme Reisen mit dem MICHELIN-Führer 2008.

Den MICHELIN-Führer finden Sie auch im Internet unter
www.ViaMichelin.com
oder schreiben Sie uns eine E-mail:
leguidemichelin-france@fr.michelin.com

Kategorien & Auszeichnungen

KOMFORTKATEGORIEN

Der MICHELIN-Führer bietet in seiner Auswahl die besten Adressen jeder Komfort- und Preiskategorie. Die ausgewählten Häuser sind nach dem gebotenen Komfort geordnet; die Reihenfolge innerhalb jeder Kategorie drückt eine weitere Rangordnung aus.

⌂⌂⌂⌂⌂	XXXXX	**Großer Luxus und Tradition**
⌂⌂⌂⌂	XXXX	**Großer Komfort**
⌂⌂⌂	XXX	**Sehr komfortabel**
⌂⌂	XX	**Mit gutem Komfort**
⌂	X	**Mit Standard-Komfort**
⌂		**Privatzimmer**
sans rest		**Hotel ohne Restaurant**
avec ch		**Restaurant vermietet auch Zimmer**

AUSZEICHNUNGEN

Um ihnen behilflich zu sein, die bestmögliche Wahl zu treffen, haben einige besonders bemerkenswerte Adressen dieses Jahr eine Auszeichnung erhalten. Die Sterne bzw. „Bib Gourmand" sind durch das entsprechende Symbol ✿ bzw. ☺ und **Rest** gekennzeichnet.
Ist ein Haus mit einem Bib Hotel ausgezeichnet, wird die Bezeichnung „**ch**" (für die Angabe der Zimmerzahl) in blau gedruckt.

DIE STERNE: DIE BESTEN RESTAURANTS

Die Häuser, die eine überdurchschnittlich gute Küche bieten, wobei alle Stilrichtungen vertreten sind, wurden mit einem Stern ausgezeichnet. Die Kriterien sind: die Auswahl der Produkte, die persönlichen Akzente der Küche, das Knowhow bei der Zubereitung und im Geschmack, das Preis-Leistungs-Verhältnis und die immer gleich bleibende Qualität.

✿✿✿ **Eine der besten Küchen: eine Reise wert**
26 Man isst hier immer sehr gut, öfters auch exzellent.

✿✿ **Eine hervorragende Küche: verdient einen Umweg**
68

✿ **Ein sehr gutes Restaurant in seiner Kategorie**
435

DIE BIB: DIE BESTEN PREISWERTEN HÄUSER

☺ **Bib Gourmand**
510 Häuser, die eine gute Küche bis 28 € bieten – in Paris : bis 35 € (Preis für eine dreigängige Mahlzeit ohne Getränke).
Außerhalb von Paris handelt es sich meist um eine regional geprägte Küche.

Bib Hotel

297 Häuser, die eine Mehrzahl ihrer komfortablen Zimmer bis 72 € anbieten – bzw. weniger als 88 € in größeren Städten und Urlaubsorten (Preis für 2 Personen ohne Frühstück).

DIE ANGENEHMSTEN ADRESSEN

Die rote Kennzeichnung weist auf besonders angenehme Häuser hin. Dies kann sich auf den besonderen Charakter des Gebäudes, die nicht alltägliche Einrichtung, die Lage, den Empfang oder den gebotenen Service beziehen.

bis **Angenehme Hotels**

Angenehme Privatzimmer

bis **Angenehme Restaurants**

BESONDERE ANGABEN

Neben den Auszeichnungen, die den Häusern verliehen werden, legen die MICHELIN-Inspektoren auch Wert auf andere Kriterien, die bei der Wahl einer Adresse oft von Bedeutung sind.

LAGE

Wenn Sie eine ruhige Adresse oder ein Haus mit einer schönen Aussicht suchen, achten Sie auf diese Symbole:

Ruhiges Hotel

Sehr ruhiges Hotel

Interessante Sicht

Besonders schöne Aussicht

WEINKARTE

Wenn Sie ein Restaurant mit einer besonders interessanten Weinauswahl suchen, achten Sie auf dieses Symbol:

Weinkarte mit besonders attraktivem Angebot

Aber vergleichen Sie bitte nicht die Weinkarte, die Ihnen vom Sommelier eines großen Hauses präsentiert wird, mit der Auswahl eines Gasthauses, dessen Besitzer die Weine der Region mit Sorgfalt zusammenstellt.

Einrichtung & Service

30 ch Anzahl der Zimmer

Garten, Liegewiese – Park – Strandbad

Garten-, Terrassenrestaurant

Freibad oder Hallenbad

Wellnessbereich

Fitnessraum – Tennisplatz

Fahrstuhl

Für Körperbehinderte leicht zugängliches Haus

Klimaanlage

Nichtraucher Zimmer vorhanden

High-Speed Internet Anschluss in den Zimmern

Veranstaltungsraum

Konferenzraum

Restaurant mit Wagenmeister-Service (Trinkgeld üblich)

Parkplatz / gesicherter Parkplatz für Gäste

Garage (wird gewöhnlich berechnet)

Hunde sind unerwünscht

Nächstgelegene U-Bahnstation

Open / Closed May-October Öffnungszeit / Schließungszeit, vom Hotelier mitgeteilt

Preise

Die in diesem Führer genannten Preise wurden uns im Herbst 2007 angegeben. Sie können sich mit den Preisen von Waren und Dienstleistungen ändern. Sie enthalten Bedienung und MwSt. Es sind Inklusivpreise, die sich nur noch durch die evtl. zu zahlende Kurtaxe erhöhen können. Die Häuser haben sich verpflichtet, die von den Hoteliers selbst angegebenen Preise den Kunden zu berechnen. Anlässlich größerer Veranstaltungen, Messen und Ausstellungen werden von den Hotels in manchen Städten und deren Umgebung erhöhte Preise verlangt. Erkundigen Sie sich bei den Hoteliers nach eventuellen Sonder- bedingungen.

RESERVATION UND ANZAHLUNG

Einige Häuser verlangen zur Bestätigung der Reservierung eine Anzahlung oder die Kreditkartennummer. Diese ist als Garantie sowohl für die Häuser als auch für den Gast anzusehen. Bitten Sie den Hotelier, dass er Ihnen in seinem Bestätigungsschreiben die genauen Bedingungen mitteilt.

KREDITKARTEN

	Akzeptierte Kreditkarten:
VISA MC AE DC	Visa – MasterCard – American Express – Diners Club

ZIMMER

ch – 🚹 50/80 €	Mindest- und Höchstpreis für ein Einzelzimmer
ch – 🚹🚹 60/100 €	Mindest- und Höchstpreis für ein Doppelzimmer
☕ 9 €	Preis für Frühstück
ch ☕	Zimmerpreis inkl. Frühstück

HALBPENSION

½ P 50/70 €	Mindest- und Höchstpreis für Halbpension (Zimmerpreis inkl. Frühstück und einer Mahlzeit) pro Person, bei einem von zwei Personen belegten Doppelzimmer für einen Aufenthalt von mindestens 3 Tagen. Falls eine Einzelperson ein Doppelzimmer belegt, kann ein Preisaufschlag verlangt werden. In den meisten Hotels wird auch Vollpension angeboten.

RESTAURANT

(13 €)	Preis für ein Menu, bestehend aus Vorspeise/Hauptgericht oder Hauptgericht/Dessert, das unter der Woche mittags serviert wird
🪙	Menu unter 18 €
Menu 15 € (déj.)	Menu wird nur mittags angeboten
Menu 17 € (sem.)	Menu wird nur unter der Woche angeboten
Menu 16/38 €	Mindest- und Höchstpreis der Menus
Carte 24/48 €	Der erste Preis entspricht einer einfachen Mahlzeit und umfasst Vorspeise, Hauptgericht, Dessert. Der zweite Preis entspricht einer reichlicheren Mahlzeit (mit Spezialität) bestehend aus Vorspeise, Hauptgang, Käse und Dessert.
bi	Getränke inklusiv

Städte

ALLGEMEINES

63300	Postleitzahl *die beiden ersten Ziffern sind gleichzeitig die Departements-Nummer*
✉ 57130 Ars	Postleitzahl und Name des Verteilerpostamtes
P SP	Präfektur – Unterpräfektur
337 E5	Nummer der Michelin-Karte « DEPARTEMENTS France » MICHELIN und Koordinatenangabe
Jura	Siehe den Grünen MICHELIN-Reiseführer Jura
1057 h. alt. 75	Einwohnerzahl (Quelle: www.insee.fr) – Höhe
Sta. therm.	Thermalbad
1200/1900	Höhe des Wintersportortes und Maximalhöhe, die mit Kabinenbahn oder Lift erreicht werden kann
2	Anzahl der Kabinenbahnen
14	Anzahl der Schlepp- oder Sessellifte
	Langlaufloipen
BY **b**	Markierung auf dem Stadtplan
9	Golfplatz und Anzahl der Löcher
	Rundblick, Aussichtspunkt
	Flughafen
	Ladestelle für Autoreisezüge *Auskunft unter der angegebenen Telefonnummer*
	Autofähre – Personenfähre
i	Informationsstelle

SEHENSWÜRDIGKEITEN

BEWERTUNG

★★★	Eine Reise wert
★★	Verdient einen Umweg
★	Sehenswert

Museen sind im allgemeinen dienstags geschlossen

LAGE

	In der Stadt
	In der Umgebung der Stadt
N, S, E, O	Die Sehenswürdigkeit befindet sich: im Norden, Süden, Osten, Westen der Stadt
② ④	Zu erreichen über die Ausfallstraße ② bzw. ④, die auf dem Stadtplan identisch gekennzeichnet sind.
6 km	Entfernung in Kilometern

Stadtpläne

Hotels
Restaurants

SEHENSWÜRDIGKEITEN

Sehenswertes Gebäude
Sehenswerte katholische bzw. evangelische Kirche

STRAßEN

Autobahn, Schnellstraße
Numerierte Anschlußstelle: Autobahneinfahrt – und/oder -ausfahrt
Hauptverkehrsstraße
Einbahnstraße – Gesperrte Straße oder mit Verkehrsbeschränkungen
Fußgängerzone – Straßenbahn
R. Pasteur — Einkaufsstraße – Parkplatz, Parkhaus – Park-and-Ride-Plätze
Tor – Passage – Tunnel
Bahnhof und Bahnlinie – Autoreisezug
Standseilbahn – Seilschwebebahn
B — Bewegliche Brücke – Autofähre

SONSTIGE ZEICHEN

Informationsstelle
Moschee – Synagoge
Turm – Ruine – Windmühle – Wasserturm
Garten, Park, Wäldchen – Friedhof – Bildstock
Stadion – Golfplatz – Pferderennbahn – Eisbahn
- Freibad – Hallenbad
Aussicht – Rundblick – Orientierungstafel
Denkmal – Brunnen – Fabrik
Einkaufszentrum – Multiplex-Kino
Jachthafen – Leuchtturm – Funk-, Fernsehturm
S.N.C.F. — Flughafen – U-Bahnstation – Autobusbahnhof
Schiffsverbindungen: Autofähre – Personenfähre
3 — Straßenkennzeichnung (identisch auf Michelin-Stadtplänen und Abschnittskarten)
Hauptpostamt (postlagernde Sendungen) u. Telefon
Krankenhaus – Markthalle – Kaserne
Öffentliches Gebäude, durch einen Buchstaben gekennzeichnet:
A C — - Landwirtschaftskammer – Handelskammer
G H J — - Gendarmerie – Rathaus – Gerichtsgebäude
M P T — - Museum – Präfektur, Unterpräfektur – Theater
U — - Universität, Hochschule
POL. — - Polizei (in größeren Städten Polizeipräsidium)
4^m4 18T 18 — Unterführung (Höhe bis 4,50 m) – Höchstbelastung (unter 19 t)

Achtung: Die Nummerierung der National-und der Landstraßen in Frankreich wird z. Zt. Geändert.

Modo de empleo

INFORMACIÓN TURÍSTICA

Distancias desde las poblaciones principales, oficinas de turismo, puntos de interés turístico locales, medios de transporte, campos de golf y ocio...

EL ALOJAMIENTO

De 🏨🏨🏨🏨🏨 a 🏨, ⌂: categorías de confort.
En rojo 🏨🏨🏨🏨🏨 ... 🏨, ⌂: los más agradables.

LAS MEJORES DIRECCIONES A PRECIOS MODERADOS

- Bib Gourmand.
- Bib Hotel.

RESTAURANTES

De XXXXX a X: categorías de confort.
En rojo XXXXX ... X: los más agradables.

ESTRELLAS

- ✿✿✿ Justifica el viaje.
- ✿✿ Vale la pena desviarse.
- ✿ Muy buena cocina.

ABBAYE DE FONTFROIDE - 03 Aude - 344 I4 - ratt

ABBAYE DE SAINT-WANDRILLE – 18 Cher – 32
Montrond

ABBEVILLE - 80 Somme - 24 567 h. - alt. 8 - ✉ 8010
Nord Pas-de-Calais Picardie
Paris 186 - Amiens 51 - Boulogne-sur-Mer
d'Avignon - ☎ 04 90 81 51 51, par N3 et N7
Office de tourisme, 1 place de l'Amiral C
risme.abbeville@wanadoo.fr - Fax 03 22
d'Abbeville, Route du Val par rte St-Val
- Fax 03 22 24 49 61 - ✉ 80132
Vitraux contemporains★★ de l'église
légiale St-Vulfran AE **D** - Musée Bouch
Vallée de la Somme★ - Château de B

Les Jardins du Château
rte du Port – ☎ 04 79 00 00 46
– welcome@hotelmandjaro.com – Fa
15 ch (1/2 P seult) – 17 suites 250/440
Rest Le Cœur d'Or – ☎ 04 79 01 46
Rest Terrasses du Cœur d'Or – (fe
◆ Lauze, pierre et bois "vieilli" comp
Superbes chambres savoyardes, é
Décor tout bois et coins "cosy" au
Terrasses.

Le Relais de la Poste
rte de Lion, D 541 : 1 km – ☎ 04 7
– Fermé 31 oct.-18 nov., 19-
42 ch – 🛉40/60 € 🛉🛉60/65 €
◆ Sur la route de la grotte de M
cadre actuel ou sous les fron

Atelier des Saveurs
10 bd Croisette – ☎ 04 92 9
– Fax 04 93 38 97 90 – Fer
Rest – (dîner seult) 75/1
Spéc. Bocal de foie gr
Mad" tiède à la vanille
◆ Élégante verrière ou
Un joli cadre pour

OTRAS PUBLICACIONES MICHELIN

Referencia del mapa MICHELIN y de la Guía Verde en los que se encuentra la localidad.

LOCALIZAR LA CIUDAD

Emplazamiento de la localidad en el mapa regional situado al final de la guía (nº del mapa y coordenadas).

LOCALIZAR EL ESTABLECIMIENTO

Localización en el plano de la ciudad (coordenadas e índice).

DESCRIPCIÓN DEL ESTABLECIMIENTO

Ambiente, estilo, carácter y especialidades.

HOTELES TRANQUILOS

Hotel tranquilo.
Hotel muy tranquilo.

PRECIOS

INSTALACIONES Y SERVICIOS

Narbonne
– rattaché à St-Amand-
22 **C4**
1 E7
uen 106
t ✆ 03 22 24 27 92 - Office.tou-
26
somme : 4 km - ✆ 03 22 24 98 58
épulcre AM **B** - Façade★ de la col-
Perthes★ BY **M**
e★
donjon
ch 35 à 70
Fermé mi-déc.-mi-avril
01 46 40 –
uplex 300 €
er seult) 70/125 €
ndi) 25 € Enf. 16 €
AX **b**
es luxueux chalets regroupés en hameau.
s high-tech et toutes dotées d'une loggia.
d'Or. Cuisine du terroir et plats simples aux
09 – *info@labastide.com* – Fax 04 75 46 10 62
merc. soir et lundi
– **Rest** 16 € (déj. en sem.) 22/52 €
évigné, une cuisine traditionnelle servie dans un
s de la terrasse. En hiver, spécialités de truffes.
ch,
– *ateliersdessaveurs@luciedurand.com*
ov.-30 déc., dim.
carte 100/140 €
nard. Canon d'agneau rôti au thym-citron. "Traou
ôtes de Provence
r le ciel azuréen et sobre décor d'inspiration Napoléon
cuisine unissant saveurs du Sud-Ouest et de Provence.
rest,
îles de Lérins
00 00 – *bellevue@free.fr* – Fax 04 93 67 81 78
voir plan d'Antibes AU **d**
ue de sable fin des Alpes-Maritimes.

Compromisos

"Esta obra aparece con el siglo y durará tanto como él".

Esta frase incluida en el prólogo de la primera Edición de la guía MICHELIN 1900 se hizo célebre a lo largo de los años y llegó a ser premonitoria. Si actualmente la guía cuenta con tantos lectores en todo el mundo, se debe en gran parte a su constante compromiso con todos ellos; compromiso que queremos reafirmar año tras año.

Compromisos de la guía MICHELIN

La visita anónima: los inspectores visitan anónima y periódicamente hoteles y restaurantes para valorar el nivel de las prestaciones que ofrecen a sus clientes. Pagan todas las facturas y sólo se dan a conocer cuando necesitan obtener datos complementarios. Por otra parte, las cartas de los lectores constituyen una valiosa fuente de información para organizar nuestras visitas.

La independencia: la selección de establecimientos se efectúa con total independencia y pensando exclusivamente en los lectores. Los inspectores y el redactor jefe adoptan las decisiones de manera colegiada. Las distinciones más destacadas se deciden a nivel europeo. La inserción de establecimientos en la guía es totalmente gratuita.

La selección: la guía ofrece una selección de los mejores hoteles y restaurantes de todas las categorías de confort y precio. Constituye el resultado de la rigurosa aplicación del mismo método por parte de todos los inspectores.

La actualización anual: al objeto de ofrecer los datos más fiables, anualmente se revisan y actualizan todas las informaciones prácticas, las clasificaciones y las distinciones.

La homogeneidad de la selección: los criterios de clasificación son idénticos en todos los países que abarca la guía MICHELIN.

... y un solo objetivo: hacer cuanto esté en nuestra mano para ayudar al lector con el fin de que cada viaje o cada salida se conviertan en un momento de placer conforme a la misión que se ha fijado MICHELIN : contribuir a una mejor movilidad.

Editorial

Estimado lector,

Tenemos el placer de presentarle la 99ª edición de la guía MICHELIN Francia. Esta guía contiene una selección de los mejores hoteles y restaurantes en cada categoría de precios, efectuada por un equipo de inspectores profesionales y formados en el sector de la hostelería. Como todos los años, han recorrido el país visitando nuevos establecimientos y comprobando el nivel de las prestaciones de los que ya figuraban en anteriores ediciones.

También anualmente, entre los establecimientos seleccionados distinguimos las mejores mesas con ✿ a ✿✿✿. Las estrellas distinguen los establecimientos que proponen la mejor calidad culinaria, en todos los estilos, teniendo en cuenta los productos utilizados, la personalidad de la cocina, el dominio de las cocciones y de los sabores, la relación calidad/precio, así como la regularidad.

Una vez más hemos detectado muchos restaurantes cuya cocina ha evolucionado muy favorablemente. Para destacar los que han mejorado su clasificación en la edición 2008, sumándose a los establecimientos con una, dos o tres estrellas, hemos añadido frente a cada uno de ellos la letra « **N** ».

Asimismo, resaltamos los establecimientos « ***con posibilidades*** » de ascender al nivel superior. Estos establecimientos, que figuran en rojo en dicha relación, y en nuestras páginas son los más destacados en su categoría. Podrán mejorar su calificación si, a lo largo del tiempo y en la mayoría de las preparaciones de la carta, progresa la regularidad de sus prestaciones. Mediante esta mención especial pretendemos dar a conocer los restaurantes que constituyen, a nuestro parecer, los valores de la gastronomía del futuro. Su opinión nos interesa y en particular en lo referente a los establecimientos « con posibilidades ». Escríbanos porque su participación es importante para orientar nuestras visitas y mejorar permanentemente su guía.

Una vez más, gracias por su fidelidad y buenos viajes con la guía MICHELIN 2008.

Consulte la guía MICHELIN en **www.ViaMichelin.com**
y escríbanos a : **leguidemichelin-france@fr.michelin.com**

Categorías y distinciones

CATEGORÍAS DE CONFORT

La guía MICHELIN incluye en su selección los mejores establecimientos en cada categoría de confort y de precio. Los establecimientos están clasificados según su confort y se citan por orden de preferencia dentro de cada categoría.

🏨🏨🏨🏨🏨	XXXXX	**Gran lujo y tradición**
🏨🏨🏨🏨	XXXX	**Gran confort**
🏨🏨🏨	XXX	**Muy confortable**
🏨🏨	XX	**Confortable**
🏨	X	**Sencillo pero confortable**
⌂		**Turismo rural**
sans rest		**El hotel no dispone de restaurante**
avec ch		**El restaurante tiene habitaciones**

DISTINCIONES

Para ayudarle a hacer la mejor selección, algunos establecimientos especialmente interesantes han recibido este año una distinción.

Para los establecimientos distinguidos por una estrella o un Bib Gourmand, la mención " **Rest** " aparece en color rojo en la descripción del establecimiento.

Para los establecimientos ditinguidos por un Bib Hotel, la mención " **ch** " aparece en color azul en la descripción del establecimiento.

LAS ESTRELLAS: LAS MEJORES MESAS

Los criterios que se han seguido son: los productos utilizados, la personalidad de la cocina, el dominio de las cocciones y de los sabores, la relación calidad/precio, así como la regularidad.

✿✿✿ 26	**Cocina de nivel excepcional, esta mesa justifica el viaje** Establecimiento donde siempre se come bien y, en ocasiones, maravillosamente.
✿✿ 68	**Excelente cocina, vale la pena desviarse**
✿ 435	**Muy buena cocina en su categoría**

LOS BIB:
LAS MEJORES DIRECCIONES A PRECIOS MODERADOS

Bib Gourmand

510 Establecimiento que ofrece una cocina de calidad, generalmente de tipo regional, a un máximo de 28 € (35 € en París). Precio de una comida sin la bebida.

Bib Hotel

297 Establecimiento que ofrece un cierto nivel de calidad con habitaciones a un máximo de 72 € (88 € en grandes ciudades y zonas turisticas). Precio para 2 personas sin el desayuno.

LAS DIRECCIONES MÁS AGRADABLES

El rojo indica los establecimientos especialmente agradables tanto por las características del edificio, la decoración original, el emplazamiento, el trato y los servicios que ofrece.

a **Hoteles agradables**

Turismos rurales agradables

a **Restaurantes agradables**

MENCIONES PARTICULARES

Además de las distinciones concedidas a los establecimientos, los inspectores de MICHELIN también tienen en cuenta otros criterios con frecuencia importantes cuando se elige un establecimiento.

SITUACIÓN

Los establecimientos tranquilos o con vistas aparecen señalados con los símbolos:

Hotel tranquilo

Hotel muy tranquilo

Vista interesante

Vista excepcional

CARTA DE VINOS

Los restaurantes con una carta de vinos especialmente interesante aparecen señalados con el símbolo:

Carta de vinos particularmente atractiva

Pero no compare la carta que presenta el sumiller de un restaurante de lujo y tradición con la de un establecimiento más sencillo cuyo propietario sienta predilección por los vinos de la zona.

Instalaciones y servicios

30 ch	Número de habitaciones
	Jardín – Parque – Playa equipada
	Comidas servidas en el jardín o en la terraza
	Piscina al aire libre o cubierta
	Espacio dedicado al bienestar y la relajación
	Gimnasio – Cancha de tenis
	Ascensor – Instalaciones adaptadas para discapacitados
	Aire acondicionado
	Habitaciones disponibles para no fumadores
	Conexión a Internet con sistema de alta velocidad
	Salones privados en los restaurantes
	Salas de reuniones
	Restaurante con servicio de aparcacoches (es costumbre dejar propina)
	Aparcamiento / Aparcamiento cerrado reservado a los clientes
	Garaje (generalmente de pago)
	No se admiten perros
	Estación de metro más próxima
Open / Closed May-October	Período de apertura comunicado por el hotelero

Precios

Los precios que indicamos en esta guía nos fueron facilitados en el otoño de 2007. Pueden sufrir modificaciones debido a las variaciones de los precios de bienes y servicios. El servicio y los impuestos están incluidos. En la factura no debe figurar ningún recargo excepto una eventual tasa de alojamiento. Los hoteles y restaurantes se han comprometido, bajo su responsabilidad, a aplicar estos precios al cliente. Durante la celebración de determinados eventos (congresos, ferias, salones, festivales, pruebas deportivas...) los precios indicados por los hoteleros pueden sufrir importantes aumentos. Por otra parte, infórmese con antelación porque muchos establecimientos aplican tarifas muy ventajosas.

RESERVAS Y ARRAS

Para confirmar la reserva, algunos establecimientos piden el número de la tarjeta de crédito o el abono de arras. Se trata de un depósito-garantía que compromete tanto al establecimiento como al cliente. Pida al hotelero confirmación escrita de las condiciones de estancia así como de todos los detalles útiles.

TARJETAS DE CRÉDITO

	Tarjetas de crédito aceptadas:
VISA MC AE D	Visa – MasterCard – American Express – Diners Club

HABITACIONES

ch – 50/80 €	Precio de las habitaciones mínimo/máximo para 1 persona
ch – 60/100 €	Precio de las habitaciones mínimo/máximo para 2 personas
9 €	Precio del desayvro
ch	Desayuno incluido

MEDIA PENSIÓN

½ P 50/70 €	Precio mínimo/máximo de la media pensión (habitación, desayuno y una comida) por persona. Precio de la habitación doble ocupada por dos personas y durante una estancia mínima de tres días. Si una persona sola ocupa una habitación doble se le suele aplicar un suplemento. La mayoría de estos hoteles ofrecen también la pensión completa.

RESTAURANTE

(13 €)	Comida compuesta por un plato fuerte del día y una entrada o un postre, servida generalmente a mediodía los días de semana
	Menú a menos de 18 €
Menu 15 € (déj.)	Menú servido sólo a mediodía
Menu 17 € (sem.)	Menú servido sólo los días de semana
Menu 16/38 €	Menú más económico / más caro
Carte 24/48 €	**Comida a la carta sin bebida.** El primer precio corresponde a una comida normal que incluye: entrada, plato fuerte del día y postre. El segundo precio se refiere a una comida más completa (con especialidad) que incluye: dos platos, queso y postre.
bi	Bebida incluida

Localidades

GENERALIDADES

63300	Código postal de la localidad *los dos primeros dígitos corresponden al número del departamento o provincia*
✉ 57130 Ars	Código postal y lugar de destino
P SP	Prefectura – Subprefectura
337 E5	Mapa Michelin "DEPARTEMENTS France" MICHELIN y coordenadas en los mapas
Jura	Ver La Guía Verde Michelin Jura
1057 h.	Población (según datos: www.insee.fr)
alt. 75	Altitud de la localidad
Sta. therm.	Balneario
1200/1900	Altitud de la estación y altitud máxima alcanzada por los remontes mecánicos
2	Número de teleféricos o telecabinas
14	Número de telesquíes o telesillas
	Esquí de fondo
BY **b**	Letras para localizar un emplazamiento en el plano
9	Golf y número de hoyos
	Panorama, vista
	Aeropuerto – Localidad con servicio Auto-Tren *Información en el número indicado*
	Transportes marítimos
	Transportes marítimos sólo para pasajeros
	Información turística

INFORMACIONES TURÍSTICAS

INTERÉS TURÍSTICO

★★★	Justifica el viaje
★★	Vale la pena desviarse
★	Interesante

Los museos cierran generalmente los martes

SITUACIÓN

	En la población
	En los alrededores de la población
	El lugar de interés está situado: al norte, al sur, al este, al oeste
② ④	Salga por la salida ② o ④ identificada por el mismo signo en el plano de la Guía y en el mapa Michelin
6 km	Distancia en kilómetros

Planos

Hoteles
Restaurantes

CURIOSIDADES

Edificio interesante
Edificio religioso interesante:
- Católico – Protestante

VÍAS DE CIRCULACIÓN

Autopista, autovía
número del acceso : completo-parcial
Vía importante de circulación
Sentido único – Calle impracticable, de uso restringido
Calle peatonal – Tranvía
R. Pasteur P R Calle comercial – Aparcamiento – Aparcamientos "P + R"
Puerta – Pasaje cubierto – Túnel
Estación y línea férrea – Auto-tren
Funicular – Teleférico, telecabina
B Puente móvil – Barcaza para coches

SIGNOS DIVERSOS

Oficina de Información de Turismo
Mezquita – Sinagoga
Torre – Ruinas – Molino de viento – Depósito de agua
Jardín, parque, bosque –Cementerio –Crucero
Estadio – Golf – Hipódromo – Pista de patinaje
Piscina al aire libre, cubierta
Vista – Panorama – Mesa de Orientación
Monumento – Fuente – Fábrica
Centro comercial – Multicines
Puerto deportivo – Faro – Torreta de telecomunicación
S.N.C.F. Aeropuerto – Boca de metro – Estación de autobuses
Transporte por barco : pasajeros y vehículos, pasajeros solamente
③ Referencia común a los planos y a los mapas detallados Michelin
Oficina central de lista de correos – Teléfonos
Hospital – Mercado cubierto – Cuartel
Edificio público localizado con letra :
A C - Cámara de Agricultura – Cámara de Comercio
G H J -Guardia civil – Ayuntamiento – Palacio de Justicia
M P T -Museo – Gobierno civil –Teatro
U -Universidad, Escuela superior
POL. - Policía (en las grandes ciudades: Jefatura)
4^m4 18T ⑱ Pasaje bajo (inf. a 4m 50) – Carga limitada (inf. a 19 t)

¡Cuidado! En Francia, nueva numeración de carreteras naciaonales y regionales en curso.

本書の使い方

観光情報

主要都市からの距離、観光局、観光名所、交通手段、ゴルフ場、レジャー施設など。

宿泊施設

🏨🏨🏨から🏨、🏠：
快適さのカテゴリー

🏨🏨🏨から🏨、🏠：
そのカテゴリーで特に快適

手頃な値段でクオリティの高いホテル・レストラン

ビブ・グルマン

ビブ・ホテル

レストラン

XXXXXから X：快適さのカテゴリー

XXXXXから X：そのカテゴリーで特に快適

星付きレストラン

✿✿✿　そのために旅行する価値がある卓越した料理

✿✿　遠回りしてでも訪れる価値がある素晴らしい料理

✿　そのカテゴリーで特に美味しい料理

ABBAYE DE FONTFROIDE - 03 Aude - **344** I4 - ratt

ABBAYE DE SAINT-WANDRILLE – 18 Cher – 3

Montrond

ABBEVILLE - 80 Somme - 24 567 h. - alt. 8 - ✉ 801

Nord Pas-de-Calais Picardie

Paris 186 - Amiens 51 - Boulogne-sur-Mer
d'Avignon - ☎ 04 90 81 51 51, par N3 et N
Office de tourisme, 1 place de l'Amiral C
risme.abbeville@wanadoo.fr - Fax 03 2
d'Abbeville, Route du Val par rte St-Va
- Fax 03 22 24 49 61 - ✉ 80132

Vitraux contemporains★★ de l'église
légiale St-Vulfran AE **D** - Musée Bouc
Vallée de la Somme★ - Château de B

Les Jardins du Château
rte du Port – ☎ 04 79 00 00 46
- welcome@hotelmandjaro.com – Fa
15 ch (1/2 P seult) – 17 suites 250/44
Rest Le Cœur d'Or – ☎ 04 79 01 46
Rest Terrasses du Cœur d'Or – (f
◆ Lauze, pierre et bois "vieilli" com
Superbes chambres savoyardes, é
Décor tout bois et coins "cosy" a
Terrasses.

Le Relais de la Poste
rte de Lion, D 541 : 1 km – ☎ 04
– Fermé 31 oct.-18 nov., 19-
42 ch – 40/60 € 60/65 €
◆ Sur la route de la grotte de
cadre actuel ou sous les fro

Atelier des Saveurs
10 bd Croisette – ☎ 04 92
– Fax 04 93 38 97 90 – Fe
Rest – (dîner seult) 75/1
Spéc. Bocal de foie g
Mad" tiède à la vanill
◆ Élégante verrière o
Un joli cadre pour

ミシュランの他の刊行物

ミシュラン地図やミシュラン、グリーンガイドにおける施設の所在地

その地名の所在地を確認

巻末に、フランスの地方別地図を掲載しており、その地名の所在地を確認することができます（図番号、経線・緯線間をアルファベット、数字で表記）。

ホテル・レストランの所在地を確認

その地名の市街地図でホテル、レストランの所在地を確認することができます（アルファベット表記）。

ホテル・レストランの簡単な説明

その雰囲気、スタイル、個性、スペシリティなどが記載されています。

静かなホテル

静かなホテル

非常に静かなホテル

設備とサービス

値段

Narbonne

– rattaché à St-Amand-

22 **C4**

E7

ıen 106

03 22 24 27 92 - Office.tou-

03 22 24 98 58

6

omme : 4 km - 03 22 24 98 58

epulcre AM **B** - Façade★ de la col-

erthes★ BY **M**

★

donjon

ch 35 à 70

Fermé mi-déc. -mi-avril

01 46 40 –

AX **b**

plex 300 €

r seult) 70/125 €

di) 25 € Enf. 16 €

es luxueux chalets regroupés en hameau.

high-tech et toutes dotées d'une loggia.

'Or. Cuisine du terroir et plats simples aux

09 – *info@labastide.com* – Fax 04 75 46 10 62

merc. soir et lundi

– **Rest** 16 € (déj. en sem.) 22/52 €

evigné, une cuisine traditionnelle servie dans un

de la terrasse. En hiver, spécialités de truffes.

ch,

ateliersdessaveurs@luciedurand.com

v.-30 déc., dim.

arte 100/140 €

ard. Canon d'agneau rôti au thym-citron. "Traou

tes de Provence

le ciel azuréen et sobre décor d'inspiration Napoléon

uisine unissant saveurs du Sud-Ouest et de Provence.

rest,

îles de Lérins

0.00 – *bellevue@free.fr* – Fax 04 93 67 81 78

voir plan d'Antibes AU **d**

ue de sable fin des Alpes-Maritimes.

ミシュランガイドの約束

「このガイドブックは、新しい世紀に誕生し、そしてその世紀とともに生き続けることだろう」

1900年のミシュランガイド創刊号の序文に記されたこの言葉は、年を追うごとに有名になっていき、そしてそれは的中しました。今日、ミシュランガイドが世界中で読まれている理由は、まさにミシュランガイドが読者に誓った約束を忠実に守り続けてきたからです。ここでもう一度、その約束を挙げてみましょう。

ミシュランガイドの5つの約束

匿名調査：調査員は、一般のお客様に提供されるサービスを評価する目的でホテル・レストランを定期的に匿名で訪問します。訪問先では宿泊や飲食の代金を支払います。時にはその後、より詳しい情報を得るために、身分を明かすこともあります。また読者から頂いた情報が調査員の訪問を方向づけるのに役立っています。

独立性：ホテル・レストランの選択は、読者の利益のみを考慮してミシュランが独自に行います。その決定は調査員たちと編集長が合議制による会議によってなされます。また、最も格式のある 星の授与はヨーロッパレベルで決められます。ホテル・レストランの掲載料は無料です。

選択：ミシュランガイドは、快適さ・値段別のすべてのカテゴリーのホテル・レストランの中から最良のものを厳選します。それは、すべての調査員が厳密に同じ方法を適用して調査した結果です。

毎年の更新：最も信頼できる情報を提供するため、ミシュランガイドでは毎年、情報、快適度、星の評価などの内容を見直し、更新します。

選択の一貫性：評価の基準は、ミシュランガイドによってカバーされている国において一貫しています。

…その目的はただ一つ。それは、ミシュラングループが掲げる「モビリティの向上への貢献」という使命に基づき、読者の皆様が移動する際に便宜を図り、できるだけ快適なひとときを過ごして頂けるよう、お手伝いしようとするものです。

読者の皆様へ

第99版「ミシュランガイド・フランス2008」をお届けいたします。ホテル・レストラン業界経験者の調査員スタッフにより、値段カテゴリー別に最良のホテル・レストランを厳選しました。調査員は毎年、その国を縦断し、新しいホテル・レストランを探して訪問します。すでにミシュランガイドに掲載されているものに関してはそのサービス内容をチェックします。また毎年、最も優れたレストランが選ばれ、✿から✿✿✿が授与されます。ミシュランガイドの星は、素材の選択、料理の個性、料理法と味付けの完成度、価格と質のバランス、料理全体の一貫性などを考慮し、あらゆるスタイルの最高の料理を提供するレストランに与えられます。

今年も多くのレストランが料理を向上させ、そして注目されました。« **N** »はミシュランガイド・フランス2008で初めて掲載されたレストランにつけられる印で、一つ星、二つ星、三つ星レストランの仲間入りしたことを告げるものです。さらに、当該カテゴリーの中で最高の « **ライジングスター** レストランが赤で表示されています。これらのレストランは、メニュー全体のクオリティと一貫性を高めることができれば、さらにその上の星への期待ができるというものです。この « ライジングスター »は、明日のガストロノミーを担った、期待されている星を読者の皆様にご紹介しようと設けられました。

特に« ライジングスター »に関するものなど、読者の皆様のご意見をお待ちしています。どんどんお寄せください。また、読者の皆様の参加は、調査員の訪問の方向づけを決定し、なによりもミシュランガイドが今後も充実した情報を提供していく上でとても貴重なものとなります。

最後になりましたが、ミシュランガイドをご愛読いただき、ありがとうございます。では、「ミシュランガイド2008」を携え、どうぞ良い旅をなさってください。

ミシュランガイドの公式サイト:
www.ViaMichelin.com

メールアドレス:
leguidemichelin-france@fr.michelin.com

Awards 2008

Distinctions 2008
Distinzioni 2008
Auszeichnungen 2008
Distinciones 2008

Starred establishments 2008

The colour corresponds to the establishment with the most stars in this location.

Paris	This location has at least one 3 star restaurant.	✻✻✻
Rouen	This location has at least one 2 star restaurant.	✻✻
Rennes	This location has at least one 1 star restaurant.	✻

Bondues
Lille
Ligny-en-Cambrésis
Rethondes
Sarreguemines
Courcelles-sur-Vesle
Zoufftgen
Phalsbourg
Untermuhlthal
Reuilly-Sauvigny
Stiring-Wendel
Lembach
Reims
Metz
Gundershoffen
Montchenot
Sarrebourg
L'Épine
Belleville
Marlenheim
Vinay
Châlons-en-Champagne
Nancy
La Wantzenau
Épernay
Obernai
Rosheim
Strasbourg
Pont-Ste-Marie
Lunéville
Illhaeusern
Colombey-les-Deux-Églises
Sens
Épinal
Vauchoux
Rixheim
C
Joigny
Mulhouse
Chablis
Riedisheim
Sierentz
Auxerre
Prenois
Landser
La Bussière-sur-Ouche
Dijon
Montbéliard
St-Père
Chamesol
Pernand-Vergelesses
Sampans
Bonnétage
Saulieu
Bouilland
Dole
Villers-le-Lac
Nevers
Beaune
Levernois
Port-Lesney
Morteau
Mercurey
Chagny
Arbois
Malbuisson
Sennecey-le-Grand
Montceau-les-Mines
Tournus
Roanne
St-Rémy
St-Priest-Bramefant
Vonnas
Veyrier-du-Lac
Vichy
Chamonix-Mont-Blanc
Mionnay
Annecy
Le Coteau
Megève
Bort-l'Étang
Lyon
St Martin-de-Belleville
Clermont-Ferrand
Le-Bourget-du-Lac
Charbonnières-les-Bains
Courchevel 1850
Vienne
D
St-Bonnet-le-Froid
Le Puy-en-Velay
Pont-de-l'Isère
Uriage-les-Bains
Corrençon-en-Vercors
Alleyras
Granges-les-Beaumont
Lamastre
Aumont-Aubrac
St-Agrève
Valence
Moustiers-Ste-Marie
Mougins
La Turbie
Les Baux-de-Provence
Eygalières
E
Tornac
Bonnieux
Grasse
Monte-Carlo
Montpellier
Ampus
Garons
Tourtour
Èze
Callas
Lorgues
Cannes
Beaulieu-sur-Mer
Marseille
Erbalunga
Grimaud
La Napoule
Béziers
Calvi
Narbonne
B
St-Tropez
Ile de Porquerolles
Aiguebelle
Perpignan
St-Cyprien
Collioure
Cala Rossa
Porto-Vecchio

Starred establishments 2008

The colour corresponds to the establishment with the most stars in this location.

Ile-de-France

Provence

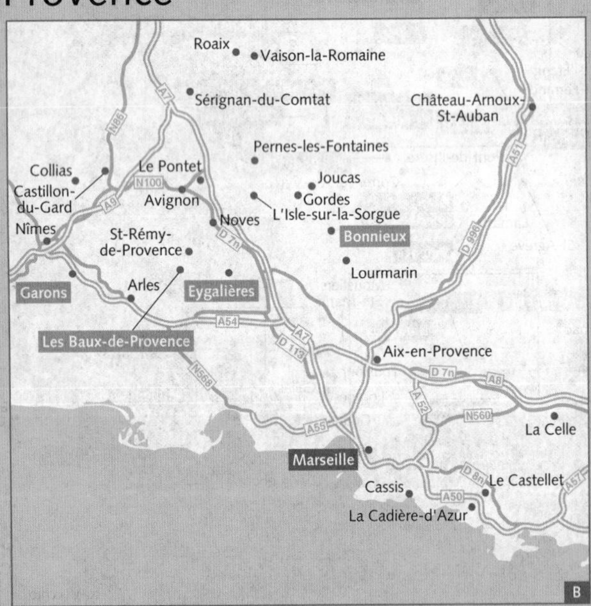

Alsace

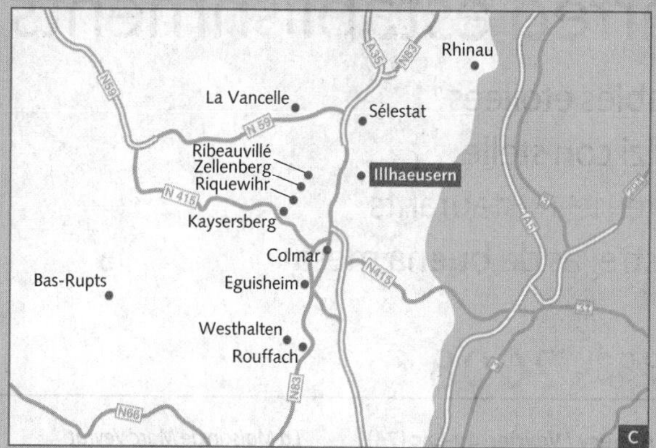

Rhône-Alpes

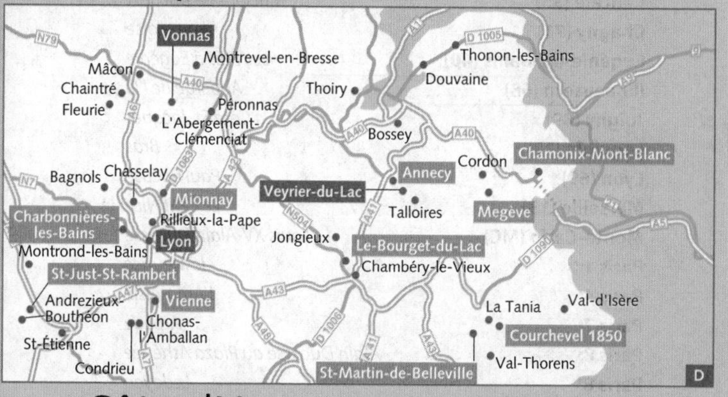

Côte-d'Azur

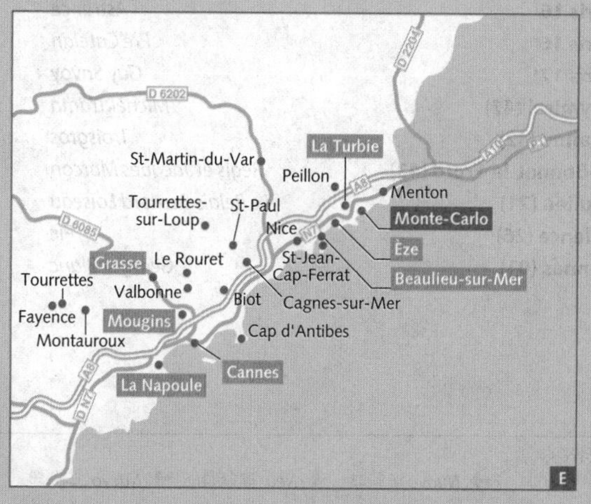

Starred establishments

Les tables étoilées

Esercizi con stelle

Die Sterne-Restaurants

Las estrellas de buena mesa

✿✿✿ 2008

Annecy / Veyrier-du-Lac (74)	*La Maison de Marc Veyrat*
Baerenthal / Untermuhlthal (57)	*L'Arnsbourg*
Cancale (35)	*Maisons de Bricourt*
Chagny (71)	*Lameloise*
Eugénie-les-Bains (40)	*Les Prés d'Eugénie*
Illhaeusern (68)	*Auberge de l'Ill*
Joigny (89)	*La Côte St-Jacques*
Laguiole (12)	*Bras*
Lyon (69)	*Paul Bocuse*
Marseille (13)	*Le Petit Nice* **N**
Monte-Carlo (MC)	*Le Louis XV-Alain Ducasse*
Paris 1er	*le Meurice*
Paris 4e	*L'Ambroisie*
Paris 7e	*Arpège*
Paris 8e	*Alain Ducasse au Plaza Athénée*
Paris 8e	*Ledoyen*
Paris 8e	*Pierre Gagnaire*
Paris 16e	*Astrance*
Paris 16e	*Pré Catelan*
Paris 17e	*Guy Savoy*
Puymirol (47)	*Michel Trama*
Roanne (42)	*Troisgros*
St-Bonnet-le-Froid (43)	*Régis et Jacques Marcon*
Saulieu (21)	*Le Relais Bernard Loiseau*
Valence (26)	*Pic*
Vonnas (01)	*Georges Blanc*

→ **N** *New* ✿✿✿

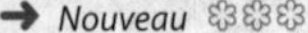

→ *Nouveau* ✿✿✿ → *Nuovo* ✿✿✿ → *Neu* ✿✿✿ → *Nuevo* ✿✿✿

✿✿ 2008

➜ **In red** *the 2008 Rising Stars for* ✿✿✿
➜ **En rouge** *les espoirs 2008 pour* ✿✿✿
➜ **In rosso** *le promesse 2008 per* ✿✿✿
➜ **In rote** *die Hoffnungsträger 2008 fur* ✿✿✿
➜ **In rojo** *las mesas 2008 con posibilidades para* ✿✿✿

Annecy (74) *Le Clos des Sens*
Arbois (39) *Jean-Paul Jeunet*
Les Baux-de-Provence (13) *L' Oustaù de Baumanière*
Beaulieu-sur-Mer (06) *La Réserve de Beaulieu*
Béthune / Busnes (62) *Le Château de Beaulieu*
Bonnieux (84) *La Bastide de Capelongue*
Le-Bourget-du-Lac (73) *Le Bateau Ivre*
Calvi (2B) *La Villa*
Cannes (06) *La Palme d'Or*
Carantec (29) *L'Hôtel de Carantec-Patrick Jeffroy*
Chamonix-Mont-Blanc (74) *Hameau Albert 1er*
Courchevel / Courchevel 1850 (73) *Le Bateau Ivre*
Courchevel / Courchevel 1850 (73) *Le Chabichou*
Eygalières (13) *Bistrot d'Eygalières "Chez Bru"*
Èze (06) *Château de la Chèvre d'Or*
Fontjoncouse (11) *Auberge du Vieux Puits*
Grasse (06) *La Bastide St-Antoine*
Gundershoffen (67) *Au Cygne*
L'Isle-Jourdain / Pujaudran (32) *Le Puits St-Jacques* **N**
Lorient (56) *L'Amphitryon*
Lyon (69) *Auberge de l'Île*
Lyon (69) *Nicolas Le Bec*
Lyon / Charbonnières-les-Bains (69) *La Rotonde*
Magescq (40) *Relais de la Poste*
Mandelieu / La Napoule (06) *L'Oasis*
Megève (74) *Flocons de Sel*
Mionnay (01) *Alain Chapel*
Monte-Carlo (MC) *Joël Robuchon Monte-Carlo*
Montpellier (34) *Le Jardin des Sens*
Mougins (06) *Alain Llorca - Le Moulin de Mougins*

Nantes / Haute-Goulaine (44) *Manoir de la Boulaie*
Nîmes / Garons (30) *Alexandre*
Obernai (67) *La Fourchette des Ducs*
Onzain (41) *Domaine des Hauts de Loire* **N**
Paris 1er *Carré des Feuillants*
Paris 1er *Le Grand Véfour*
Paris 6e *Hélène Darroze-La Salle à Manger*
Paris 6e *Relais Louis XIII*
Paris 7e *L'Atelier de Joël Robuchon* **N**
Paris 8e *Les Ambassadeurs*
Paris 8e *Apicius*
Paris 8e *Le Bristol*
Paris 8e *Le "Cinq"*
Paris 8e *Les Élysées*
Paris 8e *Lasserre*
Paris 8e *Senderens*
Paris 8e *Taillevent*
Paris 16e *La Table de Joël Robuchon*
Paris 17e *Michel Rostang*
Pau / Jurançon (64) *Chez Ruffet*
Pauillac (33) *Château Cordeillan Bages*
Reims (51) *Château les Crayères*
Reims (51) *L'Assiette Champenoise*
La Rochelle (17) *Richard et Christopher Coutanceau*
Romans-sur-Isère / Granges-les-Beaumont (26) *Les Cèdres*
Rouen (76) *Gill*
St-Émilion (33) *Hostellerie de Plaisance* **N**
St-Jean-Pied-de-Port (64) *Les Pyrénées* **N**
St-Just-St-Rambert (42) *Le Neuvième Art* **N**
St-Martin-de-Belleville (73) *La Bouitte* **N**
Sens (89) *La Madeleine*
Strasbourg (67) *Au Crocodile*
Toulouse (31) *Michel Sarran*
Toulouse / Colomiers (31) *L'Amphitryon* **N**
La Turbie (06) *Hostellerie Jérôme*
Uriage-les-Bains (38) *Grand Hôtel*
Vézelay / St-Père (89) *L'Espérance*
Vienne (38) *La Pyramide*

➜ **N** *New* ✿✿
➜ *Nouveau* ✿✿ ➜ *Nuovo* ✿✿ ➜ *Neu* ✿✿ ➜ *Nuevo* ✿✿

❀ 2008

→ **In red** *the 2008 Rising Stars for* ❀❀
→ **En rouge** *les espoirs 2008 pour* ❀❀
→ **In rosso** *le promesse 2008 per* ❀❀
→ **In rote** *die Hoffnungsträger 2008 fur* ❀❀
→ **In rojo** *las mesas 2008 con posibilidades para* ❀❀

Agen (47) *Mariottat*
Agen / Moirax (47) *Auberge le Prieuré* **N**
Ainhoa (64) *Ithurria*
Aix-en-Provence (13) *Le Clos de la Violette*
Aix-en-Provence (13) *Pierre Reboul* **N**
Albi (81) *L'Esprit du Vin*
Alleyras (43) *Le Haut-Allier*
Amboise (37) *Château de Pray* **N**
Amboise (37) *Le Choiseul*
Amiens / Dury (80) *L'Aubergade*
Ampus (83) *La Fontaine d'Ampus*
Andrézieux-Bouthéon (42) *Les Iris*
Anduze / Tornac (30) *Les Demeures du Ranquet*
Angers (49) *Le Favre d'Anne* **N**
Annecy (74) *Le Belvédère*
Annecy (74) *La Ciboulette*
Antibes / Cap d'Antibes (06) *Bacon*
Antibes / Cap d'Antibes (06) *Les Pêcheurs*
Arles (13) *L 'Atelier de Jean Luc Rabanel*
Arles (13) *Le Cilantro*
Arpajon (91) *Le Saint Clément*
Astaffort (47) *Le Square "Michel Latrille"*
Astaffort (47) *Une Auberge en Gascogne* **N**
Aulnay-sous-Bois (93) *Auberge des Saints Pères*
Aumont-Aubrac (48) *Chez Camillou*
Auxerre (89) *Barnabet*
Avignon (84) *Christian Étienne*
Avignon (84) *D'Europe*
Avignon (84) *La Mirande*
Avignon / Le Pontet (84) *Auberge de Cassagne*
Azay-le-Rideau / Saché (37) *Auberge du XIIe Siècle*
Bagnoles-de-l'Orne (61) *Le Manoir du Lys*
Bagnols (69) *Château de Bagnols*
Barneville-Carteret / Carteret (50) *De la Marine*
La Baule (44) *Castel Marie-Louise*
Les Baux-de-Provence (13) *La Cabro d'Or*
Bayeux / Audrieu (14) *Château d'Audrieu*
Bayonne (64) *Auberge du Cheval Blanc*
Beaune (21) *Le Bénaton*
Beaune (21) *Le Jardin des Remparts*
Beaune / Levernois (21) *Hostellerie de Levernois*
Beaune / Pernand-Vergelesses (21) *Charlemagne*
Béhuard (49) *Les Tonnelles*
Belcastel (12) *Vieux Pont*
Belle-Église (60) *La Grange de Belle-Eglise*
Belleville (54) *Le Bistroquet*
Beuvron-en-Auge (14) *Le Pavé d'Auge*
Les Bézards (45) *Auberge des Templiers*
Béziers (34) *L'Ambassade*
Béziers (34) *Octopus* **N**
Biarritz (64) *Du Palais*
Biarritz / Arcangues (64) *Le Moulin d'Alotz*
Bidart (64) *Table et Hostellerie des Frères Ibarboure*
Billiers (56) *Domaine de Rochevilaine* **N**
Biot (06) *Le Jarrier* **N**
Biot (06) *Les Terraillers*
Blois (41) *Au Rendez-vous des Pêcheurs*
Blois (41) *Le Médicis* **N**
Blois (41) *L'Orangerie du Château*
Bonnétage (25) *L'Etang du Moulin*
Bordeaux (33) *Le Chapon Fin*
Bordeaux (33) *Le Pavillon des Boulevards*
Bordeaux / Bouliac (33) *Le St-James*
Bordeaux / Cenon (33) *La Cape*
Bordeaux / Lormont (33) *Jean-Marie Amat* **N**
Bosdarros (64) *Auberge Labarthe*

Bougival (78) *Le Camélia*
Bouilland (21) *Hostellerie du Vieux Moulin*
Boulogne-Billancourt (92) *Au Comte de Gascogne*
Boulogne-sur-Mer (62) *La Matelote*
Le Bourg-Dun (76) *Auberge du Dun*
Bourg-en-Bresse / Péronnas (01) *La Marelle*
Bourges (18) *L'Abbaye St-Ambroix*
Le-Bourget-du-Lac (73) *Auberge Lamartine*
Le-Bourget-du-Lac (73) *La Grange à Sel*
Bracieux (41) *Bernard Robin - Le Relais de Bracieux*
Brantôme (24) *Le Moulin de l'Abbaye*
Brantôme / Champagnac-de-Belair (24) *Le Moulin du Roc*
Le Breuil-en-Auge (14) *Le Dauphin*
Briollay (49) *Château de Noirieux*
Le Buisson-de-Cadouin (24) *Le Manoir de Bellerive*
La Bussière-sur-Ouche (21) *Abbaye de la Bussière*
La Cadière-d'Azur (83) *Hostellerie Bérard*
Caen (14) *Le Pressoir*
Cagnes-sur-Mer (06) *Josy-Jo*
Cagnes-sur-Mer (06) *Le Cagnard*
Cahors / Lamagdelaine (46) *Claude et Richard Marco*
Cahors / Mercuès (46) *Château de Mercuès*
Cahuzac-sur-Vère (81) *Château de Salettes* **N**
Callas (83) *Hostellerie Les Gorges de Pennafort*
Calvinet (15) *Beauséjour*
Carcassonne (11) *De La Cité*
Carcassonne (11) *Domaine d'Auriac*
Carcassonne (11) *Le Parc Franck Putelat*
Cassis (13) *La Villa Madie* **N**
Le Castellet (83) *Du Castellet*
La Celle (83) *Hostellerie de l'Abbaye de la Celle*
Cergy-Pontoise / Cormeilles-en-Vexin (95) *Maison Cagna*
Chablis (89) *Hostellerie des Clos*
Chaintré (71) *La Table de Chaintré* **N**
Châlons-en-Champagne (51) *D'Angleterre*
Châlons-en-Champagne / L'Épine (51) *Aux Armes de Champagne*
Chalon-sur-Saône / St-Rémy (71) *Moulin de Martorey*
Chambéry / Chambéry-le-Vieux (73) *Château de Candie*
Chamesol (25) *Mon Plaisir*
Chamonix-Mont-Blanc (74) *Le Bistrot*
Champtoceaux (49) *Les Jardins de la Forge*
Chantilly (60) *Carmontelle* **N**
Chasselay (69) *Guy Lassausaie*
Château-Arnoux-St-Auban (04) *La Bonne Étape*
Châteaufort (78) *La Belle Époque*
Châtillon-sur-Chalaronne / L'Abergement-Clémenciat (01) *St-Lazare*
Chenonceaux (37) *Auberge du Bon Laboureur*
Chinon (37) *Au Plaisir Gourmand*
Chinon / Marçay (37) *Château de Marçay*
Clères / Frichemesnil (76) *Au Souper Fin*
Clermont / Étouy (60) *L'Orée de la Forêt*
Clermont-Ferrand (63) *Emmanuel Hodencq*
Clermont-Ferrand (63) *Jean-Claude Leclerc*
Collioure (66) *Le Neptune*
Colmar (68) *JY'S*
Colmar (68) *Rendez-vous de Chasse*
Colombey-les-Deux-Églises (52) *Hostellerie la Montagne*
Compiègne / Rethondes (60) *Alain Blot*
Condom (32) *La Table des Cordeliers* **N**
Condrieu (69) *Hôtellerie Beau Rivage*
Conques (12) *Le Moulin de Cambelong*
Conteville (27) *Auberge du Vieux Logis*
Cordes-sur-Ciel (81) *Le Grand Écuyer*
Cordon (74) *Les Roches Fleuries*
Couilly-Pont-aux-Dames (77) *Auberge de la Brie*
Courcelles-sur-Vesle (02) *Château de Courcelles*
Courchevel / La Tania (73) *Le Farçon*
Curzay-sur-Vonne (86) *Château de Curzay*
Dampierre-en-Yvelines (78) *Auberge du Château "Table des Blot"*
Dax (40) *Une Cuisine en Ville*
Deauville (14) *Royal-Barrière*
Dijon (21) *Hostellerie du Chapeau Rouge*

➜ **N** *New* ✿
➜ *Nouveau* ✿ ➜ *Nuovo* ✿ ➜ *Neu* ✿ ➜ *Nuevo* ✿

Dijon (21) *Le Pré aux Clercs*
Dijon (21) *Stéphane Derbord*
Dijon / Prenois (21) *Auberge de la Charme*
Dole (39) *La Chaumière* **N**
Dole / Sampans (39) *Château du Mont Joly* **N**
Douvaine (74) *Ô Flaveurs* **N**
Eguisheim (68) *Caveau d'Eguisheim*
Épernay (51) *Les Berceaux* **N**
Épernay / Vinay (51) *Hostellerie La Briqueterie*
Épinal (88) *Ducs de Lorraine*
Erbalunga (2B) *Le Pirate*
Escaldes-Engordany (AN) *Aquarius*
Èze (06) *Château Eza*
Fayence (83) *Le Castellaras*
Flers / La Ferrière-aux-Étangs (61) *Auberge de la Mine* **N**
Fleurie (69) *Le Cep*
Forbach / Stiring-Wendel (57) *La Bonne Auberge*
Gérardmer / Bas-Rupts (88) *Les Bas-Rupts*
Gordes (84) *Les Bories* **N**
La Gouesnière (35) *Maison Tirel-Guérin*
Grasse (06) *Lou Fassum "La Tourmaline"* **N**
Grenade-sur-l'Adour (40) *Pain Adour et Fantaisie*
Grimaud (83) *Les Santons*
Gujan-Mestras (33) *La Guérinière*
Hasparren (64) *Ferme Hégia*
Hennebont (56) *Château de Locguénolé*
Honfleur (14) *La Ferme St-Siméon*
Honfleur (14) *Sa. Qua. Na*
Honfleur (14) *La Terrasse et l'Assiette*
Île de Noirmoutier / L'Herbaudière (85) *La Marine*
Île de Porquerolles (83) *Mas du Langoustier*
Île de Ré / La Flotte (17) *Richelieu*
L'Isle-sur-la-Sorgue (84) *Le Vivier* **N**
Issoudun (36) *Rest. La Cognette*
Jarnac / Bourg-Charente (16) *La Ribaudière*
Jongieux (73) *Auberge Les Morainières*
Joucas (84) *Hostellerie Le Phébus*
Joucas (84) *Le Mas des Herbes Blanches*
Kaysersberg (68) *Chambard*
Lacave (46) *Château de la Treyne*
Lacave (46) *Pont de l'Ouysse*
Laguiole (12) *Grand Hôtel Auguy*
Lamastre (07) *Midi*
Langon (33) *Claude Darroze*
Lannion / la Ville Blanche (22) *La Ville Blanche*
Lastours (11) *Le Puits du Trésor*
Laval (53) *Bistro de Paris*
Le Lavandou / Aiguebelle (83) *Mathias Dandine*
Le Lavandou / Aiguebelle (83) *Le Sud*
Laventie (62) *Le Cerisier*
Lembach (67) *Auberge du Cheval Blanc*
Lezoux / Bort-l'Étang (63) *Château de Codignat*
Lièpvre / La Vancelle (67) *Auberge Frankenbourg*
Ligny-en-Cambrésis (59) *Château de Ligny*
Lille (59) *A L'Huîtrière*
Lille (59) *La Laiterie*
Lille (59) *Le Sébastopol*
Lille / Bondues **(59)** *Val d'Auge*
Limoges (87) *Amphitryon*
Limoges / St-Martin-du-Fault (87) *La Chapelle St-Martin*
Loiré (49) *Auberge de la Diligence* **N**
Lorgues (83) *Bruno*
Lorient (56) *Henri et Joseph*
Lourmarin (84) *Auberge La Fenière*
Lunéville (54) *Château d'Adoménil*
Lyon (69) *L'Alexandrin* **N**
Lyon (69) *Auberge de Fond Rose*
Lyon (69) *Christian Têtedoie*
Lyon (69) *Le Gourmet de Sèze*
Lyon (69) *Mathieu Viannay*
Lyon (69) *Pierre Orsi*
Lyon (69) *Les Terrasses de Lyon*
Lyon (69) *Les Trois Dômes*
Lyon / Rillieux-la-Pape (69) *Larivoire*
Mâcon (71) *Pierre*
Maisons-Laffitte (78) *Tastevin*
Malbuisson (25) *Le Bon Accueil*
Le Mans (72) *Beaulieu*
Marlenheim (67) *Le Cerf*
Marseille (13) *L'Épuisette*
Marseille (13) *Péron* **N**
Marseille (13) *Une Table au Sud*
Maury (66) *Pascal Borrell* **N**
Melun / Vaux-le-Pénil (77) *La Table St-Just*
Menton (06) *Mirazur*
Menton (06) *Paris Rome*
Mercurey (71) *Hôtellerie du Val d'Or*
Metz (57) *Au Pampre d'Or*
Metz (57) *La Citadelle*
Metz (57) *L'Écluse*

Meudon (92) *L'Escarbille*
Missillac (44) *La Bretesche*
Montargis (45) *La Gloire*
Montauban (82) *Crowne Plaza* **N**
Montauroux (83) *Auberge des Fontaines d'Aragon*
Montbazon (37) *Chancelière "Jeu de Cartes"*
Montbéliard (25) *Le St-Martin* **N**
Montceau-les-Mines (71) *Le France*
Monte-Carlo (MC) *Bar Bœuf et Co*
Monte-Carlo (MC) *Grill de l'Hôtel de Paris*
Monte-Carlo (MC) *Vistamar*
Montreuil (62) *Château de Montreuil*
Montreuil / La Madelaine-sous-Montreuil (62) *Auberge de la Grenouillère* **N**
Montrevel-en-Bresse (01) *Léa*
Montrond-les-Bains (42) *Hostellerie La Poularde*
Morteau (25) *Auberge de la Roche*
Mougins (06) *Le Mas Candille*
Moustiers-Ste-Marie (04) *Bastide de Moustiers*
Mulhouse (68) *Il Cortile*
Mulhouse / Landser (68) *Hostellerie Paulus*
Mulhouse / à Riedisheim (68) *La Poste*
Mulhouse / Rixheim (68) *Le Manoir*
Nancy (54) *Le Grenier à Sel*
Nantes (44) *L'Atlantide*
Narbonne (11) *La Table St-Crescent*
Neuilly-sur-Seine (92) *La Truffe Noire*
Nevers (58) *Jean-Michel Couron*
Nice (06) *Chantecler*
Nice (06) *Jouni « Atelier du Goût »* **N**
Nice (06) *Keisuke Matsushima*
Nice (06) *L'Univers-Christian Plumail*
Nîmes (30) *Le Lisita*
Noves (13) *Auberge de Noves*
Obernai (67) *Le Bistro des Saveurs*
Orange / Sérignan-du-Comtat (84) *Le Pré du Moulin*
Paris 1er *L'Espadon*
Paris 1er *Gérard Besson*
Paris 1er *Goumard*
Paris 2e *Le Céladon*
Paris 2e *Le Pur' Grill* **N**
Paris 4e *Benoit*
Paris 5e *La Tour d'Argent*
Paris 6e *Jacques Cagna*
Paris 6e *Paris*
Paris 6e *Le Restaurant* **N**
Paris 6e *Ze Kitchen Galerie* **N**
Paris 7e *Aida* **N**
Paris 7e *Auguste*
Paris 7e *Le Divellec*
Paris 7e *Les Fables de La Fontaine*
Paris 7e *Gaya Rive Gauche par Pierre Gagnaire*
Paris 7e *Il Vino d'Enrico Bernardo* **N**
Paris 7e *Vin sur Vin*
Paris 7e *Le Violon d'Ingres*
Paris 8e *L'Angle du Faubourg*
Paris 8e *Le Chiberta*
Paris 8e *Copenhague*
Paris 8e *Dominique Bouchet*
Paris 8e *Laurent*
Paris 8e *Stella Maris*
Paris 8e *La Table du Lancaster*
Paris 9e *Jean*
Paris 12e *Au Trou Gascon*
Paris 14e *Maison Courtine*
Paris 14e *Montparnasse'25*
Paris 16e *Hiramatsu*
Paris 16e *La Grande Cascade*
Paris 16e *Passiflore*
Paris 16e *Le Pergolèse*
Paris 16e *Relais d'Auteuil*
Paris 16e *La Table du Baltimore*
Paris 17e *Bath's*
Paris 17e *La Braisière*
Peillon (06) *Auberge de la Madone*
Périgueux (24) *L'Essentiel* **N**
Pernes-les-Fontaines (84) *Au Fil du Temps*
Perpignan (66) *La Galinette*
Le Perreux-sur-Marne (94) *Les Magnolias*
Perros-Guirec (22) *La Clarté*
Le-Petit-Pressigny (37) *La Promenade*
Phalsbourg (57) *Au Soldat de l'An II*
La Plaine-sur-Mer (44) *Anne de Bretagne*
Plancoët (22) *Crouzil et Hôtel L'Ecrin*
Plomodiern (29) *Auberge des Glazicks*

→ **N** *New* ✿
→ *Nouveau* ✿ → *Nuovo* ✿ → *Neu* ✿ → *Nuevo* ✿

Poitiers / St-Benoît (86) *Passions et Gourmandises* **N**
La Pomarède (11) *Hostellerie du Château de la Pomarède*
Pont-Aven (29) *Moulin de Rosmadec*
Pont-Aven (29) *La Taupinière*
Pont-du-Gard / Castillon-du-Gard (30) *Le Vieux Castillon*
Pont-du-Gard / Collias (30) *Hostellerie Le Castellas*
Port-Lesney (39) *Château de Germigney*
Port-Louis (56) *Avel Vor*
Porto-Vecchio (2A) *Belvédère*
Porto-Vecchio (2A) *Casadelmar*
Porto-Vecchio (2A) *Grand Hôtel de Cala Rossa*
Port-sur-Saône / Vauchoux (70) *Château de Vauchoux*
Le Puy-en-Velay (43) *François Gagnaire*
Questembert (56) *Le Bretagne et sa Résidence*
Quimper (29) *La Roseraie de Bel Air*
Reims (51) *Foch*
Reims (51) *Le Millénaire*
Reims / Montchenot (51) *Grand Cerf*
Rennes (35) *Coq-Gadby* **N**
Rennes (35) *La Fontaine aux Perles*
Rennes / Noyal-sur-Vilaine (35) *Auberge du Pont d'Acigné*
Rennes / St-Grégoire (35) *Le Saison*
Reuilly-Sauvigny (02) *Auberge Le Relais*
Rhinau (67) *Au Vieux Couvent*
Ribeauvillé (68) *Au Valet de Cœur et Hostel de la Pépinière*
Riquewihr (68) *Table du Gourmet*
Riquewihr / Zellenberg (68) *Maximilien*
Roanne / Le Coteau (42) *L'Auberge Costelloise*
La Roche-Bernard (56) *L'Auberge Bretonne*
La Roche-l'Abeille (87) *Le Moulin de la Gorce*
Rodez (12) *Goûts et Couleurs*
Romorantin-Lanthenay (41) *Grand Hôtel du Lion d'Or*
Roscoff (29) *Le Brittany*
Roscoff (29) *Le Temps de Vivre*
Rosheim (67) *Hostellerie du Rosenmeer*
Rouen (76) *L'Écaille*
Rouen (76) *Les Nymphéas*
Rouffach (68) *Philippe Bohrer*
Le Rouret (06) *Le Clos St-Pierre*
Roye (80) *La Flamiche*

Les Sables-d'Olonne / Anse de Cayola (85) *Cayola*
Sables-d'Or-les-Pins (22) *La Voile d'Or - La Lagune*
St-Agrève (07) *Faurie* **N**
St-Brieuc (22) *Aux Pesked*
St-Brieuc (22) *Youpala Bistrot*
St-Brieuc / Sous-la-Tour (22) *La Vieille Tour*
St-Céré (46) *Les Trois Soleils de Montal*
St-Cyprien (66) *L'Île de la Lagune*
St-Étienne (42) *Nouvelle*
St-Félix-Lauragais (31) *Auberge du Poids Public*
St-Jean-Cap-Ferrat (06) *Grand Hôtel du Cap Ferrat* **N**
St-Jean-de-Luz (64) *Grand Hôtel*
St-Julien-en-Genevois / Bossey (74) *La Ferme de l'Hospital*
St-Lyphard (44) *Auberge de Kerbourg*
St-Malo (35) *A la Duchesse Anne*
St-Malo (35) *Le Chalut*
St-Malo / St-Servan-sur-Mer (35) *Le St-Placide*
St-Martin-du-Var (06) *Jean-François Issautier*
Saint-Maur-des-Fossés / La Varenne-St-Hilaire (94) *La Bretèche*
St-Médard (46) *Gindreau*
St-Paul (06) *Le Saint-Paul*
St-Priest-Bramefant (63) *Château de Maulmont*
St-Rémy-de-Provence (13) *La Maison Jaune*
St-Rémy-de-Provence (13) *La Maison de Bournissac*
St-Savin (86) *Christophe Cadieu*
St-Sulpice-le-Verdon (85) *Thierry Drapeau Logis de la Chabotterie*
St-Tropez (83) *Résidence de la Pinède*
St-Tropez (83) *Villa Belrose*
Sarlat-la-Canéda (24) *Le Grand Bleu* **N**
Sarrebourg (57) *Mathis*
Sarreguemines (57) *Auberge St-Walfrid*
Sarreguemines (57) *Thierry Breininger - Le Vieux Moulin*
Saubusse (40) *Villa Stings*
La Saussaye (27) *Manoir des Saules*
Sauveterre-de-Rouergue (12) *Le Sénéchal*
Sélestat (67) *Hostellerie de l'Abbaye la Pommeraie*

Sénart / Pouilly-le-Fort (77)	*Le Pouilly*	**Tourtour (83)**	*Les Chênes Verts*
Sennecey-le-Grand (71)	*L'Amaryllis* **N**	**Trébeurden (22)**	*Manoir de Lan-Kerellec*
Sierentz (68)	*Auberge St-Laurent*	**Le Tremblay-sur-Mauldre (78)**	*Laurent Trochain*
Sousceyrac (46)	*Au Déjeuner de Sousceyrac* **N**	**Trémolat (24)**	*Vieux Logis*
La Souterraine (23)	*Château de la Cazine*	**Troyes / Pont-Ste-Marie (10)**	*Hostellerie de Pont-Ste-Marie*
Strasbourg (67)	*Buerehiesel* **N**	**Urt (64)**	*Auberge de la Galupe*
Strasbourg (67)	*La Casserole* **N**	**Vailly-sur-Sauldre (18)**	*Le Lièvre Gourmand*
Strasbourg (67)	*Serge and Co*	**Vaison-la-Romaine (84)**	*Le Moulin à Huile*
Strasbourg / La Wantzenau (67)	*Relais de la Poste*	**Vaison-la-Romaine / Roaix (84)**	*Le Grand Pré*
Talloires (74)	*L'Auberge du Père Bise*	**Valbonne (06)**	*Lou Cigalon*
Tarbes (65)	*L'Ambroisie*	**Val-d'Isère (73)**	*Les Barmes de l'Ours*
Terrasson-Lavilledieu (24)	*L'Imaginaire*	**Valence / Pont-de-l'Isère (26)**	*Michel Chabran*
Thoiry (01)	*Les Cépages*	**Val-Thorens (73)**	*L'Oxalys*
Thonon-les-Bains (74)	*Le Prieuré*	**Vannes / St-Avé (56)**	*Le Pressoir*
Toulouse (31)	*En Marge* **N**	**Vichy (03)**	*Jacques Decoret*
Toulouse (31)	*Metropolitan* **N**	**Vienne / Chonas-l'Amballan (38)**	*Domaine de Clairefontaine*
Toulouse / Rouffiac-Tolosan (31)	*Ô Saveurs*	**Vierzon (18)**	*La Maison de Célestin* **N**
Le Touquet-Paris-Plage (62)	*Westminster*	**Villard-de-Lans / Corrençon-en-Vercors (38)**	*du Golf* **N**
Tournus (71)	*Aux Terrasses*	**Villers-le-Lac (25)**	*Le France* **N**
Tournus (71)	*Rest. Greuze*	**Westhalten (68)**	*Auberge du Cheval Blanc*
Tourrettes (83)	*Faventia*	**Wimereux (62)**	*Epicure*
Tourrettes-sur-Loup (06)	*Les Bacchanales* **N**	**Zoufftgen (57)**	*La Lorraine*
Tours (37)	*Charles Barrier*		
Tours (37)	*La Roche Le Roy*		
Tours / Rochecorbon (37)	*Les Hautes Roches*		

→ **N** *Nouveau* ✿
→ *New* ✿ → *Nuovo* ✿ → *Neu* ✿ → *Nuevo* ✿

The 2008 Rising Stars for ✿

Les espoirs 2008 pour ✿

Le promesse 2008 per ✿

Die Hoffnungsträger fur ✿

Las mesas 2008 con posibilidades para ✿

Bourges (18)	*Le d'Antan Sancerrois*	**Lannilis (29)**	*Auberge des Abers*
Le-Bourget-du-Lac / Les Catons (73)	*Atmosphères*	**La Malène (48)**	*Château de la Caze*
Cholet (49)	*Au Passé Simple*	**Marseille (13)**	*Charles Livon*
Clermont-Ferrand (63)	*Fleur de Sel*	**Nevez (29)**	*Ar Men Du*
Grenoble (38)	*Le Fantin Latour*	**Nice (06)**	*Les Viviers*
Istres (13)	*La Table de Sébastien*	**Niederschaeffolsheim (67)**	*Au Bœuf Rouge*
		Ventabren (13)	*La Table de Ventabren*

Stars on the move

■ *Starred in the 2007 guide, several establishments have subsequently changed owner or simply changed address. In an effort to keep you informed, here is the latest information…*

➜ in Cannes (06)

At the **Villa des Lys**, the restaurant is being relocated to the entrance of the Hôtel Majestic. The opening date is yet to be announced.

➜ at Châteaumeillant (18)

The chef of the **Piet à Terre** has closed his establishment and plans to reopen in Bourges.

➜ in Lyon (69)

On the 31 December 2007, Jean-Paul Lacombe presided over the last "gastronomic" sitting at **Léon de Lyon**. His contemporary brasserie (with the same name) is due to open in March 2008.

➜ in Paris (75)

The team from the **Chamarré** has crossed the river to the Moulin de la Galette. Antoine Meerah sold his establishment on the bd Tour-Maubourg to d'Enrico Bernardo, the World's Best Sommelier 2004, who transformed it into Il Vino d'Enrico Bernardo (a second such restaurant has opened in Courchevel 1850).

➔ in Saint-Rémy de Provence (13)

Pierre Reboul has opened in Aix-en-Provence where he has regained a star at his eponymous restaurant.

➔ at Tours (37)

Chef-patron **Jean Bardet** has put his establishment up for sale.

➔ at Vence (06)

Jacques Maximin's La Table d'Amis has closed. Holder of two stars for more than a quarter of a century, the chef (Meilleur Ouvrier de France) joins the Groupe Alain Ducasse.

➔ in Versailles (78)

Gérard Vié has left **Les Trois Marches**. His successor at the Trianon Palace is Gordon Ramsay.

Bib Gourmand

Good food at moderate prices
Repas soignés à prix modérés
Pasti accurati a prezzi contenuti
Sorgfältig zubereitete, preiswerte mahlzeiten
Buenas comidas a precios moderados

Abbeville (80)	*La Corne*	N
Agde / Le Grau-d'Agde (34)	*L'Adagio*	
Agen (47)	*Le Margoton*	N
Aiguebelette-le-Lac / Novalaise (73)	*Novalaise-Plage*	
Aire-sur-la-Lys / Isbergues (62)	*Le Buffet*	
Aix-en-Provence / Le Canet (13)	*L'Auberge Provençale*	
Aizenay (85)	*La Sittelle*	N
Ajaccio (2A)	*U Licettu*	
Alès / Méjannes-lès-Alès (30)	*Auberge des Voutins*	N
Altwiller (67)	*L 'Écluse 16*	
Ambert (63)	*Les Copains*	
Ambierle (42)	*Le Prieuré*	
Ambronay (01)	*Auberge de l'Abbaye*	
Amiens (80)	*Au Relais des Orfèvres*	
Amiens / Dury (80)	*La Bonne Auberge*	
Ammerschwihr (68)	*Aux Armes de France*	
Ancenis (44)	*La Toile à Beurre*	
Angers (49)	*Le Petit Comptoir*	
Angers (49)	*Le Relais*	
Angoulême (16)	*L'Aromate*	
Angoulême (16)	*Le Terminus*	
Annecy (74)	*Contresens*	
Annonay (07)	*Marc et Christine*	N
Antibes (06)	*Oscar's*	
Antraigues-sur-Volane (07)	*La Remise*	
Argoules (80)	*Auberge du Coq-en-Pâte*	
Asnières-sur-Seine (92)	*La Petite Auberge*	
Aube (61)	*Auberge St-James*	
Aumale (76)	*Villa des Houx*	
Aumont-Aubrac (48)	*Le Compostelle*	
Aurillac (15)	*Quatre Saisons*	
Auvers-sur-Oise (95)	*Auberge Ravoux*	N
Auxerre (89)	*Le Bourgogne*	N
Auxerre / Vincelottes (89)	*Auberge Les Tilleuls*	
Avallon / Valloux (89)	*Auberge des Chenêts*	
Avignon (84)	*L'Isle Sonnante*	
Ax-les-Thermes (09)	*Le Chalet*	
Azay-le-Rideau (37)	*L'Aigle d'Or*	
Baden (56)	*Le Gavrinis*	
Bâgé-le-Châtel (01)	*La Table Bâgésienne*	
Ban-de-Laveline (88)	*Auberge Lorraine*	
Bandol (83)	*Le Clocher*	
Banyuls-sur-Mer (66)	*Al Fanal et H. El Llagut*	
Barr (67)	*Aux Saisons Gourmandes*	N
Bar-sur-Aube (10)	*La Toque Baralbine*	
Bastia (2B)	*La Corniche*	
La Bâtie-Divisin (38)	*L'Olivier*	
Bayonne (64)	*Bayonnais*	
Bayonne (64)	*François Miura*	
Beaune (21)	*La Ciboulette*	
Beaune / Ladoix-Serrigny (21)	*Les Terrasses de Corton*	
Beaune / Levernois (21)	*La Garaudière*	
Beauzac (43)	*L'Air du Temps*	
Beauzac / Bransac (43)	*La Table du Barret*	
Bédarieux / Villemagne-l'Argentière (34)	*Auberge de l'Abbaye*	
Bellême / Nocé (61)	*Auberge des 3 J.*	
Belleville (69)	*Le Beaujolais*	
Bergerac / Moulin de Malfourat (24)	*La Tour des Vents*	
Bergheim (68)	*Wistub du Sommelier*	
La Bernerie-en-Retz (44)	*L'Artimon*	N
Bernières-sur-Mer (14)	*L'As de Trèfle*	
Le Bessat (42)	*La Fondue "Chez l'Père Charles"*	
Béthune / Busnes (62)	*Le Jardin d'Alice*	N

Biarritz (64) *Le Clos Basque*
Bidarray (64) *Auberge Iparla*
Blangy-sur-Bresle (76) *Les Pieds dans le Plat*
Blienschwiller (67) *Le Pressoir de Bacchus* **N**
Bois-Colombes (92) *Le Chefson*
Bonlieu (39) *La Poutre*
Bonneuil-Matours (86) *Le Pavillon Bleu*
Bonneville / Vougy (74) *Le Bistro du Capucin*
Bonny-sur-Loire (45) *Voyageurs*
Bordeaux (33) *Gravelier*
Boudes (63) *Le Boudes La Vigne* **N**
Bourg-en-Bresse (01) *Mets et Vins* **N**
Bourg-en-Bresse (01) *Les Quatre Saisons* **N**
Bourg-Saint-Maurice (73) *L'Arssiban*
Bourth (27) *Auberge Chantecler*
Bouzel (63) *L'Auberge du Ver Luisant*
Bozouls (12) *A la Route d'Argent*
Bracieux (41) *Le Rendez vous des Gourmets* **N**
La Bresse (88) *Le Clos des Hortensias*
Brest (29) *Ma Petite Folie*
Bretenoux / Port-de-Gagnac (46) *Hostellerie Belle Rive*
Brévonnes (10) *Au Vieux Logis*
Briançon (05) *Le Péché Gourmand*
Brioude (43) *Poste et Champanne*
Brive-la-Gaillarde (19) *La Toupine*
Brou (28) *L'Ascalier*
Buellas (01) *L'Auberge Bressane* **N**
Bully (69) *Auberge du Château* **N**
Buxy (71) *Aux Années Vins*
Buzançais (36) *L'Hermitage*
Cabourg / Dives-sur-Mer (14) *Chez le Bougnat*
Caen (14) *Café Mancel*
Cahors (46) *La Garenne*
Cahors (46) *L'Ô à la Bouche*
Calais (62) *Au Côte d'Argent*
Cambrai (59) *Auberge Fontenoise*
Cancale (35) *Surcouf* **N**
Cannes (06) *Comme Chez Soi*
Carhaix-Plouguer / Port-de-Carhaix (29) *Auberge du Poher*
Carignan (08) *La Gourmandière*
Carmaux (81) *Au Chapon Tarnais*
Casteljaloux (47) *La Vieille Auberge* **N**
Castellane / La Garde (04) *Auberge du Teillon*
Castéra-Verduzan (32) *Le Florida*
Castillon-en-Couserans / Audressein (09) *L'Auberge d'Audressein*
Caussade / Monteils (82) *Le Clos Monteils* **N**
Chablis (89) *Laroche Wine Bar* **N**
Challans / La Garnache (85) *Le Petit St-Thomas*
Challans / Le Perrier (85) *Les Tendelles*
Chalon-sur-Saône (71) *L'Air du Temps*
Chalon-sur-Saône (71) *L'Auberge des Alouettes*
Chamonix-Mont-Blanc (74) *Atmosphère*
Chamonix-Mont-Blanc (74) *L'Impossible* **N**
Chamonix-Mont-Blanc (74) *La Maison Carrier*
Chamonix-Mont-Blanc / Les Praz-de-Chamonix (74) *La Cabane des Praz* **N**
Chandolas (07) *Auberge les Murets*
La Chapelle-d'Abondance (74) *L'Ensoleillé*
La Chapelle-d'Abondance (74) *Les Gentianettes*
Charette (38) *Auberge du Vernay*
Charleville-Mézières (08) *La Table d' Artur «R»* **N**
Charroux (03) *Ferme Saint-Sébastien*
Chartres (28) *St-Hilaire* **N**
Château-Arnoux-St-Auban (04) *Au Goût du Jour*
Château-Gontier / Coudray (53) *L'Amphitryon*
Châtelaillon-Plage (17) *Les Flots*
Châtellerault (86) *Bernard Gautier*
Chauffailles / Châteauneuf (71) *La Fontaine*
Chénérailles (23) *Coq d'Or*
Cherbourg-Octeville (50) *Café de Paris*
Cherbourg-Octeville (50) *Le Pily* **N**
Cherbourg-Octeville (50) *Le Vauban*
Chilleurs-aux-Bois (45) *Lancelot* **N**
Chinon (37) *L'Océanic* **N**
Chisseaux (37) *Auberge du Cheval Rouge*
Cholet (49) *La Grange*
Clères (76) *Auberge du Moulin*
Clermont-Ferrand (63) *Amphitryon Capucine*
Clermont-Ferrand / Orcines (63) *Auberge de la Baraque* **N**
Clermont-Ferrand / Puy de Dôme (63) *Mont Fraternité*
Clisson / Gétigné (44) *La Gétignière*
Col de la Schlucht (88) *Le Collet*
Coligny (01) *Au Petit Relais*

- **Colmar (68)** *Aux Trois Poissons*
- **Colmar (68)** *Chez Hansi*
- **Colmar / Ingersheim (68)** *La Taverne Alsacienne*
- **Combeaufontaine (70)** *Le Balcon*
- **Conilhac-Corbières (11)** *Auberge Côté Jardin*
- **Conques (12)** *Auberge St-Jacques*
- **Contamine-sur-Arve (74)** *Le Tourne Bride*
- **Cordon (74)** *Le Cordonant*
- **Coullons (45)** *La Canardière* **N**
- **Coulon (79)** *Le Central*
- **Le Creusot / Montcenis (71)** *Le Montcenis*
- **Le Croisic (44)** *Le Saint-Alys* **N**
- **Crozon (29)** *Le Mutin Gourmand*
- **Cucugnan (11)** *Auberge de Cucugnan*
- **Daglan (24)** *Le Petit Paris*
- **Dax (40)** *L'Amphitryon*
- **Dijon / Chenôve (21)** *Le Clos du Roy*
- **Douarnenez (29)** *Le Clos de Vallombreuse*
- **Doué-la-Fontaine (49)** *Auberge Bienvenue*
- **Dourgne (81)** *Les Saveurs de St-Avit*
- **Draguignan / Flayosc (83)** *L'Oustaou*
- **Dunes (82)** *Les Templiers*
- **Dunières (43)** *La Tour*
- **Dunkerque / Coudekerque-Branche (59)** *Le Soubise*
- **Espalion (12)** *Le Méjane*
- **Estaing (12)** *L' Auberge St-Fleuret*
- **Évron (53)** *Relais du Gué de Selle* **N**
- **Évron (53)** *La Toque des Coëvrons*
- **Eygalières (13)** *Sous Les Micocouliers* **N**
- **Les Eyzies-de-Tayac (24)** *La Métairie*
- **Faverges (74)** *Florimont*
- **Favières (80)** *La Clé des Champs* **N**
- **Fléré-la-Rivière (36)** *Le Relais du Berry*
- **Florac (48)** *Des Gorges du Tarn*
- **Florac / Cocurès (48)** *La Lozerette*
- **Fondamente (12)** *Baldy*
- **Fontvieille (13)** *Le Patio* **N**
- **Fontvieille (13)** *La Table du Meunier*
- **Fouday (67)** *Julien*
- **Fouesnant / Cap-Coz (29)** *De la Pointe du Cap Coz*
- **Francescas (47)** *Le Relais de la Hire* **N**
- **Fréjus (83)** *L'Amandier*
- **Fréjus (83)** *Les Potiers*
- **Fresnicourt (62)** *Auberge du Donjon*
- **Froncles-Buxières (52)** *Au Château*
- **Gagny (93)** *Le Vilgacy*
- **Gasny (27)** *Auberge du Prieuré Normand*
- **Gassin (83)** *Auberge la Verdoyante*
- **Geneston (44)** *Le Pélican*
- **Gigondas (84)** *Les Florets*
- **Gilette / Vescous (06)** *La Capeline*
- **Gourdon (46)** *Hostellerie de la Bouriane*
- **Grandcamp-Maisy (14)** *La Marée*
- **Grandvillers (88)** *Europe et Commerce* **N**
- **Grenoble (38)** *Le Coup de Torchon*
- **Gresse-en-Vercors (38)** *Le Chalet*
- **Grignan (26)** *Le Probus*
- **La Guerche-de-Bretagne (35)** *Calèche*
- **Guilliers (56)** *Au Relais du Porhoët*
- **Le Havre (76)** *La Petite Auberge* **N**
- **Honfleur (14)** *Le Bréard*
- **Honfleur (14)** *Entre Terre et Mer*
- **Houlgate (14)** *L'Eden*
- **Île de Noirmoutier / Noirmoutier-en-l'Île (85)** *Le Grand Four*
- **L'Isle-sur-Serein (89)** *Auberge du Pot d'Étain*
- **Les Issambres (83)** *Chante-Mer*
- **Kaysersberg (68)** *À l'Arbre Vert*
- **Lacapelle-Marival (46)** *La Terrasse*
- **Lanarce (07)** *Le Provence* **N**
- **Langeac / Reilhac (43)** *Val d'Allier*
- **Langon / St-Macaire (33)** *Abricotier*
- **Languimberg (57)** *Chez Michèle*
- **Lantosque (06)** *La Source*
- **Lapalisse (03)** *Galland*
- **Lapoutroie (68)** *Les Alisiers*
- **Largentière / Sanilhac (07)** *Auberge de la Tour de Brison* **N**
- **Larrau (64)** *Etchemaïté*
- **Lavelanet / Nalzen (09)** *Les Sapins*
- **Leutenheim (67)** *Auberge Au Vieux Couvent*
- **Libourne (33)** *Chez Servais* **N**
- **Lièpvre / La Vancelle (67)** *Elisabeth*
- **Liessies (59)** *Le Carillon*
- **Lille (59)** *La Coquille*
- **Lille / Capinghem (59)** *La Marmite de Pierrot*
- **Limoges (87)** *Le Vanteaux*
- **Longueville-sur-Scie (76)** *Le Cheval Blanc*
- **Lorris (45)** *Guillaume de Lorris*
- **Le Luc (83)** *Le Gourmandin*
- **Luçon (85)** *La Mirabelle*
- **Lyon (69)** *Le Bistrot de St-Paul*
- **Lyon (69)** *Daniel et Denise*
- **Lyon (69)** *L'Est*
- **Lyon (69)** *Le Garet*
- **Lyon (69)** *Magali et Martin*
- **Lyon (69)** *33 Cité* **N**
- **Lyon (69)** *Le Verre et l'Assiette*
- **Malbuisson / Granges-Ste-Marie (25)** *Auberge du Coude*
- **Mancey (71)** *Auberge du Col des Chèvres*
- **Mansle / Luxé (16)** *Auberge du Cheval Blanc*

Manzac-sur-Vern (24)	*Le Lion d'Or*	
Margaux / Arcins (33)	*Le Lion d'Or*	
Marseillan (34)	*Chez Philippe*	
Maussane-les-Alpilles / Paradou (13)	*Bistrot de la Petite France*	
Mazaye (63)	*Auberge de Mazayes*	
Mélisey (70)	*La Bergeraine*	
Mende (48)	*Le Mazel*	
Mende (48)	*La Safranière*	
Messery (74)	*Atelier des Saveurs*	
Meyronne (46)	*La Terrasse*	
Meyrueis (48)	*Du Mont Aigoual*	
Minerve (34)	*Relais Chantovent*	
Mittelbergheim (67)	*Am Lindeplatzel*	
Mittelbergheim (67)	*Gilg*	**N**
Les Molunes (39)	*Le Pré Fillet*	
Monestier-de-Clermont (38)	*Au Sans Souci*	
Montbrison / Savigneux (42)	*Yves Thollot*	
Montech (82)	*La Maison de l'Eclusier*	
Montmorillon (86)	*Hôtel de France et Lucullus*	
Montpellier (34)	*Prouhèze Saveurs*	**N**
Montpon-Ménestérol / Ménestérol (24)	*Auberge de l'Eclade*	**N**
Montreuil / Inxent (62)	*Auberge d'Inxent*	
Montsalvy (15)	*L'Auberge Fleurie*	
Montsoreau (49)	*Diane de Méridor*	
Mur-de-Barrez (12)	*Auberge du Barrez*	
Najac (12)	*Le Belle Rive*	
Najac (12)	*L' Oustal del Barry*	
Nancy (54)	*V Four*	
Nantes (44)	*La Divate*	
Nantes / Couëron (44)	*François II*	
Nantes / St-Herblain (44)	*Les Caudalies*	
Narbonne / Bages (11)	*Le Portanel*	
Natzwiller (67)	*Auberge Metzger*	
Neufchâtel-sur-Aisne (02)	*Le Jardin*	
Neuillé-le-Lierre (37)	*Auberge de la Brenne*	
Nevers (58)	*Le Bengy*	**N**
Nevers / Sauvigny-les-Bois (58)	*Moulin de l'Étang*	
Neyrac-les-Bains (07)	*Du Levant*	
Nice (06)	*Au Rendez-vous des Amis*	
Niedersteinbach (67)	*Cheval Blanc*	
Nîmes (30)	*Aux Plaisirs des Halles*	
Nîmes (30)	*Le Bouchon et L'Assiette*	
Nogent-le-Roi (28)	*Relais des Remparts*	
Nogent-sur-Seine (10)	*Beau Rivage*	
Notre-Dame-de-Bellecombe (73)	*Ferme de Victorine*	
Noyalo (56)	*L'Hortensia*	**N**
Nuits-St-Georges (21)	*La Cabotte*	**N**
Nyons (26)	*Le Petit Caveau*	
Obernai / Ottrott (67)	*À l'Ami Fritz*	
Oisly (41)	*St-Vincent*	**N**
Orléans (45)	*La Dariole*	
Orléans (45)	*Eugène*	
Orléans / Olivet (45)	*Laurendière*	
Ornans (25)	*Courbet*	
Oucques (41)	*Du Commerce*	
Pailherols (15)	*Auberge des Montagnes*	
Paimpol (22)	*De la Marne*	
Pamiers (09)	*De France*	
Paris 1er	*Au Gourmand*	**N**
Paris 2e	*Aux Lyonnais*	
Paris 3e	*Ambassade d'Auvergne*	
Paris 5e	*Buisson Ardent*	
Paris 5e	*Papilles*	**N**
Paris 5e	*Ribouldingue*	
Paris 6e	*L'Épi Dupin*	
Paris 6e	*Fish La Boissonnerie*	
Paris 6e	*La Rotonde*	
Paris 7e	*L'Affriolé*	
Paris 7e	*Au Bon Accueil*	
Paris 7e	*Café Constant*	**N**
Paris 7e	*Chez l'Ami Jean*	
Paris 7e	*Chez les Anges*	
Paris 7e	*Clos des Gourmets*	
Paris 7e	*P'tit Troquet*	
Paris 9e	*Carte Blanche*	
Paris 9e	*L'Oenothèque*	**N**
Paris 9e	*La Petite Sirène de Copenhague*	
Paris 9e	*Le Pré Cadet*	
Paris 9e	*Spring*	
Paris 10e	*Café Panique*	**N**
Paris 10e	*Chez Michel*	**N**
Paris 10e	*Urbane*	**N**
Paris 11e	*Auberge Pyrénées Cévennes*	
Paris 11e	*Mansouria*	
Paris 11e	*Le Temps au Temps*	
Paris 12e	*Jean-Pierre Frelet*	
Paris 14e	*La Cerisaie*	
Paris 14e	*La Régalade*	
Paris 14e	*Severo*	
Paris 15e	*Afaria*	**N**
Paris 15e	*Le Bélisaire*	
Paris 15e	*Beurre Noisette*	
Paris 15e	*Caroubier*	
Paris 15e	*Le Dirigeable*	**N**
Paris 15e	*Le Grand Pan*	**N**
Paris 15e	*Stéphane Martin*	
Paris 15e	*Thierry Burlot « Le Quinze »*	
Paris 15e	*Le Troquet*	
Paris 16e	*A et M Restaurant*	**N**
Paris 16e	*Chez Géraud*	
Paris 17e	*Caves Petrissans*	

→ **N** *New* ☺ → *Nouveau* ☺ → *Nuovo* ☺ → *Neu* ☺ → *Nuevo* ☺

Paris 17e *Chez Mathilde-Paris XVII*
Paris 17e *L'Entredgeu*
Paris 17e *Graindorge*
Paris 17e *La Soupière*
Paris 19e *La Cave Gourmande*
Paris 20e *Les Allobroges*
Pau / Lescar (64) *La Terrasse*
Péron (01) *Auberge Communale La Fruitière*
Perpignan (66) *Les Antiquaires*
La-Petite-Pierre / Graufthal (67) *Le Cheval Blanc* **N**
Phalsbourg (57) *Erckmann-Chatrian*
Plaisians (26) *Auberge de la Clue*
Pléneuf-Val-André / Le-Val-André (22) *Au Biniou*
Ploemeur / Lomener (56) *Le Vivier*
Ploubalay (22) *De la Gare*
Polliat (01) *De la Place*
Pons (17) *De Bordeaux*
Pont-de-Vaux (01) *Le Raisin*
Pontlevoy (41) *De l'École*
Les-Ponts-Neufs (22) *La Cascade*
Porto (2A) *Bella Vista*
Pouillon (40) *L'Auberge du Pas de Vent*
Puteaux (92) *La Table d'Alexandre*
Le Puy-en-Velay (43) *Tournayre*
Le Puy-en-Velay / Espaly-St-Marcel (43) *L'Ermitage*
Quarré-les-Tombes (89) *Le Morvan*
Quédillac (35) *Le Relais de la Rance*
Quiberon (56) *La Chaumine*
Quimper / Ty-Sanquer (29) *Auberge de Ti-Coz*
Réalmont (81) *Les Secrets Gourmands*
Remiremont / Girmont-Val-d'Ajol (88) *Auberge de la Vigotte* **N**
Rennes (35) *Le Four à Ban*
Rennes (35) *Le Quatre B*
Reugny (03) *Table de Reugny* **N**
Rians (83) *La Roquette*
Riom (63) *Le Flamboyant*
Riquewihr (68) *Le Sarment d'Or*
Roanne (42) *Le Central* **N**
Rodez (12) *Les Jardins de l'Acropolis*
Romorantin-Lanthenay (41) *Auberge le Lanthenay*
La Roque-Gageac (24) *La Belle Étoile*
La Roquette-sur-Siagne (06) *La Terrasse*
Roscoff (29) *L'Écume des Jours*
Rostrenen (22) *L'Eventail des Saveurs*
Rouvres-en-Xaintois (88) *Burnel*
Les Sables-d'Olonne (85) *La Pilotine*
St-Alban-les-Eaux (42) *Le Petit Prince* **N**
St-Amand-Montrond / Bruère-Allichamps (18) *Les Tilleuls* **N**
St-Amand-Montrond / Abbaye-de-Noirlac (18) *Auberge de l'Abbaye de Noirlac* **N**
St-Benoît-sur-Loire (45) *Grand St-Benoît*
St-Bonnet-le-Froid (43) *André Chatelard*
St-Bonnet-le-Froid (43) *Bistrot la Coulemelle*
St-Bonnet-le-Froid (43) *Le Fort du Pré*
St-Brieuc (22) *Ô Saveurs* **N**
St-Brieuc / Cesson (22) *La Croix Blanche*
St-Clément-les-Places (69) *L'Auberge de Saint-Clément* **N**
St-Disdier (05) *La Neyrette*
St-Dizier (52) *La Gentilhommière* **N**
St-Flour (15) *Grand Hôtel de l'Étape*
St-Georges-des-Sept-Voies (49) *Auberge de la Sansonnière* **N**
St-Germain-du-Bois (71) *Hostellerie Bressane*
St-Hilaire-des-Loges (85) *Le Pantagruelion*
St-Hippolyte (68) *Winstub Rabseppi-Stebel*
St-Jean-du-Bruel (12) *Du Midi-Papillon*
St-Julien-Chapteuil (43) *Vidal*
St-Justin (40) *France*
St-Malo (35) *La Grassinais*
St-Martin-de-Londres (34) *Auberge de Saugras*
St-Martin-en-Bresse (71) *Au Puits Enchanté*
St-Michel-en-l'Herm (85) *La Rose Trémière*
St-Michel-Mont-Mercure (85) *Auberge du Mont Mercure*
St-Palais-sur-Mer (17) *Les Agapes*
St-Pierre-sur-Dives (14) *Auberge de la Dives*
St-Quirin (57) *Hostellerie du Prieuré*
St-Suliac (35) *La Ferme du Boucanier* **N**
St-Thégonnec (29) *Auberge St-Thégonnec*
St-Vaast-la-Hougue (50) *France et Fuchsias*
St-Valery-en-Caux (76) *Du Port*
St-Vallier (26) *Le Bistrot d'Albert et Hôtel Terminus*
Ste-Cécile-les-Vignes (84) *Campagne, Vignes et Gourmandises* **N**
Ste-Croix-de-Verdon (04) *L'Olivier* **N**
Ste-Euphémie (01) *Au Petit Moulin*
Stes-Maries-de-la-Mer (13) *Hostellerie du Pont de Gau*

Salies-de-Béarn / Castagnède (64)	La Belle Auberge	
Salignac-Eyvigues (24)	La Meynardie	
Sancerre (18)	La Pomme d'Or	
Santenay (21)	Le Terroir	
Le Sappey-en-Chartreuse (38)	Les Skieurs	N
Sassetot-le-Mauconduit (76)	Le Relais des Dalles	
Saugues (43)	La Terrasse	
Saumur (49)	Gambetta	
Sauternes (33)	Saprien	
Sauxillanges (63)	Restaurant de la Mairie	
Savonnière (37)	La Maison Tourangelle	
Seillonnaz (01)	La Cigale d'Or	N
Sélestat (67)	La Vieille Tour	N
Semblançay (37)	La Mère Hamard	
Semur-en-Auxois (21)	Hostellerie d'Aussois	
Senones (88)	Au Bon Gîte	
Sérignan (34)	L 'Harmonie	
Servon (50)	Auberge du Terroir	
Sète (34)	Paris Méditerranée	
Sillé-le-Guillaume (72)	Le Bretagne	
Sochaux / Étupes (25)	Au Fil des Saisons	
Soissons (02)	Chez Raphaël	N
Sorges (24)	Auberge de la Truffe	
Sospel (06)	Des Étrangers	
La Souterraine / St-Étienne-de-Fursac (23)	Nougier	
Strasbourg (67)	Le Clou	N
Strasbourg / Fegersheim (67)	Auberge du Bruchrhein	
Tamniès (24)	Laborderie	
Tarnac (19)	Des Voyageurs	
Tharon-Plage (44)	Le Belem	
Thiais (94)	Ophélie la Cigale Gourmande	
Thonon-les-Bains / Port-de-Séchex (74)	Le Clos du Lac	
Toulouse / Castanet-Tolosan (31)	La Table des Merville	
Tourcoing (59)	La Baratte	
Tournus (71)	Le Terminus	
Tournus / Le Villars (71)	L 'Auberge des Gourmets	N
Tours (37)	L'Arche de Meslay	
Tours (37)	La Deuvalière	N
Tours (37)	Les Linottes Gourmandes	N
Tours / Vallières (37)	Auberge de Port Vallières	
Trémolat (24)	Bistrot d'en Face	
Triel-sur-Seine (78)	St-Martin	
Troyes / Pont-Ste-Marie (10)	Bistrot DuPont	
Tulle (19)	La Toque Blanche	
La Turballe (44)	Le Terminus	N
La Turbie (06)	Café de la Fontaine	
Uchaux (84)	Côté Sud	
Uchaux (84)	Le Temps de Vivre	N
Uzerche / St-Ybard (19)	Auberge St-Roch	
Uzès / St-Siffret (30)	L'Authentic	N
Valbonne (06)	L'Auberge Fleurie	
Le-Val-d'Ajol (88)	La Résidence	N
Valence (26)	L'Épicerie	
Valence (26)	Le 7	N
Valence-sur-Baïse (32)	La Ferme de Flaran	
Valloire (73)	Relais du Galibier	
Valmont (76)	Le Bec au Cauchois	N
Le Valtin (88)	Auberge du Val Joli	
Vannes (56)	Roscanvec	
Vannes (56)	La Table Alsacienne	
Varades (44)	La Closerie des Roses	
Vaux-sous-Aubigny (52)	Auberge des Trois Provinces	
Venarey-les-Laumes / Alise-Ste-Reine (21)	Cheval Blanc	
Vence (06)	Le Vieux Couvent	
Vendôme (41)	Le Terre à TR	N
Vernon (27)	Les Fleurs	
Versailles (78)	Le Potager du Roy	
Vichy (03)	L'Alambic	N
Vic-sur-Cère / Col-de-Curebourse (15)	Hostellerie St-Clément	
Vierzon (18)	Le Champêtre	N
Villard-de-Lans (38)	Les Trente Pas	
Villedieu-les-Poêles (50)	Manoir de l'Acherie	
Villefranche-de-Rouergue (12)	L'Épicurien	
Villefranche-sur-Saône (69)	Le Juliénas	N
Villeneuve-sur-Lot / Pujols (47)	Lou Calel	N
Villié-Morgon (69)	Le Morgon	
Villiers-sur-Marne (52)	La Source Bleue	
Viré (71)	Relais de Montmartre	
Viviers (07)	Le Relais du Vivarais	
Wierre-Effroy (62)	La Ferme du Vert	N
Wissembourg (67)	Le Carrousel Bleu	
Yerville (76)	Hostellerie des Voyageurs	

Bib Hôtel

Good accomodation at moderate prices outside the Paris region

Bonnes nuits à petits prix en province

Buona sistemazione a prezzi contenuti in provincia

Hier übernachten Sie gut und preiswert in der Provinz

Grato descanso a precios moderados en provincias

Aguessac (12) *Auberge le Rascalat*
Aix-les-Bains (73) *Auberge St-Simond*
Ajaccio (2A) *Kallisté* **N**
Allevard (38) *Les Alpes*
Ambonnay (51) *Auberge St-Vincent*
Angers (49) *Du Mail*
Angers (49) *Le Progrès*
Annecy (74) *Nord*
Annot (04) *L'Avenue*
Argentat (19) *Fouillade*
Aubeterre-sur-Dronne (16) *Hostellerie du Périgord*
Aubrac (12) *La Dômerie*
Aubusson (23) *Villa Adonis*
Aulnay (17) *Du Donjon*
Auray (56) *Du Loch*
Aurec-sur-Loire (43) *Les Cèdres Bleus*
Autrans (38) *Les Tilleuls* **N**
Autun (71) *La Tête Noire*
Auxerre (89) *Normandie*
Availles-Limouzine (86) *La Chatellenie*
Avignon / Île de la Barthelasse (84) *La Ferme*
Ax-les-Thermes (09) *Le Chalet*
Azay-le-Rideau (37) *De Biencourt*
Azay-le-Rideau (37) *Des Châteaux* **N**
Baerenthal (57) *Le Kirchberg*
Bagnères-de-Bigorre / Beaudéan (65) *Le Catala*
Baix (07) *Les Quatre Vents* **N**
Balot (21) *Auberge de la Baume*
Ban-de-Laveline (88) *Auberge Lorraine*
Baratier (05) *Les Peupliers*
Barbotan-les-Thermes (32) *De la Paix*
Bastelica (2A) *Chez Paul* **N**
Beaugency (45) *De la Sologne*
Beaune (21) *Grillon*
Beaune / Levernois (21) *Le Parc*
Beauzac (43) *L'Air du Temps*
Beauzac / Bransac (43) *La Table du Barret*
Bénodet (29) *Domaine de Kereven*
Berck-sur-Mer / Berck-Plage (62) *L'Impératrice*
Béthune (62) *L'Éden* **N**
Biarritz (64) *Maïtagaria*
Biarritz / Arbonne (64) *Laminak* **N**
Blienschwiller (67) *Winzenberg*
Bois-le-Roi (77) *Le Pavillon Royal*
Bollezeele (59) *Hostellerie St-Louis*
Bonifacio (2A) *Domaine de Licetto* **N**
Bonnétage (25) *L'Etang du Moulin*
Bonneval-sur-Arc (73) *A la Pastourelle*
La Bouilladisse (13) *La Fenière* **N**

→ **N** *New*
→ *Nouveau* → *Nuovo* → *Neu* → *Nuevo*

Bourges (18) *Le Berry*
Bourges (18) *Le Christina*
Bourges (18) *Les Tilleuls* **N**
Bourg-St-Maurice (73) *L'Autantic*
Bozouls (12) *A la Route d'Argent*
Bracieux (41) *De la Bonnheure*
Bretenoux / Port-de-Gagnac (46) *Hostellerie Belle Rive* **N**
Brissac-Quincé (49) *Le Castel* **N**
Le Bugue / Campagne (24) *Du Château*
Buis-les-Baronnies (26) *Les Arcades-Le Lion d'Or*
Burnhaupt-le-Haut (68) *Le Coquelicot*
Caen (14) *Des Quatrans*
Calais (62) *Métropol Hôtel*
Calais / Blériot-Plage (62) *Les Dunes* **N**
Calvinet (15) *Beauséjour*
Camaret-sur-Mer (29) *Vauban*
Cambo-les-Bains (64) *Ursula* **N**
Camiers (62) *Les Cèdres*
Cancale (35) *Le Chatellier*
Cannes (06) *Florian*
Carennac (46) *Hostellerie Fénelon* **N**
Carhaix-Plouguer (29) *Noz Vad*
Castelnaudary (11) *Du Canal*
Castres (81) *Renaissance*
Céret (66) *Les Arcades*
Chagny (71) *De la Poste*
Challans (85) *De l'Antiquité*
Chamonix-Mont-Blanc / Les Bossons (74) *Aiguille du Midi*
Champtoceaux (49) *Le Champalud*
Chandolas (07) *Auberge les Murets*
Charleville-Mézières (08) *De Paris*
Château-Gontier (53) *Parc Hôtel* **N**
Chaudes-Aigues (15) *Beauséjour*
Chaumont / Chamarandes (52) *Au Rendez-Vous des Amis* **N**
Chauvigny (86) *Lion d'Or*
Chépy (80) *L'Auberge Picarde* **N**
Cherbourg-Octeville (50) *La Renaissance*
Chézery-Forens (01) *Commerce*
Chinon (37) *Diderot*
Col de la Schlucht (88) *Le Collet* **N**
Comps-sur-Artuby (83) *Grand Hôtel Bain*
Cordon (74) *Le Cordonant*
Coti-Chiavari (2A) *Le Belvédère*
Cour-Cheverny (41) *St-Hubert* **N**
La Courtine (23) *Au Petit Breuil*
Coutras (33) *Henri IV*
Crozon (29) *La Presqu'île*
Cruis (04) *Auberge de l'Abbaye*
Dambach-la-Ville (67) *Le Vignoble*
Damgan (56) *Albatros*
Donzenac (19) *Relais du Bas Limousin*
Doué-la-Fontaine (49) *Auberge Bienvenue*
Dreux (28) *Le Beffroi*
Entraygues-sur-Truyère / Le Fel (12) *Auberge du Fel*
Épaignes (27) *L'Auberge du Beau Carré*
Erquy (22) *Beauséjour*
Espalion (12) *De France*
Estaing (12) *L' Auberge St-Fleuret*
Eymet (24) *Les Vieilles Pierres*
Le Falgoux (15) *Des Voyageurs*
La Ferté-St-Cyr (41) *Saint-Cyr* **N**
Florac / Cocurès (48) *La Lozerette*
Fouesnant / Cap-Coz (29) *Belle-Vue*
Fougères (35) *Les Voyageurs*
Gaillac (81) *La Verrerie*
Gennes (49) *Les Naulets d'Anjou*
Gérardmer (88) *Gérard d'Alsace*
La Giettaz (73) *Flor'Alpes*
Gimel-les-Cascades (19) *Hostellerie de la Vallée*
Gordes (84) *Auberge de Carcarille*
Goumois (25) *Le Moulin du Plain*
Gresse-en-Vercors (38) *Le Chalet*
Guebwiller (68) *Domaine du Lac* **N**
Guilliers (56) *Au Relais du Porhoët*
Hagetmau (40) *Le Jambon*
Hesdin (62) *Trois Fontaines*
Le Hohwald (67) *Hôtel Petite Auberge*
Les Houches (74) *Auberge Le Montagny*
Île-de-Sein (29) *Ar Men*
Île d'Yeu / Port-Joinville (85) *Atlantic Hôtel*
Illhaeusern (68) *Les Hirondelles*
L'Isle-d'Abeau (38) *Le Relais du Çatey*
L'Isle-sur-Serein (89) *Auberge du Pot d'Étain* **N**
Itxassou (64) *Le Chêne*
Jonzac / Clam (17) *Le Vieux Logis*
Jougne (25) *La Couronne* **N**
Juliénas (69) *Chez la Rose*
Juvigny-sous-Andaine (61) *Au Bon Accueil*
Kaysersberg (68) *Constantin*
Kilstett (67) *Oberlé* **N**

➜ **N** *New*
➜ *Nouveau* ➜ *Nuovo* ➜ *Neu* ➜ *Nuevo*

Labaroche (68) *La Rochette*
Lacapelle-Viescamp (15) *Du Lac*
Lac Chambon (63) *Le Grillon* **N**
Lanarce (07) *Le Provence*
Langeac / Reilhac (43) *Val d'Allier*
Largentière / Sanilhac (07) *Auberge de la Tour de Brison* **N**
Larrau (64) *Etchemaïté*
Lascelle (15) *Lac des Graves*
Locronan (29) *Le Prieuré*
Lons-le-Saunier (39) *Nouvel Hôtel*
Lorient (56) *Astoria* **N**
Luz-St-Sauveur / Esquièze-Sère (65) *Terminus*
Lyon (69) *Célestins*
Mandelieu / La Napoule (06) *Villa Parisiana*
Margès (26) *Auberge Le Pont du Chalon*
Masseret (19) *De la Tour*
Mauriac (15) *Serre*
Mazaye (63) *Auberge de Mazayes*
Métabief (25) *Étoile des Neiges* **N**
Meyrueis (48) *Family Hôtel*
Meyrueis (48) *Du Mont Aigoual*
Millau (12) *Château de Creissels*
Mittelhausen (67) *À l'Étoile*
Molsheim (67) *Le Bugatti*
Les Molunes (39) *Le Pré Fillet*
Monestier-de-Clermont (38) *Au Sans Souci*
Montargis / Amilly (45) *Le Belvédère*
Montauban (82) *Du Commerce*
Montélier (26) *La Martinière*
Montigny-la-Resle (89) *Le Soleil d'Or*
Montigny-sur-Avre (28) *Moulin des Planches*
Montlivault (41) *La Maison d'À Côté* **N**
Montluel (01) *Petit Casset*
Montmelard (71) *Le St-Cyr*
Montpellier (34) *Du Parc*
Montsalvy (15) *L'Auberge Fleurie*
Morteau / Les Combes (25) *L'Auberge de la Motte* **N**
Mulhouse / Frœningen (68) *Auberge de Froeningen*
Nantua (01) *L'Embarcadère* **N**
Natzwiller (67) *Auberge Metzger* **N**
Niederschaeffolsheim (67) *Au Bœuf Rouge* **N**
Niedersteinbach (67) *Cheval Blanc* **N**
Nogent-le-Rotrou (28) *Brit Hôtel du Perche*
Nogent-le-Rotrou (28) *Sully*
Nogent-sur-Seine (10) *Beau Rivage*
Nontron (24) *Grand Hôtel* **N**
Le Nouvion-en-Thiérache (02) *Paix*
Noyalo (56) *L'Hortensia* **N**
Oberhaslach (67) *Hostellerie St-Florent* **N**
Obersteinbach (67) *Anthon* **N**
Orbey / Pairis (68) *Le Domaine de Pairis* **N**
Orléans (45) *Marguerite* **N**
Ouistreham (14) *Du Phare*
Pailherols (15) *Auberge des Montagnes*
Paimpol / Ploubazlanec (22) *Les Agapanthes*
Paray-le-Monial / Poisson (71) *La Poste et Hôtel La Reconce*
Pau (64) *Le Bourbon*
Pégomas (06) *Le Bosquet*
Péron (01) *Auberge Communale La Fruitière*
Pierre-Buffière (87) *La Providence*
Pierrefort (15) *Du Midi*
Pont-Aven (29) *Les Ajoncs d'Or*
Pont-de-l'Arche (27) *De la Tour*
Pont-du-Bouchet (63) *La Crémaillère* **N**
Porto-Pollo (2A) *Les Eucalyptus* **N**
Le Pouldu (29) *Le Panoramique*
Prats-de-Mollo-la-Preste / La Preste (66) *Ribes*
Le Puy-en-Velay / Espaly-St-Marcel (43) *L'Ermitage*
Quarré-les-Tombes (89) *Le Morvan*
Quédillac (35) *Le Relais de la Rance*
Rânes (61) *St-Pierre*
Reipertswiller (67) *La Couronne*
Remiremont / Girmont-Val-d'Ajol (88) *Auberge de la Vigotte* **N**
Rennes (35) *Britannia*
Rennes (35) *Des Lices*
Réville (50) *Au Moyne de Saire*
Rieumes (31) *Auberge les Palmiers*
Riom-Ès-Montagnes (15) *St-Georges*
Rochefort (17) *Roca Fortis*
La Rochette (73) *Du Parc*
Romagnieu (38) *Auberge les Forges de la Massotte*
Ronchamp / Champagney (70) *Le Pré Serroux*
Roussillon (84) *Les Sables d'Ocre*
Rouvres-en-Xaintois (88) *Burnel* **N**

→ **N** *New*
→ *Nouveau* → *Nuovo* → *Neu* → *Nuevo*

Rue / St-Firmin (80) *Auberge de la Dune*
Les Sables-d'Olonne (85) *Antoine*
Les Sables-d'Olonne (85) *Les Embruns*
Saillagouse (66) *Planes (La Vieille Maison Cerdane)*
St-Agnan (58) *La Vieille Auberge*
St-Ambroix / Larnac (30) *Le Clos des Arts*
St-Bonnet-en-Champsaur (05) *la Crémaillère*
St-Chély-d'Apcher / La Garde (48) *Le Rocher Blanc* **N**
St-Disdier (05) *La Neyrette*
St-Flour (15) *Auberge de La Providence*
St-Gervais-d'Auvergne (63) *Le Relais d'Auvergne* **N**
St-Jean-de-Maurienne (73) *St-Georges*
St-Jean-du-Bruel (12) *Du Midi-Papillon*
St-Jean-en-Royans / Col de la Machine (26) *Du Col de la Machine*
St-Lary (09) *Auberge de l'Isard*
St-Malo (35) *San Pedro*
St-Rémy-de-Provence (13) *L'Amandière*
St-Sernin-sur-Rance (12) *Carayon*
St-Sorlin-d'Arves (73) *Beausoleil*
St-Vaast-la-Hougue (50) *La Granitière*
St-Valéry-en-Caux (76) *Les Remparts*
St-Valéry-sur-Somme (80) *Du Port et des Bains* **N**
Ste-Menéhould (51) *Le Cheval Rouge*
Saintes (17) *L'Avenue*
Stes-Maries-de-la-Mer (13) *Pont Blanc*
Salers (15) *Le Bailliage*
Salies-de-Béarn / Castagnède (64) *La Belle Auberge*
Sallanches (74) *Auberge de l'Orangerie*
Sarlat-la-Canéda (24) *Le Mas de Castel*
Sarlat-la-Canéda (24) *Le Mas del Pechs*
Sarrebourg (57) *Les Cèdres*
Sarreguemines (57) *Amadeus*
Sars-Poteries (59) *Marquais*
Saugues (43) *La Terrasse*
Sauveterre-de-Béarn (64) *La Maison de Navarre* **N**
Saverne (67) *Le Clos de la Garenne* **N**
Sées / Macé (61) *Île de Sées*
Semblançay (37) *La Mère Hamard*
Semur-en-Auxois (21) *Les Cymaises*
Senones (88) *Au Bon Gîte*
Servon (50) *Auberge du Terroir*
Sommières (30) *De l'Estelou*
Sondernach (68) *A l'Orée du Bois*
Souillac (46) *Le Quercy*
Sousceyrac (46) *Au Déjeuner de Sousceyrac* **N**
Stenay (55) *Du Commerce*
Strasbourg / Blaesheim (67) *Au Bœuf* **N**
Strasbourg / Entzheim (67) *Père Benoit* **N**
Strasbourg / Mittelhausbergen (67) *Tilleul* **N**
Tarnac (19) *Des Voyageurs*
Thann (68) *Aux Sapins*
Le Thillot / Le Ménil (88) *Les Sapins*
Thizy (69) *La Terrasse*
Le Touquet-Paris-Plage / Stella-Plage (62) *Des Pelouses* **N**
Tournon-sur-Rhône (07) *Les Amandiers*
Tournus (71) *Le Terminus*
Turckheim (68) *Le Berceau du Vigneron*
Uriage-les-Bains (38) *Les Mésanges*
Uzès (30) *Le Patio de Violette* **N**
Valenciennes (59) *Baudouin*
Valgorge (07) *Le Tanargue* **N**
Valleraugue (30) *Auberge Cévenole*
Vaux-sous-Aubigny (52) *Hôtel Le Vauxois* **N**
Verneuil-sur-Avre (27) *Du Saumon*
Vézelay / Pierre-Perthuis (89) *Les Deux Ponts* **N**
Viaduc-de-Garabit (15) *Beau Site*
Vichy / Abrest (03) *La Colombière* **N**
Villé (67) *La Bonne Franquette*
Villersexel (70) *La Terrasse*
Vittel (88) *Providence* **N**
Viviers (07) *Le Relais du Vivarais* **N**
Vougeot / Gilly-lès-Cîteaux (21) *L'Orée des Vignes*
Wimereux (62) *Du Centre*
Wissembourg (67) *Au Moulin de la Walk*

→ **N** *New*
→ *Nouveau* → *Nuovo* → *Neu* → *Nuevo*

Pleasant Lodging

Hébergements agréables
Alloggio ameno
Angenehme Unterbringung
Alojamientos agradables

Antibes / Cap d'Antibes (06) *Du Cap*
La Baule (44) *Hermitage Barrière*
Beaulieu-sur-Mer (06) *La Réserve de Beaulieu*
Biarritz (64) *Du Palais*
Cannes (06) *Carlton Inter Continental*
Cannes (06) *Majestic Barrière*
Cannes (06) *Martinez*
Courchevel / Courchevel 1850 (73) *Les Airelles*
Deauville (14) *Normandy-Barrière*
Deauville (14) *Royal-Barrière*
Évian-les-Bains (74) *Royal*
Monte-Carlo (MC) *Paris*
Nice (06) *Negresco*
Paris 1er *Le Meurice*
Paris 1er *Ritz*
Paris 8e *Le Bristol*
Paris 8e *Crillon*
Paris 8e *Four Seasons George V*
Paris 8e *Plaza Athénée*
Paris 9e *Intercontinental Le Grand*
Paris 16e *Raphael*
St-Jean-Cap-Ferrat (06) *Grand Hôtel du Cap Ferrat*
St-Tropez (83) *Byblos*
St-Tropez (83) *Château de la Messardière*
Tourrettes (83) *Four Seasons Resort Provence at Terre Blanche*

Ablis (78) *Château d'Esclimont*
Aix-en-Provence (13) *Villa Gallici*
Antibes / Cap d'Antibes (06) *Impérial Garoupe*
Avallon / Vault-de-Lugny (89) *Château de Vault de Lugny*
Avignon (84) *D'Europe*
Avignon (84) *La Mirande*
Bagnols (69) *Château de Bagnols*
Barbizon (77) *Hôtellerie du Bas-Bréau*
Beaune (21) *Le Cep*
Belle-Île / Port-Goulphar (56) *Castel Clara*
Béthune / Busnes (62) *Le Château de Beaulieu*
Les Bézards (45) *Auberge des Templiers*
Bidarray (64) *Ostapé*
Billiers (56) *Domaine de Rochevilaine*
Bordeaux (33) *Burdigala*
Bordeaux / Martillac (33) *Les Sources de Caudalie*
Briollay (49) *Château de Noirieux*
Brive-la-Gaillarde / Varetz (19) *Château de Castel Novel*
Cahors / Mercuès (46) *Château de Mercuès*
Calvi (2B) *La Villa*
Cannes (06) *3.14 Hôtel*
Carcassonne (11) *De La Cité*
Le Castellet / Le Castellet (83) *Du Castellet*
Cavalière (83) *Le Club de Cavalière et Spa*
Chamonix-Mont-Blanc (74) *Hameau Albert 1er*
Colroy-la-Roche (67) *Hostellerie La Cheneaudière*
Courcelles-sur-Vesle (02) *Château de Courcelles*
Courchevel / Courchevel 1850 (73) *Amanresorts Le Mélézin*
Courchevel / Courchevel 1850 (73) *Annapurna*

Courchevel / Courchevel 1850 (73) *Cheval Blanc*
Courchevel / Courchevel 1850 (73) *Le Kilimandjaro*
Curzay-sur-Vonne (86) *Château de Curzay*
Divonne-les-Bains (01) *Le Grand Hôtel*
Eugénie-les-Bains (40) *Les Prés d'Eugénie*
Évian-les-Bains (74) *Ermitage*
Èze (06) *Château de la Chèvre d'Or*
Èze-Bord-de-Mer (06) *Cap Estel*
Gordes (84) *La Bastide de Gordes et Spa*
Grasse (06) *La Bastide St-Antoine*
Honfleur (14) *La Ferme St-Siméon*
Île de Ré / La Flotte (17) *Richelieu*
Joigny (89) *La Côte St-Jacques*
Juan-les-Pins (06) *Belles Rives*
Juan-les-Pins (06) *Juana*
Lacave (46) *Château de la Treyne*
Le Lavandou / Aiguebelle (83) *Les Roches*
Ligny-en-Cambrésis (59) *Château de Ligny*
Lille (59) *L'Hermitage Gantois*
Luynes (37) *Domaine de Beauvois*
Lyon (69) *Cour des Loges*
Lyon (69) *Villa Florentine*
Lyon / Charbonnières-les-Bains (69) *Le Pavillon de la Rotonde*
Megève (74) *Les Fermes de Marie*
Megève (74) *Lodge Park*
Mirambeau (17) *Château de Mirambeau*
Montbazon (37) *Château d'Artigny*
Monte-Carlo (MC) *Hermitage*
Monte-Carlo (MC) *Monte Carlo Bay Hôtel and Resort*
Monte-Carlo (MC) *Métropole*
Monte-Carlo (MC) *Port Palace*
Monte-Carlo / Monte-Carlo-Beach (06) *Monte-Carlo Beach Hôtel*
Mougins (06) *Le Mas Candille*
Onzain (41) *Domaine des Hauts de Loire*
Paris 1er *Costes*
Paris 1er *De Vendôme*
Paris 3e *Murano*
Paris 3e *Pavillon de la Reine*
Paris 8e *Napoléon*
Paris 16e *Le Parc-Trocadéro*
Paris 16e *St-James Paris*
Perros-Guirec (22) *L'Agapa*
Pont-du-Gard / Castillon-du-Gard (30) *Le Vieux Castillon*
Porticcio (2A) *Le Maquis*
Porto-Vecchio (2A) *Casadelmar*
Porto-Vecchio (2A) *Grand Hôtel de Cala Rossa*
Pouilly-en-Auxois / Chailly-sur-Armançon (21) *Château de Chailly*
Puymirol (47) *Michel Trama*
Ramatuelle (83) *Villa Marie*
Reims (51) *Château les Crayères*
Roanne (42) *Troisgros*
Roquebrune (06) *Vista Palace*
Rouffach (68) *Château d'Isenbourg*
St-Émilion (33) *Hostellerie de Plaisance*
St-Jean-Cap-Ferrat (06) *Royal Riviera*
St-Jean-Cap-Ferrat (06) *Voile d'Or*
St-Tropez (83) *La Bastide de St-Tropez*
St-Tropez (83) *Résidence de la Pinède*
St-Tropez (83) *Villa Belrose*
Ste-Foy-la-Grande (33) *Château des Vigiers*
Ste-Maxime (83) *Le Beauvallon*
Saulieu (21) *Le Relais Bernard Loiseau*
Strasbourg (67) *Régent Petite France*
Talloires (74) *L'Auberge du Père Bise*
Val-d'Isère (73) *Christiania*
Valence (26) *Pic*
Versailles (78) *Trianon Palace*
Vienne (38) *La Pyramide*
Villeneuve-lès-Avignon (30) *Le Prieuré*
Vitrac (24) *Domaine de Rochebois*
Vonnas (01) *Georges Blanc*
Vougeot / Gilly-lès-Cîteaux (21) *Château de Gilly*

Aigues-Mortes (30) *Villa Mazarin*
Aillant-sur-Tholon (89) *Domaine du Roncemay*
Aix-en-Provence (13) *Le Pigonnet*
Aix-en-Provence / Celony (13) *Le Mas d'Entremont*
Ajaccio (2A) *Palazzu U Domu*
Albi (81) *La Réserve*
Alpe-d'Huez (38) *Au Chamois d'Or*
Amboise (37) *Le Choiseul*
Amboise (37) *Le Manoir Les Minimes*
Arles (13) *L'Hôtel Particulier*
Avignon / Montfavet (84) *Hostellerie Les Frênes*
Avignon / Le Pontet (84) *Auberge de Cassagne*
Bagnoles-de-l'Orne (61) *Le Manoir du Lys*
Bagnols-sur-Cèze (30) *Château de Montcaud*
La Baule (44) *Castel Marie-Louise*

Les Baux-de-Provence (13) *La Cabro d'Or*
Bayeux (14) *Château de Sully*
Bayeux / Audrieu (14) *Château d'Audrieu*
Beaune (21) *L'Hôtel*
Beaune / Levernois (21) *Hostellerie de Levernois*
Bénodet / Ste-Marine (29) *Villa Tri Men*
Béthune / Gosnay (62) *Chartreuse du Val St-Esprit*
Biarritz (64) *Beaumanoir*
Biarritz / Lac de Brindos (64) *Château de Brindos*
Bordeaux / Bouliac (33) *Le St-James*
Boulogne-sur-Mer (62) *La Matelote*
Le-Bourget-du-Lac (73) *Ombremont*
Boutigny-sur-Essonne (91) *Domaine de Bélesbat*
Brantôme (24) *Le Moulin de l'Abbaye*
Brantôme / Champagnac-de-Belair (24) *Le Moulin du Roc*
Le Buisson-de-Cadouin (24) *Le Manoir de Bellerive*
La Bussière-sur-Ouche (21) *Abbaye de la Bussière*
La Cadière-d'Azur (83) *Hostellerie Bérard*
Cagnes-sur-Mer (06) *Le Cagnard*
Callas (83) *Hostellerie Les Gorges de Pennafort*
Calvi (2B) *La Signoria*
Cancale (35) *De Bricourt-Richeux*
Carantec (29) *L'Hôtel de Carantec-Patrick Jeffroy*
Carcassonne (11) *Domaine d'Auriac*
Carcassonne / Cavanac (11) *Château de Cavanac*
Carpentras / Mazan (84) *Château de Mazan*
Les Carroz-d'Arâches (74) *Les Servages d'Armelle*
Cassel (59) *Châtellerie de Schoebeque*
La Celle (83) *Hostellerie de l'Abbaye de la Celle*
Chagny (71) *Lameloise*
Chambéry / Chambéry-le-Vieux (73) *Château de Candie*
Chambolle-Musigny (21) *Château André Ziltener*
Chamonix-Mont-Blanc (74) *Grand Hôtel des Alpes*
Château-Arnoux-St-Auban (04) *La Bonne Étape*
Chenonceaux (37) *Auberge du Bon Laboureur*
Chinon / Marçay (37) *Château de Marçay*
Cognac (16) *Château de l'Yeuse*
Coise-St-Jean-Pied-Gauthier (73) *Château de la Tour du Puits*
La Colle-sur-Loup (06) *Le Clos des Arts*
Colmar (68) *Les Têtes*
Colombey-les-Deux-Églises (52) *Hostellerie la Montagne*
Condrieu (69) *Hôtellerie Beau Rivage*
Connelles (27) *Le Moulin de Connelles*
Cordes-sur-Ciel (81) *Le Grand Écuyer*
Cordon (74) *Le Cerf Amoureux*
Cordon (74) *Les Roches Fleuries*
Courchevel / Courchevel 1850 (73) *La Sivolière*
Courchevel / Courchevel 1850 (73) *Le Chabichou*
Crillon-le-Brave (84) *Crillon le Brave*
Le Croisic (44) *Le Fort de l'Océan*
La Croix-Valmer / Gigaro (83) *Château de Valmer*
Crozet (01) *Jiva Hill Park Hôtel*
Cruseilles (74) *Château des Avenières*
Deauville (14) *Hostellerie de Tourgéville*
Dinard (35) *Villa Reine Hortense*
Enghien-les-Bains (95) *Grand Hôtel Barrière*
Épernay / Champillon (51) *Royal Champagne*
Épernay / Vinay (51) *Hostellerie La Briqueterie*
Les Eyzies-de-Tayac (24) *Du Centenaire*
Èze (06) *Château Eza*
Fère-en-Tardenois (02) *Château de Fère*
Gémenos (13) *Relais de la Magdeleine*
Gérardmer (88) *Le Manoir au Lac*
Gérardmer / Bas-Rupts (88) *Les Bas-Rupts*
Gordes (84) *Les Bories*
Grasse (06) *La Bastide St-Mathieu*
Le Grau-du-Roi / Port-Camargue (30) *Spinaker*
Gressy (77) *Le Manoir de Gressy*
Grignan (26) *Manoir de la Roseraie*
Hennebont (56) *Château de Locguénolé*
Honfleur (14) *Le Manoir du Butin*
Igé (71) *Château d'Igé*
Île de Porquerolles (83) *Le Mas du Langoustier*
Île de Ré / St-Martin-de-Ré (17) *De Toiras*
Île de Ré / St-Martin-de-Ré (17) *Le Clos St-Martin*
Joucas (84) *Hostellerie Le Phébus*
Joucas (84) *Le Mas des Herbes Blanches*
Lacave (46) *Pont de l'Ouysse*
Laguiole (12) *Bras*
Langeais / St-Patrice (37) *Château de Rochecotte*
Lencloître / à Savigny-sous-Faye (86) *Château Hôtel de Savigny*
Lezoux / Bort-l'Étang (63) *Château de Codignat*
Lille / Emmerin (59) *La Howarderie*
Limoges / St-Martin-du-Fault (87) *Chapelle St-Martin*
Locquirec (29) *Le Grand Hôtel des Bains*
Lorgues (83) *Château de Berne*
Lourmarin (84) *Le Moulin de Lourmarin*
Lunéville (54) *Château d'Adoménil*
Lyon (69) *Le Royal Lyon*
Magescq (40) *Relais de la Poste*
La Malène (48) *Château de la Caze*
Manigod (74) *Chalet Hôtel Croix-Fry*

Manosque / La Fuste (04) *Hostellerie de la Fuste*
Marseille (13) *Le Petit Nice*
Maussane-les-Alpilles / Paradou (13) *Le Hameau des Baux*
Megève (74) *Chalet du Mont d'Arbois*
Megève (74) *Chalet St-Georges*
Megève (74) *Le Fer à Cheval*
Megève (74) *Mont-Blanc*
Menton (06) *Grand Hôtel des Ambassadeurs*
Méribel (73) *Allodis*
Méribel (73) *Le Grand Coeur et Spa*
Méribel (73) *Le Yéti*
Missillac (44) *La Bretesche*
Moëlan-sur-Mer (29) *Manoir de Kertalg*
Moissac (82) *Le Manoir Saint-Jean*
Molitg-les-Bains (66) *Château de Riell*
Monaco (MC) *Columbus*
Montbazon (37) *Domaine de la Tortinière*
Montélimar (26) *Domaine du Colombier*
Montpellier / Castelnau-le-Lez (34) *Domaine de Verchant*
Montreuil (62) *Château de Montreuil*
Montrichard / Chissay-en-Touraine (41) *Château de Chissay*
Mougins (06) *De Mougins*
Moustiers-Ste-Marie (04) *Bastide de Moustiers*
Najac (12) *Les Demeures de Longcol*
Nancy (54) *Grand Hôtel de la Reine*
Nans-les-Pins (83) *Domaine de Châteauneuf*
Nice (06) *La Pérouse*
Nieuil (16) *Château de Nieuil*
Nîmes (30) *Jardins Secrets*
Obernai (67) *A la Cour d'Alsace*
Obernai (67) *Le Parc*
Paris 6e *D'Aubusson*
Paris 6e *Esprit Saint-Germain*
Paris 6e *L'Hôtel*
Paris 6e *Relais St-Germain*
Paris 7e *Duc de St-Simon*
Paris 7e *Pont Royal*
Paris 8e *Daniel*
Paris 8e *De Sers*
Paris 8e *François 1er*
Paris 11e *Les Jardins du Marais*
Paris 16e *Keppler*
Paris 16e *Sezz*
Paris 16e *Square*
Paris 16e *Trocadero Dokhan's*
Paris 18e *Kube*
Pau (64) *Villa Navarre*
Pauillac (33) *Château Cordeillan Bages*
Pérouges (01) *Ostellerie du Vieux Pérouges*
Poligny / Monts-de-Vaux (39) *Hostellerie des Monts de Vaux*
Pons / Mosnac (17) *Moulin du Val de Seugne*
Pornichet (44) *Sud Bretagne*
Port-en-Bessin (14) *La Chenevière*
Port-Lesney (39) *Château de Germigney*
Porto-Vecchio (2A) *Belvédère*
Propriano (2A) *Grand Hôtel Miramar*
Rayol-Canadel-sur-Mer (83) *Le Bailli de Suffren*
Reims (51) *L'Assiette Champenoise*
Ribeauvillé (68) *Le Clos St-Vincent*
Roscoff (29) *Le Brittany*
St-Arcons-d'Allier (43) *Les Deux Abbesses*
St-Bonnet-le-Froid (43) *Le Clos des Cimes*
St-Émilion (33) *Château Grand Barrail*
St-Florent (2B) *Demeure Loredana*
St-Germain-en-Laye (78) *La Forestière*
St-Jean-de-Luz (64) *Grand Hôtel*
St-Jean-de-Luz (64) *Parc Victoria*
St-Jean-de-Luz (64) *Zazpi Hôtel*
St-Jean-Pied-de-Port (64) *Les Pyrénées*
St-Omer / Tilques (62) *Château Tilques*
St-Paul (06) *La Colombe d'Or*
St-Paul (06) *Le Mas de Pierre*
St-Paul (06) *Le Saint-Paul*
St-Paul-Trois-Châteaux (26) *Villa Augusta*
St-Rémy-de-Provence (13) *Hostellerie du Vallon de Valrugues*
St-Rémy-de-Provence (13) *Le Château des Alpilles*
St-Rémy-de-Provence (13) *Les Ateliers de l'Image*
St-Tropez (83) *Le Yaca*
St-Tropez (83) *Pan Deï Palais*
Ste-Anne-la-Palud (29) *De La Plage*
Ste-Maure-de-Touraine / Noyant-de-Touraine (37) *Château de Brou*
Ste-Preuve (02) *Domaine du Château de Barive*
Saintes (17) *Relais du Bois St-Georges*
Stes-Maries-de-la-Mer (13) *Le Mas de la Fouque*
Salon-de-Provence (13) *Abbaye de Sainte-Croix*
Le Sambuc (13) *Le Mas de Peint*
Sarlat-la-Canéda (24) *Clos La Boëtie*
Sault (84) *Hostellerie du Val de Sault*
Saumur (49) *Château de Verrières*
Saumur / Chênehutte-les-Tuffeaux (49) *Le Prieuré*
La Saussaye (27) *Manoir des Saules*
Strasbourg (67) *Régent Contades*
Strasbourg / Plobsheim (67) *Le Kempferhof*
Tarbes (65) *Le Rex Hotel*
Théoule-sur-Mer / Miramar (06) *Miramar Beach*
Thuret (63) *Château de la Caniére*
Tignes (73) *Les Campanules*
Tournus (71) *Hôtel de Greuze*
Tours / Joué-lès-Tours (37) *Château de Beaulieu*
Tours / Rochecorbon (37) *Les Hautes Roches*
Tourtour (83) *La Bastide de Tourtour*
Trébeurden (22) *Manoir de Lan-Kerellec*
Trébeurden (22) *Ti al Lannec*
Trégunc (29) *Auberge Les Grandes Roches*

Trémolat (24) *Le Vieux Logis*
Trigance (83) *Château de Trigance*
Troyes (10) *La Maison de Rhodes*
Troyes (10) *Le Champ des Oiseaux*
Uriage-les-Bains (38) *Grand Hôtel*
Val-Thorens (73) *Fitz Roy*
Verdun / Les Monthairons (55) *Hostellerie du Château des Monthairons*
Verneuil-sur-Avre (27) *Hostellerie Le Clos*
Vervins (02) *Tour du Roy*
Vézelay / St-Père (89) *L'Espérance*
Ville-d'Avray (92) *Les Étangs de Corot*
Villeneuve-lès-Avignon (30) *La Magnaneraie*
Villeneuve-sur-Lot / St-Sylvestre-sur-Lot (47) *Château Lalande*
Villiers-le-Mahieu (78) *Château de Villiers le Mahieu*

Aisonville-et-Bernoville (02) *Le 1748*
Aix-en-Provence (13) *Bastide du Cours*
Ajaccio (2A) *Les Mouettes*
Alleyras (43) *Le Haut-Allier*
Amboise (37) *Château de Pray*
Anduze / Tornac (30) *Les Demeures du Ranquet*
Argelès-sur-Mer (66) *Le Cottage*
Argenton-sur-Creuse / Bouesse (36) *Château de Bouesse*
Astaffort (47) *Le Square "Michel Latrille"*
Auribeau-sur-Siagne (06) *Auberge de la Vignette Haute*
Aurillac / Vézac (15) *Château de Salles*
Auxerre (89) *Le Parc des Maréchaux*
Bagnoles-de-l'Orne (61) *Bois Joli*
Barneville-Carteret / Carteret (50) *Des Ormes*
Les Baux-de-Provence (13) *La Riboto de Taven*
Les Baux-de-Provence (13) *Mas de l'Oulivié*
Beaulieu (07) *La Santoline*
Beaune / Montagny-lès-Beaune (21) *Le Clos*
Belle-Île / Bangor (56) *La Désirade*
Bergerac (24) *Château Rauly-Saulieut*
Bergerac / St-Nexans (24) *La Chartreuse du Bignac*
Bermicourt (62) *La Cour de Rémi*
Besançon (25) *Charles Quint*
Biarritz (64) *Le Château du Clair de Lune*
Bidart (64) *L'Hacienda*
Bidart (64) *Villa L'Arche*
Bize-Minervois (11) *La Bastide Cabezac*
Bonifacio (2A) *Genovese*
Bonnat (23) *L'Orangerie*
Bonnieux (84) *Auberge de l'Aiguebrun*
Bourges (18) *D'Angleterre*
Bourgueil / Restigné (37) *Manoir de Restigné*
Cangey (37) *Le Fleuray*
Cannes (06) *Cavendish*
Carpentras / Monteux (84) *Domaine de Bournereau*
Carsac-Aillac (24) *La Villa Romaine*
Castries (34) *Disini*
Céret (66) *Le Mas Trilles*
Chablis (89) *Du Vieux Moulin*
Chablis (89) *Hostellerie des Clos*
Le Châtelet / Notre-Dame d'Orsan (18) *La Maison d'Orsan*
Châtillon-sur-Chalaronne (01) *La Tour*
La Châtre / St-Chartier (36) *Château de la Vallée Bleue*
Cogolin (83) *La Maison du Monde*
La Colle-sur-Loup (06) *L'Abbaye*
Colmar (68) *Hostellerie Le Maréchal*
Condom (32) *Les Trois Lys*
Conques (12) *Le Moulin de Cambelong*
Crépon (14) *Ferme de la Rançonnière*
Les Deux-Alpes (38) *Chalet Mounier*
Épernay (51) *Clos Raymi*
Erbalunga (2B) *Castel'Brando*
Ermenonville (60) *Le Prieuré*
Eugénie-les-Bains (40) *La Maison Rose*
Les Eyzies-de-Tayac (24) *Ferme Lamy*
Fayence (83) *Moulin de la Camandoule*
Fontaine-de-Vaucluse (84) *Du Poète*
Fort-Mahon-Plage (80) *Auberge Le Fiacre*
Fréjus (83) *L'Aréna*
Gensac (33) *Château de Sanse*
Gex / Échenevex (01) *Auberge des Chasseurs*
Goumois (25) *Taillard*
Graveson (13) *Moulin d'Aure*
Grignan (26) *Le Clair de la Plume*
Guéthary (64) *Villa Catarie*
Gundershoffen (67) *Le Moulin*
Hauteluce (73) *La Ferme du Chozal*
Le Havre (76) *Vent d'Ouest*
Honfleur (14) *L'Écrin*
Honfleur (14) *La Chaumière*
Honfleur (14) *Les Maisons de Léa*
Hossegor (40) *Les Hortensias du Lac*
Île de Noirmoutier / Noirmoutier-en-l'Île (85) *Fleur de Sel*
Île de Port-Cros (83) *Le Manoir*
L'Isle-sur-la-Sorgue (84) *Hostellerie La Grangette*
Juan-les-Pins (06) *La Villa*
Juan-les-Pins (06) *Ste-Valérie*
Jungholtz (68) *Les Violettes*
Lacabarède (81) *Demeure de Flore*
Lille (59) *Art Déco Romarin*
Limoux (11) *Grand Hôtel Moderne et Pigeon*
Lourmarin (84) *La Bastide de Lourmarin*
Lumbres (62) *Moulin de Mombreux*

Lussac-les-Châteaux (86) *Les Orangeries*
Madières (34) *Château de Madières*
La Malène (48) *Manoir de Montesquiou*
Marlenheim (67) *Le Cerf*
Marsolan (32) *Lous Grits*
Martel (46) *Relais Ste-Anne*
Maussane-les-Alpilles / Paradou (13) *Du Côté des Olivades*
Megève (74) *Au Coin du Feu*
Ménerbes (84) *La Bastide de Marie*
Meyronne (46) *La Terrasse*
Monpazier (24) *Edward 1er*
Montsoreau (49) *La Marine de Loire*
Moudeyres (43) *Le Pré Bossu*
Mougins (06) *Le Manoir de l'Étang*
Mougins (06) *Les Muscadins*
Mussidan / Sourzac (24) *Le Chaufourg en Périgord*
Nancy (54) *D'Haussonville*
Neauphle-le-Château (78) *Domaine du Verbois*
Nice (06) *Le Grimaldi*
Nîmes (30) *La Maison de Sophie*
Nitry (89) *Auberge la Beursaudière*
Nyons (26) *La Bastide des Monges*
Oradour-sur-Vayres (87) *La Bergerie des Chapelles*
Orgeval (78) *Moulin d'Orgeval*
Orgon (13) *Le Mas de la Rose*
Osthouse (67) *À la Ferme*
Paris 2e *Noailles*
Paris 3e *Du Petit Moulin*
Paris 4e *Bourg Tibourg*
Paris 4e *Caron de Beaumarchais*
Paris 6e *Des Académies et des Arts*
Paris 7e *Le Bellechasse*
Paris 8e *Le A*
Paris 8e *Centvingttrois*
Paris 8e *Chambiges Élysées*
Paris 8e *Pershing Hall*
Paris 16e *Bassano*
Paris 16e *Kléber*
Paris 17e *Banville*
Paris 17e *Waldorf Arc de Triomphe*
Peillon (06) *Auberge de la Madone*
Perros-Guirec (22) *Le Manoir du Sphinx*
Petit-Bersac (24) *Château Le Mas de Montet*
Le Pradet / Les Oursinières (83) *L'Escapade*
Puy-l'Évêque (46) *Bellevue*
Rennes (35) *Le Coq-Gadby*
Rocamadour (46) *Domaine de la Rhue*
Rodez (12) *La Ferme de Bourran*
Romans-sur-Isère (26) *L'Orée du Parc*
La Roque-sur-Pernes (84) *Château la Roque*
Saillagouse / Llo (66) *L'Atalaya*
St-Affrique-les-Montagnes (81) *Domaine de Rasigous*
St-Amour-Bellevue (71) *Auberge du Paradis*
St-Émilion (33) *Au Logis des Remparts*
St-Étienne-de-Baïgorry (64) *Arcé*
St-Flour / St-Georges (15) *Le Château de Varillettes*
St-Jean-de-Luz (64) *La Devinière*
St-Laurent-des-Arbres (30) *Le Saint-Laurent*
St-Martin-de-Belleville (73) *St-Martin*
St-Paul (06) *La Grande Bastide*
St-Paul (06) *Le Hameau*
St-Rémy-de-Provence (13) *Gounod*
St-Rémy-de-Provence (13) *La Maison de Bournissac*
St-Saud-Lacoussière (24) *Hostellerie St-Jacques*
St-Tropez (83) *Benkiraï*
St-Tropez (83) *La Maison Blanche*
St-Tropez (83) *La Mistralée*
St-Tropez (83) *Pastis*
St-Vallier (26) *Domaine des Buis*
Ste-Anne-d'Auray (56) *L'Auberge*
Salers / Le Theil (15) *Hostellerie de la Maronne*
Sare (64) *Arraya*
Saulxures (67) *La Belle Vue*
Sauternes (33) *Relais du Château d'Arche*
Sauveterre (30) *Château de Varenne*
Sélestat (67) *Auberge de l'Illwald*
Sélestat (67) *Les Prés d'Ondine*
Sézanne / Mondement-Montgivroux (51) *Domaine de Montgivroux*
Strasbourg (67) *Chut - Au Bain aux Plantes*
Toulouse (31) *Garonne*
Tournus / Brancion (71) *La Montagne de Brancion*
La Trinité-sur-Mer (56) *Le Lodge Kerisper*
La Trinité-sur-Mer (56) *Petit Hôtel des Hortensias*
Turquant (49) *Demeure de la Vignole*
Uchaux (84) *Château de Massillan*
Uzès (30) *Hostellerie Provençale*
Uzès / St-Maximin (30) *Château de St-Maximin*
Valaurie (26) *Le Moulin de Valaurie*
Vannes (56) *Villa Kerasy*
Vannes / Arradon (56) *Le Logis de Parc er Gréo*
Ygrande (03) *Château d'Ygrande*

Argenton-sur-Creuse (36) *Manoir de Boisvillers*
Avensan (33) *Le Clos de Meyre*
Beaune / Puligny-Montrachet (21) *La Chouette*
Biarritz (64) *Maison Garnier*
Bormes-les-Mimosas (83) *Hostellerie du Cigalou*
Cancale (35) *Auberge de la Motte Jean*
Clermont-l'Hérault / St-Saturnin-de-Lucian (34) *Du Mimosa*

Cliousclat (26) *La Treille Muscate*
Crest-Voland (73) *Caprice des Neiges*
Cuq-Toulza (81) *Cuq en Terrasses*
Deauville (14) *Villa Joséphine*
Eygalières (13) *Mas dou Pastré*
Florac / Cocurès (48) *La Lozerette*
Forcalquier (04) *Auberge Charembeau*
La Garde-Guérin (48) *Auberge Régordane*
Gordes (84) *La Ferme de la Huppe*
Le Grand-Bornand / Le Chinaillon (74) *Les Cimes*
Graveson (13) *Le Cadran Solaire*
Île de Ré / Ars-en-Ré (17) *Le Sénéchal*
Île de Ré / St-Martin-de-Ré (17) *La Maison Douce*
L'Isle-sur-la-Sorgue (84) *Le Mas des Grès*
Lyons-la-Forêt (27) *Les Lions de Beauclerc*
Le Mans / St-Saturnin (72) *Domaine de Chatenay*
Montauban-sur-l'Ouvèze (26) *La Badiane*
Montclus (30) *La Magnanerie de Bernas*
Moustiers-Ste-Marie (04) *La Ferme Rose*
Paris 16e *Windsor Home*
Propriano (2A) *Le Lido*
Rocamadour (46) *Troubadour*
St-Alban-sur-Limagnole (48) *Relais St-Roch*
St-Céré (46) *Villa Ric*
St-Disdier (05) *La Neyrette*
St-Laurent-du-Verdon (04) *Le Moulin du Château*
St-Malo / St-Servan-sur-Mer (35) *L'Ascott*
St-Prix (95) *Hostellerie du Prieuré*
Salers (15) *Saluces*
Sancerre / St-Thibault (18) *de la Loire*
Seignosse (40) *Villa de l'Etang Blanc*
Serre-Chevalier / Le Monêtier-les-Bains (05) *L'Alliey*
Vaison-la-Romaine / Crestet (84) *Mas de Magali*
Valberg (06) *Blanche Neige*
Val-d'Isère (73) *La Becca*
Wierre-Effroy (62) *La Ferme du Vert*

Aiguebelette-le-Lac / Lépin-le-Lac (73) *La Bageatière*
Alès / St-Hilaire-de-Brethmas (30) *Comptoir St-Hilaire*
Alleins (13) *Domaine de Méjeans*
Amboise (37) *Vieux Manoir*
Andelot-lès-St-Amour (39) *Château Andelot*
Apt / Saignon (84) *Chambre de Séjour avec Vue*
Argelès-sur-Mer (66) *Château Valmy*
Aubrac (12) *Catherine Painvin*
Aureille (13) *Le Balcon des Alpilles*
Auxerre / Appoigny (89) *Le Puits d'Athie*
Auxerre / Villefargeau (89) *Le Petit Manoir des Bruyères*
Avignon (84) *Lumani*
Ayguesvives (31) *La Pradasse*
Balazuc (07) *Château de Balazuc*
Barcelonnette / St-Pons (04) *Domaine de Lara*
Le Barroux (84) *L'Aube Safran*
Bastia (2B) *Château Cagninacci*
La Bastide-Clairence (64) *Maison Maxana*
La Baume (74) *La Ferme aux Ours*
Bazouges-la-Pérouse (35) *Le Château de la Ballue*
Beaulieu-sur-Dordogne / Brivezac (19) *Château de la Grèze*
Belle-Île / Le Palais (56) *Château de Bordenéo*
Bessonies (46) *Château de Bessonies*
Béziers / Villeneuve-lès-Béziers (34) *La Chamberte*
Biarritz (64) *Nere-Chocoa*
Biarritz (64) *Villa Le Goëland*
Biarritz / Arcangues (64) *Les Volets Bleus*
Blois / St-Denis-sur-Loire (41) *La Malouinière*
Bormes-les-Mimosas (83) *La Bastide des Vignes*
La Bourboule (63) *La Lauzeraie*
Bourg-en-Bresse / Lalleyriat (01) *Le Nid à Bibi*
Bras (83) *Une Campagne en Provence*
Le Bugue (24) *Maison Oléa*
Cabrières-d'Aigues (84) *Le Mas des Câpriers*
Cambrai (59) *Le Clos St-Jacques*
Cancon / St-Eutrope-de-Born (47) *Domaine du Moulin de Labique*
Carcassonne (11) *La Maison Coste*
Cascastel-des-Corbières (11) *Domaine Grand Guilhem*
Cassis (13) *Château de Cassis*
Cerdon (45) *Les Vieux Guays*
Cervione (2B) *Casa Corsa*
Chamonix-Mont-Blanc / Le Lavancher (74) *Les Chalets de Philippe*
Charolles (71) *Le Clos de l'Argolay*
Chassagne-Montrachet (21) *Château de Chassagne-Montrachet*
Chénérailles / Montignat (23) *La Maison Bleue*
Clémont (18) *Domaine des Givrys*
Clisson / Le Pallet (44) *Château de la Sébinière*
Collonges-la-Rouge (19) *Jeanne*
Colonzelle (26) *La Maison de Soize*
Corvol-d'Embernard (58) *Le Colombier de Corvol*
Coux-et-Bigaroque (24) *Manoir de la Brunie*
Crazannes (17) *Château de Crazannes*
Cucugnan (11) *La Tourette*
Cult (70) *Les Egrignes*
Danizy (02) *Domaine le Parc*
Derchigny (76) *Manoir de Graincourt*
Dournazac (87) *Château de Montbrun*
Drain (49) *Le Mésangeau*
Dreux / Vert-en-Drouais (28) *Château de Marsalin*

Eccica-Suarella (2A) *Carpe Diem Palazzu*
Les Échelles / St-Christophe-la-Grotte (73) *La Ferme Bonne de la Grotte*
Ennordres (18) *Les Chatelains*
Escatalens (82) *Maison des Chevaliers*
Espelette (64) *Irazabala*
Eu (76) *Manoir de Beaumont*
Farges-Allichamps (18) *Château de la Commanderie*
Fontenay-le-Comte (85) *Le Logis de la Clef de Bois*
Gramat (46) *Moulin de Fresquet*
Le Grand-Bornand / Le Bouchet (74) *Le Chalet des Troncs*
Grasse (06) *Moulin St-François*
Grez-en-Bouère (53) *Château de Chanay*
Guebwiller / Murbach (68) *Le Schaeferhof*
Hasparren (64) *Ferme Hégia*
Honfleur (14) *La Petite Folie*
Honfleur (14) *Le Clos Bourdet*
Île de Noirmoutier / Noirmoutier-en-l'Île (85) *La Maison de Marine*
Île de Ré / St-Martin-de-Ré (17) *Domaine de la Baronnie*
Île de Ré / St-Martin-de-Ré (17) *La Coursive St-Martin*
Île de Ré / St-Martin-de-Ré (17) *La Maison du Port*
Ivoy-le-Pré (18) *Château d'Ivoy*
Jarnac (16) *Château St-Martial*
Jullié (69) *Domaine de la Chapelle de Vâtre*
Landudec (29) *Château du Guilguiffin*
Lascabanes (46) *Le Domaine de Saint-Géry*
Lavannes (51) *La Closerie des Sacres*
Lestiac-sur-Garonne (33) *Les Logis de Lestiac*
Libourne / La Rivière (33) *Château de La Rivière*
Lille (59) *La Maison Carrée*
Linières-Bouton (49) *Château de Boissimon*
Lissac-sur-Couze (19) *Château de Lissac*
Lodève (34) *Domaine du Canalet*
Lorgues (83) *La Bastide du Pin*
Lyon / Écully (69) *Les Hautes Bruyères*
Mâcon / Hurigny (71) *Château des Poccards*
Manthelan (37) *Le Vieux Tilleul*
Martainville-Épreville (76) *Sweet Home*
Martigné-Briand (49) *Château des Noyers*
Maussane-les-Alpilles / Paradou (13) *La Maison du Paradou*
Meaux / Trilbardou (77) *M. et Mme Cantin*
Meauzac (82) *Manoir des Chanterelles*
Merry-sur-Yonne (89) *Le Charme Merry*
Monhoudou (72) *Château de Monhoudou*
Montbenoît / La Longeville (25) *Le Crêt l'Agneau*
Moustiers-Ste-Marie (04) *La Bouscatière*
Mutigny (51) *Manoir de Montflambert*
Nantes / La Haie-Fouassière (44) *Château du Breil*
Nantes / Pont-St-Martin (44) *Château du Plessis-Atlantique*
Neauphle-le-Château (78) *Le Clos Saint-Nicolas*
Notre-Dame-de-Livaye (14) *Aux Pommiers de Livaye*
Notre-Dame-du-Guildo (22) *Château du Val d' Arguenon*
Notre-Dame-du-Pé (72) *La Reboursière*
Oinville-sous-Auneau (28) *Caroline Lethuillier*
Ornans (25) *Le Jardin de Gustave*
Pérignac (16) *Château de Lerse*
Planguenoual (22) *Manoir de la Hazaie*
Plazac (24) *Béchanou*
Poitiers / Lavoux (86) *Logis du Château du Bois Dousset*
Poligny (05) *Le Chalet des Alpages*
Portel-des-Corbières (11) *Domaine de la Pierre Chaude*
Pouilly-en-Auxois / Créancey (21) *Château de Créancey*
Privas / Rochessauve (07) *Château de Rochessauve*
Quimperlé (29) *Château de Kerlarec*
Riantec (56) *La Chaumière de Kervassal*
Riquewihr (68) *Le B. Espace Suites*
Robion (84) *Mas la Fausseranne*
Rochefort (17) *Palmier sur Cour*
Rodez (12) *Château de Labro*
Roquebrune (06) *Le Roquebrune*
Rustrel (84) *La Forge*
St-Adjutory (16) *Château du Mesnieux*
St-André-de-Roquelongue (11) *Demeure de Roquelongue*
St-Bômer-les-Forges (61) *Château de la Maigraire*
St-Calais (72) *Château de la Barre*
St-Étienne-la-Thillaye (14) *La Maison de Sophie*
St-Front (43) *La Vidalle d'Eyglet*
St-Léon (47) *Le Hameau des Coquelicots*
St-Mathurin (85) *Le Château de la Millière*
St-Michel-Escalus (40) *La Bergerie-St-Michel*
St-Michel-Mont-Mercure (85) *Château de la Flocellière*
St-Palais-sur-Mer (17) *Ma Maison de Mer*
St-Pierre-d'Albigny (73) *Château des Allues*
St-Rémy-de-Provence (13) *La Maison du Village*
St-Silvain-Bellegarde (23) *Les Trois Ponts*
St-Sornin (17) *La Caussolière*
St-Valéry-en-Caux (76) *Château du Mesnil Geoffroy*
Ste-Mère-Église (50) *Château de L'Isle Marie*
Ste-Nathalène (24) *La Roche d'Esteil*
Segonzac (19) *Pré Laminon*
Soustons (40) *Domaine de Bellegarde*
Strasbourg (67) *La Belle Strasbourgeoise*
Toulon-la-Montagne (51) *Les Corettes*
Tournus (71) *La Tour du Trésorier*
Tourrettes-sur-Loup (06) *Histoires de Bastide*
Tourrettes-sur-Loup (06) *La Demeure de Jeanne*
Troyes / Moussey (10) *Domaine de la Creuse*
Tulette (26) *K-Za*
Uzer (07) *Château d'Uzer*
Uzès / Montaren-et-St-Médiers (30) *Clos du Léthé*
Valojoulx (24) *La Licorne*
Vals-les-Bains (07) *Château Clément*
Vence (06) *La Colline de Vence*
Vergoncey (50) *Château de Boucéel*
Verteuil-sur-Charente (16) *Le Couvent des Cordeliers*
Villemontais (42) *Domaine de Fontenay*
Villiers-sous-Grez (77) *La Cerisaie*
Vollore-Ville (63) *Château de Vollore*
Vouvray (37) *Domaine des Bidaudières*

Pleasant restaurants

Restaurants agréables
Ristoranti ameni
Angenehme Restaurants
Restaurantes agradables

XXXXX

Annecy / Veyrier-du-Lac (74) *La Maison de Marc Veyrat*
Antibes / Cap d'Antibes (06) *Eden Roc*
Les Baux-de-Provence (13) *L' Oustaù de Baumanière*
Illhaeusern (68) *Auberge de l'Ill*
Lyon (69) *Paul Bocuse*
Monte-Carlo (MC) *Le Louis XV-Alain Ducasse*
Paris 1er *L'Espadon*
Paris 1er *le Meurice*
Paris 5e *La Tour d'Argent*
Paris 8e *Alain Ducasse au Plaza Athénée*
Paris 8e *Les Ambassadeurs*
Paris 8e *Apicius*
Paris 8e *Le Bristol*
Paris 8e *Le "Cinq"*
Paris 8e *Lasserre*
Paris 8e *Ledoyen*
Paris 8e *Taillevent*

XXXX

Baerenthal / Untermuhlthal (57) *L'Arnsbourg*
Le-Bourget-du-Lac (73) *Le Bateau Ivre*
Cannes (06) *La Palme d'Or*
Lille (59) *A L'Huîtrière*
Lyon (69) *Pierre Orsi*
Lyon / Charbonnières-les-Bains (69) *La Rotonde*
Mandelieu / La Napoule (06) *L'Oasis*
Mionnay (01) *Alain Chapel*
Monte-Carlo (MC) *Grill de l'Hôtel de Paris*
Monte-Carlo (MC) *Joël Robuchon Monte-Carlo*
Montpellier (34) *Le Jardin des Sens*
Mougins (06) *Alain Llorca - Le Moulin de Mougins*
Nice (06) *Chantecler*
Paris 1er *Le Grand Véfour*
Paris 4e *L'Ambroisie*
Paris 8e *Laurent*
Paris 16e *La Grande Cascade*
Paris 16e *Pré Catelan*
La Rochelle (17) *Richard et Christopher Coutanceau*
Romans-sur-Isère / Granges-les-Beaumont (26) *Les Cèdres*
St-Bonnet-le-Froid (43) *Régis et Jacques Marcon*
Tourrettes (83) *Faventia*

Agen (47) *Mariottat*
Aix-en-Provence (13) *Le Clos de la Violette*
Antibes / Cap d'Antibes (06) *Bacon*
Antibes / Cap d'Antibes (06) *Les Pêcheurs*
Avignon (84) *Christian Étienne*
Balleroy (14) *Manoir de la Drôme*
Belle-Église (60) *La Grange de Belle-Eglise*
Bidart (64) *Table et Hostellerie des Frères Ibarboure*
Biot (06) *Les Terraillers*
Bonnieux (84) *La Bastide de Capelongue*
Boulogne-sur-Mer (62) *La Matelote*
Bourges (18) *L' Abbaye St-Ambroix*
Cancale (35) *Maisons de Bricourt*
Cassis (13) *La Villa Madie*
Chalon-sur-Saône / St-Rémy (71) *Moulin de Martorey*
Champtoceaux (49) *Les Jardins de la Forge*
Chasselay (69) *Guy Lassausaie*
Clisson (44) *La Bonne Auberge*
Compiègne / Rethondes (60) *Alain Blot*
Courchevel / Courchevel 1850 (73) *Le Bateau Ivre*
Dole / Sampans (39) *Château du Mont Joly*
Dunkerque / Coudekerque-Branche (59) *Le Soubise*
Fayence (83) *Le Castellaras*
Fontevraud-l'Abbaye (49) *La Licorne*
Fontjoncouse (11) *Auberge du Vieux Puits*
Forbach / Stiring-Wendel (57) *La Bonne Auberge*
Grenade-sur-l'Adour (40) *Pain Adour et Fantaisie*
Gundershoffen (67) *Au Cygne*
Le Lavandou / Aiguebelle (83) *Mathias Dandine*
Lourmarin (84) *Auberge La Fenière*
Lyon (69) *Les Terrasses de Lyon*
Maisons-Laffitte (78) *Tastevin*
Malbuisson (25) *Le Bon Accueil*
Monte-Carlo (MC) *Vistamar*
Montpellier / Lattes (34) *Domaine de Soriech*
Mougins (06) *La Terrasse*
Moulins (03) *Le Clos de Bourgogne*
Mulhouse / Rixheim (68) *Le Manoir*
Nantes / Haute-Goulaine (44) *Manoir de la Boulaie*
Nîmes / Garons (30) *Alexandre*
Obernai (67) *La Fourchette des Ducs*
Orléans / Olivet (45) *Le Rivage*
Ozoir-la-Ferrière (77) *La Gueulardière*
Pacy-sur-Eure / Cocherel (27) *La Ferme de Cocherel*
Pau (64) *Au Fin Gourmet*
Pont-Aven (29) *Moulin de Rosmadec*
Le Puy-en-Velay (43) *François Gagnaire*
Questembert (56) *Le Bretagne et sa Résidence*
Reims / Montchenot (51) *Grand Cerf*
Riquewihr (68) *Table du Gourmet*
La Roche-Bernard (56) *L'Auberge Bretonne*
La Roche-l'Abeille (87) *Le Moulin de la Gorce*
Les Sables-d'Olonne (85) *Beau Rivage*
St-Germain-en-Laye (78) *Cazaudehore*
St-Saturnin-lès-Apt (84) *Domaine des Andéols*
St-Valery-en-Caux (76) *Les Hêtres*
Sénart / Pouilly-le-Fort (77) *Le Pouilly*
Sierentz (68) *Auberge St-Laurent*
Strasbourg (67) *Buerehiesel*
Toulon (83) *Les Pins Penchés*
Toulouse / Colomiers (31) *L'Amphitryon*
Tournus (71) *Rest. Greuze*
Urt (64) *Auberge de la Galupe*
Valence / Pont-de-l'Isère (26) *Michel Chabran*
Vannes / Saint-Avé (56) *Le Pressoir*

Aire-sur-la-Lys / Isbergues (62) *Le Buffet*
Ajaccio (2A) *Palm Beach*
Alès / Saint-Privat-des-Vieux (30) *Le Vertige des Senteurs*
Antibes (06) *Oscar's*
Auxerre / Vincelottes (89) *Auberge Les Tilleuls*
Ay (51) *Vieux Puits*
Azay-le-Rideau / Saché (37) *Auberge du XIIe Siècle*
Bannegon (18) *Moulin de Chaméron*
Le Bar-sur-Loup (06) *La Jarrerie*
Beaune (21) *Caveau des Arches*
Béhuard (49) *Les Tonnelles*
Belcastel (12) *Vieux Pont*
Biarritz (64) *Campagne et Gourmandise*
Blainville-sur-Mer (50) *Le Mascaret*
Le-Bourget-du-Lac (73) *La Grange à Sel*
Bray-et-Lû (95) *Les Jardins d'Epicure*

Chaintré (71) *La Table de Chaintré*
Chamonix-Mont-Blanc (74) *La Maison Carrier*
Chamonix-Mont-Blanc / Les Praz-de-Chamonix (74) *La Cabane des Praz*
Charroux (03) *Ferme Saint-Sébastien*
Châtillon-sur-Chalaronne / L'Abergement-Clémenciat (01) *St-Lazare*
Clermont-l'Hérault / St-Guiraud (34) *Le Mimosa*
Couilly-Pont-aux-Dames (77) *Auberge de la Brie*
Divonne-les-Bains (01) *Le Rectiligne*
Eugénie-les-Bains (40) *La Ferme aux Grives*
Eygalières (13) *Bistrot d'Eygalières "Chez Bru"*
Falicon (06) *Parcours*
Ferrières-les-Verreries (34) *La Cour-Mas de Baumes*
Gordes (84) *L'Estellan*
Gordes (84) *Le Mas Tourteron*
Île de Ré / St-Martin-de-Ré (17) *Bô*
L'Isle-sur-Serein (89) *Auberge du Pot d'Étain*
Kilstett (67) *Au Cheval Noir*
Labaroche (68) *Blanche Neige*
Lapoutroie (68) *Les Alisiers*
Le Lavandou / Aiguebelle (83) *Le Sud*
Loiré (49) *Auberge de la Diligence*
Lyon (69) *Auberge de l'Île*
Marseille (13) *L'Épuisette*
Megève / Leutaz (74) *La Sauvageonne*
Mollégès (13) *Mas du Capoun*
Montauroux (83) *Auberge des Fontaines d'Aragon*
Montbazon (37) *Chancelière "Jeu de Cartes"*
Morteau (25) *Auberge de la Roche*
Nans-les-Pins (83) *Château de Nans*
Nantes (44) *L'Océanide*
Nice (06) *Jouni «Atelier du Goût»*
Nieuil (16) *La Grange aux Oies*
Orange (84) *Le Mas des Aigras*
Paris 6e *Le Restaurant*
Paris 7e *Il Vino d'Enrico Bernardo*
Paris 16e *Tsé Yang*
Plateau-d'Assy (74) *Les Métiers d'Art*
Le Pradet / Les Oursinières (83) *La Chanterelle*
Le Puy-en-Velay / Espaly-St-Marcel (43) *L'Ermitage*
La Rivière-Thibouville (27) *Le Manoir du Soleil d'Or*
Le Rouret (06) *Le Clos St-Pierre*
St-Agrève (07) *Domaine de Rilhac*
St-Ambroix / St-Victor-de-Malcap (30) *La Bastide des Senteurs*
St-Lyphard (44) *Auberge de Kerbourg*
St-Martin-de-Belleville (73) *La Bouitte*
Sassetot-le-Mauconduit (76) *Le Relais des Dalles*
Sessenheim (67) *Au Boeuf*
Strasbourg (67) *La Cambuse*
La Turbie (06) *Hostellerie Jérôme*
Vaison-la-Romaine (84) *Le Moulin à Huile*
Vaison-la-Romaine / Roaix (84) *Le Grand Pré*
Valbonne (06) *Daniel Desavie*
Valbonne (06) *Lou Cigalon*
Vence (06) *Le Vieux Couvent*
Verdun-sur-le-Doubs (71) *Hostellerie Bourguignonne*
Villefranche-sur-Mer (06) *L'Oursin Bleu*

Aix-en-Provence (13) *Pierre Reboul*
Arles (13) *La Chassagnette*
Auvers-sur-Oise (95) *Auberge Ravoux*
Avignon (84) *Les 5 Sens*
Bairols (06) *Auberge du Moulin*
Bédarieux / Villemagne-l'Argentière (34) *Auberge de l'Abbaye*
Biarritz (64) *Philippe*
Blois (41) *Au Rendez-vous des Pêcheurs*
Bonnieux (84) *Le Fournil*
Cagnes-sur-Mer (06) *Le Grimaldi*
Cancale (35) *La Maison de la Marine*
Chalon-sur-Saône (71) *Le Bistrot*
Cherbourg-Octeville (50) *Le Pommier*
Clermont-Ferrand (63) *Fleur de Sel*
Cormeilles (27) *Gourmandises*
Dax (40) *Une Cuisine en Ville*
Dinard / St-Lunaire (35) *Le Décollé*
Erquy / St-Aubin (22) *Relais St-Aubin*
Fontvieille (13) *Le Patio*
Gevrey-Chambertin (21) *Chez Guy*
Langon (33) *Chez Cyril*
Lavaur (24) *Auberge de Bayle Viel*
Merkwiller-Pechelbronn (67) *Auberge du Puits VI*
Notre-Dame-de-Bellecombe (73) *Ferme de Victorine*
Paris 7e *L'Atelier de Joël Robuchon*
Le Puy-en-Velay (43) *Le Poivrier*
St-Agrève (07) *Faurie*
St-Alban-sur-Limagnole (48) *La Petite Maison*
St-Marc-À-Loubaud (23) *Les Mille Sources*
St-Paul (06) *La Toile Blanche*
St-Vaast-la-Hougue (50) *Le Chasse Marée*
Ste-Cécile-les-Vignes (84) *Campagne, Vignes et Gourmandises*
Sare (64) *Olhabidea*
Tourrettes-sur-Loup (06) *Les Bacchanales*
Turenne (19) *Maison des Chanoines*
Vichy (03) *Brasserie du Casino*
Yvetot (76) *Auberge du Val au Cesne*

Further information

Pour en savoir plus

Per saperne di piú

Gut zu wissen

Para saber más

Vineyards & Regional Specialities

Vignobles & Spécialités régionales
Vini e Specialità regionali
Weinberge & regionale Spezialitäten
Viñedos y Especialidades regionales

① NORMANDIE

Demoiselles de Cherbourg à la nage,
Andouille de Vire,
Sole dieppoise,
Poulet Vallée d'Auge,
Tripes à la mode de Caen,
Canard à la rouennaise,
Agneau de pré-salé,
Camembert, Livarot, Pont-l'Évêque,
Neufchâtel,
Tarte aux pommes au calvados,
Crêpes à la normande, Douillons

② BRETAGNE

Fruits de mer, Crustacés, Huîtres de Belon,
Galettes au sarrazin/blé noir, Charcuteries,
Andouille de Guéméné, St-Jacques à la bretonne,
Homard à l'armoricaine,
Poissons : bar, turbot, lieu jaune,
maquereau, etc.,
Cotriade, Kig Ha Farz,
Légumes : artichaut, chou-fleur, etc.,
Crêpes, Gâteau breton, Far, Kouing-aman

③ VAL DE LOIRE

Rillettes de Tours, Andouillette au vouvray,
Poissons de rivière : brochet, sandre, etc.,
Saumon beurre blanc, Gibier de Sologne,
Fromages de chèvre : Ste-Maure, Valençay,
Crémet d'Angers, Macarons, Nougat glacé,
Pithiviers, Tarte tatin

④ SUD-OUEST

Garbure, Ttoro, Jambon de Bayonne,
Foie gras, Omelette aux truffes,
Pipérade, Lamproie à la bordelaise,
Poulet basquaise, Cassoulet,
Confit de canard ou d'oie,
Cèpes à la bordelaise,
Tomme de brebis, Roquefort,
Gâteau basque, Pruneaux à l'armagnac

⑤ CENTRE-AUVERGNE

Cochonnailles, Tripous,
Champignons : cèpes, girolles, etc.,
Pâté bourbonnais, Aligot, Potée auvergnate,
Chou farci, Pounti, Lentilles du Puy,
Cantal, St-Nectaire, Fourme d'Ambert,
Flognarde, Gâteau à la broche

⑬ NORD-PICARDIE

Moules, Ficelle picarde,
Flamiche aux poireaux,
Poissons : sole, turbot, etc.,
Potjevlesch, Waterzoï,
Gibier d'eau,
Lapin à la bière, Hochepot,
Boulette d'Avesnes,
Maroilles, Gaufres

⑫ BOURGOGNE

Jambon persillé,
Gougère,
Escargots de Bourgogne,
Œufs en meurette,
Pochouse, Coq au vin,
Jambon chaud à la crème,
Viande de charolais,
Bœuf bourguignon,
Époisses, Poire dijonnaise,
Desserts au pain d'épice

⑪ ALSACE-LORRAINE

Charcuterie, Presskopf,
Quiche lorraine, Tarte à l'oignon,
Grenouilles, Asperges,
Poissons : sandre, carpe, anguille,
Coq au riesling, Spaetzle,
Choucroute, Baeckeoffe,
Gibiers : biche, chevreuil, sanglier,
Munster, Kougelhopf,
Tarte aux mirabelles ou aux quetsches, Vacherin glacé

⑩ FRANCHE-COMTÉ/JURA

Jésus de Morteau, Saucisse de Montbéliard,
Croûte aux morilles, Soufflé au fromage,
Poissons de lac et rivières : brochet, truite,
Grenouilles, Coq au vin jaune, Comté, vacherin,
Morbier, Cancoillotte, Gaudes au maïs

⑨ LYONNAIS-PAYS BRESSAN

Rosette de Lyon, Grenouilles de la Dombes,
Gâteau de foies blonds, Quenelles de brochet,
Saucisson truffé pistaché, Poularde demi-deuil,
Tablier de sapeur, Cardons à la mœlle,
Volailles de Bresse à la crème,
Cervelle de canut, Bugnes

⑧ SAVOIE-DAUPHINÉ

Gratin de queues d'écrevisses,
Poissons de lac : omble chevalier, perche, féra,
Ravioles du Royans, Fondue, Raclette, Tartiflette,
Diots au vin blanc, Fricassée de caïon, Potée savoyarde,
Farçon, Farcement, Gratin dauphinois,
Beaufort, Reblochon, Tomme de Savoie,
St-Marcellin, Gâteau de Savoie, Gâteau aux noix,
Tarte aux myrtilles

⑦ PROVENCE-MÉDITERRANÉE

Aïoli, Pissaladière, Salade niçoise, Bouillabaisse,
Anchois de Collioure, Loup grillé au fenouil,
Brandade nîmoise, Bourride sétoise,
Pieds paquets à la marseillaise, Petits farcis niçois,
Daube provençale,
Agneau de Sisteron,
Picodon, Crème catalane,
Calissons, Fruits confits

⑥ CORSE

Jambon, Figatelli,
Lonzo, Coppa,
Langouste,
Omelette au brocciu,
Civet de sanglier,
Chevreau,
Fromages de brebis (Niolu),
Flan de châtaignes,
Fiadone

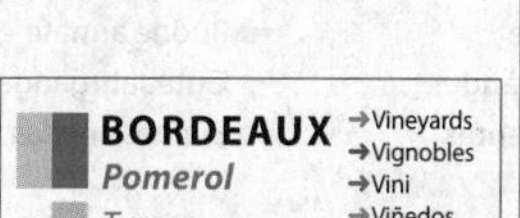

⑦ **CORSE**

Jambon

→ Regional specialities
→ Spécialités régionales
→ Vini e Specialità regionali
→ Viñedos y Especialidades regionales
→ Weinberge und regionale Spezialitäten

Choosing a good wine

Choisir le bon vin

Scegliere un buon vino

Der richtige Wein

Escoger el vino

	1995	1996	1997	1998	1999	2000	2001	2002	2003	2004	2005	2006
Alsace	Good	Good	Great	Good	Good	Great	Great	Good	Good	Good	Great	Good
White Bordeaux	Good	Great	Good	Good	Average	Great	Good	Average	Good	Good	Great	Good
Red Bordeaux	Great	Great	Average	Good	Good	Great	Good	Good	Good	Good	Great	Good
White Bourgogne	Great	Great	Great	Good	Good	Good	Average	Great	Good	Good	Great	Good
Red Bourgogne	Great	Great	Good	Good	Great	Good	Average	Great	Good	Good	Great	Good
Beaujolais	Great	Average	Great	Good	Great	Great	Good	Good	Great	Good	Great	Good
Champagne	Good	Great	Good	Good	Great	Average	Average	Good	Great	Good	Good	Good
Northern Côtes du Rhône	Good	Great	Good	Good	Great	Good	Good	Good	Good	Good	Great	Great
Southern Côtes du Rhône	Good	Great	Good	Great	Good	Great	Great	Average	Good	Good	Great	Good
Provence	Good	Good	Good	Average	Good	Good	Great	Good	Good	Good	Good	Good
Languedoc *Roussillon*	Good	Great	Good	Great	Good	Good	Good	Average	Good	Good	Good	Good
Val de Loire *Muscadet*	Great	Great	Good	Good	Good	Good	Good	Good	Great	Good	Great	Good
Val de Loire *Anjou-Touraine*	Great	Great	Good	Good	Good	Good	Good	Good	Great	Good	Great	Good
Val de Loire *Pouilly-Sancerre*	Good	Great	Great	Good	Good	Great	Good	Good	Great	Good	Great	Good

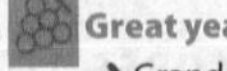
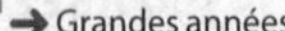

Great years
→ Grandes années
→ Grandi annate
→ Großen Jahrgänge
→ Añadas excelentes

Good years
→ Bonne années
→ Buone annate
→ Gute Jahrgänge
→ Buenas añadas

Average years
→ Années moyenne
→ Annate corrette
→ Mittlere Jahrgänge
→ Añadas correcias

The greatest vintages since 1970 : 1970 - 1975 - 1979 - 1982 - 1985 - 1989 - 1990 - 1996

→ Les grandes années depuis1970
→ Le grandi annate dal 1970
→ Dis größten Jahrgänge seit 1970
→ Las grandes añadas desde 1970

SUGGESTIONS FOR COMPLEMENTARY DISHES AND WINES

→ **Associer les mets & vins**

→ **Suggerimento per l'abbinamento tra cibo e vini**

→ **Empfehlungen welcher Wein zum welchem Gericht**

→ **Sugerencias para combinar platos y vinos**

Dishes	Region of production	Appellation
→ **SHELLFISH** Dry whites → CRUSTACÉS & COQUILLAGES : Blancs secs → CROSTACEI : Bianchi secchi → SCHALENTIERE : Trockene Weiße → CRUSTÁCEOS : Blancos seccos	Alsace Bordeaux Bourgogne Côtes du Rhône Provence Languedoc-Roussillon Val de Loire	Sylvaner/Riesling Entre-deux-Mers Chablis/Mâcon Villages St Joseph Cassis/Palette Picpoul de Pinet Muscadet/Montlouis
→ **FISH** Dry whites → POISSONS : Blancs secs → PESCI : Bianchi secchi → FISCHE : Trockene Weiße → PESCADOS : Blancos seccos	Alsace Bordeaux Bourgogne Côtes du Rhône Provence Corse Languedoc-Roussillon Val de Loire	Riesling Pessac-Léognan/Graves Meursault/Chassagne-Montrachet Hermitage/Condrieu Bellet/Bandol Patrimonio Coteaux du Languedoc Sancerre/Menetou-Salon
→ **POULTRY** Whites and light reds → VOLAILLES & CHARCUTERIES : Blancs et rouges légers → POLLAME : Bianchi e rossi leggeri → GEFLÜGEL : Weiße und leichte Rote → AVES : Blancos y tintos suaves	Alsace Champagne Bordeaux Bourgogne Beaujolais Côtes du Rhône Provence Corse Languedoc-Roussillon Val de Loire	Tokay-Pinot gris/Pinot noir Coteaux Champenois blanc et rouge Côtes de Bourg/Blaye/Castillon Mâcon/St Romain Beaujolais Villages Tavel (rosé)/Côtes du Ventoux Coteaux d'Aix-en-Provence Coteaux d'Ajaccio/Porto-Vecchio Faugères Anjou/Vouvray
→ **MEATS** Reds → VIANDES : Rouges → CARNI : Rossi → FLEISCH : Rote → CARNES : Tintos	Bordeaux/Sud-Ouest Bourgogne Beaujolais Côtes du Rhône Provence Languedoc-Roussillon Val de Loire	Médoc/St Émilion/Buzet Volnay/Hautes Côtes de Beaune Moulin à Vent/Morgon Vacqueyras/Gigondas Bandol/Côtes de Provence Fitou/Minervois Bourgueil/Saumur
→ **GAME** Hearty reds → GIBIER : Rouges corsés → SELVAGGINA : Rossi di corpo → WILD : Kräftige Rote → CAZAS : Tintos con cuerpo	Bordeaux/Sud-Ouest Bourgogne Côtes du Rhône Languedoc-Roussillon Val de Loire	Pauillac/St Estèphe/Madiran/Cahors Pommard/Gevrey-Chambertin Côte-Rotie/Cornas Corbières/Collioure Chinon
→ **CHEESES** Whites and reds → FROMAGES : Blancs et rouges → FORMAGGI : Bianchi e rossi → KÄSESORTEN : Weiße und Rote → QUESOS : Blancos y tintos	Alsace Bordeaux Bourgogne Beaujolais Côtes du Rhône Languedoc-Roussillon Jura/Savoie Val de Loire	Gewurztraminer St Julien/Pomerol/Margaux Pouilly-Fuissé/Santenay St Amour/Fleurie Hermitage/Châteauneuf-du-Pape St Chinian Vin Jaune/Chignin Pouilly-Fumé/Valençay
→ **DESSERTS** Dessert wines → DESSERTS : Vins de desserts → DESSERT : Vini da dessert → NACHTISCHE : Dessert-Weine → POSTRES : Vinos dulces	Alsace Champagne Bordeaux/Sud-Ouest Bourgogne Jura/Bugey Côtes du Rhône Languedoc-Roussillon Val de Loire	Muscat d'Alsace/Crémant d'Alsace Champagne blanc et rosé Sauternes/Monbazillac/Jurançon Crémant de Bourgogne Vin de Paille/Cerdon Muscat de Beaumes-de-Venise Banyuls/Maury/Muscats/Limoux Coteaux du Layon/Bonnezeaux

→ *Region of production* → *Région vinicole* → *Regione vinicola* → *Wein gegend* → *Regiõn vinicola*

→ *Appellation* → *Appellation* → *Denominazione* → *Appellation* → *Denominaciõn*

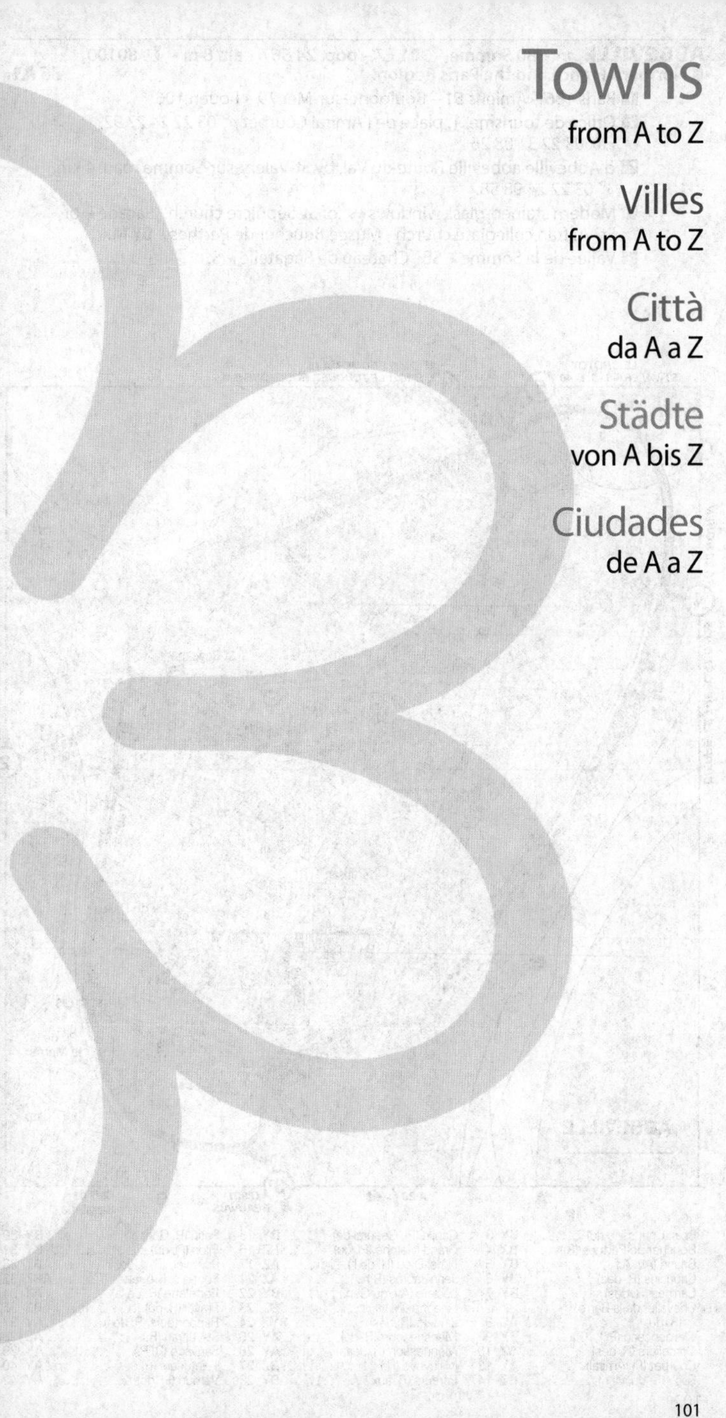

Towns
from A to Z

Villes
from A to Z

Città
da A a Z

Städte
von A bis Z

Ciudades
de A a Z

ABBEVILLE – 80 Somme – 301 E7 – pop. 24 567 – alt. 8 m – ✉ 80100

Northern France and the Paris Region 36 **A1**

- Paris 186 – Amiens 51 – Boulogne-sur-Mer 79 – Rouen 106
- Office de tourisme, 1, place de l'Amiral Courbet ☎ 03 22 24 27 92, Fax 03 22 31 08 26
- d'Abbeville abbeville Route du Val, by St-Valèry-sur-Somme road: 4 km, ☎ 03 22 24 98 58.
- Modern stained-glass windows★★ of St-Sépulcre church - Façade★ of St-Vulfran collegiate church - Musée Boucher de Perthes★ BY **M.**
- Vallée de la Somme★ SE - Château de Bagatelle★ S.

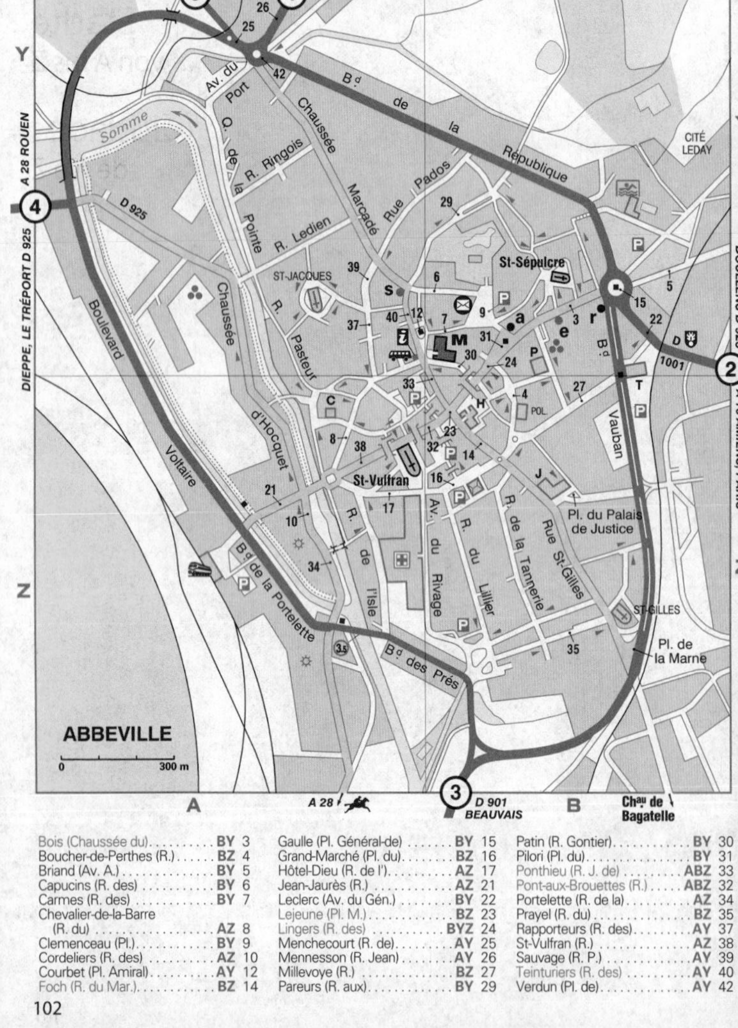

Bois (Chaussée du) . . . . BY 3	Gaulle (Pl. Général-de) . . . . BY 15	Patin (R. Gontier) . . . . BY 30
Boucher-de-Perthes (R.) . . . . BZ 4	Grand-Marché (Pl. du) . . . . BZ 16	Pilori (Pl. du) . . . . BY 31
Briand (Av. A.) . . . . BY 5	Hôtel-Dieu (R. de l') . . . . AZ 17	Ponthieu (R. J. de) . . . . ABZ 33
Capucins (R. des) . . . . BY 6	Jean-Jaurès (R.) . . . . AZ 21	Pont-aux-Brouettes (R.) . . . . ABZ 32
Carmes (R. des) . . . . BY 7	Leclerc (Av. du Gén.) . . . . BY 22	Portelette (R. de la) . . . . AZ 34
Chevalier-de-la-Barre (R. du) . . . . AZ 8	Lejeune (Pl. M.) . . . . BZ 23	Prayel (R. du) . . . . BZ 35
Clemenceau (Pl.) . . . . BY 9	Lingers (R. des) . . . . BYZ 24	Rapporteurs (R. des) . . . . AY 37
Cordeliers (R. des) . . . . AZ 10	Menchecourt (R. de) . . . . AY 25	St-Vulfran (R.) . . . . AZ 38
Courbet (Pl. Amiral) . . . . AY 12	Mennesson (R. Jean) . . . . AY 26	Sauvage (R. P.) . . . . AY 39
Foch (R. du Mar.) . . . . BZ 14	Millevoye (R.) . . . . BZ 27	Teinturiers (R. des) . . . . AY 40
	Pareurs (R. aux) . . . . BY 29	Verdun (Pl. de) . . . . AY 42

Mercure Hôtel de France rest,
19 pl. Pilori – ✆ 03 22 24 00 42 – h5440@accor.com
– Fax 03 22 24 26 15 – Closed March BY **a**
72 rm – €94/98 €110/118, €12 – **Rest** – Menu (€16), €20 – Carte €24/40
◆ This large town-centre establishment with a brick façade offers fresh, well-equipped rooms, as well as one suite with a "spa" bath. Comfortable wine bar. A bright veranda dining room with rotisserie corner; grills and traditional cuisine.

Relais Vauban without rest
4 bd Vauban – ✆ 03 22 25 38 00 – contact@relais-vauban.com
– Fax 03 22 31 75 97 – Closed 1st-9 March, 20 December-4 January BY **r**
22 rm – €48/51 €50/54, €7,50
◆ Small hotel on a busy street near the town centre, offering bright and functional rooms. Friendly service and extremely well kept.

La Fermette des Prés de Mautort without rest
10 imp. de la Croix by ⑤ – ✆ 03 22 24 57 62
– brigitte.delahaye2@wanadoo.fr – Fax 03 22 24 57 62
3 rm – €45 €50
◆ Distinctive country farm offering the promise of a good night's sleep in comfortable rooms. Breakfast on the veranda or terrace overlooking the garden (indoor pool).

L'Escale en Picardie
15 r. des Teinturiers – ✆ 03 22 24 21 51 – Fax 03 22 24 21 51
– Closed 21 August-9 September, 23 February-7 March, Thursday dinner, Sunday dinner and Monday AY **s**
Rest – Menu (€21 bi), €32/45 – Carte €42/63
◆ Succulent fish and seafood served in a rustic dining room with beams and a stone fireplace: a charming welcome awaits you in this restaurant.

La Corne
32 chaussée du Bois – ✆ 03 22 24 06 34 – mlematelot@aol.com
– Fax 03 22 24 03 65 – Closed 15-30 July, Christmas holidays, Saturday lunch and Sunday BY **e**
Rest – Menu (€15), €23 – Carte €28/49
◆ A blue façade and an attractive retro interior for this old Abbeville house, transformed into a restaurant. Generous, bistro-style cuisine, including calf's sweetbreads and *andouillette*...

in St-Riquier **9 km by ②, D 925 – pop. 1 186 – alt. 29 m – ✉ 80135**
Syndicat d'initiative, le Beffroi ✆ 03 22 28 91 72,
Fax 03 22 28 02 73

Jean de Bruges without rest
18 pl. de l'Église – ✆ 03 22 28 30 30 – jeandebruges@wanadoo.fr
– Fax 03 22 28 00 69
11 rm – €100 €110/225, €14
◆ On the square in front of the Abbey, an elegant 17C house in white stone. Rooms have lots of character and contain antique furniture. Breakfast room under a glass canopy.

in Mareuil-Caubert **4 km South by D 928 (direction hippodrome then Rouen road) – pop. 890 – alt. 12 m – ✉ 80132**

Auberge du Colvert
4 rte Rouen – ✆ 03 22 31 32 32 – Fax 03 22 31 32 32
– Closed 28 July-8 August, Sunday dinner, Tuesday dinner and Wednesday
Rest – Menu €13 (weekday lunch), €19/28 – Carte €25/30
◆ A country inn with a wood-panelled dining room, brightened by large bay windows and heated by a hanging fireplace. Traditional seasonal cuisine.

L'ABERGEMENT-CLÉMENCIAT **– 01 Ain – 328** C4 **– see Châtillon-sur-Chalaronne**

L'ABER-WRAC'H – 29 Finistère – 308 D3 – ✉ 29870 Landeda
Brittany 9 **A1**

Paris 605 – Brest 28 – Landerneau 34 – Morlaix 69 – Quimper 94

Les Abers★★.

La Baie des Anges without rest

350 rte des Anges – ☎ 02 98 04 90 04 – contact@lesanges.fr – Fax 02 98 04 92 27 – Closed February

26 rm – €90/115 €125/185, €14 – 4 suites

◆ A charming hotel facing the wild landscapes of Aber Wrac'h. Peaceful, bright and modern rooms. If possible, book those with a sea view.

La Villa Les Anges without rest l'Aber,

16 rte des Anges – Closed February

11 rm – €105/130 €105/195, €16

◆ Contemporary villa facing the sea, a stone's throw from the main hotel.

ABLIS – 78 Yvelines – 311 G4 – pop. 2 705 – alt. 151 m – ✉ 78660 18 **A2**

Paris 62 – Chartres 31 – Mantes-la-Jolie 64 – Orléans 79 – Rambouillet 14 – Versailles 49

Syndicat d'initiative, Hôtel de Ville ☎ 01 30 46 06 06, Fax 01 30 46 06 07

West 6 km by D 168 – ✉ 28700 St-Symphorien-le-Château

Château d'Esclimont

2 rue Château d'Esclimont – ☎ 02 37 31 15 15 – esclimont@grandesetapes.fr – Fax 02 37 31 57 91

52 rm – €160/890 €160/890, €22 – 5 suites – **Rest** – Menu €39 (weekday lunch), €55/89 – Carte €61/90

◆ For a taste of château life, visit this 15C and 16C residence, former home of the La Rochefoucauld family. Magnificent park with lake, river and landscaped gardens. A dining room in 18C style and another renowned for its exquisite Cordova leather.

ABRESCHVILLER – 57 Moselle – 307 N7 – pop. 1 285 – alt. 340 m – ✉ 57560
Alsace-Lorraine 27 **D2**

Paris 433 – Baccarat 46 – Lunéville 62 – Phalsbourg 23 – Sarrebourg 17 – Strasbourg 79

Office de tourisme, 78, rue Jordy ☎ 03 87 03 77 26, Fax 03 87 03 77 26

Auberge de la Forêt

276 r. des Verriers, in Lettenbach : 0,5 km – ☎ 03 87 03 71 78 – aubergedelaforet2@wanadoo.fr – Fax 03 87 03 79 96 – Closed 1st-21 January, Tuesday dinner and Monday

Rest – Menu (€18), €24/39 – Carte €33/52

◆ Smart village inn with charming dining rooms, the most recent with splendid contemporary settings. Traditional cuisine and regional specialities.

ABREST – 03 Allier – 326 H6 – see Vichy

ACCOLAY – 89 Yonne – 319 F6 – pop. 433 – alt. 125 m – ✉ 89460
Burgundy-Jura 7 **B2**

Paris 188 – Avallon 31 – Auxerre 23 – Tonnerre 40

Hostellerie de la Fontaine with rm

16 r. Reigny – ☎ 03 86 81 54 02 – hostellerie.fontaine@wanadoo.fr – Fax 03 86 81 52 78 – Open 14 February-15 November, and closed Sunday dinner from 1st October to 31 March, Tuesday lunch and Monday

11 rm – €51 €54, €9 – ½ P €60 – **Rest** – *(closed at lunchtime from Mon. to Thurs.)* Menu €26/41 – Carte €31/46

◆ A Burgundian house located in a sleepy village in the Cure valley. Meals are served in the old wine cellar or, weather permitting, in the pleasant flower garden.

ACQUIGNY – 27 Eure – 304 H6 – pop. 1 438 – alt. 19 m – ✉ 27400 33 D2

Paris 105 – Évreux 22 – Mantes-la-Jolie 54 – Rouen 38

XX L' Hostellerie

1 r. d'Evreux – ✆ 02 32 50 20 05 – Fax 02 32 50 56 04 – Closed 14 July-5 August, 23 February-10 March, Sunday dinner, Tuesday dinner and Monday

Rest – Menu (€ 19), € 28/68 bi – Carte € 38/96

◆ Well-prepared, modern food to be appreciated in a cosy and quiet atmosphere in a warm-coloured dining room with discreetly modern decorations. Charming welcome.

X La Table du Béarnais

40 r. A.-Briand – ✆ 02 32 40 37 73 – Fax 02 32 25 94 69 – Closed Thursday dinner, Sunday dinner and Monday

Rest – Menu € 12,50 (weekday lunch), € 28/49 – Carte € 55/67

◆ This pleasant house welcomes you in two dining rooms with a rustic atmosphere (exposed beams, lamps on the tables). The tasty dishes are full of flavours from Béarn and Landes.

LES ADRETS-DE-L'ESTÉREL – 83 Var – 340 P4 – pop. 2 063 – alt. 295 m – ✉ 83600 42 E2

Paris 881 – Cannes 26 – Draguignan 44 – Fréjus 17 – Grasse 30 – Mandelieu-la-Napoule 15

Office de tourisme, place de la Mairie ✆ 04 94 40 93 57

Massif de l'Estérel★★★, French Riviera

La Verrerie without rest

– ✆ 04 94 40 93 51 – reservations@laverrerie.com – Fax 04 94 44 10 35

7 rm – †€ 50/60 ††€ 65/75, ☕ €8

◆ Mediterranean-style building situated within the village, appreciated for its relaxing surroundings. Rooms are cool and spacious.

Southeast 3 km by D 237 and D N7 – ✉ 83600 Les Adrets-de-l'Esterel

Auberge des Adrets

– ✆ 04 94 82 11 82 – info@auberge-adrets.com – Fax 04 94 82 11 80 – Open 11avril-12 October

10 rm – †€ 118/230 ††€ 156/256, ☕ € 16

Rest – *(open 30 March-30 September and closed lunch from Monday to Thursday in July August, Sunday dinner and Monday off season)* Menu € 45/68 – Carte € 73/84

◆ Building with character where each room is personalised with lovely furniture. Welcoming lounge, small, pleasant swimming pool and pretty green garden with hammocks. Elegant and cosy restaurant. The terrace offers magnificent views of the Esterel Hills."

Luxury pad or humble abode?
X and 🏠 denote categories of comfort.

AFA – 2A Corse-du-Sud – 345 B8 – see Corse (Ajaccio)

AFFIEUX – 19 Corrèze – 329 L2 – pop. 349 – alt. 480 m – ✉ 19260 25 C2

Paris 472 – Limoges 83 – Tulle 39 – Brive-la-Gaillarde 64 – Ussel 66

X Le Cantou

au bourg – ✆ 05 55 98 13 67 – Fax 05 55 98 13 67 – Closed Sunday dinner and Wednesday

Rest – Menu € 16 (weekday lunch)/32 – Carte € 37/51

◆ A small romantic dining room for the winter months and a veranda for the summer. Whatever the season, enjoy a delicious mix of traditional and regional cuisine.

AGAY – 83 Var – **340** Q5 – ✉ **83530** French Riviera 42 **E2**

Paris 880 – Cannes 34 – Draguignan 43 – Fréjus 12 – Nice 65 – St-Raphaël 9

Syndicat d'initiative, place Giannetti ✆ 04 94 82 01 85, Fax 04 94 82 74 20

Massif de L'Estérel★★★.

France-Soleil without rest VISA

206 av. des Pléiades – ✆ 04 94 82 01 93 – hotelfrancesoleil@aol.com – Fax 04 94 82 73 95 – Open from Easter to October

18 rm – €85/143 €85/143, €10

◆ Set back slightly from the coast is this modest family hotel. The simple rooms are contained in three small buildings, most with sea views.

AGDE – 34 Hérault – **339** F9 – **pop. 19 988** – **alt. 5 m** – **Casino : at Cap d'Agde BY** – ✉ **34300** Languedoc-Roussillon-Tarn Gorges 23 **C2**

Paris 754 – Béziers 24 – Lodève 60 – Millau 118 – Montpellier 56 – Sète 25

Office de tourisme, 1, place Molière ✆ 04 67 94 29 68, Fax 04 67 94 03 50

du Cap-d'Agde Le Cap-d'Agde 4 avenue des Alizés, South: 4 km by D 32, ✆ 04 67 26 54 40.

Former St-Étienne cathedral ★.

Athéna without rest VISA

av. F.-Mitterrand, Cap d'Agde road, D 32[E10] – ✆ 04 67 94 21 90 – hotel.athena@free.fr – Fax 04 67 94 80 80

32 rm – €48/80 €48/80, €8

◆ Modern hotel on the outskirts of the town. Rooms are well-equipped and decorated in sober Provençal style, some with terrace or loggia. Quieter to the rear.

La Table de Stéphane VISA

2 r. des Moulins-à-Huile, (The septs fonts area) – ✆ 04 67 26 45 22 – caroline@latabledestephane.com – Fax 04 67 26 45 22 – Closed 20-30 October, 2-9 January, 16-23 February, Sunday dinner except 12 July-30 August, Saturday lunch and Monday

Rest – *(pre-book)* Menu (€ 20 bi), € 25/59 – Carte € 45/70

◆ Dishes in keeping with current tastes and good regional wine list served in a modern decor enhanced by splashes of pastels. Drinks and coffee served in the sitting room.

Larcen VISA

41 r. Brescou – ✆ 04 67 00 01 01 – restaurantlarcen@orange.fr – Closed 10-30 June, Sunday and Monday

Rest – Carte € 24/41

◆ A bay window allows you to see the kitchens from the spacious and modern dining room. Lovely terrace with pool, palm trees and bougainvilleas. Modern menu.

in Grau d'Agde 4 km Southwest by D 32[E] – ✉ **34300**

L'Adagio VISA

3 quai Cdt-Méric – ✆ 04 67 21 13 00 – contact@ladagio.fr – Fax 04 67 21 13 00 – Closed 20 December-31 January, Wednesday except dinner in season and Monday from July to September

Rest – Menu € 15 (weekday lunch), € 27/57 – Carte € 47/59

◆ Modern cuisine in a light dining room, with pretty, wrought iron furniture. The coming and going of boats on the Hérault will entertain you while you eat on the terrace.

in Cap d'Agde 5 km Southeast by D 32[E10] – ✉ **34300**

Office de tourisme, rond-point du Bon Accueil ✆ 04 67 01 04 04, Fax 04 67 26 22 99

Ephèbe d'Agde★★ at the musée de l'Ephèbe.

Plans on following pages

Du Golfe VISA

Île des Loisirs – ✆ 04 67 26 87 03 – hotel.golf@tahoe.fr – Fax 04 67 26 26 89 – Closed January and February BY **m**

50 rm – €95/185 €95/185, €20 – 3 suites

Rest *Caladoc* – see restaurant listing

◆ The ochre façade of this hotel situated on the famous island has elegant modern rooms (on the resort or pool side) and a good fitness centre.

Palmyra Golf Hôtel without rest

av. des Alizés – ✆ 04 67 01 50 15 – palmyragolf@wanadoo.fr – Fax 04 67 01 50 14 – Open 15 March-17 November AX **p**

33 rm – €95/290 €95/290, ☕ €18 – 1 suite

◆ The Palmyra's spacious, elegant and modern rooms are located around a patio and offer a balcony or terrace overlooking the golf course.

Capaô rest, rm,

r. des Corsaires – ✆ 04 67 26 99 44 – contact@capao.com – Fax 04 67 26 55 41 – Open 5 April-5 October AY **b**

55 rm – €72/130 €78/145, ☕ €12 – ½ P €72/108

Rest *Le Manhattan* – *✆ 04 67 26 21 54 (open 5 April-30 September) (dinner only)* Menu €28/59 – Carte €43/80

Rest *Capaô Beach* – *✆ 04 67 26 41 25 (open 1st May-30 September) (lunch only except July-August)* Carte €32/49

◆ This hotel complex, near the Richelieu beach, offers numerous sports facilities. Spacious rooms with balconies. At the Manhattan, large, modern dining room, terraces and sea-inspired food. The Capaô Beach serves buffet meals and grilled food by the waterside.

La Grande Conque without rest

La Grande Conque – ✆ 04 67 26 11 42 – information@hotelgrandeconque.com – Fax 04 67 26 24 15 – Open April-October CY **a**

20 rm – €79/99 €120, ☕ €13

◆ An attractive location facing the sea and the black sand beach for this hotel perched on basalt cliffs. Rooms are spacious and all have loggia.

La Bergerie du Cap without rest

4 av. Cassiopée – ✆ 04 67 01 71 35 – labergerieducap@hotmail.fr – Fax 04 67 26 14 11 – Open 21 March-5 October

12 rm – €85/200 €85/250, ☕ €12

◆ 18C sheepfold converted into a hotel with cosy rooms in various styles. Terrace opposite the pool and Jacuzzi.

Les Grenadines without rest

6 impasse Marie-Céleste – ✆ 04 67 26 27 40 – hotelgrenadines@hotelgrenadines.com – Fax 04 67 26 10 80 – Open 1st February-9 November AY **k**

20 rm – €57/98 €57/130, ☕ €10

◆ A pleasant residence, noted for its family atmosphere and its practical rooms. Its proximity to the beaches, Aqualand and to the "Île des Loisirs" will appeal to children and adults alike.

Azur without rest

18 av. Iles d'Amérique – ✆ 04 67 26 98 22 – contact@hotelazur.com – Fax 04 67 26 48 14 AX **f**

34 rm – €46/96 €46/96, ☕ €8

◆ A privileged site in the centre of the resort, well-equipped rooms – some with mezzanine – and a pleasant swimming pool are just some of the advantages of this hotel.

Caladoc – Hôtel du Golfe

Île des Loisirs – ✆ 04 67 26 87 03 – hotel.golf@tahoe.fr – Fax 04 67 26 26 89 – Open May-October and closed Sunday and Monday BY **m**

Rest – *(dinner only)* Menu €28/65

◆ Designer furnishings and wood panelling (wenge, mangrove): a "Zen" decor for a cuisine in keeping with current taste. Languedoc wines in the feature cellar.

La Pléiade

3 av. des Alizés – ✆ 04 67 01 56 12 – pleiade34@orange.fr – Fax 04 67 31 33 86 – Closed dinner from October to June AX **p**

Rest – Menu (€16), €19/31 – Carte €27/47

◆ Restaurant set in the Palmyra Golf hotel. The welcoming and refined dining room has a pleasant view of the greens. Traditional food.

LE CAP D'AGDE

Acadiens (Allée des) .... **CX** 3
Alfonse (Av. du Chevalier d') . **AX** 4
Alizés (Av. des) .... **AXY**
Antilles (Rd-Pt des) .... **AY** 6
Beaupré (Quai du) .... **CX** 7
Belle Isle (Av. de)......... **ABX**
Bon Accueil (Rd-Pt du)...... **BX** 9
Bouteillou (Rd-Pt du) .... **CX** 10
Cantinières (Av. des) .... **CX**
Capelet (Quai du) .... **AX** 12
Challiès (Av. du Passeur)... **ABY**
Chandelles (R. des) .... **BX** 15
Contrebandiers (Av. des)... **BCX**
Corsaires (R. des) .... **AY**
Courette (R. de la) .... **CX** 17
Dominico (Quai Di) .... **BX** 18
Estacade (R. de l') .... **BY** 19
Falaise (R. de la) .... **CY** 21
Flânerie (Allée de la)........ **CX** 23
Fouquet (Rd-Pt Nicolas)...... **BX** 24
Gabelle (R. de la) .... **BX** 26
Galères (Av. des) .... **CX**
Gallo-Romains (R. des) ..... **AX**
Garnison (R. de la) .... **CXY**
Gentilshommes (Cours des) **CXY**
Gouverneur (R. du).......... **CX**
Grenadiers (R. des) .... **CX** 31
Hallebardes (Av. des) .... **CX** 32
Hune (R. de la) .... **BX** 34
Iles-d'Amérique (Av. des).... **AY** 36
Ile (Av. de l') .... **BCY**
Jetée (Av. de la) .... **CY**
Joutes (Quai des) .... **BX** 39
Labech (R. du) .... **BX**
Louisiane (Allée de la) ...... **CX** 40
Miquel (Quai Jean) .... **BCX**
Outre-Mer (Av. d')........... **AY**
Pacifique (R. du) .... **AY**
Phocéens (Quai des) .... **CY** 42
Radoub (Rd-Pt du) .... **CY** 43
St-Martin-des-Vignes (R.).... **AX**
St-Martin (Quai) .... **BX** 48
Sarret-de-Coussergue (R.) . **ABX**
Sergents (Av. des) .... **BCX**
Soldats (Av. des)............ **CX**
Surintendant (Av. du) .... **BX**
Tambour (R. du) .... **BX** 51
Tirème (Quai de la) .... **CXY** 56
Tours-de-St-Martin
(Rd-Pt des) .... **AX** 53
Trinquette (Quai de la) ...... **CX** 54
Vaisseaux (R. des) .... **CX**
Vent-des-Dames (R. du)..... **BX**
Vieux Cap (Quai du) .... **BY**
Volvire-de-Brassac (R.)...... **AX**
2-Frères (R. des) .... **CY**
4-Cantons (Allée des)....... **CX** 60

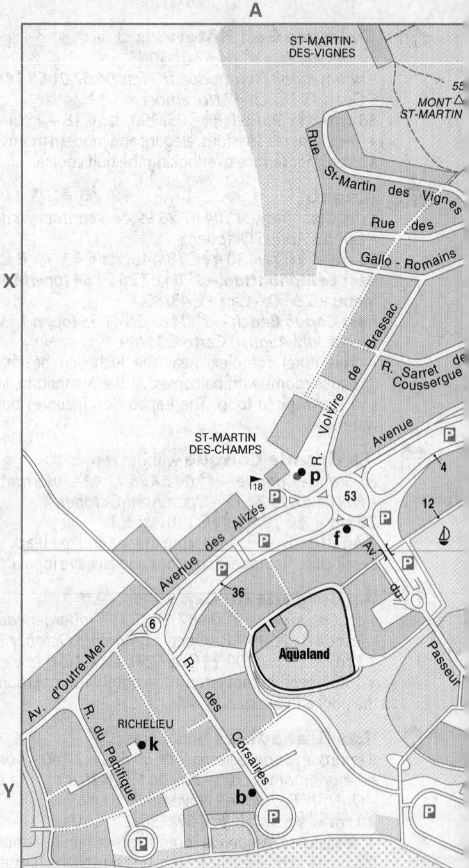

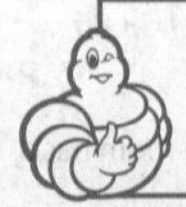

Undecided between two equivalent establishments?
Within each category,
establishments are classified in our order of preference.

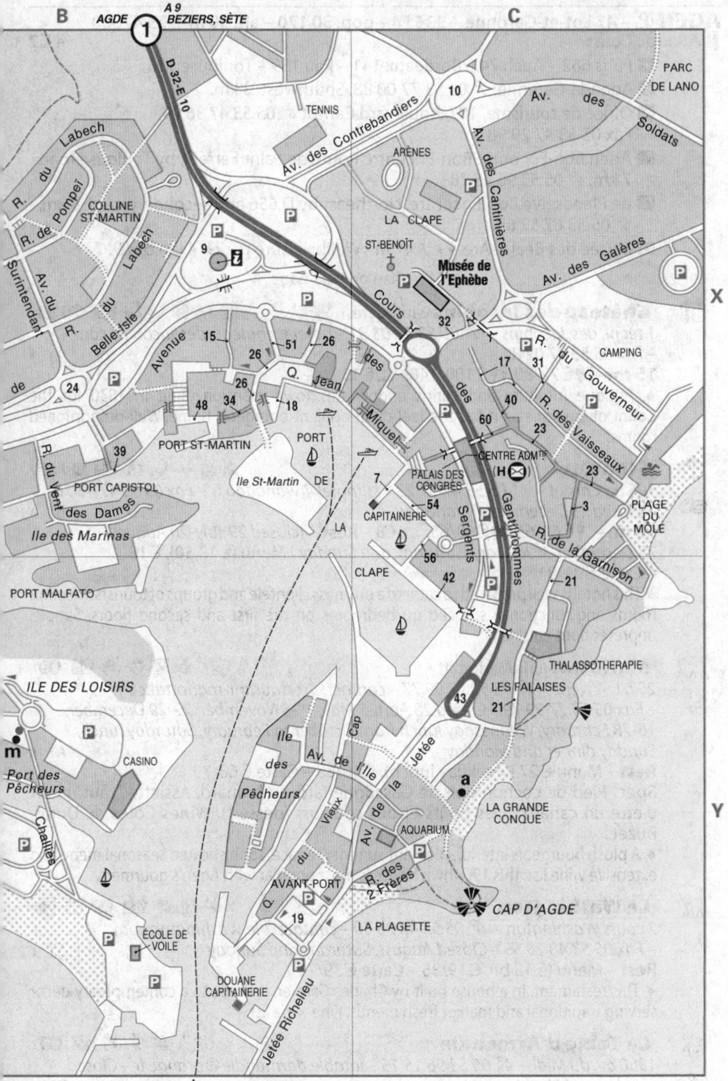

B AGDE A 9 BEZIERS, SÈTE C

1

D 32-E 10

PARC DE LANO
10
TENNIS
Av. des Soldats
Av. des Contrebandiers
ARÈNES
Av. des Cantinières
Labech
R. du
R. de Pompeï
COLLINE ST-MARTIN
LA CLAPE
ST-BENOÎT
Musée de l'Ephèbe
Av. des Galères
9
Surintendant
Av. du
R. du Labech
Belle-Isle
Cours
X
32
CAMPING
R. du Gouverneur
Avenue
15
51
26
26
26
Q. Jean Miquel
des
17
31
de
24
48
34
18
40
R. des Vaisseaux
60
23
PORT
PORT ST-MARTIN
CENTRE ADMTIF
39
R. du Vent des Dames
PORT CAPISTOL
Ile St-Martin
DE
7
PALAIS DES CONGRÈS
23
54
CAPITAINERIE
3
PLAGE DU MÔLE
Ile des Marinas
LA
Sergents
Gentilhommes
R. de la Garnison
CLAPE
56
PORT MALFATO
42
21
THALASSOTHERAPIE
ILE DES LOISIRS
LES FALAISES
43
21
m
CASINO
Port des Pêcheurs
Ile des Pêcheurs
Cap
Av. de l'Ile
Jetée
Av. de la
a
LA GRANDE CONQUE
Y
Vieux
du
AQUARIUM
Challies
Q.
AVANT-PORT
R. des 2 Frères
CAP D'AGDE
19
LA PLAGETTE
ÉCOLE DE VOILE
DOUANE CAPITAINERIE
Jetée Richelieu

B FORT DE BRESCOU C

Good food and accommodation at moderate prices?
Look for the Bib symbols: red Bib Gourmand for food,
blue Bib Hotel for hotels.

AGEN P – 47 Lot-et-Garonne – 336 F4 – pop. 30 170 – alt. 50 m – ✉ 47000

Atlantic Coast 4 **C2**

Paris 662 – Auch 74 – Bordeaux 141 – Pau 159 – Toulouse 116

Agen-la-Garenne: ✆ 05 53 77 00 88, Southwest: 3 km.

Office de tourisme, 107, boulevard Carnot ✆ 05 53 47 36 09, Fax 05 53 47 29 98

Agen Bon-Encontre Bon-Encontre Route de Saint Ferréol, by Toulouse road: 7 km, ✆ 05 53 96 95 78 ;

de Pleneselve Bon-Encontre, Northeast by D 656 and secondary road: 8 km, ✆ 05 53 67 52 65.

Musée des Beaux-Arts★★ AXY **M** - Walibi leisure park★ 4 km by ⑤.

Plan on next page

Château des Jacobins without rest

1 ter pl. des Jacobins – ✆ 05 53 47 03 31 – hotel@chateau-des-jacobins.com – Fax 05 53 47 02 80 AY **f**

15 rm – †€ 72/80 ††€ 100/140, ☕ € 13

◆ Antique furniture and curios endow this town mansion. Built in 1830 for the Count of Cassigneau, it has the feel of an opulent bourgeois home. Well-proportioned rooms.

Stim'Otel

105 bd Carnot – ✆ 05 53 47 31 23 – stimotel@wanadoo.fr – Fax 05 53 47 48 70 – Closed 23 December-1st January BY **a**

58 rm – †€ 60/65 ††€ 60/65, ☕ €8 – **Rest** – *(closed 29 July-20 August, 23 December-1st January, Saturday and Sunday)* Menu (€ 13,50), € 18 – Carte € 21/31

◆ This hotel is well prepared to cater to a business clientele and groups of tourists: meeting rooms and functional, spruced up bedrooms on the first and second floors. Simple, unpretentious cuisine.

Mariottat (Eric Mariottat)

25 r. L.-Vivent – ✆ 05 53 77 99 77 – contact@restaurant-mariottat.com – Fax 05 53 77 99 79 – Closed 28 April-5 May, 1st-5 November, 22-29 December, 16-28 February, Wednesday lunch from October to February, Saturday lunch, Sunday dinner and Monday AY **s**

Rest – Menu € 27 (weekday lunch), € 40/68 – Carte € 68/79

Spec. Pied de cochon noir de Gascogne farci au homard. Assiette "tout un art d'être un canard". Des goûts et des couleurs (dessert). **Wines** Côtes de Duras, Buzet.

◆ A plush bourgeois interior, pleasant summer terrace, sophisticated seasonal menu and extensive wine list: this 19C town house is most popular with Agen's gourmets.

Le Washington

7 cours Washington – ✆ 05 53 48 25 50 – contact@le-washington.com – Fax 05 53 48 25 55 – Closed August, Saturday and Sunday AY **r**

Rest – Menu (€ 15 bi), € 19/35 – Carte € 39/71

◆ This restaurant, in a house built by Charles Garnier, is home to a contemporary decor serving traditional and market fresh menus. Fine wine list.

La Table d'Armandie

1350 av. du Midi – ✆ 05 53 96 15 15 – latable.darmandie@orange.fr – Closed Sunday and Monday ZA **a**

Rest – Menu € 16 (weekday lunch), € 20/46 – Carte € 36/48

◆ A minimalist contemporary style, large communal table, open kitchen and a giant TV screen (sporting events). Market fresh menu and predominantly regional wine list.

Le Margoton

52 r. Richard-Cœur-de-Lion – ✆ 05 53 48 11 55 – contact@lemargoton.com – Fax 05 53 48 11 55 – Closed 25 August-1st September, 22 December-5 January, Saturday lunch, Sunday and Monday AY **e**

Rest – Menu € 16 (weekday lunch), € 23/34 – Carte € 32/54

◆ A pleasant establishment built with traditional materials in the picturesque old town. Family atmosphere. Cosy colour theme with contemporary notes. Appetising updated menu.

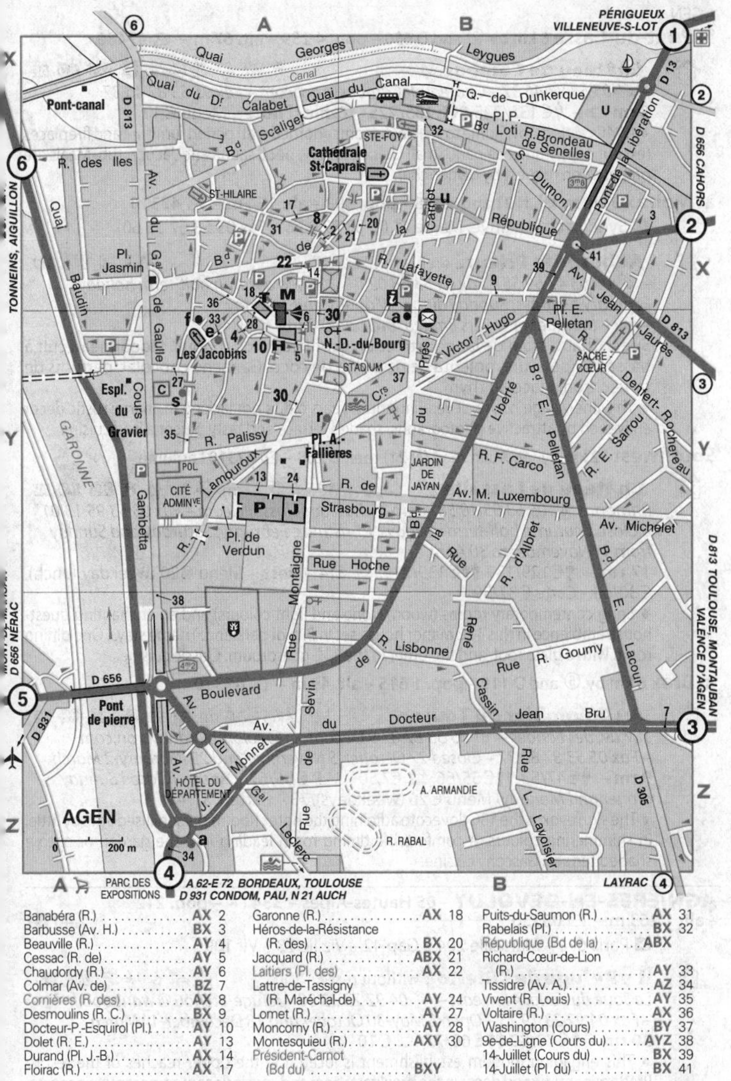

Banabéra (R.) . . . . **AX** 2
Barbusse (Av. H.) . . . . **BX** 3
Beauville (R.) . . . . **AY** 4
Cessac (R. de) . . . . **AY** 5
Chaudordy (R.) . . . . **AY** 6
Colmar (Av. de) . . . . **BZ** 7
Cornières (R. des) . . . . **AX** 8
Desmoulins (R. C.) . . . . **BX** 9
Docteur-P.-Esquirol (Pl.) . . . . . **AY** 10
Dolet (R. E.) . . . . **AY** 13
Durand (Pl. J.-B.) . . . . **AX** 14
Floirac (R.) . . . . **AX** 17
Garonne (R.) . . . . **AX** 18
Héros-de-la-Résistance (R. des) . . . . **BX** 20
Jacquard (R.) . . . . **ABX** 21
Laitiers (Pl. des) . . . . **AX** 22
Lattre-de-Tassigny (R. Maréchal-de) . . . . **AY** 24
Lomet (R.) . . . . **AY** 27
Moncorny (R.) . . . . **AY** 28
Montesquieu (R.) . . . . **AXY** 30
Président-Carnot (Bd du) . . . . **BXY**
Puits-du-Saumon (R.) . . . . **AX** 31
Rabelais (Pl.) . . . . **BX** 32
République (Bd de la) . . . . **ABX**
Richard-Cœur-de-Lion (R.) . . . . **AY** 33
Tissidre (Av. A.) . . . . **AZ** 34
Vivent (R. Louis) . . . . **AY** 35
Voltaire (R.) . . . . **AX** 36
Washington (Cours) . . . . **BY** 37
9e-de-Ligne (Cours du) . . . . . . **AYZ** 38
14-Juillet (Cours du) . . . . **BX** 39
14-Juillet (Pl. du) . . . . **BX** 41

La Part des Anges

14 r. Émile-Sentini – ✆ 05 53 68 31 00 – Fax 05 53 68 03 21

– Closed 18-30 August, February holidays, Monday from October to May and Sunday BX **u**

Rest – Menu €18/30 – Carte €31/67

◆ Cookery books and old crates of wine adorn this small town centre restaurant where you are made to feel at home. Generous regional fare at reasonable prices.

in Pont-du-Casse 6 km by ② and D 656 – pop. 4 259 – alt. 67 m – ✉ 47480

Château de Cambes – ✆ 05 53 87 46 37 – ChateaudeCambes@aol.com – Fax 05 53 87 46 37

8 rm – 🛉€ 135/225 🛉🛉€ 135/225 – **Table d'hôte** – Menu € 40

◆ A 14C castle is now home to spacious rooms adorned with period furniture and fireplaces (except one). Immense park, small chapel, library, pool, sauna and Jacuzzi tub. Meals are prepared on request by owner-chef.

at Moirax 9 km by ④, N 21 and D 268 – pop. 998 – alt. 154 m – ✉ 47310

Syndicat d'initiative, Mairie ✆ 05 53 87 03 69, Fax 05 53 67 55 60

Auberge le Prieuré (Benjamin Toursel)

– ✆ *05 53 47 59 55 – Fax 05 53 68 02 01 – Closed autumn half-term holidays, February holidays, Sunday dinner, Monday and Tuesday*

Rest – *(number of covers limited, pre-book)* Carte € 43/49

Spec. Chaud-froid de langoustines en cappuccino de fenouil. Pigeonneau cuit à basse température, polenta de riz au lait de coco. Ganache chocolat, parfums de tarte citron, glace au thym.

◆ This fine village house, several hundred years old, is not lacking in charm: rustic decor enlivened by attractive photographs, shaded terrace and tasty personalised cuisine.

Southwest 12 km by ④, Auch road (N 21) then D 268 – ✉ 47310 Laplume

Château de Lassalle rm,

Brimont – ✆ 05 53 95 10 58 – info@chateaudelassalle.com – Fax 05 53 95 13 01 – Closed autumn half-term holidays, Christmas, February, Saturday and Sunday from 1st November to 30 April

17 rm – 🛉€ 129/139 🛉🛉€ 139/219, ☕ € 14 – **Rest** – Menu € 20 (weekday lunch), € 30/60 – Carte € 37/59

◆ Snug contemporary rooms (wood, stone and light colours) and an enchanting guest-house ambience in this 18C manor house set in 8ha of parkland. Theme stays. One dining room with a glass roof, and the other in the 11C guardroom. Classic cuisine.

in Brax 6 km by ⑤ and D 119 – pop. 1 615 – alt. 49 m – ✉ 47310

Au Colombier du Touron rm,

187 av. des Landes – ✆ 05 53 87 87 91 – contact@colombierdutouron.com – Fax 05 53 87 82 37 – Closed 27 October-5 November and 23 February-2 March

9 rm – 🛉€ 47/53 🛉🛉€ 55/66, ☕ € 7,50 – ½ P € 55/62 – **Rest** – *(Closed Sunday dinner and Monday)* Menu € 26 (weekdays)/73 – Carte € 31/49

◆ The sign evokes the 18C dovecote adjoining the hotel. Rooms personalised little by little, in shimmering colours. A comfortable dining room leading into the garden or onto a shaded terrace. Gascony cuisine.

AGNIERES-EN-DEVOLUY – 05 Hautes-Alpes – 334 D4 – pop. 212 – alt. 1 263 m – ✉ 05250

40 **B1**

Paris 690 – Marseille 204 – Gap 42 – Vizille 73 – Vif 109

Le Refuge de l'Eterlou without rest

La Joue du Loup, 4 km east – ✆ 04 92 23 33 80 – refuge-eterlou@wanadoo.fr – Fax 04 92 23 19 13 – Open 8 May-30 October and 18 December-1st March

30 rm – 🛉€ 70/80 🛉🛉€ 60/75, ☕ € 10

◆ This engaging modern establishment is located in the upper reaches of the resort. Predominantly wood decor in the breakfast room and spacious contemporary style rooms.

AGUESSAC – 12 Aveyron – 338 K6 – pop. 833 – alt. 375 m – ✉ 12520

29 **D2**

Paris 628 – Florac 76 – Mende 87 – Millau 9 – Rodez 60 – Sévérac-le-Château 25

Auberge le Rascalat rest,

2 km Verrières road on D 809 – ✆ 05 65 59 80 43 – societe.exploitation.rascalat@wanadoo.fr – Fax 05 65 59 73 90 – Open 2 April-11 November

14 rm – 🛉€ 59/69 🛉🛉€ 59/69, ☕ € 10 – ½ P € 63/68 – **Rest** – *(closed Monday lunch and Tuesday lunch)* Menu € 24/46 – Carte € 33/62

◆ This former oil mill is situated in a rural setting between the causses and the river. Country-style bedrooms and an attractive swimming pool in the garden. Breakfast is served in the vaulted cellar. A rustic restaurant where lamb is roasted on a spit over the open fire in spring. Summer terrace.

AHETZE – 64 Pyrénées-Atlantiques – 342 C2 – pop. 1 452 – alt. 28 m – ✉ 64210 3 A3

Paris 767 – Bordeaux 207 – Pau 127 – Donostia-San Sebastián 52 – Irun 32

La Ferme Ostalapia with rm

chemin d' Ostalapia, 3 km south on D 855 – ✆ 05 59 54 73 79 – ostalapia@wanadoo.fr – Fax 05 59 54 98 85 – Closed December-January, Wednesday, Thursday except July-August and dinner July-August

8 rm – †€ 65/155 ††€ 65/155, ☕ € 10 – **Rest** – Carte € 26/66

◆ Regional farm with e well-earned local reputation *Terroir* cuisine served in two basque dining rooms, or outside with e view of the mountains. Cosy, country-style guest rooms.

L'AIGLE – 61 Orne – 310 M2 – pop. 8 972 – alt. 220 m – ✉ 61300 Normandy

Paris 137 – Alençon 68 – Chartres 79 – Dreux 61 – Évreux 56 – Lisieux 59

Office de tourisme, place Fulbert-de-Beina ✆ 02 33 24 12 40, Fax 02 33 34 23 77 33 C2

Du Dauphin

pl. de la Halle – ✆ 02 33 84 18 00 – regis.ligot@free.fr – Fax 02 33 34 09 28

30 rm – †€ 62/72 ††€ 62/85, ☕ € 10 – ½ P € 97/119

Rest – *(closed Sunday dinner)* Menu € 33/38 – Carte € 41/124

Rest *La Renaissance* – brasserie Menu € 11,50/15 – Carte € 15/41

◆ The older of these two buildings was already a hostelry back in 1618. Renovated guestrooms, lounge with a fireplace, and shop selling regional produce. Modern menu served in a traditional, comfortable dining room. Renaissance brasserie decorated in attractive Retro style.

Toque et Vins

35 r. L.-Pasteur, (rte d'Argentan) – ✆ 02 33 24 05 27 – Fax 02 33 24 05 27 – Closed 27 July-10 August, 25 December-3 January,Tuesday dinner, Sunday and Monday

Rest – Menu € 16/30 – Carte € 19/31

◆ The name says it all: a fine selection of wines, by the bottle and glass, to accompany traditional cuisine. A simple bistro setting. Wine-tasting evenings.

Dreux road 3.5 km east on N 26 – ✉ 61300 St-Michel-Tubœuf

Auberge St-Michel

– ✆ 02 33 24 20 12 – auberge.saint-michel@wanadoo.fr – Fax 02 33 34 96 62 – Closed Tuesday dinner, Wednesday dinner and Thursday

Rest – Menu € 17 bi/29 – Carte € 24/40

◆ This attractive Normandy façade with its sprawling Virginia creeper is home to a series of rustic, cosy little rooms with bistro-style furniture. Local food.

AIGUEBELETTE-LE-LAC – 73 Savoie – 333 H4 – pop. 191 – alt. 410 m – ✉ 73610 French Alps 46 F2

Paris 552 – Belley 34 – Chambéry 22 – Grenoble 76 – Voiron 35

Lake★ - Panorama★★ on the col de l'Épine road North.

in la Combe (East bank) 4 km by D 921ᵈ – ✉ 73610

La Combe "chez Michelon" with rm ≤ lake,

– ✆ 04 79 36 05 02 – chezmichelon@aol.com – Fax 04 79 44 11 93 – Closed 16 December-24 January, Monday except lunch May-September and Tuesday

5 rm – ††€ 60/72, ☕ € 8,50 – **Rest** – Menu (€ 19), € 24/48 – Carte € 37/56

◆ Perfect stopover for nature lovers: located between lake, mountain and forest. Modern dining room and terrace shaded by chestnut trees. Good selection of Savoyard wines.

in Lépin-le-Lac (South bank) 2.5 km by D 921ᴰ – pop. 347 – alt. 400 m – ✉ 73610

Office de tourisme, place de la Gare ✆ 04 79 36 00 02

La Bageatière

– ✆ 04 79 65 95 61 – contact@labageatiere.com

4 rm ☕ – †€ 65/85 ††€ 70/90 – **Table d'hôte** – Menu € 18 bi/24 bi

◆ Peaceful farmhouse dating from the 19C with fine, well-kept rustic bedrooms. Home-made jams at breakfast, served under a trellis overlooking gardens in summer.

in Novalaise-Lac (West bank) 7 km by D 921 – pop. 1 432 – alt. 427 m – ✉ 73470

Novalaise-Plage ← lake, VISA

Le Neyret – ☎ 04 79 36 02 19 – novalaiseplage@wanadoo.fr – Fax 04 79 36 04 22 – Closed 1st-8 December and 2 January-4 February

13 rm – †€ 57/88 ††€ 57/88, ☐ € 10 – ½ P € 58/75 – **Rest** – Menu € 28/85 – Carte € 52/112

◆ The white silhouette of this chalet is reflected in the waters of the lake. All rooms refurbished in contemporary style. Inventive and tasty food served on a shaded terrace with a panoramic view over the emerald waters and the mountains.

in St-Alban-de-Montbel (West bank) 7 km by D 921 – pop. 447 – alt. 400 m – ✉ 73610

Les Lodges du Lac VISA

La Curiaz, D 921 – ☎ 04 79 36 00 10 – bienvenue@leslodgesdulac.com – Fax 04 79 44 10 57 – Closed Sunday dinner and Monday from 15 September to 15 June

13 rm – †€ 50/70 ††€ 50/70, ☐ € 8 – 3 suites – ½ P € 76/96 – **Rest** – Menu € 12 (weekday lunch), € 19/38 – Carte € 20/44

◆ Set back from the lake, the annexe of this hotel has ground-floor rooms opening out onto the garden; the duplex rooms are particularly suitable for families. Boats available. Traditional cuisine is served in the restaurant. Special diets catered for on request.

in Attignat-Oncin 7 km South by D 921 – pop. 418 – alt. 570 m – ✉ 73610

Mont-Grêle with rm ← rm, VISA

– ☎ 04 79 36 07 06 – le-mont-grele@wanadoo.fr – Fax 04 79 36 09 54 – hotel closed 1st December-7 February and Sunday evening, Restaurant: closed 15 December-7 February, Sunday dinner, Tuesday dinner and Wednesday except June-August

10 rm – †€ 47/51 ††€ 51/57, ☐ € 8,50 – ½ P € 57/61 – **Rest** – Menu (€ 22), € 28/35 – Carte € 43/56

◆ This panoramic restaurant, bathed in natural light, has lovely views of a wooded park crossed by a small stream. Traditional and occasionally creative dishes on the menu, in addition to fish from the lake. Very simple rooms but spacious and well kept.

AIGUEBELLE – 83 Var – 340 N7 – see le Lavandou

AIGUES-MORTES – 30 Gard – 339 K7 – pop. 6 012 – alt. 3 m – ✉ 30220

Provence 23 **C2**

Paris 745 – Arles 49 – Montpellier 38 – Nîmes 42 – Sète 56

Office de tourisme, place Saint-Louis ☎ 04 66 53 73 00, Fax 04 66 53 65 94

Ramparts★★ and Tour de Constance★★: ✻★★ - Notre-Dame des Sablons church ★.

Villa Mazarin without rest VISA

35 bd Gambetta – ☎ 04 66 73 90 48 – am@villamazarin.com – Fax 04 66 73 90 49 – Closed 15 January-15 February

20 rm – †€ 89/135 ††€ 114/255, ☐ € 13

◆ This splendid mansion invites guests to enjoy the refinement of its sitting rooms and the shade of its lovely garden. Comfortable rooms, indoor pool and relaxation facilities.

St-Louis VISA

10 r. Am.-Courbet – ☎ 04 66 53 72 68 – hotel.saint-louis@wanadoo.fr – Fax 04 66 53 75 92 – Open 2 April-4 October

22 rm – †€ 62/94 ††€ 79/102, ☐ € 10 – ½ P € 65/77 – **Rest** – *(closed Saturday lunch, Tuesday and Wednesday)* Menu (€ 15), € 19/26

◆ Inside the town walls, near the Constance Tower, an elegant 18C building with comfortable, colourful rooms. Those on the 2nd floor are more spacious. Enjoy the Provençal style indoor dining area with fireplace in winter. In summer, pretty, shaded patio.

Canal without rest VISA

440 rte de Nîmes – ☎ 04 66 80 50 04 – contact@hotelcanal.fr – Fax 04 66 80 50 32 – Closed 15 November-15 December and 10 January-20 February

25 rm – †€ 65/148 ††€ 65/148, ☐ € 11

◆ At the entrance to the town, opposite the canal, is this contemporary style hotel. The functional, air-conditioned rooms are well soundproofed. Swimming pool and sun deck.

XX **Les Arcades** with rm

23 bd Gambetta – ✆ 04 66 53 81 13 – info@les-arcades.fr – Fax 04 66 53 75 46
9 rm – €99/106 €106/142 – **Rest** – *(closed 1st-19 March, 7-22 October, Tuesday lunch, Thursday lunch and Monday except dinner July-August)*
Menu (€22), €35/45 – Carte €46/59
◆ Beautiful 16C house in a refined Provençal decor of bare stone. Arcaded terrace, regional cuisine and attractive rooms. Peace and quiet guaranteed.

XX **La Salicorne**

9 r. Alsace-Lorraine – ✆ 04 66 53 62 67 – Closed January and Tuesday except school holidays
Rest – *(dinner only)* Carte €38/56
◆ Stonework, exposed beams, a fireplace, wrought iron, a pleasant summer terrace and food with a southern flavour - Provence personified to the rear of the Sablons church.

AILEFROIDE – **05 Hautes-Alpes** – **334** G3 – **see Pelvoux (District of)**

AILLANT-SUR-THOLON – **89 Yonne** – **319** D4 – **pop. 1 454** – **alt. 112 m** – ✉ **89110**

Paris 144 – Auxerre 20 – Briare 70 – Clamecy 61 – Gien 80 – Montargis 59
Office de tourisme, 1, cour de la Halle aux Grains ✆ 03 86 63 54 17, Fax 03 86 63 54 17 7 **B1**

Southwest 7 km by D 955, D 57 and secondary road – ✉ **89110 Chassy**

Domaine du Roncemay rm, rm,

– ✆ 03 86 73 50 50
– reservation@roncemay.com – Fax 03 86 73 69 46
– Open mid March-mid November and closed Tuesday lunch and Monday
18 rm – €100/280 €100/280, €18 – 3 suites – ½ P €156/175
Rest – Menu €35 (weekdays)/52 – Carte €56/64
◆ This beautiful hotel, adjoining a vast golf course, embodies the style of the region. Attractive rustic rooms. Fitness facilities and a superb Turkish bath. Modern food inspired by the traditions of Burgundy, served in a pleasant room overlooking the park.

AIMARGUES – **30 Gard** – **339** K6 – **pop. 3 442** – **alt. 6 m** – ✉ **30470** 23 **C2**

Paris 740 – Montpellier 40 – Aigues-Mortes 16 – Alès 62 – Arles 41 – Nîmes 25

XX **Un Mazet sous les platanes**

3 bd St-Louis – ✆ 04 66 51 73 03 – lemazetsouslesplatanes@wanadoo.fr – Fax 04 66 51 73 03 – Closed 23-30 December, Saturday lunch, Sunday dinner and Monday
Rest – Menu €29 – Carte €32/40
◆ Attractive house with an inner courtyard terrace offering a view of the kitchens. Smart dining rooms mixing Provençal and Oriental influences, in line with the menu.

AIME – **73 Savoie** – **333** M4 – **pop. 3 229** – **alt. 690 m** – ✉ **73210**
French Alps 45 **D2**

Paris 622 – Albertville 41 – Bourg-St-Maurice 13 – Chambéry 90 – Moûtiers 15
Syndicat d'initiative, avenue de la Tarentaise ✆ 04 79 55 67 00, Fax 04 79 55 60 01
Former St-Martin basilica★★.
Vallée de la Tarentaise★★.

Le Cormet without rest

9 chemin du Replat – ✆ 04 79 09 71 14 – hotelducormet@orange.fr – Fax 04 79 09 96 72
14 rm – €46/56 €56/65, €6
◆ Small hotel with a family atmosphere and a Savoyard name meaning mountain pass. Simple, well-kept rooms, quieter at the back. Pleasant, adjoining bar frequented by locals.

AINCILLE – **64 Pyrénées-Atlantiques** – **342** E6 – **see St-Jean-Pied-de-Port**

AINHOA – 64 Pyrénées-Atlantiques – 342 C5 – pop. 599 – alt. 130 m – ✉ 64250

Atlantic Coast 3 **A3**

Paris 791 – Bayonne 28 – Biarritz 29 – Cambo-les-Bains 11 – Pau 125 – St-Jean-de-Luz 26

Typical Basque village ★.

Ithurria (Xavier Isabal)

pl. du Fronton – ✆ 05 59 29 92 11 – hotel@ithurria.com – Fax 05 59 29 81 28 – Open 11 April-2 November

28 rm – €95/110 €135/150, €11 – ½ P €107/115

Rest – *(closed Thursday lunch except July-August and Wednesday) (pre-book Sat - Sun)* Menu €36/58 – Carte €50/77

Spec. Rossini de pied de porc. Tournedos de lapin au basilic. Délice à l'Izarra à la cerise noire d'Itxassou. **Wines** Jurançon sec, Irouléguy.

◆ Attractive 17C Basque-style house facing the pelota wall of the village. Elegant lounge and comfortable rooms adorned with antique furniture. Charming restaurant with antique ranges, exposed beams, traditional floor tiles, fireplace and copper ornaments. Delicious regional cuisine with a light touch.

Argi Eder

rest,

rte de la Chapelle – ✆ 05 59 93 72 00 – argi.eder@wanadoo.fr – Fax 05 59 93 72 13 – Open 1st April-9 November

18 rm – €95/120 €95/120, €13 – 8 suites – ½ P €89/120

Rest – *(closed Sunday dinner except July-August, Wednesday except dinner July-August and Monday)* Menu €26 (weekdays)/52 – Carte €44/55

◆ On a hillside, a large building typical of the region with a pool in the grounds overlooking the countryside. Vast redecorated rooms and a lounge/bar (fine collection of Armagnacs). Regional food in a Basque-style dining room. Excellent choice of Bordeaux wines.

Oppoca

r. Principale – ✆ 05 59 29 90 72 – oppoca@wanadoo.fr – Fax 05 59 29 81 03 – Closed 24 November-22 December, 11 January-6 February, Sunday dinner and Monday

Rest – *(closed Sunday dinner and Monday except August)* Menu €25/50 – Carte €48/55

◆ This inn has been refurbished and its rooms and lounge are now more welcoming. Traditional cuisine, rustic setting (room looking out over the garden), terrace.

AIRAINES – 80 Somme – 301 E8 – pop. 2 099 – alt. 30 m – ✉ 80270

Northern France and the Paris Region 36 **A1**

Paris 172 – Abbeville 22 – Amiens 30 – Beauvais 69 – Le Tréport 51

Syndicat d'initiative, place de la Mairie ✆ 03 22 29 34 07, Fax 03 22 29 47 50

in Allery 5 km West by D 936 – pop. 752 – alt. 50 m – ✉ 80270

Relais Forestier du Pont d'Hure

– ✆ 03 22 29 42 10 – lepontdhure@wanadoo.fr – Fax 03 22 29 27 91 – Closed 28 July-22 August, 2-23 January and dinner except Saturday

Rest – Menu €17 (weekday lunch), €21/23

◆ Dine here after a walk in the forest: food is prepared and grilled over a wood fire, in the rustic fireplace of a dining room adorned with hunting trophies.

AIRE-SUR-L'ADOUR – 40 Landes – 335 J12 – pop. 6 003 – alt. 80 m – ✉ 40800

Atlantic Coast 3 **B3**

Paris 722 – Auch 84 – Condom 68 – Dax 77 – Mont-de-Marsan 33 – Orthez 59 – Pau 51

Office de tourisme, place Général-de-Gaulle ✆ 05 58 71 64 70, Fax 05 58 71 64 70

Sarcophagus of Ste-Quitterie★ in St-Pierre-du-Mas church.

Chez l'Ahumat with rm

2 r. Mendès-France – ✆ 05 58 71 82 61 – Closed 10-18 March, 18-29 June and 1st-14 September

12 rm – €27/30 €33/39, €5 – ½ P €33/35 – **Rest** – *(closed Tuesday dinner and Wednesday)* Menu €11/29 – Carte €20/36

◆ Restaurant run by the same family for three generations. Two country-style dining rooms that display a collection of antique plates. Regional cuisine.

Bordeaux road by N 124 – ✉ 40270 Cazères-sur-l'Adour

Aliotel rm, VISA
– ✆ 05 58 71 72 72 – aliotel@free.fr – Fax 05 58 71 81 94
34 rm – €39 €44/46, €6 – **Rest** – Menu €13 bi
◆ A functional establishment offering practical, standardised rooms, that are well sound-proofed. Well-designed sports facilities in a country setting. A simple restaurant with large dining area in cafeteria style.

in Ségos (32 Gers) 9 km South-West by N 134 and D 260 – **pop. 234 – alt. 111 m** – ✉ 32400

Domaine de Bassibé VISA AE
– ✆ 05 62 09 46 71 – bassibe@relaischateaux.com – Fax 05 62 08 40 15
– Open 20 March-2 January and closed Tuesday and Wednesday except July-August
10 rm – €140 €140, €16 – 7 suites – ½ P €132 – **Rest** – *(dinner only except Saturday, Sunday and July-August)* Menu €46/58
◆ The cosy guestrooms full of charm add to the romantic air of this country property. Restaurant located in the estate's old wine press (whitewashed beams, fireplace) with quiet terrace in the shade of the plane trees.

Minvielle et les Oliviers rm, rest, VISA AE
– ✆ 05 62 09 40 90 – lminvielle@wanadoo.fr – Fax 05 62 08 48 62
18 rm – €43/49 €48/55, €10 – ½ P €50/55 – **Rest** – *(closed Sunday dinner from October to April and Saturday lunch)* Menu €13 bi (weekday lunch), €18/24 – Carte €18/40
◆ In a small village in Gers, this modern building is in a regional style. The rooms in the annex are more recent and have a smart, Provencal decor and a large balcony. Huge, rustic dining room where traditional food is served.

AIRE-SUR-LA-LYS – 62 Pas-de-Calais – 301 H4 – pop. 9 661 – alt. 30 m – ✉ 62120 Northern France and the Paris Region

30 **B2**

Paris 236 – Arras 56 – Boulogne-sur-Mer 68 – Calais 60 – Lille 62
Office de tourisme, Grand-Place ✆ 03 21 39 65 66, Fax 03 21 39 65 66
Bailiwick★ - Tower★ of St-Pierre collegiate church ★.

Hostellerie des 3 Mousquetaires VISA AE
Château de la Redoute, Béthune road (D 943) – ✆ 03 21 39 01 11 – hotel.mousquetaires@wanadoo.fr – Fax 03 21 39 50 10 – Closed 20 December-20 January
33 rm – €53/145 €53/145, €13 – 2 suites – **Rest** – Menu (€18), €23/45 – Carte €65/80
◆ A 19C house with country charm, in a park with a pond and hundred-year-old trees. Rooms with personal touches. Choose what you would like a view of: the open kitchen or the Lys valley from the bay windows.

in Isbergues 6 km Southeast by D 187 – **pop. 9 836 – alt. 25 m** – ✉ 62330

Le Buffet with rm rest, VISA
22 r. de la Gare – ✆ 03 21 25 82 40 – lebuffetisbergues@wanadoo.fr – Fax 03 21 27 86 42 – Closed 28 July-21 August, 26 February-9 March, Monday (except lunch on public holidays) and Sunday dinner
5 rm – €60 €64, €10 – **Rest** – Menu €20/85 – Carte €51/63
◆ The former station buffet is now particularly attractive with two elegant dining rooms, carefully laid tables and tasty regional, seasonal cuisine.

AISEY-SUR-SEINE – 21 Côte-d'Or – 320 H3 – pop. 196 – alt. 255 m – ✉ 21400

8 **C1**

Paris 248 – Châtillon-sur-Seine 15 – Chaumont 75 – Dijon 68 – Montbard 26

Roy with rm rest, VISA
– ✆ 03 80 93 21 63 – hotelduroy@wanadoo.fr – Fax 03 80 93 25 74 – Closed 1st-20 January and Sunday dinner
5 rm – €48 €48, €6,50 – ½ P €52 – **Rest** – Menu €17 (weekday lunch), €20/38 – Carte €34/51
◆ Exposed beams, huge fireplace and rustic furniture are all part of the slightly sombre pastoral decor of the restaurant. Small but pleasant rooms established in two adjoining Burgundian houses surrounding a tree-filled garden. Country-style bar-lounge.

AISONVILLE-ET-BERNOVILLE – 02 Aisne – 306 D3 – pop. 291 – alt. 155 m – ✉ 02110 37 C1

Paris 200 – Amiens 115 – Laon 50 – Saint-Quentin 31 – Valenciennes 65

Le 1748

9 r. de Condé – ☎ 03 23 66 85 85 – le1748@wanadoo.fr – Fax 03 23 66 85 70
16 rm – €52/89 €52/89, €12 – ½ P €55/75 – **Rest** – Menu €27/44 – Carte €26/44

◆ This outstanding hotel is housed in the old farm and stables of a château, said to be among the most beautiful in France. Cosy, individually decorated rooms. Regional produce and the local beer, Bernoville, served in a cheerful café setting.

AITON – 73 Savoie – 333 K4 – pop. 1 163 – alt. 405 m – ✉ 73220 46 F2

Paris 604 – Annecy 64 – Chambéry 38 – Lyon 138

Du Fort

rte du Fort – ☎ 04 79 36 90 27 – restofort@wanadoo.fr – Fax 04 79 36 89 61 – Closed 15 February-3 March, Tuesday dinner, Sunday dinner and Wednesday
Rest – Menu €24/44 – Carte approx. €44

◆ This restaurant enjoys an excellent location because it is built on the foundations of a former military fort! Wide bay windows opening onto the mountain. Traditional dishes.

AIX (ÎLE) – 17 Charente-Maritime – 324 C3 – see Île-d'Aix

AIX-EN-PROVENCE – 13 Bouches-du-Rhône – 340 H4 – pop. 134 222 – alt. 206 m – Casino AY – ✉ 13100 Provence 40 B3

Paris 752 – Avignon 82 – Marseille 30 – Nice 177 – Sisteron 102 – Toulon 84

Office de tourisme, 2, place du Général-de-Gaulle ☎ 04 42 16 11 61, Fax 04 42 16 11 62

Set Golf 1335 chemin de Granet, West: 6 km by D 17, ☎ 04 42 29 63 69 ;

d'Aix-Marseille Les Milles Domaine de Riquetti, by Marignane road and D 9: 8 km, ☎ 04 42 24 20 41 ;

Sainte-Victoire Golf Club Fuveau Lieu dit "Château l'Arc", by Aubagne road and D 6: 14 km, ☎ 04 42 29 83 43.

Old Aix★★ - Cours Mirabeau★★ - St-Sauveur cathedral ★: triptych of the Burning Bush★★ - Cloister★ BX B[8] - Place Albertas★ BY 3 - Place★ de l'hôtel de ville BY 37 - Courtyard ★ of the town hall BY H - Mazarin district ★: Quatre-Dauphins fountain ★ BY D - Musée Granet★ CY M[6] - Musée des Tapisseries★ BX M[2] - Vasarely Foundation ★ AV M[5].

Plans on following pages

Villa Gallici

18 bis av. de la Violette – ☎ 04 42 23 29 23 – reservation@villagallici.com – Fax 04 42 96 30 45 – Closed 21-26 December and 2 January-1st February
18 rm – €220/740 €220/740, €22 – 4 suites
Rest – *(closed Wednesday from October to May and Tuesday except July) (number of covers limited, pre-book)* Menu €45 (lunch)/90 BV **k**

◆ This high perched villa is a résumé of the best of Provence, with its plane trees, cypresses, fountain, pool, crickets, tasteful fabrics and wrought iron. Charming 19C-styled rooms. Classic Mediterranean flavoured cuisine. Tempting shaded summer terrace.

Le Pigonnet

5 av. du Pigonnet ✉ 13090 – ☎ 04 42 59 02 90 – reservation@hotelpigonnet.com – Fax 04 42 59 47 77 AV **a**
51 rm – €135/270 €175/390, €25
Rest – *(closed 23-31 December, Saturday lunch and Sunday dinner from November to March)* Menu €56 – Carte €82/90

◆ Paul Cézanne was inspired by the scents and colours of Provence in this gracious abode, set in a flower-filled park. Cosy, plush and romantic interior. Elegant dining rooms and a terrace overlooking the garden. Up-to-date menu.

AIX-EN-PROVENCE

Berger (Av. G.) .... **BV** 7
Brossolette (Av.) .... **AV** 13
Club Hippique (Av.) ...... **AV** 18
Dalmas (Av. J.) .... **AV** 23
Ferrini (Av. F.) .... **AV** 30
Fourane (Av. de la) ...... **AV** 32
Galice (Rte de) .... **AV** 33
Isaac (Av. J.) .... **BV** 41
Malacrida (Av. H.) .... **BV** 48
Minimes (Crs des) .... **AV** 52
Moulin (Av. J.) .... **BV** 56
Pigonnet (Av. du) .... **AV** 62
Poilus (Bd des) .... **BV** 67
Prados (Av. E.) .... **AV** 68
Solari (Av. Ph.) .... **AV** 76

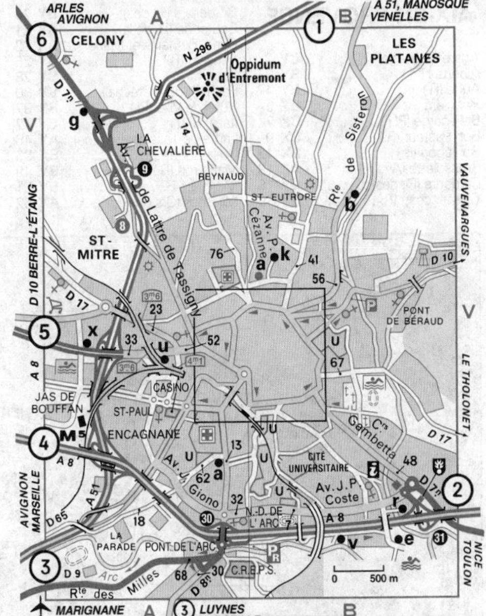

Aquabella
2 r. des Étuves – ✆ 04 42 99 15 00 – info@aquabella.fr – Fax 04 42 99 15 01 AX **a**

110 rm – †€ 149/175 ††€ 169/195, ☕ € 18 – ½ P € 119/126

Rest *L'Orangerie* – Menu (€ 21), € 26/39 – Carte € 37/62

♦ Adjoining the Sextius thermal baths this hotel has modern rooms in Provençal shades. Those on the upper floors have a terrace and overlook the old town. This contemporary restaurant is housed in a glass and steel structure and has a poolside terrace.

Grand Hôtel Mercure Roi René
24 bd du Roi-René – ✆ 04 42 37 61 00 – h1169@accor.com – Fax 04 42 37 61 11 BZ **b**

134 rm – †€ 195/235 ††€ 215/255, ☕ € 20 – 3 suites

Rest *La Table du Roi* – Menu € 36 – Carte approx. € 42

♦ Modern hotel whose exterior pays homage to the regional style, while its partially refurbished interior is distinctly contemporary and minimalist. Patio and pool. La Table du Roi is decorated with wood panelling and pretty colours; classic menu.

Des Augustins without rest
3 r. de la Masse – ✆ 04 42 27 28 59 – hotel.augustins@wanadoo.fr – Fax 04 42 26 74 87 BY **x**

29 rm – †€ 113/240 ††€ 113/240, ☕ € 10

♦ Luther the reformer stayed in this 15C convent in his time. Personalised, extremely comfortable rooms. Lobby in the 12C chapel.

Le Galice
5 rte Galice – ✆ 04 42 52 75 27 – hotelgalice@bestwestern-aix.com – Fax 04 42 52 75 28 AV **u**

90 rm – †€ 99/160 ††€ 99/160, ☕ € 12 – ½ P € 116/177

Rest – *(closed Saturday lunch and Sunday)* Menu (€ 18) – Carte € 24/35

♦ This modern, glazed hotel has spacious, comfortable and well-soundproofed rooms. Those on the pool side are the most pleasant. Classic menu with Mediterranean influences served in a cosy room or on the terrace.

AIX-EN-PROVENCE

Agard (Passage) . . . . CY 2
Albertas (Pl.) . . . . BY 3
Aude (R.) . . . . BY 4
Bagniers (R. des) . . . . BY 5
Bellegarde (Pl.) . . . . CX 7
Bon Pasteur (R.) . . . . BX 9
Boulégon (R.) . . . . BX 12
Brossolette (Av.) . . . . AZ 13
Cardeurs (Pl. des) . . . . BY 16
Clemenceau (R.) . . . . BY 18
Cordeliers (R. des) . . . . BY 20
Couronne (R. de la) . . . . BY 21
Curie (R. Pierre-et-Marie) . . . BX 22
Espariat (R.) . . . . BY 26
Fabrot (R.) . . . . BY 28
Foch (R. du Maréchal) . . . . BY 30
Hôtel de Ville (Pl.) . . . . BY 37
Italie (R. d') . . . . CY 42
Lattre-de-Tassigny (Av. de) . . AY 46
De-la-Roque (R. J.) . . . . BX 25
Matheron (R.) . . . . BY 49
Méjanes (R.) . . . . BY 51
Minimes (Crs des) . . . . AY 52
Mirabeau (Cours) . . . . BCY
Montigny (R. de) . . . . BY 55
Napoléon-Bonaparte (Av.) . . AY 57
Nazareth (R.) . . . . BY 58
Opéra (R. de l') . . . . CY 62
Pasteur (Av.) . . . . BX 64
Paul-Bert (R.) . . . . BX 66
Prêcheurs (Pl. des) . . . . CY 70
Richelme (Pl.) . . . . BY 72
Saporta (R. G.-de) . . . . BX 75
Thiers (R.) . . . . CY 80
Verdun (Pl. de) . . . . CY 85
4-Septembre (R.) . . . . BZ 87

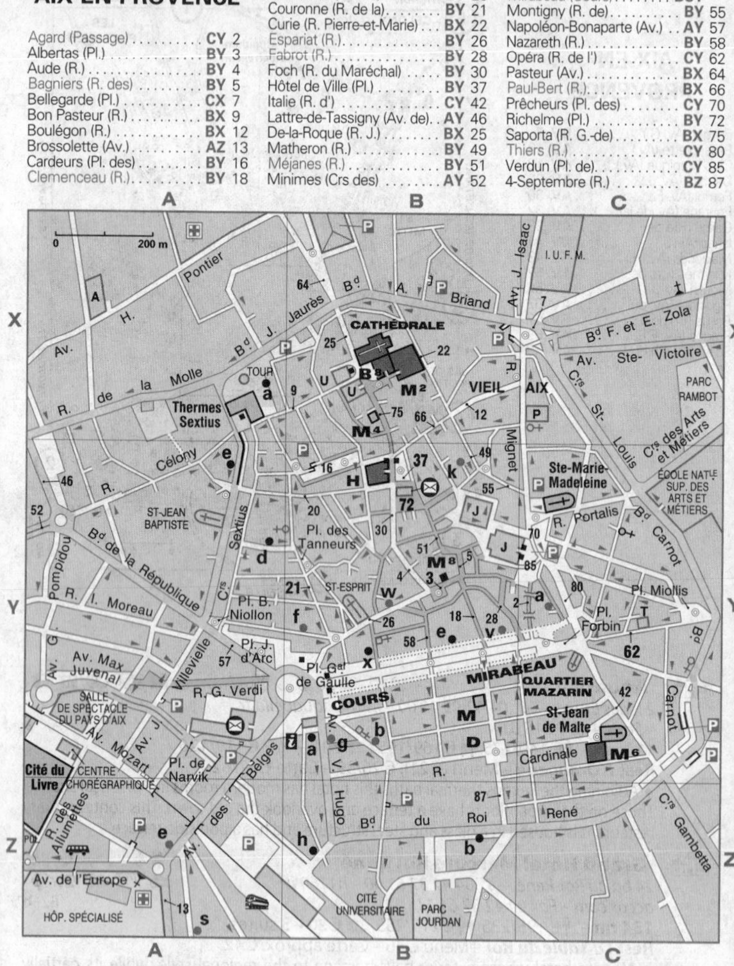

Novotel Beaumanoir

r. Marcel-Arnaud, Résidence Beaumanoir, Motorway exit 3, Sautets – ☎ 04 42 91 15 15 – h0393@accor.com – Fax 04 42 91 15 05 BV **r**

102 rm – 🚹€ 130/160 🚹🚹€ 130/160, ☕ € 12,50 – **Rest** – Carte € 22/39

◆ This establishment with its comfortable rooms (the majority refurbished) offers reasonably peaceful surroundings, including a landscaped garden and small botanical trail. Contemporary dining room extending onto a terrace overlooking the swimming pool.

Kyriad Prestige

rm, VISA

42 rte de Galice – ☎ 04 42 95 04 41 – aixenprovence@kyriadprestige.fr – Fax 04 42 59 47 29 AV **x**

84 rm – 🚹€ 102/117 🚹🚹€ 102/117, ☕ € 12 – **Rest** – Menu (€ 19), € 26 – Carte € 29/38

◆ A modern, semi-circular building by the ring road. Pleasant, soundproofed rooms, although those on the upper floors are even quieter. Small fitness centre. Buffet menus served in a marine style dining room. Poolside terrace.

Bastide du Cours rm, rm, VISA AE
43-47 cours Mirabeau – 04 42 26 10 06 – info@bastideducours.com – Fax 04 42 93 07 65 BY **e**
11 rm – €145/400, €13 – 4 suites – **Rest** – Menu €20/40 – Carte €31/58
◆ This large house offers well equipped, comfortable rooms decorated in an individual, old-fashioned spirit. Four overlook the cours Mirabeau. Up-to-date restaurant brasserie, cosy atmosphere (warm colours, sitting rooms, libraries, cane armchairs).

Cézanne without rest VISA AE
40 av. Victor-Hugo – 04 42 91 11 11 – hotelcezanne@hotelaix.com – Fax 04 42 91 11 10 BZ **h**
55 rm – €150/175 €170/195, €18 – 2 suites
◆ A business centre, Wifi, free minibar in the rooms and baskets of fruit: details that make a difference! Smart or very fashionable baroque sitting rooms.

St-Christophe rm, rest, VISA AE
2 av. Victor-Hugo – 04 42 26 01 24 – saintchristophe@francemarket.com – Fax 04 42 38 53 17 BY **a**
60 rm – €79/85 €85/98, €11 – 7 suites
Rest *Brasserie Léopold* – Menu (€22), €30 – Carte €28/44
◆ Practical rooms with a 1930s atmosphere or Provençal style charm, with or without terrace. Regional cuisine and brasserie dishes in an attractive Art Deco setting. A pavement terrace for fine weather.

Novotel Pont de l'Arc VISA AE
av. Arc-de-Meyran, Aix Pont de l'Arc motorway exit – 04 42 16 09 09 – h0394@accor.com – Fax 04 42 26 00 09 BV **v**
80 rm – €98/128 €98/128, €12,50 – **Rest** – Carte €19/42
◆ A Novotel set between the motorway and Arc. Fully renovated and soundproofed rooms, the nicest face the garden and pool. Riverside fitness track. Comfortable dining room and shaded terraces, one embellished with a fountain.

Le Globe without rest VISA AE
74 cours Sextius – 04 42 26 03 58 – contact@hotelduglobe.com – Fax 04 42 26 13 68 – Closed 20 December-20 January AY **e**
46 rm – €56/59 €68/72, €8,50
◆ A yellow building home to plain, well soundproofed, very well kept and not too expensive rooms. The lobby has been treated to a makeover. Rooftop sundeck/terrace.

Le Manoir without rest VISA AE
8 r. Entrecasteaux – 04 42 26 27 20 – msg@hotelmanoir.com – Fax 04 42 27 17 97 – Closed 9 January-2 February AY **d**
40 rm – €62/92 €75/92, €10
◆ Once a monastery, then a millinery and now an unassuming, well-kept hotel, gradually being renovated. Summer terrace in part of the old cloisters. 1940s inspired sitting room.

Le Clos de la Violette VISA AE
10 av. Violette – 04 42 23 30 71 – restaurant@closdelaviolette.fr – Fax 04 42 21 93 03 – Closed in August, Sunday and Monday BV **a**
Rest – *(number of covers limited, pre-book)* Menu €50 (weekday lunch), €90/130 – Carte €96/107
Spec. Truffes et gibier (November to March). Petits farcis provençaux (June to October). Poissons de Méditerranée.
◆ Set in a garden away from the historic centre, the Clos de la Violette now sports a modern decor and is also more moderately priced. Brown colour scheme and verdant terrace.

L'Aixquis VISA AE
22 r. Leydet – 04 42 27 76 16 – aixquis@aixquis.com – Fax 04 42 93 10 61 – Closed 9-17 August, Monday lunch and Sunday BY **f**
Rest – Carte €36/70
◆ A pleasant, modern dining room in a small street in the town centre, serving food that depends on the market produce, chalked up on a blackboard every day.

XX **Les 2 Frères**

4 av. Reine-Astrid – ✆ 04 42 27 90 32 – les-deuxfreres@wanadoo.fr – Fax 04 42 12 47 08 – Closed Sunday dinner from November to March AZ **s**

Rest – Menu € 28/35 bi – Carte € 40/72

◆ As the name suggests, this restaurant is run by two brothers: the older one prepares the delicious, modern cuisine (his labours are projected onto a screen in the dining room), while his sibling works front of house. Trendy bistro atmosphere.

XX **Amphitryon**

2 r. Paul-Doumer – ✆ 04 42 26 54 10 – amphitryon22@wanadoo.fr – Fax 04 42 38 36 15 – Closed 15 August-1st September, Sunday and Monday

Rest – Menu € 23 (weekday lunch), € 27/36 – Carte € 40/44 BY **s**

◆ Near the Cours Mirabeau, with a mix of classical and modern decor. Enjoy regional cuisine in the dining room or at the more informal counter. Enthusiastic service. Quiet patio.

X **Pierre Reboul**

11 Petite-Rue-St-Jean – ✆ 04 42 20 58 26 – restaurant-pierre-reboul@orange.fr – Fax 04 42 38 79 67 – Closed Sunday and Monday CY **a**

Rest – *(number of covers limited, pre-book)* Menu € 39/110 – Carte € 80/100

Spec. Huîtres et bulle d'iode pétillante. Mini "taureauburger" de Camargue et foie gras. Verre chocolat-menthe.

◆ In the heart of the old town, this elegant, contemporary restaurant specialises in delicious, innovative cuisine with a focus on quality produce.

X **Le Passage**

10 r. Villars – ✆ 04 42 37 09 00 – contact@le-passage.fr – Fax 04 42 37 09 09

Rest – Menu € 23/35 – Carte € 38/53 BY **b**

◆ Metal, walkways and contemporary furniture have rejuvenated this 19C confectionary. Situated on three floors it has a bistro, wine bar, tapas bar, cookery school and tearoom.

X **Le Formal**

32 r. Espariat – ✆ 04 42 27 08 31 – Fax 04 42 27 08 31 – Closed 13-21 April, 17 August-1st September, 4 – 12 January, Saturday lunch, Sunday and Monday BY **w**

Rest – Menu (€ 18), € 22 bi (weekday lunch), € 30 € (dinner)/49 (dinner) – Carte approx. € 40

◆ A restaurant occupying 15C vaulted cellars adorned with a collection of contemporary paintings. Inventive, well-presented cuisine.

X **Chez Féraud**

8 r. du Puits-Juif – ✆ 04 42 63 07 27 – marcferaud@cegetel.net – Closed August, Sunday and Monday BY **k**

Rest – Menu (€ 22), € 29 – Carte € 32/44

◆ Hidden in a back street of old Aix, this charming family-run establishment boasts a 12C well. Provençal cuisine (pistou, stew, etc.) and grilled meat are prepared in the dining room.

X **Yamato**

21 av. des Belges – ✆ 04 42 38 00 20 – yamato.koji-yuriko@wanadoo.fr – Fax 04 42 38 52 65 – Closed Tuesday lunch and Monday AZ **e**

Rest – Menu (€ 28), € 48/68 – Carte € 41/61

◆ Mrs Yuriko, the owner of this small Japanese restaurant, greets guests in traditional costume. The decor is also typically Japanese, and the restaurant has a veranda, terrace and garden. "Discovery" menus.

X **Yôji**

7 av. Victor-Hugo – ✆ 04 42 38 48 76 – Fax 04 42 38 47 01 – Closed Monday lunchtime and Sunday BY **g**

Rest – Menu € 17/30 – Carte € 22/60

◆ Take a trip from the land of sunshine to the Land of the Rising Sun: Japanese food, a Korean barbecue and sushi bar in a Zen decor.

St-Canadet road 9 km by ①, D 96 and D 13 – ✉ 13100 Aix-en-Provence

Domaine De La Brillane without rest

195 rte de Couteron, on D 13 and secondary road – ✆ 06 74 77 01 20 – domaine@labrillane.com – Fax 04 42 54 31 25 – Closed 20 December-4 January

5 rm – †€ 120/150 ††€ 150

◆ Named after wines, the snug guestrooms have a view of the vineyards or Ste Victoire Mountain. Tastings of the estate's organic wine.

in Le Canet 8 km by ② on D 7n – ✉ 13100 Beaurecueil

L'Auberge Provençale

RN 7, (Le Canet de Meyreuil) – ☎ 04 42 58 68 54 – aubergiste@aol.com – Fax 04 42 58 68 05 – Closed 15-30 July, Tuesday except lunch September-May and Wednesday

Rest – Menu € 24/48 – Carte € 54/57

◆ A pretty roadside inn with pleasant Provençal dining rooms. Generous, traditional food and a fine regional wine list.

in Beaurecueil 10 km by ②, D 7n and D 58 – **pop. 568** – **alt. 254 m** – ✉ 13100

Relais Ste-Victoire with rm

D 46, 300 av. Sylvain Gautier – ☎ 04 42 66 94 98 – relais-ste-victoire@wanadoo.fr – Fax 04 42 66 85 96 – Closed autumn half-term holidays, 2-7 January, Friday except dinner in season, Sunday dinner and Monday

15 rm – †€ 65/122 ††€ 65/122, ☕ € 14 – ½ P € 130/160 – **Rest** – *(pre-book Sat - Sun)* Menu € 27/85

◆ This estate at the foot of Ste Victoire features two plush dining rooms (ceramic collection) and an Italian style patio-veranda. Tasty modern food with a Provençal twist.

via ③ 5 km D9 or A 51, Les Milles exit– ✉13546 Aix-en-Provence

Château de la Pioline

rm, rest,

260 r. Guillaume-du-Vair – ☎ 04 42 52 27 27 – info@chateaudelapioline.fr – Fax 04 42 52 27 28 – Closed 23 February-2 March

30 rm – †€ 165/430 ††€ 165/430, ☕ € 20 – 3 suites – **Rest** – *(closed at the weekend from November to March)* Menu (€ 37), € 45/64 – Carte € 47/69

◆ A fine, listed property, housing large, attractively furnished rooms. Those in the recently built wing are smaller but boast a terrace. Formal garden. This Louis XVI style dining room is decorated with charcoal sketches. Concert dinners.

in Celony 3 km on D 7n – ✉ 13090 Aix-en-Provence

Le Mas d'Entremont

rm,

315 rte Nationale 7 – ☎ 04 42 17 42 42 – entremont@wanadoo.fr – Fax 04 42 21 15 83 – Open 15 March-31 October AV **g**

14 rm – †€ 145/150 ††€ 145/185, ☕ € 17 – 6 suites – ½ P € 127/172

Rest – *(closed Sunday evening and Monday lunchtime)* Menu € 40/45 – Carte € 55/66

◆ Handsome ochre-coloured country house tucked away in the upper part of Aix. Park, water features and antique columns. Spacious personalised rooms and suites. Welcoming winter restaurant and delightful shaded terrace for summer dining. Traditional, seasonal cuisine.

AIX-LES-BAINS – **73 Savoie** – **333** I3 – **pop. 25 732** – **alt. 200 m** – **Spa : mid Jan.-mid Dec.** – **Casinos : Grand Cercle** CZ, **New Casino** BZ – ✉ **73100** French Alps 46 **F2**

- Paris 539 – Annecy 34 – Bourg-en-Bresse 115 – Chambéry 18 – Lyon 107
- Chambéry-Savoie: ☎ 04 79 54 49 54, to Viviers-du-Lac by ③: 8 km.
- Office de tourisme, place Maurice Mollard ☎ 04 79 88 68 00, Fax 04 79 88 68 01
- d'Aix-les-Bains Avenue du Golf, by Chambéry road: 3 km, ☎ 04 79 61 23 35.
- Esplanade du Lac★ - Town hall★ staircase CZ **H** - Musée Faure★ - Roman remains★ - Casino Grand Cercle★.
- Lac du Bourget★★ - Abbaye de Hautecombe★★ - Les Bauges★.

Plan on next page

Radisson SAS

rm, rest,

av. Ch.-de-Gaulle – ☎ 04 79 34 19 19 – info.aixlesbains@radissonsas.com – Fax 04 79 88 11 49 CZ **x**

92 rm – †€ 122/167 ††€ 135/177, ☕ € 19 – 10 suites – ½ P € 72/88

Rest – brasserie *(closed Sunday dinner and Monday from November to March)* Menu (€ 26), € 32

◆ In the heart of the casino park with a pleasant Japanese garden, this imposing hotel has rooms of sober elegance that are modern and well-equipped. Small brasserie-inspired menu served in a modern setting or on the pleasant terrace.

AIX-LES-BAINS

Bains (R. des) . . . . CZ 2
Berthollet (Bd) . . . . CZ 3
Boucher (Sq. A.) . . . . CY 5
Carnot (Pl.) . . . . CZ 6
Casino (R. du) . . . . CZ 8
Chambéry (R. de) . . . . CZ 9
Charcot (Bd J.) . . . . AX 10
Clemenceau (Pl.) . . . . BY 12
Dacquin (R.) . . . . CZ 13
Davat (R.) . . . . CZ 15
Fleurs (Av. des) . . . . CZ 16
Garibaldi (Bd) . . . . AX 17
Garrod (R. Sir-A.) . . . . CZ 18
Gaulle (Av. de) . . . . CZ 19
Georges-1er (R.) . . . . CZ 21
Lamartine (R.) . . . . CZ 22
Lattre-de-Tassigny
(Av. Mar.-de) . . . . AX, BY 23
Liège (R. de) . . . . CZ 24
Marlioz (Av. de) . . . . AX 25
Mollard (Pl. M.) . . . . CZ 26
Monard (R. S.) . . . . CZ 27
Petit Port (Av. du) . . . . AX, BYZ 28
Pierpont-Morgan (Bd) . . . . . . BY 29
Près-Riants (R.) . . . . BY 30
République (R.) . . . . CY 32
Revard (Pl. du) . . . . CZ 33
Roche-du-Roi (Bd de la) . . . . CZ 34
Roosevelt (Av. F.) . . . . AX 35
Rops (Av. D.) . . . . AX 37
Russie (Bd de) . . . . AX 39
Seyssel (R. C.-de) . . . . CZ 40
Temple-de-Diane (Sq.) . . . . . CZ 45
Temple (R. du) . . . . CZ 43
Verdun (Av. de) . . . . BZ 46
Victoria (Av.) . . . . CZ 47

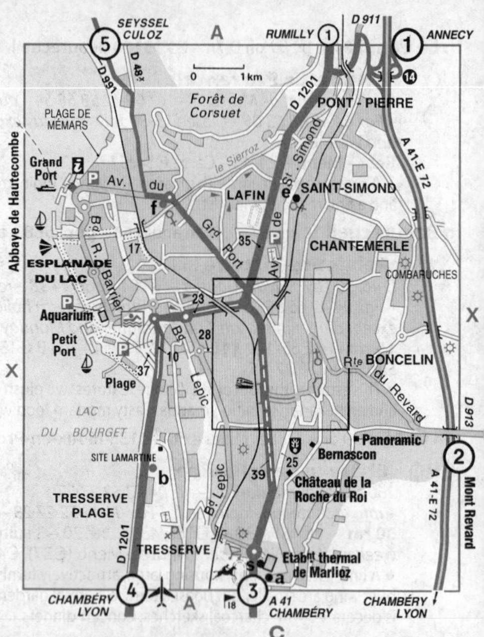

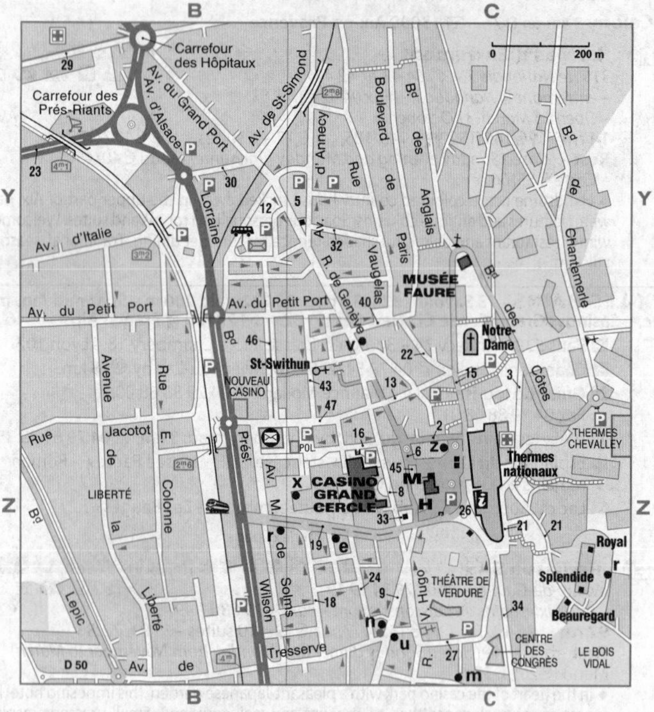

Mercure Ariana
rm, VISA
111 av. de Marlioz, at Marlioz: 1.5 km –
✆ 04 79 61 79 79 – h2945@accor.com – Fax 04 79 61 79 00 AX **a**
60 rm – †€ 90/134 ††€ 100/144, ☐ € 14 – ½ P € 78/100 – **Rest** – Menu (€ 21), € 26 – Carte € 32/40
♦ Welcoming establishment that is part of the Marlioz spa resort. Spacious rooms, sometimes with a balcony. Balneotherapy centre. Well-lit dining room and attractive terrace overlooking a park shaded by 100-year-old trees.

Astoria
rm, VISA
pl. des Thermes – ✆ 04 79 35 12 28 – hotel.astoria-savoie@wanadoo.fr
– Fax 04 79 35 11 05 – Closed 27 November-5 January CZ **z**
94 rm – †€ 62/80 ††€ 85/104, ☐ € 12 – ½ P € 58/65
Rest – Menu € 24 – Carte € 29/42
♦ This former (1905) luxury hotel opposite the thermal baths is a reminder of the sumptuous past of Aix-les-Bains. Skilfully-renovated, Belle Époque decor, modern comfort and spacious rooms. Art nouveau decor has been preserved in this large and elegant dining room.

Le Manoir
VISA
37 r. Georges-1er – ✆ 04 79 61 44 00 – Hotel-le-Manoir@wanadoo.fr
– Fax 04 79 35 67 67 – Closed 15-30 December CZ **r**
73 rm – †€ 88/128 ††€ 98/168, ☐ € 13 – ½ P € 88/138
Rest – Menu € 29/68 – Carte € 32/78
♦ Hotel located in the converted outbuildings of the former Splendide and Royal luxury hotels. Enjoy the peaceful garden, cosy rooms with personal touches and wellness centre. Dining room extending out to a veranda that opens onto an expanse of green. Pleasant terrace.

Mercure Acquaviva
VISA
111 av. de Marlioz, at Marlioz: 1.5 km – ✆ 04 79 61 77 77 – h2944@accor.com
– Fax 04 79 61 77 00 AX **s**
100 rm – †€ 74/100 ††€ 82/110, ☐ € 13 – ½ P € 67/81 – **Rest** – *(open 15 April-15 October)* Menu (€ 16), € 24 – Carte € 28/34
♦ Modern hotel with basic rooms; those facing the shady park of the Aix-Marlioz complex are quieter. Numerous facilities for meetings. A dining room designed like a winter garden, terrace-patio and traditional menu.

Agora
rm, rest, VISA
1 av. de Marlioz – ✆ 04 79 34 20 20 – reception@hotel-agora.com
– Fax 04 79 34 20 30 – Closed 19 December-4 January CZ **u**
61 rm – †€ 63/85 ††€ 75/97, ☐ € 12 – ½ P € 68/79 – **Rest** – *(closed Monday lunch, Saturday lunch and Sunday from October to April)* Menu € 22 (weekday lunch), € 24/42 – Carte € 24/42
♦ The advantages of this hotel include its central location and excellent facilities. Relaxation guaranteed with swimming pool, sauna and hammam in the basement. Modern-style dining room and cosy atmosphere. Traditional food.

Palais des Fleurs
rm, rest, rest,
VISA
17 r. Isaline – ✆ 04 79 88 35 08
– palais.des.fleurs@wanadoo.fr – Fax 04 79 35 42 79 – Closed 10 November-31 January CZ **m**
42 rm – †€ 54/66 ††€ 63/79, ☐ € 9 – 1 suite – ½ P € 49/63
Rest – *(closed 10 November-28 February)* Menu € 19/24 – Carte € 26/34
♦ Family run establishment in a quiet residential area. The rooms are spacious, sober and pleasant and amenities include attractive pool and fitness centre. Traditional cuisine caters to special diets on the mezzanine or by the pool.

Grand Hôtel du Parc
rm, rest, rest, VISA
28 r. de Chambéry – ✆ 04 79 61 29 11 – info@grand-hotel-du-parc.com
– Fax 04 79 88 33 49 – Closed 18 December-10 February CZ **n**
36 rm – †€ 49/57 ††€ 59/69, ☐ € 10 – ½ P € 73
Rest ***La Bonne Fourchette*** – *✆ 04 79 34 00 31 (closed Wednesday lunch off season, Sunday dinner and Monday)* Menu € 30/65 – Carte € 48/67
♦ 1817 building near the open-air theatre. Spacious and simple rooms. The lounge retains its attractive original decor. At the Bonne Fourchette, pleasantly retro dining room and traditional food.

Auberge St-Simond rm, VISA AE

130 av. St-Simond – 04 79 88 35 02 – auberge@saintsimond.com – Fax 04 79 88 38 45 – Closed 1st-10 November, 20 December-25 January, Monday lunch from 1st October to 30 April and Sunday dinner AX **e**

24 rm – €58/63 €58/75, €10 – ½ P €53/68 – **Rest** – Menu €25 (weekday lunch), €30/38 – Carte €31/42

◆ Smart, well-maintained guestrooms with individual touches in this hotel, renowned for its friendly atmosphere and pleasant garden with a swimming pool. Traditional cuisine served in the dining room or on the terrace, depending on the weather.

Beaulieu VISA AE

29 av. Ch.-de-Gaulle – 04 79 35 01 02 – info@hotel-beaulieu.fr – Fax 04 79 34 04 82 – Open 1st April-4 November BCZ **r**

30 rm – €38/40 €42/52, €6 – ½ P €42/58 – **Rest** – *(closed Sunday dinner, Wednesday dinner and Monday)* Menu (€12), €16

◆ A hundred-year old façade harbours old, though well-kept rooms with colourful furniture; some have received a facelift. Attractive summer terrace in a garden planted with trees or the restaurant room under a glass dome.

Savoy without rest VISA

21 av. Ch.-de-Gaulle – 04 79 35 13 33 – hotelsavoy.perrault@wanadoo.fr – Fax 04 79 88 40 10 – Open 1stApril-31 October CZ **e**

19 rm – €33/37 €36/42, €6

◆ An atmosphere and decor reminiscent of the days of our grandmothers. The well-maintained rooms are quieter in the back.

Revotel without rest VISA

198 r. de Genève – 04 79 35 03 37 – revotel@wanadoo.fr – Fax 04 79 88 82 99 – Closed 1st December-5 February CZ **v**

18 rm – €32/39 €32/39, €6

◆ A low-cost establishment near the livelier districts. Functional rooms with 1970s-style furniture. Quieter rooms towards the back.

L'Annexe VISA AE

205 bord du Lac – 04 79 35 25 64 – Fax 04 79 35 20 45 – Closed 26 October-10 November, 22-29 December, 9-23 February, Sunday dinner and Monday AX **b**

Rest – Menu €16 (weekday lunch), €24/37 – Carte €31/50

◆ A modern building overlooking the lake. Refined, contemporary dining room, plus an attractive panoramic terrace adorned with teak furniture. Modern cuisine.

Auberge du Pont Rouge VISA

151 av. du Grand-Port – 04 79 63 43 90 – Fax 04 79 63 43 90 – Closed Sunday dinner (weekday lunch), Wednesday dinner and Monday AX **f**

Rest – Menu €20, €28/32 – Carte approx. €46

◆ Leave the heart of the resort for this unassuming house with veranda and terrace. Specialities of the Southwest and fish from the lake. Friendly atmosphere.

AIZENAY – 85 Vendée – 316 G7 – pop. 6 095 – alt. 62 m – ✉ 85190 34 **B3**

Paris 435 – Challans 26 – Nantes 60 – La Roche-sur-Yon 18 – Les Sables-d'Olonne 33

Office de tourisme, rond-point de la Gare 02 51 94 62 72, Fax 02 51 94 62 72

La Sittelle VISA AE

33 r. Mar- Leclerc – 02 51 34 79 90 – Fax 02 51 94 81 77 – Closed August, 1st-7 January, Saturday lunch, Monday and dinner except Saturday

Rest – *(number of covers limited, pre-book)* Menu €22/35 (weekend)

◆ Elegant, unassuming residence with brick fireplaces, moulded ceilings and old parquet floors. The sophisticated, traditional cuisine also has a few personal touches.

AJACCIO – 2A Corse-du-Sud – 345 B8 – see Corse

ALBAN – 81 Tarn – **338** G7 – **pop. 848 – alt. 600 m** – ✉ **81250** 29 **C2**

Paris 723 – Albi 29 – Castres 54 – Toulouse 106

Syndicat d'initiative, 21, place des Tilleuls ☎ 05 63 55 93 90, Fax 05 63 55 93 90

Au Bon Accueil

49 av. de Millau – ☎ 05 63 55 81 03 – Bardyj@wanadoo.fr – Fax 05 63 55 82 97 – Closed 1st-31 January

11 rm – €39/53 €39/65, ☕ €7 – ½ P €45/50 – **Rest** – *(closed dinner and weekends in January, Friday dinner and Sunday dinner except July-August)* Menu (€13,50), €17/43 – Carte €31/52

◆ Practical for a stop-over between Albi and Millau, a small hotel with a charming façade housing renovated rooms. Pleasant, family atmosphere. Generous, traditional food to be savoured under the rustic beams of the dining room.

ALBERT – 80 Somme – **301** I8 – **pop. 10 065 – alt. 65 m** – ✉ **80300**
Northern France and the Paris Region 36 **B1**

Paris 156 – Amiens 30 – Arras 50 – St-Quentin 53

Office de tourisme, 9, rue Léon Gambetta ☎ 03 22 75 16 42, Fax 03 22 75 11 72

Royal Picardie rm,

rte d'Amiens – ☎ 03 22 75 37 00 – reservation@royalpicardie.com – Fax 03 22 75 60 19

23 rm – €78/229 €87/229, ☕ €10 – **Rest** – *(dinner only) (residents only)* Menu €32 – Carte €39/59

◆ This impressive building on the outskirts of town offers functional guestrooms with added extras such as an electric trouser press and courtesy tray. At the restaurant, traditional cuisine served in a dining room adorned with Louis XIII furniture.

in Authuille 5 km north by D 50 – **pop. 167 – alt. 85 m** – ✉ **80300**

Auberge de la Vallée d'Ancre

6 r. Moulin – ☎ 03 22 75 15 18 – Closed 18 August-3 September, 16 February-4 March, Sunday dinner, Wednesday dinner and Monday

Rest – Menu €22/31 – Carte €25/41

◆ Pleasant riverside inn with a warm welcome. Traditional dishes much appreciated by a local clientele.

ALBERTVILLE – 73 Savoie – **333** L3 – **pop. 17 340 – alt. 344 m** – ✉ **73200**
French Alps 46 **F2**

Paris 581 – Annecy 46 – Chambéry 51 – Chamonix-Mont-Blanc 64

Office de tourisme, place de l'Europe ☎ 04 79 32 04 22, Fax 04 79 32 87 09

Bourg de Conflans★, porte de Savoie ≤★ B, Grande Place★ - Fort du Mont road ★★ E.

Million rest,

8 pl. de la Liberté – ☎ 04 79 32 25 15 – hotel.million@wanadoo.fr – Fax 04 79 32 25 36 – Closed 28 April-12 May and 27 October-10 November

26 rm – €78/106 €107/151, ☕ €15 – ½ P €80

Rest – *(closed 28 July-4 August, Saturday lunch, Sunday dinner and Monday)* Menu €26/52 – Carte €63/77

◆ Imposing 18C establishment next to the Olympic Games Centre. Eclectic interior decor and personalised rooms. Modern cuisine is served in the classic and spacious dining room or on the verdant terrace.

Albert 1er rest,

38 av. Victor-Hugo – ☎ 04 79 37 77 33 – contact@albert1er.fr – Fax 04 79 37 89 01

16 rm – €59/77 €76/83, ☕ €6 – ½ P €52/56 – **Rest** – brasserie *(closed Sunday dinner)* Menu €12,50 (lunch) – Carte €21/36

◆ Next to the station, small (19C), renovated building offering cosy rooms. The best are the most recent ones. Quieter at the back. Modern bistro with veranda and pavement terrace; typical brasserie food with Savoy specialities.

at Monthion 7 km south by Chambéry road(exit 26) and D 64 – ✉ 73200

XX **Les 16 Clochers** ≤ valley and mountains, P VISA

91 chemin des 16 Clochers – ✆ 04 79 31 30 39 – Fax 04 79 31 30 39 – Closed 14-21 April, 1st-8 September, 23 December-15 January, Sunday dinner, Tuesday dinner and Monday

Rest – Menu € 19, € 26/48 – Carte € 46/67

♦ Warm welcome, panoramic terrace and attractive interior (part rustic, part Savoyard, antiques etc...) characterise this establishment, perched above the valley. Traditional dishes.

Southwest 4 km by Chambéry road (exit 28) – ✉ 73200 Albertville

Le Roma rm, rest, P VISA AE

85 chemin Pont-Albertin – ✆ 04 79 37 15 56 – hotelleroma@aol.com – Fax 04 79 37 01 31

133 rm – †€ 65/108 ††€ 80/135, ☕ € 13,50 – 10 suites – ½ P € 72

Rest – *(closed Sat. lunchtime)* Menu (€ 18), € 23/39 – Carte € 26/41

♦ Near to the bypass, a vast hotel complex where the emphasis is on relaxation and leisure. Spacious and quiet rooms; opt for the recently renovated ones. Traditional restaurant with a classic setting and pizzeria; both offer a covered terrace.

ALBI P – 81 Tarn – 338 E7 – pop. 46 274 – alt. 174 m – ✉ 81000

Languedoc-Roussillon-Tarn Gorges 29 **C2**

Paris 694 – Béziers 150 – Clermont-Ferrand 286 – Toulouse 76

Office de tourisme, place Sainte-Cécile ✆ 05 63 49 48 80, Fax 05 63 49 48 98

Albi Lasbordes Château de Lasbordes, West: 4 km by Rue de la Berchère, ✆ 05 63 54 98 07 ;

de Florentin-Gaillac Marssac-sur-Tarn Al Bosc, by Toulouse road: 11 km, ✆ 05 63 55 20 50.

Race circuit ✆ 05 63 43 23 00, 2 km by ⑤.

Ste-Cécile cathedral ★★★: Rood-screen★★★ - Palais de la Berbie★: musée Toulouse-Lautrec★★ - Le Vieil Albi★★: hôtel Reynès★ Z **C** - Pont Vieux★ - Pharmacie des Pénitents★ - ≤★ from the moulins albigeois (Albi windmills).

Plan on next page

La Réserve ≤ rm, P VISA AE

rte de Cordes, via ⑥: 3 km – ✆ 05 63 60 80 80 – reservealbi@relaischateaux.com – Fax 05 63 47 63 60 – Open 1st May-31 October

24 rm – †€ 150/328 ††€ 150/328, ☕ € 20 – 2 suites

Rest – *(closed lunch except Sunday and public holidays)* Menu € 40/65 – Carte € 64/91

♦ In gardens bordering the Tarn stands this large, welcoming villa where the rooms (with stylish contemporary furniture) offer views over the pool and the quiet river. Light dining room, fashionably decorated, with a huge terrace overlooking the water.

Hostellerie St-Antoine without rest P VISA AE

17 r. St-Antoine – ✆ 05 63 54 04 04 – courriel@hotel-saint-antoine-albi.com – Fax 05 63 47 10 47 Z **d**

42 rm – †€ 75/145 ††€ 85/185, ☕ € 15 – 2 suites

♦ In a calm location, this hotel was built in 1734 and renovated in the 1970's. Antique furniture and an old garden create a cosy, old-world atmosphere, with modern comfort.

Chiffre P VISA AE

50 r. Séré-de-Rivières – ✆ 05 63 48 58 48 – hotel.chiffre@yahoo.fr – Fax 05 63 38 11 15 – Closed 15 December-15 January Z **b**

36 rm – †€ 57/109 ††€ 88/169, ☕ € 15 – 2 suites – ½ P € 68/79

Rest – *(closed Saturday and Sunday) (dinner only)* Menu € 20/35

♦ Former post house situated around a patio. The refined and personalised rooms have mostly been refurbished. This hotel restaurant offers traditional dishes in a warm environment (wood-panelled walls, lavish surroundings and marine decor in the bar).

ALBI

Alsace-Lorraine (Bd) V
Andrieu (Bd Ed.) . . . . X 2
Archevêché (Pl. de l') . . . . . Y 3
Berchère (R. de la) . . . . Z
Bodin (Bd P.) . . . . X 5
Cantepau (R. de) V
Carnot (Bd). X
Castelviel (R. du) . . . . Y 7
Choiseul (Quai) . . . . Y 8
Croix-Blanche (R. de la) . . . . Z 9
Croix-Verte (R.) . . . . V, YZ 12
Dembourg (Av.). . . . . V 13
Dr-Camboulives (R. du) . . . . Z 14
Empeyralots (R. d') . . . . Z 15
Foch (Av. Mar.) X
Gambetta (Av.). X
Gaulle (Av. Gén.-de) X
Genève (R. de). . . . . Z 17
Gorsse (Pl. H. de) . . . . Y 18
Grand (R. E.). . . . . Y
Hôtel-de-Ville (R. de l') . . . . . Z 19
Jean-Jaurès (Pl.) . . . . Z
Joffre (Av. Mar.). . . . . X 22
Lacombe (Bd) . . . . X 23
Lamothe (R. de) . . . . V, Y
Lapérouse (Pl.). . . . . Z
Lattre-de-Tassigny (Av. Mar.-de). . . . . V 24
Loirat (Av. du). V
Lude (Bd du) X
Malroux (R. A.) . . . . Y 25
Maquis (Pl. du) . . . . X 26
Mariès (R.) . . . . Y
Montebello (Bd) . . . . X 27
Moulin (Lices J.) . . . . Z
Nobles (R. des) . . . . Z 28
Oulmet (R. de l') . . . . Z 29
Palais (Pl. du) . . . . Z 30
Palais (R. du) . . . . Z 31
Partisans (Espl. des) . . . . . . Y
Pénitents (R. des) . . . . Z 33
Peyrolière (R.) . . . . YZ 34
Pompidou (Lices G.) . . . . . . YZ
Porta (R.) . . . . Y
Porte-Neuve (R. de la) . . . . . Z 35
Puech-Bérenguier (R.) . . . . . Z 37
République (R. de la) . . . . V, Y
Rinaldi (R.) . . . . Y
Rivière (R. de la). . . . . Y 40
Roquelaure (R.) . . . . Z 41
Ste-Cécile (Pl.) . . . . Y 46
Ste-Cécile (R.) . . . . Z 47
Ste-Claire (R.) . . . . Y 48
St-Afric (R.) . . . . Y 42
St-Amarand (Pl.) . . . . V 69
St-Antoine (R.) . . . . Z 43
St-Clair (R.) . . . . Z 44
St-Julien (R.). . . . . Y 45
Saunal (R. de). . . . . Z 49
Savary (R. H.). . . . . Z 51
Sel (R. du). . . . . Z 52
Séré-de-Rivière (R.) . . . . Z 53
Sibille (Bd Gén.) . . . . Z
Soult (Bd) VX
Strasbourg (Bd de) . . . . . V, Y 54
Teyssier (Av. Col.) X
Thomas (Av. A.). . . . . V 57
Timbal (R.) . . . . Z 58
Toulouse-Lautrec (R. H.-de) Z 60
Valmy (Bd). VX
Verdier (Av. F.). . . . . X 62
Verdun (Pl. de) . . . . X 63
Verdusse (R. de) . . . . Z 64
Vigan (Pl. du) . . . . Z 65
Visitation (R. de la). . . . . Y 67
8-Mai-1945 (Pl. du) X

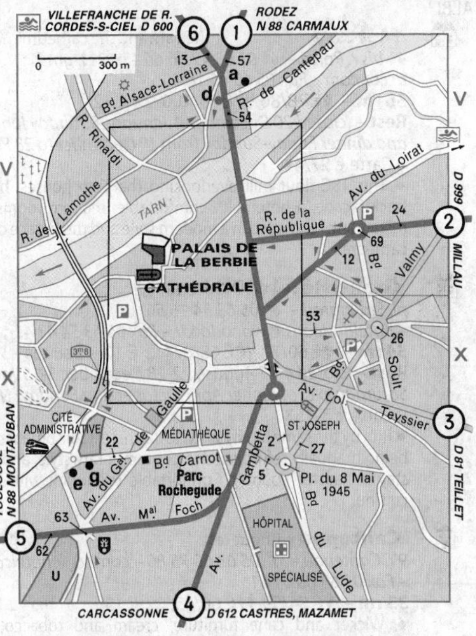

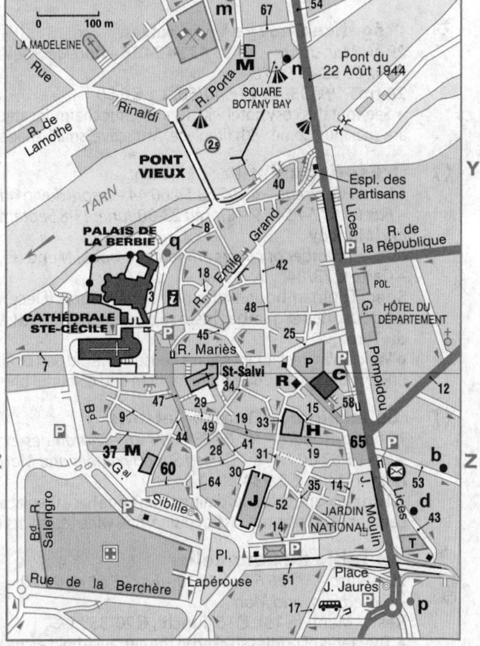

Mercure the Tarn and the cathedral, rm, rest,
41 bis r. Porta – 05 63 47 66 66 – h1211-gm@accor.com – Fax 05 63 46 18 40 Y n
56 rm – €78/86 €89/100, €12
Rest – *(closed 20 December-4 January, Saturday lunch, Sunday lunch and dinner Friday-Sunday from 1st December to 28 February)* Menu (€16), €20/35 – Carte €27/44
♦ This 18C flour mill overlooking the Tarn houses, behind the typical regional pink brick façade, a hotel with comfortable, modern rooms in subdued surroundings. The restaurant, renovated in a modern style and the terrace offer a breathtaking view over the cathedral.

Grand Hôtel d'Orléans rest,
pl. Stalingrad – 05 63 54 16 56 – hoteldorleans@wanadoo.fr – Fax 05 63 54 43 41 X e
54 rm – €60/77 €68/87, €10 – 2 suites – ½ P €60/65
Rest – *(closed 4-17 August, 22-28 December, 3-15 January, Saturday except dinner April-October and Sunday)* Menu (€17), €23/27 – Carte €31/53
♦ Run by the same family since 1902, this establishment offers functional rooms which are being gradually refurbished in contemporary style, and where you can enjoy a peaceful stay in Lautrec country. Comfortable restaurant with poolside terrace and traditional cuisine.

Cantepau without rest
9 r. Cantepau – 05 63 60 75 80 – contact@hotelcantepau.fr – Fax 05 63 60 01 61 V a
33 rm – €54/59 €60/65, €15
♦ Wicker and cane furniture, cream and tobacco shades, fans etc.: the recent complete renovation of this little family hotel is inspired by a colonial style. Friendly welcome.

Régence George V without rest
29 av. Mar.-Joffre – 05 63 54 24 16 – hotelgeorgeV@orange.fr – Fax 05 63 49 90 78 X g
24 rm – €35/45 €40/50, €6,50
♦ Seek out this cosy hotel with its authentic charm, located not far from the station. Rooms are spacious, some with fireplace. Attractive, small, shaded courtyard.

L'Esprit du Vin (David Enjalran)
11 quai Choiseul – 05 63 54 60 44 – lespritduvin@free.fr – Fax 05 63 54 54 79 – Closed 23-30 June, 1st-8 September, 19-31 January, Sunday and Monday Y q
Rest – *(number of covers limited, pre-book)* Menu (€26), €30 (lunch) – Carte €73/84
Spec. Topinambour, truffe noire et foie gras (December to beg. March). Duo de langoustines et gambas juste saisies. Pêche melba (summer). **Wines** Gaillac, Côtes du Tarn.
♦ Welcoming restaurant set in a house in the old part of Albi. Large dining room under red brick vaults and another more modern and colourful one. Creative food.

Le Jardin des Quatre Saisons
19 bd Strasbourg – 05 63 60 77 76 – lejardindes4saisons@tiscali.fr – Fax 05 63 60 77 76 – Closed Sunday dinner and Monday V d
Rest – Menu €22/34
♦ Two pleasant, colourful dining rooms: one has a fireplace, while the other is adorned with paintings and plants. Classic cuisine, fine wine list, spirits and cigars.

La Table du Sommelier
20 r. Porta – 05 63 46 20 10 – Fax 05 63 46 20 10 – Closed Sun. and Mon. Y m
Rest – Menu (€13), €16 (lunch), €20/35 bi
♦ The crates of bottles stacked in the entrance hold a clue to the importance given to wine in this establishment. References to Bacchus are displayed in the decoration. Bistro-style cuisine.

X **L'Epicurien**

42 pl. Jean-Jaurès – ✆ 05 63 53 10 70 – Fax 05 63 43 16 90 – Closed 21-27 December, Sunday and Monday Z **p**

Rest – Menu € 19 (weekday lunch), € 28/36 – Carte € 47/54

◆ This is the fashionable address of the town. Minimalist but nonetheless a welcoming setting with benches, bay windows, and a direct view of the kitchens. Modern menu.

in Castelnau-de-Lévis 7 km by ⑥, D 600 and D 1 – pop. 1 403 – alt. 221 m – ✉ 81150

XX **La Taverne** with rm rest,

r. Aubijoux – ✆ 05 63 60 90 16 – contact@tavernebesson.com – Fax 05 63 60 96 73

8 rm – †€ 58/65 ††€ 58/85, ☕ € 9 – **Rest** – *(closed 26 July-10 August, Sunday dinner and Monday off season)* Menu € 23 (weekdays)/61 – Carte € 44/63

◆ Former bakers' co-operative, with two comfortable dining rooms, one of which displays the original brick ovens. Refined cuisine focusing on local and traditional dishes.

ALENÇON Ⓟ – 61 Orne – 310 J4 – pop. 28 935 – alt. 135 m – ✉ 61000

Normandy 33 **C3**

Paris 190 – Chartres 119 – Évreux 119 – Laval 90 – Le Mans 54 – Rouen 150

Office de tourisme, place de la Magdeleine ✆ 02 33 80 66 33, Fax 02 33 80 66 32

d'Alençon-en-Arçonnay Arçonnay Le Petit Maleffre, by Mans road: 3 km, ✆ 02 33 28 56 67.

Église Notre-Dame (Notre Dame Church)★ - Musée des Beaux-Arts et de la Dentelle (Museum of Fine Arts and Lacework)★ : lace collection ★ BZ **M²**.

Plan on next page

Mercure without rest

187 av. Gén- Leclerc, 2 km on ④ – ✆ 02 33 28 64 64 – h1359@accor.com – Fax 02 33 28 64 72 – Closed 24 December-1 January

53 rm – †€ 66 ††€ 71, ☕ € 8,70

◆ Fairly recent building located in a small commercial park. Rooms are practical and well soundproofed, those on the first floor are modern and renovated. Breakfast buffet.

XX **Au Petit Vatel**

72 pl. Cdt-Desmeulles – ✆ 02 33 26 23 78 – Fax 02 33 82 64 57 – Closed 23 July-13 August, 18 February-9 March, Sunday dinner, Tuesday dinner and Wednesday BZ **s**

Rest – Menu € 20/69 – Carte € 31/57

◆ In a small square is this pretty house built in local stone, embellished with flower-covered balconies. Elegant dining room with pastel shades and rustic-style chairs.

X **Le Chapeau Rouge**

117 r. de Bretagne – ✆ 02 33 26 57 53 – Closed 1st-14 September, Saturday lunch and Sunday AY **v**

Rest – Menu (€ 13), € 16/25 – Carte € 22/30

◆ The hat on the sign is red but the dining room is all-yellow, in a Mediterranean style. The cuisine consists of a few daring combinations with a traditional base.

via ① N 138 and secondary road - ✉ 61250 Valframbert

Château de Sarceaux rest,

– ✆ 02 33 28 85 11 – chateaudesarceaux@yahoo.fr – Fax 02 33 28 85 11 – Closed 15 January-15 February

5 rm ☕ – †€ 100/145 ††€ 100/145 – **Table d'hôte** – Menu € 47 bi

◆ A 12-ha park with a pond surrounds this 17C and 19C castle with refined rooms decorated with authentic furniture and family paintings, all facing south. Candle-light dinner in the restaurant; traditional menu.

ALENÇON

Argentan (R. d') . . . . **AY** 2
Basingstoke (Av. de) . . . . . . **AY** 3
Bercail (R. du) . . . . **BZ** 4
Capucins (R. des) . . . . **CZ** 6
Clemenceau (Cours) . . . . . **BCZ**
Duchamp (Bd) . . . . **AY** 8
Écusson (R. de l') . . . . **AY** 9
Fresnay (R. de) . . . . **BZ** 13
Grandes-Poteries (R. des) . . **BZ** 14
Grande-Rue . . . . **BZ** 15
Halle-au-Blé (Pl. de la) . . . . . **BZ** 17
Lattre-de-Tassigny (R. du Mar.-de) . . . . **BCZ** 19
Leclerc (Av. du Gén.) . . . . . . **AY** 20
La Magdeleine (Pl.) . . . . **CZ** 18
Mans (R. du) . . . . **AY** 24
Marguerite-de-Lorraine (Pl.) . **BZ** 25
Porte-de-la-Barre (R.) . . . . . **BZ** 30
Poterne (R. de la) . . . . **CZ** 33
Quakenbruck (Av. de) . . . . . . **AY** 34
Rhin-et-Danube (Av.) . . . . . . **AY** 35
Sieurs (R. aux) . . . . **BZ**
Tisons (R. des) . . . . **AY** 39
1er Chasseurs (Bd) . . . . **AY** 40
14e Hussards (R. du) . . . . . . **AY** 42

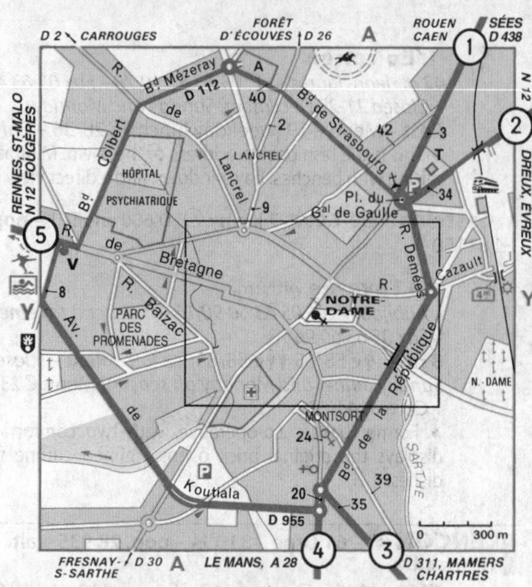

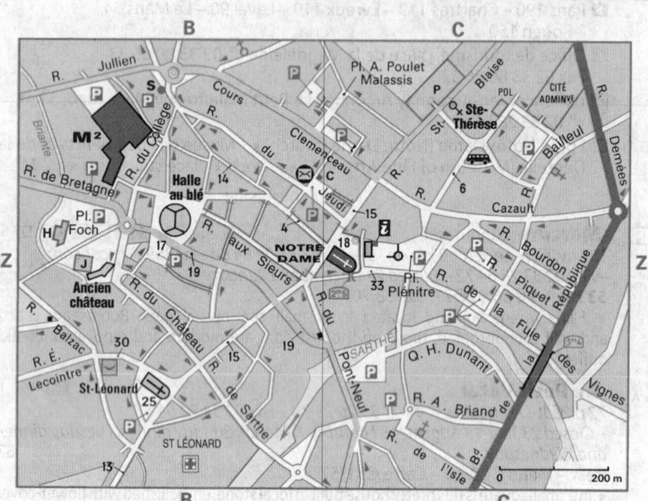

ALÉRIA – 2B Haute-Corse – **345** G7 – **see Corse**

ALÈS – 30 Gard – **339** J4 – **pop. 39 346 – alt. 136 m** – ✉ **30100**
Languedoc-Roussillon-Tarn Gorges 23 **C1**

Paris 706 – Albi 226 – Avignon 72 – Montpellier 70 – Nîmes 46

Office de tourisme, place de la Mairie ✆ 04 66 52 32 15, Fax 04 66 52 57 09

Musée minéralogique de l'Ecole des Mines★ N - Musée-bibliothèque Pierre-André-Benoit★ West: 2 km - Mine-témoin★ West: 3 km.

ALÈS

Street	Grid	No.
Albert-1er (R.)	B	2
Audibert (R. Cdt)	A	3
Avéjan (R. d')	B	
Barbusse (Pl. Henri)	B	4
Docteur-Serres (R.)	B	
Edgar-Quinet (R.)	B	
Hôtel-de-Ville (Pl. de l')	A	5
Lattre-de-Tassigny (Av. de)	B	6
Leclerc (Pl. Gén.)	B	8
Louis-Blanc (Bd)	B	
Martyrs-de-la-Résistance (Pl.)	B	9
Michelet (R.)	B	10
Paul (R. Marcel)	B	12
Péri (Pl. Gabriel)	B	13
Rollin (R.)	A	14
St-Vincent (R.)	B	15
Semard (Pl. Pierre)	B	16
Soleil (R. du Faubourg du)	B	17
Stalingrad (Av. de)	B	18
Taisson (R.)	B	19
Talabot (Bd)	B	20

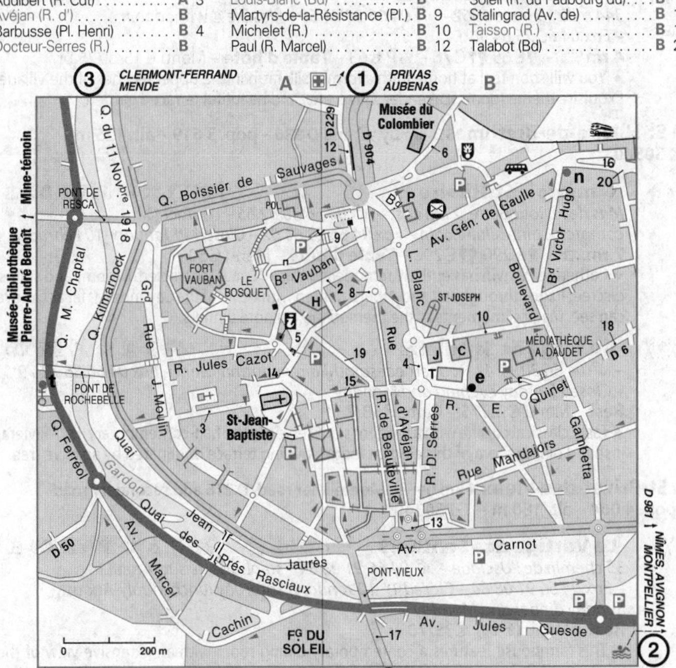

Ibis without rest

18 r. E.-Quinet – ☎ 04 66 52 27 07 – h0338@accor.com – Fax 04 66 52 36 33 B **e**

75 rm – †€ 51/67 ††€ 51/67, ☕ € 7,50

◆ A 1970s hotel in the heart of Alès. All the spacious and well-soundproofed rooms have been renovated. Lounge bar. Bicycle shed.

Le Riche with rm

42 pl. Sémard – ☎ 04 66 86 00 33 – reception@leriche.fr – Fax 04 66 30 02 63 – Closed Aug. B **n**

19 rm – †€ 46 ††€ 59, ☕ € 8 – ½ P € 50

Rest – Menu € 20/48 – Carte € 23/44

◆ Fine, early-20C building. Art Nouveau dining room with a high ceiling and brightly coloured wood panelling. Classic cuisine. Simple rooms.

L'Atelier des Saveurs

16 fbg de Rochebelle – ☎ 04 66 86 27 77 – gouny.henri@wanadoo.fr – Fax 04 66 86 27 77 – Closed 18 August-7 September, Saturday lunch, Sunday dinner and Monday

Rest – Menu (€ 16), € 23/50 – Carte € 30/43 A **t**

◆ The scene at this 'workshop of flavours' is a bright, discreetly countrified interior, inviting shaded patio, warm, friendly atmosphere and appealing up-to-date recipes full of southern flavour.

in St-Martin-de-Valgalgues 2 km by ① – pop. 4 283 – alt. 148 m – ✉ 30520

Le Mas de la Filoselle rest,
344 r. du 19 mars 1962 – ☎ 04 66 24 74 60 – filoselle@wanadoo.fr – Fax 04 66 25 64 96
4 rm – €65 €76 – ½ P €63 – **Table d'hôte** – Menu €15 bi/25 bi
◆ You will soon feel at home in this former silk farm in the upper reaches of the village. Exquisite theme rooms (Lavender, Olive, etc.) and beautiful terraced garden.

in St-Hilaire-de-Brethmas 3 km by ② and D 936 – pop. 3 619 – alt. 125 m – ✉ 30560

Comptoir St-Hilaire
Mas de la Rouquette, 2 km east – ☎ 04 66 30 82 65 – contact@comptoir-saint-hilaire.com – Fax 04 66 25 64 02 – Closed 1st January-10 February
7 rm – €290 €290 – **Table d'hôte** – Menu €50
◆ Catherine Painvin has entirely remodelled this 17C mas: characterful rooms and suites, discreet luxury throughout, and superb garden with views of the Cevennes as far as the eye can see. Magical moments at the themed table d'hôte dinners.

Auberge de St-Hilaire
– ☎ 04 66 30 11 42 – aubergedesainthilaire@hotmail.com – Fax 04 66 86 72 79 – Closed Sunday evening and Monday
Rest – Menu €25/75 – Carte €58/73
◆ Tasty classical cuisine with a modern slant served in the half-contemporary, half-Riviera-inspired dining room of this elegant lodge. Inviting terrace dominated by an olive tree.

in St-Privat-des-Vieux 4 km by ②, Montélimar road, D 216 and secondary road – pop. 4 064 – alt. 180 m – ✉ 30340

Le Vertige des Senteurs
35 chemin de l'Usclade – ☎ 04 66 91 08 84 – stephane.delsuc@neuf.fr – Fax 04 66 91 08 84 – Closed 1st-10 January, Saturday lunch in July-August, Sunday dinner and Monday
Rest – Menu (€19), €35/70
◆ This farmhouse features a contemporary dining room with an extensive view of the Cévennes. A fitting setting for the carefully prepared inventive cuisine, served by attentive staff.

in Méjannes-lès-Alès 7.5 km by ② and D 981 – pop. 905 – alt. 141 m – ✉ 30340

Auberge des Voutins
rte d'Uzès – ☎ 04 66 61 38 03 – Fax 04 66 61 04 19 – Closed Sunday dinner and Monday except public holidays
Rest – Menu €28/58 – Carte €53/62
◆ Building typical of the region, sheltered from the road by a line of trees. Traditional cuisine to be enjoyed in a countrified dining room or on the terrace shaded by a lime tree.

ALFORTVILLE – 94 Val-de-Marne – **312** D3 – **101** 27 – see Paris, Area

---

ALGAJOLA – 2B Haute-Corse – **345** C4 – see Corse

ALISE-STE-REINE – 21 Côte-d'Or – **320** G4 – see Venarey-les-Laumes

---

ALIX – 69 Rhône – **327** G4 – pop. 690 – alt. 287 m – ✉ 69380 43 **E1**
Paris 442 – L'Arbresle 12 – Lyon 28 – Villefranche-sur-Saône 12

Le Vieux Moulin
chemin du Vieux-Moulin – ☎ 04 78 43 91 66 – lemoulindalix@wanadoo.fr – Fax 04 78 47 98 46 – Closed 16 August-3 September, Monday and Tuesday
Rest – Menu €25/51 – Carte €27/51
◆ This Rhone mill, built in stone, has been converted into a village inn. Countrified interior and a peaceful shaded terrace very popular in summer. Classic fare and daily specials.

ALLAIN – 54 Meurthe-et-Moselle – **307** G7 – **pop. 387** – **alt. 306 m** – ✉ **54170** 26 **B2**

▶ Paris 305 – Nancy 34 – Neufchâteau 28 – Toul 16 – Vittel 49

La Haie des Vignes without rest

0.5 km at the A 31 interchange, Neufchâteau road – ✆ 03 83 52 81 82 – hotel.haiedesvignes@free.fr – Fax 03 83 52 04 27

39 rm – 🛉€ 41 🛉🛉€ 56, ☕ € 6

◆ Motel-style modern building located near the motorway, but in the quiet of the Lorraine countryside. Rooms are functional, subdued and well kept, with direct garden access.

ALLAS-LES-MINES – 24 Dordogne – **329** H6 – see St-Cyprien

ALLEINS – 13 Bouches-du-Rhône – **340** F3 – **pop. 2 368** – **alt. 180 m** – ✉ **13980** 42 **E1**

▶ Paris 725 – Marseille 63 – Aix-en-Provence 34 – Avignon 47

Domaine de Méjeans

R.D.71B – ✆ 04 90 57 31 74 – info@domainedemejeans.com – Fax 04 90 57 31 74

5 rm ☕ – 🛉€ 140/180 🛉🛉€ 150/210 – **Table d'hôte** – Menu € 28/40

◆ A poplar lined drive leads up to this luxurious property set in grounds complete with pond, garden and swimming pool. Comfortable, well-equipped rooms.

ALLERY – 80 Somme – **301** E8 – see Airaines

ALLEVARD – 38 Isère – **333** J5 – **pop. 3 081** – **alt. 470 m** – **Winter sports : at Collet d'Allevard 1 450/2 100 m** ⛷13 – **Spa : early March-mid Oct.** – **Casino** – ✉ **38580** ▮ French Alps 46 **F2**

▶ Paris 593 – Albertville 50 – Chambéry 33 – Grenoble 40

ℹ Office de tourisme, place de la Résistance ✆ 04 76 45 10 11, Fax 04 76 97 59 32

👁 le Collet road★★ by D525ᴬ.

ALLEVARD

Baroz (R. Emma) 2
Bir-Hakeim (R. de) 3
Charamil (R.) 5
Chataing (R. Laurent) 6
Chenal (R.) 7
Davallet (Av.) 8
Docteur-Mansord (R.) 9
Gerin (Av. Louis) 15
Grand Pont (R. du) 19
Libération (R. de la) 21
Louaraz (Av.) 22
Niepce (R. Bernard) 23
Ponsard (R.) 24
Rambaud (Pl. P.) 25
Résistance (Pl. de la) 27
Savoie (Av. de) 28
Thermes (R. des) 29
Verdun (Pl. de) 32
8-Mai-1945 (R. du) 34

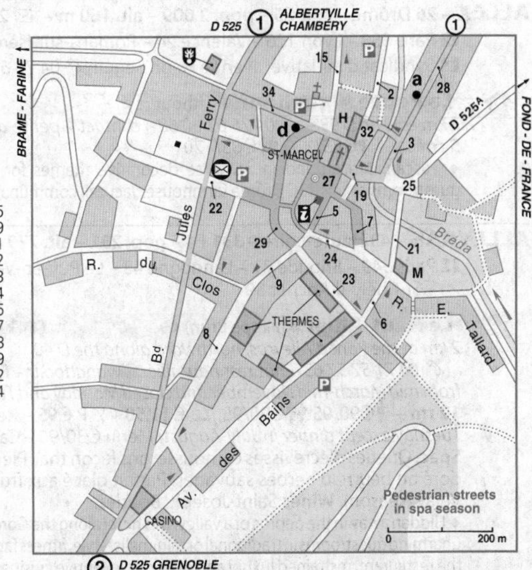

Les Alpes rest,

pl. du Temple – ✆ *04 76 45 94 10* – *hotel@lesalpesallevard.com* – *Fax 04 76 45 80 81* – *Closed 12-28 April, 25 October-6 November and Sunday dinner in winter* **d**
17 rm – €54/55 €56/62, ☕ €9 – ½ P €60/67 – **Rest** – *(closed Friday dinner off season and Sunday dinner)* Menu (€14,50), €17 (weekday lunch), €29/48 – Carte €35/57
♦ A family hotel, easily recognisable by its yellow and green facade, in the heart of the spa resort. Rather spacious, spotless rooms with personal touches. The recently renovated dining room sports a classic influence in keeping with the traditional menu.

Les Terrasses

29 av. de Savoie – ✆ *04 76 45 84 42* – *responsable@hotellesterrasses.com* – *Fax 04 76 13 57 65* – *Closed 14-27 April and 26 October-6 November* **a**
16 rm – €44 €44, ☕ €6,50 – ½ P €50/60 – **Rest** – *(Closed Sunday dinner, Tuesday dinner and Wednesday)* Menu (€14), €21/33 – Carte €22/31
♦ A friendly welcome awaits guests in this tall 1930s house, situated near the River Bréda. Functional bedrooms; those at the back facing the garden are quieter. Simple Provençal decor in the dining room; traditional dishes.

in Pinsot **7 km South by D 525 A – pop. 139 – alt. 730 m – ✉ 38580**

Pic de la Belle Étoile

– ✆ *04 76 45 89 45* – *hotel@pbetoile.com* – *Fax 04 76 45 89 46* – *Closed 12 April-9 May, 18 October-16 November, Friday dinner, Saturday and Sunday except 7 July-18 August, 25 December-4 January and 9 February-9 March*
40 rm – €63/95 €79/119, ☕ €11 – ½ P €75/97 – **Rest** – Menu €34/47
♦ This imposing local style residence, with a recent extension, offers a garden that rolls down to a stream. Choose the rooms in the recently-built wing. Classic dishes with a regional accent are served in a modern dining area or on the terrace.

South **17 km by D 525A and secondary road - ✉ 38580 Allevard**

Auberge Nemoz

au hameau "La Martinette" – ✆ *04 76 45 03 10* – *aubergenemoz@wanadoo.fr* – *Fax 04 76 45 03 10* – *Closed November and 15-30 April*
5 rm ☕ – €62/76 €72/86 – ½ P €53/65 – **Table d'hôte** – Menu €22/32
♦ In the valley of the Haut Bréda, wood and stone chalet with personalised rooms (antique furniture and family heirlooms). In summer, horseriding (reservation necessary). Rustic, convivial restaurant serving local specialities including *raclette.*

ALLEX – 26 Drôme – 332 C5 – pop. 2 009 – alt. 160 m – ✉ 26400 44 B3

Paris 588 – Lyon 126 – Valence 24 – Romans-sur-Isère 46 – Montélimar 34

Syndicat d'initiative, avenue Henri Seguin ✆ 04 75 62 73 13

La Petite Aiguebonne without rest

2 km east on D 93 – ✆ *04 75 62 60 68* – *contact@petite-aiguebonne.com*
5 rm ☕ – €85/120 €85/120
♦ Tuscan, African, Indian... Diverse decorative themes for the pretty, well-equipped guestrooms at this 13C Drôme farmhouse. Jacuzzi, communal kitchen.

ALLEYRAS – 43 Haute-Loire – 331 E4 – pop. 231 – alt. 779 m – ✉ 43580 6 C3

Paris 549 – Brioude 71 – Langogne 43 – Le Puy-en-Velay 32 – St-Chély-d'Apcher 59

Le Haut-Allier (Philippe Brun) rest, rest,

2 km at the Pont d'Alleyras, northward along the D 40 – ✆ *04 71 57 57 63* – *hot.rest.hautallier@wanadoo.fr* – *Fax 04 71 57 57 99* – *Open from mid March-mid November and closed Monday and Tuesday except July-August*
12 rm – €90/95 €90/95, ☕ €11,50 – ½ P €95 – **Rest** – *(closed Monday and Tuesday except dinner in July-August)* Menu €30/90 – Carte €57/70
Spec. Queues d'écrevisses et mousserons façon thaï. Piéce de veau de lait fermier doré au beurre d'herbes sauvages. Parfait glacé aux fruits rouges des Monts du Velay (season). **Wines** Saint-Joseph, Boudes.
♦ Hidden away in the depths of a valley, this hotel along the Gorges de l'Allier is worth a visit. Charming guestrooms in traditional or minimalist style, fitness facilities and friendly service. In the restaurant, restrained luxury and delicious inventive cuisine inspired by local produce.

ALLOS – 04 Alpes-de-Haute-Provence – **334** H7 – **pop. 637** – **alt. 1 425 m** – **Winter sports : 1 400/2 000 m** 4 29 – ✉ **04260** French Alps 41 **C2**

Paris 763 – Barcelonnette 36 – Colmars 8 – Digne-les-Bains 78

Office de tourisme, place du Presbytère ✆ 04 92 83 02 81, Fax 04 92 83 06 66

✳★★ of the col d'Allos Northwest: 15 km.

in la Foux d'Allos 9 km northwest by D 908 – ✉ **04260 Allos**

Office de tourisme, Maison de la Foux ✆ 04 92 83 80 70, Fax 04 92 83 86 27

Du Hameau

– ✆ 04 92 83 82 26 – info@hotel-du-hameau.fr – Fax 04 92 83 87 50
– Closed 20 April-13 June and 21 September-5 December
36 rm – €65/95 €85/125, €11 – 9 suites – ½ P €65/90
Rest – Menu €18/45

♦ Chalet-style hotel with comfortable panelled rooms; those with mezzanines can accommodate families. Good leisure facilities. Nice view of the mountains from this restaurant and terrace. Traditional dishes, fondues, raclettes.

LES ALLUES – 73 Savoie – **333** M5 – **see Méribel**

ALLY – 15 Cantal – **330** B3 – **pop. 700** – **alt. 720 m** – ✉ **15700** 5 **A3**

Paris 532 – Clermont-Ferrand 119 – Aurillac 46 – Tulle 71 – Ussel 69

Château de la Vigne without rest

1 km north-east on D 680 – ✆ 04 71 69 00 20 – la.vigne@wanadoo.fr
– Fax 04 71 69 00 20 – Open April-October
4 rm – €110/130 €110/130, €6

♦ In the same family since its construction (15-18C), this château offers rooms with historical decor ("Louis XV", "Troubadour", "Directoire"...).

ALOXE-CORTON – 21 Côte-d'Or – **320** J7 – **see Beaune**

ALPE D'HUEZ – 38 Isère – **333** J7 – **pop. 1 479** – **alt. 1 860 m** – **Winter sports : 1 250/3 330 m** 15 69 – ✉ **38750** French Alps 45 **C2**

Paris 625 – Le Bourg-d'Oisans 12 – Briançon 71 – Grenoble 63

Altiport ✆ 04 76 11 21 73, Southeast.

Office de tourisme, place Paganon ✆ 04 76 11 44 44

Pic du Lac Blanc ✳★★★ by cable car - Villars-Reculas road★ 4 km by D 211B.

Plan on next page

Au Chamois d'Or < pistes and mountains, rm, rest,

rd-pt des pistes – ✆ 04 76 80 31 32
– resa@chamoisdor-alpedhuez.com – Fax 04 76 80 34 90
– Open 15 December-20 April B **e**
40 rm – €250 €330, €17 – 5 suites – ½ P €220/275
Rest – Menu €35 (lunch), €53/65 – Carte €54/85

♦ Imposing chalet with a large south facing terrace at the foot of the slopes. All-wood or modern style rooms; those on the third floor are more comfortable. Some overlook the Oisans massif. Attractive mountain-chic style restaurant; classic well-prepared menu.

Le Pic Blanc rest,

r. Rif-Briant – ✆ 04 76 11 42 42 – hotel.pic.blanc@hmc-hotel.com
– Fax 04 76 11 42 43 – Open 1st June-31 August and 1st December-25 April
94 rm – €136/268 €180/435, €12 – ½ P €100/233 – **Rest** – *(dinner only) (residents only)* Menu €26

♦ Large, modern, chalet style building set at the top of the resort. Spacious, English style rooms all with a balcony. Sun deck, swimming pool and sauna. Restaurant serving traditional food.

Le Printemps de Juliette without rest

av. des Jeux – ✆ 04 76 11 44 38 – info@leprintempsdejuliette.com
– Fax 04 76 11 44 37
8 rm – €140/200 €140/200, €15 – 4 suites

♦ A gem of a hotel in the heart of the resort: eight rooms and one suite individually decorated in pastel shades (balconies). In season, a saxophonist plays live in the tea room.

ALPE D'HUEZ

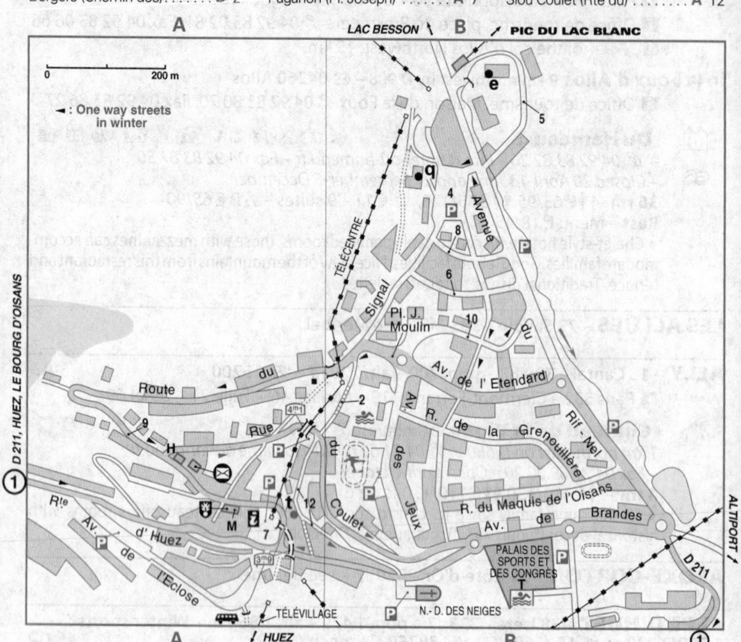

Le Dôme
Massif de l'Oisans, VISA

pl. du Cognet – 04 76 80 32 11 – info@dome-alpedhuez.com – Fax 04 76 80 66 48 – Open July-August and December- April B **q**

25 rm – €78/172 €92/187, €12 – ½ P €99/145 – **Rest** – *(open December-April)* Menu (€18), €29 – Carte €27/49

◆ The hotel, founded by the current owner's grandfather, stands on the site of a former refuge of the Touring Club. Functional rooms, gradually redone in local style. Shopping arcade. Small dining room with a mountain style atmosphere. Traditional and regional menu.

Au P'tit Creux
VISA AE

chemin des Bergers – 04 76 80 62 80 – ptit.creux@wanadoo.fr – Fax 04 76 80 39 37 – Closed 8 May-25 June, 15 November-1st December, Monday lunch, Tuesday lunch from 1st February to 8 May, Sunday dinner and Monday dinner from 1st September to 15 November A **t**

Rest – *(pre-book)* Menu €48 – Carte €29/56

◆ Old wainscoting, red and beige tablecloths and straw chairs depict the new alpine decor of this smart restaurant and veranda extension. Classic cuisine.

in Huez **3.5 km Southwest by D 211 – pop. 202 – alt. 1 495 m – 38750**

L'Ancolie
rm, VISA

av. de l'Église – 04 76 11 13 13 – forestieryves@aol.com – Fax 04 76 11 13 11 – Open 30 November-26 April, 1st June-23 August, 2-30 September

16 rm – €52/96 €56/100, €11 – ½ P €60/82 – **Rest** – *(dinner only December-April)* Menu (€11,50), €15 (weekday lunch), €18/75 – Carte €22/40

◆ Lovely local-style house situated in a preserved old village. Renovated, mountain-style interior (wood and stone decor), smart rooms and a peaceful environment. Traditional food, local specialities and pretty view of Oisans from the restaurant.

ALPUECH – 12 Aveyron – 338 J2 – pop. 79 – alt. 1 082 m – ✉ 12210 29 D1

Paris 566 – Toulouse 213 – Rodez 66 – Aurillac 81 – Onet-le-Château 64

Air Aubrac

La Violette, south 5 km on Laguiole road – ✆ 05 65 44 33 64 – airaubrac@wanadoo.fr – Fax 05 65 44 33 64 – Open 24 April-6 October and 28 December-3 January

5 rm – €53 €59/63 – ½ P €49/51 – **Table d'hôte** – Menu €20 bi

◆ This typical old farm surrounded by pastureland in the Aubrac is run by a hot-air balloon pilot (trips available). Charming, comfortable guestrooms. The owner prepares simple dishes using regional ingredients and produce from her own vegetable garden.

ALTENSTADT – 67 Bas-Rhin – 315 L2 – see Wissembourg

ALTHEN-DES-PALUDS – 84 Vaucluse – 332 C9 – pop. 1 988 – alt. 34 m – ✉ 84210 42 E1

Paris 676 – Avignon 18 – Carpentras 12 – Cavaillon 24 – Orange 22

Hostellerie du Moulin de la Roque

rte de la Roque – ✆ 04 90 62 14 62 – hotel@moulin-de-la-roque.com – Fax 04 90 62 18 50

28 rm – €72/140 €72/140, €11 – ½ P €70/105 – **Rest** – *(closed Monday except dinner in season, Saturday except dinner off season and Sunday dinner off season)* Menu €25/55

◆ A path bordered by plane trees takes you to this 17C mill. Personalised rooms look onto a park intersected by the Sorgue (fishing). Savour produce from the orchard and vegetable garden in the pleasant elegant dining room and on the shady terrace.

ALTKIRCH – 68 Haut-Rhin – 315 H11 – pop. 5 386 – alt. 312 m – ✉ 68130 Alsace-Lorraine 1 A3

Paris 457 – Basel 33 – Belfort 35 – Montbéliard 52 – Mulhouse 19 – Thann 27

Office de tourisme, 5 place Xavier Jourdain ✆ 03 89 40 02 90, Fax 03 89 40 02 90

de la Largue Seppois-le-Bas Rue du Golf, South: 23 km by D 432, ✆ 03 89 07 67 67.

in Wahlbach 10 km East by D 419 and D 19B – pop. 323 – alt. 320 m – ✉ 68130

Auberge de la Gloriette with rm

9 r. Principale – ✆ 03 89 07 81 49 – la-gloriette2@wanadoo.fr – Fax 03 89 07 40 56 – Closed 24 January-12 February

5 rm – €46/100 €58/100, €15 – ½ P €58 – **Rest** – *(closed Mon. and Tues.)* Menu €15 (weekday lunch), €28/65 – Carte €27/63

◆ This farmstead offers refined classic cuisine in the dining room with a pleasant decor mixing old and new. The rooms are more comfortable (antiques) in the main wing.

ALTWILLER – 67 Bas-Rhin – 315 F3 – pop. 399 – alt. 220 m – ✉ 67260 1 A1

Paris 412 – Metz 86 – Nancy 73 – Le Haras 10 – Strasbourg 94

L'Écluse 16

Southeast: 3.5 km – ✆ 03 88 00 90 42 – clerouxmugler@aol.com – Fax 03 88 00 91 94 – Closed 1st-10 March, 25 December-1st January, Monday and Tuesday

Rest – Menu €18 (weekdays)/42

◆ Former towpath lodge on the banks of the Houillères de la Sarre canal. Simple decor in the sunny dining room where tasty, modern food is served.

ALVIGNAC – 46 Lot – 337 G3 – pop. 573 – alt. 400 m – ✉ 46500 29 C1

Paris 529 – Brive-la-Gaillarde 52 – Cahors 65 – Figeac 43 – Rocamadour 8 – Tulle 65

Syndicat d'initiative, le bourg ✆ 05 65 33 66 42, Fax 05 65 33 60 62

Du Château

– ✆ 05 65 33 60 14 – hotel-du-chateau@wanadoo.fr – Fax 05 65 33 69 28 – Open 7 April-5 November

20 rm – ♦€ 38/42 ♦♦€ 38/42, ☐ € 7 – ½ P € 42/47 – **Rest** – *(closed Wednesday dinner and Sunday dinner except July-August)* Menu € 12 (weekday lunch), € 15/24 – Carte € 14/32

♦ This ancient building with its stone facade covered in ivy is set against the church. The functional, well-kept rooms are being gradually renovated. Pleasant garden. Simple and welcoming dining room in harmony with the local food.

AMBÉRIEU-EN-BUGEY – 01 Ain – 328 F5 – pop. 11 436 – alt. 300 m – ✉ 01500

Burgundy-Jura 44 **B1**

Paris 468 – Bourg-en-Bresse 31 – Lyon 55 – Nantua 44

Ambotel rest,

(Pragnat Nord business park), North by D1075 towards Bourg-en-Bresse – ✆ *04 74 46 42 22 – Fax 04 74 46 87 92*

35 rm – ♦€ 54 ♦♦€ 62/72, ☐ € 6,50 – **Rest** – Menu (€ 12), € 15 (weekday lunch), € 20/35 – Carte € 21/40

♦ This new construction is characterised by its contemporary architecture and smart ochre facade. Modern rooms practically furnished in lightwood. The attractive colourful dining room offers traditional, unpretentious food.

AMBÉRIEUX-EN-DOMBES – 01 Ain – 328 C5 – pop. 1 408 – alt. 296 m – ✉ 01330

43 **E1**

Paris 437 – Bourg-en-Bresse 40 – Lyon 35 – Mâcon 43 – Villefranche-sur-Saône 18

Syndicat d'initiative, Mairie ✆ 04 74 00 84 15, Fax 04 74 00 84 04

Auberge des Bichonnières

545 rte du 3-Septembre-1944 – ✆ *04 74 00 82 07 – bichonnier@wanadoo.fr – Fax 04 74 00 89 61 – Closed 20 December-30 January, Sunday dinner and Monday except July-August*

9 rm – ♦€ 49 ♦♦€ 54/64, ☐ € 9 – ½ P € 58/72 – **Rest** – *(closed Sunday dinner except July-August, Tuesday lunch and Monday) (number of covers limited, pre-book)* Menu (€ 19 bi), € 25/33 – Carte € 39/45

♦ This typical old Dombes farmhouse offers soberly rustic rooms, adorned with locally inspired murals. Flower-decked terrace located in an attractive courtyard. Traditional cooking with a regional accent served in a rustic decor.

AMBERT – 63 Puy-de-Dôme – 326 J9 – pop. 7 309 – alt. 535 m – ✉ 63600

Auvergne 6 **C2**

Paris 438 – Brioude 63 – Clermont-Ferrand 77 – Thiers 53

Office de tourisme, 4, place de Hôtel de Ville ✆ 04 73 82 61 90, Fax 04 73 82 48 36

St-Jean church ★ - La Dore valley ★ North and South - Moulin Richard-de-Bas★ 5.5 km East by D 996 - Musée de la Fourme et du fromage - Panoramic train★ (July-August).

Les Copains with rm rm,

42 bd Henri-IV – ✆ *04 73 82 01 02 – hotel.rest.les.copains@wanadoo.fr – Fax 04 73 82 67 34 – Closed 18-28 April, 6 September-6 October, 14-22 February, Sunday dinner, Saturday and dinner on public holidays*

10 rm – ♦€ 46/48 ♦♦€ 48/60, ☐ € 6,50 – ½ P € 48/67 – **Rest** – Menu € 12 (weekday lunch), € 23/48 – Carte € 31/48

♦ Opposite the picturesque rotunda (town hall) made famous by Jules Romains in his novel, Les Copains. Regional dishes and the renowned Fourme cheese served in a dining room decorated in sunny colours.

AMBIALET – 81 Tarn – 338 G7 – pop. 381 – alt. 220 m – ✉ 81430

Languedoc-Roussillon-Tarn Gorges 29 **C2**

Paris 718 – Albi 23 – Castres 55 – Lacaune 52 – Rodez 71 – St-Affrique 60

Syndicat d'initiative, le bourg ✆ 05 63 55 39 14, Fax 05 63 55 39 14

Site★.

Du Pont
– ✆ 05 63 55 32 07 – hotel-restaurant.pont@wanadoo.fr – Fax 05 63 55 37 21 – Closed 2 January-13 February, Sunday dinner and Monday from November to March
20 rm – †€ 55/57 ††€ 61/63, ☕ € 10 – ½ P € 58/61 – **Rest** – Menu € 22/48 – Carte € 39/56
♦ Traditional house with views over Ambialet located on the banks of the Tarn. Fresh rooms overlooking the countryside or the river. The dining room is furnished in rustic style. On fine days, sample traditional dishes on the panoramic terrace.

AMBIERLE – 42 Loire – **327** C3 – **pop. 1 728** – **alt. 467 m** – ✉ **42820**
Lyon - Rhone Valley 44 **A1**

Paris 379 – Lapalisse 33 – Roanne 18 – Thiers 81 – Vichy 58
Church ★.

Le Prieuré
r. de la Mairie – ✆ 04 77 65 63 24 – leprieureambierle@wanadoo.fr – Fax 04 77 65 69 90 – Closed Sunday dinner, Tuesday and Wednesday
Rest – Menu € 26/63 – Carte € 40/100
♦ Facing the former Cluny priory, this bright, modern restaurant serves inventive, contemporary cuisine. Handsome terrace in the garden and courtyard.

L'AMBITION – 28 Eure-et-Loir – **311** B6 – **see Nogent-le-Rotrou**

AMBOISE – 37 Indre-et-Loire – **317** O4 – **pop. 11 457** – **alt. 60 m** – ✉ **37400**
Châteaux of the Loire 11 **A1**

Paris 223 – Blois 36 – Loches 37 – Tours 27 – Vierzon 96
Office de tourisme, quai Gal de Gaulle ✆ 02 47 57 09 28, Fax 02 47 57 14 35
Château★★: ≤★★ from the terrace, ≤★★ of the Minimes tower - Clos-Lucé★ - Chanteloup pagoda ★ 3 km by ④.
Lussault-sur-Loire: aquarium de Touraine★ West: 8 km by ⑤.

Plan on next page

Le Choiseul
36 quai Ch.-Guinot – ✆ 02 47 30 45 45 – choiseul@grandesetapes.fr – Fax 02 47 30 46 10 B **v**
28 rm – †€ 100/280 ††€ 100/340, ☕ € 22 – 4 suites – ½ P € 130/250
Rest – *(closed lunch except Sunday and public holidays)* Menu € 60/90 – Carte € 48/86
Rest ***Le 36*** – *(closed Sunday and public holidays) (lunch only)* Menu (€ 25), € 32
Spec. Ecrevisses et grenouilles, bouillon léger et bonbon frit aux herbes. Carré d'agneau allaiton d'Aveyron caramélisé au piment doux. Chocolat "concepcion".
Wines Montlouis, Touraine-Mesland.
♦ This elegant 18C property built facing the River Loire has a beautiful flower garden and swimming pool. Classical rooms. Inventive cuisine served in a panoramic room overlooking the île d'Or. At Le 36, a conservatory setting and simple dishes.

Le Manoir Les Minimes without rest
34 quai Ch.-Guinot – ✆ 02 47 30 40 40 – reservation@manoirlesminimes.com – Fax 02 47 30 40 77 – Open 12 March-10 November B **x**
13 rm – †€ 119/190 ††€ 119/190, ☕ € 12 – 2 suites
♦ A fine 18C abode on the banks of the River Loire. Handsome sitting rooms and refined bedrooms adorned with splendid furniture from a variety of periods.

Le Manoir St Thomas without rest
1 Mail St-Thomas – ✆ 02 47 23 21 82 – info@manoir-saint-thomas.com – Fax 02 47 23 24 96 – Closed 30 November-17 December and 7-31 January
8 rm – †€ 120/170 ††€ 120/190, ☕ € 17 – 2 suites B **d**
♦ Nothing is too much trouble for guests' comfort in this Renaissance manor. Garden with pool, attractive sitting rooms and characterful bedrooms (exposed beams or painted ceilings).

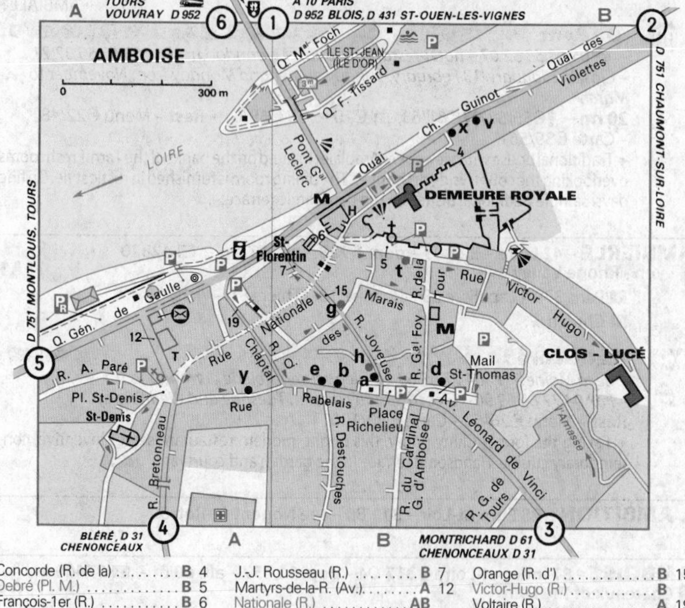

Concorde (R. de la) . . . . B 4
Debré (Pl. M.) . . . . B 5
François-1er (R.) . . . . B 6
J.-J. Rousseau (R.) . . . . B 7
Martyrs-de-la-R. (Av.) . . . . A 12
Nationale (R.) . . . . AB
Orange (R. d') . . . . B 15
Victor-Hugo (R.) . . . . B
Voltaire (R.) . . . . A 19

Novotel

2 km south via ③ Chenonceaux road – ☎ 02 47 57 42 07 – novotel.amboise@wanadoo.fr – Fax 02 47 30 40 76

121 rm – †€ 94/118 ††€ 114/138, ☕ € 13 – **Rest** – Carte € 19/36

◆ This building dominates Amboise and the Loire valley. Spacious, modern rooms in keeping with the chain's standards; some overlook the château. Contemporary dining room. A simple menu based on grills, salads and pasta.

Château de Pray

3 km, rte de Chargé via ② and D 751 – ☎ 02 47 57 23 67 – chateau.depray@wanadoo.fr – Fax 02 47 57 32 50 – Closed 15-30 November and 8-26 January

19 rm – †€ 110/185 ††€ 110/185, ☕ € 13 – 1 suite – ½ P € 110/148

Rest – *(closed Monday dinner and Tuesday except from 1st April to 30 October)* Menu € 30 (weekday lunch), € 47/60 – Carte € 49/72

Spec. Langoustines bretonnes, tomate et œuf cassé à la truffe. Suprême de géline, salsifis aux truffes, galette Maxime. Crousti-fondant vanille café, sorbet cacao.

◆ This former fortress built during the Crusades and extended in the 17C is set in a vast park. Period furnished rooms in the château, family-sized in the pavilion opposite. Renaissance style dining room and a terrace overlooking a vegetable garden. Up-to-the-minute menu.

Clos d'Amboise without rest

27 r. Rabelais – ☎ 02 47 30 10 20 – le-clos-amboise@wanadoo.fr – Fax 02 47 57 33 43 – Closed 1st December-12 February B **b**

17 rm – †€ 75/135 ††€ 75/135, ☕ € 11

◆ A lovely garden with heated pool and smart personalised rooms characterise this manor house near the château. Fitness facilities in the former stables.

Domaine de l'Arbrelle

rte des Ormeaux, on the D31 – ☎ 02 47 57 57 17 – contact@arbrelle.com – Fax 02 47 57 64 89 – Closed 30 November-11 January

21 rm – †€ 68/136 ††€ 68/145, ☕ € 14 – **Rest** – *(dinner only)* Menu € 24/40 – Carte € 39/48

◆ In the heart of a park situated on the edge of the forest, this establishment features a stylish lounge and pleasant, contemporary rooms. Small, rustic-bourgeois dining room; pergola and terrace facing the garden.

Le Vinci Loire Valley without rest
12 av. E. Gounin, 1 km south via ④ – ✆ 02 47 57 10 90 – reservation@vinciloirevalley.com – Fax 02 47 57 17 52
26 rm – €72/89 €72/89, €10
◆ In the town suburbs, this hotel has been renovated in a pleasant contemporary style. Comfortable, well-equipped rooms.

Le Blason without rest
11 pl. Richelieu – ✆ 02 47 23 22 41 – hotel@leblason.fr – Fax 02 47 57 56 18 – Closed 13 January-13 February B **a**
25 rm – €44/45 €49/58, €6,50
◆ The facade and picturesque layout of this 15C building have been preserved, giving the hotel its appealing charm. Renovated rooms in pastel shades and ceilings with beams.

Vieux Manoir without rest
13 r. Rabelais – ✆ 02 47 30 41 27 – info@le-vieux-manoir.com – Fax 02 47 30 41 27 – Open 15 February-15 November A **y**
6 rm – €125/140 €135/235
◆ A French style garden surrounds this 18C manor and the pavilion, home to a lovely apartment. "Vintage" decor in the rooms with antique wardrobes and paintings.

Au Charme Rabelaisien without rest
25 r. Rabelais – ✆ 02 47 57 53 84 – aucharmerabelaisien@wanadoo.fr – Fax 02 47 57 53 84 B **e**
3 rm – €60/80 €120/140
◆ This bourgeois mansion was formerly a bank, school and solicitors offices. It now offers tasteful rooms, a friendly welcome, tranquillity and a small garden with pool.

Le Pavillon des Lys with rm
rm,
9 r. Orange – ✆ 02 47 30 01 01 – pavillondeslys@wanadoo.fr – Fax 02 47 30 01 90 – Closed 20 November-7 December and 2-31 January
7 rm – €90/180 €90/180, €12 – 1 suite – ½ P €95
Rest – *(closed Tuesday and lunch except Saturday and Sunday)*
Menu €26/38 B **g**
◆ This 18C abode houses two small, opulent dining rooms and a lounge. In summer, the terrace is laid in the interior courtyard. Inventive market inspired menu.

L'Alliance
14 r. Joyeuse – ✆ 02 47 30 52 13 – restaurant.lalliance@wanadoo.fr – Fax 02 47 30 52 13 – Closed 2 January-13 February, Tuesday and Wednesday except dinner from June to August B **h**
Rest – Menu (€15), €20/45 – Carte €34/50
◆ A stone's throw from the town centre, this appealing restaurant is run by a young couple. Modern style dining room, wrought iron on the veranda/terrace. Contemporary cuisine.

L'Épicerie
46 pl. M-Debré – ✆ 02 47 57 08 94 – Fax 02 47 57 08 89 – Closed 15 October-15 December, Monday and Tuesday except from July to September
Rest – Menu €12 (weekday lunch), €21/38 – Carte €29/52
◆ This half-timbered 1338 house and its pleasant terrace are admirably located opposite the château. Country-style interior and tightly packed tables. Regional cuisine.

in St-Ouen-les-Vignes 6.5 km by ① and D 431 – pop. 941 – alt. 80 m – ✉ 37530

L'Aubinière with rm
rest,
29 r. Jules-Gautier – ✆ 02 47 30 15 29 – restaurant-laubiniere@wanadoo.fr – Fax 02 47 30 02 44 – Closed 1st-15 March
6 rm – €80/100 €110/135, €12 – ½ P €100
Rest – *(closed Sunday dinner from October-May, Wednesday except dinner from June-September and Monday)* Menu €26 (weekday lunch), €34/42 – Carte €43/76
◆ Beautiful dining room, terrace overlooking a pretty garden, up-to-date cuisine, rich regional wine list and cosy rooms: this inn has it all!

in Limeray 7 km by ① and D 952 – pop. 945 – alt. 70 m – ✉ 37530

XX **Auberge de Launay** with rm — rm, P VISA MC
9 r. de la Rivière – ☎ 02 47 30 16 82 – info@aubergedelaunay.com – Fax 02 47 30 15 16 – Closed 7-13 April and 19 December-11 January
15 rm – †€ 55/73 ††€ 55/73, ☕ € 14 – ½ P € 50/62
Rest – *(closed Sunday dinner from November to February and Saturday lunch)* Menu € 19 (weekday lunch), € 23/35
◆ Old 18C farm housing a rustic dining room, a veranda and a pleasant terrace. Renovated rooms in warm colours. The herbs and vegetables come from the cottage garden.

in Nazelles-Négron 4 km by ⑥ and Noizay road – pop. 3 633 – alt. 57 m – ✉ 37530

Château des Ormeaux without rest — P VISA MC
– ☎ 02 47 23 26 51 – contact@chateaudesormeaux.fr – Fax 02 47 23 19 31 – Closed 15 January-15 February
5 rm ☕ – †€ 110/155 ††€ 115/165
◆ This 1830 château, masterfully renovated in a bourgeois style, dominates the Loire Valley. Each room pays tribute to a classical composer (music available). Regional produce.

AMBONNAY – 51 Marne – 306 H8 – pop. 934 – alt. 95 m – ✉ 51150 13 **B2**

Paris 169 – Châlons-en-Champagne 24 – Épernay 19 – Reims 28 – Vouziers 65

XX **Auberge St-Vincent** with rm — AC rest, rm, VISA MC AE
1 r. St-Vincent – ☎ 03 26 57 01 98 – info@auberge-st-vincent.com – Fax 03 26 57 81 48 – Closed 18 August-3 September, 10 February-12 March, Tuesday lunch, Sunday dinner and Monday
10 rm – †€ 54 ††€ 57/68, ☕ € 10 – ½ P € 81/85 – **Rest** – Menu € 30/72 – Carte € 66/87
◆ Regional cooking is the order of the day in this elegant Champagne inn. Old kitchen utensils decorate the dining room fireplace. Renovated rooms.

AMBRONAY – 01 Ain – 328 F4 – pop. 2 146 – alt. 250 m – ✉ 01500
Burgundy-Jura 44 **B1**

Paris 463 – Belley 53 – Bourg-en-Bresse 28 – Lyon 59 – Nantua 39

X **Auberge de l'Abbaye** — VISA MC
pl. des Anciens-Combattants – ☎ 04 74 46 42 54 – lavaux.ivan@wanadoo.fr – Fax 04 74 38 82 68 – Closed 3-9 March, 30 July-7 August, 22 December-4 January, Wednesday dinner, Sunday dinner and Monday
Rest – Menu (€ 20), € 28
◆ You can enjoy a tempting market sourced set menu in this delightful retro-style inn. Lovely cellar where customers can choose their own wine.

AMÉLIE-LES-BAINS-PALALDA – 66 Pyrénées-Orientales – 344 H8 – pop. 3 475 – alt. 230 m – Spa : late Jan.-late Dec. – Casino – ✉ 66110
Languedoc-Roussillon-Tarn Gorges 22 **B3**

Paris 882 – Céret 9 – Perpignan 41 – Prats-de-Mollo-la-Preste 24

Office de tourisme, 22, avenue du Vallespir ☎ 04 68 39 01 98, Fax 04 68 39 20 20

de Falgos Saint-Laurent-de-Cerdans Domaine de Falgos, South: 4 km by D 3 and D 3A, ☎ 04 68 39 51 42.

Medieval town of Palalda★.

Palmarium Hôtel — AC rest, VISA MC
av. Vallespir – ☎ 04 68 39 19 38 – information@hotelpalmarium.fr – Fax 04 68 39 04 23 – Closed 2 December-31 January
65 rm – †€ 36/54 ††€ 51/54, ☕ € 7 – ½ P € 47/54 – **Rest** – Menu € 18/32 – Carte € 22/39
◆ This modern building on the main road is a practical option for an overnight stay. Simple accommodation and family pension atmosphere. A neo-rustic dining room with exposed beams. Regional, traditional cuisine. Theme evenings with buffet menus.

Des Bains et des Gorges VISA

pl. Arago – 04 68 39 29 02 – hotel-bains-gorges@wanadoo.fr – Fax 04 68 39 82 52 – Closed 15 December-15 February

43 rm – €30/36 €34/41, €5,50 – ½ P €32/37 – **Rest** – Menu €14/18

◆ The main advantage of this hotel is its location near the thermal baths. Simple, clean rooms, some of which have a balcony. Catalan cuisine served in a spacious dining room with rustic furniture and 1970s decor.

L'AMÉLIE-SUR-MER – **33 Gironde** – **335** E2 – **see Soulac-sur-Mer**

AMIENS P – **80 Somme** – **301** G8 – **pop. 135 501** – **Built-up area 160 815** – **alt. 34 m** – 80000 **Northern France and the Paris Region** 36 **B2**

Paris 142 – Lille 123 – Reims 173 – Rouen 122 – St-Quentin 81

Office de tourisme, 6 bis, rue Dusevel 03 22 71 60 50, Fax 03 22 71 60 51

d'Amiens Querrieu D 929, by Albert road: 7 km, 03 22 93 04 26 ;

de Salouel Salouel Rue Robert Mallet, Southwest: 5 km, 03 22 95 40 49.

Notre-Dame cathedral ★★★ (stalls ★★★) - Hortillonnages★ - Hôtel de Berny★ CY **M³** - Quartier St-Leu★ - Musée de Picardie★★ - Théâtre de marionnettes "ché cabotans d'Amiens" CY **T²**.

Plans on following pages

Carlton rest, VISA

42 r. Noyon – 03 22 97 72 22 – reservation@lecarlton.fr – Fax 03 22 97 72 00

24 rm – €75 €105/130, €10 – ½ P €75 – **Rest** – Menu (€13 bi), €18/21 bi – Carte €25/33 CZ **s**

◆ A 19C building near the station. Cosy rooms with dark wood furniture and murals. Excellent soundproofing. Friendly atmosphere and brasserie decor (banquettes, booths etc) in this restaurant which serves reasonably priced buffet-style buffet menus.

Grand Hôtel de l'Univers without rest VISA

2 r. Noyon – 03 22 91 52 51 – hotelunivers.amiens@wanadoo.fr – Fax 03 22 92 81 66 CZ **a**

41 rm – €65/150 €85/150, €12,50

◆ Old house with a renovated façade by a main road. Bourgeois reception and lovely staircase with a glass canopy leading to comfortable rooms.

Mercure Cathédrale without rest VISA

17 pl. au Feurre – 03 22 22 00 20 – mercure.amiens@escalotel.com – Fax 03 22 91 86 57 BY **r**

47 rm – €91/94 €103/118, €13

◆ This 18C post house with an attractive façade is now a hotel offering soundproofed, well-equipped rooms with attractive light-coloured wood furniture.

Le Saint-Louis VISA

24 r. des Otages – 03 22 91 76 03 – info@le-saintlouis.com – Fax 03 22 92 78 75 – Closed 24-30 March, 21 July-10 August, 22-28 December, Monday dinner, Saturday lunch and Sunday CZ **h**

15 rm – €53 €53/66, €8 – **Rest** – Menu (€15), €18/24 – Carte €26/46

◆ A warm welcome awaits you in this charming establishment on the town's doorstep. Very well-kept, cosy rooms. An attractive pastel colour scheme adorns the bright dining room serving traditional cuisine.

Ibis rm, rm, VISA

4 r. Mar.-de-Lattre-de-Tassigny – 03 22 92 57 33 – H0480@accor.com – Fax 03 22 91 67 50 BY **e**

94 rm – €59/82 €59/82, €7,50 – **Rest** – *(dinner only)* Menu €16 bi/23 bi

◆ Good location in the heart of the cultural district for this 1980s construction. Functional, air-conditioned rooms gradually renovated in line with the chain's latest standards. The wide bay windows of the restaurant let you watch what's happening in the street; buffet menus.

Victor Hugo without rest VISA

2 r. Oratoire – 03 22 91 57 91 – hotelvictorhugo@wanadoo.fr – Fax 03 22 92 74 02

10 rm – €41 €41, €6,50 CY **v**

◆ Small family hotel a stone's throw away from the Gothic cathedral and the famous Crying Angel. Lovely wooden staircase leads up to simple and well-kept rooms.

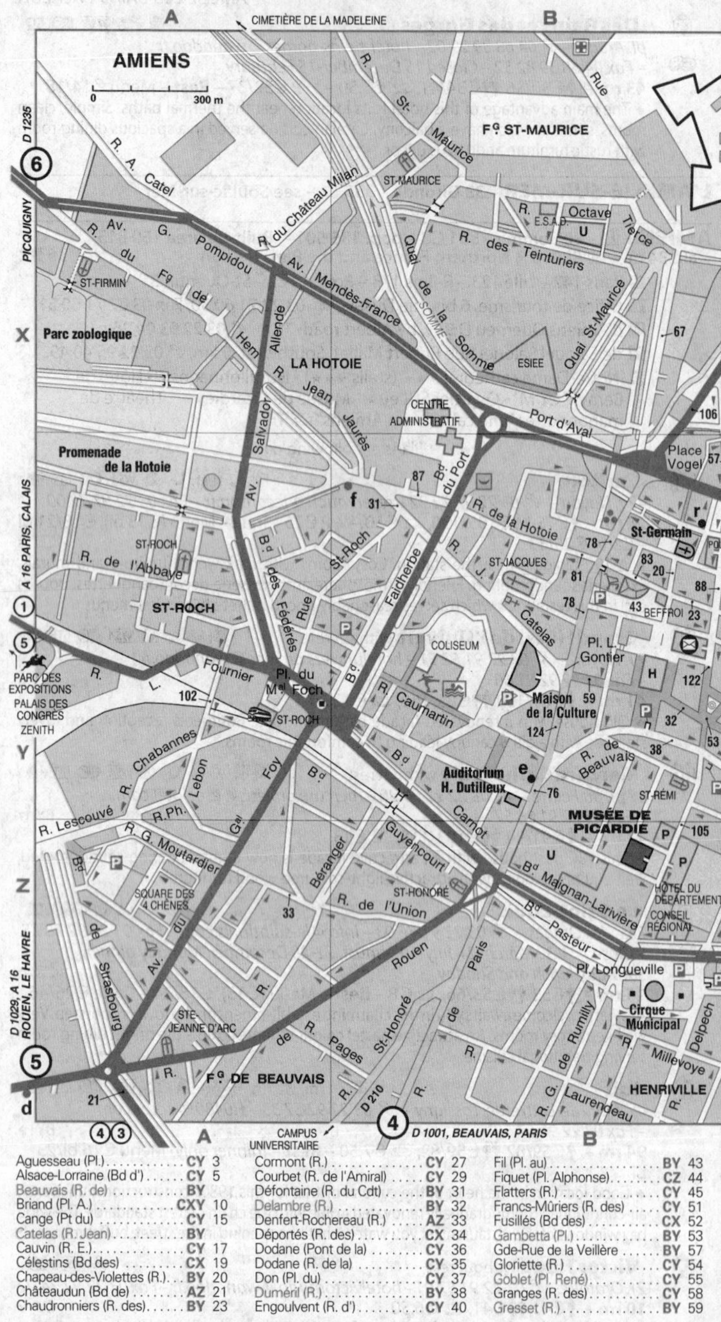
AMIENS
0
300 m
A
B
X
Y
Z
CIMETIÈRE DE LA MADELEINE
D 1235
PICQUIGNY
A 16 PARIS, CALAIS
D 1029, A 16
ROUEN, LE HAVRE
D 1001, BEAUVAIS, PARIS
D 210
CAMPUS UNIVERSITAIRE
PARC DES EXPOSITIONS
PALAIS DES CONGRÈS
ZENITH
Fg ST-MAURICE
ST-MAURICE
R. St-Maurice
R. du Château Milan
R. A. Catel
Av. G. Pompidou
Av. Mendès-France
R. du Fg de Hem
ST-FIRMIN
Parc zoologique
LA HOTOIE
Av. Salvador Allende
R. Jean Jaurès
Promenade de la Hotoie
CENTRE ADMINISTRATIF
Bd du Port
Port d'Aval
Quai de la Somme
SOMME
Quai St-Maurice
ESIEE
R. des Teinturiers
R. Octave Tierce
E.S.A.D.
Place Vogel
St-Germain
R. de la Hotoie
ST-JACQUES
R. J. Catelas
ST-ROCH
R. de l'Abbaye
Bd des Fédérés
Rue St-Roch
Bd Faidherbe
COLISEUM
Pl. L. Gontier
Maison de la Culture
BEFFROI
R. L. Fournier
Pl. du Mal Foch
R. Caumartin
R. de Beauvais
Auditorium H. Dutilleux
ST-RÉMI
MUSÉE DE PICARDIE
R. Chabannes
R. Lebon
Bd Gal Foy
Bd Guyencourt
Bd Carnot
R. Lescouvé
R. Ph.
R. G. Moutardier
SQUARE DES 4 CHÊNES
Bd de Strasbourg
Av. du
R. Béranger
ST-HONORÉ
R. de l'Union
Bd Maignan-Larivière
HÔTEL DU DÉPARTEMENT
CONSEIL RÉGIONAL
Bd Pasteur
Pl. Longueville
Cirque Municipal
R. Delpech
R. Millevoye
R. de Rouen
R. de Paris
R. de Rumilly
R. G. Laurendeau
R. St-Honoré
R. de Pages
STE-JEANNE D'ARC
Fg DE BEAUVAIS
HENRIVILLE
H
U
POL
f
r
e
n
d
6
1
5
4
3
21
31
33
67
76
78
81
83
87
88
20
23
32
38
43
53
57
59
102
105
106
122
124

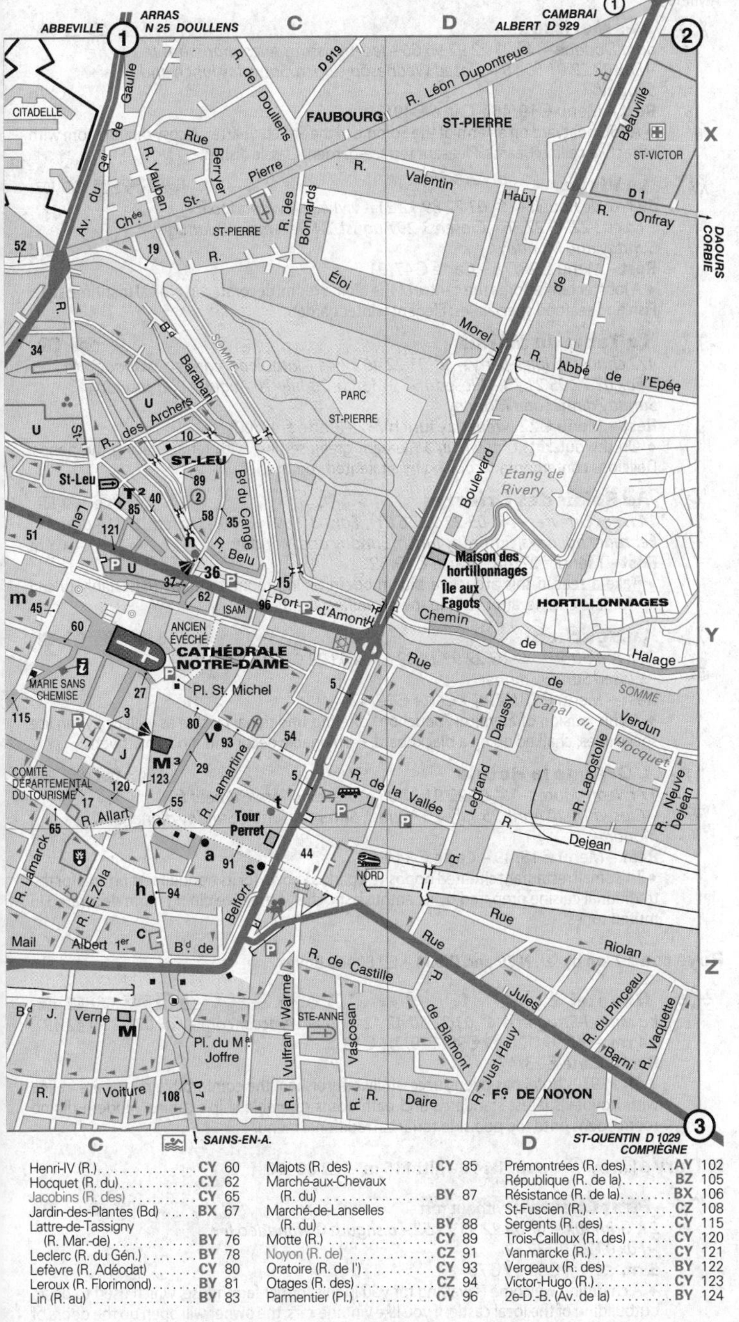

Henri-IV (R.)	CY	60
Hocquet (R. du)	CY	62
Jacobins (R. des)	CY	65
Jardin-des-Plantes (Bd)	BX	67
Lattre-de-Tassigny (R. Mar.-de)	BY	76
Leclerc (R. du Gén.)	BY	78
Lefèvre (R. Adéodat)	CY	80
Leroux (R. Florimond)	BY	81
Lin (R. au)	BY	83
Majots (R. des)	CY	85
Marché-aux-Chevaux (R. du)	BY	87
Marché-de-Lanselles (R. du)	BY	88
Motte (R.)	CY	89
Noyon (R. de)	CZ	91
Oratoire (R. de l')	CY	93
Otages (R. des)	CZ	94
Parmentier (Pl.)	CY	96
Prémontrées (R. des)	AY	102
République (R. de la)	BZ	105
Résistance (R. de la)	BX	106
St-Fuscien (R.)	CZ	108
Sergents (R. des)	CY	115
Trois-Cailloux (R. des)	CY	120
Vanmarcke (R.)	CY	121
Vergeaux (R. des)	BY	122
Victor-Hugo (R.)	CY	123
2e-D.-B. (Av. de la)	BY	124

XXX **Les Marissons**

pont Dodane – ✆ 03 22 92 96 66 – les-marissons@les-marissons.fr – Fax 03 22 91 50 50 – Closed Wednesday lunch, Saturday lunch and Sunday CY **n**

Rest – Menu € 19/46 – Carte € 49/61

◆ A 15C boatyard on an arm of the Somme in the St-Leu quarter. A cosy dining room with attractive ceiling beams. Pleasant terrace-garden. Classic dishes.

XXX **Le Vivier**

593 rte de Rouen – ✆ 03 22 89 12 21 – vivier.le@wanadoo.fr – Fax 03 22 45 27 36 – Closed 3-29 August, 24 December-5 January, Sunday and Monday AZ **d**

Rest – Menu € 28/78 – Carte € 47/91

◆ A lobster tank adorns the centre of the dining room, decorated in typical maritime style. Fish and seafood specialities. Elegant winter garden.

XX **La Table du Marais**

472 chaussée Jules-Ferry – ✆ 03 22 46 17 44 – latabledumarais@wanadoo.fr – Fax 03 22 95 21 73 – Closed 1st-12 March, 28 July-20 August, 1st-8 January, Sunday dinner and Monday

Rest – Menu € 22 (weekday lunch)/32 – Carte € 49/60

◆ On the outskirts of town, in a pleasant green setting, with terrace facing the ponds. Delicious contemporary cooking by a talented young chef.

XX **Au Relais des Orfèvres**

14 r. des Orfèvres – ✆ 03 22 92 36 01 – Fax 03 22 91 83 30 – Closed 10-31 August, February holidays, Saturday lunch, Sunday and Monday CY **m**

Rest – Menu € 27/48 – Carte € 49/52

◆ Take a seat in this attractive blue modern dining room, to enjoy reasonably-priced up-to-date cuisine, after visiting the magnificent cathedral.

XX **Le Bouchon**

10 r. A.-Fatton – ✆ 03 22 92 14 32 – Fax 03 22 91 12 58 – Closed Sunday dinner CY **t**

Rest – Menu € 18/36 bi – Carte € 22/47

◆ A chic version of a typical "bouchon" offering traditional cuisine as well as Lyonnaise specialities, chalked up on a blackboard. Fashionable decor and modern artwork.

XX **L'Orée de la Hotoie**

17 r. Jean-Jaurès – ✆ 03 22 91 37 05 – loréedelahotoie@neuf.fr – Closed 14-20 April, 25 July-20 August, Saturday lunch, Sunday dinner and Monday BY **f**

Rest – Menu € 18/49 – Carte € 34/51

◆ This small restaurant situated opposite a park is known for its tranquil setting and for the traditional cuisine prepared by its enthusiastic chef. Attractive dining room decorated in muted tones.

Roye road 7 km by ③, N 29 and D 934 – ✉ 80440 Boves

Novotel

rm,

bd Michel-Strogoff – ✆ 03 22 50 42 42 – H0396@accor.com – Fax 03 22 50 42 49

94 rm – €99/129 €99/129, €13

Rest – Carte € 23/47

◆ This 1970s hotel has been successfully refurbished: the comfortable rooms are in line with Novotel's latest standards and bathrooms resemble ship's cabins. Modern dining room opens onto the poolside terrace. Traditional menu.

in Dury 6 km by ④ – pop. 1 141 – alt. 115 m – ✉ 80480

Petit Château without rest

2 r. Grimaux – ✆ 03 22 95 29 52 – a.saguez@wanadoo.fr – Fax 03 22 95 29 52

5 rm – €55 €78

◆ A charming welcome is waiting for you in this former farmhouse, which used to be an outbuilding of the local castle. If you like vintage cars, the owner will open up the doors of his workshop for you.

XXX **L'Aubergade** (Eric Boutté)

78 rte Nationale – ✆ 03 22 89 51 41 – aubergade.dury@wanadoo.fr – Fax 03 22 95 44 05 – Closed 6-21 April, 3-18 August, 21 December-5 January, Sunday and Monday

Rest – Menu € 39/70 – Carte € 67/94

Spec. Coquilles Saint-Jacques (October to April). Chou farci "hommage à Jean Delaveyne". Agneau de lait des Pyrénées, carré rôti et épaule confite (December to May).

◆ Limed wood furniture, antique-style colonnades and pastel shades make up the dining room decor. French doors open onto the summer terrace. Tasty up-to-date menu.

X **La Bonne Auberge**

63 rte Nationale – ✆ 03 22 95 03 33 – Closed 30 June-29 July, February holidays, Sunday dinner, Monday and Tuesday

Rest – Menu (€ 20), € 25/50 – Carte € 44/56

◆ This smart regional façade is covered with flowers in summer. In the recently redecorated dining room you will be offered contemporary cuisine.

AMILLY – **45 Loiret** – **318** N4 – **see Montargis**

AMMERSCHWIHR – **68 Haut-Rhin** – **315** H8 – **pop. 1 892** – **alt. 215 m** – ✉ **68770**
Alsace-Lorraine 2 **C2**

Paris 441 – Colmar 9 – Gérardmer 49 – St-Dié 44 – Sélestat 29

A l'Arbre Vert

7 r. des Cigognes – ✆ 03 89 47 12 23 – info@arbre-vert.net – Fax 03 89 78 27 21 – Closed 15 February-13 March, Monday from November to April and Tuesday

19 rm – †€ 41 ††€ 53, ☕ € 9 – ½ P € 59/65 – **Rest** – Menu € 23/49 – Carte € 37/53

◆ Alsatian house in a village at the foot of sloping vineyards offering functional rooms, of which those in the annex are more modern. Restaurant (non-smoking) with fine wood carvings of vineyard scenes serving carefully-prepared regional dishes. Smoking room.

XXX **Aux Armes de France** with rm

1 Grand'Rue – ✆ 03 89 47 10 12 – aux.armes.de.france@wanadoo.fr – Fax 03 89 47 38 12 – Closed one week in March, Wednesday and Thursday

10 rm – †€ 69/84 ††€ 69/84, ☕ € 12 – **Rest** – Menu € 28 (weekdays), € 32/46 – Carte € 35/79

◆ Venture over the threshold of this regional hostelry to sample the traditional menu with modern touches, served in an updated cosy Alsatian decor. Summer terrace.

X **Aux Trois Merles**

5 r. de la 5e DB – ✆ 03 89 78 24 35 – info@trois-merles.com – Fax 03 89 78 13 06 – Closed in November, January and February, Sunday dinner, Wednesday dinner and Monday off season

Rest – Menu € 25/42

◆ A pleasant restaurant situated in one of the villages on the famous Wine Road. Neat, rustic interior, a shady terrace facing the garden and traditional cuisine.

AMNÉVILLE – **57 Moselle** – **307** H3 – **pop. 9 314** – **alt. 162 m** – **Spa : early March-early Dec.** – **Casino** – ✉ **57360** Alsace-Lorraine 26 **B1**

Paris 319 – Briey 17 – Metz 21 – Thionville 16 – Verdun 67

Office de tourisme, 2, rue du casino ✆ 03 87 70 10 40, Fax 03 87 71 90 94

d'Amneville BP 99, South: 2 km, ✆ 03 87 71 30 13.

Parc zoologique du bois de Coulange (zoo)★★.

Walibi-Schtroumpf Amusement Park ★ 3 km S.

at Parc de Loisirs (leisure park) **2.5 km, Bois de Coulange south – ✉ 57360 Amnéville**

Diane without rest

– ✆ 03 87 70 16 33 – accueilhotel@wanadoo.fr – Fax 03 87 72 36 72

47 rm – †€ 66 ††€ 75, ☕ € 9 – 3 suites

◆ Situated at the forest's edge, this hotel offers spacious rooms, some with balcony, equipped with coloured cane furniture. Breakfast room overlooking the countryside.

La Forêt

1 r. de la Source – 03 87 70 34 34 – resto.laforet@wanadoo.fr – Fax 03 87 70 34 25 – Closed 28 July-11 August, 22 December-6 January, Sunday dinner, Monday and dinner on public holidays

Rest – Menu € 20/45 – Carte € 33/53

◆ Bright, spacious restaurant with an abundance of flowers. The terrace facing the forest is popular in summer. Traditional dishes.

AMOU – 40 Landes – 335 G13 – pop. 1 452 – alt. 44 m – ✉ 40330 3 B3

Paris 760 – Aire-sur-l'Adour 51 – Dax 31 – Mont-de-Marsan 47 – Orthez 14 – Pau 50

Office de tourisme, 10, place de la poste 05 58 89 02 25, Fax 05 58 89 02 25

Le Commerce

(near the church) – 05 58 89 02 28 – lecommerceamou@orange.fr – Fax 05 58 89 24 45 – Closed 10 November-1st December, 9-22 February, Sunday dinner and Monday except July-August

15 rm – €45 €60, €7 – ½ P €62/65 – **Rest** – Menu €15 (weekdays)/42 – Carte €24/44

◆ Large house with Virginia creeper on the walls, refurbished in a contemporary, cosy style. Rooms with sloping ceilings on the second floor; bar on the ground floor. The house specialities in this restaurant are pâté, terrine and confit, either served in the rustic dining room or under the arbour.

AMPHION-LES-BAINS – 74 Haute-Savoie – 328 M2 – ✉ 74500
French Alps 46 F1

Paris 573 – Annecy 81 – Évian-les-Bains 4 – Genève 40 – Thonon-les-Bains 6

Office de tourisme, 215, rue de la Plage 04 50 70 00 63, Fax 04 50 70 03 03

Princes

– 04 50 75 02 94 – hotel.des.princes@wanadoo.fr – Fax 04 50 75 59 93 – Open end April-end September

33 rm – €59/85 €64/122, €11 – 2 suites – ½ P €63/110

Rest – *(closed Wednesday except 9 July-20 August)* Menu (€19), €28/36 – Carte €31/56

◆ A 19C building on the banks of the Léman. The rooms with a view of the lake are to be preferred, for the view and the peace and quiet. Charming little private port. Restaurants with panoramic views, one of which is on the waterside. Mainly fish menu.

Le Tilleul with rm

252 RN5 – 04 50 70 00 39 – letilleul@aol.com – Fax 04 50 70 05 57 – Closed 22 December-6 January, Sunday dinner and Monday except 15 July-31 August

19 rm – €61/70 €65/80, €9 – ½ P €68/78 – **Rest** – *(closed 30 June-15 July)* Menu €18 (weekdays)/42 – Carte €33/49

◆ In the restaurant: beams, regional furniture and copperware. On the table: perch and whitefish from Lake Léman. Garden service in summer.

AMPUS – 83 Var – 340 N4 – pop. 707 – alt. 600 m – ✉ 83111
French Riviera 41 C3

Paris 876 – Castellane 58 – Draguignan 15 – Toulon 93

La Fontaine d'Ampus (Marc Haye)

– 04 94 70 98 08 – Closed Monday, Tuesday and Wednesday

Rest – *(number of covers limited, pre-book)* Menu €42 (set menu)

Spec. Sablé de pois chiches au parmesan et tomates confites (July-August). Lapin, cèpes et foie gras cuit en feuille de châtaignier (September-October). Gaspacho de melon et fraise (June). **Wines** Côtes de Provence, Coteaux Varois.

◆ A small old house with an intimate and regional setting that encourages you to discover Provence through its products and recipes. Single, set menu on the board.

ANCENIS – 44 Loire-Atlantique – 316 I3 – pop. 7 010 – alt. 13 m – ✉ 44150
Châteaux of the Loire 34 **B2**

Paris 347 – Angers 55 – Châteaubriant 48 – Cholet 49 – Laval 100 – Nantes 41

Office de tourisme, 27, rue du Château ✆ 02 40 83 07 44

Akwaba
rest,

bd Dr -Moutel – ✆ 02 40 83 30 30 – hotelakwaba@yahoo.fr – Fax 02 40 83 25 10

56 rm – €59 €65, €8 – 1 suite – ½ P €55/59 – **Rest** – *(closed August and Sunday)* Menu €18/24 – Carte €19/35

◆ An Ivory Coast welcome in this hotel situated in the heart of a small shopping centre. Functional rooms. Lounge and restaurant renovated in a contemporary style serving spicy Southern style food.

La Charbonnière
la Loire,

On the banks of the Loire on Joubert boulevard – ✆ 02 40 83 25 17 – contact@restaurant-la-charbonniere.com – Fax 02 40 98 85 00 – Closed Saturday lunch October-March, Sunday dinner, Wednesday dinner and dinner on public holidays

Rest – Menu €16 bi/45 – Carte €39/56

◆ Space and tranquillity characterise this place: the veranda and terrace set in the garden offer a pretty view of the Loire and the suspension bridge. Traditional dishes.

Les Terrasses de Bel Air

1 km eastward Angers road – ✆ 02 40 83 02 87 – terrassebelair.jpg@wanadoo.fr – Fax 02 40 83 33 46 – Closed 1st-12 July, Sunday dinner and Monday

Rest – Menu €16 (weekday lunch), €27/49

◆ Located on a busy road, but facing the Loire, these two dining rooms have a homely atmosphere with fireplace, parquet and period furniture.

La Toile à Beurre

82 r. St-Pierre – ✆ 02 40 98 89 64 – latoileabeurre@wanadoo.fr – Fax 02 40 96 01 49 – Closed 17-31 March, 1st-18 September, Sunday dinner, Wednesday dinner and Monday

Rest – Menu €19 (weekday lunch), €27/55 – Carte €34/42

◆ Exposed stonework and beams, terracotta floor tiles and a fine fireplace form an authentic rustic setting in this house built in 1753. Attractive terrace. Traditional dishes and fish from the Loire.

ANCY-LE-FRANC – 89 Yonne – 319 H5 – pop. 1 108 – alt. 180 m – ✉ 89160
Burgundy-Jura 7 **B1**

Paris 215 – Auxerre 54 – Châtillon-sur-Seine 38 – Montbard 27 – Tonnerre 18

Syndicat d'initiative, 59, Grande Rue ✆ 03 86 75 03 15, Fax 03 86 75 04 41

Château★★.

Hostellerie du Centre
rm,

34 Grande-Rue – ✆ 03 86 75 15 11 – hostellerieducentre@diaphora.com – Fax 03 86 75 14 13 – Closed 20 December-31 January, Sunday dinner and Monday from 15 November to 15 March

22 rm – €44 €49, €7 – ½ P €48/54 – **Rest** – Menu €11 (weekday lunch), €16/45 – Carte €24/70

◆ Little old building offering cool, practical rooms with the more spacious ones being in the annex. The covered swimming pool can be enjoyed at any time of year. Simple dining room where you are served a traditional cuisine and some Burgundian specialities.

ANCY-SUR-MOSELLE – 57 Moselle – 307 H4 – see Metz

ANDELOT-LÈS-ST-AMOUR – 39 Jura – 321 C8 – pop. 80 – alt. 420 m – ✉ 39320

Paris 413 – Besançon 130 – Bourg-en-Bresse 34 – Mâcon 70 16 **B3**

Château Andelot
monts du Jura,

r. de l'Église – ✆ 03 84 85 41 49 – info@chateauandelot.com – Fax 03 84 85 46 74 – Open April-October

7 rm – €100/200 €100/200 – **Table d'hôte** – Menu €15/40

◆ 12C stronghold surrounded by French-style gardens. The keep houses two rooms and a suite; the other rooms open directly onto the interior courtyard. From the terrace there is a panoramic view of the Jura peaks. Local fare served in a medieval setting.

LES ANDELYS – 27 Eure – 304 I6 – pop. 9 047 – alt. 28 m – ✉ 27700

Normandy 33 **D2**

Paris 93 – Évreux 38 – Gisors 30 – Mantes-la-Jolie 54 – Rouen 40

Syndicat d'initiative, rue Philippe Auguste ✆ 02 32 54 41 93, Fax 02 32 54 41 93

Ruins of Château Gaillard★★ ≤★★ - Notre-Dame church ★.

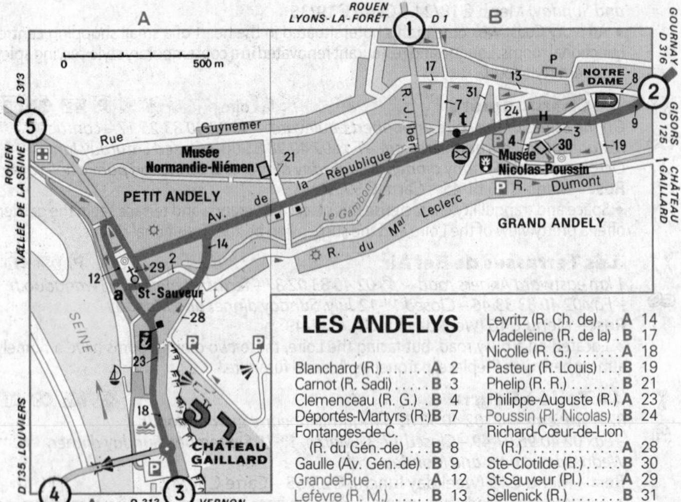

XXX **La Chaîne d'Or** with rm ≤ P VISA MC AE

25 r. Grande – ✆ 02 32 54 00 31 – chaineor@wanadoo.fr – Fax 02 32 54 05 68 – Closed autumn half-term holidays, Christmas holidays, 2-22 January, February holidays, Monday lunch and Tuesday lunch A **a**

12 rm – †€ 78/132 ††€ 78/132, ☐ € 12 – **Rest** – Menu € 29/88 – Carte € 47/82

◆ This 18C post house was also a tollhouse: a chain used to block the Seine. An elegant dining room facing the river. Contemporary cuisine.

X **De Paris** with rm P VISA MC

10 av. de la République – ✆ 02 32 54 00 33 – h.paristhierry@wanadoo.fr – Fax 02 32 54 65 92 B **t**

11 rm – †€ 55/66 ††€ 55/66, ☐ € 7,50 – ½ P € 80 – **Rest** – *(closed 2-12 January, Sunday dinner, Monday lunch and Wednesday)* Menu (€ 16), € 25/41 – Carte € 28/43

◆ An attractive mansion (1880) is the location for this small restaurant, with an elegant, yet rustic ambience. Pleasant courtyard terrace. Refurbished, simply decorated rooms. The three newest rooms occupy an annexe, which also houses a meeting room.

ANDLAU – 67 Bas-Rhin – 315 I6 – pop. 1 654 – alt. 215 m – ✉ 67140

Alsace-Lorraine 2 **C1**

Paris 501 – Erstein 25 – Le Hohwald 8 – Molsheim 25 – Sélestat 18 – Strasbourg 43

Syndicat d'initiative, 5, rue du Gen-de-Gaulle ✆ 03 88 08 22 57, Fax 03 88 08 42 22

St-Pierre and St-Paul church ★: portal★★, crypt★.

Zinckhotel without rest P VISA MC AE

13 r. de la Marne – ✆ 03 88 08 27 30 – zinck.hotel@wanadoo.fr – Fax 03 88 08 42 50

18 rm – †€ 59 ††€ 68/95, ☐ € 11

◆ An unusually decorated old mill: rooms with personal touches (zen, pop, jazz or Empire styles) and corridors resembling boat decks. The modern wing overlooks the vineyard.

Kastelberg

10 r. Gén.-Koenig – 03 88 08 97 83 – kastelberg@wanadoo.fr – Fax 03 88 08 48 34

29 rm – €58 €61/89, €10 – ½ P €60/65

Rest – *(open 12 March-2 November, 28 November-4 January) (dinner only)* Menu €19/43 – Carte €26/56

♦ A smart Alsatian façade surrounded by vineyards. The simple, practical rooms have sloping ceilings or a balcony and rustic furniture. Rustic but smart restaurant with attractively set tables. Wholesome country cooking.

Bœuf Rouge

6 r. du Dr-Stoltz – 03 88 08 96 26 – auboeufrouge@wanadoo.fr – Fax 03 88 08 99 29 – Closed 23 June-11 July, 23 February-8 March, Wednesday dinner and Thursday except 12 July-30 September

Rest – Menu (€10), €15/30 – Carte €21/58

♦ A friendly, generous and typical Alsatian restaurant housed in a former 17C post house. Traditional food in an elegant wood-panelled room.

ANDORRE (PRINCIPALITY) – 343 H9 – see end at guide

ANDREZÉ – 49 Maine-et-Loire – 317 D5 – pop. 1 798 – alt. 87 m – ✉ 49600

34 **B2**

Paris 371 – Nantes 59 – Angers 80 – Cholet 16 – Rezé 71

Le Château de la Morinière

– 02 41 75 40 30 – pringarbe.pascal@wanadoo.fr

5 rm – €69/85 €69/85 – **Table d'hôte** – Menu €30 bi

♦ Built on the ruins of a medieval château destroyed during the Vendée wars, this romantic edifice is Napoleon III in style. Personalised, very quiet rooms. Candle lit dining at the table d'hôte. Cookery lessons.

ANDRÉZIEUX-BOUTHÉON – 42 Loire – 327 E6 – pop. 9 153 – alt. 395 m – ✉ 42160

44 **A2**

Paris 460 – Lyon 76 – Montbrison 20 – Roanne 71 – St-Étienne 19

Office de tourisme, 11, rue Charles-de-Gaulle 04 77 55 37 03, Fax 04 77 55 88 46

Lac de retenue de Grangent (Grangent barrier lake)★★ S : 9 km

Auvergne-Rhone Valley.

Novotel

rest,

1 r. 18-Juin-1827 – 04 77 36 10 50 – h0435@accor.com – Fax 04 77 36 10 57

98 rm – €66/120 €66/120, €12,50

Rest – Menu €19 – Carte €15/38

♦ This chain hotel, built in 1974, is still in good condition. Spacious lobby, lounge and bar, plus a choice of meeting rooms. Ask for the more recently redecorated guestrooms. The restaurant has a simple, gay contemporary setting. A terrace opposite the swimming pool.

Les Iris (Lionel Githenay)

32 av. J.-Martouret , (towards the station) – 04 77 36 09 09 – Fax 04 77 36 09 00 – Closed 18-29 August, 2-21 January and Sunday evening

10 rm – €75 €85, €12 – ½ P €89

Rest – *(closed Sunday dinner, Monday and Tuesday)* Menu €35 (weekday lunch), €42/79 – Carte €62/67

Spec. Salade de homard aux légumes et herbes du moment (June to August). Pigeon "comme un rôti" à la coriandre, purée et chips de persil (February to April). Moelleux tiède au potimarron, crème catalane, glace aux cèpes (October-November). **Wines** Vin de pays d'Urfé, Côtes du Forez.

♦ Attractive mansion, dating from 1900, with a pink façade, and its more modern annexe, housing small guestrooms, some overlooking the garden (swimming pool). Inventive cuisine served outdoors or in two attractive dining rooms adorned with children's portraits.

ANDUZE – 30 Gard – 339 I4 – pop. 3 004 – alt. 135 m – ✉ 30140

Languedoc-Roussillon-Tarn Gorges 23 **C2**

Paris 718 – Montpellier 60 – Alès 15 – Florac 68 – Lodève 84 – Nîmes 46 – Le Vigan 52

Office de tourisme, plan de Brie ☎ 04 66 61 98 17, Fax 04 66 61 79 77

Bambouseraie de Prafrance (bamboo garden) ★★ North: 3 km by D 129.

Grottoes of Trabuc★★ Northwest: 11 km - Le Mas soubeyran: Desert Museum★ (17C-18C Protestant remembrance) Northwest: 7 km.

Northwest by St-Jean-du-Gard road – ✉ 30140 Anduze

La Porte des Cévennes

3 km – ☎ 04 66 61 99 44 – reception@porte-cevennes.com – Fax 04 66 61 73 65 – Open 1st April-15 October

34 rm – €73/80 €73/80, €9 – ½ P €65/70

Rest – *(dinner only)* Menu €23/30 – Carte €30/41

◆ A peaceful house near the bamboo plantation where the 'Wages of Fear' was filmed. Spacious, practical rooms, half of which overlook the Gardon valley. Classic menu in a countrified decor or on the panoramic terrace.

Le Moulin de Corbès with rm

4 km away – ☎ 04 66 61 61 83 – Fax 04 66 61 68 06 – Closed Sunday dinner and Monday off season

4 rm – €70/80 €70/80, €10 – **Rest** – Menu (€25), €35/60

◆ On the banks of the Gardon this inviting restaurant with three sunny dining rooms is decorated on the theme of wine (wine-tasting courses). Practical, quiet rooms.

in Générargues 5.5 km Northwest by D 129 and D 50 – pop. 639 – alt. 160 m – ✉ 30140

Auberge des Trois Barbus — Camisards valley,

rte de Mialet – ☎ 04 66 61 72 12 – les3barbus@free.fr – Fax 04 66 61 72 74 – Closed 2 January-15 March, Sunday dinner from October to April, Tuesday from November to March, Tuesday lunch from May to September and Monday except dinner from May to September

32 rm – €61/118 €61/118, €13 – ½ P €63/92 – **Rest** – Menu (€17), €27/49 – Carte €43/60

◆ This hillside hotel on the edge of the "Cevennes Desert" offers large rooms with regional furniture and overlooks the Camisards valley. Classic, market fresh repertory in a tasteful interior. Grilled dishes by the pool.

in Tornac 6 km Southeast by D 982 – pop. 718 – alt. 140 m – ✉ 30140

Les Demeures du Ranquet (Anne Majourel) — rm,

St-Hippolyte-du-Fort road : 2 km – ☎ 04 66 77 51 63 – contact@ranquet.com – Fax 04 66 77 55 62 – Open 18 March-17 November

10 rm – €130/225 €130/225, €16 – ½ P €120/165

Rest – *(closed Tuesday and Wednesday except evenings from 1st June to 15 September and Monday lunchtime in summer)* Menu (€25), €38/90 – Carte €66/77

Spec. Bonbon de brandade de morue, calmar et courgettes au piment d'Espelette. Baudroie en "aïgo bulido", lard rôti à la sauge. Agneau de lait de l'Aveyron dans tous ses états (spring). **Wines** Vin de pays du Gard, Coteaux du Languedoc.

◆ This enticing Cévennes farmhouse and its recent well-equipped outbuildings are tucked away in parkland surrounded by scrub. Peace and quiet, art exhibitions and a golf practice. The inventive regional menu has an emphasis on home-grown vegetables and herbs.

ANET – 28 Eure-et-Loir – 311 E2 – pop. 2 651 – alt. 73 m – ✉ 28260

11 **B1**

Paris 76 – Chartres 51 – Dreux 16 – Évreux 37 – Mantes-la-Jolie 28 – Versailles 58

Syndicat d'initiative, 8, rue Delacroix ☎ 02 37 41 49 09

Castle★ **Normandy.**

XX **Auberge de la Rose** with rm VISA

6 r. Ch.-Lechevrel – ✆ 02 37 41 90 64 – Fax 02 37 41 47 88 – Closed 12 Dec.-3 Jan., Sunday evening and Monday

7 rm – †€ 29/38 ††€ 29/38, ☕ € 6 – **Rest** – Menu € 25 – Carte € 40/57

◆ This restaurant is a survivor - it was already recommended in the 1900 Michelin Guide! A comfortable dining room with rafters and Louis XIII-style furniture.

XX **Manoir d'Anet** VISA

3 pl. du Château – ✆ 02 37 41 91 05 – wilfrid.beaugeard@wanadoo.fr – Fax 02 37 41 91 04 – Closed Tuesday and Wednesday

Rest – Menu € 26/46 – Carte € 53/59

◆ A restaurant in an ideal location opposite Diane de Poitiers' castle. The rustic and flowered dining room is graced by an imposing stone chimney. Bar, tea room.

ANGERS P – **49 Maine-et-Loire** – **317** F4 – **pop. 151 279** – **Built-up area 226 843** – **alt. 41 m** – ✉ **49000** Châteaux of the Loire 35 **C2**

Paris 294 – Laval 79 – Le Mans 97 – Nantes 88 – Rennes 129 – Tours 108

Aéroport d'Angers-Marcé, ✆ 02 41 33 50 20, by ①: 24 km.

Office de tourisme, 7, place Kennedy ✆ 02 41 23 50 00, Fax 02 41 23 50 09

d'Avrille Avrillé Château de la Perrière, Northwest: 5 km by D 175, ✆ 02 41 69 22 50 ;

d'Angers Brissac-Quincé Moulin de Pistrait, by Cholet road and D 751: 8 km, ✆ 02 41 91 96 56 ;

Anjou Golf & Country Club Champigné Route de Cheffes, North: 24 km by D 775 and D 768, ✆ 02 41 42 01 01.

Château★★★: hanging of the Apocalypse★★★, hanging of the Passion and Tapisseries mille-fleurs (tapestries of a thousand flowers) ★★, ≤★ from the Moulin tower - Old town★: cathedral★, Romanesque gallery★★ of the prefecture★ BZ **P**, David d'Angers gallery ★ BZ **B**, - Maison d'Adam (Adam's House) ★ BYZ **K** - Hôtel Pincé★ - Choir★★ of St-Serge church★ - Musée Jean Lurçat et de la Tapisserie contemporaine★★ in former St-Jean hospital★ - La Doutre★ AY - Musée régional de l'Air★.

Château de Pignerolle★: European Museum of Communication★★ East: 8 km by D 61.

Plans on following pages

Anjou AC VISA AE

1 bd Mar.- Foch – ✆ 02 41 21 12 11 – info@hoteldanjou.fr – Fax 02 41 87 22 21 CZ **h**

53 rm – †€ 107/117 ††€ 172/186, ☕ € 14

Rest ***La Salamandre*** – *✆ 02 41 88 99 55 (closed Sunday)* Menu € 28/78 – Carte € 47/57

◆ This building from 1845 boasts a lovely interior decor: lounges adorned with Art Deco mosaics and plush rooms furnished in a variety of periods. Captivating Renaissance-style restaurant: frescoes, French-style ceiling and salamanders.

Hôtel de France AC VISA AE

8 pl. de la Gare – ✆ 02 41 88 49 42 – hdf.angers@wanadoo.fr – Fax 02 41 87 19 50

55 rm – †€ 77/133 ††€ 77/133, ☕ € 13 – 1 suite AZ **t**

Rest ***Les Plantagenêts*** – *(closed August, Saturday lunch, Sunday dinner and Wednesday)* Menu € 20/40 – Carte € 30/54

◆ Plush, well-equipped rooms, small sitting rooms, seminar room and tasty breakfasts (local produce): equally popular with business and leisure guests. Les Plantagenêts provides a low-key atmosphere, serving up-to-date cuisine with a good local wine list.

Mercure Centre rest, AC rest, VISA AE

pl. Mendès-France, (Congressional Centre) – ✆ 02 41 60 34 81 – h0540@accor.com – Fax 02 41 60 57 84 CY **a**

84 rm – †€ 89/140 ††€ 99/150, ☕ € 14

Rest ***Le Grand Jardin*** – *(closed 23-29 December)* Menu (€ 14,50), € 20 – Carte € 19/32

◆ Situated next to a conference centre, this modern hotel offers functional, well-soundproofed rooms, some of which overlook the Jardin des Plantes. Pleasant wine bar. The restaurant opens onto leafy greenery. Contemporary decor and cuisine; Anjou wines.

Barangé (Bd Ch.)	DX	3	Estienne d'Orves (Bd)	EX	29	Monplaisir (Bd de)	EV	51
Barra (R.)	DV	4	Félix-Faure (Q.)	EV	30	Montaigne (Av.)	EX	50
Baumette (Pr. de la)	DX	6	Joxe (Av. J.)	EV	35	Moulin (Bd J.)	DEV	52
Bedier (Bd J.)	EX	7	Larevellière (R.)	EV	37	Portet (Bd J.)	DX	61
Bon-Pasteur (Bd)	DV	9	Lattre-de-Tassigny			Pyramide (Rte de la)	EX	63
Bouchemaine (Rte de)	DX	10	(Bd de)	EX	39	Rabelais (R.)	EX	65
Chalouère (R. de la)	EV	13	Letanduère (R. de)	EX	41	Ramon (Bd G.)	EV	67
Chaumin (Bd E.)	EX	17	Lizé (R. du Gén.)	DV	44	St-Jacques (R.)	DV	76
Doyenné (Bd du)	EV	24	Meignanne (R. de la)	DV	46	Saumuroise (R.)	EX	87
Dunant (Bd H.)	EV	26	Millot (Bd J.)	EX	48	Strasbourg (Bd de)	DEX	88

Du Mail without rest — VISA

8 r. des Ursules – ✆ 02 41 25 05 25 – contact@hotel-du-mail.com – Fax 02 41 86 91 20 CY **b**

28 rm – †€ 39/75 ††€ 57/85, ☕ € 15

♦ A hotel with character housed in the discreet walls of a 17C former convent. Most of the personalised rooms are spacious.

Le Progrès without rest — VISA

26 av. D.-Papin – ✆ 02 41 88 10 14 – hotel.leprogres@wanadoo.fr – Fax 02 41 87 82 93 – Closed 9-17 August and 20 December-4 January AZ **f**

41 rm – †€ 42/58 ††€ 54/64, ☕ € 8,50

♦ A welcoming hotel, opposite the railway station with modern, bright and practical rooms. Breakfast is served in a pleasant room facing a flower-decked courtyard.

Continental without rest — VISA

14 r. L.-de-Romain – ✆ 02 41 86 94 94 – reservation@hotellecontinental.com – Fax 02 41 86 96 60 BYZ **n**

25 rm – †€ 58/65 ††€ 65/75, ☕ € 9,50

♦ This centrally located hotel in an old building features bright, recently refurbished, well-kept and well-soundproofed rooms.

De l'Europe without rest — VISA

3 r. Châteaugontier – ✆ 02 41 88 67 45 – hoteldeleurope-angers@wanadoo.fr – Fax 02 41 86 17 42 CZ **a**

29 rm – †€ 50 ††€ 60/68, ☕ € 8,50

♦ This hotel with a pleasant family atmosphere is located in a shopping district. Small, brightly coloured rooms. Pleasant breakfast room.

Ibis

r. Poissonnerie – ✆ 02 41 86 15 15 – h0848-gm@accor.com – Fax 02 41 87 10 41 BY **b**

95 rm – †€ 47/81 ††€ 47/81, ☐ € 7,50 – **Rest** – *(dinner only)* Carte approx. € 20

◆ Near the cathedral and castle, this hotel is above all practical: small functional rooms, conference facilities, wifi, air conditioning. Chequered tablecloths and a zinc counter endow this restaurant with an old bistro feel. Classic menu.

Grand Hôtel de la Gare without rest

5 pl. de la Gare – ✆ 02 41 88 40 69 – info@hotel-angers.fr – Fax 02 41 88 45 41 – Closed 26 July-18 August, and 21 December-4 January BZ **a**

52 rm – †€ 46/68 ††€ 55/72, ☐ € 8

◆ The corridors and breakfast room are adorned with brightly coloured frescoes. Pretty modern rooms overlooking the fountain in front of the station.

Le Favre d'Anne (Pascal Favre d'Anne)

18 quai des Carmes – ✆ 02 41 36 12 12 – favredanne@wanadoo.fr – Closed 29 July-13 August, Sunday and Monday AY **t**

Rest – Menu € 35/80 – Carte € 46/64

Rest *L'R du Temps* – *(closed Monday in July-August and Sunday) (lunch only)* Menu (€ 20), € 24 – Carte € 34/38

Spec. Minute de bar, crémet d'Anjou au wasabi. Rouget, artichaut et lard paysan, fouace aux rillettes. Filet de bœuf "Maine-Anjou", tatin d'échalottes.

◆ An old town house serving modern, creative cuisine popular with a clientele of regulars. Contemporary decor; view of the château and the Maine. Fashionable menu and unusual concept (the price depends on the number of starters chosen).

Le Relais

9 r. de la Gare – ✆ 02 41 88 42 51 – c.noel10@wanadoo.fr – Fax 02 41 24 75 20 – Closed 27 April-5 May, 9 August-2 September, 21 December-5 January, Sunday and Monday BZ **u**

Rest – Menu (€ 18), € 22/40 – Carte € 41/60

◆ This establishment's modern, low-key, elegant decoration includes bench seating, mosaic flooring and fine murals depicting wine and the 'good life'. Appetising traditional cuisine.

Provence Caffé

9 pl. Ralliement – ✆ 02 41 87 44 15 – Fax 02 41 87 44 15 – Closed Sunday and Monday BCY **e**

Rest – *(pre-book)* Menu (€ 15), € 20/30

◆ Designer furniture, soft lighting and music: the Caffé has been treated to a trendy minimalist lounge style, without however forgoing its southern flavour (spices, fish, etc.).

Le Petit Comptoir

40 r. David-d'Angers – ✆ 02 41 88 81 57 – lepetitcomptoir@9business.fr – Fax 02 41 88 81 57 – Closed 28 July-18 August, 5-12 May, 19-31 January, Sunday and Monday CZ **d**

Rest – Menu (€ 19), € 28

◆ The crimson red façade of this Angers bistro hides a tiny but welcoming dining room. Relaxed atmosphere and generous food with a lot of creativity.

Le Crèmet d'Anjou

21 r. Delaâge – ✆ 02 41 88 38 38 – Closed 14 July-15 August, 24 December-5 January BZ **e**

Rest – Menu (€ 15), € 21/25

◆ Named after a famous local dessert, this establishment is renowned for its owner's jovial character and his generous traditional fare, prepared before your very eyes.

near Parc des Expositions 6 km by ① and N 23 – ✉ 49480 St-Sylvain-d'Anjou

Auberge d'Éventard

rd-pt du Bon-Puits – ✆ 02 41 43 74 25 – contact@auberge-eventard.com – Fax 02 41 34 89 20 – Closed 1st-12 May, 2-12 January, Saturday lunch, Sunday dinner and Monday

Rest – Menu € 23 (weekdays)/82 – Carte € 25/76

◆ A fervent champion of regional produce, the chef offers two classic menus served in an elegant welcoming interior of trinkets, collections of chinaware and carafes.

ANGERS

Street	Grid	No.
Alsace (R. d')	CZ	
Aragon (Av. Yolande d')	AY	2
Baudrière (R.)	BY	5
Beaurepaire (R.)	AY	
Bichat (R.)	AY	8
Bon-Pasteur (Bd du)	AY	9
Bout-du-Monde (Prom. du)	AY	12
Bressigny (R.)	CZ	
Chaperonnière (R.)	BYZ	15
Commerce (R. du)	CY	19
David-d'Angers (R.)	CY	21
Denis-Papin (R.)	BZ	22
Droits-de-l'Homme (Av. des)	CY	25
Espine (R. de l')	BY	27
Estoile (Sq. J. de l')	AY	28
Foch (Bd du Mar.)	BCZ	
Freppel (Pl.)	BY	31
Gare (R. de la)	BZ	32
Laiterie (Pl.)	AY	
Lenepveu (R.)	CY	40
Lices (R. des)	BZ	
Lionnaise (R.)	AY	
Lise (R. P.)	CY	43
Marceau (R.)	AZ	45
Mirault (Bd)	BY	49
Mondain-Chanlouineau (Sq.)	BY	51
Oisellerie (R.)	BY	53
Parcheminerie (R.)	BY	54
Pasteur (Av.)	CY	55
Pilori (Pl. du)	CY	56
Plantagenêt (R.)	BY	57
Pocquet-de-Livonnières (R.)	CY	58
Poëliers (R. des)	CY	59
Pompidou (Allées)	CY	60
Prés.-Kennedy (Place du)	AZ	62
Ralliement (Pl. du)	BY	66
Résistance-et-de-la-Déport. (Bd)	CY	68
Robert (Bd)	BY	69
La Rochefoucauld Liancourt (Pl.)	ABY	38
Roë (R. de la)	BY	70
Ronceray (Bd du)	AY	71
Ste-Croix (Pl.)	BZ	86
St-Aignan (R.)	AY	72
St-Aubin (R.)	BZ	73
St-Étienne (R.)	CY	75
St-Julien (R.)	BCZ	
St-Laud (R.)	BY	77
St-Lazare (R.)	AY	79
St-Martin (R.)	BZ	80
St-Maurice (Mtée)	BY	82
St-Maurille (R.)	CY	83
St-Michel (Bd)	CY	84
St-Samson (R.)	CY	85
Talot (R.)	BZ	89
Tonneliers (R. des)	AY	90
Ursules (R. des)	CY	91
Voltaire (R.)	BZ	93
8-Mai-1945 (Av. du)	CZ	94

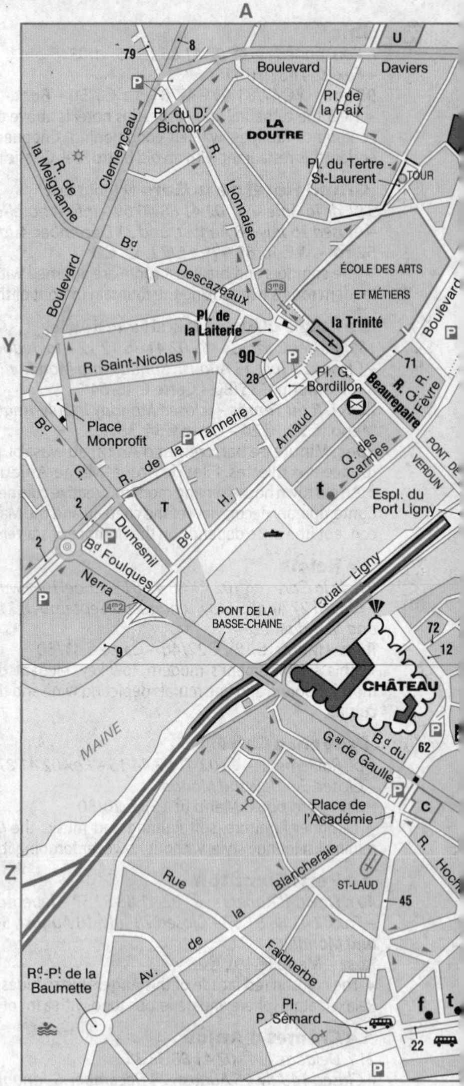

in Trélazé by ③ – pop. 11 025 – alt. 20 m – ✉ 49800

Hôtel de Loire

328 r. Jean-Jaurès – ✆ 02 41 81 89 18 – bateliers@hoteldeloire.com – Fax 02 41 81 89 20

49 rm – †€ 64/90 ††€ 71/97, ☕ € 10 – ½ P € 62/75 – **Rest** – Menu (€ 12), € 23/41 – Carte € 20/37

◆ This recent hotel on a busy road houses non-smoking rooms decorated with lovely simplicity (minimalist, mahogany-type furniture, chocolate shades...). The restaurant has modern decor with references to the Loire and a brasserie-style menu.

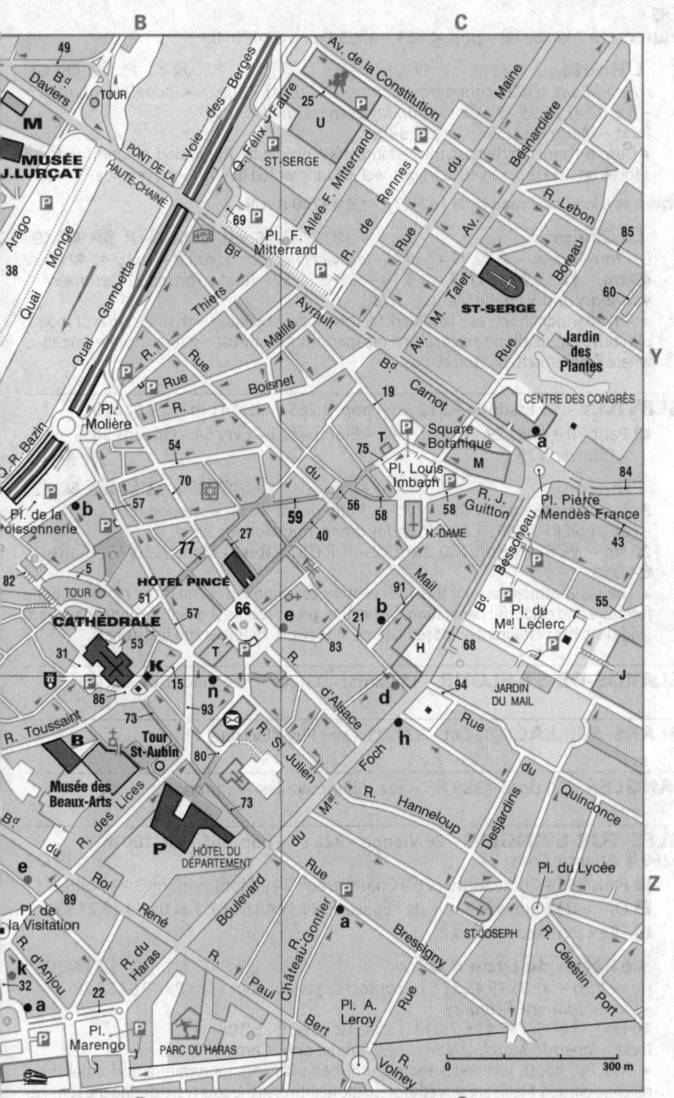

West – ✉ 49000 Angers

Mercure Lac de Maine

2 allée du Grand-Launay – ✆ 02 41 48 02 12 – h1212@accor.com – Fax 02 41 48 57 51

77 rm – †€ 75/135 ††€ 85/150, ☕ € 12,50 DX **n**

Rest *Le Diffen* – *(closed 22 December-4 January, lunch 14 July-15 August, Saturday and Sunday)* Menu € 17/31 bi – Carte € 40/45

◆ This hotel with a slightly austere front has been refurbished from top to toe: functional, well-equipped and well-soundproofed rooms. Good seminar facilities. The pleasant dining room does not have the usual chain decor; attractive menu and market-inspired set menu.

in Beaucouzé 7 km by ⑤ – **pop. 4 851 – alt. 54 m –** ✉ **49070**

XXX **L'Hoirie**

r. Henri-Faris, (D 723 commercial centre) – ✆ 02 41 72 06 09 – lhoirie@wanadoo.fr – Fax 02 41 36 35 48 – Closed Sunday evening and Monday

Rest – Menu € 23/55 – Carte € 38/60

♦ Despite the nearby bypass, this restaurant is very popular. Appetising, modern food with a focus on wild fish, served in a light, well-soundproofed dining room/veranda.

Northwest 8 km Laval road by N 162 - DV – ✉ **49240 Avrillé**

Le Cavier rest,

La Croix-Cadeau – ✆ 02 41 42 30 45 – lecavier@lacroixcadeau.fr – Fax 02 41 42 40 32

43 rm – €57 €57/72, € 10 – ½ P € 56/59 – **Rest** – *(closed 21 December-4 January and Sunday)* Menu € 21/38

♦ A 1730 windmill acts as a landmark for this modern building with three types of rooms: old and rustic, small and practical or more spacious. An unusual restaurant located in cellars where flour used to be stored.

ANGERVILLE – 91 Essonne – 312 A6 – pop. 3 265 – alt. 141 m – ✉ 91670

Paris 70 – Ablis 29 – Chartres 46 – Étampes 21 – Évry 54 – Orléans 56 – Pithiviers 29

18 **B3**

France

2 pl. du Marché – ✆ 01 69 95 11 30 – hotel-de-france3@wanadoo.fr – Fax 01 64 95 39 59 – Closed Sunday dinner and Monday lunch

20 rm – €68 €98/130, € 12 – ½ P € 87 – **Rest** – Menu € 30/40 – Carte € 42/55

♦ The rustic atmosphere of this 18th century coaching inn is enhanced by the antique furniture and colourful decoration. Distinctive, pretty rooms. A delightful inner courtyard leads into the restaurant (exposed beams, stonework, fireplace and flagstones).

ANGLARDS-DE-ST-FLOUR – 15 Cantal – 330 G5 – see Viaduc de Garabit

---

ANGLARS-JUILLAC – 46 Lot – 337 D5 – see Puy-l'Évêque

LES ANGLES – 30 Gard – 339 N5 – see Villeneuve-lès-Avignon

ANGLES-SUR-L'ANGLIN – 86 Vienne – 322 L4 – pop. 365 – alt. 100 m – ✉ 86260 Atlantic Coast

39 **D1**

Paris 336 – Châteauroux 78 – Châtellerault 34 – Montmorillon 34 – Poitiers 51

Office de tourisme, 1, rue de l'Église ✆ 05 49 48 86 87, Fax 05 49 48 27 55

Site★ - château ruins★.

Le Relais du Lyon d'Or rm,

rte de Vicq – ✆ 05 49 48 32 53 – contact@lyondor.com – Fax 05 49 84 02 28 – Closed January- February

10 rm – €75/135 €75/135, € 12 – ½ P € 78/108

Rest – *(open 16 March-2 November) (dinner only)* Carte € 32/39

♦ This 14C house has pretty rooms furnished with antique furniture and a delicious, relaxing garden. Meals are served around the hearth or in the courtyard during the summer months. Wine list put together by the owner, a former wine merchant.

ANGLET – 64 Pyrénées-Atlantiques – 342 C4 – pop. 35 263 – alt. 20 m – ✉ 64600 Atlantic Coast

3 **A3**

Paris 769 – Bayonne 5 – Biarritz 4 – Cambo-les-Bains 18 – Pau 114 – St-Jean-de-Luz 21

Biarritz-Anglet-Bayonne ✆ 05 59 43 83 83, Southwest: 2 km.

Office de tourisme, 1, avenue de la Chambre d'Amour ✆ 05 59 03 77 01, Fax 05 59 03 55 91

de Chiberta 104 boulevard des Plages, North: 5 km by D 5, ✆ 05 59 52 51 10.

Plan: see Biarritz-Anglet-Bayonne

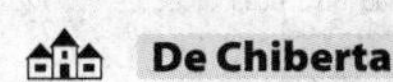

De Chiberta et du Golf rm, rm, rest,
104 bd des Plages – ☎ 05 59 58 48 48 – hotelchiberta@hmc-hotels.com – Fax 05 59 63 57 84 ABX
92 rm – €115/260 €115/260, €12 – ½ P €93/165 – **Rest** – Menu €25 – Carte €32/47
♦ This 1920s residence situated next to the prestigious Chiberta golf course has comfortable rooms offering a view of the greens and the lake. Dining room-veranda and pretty, shaded terrace; traditional menu.

Atlanthal rest,
153 bd des Plages – ☎ 05 59 52 75 75 – info@atlanthal.com – Fax 05 59 52 75 13 ABX
99 rm – €108/232 €158/384, €11 – ½ P €106/219 – **Rest** – Menu €28 – Carte €35/47
♦ A modern complex with excellent leisure facilities, including well-equipped thalassotherapy and fitness centres. Lovely views of the Atlantic. Spacious guestrooms. Traditional cuisine served in the veranda-restaurant facing the sea. Basque dishes and a tapas bar.

Novotel Biarritz Aéroport
68 av. d'Espagne, (D 810) – ☎ 05 59 58 50 50 – h0994@accor.com – Fax 05 59 03 33 55 BX**m**
121 rm – €92/140 €97/143, €13,50 – **Rest** – Carte €23/43
♦ A large establishment on the edge of a park. The standardised rooms are spacious and well equipped, those facing the woods are quieter. Pleasant dining room incorporating wood, bricks and warm colours.

La Fleur de Sel
5 av. de la Fôret – ☎ 05 59 63 88 66 – jf.fleurdesel@wanadoo.fr – Closed 16 February-12 March, 23 June-2 July, 27 October-6 November, Tuesday lunch in July-August, Sunday dinner off season, Wednesday lunch and Monday BX **a**
Rest – Menu €30/46 bi – Carte €31/43
♦ This friendly restaurant has a bright, spacious dining room overlooking a summer terrace. Modern decor and traditional, market-inspired cuisine.

ANGOULÊME P – 16 Charente – 324 K6 – pop. 43 171 – Built-up area 103 746 – alt. 98 m – ✉ 16000 Atlantic Coast 39 **C3**

Paris 447 – Bordeaux 119 – Limoges 105 – Niort 116 – Périgueux 85
Angoulême-Brie Champniers: ☎ 05 45 69 88 09, 15 km Northeast
Office de tourisme, place des Halles ☎ 05 45 95 16 84, Fax 05 45 95 91 76
de l'Hirondelle Chemin de l'Hirondelle, South: 2 km, ☎ 05 45 61 16 94.
Site★ - High town ★★ - St-Pierre cathedral ★: front★★ Y **F** - C.N.B.D.I. (Centre national de la bande dessinée et de l'image – National strip cartoon and picture centre)★ Y.

Plan on next page

Mercure Hôtel de France rm,
1 pl. des Halles-Centrales – ☎ 05 45 95 47 95 – h1213@accor.com – Fax 05 45 92 02 70 Y **e**
89 rm – €99/109 €109/119, €13 – **Rest** – *(closed Sunday lunch and Saturday)* Menu €27/37 – Carte €23/38
♦ Occupying the house where Guez de Balzac was born, this hotel is extended by a modern wing. Pleasant, modern rooms; a pretty garden overlooking the Charente. Pleasant contemporary dining room with a quiet summer terrace.

Européen without rest
1 pl. G.-Perot – ☎ 05 45 92 06 42 – europeenhotel@wanadoo.fr – Fax 05 45 94 88 29 – Closed 25 December-1st January Y **a**
31 rm – €49 €61, €8,50
♦ Within easy walking distance from the city walls, a family establishment in the process of being renovated, with well-soundproofed rooms; those on the 3rd floor have more character.

ANGOULÊME

Aguesseau (Rampe d') . . . . . Y 2
Arsenal (R. de l') . . . . Z 4
Basseau (R. de) . . . . X 6
Beaulieu (Rempart de) . . . . . Y 8
Belat (R. de) . . . . Z 10
Bouillaud (Pl.) . . . . Z 12
Briand (Bd A.) . . . . Y 14
Chabasse (Bd R.) . . . . X 17
Champs-de-Mars (Pl.) . . . . . Y 18
Churchill (Bd W.) . . . . Z 20
Corderie (R. de la) . . . . Y 24
Desaix (Rempart) . . . . Z 26
Dr-E.-Roux (Bd du) . . . . Z 28
Fontaine-du-Lizier (R.) . . . . . Y 30
Frères-Lumière (R. des) . . . . Y 32
Gambetta (Av.) . . . . Y 34
Gaulle (Av. du Gén.-de) . . . . Y 36
Guérin (R. J.) . . . . Y 37
Guillon (Pl. G.) . . . . Y 38
Iéna (R. d') . . . . Z 40
Lattre-de-Tassigny (Av. du Mar. de) . . . . . X, Y 42
Liedot (Bd) . . . . X 44
Louvel (Pl. F.) . . . . Y 46
Marengo (Pl. et R.) . . . . YZ 47
Midi (Rempart du) . . . . Y 48
Monlogis (R.) . . . . X 50
Papin (R. D.) . . . . Y 52
Paris (R. de) . . . . Y
Pasteur (Bd) . . . . Y 53
Périgueux (R. de) . . . . . . X, YZ 55
Postes (R. des) . . . . Y 57
Renoleau (R. A.) . . . . Z 58
République (Bd de la) . . . X, Y 59
La Rochefoucauld (R. de la) . Y 41
Saintes (R. de) X
St-André (R.) . . . . Y 60
St-Antoine (R.) . . . . X 61
St-Martial (Pl. et R.) . . . . Z 65
St-Roch (R.) . . . . X, Y 67
Soleil (R. du) . . . . Y 70
Tharaud (Bd J. et J.) . . . . Z 72
Turenne (R. de) . . . . Y 73
3-Fours (R. des) . . . . Y 75
8-Mai-1945 (Bd du) . . . . X 80

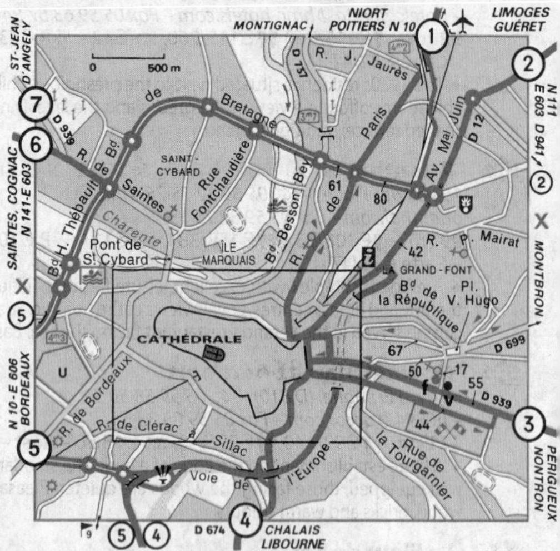

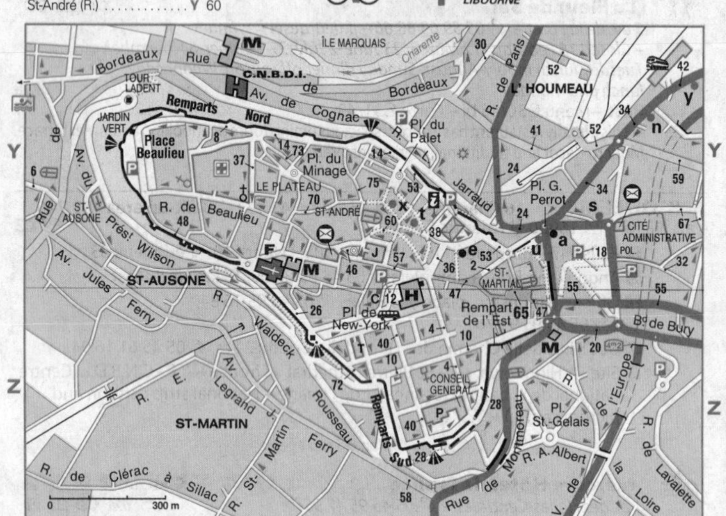

 **L'Épi d'Or** without rest

66 bd René-Chabasse
– ✆ 05 45 95 67 64
– epidor@wanadoo.fr
– Fax 05 45 92 97 23

33 rm – †€ 50/55 ††€ 55/62, ☕ € 8 X v

◆ Useful address within a short distance of the place Victor Hugo where a lively market is held. The spacious and practical rooms are quieter to the rear.

Le Palma

4 rampe d'Aguesseau – ✆ 05 45 95 22 89 – lepalma@tiscali.fr – Fax 05 45 94 26 66 – Closed 19 December-5 January, Saturday lunch and Sunday
9 rm – †€ 58 ††€ 65, ☕ € 7,50 – ½ P € 55/62 – **Rest** – Menu € 14,50/32 – Carte € 35/41 Y **u**

◆ Comfortable non-smoking rooms, tastefully decorated and graced with painted or natural wood furniture. The sober and light restaurant (traditional menu) has a room serving dishes of the day and a few Spanish specialities.

Champ Fleuri without rest

Chemin de l'Hirondelle, (at the golf course), 2 km, south of the map – ✆ 06 23 59 76 30 – entreprise2010@wanadoo.fr – Fax 05 45 23 82 02
5 rm ☕ – †€ 60/75 ††€ 65/80

◆ Lovely old house and walled garden next to the golf course. Pretty personalised rooms, panoramic view of Angoulême, terrace and swimming pool: the best of town and country.

La Ruelle

6 r. Trois-Notre-Dame – ✆ 05 45 95 15 19 – laruelle16@wanadoo.fr – Fax 05 45 92 94 64 – Closed 3-25August, Sunday and Monday Y **x**
Rest – Menu € 25 (weekday lunch), € 32/53 – Carte € 51/66

◆ Surprising interior obtained by combining two old houses, formerly separated by an alley. Old stonework, beams and fireplace form the backdrop to cuisine with an occasional southern slant.

Le Terminus

3 pl. de la Gare – ✆ 05 45 95 27 13 – Fax 05 45 94 04 09 – Closed Sun Y **n**
Rest – Menu (€ 17), € 25/31 – Carte € 46/63

◆ A chic modern brasserie all in black and white. The up-to-date menu takes Atlantic seafood and enriches it with regional touches. Lovely terrace.

Les Gourmandines

25 r. de Genève – ✆ 05 45 92 58 98 – Fax 05 45 92 58 98 – Closed February holidays, 12 August-1st September, Christmas holidays, Sunday and Monday
Rest – Menu € 30/36 – Carte € 36/46 Y **t**

◆ Pleasant small establishment in an old house near the market. Traditional cuisine with an occasional up-to-date touch of modernity.

L'Aromate

41 bd René-Chabasse – ✆ 05 45 92 62 18 – Closed 1st-8 May, August, 22 December-5 January, Tuesday dinner, Wednesday dinner, Sunday dinner and Monday
Rest – *(number of covers limited, pre-book)* Menu € 14,50 (weekdays)/38 – Carte € 27/38 X **f**

◆ This small neighbourhood bistro offers good traditional cuisine with a modern twist, a friendly welcome and unpretentious rustic decor.

Côté Gourmet

23 pl. de la Gare – ✆ 05 45 95 00 27 – fabsev.salzat@yahoo.fr – Fax 05 45 95 00 27 – Closed 4-25 August, February holidays, Tuesday dinner, Saturday lunch and Sunday
Rest – Menu (€ 14,50 bi), € 22/32 – Carte € 30/37 Y **y**

◆ Modern-bistro style upstairs and high tables on the ground floor; simple up-to-date cuisine popular with local gourmets.

La Cité

28 r. St-Roch – ✆ 05 45 92 42 69 – gicebet@aol.com – Fax 05 45 93 24 35 – Closed 28 July-19 August, 22 February-9 March, Sunday and Monday Y **s**
Rest – Menu € 13,50 (weekday lunch), € 18/28 – Carte € 24/38

◆ Country-style furniture and fresh, bright decor set the scene for this family-run establishment serving traditional cuisine dominated by fish.

in Soyaux 4 km by ③ – **pop. 10 177 – alt. 133 m – ✉ 16800**

La Cigogne

at the Town Hall take Rue A.-Briand and 1.5 km... – ✆ 05 45 95 89 23 – lacigogne16@wanadoo.fr – Closed 23 February-10 March, 20 October-12 November, 22 December-3 January, Wednesday dinner, Sunday dinner and Monday
Rest – Menu € 26/46 – Carte € 50/79

◆ Next to an old mushroom farm, this house welcomes you to its bright dining room and shaded terrace looking out over fields. The menu combines tradition and modernity.

in Roullet 14 km by ⑤ and N 10, dir. Bordeaux – pop. 3 525 – alt. 50 m – ✉ 16440

La Vieille Étable
rte Mouthiers : 1,5 km – ☎ 05 45 66 31 75 – vieille.etable@wanadoo.fr – Fax 05 45 66 47 45 – Closed Sunday dinner from October to mid May
29 rm – †€ 62/120 ††€ 62/150, ☐ € 12 – **Rest** – Menu € 17/52 – Carte € 48/57
◆ Surrounded by parkland with pond, this restored farm has neo-rustic rooms; the three new rooms are tastefully personalised. Traditional cuisine served by the fireplace or on the shaded terrace; gastronomic menu, children's meals.

ANNECY P – 74 Haute-Savoie – **328** J5 – pop. 50 348 – Built-up area 136 815 – alt. 448 m – Casino : the Impérial – ✉ 74000 French Alps 46 **F1**

Paris 536 – Aix-les-Bains 34 – Genève 42 – Lyon 138 – St-Étienne 187

Annecy-Haute-Savoie ☎ 04 50 27 30 06, by N 508 BU and D 14: 4 km.

Office de tourisme, 1, rue Jean Jaurès, Bonlieu ☎ 04 50 45 00 33, Fax 04 50 51 87 20

du Belvédère Saint-Martin-Bellevue Chef Lieu, by la Roche-sur-Foron road: 6 km, ☎ 04 50 60 31 78 ;

du Lac d'Annecy Veyrier-du-Lac Route du Golf, by Talloires road: 10 km, ☎ 04 50 60 12 89 ;

de Giez-Lac-d'Annecy Giezby Albertville road: 24 km, ☎ 04 50 44 48 41.

Old Annecy★★: Deposition★ in St-Maurice church EY **E**, Palais de l'Isle★★ EY **M²**, rue Ste-Claire★ - bridge over the Thiou ≤★ EY **N** - Musée-château d'Annecy★ - Les Jardins de l'Europe (Gardens of Europe) ★ - Lakeside★★ ≤★*.

Tour of the lake★★★ - Gorges du Fier★★: 11 km by ⑥ - Col de la Forclaz★★ - Forêt du crêt du Maure★: ≤★★ 3 km by D 41 CV.

Plans on following pages

L'Impérial Palace ≤ lake, rm, rest,
allée de l'Impérial – ☎ 04 50 09 30 00 – reservation@hotel-imperial-palace.com – Fax 04 50 09 33 33 CV **s**
91 rm – †€ 300/450 ††€ 300/450, ☐ € 25 – 8 suites
Rest *La Voile* – Carte € 39/72
◆ Magnificent views of the lake from this 1913 luxury hotel set in a park. Contemporary, well-equipped rooms, conference centre, casino, fitness facilities and beauty parlour. Pleasant dining room with a superb terrace opening onto the gardens and lake.

Les Trésoms ≤ rest,
3 bd de la Corniche – ☎ 04 50 51 43 84 – info@lestresoms.com – Fax 04 50 45 56 49 CV **f**
50 rm – †€ 119/219 ††€ 139/269, ☐ € 16 – ½ P € 110/179
Rest *La Rotonde* – *(closed Saturday lunch, Sunday dinner, Monday and lunch in July-August)* Menu € 29 (weekday lunch), € 35/87 – Carte € 65/85
Rest *La Coupole* – *(closed Tuesday dinner, Wednesday dinner, Thursday dinner and lunch except July-August) (residents only)* Menu € 29/35
◆ Situated in a tranquil garden, a restored 1930s residence retaining its Art Deco charm. Around half the warmly decorated rooms haave lake views. Spa. The rotunda serves modern dishes (panoramic terrace). Simple cuisine at la Couple.

Le Pré Carré without rest
27 r. Sommeiller – ☎ 04 50 52 14 14 – precarre@hotel-annecy.net – Fax 04 50 63 26 19 EX **b**
27 rm – †€ 145/195 ††€ 175/225, ☐ € 14 – 2 suites
◆ Recent hotel near to the old town and the lake. The very modern rooms are decorated in a mixture of soft shades. Breakfast under glass. Jacuzzi, sauna.

Novotel Atria
1 av. Berthollet – ☎ 04 50 33 54 54 – h1357@accor.com – Fax 04 50 45 50 68 DX **h**
95 rm – †€ 79/159 ††€ 79/159, ☐ € 13 – **Rest** – Carte € 23/43
◆ This glass-fronted building behind the station is next door to a well-equipped conference centre. Comfortable, soundproofed rooms and smiling staff. Functional dining room and Novotel cuisine. Small street terrace in summer.

ANNECY

Aléry (Av. d') . . . . **BV** 4
Aléry (Gde-R. d') . . . . **BV** 7
Balmettes (Fg des) . . . . **CV** 10
Beauregard (Av. de) . . . . **BV** 13
Bel-Air (R. du) . . . . **CU** 15
Bordeaux (R. Henry) . . . . . . **CU** 18
Boschetti (Av. Lucien) . . . . **BCV** 21
Chambéry (Av. de) . . . . **BV** 23
Chevêne (Av. de) . . . . **BV** 29
Corniche (Bd de la) . . . . **CV** 32
Crête (R. de la) . . . . **BU** 38
Crêt-de-Maure (Av. du) . . . . . **CV** 35
Fins Nord (Ch. des) . . . . . . **BCU** 45
Hirondelles (Av. des) . . . . . . **BV** 52
Leclerc (R. du Mar.) . . . . **BU** 59
Loverchy (Av. de) . . . . **BV** 63
Martyrs-de-la-Déportation (R. des) . . . . **CU** 64
Mendès-France (Av. Pierre) . **BV** 65
Mermoz (R. Jean) . . . . **CU** 66
Novel (Av. de) . . . . **CU** 69
Perréard (Av. Germain) . . . . **BU** 73
Pont-Neuf (Av. du) . . . . **BV** 77
Prélevet (Av. de) . . . . **BV** 79
Prés-Riants (R. des) . . . . **CU** 81
Saint-Exupéry (R. A.-de) . . . . **CU** 86
Stade (Av. du) . . . . **BCU** 92
Theuriet (R. André) . . . . **CV** 93
Thônes (Av. de) . . . . **CU** 94
Trésum (Av. de) . . . . **CV** 97
Trois-Fontaines (Av. des) . . . . **BV** 98
Val-Vert (R. du) . . . . **BV** 99

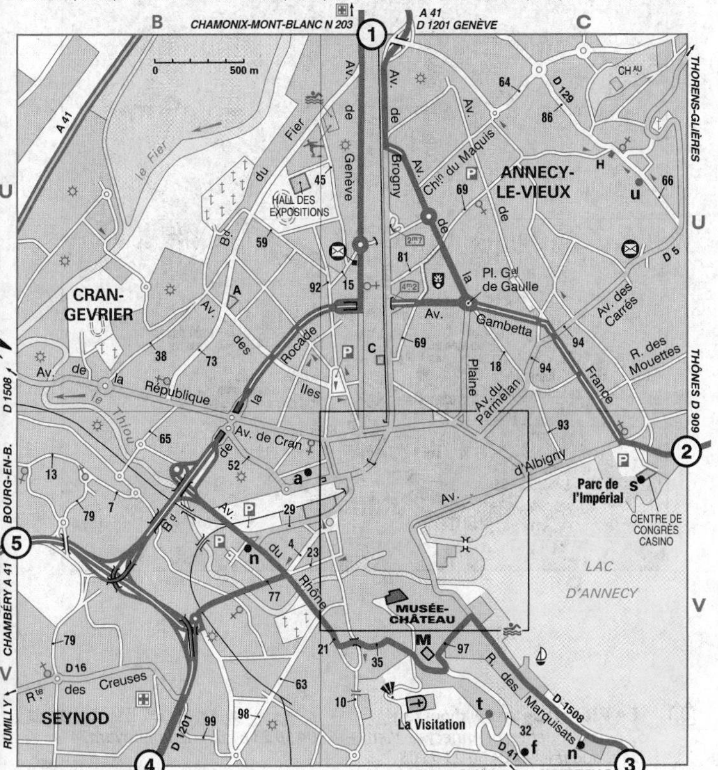

Splendid without rest

4 quai E.-Chappuis – ✆ 04 50 45 20 00 – info@splendidhotel.fr – Fax 04 50 45 52 23 EY **d**

47 rm – 🚹€ 105/134 🚹🚹€ 116/150, ☕ € 14

◆ Art Deco hotel located between the lake and the historic centre. Big practical rooms with good soundproofing; appealing to business travellers.

Carlton without rest

5 r. Glières – ✆ 04 50 10 09 09 – contact@bestwestern-carlton.com – Fax 04 50 10 09 60 DY **g**

55 rm – 🚹€ 82/124 🚹🚹€ 105/180, ☕ € 14

◆ This hotel located in a 20C building near the station and the castle has functional, spacious and comfortable rooms. 1980s decor.

ANNECY

Chambéry (Av. de) . . . . **DY** 23
Chappuis (Q. Eustache) . . . . **EY** 26
Filaterie (R.) . . . . **EY** 43
Grenette (R.) . . . . **EY** 51
Hôtel-de-Ville (Pl. de l') . . . . . **EY** 53
Jean-Jacques-Rousseau (R.) **DY** 55
Lac (R. du) . . . . **EY** 57
Libération (Pl. de la) . . . . . . **EY** 61
Pâquier (R. du) . . . . **EY** 71
Perrière (R.) . . . . **EY** 75
Pont-Morens (R. du) . . . . **EY** 76
Poste (R. de la) . . . . **DY** 78
République (R.) . . . . **DY** 83
Royale (R.) . . . . **DY** 85
Ste-Claire (Fg et R.) . . . . **DY** 91
St-François-de-Sales (Pl.) . . . **EY** 87
St-François-de-Sales (R.) . . . **DY** 89
Tour-la-Reine (Ch.) . . . . **EY** 95

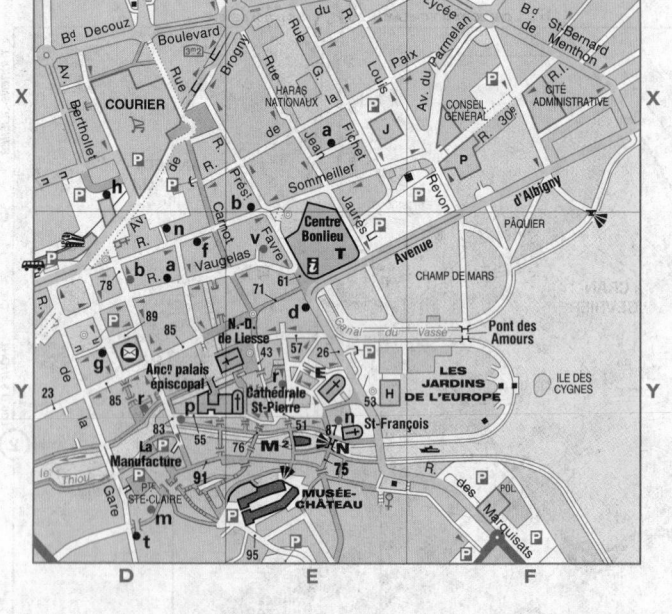

Le Flamboyant without rest
52 r. des Mouettes, at Annecy-le-Vieux – ✆ 04 50 23 61 69 – leflamboyant74@wanadoo.fr – Fax 04 50 23 05 03 CU
31 rm – €56/92 €68/115, €11,50
◆ Large, refurbished rooms – with kitchenette, balcony or terrace – in three chalet-style buildings. Bar decorated in the style of an English pub. Breakfast on the veranda.

Des Marquisats without rest
6 chemin Colmyr – ✆ 04 50 51 52 34 – reservations@marquisats.com – Fax 04 50 51 89 42 – Closed 22 - 28 Oct. CV **n**
23 rm – €67/115 €67/115, €10
◆ On a hillside close to a beach, this progressively renovated stone house has a variety of decorative styles in its comfortable rooms which face the lake or woodland.

International
19 av. du Rhône – ✆ 04 50 52 35 35 – reservation@bestwestern-hotelinternational.com – Fax 04 50 52 35 00 BV **n**
134 rm – €75/160 €75/160, €13
Rest – *(closed Friday dinner, Saturday and Sunday from November to April)*
Menu €15/35 – Carte €24/46
◆ Modern, functional rooms, some with a balcony; those facing away from the ring road are preferable. Good seminar facilities and English-style bar. Wood dominates the restaurant. Unpretentious classic menu.

Mercure without rest
26 r. Vaugelas – ✆ 04 50 45 59 80 – h2812@accor.com – Fax 04 50 45 21 99 DY **a**
39 rm – †€ 95/140 ††€ 105/140, ☐ € 13
♦ This establishment is centrally located with practical, calm rooms decorated in blue and yellow (in homage to Provence). Breakfast buffet menu.

Allobroges Park without rest
11 r. Sommeiller – ✆ 04 50 45 03 11 – info@allobroges.com – Fax 04 50 51 88 32 DY **n**
47 rm – †€ 68/89 ††€ 74/99, ☐ € 8,50 – 3 suites
♦ The sign of this town centre hotel recalls the Celtic tribe that used to inhabit the region. Modern renovated rooms in beige and brown harmonies.

Amiral
61 r. Centrale, at Annecy-le-Vieux on ② ✉ 74940 – ✆ 04 50 23 29 26 – contact@amiral-hotel.com – Fax 04 50 23 74 18
36 rm – †€ 55/60 ††€ 65/78, ☐ € 12 – 1 suite – ½ P € 60/65
Rest – Menu € 22/45 – Carte € 25/50
♦ Situated near the beaches along the lakeshore, this colonial-style hotel has small, renovated guestrooms. Shades of yellow, red banquettes and a counter bar in the dining room. Shaded terrace and a traditional menu given a contemporary twist.

Nord without rest
24 r. Sommeiller – ✆ 04 50 45 08 78 – contact@annecy-hotel-du-nord.com – Fax 04 50 51 22 04 DY **f**
30 rm – †€ 45/59 ††€ 55/66, ☐ € 7
♦ Ideally located in the centre, this small unpretentious hotel is the perfect base from which to explore the town. Cheerful and bright modern decor in the rooms.

de Bonlieu without rest
5 r. Bonlieu – ✆ 04 50 45 17 16 – info@annecybonlieuhotel.fr – Fax 04 50 45 11 48 – Closed 27 October-10 November EX **a**
35 rm – †€ 72/96 ††€ 80/104, ☐ € 11
♦ In a quiet street near the centre of town, a modern little hotel with rooms that are practical, modern and relaxing, if a little cramped.

Kyriad Centre without rest
1 fg Balmettes – ✆ 04 50 45 04 12 – annecy.hotel.kyriad@wanadoo.fr – Fax 04 50 45 90 92 DY **t**
24 rm – †€ 67/77 ††€ 67/77, ☐ € 7,50
♦ Situated near the old part of Annecy, this 16C building is undergoing a rebirth. Rooms vary in size; simply furnished and enlivened with shades of yellow and blue.

Les Terrasses rest,
15 r. L.-Chaumontel – ✆ 04 50 57 08 98 – lesterrasses@wanadoo.fr – Fax 04 50 57 05 28 BV **a**
20 rm – †€ 52/70 ††€ 56/72, ☐ € 8 – ½ P € 54/60 – **Rest** – *(closed 15 December-18 January, Saturday and Sunday except July-August and lunch)* Menu € 18
♦ In a residential area near to the train station, a good hotel with smart rooms furnished in a country style. A warm family welcome. An attractively simple partly panelled restaurant; terracing on the garden side.

Le Clos des Sens (Laurent Petit) with rm
13 r J.-Mermoz ✉ 74940 – ✆ 04 50 23 07 90 rm,
– artisanculinaire@closdessens.com – Fax 04 50 66 56 54 – Closed 27 April-7 May, 1st-23 September, Sunday except dinner in July-August, Tuesday lunch and Monday CU **u**
4 rm – †€ 170/190 ††€ 170/190, ☐ € 16 – 1 suite
Rest – Menu € 33 (weekday lunch), € 48/100 – Carte € 81/100
Spec. Cueillette d'aromates de notre jardin, légumes croquants (April to October). Truite du lac, basse température, huile d'olive cryogénisée (February to October). Féra, consommé céleri-shizo-agrumes (February to October). **Wines** Mondeuse blanche, Mondeuse d'Arbin.
♦ Thoughtful and inventive dishes beautifully presented in an elegantly contemporary setting. Terrace overlooking Annecy; original and refined rooms.

La Ciboulette (Georges Paccard)
10 r. Vaugelas, (Cour du Pré Carré) – ☎ 04 50 45 74 57 – laciboulette74@wanadoo.fr – Fax 04 50 45 76 75 – Closed 30 June-26 July, 27 October-4 November, 9-18 February, and Monday
Rest – Menu € 29 (weekday lunch), € 43/55 – Carte € 64/83 EY **v**
Spec. Féra du lac aux champignons, lait battu à l'estragon et caillou glacé (March to October). Turbot rôti sur l'arête, artichaut et croûte Savoie-Piémont. Cœur de ris de veau crousti-moelleux, bâton d'enfance et jus de gentiane. **Wines** Chignin-Bergeron, Mondeuse d'Arbin.
◆ Classic and contemporary styles combine in the thoughtful, tasteful decor of this restaurant serving classical cuisine with a modern twist.

Le Belvédère (Vincent Lugrin) with rm ← Annecy and lake,
7 chemin Belvédère, 2 km, Semnoz road south-eastward via Rue Marquisat – ☎ 04 50 45 04 90 – b@belvedere-annecy.com – Fax 04 50 45 67 25 – Closed 1st-14 December, January, Sunday dinner, Tuesday and Wednesday
5 rm – †€ 80/135 ††€ 80/135, ☕ € 10 – ½ P € 90/105 CV **t**
Rest – Menu € 26 (weekday lunch), € 35/70 – Carte € 46/91
Spec. Foie gras de canard aux perles de vanille bourbon. Omble chevalier du lac au beurre, émulsion au poivre de Séchuan. Cigare en chocolat noir fourré d'une mousse café. **Wines** Chignin-Bergeron, Mondeuse d'Arbin.
◆ Appetising modern cuisine and a view of Lake Annecy. Inviting summer terrace and quiet bedrooms, which also command a stunning view.

Le Bilboquet
14 fg Ste-Claire – ☎ 04 50 45 21 68 – eric.besson@neuf.fr – Fax 04 50 45 21 68 – Closed 1st-15 July, Sunday except dinner July-August and Monday DY **m**
Rest – Menu € 20 (weekday lunch), € 26/45 – Carte € 42/56
◆ Thick old walls guarantee a cool ambiance in this pleasant restaurant by the port of Ste-Claire. Enticing menu mixing tradition and modernity.

Auberge du Lyonnais with rm
9 r. de la République – ☎ 04 50 51 26 10 – aubergedulyonnais@wanadoo.fr – Fax 04 50 51 05 04 – Closed 20 October-7 November DY **p**
10 rm – †€ 45/70 ††€ 50/75, ☕ € 8 – **Rest** – Menu € 23/59 – Carte € 42/62
◆ Old house in the historic centre between two branches of the Thiou canal. Good brasserie-style cuisine served in a nautical setting, or better still on the fine waterside terrace. Simple mountain-style accommodation.

Auberge de Savoie
1 pl. St-François – ☎ 04 50 45 03 05 – aubergedesavoie@laposte.net – Fax 04 50 51 18 28 – Closed 16 November-3 December, 4-21 January, Tuesday except July-August and Wednesday EY **n**
Rest – Menu € 27/57 – Carte € 48/68
◆ Professional welcome and service at this warm, modern restaurant built against the church of St François. The terrace on a small square has views of the Thiou and chateau.

La Brasserie St-Maurice
7 r. Collège-Chapuisien – ☎ 04 50 51 24 49 – stmau@stmau.com – Fax 04 50 51 24 49 – Closed Sunday and Monday EY **r**
Rest – Menu € 18 (weekday lunch), € 24/39 – Carte € 31/58
◆ A low key restaurant set in a magnificent house built in 1675. The splendid timber pillars in the dining room are original. Summer terrace and traditional cuisine.

Contresens
10 r. de la Poste – ☎ 04 50 51 22 10 – Fax 04 50 51 34 26 – Closed 24 April-6 May, 9-23 August, 23 December-5 January, Sunday and Monday DY **b**
Rest – Menu (€ 19), € 26 – Carte approx. € 33
◆ Shoulder to shoulder dining in this popular restaurant serving deliciously playful contemporary fare in a modern bistro setting.

Nature et Saveur
pl. des Cordeliers – ☎ 04 50 45 82 29 – postmaster@nature-saveur.com – Closed 1st-7 May, 13-22 July, 21 December – 4 January, Sunday, Monday and Tuesday
Rest – Menu € 28 (weekday lunch), € 45/55 – Carte € 26/32 DY **r**
◆ An unusual establishment run on ecological principles with many surprises and few calories. Organic wines; teas for sale and takeaways available.

in Chavoires 4,5 km by ② – ✉ 74290 Veyrier-du-Lac

Demeure de Chavoire without rest
71 rte d'Annecy – ✆ 04 50 60 04 38 – demeure.chavoire@wanadoo.fr – Fax 04 50 60 05 36 – Closed 10 - 24 Nov.
10 rm – €130/145 €145/275, €16 – 3 suites
◆ A discreet façade for a hotel with character. Cosy, romantic rooms, antique furniture, pastel colour scheme and pleasant garden-terrace facing the lake.

in Veyrier-du-Lac 5,5 km by ② – **pop. 2 063 – alt. 504 m** – ✉ **74290**
Office de tourisme, rue de la Tournette ✆ 04 50 60 22 71, Fax 04 50 60 00 90

La Veyrolaine — lake and mountains,
30 rte Crêt des Vignes – ✆ 04 50 60 15 87 – la.veyrolaine@orange.fr – Fax 06 73 60 01 16 – Closed 27 October-8 November
3 rm – €65/115 €75/115 – **Table d'hôte** – *(closed March)* Menu €30
◆ There are many reasons to stay at this fine villa where guests are made to feel at home, among them the kind hosts, comfortable, elegant interior and proximity of the lake. Savoury, seasonal cuisine prepared by the owner, once the chef at a luxury hotel. Summer terrace.

La Maison de Marc Veyrat with rm — lake,
13 vieille rte des Pensières – ✆ 04 50 60 24 00 – reservation@marcveyrat.fr – Fax 04 50 60 23 63 – Open mid February-end October and closed Tuesday except July-August, Monday and lunch except Saturday and Sunday
9 rm – €300 €300/670, €60 – 2 suites
Rest – Menu €338
Spec. Asperge verte sauvage destructurée, fruit de la passion, écume romarin. Nouilles disparaissantes, sans farine ni œuf, sorbet cardamine. Bar en bulle de plastique, chocolat blanc, dérivé de citronnelle. **Wines** Ayze, Mondeuse d'Arbin.
◆ Brilliant food with mountain herbs and flowers, superb Savoy decor and a divine terrace facing the lake: a gastronomic genie watches over this enchanting blue house.

in Sévrier 6 km South by ③ – **pop. 3 421 – alt. 456 m** – ✉ **74320**
Office de tourisme, ✆ 04 50 52 40 56, Fax 04 50 52 48 66
Musée de la Cloche★.

Auberge de Létraz
921 rte d'Albertville – ✆ 04 50 52 40 36 – accueil@auberge-de-letraz.com – Fax 04 50 52 63 36
23 rm – €58/180 €58/180, €16 – 1 suite – ½ P €84/161
Rest – *(closed mid November-mid December, Sunday dinner and Monday October-May)* Menu €39/74 – Carte €60/89
◆ The garden of this hotel is perfectly located in front of the lake. The rooms overlooking the lake are quieter, and are refurbished in a modern vein. Traditional menu and theme evenings in this restaurant overlooking the jewel of Annecy.

Beauregard — rm, rest,
– ✆ 04 50 52 40 59 – info@hotel-beauregard.com – Fax 04 50 52 44 71 – Closed 14 November-19 January
45 rm – €50/70 €55/99, €10 – ½ P €53/73 – **Rest** – *(closed Sunday from October to April)* Menu (€16), €21/46 – Carte €28/43
◆ Large Savoyard style establishment poised between the lake and the road. Practical, well-kept rooms; good seminar facilities. The rotunda restaurant and shaded terraces offer a fine view of the lake. Simple, classic cuisine.

L'Auberge de Chuguet — rm, rest,
823 rte d'Albertville – ✆ 04 50 19 03 69 – achuguet@aol.com – Fax 04 50 52 49 42
25 rm – €54/83 €54/98, €8 – ½ P €52/75
Rest *L'Arpège* – *✆ 04 50 19 07 35 (closed Saturday lunch, Sunday dinner and Monday)* Menu €19 (weekday lunch), €25/50 – Carte €38/53
◆ An unexceptional building but the predominantly blue interior has character. Rooms offering simple comfort, with more recent duplex and studio accommodation. Contemporary nautical setting. Fine terrace shaded by plane trees with a view of the lake.

in Pringy **8 km north by ① and secondary road – pop. 2 616 – alt. 483 m – ✉ 74370**

XX **Le Clos du Château**

70 rte Cuvat, towards Promery – ✆ 04 50 66 82 23 – leclosduchateau@wanadoo.fr – Fax 04 50 66 87 18 – Closed 23 July-23 August, Sunday dinner and Monday

Rest – Menu € 18 (weekday lunch), € 28/51 – Carte € 43/53

◆ This new restaurant adjoining the château is run by three trained chefs. The contemporary decor matches the cuisine on offer.

ANNEMASSE – 74 Haute-Savoie – 328 K3 – pop. 27 253 – Built-up area 106 673 – alt. 432 m – Casino : Grand Casino – ✉ 74100

46 **F1**

Paris 538 – Annecy 46 – Bonneville 22 – Genève 8 – Thonon-les-Bains 31

Office de tourisme, place de la Gare ✆ 04 50 95 07 10, Fax 04 50 37 11 71

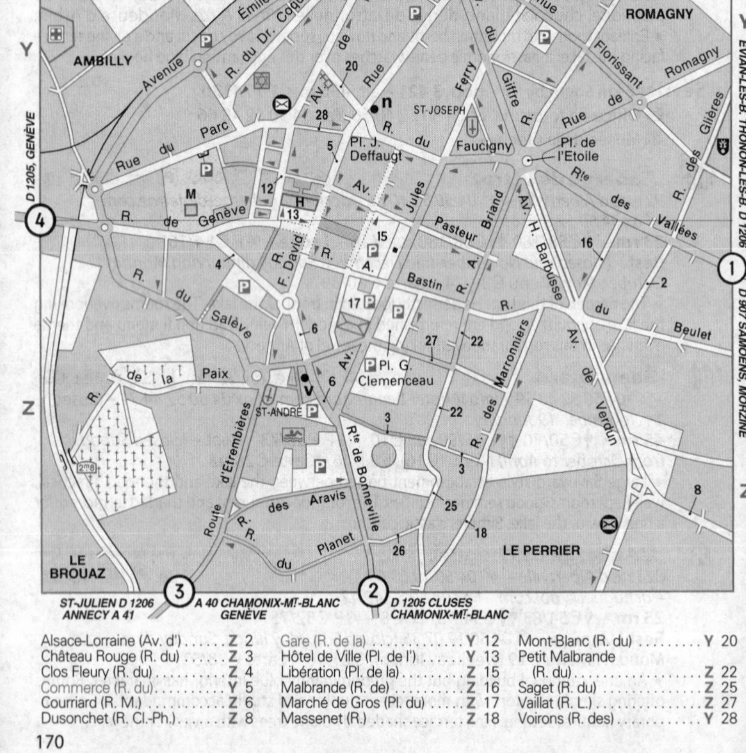

Alsace-Lorraine (Av. d') . . . . . . Z 2	Gare (R. de la) . . . . Y 12	Mont-Blanc (R. du) . . . . Y 20
Château Rouge (R. du) . . . . . . Z 3	Hôtel de Ville (Pl. de l') . . . . . . Y 13	Petit Malbrande (R. du) . . . . Z 22
Clos Fleury (R. du) . . . . Z 4	Libération (Pl. de la) . . . . Z 15	Saget (R. du) . . . . Z 25
Commerce (R. du) . . . . Y 5	Malbrande (R. de) . . . . Z 16	Vaillat (R. L.) . . . . Z 27
Courriard (R. M.) . . . . Z 6	Marché de Gros (Pl. du) . . . . . Z 17	Voirons (R. des) . . . . Y 28
Dusonchet (R. Cl.-Ph.) . . . . . . Z 8	Massenet (R.) . . . . Z 18	

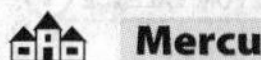

Mercure
by ③ and Gaillard road ✉ 74240 – ✆ 04 50 92 05 25 – h0343@accor.com – Fax 04 50 87 14 50
78 rm – †€ 64/145 ††€ 74/155, ☐ € 14 – **Rest** – Carte € 29/51
◆ Situated near the motorway and a river, this hotel is surrounded by greenery. Fairly spacious, comfortable and soundproofed rooms. Sober poolside dining room and terrace. Traditional dishes.

La Place without rest
10 pl. J.-Deffaugt – ✆ 04 50 92 06 44 – hotel.la.place@wanadoo.fr – Fax 04 50 87 07 45 Y **n**
43 rm – †€ 49/57 ††€ 64/75, ☐ € 8
◆ A central hotel conveniently located on the way to Switzerland. Handsome designer lounge, immaculate rooms with contemporary wooden furniture, pleasant welcome.

St-André without rest
20 r. M.-Courriard – ✆ 04 50 84 07 00 – resa@hotel-st-andre.com – Fax 04 50 84 36 22 Z **v**
40 rm – †€ 58 ††€ 68, ☐ € 8 – 2 suites
◆ Situated in an office district, this recent establishment offers spacious, light, well-equipped rooms that are ideal for business travellers (practically furnished).

ANNONAY – 07 Ardèche – 331 K2 – pop. 17 522 – alt. 350 m – ✉ 07100

Lyon - Rhone Valley 44 **B2**

Paris 529 – St-Étienne 44 – Valence 56 – Yssingeaux 57

Office de tourisme, place des Cordeliers ✆ 04 75 33 24 51, Fax 04 75 32 47 79

Annonay Gourdan Le Pelou, by Serrières road and D 820: 6 km, ✆ 04 75 67 03 84 ;

d'Albon Saint-Rambert-d'Albon Château de Senaud, East: 19 km by D 82, ✆ 04 75 03 03 90.

Plan on next page

Marc et Christine
29 av. Marc-Seguin – ✆ 04 75 33 46 97 – marc-et-christine@wanadoo.fr – Closed 18 August-2 September, 9-23 February, Sunday dinner and Monday **e**
Rest – Menu € 18/45 – Carte € 24/48
◆ This family-run gourmet bistro is a short trek from the town centre. Sample traditional cuisine made with regional produce in a delightfully provincial atmosphere.

in Golf de Gourdan 6.5 km by ① and D 1082 (St-Étienne road) – ✉ 07430 Annonay

Domaine du Golf de Saint Clair
– ✆ 04 75 67 01 00 – reception@domainestclair.fr – Fax 04 75 67 07 38
rm, rm,
54 rm – †€ 90/95 ††€ 110, ☐ € 12 – 2 suites – **Rest** – Carte € 29/36
◆ Completely renovated hotel, popular with business travellers, set in a quiet location surrounded by a golf course. Contemporary guestrooms, most with their own balcony. Modern restaurant under the beams of a large barn. Traditional cuisine.

in St-Marcel-lès-Annonay 8,5 km by ④, D 206 and D 1082 – pop. 1 223 – alt. 450 m – ✉ 07100

Auberge du Lac
Le Ternay – ✆ 04 75 67 12 03 – contact@aubergedulac.fr – Fax 04 75 34 90 20 – Closed January
12 rm – †€ 80/145 ††€ 80/145, ☐ € 12 – ½ P € 72/105
Rest – *(closed Tuesday lunch except in July-August, Sunday dinner and Monday)* Menu € 32/47
◆ Former auberge facing the dam, transformed into a luxurious and cosy hotel. Well-appointed, personalised bedrooms decorated with a floral theme. Roof terrace. Provençal dining room or outdoor tables with views of the lake and Le Pilat.

Alsace-Lorraine (Pl.) 2
Boissy-d'Anglas (R.) 3
Cordeliers (Pl. des) 4
Libération (Pl. de la) 6
Marc-Seguin (Av.) 7
Meyzonnier (R.) 8
Montgolfier (R.) 9

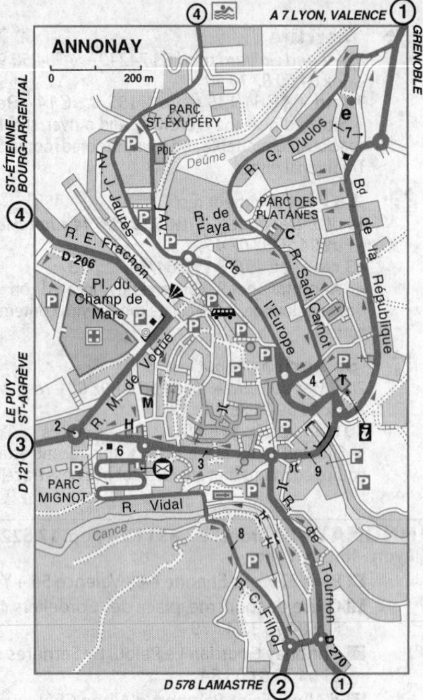

in St-Julien-Molin-Molette **10.5 km by ④, D 206 and D 1082 – pop. 1 132 – alt. 589 m – ✉ 42220**

La Rivoire
at La Rivoire, 4 km south by local road – ✆ 04 77 39 65 44 – info@larivoire.net – Fax 04 77 39 67 86
5 rm – 🚹€ 47/52 🚹🚹€ 57/62 – ½ P € 48 – **Table d'hôte** – Menu € 19 bi
◆ This noble residence with a round tower is thought to date from the 15C. The bright rooms are named after colours. Fine views of the Déome valley and the foothills of the Ardèche. Local cold meats and vegetables from the family garden are served in this restaurant.

ANNOT – 04 Alpes-de-Haute-Provence – 334 I9 – pop. 988 – alt. 708 m – ✉ 04240

French Alps 41 **C2**

Paris 812 – Castellane 31 – Digne-les-Bains 69 – Manosque 112
Office de tourisme, boulevard Saint-Pierre ✆ 04 92 83 23 03, Fax 04 92 83 30 63
Old town ★ - Clue de Rouaine★ South: 4 km.

L'Avenue VISA
av. de la Gare – ✆ 04 92 83 22 07 – contact@hotel-avenue.com – Fax 04 92 83 33 13 – Open 1st April-30 October
9 rm – 🚹€ 60/66 🚹🚹€ 60/66, ☕ € 8 – ½ P € 55 – **Rest** – *(closed lunch weekdays)* Menu € 20/30
◆ Put your suitcase down in one of the Provençal style rooms in this pleasant family-run establishment situated on a shady avenue. Extremely well kept. A pleasant dining room in a modern setting, small pavement terrace and cuisine with a regional flavour.

ANSE – 69 Rhône – 327 H4 – pop. 4 744 – alt. 170 m – ✉ 69480 43 E1

Paris 436 – Bourg-en-Bresse 57 – Lyon 27 – Mâcon 51 – Villefranche-sur-Saône 7

Office de tourisme, place du 8 mai 1945 ✆ 04 74 60 26 16, Fax 04 74 67 29 74

St-Romain

rm, VISA MC AE

rte des Graves – ✆ 04 74 60 24 46 – hotel-saint-romain@wanadoo.fr – Fax 04 74 67 12 85 – Closed Sunday dinner from November to April

24 rm – €46 €49/54, €7 – ½ P €51 – **Rest** – Menu €21/46 – Carte €41/49

◆ An old renovated farm in Beaujolais style whose rustic rooms are extremely well looked after. A country-style dining room where the menu is resolutely traditional. Good choice of local wines.

Au Colombier

VISA MC AE

126 allée Colombier – ✆ 04 74 67 04 68 – info@aucolombier.com – Fax 04 74 67 20 30 – Closed 2-8 January and Monday from October to May

Rest – Menu €27/48 – Carte €42/57

◆ Sturdy 18C residence on the banks of the River Saône. Meals are served on the terrace in summer and in front of the stone fireplace in winter. Good, innovative cuisine.

ANTHY-SUR-LÉMAN – 74 Haute-Savoie – 328 L2 – see Thonon-les-Bains

ANTIBES – 06 Alpes-Maritimes – 341 D6 – pop. 72 412 – alt. 2 m – Casino : "la Siesta" seaside by ① – ✉ 06600 French Riviera 42 E2

Paris 909 – Aix-en-Provence 160 – Cannes 11 – Nice 21

Office de tourisme, 11, place du Général-de-Gaulle ✆ 04 92 90 53 00, Fax 04 92 90 53 01

Old town ★: Promenade Amiral-de-Grasse ≤★ DXY - Château Grimaldi (Déposition de Croix★, Musée donation Picasso★) DX - Musée Peynet et de la Caricature★ DX M² - Marineland★ 4 km by ①.

Plans on following pages

Josse without rest

VISA MC AE

8 bd James-Wyllie – ✆ 04 92 93 38 38 – hotel.josse@wanadoo.fr – Fax 04 92 93 38 39 BU s

26 rm – €91/183 €102/183, €11

◆ A boulevard separates this long building from Salis beach. All the rooms have tasteful furnishings and balconies with a sea view.

Mas Djoliba

VISA MC

29 av. de Provence – ✆ 04 93 34 02 48 – hotel.djoliba@wanadoo.fr – Fax 04 93 34 05 81 – Open 1st February-31 October CY d

13 rm – €70/95 €80/168, €11 – ½ P €81/109

Rest – *(open 1st May-30 September) (dinner only) (residents only)*

◆ Relax poolside in a garden planted with palm trees and bougainvillea, or in the charming rooms of this 1920s villa; those on the top floor have a terrace overlooking the Cap.

Petit Castel without rest

VISA MC AE

22 chemin des Sables – ✆ 04 93 61 59 37 – hotel@lepetitcastel.fr – Fax 04 93 67 51 28 BU b

16 rm – €74/155 €78/175, €11

◆ A hospitable, refurbished villa on a main road in a residential district. Soundproofing and air-conditioning in the rooms, rooftop sundeck and Jacuzzi, bicycles.

Modern Hôtel without rest

VISA MC AE

1 r. Fourmilière – ✆ 04 92 90 59 05 – modernhotel@wanadoo.fr – Fax 04 92 90 59 06 – Closed 15 December-15 January CX a

17 rm – €56/68 €64/82, €5,50

◆ This hotel located at the beginning of the pedestrian area has been renovated. Soberly decorated rooms, new bedding and functional furniture.

ANTIBES

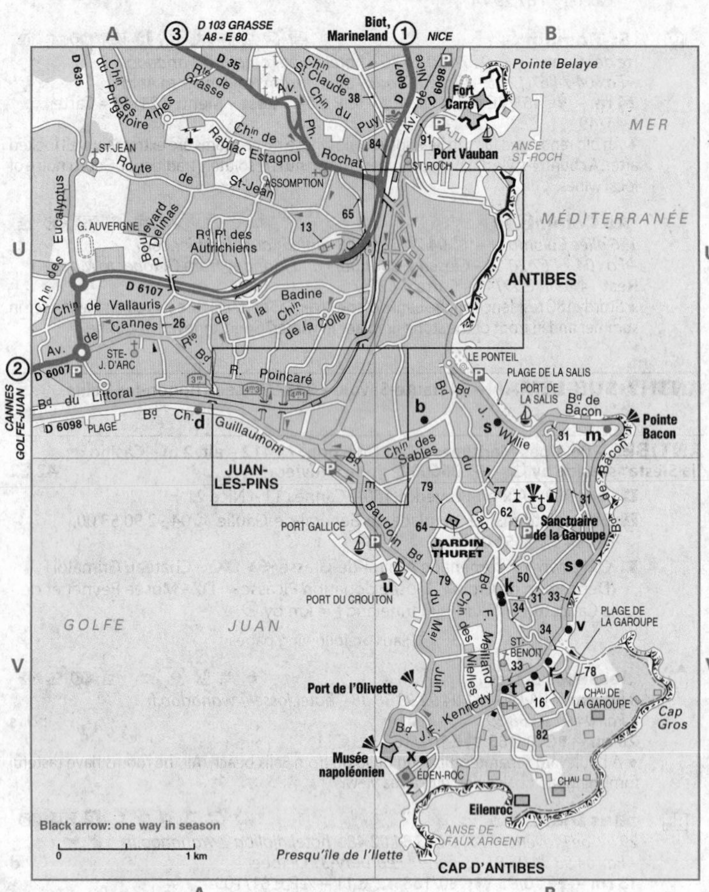

Les Vieux Murs

25 promenade Amiral-de-Grasse – ☎ 04 93 34 06 73 – lesvieuxmurs@wanadoo.fr – Fax 04 93 34 81 08 – Closed 12 January-9 February, Tuesday lunch, Monday from September to mid June and lunch mid June-end August DY **f**

Rest – Menu (€ 29), € 34 (lunch), € 42/60 – Carte € 64/87

◆ This house and terrace on the ramparts facing the sea is decorated in warm shades of orange. Tasty contemporary cuisine. Bar-lounge (art exhibitions).

Oscar's

8 r. Rostan – ☎ 04 93 34 90 14 – Fax 04 93 34 90 14 – Closed 1st-15 June, 23 December-10 January, Sunday and Monday DX **s**

Rest – *(number of covers limited, pre-book)* Menu € 28 – Carte € 63/94

◆ Enjoy the surprisingly original decor of sculptures set in niches and ancient landscapes. The restaurant owes its success to its tasty Italian/Provençal cuisine.

ANTIBES

Street	Grid	No.
Albert 1er (Bd)	CDY	
Alger (R. d')	CX	3
Arazy (R.)	DXY	4
Barnaud (Pl. Amiral)	DY	6
Barquier (Av.)	DY	8
Bas-Castelet (R. du)	DY	9
Bateau (R. du)	DX	10
Clemenceau (R. G.)	DX	14
Dames-Blanches (Av. des)	CY	19
Directeur Chaudon (R.)	CY	20
Docteur Rostan (R. du)	DX	24
Gambetta (Av.)	CX	30
Gaulle (Pl. du Gén.-de)	CXY	
Grand-Cavalier (Av. du)	CX	37
Guynemer (Pl.)	CX	40
Haut-Castelet (R. du)	DY	42
Horloge (R. de l')	DX	43
Martyrs-de-la-Résistance (Pl. des)	CDX	51
Masséna (Cours)	DX	52
Meissonnier (Av.)	CDY	54
Nationale (Pl.)	DX	55
Orme (R. de l')	DX	57
République (R. de la)	CDX	67
Revely (R. du)	DX	68
Revennes (R. des)	DY	69
St-Roch (Av.)	CX	72
Saleurs (Rampe des)	DX	75
Tourraque (R. de la)	DY	83
Vautrin (Bd. du Gén.)	CX	84
8-Mai 1945 (Square du)	DX	90
24-Août (Av. du)	CY	92

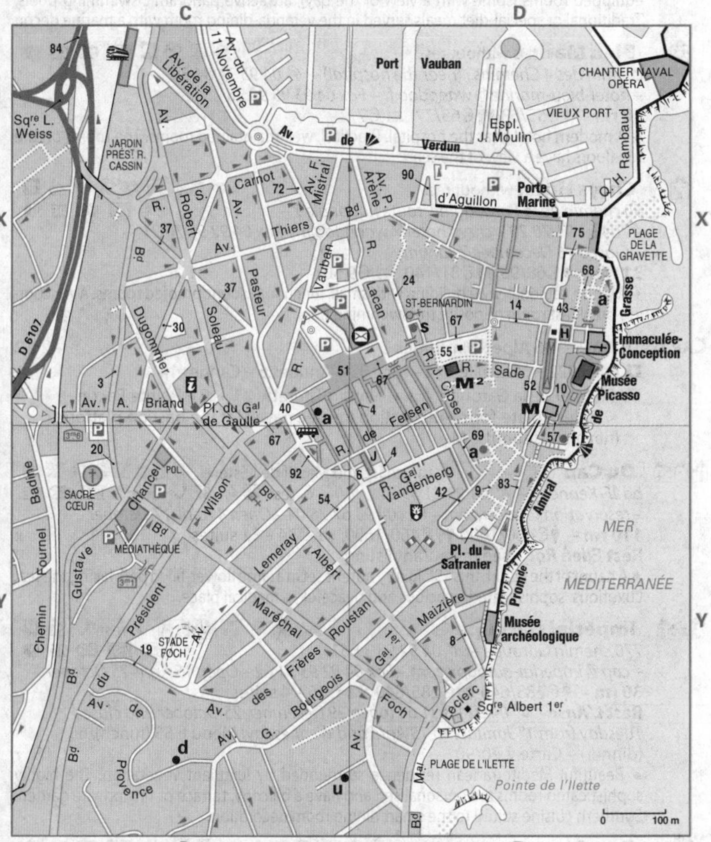

XX Le Figuier de St-Esprit

14 r. St-Esprit – ✆ 04 93 34 50 12 – Fax 04 93 34 94 25 – Closed 23 November-21 December, Wednesday lunch and Tuesday DX **a**

Rest – *(dinner only from 15 June to 31 August)* Menu € 30 (weekday lunch), € 48/75 – Carte € 48/100

◆ Set in the ramparts, attractive establishment recently taken over by Christian Morisset. Contemporary cuisine ine a light, modern dining room or on the patio, under the fig tree...

X Le Sucrier

6 r. des Bains – ✆ 04 93 34 85 40 – info@lesucrier.com – Fax 04 93 34 85 40 – Closed 17-25 November, 12-27 January, Tuesday lunch from October to May and Monday

Rest – Menu € 20/40 – Carte € 37/60 DY **a**

◆ This restaurant serves Italian specialities, such as fresh pasta and fish dishes, as well as traditional cuisine. Attractive dining rooms (one of which is vaulted) and a terrace.

Nice road by ① and D 6007 – ✉ 06600 Antibes

Baie des Anges-Thalazur ← rm, rest,
770 chemin Moyennes-Breguières, (near the hospital) – ☎ 04 92 91 82 00 – antibes@thalazur.fr – Fax 04 93 65 94 14
164 rm – €69/114 €93/139, €15 – ½ P €82/110
Rest – Menu €32 – Carte €33/56
◆ The hotel and thalassotherapy centre have just been fully renovated. Large, well-equipped rooms (some with a view of the bay); attractive panoramic swimming pools. Traditional or special-diet meals served in the veranda-dining room with a marine decor.

Bleu Marine without rest
chemin des 4 Chemins , (near the hospital) – ☎ 04 93 74 84 84 – hotel-bleu-marine@wanadoo.fr – Fax 04 93 95 90 26
18 rm – €55/63 €65/77, €7
◆ A modern hotel near the hospital. Practical, well-maintained rooms. The rooms on the top floors have a view of the sea.

Chrys Hôtel without rest
50 chemin de la Parouquine, route nationale 7 – ☎ 04 92 91 70 20 – chrys-hotel@wanadoo.fr – Fax 04 92 91 70 21 – Closed 15 December-7 January
31 rm – €68/95 €81/140, €9,50
◆ A white, regional-style building with small, functional, soundproofed rooms. A welcoming breakfast room opposite the swimming pool.

CAP D'ANTIBES – 06 Alpes-Maritimes 42 **E2**

Paris 922 – Marseille 174 – Nice 35 – Antibes 6 – Cannes 14

Plateau de la Garoupe ★★ - Jardin Thuret★ Z F - ←★ Pointe Bacon - ←★ de la plate-forme du bastion (musée naval) [of the bastion platform (naval museum)] Z **M.**

Du Cap ← the coast and Massif de l'Esterel, rest,
bd JF-Kennedy – ☎ 04 93 61 39 01 – reservation@hdcer.com – Fax 04 93 67 76 04 – Open 4 April-17 October
110 rm – €460/1600 €460/1600, €34 – 11 suites BV **x**
Rest *Eden Roc* – see restaurant listing
◆ A haunt of the jet set, this 19C luxury hotel is set in a large flower-filled park facing the sea. Luxurious, sophisticated, spacious and peaceful - a magical place.

Impérial Garoupe rest,
770 chemin Garoupe – ☎ 04 92 93 31 61 – cap@imperial-garoupe.com – Fax 04 92 93 31 62 – Open 15 April-25 October
30 rm – €285/640 €285/640, €26 – 4 suites
Rest *L'Anse* – *☎ 04 92 93 31 64 (open 29 December-25 October and closed Tuesday from 1st January to 15 April and Wednesday)* Menu €55 (lunch)/65 (dinner) – Carte €70/90 BV **r**
◆ Beautiful Mediterranean residence surrounded by luxuriant vegetation. The highly sophisticated rooms are personalised and have a balcony, terrace or tiny private garden. Southern cuisine suited to the smart dining room decoration.

Don César ← rm,
46 bd la Garoupe – ☎ 04 93 67 15 30 – hotel.don.cesar@wanadoo.fr – Fax 04 93 67 18 25 – Open 1st April-5 November BV **s**
21 rm – €165/335 €165/495, €18 – **Rest** – *(closed Tuesday lunch and Monday) (number of covers limited, pre-book)* Menu €39/45 – Carte €54/79
◆ A large modern villa with Greco-Roman architectural touches. The private terraces of the cosy rooms all overlook the sea. "Infinity edge" swimming pool. Intimate dining room. Inventive cuisine with an emphasis on regional produce.

La Baie Dorée ← sea,
579 bd la Garoupe – ☎ 04 93 67 30 67 – baiedoree@wanadoo.fr – Fax 04 92 93 76 39
18 rm – €230/510 €230/665, €20 – ½ P €235 BV **v**
Rest – *(open April-September)* Carte €64/92
◆ This bright Mediterranean villa practically has its "feet in the water". Rooms are welcoming, well cared-for, with a terrace or balcony, all have a view over the bay. Private jetty. In fine weather, the tables are laid facing the sea. Seafood cuisine.

Beau Site without rest
141 bd Kennedy – ✆ 04 93 61 53 43 – hbeausit@club-internet.fr
– Fax 04 93 67 78 16 – Closed 4 November-1st February BV **t**
28 rm – €70/135 €80/200, €12,50
◆ A neat façade, rooms with furniture painted in 18C Provençal style, a shaded terrace and the swimming pool are the attractions of this friendly hotel on a delicious peninsula.

La Garoupe et Gardiole without rest
60 chemin Garoupe – ✆ 04 92 93 33 33 – info@hotel-lagaroupe-gardiole.com
– Fax 04 93 67 61 87 – Open 6 April-21 October BV **k**
37 rm – €75/95 €98/140, €12
◆ Attractive houses restored in Provençal style enhanced by a pool, garden and splendid pergola-terrace. Fresh-looking rooms in the Garoupe and a more rustic look in the Gardiole.

Castel Garoupe without rest
959 bd la Garoupe – ✆ 04 93 61 36 51 – castel-garoupe@wanadoo.fr
– Fax 04 93 67 74 88 – Open from March to October BV **a**
25 rm – €94/142 €125/164, €10 – 3 suites
◆ The interior sports a mixture of antique furniture and ornaments and modern decoration. Comfortable rooms with balcony. Swimming pool in a lush garden; new tennis court.

Eden Roc – Hôtel du Cap — the coast and the islands,
bd JF-Kennedy – ✆ 04 93 61 39 01
– reservation@hdcer.com – Fax 04 93 67 76 04 – Open 4 April-17 October
Rest – Carte €86/196 BV **z**
◆ A superb villa, in splendid isolation on a rock by the sea: it would be difficult to find a better location for sampling the luxury of this mythical establishment where lingering at a table on the terrace is a must.

Bacon — Antibes and Baie des Anges, (dinner)
bd Bacon – ✆ 04 93 61 50 02 – contact@restaurantdebacon.com
– Fax 04 93 61 65 19 BU**m**
– Open 1st March-31 October and closed Tuesday lunchtime and Monday
Rest – Menu €49/79 (Except dinner in July and August) – Carte €69/227
Spec. Bouillabaisse. Poissons crus au citron et aux herbes. Chapon Grand-Mère aux petits oignons blancs (May to September). **Wines** Bellet, Côtes de Provence.
◆ This former "guingette" (1948) is now an elegant and soberly decorated restaurant, well-know for its seafood. A panoramic dining room and terrace combine elegance with discretion.

Les Pêcheurs — the sea and l'Esterel,
10 Bd Mar. Juin – ✆ 04 92 93 71 55
– reservation@lespecheurs-juan.com – Fax 04 92 93 15 04
– Closed 12 November-20 December, 16 February-5 March, lunch mid June-mid September, Tuesday and Wednesday from mid September to mid June
Rest – Menu €45 (lunch), €70/95 – Carte €61/117 BV **u**
Rest *La Plage* – *✆ 04 92 93 13 30 (open April-September and closed dinner except in July-August)* Carte €41/70
Spec. Spaghettini de langoustines au pistou (May to September). Petite marmite des pêcheurs en jus de bouillabaisse. Poissons de Méditerranée et des pêcheurs du port du Crouton. **Wines** Coteaux d'Aix-en-Provence-les Baux, Côtes de Provence.
◆ Attractive, modern decor, a delightful terrace with a panoramic view and subtle food using produce from the sea offered in this restaurant superbly situated at the water's edge. The Plage restaurant serves simple meals under the seaside pine trees.

ANTONY – 92 Hauts-de-Seine – **311** J3 – **101** 25 – see Paris, Area

Red = Pleasant. Look for the red and symbols.

ANTRAIGUES-SUR-VOLANE – 07 Ardèche – 331 I5 – pop. 498 – alt. 470 m – ✉ 07530 Lyon - Rhone Valley 44 A3

Paris 637 – Aubenas 15 – Lamastre 58 – Langogne 67 – Privas 42 – Le Puy-en-Velay 75

Syndicat d'initiative, le village ☎ 04 75 88 23 06, Fax 04 75 88 23 06

La Remise

au pont de l'Huile – ☎ 04 75 38 70 74

Closed 23 June-1st July, 8-16 September, 15 December – 8 January, Sunday dinner, Thursday dinner and Friday except July-August

Rest – *(pre-book)* Menu € 22/35

◆ Here, the owner of the house presents orally the choice of regional recipes which depend on the products available at the daily market. Informal service and gingham tablecloths in an old Ardèche barn.

ANZIN-ST-AUBIN – 62 Pas-de-Calais – 301 J6 – see Arras

AOSTE – 38 Isère – 333 G4 – pop. 1 715 – alt. 221 m – ✉ 38490 French Alps 45 C2

Paris 512 – Belley 25 – Chambéry 37 – Grenoble 55 – Lyon 71

in la Gare de l'Est 2 km northeast on D 1516 – ✉ 38490 Aoste

Au Coq en Velours with rm

1800 rte de St-Genix – ☎ 04 76 31 60 04 – contact@au-coq-en-velours.com – Fax 04 76 31 77 55 – Closed 19-28 August, 30 December-26 January, Thursday dinner, Sunday dinner and Monday

7 rm – †€ 65/75 ††€ 65/75, ☐ € 9 – **Rest** – Menu € 26/59 – Carte € 35/54

◆ Smart village inn run by the same family since 1900. Warm contemporary dining room decorated on a cockerel theme, flower-decked garden and terrace, tasty regional menu.

APPOIGNY – 89 Yonne – 319 E4 – see Auxerre

APREMONT – 73 Savoie – 333 I4 – pop. 890 – alt. 330 m – ✉ 73190 46 F2

Paris 569 – Grenoble 50 – Albertville 48 – Chambéry 9 – St-Jean-de-Maurienne 71

du Granier Apremont Chemin de Fontaine Rouge, North: 1 km by D 201, ☎ 04 79 28 21 26.

Col de Granier: ≤★★ from chalet-hotel terraces, Southwest: 14 km, French Alps.

Auberge St-Vincent

– ☎ 04 79 28 21 85 – aubergestvincent@yahoo.fr – Fax 04 79 71 62 06 – Closed Sunday dinner, Tuesday dinner and Wednesday

Rest – Menu € 15 (weekday lunch), € 21/29 – Carte € 34/41

◆ Welcoming and rustic atmosphere in this village famous for its wine: fine vaulted dining room and a pretty terrace looking on to the vineyards.

APT – 84 Vaucluse – 332 F10 – pop. 11 172 – alt. 250 m – ✉ 84400 Provence 42 E1

Paris 728 – Aix-en-Provence 56 – Avignon 54 – Digne-les-Bains 91

Office de tourisme, 20, avenue Ph. de Girard ☎ 04 90 74 03 18, Fax 04 90 04 64 30

Plan on next page

Le Couvent without rest

36 r. Louis-Rousset – ☎ 04 90 04 55 36 – loucouvent@wanadoo.fr – Fax 08 71 33 50 81 – Closed 11-23 February B d

5 rm ☐ – †€ 80/95 ††€ 85/120

◆ Inside the walls of this former convent (17C) you will forget that you are in the middle of the town centre. Rooms full of character, opening onto a garden. Breakfast under the refectory's vaulted ceiling.

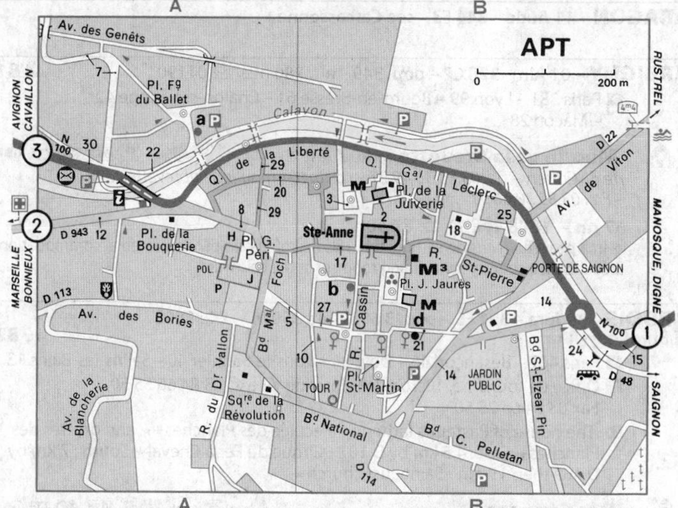

Amphithéâtre (R. de l')	B 2	Lauze-de-Perret (Crs et Pl.)	B 14	Sagy (Quai Léon)	A 22
Carnot (Pl.)	B 3	Libération (Av. de la)	B 15	Saignon (Av. de)	B 24
Cély (R.)	AB 5	Marchands (R. des)	B 17	St-Pierre (Pl.)	B 25
Cucuronne (Mtée de la)	A 7	Martyrs de la Résistance (Pl des)	B 18	St-Pierre (R.)	B
Docteur-Gros (R. du)	A 8	République (R. de la)	A 20	Scudéry (R.)	B 27
Gambetta (R.)	B 10	Rousset (R. Louis)	B 21	Sous-Préfecture (R. de la)	A 29
Girard (Av. Ph.-de)	A 12			Victor-Hugo (Av.)	A 30

XX **Auberge du Luberon** VISA

17 quai Léon-Sagy – ✆ 04 90 74 12 50 – serge.peuzin@free.fr – Fax 04 90 04 79 49 – Closed 11 November-10 December, 2-15 January, Sunday and Monday except dinner April-October and Tuesday lunch A **a**

Rest – Menu € 35/57 – Carte € 43/65

◆ Well situated on the Cavalon quayside, veranda dining room and terrace set in the shade of a plane tree. Preserved fruit, an Apt speciality, is used plentifully in the dishes.

X **La Manade** AC VISA

8 r. René-Cassin – ✆ 04 90 04 79 06 – christin.katy@neuf.fr – Closed 20 December-20 January, Sunday dinner and Thursday dinner in winter, Saturday lunch, Tuesday dinner and Wednesday B **b**

Rest – Menu € 25/35 – Carte € 33/42

◆ This restaurant, recently taken over by young people who are as welcoming as they are dynamic, includes two rustic dining rooms and a small terrace where you are offered a choice of regional dishes updated with the seasons.

in Saignon **4 km Southeast by D 48 – pop. 994 – alt. 450 m – ✉ 84400**

Auberge du Presbytère rm, VISA

pl. de la fontaine – ✆ 04 90 74 11 50 – auberge.presbytere@wanadoo.fr – Fax 04 90 04 68 51 – Closed from mid November to mid December and from mid January to end February

16 rm – †€ 58/145 ††€ 58/180, ☕ € 10,50 – **Rest** – *(closed Wednesday) (pre-book)* Menu (€ 28), € 38

◆ Antique furniture, red paving tiles, exposed beams and a fireplace preserve the spirit of this reputable house. Pleasant rooms, two of which have a terrace with a unique view. Pretty dining room and veranda, patio and terrace set up at lunch time on the village square.

Chambre de Séjour avec Vue without rest

– ✆ 04 90 04 85 01 – info@chambreavecvue.com – Fax 04 90 04 85 01 – Open from April to October

5 rm ☕ – †€ 80 ††€ 80/100

◆ This lovely house welcomes numerous artists (workshop and gallery). Colourful, well-kept rooms. Original breakfast room, pretty garden.

ARAGON – 11 Aude – 344 E3 – see Carcassonne

ARBIGNY – 01 Ain – 328 C2 – pop. 349 – alt. 280 m – ✉ 01190 44 B1

Paris 381 – Lyon 99 – Bourg-en-Bresse 61 – Chalon-sur-Saône 42 – Mâcon 28

Moulin de la Brevette without rest

rte de Cuisery – ✆ 03 85 36 49 27 – contact@moulindelabrevette.com – Fax 03 85 30 66 91

17 rm – †€ 48 ††€ 52, ☕ € 6,50

◆ In a peaceful riverside setting, this 18C mill offers simply decorated accommodation. Breakfast in a country-style dining room, or in the courtyard.

ARBOIS – 39 Jura – 321 E5 – pop. 3 698 – alt. 350 m – ✉ 39600

Burgundy-Jura 16 B2

Paris 407 – Besançon 46 – Dole 34 – Lons-le-Saunier 40 – Salins-les-Bains 13

Office de tourisme, 10, rue de l'Hôtel de Ville ✆ 03 84 66 55 50, Fax 03 84 66 25 50

The house of Pasteur's father ★ - Reculée des Planches★★ and grottes des Planches★ East : 4,5 km by D 107 - Cirque du Fer à Cheval★ South : 7 km by D 469 then 15 mn - Saint-Just church★.

Des Cépages rm, rest,

rte de Villette-les-Arbois – ✆ 03 84 66 25 25 – contact@hotel-des-cepages.com – Fax 03 84 66 08 24

33 rm – †€ 62 ††€ 70, ☕ € 10 – ½ P € 60 – **Rest** – buffet *(closed Friday, Saturday and Sunday) (dinner only)* Menu € 19/27

◆ By the N83 main road, this square building has practical rooms; those facing the road have efficient soundproofing and air-conditioning. Buffet meals and grilled meats in the recently renovated dining room.

Messageries without rest

r. de Courcelles – ✆ 03 84 66 15 45 – hotel.lesmessageries@wanadoo.fr – Fax 03 84 37 41 09 – Closed December and January

26 rm – †€ 31/53 ††€ 35/69, ☕ € 9

◆ This old post house with an ivy-clad façade is on a busy road next door to a small café. The rooms to the rear are quieter and have been refurbished.

Jean-Paul Jeunet with rm rest,

9 r. de l'Hôtel-de-Ville – ✆ 03 84 66 05 67 – jpjeunet@wanadoo.fr – Fax 03 84 66 24 20

Closed December, January, Tuesday and Wednesday except dinner July-mid September

12 rm – †€ 90/110 ††€ 110/138, ☕ € 17 – ½ P € 115/130

Rest – Menu € 53/130 – Carte € 80/99

Spec. Homard "bleu" de Bretagne en deux services. Poularde de Bresse aux morilles et vin jaune. Rhubarbe et gentiane (summer). **Wines** L'Etoile, Arbois-Trousseau.

◆ Elegantly rustic dining room, verdant patio, inventive local cuisine and a superb wine list make for a winning combination at this gourmet restaurant.

Le Prieuré

– Closed December, January, Tuesday and Wednesday from mid September to June

7 rm – †€ 72/88 ††€ 88/130, ☕ € 17

◆ 200 m away from the main residence, a comfortable 17C building where the client is well looked after. The rooms are classically furnished. Relaxing flower-decked garden.

La Balance Mets et Vins

47 r. de Courcelles – ✆ 03 84 37 45 00 – Fax 03 84 66 14 55 – Closed 23-30 June, 23 December-5 March, Tuesday dinner from September to June and Wednesday except public holidays

Rest – Menu € 23/55 – Carte € 28/55

◆ The chef of this restaurant is a wine lover and concocts his dishes using a splash of wine from the Jura region. Minimalist interior décor, pleasant terrace and fine selection of regional wines.

Le Caveau d'Arbois
3 rte de Besançon – ✆ 03 84 66 10 70 – contact@caveau-arbois.com – Fax 03 84 37 49 62
Rest – Menu € 19/48 – Carte € 32/51
◆ A regional style building on the edge of Arbois. Traditional fare, embellished with local specialities is savoured in a light and soberly decorated dining room.

ARBONNE – 64 Pyrénées-Atlantiques – 342 C4 – see Biarritz

L'ARBRESLE – 69 Rhône – 327 G4 – pop. 5 777 – alt. 230 m – ✉ 69210 43 E1

Paris 453 – Lyon 28 – Mâcon 68 – Roanne 58 – Villefranche-sur-Saône 23
Office de tourisme, 18, place Sapéon ✆ 04 74 01 48 87

Capucin
27 r. P.-Brossolette – ✆ 04 37 58 02 47 – Closed 1st-25 August, February holidays, Sunday and Monday
Rest – Menu € 13 bi (weekday lunch), € 18/30 – Carte € 24/37
◆ A 17C house bordering a pedestrian street on which it sets up its summer terrace. Exposed stone and rustic chairs indoors. Classic menu.

ARCACHON – 33 Gironde – 335 D7 – pop. 11 454 – alt. 5 m – Casino BZ – ✉ 33120 Atlantic Coast 3 B2

Paris 650 – Agen 196 – Bayonne 181 – Bordeaux 67 – Dax 145 – Royan 192
Office de tourisme, esplanade Georges Pompidou ✆ 05 57 52 97 97, Fax 05 57 52 97 77
18 d'Arcachon La Teste-de-Buch 35 boulevard d'Arcachon, ✆ 05 56 54 44 00.
Seafront★: ≤★ of the pier - Boulevard de la Mer★ - La Ville d'Hiver★ - Musée de la maquette marine: port★ BZ **M.**

Plan on next page

Park Inn without rest
4 r. Prof.-Jolyet – ✆ 05 56 83 99 91 – info.arcachon@rezidorparkinn.com – Fax 05 56 83 87 92 – Closed 5-26 December BZ **r**
57 rm – †€ 90/165 ††€ 100/231, ☕ € 15
◆ Contemporary hotel facing the sea with modern comforts. Choose rooms with a balcony and view of the Bassin d'Arcachon. Conference rooms in the adjoining congress centre.

Point France without rest
1 r. Grenier – ✆ 05 56 83 46 74 – hotel-point-france@hotel-point-france.com – Fax 05 56 22 53 24 – Open from March to beg. of November BZ **q**
34 rm – †€ 85/185 ††€ 92/185, ☕ € 12,50
◆ Pleasant 1970s hotel whose rooms have been renovated and decorated in different styles, from modern to more ethnic. Some have seafront terraces.

Les Vagues
9 bd de l'Océan – ✆ 05 56 83 03 75 – info@lesvagues.fr – Fax 05 56 83 77 16 AZ **b**
33 rm – †€ 71/184 ††€ 71/184, ☕ € 12 – ½ P € 84/137
Rest – *(open 21 March-2 November)* Menu € 26/33 – Carte € 25/49
◆ This hotel offers direct access to the beach. Spruce, well-equipped rooms; those on the top floor are enlarged by a bow-window. Panoramic view from this pleasant dining room with a nautical decor. Fish, seafood and traditional dishes.

Les Mimosas without rest
77bis av. de la République – ✆ 05 56 83 45 86 – contact.hotel@wanadoo.fr – Fax 05 56 22 53 40 – Open 15 February-15 November BZ **f**
21 rm – †€ 40/60 ††€ 45/85, ☕ € 6,50
◆ Two regional-style buildings in a quiet residential area with modest, rustic, well-kept rooms. Pleasant summer terrace and reasonable prices.

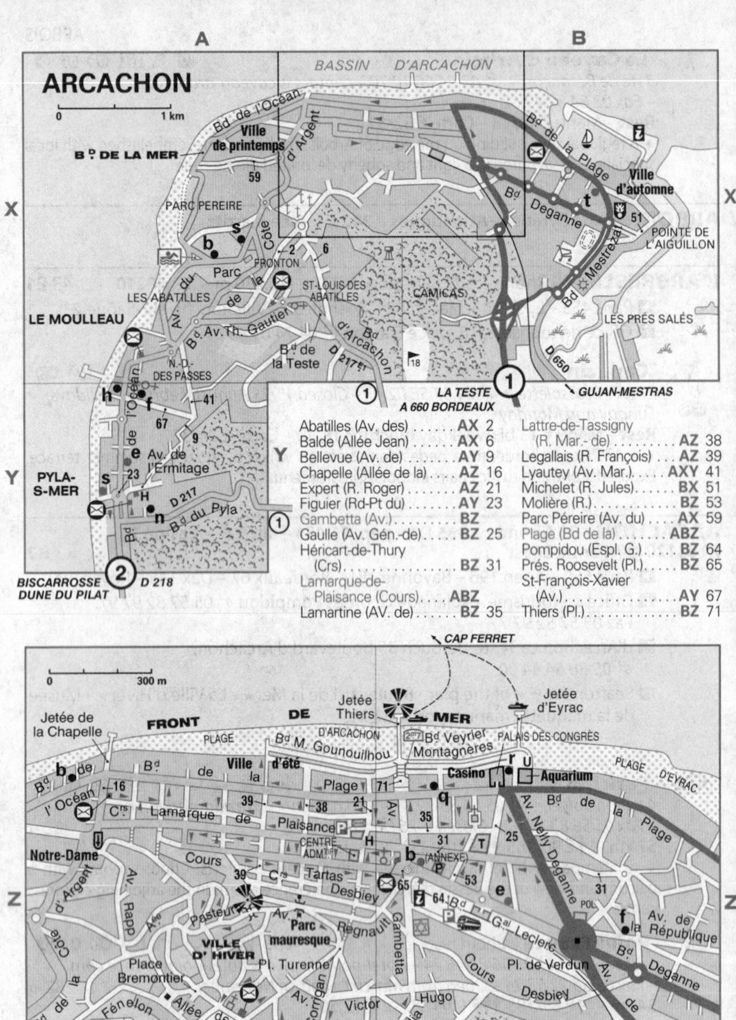

XX Le Patio

10 bd Plage – ✆ 05 56 83 02 72 – lepatio.sarl@wanadoo.fr – Fax 05 56 54 89 98 – Closed 13-26 October, 16-28 February, Sunday dinner, Thursday lunch and Wednesday BX t

Rest – Menu € 35 bi (weekday lunch), € 50/65 – Carte € 48/72

♦ Frescoes and colourful curtains bring a romantic note to this elegant dining room which opens onto a flower-decked patio terrace. Cuisine focused on fish and seafood.

Aux Mille Saveurs

25 bd Gén.-Leclerc – ✆ 05 56 83 40 28 – auxmillesaveurs@wanadoo.fr – Fax 05 56 83 12 14 – Closed 27 October-7 November, 16-25 February, Sunday dinner except July-August, Tuesday dinner except August and Wednesday

Rest – Menu € 18 (weekday lunch), € 28/45 – Carte € 41/62 BZ **e**

◆ A wide array of subtly spiced flavours with contemporary touches. The large dining room has been completely redecorated and extended by a veranda.

Chez Yvette

59 bd Gén.-Leclerc – ✆ 05 56 83 05 11 – Fax 05 56 22 51 62 BZ **b**

Rest – Menu € 20 – Carte € 30/76

◆ This restaurant renowned for its seafood is a local institution. It has been run by a family of oyster-farmers for over 30 years. Nautical setting and a lively atmosphere.

in Abatilles **2 km Southwest– ✉ 33120 Arcachon**

Novotel rest,

av. du Parc – ✆ 05 57 72 06 72 – h3382@accor.com – Fax 05 57 72 06 82 – Closed 4-17 January AX **b**

94 rm – €118/185 €148/185, €15

Rest *Côté d'Arguin* – Menu (€ 19 bi), € 29/38 – Carte € 43/60

◆ A new Novotel in a pine grove 100m from the beach, combined with a thalassotherapy centre. Modern, comfortable rooms. Solarium. Appealing menu with flavours of the sea, slimmers' menu and a good choice of Côté d'Arguin Bordeaux.

Parc without rest

5 av. du Parc – ✆ 05 56 83 10 58 – b.dronne@wanadoo.fr – Fax 05 56 54 05 30 – Open 1st May-30 September AX **s**

30 rm – €58/79 €58/90, €8,50

◆ The rooms in this 1970s building surrounded by pine trees are gradually being renovated: they are spacious, with balconies and now have a discreet, modern decor.

in Moulleau **5 km Southwest– ✉ 33120 Arcachon**

Yatt without rest

253 bd Côte-d'Argent – ✆ 05 57 72 03 72 – information@yatt-hotel.com – Fax 05 56 22 51 34 – Open April-October AY **h**

28 rm – €45/105 €45/130, €13

◆ Hotel with a bright white façade. Simple and well-kept rooms, smaller on the first floor. Buffet breakfast. Terrace.

Les Buissonnets without rest

12 r. L.-Garros – ✆ 05 56 54 00 83 – hotellesbuissonnets@wanadoo.fr – Fax 05 56 22 55 13 – Closed October and January AY **f**

13 rm – €95 €95, €9

◆ An attractive villa (1895) covered in Virginia creeper. Most of the practical, discreetly personalised rooms overlook a flower garden. Shop selling local produce.

ARCANGUES – 64 Pyrénées-Atlantiques – 342 C4 – see Biarritz

ARC-EN-BARROIS – 52 Haute-Marne – 313 K6 – pop. 898 – alt. 270 m – ✉ 52210 Northern France and the Paris Region 14 C3

Paris 263 – Bar-sur-Aube 55 – Châtillon-sur-Seine 44 – Chaumont 24 – Langres 30

Office de tourisme, place Moreau ✆ 03 25 02 52 17, Fax 03 25 02 52 17

d'Arc-en-Barrois Club House, South: 1 km by D 6, ✆ 03 25 01 54 54.

Du Parc

1 pl.Moreau – ✆ 03 25 02 53 07 – hotel.duparc@wanadoo.fr – Fax 03 25 02 42 84 – Closed 23 February-1st March, Sunday dinner and Monday from 23 March to 15 June, Tuesday dinner and Wednesday from 5 September to 22 February

16 rm – €63 €63, €7,50 – ½ P €62 – **Rest** – Menu (€ 11), € 19/42 – Carte € 27/49

◆ Former staging post, parts of which date from the 17C, housing small, renovated rooms in warm colours. Classic cuisine served in a dining room with parquet flooring and period furnishings. Contemporary decor in the brasserie.

ARCHAMPS – 74 Haute-Savoie – **328** J4 – see St-Julien-en-Genevois

ARCHINGEAY – 17 Charente-Maritime – **324** F4 – **pop. 519 – alt. 22 m** – ✉ 17380 38 **B2**

Paris 462 – La Rochelle 55 – Niort 64 – Poitiers 128

Les Hortensias rm, rm,

16 r. des Sablières – ✆ 05 46 97 85 70 – jpmt.jacques@wanadoo.fr – Fax 05 46 97 61 89 – Closed 22 December-15 January

3 rm – €49 €58 – **Table d'hôte** – Menu €22 bi

◆ This former wine-producing farm is very peaceful. The rooms and the suite have lovely Charentes, cherry wood furniture. You may have your copious breakfast whilst admiring the flower-decked garden, the vegetable plot and the small orchard. Family food.

ARCINS – 33 Gironde – **335** G4 – see Margaux

ARCIZANS-AVANT – 65 Hautes-Pyrénées – **342** L7 – see Argelès-Gazost

LES ARCS – 73 Savoie – **333** N4 – **Winter sports : 1 600/3 226 m** 7 54 – ✉ 73700 Bourg St Maurice French Alps 45 **D2**

Paris 644 – Albertville 64 – Bourg-St-Maurice 11 – Chambéry 113 – Val-d'Isère 41

Office de tourisme, Bourg-Saint-Maurice ✆ 04 79 07 12 57, Fax 04 79 07 24 90

Arc 1800 ★ - Arc 1600 ★ - Arc 2000 ★ - Le Transac cable car ★★ - La Cachette chairlift ★.

Grand Hôtel Paradiso rm, VISA

Les Arcs 1800, (Charmettoger village) – ✆ 04 79 07 65 00 – reservation@grandhotelparadiso.com – Fax 04 79 07 64 08 – Open July-August and 23 December-18 April

81 rm – €145/210 €210/310, €12 – 6 suites – ½ P €130/180

Rest – Menu €37/57 – Carte €29/37

◆ Successful combination of Savoyard decor with modern comfort in this chalet situated at the foot of the slopes. Well-equipped rooms for families. Large choice of activities and entertainment. The restaurant's panoramic terrace overlooking the valley is an invitation to sit back and relax.

LES ARCS – 83 Var – **340** N5 – **pop. 5 334 – alt. 80 m** – ✉ 83460 French Riviera 41 **C3**

Paris 848 – Cannes 59 – Draguignan 11 – Fréjus 25 – St-Raphaël 29

Polyptyque★ in the church - Ste-Roseline chapel ★ Northeast: 4 km.

Le Relais des Moines VISA

1.5 km eastward along the St. Roseline road – ✆ 04 94 47 40 93 – contact@lerelaisdesmoines.com – Fax 04 94 47 40 93 – Closed 24 November-13 December, Sunday dinner from September to June and Monday

Rest – Menu (€25 bi), €50/80 – Carte €65/97

◆ This former sheepfold built on the hillside, used to serve as a canteen for the monks. Lovely 16C stone arches in the interior and charming, shady terrace in the park.

La Vigne à Table VISA

RN 7, (Wine producers') – ✆ 04 94 47 48 47 – lavigneatable@wanadoo.fr – Fax 04 94 47 55 13 – Closed Sunday dinner and Wednesday

Rest – Menu €34/90 – Carte €53/76

◆ An address for amateurs of inventive, seasonally-inspired cuisine (featuring lots of flowers) and Côtes de Provence wines. Luminous, Provençal-style setting.

Logis du Guetteur with rm rm, VISA

au village médiéval – ✆ 04 94 99 51 10 – contact@logisduguetteur.com – Fax 04 94 99 51 29 – Closed in February

10 rm – €124/147 €124/147, €15 – 2 suites – **Rest** – Menu (€28), €40/82

◆ Picturesque establishment situated in an 11C fort. Rustic dining rooms set in superb medieval vaults, covered terrace. Modern food. Simple and very comfortable rooms.

ARC-SUR-TILLE – 21 Côte-d'Or – 320 L5 – pop. 2 332 – alt. 219 m – ✉ 21560 8 D1

Paris 323 – Avallon 119 – Besançon 97 – Dijon 13 – Langres 73

Auberge Les Marronniers

16 r. de Dijon – ✆ 03 80 37 09 62 – Fax 03 80 37 24 94
15 rm – †€ 55 ††€ 60, ☐ € 8,50 – ½ P € 72 – **Rest** – Menu € 23 (weekday lunch), € 33/65 – Carte € 36/60
◆ Large, prettily decorated rooms (wrought iron, painted wood, coloured fabrics) and with particularly well-designed bathrooms. A rustic style dining room with a shellfish tank. Pretty terrace beneath horse chestnut trees.

ARDENAIS – 18 Cher – 323 K7 – pop. 152 – alt. 233 m – ✉ 18170 12 C3

Paris 299 – Orléans 173 – Bourges 66 – Montluçon 46 – Issoudun 51

Domaine de Vilotte

4 km south on D 38 – ✆ 02 48 96 04 96 – tour.dev@wanadoo.fr – Fax 02 48 96 04 96 – Open from March to October
5 rm ☐ – †€ 75 ††€ 85 – **Table d'hôte** – Menu € 25 bi
◆ Discover the bucolic charm of this family estate set in superb parkland, complete with pond. Attractive Empire-style interior; table d'hôte in an old-fashioned kitchen (copper pans, beams). Dishes with a local flavour.

ARDENTES – 36 Indre – 323 H6 – pop. 3 323 – alt. 172 m – ✉ 36120 Dordogne-Berry-Limousin 12 C3

Paris 275 – Argenton-sur-Creuse 43 – Bourges 66 – Châteauroux 14 – La Châtre 23

Gare

2 r. de la Gare – ✆ 02 54 36 20 24 – Fax 02 54 36 92 07 – Closed 22 July-13 August, 17 February-4 March, Sunday dinner, Wednesday dinner, Monday and dinner on public holidays
Rest – Menu € 22/29
◆ Situated in a quiet area near the old station, a relatively uninteresting façade conceals a rustic and well-laid out restaurant with exposed beams. Traditional cuisine in large portions.

ARDRES – 62 Pas-de-Calais – 301 E2 – pop. 4 154 – alt. 11 m – ✉ 62610 Northern France and the Paris Region 30 A1

Paris 273 – Calais 18 – Arras 93 – Boulogne-sur-Mer 38 – Lille 90
Office de tourisme, place d'Armes ✆ 03 21 35 28 51, Fax 03 21 35 28 51

Le François 1er

pl. des Armes – ✆ 03 21 85 94 00 – lewandowski@lefrancois1er.com – Fax 03 21 85 87 53 – Closed 15-19 March, 1st-13 September, 24 December-6 January, Sunday dinner, Wednesday dinner and Monday
Rest – Menu € 25/49 – Carte € 45/71
◆ Attractive residence on the picturesque Grand Place. The white walls enhance the tastefully elegant dining room's parquet floor and fine beams. Up-to-date cuisine.

ARÊCHES – 73 Savoie – 333 M3 – alt. 1 080 m – Winter sports : 1 050/2 300 m 15 – ✉ 73270 Beaufort sur Doron French Alps 45 D1

Paris 606 – Albertville 26 – Chambéry 77 – Megève 42
Office de tourisme, route Grand Mont ✆ 04 79 38 37 57, Fax 04 79 38 16 70
Hameau de Boudin★ East: 2 km.

Auberge du Poncellamont

– ✆ 04 79 38 10 23 – Fax 04 79 38 13 98 – Open 15 June-15 September and 20 December-15 April and closed Sunday dinner, Monday lunch and Wednesday
14 rm – †€ 56 ††€ 60/65, ☐ € 9 – ½ P € 60/63 – **Rest** – Menu € 20 (weekdays)/30 – Carte € 30/36
◆ Situated in the village, a Savoy chalet (entirely non-smoking) is decked in flowers in summer. The rooms are simple and practical, some are attic rooms and some have balconies. Simple but pleasant country-style dining room and a terrace where one is gently rocked by the murmur of a fountain.

ARÈS – 33 Gironde – 335 E6 – pop. 4 680 – alt. 6 m – ✉ 33740 Atlantic Coast

Paris 627 – Arcachon 47 – Bordeaux 48 3 **B1**

Office de tourisme, esplanade G. Dartiquelongue ✆ 05 56 60 18 07, Fax 05 56 60 39 41

des Aiguilles Vertes Lanton Route de Bordeaux, Southeast: 12 km, ✆ 05 56 82 95 71.

St-Éloi with rm

11 bd Aérium – ✆ 05 56 60 20 46 – nlatour2@wanadoo.fr – Fax 05 56 60 10 37 – Closed 5 January-8 February, Wednesday dinner, Sunday dinner, Monday from September to June and Monday lunch in July-August

8 rm – †€ 60 ††€ 75, ☕ € 8 – ½ P € 85/97 – **Rest** – Menu € 32 (weekdays)/58 – Carte € 42/69

◆ White seaside house near the Bassin D'Arcachon. Pleasant contemporary dining room, terrace, traditional cuisine and ethnic-style rooms.

ARGELÈS-GAZOST – 65 Hautes-Pyrénées – 342 L6 – pop. 3 241 – alt. 462 m – Spa : mid April-late Oct. – Casino Y – ✉ 65400 Languedoc-Roussillon-Tarn Gorges

Paris 863 – Lourdes 13 – Pau 58 – Tarbes 32 28 **A3**

Office de tourisme, 15, place République ✆ 05 62 97 00 25, Fax 05 62 97 50 60

Plan on next page

Le Miramont

rm, rest, VISA

44 av. des Pyrénées – ✆ 05 62 97 01 26 – hotel-miramont@sudfr.com – Fax 05 62 97 56 67 – Closed 1st-21 December Z **n**

19 rm – †€ 55/60 ††€ 65/100, ☕ € 12 – ½ P € 49/60 – **Rest** – *(closed Wednesday except July-August) (pre-book Sat - Sun)* Menu (€ 14), € 20/34 – Carte approx. € 33

◆ This lovely white villa with a cruise liner look (1930s) is set in the middle of a garden full of flowers. The rooms are very comfortable; older and slightly simpler accommodation in the annex. Bright, non-smoking veranda-dining room surrounded by greenery. Fine, modern cuisine.

Les Cimes

rest, VISA

pl. Ourout – ✆ 05 62 97 00 10 – contact@hotel-lescimes.com – Fax 05 62 97 10 19 – Closed 2 November-25 December and 2 January-5 February Z **a**

26 rm – †€ 48/55 ††€ 69/76, ☕ € 10 – ½ P € 55/68 – **Rest** – Menu € 20/45 – Carte € 14/36

◆ A building dating from the 1950s with a modern wing made of glass and wood. Differently styled rooms, some of which have balconies overlooking a peaceful garden. Pleasant flowered patio-veranda for breakfast. A large, bright restaurant offering a traditional menu.

Soleil Levant

rest, rest, VISA

17 av. des Pyrénées – ✆ 05 62 97 08 68 – hsoleillevant@orange.fr – Fax 05 62 97 04 60 – Closed 26 November-23 December and 2 January-2 February Y **t**

35 rm – †€ 41/44 ††€ 45/50, ☕ € 8 – ½ P € 42/48 – **Rest** – Menu € 12,50/42

◆ An attractive hotel in the lower part of town with practical, well-kept rooms; some have a view of the surrounding mountains. Bar, lounge, terrace and well-kept garden. Two communicating dining rooms with a family guesthouse atmosphere. Traditional fare.

in St-Savin 3 km South by D 101 - Z – pop. 353 – alt. 580 m – ✉ 65400

Site★ of the Piétat chapel South: 1 km.

Le Viscos with rm

rest, VISA

1 r. Lamarque – ✆ 05 62 97 02 28 – leviscos.jpsaint-martin@wanadoo.fr – Fax 05 62 97 04 95 – Closed 7-29 January, Monday except dinner in season and Sunday dinner

9 rm – †€ 60/84 ††€ 60/106, ☕ € 9,50 – ½ P € 62/85 – **Rest** – Menu € 28/79 – Carte € 47/76

◆ This family-run inn has been welcoming guests since 1840. The dining room opens out onto a terrace with views of the mountains. Generous portions of regional cuisine. Cosy rooms.

ARGELÈS-GAZOST

Alicot (R. Michel) . . . . **Y** 3
Bourdette (R. Jean) . . . . **Z** 18
Bourg Neuf (R. du) . . . . **Y** 19
Coubertin (Av. P. de) . . . . **Z** 29
Dambé (Av. Jules) . . . . **Y** 30
Digoy (R. Capitaine) . . . . . . **YZ** 33
Edouard-VII (Pl.) . . . . **Z** 36
Foch (R. du Mar.) . . . . **Y** 39
Gassan (Av. Emile) . . . . **Y** 42
Joffre (Pl.) . . . . **YZ** 53
Nansouty (Av. du Gén.) . . . . . **Y** 69
Pasteur (R.) . . . . **Z** 75
Pérus (Pl.) . . . . **Y** 77
Poilus (R. des) . . . . **Y** 80
Reine Nathalie (Av.) . . . . **Y** 84
République (Pl. de la) . . . . **Z** 85
Sainte-Castere (R.) . . . . **Z** 91
Saint-Orens (R.) . . . . **Z** 88
Sassere (Av. Hector) . . . . **Y** 92
Sorbe (R.) . . . . **Y** 93
Sylvestre (Av. Armand) . . . . . **Z** 96
Victoire (Pl. de la) . . . . **Y** 100
Vieuzac (R. de) . . . . **Y** 101
8-Mai (R. du) . . . . **Y** 106

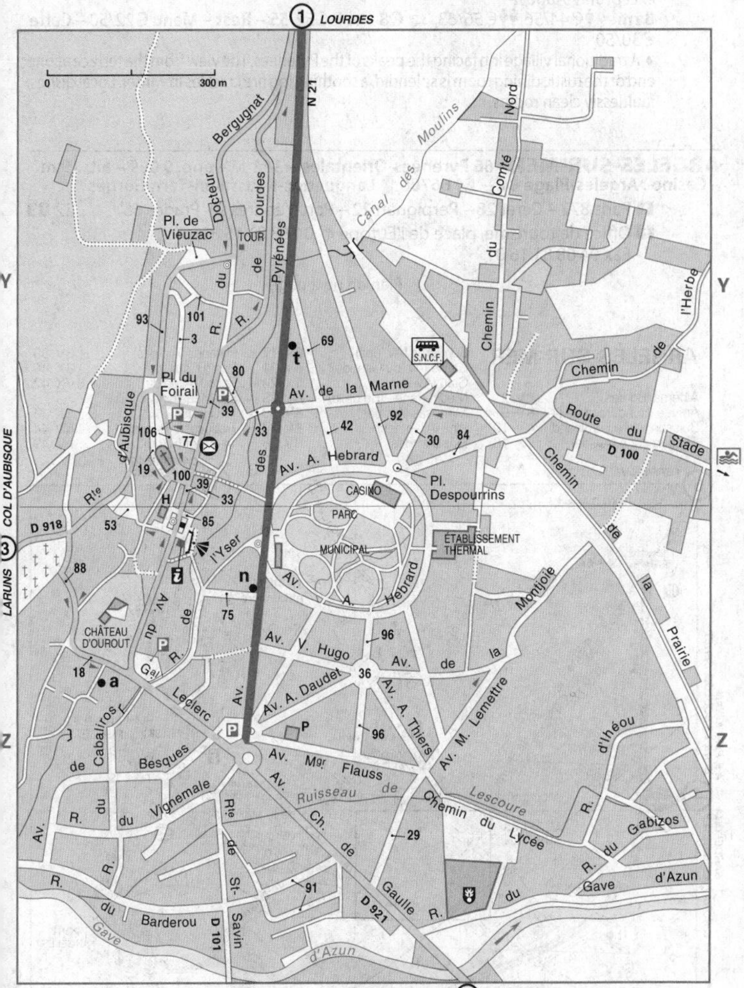

① LOURDES

LARUNS ③ COL D'AUBISQUE

COL DU TOURMALET ② CAUTERETS

A good night's sleep without spending a fortune?
Look for a Bib Hôtel .

in Arcizans-Avant **4.5 km South by D 101 and D 13 – pop. 298 – alt. 640 m – ✉ 65400**

✕ **Auberge Le Cabaliros** with rm

16 r. de l'Église – ☎ 05 62 97 04 31 – auberge.cabaliros@wanadoo.fr – Fax 05 62 97 91 48 – Closed 3 November-5 February, Tuesday and Wednesday except July-August

8 rm – †€ 44/56 ††€ 56/63, ☕ € 8 – ½ P € 52/55 – **Rest** – Menu € 22/50 – Carte € 30/50

◆ A traditional village inn facing the peaks of the Pyrenees. The view from the terrace at one end of the rustic dining room is splendid, a soothing log fire crackles in winter. Local dishes; faultlessly clean rooms.

ARGELÈS-SUR-MER – 66 Pyrénées-Orientales – 344 J7 – pop. 9 069 – alt. 19 m – Casino : Argelès-Plage BV – ✉ 66700 Languedoc-Roussillon-Tarn Gorges

Paris 872 – Céret 28 – Perpignan 22 – Port-Vendres 9 – Prades 66 22 **B3**

Office de tourisme, place de l'Europe ☎ 04 68 81 15 85, Fax 04 68 81 16 01

Plan on next page

ARGELÈS-SUR-MER

Albères (Bd des) **BV** 2
Arrivée (Rond-Point de l') **BV** 6
Buisson (Allée Ferdinand) **AV** 10
Charlemagne (Av. de) **BX** 16
Corbières (Av. des) **BV** 17
Gaulle (Av. du Gén.-de) **BV** 21
Grau (Av. du) **BX** 24
Méditerranée (Bd de la) **BV** 29
Mimosas (Av. des) **BV** 30
Pins (Allée des) **BV** 37
Pins (Av. des) **BV** 38
Platanes (Av. des) **BV** 39
Port (R. du) **BX** 40
Racou (Allée du) **BVX** 42
Ste-Madeleine (Chemin) **AX** 43
Trabucaire (R. des) **AV** 44
14-Juillet (R. du) **AV** 49

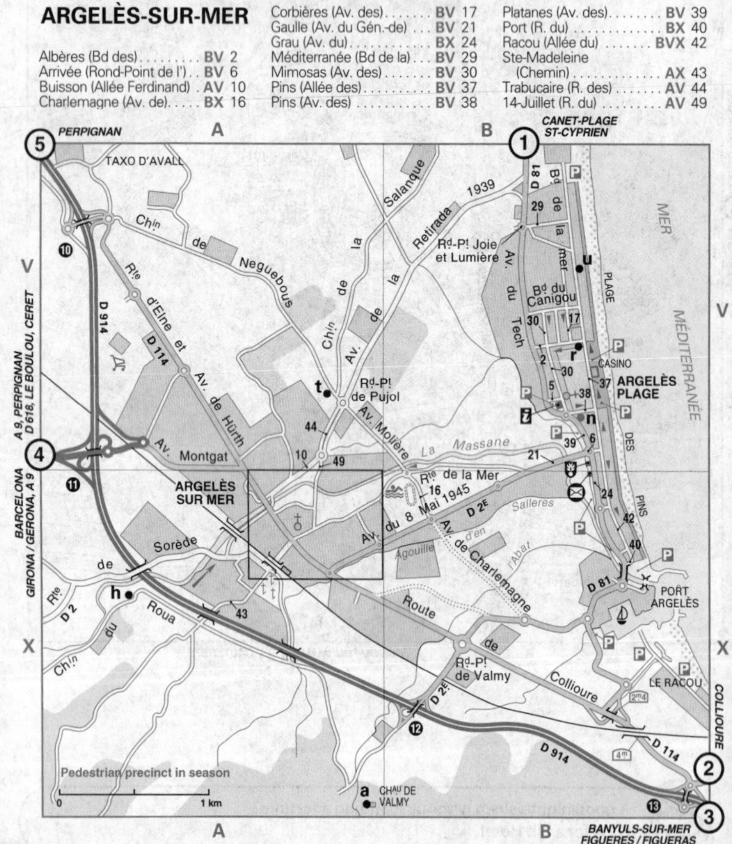

ARGELÈS-SUR-MER

Albert (R. Marcelin) . . . . **CY** 3
Bel Air (R. de) . . . . **CY** 7
Blanqui (R.) . . . . **CY** 9
Castellans (Pl. des) . . . . **CY** 13
Castellans (R.) . . . . **CY** 14
Desclot (R.) . . . . **CY** 18
Gambetta (R.) . . . . **CDZ** 20
Gendarmerie (R. de la) . . . **CDZ** 22
Jean-Jaurès (R.) . . . . **CY** 26
Libération (Av. de la) . . . **CDYZ**
Majorque (R. de) . . . . **CY** 27
Morata (R. Juan) . . . . **CY** 32
Nationale (Rte) . . . . **CYZ**
Notre-Dame-de-Vie (Rte) . . **CZ** 33
Paix (R. de la) . . . . **CY** 35
Remparts (R. des) . . . . **CY** 41
République (Pl. de la) . . . . . **CY** 42
République (R. de la) . . . . . **CY**
Travail (R. du) . . . . **CY** 45
Wilson (R.) . . . . **CZ** 47
11-Novembre (Av. du) . . . . **CY** 48

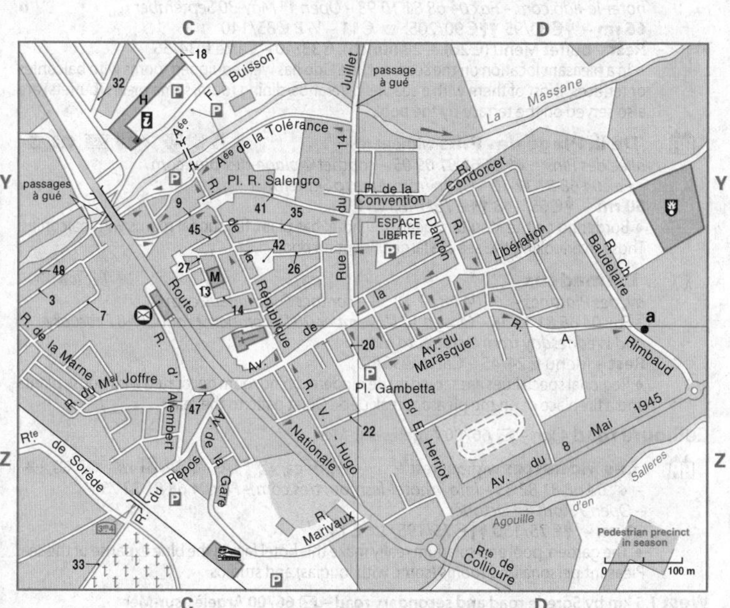

Le Cottage without rest

21 r. Arthur-Rimbaud – ✆ 04 68 81 07 33
– info@hotel-lecottage.com – Fax 04 68 81 59 69
– Open 12 April-13 October
DY **a**

33 rm – †€ 60/210 ††€ 60/305, ☕ € 14

◆ Modern building with leisure and relaxation facilities (pool, crazy golf and spa). Nice rooms with the advantages of a garden and the peace of a residential area.

Acapella without rest

chemin de Neguebous – ✆ 04 68 95 89 45
– contact@hotel-acapella.com – Fax 04 68 95 84 93
– Closed 17 November-18 December
AV **t**

30 rm – †€ 29/49 ††€ 29/74, ☕ € 7

◆ Argelès has just over 7000 inhabitants in winter and several hundred thousand in summer... so remember to book! Economical, non-smoking hotel; rooms with balconies.

Château Valmy without rest

< sea and vineyard,

chemin de Valmy – ✆ 04 68 95 95 25 – contact@chateau-valmy.com – Fax 04 68 81 15 18
– Open April-November
AX **a**

5 rm ☕ – †€ 150/350 ††€ 150/350

◆ Chateau built by a Danish architect in 1900 magnificently set among the vines. Luxurious rooms with splendid sea views and wine tasting sessions.

in Argelès-Plage 2,5 km East – ✉ 66700 Argelès-sur-Mer
Languedoc-Roussillon-Tarn Gorges

Southeast: Côte Vermeille★★.

Grand Hôtel du Lido
bd de la Mer – ✆ 04 68 81 10 32 – contact@hotel-le-lido.com – Fax 04 68 81 10 98 – Open 1st May-30 September BV **u**
66 rm – €80/95 €90/205, €11 – ½ P €85/140
Rest – buffet Menu (€26), €28 (lunch), €33/40 – Carte €34/55
◆ In a pleasant location on the sea front, the Lido has well-equipped rooms with balconies or terraces, most of them with a sea view. Veranda-dining room; some meals (buffets) are also served on the terrace by the pool.

De la Plage des Pins without rest
allée des Pins – ✆ 04 68 81 09 05 – contact@plage-des-pins.com – Fax 04 68 81 12 10 – Open from June to September BV **r**
50 rm – €65/148 €75/148, €11
◆ Bordering on the Mediterranean, the hotel has plain, functional rooms with balconies. Those overlooking the sea are larger. Beautiful pool.

L'Amadeus
av. des Platanes – ✆ 04 68 81 12 38 – contact@lamadeus.com – Fax 04 68 81 12 38 – Closed 12 November-20 December, 2 January-8 February and Wednesday from October to May BV **n**
Rest – Menu €24/45 – Carte €35/52
◆ Regional specialities are served in the modern dining room decorated with house plants and a fireplace or on the pleasant teak deck. Quiet patio to the rear.

Collioure road 4 km – ✉ 66700 Argelès-sur-Mer

Les Mouettes without rest
sea,
– ✆ 04 68 81 82 83 – info@hotel-lesmouettes.com – Fax 04 68 81 32 73 – Open 7 April-14 October
31 rm – €75/150 €75/195, €14
◆ The garden, pool and solarium really make this hotel facing the blue expanse of the sea. Pleasant personalised rooms (some with loggias) and studios.

West 1,5 km by Sorède road and secondary road – ✉ 66700 Argelès-sur-Mer

Auberge du Roua
chemin du Roua – ✆ 04 68 95 85 85 – magalie@aubergeduroua.com – Fax 04 68 95 83 50 – Open 13 February-15 November AX **h**
14 rm – €60/95 €60/189, €10 – 3 suites – ½ P €73/138
Rest – *(closed Wednesday dinner from October to April) (dinner only)*
Menu €35/75 – Carte €48/66
◆ Authentic mas dating from the 17C, sheltered from noise. The renovated rooms are all different; the clean lines of the modern decor go well with the old building. Modern, Mediterranean cuisine served under beautiful arches or on a terrace around the pool.

ARGENTAN – 61 Orne – 310 I2 – pop. 16 596 – alt. 160 m – ✉ 61200
Normandy 33 **C2**

Paris 191 – Alençon 46 – Caen 59 – Dreux 115 – Flers 42 – Lisieux 58
Office de tourisme, Chapelle Saint-Nicolas ✆ 02 33 67 12 48, Fax 02 33 39 96 61
des Haras Nonant-le-Pin Les Grandes Bruyères, East: 22 km, ✆ 02 33 27 00 19.
St-Germain church ★.

Plan on next page

De France
8 bd Carnot – ✆ 02 33 67 03 65 – contact@lapucealoreille-61.com – Fax 02 33 36 62 24 – Closed 7-21 July, 22-29 December, 16 February-2 March, Friday dinner, Sunday dinner, Monday and dinner on public holidays **r**
10 rm – €44 €46, €7 – ½ P €48 – **Rest** – Menu €13/34
◆ A warm welcome and an impeccable service are the best features of this family-run establishment situated near the station. Mechanical musical instruments decorating the dining room put on a little show created by the owner. Traditional food.

ARGENTAN

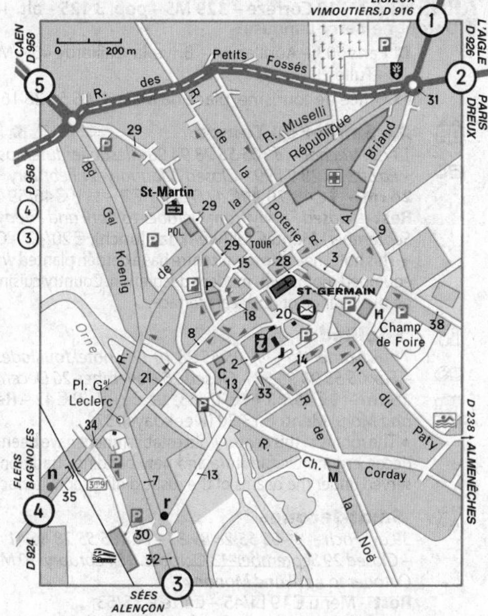

Ariès — rm, rm, VISA AE

Z.A. Beurrerie, 1 km via ④ – ✆ 02 33 39 13 13 – arieshotel@wanadoo.fr – Fax 02 33 39 34 71

43 rm – 🛉€ 46 🛉🛉€ 46, ☕ € 6,50 – **Rest** – *(closed Friday dinner, Saturday and Sunday)* Menu € 10/20 – Carte € 19/23

◆ A very well insulated hotel situated by quite a busy road. Simple and functional accommodation. Bistro-style furniture and simple table settings in a restaurant proposing classic cuisine, buffet menus and dishes of the day.

XXX **La Renaissance** with rm — VISA AE

20 av. 2e-Division-Blindée – ✆ 02 33 36 14 20 – larenaissance.viel@wanadoo.fr – Fax 02 33 36 65 50 – Closed 4-19 August, 15-23 February and Sunday dinner

14 rm – 🛉€ 59/81 🛉🛉€ 64/85, ☕ € 10 – **Rest** – *(closed 27 July-19 August, Sunday dinner and Monday)* Menu (€ 19), € 25/54 – Carte € 50/68 **n**

◆ Large bay windows overlooking the garden light up this elegant, rustic dining room, which has a lovely Renaissance-style fireplace. Innovative cuisine.

via ② 11 km by N 26 and D 729 – ✉ 61310 Silly-en-Gouffern

Pavillon de Gouffern — VISA AE

– ✆ 02 33 36 64 26 – pavillondegouffern@wanadoo.fr – Fax 02 33 36 53 81

20 rm – 🛉€ 48/160 🛉🛉€ 75/200, ☕ € 12 – ½ P € 125/145 – **Rest** – Menu (€ 25), € 38/55 bi

◆ Situated in a park surrounded by woods, a half-timbered 19C hunting lodge. Prettily renovated rooms furnished in a country style. The two dining rooms renovated in a modern style have a fine view of the estate. Traditional cuisine.

in Fontenai-sur-Orne 4,5 km by ④ – **pop. 277 – alt. 65 m – ✉ 61200**

XX **Faisan Doré** with rm — rest, VISA AE

– ✆ 02 33 67 18 11 – lefaisandore@wanadoo.fr – Fax 02 33 35 82 15 – Closed 1st-15 August, Saturday lunch and Sunday dinner

16 rm – 🛉€ 55/150 🛉🛉€ 55/150, ☕ € 9 – **Rest** – Menu € 29/65 bi – Carte € 35/55

◆ A Normandy inn situated on a busy road. The dining room with a cosy bar-lounge in front of it has a new floral décor theme. Warm welcome.

ARGENTAT – 19 Corrèze – 329 M5 – pop. 3 125 – alt. 183 m – ✉ 19400
Dordogne-Berry-Limousin 25 **C3**

Paris 503 – Aurillac 54 – Brive-la-Gaillarde 45 – Mauriac 49 – St-Céré 40 – Tulle 29

Office de tourisme, place da Maïa ✆ 05 55 28 16 05, Fax 05 55 28 45 16

Le Sablier du Temps
rest,

13 r. J.-Vachal – ✆ 05 55 28 94 90 – lesablierdutemps@wanadoo.fr – Fax 05 55 28 94 99 – Closed 7 January-11 February

24 rm – €45/70 €47/70, €7 – ½ P €46/59

Rest – *(closed Friday from October to April and Friday lunch in May, June and September)* Menu €14 (weekday lunch), €20/42 – Carte €29/54

◆ This hotel near the town centre has a garden planted with trees and a pool. Functionally equipped rooms with modern decoration. Country cuisine served in a rustic dining room, on the veranda or on a leafy terrace.

Fouillade
rest,

11 pl. Gambetta – ✆ 05 55 28 10 17 – hotel.fouillade.argentat@wanadoo.fr – Fax 05 55 28 90 52 – Closed 26 November-26 December

15 rm – €45/63 €45/63, €7 – ½ P €42 – **Rest** – *(closed Sun. evening and Mon.)* Menu €13,50 (weekdays)/37

◆ The rooms of this century-old establishment have been rejuvenated with contemporary decor, ergonomic furniture and new bedding. Traditional dishes with regional touches served under the beams of the rustic dining room; terrace at the front.

Saint-Jacques

39 av. Foch – ✆ 05 55 28 89 87 – Fax 05 55 28 86 41 – Closed 29 September-13 October, 18 February-10 March, Sunday dinner from October to April and Monday

Rest – Menu €19 bi/45 – Carte €35/53

◆ Monsieur is hard at work in the kitchen while Madame runs the show in the comfortable, elegant dining room. Veranda and verdant terrace.

Auberge des Gabariers

15 quai Lestourgie – ✆ 05 55 28 05 87 – Fax 05 55 28 69 63 – Open April-November and closed Tuesday dinner and Wednesday except July-August

Rest – Menu (€16), €27/36 – Carte €32/46

◆ A lovely 16C house on the banks of the Dordogne. Rustic atmosphere, dishes grilled on a spit, riverside terrace in the shade of a linden tree, and charming bedrooms facing the river.

ARGENTEUIL – 95 Val-d'Oise – 305 E7 – 101 14 – see Paris, Area

ARGENTIÈRE – 74 Haute-Savoie – 328 O5 – alt. 1 252 m – Winter sports : see Chamonix – ✉ 74400 French Alps 45 **D1**

Paris 619 – Annecy 106 – Chamonix-Mont-Blanc 10 – Vallorcine 10

Office de tourisme, 24, route du village ✆ 04 50 54 02 14, Fax 04 50 54 06 39

Aiguille des Grands Montets★★★: ✻★★★ - Aiguilles Rouges natural reserve ★★★ North: 3 km - Col de la Balme★★: ✻★★.

Grands Montets without rest

(near the Lognon cable car) – ✆ 04 50 54 06 66 – info@hotel-grands-montets.com – Fax 04 50 54 05 42 – Open 26 June-25 August and 19 December-5 May

45 rm – €100/180 €100/180, €10 – 3 suites

◆ This hotel has many charming attractions: It is quiet, near the cable car, sports regional decor in the lounge bar, has a pool and rooms (some nicely refurbished) with a view.

Montana
rm,

24 clos du Montana – ✆ 04 50 54 14 99 – info@hotel-montana.fr – Fax 04 50 54 03 40 – Open 15 June-30 September and 8 December-11 May

23 rm – €90/165 €90/165, €15 – ½ P €86/114

Rest – *(open 15 June-30 September) (dinner only) (residents only)* Menu €24/34

◆ Popular for its particularly friendly family ambiance. Plainly furnished rooms with balconies facing the Grands Montets. Restaurant with alpine decor and terrace facing the mountains. Traditional simple dishes.

ARGENTON-SUR-CREUSE – **36 Indre** – **323** F7 – **pop. 5 146** – **alt. 100 m** –
✉ **36200** ▮ **Dordogne-Berry-Limousin** 11 **B3**

▶ Paris 297 – Châteauroux 32 – Limoges 93 – Montluçon 103 – Poitiers 100

ℹ Office de tourisme, 13, place de la République ✆ 02 54 24 05 30, Fax 02 54 24 28 13

👁 Old bridge ⩤★ - ⩤★ from the terrace of N.-D.-des-Bancs chapel.

ARGENTON-SUR-CREUSE

Acacias (Allée des)	2
Barbès (R.)	5
Brillaud (R. Charles)	6
Chapelle-N.-D. (R. de la)	7
Châteauneuf (R.)	8
Chauvigny (R. A. de)	10
Coursière (R. de la)	12
Gare (R. de la)	14
Grande (R.)	15
Merle-Blanc (R. du)	18
Point-du-Jour (R. du)	20
Pont-Neuf (R. du)	23
Raspail (R.)	24
République (Pl. de la)	25
Rochers-St-Jean (R. des)	27
Rosette (R.)	28
Rousseau (R. Jean-J.)	29
Tanneurs (R. des)	31
Victor-Hugo (R.)	33
Villers (Impasse de)	35

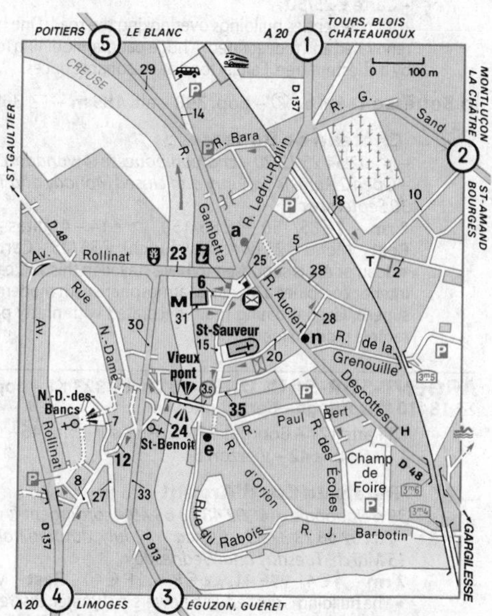

Manoir de Boisvillers without rest

11 r. Moulin-de-Bord – ✆ 02 54 24 13 88 – manoir.de.boisvillers@wanadoo.fr – Fax 02 54 24 27 83 – Closed 6 January-3 February **e**

16 rm – †€ 53/107 ††€ 57/107, ☕ € 10

◆ Fine 18C bourgeois residence in the centre of the old part of Argenton. Charming, personalised rooms, a pleasant, contemporary lounge and pretty leafy garden with a swimming pool.

Le Cheval Noir

rest, VISA

27 r. Auclert-Descottes – ✆ 02 54 24 00 06 – chevalnoirhotel@wanadoo.fr – Fax 02 54 24 11 22 – Closed Sunday dinner off season **n**

20 rm – †€ 46 ††€ 60, ☕ € 7,50 – ½ P € 57 – **Rest** – Menu € 21/29 – Carte € 25/35

◆ A former post house owned by the same family for over a century. The communal areas have been updated, as have the fresh and cosy rooms varying in size and décor. A traditional meal in a bright and modern dining room or in the flowered courtyard in summer.

La Source

9 r. Ledru-rollin – ✆ 02 54 24 30 21 – Fax 02 54 24 30 21 – Closed November and February school holidays, Tuesday evening and Wednesday **a**

Rest – Menu € 15 (weekday lunch), € 23/38 – Carte € 30/34

◆ Traditional, welcoming restaurant occupying an old post house. Two dining rooms, one rustic (exposed beams, rack and old wooden billiard table); the other is classic and quiet.

in St-Marcel 2 km by ① – **pop. 1 641 – alt. 146 m** – ✉ **36200**

Church ★ - Musée archéologique d'Argentomagus★ - Théâtre du Virou★.

Le Prieuré

– ✆ *02 54 24 05 19 – contact@restaurant-leprieure.com – Fax 02 54 24 32 28 – Closed 6-19 October, 22 February-9 March, Sunday dinner and Monday off season*

15 rm – †€ 45/50 ††€ 52/55, ☕ € 8 – ½ P € 48/57 – **Rest** – Menu € 17/50 – Carte € 25/50

◆ Two Seventies buildings overlooking the road. One has simple rooms, gradually being renovated and redecorated. A huge panoramic dining room with a garden-terrace shaded by a chestnut tree. Family food at reasonable prices.

in Bouësse 11 km by ② – **pop. 398 – alt. 185 m** – ✉ **36200**

Château de Bouesse

– ✆ *02 54 25 12 20 – chateau.bouesse@wanadoo.fr – Fax 02 54 25 12 30 – Open 2 April-1st January and closed Monday and Tuesday except 16 May-30 September*

8 rm – †€ 85/150 ††€ 85/150, ☕ € 14 – 4 suites – ½ P € 88/121

Rest – Menu € 23 (weekday lunch), € 35/45 – Carte € 54/61

◆ Joan of Arc is supposed to have stayed in this 13C castle set at the heart of a park. The interior combines a Medieval atmosphere with modern comfort. The room in the keep is superb. Elegant dining room decorated with pretty painted woodwork where you can sample modern food.

ARGENT-SUR-SAULDRE – 18 Cher – 323 K1 – pop. 2 502 – alt. 171 m – ✉ 18410 Dordogne-Berry-Limousin

12 **C2**

Paris 171 – Bourges 57 – Cosne-sur-Loire 46 – Gien 22 – Orléans 62 – Salbris 42 – Vierzon 54

Relais du Cor d'Argent with rm

39 r. Nationale – ✆ 02 48 73 63 49 – cordargent@wanadoo.fr – Fax 02 48 73 37 55 – Closed 7-12 July, autumn half-term holidays, 15 February-15 March, Tuesday and Wednesday

7 rm – †€ 41 ††€ 41, ☕ € 8 – ½ P € 40 – **Rest** – Menu € 17/58 – Carte € 37/61

◆ The building is decked with flowers in summer. Discreet dining rooms serving traditional cuisine based on the market produce available. Simple little rooms.

ARGOULES – 80 Somme – 301 E5 – pop. 335 – alt. 18 m – ✉ 80120 Northern France and the Paris Region

36 **A1**

Paris 217 – Abbeville 34 – Amiens 82 – Calais 93 – Hesdin 17 – Montreuil 21

Abbey★★ and gardens★★ of Valloires Northwest: 2 km.

Auberge du Coq-en-Pâte

37 rte de Valloires – ✆ 03 22 29 92 09 – Fax 03 22 29 92 09 – Closed 1st-8 April, 2-15 September, 6-26 January, Sunday dinner, Wednesday dinner and Monday except public holidays

Rest – *(number of covers limited, pre-book)* Menu € 20 – Carte € 27/44

◆ A charming little house near Valloires Abbey. The dining room is decorated with prints and paintings of animals. Tasty half-traditional, half-modern cuisine.

ARLEMPDES – 43 Haute-Loire – 331 F4 – pop. 114 – alt. 840 m – ✉ 43490 Lyon - Rhone Valley

6 **C3**

Paris 559 – Aubenas 67 – Langogne 27 – Le Puy-en-Velay 29

Site★★.

Le Manoir

rm

– ✆ *04 71 57 17 14 – Fax 04 71 57 19 68 – Open 15 March-25 October and closed Sunday dinner off season*

13 rm – †€ 33 ††€ 43, ☕ € 6,50 – ½ P € 42 – **Rest** – Menu € 21/40

◆ This country house with small rooms is situated in the heart of a picturesque village, dominated by a volcanic peak and a ruined castle. Classic menu of regional inspiration; stonework and a handsome fireplace in the dining room.

ARLES – 13 Bouches-du-Rhône – **340** C3 – **pop. 50 513 – alt. 13 m** – ✉ **13200**
Provence 40 **A3**

Paris 719 – Aix-en-Provence 77 – Avignon 37 – Marseille 94 – Nîmes 32

Office de tourisme, boulevard des Lices ✆ 04 90 18 41 20, Fax 04 90 18 41 29

Amphitheatre★★ - Théâtre antique★★ - St-Trophime cloister★★ and church★: portal★★ - Les Alyscamps★ - Palais Constantin★ Y **S** - Town hall: vestibule ★ vault Z **H** - Cryptoportiques★ Z **E** - Musée de l'Arles antique★★ (sarcophagus★★) - Museon Arlaten★ Z **M**[6] - Musée Réattu★ Y **M**[4] - Ruins of Montmajour abbey ★ 5 km by ①.

Plan on next page

Jules César

bd des Lices – ✆ 04 90 52 52 52 – contact@julescesar.fr – Fax 04 90 52 52 53 – Closed Saturday and Sunday from November to March Z **b**

50 rm – €130/250 €175/250, €23 – 1 suite

Rest ***Lou Marquès*** – *(closed Saturday lunch, Sunday dinner and Monday from 3 November to 13 March except public holidays)* Menu (€21), €28/60 – Carte €53/87

◆ Former Carmelite convent surrounded by a walled garden: the epitome of elegance and serenity. Beautiful antique furnished rooms, vaulted meeting rooms, cloister and chapel with a baroque altarpiece. Attractive terrace and southern flavours at the subtly modern Lou Marquès.

Nord Pinus rm,

pl. du Forum – ✆ 04 90 93 44 44 – info@nord-pinus.com – Fax 04 90 93 34 00 – Open 15 February-15 November Z **t**

25 rm – €120/160 €160/295, €20 – 1 suite

Rest – *(open 15 March-15 November and closed Monday and Tuesday)* Menu €35

◆ A veritable Arles institution with such illustrious guests as Cocteau, Picasso and Dominguin whose 'traje de luces' illuminates the bar. The decor, which is a combination of baroque and bull fighting, is a treat for the eye. A pleasant restaurant with an Art Deco touch, serving brasserie-style cuisine.

L'Hôtel Particulier rm,

4 r. de la Monnaie – ✆ 04 90 52 51 40 – contact@hotel-particulier.com – Fax 04 90 96 16 70 – Closed 18 November-26 December Z **d**

8 rm – €209/259 €209/259, €19 – 5 suites

Rest – *(dinner only) (residents only)* Menu €35/50

◆ Superb 18C mansion in the Roquette district. Fine interior combining old and new. Rooms with personal touches. Pretty courtyard garden, sauna, steam bath, etc. Dinner is made entirely from fresh produce.

D'Arlatan without rest

26 r. Sauvage, (near Place du Forum) – ✆ 04 90 93 56 66 – hotel-arlatan@wanadoo.fr – Fax 04 90 49 68 45 – Closed 5 January-5 February Y **f**

41 rm – €52/85 €85/155, €13 – 7 suites

◆ This graceful 15C residence, with 4C foundations, relives its past through exhibitions of archaeological remains. Decor with personal touches and fine antique furniture.

Mercure Arles Camargue rest,

av. 1e-Division-Française-Libre, (near the Palais des Congrés) – ✆ 04 90 93 98 80 – h2738@accor.com – Fax 04 90 49 92 76 X **t**

80 rm – €90/120 €100/130, €14

Rest – Menu (€18), €24 – Carte approx. €28

◆ Opposite the museum of ancient Arles, comfortable rooms with regional touches. Bar with wrought iron and southern colours. Good seminar facilities. Garden with water feature. Southern accents abound in the dining room and in the traditional cuisine.

Calendal without rest

5 r. Porte-de-Laure – ✆ 04 90 96 11 89 – contact@lecalendal.com – Fax 04 90 96 05 84 – Closed 4 January-4 February Z **s**

35 rm – €59/99 €59/129, €10 – 3 suites

◆ Delightful rooms in Mediterranean colours with a view of the ancient theatre, the bullring or the attractive garden. Tearoom. Provençal salads for summer lunchtimes.

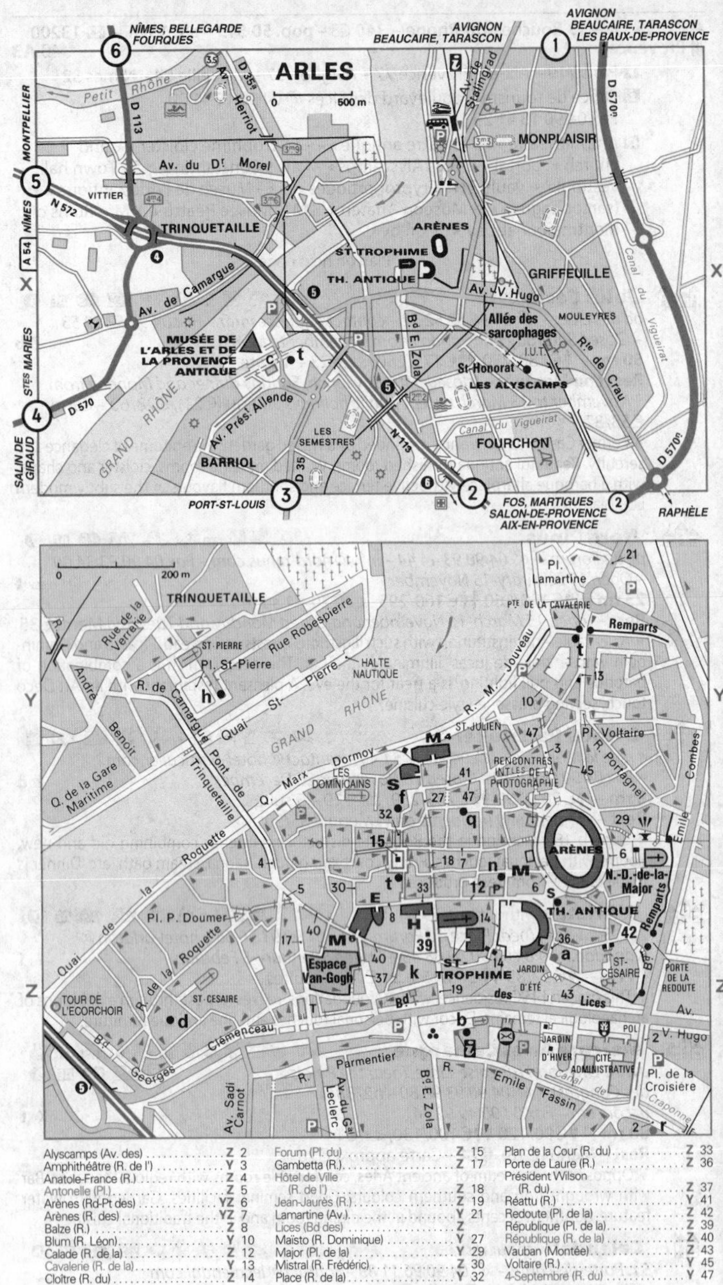

Alyscamps (Av. des)	Z 2	Forum (Pl. du)	Z 15	Plan de la Cour (R. du)	Z 33
Amphithéâtre (R. de l')	Y 3	Gambetta (R.)	Z 17	Porte de Laure (R.)	Z 36
Anatole-France (R.)	Z 4	Hôtel de Ville (R. de l')	Z 18	Président Wilson (R. du)	Z 37
Antonelle (Pl.)	Z 5	Jean-Jaurès (R.)	Z 19	Réattu (R.)	Y 41
Arènes (Rd-Pt des)	YZ 6	Lamartine (Av.)	Y 21	Redoute (Pl. de la)	Z 42
Arènes (R. des)	YZ 7	Lices (Bd des)	Z	République (Pl. de la)	Z 39
Balze (R.)	Z 8	Maïsto (R. Dominique)	Y 27	République (R. de la)	Z 40
Blum (R. Léon)	Y 10	Major (Pl. de la)	Y 29	Vauban (Montée)	Z 43
Calade (R. de la)	Z 12	Mistral (R. Frédéric)	Z 30	Voltaire (R.)	Y 45
Cavalerie (R. de la)	Y 13	Place (R. de la)	Y 32	4-Septembre (R. du)	Y 47
Cloître (R. du)	Z 14				

Mireille
2 pl. St-Pierre, (at Trinquetaille) – ✆ 04 90 93 70 74 – contact@hotel-mireille.com – Fax 04 90 93 87 28 – Closed 4 January-10 February Y **h**
34 rm – €69/150 €69/150, ☕ €13 – **Rest** – *(closed Monday lunch and Sunday)* Menu €22 (weekdays)/45 – Carte €34/53
◆ These two outlying houses stand on the right bank of the River Rhône. Stylish rooms in Provençal style. Small shop selling regional produce. Attentive hospitality. Pleasant pool-side terrace lined by mulberry trees. Classic menu.

Amphithéâtre without rest
5 r. Diderot – ✆ 04 90 96 10 30 – contact@hotelamphitheatre.fr – Fax 04 90 93 98 69
25 rm – €45/50 €49/92, ☕ €7 – 3 suites Z **n**
◆ This handsome 17C building is home to snug, revamped rooms, those in the adjoining townhouse are more spacious and comfortable. Attractive breakfast room.

Les Acacias without rest
2 r. de la Cavalerie – ✆ 04 90 96 37 88 – contact@hotel-acacias.com – Fax 04 90 96 32 51 – Open 16 March-25 October Y **t**
33 rm – €51/100 €51/100, ☕ €6
◆ Hotel with a cheerful pink facade at the foot of the Porte de la Cavalerie. Colourful and simply furnished rooms. Breakfast room brightened with a mural.

Muette without rest
15 r. des Suisses – ✆ 04 90 96 15 39 – hotel.muette@wanadoo.fr – Fax 04 90 49 73 16 – Closed 11-24 February Y **q**
18 rm – €45/54 €48/54, ☕ €8
◆ Attractive 12C facade overlooking a small square. Soberly Provençal rooms with exposed stone. Breakfast room adorned with bull-fighting photos.

Le Cilantro (Jérôme Laurent)
31 r. Porte-de-Laure – ✆ 04 90 18 25 05 – infocilantro@aol.com – Fax 04 90 18 25 10 – Closed 3-17 March, 2-17 November, 1st-18 January, Saturday lunch, Sunday and Monday Z **a**
Rest – Menu (€24), €28 (weekday lunch), €60/80 – Carte €61/66
Spec. Burger de foie gras aux pommes rôties (September to January). Arlequin d'écrevisses de Camargue sous rosace de navet (April to June). Cromesquis de cèpes au lard gras (September to December) **Wines** Costières de Nîmes, Les Baux de Provence.
◆ Behind the antique theatre and near the arenas, this unassuming establishment serves inventive cuisine in a modern, elegant setting. Pleasant summer terrace.

L'Atelier de Jean Luc Rabanel
7 r. des Carmes – ✆ 04 90 91 07 69 – jlr@cuisinetc.com – Closed Monday and Tuesday Z **k**
Rest – *(number of covers limited, pre-book)* Menu €42/65
Spec. Menu "Tapas". **Wines** Vin de pays des Bouches du Rhône
◆ Organic produce and vegetables from the cottage garden are used to create an original and subtle personalised cuisine, served as tapas. Contemporary bistro decor and friendly welcome.

Le Jardin de Manon
14 av. des Alyscamps – ✆ 04 90 93 38 68 – Fax 04 90 49 62 03 – Closed 1st-27 November, 21 February-10 March, Sunday dinner from October to March, Tuesday dinner and Wednesday Z **r**
Rest – *(closed Tues. evening and Wed.)* Menu €22/46 – Carte €33/50
◆ The contemporary style dining rooms of this restaurant offer regional, seasonal menus. Pleasant, peaceful and shaded terrace at the back.

Sambuc road 17 km by ④, D 570 and D 36 – ✉ 13200 Arles

La Chassagnette
– ✆ 04 90 97 26 96 – chassagnette@heureuse-camargue.com – Fax 04 90 97 26 95 – Closed 12-30 November, 5 January-15 February and Wednesday except 18 June-10 September
Rest – *(number of covers limited, pre-book)* Menu €34 (lunch), €59/80
◆ A finely restored Camargue farmhouse with lovely terrace. Provençal cuisine, featuring produce from the magnificent organic vegetable garden.

ARMBOUTS-CAPPEL – 59 Nord – 302 C2 – see Dunkerque

ARMOY – 74 Haute-Savoie – 328 M2 – see Thonon-les-Bains

ARNAGE – 72 Sarthe – 310 K7 – see le Mans

ARNAS – 69 Rhône – 327 H3 – see Villefranche-sur-Saône

ARNAY-LE-DUC – 21 Côte-d'Or – 320 G7 – pop. 1 829 – alt. 375 m – ✉ 21230

Burgundy-Jura 8 **C2**

Paris 285 – Autun 28 – Beaune 36 – Chagny 38 – Dijon 59 – Montbard 74 – Saulieu 29

Office de tourisme, 15, rue Saint-Jacques ✆ 03 80 90 07 55

Chez Camille

1 pl. Edouard-Herriot – ✆ 03 80 90 01 38 – chez-camille@wanadoo.fr – Fax 03 80 90 04 64

11 rm – €79 €79, €9 – ½ P €80 – **Rest** – Menu €20/86 – Carte €45/60

◆ Individual and cosy rooms, some with a small lounge, and others - on the second floor - have exposed beams. Dishes with a Burgundy flavour served in a winter garden-style dining room with a glass roof.

ARPAILLARGUES-ET-AUREILLAC – 30 Gard – 339 L4 – see Uzès

ARPAJON – 91 Essonne – 312 C4 – pop. 9 053 – alt. 51 m – ✉ 91290 18 **B2**

Paris 32 – Chartres 71 – Évry 18 – Fontainebleau 49 – Melun 45 – Orléans 94 – Versailles 39

Office de tourisme, place de l'Hôtel de Ville ✆ 01 60 83 36 51, Fax 01 60 83 80 00

de Marivaux Janvry Bois de Marivaux, Northwest: 17 km by D 97, ✆ 01 64 90 85 85.

Arpège without rest

23 av. J.-Jaurès – ✆ 01 69 17 10 22 – hotel.arpege@wanadoo.fr – Fax 01 60 83 94 20 – Closed 25 July-24 August

48 rm – €66 €73, €10

◆ This recently built, town centre hotel offers well soundproofed and well equipped, functional rooms. Photos by Doisneau on the walls.

Le Saint Clément (Jean-Michel Delrieu)

16 av. Hoche, (D 152) – ✆ 01 64 90 21 01 – le-saint-clement@wanadoo.fr – Fax 01 60 83 32 67 – Closed 5-12 May, 11-31 August, 22-29 December, Saturday lunch, Sunday dinner, Wednesday lunch and Monday

Rest – Menu €37/57 – Carte €77/88

Spec. Tarte fine aux cèpes (September to November). Saint-Jacques et parmentier de céleri (October to March). Tarte aux figues fraîches, glace figue (September-October).

◆ Neo-Classical building housing a sober and comfortable dining room; shaded summer terrace. Good classic cooking focusing on French produce.

ARPAJON-SUR-CÈRE – 15 Cantal – 330 C5 – see Aurillac

LES ARQUES – 46 Lot – 337 D4 – pop. 158 – alt. 254 m – ✉ 46250

Dordogne-Berry-Limousin 28 **B1**

Paris 569 – Cahors 28 – Gourdon 27 – Villefranche-du-Périgord 19 – Villeneuve-sur-Lot 58

St-Laurent church ★: Christ★ and Pietà★ - Frescoes★ of St-André-des-Arques church.

La Récréation

– ✆ 05 65 22 88 08 – *Open March-October and closed Wednesday and Thursday*
Rest – Menu € 31

◆ Pleasant, somewhat nostalgic restaurant established in an old village school. Classroom-dining room, schoolyard-terrace, and sculpted totem-chestnut tree in the playground. Updated menu.

ARRADON – 56 Morbihan – 308 O9 – see Vannes

ARRAS – 62 Pas-de-Calais – 301 J6 – pop. 40 590 – Built-up area 124 206 – alt. 72 m – ✉ 62000 Northern France and the Paris Region 30 B2

Paris 179 – Amiens 69 – Calais 110 – Charleville-Mézières 159 – Lille 54

Office de tourisme, place des Héros ✆ 03 21 51 26 95, Fax 03 21 71 07 34

d'Arras Anzin-Saint-Aubin Rue Briquet Taillandier, Northwest: 5 km by D 341, ✆ 03 21 50 24 24.

Grand'Place★★★ and Place des Héros★★★ - Town hall and belfry★ BY **H** - Former St-Vaast abbey★★: musée des Beaux-Arts★.

Plans on following pages

De l'Univers

rm, rest, VISA MC AE

3 pl. de la Croix-Rouge – ✆ 03 21 71 34 01 – univers.hotel@najeti.com – Fax 03 21 71 41 42 BZ **v**

38 rm – €82/123 €95/143, € 15 – **Rest** – Menu (€ 19), € 26, € 37/75 bi – Carte € 34/48

◆ Once a monastery, then a hospital and finally a hotel: this elegant, peaceful 18C property has personalised rooms, some with a Provençal atmosphere. Restaurant with pleasant decor. Contemporary cuisine served.

D'Angleterre without rest

VISA MC AE

7 pl. Foch – ✆ 03 21 51 51 16 – info@hotelangleterre.info – Fax 03 21 71 38 20 – Closed 23 December-2 January CZ **r**

20 rm – €85 €99/125, € 9

◆ A regional style brick building dating from 1929, near the TGV station. Spacious, well-equipped rooms with period furnishings. Lounge bar with a British atmosphere.

Mercure Atria

rm, VISA MC AE

58 bd Carnot – ✆ 03 21 23 88 88 – h1560-gm@accor.com – Fax 03 21 23 88 89 CZ **b**

80 rm – €74/106 €84/116, € 13 – **Rest** – *(closed lunch 20 July-25 August, Saturday lunch, Sunday lunch and lunch on public holidays)* Menu € 23 – Carte € 24/31

◆ Large brick and glass complex near the business district. Rooms renovated in a contemporary style. Light wood furniture and trendy colours. A simple restaurant with plants and floral decor.

Moderne without rest

rest, VISA MC AE

1 bd Faidherbe – ✆ 03 21 23 39 57 – contact@hotel-moderne-arras.com – Fax 03 21 71 55 42 – Closed 21December-4 January CZ **m**

50 rm – €66/100 €76/110, € 8,50

◆ Lovely building (1920) opposite the station and near the Grand Place. Rooms with simple, functional furniture, brightened with colourful soft furnishings.

Express By Holiday Inn without rest

VISA MC AE

3 r. du Dr Brassart – ✆ 03 21 60 88 88 – reservations@hiexpress-arras.com – Fax 03 21 60 89 00 CZ **y**

98 rm – €80/150 €80/150

◆ Modern building adjoining the railway station. Modern rooms with facilities well-suited to the needs of a business clientele.

Ibis without rest

VISA MC AE

11 r. de la Justice – ✆ 03 21 23 61 61 – h1567@accor.com – Fax 03 21 71 31 31 CZ **n**

63 rm – €56/75 €56/75, € 7,50

◆ Ideally located between two magnificent Arras squares. The rooms are quite small but functional and soundproofed.

ARRAS

Adam (R. Paul)	AY	2
Agaches (R. des)	BY	3
Albert-Ier-de-Belgique (R.)	BY	4
Ancien-Rivage (Pl. de l')	BY	5
Barbot (R. du Gén.)	BY	6
Baudimont (Rd-Pt)	AY	7
Carabiniers-d'Artois (R. des)	AY	8
Cardinal (R. du)	CZ	9
Delansorne (R. D.)	BZ	10
Doumer (R. P.)	BY	12
Ernestale (R.)	BZ	13
Ferry (R. J.)	AY	15
Foch (R. Maréchal)	CZ	16
Gambetta (R.)	BCZ	
Gouvernance (R. de la)	BY	18
Guy Mollet (Pl.)	CY	19
Kennedy (Av. J.)	AZ	24
Legrelle (R. E.)	BCZ	25
Madeleine (Pl. de la)	BY	28
Marché-au-Filé (R. du)	BY	30
Marseille (Pl. de)	BZ	31
Robespierre (R.)	BZ	34
Ronville (R.)	CZ	35
Ste-Claire (R.)	AZ	37
Ste-Croix (R.)	CY	39
St-Aubert (R.)	BY	
Strasbourg (Bd de)	CZ	42
Taillerie (R. de la)	CY	43
Teinturiers (R. des)	BY	45
Théâtre (Pl. et R.)	BZ	47
Verdun (Cours de)	AZ	49
Victor-Hugo (Pl.)	AZ	51
Wacquez-Glasson (R.)	CZ	52
Wetz-d'Amain (Pl. du)	BY	53
29-Juillet (R. du)	BY	54
33e (Pl. du)	BY	55

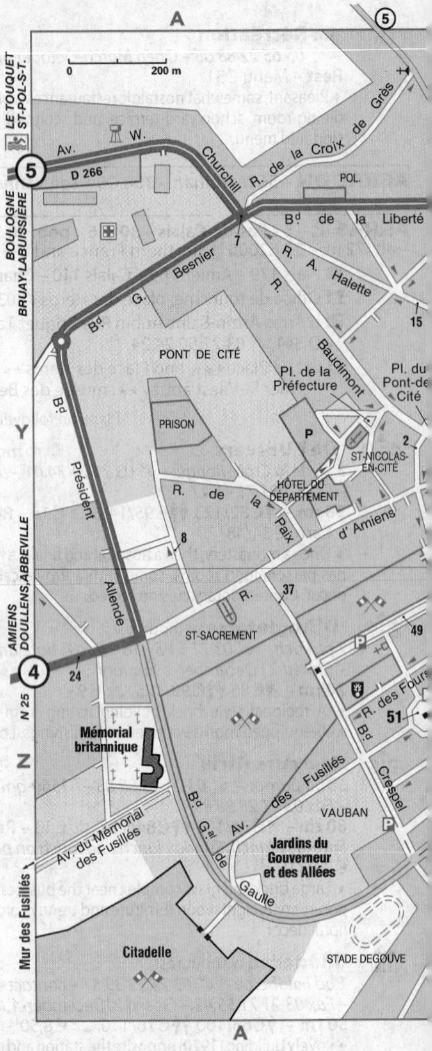

3 Luppars without rest

49 Grand'Place – ✆ 03 21 60 02 03 – contact3.luppars@wanadoo.fr – Fax 03 21 24 24 80 CY **r**

42 rm – €55 €70, €8

◆ The oldest building in Arras (1467, a superb Gothic facade) with simple rooms; those at the rear are quieter.

La Corne d'Or without rest

1 pl. Guy-Mollet – ✆ 03 21 58 85 94 – franck@lamaisondhotes.com CY **a**

3 rm – €64/77 €77/93, €7 – 2 suites

◆ Savour the romantic atmosphere and refined decor of this private mansion remodelled in the 18C. Choice of classic or contemporary bedrooms, plus attic-style loft rooms and superb cellars.

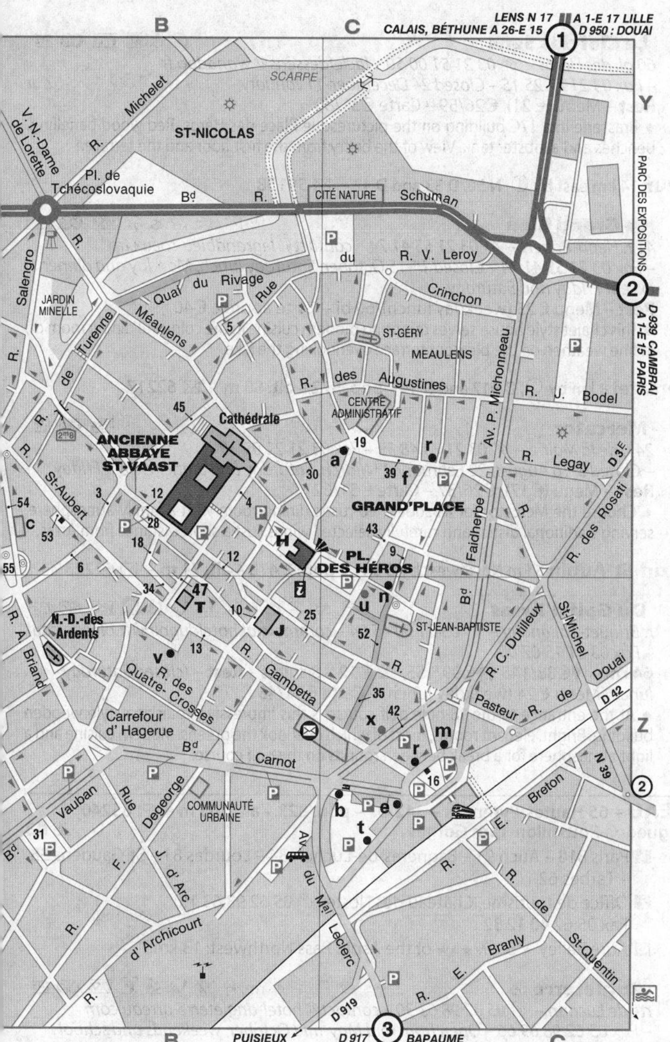

La Faisanderie VISA MC AE D

45 Grand'Place – ✆ 03 21 48 20 76 – la-faisanderie@wanadoo.fr – Fax 03 21 50 89 18 – Closed 4-18 August, 23 February-9 March, Sunday dinner, Monday and dinner on public holidays CY **f**

Rest – Menu € 23/62 – Carte € 42/85

◆ A 17C house, on the sumptuous square, with a fine cellar whose imposing stone columns support an old brick vaulted ceiling. Up-to-date cuisine.

La Coupole d'Arras VISA MC AE

26 bd de Strasbourg – ✆ 03 21 71 88 44 – lacoupoledarras@orange.fr – Fax 03 21 71 52 46 – Closed Sunday dinner from November to Easter CZ **x**

Rest – Menu (€ 29), € 34 – Carte € 28/64

◆ Large restaurant with a 1920s-type brasserie atmosphere: copies of Mucha, stained glass, Art Deco furniture, etc. Traditional dishes and good choice of home-made cakes.

XX **La Clef des Sens**

60 pl. des Héros – ✆ 03 21 51 00 50 – laclefdessens@wanadoo.fr – Fax 03 21 71 25 15 – Closed 24 December-11 January CZ **u**

Rest – Menu (€ 21), € 26/59 – Carte € 31/80

◆ Brasserie in a 17C building on the picturesque Place des Héros. Red wood panelling, benches and a lobster tank. View of the belfry from the first floor and the terrace.

in Rœux **14 km east by ①, N 50, D 33 and D 42 – ✉ 59158**

XX **Le Grand Bleu**

41 r. Henri-Robert – ✆ 03 21 55 41 74 – contact@legrandbleu-roeux.fr – Fax 03 21 55 41 74 – Closed 1st-15 October, Saturday lunch, Monday and dinner except Friday and Saturday

Rest – Menu € 25 (weekday lunch)/60 bi – Carte approx. € 40

◆ This chalet style house serves tempting modern cuisine in the colourful dining room or, in fine weather, on the pleasant terrace overlooking the lake.

in Mercatel **8 km by ③, D 917 and D 34 – pop. 572 – alt. 88 m – ✉ 62217**

X **Mercator**

24 r. de la Mairie – ✆ 03 21 73 48 33 – Fax 03 21 22 09 39 – Closed 3-16 August, 22 February-1st March, Saturday and dinner except Friday

Rest – Menu (€ 17), € 26/37 – Carte € 31/62

◆ Choose the Mercator for its sober neo-rustic dining room with a family atmosphere, serving traditional dishes and carefully-selected wines, just a short distance from Arras.

in Anzin-St-Aubin **5 km Northwest by D 341 – pop. 2 470 – alt. 71 m – ✉ 62223**

Du Golf d'Arras

r. Briquet-Tallandier – ✆ 03 21 50 45 04 – commercial.hoteldugolf@fr.oleane.com – Fax 03 21 15 07 00

64 rm – † € 88/145 †† € 99/155, ☕ € 12 – 8 suites – **Rest** – *(closed Saturday lunch)* Menu € 24 (weekday lunch) – Carte € 31/43

◆ At the entrance to the 18-hole golf course is this impressive Louisiana style wooden building. Bright, elegant rooms, most of which overlook the greens. Modern cuisine and a light atmosphere for a break between rounds on the golf course.

ARREAU – 65 Hautes-Pyrénées – 342 O7 – pop. 823 – alt. 705 m – ✉ 65240

Languedoc-Roussillon-Tarn Gorges 28 **A3**

Paris 818 – Auch 91 – Bagnères-de-Luchon 34 – Lourdes 81 – St-Gaudens 55 – Tarbes 62

Office de tourisme, Château des Nestes ✆ 05 62 98 63 15, Fax 05 62 40 12 32

Aure Valley ★ S - ✻★★★ of the Aspin Pass Northwest: 13 km.

Angleterre

rm,

rte de Luchon – ✆ 05 62 98 63 30 – contact@hotel-angleterre-arreau.com – Fax 05 62 98 69 66 – Open from mid May-mid October, weekends and school holidays from 26 December to 31 March and closed Monday in May-June and September

17 rm – † € 54/75 †† € 65/115, ☕ € 9 – ½ P € 68/92 – **Rest** – *(dinner only)* Menu € 20/38

◆ Old post house converted over the years into a hotel with character, in a small typical valley village. A lovely staircase leads to smartly renovated rooms. Traditional food and country-style setting, reviewed and updated in the restaurant. Cosy lounge-bar.

ARROMANCHES-LES-BAINS – 14 Calvados – 303 I3 – pop. 552 – ✉ 14117

Normandy 32 **B2**

Paris 266 – Bayeux 11 – Caen 34 – St-Lô 46

Office de tourisme, 2, rue du Maréchal Joffre ✆ 02 31 22 36 45, Fax 02 31 22 92 06

Musée du débarquement - La Côte du Bessin★ West.

La Marine ← Man - made port for disembarcation, rest,
1 quai du Canada – ✆ 02 31 22 34 19
– hotel.de.la.marine@wanadoo.fr – Fax 02 31 22 98 80
– Open 14 February-11 November
28 rm – †€ 61 ††€ 86, ☕ € 10 – ½ P € 68/90 – **Rest** – Menu € 22/39 – Carte € 36/64

◆ With the advantage of being situated on the coastline, this welcoming residence offers comfortable rooms a view of The English Channel. Pretty, modern décor in the restaurant and bay windows overlooking the waves.

in La Rosière **3 km Southwest by Bayeux road – ✉14117 Tracy-sur-Mer**

La Rosière without rest
14 rte de Bayeux – ✆ 02 31 22 36 17 – hotel.larosiere@wanadoo.fr
– Fax 02 31 22 19 33 – Open 15 March-10 November
24 rm – †€ 51/94 ††€ 51/94, ☕ € 8

◆ Away from the road, this welcoming hotel has functional rooms with soundproofing. Rooms in the annex are at ground floor/garden level.

ARS-EN-RÉ – 17 Charente-Maritime – 324 A2 – see Ile de Ré

ARTRES – 59 Nord – 302 J6 – see Valenciennes

ARVIEU – 12 Aveyron – 338 H5 – pop. 880 – alt. 730 m – ✉ 12120 29 D2

▶ Paris 663 – Albi 66 – Millau 59 – Rodez 31 – St-Affrique 47 – Villefranche-de-Rouergue 77

ℹ Syndicat d'initiative, Le Bourg ✆ 05 65 46 71 06, Fax 05 65 63 19 16

Au Bon Accueil
pl. du Centre – ✆ 05 65 46 72 13 – jean-pierre.pachins@wanadoo.fr
– Fax 05 65 74 28 95 – Closed 15 December-15 January
10 rm – †€ 42/46 ††€ 42/90, ☕ € 7 – ½ P € 42/43
Rest – Menu € 12 (weekdays)/34

◆ Situated on the main village square, the bar of this delightful inn is popular with the locals. Tastefully redecorated, well-kept and comfortable rooms. Simple traditional cuisine is served in this rustic restaurant as well as some regional dishes.

ARVIEUX – 05 Hautes-Alpes – 334 I4 – pop. 355 – alt. 1 550 m – ✉ 05350

French Alps 41 C1

▶ Paris 782 – Briançon 55 – Gap 80 – Marseille 254

ℹ Office de tourisme, la ville ✆ 04 92 46 75 76, Fax 04 92 46 83 03

La Ferme de l'Izoard
La Chalp, Route du Col – ✆ 04 92 46 89 00 – info@laferme.fr – Fax 04 92 46 82 37
– Closed April and 29 September-19 December
23 rm – †€ 60/161 ††€ 60/161, ☕ € 11 – 3 suites – ½ P € 59/109
Rest – *(closed Tuesday lunch and Thursday lunch during term time)*
Menu (€ 17), € 23/51 – Carte € 24/45

◆ Traditional farmhouse-style building. Spacious rooms with a balcony or South-facing terrace on the ground floor. Welcoming lounge decorated with local furniture. The restaurant offers a traditional menu with local specialities and grills.

ARZ (ÎLE) – 56 Morbihan – 308 O9 – see Île-d'Arz

ARZON – 56 Morbihan – 308 N9 – pop. 2 056 – alt. 9 m – ✉ 56640

Brittany 9 A3

▶ Paris 487 – Auray 52 – Lorient 94 – Quiberon 81 – La Trinité-sur-Mer 66 – Vannes 33

ℹ Office de tourisme, rond-point du Crouesty ✆ 02 97 53 69 69, Fax 02 97 53 76 10

◉ Tumulus de Tumiac or butte de César ✻★ East: 2 km then 30 mn.

at Port du Crouesty 2 km Southwest – ✉ 56640 Arzon

Miramar
– ✆ 02 97 53 49 00 – reservation@miramarcrouesty.com – Fax 02 97 53 49 99 – Open from March to September
112 rm – €185 €260, ☕ €19 – 12 suites
Rest *Salle à Manger* – Menu €50/90 – Carte €57/92
Rest *Ruban Bleu* – Menu €50 – Carte €40/66
♦ Anchored off the tip of the Rhuys peninsula, this hotel and thalassotherapy centre resemble an ocean liner from a distance. Spacious standard rooms with balcony. Attractive sea view and ocean liner decor at the Salle à Manger. Diet dishes at the Ruban Bleu.

Le Crouesty without rest
r. du Croisty – ✆ 02 97 53 87 91 – hotellecrouesty@wanadoo.fr – Fax 02 97 53 66 76 – Open February school holidays-15 November
26 rm – €69/81 €69/90, ☕ €8
♦ This hotel near the marina provides small, functional and soberly decorated rooms. Piano lounge adorned with a fireplace.

in Port Navalo 3 km West – ✉ 56640 Arzon

Grand Largue ← gulf of Morbihan,
à l'embarcadère – ✆ 02 97 53 71 58 – largueadam@wanadoo.fr – Fax 02 97 53 92 20 – Closed 12 November-25 December, 5 January-10 February, Tuesday except July-August and Monday
Rest – Menu €35/87
Rest *Le P'tit Zeph* – by the landing stage – Menu €28 – Carte €32/48
♦ This villa, proudly facing the entrance to the Morbihan bay, offers inventive seafood cuisine in its attractive dining room with a panoramic sea view. Fish and seafood bistro dishes chalked up on a slate.

ASNIÈRES-SUR-SEINE – 92 Hauts-de-Seine – 311 J2 – 101 15 – see Paris, Area

---

ASPRES-LES-CORPS – 05 Hautes-Alpes – 334 D4 – see Corps

ASTAFFORT – 47 Lot-et-Garonne – 336 F5 – pop. 1 880 – alt. 65 m – ✉ 47220 4 C2

Paris 674 – Agen 19 – Auvillar 29 – Condom 31 – Lectoure 20

Syndicat d'initiative, 13 place de la Nation ✆ 05 53 67 13 33, Fax 05 53 67 13 33

Le Square "Michel Latrille"
5 pl. Craste – ✆ 05 53 47 20 40 – latrille.michel@wanadoo.fr – Fax 05 53 47 10 38 – Closed 1st-26 January and Sunday except July-August
14 rm – €53 €63/140, ☕ €12
Rest – *(closed 28 April-5 May, 1st- 26 January, Tuesday lunch, Sunday dinner and Monday)* Menu (€26), €37/57 – Carte €57/97
Spec. Ravioli de langoustines au fumet de truffe. Suprêmes de pigeonneau rôtis, cuisses confites et risotto aux cèpes. Moelleux au café, glace café, sauce arabica.
Wines Vin de pays de l'Agenais, Buzet.
♦ Contemporary and antique furniture, bright colours and elegant detail. The rooms in these charming houses are full of character; two have been refurbished. A lovely dining room around a stunning arcaded patio and panoramic terrace. A rich wine list.

Une Auberge en Gascogne (Fabrice Biasiolo)
9 fg. Corné, (opposite the post office) – ✆ 05 53 67 10 27 – une-auberge-en-gascogne@wanadoo.fr – Fax 05 53 67 10 22 – Closed 1st-15 January, Sunday dinner and Monday lunch from October to May, Thursday lunch and Wednesday
Rest – Menu €23 (weekday lunch), €40/115 bi – Carte €41/49
Spec. Le petit-déjeuner Gascon. Ventrèche de thon du pays Basque. Agneau des Pyrénées (spring).
♦ The contemporary decor is the perfect foil for interesting and inventive cuisine based on local produce. Original sitting room, and quiet summer terrace in the inner courtyard.

ATTICHY – 60 Oise – 305 J4 – pop. 1 852 – alt. 73 m – ✉ 60350 37 C2

Paris 101 – Compiègne 18 – Laon 62 – Noyon 26 – Soissons 24

XX **La Croix d'Or** with rm

13 r. Tondu-de-Metz – ✆ 03 44 42 15 37 – lacroixdor60@aol.com – Fax 03 44 42 15 37

4 rm – ♦€ 35 ♦♦€ 42 – ½ P € 60 – **Rest** – *(closed Sunday dinner, Tuesday dinner and Monday)* Menu € 17, € 31/53

♦ Two regional-style houses opposite the town hall and around an enclosed courtyard. One offers a fresh, modern dining room while the other provides simple, practical rooms.

ATTIGNAT – 01 Ain – 328 D3 – pop. 1 924 – alt. 227 m – ✉ 01340 44 B1

Paris 420 – Bourg-en-Bresse 13 – Lons-le-Saunier 76 – Louhans 46 – Mâcon 35 – Tournus 42

XX **Dominique Marcepoil** with rm

481 Grande Rue, (D 975) – ✆ 04 74 30 92 24 – marcepoil@libertysurf.fr – Fax 04 74 25 93 48 – Closed 22 September-5 October, 9-22 February, Monday lunch and Sunday

11 rm – ♦€ 52 ♦♦€ 66, € 10 – ½ P € 70/75 – **Rest** – Menu € 30 bi/50 – Carte € 45/84

♦ Frogs' legs and Bresse chicken – the region's best on your plate! The house also offers a fine choice of more modern dishes. Quiet poolside rooms.

ATTIGNAT-ONCIN – 73 Savoie – 333 H4 – see Aiguebelette-le-Lac

AUBAGNE – 13 Bouches-du-Rhône – 340 I6 – pop. 42 638 – alt. 102 m – ✉ 13400

Provence 40 B3

Paris 788 – Aix-en-Provence 39 – Brignoles 48 – Marseille 18 – Toulon 48

Office de tourisme, avenue Antide Boyer ✆ 04 42 03 49 98, Fax 04 42 03 83 62

Souléia

4 cours Voltaire – ✆ 04 42 18 64 40 – contact@hotel-souleia.com – Fax 04 42 08 13 21

72 rm – ♦€ 69/84 ♦♦€ 69/84, € 8,50 – ½ P € 57

Rest – *(closed Saturday dinner, Sunday lunch and Friday)* Menu € 20 – Carte € 24/37

♦ Situated in the santon (clay figurines) capital, a modern hotel with functional rooms, some of which have a private terrace. Satellite TV. Brasserie overlooking the square on the ground floor; a panoramic restaurant (sun terrace) on the roof serves traditional cuisine.

in St-Pierre-lès-Aubagne 5 km north by D 96 or D 43 – ✉ 13400

Hostellerie de la Source without rest

– ✆ 04 42 04 09 19 – hoteldelasource@aol.com – Fax 04 42 04 58 72

26 rm – ♦€ 72/83 ♦♦€ 89/170, € 12

♦ A 17C residence with its own spring, in wooded grounds. Recently built extension. Well looked after rooms and handsome pool with a glass roof.

North 4 km by D44 and secondary road – ✉ 13400 Aubagne

XX **La Ferme**

La Font de Mai, chemin Ruissatel, (Chemin Ruissatel) – ✆ 04 42 03 29 67 – auberge-la-ferme@wanadoo.fr – Closed August, February holidays, Saturday lunch, Monday and dinner except Friday and Saturday

Rest – Menu € 50 – Carte € 47/85

♦ House typical of the region facing Mont Garlaban, much loved by Marcel Pagnol. Here copious market produce is served in the shade of an ancient oak or in a cosy, Provençal dining room.

AUBAZINE – 19 Corrèze – 329 L4 – pop. 732 – alt. 345 m – ✉ 19190
Dordogne-Berry-Limousin 25 C3

- Paris 480 – Aurillac 86 – Brive-la-Gaillarde 14 – St-Céré 50 – Tulle 17
- Office de tourisme, le bourg ✆ 05 55 25 79 93, Fax 05 55 25 79 93
- d'Aubazine Beynat Complexe Touristique Coiroux, East: 4 km, ✆ 05 55 27 25 66.
- St Etienne Cistercian Abbey★ : clocher (belltower)★, furniture★, tombeau de St-Étienne (Tomb of St Etienne)★★, armoire liturgique (liturgucal cabinet)★.

De la Tour
pl. de l'Église – ✆ 05 55 25 71 17 – hoteldelatour19@orange.fr – Fax 05 55 84 61 83 – Closed 2-20 January, Sunday dinner and Monday lunch except July-August

18 rm – †€ 48 ††€ 50, ☕ € 7 – ½ P € 58 – **Rest** – Menu (€ 18), € 21 (except Sunday lunch)/30 – Carte € 30/65

◆ Facing the abbey; an old house with character and a tower. Old rooms brightened with colourful wallpaper. Regional food served in rustic rooms decorated with copper and pewter ornaments.

AUBE – 61 Orne – 310 M2 – pop. 1 540 – alt. 230 m – ✉ 61270
Normandy 33 C3

- Paris 144 – L'Aigle 7 – Alençon 55 – Argentan 47 – Mortagne-au-Perche 32

Auberge St-James
62 rte de Paris – ✆ 02 33 24 01 40 – Fax 02 33 24 01 40 – Closed 11-28 August, Sunday dinner, Tuesday dinner and Wednesday

Rest – Menu € 16/30 – Carte € 26/39

◆ A simple, pleasant address set in the village where the countess of Ségur lived. The menu is made up of tasty little dishes from various regions of France.

AUBENAS – 07 Ardèche – 331 I6 – pop. 11 018 – alt. 330 m – ✉ 07200
Lyon - Rhone Valley 44 A3

- Paris 627 – Alès 76 – Montélimar 41 – Privas 32 – Le Puy-en-Velay 91
- Office de tourisme, 4, boulevard Gambetta ✆ 04 75 89 02 03, Fax 04 75 89 02 04
- Site★ - Façade★ of the château.

Plan on next page

Ibis without rest
rte de Montélimar – ✆ 04 75 35 44 45 – Fax 04 75 93 01 01

43 rm – †€ 67/75 ††€ 67/75, ☕ € 8

◆ Situated on the Southern outskirts of the town, this Ibis hotel has rooms in line with the chain's standards.

Le Fournil
34 r. 4-Septembre – ✆ 04 75 93 58 68 – Fax 04 75 93 58 68 – Closed 24 June-7 July, autumn half-term holidays, January, Sunday and Monday Y s

Rest – Menu € 21/40 – Carte € 26/47

◆ In a small street in the old town, this ancient house has a smart, vaulted dining room. Tasty, classic food and pretty terrace in the courtyard.

Le Coyote
13 bd Mathon – ✆ 04 75 35 01 28 – Fax 04 75 35 01 28 – Closed 1st-10 July, Sunday and Monday Y e

Rest – *(number of covers limited, pre-book)* Menu (€ 15), € 19/30 – Carte € 23/40

◆ No-frills decor at this unpretentious neighbourhood restaurant, prized by regulars for its tasty traditional dishes based on market produce.

AUBENAS

Béranger de la Tour (R.) . . . . Y 2
Bernardy (R. de) . . . . YZ 3
Bouchet (R. Auguste) . . . . Y 4
Champalbert (R.) . . . . Y 5
Cordeliers (R. des) . . . . Y 6
Couderc (R. G.) . . . . Z 7
Delichères (R.) . . . . Y 8
Gambetta (Bd) . . . . Z
Gaulle (Pl. Gén.-de) . . . . Z 9
Grand'Rue . . . . Y 10
Hoche (R.) . . . . Z 12
Hôtel de Ville (Pl.) . . . . Y 13
Jeanne d'Arc (Pl.) . . . . YZ 16
Jean-Jaurès (R.) . . . . Y 15
Jourdan (R.) . . . . Y 17
Laprade (Bd C.) . . . . Z 18
Lésin-Lacoste (R.) . . . . Y 19
Montlaur (R.) . . . . Y 21
Nationale (R.) . . . . Y 22
Parmentier (Pl.) . . . . Y 24
Radal (R.) . . . . Z 25
République (R. de la) . . . . Y 26
Réservoirs (R. des) . . . . Y 27
Roure (Pl. Jacques) . . . . Y 29
St-Benoît (Rampe) . . . . Y 30
Silhol (R. Henri) . . . . Y 32
Vernon (Bd de) . . . . Z 33
4-Septembre (R.) . . . . Y 35

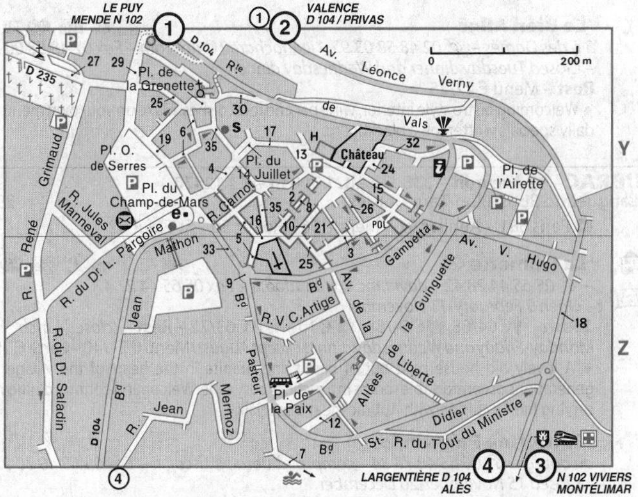

AUBETERRE-SUR-DRONNE - 16 Charente - 324 L8 - pop. 365 - alt. 72 m - ✉ 16390 Atlantic Coast 39 **C3**

▶ Paris 494 – Angoulême 48 – Bordeaux 90 – Périgueux 54

Office de tourisme, place du Château ✆ 05 45 98 57 18, Fax 05 45 98 54 13

d'Aubeterre Saint-Séverin Le Manoir de Longeveau, Northeast: 7 km by D 17 and D 78, ✆ 05 45 98 55 13.

Église monolithe★★.

Hostellerie du Périgord

rm, VISA

– ✆ 05 45 98 50 46 – hpmorel@aol.com – Fax 05 45 98 50 46 – Closed 18-31 January
12 rm – €46 €69, €7 – ½ P €65 – **Rest** – *(closed Sunday dinner and Monday)* Menu €17 (weekday lunch), €31/41

◆ A successful facelift for this small, family-run hotel at the foot of the famous village. Discreetly contemporary, well-soundproofed and well-maintained rooms. The restaurant offers a menu that is part classic, part modern. Pleasant veranda facing the garden and pool.

AUBIGNY-SUR-NÈRE - 18 Cher - 323 K2 - pop. 5 907 - alt. 180 m - ✉ 18700 Dordogne-Berry-Limousin 12 **C2**

▶ Paris 180 – Orléans 67 – Bourges 48 – Cosne-sur-Loire 41 – Gien 30 – Salbris 32 – Vierzon 44

Office de tourisme, 1, rue de l'Église ✆ 02 48 58 40 20, Fax 02 48 58 40 20

La Chaumière

rest, VISA

2 r. Paul-Lasnier – ✆ 02 48 58 04 01 – lachaumiere.hotel@wanadoo.fr – Fax 02 48 58 10 31 – Closed 11-25 August, 16 February-15 March and Sunday dinner except July-August and public holidays
11 rm – €54/68 €69/100, €8 – ½ P €62/77 – **Rest** – *(closed Sunday dinner and Monday except dinner in July-August and public holidays)*
Menu €19/54 – Carte €34/48

◆ Painstakingly maintained old building with comfortable bedrooms (wood and stone, personal touches), plus two attractive rustic dining rooms serving traditional cuisine.

Villa Stuart

12 av. de Paris – ✆ 02 48 58 93 30 – villastuart@wanadoo.fr

4 rm – € 60/70 € 70/80 – **Table d'hôte** – Menu € 25 bi

◆ This elegant residence is the perfect place for a pleasant stay. Four light and spacious guestrooms, each decorated along a particular theme (travel, art, history etc). Food enthusiasts will love this guest house, where the owner makes his own jams and run cookery classes.

Le Bien Aller

3 r. des Dames – ✆ 02 48 58 03 92 – jeanachard2@aol.com – Fax 02 48 58 00 34 – Closed Tuesday dinner and Wednesday dinner

Rest – Menu € 22/25

◆ Welcoming bistro style interior, wine bar and local dishes. Make up your own menu from daily specials written on a blackboard.

AUBRAC – 12 Aveyron – 338 J3 – alt. 1 300 m – ✉ 12470

Languedoc-Roussillon-Tarn Gorges 29 **D1**

Paris 581 – Aurillac 97 – Mende 66 – Rodez 56 – St-Flour 62

La Dômerie

– ✆ 05 65 44 28 42 – david.mc@wanadoo.fr – Fax 05 65 44 21 47 – Open 9 February-11 November

25 rm – € 64/88 € 64/88, € 10 – ½ P € 63/72 – **Rest** – *(closed lunch Monday-Friday and Wednesday dinner except August)* Menu € 21/40 – Carte € 29/51

◆ A lovely old house built out of basalt and granite in the heart of the village. Two generations of comfortable rooms in a rustic or cosy style. Welcoming country dining room serving family cuisine with Aubrac meat a speciality.

Catherine Painvin

au bourg – ✆ 05 65 48 78 84 – comptoir.aubrac@tiscali.fr – Fax 05 65 48 78 92 – Closed 15 November-20 December

5 rm – € 220/275 € 220/585 – **Table d'hôte** – Menu € 35 bi

◆ This unexpected address in the centre of Aubrac houses superb rooms decorated with furniture, objects and fabrics brought back from either India or Mongolia. There is also a home decoration shop and wine bar for testing local produce.

AUBUSSON – 23 Creuse – 325 K5 – pop. 4 662 – alt. 440 m – ✉ 23200

Dordogne-Berry-Limousin 25 **C2**

Paris 387 – Clermont-Ferrand 91 – Guéret 41 – Limoges 89 – Montluçon 64

Office de tourisme, rue Vieille ✆ 05 55 66 32 12, Fax 05 55 83 84 51

Musée départemental de la Tapisserie★ (Jean-Lurçat Cultural Centre).

AUBUSSON

Chapitre (R. du) 2
Chateaufavier (R.) 4
Dayras (Pl. M.) 5
Déportés (R. des) 7
Espagne (Pl. Gén.) 8
Fusillés (R. des) 10
Iles (Quai des) 12
Libération (Pl. de la) 15
Lissiers (Av. des) 16
Lurçat (Pl. J.) 18
Marché (Pl. du) 20
République (Av.) 23
St-Jean (R.) 24
Terrade (Pont de la) 27
Vaveix (R.) 29
Vieille (R.) 30

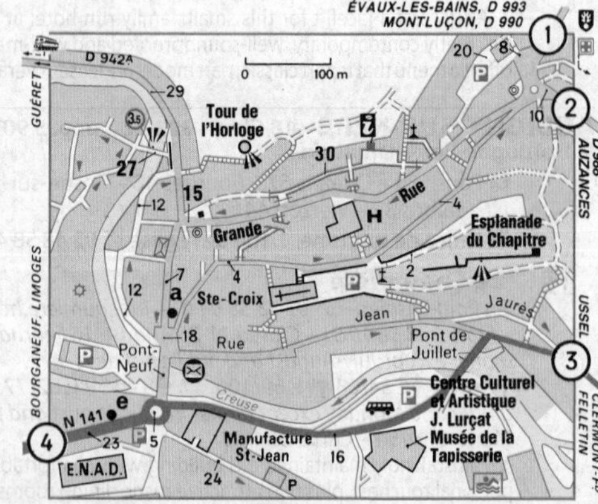

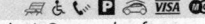

Villa Adonis without rest

14 av. de la République – ✆ 05 55 66 46 00 – villaadonis@wanadoo.fr – Fax 05 55 66 17 90 – Closed 30 December-2 January e

10 rm – 🚹€ 52 🚹🚹€ 52/57, ☕ € 7

◆ The beautiful reception hall sets the tone for this hotel with attractive bedrooms that combine modern comforts and cosy contemporary decor. Superb garden.

Le France

6 r. des Déportés – ✆ 05 55 66 10 22 – hotel.lefranceaubusson@wanadoo.fr – Fax 05 55 66 88 64 – **21 rm** – 🚹€ 59 🚹🚹€ 115, ☕ € 12 – ½ P € 60/88

Rest – *(closed Sunday dinner from 11 November to 16 March)* Menu € 22/40 – Carte € 25/49 a

◆ An 18C house between the River Creuse and the old centre with tastefully decorated guestrooms (antique furniture and carefully chosen fabrics) that are gradually being renovated. Elegant dining room and pretty summer terrace in the inside courtyard.

AUCH Ⓟ – 32 Gers – 336 F8 – pop. 21 838 – alt. 169 m – ✉ 32000

Languedoc-Roussillon-Tarn Gorges 28 **B2**

- Paris 713 – Agen 74 – Bordeaux 205 – Tarbes 74 – Toulouse 79
- Office de tourisme, 1, rue Dessoles ✆ 05 62 05 22 89, Fax 05 62 05 92 04
- d'Auch-EmbatsWest: 5 km by D 924, ✆ 05 62 61 10 11 ;
- de Gascogne Masseube Les Stournes, South: 25 km, ✆ 05 62 66 03 10.
- Ste-Marie cathedral ★★: stalls★★★, stained-glass windows★★.

AUCH

Alsace (Av. d') . . . . . BY 2
Caillou (Pl. du) . . . . . AZ 4
Caumont (R.) . . . . . AZ 5
Convention (R. de la) . . . . . AZ 7
Daumesnil (R.) . . . . . BY 9
David (Pl. J.) . . . . . AY 8
Dessoles (R.) . . . . . AY 12
Espagne (R.) . . . . . AZ 13
Fabre d'Églantine (R.) . . . . . AZ 14
Gambetta (R.) . . . . . AY
Lagarrasic (Allées) . . . . . ABZ 17
Lamartine (R.) . . . . . AY 15
Lartet (R. Ed.) . . . . . AZ 16
Lissagaray (Q.) . . . . . BYZ 18
Marceau (R.) . . . . . BY 19
Marne (Av. de la) . . . . . BY 22
Montebello (R.) . . . . . BZ 23
Pasteur (R.) . . . . . BZ 25
Pont-National (R. du) . . . . . AZ 27
Pouy (R. du) . . . . . BY 28
Prieuré (Pt du) . . . . . AZ 29
Rabelais (R.) . . . . . BZ 31
République (Pl. de la) . . . . . AZ 33
Rousseau (R. A.) . . . . . AZ 35
Salleneuve (R.) . . . . . AY 38
Somme (R. de la) . . . . . BY 40

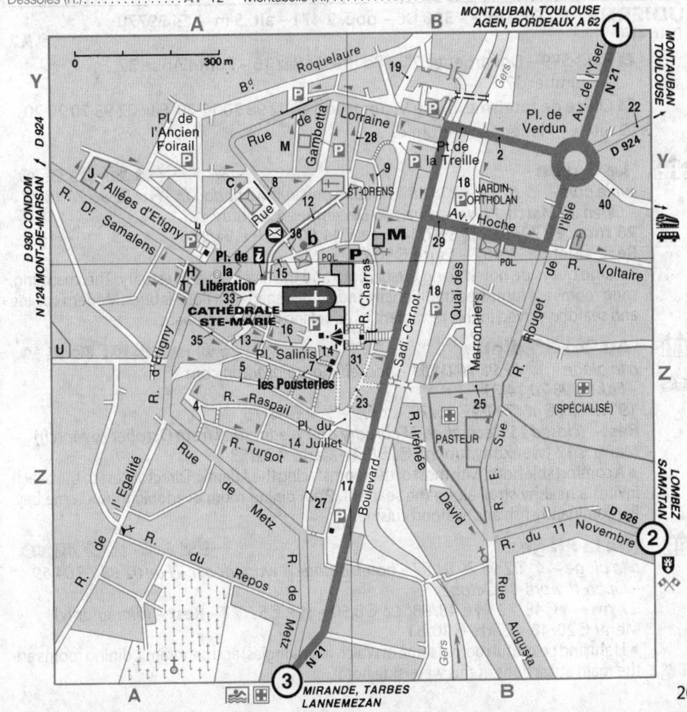

La Table d'Oste

7 r. Lamartine – ✆ 05 62 05 55 62 – latabledoste@hotmail.fr – Fax 05 62 05 55 62 – Closed 9-23 March, 7-16 June, 8-17 November, Saturday dinner in summer, Sunday and Monday lunch AY **b**

Rest – *(number of covers limited, pre-book)* Menu € 16/24 – Carte € 24/45

◆ Local specialities to be enjoyed in a small, rustic dining room (exposed beams, antique knick-knacks...) or on the summer terrace overlooking the street.

Agen road 7 km by ① – ✉ 32810 Montaux-les-Créneaux

Le Papillon

N 21 – ✆ 05 62 65 51 29 – lepapillon@wanadoo.fr – Fax 05 62 65 54 33 – Closed 25 August-8 September, 16 February-2 March, Sunday dinner and Monday

Rest – Menu € 17 (weekdays)/42 – Carte € 35/48

◆ New building away from the main road. The dining room is bright and decorated with paintings opening onto a pretty shady terrace. Classic food.

AUDERVILLE – 50 Manche – 303 A1 – pop. 283 – alt. 55 m – ✉ 50440

Normandie Cotentin 32 **A1**

Paris 382 – Caen 149 – Saint-Lô 113 – Cherbourg 29 – Équeurdreville-Hainneville 25

Office de tourisme, gare Maritime ✆ 02 33 04 50 26

Auberge de Goury

Port de Goury – ✆ 02 33 52 77 01 – auberge-de-goury@hotmail.fr – Fax 02 33 08 14 37 – Closed January and Monday in August

Rest – Menu € 16 (weekday lunch), € 25/59 – Carte € 23/82

◆ This rustic, granite building was once used as a store for goods smuggled between France and the Channel Islands. Fish and seafood on the menu. Terrace.

AUDIERNE – 29 Finistère – 308 D6 – pop. 2 471 – alt. 5 m – ✉ 29770

Brittany 9 **A2**

Paris 599 – Douarnenez 21 – Pointe du Raz 16 – Pont-l'Abbé 32 – Quimper 37

Office de tourisme, 8, rue Victor Hugo ✆ 02 98 70 12 20, Fax 02 98 70 20 20

Site★ - Planète Aquarium★★.

Le Goyen

sur le port – ✆ 02 98 70 08 88 – hotel.le.goyen@wanadoo.fr – Fax 02 98 70 18 77 – Open 20 March-11 November, 30 December-4 January

26 rm – €79/101 €87/147, ☕ €11,50 – ½ P €94/136

Rest – Menu € 25/57 – Carte € 50/65

◆ Large quayside hotel facing the harbour and the River Goyen's estuary. The charming, snug rooms are furnished traditionally and embellished with floral fabrics. Modern cuisine and seafood served in this restaurant overlooking the fishing boats.

Au Roi Gradlon

rest,

à la plage – ✆ 02 98 70 04 51 – accueil@auroigradlon.com – Fax 02 98 70 14 73

19 rm – €46/79 €46/79, ☕ €9 – ½ P €68/76

Rest – *(closed 15 December-7 February and Wednesday from October to March)* Menu € 17 (weekday lunch), € 25/54 – Carte € 32/53

◆ A comfortable hotel with most of the rooms facing the Atlantic. Direct access to the beach invites a healthy stroll along the seafront. Plain dining room overlooking Audierne bay. Predominantly fish and seafood cuisine.

De la Plage

à la plage – ✆ 02 98 70 01 07 – hotel.laplage@wanadoo.fr – Fax 02 98 75 04 69 – Open 1st April-31 October

22 rm – €48/72 €48/88, ☕ €8,50 – ½ P €57/77 – **Rest** – *(dinner only)* Menu € 20/48 – Carte € 30/51

◆ Light and colourful rooms (some of which have loggias) and panoramic dining rooms are the main attractions of this waterside hotel.

Manoir de Suguensou without rest
at 2 km on Pont-Croix road – ✆ 02 98 70 07 23 – suguensou@wanadoo.fr – Fax 02 98 70 07 23 – Closed 10 November-5 January
4 rm – €55/65 €55/65
◆ A pretty lane leads to this small 19C manor with a wild, pretty garden. Attractive lounges, large guestrooms and a family atmosphere.

L'Iroise
8 quai Camille-Pelletan – ✆ 02 98 70 15 80 – restaurant.liroise@wanadoo.fr – Fax 02 98 70 20 82 – Closed 5-31 January and Tuesday except 15 July-31 August
Rest – Menu € 19 (lunch), € 25/79
◆ A summer terrace overlooking the quayside and the port lie before this dining room brightened with pastel tones and with exposed-stone walls. Modern dishes and seafood flavours.

AUDINCOURT – 25 Doubs – 321 L2 – pop. 15 539 – alt. 323 m – ✉ 25400

Burgundy-Jura 17 **C1**

Paris 476 – Basel 96 – Belfort 21 – Besançon 75 – Montbéliard 6 – Mulhouse 59
Sacré-Coeur church: baptistry ★ AY **B.**

See plan of Montbéliard urban area.

Les Tilleuls without rest
51 r. Foch – ✆ 03 81 30 77 00 – hotel.tilleuls@wanadoo.fr – Fax 03 81 30 57 20
47 rm – €48/60 €66/74, € 7,80 Y **s**
◆ The hotel is made up of an old restored house and bungalows with wood-panelled rooms. Garden adorned with a pergola. Comfortable and pleasant atmosphere.

in Taillecourt 1.5 km North, Sochaux road – pop. 743 – alt. 330 m – ✉ 25400

Auberge La Gogoline
23 r. Croisée – ✆ 03 81 94 54 82 – jacquesferrare@orange.fr – Fax 03 81 95 20 42 – Closed 26 August-23 September, February school holidays, Saturday lunch, Sunday dinner, Monday and Tuesday Y **k**
Rest – Menu € 30/58 – Carte € 43/59
◆ Protected from the shops by its garden, this cottage-like house sports a plush, comfortable, countrified interior. Classic cuisine and fine wine list.

AUDRESSEIN – 09 Ariège – 343 E7 – see Castillon-en-Couserans

AUDRIEU – 14 Calvados – 303 I4 – see Bayeux

AUGEROLLES – 63 Puy-de-Dôme – 326 I8 – pop. 889 – alt. 540 m – ✉ 63930

6 **C2**

Paris 411 – Clermont-Ferrand 61 – Montluçon 149 – Roanne 65 – Vichy 55

Les Chênes
rte de piboulet, 1 km west via D 42 – ✆ 04 73 53 50 34 – Fax 04 73 53 52 20 – Closed 30 June-13 July, 26 December-2 January, 16-22 February, Tuesday dinner except July-August, Sunday dinner, Monday dinner and Saturday
Rest – Menu (€ 11,50 bi), € 18/39
◆ Family inn housing a smart dining room that mixes rustic and modern styles. The appetising, traditional food focuses on local produce.

AUGERVILLE-LA-RIVIÈRE – 45 Loiret – 318 L2 – pop. 197 – alt. 100 m – ✉ 45330

12 **C1**

Paris 92 – Orléans 76 – Évry 59 – Corbeil-Essonnes 62 – Melun 52

Château D'Augerville rm, rest,
pl. du Château – ✆ 02 38 32 12 07 – reservation@chateau-augerville.com – Fax 02 38 32 12 15
38 rm – €135/450 €135/450, € 15 – 2 suites – **Rest** – Carte € 37/61
◆ Comfortable rooms designed by architect Patrick Ribes, magnificent 112 ha grounds and an 18-hole golf course – this medieval château is paradise for golfers. Handsome oak panelled dining room and concise modern menu.

AULLÈNE – 2A Corse-du-Sud – **345** D9 – **see Corse**

AULNAY – 17 Charente-Maritime – **324** H3 – **pop. 1 507** – **alt. 63 m** – ✉ 17470
Atlantic Coast 38 **B2**

Paris 424 – Angoulême 66 – Niort 41 – Poitiers 87 – La Rochelle 72

Office de tourisme, 290, avenue de l'Église ✆ 05 46 33 14 44, Fax 05 46 33 15 46

St-Pierre church ★★.

Du Donjon without rest
4 r. des Hivers – ✆ 05 46 33 67 67 – hoteldudonjon@wanadoo.fr – Fax 05 46 33 67 64
10 rm – €54/65 €54/75, €6,50
◆ A charming Saintonge house, not far from the church of St Pierre. Tasteful interior: old beams and stone, rustic furniture and modern comforts. Pretty garden.

AULNAY-SOUS-BOIS – 93 Seine-Saint-Denis – **305** F7 – **101** 18 – **see Paris, Area**

AULON – 65 Hautes-Pyrénées – **342** N7 – **pop. 84** – **alt. 1 213 m** – ✉ 65240 28 **A3**

Paris 830 – Bagnères-de-Luchon 44 – Col d'Aspin 24 – Lannemezan 38 – St-Lary-Soulan 13

Auberge des Aryelets
– ✆ 05 62 39 95 59 – philipperaffie@free.fr – Fax 05 62 39 95 59 – Closed 2-15 June, 10 November-19 December, Sunday dinner, Monday dinner and Tuesday except school holidays and Monday lunch
Rest – Menu €22/36 – Carte €20/42
◆ This dressed-stone house that also houses the town hall has been able to keep its rustic and authentic character. Regional cuisine, served in pleasant atmosphere. Flower-decked terrace.

AULUS-LES-BAINS – 09 Ariège – **343** G8 – **pop. 189** – **alt. 750 m** – **Spa : late April-late Oct.** – ✉ 09140 Languedoc-Roussillon-Tarn Gorges 28 **B3**

Paris 807 – Foix 76 – Oust 17 – St-Girons 34

Office de tourisme, résidence Ars ✆ 05 61 96 00 01

Garbet Valley ★ N.

Hostellerie de la Terrasse rm,
– ✆ 05 61 96 00 98 – jeanfrancois.maurette@wanadoo.fr – Fax 05 61 96 01 42 – Open 2 May-30 October
13 rm – €45/50 €50/65, €12 – ½ P €55/65 – **Rest** – *(open 2 June-29 September) (dinner only)* Menu €19/45
◆ Beyond the river crossed by a footbridge, a family ambiance in this house nearly a century old which offers simple rooms, some with terrace. A semi-rustic, semi-classic restaurant with a shaded terrace lapped by the River Garbet.

Les Oussaillès rm,
– ✆ 05 61 96 03 68 – jcharrue@free.fr – Closed 15 November-15 December
11 rm – €34/39 €45/56, €6,50 – ½ P €43/48 – **Rest** – *(dinner only) (residents only)* Menu €14
◆ Old stone house in the Ariège style flanked by an elegant little tower, in the centre of the spa. Some of the rooms overlook the garden. A bright modern dining room and terrace facing the mountain. Home cooking and friendly ambience.

AUMALE – 76 Seine-Maritime – **304** K3 – **pop. 2 577** – **alt. 130 m** – ✉ 76390
Normandy 33 **D1**

Paris 136 – Amiens 48 – Beauvais 49 – Dieppe 69 – Rouen 74

Syndicat d'initiative, rue Centrale ✆ 02 35 93 41 68, Fax 02 35 93 41 68

Villa des Houx
6 av. Gén.-de-Gaulle – ✆ 02 35 93 93 30 – contact@villa-des-houx.com – Fax 02 35 93 03 94 – Closed 1st January-10 February and Sunday dinner from 15 September to 15 May except public holidays
22 rm – €60/70 €65/95, €9 – ½ P €70/80 – **Rest** – *(closed Sunday dinner and Monday 15 September-15 May except public holidays)* Menu €23/50 – Carte €35/57
♦ This family establishment has a pretty, half-timbered façade. You will sleep the sleep of the just in these perfectly comfortable rooms. Dining room, veranda and summer terrace give onto the peaceful garden. Classic French cuisine inspired with touches of more rustic cooking.

AUMONT-AUBRAC – 48 Lozère – 330 H6 – pop. 1 031 – alt. 1 040 m – ✉ 48130 23 C1

Paris 549 – Aurillac 115 – Espalion 57 – Marvejols 25 – Mende 40 – Le Puy-en-Velay 90

Office de tourisme, rue de l'Église ✆ 04 66 42 88 70, Fax 04 66 42 88 70

Grand Hôtel Prouhèze
2 rte du Languedoc – ✆ 04 66 42 80 07 – prouheze@prouheze.com – Fax 04 66 42 87 78 – Closed 4-30 November and 19 January-12 February
24 rm – €50 €50/90, €13 – ½ P €90
Rest *Le Compostelle* – see restaurant listing
Rest – *(open 15 March-31 October and closed lunch except Saturday, Sunday and public holidays)* Menu €51/65
♦ A pleasant mix of colour and simplicity depicts the antique and contemporary lines of this family-run establishment on the station square. Tasty regional cuisine and fine Languedoc wines served in a warm decor.

Chez Camillou (Cyril Attrazic)
10 rte du Languedoc – ✆ 04 66 42 80 22 – chezcamillou@wanadoo.fr – Fax 04 66 42 93 70 – Open 1st April-31 October
38 rm – €48/67 €48/70, €9 – 3 suites – ½ P €55/86
Rest *Cyril Attrazic* – *✆ 04 66 42 86 14 (closed 15 November-15 December, 15 January-21 February, Sunday dinner and Monday except July- August)* Menu €18/75 – Carte €47/66
Spec. Bouchées de bœuf d'Aubrac comme un tartare. Tartelette aux cèpes de pays. Millefeuille au caramel salé.
♦ Slightly off the main road, two modern buildings in a wooded area. Spacious rooms, furnished in a rustic style. Bright, contemporary dining room in beige offering updated regional cuisine.

Le Compostelle – Grand Hôtel Prouhèze
– ✆ 04 66 42 80 07 – prouheze@prouheze.com – Fax 04 66 42 87 78 – Closed 4-30 November, 19 January-12 February, Monday dinner, Wednesday lunch and Tuesday from December to March
Rest – Menu €19/28
♦ Aligot, stuffed cabbage, tripe specialities... a resume of Aubrac on your plate! Provincial recipes honoured in this bistro with a very countrified charm.

AUNAY-SUR-ODON – 14 Calvados – 303 I5 – pop. 2 902 – alt. 188 m – ✉ 14260 Normandy 32 B2

Paris 269 – Caen 36 – Falaise 42 – Flers 37 – St-Lô 53 – Vire 34

Office de tourisme, place de l'Hôtel de Ville ✆ 02 31 77 60 32, Fax 02 31 77 65 46

St-Michel with rm
r. de Caen – ✆ 02 31 77 63 16 – saint-michel-aunay@wanadoo.fr – Fax 02 31 77 05 83 – Closed 5-25 November, 5-25 January, Sunday dinner and Monday except July-August and public holidays
6 rm – €42 €42, €7 – ½ P €45 – **Rest** – Menu €15/42 – Carte €34/49
♦ A discreet little family inn where traditional dishes are prepared with a regional touch. Comfortable, well-lit dining room. Simple, practical rooms.

AUPS – 83 Var – 340 M4 – pop. 1 903 – alt. 496 m – ✉ 83630

French Riviera 41 C3

Paris 818 – Aix-en-Provence 90 – Digne-les-Bains 78 – Draguignan 29 – Manosque 59

Syndicat d'initiative, place Frédéric Mistral ☎ 04 94 84 00 69, Fax 04 94 84 00 69

Des Gourmets

5 r. Voltaire – ☎ 04 94 70 14 97 – lesgourmetsaups@aol.com – Closed 23 June-9 July, 1st-17 December, Sunday dinner except July-August and Monday

Rest – Menu € 16/34 – Carte € 47/83

◆ In the village where Var's largest truffles market is held. Very simple rustic setting serving dishes with regional flavours.

in Moissac-Bellevue 7 km West by D9 – pop. 151 – alt. 599 m – ✉ 83630

Bastide du Calalou

rte d'Aups – ☎ 04 94 70 17 91 – info@bastide-du-calalou.com – Fax 04 94 70 50 11 – Closed 15 November-20 December

32 rm – †€ 77/208 ††€ 77/259, ☕ € 15 – ½ P € 79/193 – **Rest** – Menu (€ 22), € 28 (weekdays)/60 – Carte € 28/59

◆ Taste the good life of Haute-Provence: three lounges to relax in (piano bar, video room and library) and bedrooms furnished with care. Pleasant Provençal-style dining room, a flowery and shady terrace and local cuisine.

AURAY – 56 Morbihan – 308 N9 – pop. 10 911 – alt. 35 m – ✉ 56400 Brittany

9 A3

Paris 477 – Lorient 41 – Pontivy 54 – Quimper 102 – Vannes 20

☎ 3635 (0,34 €/mn)

Office de tourisme, 20, rue du Lait ☎ 02 97 24 09 75, Fax 02 97 50 80 75

Quartier St-Goustan★ - Promenade du Loch★ - St-Gildas church ★ - Ste-Avoye: Rood-screen★ and framework★ of the church 4 km by ①.

Plan on next page

Du Loch

2 r. Guhur, (The Forest) – ☎ 02 97 56 48 33 – contact@hotel-du-loch.com – Fax 02 97 56 63 55 – Closed 15 December-4 January e

30 rm – †€ 54/72 ††€ 59/72, ☕ € 8 – **Rest** – *(closed Saturday lunch and Sunday dinner from October to Easter)* Menu (€ 17), € 28/47 – Carte € 25/46

◆ Unusual modern architecture (1970s) surrounded by preserved forestland and on the banks of the Loch. Spacious, functional rooms. Classic dishes (seafood) served in a veranda-style dining room surrounded by greenery.

Closerie de Kerdrain

20 r. L.-Billet – ☎ 02 97 56 61 27 – closerie.kerdrain@wanadoo.fr – Fax 02 97 24 15 79 – Closed 5 January-10 February, Tuesday except dinner from Easter to November and Monday s

Rest – Menu € 25 (weekday lunch)/75 – Carte € 58/83

◆ A charming little Breton manor house nestling in a garden. Elegant, wood-panelled dining rooms and a pleasant terrace complement the appetising modern cuisine.

La Table des Marées

16 r. Jeu-de-Paume – ☎ 02 97 56 63 60 – info@latabledesmarees.com – Closed 15 October-15 November, Sunday except lunch in season, Saturday lunch and Monday

Rest – Menu (€ 20 bi), € 28/48

◆ The updated menu evolves depending on the catch of the day. The snug interior sports a blend of modern furniture with old stones and a hearth.

Chebaudière

6 r. Abbé-J.-Martin – ☎ 02 97 24 09 84 – Fax 02 97 24 09 84 – Closed 22-31 October, 9-20 February, Tuesday dinner, Sunday dinner and Wednesday n

Rest – Menu € 17/37 – Carte € 33/49

◆ A small, local restaurant serving dishes in keeping with current taste. Discreetly contemporary dining room, a place for painting exhibitions as well.

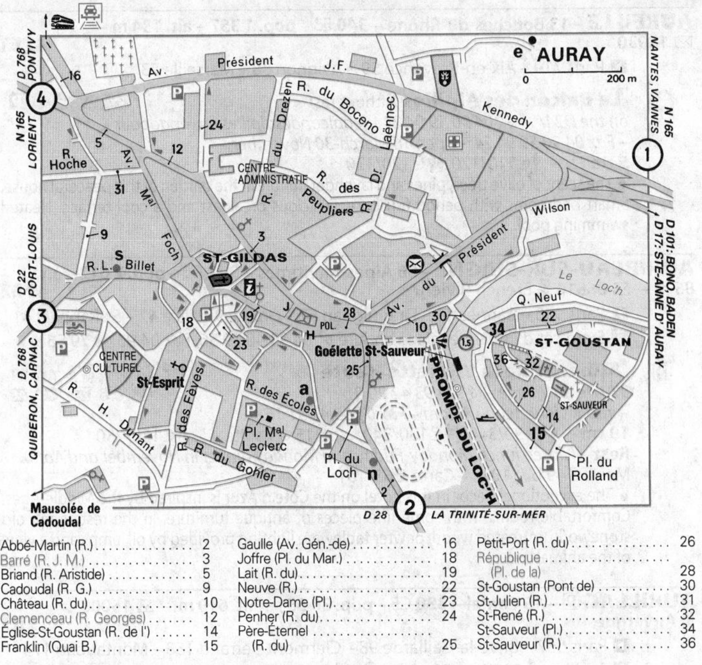

Abbé-Martin (R.)	2	Gaulle (Av. Gén.-de)	16	Petit-Port (R. du)	26
Barré (R. J. M.)	3	Joffre (Pl. du Mar.)	18	République (Pl. de la)	28
Briand (R. Aristide)	5	Lait (R. du)	19	St-Goustan (Pont de)	30
Cadoudal (R. G.)	9	Neuve (R.)	22	St-Julien (R.)	31
Château (R. du)	10	Notre-Dame (Pl.)	23	St-René (R.)	32
Clemenceau (R. Georges)	12	Penher (R. du)	24	St-Sauveur (Pl.)	34
Église-St-Goustan (R. de l')	14	Père-Éternel (R. du)	25	St-Sauveur (R.)	36
Franklin (Quai B.)	15				

at golf de St-Laurent 10 km by ③, D 22 and secondary road – ✉ 56400 Auray

Du Golf de St-Laurent rest, rest,

– *☎ 02 97 56 88 88 – hotel-golf-saint-laurent@wanadoo.fr – Fax 02 97 56 88 28 – Closed Christmas holidays*

42 rm – €62/159 €62/159, ☕ €13 – ½ P €66/114

Rest – *(closed Christmas holidays and February school holidays, Friday, Saturday and Sunday from November to February) (dinner only)* Menu €28/35 – Carte €31/44

◆ The golf course setting guarantees calm and quiet. Functional rooms with private terraces. Electronic golf course. Traditional food served in a dining room overlooking the swimming pool.

AUREC-SUR-LOIRE – 43 Haute-Loire – 331 H1 – pop. 4 895 – alt. 435 m – ✉ 43110

6 **D2**

Paris 536 – Firminy 11 – Le Puy-en-Velay 56 – St-Étienne 22 – Yssingeaux 32

Office de tourisme, Château du Moine-Sacristain ☎ 04 77 35 42 65, Fax 04 77 35 32 46

Les Cèdres Bleus rm, rest,

rte Bas-en-Basset – ☎ 04 77 35 48 48 – lescedresbleus@yahoo.fr – Fax 04 77 35 37 04 – Closed 2 January-2 February and Sunday dinner

15 rm – €42 €62/65, ☕ €8 – ½ P €60

Rest – *(closed Sunday dinner, Monday lunch and Tuesday lunch)* Menu €20 (weekdays)/80 – Carte €45/67

◆ Three wooden chalets with comfortably renovated rooms in a wooded park between the Gorges de la Loire and the Lac de Grangent. Enjoy ambitious traditional cuisine in the leafy surroundings of the panoramic dining room or the flower-decked terrace.

AUREILLE – 13 Bouches-du-Rhône – 340 E3 – pop. 1 357 – alt. 134 m – ✉ 13930 42 E1

Paris 719 – Aix-en-Provence 59 – Avignon 38 – Marseille 73

Le Balcon des Alpilles without rest
on the D24^A – ✆ 04 90 59 94 24 – lebalcondesalpilles@wanadoo.fr
– Fax 04 90 59 94 24 – Open 16 March-30 November
5 rm – €110/120 €120/130
◆ The scent of olive trees, pines and lavender mingle in the garden of this peaceful house. Smart bedrooms with period furniture. Delicious breakfast and a cool terrace. Heated swimming pool.

AURIBEAU-SUR-SIAGNE – 06 Alpes-Maritimes – 341 C6 – pop. 2 612 – alt. 85 m – ✉ 06810 French Riviera 42 E2

Paris 900 – Cannes 15 – Draguignan 62 – Grasse 9 – Nice 42 – St-Raphaël 41

Syndicat d'initiative, place en Aïre ✆ 04 93 40 79 56, Fax 04 93 40 79 56

Auberge de la Vignette Haute rm, VISA AE
370 rte du Village – ✆ 04 93 42 20 01
– info@vignettehaute.com – Fax 04 93 42 31 16
19 rm – €130/340 €130/340, €15 – 1 suite – ½ P €150/250
Rest – *(closed lunch Monday-Friday and Monday dinner in November and April)*
Menu €49 bi/110 bi – Carte €65/101
◆ The exceptional decor in this hotel on the Côte d'Azur is inspired by the Middle Ages. Comfortable rooms, with some fine pieces of antique furniture. In the restaurant: old stonework, untreated wood, pewter tableware lighting provided by oil lamps and a view of the animal pen

AURILLAC P – 15 Cantal – 330 C5 – pop. 30 551 – alt. 610 m – ✉ 15000 Auvergne 5 B3

Paris 557 – Brive-la-Gaillarde 98 – Clermont-Ferrand 158 – Montauban 174

Aurillac ✆ 04 71 64 50 00 by ③: 2 km.

Office de tourisme, place du square ✆ 04 71 48 46 58, Fax 04 71 48 99 39

18 de Haute-Auvergne Arpajon-sur-Cère La Bladade, Southwest by N 122 and D 153: 7km, ✆ 04 71 47 73 75 ;

9 de Vézac Aurillac Vézac Mairie, Southeast by D 990: 8 km, ✆ 04 71 62 44 11.

Château St-Étienne: muséum des Volcans★.

Plan on next page

Grand Hôtel de Bordeaux without rest VISA AE
2 av. de la République – ✆ 04 71 48 01 84
– bestwestern@hotel-de-bordeaux.fr – Fax 04 71 48 49 93
– Closed 20-28 December BY **r**
33 rm – €58/62 €80/135, €10
◆ Most of the rooms of this handsome early 20C building have been refurbished in a pleasant contemporary style; the others are also attractive (period or cane furniture).

Delcher rm, VISA AE
20 r. Carmes – ✆ 04 71 48 01 69 – hotel.delcher@wanadoo.fr – Fax 04 71 48 86 66
– Closed 13-21 April, 16 July-1st August and 21 December-5 January BZ **q**
23 rm – €42 €48, €7 – ½ P €46 – **Rest** – *(closed Sunday dinner)*
Menu (€12,50), €17/27 – Carte €21/28
◆ Unpretentious rooms, some with exposed beams. In one of the rooms and in the lounge there are murals by Danish artist Gorm Hansen, painted to cover his rent! Traditional no-fuss cooking served, in summer, on a courtyard-terrace.

Le Square rm, VISA AE
15 pl. du Square – ✆ 04 71 48 24 72 – hotel.le.square@cantal-hotel.com
– Fax 04 71 48 47 57 – Closed 5-21 July and Sunday dinner from November to March BZ **s**
18 rm – €46 €56, €7 – ½ P €42 – **Rest** – Menu €14 (weekdays)/38 – Carte €18/42
◆ A modern building near to the old chapel of a Franciscan nunnery. The very practical rooms are quieter to the rear. The restaurant offers traditional cooking complemented by regional dishes.

Angoulême (Cours d')	BY	2	Gambetta (Av.)	BZ	23	Pupilles de la Nation (Av. des)	AZ	33
Arbre Croumaly (R. de l')	AY	3	Gerbert (Pl.)	BY	24	République (Av. de la)	AZ	
Carmes (R. des)	BZ		Marchande (R.)	BY	25	St-Géraud (Pl.)	BY	34
Champeil (R. J.-B.)	BY	6	Maynard (R. F.)	AZ	26	St-Jacques (R.)	BY	35
Château St-Étienne (R. du)	BY	7	Monastère (R. du)	BY	27	Square (Pl. du)	BY	36
Consulat (R. du)	BY	8	Monthyon (Cours)	BY	28	Vaissière (R. Robert de la)	AY	37
Coste (R. de la)	BY	9	Mont Mouchet (R. du)	AZ	29	Vermenouze (R. Arsène)	BY	38
Duclaux (R. Émile)	BY	13	Noailles (R. de)	BY	30	Veyre (Av. J.-B.)	BY	39
Fargues (R. des)	BY	18	Pavatou (Bd du)	BY	31	14-Juillet (R. du)	BZ	40
Ferry (R. Jules)	BZ	19	Prés.-Delzons (R. du)	BY	32	139e-R.-I. (R. du)	BZ	44
Frères (R. des)	BY	22						

XX Quatre Saisons

10 r. Champeil – ✆ 04 71 64 85 38 – restaurant.les.4.saisons@orange.fr
– Closed 19-25 August, Sunday dinner and Monday BY **v**

Rest – Menu € 21/38 – Carte € 37/40

◆ On the ground floor of an old house, a contemporary and pleasant dining room embellished with greenery and a beautiful aquarium. Hearty traditional cuisine.

XX Reine Margot

19 r. G.-de-Veyre – ✆ 04 71 48 26 46 – alexandre.cayron@wanadoo.fr
– Closed 8-16 March, 13 July-4 August, 4-11 November, 2-6 January, Monday dinner, Saturday lunch and Sunday BZ **u**

Rest – Menu (€ 18), € 24/39

◆ Traditional repertoire served in dining rooms decorated with dark woodwork brightened with sketches depicting Queen Margot's amorous adventures. Ground floor brasserie.

in Arpajon-sur-Cère 2 km by ③ Rodez road (D 920) – pop. 5 545 – alt. 613 m – ✉ 15130

Les Provinciales

pl. du Foirail – ✆ 04 71 64 29 50 – info@hotel-provinciales.com – Fax 04 71 64 67 87 – Closed 27 December-5 January, Saturday lunch and Sunday from 15 September to 1st June

20 rm – †€ 46 ††€ 55/60, ☐ € 7,50 – ½ P € 46 – **Rest** – Menu € 13 (lunch)/16

◆ This slate-façaded building overlooks a tiny square. Quiet functional rooms. Pub-like bar area serving brasserie dishes. This slate-façaded building overlooks a tiny square. Quiet functional rooms. Pub-like bar area serving brasserie dishes.

in Vézac by ③, D 920 and D 990: 10 km – pop. 952 – alt. 650 m – ✉ 15130

Château de Salles

– ✆ 04 71 62 41 41 – chateaudesalles@wanadoo.fr – Fax 04 71 62 44 14 – Open 22 March-31 October

26 rm – †€ 98/110 ††€ 116/166, ☐ € 18,50 – 4 suites – ½ P € 76/106

Rest – Menu € 24/43 – Carte € 40/44

◆ 15C hilltop castle in a park. Pretty personalized rooms and two unusual split-level rooms; full range of leisure activities. Extensive view of the Cantal mountains. Countryside views from the veranda-dining room, plus a terrace overlooking the Vézac golf course.

AURON – 06 Alpes-Maritimes – 341 C2 – ✉ 06660 St-Etienne-de-Tinée

French Alps 41 **C-D2**

Paris 914 – Marseille 263 – Nice 93 – Borgo San Dalmazzo 206 – Dronero 228

Office de tourisme, Grange Cossa ✆ 04 93 23 02 66, Fax 04 93 23 07 39

Le Chalet d'Auron

– ✆ 04 93 23 00 21 – mail@chaletdauron.com – Fax 04 93 23 09 19 – Open 28 June-31 August and 6 December-5 April

15 rm – †€ 85/136 ††€ 136/357, ☐ € 15 – 2 suites – ½ P € 99/367

Rest – Carte € 42/62

◆ This chalet has been completely renovated in typical Alpine style, with a cosy lounge and guestrooms with individual touches. Terrace with views of the mountains. Swimming pool and hammam. Generous portions of fish and seafood are served in this restaurant. Wood decor in the dining room.

AUSSOIS – 73 Savoie – 333 N6 – pop. 628 – alt. 1 489 m – Winter sports : 1 500/2 750 m 11 – ✉ 73500

French Alps 45 **D2**

Paris 670 – Albertville 97 – Chambéry 110 – Lanslebourg-Mont-Cenis 17 – Modane 7

Office de tourisme, route des Barrages ✆ 04 79 20 30 80, Fax 04 79 20 40 23

Monolithe de Sardières★ Northeast: 3 km - Fortified site of Esseillon★ South: 4 km.

Du Soleil

15 r. de l'Église – ✆ 04 79 20 32 42 – hotel-du-soleil@wanadoo.fr – Fax 04 79 20 37 78 – Open 16 June-15 September and 17 December-21 April

22 rm – †€ 46/53 ††€ 65/75, ☐ € 9 – ½ P € 60/74 – **Rest** – *(dinner only) (pre-book)* Menu € 22/27

◆ The hotel's advantages include rooms with mountain views and many places to relax: the sauna, steam room, outdoor hot tub or projection room. For guests only, Savoyard specialities served in a colourful dining room.

Les Mottets

6 r. Mottets – ✆ 04 79 20 30 86 – infos@hotel-lesmottets.com – Fax 04 79 20 34 22 – Closed May and 1st November-14 December

25 rm – †€ 40/47 ††€ 59/78, ☐ € 9 – ½ P € 55/66 – **Rest** – Menu € 19/36 – Carte € 25/44

◆ 200m from the slopes, a chalet providing a beautiful view of the surrounding summits. Simple and functional rooms. Rustic dining room where regional specialities take pride of place.

AUTHUILLE – 80 Somme – 301 J7 – see Albert

AUTRANS – 38 Isère – 333 G6 – pop. 1 541 – alt. 1 050 m – Winter sports : 1 050/1 710 m 13 – ✉ 38880 French Alps 45 C2

Paris 586 – Grenoble 36 – Romans-sur-Isère 58 – St-Marcellin 47 – Villard-de-Lans 16

Office de tourisme, rue du Cinéma ✆ 04 76 95 30 70, Fax 04 76 95 38 63

La Poste VISA AE

– ✆ *04 76 95 31 03 – gerard.barnier@wanadoo.fr – Fax 04 76 95 30 17 – Open 10 May-14 October and 4 December-14 April*

29 rm – €56/80 €60/90, €8,50 – ½ P €60/73 – **Rest** – *(closed Sunday dinner and Monday except July-August and 4 December-14 March)* Menu €21/45 – Carte €34/52

◆ The same family has run this spruce hotel in the village since 1937. Progressively renovated rustic rooms. Oil paintings dotted here and there. Sauna and steam bath. Classic and regional dishes, a wainscoted interior and attractive table settings.

Les Tilleuls rest, VISA AE

la Côte – ✆ 04 76 95 32 34 – tilleuls.hotel@wanadoo.fr – Fax 04 76 95 31 58 – Closed 11-29 April, 27 October-20 November, Tuesday dinner and Wednesday off season and except school holidays

18 rm – €48/60 €55/74, €8,50 – 2 suites – ½ P €54/64

Rest – Menu (€15), €20/42 – Carte €30/43

◆ Near the centre of the resort in the Vercors nature park, this welcoming building offers practical and well-maintained rooms. Six have been renovated. Classic cuisine, game in season and the house speciality: caillette.

in Méaudre 5.5 km South by D 106c – pop. 1 039 – alt. 1 012 m – Winter sports : 1000/1600 m 10 – ✉ 38112

Office de tourisme, le Village ✆ 04 76 95 20 68, Fax 04 76 95 25 93

Auberge du Furon with rm VISA AE

– ✆ *04 76 95 21 47 – gaultier.rg@orange.fr – Fax 04 76 95 24 71 – Closed 25 November-10 December*

9 rm – €50/52 €50/54, €8 – ½ P €53/55 – **Rest** – *(closed Wednesday dinner, Sunday dinner and Monday except school holidays)* Menu €20/32 – Carte €22/31

◆ This small, alpine inspired chalet, set at the foot of the ski lifts, serves regional cuisine (fondues, raclettes). Snacks available. Rooms gradually refurbished in regional style.

AUTREVILLE – 88 Vosges – 314 D2 – pop. 124 – alt. 310 m – ✉ 88300 26 B2

Paris 313 – Nancy 45 – Neufchâteau 20 – Toul 24

Le Relais Rose VISA AE

24 r. Neufchâteau – ✆ 03 83 52 04 98 – loeffler.catherine@orange.fr – Fax 03 83 52 06 03

16 rm – €43 €64/78, €13 – ½ P €60/70 – **Rest** – Menu €16 (weekday lunch), €23/30 – Carte €24/51

◆ A comfortable, cosy family hotel. Each room is a surprising jumble of furniture and styles. Somewhat kitsch but most appealing. Classic, almost country cuisine and specialities of Southwest France. Pretty terrace.

AUTUN – 71 Saône-et-Loire – 320 F8 – pop. 16 419 – alt. 326 m – ✉ 71400 Burgundy-Jura 8 C2

Paris 287 – Avallon 78 – Chalon-sur-Saône 51 – Dijon 85 – Mâcon 111

Office de tourisme, 2, avenue Charles de Gaulle ✆ 03 85 86 80 38, Fax 03 85 86 80 49

d'Autun Le Plan d'Eau du Vallon, by Chalon-sur-Saône road: 3 km, ✆ 03 85 52 09 28.

St-Lazare cathedral ★★ (tympanum★★★, capitals★★) - Musée Rolin★ (la Eve's temptation ★★, Cardinal Rolin Nativity ★★, Autun Virgin ★★) BZ M2 - Porte St-André★ - Gates★ of lycée Bonaparte AZ B - Manuscripts★ (Town hall library) BZ H.

AUTUN

Arbalète (R. de l') . . . . **BZ** 2
Arquebuse (R. de l') . . . . **BZ** 3
Cascade (R. de la) . . . . **BZ** 4
Chauchien (Gde-Rue) . . . . **BZ** 6
Cocand (R.) . . . . **AZ** 7
Cordeliers (R. des) . . . . **BZ** 9
Cordiers (R. aux) . . . . **BZ** 12
Dijon (R. de) . . . . **BY** 13
Dr-Renaud (R.) . . . . **AZ** 15
Eumène (R.) . . . . **AY** 16
Gaillon (R. de) . . . . **BY** 18
Gaulle (Av. Ch.-de) . . . . **AYZ** 19
Grange-Vertu (Rue de la) . . . . . **AY** 21
Guérin (R.) . . . . **BY** 23
Jeannin (R.) . . . . **BZ** 26
Lattre-de-Tassigny (R. de) . . . . . **BZ** 27
Laureau (Bd) . . . . **BY** 28
Marbres (R. des) . . . . **BZ** 29
Martin (R. Maître G.) . . . . **BY** 43
Notre-Dame (R.) . . . . **AZ** 31
Paris (R. de) . . . . **ABY** 32
Passage couvert . . . . **BZ** 33
Pernette (R.) . . . . **AZ** 35
Raquette (R.) . . . . **BZ** 37
St-Saulge (R.) . . . . **AZ** 40
Vieux-Colombier (R. du) . . . . **BZ** 42

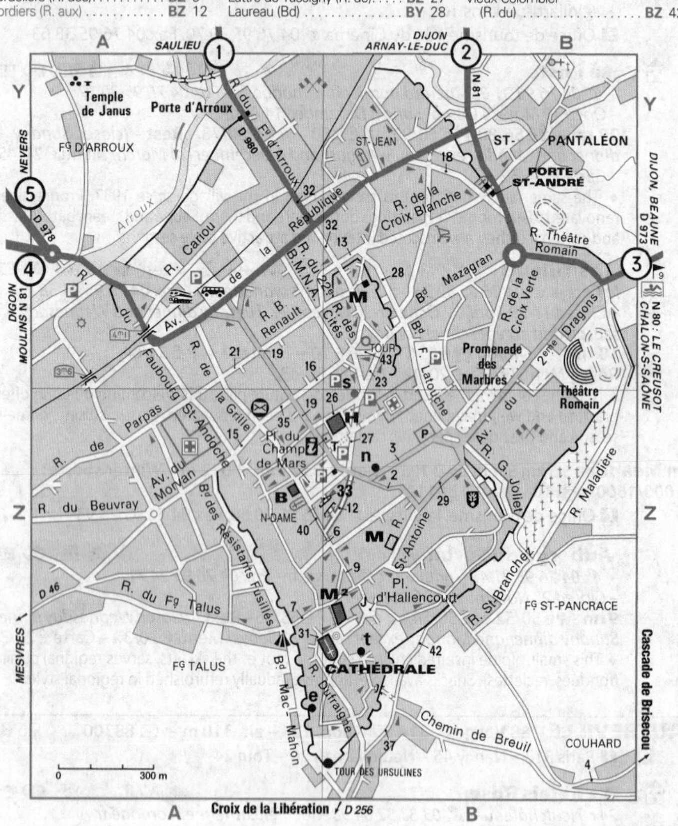

Les Ursulines

rm, VISA

14 r. Rivault – ✆ 03 85 86 58 58 – welcome@hotelursulines.fr – Fax 03 85 86 23 07
36 rm – €59/90 €69/133, ☕ €13 – 7 suites AZ **e**
Rest – *(closed Sunday dinner and Monday lunch from 2 November to 31 March)* Menu €20 bi (weekday lunch), €30/89 – Carte €38/71

◆ Former Ursuline convent, located above the old town. Quiet pastel-toned rooms. The former chapel has been turned into a banquet room. The restaurant overlooks the inner courtyard – the setting for the summer terrace. Traditional food and a good choice of Burgundy wines.

La Tête Noire

rest, VISA

3 r. Arquebuse – ✆ 03 85 86 59 99 – welcome@hoteltetenoire.fr – Fax 03 85 86 33 90 – Closed 15 December-31 January BZ **n**
31 rm – €61/74 €71/88, ☕ €10,50 – ½ P €65/72 – **Rest** – Menu (€14), €18/50 – Carte €23/55

◆ This address is being progressively renovated. The smart rooms have rustic painted wood furniture and are well soundproofed. Classic, regional cuisine served in a pleasant dining room.

Ibis
2 km rte Chalon via ③ – ✆ 03 85 52 00 00 – h3232@accor.com – Fax 03 85 52 20 20
46 rm – †€ 53/62 ††€ 53/67, ☕ € 7,50 – **Rest** – *(dinner only)* Menu (€ 11,50), € 17
◆ This Ibis on the banks of a lake that is a watersports centre overlooks the Gallo-Roman walled town. The functional rooms are up to the chain's latest standards. Panelling, paintings, and sunny tones: The restaurant dining room is pleasant and bright.

Maison Sainte-Barbe without rest
7 pl. Ste-Barbe – ✆ 03 85 86 24 77 – maison.sainte.barbe.autun@wanadoo.fr – Fax 03 85 86 19 28 BZ **t**
3 rm ☕ – †€ 58 ††€ 64
◆ Former canon's house (15-18C) at the foot of the cathedral. Large, personalised rooms, pretty breakfast room furnished with antique furniture, walled garden.

Le Chalet Bleu
3 r. Jeannin – ✆ 03 85 86 27 30 – contact@lechaletbleu.com – Fax 03 85 52 74 56 – Closed 1st-6 January, 16 February-10 March, Monday dinner, Tuesday and Sunday dinner except July-August BYZ **s**
Rest – Menu € 18/60 – Carte € 31/47
◆ Behind a glass-front, dining room with walls decorated with murals of imaginary gardens and landscapes. The menu offers a combination of traditional and local dishes; themed set menus on Friday evenings.

AUVERS – **77 Seine-et-Marne** – **312** D5 – **see Milly-la-Forêt (Essonne)**

AUVERS-SUR-OISE – **95 Val-d'Oise** – **305** E6 – **106** 6 – **101** 3 – **see Paris, Area**

AUVILLAR – **82 Tarn-et-Garonne** – **337** B7 – **pop. 876** – **alt. 141 m** – ✉ **82340**

Paris 652 – Agen 28 – Montauban 42 – Auch 62 – Castelsarrasin 22 28 **B2**

Office de tourisme, place de la Halle ✆ 05 63 39 89 82, Fax 05 63 39 89 82

L'Horloge with rm
pl. de l'Horloge – ✆ 05 63 39 91 61 – hoteldelhorloge@wanadoo.fr – Fax 05 63 39 75 20 – Closed 5 December-3 January and Friday from 15 October to 15 April
10 rm – †€ 43/45 ††€ 48/69, ☕ € 10,50 – ½ P € 52/72
Rest – *(closed Friday except dinner in July-August and Saturday lunch)*
Menu € 27/75 – Carte € 58/87
Rest *Le Bouchon* – *(closed Saturday except July-August and Friday) (lunch only)*
Menu (€ 14,50), € 18 – Carte approx. € 22
◆ Just next to the graceful Horloge, a delightful place with pretty green shutters and tables under the plane trees. Classy, modern setting. Local cuisine and wines. At lunchtime the Bouchon offers nice little bistro-style dishes with a local flavour.

in Bardigues **4 km South by D 11** – **pop. 219** – **alt. 160 m** – ✉ **82340**

Auberge de Bardigues
au bourg – ✆ 05 63 39 05 58 – info@aubergedebardigues.com – Fax 05 69 39 06 58 – Closed Monday
Rest – Menu € 15 bi (weekday lunch), € 27/42 – Carte approx. € 30
◆ Attractive rural stone building. The day's special lunchtime menu is served in the ground-floor bar and there is a brand-new dining room on the first floor. Terrace looks onto countryside.

AUVILLARS-SUR-SAÔNE – **21 Côte-d'Or** – **320** K7 – **pop. 212** – **alt. 212 m** – ✉ **21250** 7 **B3**

Paris 335 – Beaune 30 – Chalon-sur-Saône 55 – Dijon 31 – Dole 48

Auberge de l'Abbaye
1 km southward on the D 996 – ✆ 03 80 26 97 37 – auberge.abbaye@wanadoo.fr – Fax 03 80 26 97 37 – Closed Monday dinner except July-August, Tuesday dinner, Wednesday dinner and Sunday dinner
Rest – *(pre-book)* Menu € 12 (lunch except Sunday), € 21/31 – Carte € 20/36
◆ Discreet roadside inn. Two rustic dining rooms: the bigger bistro-style one offers the daily specials, the smaller and more intimate one proposes traditional dishes.

AUXERRE 🅿 – 89 Yonne – **319** E5 – pop. 37 790 – alt. 130 m – ✉ 89000

Burgundy-Jura **7 B1**

Paris 166 – Bourges 144 – Chalon-sur-Saône 176 – Dijon 152 – Sens 59

Office de tourisme, 1-2, quai de la République ☎ 03 86 52 06 19, Fax 03 86 51 23 27

St-Étienne cathedral ★★ (stained-glass windows★★, crypt★, treasure-house★) - Former St-Germain abbey ★★ (crypt★★).

Gy-l'Évêque: Christ aux Orties★ of the chapel 9.5 km by ③.

Le Parc des Maréchaux without rest

6 av. Foch – ☎ 03 86 51 43 77 – contact@hotel-parcmarechaux.com – Fax 03 86 51 31 72 AZ **u**

25 rm – 🛉€ 75/102 🛉🛉€ 86/123, ☕ € 12

◆ This Napoleon III dwelling has pretty, cosy rooms, which are fully renovated and furnished in Empire style; those opening onto the park are quietest. Muted bar decorated in red velvet.

AUXERRE

Street	Square	No.
Boucheries (R. des)	BZ	3
Bourbotte (Av.)	BY	4
Chesnez (R. M. des)	AZ	5
Coche-d'Eau (Pl. du)	BY	8
Cochois (R.)	BY	9
Diderot (R.)	AZ	10
Dr-Labosse (R. du)	BY	11
Draperie (R. de la)	AZ	12
Eckmühl (R. d')	AZ	14
Fécauderie (R.)	AZ	16
Foch (Av.)	AZ	18
Grand-Caire (R. du)	AY	20
Horloge (R. de l')	AZ	22
Hôtel-de-Ville (Pl. de l')	AZ	23
Jean-Jaurès (Av.)	BY	26
Jean-Jaurès (Pl.)	BZ	27
Leclerc (Pl. du Mar.)	AZ	34
Lepère (Pl. Ch.)	AZ	35
Maison-Fort (R.)	BY	36
Marine (R. de la)	BY	37
Mont-Brenn (R. du)	BY	38
Paris (R. de)	AY	
Puits-des-Dames (R. du)	BZ	40
St-Germain (R.)	ABY	44
St-Nicolas (Pl.)	BY	45
Schaeffer (R. René)	AZ	46
Surugue (Pl. Ch.)	AZ	47
Temple (R. du)	AZ	
Tournelle (Av. de la)	BY	48
Yonne (R. de l')	BY	52
24-Août (R. du)	AZ	54

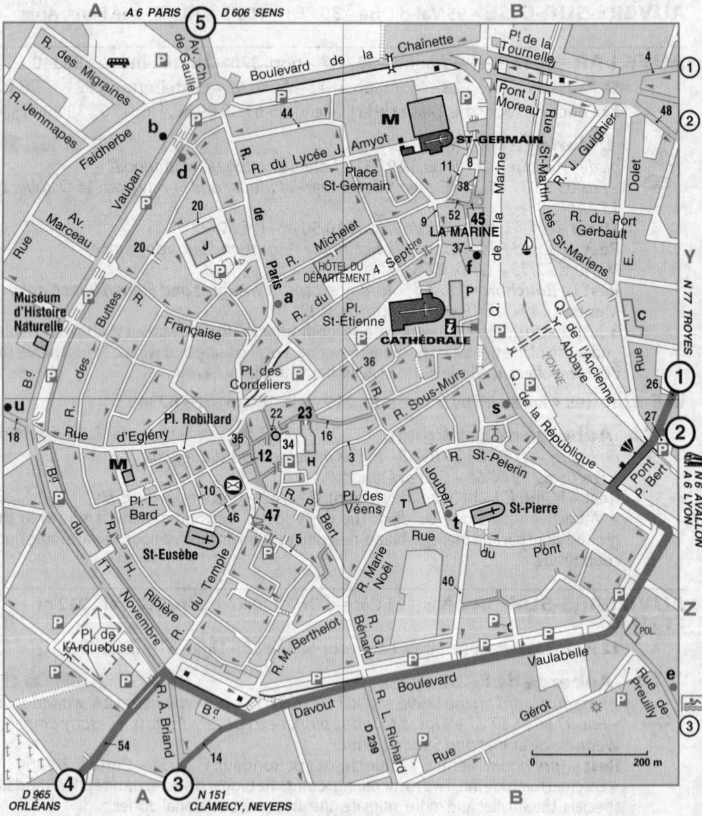

Normandie without rest

41 bd Vauban – ✆ 03 86 52 57 80 – reception@hotelnormandie.fr – Fax 03 86 51 54 33 – Closed 22 December-4 January AY **b**

47 rm – †€ 61/67 ††€ 67/95, ☕ € 8,50

◆ A peaceful courtyard terrace, comfortable rooms (preferable in the main house), an Art Deco furnished lounge bar, billiards and fitness facilities set the scene of this opulent house.

Le Maxime without rest

2 quai de la Marine – ✆ 03 86 52 14 19 – contact@lemaxime.com – Fax 03 86 52 21 70 BY **f**

26 rm – †€ 67/77 ††€ 77/113, ☕ € 10

◆ On the banks of the Yonne, this former salt warehouse was converted into a hotel in the 19C. Pleasantly renovated rooms (period furniture) overlooking the river or the quieter courtyard.

Barnabet (Jean-Luc Barnabet)

14 quai de la République – ✆ 03 86 51 68 88 – Fax 03 86 52 96 85 – Closed 22 December-13 January, Sunday dinner, Tuesday lunch and Monday

Rest – Menu (€ 29), € 46/73 bi – Carte € 75/107 BYZ **s**

Spec. Petite charlotte de lapin en gelée, foie gras et artichaut (May to October). Paillard de thon, pétales de tomate et languettes de courgettes grillées. Ris de veau doré au four aux pommes de terre sautées. **Wines** Bourgogne blanc, Irancy.

◆ A former town house opening onto a flower-decked courtyard terrace. Elegant, low-key dining room, view of the kitchen. Refined classic menu; fine choice of burgundies.

Le Jardin Gourmand

56 bd Vauban – ✆ 03 86 51 53 52 – contact@lejardingourmand.com – Fax 03 86 52 33 82 – Closed 10-19 March, 17 June-2 July, 11 November-3 December, Tuesday and Wednesday AY **d**

Rest – Menu (€ 45), € 55/65 – Carte € 82/102

◆ Smart low-key interior for this former wine grower's home where the chef whips up subtle modern dishes served with vegetables from his own garden. Faultless service.

La Salamandre

84 r. de Paris – ✆ 03 86 52 87 87 – la-salamandre@wanadoo.fr – Fax 03 86 52 05 85 – Closed Wednesday dinner, Saturday lunch, Sunday and public holidays AY **a**

Rest – Menu € 36/62 – Carte € 41/93

◆ A sought-after fish (wild) and seafood restaurant, served in a decor of shades of green, embellished by paintings and plants.

Le Bourgogne

15 r. Preuilly – ✆ 03 86 51 57 50 – contact@lebourgogne.fr – Fax 03 86 51 57 50 – Closed 4-25 August, 22 December-4 January, Thursday dinner, Sunday, Monday and public holidays BZ **e**

Rest – *(number of covers limited, pre-book)* Menu € 28

◆ Ex-garage now home to a pleasantly rustic restaurant. Market fresh recipes that are as appetising on the blackboard as they are in the plate. Lovely summer terrace.

La P'tite Beursaude

55 r. Joubert – ✆ 03 86 51 10 21 – auberge.beursaudiere@wanadoo.fr – Fax 03 86 51 10 21 – Closed 26 June-3 July, 28 August-4 September, 30 December-15 January, Tuesday and Wednesday BZ **t**

Rest – Menu (€ 18), € 24/27 – Carte € 30/62

◆ A warm, rustic interior, Burgundy dishes prepared before you and served in regional costume: the atmosphere is resolutely inviting in this unpretentious establishment.

Chablis road **8 km by ② near A 6 Auxerre-Sud interchange – ✉ 89290 Venoy**

Le Moulin de la Coudre with rm

– ✆ 03 86 40 23 79 – moulin@moulindelacoudre.com – Fax 03 86 40 23 55 – Closed 15-30 January, Sunday dinner, Monday lunch and Tuesday lunch

14 rm – †€ 62/90 ††€ 62/90, ☕ € 10 – ½ P € 80 – **Rest** – Menu (€ 20), € 23 (weekdays), € 39/62 – Carte € 35/56

◆ Old riverside mill at the bottom of a valley, where you can dine on traditional fare as you savour the peace and quiet. Tree-lined terrace. Ask for one of the family rooms.

in Champs-sur-Yonne 10 Km by ② and D 606 – pop. 1 382 – alt. 110 m – ✉ 89290

Mas des Lilas without rest
Hameau de la La Cour Barrée – ✆ 03 86 53 60 55 – hotel@lemasdeslilas.com – Fax 03 86 53 30 81 – Closed 28 October-7 November
17 rm – †€ 59 ††€ 59, ☕ € 7,50
◆ Lodges nestling in a pleasant garden dotted with flowers, housing small, well-kept, ground-floor rooms with terraces overlooking greenery.

in Vincelottes 16 km by ② D 606 and D 38 – pop. 290 – alt. 110 m – ✉ 89290

Auberge Les Tilleuls with rm
12 quai de l'Yonne – ✆ 03 86 42 22 13 – lestilleulsvincelottes@wanadoo.fr – Fax 03 86 42 23 51 – Closed 22 December-22 February, Tuesday and Wednesday
5 rm – †€ 55/66 ††€ 55/77, ☕ € 10,50 – ½ P € 64/74 – **Rest** – Menu € 26/56 – Carte € 46/79
◆ A pastoral stopover on the banks of the Yonne. Pretty rooms with work by local artists and a riverside terrace. Traditional menu and a fine choice of Burgundies.

in Chevannes 8 km by ③ and D1 – pop. 1 958 – alt. 170 m – ✉ 89240

La Chamaille with rm
4 rte Boiloup – ✆ 03 86 41 24 80 – contact@lachamaille.fr – Fax 03 86 41 34 80 – Closed 27 October-3 November, 23 February-9 March, Sunday dinner and Monday from March to September
3 rm – †€ 50/60 ††€ 60/70, ☕ € 10 – ½ P € 60/65 – **Rest** – Menu € 38/57 – Carte € 53/71
◆ An old, authentically rural farmstead tucked away in the countryside. A veranda opens onto the flower filled park through which a stream runs. Up-to-date cuisine.

in Villefargeau 5.5 km by ④ – pop. 908 – alt. 130 m – ✉ 89240

Le Petit Manoir des Bruyères
Les Bruyères, 4 km to the west – ✆ 03 86 41 32 82 – jchambord@aol.com – Fax 03 86 41 28 57
5 rm ☕ – †€ 130/220 ††€ 130/220 – **Table d'hôte** – Menu € 40
◆ This manor house, crowned with a typical glazed tile roof, is a haven of peace and tranquillity. Situated next to a forest, it offers mushroom-foraging trips in season. Stay in elegant 18C rooms or the royal "Montespan" suite. An elegant dining room with stylishly laid tables in front of a Louis XIII fireplace. Specialities from Burgundy.

near Auxerre-Nord interchange 7 km by ⑤

Mercure
D 606 – ✆ 03 86 53 25 00 – h0348@accor.com – Fax 03 86 53 07 47
77 rm – †€ 89/119 ††€ 99/129, ☕ € 12,50 – **Rest** – Menu (€ 17), € 23/25 – Carte € 20/46
◆ A motel-style construction. Simple rooms laid out around a pool and level with the garden planted with a few grape vines. Bright and pleasant modern restaurant. Traditional and regional cuisine served. Lovely terrace.

in Appoigny 8 km by ⑤ and D 606 – pop. 2 991 – alt. 110 m – ✉ 89380

Syndicat d'initiative, 4, rue du Fer à Cheval ✆ 03 86 53 20 90

Le Puits d'Athie
1 r. de l'Abreuvoir – ✆ 03 86 53 10 59 – puitsdathie@free.fr – Fax 03 86 53 10 59
4 rm ☕ – †€ 69/160 ††€ 69/160 – ½ P € 104/205 – **Table d'hôte** – *(pre-book)* Menu € 45 bi
◆ The personalised rooms of this Bourguignon house are a feast for the eyes, in particular Mykonos, decorated in blue and white and Porte d'Orient, decorated with an authentic door from Rajasthan. The proprietress rustles up southern and regional dishes.

AUXONNE – 21 Côte-d'Or – **320** M6 – **pop. 7 154 – alt. 184 m** – ✉ **21130**
Burgundy-Jura — 8 **D2**

Paris 343 – Dijon 32 – Dole 17 – Gray 38 – Vesoul 81

Office de tourisme, 11, rue de Berbis ✆ 03 80 37 34 46, Fax 03 80 31 02 34

Des Halles et Hôtel du Corbeau with rm

1 rue Berbi – ✆ 03 80 27 05 30 – sarldeshalles@wanadoo.fr – Fax 03 80 27 05 40 – Closed 26 December-18 January

9 rm – 🛉€ 50 🛉🛉€ 60/70, ☕ € 6 – **Rest** – bistrot *(closed Sunday dinner and Monday off season)* Menu (€ 13), € 20/50 – Carte € 26/49

◆ Wood, concrete and designer furniture and decor provide the contemporary backdrop for this bistro with an emphasis on daily specials and traditional cuisine based on seasonal produce. Small, attractive rooms which are ideal for an overnight stay.

in Lamarche-sur-Saône 11.5 km northwest by D 905 and D 976 – pop. 1 201 – alt. 190 m – ✉ 21760

Hostellerie St-Antoine with rm

32 r. Franche Comté – ✆ 03 80 47 11 33 – lesaintantoine@wanadoo.fr – Fax 03 80 47 13 56 – Closed Sunday dinner from 15 November to 8 March

8 rm – 🛉€ 60 🛉🛉€ 64, ☕ € 9 – 2 suites – ½ P € 66/98 – **Rest** – Menu € 14 (weekday lunch), € 26/38 – Carte € 28/65

◆ Impressive Burgundian house at the edge of the village. Two comfortable dining rooms, one under a veranda overlooking a pleasant garden. Functional rooms.

AVAILLES-LIMOUZINE – 86 Vienne – 322 J8 – pop. 1 309 – alt. 142 m – ✉ 86460

39 **C2**

Paris 413 – Chauvigny 61 – Poitiers 66 – Saint-Junien 40

Office de tourisme, 6, rue Principale ✆ 05 49 48 63 05, Fax 05 49 48 63 05

La Chatellenie

1 r. du Commerce – ✆ 05 49 84 31 31 – lachatellenie@aol.com – Fax 05 49 84 31 32 – Closed 22-29 December and February school holidays

9 rm – 🛉€ 45 🛉🛉€ 55, ☕ € 6 – ½ P € 41/46 – **Rest** – *(closed Sunday dinner and Monday)* Menu € 12 (weekdays)/25

◆ This pleasantly restored 1830 former post house has good-sized rooms with painted wooden furniture and parquet floors. Peaceful family ambiance. Traditional food served in the walled courtyard in summer.

AVALLON – 89 Yonne – 319 G7 – pop. 8 217 – alt. 250 m – ✉ 89200

Burgundy-Jura

7 **B2**

Paris 222 – Auxerre 51 – Beaune 103 – Chaumont 134 – Nevers 98

Syndicat d'initiative, 6, rue Bocquillot ✆ 03 86 34 14 19, Fax 03 86 34 28 29

Site★ - Fortified town★: Portals★ of St-Lazare church - Miserere★ du musée de l'Avallonnais **M**[1] - Cousin Valley ★ South by D 427.

Plan on following page

Hostellerie de la Poste

13 pl. Vauban – ✆ 03 86 34 16 16 – info@hostelleriedelaposte.com – Fax 03 86 34 19 19 – Closed 1st January-1st March **b**

30 rm – 🛉€ 90/110 🛉🛉€ 105/199, ☕ € 14 – ½ P € 103/113

Rest – *(open 16 March-30 November and closed Sunday and Monday)* Menu € 42/65 – Carte approx. € 42

Rest *Bistrot* – *(open 4 March-19 December and closed Sunday and Monday) (lunch only)* Menu € 14

◆ Handsome former Burgundian post house, from 1707, whose guests have included Napoleon I and John Kennedy! Pretty rooms with personal touches. The restaurant, located in converted stables, serves classic cuisine. Bistro formula at lunchtime.

Avallon Vauban without rest

53 r. de Paris – ✆ 03 86 34 36 99 – hotelavallonvauban@wanadoo.fr – Fax 03 86 31 66 31 **r**

26 rm – 🛉€ 53/54 🛉🛉€ 59/60, ☕ € 8,50

◆ By a busy crossroads, this regional style house overlooks a large shaded park around which sculpture by the owner/artist can be seen. Comfortable rooms; the quietest are to the rear.

AVALLON

Belgrand (R.)	2
Bocquillot (R.)	3
Capucins (Prom. des)	5
Collège (R. du)	6
Fontaine-Neuve (R.)	8
Fort-Mahon (R.)	9
Gaulle (Pl. Gén.-de)	12
Gde-Rue A. Briand	13
Odebert (R. des)	14
Paris (R. de)	
Porte-Auxerroise (R.)	16
Terreaux Vauban (Prom. des)	18
Vauban (Pl.)	

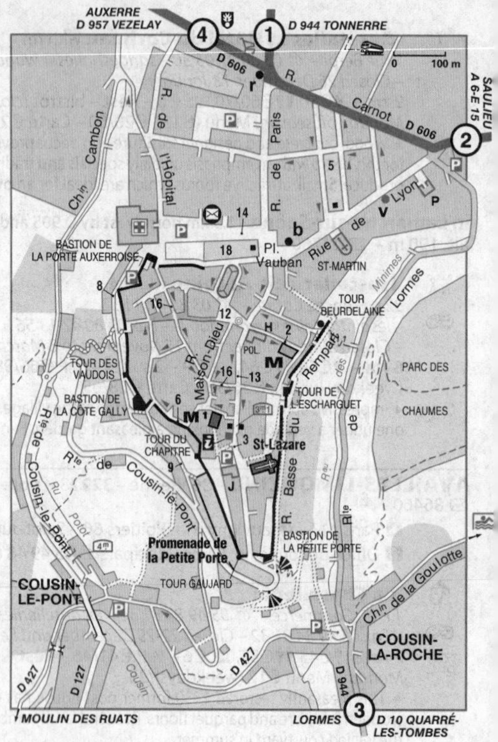

Dak'Hôtel without rest

119 r. de Lyon, Saulieu road via ② – ✆ 03 86 31 63 20 – dakhotel@yahoo.fr – Fax 03 86 34 25 28

26 rm – †€ 53 ††€ 56/58, ☕ € 8,50

◆ Cube-shaped building near the main road. Functional, well kept and soundproofed rooms. Breakfast room overlooking the garden; swimming pool.

Le Gourmillon

8 r. de Lyon – ✆ 03 86 31 62 01 – Fax 03 86 31 62 01 – Closed 5-18 January, Thursday dinner off season and Sunday dinner v

Rest – Menu € 18/32 – Carte € 25/36

◆ A little downtown address, simple but generous. Airy dining room with tasteful countrified feel. The menus give preference to rustic dishes.

Saulieu road 6 km by ② – ✉ 89200 Avallon

Le Relais Fleuri rm,

(La Cerce) – ✆ 03 86 34 02 85 – relais-fleuri@lerelais-fleuri.com – Fax 03 86 34 09 98

48 rm – †€ 79 ††€ 79/88, ☕ € 12,50 – ½ P € 80 – **Rest** – Menu € 20/62 – Carte € 36/60

◆ This hotel, on the Saulieu road, houses functional, motel-style rooms, level with the 4ha park with tennis courts and a heated pool. Elegant, rustic dining room, reinterpreted traditional menu and a wine cellar rich in Burgundies.

in Pontaubert 5 km by ④ and D 957 – pop. 377 – alt. 160 m – ✉ 89200

XX **Les Fleurs** with rm

69 rte de Vézelay – ☎ 03 86 34 13 81 – info@hotel-lesfleurs.com – Fax 03 86 34 23 32 – Closed 19 December-25 January

7 rm – †€ 51/57 ††€ 51/57, ☕ € 7,50 – ½ P € 66 – **Rest** – *(closed Thursday except from 1st July to 15 September and Wednesday)* Menu € 17/41 – Carte € 24/44

◆ A gradually refurbished family-run inn: pastel shades prevail indoors, terrace overlooking the garden, and simple rooms. Traditional and regional dishes.

In the Vallée du Cousin 6 km by ④, Pontaubert and D 427 – ✉ 89200 Avallon

Hostellerie du Moulin des Ruats

– ☎ 03 86 34 97 00 – contact@moulin-des-ruats.com – Fax 03 86 31 65 47 – Open mid February-12 November

24 rm – †€ 82/132 ††€ 82/132, ☕ € 13 – 1 suite – ½ P € 98/133 – **Rest** – *(closed Monday) (dinner only except Sunday)* Menu € 30/47 – Carte € 50/59

◆ This former 18C mill nestling in the tranquil Cousin valley invites guests to relax: pleasant bar-library with refined atmosphere and rooms with olde worlde charm. The dining room with veranda offers relaxing views over the area. Lovely terrace. Classic cuisine and decor.

in Vault-de-Lugny 6 km by ④ and D 142 – pop. 328 – alt. 148 m – ✉ 89200

Château de Vault de Lugny

rest,

11 r. du Château – ☎ 03 86 34 07 86 – hotel@lugny.fr – Fax 03 86 34 16 36 – Open 18 April-11 November

15 rm – †€ 165/530 ††€ 165/530, ☕ € 28 – **Rest** – *(closed Tuesday) (dinner only) (residents only)* Menu € 65/95 bi – Carte € 45/87

◆ This luxurious 16C chateau encourages the traditional way of life. Superb gardens and vegetable plot, pool set in a vaulted outbuilding, all in an idyllically quiet setting.

in Valloux 6 km by ④ and D 606 – ✉ 89200 Vault-de-Lugny

XX **Auberge des Chenêts**

10 rte Nationale 6 – ☎ 03 86 34 23 34 – Fax 03 86 34 21 24 – Closed 25 February-10 March, 23 June-7 July, 12 November-2 December, Tuesday from October to May, Sunday dinner and Monday

Rest – Menu (€ 18), € 23 (weekday lunch), € 26/49 – Carte € 48/62

◆ A pleasant country inn on quite a busy road. Settle yourself next to the fireplace and taste the traditional Burgundy dishes.

AVÈNE – 34 Hérault – **339** D6 – pop. 275 – alt. 350 m – Spa : early April-late Oct. – ✉ 34260 22 **B2**

Paris 705 – Bédarieux 25 – Clermont-l'Hérault 51 – Montpellier 83

Office de tourisme, le Village ☎ 04 67 23 43 38, Fax 04 67 23 16 95

Val d'Orb

rm, rest,

Les Bains-d'Avène, at the thermal baths – ☎ 04 67 23 44 45 – Fax 04 67 23 39 07 – Open April-October

58 rm – †€ 89/94 ††€ 94/100, ☕ € 8 – ½ P € 68/94 – **Rest** – Menu € 19/26 – Carte € 25/43

◆ The establishment, nestled away discreetly in a little valley, is part of a new hot springs spa. Spacious and modern lodging. Restaurant with restrained contemporary decor and terrace off the garden. Traditional menu and diet dishes.

AVENSAN – 33 Gironde – **335** G4 – pop. 1 753 – alt. 25 m – ✉ 33480 3 **B1**

Paris 589 – Bordeaux 30 – Mérignac 28 – Pessac 34 – Talence 41

Le Clos de Meyre without rest

16 rte de Castelnau – ☎ 05 56 58 22 84 – closdemeyre@wanadoo.fr – Fax 05 57 71 23 35 – Open 1st March-1st November

7 rm ☕ – †€ 90/110 ††€ 130/140 – 2 suites

◆ Situated between the Margaux and Haut Médoc vineyards, this château has been a wine estate for three centuries. Traditional and modern rooms full of character. Swimming pool in summer; tennis court.

AVESSAC – 44 Loire-Atlantique – 316 E2 – pop. 2 154 – alt. 55 m – ✉ 44460

Paris 406 – Nantes 78 – Rennes 63 – St-Nazaire 54 – Vannes 64 34 **A2**

Southeast : 3 km by D 131 (direction Plessé) – ✉ 44460 Avessac

Restaurant d'Edouard

– *02 99 91 08 89 – edouardset@wanadoo.fr – Fax 02 99 91 02 44*
– Closed 7 July-11 September, 7-31 January, and from Sunday dinner to Thursday
Rest – Menu € 35/61 – Carte € 40/47

◆ This country restaurant (former farmhouse) sports a well thought out modern interior (fireplace, stonework, designer chairs and modern tableware). Up-to-date market fresh cuisine.

AVIGNON P – 84 Vaucluse – 332 B10 – pop. 85 935 – Built-up area 253 580 – alt. 21 m – ✉ 84000 Provence 42 **E1**

Paris 682 – Aix-en-Provence 82 – Arles 37 – Marseille 98 – Nîmes 46

Avignon: 04 90 81 51 51, by ③ and N 7: 8 km.

3635 (0,34 €/mn)

Office de tourisme, 41, cours Jean Jaurès 04 32 74 32 74, Fax 04 90 82 95 03

de Châteaublanc Morières-lès-Avignon Les Plans, East: 8 km by D 58, 04 90 33 39 08 ;

du Grand Avignon Vedène Les Chênes Verts, East: 9 km by D 28, 04 90 31 49 94.

Palais des Papes★★★: ≤★★ of the terrasse des Dignitaires - Rocher des Doms ≤★★ - St-Bénézet bridge ★★ - Ramparts★ - Old mansions★ (rue Roi-René) EZ **F²** - Dome★ of Notre-Dame-des-Doms cathedral - Façade★ of the Hôtel des Monnaies (former Mint) EY **K** - Leaves ★ of St-Pierre church EY - Altar-piece★ of St-Didier church EZ - Museums: Petit Palais★★ EY, Calvet★ EZ **M²**, Lapidary ★ EZ **M⁴**, Louis Vouland (earthenware★) DYZ**M⁵** - Angladon-Dubrujeaud Foundation ★★ EZ **M¹**.

Plans on following pages

La Mirande

4 pl. Amirande – 04 90 85 93 93 – mirande@la-mirande.fr – Fax 04 90 86 26 85
20 rm – €295/380 €410/820, € 29 – 1 suite EY **g**
Rest – *(closed 5 January-12 February, Tuesday and Wednesday)* Menu € 33 (weekday lunch), € 80/105 – Carte € 94/110
Spec. Tronçon de sole doré, potimarron et champignons (autumn). Filet de bœuf poêlé, panisses aux olives et basilic. Soufflé à l'orange (winter). **Wines** Rasteau, Gigondas.

◆ Discover the mellow atmosphere of this former cardinal's palace, totally renovated in the feel of an 18C Provençal home. A great dining area with pleasant garden terrace, serving inventive cuisine. A set menu is available for evening meals, served in the former kitchen..

D'Europe

12 pl. Crillon – 04 90 14 76 76 – reservations@heurope.com – Fax 04 90 14 76 71
41 rm – €169/475 €169/475, € 17 – 3 suites EY **d**
Rest – *(closed 17 August-1st September, 23 November-1stDecember, 4-12 January, 8-23 February, Sunday and Monday)* Menu € 35 (lunch), € 48/120 – Carte € 84/139
Spec. Crémeux de parmesan aux truffes noires (December to March). Quasi d'agneau de huit heures à la lavande (summer). Le "chocolat de plantation". **Wines** Vacqueyras, Côtes du Lubéron.

◆ Elegant 16C mansion with refined decor. The top-floor suites provide glimpses of the Popes' Palace. Beautiful, elegant dining rooms enhanced by subtle modern touches. Delightful terrace with the soothing sounds of a fountain in the background. Attractive contemporary-style bar.

Avignon Grand Hôtel

rm, rm,
34 bd St-Roch, (at the station) – 04 90 80 98 09
– reservationagh@cloitre-saint-louis.com – Fax 04 90 80 98 10
22 rm – €170/220 €230/280, € 16 – 98 suites – €350/450
Rest – *(Closed Saturday and Sunday)* Carte € 38/52 EZ **t**

◆ A decor with a medieval and Provençal touch in this hotel at the foot of the ramparts. Modern rooms and spacious apartments. Round swimming pool perched on the roof. Pleasant restaurant, with southern colours. Simple brasserie style cuisine.

Cloître St-Louis rm, VISA AE
20 r. Portail-Boquier – ✆ 04 90 27 55 55 – hotel@cloitre-saint-louis.com – Fax 04 90 82 24 01 EZ **s**
80 rm – €160/380 €160/380, €16 – **Rest** – *(closed Saturday lunch)*
Menu (€27), €32 – Carte €38/52
◆ Very modern decor in a 16C cloister and its modern annexe. Spacious, elegant rooms. Roof-top terrace and swimming pool. Vaulted dining rooms and cloisters (open in summer) overlooking a peaceful courtyard with old plane trees.

Mercure Pont d'Avignon without rest VISA AE
r. Ferruce, quartier Balance – ✆ 04 90 80 93 93 – h0549@accor.com – Fax 04 90 80 93 94 EY **r**
87 rm – €90/130 €96/140, €13
◆ Recent hotel with Provençal decor; regional period pieces and warm tones brighten the bright, practical rooms. Pretty breakfast room.

Mercure Cité des Papes VISA AE
1 r. J.-Vilar – ✆ 04 90 80 93 00 – h1952@accor.com – Fax 04 90 80 93 01 EY **b**
89 rm – €90/130 €96/140, €12
Rest ***Les Domaines*** – *✆ 04 90 80 93 11* – Menu €11/25
◆ A 1970s building handy for its location in the heart of the Cité des Papes. Rooms have a simple Provençal decor. Modern setting and large terrace for the restaurant that focuses on regional dishes and wines.

Express By Holiday Inn without rest VISA AE
2 r. Mère-Térésa, TGV station – ✆ 04 32 76 88 00 – express.avignon@ihg.com – Fax 04 32 76 89 00 AX **a**
100 rm – €70/139 €70/139
◆ New construction well situated in the immediate vicinity of the TGV train station. The spacious and functional rooms have excellent sound-proofing.

Bristol without rest VISA AE
44 cours Jean-Jaurès – ✆ 04 90 16 48 48 – contact@bristol-avignon.com – Fax 04 90 86 22 72 EZ **m**
65 rm – €57/92 €77/112, €11 – 2 suites
◆ A hotel well situated on the main avenue of the walled city. Spacious and sensibly functional rooms, most overlook the inside courtyards.

De Blauvac without rest VISA AE
11 r. de la Bancasse – ✆ 04 90 86 34 11 – blauvac@aol.com – Fax 04 90 86 27 41 EY **m**
16 rm – €60/77 €65/87, €7
◆ Former residence of the Marquis of Blauvac (17C). Rustic style interior. You can often see the original stone on the walls of the rooms (some with mezzanine).

Kyriad without rest VISA AE
26 pl. de l'Horloge – ✆ 04 90 82 21 45 – hotel@kyriad-avignon.com – Fax 04 90 82 90 92 EY **p**
38 rm – €70/110 €80/110, €8
◆ Good location on one of the prettiest squares of the old town, for this renovated hotel. Small, bright, colourful rooms equipped with effective double glazing.

D'Angleterre without rest VISA AE
29 bd Raspail – ✆ 04 90 86 34 31 – info@hoteldangleterre.fr – Fax 04 90 86 86 74 – Closed 20 December-19 January DZ **a**
40 rm – €45/80 €45/80, €8
◆ This hundred-year-old building was once a pasta factory. The rooms that are getting refurbished in stages are plain, adequately equipped and well-maintained. Convenient parking.

De Garlande without rest VISA AE
20 r. Galante – ✆ 04 90 80 08 85 – hotel-de-garlande@wanadoo.fr – Fax 04 90 27 16 58 – Closed 15 January-15 February and Sunday dinner from November to March EY **f**
10 rm – €72/118 €72/118, €7
◆ A family welcome, a picturesque maze of corridors and staircases. Rooms with Provençal touches, eclectic furniture and knick-knacks: this little hotel has its own special charm.

AVIGNON

Amandier (Av. de l') CX
Aulnes (Av. des) CX
Avignon (Av. d') CX
Croix Rouge (Av. de la) BX
Docteur-Pons (Rte Touristique) . . . BV
Eisenhower (Av.) . . . . . . AX
Europe (Pont de l') . . . . AX
Ferry (Bd J.) . . . . AX
Folie (Av. de la) . . . . . BCX 29
Foncouverte (Av. de) BCX 31
Gaulle (Rocade Ch.-de) . . ABX
Lyon (Rte de) . . . . BV
Marseille (Rte de) . . . BCX 51
Monclar (Av.) . . . . AX
Monod (Bd J.) . . . . AX 58
Montfavet (Rte de) . . BCX 60
Morières (Rte de) . . . BCV
Moulin Notre-Dame (Av. du) . . . . BX 61
Réalpanier (Carr.) CV
Reine-Jeanne (Av. de la) . . . . BX 81
Royaume (Pont du) . . . AV 92
St-Chamand (Av.) . . . . . BX 95
St-Ruf (Av.) . . . . AX
Semard (Av. P.) . . . . . . BX
Sixte-Isnard (Bd) . . . . . BX 112
Souspirous (Av. de) . . . CX
Tarascon (Av. de) . . . . . AX
1re Division Blindée (Bd de la) . . . . BX 125

LES ANGLES

Pinède (Ch. de la) . . . . AV

LE PONTET

Avignon (Av. d') CV
Carpentras (Av. de) . . . CV
Delorme (Av. Th.) CV
Goutarel (Av. G.) . . . . . CV 38
Pasteur (Av. L.) CV

VILLENEUVE-LÈS-AVIGNON

Camp de Bataille (R.) . AV 15
Chartreux (Ch. des) . . . AV 16
Ducros (Bd Edmond) . AV
Fort St-André (Montée du) . . . . AV 32
Gaulle (Av. Ch.-de) . . . . AV 36
Hôpital (R. de l') . . . . . . AV 43
Joffre (Rte) . . . . AV
Leclerc (Av. Gén.) . . . . . AV
Monnaie (R. de la) . . . . AV 57
Pasteur (Av.) . . . . AV
Péri (Av. G.) . . . . AV
Ravoux (Av. Paul) . . . . . AV
République (R. de la) . . AV 87
Tour (Montée de la) . . . AV 115
Verdun (Av. de) . . . . . . AV 117

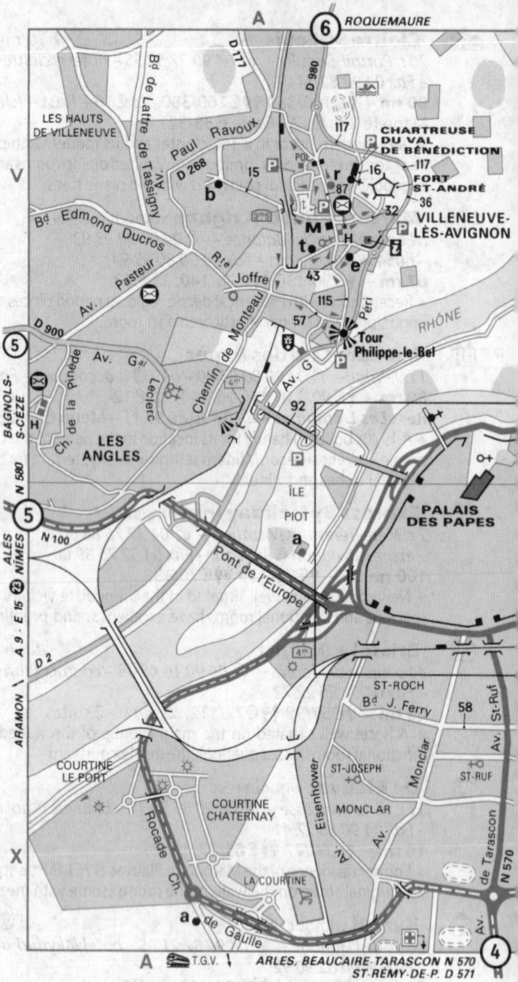

Ibis Centre Pont de l'Europe without rest
12 bd St-Dominique – ✆ 04 90 82 00 00
– ibis.avignon.centre.europe@wanadoo.fr
– Fax 04 90 85 67 16 DZ **q**
74 rm – ♦€ 49/68 ♦♦€ 49/68, ☐ € 7,50
♦ This recent structure at the foot of the ramparts offers rooms that are relatively small, but refurbished and well maintained. Breakfast buffet.

La Banasterie without rest
11 r. de la Banasterie – ✆ 04 32 76 30 78
– labanasterie@labanasterie.com
– Fax 04 32 76 30 78 EY **w**
5 rm ☐ – ♦€ 100/160 ♦♦€ 100/160
♦ This white stone residence (16C) houses gorgeous rooms whose names refer to chocolate; the owner's passion. Flower-decked terrace and patios.

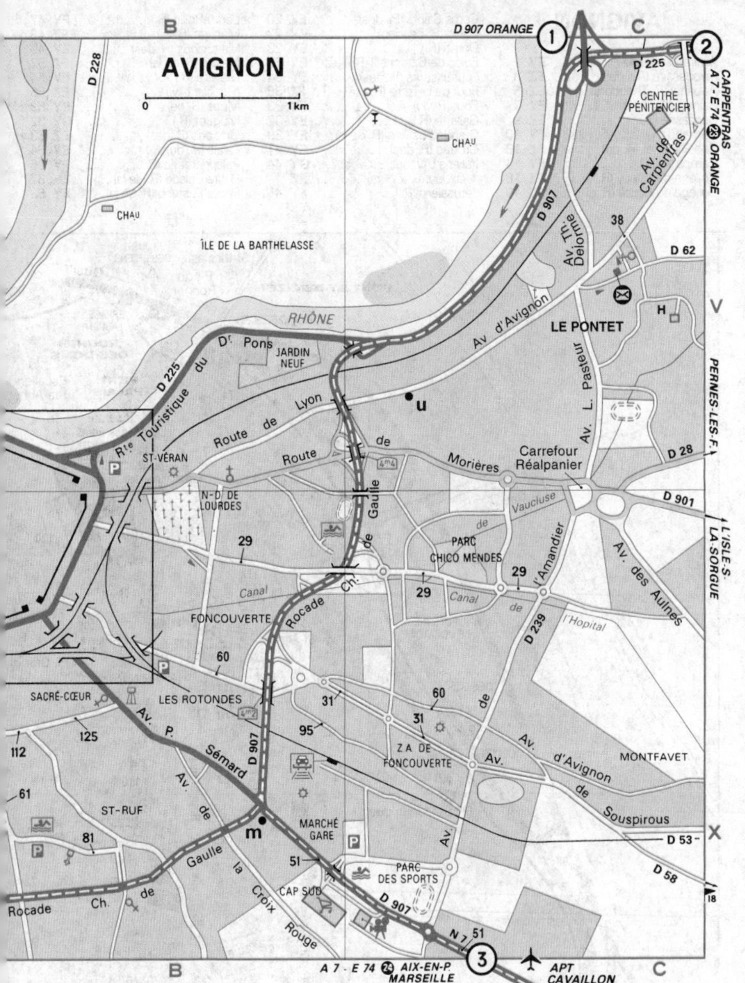

Lumani

37 Rempart St-Lazare – 𝒞 04 90 82 94 11 – lux@avignon-lumani.com
– Closed 15 November-15 December and 7 January-28 February FY **a**

5 rm – €90/160 €90/160 – **Table d'hôte** – Menu €28

◆ Artists are particularly welcome in this fine 19C manor house, which has an attractive courtyard shaded by a couple of hundred-year-old plane trees. Rooms and suites personalised with taste. Warm welcome.

Villa Agapè without rest

13 r. St-Agricol – 𝒞 04 90 85 21 92 – michele@villa-agape.com
– Fax 04 90 82 93 34 – Closed 14 June-31 July EY **x**

3 rm – €90/140 €100/150

◆ It's easy to forget the town-centre location of this attractive villa, with its verdant terrace and swimming pool. Occupying two 17C buildings, the hotel has elegant decor and a lovely lounge-library.

AVIGNON

Amirande (Pl. de l') .... EY 2
Arroussaire (Av. de l') .... FZ 3
Aubanel (R. Théodore) ...... EZ 5
Balance (R. de la) .... EY 7
Bancasse (R.) .... EY 9
Bertrand (R.) .... FY 10
Bon Martinet (R. du) .... FZ 13
Campane (R.)............... FY 14
Collège d'Annecy (R.) .... EZ 18
Collège du Roure (R. du) .... EY 19
Corps Saints (Pl. des) .... EZ 20
David (R. Félicien) .... EY 22
Dorée (R.) .... EY 23
Folco-de-Baroncelli (R.) ...... EY 28
Fourbisseurs (R. des) .... EY 34
Four de la Terre (R. du) ...... FZ 35
Four (R. du) .... FY 33
Galante (R.) .... EY 37
Grande Fusterie (R. de la).... EY 39
Grottes (R. des)............. EY 41
Italiens (Av. des)........... GY 44
Jean-Jaurès (Cours) .... EZ
Jérusalem (Pl.).............. FY 45
Ledru-Rollin (R.)............ FY 47
Manivet (R. P.).............. EFZ 48
Marchands (R. des) .... EY 49
Masse (R. de la)............. FZ 52
Molière (R.) .... EY 54
Monclar (Av.)............... EZ 55
Mons (R. de)................ EY 59
Muguet (R.) .... GY 62
Ortolans (R. des) .... EZ 63
Palais (Pl. du) .... EY 64
Palapharnerie (R.) .... FY 66
Petite Calade (R. de la) ...... EY 67
Petite Fusterie (R. de la) ..... EY 68

Street	Grid	No.
Petite Saunerie (R. de la)	FY	70
Pétramale (R.)	EZ	72
Peyrollerie (R.)	EY	73
Pont (R. du)	EY	74
Président-Kennedy (Cours)	EZ	76
Prévot (R.)	EZ	77
Rascas (R. de)	GY	79
Rempart de l'Oulle (R. du)	DY	82
Rempart du Rhône (R. du)	EY	83
Rempart St-Michel (R. du)	FZ	84
Rempart St-Roch (R. du)	DEZ	86
République (R. de la)	EYZ	
Rhône (Pte du)	EY	88
Rouge (R.)	EY	90
Ste-Catherine (R.)	FY	109
St-Agricol (R.)	EY	94
St-Christophe (R.)	FZ	97
St-Dominique (Bd)	DZ	98
St-Étienne (R.)	EY	99
St-Jean le Vieux (Pl.)	FY	101
St-Jean le Vieux (R.)	FY	102
St-Joseph (R.)	FY	104
St-Michel (R.)	EZ	105
St-Pierre (Pl.)	EY	106
St-Ruf (Av.)	FZ	108
Saraillerie (R. de la)	EYZ	110
Taulignan (R. de)	EY	113
Tour (R. de la)	GY	116
Vernet (R. Horace)	EZ	118
Vernet (R. Joseph)	EYZ	
Viala (R. Jean)	EY	119
Vice-Légat (R.)	EY	120
Vieux Sextier (R. du)	EFY	122
Vilar (R. Jean)	EY	123
Violette (R.)	EZ	124
3 Pilats (R. des)	FY	127
3 Faucons (R. des)	EZ	126

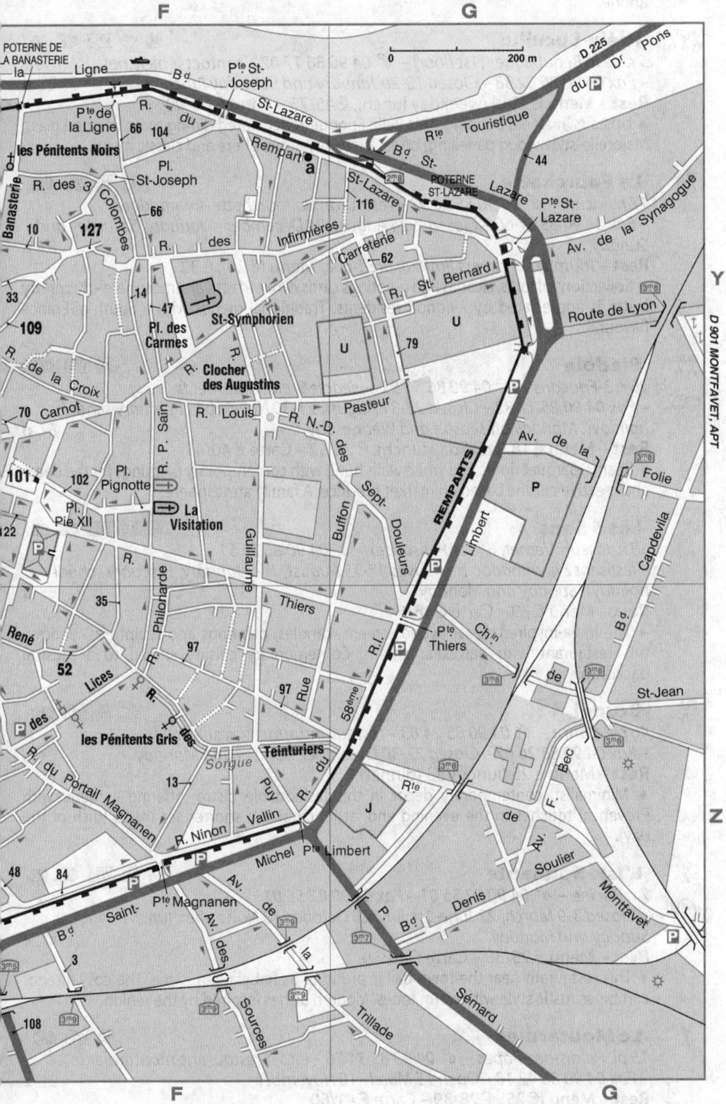

Christian Étienne

10 r. Mons – ✆ 04 90 86 16 50 – contact@christian-etienne.fr – Fax 04 90 86 67 09 – Closed Sunday and Monday except in July EY **h**

Rest – Menu € 35 (weekday lunch), € 62/117 – Carte € 65/92

Spec. Menu "homard". Menu "tomates" (June to September). Filets de rougets et légumes de saison. **Wines** Côtes du Rhône-Villages, Tavel.

◆ These 13C and 14C buildings adjoining the Palais des Papes offer period decor and a view over the square. Creative regional cuisine and a good choice of Côtes-du-Rhône.

Hiély-Lucullus

5 r. de la République, (1st floor) – ✆ 04 90 86 17 07 – contact@hiely.net – Fax 04 90 86 32 38 – Closed 13-20 January and Saturday lunch EY **n**

Rest – Menu € 35 bi (weekday lunch), € 45/75 – Carte € 60/90

◆ Upstairs in an old building. This Belle Epoque-redecorated dining room (stained glass, Majorelle-style wood panelling) offers a low-key atmosphere and classic menu.

La Fourchette

17 r. Racine – ✆ 04 90 85 20 93 – restaurant.la.fourchette@wanadoo.fr – Fax 04 90 85 57 60 – Closed 2-24 August, 24 December-4 January, Saturday and Sunday EY **u**

Rest – *(number of covers limited, pre-book)* Menu (€ 26), € 32

◆ Collections of forks, cicadas and greetings cards evoke a festival atmosphere - this pretty bistro is appreciated by Avignon residents. Traditional menus with a South-of-France flavour.

Piedoie

26 r. 3-Faucons – ✆ 04 90 86 51 53 – piedoie@club-internet.fr – Fax 04 90 85 17 32 – Closed 22-31 August, 21-30 November, February school holidays, Monday off season and Wednesday EZ **d**

Rest – Menu € 18 (weekday lunch), € 22/52 – Carte € 40/45

◆ Beams, parquet floors and white walls hung with contemporary paintings for the decor and creative cuisine based on market produce. A family atmosphere.

Les 5 Sens

18 r. Joseph-Vernet, (Place Plaisance) – ✆ 04 90 85 26 51 – les5sens2@wanadoo.fr – Closed 1st-15 August, 1st-7 January, February school holidays, Sunday and Monday EY **a**

Rest – Menu € 39 – Carte € 48/64

◆ The India-inspired decor (wood screens, candles, paintings and sculptures) endows this restaurant with particular charm. Contemporary cuisine served to a musical backdrop.

Brunel

46 r. Balance – ✆ 04 90 85 24 83 – restaurantbrunel@wanadoo.fr – Fax 04 90 86 26 67 – Closed 22-30 December, Sunday and Monday EY **e**

Rest – Menu € 25 (lunch)/33 (dinner)

◆ Minimalist, contemporary decor in this fashionable bistro; offering a menu with Provençal touches in the evening and, at lunchtime, a shorter set menu (dish of the day).

L'Isle Sonnante

7 r. Racine – ✆ 04 90 82 56 01 – Fax 04 90 82 56 01 – Closed 3-9 March, 22 June-1st July, 26 October-10 November, lunch in August, Sunday and Monday EY **v**

Rest – Menu € 25/38 – Carte € 40/50

◆ This restaurant near the town hall is proud of its Rabelaisian name. The cosy interior combines rustic style with warm tones. Modern dishes inspired by the region.

Le Moutardier

15 pl. Palais-des-Papes – ✆ 04 90 85 34 76 – info@restaurant-moutardier.fr – Fax 04 90 86 42 18 – Open 15 March-10 November EY **z**

Rest – Menu (€ 25), € 28/39 – Carte € 41/60

◆ Murals commemorating the moutardier du pape decorate the walls in this 18C house next to the palace. Wines served by the glass.

In île de la Barthelasse 5 km North by D 228 and secondary road – ✉ 84000 Avignon

La Ferme

110 chemin des Bois – ✆ 04 90 82 57 53 – info@hotel-laferme.com – Fax 04 90 27 15 47 – Open 15 March-31 October

20 rm – €64/71 €74/93, ☕ €11 – ½ P €66/77 – **Rest** – *(closed Monday lunchtime and Wednesday lunchtime)* Menu €25/40 – Carte €26/48

◆ A haven of peace near the centre of town. A beautiful restored farm offers large and airy rooms, with simple rustic furniture. Country-style dining room with beams, fireplace and old stone. Shaded terrace.

in Pontet 6 km to ② by Lyon road – **pop. 15 594 – alt. 40 m** – ✉ **84130**

Auberge de Cassagne

450 allée de Cassagne – ✆ 04 90 31 04 18 – cassagne@wanadoo.fr – Fax 04 90 32 25 09 – Closed 4-30 January

45 rm – €110/448 €130/448, ☕ €25 – 3 suites – ½ P €145/314

Rest – Menu €37 (weekday lunch), €59/106 – Carte €81/100

Spec. Grosse sole meunière. Langoustines grillées en coque et tartelette d'artichaut. Millefeuille de chocolat noir et nougat glacé à la provençale. **Wines** Côtes du Rhône.

◆ A building dating from 1850; Provençal-style rooms situated in pavilions opening onto the gardens. Non-smoking restaurant housed in an old timber-framed barn decorated in southern-French style. Terrace in the shade of an old plane tree. Modern food and good wine selection.

Les Agassins

52 av. Ch.-de-Gaulle – ✆ 04 90 32 42 91 – avignon@agassins.com – Fax 04 90 32 08 29 – Closed January and February CV **u**

26 rm – €90/200 €100/290, ☕ €19 – ½ P €105/185

Rest – *(closed Saturday lunch from January to March and from November to December)* Menu €19 (lunch), €29/68 – Carte €51/67

◆ Regional building surrounded by a flowered garden. Cane furniture and southern colours in the comfortable rooms. Sun-kissed restaurant with terrace in the shaded courtyard; Provence dishes and wines predominate.

in Montfavet - CX – ✉ **84140**

Hostellerie Les Frênes

645 av. Vertes-Rives – ✆ 04 90 31 17 93 – contact@lesfrenes.com – Fax 04 90 23 95 03 – Open 31 March-1st November

12 rm – €160/210 €210/385, ☕ €20 – 6 suites – ½ P €155/400

Rest – *(closed Saturday lunch from 15 June to 15 September and Monday except dinner from 16 June to 14 September)* Menu €30 (lunch), €50/70 – Carte €60/77

◆ This gracious old mansion (1800) and its more recent outbuildings are hidden in the greenery of its grounds. Period, contemporary, or southern styled rooms. Elegant dining room (painted wood panels, canvasses, tapestries) and a pleasant terrace overlooking the surrounding gardens.

Marseille road – ✉ **84000 Avignon**

Mercure Avignon Sud

2 r. Marie de Médicis, (Marseille road) – ✆ 04 90 89 26 26 – h0346@accor.com – Fax 04 90 89 26 27 BX **m**

105 rm – €75/120 €90/135, ☕ €13 – **Rest** – Menu (€18), €23 – Carte €22/34

◆ A hedge of trees conveniently isolates the hotel from a rather bare landscape. The rooms are large, practical and colourful. There is sufficient sound proofing. Real Provençal traditional cooking and poolside terrace dining in summer.

to the airport 8 km by ③ – ✉ **84140**

Paradou

– ✆ 04 90 84 18 30 – contact@hotel-paradou.fr – Fax 04 90 84 19 16

60 rm – €95/105 €110/160, ☕ €12 – ½ P €65/90

Rest – *(closed Sunday except dinner from 1st April to 5 October)* Menu €19 (weekday lunch)/39 – Carte €18/40

◆ Provençal-style hotel, where you should opt for one of the huge, recently created rooms; all have a mini terrace opening onto the garden or a large balcony. Southern flavoured cuisine and grills; wine list featuring local vintages.

See also hotel resources of **Villeneuve-lès-Avignon**

AVIGNON (Airport) – 84 Vaucluse – 332 C10 – see Avignon

AVOINE – 37 Indre-et-Loire – 317 K5 – pop. 1 778 – alt. 35 m – ✉ 37420 11 A2

Paris 291 – Azay-le-Rideau 28 – Chinon 7 – Langeais 27 – Saumur 23 – Tours 53

L'Atlantide

17 r. Nationale – ☎ 02 47 58 81 85 – Fax 02 47 58 81 85 – Closed Sunday dinner and Monday

Rest – *(pre-book)* Menu € 32/45

Rest *Le Casse-Croûte du Vigneron* – Menu € 13/18

♦ In a village near Chinon, regional cuisine served in a dining room reminiscent of ancient Greece, adorned with a hunting trophy and a fireplace. The wealth of local recipes and traditional dishes illustrate this restaurant's rustic authenticity: calf's head, coq au vin, etc.

AVORIAZ – 74 Haute-Savoie – 328 N3 – see Morzine

Look out for red symbols, indicating particularly pleasant establishments.

AVRANCHES – 50 Manche – 303 D7 – pop. 8 500 – alt. 108 m – ✉ 50300

Normandy 32 A3

Paris 337 – Caen 105 – Rennes 85 – St-Lô 58 – St-Malo 68

Office de tourisme, 2, rue Général-de-Gaulle ☎ 02 33 58 00 22, Fax 02 33 68 13 29

Manuscripts ★★ of the Mont-St-Michel (museum) - Jardin des Plantes: ✻★ - The "plate-forme" ✻★.

Plan on next page

La Croix d'Or

83 r. de la Constitution – ☎ 02 33 58 04 88 – hotelcroixdor@wanadoo.fr – Fax 02 33 58 06 95 – Closed 5-25 January and Sunday dinner from 15 October to 1st April BZ s

27 rm – †€ 56/63 ††€ 68/78, ☕ € 8,60 – ½ P € 70/87 – **Rest** – Menu € 17, € 26/54 – Carte € 39/59

♦ A 17C post house with an attractive half-timbered façade and splendid hall-sitting room furnished in a regional style. Most of the attractive rooms look onto the pretty flower garden. An authentic Norman feel to the dining room; a classic and regional menu.

La Ramade without rest

2 r. de la Côte, 1 km via ④ at Marcey les Grèves – ☎ 02 33 58 27 40 – hotel@laramade.fr – Fax 02 33 58 29 30 – Closed 28 December-4 February and Sunday from 16 November to 15 March

11 rm – †€ 65/86 ††€ 70/116, ☕ € 10

♦ 1950s bourgeois house with cosy personalised rooms on a floral theme. The lounge boasts a hearth. Gazebo in the garden. Non-smoking.

Jardin des Plantes

10 pl. Carnot – ☎ 02 33 58 03 68 – contact@le-jardin-des-plantes.fr – Fax 02 33 60 01 72 – Closed 8 December-12 January AZ u

25 rm – †€ 50/99 ††€ 50/99, ☕ € 10 – ½ P € 65 – **Rest** – *(closed Friday dinner, Sunday dinner and Saturday off season)* Menu € 18/42 – Carte € 35/56

♦ A family hotel at the entrance to the jardin des plantes. Reception in the bar popular with locals. Rustic rooms, more spacious in the rear building. A brasserie-style restaurant and covered terrace. Traditional cuisine.

Altos without rest

37 bd Luxembourg , par ③: 0.5 km – ☎ 02 33 58 66 64 – info@hotel-altos.com – Fax 02 33 58 40 11 – Closed 22 December-2 January

29 rm – †€ 55/69 ††€ 59/75, ☕ € 7,50

♦ A 1980s establishment by the side of a busy road with practical rooms that are gradually being done up in a more modern style.

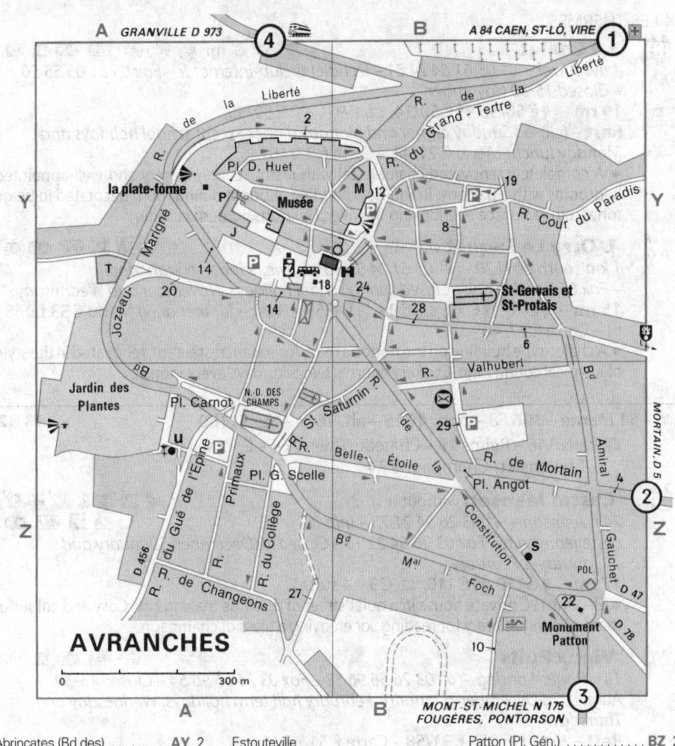

Abrincates (Bd des) . . . . AY 2
Bindel (R. du Cdt) . . . . BZ 4
Bremesnil (R. de) . . . . BY 6
Chapeliers (R. des) . . . . BY 8
Constitution (R. de la) . . . . BZ
Écoles (R. des) . . . . BZ 10
Estouteville (Pl. d') . . . . BY 12
Gaulle (R. Gén.-de) . . . . AY 14
Littré (Pl.) . . . . AY 18
Marché (Pl. du) . . . . BY 19
Millet (R. L.) . . . . AY 20
Patton (Pl. Gén.) . . . . BZ 22
Pot-d'Étain (R. du) . . . . BY 24
Puits-Hamel (R. du) . . . . AZ 27
St-Gaudens (R.) . . . . BY 28
St-Gervais (R.) . . . . BZ 29

in St-Quentin-sur-le-Homme 5 km Southeast by D 78 BZ – **pop. 1 090 – alt. 55 m – ✉ 50220**

XXX **Le Gué du Holme** with rm — rm, P VISA

14 r. des Estuaires – ✆ 02 33 60 63 76 – gue.holme@wanadoo.fr – Fax 02 33 60 06 77 – Closed 1st-11 November, 16-28 February, Saturday lunch, Sunday dinner and Monday except hotel

10 rm – €60/65 €65/100, ☕ €11 – ½ P €90 – **Rest** – Menu €27/60 – Carte €37/63

♦ The modern, wood façade contrasts with the building's stone walls. Dining rooms are elegant, the smallest opening onto a summer terrace. Seasonal menu.

AX-LES-THERMES – **09 Ariège** – **343** J8 – **pop. 1 441 – alt. 720 m – Winter sports : at Saquet via route du plateau de Bonascre★ (8km) and telecabin 1 400/2 400 m 1 15 – Spa : all year – Casino – ✉ 09110**
Languedoc-Roussillon-Tarn Gorges 29 **C3**

Paris 803 – Andorra-la-Vella 59 – Carcassonne 106 – Foix 44 – Prades 99 – Quillan 55

Puymorens Tunnel : Toll 2006, one way : cars 5.50, car and caravan 11.10, lorries 16.80 to 27.90, motorcycles 3.30. Special return rates : info ✆ 04 68 04 97 20.

Office de tourisme, 6, avenueThéophile Delcassé ✆ 05 61 64 60 60, Fax 05 61 64 68 18

Orlu Valley ★ Southeast.

Le Chalet rm, rest,

4 av. Turrel – 05 61 64 24 31 – lechalet@club-internet.fr – Fax 05 61 03 55 50 – Closed 15-30 November

19 rm – €50/56 €50/74, €9 – ½ P €52/55

Rest – *(closed Sunday dinner and Monday dinner except school holidays and Monday lunch)* Menu €21/44 – Carte €33/46

◆ A completely renovated chalet-hotel with restful, contemporary and well-appointed bedrooms with a balcony. Brand-new bedding. A bright dining room decorated in beige tones, plus a terrace overlooking the river. Delicious modern cuisine.

L'Orry Le Saquet with rm

1 km south on N 20 – 05 61 64 31 30 – sylvie.heinrich@wanadoo.fr – Fax 05 61 64 00 31 – Closed spring school holidays, November and Wednesday

15 rm – €70 €70, €9 – ½ P €59 – **Rest** – *(dinner only)* Menu €33 bi/65 bi – Carte €27/48

◆ A chalet-type building on the Andorra road. A pleasant restaurant, renovated in the style of a typical country inn. Cookery courses two Saturdays every month.

AY – **51 Marne** – **306** F8 – **pop. 4 315** – **alt. 76 m** – **51160** 13 **B2**

Paris 146 – Reims 29 – Château-Thierry 60 – Épernay 4 – Châlons-en-Champagne 34

Castel Jeanson without rest

24 r. Jeanson – 03 26 54 21 75 – info@casteljeanson.fr – Fax 03 26 54 32 19 – Closed 20 December-5 January and 20 January-5 February

17 rm – €110 €110, €9 – 4 suites

◆ Elegant 19C private house in a quiet street of the wine making city. Cosy and colourful rooms. Lounge-library for reading...or enjoying a glass of champagne.

Vieux Puits

18 r. Roger-Sondag – 03 26 56 96 53 – Fax 03 26 56 96 54 – Closed 15-30 August, 24 December-6 January, February half term holidays, Wednesday and Thursday

Rest – Menu (€25), €31/58 – Carte €51/68

◆ This restored Champagne house has a fine interior courtyard with an old well where the summer terrace is located. Three smart, rustic dining rooms.

AYGUESVIVES – **31 Haute-Garonne** – **343** H4 – **pop. 1 815** – **alt. 164 m** – **31450** Languedoc-Roussillon-Tarn Gorges 29 **C2**

Paris 704 – Colomiers 36 – Toulouse 25 – Tournefeuille 38

La Pradasse without rest

39 chemin de Toulouse, D 16 – 05 61 81 55 96 – contact@lapradasse.com – Fax 05 61 81 55 96

5 rm – €68 €80/92

◆ Designed by the owners, the rooms of this magnificently restored barn sport a delightful mixture of brick, wood and wrought iron. Fine grounds with pond.

AY-SUR-MOSELLE – **57 Moselle** – **307** I3 – **pop. 1 525** – **alt. 160 m** – **57300** 26 **B1**

Paris 327 – Briey 31 – Metz 17 – Saarlouis 56 – Thionville 16

Le Martin Pêcheur

1 rte d'Hagondange – 03 87 71 42 31 – restaurant-martin-pecheur@wanadoo.fr – Fax 03 87 71 42 31 – Closed 21-28 April, 18 August-1st September, 27 October-3 November, 16-23 February, Tuesday dinner, Saturday lunch, Sunday dinner and Monday

Rest – Menu €40 (weekday lunch), €58 €bi/100 bi – Carte €60/71

◆ Between the canal and Moselle, a former fisherman's house (1928) with a lovely garden where you can eat in summer. Warm welcome, coloured rooms, modern food and well-stocked cellar.

AYTRÉ – **17 Charente-Maritime** – **324** D3 – see La Rochelle

AZAY-LE-RIDEAU – **37 Indre-et-Loire** – **317** L5 – **pop. 3 100** – **alt. 51 m** – ✉ **37190** **Châteaux of the Loire** 11 **A2**

Paris 265 – Châtellerault 61 – Chinon 21 – Loches 58 – Saumur 47 – Tours 26

Office de tourisme, 4, rue du Château ✆ 02 47 45 44 40, Fax 02 47 45 31 46

Château★★★ - Façade★ of St-Symphorien church.

Le Grand Monarque

VISA MC AE

3 pl. de la République – ✆ 02 47 45 40 08 – monarq@club-internet.fr – Fax 02 47 45 46 25 – Closed 16 November-19 December, 4 January-10 February, Sunday (except restaurant), Tuesday lunch and Monday from 12 October to Easter

24 rm – †€ 65/135 ††€ 77/165, ☕ € 12 – ½ P € 75/119 – **Rest** – Menu (€ 15), € 29/42 – Carte € 53/87

◆ This Touraine-inspired residence consisting of two buildings separated by a leafy courtyard offers lovely rooms with beams, stonework and old furniture. Elegant, rustic dining room warmed by an imposing fireplace; superb terrace.

Des Châteaux

P VISA MC

2 rte de Villandry – ✆ 02 47 45 68 00 – info@hoteldeschateaux.com – Fax 02 47 45 68 29 – Open 15 February-15 November

27 rm – †€ 53 ††€ 57/72, ☕ € 9 – ½ P € 53/59 – **Rest** – *(closed lunch except Sunday and public holidays)* Menu € 19/26 – Carte € 24/34

◆ Prestigious châteaux are dotted along your tour route so take time to relax in one of these simple but charming little rooms. Traditional dishes prepared by the patronne at the restaurant.

De Biencourt without rest

VISA MC

7 r. Balzac – ✆ 02 47 45 20 75 – biencourt@infonie.fr – Fax 02 47 45 91 73 – Open 15 March-15 November

15 rm – †€ 48 ††€ 50, ☕ € 8

◆ Once occupied by a school (traces of which are still noticeable in the decor), this 18C house is situated near the château. Rustic and Directoire-style furniture. Breakfast served in the refurbished dining room or on the patio.

L'Aigle d'Or

AC VISA MC AE

10 av. A.-Riché – ✆ 02 47 45 24 58 – aigle-dor@wanadoo.fr – Fax 02 47 45 90 18 – Closed 1st-5 September, 15-29 November, 18 January-28 February, Monday dinner from December to Easter, Tuesday dinner except July-August, Sunday dinner and Wednesday

Rest – *(pre-book)* Menu (€ 20), € 27/62 bi – Carte € 32/54

◆ Tasty traditional dishes served in a low key dining room with exposed beams and fresh flower arrangements. Pleasant service.

in Saché **6.5 km East by D 17** – **pop. 1 004** – **alt. 78 m** – ✉ **37190**

Auberge du XIIe Siècle (Xavier Aubrun et Thierry Jimenez)

VISA MC

1 r. Château – ✆ 02 47 26 88 77 – Fax 02 47 26 88 21 – Closed 26 May-4 June, 1st-10 September, 17-26 November, 5-21 January, Sunday dinner, Tuesday lunch and Monday

Rest – *(pre-book Sat - Sun)* Menu € 30/70 – Carte € 65/77

Spec. Œufs brouillés à la crème de morilles. Sandre à la rhubarbe (June to September). Marbré au chocolat fondant. **Wines** Touraine-Azay le Rideau, Chinon.

◆ A venerable half-timbered inn often visited by Balzac not far from the château where he was often a guest. Well-preserved rustic setting. Classic recipes.

AZINCOURT – **62 Pas-de-Calais** – **301** F5 – **pop. 273** – **alt. 115 m** – ✉ **62310** 30 **A2**

Paris 225 – Arras 56 – Boulogne-sur-Mer 62 – Calais 78 – Hesdin 16 – St-Omer 40

Office de tourisme, 24, rue Charles VI ✆ 03 21 47 27 53, Fax 03 21 47 13 12

Charles VI

P VISA MC AE

12 r. Charles-VI – ✆ 03 21 41 53 00 – restaurantcharles6@wanadoo.fr – Fax 03 21 41 53 11 – Closed February school holidays and Wednesday

Rest – Menu (€ 11 bi), € 14 bi (weekday lunch), € 23/33 – Carte € 24/37

◆ Enjoy traditional cooking in an impressive country style dining room (pastel tones, beams) in the centre of this village famous for its 1415 battle.

BACCARAT – 54 Meurthe-et-Moselle – **307** L8 – **pop. 4 746 – alt. 260 m** –
✉ **54120** Alsace-Lorraine 27 **C2**

Paris 369 – Épinal 43 – Lunéville 27 – Nancy 58 – St-Dié 29 – Sarrebourg 45

Office de tourisme, 2, rue Adrien Michaut ✆ 03 83 75 13 37,
Fax 03 83 75 36 76

Stained-glass windows★ of St-Rémy church - Musée du cristal.

La Renaissance VISA

31 r. des Cristalleries – ✆ 03 83 75 11 31 – renaissance.la@wanadoo.fr
– Fax 03 83 75 21 09 – Closed 1st-7 January
16 rm – €52 €52, €10 – ½ P €62 – **Rest** – *(closed Sunday evening and Friday)* Menu €18/38 – Carte €26/51

◆ In the home of glassblowing, this handy small hotel near the Crystal Museum has functional and well soundproofed rooms. Traditional unpretentious food served in a rustic dining room or on a small flower-decked terrace.

BADEN – 56 Morbihan – **308** N9 – **pop. 3 360 – alt. 28 m** – ✉ **56870** 9 **A3**

Paris 473 – Auray 9 – Lorient 52 – Quiberon 40 – Vannes 15

Le Gavrinis rest, VISA

2 km at Toulbroch via the Vannes road – ✆ 02 97 57 00 82 – gavrinis@wanadoo.fr
– Fax 02 97 57 09 47 – Closed 17 November-4 December and 6 January-8 February
18 rm – €55/130 €55/130, €11 – ½ P €68/86
Rest – *(closed Sunday dinner off season, Monday except dinner in season, Tuesday lunch and Saturday lunch)* Menu (€19), €23/76 – Carte €39/69

◆ This recently built Breton style house, surrounded by a fine garden, is pursuing its makeover (six refurbished rooms, 12 underway) in a restrained, comfortable style. Tempting contemporary menu inspired by regional recipes. Pleasant interior and flower-decked terrace.

BAERENTHAL – 57 Moselle – **307** Q5 – **pop. 702 – alt. 220 m** –
✉ **57230** 27 **D1**

Paris 449 – Bitche 15 – Haguenau 33 – Strasbourg 62 – Wissembourg 45

Office de tourisme, 1, rue du Printemps d'Alsace ✆ 03 87 06 50 26,
Fax 03 87 06 62 31

Le Kirchberg without rest VISA

8 imp. de la Forêt – ✆ 03 87 98 97 70 – resid.hotel.kirchberg@wanadoo.fr
– Fax 03 87 98 97 91 – Closed 1st January-8 February
20 rm – €40/51 €60/64, €10

◆ A modern hotel in the heart of the Vosges Regional Park. Modern, fresh and neat rooms (ten with a small kitchen) those at the rear have a relaxing view of the fir trees. Fresh air guaranteed!

in Untermuhlthal 4 km Southeast by D 87 – ✉ 57230 Baerenthal

L'Arnsbourg (Jean-Georges Klein) VISA

– ✆ 03 87 06 50 85 – l.arnsbourg@wanadoo.fr – Fax 03 87 06 57 67
– Closed 2-17 September, 1st-28 January, Tuesday and Wednesday
Rest – *(pre-book Sat - Sun)* Menu €55 (weekday lunch), €110/140 – Carte €102/125

Spec. Emulsion de pomme de terre et truffe. Saint-Pierre infusé au laurier en croûte de sel. Pomme de ris de veau au foin, infusion à la citronnelle. **Wines** Gewurztraminer, Muscat.

◆ This imposing mansion stands alone in the forest of the Vosges and offers deliciously inventive meals in an elegant classic-modern dining room overlooking the Zinsel.

K VISA

– ✆ 03 87 27 05 60 – hotelk@orange.fr – Fax 03 87 06 88 65
– Closed 2-17 September, 1st-28 January, Tuesday and Wednesday
6 rm – €200/360 €200/360, €26 – 6 suites – €305/430

◆ The modern lines of this almost transparent edifice and its comfortable, minimalist rooms open on to a Japanese garden.

BAFFIE – 63 Puy-de-Dôme – 326 J10 – pop. 101 – alt. 850 m – ✉ 63600 6 C2

Paris 457 – Clermont-Ferrand 90 – Issoire 69 – Montbrison 44 – Thiers 71

Le Relais du Vermont

at the Col de Chemintrand – ✆ 04 73 95 34 75 – auberge-vermont@wanadoo.fr – Fax 04 73 95 93 81 – Closed 24 December-5 February, Sunday dinner, Tuesday dinner off season and Monday

Rest – Menu € 14,50/26

◆ Former coach house (1870) built on a pass from where you can enjoy a lovely view. Local dishes and inviting desserts served in a pleasant, rustic setting.

BÂGÉ-LE-CHÂTEL – 01 Ain – 328 C3 – pop. 762 – alt. 209 m – ✉ 01380 44 B1

Paris 396 – Bourg-en-Bresse 35 – Mâcon 11 – Pont-de-Veyle 7 – St-Amour 39 – Tournus 41

Syndicat d'initiative, 2, rue Marsale ✆ 03 85 30 56 66, Fax 03 85 30 56 66

La Table Bâgésienne

Gde-Rue – ✆ 03 85 30 54 22 – latablebagesienne@wanadoo.fr – Fax 03 85 30 58 33 – Closed 24 July-6 August, 20-27 December, 16-25 February, Monday dinner, Tuesday dinner and Wednesday

Rest – Menu € 19 (weekday lunch), € 24/47 – Carte € 41/59

◆ Two rustic dining rooms with a fireplace, wood panelling and antique Bresse furniture. Terrace shaded by a lime tree. Updated regional cuisine.

BAGES – 11 Aude – 344 I4 – see Narbonne

BAGNÈRES-DE-BIGORRE – 65 Hautes-Pyrénées – 342 M4 – pop. 8 048 – alt. 551 m – Spa : mid March-late Nov. – Casino – ✉ 65200

Languedoc-Roussillon-Tarn Gorges 28 A3

Paris 829 – Lourdes 24 – Pau 66 – St-Gaudens 65 – Tarbes 23

Office de tourisme, 3, allées Tournefort ✆ 05 62 95 50 71, Fax 05 62 95 33 13

de la Bigorre Pouzac Quartier Serre Devant, Northeast by D 938: 3 km, ✆ 05 62 91 06 20.

Parc thermal de Salut★ via Av. Pierre-Noguès - Grotte de Médous★★ Southeast: 2,5 km by D 935.

La Résidence

Vallon de Salut – ✆ 05 62 91 19 19 – residotel@voila.fr – Fax 05 62 95 29 88 – Open 2 May-30 September

26 rm – †€ 85/90 ††€ 85/90, ☕ € 10 – 3 suites – ½ P € 75/80 – **Rest** – *(dinner only) (residents only)* Menu € 25

◆ In the calm pastoral setting of the spa resort park. Large, renovated rooms overlooking the Salut valley. Lounge-cum-video library. Lovely, opulent dining room leading on to a pleasant terrace. Cosy and refined bar.

Hostellerie d'Asté

3.5 km Campan road (D 935) – ✆ 05 62 91 74 27 – contacts@hotel-aste.com – Fax 05 62 91 76 74 – Closed 12 November-11 December

21 rm – †€ 51/60 ††€ 51/60, ☕ € 7 – 1 suite – ½ P € 49/54 – **Rest** – *(closed Sunday dinner except school holidays)* Menu € 16/36 – Carte € 18/48

◆ An imposing building between the road and the River Adour. Small rooms, gradually being redecorated, the murmur of the river audible in those at the rear. Light dining room and waterside terrace in the garden. Traditional food focusing on produce from the sea.

Les Petites Vosges without rest

17 bd Carnot – ✆ 05 62 91 55 30 – lpv@lespetitesvosges.com – Fax 05 62 91 55 30 – Closed 12-30 November

4 rm ☕ – †€ 65 ††€ 75

◆ Next to the thermal spas and the casino, this charming house envelops a part of the ramparts of the old town. Modern décor, cosy rooms and stylish tea room. The lady of the house will give you good advice on hikes in the area.

L'Auberge Gourmande

1 bd Lyperon – 05 62 95 52 01 – Closed 21-28 September, 11-30 November, Sunday dinner off season, Monday and Tuesday

Rest – Menu € 13 (weekday lunch), € 25/50 – Carte € 38/62

♦ This family-run restaurant opposite the casino and near the baths specialises in regional cuisine. Yellow tones and copper lights in the dining room. Bar.

à Gerde South 2 km by Campan road – pop. 1 116 – alt. 570 m – ✉ 65200

Le Relais des Pyrénées without rest

1 av. 8-Mai-1945 – 05 62 44 66 67 – contact@relais-despyrenees.com – Fax 05 62 44 90 14 – Closed November

55 rm – € 66/83 € 74/119, € 10

♦ Situated on the banks of the Adour, this former textile factory now houses a modern hotel with fitness facilities and the Laurent Fignon cycling centre. Lovely views of the Pyrenees.

in Beaudéan 4.5 km South by Campan road (D 935) – pop. 378 – alt. 625 m – ✉ 65710

Office de tourisme, place de la Mairie 05 62 91 79 92

Lesponne Valley ★ Southwest.

Le Catala

– 05 62 91 75 20 – le.catala@wanadoo.fr – Fax 05 62 91 79 72 – Closed 1st-8 May, 1st-8 November, Christmas holidays and Sunday except school holidays

24 rm – € 48/50 € 52/60, € 7,50 – 3 suites – ½ P € 50 – **Rest** – *(dinner only) (residents only)*

♦ Behind the discreet façade of this Bigourdan hotel is an original interior: the decor of the rooms matches the painted frescos on the doors (sport, history, etc).

in Lesponne 8 km South by D 935 and D 29 – ✉ 65710 Campan

Domaine de Ramonjuan rest,

– 05 62 91 75 75 – ramonjuan@wanadoo.fr – Fax 05 62 91 74 54

22 rm – € 40/55 € 45/100, € 7 – ½ P € 45/60

Rest – *(closed 10-26 November, Sunday and Monday) (dinner only)*

Menu € 20/25 – Carte € 20/40

♦ This small complex offers horse riding and good leisure facilities. Rustic rooms in the farmhouse and modern studios available. A veranda dining area and summer terrace. Serving regional dishes and paella.

BAGNÈRES-DE-LUCHON – 31 Haute-Garonne – 343 B8 – pop. 2 900 – alt. 630 m – Winter sports : at Superbagnères, 1 440/2 260 m 1 14 – Spa : early March-late Oct. – Casino Y – ✉ 31110 Languedoc-Roussillon-Tarn Gorges

Paris 814 – St-Gaudens 48 – Tarbes 98 – Toulouse 141 — 28 **B3**

Office de tourisme, 18, allée d'Étigny 05 61 79 21 21, Fax 05 61 79 11 23

de Luchon Route de Montauban, 05 61 79 03 27.

Plan on next page

D'Étigny rest, rest,

opposite thermal baths – 05 61 79 01 42 – etigny@aol.com – Fax 05 61 79 80 64 – Open 1stMay-25 October — Z **k**

58 rm – € 48/78 € 48/130, € 9 – 5 suites – ½ P € 50/85

Rest – Menu € 17/43 – Carte € 25/54

♦ Opposite the thermal baths, a variety of standard quality rooms . The three renovated ones are the most comfortable. A discreet, bourgeois restaurant and shaded terrace; traditional dishes served.

Corneille

5 av. A.-Dumas – 05 61 79 36 22 – reservation.luchon@cityblue.fr – Fax 05 61 79 81 11 — Y **u**

46 rm – € 100/130 € 100/130, € 15 – 4 suites – **Rest** – Menu € 37/50

♦ This 19C construction was the first Luchon casino (period stained-glass windows). While the rooms could do with a makeover, they do command a fine view of the Pyrenees. Two dining rooms, one opening onto the garden. Traditional cuisine.

BAGNÈRES-DE-LUCHON

Alexandre-Dumas (Av.) . . . . Y 2
Bains (Allées des) . . . . Z 3
Barrau (Av. J.) . . . . Z 4
Boileau (R. P.) . . . . X 8
Boularan (Av. Jean) . . . . Y 6
Carnot (Av.) . . . . Y 9
Colomic (R.) . . . . X 12
Dardenne (Bd.) . . . . Y 13
Dr-Germès (R. du) . . . . X 14
Étigny (Allées d') . . . . YZ 16
Fontan (Bd A.) . . . . XY 17
Gambetta (R.) . . . . Y 18
Joffre (Pl. Mar.) . . . . X 20
Laity (R.) . . . . X 22
Lamartine (R.) . . . . Y 23
Nadau (R. G.) . . . . X 25
Nérée-Boubée (R.) . . . . X 26
Pyrénées (Av. des) . . . . Z 28
Quinconces (Cours des) . . . . Z 30
Rostand (Bd E.) . . . . Y 32
Thiers (R.) . . . . Y 33
Toulouse (Av. de) . . . . X 34
Victor-Hugo (R.) . . . . Y 36

D 125 (1) TOULOUSE, TARBES

D 618 COL DE PEYRESOURDE (3)

► : One way in season

SUPERBAGNÈRES

SUPERBAGNÈRES, VALLÉE DU LYS, VALLÉE DE LA PIQUE

COL DU PORTILLON (2)

Hotels and restaurants change every year, so change your Michelin guide every year!

Apsis without rest VISA AE
19 allées d'Etigny – ✆ 05 61 79 56 97 – reception.luchon@apsishotels.com – Fax 05 61 95 43 96 Y **z**
47 rm – €72/96 €90/120, ☕ €15
◆ A business clientele and skiers appreciate this brand new hotel for its central location, attractive, contemporary and well-fitted rooms, and for its "business facilities".

Royal Hôtel rest, VISA
1 cours Quinconces – ✆ 05 61 79 00 62 – Fax 05 61 79 38 35 – Open 25 May-1st October Z **v**
48 rm – €40 €45, ☕ €6 – ½ P €42/50 – **Rest** – Menu €17
◆ Hotel popular with guests taking the spa waters nearby. Rooms with diverse furnishings (rustic and classic); those on the top floor are smaller. High ceilings and mouldings give a charm typical of old-world France to the simple dining room.

Panoramic without rest P VISA AE
6 av. Carnot – ✆ 05 61 79 30 90 – hotel.panoramic@wanadoo.fr – Fax 05 61 79 32 84 – Closed 3 November-5 December X **a**
28 rm – €42/69 €50/72, ☕ €8,50
◆ A hundred-year-old building. Most of the rooms have been carefully renovated and soundproofed. Hearty buffet breakfast.

Deux Nations VISA AE
5 r. Victor-Hugo – ✆ 05 61 79 01 71 – hotel2nations@aol.com – Fax 05 61 79 27 89 Y **g**
28 rm – €26/58 €30/58, ☕ €7 – ½ P €32/43 – **Rest** – *(closed Sunday dinner and Monday except school holidays and public holidays)* Menu (€10), €15/35 – Carte €19/43
◆ The same family has been welcoming guests to this two-building establishment since 1917. Ask for one of the more recent rooms. The restaurant has its own entrance and gives onto a pleasant terrace on a pretty flower-decked patio.

La Rencluse rm, P VISA
à St-Mamet ✉ 31110 – ✆ 05 61 79 02 81 – resa@hotel-larencluse.com – Fax 05 61 79 82 99 – Closed 9 March-30 April Z **y**
24 rm – €45/52 €52/55, ☕ €7 – ½ P €41/43 – **Rest** – *(lunch only in winter)* Menu €12/25 – Carte €20/34
◆ A pleasant stopover on the road to Spain, offering rather comfortable rooms (quieter in the annex) and a 'family country home' atmosphere. Pastoral atmosphere (panelled walls, rustic furniture and checked tablecloths) and simple classic cuisine.

Pavillon Sévigné P
2 av. Jacques-Barrau – ✆ 05 61 79 31 50 – seiter@pavillonsevigne.com Z **z**
5 rm ☕ – €80 €90 – ½ P €65 – **Table d'hôte** – Menu €25 bi
◆ Frescoes, a wooden staircase and antique furniture set the scene for this stylish 19C manor house, plus modern equipment (flat screens) and a charming welcome. Pleasant dining room opening onto the garden. Single set menu served in the restaurant.

in Juzet-de-Luchon 3 km by ① – pop. 379 – alt. 625 m – ✉ 31110

Le Poujastou
r. du Sabotier – ✆ 05 61 94 32 88 – info@lepoujastou.com – Fax 05 61 94 32 88 – Closed November
5 rm ☕ – €40 €49 – **Table d'hôte** – Menu €18 bi
◆ An 18C village café which today offers simple but carefully decorated accommodation: ochre shades, cocoa floors and antique or pine furniture. Meals are served in a pleasant Pyrenean-style dining room or in the garden.

in St-Paul-d'Oueil 8 km by ③, D618 and D51 – pop. 49 – alt. 1 000 m – ✉ 31110

Maison Jeanne without rest
– ✆ 05 61 79 81 63 – Fax 05 61 79 81 63
4 rm ☕ – €64 €74/130
◆ This lovely country house looks onto a garden and the mountain. Rooms decorated with family heirlooms and homemade stencils. Very charming welcome.

BAGNEUX – 49 Maine-et-Loire – **317** I5 – **see Saumur**

BAGNOLES-DE-L'ORNE – 61 Orne – **310** G3 – **pop. 893 – alt. 140 m – Spa : mid March-late Oct. – Casino** A – ✉ **61140** **Normandy** 32 **B3**

Paris 236 – Alençon 48 – Argentan 39 – Domfront 19 – Falaise 48 – Flers 28

Office de tourisme, place du Marché ✆ 02 33 37 85 66, Fax 02 33 30 06 75

de Bagnoles-de-l'Orne Route de Domfront, ✆ 02 33 37 81 42.

Site★ - Lake★ - Thermal establishment park /I★.

BAGNOLES-DE-L'ORNE

Bois-Motté (Bd du) . . . . A 2
Casinos (R. des) . . . . A 3
Château (Av. du) . . . . A 4
Dr-Pierre-Noal (Av. du) . . . . A 7
Dr-Poulain (Av. du) . . . . A 8
Gaulle (Pl. Général-de) . . . . B 9
Hartog (Bd G.) . . . . A 13
Lemeunier-de-la-Raillère (Bd) . . . . B 14
Rozier (Av. Ph.-du) . . . . A 15
Sergenterie-de-Javains (R.) . . . . A 18

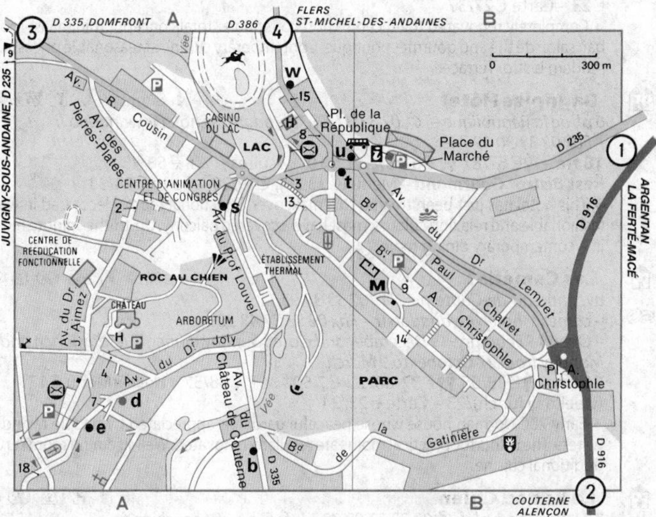

Le Manoir du Lys (Franck Quinton)

2 km rte Juvigny-sous-Andaine via ③ –
✆ 02 33 37 80 69 – manoir-du-lys@wanadoo.fr – Fax 02 33 30 05 80
– Closed 4 January-13 February, Sunday dinner, Tuesday lunch and Monday from November to April except Easter
VISA MC AE

23 rm – €75/140 €75/195, € 15 – 7 suites – ½ P € 97/190
Rest – Menu € 35/90 – Carte € 53/89
Spec. Homard bleu à la plancha. Menu "champignons" (spring and autumn). Pigeonneau rôti entier, jus clair au "sydre".

◆ In the heart of the woods in a park, a fine Norman manor. Personalised rooms in the main house; the more recent and spacious ones in an unusual outbuilding. Regional cuisine served in a superb, modern-style dining room or on an exquisite terrace.

Nouvel Hôtel

AC rest, rest, VISA MC AE

8 av. Dr-P.-Noal – ✆ 02 33 30 75 00 – contact@nouvel-hotel-bagnoles.fr
– Fax 02 33 30 75 13 – Open 8 March-2 November A **e**

30 rm – €47/58 €53/73, € 8 – ½ P € 49/59 – **Rest** – Menu € 18/32 – Carte € 25/37

◆ This pretty early 20C villa has functional, pleasant, soundproofed rooms. A lounge with piano and peaceful flower garden. Three rooms, one under a pleasant veranda; traditional, health-food and vegetarian set menus.

Bois Joli rest, VISA AE

av. Ph.-du-Rozier – ✆ 02 33 37 92 77 – boisjoli@wanadoo.fr – Fax 02 33 37 07 56 A **w**

20 rm – €72/152 €72/152, €11 – ½ P €64/106 – **Rest** – Menu €20/56 – Carte €36/65

◆ Elegant 19C Anglo-Norman villa with a half-timbered facade. Low-key interior, antique furniture of various styles and delightful, recently-renovated rooms. Park planted with trees. A welcoming dining room with fine, original wood panelling and a carved fireplace.

Ô Gayot rest, VISA

2 av. de la Ferté-Macé – ✆ 02 33 38 44 01 – contact@ogayot.com – Fax 02 33 38 47 71 – Closed 21 December-7 February, Thursday (except hotel) 1st April-9 November, Monday, Tuesday and Wednesday from 9 November to 31 March A **u**

16 rm – €45 €95, €8,50 – ½ P €48/70 – **Rest** – bistrot Menu (€16 bi), €23 – Carte €27/37

◆ Completely renovated town centre hotel offering a "total concept": minimalist rooms, bar, salon de thé and gourmet boutique. Contemporary cuisine at reasonable prices in the modern bistro. Terrace.

Bagnoles Hôtel rm, VISA

6 pl. de la République – ✆ 02 33 37 86 79 – bagnoles.hotel@wanadoo.fr – Fax 02 33 30 19 74 A **t**

18 rm – €67/87 €67/87, €10 – 2 suites – ½ P €58/73

Rest *Bistrot Gourmand* – Menu (€13,50), €19/20 – Carte €24/33

◆ This hotel has just been treated to a makeover. Functional rooms decorated in warm, fashionable and relaxing colours; most have a covered balcony. Up-to-the-minute recipes in a contemporary dining room.

Les Camélias VISA AE

av. Château-de-Couterne – ✆ 02 33 37 93 11 – cameliashotel@wanadoo.fr – Fax 02 33 37 48 32 – Open 15 February-19 December and closed Sunday dinner, Tuesday lunch and Monday from 27 October to 9 March A **b**

26 rm – €35/65 €37/68, €7,50 – ½ P €38/57 – **Rest** – Menu €17 (weekday lunch)/23 – Carte €23/34

◆ Early 20C Norman house whose peaceful garden is appreciated by people taking the waters. The colourful, practical rooms are regularly renovated. Well-lit dining room serving traditional cuisine.

Le Roc au Chien VISA AE

10 r. Prof.-Louvel – ✆ 02 33 37 97 33 – info@hotelrocauchien.fr – Fax 02 33 38 17 76 – Open 7 March-5 November A **s**

42 rm – €34/50 €48/68, €7,50 – ½ P €51/65

Rest – Menu €20/28

◆ The Countess of Ségur is said to have stayed in this hotel composed of two small adjoining buildings, one flanked by a brick turret. Rooms in rustic style. The long dining room faces the street; regional dishes and specialities for the health-conscious.

XX **Le Celtic** with rm rest, VISA AE

14 av. Dr-Noal – ✆ 02 33 37 92 11 – leceltic@club-internet.fr – Fax 02 33 38 90 27 – Closed 7 January-28 February, Sunday dinner and Monday A **d**

10 rm – €45/56 €48/56, €7,50 – ½ P €48/60 – **Rest** – Menu (€17), €19 (weekdays)/40 – Carte €32/37

◆ The attractive early-20C facade conceals a pleasant dining room decorated in pastel shades, with a fireplace and modern light-coloured wood furniture. Local dishes and charming service. Renovated rooms

BAGNOLET – 93 Seine-Saint-Denis – **305** F7 – **101** 17 – see Paris, Area

Look out for red symbols, indicating particularly pleasant establishments.

BAGNOLS – 69 Rhône – 327 G4 – pop. 701 – alt. 400 m – ✉ 69620
Lyon - Rhone Valley 43 **E1**

Paris 444 – Lyon 30 – Tarare 20 – Villefranche-sur-Saône 14

Château de Bagnols rm, rest,
– ✆ 04 74 71 40 00 – info@chateaudebagnols.fr
– Fax 04 74 71 40 49
16 rm – €396/705 €396/705, €32 – 5 suites
Rest – Menu €45 (weekday lunch), €80/120 – Carte €95/129 Reduced menu at lunchtimes
Spec. Tatin de pomme de terre au pied de cochon. Poularde de Bresse et parmentier truffé. Poitrine et rognons de veau aux herbes. **Wines** Chablis, Brouilly.
♦ Gardens open onto the Beaujolais countryside, access by drawbridge, restored Renaissance frescoes and superb rooms with personal touches - one feels to the manor born! Tempting cuisine served in a majestic guardroom with its splendid Gothic fireplace and ancestral furniture.

BAGNOLS – 63 Puy-de-Dôme – 326 C9 – pop. 532 – alt. 862 m – ✉ 63810 5 **B2**

Paris 483 – La Bourboule 23 – Clermont-Ferrand 64 – Issoire 63 – Le Mont-Dore 29

Voyageurs
au bourg – ✆ 04 73 22 20 12 – legouffet@aol.com – Fax 04 73 22 21 18 – Closed 4-22 January, Sunday dinner and Monday
20 rm – €30/45 €35/50 – ½ P €50/65 – **Rest** – Menu €19 (weekdays)/50 – Carte €41/44
♦ A 1960s building in an Auvergne village built in local style. Simple, practical rooms, gradually being renovated. A modest restaurant whose popularity is certainly due to the tasty dishes - contemporary and regional - served there!

BAGNOLS-SUR-CÈZE – 30 Gard – 339 M4 – pop. 18 103 – alt. 51 m – ✉ 30200
Provence 23 **D1**

Paris 653 – Alès 54 – Avignon 34 – Nîmes 56 – Orange 25 – Pont-St-Esprit 12

Office de tourisme, Espace Saint-Gilles ✆ 04 66 89 54 61, Fax 04 66 89 83 38

Musée d'Art moderne Albert-André★.

Site★ of Roques-sur-Cèze.

Château du Val de Cèze without rest
1 km Avignon road – ✆ 04 66 89 61 26 – hotelvaldeceze@sud-provence.com – Fax 04 66 89 97 37 – Open from March to October
22 rm – €90 €99, €7,50 – 1 suite
♦ The 17C château houses a reception area and lounges. The Provençal style rooms (wrought iron, terracotta tiles, coloured fabrics) are in houses dotted around the estate (pool and tennis court).

Alès road 5 km West by D 6 and D 143 – ✉ 30200 Bagnols-sur-Cèze

Château de Montcaud rm,
– ✆ 04 66 89 60 60 – montcaud@relaischateaux.com – Fax 04 66 89 45 04 – Open 17 April-25 October
26 rm – €170/330 €180/490, €23 – 2 suites – ½ P €180/340
Rest *Les Jardins de Montcaud* – *(closed lunch except Sunday in season)* Menu (€44), €47/77 – Carte €65/75
Rest *Bistrot de Montcaud* – *(closed Saturday and Sunday) (lunch only)* Menu €28/33 – Carte €32/37
♦ Noble 19C residence in well-tended parkland. Period furniture and warm colours personalise the attractive rooms in this haven of peace. Smart Provençal restaurant and lovely patio in the Montcaud Gardens. Simple menu in the Bistrot. Jazzy Sunday brunches in summer.

BAIE DES TRÉPASSÉS – 29 Finistère – 308 C6 – see Pointe du Raz

BAILLARGUES – 34 Hérault – 339 J7 – see Montpellier

BAILLEUL – 59 Nord – 302 E3 – pop. 14 146 – alt. 44 m – ✉ 59270
Northern France and the Paris Region 30 **B2**

Paris 244 – Armentières 13 – Béthune 31 – Dunkerque 44 – Ieper 20 – Lille 30 – St-Omer 37

Office de tourisme, 3, Grand'place ✆ 03 28 43 81 00, Fax 03 28 43 81 01

✱★ of the belfry.

Belle Hôtel without rest
19 r. de Lille – ✆ 03 28 49 19 00 – belle.hotel@wanadoo.fr – Fax 03 28 49 22 11 – Closed 4-17 August, 24 December-5 January

31 rm – €82/90 €82/150, €13

◆ Two red-brick Flemish houses. The rooms are spacious and sophisticated (period furniture) in one and more modern in the other, but both are well looked after.

BAIROLS – 06 Alpes-Maritimes – 341 D4 – pop. 114 – alt. 850 m – ✉ 06420
41 **D2**

Paris 836 – Digne-les-Bains 120 – Grasse 74 – Nice 53 – St Martin-Vésubie 40

Auberge du Moulin
4 r. Lou-Coulet – ✆ 04 93 02 92 93 – Closed 15 November-15 December and Monday

Rest – *(number of covers limited, pre-book)* Menu €25/35

◆ Former mill at the heart of a medieval hilltop village. Single Italian menu served in a pretty rustic setting and relaxed atmosphere. Bits of old machinery adorn the dining room.

BAIX – 07 Ardèche – 331 K5 – pop. 822 – alt. 80 m – ✉ 07210 44 **B3**

Paris 588 – Crest 30 – Montélimar 22 – Privas 18 – Valence 33

Les Quatre Vents without rest
Chomérac road, 2 km north-westward – ✆ 04 75 85 80 64 – Fax 04 75 85 05 30 – Closed 21 December-4 January

21 rm – €42/47 €45/50, €7

◆ An ochre façade and blue shutters for these two buildings set back a little from the busy road. Unassuming but practical rooms.

Les Quatre Vents
Chomérac road, 2 km north-westward – ✆ 04 75 85 84 49 – Fax 04 75 85 84 49 – Closed 26 December-12 January, Saturday lunch and Sunday dinner

Rest – Menu (€13,50), €21/52 – Carte €33/49

◆ This restaurant serving modern cuisine offers exposed rafters and redecorated dining rooms with paintings on display.

BALARUC-LES-BAINS – 34 Hérault – 339 H8 – pop. 5 688 – alt. 3 m – Spa : early March-mid Dec. – Casino – ✉ 34540 Languedoc-Roussillon-Tarn Gorges

Paris 781 – Agde 32 – Béziers 52 – Frontignan 8 – Lodève 54 – Montpellier 33 – Sète 9 23 **C2**

Syndicat d'initiative, Pavillon Sévigné ✆ 04 67 46 81 46, Fax 04 67 46 81 54

Le St-Clair
quai du Port – ✆ 04 67 48 48 91 – contact@restaurant-saintclair.com – Fax 04 67 18 86 96 – Closed 2-25 January

Rest – Menu €20 (weekday lunch), €30/69 – Carte €59/83

◆ Charming restaurant with a veranda-dining room overlooking the quayside and a terrace, adorned with palm trees, facing the Thau basin. A must for fish and shellfish enthusiasts.

BALAZUC – 07 Ardèche – 331 I6 – pop. 337 – alt. 170 m – ✉ 07120 44 **A3**

Paris 651 – Lyon 189 – Privas 49 – Alès 65 – Montélimar 43

Château de Balazuc
– ✆ 04 75 88 52 67 – contact@chateaudebalazuc.com – Fax 04 75 88 52 67 – Open April-October

4 rm – €130/150 €140/160 – **Table d'hôte** – Menu €38 bi

◆ Refined luxury at this beautifully restored medieval chateau in the centre of a mountain village. Ultra contemporary bedrooms (one in the old chapel), gardens and a terrace. Mediterranean cuisine served for residents.

BALDENHEIM – 67 Bas-Rhin – **315** J7 – **see Sélestat**

BALDERSHEIM – 68 Haut-Rhin – **315** I10 – **see Mulhouse**

BALLEROY – 14 Calvados – **303** G4 – **pop. 787 – alt. 70 m** – ✉ **14490**
Normandy 32 **B2**

Paris 276 – Bayeux 16 – Caen 42 – St-Lô 23 – Vire 47

Château★.

Manoir de la Drôme P VISA MC AE

– ✆ 02 31 21 60 94 – denisleclerc@wanadoo.fr – Fax 02 31 21 88 67
– Closed 25 October-6 November, 2-27 February, Sunday dinner, Tuesday lunch, Monday and Wednesday
Rest – Menu € 48/68 – Carte € 67/75

◆ This pretty 17C manor adorned with Virginia creeper invites you to savour classic dishes in an elegant dining room that opens onto the garden that meets the Drôme.

LA BALME-DE-SILLINGY – 74 Haute-Savoie – **328** J5 – **pop. 3 729 – alt. 480 m** – ✉ 74330 46 **F1**

Paris 524 – Annecy 13 – Bellegarde-sur-Valserine 30 – Belley 59 – Frangy 14 – Genève 48

Syndicat d'initiative, route de Choisy ✆ 04 50 68 78 70, Fax 04 50 68 53 29

Les Rochers AC rest, P VISA MC AE

D 1508 – ✆ 04 50 68 70 07 – hotel.restaurant.les-rochers@wanadoo.fr
– Fax 04 50 68 82 74 – Closed 1st-15 November, January, Sunday dinner and Monday except from 15 June to 15 September
24 rm – €48/52 €52/57, € 10 – ½ P € 52/59 – **Rest** – Menu € 20 (weekdays)/86 – Carte € 27/57

◆ Hotel in a small town at the foot of the Mandallaz mountain. All the rooms have been refurbished; those to the rear are quieter. A family guest-house atmosphere dominates the large dining room, furnished in Louis XIII fashion. Traditional fare.

La Chrissandière P VISA MC AE

at 400 m
10 rm – €71 €71, € 10 – ½ P € 70

◆ Thatched cottage in a 3 ha park. Refurbished, nicely decorated rooms. Park and pool: two undeniable strong points for this annexe. Reception is at Les Rochers.

LA BALME DE THUY – 74 Haute-Savoie – **328** K5 – **see Thônes**

BALOT – 21 Côte-d'Or – **320** G3 – **pop. 93 – alt. 272 m** – ✉ **21330** 8 **C1**

Paris 235 – Auxerre 74 – Chaumont 74 – Dijon 82 – Montbard 28 – Troyes 72

Auberge de la Baume rm, rm, VISA MC

– ✆ 03 80 81 40 15 – la.baume@tiscali.fr – Fax 03 80 81 62 87
– Closed 22 December-4 January
10 rm – €56 €56, € 8 – ½ P € 55/60 – **Rest** – Menu € 21/35 – Carte € 23/31

◆ Across from the church, attentive welcome and renovated rooms that are practical and well maintained. Get a taste of the local ambiance by passing by the establishment's bar. The dining room has a gallery and some fine woodwork.

BAMBECQUE – 59 Nord – **302** D2 – **pop. 655 – alt. 8 m** – ✉ **59470** 30 **B1**

Paris 271 – Calais 65 – Dunkerque 24 – Hazebrouck 26 – Lille 57 – St-Omer 36

La Vieille Forge VISA MC

38 r. Principale – ✆ 03 28 27 60 67 – lavieilleforge@voila.fr – Fax 03 28 27 60 67
– Closed 1st-15 September, Saturday lunch and dinner in winter except Friday and Saturday, Sunday dinner and Monday
Rest – Menu (€ 31), € 38/65 – Carte € 56/71

◆ A magnificent fireplace (remains of the old forge) stands in the lovely rustic dining room. The menu is made up of selections from which guests select.

BANASSAC – 48 Lozère – **330** H8 – **pop. 813** – **alt. 525 m** – ✉ **48500** 22 **B1**

Paris 588 – Florac 55 – Mende 47 – Millau 52

du Sabot La Canourgue Route des Gorges du Tarn, Southeast: 4 km by D 998, ✆ 04 66 32 84 00.

Le Calice du Gévaudan rest, VISA

– ✆ 04 66 32 94 18 – calice@wanadoo.fr – Fax 04 66 32 98 62
– Closed 22-31 August, autumn half-term holidays, Saturday dinner, Sunday and public holidays

28 rm – †€ 47/52 ††€ 50/52, ☕ € 7 – ½ P € 44 – **Rest** – Menu € 15/19 – Carte € 31/42

◆ For a place to stop on the way to your holiday, aim for this recent and functional hotel offering rather simply furnished rooms, but which have good soundproofing. A restaurant with a peaceful terrace that gives onto a garden with a children's play area.

BAN-DE-LAVELINE – 88 Vosges – **314** K3 – **pop. 1 216** – **alt. 427 m** – ✉ **88520**

Paris 411 – Colmar 59 – Épinal 67 – St-Dié 14 – Ste-Marie-aux-Mines 15 – Sélestat 39 27 **D3**

Auberge Lorraine with rm VISA

– ✆ 03 29 51 78 17 – auberge-lorraine.sarl@wanadoo.fr – Fax 03 29 51 71 72
– Closed in March, 1st-11 July, 14-24 October, Sunday and Monday

7 rm – †€ 33/48 ††€ 39/64, ☕ € 8 – ½ P € 46/56

Rest – Menu (€ 13,50), € 17, € 20/39 – Carte € 27/56

◆ A pleasant stop in the Vosges: hearty helpings of tasty regional fare served in a dolls' house decor. Faultless service. The snug, warmly decorated rooms are spacious and practical. Relaxation area.

BANDOL – 83 Var – **340** J7 – **pop. 7 905** – **alt. 1 m** – **Casino** Y – ✉ **83150** French Riviera

Paris 818 – Aix-en-Provence 68 – Marseille 48 – Toulon 18

Access to Ile de Bendor by boat (crossing 7mn) ✆ 04 94 29 44 34.

Office de tourisme, allées Vivien ✆ 04 94 29 41 35, Fax 04 94 32 50 39

de Frégate Saint-Cyr-sur-Mer Route de Bandol, by Marseille road: 4 km, ✆ 04 94 29 38 00.

Allées Jean-Moulin★. 40 **B3**

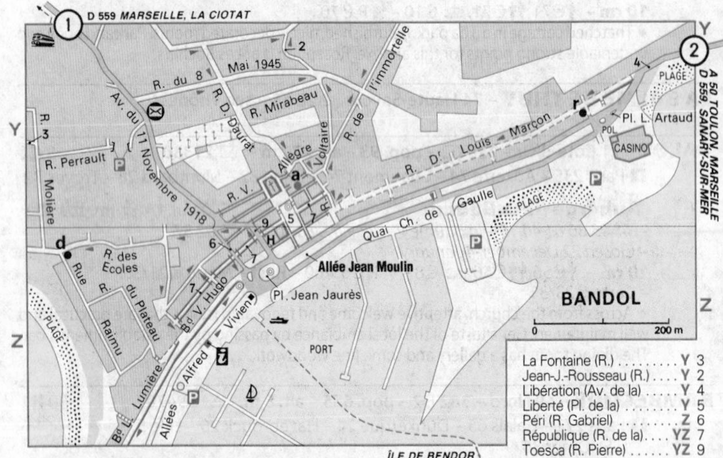

La Fontaine (R.)	Y	3
Jean-J.-Rousseau (R.)	Y	2
Libération (Av. de la)	Y	4
Liberté (Pl. de la)	Y	5
Péri (R. Gabriel)	Z	6
République (R. de la)	YZ	7
Toesca (R. Pierre)	YZ	9

De la Baie without rest VISA

62 r. Dr-Marçon – ✆ 04 94 29 40 82 – contact@hotel-baie-bandol.com – Fax 04 94 29 95 24 – Closed 20 December-30 January Y **r**

14 rm – †€ 60/95 ††€ 72/108, ☕ € 8,50

◆ After an evening at the casino, your hotel near the harbour is just a short distance away. Rather large rooms, simple but well soundproofed on the front of the hotel.

Golf Hôtel rm, rm, VISA
on Renécros beach via Blvd L. Lumière -Z – 04 94 29 45 83 – golfhotel.surplage@wanadoo.fr – Fax 04 94 32 42 47 – Open mid March-beg. November
24 rm – €54/115 €54/115, €8,50
Rest – rest. de plage *(open Easter-28 September and closed dinner except 21 June-12 September)* Menu €21 – Carte €25/40
◆ This charming villa surrounded by sand dunes has small rooms with varied furnishings, some have loggias or balconies. Meals served on the terrace overlooking the bay, where you can almost put your feet in the water!

Bel Ombra rest, VISA AE
r. de la Fontaine - Y – 04 94 29 40 90 – hotel.bel.ombra@wanadoo.fr – Fax 04 94 25 01 11 – Open 21 March-15 October
20 rm – €56/82 €56/82, €7,50 – ½ P €63/70
Rest – *(open 24 June-20 September) (dinner only) (residents only)* Menu €22
◆ Off the beaten track of the summer visitors, a villa offering small, functional, well-kept rooms. For a family stay choose those with mezzanines.

Les Galets rest, VISA AE
49 montée Voisin – 04 94 29 43 46 – info@lesgalets-bandol.com – Fax 04 94 32 44 36 – Open 15 January-5 November
20 rm – €60/65 €80/85, €8 – ½ P €63/76
Rest – *(open 1st May-30 September)* Menu €26 – Carte €30/36
◆ A hillside hotel with magnificent sea views. Most of the rather simple rooms overlook the sea. Rustic restaurant (beams and copperware) and terrace with panoramic views. Traditional cuisine.

Le Clocher VISA
1 r. de la Paroisse – 04 94 32 47 65 – le.clocher@wanadoo.fr – Closed Sunday dinner and Wednesday Y **a**
Rest – *(number of covers limited, pre-book)* Menu (€12 bi), €26/40 – Carte approx. €42
◆ A charming welcome, modern, minimalist, fashionable décor, terrace in a side street and lovely, modern food: this small restaurant in old Bandol is a good choice.

via ② 1,5 km and Sanary road – 83110 Sanary-sur-Mer

Le Castel with rm VISA AE
925 rte de la Canolle – 04 94 29 82 98 – Fax 04 94 32 53 32 – Closed 12 January-12 February and Sunday dinner from 15 November to 31 March
9 rm – €59 €69, €8 – ½ P €69 – **Rest** – *(pre-book)* Menu €32/41 – Carte €49/65
◆ Small family hotel in a flower-decked setting. Pretty little dining room, traditional cuisine and some simple rooms, for the most part on the ground floor.

BANGOR – 56 Morbihan – 063 11 – see Belle-Ile-en-Mer

BANNALEC – 29 Finistère – 308 I7 – pop. 4 785 – alt. 98 m – 29380 9 B2

Paris 535 – Carhaix-Plouguer 51 – Châteaulin 67 – Concarneau 25 – Quimper 33

Office de tourisme, Kerbail 02 98 39 43 34, Fax 02 98 39 53 44

St-Thurien road 4,5 km Northeast by D 23 and secondary road – 29380 Bannalec

Le Manoir du Ménec VISA
– 02 98 39 47 47 – merlinmenec@aol.com – Fax 02 98 39 46 17
15 rm – €80/90 €90/100, €8 – ½ P €70/75 – **Rest** – *(closed lunch except Sunday and Wednesday from mid November-mid March)* Menu €25/50
◆ Spacious old-style bedrooms in the original manor house, slightly smaller ones in its outbuildings, although with the benefit of better bathrooms. Some rooms with four-poster beds. Indoor leisure complex. Beams, old stonework and a granite fireplace give character to the dining room. Classic cuisine.

BANNAY – 18 Cher – 323 N2 – pop. 742 – alt. 148 m – ✉ 18300
Dordogne-Berry-Limousin 12 **D2**

Paris 196 – Orléans 128 – Bourges 55 – Gien 52 – Cosne-sur-Loire 6

La Buissonnière with rm rm, rm, VISA
58 r. du Canal – ✆ 02 48 72 42 07 – Fax 02 48 72 35 90
– Closed 19 January-9 February, Sunday dinner and Monday
10 rm – €52/79 €52/79, €7,50 – ½ P €55/59 – **Rest** – Menu (€12), €18/35 – Carte €25/51
◆ 1900 construction opposite the Canal de la Loire. Up-to-date cuisine served in an unfussy dining room, or under the pergola. Pratical rooms at garden level or on the first floor, the latter accessed by a gallery.

BANNEGON – 18 Cher – 323 M6 – pop. 254 – alt. 180 m – ✉ 18210 12 **D3**

Paris 284 – Bourges 43 – Moulins 70 – St-Amand-Montrond 22 – Sancoins 23

Moulin de Chaméron with rm VISA
– ✆ 02 48 61 83 80 – moulindechameron@wanadoo.fr – Fax 02 48 61 84 92
– Open 15 March-30 November and closed Tuesday lunch and Monday off season
13 rm – €69/91 €69/113, €12,50 – **Rest** – Menu €25/48 – Carte €41/53
◆ This 18C mill is home to a pleasant restaurant and milling museum in an ideal country setting. The more recent hotel section offers sober rooms.

BANYULS-SUR-MER – 66 Pyrénées-Orientales – 344 J8 – pop. 4 532 – alt. 1 m –
✉ 66650 Languedoc-Roussillon-Tarn Gorges 22 **B3**

Paris 887 – Cerbère 11 – Perpignan 37 – Port-Vendres 7

Office de tourisme, avenue de la République ✆ 04 68 88 31 58, Fax 04 68 88 36 84

✻★★ du cap Réderis East: 2 km.

Les Elmes rm, VISA
plage des Elmes – ✆ 04 68 88 03 12 – contact@hotel-des-elmes.com
– Fax 04 68 88 53 03
31 rm – €48/115 €48/115, €10 – ½ P €65/95
Rest *Littorine* – *(closed 11 November-10 December and lunch Monday-Wednesday)* Menu €33/48 – Carte €42/64
◆ Welcoming hotel on the beach. The rooms are either traditional, modern or nautical on the second floor (where they have recently been renovated). Fish and shellfish star in this restaurant with views of the Mediterranean from the terrace.

Al Fanal et H. El Llagut with rm VISA
av. Fontaulé – ✆ 04 68 88 00 81 – al.fanal@wanadoo.fr – Fax 04 68 88 13 37
– Closed 1st-15 December and 5-25 February
13 rm – €57/72 €57/72, €9 – ½ P €55/70 – **Rest** – *(closed Wednesday and Thursday from November to April)* Menu (€19), €25/38 – Carte €31/58
◆ Flavourful Catalan cooking centred on seafood. Very good regional wines to be savoured in a pleasant, nautical-style setting or on the seaside terrace. Renovated rooms.

LA BARAQUE – 63 Puy-de-Dôme – 326 F8 – see Clermont-Ferrand

BARAQUEVILLE – 12 Aveyron – 338 G5 – pop. 2 569 – alt. 792 m –
✉ 12160 29 **C1**

Paris 639 – Albi 58 – Millau 75 – Rodez 17 – Villefranche-de-Rouergue 43

Syndicat d'initiative, place du Marché ✆ 05 65 69 10 78, Fax 05 65 71 10 19

Segala Plein Ciel valley, rm, rest, VISA
rte d'Albi – ✆ 05 65 69 03 45 – infos@hotel-pleinciel.com – Fax 05 65 70 14 54 – Closed 22 December-8 January, Friday dinner and Sunday dinner except July-August
47 rm – €45/60 €45/60, €7 – ½ P €80/90 – **Rest** – Menu €20/45 – Carte €23/43
◆ A 1970s building and its grounds overlooking the small market town. The large rooms look out over the valley; most of them have been renovated in a Japanese or Canadian style. Long panoramic dining room, with nautical decor and terrace. Regional cooking.

BARATIER – 05 Hautes-Alpes – **334** G5 – **pop. 461 – alt. 855 m** – ✉ 05200 41 **C1**

Paris 705 – Gap 40 – Grenoble 143 – Marseille 215 – Valence 124

Les Peupliers

chemin de Lesdier – ☎ 04 92 43 03 47 – info@hotel-les-peupliers.com – Fax 04 92 43 41 49 – Closed 30 March-24 April and 28 September-23 October

24 rm – €42 €50/64, €7 – ½ P €49/56 – **Rest** – *(closed Tuesday lunch, Wednesday lunch, Thursday lunch and Friday lunch except July-August)* Menu €18/39 – Carte €26/40

◆ A warm and attractive chalet in a quiet verdant village setting. The roooms are a charming blend of mountain styles and Provencal decor. Some with a balcony and a view of Serre-Ponçon Lake. Pleasant Alpine dining room warmed by an open fire; shady terrace.

BARBASTE – 47 Lot-et-Garonne – **336** D4 – **pop. 1 416 – alt. 45 m** – ✉ 47230 Atlantic Coast 4 **C2**

Paris 703 – Agen 34 – Bordeaux 125 – Villeneuve-sur-Lot 50

Syndicat d'initiative, place de la Mairie ☎ 05 53 65 84 85, Fax 05 53 65 51 38

La Cascade aux Fées

r. Riberotte – ☎ 05 53 97 05 96 – gmazurier@aol.com – Open March-mid October

4 rm – €64/90 €72/100, €7 – **Table d'hôte** – *(open Monday and Saturday)* Menu €25 bi/35 bi

◆ This 18C residence in part backing on to the rock, opens onto a magnificent flowery and shady park that runs alongside the Gélise river. Rooms and lounges furnished with antique pieces are simply but tastefully decorated. Warm welcome. Market produce takes pride of place in the restaurant.

BARBAZAN – 31 Haute-Garonne – **343** B6 – **pop. 378 – alt. 464 m** – ✉ 31510 28 **B3**

Paris 779 – Bagnères-de-Luchon 32 – Lannemezan 27 – St-Gaudens 14 – Tarbes 67

Syndicat d'initiative, le village ☎ 05 61 88 35 64, Fax 05 61 88 35 64

Hostellerie de l'Aristou with rm

rte de Sauveterre – ☎ 05 61 88 30 67 – Fax 05 61 95 55 66 – Closed 17 November-13 February

6 rm – €60 €60/95, €8 – ½ P €60

Rest – *(closed lunch Monday-Thursday from May-July, Sunday dinner and Monday from September to April and Tuesday lunch from October to March)* Menu €21/45 – Carte €32/53

◆ 19C farm converted into a country inn; two welcoming dining rooms and small covered terrace. Rooms have rustic or period furniture.

LA BARBEN – 13 Bouches-du-Rhône – **340** G4 – **see Salon-de-Provence**

BARBENTANE – 13 Bouches-du-Rhône – **340** D2 – **pop. 3 645 – alt. 40 m** – ✉ 13570 Provence 42 **E1**

Paris 692 – Avignon 10 – Arles 33 – Marseille 103 – Nîmes 38 – Tarascon 16

Office de tourisme, 4, le Cours ☎ 04 90 90 85 86, Fax 04 90 95 60 02

Château★★.

Castel Mouisson without rest

– ☎ 04 90 95 51 17 – contact@hotel-castelmouisson.com – Fax 04 90 95 67 63 – Open 15 March-15 October

17 rm – €49/66 €49/66, €8

◆ This pleasant Provençal house at the foot of the Montagnette offers simple, rustic rooms overlooking an immense, beautiful garden with trees. A warm family welcome.

BARBEZIEUX-ST-HILAIRE – 16 Charente – **324** J7 – **pop. 4 819 – alt. 100 m** – ✉ 16300 Atlantic Coast 38 **B3**

Paris 480 – Bordeaux 84 – Angoulême 36 – Cognac 36 – Jonzac 24 – Libourne 70

Office de tourisme, Le Château ☎ 05 45 78 91 04, Fax 05 45 78 91 04

La Boule d'Or

9 bd Gambetta – ✆ 05 45 78 64 13 – laboule.dor@wanadoo.fr – Fax 05 45 78 63 83 – Closed 22 December-4 January, Friday dinner and Sunday dinner from October to April

18 rm – †€ 47 ††€ 47, ☕ € 5,50 – ½ P € 48 – **Rest** – Menu € 13/25 – Carte € 28/39

◆ In the capital of Cognac's Petite Champagne region, land of writer Jacques Chardonne ("Sentimental Desires"). Old building with spacious rooms. A contemporary restaurant and peaceful terrace in the shade of a chestnut tree.

BARBIZON – 77 Seine-et-Marne – 312 E5 – pop. 1 490 – alt. 80 m – ✉ 77630

Northern France and the Paris Region 19 **C3**

Paris 56 – Étampes 41 – Fontainebleau 10 – Melun 13 – Pithiviers 45

Office de tourisme, 41, Grande Rue ✆ 01 60 66 41 87, Fax 01 60 66 41 87

Cély Golf Club Cély Route de Saint Germain, West: 9 km by D64 and D11, ✆ 01 64 38 03 07.

Auberge du Père Ganne★.

Hôtellerie du Bas-Bréau

22 r. Grande – ✆ 01 60 66 40 05 – basbreau@relaischateaux.com – Fax 01 60 69 22 89

16 rm – †€ 150 ††€ 250/390, ☕ € 26 – 4 suites – **Rest** – Menu € 54 (weekday lunch)/76 – Carte € 88/120

◆ An establishment that owes its reputation to R. L. Stevenson, one of many well-known guests. Beautiful rooms with personal touches looking out on a park with thousands of flowers. Rustic-bourgeois decor in the dining room and shady terrace. Game in season.

Hostellerie La Clé d'Or

73 Grande-Rue – ✆ 01 60 66 40 96 – cle.dor@wanadoo.fr – Fax 01 60 66 42 71

16 rm – †€ 60/72 ††€ 70/170, ☕ € 11 – ½ P € 78 – **Rest** – *(closed Sunday evening from November to March)* Menu € 29/39 – Carte € 41/65

◆ Each of the rooms of this former post house is different but all are situated around an inside garden. Modern food to be enjoyed depending on the season in a cosy dining room or on the pleasant terrace.

L'Angélus

31 r. Grande – ✆ 01 60 66 40 30 – restaurant.angelus@wanadoo.fr – Fax 01 60 66 42 12 – Closed 12-29 January, Monday and Tuesday

Rest – Menu € 29/40 – Carte € 38/57

◆ In the main street, a spick and span rustic inn bears a sign in homage to one of Millet's most famous works, painted at Barbizon. Traditional menu.

BARBOTAN-LES-THERMES – 32 Gers – 336 B6 – Spa : late Feb.-late Nov. – Casino – ✉ 32150 Cazaubon

Languedoc-Roussillon-Tarn Gorges 28 **A2**

Paris 703 – Aire-sur-l'Adour 37 – Auch 75 – Condom 37 – Mont-de-Marsan 43

Office de tourisme, place Armagnac ✆ 05 62 69 52 13, Fax 05 62 69 57 71

De la Paix

24 av. des Thermes – ✆ 05 62 69 52 06 – contact@hotel-paix.fr – Fax 05 62 09 55 73 – Open 10 March-10 November

29 rm – †€ 45/49 ††€ 49/75, ☕ € 7 – ½ P € 65/70 – **Rest** – Menu (€ 13,50), € 16/35 – Carte € 19/27

◆ Recent building near the church and the hot springs spa. The spacious, well-kept rooms are equipped with functional furniture. Very discreet setting and guest house atmosphere in the restaurant: traditional cuisine and diet menus on request.

Les Fleurs de Lees

rte d'Agen – ✆ 05 62 08 36 36 – contact@fleursdelees.com – Fax 05 62 08 36 37 – Open April-October

16 rm – †€ 65/125 ††€ 65/125, ☕ € 12 – 5 suites – ½ P € 58/88

Rest – Menu (€ 21), € 39 bi (weekdays)/110 bi – Carte € 37/61

◆ Smart house in the heart of Armagnac. Quiet rooms, some with a terrace, and lovely themed suites (Africa, Asia, India, etc.) Furniture and decorative objects from Dubai in the restaurant; the cuisine blends international and local flavours.

Cante Grit rest, VISA AE

51 av. des Thermes – ✆ 05 62 69 52 12 – post@cantegrit.com – Fax 05 62 69 53 98 – Open 16 March-14 November

20 rm – †€ 40/55 ††€ 49/69, ☕ € 7 – ½ P € 48

Rest – Menu € 18 (weekdays)/38

◆ This pretty villa dating from the 1930s is covered in Virginia creeper; it has rooms that are rather large, airy and practical. The welcoming lounge is reminiscent of a family home. Welcoming dining room with fireplace and exposed beams and pleasant summer terrace.

Beauséjour VISA

6 av. des Thermes – ✆ 05 62 08 30 30 – bernard.urrutia@wanadoo.fr – Fax 05 62 09 50 78 – Open mid March-end-November

28 rm – †€ 32/70 ††€ 32/70, ☕ € 10 – ½ P € 32/55 – **Rest** – Menu € 20 (weekdays)/40

◆ Large house in the regional style, with smartly renovated rooms and a welcoming lounge in the British style. Pretty leafy garden. A restaurant in sunny shades with a terrace facing the Gers countryside. Diet meals on request.

Aubergade rest, VISA

13 av. des Thermes – ✆ 05 62 69 55 43 – aubergade2@wanadoo.fr – Fax 05 62 69 52 09 – Open 1st March-30 November

18 rm – †€ 40/48 ††€ 40/48, ☕ € 8 – ½ P € 49 – **Rest** – Menu € 12 (weekdays)/39 – Carte € 25/40

◆ At the entrance to this spa resort where exotic species of plants flourish, smart, regional-style house offering functional, well-soundproofed rooms. Pleasant dining room and traditional menu or diet dishes (for guests taking the spa waters).

BARCELONNETTE – 04 Alpes-de-Haute-Provence – 334 H6 – pop. 2 819 – alt. 1 135 m – Winter sports : Le Sauze/Super Sauze 1 400/2 000 m 23 and Pra-Loup 1 500/2 600 m 3 29 – ✉ 04400 French Alps 41 C2

Paris 733 – Briançon 86 – Cannes 161 – Digne-les-Bains 88 – Gap 68 – Nice 145

Office de tourisme, place Frédéric Mistral ✆ 04 92 81 04 71, Fax 04 92 81 22 67

St-Pons church ★ Northwest: 2 km.

Azteca without rest VISA

3 r. François-Arnaud – ✆ 04 92 81 46 36 – hotelazteca@barcelonnette.fr – Fax 04 92 81 43 92 – Closed 12 November-2 December

27 rm – †€ 59/107 ††€ 59/107, ☕ € 11

◆ An attractive villa with an original decor of Mexican furniture and handicrafts, recalling the "Barcelonnettes" who emigrated to Mexico. Three rooms continue this theme.

Le Passe-Montagne VISA AE

in 3 km, Col de la Cayolle road – ✆ 04 92 81 08 58 – Fax 04 92 81 08 58 – Open July-August, 20 December-30 April and closed Tuesday and Wednesday except school holidays

Rest – *(pre-book)* Menu € 21/29 – Carte € 29/41

◆ A warm, friendly atmosphere and rustic, alpine decor in this small chalet on the edge of the pinewoods. Regional cuisine: mountain-style in winter and Provençal in summer.

in St-Pons 2 km Northwest by D 900 and D 9 – ✉ 04400

Domaine de Lara without rest

– ✆ 04 92 81 52 81 – arlette.signoret@wanadoo.fr – Fax 04 92 81 07 76 – Closed 25 June-4 July and 12 November-19 December

5 rm ☕ – †€ 77/86 ††€ 83/92

◆ In a relaxing park, with the Pain de Sucre in the background, pretty, Provençal building converted into a guest house with character (beams, floor tiles, old stone, family furniture). Good breakfast.

in Sauze 4 km Southeast by D 900 and D 209 – ✉ 04400 Enchastrayes – Winter sports : 1 400/2 000 m 23

Office de tourisme, Immeuble Perce-Neige ✆ 04 92 81 05 61, Fax 04 92 81 21 60

L'Alp'Hôtel
– *✆ 04 92 81 05 04 – info@alp-hotel.com – Fax 04 92 81 45 84*
– Open 1st June-30 September and 15 December-15 April
14 rm – €69/120 €69/150, € 10 – ½ P €69/98 – **Rest** – Menu €23/30 – Carte €28/42

◆ The hotel is next to a chair-lift in the small ski resort dominated by the Chapeau de Gendarme; (2685m). Vaulted lounges and functional rooms, gradually being renovated, most with balconies. Fitness facilities. Dining room in Provençal tones facing the ski slopes.

in Jausiers 8 km Northeast by D 900 – pop. 896 – alt. 1 240 m – ✉ 04850

Office de tourisme, Grande Rue ✆ 04 92 81 21 45, Fax 04 92 81 59 35

Villa Morelia with rm
– *✆ 04 92 84 67 78 – inforesa@villa-morelia.com – Fax 04 92 84 65 47*
– Closed 1st March-30 April and 1st November-26 December
7 rm – €120 €150/190, €20 – 3 suites
Rest – *(closed Sunday, Monday and Tuesday except June, July and August) (dinner only from September to May) (pre-book)* Menu €35/68

◆ Elegant dining rooms at this fine "Mexican" villa (1900). Terrace overlooking the garden and swimming pool. Comfortable guestrooms.

in Pra-Loup 8.5 km Southwest by D 902, D 908 and D 109 – ✉ 04400 Uvernet Fours – Winter sports : 1 500/2 600 m 3 29

Office de tourisme, Maison de Pra-Loup ✆ 04 92 84 10 04, Fax 04 92 84 02 93

Le Prieuré de Molanès
à Molanès – ✆ 04 92 84 11 43 – info@prieure.eu – Fax 04 92 84 01 88
– Open 8 June-14 September and 21 December-13 April
13 rm – €55/65 €65/80, €10 – ½ P €55/77 – **Rest** – Menu (€14), €20, €26 – Carte €23/42

◆ Near to the chairlift, a former priory turned into a family hotel appreciated for its mountain-style atmosphere and its non-smoking rooms renovated in an Alpine style. Regional meals mostly using local produce, in a rustic, welcoming setting (beams, fireplace, farming tools).

BARCUS – 64 Pyrénées-Atlantiques – 342 H5 – pop. 774 – alt. 230 m – ✉ 64130

3 **B3**

Paris 813 – Mauléon-Licharre 14 – Oloron-Ste-Marie 18 – Pau 52 – St-Jean-Pied-de-Port 53

Chilo with rm
– *✆ 05 59 28 90 79 – martine.chilo@wanadoo.fr – Fax 05 59 28 93 10*
– Closed 3-16 March, 5-18 January, Sunday dinner, Monday dinner and Tuesday lunch from October to 15 June and Monday lunch
11 rm – €45/85 €55/105, €9 – ½ P €64/89 – **Rest** – Menu €20 (weekdays)/68 – Carte €47/64

◆ Fine house, typical of the region, in the heart of a quiet village. Regional cuisine served in a welcoming dining room (non-smoking). Pleasant garden and swimming pool with a view of the mountain.

BARDIGUES – 82 Tarn-et-Garonne – 337 B7 – see Auvillar

BARFLEUR – 50 Manche – 303 E1 – pop. 642 – alt. 5 m – ✉ 50760

Normandy

32 **A1**

Paris 355 – Carentan 48 – Cherbourg 29 – St-Lô 75 – Valognes 26

Office de tourisme, 2, rond-point le Conquérant ✆ 02 33 54 02 48, Fax 02 33 54 02 48

Pointe de Barfleur Lighthouse: ✳★★ North: 4 km - Interior★ of Montfarville church 2 km S.

Le Conquérant

18 r. St-Thomas-Becket – ✆ 02 33 54 00 82 – contact@hotel-leconquerant.com – Fax 02 33 54 65 25 – Open 15 March-15 November

10 rm – †€ 67/103 ††€ 67/103, ☕ € 10 – **Rest** – crêperie *(dinner only) (residents only)* Menu € 16/33

◆ Handsome 17C granite-built residence with French-style garden a stone's throw from the port. The six largest rooms have been redecorated and fitted with modern bathrooms. Sweet and savoury pancakes prepared traditionally, to order.

Moderne

1 pl. Gén.-de-Gaulle – ✆ 02 33 23 12 44 – cauchemez@wanadoo.fr – Fax 02 33 23 91 58 – Closed Tuesday dinner and Wednesday

Rest – Menu € 19/39 – Carte € 29/59

◆ In summer this restaurant overflows onto a pleasant terrace. Updated traditional menu featuring fine seafood.

LES BARILS – 27 Eure – 304 E9 – see Verneuil-sur-Avre

BARJAC – 30 Gard – 339 L3 – pop. 1 379 – alt. 171 m – ✉ 30430 23 D1

Paris 666 – Alès 34 – Aubenas 45 – Mende 114

Office de tourisme, place Charles Guynet ✆ 04 66 24 53 44, Fax 04 66 60 23 08

Le Mas du Terme

4 km south-eastward by D 901 and secondary road – ✆ 04 66 24 56 31 – info@masduterme.com – Fax 04 66 24 58 54 – Open 15 March-15 November

23 rm – †€ 64/104 ††€ 64/186, ☕ € 12 – ½ P € 78/141 – **Rest** – *(closed lunch except July-August and public holidays)* Menu € 34

◆ This old silkworm farm in the heart of the vineyards is quite close to the magical Orgnac pothole. Provençal rooms, apartments or furnished family holiday accommodation (gîtes). This 18C building is home to a restaurant with a vaulted ceiling and an outdoor terrace. Serves daily set menu.

BAR-LE-DUC P – 55 Meuse – 307 B6 – pop. 16 944 – alt. 188 m – ✉ 55000

Alsace-Lorraine 26 A2

Paris 255 – Metz 97 – Nancy 84 – Reims 113 – St-Dizier 26 – Verdun 56

Office de tourisme, 7, rue Jeanne-d'Arc ✆ 03 29 79 11 13, Fax 03 29 79 21 95

de Combles-en-Barrois Combles-en-Barrois 38 rue Basse, by St-Dizier road: 5 km, ✆ 03 29 45 16 03.

"le Transi" (statue)★★ in St-Étienne church AZ.

Bistro St-Jean

132 bd de La Rochelle – ✆ 03 29 45 40 40 – Fax 03 29 45 40 45 – Closed Saturday lunch and Sunday

Rest – Menu (€ 21), € 30 – Carte € 34/40

◆ Pleasant little establishment in the town centre resembling a modernised traditional bistro. Typical menu, seafood.

in Trémont-sur-Saulx 9,5 km South-West by D 3 – pop. 610 – alt. 166 m – ✉ 55000

La Source

– ✆ 03 29 75 45 22 – contact@hotel-restaurant-lasource.fr – Fax 03 29 75 48 55 – Closed 28 July-16 August, 2-19 January, Sunday dinner and Monday lunch

24 rm – †€ 65/100 ††€ 74/120, ☕ € 11 – ½ P € 80 – **Rest** – Menu € 30/55 – Carte € 35/62

◆ This Eighties motel overlooking the countryside has functional, quiet rooms for travellers, carefully renovated in pastel shades. A spit has been installed in the largest dining room, recently redecorated in a more modern style.

BARNEVILLE-CARTERET – 50 Manche – 303 B3 – pop. 2 429 – alt. 47 m – ✉ 50270 Normandy 32 A2

Paris 356 – Carentan 43 – Cherbourg 39 – Coutances 47 – St-Lô 62

Office de tourisme, 10, rue des Ecoles ✆ 02 33 04 90 58, Fax 02 33 04 93 24

de la Côte-des-Isles Saint-Jean-de-la-Rivière Chemin des Mielles, Southeast: 5 km by D 90, ✆ 02 33 93 44 85.

à Barneville-Plage

Des Isles

9 bd Maritime – ✆ 02 33 04 90 76 – hotel-des-isles@wanadoo.fr – Fax 02 33 94 53 83 – Closed February

30 rm – €69/119 €69/119, €10 – ½ P €65/90 – **Rest** – Menu (€16), €24/35 – Carte approx. €50

♦ Recently renovated hotel looking out to sea. Guestrooms of differing size, all elegantly decorated in a cosy maritime style with varying shades of blue and soft duvets. A relaxed atmosphere in which to enjoy an "all-you-can-eat" buffet of starters and desserts.

in Carteret

Office de tourisme, place des Flandres-Dunkerque ✆ 02 33 04 94 54

Viewpoint indicator ★.

De la Marine (Laurent Cesne) rest, rm,

11 r. de Paris – ✆ 02 33 53 83 31 – infos@hotelmarine.com – Fax 02 33 53 39 60 – Open 1st March-23 December

26 rm – €98/250 €98/250, €16 – ½ P €102/177

Rest – *(open 1st March-11 November and closed Sunday dinner, Thursday lunch and Monday in March, October and November, Monday lunch and Thursday lunch in April, May, June and September)* Menu €33 (weekdays)/87 – Carte €56/85

Spec. Langoustine "comme une pizza" (July-August). Soupe de homard au lait de coco. Carré d'agneau du pays rôti en croûte d'herbes.

♦ This waterfront hotel has been run by the same family since 1876. Most of the recent rooms, spacious and modern, have a terrace with views of the port. Enjoy impressive sea views from the restaurant dining room and terrace. Inventive, tasty dishes using quality ingredients.

Des Ormes rm, rest,

quai Barbey d'Aurevilly – ✆ 02 33 52 23 50 – hoteldesormes@wanadoo.fr – Fax 02 33 52 91 65 – Closed January

12 rm – €75/175 €75/175, €14 – ½ P €80/100 – **Rest** – *(closed Sunday dinner, Monday and Tuesday off season, Monday lunch and Tuesday lunch in season)* Menu €35/45 – Carte €38/102

♦ Overlooking the marina, a tastefully renovated 19C abode. Exquisite rooms, cosy sitting room and a lovely flower-decked garden in season. Elegant, romantic and contemporary dining room serving food from the land and sea.

BARON – 60 Oise – 305 H5 – pop. 777 – alt. 80 m – ✉ 60300 Northern France and the Paris Region 36 B3

Paris 65 – Amiens 110 – Argenteuil 63 – Montreuil 55

Le Domaine de Cyclone without rest

2 r. de la Gonesse – ✆ 06 08 98 05 50 – domainedecyclone@wanadoo.fr – Fax 03 44 54 26 10 – Closed 2-11 March

5 rm – €70 €80

♦ Joan of Arc is supposed to have slept in this castle. The guests now occupy rooms with very sought after décor that nearly all overlook the park. Horse riding.

BARR – 67 Bas-Rhin – 315 I6 – pop. 5 892 – alt. 200 m – ✉ 67140 Alsace-Lorraine

Paris 495 – Colmar 43 – Le Hohwald 12 – Saverne 46 – Sélestat 20 – Strasbourg 37 2 C1

Office de tourisme, place de l'Hôtel de Ville ✆ 03 88 08 66 65, Fax 03 88 08 66 51

Aux Saisons Gourmandes

23 r. Kirneck – ✆ 03 88 08 12 77 – Closed 1st-16 July, 24 February-11 March, Sunday dinner from January to April, Tuesday and Wednesday

Rest – Menu (€12), €19 (weekday lunch), €28/45 – Carte €23/47

♦ Pretty half-timbered house in the town centre sporting a tasteful, modern interior. Market fresh cuisine with traditional influences is served.

Mont Ste-Odile road by D 854 – ✉ 67140 Barr

Château d'Andlau
113 r. vallée St Ulrich, at 2 km – ✆ 03 88 08 96 78 – hotel.chateau-andlau@wanadoo.fr – Fax 03 88 08 00 93 – Closed 12-27 November and 2-26 January
22 rm – €45/51 €51/66, €11 – ½ P €59/66
Rest – *(open dinner from Tuesday to Saturday, Sunday lunch and public holidays)* Menu €26/36
◆ The simple, rustic rooms and pastoral setting of this hotel will ensure a good night's sleep. Plush dining room and classic menu. Excellent choice of international wines, unusually presented along the lines of a wine tasting manual.

LE BARROUX – 84 Vaucluse – 332 D9 – pop. 569 – alt. 325 m – ✉ 84330

Provence 42 **E1**

Paris 684 – Avignon 38 – Carpentras 12 – Vaison-la-Romaine 16

Hostellerie François-Joseph without rest
2 km via Chemin de Rabassières and Abbaye Ste-Madeleine road – ✆ 04 90 62 52 78 – hotel.f.joseph@wanadoo.fr – Fax 04 90 62 33 54 – Open from March to October
12 rm – €80/115 €80/115, €12 – 6 suites
◆ Nestled in a shady garden, a charming residence made up of several Provençal farm-houses provides a beautiful view of the surrounding countryside and Mont Ventoux.

Les Géraniums rest,
pl. de la Croix – ✆ 04 90 62 41 08 – les.geraniums@wanadoo.fr – Fax 04 90 62 56 48 – Open 1st March-1st November and 15 December-2 January
20 rm – €60/65 €60/65, €10 – ½ P €60/65 – **Rest** – *(closed Wednesday lunch and Tuesday in December)* Menu (€20), €28 (weekday lunch), €30/38 – Carte €40/45
◆ An old house in this high-perched village complete with a 12C fortress overlooking the Comtat plain. Unpretentious rooms with a rustic spirit. A pleasant restaurant with exposed rafters and a pleasant summer terrace.

L'Aube Safran
chemin du Patigiage – ✆ 04 90 62 66 91 – contact@aube-safran.com – Fax 04 90 62 66 91 – Open 15 March-15 November
5 rm – €100/145 €100/145 – **Table d'hôte** – Menu €39 bi
◆ The owners of this *mas* have opted for the good life at this idyllic location at the foot of Mt Ventoux, where they have reintroduced the culture of saffron, abandonned at the end of the 19C. Table d'hôte twice e week, with local dishes featuring the flower-spice. Boutique.

BAR-SUR-AUBE – 10 Aube – 313 I4 – pop. 6 261 – alt. 190 m – ✉ 10200

Northern France and the Paris Region 14 **C3**

Paris 230 – Châtillon-sur-Seine 60 – Chaumont 41 – Troyes 53 – Vitry-le-François 65

Office de tourisme, Place de l'Hôtel de Ville ✆ 03 25 27 24 25, Fax 03 25 27 40 02

St-Pierre church ★.

Le Saint Nicolas without rest
2 r. du Gén.-de-Gaulle – ✆ 03 25 27 08 65 – le-saintnicolas@tiscali.fr – Fax 03 25 27 60 31
27 rm – €59/62 €62/65, €8
◆ Pretty stone houses provide the setting for this quiet hotel, slightly away from the town centre. Rooms set around the swimming pool.

La Toque Baralbine
18 r. Nationale – ✆ 03 25 27 20 34 – toquebaralbine@wanadoo.fr – Fax 03 25 27 20 34 – Closed Sunday dinner except July-August and Monday
Rest – Menu €20/60 – Carte €26/50
◆ Choose to eat in the rustic rear dining room which is warmer, or on the flower-decked terrace. Tasty cuisine with a contemporary touch and the accent on local produce.

LE BAR-SUR-LOUP – 06 Alpes-Maritimes – 341 C5 – pop. 2 543 – alt. 320 m – ✉ 06620 French Riviera 42 E2

Paris 916 – Grasse 10 – Nice 31 – Vence 15

Office de tourisme, place Francis Paulet ☎ 04 93 42 72 21, Fax 04 93 42 92 60

Site★ - Danse macabre★ (paintings on wood) in St-Jacques church - ≤★ from place de l'église.

Hostellerie du Château

& rest, VISA MC AE

6 pl. Francis-Paulet – ☎ 04 93 42 41 10 – info@lhostellerieduchateau.com – Fax 04 93 42 69 32

6 rm – †€ 130 ††€ 130/180, ☐ € 14

Rest *bigaradier* – *(open 2 March-30 October and closed Tuesday lunch, Sunday dinner and Monday)* Menu € 28 (lunch), € 39/64 – Carte approx. € 45

◆ Refined Provençal bedrooms (old furniture, expensive wood, floor tiles) add to the allure of this château once owned by the Counts of Grasse. Some rooms enjoy views of the valley. Attentive service, an elegant contemporary setting and delicious modern cuisine.

La Jarrerie

VISA MC AE

– ☎ 04 93 42 92 92 – Fax 04 93 42 91 22 – Closed 2-31 January, Wednesday lunchtime and Tuesday

Rest – Menu € 27/49 – Carte € 42/53

◆ Once a monastery, then a canning factory and perfumery, this 17C regional property has a large rustic dining room with a fireplace, exposed stones and beams.

BAR-SUR-SEINE – 10 Aube – 313 G5 – pop. 3 510 – alt. 157 m – ✉ 10110 Northern France and the Paris Region 13 B3

Paris 197 – Bar-sur-Aube 37 – Châtillon-sur-Seine 36 – St-Florentin 57 – Troyes 33

Office de tourisme, 33, rue Gambetta ☎ 03 25 29 94 43, Fax 03 25 29 70 21

Interior★ of St-Étienne church.

Du Commerce with rm

AC rest, rest, P VISA MC

30 r. de la République – ☎ 03 25 29 86 36 – hotelducommerce.bar-sur-seine@wanadoo.fr – Fax 03 25 29 64 87 – Closed 27 June-7 July, 19-28 December, Friday dinner and Sunday

13 rm – †€ 41 ††€ 43, ☐ € 6,50 – ½ P € 44 – **Rest** – Menu (€ 10), € 12,50/38 – Carte € 25/42

◆ This very simple establishment is in the centre of the small town. Rustic-style dining room adorned with a fireplace. Traditional, unpretentious cuisine and modest guestrooms.

Near interchange 9 km motorway A5, Northeast by D 443 – ✉ 10110 Magnant

Le Val Moret

& rm, AC rest, P VISA MC AE

– ☎ 03 25 29 85 12 – contact@le-val-moret.com – Fax 03 25 29 70 81 – Closed 24-31 December

42 rm – †€ 50/79 ††€ 50/79, ☐ € 10 – **Rest** – Menu € 17 (weekdays)/58 – Carte € 23/53

◆ Motel-type establishment with functional and fairly spacious rooms in four buildings all on the ground floor. Lawn with playground for children. Modern dining rooms, one with a veranda: traditional menu and regional dishes.

BAS-RUPTS – 88 Vosges – 314 J4 – see Gérardmer

BASSAC – 16 Charente – 324 I6 – see Jarnac

BASSE-GOULAINE – 44 Loire-Atlantique – 316 H4 – see Nantes

BASTELICA – 2A Corse-du-Sud – 345 D7 – see Corse

BASTIA – 2B Haute-Corse – 345 F3 – see Corse

LA BASTIDE – 83 Var – 340 O3 – pop. 122 – alt. 1 000 m – ✉ 83840 41 C2

▶ Paris 813 – Castellane 25 – Digne-les-Bains 78 – Draguignan 43 – Grasse 48

Du Lachens rm,

– ☎ 04 94 76 80 01 – pepinbernard@orange.fr – Closed January- February and Tuesday except July-August

13 rm – †€ 51 ††€ 58, ☕ € 7 – ½ P € 48 – **Rest** – Menu € 24/31 – Carte € 26/41

◆ In a hamlet tucked away in the upper Var region, a traditional Provençal house with practical and well-maintained rooms. A country-style dining room and set menu where meat takes pride of place: the family butcher's is just opposite!

LA BASTIDE-CLAIRENCE – 64 Pyrénées-Atlantiques – 342 – pop. 881 – alt. 50 m – ✉ 64240 3 B3

▶ Paris 771 – Bayonne 27 – Irun 59 – Bordeaux 185

ℹ Office de tourisme, maison Darrieux ☎ 05 59 29 65 05, Fax 05 59 29 65 05

Maison Maxana rm,

r. Notre-Dame – ☎ 05 59 70 10 10 – ab@maison-maxana.com

5 rm ☕ – †€ 70/90 ††€ 80/110 – **Table d'hôte** – Menu € 35 bi

◆ Daydreams, Romance, Travel....The names of the rooms in this Basque house set the tone. A successful combination of antique furniture and African, Asian and modern touches. Regional cuisine and more exotic dishes at the table d'hôte (reservation required).

LA BASTIDE-DES-JOURDANS – 84 Vaucluse – 332 G11 – pop. 964 – alt. 412 m – ✉ 84240 40 B2

▶ Paris 762 – Aix-en-Provence 39 – Apt 40 – Digne-les-Bains 77 – Manosque 17

Auberge du Cheval Blanc with rm

– ☎ 04 90 77 81 08 – provence.luberon@wanadoo.fr – Fax 04 90 77 86 51 – Closed February and Thursday off season

4 rm – †€ 70/90 ††€ 70/90, ☕ € 10 – ½ P € 70/90 – **Rest** – Menu (€ 19 bi), € 30 – Carte € 43/54

◆ Provençal lodging in the village centre. Plush dining room in Mediterranean colours, and dishes with local savours. Pretty rooms with personal touches.

LA BÂTIE-DIVISIN – 38 Isère – 333 G4 – pop. 802 – alt. 521 m – ✉ 38490 45 C2

▶ Paris 539 – Lyon 82 – Grenoble 45 – Chambéry 41 – Saint-Martin-d'Hères 53

L'Olivier

Les Etraits – ☎ 04 76 31 00 60 – Fax 04 76 31 00 60 – Closed 24 October-5 November, Sunday dinner and Monday

Rest – Menu € 12,50 (weekday lunch), € 17/47 – Carte € 19/47

◆ The name evokes one of the favourite ingredients of the chef, who creates dishes that are updated, refined and based mainly on... olive oil. Bright dining room and garden terrace.

LA BÂTIE-NEUVE – 05 Hautes-Alpes – 334 F5 – see Gap

BATZ (ÎLE) – 29 Finistère – 308 G2 – see Île-de-Batz

BATZ-SUR-MER – 44 Loire-Atlantique – 316 B4 – pop. 3 049 – alt. 12 m – ✉ 44740 Brittany 34 A2

▶ Paris 457 – La Baule 7 – Nantes 84 – Redon 64 – Vannes 79

ℹ Syndicat d'initiative, 25, rue de la Plage ☎ 02 40 23 92 36, Fax 02 40 23 74 10

◉ ✻★★ of St-Guenolé church ★ - N.-D. du Mûrier chapel★ - guided excursions ★ in marshlands (musée des Marais salants) (museum of salt marshes) - La Côte Sauvage★.

Le Lichen without rest
Baie du Manerick - Côte Sauvage, 2 km south-east on D 45 – 02 40 23 91 92 – alain.paroux@wanadoo.fr – Fax 02 40 23 84 88
17 rm – €70/250 €70/250, €12
◆ This vast neo-Breton style villa (1956) located on the Wild Coast enjoys a unique sea view. Half the airy, fairly large rooms overlook the sea.

BAULE – **45 Loiret** – **318** H5 – **see Beaugency**

LA BAULE – **44 Loire-Atlantique** – **316** B4 – **pop. 15 831** – **alt. 31 m** – **Casino : Grand Casino** BZ – **44500** **Brittany** 34 **A2**

Paris 450 – Nantes 76 – Rennes 120 – St-Nazaire 19 – Vannes 74

Office de tourisme, 8, place de la Victoire 02 40 24 34 44, Fax 02 40 11 08 10

de Guérande Guérande Ville Blanche, by Nantes road: 6 km, 02 40 60 24 97 ;

de La Baule Saint-André-des-Eaux Domaine de Saint Denac, Northeast: 9 km, 02 40 60 46 18.

Seafront★ - Parc des Dryades★ DZ.

Plan on next page

Hermitage Barrière rm,
5 espl. Lucien-Barrière – 02 40 11 46 46 – hermitage@lucienbarriere.com – Fax 02 40 11 46 45 – Open 21 March-5 November and 25 December-2 January BZ **h**
202 rm – €192/328 €322/580, €21 – 5 suites– **Rest** ***La Terrasse*** – *(open Easter, All Saint's, Christmas holidays, public holidays and July-August)* Carte €24/87
Rest ***L' Eden Beach*** – beach restaurant – *02 40 11 46 16 (closed Monday dinner-Friday lunch 9 November-18 December and 5 January-beg. March)*
Menu €33 – Carte €35/80
◆ Imposing 1920s Anglo-Norman-style construction on the seafront. Spacious rooms with personal touches and views of the ocean or the garden. Swimming pool, hammam and fitness facilities. Sumptuous decor and classic cuisine at the Terrasse. Fish and shellfish specialities at the Eden Beach.

Royal-Thalasso Barrière rest,
6 av. P.-Loti – 02 40 11 48 48 – royalthalasso@lucienbarriere.com – Fax 02 40 11 48 45 – Closed 5-20 December BZ **t**
91 rm – €172/474 €172/474, €21 – 6 suites
Rest ***La Rotonde*** – Menu €43 – Carte €44/80
Rest ***Le Ponton*** – beach restaurant – *02 40 60 52 05 (closed evenings from October to March except Saturday and school holidays)* Carte €30/61
◆ In a park overlooking the sea, an age-old building linked to a modern thalassotherapy centre. Period furniture and glistening fabrics in the rooms. Traditional and diet food at La Rotonde. Seafront cuisine at the Ponton.

Castel Marie-Louise rest,
1 av. Andrieu – 02 40 11 48 38 – marielouise@relaischateaux.com – Fax 02 40 11 48 35 – Closed 2 January-7 February BZ **g**
31 rm – €165/535 €165/535, €20 – 2 suites – ½ P €161/372
Rest – *(closed lunch except Saturday in July-August and except Sunday)*
Menu €45 (lunch), €65/110 – Carte €83/120
Spec. Maquereaux et langoustines au xérès (spring-summer). Epaule de cochon noir au jus d'épices. Macarons basilic et thym aux fruits rouges (spring-summer).
Wines Muscadet de Sèvre et Maine, Anjou-Villages.
◆ Charming Belle Époque manor house with a cosy atmosphere, surrounded by a well-kept garden. Tasteful and quiet rooms with antique furniture. A cosy restaurant furnished in the style of an English cottage. Fine contemporary cuisine. Pine-shaded terrace.

Bellevue Plage rest,
27 bd de l'Océan – 02 40 60 28 55 – hotel@hotel-bellevue-plage.fr – Fax 02 40 60 10 18 – Closed 15 December-10 February DZ **r**
35 rm – €95/190 €95/190, €13 – **Rest** ***La Véranda*** – see restaurant listing
◆ Well-maintained hotel with a modern, designer look. The new rooms overlook either the pine forest or the sea, and are colourful and simple in style. Roof-terrace with fine views of the bay.

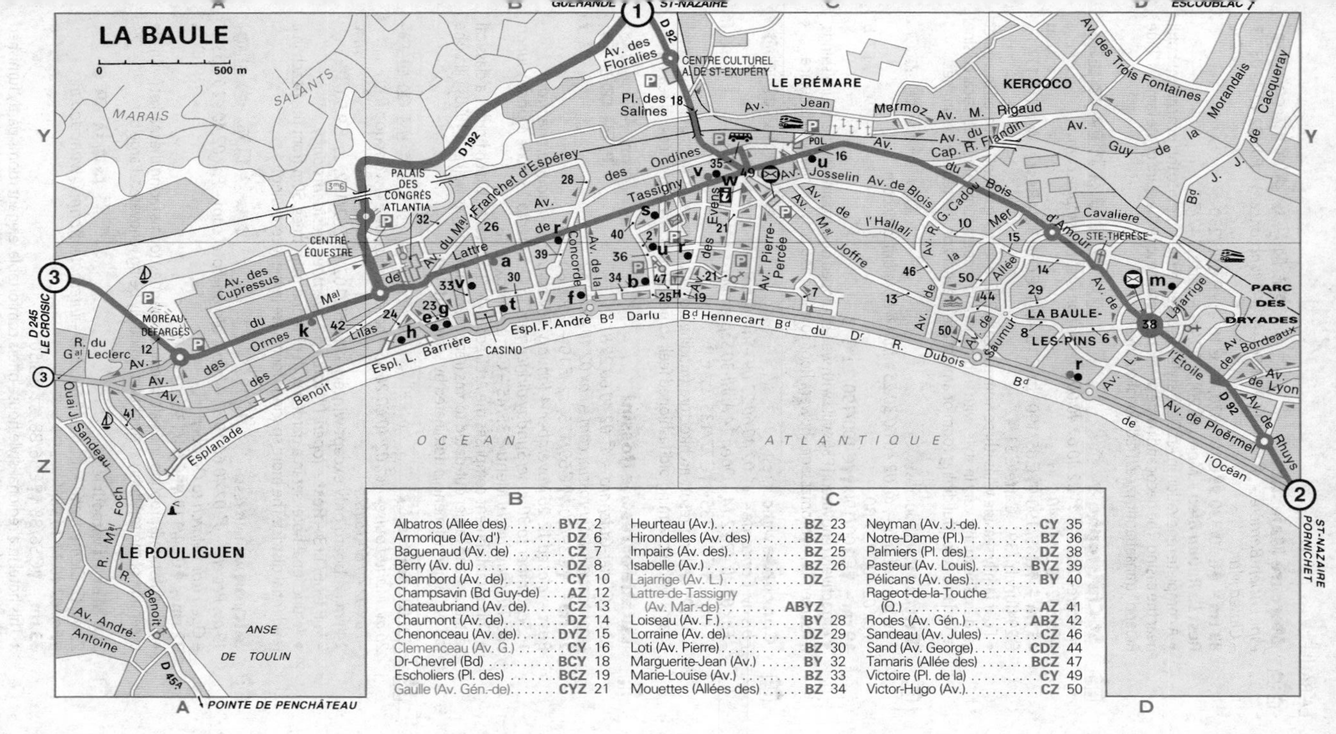

Albatros (Allée des) . . . . **BYZ** 2	Heurteau (Av.). . . . . **BZ** 23	Neyman (Av. J.-de). . . . . **CY** 35
Armorique (Av. d') . . . . **DZ** 6	Hirondelles (Av. des) . . . . **BZ** 24	Notre-Dame (Pl.) . . . . **BZ** 36
Baguenaud (Av. de) . . . . **CZ** 7	Impairs (Av. des). . . . . **BZ** 25	Palmiers (Pl. des) . . . . **DZ** 38
Berry (Av. du) . . . . **DZ** 8	Isabelle (Av.) . . . . **BZ** 26	Pasteur (Av. Louis). . . . . . . **BYZ** 39
Chambord (Av. de). . . . . **CY** 10	Lajarrige (Av. L.) . . . . **DZ**	Pélicans (Av. des). . . . . **BY** 40
Champsavin (Bd Guy-de) . . . **AZ** 12	Lattre-de-Tassigny (Av. Mar.-de) . . . . **ABYZ**	Rageot-de-la-Touche (Q.) . . . . **AZ** 41
Chateaubriand (Av. de). . . . . . **CZ** 13	Loiseau (Av. F.). . . . . **BY** 28	Rodes (Av. Gén.) . . . . **ABZ** 42
Chaumont (Av. de). . . . . **DZ** 14	Lorraine (Av. de) . . . . **DZ** 29	Sandeau (Av. Jules) . . . . **CZ** 46
Chenonceau (Av. de). . . . . . **DYZ** 15	Loti (Av. Pierre) . . . . **BZ** 30	Sand (Av. George) . . . . **CDZ** 44
Clemenceau (Av. G.) . . . . **CY** 16	Marguerite-Jean (Av.) . . . . . . **BY** 32	Tamaris (Allée des) . . . . . . **BCZ** 47
Dr-Chevrel (Bd) . . . . **BCY** 18	Marie-Louise (Av.) . . . . **BZ** 33	Victoire (Pl. de la) . . . . **CY** 49
Escholiers (Pl. des) . . . . **BCZ** 19	Mouettes (Allées des) . . . . . . **BZ** 34	Victor-Hugo (Av.). . . . . **CZ** 50
Gaulle (Av. Gén.-de). . . . . . . **CYZ** 21		

Mercure Majestic
espl. Lucien-Barrière – 02 40 60 24 86 – h5692@accor.com – Fax 02 40 42 03 13 – Closed Mar. BZ **e**
83 rm – €90/330 €100/370, €16 – ½ P €95/230
Rest *Le Ruban Bleu* – Menu (€20), €29/49 – Carte €47/73
♦ A complete renovation in Art Deco style has breathed new life into this beachfront hotel near the casino. The decor and name of this restaurant evoke the spirit of the famous "Blue Riband" transatlantic race. Traditional cuisine.

St-Christophe
pl. Notre-Dame – 02 40 62 40 00 – reception@st-christophe.com – Fax 02 40 62 40 40 BZ **u**
45 rm – €65/190 €65/190, €10 – ½ P €66/132 – **Rest** – Menu (€17), €29 (lunch)/39 – Carte €31/42
♦ Four family seaside villas (three from the early 20C, one more recent) situated in a quiet garden. The rooms vary in style, with traditional and modern furnishings. Classical cuisine served in a colourful dining room or amidst the greenery on the terrace in summer.

Brittany without rest
7 av. des Impairs – 02 40 60 30 25 – info@hotelbrittany.com – Fax 02 40 24 37 30 BZ **b**
19 rm – €100/190 €100/190, €13
♦ Attractively renovated 1930s villa with well-equipped guestrooms (modern furnishings, flatscreen TV, hydromassage shower). Roof-solarium and cosy lounge with fireplace.

Concorde without rest
1 bis av. Concorde – 02 40 60 23 09 – info@hotel-la-concorde.com – Fax 02 40 42 72 14 – Open 14 April-30 September BZ **f**
47 rm – €77/135 €77/135, €9
♦ 1900s bathing resort architecture (modified over the years) at this family-run hotel. Rooms with a charming old-fashioned feel, some with balcony or terrace and sea views.

Lutetia et rest. le Rossini rm, rest,
13 av. Olivier-Guichard – 02 40 60 25 81 – contact@lutetia-rossini.com – Fax 02 40 42 73 52 CZ **r**
26 rm – €39/60 €69/175, €10 – ½ P €80/138
Rest – *(closed 12-26 November, 4 January-20 February, Monday dinner from 1st September to 30 June, Sunday dinner from 15 October to 15 April, Monday lunch and Tuesday lunch)* Menu €35/45 – Carte approx. €48
♦ This establishment comprises the Art Deco-style "Le Lutétia", which houses a classical restaurant and rather out-dated rooms (renovation planned), as well as a 1930s villa. The rather traditional menu is dominated by seafood dishes.

La Mascotte rest, rest,
26 av. Marie-Louise – 02 40 60 26 55 – hotel.la.mascotte@wanadoo.fr – Fax 02 40 60 15 67 BZ **v**
24 rm (½ board only except winter) – €62/102 €62/102, €9,50 – ½ P €66/113 – **Rest** – *(open 1st March-5 November) (residents only)*
♦ A functional hotel set in a garden with pine and palm trees, 50m from the beach in a residential district. The more spacious rooms are in the recent wing.

Alcyon without rest
19 av. Pétrels – 02 40 60 19 37 – info@alcyon-hotel.com – Fax 02 40 42 71 33 – Open from March to October BY **s**
32 rm – €64/113 €64/136, €10
♦ Efficient sound-proofing and balconies in all the guestrooms facing the market (with the exception of the top floor) at this hotel, gradually being renovated. Large bar.

Le Marini without rest
22 av. G.-Clemenceau – 02 40 60 23 29 – interhotelmarini@wanadoo.fr – Fax 02 40 11 16 98 CY **u**
33 rm – €56/88 €56/88, €8,50
♦ This hotel in a regional-style house offers comfortable, elegant rooms partly furnished with antique furniture. British atmosphere in the bar. Attractive heated indoor swimming pool.

Hostellerie du Bois

65 av Lajarrige – ✆ 02 40 60 24 78 – hostellerie-du-bois@wanadoo.fr – Fax 02 40 42 05 88 – Open 16 March-14 November DZ **m**

15 rm – †€ 60/74 ††€ 60/74, ☕ € 7 – ½ P € 59/66 – **Rest** – *(dinner only) (residents only)*

◆ Charming half-timbered house (1923) with traditionally furnished guestrooms and public areas. Well-maintained and decorated with souvenirs from the owners' travels. Garden. Breakfast served in a quiet, rustic-style room. Evening meals available for residents.

St-Pierre without rest

124 av. de Lattre-de-Tassigny – ✆ 02 40 24 05 41 – contact@hotel-saint-pierre.com – Fax 02 40 11 03 41 BYZ **r**

19 rm – †€ 54/64 ††€ 72/82, ☕ € 9

◆ Friendly welcome and reasonable prices at this hotel housed in a typical villa with blue half-timbering. Discreet maritime decor in the rooms. Breakfast served on the veranda.

Les Dunes without rest

277 av. de Lattre-de-Tassigny – ✆ 02 51 75 07 10 – info@hotel-des-dunes.com – Fax 02 51 75 07 11 CY **w**

32 rm – †€ 45/72 ††€ 45/72, ☕ € 7

◆ A welcoming and reasonably priced family-run hotel in this busy seaside resort. Well-maintained functional rooms, with those to the rear generally quieter.

La Véranda – Hôtel Bellevue Plage

27 bd de l' Océan – ✆ 02 40 60 57 77 – courriel@restaurant-laveranda.com – Fax 02 40 24 00 22 – Closed 15 December-1st February, Wednesday from September to June and Monday except dinner in July-August DZ **r**

Rest – Menu € 22 bi (weekday lunch), € 39/85 bi – Carte € 60/105

◆ A bright, sober, two-floor modern dining room and veranda, serving tasty, modern cuisine. Most tables overlook the beach.

La Maison Blanche

20 bis av. Pavie – ✆ 02 40 23 00 00 – lamaisonblanchelabaule@orange.fr – Fax 02 40 23 03 60 – Closed Saturday lunch and Sunday dinner off season and except school holidays BZ **a**

Rest – Menu (€ 15), € 23/58 – Carte € 34/58

◆ Resolutely contemporary culinary focus at this restaurant occupying an attractive glazed rotunda (with upper floor). Chic lounge ambience and stylish modern decor.

Carpe Diem

29 av. J. Boutroux, 5 km north on Golf de la Baule road – ✆ 02 40 24 13 14 – contact@le-carpediem.fr – Closed 19 January-16 February, Sunday dinner off season and Monday

Rest – Menu (€ 15), € 20/70 bi – Carte € 34/91

◆ A pleasant rustic-style restaurant (exposed beams, stone fireplace, wood furniture) near the golf course. Carefully prepared contemporary cuisine.

La Ferme du Grand Clos

52 av. de Lattre-de-Tassigny – ✆ 02 40 60 03 30 – contact@lafermedugrandclos.com – Fax 02 40 60 03 30 – Closed 10-16 March, 24 November-21 December, Tuesday, Wednesday from October to March and Monday except school holidays AZ **k**

Rest – crêperie Carte € 17/35

◆ This farm, hidden away at the bottom of a garden, is over a hundred years old. Rustic dining room which looks onto the kitchens. Pancakes and other regional specialities.

at the Golf 7 km North by N 171 – ✉ 44117 St-André-des-Eaux

Du Golf International

– ✆ 02 40 17 57 57 – hoteldugolflabaule@lucienbarriere.com – Fax 02 40 17 57 58 – Open 28 March-26 October

119 rm – †€ 91/334 ††€ 91/334, ☕ € 18 – 55 suites

Rest *Le Green* – *(closed lunch except in July-August)* Carte € 27/46

◆ A hotel complex and park at the heart of a huge golf course. Spacious, well-designed guestrooms, plus a few villas available for rent. Children's club. Le Green, opposite the pool, offers traditional fare.

LA BAUME – 74 Haute-Savoie – 328 M3 – pop. 250 – alt. 730 m – ✉ 74430 46 **F1**

▶ Paris 597 – Lyon 214 – Annecy 95 – Genève 52 – Lausanne 138

La Ferme aux Ours

La Voagère – ✆ 04 50 72 19 88 – catherine.coulais@free.fr – Closed November
4 rm – ♦€ 75/100 ♦♦€ 85/110 – ½ P € 70/80 – **Table d'hôte** – Menu € 28
♦ Fine, remote Savoie farmhouse overlooking the valley. Cosy, well-kept rooms (teddy bear collection) and charming welcome from the owner, who is very interested in hiking.

BAUME-LES-DAMES – 25 Doubs – 321 I2 – pop. 5 384 – alt. 280 m – ✉ 25110 Burgundy-Jura 17 **C2**

▶ Paris 440 – Belfort 62 – Besançon 30 – Lure 45 – Montbéliard 45 – Pontarlier 65 – Vesoul 45

ℹ Office de tourisme, 6, rue de Provence ✆ 03 81 84 27 98, Fax 03 81 84 15 61

18 du Château de Bournel Cubry, North: 20 km by D 50, ✆ 03 81 86 00 10.

Hostellerie du Château d'As with rm

24 r. Château-Gaillard – ✆ 03 81 84 00 66 – courriel@chateau-das.com – Fax 03 81 84 39 67
6 rm – ♦€ 61/78 ♦♦€ 61/78, ☕ € 10 – ½ P € 63/71 – **Rest** – Menu € 21 (weekday lunch), € 29/69 – Carte € 39/59
♦ A large 1930s villa retaining its atmosphere of the past. Bright, elegant dining room (superb mother-of-pearl chandelier) where modern cuisine is served. Spacious rooms.

BAUME-LES-MESSIEURS – 39 Jura – 321 D6 – pop. 194 – alt. 333 m – ✉ 39210 Burgundy-Jura 16 **B3**

▶ Paris 406 – Champagnole 27 – Dole 54 – Lons-le-Saunier 12 – Poligny 21

◉ Abbey★ (altar-piece with shutter★ in the church) - Belvédère des Roches de Baume (viewpoint)★★★ overlooking cirque★★★ and grottoes★ of Baume South: 3,5 km.

Des Grottes

aux Grottes, 3 km southward – ✆ 03 84 48 23 15 – restaurantdesgrottes@wanadoo.fr – Fax 03 84 48 23 15 – Open 1st April-30 September and closed Monday except July-August
Rest – *(lunch only) (pre-book)* Menu € 15 (weekdays), € 22/35 – Carte € 28/45
♦ Rural house dating from 1900 overlooking a fine waterfall. Restaurant with Belle Epoque charm plus a less formal café. Regional fare; fresh trout available.

BAUVIN – 59 Nord – 302 F4 – pop. 5 338 – alt. 25 m – ✉ 59221 30 **B2**

▶ Paris 208 – Arras 33 – Béthune 22 – Lens 15 – Lille 26

Les Salons du Manoir

53 r. J.-Guesde – ✆ 03 20 85 64 77 – pmortreux@nordnet.fr – Fax 03 20 86 72 22 – Closed August, February holidays, Monday and Tuesday
Rest – Menu € 40 bi/70 bi
♦ In 3 ha of grounds, the main house's outbuildings have been turned into a restaurant. Light dining room with fireplace. Well-prepared traditional cuisine.

LES BAUX-DE-PROVENCE – 13 Bouches-du-Rhône – 340 D3 – pop. 434 – alt. 185 m – ✉ 13520 Provence 42 **E1**

▶ Paris 712 – Arles 20 – Avignon 30 – Marseille 86 – Nîmes 44 – St-Rémy-de-Provence 10

ℹ Office de tourisme, Maison du Roy ✆ 04 90 54 34 39, Fax 04 90 54 51 15

⛳ des Baux-de-Provence Domaine de Manville, South: 2 km, ✆ 04 90 54 40 20.

◉ Site★★★ - Village★★★: Square★ and St-Vincent church ★ - Château★: ✳★★ - Monument Charloun Rieu ≤★ - Tour Paravelle ≤★ - Musée Yves-Brayer★ - Cathédrale d'Images★ North: 1 km by D 27 - ✳★★★ on the village North: 2,5 km by D 27.

In the Vallon

La Riboto de Taven rm, rm,
– 04 90 54 34 23 – contact@riboto-de-taven.fr
– Fax 04 90 54 38 88 – Closed 5 January-5 March
5 rm – €160/280 €160/280, €18 – 1 suite – ½ P €137/191
Rest – *(closed Wednesday) (dinner only) (residents only)* Menu €54
◆ This unusual farmhouse is a delight to the eyes and offers a clear view of Les Baux. Flower garden, pleasant pool and tastefully decorated rooms (two of them are troglodyte). Handsome timbered ceiling and large fireplace in the dining room. Market-inspired cuisine.

L' Oustaù de Baumanière with rm
– 04 90 54 33 07 – oustau@relaischateaux.com
– Fax 04 90 54 40 46 – Closed Thursday lunch and Wednesday from November to March
12 rm – €230/410 €230/410, €22 – 4 suites – ½ P €295/442
Rest – Menu €120 bi (weekday lunch)/175 – Carte €135/190
Spec. Œuf de poule, eau de tomate en consommé clair, jus condiment d'un aïoli (June to September). Rouget barbet, basilic et fleur de thym. Crêpe soufflée "tradition Baumanière". **Wines** Les Baux-de-Provence.
◆ A magical establishment serving sun-drenched cuisine amidst the ancient vaults of a 16C abode. Superb terrace with the Alpilles in the background. Fine wine cellar. Comfortable rooms and stylish suites in the main house and in a small farmhouse (La Guigou).

Le Manoir
à 1 km rte d'Arles via D 27 – 04 90 54 33 07
– Closed Wednesday from November to March
7 rm – €230/340 €230/340, €22 – 7 suites – €395/555 – ½ P €195/443
◆ The rooms in this elegant farmhouse combine the comfort, refinement and charm of Provence in bygone days. Wooded park with a splendid ancient plane tree and a classical garden.

Arles road Southwest by D 27

La Cabro d'Or rm,
1 km – 04 90 54 33 21 – cabro@relaischateaux.com – Fax 04 90 54 45 98
– Closed Sunday dinner, Tuesday lunch and Monday from November to March
22 rm – €160/275 €160/275, €21 – 8 suites – ½ P €160/315
Rest – Menu €49 bi/100 – Carte €95/100
Spec. Thon rouge de Méditerranée décliné en tartare de légumes, bruschetta de tomate et confit en verrine. Dos de loup aux légumes de Provence. Carré d'agneau rôti à la broche. **Wines** Coteaux d'Aix-en-Provence-les Baux.
◆ Chic country style, with elegant rooms, a beautiful garden and many leisure activities including a riding centre. Cosy, sophisticated dining room, a terrace underneath the lime trees and fine contemporary cuisine. Provence at its best!

Mas de l'Oulivié without rest
2.5 km – 04 90 54 35 78 – contact@masdeloulivie.com – Fax 04 90 54 44 31
– Open 19 March-12 November
25 rm – €105/260 €105/260, €13 – 2 suites
◆ A relaxing break in the heart of olive groves: Provençal decorated rooms, overflow pool in the garden, and massages. Light lunches for residents only.

Auberge de la Benvengudo rm,
2 km – 04 90 54 32 54 – contact@ rest,
benvengudo.com – Fax 04 90 54 42 58 – Open 14 March-2 November
25 rm – €110/225 €110/225, €15 – 3 suites – ½ P €110/168
Rest – *(closed Sunday) (dinner only)* Menu €45
◆ This charming farmhouse, covered in Virginia creeper and surrounded by a pretty garden, lies at the foot of the citadel. Ask for a room which has been renovated. Provençal-style furniture in the dining room and one set menu, based on the market produce available.

BAVAY – 59 Nord – 302 K6 – pop. 3 581 – alt. 148 m – ✉ 59570
Northern France and the Paris Region 31 **D2**

Paris 229 – Avesnes-sur-Helpe 24 – Lille 79 – Maubeuge 15 – Mons 25

Office de tourisme, rue Saint-Maur 03 27 39 81 65, Fax 03 27 39 81 65

XX **Le Bagacum**

r. Audignies – ✆ 03 27 66 87 00 – contact@bagacum.com – Fax 03 27 66 86 44 – Closed Sunday dinner and Monday except holidays

Rest – Menu € 27 bi, € 33/49 bi – Carte € 36/77

◆ Red-brick walls, exposed roof beams, ornaments and paintings give character to this restaurant in a converted barn. Flowered terrace. Traditional cuisine.

XX **Le Bourgogne**

porte Gommeries – ✆ 03 27 63 12 58 – restaurantlebourgogne@orange.fr – Fax 03 27 66 99 74 – Closed 29 July-20 August, 5-20 January, Monday and dinner except Friday and Saturday

Rest – Menu € 20 (weekday lunch), € 35/55 – Carte € 29/52

◆ On a busy thoroughfare, this brick building is typical of northern architecture; nice summer terrace. The cuisine is a blend of tradition and invention. Burgundies feature heavily on the wine list.

BAVELLA (COL) – 2A Corse-du-Sud – 345 E9 – see Corse

BAYARD (COL) – 05 Hautes-Alpes – 334 E5 – see Col Bayard

BAYEUX – 14 Calvados – 303 H4 – pop. 14 961 – alt. 50 m – ✉ 14400

Normandy 32 **B2**

Paris 265 – Caen 31 – Cherbourg 95 – Flers 69 – St-Lô 36 – Vire 60

Office de tourisme, pont Saint-Jean ✆ 02 31 51 28 28, Fax 02 31 51 28 29

AS Bayeux Omaha Beach Golf Port-en-Bessin Ferme Saint Sauveur, by Port-en-Bessin road and D 514: 11 km, ✆ 02 31 22 12 12.

Tapestry of "la reine Mathilde" (Queen Mathilda) ★★★ - Notre-Dame cathedral ★★ - Musée-mémorial de la bataille de Normandie★ Y **M**[1] - Half-timbered house★ (rue St-Martin) Z **N.**

Plan on next page

Le Lion d'Or

71 r. St-Jean – ✆ 02 31 92 06 90 – lion.d-or.bayeux@wanadoo.fr – Fax 02 31 22 15 64 Z **e**

27 rm – †€ 78/150 ††€ 78/170, ☕ € 12 – 1 suite – ½ P € 77/133

Rest – *(closed 23 December-17 January, Monday lunch, Tuesday lunch and Saturday lunch)* Menu € 25 (lunch), € 29/50 – Carte € 51/62

◆ This old post house, part of which dates back to the 18C, with an attractive paved front courtyard, has comfortable rooms furnished in a variety of styles. Traditional cuisine served in a warm setting: beams, antique ornaments and carefully-laid tables.

Novotel

rm, rm,

117 r. St-Patrice – ✆ 02 31 92 16 11 – h0964@accor.com – Fax 02 31 21 88 76

77 rm – †€ 83/145 ††€ 95/145, ☕ € 12 – **Rest** – *(closed Sunday lunch and Saturday except 10 July-20 August)* Menu € 14/25 – Carte approx. € 30 Y **x**

◆ This establishment has been entirely renovated, bringing it up to the new standards of the chain: modern bar and lounge, practical rooms with contemporary furnishings. Beige walls, purple chairs and warm parquet floors make up the pleasant setting of the restaurant.

Château de Bellefontaine without rest

49 r. Bellefontaine – ✆ 02 31 22 00 10 – info@hotel-bellefontaine.com – Fax 02 31 22 19 09 – Closed 2 Jan.-2 Feb. Y **v**

14 rm – †€ 70/115 ††€ 90/160, ☕ € 12

◆ A pretty park with majestic trees and a pond separate this 18C château from the road. Lounge with a fine fireplace. Comfortable rooms furnished differently.

Churchill without rest

14 r. St-Jean – ✆ 02 31 21 31 80 – info@hotel-churchill.fr – Fax 02 31 21 41 66 – Open from March to November Z **h**

32 rm – †€ 75/95 ††€ 90/125, ☕ € 9

◆ Fine buildings around an inner courtyard with a veranda, where breakfast is served. Refurbished rooms with period furniture, decorated in ivory and burgundy tones. Delicatessen.

BAYEUX

Aure (Bords de l') . . . . Z 2
Bienvenu (R. du) . . . . Z 3
Bois (Pl. au) . . . . Z 4
Bouchers (R. des) . . . . Z
Bourbesneur (R.) . . . . Z 6
Bretagne (R. de la) . . . . Z
Chanoines (R. des) . . . . Z 7
Chartier (R. A.) . . . . Z 8
Churchill (Bd W.) . . . . Y
Clemenceau (Av. G.) . . . . Z
Conseil (Av.) . . . . Y
Courseulles (R. de) . . . . Y 9
Cuisiniers (R. des) . . . . Z 12
Dais (R. Gén.-de) . . . . Z
Dr-Michel (R.) . . . . Y 13
Eindhoven (Bd) . . . . Y
Eisenhower (Rond-Point) . . . . . . Y 14
Foch (R. Mar.) . . . . Z 15
Franche (R.) . . . . Z
Gaulle (Pl. Ch.-de) . . . . Z
Laitière (R.) . . . . Z 16
Larcher (R.) . . . . Z
Leclerc (Bd Mar.) . . . . Y 17
Leforestier (R. Lambert) . . . . . Z 18
Liberté (Pl. de la) . . . . Z 19
Maîtrise (R. de la) . . . . Z 20
Marché (R. du) . . . . Z 21
Montgomery (Bd Mar.) . . . . Y 23
Nesmond (R. de) . . . . Z
Pigache (R. de la) . . . . Y 24
Pont-Trubert (R. du) . . . . Y 25
Poterie (R. de la) . . . . Z 28
Royale (R.) . . . . Z
Sadi-Carnot (Bd) . . . . Y 29
St-Jean (R.) . . . . Y, Z
St-Laurent (R.) . . . . Y, Z
St-Loup (R.) . . . . Y, Z 30
St-Malo (R.) . . . . Z
St-Martin (R.) . . . . Z
St-Patrice (R. et Pl.) . . . . Z 31
St-Quentin (R.) . . . . Y 41
Schumann (R. M.) . . . . Z 42
Tardif (R.) . . . . Z
Teinturiers (R. des) . . . . Z 32
Terres (R. des) . . . . Z 33
Vaucelles (Rond-Point de) . . . . Y 35
Verdun (R. de) . . . . Y 37
Ware (Bd F.) . . . . Y 38
6-Juin (Bd du) . . . . Y

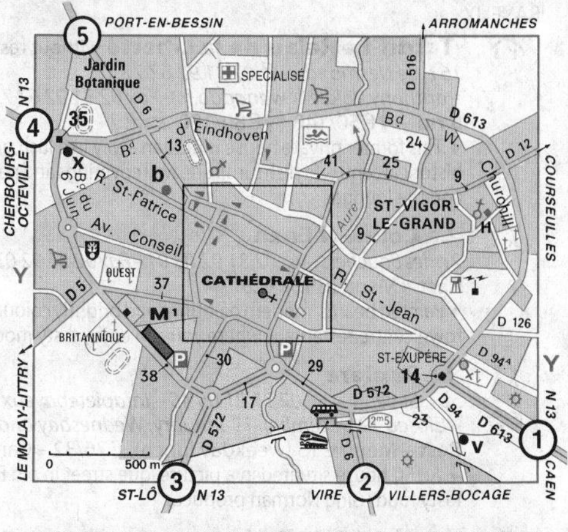

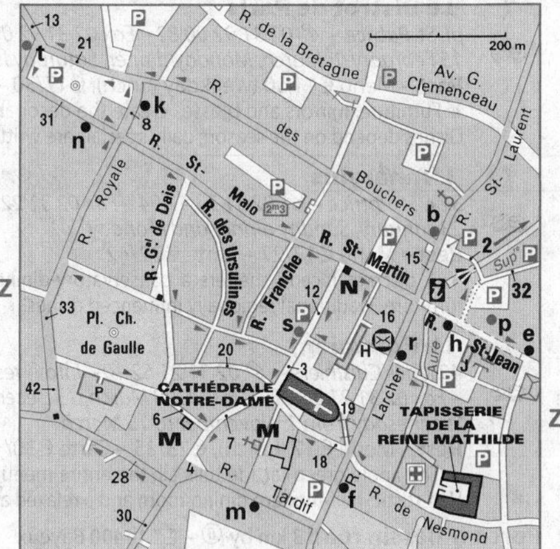

d'Argouges without rest
21 r. St-Patrice – ✆ 02 31 92 88 86 – hotel.dargouges@orange.fr – Fax 02 31 92 69 16 Z **n**
28 rm – †€ 52/84 ††€ 68/116, ☐ € 8
♦ An 18C town house, surrounded by a restful garden, in the middle of town. Rather spacious, renovated rooms with some antique furniture.

Reine Mathilde without rest
23 r. Larcher – ✆ 02 31 92 08 13 – hotel.reinemathilde@wanadoo.fr – Fax 02 31 92 09 93 – Open from mid February-mid November Z **r**
16 rm – †€ 55 ††€ 55, ☐ € 7
♦ The name of this flower-decked hotel refers to the famous tapestry. Rooms are simple but well kept and are all named afte Norman saints. Tea room.

Le Bayeux without rest
9 r. Tardif – ✆ 02 31 92 70 08 – lebayeux@wanadoo.fr – Fax 02 31 21 15 74 – Open 1st March-15 November Z **m**
29 rm – †€ 50/63 ††€ 50/63, ☐ € 7
♦ Hotel in a quiet street, with a sober façade but functional and well-kept rooms have been renovated in a modern style.

Tardif-Le Relais de la Liberté without rest
16 r. de Nesmond – 02 31 92 67 72 – anthony.voidie@wanadoo.fr – Fax 02 31 92 67 72 Z **f**
5 rm – €50/140 €80/190, €7
◆ This former private house is hidden away in a lush green garden two minutes from the historical centre. Stylish furniture, wall coverings and paintings give character to the rooms and the lounge.

La Coline d'Enzo
2 r. des Bouchers – 02 31 92 03 01 – Fax 02 31 92 03 01 – Closed Sunday and Monday
Rest – Menu (€ 15), € 24/44 Z **b**
◆ Painted beams, modern paintings and brightly coloured fabrics brighten the walls of this town centre restaurant where you can enjoy tasty modern dishes.

La Rapière
53 r. St-Jean – 02 31 21 05 45 – larapierebayeux@orange.fr – Fax 02 31 21 11 81 – Closed 19 December-19 January, Wednesday and Thursday Z **p**
Rest – Menu € 15 (weekday lunch), € 26/32 – Carte € 34/54
◆ A 15C house situated in a picturesque street in old Bayeux. A lovely, rustic interior and tasty food using Norman produce.

Le Bistrot de Paris
pl. St-Patrice – 02 31 92 00 82 – Fax 02 31 92 00 82 – Closed 10-24 August, 15 February-1st March, Monday dinner, Saturday lunch and Sunday Z **t**
Rest – Menu € 11,50 (weekday lunch), € 17/30 – Carte € 22/36
◆ Furniture, mirrors and brasses create the decor and the atmosphere of an old bistro. Dishes depend on the season; daily specials are written on the board.

L'Amaryllis
32 r. St-Patrice – 02 31 22 47 94 – Fax 02 31 22 50 03 – Closed 20 December-23 January, Sunday dinner and Monday Y **b**
Rest – Menu € 17/27 – Carte € 32/42
◆ A discreet façade shelters a conservatory-dining room furnished with bistro style furniture. Traditional regionally influenced dishes.

Le Pommier
40 r. des Cuisiniers – 02 31 21 52 10 – info@restaurantlepommier.com – Fax 02 31 21 06 01 – Closed 2-8 March, 15 December-11 January, Tuesday and Wednesday from 1st November to 15 March Z **s**
Rest – Menu € 17 (lunch), € 23/35 – Carte € 30/44
◆ The apple green façade tells all: the entire menu is based on Normandy specialities! Half-rustic, half-modern dining room and a relaxed atmosphere.

Port-en-Bessin road 3 km by ⑤ – ✉ 14400 Bayeux

Château de Sully rm,
Port en Bessin road – 02 31 22 29 48 – info@chateau-de-sully.com – Fax 02 31 22 64 77 – Open 2 March-9 December
22 rm – € 130/190 € 150/420, € 15 – ½ P € 149/274 – **Rest** – *(closed lunch except Sunday) (number of covers limited, pre-book)* Menu € 49/85
◆ This 18C château, with gardens at the front, is very attractive. Discreet luxury in the delicately personalised rooms. Two restaurant dining rooms completed by a veranda facing the garden. The dishes are a traditional and modern mix.

in Audrieu 13 km by ① and D 158 – pop. 839 – alt. 71 m – ✉ 14250

Château d'Audrieu rest,
– 02 31 80 21 52 – audrieu@relaischateaux.com – Fax 02 31 80 24 73 – Closed 7 December-1st February
25 rm – € 134/441 € 134/441, € 25 – 4 suites – ½ P € 144/282
Rest – *(closed Monday and lunch except Saturday, Sunday and public holidays)* Menu € 38 (lunch), € 54/95 – Carte € 71/98
Spec. Crevette géante snackée, vinaigre balsamique. Bar de l'ami Dominique, marinière de pomelos. Tomate-fraises-concombre, "p'tit beurre géant" (June to September).
◆ This 18C listed château lies in the middle of a huge park and offers fine rooms adorned with antique furniture. Elegant dining room serving modern cuisine and good selection of wines – a taste of the good life!

BAYONNE – 64 Pyrénées-Atlantiques – 342 D2 – pop. 40 078 – Built-up area 178 965 – alt. 3 m – ✉ 64100 Atlantic Coast 3 A3

Paris 765 – Bordeaux 183 – Biarritz 9 – Pamplona 109 – San Sebastián 53

Biarritz-Anglet-Bayonne: ✆ 05 59 43 83 83, Southwest: 5 km by N 10 AZ.

Office de tourisme, place des Basques ✆ 08 20 42 64 64, Fax 05 59 59 37 55

Makila Golf Club Biarritz Route de Cambo, South: 6 km by D 932, ✆ 05 59 58 42 42.

Ste-Marie cathedral ★ and cloister★ **B** - Fairs★ (start of August) - Musée Bonnat★★ BY **M²** - Musée basque★★★.

Access and exits: See Biarritz.

Plan on following page

Adour Hôtel

13 pl. Ste-Ursule – ✆ 05 59 55 11 31 – resa@adourhotel.net – Fax 05 59 55 86 40
12 rm – €62/90 €68/95, €7,50 – ½ P €57/70 – **Rest** – table d'hôte *(closed Friday, Saturday and Sunday) (dinner only) (residents only)* Menu €18 BY **f**

◆ A renovated hotel situated very near the train station. The décor of each of the rooms is inspired by a local theme (Espelette pepper, surfing, Basque pelota, bullfighting, chocolate...). Good soundproofing. Regional food served in the restaurant.

Auberge du Cheval Blanc (Jean-Claude Tellechea)

68 r. Bourgneuf – ✆ 05 59 59 01 33 – Fax 05 59 59 52 26 – Closed 7-17 July, 30 July-4 August, 10-20 November, 16-9 March, Sunday dinner except August, Saturday lunch and Monday BZ **b**
Rest – Menu €30/85 – Carte €54/75
Spec. Pressé de truite fumée maison, foie gras et poires au porto. Liégeois d'huîtres tièdes (15 September to 15 March). Parmentier de xamango au jus de veau truffé. **Wines** Jurançon, Irouléguy.

◆ This former post house (1715) offers the charm of a dining room in pastel shades, paintings by a Basque artist, flower arrangements, reinvented local cuisine and a fine choice of Irouléguy wine.

François Miura

24 r. Marengo – ✆ 05 59 59 49 89 – Closed in March, Christmas holidays, Sunday dinner, Thursday lunch and Wednesday BZ **r**
Rest – Menu €21/32 – Carte €41/51

◆ In old Bayonne, a vaulted restaurant with paintings and modern furniture. Modern cuisine and local produce.

El Asador

pl. Montaut – ✆ 05 59 59 08 57 – Closed 9 June-2 July, 22 December-7 January, Sunday dinner and Monday except holidays AZ **e**
Rest – *(number of covers limited, pre-book)* Menu €20 (weekdays) – Carte €27/41

◆ Beams, bullfighting posters from the Fifties, Hispano-Basque cuisine and a friendly atmosphere: this restaurant will appeal to aficionados.

Bayonnais

38 quai des Corsaires – ✆ 05 59 25 61 19 – Fax 05 59 59 00 64 – Closed 1st-16 June, 21 December-6 January, Monday except July-August and Sunday BZ **s**
Rest – Menu €16 – Carte €30/38

◆ Near the Basque museum, a good venue offering copious regional dishes. A regional-style dining room completed by a terrace facing the banks of the Nive.

La Grange

26 quai Galuperie – ✆ 05 59 46 17 84 – Closed Sunday except public holidays
Rest – Menu €19 – Carte €36/48 BZ **a**

◆ Former grocer's in the arcades with antique fittings, wood panelling and brick walls. Updated Basque specialities chalked on a blackboard; wine list set out according to price.

North 2.5 km by Bordeaux road and D308 (see map of Biarritz) – ✉ 64100 Bayonne

Le Mamelon Vert without rest

< l'Adour,

1 chemin de Laborde – ✆ 05 59 74 59 70 – info@mamelonvert.com – Closed 25 December-1st January – **5 rm** – €70 €120 BCX **t**

◆ This regional style house that overlooks the Adour offers comfortable rooms decorated with engravings and antique furniture: the Red and the Blue have a lot of character.

Argenterie (R.) AZ 3	Hugo (R. Victor) AZ 125	Orbe (R.) AZ 92
Bastion Royal (R. du) BZ 12	Jaureguiberry (Q.) AZ 57	Pannecau (Pont) BZ 93
Bernède (R.) AY 15	Lachepaillet (Bd du Rempart) AZ 64	Pelletier (R.) BZ 95
Bonnat (Av. Léon) AY 16	Laffitte (R. Jacques) BYZ 65	Port-de-Castets (R.) AZ 97
Bourgneuf (R.) BYZ 17	Lamarque (Av. du Chanoine) AZ 23	Port-Neuf (R.) AY 98
Château-Vieux (Pl.) AZ 24	Liberté (Pl. de la) BY 73	Ravignan (R.) BZ 104
Cordeliers (R. des) BZ 26	Lormand (R.) AY 74	Roquebert (Q. du Cdt) BZ 108
Corsaires (Quai des) BZ 28	Marengo (Pont et R. de) BZ 80	Ste-Catherine (R.) BY 109
Dubourdieu (Q. Amiral) BZ 31	Marines (Av. des Allées) AY 81	Thiers (R.) AY
Duvergier-de-Hauranne (Av.) BZ 32	Mayou (Pont) BY 83	Tonneliers (R. des) BZ 112
Galuperie (Quai) BZ 35	Monnaie (R. de la) AZ 86	Tour-de-Sault (R.) AZ 120
Génie (Pont du) BZ 39		11-Novembre (Av.) AY 128
Gouverneurs (R. des) AZ 41		49e (R. du) AY 129

BAY-SUR-AUBE – 52 Haute-Marne – 313 K7 – pop. 56 – alt. 320 m – ✉ 52160

Paris 312 – Châlons-en-Champagne 214 – Chaumont 65 – Langres 33 – Châtillon-sur-Seine 50 14 **C3**

La Maison Jaune

– ✆ 03 25 84 99 42 – jwjansen@club-internet.fr – Fax 03 25 87 57 65 – Open from April to October

4 rm – €70 €85 – **Table d'hôte** – Menu €30 bi

◆ Old farmhouse which will enchant lovers of art and culture: superb library, the owner's paintings, antique shop finds. Rooms which are beautiful in their simplicity. Factory lamps from the 1930s bring character to this cosy table d'hôte.

BAZAS – 33 Gironde – 335 J8 – pop. 4 357 – alt. 70 m – ✉ 33430 Atlantic Coast

Paris 637 – Agen 84 – Bergerac 105 – Bordeaux 62 – Langon 17 – Mont-de-Marsan 70 3 **B2**

Office de tourisme, 1, place de la Cathédrale ✆ 05 56 25 25 84, Fax 05 56 25 95 59

St-Jean cathedral ★ - Château de Cazeneuve★★ Southwest: 11 km by D 9 - Château de Roquetaillade★★ Northwest: 2 km - Uzeste collegiate church ★.

Domaine de Fompeyre

rest,

rte Mont-de-Marsan – ✆ 05 56 25 98 00 – resa-bazas@monalisahotels.com – Fax 05 56 25 16 25

48 rm – †€ 99/158 ††€ 99/158, ☕ € 13 – ½ P € 90/120 – **Rest** – *(closed Sunday dinner 23 November-16 March)* Menu € 35/45 – Carte € 39/64

◆ A wooded park and extensive leisure facilities (a pleasant aquatic complex) in this resort hotel. Stylish rooms, those in the manor are larger. A cosy dining room and winter-garden style veranda. Here you can try, amongst others, Bazas beef.

Les Remparts

49 pl. de la Cathédrale, (Espace Mauvezin) – ✆ 05 56 25 95 24 – contact@restaurant-les-remparts.com – Fax 05 56 25 95 24 – Closed 20 October-5 November, 2-9 February, Sunday dinner and Monday

Rest – Menu (€ 14 bi), € 17 (weekday lunch), € 23/42 – Carte € 37/53

◆ Terrace situated on the medieval town walls, looking down onto the cathedral rose garden. Spacious dining room, decorated with paintings. Tradional dishes.

in Bernos-Beaulac 6 km South by D932 – pop. 1 071 – alt. 66 m – ✉ 33430

Dousud

– ✆ 05 56 25 43 23 – info@dousud.fr – Fax 05 56 25 42 75

5 rm ☕ – †€ 50/65 ††€ 65/80 – **Table d'hôte** – Menu € 20 bi

◆ This pretty Landes farm enjoys the quiet of a 9ha park where horses are bred. The personalised rooms are situated in the outbuildings; two of them have a terrace. In the evening the meals are prepared by the lady of the house, a former restaurant owner.

BAZEILLES – 08 Ardennes – 306 L4 – see Sedan

BAZINCOURT-SUR-EPTE – 27 Eure – 304 K6 – see Gisors

BAZOUGES-LA-PÉROUSE – 35 Ille-et-Vilaine – 309 M4 – pop. 1 854 – alt. 106 m – ✉ 35560 Brittany 10 **D2**

Paris 376 – Fougères 34 – Rennes 45 – Saint-Malo 53

Office de tourisme, 2, place de l'Hôtel de Ville ✆ 02 99 97 40 94, Fax 02 99 97 40 64

Le Château de la Ballue without rest

4 km north-east – ✆ 02 99 97 47 86 – chateau@la-ballue.com – Fax 02 99 97 47 70

5 rm – †€ 170/195 ††€ 220/290, ☕ € 15

◆ Splendid Baroque, French-style gardens surround this 17C château. The elegant, spacious rooms with high ceilings are adorned with lovely period woodwork and antique furniture.

BEAUCAIRE – 30 Gard – 339 M6 – pop. 13 748 – alt. 18 m – ✉ 30300 Provence

Paris 703 – Arles 18 – Avignon 27 – Nîmes 24 23 **D2**

Office de tourisme, 24, cours Gambetta ✆ 04 66 59 26 57, Fax 04 66 59 68 51

Château★.

Les Vignes Blanches

67 rte de Nîmes – ✆ 04 66 59 13 12 – contact@lesvignesblanches.com – Fax 04 66 58 08 11 – Closed 2 January-8 February

57 rm – †€ 69/97 ††€ 69/97, ☕ € 9 – ½ P € 70/76 – **Rest** – *(closed Sunday dinner and Monday from November to January)* Menu € 14 (weekday lunch), € 18/39 – Carte € 28/49

◆ On a busy street, this well-kept hotel features an unusual lobby, colourful rooms (quieter to the rear), named after their decorative theme. Traditional dishes prepared in a wood-fired oven, served in the bistro or a cosy dining room.

L'Oliveraie rest,
Chemin Clapas de Cornut, Nîmes road – 04 66 59 16 87 – fvalota@club-internet.fr – Fax 04 66 59 08 91
39 rm – €62 €62/64, €11 – ½ P €68/75
Rest – *(closed Sunday dinner except in July-August and Saturday lunch)* Menu (€16), €19/39 – Carte €29/45
♦ A family atmosphere can be found in this establishment made up of two buildings. Comfortable rooms with a balcony or terrace; those in the recent wing are more modern. Pleasant dining room decorated with numerous knick-knacks; veranda with exposed rafters.

Southwest **6 km (St Gilles road) then left , Nouriguier lock – ✉ 30300 Beaucaire**

Mas de Lafont without rest
chemin du Mas d'Aillaud – 04 66 59 29 59 – Fax 04 66 59 29 59 – Open 1st May-1st October
3 rm – €70/80 €80/90
♦ Amid vines and apricot trees, a 17C country house with spacious rooms furnished with superb Provençal furniture, all overlook the garden. Fully equipped kitchen available.

BEAUCENS – 65 Hautes-Pyrénées – 342 L5 – pop. 350 – alt. 450 m – ✉ 65400

Languedoc-Roussillon-Tarn Gorges 28 **A3**

Paris 866 – Pau 59 – Tarbes 38 – Toulouse 191

Eth Béryè Petit
15 rte Vielle – 05 62 97 90 02 – contact@beryepetit.com – Fax 05 62 97 90 02
3 rm – €56/63 €56/63 – **Table d'hôte** – *(Open Friday dinner and Saturday dinner from November to April)* Menu €20 bi
♦ Set amid meadows and woods, this welcoming Bigourdan house (1790) has been restored with care. Its name means little orchard and the calm, cosy rooms have a splendid view of the valley. Dine and breakfast in a pretty sitting room by the fire or on the terrace.

LE BEAUCET – 84 Vaucluse – 332 D10 – see Carpentras

BEAUCOUZÉ – 49 Maine-et-Loire – 317 F4 – see Angers

BEAUDÉAN – 65 Hautes-Pyrénées – 342 M5 – see Bagnères-de-Bigorre

BEAUFORT – 73 Savoie – 333 M3 – pop. 1 985 – alt. 750 m – ✉ 73270

French Alps 45 **D1**

Paris 601 – Albertville 21 – Chambéry 72 – Megève 37
Office de tourisme, Route du Grand Mont 04 79 38 37 57, Fax 04 79 38 16 70
Beaufortain★★.

Le Grand Mont
pl. de l'Église – 04 79 38 33 36 – hoteldugrandmont2@wanadoo.fr – Fax 04 79 38 39 07 – Closed 20 April-5 May and 1st October-7 November,
15 rm – €47/49 €58/60, €8,50 – ½ P €56/59
Rest – *(closed Saturday lunch and Sunday dinner)* Menu (€13), €21/32 – Carte €22/35
♦ Pleasant ambience inside this country house in a village that is renowned for its milk and cheese. Well-kept rooms. The restaurant offers a rustic setting - quite simple - adorned with photographs of Beaufort landscapes.

La Table du Berger
Grande-Rue – 04 79 38 37 91 – Closed January, Sunday dinner and Monday
Rest – Menu €14,50 (weekday lunch), €17/43 – Carte €27/40
♦ A mural depicting Gargantuan brings a touch of fantasy to the sober, mountain-style décor of this restaurant set in a typical, regional building. Local dishes.

BEAUGENCY – 45 Loiret – **318** G5 – **pop. 7 106 – alt. 99 m** – ✉ **45190**
Châteaux of the Loire 12 **C2**

- Paris 152 – Blois 35 – Châteaudun 42 – Orléans 31 – Vendôme 65
- Office de tourisme, 3, place Dr Hyvernaud ✆ 02 38 44 54 42, Fax 02 38 46 45 31
- de Ganay Saint-Laurent-Nouan Prieuré de Ganay, South: 7 km by D 925, ✆ 02 54 87 26 24 ;
- Les Bordes Golf International Saint-Laurent-Nouan Les Petits Rondis, South: 9 km by D 925, ✆ 02 54 87 72 13.
- Notre-Dame church ★ - Keep★ - Hangings★ in the town hall **H** - Musée régional de l'Orléanais★ in the château.

BEAUGENCY

Abbaye (R. de l') 2
Bretonnerie (R. de la) 3
Change (R. du) 4
Châteaudun (R. de) 5
Cordonnerie (R. de la) 6
Dr-Hyvernaud (Pl.) 8
Dunois (Pl.) 9
Maille-d'Or (R. de la) 10
Martroi (Pl. du) . . . .
Pellieux (Passage) 12
Pont (R. du) . . . .
Puits-de-l'Ange (R. du) 14
Sirène (R. de la) 15
Traîneau (R. du) 17
Trois-Marchands (R. des) 18

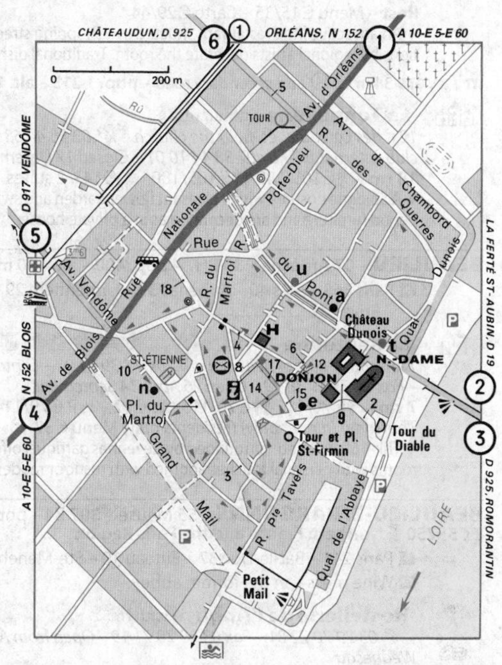

Hostellerie de l'Écu de Bretagne

pl. Martroi – ✆ *02 38 44 67 60 – ecu-de-bretagne@wanadoo.fr – Fax 02 38 44 68 07*
34 rm – †€ 60/147 ††€ 70/160, ☕ € 12 – ½ P € 65/150 – **Rest** – *(closed Sunday dinner off season)* Menu € 23/36 – Carte € 45/61 **n**
◆ This old coaching inn (1607) and annexe in the heart of town have been given a new lease of life. Pleasant guestrooms with personal touches. A friendly dining room serving traditional cuisine; fine selection of local wines.

De la Sologne without rest

6 pl. St-Firmin – ✆ *02 38 44 50 27 – hotel-de-la-sologne.beaugency@wanadoo.fr – Fax 02 38 44 90 19 – Closed 23 December-7 January* **e**
16 rm – †€ 45/63 ††€ 48/68, ☕ € 8,50
◆ Pretty, flower-decked steps lead to this Sologne-style building a stone's throw from the Tour St-Firmin. Well-maintained small rooms with individual touches.

Le Relais des Templiers without rest

– ✆ *02 38 44 53 78 – info@hotelrelaistempliers.com – Fax 02 38 46 42 55 – Closed 26 December-4 January* **a**
15 rm – †€ 47/65 ††€ 47/65, ☕ € 7,50
◆ This hotel with an attractive stone façade on the edge of the historic centre has fairly spacious rooms decorated in a simple, practical style. Bright breakfast room.

XX **Le Petit Bateau**

54 r. du Pont – ✆ 02 38 44 56 38 – lepetitbateau@wanadoo.fr – Fax 02 38 46 44 37 – Closed 17-29 November, 12-22 January, Sunday dinner and Monday **u**

Rest – Menu (€ 15), € 21 (weekdays)/38 – Carte € 41/64

♦ Two dining rooms: one has a well-kept rustic decor with exposed beams and fireplace; the other is smaller and opens onto a courtyard terrace. Traditional cuisine.

X **Le Relais du Château**

8 r. du Pont – ✆ 02 38 44 55 10 – carre-philippe45@orange.fr – Closed February, Thursday lunch July-October, Tuesday dinner and Thursday dinner October-June and Wednesday **t**

Rest – Menu € 15/35 – Carte € 29/44

♦ An attractive little restaurant situated in a shopping street near the keep (11C). Exhibitions by regional artists decorate the room. Traditional dishes.

in Tavers **3 km by ④ and secondary road – pop. 1 215 – alt. 100 m – ✉ 45190**

La Tonnellerie without rest

12 r. des Eaux-Bleues, near the church – ✆ 02 38 44 68 15 – tonelri@club-internet.fr – Fax 02 38 44 10 01 – Closed 17 December-15 January

18 rm – †€ 105/180 ††€ 105/180, ☕ € 14 – 2 suites

♦ A Sologne hostelry with a pleasant flower garden and swimming pool. The rooms have period furniture and are decorated as in a private house.

BEAULIEU – 07 Ardèche – 331 H7 – pop. 400 – alt. 130 m – ✉ 07460 44 A3

Paris 668 – Alès 40 – Aubenas 39 – Largentière 29 – Pont-St-Esprit 50 – Privas 71

La Santoline rm, rest,

1 km south-east of Beaulieu – ✆ 04 75 39 01 91 – contacts@lasantoline.com – Fax 04 75 39 38 79 – Open 26 April-14 September

7 rm – †€ 70/115 ††€ 70/115, ☕ € 12 – ½ P € 79/114 – **Rest** – *(closed Thursday) (dinner only) (residents only)* Menu € 32

♦ This 16C building, surrounded by Cévennes garrigue, offers charming service. Pleasant rooms with personal touches adorned with rustic or modern furniture.

BEAULIEU-EN-ARGONNE – 55 Meuse – 307 B4 – pop. 30 – alt. 275 m – ✉ 55250 Northern France and the Paris Region 26 A2

Paris 241 – Bar-le-Duc 37 – Futeau 10 – Ste-Menehould 23 – Verdun 38

Wine press★ in the former abbey.

X **Hostellerie de l'Abbaye** with rm

– ✆ 03 29 70 72 81 – Fax 03 29 70 71 19 – Open from April to October and closed Wednesday

8 rm – †€ 47/56 ††€ 47/56, ☕ € 5 – ½ P € 35 – **Rest** – Menu € 17/25 – Carte € 29/41

♦ Very simple restaurant with an attractive view of the Argonne countryside and surrounding woodland massifs. Discreet Sixties building which also houses a bar-tobacconist's. Most of the well-kept rooms have a view of the surrounding countryside.

BEAULIEU-SUR-DORDOGNE – 19 Corrèze – 329 M6 – pop. 1 286 – alt. 142 m – ✉ 19120 Dordogne-Berry-Limousin 25 C3

Paris 513 – Aurillac 65 – Brive-la-Gaillarde 44 – Figeac 56 – Sarlat-la-Canéda 69 – Tulle 38

Office de tourisme, place Marbot ✆ 05 55 91 09 94, Fax 05 55 91 10 97

St-Pierre church ★★: south portal ★★ - Old town ★.

Manoir de Beaulieu rest, rest,

4 pl. Champ-de-Mars – ✆ 05 55 91 01 34 – reservation@manoirdebeaulieu.com – Fax 05 55 91 23 57

25 rm – †€ 70/120 ††€ 75/130, ☕ € 10 – 1 suite – **Rest** – Menu (€ 20), € 27/80 – Carte € 51/85

♦ This impressive hotel, founded in 1912, has benefited from a recent facelift. Cosy rooms embellished with antique furniture and modern bathrooms. Modern cuisine served in a welcoming, rustic restaurant.

Le Relais de Vellinus rm, VISA AE
17 pl. du Champ-de-Mars – ☎ 05 55 91 11 04 – contact@vellinus.com – Fax 05 55 91 26 16 – Closed 22 December-4 January, Sunday dinner and Saturday lunch
20 rm – €54/115 €54/115, €9 – ½ P €64/72 – **Rest** – Menu €18 (weekday lunch)/44 – Carte €54
◆ Attractively refurbished, this hotel has undergone a major transformation. Contemporary comfort, with each bedroom devoted to a different travel theme (Moorish, zen, the sea, Africa etc). A serene ambience pervades the dining room and terrace. Traditional cuisine.

Les Charmilles with rm VISA
20 bd St-Rodolphe-de-Turenne – ☎ 05 55 91 29 29 – charme@club-internet.fr – Fax 05 55 91 29 30 – Closed 27 October-16 November
8 rm – €58 €58, €8 – ½ P €54 – **Rest** – *(closed Wednesday October-May)* Menu €20/45 – Carte €30/63
◆ A well-renovated regional-style home: pleasant dining room, charming terrace on the banks of the Dordogne, classic menu and smart rooms.

in Brivezac **8 km Argentat road by D 940 and D 12 – pop. 199 – alt. 140 m – ✉ 19120**

Château de la Grèze
– ☎ 05 55 91 08 68 – anne-odile-france@wanadoo.fr – Closed 20-27 December
5 rm – €50/98 €58/106 – **Table d'hôte** – *(closed Wednesday, Saturday and Sunday in July-August)* Menu €25 bi
◆ This elegant 18C residence is surrounded by a park. Spacious, personalised bedrooms with wonderful views of the valley. Swimming pool. Horse-trekking possible.

BEAULIEU-SUR-MER – 06 Alpes-Maritimes – 341 F5 – pop. 3 675 – Casino – ✉ 06310 French Riviera 42 E2

Paris 935 – Menton 20 – Nice 8
Office de tourisme, place Georges Clemenceau ☎ 04 93 01 02 21, Fax 04 93 01 44 04
Site★ of Villa Kerylos★ - Baie des Fourmis★.

Plan on following page

La Réserve de Beaulieu sea, VISA AE
5 bd Mar.-Leclerc – ☎ 04 93 01 00 01 – reservation@reservebeaulieu.com – Fax 04 93 01 28 99 – Closed 26 October-19 December Z **w**
28 rm – €180/960 €350/1365, €33 – 11 suites
Rest – *(closed lunch from June to October and Monday)* Menu €75 (weekday lunch), €95/230 – Carte €180/250
Spec. Coupe estivale de langoustines royales (summer). Turbot cuit au plat, aux zestes d'agrumes et amandes, lasagne de tourteau et courgettes fleurs (summer). Duo acidulé de pêche et abricot (summer). **Wines** Bellet, Côtes de Provence.
◆ Seaside luxury hotel built in 1880 in the style of Florentine Renaissance palaces with a wealth of modern-day comforts. A beauty parlour and opulent villa-suites. Refined dining room, terrace with a view over the bay and reinvented Provençal-inspired cuisine.

Carlton without rest VISA AE
7 av. Edith Cavell – ☎ 04 93 01 44 70 – info@carlton-beaulieu.com – Fax 04 93 01 44 30 – Closed 11 January-13 February Z **s**
33 rm – €74/190 €74/190, €12
◆ 1930s villa in a residential district near the beach and casino with classically furnished bedrooms and a pleasant swimming pool. Attentive staff and professional service.

Frisia without rest VISA AE
2 bd E- Gauthier – ☎ 04 93 01 01 04 – info@frisia-beaulieu.com – Fax 04 93 01 31 92 – Closed 9 November-16 December Y **r**
33 rm – €52/135 €59/135, €9 – 1 suite
◆ Half the rooms and the rooftop sundeck overlook the marina and coast. An annexe in the courtyard-garden is home to one spacious room and a suite with terrace.

Comté de Nice without rest VISA AE
bd Marinoni – ☎ 04 93 01 19 70 – contact@hotel-comtedenice.com – Fax 04 93 01 23 09 Y **a**
32 rm – €60/95 €70/105, €10
◆ In a discreet building in the town centre, generously proportioned and well-equipped rooms, most with balconies; the seaside rooms are quieter. Comfortable lounges and bar.

BEAULIEU-SUR-MER

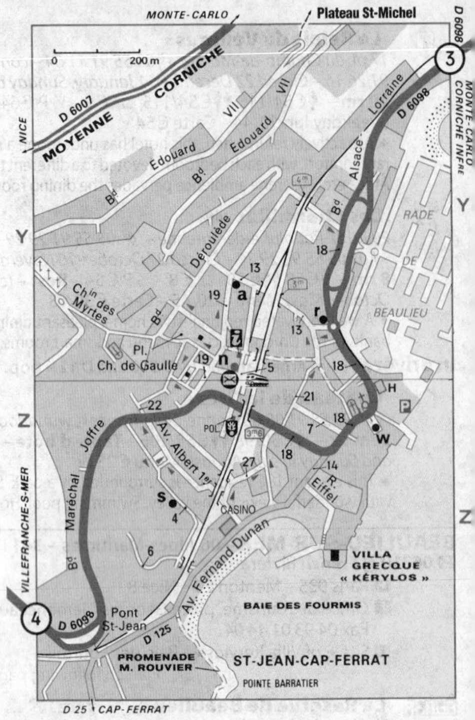

XX **Les Agaves**

4 av. Mar.-Foch – ✆ 04 93 01 13 12 – lelu.jacky@wanadoo.fr – Fax 04 93 01 65 97 – Closed 20 November-14 December Y **n**

Rest – *(dinner only)* Menu € 37 – Carte € 49/77

◆ Wood panelling, original mouldings, parquet floors and a slight Provençal touch in the decor: this discreet Beaulieu restaurant serves cuisine in line with current taste, with a regional flavour.

Other hotel resources see: **St-Jean-Cap-Ferrat**

BEAUMARCHÉS – 32 Gers – 336 C8 – pop. 588 – alt. 175 m – ✉ 32160

28 **A2**

Paris 755 – Agen 108 – Pau 64 – Mont-de-Marsan 65 – Auch 54

in Cayron 5 km East by D 946 – ✉ 32230

Relais du Bastidou

2 km southward by secondary road – ✆ 05 62 69 19 94 – lerelaisdubastidou@libertysurf.fr – Fax 05 62 69 19 94 – Closed November

8 rm – †€ 50/70 ††€ 50/70, ☕ € 8 – ½ P € 40/55 – **Rest** – *(closed Sunday dinner and Monday except July-August) (pre-book)* Menu € 20 (weekdays)/34 – Carte € 19/41

◆ This former isolated farm in the middle of the countryside guarantees you maximum quiet. The rooms, in the converted barn, offer pretty, chic, rustic décor. Sauna and jacuzzi. A country dining room heated by an attractive brick fireplace.

BEAUMES-DE-VENISE – 84 Vaucluse – 332 D9 – see Carpentras

BEAUMONT-DE-LOMAGNE – 82 Tarn-et-Garonne – 337 B8 – pop. 3 690 – alt. 400 m – ✉ 82500 Languedoc-Roussillon-Tarn Gorges 28 B2

Paris 662 – Toulouse 58 – Agen 60 – Auch 51 – Condom 64 – Montauban 35

Office de tourisme, 3, rue Pierre Fermat ✆ 05 63 02 42 32, Fax 05 63 65 61 17

Le Commerce

rest, rm, VISA MC AE

58 r. Mar.-Foch – ✆ 05 63 02 31 02 – hotelrest.lecommerce@wanadoo.fr – Fax 05 63 65 26 22 – Closed 22 December-11 January and Sunday dinner

12 rm – €42/48 €48, €7,50 – ½ P €45 – **Rest** – *(closed Friday dinner except July-August, Sunday dinner and Monday)* Menu (€9,50), €18 (weekdays)/33 – Carte €25/44

♦ Local house by the side of the road running through the village. The renovated and well-kept rooms offer all the desired comforts. The restaurant dining room has retained its country charm. Traditional cuisine.

BEAUMONT-EN-AUGE – 14 Calvados – 303 M4 – pop. 496 – alt. 90 m – ✉ 14950 Normandy 32 A3

Paris 199 – Caen 42 – Deauville 12 – Le Havre 49 – Lisieux 21 – Pont-l'Évêque 7

Auberge de l'Abbaye

VISA MC AE

– ✆ 02 31 64 82 31 – Closed 29 September-8 October, 5-28 January, Monday dinner from November to March, Tuesday except July-August and Wednesday

Rest – Menu €30/54 – Carte €45/86

♦ Fine 18C façade covered with Virginia creeper. Local dishes are served in three small, typically-Norman dining rooms decorated with antique trinkets.

BEAUNE – 21 Côte-d'Or – 320 I7 – pop. 21 923 – alt. 220 m – ✉ 21200 Burgundy-Jura 7 A3

Paris 308 – Autun 49 – Chalon-sur-Saône 29 – Dijon 45 – Dole 65

Office de tourisme, 1 rue de l'Hôtel Dieu ✆ 03 80 26 21 30, Fax 03 80 26 21 39

de Beaune Levernois Levernois, Southeast: 4 km by D 970, ✆ 03 80 24 10 29.

Hôtel-Dieu★★★ : polyptyque du Jugement dernier (polyptych of the Final Judgement)★★★, Grand'salle salle ou chambre des pauvres (Great Hall or Poor Man's Room)★★★ - Collégiale Notre-Dame (Notre Dame Collegiate Church)★ : tapestries★★ - Hôtel de la Rochepot★ AY B - ramparts★.

Plan on next page

Le Cep without rest

VISA MC AE

27 r. Maufoux – ✆ 03 80 22 35 48 – resa@hotel-cep-beaune.com – Fax 03 80 22 76 80 AZ z

49 rm – €125/204 €160/244, €20 – 13 suites

♦ 16C and 18C town houses offering rooms with personal touches and superb suites. Breakfast served in the Renaissance courtyard in summer under the shade of a venerable weeping willow.

Hostellerie Le Cèdre

rm, VISA MC AE

12 bd Mar.-Foch – ✆ 03 80 24 01 01 – info@lecedre-beaune.com – Fax 03 80 24 09 90 AY t

40 rm – €155/205 €155/205, €17 – ½ P €165/205

Rest – *(closed 23-28 December, 2-16 January, Saturday lunch and Sunday lunch)* Menu €18 (weekday lunch), €42/78 – Carte €52/95

♦ An attractive early 20C residence and garden with century-old trees. Spacious, elegant and well-soundproofed rooms. Fitness room and sauna. A bourgeois restaurant in a 19C house with a terrace in the shade of an old cedar. Up-to-date cuisine.

De la Poste

rm, rm, VISA MC AE

5 bd Clemenceau – ✆ 03 80 22 08 11 – reservation@hoteldelapostebeaune.com – Fax 03 80 24 19 71 AZ f

33 rm – €130/295 €130/295, €20 – 3 suites

Rest – *(closed Tuesday and lunch except Sunday and public holidays)* Menu €38/59 – Carte €51/63

Rest *Le Bistro* – *(closed Tuesday) (lunch only)* Menu €26 – Carte €24/37

♦ This old 19C coaching inn has recently undergone a major refurbishment. Bedrooms with old and modern furnishings. Lounge bar with Art deco feel. Elegant, classic restaurant in bright tones. A painted mural with a wine making theme in the bistro.

BEAUNE

Street	Grid	No.
Alsace (R. d')	AZ	2
Belin (R.)	AZ	4
Bourgelat (R.)	AZ	5
Carnot (Petite-Pl.)	AZ	6
Carnot (Pl.)	AZ	7
Carnot (R.)	AZ	9
Château (R. du)	BY	10
Dames (Rempart des)	AZ	13
Dr-Jorrot (Pl. du)	BY	15
Enfant (R. de l')	AY	16
Enfert (R. d')	AZ	17
Favart (R.)	AY	18
Fleury (Pl.)	AZ	19
Fraysse (R. E.)	AZ	21
Halle (Pl. de la)	AZ	23
Lorraine (R. de)	AY	
Maufoux (R.)	AZ	25
Monge (Pl.)	AY	26
Monge (R.)	AZ	28
Perpreuil (Bd.)	AZ	29
Poterne (R.)	AZ	30
Rolin (R.)	AZ	31
Rousseau-Deslandes (R.)	BY	32
Ste-Marguerite (R.)	AY	35
St-Nicolas (R. du Fg)	AY	34
Tonneliers (R. des)	AY	37
Ziem (Pl.)	AZ	40

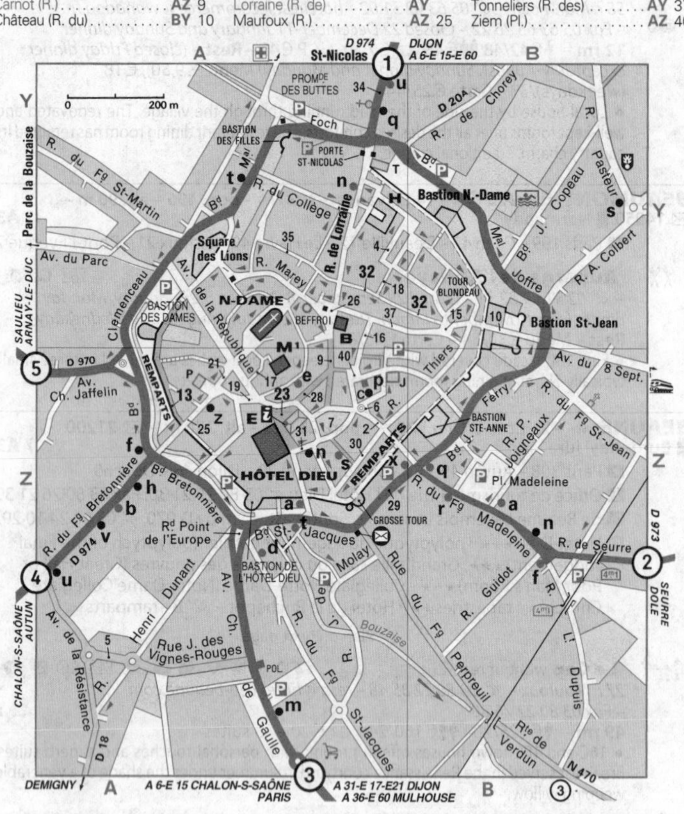

L'Hôtel without rest

5 r. Samuel-Legay – ✆ 03 80 25 94 14 – info@lhoteldebeaune.com – Fax 03 80 25 94 13 – Closed December AZ **p**

7 rm – †€ 180/335 ††€ 180/335, ☕ € 25

◆ Luxurious, Empire-style rooms, high-tech equipment and designer bathrooms: a new lease of life for this large residence, once the Louis Jadot winery.

Mercure rm,

av. Ch.-de-Gaulle – ✆ 03 80 22 22 00 – h1217@accor.com – Fax 03 80 22 91 74 AZ**m**

94 rm – †€ 90/122 ††€ 106/142, ☕ € 14 – 13 suites – **Rest** – Menu (€ 16), € 21 – Carte € 20/45

◆ This establishment on the outskirts of town is useful for business trips: functional and well-renovated rooms for work and rest, bar and swimming pool for relaxation. Traditional meals in a modern dining room and setting overlooking the terrace and swimming pool.

Henry II without rest VISA

12 r. Faubourg-St-Nicolas – ☎ 03 80 22 83 84 – info@henry2.fr – Fax 03 80 24 15 13
58 rm – €69/139 €72/249, €9,50 AY **q**

◆ The recent wing of the hotel has been designed to blend in with the part that is listed: a 16C post house. Rooms in various shapes and styles, from Louis XV to Art Deco.

La Closerie without rest VISA

via ④ Autun road D 974 – ☎ 03 80 22 15 07 – closeriehotelbeaune@wanadoo.fr – Fax 03 80 24 16 22 – Closed 23 December-15 January
47 rm – €55/85 €60/140, €12

◆ Between the town centre and the motorways, this establishment stands surrounded by greenery. The fresh and modern rooms have been redecorated. Some overlook the garden's swimming pool.

Panorama rest, VISA

74 rte Pommard, via ④ – ☎ 03 80 26 22 17 – hotel@le-panorama.com – Fax 03 80 26 22 18 – Closed 22 December-3 January and 9 February-8 March
65 rm – €65/125 €70/125, €11 – ½ P €75/93 – **Rest** – *(Open 15 March-30 November and closed Sunday off season) (dinner only)* Carte €36/46

◆ This motel-type establishment has recently been renovated. Functional and quiet rooms in two modern houses in the middle of the vineyard. The rotunda restaurant gracefully combines old (furniture) with new (metal framework). Regional cuisine.

Belle Époque without rest VISA

15 r. Fg-Bretonnière – ☎ 03 80 24 66 15 – infos@hotel-belleepoque-beaune.com – Fax 03 80 24 17 49 AZ **h**
19 rm – €82 €90/165, €9

◆ An old house with character; a 1900 glass roof, rustic rooms, some with beams or fireplaces, and overlooking the interior courtyard. Pleasantly retro bar.

De la Paix without rest VISA

45 r. Fg-Madeleine – ☎ 03 80 24 78 08 – contact@hotelpaix.com – Fax 03 80 24 10 18
22 rm – €56/72 €72/132, €9,50 BZ **n**

◆ Pleasant family stopover on a busy road. Generously-proportioned rooms furnished in a contemporary style or in painted wood. Lounge, billiards and pretty bar.

Grillon without rest VISA

21 rte Seurre, 1 km via ② – ☎ 03 80 22 44 25 – joel.grillon@wanadoo.fr – Fax 03 80 24 94 89 – Closed 2 February-3 March
17 rm – €54/95 €54/95, €9

◆ A spruce pink building with almond green shutters in an enclosed garden. Charming rooms, lounge-bar in the cellar and a flower-decked terrace for breakfast in summer.

Hostellerie de Bretonnière without rest VISA

43 r. Fg-Bretonnière – ☎ 03 80 22 15 77 – infos@hotelbretonniere.com – Fax 03 80 22 72 54 – Closed Sun evening from 1 Dec - 31 Mar except during school and public holidays AZ **v**
32 rm – €55/79 €55/110, €8,50

◆ Old post house and its annex offer rooms and duplexes, being renovated in stages, in a modern style; some open on to the garden. A warm welcome.

Central VISA

2 r. V.-Millot – ☎ 03 80 24 77 24 – hotel.central.beaune@wanadoo.fr – Fax 03 80 22 30 40 AZ **n**
20 rm – €50/60 €79/89, €10 – 1 suite
Rest *Le Cheval Blanc* – ☎ *03 80 24 69 70 (closed mid December-mid January, Tuesday and Wednesday)* Menu (€15), €23/32 – Carte approx. €34

◆ 100m from the Hotel Dieu, a corner building dating from 1595. Modern, spacious and well-soundproofed rooms. A suite is also available. Contemporary decor and classic and regional cuisine in the Cheval Blanc restaurant. Sheltered pavement terrace.

La Villa Fleurie without rest VISA

19 pl. Colbert – ☎ 03 80 22 66 00 – la.villa.fleurie@wanadoo.fr – Fax 03 80 22 45 46 – Closed January BY **s**
10 rm – €69/79 €69/99, €8,50

◆ Candy box hotel dating from the Belle Epoque with a small flower-decked garden at the front. Rooms are modern or have antique furniture. Breakfast room with a British charm.

Alésia without rest

4 av. des Sablières, 1 km rte Dijon via ① – ✆ 03 80 22 63 27 – hotel.alesia@wanadoo.fr – Fax 03 80 24 95 28

15 rm – †€ 34 ††€ 49, ☕ € 7,50

◆ On the edge of Beaune, a pleasant establishment for those on a budget. The simple, fresh rooms are well kept. Attentive service.

Beaune Hôtel without rest

55 bis r. Fg-Bretonnière – ✆ 03 80 22 11 01 – beaunehotel@aol.com – Fax 03 80 22 46 66 – Closed 18 November-12 December and 22 December-5 January

21 rm – †€ 62/90 ††€ 68/125, ☕ € 8 AZ **u**

◆ Discreet building situated near to a junction. The rooms are rather small but functional and extremely well kept; nearly all of them overlook the quiet courtyard.

Le Jardin des Remparts (Roland Chanliaud)

10 r. Hôtel-Dieu – ✆ 03 80 24 79 41 – info@le-jardin-des-remparts.com – Fax 03 80 24 92 79 – Closed 1st December-13 January, Sunday and Monday except public holidays AZ **a**

Rest – Menu € 35 (weekday lunch), € 58/88 – Carte € 60/81

Spec. Tartare de charolais aux huîtres, écume de mer. Lotte au beurre d'algues et coquillages, jus au thé. Pigeon rôti au jus et gousses de petits pois (spring-summer). **Wines** Meursault, Beaune.

◆ Charming 1930s house and delightful garden terrace along the ramparts. Modern decor, inventive cuisine and fine wines; grand piano and wine-growing utensils in the lounge.

L'Écusson

pl. Malmédy – ✆ 03 80 24 03 82 – contact@ecusson.fr – Fax 03 80 24 74 02 – Closed 2 February-2 March, Wednesday and Sunday except holidays BZ **f**

Rest – Menu € 26/62 – Carte € 53/74

◆ Up-to-date market-inspired menus concocted by the owner-chef, served in a sophisticated classical-rustic setting or on the inviting terrace. Friendly atmosphere. Excellent Burgundies.

Le Bénaton (Bruno Monnoir)

25 r. Faubourg-Bretonnière – ✆ 03 80 22 00 26 – lebenaton@club-internet.fr – Fax 03 80 22 51 95 – Closed 1st-7 July, 5-15 December, February Holidays, Saturday lunch from April to November, Thursday except dinner from April to November and Wednesday AZ **b**

Rest – Menu (€ 23), € 45/85 – Carte € 51/79

Spec. Bocal de homard à l'huile d'olive et jeunes légumes (spring and Autumn). Tête de veau rôtie, langoustines frites, bouillon gribiche. Gâteau au chocolat chaud et cassis. **Wines** Meursault.

◆ Delicious inventive cuisine served in a dining room redecorated in a contemporary, elegant style, or in summertime, on the teak-furnished terrace.

Caveau des Arches

10 bd Perpreuil – ✆ 03 80 22 10 37 – info@caveau-des-arches.com – Fax 03 80 22 76 44 – Closed 18 July-19 August, 20 December-19 January, Sunday and Monday ABZ **x**

Rest – Menu (€ 16), € 21/45 – Carte € 28/53

◆ Traditional meals served in a vaulted stone basement (18C) integrating the foundations of a bridge (15C). Modern décor; good choice of Burgundies.

Sushikai

50 fg St-Nicolas – ✆ 03 80 24 02 87 – Fax 03 80 24 79 85 – Closed 5-22 January, Wednesday and Thursday AY **u**

Rest – Menu (€ 19), € 25 (weekday lunch), € 34/54 – Carte € 40/54

◆ Dark wood, pebbles, bamboo and a garden at the rear complete with a small bridge: this restaurant with Zen and minimalist décor offers authentic Japanese food accompanied by a regional wine list.

Le Verger

21 rte de Seurre, 1 km via ② – ✆ 03 80 24 28 05 – Fax 03 80 22 78 89 – Closed 15 January-1st March, Monday lunch, Thursday lunch and Wednesday

Rest – Menu € 15 (weekday lunch), € 25/39 – Carte € 36/50

◆ Facing the pretty flowered garden, the modern dining room has a pleasant terrace. Contemporary cuisine with a regional flavour and wines from small vineyards.

XX **L'Auberge Bourguignonne** with rm rest, VISA

4 pl. Madeleine – ✆ 03 80 22 23 53 – contact@auberge-bourguignonne.fr – Fax 03 80 22 51 64 – Closed 22 November-15 December, 21 February-9 March and Monday except public holidays BZ **a**

10 rm – €56 €58/73, €8 – **Rest** – Menu €20/42 – Carte €36/55

◆ A former post house built of stone (18C) containing two country-style dining rooms for traditional meals with a local flavour. Terrace shaded by lime trees. Fresh and neat rooms with matching rustic furniture.

XX **Auberge du Cheval Noir** VISA

17 bd St-Jacques – ✆ 03 80 22 07 37 – lechevalnoir@wanadoo.fr – Fax 03 80 24 06 92 – Closed 1st-6 March, 12-28 February, Sunday dinner from November to April, Tuesday and Wednesday AZ **t**

Rest – Menu €21 (weekdays)/65 bi – Carte €27/60

◆ Near the Hotel-Dieu, alongside the ring road, a restaurant with a modern menu in a classic-modern setting. Lovely teak terrace.

XX **Loiseau des Vignes** VISA AE

31 r. Maufoux – ✆ 03 80 24 12 06 – loiseaudesvignes@bernard-loiseau.com – Fax 03 80 22 06 22 – Closed 27 January-12 February, 2-16 December, Sunday and Monday AZ **z**

Rest – Menu €28 (lunch), €75/98 – Carte €58/62

◆ Neat establishment, new to the Loiseau group. Chef's classics served in the evening with a simpler lunchtime menu. High-tech wine preservation system (all served by the glass).

X **La Ciboulette** VISA AE

69 r. de Lorraine – ✆ 03 80 24 70 72 – Fax 03 80 22 79 71 – Closed 4-20 August, 2-25 February, Monday and Tuesday AY **n**

Rest – Menu €20/26 – Carte €25/40

◆ Two dining rooms brightened by green cane furniture and woodwork. Appetising, short, traditional menu with a Burgundy flavour.

X **Ma Cuisine** VISA

passage Ste-Hélène – ✆ 03 80 22 30 22 – macuisine@wanadoo.fr – Fax 03 80 24 99 79 – Closed August, Wednesday, Saturday and Sunday AZ **s**

Rest – *(number of covers limited, pre-book)* Menu €22 – Carte €34/68

◆ In a quiet street, a pretty little restaurant in Provençal colours with a vaulted ceiling. Cuisine based on market produce displayed on a blackboard, wine list with some 800 appellations.

X **Le P'tit Paradis** VISA

25 r. Paradis – ✆ 03 80 24 91 00 – Closed 1st-16 March, 17-31 August, 17 November-1st December, Sunday and Monday AZ **e**

Rest – *(pre-book)* Menu €27/35 – Carte €37/49

◆ Situated in an old cobbled street in the town centre, this "little paradise" has a dining room charmingly decorated in shades of beige and chocolate brown. Terrace. Seasonal cuisine.

X **Le Comptoir des Tontons** VISA

22 r. Faubourg-Madeleine – ✆ 03 80 24 19 64 – lestontons@wanadoo.fr – Fax 03 80 22 34 07 – Closed 27 July-25 August, 1st-16 February, Sunday and Monday BZ **r**

Rest – Menu €25/28

◆ A friendly atmosphere reigns in this small bistro where you can enjoy, in décor dedicated to the film "Les Tontons Flingueurs", a market-based set menu that goes well with a good Burgundy.

X **Bissoh** VISA

1a r. du Faubourg-St-Jacques – ✆ 03 80 24 99 50 – bis@bissoh.com – Fax 03 80 24 99 50 – Closed 3-25 February, Tuesday and Wednesday AZ **d**

Rest – Menu €13 (weekday lunch), €28/57 – Carte €21/34

◆ The Japanese-born chef prepares traditional dishes from his country using French-sourced produce. The interior is a singular blend of rusticity and Japanese touches.

Aux Vignes rouges
4 bd Jules-Ferry – ☎ 03 80 24 71 28 – Fax 03 80 24 68 05 – Closed Tuesday and Wednesday BZ **q**
Rest – Menu € 14,50 (weekday lunch), € 18/45 – Carte € 25/70
◆ Traditional cuisine using local produce served in a welcoming dining room with well-presented tables and friendly service.

in Savigny-lès-Beaune 7 km by ①, D 18 and D 2 – pop. 1 422 – alt. 237 m – ✉ 21420

Syndicat d'initiative, 13, rue Vauchey Very ☎ 03 80 26 12 56, Fax 03 80 26 12 56

Le Hameau de Barboron without rest
– ☎ 03 80 21 58 35 – lehameaudebarboron@wanadoo.fr – Fax 03 80 26 10 59
12 rm – €100/135 €100/200, € 15
◆ In the middle of a huge hunting reserve, a series of superbly restored fortified farm buildings (16C) where you will stay in personalised rooms with a preserved country charm.

La Cuverie
5 r. Chanoine-Donin – ☎ 03 80 21 50 03 – Fax 03 80 21 50 03 – Closed 20 December-20 January, Tuesday and Wednesday
Rest – Menu € 16/39 – Carte € 25/40
◆ Rustic Burgundy furniture, exposed stone walls and a fine collection of coffee pots in this former fermenting room (18C), offering you a traditional meal based on local produce.

in Pernand-Vergelesses 7 km North by D18 – pop. 310 – alt. 275 m – ✉ 21420

Charlemagne (Laurent Peugeot)
Vergelesses road – ☎ 03 80 21 51 45 – laurentpeugeot@wanadoo.fr – Fax 03 80 21 58 52 – Closed 29 July-6 August, 29 January-4 March, Tuesday and Wednesday
Rest – Menu € 25 (weekday lunch), € 41/79 – Carte € 70/93
Spec. Escargots de Bourgogne revisités. Bar en paupiette de tapenade. Foie gras de canard "coffret surprise". **Wines** Pernand-Vergelesses, Savigny-lès-Beaune.
◆ A French-Japanese couple owns this restaurant overlooking the Charlemagne Corton vineyards. Inventive food with regional and Japanese touches; modern, fashionable, Zen décor.

Dijon road 4 km by ① – ✉ 21200 Chorey-lès-Beaune

Ermitage de Corton
– ☎ 03 80 22 05 28 – ermitage.corton@wanadoo.fr – Fax 03 80 24 64 51 – Closed 22-28 December and 8 February-10 March
4 rm – €120/145 €145/160, € 20 – 8 suites – €180/250 – ½ P € 135 – **Rest** – *(closed Wednesday and lunch except Sunday)* Menu € 45/75 – Carte € 64/79
◆ This imposing inn is situated between the main road and the vineyard. It offers spacious rooms and suites, most of them redecorated in a trendy style. Modern food based on local produce served in a large classic dining room.

in Aloxe-Corton 6 km by ① – pop. 172 – alt. 255 m – ✉ 21420

Villa Louise without rest
– ☎ 03 80 26 46 70 – hotel-villa-louise@wanadoo.fr – Fax 03 80 26 47 16 – Closed 10 January-20 February
12 rm – €96/149 €96/190, € 15
◆ A fine 17C wine-producer's house with a garden (old lime tree) overlooking the Charlemagne Corton vineyards. Cosy rooms and lounge and warm, guesthouse ambience.

in Ladoix-Serrigny 7 km by ① and D 974 – pop. 1 618 – alt. 200 m – ✉ 21550

La Buissonnière
à Buisson – ☎ 03 80 26 43 58 – restaurantlabuissonniere@wanadoo.fr – Closed 23 December-7 January, Tuesday and Wednesday
Rest – Carte € 26/61
◆ A warm welcome at this establishment where you choose the setting for your meal: modern in the glass-roofed room, or rustic in the old cellar with its press.

Les Terrasses de Corton with rm
38-40 rte de Beaune – ✆ 03 80 26 42 37 – patrice.sanchez3@wanadoo.fr – Fax 03 80 26 42 13 – Closed 1st-6 March, 21-29 December, 11 January-28 February, Tuesday dinner and Sunday dinner from October to March, Thursday lunch from March to October and Wednesday
9 rm – †€ 42 ††€ 56, ☐ € 8,50 – 1 suite – ½ P € 50 – **Rest** – Menu (€ 17), € 23/43 – Carte € 24/50
◆ In this little winegrowing village, a family guesthouse that has a menu of local dishes. Bright dining room with a shaded terrace at the rear.

in Challanges 4 km by ② then D 111 – ✉ 21200

Château de Challanges without rest
r. des Templiers – ✆ 03 80 26 32 62 – chateau.challanges@wanadoo.fr – Fax 03 80 26 32 52 – Closed 7-22 December
15 rm – †€ 80/135 ††€ 80/135, ☐ € 12 – 5 suites
◆ Fine 1870 gentleman's residence in parkland with many species of tree. Bygone charm blends with modern comfort in the rooms and suites. Hot air ballooning in summer.

Southeast near A 6 interchange 2 km by ③ – ✉ 21200 Beaune

Novotel
av. Ch.-de-Gaulle – ✆ 03 80 24 59 00 – h1177@accor.com – Fax 03 80 24 59 29
127 rm – †€ 113/128 ††€ 123/128, ☐ € 13,50 – **Rest** – Menu (€ 20), € 24/30 – Carte € 26/36
◆ Completely renovated in 2006, this simple hotel dating from the 1990s has a traditional, red-tiled roof. Modern lounge-lobby next to the swimming pool. Smart rooms. Modern dining room and teak terrace overlooking the pool. Traditional cuisine.

in Levernois 5 km Southeast by Verdun-sur-le-Doubs road, D 970 and D 111L - BZ – pop. 260 – alt. 198 m – ✉ 21200

Hostellerie de Levernois
r. du Golf – ✆ 03 80 24 73 58 – levernois@relaischateaux.com – Fax 03 80 22 78 00 – Closed 25 January-13 March
22 rm – †€ 130/305 ††€ 130/305, ☐ € 20 – 4 suites – ½ P € 150/238
Rest – *(closed Wednesday from November to March and lunch except Sunday)* Menu € 65/98 – Carte € 76/110
Rest *Le Bistrot du Bord de l'Eau* – *✆ 03 80 24 89 58 (closed Sunday) (lunch only)* Menu € 28/32
Spec. Pigeon au foie gras, navets caramélisés au cassis sauce salmis. Déclinaison de bœuf à l'échalote et à la moelle, jus à l'estragon. Variation autour du pain d'épice. **Wines** Vougeot blanc, Beaune.
◆ A spruce manor house (19C) and its outbuildings, surrounded by a park with a stream running through it. Lovely rooms with character. Elegant, modern restaurant overlooking the French-style garden. Former barn, overlooking the water, converted into a pretty, neo-rustic bistro.

Golf Hôtel without rest
rte de Combertault – ✆ 03 80 24 78 20 – hotelcolvert@wanadoo.fr – Fax 03 80 24 77 70
24 rm – †€ 65/90 ††€ 90/110, ☐ € 12
◆ A modern building opening onto the golf course. The rooms sport stained wooden furniture, a map of the vineyard on the wall, and a balcony overlooking the greens. Bright lounge with fireplace.

Le Parc without rest
13 r. du Golf – ✆ 03 80 24 63 00 – leparc@levernois.com – Fax 03 80 24 21 19 – Closed 25 January-28 February
17 rm – †€ 55/70 ††€ 55/70, ☐ € 8
◆ A flowered courtyard and a pretty park overlooking the countryside make this former farm (18C) a relaxing stop-over. Cosy rooms, classically furnished.

La Garaudière
10 Grand'Rue – ✆ 03 80 22 47 70 – Fax 03 80 22 64 01
– Closed 1st December-15 January, Saturday lunch from April to November, Sunday from mid January to end March and Monday
Rest – Menu € 16 (weekdays)/29 – Carte € 26/54
◆ A former barn converted into a pleasant inn, regional dishes and grills cooked over the fire, welcoming, rustic interior and a terrace under an arbour.

in Montagny-lès-Beaune 3 km by ③ and D 113 – pop. 715 – alt. 206 m – ✉ 21200

Le Clos without rest
22 r. Gravières – ✆ 03 80 25 97 98 – hotelleclos@wanadoo.fr – Fax 03 80 25 94 70
– Closed 25 November-18 January
24 rm – €75/115 €75/200, ☕ €11
◆ A wine-maker's style property (1779) houses you in rooms and a duplex personalised by antique furniture. Old wine-press and bread oven in the courtyard. Well-kept garden.

Adélie without rest
1 rte de Bligny – ✆ 03 80 22 37 74 – reservation@hoteladelie.com – Fax 03 80 24 23 18 – Closed 21-25 December and Sunday from 23 November to 29 March
19 rm – €53 €57, ☕ €7,50
◆ This family hotel situated in the heart of a peaceful village in Beaunois country offers small, renovated rooms brightened with pastel tones and decorated with pine furniture.

in Meursault 8 km by ④ – pop. 1 598 – alt. 243 m – ✉ 21190

Office de tourisme, place de l'Hôtel de Ville ✆ 03 80 21 25 90, Fax 03 80 21 61 62

Les Charmes without rest
10 pl. Murger – ✆ 03 80 21 63 53 – contact@hotelleschcharmes.com
– Fax 03 80 21 62 89 – 11 Mar - 1 Dec
14 rm – €85 €95/115, ☕ €10
◆ Former winegrower's property from the 18C housing spacious rooms (non-smoking) with antique furniture or rooms that are more modern and colourful. Garden.

Le Relais de la Diligence
at the station, 2.5 km south-eastward along the D 23 – ✆ 03 80 21 21 32
– diligence.la@wanadoo.fr – Fax 03 80 21 64 69
– Closed 18 December-25 January, Tuesday dinner and Wednesday off season
Rest – Menu € 11,50 (weekday lunch), € 17/39 – Carte € 26/48
◆ Former coach house made of local stone near to the station. Two dining rooms, are largely open onto the vineyards, the same goes for the terrace. Traditional menu.

Le Bouchon
pl. de l'Hôtel-de-Ville – ✆ 03 80 21 29 56 – Fax 03 80 21 29 56
– Closed 20 November-27 December, Sunday dinner and Monday
Rest – Menu € 12 (weekday lunch), € 15/35 – Carte € 25/37
◆ Near to the town hall with its shiny tiles, a little "bouchon" style bistro. Traditional menus and rustic dishes in a renovated dining room (light wood and mirrors).

in Puligny-Montrachet 12 km by ④ and D 974 – pop. 464 – alt. 227 m – ✉ 21190

Le Montrachet
– ✆ 03 80 21 30 06 – info@le-montrachet.com – Fax 03 80 21 39 06
– Closed 1st December-16 January
30 rm – €120/130 €120/200, ☕ €15 – ½ P €130/140 – **Rest** – Menu €30 (lunch), €55/75 – Carte €56/90
◆ A pretty village house (1824) and converted stables, offering comfortable rooms and suites, which are either rustic or more modern in style. Wine for sale in the cellar. Quiet atmosphere, modern menu and good selection of Burgundy white wines in the restaurant.

La Maison d'Olivier Leflaive
pl. du Monument – ✆ 03 80 21 37 65 – contact@olivier-leflaive.com
– Fax 03 80 21 33 94 – Closed 31 December-30 January
13 rm – €150/180 €150/180, ☕ €10 – **Rest** – wine bar *(closed Sunday)* Menu €39 bi/49 (a la carte in the evenings) – Carte €28/40
◆ Large house set in the centre of the village. Charming, brand new rooms decorated in different styles, including Baroque, rustic, pop, romantic and retro. Light dishes served to accompany the wine tasting (vineyard and cellar tours).

La Chouette without rest

3 bis r. des Creux de Chagny – ☎ 03 80 21 95 60 – info@la-chouette.fr – Fax 03 80 21 95 61 – Closed 19 December-3 January

6 rm – **†€ 125 ††€ 140**

◆ A quiet Burgundian house for a pleasant stay in large rooms personalised in a cosy style. Comfortable, classic-modern lounge and well-kept garden.

in Volnay by ④ and D 974 – pop. 323 – alt. 290 m – ✉ 21190

Auberge des Vignes

D 974 – ☎ 03 80 22 24 48 – elisabeth.leneuf@free.fr – Fax 03 80 22 24 48 – Closed 26 June-2 July, 16 February-9 March, Wednesday dinner, Sunday dinner and Monday

Rest – Menu € 16 (weekday lunch), € 19/40 – Carte € 28/46

◆ Former farm where traditional dishes and mellow Volnay wines can be enjoyed in a rustic setting. Comforting fire in winter; veranda and terrace facing the vineyard.

in La Montagne 3 km by ⑤ and D 970, secondary road – ✉ 21200 Beaune

La Terre d'Or without rest

r. Izembart – ☎ 03 80 25 90 90 – jlmartin@laterredor.com – Fax 08 21 47 99 67 – Closed February

6 rm – **†€ 110/205 ††€ 140/260,** € 15

◆ Huge, modern house with well-kept rooms on the hills above the town. Garden with swimming pool. Wine cellar with tasting sessions; cooking lessons available.

in Bouze-lès-Beaune 6.5 km by ⑤ and D 970 – pop. 261 – alt. 400 m – ✉ 21200

La Bouzerotte

– ☎ 03 80 26 01 37 – contact@labouzerotte.com – Fax 03 80 26 09 37 – Closed 27 August-2 September, 22 December-14 January, 23 February-10 March, Monday and Tuesday

Rest – *(pre-book Sat - Sun)* Menu (€ 13,50), € 17 (weekday lunch), € 24/40 – Carte € 24/57

◆ At the entrance to a Beaune mountain village, a nice restaurant serving modern, seasonal food in a neo-rustic setting or on a leafy, teak terrace.

See also hotel resource of **Bouilland**

BEAURECUEIL – 13 Bouches-du-Rhône – 340 I4 – see Aix-en-Provence

---

BEAUREGARD-VENDON – 63 Puy-de-Dôme – 326 F7 – see Riom

BEAUREPAIRE-EN-BRESSE – 71 Saône-et-Loire – 320 M9 – pop. 515 – alt. 147 m – ✉ 71580

8 **D3**

Paris 383 – Châlon-sur-Saône 49 – Bourg-en-Bresse 65 – Lons-le-Saunier 13 – Tournus 45

Auberge de la Croix Blanche

– ☎ 03 85 74 13 22 – aubergedelacroixblanche@libertysurf.fr – Fax 03 85 74 13 25 – Closed 9-16 June, 17 November-8 December, 7-14 January, Sunday dinner and Monday except July-August

14 rm – **†€ 36/41 ††€ 36/47,** € 11 – ½ P € 50/55 – **Rest** – Menu € 15/50 – Carte € 30/48

◆ Near a busy road, this inn has a roof that's easy to find with a white cross on it and ears of corn drying under the façade lean-to. Very clean rooms overlooking the garden. Bressan décor in the restaurant; regional produce prepared in a modern setting.

BEAUSOLEIL – 06 Alpes-Maritimes – 341 F5 – pop. 12 775 – alt. 89 m – ✉ 06240

Paris 947 – Monaco 4 – Menton 11 – Monte-Carlo 2 – Nice 21 42 **E2**

Office de tourisme, 32, boulevard de la République ☎ 04 93 78 01 55, Fax 04 93 78 85 85

See plan of Monaco (Principality of).

Olympia without rest VISA AE
17 bis bd Gén.- Leclerc – 04 93 78 12 70 – olympiahotel@hotmail.com – Fax 04 93 41 85 04 DX **t**
31 rm – €85/120 €85/160, €10 – 1 suite
◆ Fine freestone fronted building adorned with balconies and a finely worked cornice located on the French-Monegasque border. Sober, soundproofed and tasteful rooms.

LE BEAUSSET – **83 Var** – **340** J6 – **pop. 7 723** – **alt. 167 m** – ✉ **83330** 40 **B3**

Paris 817 – Aix-en-Provence 67 – Marseille 47 – Toulon 18

Office de tourisme, place Charles-de-Gaulle 04 94 90 55 10, Fax 04 94 98 51 83

Mas Lei Bancau without rest VISA AE
1 km southward along the D N8 and secondary road – 04 94 90 27 78 – leibancau@wanadoo.fr – Fax 04 94 90 29 00 – Open from March to October
7 rm – €86/111 €86/157, €10
◆ A sloping path leads to this farmhouse overlooking the Bandol vineyards. Breakfast room and bedrooms in the colours of Provence. Lovely grounds, typical of the region.

La Cigalière without rest VISA AE
1.5 km north on D N8 and secondary road – 04 94 98 64 63 – hotellacigaliere@wanadoo.fr – Fax 04 94 98 66 04
14 rm – €65/70 €65/70, €9 – 5 suites
◆ In a residential area, two local-style houses in the shade of pine trees. The studios with kitchenette and private terrace are very popular with families.

BEAUVAIS P – **60 Oise** – **305** D4 – **pop. 55 392** – **Built-up area 100 733** – **alt. 67 m** – ✉ **60000** Northern France and the Paris Region 36 **B2**

Paris 87 – Amiens 63 – Boulogne-sur-Mer 182 – Compiègne 60 – Rouen 82

Beauvais-Tillé 03 44 11 46 66, 3,5 km au Northeast

Office de tourisme, 1, rue Beauregard 03 44 15 30 30, Fax 03 44 15 30 31

du Vivier Ons-en-Bray RN 31, by Gournay-en-Bray road: 15 km, 03 44 84 24 11.

St-Pierre cathedral★★★: astronomical clock★ - St-Étienne church★: stained-glass windows★★ and Jesse tree★★★ - Musée départemental de l'Oise★ in the former bishop's palace M².

Plan on next page

Hostellerie St-Vincent rm, VISA AE
3 km by ③ (Espace St-Germain), 241 Rue de Clermont – 03 44 05 49 99 – h.st.vincent@wanadoo.fr – Fax 03 44 05 52 94
67 rm – €67/80 €67/80, €9,50 – 1 suite – ½ P €50 – **Rest** – Menu €17 (weekdays)/36 – Carte €26/40
◆ A recently-built hotel near main roads and the motorway slip road, offering redecorated, functional and soundproofed rooms. Internet access available. Spacious and light dining room; traditional menus completed by blackboard specials.

XX **La Maison Haute** VISA
128 r. de Paris, (Voisinlieu district), 1.5 km on ④ – 03 44 02 61 60 – Fax 03 44 02 15 36 – Closed 15-19 April, 13 July-30 August, 1st-8 January, Saturday lunch, Sunday and Monday
Rest – Menu (€27), €30/33
◆ Contemporary restaurant (light tones and dark wood) in e residential neighbourhood. Up-to-date cuisine and a warm welcome.

X **La Baie d'Halong** VISA
32 r. de Clermont, 1 km by ③ – 03 44 45 39 83 – ta.hoang@wanadoo.fr – Closed 15 April-1st May, 14 July-15 August, 20 December-3 January, Wednesday lunch, Saturday lunch, Sunday, Monday and public holidays
Rest – Menu (€15), €23/26
◆ Exclusively Vietnamese cuisine combining fresh ingredients with a delicate use of spices. Paintings depicting the Bay of Halong adorn the dining room.

BEAUVAIS

Beauregard (R.) 2
Brière (Bd J.) 3
Carnot (R.) ....
Clemenceau (Pl.) 4
Dr-Gérard (R.) 5
Dr-Lamotte (Bd du) 6
Dreux (R. Ph. de) 7
Gambetta ....
Grenier-à-Sel (R.) 8
Guéhengnies (R. de) 9
Hachette (Pl. J.) 10
Halles (Pl. des) 12
Leclerc (R. Mar.) 13
Lignières (R. J. de) 15
Loisel (Bd A.) 16
Malherbe (R. de) 18
Nully-d'Hécourt (R.) 19
République (Av. de la) 20
St-André (Bd) 22
St-Laurent (R.) 23
St-Pierre (R.) 24
Scellier (Cours) 27
Taillerie (R. de la) 29
Tapisserie (R. de la) 30
Villiers-de-l'Isle-Adam (R.) 35
Vincent-de-Beauvais (R.) 26
Watrin (R. du Gén.) 36
27-Juin (R. du) 38

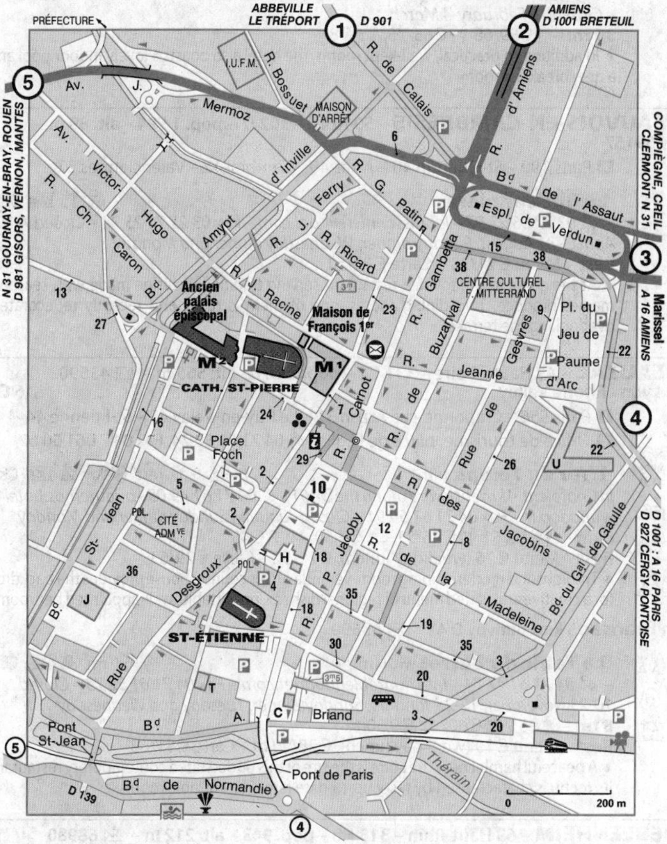

via ④ 5 km , D 1001 (towards Paris) – ✉ 60000 Beauvais

Mercure – rm, rest

21 av. Montaigne – ✆ 03 44 02 80 80 – h0350@accor.com – Fax 03 44 02 12 50
60 rm – €92 €98, €13 – **Rest** – Menu €25 – Carte €29/34
◆ A 1970s building, offering good-sized, renovated and well-soundproofed rooms. Dining room adorned with a fireplace and summer terrace by the pool. Traditional cuisine served.

XX **Le Bellevue**

3 av. Rhin-et-Danube – ✆ 03 44 02 17 11 – restaurantlebellevue@wanadoo.fr – Fax 03 44 02 54 44 – Closed 10-24 August, Saturday and Sunday
Rest – Carte €26/50
◆ This simple modern restaurant, in the centre of a shopping area, is adorned with paintings and serves classic cuisine with fresh market produce.

BEAUVOIR-SUR-MER – 85 Vendée – 316 D6 – pop. 3 399 – alt. 8 m – ✉ 85230
Atlantic Coast 34 **A3**

Paris 443 – Challans 15 – Nantes 59 – Noirmoutier-en-l'Ile 22 – La Roche-sur-Yon 59

Office de tourisme, rue Charles Gallet ✆ 02 51 68 71 13, Fax 02 51 49 05 04

Le Relais des Touristes without rest

rte de Gois – ✆ 02 51 68 70 19 – relaisdestouristes@free.fr – Fax 02 51 49 33 45 – Closed 16 February-4 March

39 rm – †€ 59/68 ††€ 65/75, ☐ € 8

◆ In addition to practical, well-kept rooms, the hotel also boasts a lovely indoor pool and a new breakfast room.

BEAUVOIS-EN-CAMBRÉSIS – 59 Nord – 302 I7 – pop. 1 994 – alt. 89 m – ✉ 59157
31 **C3**

Paris 190 – St-Quentin 40 – Arras 48 – Cambrai 12 – Valenciennes 37

La Buissonnière

– ✆ 03 27 85 29 97 – labuissonniere@aol.com – Fax 03 27 76 25 74 – Closed 7-15 April, 3-31 August, Sunday dinner, Wednesday dinner and Monday

Rest – Menu € 21/33 – Carte € 31/51

◆ At the gates to the town, a restaurant serving traditional cuisine made with seasonal market produce. Two dining rooms, one of them is rustic and recently redecorated, overlooking the terrace.

BEAUZAC – 43 Haute-Loire – 331 G2 – pop. 2 061 – alt. 565 m – ✉ 43590
Lyon - Rhone Valley 6 **C3**

Paris 556 – Craponne-sur-Arzon 31 – Le Puy-en-Velay 45 – St-Étienne 44

Office de tourisme, place de l'Église ✆ 04 71 61 50 74, Fax 04 71 61 50 62

L'Air du Temps with rm — rest,

in Confolent, 4 km eastward along the D 461 – ✆ 04 71 61 49 05 – airdutemps.hotel@wanadoo.fr – Fax 04 71 61 50 91 – Closed January, Sunday dinner and Monday

8 rm – †€ 46/51 ††€ 46/51, ☐ € 7,50 – ½ P € 45

Rest – Menu € 16 (weekday lunch), € 21/52 – Carte € 29/63

◆ The light and modern dining room-veranda of this country house provides the backdrop for a creative and varied menu of regional dishes. Comfortable, well-appointed bedrooms.

in Bransac 3 km South by D 42 – ✉ 43590

La Table du Barret with rm — rm,

– ✆ 04 71 61 47 74 – info@latabledubarret.com – Fax 04 71 61 52 73 – Closed 10-23 November, 12-25 January, Sunday dinner, Tuesday and Wednesday

8 rm – †€ 55 ††€ 60, ☐ € 9,50

Rest – Menu € 19 (weekday lunch), € 28/90 bi – Carte € 51/66

◆ A peaceful hamlet near the Loire is the site of this understated contemporary restaurant. Its menu is characterised by tasty up-to-date fare. Comfortable rooms.

BEBLENHEIM – 68 Haut-Rhin – 315 H8 – pop. 943 – alt. 212 m – ✉ 68980
Alsace-Lorraine 2 **C2**

Paris 444 – Colmar 11 – Gérardmer 55 – Ribeauvillé 5 – St-Dié 48 – Sélestat 19

Auberge Le Bouc Bleu

2 r. 5-Décembre – ✆ 03 89 47 88 21 – Fax 03 89 86 01 04 – Closed February school holidays, Wed. and Thursday

Rest – *(number of covers limited, pre-book)* Menu € 25/32 – Carte € 32/39

◆ Books, antiques and old menus endow this pleasant countrified restaurant (non-smoking) with a flea market spirit. Paved courtyard terrace and market-fresh cuisine.

LE BEC-HELLOUIN – 27 Eure – 304 E6 – pop. 406 – alt. 101 m – ✉ 27800
Normandy, G. Brittany 33 **C2**

Paris 153 – Bernay 22 – Évreux 46 – Lisieux 46 – Pont-Audemer 23 – Rouen 41

Abbey★★.

Auberge de l'Abbaye

12 pl. Guillaume-le-Conquérant – ✆ 02 32 44 86 02 – catherine-fabrice.c@wanadoo.fr – Fax 02 32 46 32 23 – Closed 20 November-10 February, Wednesday from October to March and Tuesday

8 rm – †€ 70 ††€ 80, ☕ € 10 – 1 suite – ½ P € 78 – **Rest** – Menu € 21/29 – Carte € 28/35

◆ A haven for travellers since the 18C, this smart half-timbered residence houses renovated, prettily personalised rooms. Traditional food enriched with local produce, served in country-style dining rooms.

Le Canterbury

3 r. de Canterbury – ✆ 02 32 44 14 59 – Fax 02 32 44 14 59 – Closed Sunday dinner, Tuesday dinner and Wednesday

Rest – Menu € 18 (weekday lunch), € 23/38 – Carte € 33/45

◆ In a fairly quiet street, a half-timbered façade covered with Virginia creeper. Exposed beams and whitewashed walls give a rustic character to the dining room.

BÉDARIEUX – 34 Hérault – 339 D7 – pop. 5 962 – alt. 196 m – ✉ 34600 22 B2

Paris 723 – Béziers 34 – Lodève 29 – Montpellier 70

Office de tourisme, 1, rue de la République ✆ 04 67 95 08 79, Fax 04 67 95 39 69

De l'Orb without rest

D 908, rte Hérépian – ✆ 04 67 23 35 90 – hotelorb@free.fr – Fax 04 67 23 98 46

28 rm – †€ 40/79 ††€ 40/79, ☕ € 7

◆ This new and welcoming hotel is situated at the entrance to the town. Its small, functional, air-conditioned rooms are very quiet.

La Forge

22 av. Abbé-Tarroux, (opposite the tourist information centre) – ✆ 04 67 95 13 13 – Fax 04 67 95 10 81 – Closed 17 November-1st December, 5-26 January, Sunday dinner, Wednesday dinner off season and Monday

Rest – Menu € 16/36 – Carte € 38/52

◆ These vaults from the 17C used to house a forge and stables. Unusual interior architecture, a monumental fireplace and large flower-decked, shady terrace. Traditional food.

in Villemagne-l'Argentière 8 km West by D 908 and D 922 – pop. 429 – alt. 193 m – ✉ 34600

Auberge de l'Abbaye with rm

pl. du couvent – ✆ 04 67 95 34 84 – auberge.abbaye@free.fr – Fax 04 67 95 34 84 – Closed 19 November-13 February, Monday and Tuesday off season

3 rm ☕ – †€ 130 ††€ 130 – 1 suite – **Rest** – Menu € 27/58

◆ A monastic ambience, but not an austere one in the vaulted dining room of this old convent building. Dishes are a blend of local produce, spices and sweet/savoury flavours. New themed rooms.

BÉDOIN – 84 Vaucluse – 332 E9 – pop. 2 609 – alt. 295 m – ✉ 84410

Provence 42 E1

Paris 692 – Avignon 43 – Carpentras 16 – Nyons 36 – Sault 35 – Vaison-la-Romaine 21

Office de tourisme, Espace Marie-Louis Gravier ✆ 04 90 65 63 95, Fax 04 90 12 81 55

Le Paty ≤★ Northwest: 4,5 km.

Des Pins

chemin des Crans, 1 km eastward by secondary road – ✆ 04 90 65 92 92 – hoteldespins@wanadoo.fr – Fax 04 90 65 60 66

25 rm – †€ 60/105 ††€ 60/105, ☕ € 9,50 – ½ P € 63/83

Rest – *(Open 16 March-31 October and closed weekday lunch)*

Menu € 25/38 – Carte € 31/54

◆ Regional-style house in the middle of a pine grove where cyclists are happy to make a stop. Rooms with Provençal touches, renovated, some on the garden level have terraces. Rustic lounge. Modern food in a typical interior or outside.

in Ste-Colombe 4 km East by Mont-Ventoux road – ✉ 84410

La Garance without rest

Ste-Colombe – 04 90 12 81 00 – info@lagarance.fr – Fax 04 90 65 93 05 – Open 21 March-5 November

13 rm – €50/72 €50/72, €7,50

◆ A hamlet amid vineyards and orchards, with the Ventoux in the background serves as a setting for his old farm favoured by hikers. The rooms on the ground floor have a terrace.

Mont-Ventoux road 6 km East – ✉ 84410 Bédoin

Le Mas des Vignes Lace from Montmirail and le Comtat,

au virage de St-Estève – 04 90 65 63 91 – decoetlogon@aol.com – Fax 04 90 65 63 91 – Open April-November and closed Tuesday lunchtime and Monday except July-August and at lunchtime in July-August except Sunday and public holidays

Rest – Menu €35/50 – Carte €36/43

◆ A chapel on the Ventoux road is the origin of this venerable building with a large terrace offering wide panoramic views. Elegant dining room in beige tones; regional food.

BÈGLES – 33 Gironde – 335 H5 – see Bordeaux

BEG-MEIL – 29 Finistère – 308 H7 – ✉ 29170 Brittany 9 B2

Paris 560 – Concarneau 16 – Pont-l'Abbé 23 – Quimper 20 – Quimperlé 44

Site★.

Thalamot rest,

4-6 Le Chemin Creux – 02 98 94 97 38 – resa@hotel-thalamot.com – Fax 02 98 94 49 92 – Open 6 April-6 October

30 rm – €57/74 €58/76, €8,50 – ½ P €57/75 – **Rest** – Menu €24/49 – Carte €28/77

◆ In a quiet area near the beaches, simple and modern rooms. A collection of early 20C paintings depicting scenes of Brittany. Fish and seafood served in a restaurant giving onto a garden terrace with trees.

LA BÉGUDE-DE-MAZENC – 26 Drôme – 332 C6 – pop. 1 205 – alt. 215 m – ✉ 26160 44 B3

Paris 621 – Lyon 160 – Montélimar 16 – Valence 56

Office de tourisme, avenue du Président Loubet 04 75 46 24 42, Fax 04 75 46 24 42

Le Jabron

5 av. Mme-de-Sévigné – 04 75 46 28 85 – hotel-lejabron@wanadoo.fr – Fax 04 75 46 24 31

12 rm – €52/55 €52/55, €7 – ½ P €50/55 – **Rest** – Menu €12 (weekday lunch), €18/35 – Carte €21/46

◆ In the village, a small, hotel skilfully renovated by its new owners. The bright and colourful rooms have double glazing. Classical dishes served on the terrace or in the dining room. Conference room.

BÉHEN – 80 Somme – 301 D7 – pop. 439 – alt. 105 m – ✉ 80870 36 A1

Paris 195 – Amiens 77 – Abbeville 19 – Berck 59 – Eu 30

Chateau de Béhen

8 r. du Château – 03 22 31 58 30 – info@cuvelier.com – Fax 03 22 31 58 39

6 rm – €100 €110 – **Table d'hôte** – Menu €39 bi/49 bi

◆ Live the life of Riley, at least during your stay at this fine 18C residence set in parkland. Antique or period furniture int the rooms (attic-style on the upper floor). Traditional dishes served in the rustic dining room.

BÉHUARD – 49 Maine-et-Loire – 317 F4 – pop. 110 – alt. 17 m – ✉ 49170 35 C2

Paris 310 – Angers 18 – Laval 88 – Nantes 88 – La Roche-sur-Yon 118 – Tours 124

Syndicat d'initiative, 9, rue Chevalier Buhard 02 41 72 84 11, Fax 02 41 72 84 11

Les Tonnelles (Gérard Bossé)

– *02 41 72 21 50 – lestonnelles49@free.fr – Fax 02 41 72 81 10 – Closed 4-10 March, 7-13 October, January, Wednesday except lunch from 16 March-31 October, Tuesday from 1st November-15 March, Sunday dinner and Monday*

Rest – *(number of covers limited, pre-book)* Menu (€ 27), € 47/95 bi – Carte € 59/83

Spec. Huîtres cuisinées (September to April). Poissons de Loire ou de l'Erdre au beurre blanc. Pigeonneau au jus de cabernet (February to September). **Wines** Savennières, Saumur-Champigny.

◆ An attractive restaurant on the picturesque Ile de Béhuard. Elegant modern decoration, pleasant terrace, fine local cuisine and wide choice of regional wines.

BEINHEIM – 67 Bas-Rhin – 315 M3 – pop. 1 790 – alt. 115 m – ✉ 67930 — 1 B1

Paris 504 – Haguenau 25 – Karlsruhe 37 – Strasbourg 48 – Wissembourg 27

François without rest

58 r. Principale – 03 88 86 41 26 – Fax 03 88 86 27 00 – Closed 28 July-10 August and 24 December-4 January

13 rm – €34 €48/60, €6

◆ A discreet hotel in a large regional-style villa, surrounded by a garden. Cosy and well-kept rooms, some with balconies.

BELCAIRE – 11 Aude – 344 C6 – pop. 392 – alt. 1 002 m – ✉ 11340 — 22 A3

Paris 810 – Ax-les-Thermes 26 – Carcassonne 81 – Foix 54 – Quillan 29

Office de tourisme, 22, avenue d'Ax les Thermes 04 68 20 75 89, Fax 04 68 20 79 13

Forests★★ of the Plaine and Comus Northwest.

Belvédère du Pas de l'Ours★★ East: 13 km then 15 mn,

Languedoc-Roussillon-Tarn Gorges.

Bayle with rm

38 av. des Thermes – 04 68 20 31 05 – hotel-bayle@wanadoo.fr – Fax 04 68 20 35 24 – Closed November

12 rm – €40 €40, € 5,50 – ½ P € 44 – **Rest** – Menu € 11 (weekday lunch), € 16/33 – Carte € 21/40

◆ A family restaurant in a village in the land of the Cathars. Rustic dining room with a terrace overlooking the countryside. Dishes inspired by local cuisine. Well-kept rooms.

BELCASTEL – 12 Aveyron – 338 G4 – pop. 251 – alt. 406 m – ✉ 12390

Languedoc-Roussillon-Tarn Gorges — 29 C1

Paris 623 – Decazeville 28 – Rodez 25 – Villefranche-de-Rouergue 36

Syndicat d'initiative, le bourg 05 65 64 46 11

Vieux Pont (Nicole Fagegaltier et Bruno Rouquier) with rm

– *05 65 64 52 29 – hotel-du-vieux-pont@wanadoo.fr – Fax 05 65 64 44 32 – Closed 1st January-12 March, Sunday dinner and Tuesday lunch except July-August and Monday (except hotel in July-August)*

7 rm – €80/95 €80/95, € 12 – ½ P € 95/103

Rest – *(closed Sun. evening except July - Aug., Tues. lunch and Mon.) (number of covers limited, pre-book)* Menu € 27 (weekday lunch), € 43/82 – Carte € 53/65

Spec. Foie de canard grillé. Pigeon du Mont Royal croûté de cèpes secs et d'ail. "Tout chocolat noir". **Wines** Marcillac, Vins d'Entraygues et du Fel.

◆ Two houses on either side of a 15C stone bridge. Fine contemporary, regional cuisine served in an elegant modern setting. Quiet, cosy bedrooms in an old barn on the other side of the river. Breakfast served at the water's edge in summer.

If breakfast is included the symbol appears after the number of rooms.

BELFORT Ⓟ – 90 Territoire de Belfort – 315 F11 – pop. 50 417 – Built-up area 104 962 – alt. 360 m – ✉ 90000 Burgundy-Jura 17 C1

Paris 422 – Basel 78 – Besançon 93 – Épinal 95 – Mulhouse 41

Office de tourisme, 2 bis, rue Clemenceau ✆ 03 84 55 90 90, Fax 03 84 55 90 70

de Rougemont-le-Château Rougemont-le-Château Route de Masevaux, Northeast: 16 km by D 83 and D 25, ✆ 03 84 23 74 74.

Le Lion★★ - Fortified camp ★★: ※★★ from the fort terrace - Old town★: porte de Brisach★ - Organ★ of St-Christophe cathedral Y **B** - Frescoe★ (car park: rue de l'As-de-Carreau Z 6) - Amateur's study★: Donation Maurice Jardot **M**[1].

Plan on next page

Novotel Atria

av. Espérance, (at the Congressional centre) – ✆ 03 84 58 85 00 – h1742@accor.com – Fax 03 84 58 85 01 Y **u**

79 rm – †€ 59/155 ††€ 59/155, ☕ € 13,50 – **Rest** – Menu (€ 16), € 21/45 – Carte € 20/43

◆ Elegant futuristic architecture in this hotel that is part of a conference centre. Comfortable rooms renovated according to the chain's standards; some overlook the Vauban fortifications. Typical Novotel café in a contemporary setting.

Boréal without rest

2 r. Comte-de-la-Suze – ✆ 03 84 22 32 32 – hotel.boreal@wanadoo.fr – Fax 03 84 28 15 01 – Closed 19 December-4 January Z **r**

52 rm – †€ 62/95 ††€ 62/100, ☕ € 11 – 2 suites

◆ In a quiet street on the right bank, this hotel is noted for its comfortable rooms, particularly the more recent ones, and its attentive staff.

Grand Hôtel du Tonneau d'Or

1 r. Reiset – ✆ 03 84 58 57 56 – tonneaudor@tonneaudor.fr – Fax 03 84 58 57 50 Y **e**

52 rm – †€ 105/139 ††€ 115/149, ☕ € 11

Rest – *(closed August, 1st- 7 January, Saturday and Sunday)* Menu (€ 16 bi), € 27/32 – Carte € 34/42

◆ The stunning façade and immense lobby of this 1907 building have retained their Belle Époque appeal. Spacious rooms with practical furniture. Attractive decor inspired by the Parisian brasseries of the early 20C in the restaurant.

Les Capucins

20 fg Montbéliard – ✆ 03 84 28 04 60 – hotel-des-capucins@wanadoo.fr – Fax 03 84 55 00 92 Z **n**

35 rm – †€ 53 ††€ 60, ☕ € 7,50

Rest – *(closed 27 July-18 August, 23 December-5 January, Saturday lunch and Sunday)* Menu € 15/36 – Carte € 37/45

◆ Small, snug rooms adorned with quilts and bright colours set the scene of this pleasant hotel. The rooms on the top floor are under the eaves. A traditional menu served in two somewhat rustic dining rooms.

Vauban without rest

4 r. Magasin – ✆ 03 84 21 59 37 – hotel.vauban@wanadoo.fr – Fax 03 84 21 41 67 – Closed Christmas holidays, February half-term holidays and Sunday dinner Y **h**

14 rm – †€ 69 ††€ 80, ☕ € 8,50

◆ The discreet charm of a family home whose rooms appear ready to welcome friends, and are adorned with work by local artists. Attractive garden on the banks of the Savoureuse.

Le Pot au Feu

27 bis Grand'rue – ✆ 03 84 28 57 84 – mflunois@wanadoo.fr – Fax 03 84 58 17 65 – Closed 1st-20 August, 1st-12 January, Saturday lunch, Monday lunch and Sunday Y **s**

Rest – Menu (€ 14), € 20 (weekday lunch), € 29 € bi/52 – Carte € 33/63

◆ An attractive stone cellar is the scene of this bistro where the chef rustles up dishes from his childhood, in addition to regional and market fresh recipes.

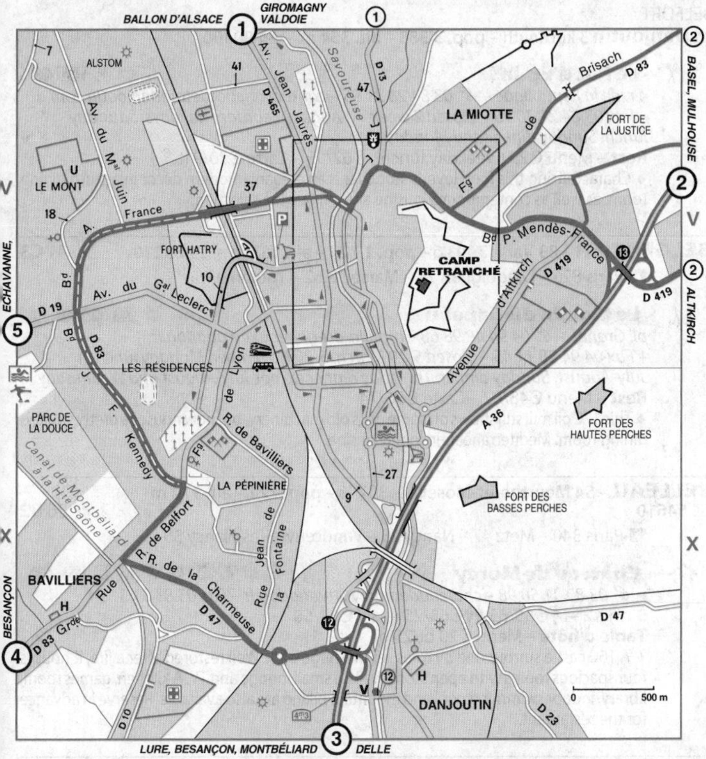

BALLON D'ALSACE
GIROMAGNY
VALDOIE
BASEL, MULHOUSE
ALTKIRCH
ECHAVANNE,
BESANÇON
LURE, BESANÇON, MONTBÉLIARD
DELLE
ALSTOM
LE MONT
LA MIOTTE
FORT DE LA JUSTICE
FORT HATRY
CAMP RETRANCHÉ
LES RÉSIDENCES
PARC DE LA DOUCE
LA PÉPINIÈRE
FORT DES HAUTES PERCHES
FORT DES BASSES PERCHES
BAVILLIERS
DANJOUTIN
Av. Jean Jaurès
Av. du Mal Juin
Av. du Gal Leclerc
Bd J. F. Kennedy
Bd P. Mendès-France
Avenue d'Altkirch
R. de Lyon
R. de Bavilliers
R. de Belfort
R. de la Charmeuse
Rue Jean de la Fontaine
Canal de Montbéliard à la Hte Saône
Rue Grde
Savoureuse
Fg de Brisach
D 83
D 13
D 465
D 419
D 19
D 47
D 23
D 10
A 36
0
500 m

BELFORT

Ancêtres (Fg des) . . . . Y 3
Armes (Pl. d') . . . . Y 5
As-de-Carreau (R. de l') . . . . Z 6
Auxelles (Via d') . . . . V 7
Besançon (R. de) . . . . X 9
Boulloche (Pt A.) . . . . V 10
Bourgeois (Pl. des) . . . . Y 12
Carnot (Bd) . . . . Z 15
Château-d'Eau (Av. du) . . . . V 18
Clemenceau (R. G.) . . . . Y 20
Denfert-Rochereau (R.) . . . . Z 21
Dr-Corbis (Pl. du) . . . . Z 23
Dr-Fréry (R. du) . . . . Y 24
Dreyfus-Schmidt (R.) . . . . Y 25
Dunant (Bd H.) . . . . X 27
Espérance (Av. de l') . . . . Y 28
Foch (Av. Mar.) . . . . Z 29
France (Fg de) . . . . Z 30
Gaulard (R. du Gén.) . . . . Z 31
Grande-Fontaine (Pl. de la) . . . . . . Z 32
Grande-Fontaine (R.) . . . . Y 33
Grand'Rue . . . . Y 34
Joffre (Bd du Mar.) . . . . VY 37
Lebleu (R. F.) . . . . Z 40
Lille (R. de) . . . . V 41
Magasin (Q. du) . . . . Y 43
Metz-Juteau (R.) . . . . Y 45
Moulin (Av. J.) . . . . V 47
Mulhouse (R. de) . . . . Y 46
Pompidou (R. G.) . . . . Y 48
République (Pl. de la) . . . . Y 49
République (R. de la) . . . . Z 50
Roussel (R. du Gén.) . . . . Y 51
Sarrail (Av. du Gén.) . . . . Z 52
Vauban (Q.) . . . . Y 60

R. P. Berger
Square E. Lechten
CENTRE DES CONGRÈS
ÉCOLE DES BEAUX-ARTS
Marché couvert Fréry
Av. Capit. de la Laurencie
Fg de Brisach
PORTE DE BRISACH
HÔTEL DU DÉPT
CITÉ ADMTIVE
LE LION
CAMP RETRANCHÉ
R. Gal Strolz
Q. Ch. Vallet
Savoureuse
Fg de Montbéliard
R. Thiers
Rue Gambetta
D 465
D 83
D 13
D 19
D 23
0
200 m

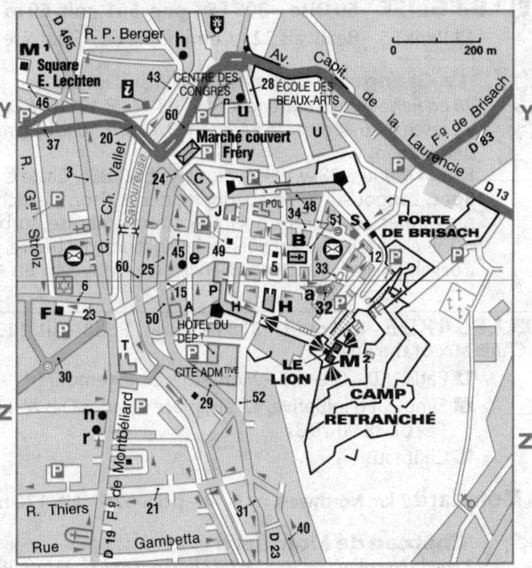

in Danjoutin 3 km South – pop. 3 383 – alt. 354 m – ✉ 90400

XXX **Le Pot d'Étain** P VISA

4 r. de la République – ✆ 03 84 28 31 95 – contact@lepotdetaindanjoutin.com – Fax 03 84 21 70 15 – Closed 2 weeks in August, February holidays, Saturday lunch, Sunday dinner and Monday X v

Rest – Menu € 29 (weekday lunch), € 62/95 – Carte € 70/91

◆ Characterising this food lover's stopover is an elegant, modern decor in a plush dining room, as well as contemporary cuisine and a fine wine selection.

BELGENTIER – 83 Var – 340 L6 – pop. 1 724 – alt. 152 m – ✉ 83210 41 **C3**

Paris 826 – Draguignan 71 – Marseille 62 – Toulon 23

XX **Le Moulin du Gapeau** AC VISA AE

pl. Granet – ✆ 04 94 48 98 68 – moulin-du-gapeau@wanadoo.fr – Fax 04 94 28 11 45 – Closed 5-20 March, 5-20 November, Monday lunch in July-August, Sunday dinner, Thursday dinner except July-August and Wednesday

Rest – Menu € 48/82 – Carte € 56/74

◆ This 17C oil mill still shows off some of its old machinery, but now houses a pretty vaulted dining room. Mediterranean-inspired cuisine.

BELLEAU – 54 Meurthe-et-Moselle – 307 I6 – pop. 722 – alt. 172 m – ✉ 54610 26 **B2**

Paris 340 – Metz 47 – Nancy 25 – Vandœuvre-lès-Nancy 35

Château de Morey rm, P VISA

– ✆ 03 83 31 50 98 – chateaudemorey@wanadoo.fr – Fax 03 83 31 51 94

5 rm – €55/65 €65/75 – ½ P €53/58

Table d'hôte – Menu € 20 bi/25 bi

◆ A 16C castle surrounded by trees set in a huge park. Well restored after a fire, it houses four spacious rooms with open stone walls, a small lounge and TV. A kitchen, games room, library, indoor swimming pool and mountain biking are also available. Reserve in advance for the restaurant.

BELLE-ÉGLISE – 60 Oise – 305 E5 – pop. 561 – alt. 69 m – ✉ 60540 36 **B3**

Paris 53 – Beauvais 32 – Compiègne 64 – Pontoise 29

XXX **La Grange de Belle-Eglise** (Marc Duval) AC P VISA

28 bd René-Aimé-Lagabrielle – ✆ 03 44 08 49 00 – Fax 03 44 08 45 97 – Closed 4-26 August, 16 February-3 March, Sunday dinner, Tuesday lunch and Monday

Rest – Menu € 28 (weekday lunch), € 60/85 – Carte € 81/139

Spec. Langoustines en spaghetti, déclinaison d'artichaut en dariole. Poitrine de pigeonneau aux petits pois. Macaron framboise, sorbet fromage blanc.

◆ This elegant restaurant offers a dining room with beams, pleasant veranda overlooking a delightful garden and fine silverware in display cabinets. Classic dishes.

BELLEGARDE – 45 Loiret – 318 L4 – pop. 1 558 – alt. 113 m – ✉ 45270
Châteaux of the Loire 12 **C2**

Paris 110 – Gien 41 – Montargis 24 – Nemours 41 – Orléans 50 – Pithiviers 30

Syndicat d'initiative, 12 bis, place Charles Desvergnes ✆ 02 38 90 25 37, Fax 02 38 90 28 32

Château★.

in Montliard 7 km Northwest by D 44 – pop. 175 – alt. 126 m – ✉ 45340

Château de Montliard P

3 rte de Nesploy – ✆ 02 38 33 71 40 – a.galizia@infonie.fr – Fax 02 38 33 86 41

4 rm – €56/80 €66/89 – **Table d'hôte** – Menu € 23 bi/33 bi

◆ In the same family since 1384, this castle surrounded by a moat still has a lovely medieval interior with a spiral staircase, thick walls and stained glass. The rooms all have a painted ceiling and fireplace. The restaurant serves one set menu in a lovely, rustic setting.

BELLEGARDE-SUR-VALSERINE – 01 Ain – 328 H4 – pop. 10 846 – alt. 350 m – ✉ 01200 Burgundy-Jura 45 C1

Paris 497 – Annecy 43 – Bourg-en-Bresse 73 – Genève 43 – Lyon 113

Office de tourisme, 24, place Victor Bérard ✆ 04 50 48 48 68, Fax 04 50 48 65 08

Banks of the Valserine North: 2 km by N84.

La Belle Époque-Maison Watami

rest, VISA

10 pl. Gambetta – ✆ 04 50 48 14 46 – Fax 04 50 56 01 71
– Closed 21 December-2 January

20 rm – €51/61 €61/68, ☕ €9 – **Rest** – *(closed Monday lunch)*
Menu €19/26 – Carte €16/35

♦ An attractive early-20C abode. Fine carved wood period staircase (1907) leading to spacious, tastefully revamped guestrooms. Enjoy the show in this Japanese style restaurant as Asian specialities are rustled up before you.

in Lancrans 3 km North by D 1084 and D 991 – pop. 935 – alt. 500 m – ✉ 01200

Le Sorgia

VISA

39 Gde-Rue – ✆ 04 50 48 15 81 – Fax 04 50 48 44 72
– Closed 1st-18 August, 20 December-12 January, Sunday and Monday

17 rm – €54 €54, ☕ €7,50 – ½ P €45

Rest – *(closed Saturday lunch, Sunday dinner and Monday)* Menu €16 (weekdays)/45 – Carte €24/49

♦ The same family has been greeting guests in this inn at the heart of the village since 1890. Simple but neat and regularly spruced up rooms A countrified dining room and flower-decked terrace facing the garden. Regularly renewed regional menu.

in Eloise (74 H.-Savoie) 5 km southeast by D 1508 and secondary road – pop. 715 – alt. 511 m – ✉ 01200

Le Fartoret

VISA

– ✆ 04 50 48 07 18 – lefartoret@wanadoo.fr – Fax 04 50 48 23 85
– Closed 23 December-3 January and Sunday dinner off season

41 rm – €40 €57/91, ☕ €10 – ½ P €64/81 – **Rest** – Menu €20 (weekdays), €27/45 – Carte €34/54

♦ In a village on the hills of Bellegarde, a hotel set in the grounds of a century-old farmhouse. The rooms, though not very modern, are well maintained. Fine collection of cockerels. View of the valley from the large dining room. Classic culinary repertory.

BELLE-ÎLE-EN-MER ★★ – 56 Morbihan – 308 L10 Brittany 9 B3

Access by sea transport for **Le Palais** (in summer **compulsory booking** for taking vehicles).

from **Quiberon** (Port-Maria) - Crossing 45 mn - Information and prices: S.M.N. ✆ 0 820 056 000 (Le Palais), Fax 02 97 31 56 81, www.smn-navigation.fr.

from **Port-Navalo** - (April-Oct.) - Crossing 1 h - Information and prices: Navix S.A. at Port-Navalo ✆ 0 825 162 120 (0,15 €/mn)

from **Vannes** - (April-Oct.) - Crossing 2 h - Information and prices: Navix S.A., Gare Maritime ✆ 0 825 162 100 ou 0 825 132 100 (0.15 €/mn), Fax 02 97 46 60 29, www.navix.fr

from **Lorient** - Seasonal service - Crossing 50 mn (passengers only, compulsory booking) - Information and prices S.M.N. ✆ 0 820 056 000 (0.12 €/mn) - For **Le Palais** and for **Sauzon** : from **Quiberon** - Seasonal service - Crossing 25 mn - Information and prices: S.M.N. ✆ 0 820 056 000 (0.12 €/mn) (Quiberon) - Information and prices: Navix S.A.

from **Locmariaquer** - ✆ 0 825 162 130 (0.15 €/mn) - **Auray Le Bono** - ✆ 0 825 162 140 (0.15 €/mn) - **La Trinité-sur-Mer** (July-August) - ✆ 0 825 162 150 (0.15 €/mn), Fax 02 97 46 60 29.

Office de tourisme, quai Bonnelle, Le Palais ✆ 02 97 31 81 93, Fax 02 97 31 56 17

Côte sauvage★★★.

BANGOR – 56 Morbihan – pop. 738 – alt. 45 m – ✉ 56360 9 **B3**

Paris 513 – Rennes 162 – Vannes 53 – Auray 34 – Larmor-Plage 12

Le Palais: Vauban citadel ★ Northeast: 3,5 km.

La Désirade rest, VISA

Le Petit Cosquet – *02 97 31 70 70* – *hotel-la-desirade@wanadoo.fr* – *Fax 02 97 31 89 63* – *Open 29 March-4 November and 28 December-3 January*

30 rm – €102/149 €122/164, €15 – 2 suites – ½ P €95/123

Rest *La Table* – Menu €29/44 – Carte €47/57

◆ This cluster of modern Breton style houses extends a warm welcome. Cosy interior and predominantly wood rooms with personal touches. Brand new wellness centre. Pleasant restaurant serving up-to-the-minute recipes.

LE PALAIS – 56 Morbihan – pop. 2 457 – alt. 7 m – ✉ 56360 9 **B3**

Paris 508 – Rennes 157 – Vannes 48 – Lorient 3 – Ploemeur 9

Citadelle Vauban (Vauban Citadel)★.

Citadelle Vauban VISA

– *02 97 31 84 17* – *reception.vauban@leshotelsparticuliers.com* – *Fax 02 97 31 89 47* – *Open end April-15 October*

40 rm – €120/300 €130/300, €15 – 3 suites – ½ P €210/350

Rest *La Table du Gouverneur* – Menu (€30), €38/48 – Carte €42/67

◆ This hotel and museum, dominating the port has won over Vauban's citadel and gardens. An Indian spirit reigns in the stylish rooms, almost all of which face the sea. Seafood cuisine served in an interior which combines 18C-19C paintings with a modern decor.

Le Clos Fleuri rest, rest, VISA

rte de Sauzon, at Bellevue – *02.97.31.45.45* – *hotel-leclosfleuri@orange.fr* – *Fax 02 97 31 45 57*

20 rm – €74 €85/130, €15 – ½ P €71/103 – **Rest** – *(dinner only) (residents only)* Menu €28

◆ On the heights of the town, this distinctive regional hotel offers small, smart rooms with country furniture and painted different colours. Set menu on a slate, served in the evenings to guests, changes daily.

Château de Bordenéo without rest VISA

2 km Sauzon Bordenéo road north-westward – *02 97 31 80 77* – *chateaudebordeneo@wanadoo.fr* – *Fax 02 97 31 50 17*

5 rm – €122/172 €134/184

◆ This elegant 19C manor house is very restful and makes the most of its park planted with century-old trees. Each of the cosy rooms decorated in pastel shades has its own atmosphere.

L' Annexe VISA

3 quai Yser – *02 97 31 81 53* – *Fax 02 97 31 81 53* – *Closed March, Monday and Tuesday from November to February and Wednesday*

Rest – *(dinner only)* Carte €26/46

◆ A pleasant atmosphere reigns among the tightly packed tables. The service is fast and informal and the quality of the seafood beyond reproach. Wood fire grilled dishes.

PORT-GOULPHAR – 56 Morbihan – ✉ 56360 Bangor 9 **B3**

Paris 517 – Rennes 166 – Vannes 57 – Auray 38 – Larmor-Plage 16

Site★: ★.

Castel Clara cove and cliffs, rest, VISA

– *02 97 31 84 21* – *castelclara@relaischateaux.com* – *Fax 02 97 31 51 69* – *Closed 13 January-13 February*

59 rm – €155/380 €155/380, €25 – 4 suites

Rest – *(dinner only)* Menu €85/135 – Carte €69/112

Rest *Le Buffet* – Menu €45 (lunch)/55 (dinner)

◆ An idyllic spot on the Wild Coast, a thalassotherapy centre, refined rooms with a panoramic view - discreet luxury at the end of the world! Elegant dining room and terrace with a view of the cliffs. Modern cuisine. The restaurant overlooks the new swimming pool.

SAUZON – 56 Morbihan – pop. 835 – alt. 35 m – ✉ 56360 9 **B3**

Paris 515 – Rennes 164 – Vannes 55 – Lorient 9 – Lanester 13

Site★ - Pointe des Poulains★★: ☀★ Northwest: 3 km then 30 mn - Port-Donnant: site★★ South: 6 km then 30 mn.

Hostellerie La Touline without rest VISA MC
r. du Port-Vihan – ☎ 02 97 31 69 69 – la-touline@libertysurf.fr – Fax 02 97 31 66 00 – Open 15 March-12 October
5 rm – €106 €106, €12
◆ Attractive hamlet of small houses perched above the small harbour. The rooms are decorated according to different themes: Brittany, Zanzibar... Relaxing garden.

Roz Avel VISA MC AE
(behind the church) – ☎ 02 97 31 61 48 – Fax 02 97 31 61 48 – Open 15 March-11 November, 16-31 December and closed Wednesday
Rest – *(number of covers limited, pre-book)* Menu € 30/46
◆ A country house with Breton furniture in the dining room and a terrace with a small garden at one end. Excellent fish and seafood prepared with care.

Le Contre Quai VISA MC
r. St-Nicolas – ☎ 02 97 31 60 60 – lucien.coquant@wanadoo.fr – Open 18 April-20 September and closed Sunday except July-August
Rest – *(dinner only)* Menu € 42 – Carte € 58/70
◆ Pleasant restaurant overlooking the picturesque harbour of Sauzon. Appetising 'surf n'turf' cuisine served in an attractive dining room with stylish nautical decor.

Café de la Cale VISA MC
– ☎ 02 97 31 65 74 – Fax 02 97 31 63 27 – Open from April to end September, autumn half-term holidays, Christmas holidays and February school holidays
Rest – *(pre-book)* Carte € 26/47
◆ An old sardine factory converted into a smart, fashionable bistro. Well known yachtsmen and tourists flock here to enjoy the appetising fish, shellfish and regional cuisine.

Les Embruns
Le Quai – ☎ 02 97 31 64 78 – Fax 02 97 31 63 32 – Open 20 March-5 November
Rest – crêperie Carte € 12/23
◆ One hundred percent organic sweet and savoury pancakes. From the flour and eggs to the fillings (salmon, etc). Built against the cliffs, the house and terrace face the port.

BELLÊME – 61 Orne – **310** M4 – pop. 1 774 – alt. 241 m – ✉ 61130
Normandy 33 **C3**

Paris 168 – Alençon 42 – La Ferté-Bernard 23 – Le Mans 55 – Mortagne-au-Perche 18

Office de tourisme, boulevard Bansard des Bois ☎ 02 33 73 09 69, Fax 02 33 83 95 17

De Bellême Saint-Martin Les Sablons, Southwest: 2 km, ☎ 02 33 73 12 79.

Forest★.

in Nocé 8 km East by D 203 – pop. 760 – alt. 120 m – ✉ 61340

Auberge des 3 J. VISA MC
– ☎ 02 33 73 41 03 – Fax 02 33 83 33 66 – Closed 15-30 September, 1st-15 January, Tuesday from September to June, Sunday dinner and Monday
Rest – Menu € 26/36 – Carte € 31/39
◆ Prettily laid tables and paintings in a rustic dining room where stone and wood dominate. Well-prepared food, both traditional and local dishes.

BELLEU – 02 Aisne – **306** C6 – see Soissons

BELLEVAUX – 74 Haute-Savoie – **328** M3 – pop. 1 158 – alt. 913 m – Winter sports : 1 100/1 800 m 23 – ✉ 74470 French Alps 46 **F1**

Paris 572 – Annecy 70 – Bonneville 29 – Genève 44 – Thonon-les-Bains 23

Office de tourisme, les Contamines ☎ 04 50 73 71 53, Fax 04 50 73 78 60

Site★.

La Cascade
– ☎ 04 50 73 70 22 – hotelacascade@wanadoo.fr – Fax 04 50 73 77 46 – Closed 24 March-12 April and October
11 rm – †€ 38 ††€ 48, ☕ € 6 – ½ P € 49
Rest – Menu € 18 (weekdays), € 22/26 – Carte € 22/30
♦ Modern building in the centre of the small resort. Spacious and bright rooms, all with balconies and views of the surrounding mountains. Very well-kept. Comfortable circular dining room with a rooftop terrace that offers a fine panoramic view.

Les Moineaux
– ☎ 04 50 73 71 11 – info@hotel-les-moineaux.com – Fax 04 50 73 75 79 – Open 16 June-9 September and 21 December-9 April
14 rm – †€ 43 ††€ 56, ☕ € 6 – ½ P € 48/51 – **Rest** – Menu € 18 (weekdays)/29
♦ Two chalet-type buildings at the bottom of the village. The functional rooms are equipped with balconies overlooking the mountains. Sober, regional décor, very well-kept. Simple restaurant with a modern setting, family-style cuisine with Savoy touches and a vegetarian set menu.

in Hirmentaz 7 km Southwest by D 26 and D 32 – ✉ 74470 Bellevaux

Le Christania
– ☎ 04 50 73 70 77 – info@hotel-christania.com – Fax 04 50 73 76 08 – Open 1st June-15 September and 20 December-1st April
35 rm – †€ 52/56 ††€ 56/58, ☕ € 8 – ½ P € 54/64 – **Rest** – Menu € 21/30 – Carte € 26/38
♦ 1970s-style family hotel at the foot of the pistes. Rustic rooms, most with balconies; sloped ceilings in those on the top floor. Restaurant facing the pool and terrace. Regional cuisine and snack menu.

BELLEVILLE – 54 Meurthe-et-Moselle – 307 H6 – pop. 1 280 – alt. 190 m – ✉ 54940

26 **B2**

Paris 359 – Metz 42 – Nancy 19 – Pont-à-Mousson 14 – Toul 36

Le Bistroquet (Marie-France Ponsard)
97 rte Nationale – ☎ 03 83 24 90 12 – le-bistroquet@wanadoo.fr – Fax 03 83 24 04 01 – Closed 16 August-3 September, Saturday lunch, Sunday dinner, Monday and Tuesday
Rest – *(number of covers limited, pre-book)* Menu € 33/75 – Carte € 54/80
Spec. Foie gras de canard lorrain poêlé. Saint-Pierre rôti, beurre blanc émulsionné. Soufflé à la liqueur de mirabelle de Lorraine. **Wines** Gris de Toul, Pinot noir des Côtes de Toul.
♦ 1900-style dining room (mirrors, posters and chandeliers) behind a discreet façade. A flower-decked terrace and skilfully prepared classic food.

La Moselle
1 r. Prosper-Cabirol – ☎ 03 83 24 91 44 – lamoselle@wanadoo.fr – Fax 03 83 24 99 38 – Closed 21 July-10 August, 16 February-1st March, Sunday dinner, Tuesday dinner and Wednesday
Rest – Menu € 22/52 – Carte € 39/82
♦ A family establishment in two welcoming rooms, separated by panels decorated with stained glass windows in the style of the School of Nancy. Pleasant shady terrace.

BELLEVILLE – 69 Rhône – 327 H3 – pop. 5 840 – alt. 192 m – ✉ 69220

Lyon - Rhone Valley

43 **E1**

Paris 416 – Bourg-en-Bresse 43 – Lyon 45 – Mâcon 31 – Villefranche-sur-Saône 15

Office de tourisme, 27, rue du Moulin ☎ 04 74 66 44 67, Fax 04 74 06 43 56

L'Ange Couronné
18 r. de la République – ☎ 04 74 66 42 00 – angecouronne@wanadoo.fr – Fax 04 74 66 49 20 – Closed 2-6 June, 29 September-7 October, 5-27 January, Tuesday lunch, Sunday dinner and Monday
15 rm – †€ 42 ††€ 46, ☕ € 7 – **Rest** – Menu (€ 12), € 17/45 – Carte € 32/40
♦ A former post house on the main road of Belleville. An atrium designed like a winter garden leads to simple, functional rooms. An attractively modern dining room where the focus is on traditional cuisine.

Le Beaujolais

40 r. Mar.-Foch, (near the station) – ✆ 04 74 66 05 31 – postmaster@restaurant-le-beaujolais.com – Fax 04 74 07 90 46 – Closed 14-20 April, 4-27 August, 22-28 December, Sunday dinner, Tuesday dinner and Wednesday

Rest – Menu (€ 13), € 17 (weekday lunch), € 25/42 – Carte € 31/39

◆ A country inn where a fine Bresse cabinet takes pride of place in the dining room. Traditional dishes and wines with a distinct Beaujolais emphasis. Friendly welcome.

in Pizay 5 km Northwest by D 18 and D 69 – ✉ 69220 St-Jean-d'Ardières

Château de Pizay

rm, rm,

– ✆ 04 74 66 51 41 – info@chateau-pizay.com – Fax 04 74 69 65 63 – Closed 19 December-4 January

62 rm – †€ 175/299 ††€ 199/299, ☕ € 19 – ½ P € 147/210

Rest – Menu € 40/65 – Carte € 59/105

◆ A beautiful château standing in the middle of the vineyards. Period bedrooms in the old stables, with more modern and spacious accommodation in the new buildings. French-style garden. Stately dining room, tables on the terrace in the main courtyard, and a classic menu.

BELLEY – 01 Ain – 328 H6 – pop. 8 004 – alt. 279 m – ✉ 01300

Burgundy-Jura 45 **C1**

Paris 507 – Aix-les-Bains 31 – Bourg-en-Bresse 83 – Chambéry 36 – Lyon 96

Office de tourisme, 34, Grande Rue ✆ 04 79 81 29 06, Fax 04 79 81 08 80

Choir★ of St-Jean cathedral - Framework★ of the château des Allymes.

Ibis

rm,

bd Mail – ✆ 04 79 81 01 20 – Fax 04 79 81 53 83

35 rm – †€ 50/59 ††€ 50/59, ☕ € 8 – **Rest** – Menu (€ 12,50 bi), € 14 bi/17 – Carte € 22/27

◆ A useful hotel for an overnight stay in the town centre. Rooms refurbished to meet the chain's latest standards. Buffet breakfast. Black and white photos of actors adorn the walls. Concise, classic menu.

Southeast 3 km on Chambéry road – ✉ 01300 Belley

Auberge La Fine Fourchette

N504 Virignin – ✆ 04 79 81 59 33 – Fax 04 79 81 55 43 – Closed 20 August-2 September, 24 December-5 January, Sunday dinner and Monday

Rest – Menu € 24/54 – Carte € 41/52

◆ A charming house overlooking the road, and facing the countryside and the Rhône Canal. The redecorated dining room's bay windows open onto a terrace. Classic cuisine.

in Contrevoz 9 km Northwest on D 32 – pop. 430 – alt. 320 m – ✉ 01300

Auberge de Contrevoz

– ✆ 04 79 81 82 54 – auberge.de.contrevoz@wanadoo.fr – Fax 04 79 81 80 17 – Closed 25 December-25 January, Sunday dinner and Monday

Rest – Menu € 25/43 – Carte € 32/47

◆ A welcoming regional house decorated in a fitting rustic style. Generous portions of updated cuisine with a regional twist (seasonal theme menus, Bugey truffles).

in Pugieu 9 km northwest on D 1504 – pop. 126 – alt. 247 m – ✉ 01510

Le Moulin du Martinet

– ✆ 04 79 87 82 03 – moulindumartinet@gmail.com – Closed 10-20 March, 10-20 October, 2-12 January, Sunday dinner except July-August, Tuesday dinner and Wednesday

Rest – Menu € 13 (weekday lunch), € 17/48 – Carte € 30/46

◆ This appealing old mill (1825) offers a garden facing the mountain, with free-range ducks, a trout pool and pleasant terrace. Modern cuisine, with meals by the fireplace in winter.

BELVES – 24 Dordogne – 329 H7 – pop. 1 431 – alt. 175 m – ✉ 24170

Paris 552 – Bordeaux 197 – Périgueux 66 – Bergerac 56 – Villeneuve-sur-Lot 66

Office de tourisme, 1, rue des Filhols ✆ 05 53 29 10 20

Clément V without rest

15 r. J.-Manchotte – ✆ 05 53 28 68 80 – contact@clement5.com – Fax 05 53 28 14 21

10 rm – €95/200 €95/200, €12

◆ Situated in an isolated setting above the village, this charming house is well worth the detour for its original guestrooms with individual touches, its 11C vaulted cellars and its beautiful winter garden.

in Sagelat 2 km north by D 53 – pop. 325 – alt. 78 m – ✉ 24170

Le Branchat

Southeast by D 710 and secondary road – ✆ 05 53 28 98 80 – info@lebranchat.com – Fax 05 53 59 22 52 – Open 28 March-26 October

3 rm – €55/72 €55/72 – **Table d'hôte** – Menu €25

◆ Horse riders can stopover in this attractive and peaceful hotel during the holiday season. The spacious upstairs rooms are adorned with antique or painted-wood furniture.

Auberge de la Nauze with rm — rest,

Fongauffier – ✆ 05 53 28 44 81 – aubergedelanauze@wanadoo.fr – Fax 05 53 29 99 18 – Closed 20-29 June, 29 November-14 December, February holidays, Monday except dinner in July-August, Tuesday dinner and Saturday lunch from September to June

8 rm – €36/38 €38/40, €6 – ½ P €38/48 – **Rest** – Menu €13,50 (weekday lunch), €21/50 – Carte €29/67

◆ Appetising, traditional food is served in this stone, local-style house with a dining room offering exposed beams and leading onto a terrace. Pastel-toned rooms.

BENFELD – 67 Bas-Rhin – 315 J6 – pop. 4 878 – alt. 160 m – ✉ 67230

Alsace-Lorraine — 1 B2

Paris 502 – Colmar 41 – Obernai 17 – Sélestat 19 – Strasbourg 36

Office de tourisme, 3, rue de l'Église ✆ 03 88 74 04 02, Fax 03 88 58 10 45

Au Petit Rempart

1 r. Petit-Rempart – ✆ 03 88 74 42 26 – Fax 03 88 74 18 58 – Closed 15 July-15 August, 15 February-15 March, Monday dinner, Tuesday dinner, Thursday dinner and Wednesday

Rest – Menu €10 (weekday lunch), €24/42 – Carte €29/49

◆ The main dining room offers a refined setting with wood carvings, coffer ceilings and Louis XIII-style chairs while the other houses a wine bar. Traditional menu.

BÉNODET – 29 Finistère – 308 G7 – pop. 2 750 – Casino – ✉ 29950

Brittany — 9 A2

Paris 563 – Concarneau 19 – Fouesnant 8 – Pont-l'Abbé 13 – Quimper 17 – Quimperlé 47

Office de tourisme, 29, avenue de la Mer ✆ 02 98 57 00 14, Fax 02 98 57 23 00

de l'Odet Clohars Fouesnant, North: 4 km by D 34, ✆ 02 98 54 87 88.

Pont de Cornouaille ≤★ - The Odet★★ by boat: 1h30.

Ker Moor — rm,

corniche de la Plage – ✆ 02 98 57 04 48 – kermoor.hotel@wanadoo.fr – Fax 02 98 57 17 96 – Closed 18 December-8 January

69 rm – €65/100 €75/130, €10 – 15 suites – ½ P €65/94

Rest – *(open 1st March-31 October)* Menu €30/75 – Carte €23/68

◆ Large 1930s building and annex (conference rooms and bar) in the middle of a wooded park. Modern rooms of various sizes and long-stay apartments. A dining room adorned with works by the artist Pierre de Belay and Sixties leatherette chairs.

Kastel rest, VISA

corniche de la Plage – ✆ 02 98 57 05 01 – hotel.kastel@wanadoo.fr – Fax 02 98 57 29 99 – Closed 7-25 December

22 rm – €67/112 €105/127, €9,50 – ½ P €86/98 – **Rest** – Menu (€20), €27/32 – Carte €34/58

♦ You just need to cross the street to reach the beach! Pleasant lobby and spacious rooms with rattan furniture, facing the park (sports facilities) or the sea. The dining room's decor is bright and colourful. Cuisine with aromatic herbs and spices.

Le Grand Hôtel Abbatiale rm, VISA

4 av. Odet – ✆ 02 98 66 21 66 – abbatiale.benodet@wanadoo.fr – Fax 02 98 66 21 50 – Closed 14-28 December

50 rm – €65/90 €75/112, €9,50 – ½ P €68/88 – **Rest** – *(closed Saturday lunch)* Menu €21/42 – Carte €29/54

♦ This hotel's major advantage is its matchless location opposite the port of this little Breton seaside resort. Practical rooms; some command a beautiful view of the sea. Traditional cuisine and seafood.

Domaine de Kereven without rest VISA

2 km Quimper road – ✆ 02 98 57 02 46 – domaine-de-kereven@wanadoo.fr – Fax 02 98 66 22 61 – Open 11 April-30 September

12 rm – €48/58 €58/75, €9

♦ A new hotel complex of traditionally designed buildings in a tranquil rural setting. Cosy guestrooms plus a number of cottages (gîtes) and maisonettes. Breton furniture in the dining room where hot crêpes are served for breakfast.

Les Bains de Mer rest, VISA

11 r. Kerguelen – ✆ 02 98 57 03 41 – bainsdemer@portdebenodet.com – Fax 02 98 57 11 07 – Closed January

32 rm – €44/59 €57/73, €8,50 – ½ P €50/67

Rest – *(closed Saturday lunch, Tuesday lunch and Friday from 1st October to Easter)* Menu (€10,50), €12,50 (weekday lunch), €21/55 – Carte €25/45

♦ After a dip in the sea, you will enjoy your smart, modern room in this welcoming hotel, in the adopted town of yachtsman Eric Tabarly. A traditional restaurant decorated in contrasting tones, with green walls and plum-coloured curtains and chairs.

in Clohars-Fouesnant **3 km Northeast by D 34 and secondary road – pop. 1 417 – alt. 30 m – ✉ 29950**

XX **La Forge d'Antan** VISA

31 rte de Nors Vraz – ✆ 02 98 54 84 00 – laforgedantan2@wanadoo.fr – Fax 02 98 54 89 11 – Closed Tuesday except dinner July-September, Wednesday lunch and Monday

Rest – Menu €39/59 – Carte €45/79

♦ An appealing countryside inn with two dining rooms: one decorated in an inviting rustic style, the other brighter, facing the garden. Classic fare, fish and shellfish.

in Ste-Marine **5 km West by pont de Cornouaille – ✉ 29120 Combrit**

Villa Tri Men rm, rest, VISA

16 r. du Phare – ✆ 02 98 51 94 94 – contact@trimen.fr – Fax 02 98 51 95 50 – Closed 16 November-18 December and 4 January-5 February

20 rm – €110/270 €110/270, €13

Rest – *(closed Sunday and Monday except from 15 June to 15 September) (dinner only)* Menu €34 – Carte €42/64

♦ Lovely 1900 villa, nestling in a leafy, seaside garden. Elegant and understated rooms with modern furniture. Pleasant dining room and attractive terrace overlooking the estuary. Up-to-the-minute menu.

BÉNOUVILLE – **14 Calvados – 303 K4 –** **see Caen**

BERCK-SUR-MER – 62 Pas-de-Calais – 301 C5 – pop. 14 378 – alt. 5 m – Casino – ✉ 62600 Northern France and the Paris Region 30 A2

- Paris 232 – Abbeville 48 – Arras 93 – Boulogne-sur-Mer 40 – Calais 83 – Montreuil 16
- Office de tourisme, 5, avenue Francis Tattegrain ☎ 03 21 09 50 00, Fax 03 21 09 15 60
- de Nampont Saint-Martin Nampont-Saint-Martin Maison Forte, by D 940 and D 901: 15 km, ☎ 03 22 29 92 90.
- Parc d'attractions de Bagatelle (amusement park)★ 5 km by ①.

in Berck-Plage – ✉ 62600

L'Impératrice rest, VISA MC

43 r. Division-Leclerc – ☎ 03 21 09 01 09 – hotel-imperatrice@wanadoo.fr – Fax 03 21 09 72 80

12 rm – †€ 60/65 ††€ 60/77, ☕ € 8 – ½ P € 80/85 – **Rest** – *(pre-book)* Menu € 22/32 – Carte € 29/37

◆ Empress Eugenie inaugurated the first naval hospital here in Berck. Pleasant small and functional rooms. A colourful restaurant with a welcoming atmosphere, serving regional cuisine and seafood dishes.

XX **La Verrière** VISA MC AE

pl. 18-Juin – ☎ 03 21 84 27 25 – nvincent@g-partouche.fr – Fax 03 21 84 14 65 – Closed 10-16 March, 17-23 November, Sunday dinner and Monday off season

Rest – Menu (€ 12,50 bi), € 20/50 – Carte € 52/58

◆ Large modern, bright and well-kept restaurant dining room, in a former bus station converted into a casino, serving savoury contemporary cuisine.

in Groffliers 4 km Southeast by D 940 – pop. 1 422 – alt. 4 m – ✉ 62600

XXX **L' Auberge de la Madelon Fleurie** ← P VISA MC

198 r. Baie d'Authie, 2 km at La Madelon port southward – ☎ 03 21 94 05 05 – auberge.madelon@wanadoo.fr – Fax 03 21 94 40 36 – Closed January, Thursday lunch and Wednesday

Rest – Menu € 18 (weekday lunch), € 29/52 – Carte € 43

◆ With a bright interior decorated in warm tones, this famous restaurant specialises in contemporary cuisine. Short menu and daily specials prepared by an enthusiastic young chef.

The sun's out – let's eat alfresco!
Look for a terrace:

BERGERAC – 24 Dordogne – 329 D6 – pop. 26 053 – alt. 37 m – ✉ 24100 Dordogne-Berry-Limousin 4 C1

- Paris 534 – Agen 91 – Angoulême 110 – Bordeaux 94 – Périgueux 48
- Bergerac-Roumanières: ☎ 05 53 22 25 25, by ③: 5 km.
- Office de tourisme, 97, rue Neuve d'Argenson ☎ 05 53 57 03 11, Fax 05 53 61 11 04
- Château les Merles Mouleydier D 660, by Sarlat road: 15 km, ☎ 05 53 63 13 42.
- Old Bergerac★★: musée du Tabac★★ (maison Peyrarède★) - Musée du Vin, de la Batellerie et de la Tonnellerie★M³.

Plan on next page

De France without rest VISA MC AE

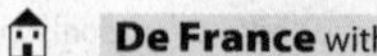

18 pl. Gambetta – ☎ 05 53 57 11 61 – hoteldefrance15@wanadoo.fr – Fax 05 53 61 25 70 AY **b**

20 rm – †€ 62/71 ††€ 62/71, ☕ € 10

◆ Opposite the shaded market square (Wednesdays and Saturdays), the De France has been fully refurbished. Simple, air-conditioned rooms, quieter on the pool side.

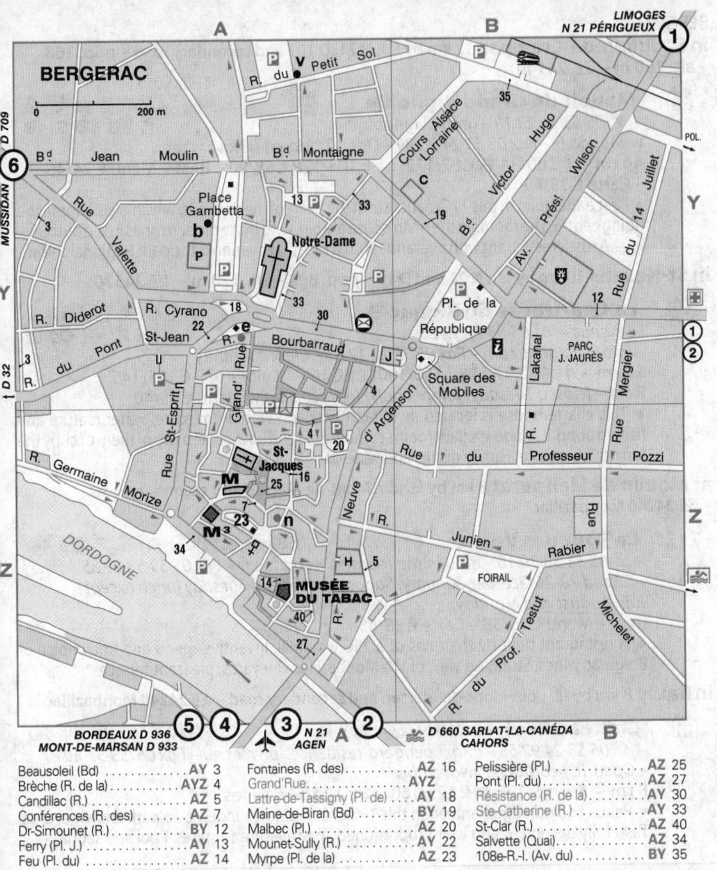

Beausoleil (Bd) . . . . AY 3	Fontaines (R. des) . . . . AZ 16	Pelissière (Pl.) . . . . AZ 25
Brèche (R. de la) . . . . AYZ 4	Grand'Rue . . . . AYZ	Pont (Pl. du) . . . . AZ 27
Candillac (R.) . . . . AZ 5	Lattre-de-Tassigny (Pl. de) . . . . AY 18	Résistance (R. de la) . . . . AY 30
Conférences (R. des) . . . . AZ 7	Maine-de-Biran (Bd) . . . . BY 19	Ste-Catherine (R.) . . . . AY 33
Dr-Simounet (R.) . . . . BY 12	Malbec (Pl.) . . . . AZ 20	St-Clar (R.) . . . . AZ 40
Ferry (Pl. J.) . . . . AY 13	Mounet-Sully (R.) . . . . AY 22	Salvette (Quai) . . . . AZ 34
Feu (Pl. du) . . . . AZ 14	Myrpe (Pl. de la) . . . . AZ 23	108e-R.-I. (Av. du) . . . . BY 35

Europ Hôtel without rest

20 r. Petit-Sol – ✆ 05 53 57 06 54 – europ.hotel.bergerac@wanadoo.fr – Fax 05 53 58 67 60 AY **v**

22 rm – 🚹€ 42 🚹🚹€ 46/56, ☕ € 7,50

◆ The poolside garden is the best feature of this hotel near the railway station. Renovated, well-kept rooms with air-conditioning and double-glazing on the road side .

L'Imparfait

8 r. Fontaines – ✆ 05 53 57 47 92 – mfernandezp@wanadoo.fr – Fax 05 53 23 43 18 – Closed 23 December-4 February, Sunday and Monday AZ **n**

Rest – Menu € 21 (weekday lunch), € 31/45 – Carte € 48/74

◆ This medieval house in the historic centre welcomes you to its large dining room where stones and exposed beams lend it character. Fine, traditional cuisine.

Le Repaire de Savinien

15 r. Mounet-Sully – ✆ 05 53 24 35 46 – Closed 1st-8 January, 24 February-10 March, Sunday and Monday from September to May AY **e**

Rest – Carte € 26/34

◆ Bistro ambience two minutes from Notre Dame Church: tightly packed tables and a slate menu. Traditional dishes that vary with the seasons and market availability.

in St-Julien-de-Crempse 12 km by ①, N 21, D 107 and secondary road – pop. 168 – alt. 150 m – ✉ 24140

Manoir du Grand Vignoble
– ✆ 05 53 24 23 18 – *grand.vignoble@wanadoo.fr* – Fax 05 53 24 20 89 – Open 21 March-8 November
44 rm – †€ 60/84 ††€ 82/112, ☕ € 10 – ½ P € 58/90 – **Rest** – Menu € 24/46 – Carte € 28/49
◆ Peace and quiet in this 17C manor set in the heart of the grounds, which is also home to a riding centre. The rooms in the main house are old, with more modern ones in the outbuildings. A rustic restaurant with a veranda and terrace that overlooks the park. Regional cuisine.

in St-Nexans 10 km by ③, N 21 and D 19 – pop. 802 – alt. 120 m – ✉ 24520

La Chartreuse du Bignac
Le Bignac – ✆ 05 53 22 12 80
– *info@abignac.com* – Fax 05 53 22 12 81 – Closed January
12 rm – †€ 140/170 ††€ 150/190, ☕ € 16 – 1 suite – ½ P € 125/145
Rest – *(closed Tuesday) (dinner only) (residents only)* Menu € 35/40
◆ This charterhouse is located in 12ha of parkland with a dovecote, water feature and fishing pond. Its huge, elegant rooms combine old and new details; two of them occupy the former wine store. Family dishes and wine bar.

at Moulin de Malfourat 8 km by ④,dir. Mont-de-Marsan and secondary road – ✉ 24240 Monbazillac

La Tour des Vents ← Bergerac valley,
– ✆ 05 53 58 30 10 – *moulin.malfourat@wanadoo.fr* – Fax 05 53 58 89 55
– Closed 20-26 October, January, Sunday dinner and Tuesday lunch except July-August and Monday
Rest – Menu € 25/58 – Carte € 38/65
◆ A restaurant built by the ruins of a 15C windmill. Inventive menu and fine choice of Bergerac wines. Stunning view of the Monbazillac vineyards; pleasant terrace.

in Rauly 8 km by ④ , dir. Mont-de-Marsan and secondary road – ✉ 24240 Monbazillac

Château Rauly-Saulieut without rest
– ✆ 05 53 24 92 55 – *info@perigord-residences-privees.eu* – Fax 05 53 57 80 87
– Open 16 February-1st November
8 rm – †€ 105/125 ††€ 125/160, ☕ € 12,50 – 6 suites
◆ Peace and quiet guaranteed in this 19C château, surrounded by a park and vineyards. Tastefully decorated and well-proportioned apartments and suites. Pool and sauna.

BERGÈRES-LÈS-VERTUS – 51 Marne – 306 F9 – see Vertus

BERGHEIM – 68 Haut-Rhin – 315 I7 – pop. 1 830 – alt. 235 m – ✉ 68750

Alsace-Lorraine 2 C2

Paris 449 – Colmar 18 – Ribeauvillé 4 – Sélestat 11

La Bacchante with rm
Grand Rue – ✆ 03 89 73 31 15 – *labacchante@wanadoo.fr* – Fax 03 89 73 60 65
– Closed 17 February-12 March, 16-27 November and Thursday in January-February
12 rm – †€ 60 ††€ 70/115, ☕ € 15 – ½ P € 70 – **Rest** – *(closed Wednesday lunch, Friday lunch and Thursday)* Menu € 22 (weekday lunch), € 28/48 – Carte € 29/41
◆ This former winery sports a rustic decor full of character. Pretty terrace in an inner courtyard. Cuisine based on local produce with dishes of the day.

Wistub du Sommelier
– ✆ 03 89 73 69 99 – *info@wistub-du-sommelier.com* – Fax 03 89 73 36 58
– Closed 15-31 July, February holidays, Sunday dinner, Tuesday dinner and Wednesday
Rest – Menu (€ 17), € 21 (weekdays)/40 – Carte € 27/47
◆ 19C parquet floor and bar, wainscoting and an earthenware stove: a pleasant but modernized Winstub decor lies behind this pretty Alsatian façade. Tasty locally sourced dishes.

BERGUES – 59 Nord – 302 C2 – pop. 4 209 – alt. 4 m – ✉ 59380

Northern France and the Paris Region 30 **B1**

Paris 279 – Calais 52 – Dunkerque 9 – Hazebrouck 34 – Lille 65 – St-Omer 31

Office de tourisme, Place Henri Billiaert ☎ 03 28 68 71 06, Fax 03 28 68 71 06

Hondschoote Crown ★.

Au Tonnelier

4 r. Mont-de-Piété , (near the church) – ☎ 03 28 68 70 05 – contact@autonnelier.com – Fax 03 28 68 21 87 – Closed 24 December-5 January

25 rm – †€ 39/46 ††€ 47/78, ☕ € 10 – ½ P € 50/53 – **Rest** – *(closed Sunday dinner)* Menu € 18/31 – Carte € 29/39

♦ In the town whose fortifications were the work of Vauban, find this small family hotel in a brick house with a profusion of flowers. Practical rooms. An inviting dining room (wood panelling and bistro furniture) serving traditional cuisine.

Cornet d'Or

26 r. Espagnole – ☎ 03 28 68 66 27 – Closed Sunday dinner and Monday

Rest – Menu € 28/40 – Carte approx. € 53

♦ Restaurant with an appealing Flemish façade and an elegant bourgeois dining room. Good simple produce takes pride of place in the generous menu of traditional fare.

BERMICOURT – 62 Pas-de-Calais – 301 G5 – pop. 128 – alt. 118 m – ✉ 62130

Paris 234 – Lille 100 – Arras 50 – Lens 61 – Liévin 58 30 **B2**

La Cour de Rémi

1 r. Baillet – ☎ 03 21 03 33 33 – sebastien@lacourderemi.com – Closed 18 February-7 March

7 rm – †€ 80 ††€ 80/130, ☕ € 10 – **Rest** – *(Closed Saturday lunch, Sunday dinner and Monday)* Menu € 17 bi (weekday lunch), € 28/33 – Carte € 33/45

♦ Charming hotel incorporating the outbuildings of a country château. Friendly service and cosy rooms with a personal touch. Enjoy modern cuisine in a bright and uncluttered contemporary style dining room, or outdoors. Daily specials on the board.

BERNAY – 27 Eure – 304 D7 – pop. 11 024 – alt. 105 m – ✉ 27300

Normandy 33 **C2**

Paris 155 – Argentan 69 – Évreux 49 – Le Havre 72 – Louviers 52 – Rouen 60

Syndicat d'initiative, 29, rue Thiers ☎ 02 32 43 32 08, Fax 02 32 45 82 68

Boulevard des Monts★.

Acropole Hôtel without rest

3 km south-west on Broglie road(D 438) – ☎ 02 32 46 06 06 – acropolehotel@wanadoo.fr – Fax 02 32 44 01 04

51 rm – †€ 54/68 ††€ 54/68, ☕ € 10

♦ Just outside the shopping area, an establishment with above all practical accommodation. Soundproofing and facilities useful for a restful stop or business stay.

Hostellerie du Moulin Fouret with rm

3.5 km southward along the St-Quentin-des-Isles road – ☎ 02 32 43 19 95 – lemoulinfouret@wanadoo.fr – Fax 02 32 45 55 50 – Closed Sunday dinner and Monday except July-August

8 rm – †€ 55 ††€ 55, ☕ € 10 – **Rest** – Menu € 40 – Carte € 60/85

♦ Elegant dining room opening onto the bar which contains the old workings of this converted mill. The peaceful terrace leads into a riverside flower garden. Modern menu.

LA BERNERIE-EN-RETZ – 44 Loire-Atlantique – 316 D5 – pop. 2 499 – alt. 24 m – ✉ 44760

34 **A2**

Paris 434 – Nantes 46 – Saint-Nazaire 38 – Saint-Herblain 46 – Rezé 43

Office de tourisme, 3, chaussée du Pays de Retz ☎ 0240827099, Fax 0251746140

L'Artimon

17 r. J. du Plessis – ☎ 02 51 74 61 60 – Closed 15-22 February, Monday except dinner in July-August, Sunday dinner and Tuesday from September to June and Wednesday

Rest – *(number of covers limited, pre-book)* Menu € 18 (weekdays)/34

♦ Well located on the market square. The restrained interior of wood and murals by a local artist pays homage to the sea. Unusual menu in a contemporary spirit.

BERNEUIL-SUR-AISNE – 60 Oise – 305 J4 – pop. 922 – alt. 45 m – ✉ 60350

37 **C2**

Paris 107 – Amiens 97 – Compiègne 17 – Creil 55

Le Manoir de Rochefort without rest

– ✆ *03 44 85 81 78 – rochefort1@orange.fr – Fax 03 44 85 81 78 – Closed January and February*

4 rm – ♦€ 75 ♦♦€ 85

◆ The former chapel (17C) of this manor houses understated and elegant rooms, all with a garden terraces. The nearby forest and quiet atmosphere are added attractions.

BERNEX – 74 Haute-Savoie – 328 N2 – pop. 854 – alt. 955 m – Winter sports : 1 000/2 000 m 13 – ✉ 74500 French Alps

46 **F1**

Paris 590 – Annecy 97 – Évian-les-Bains 10 – Morzine 32 – Thonon-les-Bains 20

Office de tourisme, le Clos du Moulin ✆ 04 50 73 60 72, Fax 04 50 73 16 17

Chez Tante Marie rm, VISA AE

– ✆ *04 50 73 60 35 – chez-tante-marie@wanadoo.fr – Fax 04 50 73 61 73 – Closed 29 March-12 April and 15 October-20 December*

27 rm – ♦€ 65/75 ♦♦€ 78/85, € 10,50 – ½ P € 70/85 – **Rest** – *(closed Sunday dinner except school holidays)* Menu € 21/56 – Carte € 23/45

◆ Nestled in the Alps, this hotel has a warm family atmosphere. The somewhat faded, rustically furnished rooms command a fine view of the peaks and the meadow-garden. Countrified dining room and panoramic terrace; classic and regional cuisine.

in La Beunaz 1,5 km Northwest by D 52 – ✉74500 Bernex – alt. 1 000 m

Bois Joli VISA AE

– ✆ *04 50 73 60 11 – hboisjoli@wanadoo.fr – Fax 04 50 73 65 28 – Open May-mid October and 20 December-end March*

29 rm – ♦€ 58/70 ♦♦€ 72/96, € 9,50 – ½ P € 60/70 – **Rest** – *(closed Sunday dinner and Wednesday)* Menu € 25/48 – Carte € 35/52

◆ A smart chalet amid a sea of greenery. Quiet rooms decorated in Alpine style with balconies facing the Dent d'Oche or Mount Billiat. Fully equipped relaxation centre. Dining room with wood-panelling and a summer terrace, both with beautiful views.

BERNIÈRES-SUR-MER – 14 Calvados – 303 J4 – pop. 1 882 – ✉ 14990 Normandy

32 **B2**

Paris 252 – Caen 20 – Hérouville-Saint-Clair 21 – Le Havre 107

Syndicat d'initiative, 159, rue Victor Tesnières ✆ 02 31 96 44 02, Fax 02 31 96 98 96

L'As de Trèfle VISA

420 r. L.-Hettier – ✆ *02 31 97 22 60 – asdetrefle3@wanadoo.fr – Fax 02 31 97 22 60 – Closed 2 January-10 February, Tuesday except July-August and Monday*

Rest – Menu € 22 (weekdays)/39 – Carte € 35/62

◆ Just off the shore, in a quiet residential area, a smart restaurant with well-spaced and well-laid tables where you can enjoy tasty, traditional food.

BERNOS-BEAULAC – 33 Gironde – 335 J8 – see Bazas

BERRIC – 56 Morbihan – 308 P9 – pop. 1 027 – alt. 65 m – ✉ 56230

10 **C3**

Paris 474 – Rennes 113 – Vannes 24 – Saint-Nazaire 73

Le Moulin du Bois VISA

3 km north-east on D 7 (Questembert road) – ✆ *02 97 67 04 44 – tgoujon@wanadoo.fr – Fax 02 97 67 06 79*

3 rm – ♦€ 84/104 ♦♦€ 90/110 – **Table d'hôte** – Menu € 40 bi/50 bi

◆ This old house on the hillside is home to tastefully decorated attractive rooms. Ideal for nature lovers (nearby forest and lake).

BERRWILLER – 68 Haut-Rhin – 315 H9 – pop. 1 058 – alt. 260 m – ✉ 68500 1 A3

Paris 467 – Belfort 45 – Colmar 31 – Épinal 99 – Guebwiller 9 – Mulhouse 20

L'Arbre Vert

96 r. Principale – ✆ 03 89 76 73 19 – rest.koenig.arbrevert@wanadoo.fr – Fax 03 89 76 73 68 – Closed 7-28 July, Sunday dinner and Monday

Rest – Menu € 12 (weekday lunch), € 22/48 – Carte € 32/55

◆ This charming flower-decked inn serves delicious regional food served in an elegant, contemporary-style dining room. Daily specials also available in the bistro.

BERRY-AU-BAC – 02 Aisne – 306 F6 – pop. 528 – alt. 62 m – ✉ 02190 37 D2

Paris 161 – Laon 30 – Reims 21 – Rethel 46 – Soissons 48 – Vouziers 66

La Cote 108

– ✆ 03 23 79 95 04 – lacote108@orange.fr – Fax 03 23 79 83 50 – Closed 28 July-12 August, 26 December-13 January, Sunday dinner, Monday and Tuesday

Rest – *(pre-book Sat - Sun)* Menu € 25/80 – Carte € 51/67

◆ A gourmet break facing Hill 108: this roadside restaurant serves modern cuisine in a refined, contemporary setting. Flower garden.

BERRY-BOUY – 18 Cher – 323 J4 – pop. 934 – alt. 136 m – ✉ 18500 12 C3

Paris 238 – Orléans 112 – Bourges 9 – Vierzon 27 – Issoudun 41

L'Ermitage without rest

– ✆ 02 48 26 87 46 – domaine-ermitage@wanadoo.fr – Fax 02 48 26 03 28 – Closed mid November-beg. January

5 rm – †€ 48/51 ††€ 61/64

◆ Set in grounds planted with century-old trees, this wine estate extends a friendly welcome (wine tasting) to guests. Attractively decorated rooms.

BERZE-LA-VILLE – 71 Saône-et-Loire – 320 I11 – pop. 530 – alt. 350 m – ✉ 71960 Burgundy-Jura 8 C3

Paris 408 – Mâcon 13 – Charolles 47 – Cluny 13 – Roanne 85

in la Croix-Blanche 2 km West – ✉ 71960

Le Relais du Mâconnais

D 17 – ✆ 03 85 36 60 72 – resa@lannuel.com – Fax 03 85 36 65 47 – Closed January, Sunday dinner and Monday

Rest – Menu € 24 (weekday lunch), € 28/80 – Carte € 46/66

◆ Fine, regional-style house in the town centre. Contemporary cuisine served in a modern dining room decorated in tones of brown and sea-green. Functional rooms.

BESANÇON P – 25 Doubs – 321 G3 – pop. 117 733 – Built-up area 134 376 – alt. 250 m – Casino BY – ✉ 25000 Burgundy-Jura 16 B2

Paris 405 – Basel 167 – Bern 180 – Dijon 91 – Lyon 225 – Nancy 204

Office de tourisme, 2, place de la 1re Armée Française ✆ 03 81 80 92 55, Fax 03 81 80 58 30

de Besançon Mamirolle La Chevillotte, East: 13 km by N 57, D 464 and D 104, ✆ 03 81 55 73 54.

Site★★★ - Citadel★★: musée d'Histoire naturelle★ M³, musée comtois★ M², musée de la Résistance et de la Déportation★ M⁴ - Old town★★ ABYZ : Palais Granvelle★, cathedral★ (Virgins with Saints★), astronomical clock★, façades of 17C houses.★ - Prefecture★ AZ P - Bibliothèque municipale (Municipal library)★ BZ B - Gate★ of St-Jacques hospital AZ - Musée des Beaux-Arts et d'Archéologie★★.

Plans on following pages

BESANÇON

Allende (Bd S.) . . . . AX 2
Belfort (R. de) . . . . BX
Brulard (R. Gén.) . . . . AX 5
Carnot (Av.) . . . . BX 7
Chaillot (R. de) . . . . BX 12
Clemenceau (Av. Georges) . AX 15
Clerc (R. F.) . . . . BX 16
Fontaine-Argent (Av.) . . . . BX 19
Jouchoux (R. A.) . . . . AX 25
Lagrange (Av. Léo) . . . . AX 27
Montrapon (Av. de) . . . . AX 34
Observatoire (Av. de l') . . . . . AX 35
Ouest (Bd) . . . . AX 37
Paix (Av. de la) . . . . BX 38
Vaite (R. de la) . . . . BX 55
Voirin (R.) . . . . BX 57

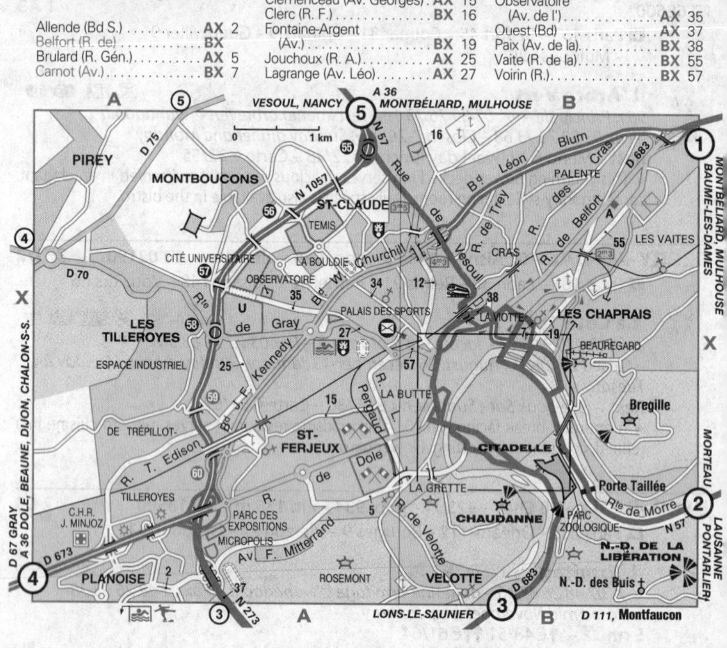

Mercure Parc Micaud

3 av. Ed.-Droz – ✆ 03 81 40 34 34 – h1220@accor.com – Fax 03 81 40 34 39

91 rm – †€ 69/126 ††€ 79/136, € 13,50 – **Rest** – *(closed Saturday lunchtime and Sunday lunchtime)* Carte € 23/35 BY **d**

♦ This hotel benefits from a lovely location facing the Doubs, near the old town where Victor Hugo was born in 1802. Renovated rooms catering for business travellers. This contemporary-style restaurant, decorated on the theme of time, has a view of the casino gardens.

Charles Quint without rest

3 r. Chapitre – ✆ 03 81 82 05 49 – hotel-charlesquint@wanadoo.fr – Fax 03 81 82 61 45 – Closed 6-12 April BZ **f**

9 rm – †€ 87 ††€ 138, € 11

♦ Successful renovation has brought a shine back to this noble 18C residence. The rooms decorated with wood panelling and mouldings overlook the cathedral or the garden.

Ibis La City

av. Louise-Michel – ✆ 03 81 85 11 70 – h3297@accor.com – Fax 03 81 85 11 77

119 rm – †€ 52/69 ††€ 52/69, € 7,50 – **Rest** – Menu (€ 11), € 21 – Carte € 17/62 AZ **m**

♦ A completely new building in the heart of the city of Besançon. You'll appreciate the spacious, modern rooms decorated in line with the latest Ibis standard. Brasserie food (seafood and sauerkraut specialities) served under a 1900-style glass roof or on the terrace.

Ibis Centre without rest

21 r. Gambetta – ✆ 03 81 81 02 02 – H1364@accor.com – Fax 03 81 81 89 65 BY

49 rm – †€ 55/71 ††€ 55/85, € 8

♦ A freestone industrial building - a 19C watch hand factory - converted into a hotel. Rooms have been renovated in the hotel chain's style.

BESANÇON

Hôtel du Nord without rest

8 r. Moncey – 03 81 81 34 56 – hoteldunord3@wanadoo.fr – Fax 03 81 81 85 96 BY **r**

44 rm – €38/43 €51/59, €5,50

◆ Leave your car in the garage and discover the old town on foot from this very central 19C building. Practical and soundproofed rooms. Considerate service.

XXX **Le Manège**

2 fg Rivotte – 03 81 48 01 48 – restaurant-le-manege@wanadoo.fr – Fax 03 81 82 74 50 – Closed 4-18 August, 2-8 January, Saturday lunch, Sunday dinner and Monday BZ **u**

Rest – Menu €25 (weekday lunch), €39/69 – Carte €46/68

◆ Delicious contemporary dishes, prepared by a young self-taught chef, and served in a modern setting.

XX **Le Poker d'As**

14 square St-Amour – ✆ 03 81 81 42 49 – Fax 03 81 81 05 59 – Closed 10 July-5 August, 23 December-3 January, Sunday dinner and Monday BY **u**

Rest – Menu € 18/46 – Carte € 28/64

◆ An amusing selection of copper and sculpted wood covers the walls of this pretty dining room. Traditional and regional specialities.

XX **Le Chaland**

promenade Micaud, near Bregille bridge – ✆ 03 81 80 61 61 – chaland@chaland.com – Fax 03 81 88 67 42 – Closed Sunday dinner BY **s**

Rest – Menu € 16/55 bi – Carte € 36/54

◆ Barge from 1904, converted into a restaurant in the 1960s. The rocking of passing boats makes for a lively meal on the Doubs. Classic and regional cuisine.

XX **Christophe Menozzi**

11 r. Jean-Petit – ✆ 03 81 81 28 01 – Fax 03 81 83 36 97 – Closed 3-26 August, 28 December-5 January, Sunday, Monday and public holidays AY **e**

Rest – Menu € 22/46 – Carte € 36/51

◆ Housed in an old, regional-style building, this restaurant, run by Christophe Menozzi, serves local cuisine accompanied by a good choice of wines.

X **La Table des Halles**

22 r. Gustave-Courbet – ✆ 03 81 50 62 74 – la.table.des.halles@orange.fr – Fax 03 81 50 66 42 – Closed 2-18 August, February school holidays, Sunday and Monday AY **f**

Rest – Menu € 16/20 – Carte € 26/36

◆ This ex-convent now houses an inviting restaurant decorated in a modern style. Updated recipes that happily mingle local and bourguignon influences.

in Chalezeule 5,5 km by ① and D 217 – pop. 952 – alt. 252 m – ✉ 25220

Les Trois Iles rest,

1 r. des Vergers – ✆ 03 81 61 00 66 – hotel.3iles@wanadoo.fr – Fax 03 81 61 73 09 – Closed 26 December-8 January

17 rm – €55/80 €55/80, € 12 – ½ P € 58/70

Rest – *(closed 23 December-10 January) (dinner only)* Menu € 20

◆ Family-run establishment renowned for its calm and green surroundings. Rooms are discreetly decorated and furnished in a rustic style. A single daily set menu served in a veranda-dining room with fireplace, period furniture and wrought iron lights.

in Roche-lez-Beaupré 8 km by ① – pop. 2 062 – alt. 242 m – ✉ 25220

X **Auberge des Rosiers**

6 r. des Rosiers – ✆ 03 81 57 05 85 – Fax 03 81 60 51 54 – Closed 20-29 October, 16 February-3 March, Monday dinner, Sunday dinner and Tuesday

Rest – Menu € 11/35 – Carte € 26/46

◆ At the gates of the village, this establishment serves traditional cuisine in a fresh and bright restaurant or on the shaded terrace.

in Montfaucon 9 km by ②, D 464 and D 146 – pop. 1 372 – alt. 491 m – ✉ 25660

XX **La Cheminée**

rte du Belvédère – ✆ 03 81 81 17 48 – restaurantlacheminee@wanadoo.fr – Fax 03 81 82 86 45 – Closed 16 February-11 March, Sunday dinner, Wednesday dinner and Monday

Rest – Menu € 22 (weekdays)/49 – Carte € 45/74

◆ In a picturesque village overlooking the town of Besançon. Two dining rooms, one with a glimpse of the surrounding hillside. Local specialities.

in Champvans-les-Moulins 8 km by ④ On D 70 – pop. 232 – alt. 252 m – ✉ 25170

X **La Source**

4 r. des Sources – ✆ 03 81 59 90 57 – lasource.ch@wanadoo.fr – Fax 03 81 59 09 39 – Closed 1st-11 September, 26 December-22 January, Wednesday dinner except June-August, Sunday dinner and Monday

Rest – Menu € 16 (weekday lunch), € 22/33 – Carte € 31/46

◆ Modern building with a garden and its pond. Traditional and local dishes served in a dining room with overhead exposed beams or on the terrace.

in Geneuille 13 km by ⑤, N 57 and D 1 – pop. 890 – alt. 220 m – ✉ 25870

Château de la Dame Blanche VISA MC AE

1 chemin de la Goulotte – ☎ 03 81 57 64 64 – contact@chateau-de-la-dame-blanche.fr – Fax 03 81 57 65 70 – Closed Sunday evening

26 rm – †€ 77 ††€ 143, ☕ € 10 – 2 suites – ½ P € 123

Rest – *(closed Sunday dinner and Monday)* Menu € 25 (weekday lunch), € 35/84 – Carte € 64/80

◆ Large mansion in the heart of an English-style park. Elegant, personalised rooms (non-smoking only). Three suites. Traditional food to be enjoyed under the moulded ceilings and crystal chandeliers of the pleasant dining rooms.

BESSANS – 73 Savoie – 333 O6 – pop. 311 – alt. 1 730 m – Winter sports : 1 750/2 050 m 4 – ✉ 73480 French Alps 45 D2

Paris 698 – Albertville 125 – Chambéry 138 – Lanslebourg-Mont-Cenis 13 – Val-d'Isère 41

Office de tourisme, rue Maison Morte ☎ 04 79 05 96 52, Fax 04 79 05 83 11

Paintings★ of St-Antoine chapel.

Avérole Valley ★★.

Le Mont-Iseran rest, VISA MC

pl. de la Mairie – ☎ 04 79 05 95 97 – Fax 04 79 05 84 67 – Open 20 June-25 September and 15 December-10 April

19 rm – †€ 37/70 ††€ 37/72, ☕ € 7 – ½ P € 51/57 – **Rest** – Menu € 12/48 – Carte € 20/40

◆ In the centre of the village and near the slopes, a chalet with regularly renovated rooms, often with balcony. Bar-tea salon. Dining room decorated with painted wainscoting and a statuette of the mythical "devil of Bessans"; classic cuisine.

LE BESSAT – 42 Loire – 327 G7 – pop. 414 – alt. 1 170 m – Winter sports : 1 170/1 427 m – ✉ 42660 44 B2

Paris 530 – Annonay 29 – St-Chamond 19 – St-Étienne 19 – Yssingeaux 65

Syndicat d'initiative, Maison Communale ☎ 04 77 20 43 76, Fax 04 77 20 46 10

La Fondue "Chez l'Père Charles" with rm VISA MC

Gde-rue – ☎ 04 77 20 40 09 – Fax 04 77 20 45 20 – Open 16 March-14 November and closed Sunday dinner and Monday lunch except school holidays

8 rm – †€ 45 ††€ 55, ☕ € 7 – **Rest** – Menu (€ 12), € 15 (weekdays), € 23/52 – Carte € 37/54

◆ Countrified dining rooms in this inn situated in the centre of the village. Tasty, traditional cuisine with a regional touch. Simple rooms.

BESSE-ET-ST-ANASTAISE – 63 Puy-de-Dôme – 326 E9 – pop. 1 672 – alt. 1 050 m – Winter sports : to Super Besse – ✉ 63610 Auvergne 5 B2

Paris 462 – Clermont-Ferrand 46 – Condat 28 – Issoire 30 – Le Mont-Dore 25

Office de tourisme, place du Dr Pipet ☎ 04 73 79 52 84, Fax 04 73 79 52 08

St-André church ★ - Rue de la Boucherie★ - Town gate★ - Pavin lake ★★ ★ and Puy de Montchal★★ ★★ Southwest: 4 km by D 978.

Les Mouflons VISA MC AE

Berthelage – ☎ 04 73 79 56 93 – info@hotel-mouflons-besse.com – Fax 04 73 79 51 18 – Closed 15 November-15 December

51 rm – †€ 75 ††€ 80, ☕ € 8,50 – ½ P € 54/60 – **Rest** – *(closed lunch except weekends)* Menu € 15/40 – Carte approx. € 36

◆ Imposing 1970s building with chalet features. Choose one of the renovated rooms. The others are simpler and slightly antiquated. A spacious restaurant partitioned by sections of lava stone. Regional cuisine.

La Gazelle 
rte Compains – 04 73 79 50 26 – marie.renaud@lagazelle.fr – Fax 04 73 79 89 03 – Closed 10 October-20 December and 20 March-20 April
35 rm – €56/70 €56/70, €8,50 – ½ P €54/64 – **Rest** – *(dinner only)* Menu €19
◆ From its imposing location, this hotel enjoys a splendid view of medieval Besse. Guestrooms decorated in Alpine style. Breakfast served on the veranda. Traditional cuisine served in a simply furnished dining room with a superb view.

Hostellerie du Beffroy with rm — rest, VISA MC AE
26 r. Abbé-Blot – 04 73 79 50 08 – lebeffroy@orange.fr – Fax 04 73 79 57 87 – Closed 1st November-20 December and Monday except July-August
13 rm – €52/58 €55/105, €11 – 1 suite – ½ P €65/85
Rest – *(Half-board only 20 December-22 Mars) (pre-book Sat - Sun)* Menu €25, €27/70 – Carte €65/66
◆ This 15C house was a former belfry keepers' residence. It has two rustic dining rooms with furniture polished by the ages. Contemporary cuisine.

BESSINES-SUR-GARTEMPE – 87 Haute-Vienne – 325 F4 – pop. 2 743 – alt. 335 m – 87250 — 24 B1

Paris 355 – Argenton-sur-Creuse 58 – Bellac 29 – Guéret 55 – Limoges 38

Office de tourisme, 6, avenue du 11 novembre 05 55 76 09 28, Fax 05 55 76 68 45

Bellevue — P VISA MC AE
2 av. de Limoges – 05 55 76 01 99 – hotel.bellevue@netcourrier.com – Fax 05 55 76 68 81 – Closed 9 January-9 February, Saturday lunch and Friday dinner from October to June
12 rm – €49 €49, €7 – ½ P €61 – **Rest** – Menu €13 (weekday lunch), €20/48 – Carte €26/35
◆ This family-run inn on the main road through the village is a practical stopover. The accommodation here is in simple, functional guestrooms. Traditional establishment whose sole vocation is to satisfy your hunger.

Château Constant — P
av. 11 novembre-1918 – 05 55 76 78 42 – chateau_constant@yahoo.com
5 rm – €69 €79 – **Table d'hôte** – Menu €22 bi
◆ Manor house set in parkland, run by a globetrotting Dutch couple. Varied furnishings (period, antique, ethnic); international cuisine served in a spacious and bright dining room.

in La Croix-du-Breuil 3 km North On D 220 – 87250 Bessines-sur-Gartempe

Manoir Henri IV — P VISA MC AE
– 05 55 76 00 56 – manoirhenriIV@free.fr – Fax 05 55 76 14 14 – Closed Monday from October to May and Sunday dinner
11 rm – €46/60 €46/60, €8 – **Rest** – Menu €23 (weekday lunch), €26/48
◆ Henry IV allegedly was the guest of this fortified farmhouse from the 16C, now with a recently added new wing. You will stay in rustic rooms. Traditional dishes to savour in the dining rooms of the manor which have retained their country charm.

BESSONIES – 46 Lot – 337 I3 – pop. 112 – alt. 520 m – 46210 — 29 C1

Paris 587 – Toulouse 215 – Cahors 95 – Aurillac 34 – Figeac 39

Château de Bessonies — P
– 05 65 11 65 25/06 03 – info@chateau-bessonies.com – Open March-mid November
4 rm – €129/159 €129/159 – **Table d'hôte** – Menu €30 bi
◆ Marshal Ney, hero of the Napoleonic Wars, sought refuge in this 1550 château before he was arrested for treason. Spacious rooms furnished in period style. A communal table serving regional fare takes pride of place in the dining room.

BÉTHUNE – 62 Pas-de-Calais – **301** I4 – **pop. 27 808** – **Built-up area 259 198 – alt. 34 m** – ✉ **62400** **Northern France and the Paris Region** 30 **B2**

Paris 214 – Arras 34 – Calais 83 – Boulogne-sur-Mer 90 – Lille 39

Office de tourisme, 42-48 rue St Pry ☎ 03 21 57 25 47, Fax 03 21 57 01 60

du Vert-Parc Illies 3 route d'Ecuelles, by Lille road: 18 km, ☎ 03 20 29 37 87.

BÉTHUNE

Albert-1er (R.) . . . . **YZ** 2
Arras (R. d') . . . . **Z** 3
Bruay (R. de) . . . . **Z** 6
Buridan (R.) . . . . **Z** 7
Clemenceau (Pl. G.) . . . . **Z**
Egalité (R. de l') . . . . **Y** 8
Gambetta (R.) . . . . **YZ** 10
Grand'Place . . . . **Z**
Haynaut (R. Eugène) . . . . **Z** 12
Juin (Av. du Mar.) . . . . **Z** 14
Kennedy (Av. du Prés.) . . . . . . **Y** 15
Lamartine (Pl.) . . . . **Y** 17
Lattre-de-Tassigny (Av. de) . . . **Z** 18
Pont de Pierre (R. du) . . . . **Y** 20
Quai du Rivage (R. du) . . . . **Y** 21
République (Pl. de la) . . . . **Y** 22
Sadi-Carnot (R.) . . . . **Y**
Treilles (R. des) . . . . **Z** 25
Vauban (Bd) . . . . **Z** 26
Zola (R. Emile) . . . . **Z** 27

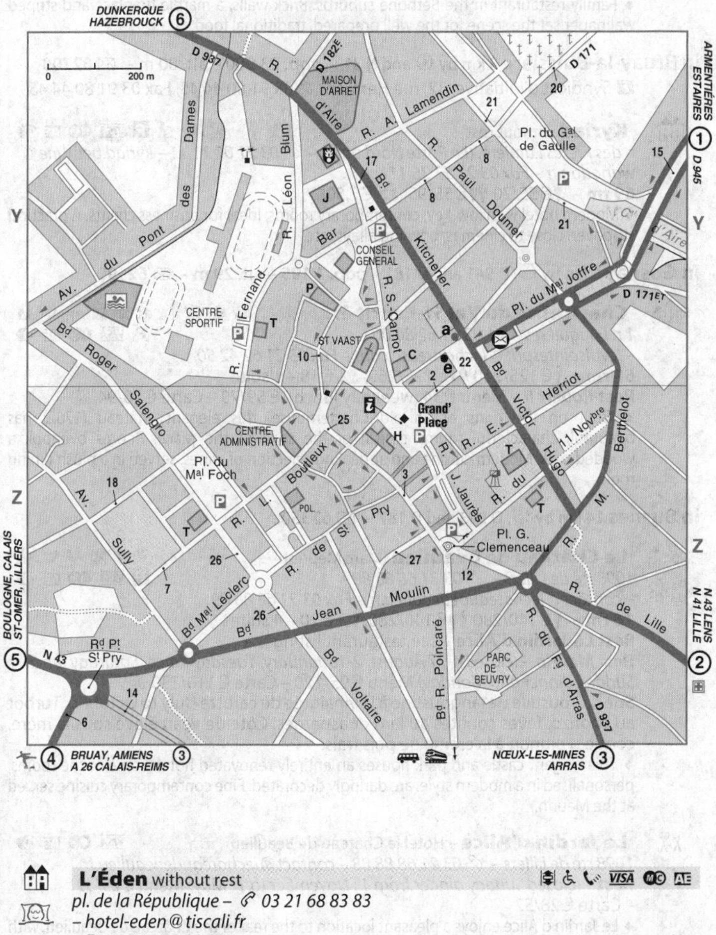

L'Éden without rest VISA MC AE
pl. de la République – ☎ *03 21 68 83 83*
– hotel-eden@tiscali.fr
– Fax 03 21 68 83 84 Y **e**
32 rm – €55/110 €55/110, ☕ €7,50
◆ A brick house in the town centre. Warm interior (light wood, colourful soft furnishings) with rooms of various sizes, some with massage-jet baths.

XXX **Au Départ**

1 r. F. Mitterand, opposite SNCF train station – ✆ 03 21 57 18 04 – jfrancois.buche@wanadoo.fr – Fax 03 21 01 18 20 – Closed 3-25 August, February holidays, Tuesday lunch, Saturday lunch, Sunday dinner and Monday
Rest – Menu € 20 (weekday lunch), € 30/60 – Carte € 48/82
◆ Opposite the railway station, a regional house that sports a daring colourful façade (black and white walls and a bow window). Warmly welcoming. Carefully prepared modern cuisine.

in Labourse **4 km by ②, D 943 and D 65 – pop. 2 028 – alt. 25 m – ✉ 62113**

XX **Terre et Mer**

16 r. A.-Larue – ✆ 03 21 64 03 57 – Closed 7-13 April, 28 July-17 August, Saturday lunch, Sunday dinner, Monday and dinner on public holidays
Rest – Menu (€ 12), € 27/50 – Carte € 35/54
◆ Family restaurant in the Béthune suburbs. Brick walls, a marble fireplace and striped wallpaper set the scene for the well prepared, traditional food.

in Bruay-la-Buissière **8 km by ④ and N 31 – pop. 23 900 – alt. 80 m – ✉ 62700**

Syndicat d'initiative, 32, rue Hermant ✆ 03 91 80 44 45, Fax 03 91 80 44 45

Kyriad without rest

r. des Frères Lumière, (La Porte Nord park) – ✆ 03 21 01 11 11 – kyriad.bethune@wanadoo.fr – Fax 03 21 57 35 11
69 rm – €55/70 €55/95, € 7,50
◆ Modern hotel with low-key, contemporary rooms, ideal for business clients. A practical stopover, close to cinemas, bowling alleys, etc.

in Gosnay **5 km by ④, D 941 and D 181 – pop. 1 195 – alt. 29 m – ✉ 62199**

Chartreuse du Val St-Esprit rm,

1 r. Fouquières – ✆ 03 21 62 80 00 – levalsaintesprit@lachartreuse.com – Fax 03 21 62 42 50
66 rm – €125/260 €125/260, € 18 – 1 suite
Rest *Robert II* – Menu € 34 (weekday lunch), € 59/79 – Carte € 50/94
◆ Built on the ruins of an old Charterhouse, this elegant château (1762) has beautiful, characterful rooms typical of the style of the place. Rooms overlook a wooded park. Modern cuisine and appealing selection of wines, served in a plush dining room.

in Busnes **14 km by ⑤, D 943 and D 187 – ✉ 62350**

Le Château de Beaulieu (Marc Meurin)

1098 rte de Lillers – ✆ 03 21 68 88 88 – contact@lechateaudebeaulieu.fr – Fax 03 21 68 88 89
16 rm – €140/280 €140/280, € 20 – 4 suites
Rest Le Jardin d'Alice – see restaurant listing
Rest *Meurin* – *(closed 4-27 August, 2-15 January, Tuesday lunch, Saturday lunch, Sunday dinner and Monday)* Menu € 95/120 – Carte € 110/130
Spec. Croustille de langoustine à la vinaigrée de carotte (July to October). Turbot au chorizo, fèves confites au lard et asperges. Côte de veau élevé sous la mère, coque d'oignon à la crème de pois frais.
◆ This elegant castle and park houses an entirely renovated hotel. Some of the rooms, personalised in a modern style, are daringly decorated. Fine contemporary cuisine served at the Meurin.

XX **Le Jardin d'Alice** – Hôtel le Château de Beaulieu

1098 rte de Lillers – ✆ 03 21 68 88 88 – contact@lechateaudebeaulieu.fr
Rest – *(closed Sunday dinner from 1st November to 1st May)* Menu € 25/32 – Carte € 28/52
◆ Le Jardin d'Alice enjoys a pleasant location to the rear of the Château de Beaulieu, with bay windows and terrace. Lounge-style atmosphere and fine traditional cuisine.

LE BETTEX – **74 Haute-Savoie** – **328** N5 – **see St-Gervais-les-Bains**

BEUIL – 06 Alpes-Maritimes – 341 C3 – pop. 334 – alt. 1 450 m – Winter sports : 1 470/2 100 m 26 – ✉ 06470 French Alps 41 D2

Paris 809 – Barcelonnette 80 – Digne-les-Bains 117 – Nice 79 – Puget-Théniers 31

Syndicat d'initiative, quartier du Pissaïre ✆ 04 93 02 32 58, Fax 04 93 02 35 72

Site★ - Church ★ paintings.

L'Escapade

Le village – ✆ 04 93 02 31 27 – hotel-escapade@wanadoo.fr – Fax 04 93 02 20 50 – Closed 24 March-4 April and 1st October-26 December

11 rm – €52 €62/78, €10 – ½ P €58/71 – **Rest** – Menu €22/27 – Carte €35/41

◆ Small, but well kept rooms decorated in a mountain style. Some are under the eaves, others have a south facing balcony. The restaurant has a nice country setting decorated with old agricultural objects. Regional cuisine.

LA BEUNAZ – 74 Haute-Savoie – 328 M2 – see Bernex

BEUVRON-EN-AUGE – 14 Calvados – 303 L4 – pop. 233 – alt. 11 m – ✉ 14430 Normandy 33 C2

Paris 219 – Cabourg 14 – Caen 32 – Lisieux 25 – Pont-l'Évêque 33

Village★ - Clermont-en-Auge★ Northeast: 3 km.

Le Pavé d'Auge (Jérôme Bansard)

– ✆ 02 31 79 26 71 – info@pavedauge.com – Fax 02 31 39 04 45 – Closed 24 November-26 December, 16-23 February, Monday and Tuesday except dinner July-August

Rest – Menu €35/58

Spec. Encornets et huîtres grillés, bœuf séché, artichaut violet et jus de viande (April to September). Escalopes de foie gras poêlé, aigre-doux de mangue, pomme et gingembre (October to March). Pommes en tatin, crème vanille, glace pomme, arlette et chantilly. **Wines** Vin de pays de Normandie.

◆ At the centre of the pretty village, restored covered markets offering the pleasure of a meal influenced by local produce and a good wine selection. Intimate and welcoming room, with beams, half-timbering and stylish red velvet covered chairs.

Auberge de la Boule d'Or

– ✆ 02 31 79 78 78 – Fax 02 31 39 61 50 – Closed mid January-mid February, Tuesday dinner and Wednesday

Rest – Menu €24/35 – Carte €29/57

◆ On the square, a half-timbered façade with two smart, rustic dining rooms. Floor tiles and bright yellow walls in the one on the ground floor, warmed up by a fireplace used for grilling meat. Traditional food with a local flavour.

BEUZEVILLE – 27 Eure – 304 C5 – pop. 3 097 – alt. 129 m – ✉ 27210 Normandy 32 A3

Paris 179 – Bernay 38 – Deauville 26 – Évreux 76 – Honfleur 16 – Le Havre 34

Office de tourisme, 52, rue Constant Fouché ✆ 02 32 57 72 10, Fax 02 32 57 72 10

Le Petit Castel without rest

32 r. Constant-Fouché – ✆ 02 32 57 76 08 – auberge-du-cochon-dor@wanadoo.fr – Fax 02 32 42 25 70 – Closed 2 January-5 February

16 rm – €60/66 €66/76, €11

◆ The hotel offers practical rooms with colourful furnishings; those overlooking the garden are quieter. The Reception service is sometimes at the Cochon d'Or inn.

Auberge du Cochon d'Or with rm

64 r. des Anciens d'AFN – ✆ 02 32 57 70 46 – auberge-du-cochon-dor@wanadoo.fr – Fax 02 32 42 25 70 – Closed 1st January-7 February

4 rm – €60/66 €66/76, €11 – ½ P €65 – **Rest** – *(closed Sunday dinner 15 September-15 April and Monday)* Menu €20 (weekdays)/42 – Carte €30/43

◆ Housed in an early-20C Norman house, this restaurant invites you to discover its two elegant dining rooms and its traditional food with a regional flavour.

West 3 km by N 175 – ✉ 14130 Quetteville

Hostellerie de la Hauquerie-Chevotel rm,
– ✆ 02 31 65 62 40 – info@ rest, VISA
chevotel.com – Fax 02 31 64 24 52 – Open 1st March-30 November
16 rm – €110/200 €110/200, €15 – 2 suites – ½ P €97/152
Rest – *(dinner only)* Menu €28/42 – Carte €39/52
◆ Cottage atmosphere in this hotel-haras dedicated to our pure-blooded friends. The rooms, whose decor evokes the names of famous studs, opens out onto an area of green. Understated elegance distinguishes the small dining room where modern food is served.

BEYNAC ET CAZENAC – 24 Dordogne – **329** H6 – **pop. 506** – **alt. 75 m** – ✉ **24220** Dordogne-Berry-Limousin 4 **D3**

Paris 537 – Brive-la-Gaillarde 63 – Gourdon 28 – Périgueux 66 – Sarlat-la-Canéda 12

Office de tourisme, La Balme ✆ 05 53 29 43 08, Fax 05 53 29 43 08

Site★★ - Village★ - Calvary ★★ - Château★★: ★★.

in Vézac 2 km southeast on Sarlat road – **pop. 594** – **alt. 90 m** – ✉ **24220**

Le Relais des Cinq Châteaux with rm rm,
– ✆ 05 53 30 30 72 rest, VISA
– 5chateaux@perigord.com – Fax 05 53 30 30 08
14 rm – €52/135 €52/135, €7 – ½ P €55/98 – **Rest** – Menu €23/37 – Carte €38/51
◆ This modern regional house has two rooms, one with a veranda. The terrace commands a fine view of the countryside and three fortified castles. Tasty classic dishes.

LES BÉZARDS – 45 Loiret – **318** N5 – ✉ **45290** 12 **D2**

Paris 136 – Auxerre 79 – Gien 17 – Joigny 58 – Montargis 23 – Orléans 75

Auberge des Templiers rm,
4 km from motorway A77, exit 19 – VISA
✆ 02 38 31 80 01 – templiers@relaischateaux.fr – Fax 02 38 31 84 51
– Closed February and Monday lunch
20 rm – €195/275 €195/275, €25 – 10 suites – ½ P €180/220
Rest – Menu €55 (lunch), €78/125 – Carte €81/145
Spec. Araignée de mer et bar à cru en marinade d'artichauts poivrade. Sandre de Loire à la lie de vin de Sancerre. Gibier de Sologne (hunting season). **Wines** Sancerre, Pouilly-Fumé.
◆ A unique hotel with personalised and refined decor. Cottages spread throughout the park house luxurious apartments. Hunting trips organised. A very chic ambiance in the restaurant and terrace surrounded by roses; updated classic menu.

BÈZE – 21 Côte-d'Or – **320** L5 – **see Mirebeau-sur-Bèze**

BÉZIERS – 34 Hérault – **339** E8 – **pop. 69 153** – **Built-up area 124 967** – **alt. 17 m** – ✉ **34500** Languedoc-Roussillon-Tarn Gorges 22 **B2**

Paris 758 – Marseille 234 – Montpellier 71 – Perpignan 93

Béziers-Vias: ✆ 04 67 80 99 09, by ③: 12 km.

Office de tourisme, 29, avenue Saint-Saëns ✆ 04 67 76 84 00, Fax 04 67 76 50 80

de Saint-Thomas Route de Pezenas, Northeast: 12 km, ✆ 04 67 39 03 09.

Former St-Nazaire cathedral ★: terrace ★ - Musée du Biterois★ BZ M³ - Jardin St Jacques ★.

Plans on following pages

Mercure without rest
33 av. Camille-St-Saëns – ✆ 04 67 00 19 96 – h5639@accor.com
– Fax 04 67 00 19 98 CY f
58 rm – €102/129 €117/140, €13
◆ New hotel built between the tourist office and the conference centre. Rooms decorated in boat-cabin style: wood panelling, portholes and rounded forms.

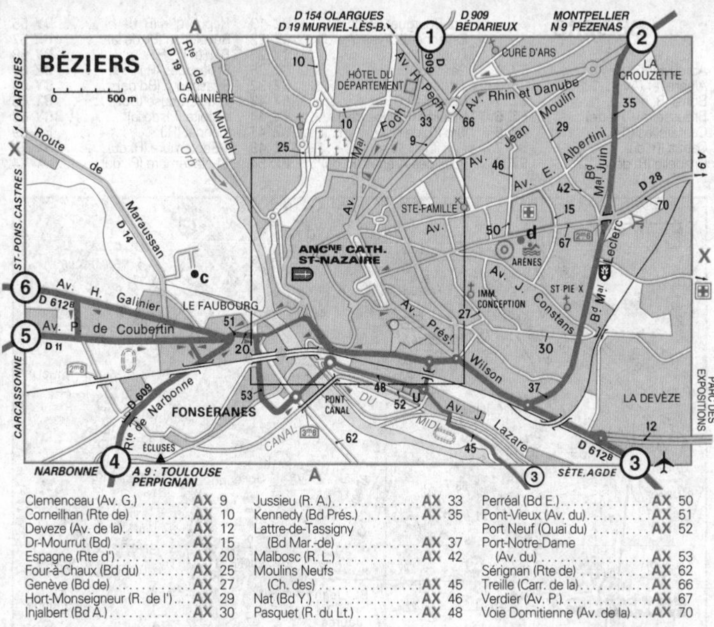

Champ de Mars without rest
17 r. de Metz – ✆ 04 67 28 35 53 – hotel-champdemars@wanadoo.fr – Fax 04 67 28 61 42 CY **v**
10 rm – €32/50 €37/50, €6
◆ Small family hotel in a quiet street away from the town centre. The rooms are of average size, well-equipped and are being gradually redecorated.

Les Jardins du Rebaut without rest
chemin rural 103, rte de Maraussan – ✆ 04 67 28 71 03 – lesjardinsdurebaut@wanadoo.fr – Fax 04 67 28 71 03 – Open 1st March-30 October AX **w**
5 rm – €75 €75/130
◆ This former wine and spirits store house benefits from a garden with a magnificent fig tree. Its new and personalised rooms offer a clear view of the cathedral (the so-called "Syrah" room is the exception).

L'Ambassade (Patrick Olry)
22 bd de Verdun, (opposite the station) – ✆ 04 67 76 06 24 – lambassade-beziers@wanadoo.fr – Fax 04 67 76 74 05 – Closed 12 July-5 August, Sunday and Monday CZ **n**
Rest – Menu €28/95 – Carte €47/94
Spec. Carpaccio de thon rouge de Méditerranée (spring-summer). Tronçon de baudroie et fleur de courgette farcie de brandade (summer). Menu dégustation "Autour du champignon" (season). **Wines** Côtes du Roussillon, Côteaux du Languedoc.
◆ Resolutely modern decoration (light wood panelling, frosted glass), appetising dishes and an exceptional wine list. Extremely popular with locals.

Le Val d'Héry
67 av. Prés.-Wilson – ✆ 04 67 76 56 73 – val-dhery@wanadoo.fr – Fax 04 67 76 56 73 – Closed 15 June-15 July, Sunday and Monday CZ **b**
Rest – Menu €21/42 – Carte €40/66
◆ Near the Plateau des Poètes, a pretty 19C park. Discreet modern decor with paintings by the chef adding a bright touch; modern cuisine that varies with the seasons.

BÉZIERS

Abreuvoir (R. de l') . . . . **BZ** 2
Albert-1er (Av.) . . . . **CY** 3
Bonsi (R. de) . . . . **BZ** 4
Brousse (Av. Pierre) . . . . **BZ** 5
Canterelles (R.) . . . . **BZ** 6
Capus (R. du) . . . . **BZ** 7
Citadelle (R. de la) . . . . **BZ** 9
Drs-Bourguet (R. des) . . . . . . **BZ** 13
Estienne-d'Orves (Av. d') . . . **BZ** 22
Flourens (R.) . . . . **BY** 23
Garibaldi (Pl.) . . . . **CZ** 26
Joffre (Av. Mar.) . . . . **CZ** 32
Massol (R.) . . . . **BZ** 43
Moulins (Rampe des) . . . . **BY** 44
Orb (R. de l') . . . . **BZ** 47
Péri (Pl. G.) . . . . **BYZ** 49
Puits-des-Arènes (R. du) . . . **BZ** 54
République (R. de la) . . . . . . **BY** 55
Révolution (Pl. de la) . . . . **BZ** 57
Riquet (R. P.) . . . . **BY** 58
St-Jacques (R.) . . . . **BZ** 60
Strasbourg (Bd de) . . . . **CY** 64
Tourventouse (Bd) . . . . **BZ** 65
Victoire (Pl. de la) . . . . **BCY** 68
Viennet (R.) . . . . **BZ** 69
4-Septembre (R. du) . . . . **BY** 72
11-Novembre (Pl. du) . . . . . . **CY** 74

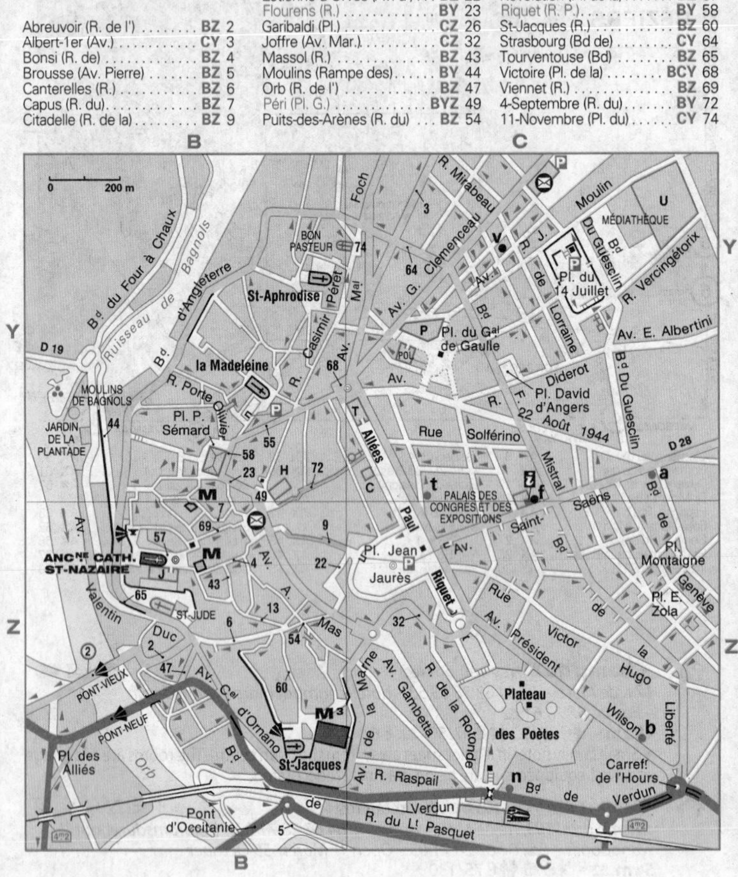

ꭗꭗ **Octopus** (Fabien Lefebvre)

12 r. Boïeldieu – ✆ 04 67 49 90 00 – Fax 04 67 28 06 73 – Closed 1st-8 May, 16 August-4 September, 24 December-6 January, Sunday and Monday CY **t**

Rest – Menu € 21 bi (weekday lunch), € 29/70 – Carte € 44/73

Spec. Langoustines rôties en coque, cardamome, citron vert. Pomme de ris de veau rôtie, jus de carotte et safran. Feuille à feuille croustillant chocolat.

◆ Choice of two modern-style dining rooms and a terrace set in the interior courtyard in which to enjoy the modern, well-presented dishes.

ꭗ **La Table de Marthe**

74 av. St-Saëns – ✆ 04 67 62 68 35 – Fax 04 67 62 68 35 – Closed 20 July-6 August, Sunday and Monday CY **a**

Rest – Carte € 27/55

◆ Rugby shirts and photographs decorate this restaurant appreciated by regular customers for its convivial atmosphere. The food is traditional and made from fresh market produce.

La Maison de Campagne

22 av. Pierre Verdier – ✆ 04 67 30 91 85 – aupauvrejacques@wanadoo.fr – Fax 04 67 30 47 32 – Closed 17 August-3 September, 28 October-3 November, Sunday, Monday and dinner Tuesday-Thursday

Rest – Menu € 40/80

◆ Hacienda-style country house with a large patio-terrace, particularly pleasant for summer dining. Rustic-chic interior, home-style cooking and tapas bar.

via ③ 6 km near A9-Béziers-Est interchange – ✉ 34420 Villeneuve-lès-Béziers

Le Pavillon

rm, rest,

Z.A la Montagnette, rte Valras 1 km – ✆ 04 67 39 40 00 – hotel.pavillon@orange.fr – Fax 04 67 39 39 61 – Closed 25 December-2 January

78 rm – € 65/85 € 65/85, € 8 – ½ P € 55 – **Rest** – Menu € 20/38 – Carte € 24/46

◆ Situated on the outskirts of town, a useful stopover on the way to Spain. Renovated, functional, air-conditioned rooms. Good sports facilities; children's playground. Large dining room serving traditional cuisine and buffet meals.

in Villeneuve-lès-Béziers 7 km by ③, D 612 and D 37 – pop. 3 434 – alt. 6 m – ✉ 34420

Office de tourisme, place de la Fontaine ✆ 04 67 39 48 83

La Chamberte

rm,

r. de la Source – ✆ 04 67 39 84 83 – contact@la-chamberte.com – Closed 1st-15 March and 1st-21 November

5 rm – € 70/78 € 96/98, € 15 – ½ P € 83 – **Table d'hôte** – *(closed Monday dinner) (pre-book)* Menu € 35 bi/53 bi

◆ A Mediterranean garden precedes this former wine cellar. The interior decoration combines Moorish, Andalusian and exotic influences in an attractive manner. Enjoy dishes made with market-fresh ingredients in a spacious, relaxing setting.

in Maraussan 6 km West by D 14 – pop. 2 782 – alt. 38 m – ✉ 34370

Parfums de Garrigues

37 r. de l'Ancienne-Poste – ✆ 04 67 90 33 76 – Fax 04 67 90 33 76 – Closed 14 April-2 May, 25-31 August, autumn half-term holidays, Tuesday and Wednesday

Rest – Menu € 25/55 – Carte € 32/57

◆ Comfortable dining room with southern colours and shady terrace in the interior courtyard of this prettily-restored building. Cuisine with the flavours of the garrigue.

Le Vieux Puits

207 av. de Cazouls – ✆ 04 67 90 05 59 – Fax 04 67 26 60 45 – Closed 2-16 January, Saturday lunch, Sunday dinner and Monday

Rest – Menu € 19/35 – Carte € 23/41

◆ "The Old Well" is named for the well at the entrance to the dining room ,decorated with murals. Pleasant summer terrace set in the interior courtyard and traditional food.

BIARRITZ – 64 Pyrénées-Atlantiques – 342 C4 – pop. 30 055 – alt. 19 m – Casino – ✉ 64200 Atlantic Coast 3 A3

Paris 772 – Bayonne 9 – Bordeaux 190 – Pau 122 – San Sebastián 47

Biarritz-Anglet-Bayonne: ✆ 05 59 43 83 83, 2 km ABX.

✆ 3635 (0,34 €/mn)

Office de tourisme, square d'Ixelles - Javalquinto ✆ 05 59 22 37 00, Fax 05 59 24 14 19

18 de Biarritz 2 avenue Edith Cavell, Northeast: 1 km, ✆ 05 59 03 71 80 ;

9 d'Ilbarritz Bidart Avenue du Château, South: 3 km by D 911, ✆ 05 59 43 81 30 ;

18 d'Arcangues Arcangues Jaureguiborde, Southeast: 8 km, ✆ 05 59 43 10 56.

<★★ from the Perspective - <★ lighthouse and Pointe St-Martin AX - Rocher de la Vierge (Virgin's Rock) ★ - Musée de la mer★.

Plans on following pages

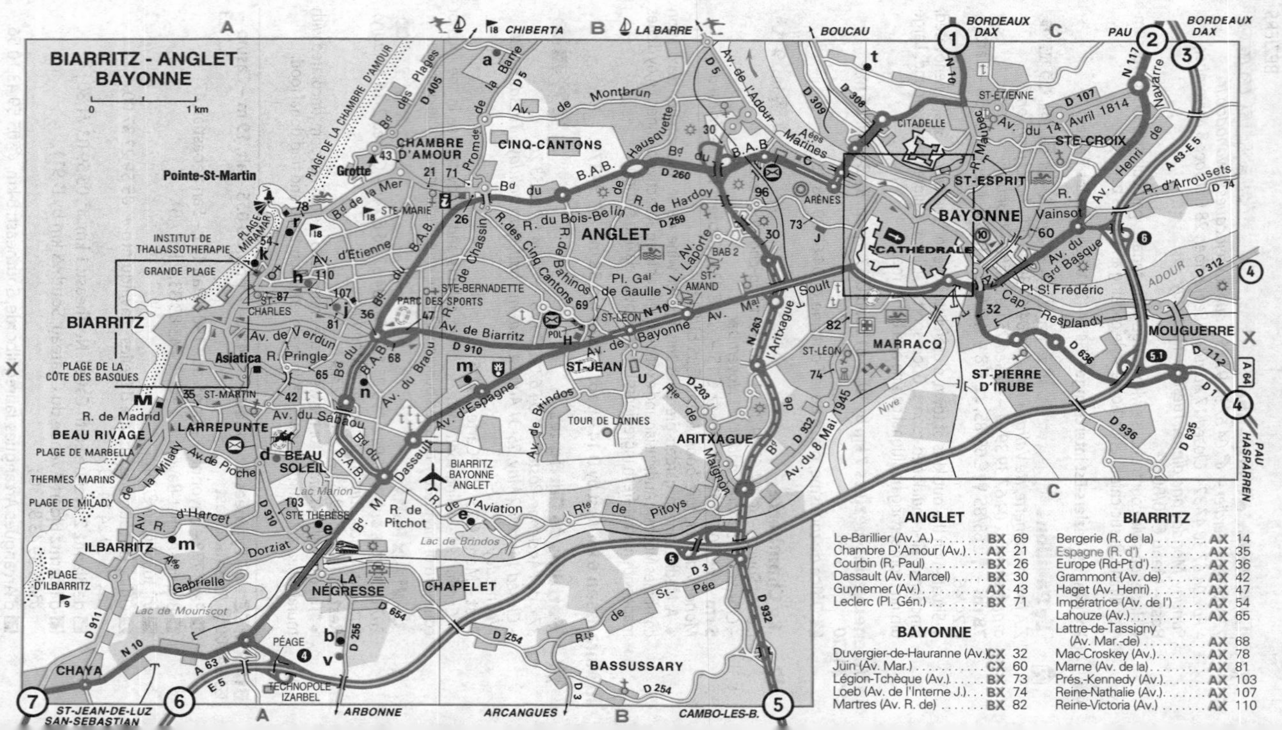
BIARRITZ - ANGLET
BAYONNE
0
1 km
BORDEAUX DAX
PAU
BOUCAU
CHIBERTA
LA BARRE
HASPARREN
CAMBO-LES-B.
ARCANGUES
ARBONNE
ST-JEAN-DE-LUZ
SAN-SEBASTIAN
BIARRITZ
ANGLET
BAYONNE
CINQ-CANTONS
CHAMBRE D'AMOUR
Pointe-St-Martin
ST-ESPRIT
STE-CROIX
CATHÉDRALE
CITADELLE
MARRACQ
ST-PIERRE D'IRUBE
MOUGUERRE
ARITXAGUE
ST-JEAN
BEAU RIVAGE
LARREPUNTE
BEAU SOLEIL
ILBARRITZ
LA NÉGRESSE
CHAPELET
BASSUSSARY
CHAYA
BIARRITZ BAYONNE ANGLET
TECHNOPOLE IZARBEL
ANGLET
Le-Barillier (Av. A.) . . . . BX 69
Chambre D'Amour (Av.) . . . AX 21
Courbin (R. Paul) . . . . BX 26
Dassault (Av. Marcel) . . . . . BX 30
Guynemer (Av.) . . . . AX 43
Leclerc (Pl. Gén.) . . . . BX 71
BAYONNE
Duvergier-de-Hauranne (Av.) CX 32
Juin (Av. Mar.) . . . . CX 60
Légion-Tchèque (Av.) . . . . . BX 73
Loeb (Av. de l'Interne J.) . . . BX 74
Martres (Av. R. de) . . . . BX 82
BIARRITZ
Bergerie (R. de la) . . . . AX 14
Espagne (R. d') . . . . AX 35
Europe (Rd-Pt d') . . . . AX 36
Grammont (Av. de) . . . . AX 42
Haget (Av. Henri) . . . . AX 47
Impératrice (Av. de l') . . . . . AX 54
Lahouze (Av.) . . . . AX 65
Lattre-de-Tassigny (Av. Mar.-de) . . . . AX 68
Mac-Croskey (Av.) . . . . AX 78
Marne (Av. de la) . . . . AX 81
Prés.-Kennedy (Av.) . . . . AX 103
Reine-Nathalie (Av.) . . . . AX 107
Reine-Victoria (Av.) . . . . AX 110

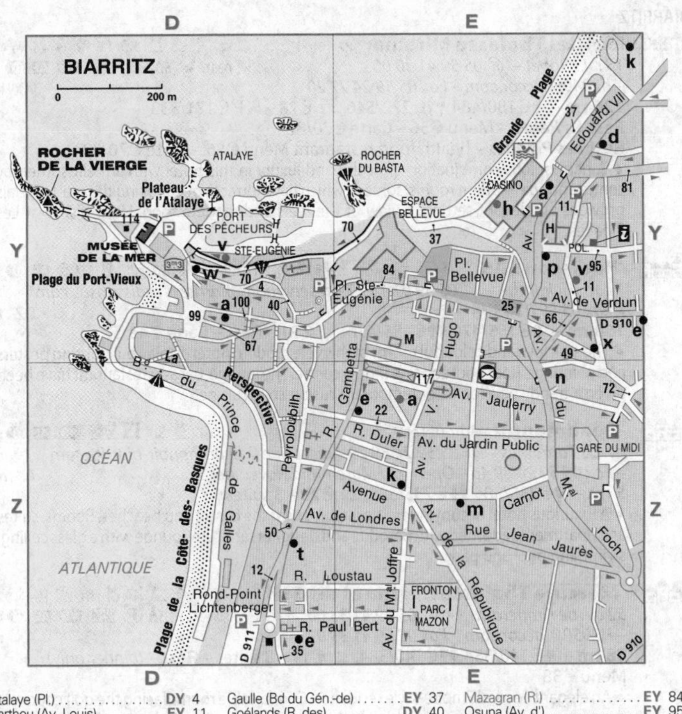

Atalaye (Pl.) .... DY 4
Barthou (Av. Louis) .... EY 11
Beaurivage (Av.) .... DZ 12
Champ-Lacombe (R.) .... EZ 22
Clemenceau (Pl.) .... EY 25
Édouard-VII (Av.) .... EY
Espagne (R. d') .... DZ 35
Foch (Av. du Mar.) .... EZ
Gambetta (R.) .... DEZ
Gaulle (Bd du Gén.-de) .... EY 37
Goélands (R. des) .... DY 40
Helder (R. du) .... EY 49
Hélianthe (Rd-Pt) .... DZ 50
Larralde (R.) .... EY 66
Larre (R. Gaston) .... DY 67
Leclerc (Bd Mar.) .... DEY 70
Libération (Pl. de la) .... EZ 72
Marne (Av. de la) .... EY 81
Mazagran (R.) .... EY 84
Osuna (Av. d') .... EY 95
Port-Vieux (Pl. du) .... DY 99
Port-Vieux (R. du) .... DY 100
Rocher de la Vierge (Espl. du) .... DY 114
Sobradiel (Pl.) .... EZ 117
Verdun (Av. de) .... EY
Victor-Hugo (Av.) .... EYZ

Du Palais rest, **P** VISA AE

1 av. de l'Impératrice – 05 59 41 64 00 – reception@hotel-du-palais.com – Fax 05 59 41 67 99 EY **k**

124 rm – €280/495 €380/570, €42 – 30 suites – ½ P €275/370

Rest *La Villa Eugénie* – *(closed 1st February-19 March, lunch in July-August, Wednesday lunch, Monday and Tuesday)* Menu €120 – Carte €97/145

Rest *La Rotonde* – *(closed February)* Menu (€48), €65 – Carte €60/86

Rest *L'Hippocampe* – poolside restaurant *(open mid April-end October and closed dinner except July-August)* Menu €57 – Carte €68/82

Spec. Rouget en filets poêlés, chipirons, riz crémeux, sauce à l'encre. Blanc de bar, fine crème au vin blanc d'Irouléguy, caviar d'Aquitaine (October to January). Agneau de lait des Pyrénées cuit au sautoir (November to May). **Wines** Irouléguy, Jurançon.

◆ This elegant seaside residence, a gift from Napoleon III to his Empress, is now a luxury hotel. Rooms have Empire furniture. Villa Eugénie offers an attractive, quiet dining room and contemporary food. From La Rotonde, you have a lovely view of the Grande Plage beach. Pool-side restaurant (in season) serving buffets and grills.

Sofitel Thalassa Miramar
13 r. L.-Bobet – 05 59 41 30 00 – h2049@accor.com – Fax 05 59 24 77 20 rest, VISA AX **k**
126 rm – €180/484 €272/546, €28 – ½ P €171/333
Rest *Le Relais* – Menu €56 – Carte €70/82
Rest *Les Piballes* – health food restaurant Menu €56 – Carte €70/82
♦ A harmonious combination of health and luxury in this hotel with a thalassotherapy centre and spa. Modern rooms, some of which have terraces overlooking the sea. Le Relais provides an elegant setting, a view of the reefs and modern food. Light dishes at Les Piballes.

Radisson SAS rm, VISA
1 carr. Hélianthe – 05 59 01 13 13 – reservations.biarritz@radissonsas.com – Fax 05 59 01 13 14 DZ **t**
150 rm – €155/470 €155/470, €21 – **Rest** – Carte €43/52
♦ The spacious and colourful rooms of this very modern hotel display bullfighting posters and paintings. Roof pool and fine fitness centre. The lounge-bar and restaurant have been given a trendy new look. Contemporary, fusion-style cuisine.

Beaumanoir without rest VISA
av. de Tamames – 05 59 24 89 29 – reception@beaumanoir-biarritz.com – Fax 05 59 24 89 46 – Open mid March-mid November AX **n**
5 rm – €235/385 €235/385, €20 – 3 suites
♦ A luxurious hotel occupying former stables near the centre and beaches. Rooms, suites and apartments adorned with Baroque and designer furniture; lounge with a glass ceiling; swimming pool and park.

Mercure Thalassa Regina et du Golf rm, VISA
52 av. de l'Impératrice – 05 59 41 33 00 – H2050@accor.com – Fax 05 59 41 33 99 AX **r**
58 rm – €140/354 €140/384, €19 – 8 suites – **Rest** – *(dinner only)* Menu €38
♦ An elegant Second Empire-style residence. Comfortable rooms facing the golf course or the ocean, reached by gangways that look down on the glass-roofed atrium. The restaurant has attractive maritime decor and a canopied area.

Mercure Plaza Centre without rest VISA
av. Édouard-VII – 05 59 24 74 00 – h5681@accor.com – Fax 05 59 22 22 01 EY **p**
69 rm – €117/235 €130/255, €16
♦ Sympathetic renovation for this hotel with its attractive Art Deco facade facing the beach and casino. Pleasant rooms. Jazz evenings.

Tonic VISA
58 av. Édouard-VII – 05 59 24 58 58 – reservation-biarritz@tonichotel.com – Fax 05 59 24 86 14 EY **d**
63 rm – €135/255 €165/355, €18 – ½ P €140/235
Rest *La Maison Blanche* – Menu (€19) – Carte €49/68
♦ Hotel near the Grande Plage (beach), offering elegant and modern rooms, all equipped with hydromassage baths for an invigorating wake-up! A fashionable colour scheme of beiges and browns in a pleasant modern dining room. Updated cuisine to match.

Édouard VII without rest VISA
21 av. Carnot – 05 59 22 39 80 – contact@hotel-edouardvii.com – Fax 05 59 22 39 71 EZ **k**
18 rm – €78/140 €78/140, €10
♦ The well-maintained rooms in this attractive 18C Biarritz villa offer a number of pleasant personal touches. Friendly service.

Alcyon without rest VISA
8 r. Maison-Suisse – 05 59 22 64 60 – contact@hotel-alcyon-biarritz.com – Fax 05 59 22 64 64 – Closed 1st-15 March EY **x**
15 rm – €75/90 €85/120, €9
♦ This hotel combines the charm of an old building with modern comforts. Contemporary-style lounge, designer breakfast room and elegant, well-renovated rooms.

Windsor
19 Bd du Gén. de Gaulle, (Grande Plage) – 05 59 24 08 52 – hotelwindsor-biarritz@wanadoo.fr – Fax 05 59 24 98 90 – Closed 13 - 30 Nov. EY a
48 rm – €65/225 €65/265, €10 – ½ P €67/137
Rest ***Le Galion*** – *05 59 24 20 32 (closed Sunday dinner from 16 November-29 February, Monday except dinner from 1st July-15 September and Tuesday lunch)*
Menu €30 – Carte €42/58
◆ Rooms with a sea view, facing the town or overlooking a courtyard at this hotel near the Grande Plage. Those renovated are simple and modern in style. Panoramic dining room facing the Atlantic; traditional food focusing on seafood.

Maïtagaria without rest
34 av. Carnot – 05 59 24 26 65 – hotel.maitagaria@wanadoo.fr – Fax 05 59 24 26 30 – Closed 24 November-15 December EZ m
15 rm – €52/60 €59/95, €8
◆ A friendly welcome awaits guests in this regional-style hotel offering functional or more comfortable rooms, most with attractive Art Deco furniture.

Maison Garnier without rest
29 r. Gambetta – 05 59 01 60 70 – maison-garnier@hotel-biarritz.com – Fax 05 59 01 60 80 – Closed 12-26 December, 5-20 January EZ e
7 rm – €90/95 €90/140, €10
◆ This 19C Biarritz mansion is pleasantly decorated in a guest house style. The antique furniture and careful decoration give character to the fairly large rooms.

Marbella
rm,
11 r. Port-Vieux – 05 59 24 04 06 – infos@hotel-marbella.fr – Fax 05 59 24 63 26 – Closed 15 January-15 February, Sunday evening and Monday evening off season, Monday lunch and Tuesday lunch DY a
29 rm – €72/110 €79/156, €12 – ½ P €67/105 – **Rest** – Menu €13 (weekday lunch)/22 – Carte €26/40
◆ A building on a shopping street, near the Rocher de la Vierge and the Musée de la Mer. Somewhat small but pleasant, well-kept rooms. Regional, simple food chalked up on the board every day and served in a rustic setting.

Oxo without rest
38 av. de Verdun – 05 59 24 26 17 – christina@biarritz-hotel.com – Fax 05 59 24 66 08 – **20 rm** – €50/70 €52/73, €7,50 EY e
◆ Complete renovation and a new name (the ***ox***ygen of the Pyrenees meets the ***o***cean) for this hotel on a busy avenue opposite the multi-media library.

Villa Vauréal without rest
14 r. Vauréal – 06 10 11 64 21 – info@villavaureal.com – Fax 05 59 22 64 19 – Closed 5-31 January – **5 rm** – €93/168 €101/176 DZ e
◆ A stone's throw from the Plage des Basques, comfortable villa in a large garden with magnificent trees. Individual touches in the guestrooms (each named after a fruit). Home-made jam.

Villa Le Goëland without rest
coast,
12 plateau de l'Atalaye – 05 59 24 25 76 – info@villagoeland.com – Fax 05 59 22 36 83 – **4 rm** – €130/250 €130/250, €10 DY w
◆ This large villa occupying one of the most attractive sites in Biarritz offers breath-taking views extending from Spain to the Landes coast. Some rooms have a terrace.

Nere-Chocoa without rest
28 r. Larreguy – 06 08 33 84 35 – maryse.cadou@wanadoo.fr – Fax 05 59 41 07 95 – **5 rm** – €65/75 €70/105, €9 AX e
◆ This house surrounded by oak trees has hosted illustrious guests such as Empress Eugénie. Huge, elegant guestrooms, a collection of paintings and a comfortable lounge for musical evenings.

La Ferme de Biarritz without rest
15 r. Harcet – 05 59 23 40 27 – info@fermedebiarritz.com – Closed 7-19 January – **5 rm** – €55/80 €55/80, €8 AX m
◆ A well-restored 17C Basque farmhouse near the beach. The smart, attic rooms (non-smoking) are furnished with antiques. Breakfast in the garden or beside the fire.

XX **Sissinou**

5 av. Mar.-Foch – ✆ 05 59 22 51 50 – restaurant.sissinou@wanadoo.fr
Fax 05 59 22 50 58 – Closed 22 June-7 July, 26 October-6 November, 15 February-2 March, Sunday and Monday except August and lunch in August EZ **n**
Rest – Menu € 53/70
◆ This fashionable restaurant offers relaxed service in a contemporary setting (aubergine bench seats, green walls and designer lighting). Both contemporary and classic dishes available.

XX **Café de la Grande Plage** ← ocean,

1 av. Edouard-VII, (casino) – ✆ 05 59 22 77 88 – casinobiarritz@lucienbarriere.com – Fax 05 59 22 77 99 EY **h**
Rest – Menu € 28 – Carte € 29/43
◆ A little hungry between two games of black-jack? On the ground floor of the casino, Art Deco style brasserie decorated with mosaics. Ideal view over the beach and the surfers.

XX **Plaisir des Mets**

5 r. de Centre – ✆ 05 59 24 34 66 – Closed 17 June-11 July, 17 November-11 December, Monday lunch and Thursday lunch in July-August, Tuesday except dinner in July-August and Wednesday EZ **a**
Rest – Carte € 36/54
◆ This contemporary restaurant serving seasonal cuisine has a refined bistro style with an ivory and chocolate decor and modern paintings.

XX **La Table d' Aranda**

87 av. de la Marne – ✆ 05 59 22 16 04 – Fax 05 59 22 16 04 – Closed 12-19 November, 6 January-4 February, Wednesday lunch and Tuesday in season AX **j**
Rest – Menu (€ 15), € 20 (lunch except Sunday) – Carte approx. € 40
◆ Word-of-mouth has brought a loyal following to this restaurant with a rustic Basque decor within the walls of a former rotisserie. Personalised, inventive cuisine combining sweet and savoury flavours.

X **Philippe**

30 av. du Lac Marion – ✆ 05 59 23 13 12 – lafargue.philippe@hotmail.com – Closed 2 weeks in November, 2 weeks in March, Monday except July-September and Tuesday except dinner in August AX **d**
Rest – *(dinner only) (number of covers limited, pre-book)* Menu € 50/75 – Carte € 30/75
◆ An open-plan kitchen, a wood-fired oven for suckling pig and lamb, inventive cooking and avant-garde decor at this surprising restaurant. Exhibition and sale of contemporary art.

X **Le Clos Basque**

12 r. L.-Barthou – ✆ 05 59 24 24 96 – Fax 05 59 22 34 46 – Closed 23 June-3 July, 27 October-17 November, 23 February-12 March, Sunday dinner except July-August and Monday EY **v**
Rest – *(number of covers limited, pre-book)* Menu € 24
◆ Exposed stone and azulejos give a Spanish air to this little dining room with a friendly atmosphere. Popular summer terrace. Regional specialities.

X **Chez Albert**

Port-des-Pêcheurs – ✆ 05 59 24 43 84 – Fax 05 59 24 20 13 – Closed 24 November-13 December, 5 January-10 February and Wednesday except July-August
Rest – Menu € 40 – Carte € 34/62 DY **v**
◆ Seafood and fish are the main focus at this busy but relaxed restaurant with a fine view of the little fishing port. Very popular terrace in summer.

at Brindos Lake 4 km Southeast – ✉ 64600 Anglet

Château de Brindos rm,

1 allée du Château – ✆ 05 59 23 89 80 – brindos@relaischateaux.com – Fax 05 59 23 89 81 – Closed 17 February-6 March
24 rm – †€ 160/270 ††€ 210/325, ☐ € 25 – 5 suites
Rest – *(closed Sunday dinner and Monday except from May to October)*
Menu € 32 (weekday lunch), € 52/70 – Carte € 59/72 BX **e**
◆ Elegant building, facing a 10-ha lake and ideal for relaxing, offering very spacious bedrooms with luxury bathrooms and lounges adorned with attractive wood panelling. A rotunda-style dining room and tree-shaded terrace by the lake. Refined modern cuisine.

Arbonne road 4 km South via La Négresse and D 255 – ✉ 64200 Biarritz

Le Château du Clair de Lune without rest
48 av. Alan-Seeger – ✆ 05 59 41 53 20 – hotel-clair-de-lune@wanadoo.fr – Fax 05 59 41 53 29 AX **b**
17 rm – †€ 80/96 ††€ 130/155, ☕ € 10
♦ Charming mansion dating from 1902 surrounded by attractive grounds. Elegant rooms, with a more rural decor in the separate lodge - ideal for gazing at the moonlight in Biarritz!

Campagne et Gourmandise
52 av. Alan-Seeger, (Arbonne road) – ✆ 05 59 41 10 11 – Fax 05 59 43 96 16 – Closed Sunday dinner except 13 July-31 August, Monday lunch and Wednesday
Rest – Menu € 45/70 AX **v**
♦ This old farmhouse, surrounded by a large garden facing the Pyrenees, specialises in regional cuisine. Smart country-style interior (attractive fireplace), veranda and pretty terrace.

in Arbonne 7 km South via La Négresse and D 255 – pop. 1 375 – alt. 37 m – ✉ 64210

Laminak without rest
rte de St-Pée – ✆ 05 59 41 95 40 – info@hotel-laminak.com – Fax 05 59 41 87 65 – Closed 15-November
12 rm – †€ 71 ††€ 71, ☕ € 10
♦ 18C farmhouse on the outskirts of this pretty village. Recently decorated rooms with personal touches. Breakfast served in the veranda facing the delightful garden. Swimming pool.

in Arcangues 8 km via La Négresse, D 254 and D 3 – pop. 2 733 – alt. 80 m – ✉ 64200

i Office de tourisme, le bourg ✆ 05 59 43 08 55, Fax 05 59 43 39 16

Les Volets Bleus without rest
chemin Etchegaraya, 2 km south on the old St Pée road – ✆ 607690385 – maisonlesvoletsbleus@wanadoo.fr – Fax 559223971 – Closed January and February
5 rm ☕ – †€ 90/144 ††€ 100/154
♦ Enjoy the peaceful garden and refinement of this Basque villa restored with antique materials. Patina-effect walls, terracotta tiles and traditional quilts in the rooms.

Maison Gastelhur without rest
chemin Gastelhur, 2 km west on secondary road – ✆ 05 59 43 01 46 – miguel.lagrolet@wanadoo.fr – Fax 05 59 43 12 96 – Closed 16 February-10 March
3 rm – †€ 110/130 ††€ 110/130, ☕ € 8
♦ Set in grounds bordering a golf course, this 18C stately home offers peace and quiet. Spacious rooms adorned with family heirlooms and antiques.

Le Moulin d'Alotz (Benoît Sarthou)
south: 3 km by Arbonne road and secondary road – ✆ 05 59 43 04 54 – Closed 24 June-1st July, 20-28 October, 23 December -29 January, Tuesday and Wednesday
Rest – *(number of covers limited, pre-book)* Menu € 55/60 – Carte € 54/64
Spec. Cannelloni de langoustines, andouille béarnaise grillée et crème de maïs. Pigeonneau rôti, poudre réglisse, girolles et petits pois. Confit de tomate aux épices, gâteau frangipane-pistache, crème glacée verveine. **Wines** Irouléguy, Madiran.
♦ Basque mill said to date from 1694. Elegant interior of whitewashed beams and wood panelling. Attractive terrace, flower-filled garden and contemporary cuisine with individual touches.

Auberge d'Achtal
pl. du Fronton , (pedestrian access) – ✆ 05 59 43 05 56 – achtal@wanadoo.fr – Fax 05 59 43 16 98 – Closed 5 January-20 March, Tuesday and Wednesday
Rest – Menu € 28 – Carte € 22/51
♦ This picturesque Basque village is the final resting place of Luis Mariano, prince of the operetta. Rustic interior and shaded terrace at the front of the building. Local dishes.

See also resources at **Anglet**

BIDARRAY – 64 Pyrénées-Atlantiques – 342 D3 – pop. 645 – alt. 110 m – ✉ 64780 Atlantic Coast 3 A3

Paris 799 – Biarritz 37 – Cambo-les-Bains 17 – Pau 127 – St-Jean-Pied-de-Port 21

Ostapé rm, VISA

Chahatoa, 4 km north on D 349 – ✆ 05 59 37 91 91 – contact@ostape.com – Fax 05 59 37 91 92 – Open 20 March-11 November

22 suites – €230/565, € 22 – **Rest** – *(closed Monday lunch and Tuesday lunch)* Menu € 55/68

◆ Splendid Basque-style villas surrounded by a 45 ha park. Spacious, elegant rooms with up-to-date facilities. Swimming pool and fitness room. Regional dishes with a contemporary twist served in an elegant 17C farmhouse.

Barberaenea rest, VISA

pl. de l'Église – ✆ 05 59 37 74 86 – hotel-restaurant-barberaenea@wanadoo.fr – Fax 05 59 37 77 55 – Closed 15 November-15 January

9 rm – €35/61 €35/61, € 6,50 – ½ P € 41/54 – **Rest** – Menu € 20/25 – Carte € 21/29

◆ A simple, authentic and friendly Basque hotel near the pelota wall. Rustic rooms with fine views over the surrounding mountains and valleys. This restaurant is decked out with country furniture and typical regional tablecloths; the dishes are made with fresh local produce.

Auberge Iparla VISA

chemin de l'Église-Bordaberria – ✆ 05 59 37 77 21 – iparla2@wanadoo.fr – Fax 05 59 37 78 84 – Open 15 March-15 November and closed Tuesday and Wednesday except July-August

Rest – Menu € 25 – Carte € 36/45

◆ Café-restaurant on a picturesque village square serving Basque specialities and meat grilled over an open fire. Rustic decor.

BIDART – 64 Pyrénées-Atlantiques – 342 C4 – pop. 4 670 – alt. 40 m – ✉ 64210 Atlantic Coast 3 A3

Paris 778 – Bayonne 17 – Biarritz 7 – Pau 122 – St-Jean-de-Luz 9

Office de tourisme, rue d'Erretegia ✆ 05 59 54 93 85, Fax 05 59 54 70 51

d'Ilbarritz Avenue du Château, North: 3 km by N 10 and D 911, ✆ 05 59 43 81 30.

Ste-Madeleine chapel ※★.

Villa L'Arche without rest Ocean, VISA AE

chemin Camboénéa – ✆ 05 59 51 65 95 – villalarche@wanadoo.fr – Fax 05 59 51 65 99 – Open 16 February-14 November

8 rm – €100/265 €100/265, € 14

◆ Between a quiet residential part of the resort and the ocean shore - a charming villa. The attractive, personalised rooms and pretty garden overlook the waves.

L'Hacienda without rest VISA

50 r. Bassilour, south on the N10, rte Ahetze and minor road: 3 km – ✆ 05 59 54 92 82 – contact@hotel-hacienda.fr – Fax 05 59 26 52 73 – Open 21 March-1st November

14 rm – €115/220 €115/220, € 12

◆ Romanticism and refinement meet in this elegant Spanish-style residence. Themed rooms, deliciously coloured and decorated. Large, flower-filled garden.

Ouessant-Ty without rest VISA

r. Erretegia – ✆ 05 59 54 71 89 – hotel.ouessant-ty@wanadoo.fr – Fax 05 59 47 58 70

12 rm – €67/103 €65/103, € 12

◆ A pleasant, fairly recent hotel which is both centrally located and a stone's throw from the beaches. Large rooms with cane furniture (three family rooms with a small kitchen). Creperie next door.

Irigoian without rest VISA

av. de Biarritz – ✆ 05 59 43 83 00 – irigoian@wanadoo.fr – Fax 05 59 41 19 07

5 rm – €80/110 €80/110, € 8

◆ This 17C farmhouse is situated by the sea and next to a golf course. Tastefully decorated rooms with spacious bathrooms.

Table et Hostellerie des Frères Ibarboure (Jean-Philippe Ibarboure) with rm rm,
chemin de Ttalienea, South by D 810, Ahetze road and secondary road: 4 km – 05 59 54 81 64 – contact@freresibarboure.com – Fax 05 59 54 75 65 – Closed 15 November-7 December and 5-20 January
12 rm – €120/160 €130/230, €14
Rest – *(closed Wednesday from 7 September to 30 June, Sunday dinner except August and Monday lunch July-beg. September)* Menu €37 (weekday lunch), €47/69 – Carte €60/79
Spec. Face à face de tourteau, carpaccio de bar et caviar d'Aquitaine (May to October). Tourteau en craquant, asperges vertes, sauce homardine. Foie chaud de canard aux agrumes. **Wines** Jurançon sec, Irouléguy.
♦ This Basque residence stands at the heart of a pleasant park. Cosy dining rooms, a garden terrace, and cuisine from the south-west. Spacious, individually furnished guestrooms.

BIEF – **25 Doubs** – **321** K3 – **see Villars-sous-Dampjoux**

BIELLE – **64 Pyrénées-Atlantiques** – **342** J6 – **pop. 436** – **alt. 448 m** – ✉ **64260**
Atlantic Coast 3 **B3**
Paris 803 – Laruns 9 – Lourdes 43 – Oloron-Ste-Marie 26 – Pau 31

L'Ayguelade rest,
Pau road: 1 km – 05 59 82 60 06 – hotel.ayguelade@wanadoo.fr – Fax 05 59 82 61 17 – Closed January, Tuesday and Wednesday except July-August
10 rm – €46 €46/56, €7 – ½ P €46/56 – **Rest** – Menu €16 (weekday lunch), €20/38 – Carte €24/44
♦ A Bearnaise house and annexe along an affluent of the Ossau mountain stream (fishing). Most of the small rooms are modern, colourful and have been renovated. Regional food served under the new veranda in fine weather, or in a rustic dining room.

BIESHEIM – **68 Haut-Rhin** – **315** J8 – **see Neuf-Brisach**

BIGNAN – **56 Morbihan** – **308** O7 – **see Locminé**

BILLÈRE – **64 Pyrénées-Atlantiques** – **342** J5 – **see Pau**

BILLIERS – **56 Morbihan** – **308** Q9 – **pop. 705** – **alt. 20 m** – ✉ **56190** 10 **C3**
Paris 461 – La Baule 42 – Nantes 87 – Redon 39 – La Roche-Bernard 17 – Vannes 28

Domaine de Rochevilaine < the coast,
at la Pointe de Pen Lan, 2 km by D 5 – rest,
02 97 41 61 61 – rochevilaine@relaischateaux.com – Fax 02 97 41 44 85
31 rm – €141/416 €141/416, €19 – 4 suites – ½ P €138/413
Rest – Menu €39 (weekday lunch), €68/100 – Carte €63/76
Spec. Huîtres creuses cuisinées en coquille au beurre de baratte. Bar de ligne en croûte de sel, béarnaise de fenouil. Kouign-amann, glace au caramel salé.
♦ A hamlet of attractive Breton houses and a balneotherapy centre anchored to the far end of a rocky point facing the ocean. Spacious and personalised rooms. Attractive rustic dining room (wainscoting, mirrors, red fabric) looking seawards. Updated classic fare.

Les Glycines without rest
17 pl. de l'Église – 06 11 86 07 52 – grimaud.veronique56@wanadoo.fr – Fax 02 97 45 69 68 – **5 rm** – €82/102 €90/110
♦ Blue and white house on the village square. Spruce, colourful interior (piano, knick-knacks, books and paintings). Children's play area.

BIOT – **06 Alpes-Maritimes** – **341** D6 – **pop. 7 395** – **alt. 80 m** – ✉ **06410**
French Riviera 42 **E2**
Paris 910 – Antibes 6 – Cagnes-sur-Mer 9 – Cannes 17 – Grasse 20 – Nice 21 – Vence 18
Office de tourisme, 46, r. Saint-Sébastien 04 93 65 78 00, Fax 04 93 65 78 04
de Biot Avenue Michard Pelissier, South: 1 km, 04 93 65 08 48.
Musée national Fernand Léger★★ - Rosaire altar-piece ★ in the church.

Domaine du Jas without rest

625 rte de la Mer, D4 – ✆ 04 93 65 50 50 – domaine-du-jas@wanadoo.fr – Fax 04 93 65 02 01 – Open 16 March-4 January – **19 rm** – †€ 90/125 ††€ 110/235, ☕ € 15

◆ Several modern villas in a local style scattered around a pool. Pretty Provence-style rooms with balconies or terraces; some have views over Biot.

Les Terraillers (Michaël Fulci)

11 rte Chemin-Neuf, at the foot of the village – ✆ 04 93 65 01 59 – lesterraillers@tiscali.fr – Fax 04 93 65 13 78 – Closed 23 October-30 November, Wednesday and Thursday

Rest – Menu € 39 (weekday lunch), € 62/110 – Carte € 86/120

Spec. Fleurs de courgettes farcies. Loup sauvage en croûte de sel, sauce à l'aneth. Banane rôtie en injection de chocolat, glace rhum-raisin. **Wines** Vin de pays des Alpes-Maritimes, Côtes de Provence.

◆ A 16C pottery workshop, the kiln has been transformed into a lounge. Lovely dining room with vaults, stone, exposed beams and fresh flowers. Menu with a Southern touch.

Le Jarrier (Sébastien Broda)

in the village, 30 passage Bourgade – ✆ 04 93 65 11 68 – info@lejarrier.com – Fax 04 93 65 50 03 – Closed Monday lunch, Saturday lunch and Sunday

Rest – Menu (€ 19), € 23 (weekday lunch), € 30/59 – Carte € 42/66

Spec. Emietté de tourteau, guacamole, émulsion d'orange. Pigeonneau rôti, cocotte de fruits de saiason, jus simple et aceto. Soufflé praliné-noisette, glace caramel.

◆ Hidden behind the façade of this discreet country house is a chic and trendy restaurant with contemporary decor and a lounge-style ambience. Refined cuisine rich in flavours.

Chez Odile

au village – ✆ 04 93 65 15 63 – Closed 1st December-31 January, lunch July-August, Wednesday dinner and Thursday off season – **Rest** – Menu € 30

◆ This attractive countrified inn is an institution in the neighbourhood. The owner, Odile, is friendly and enthusiastic, announcing the regional menu at your table.

BIOULE – 82 Tarn-et-Garonne – 337 F7 – pop. 845 – alt. 84 m – ✉ 82800 28 B2

▶ Paris 613 – Toulouse 75 – Montauban 22 – Cahors 53 – Moissac 60

Les Boissières

Caussade road – ✆ 05 63 24 50 02 – Fax 05 63 24 60 80 – Closed 10-22 August, 27 October-7 November, 9-20 February, Saturday lunch, Sunday dinner and Monday

10 rm – †€ 70/110 ††€ 70/110, ☕ € 9 – ½ P € 110/115

Rest – Menu € 22 (weekday lunch), € 33/50 – Carte € 38/40

◆ Hotel comprised of a 19C manor house and its red brick stables, set in parkland. Rooms in rustic and modern styles; dining room and pergola for fine weather. Up-to-date dishes.

BIRIATOU – 64 Pyrénées-Atlantiques – 342 B4 – see Hendaye

BIRKENWALD – 67 Bas-Rhin – 315 I5 – pop. 253 – alt. 295 m – ✉ 67440

▶ Paris 461 – Molsheim 23 – Saverne 12 – Strasbourg 34 1 A1

Au Chasseur

7 r. de l'Église – ✆ 03 88 70 61 32 – contact@chasseurbirkenwald.com – Fax 03 88 70 66 02 – Closed 6 January-5 February

23 rm – †€ 65 ††€ 86, ☕ € 14 – 3 suites – ½ P € 70/83 – **Rest** – *(closed Tuesday lunch, Thursday lunch and Monday)* Menu (€ 12), € 15 (weekday lunch), € 32/65 – Carte € 35/51

◆ The recently renovated rooms in this characterful inn are comfortable and attractively appointed. Some offer views of the Vosges. Elegant, classic regional restaurant adorned with attractive larch and burr wood panelling.

BISCARROSSE – 40 Landes – 335 E8 – pop. 9 281 – alt. 22 m – Casino – ✉ 40600

Atlantic Coast 3 B2

▶ Paris 656 – Arcachon 40 – Bayonne 128 – Bordeaux 74 – Dax 91 – Mont-de-Marsan 84

Office de tourisme, 55, pl. Georges Dufau ✆ 05 58 78 20 96, Fax 05 58 78 23 65

de Biscarrosse Route d'Ispe, East: 9 km by D 83 and D 305, ✆ 05 58 09 84 93.

La Fontaine Marsan

pl. Marsan – ✆ 05 58 82 81 29 – fontaine.marsan@wanadoo.fr – Closed Sunday dinner and Monday except July-August

Rest – Menu € 15 (weekday lunch), € 20/40 – Carte € 33/46

◆ Bright dining room with an unusual collection of miniature tricycles. Traditional, bistro-style food with a regional touch.

in Ispe 6 km North by D 652 and D 305 – ✉ 40600 Biscarosse

La Caravelle

– ✆ 05 58 09 82 67 – lacaravelle.40@wanadoo.fr – Fax 05 58 09 82 18 – Open mid February-31 October

15 rm (½ board only in season) – †€ 48 ††€ 67/102, ☕ € 7 – ½ P € 61/71

Rest – *(closed Monday lunch and Tuesday lunch except July-August)*
Menu € 16/39 – Carte € 21/56

◆ All the rooms in this hotel overlook the lake. Some have recently been renovated and those on the ground floor of the annexe are surrounded by greenery. "Holiday" atmosphere in the dining room-veranda and a pleasant shady terrace.

at the Golf 7 km Northwest by D 652 and D 305

Le Parcours Gourmand

av. du Golf – ✆ 05 58 09 84 84 – golfdebiscarrosse@wanadoo.fr – Fax 05 58 09 84 50 – Closed 7January-12 February

Rest – Menu € 35/75 – Carte € 53/72

◆ Classic menu featuring local produce in this restaurant among pines on the golf course. Elegant interior and terrace overlooking the greens.

BITCHE – 57 Moselle – 307 P4 – pop. 5 752 – alt. 300 m – ✉ 57230

Alsace-Lorraine 27 **D1**

Paris 438 – Haguenau 43 – Sarrebourg 62 – Sarreguemines 33 – Saverne 51 – Strasbourg 72

Office de tourisme, 4, rue du glacis du Château ✆ 03 87 06 16 16, Fax 03 87 06 16 17

Holigest Golf de Bitche 2 rue des Prés, East: 1 km by D 662, ✆ 03 87 96 15 30.

Citadel★ - Ligne Maginot: Heavy work of Simserhof★ West: 4 km.

Le Strasbourg with rm

24 r. Col-Teyssier – ✆ 03 87 96 00 44 – le-strasbourg@wanadoo.fr – Fax 03 87 96 11 57 – Closed 9-24 February

10 rm – †€ 48/76 ††€ 53/90, ☕ € 10 – **Rest** – *(closed Sunday dinner, Tuesday lunch and Monday)* Menu € 23/54 – Carte € 39/53

◆ In the town centre this traditional style establishment serves contemporary cuisine in a spacious dining room with a new, Art deco inspired look. Smart rooms decorated with different themes: Africa, Asia, Provence, etc.

La Tour

3 r. de la Gare – ✆ 03 87 96 29 25 – restaurant.la.tour@wanadoo.fr – Fax 03 87 96 02 61 – Closed 18 February-4 March, Tuesday dinner and Monday

Rest – Menu € 24/55 bi – Carte € 29/52

◆ Between the station and town centre, a large building with a tower. Belle Epoque-style decor for the three attractive dining rooms.

BIZE-MINERVOIS – 11 Aude – 344 I3 – pop. 872 – alt. 58 m – ✉ 11120 22 B2

Paris 792 – Béziers 33 – Carcassonne 49 – Narbonne 22 – St-Pons-de-Thomières 33

La Bastide Cabezac

au Hameau de Cabezac, South: 3 km on D 5 – ✆ 04 68 46 66 10 – contact@labastidecabezac.com – Fax 04 68 46 66 29 – Closed 23 November-15 December, 16-28 February, lunch Monday to Wednesday in season, Saturday lunch, Sunday dinner and Monday from 16 September to 14 April

12 rm – †€ 80/95 ††€ 80/130, ☕ € 10 – ½ P € 75/90 – **Rest** – Menu (€ 16), € 25/75 – Carte € 50/71

◆ An 18C post house in the heart of a hamlet. The refined setting, regional-style furniture and warm colours make this a pleasant place to stay. Elegant restaurant offering local wines and contemporary southern dishes.

BLAESHEIM – 67 Bas-Rhin – 315 J5 – see Strasbourg

BLAGNAC – 31 Haute-Garonne – 343 G3 – see Toulouse

BLAINVILLE-SUR-MER – 50 Manche – 303 C5 – pop. 1 483 – alt. 26 m – ✉ 50560

Paris 347 – Caen 116 – Saint-Lô 41 – Saint Helier 56 – Granville 36 — 32 **A2**

Syndicat d'initiative, place de la Marine ✆ 02 33 07 90 89, Fax 02 33 47 97 93

XX **Le Mascaret** with rm — rm, VISA MC AE

1 r. de Bas – ✆ 02 33 45 86 09 – le.mascaret@wanadoo.fr – Fax 02 33 07 90 01 – Closed 23 November-5 December and 2-28 January

5 rm – †€ 95/115 ††€ 115/165, ☕ € 10 – ½ P € 120/150 – **Rest** – *(closed Sunday dinner and Wednesday dinner except 15 July-30 August and Monday)* Menu (€ 25), € 29/69 – Carte € 58/85

◆ 18C mansion with courtyard and herb garden. Inventive cuisine to savour in a colourful, plush and intimate setting. Original, baroque-style decor in the rooms (contrasting patterns, pedestal baths); relaxation area.

LE BLANC – 36 Indre – 323 C7 – pop. 6 998 – alt. 85 m – ✉ 36300

Dordogne-Berry-Limousin — 11 **B3**

Paris 326 – Bellac 62 – Châteauroux 61 – Châtellerault 52 – Poitiers 62

Office de tourisme, pl. de la Libération ✆ 02 54 37 05 13, Fax 02 54 37 31 93

XX **Le Cygne** — AC VISA MC

8 av. Gambetta – ✆ 02 54 28 71 63 – Closed 16 June-9 July, 24 August-3 September, 2-25 January, Sunday dinner, Monday and Tuesday

Rest – *(number of covers limited, pre-book)* Menu € 19/60 – Carte € 31/84

◆ Near the church renowned for its miraculous cures, a pleasant restaurant with well-laid tables. Modern cuisine that varies with the market produce available.

LE BLANC-MESNIL – 93 Seine-Saint-Denis – 305 F7 – 101 17 – see Paris, Area

BLANGY-SUR-BRESLE – 76 Seine-Maritime – 304 J2 – pop. 3 405 – alt. 70 m – ✉ 76340

33 **D1**

Paris 156 – Abbeville 29 – Amiens 56 – Dieppe 55 – Neufchâtel-en-Bray 31 – Le Tréport 26

Syndicat d'initiative, 1, rue Checkroun ✆ 02 35 93 52 48, Fax 02 35 94 06 14

X **Les Pieds dans le Plat** — AC VISA MC AE

27 r. St-Denis – ✆ 02 35 93 38 36 – Fax 02 35 93 43 64 – Closed February holidays, Thursday dinner and Sunday dinner from September to May and Monday

Rest – Menu € 16 (weekdays)/30 – Carte € 25/44

◆ Smart and light dining room brightened with paintings by a local artist and unusual glass flowers. Service with a smile and local, generous, well-made cuisine.

BLANQUEFORT – 33 Gironde – 335 H5 – see Bordeaux

BLENDECQUES – 62 Pas-de-Calais – 301 G3 – see St-Omer

BLÉNEAU – 89 Yonne – 319 A5 – pop. 1 459 – alt. 200 m – ✉ 89220 — 7 **A1**

Paris 156 – Auxerre 56 – Clamecy 59 – Gien 30 – Montargis 42

Syndicat d'initiative, 2, rue Aristide Briand ✆ 03 86 74 82 28, Fax 03 86 74 82 28

Château de St Fargeau★★ **G. Burgundy-Jura.**

Blanche de Castille — P VISA MC AE

17 r. d'Orléans – ✆ 03 86 74 92 63 – daniel.gaspard@wanadoo.fr – Fax 03 86 74 94 43 – Closed Sunday evening

12 rm – †€ 45 ††€ 52/65, ☕ € 8,50 – 1 suite – ½ P € 55

Rest – *(closed 8-21 September, 31 December-18 January, Sunday and Thursday)* Menu € 15 (weekdays)/25 – Carte € 20/34

◆ A family-run hotel in a former post house with well-kept rooms; each one has a girl's name. Those on the top floor have sloping roofs. A plush restaurant and a terrace on the inner courtyard, serving updated fare.

Auberge du Point du Jour
pl. de la Mairie – ✆ 03 86 74 94 38 – auberge-point-du-jour@orange.fr – Fax 03 86 74 85 92 – Closed 1st-8 January, Sunday dinner, Monday and Tuesday
Rest – Menu € 17 (weekday lunch), € 24/49 – Carte € 35/58
♦ Exposed beams, woodwork and fresh flowers set the welcoming scene in this small establishment. Traditional cuisine with a regional twist.

BLÉNOD-LÈS-PONT-À-MOUSSON – 54 Meurthe-et-Moselle – 307 H5 – see Pont-à-Mousson

BLÉRÉ – 37 Indre-et-Loire – 317 O5 – pop. 4 576 – alt. 59 m – ✉ 37150
Châteaux of the Loire 11 **A1**

Paris 234 – Blois 48 – Château-Renault 36 – Loches 25 – Montrichard 16 – Tours 27

Office de tourisme, 8, rue Jean-Jacques Rousseau ✆ 02 47 57 93 00, Fax 02 47 57 93 00

Cheval Blanc rest,
pl. de l'Église – ✆ 02 47 30 30 14 – le.cheval.blanc.blere@wanadoo.fr – Fax 02 47 23 52 80 – Closed 1st January-14 February
12 rm – €59/61 €62/65, ☕ €9 – ½ P €82/85 – **Rest** – *(closed Sunday dinner except July-August, Friday lunch and Monday) (pre-book)* Menu (€22), €43/62 – Carte €53/58
♦ A 17C residence whose rooms mostly overlook a peaceful flower-decked courtyard. Pool and garden. Pleasant restaurant with a rustic style dining room to the rear and a brighter area at the front. Classic cooking.

BLÉRIOT-PLAGE – 62 Pas-de-Calais – 301 E2 – see Calais

BLESLE – 43 Haute-Loire – 331 B2 – pop. 660 – alt. 520 m – ✉ 43450
Auvergne 5 **B3**

Paris 484 – Aurillac 92 – Brioude 23 – Issoire 39 – Murat 45 – St-Flour 39

Office de tourisme, place de l'Église ✆ 04 71 76 26 90, Fax 04 71 76 28 17

St-Pierre church ★.

La Bougnate rm,
pl. Vallat – ✆ 04 71 76 29 30 – contact@labougnate.com – Fax 04 71 76 29 39 – Closed December-January and Monday from October to March
8 rm – €55/90 €55/90, ☕ €9 – ½ P €70 – **Rest** – Menu €19/31 – Carte €27/36
♦ This peaceful attractive inn is located in one of the village's houses. Smart simple rooms; those in the small tower are more picturesque. Craft shop. Pretty, rustic interior, Aubrac beef specialities and a fine wine list.

BLIENSCHWILLER – 67 Bas-Rhin – 315 I6 – pop. 288 – alt. 230 m – ✉ 67650

Paris 504 – Barr 51 – Erstein 26 – Obernai 19 – Sélestat 11 – Strasbourg 47

Syndicat d'initiative, 4, rue du Winzenberg ✆ 03 88 92 40 16, Fax 03 88 92 40 16 2 **C1**

Winzenberg without rest
58 rte des Vins – ✆ 03 88 92 62 77 – winzenberg@wanadoo.fr – Fax 03 88 92 45 22 – Closed 24 December-3 January and 11 February-9 March
13 rm – €42/45 €45/53, ☕ €7
♦ This family-run hotel, in a former winegrower's home, has character with its flower-filled, pink facade, pretty inner courtyard and stylish rooms (painted wooden furniture).

Le Pressoir de Bacchus
50 rte des Vins – ✆ 03 88 92 43 01 – lepressoirdebacchus@wanadoo.fr – Closed 30 June-17 July, 23 February-11 March, Wednesday except dinner from April to December and Tuesday
Rest – Menu (€15), €25/60 bi – Carte €30/43
♦ Simple and well-kept setting combining Alsatian style and bistro atmosphere. Regional food and wine exclusively from the village. Warm welcome.

BLOIS P – 41 Loir-et-Cher – **318** E6 – **pop. 49 171** – **Built-up area 116 544** – **alt. 73 m** – ✉ **41000** **Châteaux of the Loire** 11 **A1**

Paris 182 – Le Mans 111 – Orléans 61 – Tours 66

Office de tourisme, 23, place du Château ✆ 02 54 90 41 41, Fax 02 54 90 41 48

du Château de Cheverny Cheverny La Rousselière, by Cheverny road: 15 km, ✆ 02 54 79 24 70.

Château★★★: musée des Beaux-Arts★ - Old Blois★: St-Nicolas church ★ - Courtyard with galleries★ of the Hôtel d'Alluye YZ **E** - Jardins de l'Evêché ≤★ - Jardin des simples et des fleurs royales ≤★ **L** - Maison de la Magie Robert-Houdin★.

Plan on next page

Mercure Centre

28 quai St-Jean – ✆ 02 54 56 66 66 – h1621@accor.com – Fax 02 54 56 67 00 Y **f**

96 rm – †€ 95 ††€ 113/120, ☕ € 11,50 – **Rest** – Menu € 23/27 – Carte € 30/40

◆ Practical, modern rooms, some of which are reached by a gangway that leads into a lounge bar. View of the Loire from some rooms. The bright dining room overlooks the Loire. Interesting selection of wines by the glass.

Holiday Inn Garden Court

rm,

26 av. Maunoury – ✆ 02 54 55 44 88 – holiblois@wanadoo.fr – Fax 02 54 74 57 97 Y **t**

78 rm – †€ 78/98 ††€ 78/98, ☕ € 10 – **Rest** – *(closed Saturday lunch, Sunday lunch and lunch on public holidays)* Menu € 18/27 – Carte € 29/38

◆ This hotel is slightly outside the town centre but near the corn market (now a concert and exhibition hall). Well equipped, spacious rooms. Winter garden-style restaurant. Indoor terrace serving grilled meat and salads in summer.

Anne de Bretagne without rest

31 av. J.-Laigret – ✆ 02 54 78 05 38 – annedebretagne@free.fr – Fax 02 54 74 37 79 – Closed 5 January-8 February – **27 rm** – †€ 46/51 ††€ 54/59, ☕ € 7 Z **k**

◆ This family establishment on a tree lined square near the château is well worth the stay: cosy sitting room, simple, brightly decorated rooms and summer breakfast terrace.

Monarque

61 r. Porte-Chartraine – ✆ 02 54 78 02 35 – lemonarque@free.fr – Fax 02 54 74 82 76 – Closed 8 December-6 January Y **a**

22 rm – †€ 38/57 ††€ 55/57, ☕ € 6,50 – ½ P € 50 – **Rest** – *(closed Mon. from Oct. to Mar.)* Menu € 25/28 – Carte € 16/29

◆ This 19C building, home to a welcoming hotel, is a few minutes from the pedestrian streets. All the small, well-kept, tasteful rooms are air-conditioned. A central well of light and a few works of art adorn this restaurant that serves modern cuisine.

Ibis without rest

3 r. Porte-Côté – ✆ 02 54 74 01 17 – H0920@accor.com – Fax 02 54 74 85 69

56 rm – †€ 52/71 ††€ 52/71, ☕ € 7,50 Z **x**

◆ A central address combining the style of an old private residence (mosaic in the hall, stucco, mouldings) and the functionality of renovated and well-soundproofed rooms.

Le Plessis without rest

195 r. Albert-1er – ✆ 02 54 43 80 08 – leplessisblois@wanadoo.fr – Fax 02 54 43 95 24 – **5 rm** ☕ – †€ 100/120 ††€ 110/130 X **e**

◆ A stylishly converted winegrowing property: reading room and brunch-style breakfasts in the main 18C house, while elegant bedrooms are in the former wine press.

L'Orangerie du Château (Jean-Marc Molveaux)

1 av. J.-Laigret – ✆ 02 54 78 05 36 – contact@orangerie-du-chateau.fr – Fax 02 54 78 22 78 – Closed 18-24 August, 3-9 November, 15 February-15 March, Monday lunch from May to October, Tuesday dinner from November to April, Sunday dinner and Wednesday

Rest – Menu € 34 (except Saturday dinner)/72 – Carte € 73/93 Z **e**

Spec. Huîtres spéciales, tourteau, chou-fleur et foie gras cru. Selle et carré d'agneau rôtis sur tranche d'aubergine confite (April to October). "Atout framboise" (June to September). **Wines** Cour-Cheverny, Touraine.

◆ A handsome outbuilding of the 15C château and a terrace with a clear view of Francois I's noble abode. Contemporary cuisine. Bright refined dining room.

BLOIS

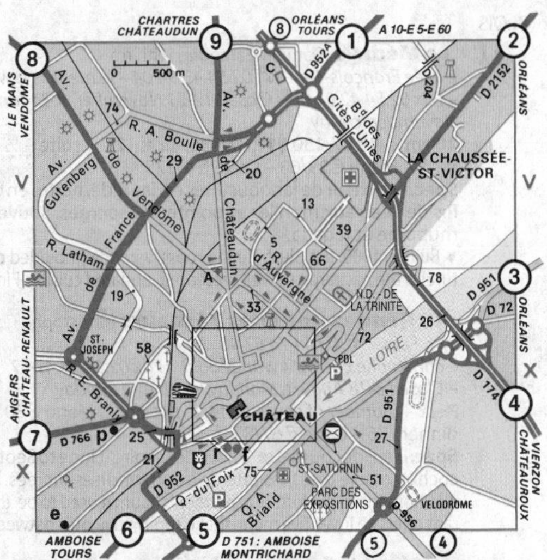

CHARTRES CHÂTEAUDUN
ORLÉANS TOURS
A 10-E 5-E 60
LE MANS VENDÔME
ORLÉANS
LA CHAUSSÉE-ST-VICTOR
N.D.-DE LA TRINITÉ
LOIRE
CHÂTEAU
ST-SATURNIN
PARC DES EXPOSITIONS
VELODROME
ANGERS CHÂTEAU-RENAULT
AMBOISE TOURS
D 751 : AMBOISE MONTRICHARD
VIERZON CHÂTEAUROUX
ST-JOSEPH
R. A. Boulle
Av. de Vendôme
Av. de France
Av. Gutenberg
R. Latham
R. d'Auvergne
Av. de Châteaudun
Bd des Cités Unies
Q. du Foix
Q. A. Briand

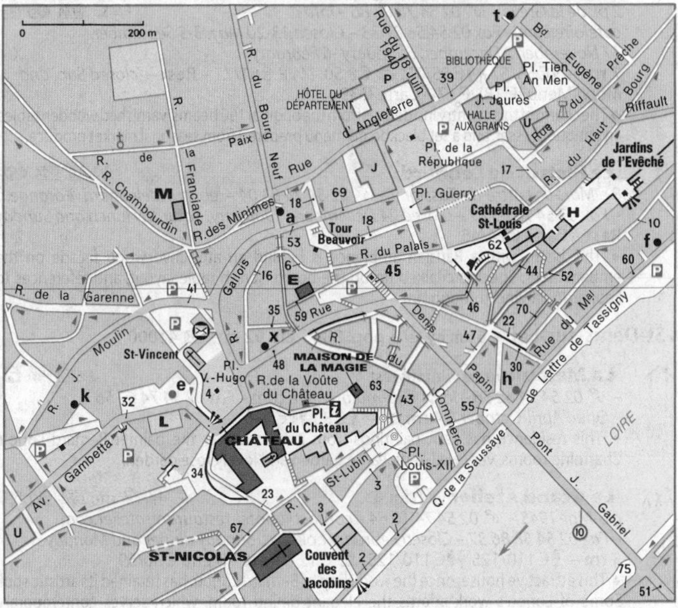

XXX **Le Médicis** (Damien Garanger) with rm

2 allée François-1er – 02 54 43 94 04 – le.medicis@wanadoo.fr – Fax 02 54 42 04 05 – Closed 12-21 November, 8-31 January, Sunday dinner from November to May X **p**

10 rm – €87/130 €87/130, €12 – 1 suite – ½ P €87

Rest – Menu €29/68 – Carte €47/75

Spec. Fraîcheur de langoustines et daurade, huître en gelée et caviar d'Aquitaine. Ris de veau aux morilles et pointes d'asperges. Souvenir sucré d'enfance, fraise, rhubarbe et tagada.

◆ Built in 1900, the plush dining room/veranda (moulded ceilings, Second Empire furniture) is the backdrop to well presented, updated cuisine. Fine wine list. Stylish bedrooms.

X **Au Rendez-vous des Pêcheurs** (Christophe Cosme)

27 r. Foix – 02 54 74 67 48 – christophe.cosme@wanadoo.fr – Fax 02 54 74 47 67 – Closed 3-18 August, Monday lunch and Sunday X **r**

Rest – *(number of covers limited, pre-book)* Menu €30 (except Saturday dinner)/76 – Carte €67/87

Spec. Fleur de courgette "Vallée de la Loire" (June to September). Anguille au pied de cochon et foie gras. Assiette de gourmandises sucrées. **Wines** Jasnières, Touraine.

◆ In homage to the former fishermen's haunt it used to be, this friendly bistro-style restaurant offers an inventive menu that happily navigates between land and sea.

X **Côté Loire " Auberge Ligérienne"** with rm

2 pl. de la Gréve – 02 54 78 07 86 – info@coteloire.com – Fax 02 54 56 87 33 – Closed 13-20 May, 3-9 September, 17 November-2 December, 6 January -6 February X **f**

7 rm – €55/57 €55/75, €8,50 – ½ P €61/71 – **Rest** – *(closed Sun. and Mon.)* Menu (€18), €27 – Carte €39

◆ The charm of this country inn derives from the original 16C beams, varnished wooden tables, an antique dresser, and a set blackboard menu prepared from seasonal market produce.

X **Le Bistrot de Léonard**

8 r. Mar.-de Lattre-de-Tassigny – 02 54 74 83 04 – lebistrotdeleonard@orange.fr – Fax 02 54 74 85 87 – Closed 24 December-1st January, Saturday lunch and Sunday

Rest – Carte €24/46 Z **h**

◆ This bistro with a Parisian ambience is behind an attractive wood façade on the embankment. Specials chalked up on the board, stylish table layout, and references to Leonardo da Vinci throughout.

in St-Denis-sur-Loire 6 km by ② – pop. 884 – alt. 92 m – ✉ 41000

La Malouinière without rest

– 02 54 74 62 56 – infos@la-malouiniere.com – Fax 02 54 74 62 56 – Open April-October – **4 rm** – €80 €130

◆ This residence has kept paintings from its first owner the painter Bernard Lorjou. Charming rooms, very well-kept. Large garden and lovely rose garden.

XXX **Le Grand Atelier** with rm

r. 8-Mai-1945 – 02 54 74 10 64 – contact@hotel-restaurant-atelier.com – Fax 02 54 58 86 37 – Closed February holidays, Sunday dinner and Monday

5 rm – €110/125 €110/125, €12 – **Rest** – Menu €30/59

◆ This attractive house, once the workshop of Bernard Lorjou, has retained its artistic soul. Some of Lorjou's work adorns the elegant dining room, which serves contemporary cuisine. Terrace. Quite cosy rooms.

in Molineuf 9 km by ⑦ – pop. 801 – alt. 115 m – ✉ 41190

XX **Poste**

11 av. de Blois – 02 54 70 03 25 – contact@restaurant-poidras.com – Fax 02 54 70 12 46 – Closed 17 November-5 December, 23 February-13 March, Tuesday October-April, Sunday dinner September-June and Wednesday

Rest – Menu €18/34

◆ Country inn on the edge of Blois forest, housing a colourful modern dining room extended by a bright veranda. Contemporary cuisine.

BLONVILLE-SUR-MER – **14 Calvados** – **303** M3 – **pop. 1 341** – **alt. 10 m** – ✉ **14910**

Paris 205 – Caen 46 – Deauville 5 – Le Havre 50 – Lisieux 34 – Pont-l'Évêque 18 32 **A3**

Office de tourisme, 32 bis, avenue Michel d'Ornano ✆ 02 31 87 91 14, Fax 02 31 87 11 38

L'Épi d'Or rest, VISA MC AE

23 av. Michel-d'Ornano – ✆ 02 31 87 90 48 – epidor@hotel-normand.com – Fax 02 31 87 08 98 – Closed 15-26 December and 14 January-19 February

40 rm – €50/70 €55/160, €8 – ½ P €65/95

Rest – *(closed Wednesday and Thursday except July-August)* Menu €19/45 – Carte €30/92

◆ A pleasant, recently renovated, Norman-style house. The rooms are all the same and are above all practical. A tasteful modern dining room and traditional menu: quick meals are served in a rustic setting.

BOIS-COLOMBES – **92 Hauts-de-Seine** – **311** J2 – **101** 15 – **see Paris, Area**

BOIS DE BOULOGNE – **75 Ville-de-Paris** – **see Paris (Paris 16e)**

BOIS DE LA CHAIZE – **85 Vendée** – **316** C5 – **see Île de Noirmoutier**

BOIS-DU-FOUR – **12 Aveyron** – **338** J5 – ✉ **12780** 29 **D1**

Paris 627 – Aguessac 16 – Millau 23 – Pont-de-Salars 25 – Rodez 45 – Sévérac-le-Château 18

Relais du Bois du Four VISA MC

– ✆ 05 65 61 86 17 – contact@bois-du-four.com – Fax 05 65 58 81 37 – Open 1st April-27 June, 8 July-15 November and closed Sunday dinner and Wednesday

26 rm – €50 €50, €7 – ½ P €51/56 – **Rest** – Menu €16/31 – Carte €20/43

◆ Fishing enthusiasts will want to cast a few lines in the pond opposite this former post house. The practical tasteful first floor rooms have been treated to a facelift. Impeccably well-kept. A largey countrified restaurant and cuisine with an Aveyron bias.

BOIS-LE-ROI – **77 Seine-et-Marne** – **312** F5 – **pop. 5 292** – **alt. 80 m** – ✉ **77590** 19 **C2**

Paris 58 – Fontainebleau 10 – Melun 10 – Montereau-Fault-Yonne 26

U.C.P.A. Bois-le-Roi Base de loisirs, Northwest: 2 km, ✆ 01 64 81 33 31.

Le Pavillon Royal without rest VISA MC AE

40 av. Gallieni – ✆ 01 64 10 41 00 – hotel-le-pavillon-royal@wanadoo.fr – Fax 01 64 10 41 10

33 rm – €65 €65, €6,50

◆ A little outside the town centre, a modern hotel with practical and modern rooms, some with cane furniture. Well soundproofed and maintained.

La Marine VISA MC

52 quai O.-Metra, (near the lock) – ✆ 01 60 69 61 38 – Fax 01 60 66 38 59 – Closed 15 October-7 November, 16-28 February, Monday and Tuesday except public holidays

Rest – Menu €28/33 – Carte €48/63

◆ This pleasant guesthouse is well placed on the banks of the Seine. Rustic style dining room and peaceful summer terrace. Traditional cuisine.

BOIS-PLAGE-EN-RÉ – **17 Charente-Maritime** – **324** B2 – **see Île de Ré**

BOISSERON – **34 Hérault** – **339** J6 – **see Sommières**

BOISSET – **15 Cantal** – **330** B6 – **pop. 653** – **alt. 426 m** – ✉ **15600** 5 **A3**

Paris 559 – Aurillac 31 – Calvinet 18 – Entraygues-sur-Truyère 48 – Figeac 36 – Maurs 14

Auberge de Concasty rm, P VISA MC AE
Northeast : 3 km via D 64 – ✆ 04 71 62 21 16 – info@auberge-concasty.com – Fax 04 71 62 22 22 – Open 1st April- 30 November
12 rm – †€ 61/71 ††€ 61/119, ☕ € 16 – 1 suite – ½ P € 70/114 – **Rest** – *(dinner only) (pre-book)* Menu € 32/43
◆ Fresh air and a restful stay are guaranteed on this estate in the Cantal countryside. Stylish modern rooms, with those in the outbuildings offering more space. Auvergne-style brunch available on request. One set menu marrying tradition and local produce, served in a pleasant, rustic dining room.

BOISSIÈRES – 46 Lot – 337 E4 – pop. 312 – alt. 229 m – ✉ 46150 28 B1

Paris 573 – Toulouse 137 – Cahors 14 – Sarlat-la-Canéda 63 – Caussade 64

Michel & Lydia P
East 1 km on secondary road – ✆ 05 65 21 43 29 – Fax 05 65 21 43 29 – Closed 3 December-3 January
4 rm ☕ – †€ 56/71 ††€ 61/75 – **Table d'hôte** – Menu € 22 bi
◆ The Belgian owners take great care over their delightful modern home. Comfortable, individually decorated rooms (antiques and family heirlooms). The chef, a former baker, prepares traditional cuisine. Home-made bread and pastries.

BOLLENBERG – 68 Haut-Rhin – 315 H9 – see Rouffach

BOLLEZEELE – 59 Nord – 302 B2 – pop. 1 382 – alt. 40 m – ✉ 59470 30 B1

Paris 274 – Calais 45 – Dunkerque 24 – Lille 68 – St-Omer 18

Hostellerie St-Louis P VISA MC AE
47 r. de l'Église – ✆ 03 28 68 81 83 – contact@hostelleriesaintlouis.com – Fax 03 28 68 01 17 – Closed 30 June-11 July, 23 December-18 January and Sunday dinner
27 rm – †€ 42/50 ††€ 55/80, ☕ € 9 – ½ P € 58/63 – **Rest** – *(closed lunch from Monday to Saturday and Sunday dinner)* Menu € 24/50 – Carte approx. € 45
◆ This lovely early-19C house has a pleasant garden with a water feature. The modern rooms are spacious and practical. Period furniture and pastel shades in a bourgeois setting; classic generous menu served with a smile.

BONDUES – 59 Nord – 302 G3 – see Lille

BONIFACIO – 2A Corse-du-Sud – 345 D11 – see Corse

BONLIEU – 39 Jura – 321 F7 – pop. 225 – alt. 785 m – ✉ 39130

Burgundy-Jura 16 B3

Paris 439 – Champagnole 23 – Lons-le-Saunier 32 – Morez 24 – St-Claude 42

La Poutre with rm P VISA MC
– ✆ 03 84 25 57 77 – Fax 03 84 25 51 61 – Open 7 May-1st November and closed Monday dinner, Tuesday except July-August and Monday lunch
8 rm – †€ 46 ††€ 58, ☕ € 8 – ½ P € 60 – **Rest** – Menu € 25/68 – Carte € 51/79
◆ A 1740 farmhouse in the market town centre. Stylish blue and yellow rustic dining room with beams, old stonework and a lovely fireplace. Regional menu.

BONNAT – 23 Creuse – 325 I3 – pop. 1 348 – alt. 330 m – ✉ 23220 25 C1

Paris 329 – Châtre 37 – Guéret 20 – Montluçon 72 – Souterraine 53

L'Orangerie P VISA MC AE
3 bis r. de la Paix – ✆ 05 55 62 86 86 – reception@hotel-lorangerie.fr – Fax 05 55 62 86 87 – Closed from January to March, Tuesday lunch, Sunday dinner and Monday from November to April
30 rm – †€ 80/110 ††€ 80/110, ☕ € 12 – **Rest** – *(closed Sun. evening and Mon. from 10 Oct. to 31 Mar.)* Menu € 20 (weekday lunch), € 28/65 – Carte € 51/89
◆ Pleasant lounges and attractive, comfortable bedrooms adorned with Louis XV-style furniture. Breakfasts on the terrace. In summer, traditional gourmet cuisine is served facing the garden (a French-style vegetable garden).

BONNATRAIT – 74 Haute-Savoie – 328 L2 – see Thonon-les-Bains

BONNE – 74 Haute-Savoie – 328 K3 – pop. 2 098 – alt. 457 m – ✉ 74380 46 F1

Paris 545 – Annecy 45 – Bonneville 16 – Genève 18 – Thonon-les-Bains 31

Baud with rm — rest, P VISA MC AE D
– *04 50 39 20 15 – info@hotel-baud.com – Fax 04 50 36 28 96*
13 rm – €95/230 €95/230, € 14 – **Rest** – *(closed Sunday dinner)*
Menu (€ 24), € 26 (weekday lunch), € 36/68 – Carte € 41/73
◆ Cosy, elegant, contemporary dining rooms, updated bistro menu, tempting wine list, plush sitting rooms and a secret garden on the banks of the Ménoge.

at Pont-de-Fillinges 2,5 km East – ✉ 74250

Le Pré d'Antoine — A/C P VISA MC
rte Boëge – 04 50 36 45 06 – lepredantoine@aol.com – Fax 04 50 31 12 28 – Closed 1st to 8 January, Tuesday dinner and Wednesday
Rest – Menu € 21, € 35/49 – Carte € 38/58
◆ A modern building in chalet style with a large wood-panelled dining room and a well-exposed terrace. Classic cuisine with dishes varying between country and tradition.

BONNE-FONTAINE – 57 Moselle – 307 O6 – see Phalsbourg

BONNÉTAGE – 25 Doubs – 321 K3 – pop. 674 – alt. 960 m – ✉ 25210 17 C2

Paris 468 – Belfort 69 – Besançon 65 – Biel/Bienne 62 – La Chaux-de-Fonds 29

L'Etang du Moulin (Jacques Barnachon) with rm — rest, P VISA MC AE
1.5 km via D 236 and private road – 03 81 68 92 78 – etang.du.moulin@wanadoo.fr – Fax 03 81 68 94 42 – Closed 22-29 December, 5 January-12 February, Sunday dinner and Monday from 18 November to 15 March, Tuesday except dinner in July-August and Wednesday lunch
19 rm – €55/70 €60/80, € 8,50 – ½ P € 54/64
Rest – Menu € 23/95 – Carte € 32/73
Spec. Palette de foies gras de canard et d'oie. Ragoût de morilles au vin jaune à la crème de Bonnétage. Indispensable de la maison, fraîcheur de gentiane, extrait de bourgeons de sapin et croquant de fruits secs. **Wines** Arbois-Savagnin, Charcennes.
◆ A large chalet in the middle of the countryside, near a small lake. Comfortable, modern dining room serving delicious local dishes (selection of foie gras) and fine wine list.

Les Perce-Neige with rm — A/C rest, P VISA MC
D 437 – 03 81 68 91 51 – patrick-bole@wanadoo.fr – Fax 03 81 68 95 25 – Closed 20-30 January – **12 rm** – €41 €50, € 6,50 – ½ P € 50
Rest – *(closed Sunday dinner)* Menu € 14,50 (weekdays)/44 – Carte € 28/56
◆ Traditional dishes served in a rustic setting; chalet ambiance perfect for sampling the fondue. Functional rooms in a building next to a road that is fairly quiet at night.

BONNEUIL-MATOURS – 86 Vienne – 322 J4 – pop. 1 708 – alt. 60 m – ✉ 86210

Paris 322 – Bellac 79 – Le Blanc 51 – Châtellerault 17 – Montmorillon 42 – Poitiers 25 39 C1

Office de tourisme, Carrefour Maurice Fombeure 05 49 85 08 62, Fax 05 49 85 08 62

Le Pavillon Bleu — VISA MC
D 749, (opposite the bridge) – 05 49 85 28 05 – c.ribardiere@wanadoo.fr – Fax 05 49 21 61 94 – Closed 29 September-15 October, Wednesday dinner, Sunday dinner and Monday
Rest – Menu (€ 13), € 19/36 – Carte approx. € 30
◆ Take the suspension bridge across the Vienne to this pretty family inn popular for its relaxing atmosphere and tasty traditional fare.

BONNEVAL – 28 Eure-et-Loir – 311 E6 – pop. 4 285 – alt. 128 m – ✉ 28800

Châteaux of the Loire 11 B1

Paris 121 – Chartres 31 – Lucé 34 – Orléans 66

Office de tourisme, 2, square Westerham 02 37 47 55 89, Fax 02 37 96 28 62

Hostellerie du Bois Guibert

in Guibert, 2 km south-west – ✆ 02 37 47 22 33 – bois-guibert@wanadoo.fr – Fax 02 37 47 50 69

20 rm €69 €160, ☕ €12, ½ P €72/126 – **Rest** Menu €28/64 – Carte €53/86

◆ In a tranquil setting at the heart of a delightful park, this 18C country house offers guests comfortable rooms embellished with period furniture. An elegant restaurant and a pleasant terrace looking onto the garden. Classical food and a vegetarian menu.

BONNEVAL-SUR-ARC – 73 Savoie – 333 P5 – pop. 242 – alt. 1 800 m – Winter sports : 1 800/3 000 m 10 – ✉ 73480 French Alps 45 D2

Paris 706 – Albertville 133 – Chambéry 146 – Lanslebourg 21 – Val-d'Isère 30

Syndicat d'initiative, la Ciamarella ✆ 04 79 05 95 95, Fax 04 79 05 86 87

Old village★★.

A la Pastourelle

– ✆ 04 79 05 81 56 – hotel.pastourelle@wanadoo.fr – Fax 04 79 05 85 44 – Closed 1 week in June and autumn half-term holidays

12 rm – €54/58 €58/62, ☕ €7 – ½ P €55

Rest – *(open 20 December-20 April)* Menu €11,50/21 – Carte €11/32

◆ Quiet and cosy comfort in this family establishment typical of the charming old village. Restaurant-creperie with beams, fireplace, stone arch and photos of ancestors. On the menu are raclettes, fondues, crêpes and "diot", the regional speciality.

La Bergerie

– ✆ 04 79 05 94 97 – Fax 04 79 05 93 24 – Open 15 June-25 September and 20 December-25 April

22 rm – €41/50 €55/62, ☕ €11 – ½ P €57/62 – **Rest** – Menu €16/26 – Carte €23/42

◆ Enter the Bergerie and relax in its peace and quiet in bright rooms with fine views of the Évettes massif. The numerous copper pans and country objects on the walls give the dining room a rustic feel.

BONNEVILLE – 74 Haute-Savoie – 328 L4 – pop. 10 463 – alt. 450 m – ✉ 74130 French Alps 46 F1

Paris 556 – Annecy 42 – Chamonix-Mont-Blanc 54 – Nantua 87 – Thonon-les-Bains 45

Office de tourisme, 148, place de l'Hôtel de Ville ✆ 04 50 97 38 37, Fax 04 50 97 19 33

Bellevue

à Ayze, 2.5 km east by D 6 – ✆ 04 50 97 20 83 – Fax 04 50 25 28 38 – Open 5 May-28 September, February holidays and closed Sunday evening except July-August

20 rm €45/47 €50/56, ☕ €7 – ½ P €48/50 – **Rest** *(open 11 June-31 August and closed Sunday dinner and lunch except 1st July-24 August)* Menu €18/34

◆ Built in the 1960s, this family establishment has simple rooms; some overlook the Ayze vines. At garden level, a panoramic dining room and terrace commanding a view over the Arve plain; traditional food.

in Vougy 5 km east by D 1205 – pop. 958 – alt. 471 m – ✉ 74130

Le Capucin Gourmand

1520 rte de Genève, D 1205 – ✆ 04 50 34 03 50 – lecapucingourmand@wanadoo.fr – Fax 04 50 34 57 57 – Closed 1st-24 August, 1st-7 January, Saturday lunch, Sunday and Monday

Rest – Menu €36/55 – Carte €46/72

Rest *Le Bistro du Capucin* – Menu (€21 bi), €27 – Carte €28/39

◆ Walls decorated with stencilling, stylish furniture and trinkets set the scene in the restaurant where guests can enjoy modern cuisine and a good wine list. Plain decor, informal ambiance and a typical, traditional bistro-type menu.

BONNIEUX – 84 Vaucluse – 332 E11 – pop. 1 417 – alt. 400 m – ✉ 84480 Provence

Paris 721 – Aix-en-Provence 49 – Apt 12 – Carpentras 42 – Cavaillon 27

Office de tourisme, 7, place Carnot ✆ 04 90 75 91 90, Fax 04 90 75 92 94

Terrace ★. 42 E1

La Bastide de Capelongue (Edouard Loubet) with rm
rte de Lourmarin, then D 232 and minor road: 1,5 km – ✆ 04 90 75 89 78 – contact@capelongue.com – Fax 04 90 75 93 03 – Open from mid March to mid November
17 rm – €160/380 €190/380, €22 – ½ P €215/275
Rest – *(closed Wednesday except July-August)* Menu €70 (weekday lunch), €140/190 – Carte €107/182
Spec. Boudin de volaille truffé à la pistache, jus à la mauve des prés (June-July). Oursins en coque au beurre d'oursin, salade d'algues de wakamé (October to November). Ananas Victoria. **Wines** Côtes du Lubéron.
♦ Large residence with a traditional feel set in the countryside. Elegant dining room (beige shades) and pleasant terrace with wrought iron furnishings. Inventive food. Provençal rooms; some enjoy a pretty view of the village.

La Ferme de Capelongue
10 suites – €220/420, €22
♦ Opposite the Bastide, in a small renovated hamlet, apartments and studios with minimalist décor making the most of the old stone walls. Huge garden with a swimming pool.

Le Fournil
pl. Carnot – ✆ 04 90 75 83 62 – Fax 04 90 75 96 19 – Closed 20 November-20 December, 6 January-20 February, Saturday lunch and Tuesday except dinner from April to September and Monday
Rest – *(number of covers limited, pre-book)* Menu €28 (lunch), €42 € (dinner)/48 (dinner)
♦ House set against the hillside offering you a terrace on the small square or an unusual, naturally cool dining room cut into the cliff, with modern decor.

Southeast **6 km by D 36 and D 943 – ✉ 84480 Bonnieux**

Auberge de l'Aiguebrun
– ✆ 04 90 04 47 00 – resa@aubergedelaiguebrun.fr – Fax 04 90 04 47 01 – Closed 2 January-15 March
11 rm – €125/155 €140/200 – ½ P €120/150 – **Rest** – *(closed Tuesday and Wednesday except dinner 1st July-15 September)* Menu €35 (weekday lunch), €55/65 – Carte €56/60
♦ Nestling in a hollow in the Luberon Valley, a Provençal house with neat rooms, four of them in 'cabins'. An attractive country dining room opening onto a terraced garden near the river.

BONNY-SUR-LOIRE – 45 Loiret – 318 O6 – pop. 1 924 – alt. 190 m – ✉ 45420

12 **D2**

Paris 167 – Auxerre 64 – Cosne-sur-Loire 25 – Gien 24 – Montargis 57
Office de tourisme, 29, Grande Rue ✆ 02 38 31 57 71, Fax 02 38 31 57 71

Voyageurs with rm
rest,
10 Grande-Rue – ✆ 02 38 27 01 45 – hotel-des-voyageurs9@wanadoo.fr – Fax 02 38 27 01 46 – Closed 25 August-9 September, 2-13 January, 23 February-10 March and Sunday evening
6 rm – €39 €39/46, €6 – ½ P €54
Rest – *(closed Sunday dinner, Tuesday lunch and Monday)* Menu €19 (weekdays)/44 – Carte €28/48
♦ Entirely renovated establishment with exhibition of paintings by a family artist. Well-prepared cuisine in keeping with current taste. Functional rooms.

BONS-EN-CHABLAIS – 74 Haute-Savoie – 328 L3 – pop. 3 980 – alt. 565 m – ✉ 74890

46 **F1**

Paris 552 – Annecy 60 – Bonneville 30 – Genève 25 – Thonon-les-Bains 16

Progrès
rm,
r. Annexion – ✆ 04 50 36 11 09 – hotelleprogres2@wanadoo.fr – Fax 04 50 39 44 16 – Closed 15 June-4 July, 1st-18 January, Sunday evening and Monday
10 rm – €50 €59, €9 – ½ P €56 – **Rest** – Menu (€13), €18 (weekdays)/48 – Carte €29/47
♦ Two village houses, one with comfortable modern rooms. An ideal base for walks around the Grand Signal des Voirons. Part rustic, part elegant, this restaurant has been decorated with care. Classic cuisine.

Le pont de Pierre

BORDEAUX

🅿 **Department:** 33 Gironde
Michelin LOCAL map: n° **335** H5
Paris 579 – Lyon 537 – Nantes 323 – Strasbourg 970 – Toulouse 244

Population: 215 363 — 3 **B1**
Pop. built-up area: 753 931
Altitude: 4 m – **Postal Code:** ✉ 33000
Atlantic Coast

USEFUL INFORMATION

TOURIST OFFICE

12 cours du 30 juillet ✆ 05 56 00 66 00, Fax 05 56 00 66 01

MAISON DU VIN DE BORDEAUX

(information, tastings)
(closed weekends and public holidays)
1 cours 30 Juillet ✆ 05 56 00 22 88
wine bar open daily 11 h à 22 h.

TRANSPORT

Auto-train ✆ 3635 et tapez 42 (0,34 €/mn)

AIRPORT

Bordeaux-Mérignac: ✆ 05 56 34 50 50, **AU** : 11 km

LEISURE

CASINO

Bordeaux-Lac, r. Cardinal Richaud ✆ 05 56 69 49 00 BT

A FEW GOLF COURSES

36 de Bordeaux-Lac Avenue de Pernon, North: 5 km by D 209, ✆ 05 56 50 92 72 ;
36 du Médoc Le Pian-Médoc Chemin de Courmateau, by Castelnau road: 16 km, ✆ 05 56 70 11 90 ;
27 de Pessac Pessac Rue de la Princesse, Southwest: 16 km by D 1250, ✆ 05 57 26 03 33.

TO BE SEEN

18C BORDEAUXe S.

Grand théâtre★★ - Place de la Comédie - Place Gambetta - Cours de l'intendance - Notre-Dame church ★ DX - Place de la Bourse★★ - Place du Parlement★ - St-Michel basilica ★ Porte de la Grosse Cloche★ EY Fountains★ of the Girondins monument, Esplanade des Quinconces.

QUARTIER DES CHARTRONS

Wine warehouses - Balconies★ of cours Xavier-Arnozan - Entrepôt Lainé★ : musée d'Art contemporain (Modern Art Museum)★ **BU M2** Musée des Chartrons BU M5 - Colbert cruiser★★

QUARTIER PEY BERLAND

St-André Cathedral ★ - Town hall DY **H** - ≤★★ of the Pey Berland Tower ★ DY **Q** Museum: Beaux-Arts (fine arts)★ DY M4 - Aquitaine★★ DY M1 - Arts décoratifs★ DY M3

CONTEMPORARY BORDEAUX

Quartier Mériadeck CY : green spaces, glass and concrete building (Caisse d'Épargne (savings bank), Bibliothèque (library), Hôtel de Région (regional authorities building), Hôtel des Impôts (tax office).

Burdigala
115 r. G.-Bonnac – 05 56 90 16 16 – burdigala@burdigala.com – Fax 05 56 93 15 06 *p. 6* CX **r**
77 rm – €200/305 €200/305, €20 – 6 suites
Rest *Le Jardin de Burdigala* – – Menu (€29), €38 – Carte €55/67
◆ The elegant and quiet rooms of this luxury hotel have period and modern furniture, fine materials, the latest equipment and are perfectly soundproofed. The Jardin de Burdigala has a refined rotunda dining room, with a central structure and a skylight.

Seeko'o without rest
54 quai de Bacalan – 05 56 39 07 07 – contact@seekoo-hotel.com – Fax 05 56 39 07 09 *p. 5* BT **h**
45 rm – €180/360 €180/360, €14
◆ The name, "iceberg" in Inuit, sets the tone! A Corian covered façade and "pop" style rooms on the banks of the Gironde.

Mercure Cité Mondiale
18 parvis des Chartrons – 05 56 01 79 79 – h2877@accor.com – Fax 05 56 01 79 00 *p. 5* BU **k**
96 rm – €102/122 €112/260, €14
Rest *Le 20* – *05 56 01 78 78 (closed 28 July-18 August, 22 December-2 January, Friday dinner, Saturday and Sunday)* Menu €19/38 – Carte €24/37
◆ Contemporary rooms, meeting facilities and a roof-terrace with a view over Bordeaux where breakfast is served in the summer. Situated in the Cité Mondiale complex. At the 20: tasting of wines to accompany the bistro-type meals. Smart decor.

Mercure Mériadeck
5 r. R.-Lateulade – 05 56 56 43 43 – h1281@accor.com – Fax 05 56 96 50 59 *p. 6* CY **v**
194 rm – €118 €128, €14 – 2 suites – **Rest** – *(closed Saturday and Sunday) (dinner only)* Menu (€22) – Carte €30/46
◆ Cinematic decor with posters, photos and objects relating to films. Rooms are practical, in usual chain style. Well-equipped conference rooms. This restaurant celebrates the Cannes Film Festival. Traditional menu.

Bayonne Etche-Ona without rest
4 r. Martignac – 05 56 48 00 88 – bayetche@bordeaux-hotel.com – Fax 05 56 48 41 60 – Closed 22 December-6 January *p. 6* DX **f**
62 rm – €138/154 €159/180, €12 – 1 suite
◆ In the "Golden Triangle", this hotel on two floors of an 18C building mingles tradition and elegance in its personalised, well-cared for rooms with modern fixtures and fittings.

Novotel Bordeaux-Centre
rm, rest,
45 cours Mar- Juin – 05 56 51 46 46 – h1023@accor.com – Fax 05 56 98 25 56 *p. 6* CY **m**
137 rm – €88/117 €88/147, €14 – **Rest** – Carte €19/38
◆ Architecture that blends well into the Meriadeck district; big functional rooms, regularly redecorated and well-soundproofed in this Novotel. A discreet dining room and a terrace overlooking the city. New café.

De Normandie without rest
7 cours 30-Juillet – 05 56 52 16 80 – info@hotel-de-normandie-bordeaux.com – Fax 05 56 51 68 91 *p. 6* DX **z**
100 rm – €59/110 €98/240, €14
◆ An immense elegant hall leads to a variety of functional rooms decorated in pastel shades, those on the top floor have been redone (contemporary, comfortable and with balconies).

Majestic without rest
2 r. Condé – 05 56 52 60 44 – mail-majestic@hotel-majestic.com – Fax 05 56 79 26 70 *p. 6* DX **a**
48 rm – €75 €200, €9 – 1 suite
◆ This elegant 18C building typical of the Bordeaux region is home to well-maintained and varied guestrooms, a cosy lounge, and a stylish breakfast room.

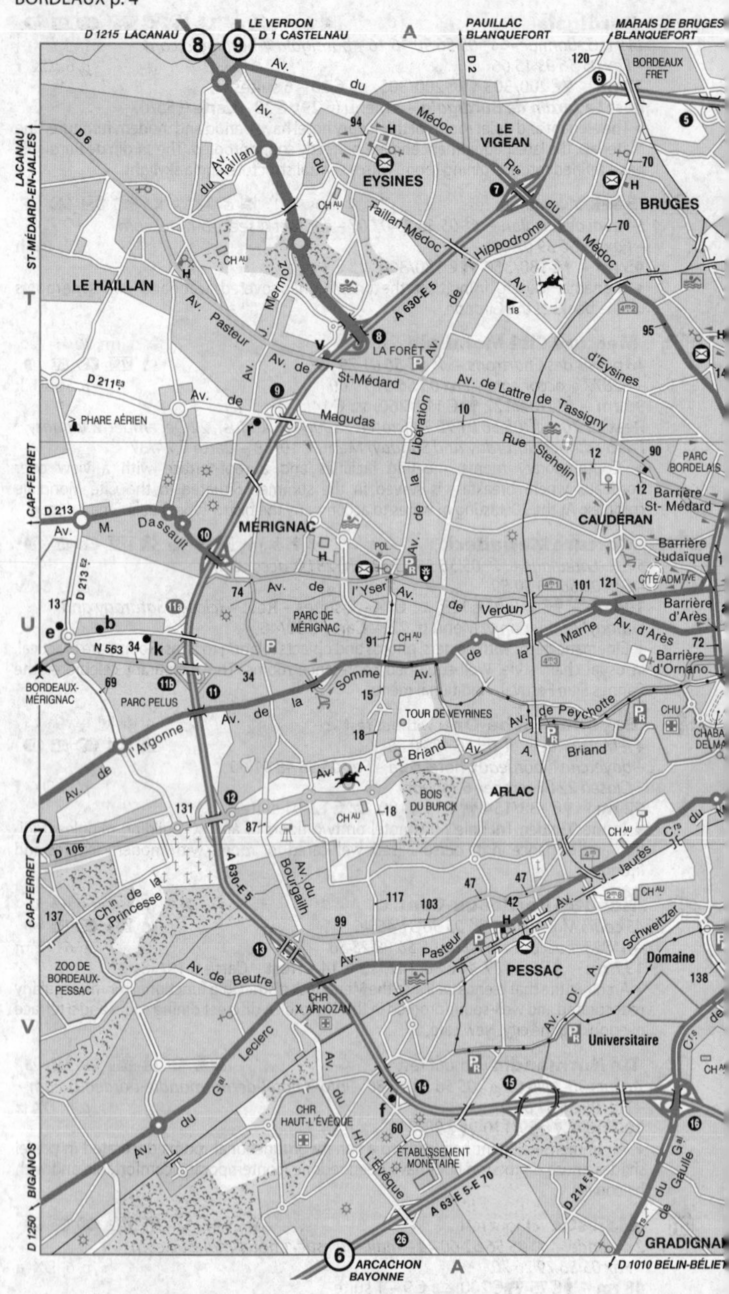
LE VERDON
D 1 CASTELNAU
D 1215 LACANAU
PAUILLAC
BLANQUEFORT
MARAIS DE BRUGES
BLANQUEFORT
BORDEAUX FRET
LE VIGEAN
EYSINES
BRUGES
LE HAILLAN
LA FORÊT
MÉRIGNAC
CAUDÉRAN
PHARE AÉRIEN
PARC BORDELAIS
PARC DE MÉRIGNAC
BORDEAUX-MÉRIGNAC
PARC PELUS
TOUR DE VEYRINES
BOIS DU BURCK
ARLAC
PESSAC
ZOO DE BORDEAUX-PESSAC
CHR X. ARNOZAN
CHR HAUT-L'ÉVÊQUE
ÉTABLISSEMENT MONÉTAIRE
Domaine Universitaire
GRADIGNAN
ARCACHON
BAYONNE
D 1010 BÉLIN-BÉLIET
LACANAU
ST-MÉDARD-EN-JALLES
CAP-FERRET
BIGANOS
A 630-E 5
A 63-E 5-E 70

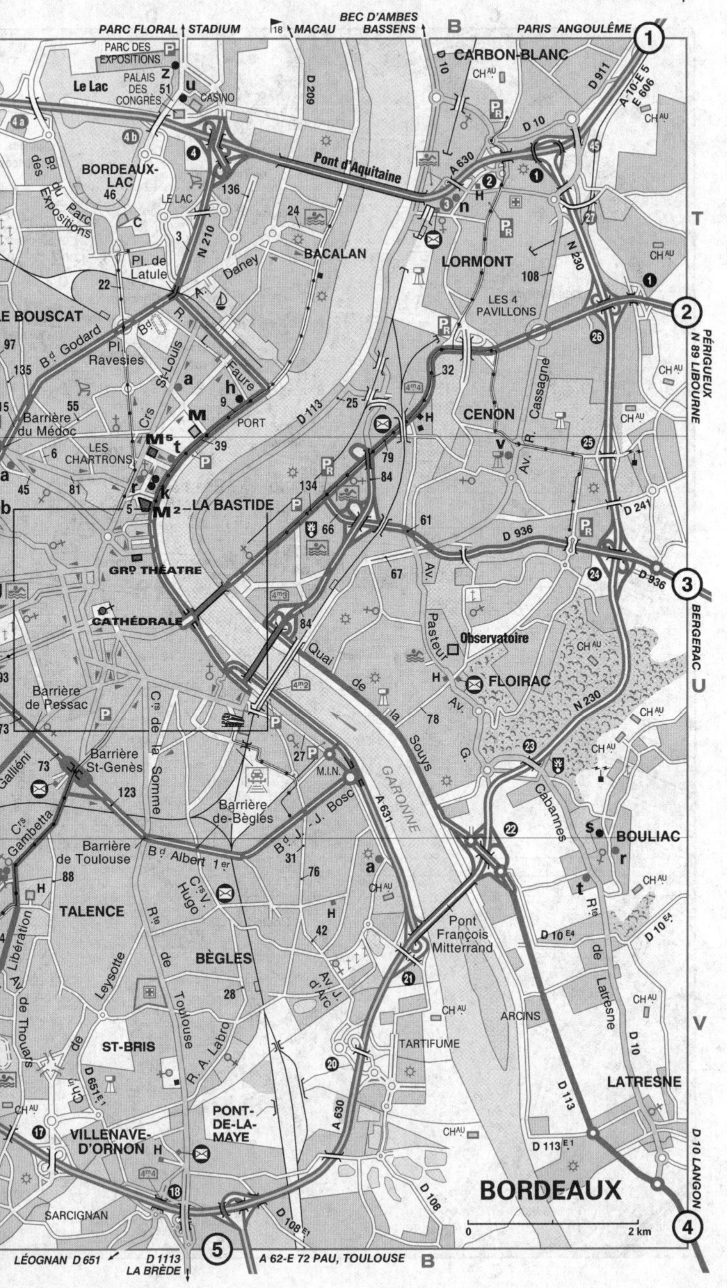
PARC FLORAL
STADIUM
MACAU
BEC D'AMBES
BASSENS
PARIS ANGOULÊME
CARBON-BLANC
PARC DES EXPOSITIONS
Le Lac
PALAIS DES CONGRÈS
CASINO
BORDEAUX-LAC
LE LAC
Bd des Parc Expositions
Pont d'Aquitaine
BACALAN
LORMONT
LES 4 PAVILLONS
Pl. de Latule
A. Daney
E BOUSCAT
Bd Godard
Pl. Ravesies
Crs St-Louis
R. L. Faure
PORT
Barrière du Médoc
LES CHARTRONS
LA BASTIDE
CENON
Av. R. Cassagne
GRD THÉATRE
CATHÉDRALE
Barrière de Pessac
Quai de la Souys
Av. Pasteur
Observatoire
FLOIRAC
Av. G. Cabannes
GARONNE
M.I.N.
Barrière St-Genès
Crs de la Somme
Barrière de-Bègles
Bd J. J. Bosc
Crs Gambetta
Barrière de Toulouse
Bd Albert 1er
Crs V. Hugo
TALENCE
BÈGLES
BOULIAC
Pont François Mitterrand
Rte de Latresne
Av. de la Libération
Av. de Thouars
Leysotte
Rte de Toulouse
R. A. Labro
Av. J. d'Arc
ARCINS
TARTIFUME
ST-BRIS
LATRESNE
PONT-DE-LA-MAYE
VILLENAVE-D'ORNON
SARCIGNAN
BORDEAUX
0
2 km
LÉOGNAN D 651
D 1113 LA BRÈDE
A 62-E 72 PAU, TOULOUSE
PÉRIGUEUX N 89 LIBOURNE
BERGERAC
D 10 LANGON
A 10-E 5 E 606
A 630
A 631
N 230
N 210
D 936
D 113
D 10
D 108
D 209
D 911
D 241
D 113 E1
D 10 E4
D 108 E1
D 651 E1

C
D
X
Y
Z
Turenne
Rue Turenne
Fondaudège
Pl. de Tourny
Espl. des Quinconces
MAISON DU VIN DE BORDEAUX
St-Seurin
Pl. des Martyrs de la Résistance
Pl. du Chapelet
N.-DAME
GRAND THÉATRE
l'Intendance
Rue Judaïque
Pl. Gambetta
Pte Dijeaux
Bonnac
PEY BERLAND
VIEUX BORDEAUX
Centre Jean Moulin
Bonnier
MÉRIADECK
HÔTEL DU DÉPT
Esplanade Ch. de Gaulle
CATH. ST-ANDRÉ
d' Alsace
ST-BRUNO
Hôtel de Région
ST-PAUL
PALAIS DES SPORTS
ÉCOLE NATle DE LA MAGISTRATURE
Pl. de la République
R. de Cursol
STE-EULALIE
Cours de la Libération
Pl. de Pressensé
Porte d'Aquitaine
R. Ed. Costedoat
Villedieu
Pl. de la Victoire
ST-VICTOR
ST-NICOLAS
N.-D. DES ANGES
Barrière de Pessac
R. A. Bayssela nce
Cadroin
St-Nicolas
Duhen
Treuils
Mouneyra
Belleville
Tondu
Pessac
Sourdis
R. F. Audeguil
Lamourous
St-Genès
Mazarin
Leberthon
l'Argonne
Somme
Pasteur
Catherine
Lande
R. G. Rioux
Belfort
d'Albret
Juin
François
Lachassaigne
Allo
Barraud
Abbé
Thiac
Palais
Gallien
l'Épée
Clemenceau
Huguerie
Tourny
Remparts
Carles
Joffre
Burguet
Conils
Pl. C Jullia
Grassi
Dijeaux

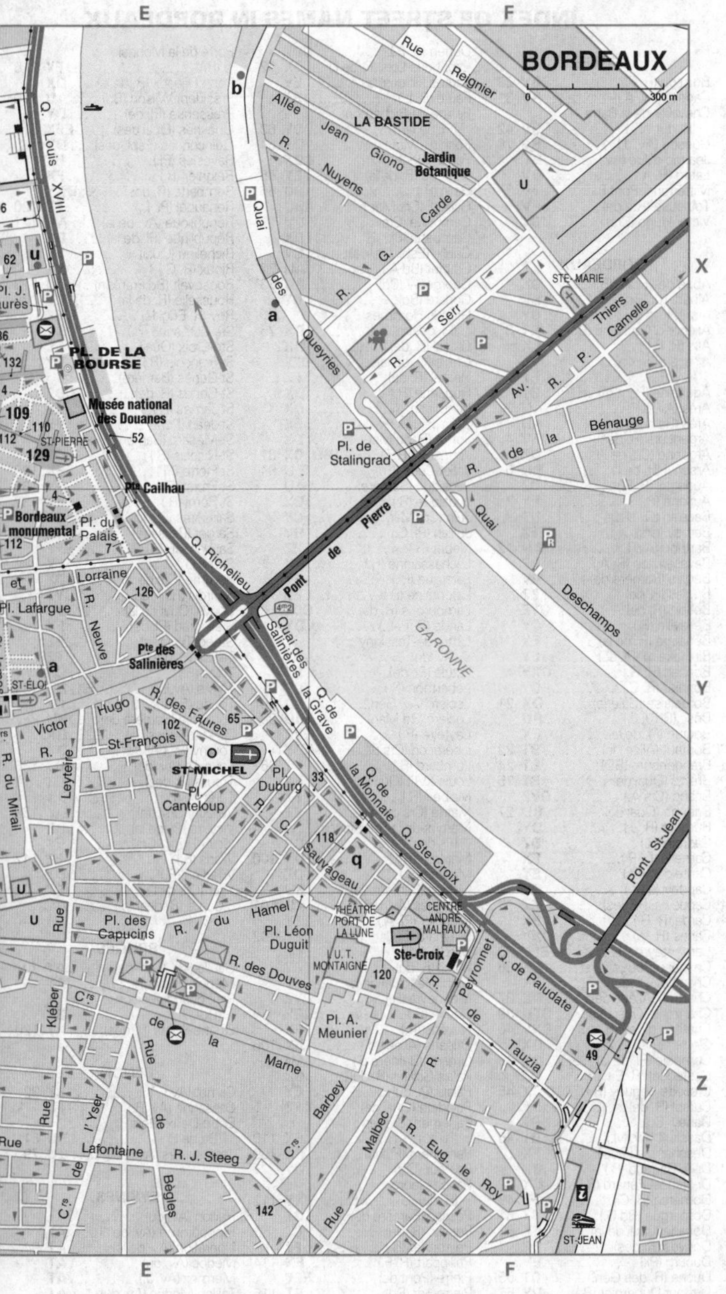

BORDEAUX
0
300 m
E
F
X
Y
Z
LA BASTIDE
Jardin Botanique
PL. DE LA BOURSE
Musée national des Douanes
ST-PIERRE
Pte Cailhau
Bordeaux monumental
Pl. du Palais
Pont de Pierre
Pl. de Stalingrad
STE-MARIE
GARONNE
Pte des Salinières
ST-ÉLOI
ST-MICHEL
Pl. Duburg
Pl. Canteloup
THÉÂTRE PORT DE LA LUNE
CENTRE ANDRÉ MALRAUX
Ste-Croix
I.U.T. MONTAIGNE
Pl. des Capucins
Pl. Léon Duguit
Pl. A. Meunier
Pont St-Jean
ST-JEAN
Q. Louis XVIII
Q. Richelieu
Quai des Salinières
Q. de la Grave
Q. de la Monnaie
Q. Ste-Croix
Q. de Paludate
Quai des Queyries
Quai Deschamps
Allée Jean Giono
R. Nuyens
Rue Reignier
R. G. Carde
R. Serr
Av. Thiers
R. P. Camelle
R. de la Bénauge
Pl. Lafargue
R. Neuve
Lorraine
R. des Faures
Victor Hugo
R. St-François
R. Leyteire
R. du Mirail
R. C. Sauvageau
R. du Hamel
R. des Douves
R. Peyronnet
R. de Tauzia
Crs de la Marne
Rue Kléber
Rue de Bègles
Rue de l'Yser
Crs de Lafontaine
R. J. Steeg
Crs Barbey
Rue Malbec
R. Eug. le Roy
4m2

INDEX OF STREET NAMES IN BORDEAUX

Grand Hôtel Français without rest

12 r. du Temple – ☎ 05 56 48 10 35 – infos@grand-hotel-francais.com – Fax 05 56 81 76 18 *p. 6* DX **v**

35 rm ☐ – **†€ 106/144 ††€ 131/176**

♦ A fine, 18C house with ironwork balconies on the façade. The lounges and staircase have retained their original character. The comfortable rooms are in a more modern vein.

De la Presse without rest

6 r. Porte-Dijeaux – ☎ 05 56 48 53 88 – info@hoteldelapresse.com – Fax 05 56 01 05 82 – Closed 24 December-11 January *p. 6* DX **k**

27 rm – **†€ 65/83 ††€ 74/93,** ☐ **€ 9**

♦ In the centre of the pedestrian area, a stone façade fronts a recently renovated and well-kept hotel. Functional rooms. Regulated car access.

Des Quatre Sœurs without rest

6 cours 30-Juillet – ☎ 05 57 81 19 20 – 4soeurs@mailcity.com – Fax 05 56 01 04 28

34 rm – **†€ 80 ††€ 90,** ☐ **€ 8** *p. 6* DX **u**

♦ This venerable hotel is proud to say that the musician Richard Wagner and the writer John Dos have stayed there. Today it houses well-soundproofed rooms, personalised with pretty painted furniture.

Continental without rest

10 r. Montesquieu – ☎ 05 56 52 66 00 – continental@hotel-le-continental.com – Fax 05 56 52 77 97 *p. 6* DX **b**

50 rm – **†€ 72/89 ††€ 79/104,** ☐ **€ 8,50 – 1 suite**

♦ Former 18C mansion near the galerie des Grands Hommes. Pleasant rooms of various sizes with bright colours. Cosy, well-furnished salon.

De l'Opéra without rest

35 r. Esprit-des-Lois – ☎ 05 56 81 41 27 – hotel.opera.bx@wanadoo.fr – Fax 05 56 51 78 80 *p. 6* DX **n**

28 rm – **†€ 45/55 ††€ 55/60,** ☐ **€ 6**

♦ Family hotel in an 18C building near the historic district. Well-kept, simple rooms, with sloping ceilings on the top floor; non-smoking.

Notre-Dame without rest

36 r. Notre-Dame – ☎ 05 56 52 88 24 – contact@hotelnotredame33.com – Fax 05 56 79 12 67 *p. 5* BU **k**

22 rm – **†€ 41 ††€ 51,** ☐ **€ 6**

♦ Lovers of antiques will enjoy this small hotel in a quarter brimming over with shops selling antique furniture and objects. Practical rooms at a reasonable price.

Une Chambre en Ville without rest

35 r. Bouffard – ✆ 05 56 81 34 53 – ucev@bandb-bx.com – Fax 05 56 81 34 54 p. 6 DXY **t**

5 rm – €89 €99, €9

◆ In the heart of the historic town centre, impeccable rooms decorated with varied themes and called Bordelais, Nautical, Oriental... Breakfast is served in a modern lounge.

Le Chapon Fin

5 r. Montesquieu – ✆ 05 56 79 10 10 – contact@chapon-fin.com – Fax 05 56 79 09 10 – Closed 20 July-18 August, 15 February-2 March, Sunday, Monday and public holidays p. 6 DX **p**

Rest – Menu €32 (lunch), €55/85 – Carte €88/95

Spec. Longuets toastés aux huîtres et farce crépinette, jus lie de vin. Duo de rougets, émulsion de soupe de roche (winter). Pigeon à la nougatine de cumin (autumn-winter). **Wines** Côtes de Blaye, Saint-Estèphe.

◆ A genuine Bordeaux institution popular among gourmets for its updated cuisine, fine wine list and original 1900s decor.

Le Pavillon des Boulevards (Denis Franc)

120 r. Croix-de-Seguey – ✆ 05 56 81 51 02 – pavillon.des.boulevards@wanadoo.fr – Fax 05 56 51 14 58 – Closed 6-26 August, 3-10 January, Saturday lunch, Monday lunch and Sunday p. 5 BU **a**

Rest – Menu €40 (lunch), €65/100 – Carte €78/98

Spec. Liégeois de caviar, homard à la crème de châtaigne. Sole dorée au beurre demi-sel, jus au combawa. Effeuillé de pommes confites au caramel. **Wines** Graves blanc, Pessac-Léognan.

◆ Cooking utensils fixed to the walls make for surprising decor in this contemporary restaurant with a lovely green terrace. Thoughtful, inventive cuisine.

Jean Ramet

7 pl. J.-Jaurès – ✆ 05 56 44 12 51 – jean.ramet@free.fr – Fax 05 56 52 19 80 – Closed 28 April-4 May, 3-26 August, Sunday and Monday p. 7 EX **u**

Rest – Menu €35 (lunch), €60/70 – Carte €60/74

◆ Local gourmets enjoy the classic, updated cuisine in this restaurant near the Garonne, decorated in sunny shades that match the fittings and furnishings.

Le Vieux Bordeaux

27 r. Buhan – ✆ 05 56 52 94 36 – Fax 05 56 44 25 11 – Closed 5-25 August, 17 February-2 March, Sunday, Monday and holidays p. 7 EY **a**

Rest – Menu (€20 bi), €29/52 – Carte €40/80

◆ Two dining rooms tastefully redecorated in shades of grey, period and contemporary furniture. One opens onto a pleasant patio. Generous portions of classic cooking.

L'Alhambra

111bis r. Judaïque – ✆ 05 56 96 06 91 – Fax 05 56 98 00 52 – Closed 14 July-15 August, Saturday lunch, Monday lunch and Sunday p. 6 CX **e**

Rest – Menu €20/40 – Carte €40/60

◆ Attractively laid out in a winter-garden style; shades of green and comfortable cane furniture. Flavoursome traditional cuisine varies with the seasons and market availability.

La Table Calvet

81 cours Médoc – ✆ 05 56 39 62 80 – tablecalvet@calvet.com – Fax 05 56 39 62 80 – Closed 1st-28 August, 24 December-2 January, 23-31 March, Saturday lunch, Sunday and Monday p. 5 BT **a**

Rest – Menu €20 (lunch), €28/55 – Carte €42/54

◆ The Calvet wine merchants have opened a gourmet restaurant with creative, seasonal cuisine. Food is served in the attractive setting of a former 19C wine and spirit storehouse.

Le Clos d'Augusta

339 r. Georges-Bonnac – ✆ 05 56 96 32 51 – leclosdaugusta@wanadoo.fr – Fax 05 56 51 80 46 – Closed 2-25 August, 21-29 December, Saturday lunch, Sunday and holidays p. 4 AU **a**

Rest – Menu €20 (weekday lunch), €43/65 – Carte €50/69

◆ The restaurant is named after a famous American golf course. The chef has two passions: cooking and golf. Pleasant garden-terrace at the rear. Modern recipes.

XX **La Tupina**

6 r. Porte-de-la-Monnaie – ✆ 05 56 91 56 37 – latupina@latupina.com – Fax 05 56 31 92 11 p. 7 FY **q**

Rest – Menu (€ 18), € 34 bi/58 – Carte € 26/90

◆ Relaxed atmosphere at this country-style house. Dishes from the southwest roast on the fireplace or on the stove as in the olden days. Good wine list.

XX **Gravelier**

114 cours Verdun – ✆ 05 56 48 17 15 – restogravelier@yahoo.fr – Fax 05 56 51 96 07 – Closed 26 July-24 August, February holidays, Saturday and Sunday p. 5 BU **r**

Rest – Menu € 20 (weekday lunch), € 28/50 – Carte € 55/61

◆ Teak and zinc furniture, striking colours and a view of the kitchens. Inventive menu with Asian influences concocted by a creative chef.

X **L'Estaquade** ← old Bordeaux,

quai Queyries – ✆ 05 57 54 02 50 – Fax 05 57 54 02 51 – Closed 25 December-2 January p. 7 EX **a**

Rest – *(pre-book)* Menu € 16 (weekday lunch) – Carte € 37/66

◆ By the Garonne, this unusual construction on piles overlooks old Bordeaux. Deliberately sparse decor, daily specials and a seasonal menu: a popular spot.

X **Auberge ' Inn**

245 r. de Turenne – ✆ 05 56 81 97 86 – auberge-inn@orange.fr – Fax 05 56 81 34 71 – Closed 2-25 August, 20-29 December, 15-23 February, Saturday, Sunday and public holidays p. 5 BU **b**

Rest – Menu € 19 (lunch), € 27/46 – Carte € 35/54

◆ Aubergine and aniseed-green coloured walls, minimalist modern furniture, a small, pretty terrace and up-to-date food: a very in inn!

X **La Petite Gironde**

75 quai Queyries – ✆ 05 57 80 33 33 – Fax 05 57 80 33 31 – Closed 24 December-1st January, Saturday lunch and Sunday dinner p. 7 EX **b**

Rest – Menu € 16/32 – Carte € 28/41

◆ This riverside restaurant on the Garonne's right bank has pleasantly trendy decor. The waterside terrace is very popular; traditional menu.

X **Quaizaco**

80 quai des Chartrons – ✆ 05 57 87 67 72 – quaizaco@orange.fr – Fax 05 57 87 34 42 – Closed 8-18 August, Saturday lunch and Sunday p. 5 BU **t**

Rest – Menu (€ 11), € 14 – Carte € 30/41

◆ Behind the façade of these 18C warehouses is a striking interior adorned with contemporary furnishings and temporary exhibitions of modern art. Up-to-date cuisine.

in Bordeaux-Lac (near the parc des expositions) (exhibition centre) - ✉ 33300 Bordeaux

Sofitel Aquitania rm,

av. J.-G.-Domergue – ✆ 05 56 69 66 66 – h0669@accor.com – Fax 05 56 69 66 00 p. 5 BT **u**

166 rm – € 200/350 € 210/350, € 22 – 19 suites

Rest *l'Aquitania* – Menu (€ 26 bi), € 31 bi – Carte € 34/61

◆ A hotel popular with business clients due to its direct access to the Convention Centre, 2000m² meeting facilities and comfortable designer rooms; all in all a successful renovation. Contemporary decor and a summer terrace overlooking the lake.

Novotel-Bordeaux Lac rm,

av. J.-G.-Domergue – ✆ 05 56 43 65 00 – h0403@accor.com – Fax 05 56 43 65 01 p. 5 BT **z**

175 rm – € 95/135 € 95/135, € 14

Rest – *(closed Friday dinner, Sunday lunch and Saturday from October to March)* Carte € 21/40

◆ Near the exhibition centre; the rooms (ask for one on the lake side), have been partly renovated in keeping with the chain's latest standards. Garden with children's area. Dine in the ultra fashionable interior or on the poolside terrace.

via A 630 bypass:

in Blanquefort 3 km north, exit 6 – pop. 13 901 – alt. 17 m – ✉ 33290

Les Criquets rm,
130 av. 11-Novembre (D 210) – ✆ 05 56 35 09 24 – hotel@lescriquets.com – Fax 05 56 57 13 83
21 rm – †€ 60 ††€ 82/125, ☕ € 12 – ½ P € 79 – **Rest** – *(closed Saturday lunch, Sunday dinner and Monday)* Menu € 20 (weekday lunch), € 40/65 – Carte € 53/72
◆ A pleasant country home feel pervades this old farmstead and its smart modern rooms (wood, wrought iron and bright fabrics). Pleasant dining room, terrace facing the garden and tasty updated menu.

in Lormont Northeast, exit 2 – pop. 21 100 – alt. 60 m – ✉ 33310

Office de tourisme, 4, avenue de la Libération ✆ 05 56 74 29 17

Jean-Marie Amat
26 r. Raymond-Lis – ✆ 05 56 06 12 52 – Fax 05 56 74 77 89 – Closed 14 July-15 August, 23 December-2 January, Sunday and Monday
Rest – Menu € 30 (weekday lunch) – Carte € 63/105 p. 5 BT **n**
Spec. Foie frais aux fruits de saison. Pigeon grillé aux épices, cuisses en pastilla. Pêche pochée et sorbet au "Lillet" (summer).
◆ This contemporary restaurant in a renovated château signals the return of the "enfant terrible". Fine modern cuisine, elegant veranda, views of the countryside and the Pont d'Aquitaine.

in Cenon East, exit 25 – pop. 21 283 – alt. 50 m – ✉ 33150

La Cape (Nicolas Magie)
allée Morlette – ✆ 05 57 80 24 25 – Fax 05 56 32 37 46 – Closed 1st-21 August, Christmas holidays, Saturday, Sunday and public holidays p. 5 BU **v**
Rest – Menu (€ 23), € 37
◆ This establishment is often full thanks to its delicious inventive cuisine, highly original and strikingly colourful decor and its pleasant garden-terrace.

in Bouliac Southeast, exit n° 23 – pop. 3 248 – alt. 74 m – ✉ 33270

Le St-James < Bordeaux, rm,
pl. C.-Hostein, (at Bouliac), near the church – ✆ 05 57 97 06 00 – stjames@relaischateaux.com – Fax 05 56 20 92 58 – Closed 1st-15 January p. 5 BU **s**
15 rm – †€ 185/290 ††€ 185/290, ☕ € 23 – 3 suites
Rest – *(closed 21 April-5 May, 27 October-5 November, 1st- 15 January, Sunday and Monday)* Menu (€ 30), € 59 bi/125 – Carte € 90/121
Rest *Côté Cour* – *✆ 05 57 97 06 06 (closed 2-24 August, 17 January-1st February, Saturday and Sunday) (lunch only)* Menu (€ 19), € 26
Spec. Makis de légumes croquants, crème glacée boquerone et langoustines (summer). Jeune poulette rôtie en cocotte, déglaçage iodé (October to February.). Crêpes croustillantes à l'orange safranée, sorbet orange sanguine (winter). **Wines** Saint-Estèphe, Saint-Emilion.
◆ Wine-grower's house and tobacco-drying outbuildings designed by J. Nouvel, with fine views of Bordeaux. Designer rooms, one of which boasts a Harley Davidson. Fine, creative cuisine at the restaurant. Seasonal market produce at the Côté Cour brasserie.

Auberge du Marais
22 rte de Latresne – ✆ 05 56 20 52 17 – Fax 05 56 20 98 06 – Closed 4-10 March, 4-26 August, Sunday dinner and Monday p. 5 BV **t**
Rest – Menu € 14,50 (weekday lunch), € 20/48 – Carte € 28/50
◆ In summer, diners can choose between a lovely shaded terrace or rustic-bourgeois dining room, now air-conditioned. Traditional menu.

Café de l'Espérance
(behind the church) – ✆ 05 56 20 52 16 – saintjames@relaischateaux.com – Fax 05 56 20 92 58 p. 5 BV **r**
Rest – Carte € 24/44
◆ Fans of the little village café will love this bistro, where you can take your time over a drink under the trellis. Traditional cuisine and grills listed on the blackboard.

in Bègles Southeast, exit 21 – pop. 24 500 – alt. 6 m – ✉ 33130

Chiopot
281 r. des Quatre-Castera – ✆ 05 56 85 62 41 – chiopot@free.fr – Fax 05 56 85 07 24 – Closed Saturday lunch and Sunday p. 5 BV a
Rest – Menu € 22 bi – Carte € 26/78
◆ In bistro-brasserie style, conviviality is guaranteed whether in the dining room or on the shaded terrace. Traditional dishes, grills, fine wines (on sale in the boutique).

in Martillac 9 km south, exit 18, D 1113 and secondary road – pop. 2 020 – alt. 40 m – ✉ 33650

Les Sources de Caudalie rm, rest,
chemin de Smith-Haut-Lafitte – ✆ 05 57 83 83 83 – sources@sources-caudalie.com – Fax 05 57 83 83 84
43 rm – †€ 200/250 ††€ 235/285, ☕ € 22 – 7 suites
Rest *La Grand'Vigne* – *(closed Monday and Tuesday from November to April)* Menu € 85 – Carte € 67/102
Rest *La Table du Lavoir* – Menu (€ 26), € 35
◆ This estate has a vinotherapy institute and offers luxury, relaxation and health farm facilities in the heart of the vineyards. Up-to-date menu and good choice of wine at the 18C Grand'Vigne. La Table was once the wash house for grape pickers.

Château de Lantic without rest
10 rte de Lartigue – ✆ 05 56 72 58 68 – mginebre@wanadoo.fr – Fax 05 56 72 58 67
8 rm ☕ – †€ 79/159 ††€ 79/159
◆ This adorable castle offers rooms with antique furniture often decorated with a romantic feel. Some have a small kitchen. There are exhibitions in an outbuilding.

Southwest Exit 14 - ✉ 33600 Pessac

Holiday Inn Bordeaux Sud
10 av. Antoine Becquerel – ✆ 05 56 07 59 59 – contact@hi-pessac.com – Fax 05 56 07 59 69 p. 4 AV f
90 rm – †€ 75/150 ††€ 75/150, ☕ € 15 – **Rest** – *(Closed Saturday, Sunday and public holidays)* Menu (€ 17), € 21/27 – Carte € 24/41
◆ Near a motorway ring road, this hotel's rooms are comfortable, modern and have king-size beds. State-of-the-art conference and meeting facilities. Welcoming, bistro-style dining room offering traditional food.

in Mérignac West, exit n° 9 – pop. 61 992 – alt. 35 m – ✉ 33700

Kyriad Prestige rm,
116 av. Magudas – ✆ 05 57 92 00 00 – kprestige@bordeaux-hotels.net – Fax 05 57 92 00 60 p. 4 AT r
75 rm – †€ 80/115 ††€ 80/115, ☕ € 12,50 – 2 suites – **Rest** – *(closed Sunday)* Menu € 26 – Carte € 29/43
◆ Spacious, well-soundproofed rooms of various categories: relatively plain standard rooms, more contemporary executive rooms (teak furnishings) and family rooms with a mezzanine. Cold or hot buffets in a dining room with a fireplace and exposed beams.

in Eysines West, exit n° 9 – pop. 18 407 – alt. 15 m – ✉ 33320

Les Tilleuls
à La Forêt, 205 av. St-Médard – ✆ 05 56 28 04 56 – restotilleuls@wanadoo.fr – Fax 05 56 28 93 22 – Closed 18-24 February, Saturday lunch, Sunday dinner and Monday p. 4 AT v
Rest – Menu € 19 (weekday lunch), € 28/47 – Carte € 44/64
◆ A pleasant restaurant serving classical dishes and regional specialities. A rustic dining room decorated in warm, bright colours, and a pretty terrace in the summer.

to Bordeaux-Mérignac Airport West, exit 11 from the south, exit 11b from the north – ✉ 33700 Mérignac

Quality Suites Aéroport without rest
83 av. J.F.-Kennedy – ✆ 05 57 53 21 22 – reservation@qualitybordeaux.com – Fax 05 57 53 21 23 p. 4 AU b
245 rm – †€ 95/160 ††€ 95/290, ☕ € 17 – 14 suites
◆ New building with minimalist lines. Home entertainment equipment and Wifi in the large contemporary, soundproofed rooms. Lighter meals served at the bar.

Mercure Bordeaux Aéroport rm,

1 av. Ch.-Lindbergh – ✆ 05 56 34 74 74 – h1508@accor.com – Fax 05 56 34 30 84 *p. 4* AU **e**

149 rm – †€ 95/130 ††€ 105/140, ☕ € 14 – **Rest** – Menu € 21/34 – Carte € 23/54

◆ Hotel designed for a good rest between flights. English-style bar, meeting rooms and well-updated rooms (decor on the theme of the five continents). Traditional cuisine served in an elegant dining room overlooking a terrace.

Novotel Aéroport rm,

av. J.F.-Kennedy – ✆ 05 57 53 13 30 – h0402@accor.com – Fax 05 56 55 99 64

137 rm – †€ 95/135 ††€ 95/135, ☕ € 13,50 – **Rest** – Menu € 19/25 – Carte € 22/40 *p. 4* AU **k**

◆ This hotel has updated its image with trendier renovated rooms and a café in line with the chain's latest specifications. Pine wood and outside play area for children. Simple cuisine based mainly on grills and a pleasant view of the garden.

L' Iguane

83 av. J.F.-Kennedy – ✆ 05 56 34 07 39 – iguane.rest@wanadoo.fr – Fax 05 56 34 41 37 *p. 4* AU **b**

Rest – *(closed 27 July-24 August, Saturday lunch and Sunday)* Menu (€ 21), € 32/40 bi – Carte € 40/57

Rest *L'Olive de Mer* – *✆ 05 56 12 99 99 (closed Friday dinner, Sunday lunch and Saturday)* Menu € 22/37 – Carte € 25/38

◆ Bright, contemporary long dining room, with parquet flooring and slatted blinds). Attentive service, white tablecloths and seasonal menu. Sea-inspired menu at the Olive de Mer (designer furniture and fashionable decor).

LES BORDES – 45 Loiret – 318 L5 – see Sully-sur-Loire

BORMES-LES-MIMOSAS – 83 Var – 340 N7 – pop. 6 324 – alt. 180 m –

✉ 83230 French Riviera 41 **C3**

Paris 871 – Fréjus 57 – Hyères 21 – Le Lavandou 4 – St-Tropez 35 – Toulon 39

Office de tourisme, 1, place Gambetta ✆ 04 94 01 38 38, Fax 04 94 01 38 39

de Valcros La Londe-les-MauresNorthwest: 12 km, ✆ 04 94 66 81 02.

Site★ - Old streets★ - ← ★ of the château.

Hostellerie du Cigalou without rest

pl. Gambetta, In the old village – ✆ 04 94 41 51 27 – resas@hostellerieducigalou.com – Fax 04 94 46 20 73

17 rm – †€ 100/230 ††€ 100/230, ☕ € 13,50 – 3 suites

◆ The owner of this pretty house has decorated the rooms with sophistication, mixing different styles and atmospheres. Meals served in the charming Provençal café downstairs.

La Bastide des Vignes rm,

464 chemin Patelin – ✆ 04 94 71 20 29 – bastidedesvignes@wanadoo.fr – Fax 04 94 15 12 71

5 rm ☕ – †€ 105/129 ††€ 105/129 – **Table d'hôte** – Menu € 40 bi

◆ A charming bastide set amid the vineyards. The cosy, very Provençal rooms (floor tiles, ochre shades) don't have TVs and are exceptionally quiet. Lovely swimming pools. Regional wine tasting in the restaurant, offered every other day, reservations necessary.

Les Plumbagos without rest ← sea,

88 impasse du Pin, quartier Le Pin, le Mont Roses – ✆ 06 09 82 42 86 – plumbagos@wanadoo.fr – Open March-October

3 rm ☕ – †€ 90/125 ††€ 90/125

◆ The attractions of this lovely 1920s building include a splendid, tranquil location overlooking the bay, pretty Provençal-style guestrooms and a delightful garden.

Lou Portaou

r. Cubert-des-Poètes – ✆ 04 94 64 86 37 – lou.portaou@wanadoo.fr – Fax 04 94 64 81 43 – Closed 15 November-20 December, Saturday lunch in season, Sunday dinner and Monday off season

Rest – *(pre-book)* Menu € 32/39 – Carte approx. € 41

◆ Unusual "restaurant-museum" that has kept the soul of this old medieval residence: objects and furniture from this period are reunited in the two little vaulted rooms.

La Tonnelle de Gil Renard

pl. Gambetta – ☎ 04 94 71 34 84 – restau.la.tonnelle@free.fr – Closed 1 week in March, 1st November-7 December, Thursday from October to March, Thursday lunch in May, June and September and Wednesday except July-August

Rest – *(dinner only in July-August)* Menu (€ 27), € 38/42 – Carte € 41/49

♦ Old house next to the tourist office. Dining room and veranda feature the colours of the south; a fireplace provides welcome warmth in the.

La Rastègue

48 bd Levant, to the south, Le Pin district: 2km – ☎ 04 94 15 19 41 – Closed January, Monday and lunch except Sunday.

Rest – Menu € 39

♦ This welcoming restaurant sets itself apart with its pleasant terrace and its gleaming kitchen opening on to the dining room. Single set menu announced to you (regionally inspired food).

South 1 km – ✉ 83230 Bormes-les-Mimosas

Le Domaine du Mirage

rm, rest,

38 r. Vue-des-Iles – ☎ 04 94 05 32 60 – resas@domainedumirage.com – Fax 04 94 64 93 03 – Open 29 March-5 November

35 rm – 🚹€ 126/256 🚹🚹€ 126/256, ☕ € 13,50 – ½ P € 107/173

Rest – Menu € 34 – Carte € 34/42

♦ Pleasant hotel on the heights of Bormes, in the midst of lush vegetation. Pretty Provençal-style furnished rooms with a balcony or terrace. Restaurant in a pleasant setting of wrought iron, southern shades and murals.

in la Favière 4 km south – ✉ 83230 Bormes-les-Mimosas

Plage

rest,

– ☎ 04 94 71 02 74 – hoteldelaplage.bormes@wanadoo.fr – Fax 04 94 71 77 22 – Open 1st April-30 September

45 rm – 🚹€ 55/79 🚹🚹€ 55/79, ☕ € 8 – ½ P € 55/66 – **Rest** – *(dinner only except Sunday)* Menu € 22/29 – Carte € 22/40

♦ A stone's throw from Cap Bénat and the Brégançon Fort, this hotel has simple, well-soundproofed rooms adorned with pictures and old curios. Dining room exuding a genteel guesthouse ambiance and a shaded terrace with Provençal fountain.

in Cabasson 8 km south – ✉ 83230 Bormes-les-Mimosas

Les Palmiers

240 Chemin du Petit-Fort – ☎ 04 94 64 81 94 – les.palmiers@wanadoo.fr – Fax 04 94 64 93 61 – Closed 10 November-1st February

17 rm – 🚹€ 60/140 🚹🚹€ 160/200, ☕ € 15 – ½ P € 100/180

Rest – Menu € 33/62 – Carte € 37/65

♦ Brégançon Fort and the beach are close to this establishment. The majority of the bedroom balconies overlook the garden. Bright dining room and poolside terrace. Bouillabaisse on request.

BORNY – 57 Moselle – 307 I4 – see Metz

BORT-L'ÉTANG – 63 Puy-de-Dôme – 326 H8 – see Lezoux

BOSDARROS – 64 Pyrénées-Atlantiques – 342 J5 – pop. 937 – alt. 370 m – ✉ 64290

3 **B3**

Paris 790 – Pau 14 – Lourdes 36 – Oloron-Ste-Marie 29 – Tarbes 50

Auberge Labarthe (Eric Dequin)

1 r. P.-Bidau – ☎ 05 59 21 50 13 – auberge-labarthe@wanadoo.fr – Fax 05 59 21 68 55 – Closed 22 June-7 July, 18-31 January, Sunday dinner, Monday and Tuesday

Rest – *(pre-book Sat - Sun)* Menu € 23/62 – Carte € 58/70

Spec. Ventrèche de thon rouge (spring-summer). Palombe entière rôtie, flambée au capucin (October-November). Baba au vieux rhum (spring-summer). **Wines** Jurançon, Béarn.

♦ A smart flower-decked house behind the church. Elegant, rustic-style dining room decorated in subtle tones of pink and pale green. Generous portions of regional cuisine.

BOSSEY – 74 Haute-Savoie – **328** J4 – see St-Julien-en-Genevois

LES BOSSONS – 74 Haute-Savoie – **328** O5 – see Chamonix

BOUAYE – 44 Loire-Atlantique – **316** F5 – see Nantes

BOUC-BEL-AIR – 13 Bouches-du-Rhône – **340** H5 – pop. 12 297 – alt. 259 m – ✉ 13320 40 **B3**

Paris 758 – Aix-en-Provence 10 – Aubagne 41 – Marseille 22 – Salon-de-Provence 43

L'Étape Lani rm, rm, rm, VISA MC AE D

south on D 6 Gardane-Marseille road – ✆ 04 42 22 61 90 – etapelani@worldonline.fr – Fax 04 42 22 68 67 – Closed Sunday

31 rm – €64/72 €70/82, €17 – ½ P €58/89

Rest – *(closed lunch 23-31 December, Monday lunch, Sunday lunch in July-August, Saturday lunch and Sunday dinner)* Menu €17 (weekday lunch), €26/52

◆ The warm welcome and well-soundproofed rooms in the main building and the pleasant Provençal decor in the new annexe quickly make guests forget about the busy nearby road. Charming restaurant in sunny tones, serving cuisine with a distinct Southern flavour.

BOUCÉ – 03 Allier – **326** H5 – see Varennes-sur-Allier

LE BOUCHET – 74 Haute-Savoie – **328** L5 – see Le Grand-Bornand

BOUDES – 63 Puy-de-Dôme – **326** G10 – pop. 252 – alt. 466 m – ✉ 63340 5 **B2**

Paris 462 – Brioude 29 – Clermont-Fd 52 – Issoire 16 – St-Flour 62

Le Boudes La Vigne with rm rest, VISA MC AE D

– ✆ 04 73 96 55 66 – Fax 04 73 96 55 55 – Closed 30 June-8 July, 25 August-3 September, 2-22 January, Sunday dinner, Tuesday lunch and Monday

10 rm – €38 €38/85, €6 – ½ P €60 – **Rest** – Menu (€17), €22/45

◆ A house built on the old fortifications. Updated cuisine served in a refurbished room decorated in pastel shades with stone walls. Fine selection of local vintages.

BOUËSSE – 36 Indre – **323** G7 – see Argenton-sur-Creuse

BOUGIVAL – 78 Yvelines – **311** I2 – **101** 13 – see Paris, Area

LA BOUILLADISSE – 13 Bouches-du-Rhône – **340** I5 – pop. 4 904 – alt. 220 m – ✉ 13720 40 **B3**

Paris 776 – Aix-en-Provence 27 – Brignoles 43 – Marseille 31 – Toulon 60

Syndicat d'initiative, place de la Libération ✆ 04 42 62 97 08, Fax 04 42 62 98 65

La Fenière rm, rest, VISA MC AE

– ✆ 04 42 72 38 38 – la.feniere@wanadoo.fr – Fax 04 42 62 30 54 – Closed Saturday lunch and Sunday

10 rm – €50/60 €58/63, €7 – ½ P €51/55 – **Rest** – Menu €16/25 – Carte €24/43

◆ Establishment housed in two buildings. On the garden/swimming pool side you will find small, practical and meticulously well-kept rooms. A Provençal style restaurant (exposed beams and fireplace) leading onto a terrace serving regional cuisine.

BOUILLAND – 21 Côte-d'Or – 320 I7 – pop. 168 – alt. 400 m – ✉ 21420
Burgundy-Jura 8 **C2**

Paris 295 – Autun 54 – Beaune 17 – Bligny-sur-Ouche 13 – Dijon 41 – Saulieu 57

Hostellerie du Vieux Moulin
1 r. de la Forge – ☎ 03 80 21 51 16 – le-moulin@le-moulin-de-bouilland.com – Fax 03 80 21 59 90 – Open 13 March-1st December and 17 December-2 January
23 rm – €85/160 €85/160, ☕ €16 – 3 suites
Rest – *(closed lunch Monday-Thursday and Wednesday dinner October-May)* Menu €39/105 – Carte €81/102
Spec. Homard du vivier. Côtes et selle d'agneau, jus à la réglisse (April to July). Filet de bœuf charolais, jus à l'anchois. **Wines** Savigny-les-Beaune, Ladoix.
♦ Older rooms in the mill; more modern in the outbuildings. Peace and quiet only two minutes from the A6 motorway and Burgundy's vineyards! Fitness centre and swimming pool. Refined seasonal menu which celebrates local produce. Contemporary dining room.

Auberge Saint-Martin
17 rte de Beaune – ☎ 03 80 21 53 01 – Fax 03 80 21 53 01 – Closed 1st-9 July, 3 December-7 February, Tuesday and Wednesday
Rest – Menu €20/28 – Carte €23/31
♦ The small, country-style dining room in this welcoming 18C inn looks onto a pretty wooden terrace. Appetising traditional dishes alongside specialities from Burgundy.

LA BOUILLE – 76 Seine-Maritime – 304 F5 – pop. 791 – alt. 5 m – ✉ 76530
Normandy 33 **D2**

Paris 132 – Bernay 44 – Elbeuf 12 – Louviers 32 – Pont-Audemer 35 – Rouen 21

Le Bellevue
13 quai Hector-Malot – ☎ 02 35 18 05 05 – bellevue@hotel.wanadoo.fr – Fax 02 35 18 00 92 – Closed 3-10 August and 24 December-4 January
20 rm – €53/86 €53/86, ☕ €8 – ½ P €49/53 – **Rest** – *(closed Sunday dinner from 15 October to 15 April)* Menu €15/41 – Carte €35/79
♦ On a bank of the Seine. Rooms variously furnished (colourful cane or seventies style); some have fine views of the river. The pleasant dining room is typical of Normandy, with beams and half-timbering.

St-Pierre
4 pl. du Bateau – ☎ 02 35 68 02 01 – blanchardlau@wanadoo.fr – Fax 02 35 68 04 26 – Closed 25 August-9 September, 3-11 November, 18 February-4 March, Sunday dinner from October to Easter, Monday and Tuesday
Rest – Menu (€20), €27/65 – Carte €54/70
♦ A bright, modern dining room and pleasant terrace with the Seine as a backdrop. Contemporary cuisine and friendly, efficient service.

De la Poste
6 pl. du Bateau – ☎ 02 35 18 03 90 – Fax 02 35 18 18 91 – Closed 17 December-9 January, Sunday dinner, Monday dinner and Tuesday
Rest – Menu €29/42 – Carte €50/62
♦ 18C post house with pretty, half-timbered façade, anchored along the quays. Rustic dining room or, on the first floor, more modern and brighter decor with a view of the Seine.

Les Gastronomes
1 pl. du Bateau – ☎ 02 35 18 02 07 – Fax 02 35 18 14 49 – Closed 24 October-13 November, 20 February-5 March, Wednesday and Thursday except public holidays
Rest – Menu €20/41 – Carte €42/50
♦ Next to the church, a family restaurant with two dining rooms; the one on the ground floor is like a Belle Époque bistro; rustic touches and a panormaic view upstairs.

BOUIN – 85 Vendée – 316 E6 – pop. 2 242 – alt. 5 m – ✉ 85230 34 **A3**

Paris 435 – Challans 22 – Nantes 51 – Noirmoutier-en-l'Ile 29 – La Roche-sur-Yon 66

Office de tourisme, boulevard Sébastien Luneau ☎ 02 51 68 88 85

Du Martinet rm, rest, VISA MC AE
pl. du Gén.-Charette – 02 51 49 08 94 – hotel.martinet@wanadoo.fr – Fax 02 51 49 83 08
30 rm – €49/56 €56/74, €7 – ½ P €56/65 – **Rest** – *(closed Monday lunch and Tuesday lunch)* Menu €24/36 – Carte €22/42
◆ Old house with a family ambiance in a quiet village in the Breton Vendée marshland. The rooms on the garden level are pleasant and cosy. Characterful dining room (furniture and antique objects) and pretty veranda. Local seafood.

BOULIAC – 33 Gironde – 335 H6 – see Bordeaux

BOULIGNEUX – 01 Ain – 328 C4 – see Villars-les-Dombes

BOULOGNE-BILLANCOURT – 92 Hauts-de-Seine – 311 J2 – 101 24 – see Paris, Area

BOULOGNE-SUR-MER – 62 Pas-de-Calais – 301 C3 – pop. 44 859 – Built-up area 135 116 – alt. 58 m – Casino (private) Z – ✉ 62200

Northern France and the Paris Region 30 **A2**

Paris 265 – Amiens 130 – Arras 122 – Calais 35 – Lille 118 – Rouen 185

Office de tourisme, 24, quai Gambetta 03 21 10 88 10, Fax 03 21 10 88 11

de Wimereux Wimereux Avenue François Mitterrand, by Wimereux road: 8 km, 03 21 32 43 20.

Nausicaa★★★ - Ville haute★★: crypt and treasure-house★ of the basilica ≤★ of the belfry Y **H** - Views★ from the ramparts - Calvaire des marins ≤★ Y - Château-museum ★: Greek vases★★, Inuit and Aleout masks ★★ - Colonne de la Grande Armée★: ✵★★ 5 km by ① - Côte d'Opale★ by ①.

Plan on next page

La Matelote ≤ VISA MC AE
70 bd Ste-Beuve – 03 21 30 33 33 – tony.lestienne@la-matelote.com – Fax 03 21 30 87 40 Y **q**
35 rm – €80/115 €95/170, €15
Rest ***La Matelote*** – see restaurant listing
◆ An elegant 1930s building on the seafront, opposite Nausicaa. Comfortable rooms, warm atmosphere, attentive service and a new relaxation centre.

Métropole without rest VISA MC AE
51 r. Thiers – 03 21 31 54 30 – hotel.metropol@wanadoo.fr – Fax 03 21 30 45 72 – Closed 20 December-12 January Z **e**
25 rm – €69/75 €87/94, €10,50
◆ Town-centre family hotel. The spacious rooms offer modern facilities (new bedding). Attractive breakfast room overlooking the garden.

Hamiot VISA MC AE
1 r. Faidherbe – 03 21 31 44 20 – hotelrestauranthamiot@wanadoo.fr – Fax 03 21 83 71 56 Z **h**
12 rm – €65/95 €80/100, €12 – ½ P €90/120
Rest ***Grand Restaurant*** – *(closed 23 June-6 July, 1st-15 September, 1st-15 January, Sunday dinner and Wednesday)* Menu €20/38 – Carte €43/56
Rest ***Brasserie*** – Menu €13,50/30 – Carte €18/36
◆ This post-war building overlooks the port and has renovated rooms (fine wooden furniture) that are comfortable and well soundproofed. The Grand Restaurant offers a low-key atmosphere and overlooks the harbour. Brasserie with a lively atmosphere and summer terrace.

H. de la Plage without rest ≤ VISA MC AE
168 bd Ste-Beuve – 03 21 32 15 15 – hoteldelaplage4@wanadoo.fr – Fax 03 21 30 47 97 X **u**
42 rm – €45/55 €55/75, €7
◆ The hotel is right on the seafront, hence the name ("Beach"). Functional rooms; those at the back are quiet and those at the front from the third floor up are best for views.

BOULOGNE-SUR-MER

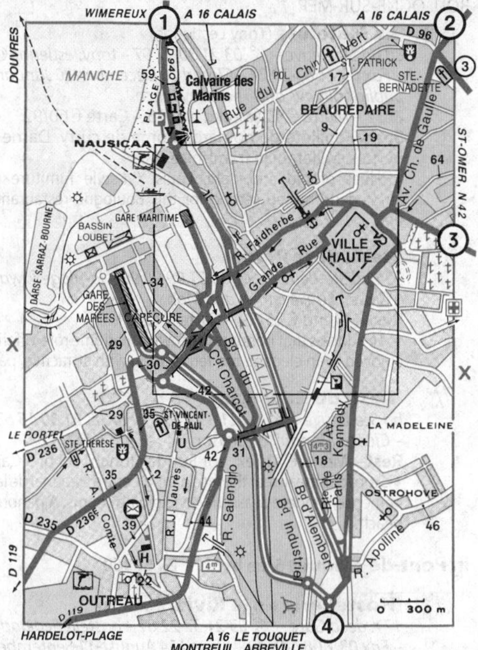

NAUSICAA
GARE MARITIME
PORT
BASSIN NAPOLÉON
CAPÉCURE
ST-PIERRE
ST-MICHEL
Musée San Martin
CASINO
St-Nicolas
Basilique
CHÂTEAU MUSÉE
VILLE HAUTE
ST-FRANÇOIS DE-SALES
VIADUC J-JAURÈS
LE TOUQUET MONTREUIL
CENTRALE
0 200 m

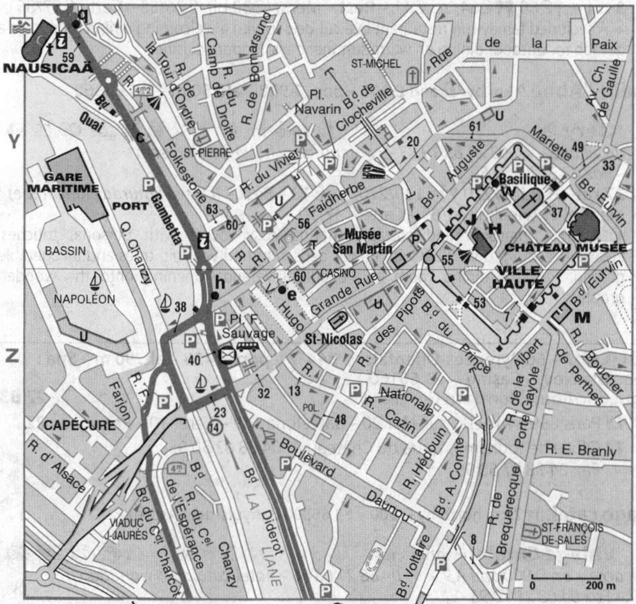

La Matelote (Tony Lestienne)
80 bd Ste Beuve – ☎ 03 21 30 17 97 – tony.lestienne@la-matelote.com – Fax 03 21 83 29 24 – Closed 20 December-20 January, Sunday dinner except public holidays and Thursday lunch Y **q**
Rest – Menu € 35 (weekdays)/75 – Carte € 60/92
Spec. Feuilleté de homard, arôme de curry. Darne de turbot, sabayon de fines herbes. Millefeuille framboise.
◆ Hues of red and gold, Louis XVI-style furniture and nautical ornaments form an elegant, muted setting for this Boulogne restaurant. Seafood prepared to perfection.

Rest. de la Plage
124 bd Ste-Beuve – ☎ 03 21 99 90 90 – la-plage@wanadoo.fr – Fax 03 21 87 23 14 – Closed Sun. evening and Mon. X **v**
Rest – Menu € 25/59 – Carte € 42/81
◆ An address that honours the town's maritime role, offering a menu rich in seafood, to be enjoyed in an elegant, modern setting with attractive, pastel shades.

Rest. de Nausicaa
bd Ste-Beuve – ☎ 03 21 33 24 24 – Fax 03 21 30 15 63 – Closed Monday off season Y **t**
Rest – Menu € 21 (except Sunday lunch)/35 bi – Carte € 29/56
◆ Stop for a meal near the fascinating Centre National de la Mer. A lively atmosphere in two immense, modern brasserie-style dining rooms. A panoramic view over the harbour and beach.

in Pont-de-Briques 5 km by ④ – ✉ 62360

Hostellerie de la Rivière with rm
17 r. de la Gare – ☎ 03 21 32 22 81 – hostelleriedelariviere@wanadoo.fr – Fax 03 21 87 45 48 – Closed 24 August-11 September, 7-28 January, Sunday dinner, Tuesday lunch and Monday
8 rm – †€ 60 ††€ 64, ☕ € 11 – **Rest** – Menu (€ 30 bi), € 36/55 – Carte € 57/85
◆ A secluded family-run restaurant in a cul-de-sac with a welcoming dining room plus a garden for outdoor dining on warm summer days. Modern cuisine.

in Hesdin-l'Abbé 9 km by ④ and D 901 – pop. 1 998 – alt. 50 m – ✉ 62360

Cléry
au village – ☎ 03 21 83 19 83 – chateau-clery.hotel@najeti.com – Fax 03 21 87 52 59
27 rm – †€ 130/270 ††€ 130/270, ☕ € 18 – **Rest** – *(closed Saturday lunchtime)* Menu € 29 (weekdays)/69 – Carte € 47/59
◆ An 18C mansion and cottage offering cosy rooms with personal touches. Pleasant reading room. Park with flower beds, hundred-year-old trees and a vegetable garden. Pleasant dining room and beautiful veranda opening onto the wooded grounds.

LE BOULOU – **66 Pyrénées-Orientales – 344** I7 – **pop. 4 428 – alt. 90 m – Spa : mid Feb.-late Nov. – Casino – ✉ 66160**
Languedoc-Roussillon-Tarn Gorges 22 **B3**

Paris 869 – Argelès-sur-Mer 20 – Barcelona 169 – Céret 10 – Perpignan 22

Office de tourisme, 1, rue du Château ☎ 04 68 87 50 95, Fax 04 68 87 50 96

at village catalan 7 km north by D 900 – ✉ 66300 Banyuls-dels-Aspres

Village Catalan without rest
access on D 900 and A 9 – ☎ 04 68 21 66 66 – hotel-catalan@wanadoo.fr – Fax 04 68 21 70 95
77 rm – †€ 60/70 ††€ 70/84, ☕ € 10
◆ On a motorway service area, functional, well-soundproofed rooms, some of which overlook the garden and pool; eight have a private garage.

Southeast 4.5 km by D 900, D 618 and secondary road – ✉ 66160 Le Boulou

Relais des Chartreuses — rm, VISA MC AE
106 av. d'En-Carbouner – ✆ 04 68 83 15 88 – contact@relais-des-chartreuses.fr – Fax 04 68 83 26 62 – Closed 2 January-15 February
10 rm – †€ 60/150 ††€ 60/150, ☕ € 10 – ½ P € 65/170
Rest – *(closed Wednesday) (dinner only) (residents only)* Menu € 26
◆ Built on a hillside, a stone farmhouse from the 17C that has been entirely restored. Spacious personalised rooms. Sauna, jacuzzi and terrace under the lime trees.

in Vivès 5 km West by D 115 and D 73 – **pop. 128** – **alt. 228 m** – ✉ 66490

L'Hostalet de Vivès with rm — A/C rm, VISA MC
r. de la Mairie – ✆ 04 68 83 05 52 – hostalet.de.vives@free.fr – Fax 04 68 83 51 91 – Closed 13 January-5 March, Tuesday off season and Wednesday
3 rm – †€ 60/95 ††€ 60/95, ☕ € 11 – **Rest** – Menu € 22 (weekday lunch)/32 – Carte € 29/52
◆ This fine 12C stone house has preserved all its old charm. Staff wear traditional costumes and serve huge Catalan dishes. A few functional guest rooms.

BOURBACH-LE-BAS – 68 Haut-Rhin – 315 G10 – pop. 563 – alt. 340 m – ✉ 68290 1 A3

▶ Paris 451 – Altkirch 27 – Belfort 26 – Mulhouse 25 – Thann 10

A la Couronne d'Or with rm — P VISA MC AE
9 r. Principale – ✆ 03 89 82 51 77 – Fax 03 89 82 58 03 – Closed 18 February-2 March
7 rm – †€ 42 ††€ 58, ☕ € 7 – **Rest** – *(Closed Monday and Tuesday)* Menu € 19/50 – Carte € 25/49
◆ In a little village in the Doller Valley. Long cottage with a sectional rustic dining room and a smaller room with a stove. Simple, well-soundproofed rooms.

BOURBON-LANCY – 71 Saône-et-Loire – 320 C10 – pop. 5 634 – alt. 240 m – Spa : early April-late Oct. – Casino – ✉ 71140 Burgundy-Jura 7 B3

▶ Paris 308 – Autun 62 – Mâcon 110 – Montceau-les-Mines 55 – Moulins 36

ℹ Office de tourisme, place d'Aligre ✆ 03 85 89 18 27, Fax 03 85 89 28 38

⛳ de Givalois Givallois, East: 3 km, ✆ 03 85 89 05 48.

◉ Wooden house and Clock tower ★ B.

BOURBON-LANCY

Aligre (Pl. d') 2
Autun (R. d') 3
Châtaigneraie (R. de la) 4
Commerce (R. du) 5
Dr-Gabriel-Pain (R. du) 6
Dr-Robert (R. du) 7
Gaulle (Av. du Gén.-de) . . . . .
Gueugnon (R. de) 12
Horloge (R. de l') 13
Libération (Av. de la) 15
Musée (R. du) 16
Prébendes (R. des) 18
République (Pl. de la) 22
St-Nazaire (R.) 23

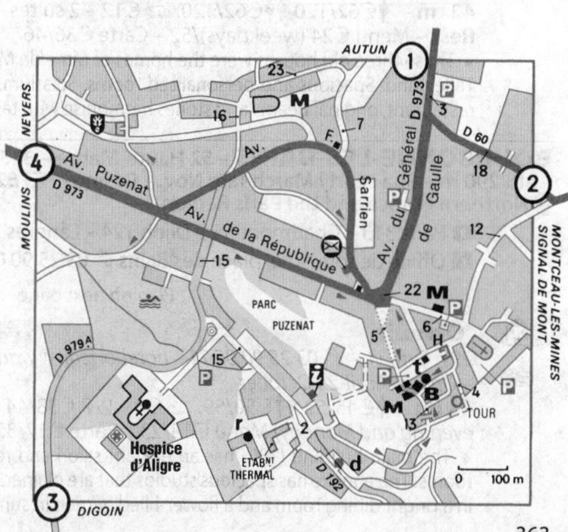

Le Manoir de Sornat rest, VISA AE

allée Sornat , 2 km Moulins road via ④ – ☎ 03 85 89 17 39 – manoir-de-sornat@wanadoo.fr – Fax 03 85 89 29 47 – Closed 2 January-10 February, Sunday dinner except July-August and public holidays, Monday lunch and Tuesday lunch

13 rm – €62/110 €62/140, €12 – ½ P €80/110 – **Rest** – Menu (€ 19), €25 (weekday lunch), €28 € (dinner)/90 – Carte €55/93

◆ Normandy mansion in a pleasant wooded park. Fine woodwork in the hall and sitting room. Spacious rooms furnished in contemporary style. The decoration of the plush dining room pays homage to Monet; updated classic cuisine.

Le Grand Hôtel VISA

1 parc Thermal – ☎ 03 85 89 08 87 – ghthermal@stbl.fr – Fax 03 85 89 32 23 – Open 1st March-15 December and closed Tuesday and Wednesday from 27 October to 15 December **r**

28 rm – €56 €70/78, €6 – ½ P €53/56 – **Rest** – Menu €21/25 – Carte €21/42

◆ Old convent bordering the park of the spa. Spacious rooms, with modern or period furniture. The restaurant is rather austere - a bit like a "pension de famille". There is a pretty terrace in the former convent's cloister; special dietary meals on request.

La Tourelle du Beffroi without rest VISA

pl. de la Mairie – ☎ 03 85 89 39 20 – contact@hotellatourelle.fr – Fax 03 85 89 39 29 – **8 rm** – €55 €73, €9 **t**

◆ Good spot by the belfry for this lovely 1900 house with a tower and balustraded terrace. Rooms decorated with care. Guesthouse ambiance.

XX **Villa du Vieux Puits** with rm rest, VISA

7 r. Bel-Air – ☎ 03 85 89 04 04 – Fax 03 85 89 13 87 – Closed 22 January-10 March, 23 December-6 January and Sunday **d**

7 rm – €48/50 €50/60, €10 – ½ P €65/72 – **Rest** – *(dinner only)* Menu €20/40 – Carte €31/42

◆ Pretty guesthouse in the walls of a former tannery hidden away in a garden below the road. Country-style restaurant and cosy rooms.

BOURBON-L'ARCHAMBAULT – 03 Allier – 326 F3 – pop. 2 564 – alt. 367 m – Spa : early March-early Nov. – Casino – ✉ 03160 Auvergne 5 **B1**

Paris 292 – Montluçon 53 – Moulins 24 – Nevers 54

Office de tourisme, 1, place de l'Hotel de Ville ☎ 04 70 67 09 79, Fax 04 70 67 15 20

New park ←★ - Château ←★.

Grand Hôtel Montespan-Talleyrand rest, VISA AE

pl. des Thermes – ☎ 04 70 67 00 24 – hotelmontespan@wanadoo.fr – Fax 04 70 67 12 00 – Open 1st April-19 October

42 rm – €62/120 €62/120, €12 – 2 suites – ½ P €64/83

Rest – Menu €24 (weekdays)/52 – Carte €36/46

◆ These three old houses were the homes of Mme de Montespan, Mme de Sévigné and Talleyrand. Spacious and personalised rooms. Solarium, classical interior garden. In the restaurant, original beams and stones harmonise with tasteful contemporary decoration.

BOURBONNE-LES-BAINS – 52 Haute-Marne – 313 O6 – pop. 2 495 – alt. 290 m – Spa : early March-late Nov. – Casino – ✉ 52400 Northern France and the Paris Region 14 **D3**

Paris 313 – Chaumont 55 – Dijon 124 – Langres 39 – Neufchâteau 53

Office de tourisme, place des Bains ☎ 03 25 90 01 71, Fax 03 25 90 14 12

Plan on next page

Orfeuil rest, VISA

29 r. Orfeuil – ☎ 03 25 90 05 71 – hotel-orfeuil@wanadoo.fr – Fax 03 25 84 46 25 – Open 6 April-25 October **a**

43 rm – €45/52 €50/59, €8 – ½ P €38/44 – **Rest** – *(closed Sunday evening and Monday)* Menu €13/23 – Carte €17/32

◆ The main building (18C) has an elegant salon and regularly renovated, comfortable rooms. The annexe has spacious studios that are plainer. Sixties furnishings and greenery in a bright dining room and a flower-filled garden in summer.

BOURBONNE-LES-BAINS

Bains (R. des) 2
Bassigny (R. du) 3
Capucins (R. des) 4
Daprey Blache (R.) 5
Écoles (R. des) 6
Gouby (Av. du Lieutenant) 7
Grande-Rue 9
Hôtel-Dieu (R. de l') 12
Lattre-de-Tassigny
(Av. Maréchal-de) 14
Maistre (R. du Gén.) 15
Pierre (R. Amiral) 22
Porte Galon (R.) 23
Verdun (Pl. de) 25
Walferdin (R.) 26

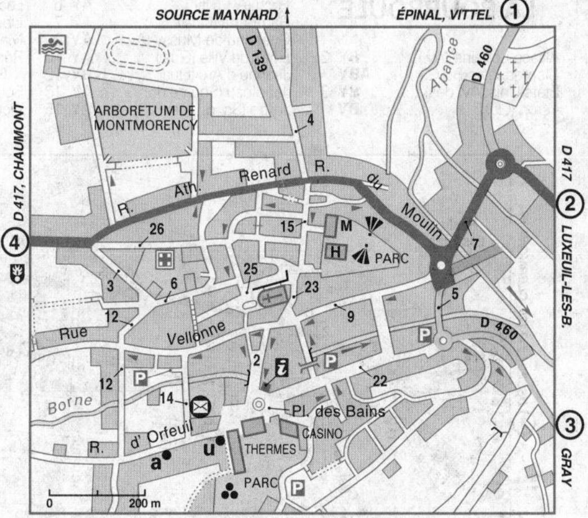

Des Sources

rm, rest, VISA

pl. des Bains – *03 25 87 86 00* – *hotel-des-sources@wanadoo.fr* – *Fax 03 25 87 86 33* – *Open 6 April-29 November* **u**

23 rm – €45/55 €50/65, €8 – ½ P €40/46 – **Rest** – *(closed Wed. evening)* Menu €13/30 – Carte €21/41

◆ Family establishment near the baths, with simple, functional and well-kept rooms. The dining room opens up onto a pretty verdant patio with a small pool, where tables are set in good weather.

LA BOURBOULE – 63 Puy-de-Dôme – 326 D9 – pop. 2 043 – alt. 880 m – Spa : early Feb.-early Oct. – Casino AZ – ✉ 63150 Auvergne 5 B2

Paris 469 – Aubusson 82 – Clermont-Ferrand 50 – Mauriac 71 – Ussel 51

Office de tourisme, place de la République 04 73 65 57 71, Fax 04 73 65 50 21

Parc Fenêstre★ - Murat-le-Quaire: musée de la Toinette★ North: 2 km.

Plan on next page

Régina

VISA

av. Alsace-Lorraine – *04 73 81 09 22* – *reservation@hotelregina-labourboule.com* – *Fax 04 73 81 08 55* – *Closed 1st-20 December and 5 January-1st February* BY **v**

24 rm – €58/65 €70/140, €7,50 – ½ P €55/75

Rest – *(closed lunchtime from 11 - 30 Nov and from 20 Jan - 3 Feb)* Menu €13/30 – Carte €23/40

◆ A 19C residence on the banks of the Dordogne. Rooms are modern and well equipped. Leisure area. Two dining rooms: one Art Deco with moulded ceiling and old parquet flooring, the other is modern. The new chef prepares wholesome traditional recipes.

Le Charlet

rest, VISA

bd L.-Choussy – *04 73 81 33 00* – *contact@lecharlet.fr* – *Fax 04 73 65 50 82* – *Closed 10 November-20 December* AZ **g**

36 rm – €45/70 €50/75, €9 – ½ P €45/62 – **Rest** – Menu €18/35 – Carte €23/43

◆ Hotel in a fairly quiet district, offering small, clean rooms in perfect condition. Full relaxation and sports facilities. A restaurant with bistro style furniture, green plants and screens. Extensive, traditional and regional menu.

LA BOURBOULE

Alsace-Lorraine (Av.) . . . . BY 2
Clemenceau (Bd G.) . . . . . ABY
États-Unis (Av. des) . . . . BY 3
Féron (Quai) . . . . BY
Foch (Av. Mar.) . . . . AY 6
Gambetta (Quai) . . . . AZ 7
Guéneau-de-Mussy (Av.) . . . AY 8
Hôtel de Ville (Quai) . . . . AY 10
Jeanne-d'Arc (Quai) . . . . BY 12
Jet-d'eau (Square du) . . . . . . AY 13
Joffre (Sq. du Mar.). . . . . BY 15
Lacoste (Pl. G.) . . . . AY 16
Libération (Q. de la) . . . . AZ 17
Mangin (Av. du Général). . . . AZ 19
République (Pl. de la) . . . . AZ 21
Souvenir (Pl. du) . . . . BY 22
Victoire (Pl. de la). . . . . AY 23

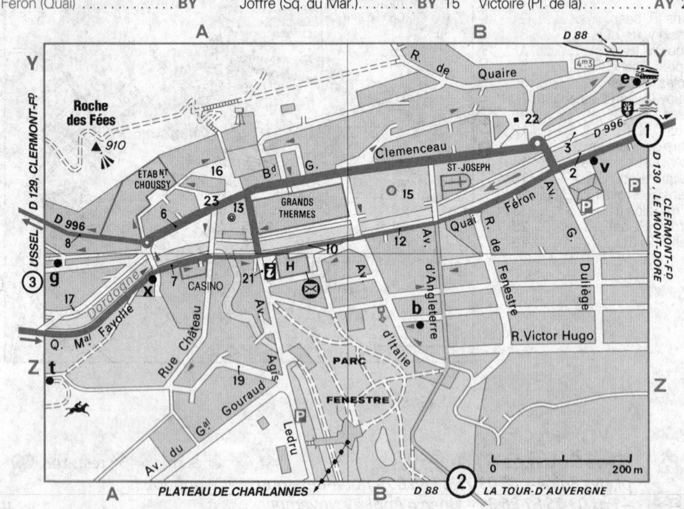

Le Parc des Fées
rest, VISA AE
107 quai Mar.-Fayolle – ✆ 04 73 81 01 77 – info@parcdesfees.com – Fax 04 73 81 30 40 – Closed 6 November-20 December and 8 January-1st February
42 rm – 🛉€ 49/56 🛉🛉€ 61/67, ☕ € 9 AZ **x**
Rest – Menu (€ 10), € 18 – Carte € 20/29
◆ Half of the rooms in this century-old building overlook the Dordogne. Space, modern decoration and comfort are on the menu. Games room for children. Welcoming restaurant where pastel tones and mirrors abound. Traditional menu.

Aviation
rest, VISA AE
r. de Metz – ✆ 04 73 81 32 32 – aviation@nat.fr – Fax 04 73 81 02 85 – Closed 1st October-21 December BZ **b**
44 rm – 🛉€ 49/64 🛉🛉€ 49/64, ☕ € 7 – ½ P € 46/57 – **Rest** – Menu € 16/19 – Carte € 15/28
◆ Hotel in an early-20C house near the Fenestre park. Home to functional rooms and a wide range of leisure facilities: pool, fitness, games room, billiards, etc. Classic, regional meals served in a tasteful dining room with well-spaced tables.

Au Val Doré
VISA AE
r. de Belgique – ✆ 04 73 81 06 14 – valdore@wanadoo.fr – Fax 04 73 65 58 79 – Closed 11 November-25 December BY **e**
29 rm – 🛉€ 41/57 🛉🛉€ 43/69, ☕ € 7 – ½ P € 45/52 – **Rest** – Menu € 12 (weekday lunch), € 17/21 – Carte € 15/29
◆ A family-run hotel near the railway station. The rooms are decorated in a low-key modern fashion. Small indoor pool and fitness facilities. Have a drink before dinner in the lounge (fireplace) followed by simple dishes in the spacious, sunny dining room decorated with flowers.

La Lauzeraie without rest
P
577 chemin de la Suchère – ✆ 04 73 81 15 70 – goigoux.martine@wanadoo.fr – Closed 15 October-1st December AZ **t**
4 rm ☕ – 🛉€ 75 🛉🛉€ 105/125
◆ Serenity and comfort await you in this recent house built using old materials. Lovely rooms decorated with antiques or period furniture. Indoor pool, fitness facilities and steam bath.

in St-Sauves-d'Auvergne 5 km by ③ – **pop. 1 052 – alt. 791 m** – ✉ **63950**

Office de tourisme, le bourg ✆ 04 73 65 50 40

De la Poste

pl. du Portique – ✆ 04 73 81 10 33 – hoteldelaposte63@aol.com – Fax 04 73 81 02 27

15 rm – €38/42 €40/46, ☕ €6 – ½ P €41/44 – **Rest** – *(closed 5-28 January)* Menu €15/28 – Carte €17/44

♦ This old post house is also a bar and newsagents. Rustic rooms with a somewhat old feel but well kept. Two country dining rooms with exposed beams. Traditional menu and Auvergne specialities.

BOURDEILLES – **24 Dordogne** – **329** E4 – see Brantôme

BOURG-ACHARD – **27 Eure** – **304** E5 – **pop. 2 517** – **alt. 124 m** – ✉ **27310**
Normandy 33 **C2**

Paris 141 – Bernay 39 – Évreux 62 – Le Havre 62 – Rouen 30

L'Amandier

581 rte Rouen – ✆ 02 32 57 11 49 – restaurant.amandier@wanadoo.fr – Fax 02 32 57 11 49 – Closed 4-10 August, 5-16 January, Sunday dinner, Monday dinner, Wednesday dinner and Tuesday

Rest – Menu €19 (weekday lunch), €28/37 – Carte €56/75

♦ In the centre of the village, pleasant restaurant redecorated in contemporary style (view of the garden). Friendly welcome and generously served updated cuisine.

Red = Pleasant. Look for the red and symbols.

BOURG-CHARENTE – **16 Charente** – **324** I5 – see Jarnac

LE BOURG-DUN – **76 Seine-Maritime** – **304** F2 – **pop. 440** – **alt. 17 m** – ✉ **76740**
Normandy 33 **C1**

Paris 188 – Dieppe 20 – Fontaine-le-Dun 7 – Rouen 56 – St-Valery-en-Caux 15

Office de tourisme, 6, place du Village ✆ 02 35 97 63 05, Fax 02 35 57 24 51

Church ★ tower.

Auberge du Dun (Pierre Chrétien)

(opposite the church) – ✆ 02 35 83 05 84 – Fax 02 35 83 05 84 – Closed 22 September-6 October, 16 February-1st March, Wednesday except lunch from 1st March to 15 September, Sunday dinner and Monday

Rest – *(pre-book Sat - Sun)* Menu €30 (weekdays)/46 – Carte €69/97

Spec. Marmite de homard, risotto aux champignons (15 June to 31 August). Chinoiseries de Saint-Jacques au chou (15 October to 30 April). Crêpes soufflées au calvados.

♦ Pretty inn with two, rustic dining rooms, with a glass window separating them from the busy kitchens. Modern cuisine prepared with care.

BOURG-EN-BRESSE Ⓟ – **01 Ain** – **328** E3 – **pop. 40 666** – **Built-up area 101 016** – **alt. 251 m** – ✉ **01000** **Burgundy-Jura** 44 **B1**

Paris 424 – Annecy 113 – Genève 112 – Lyon 82 – Mâcon 38

Office de tourisme, 6, avenue Alsace Lorraine ✆ 04 74 22 49 40, Fax 04 74 23 06 28

de Bourg-en-Bresse Parc de Loisirs de Bouvent, by Nantua road: 2 km, ✆ 04 74 24 65 17.

Brou church ★★ (tombs★★★, stalls★★, rood-screen★★, stained-glass wwindows★★, chapel and oratories★★★, portal★) X **B** - Stalls★ of Notre-Dame church Y - Musée du monastère★ X **E.**

BOURG-EN-BRESSE

Street	Grid	No.
Anciens Combattants (Av. des)	Z	3
Arsonval (Av. A. d')	X	4
Bad-Kreuznach (Av. de)	X	5
Basch (R. Victor)	Z	6
Baudin (Av. A.)	Z	7
Belges (Av. des)	Y	9
Bernard (Pl.)	Y	10
Bons Enfants (R. des)	YZ	12
Bouveret (R.)	Y	13
Champ-de-Foire (Av. du)	Y	14
Citadelle (R. de la)	X	15
Crêts (R. des)	X	16
Debeney (R. Général)	Y	17
Europe (Car. de l')	X	19
Foch (R. Maréchal)	Y	20
Gambetta (R.)	Z	21
Huchet (Bd E.)	X	22
Jean-Jaurès (Av.)	X, Z	23
Joliot-Curie (Bd Irène)	X	24
Juin (Av. Maréchal)	X	26
Lévrier (Bd A.)	X	27
Lyon (Pont de)	X	28
Mail (Av. du)	X	30
Migonney (R. J.)	Z	31
Morgon (R. J.)	X	32
Muscat (Av. A.)	Z	33
Neuve (Pl.)	Y	34
Notre-Dame (R.)	Y	35
Palais (R. du)	Y	36
St-Nicolas (Bd)	X	37
Samaritaine (R.)	Z	38
Semard (Av. P.)	X	40
Teynière (R.)	Z	42
Valéry (Bd P.)	X	43
Verdun (Cours de)	Y	44
Victoire (Av. de la)	Z	45
4-Septembre (R. du)	Y	48
23e-R.I. (R. du)	X	50

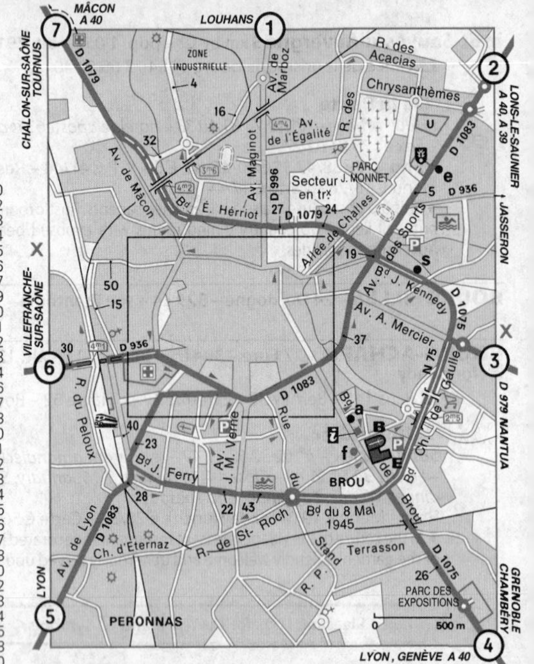

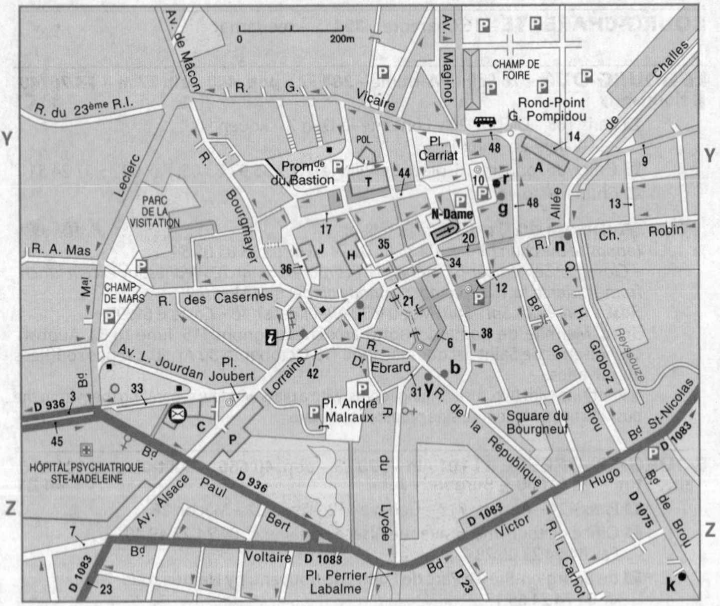

Mercure rm, rm, rest, VISA AE
10 av. Bad-Kreuznach – ✆ 04 74 22 44 88 – h1187@accor.com – Fax 04 74 23 43 57 X e
60 rm – †€ 86/93 ††€ 94/105, ☕ € 12,50 – **Rest** – *(closed Sunday lunch and Saturday)* Menu (€ 17), € 23 (lunch), € 26/39 – Carte € 30/45
◆ This Mercure offers several types of comfortable rooms; all are comfortable and well equipped. This restaurant features a contemporary style but has lost none of its refined charm. Covered terrace and view of the garden. Traditional cuisine.

De France without rest VISA AE
19 pl. Bernard – ✆ 04 74 23 30 24 – infos@grand-hoteldefrance.com – Fax 04 74 23 69 90 Y r
44 rm – †€ 77/85 ††€ 86/94, ☕ € 12 – 1 suite
◆ This hotel near Notre Dame Church sports a stylish mixture of cosy and modern details: spacious, attractive rooms and a lobby restored to its original 1900 glory.

Ariane rm, rm, rest, VISA AE
bd Kennedy – ✆ 04 74 22 50 88 – hotel.ariane.bourg@wanadoo.fr – Fax 04 74 22 51 57 X s
40 rm – †€ 80 ††€ 90, ☕ € 11 – **Rest** – *(closed Sunday and public holidays) (dinner only)* Menu € 28/48
◆ A 1980s hotel, slightly set back from the ring road, with modern rooms and simple, functional furniture, as well as colourful decoration. The dining room and terrace both overlook the garden and pool.

Du Prieuré without rest VISA AE
49 bd de Brou – ✆ 04 74 22 44 60 – hotel-du-prieure@wanadoo.fr – Fax 04 74 22 71 07 X a
14 rm – †€ 75/87 ††€ 78/90, ☕ € 9,50
◆ A fresh lease of life has been given to this hotel. Choice between first floor, modernised rooms or others with a slightly antiquated charm (Louis XV, Louis XVI or Bresse period furniture).

Logis de Brou without rest VISA AE
132 bd de Brou – ✆ 04 74 22 11 55 – citotel@logisdebrou.com – Fax 04 74 22 37 30 Z k
30 rm – †€ 54/65 ††€ 61/72, ☕ € 9
◆ This 1970s hotel is gradually being revamped. The colourful rooms, with balconies, sport a variety of styles. Attractive flower garden and delicious breakfasts.

L'Auberge Bressane VISA AE
166 bd de Brou – ✆ 04 74 22 22 68 – info@aubergebressane.fr – Fax 04 74 23 03 15 – Closed Tuesday X f
Rest – Menu (€ 20), € 26 (weekdays)/73 – Carte € 60/84
◆ Well-known establishment: classic updated cuisine and fine choice of Burgundy wines. Collection of cockerels, Bresse furnishings. Terrace overlooking Brou church.

La Reyssouze VISA AE
20 r. Ch.-Robin – ✆ 04 74 23 11 50 – Fax 04 74 23 94 32 – Closed 11-20 April, 4-18 August, Sunday dinner and Monday Y n
Rest – Menu € 25 (weekday lunch), € 35/54 – Carte € 41/64
◆ This redecorated, low key and intimate restaurant takes its name from the nearby river. Enjoy its tasty regional dishes made according to tradition.

Chez Blanc VISA AE
19 pl. Bernard – ✆ 04 74 45 29 11 – chezblanc@georgesblanc.com – Fax 04 74 24 73 69 Y g
Rest – Menu € 20 (weekday lunch), € 24/45 – Carte € 36/51
◆ A 1900s house, decorated in a smart bistro style: bright colours, red bench seating, antiques and a 1940s veranda. Regional produce takes pride of place on the menu.

Le Français VISA AE
7 av. Alsace-Lorraine – ✆ 04 74 22 55 14 – Fax 04 74 22 47 02 – Closed 28 July-20 August, Saturday dinner and Sunday Z r
Rest – Menu € 24/51 – Carte € 29/61
◆ Since 1932, the same family has been welcoming guests to this local institution with a Belle Epoque setting. Oyster bar and brasserie-type dishes with Bresse touches.

Mets et Vins

11 r. de la République – ✆ 04 74 45 20 78 – Fax 04 74 45 20 78 – Closed Monday and Tuesday Z b

Rest – Menu € 14 bi (weekday lunch), € 18/45 – Carte € 28/50

◆ This restaurant stands out from the surrounding competition thanks to its appetising updated food. The dining room sports a retro feel (salmon pink colour scheme).

Chalet de Brou

(opposite Brou church) – ✆ 04 74 22 26 28 – Fax 04 74 24 72 42 – Closed 1st-12 July, 22 December-20 January, Monday dinner, Thurday dinner and Friday X f

Rest – Menu € 16 (weekdays)/45 – Carte € 22/47

◆ An architectural gem opposite Brou church, this family restaurant serves tasty little traditional dishes with an emphasis on local produce in a charming old-fashioned setting.

Les Quatre Saisons

6 r. de la République – ✆ 04 74 22 01 86 – Fax 04 74 21 10 35 – Closed 1st-10 May, 15-30 August, 2-10 January, Saturday lunch, Sunday and Monday Z y

Rest – Menu € 19/55 – Carte € 28/51

◆ The chef, a fan of local wines and produce, will set your taste buds tingling with his generous, cleverly reinterpreted regional recipes. Friendly and informal atmosphere.

Lons-le-Saunier road 6,5 km by ② N 83 – ✉ 01370 St-Étienne-du-Bois

Les Mangettes

– ✆ 04 74 22 70 66 – Fax 04 74 22 70 66 – Closed 18-26 June, 1st-10 October, 7-22 January, Sunday dinner, Monday dinner and Tuesday

Rest – *(number of covers limited, pre-book)* Menu € 18 (weekday lunch), € 23/36 – Carte € 23/36

◆ A country house with a simple rustic interior. Tasty regional cuisine, lovely desserts. Interior of stuffed animals, old postcards and fireplace.

in Péronnas 3 km by ⑤, D 1083 – pop. 5 534 – alt. 281 m – ✉ 01960

La Marelle (Didier Goiffon)

1593 av. de Lyon – ✆ 04 74 21 75 21 – contact@lamarelle.fr – Fax 04 74 21 06 81 – Closed 28 April-8 May, 18 August-10 September, 2-14 January, Sunday dinner, Tuesday and Wednesday

Rest – Menu € 28 (weekday lunch), € 39/75 – Carte € 52/82

Spec. Menu "Délicate Vénus" autour de la Saint-Jacques (October to April). Volailles locales. Poire tapée aux morilles et vin jaune. **Wines** Manicle, Pouilly-Fuissé.

◆ La Marelle can be relied upon to rustle up inventive, mouth watering dishes served in a smart, warm interior that mixes country chic with contemporary.

in Lalleyriat 7 km by ⑤, N 83 and D 22 – ✉ 01960

Le Nid à Bibi

– ✆ 04 74 21 11 47 – lenidabibi@wanadoo.fr – Fax 04 74 21 02 83

5 rm – †€ 85/110 ††€ 100/130 – ½ P € 70/90 – **Table d'hôte** – Menu € 20 (weekday dinner), € 30/45

◆ This guesthouse provides quiet, attractive rooms, delicious breakfasts and a host of leisure activities. Faultless welcome. Home from home! Delicious regional produce turned into tasty recipes.

BOURGES Ⓟ – 18 Cher – 323 K4 – pop. 72 480 – Built-up area 123 584 – alt. 153 m – ✉ 18000 Dordogne-Berry-Limousin 12 C3

Paris 244 – Châteauroux 65 – Dijon 254 – Nevers 69 – Orléans 121

Office de tourisme, 21, rue Victor Hugo ✆ 02 48 23 02 60, Fax 02 48 23 02 69

Bourges Golf Club Route de Lazenay, South: 5 km by D 106, ✆ 02 48 20 11 08.

St-Étienne cathedral ★★★: North Tower ≤★★ Z - Jardins de l'Archevêché★ - Palais Jacques-Cœur★★ - Jardins des Prés-Fichaux★ - Half-timbered houses★ - Hôtel des Échevins★: musée Estève★ Y M² - Hôtel Lallemant★ Y M³ - Hôtel Cujas★: Musée du Berry★ Y M¹ - Muséum d'histoire naturelle★ Z - Marshlands★ V - Ramparts walkway★.

BOURGES

Street	Grid	No.
Armuriers (R. des)	Z	2
Auron (Bd d')	Z	
Barbès (R.)	Z	4
Beaux-Arts (R. des)	Y	5
Bourbonnoux (Prom.)	YZ	
Calvin (R.)	Y	7
Cambournac (R.)	Y	8
Champ-de-Foire (R. du)	Z	12
Commerce (R. du)	Y	13
Coursarlon (R.)	Y	
Cujas (Pl.)	Y	15
Dr-Témoin (R. du)	Y	17
Dormoy (Av. Marx)	Y	19
Équerre (R. de l')	Z	20
George-Sand (Escalier)	Y	27
Hémerettes (R. des)	Z	29
Jacobins (Cour des)	Z	31
Jacques-Coeur (R.)	Y	32
Jean-Jaurès (Av.)	Y	
Joyeuse (R.)	Y	35
Juranville (Pl.)	Z	36
J.-J. Rousseau (R.)	Z	33
Leblanc (R. N.)	YZ	40
Linières (R. de)	Z	42
Louis XI (Av.)	Z	43
Mallet (R. L.)	Z	44
Marceau (Rampe)	Z	45
Mirebeau (R.)	Y	
Moyenne (R.)	YZ	
Orléans (Av. d')	Y	48
Pelvoysin (R.)	Y	50
Poissonnerie (R. de la)	Y	52
Prinal (R. du)	Y	55
Rimbault (R. J.)	Z	61
Strasbourg (Bd de)	Z	71
Thaumassière (R. de la)	Y	72
Tory (R. G.)	Y	73
Victor-Hugo (R.)	Z	74
3-Maillets (R. des)	Z	75
4-Piliers (Pl. des)	Z	76
95e-de-Ligne (Av. du)	Z	78

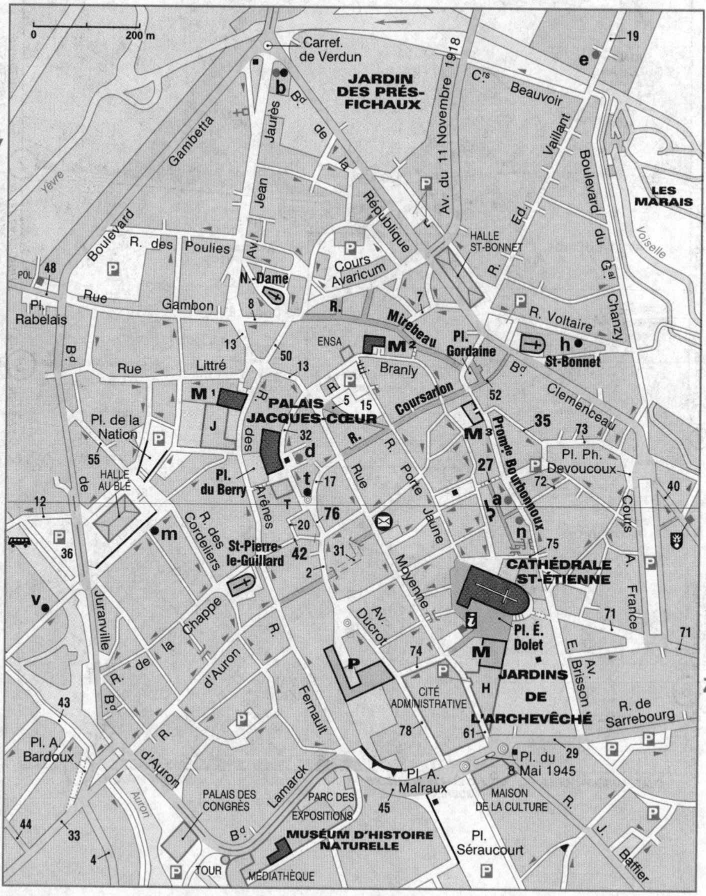

De Bourbon

bd de la République – ✆ 02 48 70 70 00 – contact@hoteldebourbon.fr – Fax 02 48 70 21 22

Y **b**

58 rm – 🚹€ 95/220 🚹🚹€ 110/235, ☕ € 15

Rest *L'Abbaye St-Ambroix* – see restaurant listing

◆ The De Bourbon occupies a former 17C abbey near the town centre. All the hotel's bedrooms have been recently refurbished. Elegant lounge-bar.

BOURGES

Street	Map	No.
Baffier (R. J.)	X	3
Bérégovoy (Av. P.)	X	6
Deux-Ponts (R. des)	V	16
Dormoy (Av. M.)	V	19
Farman (Rd-Pt H.)	X	21
Foch (Bd du Mar.)	X	23
Frères-Voisin (Av. des)	X	25
Industrie (Bd de l')	X	30
Joffre (Bd du Mar.)	X	34
J.-J.-Rousseau (R.)	X	33
Laudier (Av. H.)	V	38
Liberté (Bd de la)	X	41
Mitterrand (Av. F.)	X	47
Orléans (Av. d')	V	48
Pignoux (R. de)	X	51
Près-le-Roi (Av. des)	V	53
Prospective (Av. de la)	V	56
Pyrotechnie (Pl. de la)	X	57
Santos-Dumont (Bd)	X	65
Sellier (R. H.)	X	66
Semard (Av. P.)	V	68

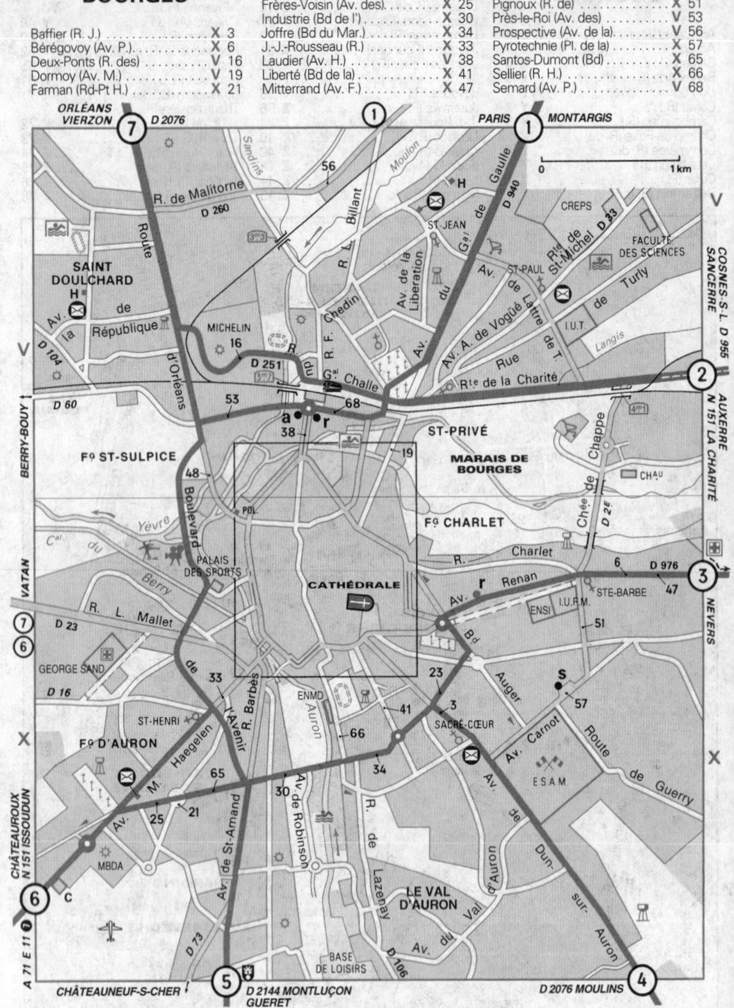

Le Berry

3 pl. Gén.-Leclerc – ☎ 02 48 65 99 30
– leberry.bourges@wanadoo.fr
– Fax 02 48 24 29 17 V a

64 rm – †€ 49 ††€ 66, ☐ € 8,50

Rest – *(closed 24 December-1st January, Saturday lunch and Sunday)*
Menu € 16/22 – Carte € 20/42

◆ A large modern building opposite the station with rooms that are being renovated in stages. Bright colours, painted wood panelling and African artwork. Restaurant with exotic decoration and world cuisine.

D'Angleterre without rest
1 pl. Quatre-Piliers – ✆ 02 48 24 68 51 – hotel@bestwestern-angleterre-bourges.com – Fax 02 48 65 21 41 – Closed 28 December-4 January Y **t**
31 rm – €82/115 €92/135, €10
◆ This hotel, which has benefited from a recent facelift, enjoys a good location near the Palais Jacques Cœur. A pleasant and comfortable base for your stay.

Le Christina without rest
5 r. de la Halle – ✆ 02 48 70 56 50 – info@le-christina.com – Fax 02 48 70 58 13
71 rm – €45/80 €50/80, €8 Z**m**
◆ A practical location near the centre of town, opposite the impressive 19C corn exchange *(halle au blé)*. Functional guestrooms decorated with Basque furniture and warm tones.

Les Tilleuls without rest
7 pl. Pyrotechnie – ✆ 02 48 20 49 04 – lestilleuls.bourges@wanadoo.fr – Fax 02 48 50 61 73 – Closed 26 Dec. - 3 Jan. X **s**
39 rm – €56 €64, €7
◆ Flower-decked hotel with air-conditioned guestrooms, either rustic or more classical in style. Those in the annexe have been renovated. Swimming pool and small fitness room.

Ibis
quartier Prado – ✆ 02 48 65 89 99 – h0819@accor-hotels.com – Fax 02 48 65 18 47 Z **v**
86 rm – €50/69 €50/69, €7,50 – **Rest** – *(dinner only)* Menu €12,50/18
◆ A practical choice just 10 minutes' walk from the cathedral and palace. Well-maintained guestrooms and friendly staff. Bar, lounge and dining room separated by partitions. Buffet-style menus.

Arcane without rest
2 pl. du Gén.-Leclerc – ✆ 02 48 24 20 87 – arcane.bourges@wanadoo.fr – Fax 02 48 69 00 67 V **r**
30 rm – €35/39 €42/45, €6,50
◆ This completely renovated hotel facing the railway station offers affordably priced, functional guestrooms and a good buffet breakfast.

Le Cèdre Bleu without rest
14 r. Voltaire – ✆ 02 48 25 07 37 – lecedre-bleu@wanadoo.fr Y **n**
3 rm – €53/70 €58/75 – 1 suite
◆ A rare pearl in the centre of the town, this impressive Napoleon III-style residence with its pleasant garden offers beautifully maintained and individually decorated bedrooms.

L'Abbaye St-Ambroix – Hôtel de Bourbon
60 av. J.-Jaurès – ✆ 02 48 70 80 00 – contact@abbayesaintambroix.fr – Fax 02 48 70 21 22 – Closed Sunday dinner from November to March, Monday and Tuesday Y **b**
Rest – Menu (€30 bi), €42 bi (weekday lunch), €49/80 – Carte €77/81
Spec. Foie gras de canard en copeaux sur salade frisée (spring-summer). Cuisses de grenouilles au beurre d'ail et persil (spring and autumn). Noix de ris de veau croustillante. **Wines** Menetou-Salon, Reuilly.
◆ The abbey's former chapel (17C) with its huge vaulted ceiling has been magnificently renovated in contemporary style. A superb setting for fine up-to-date cuisine.

Le Jardin Gourmand
15 bis av. E.-Renan – ✆ 02 48 21 35 91 – Fax 02 48 20 59 75 – Closed 20 December-20 January, Sunday dinner, Tuesday lunch and Monday X **r**
Rest – Menu €16/40 – Carte €30/53
◆ Tasteful mansion on a boulevard outside the town centre with three small, classically furnished dining rooms. Attractive lounge with wooden fireplace. Traditional cuisine.

Beauvoir
1 av. Marx-Dormoy – ✆ 02 48 65 42 44 – didier-guyot@club-internet.fr – Fax 02 48 24 80 84 – Closed 5-25 August and Sunday dinner Y **e**
Rest – Menu €19/43 – Carte €42/73
◆ A contemporary, bright interior decorated in warm tones adds to the charm of this delightful suburban restaurant. Modern cuisine and an impressive wine list.

XX **Le Jacques Cœur**

3 pl. J.-Coeur – ✆ 02 48 26 53 01 – restaurant.jacquescoeur@wanadoo.fr – Fax 02 48 26 58 05 – Closed 26-30 December, Monday lunch, Saturday lunch and Sunday except July-August Y **d**

Rest – Menu € 20/60 – Carte € 50/84

◆ An old Berruryère residence opposite the Jacques Cœur palace. The decor of the elegant dining rooms is faintly reminiscent of the Middle Ages (stained glass, fleur de lis). Modern food.

XX **Le Bourbonnoux**

44 r. Bourbonnoux – ✆ 02 48 24 14 76 – restaurant-bourbonnoux@wanadoo.fr – Fax 02 48 24 77 67 – Closed 11-21 April, 15 August-5 September, 27 February-8 March, lunch, Sunday dinner and Friday Y **a**

Rest – Menu € 13/32 – Carte € 26/40

◆ Bright colours and half-timbered walls make up the pleasant interior of this restaurant, situated in a street lined with craft shops. Friendly service. Updated classic cuisine.

XX **Le d'Antan Sancerrois**

50 r. Bourbonnoux – ✆ 02 48 65 96 26 – dantan.sancerrois@wanadoo.fr – Fax 02 48 70 50 82 – Closed 5-23 August, 23 December-5 January, Sunday, Monday and public holidays Z **n**

Rest – Carte € 34/51

◆ A narrow paved street leads to this old house with a semi-retro, semi-contemporary feel. Modern cuisine full of originality, served in a relaxed atmosphere.

Châteauroux road 7 km by ⑥, near A 71 interchange – ✉ 18570 Le Subdray

Novotel

– ✆ 02 48 26 53 33 – h1302@accor.com – Fax 02 48 26 52 22

93 rm – €108/115 €130/145, ☕ €13 – **Rest** – Menu (€18), €23/25 – Carte €27/32

◆ This Novotel near a motorway toll booth has been given a facelift in keeping with the hotel chain's new Novation look. Buffet breakfast. This simple, contemporary dining room opens onto a garden and a terrace by the swimming pool.

in St-Doulchard -V-to ⑦ – **pop. 9 018 – alt. 158 m – ✉ 18230**

Logitel without rest

r. de Malitorne – ✆ 02 48 70 07 26 – hotel.logitel@wanadoo.fr – Fax 02 48 24 59 94

30 rm – €48 €48, ☕ €7

◆ Basic rooms furnished in the 1980s style, well kept up and at reasonable prices; a simple place to stop at the edge of Bourges. Family-style welcome.

LE BOURGET – 93 Seine-Saint-Denis – 305 F7 – 101 17 – see Paris, Area

---

BOURG-ET-COMIN – 02 Aisne – 306 D6 – pop. 678 – alt. 55 m – ✉ 02160

37 **D2**

Paris 141 – Reims 40 – Château-Thierry 54 – Laon 25 – Soissons 27

De la Vallée

rm,

6 r. d'Oeuilly – ✆ 03 23 25 81 58 – lavallee02@aol.com – Fax 03 23 25 38 10 – Closed 9-16 April, 18-24 September, January, Tuesday dinner and Wednesday

9 rm – €48 €48/60, ☕ €8 – ½ P €52/60 – **Rest** – Menu (€13), €17/38 – Carte €22/48

◆ A pretty stop-off on the Chemin des Dames circuit. The functional, well-kept rooms have been recently renovated. Warm welcome. Traditional food served in a bright dining room-veranda.

LE BOURGET-DU-LAC – 73 Savoie – 333 I4 – pop. 3 945 – alt. 240 m – ✉ 73370 French Alps

46 **F2**

Paris 531 – Aix-les-Bains 10 – Annecy 44 – Belley 23 – Chambéry 13 – La Tour-du-Pin 52

Office de tourisme, place Général Sevez ✆ 04 79 25 01 99, Fax 04 79 26 10 76

Lake★★ - Church: carved frieze ★ in choir.

Ombremont — lake and mountains,
2 km north on D 1504 – ✆ 04 79 25 00 23
– ombremontbateauivre@wanadoo.fr – Fax 04 79 25 25 77 – Closed 14-30 April, November, Monday and Tuesday from December to April except public holidays
17 rm – €140/255 €140/255, €22 – ½ P €150/210
Rest *Le Bateau Ivre* – see restaurant listing
◆ In a tree-lined, flower-decked park, vast 1930 property with pretty personalised rooms, nearly all of which command a superb view of the lake. Lovely pool; sauna.

Le Bateau Ivre (Jean-Pierre Jacob) – Hôtel Ombremont — lake and mountains,
2 km north on D 1504 –
✆ 04 79 25 00 23 – ombremontbateauivre@wanadoo.fr – Fax 04 79 25 25 77
– Closed 14-30 April, November, Monday except dinner from mid June to mid September, Tuesday except dinner from May to October and Thursday lunch from May to October
Rest – Menu €55 (lunch), €85/170 – Carte €95/137
Spec. Brochet en quenelles, émulsion d'écrevisses (May to October). Cuisses de grenouilles rôties et désossées, mousseline à l'ail doux (May to October). Ris de veau braisé, jus aux pamplemousses confits (May to October). **Wines** Chignin-Bergeron, Roussette de Monterminod.
◆ Superb panoramic views of the lake and Mount Revard can be had from the elegant and understated dining room or the delightful terrace. Wildly inventive cuisine.

Auberge Lamartine (Pierre Marin) — lake and mountains,
3.5 km north by D 1504 – ✆ 04 79 25 01 03
– aubergelamartine@wanadoo.fr – Fax 04 79 25 20 66
– Closed 21 December-15 January, Sunday dinner and Monday except public holidays
Rest – Menu €26 (weekday lunch), €37/80 – Carte €65/94
Spec. Pressé de lavaret aux légumes. Omble chevalier du lac. Pigeon du Vercors farci au foie gras. **Wines** Chignin, Chignin-Bergeron.
◆ Delicate cuisine, warm dining room (glass-enclosed wine cellar, paintings, fireplace, etc.) and terrace looking out onto the "Lamartine Lake": O time, suspend thy flight!

La Grange à Sel
– ✆ 04 79 25 02 66 – info@lagrangeasel.com – Fax 04 79 25 25 03
– Closed 2 January-10 February, Sunday dinner and Wednesday
Rest – Menu €27 (weekday lunch), €38/80 – Carte €55/89
Spec. Langoustines lardées sur chutney de fruits d'ici et d'ailleurs. Homard en raviole, mousseline d'ail doux. Filet de bœuf, pommes fondantes à la moelle. **Wines** Chignin-Bergeron, Mondeuse.
◆ Former salt barn with original stonework and open beams. On fine days take a table in the pretty garden to enjoy fine, personalised cuisine.

Beaurivage with rm — rm,
– ✆ 04 79 25 00 38 – webmaster@beaurivage-bourget-du-lac.com
– Fax 04 79 25 06 49 – Closed 20 October-21 November, 16-23 February, Wednesday dinner except July-August, Sunday dinner and Monday
7 rm – €65 €65, €9 – **Rest** – Menu (€20), €23 (weekday lunch), €33/40 – Carte €40/55
◆ The dining room opens out onto a pleasant terrace shaded by plane trees from where the eye wanders to the romantic lake. Classic cuisine. Renovated and well-equipped rooms.

in Catons **2,5 km Northwest by D 42 – ✉ 73370**

Atmosphères with rm — lake and mountains,
618 rte des Tournelles – ✆ 04 79 25 01 29
– info@atmospheres-hotel.com – Fax 04 79 25 26 19
– Closed 15 October-15 November, Tuesday and Wednesday, except hotel from October to April
4 rm – €95/115 €95/115, €13
Rest – Menu €21 (weekday lunch), €37/62
◆ Carefully prepared cuisine based on fresh market produce. Stylish, modern interior, superb view of the lake, lovely panoramic terrace: a chalet of untold appeal. Rooms have a minimalist decor, contemporary colour scheme and state of the art facilities.

BOURG-LA-REINE – **92 Hauts-de-Seine** – **311** J3 – **101** 25 – **see Paris, Area**

BOURGOIN-JALLIEU – 38 Isère – 333 E4 – pop. 22 947 – alt. 235 m – ✉ 38300
Lyon - Rhone Valley 44 **B2**

- Paris 503 – Bourg-en-Bresse 81 – Grenoble 66 – Lyon 43 – La Tour-du-Pin 16
- Syndicat d'initiative, 1, place Carnot ☎ 04 74 93 47 50, Fax 04 74 93 76 01
- de L'isle-d'Abeau L'Isle-d'Abeau Le Rival, by Lyon road (D 1006): 5 km, ☎ 04 74 43 28 84.

Des Dauphins without rest
8 r. François-Berrier, 1.5 km on ④ – ☎ 04 74 93 00 58 – direction@hoteldesdauphins.fr – Fax 04 74 28 27 39
20 rm – †€ 45/55 ††€ 45/55, ☕ € 7
◆ The comfortable house (1910) and two wings are home to well kept pleasant rooms. On the leisure side: terrace overlooking the garden and giant sequoia tree, pool and small sauna.

BOURGOIN-JALLIEU

Street	Grid	No.
Alpes (Av. des)	A	2
Belmont (R. Robert)	B	4
Carnot (Pl.)	B	5
Champ de Mars (Pl. du)	B	6
Clemenceau (R. Georges)	A	9
Diéderichs (Pl. Ch.)	B	10
Dos de l'Âne (R. du)	B	12
Gambetta (Av.)	A	13
Génin (Av. Ambroise)	A	15
Halle (Pl. de la)	B	16
Libération (R. de la)	B	
Liberté (R. de la)	B	19
Moulins (R. des)	B	22
Moulin (R. J.)	B	21
Nations-Unies (Av. des)	B	23
Paix (R. de la)	A	25
Pontcottier (R.)	B	
Pouchelon (R. de)	B	26
République (Pl. de la)	A	29
République (R. de la)	AB	31
St-Michel (Pl.)	B	32
Seigner (R. Joseph)	A	35
Victor-Hugo (R.)	B	36
1er Atelier (R. du)	A	37
19-Mars-1962 (R. du)	AB	39
23-Août-1944 (Pl. du)	B	41

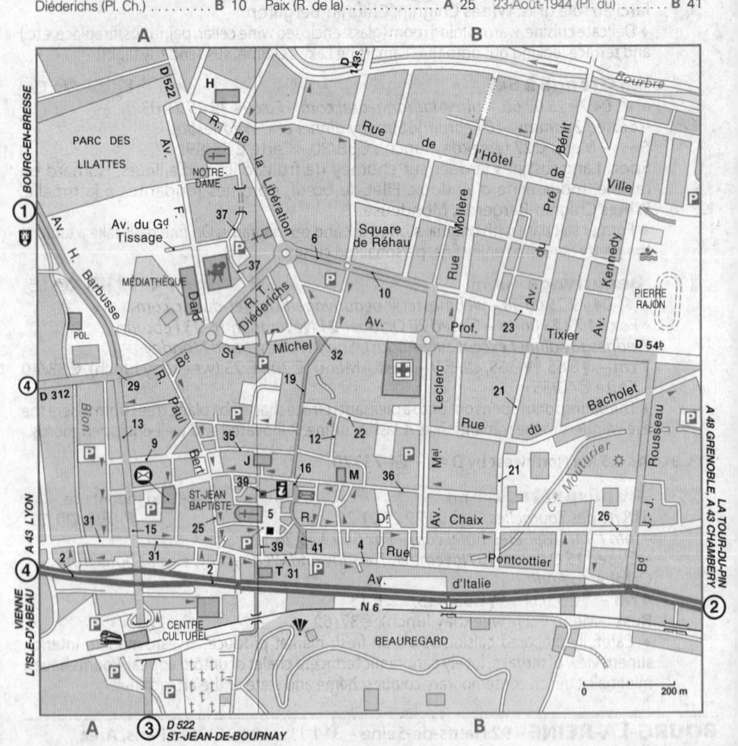

via ② 2 km by D 1006 and Boussieu road – ✉ 38300 Bourgoin-Jallieu

Domaine des Séquoias rest, VISA

54 Vie-de-Boussieu – ✆ 04 74 93 78 00 – info@domaine-sequoias.com – Fax 04 74 28 60 90 – Closed 9 Aug. - 7 Sept., 21 Dec. - 4 Jan., Sun. evening, Tues. lunchtime, Mon. and bank holiday evenings

19 rm – † € 110/200 †† € 110/200, ☕ € 18 – **Rest** – *(closed 27 July-1st September, Sunday dinner, Tuesday lunch and Monday)* Menu (€ 30), € 36/78 – Carte € 44/100

◆ Tasteful, designer rooms in the wing. An elegant 18C mansion hides a smart contemporary dining room opening into a tree lined garden. Traditional menu and fine choice of Côtes du Rhône wines.

in La Grive **4.5 km by ④ – ✉38300 Bourgoin-Jallieu**

Bernard Lantelme VISA

D 312 – ✆ 04 74 28 19 12 – b.lantelme@free.fr – Fax 04 74 93 78 88 – Closed 26 July-25 August, Saturday and Sunday

Rest – Menu € 22/54 – Carte € 38/46

◆ A 19C farmhouse converted into a restaurant. The modern paintings bring a colourful touch to the rustic dining room and form a pleasant contrast with the traditional cuisine.

BOURG-ST-ANDÉOL – 07 Ardèche – 331 J7 – pop. 7 768 – alt. 36 m – ✉ 07700

Lyon - Rhone Valley 44 **B3**

▶ Paris 640 – Aubenas 57 – Montélimar 26 – Orange 34 – Pont-Saint-Esprit 16

ℹ Office de tourisme, place du champs de Mars ✆ 04 75 54 54 20, Fax 04 75 49 10 57

Le Clos des Oliviers rest, VISA

pl. Champ-de-Mars – ✆ 04 75 54 50 12 – contact@closdesoliviers.fr – Fax 04 75 54 63 26 – Closed 29 September-5 October, 1st-25 January, Sunday and Monday from September to June and Monday lunch in July-August

24 rm – † € 32/43 †† € 40/48, ☕ € 6 – ½ P € 38/44 – **Rest** – Menu € 12,50 (weekday lunch), € 15/35 – Carte € 20/37

◆ This old house has had a welcome overhaul offering small, functional and colourful rooms plus new bathrooms; quieter annexe. Summer terrace surrounded by some olive trees; contemporary cuisine and Southern flavours.

BOURG-STE-MARIE – 52 Haute-Marne – 313 N4 – pop. 110 – alt. 329 m – ✉ 52150

14 **C3**

▶ Paris 302 – Chaumont 39 – Langres 45 – Neufchâteau 24 – Vittel 43

Le St-Martin rm, VISA

46 r. Grande-Fontaine – ✆ 03 25 01 10 15 – f1253@aol.com – Fax 03 25 03 91 68 – Closed 21 December-5 January and Sunday dinner 15 October-30 March

8 rm – † € 39 †† € 49/55, ☕ € 8 – ½ P € 66 – **Rest** – Menu € 16/38 – Carte € 23/38

◆ You will find colourful, well-renovated rooms named after flowers in this old house near a busy road. Pleasant little lounge with wrought iron furniture. Traditional cuisine served in the warm environs of the restaurant.

BOURG-ST-MAURICE – 73 Savoie – 333 N4 – pop. 6 747 – alt. 850 m – Winter sports : see "aux Arcs" – ✉ 73700

French Alps 45 **D2**

▶ Paris 635 – Albertville 54 – Aosta 79 – Chambéry 103 – Chamonix-Mont-Blanc 74

ℹ Office de tourisme, 105, place de la Gare ✆ 04 79 07 12 57, Fax 04 79 07 24 90

⛳ des Arcs Chalet des Villards, South: 20 km, ✆ 04 79 07 43 95.

Frescoes★ of the St-Grat chapel in Vulmix South: 4 km.

L'Autantic without rest VISA

69 rte Hauteville – ✆ 04 79 07 01 70 – bonjour@hotel-autantic.fr – Fax 04 79 07 51 55

29 rm – † € 40/70 †† € 80/130, ☕ € 8

◆ Welcoming hotel built like a Tarentais chalet. Its smart rooms have wooden or wrought iron furniture and overlook the countryside; ten or so have a terrace or a balcony. Breakfast area on a veranda. Indoor pool.

L'Arssiban

253 av. Antoine-Borrel – ✆ 04 79 07 77 35 – Fax 04 79 07 77 35 – Closed 22 June-13 July, 26 October-3 November, 4-8 January, Wednesday from September to June and Sunday dinner

Rest – Menu € 25/35 – Carte € 34/60

◆ Stone vaults, old tiling, and well-waxed, wooden tables: authentic decor that goes well with the generous, contemporary cuisine.

Le Montagnole

26 av. du Stade – ✆ 04 79 07 11 52 – Fax 04 79 07 11 52 – Closed 26 May-13 June, 17 November-10 December, Monday dinner and Tuesday off season

Rest – Menu (€ 15), € 17/37 – Carte € 28/49

◆ The welcoming painter and poet owners of this establishment lovingly cover the walls and menus with their most successful works. They are just as artistic in the kitchen, where they give a zest of originality to traditional dishes. Savoyard menu.

BOURGUEIL – 37 Indre-et-Loire – 317 J5 – pop. 4 109 – alt. 42 m – ✉ 37140

Châteaux of the Loire — 11 **A2**

Paris 281 – Angers 81 – Chinon 16 – Saumur 23 – Tours 45

Syndicat d'initiative, 16, place de l'église ✆ 02 47 97 91 39, Fax 02 47 97 91 39

La Rose de Pindare

4 pl. Hublin – ✆ 02 47 97 70 50 – Fax 02 47 97 70 50 – Closed 24 June-2 July, 26 August-3 September, 11-19 November, 27 January-4 February, Tuesday and Wednesday

Rest – Menu € 18/29 – Carte € 32/53

◆ A simple interior of white walls, flowers and bare beams form a backdrop to classic fare with a fine Bourgueil wine list. Pleasant terrace. The name is an anagram of Pierre Ronsard.

Le Moulin Bleu

7 rte du Moulin-Bleu, 2 km northward via rte de Courléon – ✆ 02 47 97 73 13 – Fax 02 47 97 79 66 – Closed mid December-end February, Sunday dinner and Monday dinner in winter, Tuesday dinner and Wednesday

Rest – Menu (€ 16 bi), € 19/37 – Carte € 30/47

◆ A 15C regional style mill. Vaulted dining rooms and a terrace overlooking the vineyards. Traditional dishes and local wines.

in Restigné 5 km east by D 35 – pop. 1 158 – alt. 32 m – ✉ 37140

Manoir de Restigné

15 rte de Tours – ✆ 02 47 97 00 06 – contact@manoirderestigne.com – Fax 02 47 97 01 43 – Closed 1st January-10 February

6 rm – € 205/345 € 205/345, € 15 – ½ P € 235 – **Rest** – *(closed Tuesday dinner and Wednesday)* Menu € 35 (lunch), € 55/75

◆ This well-restored, 17-18C manor is set amidst vineyards and home to pleasant, refined rooms, decorated on the theme of grape varieties. Wine bar. Meals served in the former cellar with its prettily-dressed tables. Terrace in fine weather.

BOURNEVILLE – 27 Eure – 304 D5 – pop. 736 – alt. 124 m – ✉ 27500 — 32 **B3**

Paris 155 – Le Havre 45 – Rouen 43 – Brionne 25 – Caudebec-en-Caux 25

Office de tourisme, le Bourg ✆ 02 32 57 32 23, Fax 02 32 57 15 48

Risle Seine

– ✆ 02 32 42 30 22 – risle-seine@free.fr – Closed February half-term holidays, Tuesday dinner and Wednesday

Rest – Menu (€ 11,50), € 18/29 – Carte € 19/30

◆ This little inn in the centre of the village has a rustic dining room and a veranda overlooking a green setting. Traditional, carefully prepared cuisine.

For a pleasant stay in a charming hotel, look for the red … symbols.

BOURRON-MARLOTTE – 77 Seine-et-Marne – 312 F5 – pop. 2 737 – alt. 71 m – ✉ 77780 19 C3

Paris 72 – Fontainebleau 9 – Melun 26 – Montereau-Fault-Yonne 26 – Nemours 11

Office de tourisme, 37, rue Murger ✆ 01 64 45 88 86, Fax 01 64 45 86 80

XXX **Les Prémices** P VISA MC AE

Château de Bourron – ✆ 01 64 78 33 00 – lespremices@aol.com – Fax 01 64 78 36 00 – Closed 1st-15 August, 25 December-1st January, February holidays, Sunday dinner, Monday and Tuesday

Rest – Menu € 38/145 – Carte € 67/117

◆ Matching soft furnishings and designer furniture elegantly decorate this restaurant in an outbuilding of a 16C Bourron castle. Creative cuisine using many exotic products.

BOURTH – 27 Eure – 304 E9 – pop. 1 124 – alt. 182 m – ✉ 27580 33 C2

Paris 125 – L'Aigle 16 – Alençon 78 – Évreux 46 – Verneuil-sur-Avre 11

XX **Auberge Chantecler** VISA MC AE

opposite the church – ✆ 02 32 32 61 45 – Fax 02 32 32 61 45 – Closed 3 weeks in August, 2 weeks in January, Thursday dinner, Sunday dinner and Monday

Rest – Menu € 16 (weekday lunch), € 27/44 – Carte € 33/47

◆ This limed-brick façade is covered with flowers in summer. A collection of cockerels, regularly added to by the locals, is on display in the two dining rooms. Local food.

BOUSSAC – 23 Creuse – 325 K2 – pop. 1 602 – alt. 376 m – ✉ 23600
Dordogne-Berry-Limousin 25 C1

Paris 333 – Aubusson 50 – La Châtre 37 – Guéret 41 – Montluçon 38

Office de tourisme, place de l'Hôtel de Ville ✆ 05 55 65 05 95, Fax 05 55 65 00 94

Site★.

in Nouzerines 10 km Northwest by D97 – pop. 261 – alt. 407 m – ✉ 23600

XX **La Bonne Auberge** with rm VISA MC AE

1 r. Lilas – ✆ 05 55 82 01 18 – labonneauberge-23@orange.fr – Closed 6-21 October, 16 February-10 March, Sunday evening (except hotel) and Monday

6 rm – †€ 42/50 ††€ 42/58, ☕ € 7 – ½ P € 33/37 – **Rest** – Menu € 16/41 – Carte € 31/53

◆ A country restaurant serving traditional cuisine with a local flavour. With its postal service and bar serving daily specials, this discreet house is the focal point of this small Creuse village.

BOUT-DU-PONT-DE-LARN – 81 Tarn – 338 G9 – see Mazamet

BOUTIGNY-SUR-ESSONNE – 91 Essonne – 312 D5 – pop. 3 002 – alt. 61 m – ✉ 91820 18 B3

Paris 58 – Corbeil-Essonnes 29 – Étampes 19 – Fontainebleau 29 – Melun 33

Domaine de Bélesbat rm, P VISA MC AE

– ✆ 01 69 23 19 00 – reception@belesbat.com – Fax 01 69 23 19 01 – Closed 14 December-2 January and February

59 rm ☕ – †€ 370 ††€ 370 – 1 suite

Rest *L'Orangerie* – , *✆ 01 69 23 19 30* – Menu € 20 (lunch), € 60 € (dinner)/100 (dinner) – Carte € 70/95

◆ Henry IV and Voltaire stayed in this 15 and 18C château which now offers luxury contemporary or classic rooms. A branch of the Essonne runs through the fine park; 18-hole golf course. Short traditional menu served in a superb horticultural greenhouse.

BOUZEL – 63 Puy-de-Dôme – 326 G8 – pop. 507 – alt. 320 m – ✉ 63910 6 C2

Paris 432 – Ambert 57 – Clermont-Ferrand 23 – Issoire 38 – Thiers 25 – Vichy 47

L'Auberge du Ver Luisant

2 r. Breuil – ✆ 04 73 62 93 83 – Fax 04 73 62 93 83 – Closed 21-28 April, 18 August-8 September, 1st-9 January, Sunday dinner, Wednesday dinner and Monday

Rest – Menu € 15 (weekday lunch), € 25/48 – Carte € 30/52

◆ Take the time to seek out this discreet village house of rustic inspiration, and sample the traditional cuisine that varies with the seasons.

BOUZE-LÈS-BEAUNE – 21 Côte-d'Or – 320 I7 – see Beaune

BOUZIGUES – 34 Hérault – 339 G8 – see Mèze

BOUZON-GELLENAVE – 32 Gers – 336 C7 – pop. 167 – alt. 124 m – ✉ 32290 28 A2

Paris 745 – Auch 60 – Mont-de-Marsan 53 – Toulouse 135

Château du Bascou

Lieu dit St-Go – ✆ 05 62 69 04 12 – chateau.du.bascou@free.fr – Fax 05 62 69 06 09 – Closed 23-31 August and 20-28 December

3 rm – †€ 74 ††€ 74 – **Table d'hôte** – *(closed Wednesday)* Menu € 20 bi/28 bi

◆ This lovely, 19C residence hidden away in a park is surrounded by 5 ha of vineyards. The rooms, in a chic, rustic style are named after grape varieties. Seawater swimming pool. Carefully prepared food in the restaurant. Possibility of tasting estate wines (cellar).

BOUZY – 51 Marne – 306 G8 – pop. 997 – alt. 111 m – ✉ 51150 13 B2

Paris 168 – Châlons-en-Champagne 29 – Épernay 21 – Reims 27

Les Barbotines without rest

1 pl. A.-Tritant – ✆ 03 26 57 07 31 – contact@lesbarbotines.com – Fax 03 26 58 26 36 – Closed 1st-12 August and 15 December-1st February

5 rm – †€ 70 ††€ 90

◆ You can contemplate the prestigious Champagne route from this lovely, 19C wine producer's house. Smart, personalised rooms with antique furniture.

BOYARDVILLE – 17 Charente-Maritime – 324 C4 – see île d'Oléron

BOZOULS – 12 Aveyron – 338 I4 – pop. 2 329 – alt. 530 m – ✉ 12340

Languedoc-Roussillon-Tarn Gorges 29 D1

Paris 603 – Espalion 11 – Mende 94 – Rodez 22 – Sévérac-le-Château 41

Office de tourisme, 2 bis, place de la Mairie ✆ 05 65 48 50 52, Fax 05 65 51 28 01

Trou de Bozouls ★.

A la Route d'Argent rm, rest,

rte d' Espalion – ✆ 05 65 44 92 27 – yves.catusse@wanadoo.fr – Fax 05 65 48 81 40 – Closed 2 January-31 March

21 rm – †€ 42 ††€ 42, € 7 – ½ P € 49

Rest – *(closed Monday except dinner July-August and Sunday dinner off season)* Menu € 18 (weekdays)/39

◆ Modern (late 20C) hotel with rooms overlooking the road or swimming pool and car park. Six new rooms of the same standard in a nearby villa. Traditional cuisine that varies according to market availability, served in a contemporary-style dining room with frosted glass panels, subdued lighting and modern paintings on the walls.

Les Brunes without rest

5 km south along the D 920 and secondary road – ✆ 05 65 48 50 11 – lesbrunes@wanadoo.fr

5 rm – †€ 74/117 ††€ 81/124

◆ Quiet, cosy accommodation in this attractive, 18C turreted manor house. Elegant interior decor, breakfast served by the fireplace, garden-orchard and open countryside as a backdrop.

Le Belvédère with rm
St Julien road – ✆ 05 65 44 92 66 – belvedere.bozouls@wanadoo.fr – Fax 05 65 44 46 26 – Closed 3-21 March, 29 September-24 October, Sunday dinner and Monday lunch
12 rm – †€ 39/59 ††€ 39/59, ☕ € 7 – ½ P € 40 – **Rest** – Menu € 16, € 19/38 – Carte € 32/49
◆ This house overlooking the Gorge du Dourdou is full of rustic character. Try the Aubrac beef, barbecued over the open fireplace. The hotel has two types of guestrooms.

BRACIEUX – 41 Loir-et-Cher – 318 G6 – pop. 1 158 – alt. 70 m – ✉ 41250

Châteaux of the Loire 11 **B1**

Paris 185 – Blois 19 – Montrichard 39 – Orléans 64 – Romorantin-Lanthenay 30

Syndicat d'initiative, 10 Les Jardins du Moulin ✆ 02 54 46 09 15, Fax 02 54 46 09 15

De la Bonnheure without rest
– ✆ 02 54 46 41 57 – Fax 02 54 46 05 90 – Open mid March-beg. December
11 rm – †€ 55 ††€ 55, ☕ € 8,50 – 2 suites
◆ This delightful hotel offers rustic rooms, a garden displaying farm tools, carefully-prepared breakfasts and services for cyclists and hikers. Rise and shine!

Du Cygne without rest
5 r. René-Masson – ✆ 02 54 46 41 07 – autebert@wanadoo.fr – Fax 02 54 46 04 87 – Closed 20 December-10 February, Sunday and Monday off season
19 rm – †€ 52 ††€ 60/68, ☕ € 7,40
◆ Simple, functional rooms spread over several typical local buildings in the town centre. Some rooms have been modernised. Quiet pool to the rear.

Bernard Robin - Le Relais de Bracieux
1 av. de Chambord – ✆ 02 54 46 41 22 – robin@relaischateaux.com – Fax 02 54 46 03 69 – Closed 22 December-29 January, Wednesday except July-August and Tuesday
Rest – *(number of covers limited, pre-book)* Menu € 30 (weekday lunch), € 60/98 – Carte € 66/104
Spec. "Noir et blanc-manger" de sole au caviar. Cuisses de grenouilles en fricassée d'aromates. Lièvre à la royale (season). **Wines** Cour-Cheverny, Touraine.
◆ Old paintings and tapestries adorn this elegant dining room overlooking the garden. Classic cuisine and very fine wine list.

Le Rendez vous des Gourmets
20 r. Roger-Brun – ✆ 02 54 46 03 87 – r.d.v. desgourmets@orange.fr – Fax 02 54 56 88 32 – Closed 7-17 April, 24 December-10 January, Sunday dinner except July-August and Wednesday
Rest – Menu € 17 (weekday lunch), € 20/49 – Carte € 36/71
◆ This simple, rustic restaurant has the charm of a family inn. The chef/owner prepares contemporary cuisine. Small courtyard terrace in fine weather.

BRAM – 11 Aude – 344 D3 – pop. 3 156 – alt. 134 m – ✉ 11150 22 **A2**

Paris 749 – Montpellier 173 – Carcassonne 24 – Castres 67 – Pamiers 86

North Castelnaudary road: 4 km by D 4, N 113 and secondary road - ✉ 11150 Bram

Château de la Prade
– ✆ 04 68 78 03 99 – chateaulaprade@wanadoo.fr – Fax 04 68 24 96 31 – Open April-October
4 rm ☕ – †€ 70/85 ††€ 80/95 – **Table d'hôte** – Menu € 19
◆ Comfortable rooms at this manor house set in parkland complete with ancient trees, peacocks, geese and a swimming pool. Delicious breakfast with homemade jam, served in the sitting room or on the terrace.

BRANCION – 71 Saône-et-Loire – 320 I10 – see Tournus

LA BRANDE – 36 Indre – 323 H7 – see Montipouret

BRANSAC – 43 Haute-Loire – 331 G2 – see Beauzac

BRANTÔME – 24 Dordogne – 329 E3 – pop. 2 043 – alt. 104 m – ✉ 24310

Dordogne-Berry-Limousin 4 C1

Paris 470 – Angoulême 58 – Limoges 83 – Nontron 23 – Périgueux 27 – Thiviers 26

Syndicat d'initiative, boulevard Charlemagne ✆ 05 53 05 80 52, Fax 05 53 05 80 52

Steeple★★ of the abbey church - Banks of the Dronne★★.

Le Moulin de l'Abbaye

rm, rest,

– ✆ *05 53 05 80 22*
– *moulin@relaischateaux.com – Fax 05 53 05 75 27*
– *Open 15 April-15 November*

16 rm – €210/245 €210/245, €20 – 3 suites – ½ P €200/240

Rest – *(closed Monday except July-September and lunch except week-ends and public holidays)* Menu €58/78 – Carte €75/90

Spec. Lobe de foie gras de canard froid, poché au vin de noix. Dodine de pigeonneau au foie gras. Gratin de fraises. **Wines** Montravel, Pécharmant.

◆ Individually decorated guestrooms in a choice of three buildings: the charming mill, or the former houses of the miller and abbot, to the background murmur of a waterfall. Enjoy delightfully bucolic views of the Dronne from the elegant restaurant and riverside terrace. Regional cuisine.

Chabrol

– ✆ *05 53 05 70 15 – charbonnel.freres@wanadoo.fr – Fax 05 53 05 71 85*
– *Closed 15 November-15 December, 1st February-10 March, Sunday dinner except from July to September and Monday*

19 rm – €55 €90, €12 – ½ P €70/100 – **Rest** – Menu €29 (weekdays)/65 – Carte €36/98

◆ The expression "traditional house" applies perfectly to the Chabrol hotel. The bedrooms, which have been renovated gradually are now more comfortable. A dining room with a provincial setting and panoramic terrace overlooking the River Dronne.

Au Fil du Temps

1 chemin du Vert Galand – ✆ 05 53 05 24 12
– *fildutemps@fildutemps.fr – Fax 05 53 05 18 01*
– *Closed 10 December-12 February, Monday and Tuesday*

Rest – Menu (€12), €24/35 – Carte €26/38

◆ One dining room with a rotisserie, a second with an open fire, and a terrace beneath the shade of a lime tree: three delightful settings in which to enjoy local specialities and grilled meats.

Au Fil de l'Eau

21 quai Butin – ✆ 05 53 05 73 65 – fildeleau@fildeleau.fr – Fax 05 53 35 04 81
– *Open 16 April-19 October and closed Sunday dinner and Tuesday from April to June*

Rest – Menu €24/31

◆ Attractive café with terrace beneath weeping willows on the banks of the Dronne. Fried fish and *matelote* (fish stew) to a backdrop of fishing-inspired decor.

in Champagnac de Belair 6 km Northeast by D 78 and D 83 – pop. 685 – alt. 135 m – ✉ 24530

Le Moulin du Roc (Alain Gardillou)

– ✆ *05 53 02 86 00 – info@moulinduroc.com*
– *Fax 05 53 54 21 31 – Open 8 May-12 October*

13 rm – €160 €160, €18 – ½ P €160 – **Rest** – *(closed Wednesday lunch and Tuesday)* Menu €40 bi/65

Spec. Soupe glacée aux herbes de notre jardin. Blanc de pintade fermière rôtie, tartine de légumes, foie gras poêlé. Tarte fondante au chocolat mi-amer. **Wines** Montravel, Bergerac.

◆ A magical place: an old oil mill on the Dronne surrounded by countryside. The interior has personalised characterful rooms. Waterside garden. Modern, regional cuisine (set menu) served in two rustic-style dining rooms. Terrace overlooking the river.

in Bourdeilles 10 km Southwest by D 78 – pop. 777 – alt. 103 m – ✉ 24310

Syndicat d'initiative, place des Tilleuls ☏ 05 53 03 42 96, Fax 05 53 54 56 27

Château★: furniture★★, dining room★★ fireplace.

Hostellerie Les Griffons

Le Pont – ☏ 05 53 45 45 35 – griffons@griffons.fr – Fax 05 53 45 45 20 – Open 1st April-30 November

10 rm – €95/105 €105/115, €11 – **Rest** – *(open 1st April-15 October and closed lunch except July-August, Sunday and holidays)* Menu (€20 bi), €24 bi (weekday lunch)/35

◆ At the foot of the castle, a 16C bourgeois house overlooking the Dronne. Rooms have antique furniture, stonework, beams and attractive roof beams on the top floor. Comfortable lounge, bright veranda facing the river, and terrace overlooking the garden. Classical cuisine.

BRAS – 83 Var – 340 K5 – pop. 1 298 – alt. 280 m – ✉ 83149 41 **C3**

Paris 814 – Aix-en-Provence 55 – Marseille 62 – Toulon 61

Syndicat d'initiative, place du 14 juillet ☏ 04 94 69 98 26

Une Campagne en Provence

Domaine Le Peyrourier, 3 km south-westward along the D 28 and secondary road – ☏ 04 98 05 10 20 – info@provence4u.com – Fax 04 98 05 10 21 – Closed 7 January-3 March

6 rm – €80/110 €85/115, €10 – **Table d'hôte** – Menu €26 bi/32 bi

◆ Huge estate surrounded by prairies and vineyards. The rooms, tastefully furnished, in the old buildings whose origins go back to the Templars, each have their own personality and benefit from a garden or the view of the hills. Provençal cuisine in the restaurant and estate wines.

BRAX – 47 Lot-et-Garonne – 336 F4 – see Agen

BRAY-ET-LU – 95 Val-d'Oise – 305 A6 – 106 – pop. 753 – alt. 28 m – ✉ 95710 18 **A1**

Paris 70 – Rouen 61 – Gisors 26 – Pontoise 36 – Vernon 18

Les Jardins d'Epicure with rm

16 Grande-Rue – ☏ 01 34 67 75 87 – info@lesjardinsdepicure.com – Fax 01 34 67 90 22 – Closed 2 January-8 February, Thursday lunch, Tuesday and Wednesday from November to March, Tuesday lunch in April-May and September-October, Sunday dinner and Monday from September to May

13 rm – €110/250 €110/250, €25 – 2 suites – ½ P €75/225

Rest – Menu €30 (weekday lunch), €39/105 – Carte €67/74

◆ A handsome mansion (1852) nestling in a pretty park with river. Plush dining room opening onto a veranda and a pool. Rooms with character.

BREBIÈRES – 62 Pas-de-Calais – 301 L5 – see Douai

BRÉDANNAZ – 74 Haute-Savoie – 328 K6 – alt. 450 m – ✉ 74210 46 **F1**

Paris 550 – Albertville 31 – Annecy 15 – Megève 46

in Chaparon 1.5 km south by secondary road - ✉ 74210 - Doussard

La Châtaigneraie

325 chemin des Fontaines – ☏ 04 50 44 30 67 – info@hotelchataigneraie.com – Fax 04 50 44 83 71 – Open 1st April-1st October and closed Sunday dinner and Monday except from May to September

Rest – Menu €21 (weekdays)/48 – Carte €28/42

◆ Regional cuisine served in a large, country-style dining room with a fireplace, on a quiet terrace at the back of the restaurant, or in a shaded garden facing the mountains.

BRÉHAT (ÎLE) – 22 Côtes-d'Armor – **309** D1 – see Île-de-Bréhat

BRELES – 29 Finistère – **308** C4 – **pop. 749 – alt. 52 m –** ✉ **29810** 9 **A1**

Paris 616 – Rennes 264 – Quimper 99 – Brest 25 – Landerneau 47

Auberge de Bel Air rm,

Lanildut road – ✆ 02 98 04 36 01 – info.belair@aumoulindebelair.com – Fax 02 98 04 36 01 – Closed 1st-21oct., 10 January-1st February

3 rm – €60 €60/66 – **Table d'hôte** – *(closed Tuesday and Wednesday except school holidays and Monday season)* Menu €27 bi

◆ This old granite farm in a verdant setting next to the Aber Ildut looks onto a large garden and pond. Cosy, comfortable bedrooms; riverside terrace. Market fresh menus served in a rustic setting. Cooking lessons from the owner.

LA BRESSE – 88 Vosges – **314** J4 – **pop. 4 928 – alt. 636 m – Winter sports : 650/1 350 m 31 –** ✉ **88250** Alsace-Lorraine 27 **C3**

Paris 437 – Colmar 52 – Épinal 52 – Gérardmer 13 – Thann 39 – Le Thillot 20

Office de tourisme, 2a, rue des Proyes ✆ 03 29 25 41 29, Fax 03 29 25 64 61

Les Vallées VISA AE

31 r. P.-Claudel – ✆ 03 29 25 41 39 – hotel.lesvallees@remy-loisirs.com – Fax 03 29 25 64 38

56 rm – €40/65 €50/85, €10 – ½ P €50/74 – **Rest** – Menu €17, €22/49 – Carte €23/40

◆ Functional rooms of varying sizes, and extensive conference and leisure facilities, mean that this hotel is fully booked winter come summer. The restaurant consists of a tall, light coloured, timber structure, huge bay windows and regionally sourced dishes.

South 3 km, Cornimont road by D 486 – ✉ 88250 La Bresse

Le Clos des Hortensias VISA

51 rte de Cornimont – ✆ 03 29 25 41 08 – Fax 03 29 25 65 34 – Closed 11-24 November, Sunday dinner and Monday

Rest – *(pre-book)* Menu €15 (weekday lunch), €22/39

◆ A mural representing hydrangeas decorates the façade of this family restaurant (non-smoking). Traditional, carefully prepared cuisine served in a decor that is as pleasant as the service.

BRESSIEUX – 38 Isère – **333** E6 – **pop. 89 – alt. 510 m –** ✉ **38870** 43 **E2**

Paris 533 – Grenoble 50 – Lyon 76 – Valence 73 – Vienne 45 – Voiron 30

Auberge du Château VISA AE

– ✆ 04 74 20 91 01 – Fax 04 74 20 54 69 – Closed 20 October-13 November, 16 February-12 March, Sunday dinner off season, Tuesday and Wednesday

Rest – Menu (€21), €30/68 – Carte €39/46

◆ In an old mountain village, this friendly establishment has been admirably restored. The shaded terrace offers a beautiful view of the valley and the Lyonnais mountains.

BRESSON – 38 Isère – **333** H7 – see Grenoble

BRESSUIRE – 79 Deux-Sèvres – **322** D3 – **pop. 17 799 – alt. 186 m –** ✉ **79300** Atlantic Coast 38 **B1**

Paris 364 – Angers 84 – Cholet 45 – Niort 64 – Poitiers 82 – La Roche-sur-Yon 87

Office de tourisme, place de l'Hotel de Ville ✆ 05 49 65 10 27, Fax 05 49 80 41 49

La Boule d'Or VISA AE

15 pl. E.-Zola – ✆ 05 49 65 02 18 – hotel-labouledor@wanadoo.fr – Fax 05 49 74 11 19 – Closed 26 July-18 August and 1st-8 March

20 rm – €45/47 €47, €7 – ½ P €42/64 – **Rest** – *(closed Sunday dinner and Monday lunch)* Menu €13,50/35 – Carte €35/46

◆ Regional building close to the station. Various bedroom sizes, adequately furnished; the more modern bedrooms have better sound-proofing. Brand new interior; classic cuisine.

BREST – 29 Finistère – **308** E4 – **pop. 149 634** – **Built-up area 210 055** – **alt. 35 m** – ✉ **29200** Brittany 9 **A2**

- Paris 596 – Lorient 133 – Quimper 72 – Rennes 246 – St-Brieuc 145
- Brest-Bretagne ✆ 02 98 32 01 00, 10 km Northeast
- Office de tourisme, Place de la Liberté ✆ 02 98 44 24 96, Fax 02 98 44 53 73
- de Brest les Abers Plouarzel Kerhoaden, Northeast: 24 km by D 5, ✆ 02 98 89 68 33.
- Océanopolis★★★ - Cours Dajot ≤★★ - Crossing the harbour★ - Arsenal and naval base ★ DZ - Musée des Beaux-Arts★ EZ **M**[1] - Musée de la Marine★ DZ **M**[2] - Botanic Conservatory of vallon du Stang-Alar★.
- Les Abers ★★

Le Continental without rest

41 r. E.-Zola – ✆ 02 98 80 50 40 – continental.brest@oceaniahotels.com – Fax 02 98 43 17 47 EY **f**

73 rm – †€ 130 ††€ 130/190, ☕ € 13

◆ This hotel is popular with Brest's visiting dignitaries. Bernard Buffet reproductions in the hall and spacious and cosy, modern or Art Deco rooms.

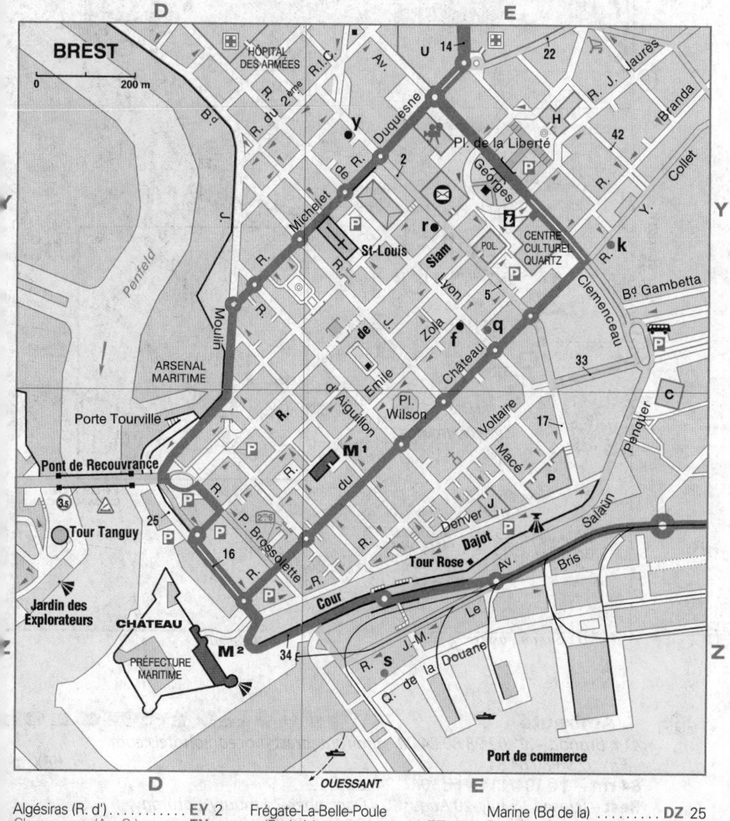

Algésiras (R. d') . . . . **EY** 2
Clemenceau (Av. G.) . . . . **EY**
Colbert (R.) . . . . **EY** 5
Foch (Av. Mar.) . . . . **EY** 14
Français-Libres (Bd des) . . . . **DZ** 16
Frégate-La-Belle-Poule (R. de la) . . . . **EZ** 17
Jean-Jaurès (R.) . . . . **EY**
Kérabécam (R. de) . . . . **EY** 22
Liberté (Pl. de la) . . . . **EY**
Lyon (R. de) . . . . **DEY**
Marine (Bd de la) . . . . **DZ** 25
Réveillère (Av. Amiral) . . . . . **EY** 33
Roosevelt (Av. Fr.) . . . . **DZ** 34
Siam (R. de) . . . . **EY**
11-Martyrs (R. des) . . . . **EY** 42

BREST

Aiguillon (R. d') . . . . EZ
Albert-1er (Pl.) . . . . BZ
Algésiras (R. d') . . . . EY 2
Anatole-France (R.) . . . . AX
Beaumanoir (R.) . . . . AX 3
Blum (Bd Léon) . . . . BV
Botrel (R. Th.) . . . . BV
Bot (R. du) CV
Le Bris (R. J.-M.) . . . . EZ
Brossolette (R. Pierre) . . . . . DZ
Bruat (R.) . . . . BX
Caffarelli (Porte) . . . . AX
Château (R. du) . . . . EYZ
Clemenceau (Av. G.) . . . . EY
Colbert (R.) . . . . EY 5
Collet (R. Yves) . . . . BX
Corniche (Rte de la) . . . . AX
Dajot (Cours) . . . . EZ
Denvers (R.) . . . . EZ

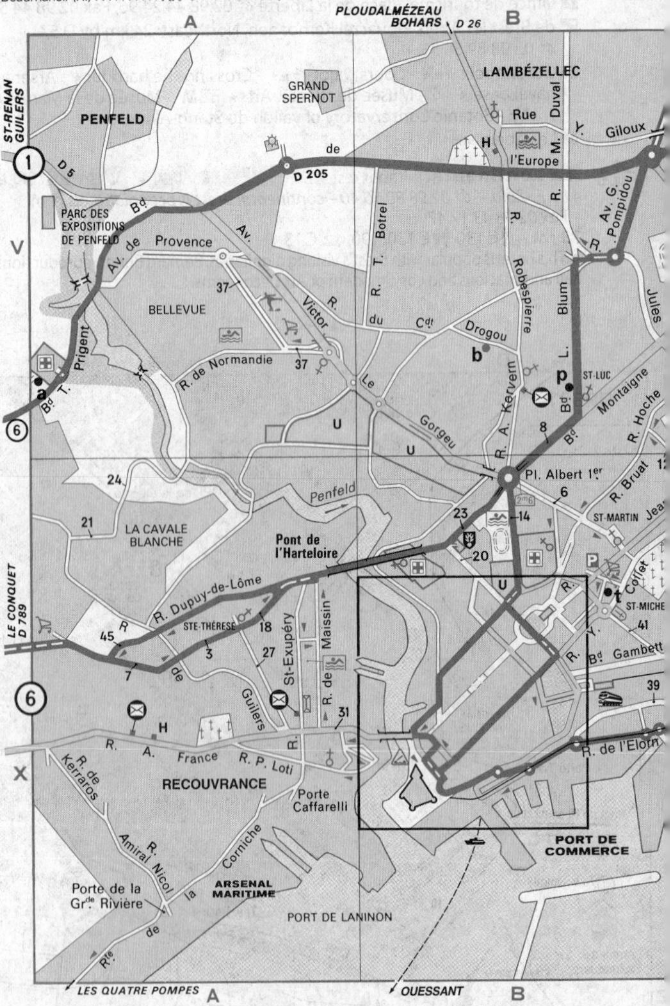

L'Amirauté

41 r. Branda – ✆ 02 98 80 84 00 – amirautebrest@oceaniahotels.com – Fax 02 98 80 84 84 BX **t**

84 rm – €104/114 €104/124, ☕ €12

Rest – *(closed 15 July-20 August, 24 December-7 January, Saturday, Sunday and public holidays)* Menu (€20), €28/50

◆ Modern architecture with elegant lines. Rooms are well soundproofed and have tasteful modern furniture. A restaurant in a brasserie style. Modern cuisine made with regional produce.

Desmoulins (Av. C.) . . . . BX 6
Dr-Kerrien (R. du) . . . . AX 7
Doumer (R. Paul) . . . . BV 8
Dourjacq (Rte du) CV
Drogou (R. Com.) . . . . BV
Dupuy-de-Lôme (R.) . . . . AX
Duquesne (R.) . . . . EY 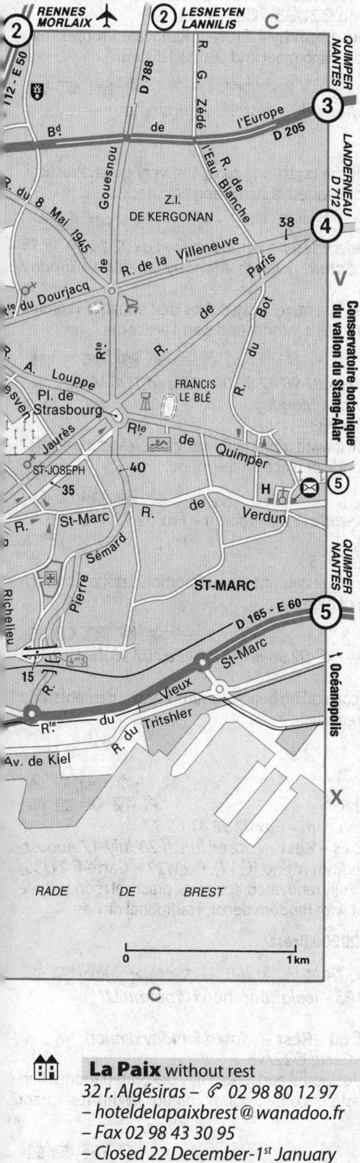
Duval (R. Marcellin) . . . . BV
Eau-Blanche (R. de l') CV
Elorn (R. de l') . . . . BX
Europe (Bd de l') . . . . ACV
Ferry (R. J.) . . . . BCX 12
Foch (Av. Mar.) . . . . BX 14
Forestou (Pont du) . . . . CX 15
Français-Libres (Bd des) . . . . DZ 16
Frégate-La-Belle-Poule (R. de la) . . . . EZ 17
Gallieni (R. du Mar.) . . . . AX 18
Gambetta (Bd) . . . . BX
Le Gorgeu (Av. Victor) . . . . AV
Gouesnou (Rte de) CV
Grande-Rivière (Porte de la) . . . . AX
Guilers (R. de) . . . . AX
Harteloire (Pt. de l') . . . . AX
Harteloire (R. de l') . . . . AX 20
Hoche (R.) . . . . BV
Jean-Jaurès (R.) . . . . EY
Kent (R. de) . . . . AX 21
Kérabécam (R. de) . . . . EY 22
Kérraros (R. de) . . . . AX
Kervern (R. Auguste) . . . . BV
Kiel (Av. de) CX
Lamotte-Picquet (R.) . . . . BX 23
Lesven (R. Jules) . . . . BCV
Libération (Av. de la) . . . . AX 24
Liberté (Pl. de la) . . . . EY
Loti (R. Pierre) . . . . AX
Louppe (R. Albert) CV
Lyon (R. de) . . . . DEY
Macé (R. Jean) . . . . EZ
Maissin (R. de) . . . . AX
Marine (Bd de la) . . . . DZ 25
Michelet (R.) . . . . DV
Montaigne (Bd) . . . . BV
Mouchotte (Bd Cdt) . . . . AX 27
Moulin (Bd Jean) . . . . DY
Nicol (R. de l'Amiral) . . . . AX
Normandie (R. de) . . . . AV
Paris (R. de) CV
Pompidou (R. G.) . . . . BV
Porte (R. de la) . . . . AX 31
Prigent (Bd T.) . . . . AV
Provence (Av. de) . . . . AV
Quimper (Rte de) CV
Recouvrance (Pt de) . . . . DZ
Réveillère (Av. Amiral) . . . . EY 33
Richelieu (R.) CX
Robespierre (R.) . . . . BY
Roosevelt (Av. Fr.) . . . . DZ 34
Saint-Exupéry (R.) . . . . AX
St-Marc (R.) CX
Salaün-Penquer (Av.) . . . . EZ
Sébastopol (R.) . . . . CX 35
Semard (R. Pierre) CX
Siam (R. de) . . . . EY
Strasbourg (Pl. de) CV
Tarente (Av. de) . . . . AV 37
Tourbihan (R. de) . . . . CV 38
Tourville (Porte) . . . . DZ
Tritshler (R. du) CX
Troude (R. Amiral) . . . . BX 39
Valmy (R. de) . . . . CX 40
Verdun (R. de) CX
Victor-Hugo (R.) . . . . BX 41
Vieux-St-Marc (R. du) CX
Villeneuve (R. de la) CV
Voltaire (R.) . . . . EZ
Wilson (Pl.) . . . . EZ
Zédé (R. G.) CV
Zola (R. Émile) . . . . EY
2e-R.C.I. (R. du) . . . . DY
8-Mai-1945 (R. du) CV
11-Martyrs (R. des) . . . . EY 42
19-Mars-1962 (R. du) . . . . AX 45

La Paix without rest

32 r. Algésiras – ✆ 02 98 80 12 97
– hoteldelapaixbrest@wanadoo.fr
– Fax 02 98 43 30 95
– Closed 22 December-1st January

EY **y**

29 rm – 🛉€ 68/72 🛉🛉€ 82/115, ☕ € 10

◆ Small, town centre hotel entirely redecorated in a minimalist, modern style. Brand new, well equipped, soundproofed rooms. Generous buffet breakfast.

Océania rest,

82 r. Siam – 02 98 80 66 66 – oceania.brest@oceaniahotels.com – Fax 02 98 80 65 50 EY **r**

82 rm – €98/128 €98/128, €13 – **Rest** – *(closed 28 July-18 August, Saturday lunch and Sunday lunch)* Menu €21/33 – Carte €23/39

♦ In Rue de Siam, mentioned in a famous poem by J. Prévert. Renovated rooms (two categories) and contemporary restaurant serving meat and seafood dishes.

Du Questel without rest

120 r. F.-Thomas – 02 98 45 99 20 – hotel-du-questel@wanadoo.fr – Fax 02 98 45 94 02 AV **a**

30 rm – €39/45 €48, €7

♦ A brand new, very handy hotel just off the north ring-road, but very quiet. Practical, well-kept rooms, reasonable prices and, on request, a small range of snacks.

La Fleur de Sel

15 bis r. de Lyon – 02 98 44 38 65 – lafleurdesel@wanadoo.fr – Fax 02 98 44 38 53 – Closed 1st-24 August, 1st-10 January, Saturday lunch, Monday lunch and Sunday

Rest – Menu €29/41 – Carte €45/66 EY **q**

♦ The chef of this establishment prepares inventive, tasty dishes that enhance regional produce, herbs and flavours. Modern, minimalist interior and warm welcome.

Le Nouveau Rossini

22 r. Cdt-Drogou – 02 98 47 90 00 – Fax 02 98 47 90 00 – Closed 1st-8 March, 24 August-3 September, Sunday dinner and Monday BV **b**

Rest – Menu (€28), €43/69 – Carte €40/83

♦ Adorable, hundred-year-old Breton house with a pretty flower garden and a cellar for wine-tasting. Seafood and shellfish take pride of place on the menu.

Le Ruffé

1 bis r. Y.-Collet – 02 98 46 07 70 – le-ruffe@wanadoo.fr – Fax 02 98 44 31 46 – Closed Sunday dinner and Monday EY **k**

Rest – Menu (€14), €20/36 – Carte €27/55

♦ In a boat-cum-brasserie inspired decor, this restaurant serves traditional dishes in which regional produce and seafood take pride of place.

La Maison de l'Océan

2 quai de la Douane, (commercial port) – 02 98 80 44 84 – Fax 02 98 46 19 83

Rest – Menu €16/38 EZ **s**

♦ "L'Océan" celebrates the ocean in its decor (scaling bench, furniture and ornaments) and menu (seafood). Substantial clientele of regulars.

North 5 km by D 788 CV – ✉ 29200 Brest

Oceania Brest Aéroport rm, rest,

32 av. Baron Lacrosse – 02 98 02 32 83 – oceania.brestaeroport@oceaniahotels.com – Fax 02 98 41 69 27

82 rm – €98/128 €98/128, €13 – **Rest** – *(closed lunch 28 July-17 August, Saturday lunch, Sunday lunch and holidays)* Menu (€17), €21/27 – Carte €21/35

♦ A Seventies building in a green setting. Fully renovated, spacious, practical rooms; some look onto the swimming pool. Restaurant with modern decor. Traditional dishes.

at Port du Moulin Blanc 7 km by ⑤ – ✉ 29200 Brest

Plaisance Hôtel rest,

37 r. du Moulin Blanc – 02 98 42 33 33 – leplaisancehotel@hotmail.fr – Fax 02 98 02 59 34

46 rm – €65 €72, €7 – ½ P €80 – **Rest** – *(closed Sunday dinner)* Menu (€13 bi), €16 (weekdays)/35 – Carte €22/48

♦ Well-located hotel offering functional, colourful and identically decorated rooms. Perfect for an excursion to Oceanopolis. Tasteful contemporary interior in this restaurant serving brasserie style cuisine.

Ma Petite Folie

– 02 98 42 44 42 – Fax 02 98 41 43 68 – Closed 1 - 10 Jan

Rest – Menu €22/28 – Carte €32/54

♦ The upper and lower decks are now dining rooms - an original nautical decor and delicious fish/seafood cuisine have given this old lobster boat (1952) a new lease of life.

BRETENOUX – 46 Lot – 337 H2 – pop. 1 231 – alt. 136 m – ✉ 46130
Dordogne-Berry-Limousin 29 **C1**

Paris 521 – Brive-la-Gaillarde 44 – Cahors 83 – Figeac 48 – Sarlat-la-Canéda 65 – Tulle 47

Office de tourisme, avenue de la Libération ☎ 05 65 38 59 53, Fax 05 65 39 72 14

Château of Castelnau-bretenoux★★: ≤★ Southwest: 3,5 km.

Domaine de Granval with rm

rte de St-Céré – ☎ 05 65 38 63 99 – domainedegranval@wanadoo.fr – Fax 05 65 39 77 06 – Closed 28 October-11 November

7 rm – €54/60 €60/65, €9 – ½ P €56/62

Rest – *(closed Monday lunchtime, Saturday lunchtime and Sunday)* Menu €19/26 – Carte €40/51

◆ The chef of this restaurant updates his recipes every day depending on the market. Welcoming, rustic setting with fireplace, stone walls, beams and country view.

at Port de Gagnac 6 km northeast by D 940 and D 14 – ✉ 46130 Gagnac-sur-Cère

Hostellerie Belle Rive

rm, VISA MC AE

Port de Gagnac – ☎ 05 65 38 50 04 – hostelleriebellerive@yahoo.fr – Fax 05 65 38 47 72 – Closed 20 December-5 January

12 rm – €45 €60, €7 – 1 suite – ½ P €56/58

Rest *(closed Friday dinner and Sunday dinner 15 April-7 July and 1st September-15 October, Saturday except dinner 15 April-15 October and Sunday from mid October to mid April)* Menu €16 (weekday lunch), €25/41 – Carte €38/59

◆ This old house in typical regional style, in a hamlet on the banks of the River Cère, offers renovated, warm and well-kept rooms. Attractive dining room in a contemporary style, with the original fireplace and a 19C wooden wine press. Updated traditional cuisine.

BRETEUIL – 27 Eure – 304 F8 – pop. 3 473 – alt. 168 m – ✉ 27160 Normandy

Paris 117 – L'Aigle 25 – Alençon 88 – Évreux 31 – Verneuil-sur-Avre 12 33 **C2**

Syndicat d'initiative, 60, place Lafitte ☎ 02 32 67 88 18, Fax 02 32 67 88 18

Grain de Sel

VISA MC

76 pl. Laffitte – ☎ 02 32 29 70 61 – Fax 02 32 29 70 61 – Closed 1st-15 August, Sunday dinner, Tuesday dinner and Monday

Rest – Menu €16/28

◆ A traditional menu awaits in this small restaurant in the market square. Art exhibitions brighten up the smart dining rooms.

BRÉTIGNOLLES-SUR-MER – 85 Vendée – 316 E8 – pop. 2 686 – alt. 14 m – ✉ 85470
34 **A3**

Paris 465 – Challans 30 – La Roche-sur-Yon 44 – Nantes 86

Office de tourisme, 1, boulevard du Nord ☎ 02 51 90 12 78, Fax 02 51 22 40 72

J.-M. Pérochon et Hôtellerie des Brisants with rm

63 av. de la Grand'Roche – ☎ 02 51 33 65 53 ≤ rest, VISA MC

– perochonjeanmarc@wanadoo.fr – Fax 02 51 33 89 10 – Closed 12-26 November, 2-24 February

15 rm – €41/75 €45/80, €9 – ½ P €57/75 – **Rest** – *(closed Monday except dinner July-August, Sunday dinner September-June, and Tuesday lunch)* Menu €31/68 bi – Carte €51/99

◆ Pretty view of the Atlantic from this large dining room, spruced up in a contemporary minimalist spirit. Updated seafood menu. Redecorated rooms.

BRETTEVILLE-SUR-LAIZE – 14 Calvados – 303 C2 – pop. 1 504 – alt. 54 m – ✉ 14680

Paris 245 – Caen 18 – Hérouville-Saint-Clair 23 – Lisieux 52 32 **B2**

Château des Riffets

– ☎ 02 31 23 53 21 – chateau.riffets@wanadoo.fr – Fax 02 31 23 75 14

4 rm – €110 €110/160 – **Table d'hôte** – Menu €45 bi

◆ Dominating a huge wooded park, this pretty manor houses spacious and elegant rooms. Period furniture and modern fittings make it a comfortable place to stay. Family food inspired by the region, prepared with market-fresh produce, and served in a dining room with character.

LE BREUIL – 71 Saône-et-Loire – 320 G9 – see le Creusot

LE BREUIL-EN-AUGE – 14 Calvados – 303 N4 – pop. 846 – alt. 38 m – ✉ 14130

Paris 196 – Caen 55 – Deauville 21 – Lisieux 10 33 **C2**

XX **Le Dauphin** (Régis Lecomte) VISA MC AE

2 r. de l'Église – ☎ 02 31 65 08 11 – dauphin.le@wanadoo.fr – Fax 02 31 65 12 08 – Closed 12 November-2 December, Sunday dinner and Monday

Rest – Menu € 37/45 (a la carte on Saturday evening) – Carte € 65/77

Spec. Escalope de foie gras normand aux poires et caramel de cidre. Tajine de homard breton aux girolles (May to October). Tartelette aux pralines roses, glace plombières.

◆ Norman restaurant appreciated as much for its personalised cuisine as for its welcoming, country chic decor (coat of arms, chrome plated stove, and watercolours).

in St-Philbert-des-Champs 2.5 km northeast by D 264 – pop. 606 – alt. 143 m – ✉ 14130

Le Bonheur est dans le Pré rest, P

Le Montmain – ☎ 02 31 64 29 79 – lebonheurdanslepre@wanadoo.fr

3 rm – €80/98 €80/98 – **Table d'hôte** – Menu € 20 bi/25 bi

◆ Nicely-restored farm with a modern extension and villas next to a meadow. Spacious, tastefully decorated rooms and pleasant garden. Cosy dining room where the owner serves market-inspired dishes.

BREUILLET – 17 Charente-Maritime – 324 D5 – pop. 2 178 – alt. 28 m – ✉ 17920

Paris 509 – Poitiers 176 – La Rochelle 69 – Rochefort 39 – Saintes 38 38 **A3**

XX **L'Aquarelle** VISA MC

22 rte du Candé – ☎ 05 46 22 11 38 – aurelpain@wanadoo.fr – Closed 2-15 June, 1 week in October, Tuesday lunch and Monday

Rest – Menu € 24/46 – Carte € 38/48

◆ Low-key contemporary interior decorated in natural shades; up-to-date menu in which the chef lets his creativity run wild. Definitely worth a visit.

BRÉVONNES – 10 Aube – 313 G3 – pop. 584 – alt. 120 m – ✉ 10220 13 **B3**

Paris 198 – Bar-sur-Aube 30 – St-Dizier 59 – Troyes 28 – Vitry-le-François 51

XX **Au Vieux Logis** with rm rest, P VISA MC

1 r. Piney – ☎ 03 25 46 30 17 – logisbrevonnes@wanadoo.fr – Fax 03 25 46 37 20 – Closed 18 February-13 March, Monday except dinner May-September and Sunday dinner

5 rm – €46/55 €46/55, € 7,50 – ½ P € 57/63 – **Rest** – Menu € 17 (weekdays), € 21/43 – Carte € 31/46

◆ The family atmosphere is jealously guarded in the rustic decor filled with all the charm of the houses of our grandmothers. Tasty traditional menu.

BRIANÇON – 05 Hautes-Alpes – 334 H3 – pop. 10 737 – alt. 1 321 m – Winter sports : 1 200/2 800 m 9 67 – Casino – ✉ 05100 French Alps 41 **C1**

Paris 681 – Digne-les-Bains 145 – Gap 89 – Grenoble 119 – Torino 109

☎ 3635 (0,34 €/mn)

Office de tourisme, 1, place du Temple ☎ 04 92 21 08 50, Fax 04 92 20 56 45

de Montgenèvre Montgenèvre Route d'Italie, Northeast: 12 km, ☎ 04 92 21 94 23.

High town★★: Grande Gargouille★, Statue "La France"★**B** - Upper covered way ★, ≤★ of porte de la Durance - Puy St-Pierre ✻★★ of the church Southwest: 3 km via Rte de Puy St-Pierre.

Croix de Toulouse ≤★★ via Av. de Toulouse and D232ᵀ : 8,5 km.

Plan on next page

Parc Hôtel without rest P VISA MC AE

Central Parc – ☎ 04 92 20 37 47 – resa-serre-che1@monalisahotels.com – Fax 04 92 20 53 74 A **a**

60 rm – €89/114 €89/114, € 10

◆ This recently built downtown construction offers renovated rooms, comfortable and brightened with fabrics in Provençal colours.

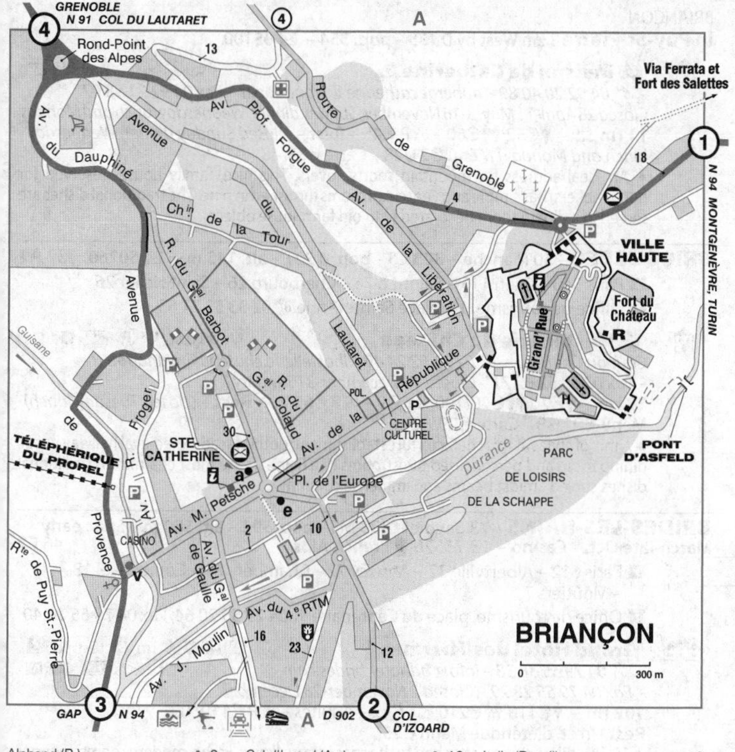

Alphand (R.)	A 2	Col-d'Izoard (Av.)	A 12	Italie (Rte d')	A 18
Baldenberger (Av. P.)	A 4	Daurelle (Av. A.)	A 13	Pasteur (R.)	A 23
Centrale (R.)	A 10	Gaulle (Av. Gén.-de)	A 16	159e-R.-I.-A. (Av.)	A 30

La Chaussée

4 r. Centrale – ✆ 04 92 21 10 37 – hotel.de.la.chaussee@wanadoo.fr – Fax 04 92 20 03 94 – Closed 1st-24 May and 1st-20 October A **e**

13 rm – €60/75 €60/80, ☕ €7,50 – ½ P €57/67 – **Rest** – *(closed 20 April-31 May, 1st-25 October, Monday lunch, Tuesday lunch and Wednesday lunch)* Menu €20/37 – Carte €27/38

◆ For five generations the same family has welcomed visitors to this hotel located in the lower town. Simple soundproofed bedrooms, some with a balcony or terrace on the south side. The restaurant decor resembles the inside of a chalet. Dishes with a local flavour.

Le Péché Gourmand

2 rte de Gap – ✆ 04 92 21 33 21 – Fax 04 92 21 33 21 – Closed 1st-16 May, 10-25 October, Sunday dinner and Monday A **v**

Rest – Menu €19 (weekday lunch), €25/48 – Carte €38/62

◆ A restaurant in the cellars of an old pasta factory on the River Guisane. Warm decor, with an exhibition of paintings and modern cuisine made with care.

in La Vachette 3 km by ① – ✉ 05100

Le Vach' tin

rte d'Italie – ✆ 04 92 46 93 13 – Fax 04 92 20 13 61 – Closed 27 October-30 November, Sunday and Monday except July-August

Rest – *(pre-book)* Menu €20 – Carte €24/43

◆ The façade is not particularly attractive but the vaulted dining room of this old farm building has a mountainous rustic charm. Up-to-date cuisine.

in Puy-St-Pierre 3 km West by D 135 – pop. 354 – ✉ 05100

La Maison de Catherine
– ✆ 04 92 20 40 89 – aubergecatherine@wanadoo.fr – Fax 04 92 21 98 07
Closed 28 April-11 May, 3-16 November, Sunday dinner, Wednesday lunch and Monday
11 rm – €52 €60 – ½ P €45 – **Rest** – *(closed Sunday dinner, Wednesday lunch and Monday)* Menu €21/28 – Carte €35/48
♦ An ideal address for mountain sports' lovers. This nice, family house (reserved for non-smokers) has simple and very clean rooms furnished in pine. The traditional dishes are served in a dining room decorated with old farmhouse objects.

BRICQUEBEC – 50 Manche – 303 C3 – pop. 4 221 – alt. 145 m – ✉ 50260 32 A1

Paris 348 – Caen 115 – Saint-Lô 76 – Cherbourg 26 – Saint Helier 26
Office de tourisme, 13, place Sainte-Anne ✆ 02 33 52 21 65

L'Hostellerie du Château rest,
Cour du Château – ✆ 02 33 52 24 49 – lhostellerie.chateau@wanadoo.fr – Fax 02 33 52 62 71 – Closed 15 December-31 January
17 rm – €70 €70/100, €9 – ½ P €65/80 – **Rest** – *(closed Tuesday lunch)* Menu €21/38 – Carte €29/82
♦ A mix of styles at this characterful establishment: gothic façade, medieval hallway, rustic dining room and personalised guestrooms ("La Reine" is the most charming). Traditional dishes served amidst beams and immense columns.

BRIDES-LES-BAINS – 73 Savoie – 333 M5 – pop. 593 – alt. 580 m – Spa : early March-late Oct. – Casino – ✉ 73570 French Alps 46 F2

Paris 612 – Albertville 32 – Annecy 77 – Chambéry 81 – Courchevel 18 – Moûtiers 7
Office de tourisme, place du Centenaire ✆ 04 79 55 20 64, Fax 04 79 55 20 40

Grand Hôtel des Thermes rm, rest,
– ✆ 04 79 55 38 38 – info@gdhotel-brides.com
– *Fax 04 79 55 28 29 – Closed 2 November-28 December*
102 rm – €110 €210, €12 – 4 suites – ½ P €119/160
Rest – rest. diététique Menu €25
♦ 19C building directly attached to the spas by a walkway. Large, modern rooms, lounges and fitness facilities under a glass dome. Slightly old-fashioned dining room, (preserved high ceiling) with paintings and plants. Modern menu and set menus especially for those taking a cure.

Golf-Hôtel rest,
– ✆ 04 79 55 28 12 – golfhotel-brides@wanadoo.fr – Fax 04 79 55 24 78
– *Closed 1st November-25 December*
55 rm – €69/138 €82/138, €9 – ½ P €68/150
Rest – *(closed lunch 26 December-9 March)* Menu €25 – Carte €20/33
♦ This elegant 1920s hotel has had a facelift. Superb reception area, spacious and modern rooms, some with a pretty view over the Vanoise mountain. A fountain decorated with a statue stands in the centre of this restaurant with two dining rooms.

Amélie rm,
r. Émile-Machet – ✆ 04 79 55 30 15 – info@hotel-amelie.com – Fax 04 79 55 28 08 – Closed 2 November-20 December
40 rm – €80/95 €115/125, €11 – ½ P €62/95
Rest *Les Cerisiers* – – Menu €23/40 – Carte €48/61
♦ Modern building situated within easy reach of the cable-car station and the spa centre. Functional, well soundproofed rooms with marble bathrooms. Savoyard specialities and diet menus served in a modern dining room.

Altis Val Vert
Quartier de l'Olympe – ✆ 04 79 55 22 62 – altisvalvert@wanadoo.fr – Fax 04 79 55 29 12 – Closed 30 October-20 December
28 rm – €50/62 €68/75, €10 – ½ P €62/65 – **Rest** – *(closed lunch mid December-beg. April)* Menu (€17), €22 (weekdays)/26 – Carte €25/38
♦ At the centre of the resort, two chalets separated by a delightful garden in full bloom in summer. The rooms are comfortable and colourful. Neo-rustic restaurant with a charming summer garden terrace full of colour on sunny days.

Des Sources
av. des Marronniers – ✆ 04 79 55 29 22 – les.sources.1@wanadoo.fr – Fax 04 79 55 27 06 – Closed 2 November-20 December
70 rm – †€ 53/63 ††€ 55/65, ☐ € 6 – ½ P € 65 – **Rest** – Menu € 19
◆ Stately buildings set around a main building. The bedrooms, which have been slowly done over, boast balconies offering views over the spa gardens. Exposed beams, country furniture and a fresco give this spacious dining room a rustic air.

Le Belvédère without rest
r. Émile-Machet, quartier des Sources – ✆ 04 79 55 23 41 – hotel.belvedere@wanadoo.fr – Fax 04 79 55 24 96 – Closed end October-mid December
28 rm – †€ 37/43 ††€ 52/66, ☐ € 5
◆ Here you will enjoy a pleasant stay opposite the Vanoise mountains in this small Savoy "castel". Simple decor and alpine furniture in the rooms.

BRIE-COMTE-ROBERT – 77 Seine-et-Marne – 312 E3 – 101 39 – see Paris, Area

BRIGNAC – 34 Hérault – 339 F7 – see Clermont-L'Hérault

BRIGNOGAN-PLAGES – 29 Finistère – 308 F3 – pop. 849 – alt. 17 m – ✉ 29890

9 **A1**

Paris 585 – Brest 41 – Landerneau 27 – Morlaix 49 – Quimper 89

Office de tourisme, 7, avenue du Général-de-Gaulle ✆ 02 98 83 41 08, Fax 02 98 83 41 08

Castel Régis without rest
Prom. du Garo – ✆ 02 98 83 40 22 – castel-regis@wanadoo.fr – Fax 02 98 83 44 71 – Open 26 April-30 September
22 rm – †€ 78/115 ††€ 78/115, ☐ € 10
◆ The enchanting setting in a large garden bordering the Pontusva cove is the main attraction of this hotel made up of several buildings. Sober, nautical-style rooms.

LA BRIGUE – 06 Alpes-Maritimes – 341 G3 – see Tende

BRINON-SUR-SAULDRE – 18 Cher – 323 J1 – pop. 1 089 – alt. 147 m – ✉ 18410

12 **C2**

Paris 190 – Bourges 66 – Cosne-sur-Loire 59 – Gien 37 – Orléans 53 – Salbris 25

La Solognote
rest,
34 Grande-Rue – ✆ 02 48 58 50 29 – lasolognote@wanadoo.fr – Fax 02 48 58 56 00 – Closed 18 February-19 March, Thursday lunch, Tuesday and Wednesday from 11 November to 30 March
13 rm – †€ 58 ††€ 76, ☐ € 10 – 1 suite – ½ P € 85 – **Rest** – Menu € 23/30 – Carte € 40/53
◆ A family hotel made up of several small houses containing tastefully decorated rustic or modern rooms, all overlooking an attractive courtyard terrace. Elegant, cosy restaurant: antique furniture and knick-knacks. The bar has been redone.

Les Bouffards
– ✆ 02 48 58 59 88 – bouffards@wanadoo.fr – Fax 02 48 58 32 11
5 rm ☐ – †€ 60/150 ††€ 60/150 – **Table d'hôte** – *(closed Sunday)* Menu € 25 bi
◆ Welcoming family home in attractive parkland complete with pool. Spacious comfortable rooms ensure you will make the most of the peaceful setting.

BRIOLLAY – 49 Maine-et-Loire – 317 F3 – pop. 2 282 – alt. 20 m – ✉ 49125

35 **C2**

Paris 288 – Angers 15 – Château-Gontier 44 – La Flèche 45

Syndicat d'initiative, 6, rue de la Mairie ✆ 02 41 42 16 84, Fax 02 41 37 92 89

Ceiling★★★ of the Guards' Room of the chateau de Plessis-Bourré Northwest: 10 km **Châteaux of the Loire.**

via Soucelles road 3 km (D 109) – ✉ 49125 Briollay

Château de Noirieux 🐿 VISA

26 rte du Moulin – ☎ 02 41 42 50 05
– noirieux@relaischateaux.com – Fax 02 41 37 91 00
– Closed from mid February to mid March and November, Sunday and Monday from October to May
19 rm – 🛉€ 175/370 🛉🛉€ 175/370, ☕ € 22 – ½ P € 160/246
Rest – *(closed Sunday dinner October-May, Tuesday except dinner from October-May and Monday)* Menu € 47 (weekday lunch), € 59/110 – Carte € 98/133
Rest *Côté Véranda* – *(closed Tuesday from October-May, Sunday and Monday) (lunch only)* Menu € 32/48
Spec. Lasagne d'araignée de mer à la truffe. Escalopes de turbot côtier grillées, asperges vertes et artichauts poivrades (April to October). "Petites folies" de desserts gourmands de Mireille. **Wines** Saumur, Anjou.
◆ This magnificent estate includes a 17C château, 15C manor and a chapel in a park overlooking the River Loir. Refined rooms. Elegant dining room and shady terrace; lovely, contemporary cuisine. The Côté Véranda is only open for lunch.

BRION – 01 Ain – **328** G3 – **see Nantua**

BRIONNE – 27 Eure – **304** E6 – **pop. 4 449** – **alt. 56 m** – ✉ **27800**
Normandy 33 **C2**

- Paris 156 – Bernay 16 – Évreux 40 – Lisieux 40 – Pont-Audemer 27 – Rouen 44
- Office de tourisme, 1, rue du Général-de-Gaulle ☎ 02 32 45 70 51
- du Champ de Bataille Le Neubourg Château du Champ de Bataille, West: 18 km by D 137 and D 39, ☎ 02 32 35 03 72.
- Bec-Hellouin abbey ★★ North: 6 km - Harcourt: château★ and arboretum★ Southeast: 7 km.

Le Logis with rm VISA

pl. St-Denis – ☎ 02 32 44 81 73 – lelogisdebrionne@free.fr – Fax 02 32 45 10 92
– Closed 18 August-2 September, 3-9 November, February holidays, Saturday lunch, Sunday dinner and Monday
12 rm – 🛉€ 70 🛉🛉€ 72, ☕ € 11,50 – **Rest** – Menu € 19 (weekday lunch), € 25/46 – Carte approx. € 56
◆ A contemporary dining room with numerous green plants, serving food in keeping with current tastes and local specialities. Rooms decorated with old-fashioned furniture.

BRIOUDE – 43 Haute-Loire – **331** C2 – **pop. 6 820** – **alt. 427 m** – ✉ **43100**
Auvergne 6 **C3**

- Paris 479 – Clermont-Ferrand 69 – Le Puy-en-Velay 62 – St-Flour 52
- Office de tourisme, place Lafayette ☎ 04 71 74 97 49, Fax 04 71 74 97 87
- St-Julien basilica★★ (apse★★, capitals★★).
- Lavaudieu: frescoes★ in the church and cloisters★★ of the former abbey 9.5 km by ①.

Plan on next page

La Sapinière 🐿 rest, VISA

av. P.-Chambriard – ☎ 04 71 50 87 30 – hotel.la.sapiniere@wanadoo.fr
– Fax 04 71 50 87 39 – Closed February, November school holidays and Sunday dinner except July-August m
11 rm – 🛉€ 80/85 🛉🛉€ 96/104, ☕ € 10 – ½ P € 78
Rest – *(open from Easter to 31 December and closed autumn half-term holidays, Sunday dinner, Monday and lunch except Sunday)* Menu € 26/45 – Carte € 33/45
◆ An attractive modern building in the heart of the town yet quiet with a pleasant garden, with spacious countrified rooms. Lovely indoor swimming pool; Jacuzzi. Exposed rafters and light-coloured wood in this pleasantly bright restaurant.

BRIOUDE

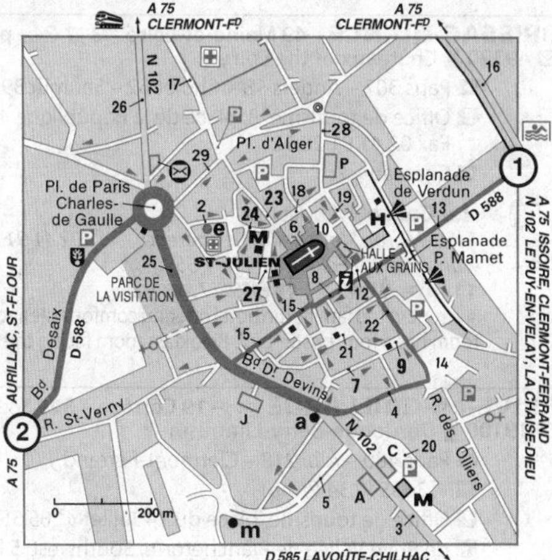

Artemis rm, VISA
Parc des Conchettes, Rocade N102: 2 km northwest – ✆ 04 71 50 45 04 – info@artemis-hotel.com – Fax 04 71 50 45 05
40 rm – €60/74 €60/74, €9,50 – ½ P €57/59 – **Rest** – Menu (€13,50), €17/39 – Carte €25/57
◆ By the main road bypassing Brioude, this hotel offers rooms, garden, swimming pool and seminar room. Contemporary modern fittings and well soundproofed. Modern dining room in shades of cream serving traditional cuisine.

Poste et Champanne rest, VISA
1 bd Dr-Devins – ✆ 04 71 50 14 62 – hpbrioude@wanadoo.fr – Fax 04 71 50 10 55 – Closed autumn half-term holidays, 26 January-3 March, Sunday dinner and Monday lunch a
20 rm – €32/48 €48/56, €7 – ½ P €48 – **Rest** – Menu €15 (weekdays), €23/42
◆ A town-centre family establishment. Refurbished rooms, functional in the main building and quieter and more comfortable in the annexe. The rustic old-fashioned restaurant is very authentic, as is its generous "one hundred percent" tasty Auvergne cuisine.

BRIOUZE – 61 Orne – **310** G2 – **pop. 1 620** – **alt. 210 m** – ✉ **61220** 32 **B3**
Paris 218 – Alençon 58 – Argentan 26 – La Ferté-Macé 13 – Flers 17

Sophie with rm rest, VISA
5 pl. Albert-1er – ✆ 02 33 62 82 82 – Fax 02 33 62 82 83 – Closed 10 August-8 September, 20 December-4 January, Sunday dinner, Friday dinner and Saturday
9 rm – €40 €40/65, €6 – **Rest** – Menu €12/25 – Carte €19/35
◆ On the village square, which is extremely lively on cattle market days, this small family restaurant has two simple, rustic dining rooms. Practical rooms.

BRISSAC – 34 Hérault – **339** H5 – **pop. 442** – **alt. 145 m** – ✉ **34190** 23 **C2**
Paris 732 – Alès 55 – Montpellier 41 – Le Vigan 25

Jardin aux Sources with rm rm, rm, VISA
30 av. du Parc – ✆ 04 67 73 31 16 – isaje@club-internet.fr – Fax 04 67 73 31 16 – Closed 27 October-14 November, 5-23 January, Sunday dinner and Wednesday off season and Monday
5 rm – €85/100 €100/135 – **Rest** – *(number of covers limited, pre-book)* Menu (€19), €26 (weekday lunch), €31/64 – Carte €47/53
◆ Stone house in a picturesque village. Vaulted restaurant overlooking the kitchen, delightful terrace and inventive cuisine. Charming rooms.

BRISSAC-QUINCÉ – 49 Maine-et-Loire – 317 G4 – pop. 2 296 – alt. 65 m – ✉ 49320 Châteaux of the Loire

35 **C2**

Paris 307 – Angers 18 – Cholet 62 – Saumur 39

Office de tourisme, 8, place de la République ✆ 02 41 91 21 50, Fax 02 41 91 28 12

Château★★.

Le Castel without rest

1 r. L.-Moron , (opposite the château) – ✆ 02 41 91 24 74 – le.castel.brissac@wanadoo.fr – Fax 02 41 91 71 55

11 rm – 🛉€ 45/77 🛉🛉€ 45/77, ☕ € 8

◆ A renovated family-run hotel offering comfortable and spruce rooms. The most luxurious room has a four-poster bed. Breakfast room facing the garden.

BRIVE-LA-GAILLARDE – 19 Corrèze – 329 K5 – pop. 49 141 – alt. 142 m – ✉ 19100 Dordogne-Berry-Limousin

24 **B3**

Paris 480 – Albi 218 – Clermont-Ferrand 170 – Limoges 92 – Toulouse 201

✆ 3635 (0,34 €/mn)

Office de tourisme, place du 14 Juillet ✆ 05 55 24 08 80, Fax 05 55 24 58 24

de Brive Vallée de Planchetorte, Southwest: 5 km, ✆ 05 55 87 57 57.

Musée de Labenche★.

BRIVE-LA-GAILLARDE

Blum (Av. L.) .... **AX** 4
Clemenceau (Bd) ...... **AX** 6
Dalton (R. Gén.) .... **AX** 7
Dellessert (R. B.) ...... **AX** 9
Dr-Marbeau (Bd) .... **AX** 10
Dormoy (Bd M.) .... **AX** 13
Dubois (Bd Cardinal) ... **AX** 15
Foch (Av. du Mar.) ..... **AX** 17
Germain (Bd Colonel) ... **AX** 20
Grivel (Bd Amiral) ...... **AX** 22
Hériot (Av. E.) .... **AX** 24
Leclerc (Av. Mar.) ...... **AX** 31
Michelet (Bd) .... **AX** 33
Paris (Av. de) .... **AX** 34
Pasteur (Av.) .... **AX** 35
Pompidou (Av. G.) ..... **AX** 37

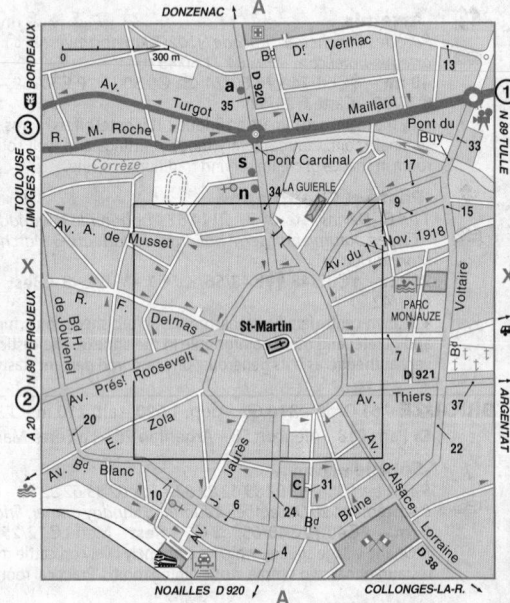

La Truffe Noire

22 bd A.-France – ✆ 05 55 92 45 00 – contact@la-truffe-noire.com – Fax 05 55 92 45 13

CY **v**

27 rm – 🛉€ 85/100 🛉🛉€ 100/125, ☕ € 19 – **Rest** – Menu (€ 26), € 38/80 – Carte € 52/72

◆ Large regional 19C home located on the threshold of the old town. Welcoming lounge with imposing fireplace and beautiful bedrooms with modern decor. Truffles and Corrèze specialities served in the attractive dining room or on the shady terrace.

BRIVE-LA-GAILLARDE

Alsace-Lorraine (Av. d') . . . . . **CZ** 2
Anatole-France (Bd) . . . . **CY** 3
Dalton (R. Gén.) . . . . **CY** 7
Dauzier (Pl. J.-M.) . . . . **CY** 8
Dellessert (R. B.) . . . . **CY** 9
Dr-Massénat (R.) . . . . **CY** 12
Échevins (R. des) . . . . **CZ** 14
Faro (R. du Lt-Colonel) . . . . . **CZ** 16
Gambetta (R.) . . . . **CZ**
Gaulle (Pl. Ch. de) . . . . **CZ** 18
Halle (Pl. de la) . . . . **CY** 23
Herriot (Av. E.) . . . . **CZ** 24
Hôtel-de-Ville (Pl. de l') . . . . . **CY** 26
Hôtel-de-Ville (R. de l') . . . . . **BZ** 27
Latreille (Pl.) . . . . **CZ** 30
Lattre-de-Tassigny (Pl. de) . . . . **CZ** 29
Leclerc (Av. Mar.) . . . . **CZ** 31
Lyautey (Bd Mar.) . . . . **BZ** 32
Majour (R.) . . . . **BYZ** 36
Paris (Av. de) . . . . **BY**
Puyblanc (Bd de) . . . . **CZ** 19
Raynal (R. B.) . . . . **CZ** 40
République (Pl. de la) . . . . . . **BZ** 42
République (R. de la) . . . . . . **BZ** 43
Salan (R. du) . . . . **CZ** 45
Ségéral-Verninac (R.) . . . . **BY** 46
Teyssier (R.) . . . . **CY** 47
Toulzac (R.) . . . . **CY** 48
14 Juillet (Av. du) . . . . **CY** 21

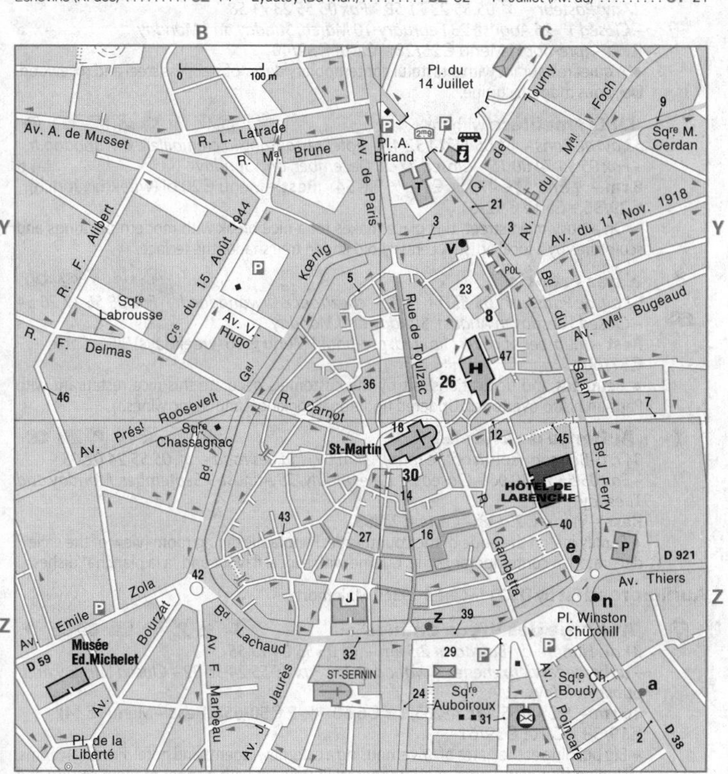

Le Collonges without rest
3 pl. W.-Churchill – ✆ 05 55 74 09 58 – lecollonges@wanadoo.fr – Fax 05 55 74 11 25 CZ **n**
24 rm – 🚹€ 50/52 🚹🚹€ 52/59, ☕ € 8,50
◆ This family-run hotel is located just off the ring road round the town centre. A smart lounge bar and soberly modern rooms assure the well being of travellers.

Le Coq d'Or without rest
16 bd Jules-Ferry – ✆ 05 55 17 12 92 – marc.belacel@wanadoo.fr – Fax 05 55 88 39 90 – Closed 23 December-2 January CZ **e**
8 rm – 🚹€ 50 🚹🚹€ 55, ☕ € 8
◆ A renovated hotel on the ring road, just a short distance from the centre. Small bedrooms adorned with antique furniture. Bar-tabac and pavement terrace beneath the shade of the plane trees.

XXX **Les Arums**

15 av. Alsace-Lorraine – ✆ 05 55 24 26 55 – Fax 05 55 17 13 22 – Closed 25 August-1st September, Saturday lunch, Sunday dinner and Monday
Rest – Menu (€ 27 bi), € 38/85 – Carte € 47/51 CZ **a**
◆ Minimalist, contemporary dining room enhanced by colourful modern art. Creative cuisine. Leafy terrace.

XX **La Toupine**

27 av. Pasteur – ✆ 05 55 23 71 58 – Fax 05 55 23 71 58 – Closed 1st-26 August, 23 February-10 March, Sunday and Monday AX **a**
Rest – *(pre-book)* Menu € 25/28 – Carte € 32/40
◆ A quiet restaurant with a tasteful contemporary decor of stainless steel and rosewood. Delicious modern cuisine.

XX **La Crémaillère** with rm

53 av. de Paris – ✆ 05 55 74 32 47 – hotel.restaurant-la.cremaillere@wanadoo.fr – Fax 05 55 74 00 15 – Closed 22-28 December, and Sunday AX **n**
8 rm – €44 €47, € 7 – ½ P € 54 – **Rest** – Menu € 20 bi (weekday lunch), € 29/36 – Carte € 52/61
◆ On a busy main street, this place makes for a nice break with modern paintings and sculptures by a local artist. A century-old linden tree shades the terrace.

X **Chez Francis**

61 av. de Paris – ✆ 05 55 74 41 72 – chezfrancis@wanadoo.fr – Fax 05 55 17 20 54 – Closed Tuesday in August, Sunday and Monday AX **s**
Rest – *(number of covers limited, pre-book)* Menu € 16 (weekdays)/25 – Carte € 37/60
◆ Retro ads and dedications left by the customers decorate this nice restaurant with Parisian bistro overtones. Updated traditional cooking; Languedoc wines.

X **Auberge de Chanlat**

34 r. G-Buisson, (south of the map), 2 km by Noailles road – ✆ 05 55 24 02 03 – Fax 05 55 74 39 06 – Closed 23 June-1st July, 25 August-9 September, Monday and Tuesday
Rest – Menu € 22/38 – Carte € 27/53
◆ Family inn on the edge of the countryside. Panoramic dining room (view of the valley) decorated in contemporary style. Cuisine with a local flavour and "à la plancha" dishes.

Aurillac road Est by D 921 CZ – ✉ 19360 Malemort

Auberge des Vieux Chênes

31 av. Honoré-de-Balzac, at 2.5 km – ✆ 05 55 24 13 55 – aubergedesvieuxchenes@wanadoo.fr – Fax 05 55 24 56 82 – Closed Sunday and public holidays
16 rm – €45/55 €48/65, € 6,50 – ½ P € 50/65 – **Rest** – Menu (€ 14), € 19/38 – Carte € 39/61
◆ Big building at the gates of Brive, housing a café, newsagents and hotel. Practical rooms, including four new, larger, modern rooms. Restaurant with a sober modern setting and classical cuisine with a regional accent.

in Varetz 10 km by ③, D 901 and D 152 – pop. 1 918 – alt. 109 m – ✉ 19240

Château de Castel Novel

in Varetz – ✆ 05 55 85 00 01 – novel@relaischateaux.com – Fax 05 55 85 09 03 – Closed 26 December-20 January, Sunday dinner and Monday except July-August
32 rm – €84/300 €104/320, € 19 – 5 suites – ½ P € 144/220
Rest – *(closed Sunday dinner and Monday dinner except July-August, Saturday lunch and Monday lunch)* Menu (€ 24), € 32, € 41/71 – Carte € 66/90
◆ Colette loved the amazing peacefulness of this 13C château built in red sandstone and its surrounding park. Bedrooms of real character in which you can be the lord or lady of the manor for a night. One of the dining rooms is in the novelist Colette's old library.

BRIVEZAC – 19 Corrèze – 329 M5 – see Beaulieu-sur-Dordogne

BRON – 69 Rhône – 327 I5 – see Lyon

BROU – 28 Eure-et-Loir – **311** C6 – **pop. 3 713 – alt. 150 m** – ✉ **28160** 11 **B1**

Paris 142 – Chartres 38 – Châteaudun 22 – Le Mans 86 – Nogent-le-Rotrou 33

Office de tourisme, rue de la Chevalerie ☎ 02 37 47 01 12, Fax 02 37 47 01 12

L'Ascalier VISA

9 pl. Dauphin – ☎ 02 37 96 05 52 – Fax 02 37 47 02 41 – Closed Sunday dinner, Monday dinner and Tuesday dinner

Rest – *(pre-book)* Menu (€ 14), € 19/40

◆ The lovely 16C "ascalier" (staircase, in local parlance) leads to the upstairs dining room. A rustic interior, flowered terrace and good traditional dishes: the address is very popular.

BROUAINS – 50 Manche – **303** G7 – see Sourdeval

BROUCKERQUE – 59 Nord – **302** B2 – **pop. 1 165 – alt. 2 m** – ✉ **59630** 30 **B1**

Paris 283 – Calais 37 – Cassel 26 – Dunkerque 14 – Lille 74 – St-Omer 28

Middel Houck VISA AE

pl. du Village – ☎ 03 28 27 13 46 – middelhouck@wanadoo.fr – Fax 03 28 27 19 19 – Closed 3-16 August, dinner from Sunday to Friday and Saturday

Rest – Menu € 18 (weekday lunch), € 26/55 bi – Carte € 37/50

◆ Brick walls, exposed beams and freshly cut flowers set the scene in this friendly former post house. Traditional menu with regional accents.

BROUILLA – 66 Pyrénées-Orientales – **344** I7 – **pop. 918 – alt. 45 m** – ✉ **66620** 22 **B3**

Paris 873 – Montpellier 176 – Perpignan 20 – Figueres 47 – Roses 66

L'Ancienne Gare without rest

at "Le Millery", 1 km north by D 8 B – ☎ 04 68 89 88 21 – anciennegare@yahoo.fr

5 rm – €55 €65

◆ A stone's throw from the Spanish border, former railway station transformed into a friendly guesthouse. Romantic guestrooms, antique charm, terrace and view of the Canigou.

BROUILLAMNON – 18 Cher – **323** I4 – see Charost

BROUSSE-LE-CHÂTEAU – 12 Aveyron – **338** H7 – **pop. 163 – alt. 239 m** – ✉ **12480** Languedoc-Roussillon-Tarn Gorges 29 **D2**

Paris 696 – Albi 54 – Cassagnes-Bégonhès 35 – Lacaune 50 – Rodez 61 – St-Affrique 29

Perched village★.

Le Relays du Chasteau rest, VISA

– ☎ 05 65 99 40 15 – lerelaysduchasteau@wanadoo.fr – Fax 05 65 99 21 25 – Closed 20 December-20 January, Friday dinner and Saturday from October to May

12 rm – €37/48 €37/48, € 6,50 – ½ P € 42/44 – **Rest** – Menu € 16 (weekdays)/33 bi – Carte € 15/28

◆ Pretty Aveyron house with simple functional rooms, all facing the medieval château. A fireplace heats the country-style dining room (copper pots and bare wood). Regionally inspired menu.

LES BROUZILS – 85 Vendée – **316** I6 – **pop. 2 031 – alt. 64 m** – ✉ **85260** 34 **B3**

Paris 427 – Nantes 46 – La Roche-sur-Yon 37 – Cholet 77 – Saint-Herblain 53

Manoir de la Thébline without rest

l'Herbergement road – ☎ 02 51 42 99 98 – contact@manoirthebline.com

3 rm – €90 €90

◆ Elegant old furniture adds style to the cosy guestrooms in this attractive 19C residence. Pleasant flower garden, billiard room and library. Very well-maintained.

BRUAY-LA-BUISSIERE – 62 Pas-de-Calais – 301 I5 – see Béthune

BRUÈRE-ALLICHAMPS – 18 Cher – 323 K6 – see St-Amand-Montrond

BRUMATH – 67 Bas-Rhin – 315 K4 – pop. 8 930 – alt. 145 m – ✉ 67170 1 B1

Paris 472 – Haguenau 14 – Molsheim 45 – Saverne 35 – Strasbourg 19

À L'Écrevisse

4 av. de Strasbourg – ✆ 03 88 51 11 08 – ecrevisse@wanadoo.fr – Fax 03 88 51 89 02 – Closed 25 July-8 August, Monday dinner and Tuesday

Rest – Menu € 18/49 – Carte € 32/62

Rest *Krebs'Stuebel* – *(Closed Monday dinner and Tuesday)* Menu (€ 12,50 bi), € 18/38 – Carte € 26/46

◆ The same family has run this Alsatian establishment for seven generations. Elegant restaurant dining room serving classic cuisine. Old but well-kept rooms At the Krebs'Stuebel, the atmosphere and decor is winstub-style; spur-of-the-moment cuisine and tapas.

LE BRUSC – 83 Var – 340 J7 – see Six-Fours-les-Plages

BRY-SUR-MARNE – 94 Val-de-Marne – 312 E2 – 101 18 – see Paris, Area

BUELLAS – 01 Ain – 328 D3 – pop. 1 288 – alt. 225 m – ✉ 01310 43 E1

Paris 424 – Annecy 120 – Bourg-en-Bresse 9 – Lyon 69 – Mâcon 32

L'Auberge Bressane

pl. du Prieuré – ✆ 04 74 24 20 20 – Fax 04 74 24 20 20 – Closed 27 October-5 November, 16 February-4 March, Sunday dinner, Tuesday and Wednesday

Rest – Menu € 11,50 (weekday lunch), € 20/38 – Carte € 29/38

◆ Tasty regional fare, a zest of southern flavours and a sprinkling of creativity to tempt the palate in this former bakery, now a Provençal-inspired restaurant. Attentive staff.

LE BUGUE – 24 Dordogne – 329 G6 – pop. 2 778 – alt. 62 m – ✉ 24260

Dordogne-Berry-Limousin 4 C3

Paris 522 – Bergerac 47 – Brive-la-Gaillarde 72 – Périgueux 42 – Sarlat-la-Canéda 32

Office de tourisme, porte de la Vézère ✆ 05 53 07 20 48, Fax 05 53 54 92 30

de La Marterie Saint-Félix-de-Reillac-et-Mortemart Domaine de la Marterie, North: 13 km by D 710, ✆ 05 53 05 61 00.

Gouffre de Proumeyssac★★ South: 3 km.

Domaine de la Barde

rm,

rte de Périgueux – ✆ 05 53 07 16 54 – hotel@domainedelabarde.com – Fax 05 53 54 76 19 – Closed 3 January-15 March

18 rm – †€ 95/198 ††€ 95/240, ☕ € 15 – ½ P € 146/291

Rest *Le Vélo Rouge* – *(closed lunch Tuesday-Friday and Monday)* Menu € 39 – Carte € 47/51

◆ Beautiful 18C Périgord mansion overlooking a French style garden. Two converted outhouses, an old mill and forge are home to spacious, tastefully decorated rooms. Traditional dishes take pride of place on the table without forgetting regional specialities.

Sarlat road 3 km East by D 703 and secondary road ✉ 24260

Maison Oléa without rest

< la Vézère valley,

La Combe de Leygue – ✆ 05 53 08 48 93 – info@olea-dordogne.com – Fax 05 53 08 48 93 – Closed 21 December-4 January

5 rm – †€ 55/70 ††€ 65/75, ☕ € 5

◆ The rooms of this guesthouse have south-facing balconies with a view of the Vézère valley. Tasteful interior. Open air summer pool and vegetable garden.

in Campagne 4 km Southeast by D 703 – pop. 310 – alt. 60 m – ✉ 24260

Du Château rm, VISA
– ✆ *05 53 07 23 50 – hotduchateau@aol.com – Fax 05 53 03 93 69*
– Open 16 March-15 October
12 rm – €55/60 €55/60, ☕ €8 – ½ P €55/60 – **Rest** – Menu €22/50
– Carte €33/47
◆ In the heart of the Périgord Noir, a house of character, kept cool in summer by the thickness of its walls. A countrified atmosphere abounds in the simply furnished rooms. Rustic style decor in the dining room and veranda; unpretentious menu.

BUIS-LES-BARONNIES – 26 Drôme – 332 E8 – pop. 2 226 – alt. 365 m – ✉ 26170 French Alps

44 **B3**

Paris 685 – Carpentras 39 – Nyons 29 – Orange 50 – Sault 38 – Sisteron 72 – Valence 130
Office de tourisme, 14, boulevard Eysserie ✆ 04 75 28 04 59, Fax 04 75 28 13 63
Old town ★.

Les Arcades-Le Lion d'Or without rest VISA
pl. du Marché – ✆ 04 75 28 11 31 – info@hotelarcades.fr – Fax 04 75 28 12 07
– Open from March to November
15 rm – €41/66 €47/70, ☕ €7,50 – 1 suite
◆ The entrance to the hotel is found beneath the 15C arcades in the central square. Renovated, prettily personalised rooms. The charming interior garden is worth seeing.

LE BUISSON-CORBLIN – 61 Orne – 310 F2 – see Flers

LE BUISSON-DE-CADOUIN – 24 Dordogne – 329 G6 – pop. 2 075 – alt. 63 m – ✉ 24480

4 **C3**

Paris 532 – Bergerac 38 – Brive-la-Gaillarde 81 – Périgueux 52 – Sarlat-la-Canéda 36
Office de tourisme, place André Boissière ✆ 05 53 22 06 09, Fax 05 53 22 06 09

Le Manoir de Bellerive rm, rm, VISA AE
Siorac road: 1.5 km – ✆ 05 53 22 16 16
– manoir.bellerive@wanadoo.fr – Fax 05 53 22 09 05 – Closed 2 January-15 March
21 rm – €155/240 €155/240, ☕ €18
Rest ***Les Délices d'Hortense*** – *(closed Monday except July-August, Tuesday October-May and lunch Monday-Thursday)* Menu €48/90 – Carte €78/88
Rest ***La Table de Louis*** – bistrot *(closed Monday lunch)* Carte approx. €31
Spéc. Velouté de langoustines, girolles, chair de crabe. Agneau du Quercy dans "toute sa splendeur". "Chaud...colat" périgourdin. **Wines** Bergerac, Pécharmant.
◆ This Napoleon III manor house sports a countrified spirit: large mirrors, floral wallpaper, period furniture and views of the English style park or the Dordogne region. Elegant dining rooms and personalised classic cuisine. Traditional fare in the bistro.

in Paleyrac 4 km southeast by D 25 and secondary road – ✉ 24480

Le Clos Lascazes without rest VISA
– ✆ 05 53 74 33 94 – clos-lascazes@wanadoo.fr – Fax 05 53 74 03 22 – Open March-mid November
5 rm – €68/89 €68/105, ☕ €8
◆ Three houses built in different centuries extend an invitation to relax and wind down (park, salt water pool). White walls, embroidered bed linen and prints set the scene in the bright rooms.

BULGNEVILLE – 88 Vosges – 314 D3 – pop. 1 286 – alt. 350 m – ✉ 88140 Alsace-Lorraine

26 **B3**

Paris 342 – Belfort 133 – Épinal 55 – Langres 71 – Vesoul 92
Syndicat d'initiative, 105, rue de l'Hôtel de Ville ✆ 03 29 09 14 67, Fax 03 29 09 14 67

Benoit Breton without rest

74 r. des Récollets – 03 29 09 21 72 – benoitbreton.chambresdhotes@wanadoo.fr – Fax 03 29 09 21 72

4 rm – €65 €70

◆ An antique dealer by profession, Mr Breton has left his stamp on the spacious rooms furnished stylishly with antiques and ornaments. Chickens, ducks and a goat roam free in the garden.

La Marmite Beaujolaise

34 r. de l'Hôtel-de-Ville – 03 29 09 16 58 – Fax 03 29 07 83 99 – Closed Sunday dinner and Monday

Rest – Menu € 13 (weekday lunch), € 20/38 – Carte € 34/47

◆ 17C inn serving tasty, traditional food with a regional slant. Stylish rustic décor of beams, bare stonewalls and fireplace.

BULLY – 69 Rhône – 327 G4 – pop. 1 739 – alt. 313 m – 69210 43 E1

Paris 471 – Lyon 32 – Saint-Étienne 92 – Villeurbanne 41 – Lyon 03 34

Auberge du Château

pl. de l'Église – 04 74 01 25 36 – aubergeduchateau@yahoo.fr – Fax 04 74 72 50 95 – Closed 15-30 September, 5-27 January, Saturday lunch, Sunday dinner and Monday

Rest – Menu € 17 (weekday lunch), € 27/49

◆ Opposite the village church, venerable inn (1749) with a tasteful, surprisingly contemporary restaurant. Open kitchen and up-to-date cuisine.

BURLATS – 81 Tarn – 338 F9 – see Castres

BURNHAUPT-LE-HAUT – 68 Haut-Rhin – 315 G10 – pop. 1 505 – alt. 300 m – 68520 1 A3

Paris 454 – Altkirch 16 – Belfort 32 – Mulhouse 17 – Thann 12

Le Coquelicot rm, rest,

at the Pont d'Aspach, 1 km northward – 03 89 83 10 10 – info@aigleor.com – Fax 03 89 83 10 33

26 rm – €68 €68/84, € 11 – ½ P € 61/69

Rest – *(closed 26 July-11 August, 27 December-5 January, Saturday lunch and Sunday dinner)* Menu € 11,50 (weekday lunch), € 23/55 – Carte € 29/48

◆ The village is situated at the edge of the picturesque region of Sundgau. Well located for the road network, this hotel has practical, comfortable bedrooms. Pastel colours and floral prints create a spring atmosphere in the Coquelicot dining room.

BUSNES – 62 Pas-de-Calais – 301 I4 – see Béthune

BUSSEAU-SUR-CREUSE – 23 Creuse – 325 J4 – 23150 Ahun 25 C1

Paris 368 – Aubusson 27 – Guéret 17

Moutier d'Ahun: panelling★★ of the church Southeast: 5,5 km - Ahun: panelling★ of the church Southeast: 6 km, G. Dordogne-Berry-Limousin.

Le Viaduc with rm

9 Busseau Gare – 05 55 62 57 20 – ch-cl-lemestre@wanadoo.fr – Fax 05 55 62 55 80 – Closed 5-25 January, Sunday dinner and Monday

7 rm – €38 €41, € 6 – ½ P € 48 – **Rest** – Menu € 15 (weekday lunch), € 25/35 – Carte € 34/46

◆ This auberge makes the most of its commanding position. The rustic dining room and terrace offer a beautiful view over the 1863 viaduct straddling the River Creuse. Well-maintained rooms.

LA BUSSIÈRE – 45 Loiret – 318 N5 – pop. 749 – alt. 160 m – 45230

Burgundy-Jura 12 D2

Paris 142 – Auxerre 74 – Cosne-sur-Loire 46 – Gien 14 – Montargis 29 – Orléans 79

Château des pêcheurs★.

Le Nuage
r. Briare – ✆ 02 38 35 90 73 – contact@lenuage.com – Fax 02 38 35 90 62 – Closed 24 December-2 January
16 rm – †€ 48 ††€ 52, ☕ € 7 – 1 suite – ½ P € 43 – **Rest** – *(dinner only except weekends) (residents only weekdays)* Menu € 12/18 – Carte € 22/34
◆ New motel-type establishment located at the entrance to the town. Practical, well laid-out bedrooms. Relaxing setting with a gym. Classic recipes and grilled food served in an all-pink dining room topped with a mezzanine lounge.

LA BUSSIÈRE-SUR-OUCHE – 21 Côte-d'Or – 320 I6 – pop. 190 – alt. 320 m – ✉ 21360 Burgundy-Jura 8 C2

Paris 297 – Dijon 34 – Chalon-sur-Saône 63 – Beaune 34 – Autun 59

Abbaye de la Bussière
– ✆ 03 80 49 02 29 – info@abbayedelabussiere.fr – Fax 03 80 49 05 23 – Closed 1st January-15 February
15 rm – †€ 160/375 ††€ 160/375, ☕ € 29
Rest – *(closed Monday, Tuesday and lunch except Sunday)* Menu € 60/95 (dinner) – Carte € 83/117
Rest *Le Bistrot* – *(closed Monday and Tuesday) (lunch only)* Menu € 29/33
Spec. L'artichaut en dégustation (except winter). La grosse langoustine sur la braise (May to September). L'échine de cochon cul noir aux oignons blancs, jus au poivre de Tasmanie. **Wines** Saint-Romain, Corton-Charlemagne.
◆ A carefully restored 12C Cistercian abbey. Cosy lounges and luxurious guestrooms with all modern comforts. The hotel is surrounded by magnificent parkland. Fine modern cuisine served in an aristocratic ambience. The bistro offers a concise lunchtime menu.

BUSSY-ST-GEORGES – 77 Seine-et-Marne – 312 F2 – 101 20 – see Paris, Area (Marne-la-Vallée)

BUXY – 71 Saône-et-Loire – 320 I9 – pop. 2 098 – alt. 263 m – ✉ 71390 8 C3

Paris 351 – Chagny 25 – Chalon-sur-Saône 17 – Montceau-les-Mines 33
Office de tourisme, place de la gare ✆ 03 85 92 00 16, Fax 03 85 92 00 57

Fontaine de Baranges without rest
r. Fontaine-de-Baranges – ✆ 03 85 94 10 70 – hotel.fontaine.de.baranges@wanadoo.fr – Fax 03 85 94 10 79
18 rm – †€ 67/107 ††€ 67/107, ☕ € 9 – 3 suites
◆ A master winemaker occupied this elegant residence that has retained its 19C charm. Personalised and spacious rooms, a third with a private terrace overlooking the romantic garden. Enjoy breakfast in the beautiful vaulted cellar

Relais du Montagny without rest
– ✆ 03 85 94 94 94 – le.relais.du.montagny@wanadoo.fr – Fax 03 85 92 07 19 – Closed January, Friday dinner and Sunday dinner off season
30 rm – †€ 52/60 ††€ 54/64, ☕ € 10
◆ This establishment, waiting to be renovated, houses identical functional bedrooms, a bar and billiards. The Voie Verte, an old railway line converted into a walking route makes for a great excursion.

Aux Années Vins
2 Grande-Rue – ✆ 03 85 92 15 76 – aux.annees.vins@wanadoo.fr – Fax 03 85 92 12 20 – Closed 15-25 September, 19 January-19 February, Wednesday except dinner 1st April-11 November, Monday dinner 11 November-31 March and Tuesday
Rest – Menu (€ 15), € 20/59 – Carte € 35/53
◆ Well-situated right in the centre of the village, large dining room decorated with a stone fireplace. Interior terrace underneath the arches. Traditional cuisine made with care.

BUZANÇAIS – 36 Indre – 323 E5 – pop. 4 581 – alt. 111 m – ✉ 36500 11 B3

Paris 286 – Le Blanc 47 – Châteauroux 25 – Chatellerault 78 – Tours 91
Syndicat d'initiative, 11, passage du Marché ✆ 02 54 84 22 00, Fax 02 54 02 13 45

L'Hermitage rest, VISA

1 chemin de Vilaine – ✆ 02 54 84 03 90 – logis-hermitage@wanadoo.fr – Fax 02 54 02 13 19 – Closed 2-25 January, Sunday dinner and Monday except July-August, Monday lunch in July-August

12 rm – ♦€ 59 ♦♦€ 71, ☕ € 7,50 – ½ P € 67/85 – **Rest** – *(pre-book Sat - Sun)* Menu € 16 (weekday lunch), € 22/51 – Carte € 34/55

♦ Welcoming property with a leafy garden where the River Indre runs; the rooms nearly all have this peaceful setting and are gradually being renovated. Contemporary cuisine in a comfortable dining room or on the veranda facing the countryside.

Northeast **3 km by D 926 (Levroux road) ✉ 36500 Buzançais**

Le Boisrenault without rest VISA

– ✆ 02 54 84 03 01 – boisrenault@wanadoo.fr – Fax 02 54 84 10 57

5 rm ☕ – ♦€ 73/94 ♦♦€ 79/105

♦ 19C castle surrounded by a park. Quiet lounges with old family furniture and the same goes for the comfortable rooms (two with a small kitchen) decorated in an eclectic style.

Good food without spending a fortune?
Look out for the Bib Gourmand

CABANAC-SÉGUENVILLE – 31 Haute-Garonne – 343 E2 – pop. 128 – alt. 200 m – ✉ 31480

28 **B2**

Paris 668 – Colomiers 39 – Montauban 46 – Toulouse 51

Château de Séguenville

via D 1 and D 89A – ✆ 05 62 13 42 67 – info@chateau-de-seguenville.com – Fax 05 62 13 42 68 – Closed 15 December-15 January

5 rm ☕ – ♦€ 100 ♦♦€ 120/125 – **Table d'hôte** – *(closed Saturday in July-August and Sunday)* Menu € 25

♦ This pretty 19C Gascon castle is surrounded by century-old trees. It houses vast, tastefully furnished rooms, one of which boasts an enormous terrace with sweeping views of the countryside. Regional food.

CABASSON – 83 Var – 340 M7 – see Bormes-les-Mimosas

CABESTANY – 66 Pyrénées-Orientales – 344 I6 – see Perpignan

CABOURG – 14 Calvados – 303 L4 – pop. 3 520 – alt. 3 m – Casino – ✉ 14390

Normandy

32 **B2**

Paris 220 – Caen 24 – Deauville 23 – Lisieux 35 – Pont-l'Évêque 34

Office de tourisme, jardins de l'Hotel de Ville ✆ 02 31 06 20 00, Fax 02 31 06 20 10

Public de Cabourg Avenue de l'Hippodrome, 1 km by Ave de l'Hippodrome, ✆ 02 31 91 70 53 ;

de Cabourg Le Home Varaville 38 avenue du Pdt René Coty, by Caen road: 3 km, ✆ 02 31 91 25 56.

Plan on next page

Grand Hôtel ← Sea, VISA

prom. M.-Proust – ✆ 02 31 91 01 79 – h1282@accor.com – Fax 02 31 24 03 20

A s

68 rm – ♦€ 205/305 ♦♦€ 215/315, ☕ € 18 – 2 suites – ½ P € 173/223

Rest – *(closed January, Monday and Tuesday except July-August)* Menu € 44 – Carte € 53/65

♦ Palace on the sea front haunted by the memory of Marcel Proust: his room has been entirely reconstituted. The others remain personalised and comfortable. Traditional food and refined atmosphere in the elegant dining room opening onto the beach.

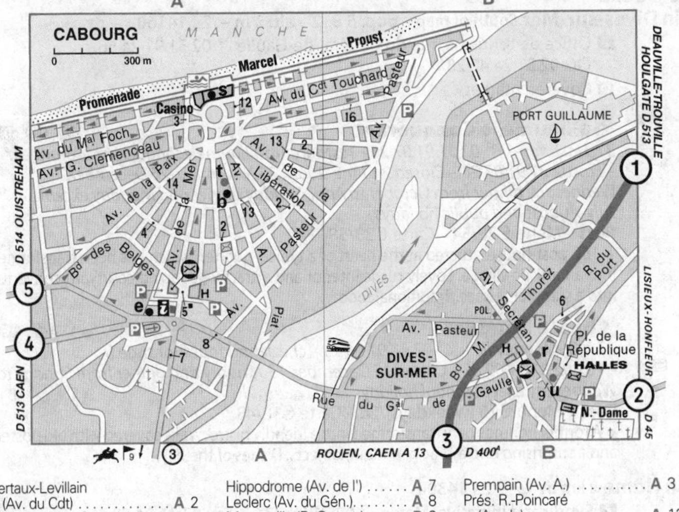

Bertaux-Levillain (Av. du Cdt) . . . . A 2
Castelnau (Av. Gén.-de) . . . . . A 4
Coquatrix (Pl. B.) . . . . A 5
Hastings (R. d') . . . . B 6
Hippodrome (Av. de l') . . . . . . A 7
Leclerc (Av. du Gén.). . . . . A 8
Manneville (R. Gaston) . . . . . . B 9
Mermoz (Av. Jean) . . . . A 12
Mer (Av. de la). . . . . A
Prempain (Av. A.) . . . . A 3
Prés. R.-Poincaré (Av. du). . . . . A 13
République (Av. de la). . . . . . . A 14
Roi-Albert-1er (Av. du). . . . . . . B 16

Mercure Hippodrome

rm,

av. M.-d'Ornano, on av. Hippodrome A –

02 31 24 04 04 – mercurecabourghippodrome@wanadoo.fr – Fax 02 31 91 03 99

75 rm – €98/144 €98/260, € 12 – **Rest** – *(closed 6 January-4 February, Sunday and Monday October-Easter)* Menu € 15/19 – Carte € 20/32

♦ These two new Norman-style buildings are near the racecourse. The rooms are decorated in a modern and practical style. A welcoming, comfortable dining room with an excellent view of the racecourse.

Du Golf

rm,

av. M.-d'Ornano, via av. Racecourse A – 02 31 24 12 34 – hoteldugolfcabourg@yahoo.fr – Fax 02 31 24 18 51 – Open 16 March-15 November

39 rm – €60/78 €60/78, € 8 – **Rest** – *(closed lunch 15 October-15 November)* Menu € 17/35

♦ A motel-type establishment, on the edge of the golf course, offering simple, functional ground-floor rooms overlooking the garden or terrace. A comfortable, discreetly contemporary dining room overlooking the greens.

Castel Fleuri without rest

4 av. Alfred-Piat – 02 31 91 27 57 – info@castel-fleuri.com – Fax 02 31 24 03 48 – Closed 5-24 January A **b**

22 rm – €74 €85

♦ Charming house with a pretty garden in front where breakfast is served when the weather permits. Smart, fresh rooms; lounge both simple and cosy.

Le Cottage without rest

24 av. Gén.-Leclerc – 02 31 91 65 61 – r.dany@wanadoo.fr – Fax 02 31 28 78 82 – Closed January – **14 rm** – €50/58 €60/110, € 8 A **e**

♦ A guesthouse atmosphere in this 1900s cottage with a small garden at the front. Rooms are simple but regularly renovated, all have different décor.

Le Baligan

8 av. Alfred Piat – 02 31 24 10 92 – info@lebaligan.fr – Fax 02 31 28 99 09 – Closed 8 December-12 January, 9-15 February and Wednesday except public holidays A **t**

Rest – Menu € 17 (weekday lunch)/24 – Carte € 28/41

♦ Recent, bistro-style address in the town centre. Open kitchen where the chef prepares fresh seafood-based dishes in a regularly changing menu.

in Dives-sur-Mer South of map – pop. 5 812 – alt. 3 m – ✉ 14160

Office de tourisme, rue du Général-de-Gaulle ✆ 02 31 91 24 66, Fax 02 31 24 42 28

Covered market★.

XX **Guillaume le Conquérant**

2 r. Hastings – ✆ 02 31 91 07 26 – restaurantguillaumeleconquerant@orange.fr – Fax 02 31 91 07 26 – Closed 24 June-2 July, 25 November-26 December, Wednesday dinner from October to April, Sunday dinner and Monday except July-August and public holidays B **r**

Rest – Menu € 28/54 – Carte € 33/58

◆ 16C post-house situated at the heart of a typical quarter, which has been transformed into an artistic village. Lovely rustic interior and attractive cobbled courtyard converted into a summer terrace. Traditional food.

X **Chez le Bougnat**

27 r. G.-Manneville – ✆ 02 31 91 06 13 – chezlebougnat@orange.fr – Fax 02 31 91 09 87 – Closed 15 December-15 January and dinner from Sunday to Wednesday execpt school holidays B **u**

Rest – Menu € 16 (weekdays)/26 – Carte € 18/43

◆ A former ironmongery transformed into a friendly bistro. Walls covered with old posters and a surprising bric-a-brac of antique objects. Dishes of the day.

in Hôme 2 km by ⑤ – ✉ 14390

Syndicat d'initiative, Mairie ✆ 02 31 24 73 83, Fax 02 31 24 72 41

Manoir de la Marjolaine without rest

5 av. du Prés.-Coty – ✆ 02 31 91 70 25 – eric.faye@orange.fr – Fax 02 31 91 77 10

5 rm – †€ 70/110 ††€ 80/120

◆ After having fallen under the charm of the small leafy park, you will discover the manor and its spacious rooms decorated with original paintings. Pleasant welcome.

XX **Au Pied des Marais**

26 av. du Prés.-Coty – ✆ 02 31 91 27 55 – au-pied-des-marais@orange.fr – Fax 02 31 91 86 13 – Closed 24 June-2 July, 16-26 December, 27 January-12 February, Tuesday and Wednesday except dinner in July-August

Rest – Menu € 20 bi (weekday lunch), € 30/50 – Carte € 36/61

◆ Contemporary cuisine made with regional produce. Grilled dishes cooked in front of you in the dining room's fireplace. Rustic decor and veranda.

CABRERETS – 46 Lot – 337 F4 – pop. 203 – alt. 130 m – ✉ 46330

Dordogne-Berry-Limousin 29 **C1**

Paris 565 – Cahors 26 – Figeac 44 – Gourdon 42 – St-Céré 58 – Villefranche-de-Rouergue 44

Office de tourisme, place du Sombral ✆ 05 65 31 29 06, Fax 05 65 31 29 06

Château de Gontaut-Biron★ - ≤★ of the left bank of the Célé.

Grotte du Pech Merle★★★ Northwest: 3 km.

Auberge de la Sagne

rte grotte de Pech Merle – ✆ 05 65 31 26 62 – contact@hotel-auberge-cabrerets.com – Fax 05 65 30 27 43 – Open 15 May-15 September

8 rm – †€ 48/54 ††€ 48/54, € 7 – ½ P € 46/49 – **Rest** – *(dinner only) (number of covers limited, pre-book)* Menu € 16/23 – Carte € 25/33

◆ Building inspired by regional design with simple but cosy bedrooms, in a country style. The bedrooms on the top floor have sloping roofs. Attractive shaded garden. Lot specialities in this discreetly rustic restaurant warmed by an open fireplace.

Undecided between two equivalent establishments? Within each category, establishments are classified in our order of preference.

CABRIÈRES – 30 Gard – 339 L5 – pop. 1 117 – alt. 120 m – ✉ 30210 23 D2

Paris 695 – Avignon 33 – Alès 64 – Arles 40 – Nîmes 15 – Orange 45 – Pont-St-Esprit 52

L'Enclos des Lauriers Roses rm, VISA MC AE

71 r. du 14-Juillet – ✆ 04 66 75 25 42 – hotel-lauriersroses@wanadoo.fr – Fax 04 66 75 25 21 – Open 14 March-7 November

18 rm – €80/110 €80/110, €12 – 2 suites – ½ P €65/95

Rest – Menu €23/42 – Carte €32/50

◆ Buildings typical of the Gard region in the village overlooking an attractive garden with five varieties of oleander. Stylish, Provençal rooms, most of which have a terrace. A restaurant decorated in Provençal style serving classic and regional cuisine.

CABRIÈRES-D'AIGUES – 84 Vaucluse – 332 F11 – pop. 651 – alt. 425 m – ✉ 84240 40 B2

Paris 755 – Marseille 63 – Avignon 82 – Aix-en-Provence 35 – Salon-de-Provence 75

Le Mas des Câpriers without rest VISA MC AE

chemin Raouk – ✆ 04 90 77 69 68 – masdescapriers@orange.fr – Fax 04 90 77 69 68 – Closed 20 December-10 February

4 rm – €95/165 €95/165

◆ Beautiful 18C house among vineyards and countryside. The rooms exude charm (one occupies an 1897 caravan and is superb). A slice of paradise.

CABRIÈRES-D'AVIGNON – 84 Vaucluse – 332 D10 – pop. 1 422 – alt. 167 m – ✉ 84220 Provence 42 E1

Paris 715 – Aix-en-Provence 74 – Avignon 34 – Marseille 88

La Bastide de Voulonne rest, VISA MC AE

D 148 – ✆ 04 90 76 77 55 – contact@bastide-voulonne.com – Fax 04 90 76 77 56 – Open from mid February to mid November

13 rm – €90/145 €90/145, €11 – ½ P €78/105 – **Rest** – *(closed Sunday) (dinner only) (resident only)* Menu €30

◆ In open country, this 1764 farmhouse among vines and fruit trees has been well restored. Smart, well-presented rooms, friendly welcome and themed itineraries. Evenings only set menu (regional fare) served at communal tables; shady terrace.

Le Vieux Bistrot with rm rm, VISA MC

Grande-Rue – ✆ 04 90 76 82 08 – levieuxbistrot@wanadoo.fr – Fax 04 90 76 98 98 – Closed Monday

6 rm – €65/100 €65/100, €8 – **Rest** – Carte €29/41

◆ This authentic bistro occupies a charming village house. Well-preserved decor which pays homage to the glory of wine. The set menu only offers a choice of hot dishes (the rest is a surprise). Smart, personalised rooms with a terrace on the top floor.

CABRIS – 06 Alpes-Maritimes – 341 C6 – see Grasse

CADENET – 84 Vaucluse – 332 F11 – pop. 3 883 – alt. 170 m – ✉ 84160 Provence 42 E1

Paris 742 – Apt 24 – Cavaillon 34 – Manosque 48 – Salon-de-Provence 36

Office de tourisme, 11, place du Tambour d'Arcole ✆ 04 90 68 38 21, Fax 04 90 68 24 49

La Tuilière VISA MC

chemin de la Tuilière – ✆ 04 90 68 24 45 – clo@latuiliere.com – Fax 04 90 68 24 45

5 rm – €54/69 €54/85 – **Table d'hôte** – Menu €22 bi

◆ This 18C country house has a wine estate and offers five Provençal style rooms where you can enjoy the fragrant peace and quiet of the Luberon nature reserve. Regional food and garden produce are served in the restaurant (reserve in advance). Pretty terrace overlooking the village.

La Cour

3 r. Hoche – ✆ 04 90 08 57 66 – la.cour.restaurant@free.fr – Fax 04 90 08 57 66 – Closed 10-20 November, 11 January-12 February, Thursday and Friday except dinner from September to June, lunch in July-August and Wednesday

Rest – Menu € 25/55 – Carte € 48/59

◆ Former wicker workshop converted into a pleasant restaurant serving modern food. Smart rustic dining room and pleasant terrace.

LA CADIÈRE-D'AZUR – 83 Var – 340 J6 – pop. 4 239 – alt. 144 m – ✉ 83740

French Riviera 40 **B3**

Paris 815 – Aix-en-Provence 66 – Brignoles 53 – Marseille 45 – Toulon 22

Office de tourisme, place Général-de-Gaulle ✆ 04 94 90 12 56, Fax 04 94 98 30 13

≤★ - Le Castelet: Village★ Northeast: 4 km.

Hostellerie Bérard (René et Jean-François Bérard)

av. Gabriel-Péri –

✆ 04 94 90 11 43 – berard@hotel-berard.com – Fax 04 94 90 01 94 – Closed 4 January-10 February

32 rm – †€ 91/169 ††€ 91/169, ☕ € 19 – 5 suites

Rest – *(closed Tuesday except dinner from 15 April-1st October and Monday)* Menu € 49/140 – Carte € 79/133

Rest *Le Petit Jardin* – *(closed Wednesday and Thursday)* Menu (€ 35) – Carte € 29/60

Spec. Rouget de roche juste saisi, petits calamars et risotto (spring-summer). Poulette de Bresse rôtie, fourrée à la brousse d'herbes. Assiette gourmande. **Wines** Bandol, Côtes de Provence.

◆ A hotel made up of several houses with character including an 11C convent in which beautiful Provençal rooms have been created. Elegant dining room facing the Bandol vineyard, pretty terrace and delicious contemporary cuisine. Le Petit Jardin is a Southern bistro ideal, for a quick bite.

CADILLAC – 33 Gironde – 335 J7 – pop. 2 365 – alt. 16 m – ✉ 33410

Atlantic Coast 3 **B2**

Paris 607 – Bordeaux 41 – Langon 12 – Libourne 40

Office de tourisme, 9, place de la Libération ✆ 05 56 62 12 92, Fax 05 56 76 99 72

Du Château de la Tour rm,

av. de la libération, (D 10) – ✆ 05 56 76 92 00 – contact@hotel-restaurant-chateaudelatour.com – Fax 05 56 62 11 59

32 rm – †€ 75/105 ††€ 90/230, ☕ € 12 – ½ P € 80/90 – **Rest** – *(closed Sunday dinner from November to February)* Menu € 15 (weekday lunch), € 28/55 – Carte € 35/55

◆ This gradually updated hotel built in the old kitchen garden of the Dukes of Épernon offers modern rooms, sauna and jacuzzi. Riverside park. A restaurant with roof beams, summer terrace, traditional menu and regional specialities.

CAEN P – 14 Calvados – 303 J4 – pop. 113 987 – Built-up area 199 490 – alt. 25 m – ✉ 14000 Normandy 32 **B2**

Paris 236 – Alençon 105 – Cherbourg 125 – Le Havre 91 – Rennes 189

Caen-Carpiquet: ✆ 02 31 71 20 10, by D 9: 7 km.

Office de tourisme, 12, place Saint-Pierre ✆ 02 31 27 14 14, Fax 02 31 27 14 13

27 de Caen Biéville-Beuville Le Vallon, North: 5 km by D 60, ✆ 02 31 94 72 09 ;

18 de Garcelles Garcelles-Secqueville Route de Lorguichon, by Falaise road: 15 km, ✆ 02 31 39 09 09.

Abbaye aux Hommes★★: St-Etienne church ★★ - Abbaye aux Dames★: La Trinité church ★★ - Apse★★, frieze★★ and vaults★★ of St-Pierre church ★ - St-Nicolas church and cemetery ★ - Lantern tower★ St-Jean church EZ - Hôtel d'Escoville★ DY **B** - Old houses★ (nº 52 and 54 rue St-Pierre) DY **K** - Musée des Beaux-Arts★★ in the château★ DX **M**1 - Memorial★★★ AV - Musée de Normandie★ DX **M**2.

CAEN

Baladas (Bd des) . . . . AV 6
Chemin-vert (R. du) . . . . AV 19
Chéron (Av. Henri) . . . . AV 20
Clemenceau (Av. G.) . . . . . . BV 22
Copernic (Av. N.) . . . . ABV 23
Côte-de-Nacre (Av. de la) . . . AV 24
Courseulles (Av. de) . . . . AV 25
Délivrande (R. de la) . . . . AV 29
Demi-Lune (Pl. de la) . . . . . . BV 30
Lyautey (Bd Mar.) . . . . AV 53
Montalivet (Cours) . . . . BV 59
Montgomery (Av. Mar.) . . . . AV 60
Mountbatten (Av. Am.) . . . . AV 62
Pasteur (R. L.) . . . . BV 63
Père-Ch.-de-Foucault (Av.) . . . . AV 64
Poincaré (Bd R.) . . . . BV 66
Pompidou (Bd G.) . . . . AV 67
Rethel (Bd de) . . . . BV 70
Richemond (Bd) . . . . AV 71
Trouville (Rte de) . . . . BV 84

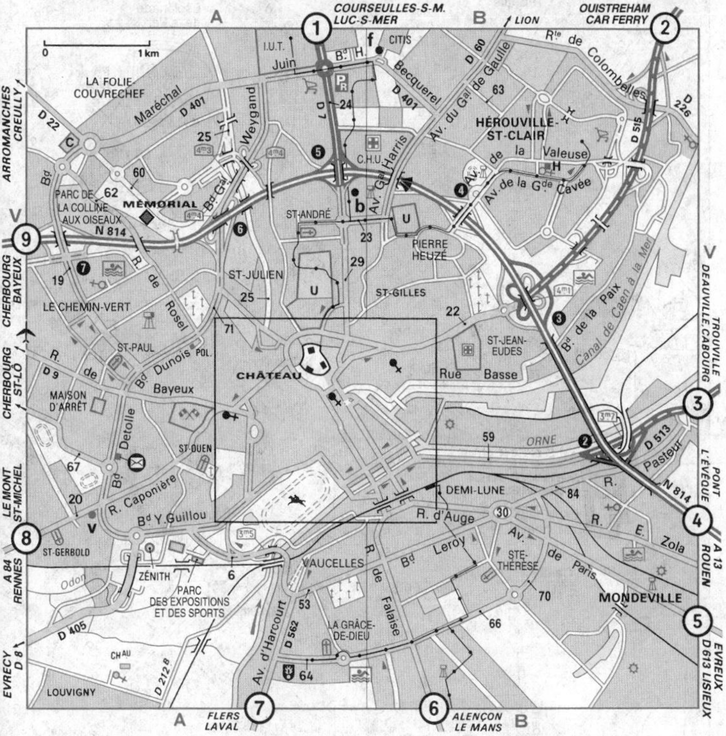

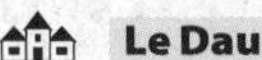

Le Dauphin

29 r. Gemare – ☎ 02 31 86 22 26
– dauphin.caen@wanadoo.fr – Fax 02 31 86 35 14
– Closed 25 October-5 November and 15-22 February DY **a**

37 rm – 🛉€ 75/185 🛉🛉€ 85/190, ☕ € 14 – ½ P € 75/125

Rest – *(closed 21 July-4 August, 25 October-5 November, 15-22 February, Saturday lunch and Sunday)* Menu (€ 16), € 20 (weekdays)/49 – Carte € 49/63

◆ An old priory near the château walls. Personalised rooms, some with age-old beams and period furniture. A pleasant stylish dining room and classic cuisine with a regional touch. A Norman setting in the adjoining lounge bar.

Mercure Port de Plaisance without rest

1 r. Courtonne – ☎ 02 31 47 24 24
– h0869@accor.com – Fax 02 31 47 43 88 EY **b**

126 rm – 🛉€ 78/200 🛉🛉€ 98/200, ☕ € 13 – 3 suites

◆ This chain hotel facing the marina has recently been enlarged. Tastefully furnished bedrooms and a cosy ambience. Business centre.

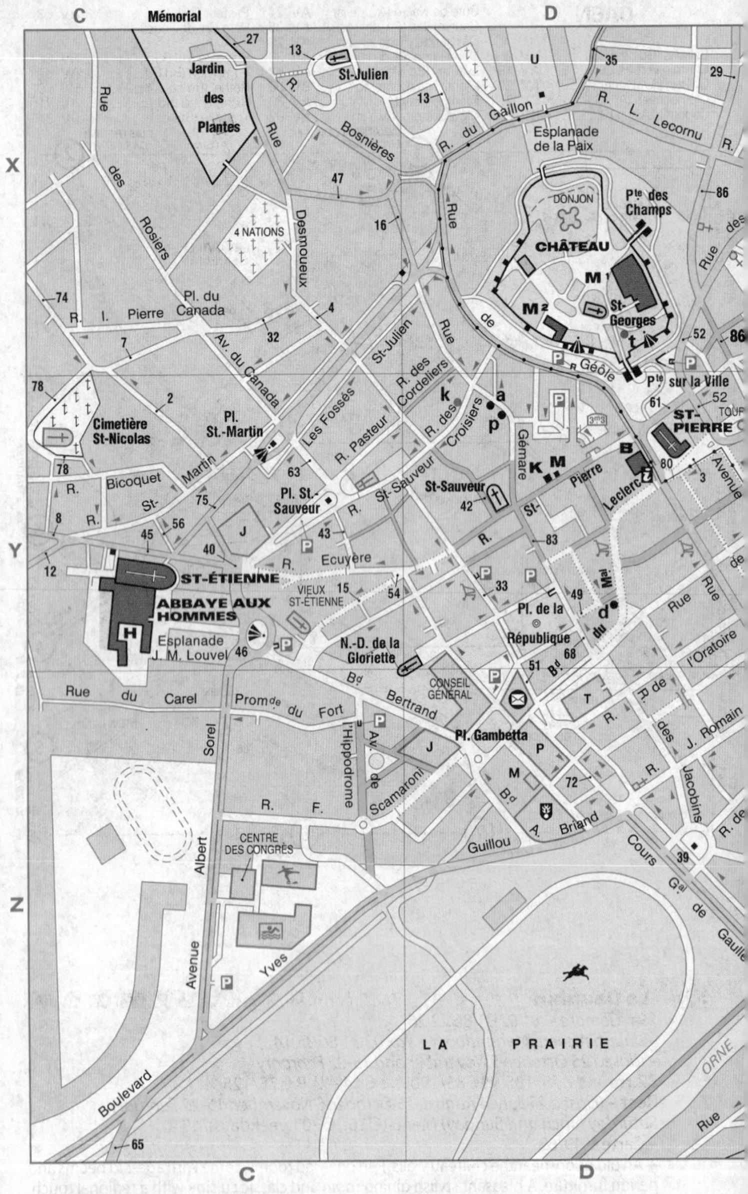

<table>
<tr><td>Moderne without rest</td></tr>
</table>

Moderne without rest

116 bd Mar.-Leclerc – ✆ 02 31 86 04 23 – info@hotel-caen.com – Fax 02 31 85 37 93

40 rm – €75/110 €95/250, ☕ €13 DY **d**

◆ Discreet post war building with regularly spruced up rooms. A view over the town rooftops from the 5th floor breakfast room.

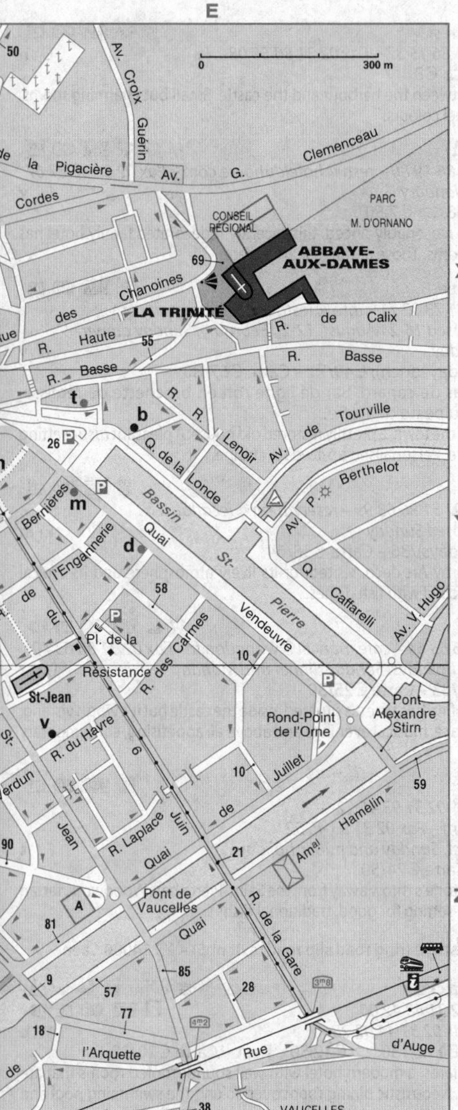

CAEN

Académie (R. de l')	CY	2
Alliés (Bd des)	DY	3
Bagatelle (Av. de)	CX	4
Barbey-d'Aurevilly (R.)	CX	7
Bayeux (R. de)	CX	8
Bir-Hakeim (Pont de)	EZ	9
Brunet (R. H.)	EYZ	10
Caponière (R.)	CY	12
Carrières-St-Julien (R. des)	CDX	13
Caumont (R. A. de)	CY	15
Chanoine X. de St-Paul (R.)	CDX	16
Chaussée-Ferrée (R. de la)	EZ	18
Churchill (Pont)	EZ	21
Courtonne (Pl.)	EY	26
Creully (R. de)	CX	27
Decaen (R. Gén.)	EZ	28
Délivrande (R. de la)	DX	29
Docteur-Rayer (R.)	CX	32
Doumer (R. Paul)	DY	33
Écuyère (R.)	CY	
Édimbourg (Av. d')	DX	35
Falaise (R. de)	EZ	38
Foch (Pl. Mar.)	DZ	39
Fontette (Pl.)	CY	40
Froide (R.)	DY	42
Fromages (R. aux)	CY	43
Guillaume-le-Conquérant (R.)	CY	45
Guillouard (Pl. L.)	CY	46
Juifs (R. aux)	CX	47
Lair (R. P.-A.)	DY	49
Lebisey (R. de)	EX	50
Lebret (R. G.)	DYZ	51
Leclerc (Bd Mar.)	DYZ	
Libération (Av. de la)	DXY	52
Malherbe (Pl.)	CDY	54
Manissier (R.)	EX	55
Marot (R. J.)	CY	56
Meslin (Q. E.)	EZ	57
Miséricorde (R. de la)	EYZ	58
Montalivet (Cours)	EZ	59
Montoir-Poissonnerie (R.)	DY	61
Pémagnie (R.)	CX	63
Petit-Vallerent (Bd du)	CZ	65
Pont-St-Jacques (R. du)	DY	68
Reine-Mathilde (Pl.)	EX	69
Sadi-Carnot (R.)	DZ	72
St-Gabriel (R.)	CX	74
St-Jean (R.)	DEYZ	
St-Manvieu (R.)	CY	75
St-Michel (R.)	EZ	77
St-Nicolas (R.)	CY	78
St-Pierre (Pl.)	DY	80
St-Pierre (R.)	DY	
Sévigné (Prom. de)	EZ	81
Strasbourg (R. de)	DY	83
Vaucelles (R. de)	EZ	85
Vaugueux (R. du)	DX	86
6-Juin (Av. du)	DEYZ	
11-Novembre (R. du)	DEZ	90

Des Quatrans without rest

17 r. Gemare – ✆ 02 31 86 25 57 – hotel-des-quatrans@wanadoo.fr – Fax 02 31 85 27 80 DY **p**

47 rm – €55 €64, €7,50

◆ Well-renovated hotel near the town centre. Pleasant hallway, cosy bar and colourful rooms. Those at the back are quieter.

Du Château without rest
5 av. du 6-Juin – ✆ 02 31 86 15 37 – Fax 02 31 86 58 08 EY **n**
24 rm – †€ 50 ††€ 60, ☕ € 8
◆ A well-situated hotel, between the harbour and the castle. Small but charming rooms, decorated in soothing pastel colours.

Du Havre without rest
11 r. du Havre – ✆ 02 31 86 19 80 – resa@hotelduhavre.com – Fax 02 31 38 87 67 – Closed 13 December-4 January EZ **v**
19 rm – †€ 46 ††€ 53/58, ☕ € 7,50
◆ Extremely well kept and reasonably priced, this recently redecorated family hotel has practical if not luxurious rooms. Those at the rear are quieter.

Le Pressoir (Ivan Vautier)
3 av. H.-Chéron – ✆ 02 31 73 32 71 – info@restaurant-le-pressoir.com – Fax 02 31 26 76 64 – Closed 16-24 August, 12-20 February, Sunday dinner, Saturday lunch and Monday AV **v**
Rest – Menu € 32 (weekday lunch), € 49/71 – Carte € 67/80
Spec. Poêlée de foie gras de canard. Bar de ligne rôti en brochette de réglisse. Pomme de ris de veau au pesto de truffe.
◆ Located in the suburbs of the town, a prettily restored old house. A pleasant rustic setting and contemporary furniture. Personalised up-to-date cuisine.

Le Carlotta
16 quai Vendeuvre – ✆ 02 31 86 68 99 – reservation@lecarlotta.fr – Fax 02 31 38 92 31 – Closed Sunday EY**m**
Rest – Menu € 22 (weekdays)/36 – Carte € 38/64
◆ Large brasserie inspired by Art deco, visited for its lively atmosphere and its typical brasserie style cuisine, enriched with fish dishes.

Café Mancel
au Château – ✆ 02 31 86 63 64 – cafe.mancel@wanadoo.fr – Fax 02 31 86 63 40 – Closed February school holidays, Sunday dinner and Monday DX **t**
Rest – Menu (€ 17), € 23/33 – Carte € 25/39
◆ Café Mancel is not easy to find because it's situated inside the castle but it's worth visiting: sober, modern setting, terrace, musical evenings and above all appetising, contemporary dishes.

Pub William's
13 r. Prairies-St-Gilles – ✆ 02 31 93 45 52 – pubwilliams14@aol.com – Fax 02 31 93 45 52 – Closed 14 July-15 August, Sunday and public holidays EY **t**
Rest – Menu € 15/28 – Carte € 24/50
◆ This welcoming pub is a stone's throw away from the Saint-Pierre bay. Woodwork, tartan and a fireplace provide the setting for good, traditional dishes.

to Caen-Université interchange (ring road slip road, exit n° 5) – ✉ 14000 Caen

Novotel Côte de Nacre
av. Côte-de-Nacre – ✆ 02 31 43 42 00 – h0405@accor.com – Fax 02 31 44 07 28 AV **b**
126 rm – †€ 98/130 ††€ 112/130, ☕ € 12,50 – **Rest** – Carte € 20/28
◆ Near the main thoroughfares, a modern hotel with well soundproofed rooms that are being gradually renovated. Neo-rustic dining room overlooking the swimming pool and pleasant lounge bar around a flat screen television.

in Hérouville St-Clair 3 km Northeast – pop. 24 025 – alt. 20 m – ✉ 14200

Mercure Côte de Nacre
2 pl. Boston-Citis – ✆ 02 31 44 05 05 – h5712@accor.com – Fax 02 31 44 95 94 BV **f**
88 rm – †€ 80/85 ††€ 98/105, ☕ € 11 – **Rest** – *(closed 24 December-1st January, lunch Saturday and Sunday)* Menu € 20 – Carte € 24/46
◆ At the heart of the office district, well-groomed, spacious rooms with good soundproofing, all of which have been treated to a makeover. English-inspired restaurant and a traditional menu that features regional specialities.

in Bénouville 10 km by ② – pop. 1 741 – alt. 8 m – ✉ 14970

Château★: main staircase★★ - Pegasus Bridge★.

La Glycine rest, P VISA AE

11 pl. Commando-nº 4, (opposite the church) – ✆ 02 31 44 61 94 – la-glycine@wanadoo.fr – Fax 02 31 43 67 30 – Closed 20 Dec.-10 Jan.

35 rm – €55 €65, €8 – ½ P €65 – **Rest** – *(closed Sunday dinner October-April)* Menu €20/30 – Carte €35/75

◆ The famous Pegasus Bridge disputed during D Day is near these two houses linked by a flowered patio. Functional identical rooms. A contemporary dining room. Traditional dishes favoured by the chefs.

Le Manoir d'Hastings et la Pommeraie with rm rm, P VISA

18 av. Côte-de-Nacre, (near the church) – ✆ 02 31 44 62 43 – contact@manoirhastings.com – Fax 02 31 44 76 18 – Closed January

15 rm – €75 €90, €10 – ½ P €95/110 – **Rest** – *(closed Sunday dinner and Monday)* Menu €28 (weekday lunch), €35/48 – Carte €52/90

◆ A rustic dining room, veranda and charming rooms on the priory side (17C), more functional facilities in the more recent building. Traditional cuisine. Tree-lined garden.

in Fleury-sur-Orne 4 km by ⑦ – pop. 4 231 – alt. 33 m – ✉ 14123

Auberge de l'Ile Enchantée VISA

1 r. St-André, (beside the Orne) – ✆ 02 31 52 15 52 – aubergeileenchantee@wanadoo.fr – Fax 02 31 72 67 17 – Closed 4-10 August, 9-15 February, Sunday dinner, Monday dinner and Wednesday

Rest – Menu €26/42 – Carte €38/53

◆ Two welcoming dining rooms in a half-timbered house. The one on the first floor is lighter and overlooks the peaceful river. Contemporary cuisine.

CAGNES-SUR-MER – 06 Alpes-Maritimes – 341 D6 – pop. 43 942 – alt. 20 m – Casino – ✉ 06800 French Riviera 42 E2

Paris 915 – Antibes 11 – Cannes 21 – Grasse 25 – Nice 13 – Vence 9

Office de tourisme, 6, boulevard Maréchal Juin ✆ 04 93 20 61 64, Fax 04 93 20 52 63

Haut-de-Cagnes★ - Château-museum★: patio★★, ★ of the tower - Musée Renoir.

Plan on next page

Domaine Cocagne rm, P VISA AE

colline de la rte de Vence, via ①, D 36 and minor road: 2 km – ✆ 04 92 13 57 77 – hotel@domainecocagne.com – Fax 04 92 13 57 89

19 rm – €175/210 €180/275, €12 – 9 suites – ½ P €124/175

Rest – *(closed 30 November-19 December and 5-18 January)* Menu €40/62 – Carte €33/50

◆ An idyllic setting (garden, swimming pool and palm trees), luxurious rooms with a balcony or terrace, beautiful contemporary interior by Jan des Bouvrie and painting exhibitions. Gourmet cuisine in a setting that is both cosy and designer inspired. New bistro.

Splendid without rest P VISA AE

41 bd Mar.-Juin – ✆ 04 93 22 02 00 – hotel.splendid.riviera@orange.fr – Fax 04 93 20 12 44 BX **x**

26 rm – €63/72 €79/89, €8

◆ This town-centre hotel adjoins a recent building. Bright, functional bedrooms; almost all of them overlook the quiet rear.

Le Chantilly without rest P VISA AE

31 chemin Minoterie – ✆ 04 93 20 25 50 – hotel.chantilly.cagnes@wanadoo.fr – Fax 04 92 02 82 63 BX **b**

18 rm – €59/65 €66/75, €8

◆ A flower-decked seaside villa. The lobby and lounge have the charm of a family house. Some of the individually furnished rooms have a balcony.

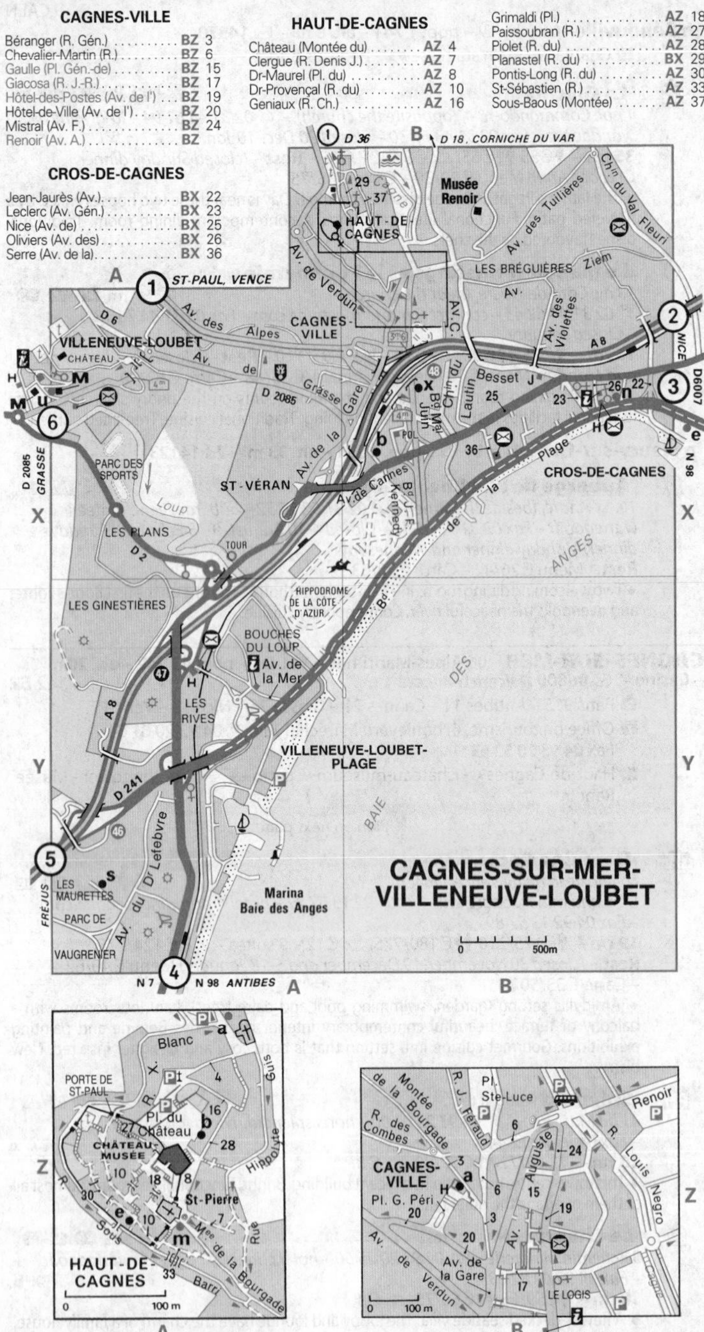
CAGNES-VILLE
Béranger (R. Gén.) .... BZ 3
Chevalier-Martin (R.) .... BZ 6
Gaulle (Pl. Gén.-de) .... BZ 15
Giacosa (R. J.-R.) .... BZ 17
Hôtel-des-Postes (Av. de l') ... BZ 19
Hôtel-de-Ville (Av. de l') ...... BZ 20
Mistral (Av. F.) .... BZ 24
Renoir (Av. A.) .... BZ
CROS-DE-CAGNES
Jean-Jaurès (Av.) .... BX 22
Leclerc (Av. Gén.) .... BX 23
Nice (Av. de) .... BX 25
Oliviers (Av. des) .... BX 26
Serre (Av. de la) .... BX 36
HAUT-DE-CAGNES
Château (Montée du) .... AZ 4
Clergue (R. Denis J.) .... AZ 7
Dr-Maurel (Pl. du) .... AZ 8
Dr-Provençal (R. du) .... AZ 10
Geniaux (R. Ch.) .... AZ 16
Grimaldi (Pl.) .... AZ 18
Paissoubran (R.) .... AZ 27
Piolet (R. du) .... AZ 28
Planastel (R. du) .... BX 29
Pontis-Long (R. du) .... AZ 30
St-Sébastien (R.) .... AZ 33
Sous-Baous (Montée) .... AZ 37
D 36
D 18, CORNICHE DU VAR
Musée Renoir
HAUT-DE-CAGNES
ST-PAUL, VENCE
CAGNES-VILLE
VILLENEUVE-LOUBET
CHÂTEAU
LES BRÉGUIÈRES
NICE
D6007
GRASSE
PARC DES SPORTS
ST-VÉRAN
CROS-DE-CAGNES
LES PLANS
HIPPODROME DE LA CÔTE D'AZUR
LES GINESTIÈRES
BOUCHES DU LOUP
LES RIVES
VILLENEUVE-LOUBET-PLAGE
BAIE DES ANGES
LES MAURETTES
PARC DE VAUGRENIER
FRÉJUS
Marina Baie des Anges
CAGNES-SUR-MER-
VILLENEUVE-LOUBET
N 7
N 98 ANTIBES
PORTE DE ST-PAUL
Pl. du Château
CHÂTEAU-MUSÉE
St-Pierre
HAUT-DE-CAGNES
Pl. Ste-Luce
CAGNES-VILLE
Pl. G. Péri
LE LOGIS

in Haut-de-Cagnes

Le Cagnard rm, VISA AE
45 r. Sous-Barri – 04 93 20 73 21 – cagnard@relaischateaux.com – Fax 04 93 22 06 39 AZ **e**
20 rm – €100/140 €135/300, €18 – 6 suites
Rest – *(closed mid November-mid December, Monday lunch, Tuesday lunch and Thursday lunch)* Menu €55 bi (weekday lunch), €75/95 – Carte €90/128
Spec. Fine lasagne de truffe d'Aups. Risotto de gambas et calamar à l'italienne. Petite pêche de Méditerranée aux saveurs de la Ligure. **Wines** Bellet, Côtes de Provence.
♦ Simenon, Renoir, Soutine, Modigliani, etc. stayed in this lovely historic abode. Some of the distinctive rooms have terraces and a sea view. In summer, the panelled ceiling of the restaurant opens to the sky. Personalised southern cuisine.

Villa Estelle without rest VISA
5 montée de la Bourgade – 04 92 02 89 83 – info@villa-estelle.com – Fax 04 92 02 88 28 BZ **a**
5 rm – €100/130 €100/195
♦ The proprietress's tasteful revamp has brought this inn back to life. Personalised rooms, some with a sea view, cosy lounge, pretty courtyard terrace and lovely garden.

Le Grimaldi with rm VISA AE
6 pl. du Château – 04 93 20 60 24 – reservation@hotelgrimaldi.com – Fax 04 93 22 82 19 – Closed 2-19 December and 6-31 January AZ **b**
5 rm – €120/135 €120/135 – ½ P €155/170 – **Rest** – *(closed lunch from Monday to Thursday in July-August and Tuesday off season) (number of covers limited, pre-book)* Menu €30 bi (weekday lunch), €35/59 – Carte €45/69
♦ A contemporary restaurant which is both simple and warm, with delectable summer terrace. In the kitchen, the chef mastefully reinterprets a regional repertoire. Charming historical allusions feature throughout.

Fleur de Sel VISA
85 montée de la Bourgade – 04 93 20 33 33 – contact@restaurant-fleurdesel.com – Fax 04 93 20 33 33 – Closed 4-11 June, 27 October-12 November, 5-21 January, Thursday lunch, Wednesday and lunch July-August AZ **m**
Rest – Menu €32/55 – Carte €44/59
♦ Pleasant little restaurant next to the church. Kitchen fully visible from the rustic/Provençal dining room (numerous copper utensils and paintings). Appetising menu.

Josy-Jo (Josy Bandecchi) VISA AE
2 r. Planastel – 04 93 20 68 76 – info@restaurant-josyjo.com – Closed 17 November -26 December, Saturday lunch and Sunday AZ **a**
Rest – Menu €29 bi (lunch)/40 – Carte €42/69
Spec. Farcis grand-mère. Selle d'agneau grillée au charbon de bois. Homard bleu grillé. **Wines** Bellet, Côtes de Provence.
♦ A simple yet friendly setting decorated with paintings, ironware and offering view of the kitchens, no-fuss service, fine grills and good little Provençal dishes.

in Cros-de-Cagnes 2 km southeast – ✉ 06800 Cagnes-sur-Mer

La Bourride VISA AE
(port du Cros) – 04 93 31 07 75 – Fax 04 93 31 89 11 – Closed 15-31 October, 15 February-10 March, Tuesday dinner and Sunday dinner off season, Tuesday lunch in July-August and Wednesday BX **e**
Rest – Menu €38/80 – Carte €53/81
♦ A dining room decorated with a mural depicting the sea, a patio with umbrella pines and a terrace opposite the harbour: three delightful spaces to taste fish and seafood.

Réserve "Loulou" VISA AE
91 bd de la Plage – 04 93 31 00 17 – louloulareserve@wanadoo.fr – Fax 04 93 22 09 26 – Closed 10-25 May, lunch 15 July-6 September, Saturday lunch and Sunday BX **n**
Rest – Menu €41/47 – Carte €45/132
♦ A pretty regional setting, paintings and lithographs as decoration, fish and grills prepared in front of you: an enticingly relaxed establishment.

Paris 575 – Agen 85 – Albi 110 – Brive-la-Gaillarde 98 – Montauban 64

Office de tourisme, place François Mitterrand ✆ 05 65 53 20 65, Fax 05 65 53 20 74

Pont Valentré★★ - North portal ★★ and cloister★ of St-Etienne cathedral ★ BY **E** - ≤★ of Cabessut bridge - Croix de Magne ≤★ West: 5 km by D 27 - Barbican and tour St-Jean★ - ≤★ from north of town.

Plan on next page

Terminus

5 av. Ch.-de-Freycinet – ✆ 05 65 53 32 00 – terminus.balandre@wanadoo.fr – Fax 05 65 53 32 26 – Closed 15-30 November AY **s**

22 rm – €50/95 €60/130, €12

Rest *Le Balandre* – see restaurant listing

◆ In theory, everyone should end up at The Terminus! An impressive 1910 house home to large, clean and soundproofed rooms. Art Deco lounge bar.

Jean XXII without rest

5 bd Gambetta – ✆ 05 65 35 07 66 – Fax 05 65 53 92 38 – Closed 20-31 October, February holidays and Sunday October-May BY **v**

9 rm – €45 €55, €7

◆ Hotel near the John XXII tower (Jacques Duèze, elected Pope in 1322, came from Cahors), within the walls of the former palace built by his family. Functional rooms.

De la Paix without rest

30 pl. St-Maurice – ✆ 05 65 35 03 40 – hoteldelapaix-cahors@wanadoo.fr – Fax 05 65 35 40 88 BZ **t**

21 rm – €48 €54/75, €6

◆ In the wake of a full makeover, this small central hotel is once again proud to offer quiet, simple and practical rooms. The most cheerful overlook the market.

Le Balandre – Hôtel Terminus

5 av. Ch.-de-Freycinet – ✆ 05 65 53 32 00 – terminus.balandre@wanadoo.fr – Fax 05 65 53 32 26 – Closed 15-30 November, Monday except dinner 1st August-15 September and Sunday AY **s**

Rest – Menu (€42), €60/88 – Carte €72/83

◆ The chef enthusiastically prepares up-to-date dishes, served in an elegant room adorned with stained glass. Magnificent wine list and a simpler lunchtime menu.

L'Ô à la Bouche

134 r. Ste-Urcisse – ✆ 05 65 35 65 69 – Fax 05 65 35 65 69 – Closed Easter holidays, autumn half-term holidays, Sunday and Monday BZ **a**

Rest – Menu (€19), €25/28 – Carte €31/36

◆ Up-to-date menu to the delight of gourmets! Old stone, brickwork, beams and a fireplace lend undeniable character to this restaurant, renowned for its mouth-watering fare.

Le Marché

27 pl. Chapou – ✆ 05 65 35 27 27 – restaurant.le.marche@cegetel.net – Fax 05 65 21 09 98 – Closed 14-20 April, 26 October-4 November, Monday except August and Sunday BZ **b**

Rest – Menu (€23), €28

◆ An in vogue establishment, as much for its elongated room with beige and plum bench seating, a wall of light and one of slate, as for its fashionable and inspired cuisine.

Au Fil des Douceurs

90 quai Verrerie – ✆ 05 65 22 13 04 – Fax 05 65 35 61 09 – Closed 23 June-7 July, 1st-19 January, Sunday and Monday BY **x**

Rest – Menu €14 (lunch), €23/50 – Carte €30/87

◆ Climb on board this boat and enjoy the stunning view of the Lot and old Cahors. Traditional fare served in two dining rooms, one above the other.

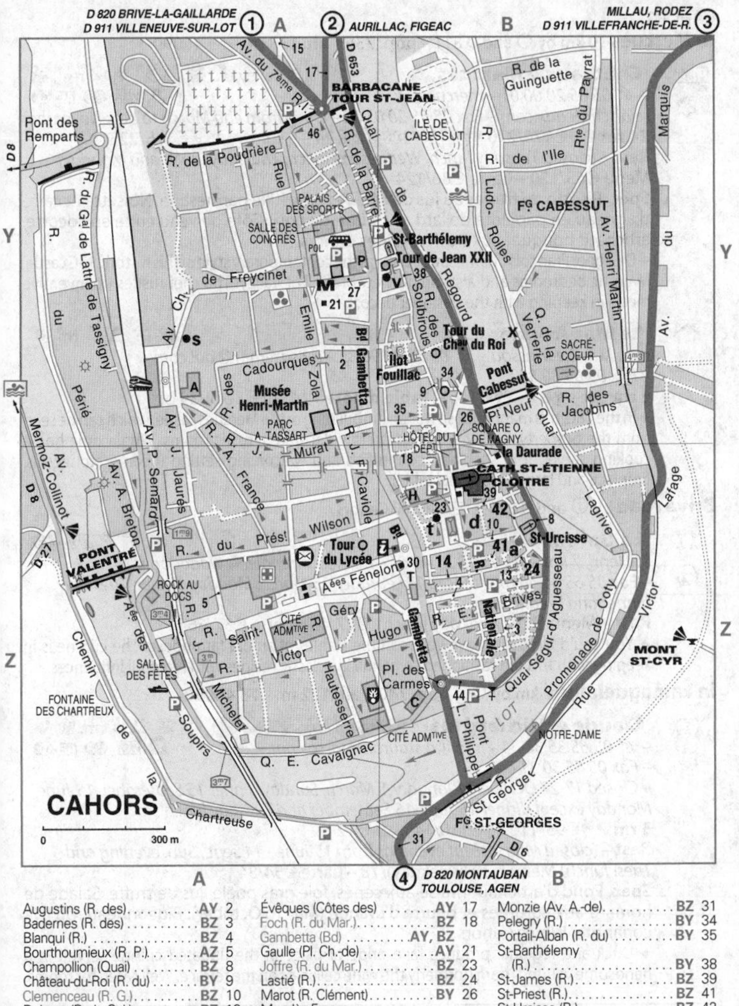

Augustins (R. des). . . . . AY 2	Évêques (Côtes des) . . . . AY 17	Monzie (Av. A.-de). . . . . BZ 31
Badernes (R. des). . . . . BZ 3	Foch (R. du Mar.). . . . . BZ 18	Pelegry (R.) . . . . BY 34
Blanqui (R.) . . . . BZ 4	Gambetta (Bd) . . . . AY, BZ	Portail-Alban (R. du) . . . . . . BY 35
Bourthoumieux (R. P.). . . . . . AZ 5	Gaulle (Pl. Ch.-de) . . . . AY 21	St-Barthélemy (R.) . . . . BY 38
Champollion (Quai) . . . . BZ 8	Joffre (R. du Mar.) . . . . BZ 23	St-James (R.) . . . . BZ 39
Château-du-Roi (R. du) . . . . . BY 9	Lastié (R.). . . . . BZ 24	St-Priest (R.). . . . . BZ 41
Clemenceau (R. G.). . . . . BZ 10	Marot (R. Clément) . . . . BY 26	St-Urcisse (R.) . . . . BZ 42
Delmas (R. du Col.). . . . . BZ 13	Mendès-France (R. P.) . . . . AY 27	Vaxis (Cours) . . . . BZ 44
Dr-Bergounioux (R.) . . . . BZ 14	Mitterrand (Pl. F.). . . . . BZ 30	Villars (R. René). . . . . AY 46
Dr-J.-Ségala (R. du) . . . . AY 15		

in Caillac 13 km by ①, **Villeneuve-sur-Lot road and D145 – pop. 533 – alt. 161 m –** ✉ **46140**

XX **Le Vinois** with rm — rm, rm, VISA

Le bourg – ✆ 05 65 30 53 60 – contact@levinois.com – Fax 05 65 21 67 27 – Closed 6-13 October, 12 January-9 February

10 rm – †€ 70/79 ††€ 86/135, ☕ € 12 – ½ P € 106/161 – **Rest** – *(closed Sunday dinner 15 September-13 July, Monday except dinner 14 July-14 September and Tuesday lunch)* Menu € 17 (weekday lunch), € 30/53

◆ In the heart of the Cahors vineyards, don't miss this stunning inn that sports a minimalist contemporary style in keeping with the cuisine. Jazz in the background. The hotel's rooms display a smart sobriety: personalised detail and a designer spirit.

in Mercuès 10 km by ① and D 811 – pop. 736 – alt. 133 m – ✉ 46090

Château de Mercuès ≤ Lot valley, rest, VISA AE
– ✆ *05 65 20 00 01 – mercues@relaischateaux.com – Fax 05 65 20 05 72 – Open from end March to beg. November*
24 rm – †€ 170/270 ††€ 180/280, ☐ € 24 – 6 suites – ½ P € 175/225
Rest – *(closed Tuesday lunch, Wednesday lunch, Thursday lunch and Monday)* Menu € 65/120 – Carte € 86/124
Spec. Risotto de truffes au jus de céleri et croustille parmesane. Noisette et carré d'agneau en papillote de lard au beurre de noix. Côte de veau cuite en cocotte, artichaut bouquet aux truffes. **Wines** Cahors.
◆ Designer François Champsaur is behind the contemporary style of this historic 13C castle. Majestic bedrooms and a stunning view of the Lot Valley. The chef rustles up inventive meals in keeping with the designer decor.

Le Mas Azemar rm,
r. du Mas-de-Vinssou – ✆ 05 65 30 96 85 – masazemar@aol.com – Fax 05 65 30 53 82
6 rm ☐ – †€ 75 ††€ 105 – **Table d'hôte** – Menu € 32 bi/39 bi
◆ In the 18C, this manor house was an outbuilding of the Mercuès castle, which can be seen from the property. Today it houses prettily decorated, rustic rooms. Wholesome home cooking served in a spacious, countrified and welcoming setting (beams, stonewalls, fireplace and large communal table).

Brive road by ① and D 820 – ✉ 46000 Cahors

La Garenne VISA
St-Henri, 7 km – ✆ 05 65 35 40 67 – michel.carrendier@wanadoo.fr – Fax 05 65 35 40 67 – Closed 1st February-15 March, Monday dinner, Tuesday dinner and Wednesday
Rest – Menu € 20 (weekday lunch), € 27/48 – Carte € 37/66
◆ You could almost believe you're in the stables of an old farmhouse! The cuisine is in keeping with this old-fashioned spirit, mixing classic recipes with regional influences.

in Lamagdelaine 7 km by ② – pop. 740 – alt. 122 m – ✉ 46090

Claude et Richard Marco with rm rm, VISA AE
– ✆ *05 65 35 30 64 – info@restaurantmarco.com – Fax 05 65 30 31 40 – Closed 17-27 October, 4 January-5 March, Sunday dinner 15 September-15 June, Monday except dinner 15 June-15 September and Tuesday lunch*
5 rm – †€ 95/110 ††€ 110/145, ☐ € 12
Rest – *(closed Mon. except evenings from 15 June - 14 Sept., Sun. evening and Tues. lunch)* Menu € 30 (weekday)/78 – Carte € 54/84
Spec. Fond d'artichaut braisé aux cèpes, foie gras poêlé, jus de truffe. Salade de homard aux agrumes et beurre d'orange (May to October). Pigeonneau rôti à la coriandre. **Wines** Cahors.
◆ Duck and regional produce take pride of place in the updated cuisine served in a handsome vaulted room (formerly the wine cellar) or on the terrace. Well cared for rooms.

CAHUZAC-SUR-VÈRE – 81 Tarn – 338 D7 – pop. 1 027 – alt. 240 m – ✉ 81140

Paris 655 – Albi 28 – Gaillac 11 – Montauban 60 – Rodez 86 – Toulouse 69
Syndicat d'initiative, Mairie ✆ 05 63 33 68 91, Fax 05 63 33 68 92 29 **C2**

Château de Salettes ≤ rm, VISA AE
south: 3 km on the D 922 – ✆ 05 63 33 60 60 – salettes@chateaudesalettes.com – Fax 05 63 33 60 61 – Closed 6-23 January and 17 February-5 March
18 rm – †€ 131/185 ††€ 131/330, ☐ € 16 – ½ P € 185/239
Rest *(closed Wednesday lunch, Monday, Tuesday from October-May, Monday lunch and Tuesday lunch from May-July and September)* Menu € 35/80 – Carte € 73/87
Spec. Grillade d'une aiguillette de foie gras. Tronçons de Saint-Pierre sur crumble d'ail et gingembre. Tube chocolat au grué de cacao, glace cacahuète, caramel salé.
◆ 13C chateau, in the middle of the vineyards, which has been entirely rebuilt. Beautiful modern decoration and designer furniture. Large rooms, some with water-jet bathtubs. The exposed stone walls and elegant decor provide an attractive backdrop for the chef's interesting cuisine.

XX **La Falaise**

rte de Cordes – ✆ 05 63 33 96 31 – guillaume.salvan@wanadoo.fr – Closed Sunday dinner, Tuesday lunch and Monday
Rest – Menu € 19 (weekday lunch), € 33/50 – Carte € 44/62

◆ Old wine warehouse converted into a restaurant. Smart, rustic dining room with a summer veranda and terrace beneath the willows. Personalised menu and a good selection of Gaillac wines.

CAILLAC – **46 Lot** – **337** E5 – **see Cahors**

CAILLY-SUR-EURE – **27 Eure** – **304** H7 – **pop. 233** – **alt. 23 m** – ✉ **27490** 33 **D2**

Paris 101 – Évreux 13 – Louviers 13 – Rouen 45 – Vernon 30

Les Deux Sapins rm, rm, VISA

24 r. de la Mairie – ✆ 02 32 67 75 13 – juhel.eric@wanadoo.fr – Fax 02 32 67 73 62 – Closed 8 August-1st September and Sunday dinner
15 rm – € 50/58 € 53/60, € 6,50 – ½ P € 48/50 – **Rest** – *(closed Sunday dinner and Monday)* Menu € 15 (weekday)/29 – Carte € 23/45

◆ A modern, welcoming motel-type establishment. Simple, functional rooms reached by a covered arcade. Small lounge beneath a glass roof. A brick-walled dining room, opening onto the inner courtyard of the hotel.

If breakfast is included the symbol appears after the number of rooms.

CAIRANNE – **84 Vaucluse** – **332** C8 – **pop. 850** – **alt. 136 m** – ✉ **84290** 40 **A2**

Paris 650 – Avignon 43 – Bollène 47 – Montélimar 51 – Nyons 25 – Orange 18

Office de tourisme, route de Sainte-Cécile ✆ 04 90 30 76 53

Auberge Castel Miréïo rm, VISA

Carpentras road by D 8 – ✆ 04 90 30 82 20 – info@castelmireio.fr – Fax 04 90 30 78 39 – Closed 31 December-14 February
8 rm – € 58/61 € 60/64, € 7,50 – 1 suite – ½ P € 58 – **Rest** – *(closed Wednesday dinner, Sunday dinner from September to June, Tuesday lunch and Saturday lunch in July-August and Monday lunch)* Menu € 19 (weekday lunch), € 22/30 – Carte € 26/37

◆ This former family residence has a recently built annexe with simple rooms enhanced by Provençal fabrics. A rustic dining room proud of its attractive hundred-year-old tiling. Traditional cuisine.

CAJARC – **46 Lot** – **337** H5 – **pop. 1 114** – **alt. 160 m** – ✉ **46160**
Dordogne-Berry-Limousin 29 **C1**

Paris 586 – Cahors 52 – Figeac 25 – Rocamadour 59 – Villefranche-de-Rouergue 27

Office de tourisme, La Chapelle ✆ 05 65 40 72 89, Fax 05 65 40 39 05

La Ségalière VISA

rte de Capdenac – ✆ 05 65 40 65 35 – hotel@lasegaliere.com – Fax 05 65 40 74 92 – Open 15 March-4 November and 15 December-31 January
24 rm – € 49/80 € 65/95, € 10 – ½ P € 65/80 – **Rest** – *(closed Sunday dinner, Monday, Tuesday and Wednesday December and January and lunch except weekends and holidays)* Menu € 28/38

◆ Françoise Sagan was born in this village. This modern hotel offers very pleasant rooms with balconies. The large pool and garden are greatly appreciated. The menu features traditional fare with a creative twist. Summer terrace.

CALACUCCIA – 2B Haute-Corse – **345** D5 – see Corse

CALAIS – 62 Pas-de-Calais – **301** E2 – **pop. 77 333** – **Built-up area 104 852** – **alt. 5 m** – **Casino** CX – ✉ **62100** **Northern France and the Paris Region** 30 **A1**

Paris 290 – Boulogne-sur-Mer 35 – Dunkerque 46 – St-Omer 43

Channel Tunnel : Coquelles Terminal AU, info **"Shuttle"** ☎ 03 21 00 61 00.

☎ 3635 (0,34 €/mn)

Office de tourisme, 12, boulevard Clemenceau ☎ 03 21 96 62 40, Fax 03 21 96 01 92

Monument of the Bourgeois de Calais (Rodin)★★ - Lighthouse ✳★★ DX - Musée des Beaux-Arts et de la Dentelle★ CX **M²**.

Cap Blanc Nez★★: 13 km by ④.

CALAIS

Bossuet (R.) .... **BT** 9
Cambronne (R.) .... **AU** 12
Chateaubriand (R.) .... **BT** 15
Égalité (Bd de l') .... **BT** 18
Einstein (Bd) .... **AU** 19
La-Fayette (Bd) .... **AT** 39
Fontinettes (R. des) .... **ATU** 25
Four-à-Chaux (R. du) .... **AU** 27
Gambetta (Bd Léon) .... **AT** 28
Gaulle (Bd du Gén.-de) .... **AT** 30
Hoche (R.) .... **ATU** 33
Jacquard (Bd) .... **AT** 34
Lattre-de-Tassigny (R. Mar.-de) .... **AT** 40
Lheureux (Quai L.) .... **BU** 41
Maubeuge (R. de) .... **BT** 43
Phalsbourg (R. de) .... **BT** 51
Prairies (R. des) .... **AU** 52
Ragueneau (R. de) .... **BTU** 57
Valenciennes (R. de) .... **AU** 69
Verdun (R. de) .... **AT** 73

Meurice

5 r. E.-Roche – ☎ 03 21 34 57 03 – meurice@wanadoo.fr – Fax 03 21 34 14 71 CX **v**

41 rm – †€ 60/150 ††€ 60/150, ☐ € 12 – ½ P € 66/89 – **Rest** – *(closed Saturday lunch)* Menu (€ 15), € 18 (weekdays)/50

◆ Traditional hotel with a huge lobby steeped in the atmosphere of 'Old France'. Delightfully antiquated large rooms; modern decor in the more recent wing. Beams, carved wood and period furniture form the cosy setting for this restaurant.

CALAIS

Rue	Carré	N°
Amsterdam (R. d')	DXY	3
Angleterre (Pl. d')	DX	4
Barbusse (Pl. Henri)	DX	6
Bonnigue (R. du Cdt)	DX	7
Bruxelles (R. de)	DX	10
Chanzy (R. du Gén.)	DY	13
Commune-de-Paris (R. de la)	CDY	16
Escaut (Quai de l')	CY	21
La-Fayette (Bd)	DY	
Foch (Pl. Mar.)	CXY	22
Fontinettes (R. des)	CDY	24
Gambetta (Bd Léon)	CY	
Georges-V (Pont)	CY	31
Jacquard (Bd)	CDY	
Jacquard (Pont)	CY	36
Jean-Jaurès (R.)	DY	37
Londres (R. de)	DX	42
Mer (R. de la)	CX	45
Notre-Dame (R.)	CDX	46
Paix (R. de la)	CX	48
Pasteur (Bd)	DY	
Paul-Bert (R.)	CDY	49
Prés.-Wilson (Av. du)	CY	54
Quatre-Coins (R. des)	CY	55
Rhin (Quai du)	CY	58
Richelieu (R.)	CX	60
Rome (R. de)	CY	61
Royale (R.)	CX	63
Soldat-Inconnu (Pl. du)	DY	64
Tamise (Quai de la)	CDY	66
Thermes (R. des)	CX	67
Varsovie (R. de)	DY	70
Vauxhall (R. du)	CY	72

Holiday Inn

bd des Alliés – 03 21 34 69 69 – holidayinn@holidayinn-calais.com – Fax 03 21 97 09 15 CX **a**

63 rm – €128/165 €138/185, €13,50

Rest – *(closed Saturday lunch, Sunday lunch and holidays lunch)* Menu €17 bi/24 – Carte €24/40

◆ Pleasantly located opposite the marina, this imposing hotel, renovated in 2005, has spacious, comfortable rooms, half of which have sea views. The bay windows of the restaurant overlook the masts of the yachts. Contemporary decor.

Métropol Hôtel without rest

43 quai du Rhin – 03 21 97 54 00 – metropol@metropolhotel.com – Fax 03 21 96 69 70 – Closed 21 December-11 January CY **h**

40 rm – €46 €67, €10 – 1 suite

◆ An old, red-brick façade. Practical, soundproofed rooms, some with an English decorative note, like the bar which has a distinctly British design.

Mercure Centre

36 r. Royale – 03 21 97 68 00 – h6739@accor.com – Fax 03 21 97 34 73 CX **d**

41 rm – €75/95 €85/115, €13 – **Rest** – *(closed Saturday lunch and Sunday)* Menu €16/35 – Carte €31/49

◆ This hotel is on a main shopping street, near the casino. Rooms have been renovated or are in Eighties style. A quiet atmosphere, upright wine cellar and classic cuisine or dishes of the day.

Aquar'aile beach and port,

255 r. J.-Moulin, (4th Floor) – 03 21 34 00 00 – f.leroy@aquaraile.com – Fax 03 21 34 15 00 – Closed Sunday evening AT **s**

Rest – Menu (€25 bi), €28/43 – Carte €46/76

◆ A unique view of the English Channel, the North Sea, and the English coastline on the horizon from this pleasant fish restaurant on the fouth floor of a building.

Au Côte d'Argent

1 digue G.-Berthe – 03 21 34 68 07 – lefebvre@cotedargent.com – Fax 03 21 96 42 10 – Closed 18 August-9 September, 22 December-6 January, 23 February-10 March, Wednesday dinner from September to April, Sunday dinner and Monday CX **f**

Rest – Menu €18 (weekdays)/40 – Carte €32/56

◆ All on board for a gourmet voyage with a fish and seafood flavour. A ship's cabin decor with a view of the busy ferry traffic in the background.

Channel

3 bd de la Résistance – 03 21 34 42 30 – contact@restaurant-lechannel.com – Fax 03 21 97 42 43 – Closed 26 July-9 August, 22 December-20 January, Sunday dinner and Tuesday CX **e**

Rest – Menu €22/52 – Carte €45/85

◆ Elegant, modern décor, first-rate fish and seafood and an appealing wine list (cellar opening on to the room): a pleasant stop-off before crossing the channel.

La Pléiade

32 r. J.-Quehen – 03 21 34 03 70 – e.memain@lapleiade.com – Fax 03 21 34 03 13 – Closed 28 July-17 August, February holidays, Sunday dinner and Monday CX **r**

Rest – Menu €28/58 – Carte €37/76

◆ Restaurant with an appealing facade, whose elegant interior is adorned with a collection of paintings by regional artists. Modern fish and market cuisine.

Histoire Ancienne

20 r. Royale – 03 21 34 11 20 – p.comte@histoire-ancienne.com – Fax 03 21 96 19 58 – Closed 1st-15 August, Monday dinner and Sunday CX **x**

Rest – Menu €11,50/36 – Carte €25/51

◆ This charming dining room has carefully preserved its bistro style: bench seating, wooden chairs and old zinc. Grilled food, traditional dishes and local produce.

Le Grand Bleu
quai de la Colonne – ✆ 03 21 97 97 98 – legrandbleu-calais@wanadoo.fr – Fax 03 21 82 53 03 – Closed 26 August-11 September, 18 February-4 March, Tuesday dinner and Wednesday CX **n**
Rest – Menu € 18/45 – Carte € 34/51
◆ The name says it all: this restaurant celebrates all aspects of the sea, both in its decor and its predominantly seafood menu.

in Coquelles **6 km West by Avenue R. Salengro** AT – **pop. 2 370 – alt. 5 m –** ✉ **62231**

Holiday Inn rm, rest, VISA AE
– ✆ 03 21 46 60 60 – info@holidayinncoquelles.com – Fax 03 21 85 76 76
118 rm – €105/125 €125/260, ☕ €15 – **Rest** – *(closed Saturday lunch)* Menu € 25/42 – Carte € 26/46
◆ This modern hotel complex 3km from the Calais Fréthun Eurostar station has comfortable rooms. Sauna, hammam, indoor pool, fitness centre and squash courts. Fine furniture in the dining room, recently redecorated in modern style.

Suitehotel without rest VISA AE
pl.de Cantorbery – ✆ 03 21 19 50 00 – h3335@accor.com – Fax 03 21 19 50 05 AU
100 rm – €92/120 €92/120, ☕ €12
◆ Large suites (over 30m²), including an office and lounge, a bedroom that can be partitioned, and a fully equipped bathroom (shower and bath).

in Blériot-Plage AT – ✉**62231 Sangatte**
Office de tourisme, route nationale ✆ 03 21 34 97 98, Fax 03 21 97 75 13

Les Dunes rest, VISA AE
48 rte Nationale – ✆ 03 21 34 54 30 – p.mene@les-dunes.com – Fax 03 21 97 17 63 – Closed 13 October-2 November and 17-30 March
9 rm – €52/66 €52/66, ☕ €8 – **Rest** – *(closed Sunday dinner except holidays and Monday September-13 July)* Menu € 18/39 – Carte € 36/57 AT **z**
◆ In the town that saw Louis Blériot fly off on the 25th July 1909 for his crossing of the Channel. Well-kept rooms that are simple and practical, with little balconies. A spacious, attractively-laid-out dining room. Fish, seafood, game in season.

CALALONGA (PLAGE) – **2A Corse-du-Sud** – **345** E11 – **see Corse (Bonifacio)**

CALA-ROSSA – **2A Corse-du-Sud** – **345** F10 – **see Corse (Porto-Vecchio)**

CALÈS – **46 Lot** – **337** F3 – **pop. 149** – **alt. 273 m** – ✉ **46350** 29 **C1**
Paris 528 – Sarlat-la-Canéda 42 – Cahors 52 – Gourdon 21 – Rocamadour 15 – St-Céré 43

Le Petit Relais rm, VISA AE
au bourg – ✆ 05 65 37 96 09 – Fax 05 65 37 95 93 – Closed 19-26 December and 3-24 January
13 rm – €48/52 €55/60, ☕ €8 – ½ P € 115/140 – **Rest** – *(closed Saturday lunch, Sunday dinner and Monday October- February)* Menu (€ 13 bi), € 17/36 – Carte € 33/44
◆ The same family has run this old Quercy establishment in the heart of a picturesque village for three generations. Rooms have been well renovated and soundproofed. A rustic restaurant (beams, fireplace, copper utensils), shady terrace and dishes prepared with local produce.

CALLAS – **83 Var** – **340** O4 – **pop. 1 388** – **alt. 398 m** – ✉ **83830**
French Riviera 41 **C3**
Paris 872 – Castellane 51 – Draguignan 14
Office de tourisme, place du 18 juin 1940 ✆ 04 94 39 06 77, Fax 04 94 39 06 79

Muy road 7 km Southeast by D 25 – ✉ 83830 Callas

Hostellerie Les Gorges de Pennafort rest,
D 25 – ☎ 04 94 76 66 51
– info@hostellerie-pennafort.com – Fax 04 94 76 67 23
– Closed from mid January to mid March
16 rm – €135/150 €185/220, €18 – 4 suites – ½ P €165/180
Rest – *(closed Sunday dinner except July-August, Monday except dinner in July-August and Wednesday lunch)* Menu (€45), €56/135 – Carte €99/154
Spec. Ravioli de foie gras et parmesan, sauce aux truffes. Carré d'agneau rôti, jus au thym. Chocolat noir amer, pain de Gênes, parfait fruit de la passion. **Wines** Côtes de Provence, Coteaux Varois.
◆ This traditional Provençal manor blends harmoniously with the landscape; the colour scheme and decor create a refined ambience . In the evening, the red walls of the gorges are dramatically lit. A revamped dining room facing a pretty water feature. Tasty food and a well-stocked cellar.

"Rest" appears in red for establishments with a (star) or (Bib Gourmand).

CALVI – 2B Haute-Corse – **345** B4 – **see Corse**

CALVINET – 15 Cantal – **330** C6 – **pop. 432 – alt. 600 m** – ✉ **15340** 5 **A3**

Paris 576 – Aurillac 34 – Entraygues-sur-Truyère 32 – Figeac 40 – Maurs 19 – Rodez 56

Beauséjour (Louis-Bernard Puech) with rm
– ☎ 04 71 49 91 68 – beausejour.puech@wanadoo.fr – Fax 04 71 49 98 63
– Closed 23-27 June, 24 November-5 December, 5 January-14 February, Sunday dinner October-May, Monday except dinner July-August, Tuesday except dinner March-September and Wednesday except dinner June-September
8 rm – €60/100 €60/100, €15 – ½ P €60/80
Rest – *(number of covers limited, pre-book)* Menu €26/60
Spec. Oeuf au pot gourmand de saison. Charlotte d'agneau allaiton d'Aveyron aux aubergines confites (June to October). Sablé à la châtaigne, pommes caramélisées. **Wines** Marcillac, Côte d'Auvergne.
◆ A country property that seeks to combine inventive recipes with locally sourced produce. Reasonably priced regional wines. Modern rooms. Non-smoking.

CAMARET-SUR-MER – 29 Finistère – **308** D5 – **pop. 2 668 – alt. 4 m** – ✉ **29570**
Brittany 9 **A2**

Paris 597 – Brest 4 – Châteaulin 45 – Crozon 11 – Morlaix 91 – Quimper 60

Office de tourisme, 15, quai Kleber ☎ 02 98 27 93 60, Fax 02 98 27 87 22

Pointe de Penhir★★★ Southwest: 3,5 km.

De France rest,
quai G.-Toudouze – ☎ 02 98 27 93 06 – hotel-france-camaret@wanadoo.fr
– Fax 02 98 27 88 14 – Open Easter-1st November
20 rm – €42/52 €51/92, €8 – ½ P €50/70
Rest – *(open 12 April-1st November)* Menu (€14), €18/42 – Carte €28/114
◆ Decorated with a seafaring theme, the rooms are well kept and soundproofed. Half enjoy a view of the sea; the others are smaller but quieter. This restaurant spread over two floors offers seafood specialities with the harbour as a backdrop.

Bellevue the port,
– ☎ 02 98 17 12 50 – hotel-france-camaret@wanadoo.fr – Fax 02 98 27 88 14
– Closed 15 January-15 February
15 rm – €65/85 €65/140, €10 – ½ P €60/85
◆ The annexe to this hotel enjoys panoramic views of the port. Quiet, functional guestrooms, all of which are equipped with kitchenettes.

Vauban without rest

4 quai du Styvel – ✆ 02 98 27 91 36 – Fax 02 98 27 96 34 – Closed December and January
16 rm – €32/45 €32/45, €6

◆ Travellers can't go wrong if they make a stop here: the hotel is rather modest but its reasonable prices and warm welcome justify making a detour!

LA CAMBE – 14 Calvados – 303 F3 – pop. 518 – alt. 25 m – ✉ 14230 32 B2

Paris 289 – Bayeux 26 – Caen 56 – Saint-Lô 31

Ferme Savigny without rest

2.5 km on D 613 and D113 – ✆ 02 31 21 12 33 – re.ledevin@libertysurf.fr
4 rm – €40 €48

◆ This former farmhouse offers comfortable and tastefully decorated rooms. If weather permits, breakfast is served under the arbour of the pretty courtyard planted with a weeping willow.

For a pleasant stay in a charming hotel,
look for the red ... symbols.

CAMBO-LES-BAINS – 64 Pyrénées-Atlantiques – 342 D4 – pop. 4 416 – alt. 67 m – Spa : early March-mid Dec. – ✉ 64250 Atlantic Coast 3 A3

Paris 783 – Biarritz 21 – Pau 115

Syndicat d'initiative, avenue de la Mairie ✆ 05 59 29 70 25, Fax 05 59 29 90 77

Epherra Souraïde Urloko Bidea, West: 13 km by D 918, ✆ 05 59 93 84 06.

Villa Arnaga★★ M.

Ursula without rest

quartier Bas-Cambo, to the North : 2 km – ✆ 05 59 29 88 88 – hotel.ursula@wanadoo.fr – Fax 05 59 29 22 15 – Closed December and January
15 rm – €44/49 €49/55, €9,50

◆ This small hotel situated in the picturesque quarter or Bas-Cambo offers you large, well-kept rooms functionally furnished.

Le Trinquet without rest

r. Trinquet – ✆ 05 59 29 73 38 – trinquet@hotel-trinquet-cambo.com – Fax 05 59 29 25 61 – Closed 3 November-9 December and Tuesday except 2 July-15 September
12 rm – €27/48 €27/48, €6,50

◆ This large house takes its name from a variant of Basque pelota. The simple and well-kept rooms lie above a café. Family atmosphere.

Le Bellevue with rm

rest,

r. des Terrasses – ✆ 05 59 93 75 75 – contact@hotel-bellevue64.com – Fax 05 59 93 75 85 – Closed 6 January-10 February
1 rm – €60/70 €80/95, €7 – 6 suites – €70/95
Rest – *(closed Thursday dinner except July-September, Sunday dinner and Monday)* Menu €12 (weekday lunch), €19/34

◆ Contemporary furniture and immaculate walls hung with modern paintings provide the decor in this restaurant serving modern cuisine. This charming, well-renovated 19C house has attractive, contemporary-style family suites.

Chez Tante Ursule with rm

quartier Bas-Cambo, to the North : 2 km ✉ 64250 – ✆ 05 59 29 78 23 – chez.tante.ursule@wanadoo.fr – Fax 05 59 29 28 57 – Closed 15-30 November, 15 February-15 March and Tuesday
7 rm – €29 €44, €7 – ½ P €55 – **Rest** – Menu €16 (weekday lunch), €20/35 – Carte €21/58

◆ This establishment situated near to the Bas Cambo fronton has a smart dining room with a pretty dresser. Food focuses on the Basque region. Rustic, well-kept rooms.

CAMBRAI – 59 Nord – 302 H6 – pop. 33 738 – alt. 53 m – ✉ 59400 Northern France and the Paris Region 31 C3

- Paris 179 – Amiens 98 – Arras 36 – Lille 77 – St-Quentin 51
- Office de tourisme, 48, rue du Noyon ✆ 03 27 78 36 15, Fax 03 27 74 82 82
- Burial ★★ by Rubens in St-Géry church AY - Musée Beaux-Arts: choir railings★, procession float★ AZ **M.**

CAMBRAI

Street	Grid	No.
Albert-1er (Av.)	BY	2
Alsace-Lorraine (R. d')	BYZ	4
Berlaimont (Bd de)	BZ	5
Briand (Pl. A.)	AYZ	6
Cantimpré (R. de)	AY	7
Capucins (R. des)	AY	8
Château-de-Selles (R. du)	AY	10
Clefs (R. des)	AY	12
Épée (R. de l')	AZ	13
Fénelon (Gde-R.)	AY	15
Fénelon (Pl.)	AY	16
Feutriers (R. des)	AY	17
Gaulle (R. Gén.-de)	BZ	18
Grand-Séminaire (R. du)	AZ	19
Lattre-de-Tassigny (R. Mar.-de)	BZ	21
Leclerc (Pl. du Mar.)	BZ	22
Lille (R. de)	BY	23
Liniers (R. des)	AZ	24
Moulin (Pl. J.)	AZ	25
Nice (R. de)	AY	27
Pasteur (R.)	AY	29
Porte-de-Paris (Pl. de la)	AZ	32
Porte-Notre-Dame (R.)	BY	31
Râtelots (R. des)	AZ	33
Sadi-Carnot (R.)	AY	35
St-Aubert (R.)	AY	36
St-Géry (R.)	AY	37
St-Ladre (R.)	BZ	39
St-Martin (Mail)	AZ	40
St-Sépulcre (Pl.)	AZ	41
Selles (R. de)	AY	43
Vaucelette (R.)	AZ	45
Victoire (Av. de la)	AZ	46
Watteau (R.)	BZ	47
9-Octobre (Pl. du)	AY	48

Château de la Motte Fénelon rm, VISA AE
square du Château, via allée St Roch - north of the map BY – 03 27 83 61 38 – contact@cambrai-chateau-motte-fenelon.com – Fax 03 27 83 71 61
10 rm – €90/260 €90/260, €10 – ½ P €120/150 – **Rest** – Menu €24 bi (weekday lunch), €26/40 – Carte €23/45
◆ This château, built by Hittorff in 1850, has green surroundings and houses rooms with character, adorned by period or limed furniture. Century-old brick vaults, tasteful decor and traditional menu are the characteristics of this restaurant.

Orangerie Parc VISA AE
30 rm – €59/103 €59/103, €10 – ½ P €89/130
◆ The orangery offers comfortable accommodation just a few steps from the castle. Simpler service in the bungalows set in an 8-ha park.

Beatus rest, VISA AE
718 av. de Paris, via ⑤ : 1,5 km – 03 27 81 45 70 – hotel.beatus@wanadoo.fr – Fax 03 27 78 00 83
33 rm – €65/69 €77/82, €9,50 – **Rest** – *(closed August, 24 December-4 January and week-ends) (dinner only) (resident only)* Menu €19 – Carte €25/54
◆ Shaded by tall trees, a white building whose superb staircase leads up to spacious modern or classical style bedrooms, all of which are different. Snug lounge-bar.

Le Clos St-Jacques VISA
9 r. St-Jacques – 03 27 74 37 61 – rquero@wanadoo.fr – Fax 03 27 74 37 61 – Closed 21 December-4 January BY **e**
6 rm – €65 €72, €8,50 – **Table d'hôte** – *(closed Friday, Saturday and Sunday)* Menu €22
◆ Monsieur happily relates the history of this lovely mansion that Madame has superbly redecorated whilst respecting its original character. Delicious breakfasts, charming welcome.

L'Escargot VISA AE
10 r. Gén.-de-Gaulle – 03 27 81 24 54 – restaurantlescargot@wanadoo.fr – Fax 03 27 83 95 21 – Closed 15-31 July, 21-26 December, Friday dinner and Wednesday BZ **n**
Rest – Menu €23/38 – Carte €30/47
◆ A discreet restaurant in the centre of this town famous for its sweets. Rustic dining rooms, including a mezzanine, serving traditional cuisine in an informal atmosphere.

Au Fil de l'Eau VISA AE
1 bd Dupleix – 03 27 74 65 31 – Fax 03 27 74 65 31 – Closed 15 July-14 August, 19-26 February, Sunday dinner, Wednesday dinner and Monday AY **f**
Rest – Menu €22/47 – Carte €27/43
◆ Pleasant little restaurant near a lock on the St Quentin Canal. Fresh and colourful dining room with tasty traditional cuisine and seafood.

Bapaume road **4 km by ⑥ – ✉ 59400 Fontaine-Notre-Dame**

Auberge Fontenoise VISA AE
543 rte de Bapaume – 03 27 37 71 24 – auberge.fontenoise@wanadoo.fr – Fax 03 27 70 34 91 – Closed Sunday dinner and Monday dinner
Rest – Menu €24/44 – Carte €38/52
◆ This discreet family inn has a rustic dining room where diners savour appetising regional food masterfully prepared with quality produce.

CAMBREMER – 14 Calvados – 303 M5 – pop. 1 092 – alt. 100 m – ✉ 14340

33 **C2**

Paris 211 – Caen 38 – Deauville 28 – Falaise 38 – Lisieux 15 – Saint-Lô 110
Syndicat d'initiative, rue Pasteur 02 31 63 08 87, Fax 02 31 63 08 21

Château Les Bruyères rm, rest, VISA AE
Cadran road (D 85) – 02 31 32 22 45 – reception@chateaulesbruyeres.com – Fax 02 31 32 22 58 – Closed 3 January-2 February
13 rm – €95 €150/220, €22 – 1 suite – ½ P €135/170 – **Rest** – *(closed Monday and Tuesday off season) (dinner only)* Menu €39/75 – Carte €52/93
◆ This noble establishment is set in a wooded park. An elegant bourgeois dining room and attractive personalised rooms for a peaceful stay. Seasonal market surf and turf dishes with savoury herbs and vegetable garden produce.

CAMIERS – 62 Pas-de-Calais – 301 C4 – pop. 2 252 – alt. 23 m – ✉ 62176 30 A2

Paris 244 – Arras 101 – Boulogne-sur-Mer 21 – Calais 58 – Le Touquet 10

Office de tourisme, esplanade Ste-Cécile-Plage ✆ 03 21 84 72 18, Fax 03 21 84 72 18

Les Cèdres

64 r. Vieux-Moulin – ✆ 03 21 84 94 54 – hotel-cedres@wanadoo.fr – Fax 03 21 09 23 29 – Closed December and January

27 rm – €55/88 €55/88, €8 – ½ P €58/70

Rest *L'Orangeraie* – *(dinner only)* Menu €24/40

◆ Two town-centre houses separated by a pleasant terrace courtyard. Modest but well-kept rooms, livened up by bright colours. Charming lounge-library. A veranda-dining room opening onto a summer terrace. Traditional and regional cuisine.

CAMON – 09 Ariège – 343 J6 – pop. 144 – alt. 349 m – ✉ 09500

Languedoc-Roussillon-Tarn Gorges 29 C3

Paris 780 – Carcassonne 63 – Pamiers 37 – Toulouse 103

Office de tourisme, 10, rue Georges d'Armagnac ✆ 05 61 68 88 26, Fax 05 61 68 88 26

L'Abbaye-Château de Camon

– ✆ 05 61 60 31 23 – peter.katielawton@wanadoo.fr – Fax 05 61 60 31 23 – Closed 2 January-15 March – **6 rm** – €100/160 €120/180, €18 – **Table d'hôte** – *(closed Wednesday)* Menu €38

◆ Time seems to have stopped in this enchanting location where the garden offers many secluded spots. The personalised rooms are in former monks' cells. In the evening you can return to the cloister where nice, regional dishes await you.

CAMPAGNE – 24 Dordogne – 329 G6 – see le Bugue

CAMPIGNY – 27 Eure – 304 D6 – see Pont-Audemer

LE CAMP-LAURENT – 83 Var – 340 K7 – see Toulon

CANAPVILLE – 14 Calvados – 303 M4 – see Deauville

CANCALE – 35 Ille-et-Vilaine – 309 K2 – pop. 5 203 – alt. 50 m – ✉ 35260 Brittany

Paris 398 – Avranches 61 – Dinan 35 – Fougères 73 – St-Malo 16 10 D1

Office de tourisme, 44, rue du Port ✆ 02 99 89 63 72, Fax 02 99 89 75 08

Site★ - Port de la Houle★ - ※★ from St-Méen church tower - Pointe du Hock and sentier des Douaniers ≤★.

Pointe du Grouin★★.

Plan on next page

De Bricourt-Richeux

≤ Mont - St - Michel bay,

Mont-St_Michel road: 6.5 km via D76, D155 and minor road – ✆ 02 99 89 64 76 – bricourt@relaischateaux.com – Fax 02 99 89 88 47

11 rm – €165/310 €165/310, €21 – 2 suites

Rest *Maisons de Bricourt* – see restaurant listing

Rest *Le Coquillage* – ✆ *02 99 89 25 25 (closed January, Friday lunch off season, Monday and Tuesday)* Menu €29/58

◆ This superb 1922 villa, where Léon Blum once stayed, is in a park (aromatic plants and livestock) overlooking the Bay of Mont St Michel. Extremely refined rooms. Faultless welcome. Tasty seafood served in a panoramic dining room. Heavenly summer terrace under the pine trees.

Le Continental

quai Thomas – ✆ 02 99 89 60 16 – hotel-conti@wanadoo.fr – Fax 02 99 89 69 58 – Closed 5 January-5 February Z s

16 rm – €48/88 €70/148, €12,50 – ½ P €79/109

Rest – *(closed Wednesday except dinner June-September and Tuesday)* Menu €17 (weekday lunch), €23/42 – Carte €21/50

◆ Exceptionally located opposite the quaint little fishing port. Comfortable bedrooms decorated in pastel shades. A pleasant welcome. Beautiful wainscoting hung with seascapes in a dining room with veranda. View of the fishing fleet.

CANCALE

Bricourt (Pl.) . . . . Y 3
Calvaire (Pl. du) . . . . Z 4
Duguay-Trouin (Quai). . . . . Z 9
Duquesne (R.) . . . . Y 10
Du-Guesclin (R.) . . . . Y 8
Fenêtre (Jetée de la) . . . . Z 12
Gallais (R.) . . . . Y 13
Gambetta (Quai) . . . . Z 14
Hock (R. du) . . . . Z 16
Jacques-Cartier (Quai). . . . . . . Z 17
Juin (R. du Mar.) . . . . Z 18
Kennedy (Quai) . . . . Z 19
Leclerc (R. Gén.) . . . . YZ 20
Mennais (R. de la) . . . . Y 22
Port (R. du) . . . . Z
République (Pl. de la). . . . . Z 23
Rimains (R. des) . . . . Y 24
Roulette (R. de la) . . . . Z 25
Stade (R. du) . . . . Y 27
Surcouf (R.) . . . . Y 28
Thomas (Quai) . . . . Z 30

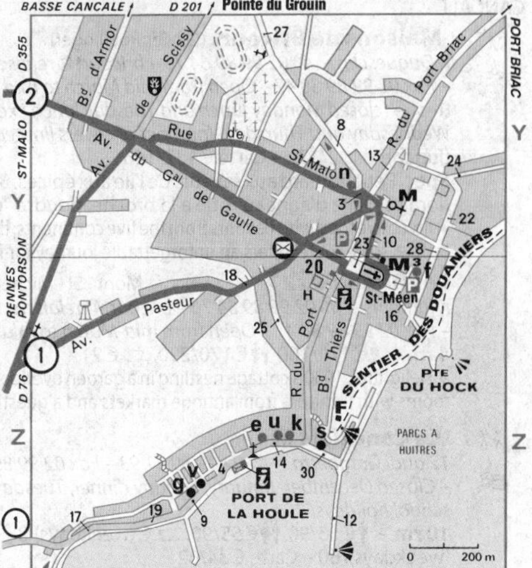

Le Querrien — rest, VISA

7 quai Duguay-Trouin – ✆ 02 99 89 64 56 – le-querrien@wanadoo.fr – Fax 02 99 89 79 35 Z v

15 rm – †€ 59/79 ††€ 59/79, ☕ € 9 – ½ P € 55/99 – **Rest** – Menu € 16,50/28 – Carte € 23/58

◆ Breton House with a wooden veranda on the quayside. The spacious rooms, all named after ships, are decorated in the colours of the sea. Nine overlook the waves. A restaurant that pays homage to the ocean in its menu and decor (fish tank, wainscoting and fresco).

Auberge de la Motte Jean without rest — VISA

via ②: 2 km on D 355 – ✆ 02 99 89 41 99 – hotel-pointe-du-grouin@wanadoo.fr – Fax 02 99 89 92 22 – Closed January and February

13 rm – †€ 65/78 ††€ 75/88, ☕ € 7

◆ The main building of a former farm lost in the Cancale countryside. Very quiet, well-cared-for garden with a pond. Rooms with personal touches and antique furniture. Personalised service.

Duguay Trouin without rest — VISA

11 quai Duguay-Trouin – ✆ 02 23 15 12 07 – leduguaytrouin1@aol.com – Fax 02 99 89 75 20 Z g

7 rm – †€ 75/85 ††€ 85/125, ☕ € 9

◆ Guests are received simply and cordially in this fully renovated hotel in a fishing port. A low-key nautical theme in the rooms (sea chests) overlooking the bay or the cliffs.

Le Chatellier without rest — VISA

1 km via ② on D 355 – ✆ 02 99 89 81 84 – hotelchatel@aol.com – Fax 02 99 89 61 69 – Closed December and January

13 rm – †€ 50/55 ††€ 60/82, ☕ € 8,50

◆ Lovely traditional Breton house whose homely charm continues to prevail. Country chic rooms under the eaves upstairs. Some overlook the garden.

Le Manoir des Douets Fleuris without rest — VISA

by ②: 1.5 km by D 365 – ✆ 02 23 15 13 81 – manoirdesdouetsfleuris@wanadoo.fr – Fax 02 23 15 13 81 – Closed January

5 rm – †€ 79/90 ††€ 79/130, ☕ € 12

◆ A 17C manor and garden. The bedrooms are individually decorated, and one sports a canopied bed and granite fireplace. Monumental hearth in the lounge.

XXX **Maisons de Bricourt** (Olivier Roellinger) P VISA MC AE D

r. Duguesclin – 02 99 89 64 76 – bricourt@relaischateaux.com – Fax 02 99 89 88 47 – Open from mid March to mid December Y n

Rest – (closed Monday lunch and Tuesday lunch except from May to September, Wednesday and Thursday) (number of covers limited, pre-book) Menu € 100 (lunch), € 122/172 – Carte € 132/146

Spec. Petit homard aux saveurs de l'île aux épices. Bar en cuisson douce aux huiles florales. Selle d'agneau rôtie à la broche, poudre "grande caravane".

◆ Inventive food with flavours from the five continents: this delicious 18C Saint Malo house on the 'spice route' offers an unforgettable journey for food lovers.

Les Rimains < Mont-St-Michel bay, P VISA MC AE D

r. Rimains – 02 99 89 64 76 – bricourt@relaischateaux.com – Fax 02 99 89 88 47 – Open from mid-March to mid-December

4 rm – €170/180 €170/290, € 21

◆ Delightful; 1930's cottage nestling in a garden overlooking the sea. Tastefully decorated rooms with furniture from antique markets and a guesthouse atmosphere.

XX **Le Cancalais** with rm < AC rest, rm, VISA MC

12 quai Gambetta – 02 99 89 61 93 – Fax 02 99 89 89 24 – Closed December-January, Sunday dinner, Tuesday lunch and Monday except school holidays Z u

10 rm – €55/90 €55/90, € (weekdays) 8 – **Rest** – Menu € 18 (weekdays)/60 – Carte € 34/62

◆ This Cancale institution serves a half-classic and half-seafood menu. It has a rustic interior of Breton inspiration and a panoramic veranda. Attractive rooms.

X **Surcouf** < VISA MC

7 quai Gambetta – 02 99 89 61 75 – Fax 02 99 89 76 41 – Closed December, January, Wednesday except July-August and Tuesday Z k

Rest – Menu € 16 (weekdays)/42 – Carte € 44/60

◆ This spruce nautical bistro stands out from the others lining the port of Cancal. Find a view of the jetty (even better upstairs) and delicious seafood cuisine.

X **Le Troquet** < VISA MC

19 quai Gambetta – 02 99 89 99 42 – Closed 12 November-31 January, Thursday and Friday Z e

Rest – Menu € 18 (weekdays)/38 – Carte € 31/55

◆ A pleasant little bistro, well worth tracking down amidst all the others along the quayside. Fish and seafood take pride of place, including the renowned Cancale oysters.

X **La Maison de la Marine** with rm rest, VISA MC

23 r. Marine – 02 99 89 88 53 – courrier@maisondelamarine.com – Fax 02 99 89 83 27 – Closed February holidays Z f

5 rm – €80/90 €90/110, € 12 – 3 suites – **Rest** – (closed Sunday dinner and Monday off season) Menu € 32/54 – Carte € 47/59

◆ A superbly converted former shipping office: intimate buccaneering-inspired decor, terrace facing the garden, sitting room with British accents. The menu mixes Breton and Mediterranean cuisine. Well-worn antiques and luxurious fixtures and fittings make the bedrooms irresistible.

at Pointe du Grouin ★★ 4.5 km north by D 201 – ✉ 35260 Cancale

La Pointe du Grouin

< islands and bay of Mont-St-Michel, rest, P VISA MC

02 99 89 60 55 – hotel-pointe-du-grouin@wanadoo.fr – Fax 02 99 89 92 22 – Open 25 March-15 November

16 rm – €85 €115, € 8 – ½ P € 83/95 – **Rest** – (closed Thursday lunch except 15 July-31 August and Tuesday) Menu € 23/75 – Carte € 37/61

◆ A marvellous windswept location for this cliff top Breton house with a magnificent view of the islands and Mont St Michel. Countrified, well-equipped rooms. Reserve a table by the windows and enjoy an exceptional view of the open sea.

CANCON – **47 Lot-et-Garonne** – **336** F2 – **pop. 1 287** – **alt. 199 m** – ✉ **47290** 4 **C2**

Paris 581 – Agen 51 – Bergerac 40 – Bordeaux 134

Syndicat d'initiative, place de la Halle 05 53 01 09 89, Fax 05 53 01 64 70

in St-Eutrope-de-Born 9 km Northeast by D 124, D 153 – pop. 609 – alt. 95 m – ✉ 47210

Domaine du Moulin de Labique
Villeréal road – ✆ 05 53 01 63 90 – moulin-de-labique@wanadoo.fr – Fax 05 53 01 73 17 – Closed 17-23 November
6 rm – €75 €90, ☕ €10 – ½ P €83 – **Table d'hôte** – Menu €25/31
◆ A brook runs alongside this large estate where ponies are bred. The rooms, set in the former stables, the barn or the main house, are tastefully decorated. Family food and homemade foie gras is served.

CANDES-ST-MARTIN – 37 Indre-et-Loire – 317 J5 – pop. 227 – alt. 35 m – ✉ 37500 Châteaux of the Loire 11 A2

Paris 290 – Angers 76 – Chinon 16 – Saumur 13 – Tours 54
Collegiate church ★.

Auberge de la Route d'Or
2 pl. de l'Église – ✆ 02 47 95 81 10 – routedor@clubinternet.fr – Fax 02 47 95 81 10 – Open 22 March-10 November, closed Tuesday except lunch July-August and Wednesday
Rest – *(number of covers limited, pre-book)* Menu €17 (weekday lunch), €23/35 – Carte €33/45
◆ A rustic inn located in two old houses, one of which dates from the 17C. Cosy dining room with a fireplace. Regionally inspired, classic cuisine.

CANDÉ-SUR-BEUVRON – 41 Loir-et-Cher – 318 E7 – pop. 1 208 – alt. 70 m – ✉ 41120 11 A1

Paris 199 – Blois 15 – Chaumont-sur-Loire 7 – Montrichard 21 – Orléans 78 – Tours 51
Syndicat d'initiative, 10, route de Blois ✆ 02 54 44 00 44, Fax 02 54 44 00 44

La Caillère
36 rte de Montils – ✆ 02 54 44 03 08 – lacaillere2@wanadoo.fr – Fax 02 54 44 00 95 – Closed January and February
14 rm – €60 €65, ☕ €11 – ½ P €66 – **Rest** – *(closed Monday lunch, Thursday lunch and Wednesday)* Menu (€20), €30/46 – Carte €50/60
◆ Old farmhouse, extended by a modern wing and separated from the road by a curtain of greenery. Plain, well kept rooms. A pleasant dining room which has kept its country atmosphere. Modern, seasonal cuisine and tables decorated with old soup tureens.

Auberge du Lion d'Or with rm
1 rte de Blois – ✆ 02 54 44 04 66 – joel.doublet41@orange.fr – Fax 02 54 44 06 19 – Closed 1st January-11 February, Monday and Tuesday
8 rm – €35/46 €35/46, ☕ €6,50 – ½ P €39/58 – **Rest** – Menu €17 (weekday)/46 – Carte €38/54
◆ A rustic atmosphere at this village inn. Find a shaded terrace where traditional, home-made food is served depending on the choice at the market. Simple rooms.

LE CANET – 13 Bouches-du-Rhône – 340 I5 – see Aix-en-Provence

CANET-EN-ROUSSILLON – 66 Pyrénées-Orientales – 344 J6 – pop. 10 182 – alt. 11 m – Casino BZ – ✉ 66140 22 B3

Paris 849 – Argelès-sur-Mer 21 – Narbonne 66 – Perpignan 11
Office de tourisme, espace Méditerranée ✆ 04 68 86 72 00, Fax 04 68 86 72 12

Plan on next page

in Canet-Plage – ✉ 66140

Les Flamants Roses
1 voie des Flamants-Roses – ✆ 04 68 51 60 60 – contact@hotel-flamants-roses.com – Fax 04 68 51 60 61
59 rm – €140/225 €170/270, ☕ €18 – 4 suites – ½ P €120/180
Rest *L'Horizon* – health-conscious cuisine *(closed Monday lunch and Tuesday lunch)* Menu €29 (weekday lunch), €44/62
Rest *Le Canotier* – buffet *(lunch only)* Menu €29 bi
◆ A modern establishment joined to a thalassotherapy centre situated next to the beach. The rooms, mostly opening onto the sea, are warm and welcoming. Modern and "light" food is served at this restaurant overlooking the sea. Brasserie-type food is served at Le Canotier.

CANET-PLAGE

Street	Grid	No.
Aigues Marines (R. des)	BZ	2
Albères (R. des)	BY	5
Amandiers (R. des)	BY	6
Anémones (Bd des)	AYZ	7
Balcons du Front de Mer (Av. des)	BZ	8
Bourgogne-Morvan (R.)	BZ	9
Capcir (Galerie du)	BY	12
Cassanyes (Galerie)	BY	14
Catalogne (Av. de la)	BY	15
Cerdagne (R. de)	BY	18
Cerisiers (R. des)	BY	20
Champagne (R. de)	BZ	22
Coquillages (R. des)	BZ	25
Corbières (R. des)	BY	28
Grande-Bretagne (R. de)	BYZ	29
Gratia (Av. Edmond)	BZ	30
Île-de-France (R.)	BZ	32
Jouy d'Arnaud (R.)	BY	33
Pountarrou (Av. du)	AY	34
Pyrénées (R. des)	BY	35
Sardane (R. de la)	ABY	36

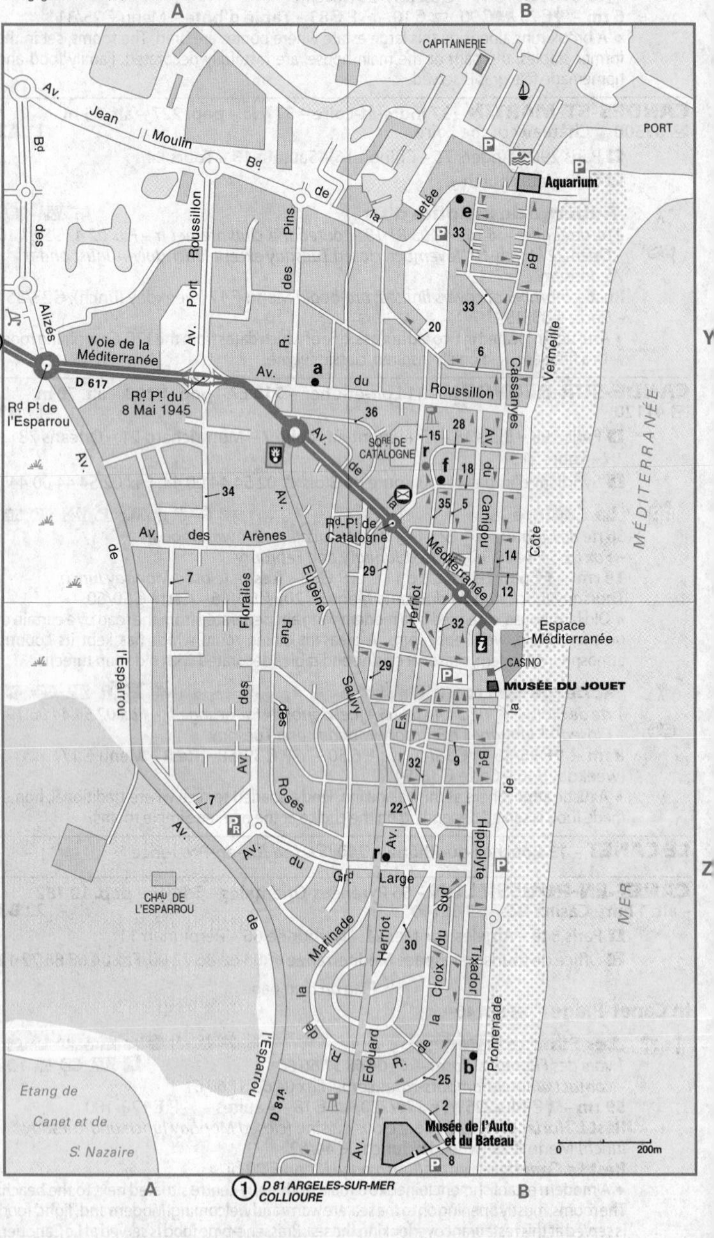

Le Mas de la Plage rm, VISA
34 av. Roussillon – ✆ 04 68 80 32 63 – contact@closdespins.com – Fax 04 68 80 49 19 – Open 2 April-30 October AY **a**
16 rm – †€ 85/120 ††€ 95/150, ☐ € 7,50 – 1 suite – ½ P € 80/95
Rest – *(dinner only) (resident only)* Menu € 35
◆ Surrounded by pine trees and ancient parkland, this charming 19C Catalan villa offers comfortable rooms painted in sunny southern shades. Lovely Mediterranean garden.

Mercure without rest < sea, VISA
120 prom. de la Côte-Vermeille – ✆ 04 68 80 28 59 – h3590@accor.com – Fax 04 68 80 80 60 BZ **b**
48 rm – †€ 89/119 ††€ 99/129, ☐ € 10
◆ Right on the seashore, this hotel offers contemporary rooms (king size beds), half of which face the sea and have balconies. Buffet breakfast.

Le Galion VISA
20 bis av. Grand-large – ✆ 04 68 80 28 23 – contact@hotel-le-galion.com – Fax 04 68 80 20 46 – Closed Sun. evening and Mon. lunch from 20 Oct. - 15 Mar. BZ **r**
28 rm – †€ 55/80 ††€ 62/128, ☐ € 10 – ½ P € 62/95 – **Rest** – *(closed Sun. evening and Mon. lunch from 20 Oct. - 15 Mar.)* Menu (€ 18), € 26/30 – Carte € 31/45
◆ This galleon is situated some 150m from the waves. Family-run establishment; most of the progressively refurbished rooms have a balcony. The restaurant opens onto the swimming pool and terrace (barbecues in summertime). Regional specialities.

Du Port rm, rest, VISA
21 bd de la Jetée – ✆ 04 68 80 62 44 – info@hotel-du-port.net – Fax 04 68 73 28 83 – Hotel: open May-October; restaurant: open June-September BY **e**
35 rm (½ board only) – ½ P € 50/70 – **Rest** – *(dinner only) (resident only)*
◆ A 1980s building, half-way between the harbour and beach. Enjoy the calm and comfort of its simple bedrooms, all with balconies. The dining room has been refurbished in a nautical style. Traditional unpretentious cuisine.

La Frégate without rest VISA
12 r. Cerdagne – ✆ 04 68 80 22 87 – contact@hotel-lafregate.fr – Fax 04 68 73 82 72 – Closed 3 January-25 March BY **f**
26 rm – †€ 50/82 ††€ 50/86, ☐ € 7,50
◆ Situated 100m from the beach, this hotel has small bedrooms, all with pleasant regional-style rustic furniture. Excellent soundproofing and faultless upkeep.

XX **Le Don Quichotte** VISA
22 av. de Catalogne – ✆ 04 68 80 35 17 – ledonquichotte@wanadoo.fr – Closed mid January-mid February, Monday and Tuesday except public holidays BY **r**
Rest – Menu € 20 (weekday lunch)/45 – Carte € 38/58
◆ The proprietor of this friendly restaurant supports the local wine growers by offering a fine choice of their production to accompany his semi-traditional, semi-regional menu.

CANGEY – 37 Indre-et-Loire – 317 P4 – pop. 773 – alt. 85 m – ✉ 37530 11 A1

Paris 210 – Amboise 12 – Blois 28 – Montrichard 26 – Tours 35
de Fleuray Route de Dame-Marie-les-Bois, North: 8 km by D 74, ✆ 02 47 56 07 07.

Le Fleuray VISA
7 km north, on D 74 Dame-Marie-les-Bois road – ✆ 02 47 56 09 25 – lefleurayhotel@wanadoo.fr – Fax 02 47 56 93 97 – Closed 5-11 November and 19 December-7 January
18 rm – †€ 78/124 ††€ 78/124, ☐ € 13 – ½ P € 81/114 – **Rest** – *(closed Monday dinner from November to February) (dinner only) (number of covers limited, pre-book)* Menu € 29/48 – Carte € 43/67
◆ This old restored farm has a great deal of charm. It has exquisitely decorated snug rooms, a garden planted with fruit trees, and a swimming pool. Updated traditional cuisine served in a well-lit country chic dining room or on a pretty summer terrace.

CANNES – 06 Alpes-Maritimes – **341** D6 – **pop. 67 304 – alt. 2 m – Casinos : Palm Beach** X, **Croisette** BZ – ✉ **06400** **French Riviera** 42 **E2**

Paris 898 – Aix-en-Provence 149 – Marseille 160 – Nice 33 – Toulon 120

Office de tourisme, 1, boulevard de La Croisette ✆ 04 92 99 84 22, Fax 04 92 99 84 23

Riviera Golf Club Mandelieu Avenue des Amazones, by la Napoule road: 8 km, ✆ 04 92 97 49 49 ;

de Cannes Mougins Mougins 175 avenue du Golf, Northwest: 9 km, ✆ 04 93 75 79 13 ;

Royal Mougins Golf Club Mougins 424 avenue du Roi, by Grasse road: 10 km, ✆ 04 92 92 49 69.

Site★★ - Seafront★★: boulevard★★ and pointe★ de la croisette - ≤★ from the tour du Mont-Chevalier AZ - Musée de la Castre★★ AZ - Chemin des Collines★ Northeast: 4 km V - La Croix des Gardes X ≤★ West: 5 km then 15 mn.

Plans on following pages

Carlton InterContinental

rm, rest,

58 bd de la Croisette – ✆ 04 93 06 40 06 – carlton@hotelsgroupe.com – Fax 04 93 06 40 25 CZ **e**

338 rm – €160/1010 €160/1010, €35 – 36 suites

Rest *Brasserie Carlton* – Menu €43/55 – Carte €63/101

Rest *La Plage* – rest. de plage – ✆ *04 93 06 44 94 (open 16 March-14 October) (lunch only)* Carte €55/88

◆ Hitchcock filmed scenes from the film To Catch a Thief in this famous hotel with its twin cupolas. Luxurious Belle Epoque interior, superb suites and an interesting history. Elegant decor, seasonal cuisine and a view of the Croisette at the Brasserie Carlton.

Martinez

rm,

73 bd de la Croisette – ✆ 04 92 98 73 00 – martinez@concorde-hotels.com – Fax 04 93 39 67 82 DZ **n**

396 rm – €285/2900 €285/2900, €34 – 16 suites

Rest *La Palme d'Or* – see restaurant listing

Rest *Relais Martinez* – ✆ *04 92 98 74 12* – Carte €48/94

Rest *Z. Plage* – beach rest. – ✆ *04 92 98 74 22 (open May-September) (lunch only)* Carte €50/118

◆ Popular with the stars at festival time; Art Deco or contemporary style rooms, sumptuous suites, modern facilities, Givenchy spa and superb fitness centre. A smart, relaxed atmosphere, gourmet cuisine and summer terrace at the Relais Martinez.

Majestic Barrière

rm,

10 bd de la Croisette – ✆ 04 92 98 77 00 – majestic@lucienbarriere.com – Fax 04 93 38 97 90 – Closed mid November-end December BZ **n**

282 rm – €225/530 €500/970, €34 – 23 suites

Rest *La Villa des Lys* – *(closed for refurbishment)*

Rest *Fouquet's* – brasserie – ✆ *04 92 98 77 05* – Menu €50 (lunch) – Carte €52/106

Rest *B. Sud* – beach rest. – ✆ *04 92 98 77 30 (open June to September) (lunch only)* Carte €48/84

◆ The immaculate majestic façade dates from the Twenties. Luxury and refinement on all floors. The best rooms look onto the sea. Well-lit and inviting dining room/veranda overlooking the Croisette: take your time and bask in the sun!

Sofitel Le Méditerranée

1 bd J.-Hibert – ✆ 04 92 99 73 00 – h0591-re@accor.com – Fax 04 92 99 73 29 AZ **n**

149 rm – €165/370 €165/750, €25 – 6 suites

Rest *Le Méditerranée* – on 7rd floor, ✆ *04 92 99 73 02* – Menu €42, €52/72 – Carte €69/88

Rest *Chez Panisse* – bistrot – ✆ *04 92 99 73 10* – Menu (€20 bi), €29 bi/27 bi – Carte €36/51

◆ A 1930s hotel, attractively decorated in Provençal style. Most of the rooms and the rooftop swimming pool enjoy a splendid view of Cannes and the bay. New seminar area. A superb panoramic view from the Méditerranée. Chez Panisse, Provence is omnipresent.

3.14 Hôtel
5 r. F.-Einesy – ✆ 04 92 99 72 00 – info@3-14hotel.com – Fax 04 92 99 72 12
80 rm – €150/880 €150/880, ☕ €25 – 15 suites – **Rest** – *(closed Sunday and Monday) (dinner only)* Menu €42 – Carte approx. €52 CZ **u**
◆ Striking multi-ethnic ambiance in this superb hotel, where the decor of the rooms, the music and the fragrances evoke all 5 continents. Lovely rooftop pool. The restaurant takes us on a tour of the world's food; enriched with spices.

Gray d'Albion rm,
38 r. des Serbes – ✆ 04 92 99 79 79 – graydalbion@lucienbarriere.com – Fax 04 93 99 26 10 – Closed 12-28 December BZ **d**
191 rm – €170/970 €170/970, ☕ €22 – 8 suites
Rest *38* – *✆ 04 92 99 79 60 (Closed Sunday and Monday)* Menu €38 bi – Carte €40/60
◆ This 1970s building has a shopping arcade and progressively renovated practical accommodation. Private beach on the Croisette. A minimalist but welcoming decor and updated cuisine.

Le Grand Hôtel rest,
45 bd de la Croisette – ✆ 04 93 38 15 45 – info@grand-hotel-cannes.com – Fax 04 93 68 97 45 – Closed 9-28 December CZ **s**
74 rm – €200/460 €200/460, ☕ €28 – 2 suites
Rest – Menu €40/55
Rest *La Plage* – beach rest. – *✆ 04 93 38 19 57 (open 9 April-7 October) (lunch only)* Carte €36/83
◆ A mixture of 1970s and contemporary interior design lend this building next-door to Malmaison an unusual but well cared for air. Pretty view of the sea. Find traditional cuisine with a regional slant at the Pré Carré. Summer fare at La Plage.

Novotel Montfleury rm, rest,
25 av. Beauséjour – ✆ 04 93 68 86 86 – h0806@accor.com – Fax 04 93 68 87 87 DY **m**
182 rm – €135/220 €135/220, ☕ €20 – 1 suite
Rest *L'Olivier* – Menu (€18 bi), €23 (weekday lunch) – Carte €31/45
◆ On the edge of the Californie district with its luxurious villas, this hotel has comfortable rooms in nautical or Provençal style. An attractive swimming pool and terrace in the shade of palm trees. Pleasant sunny decor, view of the kitchens and Mediterranean style menu at the Olivier.

Croisette Beach without rest
13 r. du Canada – ✆ 04 92 18 88 00 – H1284@accor.com – Fax 04 93 68 35 38 – Closed 8-28 December DZ **y**
94 rm – €114/635 €114/790, ☕ €20
◆ Generally spacious rooms (mostly with terrace); those on the fifth and sixth floors are the freshest. New private beach on the Croisette.

Sun Riviera without rest
138 r. d'Antibes – ✆ 04 93 06 77 77 – info@sun-riviera.com – Fax 04 93 38 31 10 – Closed 5-27 December and 1st-21 February CZ **h**
40 rm – €98/165 €132/265, ☕ €16 – 2 suites
◆ On a street lined with luxury boutiques, this hotel boasts large, stylish and well-equipped rooms; those overlooking the garden are quieter and have a balcony.

Eden Hôtel
133 r. d'Antibes – ✆ 04 93 68 78 00 – reception@eden-hotel-cannes.com – Fax 04 93 68 78 01 – Closed 10-28 December DZ **d**
116 rm – €125/280 €125/280, ☕ €20 – ½ P €98/183
Rest – *(closed Sunday and Monday)* Menu €29/45 (week-end) – Carte €32/49
◆ Ideal for shoppers: the hotel is in the prestigious Rue d'Antibes. The renovated rooms have parquet floors and contemporary furnishings.

Belle Plage without rest
6 r. J.-Dollfus – ✆ 04 93 06 25 50 – belleplage@wanadoo.fr – Fax 04 93 99 61 06 – Open 1st March-15 Nov. AZ **u**
48 rm – €120/250 €150/280, ☕ €14
◆ At the foot of the old town; film star photos hang in the rooms with balconies, around half of which overlook the sea. Roof terrace with small pool.

CANNES

Albert-Édouard (Jetée) . . . . BZ
Alexandre-III (Bd) . . . . X 2
Alsace (Bd) . . . . BDY
Anc.-Combattants-d'Afrique-du-Nord (Av.) . . . . AYZ 4
André (R. du Cdt) . . . . CZ
Antibes (R. d') . . . . BCY
Bachaga-Saïd-Boualam (Av.) . . . AY 5
Beauséjour (Av.) . . . . DYZ
Beau-Soleil (Bd) . . . . X 10
Belges (R. des) . . . . BZ 12
Blanc (R. Louis) . . . . AYZ
Broussailles (Av. des) . . . . V 16
Buttura (R.) . . . . BZ 17
Canada (R. du) . . . . DZ
Carnot (Bd) X
Carnot (Square) . . . . V 20
Castre (Pl. de la) . . . . AZ 21
Chabaud (R.) . . . . CY 22
Clemenceau (R. G.) . . . . AZ
Coteaux (Av. des) V
Croisette (Bd de la) . . . . BDZ
Croix-des-Gardes (Bd) . . . . . . VX 29
Delaup (Bd) . . . . AY 30
Dr-Pierre Gazagnaire (R.) . . . . AZ 32
Dr-R. Picaud (Av.) X
Dollfus (R. Jean) . . . . AZ 33
États-Unis (R. des) . . . . CZ 35
Favorite (Av. de la) . . . . X 38
Félix-Faure (R.) . . . . ABZ
Ferrage (Bd de la) . . . . ABY 40
Fiesole (Av.) . . . . X 43
Foch (R. du Mar.) . . . . BY 44
Gallieni (R. du Mar.) . . . . BY 48
Gaulle (Pl. Gén.-de) . . . . BZ 51
Gazagnaire (Bd Eugène) X
Grasse (Av. de) . . . . VX 53
Guynemer (Bd) . . . . AY
Hespérides (Av. des) . . . . X 55
Hibert (Bd Jean) . . . . AZ
Hibert (R.) . . . . AZ
Isola-Bella (Av. d') X
Jean-Jaurès (R.) . . . . BCY
Joffre (R. du Mar.) . . . . BY 60
Juin (Av. Mar.) . . . . DZ
Koening (Av. Gén.) . . . . DY
Lacour (Bd Alexandre) . . . . X 62
Latour-Maubourg (R.) . . . . DZ
Lattre-de-Tassigny (Av. de) . . . . AY 63
Laubeuf (Quai Max) . . . . AZ
Leader (Bd) . . . . VX 64
Lérins (Av. de) . . . . X 65
Liberté-Charles de Gaulle (A. de la) . . . . AZ 70
Lorraine (Bd de) . . . . CDY
Macé (R.) . . . . CZ 66
Madrid (Av. de) . . . . DZ
Meynadier (R.) . . . . ABY
Midi (Bd du) X
Mimont (R. de) . . . . BY
Montfleury (Bd) . . . . CDY 74
Monti (R. Marius) . . . . AY 75
Mont-Chevalier (R. du) . . . . AZ 72
Noailles (Av. J.-de) X
Observatoire (Bd de l') . . . . X 84
Oxford (Bd d') . . . . V 87
Pantiero (La) . . . . ABZ
Paradis-Terrestre (Corniches du) V 88
Pasteur (R.) . . . . DZ
Pastour (R. Louis) . . . . AY 90
Perier (Bd du) . . . . V 91
Perrissol (R. Louis) . . . . AZ 92
Petit-Juas (Av. du) VX
Pins (Bd des) . . . . X 95
Pompidou (Espl. G.) . . . . BZ
Prince-de-Galles (Av. du) . . . . . . X 97
République (Bd de la) X
Riouffe (R. Jean de) . . . . BY 98
Riou (Bd du) VX
Roi-Albert 1er (Av.) X
Rouguière (R.) . . . . BY 100
St-Antoine (R.) . . . . AZ 102
St-Nicolas (Av.) . . . . BY 105
St-Pierre (Quai) . . . . AZ
Sardou (R. Léandre) . . . . X 108
Serbes (R. des) . . . . BZ 110
Source (Bd de la) . . . . X 112
Stanislas (Pl.) . . . . AY
Strasbourg (Bd de) . . . . CDY
Teisseire (R.) . . . . CY 114
Tuby (Bd Victor) . . . . AYZ 115
Vallauris (Av. de) . . . . VX 116
Vallombrosa (Bd) . . . . AY 118
Vautrin (Bd Gén.) . . . . DZ
Vidal (R. du Cdt) . . . . CY 120
Wemyss (Av. Amiral Wester) . . . X 122

LE CANNET

Aubarède (Ch. de l') . . . . V 8
Bellevue (Pl.) . . . . V 13
Bréguières (Rte des) . . . . V 14
Cannes (R. de) . . . . V 19
Carnot (Bd) V
Cheval (Av. Maurice) . . . . V 23
Collines (Ch. des) V
Doumer (Bd Paul) . . . . V 31
Écoles (Av. des) . . . . V 34
Four-à-Chaux (Bd du) . . . . V 45
Gambetta (Bd) . . . . V 50
Gaulle (Av. Gén.-de) V
Jeanpierre (Av. Maurice) . . . . . . V 58
Mermoz (Av. Jean) . . . . V 67
Monod (Bd Jacques) . . . . V 68
Mont-Joli (Av. du) . . . . V 73
N.-D.-des-Anges (Av.) . . . . V 79
Olivetum (Bd d') . . . . V 86
Olivet (Ch. de l') . . . . V 85
Paris (R. de) . . . . V 89
Pinède (Av. de la) . . . . V 94
Pompidou (Av. Georges) . . . . V 96
République (Bd de la) V
Roosevelt (Av. Franklin) . . . . V 99
St-Sauveur (R.) . . . . V 106
Victoria (Av.) V
Victor-Hugo (R.) . . . . V 119

VALLAURIS

Cannes (Av. de) . . . . V 18
Clemenceau (Av. G.) . . . . V 25
Golfe (Av. du) . . . . V 52
Isnard (Pl. Paul) . . . . V 56
Picasso (Av. Pablo) . . . . V 93
Rouvier (Bd Maurice) . . . . V 102
Tapis-Vert (Av. du) . . . . V 113

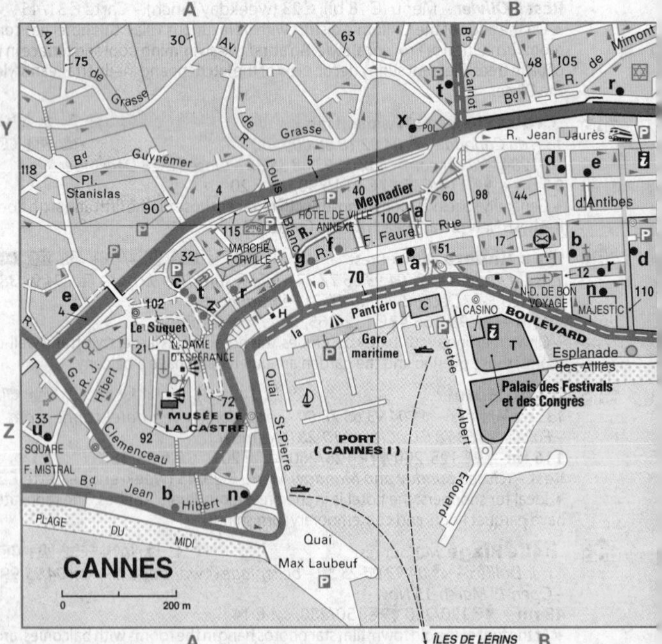

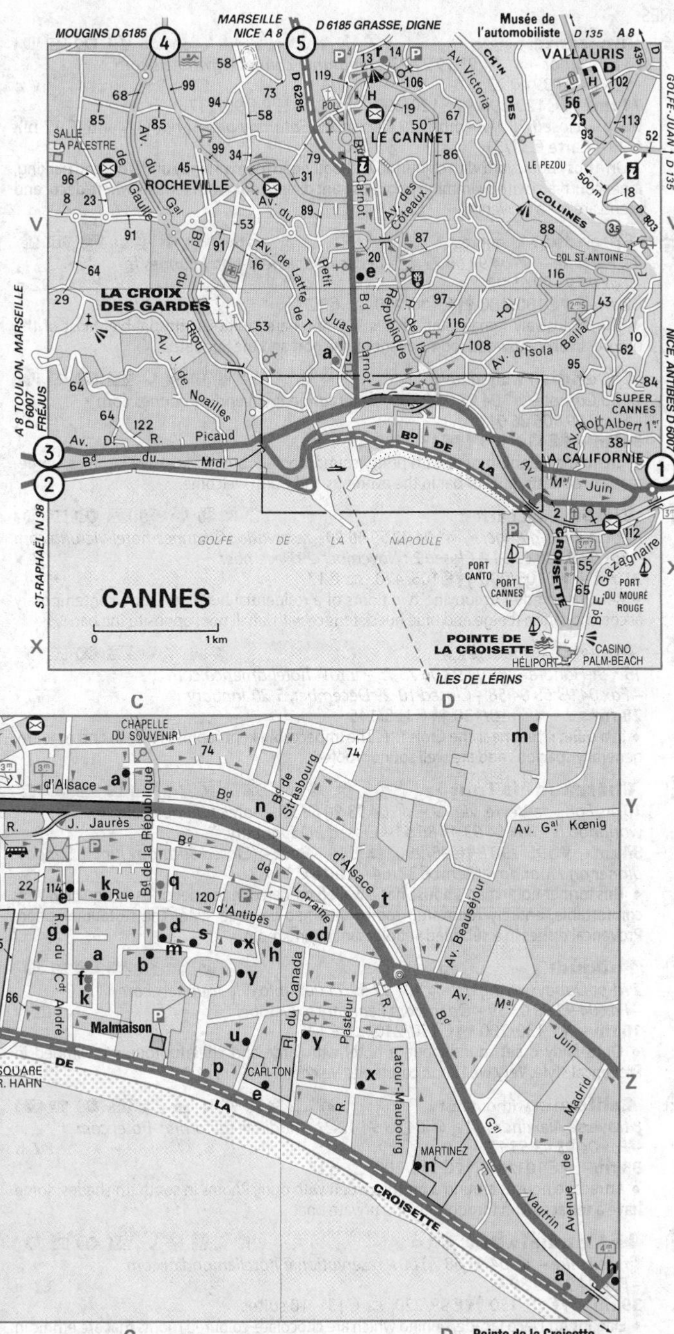
CANNES
LE CANNET
ROCHEVILLE
LA CROIX DES GARDES
VALLAURIS
LA CALIFORNIE
SUPER CANNES
GOLFE DE LA NAPOULE
POINTE DE LA CROISETTE
ÎLES DE LÉRINS
PORT CANTO
PORT CANNES II
PORT DU MOURÉ ROUGE
CASINO PALM-BEACH
HÉLIPORT
COL ST-ANTOINE
LE PEZOU
SALLE LA PALESTRE
MOUGINS D 6185
MARSEILLE NICE A 8
D 6185 GRASSE, DIGNE
Musée de l'automobiliste
D 135
A 8
GOLFE-JUAN D 135
NICE, ANTIBES D 6007
A 8 TOULON, MARSEILLE D 6007 FRÉJUS
ST-RAPHAËL N 98
CHAPELLE DU SOUVENIR
Malmaison
CARLTON
MARTINEZ
SQUARE R. HAHN
Bd de la Croisette
Pointe de la Croisette

Amarante
78 bd Carnot – ✆ 04 93 39 22 23 – amarante-cannes@jjwhotels.com – Fax 04 93 39 40 22 V **e**
71 rm – 🚹€ 120/390 🚹🚹€ 120/390, ☕ € 20 – ½ P € 90/237
Rest – *(closed 28 November-29 December, Saturday and Sunday)* Menu (€ 17 bi), € 35 – Carte € 31/51
◆ On a busy boulevard with colourful, well-equipped rooms. Handy underground parking; inner courtyard with swimming pool. Pleasant dining room with terrace, where decor and menu are both Provençal.

Splendid without rest ← the Port,
4 r. F.-Faure – ✆ 04 97 06 22 22 – accueil@splendid-hotel-cannes.fr – Fax 04 93 99 55 02 BZ **a**
62 rm – 🚹€ 100/180 🚹🚹€ 100/240, ☕ € 12
◆ The exclusively female staff of this 19C hotel are faultlessly hospitable. Most of the progressively renovated rooms overlook the port and the Suquet.

Cavendish without rest
11 bd Carnot – ✆ 04 97 06 26 00 – reservation@cavendish-cannes.com – Fax 04 97 06 26 01 BY **t**
34 rm – 🚹€ 110/160 🚹🚹€ 130/280, ☕ € 20
◆ Charming establishment with pretty soundproofed rooms, extensive facilities, home-made breakfasts, guests' bar in the evenings and warm welcome.

Victoria without rest
rd-pt Duboys-d'Angers – ✆ 04 92 59 40 00 – reservation@cannes-hotel-victoria.com – Fax 04 93 38 03 91 – Closed 23 November-29 December CZ **x**
25 rm – 🚹€ 105/290 🚹🚹€ 105/420, ☕ € 17
◆ Renovated hotel occupying two floors of a residential building. Light, contemporary accommodation (beige and blue hues); terrace with small pool opposite the bar.

America without rest
13 r. St-Honoré – ✆ 04 93 06 75 75 – info@hotel-america.com – Fax 04 93 68 04 58 – Closed 10-29 December, 5-20 January BZ **r**
28 rm ☕ – 🚹€ 110/130 🚹🚹€ 125/145
◆ In a quiet street near the Croisette. The impeccably-kept rooms are fresh and modern, generally spacious and are well soundproofed.

Château de la Tour
10 av. Font-de-Veyre, via ③ – ✆ 04 93 90 52 52 – hotelchateaulatour@wanadoo.fr – Fax 04 93 47 86 61 – Closed 2-25 January
34 rm – 🚹€ 95/290 🚹🚹€ 95/290, ☕ € 14 – **Rest** – *(Closed Saturday lunch, Sunday dinner and Monday)* Menu € 37/64 – Carte € 36/62
◆ This former nobleman's house has a walled garden offering delicious tranquillity. Very comfortable, entirely renovated rooms in a neo-baroque style. The restaurant offers Provençal dishes in a subdued yet pleasant dining room.

Fouquet's without rest
2 rd-pt Duboys-d'Angers – ✆ 04 92 59 25 00 – info@le-fouquets.com – Fax 04 92 98 03 39 – Open from February to October CZ **y**
10 rm – 🚹€ 130/200 🚹🚹€ 150/240, ☕ € 14
◆ On a fairly quiet roundabout, a hotel with large and cheerful rooms revamped in Provençal style. Very well kept; courteous welcome.

California without rest
8 traverse Alexandre-III – ✆ 04 93 94 12 21 – nadia@californias-hotel.com – Fax 04 93 43 55 17 DZ **h**
33 rm – 🚹€ 101/148 🚹🚹€ 116/300, ☕ € 18
◆ Attractive houses around a pretty garden with pool. Rooms in southern shades; some have a terrace. Wi-fi throughout and private boat.

Le Mondial without rest
1 r. Teisseire – ✆ 04 93 68 70 00 – reservation@hotellemondial.com – Fax 04 93 99 39 11 CY **e**
39 rm – 🚹€ 79/150 🚹🚹€ 99/220, ☕ € 13 – 10 suites
◆ Elagant Art Deco façade, behind which are chocolate-coloured rooms that are ethnic in style; some have balcony with sea view (upper floors).

Cannes Riviera without rest
16 bd d'Alsace – ☎ 04 97 06 20 40 – reservation@cannesriviera.com – Fax 04 93 39 20 75 BY **r**
58 rm – 🛉€ 70/140 🛉🛉€ 85/190, ☕ € 14 – 5 suites
◆ An eye-catching façade decorated with a giant portrait of Marilyn Monroe hides a distinctly Provençal-style interior. Soundproofed rooms and a rooftop swimming pool with fine views.

De Paris without rest
34 bd d'Alsace – ☎ 04 97 06 98 81 – reservation@hoteldeparis.fr – Fax 04 93 39 04 61 – Closed 9-25 December CY **a**
47 rm – 🛉€ 70/135 🛉🛉€ 90/150, ☕ € 15 – 3 suites
◆ A 19C town house near a busy road but with first-rate soundproofing. Elegant and well-kept rooms (non-smoking). Pool surrounded by palm trees.

Régina without rest
31 r. Pasteur – ☎ 04 93 94 05 43 – reception@hotel-regina-cannes.com – Fax 04 93 43 20 54 – Closed 18 November-28 December DZ **x**
19 rm – 🛉€ 98/185 🛉🛉€ 98/185, ☕ € 12
◆ Close to the Croisette, well-kept rooms (new linen and carpets) decorated in local style, most with balcony. Wi-fi.

Renoir without rest
7 r. Edith-Cavell – ☎ 04 92 99 62 62 – contact@hotel-renoir-cannes.com – Fax 04 92 99 62 82 BY **x**
14 rm – 🛉€ 125/200 🛉🛉€ 125/200, ☕ € 15 – 12 suites – 🛉🛉€ 225/620
◆ Everything behind the characterful 1913 façade is brand new. A Hollywood look in the rooms, but the modern suites sport a baroque style.

Cézanne without rest
40 bd d'Alsace – ☎ 04 92 59 41 00 – contact@hotel-cezanne.com – Fax 04 92 99 20 99
29 rm – 🛉€ 120/200 🛉🛉€ 120/200, ☕ € 17 CY **n**
◆ Stylish contemporary rooms, each of which matches grey with another livlier colour (yellow, turquoise). Fitness facilties, hammam and breakfast under the palm trees. Enchanting!

Villa de l'Olivier without rest
5 r. Tambourinaires – ☎ 04 93 39 53 28 – reception@hotelolivier.com – Fax 04 93 39 55 85 – Closed 22 November-25 December AZ **e**
23 rm – 🛉€ 80/145 🛉🛉€ 90/260, ☕ € 12
◆ Near the town centre and the Suquet, this family villa has smart, well-soundproofed rooms. Buffet breakfast on the veranda or on the terrace in summer.

Festival without rest
3 r. Molière – ☎ 04 97 06 64 40 – infos@hotel-festival.com – Fax 04 97 06 64 45 – Closed 23-27 December CZ **m**
14 rm – 🛉€ 59/119 🛉🛉€ 69/159, ☕ € 9,50
◆ Breakfast served in the rooms at this recently revamped hotel; lively colours and good soundproofing. Sauna, Jacuzzi.

La Villa Tosca without rest
11 r. Hoche – ☎ 04 93 38 34 40 – contact@villa-tosca.com – Fax 04 93 38 73 34 – Closed 12-28 December BY **e**
22 rm – 🛉€ 61/98 🛉🛉€ 82/186, ☕ € 14
◆ Fine Italianate façade behind which is a lemon yellow contemporary interior mixing old and new furnishings. Prettily renovated little rooms.

L'Estérel without rest
15 r. du 24-Août – ☎ 04 93 38 82 82 – reservation@hotellesterel.com – Fax 04 93 99 04 18 – **55 rm** – 🛉€ 49/64 🛉🛉€ 61/88, ☕ € 8 BY **d**
◆ Brand new hotel near the station offering compact but well-equipped rooms. Breakfast on the veranda with views of l'Estérel, the rooftops and the sea.

Le Mistral without rest
13 r. des Belges – ☎ 04 93 39 91 46 – contact@mistral-hotel.com – Fax 04 93 38 35 17 – Closed 13-26 December BZ **b**
10 rm – 🛉€ 77/117 🛉🛉€ 77/117, ☕ € 9
◆ Brand new small hotel behind the Palais des Festivals with pretty little rooms named after the winds. Attentive family welcome.

De Provence without rest

9 r. Molière – ✆ 04 93 38 44 35 – contact@hotel-de-provence.com – Fax 04 93 39 63 14 – Closed 1st-27 December CZ **s**

30 rm – †€ 62/79 ††€ 79/119, ☐ € 10

◆ A charming garden with palm trees fronts this hotel that is ideally located near the Croisette. Small yet smart rooms in Provençal style (some with balcony).

Florian without rest

8 r. Cdt-André – ✆ 04 93 39 24 82 – contact@hotel-leflorian.com – Fax 04 92 99 18 30 – Closed 1st December-10 January CZ **g**

20 rm – †€ 48/67 ††€ 58/77, ☐ € 6

◆ A smiling welcome at this family hotel offering simple yet well-kept rooms.Some with balcony where a good breakfast can be enjoyed.

De France without rest

85 r. d'Antibes – ✆ 04 93 06 54 54 – infos@h-de-france.com – Fax 04 93 68 53 43 – Closed 22 November-25 December CY **k**

33 rm – †€ 65/145 ††€ 67/150, ☐ € 11

◆ Discreet entrance on a street packed with luxury boutiques. Small soundproofed rooms, Art Deco style and rooftop sun terrace overlooking the bay.

La Palme d'Or – Hôtel Martinez

73 bd de la Croisette – ✆ 04 92 98 74 14 – lapalmedor@concorde-hotels.com – Fax 04 93 39 03 38 – Closed 2 January-28 February, Sunday and Monday

Rest – Menu € 61 bi (lunch), € 79/180 – Carte € 113/279 DZ **n**

Spec. "La Main tendue", caviar d'Iran, crème de concombre aux condiments. "La Balançoire", lapin cuit à la broche en gourmandise de langoustine. Chocolat "Palme d'Or" aux éclats de noisette et gelée de rose. **Wines** Côtes de Provence.

◆ An Art Deco interior featuring photos of stars and fine woods, with views of the Croisette. Fine panoramic terrace; excellent sunny cuisine.

Le Mesclun

16 r. St-Antoine – ✆ 04 93 99 45 19 – mesclun.cannes@wanadoo.fr – Fax 04 93 49 29 11 – Closed 29 June-9 July, 1st February-2 March and Sunday AZ **t**

Rest – *(dinner only)* Menu € 39 – Carte € 60/106

◆ Subtle lighting, woodwork, paintings and warm tones comprise the ideal setting in which to enjoy well-prepared tasty Mediterranean cuisine. Competent and friendly service.

Le Festival

52 bd de la Croisette – ✆ 04 93 38 04 81 – contact@lefestival.fr – Fax 04 93 38 13 82 – Closed 17 November-26 December CZ **p**

Rest – Carte € 37/58

Rest *Grill* – Carte € 41/58

◆ Drawings of ships brighten the pale-wainscoting in this large retro brasserie. Terrace opposite the Croisette with an awe-inspiring view that must be seen! At the Grill, the ambience is friendly, the setting discreet. Salads, daily specials, diet dishes etc.

Mantel

22 r. St-Antoine – ✆ 04 93 39 13 10 – noel.mantel@wanadoo.fr – Fax 04 93 39 13 10 – Closed 1st-15 July, 23-29 December, Thursday lunch, Wednesday and lunch July-August AZ **c**

Rest – Menu € 25 (lunch), € 36/58 – Carte € 43/80

◆ One of many restaurants in a picturesque street on the Suquet. This one stands out for its carefully prepared Provençal dishes and intimate decor.

Il Rigoletto

60 bd d'Alsace – ✆ 04 93 43 32 19 – Closed 24 November-15 December and Tuesday dinner in July-August DY **t**

Rest – Menu (€ 24), € 33/49 – Carte € 46/68

◆ Retro dining room serving reasonably priced fine Italian cuisine made with fresh produce; a charming family establishment off the beaten track.

Comme Chez Soi
4 r. Batéguier – ✆ 04 93 39 62 68 – info@commechezsoi.net – Fax 04 93 38 20 65 – Closed 22-27 December and Monday CZ **k**
Rest – *(dinner only)* Menu € 27/80 – Carte € 58/90
◆ A homely atmosphere with knick-knacks from around the world and eclectic furnishings. Tasty, well prepared regional fare and a choice of traditional recipes.

Rest. Arménien
82 bd de la Croisette – ✆ 04 93 94 00 58 – christian@lerestaurantarmenien.com – Fax 04 93 94 56 12 – Closed 10-27 December, Monday off season and lunch except Sunday DZ **a**
Rest – Menu € 42
◆ No choice but copious servings; a slice of Armenia's culinary heritage. Slightly kitsch setting, light with stained glass, open until late and plenty of regulars.

Relais des Semailles
9 r. St-Antoine – ✆ 04 93 39 22 32 – cannessemailles@orange.fr – Fax 04 93 39 84 73 – Closed Monday lunch, Thursday lunch and Saturday lunch AZ **z**
Rest – Menu € 22 (lunch)/34 – Carte € 49/83
◆ Paintings, antique furniture and ornaments create a cosy atmosphere in this restaurant in an old-town alleyway. Regional dishes.

Le Madeleine
13 bd Jean-Hilbert – ✆ 04 93 39 72 22 – lemadeleine@fr.st – Fax 04 93 94 61 57 – Closed 15 December-15 January, Sunday dinner 15 September-15 June, Wednesday lunch 16 June-14 September and Tuesday AZ **b**
Rest – Menu (€ 23), € 25/56 – Carte € 43/82
◆ The scene is set for this restaurant by a characteristic seaside colour scheme and a great view over Esterel and the Lérins islands. Seafood (bouillabaisse, grilled fish) menu!

3 Portes
16 r. Frères-Pradignac – ✆ 04 93 38 91 70 – roussel3portes@aol.com – Closed 24 December-1st January and Sunday off season CZ **f**
Rest – *(dinner only)* Menu € 29/55 bi – Carte € 41/62
◆ An elegant design interior and contemporary Mediterranean cuisine; trendy background music. Summer terrace and friendly welcome.

Côté Jardin
12 av. St-Louis – ✆ 04 93 38 60 28 – cotejardin.com@wanadoo.fr – Fax 04 93 38 60 28 – Closed 27 October-5 November, Sunday and Monday
Rest – Menu (€ 23), € 29/37 X **a**
◆ Restaurant located in a residential area. Dining room/veranda and small garden with shaded terrace. Family, market sourced cooking, chalked up on a blackboard.

L'Affable
5 r. la Fontaine – ✆ 04 93 68 02 09 – laffable@wanadoo.fr – Fax 04 93 68 19 09 – Closed Saturday lunch and Sunday CZ **d**
Rest – Menu (€ 20), € 24/38 – Carte € 54/71
◆ Minimalist decor, tribal art and an open kitchen in this contemporary bistro with a brief yet thoughtful and appetising menu.

Caveau 30
45 r. F.-Faure – ✆ 04 93 39 06 33 – lecaveau30@wanadoo.fr – Fax 04 92 98 05 38 AZ **f**
Rest – brasserie Menu (€ 17), € 23/35 – Carte € 34/64
◆ 1930s brasserie style in the two large dining rooms. Terrace opening onto a large shaded square. Seafood and traditional fare.

La Mère Besson
13 r. Frères-Pradignac – ✆ 04 93 39 59 24 – lamerebesson@wanadoo.fr – Fax 04 92 18 93 11 – Closed Sunday CZ **a**
Rest – *(dinner only)* Menu € 29/34 – Carte € 31/48
◆ This modest establishment has become an institution for Provençal cuisine, serving homemade specialities such as pieds et paquets and farcis niçois.

Rendez-Vous
35 r. F.-Faure – ✆ 04 93 68 55 10 – Fax 04 93 38 96 21 – Closed 5-20 January
Rest – Menu (€ 17), € 22/31 – Carte € 34/61 AZ **g**
◆ Meet up in this smart bistro restaurant beneath its Art Deco-style moulded ceiling. Sample seafood, shellfish and traditional fare with a Mediterranean twist.

La Cave
9 bd de la République – ✆ 04 93 99 79 87 – restaurantlacave@free.fr – Fax 04 93 68 91 19 – Closed Saturday lunch and Sunday CY **q**
Rest – bistrot Menu € 30 – Carte € 40/62
◆ An authentic bistro with a modern, lively ambiance, dishes of the day on the blackboard and a well-compiled wine list. Non-smoking.

Aux Bons Enfants
80 r. Meynadier – Closed December, Monday off season and Sunday AZ **r**
Rest – *(number of covers limited, pre-book)* Menu € 22
◆ This old-fashioned looking, family establishment has perfected the art of hospitality. Tasty regional cuisine and house specialities. The restaurant does not have a phone and only takes cash.

at Cannet **3 km North** - V – **pop. 42 158 – alt. 80 m** – ✉ **06110**

Office de tourisme, avenue du Campon ✆ 04 93 45 34 27, Fax 04 93 45 28 06

Pézou
346 r. St-Sauveur – ✆ 04 93 69 32 50 – Fax 04 93 43 69 14 – Closed 23 June-2 July, November, Monday lunch in July-August, Sunday dinner from September to June and Wednesday V **r**
Rest – Menu (€ 12), € 18 (lunch), € 24/30 – Carte € 25/31
◆ For a break from the Croisette, a pleasant restaurant by a pretty little square with a summer terrace. Provençal-inspired fare.

LE CANNET – 06 Alpes-Maritimes – 341 D6 – see Cannes

LE CANNET-DES-MAURES – 83 Var – 340 N5 – pop. 3 478 – alt. 124 m – ✉ 83340

41 **C3**

Paris 834 – Brignoles 31 – Cannes 73 – Draguignan 27 – Fréjus 39 – Toulon 54

Le Mas de Causserène
D N7 – ✆ 04 94 60 74 87 – l-oustalet@wanadoo.fr – Fax 04 94 60 95 97
49 rm – †€ 55/75 ††€ 58/90, ☕ € 10
Rest ***L'Oustalet*** – *(Closed Sunday dinner except July-August)* Menu € 19 (weekday lunch), € 23/36 – Carte € 22/48
◆ Near the motorway, and before the Coast beaches, a practical hotel with functional rooms. The enormous dining room, overlooking the countryside, is attractively decorated in Provençal style. Traditional cuisine, also served on the terrace.

CAPBRETON – 40 Landes – 335 C13 – pop. 6 659 – alt. 6 m – Casino – ✉ 40130

Atlantic Coast 3 **A3**

Paris 749 – Bayonne 22 – Biarritz 29 – Mont-de-Marsan 90 – St-Vincent-de-Tyrosse 12

Office de tourisme, avenue Georges Pompidou ✆ 05 58 72 12 11, Fax 05 58 41 00 29

de Seignosse Seignosse Avenue du Belvédère, North: 8 km by D 152, ✆ 05 58 41 68 30.

quartier de la plage (beach area)

Cap Club Hôtel
85 av. Mar.-de-Lattre-de-Tassigny – ✆ 05 58 41 80 00 – contact@capclubhotel.com – Fax 05 58 41 80 41
75 rm – †€ 69/151 ††€ 69/151, ☕ € 13,50 – ½ P € 98/176 – **Rest** – Menu € 22 (weekday lunch) – Carte € 26/40
◆ Sport, fitness or relaxation: you can choose the theme of your stay in this hotel opposite the beach. Modern rooms and many sports facilities. This restaurant has a contemporary setting, lovely view of the ocean and traditional food.

L'Océan rest, VISA MC AE
85 av. G.-Pompidou – 05 58 72 10 22 – hotel-capbreton@wanadoo.fr – Fax 05 58 72 08 43 – Closed 1st-20 December and 5-31 January
25 rm – €45/88 €55/106, €8,50 – **Rest** – Menu €15/25 – Carte €28/41
◆ On the banks of the channel, an immaculate façade housing rooms with balconies. Opt for the quieter ones at the back. The Atlantic has place of honour here, in terms of both decor and food. Pizzeria for snacks.

quartier la Pêcherie

Le Regalty VISA MC AE
port de plaisance – 05 58 72 22 80 – leregalty@cegetel.net – Fax 05 58 72 22 80 – Closed 15-30 November, 15-31 January, Sunday dinner and Monday
Rest – Menu €28 – Carte €35/50
Rest *Le Bistrot de la Mer* – Carte approx. €27
◆ Restaurant on the ground floor of a modern building. A nautical atmosphere in the panelled dining room. Meals feature fish and seafood. At Le Bistrot there is an oyster bar, simple comfort and a small menu concentrating on fish and seafood.

Le Pavé du Port VISA MC
port de plaisance – 05 58 72 29 28 – Fax 05 58 72 29 28 – Closed Christmas holidays, Monday lunch July-August, Tuesday October-April and Wednesday except dinner July-August
Rest – Menu €18 (weekdays)/27 – Carte €28/45
◆ Very freshly caught fish is on the menu at this restaurant overlooking the harbour. Dining rooms with discreet nautical touches and terrace-veranda.

CAP COZ – 29 Finistère – 308 H7 – see Fouesnant

CAP-d'AGDE – 34 Hérault – 339 G9 – see Agde

CAP d'AIL – 06 Alpes-Maritimes – 341 F5 – pop. 4 532 – alt. 51 m – ✉ 06320

Paris 945 – Monaco 3 – Menton 14 – Monte-Carlo 4 – Nice 18 42 **E2**

Office de tourisme, 87, avenue du 3 Septembre 04 93 78 02 33, Fax 04 92 10 74 36

See plan of Monaco (Principality of)

Marriott Riviera la Porte de Monaco rm, rest, VISA MC AE
au port – 04 92 10 67 67 – thierry.derrien@marriotthotels.com – Fax 04 92 10 67 00 AV **n**
186 rm – €149/329 €149/329, €21 – 15 suites – **Rest** – Menu €20 (weekday lunch), €39/49 – Carte €34/55
◆ Modern building facing the Cap d'Ail marina. Very comfortable rooms in compliance with its chain standards. Most of them have loggias overlooking the sea. Elegant brasserie-style restaurant. Traditional cuisine.

CAP d'ANTIBES – 06 Alpes-Maritimes – 341 D6 – see Antibes

CAPDENAC-GARE – 12 Aveyron – 338 E3 – pop. 4 587 – alt. 175 m – ✉ 12700

Paris 587 – Aurillac 65 – Rodez 59 – Villefranche-de-Rouergue 31 29 **C1**

Office de tourisme, place du 14 juillet 05 65 64 74 87, Fax 05 65 80 88 15

in St-Julien-d'Empare 2 km South by D 86 and D 558 – ✉ 12700 Capdenac- railway station

Auberge La Diège rm, VISA MC AE
– 05 65 64 70 54 – hotel@diege.com – Fax 05 65 80 81 58 – Closed 16 December-7 January
28 rm – €45/55 €52/60, €7,50 – 2 suites – ½ P €50/63
Rest – *(closed Friday dinner, Sunday dinner and Saturday from 1st October to 1st April)* Menu €19/35 – Carte €25/50
◆ A bold marriage between a resolutely contemporary building (home to functional, stylish and well-kept rooms) and an old sandstone farmhouse where the restaurant is located. Beams, stonework and a fireplace make for a rustic ambiance; regional cuisine.

CAPDENAC-LE-HAUT – 46 Lot – 337 I4 – see Figeac

CAP FERRET – 33 Gironde – 335 D7 – alt. 11 m – ✉ 33970

Atlantic Coast 3 B2

Paris 650 – Arcachon 66 – Bordeaux 71 – Lacanau-Océan 55 – Lesparre-Médoc 88

✻★ of the lighthouse.

La Frégate without rest

34 av. de l'Océan – ✆ 05 56 60 41 62 – resa@hotel-la-fregate.net – Fax 05 56 03 76 18 – Closed December and January

29 rm – †€ 47/154 ††€ 47/154, ☕ € 9

◆ Seaside houses set around the swimming pool. The rooms are gradually being updated and are simple, modern and chic.

Le Pinasse Café

2 bis av. de l'Océan – ✆ 05 56 03 77 87 – pinassecafe@wanadoo.fr – Fax 05 56 60 63 47 – Open 2 March-11 November

Rest – Menu (€ 31), € 38 – Carte € 37/59

◆ This pleasant bistro favours the sea in its decor (works with a nautical theme) and in its cooking (fish and shellfish). Terrace view of the water and Pilat Dune.

CAP FRÉHEL – 22 Côtes-d'Armor – 309 I2 – ✉ 22240 FREHEL

Brittany 10 C1

Paris 438 – Dinan 43 – Dinard 36 – Lamballe 36 – Rennes 96 – St-Brieuc 48 – St-Malo 42

Site★★★ - ✻★★★ - Fort La Latte: site★★, ✻★★ Southeast: 5 km.

La Fauconnière

sea and coast

à la Pointe – ✆ 02 96 41 54 20 – Open 1st April-5 November and closed Wednesday from September to October

Rest – *(lunch only)* Menu € 20/28 – Carte € 23/42

◆ This restaurant situated in a protected site accessible on foot, is solidly anchored on the purplish red rocks of La Fauconnière. Very simple decor, but a fantastic view.

CAP GRIS-NEZ ★★ – 62 Pas-de-Calais – 301 C2 – ✉ 62179 AUDINGHEN

Northern France and the Paris Region 30 A1

Paris 288 – Arras 139 – Boulogne-sur-Mer 21 – Calais 32 – Marquise 13 – St-Omer 61

La Sirène

sea

– ✆ 03 21 32 95 97 – Fax 03 21 32 74 75 – Closed 15 December-25 January, dinner except from May to August and Saturday from September to April, Sunday dinner and Monday

Rest – Menu € 24/42 – Carte € 29/58

◆ No mermaids in sight but lobsters and fish to charm your palate in this waterside restaurant, facing the English coastline which is visible in fine weather.

CAPINGHEM – 59 Nord – 302 F4 – see Lille

CAPPELLE-LA-GRANDE – 59 Nord – 302 C2 – see Dunkerque

CARANTEC – 29 Finistère – 308 H2 – pop. 2 724 – alt. 37 m – ✉ 29660

Brittany 9 B1

Paris 552 – Brest 71 – Lannion 53 – Morlaix 14 – Quimper 90 – St-Pol-de-Léon 10

Office de tourisme, 4, rue Pasteur ✆ 02 98 67 00 43, Fax 02 98 67 90 51

de Carantec Rue de Kergrist, South: 1km by D 73, ✆ 02 98 67 09 14.

Procession cross ★ in the church - "Chaise du Curé" (platform) ⋞★.

Pointe de Pen-al-Lann ⋞★★ East: 1.5 km then 15 mn.

L'Hôtel de Carantec-Patrick Jeffroy ← Bay of Morlaix,
r. du Kelenn – ✆ 02 98 67 00 47
– patrick.jeffroy@wanadoo.fr – Fax 02 98 67 08 25
– Closed 17 November-10 December, 19 January-3 February, Sunday dinner, Monday and Tuesday except public holidays and except school holidays 14 September-16 June, Monday lunch, Tuesday lunch and Thursday lunch 17 June-13 September
12 rm – €116/185 €150/226, €21 – ½ P €160/198
Rest – *(pre-book)* Menu €40 (weekday lunch), €64/135 – Carte €82/150
Spec. Saint-Jacques de la baie et foie gras snacké. Bar de ligne à la marmelade d'oignons de Roscoff au citron confit. Crêpes dentelles en millefeuille, crème à la bergamote et fruits frais.
◆ This charming hotel, built in 1936, overlooks the marvellous Morlaix Bay. The contemporary welcoming rooms (with terrace on the first floor) all overlook the English Channel. A panoramic restaurant where you can enjoy creative 'surf and turf' dishes.

Le Manoir de Kervézec without rest
– ✆ 02 98 67 00 26 – gerardbohic@wanadoo.fr – Fax 02 98 67 00 52 – Open April to September
5 rm – €40/58 €48/66, €6
◆ Fine 19C manor house in the centre of a huge garden overlooking the sea. Family heirlooms, century-old trees, delicious breakfasts (organic products) and utter peace and quiet.

Le Cabestan ← VISA
au port – ✆ 02 98 67 01 87 – godec.michel@wanadoo.fr
– Fax 02 98 67 90 49 – Closed 5 November-5 December, Tuesday except dinner in season and Monday
Rest – Menu €19/33 – Carte €27/42
◆ A rustic-style dining room with fine views of Callot island from the first floor. Brasserie cuisine, with the emphasis on seafood.

CARCASSONNE P – 11 Aude – 344 F3 – pop. 43 950 – alt. 110 m – ✉ 11000

Languedoc-Roussillon-Tarn Gorges 22 **B2**

- Paris 768 – Albi 110 – Narbonne 61 – Perpignan 114 – Toulouse 92
- Carcassonne-Salvaza: ✆ 04 68 71 96 46, by ④: 3 km.
- Office de tourisme, 28, rue de Verdun ✆ 04 68 10 24 30, Fax 04 68 10 24 38
- 18 de Carcassonne Route de Saint Hilaire, South: 4 km by D 118 and D 104, ✆ 06 13 20 85 43.
- La Cité★★★ - St-Nazaire basilica★ : stained-glass windows ★★, statues★★ - Musée du château Comtal : Calvary ★ of Villanière - Montolieu★ (book village) - Châteaux de Latours★- Cité des oiseaux et des loups ★ .

Plan on next page

La Maison Coste VISA AE
40 r. Coste-Reboulh – ✆ 04 68 77 12 15 – contact@maison-coste.com
– Fax 04 68 77 59 91 – Closed 20 January-10 February BZ **n**
5 rm – €87/97 €97/160 – **Table d'hôte** – Menu €25
◆ Every effort has been made to ensure that guests enjoy this tasteful, welcoming, contemporary-style establishment. Garden-terrace, Jacuzzi and sun deck. Single set menu changed nightly at the table d'hôte; aperitif and coffee on the house.

Le Parc Franck Putelat P VISA AE
80 chemin des Anglais, South of the Cité – ✆ 04 68 71 80 80
– fr.putelat@wanadoo.fr – Fax 04 68 71 80 79
– Closed January, Sunday and Monday except public holidays
Rest – Menu €27 bi (weekday lunch), €42/110 bi – Carte €66/85
Spec. Tartine de haricots de Castelnaudary confits à la sauge et mozarella à la truffe d'été (June to August). Filet de bœuf "Bocuse d'Or 2003". Sphère au chocolat Guanara, ananas et fruits de la passion.
◆ The restaurant below Carcassonne is as sophisticated as its inventive modern cuisine. Bright minimalist dining room overlooking the countryside.

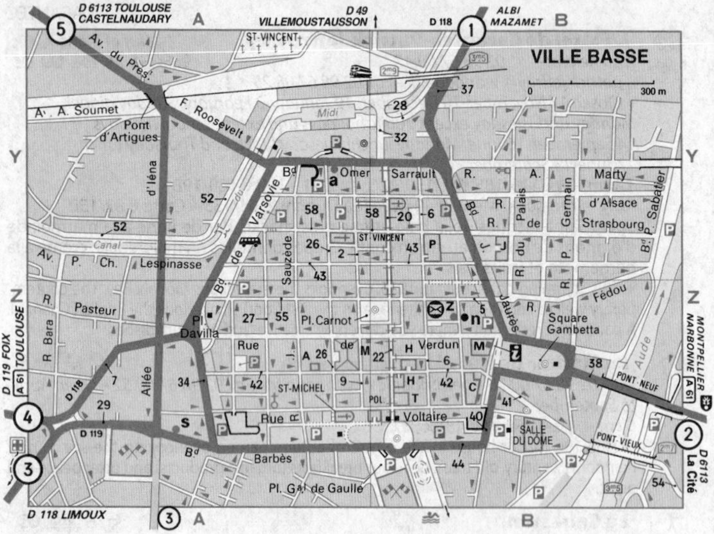

D 6113 TOULOUSE CASTELNAUDARY
A
D 49 VILLEMOUSTAUSSON
D 118
ALBI MAZAMET
B

VILLE BASSE

0 300 m

ST-VINCENT
Av. du Presᵗ F. Roosevelt
A. A. Soumet
Pont d'Artigues
d'Iéna
Allée
Midi
Bᵈ Omer Sarrault
R. A. Marty
R. d'Alsace
R. de Strasbourg
Palais
Germain
Bᵈ P. Sabatier
Bᵈ de Varsovie
Sauzède
ST-VINCENT
Canal
Av. P. Ch. Lespinasse
R. Pasteur
R. Bara
Pl. Davilla
Pl. Carnot
Rue de Verdun
R. J. Jaurès
Fédou
Square Gambetta
Aude
PONT NEUF
PONT VIEUX
SALLE DU DÔME
ST-MICHEL
Rue Voltaire
Bᵈ Barbès
Pl. Gᵃˡ de Gaulle
D 119
D 118
D 119 FOIX TOULOUSE A 61
MONTPELLIER NARBONNE A 61
D 6113 La Cité
D 118 LIMOUX
A
B
Y
Z

CARCASSONNE

Armagnac (R. A.) . . . **AY** 2
Barbès (R.) . . . . **BZ** 5
Bringer (R. Jean) . . **BYZ** 6
Bunau-Varilla (Av.) . . . **AZ** 7
Chartran (R.) . . . . **AZ** 9
Clemenceau (R. G.) . **BY** 20
Combéléran (Mtée G.) **D** 21
Courtejaire (R.) . . . . . **BZ** 22
Cros-Mayrevieille (R.) . **D** 24
Dr-A.-Tomey (R.) . . . **AYZ** 26
Études (R. des) . . . . . **AZ** 27
Foch (Av. du Mar.) . . **BY** 28
Gout (Av. Henri) . . . . **AZ** 29
Grand-Puits (R. du) . . **CD** 30
Joffre (Av. du Mar.) . **BY** 32
Marcou (Bd) . . . . **AZ** 34
Médiévale (Voie) . . . . . **D** 36
Minervoise (Rte) . . . **BY** 37
Mullot (Av. Arthur) . . **BZ** 38
Pelletan (Bd C.) . . . . . **BZ** 40
Pont-Vieux (R. du) . . . **BZ** 41
Ramon (R. A.) . . . . **ABZ** 42
République (R. de la) . . . . **ABY** 43
Roumens (Bd du Cdt) . . . . . . **BZ** 44
St-Jean (R.) . . . . **C** 46
St-Saëns (R. C.) . . . . . . **D** 48
St-Sernin (R.) . . . . **D** 49
Semard (Av. Pierre) . **AY** 52
Trivalle (R.) . . . . **BZ** 54
Verdun (R. de) . . . . **ABZ**
Victor-Hugo (R.) . . . . . **AZ** 55
Viollet-le-Duc (R.) . . . . . **C** 56
4-Septembre (R. du) . . . . **ABY** 58

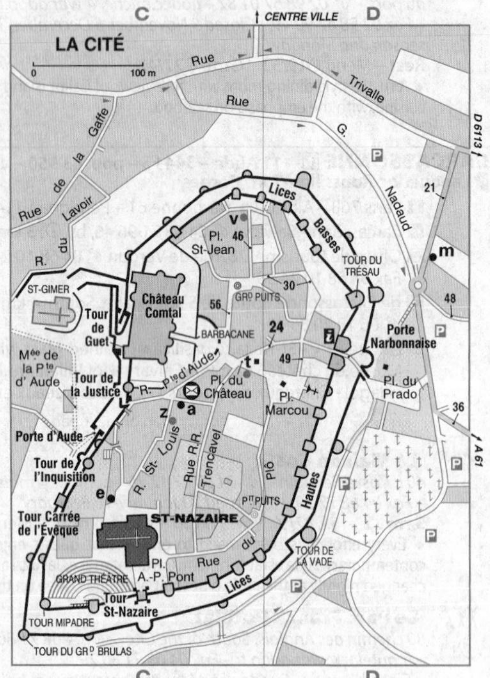

XX **Robert Rodriguez**

39 r. Coste-Reboulh – ✆ 04 68 47 37 80 – rodriguezro@wanadoo.fr – Fax 04 68 47 37 80 – Closed Wednesday except July-August and Sunday

Rest – *(number of covers limited, pre-book)* Menu € 20 bi (weekday lunch), € 39/85 bi – Carte € 64/113 BZ **z**

◆ Ring the bell to gain admittance to this discreet house and take a seat in the small (seats only 10) welcoming dining room. Regional specialities reinterpreted by the chef.

XX **Le Clos Occitan**

68 bd Barbès – ✆ 04 68 47 93 64 – Fax 04 68 72 46 91 – Closed 10-31 January, Saturday lunch, Sunday dinner and Monday AZ **s**

Rest – Menu € 16 bi (weekday lunch), € 21/40 – Carte € 29/45

◆ Former garage converted into a restaurant: warm sunny colours, a mezzanine used mainly for banquets, and a wrought iron furnished terrace. Extensive traditional menu made with market produce.

to Cité entrance near porte Narbonnaise

Mercure Porte de la Cité

18 r. Camille-St-Saens – ✆ 04 68 11 92 82 – h1622@accor.com – Fax 04 68 71 11 45

56 rm – €100/125 €110/140, € 13 – **Rest** – Menu € 17/22 – Carte € 18/39

◆ Comfort and privacy take pride of place in this Mediterranean decor that is being refurbished in a more modern spirit. View of the citadel from some rooms. Elegantly understated dining room overlooking a lush green terrace.

Du Château without rest

2 r. Camille-St-Saens – ✆ 04 68 11 38 38 – contact@hotelduchateau.net – Fax 04 68 11 38 39 D**m**

15 rm – €110/180 €110/180, € 10 – 1 suite

◆ At the foot of the city, a fully-renovated hotel with refined rooms, a pleasant contemporary decor of medieval inspiration, marble bathrooms, a lovely pool and terrace.

Montmorency without rest

2 r. Camille-St-Saens – ✆ 04 68 11 96 70 – le.montmorency@wanadoo.fr – Fax 04 68 11 96 79

20 rm – €65/85 €65/95, € 7

◆ The rooms are simpler but just as appealing and well kept as those in the main building.

In the Cité - Regulated traffic in summer

De La Cité

pl. Auguste-Pierre-Pont – ✆ 04 68 71 98 71 – reservations@hoteldelacite.com – Fax 04 68 71 50 15 – Closed 20 January-8 March C **e**

53 rm – €295/545 €295/545, € 33 – 8 suites

Rest ***La Barbacane*** – *(closed Tuesday and Wednesday) (dinner only)* Menu € 74/160 bi – Carte € 77/122

Rest ***Brasserie Chez Saskia*** – Menu € 28 (weekday lunch), € 35/50 – Carte € 35/50

Spec. Légumes en fricassée aux truffes de saison. Pavé de loup braisé aux artichauts, tomates et courgettes. Filet de charolais au foie gras, joue de bœuf braisée, sauce périgourdine. **Wines** Vin de pays des Coteaux de la Cité de Carcassonne, Limoux.

◆ A prestigious, neo-Gothic establishment with a garden and swimming pool on the ramparts side. Luxuriously appointed individually decorated rooms, a few balconies and terraces overlooking the city. Modern cuisine and a refined medieval setting at the Barbacane. Chez Saskia – a brasserie with a relaxed atmosphere.

Le Donjon

2 r. Comte-Roger – ✆ 04 68 11 23 00 – info@bestwestern-donjon.fr – Fax 04 68 25 06 60 C **a**

62 rm – €105/210 €105/210, € 11 – 2 suites

Rest – ✆ 04 68 25 95 72 *(closed Sunday evening from November to March)* Menu (€ 16), € 20/28 – Carte € 31/46

◆ An orphanage in the 15C, this medieval house with two villas in the garden is now a fully renovated hotel. Personalised rooms, some of which have a tiny terrace. Traditional cuisine in a bright, contemporary brasserie setting. Wine shop.

Comte Roger

14 r. St-Louis – ✆ 04 68 11 93 40 – restaurant@comteroger.com – Fax 04 68 11 93 41 – Closed 1st-10 March, Sunday and Monday C **z**

Rest – Menu (€ 20), € 33/60 – Carte € 41/60

♦ You may come across this shady terrace on a lively street as you walk around the historic town. Modern minimalist interior and market-fresh menu.

La Marquière

13 r. St-Jean – ✆ 04 68 71 52 00 – lamarquiere@wanadoo.fr – Fax 04 68 71 30 81 – Closed 15 January-12 February, Thursday except July-August and Wednesday

Rest – Menu (€ 18 bi), € 23/50 – Carte € 24/57 C **v**

♦ Located near the northern ramparts, this house has a restrained provincial interior and a pretty little courtyard terrace. Simple, tasty traditional cooking.

Auberge de Dame Carcas

3 pl. du Château – ✆ 04 68 71 23 23 – contact@damecarcas.com – Fax 04 68 72 46 17 – Closed 20-30 December and Wednesday C **t**

Rest – Menu € 14,50/26

♦ The sign outside depicts Dame Carcas, who according to legend ended the siege of the town, carrying a pig. So you will not be surprised to learn that the menu has a strong pork bias.

in Aragon **10 km by ① D 118 and D 935 – pop. 453 – alt. 195 m – ✉ 11600**

La Bergerie

rm, rm,

allée Pech-Marie – ✆ 04 68 26 10 65 – info@labergeriearagon.com – Fax 04 68 77 02 23 – Closed 6-22 October and 2-23 January

8 rm – €60/80 €90/110, € 10 – ½ P € 73/98

Rest – *(closed Monday and Tuesday except dinner July-August)* Menu € 25 bi (weekday lunch), € 35/60 – Carte € 56/64

♦ This new house built in the local style is situated in a picturesque high-perched village. The pleasant and colourful rooms offer a pretty view of the Cabardès vineyard. Smart dining room in sunny colours; inventive menu using high quality regional produce.

at Montredon hamlet **4 km Northeast by A. Marty road** BY – ✉ **11000 Carcassonne**

Hostellerie St-Martin

– ✆ 04 68 47 44 41 – hostellerie@chateausaintmartin.net – Fax 04 68 47 74 70 – Open 15 March-15 November – **15 rm** – €65 €95, € 9

Rest ***Château St-Martin*** – see restaurant listing

♦ This recent regional-style building is set in a peaceful park in the heart of the countryside. Pleasant rooms with a Provençal-cum-rustic decor

Château St-Martin "Trencavel"

– ✆ 04 68 71 09 53 – restaurant@chateausaintmartin.net – Fax 04 68 25 46 55 – Closed 21-27 February, Sunday evening and Wednesday

Rest – Menu € 32/56 – Carte € 47/60

♦ An attractive 14C/17C building in parkland, flanked by a 12C tower. Discreet interior decorated with a mural and pleasant summer terrace. Classic cuisine.

in Trèbes **4 km east by ② and N 113 – ✉ 11800**

Syndicat d'initiative, 12, avenue Pierre Curie ✆ 04 68 78 89 50

La Tuilerie du Bazalac without rest

7 bis rte des Corbières – ✆ 04 68 78 10 82 – info@latuileriedubazalac.com

4 rm – €75/95 €115/135

♦ Modern establishment set in a former tile works. Minimalist décor, terrace and benches beneath the arcades for lazing by the pool.

in Floure **11 km by ② and D 6113 – pop. 318 – alt. 77 m – ✉ 11800**

Château de Floure

rm, rest,

1 allée Gaston-Bonheur – ✆ 04 68 79 11 29 – contact@chateau-de-floure.com – Fax 04 68 79 04 61 – Closed 15 November-15 December and 4 January-14 February

21 rm – €110 €110/190, € 16 – 4 suites – ½ P € 116/156

Rest – *(dinner only)* Menu € 49/79 – Carte € 62/90

♦ Formerly a Roman villa, then a monastery, this 12C castle sports a plush decor of gilding and tapestries. The characterful rooms overlook the formal French gardens. Elegant wood-panelled dining room with 17C statuettes; a veranda doubles as a bar.

South via ③ 3 km and by D104 – ✉ 11000 Carcassonne

Domaine d'Auriac
– ✆ *04 68 25 72 22 – auriac@relaischateaux.com*
– Fax 04 68 47 35 54 – Closed 27 April-1st May, 9-17 November, 4 January-9 February, Sunday and Monday 5 October-21 April except holidays
23 rm – 🛉€ 100/450 🛉🛉€ 100/450, ☕ € 20 – ½ P € 145/320
Rest – *(closed Sunday evening and Monday from October to April, Monday lunch, Tuesday lunch and Wednesday lunch from May to September except public holidays)* Menu € 70/150 – Carte € 73/81
Rest *Bistrot d'Auriac* – ✆ *04 68 25 37 19 (closed 24 November-1st December, Monday and Tuesday dinner to Thursday October-April and Sunday dinner except public holidays)* Menu € 17 (lunch), € 24/45 – Carte € 26/30
Spec. Assiette de dégustation autour de l'anchois de Collioure. Cassoulet. Gibier (October to January). **Wines** Corbières, Saint-Chinian.
◆ A stylish 19C abode in parkland complete with an 18-hole golf course. Personalised rooms in the chateau, larger and more Provençal in spirit in the outhouses. Tasty local dishes served in a plush dining room that leads onto a terrace. Bistro-style clubhouse.

in Cavanac 7 km by ③ and St-Hilaire road – **pop. 665 – alt. 138 m** – ✉ **11570**

Château de Cavanac
rm, rm, rm,
– ✆ *04 68 79 61 04*
– infos@chateau-de-cavanac.fr – Fax 04 68 79 79 67
– Closed 12-26 November, January and February
24 rm – 🛉€ 65/120 🛉🛉€ 100/150, ☕ € 10 – 4 suites – **Rest** – *(closed Monday and lunch except Sunday)* Menu € 40 bi – Carte approx. € 37
◆ This 17C château is set on a winegrowing estate in the heart of the countryside. The attractive rooms are named after flowers. Breakfast is served on the veranda-terrace. A rustic-style restaurant set in the former stables. Traditional dishes and grills; wines from the estate.

CARENNAC – 46 Lot – 337 G2 – pop. 373 – alt. 123 m – ✉ 46110

Dordogne-Berry-Limousin 29 **C1**

Paris 520 – Brive-la-Gaillarde 39 – Cahors 79 – Martel 16 – St-Céré 17 – Tulle 51
Office de tourisme, le bourg ✆ 05 65 10 97 01, Fax 05 65 10 51 22
Portal★ of St Pierre church - Burial★ in the cloister chapter house.

Hostellerie Fénelon
– ✆ *05 65 10 96 46 – contact@hotel-fenelon.com – Fax 05 65 10 94 86*
– Closed 17 November-20 December, 7 January-15 March and Friday 15 October-Easter
15 rm – 🛉€ 50/56 🛉🛉€ 54/66, ☕ € 10 – ½ P € 57/67
Rest – *(closed Monday lunch, Friday lunch and Saturday lunch except July-August and Friday 10 October-30 April)* Menu (€ 17), € 23/50 – Carte € 32/57
◆ A large Quercy house with a family atmosphere where you may prefer the bedrooms with a view of the Dordogne. Beams and stonework, a fireplace and country ornaments give character to this dining room with views of the surrounding countryside.

CARGÈSE – 2A Corse-du-Sud – 345 A7 – see Corse

CARHAIX-PLOUGUER – 29 Finistère – 308 J5 – pop. 7 648 – alt. 138 m – ✉ 29270

Brittany 9 **B2**

Paris 506 – Brest 86 – Guingamp 49 – Lorient 74 – Morlaix 51 – Pontivy 59 – Quimper 61
Office de tourisme, rue Brizeux ✆ 02 98 93 04 42, Fax 02 98 93 23 83

Noz Vad without rest
12 bd de la République – ✆ 02 98 99 12 12 – aemcs@nozvad.com
– Fax 02 98 99 44 32 – Closed 15 December-18 January
44 rm – 🛉€ 49/87 🛉🛉€ 55/93, ☕ € 8,50
◆ Local artists took part in the renovation of this hotel which now has an attractive Breton decor: paintings, photos, fresco. Practical, modern rooms.

in Port de Carhaix **6 km southwest by Lorient road – ✉ 29270 Carhaix-Plouguer**

Auberge du Poher
– ✆ 02 98 99 51 18 – Fax 02 98 99 55 98 – Closed 1st-13 July, 2-15 February, Tuesday dinner, Wednesday dinner and Sunday dinner off season and Monday
Rest – Menu € 15 (weekdays), € 20/46 – Carte € 21/48
◆ Appealing inn with a pleasant rustic dining room facing the garden. Copious portions of conventional fare cooked according to tradition; very reasonably priced.

CARIGNAN – 08 Ardennes – 306 N5 – pop. 3 259 – alt. 174 m – ✉ 08110

14 **C1**

Paris 264 – Charleville-Mézières 43 – Mouzon 8 – Montmédy 24 – Sedan 20 – Verdun 70

La Gourmandière
19 av. Blagny – ✆ 03 24 22 20 99 – la-gourmandiere2@wanadoo.fr – Fax 03 24 22 20 99 – Closed Monday except public holidays
Rest – Menu (€ 20), € 29/50 – Carte € 53/74
◆ A bourgeois house made from stone with a simple, rustic dining room. In summer enjoy the terrace in the garden. Tasty food using vegetable garden produce and a nice wine list.

CARMAUX – 81 Tarn – 338 E6 – pop. 10 231 – alt. 241 m – ✉ 81400

29 **C2**

Paris 673 – Rodez 59 – Toulouse 96 – Cordes-sur-Ciel 22 – St-Affrique 90

Office de tourisme, place Gambetta ✆ 05 63 76 76 67, Fax 05 63 36 84 51

Au Chapon Tarnais
3 bd Augustin-Malroux, (N 88) – ✆ 05 63 36 60 10 – auchapontarnais@free.fr – Fax 05 63 36 60 10 – Closed 2-20 January, Saturday lunch, Sunday dinner, Tuesday dinner and Monday
Rest – Menu (€ 22), € 24/45
◆ A discreet little house on the side of the main road. Pleasant, renovated dining room with carefully laid tables offering generous, modern cuisine and a charming family welcome.

CARNAC – 56 Morbihan – 308 M9 – pop. 4 444 – alt. 16 m – Casino Z – ✉ 56340

Brittany

9 **B3**

Paris 490 – Auray 13 – Lorient 49 – Quiberon 19 – Vannes 33

Office de tourisme, 74, avenue des Druides ✆ 02 97 52 13 52, Fax 02 97 52 86 10

de Villarceaux Auray Ploemel, North: 8 km by D 196, ✆ 02 97 56 85 18.

Musée de préhistoire★★ **M** - St-Cornély church ★ **E** - St-Michel tumulus **l**★: ≤★ - Le Ménec alignments ★★ by D 196: 1.5 km - Kermario alignments ★★ y ②: 2 km - Kerlescan alignments ★ by ②: 4.5 km.

Plan on next page

Le Diana rm, VISA
21 bd de la Plage – ✆ 02 97 52 05 38 – contact@lediana.com – Fax 02 97 52 87 91 – Open 20 March-7 November Z **r**
35 rm – €105/248 €120/248, € 20 – 3 suites – ½ P € 113/177
Rest – *(open 30 April-5 October and closed Wednesday dinner off season and lunch except Sunday and public holidays)* Menu (€ 25), € 28, € 38/65 – Carte € 50/70
◆ Large building with an elegant atmosphere, housing rather spacious rooms with a sea view. Those overlooking the mini golf course are quieter. Wellness centre. A veranda and terrace facing the beach. Regionally inspired cuisine with extensive wine and rum list.

Novotel rest, VISA
av. de l'Atlantique – ✆ 02 97 52 53 00 – h0406@accor.com – Fax 02 97 52 53 55 – Closed 5-20 January Z **s**
109 rm – €99/191 €115/191, € 14 – 1 suite – ½ P € 97/135
Rest *Le Clipper* – Menu (€ 22), € 29 – Carte € 28/51
Rest *Diététique* – Menu € 30
◆ Direct access to the thalassotherapy centre, seawater swimming pool, fitness centre and tennis court. The rooms have been renovated in the usual dynamic Novotel spirit! The Clipper offers traditional dishes and a nautical setting. The Diététique offers set menus for those taking a cure, based on the advice of a dietician.

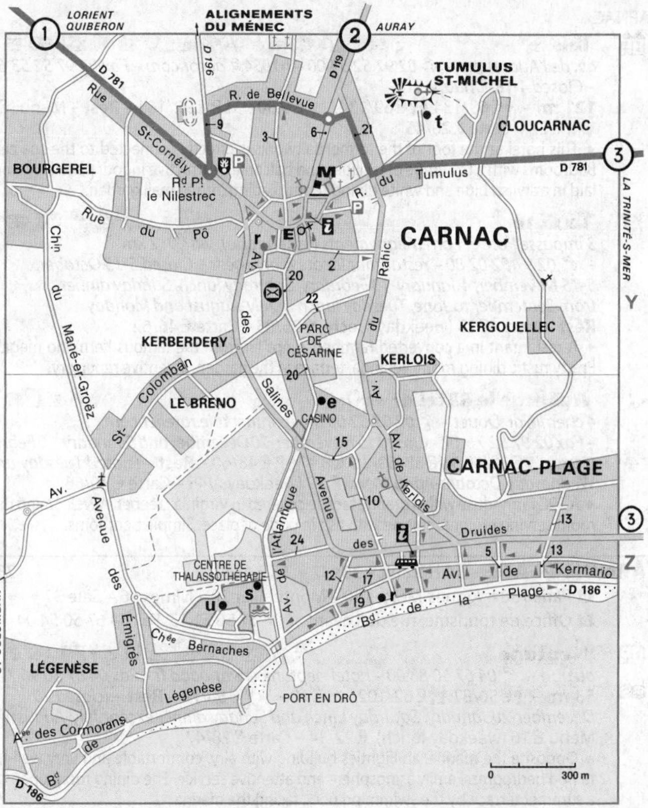

Street	Square	No.
Colary (R.)	Y	2
Courdiec (R. de)	Y	3
Cromlech (Allée du)	Z	5
Korrigans (R. des)	Y	6
Ménec (R. du)	Y	9
Menhirs (Av. des)	Z	10
Miln (Av.)	Z	12
Montagne (Allée de la)	Z	13
Palud (Av. du)	Z	15
Parc (Allée du)	Z	17
Port en Dro (Av. de)	Z	19
Poste (Av. de la)	Y	20
Poul Person (R. de)	Y	21
Roer (Av. du)	Y	22
Talleyrand (R. de)	Z	24

Celtique rest, VISA AE

82 av. des Druides – ✆ 02 97 52 14 15 – reservation@hotelceltique.com – Fax 02 97 52 71 10 Z **h**

71 rm – †€ 69/139 ††€ 69/159, ☕ € 12 – 2 suites – ½ P € 139/209

Rest – *(dinner only off season)* Menu € 25/50 – Carte € 31/70

◆ A recent building in the midst of old pine trees houses modern and light rooms decorated in a Breton fashion. Near the beach, pool with a sliding roof, Jacuzzi and fitness centre. A classic menu enriched by fish and seafood dishes to the delight of its regulars.

Tumulus rest, VISA AE

chemin du Tumulus – ✆ 02 97 52 08 21 – info@hotel-tumulus.com – Fax 02 97 52 81 88 – Closed from mid November to mid February Y **t**

23 rm – †€ 75/170 ††€ 85/295, ☕ € 15

Rest – *(closed Sunday dinner and Tuesday lunch except July-August and Monday)* Menu € 27/35 – Carte € 40/56

◆ 1920s hillside hotel, renovated in 2006, with a great view of the coast. Rooms upstairs, bungalows with terrace, pool and Jacuzzi in the garden. Unpretentious classic menu in this restaurant facing the bay of Quiberon.

Ibis rest, VISA

av. de l'Atlantique – 02 97 52 54 00 – h1054@accor.com – Fax 02 97 52 53 66 – Closed 4-18 January Z **u**

121 rm – €63/134 €69/134, €9,50 – ½ P €92/164 – **Rest** – Menu (€ 17), €22 – Carte €20/45

◆ This hotel at the foot of the former saltworks is directly connected to the spa centre. Bedrooms with a full range of facilities and balconies. Attractive indoor pool. Large buffet laid in a stylish blue and white dining room, leading into a small garden.

La Côte VISA

3 impasse Parc er Forn (Alignements de Kermario), via ②: 2 km – 02 97 52 02 80 – restaurant.lacote@orange.fr – Closed 5-15 October, 5-15 November, 4 January-10 February, Saturday lunch, Sunday dinner from September to June, Tuesday lunch in July-August and Monday

Rest – Menu €23 (weekday lunch), €35/85 – Carte €46/62

◆ A restaurant in a converted farmhouse not far from the famous Kermario megaliths. Pretty rustic dining room, veranda, terrace in the garden. Inventive repertory.

Auberge le Râtelier with rm VISA

4 chemin du Douet – 02 97 52 05 04 – contact@le.ratelier.com – Fax 02 97 52 76 11 – Closed 15 November-20 December and 5 January-10 February

9 rm – €38/60 €38/60, €8 – ½ P €48/60 – **Rest** – *(closed Tuesday and Wednesday October-April)* Menu €19 (weekdays)/45 – Carte €30/66 Y **r**

◆ A 19C farmhouse with a granite façade covered in Virginia creeper. A welcoming dining room serving regional cuisine with fish in pride of place. Simple bedrooms.

CARNON-PLAGE – 34 Hérault – 339 I7 – ✉ 34280 23 C2

Paris 758 – Aigues-Mortes 20 – Montpellier 20 – Nîmes 56 – Sète 37

Office de tourisme, rue du Levant 04 67 50 51 15, Fax 04 67 50 54 04

Neptune VISA

au port – 04 67 50 88 00 – hotel-neptune@wanadoo.fr – Fax 04 67 50 96 72

53 rm – €50/87 €62/102, €10 – ½ P €58/78 – **Rest** – *(closed 20 December-20 January, Saturday lunch and Sunday dinner except July-August)* Menu €16 (weekday lunch), €22/34 – Carte €28/47

◆ Opposite the marina, an Eighties building with airy, comfortable and very well-maintained bedrooms. Family atmosphere and attentive service. The dining room opens onto a summer terrace by the swimming pool, facing the marina.

CARNOULES – 83 Var – 340 M6 – pop. 2 594 – alt. 205 m – ✉ 83660 41 C3

Paris 831 – Brignoles 23 – Draguignan 48 – Hyères 34 – Toulon 34

Syndicat d'initiative, place Gabriel Péri 04 94 28 32 96

Tuilière with rm VISA

2 km on D 97 Toulon road – 04 94 48 32 39 – guillaume.astesiano@wanadoo.fr – Fax 04 94 48 36 06

3 rm – €50 €60/75, €7,50 – **Rest** – *(closed dinner winter except Friday-Saturday, lunch Tuesday-Thursday summer, Wednesday off season and Monday season) (number of covers limited, pre-book)* Menu €19 (weekdays)/36 – Carte €29/48

◆ Isolated in the middle of a vineyard, an old mas is home to a rustic restaurant with small, delightful Provençal dining rooms. Pleasant terrace at the front. Regional cuisine. Personalised rooms refurbished in colourful fabrics.

CARPENTRAS – 84 Vaucluse – 332 D9 – pop. 26 090 – alt. 102 m – ✉ 84200 Provence 42 E1

Paris 679 – Avignon 30 – Digne-les-Bains 139 – Gap 146 – Marseille 105

Office de tourisme, place Aristide Briand 04 90 63 00 78, Fax 04 90 60 41 02

Provence Country Club Saumane-de-Vaucluse Route de Fontaine de Vaucluse, by Cavaillon road: 18 km, 04 90 20 20 65.

Former St-Siffrein cathedral ★: Synagogue★.

Plan on next page

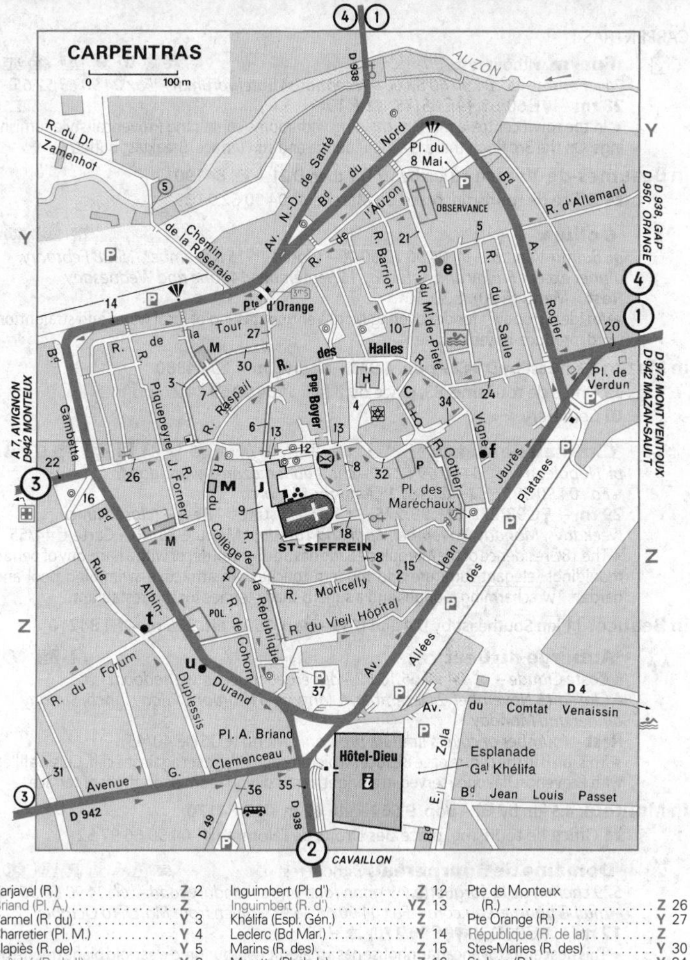

Barjavel (R.)	Z	2	Inguimbert (Pl. d')	Z	12	Pte de Monteux (R.)	Z	26
Briand (Pl. A.)	Z		Inguimbert (R. d')	YZ	13	Pte Orange (R.)	Y	27
Carmel (R. du)	Y	3	Khélifa (Espl. Gén.)	Z		République (R. de la)	Z	
Charretier (Pl. M.)	Y	4	Leclerc (Bd Mar.)	Y	14	Stes-Maries (R. des)	Y	30
Clapiès (R. de)	Y	5	Marins (R. des)	Z	15	St-Jean (R.)	Y	34
Évêché (R. de l')	Y	6	Marotte (Pl. de la)	Z	16	Sémard (Av. Pierre)	Z	31
Frères-Laurens (R. des)	Y	7	Mercière (R.)	Z	18	Sous-Préfecture (R.)	Z	32
Gaudibert-Barret (R.)	Z	8	Mont Ventoux (Av. du)	Y	20	Victor-Hugo (Av.)	Z	35
Gaulle (Pl. du Gén.-de)	Z	9	Observance (R. de l')	Y	21	Wilson (Av.)	Z	36
Guillabert (R. D.)	Y	10	Pétrarque (Av.)	Z	22	25-Août-1944 (Pl. du)	Z	37
Halles (R. des)	Y		Pte de Mazan (R.)	Y	24			

Le Comtadin rm, rest, VISA AE
65 bd Albin-Durand – 04 90 67 75 00 – reception@le-comtadin.com – Fax 04 90 67 75 01 – Closed 20 December-7 January, February holidays and Sunday from October to February Z **u**
19 rm – †€ 54/91 ††€ 73/99, ☕ € 11 – 1 suite – ½ P € 76/90
Rest – *(closed Saturday, and Sunday)* Carte € 20/30
◆ Completely refurbished late 18th century mansion. The majority of the rooms, which are light and well- soundproofed, overlook the patio where you can have your breakfast in summer (buffets).

Du Fiacre without rest VISA AE
153 r. de la Vigne – 04 90 63 03 15 – contact@hotel-du-fiacre.com – Fax 04 90 60 49 73
18 rm – †€ 60/85 ††€ 68/110, ☕ € 10 Z **f**
◆ This 18C private house in the old town has retained its original bourgeois atmosphere. The warm and comfortable rooms are quieter on the patio side.

Forvm without rest

24 r. Forum – ☎ 04 90 60 57 00 – reception@hotel-forum.fr – Fax 04 90 63 52 65
28 rm – †€ 60/65 ††€ 65/75, ☕ € 10 Z t

♦ In the town centre, a modern building with rooms containing Provençal-style furnishings. On the 3rd floor, there is a mini-lounge and sun terrace. Breakfast buffet.

in Beaumes-de-Venise **10 km by ① D 7 then D 21 – ✉ 84190**

Office de tourisme, place du Marché ☎ 04 90 62 94 39

Dolium

pl. Balma-Vénitia – ☎ 04 90 12 80 00 – Closed 1st-15 November, 15-28 February, dinner except Friday and Saturday 16 September-14 June and Wednesday
Rest – Menu (€ 20), € 30/50

♦ An ideal stopover for discovering Mont Ventoux: tasting of local wines and straightforward, produce-based cuisine.

in Mazan **7 km East by D 942 – pop. 4 943 – alt. 100 m – ✉ 84380**

Office de tourisme, 83, place du 8 Mai ☎ 04 90 69 74 27

Cemetery ≤★.

Château de Mazan

pl. Napoléon – ☎ 04 90 69 62 61 – chateaudemazan@wanadoo.fr – Fax 04 90 69 76 62 – Closed 1st January-1st March
29 rm – †€ 98/275 ††€ 98/275, ☕ € 15 – 2 suites – **Rest** – *(closed lunch weekdays, Monday November-April and Tuesday)* Menu € 35/46 – Carte € 44/55

♦ The 18C residence of the Marquis de Sade has a delightful decor with a harmony of period mouldings, elegant furniture and modern touches. An attractive swimming pool and garden. Two charming lounges and a superb shady terrace for this restaurant.

in Beaucet **11 km Southeast by D 4 and D 39 – pop. 352 – alt. 275 m – ✉ 84210**

Auberge du Beaucet

r. Coste Claude – ☎ 04 90 66 10 82 – aubergebeaucet@wanadoo.fr – Closed 15 November-2 December, 6 January-6 February, Friday lunch, Sunday dinner and Monday
Rest – *(number of covers limited, pre-book)* Menu (€ 35), € 40/45

♦ This inn is in the centre of Le Beaucet, a picturesque village set against a cliff. Cuisine filled with Provençal flavours, served in a bright, rustic dining room or on the roof terrace.

in Monteux **4,5 km by ③ – pop. 9 564 – alt. 42 m – ✉ 84170**

Office de tourisme, place des Droits de l'Homme ☎ 04 90 66 97 52

Domaine de Bournereau without rest

579 chemin de la Sorguette, Avignon road and secondary road – ☎ 04 90 66 36 13 – mail@bournereau.com – Fax 04 90 66 36 93 – Open from March to October
12 rm – †€ 90/120 ††€ 90/170, ☕ € 10

♦ This peaceful Provençal farmhouse has a majestic two-hundred-year-old plane tree in the middle of its courtyard. Spacious, comfortable rooms with antique and modern furniture.

Avignon road **10 km by ③ D 942 – ✉ 84180 Monteux**

Le Saule Pleureur

145 chemin de Beauregard – ☎ 04 90 62 01 35 – contact@le-saule-pleureur.fr – Fax 04 90 62 10 90 – Closed 3-17 March, 27 October-10 November, 5-12 January, Saturday lunch, Sunday dinner and Monday except public holidays
Rest – Menu € 29 (weekday lunch), € 59/119 bi – Carte € 75/120

♦ Near a busy road, this villa, surrounded by a garden, welcomes its guests into a modern dining room or onto a delightful veranda. Creative cuisine.

CARQUEIRANNE – 83 Var – 340 L7 – pop. 8 436 – alt. 30 m – ✉ 83320

Paris 849 – Draguignan 80 – Hyères 7 – Toulon 16 41 **C3**

La Maison des Saveurs

18 av. J.-Jaurès, (town centre) – ☎ 04 94 58 62 33 – restaurant@maisondessaveurs.com – Closed Sunday dinner, Tuesday lunch and Monday
Rest – Menu € 26

♦ In a local-style house in the town centre, this modest restaurant has two advantages: a pretty terrace shaded by a plane tree and a reasonably priced menu.

West 2 km by D 559 ✉83320 Carqueiranne

Val d'Azur without rest
3 impasse de la Valérane – ✆ 04 94 48 07 16 – valdazur@hotmail.fr – Fax 04 94 48 07 16
5 rm – €75/135 €75/135
◆ Near the sea, this new building offers personalised rooms decorated in bright colours with pretty, modern furniture and balconies.

CARRIÈRES-SUR-SEINE – **78 Yvelines** – **311** J2 – **101** 14 – **see Paris, Area**

LES CARROZ-D'ARÂCHES – **74 Haute-Savoie** – **328** M4 – **alt. 1 140 m** – **Winter sports : 1 140/2 500 m** 5 70 – ✉ **74300** French Alps 46 **F1**

Paris 580 – Annecy 67 – Bonneville 25 – Chamonix-Mont-Blanc 47 – Thonon-les-Bains 70

Office de tourisme, 9, place Ambiance ✆ 04 50 90 00 04, Fax 04 50 90 07 00

de Pierre Carrée Flaine, East: 12 km by D 106, ✆ 04 50 90 85 44.

Les Servages d'Armelle ← mountains, rm, VISA
841 rte des Servages – ✆ 04 50 90 01 62 – servages@wanadoo.fr – Fax 04 50 90 39 41 – Closed May and November
6 rm – €155/330 €155/330, €30 – 2 suites
Rest – *(closed Tuesday and Wednesday off season and Monday)*
Carte €44/74
◆ Venerable woodwork, hi-tech facilities and designer interior combined; refined accommodation at this superb sensitively restored chalet. Stylish mountain restaurant with a view of hyper-modern kitchens. Regional cuisine.

Les Airelles VISA
346 rte Moulins – ✆ 04 50 90 01 02 – lesairelles@free.fr – Fax 04 50 90 03 75 – Open 22 June-30 September and 15 December-22 April
12 rm – €50/55 €59/90, €9,50 – 3 suites – ½ P €73/98
Rest – Menu €24/36 – Carte €33/48
◆ The rooms in the first chalet are small but truly delightful (wood, warm colour scheme); the brand new second chalet offers comfortable apartments. Distinctive alpine restaurant in terms of decor and cuisine (house speciality: mountain sausages with cabbage).

La Croix de Savoie ← mountains, VISA
768 rte du Pernand – ✆ 04 50 90 00 26 – info@lacroixdesavoie.fr – Fax 04 50 90 00 63 – Closed 1st May-14 June and 6 October-24 November
Rest – Menu €19/41 – Carte approx. €38
◆ A rustic dining room (non-smoking), interesting regional dishes and a family welcome await at this restaurant. Superb view of the mountains and the valley.

CARRY-LE-ROUET – **13 Bouches-du-Rhône** – **340** F6 – **pop. 6 009** – **alt. 5 m** – **Casino** – ✉ **13620** Provence 40 **B3**

Paris 765 – Aix-en-Provence 39 – Marseille 34 – Martigues 20 – Salon-de-Provence 45

Office de tourisme, avenue Aristide Briand ✆ 04 42 13 20 36, Fax 04 42 44 52 03

Le Madrigal ← VISA
4 av. Dr G. Montus – ✆ 04 42 44 58 63 – Fax 04 42 44 58 63 – Closed from mid November to beg. January, Sunday dinner and Monday from September to April
Rest – Menu €29/38 – Carte €40/51
◆ In the upper section of Carry, overlooking the harbour, this pink house has a pleasant terrace offering picture postcard views. Traditional cuisine and fish dishes.

CARSAC-AILLAC – 24 Dordogne – 329 I6 – pop. 1 217 – alt. 80 m – ✉ 24200

Dordogne-Berry-Limousin 4 **D3**

Paris 536 – Brive-la-Gaillarde 59 – Gourdon 18 – Sarlat-la-Canéda 9

La Villa Romaine

St-Rome, 3 km on Gourdon road – ✆ 05 53 28 52 07 – contact@lavillaromaine.com – Fax 05 53 28 58 10

17 rm – €110/160 €110/160, ☕ €13 – 2 suites – ½ P €91/118

Rest – *(open 2 April-10 November and closed Wednesday dinner 23 March-10 November except July-August) (dinner only)* Menu €27/37 – Carte €34/58

◆ Attractively restored old farmhouse built on a Gallo-Roman site near the Dordogne. Spacious, well-kept rooms. Pleasant terraces, garden and pool. Pleasant, rustic setting, wrought iron furniture and contemporary cuisine.

Domaine Lacoste with rm

rest, rm,

– ✆ 05 53 59 58 81 – info@domainelacoste.com – Closed February and autumn half-term holidays

5 rm ☕ – €60/70 €60/75 – **Rest** – *(closed lunch June-September, Sunday dinner, Thursday dinner and Wednesday) (number of covers limited, pre-book)* Menu €20/30

◆ Appetising cuisine combining southern and Périgord influences. Pretty countrified decor and covered terrace by the pool. Smart simple rooms.

CARTERET – 50 Manche – 303 B3 – see Barneville-Carteret

CARVIN – 62 Pas-de-Calais – 301 K5 – pop. 17 772 – alt. 31 m – ✉ 62220

31 **C2**

Paris 204 – Arras 35 – Béthune 28 – Douai 23 – Lille 24

Parc Hôtel

Z.I. du Château – ✆ 03 21 79 65 65 – customer@parc-hotel.com – Fax 03 21 79 80 00

46 rm – €42/68 €52/80, ☕ €12 – ½ P €55/65 – **Rest** – *(closed Sunday dinner and public holiday dinner)* Menu (€19), €24/35 bi – Carte €28/36

◆ Near the motorway, a modern establishment offering functional, well-soundproofed rooms decorated in pastel colours; those overlooking the countryside are quieter. A light, spacious dining room where meals can be served buffet style.

Le Charolais

Domaine de la Gloriette, 143 bis r. Mar.-Foch – ✆ 03 21 40 12 98 – lecharolais@wanadoo.fr – Fax 03 21 40 41 15 – Closed 5-25 August, Tuesday dinner, Sunday dinner and Monday

Rest – Menu (€16), €36/68 bi – Carte €33/58

◆ This house is very much in the regional style with its brick facade. In the soberly laid out dining room you can try classic dishes and Charolais beef specialities.

CASAMOZZA – 2B Haute-Corse – 345 F4 – see Corse

CASCASTEL-DES-CORBIÈRES – 11 Aude – 344 H5 – pop. 196 – alt. 140 m – ✉ 11360

22 **B3**

Paris 835 – Perpignan 52 – Carcassonne 70 – Narbonne 48

Domaine Grand Guilhem without rest

chemin du Col-de-la-Serre – ✆ 04 68 45 86 67 – gguilhem@aol.com – Fax 04 68 45 29 58 – Closed February holidays

4 rm ☕ – €78 €85

◆ This renovated, 19C, stone residence has kept all its authenticity. The charming rooms are very well kept. Wine tasting in the cellar.

Le Clos de Cascastel

quai de la Berre – ✆ 04 68 45 06 22 – leclosdecascastel@orange.fr – Fax 04 68 45 06 22 – Closed mid November-mid December, mid January-beg. February and Tuesday

Rest – Menu €17/39 bi – Carte €24/38

◆ A village surrounded by Corbières vineyards and close to the 'citadelles du vertige'. Simple, rustic interior and pleasant terrace. Regional cuisine and wines.

CASSEL – 59 Nord – 302 C3 – pop. 2 290 – alt. 175 m – ✉ 59670
Northern France and the Paris Region 30 **B2**

Paris 250 – Calais 58 – Dunkerque 30 – Hazebrouck 11 – Lille 52 – St-Omer 21

Syndicat d'initiative, 20, Grand'Place ✆ 03 28 40 52 55, Fax 03 28 40 59 17

Site★.

Châtellerie de Schoebeque without rest

32 r. du Maréchal Foch – ✆ 03 28 42 42 67
– contact@schoebeque.com – Fax 03 28 42 21 86
14 rm – €155/299 €155/299, €15

◆ Luxury, charm and peace and quiet in this historic 18C abode. Fine rooms, spa (beauty centre) and a matchless view of Flanders from the breakfast veranda.

Au Petit Bruxelles

at the Petit-Bruxelles, south-east: 3.5 km on D 916 – ✆ 03 28 42 44 64
– aupetitbruxelles@wanadoo.fr – Fax 03 28 40 58 13 – Closed Sunday dinner, Tuesday dinner, Wednesday dinner and Monday
Rest – Menu €26/56 – Carte €31/62

◆ An old coaching inn with a spruce, red-brick façade typical of the region. Warm rustic dining room, informal ambience and sophisticated updated cuisine.

in St-Sylvestre-Cappel 6 km Northeast by D 916 – pop. 1 093 – alt. 55 m – ✉ 59114

Le St Sylvestre

57 rte Nationale – ✆ 03 28 42 82 13 – restaurantlesaintsylvestre@wanadoo.fr
– Closed 4-31 August, 23 February-4 March, Monday dinner, Saturday lunch, Sunday dinner and Wednesday
Rest – Menu €28/49 – Carte €39/49

◆ The black façade of this establishment hides a very trendy decor; designer furniture, bright colours and Chaplin films, a setting in keeping with the minimalist cuisine based on spices.

CASSIS – 13 Bouches-du-Rhône – 340 I6 – pop. 8 001 – alt. 10 m – Casino – ✉ 13260 Provence 40 **B3**

Paris 800 – Aix-en-Provence 51 – La Ciotat 10 – Marseille 30 – Toulon 42

Office de tourisme, Quai des Moulins ✆ 08 92 25 98 92, Fax 04 42 01 28 31

Site★ - Les Calanques★★ (1h by boat) - Mt de la Saoupe ✻★★: 2 km by D 41A.

Cap Canaille, Europe's highest sea cliff, ←★★★ 5 km by D41A - Semaphore ✻★★★ - Corniche des Crêtes★★ de Cassis à la Ciotat.

CASSIS

Abbé-Mouton (R.) 2
Arène (R. de l') 4
Autheman (R. V.) 5
Baragnon (Pl.) 6
Barthélemy (Bd) 7
Barthélemy (Quai Jean-Jacques) 8
Baux (Quai des) 9
Ciotat (R. de la) 10
Clemenceau (Pl.) 12
Ganteaume (Av. de l'Amiral) . 14
Jean-Jaurès (Av.) 16
Leriche (Av. Professeur) 17
Mirabeau (Pl.) 22
Moulins (Quai des) 23
République (Pl.) 25
Revestel (Av. du) 26
St-Michel (Pl.) 27
Thiers (R. Adolphe) 29
Victor-Hugo (Av.) 32

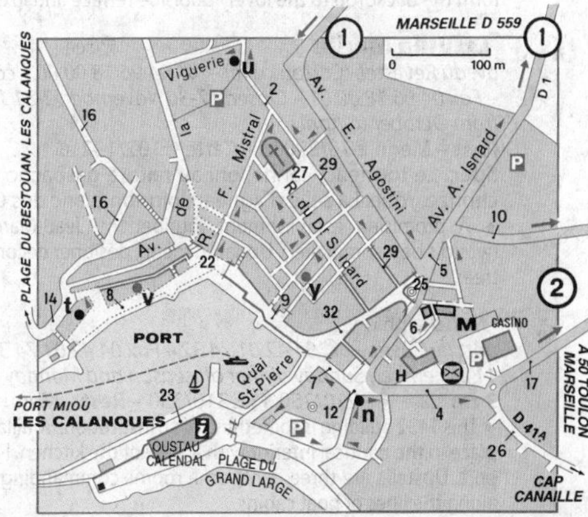

Royal Cottage without rest
6 av. 11 Novembre by ① – ✆ 04 42 01 33 34
– info@royal-cottage.com – Fax 04 42 01 06 90 – Closed 12-27 December
25 rm – €80/204 €80/204, €12
◆ A small Provençal paradise flourishing amid lush exotic vegetation. A contemporary interior. The terraces of some rooms command a fine view of the harbour.

Les Jardins de Cassis without rest
r. A. Favier, 1 km via ① – ✆ 04 42 01 84 85
– contact@lesjardinsdecassis.com – Fax 04 42 01 32 38 – Open April-October
36 rm – €60/123 €60/234, €15
◆ A series of ochre coloured buildings on the heights of Cassis. Smart rooms, often with private terraces. Attractive Mediterranean garden and pool. Jacuzzi tub.

Le Golfe without rest
3 pl. Grand Carnot – ✆ 04 42 01 00 21 – contact@hotel-le-golfe-cassis.com
– Fax 04 42 01 92 08 – Open 21 March-10 November **t**
30 rm – €70/95 €70/95, €11
◆ This appealing, unpretentious hotel has small, practical, air-conditioned rooms, some with a sea view and a terrace shaded by plane trees overlooking the harbour.

Le Clos des Arômes
10 r. Paul Mouton – ✆ 04 42 01 71 84 – closdesaromes@orange.fr
– Fax 04 42 01 31 76 – Closed 3 January-28 February **u**
14 rm – €52 €69/89, €9 – **Rest** – *(closed Tuesday lunch, Wednesday lunch and Monday except dinner in July-August)* Menu €29/40 – Carte €37/56
◆ The doors of this charming house open onto a flower-decked garden. Rooms, both discreet and contemporary, are gaily and tastefully decorated. A tiny dining room and delightful terrace, Southern cuisine: fish stews such as bourride or bouillabaisse.

Cassitel without rest
pl. Clemenceau – ✆ 04 42 01 83 44 – cassitel@hotel-cassis.com
– Fax 04 42 01 96 31 **n**
32 rm – €63/68 €71/90, €8
◆ A hotel near the beach but also in the centre of the lively part of Cassis and its nightlife (discotheques and bars). Practical rooms, renovated on the harbour side. Provençal breakfast room.

Château de Cassis without rest
Traverse du Château, (via the Traverse des Lombards) – ✆ 04 42 01 63 20
– chateaudecassis@free.fr – Fax 04 42 01 73 58
5 rm – €300/690 €300/690
◆ This 18C walled stronghold overlooks the bay of Cassis. Old stonewalls and cypress trees form the backdrop to the lovely poolside terrace and luxurious romantic rooms.

La Villa Madie sea,
av. du Revestel, (Corton cove) – ✆ 04 96 18 00 00 – contact@lavillamadie.com
– Fax 04 96 18 00 01 – Closed 17-30 November, 2-31 January, Monday and Tuesday from October to April
Rest – Menu €70/220 bi – Carte €102/132
Spec. Le tourteau, cannelloni au raifort, gaspacho de laitue. La lotte piquée au chorizo, rôtie. La selle d'agneau, oignon blanc des Cévennes farci aux céréales.
◆ A promising establishment founded by Jean-Marc Banzo and Enrico Bernardo (world's best sommelier). Updated menu, designer decor, terraces, view of the sea and fir trees.

Nino with rm
port de Cassis – ✆ 04 42 01 74 32 – Fax 04 42 01 74 32 – Closed 27 November-11 December, Sunday dinner off season and Monday **v**
3 rm – €210/250 €310/350 – **Rest** – Menu €35
◆ This 1432 building is something of an institution. Bouillabaisse and seafood take pride of place in the nautical interior with a view of the kitchen. Flower-decked terrace facing the port. Upstairs are three handsome rooms commanding a fine view. They are designed along the lines of boat cabins.

Fleurs de Thym

5 r. Lamartine – ✆ 04 42 01 23 03 – fleurdethym3@wanadoo.fr – Fax 04 42 03 95 28 – Closed mid December-mid January y

Rest – *(dinner only)* Menu € 29 (weekdays)/42

◆ Fireplace, painted wood, Souleiado fabrics, Mousiers ceramics: a cosy southern French setting in a former stone-built chapel. Updated regional fare.

CASTAGNÈDE – 64 Pyrénées-Atlantiques – 342 G4 – see Salies-de-Béarn

---

CASTAGNIERS – 06 Alpes-Maritimes – 341 E5 – pop. 1 359 – alt. 350 m – ✉ 06670

42 **E2**

Paris 938 – Antibes 34 – Cannes 44 – Contes 31 – Levens 16 – Nice 18 – Vence 22

Aspremont: ✳★ from the terrace of the former château Southeast: 4 km, **French Riviera.**

Chez Michel with rm

1 pl. St Michel – ✆ 04 93 08 05 15 – hotel.restaurant.chez-michel@wanadoo.fr – Fax 04 93 08 05 38 – Closed 26 October-7 December

20 rm – €52 €52, ☕ €8 – ½ P €60 – **Rest** – *(closed Sunday dinner and Monday)* Menu (€ 13), € 19 (weekdays)/38 – Carte € 21/48

◆ Rustic restaurant adorned with farm tools. Recipes from Nice, notably daubes and raviolis. A few simple, well-kept rooms in the annexe.

CASTANET-TOLOSAN – 31 Haute-Garonne – 343 H3 – see Toulouse

LE CASTELET – 09 Ariège – 343 I8 – see Ax-les-Thermes

CASTELJALOUX – 47 Lot-et-Garonne – 336 C4 – pop. 4 755 – alt. 52 m – ✉ 47700 Atlantic Coast

4 **C2**

Paris 674 – Agen 55 – Langon 55 – Marmande 23 – Mont-de-Marsan 73 – Nérac 30

Office de tourisme, Maison du Roy ✆ 05 53 93 00 00, Fax 05 53 20 74 32

de Casteljaloux Route de Mont de Marsan, South: 4 km by D 933, ✆ 05 53 93 51 60.

Les Cordeliers

rest,

r. Cordeliers – ✆ 05 53 93 02 19 – hotel.lescordeliers@wanadoo.fr – Fax 05 53 93 55 48 – Closed 23 December-13 January

24 rm – €40/42 €45/70, ☕ €7 – ½ P €45 – **Rest** – *(closed Sunday dinner)* Menu (€ 12), € 16 (weekdays)/29 – Carte € 26/43

◆ A warm welcome awaits at this establishment situated in an alley off the main square. The functional, well-kept rooms have been recently renovated. The restaurant is decorated in a modern, sober style, the tables are laid with care and the food is traditional.

La Vieille Auberge

11 r. Posterne – ✆ 05 53 93 01 36 – la.vieille.auberge.47@wanadoo.fr – Fax 05 53 93 18 89 – Closed 23 June-6 July, 24 November-10 December, 18-27 February, Sunday dinner, Tuesday dinner and Wednesday

Rest – Menu € 20/38 – Carte € 41/61

◆ A charming stone house in a tiny street in the old town. Bright, colourful dining room with lots of flowers. Fine, classical cuisine.

CASTELLANE – 04 Alpes-de-Haute-Provence – 334 H9 – pop. 1 508 – alt. 730 m – ✉ 04120 French Alps

41 **C2**

Paris 797 – Digne-les-Bains 54 – Draguignan 59 – Grasse 64 – Manosque 92

Office de tourisme, rue Nationale ✆ 04 92 83 61 14, Fax 04 92 83 76 89

de Taulane La Martre Le Logis du Pin, East: 17 km by D 4085, ✆ 04 93 60 31 30.

Site★ - Chaudanne lake ★ 4 km by ①.

Grand canyon du Verdon★★★.

in la Garde 6 km by ① D 559 and D 4085 – pop. 56 – alt. 928 m – ✉ 04120

Auberge du Teillon with rm
rte Napoléon – ✆ 04 92 83 60 88 – contact@auberge-teillon.com – Fax 04 92 83 74 08 – Open 15 March-15 November and closed Sunday dinner and Monday except July-August and public holidays, Tuesday lunch in July-August
8 rm – €50/55 €50/55, €8 – ½ P €55/57 – **Rest** – Menu €22/48 – Carte €36/52
◆ A smiling welcome and friendly atmosphere in this rustic roadside inn. Tasty, traditional cuisine with a modern touch; selection of Provençal dishes.

LE CASTELLET – 83 Var – 340 J6 – pop. 3 799 – alt. 252 m – ✉ 83330 40 B3

Paris 816 – Marseille 46 – Toulon 23 – Aubagne 30 – Bandol 11
Paul Ricard race circuit ✆ 04 94 98 36 66

Castel Lumière St-Cyr -sur- Mer bay, rm,
au vieux village – ✆ 04 94 32 62 20 – infos@castellumiere.com – Fax 04 94 32 70 33 – Hotel : open March-September; restaurant: closed January and February
6 rm – €85/100 €85/100, €10 – ½ P €75/85 – **Rest** – *(closed Tuesday and Wednesday 1st September-30 June and Monday lunch July-August)*
Menu €36/47 – Carte €36/52
◆ The new owners have given this old building overlooking the valley and the sea a modern look. Attractive, colourful contemporary-style rooms, six of which have a view. Contemporary-style panoramic restaurant serving Provençal cuisine.

in Ste-Anne-du-Castellet 4,5 km North by D 226 and D 26 – ✉ 83330

Castel Ste-Anne without rest
81 chemin Chapelle – ✆ 04 94 32 60 08 – hotelcastelstanne@wanadoo.fr – Fax 04 94 32 68 16
17 rm – €55 €65/70, €7,50
◆ Peace and quiet, a flower garden and attractive swimming pool form the setting for this family hotel. New rooms in the annexe have terraces; others are plainer.

at Circuit Paul Ricard 11 km North by D 226, D 26 and D N8 – ✉ 83330 Le Beausset

Du Castellet
3001 rte Hauts du Camp – ✆ 04 94 98 37 77 – welcome@hotelducastellet.com – Fax 04 94 98 37 78
34 rm – €320/380 €320/380, €32 – 13 suites
Rest *Monte Cristo* – Menu €50 (weekday lunch)/100 – Carte €89/132
Spec. "Yin et Yang" de langoustines, fraîcheur de tourteau, soupe de petits pois (spring). Saint-Pierre, seiche et casserons au saté. Carré d'agneau frotté de cumin, courgette fleur. **Wines** Bandol.
◆ Close to the track, a fine residence facing south, set in a pretty enclosed park. Decor is midway between Provençal and Tuscan; luxurious facilities and a 4-hole golf course. An elegant restaurant where the chef adds a personal note to classic Mediterranean cuisine.

Résidence des Équipages without rest
3100 rte des Hauts du Camp – ✆ 04 94 98 37 77 – welcome@hotelducastellet.com – Fax 04 94 98 37 78
19 rm – €130/160 €130/160, €15
◆ Ultramodern furniture, efficient soundproofing, flat-screen TV, Internet connection: this hotel next to the air terminal will appeal to air crew and transit passengers.

CASTELNAUDARY – 11 Aude – 344 C3 – pop. 10 851 – alt. 175 m – ✉ 11400

Languedoc-Roussillon-Tarn Gorges 22 A2

Paris 735 – Carcassonne 42 – Foix 70 – Pamiers 49 – Toulouse 60
Office de tourisme, place de Verdun ✆ 04 68 23 05 73, Fax 04 68 23 61 40

Plan on next page

Du Canal without rest
2 ter av. A. Vidal – ✆ 04 68 94 05 05 – hotelducanal@wanadoo.fr – Fax 04 68 94 05 06 AZ **b**
38 rm – €48/57 €55/66, €8
◆ A beautiful ochre building, once a lime kiln, by the Canal du Midi. Practical, well soundproofed rooms. Breakfast served at the water's edge. Pretty garden.

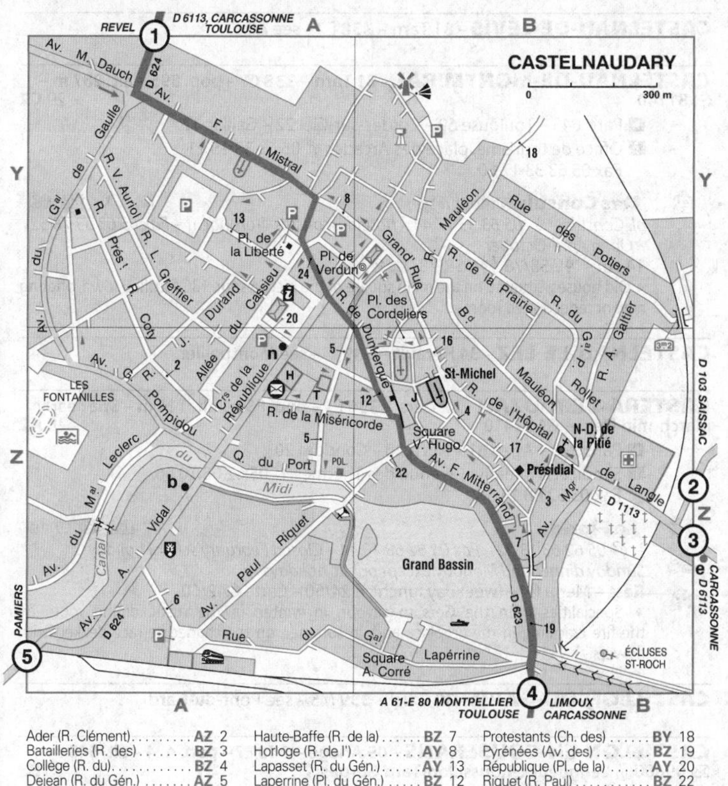

Ader (R. Clément) . . . . AZ 2
Batailleries (R. des) . . . . BZ 3
Collège (R. du) . . . . BZ 4
Dejean (R. du Gén.) . . . . AZ 5
Dunkerque (R. de) . . . . AYZ
Gare (Av. de la) . . . . AZ 6
Haute-Baffe (R. de la) . . . . . . BZ 7
Horloge (R. de l') . . . . AY 8
Lapasset (R. du Gén.) . . . . . . AY 13
Laperrine (Pl. du Gén.) . . . . . BZ 12
Pasteur (R. Louis) . . . . BZ 16
Présidial (Rampe du) . . . . BZ 17
Protestants (Ch. des) . . . . . . BY 18
Pyrénées (Av. des) . . . . BZ 19
République (Pl. de la) . . . . . . AY 20
Riquet (R. Paul) . . . . BZ 22
11-Novembre (R. du) . . . . AY 24

du Centre et du Lauragais

31 cours République – ✆ 04 68 23 25 95 – Fax 04 68 94 01 66 – Closed 1st-27 January and Sunday dinner AZ **n**

16 rm – €50/55 €50/70, ☕ €7 – ½ P €65 – **Rest** – Menu €18 (weekdays)/51 – Carte €31/60

◆ Attractive town house on Castelnaudary's main street. Practical rooms with cane furnishings. Well-lit dining room serving a traditional menu plus local specialities including the renowned cassoulet.

Le Clos Fleuri St-Siméon

134 av. Mgr. de Langle, via ③ – ✆ 04 68 94 01 20 – leclos@hotmail.fr – Fax 04 68 94 05 47 – Closed 22 December-6 January and week-end November-April

31 rm – €52/57 €55/60, ☕ €6 – ½ P €48 – **Rest** – Menu €14, €20/30 – Carte €18/36

◆ Isolated from the commercial buildings by its walled garden, this hotel has well-kept rooms in pastel colours and double-glazing. The restaurant has a terrace giving onto a small garden and the swimming pool. Simple meals and home-made cassoulet.

Le Tirou

90 av. Mgr de Langle – ✆ 04 68 94 15 95 – letirou@wanadoo.fr – Fax 04 68 94 15 96 – Closed 23-30 June, 20 December-20 January, dinner and Monday

Rest – Menu €18 (weekdays)/33 – Carte €30/53 BZ **e**

◆ The chef uses only farm-reared pork in his cassoulet. Fine choice of local wines and pleasant dining room facing the garden given over to donkeys and goats.

CASTELNAU-DE-LÉVIS – 81 Tarn – 338 E7 – see Albi

CASTELNAU-DE-MONTMIRAL – 81 Tarn – 338 C7 – pop. 895 – alt. 287 m – ✉ 81140 29 C2

Paris 645 – Toulouse 69 – Cordes-sur-Ciel 22 – Gaillac 12

Office de tourisme, place des Arcades ✆ 05 63 33 15 11, Fax 05 63 33 17 60

Des Consuls without rest VISA MC

pl. Consuls – ✆ 05 63 33 17 44 – hoteldesconsuls@orange.fr – Fax 05 63 33 78 52 – Open April-October

14 rm – †€ 58/78 ††€ 58/78, ☕ € 9

◆ Old houses, situated on the main square of the picturesque 13C fortified town, offering new or redecorated rooms.

CASTELNAU-LE-LEZ – 34 Hérault – 339 I7 – see Montpellier

CASTÉRA-VERDUZAN – 32 Gers – 336 E7 – pop. 830 – alt. 114 m – Spa : early March-mid Dec. – ✉ 32410 28 A2

Paris 720 – Agen 61 – Auch 26 – Condom 20

Syndicat d'initiative, avenue des Thermes ✆ 05 62 68 10 66, Fax 05 62 68 14 58

XX **Le Florida** VISA MC AE

– ✆ 05 62 68 13 22 – Fax 05 62 68 10 44 – Closed February school holidays, Sunday dinner and Monday except public holidays

Rest – Menu € 14 (weekday lunch), € 24/50 – Carte € 42/60

◆ Specialities from the Gers to savour, in winter, in the rustic dining room by the fire crackling in the fireplace and, in summer, on the shaded terrace decked with flowers.

CASTILLON-DU-GARD – 30 Gard – 339 M5 – see Pont-du-Gard

CASTILLON-EN-COUSERANS – 09 Ariège – 343 E7 – pop. 424 – alt. 543 m – ✉ 09800 Languedoc-Roussillon-Tarn Gorges 28 B3

Paris 787 – Bagnères-de-Luchon 61 – Foix 58 – St-Girons 14

Office de tourisme, rue Noël Peyrevidal ✆ 05 61 96 72 64, Fax 05 34 14 06 82

in Audressein 1 km by Bagnères-de-Luchon road – pop. 107 – alt. 509 m – ✉ 09800

XX **L'Auberge d'Audressein** with rm AC rest, VISA MC AE

– ✆ 05 61 96 11 80 – aubergeaudressein@club-internet.fr – Fax 05 61 96 82 96 – Closed 22 September-12 October, 5 January-2 February, Sunday dinner and Monday

7 rm – †€ 45/65 ††€ 45/65, ☕ € 9 – ½ P € 45/60 – **Rest** – Menu € 16/85 – Carte € 38/61

◆ These old stonewalls shelter a 19C forge. A warm-toned dining room, pleasant veranda overhanging the river and appetising food inspired by the region.

CASTRES – 81 Tarn – 338 F9 – pop. 43 496 – alt. 170 m – ✉ 81100 Languedoc-Roussillon-Tarn Gorges 29 C2

Paris 718 – Albi 43 – Béziers 107 – Carcassonne 70 – Toulouse 79

Castres-Mazamet: ✆ 05 63 70 34 77 by ③: 8 km.

Office de tourisme, 2, place de la Republique ✆ 05 63 62 63 62, Fax 05 63 62 63 60

de Castres Gourjade Domaine de Gourjade, North: 3 km by Roquecourbe road, ✆ 05 63 72 27 06.

Musée Goya★ - Hôtel de Nayrac★ AY - Centre national et musée Jean-Jaurès (Jean-Jaurès National Centre and Museum) AY.

Le Sidobre★ 9 km by ① - Musée du Protestantisme at Ferrières.

Plan on next page

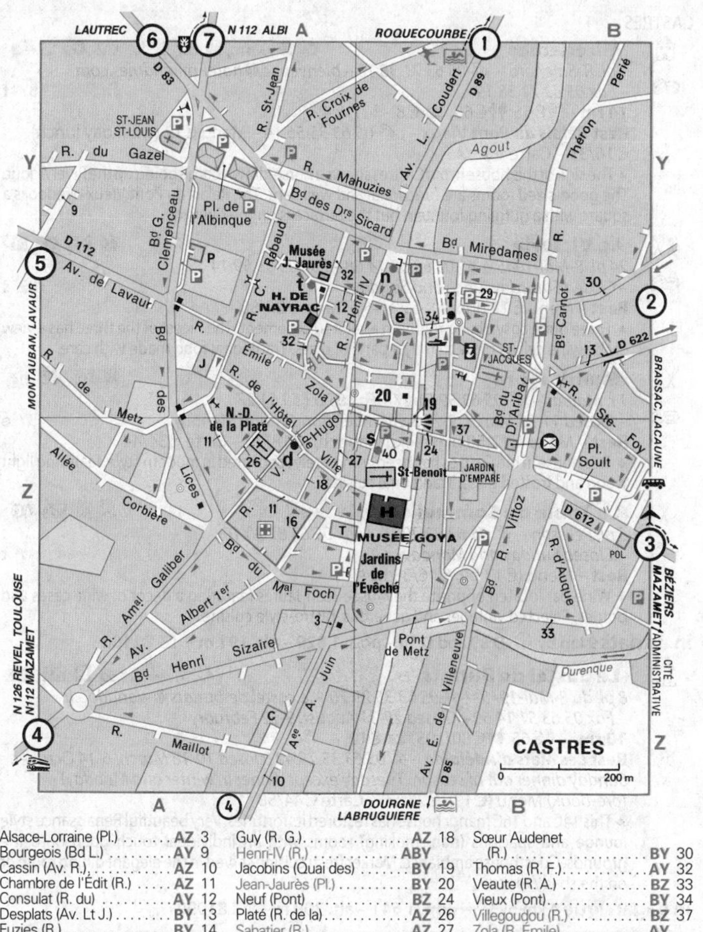

Alsace-Lorraine (Pl.)	AZ 3	Guy (R. G.)	AZ 18	Sœur Audenet (R.)	BY 30
Bourgeois (Bd L.)	AY 9	Henri-IV (R.)	ABY	Thomas (R. F.)	AY 32
Cassin (Av. R.)	AZ 10	Jacobins (Quai des)	BY 19	Veaute (R. A.)	BZ 33
Chambre de l'Édit (R.)	AZ 11	Jean-Jaurès (Pl.)	BY 20	Vieux (Pont)	BY 34
Consulat (R. du)	AY 12	Neuf (Pont)	BZ 24	Villegoudou (R.)	BZ 37
Desplats (Av. Lt J.)	BY 13	Platé (R. de la)	AZ 26	Zola (R. Émile)	AY
Fuzies (R.)	BY 14	Sabatier (R.)	AZ 27	8-Mai-1945 (Pl. du)	BZ 40
Gambetta (R.)	AZ 16	Ste-Claire (Pl.)	BY 29		

Renaissance without rest

17 r. V. Hugo – ☎ 05 63 59 30 42 – hotel.renaissance.europe@wanadoo.fr – Fax 05 63 72 11 57 AZ **d**

22 rm – €55/60 €60/70, ☕ €8

◆ A lovely half-timbered 17C façade housing personalised rooms (Empire, Napoleon III, African styles, etc.) where paintings and trinkets abound. Very cosy lounge.

Occitan

201 av. Ch. de Gaulle, via ③ – ☎ 05 63 35 34 20 – hotel-occitan@wanadoo.fr – Fax 05 63 35 70 32 – Closed 20-28 December

62 rm – €59/83 €65/90, ☕ €10 – ½ P €55/70

Rest – *(closed 20 December-4 January, Sunday lunch in August and Saturday lunch)* Menu €14 (weekdays)/40 – Carte €28/48

◆ Practical location for a stopover on the outskirts of town. All the rooms have air-conditioning and have been renovated; some occupy a new wing. Sauna and jacuzzi. Traditional food served in a contemporary setting or on the terrace opposite the swimming pool.

Miredames rm, rm, VISA AE
1 pl. R. Salengro – ✆ 05 63 71 38 18 – bienvenue@hotel-miredames.com – Fax 05 63 71 38 19 BY **f**
14 rm – €55 €63, ☕ €8 – ½ P €49
Rest *Relais du Pont Vieux* – , *✆ 05 63 35 56 14* – Menu € 12 (weekday lunch), € 16/33 – Carte € 21/45
◆ The sign of this house in old Castres shows a horse-drawn barge going up the River Agout. The good-sized rooms are functional and well kept. The Relais du Pont Vieux overlooks a square with a gurgling fountain but the terrace is on the riverside.

Le Victoria VISA AE
24 pl. 8-Mai-1945 – ✆ 05 63 59 14 68 – Fax 05 63 59 14 68 – Closed Saturday lunch and Sunday BZ **s**
Rest – Menu € 12 (lunch), € 23/46 – Carte € 26/50
◆ Three quite cosy dining rooms in a vaulted basement. The nicest of the three has a view of the wine cellars protected by a pane of glass. Traditional food made with care.

Mandragore VISA
1 r. Malpas – ✆ 05 63 59 51 27 – Fax 05 63 59 51 27 – Closed 11-25 March, 9-23 September, Sunday and Monday BY **e**
Rest – Menu € 12,50 bi (weekday lunch), € 18/26 – Carte € 34/44
◆ This house in old Castres has been completely renovated in modern style, featuring light wood and frosted glass. Traditional cuisine.

La Table du Sommelier VISA
6 pl. Pélisson – ✆ 05 63 82 20 10 – Fax 05 63 82 20 10 – Closed Sunday and Monday AY **t**
Rest – Menu (€ 13 bi), € 16/35 bi
◆ Wine bar located opposite the Musée Jean Jaurès featuring a decor of wine cases and bottles. Selected vintages and generous, bistro-style cuisine.

in Burlats **9 km by ①, D 89 and D 58 – pop. 1 829 – alt. 191 m – ✉ 81100**

Le Castel de Burlats VISA
8 pl. du 8-Mai-1945 – ✆ 05 63 35 29 20 – le.castel.de-burlats@wanadoo.fr – Fax 05 63 51 14 69 – Closed 25-31 August, 9-22 February
10 rm – €65 € 80/105, ☕ € 10
Rest *Les Mets d'Adélaïde* – *✆ 05 63 35 78 42 (closed 10-18 March, 6-14 October, Sunday dinner out of season, Tuesday except dinner in winter and Monday) (pre-book)* Menu (€ 19), € 23/55 – Carte € 44/58
◆ This 14C and 16C manor house has restored its fortunes: very beautiful Renaissance style lounge and spacious (non-smoking) rooms with an individual touch open onto the grounds. Guesthouse ambiance. Market fresh cuisine served in the elegant dining room or on the shady terrace.

in Lagarrigue **4 km by ③ – pop. 1 641 – alt. 200 m – ✉ 81090**

Montagne Noire without rest VISA AE
29 av. Castres, on RN 112 – ✆ 05 63 35 52 00 – contact@lamontagnenoire.com – Fax 05 63 35 25 59 – Closed 24 December-2 January, Saturday and Sunday
30 rm – € 83/99 € 93/110, ☕ € 11,50
◆ By a busy road, a hotel with well soundproofed rooms, furnished in Art Deco style. Sauna and small indoor swimming pool.

CASTRIES – 34 Hérault – 339 I6 – pop. 5 146 – alt. 70 m – ✉ 34160

Languedoc-Roussillon-Tarn Gorges 23 **C2**

Paris 746 – Lunel 15 – Montpellier 19 – Nîmes 44

Syndicat d'initiative, 19, rue Sainte Catherine ✆ 04 99 74 01 77, Fax 04 99 74 01 77

Disini VISA AE
1 r. des Carrières – ✆ 04 67 41 97 86 – contact@disini-hotel.com – Fax 04 67 41 97 16
15 rm – € 120/180 € 120/180, ☕ € 15 – 1 suite – **Rest** –*(closed Saturday lunch, Sunday dinner and Monday)* Menu € 32/75 – Carte € 57/66
◆ A brand-new hotel set amid a tranquil forest of evergreen oak. Individually furnished guestrooms with ethnic touches (Asia and Africa), soft lighting and high-tech comforts. Contemporary dishes in an eastern-inspired setting at the restaurant.

LE CATEAU-CAMBRÉSIS – 59 Nord – 302 J7 – pop. 7 460 – alt. 123 m – ✉ 59360 Northern France and the Paris Region 31 C3

Paris 202 – Cambrai 24 – Hirson 44 – Lille 86 – St-Quentin 41 – Valenciennes 33

Office de tourisme, 9, place du Commandant Richez ✆ 03 27 84 10 94, Fax 03 27 77 81 52

Le Relais Fénelon with rm

21 r. Mar. Mortier – ✆ 03 27 84 25 80 – Fax 03 27 84 38 60 – Closed 1st-23 August, Sunday dinner and Monday except public holidays

5 rm – €44 €44/51, €6,50 – **Rest** – Menu €20/30 – Carte €31/41

◆ The dining room of this 19C abode is full of the charm of provincial France and the comfortable lounge is equally bourgeois in style. A pleasant summer terrace facing a tree-lined garden.

LE CATELET – Aisne – 306 B2 – pop. 218 – alt. 90 m – ✉ 02420 37 C1

Paris 170 – Cambrai 22 – Le Cateau-Cambrésis 29 – Laon 66 – Péronne 28 – St-Quentin 19

La Coriandre

68 r. du Gén. Augereau – ✆ 03 23 66 21 71 – sebastien.monatte@wanadoo.fr – Fax 03 23 66 84 23 – Closed 28 July-19 August, 2-9 January, dinner except Saturday and Monday

Rest – Menu €23 (weekdays)/47 – Carte €49/56

◆ An innocuous façade bordering the main road houses this lovely rustic restaurant with provincial chairs and red flag stones. Contemporary cuisine.

LES CATONS – 73 Savoie – 333 I4 – see le Bourget-du-Lac

CAUDEBEC-EN-CAUX – 76 Seine-Maritime – 304 E4 – pop. 2 342 – alt. 6 m – ✉ 76490 Normandy 33 C1

Paris 162 – Lillebonne 17 – Le Havre 53 – Rouen 37 – Yvetot 14

Office de tourisme, place du General de Gaulle ✆ 02 32 70 46 32, Fax 02 32 70 46 31

Notre-Dame church★.

Vallon de Rançon★ Northeast: 2 km.

Normotel La Marine

18 quai Guilbaud – ✆ 02 35 96 20 11 – lamarine@libertysurf.fr – Fax 02 35 56 54 40

31 rm – €57/97 €57/97, €12 – ½ P €54/70 – **Rest** – *(closed Saturday lunch, Sunday dinner and Friday)* Menu €20 (weekdays)/44 – Carte €35/73

◆ On the banks of the Seine, where boats come and go, the best rooms in this large hotel building have a balcony overlooking the river. Panoramic restaurant dining room where traditional dishes are served. There is a summer terrace overlooking the water.

Le Normandie

19 quai Guilbaud – ✆ 02 35 96 25 11 – info@le-normandie.fr – Fax 02 35 96 68 15

16 rm – €55 €80, €7,50 – ½ P €60 – **Rest** – *(closed Monday lunch, Wednesday lunch and Sunday dinner)* Menu (€11), €18/40

◆ On the banks of the Seine, functional rooms, some furnished in a rustic style. The largest, at the front, have a small balcony and offer a view of the river. A captivating view from the restaurant bay windows; traditional and Norman dishes.

Le Cheval Blanc

4 pl. R. Coty – ✆ 02 35 96 21 66 – le-cheval-blanc-info@wanadoo.fr – Fax 02 35 95 35 40

14 rm – €56/63 €58/65, €6,50 – ½ P €67/71

Rest – *(closed 21 December-1st January, Saturday lunch, Sunday dinner and Friday)* Menu (€13), €16 (weekdays)/37 – Carte €27/49

◆ Bright and fresh, all the rooms of this town-centre establishment have been renovated and have good soundproofing; the ones on the second floor have an attic roof. A modern menu influenced by local produce is presented in the restaurant.

CAUREL – 22 Côtes-d'Armor – **309** D5 – **pop. 387 – alt. 188 m –** ✉ **22530** 10 **C2**

Paris 461 – Carhaix-Plouguer 45 – Guingamp 48 – Loudéac 24 – Pontivy 22 – St-Brieuc 48

XX **Beau Rivage** with rm

au Lac de Guerlédan , 2 km on D 111 – ✆ 02 96 28 52 15 – stefetcie@orange.fr – Fax 02 96 26 01 16 – Closed 15-30 March, Monday off season and Sunday dinner

4 rm – €56 €56, €8,50 – ½ P €60 – **Rest** – Menu €19 (weekdays)/66 – Carte €42/62

◆ This modern house has taken full advantage of its lakeside location by installing wide bay windows in the dining room and a terrace. A few practical rooms.

CAURO – **2A Corse-du-Sud** – **345** C8 – **see Corse**

CAUSSADE – 82 Tarn-et-Garonne – **337** F7 – **pop. 5 971 – alt. 109 m –** ✉ **82300** 29 **C2**

Paris 606 – Cahors 38 – Gaillac 51 – Montauban 28 – Villefranche-de-Rouergue 52

Office de tourisme, 11, rue de la République ✆ 05 63 26 04 04, Fax 05 63 26 04 04

Dupont rm,

r. Récollets – ✆ 05 63 65 05 00 – hotel-resto-dupont@cegetel.fr – Fax 05 63 65 12 62 – Closed 1st-8 January and Sunday dinner

30 rm – €44/60 €44/60, €8,50 – ½ P €43/53

Rest – *(closed Friday and Saturday except dinner season)* Menu €12 (weekday lunch), €16/26 – Carte €16/41

◆ This former 18C post house lies in this town known as "the capital of straw hats"! Choose the more modern rooms at the back. Pleasant rustic dining room and regional cuisine.

in Monteils 3 km Northeast by D 17 – **pop. 1 075 – alt. 120 m –** ✉ **82300**

X **Le Clos Monteils**

– ✆ 05 63 93 03 51 – Fax 05 63 93 03 51 – Closed 1st-7 November, 15 January-15 February, Tuesday from November to May, Saturday lunch, Sunday dinner and Monday

Rest – *(number of covers limited, pre-book)* Menu €17 (weekday lunch), €28/51

◆ The former presbytery (1771) of this Quercy village, converted into a restaurant, is decorated in the style of a private house. Pleasant terrace. Regional cooking with a contemporary touch.

CAUTERETS – 65 Hautes-Pyrénées – **342** L7 – **pop. 1 305 – alt. 932 m – Winter sports : 1 000/2 350 m 3 18 – Spa : early Feb.-late Nov. – Casino –** ✉ **65110**
Languedoc-Roussillon-Tarn Gorges 28 **A3**

Paris 880 – Argelès-Gazost 17 – Lourdes 30 – Pau 75 – Tarbes 49

Office de tourisme, place Foch ✆ 05 62 92 50 50, Fax 05 62 92 11 70

La station★ - Pont d'Espagne road and site ★★★ (chutes du Gave) (waterfall) South by D 920 - Cascade★★ and Lutour valley★ South: 2.5 km by D 920.

Cirque du Lys★★.

Plan on next page

Astérides-Sacca rest, rest,

bd Latapie-Flurin – ✆ 05 62 92 50 02 – hotel.le.sacca@wanadoo.fr – Fax 05 62 92 64 63 – Closed 15 October-15 December a

56 rm – €38/58 €47/71, €7 – ½ P €46/60 – **Rest** – Menu €16/42 – Carte €28/40

◆ Rooms with balconies furnished in a functional, contemporary style. Hall decorated with pale wood. Welcoming dining room with pale woodwork, modern furniture and warm colours; traditional recipes.

CAUTERETS

Benjamin-Dulau (Av.) 2
Bordenave (Pl.) 3
Clemenceau (Pl. G.) 4
Etigny (R. d') 5
Féria (R. de la) 6
Foch (Pl. Mar.) 8
Jean-Moulin (Pl.) 10
Latapie-Flurin (Bd) 12
Mamelon Vert (Av.) 13
Pont-Neuf (R. du) 15
Richelieu (R. de) 16
Victoire (Pl. de la) 18

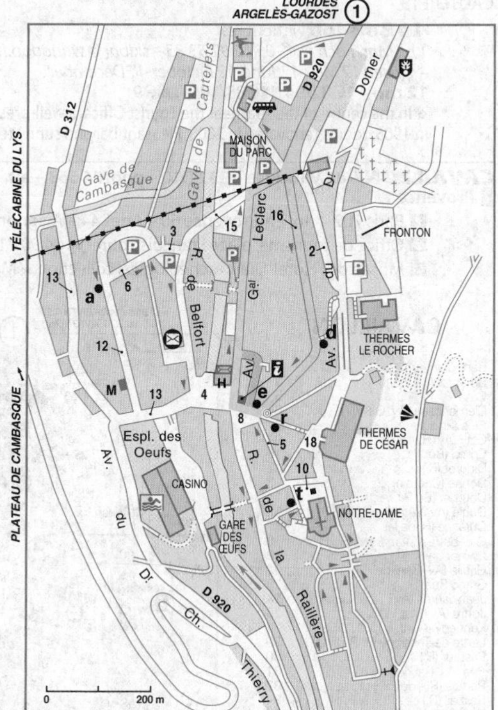

César rm, VISA

r. César – ✆ 05 62 92 52 57 – charles.fontan@wanadoo.fr – Fax 05 62 92 08 19 – Closed 27 April-22 May and 28 September-22 October **r**

17 rm – 🚹€ 46/56 🚹🚹€ 46/56, ☕ € 7 – ½ P € 50 – **Rest** – *(closed Wednesday in winter except school holidays) (dinner only From December to April)* Menu € 18/23

◆ Near the spa baths of the same name, a colourful façade and fairly large rooms, rather more attractive and modern on the 3rd floor. Traditional dishes; "garbure" (a vegetable soup served to order) is the speciality; a rather old-fashioned setting.

Welcome Cauterets rm, VISA

3 r. V. Hugo – ✆ 05 62 92 50 22 – hotelwelcomecauterets@wanadoo.fr – Fax 05 62 92 02 90 – Closed 7-25 April and 3 November-1st December **t**

26 rm – 🚹€ 41/45 🚹🚹€ 54/59, ☕ € 7 – ½ P € 45/48

Rest – *(closed 21 October-1st December)* Menu € 14 (weekdays)/24 – Carte € 17/44

◆ On a peaceful street near the church, a hotel with practical and very well-maintained rooms. Those in the annex 50m away are slightly older. The restaurant has a rustic atmosphere with exposed beams, rural furnishings and copperware. Traditional dishes.

Du Lion d'Or VISA

12 r. Richelieu – ✆ 05 62 92 52 87 – hotel.lion.dor@wanadoo.fr – Fax 05 62 92 03 67 – Closed12-24 May and 5 October-19 December **d**

19 rm – 🚹€ 65/100 🚹🚹€ 65/100, ☕ € 10 – ½ P € 57/75 – **Rest** – *(dinner only) (resident only)* Menu € 20/27 – Carte € 23/28

◆ Pleasant hotel run by the same family for 4 generations and recognisable by its lovely (19C) façade, the glass doors open out onto small wrought iron balconies. Cosy rooms personalised with objects from antique shops. Small patio decked with flowers in the summer.

Le Bois Joli without rest

1 pl. Mar. Foch – ✆ 05 62 92 53 85 – skibar@wanadoo.fr – Fax 05 62 92 02 23 – Closed 12 May-1st June, 12 October-1st December e

12 rm – 🛉€ 82/94 🛉🛉€ 85/105, ☕ € 9

◆ In the centre of the spa, near the Tourist Office, a well-preserved, distinctive hotel built in 1905; rooms renovated in 2005. Pleasant bar and sunny terrace.

CAVAILLON – 84 Vaucluse – 332 D10 – pop. 24 563 – alt. 75 m – ✉ 84300

Provence 42 **E1**

Paris 702 – Aix-en-Provence 60 – Arles 44 – Avignon 25 – Manosque 70

Office de tourisme, place Francois Tourel ✆ 04 90 71 32 01, Fax 04 90 71 42 99

Musée de l'Hôtel-Dieu: archeological collection ★ M - ≤★ from St-Jacques hill.

CAVAILLON

Berthelot (Av.) 2
Bournissac (Cours) 3
Castil-Blaze (Pl.) 5
Clemenceau (Av. G.) 6
Clos (Pl. du) 7
Coty (Av. R.) 9
Crillon (Bd) 10
Diderot (R.) 12
Donné (Chemin) 13
Doumer (Bd P.) 14
Dublé (Av. Véran) 15
Durance (R. de la) 17
Gambetta (Cours L.) 18
Gambetta (Pl. L.) 19
Gaulle (Av. Gén.-de) 22
Grand-Rue 23
Jean-Jaurès (Av.) 24
Joffre (Av. Mar.) 26
Kennedy (Av. J.-F.) 27
Lattre-de-Tassigny (R. P.-J. de) 29
Pasteur (R.) 30
Péri (Av. Gabriel) 31
Pertuis (Rte de) 32
Raspail (R.) 34
Renan (Cours E.) 35
République (R. de la) 37
Sarnette (Av. Abel) 38
Saunerie (R.) 40
Sémard (Av. P.) 41
Tourel (Pl. F.) 42
Victor-Hugo (Cours) 43

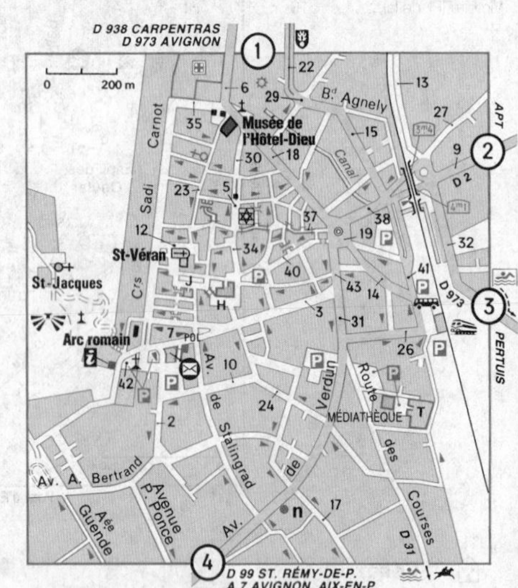

Mercure

601 av. Boscodomini, via ④: 2 km – ✆ 04 90 71 07 79 – h1951@accor.com – Fax 04 90 78 27 94

43 rm – 🛉€ 91/123 🛉🛉€ 101/133, ☕ € 12 – **Rest** – *(closed Saturday lunch and Sunday lunch October-April)* Menu (€ 15), € 20, € 23 – Carte € 18/33

◆ Recently refurbished 1970s building in a southern style. Practical bedrooms with balconies, those facing south are quieter. Attractive Provençal decor in the restaurant. The menu is based on local Comtadin ingredients.

Prévôt

353 av. Verdun – ✆ 04 90 71 32 43 – jean-jacques@restaurant-prevot.com – Closed Sunday and Monday except public holidays n

Rest – Menu € 25 (weekday lunch), € 35/85 – Carte € 64/77

◆ The decor celebrates the melon in all forms: pictures, knick-knacks, chandeliers, crockery and so on. Of course an entire menu is dedicated to the melon family!

in Cheval-Blanc 5 km by ③ – **pop. 3 524 – alt. 83 m – ✉ 84460**

L'Auberge de Cheval Blanc

481 av. de la Canebière – ✆ 04 32 50 18 55 – contact@auberge-de-chevalblanc.com – Fax 04 32 50 18 52 – Closed autumn half-term holidays, Saturday lunch, Sunday dinner and Monday except July-August

Rest – *(number of covers limited, pre-book)* Menu € 23 bi (weekday lunch), € 28/68 – Carte € 45/54

◆ This unassuming roadside inn is a pleasant stopover. Elegant decor of leather chairs, mirrors and pale colours. Contemporary, seasonal cuisine.

CAVALAIRE-SUR-MER – 83 Var – 340 O6 – pop. 5 237 – alt. 2 m – Casino – ✉ 83240 French Riviera 41 C3

Paris 880 – Draguignan 55 – Fréjus 41 – Le Lavandou 21 – St-Tropez 20 – Toulon 61

Office de tourisme, Maison de la Mer ☎ 04 94 01 92 10, Fax 04 94 05 49 89

Massif des Maures★★★.

La Calanque

sea and deep rocky inlet,

r. Calanque – ☎ 04 94 00 49 00

– mario.lacalanque@wanadoo.fr – Fax 04 94 64 66 20 – Closed 2 January-15 March

24 rm – †€ 160/275 ††€ 160/275, ☕ € 19 – 4 suites – ½ P € 130/170

Rest – Menu € 25/55 – Carte € 56/82

◆ At the foot of the hotel lie the superb beach at Cavalaire (4km), the coves and the Maures Massif. Spacious and prettily furnished guest rooms overlook the Mediterranean. The dining rooms and panoramic terrace have a pretty sea view. Local specialities.

Golfe Bleu

rm,

rte de la Croix-Valmer, 1 km by D 559 – ☎ 04 94 00 42 81 – le.golfe-bleu@wanadoo.fr – Fax 04 94 05 48 79 – Closed 1st December-15 January

15 rm – †€ 48/84 ††€ 48/84, ☕ € 7 – ½ P € 73/108 – **Rest** – *(open May-October) (dinner only)* Menu € 23

◆ Despite the proximity of the road, nights are relatively peaceful thanks to double-glazing. Simple and practical yet welcoming. The refurbished dining room opens onto a street terrace. The traditional cuisine features fish and shellfish.

LA CAVALERIE – 12 Aveyron – 338 K6 – pop. 813 – alt. 800 m – ✉ 12230 29 D2

Paris 655 – Montpellier 96 – Millau 20 – Rodez 87

De la Poste

rest, rm,

D 809 – ☎ 05 65 62 70 66 – contact@hotel-larzac.com – Fax 05 65 62 78 24

– Closed 23 December-8 January, Sunday dinner from autumn half-term holidays to Easter, Friday dinner and Saturday from November to March

31 rm – †€ 49 ††€ 49, ☕ € 7 – ½ P € 55/59 – **Rest** – Menu € 18 (weekday lunch)/55 – Carte € 23/57

◆ Convenient hotel for a stopover on the way to your holiday destination, in the heart of the Grands Causses regional nature reserve. Functional, colourful and relatively spacious rooms. Minimalist dining room and air-conditioned patio; traditional and regional dishes. Very hospitable welcome.

CAVALIÈRE – 83 Var – 340 N7 – alt. 4 m – ✉ 83980 Le Lavandou French Riviera 41 C3

Paris 880 – Draguignan 68 – Fréjus 55 – Le Lavandou 7 – St-Tropez 33 – Toulon 48

Massif des Maures★★★.

Le Club de Cavalière & Spa

sea and the islands,

30 av. Cap Nègre – rm,

☎ 04 98 04 34 34 – cavaliere@relaischateaux.com – Fax 04 94 05 73 16

– Open 19 April-28 September

32 rm – †€ 280/390 ††€ 365/735, ☕ € 20 – 5 suites – ½ P € 263/445

Rest – Menu € 45 (lunch), € 60/85 – Carte € 83/142

◆ Overlooking the sea, an elegant residence with magnificent, modern rooms and superb leisure facilities: pool, private beach, spa, sauna, Jacuzzi, fitness centre, hammam, etc. Provençal-inspired restaurant with a sliding glass roof overlooking the beach.

CAVANAC – 11 Aude – 344 E3 – see Carcassonne

CEILLAC – 05 Hautes-Alpes – 334 I4 – pop. 276 – alt. 1 640 m – Winter sports : 1 700/2 500 m 6 – ✉ 05600 French Alps 41 C1

Paris 729 – Briançon 50 – Gap 75 – Guillestre 14

Office de tourisme, le village ☎ 04 92 45 05 74, Fax 04 92 45 47 05

Site★ - St-Sébastien church ★.

Vallon du Mélezet★ - Lac Ste-Anne★★.

La Cascade
at the foot of the Mélezet south-east: 2 km – 04 92 45 05 92 – info@hotel-la-cascade.com – Fax 04 92 45 22 09 – Open 1st June-15 September and 20 December-2 April
22 rm – €43/60 €51/72, €9 – ½ P €54/64 – **Rest** – Menu €16/28 – Carte €28/35
◆ Located on a remote, beautiful alpine site, the hotel will appeal to nature lovers. Rooms have pine furniture with carvings, typical of the Queyras region. The dining room and terrace offer an attractive view of the mountains. Regional cuisine.

CEILLOUX – 63 Puy-de-Dôme – 326 I9 – pop. 151 – alt. 615 m – ✉ 63520

Paris 464 – Clermont-Ferrand 50 – Cournon-d'Auvergne 36 – Riom 62 6 **C2**

Domaine de Gaudon without rest
4 km north on the D 304 – 04 73 70 76 25 – domainedegaudon@wanadoo.fr
5 rm – €80 €98
◆ This 19C house bordered by a park and a fishing pond is a rare find. The rooms and the dining room, where breakfast is served, are superb.

LA CELLE – 83 Var – 340 L5 – pop. 1 082 – alt. 260 m – ✉ 83170 41 C3

Paris 812 – Aix-en-Provence 63 – Draguignan 62 – Marseille 65 – Toulon 48
Office de tourisme, place des Ormeaux 04 94 59 19 05

Hostellerie de l'Abbaye de la Celle rm, rm,
10 pl. du Gén. de Gaulle – 04 98 05 14 14 – contact@abbaye-celle.com – Fax 04 98 05 14 15 – Closed 14 January-7 February
10 rm – €205/275 €205/370, €20
Rest – *(closed Tuesday and Wednesday mid October-end March)* Menu €42 (weekdays)/78 – Carte €51/73
Spec. Petits farcis de légumes d'été (season). Baudroie en bourride, blanquette de légumes et safran de Provence. Tendron de veau cuit longuement puis caramélisé à la broche. **Wines** Coteaux Varois en Provence.
◆ This delightful 18C Provençal house, surrounded by a tree-filled park and a vegetable garden, has played host to General de Gaulle. Spacious and refined rooms. Dining rooms full of character and a beautiful shaded terrace. Delightful Southern cooking.

LA CELLE-LES-BORDES – 78 Yvelines – 311 H4 – 106 28 – 101 31 – see Paris, Area (Cernay-la-Ville)

CELLES-SUR-BELLE – 79 Deux-Sèvres – 322 E7 – pop. 3 480 – alt. 117 m – ✉ 79370 Atlantic Coast 38 B2

Paris 400 – Couhé 37 – Niort 22 – Poitiers 69 – St-Jean-d'Angély 52
Office de tourisme, 9, rue des Halles 05 49 32 92 28, Fax 05 49 32 92 28
Portal★ of Notre-Dame church.

Hostellerie de l'Abbaye
1 pl. Epoux-Laurant – 05 49 32 93 32 – hostellerie.abbaye@wanadoo.fr – Fax 05 49 79 72 65
20 rm – €48 €50, €7 – ½ P €48/50 – **Rest** – Menu €13 (weekdays)/45 – Carte €31/46
◆ In the shadow of the tall steeple of the abbey church, this local-style house has functional rooms, being renovated in stages. A semi-bourgeois, semi-rustic dining room and a terrace facing the courtyard; traditional food inspired from the Charente region. Fine selection of Armagnac.

CELLETTES – 41 Loir-et-Cher – 318 F6 – pop. 2 138 – alt. 78 m – ✉ 41120 11 A1

Paris 189 – Blois 9 – Orléans 68 – Romorantin-Lanthenay 36 – Tours 73
Syndicat d'initiative, 2, rue de la Rozelle 02 54 70 30 46, Fax 02 54 70 30 46

La Vieille Tour
7 r. Nationale – ✆ 02 54 70 46 31 – lavieilletour@yahoo.fr – Fax 02 54 70 46 31 – Closed 23-29 June, January, Wednesday from September to June and Tuesday
Rest – Menu € 18 (weekdays)/46 – Carte € 33/57
◆ An attractive 15C building recognisable by its old tower. Muted atmosphere and updated rustic decor in the dining room, where the emphasis is on refined traditional cuisine.

CELONY – **13 Bouches-du-Rhône** – **340** H4 – **see Aix-en-Provence**

CÉLY – **77 Seine-et-Marne** – **312** E5 – **pop. 1 010** – **alt. 62 m** – ✉ **77930**
Paris 56 – Melun 15 – Boulogne-Billancourt 56 – Montreuil 57 – Créteil 47

Chateau de Cély rest, VISA MC AE
rte de St Germain – ✆ 01 64 38 03 07 – cely@club-albatros.com – Fax 01 64 38 08 78
4 rm – †€ 260/300 ††€ 260/300, ☕ € 30 – 10 suites – ††€ 260/300 – ½ P € 220/260 – **Rest** – *(pre-book dinner)* Carte € 31/59
◆ A 14C château surrounded by parkland. The contemporary, well-equipped bedrooms enjoy splendid views of the golf course surrounded by landscaped gardens. An ideal seminar venue. Housed in a large conservatory with views of the gardens, this restaurant serves traditional cuisine.

CÉNAC-ET-ST-JULIEN – **24 Dordogne** – **329** I7 – **pop. 1 193** – **alt. 70 m** – ✉ **24250** 4 **D1**
Paris 547 – Bordeaux 205 – Périgueux 73 – Cahors 71 – Sarlat-la-Canéda 12

La Guérinière
on D 46 – ✆ 05 53 29 91 97 – contact@la-gueriniere-dordogne.com – Fax 05 53 29 91 97 – Open from Easter to October
5 rm – †€ 54/79 ††€ 54/79, ☕ € 8 – ½ P € 58/71 – **Table d'hôte** – *(closed Wednesday and Sunday except public holidays)* Menu € 23
◆ A driveway lined by plane trees leads to this Périgord Carthusian monastery. Carefully decorated rooms with parquet floors. In the evening, the owner, a former restaurateur, serves a choice of succulent local dishes in the spacious dining hall warmed in winter by a lovely open fireplace.

Le Moulin Rouge without rest VISA MC
– ✆ 05 53 28 23 66 – lemoulinrouge@perigord.com – Open 1st April-30 October
4 rm – †€ 45/50 ††€ 58/65, ☕ € 7
◆ Bucolic setting for this mill by a pond (swimming allowed). The charming owners will gladly retrace its history for you. Cosy bedrooms.

CENON – **33 Gironde** – **335** H5 – **see Bordeaux**

CERDON – **01 Ain** – **328** F4 – **pop. 672** – **alt. 300 m** – ✉ **01450** 44 **B1**
Paris 460 – Ambérieu-en-Bugey 25 – Bourg-en-Bresse 32 – Nantua 20 – Oyonnax 32
Syndicat d'initiative, place F. Allombert ✆ 04 74 39 93 02, Fax 04 74 39 93 02

Vieille Côte VISA MC AE
pl. Mairie – ✆ 04 74 39 96 86 – c.b.france@wanadoo.fr – Fax 04 74 39 93 42 – Closed 2-27 February, Tuesday and Wednesday off season
Rest – Menu € 18/43 – Carte € 24/47
◆ Madame rustles up regional dishes using home-grown herbs, while Monsieur jovially welcomes guests into two countrified dining rooms. Bugey wines.

CERDON – **45 Loiret** – **318** L6 – **pop. 1 009** – **alt. 145 m** – ✉ **45620** 12 **C2**
Paris 185 – Orléans 73 – Fleury-les-Aubrais 63 – Olivet 59 – St-Jean-de-Braye 60

Les Vieux Guays without rest
Rte des Hauteraults – ✆ 02 38 36 03 76 – lvg45@orange.fr – Fax 02 38 36 03 76 – Closed 23 February-7 March – **5 rm** ☕ – †€ 60 ††€ 75
◆ Superb unspoilt property complete with lake, pool and tennis court. This former hunting lodge offers comfortable rooms whose tasteful decoration upholds local traditions.

CÉRET – 66 Pyrénées-Orientales – 344 H8 – pop. 7 291 – alt. 153 m – ✉ 66400

Languedoc-Roussillon-Tarn Gorges 22 **B3**

Paris 875 – Gerona 81 – Perpignan 34 – Port-Vendres 37 – Prades 72

Office de tourisme, 1, avenue Georges Clemenceau ✆ 04 68 87 00 53, Fax 04 68 87 00 56

Old bridge★ - Musée d'Art Moderne★★.

La Terrasse au Soleil ≤ le Canigou and Roussillon plain, rm, rm, P VISA MC AE

West: 1.5 km along rte Fontfrède – ✆ 04 68 87 01 94 – terrasse-au-soleil.hotel@wanadoo.fr – Fax 04 68 87 39 24 – Open March-November

39 rm – ♦€ 93/210 ♦♦€ 130/249 – 2 suites – ½ P € 97/156

Rest – Menu € 31/62 – Carte € 44/70

◆ Charles Trenet lived in this isolated Catalan house on the green hills of Céret. Functional rooms to the back of the hotel. Swimming pool, jacuzzi and spa. Bright dining room adorned with earthenware and regional furniture. Terrace overlooking the Pic du Canigou.

Le Mas Trilles without rest P VISA MC

at Pont de Reynès: 3 km after Céret, towards Amélie Les Bains – ✆ 04 68 87 38 37 – mastrilles@free.fr – Fax 04 68 87 42 62 – Open 27 April-7 October

8 rm – ♦€ 85/100 ♦♦€ 108/205 – 2 suites

◆ A 17C house hidden in a small valley. Delightful rooms in Mediterranean colours, many with a terrace or private garden. Swimming pool overlooking the River Tech.

Les Arcades without rest VISA MC

1 pl. Picasso – ✆ 04 68 87 12 30 – hotelarcades.ceret@wanadoo.fr – Fax 04 68 87 49 44

30 rm – ♦€ 42/57 ♦♦€ 42/57, € 7

◆ Pleasant hotel adorned with works of art by the Céret School. Bright rooms with Catalan-style furnishings. Good breakfast including local produce.

Le Chat qui Rit P VISA MC

at la Cabanasse: 1.5 km on Amélie road – ✆ 04 68 87 02 22 – lechatquirit@wanadoo.fr – Fax 04 68 87 43 40 – Closed 5 January-10 February, Tuesday except July-August, Sunday dinner and Monday

Rest – buffet Menu (€ 15 bi), € 24/36 – Carte € 31/47

◆ As the name of this restaurant suggests, cats play an integral part in its modern decor. Large, central buffet table laid out with Catalan specialities.

Del Bisbe with rm VISA MC

4 pl. Soutine – ✆ 04 68 87 00 85 – bisbe@club-internet.fr – Fax 04 68 87 62 33 – Closed November, Tuesday and Wednesday

10 rm – ♦€ 40 ♦♦€ 40, € 6 – ½ P € 75 – **Rest** – Menu € 28

◆ This 18C residence, whose Catalan name translates as "Bishop's House", is decorated in an authentic, rustic style. Attractive vine-covered terrace. Regional cuisine and tapas bar. The reasonably priced rooms on the first floor have been refurbished. New bedding.

LE CERGNE – 42 Loire – 327 E3 – pop. 698 – alt. 640 m – ✉ 42460 44 **A1**

Paris 414 – Charlieu 17 – Chauffailles 15 – Lyon 78 – Mâcon 72 – Roanne 27 – St-Étienne 107

Bel'Vue with rm ≤ rm, VISA MC AE

– ✆ 04 74 89 87 73 – lebelvue@wanadoo.fr – Fax 04 74 89 78 61 – Closed 17-24 February, 11-24 August, Friday dinner, Sunday dinner and Monday lunch

15 rm – ♦€ 50 ♦♦€ 53/90, € 8 – ½ P € 58 – **Rest** – Menu € 19 (weekday lunch), € 24 € bi/60 – Carte € 32/54

◆ A spruce inn with, as its name indicates, a fine view of the valley from the dining room, decorated with plants. Traditional cuisine. New rooms.

CERGY – 95 Val-d'Oise – 305 D6 – 106 5 – 101 2 – see Paris, Area (Cergy-Pontoise)

CÉRILLY – 03 Allier – 326 D3 – pop. 1 568 – alt. 340 m – ✉ 03350

Auvergne 5 **B1**

Paris 298 – Bourges 66 – Montluçon 41 – Moulins 47 – St-Amand-Montrond 33

Office de tourisme, place du Champ de Foire ✆ 04 70 67 55 89, Fax 04 70 67 31 73

Chez Chaumat

pl. Péron – ✆ 04 70 67 52 21 – chezchaumat@alicepro.fr – Fax 04 70 67 35 28 – Closed 15-25 June, 5-15 September, 20 December-10 January, Sunday dinner and Monday

8 rm – †€ 40/43 ††€ 43/46, ☕ € 7 – ½ P € 48/52 – **Rest** – Menu € 12 (weekday lunch), € 19/39 – Carte € 24/37

♦ A family hotel a few metres from the superb Tronçais forest. Rooms are simple but have been refurbished and soundproofed. Two dining rooms: one a country-style bistro, the other wood-panelled and furnished in Louis XIII style.

CERNAY – 68 Haut-Rhin – 315 H10 – pop. 10 446 – alt. 275 m – ✉ 68700

Alsace-Lorraine 1 **A3**

Paris 461 – Altkirch 26 – Belfort 39 – Colmar 37 – Guebwiller 15 – Mulhouse 18 – Thann 6

Office de tourisme, 1, rue Latouche ✆ 03 89 75 50 35, Fax 03 89 75 49 24

Hostellerie d'Alsace with rm

rest,

61 r. Poincaré – ✆ 03 89 75 59 81 – hostellerie.alsace@wanadoo.fr – Fax 03 89 75 70 22 – Closed 21 July-11 August, 26 December-11 January, Saturday and Sunday

10 rm – †€ 51 ††€ 63, ☕ € 8 – ½ P € 62 – **Rest** – Menu € 19/58 – Carte € 43/60

♦ Large half-timbered hoouse in the Alsatian tradition. By contrast, the dining room and renovated accommodation are contemporary and functional.

CERNAY-LA-VILLE – 78 Yvelines – 311 H3 – 106 29 – 101 31 – see Paris, Area

CERVIONE – 2B Haute-Corse – 345 F6 – see Corse

CESSON – 22 Côtes-d'Armor – 309 F3 – see St-Brieuc

CESSON-SÉVIGNÉ – 35 Ille-et-Vilaine – 309 M6 – see Rennes

CESTAYROLS – 81 Tarn – 338 D7 – pop. 451 – alt. 233 m – ✉ 81150 29 **C2**

Paris 660 – Albi 19 – Castres 59 – Toulouse 71

Lou Cantoun

Le village – ✆ 05 63 53 28 39 – lou.cantoun@orange.fr – Fax 05 63 53 12 77 – Closed 2 January-5 February, Tuesday dinner and Wednesday

Rest – Menu € 12 bi (weekday lunch), € 22/37 – Carte € 27/43

♦ Choose between a pleasant shaded terrace and two rustic dining rooms (exposed stone, fireplace) in this restaurant which also houses the village grocery store. Traditional cuisine full of flavour.

CETTE-EYGUN – 64 Pyrénées-Atlantiques – 342 I7 – pop. 95 – alt. 700 m – ✉ 64490

3 **B3**

Paris 844 – Pau 68 – Lescun 10 – Lurbe-St-Christau 25 – Urdos 10

Au Château d'Arance

rm,

r. Centrale – ✆ 05 59 34 75 50 – didier.ziane@orange.fr – Fax 05 59 34 57 62 – Closed 12 November-7 December, 7 January-15 February and Tuesday from October to April

8 rm – †€ 50/65 ††€ 50/65, ☕ € 8 – ½ P € 52/58 – **Rest** – Menu € 17/28 – Carte approx. € 35

♦ This 13C "castel" overlooking the Aspe Valley offers a successful combination of old and new. Rooms have simple decor of parquet flooring, white walls and contemporary furniture. The old château stables house a modern dining room. Panoramic terrace.

CEVINS – 73 Savoie – **333** L4 – **pop. 687** – **alt. 400 m** – ✉ **73730** 46 **F2**

Paris 629 – Lyon 172 – Chambéry 63 – Annecy 57 – Aix-les-Bains 79

La Fleur de Sel

Les Marais – ✆ 04 79 37 49 98 – restaufleurdesel@aol.com – Fax 04 79 37 40 44 – Closed 30 June-12 July, Monday dinner, Tuesday dinner and Wednesday

Rest – Menu € 19 bi (weekday lunch), € 39/58 – Carte € 50/61

◆ Situated between the road and the vineyards, this large chalet serves contemporary cuisine in a modern, rustic-style dining room with exposed stonework, wrought-iron chairs and a fireplace. Verdant terrace.

CHABLIS – 89 Yonne – **319** F5 – **pop. 2 594** – **alt. 135 m** – ✉ **89800**

Burgundy-Jura 7 **B1**

Paris 181 – Auxerre 21 – Avallon 39 – Tonnerre 18 – Troyes 76

Office de tourisme, 1, rue du Maréchal de Lattre ✆ 03 86 42 80 80, Fax 03 86 42 49 71

Du Vieux Moulin

18 r. des Moulins – ✆ 03 86 42 47 30 – vieuxmoulin@larochewines.com – Fax 03 86 42 84 44 – Closed January and Sunday dinner off season

7 rm – €90/255 €90/255, € 12 – 2 suites

Rest *Laroche Wine Bar* – *(closed dinner Monday-Wednesday and Sunday)* Menu (€ 15 bi), € 25 – Carte € 24/43

◆ A subtle blend of tradition (bare beams and stonework) and modernity (hi-tech bathrooms and wifi): understated luxury at its best! Authentic country dishes that are well suited to the wines of the estate. Wine tasting courses run in the shop.

Hostellerie des Clos (Michel Vignaud) rest,

18 r. Jules Rathier – ✆ 03 86 42 10 63 – host.clos@wanadoo.fr – Fax 03 86 42 17 11 – Closed 23 December-23 January

32 rm – €59 €76, € 11 – 4 suites – ½ P € 100/135

Rest – Menu € 40/75 – Carte € 62/97

Spec. Nage d'huîtres spéciales d'Isigny au chablis. Dos de sandre saisi sur peau au beurre de légumes. Rognon de veau saisi dans sa graisse, jus au chablis. **Wines** Chablis, Irancy.

◆ This elegant hostelry, located in a former hospice, offers well-kept rooms (larger at the Résidence), plush sitting rooms, a smoking room and wine tasting cellar. The restaurant opens onto a garden. Classic and regional fare; good choice of local wines.

CHAGNY – 71 Saône-et-Loire – **320** I8 – **pop. 5 591** – **alt. 215 m** – ✉ **71150** 7 **A3**

Paris 327 – Autun 44 – Beaune 15 – Chalon-sur-Saône 20 – Mâcon 77

Office de tourisme, 2, place des Halles ✆ 03 85 87 25 95, Fax 03 85 87 14 44

Lameloise (Jacques Lameloise)

36 pl. d'Armes – ✆ 03 85 87 65 65 – lameloise@relaischateaux.com – Fax 03 85 87 03 57 – Closed 8-14 July, 22 December-22 January and Wednesday

16 rm – €135 €295, € 22

Rest – *(closed Monday lunch, Tuesday lunch, Thursday lunch and Wednesday) (pre-book)* Menu € 95/150 – Carte € 90/148

Spec. Pommes de terre ratte grillées aux escargots de Bourgogne. Millefeuille de filet de bœuf et foie gras poêlé, pommes de terre soufflées. Grande assiette du chocolatier. **Wines** Rully blanc, Chassagne-Montrachet rouge.

◆ This large Burgundy house has a refined interior with spacious rooms. Rustic elegance and a perfect welcome: the restaurant is a food lover's institution.

De la Poste without rest

17 r. de la Poste – ✆ 03 85 87 64 40 – hoteldelaposte-chagny71@tiscali.fr – Fax 03 85 87 64 41 – Closed 26 December-11 January

11 rm – €42/50 €44/58, € 6,50

◆ This establishment is in the centre of the village in a quiet cul-de-sac. All the renovated and well-kept rooms are at garden level.

La Ferté without rest
bd Liberté – 03 85 87 07 47 – reservation@hotelferte.com – Fax 03 85 87 37 64 – Closed 7-29 December
13 rm – €39/55 €49/62, €7
◆ A warm welcome, impeccably kept rooms and a garden full of the scent of wisteria and roses are some of the attractions of this hotel in a village in the Chalon hills.

Chalon road **2 km Southeast by N 6 and secondary road – 71150 Chagny**

Hostellerie du Château de Bellecroix
– 03 85 87 13 86 – info@chateau-bellecroix.com – Fax 03 85 91 28 62 – Closed 18 December-13 February and Wednesday except from June to September
19 rm – €85/220 €85/220, €18,50 – 1 suite – ½ P €106/190
Rest – *(closed Mon. lunch, Thurs. lunch and Wed.)* Menu €25 (weekday lunch), €49/63 – Carte €56/88
◆ Thos former home of the Knights of Malta is set in a park. The rooms, with an individual touch, are very large in the 12C commander's residence and smaller in the 18C château. This restaurant has a stylish look: Chimney, woodwork and period-style furniture.

in Chassey-le-Camp **6 km Southwest by D 974 and D 109 – pop. 277 – alt. 300 m – 71150**

Auberge du Camp Romain rm, rest,
au bourg – 03 85 87 09 91 – contact@auberge-du-camp-romain.com – Fax 03 85 87 11 51
41 rm – €70/95 €70/95, €12 – 1 suite – ½ P €75/82
Rest – Menu €19 (weekday lunch), €26/46 – Carte €26/50
◆ Amid vines and woods, close to a Neolithic camp. The main building has simple rooms; those in the annexe are larger and more modern. Copious traditional cuisine served in a rustic dining room or on the veranda.

CHAILLES – 73 Savoie – 333 H5 – see les Échelles

CHAILLY-SUR-ARMANÇON – 21 Côte-d'Or – 320 G6 – see Pouilly-en-Auxois

---

CHAINTRÉ – 71 Saône-et-Loire – 320 I12 – pop. 503 – alt. 284 m – 71570

8 **C3**

Paris 397 – Bourg-en-Bresse 45 – Lyon 70 – Mâcon 10

La Table de Chaintré (Sébastien Grospellier)
– 03 85 32 90 95 – sebastien.grospellier@yahoo.fr – Fax 03 85 32 91 04 – Closed 28 July-10 August, Monday and Tuesday except public holidays
Rest – *(number of covers limited, pre-book)* Menu €38/50
Spec. Marbré de foie gras de canard et poule faisane. Quasi de veau fermier, fricassée de cerfeuil tubéreux et mousseline de panais. Assiette des desserts.
◆ Welcoming house in the Pouilly vineyards where French Resistance heroine, Lucie Aubrac, was born. Elegant dining room and delicious market fresh menu. Game and truffles in season.

LA CHAISE-DIEU – 43 Haute-Loire – 331 E2 – pop. 772 – alt. 1 080 m – 43160

Auvergne

6 **C3**

Paris 503 – Ambert 29 – Brioude 35 – Issoire 59 – Le Puy-en-Velay 42 – St-Étienne 81

Office de tourisme, place de la Mairie 04 71 00 01 16, Fax 04 71 00 03 45

St-Robert abbey church ★★: tapestries ★★★.

Casadeï
pl. Abbaye – 04 71 00 00 58 – lacasadei@msn.com – Fax 04 71 00 01 67 – Open 2 May-end October
9 rm – €39/49 €49/53, €9 – ½ P €58/70 – **Rest** – *(dinner only) (resident only)* Menu (€23), €28 – Carte €37/40
◆ At the foot of the abbey, a family hotel with sober practical rooms. A local craft and regional produce shop; art gallery with works by local and other artists. Delightful antique-shop ambiance in this restaurant which serves authentic country recipes.

L'Écho et l'Abbaye with rm

pl. Écho – ✆ 04 71 00 00 45 – hoteldelecho@orange.fr – Fax 04 71 00 00 22 – Open 16 March-11 November and closed Wednesday except July-August
10 rm – 🛉€ 44 🛉🛉€ 49/65, ☕ € 8,50 – ½ P € 59 – **Rest** – *(number of covers limited, pre-book)* Menu € 17/40 – Carte € 27/57
◆ Attractive dining room, traditional cuisine, large wine list and V.I.P. guests during the music festival. Some rooms overlook the cloister.

CHALAIS – 16 Charente – 324 K8 – pop. 2 027 – alt. 70 m – ✉ 16210 Atlantic Coast

Paris 494 – Angoulême 47 – Bordeaux 83 – Périgueux 66 39 **C3**

Office de tourisme, 8, rue de Barbezieux ✆ 05 45 98 02 71, Fax 05 45 78 54 17

Relais du Château

au château – ✆ 05 45 98 23 58 – relaisduchateautalleyrand@wanadoo.fr – Fax 05 45 98 00 53 – Closed 2-30 November, Sunday dinner, Tuesday lunch and Monday
Rest – Menu € 17 (weekday lunch), € 24/31 – Carte € 32/37
◆ Guests cross a footbridge to reach this restaurant with a digniified vaulted room in a château built on the heights of Chalais. Medieval setting, pleasant courtyard-terrace.

CHALEZEULE – 25 Doubs – 321 G3 – see Besançon

CHALLANGES – 21 Côte-d'Or – 320 J7 – see Beaune

CHALLANS – 85 Vendée – 316 E6 – pop. 16 132 – alt. 8 m – ✉ 85300 Atlantic Coast

Paris 436 – Cholet 84 – Nantes 58 – La Roche-sur-Yon 42 34 **A3**

Office de tourisme, place de l'Europe ✆ 02 51 93 19 75, Fax 02 51 49 76 04

De l'Antiquité without rest

14 r. Galliéni – ✆ 02 51 68 02 84 – hotelantiquite@wanadoo.fr – Fax 02 51 35 55 74
16 rm – 🛉€ 52/80 🛉🛉€ 55/85, ☕ € 7 B **a**
◆ A Vendée-style modern house. Antique furniture personalises the rooms, all of which face the courtyard; the ones in the annexe are very well kept.

CHALLANS

Baudry (R. P.) . . . . A
Bazin (Bd R.) . . . . A
Biochaud (Av.) . . . . B
Bois de Céné (R. de) . . . A 2
Bonne Fontaine (R.) . . . . B
Briand (Pl. A.) . . . . A 3
Calmette (R.) . . . . B
Carnot (R.) . . . . A
Champ de Foire (Pl. du) . B 4
Cholet (R. de) . . . . B 5
Clemenceau (Bd) . . . . . . A
Dodin (Bd L.) . . . . B
F.F.I. (Bd des) . . . . A 6
Gambetta (R.) . . . . B
Gare (Bd de la) . . . . B
Gaulle (Pl. du Gén.-de) . A 7
Guérin (Bd) . . . . B
Leclerc (R. du Général) . A 8
Lézardière (R. P. de) . . . . A 10
Lorraine (R. de) . . . . A 12
Marzelles (R. des) . . . . . B 13
Monnier (R. P.) . . . . A 15
Nantes (R. de) . . . . AB
Roche-sur-Yon (R. de la) B 16
Sables (R. des) . . . . B 17
Strasbourg (Bd de) . . . . A
Viaud Grand Marais (Bd) B
Yole (Bd J.) . . . . AB

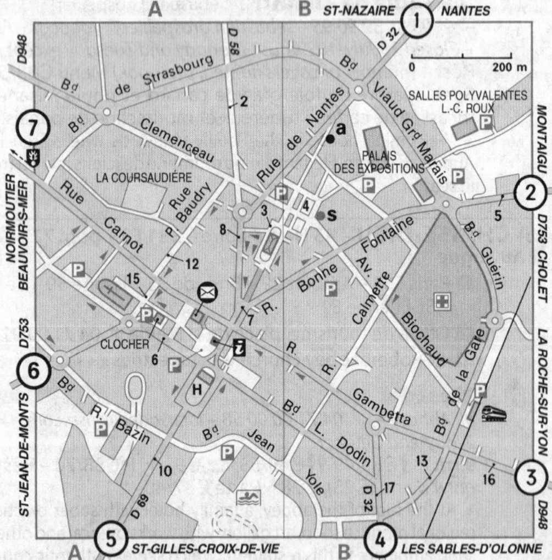

Chez Charles

8 pl. Champ de Foire – ✆ 02 51 93 36 65 – chezcharles85@aol.com – Fax 02 51 49 31 88 – Closed 23 December-24 January, Sunday dinner and Monday B s

Rest – Menu € 20 (weekdays)/55 – Carte € 24/43

♦ A nice little family restaurant in a bistro style. Classic cuisine inspired by market availability and regional produce.

in la Garnache 6,5 km by ① – pop. 3 576 – alt. 28 m – ✉ 85710

Le Petit St-Thomas

25 r. de Lattre-de-Tassigny – ✆ 02 51 49 05 99 – bienvenue@restaurant-petit-st-thomas.com – Closed 23 June-9 July, 7-28 January, Sunday dinner, Wednesday dinner and Monday

Rest – Menu € 22 (weekdays)/59 – Carte € 39/75

♦ A typical auberge from the region serving traditional, well-prepared dishes based on market produce. The veranda overlooks a small courtyard.

St-Gilles-Croix-de-Vie road by ⑤ – ✉ 85300 Challans

Château de la Vérie

2.5 km on D 69 – ✆ 02 51 35 33 44 – info@chateau-de-la-verie.com – Fax 02 51 35 14 84

21 rm – †€ 56/96 ††€ 72/158, ☕ € 10 – ½ P € 71/122 – **Rest** – *(closed Sunday dinner, Tuesday lunch and Monday off season)* Menu (€ 15 bi), € 25/55 bi – Carte € 38/74

♦ This 16C house offers guests spacious rooms with antique furniture. Country walks in the grounds, by the river and marshes. Dining room redecorated in Provence colours, complete with period mouldings and fireplace.

in Perrier 10 km by ⑥ – pop. 1 506 – alt. 4 m – ✉ 85300

Les Tendelles

lieu-dit Les Hautes Tendes, rte de Challans : 4 km – ✆ 02 51 35 36 94 – restaurant-les-tendelles@wanadoo.fr – Closed 1st-18 March, 29 September-12 October, Tuesday dinner, Wednesday dinner and Thursday dinner from October to February, Sunday dinner and Monday

Rest – Menu (€ 19), € 23 (weekdays)/47 – Carte € 35/57

♦ Inviting rustic restaurant brightened by a modern colour scheme. Modern seasonal menu and fine choice of local wines.

CHALLES-LES-EAUX – 73 Savoie – 333 I4 – see Chambéry

CHALLEX – 01 Ain – 328 I3 – pop. 1 057 – alt. 500 m – ✉ 01630 45 C1

Paris 519 – Bellegarde sur Valserine 22 – Bourg en Bresse 94 – Gex 20 – Lons le Saunier 113

Chalet l'Ecureuil

rte de la Plaine – ✆ 04 50 56 40 82 – Fax 04 50 41 24 58 – Closed Monday, Tuesday, Wednesday and lunch except Sunday

Rest – Menu € 39 – Carte € 45/64

♦ Pleasant chalet restaurant located away from the village. Rustic dining room decorated with old utensils, veranda, and traditional cuisine with inventive touches.

CHÂLONS-EN-CHAMPAGNE P – 51 Marne – 306 I9 – pop. 47 339 – alt. 83 m – ✉ 51000 Northern France and the Paris Region 13 B2

Paris 188 – Dijon 259 – Metz 157 – Nancy 162 – Reims 47 – Troyes 82

Office de tourisme, 3, quai des Arts ✆ 03 26 65 17 89, Fax 03 26 65 35 65

de la Grande-Romanie Courtisols Route Départementale 994, by Verdun road: 15 km, ✆ 03 26 66 65 97.

St-Étienne cathedral ★★ - N.-D.-en-Vaux church ★: interior★★ **F** - Statues-columns★★ of the musée du cloître in N.-D.-en-Vaux★ AY **M**1.

Basilica of N.-D.-de-l'Épine★★.

Plan on next page

CHÂLONS-EN-CHAMPAGNE

Arche-de-Mauvillain (Pt de l') . BZ 2
Bourgeois (R. Léon)....... ABY
Brossolette (Av. Pierre)....... X 4
Chastillon (R. de) .... ABZ 6
Croix-des-Teinturiers (R.) .... AZ 9
Dr-Pellier (R. du)............ X 11
Flocmagny (R. du).......... BY 12
Foch (Pl. du Maréchal) ...... AY 13
Gantelet (Rue du) .... AY 14
Gaulle
(Av. du Gén. Charles-de) .. BZ 15
Godart (Pl.)................ AY 17
Jacquiert (R. Clovis)........... X 18
Jeanne-d'Arc (Av.)............ X 21
Jean-Jaurès (R.) .... AZ 20
Jessaint (R. de) .... BZ 22
Libération (Pl. de la) .... AZ 24
Mariniers (Pt des) .... AY 26
Marne (R. de la)............. AY
Martyrs-de-la-Résistance
(R. des) .... BY 29
Orfeuil (R. d') .... AZ 31
Ormesson (Cours d') .... AZ 32
Prieur-de-la-Marne (R.) ...... BY 36
Récamier (R. Juliette)........ AZ 38
République (Pl. de la) .... AZ 39
Roosevelt (Av. du Prés.)...... X 41
Simon (Av. Jacques)......... X 45
Vaux (R. de) .... AY 47
Vieilles-Postes (R. des) .... X 48
Vinetz (R. de) .... BZ 49
Viviers (Pt des)............. AY 50

D'Angleterre (Jacky Michel) rm, VISA
19 pl. Mgr Tissier – ✆ 03 26 68 21 51
– hot.angl@wanadoo.fr – Fax 03 26 70 51 67
– Closed 27 July-19 August, Christmas holidays and Sunday BY **g**
25 rm – €75/130 €85/160, €15
Rest *Jacky Michel* – *(closed Saturday lunch, Monday lunch, Sunday and public holidays)* Menu €35, €45/95 – Carte €57/100
Rest *Les Temps changent* – *✆ 03 26 66 41 09 (closed Saturday lunch, Monday lunch, Sunday and public holidays)* Menu €23 – Carte €27/42
Spec. Langoustines royales à la nage de chardonnay. Mignon d'agneau cuit rosé aux champignons des bois (autumn). Soufflé au chocolat. **Wines** Champagne, Bouzy.
◆ A discreet building with well-appointed rooms with a personal touch, many with beautiful marble bathrooms. An elegant dining room decorated with light wood and floor tiles; tasty classic cuisine. The brasserie has modern décor and serves market-fresh dishes.

Le Renard VISA
24 pl. République – ✆ 03 26 68 03 78 – lerenard51@wanadoo.fr
– Fax 03 26 64 50 07 – Closed 19 December-5 January AZ **r**
35 rm – €65 €75, €11 – 1 suite – ½ P €67
Rest – *(closed Saturday lunch and Monday lunch)* Menu (€14,50), €19/37 – Carte €23/41
◆ These two 15C houses linked by a patio winter garden offer unusual, contemporary rooms (bed in the middle of the room, minimalist decor). A decor of wood panelling, straw chairs and bright colours at the restaurant. Friendly service.

Le Pot d'Étain without rest VISA
18 pl. République – ✆ 03 26 68 09 09 – hotellepotdetain51@wanadoo.fr
– Fax 03 26 68 58 18 AZ **u**
30 rm – €65 €70, €9
◆ Old building on a busy square offering spruce, soundproofed rooms adorned with rustic, neo-colonial or modern furniture. Homemade breakfast pastries.

Les Caudalies VISA
2 r. de l'Abbé-Lambert – ✆ 03 26 65 07 87 – caudalies@orange.fr
– Fax 03 26 65 07 87 – Closed 1st-4 May, 8-12 May, 10-24 August, 1st-11 November, 24 December-4 January, Saturday lunch and Sunday AY **v**
Rest – Menu €30/48 – Carte €36/49
◆ This delightful late 19C building (magnificent stained glass windows, Art Nouveau light fixtures) stands in the town centre. Updated traditional menu. Courtyard terrace.

Les Ardennes VISA
34 pl. République – ✆ 03 26 68 21 42 – Fax 03 26 21 34 55 – Closed Sunday dinner and Monday AZ **s**
Rest – Menu (€23), €29/45 – Carte €25/48
◆ The decor is a combination of copperware, rustic furniture, brick fireplace and a fish and lobster tank. The cuisine features local produce and seafood. Pleasant summer terrace.

Au Carillon Gourmand VISA
15 bis pl. Mgr Tissier – ✆ 03 26 64 45 07 – Fax 03 26 21 06 09
– Closed 7-13 April, 4-25 August, 2-7 March, Sunday dinner, Wednesday dinner and Monday BY **e**
Rest – Menu (€19), €32 – Carte €32/43
◆ A welcoming, contemporary dining room with a veranda overlooking the street. Traditional cuisine plus dishes of the day, depending on the market produce available.

Le Petit Pasteur VISA
42 r. Pasteur – ✆ 03 26 68 24 78 – restaurant.petitpasteur@orange.fr
– Fax 03 26 68 25 97 – Closed 2-24 August, 27 December-4 January, Sunday dinner, Saturday lunch and Monday BY **t**
Rest – Menu €19 (weekdays)/33 – Carte €35/51
◆ A pleasant restaurant with a modern setting and a pretty, flowery terrace in fine weather. Traditional dishes.

in l'Épine 8,5 km by ③ – pop. 648 – alt. 153 m – ✉ 51460

N.-Dame basilica ★★.

Aux Armes de Champagne (Philippe Zeiger) rest,

31 av. du Luxembourg – ✆ 03 26 69 30 30
– accueil@aux-armes-de-champagne.com – Fax 03 26 69 30 26
– Closed 12 January-9 February (except hotel), Sunday dinner and Monday November-April

35 rm – †€ 85/168 ††€ 85/168, ☕ € 14 – 2 suites – ½ P € 139

Rest – Menu € 25, € 45/92 – Carte € 59/98

Spec. Saint-Jacques aux truffes (15 November to 15 February). Tranche d'aubergine rôtie au pied de cochon (15 June to 15 August). Soufflé à l'estragon, sorbet groseille à maquereau (15 June to 15 August). **Wines** Champagne, Coteaux Champenois.

◆ Smart Champagne inn coupled to a comfortable, refined hotel. Cosy rooms with a personal touch. Comfortable lounge bar. The bay windows of the pretty dining room open onto the cathedral; classic cooking with a modern flair based on ingredients from the vegetable garden.

CHALON-SUR-SAÔNE – 71 Saône-et-Loire – 320 J9 – pop. 50 124 – Built-up area 130 825 – alt. 180 m – ✉ 71100 Burgundy-Jura 8 C3

Paris 335 – Besançon 132 – Dijon 68 – Lyon 125 – Mâcon 59

Office de tourisme, boulevard de la République ✆ 03 85 48 37 97, Fax 03 85 48 63 55

de Chalon-sur-Saône Châtenoy-en-Bresse Parc de Loisirs Saint Nicolas, ✆ 03 85 93 49 65.

Museums: Denon★ BZ **M¹**, Nicéphore Niepce★★ BZ **M²** - Roseraie St-Nicolas (rose garden) ★ Southeast: 4 km X.

Plan on next page

St-Régis

22 bd République – ✆ 03 85 90 95 60 – saint-regis@saint-regis-chalon.fr – Fax 03 85 90 95 70 BZ **v**

36 rm – †€ 78/90 ††€ 98/175, ☕ € 13,50 – **Rest** – *(closed Saturday lunch and Sunday dinner)* Menu € 22 (weekdays)/54 – Carte € 39/63

◆ On a busy avenue, an early 20C building with provincial charm. Grand, often spacious, rooms. Pleasant lounge furnished in leather. Bright dining room with prettily laid tables. A fine selection of wines from the Chalon valley.

St-Georges

32 av. J. Jaurès – ✆ 03 85 90 80 50 – reservation@le-saintgeorges.fr – Fax 03 85 90 80 55

50 rm – †€ 75/138 ††€ 75/138, ☕ € 11 – ½ P € 72 AZ **s**

Rest – *(closed 21 July-17 August, Saturday lunch and Sunday dinner)* Menu (€ 19), € 26/44 – Carte € 45/67

Rest *Le Petit Comptoir d'à Côté* – *✆ 03 85 90 80 52 (closed Saturday lunch, Sunday and public holidays)* Menu (€ 14), € 15/18 – Carte € 21/32

◆ A pleasant, colourful façade near the station. Welcoming and well soundproofed rooms; some decorated in a modern style. Cheerful restaurant with painted woodwork; tasty classic cuisine. Elegant brasserie decor combining leather and wood at the Petit Comptoir d'à Côté.

St-Jean without rest

24 quai Gambetta – ✆ 03 85 48 45 65 – reservation@hotelsaintjean.fr – Fax 03 85 93 62 69 BZ **s**

25 rm – †€ 42 ††€ 56, ☕ € 6

◆ This family hotel, in a nice location on the banks of the Saône, offers you a very warm welcome. Well-kept rooms decorated with floral motifs and breakfast room under a glass roof in a conservatory style.

Le Bourgogne

28 r. Strasbourg – ✆ 03 85 48 89 18 – restaurant.lebourgogne@orange.fr – Fax 03 85 93 39 10 – Closed 5-11 May, 6-21 July, 9-17 November, Saturday lunch, Sunday dinner and Monday CZ **t**

Rest – Menu € 18/47 – Carte € 43/65

◆ The high open beam ceiling and Louis XIII-style furniture in the dining room are part of the setting in this rustic, Burgundy-style restaurant. Traditional cuisine.

CHALON-SUR-SAÔNE

Arnal (R. R.) . . . . X 2
Banque (R. de la) . . . . BZ 3
Blum (Av. L.). . . . . X 4
Châtelet (Pl. du) . . . . BZ 5
Châtelet (R. du) . . . . CZ 6
Citadelle (R. de la) . . . . BY 7
Coubertin (R. P. de) . . . . X 8
Couturier (R. Ph.-L.) . . . . BZ 9
Duhesme (R. du Gén.) . . . . AY 12
Europe (Av. de l') . . . . X 14
Evêché (R. de l') . . . . CZ 15
Fèvres (R. aux) . . . . CZ 16
Gaulle (Pl. Gén.-de) . . . . BZ 17
Grande-R. . . . . BCZ 18
Hôtel-de-Ville (Pl. de l') . . . . BZ 19
Lardy (Av. P.) . . . . X 20
Leclerc (R. Gén.) . . . . BZ
Lyon (R. de) . . . . BZ 21
Mac-Orlan (R. P.) . . . . X 22
Messiaen (R. O.) . . . . AZ 24
Nugues (Av. P.) . . . . X 25
Obélisque (Pl. de l') . . . . BY 27
Pasteur (R.) . . . . BZ 28
Poilus-d'Orient (R.) . . . . X 29
Poissonnerie (R. de la) . . . . CZ 31
Pompidou (Av. G.) . . . . AZ 32
Pont (R. du) . . . . CZ 35
Porte-de-Lyon (R.) . . . . BZ 36
Port-Villiers (R. du) . . . . BZ 37
Poterne (Q. de la) . . . . CZ 38
Pretet (R. René) . . . . AZ 40
République (Bd) . . . . ABZ 42
Ste-Marie (Prom.) . . . . CZ 47
St-Georges (R.) . . . . BZ 45
St-Vincent (Pl. et R.) . . . . CZ 46
Strasbourg (R. de) . . . . CZ 48
Thénard (R. L.-J.) . . . . X 49
Trémouille (R. de la) . . . . BCY 51
8-Mai-1945 (Av.) . . . . X 52
56e-R.I. (R. du) . . . . X 54
134e-R.I. (R. du) . . . . X 58

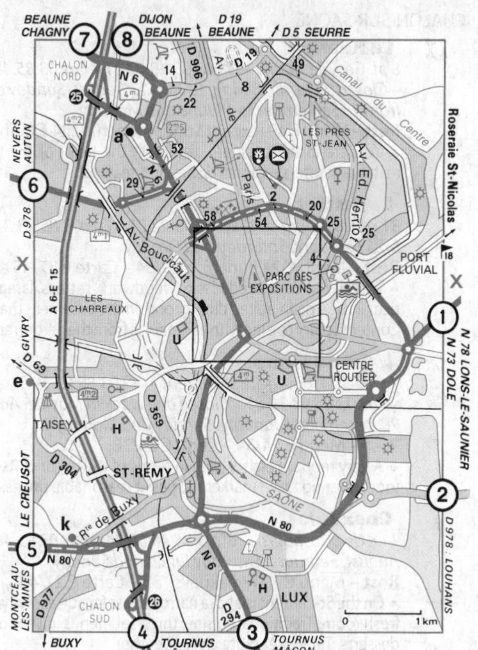

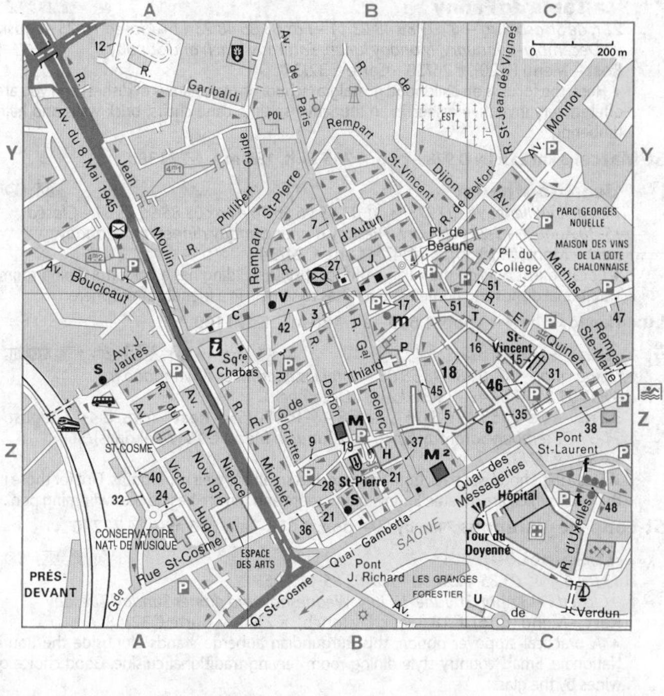

XX **La Réale**

8 pl. Gén. de Gaulle – ☎ 03 85 48 07 21 – Fax 03 85 48 57 77 – Closed 28 April-13 May, 13 July-12 August, Sunday except lunch from 1st September to 1st June and Monday BZ **m**

Rest – Menu € 19 (except Sunday lunch), € 24 € (Sunday lunch)/34 – Carte € 29/48

♦ You are in the business district, in the heart of the town, where this brasserie-style restaurant offers regional dishes and seafood.

X **Le Bistrot**

31 r. Strasbourg – ☎ 03 85 93 22 01 – Fax 03 85 93 27 05 – Closed 18-31 August, 5-25 February, Saturday and Sunday CZ **f**

Rest – Menu € 24 (lunch), € 29/34 – Carte € 37/45

♦ This all-red decorated bistro (woodwork, settees, lamps, etc.) is really tempting, in particular the small, vaulted dining room in the basement that opens into a glass-walled cellar. Contemporary cuisine with vegetables from the garden and a nice selection of Burgundies.

X **L'Air du Temps**

7 r. de Strasbourg, Ile St Laurent – ☎ 03 85 93 39 01 – lair.du.temps@wanadoo.fr – Fax 03 85 93 39 01 – Closed one week in May, 25 August-7 September, 20 December-4 January, Sunday and Monday CZ **f**

Rest – Menu € 24/34 – Carte € 34/38

♦ A very modern bistro, both in terms of the decor of its two small dining rooms and the food, offering tasty, market recipes at reasonable prices.

X **Chez Jules**

11 r. de Strasbourg – ☎ 03 85 48 08 34 – Fax 03 85 48 55 48 – Closed 3 weeks in August, February, Saturday lunch and Sunday CZ **f**

Rest – Menu € 19 (weekdays)/35 – Carte € 27/45

♦ On the St-Laurent Island, a narrow glass façade allows you to see into a rustic, simple and fresh room. Traditional cuisine; three set menus, dishes of the day and a wide selection of desserts. Tables set quite close together.

X **La Table de Fanny**

21 r. de Strasbourg – ☎ 03 85 48 23 11 – Fax 03 85 48 23 11 – Closed 16-25 August, 27 December-5 January, Monday lunch, Saturday lunch and Sunday CZ **f**

Rest – Menu (€ 20), € 26/30 – Carte € 32/37

♦ Here, the focus is on childhood nostalgia (school photos, names of dishes) and you are offered very inventive dishes in an attractive setting; cane chairs, brick walls and half-timbering.

in St-Marcel 3 km East by D 978 – pop. 4 705 – alt. 185 m – ✉ 71380

XX **Jean Bouthenet**

19 r. de la Villeneuve, (D 978) – ☎ 03 85 96 56 16 – Fax 03 85 96 75 81 – Closed 15-30 August, 15-28 February, Tuesday dinner, Sunday dinner and Monday

Rest – Menu (€ 18,50), € 24/47 – Carte € 24/34

♦ Located just outside the village, this local-style building has a colourful dining room. Traditional dishes and homemade terrines to sample in a friendly atmosphere.

in Lux 4 km to ③ by N 6 – pop. 1 620 – alt. 180 m – ✉ 71100

Les Charmilles rest,

r. Libération – ☎ 03 85 48 58 08 – hotel.les.charmilles@wanadoo.fr – Fax 03 85 93 04 49 – Closed 21-31 December

32 rm – €45/53 €51/61, € 8 – ½ P € 50/55 – **Rest** – *(closed 4-17 August, 21-31 December, Saturday lunch and Sunday)* Menu € 15 (weekdays)/36 – Carte € 27/37

♦ This 1970s hotel, set back from the road, has small but well kept rooms. Opt for those in the back, which are quieter. Sunny dining room and terrace beside the swimming pool.

in St-Loup-de-Varennes 7 km by ③ – pop. 1 018 – alt. 186 m – ✉ 71240

XX **Le Saint Loup**

13 RN 6 – ☎ 03 85 44 21 58 – Fax 03 85 44 21 58 – Closed 7-13 April, 30 June-12 July, Wednesday and dinner Sunday-Tuesday

Rest – Menu (€ 16), € 18 (weekday lunch), € 21/44 – Carte € 32/48

♦ A practical stopover option, this Burgundian auberge stands alongside the Route Nationale. Smart country-style dining room serving traditional cuisine. Good choice of wines by the glass.

in St-Rémy 4 km to ⑤ (Le Creusot road) N 6, N 80 and secondary road – pop. 5 961 – alt. 187 m – ✉ 71100

XXX ✿ **Moulin de Martorey** (Jean-Pierre Gillot)
– ✆ *03 85 48 12 98 – moulindemartorey@wanadoo.fr – Fax 03 85 48 73 67 – Closed 4-21 August, 5-22 January, Sunday dinner, Tuesday lunch and Monday except public holidays* X **k**
Rest – Menu € 30 (weekdays)/84
Spec. Lièvre à la royale (15 October to 31 December). Opéra de foie gras de canard à l'échalote confite et anguille fumée. Fondant au chocolat guanaja et pralin feuilleté. **Wines** Montagny, Givry.
♦ A tranquil 19C flour mill overlooking the mill race. Delightful rustic interior (stone flooring) set around the old machinery. Personalised cuisine and a fine wine list.

Givry road 4 km west on D 69 – ✉ 71880 Châtenoy-le-Royal :

XX **L'Auberge des Alouettes**
1 rte de Givry – ✆ 03 85 48 32 15 – Fax 03 85 93 12 96 – Closed 16 July-7 August, 7-21 January, Sunday dinner, Tuesday dinner and Wednesday X **e**
Rest – Menu € 20/31 – Carte € 28/70
♦ Inn with a warm atmosphere on a busy main road. Take a table near the elegant stone fireplace to sample the daily specials.

in Dracy-le-Fort 6 km by ⑥ and D 978 – pop. 1 092 – alt. 180 m – ✉ 71640

Le Dracy
4 r. du Pressoir – ✆ 03 85 87 81 81 – info@ledracy.com – Fax 03 85 87 77 49
47 rm – †€ 66/125 ††€ 66/125, ☕ € 11 – ½ P € 68/100
Rest *La Garenne* – Menu € 20 (weekday lunch), € 28/45 – Carte € 37/45
♦ Ideal for a peaceful break away from it all in the countryside. Cosy, refurbished rooms; those overlooking the garden have a private terrace. Brand new pool. Attractive dining room decorated in contemporary style. Regional cuisine.

near A6 Chalon-Nord interchange – ✉ 71100 Chalon-sur-Saône

Mercure
av. Europe – ✆ 03 85 46 51 89 – H368@accor.com – Fax 03 85 46 08 96
85 rm – †€ 84/116 ††€ 91/141, ☕ € 13 – **Rest** – *(closed Saturday, Sunday lunch)* Menu (€ 11), € 21 X **a**
♦ Well-placed for access to the motorway, an imposing 1970s- building with colourful, well-soundproofed rooms. Decoration based on the themes of wine and photos, the dining room opens its large bay windows onto the swimming pool.

in Sassenay 9 km Northeast by D 5 – pop. 1 402 – alt. 178 m – ✉ 71530

XX **Le Magny**
29 Grande rue – ✆ 03 85 91 61 58 – salognon.pierre@wanadoo.fr – Fax 03 85 91 77 28 – Closed 7-13 April, 1st-13 August, 1st-8 January, Sunday dinner, Tuesday dinner and Monday
Rest – Menu € 21 (weekdays)/44 – Carte € 46/52
♦ With its yellow façade with green shutters and its provincial interior (Bressan wardrobes, parquet, fireplace), this village inn provides a welcoming setting. Regional food.

CHAMAGNE – 88 Vosges – 314 F2 – see Charmes

CHAMALIÈRES – 63 Puy-de-Dôme – 326 F8 – see Clermont-Ferrand

CHAMARANDES – 52 Haute-Marne – 313 K5 – see Chaumont

CHAMBERET – 19 Corrèze – 329 L2 – pop. 1 304 – alt. 450 m – ✉ 19370

25 **C2**

Paris 453 – Guéret 84 – Limoges 66 – Tulle 45 – Ussel 64

Syndicat d'initiative, 5, place du Marché ✆ 05 55 98 30 14, Fax 05 55 98 79 34

Mont Gargan ✻★★ Northwest: 9 km, **Dordogne-Berry-Limousin.**

De France rest,

– 05 55 98 30 14 – sylvie.pouget@wanadoo.fr – Fax 05 55 73 47 15 – Closed 16-22 June, 22 December-31 January, Friday dinner, Sunday dinner and Monday

15 rm – €40/52 €40/52, €7,50 – ½ P €49 – **Rest** – Menu €13 (weekday lunch), €26/33 – Carte €28/40

◆ Family atmosphere in a smart stone house with renovated rooms. Bar with a local clientele. A stylish restaurant with its old furniture, beams and murals representing Corrèze chateaux and villages. Traditional cuisine and dishes based on local produce.

CHAMBÉRY – 73 Savoie – 333 I4 – pop. 55 786 – Built-up area 113 457 – alt. 270 m – Casino : at Challes-les-Eaux – 73000 French Alps 46 F2

Paris 562 – Annecy 50 – Grenoble 55 – Lyon 101 – Torino 205

Chambéry-Aix-les-Bains: 04 79 54 49 54, Viviers-du-Lac by ④: 8 km.

Office de tourisme, 24, boulevard de la Colonne 04 79 33 42 47, Fax 04 79 85 71 39

du Granier Apremont Apremont Chemin de Fontaine Rouge, Southeast: 8 km by D 201, 04 79 28 21 26.

Old Town★★ : Château (Castle)★, place St-Léger★, railings ★ of the Hôtel de Châteauneuf (18 Rue de la Croix-d'Or) - Crypt ★ of the Eglise St-Pierre-de-Lémenc (St Pierre de Lémenc church) - Rue Basse-du-Château★ - Cathédrale métropolitaine St-François-de-Sales (St François de Sales cathedral)★ - Musée Savoisien (Savoy Museum)★ M¹ - Musée des Beaux-Arts (Fine Arts Museum)★ M².

Plan on next page

Mercure without rest

183 pl. de la Gare – 04 79 62 10 11 – h1541@accor.com – Fax 04 79 62 10 23 A s

81 rm – €68/145 €75/160, €13,50

◆ Across from the station, determinedly modern architecture, alternating between concrete and glass. Pleasant lobby, modern lounge-bar, spacious, soundproofed rooms.

Des Princes without rest

4 r. Boigne – 04 79 33 45 36 – hoteldesprinces@wanadoo.fr – Fax 04 79 70 31 47 B r

45 rm – €75 €90, €9

◆ This charming hotel, near the Elephant Fountain, offers pleasant rooms with theme decor (music, film and poetry), select furniture, etc.

Le France without rest

22 fg Reclus – 04 79 33 51 18 – info@le-france-hotel.com – Fax 04 79 85 06 30

48 rm – €75/80 €88/95, €10 B z

◆ This imposing 1960s building has well-kept rooms with balconies, being renovated in stages. Good soundproofing.

Le St-Réal

Pl. Pierre Dumas – 04 79 70 09 33 – info@restaurant-saint-real.com – Fax 04 79 33 49 65 – Closed 1st-15 August and Sunday B x

Rest – Menu €40/95 – Carte €58/91

◆ This 17C house, formerly a church of the White Penitents, contains a stylish dining room (subdued lighting, paintings, exposed beams and stone walls). Nice selection of wines.

L'Hypoténuse

141 Carré Curial – 04 79 85 80 15 – resto-hypo@wanadoo.fr – Fax 04 79 85 80 18 – Closed spring school holidays, 17 July-17 August, Sunday and Monday B v

Rest – Menu (€18), €22/44 – Carte €38/51

◆ The "Hypotenuse in the Carré (square)" adds a few pieces of period furniture to a contemporary decor, plus paintings for a splash of colour, and the copious cuisine multiplies the pleasure.

CHAMBÉRY

Allobroges (Q. des) . . . . A 2
Banque (R. de la) . . . . B 3
Basse-du-Château (R.) . . . . . . A 4
Bernardines (Av. des) . . . . A 6
Boigne (R. de) . . . . B
Borrel (Q. du Sénateur A.) . . . B 7
Charvet (R. F.) . . . . B 9
Château (Pl. du) . . . . A 10
Colonne (Bd de la) . . . . B 12
Ducis (R.) . . . . B 13
Ducs-de-Savoie (Av. des) . . . . B 14
Europe (Espl. de l') . . . . B 16
Freizier (R.) . . . . AB 17
Gaulle (Av. Gén.-de) . . . . B 18
Italie (R. d') . . . . B 20
Jean-Jaurès (Av.) . . . . A 21
Jeu-de-Paume (Q. du) . . . . A 23
Juiverie (R.) . . . . A
Lans (R. de) . . . . A 24
Libération (Pl. de la) . . . . B 25
Maché (Pl.) . . . . A 27
Maché (R. du Fg) . . . . A 28
Martin (R. Cl.) . . . . B 30
Métropole (Pl.) . . . . B 31
Michaud (R.) . . . . B 32
Mitterrand (Pl. F.) . . . . B 33
Musée (Bd. du) . . . . AB 34
Ravet (Q. Ch.) . . . . B 35
St-François (R.) . . . . B 38
St-Léger (Pl.) . . . . B
St- Antoine (R.) . . . . A 36
Théâtre (Bd du) . . . . B 39
Vert (Av. du Comte) . . . . A 40

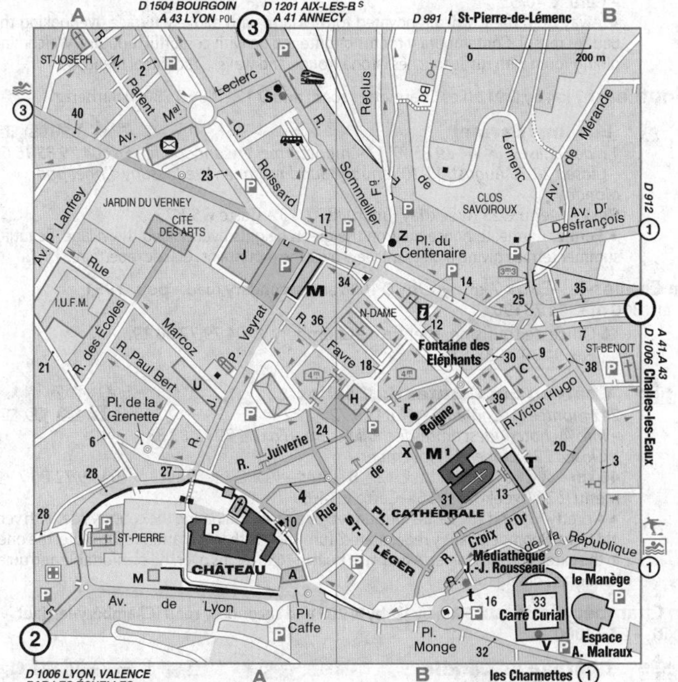

Les Comptoirs

183 pl. de la Gare – ✆ 04 79 96 97 27 – bouviergastronomie@orange.fr – Fax 04 79 96 17 78 – Closed Saturday lunch and Sunday — A s

Rest – Menu € 15 (weekday lunch), € 24/45 – Carte approx. € 35

◆ Elegant, modern dining room set in a glass pyramid structure, decorated in green and cocoa. Traditional cuisine, 'sucré-salé' served in the lounge bar in the evening. Inexpensive.

L'Atelier

59 r. de la République – ✆ 04 79 70 62 39 – contact@atelier-chambery.com – Closed Sunday and Monday — B t

Rest – Menu € 13/27 – Carte € 23/34

◆ Although set in a former post house this restaurant has modern decoration in its two rooms (one of which is non-smoking) and wine bar. Inventive food.

in Sonnaz 8 km by ① On D 991 – pop. 1 222 – alt. 370 m – ✉ 73000

Auberge Le Régent

453 rte d'Aix-les-Bains – ✆ 04 79 72 27 70 – pascal.vichard@wanadoo.fr – Fax 04 79 72 27 70 – Closed 16 August-10 September, February holidays, Sunday dinner and Wednesday

Rest – Menu (€ 19), € 27/45 – Carte € 39/57

◆ 19C Savoyard farmhouse turned into a restaurant. Stylish rustic dining rooms and a pleasant terrace facing the peaceful garden. Warm and personal service.

in St-Alban-Leysse 4 km by ①, D 1006 and secondary road – pop. 5 071 – alt. 285 m – ✉ 73230

L'Or du Temps

814 rte de Plainpalais – ☎ 04 79 85 51 28 – or.du.temps@free.fr – Fax 04 79 85 83 87 – Closed 13 August-2 September and 2-10 January

18 rm – 🛉€ 39/44 🛉🛉€ 45/50, ☕ € 6,50 – ½ P € 56/60 – **Rest** – *(closed Saturday lunch, Sunday dinner and Monday)* Menu € 13,50 (weekday lunch), € 29/46 – Carte € 40/55

◆ Away from the town, a renovated former farm with a lovely terrace overlooking the Bauges massif. Contemporary rooms brightened up with colourful furniture. Welcoming dining room with rustic touches (stone trough and walls). Traditional menu.

Southeast 2 km by D 912 (Les Charmettes road) and D 12 - B – ✉ 73000 Barberaz

Le Mont Carmel

1 r. de l'Eglise – ☎ 04 79 85 77 17 – montcarmel@wanadoo.fr – Fax 04 79 85 16 65 – Closed 20-30 August, 1st-10 January, Sunday dinner, Wednesday dinner and Monday

Rest – Menu € 25 (weekday lunch), € 37/75 – Carte € 52/72

◆ Former Carmelite house built on the green heights overlooking the village. Beautiful summer terrace giving a pleasant view over the mountains. Classic repertoire.

in Challes-les-Eaux 7 km by ②by D 1006 and secondary road – pop. 3 931 – alt. 310 m – ✉ 73190

Office de tourisme, avenue de Chambéry ☎ 04 79 72 86 19, Fax 04 79 71 38 51

Château des Comtes de Challes

247 montée du Château – ☎ 04 79 72 72 72 – info@chateaudescomtesdechalles.com – Fax 04 79 72 83 83 – Closed 29 October-12 November

46 rm – 🛉€ 60 🛉🛉€ 84, ☕ € 12 – 8 suites – ½ P € 72 – **Rest** – ☎ 04 79 72 86 71 – Menu € 26 (weekdays)/56 – Carte € 54/69

◆ A pretty 13C and 15C castle surrounded by a park dominating the countryside, with very old trees. Rooms elegantly redecorated, furnished with lovely antique furniture, the ones in the extension are plainer. A fireplace built in 1650 reigns over the comfortable and quiet restaurant dining room.

in Chambéry-le-Vieux 5 km by ③ by N 201 and secondary road (Chambéry-le-Haut exit) – ✉ 73000

Château de Candie

r. Bois de Candie – ☎ 04 79 96 63 00 – candie@icor.fr – Fax 04 79 96 63 10 – Closed 14-27 April and 26 October-5 November

15 rm – 🛉€ 130/230 🛉🛉€ 130/230, ☕ € 15 – 5 suites

Rest – *(closed Sunday dinner, Saturday lunch and Monday)* Menu € 32 (weekday lunch), € 50/75 – Carte € 73/129

Spec. Foie gras de canard en gelée de fraise et rhubarbe fondante (spring). Huîtres en gelée d'eau de mer au raifort et tartare de crevette au piment d'Espelette (autumn). Oeuf cassé, salade de pomme de terre et truffe (winter). **Wines** Manicle, Mondeuse.

◆ This 14C fortified house, built by the Crusaders, has been elegantly restored. It overlooks the Chambéry valley and is decorated with antique furniture, ornaments and rare objects. Contemporary cuisine which cleverly plays around with tastes and textures.

CHAMBOLLE-MUSIGNY – 21 Côte-d'Or – 320 J6 – pop. 313 – alt. 280 m – ✉ 21220

8 **D1**

Paris 326 – Beaune 28 – Dijon 17

Château André Ziltener without rest

– ☎ 03 80 62 41 62 – chateau.ziltener@wanadoo.fr – Fax 03 80 62 83 75 – Closed 10 December-28 February

8 rm – 🛉€ 180/220 🛉🛉€ 200/285, ☕ € 15 – 2 suites

◆ This 18C residence invites you to share in the discreet luxury of its spacious Louis XV-style rooms, a successful blend of old and new. Small wine museum.

Le Chambolle
28 r. Basse – ✆ 03 80 62 86 26 – Fax 03 80 62 86 26 – Closed 25 June-17 July, 22 December-22 January, Sunday dinner from December to March, Wednesday and Thursday
Rest – Menu € 26/40 – Carte € 23/52
◆ A smiling welcome in this small, simple, neat dining room serving dishes based on local produce, prepared with the greatest of care.

CHAMBON-LA-FORÊT – 45 Loiret – 318 K3 – pop. 625 – alt. 117 m – ✉ 45340 12 C2

Paris 96 – Châteauneuf-sur-Loire 26 – Montargis 43 – Orléans 43 – Pithiviers 15

Auberge de la Rive du Bois
1 km north by Pithiviers road – ✆ 02 38 32 28 44 – aubergedelarivedubois@wanadoo.fr – Fax 02 38 32 02 61 – Closed 30 July-19 August, 23 December-6 January, Monday dinner, Tuesday dinner and Wednesday
Rest – Menu € 15 (weekdays)/46 – Carte € 26/41
◆ This peaceful hamlet's welcoming inn is ideal for family and business get-togethers: countrified dining rooms, flower-decked terrace and veranda. Classic menu.

LE CHAMBON-SUR-LIGNON – 43 Haute-Loire – 331 H3 – pop. 2 642 – alt. 967 m – ✉ 43400 Lyon - Rhone Valley 6 D3

Paris 573 – Annonay 48 – Lamastre 32 – Privas 75 – Le Puy-en-Velay 45 – St-Étienne 60

Office de tourisme, 1, rue des Quatre Saisons ✆ 04 71 59 71 56, Fax 04 71 65 88 78

du Chambon-sur-Lignon La Pierre de la Lune, Southeast: 5 km by D 103, ✆ 04 71 59 28 10.

Bel Horizon rm, rest,
chemin de Molle – ✆ 04 71 59 74 39 – info@belhorizon.fr – Fax 04 71 59 79 81 – Closed 2-24 January, Monday (except hotel) and Sunday dinner 1st October-30 April
30 rm – €55/94 €55/100, € 10 – ½ P € 66/84 – **Rest** – Menu € 18 (weekdays)/40 – Carte € 27/46
◆ A relaxed atmosphere in this hotel that focuses on relaxation and leisure (well-being centre). Well kept, light, practical rooms. Restaurant in sunny tones and terrace overlooking the garden. Classic menu.

South 3 km by D 151, La Suchère road and secondary road – ✉ 43400 Chambon-sur-Lignon

Le Bois Vialotte rest,
La Suchère road – ✆ 04 71 59 74 03 – crosde@wanadoo.fr – Fax 04 71 65 86 32 – Open 20 May-30 September
17 rm – €52/65 €52/65, € 9 – ½ P € 54/62 – **Rest** – Menu € 15/26
◆ Those seeking quiet will enjoy this family-run hotel located on the edge of a wood. The rooms look out over open countryside and are very well kept. Guesthouse-type, somewhat antiquated, dining room and traditional home cooking.

East 3,5 km by D 157 and D 185 – ✉ 43400 Chambon-sur-Lignon

Clair Matin rm, rest,
Les Barandons – ✆ 04 71 59 73 03 – clairmatin@hotelclairmatin.com – Fax 04 71 65 87 66 – Closed 15 November-10 February, Monday and Tuesday off season
25 rm – €50/130 €50/130, € 11 – 2 suites – ½ P € 55/89
Rest – Menu € 15 (weekdays)/40 – Carte € 34/53
◆ 'On a clear day' you will enjoy a wide view of the Cévennes from this welcoming chalet. Practical rooms, many leisure activities in the park and fresh air guaranteed! The restaurant and terrace have a beautiful panoramic view of the Mézenc and Gerbier-de-Jonc peaks.

CHAMBORD – 41 Loir-et-Cher – 318 G6 – pop. 185 – alt. 71 m – ✉ 41250 11 B1

Paris 176 – Blois 18 – Châteauroux 101 – Orléans 56 – Romorantin-Lanthenay 38 – Salbris 55

Château★★★, G. Châteaux of the Loire

Du Grand St-Michel

pl. St-Louis – ✆ 02 54 20 31 31 – *hotelsaintmichel@wanadoo.fr* – *Fax 02 54 20 36 40* – *Closed mid November-mid December*

40 rm – †€ 52/110 ††€ 52/110, ☕ € 8 – **Rest** – Menu € 22/35 – Carte € 37/53

◆ On the marvellous Chambord estate overlooking the castle. Ask for one of the modern, renovated rooms. Vast restaurant decorated with trophies and paintings devoted to hunting. The terrace faces the royal hunting lodge, lit up at night.

CHAMBRAY-LÈS-TOURS – 37 Indre-et-Loire – 317 N4 – see Tours

CHAMBRETAUD – 85 Vendée – 316 K6 – pop. 1 275 – alt. 214 m – ✉ 85500 34 B3

Paris 373 – Angers 85 – Bressuire 50 – Cholet 21 – Nantes 76 – La Roche-sur-Yon 55

Château du Boisniard

rm, rm,

– ✆ 02 51 67 50 01 – *contact@chateau-boisniard.com* – *Fax 02 51 67 53 81*

17 rm – †€ 130/320 ††€ 130/390, ☕ € 27 – **Rest** – *(closed Sunday dinner 30 September-31 March)* Menu (€ 28), € 36/58 – Carte € 47/57

◆ A beautiful 15C manor (entirely non-smoking) with attractive rooms redone in a medieval style; those in the outbuildings are new and comfortable. Vast wooded estate and spa. Elegant restaurant with a view of the park. Cuisine based on fresh market produce.

CHAMESOL – 25 Doubs – 321 K2 – pop. 328 – alt. 730 m – ✉ 25190 17 C2

Paris 453 – Besançon 91 – Belfort 43 – Montbéliard 30 – Morteau 50

Mon Plaisir (Christian Pilloud)

– ✆ 03 81 92 56 17 – *mon-plaisir@wanadoo.fr* – *Fax 03 81 92 52 67* – *Closed 3-11 March, 1st-16 September, 22-30 December, Sunday dinner, Monday and Tuesday except lunch public holidays*

Rest – Menu € 38/70

Spec. Foie gras en terrine ou en escalope. Escargots en cappuccino. La farandole de desserts. **Wines** Arbois-Chardonnay, Arbois-Savagnin.

◆ A mixture of styles, numerous knick-knacks, paintings and floral arrangements make up the decor of this family restaurant with old-fashioned charm. Tempting modern cuisine.

CHAMONIX-MONT-BLANC – 74 Haute-Savoie – 328 O5 – pop. 9 830 – alt. 1 040 m – Winter sports : 1 035/3 840 m 14 36 – Casino AY – ✉ 74400 French Alps 45 D1

Paris 610 – Albertville 65 – Annecy 97 – Aosta 57 – Genève 82

Mont-Blanc Tunnel : toll 2006, one way : cars 31.90, car and caravan 42.10, lorries 115.40 to 245.40, motorcycles 21.10. Info ATMB ✆ 04 50 55 55 00 and ✆ 04 50 55 39 36.

Office de tourisme, 85, place du Triangle de l'Amitié ✆ 04 50 53 00 24, Fax 04 50 53 58 90

18 de Chamonix Les Praz-de-Chamonix 35 route du Golf, North: 3 km, ✆ 04 50 53 06 28.

East: Mer de glace★★★ and Le Montenvers★★★ by rack railway - Southeast: Aiguille du midi ❋★★★ by cable car (intermediate station: plan de l'Aiguille★★) - Northwest: Le Brévent ❋★★★ by cable car (intermediate station: Planpraz★★) - North: Col de Balme (Balme Pass)★★(Alpages de Charamillon [Charamillon Pastures]).

Plan on next page

CHAMONIX-MONT-BLANC

Aiguille-du-Midi (Av.)	AY	2
Angeville (Rte H. d')	AX	3
Balmat (Pl. Jacques)	AY	5
Blanche (Rte)	AY	
Bois-du-Bouchet (Av. du)	AX	6
Cachat-le-Géant (Av.)	AX	7
Courmayeur (Av. de)	AY	9
Cour (Pont de)	AY	8
Cristalliers (Ch. des)	AX	10
Croix-des-Moussoux (Montée)	AZ	12
Croz (Av. Michel)	AY	13
Devouassoux (Ch. F.)	AY	14
Gaillands (Rte des)	AZ	18
Gare (Pl. de la)	AY	20
Helbronner (R.)	AY	
Lyret (R.)	AY	
Majestic (Allée du)	AY	21
Mollard (Ch. de la)	AX	23
Mont-Blanc (Av. et Pl.)	AX	24
Moussoux (Rte des)	AZ	26
Mummery (R.)	AX	27
Nants (Rte des)	AZ	
Paccard (R. du Dr)	AY	28
Pècles (Rte des)	AZ	29
Pèlerins (Rte des)	AZ	
Plage (Av. de la)	AX	
Ravanel-le-Rouge (Av.)	AY	31
Recteur-Payot (Allée)	AXY	32
Roumnaz (Rte de la)	AZ	33
Triangle-de-l'Amitié (Pl. du)	AX	34
Tunnel (Rte du)	AZ	
Vallot (R. J.)	AX	
Whymper (R.)	AX	37

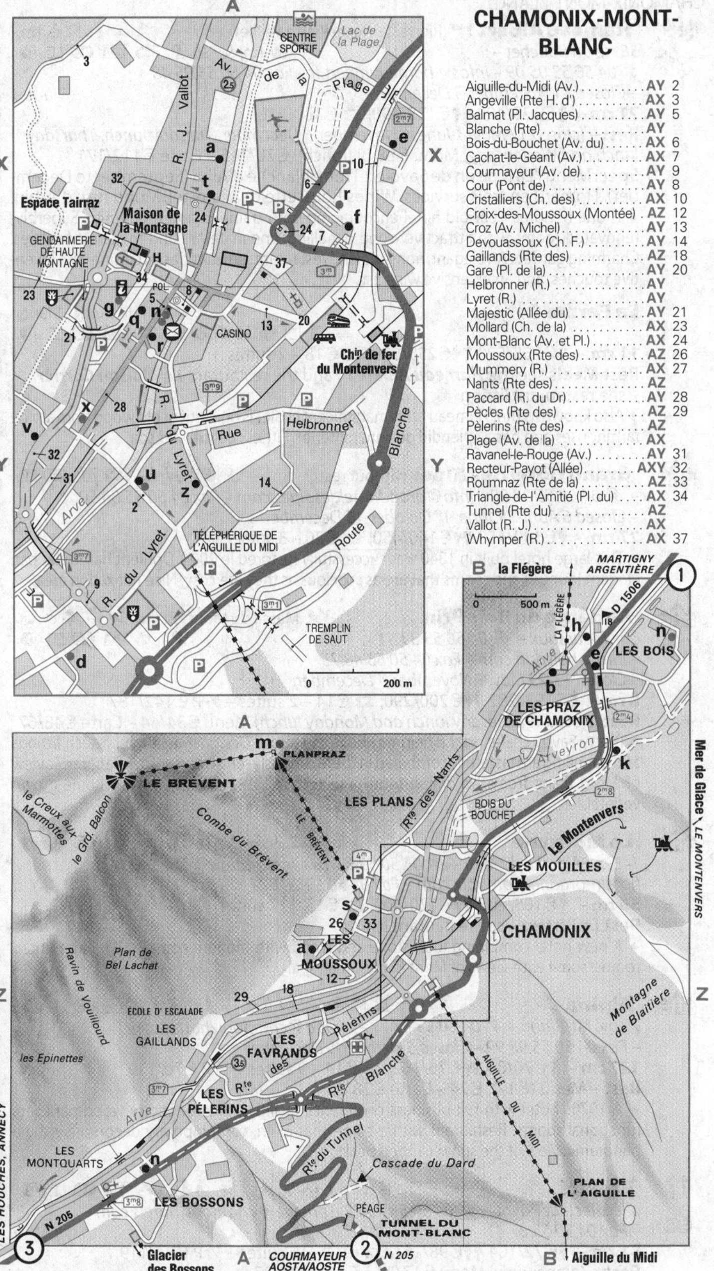

Hameau Albert 1er (Pierre Carrier et Pierre Maillet) rm, rm,
38 rte du Bouchet – 04 50 53 05 09 – infos@hameaualbert.fr – Fax 04 50 55 95 48 – Closed 11 November-3 December AX **f**
21 rm – €125/490 €125/490, €18
Rest – *(closed 12 May-3 June, 5 November-3 December, Tuesday lunch, Thursday lunch and Wednesday)* Menu €68 bi (lunch), €70/145 – Carte €112/171
Spec. Menu "La Maison de Savoie". Truffe blanche d'Alba (September to December). Homard en trois services. **Wines** Roussette de Marestel, Mondeuse d'Arbin.
◆ A one-hundred-year-old hotel encouraging both tradition and modernity. Superbly-renovated rooms with attractive wood panelling, fine materials and the latest facilities. Charming garden. An elegant, non-smoking restaurant, brilliant classic cuisine with inventive touches, and an extensive wine list.

La Ferme Massif du Mont - Blanc,
11 rm – €255/520 €255/520, €18 – 2 suites AX **f**
Rest Meals see ***the Hameau Albert 1st*** and the restaurant ***La Maison Carrier*** – see restaurant listing
◆ Also known as the "Hameau", this magnificent chalet is built out of old wood from alpine farmhouses and has a splendid designer interior. Fitness centre and spa.

Grand Hôtel des Alpes without rest
– 04 50 55 37 80 – info@grandhoteldesalpes.com – Fax 04 50 55 88 50 – Closed 6 April-15 June, 1st October-15 December AY **r**
27 rm – €140/450 €140/450, €20 – 3 suites
◆ This large hotel built in 1840 was successfully restored in 2004. Opulent hall, quiet bar, elegant lounges and rooms that are as spacious as they are cosy. Nice relaxation area.

Auberge du Bois Prin Massif du Mont - Blanc,
aux Moussoux – 04 50 53 33 51 – info@boisprin.com – Fax 04 50 53 48 75 – Closed 13-29 May, 3 November-4 December AZ **a**
8 rm – €198/282 €200/290, €14 – 2 suites – ½ P €142/187
Rest *(closed Wednesday lunch and Monday lunch)* Menu €34/44 – Carte €48/67
◆ Pretty Savoy chalet on the heights above the resort. Designer decor, high-tech fittings and panelling are tastefully combined in the luxuriously renovated rooms. Panoramic view of Mont Blanc from the dining room and terrace. Market produce and home-grown vegetables.

Le Morgane
145 av. Aiguille du Midi – 04 50 53 57 15 – reservation@hotelmorganechamonix.com – Fax 04 50 53 28 07 AY **u**
56 rm – €105/205 €120/400, €15 – 17 suites
Rest *Le Bistrot* – see restaurant listing
◆ A new hotel combining local stone and wood with modern comfort. Well-appointed rooms, some with views of Mont Blanc. Small spa.

Alpina rm, rest,
79 av. Mt-Blanc – 04 50 53 47 77 – alpina@chamonixhotels.com – Fax 04 50 55 98 99 – Closed 5 October-5 December AX **t**
127 rm – €70/84 €76/162, €14 – 9 suites – ½ P €76/119
Rest – Menu (€17), €24 – Carte €28/35
◆ A 1970s hotel with full business conference facilities. Pine or cherry wood-panelled, functional rooms. Restaurant with a somewhat plain, contemporary decor, offset by a panoramic view of the snow-capped peaks.

Prieuré rm, rest,
allée Recteur Payot – 04 50 53 20 72 – prieure@chamonixhotels.com – Fax 04 50 55 87 41 AY **v**
81 rm – €72/104 €98/162, €14 – 10 suites – ½ P €87/119
Rest – *(dinner only)* Menu €17/24 – Carte €26/37
◆ This large chalet-style hotel has soundproofed and renovated rooms in an updated Savoy style: panels, pine furniture and colourful fabrics. Wellness centre and massages. Traditional menu and a few regional dishes served in an attractive alpine setting.

Chalet Hôtel Hermitage rest,
63 chemin du Cé – 04 50 53 13 87
– info@hermitage-paccard.com – Fax 04 50 55 98 14
– Open 20 June-15 September and 21 December-6 April AX **e**
24 rm – €89/118 €97/252, €13,50 – 4 suites – **Rest** – *(closed Tuesday) (dinner only) (resident only)* Menu €24 – Carte €26/31
◆ Large, spacious panelled rooms perfect for family stays. The apartments in the annexe could come in handy. Family cuisine served in a dining room where wood prevails.

L'Oustalet without rest
330 r. Lyret – 04 50 55 54 99 – infos@hotel-oustalet.com – Fax 04 50 55 54 98
– Closed 27 May-10 June, 6 November-18 December AY **z**
15 rm – €90/114 €106/160, €13
◆ Recently-built chalet at the foot of the Aiguille du Midi (near the ski-lift) with a warm decor. Spacious, smart rooms overlooking Mont Blanc. Cosy lounge where you can relax by the fire. Hammam, sauna and jacuzzi.

Park Hotel Suisse rest,
75 allée du Majestic – 04 50 53 07 58 – reservation@chamonix-park-hotel.com
– Fax 04 50 55 99 32 – Open 31 May-30 September and
16 December-29 April AY **q**
64 rm – €76/125 €99/175, €10 – 2 suites – ½ P €68/121
Rest – Menu €18 (lunch), €28/35 – Carte €48/64
◆ Entirely renovated, this hotel allies mountain-style character with modern comfort. Attractive solarium terrace on the roof, overlooking the Mont-Blanc chain. Traditional cuisine and Savoyarde specialities served in a chalet-style setting.

De l'Arve rm, rest,
60 impasse Anémones – 04 50 53 02 31 – contact@hotelarve-chamonix.com
– Fax 04 50 53 56 92 – Closed from mid October-mid December AX **a**
37 rm – €49/85 €59/114, €9 – 1 suite – ½ P €52/79
Rest – *(open mid June-mid September, mid December-mid April and closed Tuesday and Wednesday) (dinner only) (resident only)*
Menu €18
◆ A large, local style building with rooms renovated in a Savoy style. Small garden facing the Mont Blanc range. Fitness facilities including a climbing wall. Discreet modern dining room, with bay windows facing the Arve.

Arveyron rm, rest,
1650 rte du Bouchet, 2 km – 04 50 53 18 29
– hotelarveyron@wanadoo.fr – Fax 04 50 53 06 43
– Open 14 June-28 September and 20 December-6 April BZ **k**
30 rm – €42/45 €72/78, €9 – ½ P €60/75 – **Rest** – *(closed Monday and Wednesday)* Menu €22/25 – Carte €17/26
◆ This pleasant family hotel houses mountain style rooms, quieter on the forest side. Bar-lounge, billiards and a garden...under the Chamonix icicles! Dining room which has been newly refurbished with lots of wood. Pleasant terrace. Traditional, locally inspired cuisine.

La Savoyarde rest,
28 rte Moussoux – 04 50 53 00 77 – lasavoyarde@wanadoo.fr
– Fax 04 50 55 86 82 – Closed May and November AZ **s**
14 rm – €56/76 €74/135, €12 – ½ P €74/102 – **Rest** – *(closed Tuesday and Thursday) (dinner only)* Carte €27/63
◆ A stylish 19C Chamonix house, 50 m from the Brévent cable car. Simple, panelled rooms, some with sloping roofs or with a mezzanine. The dining rooms enjoy a fine view of the mountains. Traditional fare with regional touches.

Les Jardins du Mont Blanc
62 allée du Majestic – 04 50 53 05 64 – mont-blanc@chamonixhotels.com
– Fax 04 50 55 89 44 – Closed 5 October-5 December AY **g**
Rest – *(pre-book)* Menu €19 (lunch), €33/74 – Carte €46/65
◆ A talented new chef for this town centre institution. Gastronomic meals in the evening in the comfortable, retro-style dining room; simpler offerings at lunchtime in the garden or bar.

XX **La Maison Carrier** – Hôtel Hameau Albert 1er VISA AE

44 rte du Bouchet – 04 50 53 00 03 – infos@hameaualbert.fr – Fax 04 50 55 95 48 – Closed 4-24 June, 11 November-11 December, Monday except July-August and public holidays AX **r**

Rest – Menu € 24 (weekday lunch), € 28/39 – Carte € 38/58

◆ Room for the guides; towering fireplace where the house pork meats are smoked. A pretty farmhouse rebuilt with old wood from alpine chalets. Good local cuisine.

XX **Atmosphère** VISA AE

123 pl. Balmat – 04 50 55 97 97 – info@restaurant-atmos.fr – Fax 04 50 53 38 96 AY **n**

Rest – Menu (€ 18), € 21/30 – Carte € 31/59

◆ Mountain style decor, veranda overlooking the Arve, tightly-packed tables, an extensive wine list, traditional food and regional specialities: a restaurant with atmosphere!

XX **L'Impossible** VISA AE

9 chemin du Cry – 04 50 53 20 36 – wim@nerim.fr – Fax 04 50 53 58 91 – Closed November AY **d**

Rest – Menu € 23/30 – Carte € 29/60

◆ In this old 18C farm the chef prepares lovely traditional dishes with regional touches. Cosy dining room with eclectic decoration.

XX **Le Bistrot** (Mickael Bourdillat) – Hôtel Le Morgane VISA AE

151 av. Aiguille du Midi – 04 50 53 57 64 – info@lebistrotchamonix.com – Fax 04 50 53 28 07 AY **u**

Rest – Menu € 33 (lunch), € 41/53 – Carte € 39/45

Spec. Menu du marché. **Wines** Chignin-Bergeron, Mondeuse.

◆ An uncluttered contemporary look for the "Bistrot". The menu, based on high-quality products, is accompanied by an enticing choice of wines (attractive etched glass cabinet).

X **Le Panier des Quatre Saisons** VISA AE

24 galerie Blanc-Neige, (Rue Dr Paccard) – 04 50 53 98 77 – e-panier@wanadoo.fr – Fax 04 50 53 98 77 – Closed 29 May-15 June, 10-20 November, Thursday lunch and Wednesday AY **x**

Rest – Menu (€ 15 bi), € 24/44 – Carte € 45/55

◆ This restaurant, hidden away in a narrow street, is a delightful house with a country decor. Seasonal dishes and good choice of wines by the glass (40 to choose from).

X **Le National** VISA

3 r. Dr-Paccard – 04 50 53 02 23 – Fax 04 50 53 71 94 – Closed 15 November-15 December and Monday in October-November AY **n**

Rest – Menu € 20/30 – Carte € 21/60

◆ Wood panelling, exposed stones and old photos of the resort make up the setting for traditional cuisine including Savoyard specialities. Large, busy terrace.

in Praz-de-Chamonix 2.5 km north – ✉ 74400 Chamonix-Mont-Blanc – alt. 1 060 m

La Flégère ≤★★ by cable car BZ.

Le Labrador without rest ≤ Mont - Blanc and golf, [P] VISA AE

au golf – 04 50 55 90 09 – info@hotel-labrador.com – Fax 04 50 53 15 85 – Closed 20 April-1st May and 19 October-6 December BZ **h**

31 rm – †€ 75/190 ††€ 90/250, € 10 – 1 suite

◆ A chalet of Scandinavian inspiration. All the rooms command a splendid view of the Mont Blanc and Chamonix Valley. Snug sitting rooms.

Eden ≤ [P] VISA AE

– 04 50 53 18 43 – relax@hoteleden-chamonix.com – Fax 04 50 53 51 50 – Closed 5 November-5 December BZ **e**

31 rm – †€ 65/121 ††€ 72/247, € 11 – ½ P € 74/161

Rest – *(closed 15 October-13 December and Tuesday) (dinner only)* Menu € 27/68 – Carte € 33/43

◆ The Scandinavian-born owners have redecorated this two-hundred-year-old house in a Nordic style: unusual and appealing throughout, from lounge to rooms. The restaurant is graced by a fine exhibition of photos and serves Franco-Swedish fusion cuisine.

Les Lanchers
1459 rte des Praz – 04 50 53 47 19 – vacances@hotel-lanchers-chamonix.com – Fax 04 50 53 66 14 – Closed 10 November-12 December BZ **b**
11 rm – €58/98 €58/98, €8 – ½ P €56/78 – **Rest** – Menu (€14), €18/23 – Carte €23/29
◆ Behind this façade enlivened by colourful frescoes are cool and simple rooms, and a bar frequented by the locals. Dining room-veranda offering a bistro-type setting; traditional fare, Savoyard and Italian specialities.

La Cabane des Praz
23 rte du Golf – 04 50 53 23 27 – restaurantlacabane@orange.fr – Fax 04 50 91 15 28 BZ **v**
Rest – Menu (€19), €28 – Carte €31/61
◆ This elegant log cabin has been superbly refurbished to offer a smart, relaxed ambience with a cosy lounge-bar, terrace with views of the golf-course and traditional cuisine.

in Tines 4 km by ①, D 1506 and secondary road – ✉ 74400 Chamonix-Mont-Blanc

Excelsior
251 chemin de St-Roch – 04 50 53 18 36 – excelsior@hotelchamonix.info – Fax 04 50 53 56 16 – Closed 11-25 May and 5 November-15 December
36 rm – €40/61 €65/91, €8 – ½ P €56/69 – **Rest** – *(closed Wednesday lunch 15 December-11 May)* Menu €16/42 – Carte €29/45
◆ Run by the same family since 1910, this pleasant establishment is at the foot of the Verte et du Dru peak. Good renovated rooms with light-wood wainscoting. Garden and pool. The windows of the restaurant command views of the peaks. Updated and alpine menu.

in Bois 3,5 km North – ✉ 74400 Chamonix-Mont-Blanc

Sarpé
– 04 50 53 29 31 – couttety@hotmail.fr – Closed 12 May-11 June, 5 November-5 December, Monday except school holidays BZ **n**
Rest – *(dinner only except school holidays)* Menu €22/44 – Carte €26/52
◆ A former carpenter's workshop converted into a restaurant with a rustic setting, typically Savoyard atmosphere and two small terraces. Traditional and Alpine dishes.

in Lavancher 6 km by ①, D 1506 and secondary road – ✉ 74400 Chamonix-Mont-Blanc – Winter sports : see Chamonix

★★.

Le Jeu de Paume
705 rte Chapeau – 04 50 54 03 76 – jeudepaumechamonix@wanadoo.fr – Fax 04 50 54 10 75 – Open 16 June-24 September and 6 December-14 May
24 rm – €150/255 €150/255, €14 – ½ P €124/176
Rest – *(closed Tuesday lunch and Wednesday lunch)* Menu €35/58 – Carte €40/59
◆ Wood and antique furniture throughout make for a refined setting in this traditional chalet at the foot of the Aiguille Verte. A pleasant place to relax. Somewhat baroque alpine decor and world cuisine.

Beausoleil
– 04 50 54 00 78 – info@hotelbeausoleilchamonix.com – Fax 04 50 54 17 34 – Closed 26 May-6 June and 21 September-21 December
17 rm – €46/65 €70/120, €10 – ½ P €60/85 – **Rest** – *(closed Wednesday lunch and Thursday lunch in July-August) (dinner only except July-August)* Menu €15 (lunch)/30 – Carte €23/42
◆ This (non-smoking) family chalet with an inviting façade has simple wainscoted rooms; some have been refurbished. Flower-decked garden in summer. A rustic alpine restaurant and lovely terrace; regional and cheese specialities.

Les Chalets de Philippe without rest
700-718 rte Chapeau – 06 07 23 17 26 – contact@chamonixlocations.com – Fax 04 50 54 08 28
8 rm – €84/620 €91/1215, €15
◆ Several hillside chalets dotted among the fir trees. Old wood, antique furniture, rare objects, state-of-the-art fixtures and fittings and matchless luxury. Sheer extravagance!

in Bossons 3.5 km south – ✉ 74400 Chamonix-Mont-Blanc – alt. 1 005 m

Aiguille du Midi rest, rest,
479 chemin Napoléon – ☎ 04 50 53 00 65
– hotel-aiguille-du-midi@wanadoo.fr – Fax 04 50 55 93 69
– Open 11 May-19 September and 21 December-6 April AZ **n**
40 rm – €70/80 €72/88, €13 – ½ P €70/82 – **Rest** – Menu €23/47 – Carte €28/51
◆ Tyrolean-style frescoes adorn the exterior of this hotel built in 1908. Diversely furnished rooms, park facing the Bossons Glacier and well-equipped leisure facilities. Rotunda restaurant, pleasant terrace overlooking the garden. Traditional and Savoy cuisine.

in Planpraz by cable car – ✉ 74400 Chamonix-Mont-Blanc

La Bergerie de Planpraz Mont-Blanc and peaks,
– ☎ 04 50 53 05 42 – contact@serac.biz – Fax 04 50 53 93 40
– Open beg. June-end August and mid December-end April AZ **m**
Rest – *(lunch only)* Carte €34/54
◆ Breathtaking view of the Mont Blanc range from the terrace of this mountain chalet. Rustic stone and wood interior, tasty generous dishes made with local produce.

CHAMOUILLE – 02 Aisne – 306 D6 – see Laon

CHAMOUILLEY – 52 Haute-Marne – 313 K2 – see St-Dizier

CHAMOUSSET – 73 Savoie – 333 K4 – pop. 383 – alt. 215 m – ✉ 73390

46 **F2**

Paris 588 – Albertville 26 – Allevard 25 – Chambéry 28 – Grenoble 61

Christin with rm rest,
– ☎ 04 79 36 42 06 – Fax 04 79 36 45 43 – Closed Saturday
16 rm – €42 €57, €7 – ½ P €54
Rest – *(closed Sunday dinner, Monday dinner and Saturday)* Menu €12,50 (weekday lunch), €22/38 – Carte €20/40
◆ Traditional cuisine made up of produce from the kitchen garden, rustic and friendly atmosphere. Near a little-used railway and the confluence of the Arc and Isère rivers. Rooms divided between two buildings, opening onto a big, beautiful garden.

CHAMPAGNAC-DE-BELAIR – 24 Dordogne – 329 F3 – see Brantôme

CHAMPAGNÉ – 72 Sarthe – 310 L6 – pop. 3 294 – alt. 53 m – ✉ 72470

35 **D1**

Paris 205 – Alençon 67 – Le Mans 14 – Nantes 204
Office de tourisme, place de l'Église ☎ 02 43 89 89 89, Fax 02 43 89 58 58

Le Cochon d'Or
49 rte de Paris, D 323 – ☎ 02 43 89 50 08 – Fax 02 43 89 79 34
– Closed 28 July-19 August, Monday and dinner except Saturday
Rest – Menu (€16), €20 (weekdays), €29/47 – Carte €41/53
◆ This imposing house bordering a busy road is valued in the region: here you are served good, classic food in a light and prettily decorated dining room.

CHAMPAGNE-AU-MONT-D'OR – 69 Rhône – 327 H5 – see Lyon

CHAMPAGNEUX – 73 Savoie – 333 G4 – see St-Genix-sur-Guiers

CHAMPAGNEY – 70 Haute-Saône – 314 I6 – see Ronchamp

CHAMPAGNOLE – 39 Jura – 321 F6 – pop. 8 616 – alt. 541 m – ✉ 39300
Burgundy-Jura 16 **B3**

Paris 420 – Besançon 66 – Dole 68 – Genève 86 – Lons-le-Saunier 34

Office de tourisme, rue Baronne Delort ✆ 03 84 52 43 67, Fax 03 84 52 54 57

Musée archéologique: buckle plates★ **M.**

Le Bois Dormant
rm, VISA

rte de Pontarlier, 1.5 km – ✆ 03 84 52 66 66 – hotel@bois-dormant.com – Fax 03 84 52 66 67 – Closed 20-27 December

40 rm – †€ 59/62 ††€ 67/70, ☐ € 10 – ½ P € 57/60 – **Rest** – Menu € 18 (lunch)/43 – Carte € 27/55

◆ Situated in the heart of wooded grounds, this hotel has a warm, modern decor. Functional bedrooms adorned with light wood and shades of pink. Fitness centre and swimming pool in the garden. A large veranda-dining room and quiet terrace. Traditional menu accompanied by wines from the Jura.

Genève road 8 km South – ✉39300 Champagnole

Auberge des Gourmets with rm
VISA

on N 5 – ✆ 03 84 51 60 60 – aubergedesgourmets@wanadoo.fr – Fax 03 84 51 62 83 – Closed 15 December-5 February, Sunday dinner and Monday except school holidays

7 rm – †€ 69 ††€ 74/88, ☐ € 8 – ½ P € 76 – **Rest** – Menu € 15 (weekdays)/48 – Carte € 33/62

◆ Tasty, home cooking served in several smart, rustic dining rooms (one of which is a veranda). The hotel rooms on the terrace side are quieter.

CHAMPAGNY-EN-VANOISE – 73 Savoie – 333 N5 – pop. 585 – alt. 1 240 m – ✉ 73350 French Alps 45 **D2**

Paris 625 – Albertville 44 – Chambéry 94 – Moûtiers 19

Office de tourisme, Le Centre ✆ 04 79 55 06 55, Fax 04 79 55 04 66

Altar-piece★ in the church - Champagny cable car ★: ≤★ - Champagny-le-Haut★★.

L'Ancolie
rm, rest, VISA

Les Hauts du Crey – ✆ 04 79 55 05 00 – contact@hotel-ancolie.com – Fax 04 79 55 04 42 – Open 21 June-6 September and 21 December-12 April

31 rm – †€ 59/96 ††€ 59/123, ☐ € 9 – ½ P € 56/90 – **Rest** – Menu € 18/20 – Carte € 27/42

◆ Hotel perched on the heights above an authentic village-resort and named after an alpine flower. Most of the rooms are decorated in Savoyard style and face south. Inviting dining room. Simple regional cuisine.

Les Glières
VISA

– ✆ 04 79 55 05 52 – accueil@hotel-glieres.com – Fax 04 79 55 04 84 – Open 5 July-24 August and 20 December-18 April

20 rm – †€ 46/86 ††€ 46/86, ☐ € 9,50 – ½ P € 46/78 – **Rest** – *(closed Tuesday in summer)* Menu (€ 15), € 18 – Carte € 21/37

◆ This modern chalet enjoys peaceful surroundings, while also being close to the centre of the village. Simple rooms, renewed in stages, sitting room with fireplace, sauna and game room. Rustic restaurant with a south-facing terrace. Typical Savoyard dishes.

CHAMPCEVINEL – 24 Dordogne – 329 F4 – see Périgueux

CHAMPEAUX – 50 Manche – 303 C7 – pop. 320 – alt. 80 m – ✉ 50530 32 **A2**

Paris 353 – Avranches 19 – Granville 17 – St-Lô 69 – St-Malo 85

Au Marquis de Tombelaine et H. les Hermelles with rm
VISA

D 911 – ✆ 02 33 61 85 94 – claude.giard@wanadoo.fr – Fax 02 33 61 21 52 – Hotel: closed 20-30 November and 20-30 January; restaurant: open April to end October

6 rm – †€ 55 ††€ 64, ☐ € 9 – ½ P € 68/71 – **Rest** – *(closed Tuesday dinner and Wednesday)* Menu € 25/65 – Carte € 38/78

◆ Fish, seafood and local produce come together in the food served in this restaurant perched on a cliff opposite the Mont St. Michel. Rooms with a view over the famous bay.

CHAMPEIX – 63 Puy-de-Dôme – 326 F9 – pop. 1 135 – alt. 456 m – ✉ 63320
Auvergne 5 **B2**

Paris 440 – Clermont-Ferrand 30 – Condat 49 – Issoire 14 – Le Mont-Dore 35 – Thiers 63

Syndicat d'initiative, place du Pré ✆ 04 73 96 26 73, Fax 04 73 96 21 77

Église de St-Saturnin★★ North: 10 km.

La Promenade

3 r. Halle – ✆ 04 73 96 70 24 – h.r.lapromenade@wanadoo.fr – Fax 04 73 96 71 76 – Closed October, Tuesday dinner, Thursday dinner and Wednesday from September to June, Wednesday lunch in July-August
Rest – Menu € 15/29 – Carte € 23/36

◆ Small village inn in a time-worn rustic setting. Local atmosphere in harmony with cuisine featuring Auvergne flavours.

in Montaigut-le-Blanc 3 km west by D 996 – pop. 601 – alt. 500 m – ✉ 63320

Le Chastel Montaigu without rest

< the Monts du Forez and the Monts Dore chain,
au château – ✆ 04 73 96 28 49 – Fax 04 73 96 21 60 – Open 1st May-30 September
4 rm – €120 €133

◆ The appeal of this high-perched guesthouse lies in its superb rooms (four-poster beds) located in the crenelated keep. All enjoy a view of the Dore and Forz mountains.

CHAMPENOUX – 54 Meurthe-et-Moselle – 307 J6 – pop. 1 124 – alt. 234 m – ✉ 54280 27 **C2**

Paris 332 – Château-Salins 18 – Nancy 20 – Pont-à-Mousson 40 – St-Avold 61

La Lorette

rm, VISA

52 rue St Barthélémy – ✆ 03 83 39 91 91 – la.lorette@wanadoo.fr – Fax 03 83 31 71 04 – Closed 14 July-5 August and 7-17 February
10 rm – €52 €57, €7 – ½ P €54 – **Rest** – *(closed Saturday lunch, Sunday dinner and Monday)* Menu (€13), €24/35 bi

◆ The name refers to the laurel hedges that used to grow around the family orchard near this old farmhouse converted into a hotel. Functional, quiet rooms. Two dining rooms, one a veranda. Traditional and regional fare.

CHAMPIGNÉ – 49 Maine-et-Loire – 317 F3 – pop. 1 501 – alt. 25 m – ✉ 49330 35 **C2**

Paris 287 – Angers 24 – Château-Gontier 24 – La Flèche 41

Anjou Golf & Country Club Route de Cheffes, South: 3 km by D 190, ✆ 02 41 42 01 01.

Northwest 3 km by D 768 and D 190 - ✉ 49330 Champigné

Château des Briottières

VISA

– ✆ 02 41 42 00 02 – briottieres@wanadoo.fr – Fax 02 41 42 01 55 – Closed 21 December-4 January and 9-22 February
14 rm – €120/160 €160/350, €15 – **Rest** – *(dinner only) (resident only)* Menu €50

◆ 18C style refinement can be found in this family castle surrounded by a park. Spacious rooms furnished with antique furniture and objects. Lounges and a library. 18C style and refinement can be found in this family château surrounded by a park. Spacious rooms furnished with antique objects. Lounges and a library.

CHAMPILLON – 51 Marne – 306 F8 – see Épernay

CHAMPSANGLARD – 23 Creuse – pop. 228 – alt. 360 m – ✉ 23220 25 **C1**

Paris 406 – Limoges 104 – Guéret 16 – La Souterraine 51 – Argenton-sur-Creuse 104

Office de tourisme, le bourg ✆ 05 55 51 21 18

La Villa des Cagnes without rest

à 600 m, le Villard Ouest – ✆ 05 55 51 98 95 – lescagne@wanadoo.fr

4 rm – €85 €90

◆ Late 19C hunting and fishing lodge set in a quiet garden with pool. The rooms sport a classic influence and are decorated in pastel shades with antique and period furniture.

CHAMPS-SUR-TARENTAINE – 15 Cantal – 330 D2 – pop. 1 044 – alt. 450 m – ✉ 15270

5 **B2**

Paris 500 – Aurillac 90 – Clermont-Ferrand 82 – Condat 24 – Mauriac 38 – Ussel 36

Syndicat d'initiative, Mairie ✆ 04 71 78 72 75, Fax 04 71 78 75 09

Gorges de la Rhue★★ Southeast: 9 km, **Auvergne-Rhone Valley.**

Auberge du Vieux Chêne

34 rte des Lacs – ✆ 04 71 78 71 64 – danielle.moins@wanadoo.fr – Open 21 April-30 September and closed Sunday dinner and Monday except 15 June-15 September

15 rm – €56/61 €60/86, €9 – ½ P €52/68 – **Rest** – *(dinner only)* Menu €24 – Carte €32/53

◆ A delightful country stopover in an authentic 19C farmhouse. Simple, warm rooms, suitable for a peaceful stay. The former barn has been converted into a restaurant whose centre-piece is the enormous fireplace. Bucolic terrace facing the pretty garden.

CHAMPS-SUR-YONNE – 89 Yonne – 319 E5 – see Auxerre

CHAMPTOCEAUX – 49 Maine-et-Loire – 317 B4 – pop. 1 748 – alt. 68 m – ✉ 49270 Châteaux of the Loire

34 **B2**

Paris 357 – Ancenis 9 – Angers 65 – Beaupréau 30 – Cholet 50 – Clisson 35 – Nantes 32

Office de tourisme, Le Champalud ✆ 02 40 83 57 49, Fax 02 40 83 54 73

de l'Ile d'Or La VarenneWest: 5 km by D 751, ✆ 02 40 98 58 00.

Site★ - Promenade de Champalud★★.

Le Champalud rm, VISA

pl. de l'Église – ✆ 02 40 83 50 09 – le-champalud@wanadoo.fr – Fax 02 40 83 53 81

13 rm – €58/72 €58/72, €8,50 – ½ P €57 – **Rest** – *(closed Sunday dinner from 1st October to 30 March)* Menu (€13 bi), €17/41 – Carte €28/34

◆ Exposed beams and stone walls blend in well with the modern décor of this renovated house opposite the church. Completely renovated rooms, which are well-equipped. A restaurant with rural character; traditional cuisine based on local produce. Pub bar.

Les Jardins de la Forge (Paul Pauvert) with rm rm, rm, rm, VISA

1 pl. des Piliers – ✆ 02 40 83 56 23 – jardins.de.la.forge@wanadoo.fr – Fax 02 40 83 59 80 – Closed 7-15 July, 27 October-12 November and 16 February-4 March

7 rm – €80/95 €110/165, €14

Rest – *(closed Wednesday from October-April, Sunday dinner, Monday and Tuesday) (pre-book Sat-Sun)* Menu €30 (weekdays)/92 – Carte €69/97

Spec. Duo de sandre et alose de Loire poêlés au beurre d'oseille (March to May). Dos de sandre de Loire à la crème d'asperges (spring-summer). Pigeonneau rôti sauce morilles. **Wines** Muscadet sur lie, Anjou-Villages.

◆ This restaurant, set inside the walls of the family forge, enjoys a view over the château ruins. Classic cuisine. Fine modern rooms. Garden and pool.

CHAMPVANS-LES-MOULINS – 25 Doubs – 321 F3 – see Besançon

CHANAS – 38 Isère – 333 B6 – pop. 1 931 – alt. 150 m – ✉ 38150

43 **E2**

Paris 512 – Grenoble 89 – Lyon 57 – St-Étienne 75 – Valence 51

Mercure VISA

à l'échangeur A 7 – ✆ 04 74 84 27 50 – h61486@accor.com – Fax 04 74 84 36 61

42 rm – €70/84 €78/92, €11 – **Rest** – *(closed Saturday lunch and Sunday)* Menu (€12,50), €16 – Carte €22/39

◆ For a stopover on a holiday journey, a hotel with recently renovated, practical rooms, with good soundproofing. Bright restaurant divided up by partitions and green plants. Traditional cuisine.

CHANCEAUX-SUR-CHOISILLE – 37 Indre-et-Loire – 317 N4 – pop. 2 821 – alt. 104 m – ✉ 37390 11 B2

Paris 237 – Orléans 113 – Tours 11 – Joué-lès-Tours 25 – Vendôme 50

Le Relais du Moulin de la Planche

à Langennerie, 2 km north – ✆ 02 47 55 11 96 – contact@moulindelaplanche.com – Fax 02 47 55 24 34 – Closed 10-25 January, Sunday dinner, Monday dinner and Tuesday dinner

Rest – Menu € 25 (weekday lunch), € 33/76 bi – Carte € 46/57

◆ In a calm and bucolic setting (garden, pond), 15C mill with outbuildings housing an art gallery. Rustic restaurant and fine up-to-date cuisine.

CHANCELADE – 24 Dordogne – 329 E4 – see Périgueux

CHANDAI – 61 Orne – 310 N2 – pop. 532 – alt. 200 m – ✉ 61300 33 C3

Paris 129 – L'Aigle 10 – Alençon 72 – Chartres 71 – Dreux 53 – Évreux 57 – Lisieux 66

L'Écuyer Normand

D 626 – ✆ 02 33 24 08 54 – ecuyer-normand@wanadoo.fr – Fax 02 33 34 75 67 – Closed Wednesday dinner, Sunday dinner and Monday

Rest – Menu € 25/38 – Carte € 49

◆ Equine-inspired ornaments and paintings, exposed beams, rustic furnishings and a fireplace lend character to this Norman inn; classic cuisine that follows the seasons.

CHANDOLAS – 07 Ardèche – 331 H7 – pop. 342 – alt. 115 m – ✉ 07230 44 A3

Paris 662 – Alès 43 – Aubenas 34 – Privas 66

Auberge Les Murets rm,

D 104, quartier Langarnayre – ✆ 04 75 39 08 32 – dominique.rignanese@wanadoo.fr – Fax 04 75 39 39 90 – Closed 1st-14 December, 5 January-7 February, Monday and Tuesday from 10 November-31 March

7 rm – € 58 € 58, € 8 – ½ P € 53

Rest – *(closed Monday except dinner from April-9 November and Tuesday from 10 November-31 March)* Menu € 16 (weekdays)/29 – Carte € 24/29

◆ An 18C Cévennes farmhouse surrounded by a park in the countryside and among vineyards. Spruce and pleasant rooms with cane furniture. A restaurant in two vaulted cellars. A mulberry tree over a hundred years old provides shade for the attractive terrace.

CHANTELLE – 03 Allier – 326 F5 – pop. 1 040 – alt. 324 m – ✉ 03140 Auvergne 5 B1

Paris 339 – Gannat 17 – Montluçon 61 – Moulins 47 – St-Pourçain-sur-Sioule 15

Poste with rm

5 r. de la République – ✆ 04 70 56 62 12 – Fax 04 70 56 62 12 – Closed 20 September-15 October, 20 February-12 March, Tuesday dinner off season and Wednesday

12 rm – € 30/40 € 40/46, € 5,50 – ½ P € 34/38 – **Rest** – Menu (€ 9,50), € 17 (weekdays)/36 – Carte € 31/33

◆ Subdued countrified dining room and charming, shaded courtyard-terrace. Traditional meals and friendly service. This old coaching inn has simple but well-maintained rooms, with predominantly rustic, eclectic furnishings.

CHANTEMERLE – 05 Hautes-Alpes – 334 H3 – see Serre-Chevalier

CHANTEPIE – 35 Ille-et-Vilaine – 309 M6 – see Rennes

CHANTILLY – 60 Oise – 305 F5 – pop. 10 902 – alt. 59 m – ✉ 60500

Northern France and the Paris Region 36 **B3**

- Paris 51 – Beauvais 55 – Compiègne 44 – Meaux 53 – Pontoise 41
- Office de tourisme, 60, avenue du Maréchal Joffre ✆ 03 44 67 37 37, Fax 03 44 67 37 38
- Dolce Chantilly Vineuil-Saint-Firmin Route d'Apremont, by Apremont road: 3 km, ✆ 03 44 58 47 74 ;
- d'Apremont Apremont CD 606, North: 7 km by D 606, ✆ 03 44 25 61 11 ;
- Les Golfs de Mont-Griffon Luzarches Route Départementale 909, South: 11km by N 16, ✆ 01 34 68 10 10.
- Château★★★ - Park★★ - Grandes Écuries★★: musée vivant du Cheval★★ - L'Aérophile★ (captive balloon flight): <★.
- Site★ du château de la Reine-Blanche South: 5,5 km.

CHANTILLY

Berteux (Av. de) . . . . . A 2
Canardière (Quai de la) . . . . . A 3
Cascades (R. des) . . . . . A 4
Chantilly (R. de) . . . . . B 5
Condé (Av. de) . . . . . B 6
Connétable (R. du) . . . . . AB
Embarcadère (R. de l') . . . . . A 8
Faisanderie (R. de la) . . . . . B 9
Gaulle (Av. du Gén.-de) . . . . . A 10
Joffre (Av. du Mar.) . . . . . A
Leclerc (Av. du Gén.) . . . . . A 12
Libération Maurice Schumann (Bd de la) . . . . . A 18
Orgemont (R. d') . . . . . A 15
Paris (R. de) . . . . . A 16
Vallon (Pl. Omer) . . . . . A 21
Victor-Hugo (R.) . . . . . A 22

Hotel du Parc without rest

36 av. Mar. Joffre – ✆ 03 44 58 20 00 – bwhotelduparc@wanadoo.fr – Fax 03 44 57 31 10 A **a**

57 rm – 🚹€ 100 🚹🚹€ 130/150, ☕ € 11

◆ A new hotel with quite spacious, bright and functional rooms, some of which have a terrace. The quietest overlook the garden. English bar.

Apremont road by ① and D 606

Dolce Chantilly rm, rest,
3 km ✉ 60500 Vineuil-St-Firmin – *☎ 03 44 58 47 77*
– info_chantilly@dolce.com – Fax 03 44 58 50 11 – Closed 21 December-2 January
196 rm – €150/300 €150/300, €40 – 4 suites
Rest *Carmontelle* – *☎ 03 44 58 47 57 (closed lunch 26 July-18 August, Saturday lunch, Sunday and Monday) (number of covers limited, pre-book)* Menu €49 bi (weekday lunch), €66 € bi/130 bi – Carte €92/102
Rest *L'Étoile* – *(dinner only except Sunday)* Menu €42 bi/55 bi – Carte €41/50
Spec. Jambonnettes de grenouilles. Ris de veau braisé au vin jaune. Pain de Gênes à la framboise et moelleux au chocolat.
♦ Large Ile de France style hotel on a golf course, offering spacious, practical rooms. Good fitness centre and high quality conference facilities. Inventive gourmet food served in a plush modern setting; attentive staff. At L'Étoile, you are offered a traditional menu in an attractive circular room.

Auberge La Grange aux Loups with rm
in Apremont, 6 km ✉ *60300 – ☎ 03 44 25 33 79 – lagrangeauxloups@wanadoo.fr – Fax 03 44 24 22 22 – Closed 1st-15 September and Sunday*
4 rm – €80 €80, €10 – **Rest** – *(closed Monday)* Menu (€20), €29 (weekdays)/55 – Carte €61/81
♦ Village inn with a rustic dining room and peaceful summer terrace. Classic cuisine. Four quiet rooms in an outbuilding.

in Montgrésin 5 km by ② – ✉ **60560 Orry-la-Ville**

Relais d'Aumale rm,
– ☎ 03 44 54 61 31 – relaisd.aumale@wanadoo.fr – Fax 03 44 54 69 15 – Closed 22 December-3 January
22 rm – €115/132 €130/156, €13 – 2 suites – ½ P €114/122
Rest – *(closed Sunday dinner in Winter)* Menu €28 (weekday lunch)/44 – Carte €55/80
♦ The Duke of Aumale's former hunting lodge nestles in a garden at the edge of the forest. Comfortable, tastefully appointed rooms. Two dining rooms: one modern, the other more château-like, with panelling, a French style ceiling and paintings. Traditional fare.

in Gouvieux 4 km by ④ – **pop. 9 406 – alt. 26 m** – ✉ **60270**

Château de Montvillargenne rm,
6 av. F. Mathet – ☎ 03 44 62 37 37
– info@chmvt.com – Fax 03 44 57 28 97
120 rm – €175/380 €175/380, €23 – ½ P €130/207
Rest – Menu €42/83 – Carte €46/98
♦ This 19C château, nestling in a large park, offers four categories of comfortable rooms with pleasant personal touches. Large dining room, complemented by a mezzanine and several small wainscoted sitting rooms. Pleasant terrace.

Château de la Tour rm,
chemin de la Chaussée – ☎ 03 44 62 38 38
– reception@lechateaudelatour.fr – Fax 03 44 57 31 97
41 rm – €140/225 €140/225, €13 – ½ P €100/120
Rest – Menu €39/75 – Carte €53/70
♦ Fine early-20C residence and contemporary extension overlooking a pretty 5 ha park. Elegant, refined interior. Old parquet flooring and fireplaces provide a setting for the restaurant; superb terrace. Classic menu.

Le Pavillon St-Hubert
à Toutevoie – ☎ 03 44 57 07 04 – pavillon.sthubert@wanadoo.fr
– Fax 03 44 57 75 42 – Closed 2-20 January
18 rm – €55 €80, €8 – ½ P €70/90
Rest – *(closed 2 January-8 February, Sunday dinner and Monday)* Menu €25 (weekdays), €33/50 – Carte €42/64
♦ A former hunting lodge and pretty garden on the banks of the River Oise. Small comfortable rooms. This restaurant furnished in Louis XIII style serves traditional cuisine. In summer it offers a pleasant terrace shaded by lime trees, overlooking the canal.

XX **La Renardière**

2 r. Frères Segard, (La Chaussée) – ✆ 03 44 57 08 23 – Fax 03 44 57 30 37 – Closed 4-19 August, Sunday dinner and Monday

Rest – Menu € 16 (weekday lunch), € 28/48 – Carte € 48/89

◆ An attractive inn sporting a pleasant rustic decor. Traditional cooking and an impressive wine list selected by the wine-expert owner.

Creil road 4 km by ⑤ – ✉ 60740 St-Maximin

XXX **Le Verbois**

rd-pt Verbois, (D 1016) – ✆ 03 44 24 06 22 – Fax 03 44 25 76 63 – Closed 16 August-1st September, 2-15 January, Monday except public holidays and Sunday dinner

Rest – Menu (€ 29), € 35/60 – Carte € 52/68

◆ Former coaching inn fronted by a pretty garden, on the edge of the forest. Plush dining rooms. Updated cuisine with a classic base; game in season.

CHANTONNAY – 85 Vendée – 316 J7 – pop. 7 541 – alt. 58 m – ✉ 85110

34 **B3**

Paris 410 – Nantes 79 – La Roche-sur-Yon 34 – Cholet 53 – Bressuire 53

Office de tourisme, place de la Liberté ✆ 02 51 09 45 77, Fax 02 51 09 45 78

Manoir de Ponsay

5 km east along the Pouzauges road and secondary road – ✆ 02 51 46 96 71 – manoir.de.ponsay@wanadoo.fr – Fax 02 51 46 80 07

5 rm – €62/115 €62/115, € 9 – ½ P € 66/93

Table d'hôte – Menu € 32 bi

◆ The perfect place in which to experience château life, this manor house has been in the same family since 1644. Spacious guestrooms decorated with objects collected over the centuries. Park and swimming pool. Attractive dining room, and evening meals on request.

CHAOURCE – 10 Aube – 313 E5 – pop. 1 092 – alt. 150 m – ✉ 10210

Northern France and the Paris Region

13 **B3**

Paris 196 – Auxerre 66 – Bar-sur-Aube 58 – Châtillon-sur-Seine 52 – Troyes 33

Office de tourisme, 2, Place de l'Échiquier ✆ 03 25 40 97 22, Fax 03 25 40 97 22

St-Jean-Baptiste church ★: sepulchre★★.

in Maisons-lès-Chaource 6 km southeast by D 34 – pop. 188 – alt. 235 m – ✉ 10210

Aux Maisons

– ✆ 03 25 70 07 19 – accueil@logis-aux-maisons.com – Fax 03 25 70 07 75

23 rm – €63 €68, € 10 – ½ P € 72

Rest – *(closed Sunday dinner from 15 October to 15 March)* Menu (€ 16), € 19 (weekday lunch), € 31/68 – Carte € 40/61

◆ A restored Champagne farmhouse makes up part of this hotel for non-smokers only. Spa showers in the best rooms. Good sound-proofing. Countrified dining room; summer terrace by the swimming pool.

CHAPARON – 74 Haute-Savoie – 328 K6 – see Bredannaz

LA CHAPELLE-AUX-CHASSES – 03 Allier – 326 I2 – pop. 216 – alt. 225 m – ✉ 03230

6 **C1**

Paris 294 – Moulins 21 – Bourbon-Lancy 22 – Decize 25 – Digoin 50

XX **Auberge de la Chapelle aux Chasses**

– ✆ 04 70 43 44 71 – aubergechapelle@aol.com – Closed 15-25 July, 20 October-7 November, 5-25 February, Tuesday and Wednesday

Rest – *(pre-book)* Menu € 15 bi, € 21/68 – Carte € 39/51

◆ Appetising seasonal up-to-date cuisine served in a sober half-rustic, half-modern setting. Carefully-laid tables and friendly hospitality.

LA CHAPELLE-D'ABONDANCE – 74 Haute-Savoie – 328 N3 – pop. 719 – alt. 1 020 m – Winter sports : 1 000/1 850 m 1 11 – ✉ 74360

French Alps 46 **F1**

Paris 600 – Annecy 108 – Châtel 6 – Évian-les-Bains 29 – Morzine 32 – Thonon-les-Bains 34

Syndicat d'initiative, Chef-lieu ✆ 04 50 73 51 41, Fax 04 50 73 56 04

Les Cornettes

rest, VISA

– ✆ 04 50 73 50 24 – lescornettes@valdabondance.com – Fax 04 50 73 54 16 – Open mid April mid October and mid December-end March

42 rm – €70/95 €100/145, €12 – ½ P €75/115 – **Rest** – Menu €23 (weekdays)/70

◆ Run by the same family since 1894, these buildings, linked by an underground passage, have comfortable panelled rooms. Leisure facilities and a small Savoy museum. Immense mountain-style dining room decorated with bric-a-brac. Local cuisine.

Les Gentianettes

rm, rest, VISA AE

rte de Chevenne – ✆ 04 50 73 56 46 – bienvenue@gentianettes.fr – Fax 04 50 73 56 39 – Open 13 June-15 September and 20 December-5 April and closed Wednesday in June, September, January and March

36 rm – €90/130 €95/145 – ½ P €69/115 – **Rest** – Menu €19 (weekdays)/69 – Carte €29/53

◆ A golden chalet with pleasant balcony rooms, warmly decorated with wood panelling. Sauna, hammam, jacuzzi. Tasty regional cuisine and a cosy atmosphere in this elegant restaurant with wood panelling, coppers, and farming objects.

L'Ensoleillé

rest, VISA

– ✆ 04 50 73 50 42 – info@hotel-ensoleille.com – Fax 04 50 73 52 96 – Open from June to mid September and from mid December to end March

35 rm – €60/75 €70/120, €10 – ½ P €60/95 – **Rest** – *(closed Tuesday)* Menu €20 (weekdays)/52 – Carte €28/59

◆ These two neighbouring chalets provide rooms with balconies and a fully-equipped fitness centre. Hearty Savoyard cuisine served in a dining area with wooden decor, paintings of the village and furniture and decorative objects from the region.

Le Vieux Moulin

rm, VISA AE

rte de Chevenne – ✆ 04 50 73 52 52 – maxit-levieuxmoulin@wanadoo.fr – Fax 04 50 73 55 62 – Open 1st June-30 September, 20 December-15 April and closed Wednesday

15 rm – €45/60 €60/70, €8 – ½ P €55/59 – **Rest** – Menu €22 (weekdays), €38/45 – Carte €25/44

◆ Hotel surrounded by a garden outside the town centre. Functional rooms with wooden panelling and sloping ceiling on the top floor. Regionally and traditionally influenced menu and beautiful vista over the valley from this restaurant.

LA CHAPELLE-DE-GUINCHAY – 71 Saône-et-Loire – 320 I12 – pop. 2 595 – alt. 200 m – ✉ 71570

8 **C3**

Paris 412 – Bourg-en-Bresse 50 – Caluire-et-Cuire 64 – Dijon 142

La Poularde

VISA

pl. de la Gare – ✆ 03 85 36 72 41 – restlapoularde@aol.com – Fax 03 85 33 83 25 – Closed 1st-17 August, February school holidays, Sunday dinner, Tuesday dinner and Wednesday

Rest – Menu €18 (weekday lunch), €30/45 – Carte €42/51

◆ This old house has exchanged its pink façade and rustic interior for a markedly more updated style (designer chairs and modern paintings). Contemporary cuisine.

LA CHAPELLE-EN-VALGAUDEMAR – 05 Hautes-Alpes – 334 F4 – pop. 129 – alt. 1 083 m – ✉ 05800 French Alps

41 **C1**

Paris 653 – Gap 48 – Grenoble 91 – La Mure 51

Syndicat d'initiative, La Chapelle en Valgaudemar ✆ 04 92 55 23 21, Fax 04 92 55 23 21

Les "Oulles du Diable"★★ (marmites des géants) - Cascade du Casset★ Northeast: 3,5 km.

Gioberney Chalet-hotel: cirque★★.

Du Mont-Olan rm, VISA

– ✆ *04 92 55 23 03 – info@hoteldumontolan.com – Fax 04 92 55 34 58*
– Open 1st May-15 October
14 rm – †€ 41 ††€ 49, ☕ € 7,50 – ½ P € 47 – **Rest** – Menu (€ 12), € 19/22
◆ A welcoming establishment run by the same family for 4 generations in this pretty village isolated at the foot of the Ecrins massif. Distinctive areas for guests and small rustic rooms. A rural atmosphere and traditional cuisine focusing on local produce is found in the restaurant, with quick meals offered in the bar.

LA CHAPELLE-EN-VERCORS – **26 Drôme** – **332** F4 – **pop. 662** – **alt. 945 m** – **Winter sports : to Col de Rousset 1 255/1 700 m** 8 – ✉ **26420** French Alps

Paris 604 – Die 41 – Grenoble 60 – Romans-sur-Isère 47 – St-Marcellin 35 – Valence 63 — 43 **E2**

Office de tourisme, place Piétri ✆ 04 75 48 22 54, Fax 04 75 48 13 81

Chapelle-en-Vercors South: 2 km, ✆ 04 75 48 19 86.

Grotte de la Draye blanche★, 5 km South by D 178.

Bellier VISA

– ✆ *04 75 48 20 03 – hotel-bellier@wanadoo.fr – Fax 04 75 48 25 31 – Open April-mid October and closed Wednesday dinner and Thursday off season*
13 rm – †€ 29/32 ††€ 48/65, ☕ € 7 – ½ P € 46/60 – **Rest** – Menu € 16/32 – Carte € 16/33
◆ For five generations, the same family has been running this chalet built on an outcrop overlooking the road. Half the rooms have a balcony. Rustic styled dining room with Savoyard furniture. Tree lined terrace.

Des Sports VISA

av. des Grands Goulets – ✆ *04 75 48 20 39 – hotel.des.sports@wanadoo.fr – Fax 04 75 48 10 52 – Closed 12 November-26 December, 4 January-1st February, Sunday dinner Monday*
11 rm – †€ 54/57 ††€ 54/57, ☕ € 8 – ½ P € 57/59 – **Rest** – Menu € 20/35 – Carte € 28/45
◆ In a shopping street on the way into the village, a real pied-à-terre for cyclists and hikers visiting the Vercours area. Colourful, very well-renovated rooms. The rustic decor of the restaurant has been treated to a facelift. Traditional and regional dishes.

LA CHAPELLE-ST-MESMIN – **45 Loiret** – **318** H4 – **see Orléans**

CHARBONNIÈRES-LES-BAINS – **69 Rhône** – **327** H5 – **see Lyon**

CHARENTON-LE-PONT – **94 Val-de-Marne** – **312** D3 – **101** 26 – **see Paris, Area**

CHARETTE – **38 Isère** – **333** F3 – **pop. 281** – **alt. 250 m** – ✉ **38390** — 44 **B1**

Paris 479 – Aix-les-Bains 68 – Belley 39 – Grenoble 100 – Lyon 63

Auberge du Vernay VISA

rte Optevoz, (D 52) – ✆ *04 74 88 57 57 – reservation@auberge-du-vernay.fr – Fax 04 74 88 58 57*
7 rm – †€ 55/65 ††€ 80/100, ☕ € 9 – ½ P € 88 – **Rest** – *(closed 23-29 June, January, Sunday dinner and Monday) (number of covers limited, pre-book)* Menu € 28/69 – Carte € 35/75
◆ Charming rooms with a personal touch and the quiet of the surrounding countryside are the great strong features of this nicely refurbished, attractive 18C farm. This half-rustic, half-contemporary restaurant sports a fine fireplace and serves modern, flavoursome food.

LA CHARITÉ-SUR-LOIRE – **58 Nièvre** – **319** B8 – **pop. 5 460** – **alt. 170 m** – ✉ **58400** Burgundy-Jura — 7 **A2**

Paris 212 – Auxerre 109 – Bourges 51 – Montargis 102 – Nevers 25

Syndicat d'initiative, 5, place Sainte-Croix ✆ 03 86 70 15 06, Fax 03 86 70 21 55

N.-Dame church ★★: ≤★★ on the apse - Esplanade rue du Clos ≤★.

Auberge de Seyr VISA MC

4 Grande Rue – ✆ 03 86 70 03 51 – Fax 03 86 70 03 51 – Closed 10-17 March, 17 August-4 September, Sunday dinner and Monday

Rest – Menu € 12 (weekdays)/33 – Carte € 25/36

◆ Take time for a relaxing meal in this unpretentions restaurant made up of two dining rooms with painted beams. Traditional cuisine prepared by the chef.

CHARLEVILLE-MÉZIÈRES P – 08 Ardennes – 306 K4 – pop. 55 490 – Built-up area 107 777 – alt. 145 m – ✉ 08000 Northern France and the Paris Region

Paris 230 – Luxembourg 168 – Reims 85 – Sedan 26 13 **B1**

Office de tourisme, 4, place Ducale ✆ 03 24 55 69 90, Fax 03 24 55 69 89

des Sept-Fontaines Fagnon Abbaye de Sept Fontaines, Southwest: 10 km by D 139, ✆ 03 24 37 38 24 ;

des Ardennes Villers-le-Tilleul Base de Loisirs des Poursaudes, South: 21 km by D 764 and D 33, ✆ 03 24 35 64 65.

Place Ducale★★ - Musée de l'Ardenne★ BX **M**[1] - Musée Rimbaud BX **M**[2] - N.-D.-d'Espérance basilica : stained-glass windows ★★ BZ.

Plan on next page

De Paris without rest P VISA MC AE

24 av. G. Corneau – ✆ 03 24 33 34 38 – hotel.de.paris.08@wanadoo.fr – Fax 03 24 59 11 21 BY **n**

27 rm – €45/50 €55/75, €7

◆ Arthur Rimbaud welcomes you into this hotel made up of three early 20C buildings. Fireplace in the suites and soundproofing for the street-side rooms; smaller and quieter rooms to the rear.

Le Pélican without rest P VISA MC AE

42 av. Maréchal Leclerc – ✆ 03 24 56 42 73 – hotelpelican@wanadoo.fr – Fax 03 24 59 26 16 – Closed 27 December-2 January

20 rm – €45 €48, €8

◆ This red brick house has been skilfully renovated. Some personalised rooms and double-glazing greatly reduces street noises. Particularly attractive breakfast room.

La Clef des Champs A/C VISA MC AE

33 r. Moulin – ✆ 03 24 56 17 50 – courrier@laclefdeschamps.fr – Fax 03 24 59 94 07 – Closed Sunday dinner BX **e**

Rest – Menu € 23/60 – Carte € 43/58

◆ Near Place Ducale, Charleville's "Place de Vosges", this 17C house has a discreet dining room (non-smoking) with a brick and wood fireplace. Updated cuisine.

Le Manoir du Mont Olympe VISA MC

139 r. Pâquis – ✆ 03 24 33 43 20 – lemanoirdelolympe@orange.fr – Fax 03 24 37 12 25

Rest – Menu € 23 (weekdays)/45 – Carte € 32/42 BX **v**

◆ A one hundred-year-old, red-brick villa set against Mount Olympe. Pleasant dining room in pastel colours and a shaded terrace where meals and refreshments are served.

La Côte à l'Os A/C VISA MC AE

11 cours A. Briand – ✆ 03 24 59 20 16 – la.cote.a.l.os@orange.fr – Fax 03 24 22 04 99

Rest – Menu (€ 13), € 20/28 – Carte € 26/44 BY **e**

◆ Bistro-style dining featuring seafood. Choose the long, brightly coloured dining room or the cosy setting of the 1st floor restaurant imbued with the atmosphere of Alsace. Game can be enjoyed in season.

La Table d' Artur "R" MC

9 r. Bérégovoy – ✆ 03 24 57 05 64 – Fax 03 24 27 65 60 – Closed Easter holidays, 10-31 August, Monday dinner, Wednesday dinner, Sunday and holidays

Rest – Menu (€ 20), € 26 BX **a**

◆ Down a dead-end street, a universe dedicated to wine and good food. After discovering a few choice bottles, head down to the cellar ... for a frank and sincere cuisine.

Amorini VISA MC

46 pl. Ducale – ✆ 03 24 37 48 80 – Closed 28 July-18 August, Sunday and Monday

Rest – *(lunch only)* Carte € 22/25 BX **t**

◆ The setting in this Charleville trattoria is typically Italian with cherub frescoes. Italian dishes and wine served in the dining room or on sale in the grocery store.

CHARLEVILLE-MÉZIÈRES

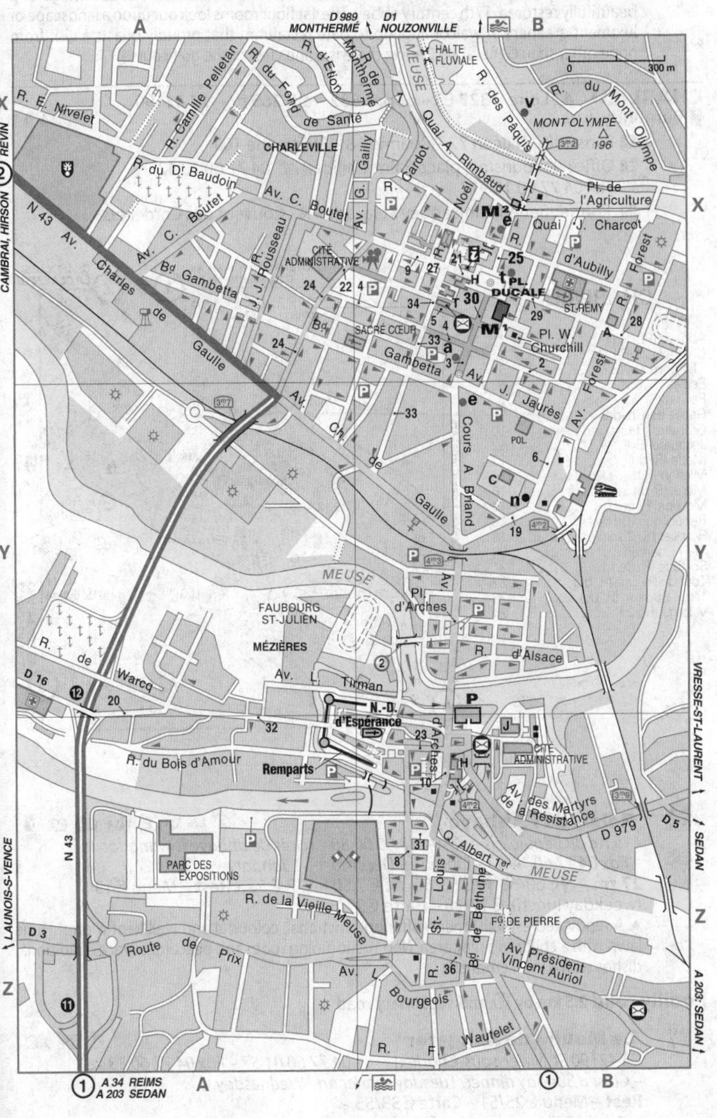

in Fagnon 8 km by D 3 AZ and D 39 – pop. 345 – alt. 171 m – ✉ 08090

Abbaye de Sept Fontaines rest,
– ✆ 03 24 37 38 24
– *abbaye-7-fontaines@wanadoo.fr – Fax 03 24 37 58 75*
23 rm – †€ 89/195 ††€ 98/199, ☕ € 14 – ½ P € 92/109 – **Rest** – Menu € 29/56 – Carte € 45/52

◆ Located in parkland that includes a gold course, this hotel takes full advantage of a beautifully restored, 17th century abbey. The 1st floor rooms look out upon a landscape of luxuriant greenery. A welcoming, up to date restaurant that proudly boasts a visit from none other than Général De Gaulle; there is a fine view of the golf course.

CHARLIEU – 42 Loire – 327 E3 – pop. 3 582 – alt. 265 m – ✉ 42190

Burgundy-Jura 44 **A1**

- Paris 398 – Mâcon 77 – Roanne 18 – St-Étienne 102
- Office de tourisme, place Saint-Philibert, ✆ 04 77 60 12 42, Fax 04 77 60 16 91
- Former Benedictine abbey★: façade★★ - Couvent des Cordeliers★.

CHARLIEU

Abbaye (Pl. de l') 2
Chanteloup (R.) 4
Chantemerle (R.) 5
Écoles (R. des) 6
Farinet (R. A.) 7
Gaulle (R. Ch.-de) 9
Grenette (R.) 10
Jacquard (Bd) 12
Merle (R. du) 13
Michon (R.) 15
Morel (R. J.) 16
Moulins (R. des) 17
République (Bd de la) 18
Rouillier (R. C.) 19
St-Philibert (Pl.) 20
Solitude (R. de la) 21
Tour-de-l'église (R. du) 22
Treuil-Buisson (R. du) 23
Valorge (Bd L.) 24

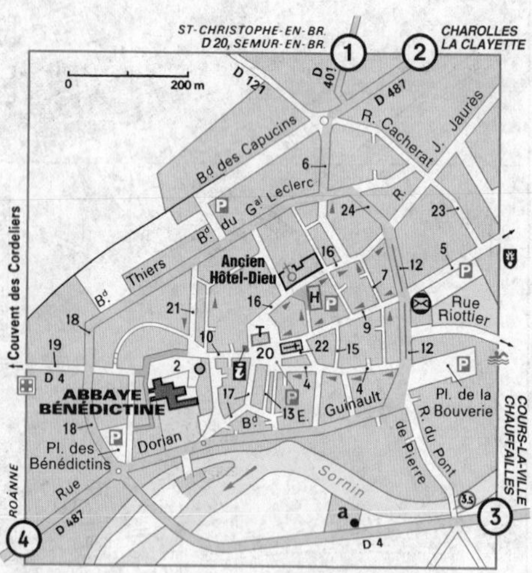

Relais de l'Abbaye
415 rte du Beaujolais – ✆ 04 77 60 00 88 – relais.de.abbaye@wanadoo.fr – Fax 04 77 60 14 60 – Closed 19 December-11 January **a**
27 rm – †€ 60/68 ††€ 68/69, ☕ € 7,50 – ½ P € 53 – **Rest** – Menu € 13 (weekday lunch), € 17/38 – Carte € 27/67

◆ A renovated establishment, offering functional, colourful and well-kept rooms. Huge lawn with a children's play area. Neo-rustic dining room and peaceful terrace. Traditional dishes with a local emphasis.

Pouilly road 2.5 km by ④ and secondary road

Le Moulin de Rongefer
✉ 42190 St-Nizier-sous-Charlieu – ✆ 04 77 60 01 57 – Fax 04 77 60 33 28 – Closed Sunday dinner, Tuesday dinner and Wednesday
Rest – Menu € 25/51 – Carte € 33/55

◆ An old mill on the banks of the Sornin with a country-style dining room and pleasant flower-decked terrace. Modern cuisine accompanied by an excellent wine list focusing on Burgundy.

in St-Pierre-la-Noaille 5.5 km Northwest by secondary road – pop. 323 – alt. 287 m – ✉ 42190

Domaine du Château de Marchangy without rest
– ✆ 04 77 69 96 76 – contact@marchangy.com – Fax 04 77 60 70 37
3 rm – 🛉€ 77/99 🛉🛉€ 85/110
◆ A splendid, 18th century chateau stands next door to an attractive wine grower's residence where tastefully decorated rooms offfer views of the Forez mountains and surrounding countryside.

CHARMES – 88 Vosges – 314 F2 – pop. 4 665 – alt. 282 m – ✉ 88130

Alsace-Lorraine 27 **C3**

Paris 381 – Épinal 31 – Lunéville 40 – Nancy 43 – St-Dié 59 – Toul 62 – Vittel 40

Office de tourisme, 2, place Henri Breton ✆ 03 29 38 17 09, Fax 03 29 38 17 09

Dancourt with rm
6 pl. Henri Breton – ✆ 03 29 38 80 80 – contact@hotel-dancourt.com – Fax 03 29 38 09 15 – Closed 18 December-18 January, Sunday dinner October-May, Saturday lunch and Friday
16 rm – 🛉€ 40/50 🛉🛉€ 45/57, € 8 – ½ P € 44/51 – **Rest** – Menu (€ 16), € 18/40 – Carte € 30/62
◆ Hotel near the house where M Barrès was born. Antiquated charm, combining Greek columns and busts, sober modern furniture and plants. Simple, practical rooms.

in Chamagne 4 km North by D 9 – pop. 416 – alt. 265 m – ✉ 88130

Le Chamagnon
236 r. du Patis – ✆ 03 29 38 14 74 – charlesvincent038@orange.fr – Fax 03 29 38 14 74 – Closed 7-28 July, 27 October-5 November, Sunday dinner, Tuesday dinner, Wednesday dinner and Monday
Rest – Menu € 10 (weekday lunch), € 19/53 – Carte € 28/46
◆ Birthplace of artist Claude Gellée (known as Le Lorrain). Hospitable restaurant with a decorative cellar. Menu influenced by flavours from Corsica, Provence and Asia.

in Vincey 4 km Southeast by N 57 – pop. 2 159 – alt. 297 m – ✉ 88450

Relais de Vincey
33 r. de Lorraine – ✆ 03 29 67 40 11 – relais.de.vincey@wanadoo.fr – Fax 03 29 67 36 66 – Closed 18-31 August
34 rm – 🛉€ 58/68 🛉🛉€ 73/81, € 9 – ½ P € 61/72 – **Rest** – *(closed Saturday lunch and Sunday dinner)* Menu (€ 21), € 25/34 – Carte € 30/53
◆ The functional rooms of this hotel are in the annexe and overlook the garden. Tennis courts, fitness centre and indoor pool. The main building houses a restaurant with pleasant modern decor where a traditional menu is served. Quick meals served in the bar.

CHARNAY-LÈS-MÂCON – 71 Saône-et-Loire – 320 I12 – see Mâcon

CHARNY-SUR-MEUSE – 55 Meuse – 307 D3 – see Verdun

CHAROLLES – 71 Saône-et-Loire – 320 F11 – pop. 3 027 – alt. 279 m – ✉ 71120

Burgundy-Jura 8 **C3**

Paris 374 – Autun 80 – Chalon-sur-Saône 67 – Mâcon 55 – Moulins 81 – Roanne 61

Office de tourisme, 24, rue Baudinot ✆ 03 85 24 05 95, Fax 03 85 24 28 12

Le Téméraire without rest
3 av. J. Furtin – ✆ 03 85 24 06 66 – guinet.suzane.@wanadoo.fr – Fax 03 85 24 05 54 – Closed 23 June-6 July
10 rm – 🛉€ 43/49 🛉🛉€ 50/59, € 6,50
◆ This hotel, named after Charles le Téméraire, is home to well-soundproofed rooms. Small lobby embellished with Charolles faience.

Le Clos de l'Argolay without rest
21 quai de la Poterne – ✆ 03 85 24 10 23 – closdelargolay@orange.fr – Closed January and February
3 rm – €89 €99 – 2 suites
◆ This 18C house in the little Venice of Charolais is surrounded by a well-tended enclosed garden. Beautiful suites (period furniture) and modern duplex in the annexe. Quality homemade produce.

De la Poste with rm
av. Libération, (near the church) – ✆ 03 85 24 11 32 – hotel-de-la-liberation-doucet@wanadoo.fr – Fax 03 85 24 05 74 – Closed 23-30 June, 17-30 November, 23 February-9 March, Sunday dinner, Thursday dinner and Monday
14 rm – €55/120 €55/120, €10 – 2 suites – **Rest** – Menu €25 (weekdays)/70 – Carte €50/76
◆ Sample modern cuisine in the refined decor of this regional style house or amid the greenery of the terrace. Comfortable rooms, some located in the recently opened annex.

Southwest 11 km by D 985 and D 270 – ✉ 71120 Changy

Le Chidhouarn
– ✆ 03 85 88 32 07 – Fax 03 85 88 01 23 – Closed 1st-11 September, 12 January-6 February, Monday and Tuesday
Rest – Menu €12,50 (weekday lunch), €20/50 – Carte €18/32
◆ A collection of sea shells enlivens this rustic building tucked away in the Charolais countryside. Fireplace to warm the lounge. Specialties based around Breton produce.

CHAROST – 18 Cher – 323 I5 – pop. 1 069 – alt. 137 m – ✉ 18290
Dordogne-Berry-Limousin 12 **C3**

Paris 239 – Châteauroux 39 – Bourges 26 – Dun-sur-Auron 42 – Issoudun 11 – Vierzon 31

in Brouillamnon 3 km northeast by N 151 and D 16E - ✉ 18290 Plou

L'Orée du Bois
– ✆ 02 48 26 21 40 – loreeduboisplou@orange.fr – Fax 02 48 26 27 81 – Closed 29 July-13 August, 12 January-13 February, Sunday dinner and Monday
Rest – Menu €15 (weekdays)/36 – Carte €33/44
◆ This country inn and pleasant garden are in a quiet hamlet. Local dishes served in a bright dining room or on the terrace in summer.

CHARQUEMONT – 25 Doubs – 321 K3 – pop. 2 209 – alt. 864 m – ✉ 25140

Paris 478 – Basel 98 – Belfort 66 – Besançon 75 – Montbéliard 49 – Pontarlier 59 17 **C2**

Au Bois de la Biche with rm ← Swiss Jura,
4.5 km southeast by D 10E and secondary road – ✆ 03 81 44 01 82 – thierry.marcelpoix@wanadoo.fr – Fax 03 81 68 65 09 – Closed 2 January-3 February and Monday
3 rm – €45 €45, €7 – ½ P €49 – **Rest** – Menu €20 (weekdays)/41 – Carte €26/52
◆ This former farmhouse, surrounded by woods, is a meeting point for hikers and overlooks the Doubs gorges. Family restaurant with views; regional cuisine. Simple bedrooms.

CHARRECEY – 71 Saône-et-Loire – 320 H8 – pop. 313 – alt. 350 m – ✉ 71510
8 **C3**

Paris 341 – Autun 36 – Beaune 29 – Chalon-sur-Saône 18 – Mâcon 77

Le Petit Blanc
2 km east by D 978, Chalon-sur-Saône road – ✆ 03 85 45 15 43 – lepetitblanc@orange.fr – Fax 03 85 45 19 80 – Closed 13-21 April, 17 August-1st September, 21 December-12 January, Sunday dinner and Thursday dinner 7 October-22 June, Sunday 23 June-6 October and Monday
Rest – Menu €15 (weekdays lunch), €22/32 – Carte €32/39
◆ This roadside inn may not appear alluring, but its local renown is deserved: a pleasant country bistro interior and very generous traditional cuisine.

CHARROUX – 03 Allier – 326 F5 – pop. 330 – alt. 420 m – ✉ 03140

Auvergne 5 **B1**

Paris 344 – Clermont-Ferrand 61 – Montluçon 68 – Moulins 52 – Vichy 30

Office de tourisme, rue de l'Horloge ✆ 04 70 56 87 71, Fax 04 70 56 87 71

La Maison du Prince de Condé without rest

pl. d'Armes – ✆ 04 70 56 81 36 – jspeer@club-internet.fr

6 rm – €50 €66

◆ This guesthouse offers personalised rooms. The duplex, called Porte d'Orient, is situated in the tower. Breakfast is served in a pretty, vaulted, 13C room.

Ferme Saint-Sébastien

chemin de Bourion – ✆ 04 70 56 88 83 – ferme.saint.sebastien@wanadoo.fr – Fax 04 70 56 86 66 – Closed 30 June-9 July, 22 September-2 October, 15 December-3 February, Tuesday except July-August and Monday

Rest – *(pre-book)* Menu €24/53 – Carte €39/71

◆ This authentic Bourbon farmhouse has been renovated and houses an attractive dining room with painted rafters and herbariums. Regionally inspired contemporary cuisine.

in Valignat 8 km West On D 183 – pop. 57 – alt. 420 m – ✉ 03330

Château de l'Ormet without rest

L'Ormet – ✆ 04 70 58 57 23 – lormet@wanadoo.fr – Fax 04 70 58 57 19 – Open April-mid November

4 rm – €64/75 €72/83

◆ Rustic, "gothic" or romantic: the rooms of this 18C Bourbonnais manor each have their own character. All overlook the park where a miniature train is set up – it's the owner's hobby.

CHARTRES Ⓟ – 28 Eure-et-Loir – 311 E5 – pop. 40 361 – Built-up area 130 681 – alt. 142 m – Great Student Pilgrimage (end April-early May) – ✉ 28000

Northern France and the Paris Region 11 **B1**

Paris 89 – Évreux 78 – Le Mans 120 – Orléans 80 – Tours 138

Office de tourisme, place de la Cathédrale ✆ 02 37 18 26 26, Fax 02 37 21 51 91

du Bois d'Ô Saint-Maixme-Hauterive Ferme de Gland, by Verneuil-sur-Avre road: 26 km, ✆ 02 37 51 04 61.

Notre-Dame cathedral ★★★: Royal portal ★★★, stained-glass windows★★★ - Old Chartres★: St-Pierre church ★, ≤★ on St-André church, banks of the Eure - Musée des Beaux-Arts: enamels★ Y **M²** - COMPA★ (Conservatoire du Machinisme agricole et des Pratiques Agricoles(Conservatory of farming mechanisation and practices)2 km by D24.

Plan on following page

Le Grand Monarque

rest, VISA

22 pl. Épars – ✆ 02 37 18 15 15 – info@bw-grand-monarque.com – Fax 02 37 36 34 18 Z **e**

50 rm – €101 €145, €14 – 5 suites

Rest *Georges* – *(closed 2-7 January, Sunday dinner and Monday)* Menu €48 – Carte €47/64

Rest *Le Madrigal* – Menu (€24 bi), €28

◆ This former 16C coaching inn has featured in the Michelin Guide since 1900! The rooms here are spacious, personalised and cosy. The restaurant offers a classic, varied menu presented in chic and quiet surroundings. Good wine selection. A friendly atmosphere and bistro-style cuisine are the hallmarks of Le Madrigal.

Ibis Centre

14 pl. Drouaise – ✆ 02 37 36 06 36 – h0917@accor.com – Fax 02 37 36 17 20 X **b**

79 rm – €50/79 €50/79, €7,50 – **Rest** – Menu (€14), €19 – Carte €20/26

◆ This hotel near the historic district and cathedral is gradually being renovated and offers functional and well-kept rooms. The restaurant terrace on the banks of the Eure is very busy in fine weather.

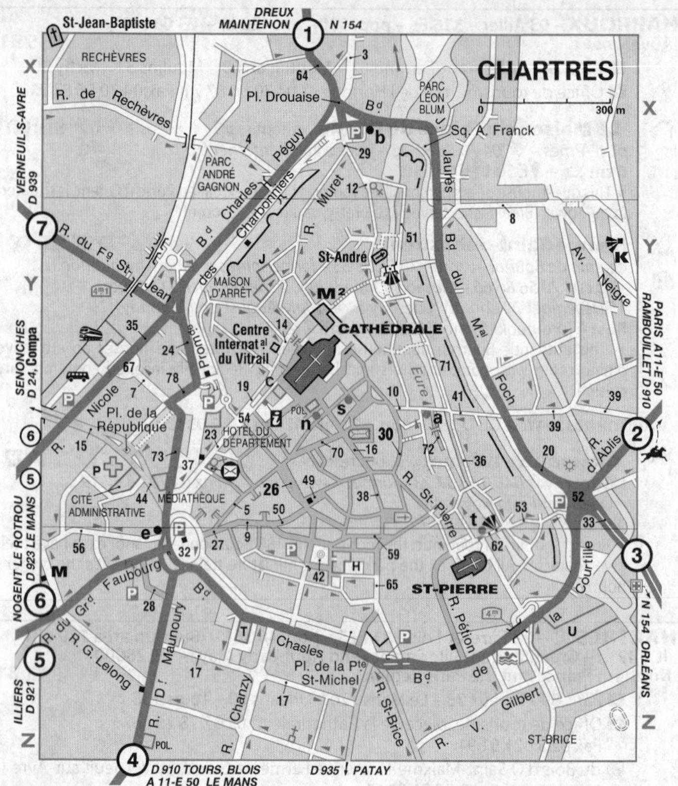

Aligre (Av. d') . . . X 3
Alsace-Lorraine (Av. d') . . . X 4
Ballay (R. Noël) . . . Y 5
Beauce (Av. Jehan-de) . . . Y 7
Bethouard (Av.) . . . Y 8
Bois-Merrain (R. du) . . . Y 9
Bourg (R. du) . . . Y 10
Brèche (R. de la) . . . X 12
Cardinal-Pie (R. du) . . . Y 14
Casanova (R. Danièle) . . . Y 15
Changes (R. des) . . . Y 16
Châteaudun (R. de) . . . Z 17
Châtelet (Pl.) . . . Y 18
Cheval-Blanc (R. du) . . . Y 19
Clemenceau (Bd) . . . Y 20
Collin-d'Harleville (R.) . . . Y 23
Couronne (R. de la) . . . Y 24
Cygne (Pl. du) . . . Y 26
Delacroix (R. Jacques) . . . Y 27
Dr-Gibert (R. du) . . . Z 28
Drouaise (R. Porte) . . . X 29
Écuyers (R. des) . . . Y 30
Épars (Pl. des) . . . Z 32
Faubourg La Grappe (R. du) . . . Y 33
Félibien (R.) . . . Y 35
Fessard (R. G.) . . . Y 78
Foulerie (R. de la) . . . Y 36
Gaulle (Pl. Gén.-de) . . . Y 37
Grenets (R. des) . . . Y 38
Guillaume (R. du Fg) . . . Y 39
Guillaume (R. Porte) . . . Y 41
Halles (Pl. des) . . . Z 42
Koenig (R. du Gén.) . . . Y 44
Marceau (Pl.) . . . Y 49
Marceau (R.) . . . Y 50
Massacre (R. du) . . . Y 51
Morard (Pl.) . . . Y 52
Morard (R. de la Porte) . . . Y 53
Moulin (Pl. Jean) . . . Y 54
Péri (R. Gabriel) . . . Z 56
Poêle-Percée (R. de la) . . . Z 59
St-Hilaire (R. du Pont) . . . Z 62
St-Maurice (R.) . . . X 64
St-Michel (R.) . . . Z 65
Semard (Pl. Pierre) . . . Y 67
Soleil-d'Or (R. du) . . . Y 70
Tannerie (R. de la) . . . Y 71
Teinturiers (Q. des) . . . Y 72
Violette (Bd Maurice) . . . Y 73

XXX **La Vieille Maison** VISA MC

5 r. au Lait – ✆ 02 37 34 10 67 – Fax 02 37 91 12 41 – Closed Sunday dinner, Tuesday lunch and Monday Y **s**

Rest – Menu (€ 29), € 35/48

◆ Exposed stonework and beams, rustic furniture and a fireplace lend style to this venerable residence, which is several hundred years old. Traditional cooking.

XX **St-Hilaire** VISA MC

11 r. Pont-St-Hilaire – ✆ 02 37 30 97 57 – Fax 02 37 30 97 57 – Closed 27 July-18 August, Sunday and Monday YZ **t**

Rest – *(number of covers limited, pre-book)* Menu € 26/42 – Carte € 39/50

◆ Red floor tiles, wooden beams, painted furniture and paintings by a local artist bestow particular charm upon this 16C building. Classical cuisine with clever touches.

Les Feuillantines

4 r. du Bourg – ✆ 02 37 30 22 21 – Fax 02 37 30 22 21 – Closed 7-16 April, 3-25 August, Christmas holidays, Sunday and Monday Y **a**

Rest – Menu (€ 18), € 25 – Carte € 41/52

◆ The chef of this attractive little restaurant in the historic quarter of town is careful to use the season's specialties in the preparation of an authentically traditional cuisine; the décor is colourful and there is a lovely terrace for summer dining.

Le Bistrot de la Cathédrale

1 Cloître Notre Dame – ✆ 02 37 36 59 60 – jalleratbertrand@wanadoo.fr – Fax 02 37 36 59 60 – Closed Wednesday Y **n**

Rest – Menu € 21/30 bi – Carte € 26/39

◆ This bistro, in the immediate vicinity of the cathedral, is popular for the cuisine created by its young, enthusiastic chef, as well as its great location.

via ② 4 km by D 910 – ✉ 28000 Chartres

Novotel rm, VISA AE

av. Marcel Proust – ✆ 02 37 88 13 50 – h0413@accor.com – Fax 02 37 30 29 56

112 rm – €88/96 €100/125, € 12,50 – **Rest** – Menu (€ 22), € 27/30 – Carte € 25/41

◆ A 1970s building located between a business estate and express roads. Choose one of the practical and bright renovated rooms. Pleasant patio-garden and children's play area. A contemporary restaurant overlooking the swimming pool. Novotel menu.

Z. A. de Barjouville **4 km by ④ – ✉ 28630 Barjouville**

Mercure rm, VISA AE

4 km, via ④ – ✆ 02 37 35 35 55 – h3481@accor.com – Fax 02 37 34 72 12

73 rm – €72 €82, € 12 – 1 suite – **Rest** – *(closed Saturday lunch and Sunday)* Menu (€ 22), € 26

◆ A chain hotel, located in a business park, whose comfortable rooms are gradually being equipped with air-conditioning. Traditional cuisine and smart bistro decor.

in Chazay **12 km west by D 24 and D 121 – ✉ 28300 St-Aubin-des-Bois**

L' Erablais without rest

38 r. Jean Moulin – ✆ 02 37 32 80 53 – jmguinard@aol.com – Fax 02 37 32 80 53 – Closed 21 December-4 January

3 rm – €35 €47

◆ The former stables of this 19C farmhouse have today been converted into stylish rooms decorated with floral motifs; the pleasant garden looks onto fields sown with rapeseed.

Northwest **8 km by ① and D121 [9] - ✉ 28300 Bailleau-l'Évêque**

Ferme du Château without rest

à Levesville – ✆ 02 37 22 97 02 – Fax 02 37 22 97 02 – Closed 25 December-1st January

3 rm – €45 €55/60

◆ Those who seek the tranquillity of natural surroundings will find it here in this fine farmhouse of Berry nestling in its delightful garden. Rooms are spacious and brightly coloured; meals available by reservation.

CHARTRES-DE-BRETAGNE – 35 Ille-et-Vilaine – 309 L6 – see Rennes

---

LA CHARTRE-SUR-LE-LOIR – 72 Sarthe – 310 M8 – pop. 1 547 – alt. 55 m –

✉ 72340 Châteaux of the Loire 35 **D2**

Paris 217 – La Flèche 57 – Le Mans 49 – St-Calais 30 – Tours 42 – Vendôme 42

Office de tourisme, Parking Central ✆ 02 43 44 40 04, Fax 02 43 44 40 04

De France
20 pl. de la République – 02 43 44 40 16 – hoteldefrance@worldonline.fr – Fax 02 43 79 62 20 – Closed Christmas holidays, February, Sunday dinner and Monday except dinner July-August
24 rm – €45 €59, €8,50 – ½ P €48 – **Rest** – *(pre-book Sat - Sun)* Menu €16/40 – Carte €30/55
◆ This former 19C coaching inn, with rooms that are gradually being renovated, has a heated swimming pool and views of the Loir and the surrounding countryside. A rustic setting and old France atmosphere characterise this restaurant serving traditional cuisine.

CHARTRETTES – 77 Seine-et-Marne – 312 F5 – pop. 2 391 – alt. 75 m – ✉ 77590 19 C2

Paris 66 – Créteil 44 – Montreuil 60 – Vitry-sur-Seine 48

Château de Rouillon without rest
41 av. Charles de Gaulle – 01 60 69 64 40 – chateau.de.rouillon@club.fr – Fax 01 60 69 64 55
5 rm – €74/96 €82/104
◆ This 17C chateau and its splendid park border the Seine; stylish furniture and antiques make up a subtly refined décor both in the lounges and in the rooms.

CHASSAGNE-MONTRACHET – 21 Côte-d'Or – 320 I8 – pop. 472 – alt. 200 m – ✉ 21190 7 A3

Paris 327 – Amboise 343 – Beaune 16 – Blois 69 – Chalon-sur-Saône 23

Château de Chassagne-Montrachet without rest
5 r. du Château – 03 80 21 98 57 – contact@michelpicard.com – Fax 03 80 21 98 56 – Closed 23 December-3 January
5 rm – €250/300 €250/300
◆ The 18C chateau and cellars of this prestigious vineyard estate opens its doors to guests. Fine, very contemporary bedrooms and bathrooms designed by the sculptor Argueyrolles.

Le Chassagne
4 imp. Chenevottes – 03 80 21 94 94 – lechassagne@wanadoo.fr – Fax 03 80 21 97 77 – Closed 1st-14 August, 31 December-14 January, Sunday dinner, Wednesday dinner and Monday
Rest – Menu €29 (weekdays)/89 – Carte €81/106
◆ Modern colourful decor, contemporary cuisine and a good selection of Chassagne-Montrachet wines. A pleasant restaurant in the heart of the great white wine region of France.

CHASSELAY – 69 Rhône – 327 H4 – pop. 2 590 – alt. 220 m – ✉ 69380 43 E1

Paris 443 – L'Arbresle 15 – Lyon 21 – Villefranche-sur-Saône 18

Guy Lassausaie
r. de Belle Sise – 04 78 47 62 59 – guy.lassausaie@wanadoo.fr – Fax 04 78 47 06 19 – Closed 4-28 August, 9-18 February, Tuesday and Wednesday
Rest – Menu €45/90 – Carte €60/72
Spec. Langoustines en cheveux d'ange, beurre blanc à la vanille. Vapeur de barbue au citron, tartare d'huîtres et Saint-Jacques (season). Poitrine de caille et foie gras en coque d'épices. **Wines** Viré-Clessé, Fleurie.
◆ Classic personalised cuisine served in spacious contemporary dining rooms, decorated with silk scarves from Lyon. Smoking room and shop selling home-made produce.

CHASSENEUIL-DU-POITOU – 86 Vienne – 322 I5 – see Poitiers

CHASSE-SUR-RHÔNE – 38 Isère – 333 B4 – see Vienne

CHASSEY-LE-CAMP – 71 Saône-et-Loire – 320 I8 – see Chagny

LA CHÂTAIGNERAIE – 85 Vendée – 316 L8 – pop. 2 762 – alt. 155 m – ✉ 85120

35 **C3**

Paris 408 – Bressuire 32 – Fontenay-le-Comte 23 – Parthenay 43 – La Roche-sur-Yon 59

Office de tourisme, rond-point des Sources ☎ 02 51 52 62 37, Fax 02 51 52 69 20

Auberge de la Terrasse

7 r. Beauregard – ☎ 02 51 69 68 68 – contact@aubergedelaterrasse.com – Fax 02 51 52 67 96 – Closed 26 April-4 May, 25 October-2 November

14 rm – €53 €67 – ½ P €52/71 – **Rest** – *(closed Sunday dinner, Friday dinner, and Saturday lunch 15 September-31 May and Sunday lunch July-August)* Menu (€12), €18 – Carte €20/40

◆ In a rather quiet district far from the town centre. The hotel has well-maintained, simple and above all practical rooms. Friendly welcome. Small rustic restaurant area decorated with paintings and prints offering a traditional à la carte and fixed-price menus.

CHÂTEAU-ARNOUX-ST-AUBAN – 04 Alpes-de-Haute-Provence – 334 E8 – pop. 4 970 – alt. 440 m – ✉ 04160 French Alps

41 **C2**

Paris 719 – Digne-les-Bains 26 – Forcalquier 30 – Manosque 42 – Sault 71 – Sisteron 15

Syndicat d'initiative, 4, place de la carrière ☎ 02 96 73 49 57
Office de tourisme, Font Robert ☎ 04 92 64 02 64, Fax 04 92 64 54 55

Église St-Donat★ - St-Jean chapel viewpoint★ - Site★ of Montfort.

La Bonne Étape (Jany Gleize)

Chemin du lac – ☎ 04 92 64 00 09 – bonneetape@relaischateaux.com – Fax 04 92 64 37 36 – Closed 4 January-12 February

18 rm – €152/172 €168/370, €19 – ½ P €161/270

Rest – *(closed 17 November-2 December, 4 January-12 February, Monday and Tuesday off season except public holidays)* Menu €42/100 – Carte €64/117

Spec. Menu "Provence". Agneau de Sisteron. Crème glacée au miel de lavande dans sa ruche. **Wines** Coteaux de Pierrevert, Palette.

◆ Difficult not to succumb to the charm of this 18C house with a Provençal flavour. Delightful rooms with antique furniture. The restaurant is embellished by an attractively rustic décor and offers classic cuisine accompanied by a wide choice of French wines.

L'Oustaou de la Foun

North : 1.5 km on N 85 – ☎ 04 92 62 65 30 – loustaoudela-foun@wanadoo.fr – Fax 04 92 62 65 32 – Closed Sunday dinner and Monday

Rest – Menu €20 bi (weekday lunch), €30/55 – Carte €54/62

◆ A restaurant serving local cuisine in a former 16C coaching inn alongside a main road. Modernised dining rooms, one of which is vaulted, the other with exposed beams. Outdoor dining in summer.

La Magnanerie with rm

North : 2 km on N 85 ✉ 04200 Aubignosc – ☎ 04 92 62 60 11 – stefanparoche@aol.com – Fax 04 92 62 63 05 – Closed 1st-8 September and 22-30 December

8 rm – €49/75 €49/75, €8 – ½ P €50/70 – **Rest** – *(closed Sunday dinner and Monday)* Menu €15 (lunch)/39 – Carte €38/72

◆ Completely refurbished with colourful designer decor in keeping with the inventive cuisine. Spacious rooms, a new bar, plus a terrace-garden.

Au Goût du Jour

14 av. Gén. de Gaulle – ☎ 04 92 64 48 48 – goutdujour@bonneetape.com – Fax 04 92 64 37 36 – Closed 4 January-12 February

Rest – Menu (€18), €25

◆ This small and cosy dining room, decorated in Provençal colours, is the place to sample a range of tasty local dishes, chalked up on the blackboard bistro-style.

CHÂTEAUBOURG – 35 Ille-et-Vilaine – 309 N6 – pop. 4 877 – alt. 50 m – ✉ 35220

10 **D2**

Paris 329 – Angers 114 – Châteaubriant 52 – Fougères 44 – Laval 57 – Rennes 24

Ar Milin' ✎

– ✆ 02 99 00 30 91 – resa.armilin@wanadoo.fr – Fax 02 99 00 37 56
– *Closed 21 December-7 January and Sunday dinner from 1st November to 28 February*
32 rm – †€ 71/126 ††€ 80/200, ☕ € 12 – ½ P € 93/116
Rest – *(closed Tuesday lunch, Monday in July-August and Saturday lunch)*
Menu € 28/99 bi – Carte € 35/70
Rest *Bistrot du Moulin* – *(closed Sunday and public holidays) (lunch only)* Carte € 16/26

◆ This former 19C flour mill stands in a park adorned with immense contemporary works of art. Welcoming rooms (those in the wing are smaller). Light dining room (white colour scheme) and view of the river; traditional cuisine. Elegant decor and relaxed ambience at the Bistrot.

in St-Didier **6 km East by D 33 – pop. 1 275 – alt. 49 m – ✉ 35220**

Pen'Roc ✎

à La Peinière, (D 105) – ✆ 02 99 00 33 02 – hotellerie@penroc.fr
– Fax 02 99 62 30 89 – *Closed 22 December-5 January, 16-22 February*
29 rm – †€ 87/231 ††€ 101/231, ☕ € 12,50 – ½ P € 95/160
Rest – *(closed Friday dinner and Sunday dinner out of season)* Menu (€ 18), € 24 (weekday)/85 – Carte € 56/96

◆ Country hotel, near a place of pilgrimage. Rooms are attractively decorated in contemporary or Asian style. Some are equipped with jacuzzi baths or have a terrace. Small, stylish dining rooms serving an up-to-date menu.

CHÂTEAUBRIANT – 44 Loire-Atlantique – 316 H1 – pop. 12 065 – alt. 70 m – ✉ 44110 Brittany

34 **B2**

Paris 354 – Angers 72 – Laval 65 – Nantes 62 – Rennes 61

Office de tourisme, 22, rue de Couëré ✆ 02 40 28 20 90, Fax 02 40 28 06 02

Château★.

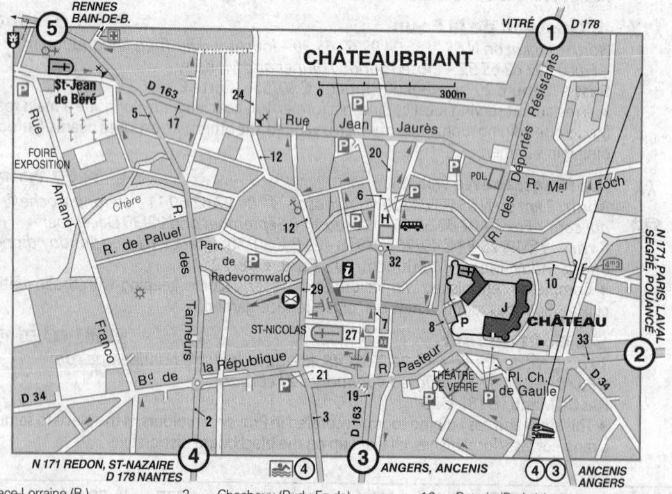

La Ferrière

Moisdon-la-Rivière road, D 178 on ④ – ✆ 02 40 28 00 28 – hostellerie-laferriere@wanadoo.fr – Fax 02 40 28 29 21
19 rm – €92 €92, €10,50 – ½ P €62/72 – **Rest** – *(closed Sunday dinner)* Menu €20 (weekday)/40 – Carte €40/56
♦ Lovely 1840 home surrounded by parkland. Comfortable, upstairs rooms in the main house, not as spacious in the adjacent pavilion. Classic culinary repertory served in characterful dining rooms or in the light veranda.

CHÂTEAU-CHALON – 39 Jura – 321 D6 – pop. 160 – alt. 420 m – ✉ 39210

Burgundy-Jura 16 **B3**

Paris 409 – Besançon 73 – Dole 51 – Lons-le-Saunier 14

Le Relais des Abbesses

r. de la Roche – ✆ 03 84 44 98 56 – relaisdesabbesses@wanadoo.fr – Fax 03 84 44 98 56 – Open February-mid November
4 rm – €62 €65/70
Table d'hôte – Menu €24 bi/32 bi
♦ It is easy to see why the owners fell in love with this village residence at first sight! Rooms, christened Agnès, Marguerite and Eugénie, have a splendid view of la Bresse, while Violette faces Château-Chalon. Home-made regional cuisine.

CHÂTEAU D'IF – 13 Bouches-du-Rhône – 340 G6 Provence 40 **B3**

from **Marseille** for Château d'If★★ (✱★★★) 20 mn.

LE CHÂTEAU D'OLÉRON – 17 Charente-Maritime – 324 C4 – see Île d'Oléron

---

CHÂTEAUDOUBLE – 83 Var – 340 N4 – pop. 381 – alt. 540 m – ✉ 83300

French Riviera 41 **C3**

Paris 875 – Castellane 50 – Draguignan 14 – Fréjus 43 – Toulon 98

Site★ - ≤★ of the "sarrasine"tower - Gorges de Châteaudouble★.

Du Château

pl. Vieille – ✆ 04 94 70 90 05 – Fax 04 94 70 90 05 – Closed Monday, Tuesday and Wednesday from 1st November to 1st March
Rest – Menu €25/40
♦ Designer-inspired seating, modern paintings and typical Provençal colours contribute to the charming atmosphere; there is a shaded terrace and the cuisine is local with an inventive flair.

CHÂTEAU-DU-LOIR – 72 Sarthe – 310 L8 – pop. 5 148 – alt. 50 m – ✉ 72500

35 **D2**

Paris 235 – La Flèche 41 – Langeais 47 – Le Mans 43 – Tours 42 – Vendôme 59

Office de tourisme, 2, avenue Jean Jaurès ✆ 02 43 44 56 68, Fax 02 43 44 56 95

Le Grand Hôtel

pl. Hôtel de Ville – ✆ 02 43 44 00 17 – avel5@wanadoo.fr – Fax 02 43 44 37 58 – Closed autumn half-term holidays, Friday dinner and Saturday lunch November-February
18 rm – €51 €51/59, €9 – ½ P €66 – **Rest** – Menu €21/39 – Carte €26/52
♦ Formerly a 19th century guest house, this limestone building today offers well-equipped, rustic or modern style rooms; the more restful areas are in the annexe (former stables). The dining room is old-fashioned and the terrace is draped in wisteria. Traditional cuisine.

CHÂTEAUDUN – 28 Eure-et-Loir – 311 D7 – pop. 14 543 – alt. 140 m – ✉ 28200 Châteaux of the Loire

11 B2

Paris 131 – Blois 57 – Chartres 45 – Orléans 53 – Tours 94

Office de tourisme, 1, rue de Luynes ✆ 02 37 45 22 46, Fax 02 37 66 00 16

Château★★ - Old town★: La Madeleine church ★ - Promenade du Mail ≤★ - Musée des Beaux-Arts et d'Histoire naturelle: Bird collection ★ M.

CHÂTEAUDUN

Cap-de-la-Madeleine (Pl.) . . . . A 3
Château (R. du) . . . . A 4
Cuirasserie (R. de la) . . . . A 5
Dunois (Pl. J.-de) . . . . A 6
Gambetta (R.) . . . . AB
Guichet (R. du) . . . . A 7
Huileries (R. des) . . . . A 8
Luynes (R. de) . . . . A 10
Lyautey (R. du Mar.) . . . . A 12
Porte d'Abas (R. de la) . . . . A 14
République (R.) . . . . AB
St-Lubin (R.) . . . . A 18
St-Médard (R.) . . . . A 19
18-Octobre (Pl. du) . . . . A 21

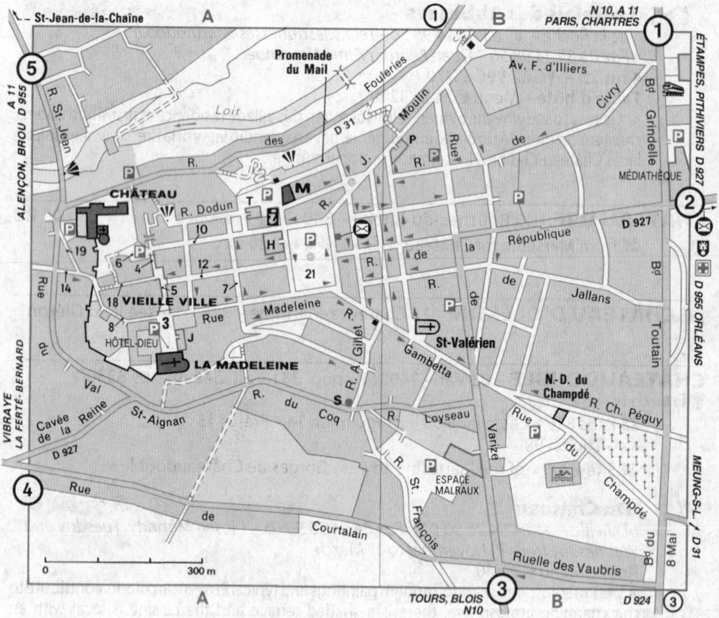

Aux Trois Pastoureaux

31 r. A Gillet – ✆ 02 37 45 74 40 – j-f.lucchese@wanadoo.fr – Fax 02 37 66 00 32 – Closed 7-21 July, 28 December-5 January, 22 February-2 March, Sunday and Monday

A s

Rest – Menu (€ 19), € 20/44 – Carte € 30/60

◆ The new décor of this restaurant features warm-toned colours and paintings by a local artist. The menus are traditional and wines may be ordered by the glass.

in Flacey 8 km North by ① – ✉ 28800 – pop. 193 – alt. 157 m – ✉ 28800

Domaine de Moresville without rest

rte de Brou, Northwest by D 110 – ✆ 02 37 47 33 94 – resa@domaine-moresville.com – Fax 02 37 47 56 40

16 rm – €70/100 €80/160, € 12 – 1 suite

◆ A fine, 18th century chateau in an attractive park with a small lake. The décor features antique furnishings and parquet flooring; rooms are restful and personalised in style; sauna and Jacuzzi.

CHÂTEAUFORT – 78 Yvelines – 311 I3 – 101 22 – see Paris, Area

CHÂTEAU-GONTIER – 53 Mayenne – 310 E8 – pop. 11 131 – alt. 33 m – ✉ 53200 Châteaux of the Loire
35 C1

Paris 288 – Angers 50 – Châteaubriant 56 – Laval 30 – Le Mans 95

Office de tourisme, place André Counord ✆ 02 43 70 42 74, Fax 02 43 70 95 52

Romanesque interior ★ of St-Jean-Baptiste church.

CHÂTEAU-GONTIER

Alsace-Lorraine (R. d') . . . . B 2
Anjou (R. René d') . . . . A
Bourg-Roussel (R. du) . . . . A 5
Chevreul (R.) . . . . A
Coubertin (Q. P. de) . . . . B 7
Doumer (Pl. Paul) . . . . A
Enfer (R. d') . . . . B 8
Foch (Av. Mar.) . . . . B 9
Fouassier (R.) . . . . A 10
Français-Libres (Rond-Point des) . . . . A 12
Gambetta (R.) . . . . A 14
Garnier (R.) . . . . A
Gaulle (Quai Ch. de) . . . . B 15
Homo (R. rené) . . . . A 18
Joffre (Av. Mar.) . . . . A 20
Leclerc (R. de la Division) . . . . A 22
Lemonnier (R. du Gén.) . . . . . . B 24
Lierru (R. de) . . . . B 25
Olivet (R. d') . . . . A 29
Pasteur (Quai) . . . . B 31
Pilori (Pl. du) . . . . A 33
Razilly (Av. de) . . . . A
République (Pl. de la) . . . . A 36
St-Jean (Pl.) . . . . A 39
St-Just (Pl.) . . . . B 40
St-Rémi (Pl.) . . . . A
Thiers (R.) . . . . B
Thionville (R. de) . . . . B 45

 **Le Jardin des Arts**

5 r. A. Cahour – ✆ 02 43 70 12 12 – jardin@art8.com – Fax 02 43 70 12 07 – Closed 28 July-17 August, 22 December-4 January and public holidays
A e

20 rm – 🚹€ 60/72 🚹🚹€ 68/88, ☕ € 8 – ½ P € 47/70 – **Rest** – *(closed Friday dinner, Saturday and Sunday)* Menu € 19/25 – Carte € 24/35

◆ A former 'sub-prefecture', with a garden overlooking the Mayenne. Spacious rooms, lounges with unusual billiard tables, computer equipment and an auditorium. Parquet flooring, a fireplace, original wood panelling and modern decoration in the restaurant.

Parc Hôtel without rest
46 av. Joffre, via ③ – ✆ 02 43 07 28 41 – contact@parchotel.fr – Fax 02 43 07 63 79 – Closed 6-22 February
21 rm – 🚹€ 56/70 🚹🚹€ 63/78, ☕ € 12
◆ A 19C mansion and outhouses set in parkland, complete with swimming pool. Attractive, individually decorated rooms, more spacious in the main house. Warm hospitality.

L'Aquarelle ← Mayenne,
2 r. Félix Marchand, (in Saint-Fort), 1 km south on D 267 (Ménil road) B – ✆ 02 43 70 15 44 – l.aquarelle@laposte.net – Closed 6-15 October, 16-25 February, Tuesday dinner and Sunday dinner October-April and Wednesday
Rest – Menu € 14 (weekday lunch), € 22/55 bi – Carte € 32/50
◆ This relaxing restaurant, on the banks of the Mayenne, serves contemporary cuisine. The bright, panoramic dining room is decorated in light green; pleasant summer terrace.

in Coudray **7 km Southeast by D 22 – pop. 640 – alt. 68 m – ✉ 53200**

L'Amphitryon
2 rte Daon – ✆ 02 43 70 46 46 – lamphitryon@wanadoo.fr – Fax 02 43 70 42 93 – Closed autumn half-term holidays, 22-26 December, Tuesday lunch, Sunday dinner and Monday
Rest – Menu (€ 13), € 17 (weekdays)/27 – Carte € 37/58
◆ A 19C house, opposite the village church, with a pleasantly refined atmosphere. Well-set tables, traditional and local cuisine.

in Ruillé-Froid-Fonds **12,5 km by ① and D605 – pop. 436 – alt. 87 m – ✉ 53170**

Logis Villeprouvée
rte du Bignon-du-Maine – ✆ 02 43 07 71 62 – christ.davenel@orange.fr – Fax 02 43 07 71 62
4 rm ☕ – 🚹€ 33 🚹🚹€ 43/48 – ½ P € 33/35 – **Table d'hôte** – Menu € 13
◆ The refined decor of this former 14C-17C priory takes you back to the days of chivalry with its displays of armour, medieval tapestries and four-poster beds. The rustic flavour of the table d'hôte dining room is perfectly suited to the dishes concocted with farm produce.

CHÂTEAUNEUF – 71 Saône-et-Loire – 320 F12 – see Chauffailles

CHÂTEAUNEUF-DE-GADAGNE – 84 Vaucluse – 84 C10 – pop. 2 838 – alt. 90 m – ✉ 84470

42 **E1**

▶ Paris 694 – Arles 47 – Avignon 13 – Marseille 95

ℹ Office de tourisme, Place de la Liberté ✆ 04 90 38 04 78, Fax 04 90 38 35 43

in Jonquerettes **4 km North by D 6 – pop. 1 236 – alt. 60 m – ✉ 84450**

Le Clos des Saumanes without rest
chemin des Saumanes – ✆ 04 90 22 30 86 – closaumane@aol.com – Fax 04 86 34 04 46 – Open from Easter to autumn half-term holidays
5 rm ☕ – 🚹€ 80 🚹🚹€ 130
◆ This stately 18C building is surrounded by a pinewood and vineyards; rooms are charmingly Provençal with old-style furnishings; one of them has a splendid terrace. Warm welcome.

CHÂTEAUNEUF-DE-GALAURE – 26 Drôme – 332 C2 – pop. 1 276 – alt. 253 m – ✉ 26330

43 **E2**

▶ Paris 531 – Beaurepaire 19 – Romans-sur-Isère 27 – Tournon-sur-Rhône 25 – Valence 41

Yves Leydier
1 r. Stade – ✆ 04 75 68 68 02 – Fax 04 75 68 66 19 – Closed February, Sunday dinner, Tuesday dinner and Wednesday
Rest – Carte € 25/47
◆ This lovely Galaure pebble-fronted building offers a choice of a cosy dining room, a veranda with large bay windows or a shady terrace overlooking the garden. Seasonal menus.

CHÂTEAUNEUF-DU-FAOU – 29 Finistère – 308 I5 – pop. 3 595 – alt. 130 m – ✉ 29520 Brittany 9 **B2**

Paris 526 – Brest 65 – Carhaix-Plouguer 23 – Châteaulin 24 – Morlaix 51 – Quimper 38

Syndicat d'initiative, 17, rue de la Mairie ✆ 02 98 81 83 90, Fax 02 98 81 79 30

Domaine de Trévarez★ South: 6 km.

Le Relais de Cornouaille

9 r. Paul-Sérusier, Carhaix road – ✆ 02 98 81 75 36 – relaiscornouaille@wanadoo.fr – Fax 02 98 81 81 32 – Closed October, Sunday dinner and Saturday off season

30 rm – €42/45 €50/53, €7 – ½ P €46/48 – **Rest** – *(closed Sunday dinner and Saturday off season)* Menu (€10), €14,50 (weekdays)/37 – Carte €18/48

◆ A family atmosphere in this hotel, whose bar is popular with locals. The bedrooms are a touch on the small side, but are functional and well-maintained. A rustic dining area, friendly service and traditional cuisine with numerous seafood specialities.

CHÂTEAUNEUF-DU-PAPE – 84 Vaucluse – 332 B9 – pop. 2 078 – alt. 87 m – ✉ 84230 Provence 42 **E1**

Paris 667 – Alès 82 – Avignon 19 – Carpentras 22 – Orange 10 – Roquemaure 10

Syndicat d'initiative, place du Portail ✆ 04 90 83 71 08, Fax 04 90 83 50 34

≤★★ of the château des Papes.

Hostellerie Château des Fines Roches

≤ the vines,

rte de Sorgues et voie privée – ✆ 04 90 83 70 23 – reservation@chateaufinesroches.com – Fax 04 90 83 78 42 – Closed November and Sunday dinner to Tuesday lunch December-April

11 rm – €99/309 €119/309, €16 – ½ P €120/215

Rest – Menu €33 bi (weekday lunch), €52/65

◆ Remarkable crenellated castle (19C) dominating the vineyard. Small elegantly decorated dining rooms where regional dishes are served. Pleasant and spacious rooms.

Le Verger des Papes

≤ the vineyard, the Luberon and Avignon,

au château – ✆ 04 90 83 50 40 – vergerdespapes@wanadoo.fr – Fax 04 90 83 50 49 – Closed 21 December-1st March, Sunday dinner, Monday dinner, Tuesday dinner and Wednesday dinner October-March

Rest – Menu €20 (weekday lunch)/29 – Carte €30/57

◆ A pleasant restaurant on the ramparts of a château. A shady terrace from which to admire a splendid panoramic view. Gallo-Roman cellars carved from the rock. Provençal cuisine.

Le Pistou

15 r. Joseph Ducos – ✆ 04 90 83 71 75 – charlotte.ledoux@tiscali.fr – Closed January, Sunday dinner and Monday

Rest – Menu €15/28 – Carte €26/35

◆ This little bistro-type restaurant is in a narrow street leading to the Papal fortress. Nice rustic decor and terrace. Traditional and regional dishes plus daily specials chalked up on the board.

West 4 km by D 17 – ✉ 84230 Châteauneuf-du-Pape

La Sommellerie

rest,

rte de Roquemaure – ✆ 04 90 83 50 00 – la-sommellerie@wanadoo.fr – Fax 04 90 83 51 85 – Closed 2 January-10 February

16 rm – €74/117 €74/175, €12 – ½ P €90/113 – **Rest** – *(closed Monday dinner and Sunday from November to April, Saturday lunch and Monday lunch)* Menu €30 (weekday lunch), €45/62 – Carte €48/103

◆ This restored shepherd's dwelling (17C) is in the heart of the Châteauneuf vineyard. Rooms are bright and attractively furnished in country style. There is a fine, well-wooded garden. This prettily ornamented, Provençal style dining room has a terrace looking onto the swimming-pool; the cuisine is regional and offers charcoal broiled specialties in summer.

CHÂTEAUNEUF-EN-THYMERAIS – 28 Eure-et-Loir – 311 D4 – pop. 2 423 – alt. 204 m – ✉ 28170 11 B1

Paris 98 – Chartres 26 – Dreux 21 – Nogent-le-Rotrou 44 – Verneuil-sur-Avre 32

du Bois d'Ô Saint-Maixme-Hauterive Ferme de Gland, West: 2 km by D 140, ✆ 02 37 51 04 61.

Le Relais D'Aligre

25 r. Jean Moulin – ✆ 02 37 51 69 59 – Fax 02 37 51 80 49 – Closed 7-28 July, Sunday dinner and Monday

Rest – Menu € 16 (weekdays)/44 – Carte € 25/75

◆ Fish, shellfish and crustaceans are the specialities of this lavender-coloured restaurant situated in the main street. The interior decor has a maritime feel. Family atmosphere.

CHÂTEAURENARD – 13 Bouches-du-Rhône – 340 E2 – pop. 12 999 – alt. 37 m – ✉ 13160 Provence 42 E1

Paris 692 – Avignon 10 – Carpentras 37 – Cavaillon 23 – Marseille 95 – Nîmes 44 – Orange 40

Syndicat d'initiative, 11, cours Carnot ✆ 04 90 24 25 50, Fax 04 90 24 25 52

Château féodal: ⁕★ of the Griffon tower.

Les Glycines with rm

14 av. V. Hugo – ✆ 04 90 94 10 66 – lesglycines3@wanadoo.fr – Fax 04 90 94 78 10 – Closed February holidays, Sunday dinner and Monday

10 rm – €47 €47, ☕ €6 – ½ P €53

Rest – Menu € 18 (weekdays)/27 – Carte € 30/46

◆ There are three dining rooms, one adjacent to the other, a covered patio and a small, attractive terrace for summer dining; regional specialities and bouillabaisse (prepared to order).

CHÂTEAUROUX P – 36 Indre – 323 G6 – pop. 49 632 – alt. 155 m – ✉ 36000 Dordogne-Berry-Limousin 12 C3

Paris 265 – Blois 101 – Bourges 65 – Limoges 125 – Tours 115

Office de tourisme, 1, place de la Gare ✆ 02 54 34 10 74, Fax 02 54 27 57 97

du Val de l'Indre Villedieu-sur-Indre Parc du Château, by Loches road: 13 km, ✆ 02 54 26 59 44.

Déols: steeple★ of the former abbey, sarcophagus★ in St-Etienne church.

Plan on next page

Colbert

4 r. Colbert – ✆ 02 54 35 70 00 – contact@hotel-colbert.fr – Fax 02 54 27 45 88

44 rm – €92 €102, ☕ €11 – 6 suites – **Rest** – Menu € 18/27 – Carte € 29/41 Z a

◆ A former tobacco factory now houses this recent and functional hotel with designer touches. Some duplexes. Bread, wine and rotisserie dishes are the themes for the modern style brasserie.

Ibis

r. V. Hugo – ✆ 02 54 34 61 61 – h1080@accor.com – Fax 02 54 27 69 51

60 rm – €72 €72/77, ☕ €8 BY v

Rest – *(closed Saturday and Sunday except July-August)* Carte € 26/37

◆ A useful stopover, this central hotel has spacious, functional rooms with good sound-proofing. A pleasant dining room with pretty chairs, wrought-iron lights, net curtains and blinds in sunny colours. Traditional cuisine.

Elysée Hôtel without rest

2 r. République – ✆ 02 54 22 33 66 – elysee36@wanadoo.fr – Fax 02 54 07 34 34

18 rm – €61 €68, ☕ €8,50 AY s

◆ A hundred-year-old hotel with well-maintained rooms with a personal touch. Freshly squeezed orange juice and home-made jam for breakfast.

Boischaut without rest

135 av. la Châtre, via ④ – ✆ 02 54 22 22 34 – boischaut@hotel-chateauroux.com – Fax 02 54 22 64 89 – Closed 28 December-5 January X v

27 rm – €44/54 €48/64, ☕ €7

◆ This establishment invites you to enjoy the comfort of its functional rooms, furnished in rustic style or with wrought iron. The breakfast room, on two levels, is light and modern.

CHÂTEAUROUX

Street	Grid	No.
Albert 1er (R.)	BY	2
Argenton (Av. d')	X	4
Augras (R. E.)	X	5
Auvergne (R. d')	X	7
Bourdillon (R.)	BZ	8
Bryas (Bd de)	X	9
Cantrelle (R.)	ABZ	10
Château-Raoul (R. du)	AY	13
Châtre (Av. de la)	X, BZ	14
Croix-Normand (Bd)	BZ	17
Duchâteau (Av. G.)	X	18
États-Unis (R. des)	X, BY	20
Fontaine-St-Germain (R.)	X	22
Fournier (R. A.)	BY	23
Gallieni (R.)	BZ	24
Gambetta (Pl.)	BY	25
Gare (R. de la)	BY	
Gaulle (Av. du Gén.-de)	X	26
Grande (R.)	BY	27
Jeux-Marins (Av. des)	AY	29
J.-J.-Rousseau (R.)	AY	28
Kennedy (Av. J.-F.)	X, AZ	30
Ledru-Rollin (R.)	BY	31
Lemoine (Av. Marcel)	X, BY	32
Marins (Av. des)	X, AY	33
Marins (Bd des)	X	34
Mitterrand (Av. F.)	X, AY	35
Moulin-Neuf (Bd du)	X	36
Palais-de-Justice (R. du)	ABZ	37
Pont-Neuf (Av. du)	X, AY	40
République (Pl. de la)	AY	44
Ste-Hélène (Pl.)	BY	48
St-Denis (Bd)	X	45
St-Luc (R.)	BY	46
Tours (Av. de)	X	50
Valle (Bd de la)	X	51
Verdun (Av. de)	X	52
Victoire et des Alliés (Pl. de la)	AY	53
Victor-Hugo (R.)	ABY	54
3e-Rég.-Aviation-de-Chasse (R. du)	X	55
6-Juin 1944 Débarquement Allié (Av. du)	AY	58

XX **Le Lavoir de la Fonds Charles**

26 r. Château-Raoul – ✆ 02 54 27 11 16 – Fax 02 54 60 02 22 – Closed 11-24 August, 26 December-11 January, Saturday lunch, Sunday dinner and Monday AY **n**

Rest – Menu € 19 (weekdays)/48 – Carte € 51/65

◆ This neo-rustic style family restaurant is located in a former washhouse at the foot of the 18C Raoul chateau; spices feature prominently in the traditional menus; there is an attractive veranda and a terrace overlooking the river.

X **Le Sommelier**

5 pl. Gambetta – ✆ 02 54 07 45 52 – Fax 02 54 08 68 46 – Closed 27 April-12 May, 3-18 August, Monday dinner and Sunday BY **t**

Rest – Menu (€ 12) – Carte € 28/47

◆ This old house has been tastefully renovated without losing its inimitable Berry character: modern interior and rustic furniture. The cuisine is traditional.

Paris road 6 km near Céré by ① – ✉ 36130 Déols

Relais St-Jacques rm, rest,

D 920 – ✆ 02 54 60 44 44 – saint-jacques@wanadoo.fr – Fax 02 54 60 44 00

46 rm – †€ 63 ††€ 70, ☕ € 9,50 – ½ P € 55/59 – **Rest** – *(closed Sunday dinner)* Menu € 22 (weekdays)/53 – Carte € 26/76

◆ Near the Déols aerodrome to the north of the lively Berry town, a 1970s building with rooms equipped with functional furniture. The restaurant is endowed with an attractively restful atmosphere and the cuisine is traditional with a choice of local specialties.

Le Poinçonnet 6 km by ⑤ – pop. 5 021 – alt. 160 m – ✉ 36330

XXX **Le Fin Gourmet**

73 av. Forêt – ✆ 02 54 35 40 17 – franck.gatefin@wanadoo.fr – Fax 02 54 35 47 20 – Closed August, Sunday dinner, Tuesday dinner and Monday

Rest – Menu € 16 (weekday lunch), € 32/42 – Carte € 41/75

◆ This discreet building on the outskirts has an elegant contemporary interior in shades of ochre and blue, modern paintings and neat table settings. Contemporary cuisine.

CHÂTEAU-THÉBAUD – 44 Loire-Atlantique – 316 H5 – see Nantes

CHÂTEAU-THIERRY – 02 Aisne – 306 C8 – pop. 14 967 – alt. 63 m – ✉ 02400 Northern France and the Paris Region 37 C3

Paris 95 – Épernay 56 – Meaux 48 – Reims 58 – Soissons 41 – Troyes 113

Syndicat d'initiative, 9, rue Vallée ✆ 03 23 83 51 14, Fax 03 23 83 14 74

du Val Secret Le Val Secret, North: 5 km, ✆ 03 23 83 07 25.

Native house of La Fontaine A **M** - Marne Valley ★.

Ile de France

37 rte de Soissons – ✆ 03 23 69 10 12 – contact@hotel-iledefrance.fr – Fax 03 23 83 49 70 – Closed 22-28 December

34 rm – †€ 82 ††€ 92, ☕ € 12 – ½ P € 85/145 – **Rest** – *(closed Sunday dinner)* Menu € 25/54

◆ Overlooking the Marne valley, this hotel has been reborn. The revamped rooms are relaxing and comfortable. Modern fitness centre and spa. Restaurant with seasonally varying menu; pleasant panoramic terrace.

Ibis rm,

60 av. du Gén. de Gaulle, in Essômes-sur-Marne, 2 km south on D 969 – ✆ 03 23 83 10 10 – ibis@groupebachelet.com – Fax 03 23 83 45 23

55 rm – †€ 47/57 ††€ 47/57, ☕ € 7,50 – **Rest** – Menu € 17

◆ Rooms conform to the latest standards of the chain; the quietest are at the rear while others give a view of the American Côte 204 monument commemorating the battles of 1918. The restaurant and the terrace overlook a pool: traditional menu.

CHÂTEL – 74 Haute-Savoie – **328** O3 – **pop. 1 190 – alt. 1 180 m – Winter sports : 1 200/2 100 m** 2 52 – ✉ **74390** **French Alps** 46 **F1**

Paris 578 – Annecy 113 – Évian-les-Bains 34 – Morzine 38 – Thonon-les-Bains 39

Office de tourisme, Chef-Lieu ✆ 04 50 73 22 44, Fax 04 50 73 22 87

Site★ - Pas de Morgins lake★ South: 3 km.

Macchi rest, rest, VISA MC AE

94 chemin de l'Etringa – ✆ 04 50 73 24 12 – contact@hotelmacchi.com – Fax 04 50 73 27 25 – Open 20 June-20 September and 20 December-20 April

32 rm – †€ 77/212 ††€ 77/212, ☕ € 13

Rest – *(dinner only)* Menu € 23 – Carte € 37/57

Rest *Le Cerf* – *(dinner only)* Menu € 22/50 – Carte € 37/57

◆ Pleasant chalet whose finely carved balconies look over the Abondance valley. Tastefully refurbished rooms, adorned with a local artist's fresco. Raclettes and fondues in a Savoyard setting. Varied traditional menu at Le Cerf.

Fleur de Neige VISA MC AE

564 rte Vonnes – ✆ 04 50 73 20 10 – information@hotel-fleurdeneige.fr – Fax 04 50 73 24 55 – Open 21 December-4 April and 29 June-30 August

34 rm – †€ 59/88 ††€ 88/150, ☕ € 12 – ½ P € 57/110

Rest *La Grive Gourmande* – *(closed lunch and Monday winter)* Menu (€ 20), € 26/54 – Carte € 52/72

◆ Mountainside chalet. The rooms are of various sizes and have diverse furnishings. Bar with fireplace; spa. At the Grive Gourmande, comfortable, round dining room, a panoramic view over the Alps and modern cooking.

Le Kandahar rm, VISA MC

1.5 km southwest by Béchigne road – ✆ 04 50 73 30 60 – lekandahar@wanadoo.fr – Fax 04 50 73 25 17 – Closed mid April-mid May, 22 June-9 July, 2 November-19 December and Wednesday off season

8 rm – †€ 46/57 ††€ 49/84, ☕ € 8 – ½ P € 40/65 – **Rest** – *(closed Sunday dinner, Tuesday dinner and Wednesday in low season)* Menu € 13 (weekday lunch), € 19/38 – Carte € 21/47

◆ Welcoming, family-run chalet-hotel, which is rustic in style. Small, functional guestrooms with wood panelling. Shuttle buses to Le Linga. Regional cuisine served in a warm and welcoming decor. Rustic furniture, grandfather clock, gleaming coppers and fireplace.

Belalp VISA MC

– ✆ 04 50 73 24 39 – belalpchatel@aol.com – Fax 04 50 73 38 55 – Open 1st July-31 August and 20 December-31 March

26 rm – †€ 49/73 ††€ 69/94, ☕ € 9 – ½ P € 59/72 – **Rest** – *(closed Tuesday)* Menu € 20/33 – Carte € 22/45

◆ This chalet has a smart façade in light wood brightened with green shutters. The attractive bedrooms have been renovated in Alpine style; ask for one of the rooms overlooking the valley. Savoy specialities are served in front of the fireplace or in the panoramic dining room (for hotel guests).

Le Choucas without rest VISA MC

303 rte Vonnes – ✆ 04 50 73 22 57 – info@hotel-lechoucas.com – Fax 04 50 81 36 70 – Open 18 June-21 September and 17 December-20 April

12 rm – †€ 59 ††€ 59, ☕ € 7,50

◆ Entirely renovated hotel in the style of a modern chalet and with an abundantly flowered façade. Sober, alpine styled rooms, most with balcony.

Les Triolets with rm valley and mountains, rest, VISA MC AE

rte Petit Châtel – ✆ 04 50 73 20 28 – info@lestriolets.com – Fax 04 50 73 24 10 – Open 28 June-31 August and 20 December-4 April

20 rm – †€ 56/70 ††€ 84/130, ☕ € 11 – ½ P € 70/90 – **Rest** – *(dinner only)* Menu € 24

◆ Overlooking the resort in a quiet location, this attractive chalet has a south-facing, panoramic dining room. Typical dishes of the region.

Le Vieux Four VISA MC

55 rte du Boude – ✆ 04 50 73 30 56 – Fax 04 50 73 38 12 – Open 1st December-19 April, 7 June-6 September and closed Monday

Rest – Menu € 16/42 – Carte € 30/51

◆ The rustic decor of this farm (1852) is embellished by objects and figurines placed in the feeding troughs of the cowshed. Traditional and Savoyard cuisine. Large terrace.

CHÂTELAILLON-PLAGE – 17 Charente-Maritime – 324 D3 – pop. 5 625 – alt. 3 m – Casino – ✉ 17340 Atlantic Coast

38 **A2**

Paris 482 – Niort 74 – Rochefort 22 – La Rochelle 19 – Surgères 29

Office de tourisme, 5, avenue de Strasbourg ✆ 05 46 56 26 97, Fax 05 46 56 58 50

Ibis

rm, rest, VISA

à la Falaise, 1.5 km – ✆ 05 46 56 35 35 – Fax 05 46 56 33 44
70 rm – €74/114 €89/114, €10 – **Rest** – Menu (€16), €19 – Carte €18/31

◆ Away from the tourist bustle, this modern building overlooking the sea contains a thalassotherapy centre. Largish functional rooms. The restaurant and terrace face towards the Atlantic. Diet and traditional cuisine.

Majestic Hôtel

VISA

bd République – ✆ 05 46 56 20 53 – majestic.chatelaillon@wanadoo.fr – Fax 05 46 56 29 24
34 rm – €48/150 €48/150, €8 – ½ P €56/106
Rest – *(closed 2-15 January, Monday lunch and Sunday dinner except 1st June-30 September, Saturday lunch and Friday)* Menu €18/25 – Carte €37/51

◆ In the heart of the resort, an attractive 1920s façade behind which are simply furnished, very well kept rooms of varying sizes. Rattan furniture and a retro look in the dining room. Menu based on seafood.

XX Le Relais de la Bernache

VISA

1 r. Félix Faure – ✆ 05 46 56 20 19 – Closed Monday, Tuesday and Wednesday from 1st January to 15 March
Rest – Menu €25/72 – Carte €44/59

◆ Regional-style house two minutes from the beach. Classic chic interior, enhanced by exotic features (mahogany chairs and ethnic masks), terrace and traditional menu.

X L'Acadie St-Victor with rm

VISA

35 bd de la Mer – ✆ 05 46 56 25 13 – stvictor@wanadoo.fr – Fax 05 46 56 25 12 – Closed 19 October-15 November, 3-28 February, Friday dinner 20 October-31 March, Sunday dinner and Monday except 15 June-15 September
13 rm – €45/64 €45/64, €7,50 – ½ P €53/64
Rest – *(closed Sunday dinner, Monday except 15 June-15 September and Friday dinner November-March)* Menu (€15,50), €21 (weekdays), €38/41 – Carte €28/47

◆ A beautiful view of the ocean from this seaside restaurant. Contemporary and bright with the emphasis on seafood. Also has basic, practical accommodation.

X Les Flots with rm

rm, VISA

52 bd de la Mer – ✆ 05 46 56 23 42 – contact@les-flots.fr – Fax 05 46 56 99 37 – Closed 15 December-29 January
11 rm – €54/95 €54/95, €8,50 – ½ P €58/80
Rest – *(closed Tuesday from October to March)* Menu €25 – Carte €29/51

◆ Nautical decor in this pleasant bistro-style restaurant overlooking the huge beach. Simple, tasty dishes made with market fresh produce announced on a slate. Modern rooms.

CHÂTELAIS – 49 Maine-et-Loire – 317 D2 – pop. 576 – alt. 65 m – ✉ 49520

34 **B2**

Paris 326 – Nantes 93 – Angers 53 – Laval 43 – Vitré 68

Le Frêne

22 r. St-Sauveur – ✆ 02 41 61 16 45 – lefrene@free.fr – Fax 02 41 61 16 45
4 rm – €55 €55 – **Table d'hôte** – Menu €19

◆ A pleasant garden ensures the tranquillity of this 17C and 19C mansion. Paintings adorn the rooms. Watercolour courses and gallery. Meals are served in a plush dining room.

LE CHÂTELET – 18 Cher – 323 J7 – pop. 1 104 – alt. 200 m – ✉ 18170 12 C3

Paris 301 – Argenton-sur-Creuse 66 – Bourges 54 – Châteauroux 55

in Notre-Dame d'Orsan 7 km northwest by D 951 and D 65, Lignères road – ✉ 18170 Rezay

La Maison d'Orsan

– ✆ 02 48 56 27 50 – prieuredorsan@wanadoo.fr – Fax 02 48 56 39 64 – Open 21 March-11 November

6 rm – †€ 180/280 ††€ 180/280, ☕ € 18 – **Rest** – *(closed lunch Monday-Friday except May-August)* Menu € 40 (lunch)/62

♦ This 17C priory makes for a delightful stop; the refectory and dormitory have been turned into wonderful contemporary rooms; exquisite arbour and re-created monastic gardens. Dishes made with produce from the vegetable garden and the market. Shop and tea room.

CHÂTELGUYON – 63 Puy-de-Dôme – 326 F7 – pop. 5 241 – alt. 430 m – Spa : early May-late Sept. – Casino B – ✉ 63140 Auvergne 5 B2

Paris 411 – Clermont-Ferrand 21 – Gannat 31 – Vichy 43 – Volvic 11

Office de tourisme, 1, avenue de l'Europe ✆ 04 73 86 01 17, Fax 04 73 86 27 03

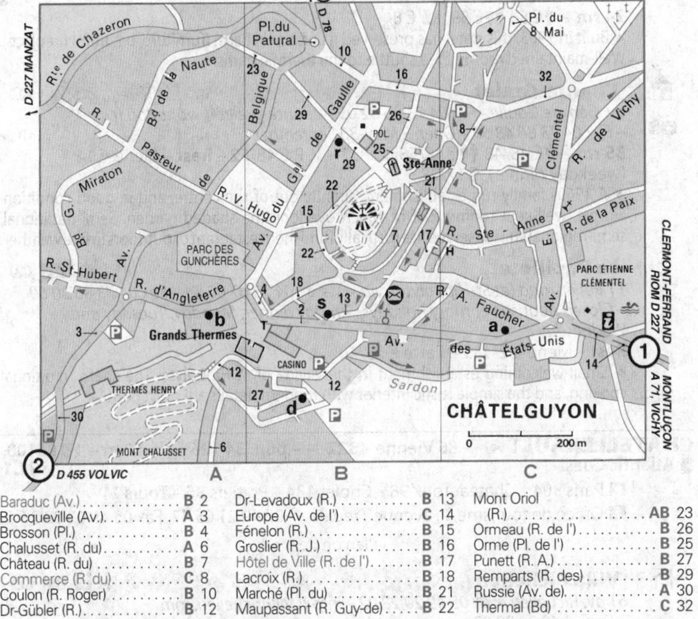

Baraduc (Av.)	B 2	Dr-Levadoux (R.)	B 13	Mont Oriol (R.)	AB 23
Brocqueville (Av.)	A 3	Europe (Av. de l')	C 14	Ormeau (R. de l')	B 26
Brosson (Pl.)	B 4	Fénelon (R.)	B 15	Orme (Pl. de l')	B 25
Chalusset (R. du)	A 6	Groslier (R. J.)	B 16	Punett (R. A.)	B 27
Château (R. du)	B 7	Hôtel de Ville (R. de l')	B 17	Remparts (R. des)	B 29
Commerce (R. du)	C 8	Lacroix (R.)	B 18	Russie (Av. de)	A 30
Coulon (R. Roger)	B 10	Marché (Pl. du)	B 21	Thermal (Bd)	C 32
Dr-Gübler (R.)	B 12	Maupassant (R. Guy-de)	B 22		

Splendid

5-7 r. Angleterre – ✆ 04 73 86 04 80 – contact@splendid-resort.com – Fax 04 73 86 17 56 – Closed 20 December-4 January, Friday dinner, Saturday, Sunday and Monday lunch 3 October-23 March A b

71 rm – †€ 57/100 ††€ 57/100, ☕ € 10 – 2 suites – ½ P € 63/84

Rest – Menu € 17 (weekdays)/37 – Carte € 39/64

♦ Guy de Maupassant regularly stayed in this old luxury hotel, built in 1872. A living room is named after him. The bedrooms, with a delightful pre-1940s atmosphere, are gradually being renovated. A majestic 19C dining area with columns and a beautiful carved wood fireplace.

Le Bellevue

4 r. A. Punett – ✆ 04 73 86 07 62 – bellevue63@wanadoo.fr – Fax 04 73 86 02 56 – Open 1st April-15 October B **d**

38 rm – ♦€ 55 ♦♦€ 75, ☕ € 12 – ½ P € 57/67 – **Rest** – *(open 1st June-20 September) (dinner only) (resident only)* Menu (€ 20), € 30 – Carte approx. € 36

♦ This 1930s hotel looks down on the small spa resort in the Brayaud countryside. The rooms, functional and fresh, are bigger to the front. A pleasant view over Châtelguyon from the restaurant. Traditional cuisine.

De Paris rest, VISA MC AE

1 r. Dr Levadoux – ✆ 04 73 86 00 12 – hotel.de.paris@wanadoo.fr – Fax 04 73 86 43 55 – Closed 10-31 October B **s**

59 rm – ♦€ 40/47 ♦♦€ 50/61, ☕ € 7,50 – ½ P € 50/55 – **Rest** – *(closed lunch from Monday to Thursday from 15 October to 15 April and Sunday dinner)* Menu € 20 (weekdays)/54 – Carte € 23/33

♦ The well dimensioned rooms are located in the main building of the establishment and in a former chapel at the rear. Sauna available. Dining area with a mixture of old and new decor. Serves traditional and regional cooking.

Régence without rest VISA MC AE

31 av. États-Unis – ✆ 04 73 86 02 60 – hotel-regence3@wanadoo.fr – Fax 04 73 86 12 49 – Closed 1st January-15 February and Wednesday from 15 October to 15 April C **a**

24 rm – ♦€ 50 ♦♦€ 59, ☕ € 8

♦ Built in 1903, this hotel has preserved its original charm (furniture, beautiful fireplace). Well-maintained rooms. Free shuttle to the thermal baths.

Chante-Grelet rest, VISA MC

av. Gén. de Gaulle – ✆ 04 73 86 02 05 – chante-grelet@wanadoo.fr – Fax 04 73 86 48 58 – Open 2 May-30 September B **r**

35 rm – ♦€ 45/48 ♦♦€ 48/55, ☕ € 7 – ½ P € 48/52 – **Rest** – Menu € 14 (weekday dinner), € 17/28

♦ A 1960s family-run establishment, slightly out of the centre, and in good condition. Simple, well-kept rooms; half of which overlook the shaded garden. Semi-traditional, semi-regional cuisine served in a rustically furnished restaurant or outdoors in fine weather.

La Papillote VISA MC

11 Volvic road (at St-Hippolyte), via ② – ✆ 04 73 67 00 64 – Fax 04 73 86 20 60 – Closed August, February holidays, Sunday dinner, Monday, Tuesday and Wednesday

Rest – Menu € 21/35 – Carte € 25/40

♦ Small welcoming establishment in the village of St Hippolyte. The chef's traditional cooking, and the simple rustic interior with modern details are most popular.

CHÂTELLERAULT – 86 Vienne – 322 J4 – pop. 34 126 – alt. 52 m – ✉ 86100

Atlantic Coast 39 **C1**

Paris 304 – Châteauroux 98 – Cholet 134 – Poitiers 36 – Tours 71

Office de tourisme, 2, avenue Treuille ✆ 05 49 21 05 47, Fax 05 49 02 03 26

Plan on next page

Villa Richelieu VISA MC

61 av. Richelieu – ✆ 05 49 20 28 02 – info@villarichelieu.com – Fax 05 49 20 28 02 AY **e**

5 rm ☕ – ♦€ 73/115 ♦♦€ 90/115 – **Table d'hôte** – *(closed weekend)* Menu € 20 bi

♦ Guest accommodation in a quiet, courtyard-facing building made of tufa, separate from the owner's house. Cosy bedrooms with lots of individual touches.

La Gourmandine VISA MC

22 av. Président Wilson – ✆ 05 49 21 05 85 – la-gourmandine@wanadoo.fr – Fax 05 49 21 05 85 – Closed 3-23 November, 2-11 January, Sunday dinner and Monday lunch AZ **x**

Rest – Menu (€ 18), € 24 (weekdays)/54 – Carte € 44/65

♦ Beautifully restored bourgeois home whose high ceilings, mouldings and original fireplace are mingled with contemporary touches and bright colours. Garden-terrace and modern menu.

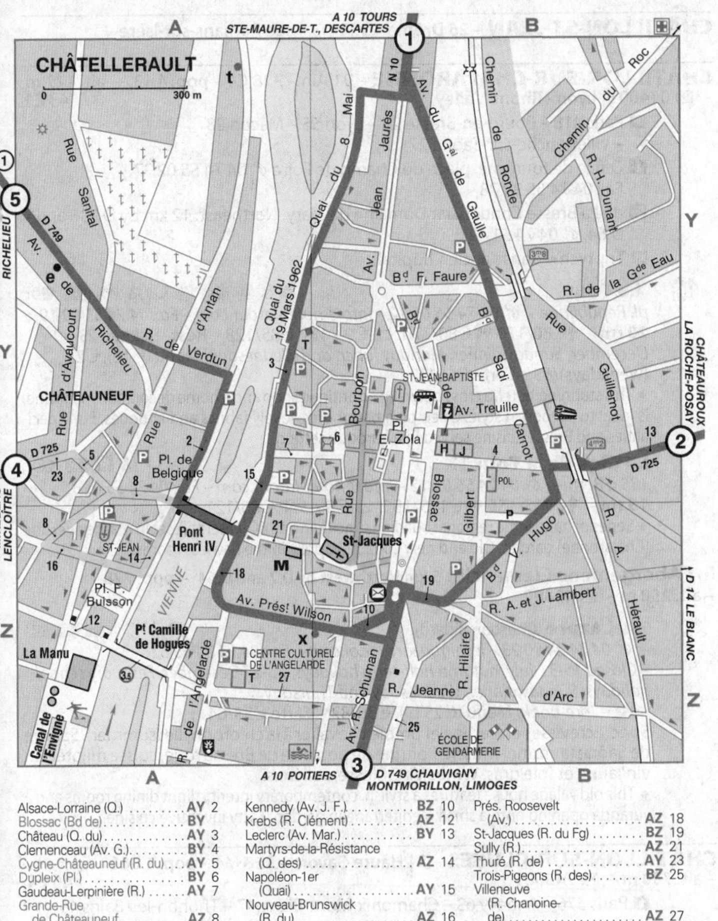

Alsace-Lorraine (Q.) . . . . **AY** 2	Kennedy (Av. J. F.) . . . . **BZ** 10	Prés. Roosevelt (Av.) . . . . **AZ** 18
Blossac (Bd de) . . . . **BY**	Krebs (R. Clément) . . . . **AZ** 12	St-Jacques (R. du Fg) . . . . **BZ** 19
Château (Q. du) . . . . **AY** 3	Leclerc (Av. Mar.) . . . . **BY** 13	Sully (R.) . . . . **AZ** 21
Clemenceau (Av. G.) . . . . **BY** 4	Martyrs-de-la-Résistance (Q. des) . . . **AZ** 14	Thuré (R. de) . . . . **AY** 23
Cygne-Châteauneuf (R. du) . . . . . **AY** 5	Napoléon-1er (Quai) . . . . **AY** 15	Trois-Pigeons (R. des) . . . . **BZ** 25
Dupleix (Pl.) . . . . **BY** 6	Nouveau-Brunswick (R. du) . . . . . . **AZ** 16	Villeneuve (R. Chanoine-de) . . . . . . **AZ** 27
Gaudeau-Lerpinière (R.) . . . . . . **AY** 7		
Grande-Rue de Châteauneuf . . . . . . **AZ** 8		

Bernard Gautier
189 r. d'Antran – ✆ 05 49 90 24 74 – Fax 05 49 90 27 85 – Closed 25 August-7 September, 15 February-7 March, Saturday, Sunday and Monday AY t

Rest – Menu (€ 17 bi), € 23/32 – Carte € 31/57

♦ The smart-rustic decor of this restaurant is reminiscent of a family inn, as is the chef's traditional hearty cuisine.

in Usseau 7 km by ⑤, D 749 and D 75 – **pop. 573** – **alt. 82 m** – ✉ **86230**

Château de la Motte
– ✆ 05 49 85 88 25 – chateau.delamotte@wanadoo.fr – Fax 05 49 85 88 25 – Open 24 March-2 November

5 rm – †€ 75/120 ††€ 75/120 – ½ P € 95/138 – **Table d'hôte** – *(closed Sunday)* Menu € 28 bi

♦ Run by a couple of history enthusiasts, this 15C castle dominating the valley. Comfort and authenticity galore, from the four-poster beds to the high ceilings. "Forgotten" vegetables from the cottage garden and produce from the orchard on the table.

CHÂTILLON-ST-JEAN – 26 Drôme – 332 D3 – see Romans-sur-Isère

CHÂTILLON-SUR-CHALARONNE – 01 Ain – 328 C4 – pop. 4 137 – alt. 177 m – ✉ 01400 Lyon - Rhone Valley 43 **E1**

Paris 418 – Bourg-en-Bresse 28 – Lyon 55 – Mâcon 28 – Villefranche-sur-Saône 27

Office de tourisme, place du Champ de Foire ☎ 04 74 55 02 27, Fax 04 74 55 34 78

de La Bresse Condeissiat Domaine de Mary, Northeast: 12 km by D 936 and D 64, ☎ 04 74 51 42 09.

Triptych★ dans l'ancien hôpital.

La Tour rest, VISA

pl. République – ☎ 04 74 55 05 12 – info@hotel-latour.com – Fax 04 74 55 09 19
20 rm – €80/170 €80/170, €9 – ½ P €85/128 – **Rest** – *(closed 23-30 December, Sunday dinner, Monday lunch and Wednesday)* Menu (€18), €23 (weekdays)/65 – Carte €60/72

◆ This stunning hotel, a cross between an antique shop and a home decoration magazine, is ideal to cocoon in style. Open plan bathrooms, lovely fabrics and antiques. Fish specialities and Bresse cuisine served in a baroque setting.

Le Clos de la Tour P VISA

135 r. Barrit – ☎ 04 74 55 05 12 – info@hotel-latour.com – Fax 04 74 55 09 19
15 rm – €115/155 €115/155, €9 – ½ P €86/121

◆ Series of handsome regional buildings, including a 16C watermill, set in a large riverside (Chalaronne) garden. Old and new cohabit happily in the flawless rooms.

in l'Abergement-Clémenciat 5 km Northwest by D 7 and D 64[c] – pop. 728 – alt. 250 m – ✉ 01400

St-Lazare (Christian Bidard) VISA AE

– ☎ 04 74 24 00 23 – lesaintlazare@aol.com – Fax 04 74 24 00 62 – Closed 15-31 July, autumn half-term holidays, 20-27 December, February school holidays, Sunday dinner, Wednesday and Thursday
Rest – *(pre-book)* Menu (€25 bi), €36/82 – Carte €53/64

Spec. Ecrevisses en verrine et omble chevalier à la chlorophylle (summer). Sandre de Saône (autumn-winter). Poitrine de poulette de Bresse rôtie, cuisse mijotée au vin jaune et foie gras. **Wines** Viré-Clessé, Juliénas.

◆ This old village house features a stylish, contemporary interior: light dining rooms and a veranda opening onto a small Mediterranean garden. Tasty inventive cuisine.

CHÂTILLON-SUR-CLUSES – 74 Haute-Savoie – 328 M4 – pop. 1 061 – alt. 730 m – ✉ 74300 46 **F1**

Paris 576 – Annecy 63 – Chamonix-Mont-Blanc 47 – Thonon-les-Bains 49

Le Bois du Seigneur P VISA AE

rte Taninges – ☎ 04 50 34 27 40 – leboisduseigneur@wanadoo.fr – Fax 04 50 34 80 20 – Closed 29 September-12 October and Sunday dinner
12 rm – €55 €55, €7 – ½ P €49 – **Rest** – *(closed 2-6 January, Tuesday lunch and Monday)* Menu (€13 bi), €16 (weekdays)/39 – Carte €37/58

◆ Savoy building overlooking a through road in a village located above Cluses. Very well kept, simple rustic style rooms. Warm welcome. Traditional fare served by the fireplace in the dining room or out on the veranda.

CHÂTILLON-SUR-INDRE – 36 Indre – 323 D5 – pop. 2 909 – alt. 115 m – ✉ 36700 11 **B3**

Paris 261 – Orléans 175 – Châteauroux 47 – Déols 51 – Le Blanc 43

Office de tourisme, boulevard du Général Leclerc ☎ 02 54 38 74 19

La Poignardière P

4 km north-east on D 975 and D 28 direction Le Tranger – ☎ 02 54 38 78 14 – maryse_lheureux@yahoo.fr – Fax 02 54 38 95 34 – Open March-November
5 rm – €70/80 €80/90 – **Table d'hôte** – Menu €25 bi

◆ 1900 style castle surrounded by a 12 ha park with 300-year-old-trees. Swimming pool, boat trips on the lake and tennis court. Bright rooms, either classic or contemporary. Traditional cuisine, fine wooden fireplace and conservatory.

CHÂTILLON-SUR-SEINE – 21 Côte-d'Or – 320 H2 – pop. 6 269 – alt. 219 m – ✉ 21400 Burgundy-Jura 8 C1

Paris 233 – Auxerre 85 – Chaumont 60 – Dijon 83 – Langres 74 – Saulieu 79 – Troyes 69

Office de tourisme, place Marmont ✆ 03 80 91 13 19, Fax 03 80 91 21 46

Source de la Douix★ - Musée★ du Châtillonnais: treasure-house of Vix★★.

in Montliot-et-Courcelles 4 km northwest by D 971 – pop. 278 – alt. 224 m – ✉ 21400

Le Magiot without rest

– *✆ 03 80 91 20 51 – lemagiot@wanadoo.fr – Fax 03 80 91 30 20*

22 rm – €40 €48, €6

◆ A new, motel style establishment. Practical rooms in the two wings enclosing the terrace-solarium. Veranda laid out as a lounge.

CHATOU – 78 Yvelines – 311 I2 – 101 13 – see Paris, Area

LA CHÂTRE – 36 Indre – 323 H7 – pop. 4 547 – alt. 210 m – ✉ 36400 Dordogne-Berry-Limousin 12 C3

Paris 298 – Bourges 69 – Châteauroux 37 – Guéret 53 – Montluçon 65

Office de tourisme, 134, rue Nationale ✆ 02 54 48 22 64, Fax 02 54 06 09 15

les Dryades Pouligny-Notre-Dame Hôtel des Dryades, South: 9 km by D 940, ✆ 02 54 06 60 67.

in St-Chartier 9 km North by D 943 and D 918 – pop. 540 – alt. 195 m – ✉ 36400

Vic: frescoes★ of the church Southwest: 2 km.

Château de la Vallée Bleue

rte Verneuil – ✆ 02 54 31 01 91 – valleebleu@aol.com – Fax 02 54 31 04 48 – Open mid March-mid November and closed Sunday dinner except June-September

14 rm – €85/140 €100/150, €12 – 1 suite – ½ P €90/115

Rest – *(closed lunch except weekends)* Menu €29/45 – Carte €38/60

◆ This beautiful 19C mansion has individually decorated rooms, while the dovecote has been converted into a pleasant duplex. The decor of this restaurant is part rustic, part conventional; menus offer fine traditional recipes and there is a highly tempting wine list.

CHÂTRES – 77 Seine-et-Marne – 312 F3 – pop. 555 – alt. 116 m – ✉ 77610 19 C2

Paris 49 – Boulogne-Billancourt 57 – Montreuil 44 – Saint-Denis 62

Le Portail Bleu

2 rte de Fontenay – ✆ 01 64 25 84 94 – leportailbleu@voila.fr – Fax 01 64 25 84 94

4 rm – €50 €60 – **Table d'hôte** – Menu €21 bi

◆ This group of old buildings has benefited from some fine restoration work; the mansard rooms are cosy with old-style furnishings.

CHAUBLANC – 71 Saône-et-Loire – 320 J8 – see St-Gervais-en-Vallière

CHAUDES-AIGUES – 15 Cantal – 330 G5 – pop. 986 – alt. 750 m – Spa: early April-late Nov. – Casino – ✉ 15110 Auvergne 5 B3

Paris 538 – Aurillac 94 – Espalion 54 – St-Chély-d'Apcher 30 – St-Flour 27

Syndicat d'initiative, 1, avenue Georges Pompidou ✆ 04 71 23 52 75, Fax 04 71 23 51 98

Beauséjour

9 av. G. Pompidou – ✆ 04 71 23 52 37 – beausejour@wanadoo.fr – Fax 04 71 23 56 89 – Open 1st April-25 November

39 rm – €45/53 €57/63, €6,50 – ½ P €48/53 – **Rest** – Menu €14/33 – Carte €25/41

◆ A stone's throw from the thermal baths, behind the white façade of this 1960s building you will find functional well-kept rooms with double-glazing. Pleasant dining areas and terrace overlooking the heated swimming pool. Regional cuisine.

in Maisonneuve 10 km southwest by D 921 – ✉ 15110 Jabrun

Moulin des Templiers with rm

– ✆ *04 71 73 81 80 – les-templiers2@wanadoo.fr – Fax 04 71 73 81 80 – Closed 10-25 October, Sunday dinner and Monday except hotel July-August*

5 rm – †€ 37/38 ††€ 37/38, ☕ € 7 – ½ P € 37/38 – **Rest** – Menu € 12,50 (weekday dinner), € 20/35 – Carte € 19/31

◆ Friendly inn by the roadside serving traditional Aubrac cooking. Pleasantly rustic dining room and a few functional rooms.

CHAUFFAILLES – 71 Saône-et-Loire – 320 G12 – pop. 4 119 – alt. 405 m – ✉ 71170 Burgundy-Jura 8 **C3**

Paris 404 – Charolles 32 – Lyon 77 – Mâcon 64 – Roanne 33

Office de tourisme, 1, rue Gambetta ✆ 03 85 26 07 06, Fax 03 85 26 03 92

in Châteauneuf 7 km West by D 8 – pop. 110 – alt. 370 m – ✉ 71740

La Fontaine

– ✆ *03 85 26 26 87 – Fax 03 85 26 26 87 – Closed 12-20 November, 5 January-6 February, Sunday dinner off season, Monday and Tuesday*

Rest – Menu € 16 bi (weekday lunch), € 20/45 – Carte € 37/46

◆ An old cloth mill covered in wisteria. The dining room is laid out like a retro-style conservatory with a fountain and decorative mosaic tiles. Local dishes.

CHAUFFAYER – 05 Hautes-Alpes – 334 E4 – pop. 334 – alt. 910 m – ✉ 05800

Paris 639 – Gap 27 – Grenoble 77 – St-Bonnet-en-Champsaur 13 40 **B1**

Château des Herbeys

2 km north by N 85 and secondary road – ✆ 04 92 55 26 83 – delas-hotel-restaurant@wanadoo.fr – Fax 04 92 55 29 66 – Open 1st April-15 November and closed Tuesday except school holidays

12 rm – †€ 65 ††€ 100/130, ☕ € 16 – ½ P € 65/85 – **Rest** – Menu € 20/38 – Carte € 36/50

◆ Deer and llamas graze in the pleasant grounds of this 13C residence. The spacious rooms have high ceilings and are enhanced by antique furnishings. The establishment lends itself ideally to banquets and open air activities. The decor here is eclectic but full of character (period furniture and bric-a-brac ornamentation).

CHAUFOUR-LÈS-BONNIÈRES – 78 Yvelines – 311 E1 – pop. 413 – alt. 157 m – ✉ 78270 18 **A1**

Paris 74 – Évreux 27 – Mantes-la-Jolie 21 – Rouen 64 – Vernon 10 – Versailles 64

Les Nymphéas without rest

RN 13 – ✆ 01 34 76 09 44 – contact@hotelnympheas.com – Fax 01 34 76 09 45

24 rm – †€ 58 ††€ 65, ☕ € 8

◆ Recent building. A hall in a rustic setting with a fireplace, and new, discreetly-decorated, well-soundproofed rooms.

Au Bon Accueil with rm

rest,

N 13 – ✆ 01 34 76 11 29 – Fax 01 34 76 00 36 – Closed 20 July-20 August, 22 December-3 January, Friday dinner, Sunday dinner and Saturday

15 rm – †€ 27 ††€ 45, ☕ € 5 – ½ P € 47 – **Rest** – Menu € 15 (weekdays)/42 – Carte € 23/46

◆ Simple location where you are guaranteed a warm welcome. Relaxed atmosphere and traditional dishes. The place also serves as a transport café.

CHAULGNES – 58 Nièvre – 319 B9 – pop. 1 262 – alt. 240 m – ✉ 58400 Burgundy-Jura

Paris 227 – Cosne-sur-Loire 40 – Dijon 201 – Nevers 21 7 **A2**

Beaumonde

Le Margat – ✆ 03 86 37 86 16 – cheryl.jj.trinquard@wanadoo.fr – Fax 03 86 37 86 16 – Open March-mid November

4 rm ☕ – †€ 60 ††€ 65 – **Table d'hôte** – Menu € 24 bi

◆ Extensive grounds surround this pink house that offers comfortable, well-furnished rooms. The most luxurious room, called Cristal, has a large corner bath and a terrace of its own. The owner hails from Australia and excels in the preparation of her own country's culinary delights.

CHAUMONT P – 52 Haute-Marne – **313** K5 – **pop. 25 996 – alt. 318 m** – ✉ **52000**
Northern France and the Paris Region 14 **C3**

Paris 264 – Épinal 128 – Langres 35 – St-Dizier 74 – Troyes 101

Office de tourisme, place du Général-de-Gaulle ✆ 03 25 03 80 80, Fax 03 25 32 00 99

Viaduct ★ - St-Jean-Baptiste basilica ★.

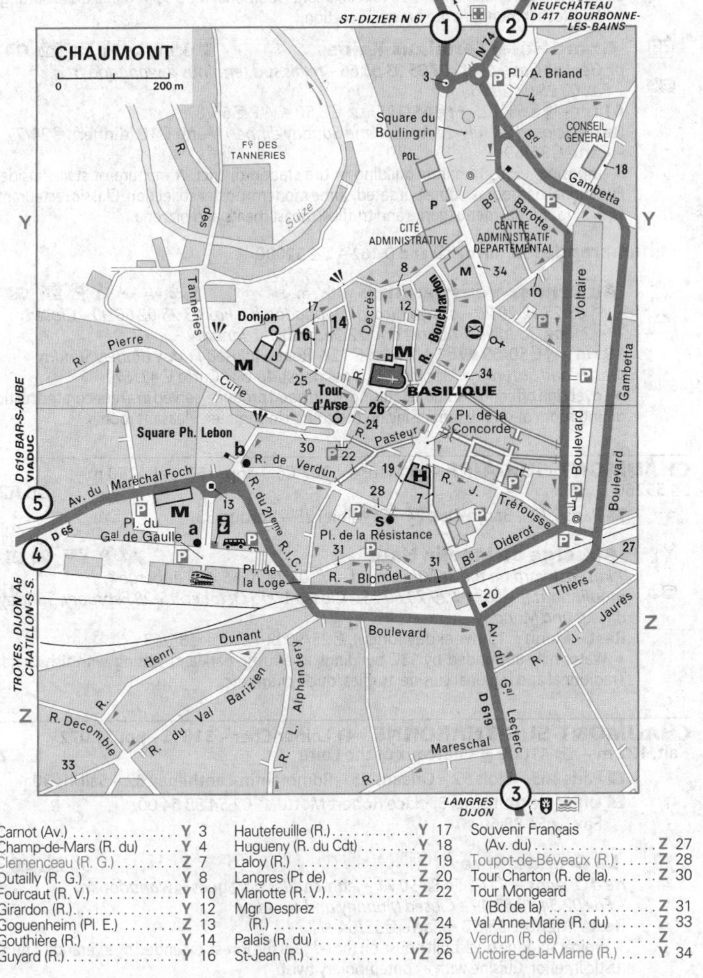

Carnot (Av.) . . . . **Y** 3
Champ-de-Mars (R. du) . . . . . **Y** 4
Clemenceau (R. G.) . . . . **Z** 7
Dutailly (R. G.) . . . . **Y** 8
Fourcaut (R. V.) . . . . **Y** 10
Girardon (R.) . . . . **Y** 12
Goguenheim (Pl. E.) . . . . **Z** 13
Gouthière (R.) . . . . **Y** 14
Guyard (R.) . . . . **Y** 16
Hautefeuille (R.) . . . . **Y** 17
Hugueny (R. du Cdt) . . . . **Y** 18
Laloy (R.) . . . . **Z** 19
Langres (Pt de) . . . . **Z** 20
Mariotte (R. V.) . . . . **Z** 22
Mgr Desprez (R.) . . . . **YZ** 24
Palais (R. du) . . . . **Y** 25
St-Jean (R.) . . . . **YZ** 26
Souvenir Français (Av. du) . . . . **Z** 27
Toupot-de-Béveaux (R.) . . . . . **Z** 28
Tour Charton (R. de la) . . . . . . **Z** 30
Tour Mongeard (Bd de la) . . . . **Z** 31
Val Anne-Marie (R. du) . . . . . . **Z** 33
Verdun (R. de) . . . . **Z**
Victoire-de-la-Marne (R.) . . . . **Y** 34

De France rm, VISA

25 r. Toupot de Béveaux – ✆ 03 25 03 01 11
– contact@hotel-france-chaumont.com – Fax 03 25 32 35 80 Z **s**
13 rm – †€ 70/95 ††€ 76/101, ☕ € 10 – 7 suites – ½ P € 72
Rest – *(closed 21 July-16 August, Sunday and public holidays) (dinner only)*
Menu € 16/36 – Carte € 29/41

◆ An inn since the 16C, this hotel offers personalised rooms with individual exotic touches. Good soundproofing and new bedding. A contemporary, welcoming makeover in the restaurant. Traditional dishes.

Les Remparts rm, VISA

72 r. Verdun – ✆ 03 25 32 64 40 – hotel.rest.des.remparts@wanadoo.fr – Fax 03 25 32 51 70 – Closed Sunday dinner from 1st November to 31 March Z **b**

17 rm – †€ 65/72 ††€ 92, ☕ € 12 – **Rest** – Menu (€ 17), € 28/49 – Carte € 33/72

◆ Family hotel near the train station offering rooms of varying sizes, renovated in stages. Small lounge and bar conducive to relaxation. Traditional food served in a quiet setting, and buffet set menus in the brasserie section.

Grand Hôtel Terminus-Reine rm, VISA

pl. Gén. de Gaulle – ✆ 03 25 03 66 66 – relais.sud.terminus@wanadoo.fr – Fax 03 25 03 28 95 Z **a**

61 rm – †€ 65/125 ††€ 65/125, ☕ € 8,50 – ½ P € 66/87

Rest – *(closed 28 July-27 August and Sunday dinner)* Menu € 16 (dinner), € 24/77 – Carte € 36/59

◆ Imposing 1950s terminus building in the station district. A mixture of styles inside. Functional bedrooms, some outdated, some modern; poster collection. Classic restaurant with a traditional menu (game and truffles). Roast meats and pizzeria.

in Chamarandes **3,5 km by ③ and D 162 – ✉ 52000**

Au Rendez-vous des Amis with rm VISA

– ✆ 03 25 32 20 20 – pascal.nicard@wanadoo.fr – Fax 03 25 02 60 90 – Closed 1st-12 May, 28 July-21 August and 22 December-2 January

19 rm – †€ 50/65 ††€ 54/73, ☕ € 12 – **Rest** – *(closed Friday dinner, Sunday dinner and Saturday)* Menu € 21 (weekdays)/48 bi – Carte € 47/67

◆ Lovely inn offering traditional cuisine using good produce, served in a redecorated rustic dining room or on the terrace facing the church in summer. Pleasant rooms.

CHAUMONT-SUR-AIRE – 55 Meuse – 307 C5 – pop. 157 – alt. 250 m – ✉ 55260 26 **A2**

Paris 270 – Bar-le-Duc 24 – St-Mihiel 25 – Verdun 33

Auberge du Moulin Haut P VISA

1 km eastward on the St-Mihiel road – ✆ 03 29 70 66 46 – auberge@moulinhaut.fr – Fax 03 29 70 60 75 – Closed 1st-15 October, 15-28 February, Sunday dinner and Monday

Rest – Menu € 15 (weekday lunch), € 25/90 bi – Carte € 35/63

◆ Watermill surrounded by 18C buildings in a rustic parkland setting with fish pond. Traditional and regional cuisine; truffles, duck, plums etc.

CHAUMONT-SUR-THARONNE – 41 Loir-et-Cher – 318 I6 – pop. 1 072 – alt. 122 m – ✉ 41600 Châteaux of the Loire 12 **C2**

Paris 165 – Blois 52 – Orléans 35 – Romorantin-Lanthenay 32 – Salbris 30

Office de tourisme, 3, place Robert Mottu ✆ 02 54 88 64 00, Fax 02 54 88 60 40

La Grenouillère P VISA

rte d'Orléans – ✆ 02 54 88 50 71 – jean-charles.dartigues@wanadoo.fr – Fax 02 54 88 53 49 – Closed Monday and Tuesday

Rest – Menu € 38/50 – Carte € 55/64

◆ Typical Sologne brick built house on the edge of the forest, extended by a veranda. Snug, rustic interior. Cuisine with a contemporary twist.

CHAUMOUSEY – 88 Vosges – 314 G3 – see Épinal

CHAUNY – 02 Aisne – 306 B5 – pop. 12 523 – alt. 50 m – ✉ 02300 37 **C2**

Paris 124 – Compiègne 46 – Laon 35 – Noyon 18 – St-Quentin 31 – Soissons 32

Syndicat d'initiative, place du Marché Couvert ✆ 03 23 52 10 79, Fax 03 23 39 38 77

Toque Blanche with rm — rest,

24 av. V. Hugo – 03 23 39 98 98 – info@toque-blanche.fr – Fax 03 23 52 32 79 – Closed 5-24 August, 1st-4 January, 21 February – 8 March, Saturday lunch, Sunday dinner and Monday

7 rm – €62/88 €72/88, €12 – **Rest** – Menu €33 (weekdays)/73 – Carte €60/78

♦ This 1920s house is surrounded by parkland. Sample tasty contemporary cooking in a recently spruced up romantic interior.

in Ognes **2 km West by Noyon road – pop. 1 120 – alt. 55 m – ✉ 02300**

L'Ardoise

26 av. Liberté – 03 23 52 15 77 – lardoise@yahoo.fr – Fax 03 23 39 91 52 – Closed 24-31 August, 1st-8 February, Sunday dinner, Monday dinner and Thursday

Rest – Carte €20/37

♦ This family-run inn serves bistro-style cuisine with the menu chalked up on a blackboard. Contemporary, monochrome decor, plus views of the kitchens. Terrace facing the garden.

in Rond-d'Orléans **8 km southeast by D 937 and D 1750 – ✉ 02300 Sinceny**

Auberge du Rond d'Orléans

– 03 23 40 20 10 – aubergedurondorleans@orange.fr – Fax 03 23 52 36 80

21 rm – €48 €55/96, €7 – ½ P €64 – **Rest** – *(Closed Sunday dinner)* Menu (€15 bi), €19/60 – Carte €38/69

♦ In the heart of the state-owned Coucy-Basse forest, a motel-style establishment with functional, well-kept rooms. Breakfast is served in a separate building. Spacious dining rooms with rustic decor, and traditional meals with regional touches.

CHAUSEY (ÎLES) – 50 Manche – 303 B6 – see Îles Chausey

LA CHAUSSÉE D'IVRY – 28 Eure-et-Loir – 311 E2 – pop. 924 – alt. 57 m – ✉ 28260 11 B1

Paris 75 – Orléans 141 – Chartres 60 – Cergy 59 – Évreux 35

Gingko without rest

Golf Parc de Nantilly – 02 37 64 01 11 – contact@hotel-gingko.com – Fax 02 37 64 32 85

20 rm – €75/160 €75/160, €8

♦ Directly overlooking the golf course, this hotel occupying an old house and its outbuildings offers guests spacious and comfortable rooms that are contemporary in style.

LA CHAUSSÉE-ST-VICTOR – 41 Loir-et-Cher – 318 F6 – see Blois

CHAUSSIN – 39 Jura – 321 C5 – pop. 1 579 – alt. 191 m – ✉ 39120 16 A2

Paris 354 – Beaune 52 – Besançon 76 – Chalon-sur-Saône 56 – Dijon 62 – Dole 21

Chez Bach

pl. Ancienne Gare – 03 84 81 80 38 – hotel-bach@wanadoo.fr – Fax 03 84 81 83 80 – Closed 22 December-6 January, Friday dinner except 14 July-31 August, Sunday dinner and Monday lunch except public holidays

22 rm – €58 €60, €11 – ½ P €68 – **Rest** – *(pre-book Sat - Sun)* Menu €18/60 – Carte €46/66

♦ In a village on the borders of the Bresse, Burgundy and the Jura. The rooms in the new building are modern and comfortable. Family hospitality. A contemporary dining area serving traditional meals and a good choice of regional wines.

Val d'Orain

34 r. S.-M. Lévy – 03 84 81 82 15 – aubergevaldorain@wanadoo.fr – Fax 03 84 81 75 24 – Closed 21-29 June, 23-31 August, 24 October-5 November, Friday dinner, Saturday lunch and Sunday dinner

10 rm – €35 €45, €6 – ½ P €42 – **Rest** – Menu €12,50 bi (weekday lunch), €17/28 – Carte €17/36

♦ An inn by the side of the main road through the village, which is on the River Orain, a tributary of the Doubs. Simple, extremely well kept rooms. Rustic dining room with a veranda, and a terrace in the courtyard. Local cuisine and Jura wines.

CHAUVIGNY – 86 Vienne – 322 J5 – pop. 7 025 – alt. 65 m – ✉ 86300
Atlantic Coast 39 **C1**

Paris 333 – Bellac 64 – Le Blanc 36 – Châtellerault 30 – Montmorillon 27 – Poitiers 26

Office de tourisme, Mairie ✆ 05 49 45 99 10, Fax 05 49 45 99 10

High town ★ - St-Pierre church ★: choir capitals★★ - Donjon de Gouzon★.

St-Savin: abbey★★ (wall paintings★★★).

Lion d'Or
rm, rest, VISA

8 r. Marché, (near the church) – ✆ 05 49 46 30 28 – Fax 05 49 47 74 28 – Closed 24 December-12 January

26 rm – €45 €45, €6,50 – ½ P €43 – **Rest** – Menu (€12), €18/39 – Carte €22/45

◆ In the lower part of town, this establishment sports a bright interior and individually decorated, comfortable and well-kept rooms. Decorative wrought iron and Art Nouveau-style chairs set the scene in this southern restaurant. Tasty classic menu.

CHAUX-NEUVE – 25 Doubs – 321 G6 – pop. 223 – alt. 992 m – ✉ 25240
16 **B3**

Paris 450 – Besançon 94 – Genève 78 – Lons-le-Saunier 68 – Pontarlier 35 – St-Claude 53

Auberge du Grand Gît
rm, VISA

– ✆ 03 81 69 25 75 – nicod@aubergedugrandgit.com – Fax 03 81 69 15 44 – Open 1st May-12 October, 20 December-29 March and closed Sunday dinner and Monday off season

8 rm – €37/42 €46/49, €8 – ½ P €47/50 – **Rest** – *(dinner only)* Menu €18/23 – Carte €24/35

◆ Find a family atmosphere and peaceful, wood panelled rooms in this recently built chalet near the ski jump area. The owner prepares appetising regional cuisine served in a pleasant country dining room.

CHAVIGNOL – 18 Cher – 323 M2 – see Sancerre

CHAVOIRES – 74 Haute-Savoie – 328 K5 – see Annecy

CHAZAY – 28 Eure-et-Loir – 311 E5 – see Chartres

CHAZEY-SUR-AIN – 01 Ain – 328 E5 – pop. 1 200 – alt. 235 m – ✉ 01150
44 **B1**

Paris 469 – Bourg-en-Bresse 45 – Chambéry 87 – Lyon 43 – Nantua 57

La Louizarde
VISA

3 km south by D 62 and secondary road – ✆ 04 74 61 53 23 – Fax 04 74 61 58 47 – Closed 1st-12 September, 23-30 December, 10-22 February, Tuesday dinner, Wednesday dinner and Thursday dinner from October to May, Saturday lunch, Sunday dinner and Monday

Rest – Menu €17 bi/41 – Carte €37/49

◆ The outline of this house recalls the architecture of Louisiana. Subtle colonial-style interior decor and attractive terrace opening onto the garden.

CHECY – 45 Loiret – 318 J4 – pop. 7 221 – alt. 112 m – ✉ 45430
12 **C2**

Paris 142 – Orléans 10 – Fleury-les-Aubrais 13 – Olivet 28 – Saint-Jean-de-Braye 6

Le Week End
VISA

1 pl. du Cloître – ✆ 02 38 86 84 93 – info@restaurant-leweekend.com – Fax 02 38 86 81 30 – Closed Sunday dinner and Monday

Rest – Menu €25 (weekdays)/65 – Carte €52/59

◆ On the main square, attractive house with comfortable and bright interior. Carefully prepared seasonal dishes and good selection of Loire wines (tastings in the cellar).

CHELLES – 60 Oise – 305 J4 – see Pierrefonds

CHÉNAS – 69 Rhône – 327 H2 – pop. 442 – alt. 253 m – ✉ 69840 43 E1

Paris 407 – Mâcon 18 – Bourg-en-Bresse 45 – Lyon 59 – Villefranche-sur-Saône 28

Les Platanes de Chénas
in Deschamps, 2 km north by D 68 – ☎ 03 85 36 79 80 – chgerber@wanadoo.fr – Fax 03 85 36 78 33 – Closed 22 December-6 January, February, dinner 15 November-15 April, Tuesday and Wednesday
Rest – Menu € 17 (weekday lunch), € 24/68 – Carte € 35/57
◆ Beams, parquet floor and a fireplace in this restaurant which was once a farmhouse. The terrace in the shade of the plane trees has a fine view of the Beaujolais region. Good wine list.

CHÊNEHUTTE-LES-TUFFEAUX – 49 Maine-et-Loire – 317 I5 – see Saumur

CHÉNÉRAILLES – 23 Creuse – 325 K4 – pop. 759 – alt. 537 m – ✉ 23130
Dordogne-Berry-Limousin 25 C1

Paris 369 – Aubusson 19 – La Châtre 63 – Guéret 32 – Montluçon 46
Syndicat d'initiative, 32, route de gouzon ☎ 05 55 62 91 22
High relief★ in the church.

Coq d'Or
7 pl. du Champ de Foire – ☎ 05 55 62 30 83 – Fax 05 55 62 95 18 – Closed 21 June-2 July, 20 September-2 October, 31 December-20 January, Sunday dinner, Wednesday dinner and Monday
Rest – Menu (€ 14), € 21/45 – Carte € 32/45
◆ The window at the entrance to this restaurant displays cockerels brought back from around the world by customers. Tasty contemporary cuisine.

in Montignat 10 km Northwest by D 990 and D 50 – ✉ 23140

La Maison Bleue
3 km by N 145 – ☎ 05 55 81 88 80 – lamaisonbleue2002@yahoo.fr – Fax 05 55 81 86 69 – Closed 10-21 March
4 rm – €50 €70/80 – **Table d'hôte** – Menu € 25 bi
◆ This old farmhouse has been superbly restored and offers delightfully original rooms decorated with objects from all over the world. One is even in an old gypsy caravan! 100% local cuisine, served by the open fireplace or on the spacious terrace.

CHENNEVIÈRES-SUR-MARNE – 94 Val-de-Marne – 312 E3 – 101 28 – see Paris, Area

CHENONCEAUX – 37 Indre-et-Loire – 317 P5 – pop. 325 – alt. 62 m – ✉ 37150
Châteaux of the Loire 11 A1

Paris 234 – Amboise 12 – Château-Renault 36 – Loches 31 – Montrichard 8 – Tours 33
Syndicat d'initiative, 1, rue Bretonneau ☎ 02 47 23 94 45, Fax 02 47 23 82 41
Château of Chenonceau★★★.

Auberge du Bon Laboureur (Antoine Jeudi) rm,
6 r. Dr Bretonneau – ☎ 02 47 23 90 02 – laboureur@wanadoo.fr – Fax 02 47 23 82 01 – Closed 11 November-19 December, 4 January-14 February and Tuesday lunch
22 rm – €95/155 €115/155, € 13 – 4 suites
Rest – Menu € 30 (weekday lunch), € 48/85 – Carte € 67/98
Spec. Crème onctueuse d'écrevisses et concassé de tomate (June to September). Conjugaison de ris et tête de veau sauce gribiche. Dessert autour de la figue (September to March). **Wines** Montlouis, Bourgueil.
◆ A group of charming houses, near the famous Château des Dames offering attractive, peaceful, renovated rooms which are all different. Park with a vegetable garden. Elegant, comfortable dining rooms and attractive, shady terrace on the edge of the garden. Traditional fare.

La Roseraie rm, VISA

7 r. Dr. Bretonneau – ☎ 02 47 23 90 09 – sfiorito@wanadoo.fr – Fax 02 47 23 91 59 – Open 15 March-12 November

17 rm – †€ 52/55 ††€ 62/67, ☕ € 11,50 – **Rest** – *(closed Monday and lunch except Sunday and public holidays)* Menu € 25/43 – Carte € 33/50

♦ A long building covered in Virginia creeper with spacious, air-conditioned guestrooms. Rustic decor and a welcoming feel. Garden and swimming pool. A country restaurant with a lounge with open fire and an emphasis on traditional cuisine.

CHENÔVE – 21 Côte-d'Or – 320 K6 – see Dijon

CHÉPY – 80 Somme – 301 C7 – pop. 1 277 – alt. 96 m – ✉ 80210 — 36 **A1**

Paris 207 – Abbeville 17 – Amiens 72 – Le Tréport 23

L'Auberge Picarde — rm, VISA

at the station – ☎ 03 22 26 20 78 – auberge-picarde@wanadoo.fr – Fax 03 22 26 33 34 – Closed 2 weeks in August and 1st-10 January

25 rm – †€ 46/63 ††€ 51/68, ☕ € 6,50 – ½ P € 60 – **Rest** – *(closed Saturday lunch and Sunday dinner)* Menu € 15 (weekdays)/39 – Carte € 23/37

♦ The comfortable rooms in old or modern style are located opposite a disused station, in a rural environment. Billiards. A covered gallery converted into a winter garden leads to the rustic style restaurant. "Tradition et terroir" offerings on the menu.

CHÉRAC – 17 Charente-Maritime – 324 H5 – pop. 1 006 – alt. 54 m – ✉ 17610

Paris 495 – Angoulême 59 – Poitiers 162 – Saintes 19 — 38 **B3**

La Pantoufle

5 imp. des Dîmiers – ☎ 05 46 95 37 10 – lapantoufle@free.fr

3 rm ☕ – †€ 45 ††€ 50 – **Table d'hôte** – Menu € 20 bi

♦ This typical Charente guesthouse with its comfortable rooms and pleasant lounge area with sofas and deckchairs in the enclosed garden constitutes a standing invitation to restful indolence. In the restaurant, the owner, an authentic cordon bleu cook, invariably delights her guests with culinary pleasures based on garden-fresh vegetables and local products.

CHERBOURG-OCTEVILLE – 50 Manche – 303 C2 – pop. 25 370 – Built-up area 117 855 – alt. 10 m – Casino BY – ✉ 50100 Normandy — 32 **A1**

Paris 359 – Brest 399 – Caen 125 – Laval 224 – Le Mans 284 – Rennes 210

Cherbourg-Maupertus: ☎ 02 33 88 57 60, by ①: 13 km.

Office de tourisme, 2 quai Alexandre III ☎ 02 33 93 52 02, Fax 02 33 53 66 97

de Cherbourg La Glacerie Domaine des Roches, by Valognes road and D 122: 7 km, ☎ 02 33 44 45 48.

Fort du Roule ←★ - Château de Tourlaville: park★ 5 km by ①.

Plan on next page

Le Louvre without rest — VISA

2 r. H. Dunant – ☎ 02 33 53 02 28 – inter.hotel.le.louvre@wanadoo.fr – Fax 02 33 53 43 88 – Closed 24 December-4 January — AX **e**

42 rm – †€ 52/58 ††€ 58/63, ☕ € 8

♦ A central location, comfortable rooms, good soundproofing and a buffet breakfast are among the attractions of this family hotel.

La Renaissance without rest — VISA

4 r. de l'Église – ☎ 02 33 43 23 90 – contact@hotel-renaissance-cherbourg.com – Fax 02 33 43 96 10 — ABX **a**

12 rm – †€ 46/60 ††€ 52/66, ☕ € 8 – 1 suite

♦ Cheerful, faultlessly kept rooms, smiling service, delicious breakfasts and reasonable prices.

Ambassadeur without rest — VISA

22 quai Caligny – ☎ 02 33 43 10 00 – ambassadeur.hotel@wanadoo.fr – Fax 02 33 43 10 01 – Closed 19 December-4 January — BX **v**

40 rm – †€ 36/53 ††€ 47/63, ☕ € 6

♦ This quayside hotel provides well-equipped rooms. Those at the front overlook the port.

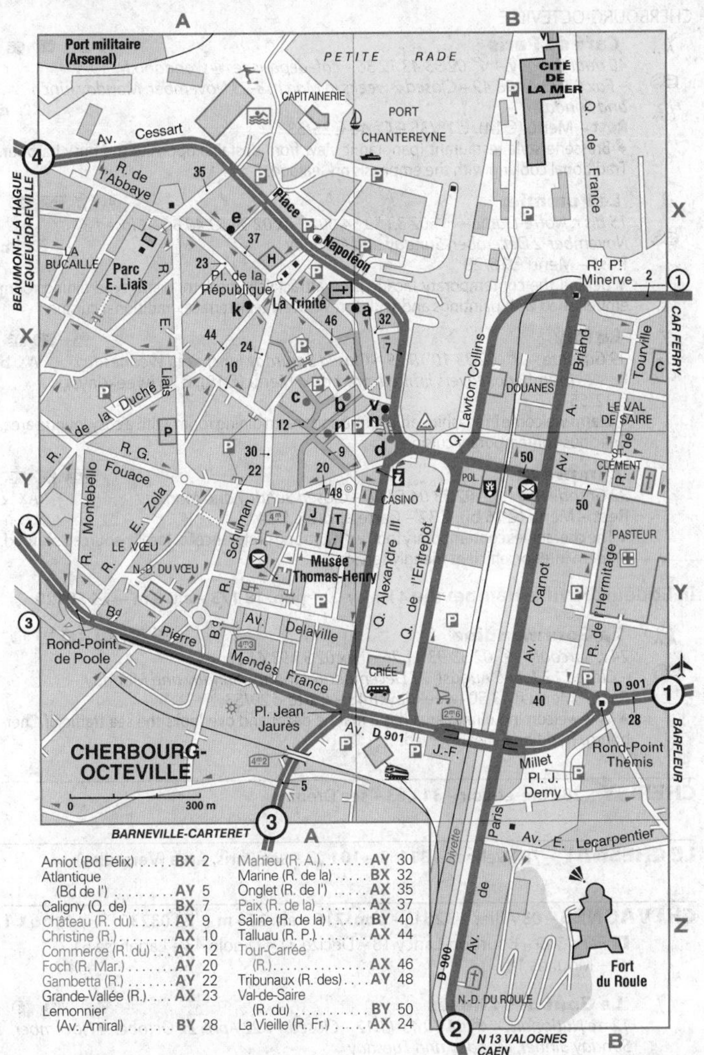

Amiot (Bd Félix) . . . . . BX 2
Atlantique (Bd de l') . . . . AY 5
Caligny (Q. de) . . . . . . BX 7
Château (R. du) . . . . . . AY 9
Christine (R.) . . . . AX 10
Commerce (R. du) . . . AX 12
Foch (R. Mar.) . . . . AY 20
Gambetta (R.) . . . . AY 22
Grande-Vallée (R.) . . . . AX 23
Lemonnier (Av. Amiral) . . . . BY 28
Mahieu (R. A.) . . . . AY 30
Marine (R. de la) . . . . . BX 32
Onglet (R. de l') . . . . . AX 35
Paix (R. de la) . . . . AX 37
Saline (R. de la) . . . . . . BY 40
Talluau (R. P.) . . . . AX 44
Tour-Carrée (R.) . . . . AX 46
Tribunaux (R. des) . . . . AY 48
Val-de-Saire (R. du) . . . . BY 50
La Vieille (R. Fr.) . . . . . AX 24

Angleterre without rest

8 r. P. Talluau – ✆ 02 33 53 70 06 – contact@hotelangleterre-fr.com – Fax 02 33 53 74 36 AX **k**

23 rm – †€ 35/45 ††€ 40/50, ☕ € 6

◆ Near the town centre, a pleasant hotel with a family atmosphere and practical, neat little rooms. Entirely non-smoking.

Le Vauban

22 quai Caligny – ✆ 02 33 43 10 11 – Fax 02 33 43 15 18 – Closed autumn half-term holidays, February school holidays, Saturday lunch, Sunday dinner and Monday

Rest – Menu € 22 (weekdays)/59 – Carte € 44/55 BX **n**

◆ Contemporary restaurant painted in light colours, pleasantly overlooking the quaysides of the harbour. View of the kitchen from the dining room; seafood menu.

XX **Café de Paris** AC VISA MC AE

40 quai Caligny – ☎ 02 33 43 12 36 – cafedeparis.res@wanadoo.fr – Fax 02 33 43 98 49 – Closed 2 weeks in March, 3-23 November, Monday lunch and Sunday BXY **d**

Rest – Menu (€ 14), € 18/35 – Carte € 25/53

♦ Brasserie-style restaurant (panoramic view from upstairs) opposite the busy harbour. Traditional cooking with the emphasis on seafood.

X **Le Pommier** AC VISA MC

15 bis r. Notre-Dame – ☎ 02 33 53 54 60 – Fax 02 33 53 40 86 – Closed 8 November-2 December, Sunday and Monday AXY **n**

Rest – Menu € 16/28

♦ Behind the contemporary façade is an attractively modern, bistro-type dining room embellished with paintings and sculptures. Lovely teak terrace; traditional cuisine.

X **Le Pily** VISA MC AE

39 Gde Rue – ☎ 02 33 10 19 29 – Closed Saturday lunch and Wednesday AX **b**

Rest – *(number of covers limited, pre-book)* Menu (€ 15), € 28 (weekdays), € 32/55

♦ Warm welcome in a fashionable prune and cream dining room, with a cosy lounge area. Delicious contemporary cuisine.

X **L'Imprévu** VISA MC AE

32 Grande Rue – ☎ 02 33 04 53 90 – Closed Sunday and Monday AX **c**

Rest – Menu (€ 16 bi), € 32 – Carte approx. € 34

♦ The chef serves contemporary food with a strong preference for locally-sourced seafood. Modern interior, efficient friendly service.

in Equeurdreville-Hainneville 4 km by ④ – pop. 18 173 – alt. 8 m – ✉ 50120

XX **La Gourmandine** AC VISA MC AE

24 r. Surcouf – ☎ 02 33 93 41 26 – Fax 02 33 93 41 26 – Closed 12 July-5 August, 21 December-6 January, Sunday and Monday

Rest – Menu € 13,50 (weekdays)/48 – Carte € 29/53

♦ This welcoming dining area has a marine decor and overlooks the sea traffic of Cherbourg. Traditional meals served.

CHERISY – 28 Eure-et-Loir – 311 E3 – see Dreux

LE CHESNAY – 78 Yvelines – 311 I3 – 101 23 – see Paris, Area (Versailles)

CHEVAGNES – 03 Allier – 326 I3 – pop. 716 – alt. 224 m – ✉ 03230 6 C1

Paris 309 – Bourbon-Lancy 18 – Decize 31 – Digoin 43 – Lapalisse 51 – Moulins 18

XX **Le Goût des Choses** VISA MC

12 rte Nationale – ☎ 04 70 43 11 12 – Closed 14-22 April, 27 October-4 November, Sunday dinner, Monday and Tuesday

Rest – Menu € 22/48 – Carte € 35/59

♦ Here, good taste is shown both by the food, prepared with seasonal market produce, and the dining room with its attractive decor and well-laid tables. Small inner courtyard terrace.

CHEVAL-BLANC – 84 Vaucluse – 332 D11 – see Cavaillon

CHEVANNES – 89 Yonne – 319 D5 – see Auxerre

CHEVERNY – 41 Loir-et-Cher – 318 F7 – see Cour-Cheverny

CHEVIGNY – 21 Côte-d'Or – 320 K6 – see Dijon

LE CHEYLARD – 07 Ardèche – 331 I4 – pop. 3 514 – alt. 450 m – ✉ 07160 44 **A3**

Paris 598 – Aubenas 50 – Lamastre 21 – Privas 47 – Le Puy-en-Velay 62 – Valence 59

Office de tourisme, rue du 5 Juillet 44 ☎ 04 75 29 18 71, Fax 04 75 29 46 75

Le Provençal rest, rm, VISA MC

17 av. de la Gare – ☎ 04 75 29 02 08 – contact@hotelrestaurantleprovencal.com – Fax 04 75 29 35 63 – Closed 28 March-16 April, 26 September-15 October, 26 December-14 January, Friday dinner, Sunday dinner and Monday

10 rm – †€ 46 ††€ 62, ☕ € 8,50 – **Rest** – Menu (€ 16), € 22/51 bi

◆ A stone building housing small, simple, well-kept rooms. The bicycle shed is popular with cyclists biking along the corniche road above the Eyrieux. Sober, rustic dining rooms, traditional cuisine inspired by local produce and a selection of local wines.

CHÉZERY-FORENS – 01 Ain – 328 I3 – pop. 369 – alt. 585 m – ✉ 01200 45 **C1**

Paris 506 – Bellegarde-sur-Valserine 17 – Bourg-en-Bresse 82 – Gex 39 – Nantua 30

Commerce with rm VISA MC

– ☎ 04 50 56 90 67 – Fax 04 50 56 92 54 – Open 7 February-28 September and closed 21-29 April, 9 June-6 July, Tuesday dinner and Wednesday except school holidays

8 rm – †€ 50/60 ††€ 50/60, ☕ € 7,50 – ½ P € 46/50 – **Rest** – Menu € 15/39 – Carte € 19/42

◆ An endearing establishment serving generous regional cuisine in a smart country decor or out on the terrace overlooking the fast-flowing Valserine. Small, well-kept rooms and warm hospitality.

CHILLE – 39 Jura – 321 D6 – see Lons-le-Saunier

CHILLEURS-AUX-BOIS – 45 Loiret – 318 J3 – pop. 1 703 – alt. 125 m – ✉ 45170 12 **C2**

Paris 96 – Orléans 30 – Chartres 71 – Étampes 47 – Pithiviers 14

Lancelot VISA MC AE

12 r. des Déportés – ☎ 02 38 32 91 15 – info@restaurant-le-lancelot.com – Fax 02 38 32 92 11 – Closed 4-24 August, 23 February-8 March, Wednesday dinner, Sunday dinner and Monday

Rest – *(pre-book Sat - Sun)* Menu (€ 14), € 20 (weekdays), € 29/65 – Carte € 48/82

◆ Welcoming flower-decked, countrified restaurant in a rustic house situated in the centre of the village. Generous updated cuisine often inspired by old family recipes.

CHINAILLON – 74 Haute-Savoie – 328 L5 – see le Grand-Bornand

CHINDRIEUX – 73 Savoie – 333 I3 – pop. 1 092 – alt. 300 m – ✉ 73310 45 **C1**

Paris 520 – Aix-les-Bains 16 – Annecy 48 – Bellegarde-sur-Valserine 39 – Chambéry 33

Abbaye de Hautecombe★★ Southwest: 10 km, **G. French Alps.**

Relais de Chautagne rm, VISA MC

– ☎ 04 79 54 20 27 – Fax 04 79 54 51 63 – Closed 24 Dec.-10 Feb., Sunday dinner and Monday

25 rm – †€ 45/48 ††€ 45/50, ☕ € 9 – **Rest** – Menu € 15 (weekdays), € 22/35 – Carte € 25/57

◆ La Chautagne is the name of this small part of Savoy through which the Rhône flows. Modern or older-style rooms, all well-maintained. Dining rooms in a neo-rustic style serving traditional cuisine, Savoyard specialities and game in season.

CHINON – 37 Indre-et-Loire – 317 K6 – pop. 8 716 – alt. 40 m – ✉ 37500

Châteaux of the Loire 11 **A3**

Paris 285 – Châtellerault 51 – Poitiers 80 – Saumur 29 – Tours 46

Office de tourisme, place Hofheim ✆ 02 47 93 17 85, Fax 02 47 93 93 05

Old Chinon★★: Grand Carroi★★ A **E** - Château★★: ≤★★.

Château d'Ussé★★ 14 km by ①.

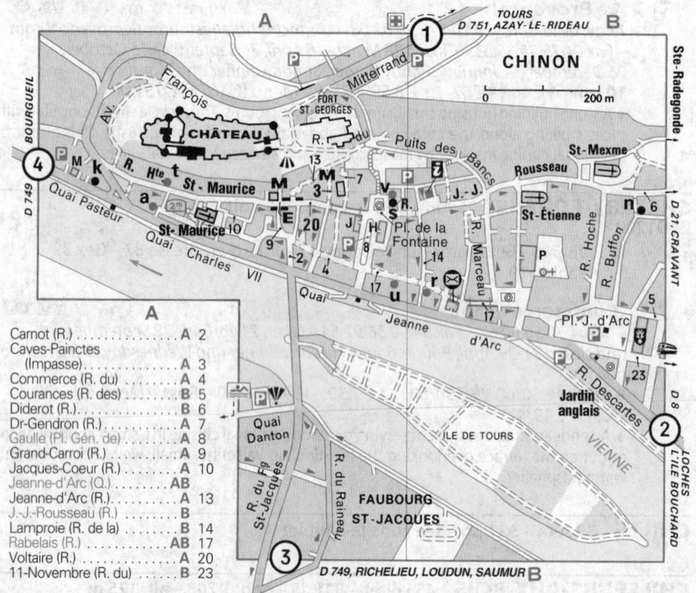

De France without rest

47 pl. Gén. de Gaulle – ✆ 02 47 93 33 91 – elmachinon@aol.com – Fax 02 47 98 37 03 – Closed 16 February-10 March, 8-28 November, Sunday dinner and Monday from November to March A **s**

30 rm – €72/80 €80/140, ☕ €10 – 3 suites

◆ Two semi-detached 16C houses with comfortable, well soundproofed, period furnished rooms. Some overlook the square and the castle. Pretty inner courtyard.

Diderot without rest

4 r. de Buffon – ✆ 02 47 93 18 87 – hoteldiderot@hoteldiderot.com – Fax 02 47 93 37 10

26 rm – €43/53 €53/75, ☕ €8 B **n**

◆ A fine 18C abode providing regularly spruced up rooms furnished in an old-fashioned manner. Table d'hôte style breakfast: farm produce and home-made jam.

Agnès Sorel without rest

4 q. Pasteur – ✆ 02 47 93 04 37 – info@agnes-sorel.com – Fax 02 47 93 06 37

10 rm – €47/98 €47/98, ☕ €9 A **k**

◆ Set in the shadow of the medieval castle, this charming hotel bordering the Vienne has individually decorated rooms. The ones in the wing are larger and quieter. Courtyard garden. Bicycle shed.

Au Plaisir Gourmand (Jean-Claude Rigollet)

quai Charles VII – ✆ 02 47 93 20 48 – Fax 02 47 93 05 66 – Closed 15 February-15 March, Sunday dinner, Monday and Tuesday A **a**

Rest – *(number of covers limited, pre-book)* Menu €28/64 – Carte €46/77

Spec. Salade de langoustines aux épices. Sandre au beurre blanc. Gratin de framboises aux amandes (May to September). **Wines** Vouvray, Chinon.

◆ This stylish and restrained 16-17C house is reached through a lovely flower-decked courtyard. Fine classic cuisine.

Au Chapeau Rouge

49 pl. du Gén. de Gaulle – ✆ 02 47 98 08 08 – chapeau.rouge@club-internet.fr – Fax 02 47 98 08 08 – Closed 26 October-18 November, 16 February-10 March, Sunday dinner and Monday A **v**

Rest – Menu € 21 (weekday lunch), € 26/56 – Carte € 39/82

◆ A stylish dining room opening onto a shaded square. Appetising dishes with a contemporary touch that vary with the seasons (truffles in winter).

L'Océanic

13 r. Rabelais – ✆ 02 47 93 44 55 – oceanic.restaurant@club-internet.fr – Fax 02 47 93 38 08 – Closed 24 March-6 April, 25-31 August, Sunday dinner and Monday A **u**

Rest – Menu € 16 bi (weekday lunch), € 24/68 bi – Carte € 35/79

◆ Friendly seafood restaurant in a pedestrian street in the town centre. A lobster tank sits imposingly in the middle of the comfortable modern dining room.

Les Années Trente

78 r. Voltaire – ✆ 02 47 93 37 18 – lebeaucharles@wanadoo.fr – Fax 02 47 93 33 72 – Closed 21-29 June, 26 November-9 December, 2-12 January, Tuesday Easter-1st November and Wednesday A **t**

Rest – Menu € 27/40 – Carte € 37/54

◆ In this restaurant in old Chinon, knick-knacks, small paintings and photos from the 1930s decorate the dining rooms. Contemporary repertory using fresh produce.

in Marçay 9 km by ③ and D 116 – pop. 448 – alt. 65 m – ✉ 37500

Château de Marçay

– *✆ 02 47 93 03 47 – marcay@relaischateaux.fr – Fax 02 47 93 45 33 – Closed 16-28 November and 6 January-1st March*

33 rm – €130 €285, ☕ €21 – 4 suites

Rest – *(closed Monday lunch, Wednesday lunch and Tuesday)* Menu € 58/115 – Carte € 86/108

Spec. (15 April-15 October) Petits légumes du "jardin de la France" cuits et crus. Petit bar de ligne cuit au plat. Agneau du Poitou-Charente, sa noisette laquée et épaule confite. **Wines** Vouvray, Chinon.

◆ This chateau remodelled in the 15C is all that remains of the original 12C military fortress. Wooded parkland with views over the vineyards creates a charming setting (wine tasting). Elegant decor, fine cuisine with a contemporary touch, and a selection of Loire wines.

CHIROUBLES – 69 Rhône – pop. 349 – alt. 430 m – ✉ 69115 43 E1

Paris 422 – Lyon 59 – Villeurbanne 67 – Bourg-en-Bresse 60 – Caluire-et-Cuire 63

La Tour

1 km away, Bridge (Fleurie road) – ✆ 04 74 04 20 26 – mfjp.bernard@free.fr

4 rm ☕ – €70 €80 – **Table d'hôte** – Menu € 25 bi

◆ Comfortable accommodation in a building full of character. The guestrooms are themed: Romantic and Floral (in the tower), Retro and Pastoral (in the main building). Views of the vineyards.

CHISSAY-EN-TOURAINE – 41 Loir-et-Cher – 318 D7 – see Montrichard

---

CHISSEAUX – 37 Indre-et-Loire – 317 P5 – pop. 575 – alt. 58 m – ✉ 37150 11 A1

Paris 235 – Tours 37 – Amboise 14 – Loches 33 – Romorantin-Lanthenay 63

Auberge du Cheval Rouge

30 r. Nationale – ✆ 02 47 23 86 67 – Fax 02 47 23 92 22 – Closed 2-10 June, 10-26 November, Sunday dinner from October to May, Monday and Tuesday

Rest – Menu € 20 (weekday lunch), € 26/50 – Carte € 42/58

◆ The former village café now houses a stylish restaurant (non-smoking) whose rustic setting is brightened up by Provençal shades. Charming leafy terrace.

CHITENAY – 41 Loir-et-Cher – 318 F7 – pop. 989 – alt. 90 m – ✉ 41120 11 A1

Paris 196 – Orléans 72 – Blois 15 – Romorantin-Lanthenay 39 – Vendôme 47

Auberge du Centre

pl. de l'Église – ☎ 02 54 70 42 11 – aub-centre@wanadoo.fr – Fax 02 54 70 35 03 – Closed 26 January-5 March

26 rm – †€ 55/82 ††€ 62/92, ☐ € 9,50 – ½ P € 60/79 – **Rest** – *(closed Sunday dinner off season, Tuesday lunch and Monday)* Menu € 23 (weekdays), € 29/47 – Carte € 34/44

◆ Village inn covered in Virginia creeper near the chateaux of the Loire. Plain, modern bedrooms. Bright, Provencal style restaurant offering a traditional menu. Small garden to the rear.

CHOISY-AU-BAC – 60 Oise – 305 I4 – see Compiègne

CHOLET – 49 Maine-et-Loire – 317 D6 – pop. 54 204 – alt. 91 m – ✉ 49300

Châteaux of the Loire 34 B2

Paris 353 – Ancenis 49 – Angers 64 – Nantes 60 – La Roche-sur-Yon 70

Office de tourisme, 14, avenue Maudet ☎ 02 41 49 80 00, Fax 02 41 49 80 09

de Cholet Allée du Chêne Landry, ☎ 02 41 71 05 01.

Musée d'Art et d'Histoire★ Z M.

Plan on next page

All Seasons

rest,

45 av. d'Angers – ☎ 02 41 71 08 08 – Fax 02 41 71 96 96 BX t

57 rm ☐ – †€ 98/108 ††€ 106/116 – **Rest** – *(closed Saturday and Sunday)* Carte € 27/40

◆ Once inside, you will forget the business zone next door. Find a warm interior in which old wood (from Canadian cabins) features prominently; modern, comfortable, well soundproofed rooms. Pleasant room topped with a glass roof, contemporary interior and classic menu.

Du Parc without rest

4 av. A. Manceau – ☎ 02 41 62 65 45 – hotel.parc.cholet@wanadoo.fr – Fax 02 41 58 64 08 – Closed 21 December-6 January and public holidays AY x

46 rm – †€ 57/58 ††€ 57/58, ☐ € 8

◆ This practical hotel is near Cholet Ice Rink. Pleasant, functional and well-soundproofed rooms. Large conference rooms. Buffet breakfast.

Demeure l'Impériale without rest

28 r. Nationale – ☎ 02 41 58 84 84 – demeure.imperiale@wanadoo.fr – Fax 02 41 63 17 03 Z t

4 rm ☐ – †€ 65/69 ††€ 69/176

◆ This 1860 mansion extends a warm welcome. Bright rooms adorned with flowers, luxurious linen and parquet floors. Breakfasts beneath a glass roof: homemade jams and cakes.

La Grange

64 r. de Saint-Antoine – ☎ 02 41 62 09 83 – Fax 02 41 62 32 89 – Closed 28 July-20 August, 9-24 February, Wednesday dinner, Sunday dinner and Monday

Rest – Menu € 18 (weekday lunch), € 27/40 – Carte € 38/43 AY g

◆ Rural objects, exposed beams and a fireplace testify to the past history of the farmhouse where you can now enjoy carefully-prepared food with a contemporary touch at a reasonable price.

La Touchetière

41 bd. Roux – ☎ 02 41 62 55 03 – latouchetiere@orange.fr – Fax 02 41 58 82 10 – Closed 28 July-19 August, Saturday lunch, Sunday dinner and Monday dinner

Rest – Menu (€ 18), € 21/36 – Carte € 39/48 AX b

◆ This inn, said to date from the 16C, has retained its rustic character. Dining room with exposed beams and a fine fireplace. Flower-decked summer terrace.

Au Passé Simple

181 r. Nationale – ☎ 02 41 75 90 06 – aupassesimple2@wanadoo.fr – Fax 02 41 75 90 06 – Closed 11-31 August, 22 December-4 January, Sunday dinner, Tuesday lunch and Monday Z v

Rest – Menu (€ 15 bi), € 18 bi (weekday lunch), € 33/68 bi – Carte € 47/51

◆ The chef skilfully prepares inventive, seasonal cuisine. Decor pleasantly combining old and new. Fine choice of regional wines.

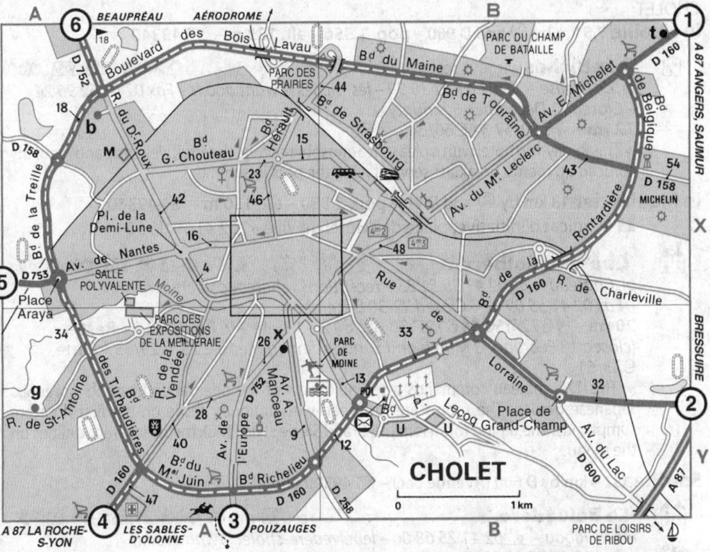

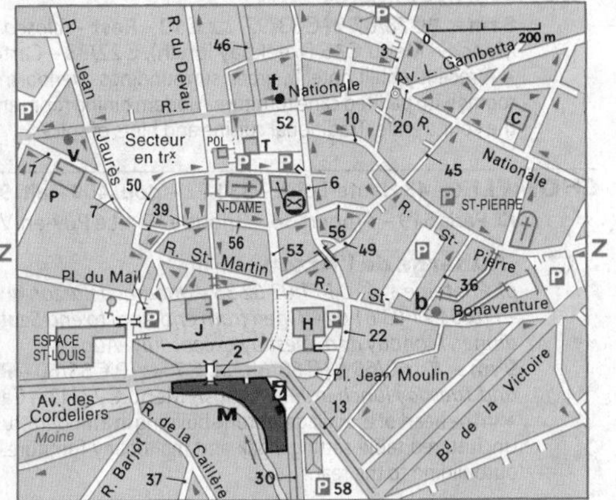

L'Ourdissoir VISA MC AE

40 r. St-Bonaventure – ✆ 02 41 58 55 18 – ourdissoir@wanadoo.fr – Fax 02 41 58 55 18 – Closed 26 July-14 August, 15-22 February, Sunday dinner, Monday dinner and Wednesday Z **b**

Rest – Menu € 18 (weekday lunch), € 22/45 bi – Carte approx. € 39

◆ In a town famous for its handkerchiefs are these two stone walled rustic dining rooms – one of which was a weaver's workshop. Generous updated cuisine, local dishes available. Reasonable prices.

in Nuaillé 7,5 km by ① and D 960 – pop. 1 356 – alt. 133 m – ✉ 49340

Les Biches without rest
pl. de l'Eglise – ✆ 02 41 62 38 99 – les-biches@wanadoo.fr – Fax 02 41 62 96 24 – Closed 21 December-6 January
12 rm – †€ 52/57 ††€ 60/64, ☕ € 8
◆ This family-run hotel with a pleasant atmosphere offers cheerful, well kept, and regularly spruced up rooms. Breakfast served facing the pool in summer.

in Maulévrier 13 km by ② and D 20 – pop. 2 830 – alt. 130 m – ✉ 49360
Syndicat d'initiative, place de l'Hôtel de Ville ✆ 02 41 55 06 50

Château Colbert
pl. Château – ✆ 02 41 55 51 33 – reception@chateaucolbert.com – Fax 02 41 55 09 02 – Closed 22-30 December
20 rm – †€ 72/150 ††€ 72/150, ☕ € 12 – 1 suite – ½ P € 77/116 – **Rest** – *(closed 18 February-3 March and Sunday dinner)* Menu € 25, € 29/65 – Carte € 53/61
◆ This 17C château commands a splendid view of the oriental park and its gorgeous Japanese garden. The rooms are furnished with antiques; those on the first floor are sumptuous. The dining room is in the Grand Siècle style (17C); try the local specialities on the menu.

Southeast 4 km by D 600 (Avenue Lac) – ✉ 49300 Cholet

Le Belvédère rest, rm,
lac de Ribou – ✆ 02 41 75 68 00 – lebelvedere-cholet@wanadoo.fr – Fax 02 41 75 68 09
8 rm – †€ 78/87 ††€ 83/92, ☕ € 10 – **Rest** – *(closed Sunday dinner and Monday)* Menu € 15 (weekday lunch), € 22/33 – Carte € 31/63
◆ A recently built hotel in green surroundings overlooking Lake Ribou. Spacious, bright rooms with painted cane furniture. Modern dining room and pleasant terrace overlooking the countryside. Traditional cuisine and hints of spices.

CHOMELIX – 43 Haute-Loire – 331 E2 – pop. 409 – alt. 910 m – ✉ 43500 6 C3

Paris 519 – Ambert 36 – Brioude 52 – Le Puy-en-Velay 30 – St-Étienne 77

Auberge de l'Arzon with rm rm, rest,
pl. Fontaine – ✆ 04 71 03 62 35 – aubergedelarzon@wanadoo.fr – Fax 04 71 03 61 62 – Open from end April to end September and closed Sunday dinner, Monday and Tuesday except July -August
9 rm – †€ 60/65 ††€ 60/65, ☕ € 7 – ½ P € 55/60 – **Rest** – *(closed Monday lunch and Tuesday lunch in July-August)* Menu € 23/47 – Carte € 25/42
◆ In the heart of the village, a stone building in a modern-rustic style serving classic cuisine. Uncluttered table settings; oak and mahogany furniture. Quiet, functional rooms in an outbuilding to the rear.

CHOMÉRAC – 07 Ardèche – 331 J5 – see Privas

CHONAS-L'AMBALLAN – 38 Isère – 333 B5 – see Vienne

CHORANCHE – 38 Isère – 333 F7 – pop. 130 – alt. 280 m – ✉ 38680
French Alps 43 E2

Paris 588 – Grenoble 52 – Valence 48 – Villard-de-Lans 20
Grotte de Coufin★★.

Le Jorjane
– ✆ 04 76 36 09 50 – info@lejorjane.com – Fax 04 76 36 00 80 – Closed 15-30 November, Sunday dinner off season and Monday
7 rm – †€ 37 ††€ 48, ☕ € 7 – ½ P € 60/72 – **Rest** – Menu (€ 8,50), € 14,50/22 – Carte € 19/28
◆ This small family-run inn in the famous village with seven caves has practical, well-kept rooms. Motor cyclists are made very welcome here. A rustic restaurant decorated with antiques. Covered roadside terrace. Traditional dishes, grills, salads, and pizzas.

CIBOURE – 64 Pyrénées-Atlantiques – 342 C4 – see St-Jean-de-Luz

CINQ CHEMINS – 74 Haute-Savoie – 328 L2 – see Thonon-les-Bains

LA CIOTAT – 13 Bouchés-du-Rhône – 340 I6 – pop. 31 630 – Casino – ✉ 13600
Provence 40 **B3**

Paris 802 – Aix-en-Provence 53 – Brignoles 62 – Marseille 32 – Toulon 36

Office de tourisme, boulevard Anatole France ☎ 04 42 08 61 32, Fax 04 42 08 17 88

Calanque de Figuerolles★ Southwest: 1.5 km then 15 mn by D141 - N.-D. de la Garde chapel ⋞★★ West: 2.5 km then 15 mn.

to Ile Verte ⋞★ by boat 30 mn .

X **La Sardine** VISA MC AE

18 r. des Combattants – ☎ 04 42 08 00 60 – contact@lasardinedemarseille.com – Fax 04 42 73 87 23 – Closed January, Sunday dinner from September to June, Tuesday lunch in July-August and Monday
Rest – Menu (€ 15), € 29/35 – Carte € 33/51
◆ This restaurant/shop offers a series of recipes made with Marseilles sardines. Eye-catching green decor and 1858 ceiling fresco. Pleasant shaded terrace facing the port.

in Liouquet 6 km east by D 559 (Bandol road) – ✉ 13600 La Ciotat

XX **Auberge Le Revestel** with rm ⋞ AC rest, P VISA MC

– ☎ 04 42 83 11 06 – revestel@wanadoo.fr – Fax 04 42 83 29 50 – Closed 17-30 November and 5 January-9 February
6 rm – †€ 65 ††€ 65, ☕ € 8 – ½ P € 75 – **Rest** – *(closed Sunday dinner and Wednesday)* Menu (€ 25 bi), € 27 bi (weekday lunch), € 38/55 – Carte € 59/64
◆ This small colourful restaurant is well located on the coast road. The dining room's wide bay windows offer a clear view of the sea. Regional cuisine with a contemporary touch.

CIRES-LÈS-MELLO – 60 Oise – 305 F5 – pop. 3 585 – alt. 39 m –
✉ 60660 36 **B3**

Paris 65 – Beauvais 32 – Chantilly 17 – Compiègne 47 – Clermont 16 – Creil 12

Relais du Jeu d'Arc P VISA MC

pl. Jeu-d'Arc , 1 km east – ☎ 03 44 56 85 00 – jeudarc@cdno.org – Fax 03 44 56 85 19 – Closed August and 21 December-1st January
14 rm – †€ 60/120 ††€ 60/120, ☕ € 8 – ½ P € 75 – **Rest** – *(closed Sunday and Monday)* Menu € 16 (weekday lunch), € 23/39 – Carte € 39/48
◆ Former post house dating back to the 17C. The rooms are modern and comfortable, some with sloping ceilings. Traditional dishes served by the fireside in a pleasant dining room set up in the former stables. Terrace with a view of the castle.

CLAIRAC – 47 Lot-et-Garonne – 336 E3 – pop. 2 385 – alt. 52 m – ✉ 47320

Paris 690 – Agen 42 – Marmande 24 – Nérac 35 4 **C2**

Office de tourisme, 16, place Viçoze ☎ 05 53 88 71 59, Fax 05 53 88 71 59

X **L'Auberge de Clairac** AC VISA MC AE

12 rte Tonneins – ☎ 05 53 79 22 52 – aubergedeclairac@orange.fr – Closed February holidays, Sunday dinner, Tuesday dinner and Wednesday
Rest – Menu € 28 bi – Carte € 27/39
◆ This 19C regional house is next to a former tobacco-curing barn. Local dishes with a contemporary touch are served in a pleasant dining room and on a pretty flower-filled terrace.

CLAIX – 38 Isère – 333 H7 – see Grenoble

CLAM – 17 Charente-Maritime – 324 H7 – see Jonzac

CLAMART – 92 Hauts-de-Seine – 311 J3 – 101 25 – see Paris, Area

CLAMECY – 58 Nièvre – 319 E7 – pop. 4 806 – alt. 144 m – ✉ 58500
Burgundy-Jura 7 B2

Paris 208 – Auxerre 42 – Avallon 38 – Cosne-sur-Loire 52 – Dijon 145 – Nevers 69
Office de tourisme, rue du Grand Marché ✆ 03 86 27 02 51, Fax 03 86 27 20 65
St-Martin church ★.

Hostellerie de la Poste
9 pl. E. Zola – ✆ 03 86 27 01 55 – hotelposteclamecy@wanadoo.fr – Fax 03 86 27 05 99
17 rm – †€ 52/74 ††€ 56/74, ☕ € 10 – ½ P € 57/65 – **Rest** – Menu € 24 (weekdays)/35 – Carte approx. € 42
◆ A former coaching inn in a small town where logs used to be spectacularly floated down the river. Smart, small bedrooms (new bathrooms), quieter to the rear. Comfortable dining room in part-classical, part-modern style. Dishes with a contemporary touch.

LES CLAUX – 05 Hautes-Alpes – 334 I5 – see Vars

CLELLES – 38 Isère – 333 G9 – pop. 378 – alt. 746 m – ✉ 38930 45 C3

Paris 614 – Die 60 – Gap 72 – Grenoble 52 – La Mure 29 – Serres 57
Office de tourisme, le bourg ✆ 04 76 34 43 09, Fax 04 76 34 43 09

Ferrat
at the railway station – ✆ 04 76 34 42 70 – hotel.ferrat@wanadoo.fr – Fax 04 76 34 47 47 – Closed 7-22 February and Tuesday off season
23 rm – †€ 40/42 ††€ 52/54, ☕ € 9 – ½ P € 58/63 – **Rest** – Menu € 21/38
◆ At the foot of Mount Aiguille, rustic or contemporary style rooms, some with small balconies. Good soundproofing. Warm and welcoming dining room in winter. In the summer, you can enjoy the veranda or the snack-bar near the swimming pool.

CLÉMONT – 18 Cher – 323 J1 – pop. 642 – alt. 141 m – ✉ 18410 12 C2

Paris 187 – Orléans 72 – Bourges 62 – Vierzon 71 – Olivet 59

Domaine des Givrys
– ✆ 02 48 58 80 74 – givrys@wanadoo.fr – Fax 02 48 58 80 74
5 rm – †€ 57 ††€ 65, ☕ € 8 – **Table d'hôte** – Menu € 30 bi
◆ For nature lovers, an ancient farm on a vast domain by lake and river. Romantic rooms. *Terroir* and conviviality are honoured at the vast oak table d'hôte.

CLÈRES – 76 Seine-Maritime – 304 G4 – pop. 1 266 – alt. 113 m – ✉ 76690
Normandy 33 D1

Paris 155 – Dieppe 45 – Forges-les-Eaux 35 – Neufchâtel-en-Bray 36 – Rouen 25 – Yvetot 39
Syndicat d'initiative, 59, avenue du Parc ✆ 02 35 33 38 64, Fax 02 35 33 38 64
Parc zoologique (zoo) ★.

in Frichemesnil 4 km Northeast by D 6 and D 100 – pop. 402 – alt. 150 m – ✉ 76690

Au Souper Fin (Eric Buisset) with rm
1 rte de Clères – ✆ 02 35 33 33 88 – buisset.eric@wanadoo.fr – Fax 02 35 33 50 42 – Closed 6-28 August, 22-30 December, Sunday dinner, Wednesday and Thursday
3 rm – †€ 52 ††€ 60, ☕ € 10 – ½ P € 70/92
Rest – Menu € 30 (weekdays)/52 – Carte € 55/74
Spec. Grillade de langoustines de Bretagne (April to September). Saint-Pierre meunière à l'amande. Millefeuille à la vanille.
◆ A pleasant restaurant with an elegant, modern decor. Well-prepared, up-to-date cuisine and a fine choice of wines. Terrace-pergola facing the garden side. Small, attractive rooms.

South 2 km on D 155 – ✉ 76690 Clères

Auberge du Moulin
36 r. des Moulins du Tot – ✆ 02 35 33 62 76 – marc.halbourg@wanadoo.fr – Fax 02 35 33 62 76 – Closed 18 August-3 September, Tuesday except dinner February-October, Sunday dinner and Monday
Rest – Menu (€ 16), € 26/39 – Carte € 34/49
◆ This friendly inn faces an old mill on the banks of a little river interspersed with watercress beds. The cuisine has a contemporary touch, offering a choice of local specialities. Terrace.

CLERMONT – 60 Oise – 305 F4 – pop. 9 699 – alt. 125 m – ✉ 60600
Northern France and the Paris Region 36 **B2**

Paris 79 – Amiens 83 – Beauvais 27 – Compiègne 34 – Mantes-la-Jolie 101 – Pontoise 62

Syndicat d'initiative, 19, place de l'Hôtel de Ville ✆ 03 44 50 40 25, Fax 03 44 50 40 25

in Gicourt-Agnetz 2 km west by old Beauvais road – ✉ 60600 Agnetz

XX **Auberge de Gicourt** VISA MC AE

466 av. Philippe Courtial – ✆ 03 44 50 00 31 – aubergedegicourt@wanadoo.fr – Fax 03 44 50 42 29 – Closed 26 July-15 August, Sunday dinner, Tuesday dinner and Wednesday

Rest – Menu € 19/46 – Carte € 44/62

♦ Close to a forest, spruce rural inn serving traditional cuisine. Recently revamped country-style dining room. Inviting flower-decked summer terrace.

in Étouy 7 km Northwest by D 151 – pop. 772 – alt. 85 m – ✉ 60600

XXX **L'Orée de la Forêt** (Nicolas Leclercq) P VISA MC AE

255 r. Forêt – ✆ 03 44 51 65 18 – info@loreedelaforet.fr – Fax 03 44 78 92 11 – Closed 2 August-2 September, 3-13 January, Saturday lunch, Sunday dinner, Friday and dinners public holidays

Rest – Menu € 29 (weekday lunch), € 48/78 – Carte € 68/82

Spec. Foie gras poêlé au sirop de betterave. Pigeonneau rôti à la badiane. Mille-feuille vanillé.

♦ Fine early-20C mansion, with attractive, elegant dining rooms and a peaceful park planted with trees. Charming service and good cuisine with a contemporary touch.

CLERMONT-EN-ARGONNE – 55 Meuse – 307 B4 – pop. 1 767 – alt. 229 m – ✉ 55120 Northern France and the Paris Region 26 **A1**

Paris 236 – Bar-le-Duc 49 – Dun-sur-Meuse 41 – Ste-Menehould 15 – Verdun 29

Syndicat d'initiative, place de la république ✆ 03 29 88 42 22, Fax 03 29 88 42 43

XX **Bellevue** with rm rm, P VISA MC AE

r. Libération – ✆ 03 29 87 41 02 – hotel.bellevuevpc@wanadoo.fr – Fax 03 29 88 46 01 – Closed 23 December-10 January and Sunday dinner

7 rm – †€ 42 ††€ 50/55, ☕ € 7,50 – ½ P € 56/60 – **Rest** – Menu € 17/48 – Carte € 27/43

♦ The dining room ceiling is decorated with wooden laths forming a wave. The banqueting hall dates back to 1925 and there is a terrace overlooking the garden. The rooms are simple, a little antiquated, and well-kept.

CLERMONT-FERRAND P – 63 Puy-de-Dôme – 326 F8 – pop. 137 140 – Built-up area 258 541 – alt. 401 m – ✉ 63000 Auvergne 5 **B2**

Paris 420 – Lyon 172 – Moulins 106 – St-Étienne 147

Clermont-Ferrand-Auvergne: ✆ 04 73 62 71 00 by D 766 CY : 6 km.

Office de tourisme, place de la Victoire ✆ 04 73 98 65 00, Fax 04 73 90 04 11

Nouveau Golf de Charade RoyatWest by D 5: 8 km, ✆ 04 73 35 73 09 ;

des Volcans Orcines La Bruyère des Moines, Northwest: 9 km, ✆ 04 73 62 15 51.

Charade race circuit, St Genès-Champanelle ✆ 04 73 29 52 95 AZ.

Old Clermont ★ EFVX : N.-D.-du-Port basilica ★★ (choir ★★★), Cathedral ★★ (stained-glass windows ★★), Amboise fountain ★, cour★ of the maison de Savaron EV - Courtyard ★ in the Hôtel de Fonfreyde EV **M**[1], musée d'archéologie Bargoin★ FX - Old Montferrand★★ : hôtel de Lignat★, hôtel de Fontenilhes★, maison de l'Éléphant★, Courtyard ★ of hôtel Regin, door ★ of hôtel d'Albiat, - Bas-relief★ of Adam and Eve's house - Musée d'art Roger-Quilliot - Viewpoint of the D 941A ≤★★ AY.

Puy de Dôme ✻★★★ 15 km by ⑥ - Vulcania (Centre Européen du Vulcanisme). Parc Naturel régional des volcans d'Auvergne (Auvergne volcano nature park)★★★.

Plans on following pages

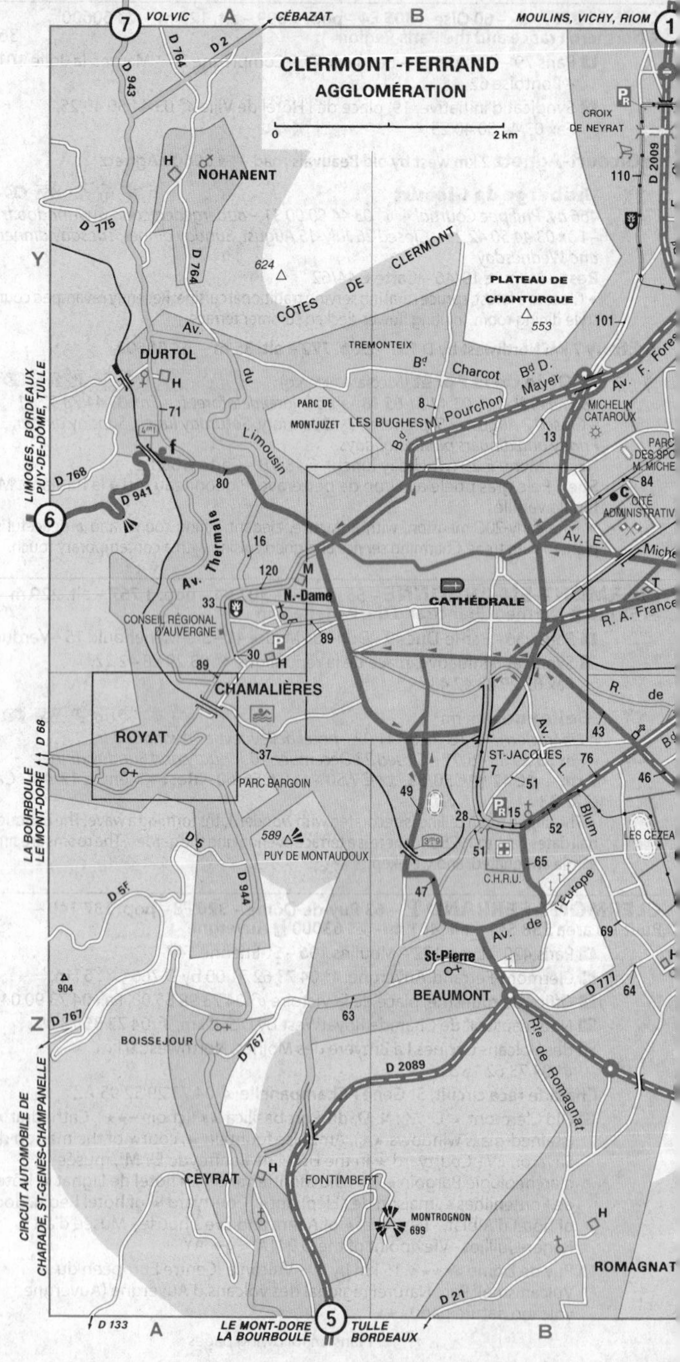

CLERMONT-FERRAND
AGGLOMÉRATION
0
2 km
VOLVIC
CÉBAZAT
MOULINS, VICHY, RIOM
NOHANENT
DURTOL
CÔTES DE CLERMONT
PLATEAU DE CHANTURGUE
TREMONTEIX
CROIX DE NEYRAT
PARC DE MONTJUZET
LES BUGHES
MICHELIN CATAROUX
CITÉ ADMINISTRATIV
N.-Dame
CATHÉDRALE
CONSEIL RÉGIONAL D'AUVERGNE
CHAMALIÈRES
ROYAT
PARC BARGOIN
ST-JACQUES
PUY DE MONTAUDOUX
C.H.R.U.
LES CÉZEA
St-Pierre
BEAUMONT
BOISSEJOUR
CEYRAT
FONTIMBERT
MONTROGNON
ROMAGNAT
LIMOGES, BORDEAUX PUY-DE-DÔME, TULLE
LA BOURBOULE LE MONT-DORE
CIRCUIT AUTOMOBILE DE CHARADE, ST-GENÈS-CHAMPANELLE
LE MONT-DORE LA BOURBOULE
TULLE BORDEAUX

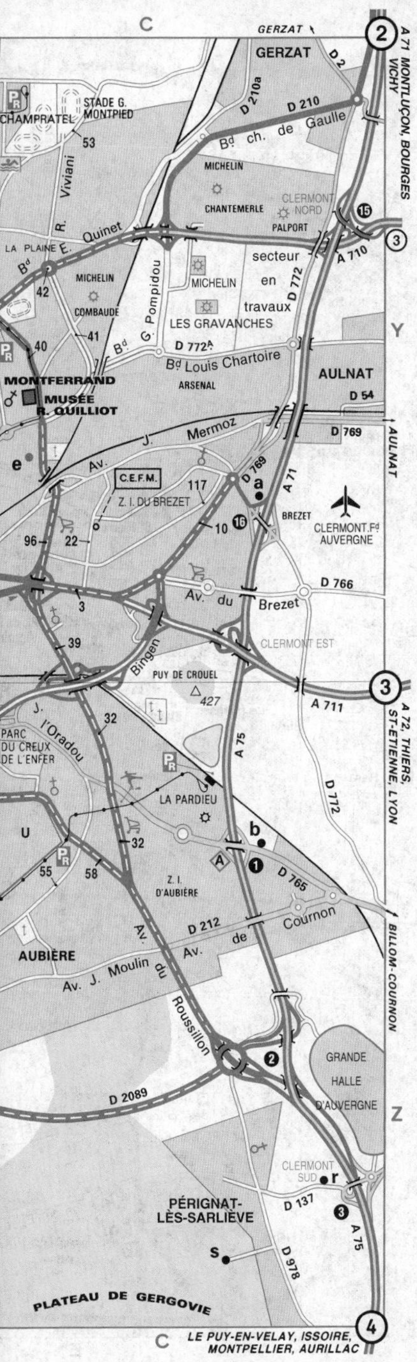

AUBIÈRE

Cournon (Av. de) . . . . **CZ**
Maerte (Av. R.) . . . . **CZ** 55
Mont Mouchet (Av. du) . . **BZ** 64
Moulin (Av. Jean) . . . . **CZ**
Noellet (Av. J.) . . . . **BZ** 69
Roussillon (Av. du) . . . . . . **CZ**

BEAUMONT

Europe (Av. de l') . . . . **BZ**
Leclerc (Av. du Mar.) . . . . . **BZ** 47
Mont Dore (Av. du) . . . . **ABZ** 63
Romagnat (Rte de) . . . . . . **BZ**

CHAMALIÈRES

Claussat (Av. J.) . . . . **AY** 16
Europe (Carrefour de l') . . **AY** 30
Fontmaure (Av. de) . . . . . . **AY** 33
Gambetta (Bd) . . . . **AZ** 37
Royat (Av. de) . . . . **AY** 89
Thermale (Av.) . . . . **AY**
Voltaire (R.) . . . . **AY** 120

CLERMONT-FERRAND

Agriculture (Av. de l') . . . . . **CY** 3
Anatole-France (R.) . . . . . . **BY**
Bernard (Bd Cl.) . . . . **BZ** 7
Bingen (Bd J.) . . . . **BCYZ**
Blanzat (R. de) . . . . **BY** 8
Blériot (R. L.) . . . . **CY** 10
Blum (Av. L.) . . . . **BZ**
Brezet (Av. du) . . . . **CY**
Champfleuri (R. de) . . . . . **BY** 13
Charcot (Bd) . . . . **BY**
Churchill (Bd Winston) . . . **BZ** 15
Clementel (Bd E.) . . . . **BY**
Cugnot (R. N.-J.) . . . . **CY** 22
Dunant (Pl. H.) . . . . **BZ** 28
La-Fayette (Bd) . . . . **BZ** 43
Flaubert (Bd G.) . . . . **CZ** 32
Forest (Av. F.) . . . . **BY**
Jean-Moulin (Bd) . . . . **CY** 39
Jouhaux (Bd L.) . . . . **CY** 40
Kennedy (Bd J.-F.) . . . . **CY** 41
Kennedy (Carrefour) . . . . . **CY** 42
Landais (Av. des) . . . . . . **BCZ** 46
Libération (Av. de la) . . . . . **BZ** 49
Limousin (Av. du) . . . . **AY**
Liondards (Av. des) . . . . **BZ** 51
Loucheur (Bd Louis) . . . . . **BZ** 52
Mabrut (R. A.) . . . . **CY** 53
Margeride (Av. de la) . . . . . **CZ** 58
Mayer (Bd D.) . . . . **BY**
Mermoz (Av. J.) . . . . **CY**
Michelin (Av. Édouard) . . . **BY**
Montalembert (R.) . . . . . . **BZ** 64
Oradour (R. de l') . . . . . . **BCZ**
Pochet-Lagaye (Bd P.) . . . . **BZ** 76
Pompidou (Bd G.) . . . . **CY**
Pourchon (Bd M.) . . . . **BY**
Puy de Dôme (Av. du) . . . . **AY** 80
Quinet (Bd Edgar) . . . . **CY**
République (Av. de la) . . . . **BY** 84
St-Jean (Bd) . . . . **CY** 96
Sous les Vignes (R.) . . . . . **BY** 101
Torpilleur Sirocco (R. du) . . **BY** 110
Verne (R. Jules) . . . . **CY** 117
Viviani (R.) . . . . **CY**

DURTOL

Paix (Av. de la) . . . . **AY** 71

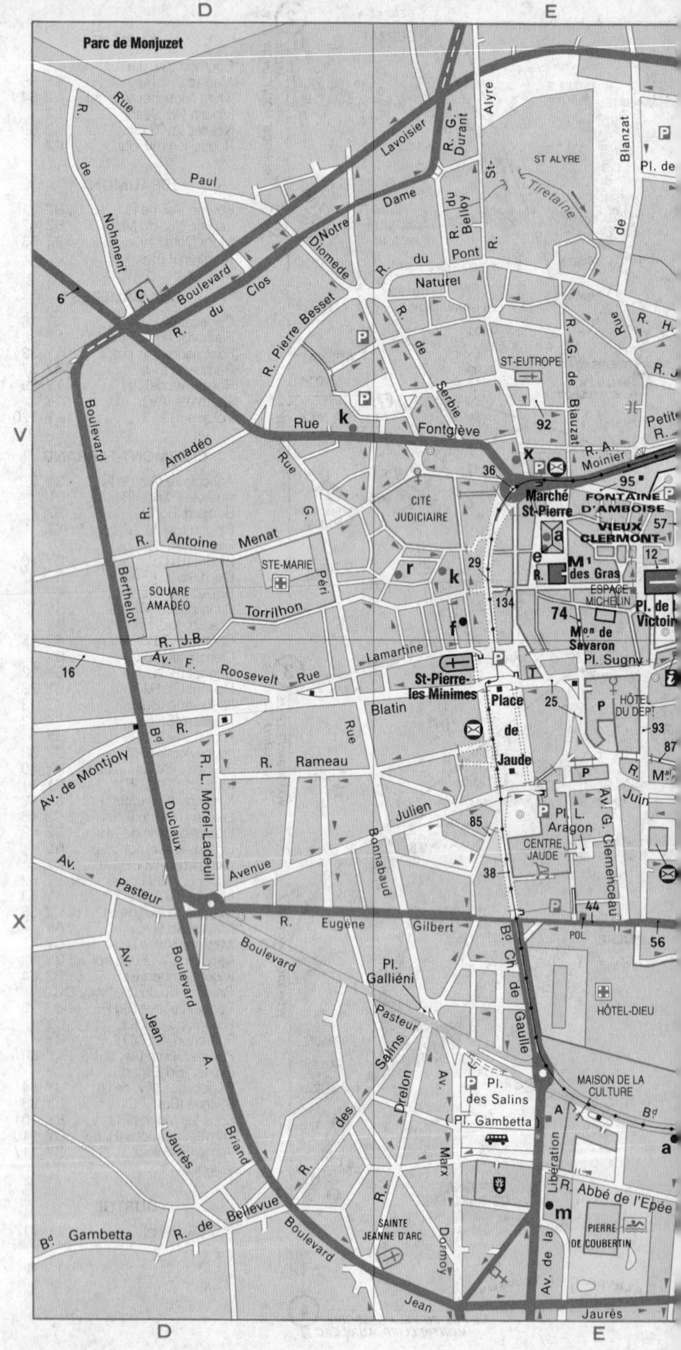
D
E
Parc de Monjuzet
Rue Paul
R. de Nohanent
Boulevard Lavoisier
R. G. Durant
St-Alyre
ST ALYRE
Tiretaine
Blanzat
Pl. de
Notre Dame
R. du Belloy
R. du Pont
Diomede
R. du Clos
Boulevard
Naturel
Rue de
R. G. de Blauzat
R. Pierre Besset
R. de Serbie
ST-EUTROPE
Boulevard
Amadéo
Rue
Fontgléve
92
Rue G.
R. A. Moinier
36
Marché St-Pierre
FONTAINE D'AMBOISE
VIEUX CLERMONT
95
57
CITÉ JUDICIAIRE
R. Antoine Menat
STE-MARIE
Péri
29
M¹ des Gras
12
SQUARE AMADÉO
Berthelot
Torrilhon
134
ESPACE MICHELIN
Pl. de Victoire
74
Mon de Savaron
R. J.B.
Lamartine
Av. F. Roosevelt
Rue
16
St-Pierre-les Minimes
Place de Jaude
Pl. Sugny
25
HÔTEL DU DEPT
93
87
Blatin
Bd R.
Rue
R. Rameau
Av. de Montjoly
R. L. Morel-Ladeuil
Duclaux
Julien
Bonnabaud
Juin
Pl. L. Aragon
85
CENTRE JAUDE
Av. G. Clemenceau
Av. Pasteur
Avenue
38
44
R. Eugène Gilbert
POL.
56
X
V
Boulevard
Pl. Galliéni
Bd Ch. de Gaulle
Av. Jean Jaurès
Boulevard A. Briand
Pasteur
Salins
HÔTEL-DIEU
MAISON DE LA CULTURE
Drelon
Av. Marx
Pl. des Salins
(Pl. Gambetta)
R. des
Libération
Bd
R. Abbé de l'Epée
R. de Bellevue
Bd Gambetta
Boulevard
SAINTE JEANNE D'ARC
Dormoy
PIERRE DE COUBERTIN
Av. de la
Jean
Jaurès
D
E

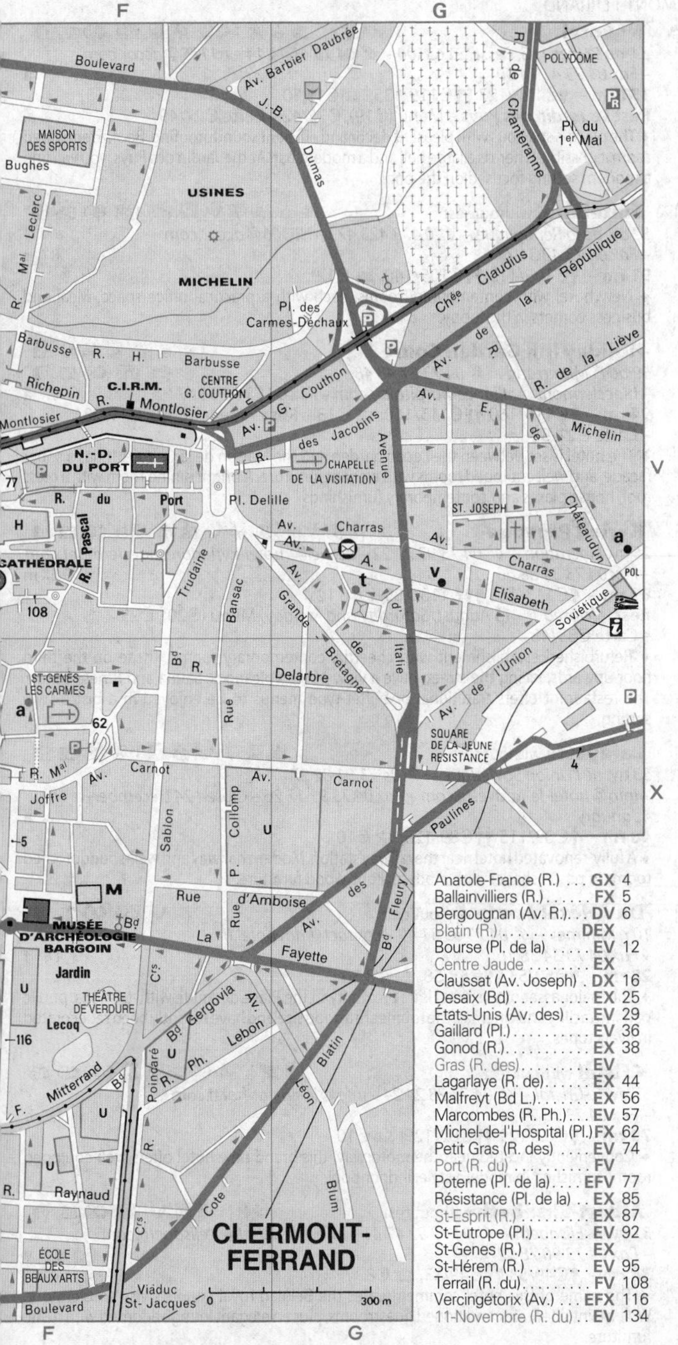

Anatole-France (R.) . . . **GX** 4
Ballainvilliers (R.) . . . . . . **FX** 5
Bergougnan (Av. R.). . . **DV** 6
Blatin (R.) . . . . **DEX**
Bourse (Pl. de la) . . . . . **EV** 12
Centre Jaude . . . . **EX**
Claussat (Av. Joseph) . **DX** 16
Desaix (Bd) . . . . **EX** 25
États-Unis (Av. des) . . . **EV** 29
Gaillard (Pl.) . . . . **EV** 36
Gonod (R.). . . . . **EX** 38
Gras (R. des). . . . . **EV**
Lagarlaye (R. de). . . . . . **EX** 44
Malfreyt (Bd L.). . . . . . . **EX** 56
Marcombes (R. Ph.) . . . **EV** 57
Michel-de-l'Hospital (Pl.) **FX** 62
Petit Gras (R. des) . . . . **EV** 74
Port (R. du) . . . . **FV**
Poterne (Pl. de la). . . . . **EFV** 77
Résistance (Pl. de la) . . **EX** 85
St-Esprit (R.) . . . . **EX** 87
St-Eutrope (Pl.) . . . . **EV** 92
St-Genes (R.) . . . . **EX**
St-Hérem (R.) . . . . **EV** 95
Terrail (R. du). . . . . **FV** 108
Vercingétorix (Av.) . . . **EFX** 116
11-Novembre (R. du) . . **EV** 134

Novotel
Z.I. du Brézet, r. G. Besse ✉ *63100 – ✆ 04 73 41 14 14 – h1175@accor.com – Fax 04 73 41 14 00* CY **a**
131 rm – †€ 112/127 ††€ 119/135, ☐ € 13,50
Rest *Le Jardin des Puys* – Menu (€ 19), € 25/42 – Carte € 27/49
♦ The place is spacious with pleasant decor and efficient soundproofing. Book a renovated room if possible. There is a large hall and a modern bar. At the Jardin des Puys, you will find a modern setting focused on the pool.

Suitehotel without rest
52 av. de la République – ✆ 0 473 423 473 – H6306@accor.com – Fax 04 73 42 34 77 BY **c**
91 rm – †€ 105/115 ††€ 105/140, ☐ € 12
♦ New hotel with contemporary rooms, each with a practical office space. Meal and business corners in the lobby.

Holiday Inn Garden Court
59 bd F. Mitterrand – ✆ 04 73 17 48 48 – higcclermont@alliance-hospitality.com – Fax 04 73 35 58 47 EX **a**
94 rm – †€ 115/160 ††€ 115/160, ☐ € 13 – **Rest** – Menu (€ 14), € 19/28 – Carte € 21/32
♦ The hotel is set between the Lecoq garden and the Maison de la Culture. It has a sober facade, and well equipped rooms with elegant furniture. A bright dining room with a glass roof, house plants and contemporary furnishings.

Kyriad Prestige
25 av. Libération – ✆ 04 73 93 22 22 – accueil@hotel-kyriadprestigeclermont.com – Fax 04 73 34 88 66 EX **m**
87 rm – †€ 113/185 ††€ 113/185, ☐ € 12
Rest – *(closed 1st- 15 August, Saturday and Sunday)* Menu (€ 20), € 25 – Carte € 33/48
♦ Refurbished establishment with cheerful, contemporary rooms. Those on the third floor upwards, facing the street, have a view of the volcanoes. Sauna and fitness centre. The restaurant offers traditional or buffet-type menus to be enjoyed in a bistro-style setting.

Lafayette without rest
53 av. de l'Union Soviétique – ✆ 04 73 91 82 27 – info@hotel-le-lafayette.com – Fax 04 73 91 17 26 – Closed 24 December-4 January GV **a**
48 rm – †€ 89/115 ††€ 89/125, ☐ € 10
♦ A fully-renovated hotel near the railway station. Modern hallway and well-soundproofed rooms in pastel shades with modern, light-wood furniture.

Dav'Hôtel Jaude without rest
10 r. Minimes – ✆ 04 73 93 31 49 – contact@davhotel.fr – Fax 04 73 34 38 16 EV **f**
28 rm – †€ 50/53 ††€ 53/58, ☐ € 8,50
♦ The major asset of this hotel is its proximity to the Place de Jaude with its shops, public parking facility and cinemas; the rooms are a good size and have recently been redecorated in lively tones.

Cristal without rest
37 av. E.-Cristal – ✆ 04 73 28 24 24 – info@le-cristal-hotel.com – Fax 04 73 28 24 20 CZ **b**
79 rm – †€ 82/129 ††€ 82/129, ☐ € 10
♦ Conveniently located near the motorway, this brand new hotel offers well-equipped rooms furnished in modern style. Indoor pool.

Albert-Élisabeth without rest
37 av. A. Élisabeth – ✆ 04 73 92 47 41 – info@hotel-albertelisabeth.com – Fax 04 73 90 78 32 GV **v**
38 rm – †€ 49/53 ††€ 49/53, ☐ € 8
♦ The name of this hotel commemorates the Belgian royal couple's visit to Clermont. Well-maintained, air-conditioned guestrooms, plus an elegant lounge adorned with rustic furniture.

Emmanuel Hodencq

pl. Marché St-Pierre, (1st floor) – ✆ 04 73 31 23 23 – emmanuel.hodencq@wanadoo.fr – Fax 04 73 31 36 00 – Closed 10-28 August, Monday lunch and Sunday
Rest – Menu (€ 27 bi), € 36 (weekdays)/135 bi – Carte € 76/97 EV **a**
Spec. Tarte fine de homard aux tomates et aromates (May to August). Noix de ris de veau dorée au sautoir, morilles étuvées au vin jaune (April-May). Macaron citron/fraises des bois, sorbet basilic (May to August). **Wines** Vin de Pays d'Urfé, Vin de pays du Puy de Dôme.
◆ This inviting modern restaurant, set above the covered market, opens onto a fine leafy terrace. Tasty cuisine with a contemporary touch.

Jean-Claude Leclerc

12 r. St-Adjutor – ✆ 04 73 36 46 30 – Fax 04 73 31 30 74 – Closed 28 April-6 May, 10 August-2 September, 2-9 January, Sunday and Monday EV **k**
Rest – Menu € 26 (weekday lunch), € 36/80 – Carte € 68/89
Spec. Délice de cèpes (autumn). Lotte aux coquillages, légumes et champignons (summer). Faux-filet de Salers, pommes de terre fondantes au cantal, sauce périgueux. **Wines** Saint-Pourçain, Châteaugay.
◆ Take a seat in this elegant modern dining room, close to the legal district, and sample unusual, up-to-date dishes. Pleasant shaded terrace.

Amphitryon Capucine

50 r. Fontgiève – ✆ 04 73 31 38 39 – kovacs.christophe557@orange.fr – Fax 04 73 31 38 44 – Closed 27 July-17 August, Sunday except public holidays and Monday
Rest – Menu € 21 (weekday lunch), € 27/75 – Carte € 51/65 DV **k**
◆ This small restaurant with a wooden façade has a renovated dining area with beams and a fireplace. Menus reflect current taste and change with the seasons.

Goûts et Couleurs

6 pl. du Changil – ✆ 04 73 19 37 82 – Fax 04 73 19 37 83 – Closed 1st-8 May, 10 August-1st September and Sunday DV **r**
Rest – Menu (€ 18), € 26/55 – Carte € 36/64
◆ Contemporary cuisine served in an attractive restaurant on a small square. Simple white and mauve decor, with paintings on the walls and a vaulted ceiling.

Brasserie Danièle Bath

pl. Marché St-Pierre – ✆ 04 73 31 23 22 – Closed 1st-10 March, 18 August-1st September, 9 February-2 March, Sunday, Monday and public holidays EV **e**
Rest – Menu € 25/42 – Carte € 42/58
◆ This fine-looking dining room with its bistro-style decor is embellished with contemporary artworks. In summer, one can enjoy the terrace facing onto the square. The cuisine is traditional and wines may be ordered by the glass.

Fleur de Sel

8 r. Abbé Girard – ✆ 04 73 90 30 59 – fleurdesel63@wanadoo.fr – Fax 04 73 90 37 49 – Closed August, Christmas holidays, Sunday, Monday and public holidays FX **a**
Rest – *(number of covers limited, pre-book)* Menu € 28/68 – Carte € 63/68
◆ Seafood and the day's special served in a sunny dining room with contemporary furniture: this place has the wind in its sails.

Le Moulin Blanc

48 r. Chandiots – ✆ 04 73 23 06 81 – restaurant.lemoulinblanc@wanadoo.fr – Fax 04 73 23 29 76 – Closed 4-11 August, 18-23 August, 2-10 January, dinner during weekdays, Saturday lunch, Sunday dinner CY **e**
Rest – Menu (€ 13), € 17 (weekday lunch), € 21/42 – Carte € 23/46
◆ Comfortable, colourful dining room where modern decor and Louis XIII style chairs come together joyfully. Traditional food with a contemporary twist.

Le Comptoir des Saveurs

5 r. Ste-Claire – ✆ 04 73 37 10 31 – lecomptoirdessaveurs63@neuf.fr – Fax 04 73 37 10 31 – Closed August, 15-23 February, Tuesday dinner, Wednesday dinner, Thursday dinner, Sunday and Monday EV **x**
Rest – Menu € 23 (lunch), € 31/41 – Carte € 37/64
◆ Savour a daily-changing and varied menu, served in mini portions. An interesting dining concept in a contemporary setting.

L'Annexe
1 r. de Coupière – ☎ 04 73 92 50 00 – croixmama@wanadoo.fr – Fax 04 73 92 92 03 – Closed Saturday lunch, Sunday, Monday and public holidays GV **t**
Rest – Menu (€ 16), € 34 – Carte € 33/69
◆ Lounge ambiance and contemporary dishes set the tone for this restaurant in a former warehouse. Large dining room, mezzanine, open kitchen, modern furniture and art exhibitions.

in Chamalières – pop. 18 136 – alt. 450 m – ✉ 63400

Radio
43 av. P. et M.-Curie – ☎ 04 73 30 87 83 – resa@hotel-radio.fr – Fax 04 73 36 42 44 – Closed 1st-8 May, 27 October-12 November and 2-9 January *Map of Royat* B **w**
26 rm – €82/125 €92/139, € 14 – ½ P € 104/130
Rest – *(closed Monday lunch, Saturday lunch and Sunday)* Menu € 40 bi (weekday lunch), € 48/92 – Carte € 62/88
◆ Elegant 1930s Art Deco establishment. The large comfortable rooms are more contemporary. Original cuisine, a fine wine list and smart renovated decor that remains full of character.

in Pérignat-lès-Sarliève 8 km – pop. 2 221 – alt. 364 m – ✉ 63170
Plateau de Gergovie★: ✻★★ South: 8 km.

Hostellerie St-Martin
– ☎ 04 73 79 81 00 – reception@hostelleriestmartin.com – Fax 04 73 79 81 01 CZ **s**
32 rm – €90/150 €90/195, € 13 – 1 suite – ½ P € 81/108
Rest – *(closed Sunday dinner from November to March)* Menu € 26/49 – Carte € 32/51
◆ The buildings of this 14C Cistercian abbey, surrounded by a pretty park, now house comfortable rooms with personal touches. Those in the annexe are more basic. An elegant restaurant with classic decor and period furniture. Terrace in the garden.

Gergovie
25 allée du Petit Puy – ☎ 04 73 79 09 95 – hotelgergovie@bestwestern.fr – Fax 04 73 79 08 76 CZ **b**
59 rm – €105/135 €105/135, € 11 – 3 suites – **Rest** – *(closed Saturday and Sunday)* Menu € 16 (lunch)/25 – Carte € 27/40
◆ Large modern hotel, recently built on the outskirts of town. Well-appointed, sober, designer-style rooms with air conditioning. Contemporary restaurant serving traditional cuisine. Attractive teak terrace for summer dining.

La Baraque road to ⑥ – ✉ 63830 Durtol

Bernard Andrieux
– ☎ 04 73 19 25 00 – andrieuxbe@wanadoo.fr – Fax 04 73 19 25 04 – Closed 1st-7 May, 3-21 August, autumn half-term holidays, 1st-10 January, 18-24 February, Saturday lunch, Wednesday lunch, Sunday dinner and Monday AY **f**
Rest – Menu (€ 28), € 52/73 – Carte € 57/76
◆ This flower-decked restaurant with its elegant, comfortable little dining rooms is a popular destination en route for the Puy de Dôme. Contemporary cuisine.

in La Baraque 6 km by ⑥ - ✉ 63870 Orcines

Le Relais des Puys
– ☎ 04 73 62 10 51 – info@relaisdespuys.com – Fax 04 73 62 22 09 – Closed 19 December-2 February, Sunday dinner October-March and Monday lunch
36 rm – €58/70 €58/70, € 8,50 – ½ P € 57/63 – **Rest** – Menu (€ 14,50), € 18 (weekdays)/43 – Carte € 27/53
◆ For seven generations, the same family has run this former stage-coach inn. The successfully renovated rooms offer every modern comfort. A large Volvic-stone fireplace helps to create an ideal environment in which to enjoy traditional fare and recipes from Auvergne.

in Orcines 8 km by ⑥ – pop. 3 067 – alt. 810 m – ✉ 63870

Office de tourisme, place de la Liberté ✆ 04 73 62 20 08, Fax 04 73 62 73 00

Les Hirondelles

34 rte de Limoges – ✆ 04 73 62 22 43 – info@hotel-leshirondelles.com – Fax 04 73 62 19 12 – Open 13 February-11 November and closed Sunday dinner, Tuesday lunch and Monday from October to April

30 rm – €52/69 €52/69, €8 – ½ P €52/62 – **Rest** – Menu €19/44 – Carte €25/36

◆ Former farmhouse, with a pretty name, on the edge of the Volcano Natural Park. Small, discreetly-decorated and well-soundproofed rooms. Dining room laid out in a converted stable with a vaulted ceiling. Auvergne cuisine.

Domaine de Ternant without rest ← Limagne plain,

Ternant, 5.5 km north – ✆ 04 73 62 11 20 – domaine.ternant@free.fr – Fax 04 73 62 29 96 – Open from mid March-mid November

5 rm – €70/82 €78/90

◆ This 19C residence, at the foot of the Dôme mountains, stands in a park with more than 200 rose bushes. The rooms have family-type furnishings and colourful patchwork quilts. Tennis and billiards.

Auberge de la Baraque

2 rte de Bordeaux – ✆ 04 73 62 26 24 – geraldine@laubrieres.com – Fax 04 73 62 26 26 – Closed 7-23 October, 5-22 January, Monday, Tuesday, Wednesday and public holidays

Rest – Menu €24/50 – Carte €31/57

◆ The food prepared by the young owner of this former coaching inn (1800) with a classic decor is modern, simple and regularly changing. Worth a detour.

at the top of Puy-de-Dôme 13 km by ⑥ – ✉ 63870 Orcines – alt. 1 465 m

Mont Fraternité ← volcanos and Sancy,

– ✆ 04 73 62 23 00 – Fax 04 73 62 10 30 – Open beg. April-end October and closed Sunday dinner and Monday

Rest – Menu €25/48 – Carte €39/47

◆ This modern restaurant, brightened by wide picture windows, is in a building also home to a museum, souvenir shop and bar. Tasty cuisine with a contemporary touch.

at col de Ceyssat 12 km by ⑥ and Puy-de-Dôme road– ✉ 63210 Ceyssat – pop. 467 – alt. 800 m

Auberge des Muletiers

– ✆ 04 73 62 25 95 – Fax 04 73 62 28 03 – Closed 5 November-19 December, 7 January-12 February, Tuesday from October to March, Sunday dinner and Monday

Rest – Menu €25/28 – Carte €27/36

◆ A chalet-type building at the foot of the Puy de Dôme. Warm, rustic decor with a dresser and fireplace. Panoramic terrace. Regional dishes.

CLERMONT-L'HÉRAULT – 34 Hérault – 339 F7 – pop. 6 532 – alt. 92 m – ✉ 34800 Languedoc-Roussillon-Tarn Gorges

23 **C2**

Paris 718 – Béziers 46 – Lodève 24 – Montpellier 42 – Pézenas 22 – Sète 55

Office de tourisme, 9, rue René Gosse ✆ 04 67 96 23 86, Fax 04 67 96 98 58

St-Paul church ★.

Tournesol

2 r. Roger Salengro – ✆ 04 67 96 99 22 – azemard.christophe@wanadoo.fr – Fax 04 67 88 12 53 – Closed Sunday dinner and Monday from October to April

Rest – Menu €16 (weekday lunch), €21/34 – Carte €37/68

◆ A traditional repertoire drawing on local influences from the chef; non-smoking dining room, pretty veranda and terrace surrounded by tropical vegetation.

Le Fontenay

1 r. Georges-Brasssens, Lac du Salagou road – ✆ 04 67 88 04 06 – Fax 04 67 88 04 06 – Closed Sunday dinner and Wednesday

Rest – Menu €15 (weekday lunch), €26/49 – Carte €48/65

◆ Recent building in a residential area. Modern, colourful dining room with a pleasant inner terrace. Cuisine in keeping with current taste and regional wines.

in St-Guiraud 7.5 km north by D 609, D 908, D 141 and D 130ᴱ – pop. 184 – alt. 120 m – ✉ 34725

Le Mimosa

– 04 67 96 67 96 – le.mimosa@free.fr – Fax 04 67 96 61 15
– Open 14 March-2 November and closed lunch except Sunday, Sunday dinner except July-August and Monday
Rest – Menu € 56/84 bi – Carte € 55/90

◆ Set in the heart of the village in a house once owned by a wine-grower. Agreeably modern interior where one can enjoy dishes based on market-fresh, Mediterranean produce. Fine choice of Languedoc wines.

in St-Saturnin-de-Lucian 10 km north by D 609, D 908, D 141 and D 130 – pop. 229 – alt. 150 m – ✉ 34725

Grotte de Clamouse★★ Northeast: 12 km - St-Guilhem-le-Désert: site★★, abbey church★ Northeast: 17 km.

Du Mimosa without rest

10 pl. de la Fontaine – 04 67 88 62 62 – ostalaria.cardabela@wanadoo.fr – Fax 04 67 88 62 82 – Open mid March-beg. November
7 rm – € 68/95 € 68/95, € 9,50

◆ Delightful hundred-year-old house on the village square. Spacious rooms with a blend of ultramodern furniture, old stonework and original fireplaces. Reception open from 5 pm on.

in Brignac 3 km east by D 4 – pop. 345 – alt. 60 m – ✉ 34800

La Missare without rest

9 rte de Clermont – 04 67 96 07 67 – la.missare@free.fr
4 rm – € 70 € 70

◆ *Missare* (dormouse in *languedocien*) allies charm and serenity : large rooms, antique furniture and objects, flower-filled garden, swimming pool and homemade breakfast.

CLICHY – 92 Hauts-de-Seine – 311 J2 – 101 15 – see Paris, Area

---

CLIOUSCLAT – 26 Drôme – 332 C5 – pop. 641 – alt. 235 m – ✉ 26270 44 B3

Paris 586 – Valence 31 – Montélimar 24

La Treille Muscate

Le Village – 04 75 63 13 10 – latreillemuscate@wanadoo.fr – Fax 04 75 63 10 79 – Closed December and January
11 rm – € 65/150 € 65/150, € 10 – 1 suite – **Rest** – *(closed Mon.)*
Menu (€ 15), € 20 (weekday lunch)/28 – Carte € 25/40

◆ This smart inn has plenty of charm: Provençal atmosphere, prettily individualised rooms and large orchards as a backdrop. Cliouscat pottery and furnishings from antique markets: the decor of the vaulted dining room is delightful. Cuisine with a southern flavour.

CLISSON – 44 Loire-Atlantique – 316 I5 – pop. 5 939 – alt. 34 m – ✉ 44190

Atlantic Coast 34 B2

Paris 396 – Nantes 31 – Niort 130 – Poitiers 151 – La Roche-sur-Yon 54

Office de tourisme, place du Minage 02 40 54 02 95, Fax 02 40 54 07 77

Site★ - Domaine de la Garenne-Lemot★.

La Bonne Auberge

1 r. O. de Clisson – 02 40 54 01 90 – labonneauberge2@wanadoo.fr – Fax 02 40 54 08 48 – Closed 11 August-3 September, 1st-20 January, Tuesday lunch, Wednesday dinner and Monday
Rest – Menu € 24 (weekday lunch), € 40/60 – Carte € 63/79

◆ Comfortable house with three pleasant, well kept dining rooms (light wood), one of which is a veranda giving onto the small garden. Traditional menu.

in Gétigné 3 km southeast by D 149 and secondary road – pop. 3 076 – alt. 26 m – ✉ 44190

La Gétignière
3 r. Navette – ✆ 02 40 36 05 37 – la.getigniere@wanadoo.fr – Fax 02 40 54 24 76 – Closed 1st-14 August, Christmas holidays, Sunday dinner, Tuesday dinner and Monday
Rest – Menu € 21 (weekday lunch)/28
◆ Wooden panelling, white boat style awnings and a profusion of plants and flowers. Enjoy modern cuisine in a contemporary dining room.

in Pallet 7 km northwest by D 149 and private road – ✉ 44330

Château de la Sébinière without rest
– ✆ 02 40 80 49 25 – info@chateausebiniere.com – Fax 02 40 80 49 25
3 rm – €80/110 €80/110
◆ Warmth and cordiality are the hallmarks of this château, set amidst woodland and vineyards. Quality furnishings in the very comfortable rooms; splendid, old style bathrooms.

CLOHARS-FOUESNANT – 29 Finistère – 308 G7 – see Bénodet

CLOYES-SUR-LE-LOIR – 28 Eure-et-Loir – 311 D8 – pop. 2 636 – alt. 97 m – ✉ 28220 Châteaux of the Loire 11 B2

Paris 146 – Blois 54 – Orléans 64 – Vendôme 30

Office de tourisme, 11, place Gambetta, Fax 02 37 98 55 27

Le Saint-Jacques
rm, rm,
pl. du Marché aux Oeufs – ✆ 02 37 98 40 08 – info@lesaintjacques.fr – Fax 02 37 98 32 63 – Closed 5-15 March, 22 December-19 January and Sunday from November to March
20 rm – €65/160 €65/160, € 12 – ½ P € 66/106
Rest – Menu € 33/50 – Carte € 35/57
Rest *Le P'tit Bistrot* – *(closed Sunday dinner and Monday)* Menu € 18/30 – Carte € 23/31
◆ Tucked away in a garden on the banks of the Loire, this former post house dating from the 16C offers restful rooms that are gradually being renovated. Cuisine with a contemporary touch is served in the restaurant or out on the well-shaded terrace. The P'tit Bistrot offers local dishes in a pre-1940s style setting.

CLUNY – 71 Saône-et-Loire – 320 H11 – pop. 4 376 – alt. 248 m – ✉ 71250 Burgundy-Jura 8 C3

Paris 384 – Mâcon 25 – Chalon-sur-Saône 49 – Montceau-les-Mines 44 – Tournus 33

Office de tourisme, 6, rue Mercière ✆ 03 85 59 05 34, Fax 03 85 59 06 95

Former abbey★★ : clocher de l'Eau Bénite (Eau Bénite belltower)★★ - Musée Ochier (Ochier Museum)★ **M** - Clocher (Belltower)★ of the église St-Marcel (St Marcel's Church).

Château de Cormatin★★ (St-Cécile study ★★★) North: 13 KM - Taizé Community North: 10 km.

Plan on following page

De Bourgogne
rm,
pl. l'Abbaye – ✆ 03 85 59 00 58 – contact@hotel-cluny.com – Fax 03 85 59 03 73 – Closed 1st December-31 January n
14 rm – €85 €95, € 10,50 – 2 suites – ½ P € 121 – **Rest** – *(closed Tuesday and Wednesday)* Menu € 25/42 – Carte € 37/58
◆ Lamartine stopped over in this interesting town house facing the Benedictine abbey. There is a pleasant lounge and a choice of diversely furnished rooms. Chequered flooring, light coloured walls, Louis XVI chairs and a stone fireplace make up the decor of the restaurant. The cuisine is traditional.

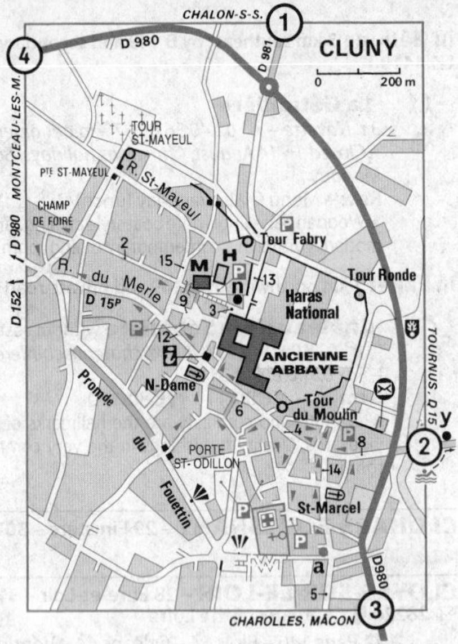

St-Odilon without rest

rte d'Azé – ✆ 03 85 59 25 00 – contact@hotelsaintodilon.com – Fax 03 85 59 06 18 **y**

36 rm – €52 €52, €7

◆ You will appreciate the country atmosphere in this motel near the Grosne bridge. Small, discreet bedrooms decorated with functional furniture.

Auberge du Cheval Blanc

1 r. Porte de Mâcon – ✆ 03 85 59 01 13 – chevalblanc.auberge@orange.fr – Fax 03 85 59 13 32 – Open mid March-November and closed 1st-13 July, Friday dinner and Saturday **a**

Rest – Menu € 17/40 – Carte € 27/36

◆ This inn designed in the local style stands at the entrance to the town. Traditional dishes are served in the restaurant, which features rafters and a high, turquoise-tinted ceiling; the walls are enlivened by festive countryside murals.

LA CLUSAZ – 74 Haute-Savoie – 328 L5 – pop. 2 023 – alt. 1 040 m – Winter sports : 1 100/2 600 m 6 49 – ✉ 74220 French Alps 46 F1

Paris 564 – Albertville 40 – Annecy 32 – Chamonix-Mont-Blanc 60

Office de tourisme, 161, place de l'église ✆ 04 50 32 65 00, Fax 04 50 32 65 01

East: Vallon des Confins★ - Manigod Valley ★ S - Col des Aravis ≤★★ by ②: 7.5 km.

Plan on next page

Beauregard

90 sentier du Bossonet – ✆ 04 50 32 68 00 – info@hotel-beauregard.fr – Fax 04 50 02 59 00 – Closed 20 October-24 November **k**

rm, rest, VISA MC AE

95 rm – €104/415 €104/415, €13 – ½ P €87/245

Rest – Menu € 25/40 – Carte € 28/45

◆ Large, comfortable, well-equipped chalet at the foot of the ski runs; spacious lounge-bar (billiards), indoor pool and fitness facilities. Light-coloured wood interior, rooms with balcony. Simple, traditional dishes served on the south-facing terrace, weather permitting.

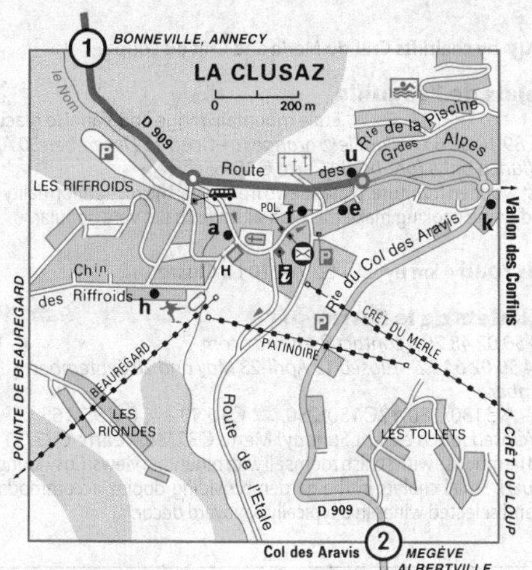

Les Sapins
– 04 50 63 33 33 – sapins@clusaz.com – Fax 04 50 63 33 34
– *Open 15 June-10 September and 20 December-10 April* **h**
24 rm – €50/80 €60/110, €10 – ½ P €56/118 – **Rest** – Menu €21/24
♦ Facing the Aravis mountains, this chalet's alpine-style rooms feature light-coloured woodwork and lively colours; many have a balcony. Direct access to the slopes. Dig into tartiflettes and fondues served against a backdrop of snow-capped peaks.

Alp'Hôtel
192 rte col des Aravis – 04 50 02 40 06 – alphotel@clusaz.com
– Fax 04 50 02 60 16 – *Open 1st June-29 September and 2 December-24 April*
15 rm – €60/210 €70/260, €10 – **Rest** – Carte €36/61 **e**
♦ Situated in the centre of La Clusaz, this chalet has rooms furnished in typical Savoy style, each with its own balcony. Lounge with an open fireplace. Regional cuisine with personal touches, served on the south-facing terrace in summer.

La Montagne
– 04 50 63 38 38 – montagne@clusaz.com – Fax 04 50 63 38 39 **u**
27 rm – €60/160 €65/200, €10 – ½ P €56/128 – **Rest** – *(closed Sunday dinner off season)* Menu (€19), €25 – Carte €30/33
♦ Standard winter-sports resort architecture. All-wood interior with cosy, generously proportioned rooms, nice vaulted bar with fireplace and lounge with billiards table. Restaurant with a panoramic view and terrace. Traditional and regional cooking.

Christiania
– 04 50 02 60 60 – contact@hotelchristiania.fr – Fax 04 50 32 66 98
– *Open 4 July-14 September and 20 December-15 April* **f**
28 rm – €44/80 €52/130, €9 – ½ P €52/98 – **Rest** – *(closed Tuesday in Winter) (dinner only in summer)* Menu (€18), €20/26 – Carte €26/33
♦ A well-maintained family-run country hotel. Practical, renovated, panelled rooms, some with a terrace. Traditional food and cheese recipes served in a simple rustic dining room.

Les Airelles
33 pl. de l'Église – 04 50 02 40 51 – airelles@clusaz.com – Fax 04 50 32 35 33
– *Closed 28 April-12 May and 17 November-7 December* **a**
14 rm – €55/100 €55/100, €9 – ½ P €55/113 – **Rest** – *(closed Sunday dinner 12 May-30 June and 15 September-15 December)* Menu €20/26 – Carte €20/40
♦ A well located unpretentious hotel near the church and at the foot of the slopes. Small rooms, most have balconies with flowers in the summer. Sauna, Jacuzzi. Restaurant popular for its rustic interior, friendly atmosphere and delicious Savoy cooking.

in Crêt du Loup by chairlifts Crêt du Merle and Crêt du Loup

Le Relais de l'Aiguille

Etale mountain range and Vanoise glacier, VISA MC
– 06 89 10 82 63 – aiguille@orange.fr – *Open 15 December-30 April*
Rest – *(lunch only) (pre-book)* Carte € 28/65
◆ Robust wooden furniture, plates hewn from slate: the rustic informality of its setting and the good home cooking make this high-altitude chalet very popular.

Col des Aravis road 4 km by ② – ✉ 74220 La Clusaz

Les Chalets de la Serraz

rest, P VISA MC AE
– 04 50 02 48 29 – contact@laserraz.com
– Fax 04 50 02 64 12 – *Closed 13 April-23 May and 28 September-7 November*
10 rm – €130/180 €130/250, € 16,50 – ½ P € 95/165
Rest – *(closed lunch except Sunday)* Menu € 32/38 – Carte € 33/51
◆ An old farmhouse with stylish rooms all with mountain views. Cosy lounge-bar, hammam and Jacuzzi. Small chalets in the garden providing duplex accommodation. Traditional cuisine and selected wines in a typically Savoyard decor.

LA CLUSE – 01 Ain – 328 G3 – see Nantua

CLUSES – 74 Haute-Savoie – 328 M4 – pop. 17 711 – alt. 486 m – ✉ 74300

French Alps 46 F1

Paris 570 – Annecy 56 – Chamonix-Mont-Blanc 41 – Thonon-les-Bains 59

Office de tourisme, 100, place du 11 Novembre 04 50 98 31 79, Fax 04 50 96 46 99

Church★ font.

Plan on next page

4 C

rm, P VISA MC AE
301 bd Chevran – 04 50 98 01 00 – hotel.4c@orange.fr
– Fax 04 50 98 32 20 BY **a**
38 rm – €73/84 €80/102, € 11 – ½ P € 65/73
Rest – *(closed Saturday and Sunday)* Menu (€ 13), € 20/32 – Carte € 16/41
◆ Slightly away from the centre, this hotel has functional rooms with small balconies (except three) overlooking the countryside. Outdoor Jacuzzi. A large restaurant with sober modern decoration and a fine terrace serving pizzas, pasta and traditional dishes.

Le Bargy

P VISA MC AE
28 av. Sardagne – 04 50 98 01 96 – le.bargy@wanadoo.fr
– Fax 04 50 98 23 24 AY **b**
30 rm – €62/68 €62/68, € 8 – ½ P € 55/58
Rest *Le Cercle des Songes* – *(closed 5-11 May, 4-24 August, 24 December-1st January, Saturday except from January to March and Sunday)* Menu (€ 13), € 15/27 – Carte € 31/43
◆ Near the town centre, this family establishment has spacious, well-soundproofed rooms, all with a sofa to sit and unwind. Full range of traditional dishes served in a comfortable and subdued setting. Brasserie-bar for quick meals.

Saint-Vincent

VISA MC AE
14 r. Faubourg St Vincent, via ②: 200 m – 04 50 96 17 47
– restaurant@le-saint-vincent.com – Fax 04 50 96 83 75 – *Closed 10-25 August, Saturday lunch and Sunday* BZ **d**
Rest – Menu € 20, € 31/58
◆ Old regional-style inn with a warm interior, semi-rustic, semi-modern. Serves seasonal cuisine based on local produce.

CLUSES

Bargy (R. du) .... **AZ** 3
Berthelot (R. M.) .... **BZ** 4
Chautemps (R. E.) .... **BZ** 7
Colomby (Av. de) .... **AY** 9
Deuxième Div. Blindée
(R. de la) .... **BY** 12
Europe (Carrefour de l') ..... **BY** 13
Ferrié (R. du Gén.) .... **BZ** 15
Gaillard (Av. A.) .... **AY** 18
Gare (Av. de la) .... **BZ** 19
Gaulle (Pl. Ch.-de) .... **BZ** 20
Grande Rue .... **BZ** 22
Grands Champs (R. des) .... **BY** 24
Grand Massif (Av. du) ...... **BY** 21
Hugard (R. Cl.) .... **BZ** 25
Lattre-de-Tassigny
(R. du Mar.-de) .... **AY** 27
Leclerc (R. du Mar.) .... **BZ** 28
Libération (Av. de la) .... **BZ** 30
Louis Armand (R.) .... **AY** 31
Luther King (R. M.) .... **AY** 33
Lycée (R. du) .... **BZ** 34
Mont-Blanc (Rd-Pt du) ...... **BZ** 37
Pasteur (R.) .... **BZ** 39
Pointe de la Cupoire (R. de la) **BY** 43
Pointe de la Lanche (R. de la) **BY** 40
Pointe du Criou (R. de la) ... **BY** 42
Pont (R. du) .... **AY** 51
Prairie (R. de la) .... **BY** 48
Pré Benevix (R. du) .... **BZ** 49
Tête de Colonney (R. de la) . **BY** 52
Trappier (R. P.) .... **AY** 57
8-Mai-1945 (R. du) .... **BZ** 59

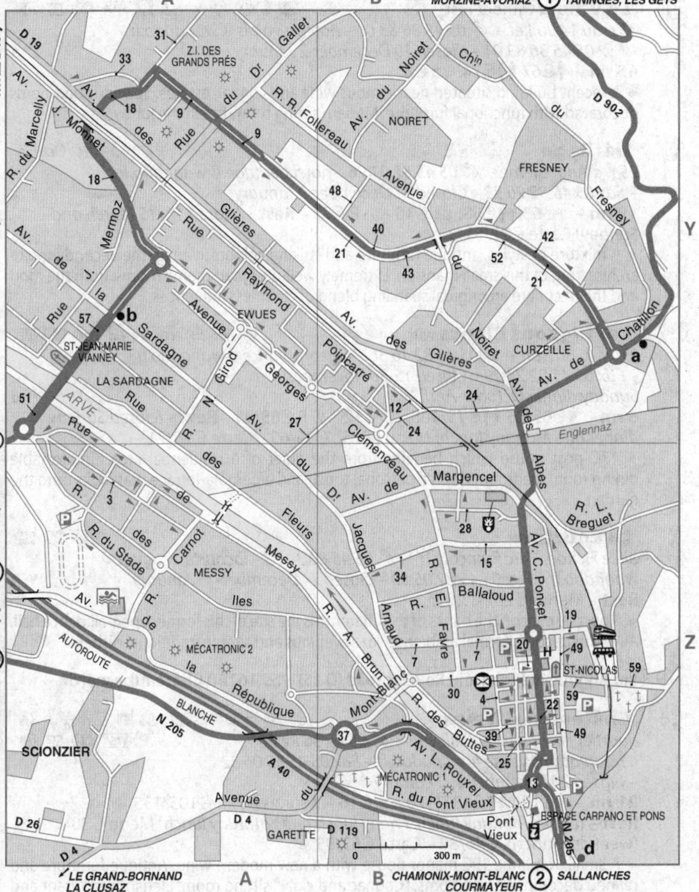

COCHEREL – 27 Eure – 304 I7 – see Pacy-sur-Eure

COCURÈS – 48 Lozère – 330 J8 – see Florac

COEX – 85 Vendée – 316 E7 – see St-Gilles-Croix-de-Vie

COGNAC – 16 Charente – 324 I5 – pop. 19 534 – alt. 25 m – ✉ 16100

Atlantic Coast 38 **B3**

Paris 478 – Angoulême 45 – Bordeaux 120 – Niort 83 – Saintes 27

Office de tourisme, 16, rue du 14 juillet ☎ 05 45 82 10 71, Fax 05 45 82 34 47

Du Cognac Saint-Brice La Maurie, East: 8 km Bourg-de-Charente road, ☎ 05 45 32 18 17.

Plan on next page

Le Valois without rest

35 r. du 14-Juillet – ☎ 05 45 36 83 00 – hotel.le.valois@wanadoo.fr – Fax 05 45 36 83 01 – Closed 19 December-2 January Z **a**

45 rm – €67 €74, €8

◆ A recent building situated near famous wine and cognac estates. Spacious bedrooms decorated with functional furniture. Modern sitting room-bar in the lobby.

Héritage

25 r. d'Angoulême – ☎ 05 45 82 01 26 – hotel.heritage@wanadoo.fr – Fax 05 45 82 20 33 – Closed 31 December-2 January Y **z**

19 rm – €63 €68, €10 – ½ P €77 – **Rest** – *(closed 1st- 15 March and Sunday)* Carte €22/51

◆ A mixture of styles, antique furniture and striking colours liven up the Second Empire architecture of this small mansion. Extremely well-designed theme rooms. Both the food and the decor are an original sparkling blend of countless influences.

Les Pigeons Blancs with rm

110 r. J.-Brisson – ☎ 05 45 82 16 36 – pigeonsblancs@wanadoo.fr – Fax 05 45 82 29 29 – Closed 15-30 November, Sunday dinner October-April Y **d**

6 rm – €65/85 €75/105, €12 – ½ P €85/95 – **Rest** – *(closed Sunday dinner and Monday lunch)* Menu (€25), €35/69 – Carte €58/71

◆ 17C post house which benefits from the quiet of a residential area. Comfortable dining room, bedrooms with a personal touch and a pergola-terrace that looks onto the garden.

La Courtine

allée Fichon, Parc François 1er – ☎ 05 45 82 34 78 – lacourtinecognac@wanadoo.fr – Fax 05 45 82 05 50 – Closed 24 December-15 January Y **t**

Rest – Menu (€20), €26 bi

◆ A bucolic park on the banks of the Charente is the site of this former open-air dance hall. All wood decor, informal ambience, jazz evenings and simple traditional dishes.

via ① 3 km Angoulême road and Rouillac road (D 15) – ✉ 16100 Châteaubernard

Château de l'Yeuse

quartier l'Échassier, r. Bellevue – ☎ 05 45 36 82 60 – reservations.yeuse@wanadoo.fr – Fax 05 45 35 06 32 – Closed 20 December-12 February

21 rm – €100 €137/170, €16 – 3 suites – ½ P €105/135

Rest – *(closed Monday lunch, Friday lunch and Saturday lunch)* Menu €30 (weekday lunch), €46/80 – Carte €63/95

◆ A small, romantic 19C manor house with a new modern wing. Antique furniture and refined decor in the bedrooms. "Cognac and cigar" sitting room. Elegant restaurant and terrace dominating the Charente valley. Excellent creative cuisine.

Domaine de l'Échassier

quartier l'Échassier, 72 r. Bellevue – ☎ 05 45 35 01 09 – echassier@wanadoo.fr – Fax 05 45 32 22 43 – Closed 21-29 December and Sunday off season

22 rm – €78/95 €95/115, €13 – ½ P €110/125

Rest – *(closed 26 October-5 November and 22 February-7 March) (dinner only)* Menu €34/45

◆ This recent establishment, located in a delightful garden, has snug, contemporary style rooms whose decor evokes wine producing activities. A few terraces and balconies. A stylish inviting dining room in a restaurant meets table d'hôte ambiance.

COGNAC

Angoulême (R. d') . . . . Y
Armes (Pl. d') . . . . Y
Bazoin (R. Abel) . . . . Y 6
Boucher (R. Cl.) . . . . Y 7
Briand (R. A.) . . . . Y
Canton (R. du) . . . . Y 8
Champ de Mars (Allées du) . . Z 9
Château (Quai du) . . . . Y 10
Cordeliers (R. des) . . . . Y 11
Corderie (Allées de la) . . . . . . Z 12
François-1er (R.) . . . . Y 13
Germain (R. H.) . . . . Y 14
Grande Rue . . . . Y 15
Isle d'Or (R. de l') . . . . Y 16
Lusignan (R. de) . . . . Y 20
Magdeleine (R.) . . . . Y 21
Martell (Pl. Ed.) . . . . Z 22
Monnet (Pl. Jean) . . . . Z 23
Palais (R. du) . . . . Y 24
Victor-Hugo (Av.) . . . . Z
14-Juillet (R. du) . . . . Z 26

Look out for red symbols, indicating particularly pleasant establishments.

COGOLIN – 83 Var – 340 O6 – pop. 9 079 – alt. 20 m – ✉ 83310 41 C3

Paris 864 – Fréjus 33 – Ste-Maxime 13 – Toulon 60

Office de tourisme, place de la République ☎ 04 94 55 01 10, Fax 04 94 55 01 11

La Maison du Monde without rest

63 r. Carnot – ☎ 04 94 54 77 54 – info@lamaisondumonde.fr – Fax 04 94 54 77 55 – Closed 1st-14 March, 16 November-31 December

12 rm – €75/185 €75/185, ☕ €13

◆ A fine, large 19C house set in a garden with palm and plane trees. Rooms with character, with furniture from all over the world.

Grain de Sel

6 r. 11-Novembre, (behind the town hall) – ☎ 04 94 54 46 86 – phianne2@orange.fr – Closed 25-31 August, 24-31 December, February holidays, Monday September-June and Sunday

Rest – *(dinner only in July-August)* Menu €31 – Carte €37/46

◆ A tiny Provençal bistro that certainly doesn't lack spice. The chef prepares the dishes before your very eyes, using ingredients fresh from the market.

Carré des Oliviers

16 r. Carnot – ☎ 04 94 54 64 21 – Closed 30 June-17 July, 22-29 December, Sunday dinner October-May and Monday

Rest – Menu €30 – Carte €42/49

◆ The dining room is undoubtedly small but this is amply compensated for by the simple, bistro-style decor. The appetising menus, chalked-up on the slate, feature Provençal specialities.

Southeast 5 km on D 98, towards Toulon – ✉ 83310

La Ferme du Magnan

– ☎ 04 94 49 57 54 – sales@alpazurhotels.com – Fax 04 94 49 57 54 – Open from February to November

Rest – Menu €35/55 – Carte €35/69

◆ A bastide in the 16C, a silkworm nursery in the 19C, and now a quaint country restaurant. Copious cuisine based on farm produce. Panoramic terrace adorned with earthenware jars.

COIGNIÈRES – 78 Yvelines – 311 H3 – pop. 4 231 – alt. 160 m – ✉ 78310 18 A2

Paris 39 – Rambouillet 15 – St-Quentin-en-Yvelines 7 – Versailles 21

Le Capucin Gourmand

170 Nationale 10 – ☎ 01 34 61 46 06 – capucingourmand@wanadoo.fr – Fax 01 34 61 46 06 – Closed Sunday evening and Monday

Rest – Carte €46/66

◆ An old post house in a business park with charm intact. Dining room both rustic and stylish, heated by an open fire in winter. Quiet flowery terrace.

Le Vivier

N 10 – ☎ 01 34 61 64 39 – k-vivier@wanadoo.fr – Fax 01 34 61 94 30 – Closed Sunday evening and Monday

Rest – Menu €36 – Carte €43/65

◆ As the sign indicates, the cuisine served is fish and seafood-based. Two beautiful rustic dining rooms, brightened with some nautical touches.

COISE-ST-JEAN-PIED-GAUTHIER – 73 Savoie – 333 J4 – pop. 945 – alt. 292 m – ✉ 73800 46 F2

Paris 582 – Albertville 32 – Chambéry 23 – Grenoble 55

Château de la Tour du Puits

du Puits road: 1 km – ☎ 04 79 28 88 00 – info@chapeaupuit.fr – Fax 04 79 28 88 01 – Closed 15 October-30 November

7 rm – €100/270 €100/270, ☕ €20 – ½ P €116/191

Rest – *(closed Tuesday lunch and Monday)* Menu €25 (weekday lunch), €42/70 – Carte €65/79

◆ This graceful château rebuilt in the 18C has a pepper-pot tower and stands in the middle of a wooded park. Delightfully decorated rooms. Heliport. The warm, intimate restaurant has great charm. Fine terrace under the plane trees.

COL BAYARD – 05 Hautes-Alpes – 334 E5 – alt. 1 248 m – ✉ 05000 GAP
French Alps 41 **C1**

Paris 658 – Gap 7 – La Mure 56 – Sisteron 60

in Laye 2,5 km North by N 85 – pop. 212 – alt. 1 170 m – ✉ 05500

La Laiterie du Col Bayard

– ☎ 04 92 50 50 06 – col.bayard@wanadoo.fr – Fax 04 92 50 19 91 – Closed 16 November-19 December, Tuesday dinner, Wednesday dinner, Thursday dinner and Monday except school holidays and holidays

Rest – Menu € 17/36 – Carte € 11/42

♦ This surprisingly original restaurant includes a shop for the sale of local products. It adjoins a dairy farm and cheese-makers. From the terrace one has a fine view of the mountains. A variety of cheeses takes pride of place on the menus.

COL DE BAVELLA – 2A Corse-du-Sud – 345 E9 – see Corse

COL DE CEYSSAT – 63 Puy-de-Dôme – 326 E8 – see Clermont-Ferrand

COL DE CUREBOURSE – 15 Cantal – 330 D5 – see Vic-sur-Cère

COL DE LA CROIX-FRY – 74 Haute-Savoie – 328 L5 – see Manigod

COL DE LA CROIX-PERRIN – 38 Isère – 333 G7 – see Lans-en-Vercors

COL DE LA FAUCILLE ★★ – 01 Ain – 328 J2 – alt. 1 320 m – Winter sports : (Mijoux-Lelex-la Faucille) 900/1 680 m 3 29 – ✉ 01170 Gex
Burgundy-Jura 46 **F1**

Paris 480 – Bourg-en-Bresse 108 – Genève 29 – Gex 11 – Morez 28 – Nantua 58

Downhill to Gex★★ (N 5) ✻★★ Southeast: 2 km - Mont-Rond★★ (access by cable car – railway station at 500 m Southwest of the pass).

La Mainaz
lake Geneva and the Alps,

col de la Faucille, 1 km south on D 1005 – ☎ 04 50 41 31 10 – mainaz@club-internet.fr – Fax 04 50 41 31 77 – Closed 15 June-2 July, 27 October-11 December, Sunday dinner and Monday except school holidays

23 rm – €77/97 €77/97, € 12,50 – ½ P € 82/107 – **Rest** – Menu € 32/65 – Carte € 45/68

♦ This large wooden chalet's undisputed asset is the exceptional view of Lake Léman and the Alps. Spacious rooms, some with a balcony. Some have been renovated. Magnificent panoramic terrace overlooking the region; classic dishes.

La Petite Chaumière

Col de la faucille – ☎ 04 50 41 30 22 – info@petitechaumiere.com – Fax 04 50 41 33 22 – Closed 1st-25 April and 11 October-19 December

54 rm – €48/55 €55/69, € 10 – ½ P € 63/71 – **Rest** – Menu (€ 15), € 20 (weekdays)/32 – Carte € 30/43

♦ A 1960s Jura chalet at the foot of the ski slopes. Small, simple, wainscoted rooms, some with a balcony. Family flats in the new wing. Look out for the owner's collection of old bellows on your way into this warm, rustic restaurant.

La Couronne

– ☎ 04 50 41 32 65 – hotel-de-la-couronne@wanadoo.fr – Fax 04 50 41 32 47 – Open 15 May-30 September and 15 December-31 March

15 rm – €65 €70, € 10 – ½ P € 65/71 – **Rest** – *(closed Wednesday in June)* Menu € 27/41 – Carte € 34/56

♦ A breath of fresh air! Most of the 1970s style rooms boast a balcony. Some have been refurbished with light wood panelling. Classic menu in the restaurant adorned with beams, knick-knacks and a mural. Open-air terrace.

COL DE LA MACHINE – 26 Drôme – 332 F4 – see St-Jean-en-Royans

COL DE LA SCHLUCHT – 88 Vosges – 314 K4 – alt. 1 258 m – Winter sports : 1 150/1 250 m Alsace-Lorraine 27 D3

Paris 441 – Colmar 37 – Épinal 56 – Gérardmer 16 – Guebwiller 46 – St-Dié 37 – Thann 43

Route des Crêtes★★★ North and South - Le Hohneck ※★★★ South: 5 km.

Le Collet rest, VISA AE

au Collet, 2 km on Gérardmer road – 03 29 60 09 57 – hotcollet@aol.com – Fax 03 29 60 08 77 – Closed 2 November-3 December

25 rm – €65 €75, €12 – 6 suites – ½ P €74/84

Rest – *(closed Thursday lunch and Wednesday except school holidays)* Menu €17 (weekday lunch), €25/28 – Carte €32/49

◆ Large, friendly chalet, surrounded by fir trees. Attractive interior decor, cosy rooms and stylish details (embroidered linen and prevalence of wood). Tasty, local food served in a welcoming dining room.

COL D'ÈZE – 06 Alpes-Maritimes – 341 F5 – see Èze

COL DU DONON – 67 Bas-Rhin – 315 G5 – alt. 718 m – ✉ 67130 Grandfontaine Alsace-Lorraine 1 A2

Paris 402 – Lunéville 61 – St-Dié 41 – Sarrebourg 39 – Sélestat 67 – Strasbourg 61

※★★ on the chain of the Vosges.

Du Donon VISA

– 03 88 97 20 69 – hotelrestdudonon@wanadoo.fr – Fax 03 88 97 20 17 – Closed 17-23 March and 12 November-3 December

22 rm – €50 €62, €9,50 – 1 suite – ½ P €64 – **Rest** – Menu €18/37 – Carte €25/40

◆ In a country setting, at an altitude of 727m/2 385ft, the Du Dunon's recently renovated rooms are adorned with painted or rustic furniture, with some having their own kitchenette. Non-smoking dining rooms and flower-decked terraces in summer.

COL DU LAUTARET – 05 Hautes-Alpes – 334 G2 – alt. 2 058 m – ✉ 05480 Villar-d'Arêne 41 C1

Paris 653 – Briançon 27 – Les Deux-Alpes 38 – Valloire 25

Des Glaciers mountains and glaciers, rm, VISA AE

– 04 92 24 42 21 – bonnabel@hotel-bonnabel.com – Fax 04 92 24 44 81 – Open 1st May-30 September and 20 December-30 March

23 rm – €165/352 €165/352, €20 – 2 suites – ½ P €133/226

Rest – *(dinner only)* Menu €35/50 – Carte €41/59

◆ An exceptional view over mountains and glaciers from this hotel at the top of a pass (2058 m). Large, chalet-style rooms, attractive fitness room. Traditional cuisine is served in the evening, and midday luncheons are of the brasserie-type. There is also a bar-games room.

COL DU PAVILLON – 69 Rhône – 327 F3 – see Cours

COLIGNY – 01 Ain – 328 F2 – pop. 1 091 – alt. 298 m – ✉ 01270 44 B1

Paris 407 – Bourg-en-Bresse 24 – Lons-le-Saunier 39 – Mâcon 57 – Tournus 48

Au Petit Relais VISA AE

Grande rue – 04 74 30 10 07 – Fax 04 74 30 10 07 – Closed 27 March-4 April, 23 September-3 October, 8-11 December, Wednesday dinner and Thursday

Rest – *(number of covers limited, pre-book)* Menu €16 (weekday lunch), €26/56 bi – Carte €38/89

◆ Neat, recently refurbished dining room serving tasty cuisine, including Bresse specialities and select wines. Inner courtyard summer terrace.

COLLÉGIEN – 77 Seine-et-Marne – **312** F2 – **101** 19 – see Paris, Area (Marne-la-Vallée)

LA COLLE-SUR-LOUP – 06 Alpes-Maritimes – **341** D5 – pop. 6 697 – alt. 90 m –
✉ **06480** French Riviera 42 **E2**

Paris 919 – Antibes 15 – Cagnes-sur-Mer 7 – Cannes 26 – Grasse 19 – Nice 18 – Vence 7

Syndicat d'initiative, 28, rue Maréchal Foch ✆ 04 93 32 68 36, Fax 04 93 32 05 07

Le Clos des Arts
350 Route de St-Paul – ✆ 04 93 32 40 00 – info@closdesarts.fr – Fax 04 93 32 69 98
8 rm – †€ 190/430 ††€ 190/430, ☕ € 26
Rest – *(closed 15 November-20 December, Tuesday lunch, Sunday dinner and Monday from 1st November to 28 February)*
Menu € 45/89 – Carte € 52/104
◆ A magnificent hotel revamped in 2006 comprising two Provençal villas with elegant and personalised junior suites, some with their own terrace. Contemporary cuisine served outdoors or beneath a painted ceiling. Seafood tank, rotisserie and grill.

Marc Hély without rest
535 rte de Cagnes, 800 m south-east on D 6 – ✆ 04 93 22 64 10 – contact@hotel-marc-hely.com – Fax 04 93 22 93 84 – Closed 9-23 November and 25 January-8 February
12 rm – †€ 69/80 ††€ 69/135, ☕ € 11
◆ Most of the bedrooms in this large house enjoy fine views over Saint-Paul-de-Vence. Functional comfort, with breakfast taken on the veranda. Swimming pool. Peace and quiet guaranteed.

L'Abbaye rm, rest,
541 bd Teisseire, (Grasse road) – ✆ 04 93 32 68 34 – contact@hotelabbaye.com – Fax 04 93 32 85 06
14 rm – †€ 85/280 ††€ 85/280, ☕ € 12 – **Rest** – *(closed Monday mid September-mid June)* Menu (€ 15), € 20 (weekday lunch), € 35/55 – Carte € 34/48
◆ Attractive guestrooms with personal touches now stand within the noble walls of this old abbey once occupied by the monks of the Ile St-Honorat. 10C chapel. The vaulted restaurant has a new trendy designer decor. Shaded terrace in the old cloister.

Le Blanc Manger
1260 rte de Cagnes – ✆ 04 93 22 51 20 – leblancmanger@wanadoo.fr – Fax 04 92 02 00 46 – Closed 12 November-12 December, Tuesday except dinner from 1st May to 15 September, Wednesday lunch from 1st May to 15 September and Monday
Rest – *(number of covers limited, pre-book)* Menu € 26/38
◆ Delicate cuisine with a southern accent is on offer in Le Blanc Manger's bijou, rustic-influenced dining room, or on the attractive, wood-furnished terrace.

COLLEVILLE-SUR-MER – 14 Calvados – **303** G3 – pop. 172 – alt. 42 m –
✉ **14710** Normandy 32 **B2**

Paris 281 – Cherbourg 84 – Caen 49 – Saint-Lô 39

Domaine de L'Hostréière without rest
rte Cimetière Américain – ✆ 02 31 51 64 64 – hotelhostreiere@wanadoo.fr – Fax 02 31 51 64 65 – Open 1st April-15 November
19 rm – †€ 75/110 ††€ 75/180, ☕ € 16
◆ The outbuildings of this old farmhouse, close to the American cemetery in St-Laurent-sur-Mer, have modern rooms, some with a terrace. Fitness centre, swimming pool and tea room.

COLLIAS – 30 Gard – **339** L5 – see Pont-du-Gard

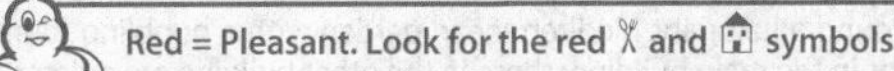

Red = Pleasant. Look for the red and symbols.

COLLIOURE – 66 Pyrénées-Orientales – **344** J7 – pop. 2 763 – alt. 2 m – Casino – ✉ 66190 Languedoc-Roussillon-Tarn Gorges 22 **B3**

Paris 879 – Argelès-sur-Mer 7 – Céret 36 – Perpignan 30 – Port-Vendres 3

Office de tourisme, place du 18 Juin ✆ 04 68 82 15 47, Fax 04 68 82 46 29

Site★★ - Altar-pieces★ in Notre-Dame-des-Anges church.

COLLIOURE

Aire (R. de l') . . . . **B** 2
Amirauté (Q. de l') . . . . **B** 3
Arago (R. François) . . . . **B** 4
Argelès (Rte d') . . . . **A**
Dagobert (R.) . . . . **B** 7
Démocratie (R. de la) . . . . **B** 8
Égalité (R. de l') . . . . **B** 9
Ferry (R. Jules) . . . . **AB** 13
Galère (R. de la) . . . . **A**
Gaulle (Av. du Gén.) . . . . **B**
Jean-Jaurès (Pl.) . . . . **B** 14
Lamartine (R.) . . . . **B** 15
Leclerc (Pl. Gén.) . . . . **AB** 17
Maillol (Av. Aristide) . . . . **A**
Mailly (R.) . . . . **B** 19
Michelet (R. Jules) . . . . **A** 20
Miradou (Av. du) . . . . **A** 23
Pasteur (R.) . . . . **B**
Pla de Las Fourques (R. du) . . . . **A**
République (R. de la) . . . . . . **AB**
Rolland (R. Romain) . . . . **A**
Rousseau (R. J.-J.) . . . . **AB** 29
St-Vincent (R.) . . . . **B** 30
Soleil (R. du) . . . . **B** 33
La Tour d'Auvergne (R. de) . . . **B** 16
Vauban (R.) . . . . **B** 34
8 Mai 1945 (Pl. du) . . . . **B** 35
18-Juin (Pl. du) . . . . **B** 40

Relais des Trois Mas ← Port and Collioure,
rte Port-Vendres – ✆ 04 68 82 05 07
– balette.restaurant@tiscali.fr – Fax 04 68 82 38 08
– Closed 30 November-7 February
23 rm – €100/160 €150/460, ☕ €18 – ½ P €148/303
Rest ***La Balette*** – *(closed Tuesday and Wednesday 1st October-1st April)*
Menu €37/74 – Carte €66/119
◆ Three renovated mas with wonderful views of the town and harbour. The individually decorated rooms are named after painters. Garden, pool and Jacuzzi. Updated regional cuisine served in summer on the pleasant panoramic terrace.

Casa Païral without rest
imp. Palmiers – ✆ 04 68 82 05 81 – contact@hotel-casa-pairal.com
– Fax 04 68 82 52 10 – Open 22 March-2 November A **b**
27 rm – €89/100 €122/198, ☕ €11
◆ A 19C home set around a luxuriant Mediterranean garden with a bubbling fountain. Characterful bedrooms in the main building; those in the other building are quieter.

L'Arapède

rte Port-Vendres – 04 68 98 09 59 – hotelarapede@yahoo.fr – Fax 04 68 98 30 90 – Closed 30 November-7 February

20 rm – €55/80 €65/110, €11 – ½ P €65/87

Rest – *(closed lunch except Sunday)* Menu €25/48 – Carte €35/53

◆ Modern hotel on the side of a hill. Attractive Catalan style furniture in the large bedrooms which face the sea and overflow pool. Restaurant decorated with old photos of Collioure, terrace overlooking the sea, and local dishes.

Madeloc without rest

r. R. Rolland – 04 68 82 07 56 – hotel@madeloc.com – Fax 04 68 82 55 09 – Open 15 March-5 November A **e**

27 rm – €65/108 €65/108, €11 – 5 suites

◆ A hotel on the heights of the town, with rooms furnished in rattan, many with terraces. Roof pool and hillside garden. Painting and sculpture exhibitions.

La Frégate

24 quai de l'Amirauté – 04 68 82 06 05 – hotel.lafregate@orange.fr – Fax 04 68 82 55 00 – Closed 30 November-7 February B **a**

26 rm – €50/70 €70/115, €8 – 1 suite – ½ P €65/88 – **Rest** – *(closed Tuesday and Wednesday October-March)* Menu €24/40 – Carte €30/45

◆ A refurbished hotel in an ideal position opposite the chateau. Small Catalan-inspired rooms which are well-kept and have been gradually updated. Two dining rooms with earthenware decoration serving good, simple local dishes.

Méditerranée without rest

av. A. Maillol – 04 68 82 08 60 – mediterraneehotel@free.fr – Fax 04 68 82 28 07 – Open April-November A **h**

23 rm – €63/92 €63/97, €10

◆ This 1970s building has functional rooms, all with balconies, which are gradually being updated in local colours. Terraced garden. Solarium.

Le Neptune (Jean-Claude Mourlane) old port,

rte Port-Vendres – 04 68 82 02 27 – smourlane@yahoo.fr – Fax 04 68 82 50 33 – Closed 5-23 December, 1st January-28 February, Tuesday and Wednesday October-June, Tuesday lunch and Monday July-September B **v**

Rest – Menu (€30), €38/105 – Carte €47/109

Spec. Anchois de Collioure selon la recette du moment. Homard bleu en coque (summer). Filet de bœuf Salers ou Aubrac. **Wines** Côtes du Roussillon-Villages, Banyuls.

◆ The superb terraces of this restaurant cling to the rock. Mediterranean decor and modern paintings on display. Regional dishes and seafood.

Le 5ème Péché

– 04 68 98 09 76 – contact@le5peche.com B **y**

Rest – *(number of covers limited, pre-book)* Menu €23 (lunch), €34/50 – Carte €46/54

◆ Japan meets Catalonia at this small restaurant in the old town. The Tokyo-born chef prepares fine fusion food with ultra-fresh fish to the fore.

Look out for red symbols, indicating particularly pleasant establishments.

COLLONGES-AU-MONT-D'OR – 69 Rhône – 327 I5 – see Lyon

COLLONGES-LA-ROUGE – 19 Corrèze – 329 K5 – pop. 413 – alt. 230 m – 19500 Dordogne-Berry-Limousin 25 C3

Paris 505 – Brive-la-Gaillarde 21 – Cahors 105 – Figeac 75 – Tulle 35

Office de tourisme, avenue de l'Auvitrie 05 55 25 47 57

Village★★: tympanum★ and steeple★ of the church, castel de Vassinhac★ - Saillac: tympanum★ of the church South: 4 km.

Le Relais de St-Jacques de Compostelle

– 05 55 25 41 02 – sarlmanalese@orange.fr – Fax 05 55 84 08 51 – Closed January, February, Tuesday except July-August and Monday

11 rm – €59 €51/64, €7,50 – ½ P €51/80 – **Rest** – Menu €17/43 – Carte €30/79

◆ An ideal spot to enjoy the bright village built of red sandstone. The rooms are not very large but are well kept and look out over the manor houses or the countryside. The dining room decor is rural and there is a pleasant terrace. Cuisine from the South-West.

Jeanne

au bourg – 05 55 25 42 31 – info@jeannemaisondhotes.com – Fax 05 55 25 47 80

5 rm – €90 €90 – **Table d'hôte** – Menu €32 bi

◆ A noble red-brick residence flanked by a 15C tower. Neo-rustic bedrooms tastefully furnished with a personal touch. Lounge with fireplace. Terrace and walled garden. Evening menus include a choice of typical family dishes.

COLMAR P – 68 Haut-Rhin – 315 I8 – pop. 65 136 – Built-up area 116 268 – alt. 194 m – ✉ 68000 Alsace-Lorraine 2 **C2**

Paris 450 – Basel 68 – Freiburg-im-Breisgau 51 – Nancy 140 – Strasbourg 78

Office de tourisme, 4, rue d'Unterlinden 03 89 20 68 92, Fax 03 89 20 69 14

d'Ammerschwihr Ammerschwihr Allée du Golf, Northwest: 9 km by D 415 then D 11, 03 89 47 17 30.

Musée d'Unterlinden★★★ (Issenheim altar-piece ★★★) - Old town★★: Maison Pfister★★ BZ **W**, St-Martin collegiate church ★ BY, Maison des Arcades★ CZ**K**, Maison des Têtes★ BY **Y** - Ancienne Douane★ BZ **D**, Ancien Corps de Garde★ BZ **B** - Virgin with rose bush★★ and stained-glass windows★ of the Dominicains church BY - Window of the Great Crucifixion★ of St-Matthieu temple CY - " Little Venice "★: ★ of St-Pierre bridge BZ , quartier de la Krutenau★, rue de la Poissonnerie★, façade of the civil court ★ BZ **J** - Maison des vins d'Alsace by ①.

Plans on following pages

Les Têtes

19 r. Têtes – 03 89 24 43 43 – les-tetes@calixo.net.fr – Fax 03 89 24 58 34 – Closed February BY **y**

21 rm – €95/112 €112/234, €14 – 1 suite

Rest *La Maison des Têtes* – see restaurant listing

◆ The historic appeal of this splendid abode, built in the 17C on the remains of the ramparts around Colmar is enhanced by its elegant Alsatian interior. Delightful inner courtyard.

Le Colombier without rest

7 r. Turenne – 03 89 23 96 00 – info@hotel-le-colombier.fr – Fax 03 89 23 97 27 – Closed 24 December-2 January BZ **u**

28 rm – €81/195 €81/195, €12

◆ A contemporary setting, Italian designer furniture, a Renaissance staircase and peaceful patio are among the treasures of this attractive 15C establishment.

Grand Hôtel Bristol

rm, rest,

7 pl. Gare – 03 89 23 59 59 – reservation@grand-hotel-bristol.com – Fax 03 89 23 92 26 AZ **g**

91 rm – €93/149 €100/149, €13,50

Rest *Rendez-vous de Chasse* – see restaurant listing

Rest *L'Auberge* – brasserie – *03 89 23 17 57* – Menu (€14), €20/29 – Carte €28/40

◆ Not far from the TGV railway station, twenty brand new rooms, fitness facilities and seminar rooms have been added to this hotel with a pleasant Belle Époque atmosphere. A stylish 1900s setting and attractive menu specialising in dishes and wines of Alsace can be found at the Auberge.

Mercure Champ de Mars without rest

2 av. Marne – 03 89 21 59 59 – h1225@accor.com – Fax 03 89 21 59 00 BZ **n**

75 rm – €111/121 €125/135, €14,50

◆ This 1970s building on the edge of Champ-de-Mars Park stands between the station and the town centre. Functional and relatively modern (wifi) rooms in the process of renovation.

Hostellerie Le Maréchal
4 pl. Six Montagnes Noires – ☎ 03 89 41 60 32 – info@le-marechal.com – Fax 03 89 24 59 40 BZ **b**
30 rm – †€ 85/95 ††€ 105/255, ☕ € 14 – ½ P € 108/189
Rest *A l'Échevin* – *(closed 14 January-1st February)* Menu € 28 (weekday lunch), € 38/78 – Carte € 43/79
♦ The rooms of these delightful Alsatian houses in Little Venice have a candy-box charm (except two which are more old-fashioned). Splendid regional breakfast. At the Échevin, a cosy decor on a musical theme and enchanting river view.

Mercure Unterlinden without rest
15 r. Golbery – ☎ 03 89 41 71 71 – h0978@accor.com – Fax 03 89 23 82 71 BY **v**
72 rm – †€ 109/129 ††€ 119/139, ☕ € 14 – 4 suites
♦ Close to the Unterlinden museum, a non-smoking establishment with comfortable, functional and modern rooms. The town centre garage is most appreciated.

St-Martin without rest
38 Grand'Rue – ☎ 03 89 24 11 51 – colmar@hotel-saint-martin.com – Fax 03 89 23 47 78 – Closed 23-26 December and 1st January-8 March CZ **e**
40 rm – †€ 79/99 ††€ 89/149, ☕ € 11
♦ Three 14C and 17C houses in the old quarter, set around an inner courtyard with a turret and a Renaissance staircase. Cosy rooms with personal touches.

Amiral without rest
11a bd du Champ-de-Mars – ☎ 03 89 23 26 25 – hotelamiralcolmar@wanadoo.fr – Fax 03 89 23 83 64 BZ **d**
47 rm – †€ 55/83 ††€ 55/99, ☕ € 12
♦ This old malthouse is home to pleasant contemporary rooms (larger on the ground floor). Hospitable sitting room with fireplace and cane furniture.

Turenne without rest
10 rte Bâle – ☎ 03 89 21 58 58 – infos@turenne.com – Fax 03 89 41 27 64 CZ **x**
83 rm – †€ 49/72 ††€ 62/82, ☕ € 8,50 – 2 suites
♦ Architecture and furniture with a regional flavour in this hotel near Little Venice. Practical rooms, generous breakfasts and reasonable prices.

La Maison des Têtes – Hôtel Les Têtes
19 r. Têtes – ☎ 03 89 24 43 43 – les-tetes@calixo.net – Fax 03 89 24 58 34 – Closed February, Sunday dinner, Tuesday lunch and Monday BY **Y**
Rest – Menu € 29/60 – Carte € 36/61
♦ This fine Renaissance house is one of the gems of Colmar's architectural heritage. Dining room (19C) lined with light wood, traditional cuisine and fine selection of local wines.

Rendez-vous de Chasse – Grand Hôtel Bristol
7 pl. de la Gare – ☎ 03 89 23 15 86 – reservation@grand-hotel-bristol.com – Fax 03 89 23 92 26 AZ **g**
Rest – Menu (€ 29), € 45/80 – Carte € 64/78
Spec. Terrine de foie gras d'oie, marmelade aux mirabelles (15 August-15 September). Omble chevalier cuit à l'huile d'olive, poêlée de girolles, cuisses de grenouille en tempura (mid June to end August). Dos de chevreuil d'Alsace, nems aux fruits, sauce épicée (15 May to 15 January). **Wines** Riesling, Pinot noir.
♦ A plush restaurant with a fireplace, stonework and ceiling beams. Original Daumier drawings on display. Updated, gourmet meals and a fine wine list.

JY'S (Jean-Yves Schillinger)
17 r. Poissonnerie – ☎ 03 89 21 53 60 – Fax 03 89 21 53 65 – Closed February school holidays, Monday lunchtime and Sunday BZ **g**
Rest – Menu € 30 (weekday lunch), € 51/68 – Carte € 57/63
Spec. Cocktail de chair de tourteau. Pavé de cabillaud rôti, tomates confites et olives noires. Canon d'agneau rôti à la fleur de sel. **Wines** Riesling, Pinot gris.
♦ Highly inventive menu and ultra-modern decor, by Olivier Gagnère: this pretty 1750 house on the banks of the Lauch is Colmar's trendiest spot.

COLMAR

Agen (R. d') . . . BY
Alsace (Av. d') . . . CYZ
Ancienne Douane (Pl. de l') . . . CZ 2
Augustins (R. des) . . . BZ 3
Bagatelle (R. de la) . . . AY
Bains (R. des) . . . BY 5
Bâle (Route de) . . . CZ
Bartholdi (R.) . . . BCZ
Blés (R. des) . . . BZ 9
Boulangers (R. des) . . . BY 12
Brasseries (R. des) . . . CY 13
Bruat (R.) . . . BZ 14
Cathédrale (Pl. de la) . . . BY 17
Cavalerie (R. de la) . . . BCY
Champ-de-Mars (Bd du) . . . BYZ 18
Chauffour (R.) . . . BZ 20
Clefs (R. des) . . . BCY
Clemenceau (Av. Georges) . . . BCZ
Écoles (R. des) . . . BZ 22
Est (R. de l') . . . CYZ
Fleischhauer (R.) . . . BCY
Fleurent (R. J.-B.) . . . BY 24
Fleurs (R. des) . . . CZ
Florimont (R. du) . . . AY 25
Foch (Av.) . . . BZ
Fribourg (Av. de) . . . CZ
Gare (Pl. et R. de la) . . . AZ
Gaulle (Av. Gén.-de) . . . ABYZ
Golbéry (R.) . . . BY
Grad (R. Charles) . . . AY
Grand'Rue . . . BCZ 31
Grenouillère (R. de la) . . . CYZ 32
Herse (R. de la) . . . BZ 33
Ingersheim (Rte d') . . . ABY
Jeanne d'Arc (Pl.) . . . CY
Joffre (Av.) . . . BZ
Kléber (R.) . . . BY 35
Ladhof (R. du) . . . CY 36
Lasch (R. Georges) . . . AZ 37
Lattre-de-Tassigny (Av. J. de) . . . ABY 43
Leclerc (Bd du Gén.) . . . BZ 45
Liberté (Av. de la) . . . AZ
Logelbach (R. du) . . . AY
Manège (R. du) . . . BZ 49
Marchands (R. des) . . . BYZ 50
Marché-aux-Fruits (Pl. du) . . . BZ 51
Marne (Av. de la) . . . BZ
Messimy (R.) . . . ABZ 52
Molly (R. Berthe) . . . BYZ 54
Mouton (R. du) . . . CY 57
Mulhouse (R. de) . . . AZ
Neuf-Brisach (Rte de) . . . CY
Nord (R. du) . . . BCY
Poincaré (Av. Raymond) . . . ABZ
Poissonnerie (R. et Q. de la) . . . BCZ 62
Preiss (R. Jacques) . . . ABZ 63
Rapp (Pl.) . . . BZ
Rapp (R.) . . . BCY
Reims (R. de) . . . BZ 65
République (Av. de la) . . . ABZ
Ribeauvillé (R. de) . . . BY 67
Roesselman (R.) . . . BY 69
Rouffach (Rte de) . . . AZ
St-Jean (R.) . . . BZ 71
St-Joseph (Pl. et R.) . . . AY
St-Josse (R.) . . . CZ
St-Léon (R.) . . . AY
St-Nicolas (R.) . . . BY 73
St-Pierre (Bd et Pont) . . . BCZ
Schlumberger (R. Camille) . . . ABZ
Schwendi (R.) . . . CZ
Sélestat (Rte de) . . . CY
Semm (R. de la) . . . CZ
Serruriers (R. des) . . . BY 75
Sinn (Quai de la) . . . BY 77
Six-Montagnes-Noires (Pl. des) . . . BZ 79
Stanislas (R.) . . . BY
Tanneurs (R. des) . . . CZ 82
Têtes (R. des) . . . BY 83
Thann (R. de) . . . CY
Tir (R. du) . . . AZ
Turckheim (R. de) . . . AY
Turenne (R.) . . . BCZ
Unterlinden (Pl. d') . . . BY 85
Val St-Grégoire (R. du) . . . AY
Vauban (R.) . . . CY
Voltaire (R.) . . . ABZ
Weinemer (R.) . . . BZ 86
1ère Armée Française (R. de la) . . . BY
2 Février (Pl. du) . . . CY 87
5e Division-Blindée (R. de la) . . . BY 95
18 Novembre (Pl. du) . . . BY 97

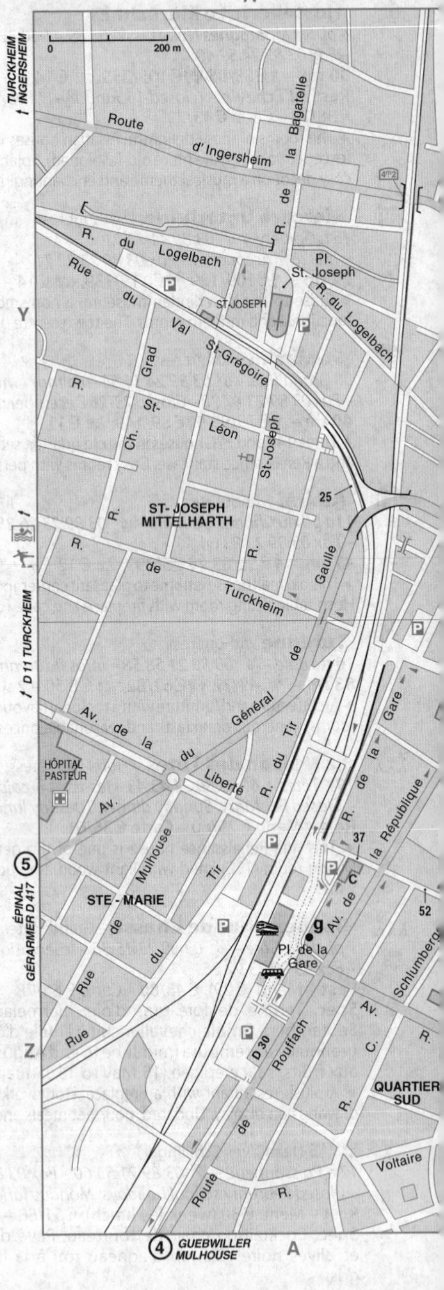

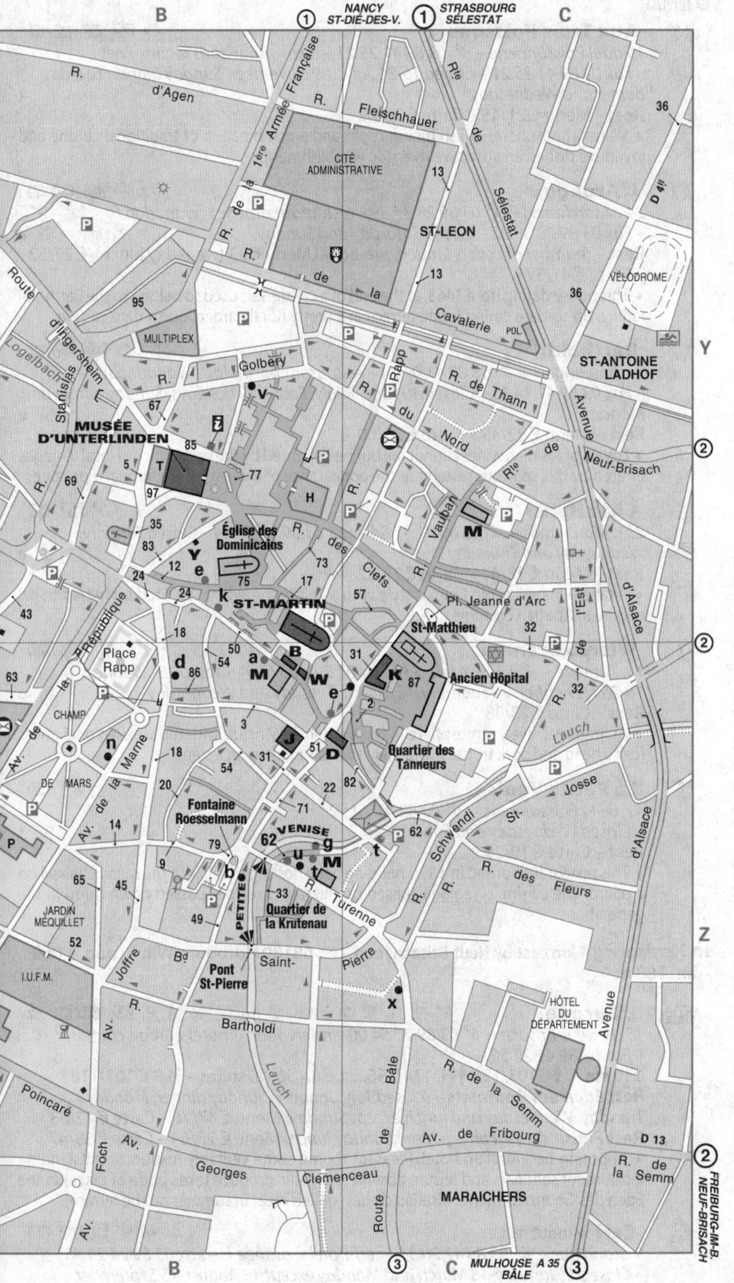
NANCY ST-DIÉ-DES-V.
STRASBOURG SÉLESTAT
CITÉ ADMINISTRATIVE
ST-LEON
VÉLODROME
MULTIPLEX
ST-ANTOINE LADHOF
MUSÉE D'UNTERLINDEN
Église des Dominicains
ST-MARTIN
St-Matthieu
Ancien Hôpital
Pl. Jeanne d'Arc
Place Rapp
CHAMP DE MARS
Quartier des Tanneurs
Fontaine Roesselmann
VENISE
PETITE
Quartier de la Krutenau
Pont St-Pierre
JARDIN MÉQUILLET
I.U.F.M.
HÔTEL DU DÉPARTEMENT
MARAICHERS
FREIBURG-IM-B. NEUF-BRISACH
MULHOUSE A 35 BÂLE

Aux Trois Poissons

15 quai Poissonnerie – 03 89 41 25 21 – auxtroispoissons@calixo.net – Fax 03 89 41 25 21 – Closed 15-31 July, 3-9 November, Sunday dinner, Tuesday dinner and Wednesday CZ **t**

Rest – Menu € 21/45 – Carte € 30/68

◆ Warm atmosphere, stylish dining room and a combination of traditional cuisine and inventive dishes: an attractive riverside establishment.

L'Arpège

24 r. Marchands – 03 89 23 37 89 – restaurant.arpege@wanadoo.fr – Fax 03 89 23 39 22 – Closed Saturday and Sunday BZ **a**

Rest – *(number of covers limited, pre-book)* Menu € 23 (weekday lunch), € 27/52 – Carte € 41/57

◆ This house dating from 1463, at the end of a cul-de-sac, used to belong to the Bartholdi family. Up-to-date dining room, terrace in a pretty floral garden, up-to-date cuisine.

Bartholdi

2 r. Boulangers – 03 89 41 07 74 – restaurant.bartholdi@wanadoo.fr – Fax 03 89 41 14 65 – Closed 30 June-7 July, February holidays, Sunday dinner and Monday BY **e**

Rest – Menu € 22/49 – Carte € 22/60

◆ Lovers of Alsatian wines cannot fail but be delighted by the vast choice of local vintages offered by this spacious restaurant the appearance of a Winstub. Traditional repertoire.

Chez Hansi

23 r. Marchands – 03 89 41 37 84 – Fax 03 89 41 37 84 – Closed January, Wednesday and Thursday BZ **e**

Rest – Menu € 18/44 – Carte € 22/52

◆ A tavern in typical old Colmar style with a half-timbered façade. Staff serve traditional cuisine in Alsatian costume.

Wistub Brenner

1 r. Turenne – 03 89 41 42 33 – Fax 03 89 41 37 99 – Closed 15-25 June, 16-25 November, 22 February-12 March, Tuesday and Wednesday BZ **u**

Rest – Carte € 28/38

◆ An informal, lively atmosphere in this authentic Winstub with terrace. Regional meals (calf's head and pork trotters) and daily specials marked on a slate.

La Petite Venise

4 r. de la Poissonnerie – 03 89 41 72 59 – Closed Wednesday and Sunday BZ **t**

Rest – Carte € 19/29

◆ This restaurant housed in a 17C building has a nostalgic feel, with the menu chalked on a board. The cuisine is regional, based on old family recipes passed down through the generations.

in Horbourg 4 km east by Neuf-Brisach road – ✉ 68180 Horbourg Wihr – pop. 5 060 – alt. 188 m

L'Europe

15 rte Neuf-Brisach – 03 89 20 54 00 – reservation@hotel-europe-colmar.fr – Fax 03 89 41 27 50

130 rm – € 103/125 € 134/156, € 14,50 – 6 suites – ½ P € 107/118

Rest *Eden des Gourmets* – *(closed July, January, Sunday dinner, Monday, Tuesday, Wednesday and lunch except Sunday)* Menu € 47/76 – Carte € 42/63

Rest *Plaisir du Terroir* – *(closed Sunday lunch)* Menu € 25/64 – Carte € 33/47

◆ Imposing neo-Alsatian hotel. Pleasant rooms, some veritably luxurious. Outstanding facilities for seminars and leisure activities. Organic produce takes pride of place on the Eden des Gourmets menu. Alsatian dishes (grilled meat in summer on the terrace).

Cerf without rest

9 Grand'Rue – 03 89 41 20 35 – cerf-hotel@orange.fr – Fax 03 89 24 24 98 – Closed 1st January-15 March and Monday except 15 August-15 September

25 rm – € 63/75 € 68/80, € 9,50

◆ A spruce, pink, half-timbered building. The comfortable, if not huge rooms are more peaceful on the garden side. Bar and sitting room in Belle Epoque style.

in Logelheim 9 km Southeast by D 13 and D 45 - CZ – **pop. 585 – alt. 195 m –** ✉ **68280**

A la Vigne rm, VISA MC

5 Grand'Rue – ✆ 03 89 20 99 60 – restaurant.alavigne@calixo.net – Fax 03 89 20 99 69 – Closed 27 June-9 July and 24 December-5 January

9 rm – €51/53 €54/72, ☕ €6,50 – ½ P €53 – **Rest** – *(closed Saturday lunch, Monday dinner and Sunday except public holidays)* Menu €11,50 (weekday lunch), €22/28 – Carte €21/36

♦ A simple, welcoming building in the regional style situated at the heart of a peaceful village. Rooms are modern, quiet and well equipped. Countrified dining room; regional fare (tartes flambées, sauerkrauts and spaetezele) and a slate of daily specials.

in Ste-Croix-en-Plaine 10 km by ③ – **pop. 2 121 – alt. 192 m –** ✉ **68127**

Au Moulin P VISA MC

rte d'Herrlisheim, on D 1 – ✆ 03 89 49 31 20 – hotelaumoulin@wanadoo.fr – Fax 03 89 49 23 11 – Open 1st April-20 December

16 rm – €49 €62/80, ☕ €10 – **Rest** – *(closed Sunday) (dinner only) (residents only)* Carte €24/35

♦ The comfortable rooms of this converted mill command a view of the Vosges. Small museum of old Alsatian objects. Snacks available (local dishes).

in Wettolsheim 4,5 km by ⑤ and D 1bis II – **alt. 220 m –** ✉ **68920**

La Palette with rm P VISA MC AE

9 r. Herzog – ✆ 03 89 80 79 14 – lapalette@lapalette.fr – Fax 03 89 79 77 00 – Closed 2-8 January

16 rm – €64/70 €70/74, ☕ €11 – 1 suite – ½ P €71 – **Rest** – *(closed Sunday dinner, Tuesday lunch and Monday)* Menu €14, €32/59 – Carte €38/50

♦ The dining rooms in this hotel are embellished by a rich palette of styles and colours. Cuisine with a contemporary touch. Attractive, renovated rooms.

in Ingersheim 4 km Northwest – **pop. 4 170 – alt. 220 m –** ✉ **68040**

La Taverne Alsacienne VISA MC AE

99 r. République – ✆ 03 89 27 08 41 – tavernealsacien@aol.com – Fax 03 89 80 89 75 – Closed 14-21 April, 21 July-7 August, 1st-10 January, Thursday dinner except December, Sunday dinner and Monday

Rest – Menu €16 (weekdays)/53 – Carte €28/58

♦ On the banks of the Fecht, this contemporary airy restaurant and bar serve daily specials as well as regional and traditional meals. Good selection of wines from Alsace.

COLOMBES – 92 Hauts-de-Seine – 312 C2 – see Paris and Area

COLOMBEY-LES-DEUX-ÉGLISES – 52 Haute-Marne – 313 J4 – pop. 650 – alt. 353 m – ✉ 52330 Northern France and the Paris Region 14 C3

Paris 248 – Bar-sur-Aube 16 – Châtillon-sur-Seine 63 – Chaumont 26 – Neufchâteau 71

Syndicat d'initiative, 68, rue du Général-de-Gaulle ✆ 03 25 01 52 33, Fax 03 25 01 98 61

Mémorial du Général-de-Gaulle and la Boisserie (museum).

Hostellerie la Montagne (Jean-Baptiste Natali) rm, VISA MC AE

r. Pisseloup – ✆ 03 25 01 51 69 – contact@hostellerielamontagne.com – Fax 03 25 01 53 20 – Closed 1st-15 October, 22-30 December, 26 January-10 February, Monday and Tuesday

9 rm – €110/160 €110/160, ☕ €13 – 1 suite

Rest – Menu €28/85 – Carte €80/103

Spec. Ravioles d'anguille fumée aux zestes de citron. Cabillaud confit au jus de morille et ail des ours. Abricots pochés et sorbet à la reine des prés. **Wines** Coteaux Champenois, Vin de Pays des Coteaux de Coiffy.

♦ Fine inventive cuisine and contemporary dining rooms. Ask for the 'chef's table' with view over the kitchens.

COLOMBIERS – 34 Hérault – 339 D9 – pop. 2 065 – alt. 25 m – ✉ 34440
Languedoc-Roussillon-Tarn Gorges 22 **B2**

Paris 779 – Béziers 10 – Montpellier 78 – Narbonne 23

Château de Colombiers

1 r. du Château – ✆ 04 67 37 06 93 – chateaudecolombiers@wanadoo.fr – Fax 04 67 37 63 11 – Closed 1st-10 January and Sunday dinner

Rest – Menu € 20 (weekday lunch), € 25/55 – Carte € 31/54

◆ This 18C château has a number of comfortable, modern dining rooms. There is also a huge terrace dotted with chestnut trees. The cuisine has a contemporary touch.

COLOMIERS – 31 Haute-Garonne – 343 F3 – see Toulouse

COLONZELLE – 26 Drôme – 332 C7 – pop. 432 – alt. 179 m – ✉ 26230 44 **B3**

Paris 642 – Lyon 180 – Montélimar 33 – Orange 37

La Maison de Soize rm, VISA

pl. de l'Église – ✆ 04 75 46 58 58 – Fax 04 75 46 58 58 – Open Easter-30 October

5 rm – €80 €90 – **Table d'hôte** – Menu € 30 bi

◆ The rooms of this old house are named after flowers. Attractive, fresh, colourful decor, modern bathrooms and excellent bedding. Home-grown vegetables feature in dishes served in the shaded garden or in a room decorated with family mementoes.

COLROY-LA-ROCHE – 67 Bas-Rhin – 315 H6 – pop. 455 – alt. 475 m – ✉ 67420

Paris 412 – Lunéville 70 – St-Dié 33 – Sélestat 31 – Strasbourg 66 1 **A2**

Hostellerie La Cheneaudière rest, VISA

3 r. Vieux Moulin – ✆ 03 88 97 61 64 – cheneaudiere@relaischateaux.com – Fax 03 88 47 21 73

32 rm – €90/260 €90/260, € 21 – 7 suites – ½ P € 99

Rest – *(closed lunch Monday-Friday from November-March)* Menu € 49 bi (lunch)/110 (dinner) – Carte € 45/112

◆ A luxury establishment set in a forest of fir trees. The spacious rooms have been refurbished in a soothing, light colour scheme. Indoor pool, massages and sauna. A gourmet menu and regional recipes to be enjoyed in two stylish dining rooms.

COLY – 24 Dordogne – 329 I5 – see le Lardin-St-Lazare

LA COMBE – 73 Savoie – 333 H4 – see Aiguebelette-le-Lac

COMBEAUFONTAINE – 70 Haute-Saône – 314 D6 – pop. 496 – alt. 259 m – ✉ 70120 16 **B1**

Paris 336 – Besançon 72 – Épinal 83 – Gray 40 – Langres 52 – Vesoul 24

Syndicat d'initiative, Mairie ✆ 03 84 92 11 80, Fax 03 84 92 15 23

Le Balcon with rm rm, VISA

– ✆ 03 84 92 11 13 – lebalcon@aol.com – Fax 03 84 92 15 89 – Closed 23 June-3 July, 29 September-4 October, 26 December-15 January, Sunday dinner, Tuesday lunch and Monday

14 rm – €45 €55/65, € 9 – ½ P € 54 – **Rest** – Menu € 24/60 – Carte € 39/72

◆ This ivy-clad inn has a rustic style dining room with copper ornamentation and polished antique furniture. Tasty, traditional cuisine. Book one of the quieter rooms at the back.

LES COMBES – 25 Doubs – 321 J4 – see Morteau

COMBLOUX – 74 Haute-Savoie – 328 M5 – pop. 1 976 – alt. 980 m – Winter sports : 1 000/1 850 m 1 24 – ✉ 74920 French Alps 46 **F1**

Paris 593 – Annecy 80 – Bonneville 37 – Chamonix-Mont-Blanc 31 – Megève 6 – Morzine 50

Office de tourisme, 49, chemin des Passerands ✆ 04 50 58 60 49, Fax 04 50 93 33 55

❄★★★ - Viewpoint indicator★ of the Cry.

Aux Ducs de Savoie Mont-Blanc, rest,
au Bouchet – 04 50 58 61 43 – info@ducs-de-savoie.com – Fax 04 50 58 67 43 – Open 1st June-6 October and 15 December-25 April
50 rm – €130/190 €130/190, €18 – ½ P €110/150
Rest – Menu €32/45 – Carte €40/52
♦ Nature lovers could wish for nothing better than this huge chalet. Ask for a room with a view, to better admire the panorama from the comfort of your bed! Pool overlooking the valley. Home cooking and Savoy specialities in the "all-wood" panoramic dining room.

Au Cœur des Prés Aravis and Mont-Blanc,
152 chemin du Champet – 04 50 93 36 55 – hotelaucoeurdespres@wanadoo.fr – Fax 04 50 58 69 14 – Open end May-end September and mid December-beg. April
33 rm – €80/90 €100/170, €12 – ½ P €77/97 – **Rest** – Menu €28 (weekdays)/36
♦ On the heights overlooking Combloux, simple accommodation but bright, wood panelled and fairly spacious with views of the peaks. Pleasant sitting room with fireplace. Extensive view, tasteful decor and classic menu in the restaurant.

Joly Site
81 rte de Sallanches – 04 50 58 60 07 – joly-site@joly-site.com – Fax 04 50 93 38 09 – Closed Monday off season
10 rm – €75/95 €75/120, €9 – ½ P €75/85 – **Rest** – Menu €19/26 – Carte €26/51
♦ Entirely renovated by an enthusiastic young team, the hotel offers rooms that are both traditional and modern, many of which have direct access to the garden. Alpine and southern recipes take pride of place in the restaurant, served around the central fireplace.

Coin Savoyard
300 rte Cry, Cuchet – 04 50 58 60 27 – coin-savoyard@wanadoo.fr – Fax 04 50 58 64 44 – Open 8 June-20 September and 15 December-12 April
14 rm – €92 €112/145, €10 – ½ P €90/105 – **Rest** – *(closed Monday lunch in winter except school holidays and Monday in June and September)* Carte €20/52
♦ Friendly 19C farmhouse next to the church. Despite its traditional alpine inn appearance it offers comfortably renovated rooms with views of the peaks. Regional specialities served by the poolside in fine weather.

COMBOURG – 35 Ille-et-Vilaine – 309 L4 – pop. 4 850 – alt. 45 m – ✉ 35270
Brittany 10 **D2**

Paris 387 – Avranches 58 – Dinan 25 – Fougères 49 – Rennes 41 – St-Malo 36 – Vitré 56
Office de tourisme, 23, place Albert Parent 02 99 73 13 93, Fax 02 99 73 52 39
des Ormes Dol-de-Bretagne Epiniac, North: 13 km by D 795, 02 99 73 54 44.
Château★.

Du Château
– 02 99 73 00 38 – hotelduchateau@wanadoo.fr – Fax 02 99 73 25 79 – Closed 19 December-27 January, Sunday dinner except July-August, Monday lunch and Saturday lunch
33 rm – €56/146 €56/146, €12 – 1 suite – ½ P €59/106
Rest – Menu (€16), €21 (weekdays)/57 – Carte €34/65
♦ At the foot of the château and lake made famous by Chateaubriand, is this attractive old house and outbuildings. Personalised, partly refurbished rooms. Menu combining traditional and regional dishes with Chateaubriand steak in pride of place. Summer garden-terrace.

L'Écrivain
pl. St-Gilduin, (opposite the church) – 02 99 73 01 61 – l-ecrivain@orange.fr – Fax 02 23 16 46 31 – Closed 20-30 June, 15-30 October, Sunday dinner, Wednesday dinner except from 15 July to 15 August and Thursday
Rest – Menu €16 (weekday lunch), €23/37
♦ Whether in the rustic or classic interior or on the terrace-garden, the bucolic charm of this establishment would have appealed to even the most famous Romantics. Updated, Breton fare.

COMBREUX – 45 Loiret – 318 K4 – pop. 202 – alt. 130 m – ✉ 45530 12 C2

Paris 113 – Bellegarde 12 – Châteauneuf-sur-Loire 14 – Orléans 41 – Pithiviers 31

Auberge de Combreux

– ✆ 02 38 46 89 89 – contact@auberge-de-combreux.fr – Fax 02 38 59 36 19 – *Closed mid December-25 January and Sunday dinner November-April*

19 rm – †€ 60/79 ††€ 60/79, ☕ € 9 – ½ P € 68/78 – **Rest** – *(closed mid December-20 January, Friday lunch May-October, Sunday dinner November-April and Monday lunch)* Menu € 19 (weekdays)/36 – Carte € 35/51

◆ Near the forest, an ivy-clad former post house and its annexe consisting of three small houses set in a garden. Rustic-style rooms, two with Jacuzzis. A welcoming dining room with countrified decor, leafy terrace and cuisine with a contemporary touch.

COMMELLE-VERNAY – 42 Loire – 327 D4 – see Roanne

COMMERCY – 55 Meuse – 307 E6 – pop. 6 324 – alt. 240 m – ✉ 55200 26 B2

Paris 269 – Bar-le-Duc 40 – Metz 73 – Nancy 53 – Toul 31 – Verdun 56

Office de tourisme, Château Stanislas ✆ 03 29 91 33 16

Côté Jardin

rm, rest, VISA

40 r. St-Mihiel – ✆ *03 29 92 09 09* – *bernard.bou794@orange.fr* – *Fax 03 29 92 09 10* – *Closed 15-31 August*

11 rm – †€ 55/70 ††€ 66/150, ☕ € 11 – ½ P € 93 – **Rest** – *(closed July-August, Friday, Saturday and Sunday) (dinner only) (resident only)* Menu € 20/25

◆ An attractively-renovated facade on the street side; on the garden side, a comfortable restaurant overlooking the terrace and the greenery. Cuisine based on seasonal produce.

De la Madeleine

La Louvière, (Nancy road) – ✆ *03 29 91 51 25* – *hotelmadeleine@free.fr* – *Fax 03 29 91 09 59*

26 rm – †€ 42/61 ††€ 56/69, ☕ € 6 – ½ P € 48/52

Rest – *(closed 24 December-1st January and Sunday dinner)* Menu € 12/32 – Carte € 17/36

◆ A modern building in the land of the famous madeleine cake, with up-to-date, soundproofed rooms, with wood and wrought iron furniture. A discreet dining room lit by wide bay windows.

COMPIÈGNE – 60 Oise – 305 H4 – pop. 41 254 – Built-up area 108 234 – alt. 41 m – ✉ 60200 Northern France and the Paris Region 36 B2

Paris 81 – Amiens 80 – Beauvais 61 – St-Quentin 74 – Soissons 39

Office de tourisme, place de l'Hôtel de Ville ✆ 03 44 40 01 00, Fax 03 44 40 23 28

de Compiègne Avenue Royale, East: by Avenue Royale, ✆ 03 44 38 48 00 ;

du Château d'Humières Monchy Humières Rue de Gournay, Northwest: 9 km by D202, ✆ 03 44 86 48 22.

Palace★★★: musée de la voiture★★, musée du Second Empire★★ - Town hall★ BZ **H** - Musée de la Figurine historique★ BZ **M** - Musée Vivenel: Greek vases ★★ AZ **M**[1].

Forêt★★ (les Beaux Monts) - Rethondes: Clairière de l'Armistice (Armistice Clearing)★★ (statue of Marshal Foch, memorial stone, Marshal Foch carriage).

Plan on next page

Les Beaux Arts without rest

VISA

33 cours Guynemer – ✆ *03 44 92 26 26* – *hotel@bw-lesbeauxarts.com* – *Fax 03 44 92 26 00* AY **v**

36 rm – †€ 69/99 ††€ 79/109, ☕ € 10 – 14 suites

◆ Pleasant teak furniture, sunny colours and modern comfort; the rooms in this quayside hotel, some with a small kitchenette, are particularly welcoming.

De Flandre without rest

VISA

16 quai République – ✆ *03 44 83 24 40* – *hoteldeflandre@wanadoo.fr* – *Fax 03 44 90 02 75* AY **u**

42 rm – †€ 50 ††€ 60, ☕ € 8

◆ Near the station on the right bank of the Oise. Rustic-style rooms, gradually being modernised. Efficient soundproofing counters the noise from the crossroad traffic.

COMPIÈGNE

Austerlitz (R. d') . . . . AZ 2
Boucheries (R. des) . . . . AZ 3
Capucins (R. des) . . . . AZ 4
Change (Pl. du) . . . . AZ 5
Clemenceau (Av. G.) . . . . BY 6
Harlay (R. de) . . . . AY 8
Hôtel-de-Ville (Pl. de l') . . . . . . AZ 10
Legendre (R. J.) . . . . BZ 12
Lombards (R. des) . . . . BZ 13
Magenta (R.) . . . . BZ 14
Notre-Dame-de-Bon-Secours (R.) . . . . AZ 15
Noyon (R. de) . . . . AY 16
Paris (R. de) . . . . AZ 17
Pierrefonds (R. de) . . . . BZ 18
St-Antoine (R.) . . . . AZ 19
St-Corneille (R.) . . . . AZ 20
St-Jacques (Pl.) . . . . BZ 22
Soissons (R. de) . . . . BY 24
Solferino (R.) . . . . AYZ 25
Sorel (R. du Prés.) . . . . AZ 26
Sous-Préfecture (R. de la) . . . BZ 27
54e-Rgt.-d'Infanterie (Pl.) . . . . AY 30

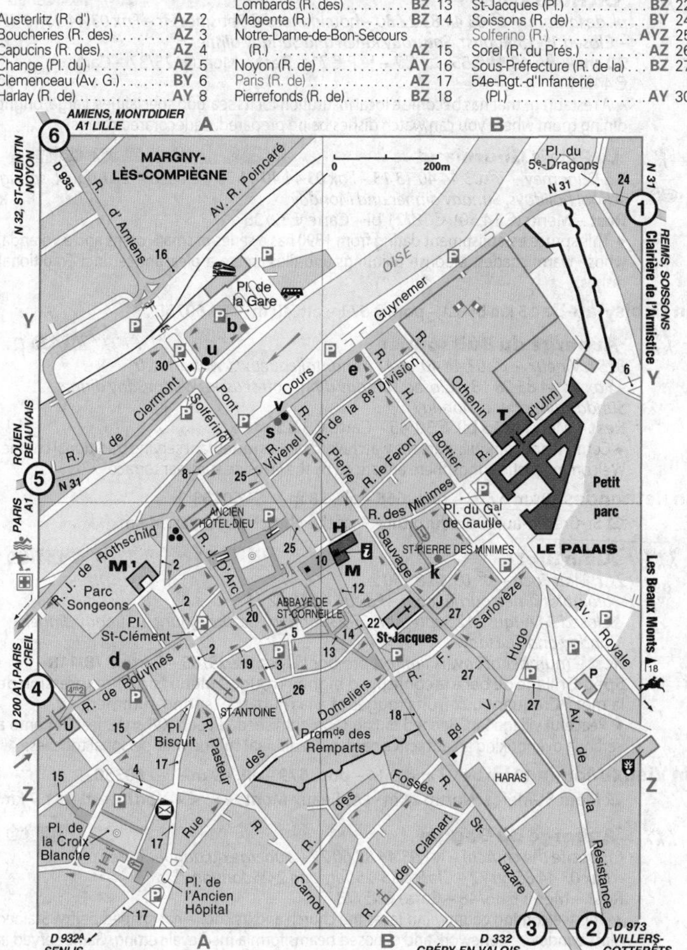

XXX Rive Gauche

AC VISA MC AE

13 cours Guynemer – ☎ 03 44 40 29 99 – rivegauche@orange.fr – Fax 03 44 40 38 00 – Closed Monday and Tuesday BY **e**

Rest – Menu € 38/45 – Carte € 73/99

◆ A sober but elegant modern dining room, enlivened by paintings, on the left bank of the Oise. Cuisine with a contemporary touch, and select wines.

XXX La Part des Anges

AC P VISA MC AE

18 r. Bouvines – ☎ 03 44 86 00 00 – lapartdesanges60@wanadoo.fr – Fax 03 44 86 09 00 – Closed August, Saturday lunch, Sunday dinner and Monday

Rest – Menu (€ 28 bi), € 33/48 – Carte € 39/51 AZ **d**

◆ A dining room in two parts (one modern, the other more intimate), adorned with a fresco depicting the 'Angels' share' and cherubs. Carefully prepared cuisine with a contemporary touch.

XX **Du Nord** with rm

pl. de la Gare – 03 44 83 22 30 – hoteldunord@9business.fr – Fax 03 44 90 11 87 – Closed 1st-15 August, Saturday lunch and Sunday dinner AY **b**

20 rm – €49 €55, €7 – ½ P €71 – **Rest** – Menu €25/37 – Carte €44/111

◆ A restaurant that has become a local institution for its seafood specialities. Large, bright dining room where you can watch dishes being prepared. Redecorated rooms.

X **Le Palais Gourmand**

8 r. Dahomey – 03 44 40 13 13 – Fax 03 44 40 41 36 – Closed 4-23 August, spring school holidays, Sunday dinner and Monday BZ **k**

Rest – Menu (€14,50), €18/21 bi – Carte €32/36

◆ This spruce establishment dating from 1890 has a series of small rooms and a veranda, whose warm shades, Moorish paintings and tiles create a pleasant setting. Traditional dishes.

in Choisy-au-Bac 5 km by ② – pop. 3 571 – alt. 40 m – ✉ 60750

XX **Auberge du Buissonnet**

825 r. Vineux – 03 44 40 17 41 – chantallequeux@wanadoo.fr – Fax 03 44 85 28 18 – Closed Tuesday dinner off season, Wednesday dinner, Sunday dinner and Monday

Rest – Menu (€15 bi), €30/45 – Carte €34/50

◆ Comfort and tranquility are the watchwords at this restaurant serving traditional cuisine. Welcoming rustic atmosphere enhanced by the lakeside summer terrace.

in Rethondes 10 km by ② – pop. 668 – alt. 38 m – ✉ 60153

St-Crépin-aux-Bois: furniture ★ of the church Northeast: 4 km.

XXX **Alain Blot**

21 r. Mar. Foch – 03 44 85 60 24 – alainblot@netcourrier.com – Fax 03 44 85 92 35 – Closed 24 August-12 September, 5-23 January, Saturday lunch, Sunday dinner, Monday and Tuesday

Rest – *(number of covers limited, pre-book)* Menu €29/85 – Carte €78/118

Spec. Grillade de bar à la confiture d'oignons rouges. Menu "simple expression de la mer". Craquant aux fruits rouges et à la rhubarbe (spring-summer).

◆ Peaceful village inn. Refined dining room furnished in Louis XVI style, leading onto a veranda overlooking an attractive garden. Traditional cuisine with personal touches.

in Vieux-Moulin 10 km by ③ and D 14 – pop. 579 – alt. 49 m – ✉ 60350

Mont St-Marc★ North: 2 km - Les Beaux-Monts★★: ≤★ NorthwestWest: 7 km.

XXX **Auberge du Daguet**

(opposite the church) – 03 44 85 60 72 – auberge.du.daguet@free.fr – Fax 03 44 85 60 72 – Closed 15-25 July and 2-25 January

Rest – Menu €36/48 – Carte €45/73

◆ This welcoming country inn faces the church and its coolie-hat shaped belfry. Stained glass windows, stonework and exposed beams form a medieval setting. Game served in season.

XX **Auberge du Mont St-Pierre**

28 rte des Étangs – 03 44 85 60 00 – safajo-js@wanadoo.fr – Fax 03 44 85 23 03 – Closed 3-18 August, February holidays, Sunday dinner, Thursday dinner and Monday except holidays

Rest – Menu €25/38 – Carte €50/65

◆ This local-style inn, on the edge of the forest, has a veranda dining room with hunting decor and a peaceful summer terrace. Seasonal produce and game.

Z.A.C. de Mercières 6 km by ⑤ and D 200 – ✉ 60472 Compiègne

Mercure rm, rest,

carrefour J. Monnet – 03 44 30 30 30 – h1623@accor.com – Fax 03 44 30 30 44

92 rm – €106/113 €113/124, €12 – **Rest** – *(closed Saturday and Sunday except July-August)* Menu €21 – Carte €28/41

◆ This hotel between the town and the motorway has been designed for the wellbeing of the traveller: comfort, space, good soundproofing and a convivial bar, perfect for relaxation. Large, discreet modern dining room with a summer terrace. "Mercure" menu and grills.

in Meux 11 km by ⑤, D 200 and D 98 – pop. 1 708 – alt. 50 m – ✉ 60880

Auberge de la Vieille Ferme rest, VISA AE
– *03 44 41 58 54 – auberge.vieille.ferme@wanadoo.fr – Fax 03 44 41 23 50 – Closed 28 July-19 August, 22 December-6 January and Sunday dinner*
14 rm – €59 €63, €8 – ½ P €80 – **Rest** – *(closed Saturday lunch, Sunday dinner and Monday)* Menu €22 bi/44 bi – Carte €29/43
◆ Old farmhouse in red brick from the Oise Valley. Simple, functional and well-kept rooms on either side of two inner courtyards. A restaurant with a country atmosphere serving traditional food based on local products.

L'Annexe VISA AE
1 r. République – 03 44 91 10 10 – restaurantlannexe@orange.fr – Fax 03 44 40 38 00 – Closed Monday and Tuesday
Rest – Menu €24/35
◆ Family-run restaurant in a brick house where well-chosen furniture and pastel colours make an intimate setting. Traditional cuisine.

COMPS-SUR-ARTUBY – 83 Var – 340 O3 – pop. 280 – alt. 898 m – ✉ 83840

French Alps 41 **C2**

Paris 892 – Castellane 29 – Digne-les-Bains 82 – Draguignan 31 – Grasse 60 – Manosque 97

Balcons de la Mescla★★★ Northwest: 14,5 km - Tunnels de Fayet ≤★★★ West: 20 km.

Grand Hôtel Bain VISA AE
– *04 94 76 90 06 – reservation@grand-hotel-bain.fr – Fax 04 94 76 92 24 – Closed 11 November-26 December*
17 rm – €55/60 €55/78, €8,50 – ½ P €53/56 – **Rest** – Menu €17/38 – Carte €29/65
◆ Hotel mentioned in the Book of Records. It has been run by the same family since 1737. Functional rooms gradually being redecorated in the regional style. Dining room with a panoramic view brightened up with Provençal touches. Local cuisine.

CONCARNEAU – 29 Finistère – 308 H7 – pop. 19 453 – alt. 4 m – ✉ 29900 Brittany

Paris 546 – Brest 96 – Lorient 49 – Quimper 22 – Vannes 102 9 **B2**

for **Beg Meil** - (July-August) Crossing 25 mn - Information and prices: Vedettes Glenn, opposite yachting harbour at Concarneau 02 98 97 10 31, Fax 02 98 60 49 70

for Iles Glénan - (April to Sept.) Crossing 1 h 10 mn - Information and prices: Vedettes de l'Odet for Glénan isles and Rivière de l'Odet - Vieux Port Bénodet

for **La Rivière de l'Odet** - (April to Sept.) Crossing 4 h return - Information and prices: see above (Vedettes Glenn), at Port de pêche of Bénodet.

Office de tourisme, quai d'Aiguillon 02 98 97 01 44, Fax 02 98 50 88 81

Enclosed town★★ C - Musée de la Pêche★ **M¹** - Pont du Moros ≤★ B - Fête des Filets bleus (Blue nets fair)★ (end of August).

Plan on next page

L'Océan ≤ rest, VISA
plage des Sables Blancs – 02 98 50 53 50 – hotel-ocean@wanadoo.fr – Fax 02 98 50 84 16 – Closed 24 December-31 January, A **r**
71 rm – €75/120 €115/175, €12 – ½ P €72/95 – **Rest** – *(closed Sunday dinner, Monday lunch and Saturday October-March)* Menu €26/45 – Carte €40
◆ Impressive modern building overlooking the sea. Spacious practical rooms: those at the front have large balconies and an attractive sea view. Large restaurant opposite the bay of Concarneau. Contemporary setting and traditional cuisine.

Les Sables Blancs ≤ the sea, rm, VISA AE
plage des Sables Blancs – 02 98 50 10 12 – contact@hotel-les-sables-blancs.com – Fax 02 98 97 20 92 A
18 rm – €95/160 €105/190, €14 – ½ P €120/160 – **Rest** – *(closed 11 November-11 December)* Menu €25 (weekday lunch), €32/85 – Carte €43/87
◆ Beautiful hotel on the water's edge with direct access to the beach. Refurbished in a chic, contemporary style. Low key decor in the bedrooms endowed with terraces. Seafood served in the lounge restaurant with ocean views as far as the eye can see.

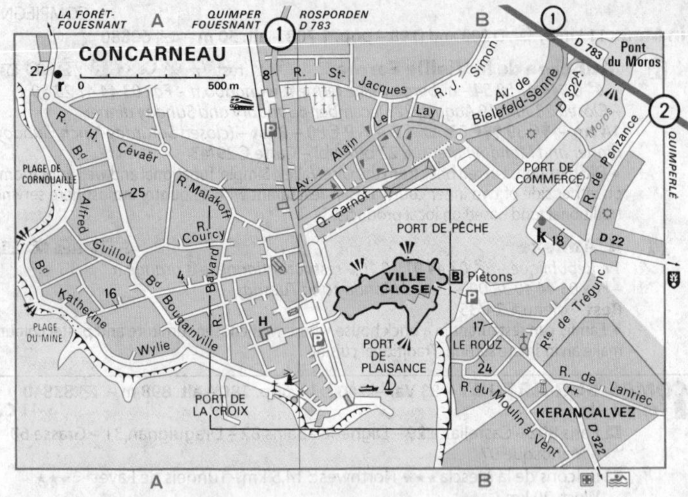

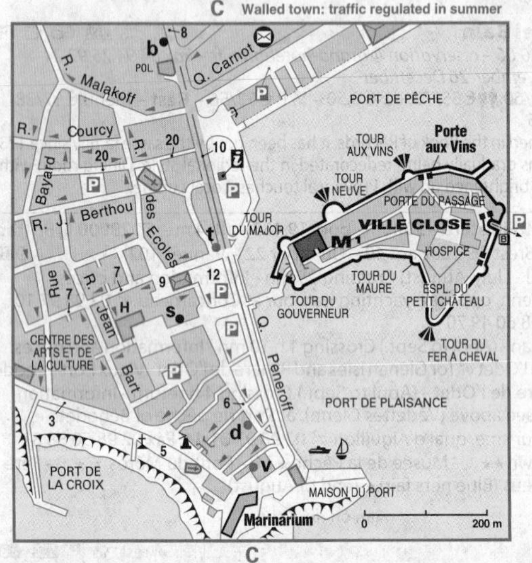

Bougainville (Bd) C 3
Courbet (R. Amiral) . . . . A 4
Croix (Quai de la) C 5
Dr-P.-Nicolas (Av. du) . . . . . C 6
Dumont-d'Urville (R.) . . . . C 7
Gare (Av. de la) AC 8
Gaulle (Pl. Gén.-de) . . C 9
Guéguin (Av. Pierre) . . . C 10
Jean-Jaurès (Pl.) . C 12
Le Lay (Av. Alain) B
Libération (R. de la) . . . . . A 16
Mauduit-Duplessis (R.) . . . . B 17
Moros (R. du) . . . B 18
Morvan (R. Gén.) C 20
Pasteur (R.) . . . . B 24
Renan (R. Ernest) A 25
Sables-Blancs (R. des) . . . . . . A 27
Vauban (R.) . . . . . C 29

Des Halles without rest

pl. de l'Hôtel de Ville – ✆ 02 98 97 11 41 – contact@hoteldeshalles.com – Fax 02 98 50 58 54 C **s**

25 rm – †€ 44/46 ††€ 53/78, ☕ € 8,50

◆ A family quality characterises this hotel (non-smokers only); personalised rooms of varying sizes, most of which sport a bright and colourful marine style.

France et Europe without rest

9 av. de la Gare – ✆ 02 98 97 00 64 – hotel.france-europe@wanadoo.fr – Fax 02 98 50 76 66 – Closed 19 December-12 January and Saturday mid November-mid March C **b**

25 rm – †€ 54/67 ††€ 54/77, ☕ € 10

◆ The location of the building on a main road does not affect the tranquillity of its functional rooms fitted with double-glazing. Nautical-inspired breakfast room.

XX **La Coquille**

1 quai du Moros – ☏ 02 98 97 08 52 – sicallac@wanadoo.fr – Fax 02 98 50 69 13 – Closed 10-20 November, Saturday lunch, Sunday dinner off season and Monday
Rest – Menu € 29/100 – Carte € 50/77 B **k**
Rest *Le Bistrot* – *(lunch only)* Menu € 20

◆ Facing the port, this rustic restaurant is decorated with light colours and a collection of maritime photos and lithographs. Fish and seafood specialities. This bistro has an attractive, maritime atmosphere. Limited menu at lunchtime.

XX **Chez Armande**

15 bis av. Dr Nicolas – ☏ 02 98 97 00 76 – Fax 02 98 97 00 76 – Closed 6-30 November, Tuesday except July-August and Wednesday C **d**
Rest – Menu (€ 12,50), € 20/36 – Carte € 31/68

◆ Generous portions of traditional cuisine in which seafood takes pride of place await you in this house opposite the walled city. Attractive, typically Breton dining room.

X **L'Amiral**

1 av. P. Guéguin – ☏ 02 98 60 55 23 – info@restaurant-amiral.com – Fax 02 98 50 66 23 – Closed 21 September-6 October, 8-23 February, Sunday dinner and Monday from October to March C **t**
Rest – Menu (€ 15), € 22/39 – Carte € 32/47

◆ Handy location between the tourist office and walled town. Pleasant wood and nautical-inspired decoration and traditional menu.

X **Le Buccin**

1 r. Duguay-Trouin – ☏ 02 98 50 54 22 – Fax 02 98 50 70 37 – Closed 17 November-12 December, Monday lunch from July to September, Saturday lunch, Sunday dinner and Thursday off season C **v**
Rest – Menu € 20, € 25/39 – Carte € 35/50

◆ Off the tourist track, this very popular restaurant serves traditional meals with an emphasis on fish in a warm atmosphere (orange and yellow colour scheme and works of art).

If breakfast is included the ☕ symbol appears after the number of rooms.

CONCHES-EN-OUCHE – 27 Eure – 304 F8 – pop. 4 280 – alt. 123 m – ✉ 27190

Normandy 33 **D2**

Paris 118 – Bernay 34 – Dreux 49 – Évreux 18 – Rouen 61

Syndicat d'initiative, place A. Briand ☏ 02 32 30 76 42, Fax 02 32 60 22 35

Ste-Foy church ★.

X **La Grand'Mare**

13 av. Croix-de-Fer – ☏ 02 32 30 23 30 – Closed Sunday evening, Tuesday evening and Monday
Rest – Menu (€ 11), € 13/27 – Carte € 16/27

◆ Open the door of this old inn and discover its elegant dining room entirely covered in wood panelling. Traditional culinary repertoire.

CONCHY-LES-POTS – 60 Oise – 305 H3 – pop. 522 – alt. 106 m – ✉ 60490

36 **B2**

Paris 100 – Compiègne 28 – Amiens 55 – Beauvais 68 – Montdidier 14 – Roye 13

XX **Le Relais**

D 1017 – ☏ 03 44 85 01 17 – Fax 03 44 85 00 58 – Closed 28 July-13 August, 23 February-4 March, Sunday dinner, Tuesday dinner, Monday and Wednesday
Rest – Menu € 27/84 – Carte € 41/68

◆ You should have no hesitation in entering this former transport café with its facade painted yellow. The dining room is bright and stylish and you can enjoy generous, traditional cuisine.

CONDÉ-NORTHEN – 57 Moselle – 307 J4 – pop. 526 – alt. 208 m – ✉ 57220

27 **C1**

▶ Paris 350 – Metz 21 – Pont-à-Mousson 52 – Saarlouis 38 – Saarbrücken 52 – Thionville 49

La Grange de Condé

41 r. Deux-Nieds – ✆ 03 87 79 30 50 – lagrangedeconde@wanadoo.fr – Fax 03 87 79 30 51

17 rm – €88/95 €88/95, ☕ €12 – 3 suites – **Rest** – Menu (€16), €22/48 – Carte €30/49

◆ Additional hotel accommodation has been added to this family farmhouse dating back to 1682. The rooms are comfortable and there is a sauna, Jacuzzi and Turkish bath. Spit-roasts and garden-fresh vegetables are served in the pleasant rustic Lorraine-style dining room.

CONDOM – 32 Gers – 336 E6 – pop. 7 251 – alt. 81 m – ✉ 32100

Languedoc-Roussillon-Tarn Gorges

28 **A2**

▶ Paris 729 – Agen 41 – Mont-de-Marsan 80 – Toulouse 121 – Auch 46

ℹ Office de tourisme, place Bossuet ✆ 05 62 28 00 80, Fax 05 62 28 45 46

◉ St-Pierre cathedral ★: Cloister★ BZ.

Les Trois Lys

38 r. Gambetta – ✆ 05 62 28 33 33 – hoteltroislys@wanadoo.fr – Fax 05 62 28 41 85 – Closed February

Y **a**

10 rm – €50/60 €110/170, ☕ €9 – ½ P €150/210 – **Rest** – *(closed Monday lunch, Thursday lunch and Sunday except July-August)* Menu €29/39 – Carte €40/57

◆ An elegant 18C residence with individually decorated rooms. Many have fine antique furniture and some have a fireplace. Attractive swimmingpool at the rear. A refurbished dining room, teak courtyard terrace, plus a cosy bar.

CONDOM

Aquitaine (Av. d') . . . . . . Y 2
Armuriers (R. des) . . . . . . Y 5
Barlet (Pont) . . . . . . Y 7
Bonnamy (R.) . . . . . . YZ 8
Buzon (R. et Quai) . . . . . . Z 12
Carmes (Pont des) . . . . . . Z 14
Cazaubon (R. H.) . . . . . . Z 16
Charron (R.) . . . . . . Y 19
Cordeliers (R. des) . . . . . . Z 21
Foch (R. Mar.) . . . . . . Y 22
Gaichies (R.) . . . . . . Y 24
Gambetta (R. L.) . . . . . . Y 26
Jean-Jaurès (R.) . . . . . . Z 28
Lannelongue (Pl.) . . . . . . Y 31
Lion-d'Or (Pl. du) . . . . . . Y 35
Monnaie (R. de la) . . . . . . YZ 38
Paix (R. de la) . . . . . . Z 40
Roquepine (R. de) . . . . . . Z 44
Roques (R.) . . . . . . Y 47
Saint-Exupéry (R.) . . . . . . Z 50
St-Pierre (Pl.) . . . . . . Y 53

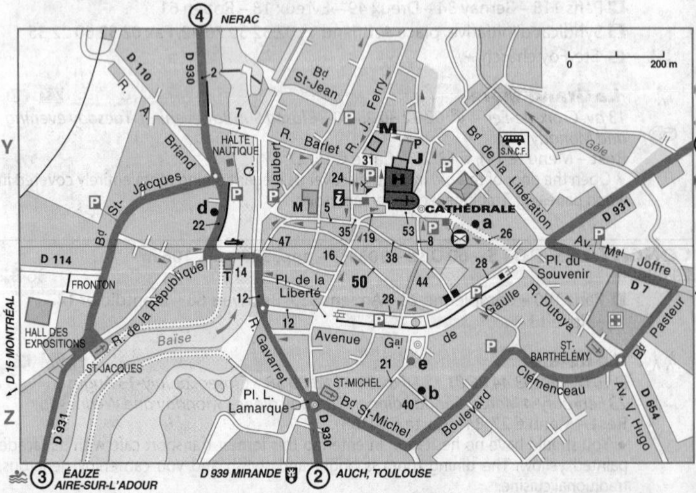

Continental rm, rm, VISA AE

20 r. Mar. Foch – ✆ 05 62 68 37 00 – lecontinental@lecontinental.net – Fax 05 62 68 23 71 – Closed 16 February-3 March, Y **d**

25 rm – †€ 42/66 ††€ 42/125, ☕ € 10 – ½ P € 90 – **Rest** – *(closed Saturday lunchtime, Sunday evening and Monday)* Menu € 13, € 20/37 – Carte € 28/49

◆ The River Baïse flows at the foot of this fully refurbished hotel. Comfortable rooms, decorated with old engravings; most of them overlook a small garden. Spruce dining room in shades of yellow and orange with a summer terrace in the courtyard. Traditional and regional dishes.

Logis des Cordeliers without rest VISA AE

r. de la Paix – ✆ 05 62 28 03 68 – info@logisdescordeliers.com – Fax 05 62 68 29 03 – Closed 2 January-3 February Z **b**

21 rm – †€ 47/64 ††€ 47/64, ☕ € 8

◆ New building located in a peaceful district. Functional rooms; opt for those on the swimming-pool side which have small flower-filled balconies. Friendly welcome.

La Table des Cordeliers (Eric Sampietro) VISA AE

1 r. des Cordeliers – ✆ 05 62 68 43 82 – info@latabledescordeliers.fr – Fax 05 62 28 15 92 – Closed 5-28 January, Sunday dinner off season, Tuesday lunch, Wednesday lunch in season and Monday Z **e**

Rest – Menu € 22 (weekdays)/58 – Carte € 48/68

Spec. Cèpe en tarte fine (autumn). Assiette des Cordeliers (duck). Croustade aux pommes, nougat glacé aux pruneaux.

◆ Housed in the cloisters and chapel of a tranquil 13C convent, this modern-style restaurant serves contemporary cuisine centred on locally sourced produce.

CONDRIEU – 69 Rhône – 327 H7 – pop. 3 424 – alt. 150 m – ✉ 69420 Lyon - Rhone Valley 44 B2

Paris 497 – Annonay 34 – Lyon 41 – Rive-de-Gier 21 – Tournon-sur-Rhône 55 – Vienne 12

Office de tourisme, place du Séquoïa ✆ 04 74 56 62 83, Fax 04 74 56 65 85

Calvary ≤★.

Hôtellerie Beau Rivage (Reynald Donet) ≤ VISA

r. Beau Rivage – ✆ 04 74 56 82 82 – infos@hotel-beaurivage.com – Fax 04 74 59 59 36

18 rm – †€ 110/160 ††€ 110/160, ☕ € 17 – 10 suites

Rest – Menu € 36 (weekday lunch), € 58/79 – Carte € 68/131

Spec. Quenelle de brochet au salpicon de homard. Fleur de courgette farcie, beurre d'estragon (15 May to 15 October). Côte de veau de lait rôtie à l'os, sauce Choron. **Wines** Condrieu, Saint-Joseph.

◆ Charming stop for connoisseurs in one of the most prestigious vineyards of the Côtes du Rhône. Elegant rustic or bourgeois rooms, all of which are resolutely cosy. Restaurant with riverside terrace serving traditional southern French cuisine.

CONFLANS-STE-HONORINE – 78 Yvelines – 311 I2 – 101 3 – see Paris, Area

CONFLANS-SUR-LOING – see MONTARGIS

CONILHAC CORBIERES – 11 Aude – 344 H3 – pop. 601 – alt. 125 m – ✉ 11200 22 B3

Paris 802 – Montpellier 120 – Carcassonne 31 – Béziers 59 – Narbonne 29

Auberge Coté Jardin with rm rm, VISA AE

D 6113 – ✆ 04 68 27 08 19 – sophie.prevel@club-internet.fr – Fax 04 68 48 64 60 – Closed 13-26 October, 19 January-2 February and Monday from October to May

8 rm – †€ 60/115 ††€ 60/115, ☕ € 10 – ½ P € 70/90 – **Rest** – *(closed Sunday dinner from September to June and Monday)* Menu (€ 18), € 27/48 – Carte € 46/57

◆ An enchanting setting which mingles stone, greenery and flowers awaits on the terrace of this smart inn. Good quality produce and tasty, fresh and simple cooking. Pretty, quiet, contemporary rooms.

CONLEAU – 56 Morbihan – 308 O9 – see Vannes

CONNELLES – 27 Eure – 304 H6 – pop. 188 – alt. 15 m – ✉ 27430 33 D2

Paris 111 – Les Andelys 13 – Évreux 34 – Rouen 33 – Vernon-sur-Eure 40

Le Moulin de Connelles

– ✆ 02 32 59 53 33 – moulindeconnelles@moulindeconnelles.com
– Fax 02 32 59 21 83

8 rm – †€ 130/200 ††€ 130/200, ☕ € 15 – 5 suites – ½ P € 109/195

Rest – *(closed lunch July-August, Sunday dinner and Monday October-April)*
Menu € 33/56 – Carte € 41/58

◆ Nestling in the heart of a park on an island in the Seine, this ravishing Anglo-Norman mansion is a haven of peace and quiet poised between romanticism and impressionism. An elegant dining room, as well as a veranda overlooking the river and delightful terrace.

CONQUES – 12 Aveyron – 338 G3 – pop. 302 – alt. 350 m – ✉ 12320

Languedoc-Roussillon-Tarn Gorges 29 C1

Paris 601 – Aurillac 53 – Espalion 42 – Figeac 43 – Rodez 37

Office de tourisme, Le Bourg ✆ 08 20 82 08 03, Fax 05 65 72 87 03

Site★★ - Village★ - Ste-Foy abbey church ★★: tympanum of the west portal ★★★ and Conques treasure-house ★★★ - Le Cendié★ West: 2 km by D 232 - Site du Bancarel★ South: 3 km by D 901.

Ste-Foy

r. Principale – ✆ 05 65 69 84 03 – hotelsaintefoy@hotelsaintefoy.fr
– Fax 05 65 72 81 04 – Open 26 April-24 October

17 rm – †€ 110/169 ††€ 115/227, ☕ € 13,50 – **Rest** – Menu (€ 18), € 38/53
– Carte € 48/67

◆ 17C house typical of Rouergue, with view of the magnificent abbey. Old stone, beams and rustic or period furniture add character to the rooms. Dining rooms with character and two rustic terraces. Contemporary menu.

Auberge St-Jacques with rm

– ✆ 05 65 72 86 36 – info@aubergestjacques.fr – Fax 05 65 72 82 47
– Closed 3 January-3 February

13 rm – †€ 50/70 ††€ 50/70, ☕ € 8 – ½ P € 48 – **Rest** – *(closed Sunday dinner and Monday from November to April)* Menu € 18/60 – Carte € 25/66

◆ The chef of this rustic restaurant prepares generous dishes of regional inspiration with creative touches. Countrified, deliciously calm rooms.

South 3 km on D 901 – ✉ 12320 Conques

Le Moulin de Cambelong (Hervé Busset)

– ✆ 05 65 72 84 77
– domaine-de-cambelong@wanadoo.fr – Fax 05 65 72 83 91
– Open 16 March-1st November and closed Monday off season

10 rm – †€ 120/210 ††€ 120/240, ☕ € 15 – ½ P € 125/165

Rest – *(dinner only except Saturday, Sunday and holidays)* Menu € 55/85 bi

Spec. "Oeuf Louisette". Filet de truite fario d'Estaing, boulgour au sureau. Morceau de cochon fermier, croustillant de gnocchi à l'amaranthe. **Wines** Marcillac.

◆ In one of the last remaining 18C watermills on the Dourdou. Pretty rooms with personal touches, fabric hangings on the walls and period furniture. The food is a creative blend of flowers and local produce (single set menu), served against the backdrop of a waterfall.

CONQUES-SUR-ORBIEL – 11 Aude – 344 F3 – pop. 2 061 – alt. 127 m – ✉ 11600 22 B2

Paris 777 – Montpellier 155 – Carcassonne 12 – Castres 62
– Castelnaudary 43

La Maison Pujol without rest

17 r. F.-Mistral – ✆ 04 68 26 98 18 – postmaster@lamaisonpujol.com – Closed January- February

4 rm ☕ – †€ 70/80 ††€ 80/90

◆ Immaculate white modern interior with raw finishes, designer objects, artworks and a colourful bedroom especially for children. Swimming pool.

LE CONQUET – 29 Finistère – 308 C4 – pop. 2 408 – alt. 30 m – ✉ 29217 Brittany

Paris 619 – Brest 24 – Brignogan-Plages 59 – St-Pol-de-Léon 85 9 **A2**

Office de tourisme, parc de Beauséjour ✆ 02 98 89 11 31, Fax 02 98 89 08 20

Site★.

Île d'Ouessant★★ - Les Abers★★.

in la Pointe de St-Mathieu 4 km south – ✉ 29217 Plougonvelin

Lighthouse ✲★★ – Ruins of the abbey church★.

Hostellerie de la Pointe St-Mathieu rm, VISA MC AE
– ✆ 02 98 89 00 19 – saintmathieu.hotel@wanadoo.fr – Fax 02 98 89 15 68 – Closed February
27 rm – †€ 55/150 ††€ 60/170, ☕ € 11 – ½ P € 68/123 – **Rest** – *(closed Sunday dinner)* Menu € 25 (weekday lunch), € 33/73 – Carte € 41/104
◆ An unbeatable end-of-the-world location between the lighthouses and the remains of an abbey. Two generations of guestrooms (ultra-modern or traditional), some with a balcony. Two dining rooms, one with designer decor, the other more rustic in style. The menu here is based on fish and seafood.

LES CONTAMINES-MONTJOIE – 74 Haute-Savoie – 328 N6 – pop. 1 129 – alt. 1 164 m – Winter sports : 1 165/2 500 m 4 22 – ✉ 74170 French Alps 46 **F1**

Paris 606 – Annecy 93 – Bonneville 50 – Chamonix-Mont-Blanc 33 – Megève 20

Office de tourisme, 18, route de Notre-Dame de la Gorge ✆ 04 50 47 01 58, Fax 04 50 47 09 54

Le Signal★ (by cable car).

L'Ô à la Bouche VISA MC
510 rte Notre-Dame de la Gorge – ✆ 04 50 47 81 67 – Open 15 June-30 September and 14 December-15 May
Rest – *(pre-book)* Menu € 16 (lunch), € 26/32
◆ Considered the best in the valley, this restaurant owes its success to its simple, elegant and contemporary mountain decor, and its traditional cuisine (meat specialities). Gastronomic dinners available.

La Chemenaz rest, P VISA MC AE
près de la télécabine du Lay – ✆ 04 50 47 02 44 – info@chemenaz.com – Fax 04 50 47 12 73 – Open 15 June-15 September and 15 December-15 April
39 rm – †€ 66/87 ††€ 100/160, ☕ € 10 – ½ P € 75/88
Rest *La Trabla* – Menu € 15 (lunch), € 21/45 – Carte € 22/42
◆ Modern chalet with large glass windows, located in the Lay hamlet opposite the cable car. Bright, well-equipped alpine style rooms (drying room). The Trabla means a shelf for cheese in Savoy dialect. Large central fireplace and home-made smoked dishes.

Gai Soleil rest, P VISA MC
288 chemin des Loyers – ✆ 04 50 47 02 94 – gaisoleil2@wanadoo.fr – Fax 04 50 47 18 43 – Open 16 June-15 September and 21 December-19 April
19 rm – †€ 58/62 ††€ 65/75, ☕ € 12 – ½ P € 58/70 – **Rest** – *(closed lunch winter)* Menu € 22 (lunch)/31
◆ Here they look after all the needs of the clientele. Overlooking the resort, this old farm with its roof covered in shingle board, is filled with beautiful flowers in season. Personalised rooms. Pleasant, rustic dining room with a family guesthouse atmosphere. Fondue evening on Tuesdays.

Le Grizzli without rest P VISA MC AE
148 rte de Notre-Dame de la Gorge – ✆ 04 50 91 56 55 – grizzlihotel@grizzli.com – Fax 04 50 91 57 00 – Closed 26 April-2 June and 15 October-15 December
16 rm – †€ 68 ††€ 68, ☕ € 8
◆ Hotel located in the town centre. Wood and colourful fabrics adorn the simple rooms which are more peaceful at the back. View of Mont Joly.

CONTAMINE-SUR-ARVE – 74 Haute-Savoie – 328 L4 – pop. 1 343 – alt. 450 m – ✉ 74130 46 **F1**

Paris 547 – Annecy 46 – Chamonix-Mont-Blanc 63 – Genève 20 – Thonon-les-Bains 36

Le Tourne Bride with rm — rest, VISA

94 rte d'Annemasse – ☎ 04 50 03 62 18 – hotel-tourne-bride@wanadoo.fr – Fax 04 50 03 91 99 – Closed 14 July-4 August, 5-25 January, Sunday dinner and Monday

7 rm – †€ 45/47 ††€ 57/60, ☕ € 7,50 – ½ P € 55 – **Rest** – Menu € 14 (weekday lunch), € 23/45 – Carte € 29/49

◆ The spruce facade of this old post house is eye catching. The stables now house a stylish country dining room serving well-prepared traditional cuisine.

CONTES – **06 Alpes-Maritimes** – **341** E5 – **pop. 6 551** – **alt. 250 m** – ✉ **06390** 41 **D2**

Paris 954 – Marseille 206 – Nice 21 – Antibes 43 – Cannes 55

Syndicat d'initiative, 13, place Jean Allardi ☎ 04 93 79 13 99

La Fleur de Thym — VISA

3 bd Charles Alunni – ☎ 04 93 79 47 33 – restaurantlafleurdethym@wanadoo.fr – Fax 04 93 79 47 33 – Closed 14-26 August, 24-10 January, Tuesday dinner and Wednesday

Rest – Menu € 18 (weekday lunch), € 26/29 – Carte € 30/51

◆ This small, rustic restaurant has a real feel of Provence, with its orange and yellow tones, fresh flowers, and large, open fireplace. Hearty, traditional cuisine and friendly service.

CONTEVILLE – **27 Eure** – **304** C5 – **pop. 726** – **alt. 33 m** – ✉ **27210** 32 **A3**

Paris 181 – Évreux 102 – Le Havre 34 – Honfleur 15 – Pont-Audemer 14 – Pont-l'Évêque 28

Auberge du Vieux Logis (Guillaume Louet) — VISA

– ☎ 02 32 57 60 16 – Fax 02 32 57 45 84 – Closed 10-27 November, Tuesday from September to June, Sunday dinner and Monday

Rest – *(closed Sun. evening except Aug., Tues. from Oct. to Apr. and Mon.)* Menu € 45 (weekdays)/85 – Carte € 66/104

Spec. Foie gras de canard poêlé sur lit de pommes sauce aigre-douce. Gratin de homard, langoustines et Saint-Jacques au coulis de crustacés (October to April). Aile de pigeon et cuisse en croûte sauce périgueux.

◆ A charming timber-framed facade and characterful Norman interior (half-timbering and brick walls). Personalised cuisine based on classic local dishes with an inventive touch.

in Marais Vernier 8 km East by D 312 and D 90 – **pop. 455** – **alt. 10 m** – ✉ **27680**

Auberge de l'Etampage with rm — rm, VISA

– ☎ 02 32 57 61 51 – etampage.blaize@wanadoo.fr – Fax 02 32 57 23 47 – Closed 23 December-1st February, Sunday dinner and Wednesday

3 rm – †€ 39 ††€ 39, ☕ € 8 – ½ P € 55 – **Rest** – Menu € 19/29 – Carte € 34/39

◆ This half-timbered village residence offers local specialities prepared with fresh, local produce. Interiors are in bistro-style and the three rooms are attractively furnished and well-kept.

in Foulbec 4 km Southeast by D 312 – **pop. 467** – **alt. 30 m** – ✉ **27210**

L'Eau-Asis without rest

La Valllée Guillemard – ☎ 02 32 56 59 92 – alain-ratiskol@wanadoo.fr – Open 1st April-30 September

3 rm – †€ 55 ††€ 55, ☕ € 6

◆ This recently constructed establishment stands in splendid parkland enhanced by a small lake with swans and ducks. The rooms, many with terraces, are personalised. The environment is one of absolute tranquillity.

CONTRES – **41 Loir-et-Cher** – **318** F7 – **pop. 3 268** – **alt. 98 m** – ✉ **41700** 11 **A1**

Paris 203 – Blois 22 – Châteauroux 79 – Montrichard 23 – Tours 66

De France — rm, rest, VISA

rte de Blois – ☎ 02 54 79 50 14 – metivier@mond.net – Fax 02 54 79 02 95 – Closed 25 January-10 March, Sunday dinner, Tuesday lunch and Monday

35 rm – †€ 54/83 ††€ 54/83, ☕ € 10 – 2 suites – ½ P € 54/81

Rest – Menu € 22 (weekdays)/50 – Carte € 37/50

◆ A good, family address located in the centre of Contres. Comfortable rooms, mostly facing the pool and garden, which are regularly renovate. Cane furniture in the annexe. Elegant, well turned out restaurant serving careful, traditional cuisine.

La Botte d'Asperges

– ✆ 02 54 79 50 49 – Fax 02 54 79 08 74 – *Closed 18-24 August, 2-15 January, Sunday dinner and Monday*

Rest – Menu € 22/49 – Carte € 36/51

◆ Behind the half-timbered facade, this bistro style restaurant has two bright dining rooms decorated with frescos of food and wine. Modern menu.

CONTREVOZ – 01 Ain – **328** G6 – see Belley

CONTREXÉVILLE – 88 Vosges – **314** D3 – pop. 3 708 – alt. 342 m – Spa : early April-early Oct. – Casino Y – ✉ 88140 Alsace-Lorraine 26 **B3**

Paris 337 – Épinal 47 – Langres 75 – Nancy 83 – Neufchâteau 28

Office de tourisme, 116, rue du Shah de Perse ✆ 03 29 08 08 68, Fax 03 29 08 25 40

de Vittel Ermittage Vittel Hôtel Ermitage, North: 7 km, ✆ 03 29 08 81 53 ;

du Bois de Hazeau Centre Préparation Olympique, by D 429: 4 km, ✆ 03 29 08 20 85.

Cosmos rm, rest,

13 r. Metz – ✆ *03 29 07 61 61*

– contact@cosmos-hotel.com – Fax 03 29 08 68 67 Y **u**

77 rm – €95 €115, €11 – 6 suites – ½ P €92/105 – **Rest** – Menu €35

◆ The comfortable rooms of this Belle Époque hotel sport a pleasant old France atmosphere. Ideal for fitness and spa fans. Large dining room with charming 1940s decor. Traditional menus and diet meals.

CONTREXÉVILLE

Daudet (R.)	Y	2
Hazau (Av. du Bois d')	Y	5
Hirschauer (R. du Gén.)	Y	6
Moulin (R. Jean)	Z	9
Shah-de-Perse (R. du)	Y	10
Stanislas (R. du Roi)	Z	12
Thomson (R. Gaston)	Z	13
Victoire (R. de la)	Y	15
Wladimir (R. Grande-Duchesse)	Z	16
Ziwer-Pacha (R.)	Z	18
11-Septembre (R. du)	Y	19

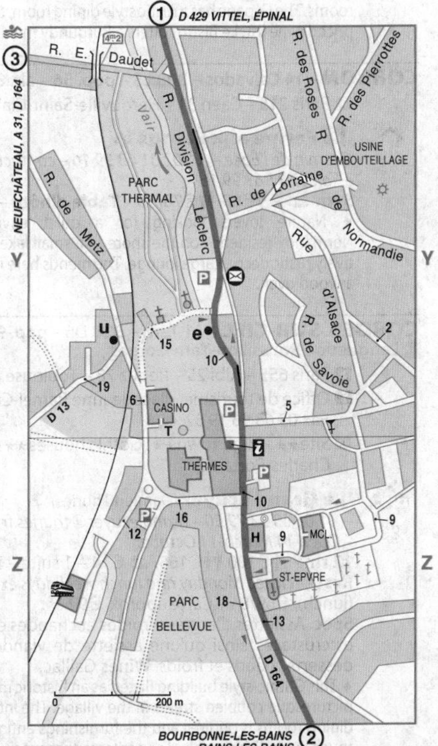

Souveraine without rest
Parc Thermal – ✆ 03 29 08 09 59 – contact@souveraine-hotel.com – Fax 03 29 08 16 39 – Open 1st April-14 September Y e
31 rm – †€ 75 ††€ 89, ☕ € 9,50
◆ The former residence of Grand-Duchess Wladimir, aunt of Nicolas II, is full of old-world charm. High ceilings, mouldings and brass bedsteads. The quietest rooms overlook the park.

COQUELLES – 62 Pas-de-Calais – 301 D2 – see Calais

CORBEIL-ESSONNES – 91 Essonne – 312 D4 – 101 37 – see Paris, Area

CORBIGNY – 58 Nièvre – 319 F8 – pop. 1 709 – alt. 203 m – ✉ 58800

Burgundy-Jura 7 **B2**

Paris 236 – Autun 76 – Avallon 38 – Clamecy 28 – Nevers 58

Office de tourisme, 8, rue de l'Abbaye ✆ 03 86 20 02 53

Hôtel de L'Europe rm, VISA AE
7 Grande Rue – ✆ 03 86 20 09 87 – hoteleuropelecepage@tiscali.fr – Fax 03 86 20 06 40 – Closed 22 December-4 January and 23 February-8 March
18 rm – †€ 48 ††€ 54, ☕ € 8 – ½ P € 56/70
Rest *Le Cépage* – *(closed Sunday dinner, Wednesday dinner and Thursday)* Menu € 28/62 – Carte € 26/59
Rest *Le Bistrot* – *(closed Sunday dinner, Wednesday dinner and Thursday)* Menu € 11/19 – Carte € 21/37
◆ This friendly, family-run hotel has colourful, well-equipped rooms with lovely bathrooms. The Cépage has a rustic style dining room, traditional cuisine and a very reasonably priced wine list. Le Bistrot offers a Burgundy menu and local dishes.

CORBON – 14 Calvados – 303 L5 – pop. 56 – alt. 8 m – ✉ 14340 33 **C2**

Paris 215 – Caen 31 – Hérouville-Saint-Clair 30 – Le Havre 70

La Ferme aux Étangs P VISA
Chemin de l'Épée – ✆ 02 31 63 99 16 – contact@lafermeauxetangs.com – Fax 02 31 63 99 16
5 rm ☕ – †€ 68 ††€ 78/98 – **Table d'hôte** – Menu € 30
◆ Nature lovers looking for a quiet environment will enjoy this splendid Normandy residence on the shore of a small lake. Spacious rooms with modern, attractively rustic decor. Large lounge. The menus here include a variety of specialities baked in a wood oven.

CORDES-SUR-CIEL – 81 Tarn – 338 D6 – pop. 996 – alt. 279 m – ✉ 81170

Languedoc-Roussillon-Tarn Gorges 29 **C2**

Paris 655 – Albi 25 – Rodez 78 – Toulouse 82 – Villefranche-de-Rouergue 47

Office de tourisme, place Jeanne Ramel-Cals ✆ 05 63 56 00 52, Fax 05 63 56 19 52

Site★★ - High town★★: Gothic houses★★ - musée d'Art et d'Histoire Charles-Portal★.

Le Grand Écuyer (Damien Thuriès) ← valley, VISA AE
– ✆ 05 63 53 79 50 – grand.ecuyer@thuries.fr – Fax 05 63 53 79 51 – Open 14 March-11 October
12 rm – †€ 100 ††€ 165, ☕ € 14 – 1 suite – ½ P € 120/135
Rest – *(closed Monday and lunch weekdays except July-August)* Menu € 49 (lunch), € 69/84 – Carte approx. € 92
Spec. Assiettes d'entrées froides et chaudes en trilogie. Une assiette de poissons et crustacés ainsi qu'une assiette de viandes et volailles en dégustation. Six desserts chauds et froids. **Wines** Gaillac.
◆ This Gothic-style building (listed as an historic monument) is located in one of the most picturesque cobbled streets in the village. The interior is very attractive. The style of the dining rooms is original and the furnishings antique. Traditional cuisine with a personal touch, with dishes cooked as a trilogy (three recipes, three products, three tastes).

Hostellerie du Vieux Cordes

21 r. St-Michel – ✆ 05 63 53 79 20 – vieux.cordes@thuries.fr – Fax 05 63 56 02 47 – Closed 1st January-13 February

18 rm – €49/155 €49/155, € 10 – 1 suite – ½ P € 78 – **Rest** – *(closed Sunday dinner and Tuesday from November to April, Tuesday lunch in May-June and in September-October, and Monday except July-August)* Menu € 22/46 – Carte approx. € 37

◆ Within the walls of an old monastery with an attractive spiral staircase leading to personalised bedrooms, some of which have been refurbished. The terrace-dining room looks out across the valley. A menu dominated by two main items: salmon and duck.

La Cité

– ✆ 05 63 56 03 53 – vieux.cordes@thuries.fr – Fax 05 63 56 02 47 – Open 1st May-14 September

8 rm – €59/72 €59/72, € 9

◆ Rooms being gradually refurbished in this 13C house at the rear of an inner courtyard.

Albi road

L'Envolée sauvage

La Borie – ✆ 05 63 56 88 52 – info@lenvolee-sauvage.com – Closed March

4 rm – €75/88 €85/88 – ½ P € 72/74

Table d'hôte – Menu € 30/40

◆ There is a truly authentic local flavour to this stylish 18C farmhouse still engaged in raising geese. The rooms are individually decorated and there is a large lounge-reading room. Farm produce garnishes the simple but flavoursome cuisine. Cooking lessons are available and visitors are guaranteed a warm welcome.

CORDON – 74 Haute-Savoie – **328** M5 – **pop. 881** – **alt. 871 m** – ✉ **74700**
French Alps 46 **F1**

Paris 589 – Annecy 76 – Bonneville 33 – Chamonix-Mont-Blanc 32 – Megève 10

Office de tourisme, route de Cordon ✆ 04 50 58 01 57, Fax 04 50 91 25 36

Site★.

Les Roches Fleuries Mont-Blanc chain, rest,

rte de la Scie – ✆ 04 50 58 06 71 – info@rochesfleuries.com – Fax 04 50 47 82 30 – Open 10 May-25 September and 16 December-10 April

20 rm – € 150/240 € 150/240, € 17 – 5 suites – ½ P € 120/175

Rest – *(closed Tuesday lunch, Sunday dinner and Monday except school holidays)* Menu € 35 (weekday lunch), € 52/78 – Carte € 64/88

Rest *La Boîte à Fromages* – *(open 2 July-31 August, 16 December-30 March and closed Sunday and Monday) (dinner only) (pre-book)* Menu € 33

Spec. Carpaccio de tête de veau aux langoustines croustillantes. Omble chevalier de nos lacs aux lentilles vertes. Poire pochée au pain d'épice en nage de vin chaud.

Wines Roussette de Marestel, Mondeuse d'Arbin.

◆ Stunning floral chalet perched on the heights of the "Balcon du Mont Blanc". A warm, wooden interior and elegant old Savoy furniture. Restaurant with a subdued alpine setting and a creative flavoursome cuisine. Regional recipes at the Boîte à Fromages.

Le Cerf Amoureux

à Nant-Cruy, 2km south (Combloux road) ✉ 74700 Sallanches – ✆ 04 50 47 49 24 – contact@lecerfamoureux.com – Fax 04 50 47 49 25 – Closed 4-18 May and 21 September-6 October

11 rm – € 130/360 € 130/360, € 17 – ½ P € 113/228

Rest – *(closed Sunday and Monday except school holidays) (dinner only) (residents only)* Menu € 36

◆ Wood and stone feature in this chalet's cosy interior. Attractive rooms with balconies facing the Aravis massif or Mont Blanc. The delightful dining room is the backdrop for good quality home cooking.

Le Chamois d'Or – Mont-Blanc chain,
– ✆ 04 50 58 05 16 – hotellechamoisdor@wanadoo.fr – Fax 04 50 93 72 96 – *Open 1st June-mid September and 20 December- beg. April*
26 rm – †€ 80/125 ††€ 115/180, ☐ € 15 – 2 suites – ½ P € 82/120
Rest – *(closed Wednesday lunch and Thursday lunch)* Menu (€ 22), € 26 (weekdays), € 32/45 – Carte € 33/58
♦ Austrian style chalet, regularly renovated, with good leisure facilities. Elegant rooms enlivened with pretty fabrics. Comfortable lounge. Antique decor in the dining room with panoramic view. Good traditional cuisine.

Le Cordonant – Mont-Blanc chain, rest,
– ✆ 04 50 58 34 56 – lecordonant@wanadoo.fr – Fax 04 50 47 95 57 – *Open mid May-end September and mid December-mid April*
16 rm – †€ 63/68 ††€ 85/90, ☐ € 9 – ½ P € 70/82
Rest – Menu € 24 (weekdays)/32 – Carte € 36/46
♦ An elegant chalet with a warm, friendly atmosphere. Lovely wooden furnishings in well-kept rooms; some with balcony on the valley side. Delicious traditional cuisine and a splendid view of the mountain tops from the rustic dining room.

CORENC – 38 Isère – 333 H6 – see Grenoble

CORMEILLES – 27 Eure – 304 C6 – pop. 1 191 – alt. 80 m – ✉ 27260 32 A3

Paris 181 – Bernay 441 – Lisieux 19 – Pont-Audemer 17 – Pont-l'Évêque 17
Office de tourisme, 14, place du Mont Mirel ✆ 02 32 56 02 39, Fax 02 32 42 32 66

L'Auberge du Président rest,
– ✆ 02 32 57 80 37 – aubergedupresident@wanadoo.fr – Fax 02 32 57 88 31
14 rm – †€ 50 ††€ 52/80, ☐ € 9,50 – ½ P € 55/65 – **Rest** – *(closed Tuesday lunch, Wednesday lunch, Thursday lunch from October-March, Monday lunch and Sunday dinner)* Menu € 18 (weekdays)/35 – Carte € 25/60
♦ The name is intended as a tribute to René Coty, former President of France, who stayed in this hotel. The rooms have recently been renovated. The pleasant Norman decor in the restaurant with beams and fireplace wins all the votes!

Gourmandises
29 r. de l'Abbaye – ✆ 02 32 42 10 96 – Fax 02 32 56 98 13 – Closed 23-30 June, January, February, Monday, Tuesday and Wednesday
Rest – Carte € 30/43
♦ The conversion of this former cheese-making establishment is a great success; the atmosphere is strikingly convivial and the pretty dining room decor is very fashionable – just the place to enjoy some delicious bistro specialities.

CORMEILLES-EN-VEXIN – 95 Val-d'Oise – 305 D6 – 106 5 – see Paris, Area (Cergy-Pontoise)

CORMERY – 37 Indre-et-Loire – 317 N5 – pop. 1 542 – alt. 59 m – ✉ 37320
Châteaux of the Loire 11 B2

Paris 254 – Blois 63 – Château-Renault 48 – Loches 22 – Montrichard 33 – Tours 21
Syndicat d'initiative, 13, rue Nationale ✆ 02 47 43 30 84, Fax 02 47 43 18 73

Auberge du Mail
pl. Mail – ✆ 02 47 43 40 32 – aubergedumail@wanadoo.fr – Fax 02 47 43 08 72 – Closed 12-20 April, 26-31 December, dinner mid October-end March, Saturday lunch and Thursday
Rest – Menu (€ 17), € 19 (except Sunday)/39 – Carte € 28/52
♦ Local-style inn near the abbey famous for its macaroons. The dining room has a comfortable rustic-style setting, and the terrace is relaxing with its lime trees and wisteria.

Auberge des 2 Cèdres
av. de la Gare – ✆ 02 47 43 03 09 – Fax 02 47 43 03 09 – Closed 7-22 July, 19-31 January, 1st-8 February, dinner Sunday-Thursday and Monday
Rest – Menu € 13,50 (weekday lunch), € 19/28 – Carte € 19/31
♦ This regional-style building near the railway station provides an open air café atmosphere. Very simple setting and terrace in a tiny garden. Friendly welcome and family cooking.

CORNILLON – 30 Gard – 339 L3 – pop. 689 – alt. 168 m – ✉ 30630

Provence 23 **D1**

Paris 666 – Avignon 50 – Alès 47 – Bagnols-sur-Cèze 17 – Pont-St-Esprit 25

La Vieille Fontaine with rm — Cèze valley, VISA

– *04 66 82 20 56 – lavieillefontaine400@orange.fr – Fax 04 66 82 33 64 – Open April-October and closed Monday, Tuesday and Wednesday in April and October*
8 rm – €155 €155, €10 – ½ P €115 – **Rest** – *(closed Mon., Tues. and Wed. from Oct. to Apr.)* Menu €35/55

◆ A house with character built against the medieval walls. Smart rooms, vaulted dining room, traditional cuisine, terraced garden and pool overlooking the valley.

CORPS – 38 Isère – 333 I9 – pop. 453 – alt. 939 m – ✉ 38970 French Alps

Paris 626 – Gap 39 – Grenoble 64 – La Mure 24 45 **C3**

Office de tourisme, Route Napoléon 04 76 30 03 85, Fax 04 76 30 03 85

Dam★★ and bridge★ of Le Sautet West: 4 km.

Du Tilleul VISA AE

r. des Fosses – 04 76 30 00 43 – jourdan@hotel-restaurant-du-tilleul.com – Fax 04 76 30 06 12 – Closed 2 November-22 December
19 rm – €38/44 €44/68, €7 – ½ P €49/60 – **Rest** – Menu €14/35 – Carte €18/28

◆ On the imperial Napoleonic road and in the heart of the old village which is very lively in the summer. Cool well-kept rooms, more peaceful in the annexe. Friendly welcome. The dining room is a little dark but has a pleasant country atmosphere. Traditional cuisine.

in Aspres-les-Corps 5 km Southeast by N 85 and D 58 – pop. 121 – alt. 930 m – ✉ 05800

Château d'Aspres VISA AE

– *04 92 55 28 90 – snc.charpentier@wanadoo.fr – Fax 04 92 55 48 48 – Open 1st March-15 November, 30 December-2 January and closed Sunday dinner*
6 rm – €80 €110, €11 – 2 suites – ½ P €70/140 – **Rest** – Menu €22/38 – Carte €29/58

◆ This stately12C-17C residence overlooks the Champsaur valley. The rooms are full of character with splendid antique furnishings. You dine in the company of old portraits in this stylishly furnished dining room. The cuisine is traditional.

CORRENÇON-EN-VERCORS – 38 Isère – 333 G7 – see Villard-de-Lans

CORRÈZE – 19 Corrèze – 329 M3 – pop. 1 152 – alt. 455 m – ✉ 19800

Dordogne-Berry-Limousin 25 **C3**

Paris 480 – Aubusson 96 – Brive-la-Gaillarde 45 – Tulle 19 – Uzerche 35

Office de tourisme, place de la Mairie 05 55 21 32 82, Fax 05 55 21 63 56

Mercure Seniorie — rest, VISA AE

– *05 55 21 22 88 – h5711@accor.com – Fax 05 55 21 24 00 – Closed 20 December-7 January*
29 rm – €53/125 €60/135, €12 – **Rest** – Menu (€21), €26/40

◆ This majestic 19C building, formerly a boarding establishment for young women looks over the medieval town. Very spacious rooms, most of which have been renovated. Comfortable dining rooms extended by a large terrace. Short menu of traditional dishes.

Le Parc des 4 Saisons

av. de la Gare – 05 55 21 44 59 – annick.peter@wanadoo.fr – Open 16 March-30 November
5 rm – €53/78 €60/85 – **Table d'hôte** – Menu €25 bi

◆ Owned by a young Belgian couple, this house and its grounds once belonged to a notary public. Smart, comfortable rooms, an attractive lounge, summer pool, sauna and massages. Country-style dining four nights a week (reservation required).

Good food and accommodation at moderate prices?
Look for the Bib symbols: red Bib Gourmand for food, blue Bib Hotel for hotels.

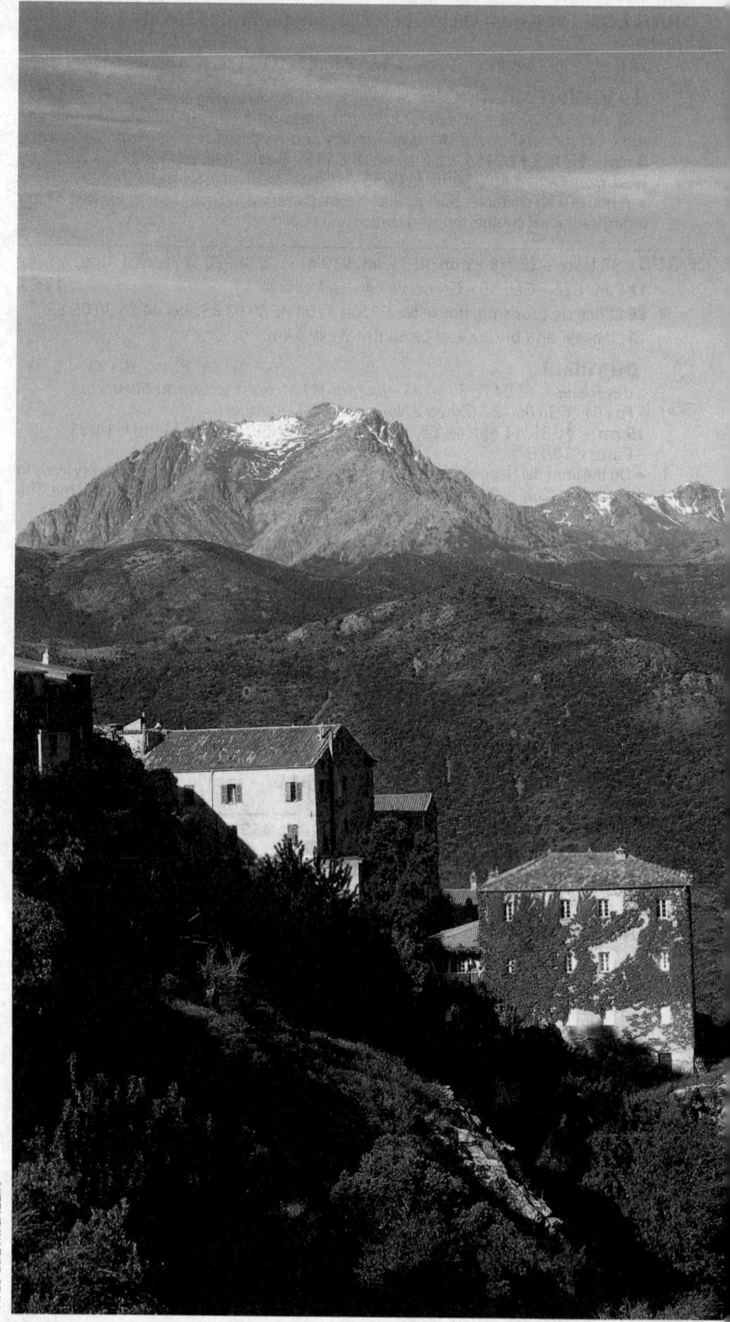

H. Le Gac/MICHELIN

La Balagne : Village de Lama

CORSE

P **Department:** Corse
Michelin LOCAL map: n° **345**

Population: 249 729
Corse

USEFUL INFORMATION

Sea transport

Crossings from mainland France to Corsica leave from Marseilles, Nice and Toulon.
from Marseilles: SNCM - 61 bd des Dames (2e) ✆ 0 825 888 088 (0.15 €/min) and 3260 quoting "SNCM", Fax 04 91 56 36 36. CMN - 4 quai d'Arenc (2e) ✆ 0 810 201 320, Fax 04 91 99 45 95.
from Nice: SNCM - Ferryterranée quai du Commerce ✆ 0 825 888 088 (0.15 €/min). CORSICA FERRIES - Port de Commerce ✆ 0 825 095 095 (0.15 €/min), Fax 04 92 00 42 94.
from Toulon: SNCM - 49 av. Infanterie de Marine (15 Mar.-15 Sep.) ✆ 0 825 888 088 (0.15 €/min). CORSICA FERRIES - Gare Maritime ✆ 0 825 095 095 (0.15 €/min).

Airports

Corsica has four airports serving Continental France, Italy and part of Europe: Ajaccio ✆ 04 95 23 56 56, Calvi ✆ 04 95 65 88 88, Bastia ✆ 04 95 54 54 54, and Figari-Sud-Corse ✆ 04 95 71 10 10 (Bonifacio and Porto-Vecchio).
See also text for these towns.

A few golf courses

9 Bastia (see the locality), ✆ 04 95 38 33 99 ;
18 de Sperone à Bonifacio(see the locality), ✆ 04 95 73 17 13.

AJACCIO 🅿 – **2A Corse-du-Sud** – **345** B8 – **pop. 52 880** – **Casino** Z – ✉ **20000** 15 **A3**

Bastia 147 – Bonifacio 131 – Calvi 166 – Corte 80 – L'Ile-Rousse 141

Ajaccio-Campo dell'Oro: ✆ 04 95 23 56 56, by ①: 7 km.

Office de tourisme, boulevard du Roi Jérôme ✆ 04 95 51 53 03, Fax 04 95 51 53 01

Old town ★ - Musée Fesch★★: Italian paintings★★★ - Bonaparte House ★ - Napoleonic room★ (1st floor of the town hall) - Jetée de la Citadelle ⋞★ - Place Gén.-de-Gaulle ou Place du Diamant ⋞★.

Golfe d'Ajaccio★★, to Iles sanguinaires★★

Albert-1er (Bd) . . . . Y 2
Bévérini Vico (Av.) . . . . Y 4
Colonna d'Ornano (Av. du Col.) . . . . Y 10
Griffi (Square P.) . . . . Y 22
Leclerc (Cours Gén.) . . . . Y 25
Madame-Mère (Bd) . . . . Y 29
Maillot (Bd H.) . . . . Y 30
Masséria (Bd) . . . . Y 32
Napoléon-III (Av.) . . . . Y 37
Napoléon (Cours) . . . . Y
Nicoli (Cours J.) . . . . Y 38
Paoli (Bd D.) . . . . Y 41
St-Jean (Montée) . . . . Y 51

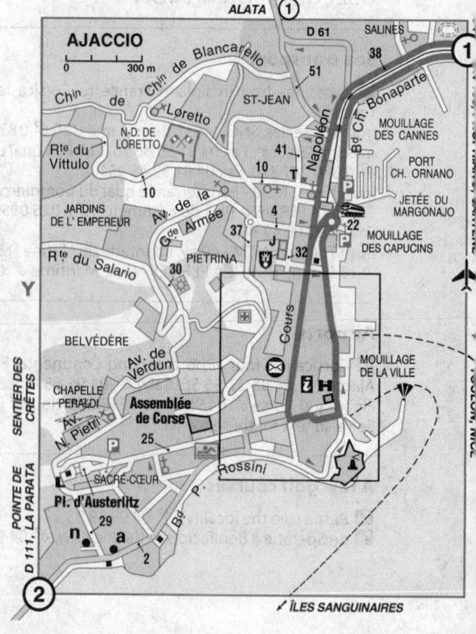

Palazzu U Domu without rest

17 r. Bonaparte – ✆ 04 95 50 00 20 – reservation@palazzu-domu.com – Fax 04 95 50 02 10 Z **e**

45 rm – †€ 180/760 ††€ 180/760, ☕ € 22

◆ Fully restored 18C palace, once home to Count Pozzo di Borgo. Luxurious feel combining modernity and tradition. Chic rooms decorated in a soft contemporary style.

Les Mouettes without rest

9 cours Lucien-Bonaparte – ✆ 04 95 50 40 40 – info@hotellesmouettes.fr – Fax 04 95 21 71 80 – Closed 5 January-6 March

28 rm – †€ 99/275 ††€ 99/275, ☕ € 14

◆ Charming residence dating from 1880 with views over the bay, Mediterranean garden and private beach. Spacious, well-decorated rooms, most of them with small balconies.

Napoléon without rest

4 r. Lorenzo Vero – ✆ 04 95 51 54 00 – info@hotel-napoleon-ajaccio.com – Fax 04 95 21 80 40 – Closed 16 December-1st January Z **s**

62 rm – †€ 72/97 ††€ 82/114, ☕ € 8

◆ Warm welcome at this hotel in a street perpendicular to Cours Napoléon. The rooms have recently been redecorated in a modern style.

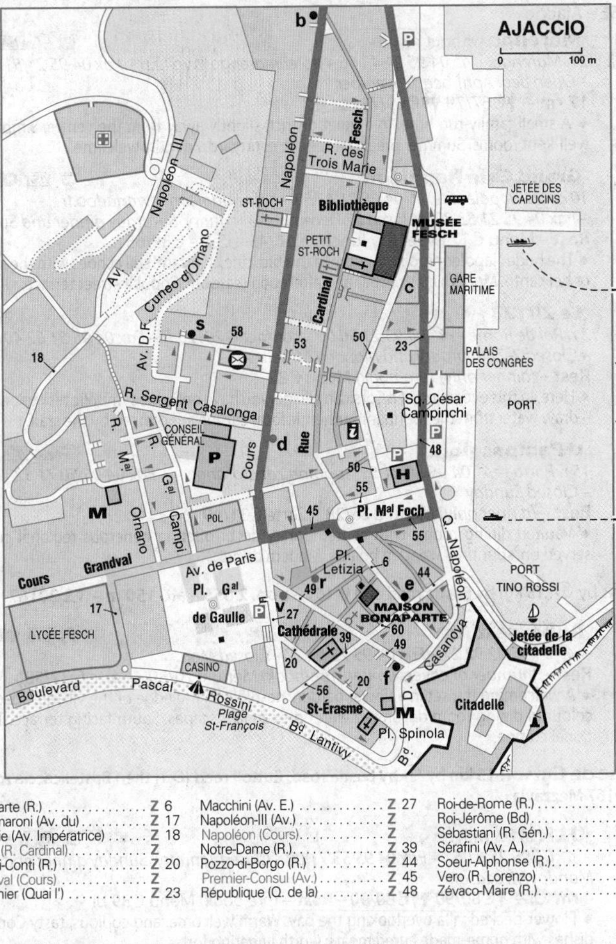

Bonaparte (R.)	Z 6	Macchini (Av. E.)	Z 27	Roi-de-Rome (R.)	Z 49
Dr-Ramaroni (Av. du)	Z 17	Napoléon-III (Av.)	Z	Roi-Jérôme (Bd)	Z 50
Eugénie (Av. Impératrice)	Z 18	Napoléon (Cours)	Z	Sebastiani (R. Gén.)	Z 53
Fesch (R. Cardinal)	Z	Notre-Dame (R.)	Z 39	Sérafini (Av. A.)	Z 55
Forcioli-Conti (R.)	Z 20	Pozzo-di-Borgo (R.)	Z 44	Soeur-Alphonse (R.)	Z 56
Grandval (Cours)	Z	Premier-Consul (Av.)	Z 45	Vero (R. Lorenzo)	Z 58
Herminier (Quai l')	Z 23	République (Q. de la)	Z 48	Zévaco-Maire (R.)	Z 60

San Carlu without rest

8 bd Casanova – ✆ 04 95 21 13 84 – hotel-san-carlu@wanadoo.fr
– Fax 04 95 21 09 99 – Closed 22 December-end January Z **f**

40 rm – €69/120 €89/140, €9

◆ Large, well-equipped, air-conditioned rooms 100 metres from St François beach. Some command a view of the citadel (military zone).

Impérial without rest

6 bd Albert 1er – ✆ 04 95 21 50 62 – info@hotelimperial-ajaccio.fr
– Fax 04 95 21 15 20 – Open 11 March-4 November and 15 December-5 January

44 rm – €70/140 €70/140, €9 Y **a**

◆ A small building on the edge of the town separated from the sea by a small square. The hotel's huge lobby is completely devoted to Napoleon. Bright, functional rooms.

Kallisté without rest

51 cours Napoléon – ✆ 04 95 51 34 45 – info@hotel-kalliste-ajaccio.com

– Fax 04 95 21 79 00 Z **b**

45 rm – €56/69 €64/79, €8

◆ This 19C building was built during the reign of Napoleon and has been refurbished with its original vaults cleverly retained. Small, comfortable rooms.

Marengo without rest

2 r. Marengo – 04 95 21 43 66 – hotel.marengo@voila.fr – Fax 04 95 21 51 26 – Open beg. April-beg. November Y **n**

17 rm – €67/79 €69/79, €7

◆ A small family-run hotel in a quiet district, slightly away from the centre. Simple but well-kept rooms. Summer breakfast terrace courtyard. Friendly welcome.

Grand Café Napoléon

10 cours Napoléon – 04 95 21 42 54 – cafe.napoleon@wanadoo.fr – Fax 04 95 21 53 32 – Closed 22 December-2 January, Saturday dinner and Sunday

Rest – Menu €17 (weekday lunch), €30/45 – Carte €39/65 Z **d**

◆ The huge Napoleonic dining room in this old 'café chantant' still echoes with the strains of bel canto. Modern cuisine. Bar and afternoon tearoom. Popular street terrace.

Le 20123

2 r. Roi de Rome – 04 95 21 50 05 – contact@20123.fr – Fax 04 95 51 02 40 – Closed 2-27 February and Monday off season Z **v**

Rest – *(dinner only) (pre-book)* Menu €32

◆ Here, in this evocation of a Corsican village, you have only one symbolic task to perform – draw water from the fountain! Authentic local cuisine announced by the staff.

U Pampasgiolu

15 r. Porta – 04 95 50 71 52 – pampa.zdt@orange.fr – Fax 04 95 50 71 52 – Closed Sunday Z **r**

Rest – *(dinner only)* Menu €26/28 – Carte €31/49

◆ Vaulted dining rooms with contemporary decor offering generous regional cuisine served on 'spuntinu' wooden boards. Modern dishes.

in Afa by ①: 15 km by Bastia road and D 161 – pop. 2 055 – alt. 150 m – ✉ 20167

Auberge d'Afa

– 04 95 22 92 27 – Fax 04 95 22 92 27 – Closed Mon.

Rest – *(number of covers limited, pre-book)* Menu €20/30 – Carte €37/58

◆ A welcoming inn set in a flower garden, nestling on the edge of the village. Spacious, colourful dining room decorated with Corsican landscapes. South-facing terrace. Traditional cuisine.

Plaine de Cuttoli 15 km by ① by Bastia road, Cuttoli road (D 1) then Bastelicaccia road – ✉ 20167 Mezzavia

U Licettu with rm

– 04 95 25 61 57 – Fax 04 95 53 71 00 – Closed January, Sunday dinner and Monday off season

4 rm – €80/90 €80/90 – **Rest** – *(pre-book)* Menu €39 bi

◆ Flower-decked villa overlooking the bay. Warm welcome, and copious, tasty Corsican dishes with home-made cured meats: worth lingering for!

in Pisciatello 12 km by ① and N 196 – ✉ 20117 Cauro

Auberge du Prunelli

– 04 95 20 02 75 – Closed Tuesday

Rest – Menu €20/31 bi – Carte €26/39

◆ 19C Corsican inn by the old bridge which crosses the Prunelli. Cuisine based on local dishes using produce fresh from the orchard and vegetable garden, served in a pleasant rustic setting.

îles Sanguinaires road by ② – ✉ 20000 Ajaccio

Dolce Vita Sanguinaires islands and the gulf, rm,

9 km – 04 95 52 42 42 – reservation@hotel-dolcevita.com – Fax 04 95 52 07 15 – Open end March-beg. November

32 rm (½ board only in season) – €115/262 €186/262, €18 – ½P €173/231

Rest *La Mer* – Menu (€25), €30/40 – Carte €73/86

◆ La Dolce Vita... and what if Anita Ekberg should rise out of the pool? An understandably popular holiday establishment, offering attractive rooms with sea views. Original food can be enjoyed in the huge dining room or on the lovely terrace facing the bay.

Cala di Sole ≤ sea, rest,

6 km – ✆ 04 95 52 01 36 – caladisole@annuaire-corse.com – Fax 04 95 52 00 20 – Open 1st April-30 October

31 rm – €120 €168, ☐ €12 – ½ P €155 – **Rest** – *(open 15 June-15 September) (dinner only)* Menu €30/40

◆ An energetic stay in a 1960s hotel at the water's edge: private beach, pool, gym, diving, jet-ski and windsurfing available. Rooms with terrace. Simple, traditional cuisine with an emphasis on fish, served overlooking the sea.

La Pinède without rest

3.5 km – ✆ 04 95 52 00 44 – hotellapinede@wanadoo.fr – Fax 04 95 52 09 48 – Closed 13 December-15 January

38 rm – €96/174 €103/174, ☐ €7

◆ This modern building's garden and pool bordered with pine trees offer a relaxing setting. Most of the modern rooms overlook the bay. Barbicaja beach nearby.

Palm Beach with rm rest,

at 5 km – ✆ 04 95 52 01 03 – hotel@palm-beach.fr – Closed 1st-30 December, Sunday dinner, Monday lunch and lunch July-August

9 rm – €90/160 €90/230, ☐ €14 – **Rest** – Menu €31/60 – Carte €62/84

◆ Predominantly fish menu in this smart Mediterranean style restaurant. Superb terrace overlooking the beach and the sea. Simple, elegant furnishings in bedrooms inspired by the fresh sea air. State of the art facilities.

ALÉRIA – **2B Haute-Corse** – **345** G7 – **pop. 1 966** – **alt. 20 m** – ✉ **20270** 15 **B2**

Bastia 71 – Corte 50 – Porto Vecchio 72

Office de tourisme, Casa Luciana ✆ 04 95 57 01 51, Fax 04 95 57 03 79

Fort de Matra (Matra Fort) ★ - Musée Jérôme-Carcopino (Jérôme Carcopino Museum) collection of Attican ceramics ★★ - Old Town★.

L'Atrachjata without rest

– ✆ 04 95 57 03 93 – info@hotel-atrachjata.net – Fax 04 95 57 08 03

29 rm – €49/89 €59/134, ☐ €11 – 1 suite

◆ This family-run hotel in the heart of Aléria (the first metropolis in Corsica's history) has been completely renovated. Large modern rooms with new bathrooms and efficient soundproofing.

L'Empereur

lieu-dit Cateraggio , (N 198) – ✆ 04 95 57 02 13 – hotel.empereur@tiscali.fr – Fax 04 95 57 02 33

22 rm – €45/77 €62/91, ☐ €6,50 – ½ P €43/59

Rest – *(closed Sunday October-April)* Menu €14/24 – Carte €26/32

◆ Motel-type accommodation in this establishment only 3 minutes from the beach. The rooms are spacious, functional and face the swimming-pool; some have a mezzanine. Tasty, traditional Corsican dishes are served here in an attractively bright dining room.

ALGAJOLA – **2B Haute-Corse** – **345** C4 – **pop. 216** – **alt. 2 m** – ✉ **20220** 15 **A1**

Bastia 76 – Calvi 16 – L'Ile-Rousse 10

Office de tourisme, rue Droite ✆ 04 95 62 78 32

Citadel★.

Stellamare without rest

chemin Santa Lucia – ✆ 04 95 60 71 18 – info@stellamarehotel.com – Fax 04 95 60 69 39 – Open from May to September

16 rm – €70/115 €70/115, ☐ €10

◆ Standing back from the sea, in the upper part of the resort, a hotel that you reach via a lovely garden. Pleasant rooms, redecorated on a regular basis.

AULLÈNE – **2A Corse-du-Sud** – **345** D9 – **pop. 138** – **alt. 825 m** – ✉ **20116** 15 **B3**

Ajaccio 73 – Bonifacio 84 – Corte 103 – Porto-Vecchio 59 – Propriano 37 – Sartène 35

San Larenzu without rest

Pasta di Grano – ✆ 04 95 78 63 12 – sanlaurenzu@hotmail.fr – Fax 04 95 74 24 83 – Open from February to October

6 rm – **♦€55 ♦♦€58**

♦ Heading for the GR 20? Laurent offers modern, well-kept rooms. The delicious breakfast (including Corsican honey and jams) is served on the terrace in good weather.

BASTELICA – **2A Corse-du-Sud** – **345** D7 – **pop. 460** – **alt. 800 m** – ✉ **20119** 15 **B2**

Ajaccio 43 – Corte 69 – Propriano 70 – Sartène 82

Panoramic road ★ of the plateau d'Ese.

400 m from col de Mercujo: belvédère ≤★★ and Southwest: 13,5 km.

Chez Paul with rm

– ✆ 04 95 28 71 59 – Fax 04 95 28 73 13

6 rm – **♦€50 ♦♦€50** – **Rest** – Menu €15/24

♦ Views of the village and Prunelli Valley from the dining room, which is separated from the kitchens by the road! Corsican cuisine; cold meat platters. Spacious apartments.

BASTIA – **2B Haute-Corse** – **345** F3 – **pop. 37 884** – ✉ **20200** 15 **B1**

Ajaccio 148 – Bonifacio 171 – Calvi 92 – Corte 69 – Porto 136

Bastia-Poretta ✆ 04 95 54 54 54, by ②: 20 km.

Office de tourisme, place Saint-Nicolas ✆ 04 95 54 20 40, Fax 04 95 54 20 41

Bastia Golf Club Borgo Castellarese, South: 20 km by Airport road, ✆ 04 95 38 33 99.

Terra-Vecchia★: Old harbour★★, Immaculate Conception oratory★ - Terra-Nova★: Assumption of the Virgin★★ in Ste-Marie church, Rococo decor★★ in Ste-Croix chapel .

Ste-Lucie church ≤★★ 6 km Northwest by D 31 X - ✻★★★ of Serra di Pigno 14 km by ③ - ≤★★ of col de Teghime 10 km by ③.

Plan on next page

Les Voyageurs without rest

9 av. Mar. Sébastiani – ✆ 04 95 34 90 80 – info@hotel-lesvoyageurs.com – Fax 04 95 34 00 65 X **r**

24 rm – **♦€70/75 ♦♦€80/95**, €8

♦ This hotel just by the station has been successfully renovated with yellow and blue colours in the rooms and good soundproofing.

Corsica Hôtels Bastia Centre without rest

av. J. Zuccarelli , via ③ – ✆ 04 95 55 10 00 – contact@corsica-hotels.fr – Fax 04 95 55 05 11

71 rm – **♦€59/79 ♦♦€71/91**, €8

♦ A well-equipped modern building. Comfortable, soundproofed and well-designed rooms. Breakfast buffet and snack-bar.

Posta Vecchia without rest

r. Posta Vecchia – ✆ 04 95 32 32 38 – info@hotel-postavecchia.com – Fax 04 95 32 14 05 Y **s**

50 rm – **♦€40/80 ♦♦€40/92**, €6,50

♦ This building with its blue shutters is in the heart of Terra-Vecchia, the old quarter of Bastia. The rooms are smallish but well-kept; those in the annexe are more spacious and attractive.

Chez Huguette

quai Sud, au Vieux-Port – ✆ 04 95 31 37 60 – panta@wanadoo.fr – Fax 04 95 31 37 60 – Closed 8-29 December, Sunday except dinner 16 June-14 September, Monday lunch 16 June-14 September and Saturday lunch Z **t**

Rest – Carte €38/65

♦ Family-run restaurant overlooking the boats in the old harbour. This pleasant neighbourhood is reflected in the fresh seafood and fish dishes.

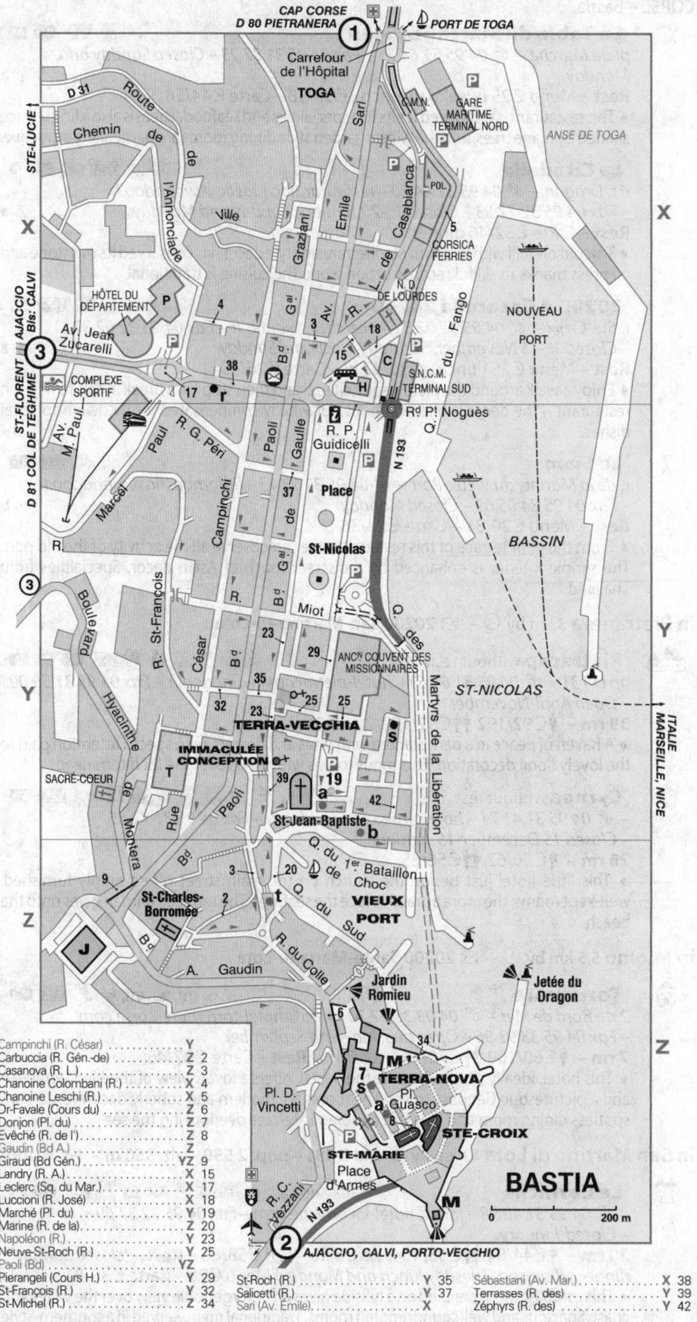

Campinchi (R. César) . . . . Y
Carbuccia (R. Gén.-de) . . . . Z 2
Casanova (R. L.) . . . . Z 3
Chanoine Colombani (R.) . . . . X 4
Chanoine Leschi (R.) . . . . X 5
Dr-Favale (Cours du) . . . . Z 6
Donjon (Pl. du) . . . . Z 7
Evêché (R. de l') . . . . Z 8
Gaudin (Bd A.) . . . . Z
Giraud (Bd Gén.) . . . . YZ 9
Landry (R. A.) . . . . X 15
Leclerc (Sq. du Mar.) . . . . X 17
Luccioni (R. José) . . . . X 18
Marché (Pl. du) . . . . Y 19
Marine (R. de la) . . . . Z 20
Napoléon (R.) . . . . Y 23
Neuve-St-Roch (R.) . . . . Y 25
Paoli (Bd) . . . . YZ
Pierangeli (Cours H.) . . . . Y 29
St-François (R.) . . . . Y 32
St-Michel (R.) . . . . Z 34
St-Roch (R.) . . . . Y 35
Salicetti (R.) . . . . Y 37
Sari (Av. Emile) X
Sébastiani (Av. Mar.) . . . . X 38
Terrasses (R. des) . . . . Y 39
Zéphyrs (R. des) . . . . Y 42

La Table du Marché St Jean

pl du Marché – ✆ 04 95 31 64 25 – Fax 04 95 31 87 23 – Closed Sunday and Monday Y **a**
Rest – Menu € 25 (weekday lunch), € 38/58 – Carte € 44/58
♦ This restaurant is renowned for its fish specialities and seafood. There is also a fine terrace shaded by plane trees, and the winter garden style dining rooms are particularly attractive.

La Citadelle

6 r. Dragon – ✆ 04 95 31 44 70 – restaurantlacitadelle@wanadoo.fr – Fax 04 95 32 77 53 – Closed 1st-20 January, Sunday and Monday Z **a**
Rest – Carte € 32/46 dinner
♦ This old oil-mill with its warm Mediterranean style decor has conserved its millstone and oil press thanks to skilful reconstruction work. The cuisine is traditional.

20200 A Casarella 20200

r. Ste-Croix – ✆ 04 95 32 02 32 – acerchef@yahoo.fr – Fax 04 95 32 02 32 – Closed 1st-15 November, Saturday lunch and Sunday Z **s**
Rest – Menu € 25 (lunch), € 30/42 bi – Carte € 26/45
♦ Enjoy a walk around the picturesque citadel and then stop for a break in this family-run restaurant – the decor is unpretentious but wholly compensated for by delightful local dishes.

Le Siam

r. de la Marine, au Vieux-Port – ✆ 04 95 31 72 13 – lesiambastia@wanadoo.fr – Fax 04 95 34 05 62 – Closed Monday Y **b**
Rest – Menu € 20/31 – Carte € 24/38
♦ From the mini-terrace of this restaurant one can observe all the activity of the old port. The simple interior is enhanced by a discreet touch of Asian decor. Specialities from Thailand.

in Pietranera 3 km by ① – ✉ 20200 San-Martino-di-Lota

Pietracap without rest

on D 131 – ✆ 04 95 31 64 63 – hotel-pietracap@wanadoo.fr – Fax 04 95 31 39 00 – Open April-November
39 rm – †€ 92/192 ††€ 92/192, ☕ € 12
♦ A haven of peace in a park planted with trees and flowers, with special attention paid to the lovely floral decoration. Enormous rooms with views over the Mediterranean.

Cyrnea without rest

– ✆ 04 95 31 41 71 – hotelcyrnea@wanadoo.fr – Fax 04 95 31 72 65 – Closed 15 December-15 January
20 rm – †€ 50/62 ††€ 56/85, ☕ € 6
♦ This little hotel just beside the church on the main street offers simply furnished, well-kept rooms; the more attractive face the seafront. The terraced garden gives onto the beach.

in Miomo 5,5 km by ① – ✉ 20200 Santa-Maria-di-Lota

Torremare

rm, rm,

2 rte Bord de Mer – ✆ 04 95 33 47 20 – info@hotel-torremare-corse.com – Fax 04 95 33 93 96 – Open beg. May-end September
7 rm – †€ 60/109 ††€ 75/147, ☕ € 10 – **Rest** – Carte € 37/46
♦ This hotel, ideally situated beside the beach, offers a lovely view of the Mediterranean and a picturesque Genoese tower. The rooms are modern and soberly decorated. Smart, spotless dining room and pleasant panoramic terrace overlooking the sea.

in San Martino di Lota 13 km by ① and D 131 – pop. 2 530 – alt. 350 m – ✉ 20200

La Corniche

sea and valley,

– ✆ 04 95 31 40 98 – info@hotel-lacorniche.com – Fax 04 95 32 37 69 – Closed January
20 rm – †€ 44/84 ††€ 53/104, ☕ € 8,50 – ½ P € 58/86 – **Rest** – *(closed Sunday dinner off season, Tuesday lunch and Monday)* Menu € 28 – Carte € 38/51
♦ This establishment perched on a hillside gives an unforgettable view over the valley and coast. Spacious and well soundproofed rooms. Traditional menu served in a southern-style dining area. Outdoor terrace with panoramic views.

Château Cagninacci without rest
– ✆ *06 78 29 03 94 – info@chateaucagninacci.com – Open 15 May-1st October*
4 rm – €86/108 €90/112
◆ This former convent dating from the 17C rightly boasts some of the finest rooms in all of Corsica – large, bright and tastefully furnished, all overlooking the sea and the island of Elba.

Ajaccio road 4 km by ② – ✉ 20600 Bastia

Ostella rm, rm,
– ✆ *04 95 30 97 70 – hotel.ostella@wanadoo.fr – Fax 04 95 33 11 70*
52 rm – €60/110 €76/290, € 12 – **Rest** – *(closed Sunday)* Menu € 23/30 – Carte € 34/58
◆ New hotel with functional rooms. Some have a small balcony overlooking the sea. Original garden with a waterfall. Fine fitness centre. A dining room with marble columns, a terrace and traditional cuisine.

Bastia-Poretta Airport road 18 km by ②, N 193 and D 507 ✉ 20290 Lucciana

Poretta without rest
rte de l'aéroport – ✆ 04 95 36 09 54 – hotel-poretta@wanadoo.fr
– Fax 04 95 36 15 32
45 rm – €57/69 €59/72, € 7
◆ This modern building stands some distance back from the road and is flanked by splendid palm trees. The rooms vary in size but are fresh and functional. Duplex suites available for families.

BOCOGNANO – 2A Corse-du-Sud – 345 D7 – pop. 343 – alt. 600 m – ✉ 20136 15 B2

Ajaccio 39 – Bonifacio 155 – Corte 43
Cascade du Voile de la Mariée ★ 3.5 km South.

Beau Séjour with rm
– ✆ *04 95 27 40 26 – ferripisani@wanadoo.fr – Fax 04 95 27 40 95*
– Open 15 April-7 October
17 rm – €43/50 €53/61, € 6,50 – ½ P € 59 – **Rest** – Menu € 16 (week), € 30/45 – Carte € 20/36
◆ This building dating from 1890 stands among chestnut trees and is a favourite haunt of walkers and nature lovers. Hearty island specialities are served in a restful flower-filled setting. The rooms here are simply furnished and some offer a fine view of Monte d'Oro.

BONIFACIO – 2A Corse-du-Sud – 345 D11 – pop. 2 658 – alt. 55 m – ✉ 20169 15 B3

Ajaccio 132 – Corte 150 – Sartène 50
Figari-Sud-Corse: ✆ 04 95 71 10 10, North: 21 km.
Office de tourisme, 2, rue Fred Scamaroni ✆ 04 95 73 11 88, Fax 04 95 73 14 97
de Sperone Domaine de Sperone, East: 6 km, ✆ 04 95 73 17 13.
Site★★★ - High town★★: Place du marché ≤★★ - Treasure-houses r★ of Bonifacio churches (Palazzu Publicu) - St-Dominique church★ - Esplanade St-Francois ≤★★ - Marine cemetery n★.
Sea grottoes and the coast★★.

Genovese rm,
Haute Ville – ✆ 04 95 73 12 34 – info@hotel-genovese.com – Fax 04 95 73 09 03
15 rm – €140/285 €140/285, € 20 – 3 suites
Rest – *(Open April-October)* Menu € 40 (lunch) – Carte € 63/79
◆ The chic and modern minimalist architecture of this place make it conductive to relaxation. Stunning rooms set around a courtyard facing the citadel or harbour. Local produce cooked in line with the restaurant's modish setting, overlooking the pool.

Santa Teresa without rest
quartier St-François, (upper town) – ✆ 04 95 73 11 32 – hotel.santateresa@wanadoo.fr – Fax 04 95 73 15 99 – Open 11 April-14 October
46 rm – €105/280 €105/280, € 15
◆ An imposing building overhanging the cliffs. Well-kept, contemporary rooms, some with a dramatic view of the sea and Sardinia.

La Caravelle

35 quai Comparetti – 04 95 73 00 03 – restaurant.la.caravelle@wanadoo.fr – Fax 04 95 73 00 41 – Open 22 March-mid October

28 rm – €97/300 €97/300, € 16 – **Rest** – *(open from May to September)* Menu € 24/60 – Carte € 44/261

◆ Sunny harbour side hotel with intimate atmosphere (shabby chic furniture). Large, comfortable and simple rooms. Menu bursting with very fresh, good quality fish. Pleasant terrace. There are two bars: one in the former chapel, the other outside.

A Trama

2 km east by Santa Manza road – 04 95 73 17 17 – hotelatrama@aol.com – Fax 04 95 73 17 79 – Closed 6 January-4 February

25 rm – €88/188 €88/188, € 14 – **Rest** – *(open 1st April-31 October) (dinner only)* Menu € 30

◆ Rooms in five bungalows in attractive grounds with olive and palm trees; they are all well decorated (mosaics) and have a private terrace. Fish of the day is on the menu, served on the veranda overlooking the pool.

A Cheda

rte Porto Vecchio, 2 km northeast on N198 – 04 95 73 03 82 – acheda@acheda-hotel.com – Fax 04 95 73 17 72

16 rm – €99/439 €99/439, € 20 – 3 suites – **Rest** – *(closed 2 January-15 February, lunch and Tuesday except 1st June-15 September)* Menu € 51/79 – Carte € 58/72

◆ A garden with a wide variety of plants surrounds the pretty, ground floor rooms of this hotel. They are decorated with wood, stone, mosaic and Mediterranean colours. Intimate restaurant and terrace overlooking the pool. Modern cuisine using local produce.

Roy d'Aragon without rest

13 quai Comparetti – 04 95 73 03 99 – info@royaragon.com – Fax 04 95 73 07 94 – Closed February

31 rm – €54/90 €140/197, € 9 – 4 suites

◆ This 18C building offers practical, colourful bedrooms, some overlooking the harbour. Fourth floor rooms on the front have a balcony. Breakfast terrace.

Le Voilier

quai Comparetti – 04 95 73 07 06 – lautrerestaurant@wanadoo.fr – Fax 04 95 73 14 27 – Closed 7 January-24 February, Sunday dinner and Wednesday off season

Rest – Menu (€ 25), € 30/35 – Carte € 55/100

◆ Terrace directly overlooking the quayside. Dining room decorated in cream tones, dark wood furniture, pictures of sailboats and appetising modern seafood cuisine.

Stella d'Oro

7 r. Doria, (upper town) – 04 95 73 03 63 – stella.oro@bonifacio.com – Fax 04 95 73 03 12 – Open April-September

Rest – Menu € 25 (lunch) – Carte € 39/70

◆ A very pleasant and attractively decorated restaurant (exposed beams, olive press and millstone). Tasty cuisine with fish to the fore. Warm matriarchal welcome.

Domaine de Licetto with rm

rte Pertusato – 04 95 73 19 48 – denisefaby@aol.com – Fax 04 95 72 11 92

7 rm – €39/70 €49/80, € 7 – **Rest** – *(open 1st April-30 October and closed Sunday except August) (dinner only) (number of covers limited, pre-book)* Menu € 33 bi (set menu)

◆ Rustic style dining room and flower-decked terrace serving Corsican family dishes made with home-grown veg. Spacious rooms. Superb view of the region from the property.

in Gurgazu **6 km Northeast by Santa-Manza road – 20169 Bonifacio**

Du Golfe

Golfe Santa Manza – 04 95 73 05 91 – golfe.hotel@wanadoo.fr – Fax 04 95 73 17 18 – Open from mid March-mid October

12 rm (½ board only) – ½ P € 55/80 – **Rest** – Menu € 21/28 – Carte € 26/42

◆ Family-run establishment nestling on a wild stretch of land in Santa Manza Bay, 50m from the sea. An ideal spot for peace, quiet and simplicity. Convivial dining room and terrace with views of the coast. Appetising, unpretentious regional food.

Northeast 10 km by Porto-Vecchio road N 198 and secondary road – ✉ 20169 Bonifacio

U Capu Biancu ← rm, rest, P VISA
Domaine de Pozzoniello – ✆ 04 95 73 05 58 – info@ucapubiancu.com – Fax 04 95 73 18 66 – Open 3 April-autumn half-term holidays and Christmas holidays
42 rm – †€ 190/640 ††€ 190/640, ☕ € 20 – 4 suites – ½ P € 164/389
Rest – Menu € 43 (lunch), € 85/195 – Carte € 81/151
◆ A rough track leads to this hotel, set in a lonely spot facing the Santa Manza gulf. Delightfully personalised rooms, overlooking the sea or the heath. Water sports. The chef originally hails from Senegal and skilfully combines Corsican and African flavours.

in la plage de Calalonga 6 km East by D 258 and secondary road – ✉ 20169 Bonifacio

Marina di Cavu ← Lavezzi and Cavallo islands, rm, P VISA
– ✆ *04 95 73 14 13 – info@marinadicavu.com – Fax 04 95 73 04 82*
6 rm – †€ 100/410 ††€ 100/410, ☕ € 21 – 3 suites – ½ P € 195/495
Rest – *(open mid March-end October) (number of covers limited, pre-book)*
Menu € 64 – Carte € 71/85
◆ Set in the Corsican scrub, this hotel looks out towards the islands of Lavezzi and Cavallo. Huge granite boulders feature in the large rooms (mosaics and North African furniture). Access the restaurant via the pool for a superb view. Fine modern menu.

CALACUCCIA – 2B Haute-Corse – **345** D5 – **pop. 340** – **alt. 830 m** – ✉ **20224** 15 **A2**

Bastia 78 – Calvi 97 – Corte 35 – Piana 68 – Porto 58

Office de tourisme, avenue Valdoniello ✆ 04 95 47 12 62, Fax 04 95 47 12 62

Calacuccia Lake ★ - Tour of the dam lake ← ★★ - Defile of la Scala di Santa Regina★★ Northeast: 5 km.

Acqua Viva without rest P VISA
– ✆ *04 95 48 06 90 – stella.acquaviva@wanadoo.fr – Fax 04 95 48 08 82*
14 rm – †€ 55/69 ††€ 55/74, ☕ € 9
◆ This hotel at the mouth of the Scala di Santa Regina gorge, which, legend has it, was hewn by the Holy Virgin herself, has modern and impeccably kept rooms. Friendly welcome.

Auberge Casa Balduina P VISA
lieu-dit Le Couvent – ✆ 04 95 48 08 57 – jeannequilichini@aol.com – Closed Christmas holidays
7 rm – †€ 57/71 ††€ 57/76, ☕ € 7 – ½ P € 63/72 – **Rest** – *(dinner guests only)*
◆ This pleasant, recently-built hotel set in a garden offers small, light and soberly decorated rooms. Breakfast is served under the pretty pergola.

CALVI – 2B Haute-Corse – **345** B4 – **pop. 5 177** – ✉ **20260** 15 **A1**

Bastia 92 – Corte 88 – L'Ile-Rousse 25 – Porto 73

Calvi-Ste-Catherine: ✆ 04 95 65 88 88, by ①.

Office de tourisme, Port de Plaisance ✆ 04 95 65 16 67, Fax 04 95 65 14 09

Citadel★★: fortifications★ - La Marine★.

Interior★ of St John the Baptist church - La Balagne★★★.. La Balagne★★★.

Plan on next page

La Villa ← Calvi and the sea, rm, P
chemin de Notre Dame de la Serra, 1 km via ① VISA
– ✆ *04 95 65 10 10 – la-villa.reservation@wanadoo.fr – Fax 04 95 65 10 50 – Open 1st April-31 October*
38 rm – †€ 250/700 ††€ 250/700, ☕ € 33 – 13 suites
Rest ***L'Alivu*** – *(closed Monday and Tuesday) (dinner only)* Menu € 90/195 – Carte € 137/208
Rest ***Le Bistrot*** – *(dinner only)* Carte € 65/75
Spec. Langoustines de nos côtes aux trois saveurs (June to mid September). Rougets de pêche locale en filets saisis à l'huile d'olive (August to October). Quasi de veau corse cuit au sautoir, tarte feuilletée aux champignons sauvages (April to October). **Wines** Ajaccio, Vin de Corse-Calvi.
◆ This contemporary luxury hôtel sits on the hillside, as if bowing to the sea. Wrought iron, mosaics, cane furnishings, terra-cotta... It's a hidden jewel! Tasty Mediterranean cuisine served at dinner by an award winning chef.

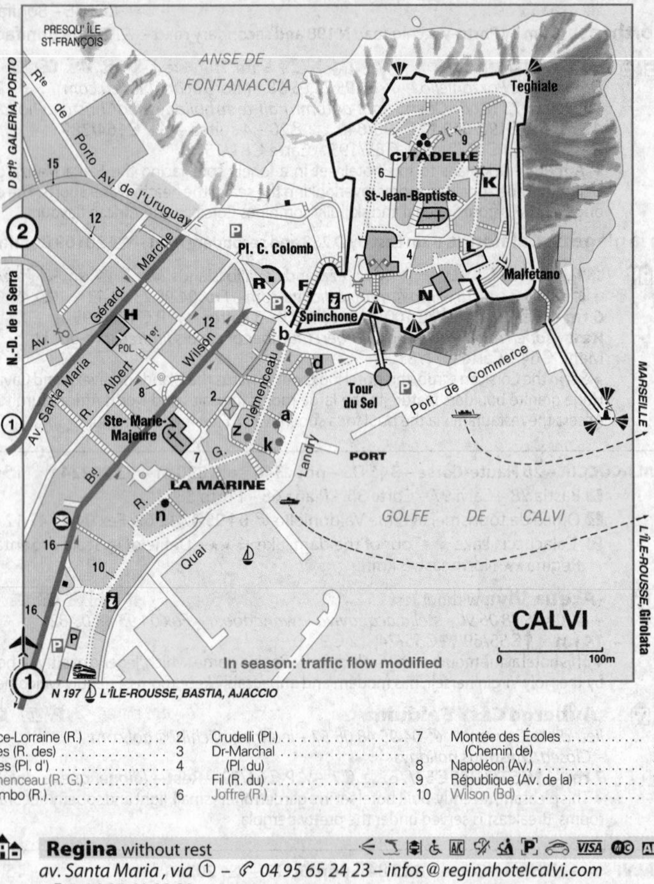

CALVI

In season: traffic flow modified

Alsace-Lorraine (R.)	2	Crudelli (Pl.)	7	Montée des Écoles (Chemin de)	12
Anges (R. des)	3	Dr-Marchal (Pl. du)	8	Napoléon (Av.)	15
Armes (Pl. d')	4	Fil (R. du)	9	République (Av. de la)	16
Clemenceau (R. G.)		Joffre (R.)	10	Wilson (Bd)	
Colombo (R.)	6				

Regina without rest

av. Santa Maria , via ① – ✆ 04 95 65 24 23 – infos@reginahotelcalvi.com – Fax 04 95 61 00 09

44 rm – 🚹€ 67/320 🚹🚹€ 67/320, ☕ € 12

◆ New hotel set high up overlooking the harbour and Bay of Calvi. Large modern rooms facing the sea or the attractive pool.

Balanea without rest

6 r. Clemenceau – ✆ 04 95 65 94 94 – info@hotel-balanea.com – Fax 04 95 65 29 71

38 rm – 🚹€ 79/219 🚹🚹€ 79/299, ☕ € 12 **n**

◆ Access via a pedestrian street. The rooms are characterised by a touch of originality with lively colours and neo-rustic or designer furniture; some have a fine panoramic view of the harbour.

Mariana without rest

av. Santa Maria – ✆ 04 95 65 31 38 – mariana-hotel-calvi@orange.fr – Fax 04 95 65 32 72

43 rm – 🚹€ 55/110 🚹🚹€ 65/160, ☕ € 10

◆ Modern hotel complex on the heights of the "ever faithful" city. Private loggia and sea view for the rooms (except for four new ones). Friendly welcome.

L'Onda without rest

av. Christophe Colomb, 1 km on ① – ✆ 04 95 65 35 00 – hotelonda@yahoo.fr – Fax 04 95 65 16 26 – Open 23 April-4 November

24 rm – 🚹€ 50/90 🚹🚹€ 65/130, ☕ € 7

◆ This small 1990s building stands near the beach and a pinewood planted towards the end of the 19C. Its rooms are functional and all have an attractive loggia.

Revellata without rest
av. Napoléon, rte d'Ajaccio via ②: 0.5 km – ✆ 04 95 65 01 89 – Fax 04 95 65 29 82 – Open 1st April-15 October
55 rm – †€ 80/115 ††€ 90/135, ☐ € 5
◆ The sea is less than 100m away, only separated from the establishment by the Porto road. The rooms have sturdy furnishings and lovely views over the "big blue".

Emile's
quai Landry – ✆ 04 95 65 09 60 – info@restaurant-emiles.com – Fax 04 95 60 56 40 – Open 15 March-15 October **k**
Rest – Menu € 40/100 – Carte € 74/135
◆ A hidden staircase leads to a terrace and veranda dining room overlooking the port and the bay. Modern cuisine focused on seafood.

L'Ile de Beauté
quai Landry – ✆ 04 95 65 00 46 – restaurantiledebeauté@orange.fr – Fax 04 95 65 27 34 – Closed 5 January-25 March and Monday October-December **a**
Rest – Menu € 21/45 – Carte € 46/67
◆ Furnished with Stark chairs, the restaurant's large, pleasant terrace faces the port. Modern cuisine with an emphasis on fish dishes and top-quality tapas.

E.A.T.
r. Clemenceau, Port ascent – ✆ 04 95 38 21 87 – remi.robert636@orange.fr – Closed 1st-15 November, 1st-15 February, Monday, Tuesday and Wednesday from November to March **b**
Rest – Menu € 33 – Carte € 35/68
◆ Unusual concept at this lounge style restaurant: diners choose either large or extra large portions of the refined modern dishes. Terrace at the foot of the citadel.

Calellu
quai Landry – ✆ 04 95 65 22 18 – calellu@wanadoo.fr – Open 1st April-31 October and closed Monday off season **d**
Rest – Menu € 22 – Carte € 42/55
◆ Small welcoming façade; beige dining room decorated with Corsican flora and offering a view of the boats in the bay. Fish specialities on the menu.

Aux Bons Amis
r. Clemenceau – ✆ 04 95 65 05 01 – Open 16 March-14 October and closed Wednesday dinner off season, Saturday lunch in season and Wednesday lunch **z**
Rest – Menu € 22 – Carte € 43/66
◆ This friendly little restaurant in a pedestrian street has a fishing theme as decoration, with nets and ornaments. Crayfish and lobster tank. Fish and seafood specialities.

via ① 5 km airport road and private lane – ✉ 20260 Calvi

La Signoria
rte de la fôret de Bonifato – ✆ 04 95 65 93 00 – info@auberge-relais-lasignoria.com – Fax 04 95 65 38 77 – Open 1st April-30 October
24 rm – †€ 180/390 ††€ 230/390, ☐ € 28 – 2 suites
Rest – *(dinner only)* Menu € 80/120 – Carte € 85/101
◆ A Mediterranean pulse throbs in this 18C building nestling in a pinewood: walls coloured in blue and ochre, Corsican period furniture...a place of warm scents and sunlight! Good modern fare, served in a southern-style dining room or on the pretty terrace.

CARGÈSE – **2A Corse-du-Sud** – **345** A7 – **pop. 982** – **alt. 75 m** – ✉ **20130** 15 **A2**

Ajaccio 51 – Calvi 106 – Corte 119 – Piana 21 – Porto 33

Office de tourisme, rue du Dr Dragacci ✆ 04 95 26 41 31, Fax 04 95 26 48 80

Greek church ★ - Site ★★ from the belvédère de la pointe Molendino (viewpoint) East: 3 km.

Thalassa rm, rest,

plage du Pero, 1.5 km north – 04 95 26 40 08 – Fax 04 95 26 41 66 – Open 1st May-30 September

25 rm – €68/90 €90/100, €6 – ½ P €73/95 – **Rest** – *(open 1st June-18 September) (dinner only) (resident only)*

◆ Pleasant family guesthouse atmosphere at this beachside hotel. The rather small but bright and well-kept rooms mostly face the sea. Pleasant dining room and leafy terrace. Traditional food.

CASAMOZZA – **2B Haute-Corse** – **345** F4 – ✉ **20290 Lucciana** 15 **B1**

Bastia 20 – Corte 49 – Vescovato 6

Chez Walter rm, rm, VISA MC AE

N 193 – 04 95 36 00 09 – hotel.chez.walter@wanadoo.fr – Fax 04 95 36 18 92

64 rm – €63/90 €85/120, €8 – 2 suites – ½ P €69/73

Rest – *(closed 15 December-6 January and Sunday except dinner in August)* Menu €20 – Carte €30/47

◆ A modern hotel complex near to Bastia Poretta airport with well-equipped rooms that have all been renovated. The style of this vast dining room is neo-rustic, the cuisine is traditional and the menus include buffet-type lunches and pizzas.

CAURO – **2A Corse-du-Sud** – **345** C8 – **pop. 1 060** – **alt. 450 m** – ✉ **20117** 15 **A3**

Ajaccio 22 – Sartène 63

Auberge Napoléon VISA MC

– 04 95 28 40 78 – Open 15 July-15 September and week-ends off season

Rest – *(dinner only except Saturday and Sunday) (pre-book)* Menu €28 – Carte €28/43

◆ Pleasant inn standing on the main street in the village. A rustic dining room serving dishes with a regional flavour. A relaxed family welcome.

CERVIONE – **2B Haute-Corse** – **345** F6 – **pop. 1 452** – **alt. 350 m** – ✉ **20221** 15 **B2**

Paris 999 – Ajaccio 140 – Bastia 52 – Corte 78 – Biguglia 45

in Prunete **5,5 km East by D 71** – ✉ **20221**

Casa Corsa without rest

Acqua Nera – 04 95 38 01 40 – casa.corsa@free.fr – Fax 04 95 33 39 27

6 rm – €56/62 €56/62

◆ You will be anything but disappointed by your warm and lively welcome to this guesthouse. Charm pervades the comfortable rooms with their spacious bathrooms. Lovely garden.

COL DE BAVELLA – **2A Corse-du-Sud** – **345** E9 – **alt. 1 218 m** – ✉ **20124 Zonza** 15 **B3**

Ajaccio 102 – Bonifacio 76 – Porto-Vecchio 49 – Propriano 49 – Sartène 47

Col and aiguilles de Bavella (pass and peaks)★★★ - Bavella forest ★★.

Auberge du Col de Bavella VISA MC AE

– 04 95 72 09 87 – auberge-bavella@wanadoo.fr – Fax 04 95 72 16 48 – Open April-October

Rest – Menu €22 – Carte €20/43

◆ A handy inn close to the GR 20 amid Laricio pines, near the majestic Bavella peaks. Large rustic dining room (fireplace). Corsican specialities and home-made cooked pork products.

CORTE – **2B Haute-Corse** – **345** D6 – **pop. 6 329** – **alt. 396 m** – ✉ **20250**

Corse 15 **B2**

Bastia 69 – Bonifacio 150 – Calvi 88 – L'Ile-Rousse 63 – Porto 93 – Sartène 149

Office de tourisme, la Citadelle 04 95 46 26 70, Fax 04 95 46 34 05

High town★: Ste-Croix chapel ★, citadel★ ≤★, Viewpoint ✻★ - Musée de la Corse★★.

✻★★ du Monte Cecu North: 7 km - Southwest: gorges de la Restonica★★.

In the Gorges de La Restonica Southwest on D 623 – ✉ **20250 Corte**

Dominique Colonna without rest
2 km – ✆ 04 95 45 25 65 – info@dominique-colonna.com – Fax 04 95 61 03 91 – Open 11 March-11 November
28 rm – †€ 65/180 ††€ 65/180, ☕ € 11,50 – 1 suite
◆ A group of modern, ivy-clad buildings stands at the entrance to the gorges and pinewoods of Corte. The rooms are modern and comfortable and there is a heated swimming-pool.

COTI-CHIAVARI – **2A Corse-du-Sud** – **345** B9 – **pop. 490** – **alt. 625 m** – ✉ **20138**
Ajaccio 42 – Propriano 38 – Sartène 50 — 15 **A3**

Le Belvédère — ≤ gulf of Ajaccio,
– ✆ 04 95 27 10 32 – Fax 04 95 27 12 99 – Open 2 March-10 November
13 rm – †€ 55 ††€ 55/71, ☕ € 5 – ½ P € 48/56 – **Rest** – *(closed lunch except Sunday 1st March-31 May) (pre-book)* Menu € 26/28
◆ Perched like an eagle's nest on the heath with an astounding view of the Gulf of Ajaccio. The rooms are spacious and functional. The glazed dining room and terrace have fantastic views. Regional cuisine (superb produce).

ECCICA-SUARELLA – **2A Corse-du-Sud** – **345** C8 – **pop. 828** – **alt. 300 m** – ✉ **20117**
Paris 964 – Ajaccio 19 – Corte 87 – Ghisonaccia 129 – Propriano 52 — 15 **A3**

Carpe Diem Palazzu — rm,
– ✆ 04 95 10 96 10 – info@carpediem-palazzu.com – Fax 04 95 23 80 83 – Closed 12 January-27 February
6 rm – †€ 270/400 ††€ 270/400, ☕ € 19 – **Table d'hôte** – *(closed Monday except school holidays)* Menu € 45/70
◆ Bare stone and wood, period and antique furniture, well-equipped bathrooms – sophisticated suites whose every detail conveys the desire for wellbeing. Turkish bath. Regional cuisine (top quality produce) served on the terrace or in the garden facing the pool.

ERBALUNGA – **2B Haute-Corse** – **345** F3 – ✉ **20222** — 15 **B1**
Bastia 11 – Rogliano 30
N.-D. des Neiges chapel ★ 3 km West.

Castel'Brando without rest — rest,
– ✆ 04 95 30 10 30 – info@castelbrando.com – Fax 04 95 33 98 18 – Closed January and February
39 rm – †€ 105/145 ††€ 105/145, ☕ € 13 – 6 suites
◆ This imposing manor house owes its origin to a doctor serving with the Napoleonic armies. All the rooms are simply but pleasantly furnished but the more modern and comfortable ones are in the recently constructed villa. Fine garden with swimming-pools.

Le Pirate
au port – ✆ 04 95 33 24 20 – jeanpierrericci@aol.com – Fax 04 95 33 18 97 – Closed 7 January-28 February, Monday and Tuesday except from June to September
Rest – Menu € 29 (weekday lunch), € 60/90 – Carte € 66/84
Spec. Tortellini d'araignée de mer sur crème de crustacés (May to June). Déclinaison autour du veau "bio" corse. Palet fondant aux framboises, sorbet agrumes (May to September). **Wines** Vin de Corse-Figari, Patrimonio.
◆ This old stone building has a pleasant terrace facing the little harbour. Adding to the charm are the stylish, renovated dining rooms and the appetising cuisine with a contemporary touch.

ÉVISA – **2A Corse-du-Sud** – **345** B6 – **pop. 196** – **alt. 850 m** – ✉ **20126** — 15 **A2**
Ajaccio 71 – Calvi 96 – Corte 70 – Piana 33 – Porto 23
Aïtone forest★★ - Cascades of Aïtone★ Northeast: 3 km then 30 mn.
Col de Vergio ≤★★ Northeast: 10 km.

Scopa Rossa rest, VISA
– ✆ *04 95 26 20 22 – scopa-rossa@wanadoo.fr – Fax 04 95 26 24 17 – Open March-November*
28 rm – †€ 43/56 ††€ 56/76, ☕ € 7 – **Rest** – Menu € 21 (weekday lunch), € 25/30
◆ The ideal hotel for a family holiday in the centre of this resort. The simple, well-kept bedrooms are divided between the main building and an annexe. The rifles decorating the rustic dining room are no longer used. Dishes based on local produce.

FAVONE – 2A Corse-du-Sud – 345 F9 – ✉ 20135 Conca 15 B3

Ajaccio 128 – Bonifacio 58

U Dragulinu rest, VISA
– ✆ *04 95 73 20 30 – hoteludragulinu@wanadoo.fr – Fax 04 95 73 22 06 – Open 11 April-30 October*
34 rm – †€ 80/210 ††€ 90/220, ☕ € 12 – **Rest** – *(open 1st June-30 September and closed lunch from 1st June to 15 July and in September, dinner from 15 July to 30 August)* Carte € 35/54
◆ This hotel run by two sisters enjoys an idyllic location opposite the beach, ideal for a seaside holiday. Well kept, practical bedrooms, mostly located on the ground floor. Simple family cooking using fresh produce in the restaurant. Pretty terrace.

FELICETO – 2B Haute-Corse – 345 C4 – pop. 162 – alt. 350 m – ✉ 20225 15 A1

Bastia 76 – Calvi 26 – Corte 72 – L'Ile-Rousse 15

Mare E Monti without rest VISA
– ✆ *04 95 63 02 00 – mare-e-monti@wanadoo.fr – Fax 04 95 63 02 01 – Open 2 April-30 October*
16 rm – †€ 70/126 ††€ 70/126, ☕ € 8
◆ Their fortune made in sugar-cane, the ancestors of this family returned from Porto Rico and built this "American Palace" between the sea and the mountain in the 19C.

GALÉRIA – 2B Haute-Corse – 345 A5 – pop. 302 – alt. 30 m – ✉ 20245 15 A2

Bastia 118 – Calvi 34 – Porto 48
Syndicat d'initiative, Carrefour ✆ 04 95 62 02 27, Fax 04 95 62 02 27
Bay of Galéria★.

in Ferayola 13 km North by D 351 and D 81B – ✉ 20245 Galeria

Auberge Ferayola VISA
– ✆ *04 95 65 25 25 – ferayola@wanadoo.fr – Fax 04 95 65 20 78 – Open from May to end September*
14 rm – †€ 50/97 ††€ 55/120, ☕ € 8 – ½ P € 57/83 – **Rest** – Menu € 21/23 – Carte € 24/38
◆ The hotel stands alone in the heart of the maquis with only the coast road between it and the sea – thus assuring tranquillity and restfulness. The rooms are simply but pleasantly furnished, and there are also chalets available. View of the sea and the mountain from the rustic style dining room and terrace.

L'ILE-ROUSSE – 2B Haute-Corse – 345 C4 – pop. 2 774 – ✉ 20220 15 A1

Bastia 67 – Calvi 25 – Corte 63
Syndicat d'initiative, 7, place Paoli ✆ 04 95 60 04 35, Fax 04 95 60 24 74
Covered market★ - Pietra island ★.
La Balagne★★★.

Santa Maria without rest VISA
rte du Port – ✆ 04 95 63 05 05 – infos@hotelsantamaria.com – Fax 04 95 60 32 48
56 rm ☕ – †€ 79/190 ††€ 90/200
◆ The hotel is located before the bridge leading to the island of Pietra. Pleasant rooms, modern design. Some offer apocalyptic views of the sea during stormy weather.

Funtana Marina without rest — sea, VISA

1 km on Monticello road and secondary road – ✆ 04 95 60 16 12 – hotel-funtana-marina@wanadoo.fr – Fax 04 95 60 35 44

29 rm – †€ 55/105 ††€ 55/105, ☕ € 9

◆ Building on a hillside surrounded by rich vegetation. The rooms, nearly all of which have been renovated, overlook the lovely pool, beyond which are the sea and town.

Cala di l'Oru without rest — VISA

bd Pierre Pasquini – ✆ 04 95 60 14 75 – hotelcaladiloru@wanadoo.fr – Fax 04 95 60 36 40 – Open from March to October

26 rm – †€ 56/106 ††€ 59/107, ☕ € 8,50

◆ The sons of the owner display photos and works of modern art in this hotel. Minimalist rooms with views of the sea or the mountains. Attractive Mediterranean garden.

L'Amiral without rest — VISA

bd Ch.-Marie Savelli – ✆ 04 95 60 28 05 – info@hotel-amiral.com – Fax 04 95 60 31 21 – Open April-September

19 rm – †€ 65/100 ††€ 65/100, ☕ € 10

◆ A small building on two floors only 25 metres from the sandy beach of the holiday resort. The rooms are of medium size, functional, and well-kept.

Le Grillon — VISA

av. P. Doumer – ✆ 04 95 60 00 49 – hr-le-grillon@wanadoo.fr – Fax 04 95 60 43 69 – Open 1st March-31 October

16 rm – †€ 35/56 ††€ 36/58, ☕ € 5,60 – ½ P € 38/49

Rest – Menu € 13,50/17 – Carte € 20/24

◆ The quality of the hospitality here eclipses the simplicity of the place. Bright, well-kept little rooms. A classic style restaurant serving family cooking with regional touches.

La Pietra — VISA

Chemin du Phare – ✆ 04 95 63 02 30 – hotellapietra@wanadoo.fr – Fax 04 95 60 15 92 – Open April-October

42 rm – †€ 64/109 ††€ 65/110, ☕ € 9 – ½ P € 64/86

Rest – Menu € 21/29 – Carte € 42/48

◆ Waterfront location on the port for this 1970s hotel with well-renovated rooms, all with balconies overlooking either the sea or the 15C Genoese tower. Local cuisine and dishes of the day against the broad backdrop of the sea.

in Monticello 4,5 km Southeast by D 63 – pop. 1 253 – alt. 220 m – ✉ 20220

A Pasturella with rm — VISA

– ✆ 04 95 60 05 65 – a.pasturella@wanadoo.fr – Fax 04 95 60 21 78 – Closed 8 November-21 December, 17-24 February and Sunday dinner from 21 December to 31 March

14 rm – †€ 80/90 ††€ 90/100, ☕ € 11 – ½ P € 88/95 – **Rest** – Menu € 33/48 – Carte € 40/65

◆ Restaurant located in a picturesque village on the Paoli corniche. Fish of the day and traditional meals served in the renovated dining area or on the lovely terrace.

LEVIE – 2A Corse-du-Sud – 345 D9 – pop. 696 – alt. 645 m – ✉ 20170 — 15 B3

Ajaccio 101 – Bonifacio 57 – Porto-Vecchio 39 – Sartène 28

Office de tourisme, rue Sorba ✆ 04 95 78 41 95, Fax 04 95 78 46 74

Musée de l'Alta Rocca★: Christ in ivory★.

Sites★★ of Cucuruzzu and Capula West: 7 km.

La Pergola

r. Sorba – ✆ 04 95 78 41 62

Rest – *(number of covers limited, pre-book)* Menu € 16/18

◆ After visiting the Alta Rocca Museum, return to the present under a welcoming bower where they serve Corsican specialities for a reasonable price.

LUMIO – **2B Haute-Corse** – **345** B4 – **pop. 1 040** – **alt. 150 m** – ✉ **20260** 15 **A1**

Bastia 82 – Calvi 10 – L'Ile-Rousse 16

Chez Charles with rm

– ✆ *04 95 60 61 71 – reservations@hotel-chezcharles.com – Fax 04 95 60 62 51 – Open 16 March-29 October*

16 rm – €45/115 €48/120, €12 – ½ P €75/100 – **Rest** – Menu (€24), €36/55 – Carte €43/61

◆ Pleasant, light dining room, well shaded panoramic terrace, up-to-date menu and comfortable rooms of southern inspiration. Handsome infinity pool.

MACINAGGIO – **2B Haute-Corse** – **345** F2 – ✉ **20248** 15 **B1**

Bastia 37

Syndicat d'initiative, port de plaisnce ✆ 04 95 35 40 34, Fax 04 95 35 40 34

U Libecciu rest, rm,

– ✆ *04 95 35 43 22 – info@u-libecciu.com – Fax 04 95 35 46 08 – Open 1st April-15 October*

30 rm – €48/94 €55/115, €7 – ½ P €70/125 – **Rest** – *(dinner only)* Menu €20/25 – Carte €25/33

◆ The Macinaggio mooring ground has been famous since Antiquity. The modern port is less than 100m away from this family guesthouse dating back to the 1980s. Spacious rooms. The restaurant menu offers Corsican specialities including a terrine of wild mountain sheep (in season).

U Ricordu rm,

– ✆ *04 95 35 40 20 – info@hotel-uricordu.com – Fax 04 95 35 41 88 – Open 22 March-6 November*

54 rm – €73/163 €76/166, €6 – **Rest** – *(open 15 April-15 October)* Menu €15/18 – Carte €26/37

◆ Fresh modern rooms await you after an invigorating trek along the coastguard path. The lovely swimming-pool is open in summertime. Discreet dining room and traditional cuisine.

MOROSAGLIA – **2B Haute-Corse** – **345** E5 – **pop. 1 008** – **alt. 800 m** – ✉ **20218** 15 **B2**

Bastia 53 – Corte 36

Osteria di U Cunventu

– ✆ *04 95 47 11 79 – cunventu@wanadoo.fr – Closed 20 December-1st February*

Rest – Menu €25/45 – Carte €28/51

◆ This small chalet is in the middle of the hamlet where the famous advocate for Corsican independence, Pascal Paoli was born. The dining room is panoramic and the cuisine is based on market-fresh Corsican produce.

NONZA – **2B Haute-Corse** – **345** F3 – **pop. 67** – **alt. 100 m** – ✉ **20217** 15 **B1**

Bastia 33 – Rogliano 49 – Saint-Florent 20

Casa Maria without rest

at the foot of the génoise tower – ✆ *04 95 37 80 95 – casamaria@wanadoo.fr – Fax 04 95 37 80 95 – Open April-October*

5 rm – €70/90 €70/90

◆ This old mansion with its comfortable, air-conditioned and soberly elegant rooms stands at the foot of a Genoese tower. Warm welcome and a splendid view of the sea.

OLETTA – **2B Haute-Corse** – **345** F4 – **pop. 830** – **alt. 250 m** – ✉ **20232** 15 **B1**

Bastia 18 – Calvi 78 – Corte 72 – L'Ile-Rousse 53

Auberge A Magina Nebbio and gulf of St-Florent,

– ✆ *04 95 39 01 01 – Open 1st April-15 October and closed Monday*

Rest – Menu €25 – Carte €31/49

◆ A breathtaking view and Corsican cuisine, prepared and served in family style in a pleasant dining room. Don't miss the magnificent sunset from the terrace.

OLMETO – 2A Corse-du-Sud – **345** C9 – **pop. 1 115 – alt. 320 m** – ✉ **20113** 15 **A3**

Ajaccio 64 – Propriano 8 – Sartène 20

Syndicat d'initiative, Village ☎ 04 95 74 65 87, Fax 04 95 74 62 86

Santa Maria rm, VISA MC

pl. de l'Église – ☎ 04 95 74 65 59 – ettorinathalie@aol.com – Fax 04 95 74 60 33 – Closed November and December

12 rm (½ board only in August) – €45/58 €45/58, €6 – ½ P €44/56 –
Rest – Menu €16/23 – Carte €29/38

♦ A former oil mill with a family atmosphere, near the church. A flight of stairs leading to the functional rooms gives the building character. The restaurant has a lovely, century-old vaulted ceiling and a pretty flower-filled terrace facing the gulf. Corsican dishes.

in Olmeto-Plage 9 km Southwest by D 157 – ✉ 20113

Ruesco P VISA MC

– ☎ 04 95 76 70 50 – info@hotel-ruesco.com – Fax 04 95 76 70 51 – Open 19 April-11 October

25 rm – €61/101 €101/139, €8,50 – **Rest** – *(open 15 May-30 September)* Carte €30/52

♦ Modern buildings housing spacious rooms. All the rooms, apart from two, have balconies overlooking the water. A garden leads up to the restaurant which specialises in grilled food and pizzas cooked over a wood fire. The terrace looks onto the beach.

South 5 km by N 196 and secondary road – ✉ 20113 Olmeto

Marinca Valinco and Propriano gulf, rm, P VISA MC AE

Lieu dit Vintricella – ☎ 04 95 70 09 00 – info@hotel-marinca.com – Fax 04 95 76 19 09 – Open April-October

53 rm – €165/620 €190/540, €25 – 3 suites – ½ P €95/500
Rest – Menu €35/55 – **Rest *Le Diamant Noir*** – *(dinner only)* Carte €53/83

♦ Hotel with views of the gulf and surrounded by gardens. Three tiered infinity pools flow towards the private beach. Large rooms with individual touches; balconies on the beach side. Spa. Lovely, Moorish style terrace; traditional cuisine. The Diamant Noir serves more elaborate meals at dinner.

PATRIMONIO – 2B Haute-Corse – **345** F3 – **pop. 645 – alt. 100 m** – ✉ **20253** 15 **B1**

Bastia 16 – St-Florent 6 – San-Michele-de-Murato 22

St-Martin church ★.

Osteria di San Martinu P VISA MC

– ☎ 04 95 37 11 93 – Open 1st May-30 September and closed Wednesday in September

Rest – Menu €22 – Carte €19/37

♦ In summer, it's all systems go on the terrace under the pergola. Corsican dishes and grills are served with Patrimonio wine, produced by the owner's brother.

PERI – 2A Corse-du-Sud – **345** C7 – **pop. 1 140 – alt. 450 m** – ✉ **20167** 15 **A2**

Ajaccio 26 – Corte 71 – Propriano 82 – Sartène 94

Chez Séraphin

– ☎ 04 95 25 68 94 – Closed 1st October-7 December, Thursday, Tuesday and Wednesday except dinner off season and Monday

Rest – Menu €42 bi

♦ Typical Corsican building in a charming village clinging to the mountainside. Terrace overlooking the valley. Warm welcome and good hearty meals.

PETRETO-BICCHISANO – 2A Corse-du-Sud – **345** C9 – **pop. 549 – alt. 600 m** – ✉ **20140**

Ajaccio 52 – Sartène 35 15 **A3**

De France P VISA MC

à Bicchisano – ☎ 04 95 24 30 55 – Fax 04 95 24 30 55 – Open from March to November

Rest – *(pre-book)* Menu €15 (weekday lunch), €21/50 – Carte €41/62

♦ Corsican specialities and home-made products such as cooked meats, jams and liqueurs are served in this well-kept rural style dining room or under the cool arbour.

PIANA – 2A Corse-du-Sud – **345** A6 – **pop. 428 – alt. 420 m** – ✉ **20115** 15 **A2**

Ajaccio 72 – Calvi 85 – Évisa 33 – Porto 13
Syndicat d'initiative, ✆ 04 95 27 84 42, Fax 04 95 27 82 72
Bay of Porto★★★.

Capo Rosso ← Gulf and Les Calanche, rm,
– *✆ 04 95 27 82 40 – info@caporosso.com*
– Fax 04 95 27 80 00 – Open 1st April-20 October VISA MC AE
50 rm (½ board only in season) – €90 €110, €20 – ½ P €105/130 –
Rest – Menu €28/38 – Carte €47/60
◆ Unrestricted views of Porto Bay and the Calanche from the swimming pool and the huge rooms (with balconies). Mostly contemporary decor. Restaurant with views, serving family seafood cuisine using the local catch.

Le Scandola ← rm, P VISA MC
rte Cargèse – ✆ 04 95 27 80 07 – infos@hotelscandola.com – Fax 04 95 27 83 88
– Closed 17 November-1st February
12 rm – €40/76 €40/76, €10 – ½ P €50/68 – **Rest** – *(dinner only)*
Menu €30
◆ With views of the Scandola peninsula and the Piana gulf, this hotel enjoys an exceptional location. Warm, colourful rooms and balconies facing the sea. Cuisine from around the world served in the lounge restaurant with views.

PORTICCIO – 2A Corse-du-Sud – **345** B8 – ✉ **20166** 15 **A3**

Ajaccio 19 – Sartène 68
Office de tourisme, les Marines ✆ 04 95 25 01 01, Fax 04 95 25 11 12

Le Maquis ← Ajaccio and gulf, rm,
– *✆ 04 95 25 05 55 – info@lemaquis.com* P VISA MC AE
– Fax 04 95 25 11 70 – Closed January and February
20 rm – €155/680 €175/680, €26 – 5 suites – ½ P €184/396
Rest – Menu €70 – Carte €81/133
◆ A pretty Genoese-style building nestling in a luxuriant seaside garden. Spacious rooms with attractive antique furniture. Splendid swimming pools. Inventive cuisine, selected wines and a fine view from the dining room and superb terrace.

Sofitel Thalassa ← gulf,
– *✆ 04 95 29 40 40 – h0587@accor.com* P VISA MC AE
– Fax 04 95 25 00 63 – Closed December and January
96 rm – €149/452 €195/519, €23 – 2 suites
Rest – Menu €49 – Carte €56/89
◆ A hotel complex devoted to Neptune: an isolated location on the tip of Cape Porticcio, a thalassotherapy centre, watersports facilities and rooms facing the sea. Dishes with a contemporary touch and light meals served in a naval decor or outside with a view of the waves.

in Agosta-Plage 2 km South – ✉ **20166 Porticcio**

Kallisté without rest ← gulf of Ajaccio, P VISA MC
rte du Vieux Molini – ✆ 04 95 25 54 19 – info@hotels-kalliste.com
– Fax 04 95 25 59 25 – Open 21 March-11 November
8 rm – €75/105 €75/180, €12 – 1 suite
◆ A quiet villa thanks to its pretty walled garden, in a residential area. Soberly-decorated rooms of various sizes with a view of the sea or the greenery.

PORTO – 2A Corse-du-Sud – **345** B6 – ✉ **20150 Ota** 15 **A2**

Ajaccio 84 – Calvi 73 – Corte 93 – Évisa 23
Office de tourisme, place de La Marine ✆ 04 95 26 10 55,
Fax 04 95 26 14 25
Tour génoise★.
Bay of Porto★★★: les Calanche★★★ - Northwest: Scandola reserve ★★★, Bay ★★ of Girolata.

Capo d'Orto without rest
– ✆ 04 95 26 11 14 – hotel.capo.d.orto@wanadoo.fr – Fax 04 95 26 13 49 – Open 10 April-20 October
39 rm – €75/139 €75/159
♦ This hotel has three room types, all well sized with balconies facing the sea. Choose one in the recently built extension with a more modern decor.

Le Subrini without rest
at la Marine – ✆ 04 95 26 14 94 – subrini@hotels-porto.com – Fax 04 95 26 11 57 – Open from March to October
23 rm – €60/90 €100/140, €10
♦ A freestone building on the main square on the seafront. The large rooms, all recently renovated, are functional and bright. View over the bay.

Le Belvédère without rest
à la Marine – ✆ 04 95 26 12 01 – info@hotel-le-belvedere.com – Fax 04 95 26 11 97
20 rm – €45/110 €45/110, €7,50
♦ At the foot of the famous Genoese tower stalwartly resisting poundings by the sea. This modern red stone building offers well-equipped rooms; choose one facing the harbour.

Bella Vista rest,
– ✆ 04 95 26 11 08 – info@hotel-bellavista.net – Fax 04 95 26 15 18 – Open April-October
17 rm (½ board only in season) – €60/85 €65/140, €11 – 4 suites – ½ P €60/110
Rest – *(open 15 April-30 September) (dinner only)* Menu €19/29 – Carte €40/61
♦ A hotel with a family atmosphere and carefully decorated rooms. Unforgettable views of the Capo d'Orto at sunset and good breakfast. Modern dishes with Corsican touches served on a panoramic dining room and terrace.

Romantique without rest
à la Marine – ✆ 04 95 26 10 85 – info@hotel-romantique-porto.com – Fax 04 95 26 14 04 – Open 15 April-15 October
8 rm – €64/92 €64/92, €8
♦ Spacious rooms with roughcast walls, tiles and handcrafted furniture. All the balconies look onto a little marina and eucalyptus wood.

La Mer
à la Marine – ✆ 04 95 26 11 27 – laora5@wanadoo.fr – Fax 04 95 96 11 27 – Open mid March-beg. November
Rest – Menu €19 (lunch)/29 – Carte €34/67
♦ At the end of the marina, the terrace of this blue-shuttered house is ideal for viewing the mountain as it plunges into the sea. Fish specialities and wood-fire grills.

PORTO-POLLO – 2A Corse-du-Sud – **345** B9 – **alt. 140 m** – ✉ 20140 15 **A3**
Ajaccio 52 – Sartène 31

Les Eucalyptus without rest
– ✆ 04 95 74 01 52 – portopollo@hotmail.com – Fax 04 95 74 06 56 – Open 5 April-14 October
32 rm – €50/82 €58/82, €8
♦ A 1960s hotel overlooking the Gulf of Valinco. Most of the functional rooms have balconies (five have been opened only recently and are more comfortable) with gulf views.

Le Kallisté
– ✆ 04 95 74 02 38 – lekalliste@free.fr – Fax 04 95 74 06 26 – Open Easter-15 October
19 rm – €58/66 €58/66, €8,50 – ½ P €55/70 – **Rest** – *(dinner only)* Carte €29/40
♦ The rooms here are modern with functional fittings and furniture. Some have a terrace giving a view of the sea. Seasonal family cooking served in a fresh, colourful dining room or out on the terrace.

PORTO-VECCHIO – 2A Corse-du-Sud – 345 E10 – pop. 10 326 – alt. 40 m – ✉ 20137

Ajaccio 141 – Bonifacio 28 – Corte 121 – Sartène 59 15 **B3**

Figari-Sud-Corse: ✆ 04 95 71 10 10, Southwest: 23 km.

Office de tourisme, rue du Docteur Camille de Rocca Serra ✆ 04 95 70 09 58, Fax 04 95 70 03 72

The Citadel ★.

Bay of Porto-Vecchio★★ - Castellu d'Arraghju★ ≤★★ North: 7.5 km.

Casadelmar ≤ Porto Vecchio gulf, rest,
7 km p on Palombaggia road – ✆ 04 95 72 34 34
– info@casadelmar.fr – Fax 04 95 72 34 35 – Open 1st April-2 November
14 rm – €350/890 €350/890, €31 – 20 suites – €470/3000
Rest – *(dinner only)* Menu €170 – Carte €116/166
Spec. Baccala séchée au vent, gambas de San Remo en sashimi, jus de poivron rouge. Risotto au citron vert, basilic, mascarpone et langoustines au gingembre. Loup de ligne en croûte de sel gris, vongole à la verveine. **Wines** Vin de Corse-Figari, Patrimonio.
♦ This luxurious, ultra modern hotel set on the hill blends into the countryside. Dramatic sea views. Designer rooms, infinity pool and superb spa. Delicious modern cuisine served in an exceptional setting.

Belvédère ≤ rm, rm, rm,
Palonbaggia beach road: 5 km – ✆ 04 95 70 54 13
– info@hbcorsica.com – Fax 04 95 70 42 63 – Open 15 March-2 January
15 rm – €100/410 €100/410, €20 – ½ P €130/285
Rest – *(closed Monday and Tuesday from 6 October-6 April)* Menu €60 (weekday lunch), €89/125 – Carte €86/126
Rest *Mari e Tarra* – rest.-terrasse *(open mid April-4 October)* Carte €39/66
Spec. Nougat froid d'huîtres, caviar avruga (October to April). Dos de denti de palangre fumé (May to September). Ris de veau glacé à la myrte. **Wines** Ajaccio, Patrimonio.
♦ Fine group of buildings with a pool and panoramic terrace set in an oasis of greenery at the water's edge. Private beach and partly refurbished rooms in quiet bungalows. Warm restaurant overlooking the sea; refined cuisine. Simplified summer menu.

Le Goéland ≤
à la Marine – ✆ 04 95 70 14 15 – contact@hotelgoeland.com – Fax 04 95 72 05 18
– Open end March-beg. November
28 rm – €65/260 €75/270, €11 – ½ P €75/170 – **Rest** – Menu €25/46
♦ This hotel has been completely refurbished and offers pleasant rooms in a maritime style with storm lamps and painted furniture. Large restaurant with views of the golf course and garden. Corsican and Mediterranean dishes on the daily specials board.

Le Syracuse without rest ≤
6 km on Palombaggia road – ✆ 04 95 70 53 63 – contact@
corse-hotelsyracuse.com – Fax 04 95 70 28 97 – Open 1st April-1st October
18 rm – €110/261 €116/275, €9
♦ Several modern buildings separated from the sea by lush vegetation. Ground floor garden rooms and others with loggias. Beach and swimming-pool.

Golfe Hôtel rm, rest,
r. du 9 Septembre 1943 – ✆ 04 95 70 48 20 – info@golfehotel.com
– Fax 04 95 70 92 00 – Closed 1st December-11 January
39 rm – €69/301 €76/320, €8 – ½ P €70/198 – **Rest** – *(closed 12 November-28 February, Friday, Saturday and Sunday off season) (dinner only)* Menu €25/30
♦ Hotel set on the road leading to the harbour. Bedrooms with contemporary decor are arranged around a pool. Those in the main building are more basic. Bright, simple dining room serving modern cuisine.

Alcyon without rest
9 r. Mar. Leclerc, (opposite the post office) – ✆ 04 95 70 50 50 – info@
hotel-alcyon.com – Fax 04 95 70 25 84 – Closed 23-26 December
40 rm – €52/153 €66/272, €10
♦ Modern building in the town centre. Plain, functional rooms, all of which have been renovated. Those at the front have sea views, the others are quieter.

San Giovanni rest,

rte Arca, 3 km south-west on D 659 – ✆ 04 95 70 22 25
– info@hotel-san-giovanni.com – Fax 04 95 70 20 11
– Open 1st March-1st November
30 rm – €60/100 €70/127, €9 – ½ P €60/78
Rest – *(dinner only) (resident only)*
◆ Guesthouse in a fine park planted with trees and flowerbeds and adorned with a pond. Rooms on the ground floor lead onto a small private garden. Pool and jacuzzi. Breakfasts and simple family meals served under the pagoda.

L'Orée du Maquis

à la Trinité, 5 km north by Chemin de la Lézardière – ✆ 04 95 70 22 21
– daniellec201@orange.fr – Fax 04 95 70 22 21
– Open 15 June-15 September and closed Monday
Rest – *(dinner only) (number of covers limited, pre-book)* Menu €65/70
◆ You reach this isolated villa by a steep road. Open air restaurant with tables shaded by a canopy and views of the coast. Fish, seafood and foie gras feature on the menu.

Le Troubadour

13 r. Gén. Leclerc, (near the Post Office) (1st floor) – ✆ 04 95 70 08 62
– bertrand.tilloux@wanadoo.fr – Fax 04 95 70 92 80
– Closed 1st-21 January and Sunday lunch
Rest – *(dinner only from mid June to September)* Menu €19 (lunch)/29
– Carte €35/57
◆ The upstairs dining room of this restaurant is decorated with panelling and brass saucepans and leads onto a pleasant flower-decked terrace. Updated Corsican cuisine.

at Santa Giulia bay **8 km South by N 198 and secondary road – ✉ 20137 Porto-Vecchio**

Moby Dick rm, rm,

– ✆ 04 95 70 70 00 – mobydick@sud-corse.com – Fax 04 95 70 70 01
– Open mid April-mid October
44 rm (½ board only) – ½ P €105/230
Rest – Menu €38 (weekday lunch)/55 – Carte €54/87
◆ Idyllic location on the lagoon, isolated from the Polynesian coloured gulf by a sandy beach. Spacious rooms on the sea and garden sides. Mediterranean cuisine and local produce to the fore in the restaurant.

Castell' Verde Gulf of Santa Giulia,

– ✆ 04 95 70 71 00
– castellverde@sud-corse.com – Fax 04 95 70 71 01
– Open 26 April-18 October
30 rm (½ board only in season) – €109/252 €120/300
– ½ P €90/150
Rest ***Le Costa Rica*** – see restaurant listing
◆ Spacious bungalows within reach of the sea, set in a protected 5h site. Colourful linen and wooden furniture in the bedrooms. Pool and direct access to the beach.

U Santa Marina with rm sea, rm, rm,

Marina Di Santa Giulia – ✆ 04 95 70 45 00
– santamarina@wanadoo.fr – Fax 04 95 70 45 00
– Open 1st April-15 November
10 rm – €144/348 €174/378, €15
Rest – *(dinner only)* Menu €55/95 – Carte €60/88
◆ Good cuisine using local fish served in colourful surroundings redolent of the south or on one of several terraces with fine views of the sea.

Le Costa Rica – H. Castell' Verde Gulf of Santa Giulia,

– ✆ 04 95 72 24 51 – castellverde@sud-corse.com
– Fax 04 95 70 05 66 – Open 1st May-15 October
Rest – Menu €35 (dinner) – Carte €39/57
◆ The pleasant terrace has a unique view overlooking the bay. Simple decor in the restaurant; contemporary menu focused on the sea.

in Cala Rossa 10 km Northeast by N 198 and D 468 – ✉ 20137 Lecci

Grand Hôtel de Cala Rossa
– ✆ 04 95 71 61 51
– *calarossa@relaischateaux.fr – Fax 04 95 71 60 11*
– *Open 1st April-2 January*
40 rm (½ board only from 1st June to 15 September) – †€ 275/535 ††€ 315/725, ☕ € 40 – 8 suites – ½ P € 230/680
Rest – *(dinner only)*
Menu € 120/160 – Carte € 130/195
Spec. Cannelloni de seiche, crevettes rouges de Méditerranée à la plancha. Saint-Pierre en aiguillettes, artichauts poivrade au tourteau. Carré d'agneau en cocotte lutée, parfums du maquis. **Wines** Vin de Corse-Figari, Patrimonio.
♦ Beneath the pine trees, a luxurious garden facing the beach and a private landing stage. An exceptional hotel in a splendid setting. Wonderful spa. Elegant and subtly rustic dining room with luxurious shaded terrace, serving creative dishes.

in la presqu'île du Benedettu 10 km Northeast by N 198 and D 468 – ✉ 20137 Porto-Vecchio

U Benedettu rm,
– ✆ *04 95 71 62 81 – benedettu@wanadoo.fr – Fax 04 95 71 66 37 – Open end March-end October*
20 rm – †€ 65/250 ††€ 65/250, ☕ € 15 – 3 suites – **Rest** – Carte € 25/45
♦ Ideal position: houses spread out around a peninsula along the beach, commanding a fine view of the Gulf of Porto-Vecchio. Regional recipes and fish dishes top the menu in this restaurant standing at the water's edge.

PROPRIANO – 2A Corse-du-Sud – 345 C9 – pop. 3 166 – alt. 5 m – ✉ 20110 15 **A3**

Ajaccio 74 – Bonifacio 62 – Corte 139 – Sartène 13

Office de tourisme, Port de Plaisance ✆ 04 95 76 01 49, Fax 04 95 76 00 65

Grand Hôtel Miramar gulf of Valinco, rm, rest,
rte Corniche – ✆ *04 95 76 06 13*
– *info@grandhotelmirarmar.com – Fax 04 95 76 13 14*
– *Open 7 May to end October*
22 rm – †€ 200/490 ††€ 200/490, ☕ € 20 – 4 suites
Rest – Menu € 39 (lunch)/75 – Carte € 45/80
♦ Villa with whitewashed walls set in lush gardens overlooking the Gulf of Valinco. Lounge decorated with antique shop finds; smart, spacious bedrooms (with balcony). Refined menu and local produce offered in a smart setting or in the shade of mulberry trees.

Loft Hôtel without rest
3 r. Pandolfi – ✆ *04 95 76 17 48 – loft-hotel@wanadoo.fr – Fax 04 95 76 22 04*
– *Open 16 March-29 October*
25 rm – †€ 48/70 ††€ 48/70, ☕ € 6
♦ Harbourside hotel with large rooms (sloping ceilings on the upper floor). Personalised welcome from the owner; breakfast served on the terrace in fine weather.

Le Lido rm, rm,
– ✆ *04 95 76 06 37 – le.lido@wanadoo.fr – Fax 04 95 76 31 18*
– *Open 15 April-30 October*
15 rm – ††€ 105/225, ☕ € 12 – **Rest** – *(open 15 April-30 September, and closed Tuesday lunch and Monday except August)* Menu (€ 24) – Carte € 53/69
♦ Hotel on a peninsula at the water's edge: well-decorated rooms (exotic woods, antiques, Portuguese mosaics), some with beachside terraces. Seafood to the fore in the restaurant, with waterside terrace on a promontory.

Le Tout va Bien "Chez Parenti"
13 av. Napoléon – ✆ *04 95 76 12 14 – mathieu.andrei@wanadoo.fr*
– *Fax 04 95 76 27 11 – Closed 1st-15 December, 2 January-28 February, Sunday dinner and Monday except dinner in season*
Rest – Menu € 21 (weekday lunch), € 30/52 – Carte € 52/84
♦ This friendly restaurant run by the Parenti family since 1935 has a pleasant terrace facing the port. Cuisine with a contemporary touch; dishes change depending on the catch of the day.

QUENZA – 2A Corse-du-Sud – **345** D9 – **pop. 215** – **alt. 840 m** – ✉ **20122** 15 **B3**

Ajaccio 85 – Bonifacio 75 – Porto-Vecchio 47 – Sartène 38

Frescoes★ of Santa-Maria-Assunta chapel.

Sole e Monti

– *04 95 78 62 53 – sole.e.monti@wanadoo.fr – Fax 04 95 78 63 88 – Open 15 April-30 September*

19 rm – †€ 70/135 ††€ 80/190, ☕ € 10 – ½ P € 70/125

Rest – *(closed Mon. lunch and Tues. lunch)* Menu € 28 (weekdays)/36 – Carte € 35/51

◆ Rustic rooms in this village dominated by the majestic Bavella peaks (two of them recently renovated exactly as they were). Choose the ones to the front overlooking the valley. Wild boar, goat, Corsican cooked meats and other local delicacies on the menu.

ST-FLORENT – 2B Haute-Corse – **345** E3 – **pop. 1 474** – ✉ **20217** 15 **B1**

Bastia 22 – Calvi 70 – Corte 75 – L'Ile-Rousse 45

Office de tourisme, centre Administratif ✆ 04 95 37 06 04, Fax 04 95 35 30 74

Santa Maria Assunta church ★★ - Old town★.

Les Agriates★.

Demeure Loredana without rest

Cisterninu Suttanu – ✆ 04 95 37 22 22 – info@demeureloredana.com – Fax 04 95 37 41 91

13 rm – †€ 230/440 ††€ 230/490, ☕ € 26 – 4 suites

◆ An exceptional break awaits guests of this hotel. Luxurious attention to detail, opulent rooms, Indian influenced decor (monumental 17C Indian balcony), sea views and pool.

La Roya ← Golfe and St Florent, rm,

1 km on Calvi road and secondary road – ✆ 04 95 37 00 40 – michel@hoteldelaroya.com – Fax 04 95 37 09 85 – Open 29 March-12 November

31 rm – †€ 140/390 ††€ 140/560, ☕ € 15 – ½ P € 110/235

Rest – *(open 29 March-2 November)* Menu € 45 – Carte € 34/60

◆ A modern building facing Roya Beach (direct access). The rooms, many with balconies overlooking the sea, are decorated with Mediterranean or Asian-style furniture. Bright dining room and terrace opening onto a delightful garden and pool.

Dolce Notte without rest ← gulf,

– *✆ 04 95 37 06 65 – info@hotel-dolce-notte.com – Fax 04 95 37 10 70 – Open April-October*

20 rm – †€ 67/122 ††€ 67/164, ☕ € 8

◆ A long low building beside the sea on the way out of the town on the road to Cap Corse. Rooms facing the Mediterranean, with terrace or loggia.

Tettola without rest

1 km north on D 81 – ✆ 04 95 37 08 53 – info@tettola.com – Fax 04 95 37 09 19 – Open April-October

30 rm – †€ 50/130 ††€ 55/160, ☕ € 8

◆ A recently built hotel on a pebble beach, with rooms facing the mountain and quieter and brighter rooms facing the sea. Warm welcome.

Le Bellevue without rest

– *✆ 04 95 37 00 06 – hotel-bellevue@wanadoo.fr – Fax 04 95 37 14 83 – Open April-October*

28 rm – †€ 65/116 ††€ 71/155, ☕ € 7

◆ A choice place in the middle of an attractive park overlooking the sea, opposite Cap Corse. The blue and white rooms have wrought-iron beds, some of them four-posters.

Les Galets without rest

rte du Front de Mer – ✆ 04 95 37 09 09 – hotellesgalets@wanadoo.fr – Fax 04 95 37 48 88 – Open April-October

16 rm – †€ 47/99 ††€ 47/128, ☕ € 7

◆ Next to a residence but independent, this recent hotel has large, functional rooms with a sea-view and balcony. A pleasant garden and friendly welcome.

Maxime without rest
St Florent – ✆ 04 95 37 05 30 – Fax 04 95 37 13 07 – Closed December and January
19 rm – †€ 48/75 ††€ 48/75, ☕ € 7
◆ A white building with blue shutters standing on the banks of a small canal (mooring is possible); most of the rooms have a loggia or balcony.

La Rascasse
promenade des Quais – ✆ 04 95 37 06 09 – atrium-saintflorent@wanadoo.fr – Fax 04 95 37 06 99 – Open April-September and closed Monday except from June to August
Rest – Menu € 38 – Carte € 43/62
◆ Following a visit to the old cathedral of Nebbio, this is just the place to enjoy some fine cuisine with a contemporary touch. There are two attractive terraces, one of which overlooks the port.

STE-LUCIE-DE-PORTO-VECCHIO – 2A Corse-du-Sud – 345 F9 – ✉ 20144

Corse 15 **B3**

Paris 942 – Ajaccio 157 – Porto-Vecchio 16 – Sartène 76 – Ghisonaccia 42
Syndicat d'initiative, Mairie annexe ✆ 04 95 71 48 99, Fax 04 95 71 48 99

Le Pinarello without rest — sea,
Pinarello – ✆ 04 95 71 44 39 – contact@lepinarello.com – Fax 04 95 70 66 87 – Open mid April-mid October
31 rm – †€ 214/535 ††€ 230/1102, ☕ € 22
◆ This beach hotel situated right on the seafront offers modern, elegant accommodation with a splendid view of the bay of the same name. Luxurious bar and terrace.

STE-LUCIE-DE-TALLANO – 2A Corse-du-Sud – 345 D9 – pop. 392 – alt. 450 m – ✉ 20112

Ajaccio 92 – Bonifacio 68 – Porto-Vecchio 48 – Sartène 19 15 **B3**

Santa Lucia
– ✆ 04 95 78 81 28 – santalucia@alicepro.fr – Fax 04 95 78 81 28 – Closed January and Sunday off season
Rest – Menu € 17/23 – Carte € 25/31
◆ Soothed by the murmer of the fountain, come linger on the shady terrace under the lime and acacia trees, opposite the main square in this picturesque village. Corsican home cooking.

STE-MARIE-SICCHÉ – 2A Corse-du-Sud – 345 C8 – pop. 357 – alt. 420 m – ✉ 20190

Ajaccio 36 – Sartène 51 15 **A3**

Santa Maria
– ✆ 04 95 25 72 65 – info@santa-maria-hotel.com – Fax 04 95 25 71 34
22 rm – †€ 45/50 ††€ 50/55, ☕ € 7 – ½ P € 50/59
Rest – *(closed 15 Dec. - 15 Feb.)* Menu (€ 15 bi), € 17/25
◆ A family guesthouse atmosphere pervades this 1970s building. Simple but well-kept rooms; some have balconies. A rustic dining area where home-cured cold meats and Corsican dishes are served. Regularly changing menu.

SANT'ANTONINO – 2B Haute-Corse – 345 C4 – pop. 77 – alt. 500 m – ✉ 20220

Paris 959 – Ajaccio 155 – Bastia 99 – Corte 74 – Calvi 21 15 **A1**

I Scalini — mountains and sea,
top of the village – ✆ 04 95 47 12 92 – Open end April-beg. October, closed Monday except dinner in July August and Tuesday lunch off season
Rest – *(number of covers limited, pre-book)* Carte € 31/42
◆ A narrow stone stairway leads to this restaurant perched in the upper part of the village. The interior is highly original (especially the washrooms!) and there are four small, superbly panoramic terraces; one can enjoy delicious specialities in a zen atmosphere.

SARTÈNE – 2A Corse-du-Sud – 345 C10 – pop. 3 410 – alt. 310 m – ✉ 20100

Ajaccio 84 – Bonifacio 50 – Corte 149 15 **A3**
Office de tourisme, 6, rue Borgo ✆ 04 95 77 15 40, Fax 04 95 77 15 40
Old town ★★ - Musée de Préhistoire corse★.

La Villa Piana without rest

Propriano road – 04 95 77 07 04 – info@lavillapiana.com – Fax 04 95 73 45 65 – Open 5 October-17 March – **32 rm** – €62/115 €62/115, €9

◆ The hotel grounds command a fine panoramic view of "the most typical of Corsican towns", as Mérimée put it. Overflow swimming pool overlooking the Rizzanèse valley. Pleasant rooms.

SOLENZARA – 2A Corse-du-Sud – 345 F8 – alt. 310 m – ✉ 20145 15 B3

Ajaccio 118 – Bonifacio 68 – Sartène 77

Office de tourisme, Anciennes ecoles 04 95 57 43 75, Fax 04 95 57 43 59

La Solenzara without rest

quartier du Palais – 04 95 57 42 18 – info@lasolenzara.com – Fax 04 95 57 46 84 – Open 15 March-30 October

28 rm – €60/95 €65/100

◆ Impressive Genoese style building dating from the 18C and surrounded by a garden. Spacious rooms which are bright and simple; those to the rear have sea views. Infinity pool; outdoor jacuzzi.

Francine et Sébastien without rest

Scaffa Rossa, 1.5 km north – 04 95 57 44 41 – sebastien.roccaserradeperetti@orange.fr – Fax 04 95 57 46 73 – **4 rm** – €90 €90

◆ Pretty modern house on the coast, set in a meticulously maintained garden with access to three small coves. Inside, there are plenty of knick-knacks and family antiques.

A Mandria

1 km north – 04 95 57 41 95 – marcantoine.roccaserra@orange.fr – Fax 04 95 57 45 96 – Closed January and February, Sunday dinner and Monday from September to June, Monday lunch and Wednesday in July and August-

Rest – Menu (€16), €22/26 – Carte €27/36

◆ Pleasantly rustic restaurant (exposed stone and beams, old tools which remind us that this was once a sheepfold) serving Corsican dishes. Pergola near a small vegetable plot.

ZONZA – 2A Corse-du-Sud – 345 E9 – pop. 1 802 – alt. 780 m – ✉ 20124 15 B3

Ajaccio 93 – Bonifacio 67 – Porto-Vecchio 40 – Sartène 38

Col and aiguilles de Bavella (Bavella pass and peaks) ★★★ Northeast: 9 km.

Le Tourisme without rest

– 04 95 78 67 72 – letourisme@wanadoo.fr – Fax 04 95 78 73 23 – Open April-October – **16 rm** – €75/100 €90/185

◆ This old coaching inn dating from 1875 retains its original fountain. Bright rooms with balconies. Garden, attractive heated pool with views, gym, sauna and jacuzzi.

CORTE – 2B Haute-Corse – 345 D6 – see Corse

CORVOL-D'EMBERNARD – 58 Nièvre – 319 D8 – pop. 112 – alt. 260 m – ✉ 58210

Paris 236 – Cosne-sur-Loire 48 – Dijon 168 – Nevers 45 7 B2

Le Colombier de Corvol

– 03 86 29 79 60 – robert.collet1@wanadoo.fr – Fax 03 86 29 79 33

5 rm – €97/107 €97/107 – **Table d'hôte** – Menu €47 bi

◆ This farmhouse dating from 1812 is home to charming bed & breakfast accommodation as well as an art gallery displaying works by contemporary artists from April to September. Lovely swimming pool in the courtyard. The menu here is based on traditional recipes.

COSNE-COURS-SUR-LOIRE – 58 Nièvre – 319 A7 – pop. 11 399 – alt. 150 m – ✉ 58200 Burgundy-Jura 7 A2

Paris 186 – Auxerre 83 – Bourges 61 – Montargis 76 – Nevers 54

Office de tourisme, pl. de l'Hôtel de Ville 03 86 28 11 85, Fax 03 86 28 11 85

du Sancerrois Sancerre, North: 10 km by D 955, 02 48 54 11 22.

Museum★ fireplace.

Le Vieux Relais
11 r. St-Agnan – ✆ 03 86 28 20 21 – contacts@le-vieux-relais.fr – Fax 03 86 26 71 12 – Closed 23 December-13 January, Friday dinner and Sunday dinner 15 September-30 April and Saturday lunch
10 rm – †€ 73/84 ††€ 80/91, ☕ € 10,50 – ½ P € 93 – **Rest** – Menu € 21 (weekdays)/41 – Carte € 31/57
♦ This centuries-old post house is between the Loire and the Nohain. The pleasant rooms lead off from a flower-decked courtyard and are named after birds. Old beams and bright colours adorn the refurbished dining room. Traditional repertory.

XX **Les Forges** with rm — AC rest, VISA MC AE
21 r. St-Agnan – ✆ 03 86 28 23 50 – denis-cathye@wanadoo.fr – Fax 03 86 28 91 60 – Closed 1 - 6 Jul, 22 - 29 Dec
7 rm – †€ 53/59 ††€ 59/68, ☕ € 8 – **Rest** – *(closed 22-28 December, Sunday dinner and Monday)* Menu (€ 19), € 26/60 – Carte € 38/49
♦ This welcoming establishment has a warm comfortable dining room serving a concise, regional menu. Attractively decorated and well-kept rooms.

COSQUEVILLE – 50 Manche – 303 D1 – pop. 491 – alt. 22 m – ✉ 50330 — 32 A1

Paris 358 – Caen 124 – Carentan 51 – Cherbourg 21 – St-Lô 79 – Valognes 27

XX **Au Bouquet de Cosqueville** with rm — P VISA MC
38 hameau Remond – ✆ 02 33 54 32 81 – aubouquet.decosqueville@orange.fr – Fax 02 33 54 63 38 – Closed January, Wednesday except July and Tuesday
7 rm – †€ 47 ††€ 52, ☕ € 6,50 – ½ P € 56
Rest – Menu € 20/65 – Carte € 45/56
♦ An old village house covered with Virginia creeper serving seafood and local dishes in an intimate, discreetly rustic setting.

LE COTEAU – 42 Loire – 327 D3 – see Roanne

LA CÔTE-ST-ANDRÉ – 38 Isère – 333 E5 – pop. 4 240 – alt. 370 m – ✉ 38260 — 44 B2

Lyon - Rhone Valley

Paris 525 – Grenoble 50 – Lyon 67 – La Tour-du-Pin 33 – Valence 75 – Vienne 36 – Voiron 32

Office de tourisme, place Hector Berlioz ✆ 04 74 20 61 43, Fax 04 74 20 56 25

XX **France** with rm — AC VISA MC AE
16 pl. de l'Église – ✆ 04 74 20 25 99 – Fax 04 74 20 35 30
14 rm – †€ 58 ††€ 60/75, ☕ € 10 – ½ P € 82 – **Rest** – *(closed Sunday dinner and Monday except holidays)* Menu € 30 (weekdays)/85 – Carte € 44/96
♦ An old building in the heart of Berlioz's hometown. Delectable cuisine based on traditional recipes. Small, simple, refurbished rooms.

COTI-CHIAVARI – 2A Corse-du-Sud – 345 B9 – see Corse

COTIGNAC – 83 Var – 340 L4 – pop. 2 026 – alt. 262 m – ✉ 83570 — 41 C3

Paris 834 – Marseille 84 – Toulon 69 – Hyères 73 – Draguignan 37

Syndicat d'initiative, 2, rue Bonaventure ✆ 04 94 04 61 87

XX **L'Ensouleillado** — AC P VISA MC AE
1 km north on D 13 – ✆ 04 94 04 61 61 – francoise.perie@wanadoo.fr – Fax 04 94 78 01 89 – Closed 17 November-3 December, 12-28 January Monday and Tuesday
Rest – *(dinner only except Saturday and Sunday)* Menu € 45 – Carte € 46/75
♦ The terrace of this attractive country house on a hill boasts an impressive view of the village. Sober, contemporary interior and market-inspired cuisine.

COTINIÈRE – 17 Charente-Maritime – 324 C4 – see île d'Oléron

LA COUARDE-SUR-MER – 17 Charente-Maritime – 324 B2 – see Île de Ré

COUCHES – 71 Saône-et-Loire – 320 H8 – pop. 1 409 – alt. 320 m – ✉ 71490
Burgundy-Jura 8 **C3**

Paris 328 – Autun 26 – Beaune 31 – Le Creusot 16 – Chalon-sur-Saône 26

Syndicat d'initiative, 3, Grande Rue ☎ 03 85 49 69 47, Fax 03 85 49 69 47

Les 3 Maures rm, VISA MC AE

4 pl. de la République – ☎ 03 85 49 63 93 – tolfotel@wanadoo.fr – Fax 03 85 49 50 29 – Closed 1st-18 March, 22-29 December and Monday off season

35 rm – €54/58 €54/58, €7 – ½ P €54 – **Rest** – *(closed 1st-18 March, 22-29 December, 15-28 February, Tuesday lunch and Monday off season)* Menu €16/40 – Carte €25/37

◆ Choose a room in the new wing of this former post house. There is a bar for local clients and a large vaulted cellar for the sale of Burgundy wines. The rustic dining room with an attractive French style ceiling extends onto a veranda.

COUDEKERQUE-BRANCHE – 59 Nord – 302 C1 – see Dunkerque

COUDRAY – 53 Mayenne – 310 F8 – see Château-Gontier

LE COUDRAY-MONTCEAUX – 91 Essonne – 312 D4 – 106 44 – see Paris, Area (Corbeil-Essonnes)

COUERON – 44 Loire-Atlantique – 316 F4 – see Nantes

COUILLY-PONT-AUX-DAMES – 77 Seine-et-Marne – 312 G2 – pop. 1 897 – alt. 50 m – ✉ 77860 Northern France and the Paris Region 19 **C2**

Paris 45 – Coulommiers 20 – Lagny-sur-Marne 12 – Meaux 9 – Melun 45

Auberge de la Brie (Alain Pavard) AC P VISA MC AE

14 av. Boulingre, (D 436) – ☎ 01 64 63 51 80 – Fax 01 60 04 69 82 – Closed 27 April-5 May, 2-26 August, 21 December-6 January, Sunday and Monday

Rest – *(number of covers limited, pre-book)* Menu (€33), €50/68 – Carte €62/85

Spec. Homard et tomates confites en millefeuille (beg. May to mid October). Saint-Jacques rôties, émulsion de citron et huile d'olive (mid October to end April). Profiteroles "minute", crème glacée et chantilly vanille, sauce tiède chocolat.

◆ Among the attractions of this smart local establishment: refined contemporary ambiance, delicious food with personal touches and a friendly welcome.

COUIZA – 11 Aude – 344 E5 – pop. 1 194 – alt. 228 m – ✉ 11190
Languedoc-Roussillon-Tarn Gorges 22 **B3**

Paris 785 – Carcassonne 41 – Foix 75 – Perpignan 88 – Toulouse 110

Château des Ducs de Joyeuse rest, VISA MC AE

allée du Château – ☎ 04 68 74 23 50 – reception@chateau-des-ducs.com – Fax 04 68 74 23 36 – Open 1st March-15 November

35 rm – €90/105 €90/205, €13 – **Rest** – *(closed Sunday and Monday except July-August and lunch September-April)* Menu (€26 bi), €29 (lunch)/55 – Carte €49/67

◆ The towers of this splendid 16C fortified château is home to medieval-inspired rooms (stonework, beams, canopied beds); the others are more rustic in style. Elegant vaulted dining room; the menu varies with the seasons and availability of local produce.

COULANDON – 03 Allier – 326 G3 – see Moulins

COULANGES-LA-VINEUSE – 89 Yonne – 319 E5 – pop. 916 – alt. 193 m – ✉ 89580 7 **B1**

Paris 180 – Auxerre 15 – Avallon 42 – Clamecy 33 – Cosne-sur-Loire 67

in Val-de-Mercy 4 km South by D 165 and D 38 – pop. 369 – alt. 115 m – ✉ 89580

XX **Auberge du Château** with rm — rest, VISA MC
3 r. du pont – ☎ 03 86 41 60 00 – delfontaine.j@wanadoo.fr – Fax 03 86 41 73 28 – Closed 15 January-5 March, Monday and Tuesday 16 September-14 June
6 rm – †€ 60/66 ††€ 69/91, ☕ € 10 – ½ P € 77/80 – **Rest** – *(number of covers limited, pre-book)* Menu € 25 (lunch), € 36/42 – Carte € 43/67
♦ This old farmhouse has become a stylish country inn. The restaurant is made up of two comfortable dining areas with parquet floors and walls decorated with paintings. Quiet rooms.

COULLONS – 45 Loiret – 318 L6 – pop. 2 274 – alt. 166 m – ✉ 45720 12 C2

Paris 165 – Aubigny-sur-Nère 18 – Gien 16 – Orléans 60 – Sully-sur-Loire 22

XX **La Canardière** VISA MC
1 r. de la Mairie – ☎ 02 38 29 23 47 – la.canardiere@wanadoo.fr – Fax 02 38 29 27 33 – Closed 11 August-2 September, 22 December-6 January, Sunday dinner, Wednesday dinner, Monday and Tuesday
Rest – Menu (€ 20), € 28/69 – Carte € 47/76
Rest *Brasserie* – Menu € 11 bi (weekday lunch)/18 – Carte € 15/42
♦ The restaurant decor is elegant and rustic with exposed beams, a fine copper fireplace, hunting trophies and stuffed animals. Traditional cuisine, with game in season. The Brasserie has a welcoming atmosphere, simple amenities and a menu chalked up daily on the board.

COULOMBIERS – 86 Vienne – 322 H6 – pop. 1 017 – alt. 141 m – ✉ 86600 39 C2

Paris 352 – Couhé 25 – Lusignan 8 – Parthenay 44 – Poitiers 19 – Vivonne 10

Auberge le Centre Poitou rm, VISA MC
– ☎ 05 49 60 90 15 – hotelcentre-poitou@wanadoo.fr – Fax 05 49 60 53 70 – Closed 20 October-3 November, 23 February-2 March, Sunday dinner and Monday 15 September-June
14 rm – †€ 48/65 ††€ 55/130, ☕ € 15 – ½ P € 56/90 – **Rest** – Menu € 26/75 – Carte € 63/80
♦ Hotel on the Compostelle road, this regional house has pleasantly furnished rooms in the style of Louis-Philippe. Piano-lounge, luxuriant garden. Welcoming inn-style restaurant, terrace arbour and well-planned up-to-date menu.

COULOMMIERS – 77 Seine-et-Marne – 312 H3 – pop. 13 852 – alt. 85 m – ✉ 77120 Northern France and the Paris Region 19 D2

Paris 62 – Châlons-en-Champagne 111 – Meaux 26 – Melun 46 – Provins 39

Office de tourisme, 7, rue du Général-de-Gaulle ☎ 01 64 03 88 09, Fax 01 64 03 88 09

XX **Les Échevins** VISA MC AE
quai de l'Hôtel-de-Ville – ☎ 01 64 20 75 85 – les.echevins@wanadoo.fr – Fax 01 64 20 03 32 – Closed August, January, Sunday and Monday
Rest – Menu (€ 13), 17 (weekdays) – Carte € 23/54
♦ The facade reminds one of a chalet. Inside, the modern restaurant is decorated with lithographs of fruits, vegetables and wines. Summer terrace. Cuisine in keeping with current taste.

in Pommeuse West: 6.5 km – pop. 2 476 – alt. 67 m – ✉ 77515

Le Moulin de Pommeuse VISA MC
32 av. Gén. Herne – ☎ 01 64 75 29 45 – info@le-moulin-de-pommeuse.com – Fax 01 64 75 29 45
6 rm ☕ – †€ 53 ††€ 64 – **Table d'hôte** – Menu € 25 bi/35 bi
♦ This 14C watermill has stylish rooms with evocative names – such as Semailles (sowing), Moisson (harvesting) and Batteuse (thresher). The former machine room is now a lounge and there is a small island in the grounds. The restaurant offers a table d'hôte menu on certain days only.

COULON – 79 Deux-Sèvres – 322 C7 – pop. 2 074 – alt. 6 m – ✉ 79510 Atlantic Coast

Paris 418 – Fontenay-le-Comte 25 – Niort 11 – La Rochelle 63 – St-Jean-d'Angély 58 — 38 **B2**

Office de tourisme, 31, rue Gabriel Auchier ✆ 05 49 35 99 29, Fax 05 49 35 84 31

Marais poitevin★★.

Au Marais without rest

quai L. Tardy – ✆ 05 49 35 90 43 – information@hotel-aumarais.com – Fax 05 49 35 81 98 – Closed 15 December-1st February

18 rm – €65 €75, ☕ €12

◆ Two former ferrymen's homes opposite the embarkation point of the moored Marais. Pleasant, colourful rustic-style rooms; some have a view of the Sèvre. Friendly welcome.

Le Central with rm

4 r. d'Autrement – ✆ 05 49 35 90 20 – le-central-coulon@wanadoo.fr – Fax 05 49 35 81 07 – Closed 9-28 February and Sunday dinner from October to March

13 rm – €49/53 €56/70, ☕ €9 – ½ P €55/62

Rest – *(closed 29 September-13 October, 9-28 February, Sunday dinner and Monday)* Menu €19 (weekdays)/40 – Carte €34/48

◆ This inn on a pretty square has a stylish dining room with exposed beams, country-type furniture, warm colours and faience ornamentation. Patio terrace. Carefully prepared traditional cuisine.

COUPELLE-VIEILLE – 62 Pas-de-Calais – 301 F4 – pop. 494 – alt. 147 m – ✉ 62310

Paris 232 – Abbeville 58 – Arras 64 – Boulogne-sur-Mer 48 – Calais 68 – Lille 90 — 30 **A2**

Le Fournil

r. St- Omer – ✆ 03 21 04 47 13 – glefournil@wanadoo.fr – Fax 03 21 47 16 06 – Closed Tuesday dinner, Sunday dinner, dinners holidays and Monday

Rest – Menu (€14,50), €17 (weekdays)/40 – Carte €40/55

◆ A restaurant near the Moulin de la Tour amusement park. Warm dining room with carefully-chosen decor, serving cuisine with a contemporary touch. Good wine selection.

COURBEVOIE – 92 Hauts-de-Seine – 311 J2 – 101 15 – see Paris, Area

COURCELLES-DE-TOURAINE – 37 Indre-et-Loire – 317 K4 – pop. 325 – alt. 85 m – ✉ 37330 — 11 **A2**

Paris 267 – Angers 74 – Chinon 46 – Saumur 46 – Tours 35

du Château des Sept-ToursEast: 7 km, ✆ 02 47 24 69 75.

at the Golf 7 km East dir. Ambillou then Château La Vallière – ✉ 37330 Courcelles-de-Touraine

Château des Sept Tours

– ✆ 02 47 24 69 75 – info@7tours.com – Fax 02 47 24 23 74 – Closed February

44 rm – €150/265 €150/265, ☕ €18 – 2 suites

Rest *Notaboo* – *(closed Sunday dinner and Monday from 1er November to 31 January and lunch from Monday to Thursday)* Menu €85/130 – Carte €60/76

Rest *Club House* – ✆ 02 47 24 59 67 *(closed Tuesday 1st December-28 February) (lunch only)* Menu €19/40 – Carte €24/28

◆ A 15C chateau surrounded by an 18-hole golf course. Large, simply decorated bedrooms; the Orangerie has a functional decor. The chef concocts inventive cuisine served in a tasteful dining room with a veranda terrace looking out over gardens. Modern menu in the Club House, set in an old chapel.

COURCELLES-SUR-VESLE – 02 Aisne – 306 D6 – pop. 295 – alt. 75 m – ✉ 02220 — 37 **C2**

Paris 122 – Fère-en-Tardenois 20 – Laon 35 – Reims 39 – Soissons 21

Château de Courcelles — ← rm, rest,
rest, VISA
– ✆ 03 23 74 13 53
– reservation@chateau-de-courcelles.fr – Fax 03 23 74 06 41
15 rm – †€ 180/355 ††€ 180/450, ☕ € 21 – 3 suites – ½ P € 175/265
Rest – Menu € 45/195 – Carte € 81/137
Spec. Langoustines à l'émietté de tourteau. Daurade grise cuite en croûte de sel aux algues (October to July). Côte de bœuf charolais grillée à la fondue de poireaux et légumes croustillants (April to October). **Wines** Champagne.
◆ A 17C chateau in a 20-hectare park with a small lake. Crébillon, Rousseau and Cocteau all stayed here, thus confirming the status of this prestigious hotel. Individually decorated rooms. Elegant dining room and fine veranda, furnished in the Napoleon III style. Cuisine in keeping with current taste.

COURCHEVEL – 73 Savoie – 333 M5 – Winter sports : 1 100/2 750 m 11 54 – ✉ 73120 French Alps 45 D2

Paris 660 – Albertville 52 – Chambéry 99 – Moûtiers 25
Altiport ✆ 04 79 08 31 23, South : 4 km
Office de tourisme, de Courchevel 1850 ✆ 04 79 08 00 29, Fax 04 79 08 15 63

Plan on next page

in Courchevel 1850 – alt. 1 850 m – ✉ 73120

✻★ - Belvédère la Saulire (viewpoint)★★★ (cable car).

Les Airelles — ← rm, rest,
VISA
au Jardin Alpin – ✆ 04 79 00 38 38
– info@airelles.fr – Fax 04 79 00 38 39 – Open 14 December-12 April Z **h**
52 rm – †€ 725/2200 ††€ 800/2200, ☕ € 50 – 7 suites
Rest *Pierre Gagnaire pour les Airelles* – *(dinner only)* Carte € 340/590
Rest *Le Coin Savoyard* – *(dinner only)* Menu € 100/130 – Carte € 110/165
◆ This large Tyrolean style chalet is full of mountain exoticism, with its oriel window, finely-worked balconies, coloured facades, faience stove... and staff in Austrian costume! Good news for gourmet skiers - Pierre Gagnaire has relocated to Savoie! Like the name, the decor and cuisine here are very much Savoyard in feel.

Cheval Blanc — ← rest,
VISA
au Jardin Alpin – ✆ 04 79 00 50 50
– info@chevalblanc.com – Fax 04 79 00 50 51
– Open 13 December-12 April Z **m**
33 rm (½ board only) - 1 suite – ½ P € 950/2250
Rest *Le 1947* – Carte € 155/210
◆ Givenchy spa, magnificent waterfall pool, boutiques, hair salon, luxurious designer rooms and a 650m2 apartment: an haute couture style mountain chalet. Tasty, updated cuisine, fine choice of Bordeaux wines and contemporary decor at 1947.

Annapurna — ← pistes and la Saulire, rest,
VISA
rte Altiport – ✆ 04 79 08 04 60
– info@annapurna-courchevel.com – Fax 04 79 08 15 31
– Open mid-December to mid-April
55 rm ☕ – †€ 495/1124 ††€ 625/1140 – 8 suites
Rest – Menu € 64 (lunch)/72 (dinner) – Carte € 52/258
◆ Of all the hotels in Courchevel this stands nearest to the peaks. It has a sober design using light-coloured wood, and is set against a backdrop of rock. Most of the rooms face south. Large dining room and terrace looking towards the ski slopes. Traditional cooking.

Le Kilimandjaro — ← pistes and mountains,
VISA
rte Altiport – ✆ 04 79 01 46 46
– welcome@hotelkilimandjaro.com – Fax 04 79 01 46 40
– Open mid December to mid April
32 rm – †€ 690/3190 ††€ 690/3190, ☕ € 45 – 3 suites
Rest *Le Cœur d'Or* – Carte € 90/245
◆ Luxurious chalets forming a small village, built with stone, aged wood and stone roof tiles. Superb, high tech Savoyard rooms, all with a loggia. Savour modern cuisine in a snug, welcoming setting.

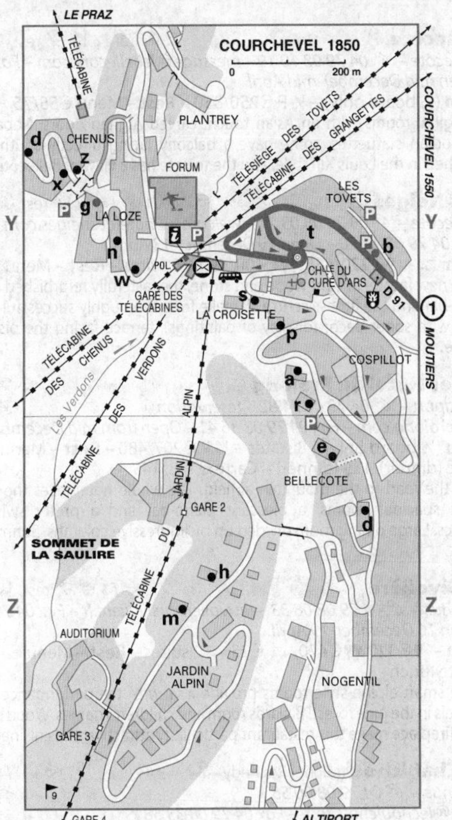

Amanresorts Le Mélézin

r. Bellecôte – ✆ 04 79 08 01 33 – lemelezin@amanresorts.com – Fax 04 79 08 08 96 – Open 19 December-13 April Y **r**

23 rm – € 680 € 1050, ☕ € 28 – 8 suites – **Rest** – Carte € 67/91

◆ Behind the facade with its "troubadour" influence is a delightful contemporary interior with attractive bronze works of art. Elegant rooms, most of which face directly south. Refined restaurant and pleasant terrace serving cuisine with a contemporary touch.

Le Carlina

rest, VISA AE

– ✆ 04 79 08 00 30 – message@hotelcarlina.com – Fax 04 79 08 04 03 – Open mid December-mid April Y **a**

58 rm (½ board only) – 5 suites – ½ P € 295/400 – **Rest** – Menu € 55/75

◆ An impressive red-brown chalet with large, quiet rooms with a view over the slopes (south) or over the valley (north). Fully-equipped balneotherapy centre. Attractive view over the snow-covered slopes from the dining room and the sunlit terrace.

Le Lana

rest, VISA AE

– ✆ 04 79 08 01 10 – info@lelana.com – Fax 04 79 08 36 70 – Open 15 December-15 April Y **p**

59 rm (½ board only) – 20 suites – ½ P € 320/1130

Rest *La Table du Lana* – Menu € 40 (lunch)/90 – Carte € 59/145

◆ Fine individualised rooms, bronzes, and superb Roman style pool: the interior of this dark wooden chalet is both stylish and distinctive. Beauty centre. An attractive dining room with decor inspired by the mountains. Sunny terrace. Traditional cuisine.

Bellecôte rest, VISA AE

r. Bellecôte – 04 79 08 10 19 – message@lebellecote.com – Fax 04 79 08 17 16 – Open mid December-mid April Z **d**

50 rm (½ board only) – ½ P € 250/350 – **Rest** – Menu € 55/75

◆ Original rooms with an Asian touch: carved Afghan doors, Nepalese furniture and Cambodian statuettes; some have a balcony facing directly south. The restaurant is furnished in the Louis XIII style, and the terrace has a view of Bellecôte peak.

Des Neiges rest, P VISA AE

r. Bellecôte – 04 79 08 03 77 – welcome@hoteldesneiges.com – Fax 04 79 08 18 70 – Open 15 December-13 April Z **e**

42 rm – †€ 220/455 ††€ 400/790 – 6 suites – **Rest** – Menu € 50, € 72/150

◆ The new facade in light wood and stone, the tastefully refurbished rooms, the discreet piano-bar and the fitness centre all make for a thoroughly successful renovation. Dining room with sober decor (display of paintings), terrace facing the pistes and traditional cuisine.

Alpes Hôtel du Pralong P VISA AE

rte Altiport – 04 79 08 24 82 – reservation@hotelpralong.com – Fax 04 79 08 36 41 – Open from mid December-mid April

57 rm (½ board only) – 8 suites – ½ P € 207/480 – **Rest** – Menu € 58 (lunch), € 75 € (dinner)/125 (dinner) – Carte € 113/145

◆ On the road to the mountain airfield. The whole hotel faces the mountain and has bright spacious rooms, a pleasant piano-bar and a pretty swimming pool with mosaics. Large dining room divided up by impressive columns. Sunny terrace facing the slopes.

La Sivolière rest, VISA AE

r. Chenus – 04 79 08 08 33 – lasivoliere@sivoliere.fr – Fax 04 79 08 15 73 – Open 16 December-19 April Y **d**

27 rm – †€ 320 ††€ 470, € 25 – 12 suites – **Rest** – Menu € 100 (dinner) – Carte lunch

◆ The smart alpine-style rooms provide a view of the performance offered up by the squirrels in the pine forest! Billiards room and children's games. Wood panelling and a fine open fireplace make this restaurant particularly attractive; the cuisine is traditional.

Le Chabichou (Michel Rochedy) rm, VISA AE

r. Chenus – 04 79 08 00 55 – info@lechabichou.com – Fax 04 79 08 33 58 – Open beg. July to beg. September and beg. December to end April Y **z**

22 rm (½ board only) – 18 suites – ½ P € 240/625

Rest – Menu (€ 60), € 100/220 – Carte € 130/220

Spec. Croque-monsieur de homard bleu, fondant de céleri. Blanquette de grenouilles aux cèpes en corolle de pommes de terre. A la rencontre du chocolat. **Wines** Chignin-Bergeron, Mondeuse d'Arbin.

◆ Attractive twin chalets all in white. The rooms have been renovated and warmly furnished in alpine style. A pleasant dining room, small cosy lounges, and two stars for the inventively flavoursome cuisine!

Les Grandes Alpes rest, VISA AE

r. de l'Église – 04 79 00 00 00 – welcome@lesgrandesalpes.com – Fax 04 79 08 12 52 – Open from beg. December to end April Y **s**

43 rm – †€ 350/680 ††€ 380/710, € 25 – 5 suites – ½ P € 190/650

Rest – Menu € 38 (lunch), € 55/68 – Carte € 39/84

◆ Chalet with an attractive stone facade situated above a luxurious shopping mall. Smart spacious rooms, the nicer ones are on the south side (quiet and view of the slopes). At midday, fast food menus. In the evening, traditional menu and Savoyard dishes.

De la Loze without rest VISA AE

r. Park City – 04 79 08 28 25 – info@la-loze.com – Fax 04 79 08 39 29 – Open 14 December-12 April Y **w**

28 rm – †€ 240/500 ††€ 240/500, € 20 – 1 suite

◆ An elegant hotel next to the cable-cars. Wall paintings in the comfortable rooms, renovated bathrooms and a lounge decorated in Austrian style for afternoon tea.

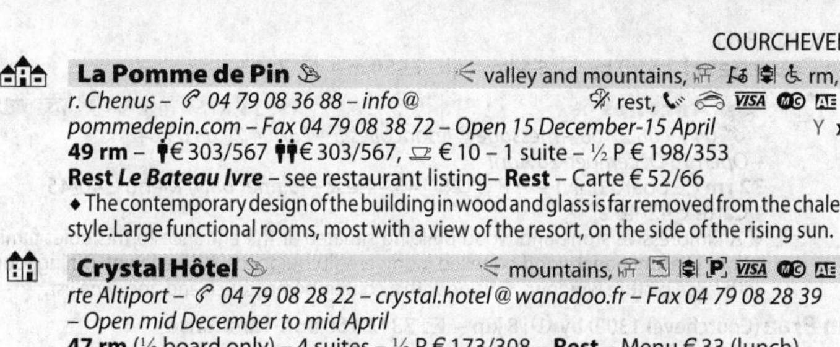

La Pomme de Pin < valley and mountains, rm, rest, VISA MC AE

r. Chenus – ✆ 04 79 08 36 88 – info@pommedepin.com – Fax 04 79 08 38 72 – Open 15 December-15 April Y **x**

49 rm – †€ 303/567 ††€ 303/567, ☐ € 10 – 1 suite – ½ P € 198/353

Rest *Le Bateau Ivre* – see restaurant listing– **Rest** – Carte € 52/66

◆ The contemporary design of the building in wood and glass is far removed from the chalet style.Large functional rooms, most with a view of the resort, on the side of the rising sun.

Crystal Hôtel < mountains, P VISA MC AE

rte Altiport – ✆ 04 79 08 28 22 – crystal.hotel@wanadoo.fr – Fax 04 79 08 28 39 – Open mid December to mid April

47 rm (½ board only) – 4 suites – ½ P € 173/308 – **Rest** – Menu € 33 (lunch), € 45/58 (dinner) – Carte € 67/80

◆ A hotel at the foot of the ski slopes away from the centre. Practical, renovated rooms, bathed in light (view of the mountain or the valley). Nice fitness centre. Restrained, up-to-date decor in a spacious wainscoted dining room. Traditional recipes.

Courcheneige < mountains, rest, VISA MC AE

r. de Nogentil – ✆ 04 79 08 02 59 – info@courcheneige.com – Fax 04 79 08 11 79 – Open 20 December-15 April – **85 rm** – †€ 172/265 ††€ 264/526, ☐ € 13 – ½ P € 132/189 – **Rest** – Menu € 25 (lunch)/35 – Carte € 32/55

◆ The chalet is located in the middle of the ski runs and is a good example of the 'get around on skis' concept. The rooms are small but functional. Rustic style dining room warmed by a great open fireplace. Fine terrace. Traditional menus.

Le Bateau Ivre (Jean-Pierre Jacob) – Hôtel La Pomme de Pin -

r. Chenus – < station and Massif de la Vanoise, VISA MC AE

✆ 04 79 00 11 71 – pommedepin.courchevel@wanadoo.fr – Fax 04 79 08 38 72 – Open mid December-mid April and closed lunch Monday-Friday Y **x**

Rest – Menu € 60 (lunch), € 95/190 – Carte € 108/215

Spec. Saint-Jacques rôties, émulsion crémeuse d'oignons. Cuisses de grenouilles rôties, mousseline à l'ail doux. Fricassée de ris de veau aux écrevisses et aux asperges de Pertuis (mid February to mid April). **Wines** Roussette de Savoie, Chignin-Bergeron.

◆ Creative cuisine, a good selection of wines, a warm modern environment and splendid views of the Vanoise and the ski resort.

La Saulire VISA MC AE

pl. Rocher – ✆ 04 79 08 07 52 – info@lasaulire.com – Fax 04 79 08 02 63 – Open 1st December-30 April Y **t**

Rest – Menu (€ 29), € 42 (lunch) – Carte € 67/98 dinner

◆ The chalet's alpine interior is stylish with Savoyard all-wood decor, old posters and mountain tools. Traditional menu and daily special chalked up on the board.

Le Genépi VISA MC AE

r. Park City – ✆ 04 79 08 08 63 – le-genepi@wanadoo.fr – Fax 04 79 06 51 43 – Open September to April and closed Saturday and Sunday from September to November

Rest – Menu € 25 (lunch), € 30/65 – Carte € 52/83 Y **g**

◆ The pleasant lounge-bar with an open fireplace gives onto two small warm, rustic-style dining rooms. Regional cuisine based on local produce.

La Fromagerie VISA MC

La Porte de Courchevel – ✆ 04 79 08 27 47 – Fax 04 79 08 20 91 – Open beg. December-end April Y **b**

Rest – *(dinner only)* Menu € 26/38 – Carte € 33/70

◆ Enjoy regional cheese specialities in a mountain style dining room decorated with objects from the Savoy region chosen at the flea market. Dinner by candlelight.

in Courchevel 1650 by ①: 4 km – ✉ 73120

Le Seizena VISA MC

– ✆ 04 79 08 26 36 – welcome@hotelseizena.com – Fax 04 79 08 38 83 – Open mid December-mid April – **20 rm** – †€ 180/350 ††€ 180/350, ☐ € 15 – **Rest** – *(dinner only)* Menu € 38/60 – Carte € 35/50

◆ This centrally located establishment has an attractive facade of wood and stone. The rooms are spacious, modern and fitted out with state of the art furnishings. A lounge bar restaurant on an aviation theme. Fine wine list and internationally inspired cuisine.

in Courchevel 1550 by ①: 5.5 km – alt. 1 550 m – ✉ 73120

Les Ancolies rest, P VISA MC
– ✆ 04 79 08 27 66 – message@lesancolies.fr – Fax 04 79 08 05 64
– *Open 15 December-20 April*
32 rm (½ board only) – ½ P € 126/143 – **Rest** – *(dinner only)* Menu € 40/45
– Carte € 42/48
◆ An impressive stone and wood building situated at the entrance to this quiet family resort. The functional wood-panelled rooms are all equipped with balconies. Dining room with large picture windows. Cuisine with a contemporary touch and fine wine list.

in Praz (Courchevel 1300) by ①: 8 km – ✉ 73120 St-Bon-Tarentaise

Les Peupliers P VISA MC AE
– ✆ 04 79 08 41 47 – infos@lespeupliers.com – Fax 04 79 08 45 05
– *Closed May and June*
33 rm – †€ 85/145 ††€ 95/250, ☕ € 11 – 2 suites – ½ P € 105/160
Rest ***La Table de mon Grand-Père*** – Menu € 25 (weekday lunch)/37
– Carte € 33/58
◆ Set next to a small lake and the Olympic ski jump, this welcoming hotel offers mountain-inspired guestrooms, those facing south with balconies. La Table de mon Grand-Père offers traditional dishes in a pleasant Savoyard setting.

IN LA TANIA – ✉ 73120 46 **F2**

Paris 661 – Lyon 195 – Chambéry 95 – Albertville 46 – Saint-Jean-de-Maurienne 104

Office de tourisme, Maison de la Tania ✆ 04 79 08 40 40, Fax 04 79 08 45 71

Le Farçon (Julien Machet) VISA MC
– ✆ *04 79 08 80 34 – Fax 04 79 08 38 51 – Open mid June-mid September, beg. December-mid April and closed Sunday dinner and Monday in summer*
Rest – Menu € 30 (lunch), € 50/120 – Carte € 58/122
Spec. Mille et trois façons de déguster les œufs et truffes. Foie de canard chaud en raviole ouverte de chocolat. Râble de lapin farci au beaufort, polenta. **Wines** Vin de Savoie, Mondeuse.
◆ Although the outdoor sign and stylish interior decor of this restaurant pay tribute to Savoie, the delicious cuisine ventures into recipes from further abroad, and is highly inventive.

COUR-CHEVERNY – 41 Loir-et-Cher – **318** F6 – pop. 2 555 – alt. 86 m – ✉ 41700

Paris 194 – Blois 14 – Châteauroux 88 – Orléans 73
– Romorantin-Lanthenay 28 11 **AB1**

Office de tourisme, 12, rue du Chêne des Dames ✆ 02 54 79 95 63, Fax 02 54 79 23 90

Château de Cheverny★★★ South: 1 km - Porte★ from the château de Troussay chapel Southwest: 3,5 km - Château de Beauregard★, **Châteaux of the Loire**

St-Hubert P VISA MC AE
– ✆ *02 54 79 96 60 – hotel-sthubert@wanadoo.fr – Fax 02 54 79 21 17*
21 rm – †€ 40 ††€ 49, ☕ € 8,50 – ½ P € 52 – **Rest** – *(closed Sunday dinner from November to March)* Menu € 16 (weekday lunch), € 22/38 – Carte € 29/45
◆ A small hotel owned by the head of the local hunting association in a town with a great hunting tradition. Pleasant provincial ambiance, hearthside lounge and modern guestrooms. Bright, colourful dining room. Traditional menu and game in season.

in Cheverny 1 km South – pop. 986 – alt. 110 m – ✉ 41700

Office de tourisme, 12, rue du Chêne des Dames ✆ 02 54 79 95 63, Fax 02 54 79 23 90

Château du Breuil P VISA MC AE
West : 3 km on the D 52 and private road – ✆ *02 54 44 20 20 – info@chateau-du-breuil.fr – Fax 02 54 44 30 40 – Closed January*
16 rm – †€ 106/140 ††€ 106/185, ☕ € 14 – 2 suites – **Rest** – *(dinner only) (resident only)* Menu € 40
◆ Visit Cheverny and stay at the 18C Château du Breuil, shielded from the outside world by a 30-hectare park planted with trees. Attractive sitting rooms and spacious bedrooms with fine furniture.

COURCOURONNES – 91 Essonne – **312** D4 – **101** 36 – **see Paris, Area (Évry)**

COURRUERO – 83 Var – **340** O6 – **see Plan-de-la-Tour**

COURS – 69 Rhône – **327** E3 – **pop. 4 241 – alt. 543 m** – ✉ **69470** 44 **A1**

Paris 416 – Chauffailles 17 – Lyon 75 – Mâcon 70 – Roanne 28 – Villefranche-sur-Saône 50

at col du Pavillon 4 km East by D 64 – alt. 755 m – ✉ 69470 Cours-la-Ville

Le Pavillon rm, **P** VISA

– *04 74 89 83 55 – hotel-pavillon@wanadoo.fr – Fax 04 74 64 70 26 – Closed 15-28 February, Sunday dinner and Saturday from September to April*

21 rm – †€ 46 ††€ 57, ☕ € 8,50 – ½ P € 63 – **Rest** – Menu € 19 (weekday lunch), € 24/35 – Carte € 33/38

♦ At the top of the pass on the edge of the forest, the peaceful environment, Scandinavian inspired architecture and comfortable rooms are most appreciated. Classic fare in a contemporary dining room with a pleasant veranda.

COUR-ST-MAURICE – 25 Doubs – **321** K3 – **pop. 157 – alt. 500 m** – ✉ **25380**

Paris 481 – Baume-les-Dames 50 – Besançon 68 – Montbéliard 44 – Maiche 12 – Morteau 37 17 **C2**

Le Moulin rest, **P** VISA

à Moulin du Milieu, East: 3 km on D 39 – 03 81 44 35 18 – hotel.lemoulin@yahoo.fr – Open March-September

6 rm – †€ 45 ††€ 76, ☕ € 6,50 – ½ P € 58/63 – **Rest** – *(closed Wednesday off season) (number of covers limited, pre-book)* Menu € 20/30 – Carte € 29/53

♦ This unusual 1930s villa was built for a miller from the valley. Retro rooms and modern lounge. Pleasant shady garden and fishing stretch reserved for guests. Traditional menu served in a smart dining room facing the river.

COURSAN – 11 Aude – **344** J3 – **see Narbonne**

COURSEULLES-SUR-MER – 14 Calvados – **303** J4 – **pop. 3 886** – ✉ **14470** Normandy 32 **B2**

Paris 252 – Arromanches-les-Bains 14 – Bayeux 24 – Cabourg 41 – Caen 20

Office de tourisme, 5, rue du 11 novembre 02 31 37 46 80, Fax 02 31 37 29 25

Steeple ★ of Bernières-sur-Mer church East: 2.5 km - Tower ★ of Ver-sur-Mer church West: 5 km by D 514.

Château ★★ de Fontaine-Henry South: 6.5 km.

La Pêcherie with rm **P** VISA

pl. 6-Juin – 02 31 37 45 84 – pecherie@wanadoo.fr – Fax 02 31 37 90 40

6 rm – †€ 60/90 ††€ 74/90, ☕ € 9 – ½ P € 74/84 – **Rest** – Menu € 21/38 – Carte € 34/71

♦ Storm lamps, oars and porthole windows give the dining room a seafaring touch. Seafood and fish served here. Boat cabin-styled rooms.

COURTENAY – 45 Loiret – **318** P3 – **pop. 3 437 – alt. 146 m** – ✉ **45320** 12 **D2**

Paris 118 – Auxerre 56 – Nemours 44 – Orléans 101 – Sens 25

Syndicat d'initiative, 5, rue du Mail 02 38 97 00 60, Fax 02 38 97 39 12

de Clairis Savigny-sur-Clairis Domaine de Clairis, North: 7 km, 03 86 86 33 90.

Auberge La Clé des Champs with rm **P** VISA AE

rte de Joigny, 1 km – 02 38 97 42 68 – info@hotel-lacledeschamps.fr – Fax 02 38 97 38 10 – Closed 13-30 October, 12-29 January, Tuesday and Wednesday

7 rm – †€ 73/131 ††€ 73/131, ☕ € 10 – **Rest** – *(number of covers limited, pre-book)* Menu € 25/45 – Carte € 37/77

♦ 17C farmhouse and flower-filled garden. Country-style rooms and an elegant rustic dining area. Private heliport.

COURTENAY
in Ervauville 9 km Northwest by N 60, D 32 and D 34 – pop. 389 – alt. 152 m – ✉ 45320

XXX **Le Gamin**
– ☎ 02 38 87 22 02 – restaurantlegamin@wanadoo.fr – Fax 02 38 87 25 40
– Closed 23 June-4 July, 10-25 November, 26 January-3 February, Sunday dinner, Monday and Tuesday
Rest – *(number of covers limited, pre-book)* Menu € 46/56
◆ This former grocery store-cum-bar has become a stylish inn (non-smokers only). The decor is original with large mirrors, fired bricks and curios. The terrace opens onto an attractive garden. Appetising cuisine with a contemporary touch.

LA COURTINE – 23 Creuse – 325 K6 – pop. 971 – alt. 789 m – ✉ 23100

Paris 424 – Aubusson 38 – La Bourboule 53 – Guéret 80 – Ussel 21
Syndicat d'initiative, Mairie ☎ 05 55 66 76 58, Fax 05 55 66 70 69 — 25 **D2**

Au Petit Breuil — rm, VISA
rte Felletin – ☎ 05 55 66 76 67 – le.petit.breuil@wanadoo.fr – Fax 05 55 66 71 84
– Closed 22 December-7 January, Monday (except hotel), Friday dinner 15 September-15 April and Sunday dinner
11 rm – †€ 42 ††€ 51, ☕ € 7 – ½ P € 58 – **Rest** – Menu € 14 (weekdays)/39 – Carte € 22/42
◆ A family residence over a century old with simply furnished but adequately appointed bedrooms; those to the rear are generally quieter. The decor of stonework, straw-bottomed chairs, antique furniture and copperware brings a rustic feel to the restaurant. Terrace overlooking the swimming pool.

COUSSEY – 88 Vosges – 314 C2 – pop. 707 – alt. 280 m – ✉ 88630 — 26 B3

Paris 290 – Metz 116 – Toul 48 – Vandœuvre-lès-Nancy 56

La Demeure du Gardien du Temps qui passe
47 Grand Rue – ☎ 03 29 06 99 83 – Fax 03 29 06 99 83
5 rm ☕ – †€ 55 ††€ 75 – **Table d'hôte** – Menu € 20
◆ An authentic charm floats about this former post house dating back to the 18C. The spacious rooms and the lounge-library are dotted with antiques. The island-inspired cuisine is a tropical holiday for the palate.

COUSTELLET – 84 Vaucluse – 332 D10 – alt. 243 m – ✉ 84220 Cabrieres d Avignon ▮ Provence — 42 E1

Paris 705 – Avignon 31 – Apt 23 – Carpentras 26 – Cavaillon 10

X **Maison Gouin** — VISA
D 900 – ☎ 04 90 76 90 18 – lamaisongouin@wanadoo.fr
– Closed 1st-23 November, 11-25 February, Wednesday and Sunday
Rest – Menu € 13 bi (weekdays lunch)/36 – Carte € 44/60
◆ Family-run restaurant in a village in the Petit Luberon, set up in the back shop of a butcher's opened in 1928. You choose your own wine straight from the cellar!

COUTANCES – 50 Manche – 303 D5 – pop. 9 522 – alt. 91 m – ✉ 50200 ▮ Normandy — 32 A2

Paris 335 – Avranches 52 – Cherbourg 76 – St-Lô 28 – Vire 66
Office de tourisme, place Georges Leclerc ☎ 02 33 19 08 10, Fax 02 33 19 08 19
Cathedral★★★: lantern tower★★★, high sections★★ - Jardin des Plantes★.

Plan on next page

Cositel — rm, VISA
r. St-Malo – ☎ 02 33 19 15 00 – accueil@cositel.fr – Fax 02 33 19 15 02
55 rm – †€ 59/81 ††€ 59/81, ☕ € 9 – ½ P € 53/60 – **Rest *Pommeau*** – *(closed Saturday lunch and Sunday lunch)* Menu (€ 15 bi), € 21/29 – Carte € 23/44
◆ Modern building on a hillside overlooking the town. Rooms are light and have functional furnishings. Traditional cuisine and summer terrace overlooking small ponds.

Manoir de L'Ecoulanderie without rest
r. de la Broche – ☎ 02 33 45 05 05 – contact@l-b-c.com — Y **b**
4 rm ☕ – †€ 90/110 ††€ 110/130
◆ Wooded parkland, an indoor pool, Coutances and its cathedral in the distance: all add to the charm of this fine 18C manor and its outbuildings. Personalised rooms.

COUTANCES

bert-1er (Av.) . . . . Z 2
roûte (R. de la) . . . . YZ 3
aniel (R.) . . . . Y 5
uhamel (R.) . . . . Z 6
cluse-Chette (R. de l') . . . . . Y 8
ncoignard (Bd) . . . . Z 9
och (R. Mar.) . . . . Z 10
ambetta (R.) . . . . Y 12
erbert (R. G.) . . . . Z 13
eclerc (Av. Division) . . . . . . Y 15
egentil-de-la-Galaisière (Bd) . Z 16
ycée (R. du) . . . . Z 17
larest (R. Thomas-du) . . . . . Y 18
lilon (R.) . . . . Y 19
lontbray (R. G.-de) . . . . Z 20
ormandie (R. de) . . . . Y 21
alais-de-Justice (R. du) . . . . Y 23
aynel (Bd J.) . . . . Y 24
uesnel-Morinière (R.) . . . . . . Z 26
épublique (Av. de la) . . . . . . Y 27
-Dominique (R.) . . . . Y 29
-Nicolas (R.) . . . . Y 30
ancrède (R.) . . . . Y 32
ourville (R.) . . . . Y 33

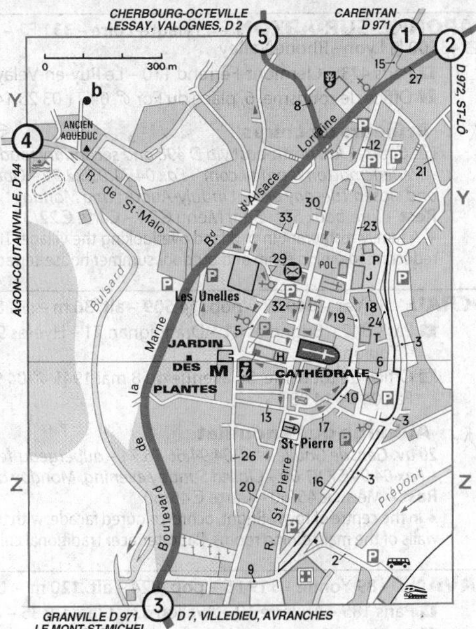

in Gratot 4 km by ④ and D 244 – **pop. 612 – alt. 83 m –** ✉ **50200**

Le Tourne-Bride

85 r. d'Argouges – ✆ 02 33 45 11 00 – Fax 02 33 45 11 00 – Closed February holidays, Sunday dinner and Monday

Rest – Menu (€ 15), € 20/52 – Carte € 36/56

◆ Traditional fare holds sway in this smart 19C post house near Château de Gratot and the Fairy-tale Tower. Warm and rustic ambiance.

COUTRAS – 33 Gironde – 335 K4 – pop. 7 003 – alt. 15 m – ✉ 33230 4 C1

Paris 527 – Bergerac 67 – Blaye 50 – Bordeaux 51 – Jonzac 58 – Libourne 18 – Périgueux 87

Office de tourisme, 17, rue Sully ✆ 05 57 69 36 53, Fax 05 57 69 36 43

Henri IV without rest

pl. du 8 Mai 1945, (opposite the station) – ✆ 05 57 49 34 34 – contact@hotelcoutras.com – Fax 05 57 49 20 72

16 rm – €50/53 €56/61, € 11

◆ Henri of Navarre waged here a battle that gave Coutras a place in history. This 19C manor has comfortable, attractively renovated rooms, some directly under the eaves.

COUX-ET-BIGAROQUE – 24 Dordogne – 329 G7 – pop. 818 – alt. 85 m – ✉ 24220 Dordogne-Berry-Limousin 4 C3

Paris 557 – Bergerac 46 – Bordeaux 180 – Périgueux 55

Manoir de la Brunie

– ✆ 05 53 31 95 62 – manoirdelabrunie@wanadoo.fr – Fax 05 53 31 95 62 – Closed December-January

5 rm – €62/97 €62/97, € 12 – **Table d'hôte** – Menu € 27 bi

◆ The scent of magnolias perfumes the garden of this fine mansion whose interior has been carefully restored. The rooms, that sport antique furniture, are each named after a local château. Périgord recipes take pride of place on the table d'hôte.

CRAPONNE-SUR-ARZON – 43 Haute-Loire – 331 F2 – pop. 2 653 – alt. 915 m – ✉ 43500 Lyon - Rhone Valley 6 C2

Paris 473 – Clermont-Ferrand 110 – Le Puy-en-Velay 39 – St-Etienne 60

Office de tourisme, 6, place du For ✆ 04 71 03 23 14, Fax 04 71 01 24 19

Brûleurs de Loups

Les Cours, 1 km north-east via D 498 and secondary road – ✆ 04 71 03 22 99 – fredericmatton@gmail.com – Fax 04 71 03 22 99 – Open 1st May-5 September and closed Tuesday except in July-August and Monday

Rest – *(pre-book Sat - Sun)* Menu € 24 – Carte € 22/37

◆ A family restaurant in parkland overlooking the village. Traditional cuisine served in a redecorated dining room and outdoor summer house-terrace.

LA CRAU – 83 Var – 340 L7 – pop. 14 509 – alt. 36 m – ✉ 83260 41 C3

Paris 847 – Brignoles 41 – Draguignan 71 – Hyères 9 – Marseille 77 – Toulon 15

Office de tourisme, 37 avenue du 8 mai 1945 ✆ 04 94 66 14 48, Fax 04 94 14 03 15

Auberge du Fenouillet

20 av. Gén. de Gaulle – ✆ 04 94 66 76 74 – aubergedu-fenouillet@orange.fr – Fax 04 94 57 81 09 – Closed Sunday evening, Monday and Tuesday

Rest – Menu € 45/60 – Carte € 45/60

◆ In the centre of town. Bright, ochre-coloured façade, with the same colour adorning the walls of the main dining rooms. Patio-terrace. Traditional cuisine.

CRAVANT – 89 Yonne – 319 F5 – pop. 824 – alt. 120 m – ✉ 89460 7 B1

Paris 185 – Auxerre 19 – Avallon 33 – Clamecy 35 – Montbard 65

Syndicat d'initiative, 4, rue d'Orléans ✆ 03 86 42 25 71

Hostellerie St-Pierre

5 r. Église – ✆ 03 86 42 31 67 – hostellerie-st-pierre@wanadoo.fr – Fax 03 86 42 37 43 – Closed 20 December-10 January and Sunday

9 rm – †€ 58 ††€ 63, ☕ € 9 – ½ P € 71 – **Rest** – *(dinner only) (number of covers limited, pre-book)* Menu € 32

◆ This family hotel extends a warm welcome to guests and offers small rooms, laid out around a delightful flower filled courtyard. Smoking lounge and wine tasting cellar. Up-to-date cuisine and good wines (vintages) at reasonable prices served in a light dining room/veranda.

CRAVANT-LES-CÔTEAUX – 37 Indre-et-Loire – 317 L6 – pop. 751 – alt. 50 m – ✉ 37500 11 A3

Paris 284 – Orléans 160 – Tours 45 – Joué-lès-Tours 37 – Châtellerault 57

Manoir des Berthaisières

– ✆ 02 47 98 35 07 – lesberthaisieres@wanadoo.fr – Fax 02 47 98 35 07

3 rm ☕ – †€ 65 ††€ 75/125 – **Table d'hôte** – Menu € 30 bi

◆ In the heart of a huge estate with vineyards, this manor offers three rooms (two in the villa, one dog-friendly). Swimming pool, fitness room and Jacuzzi. Traditional cuisine at the table d'hôte and cooking classes for guests.

CRAZANNES – 17 Charente-Maritime – 324 F4 – pop. 409 – alt. 25 m – ✉ 17350 Atlantic Coast 38 B2

Paris 468 – Poitiers 134 – Rochefort 37 – Saintes 18

Château de Crazannes

– ✆ 06 80 65 40 96 – crazannes@worldonline.fr – Fax 05 46 91 34 46

6 rm – †€ 90/180 ††€ 90/180, ☕ € 12 – **Table d'hôte** – Menu € 35

◆ This 15C château surrounded by 8 hectares of parkland is classified as an historic monument. Luxurious rooms in the keep; other rooms are decorated with fine antique furnishings.

CREANCEY – 21 Côte-d'Or – 320 H6 – see Pouilly-en-Auxoix

CRÈCHES-SUR-SAÔNE – 71 Saône-et-Loire – 320 I12 – see Mâcon

CRÉCY-LA-CHAPELLE – 77 Seine-et-Marne – 312 G2 – pop. 3 851 – alt. 50 m – ✉ 77580 Northern France and the Paris Region 19 C2

Paris 48 – Boulogne-Billancourt 56 – Montreuil 43 – Saint-Denis 60

Office de tourisme, 1, place du Marché ☎ 01 64 63 70 19, Fax 01 64 63 70 39

de la Brie Ferme de Montpichet, Southeast: 2km by D 934, ☎ 01 64 75 34 44.

La Hérissonière without rest

4 r. Barrois – ☎ 01 64 63 00 72 – laherissoniere@free.fr – Fax 01 64 63 00 72

4 rm – †€ 50 ††€ 60

◆ This charming 18C residence is admirably located on the banks of the Morin. The rooms are comfortable with original family furniture, and all look over the river.

CRÉDIN – 56 Morbihan – 308 O6 – pop. 1 421 – alt. 124 m – ✉ 56580 10 C2

Paris 451 – Rennes 100 – Vannes 49 – Pontivy 19 – Hennebont 64

La Maison Blanche aux Volets Bleus

à Blézouan, 2.5 km east on D11 and secondary road – ☎ 02 97 38 58 61 – info@lamaisonblancheauxvoletsbleus.com

4 rm – †€ 88 ††€ 126 – ½ P € 95 – **Table d'hôte** – Menu € 50 bi

◆ This engaging house stands on the edge of a hamlet lost in the countryside. The spruce rooms are decorated on the theme of Brittany. Bicycles for rent and cookery courses. Tasty home cooking served on a large teak table.

CREIL – 60 Oise – 305 F5 – pop. 30 675 – alt. 30 m – ✉ 60100 Northern France and the Paris Region 36 B3

Paris 63 – Beauvais 45 – Chantilly 9 – Clermont 17 – Compiègne 37

Syndicat d'initiative, 41, place du Général-de-Gaulle ☎ 03 44 55 16 07, Fax 03 44 55 05 27

d'Apremont Apremont CD 606, Southeast: 6 km by D 1330, ☎ 03 44 25 61 11.

La Ferme de Vaux

à Vaux, (on D 120 direction Verneuil) – ☎ 03 44 64 77 00 – joly.eveline@wanadoo.fr – Fax 03 44 26 81 50

28 rm – †€ 64 ††€ 72, € 7,50 – ½ P € 62 – **Rest** – *(closed Saturday lunch and Sunday dinner)* Menu (€ 17), € 25/36 – Carte € 41/53

◆ An old Ile-de-France-style farmhouse set around an inner courtyard. Modern comfort in the rooms; those on the ground floor are more spacious. Exposed-stone walls and modernised furnishings make up the decor of the dining room. Traditional menu and attentive service.

CRÉMIEU – 38 Isère – 333 E3 – pop. 3 169 – alt. 200 m – ✉ 38460 Lyon - Rhone Valley 44 B2

Paris 488 – Belley 49 – Bourg-en-Bresse 64 – Grenoble 86 – Lyon 36 – La Tour-du-Pin 28

Office de tourisme, 9, place de la Nation ☎ 04 74 90 45 13, Fax 04 74 90 02 25

Covered market★.

Auberge de la Chaite with rm

pl. des Tilleuls – ☎ 04 74 90 76 63 – aubergedelachaite@wanadoo.fr – Fax 04 74 90 88 08 – Closed 12-28 April, 25-31 August, 23 December-12 January, Sunday dinner, Wednesday lunch and Monday

10 rm – †€ 51 ††€ 51, € 7,50 – **Rest** – Menu € 18 (weekdays)/37 – Carte € 28/53

◆ This country house opposite the Porte de la Loi serves traditional dishes in a rustic-style dining room or on the shaded terrace. Unpretentious rooms.

CREON – 33 Gironde – 335 I6 – pop. 2 856 – alt. 110 m – ✉ 33670 Atlantic Coast 3 B1

Paris 597 – Bordeaux 25 – Arcachon 88 – Langon 32 – Libourne 22

Office de tourisme, 62, boulevardd Victor Hugo ☎ 05 56 23 23 00

Hostellerie Château Camiac rm, rest,
rte de Branne, (D 121) – 05 56 23 20 85
– info@chateaucamiac.com – Fax 05 56 23 38 84 – Open 1st May-30 September
12 rm – € 160/200 € 200/250, € 16 – 2 suites – **Rest** – *(closed Tues.)*
Menu € 32/68 – Carte € 43/71
◆ A charming stopover in this Bordelaise vineyard estate built in the 18C. Some of the rooms, decorated with antiques, have unusual windowed bathrooms. Swimming pool, tennis court. The plush cosy atmosphere of this restaurant is enhanced by paintings; the cuisine is modern in style.

CRÉON-D'ARMAGNAC – 40 Landes – 335 K11 – pop. 282 – alt. 130 m – ✉ 40240

Paris 700 – Bordeaux 122 – Condom 47 – Mont-de-Marsan 36 4 **C2**

Le Poutic
rte de Cazaubon – 05 58 44 66 97 – lepoutic@wanadoo.fr
3 rm – € 45/53 € 50/62 – **Table d'hôte** – *(closed Sunday in July-August)*
Menu € 20 bi/30 bi
◆ Oaks and lime trees shade the park that surrounds this fully restored farmhouse in the Landes. The well furnished rooms have an independent entrance. Many theme stays are available (golf, horse riding and wood pigeon shooting). Traditional and regional dishes.

CREPON – 14 Calvados – 303 I4 – pop. 199 – alt. 52 m – ✉ 14480 Normandy

Paris 257 – Bayeux 13 – Caen 23 – Deauville 66 32 **B2**

Ferme de la Rançonnière
rte Arromanches-les-Bains – 02 31 22 21 73 – ranconniere@wanadoo.fr
– Fax 02 31 22 98 39
35 rm – € 55/170 € 55/170, € 11 – ½ P € 65/125
Rest – *(closed 5-28 January)* Menu € 22 (weekdays)/48 – Carte € 34/53
◆ Wonderful medieval fortified farmhouse. Rooms with beams, antique furniture and curios. The country setting of the dining room has been carefully preserved: fireplace, stone walls and attractive vaulted ceiling.

Ferme de Mathan
800 m. further on – ranconniere@wanadoo.fr
22 rm – € 110/170 € 110/250, € 11 – ½ P € 90/240
◆ Rooms recently fitted out in an 18C smallholding; spacious, attractively decorated and furnished with finds from antique markets. Peace and quiet guaranteed.

CRESSERONS – 14 Calvados – 303 J4 – see Douvres-la-Délivrande

CREST – 26 Drôme – 332 D5 – pop. 7 739 – alt. 196 m – ✉ 26400 Lyon - Rhone Valley

Paris 585 – Die 37 – Gap 129 – Grenoble 114 – Montélimar 37 – Valence 28
Office de tourisme, place du Docteur Rozier 04 75 25 11 38, Fax 04 75 76 79 65
du Domaine de Sagnol Gigors-et-Lozeron Domaine de Sagnol, Northeast: 19 km by D 731, 04 75 40 98 00. 44 **B3**
Keep★: ✻★.

Kléber with rm rest,
6 r. A. Dumont – 04 75 25 11 69 – Fax 04 75 76 82 82 – Closed 1st-15 January, Monday dinner and Tuesday lunch Z **e**
7 rm – € 34/54 € 34/54, € 7 – **Rest** – Menu € 25/46
◆ This lends a transalpine touch to the little walled town with its keep: attractive sponge-work on the walls, and red Italian leather seats. Traditional cuisine.

in La Répara-Auriples 8 km south by D 538 and D 166 Autichamp road – pop. 222 – alt. 350 m – ✉ 26400

Le Prieuré des Sources
– 04 75 25 03 46 – leprieuredessources@wanadoo.fr – Fax 04 75 25 53 07
10 rm – € 100/195 € 100/195, € 13,50 – ½ P € 90/135
Table d'hôte – Menu € 22/43
◆ Venture through the well-kept garden to this former priory. Admire the vaulted sitting and dining rooms, as well as the spacious guestrooms decorated in an African or Asian style. Contemporary cuisine served to residents, evenings only.

LE CRESTET – 84 Vaucluse – **332** D8 – see Vaison-la-Romaine

CREST-VOLAND – 73 Savoie – **333** M3 – **pop. 418** – **alt. 1 230 m** – **Winter sports : 1 230/2 000 m** 17 – ✉ 73590 **French Alps** 46 **F1**

Paris 588 – Albertville 24 – Annecy 53 – Chamonix-Mont-Blanc 47 – Megève 15

Office de tourisme, Maison de Crest-Voland ☎ 04 79 31 62 57, Fax 04 79 31 85 36

Caprice des Neiges rest, VISA AE

rte du Col des Saisies: 1 km – ☎ 04 79 31 62 95 – info@hotel-capricedesneiges.com – Fax 04 79 31 79 30 – Closed mid April to mid June

16 rm – €78/130 €78/130, €10 – ½ P €62/92

Rest – Menu €15/40 – Carte €24/49

◆ A chalet with flower-decked balconies at the foot of the slopes slightly away from the village. A welcoming interior renovated in modern Savoie style. A pleasant, mountain-style dining room featuring lots of wood and stone. Regional cuisine. Children's play area.

Mont Bisanne VISA

– ☎ 04 79 31 60 26 – hotelmontbisanne@yahoo.fr – Fax 04 79 31 89 58 – Open 18 December-3 May

14 rm – €50 €65, €9 – ½ P €61/76

Rest – Menu (€15), €22 – Carte €22/28

◆ In the heart of this little village, a renovated chalet in charming *Savoyard* spirit. Comfortable and well-kept rooms, some with balconies. Traditional and regional dishes served in two dining rooms.

Les Campanules

chemin de la Grange – ☎ 04 79 31 81 43 – chanteline@wanadoo.fr

3 rm – €51/67 €61/67 – **Table d'hôte** – *(open from December to March)* Menu €21 bi

◆ This chalet facing the Aravis chain and Mont Charvin is a peaceful spot for nature lovers. Well-kept, comfortable rooms, a sitting room with a fireplace, and hearty breakfasts. The menus feature specialities from Savoie based on fresh local produce.

CRÉTEIL – 94 Val-de-Marne – **312** D3 – **101** 27 – see Paris, Area

CREULLY – 14 Calvados – **303** I4 – **pop. 1 426** – **alt. 27 m** – ✉ 14480 32 **B2**

Paris 253 – Bayeux 14 – Caen 20 – Deauville 62

Hostellerie St-Martin with rm VISA AE

– ☎ 02 31 80 10 11 – hostellerie.st.martin@wanadoo.fr – Fax 02 31 08 17 64

12 rm – €48 €48, €6 – ½ P €49 – **Rest** – Menu €14 (weekdays)/42

◆ These fine 16C vaulted dining rooms with sculptures by a regional artist were once the village market. Traditional dishes. Rooms available.

LE CREUSOT – 71 Saône-et-Loire – **320** G9 – **pop. 26 283** – **alt. 348 m** – ✉ 71200 **Burgundy-Jura** 8 **C3**

Paris 316 – Autun 30 – Beaune 46 – Chalon-sur-Saône 38 – Mâcon 89

Office de tourisme, château de la Verrerie ☎ 03 85 55 02 46, Fax 03 85 80 11 03

Château de la Verrerie★.

Mont St-Vincent★ ★★.

La Petite Verrerie VISA AE

4 r. J. Guesde – ☎ 03 85 73 97 97 – petiteverrerie@hotelfp-lecreusot.com – Fax 03 85 73 97 90 – Closed 20 December-5 January

43 rm – €93 €113, €12 – 6 suites – **Rest** – *(closed Saturday lunch and Sunday)* Menu €26/31

◆ From factory pharmacy to employees' association, then a VIP guesthouse and now a comfortable hotel – all steeped in the fascinating history of the town. Renovated rooms. A comfortable dining room with paintings on the subject of metallurgy. Adjoining bar.

in Breuil **5,5 km East by rue principale and direction Centre équestre – pop. 3 667 – alt. 337 m – ✉ 71670**

Le Domaine de Montvaltin without rest
– *03 85 55 87 12 – domainedemontvaltin@hotmail.com – Fax 03 85 55 54 72 – Closed February*
4 rm – €65/85 €70/90
◆ This 20C farmhouse is only 5 minutes from Le Creusot. It has been renovated and now offers three types of individually decorated rooms with a fresh, feminine touch. Tennis court, covered swimming-pool, carefully tended garden and a pond teeming with carp.

in Montcenis **3 km West by D 784 – pop. 2 352 – alt. 400 m – ✉ 71710**

Le Montcenis
2 pl. Champ de Foire – 03 85 55 44 36 – restaurant.le-montcenis@wanadoo.fr – Fax 03 85 55 89 52 – Closed 13 July-4 August, 2 weeks in February, Sunday dinner and Monday
Rest – *(number of covers limited, pre-book)* Menu (€ 13), € 19 (weekday lunch), € 26/40 – Carte € 41/51
◆ A welcoming setting consisting of a fine lounge, a vaulted cellar for aperitifs and a neo-Burgundian style dining room with exposed beams. Hearty cuisine with a personal touch.

in Torcy **4 km South by D 28 – pop. 3 554 – alt. 310 m – ✉ 71210**

Le Vieux Saule
– *03 85 55 09 53 – restaurant.levieuxsaule@wanadoo.fr – Fax 03 85 80 39 99 – Closed Sunday dinner and Monday*
Rest – Menu € 16, € 26/67 – Carte € 45/65
◆ Traditional specialities, some with a contemporary touch, are served here in the muted environment of a purple-walled dining room. The chairs bear motifs that pay tribute to a number of famous Burgundy wines.

CREUTZWALD – **57 Moselle** – **307** L3 – **pop. 14 360** – **alt. 210 m** – ✉ **57150** 27 **C1**

Paris 376 – Metz 53 – Neunkirchen 61 – Saarbrücken 37
Syndicat d'initiative, Hôtel de Ville 03 87 81 89 89, Fax 03 87 82 08 15

Auberge Richebourg
17 r. de la Houve – 03 87 90 17 54 – richebourg@wanadoo.fr – Fax 03 87 90 28 56 – Closed 1st-21 August, Saturday lunch, Sunday dinner and Monday
Rest – Menu € 20 (weekdays)/55 – Carte € 40/55
◆ Modern dining room with a terrace opening onto a small vegetable garden. Traditional cuisine and, on Tuesday and Friday evenings, grilled dishes cooked in front of you on the open fire.

CRICQUEBŒUF – **14 Calvados** – **303** M3 – **see Honfleur**

CRILLON – **60 Oise** – **305** C3 – **pop. 433** – **alt. 110 m** – ✉ **60112** 36 **A2**

Paris 103 – Aumale 33 – Beauvais 16 – Breteuil 33 – Compiègne 75 – Gournay-en-Bray 18

La Petite France
7 r. Moulin – 03 44 81 01 13 – lapetitefrance@wanadoo.fr – Fax 03 44 81 01 13 – Closed 21 July-3 August, Tuesday dinner, Sunday dinner and Monday except holidays
Rest – Menu (€ 13,50), € 23 bi/34 – Carte € 33/60
◆ This welcoming inn in a little Beauvaisis village has two rustic dining rooms. Traditional menu, including the house speciality of "tête de veau ravigote" (calf's head).

CRILLON-LE-BRAVE – 84 Vaucluse – 332 D9 – pop. 398 – alt. 340 m – ✉ 84410

42 **E1**

Paris 687 – Avignon 41 – Carpentras 14 – Nyons 37 – Vaison-la-Romaine 22

Crillon le Brave rm, VISA AE

pl. de l'Église – ☎ 04 90 65 61 61 – crillonbrave@relaischateaux.com – Fax 04 90 65 62 86 – Open April-December

28 rm – €200/700 €200/700, €19 – 4 suites – **Rest** – Carte €44/75

◆ The accommodation in this hilltop village facing Mont Ventoux is in seven typical old houses. The terraced Italian garden slopes down to the swimming-pool. Charming Provençal bedrooms. Cuisine infused with the delightful flavours of the south. Lunch snack menu also available.

CRIQUETOT-L'ESNEVAL – 76 Seine-Maritime – 304 B4 – pop. 2 149 – alt. 127 m – ✉ 76280

33 **C1**

Paris 197 – Fécamp 19 – Le Havre 28 – Rouen 81

Le Manoir

5 pl. des Anciens Élèves, (near the church) – ☎ 02 35 29 31 90 – serge.quevilly@wanadoo.fr – Fax 02 35 29 31 90

6 rm – €50/52 €62/66 – ½ P €50 – **Table d'hôte** – Menu €17

◆ Splendid Normandy wardrobes embellish the spacious rooms in this manor house with its stylish facade in stone and brick. Large flower-filled grounds planted with trees.

CRISENOY – 77 Seine-et-Marne – 312 F4 – see Melun

LE CROISIC – 44 Loire-Atlantique – 316 A4 – pop. 4 278 – alt. 6 m – ✉ 44490

Brittany

34 **A2**

Paris 459 – La Baule 9 – Nantes 86 – Redon 66 – Vannes 81

Office de tourisme, place du 18 Juin 1940 ☎ 02 40 23 00 70, Fax 02 40 23 23 70

du Croisic Golf de la Pointe, West: 3 km, ☎ 02 40 23 14 60.

Océarium★ - ★ of Mont-Lénigo.

Plan on next page

Le Fort de l'Océan rm, VISA AE

pointe du Croisic – ☎ 02 40 15 77 77 – fortocean@relaischateaux.com – Fax 02 40 15 77 80

9 rm – €200 €280/300, €18 – ½ P €165/220

Rest – *(closed 11 November-20 December, 4 January-7 February, Wednesday and Thursday lunch 14 July-31 August, Monday and Tuesday)* Menu €32 (weekday lunch), €45/78 – Carte €76/103

◆ A small, Vauban-type, 17C fort overlooking the ocean. Wonderful view of the Côte Sauvage from all the individually decorated rooms. Bikes available. Carefully prepared fish dishes to be enjoyed in an elegant veranda-dining room.

Les Vikings without rest VISA AE

à Port-Lin – ☎ 02 40 62 90 03 – vikings@fr.oleane.com – Fax 02 40 23 28 03

24 rm – €71/111 €71/111, €12 AZ **e**

◆ A holiday spirit pervades this hotel offering spacious rooms, individually decorated with traditional modern furniture. Some have a bow window with a view of the Côte Sauvage.

Les Nids without rest VISA AE

15 r. Pasteur à Port-Lin – ☎ 02 40 23 00 63 – hotellesnids@worldonline.fr – Fax 02 40 23 09 79 – Open April-September AZ **f**

24 rm – €61/77 €61/89, €9

◆ Small, well-kept hotel offering colourful rooms with painted furniture. Breakfast is served beside the covered pool. Children's playground in the garden.

Castel Moor VISA AE

Baie Castouillet, 1.5 km northwest by D 45 – ☎ 02 40 23 24 18 – castel@castel-moor.com – Fax 02 40 62 98 90

18 rm – €58/63 €64/70, €8 – ½ P €92/110 – **Rest** – *(closed Sunday dinner October- February)* Menu €24/41 – Carte €31/50

◆ Imposing modern villa on the coast road running along the Côte Sauvage. Most of the rooms boast a balcony or a terrace. A semi-circular dining room and veranda directly overlooking the sea. The menu favours fish and seafood.

LE CROISIC

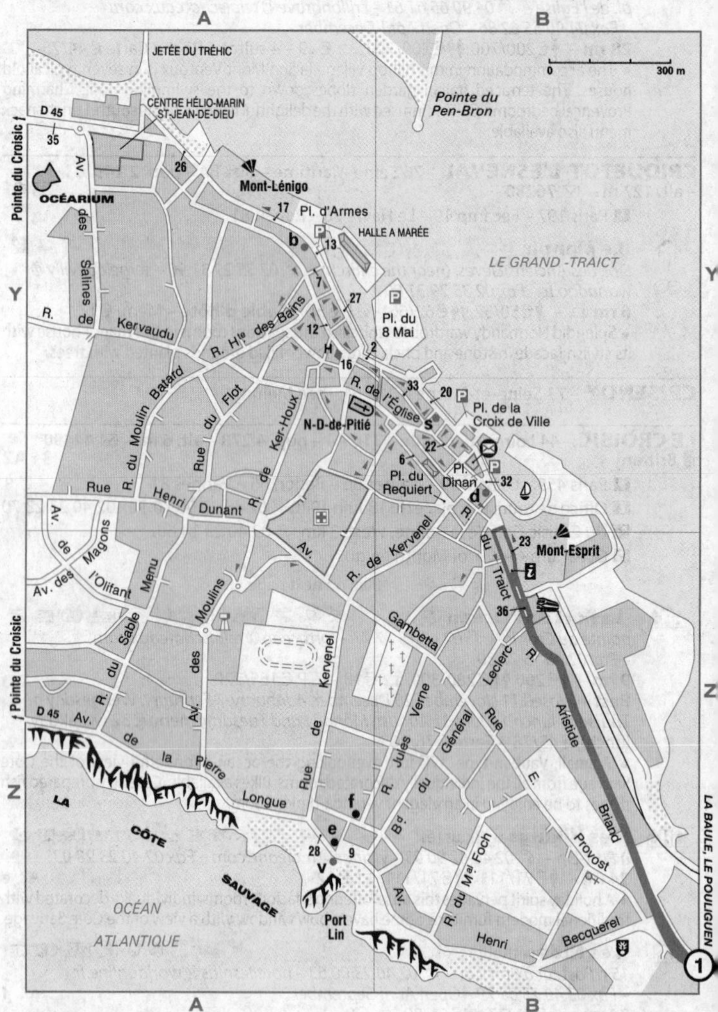

L'Océan

sea and coast, VISA

in Port-Lin – 02 40 62 90 03 – vikings@fr.oleane.com – Fax 02 40 23 28 03

Rest – Carte € 51/110 — AZ **v**

Rest *Le Bistrot de l'Océan* – Carte € 25/45

◆ The main asset of this restaurant clinging to the rocks is its panoramic sea view. Freshly caught fish and seafood. The main asset of this restaurant clinging to the rocks is its panoramic sea view. Freshly-caught fish and seafood.

XX **La Bouillabaisse Bretonne** VISA MC
au port – ✆ 02 40 23 06 74 – Fax 02 40 15 71 43 – Closed 2 January-20 March, Sunday dinner and Tuesday except July-August and Monday BY **s**
Rest – Menu € 20 bi/33 bi – Carte € 30/53
◆ The name of the place may surprise visitors from Marseille, but the view over the sea will reconcile Bretons and Provençaux. Lobsters and crayfish welcome you with open pincers.

XX **Le Lénigo** VISA MC AE
11 quai Lénigo – ✆ 02 40 23 00 31 – le.lenigo@wanadoo.fr – Fax 02 40 23 01 01 – Open 15 February-15 November and closed Monday and Tuesday except August AY **b**
Rest – Menu € 22/34 – Carte € 30/59
◆ Opposite the fish market, this restaurant is decorated in nautical style (varnished wood, portholes, ropes, etc). Simple but tasty menu with an emphasis on fish and seafood.

X **Le Saint-Alys** A/C VISA MC
3 quai Hervé-Rielle – ✆ 02 40 23 58 40 – Fax 02 40 23 58 40 – Closed 3-9 November, 23-26 December, 12-24 February, Sunday dinner, Tuesday dinner and Wednesday BY **d**
Rest – Menu € 17 (weekdays)/35 – Carte € 30/45
◆ A faultless welcome awaits you in this small well-located house opposite the marina. Restrained, tasteful interior in which to sample a modern, predominantly seafood menu.

LA CROIX-BLANCHE – 71 Saône-et-Loire – 320 I11 – see Berzé-la-Ville

LA CROIX-DU-BREUIL – 87 Haute-Vienne – 325 F4 – see Bessines-sur-Gartempe

LA CROIX-FRY (COL) – 74 Haute-Savoie – 328 L5 – see Manigod

LA CROIX-VALMER – 83 Var – 340 O6 – pop. 2 734 – alt. 120 m – ✉ 83420

French Riviera 41 **C3**

- Paris 873 – Draguignan 48 – Fréjus 35 – Le Lavandou 27 – Ste-Maxime 15 – Toulon 68
- Office de tourisme, esplanade de la Gare ✆ 04 94 55 12 12, Fax 04 94 55 12 10
- Gassin Golf Country Club Gassin Route de Ramatuelle, North: 8 km, ✆ 04 94 55 13 44.

Southwest **3,5 km by D 559 then secondary road by Débarquement roundabout – ✉ 83420 La Croix-Valmer**

X **La Petite Auberge de Barbigoua** P VISA MC
quartier Barbigoua – ✆ 04 94 54 21 82 – Open Easter-30 September and closed from Monday to Thursday from Easter to May, Monday and Tuesday from June to September
Rest – *(dinner only)* Menu (€ 30) – Carte € 39/48
◆ A discreet small restaurant with a pleasant terrace-garden. Friendly atmosphere, with a regional menu dominated by fish dishes.

in Gigaro **5 km Southeast by secondary road – ✉ 83420 La Croix-Valmer**

Château de Valmer A/C rm, P VISA MC AE D
plage de Gigaro – ✆ 04 94 55 15 15 – info@chateauvalmer.com – Fax 04 94 55 15 10 – Open beg. April-mid October
41 rm – €197/282 €345/494, € 27 – 1 suite – **Rest** – *(closed Tues.) (dinner only)* Menu € 65 – Carte € 77/98
◆ In the heart of a wine growing estate, an old mansion house with vast, regional style rooms. Pool with palm trees. New, totally comprehensive spa. In the restaurant the colours of Provence feature in the decor and on your plate!

La Pinède-Plage rm, VISA AE
plage de Gigaro – ☎ 04 94 55 16 16 – info@pinedeplage.com – Fax 04 94 55 16 10 – Open from May to the beg. October
33 rm – †€ 197/282 ††€ 340/486, ☕ € 27 – **Rest** – Menu € 56 (dinner) – Carte € 50/92
◆ Modern building by the water's edge and shaded by umbrella pine trees. Pleasant decor (beige tones). Cosy rooms with terrace or balcony. Veranda dining room with cane furniture, or tables set up next to the pool, facing the sea.

Souleias sea and islands, rm, rest, VISA AE
plage de Gigaro – ☎ 04 94 55 10 55 – infos@hotel-souleias.com – Fax 04 94 54 36 23 – Open 21 March-14 October
48 rm – †€ 100/464 ††€ 100/464, ☕ € 20 – ½ P € 125/307
Rest – *(open 2 May-5 October and closed Tuesday dinner)* Menu € 38 (weekday lunch), € 52/89
◆ Lovely property under the pine trees at the top of a hill overlooking the coast. Soberly decorated and furnished rooms, a garden with the scents of Provence, tennis courts and sailing. The restaurant – with a terrace overlooking the bar-swimming pool – organises musical evenings every Tuesday. Regional cuisine.

CROS-DE-CAGNES – **06 Alpes-Maritimes** – **341** D6 – **see Cagnes-sur-Mer**

LE CROTOY – **80 Somme** – **301** C6 – **pop. 2 439** – **alt. 1 m** – ✉ **80550**
Northern France and the Paris Region 36 **A1**

Paris 210 – Abbeville 22 – Amiens 75 – Berck-sur-Mer 29 – Hesdin 41
Office de tourisme, 1, rue Carnot ☎ 03 22 27 05 25, Fax 03 22 27 90 58

Les Tourelles VISA
2 et 4 r. Pierre Guerlain – ☎ 03 22 27 16 33 – info@lestourelles.com – Fax 03 22 27 11 45 – Closed 6 January-1st February
33 rm – †€ 41/51 ††€ 61/89, ☕ € 9
Rest – Menu € 21/31 – Carte € 25/50
◆ A fine 19C mansion facing the Bay of the Somme. Individually decorated rooms, an original dormitory for children and a cosy lounge. Numerous activities and exhibitions. Local cuisine with an emphasis on seafood served in a simple dining room.

CROZANT – **23 Creuse** – **325** G2 – **pop. 581** – **alt. 263 m** – ✉ **23160**
Dordogne-Berry-Limousin 25 **C1**

Paris 329 – Argenton-sur-Creuse 31 – La Châtre 46 – Guéret 41 – Montmorillon 68
Ruins★.

Auberge de la Vallée VISA
– ☎ 05 55 89 80 03 – Fax 05 55 89 83 22 – Closed 2 January-2 February, Monday dinner and Tuesday
Rest – Menu € 17/41 – Carte € 29/37
◆ This small country guesthouse offers traditional cuisine based on carefully selected local produce; the dining room is quietly rustic in style.

CROZET – **01 Ain** – **328** J3 – **pop. 1 349** – **alt. 540 m** – ✉ **01170** 46 **F1**

Paris 537 – Lyon 153 – Bourg-en-Bresse 105 – Genève 16 – Annecy 57

Jiva Hill Park Hôtel VISA AE
rte d'Harée – ☎ 04 50 28 48 48 – welcome@jivahill.com – Fax 04 50 28 48 49
34 rm – †€ 265/365 ††€ 305/405, ☕ € 20 – 6 suites
Rest *Shamwari* – Menu € 35 (lunch), € 45/65 – Carte € 60/68
◆ Sophisticated, contemporary luxury only 10min from Geneva airport. Designed along the lines of a South African hunting lodge, this hotel is the ultimate in chic elegance. Cosy restaurant whose terrace faces Mont Blanc. Up-to-date cuisine.

CROZON – 29 Finistère – 308 E5 – pop. 7 535 – alt. 85 m – ✉ 29160
Brittany 9 **A2**

Paris 587 – Brest 60 – Châteaulin 35 – Douarnenez 40 – Morlaix 81 – Quimper 49

Office de tourisme, boulevard de Pralognan ✆ 02 98 27 07 92, Fax 02 98 27 24 89

Church★ altar-piece.

Circuit des Pointes★★★.

La Presqu'île
pl. de l'Église – ✆ 02 98 27 29 29 – mutin.gourmand1@wanadoo.fr – Fax 02 98 26 11 97 – Closed 6-26 October, 24 March-6 April, Sunday dinner and Monday off season

12 rm – †€ 46/75 ††€ 46/75, ☕ € 10 – ½ P € 56/90

Rest ***Le Mutin Gourmand*** – see restaurant listing

◆ The old Crozon town hall has recently been turned into a hotel with soundproofed rooms decorated in a modern, Breton style. Shop selling wine and regional products.

Le Mutin Gourmand
pl. de l'Église – ✆ 02 98 27 06 51 – mutin.gourmand1@wanadoo.fr – Fax 02 98 26 11 97 – Closed 6-26 October, 24 March-6 April, Monday except dinner in season, Tuesday lunch and Sunday dinner

Rest – Menu € 23/59 – Carte € 42/73

◆ Friendly service in this Breton restaurant with modern decor, exposed stone, watercolour paintings and accompanied by lobster tank. Fine, regional cuisine, wines from the Languedoc and the Loire.

at Fret 5.5 km north by D 155 and D 55 – ✉ 29160 Crozon

Hostellerie de la Mer
11 quai du Fret – ✆ 02 98 27 61 90 – hostellerie.de.la.mer@wanadoo.fr – Fax 02 98 27 65 89 – Closed Saturday and Sunday in January

25 rm – †€ 44/70 ††€ 44/95, ☕ € 9 – ½ P € 54/67 – **Rest** – *(closed 2 January-8 February)* Menu € 25/69 – Carte € 41/80

◆ An attractive, family-run hotel overlooking the harbour in Brest, with small, simple and well-maintained rooms, some of which have a view. Breton furniture and sea views go hand in hand with a cuisine which has a distinctly maritime flavour.

CRUGNY – 51 Marne – 306 E7 – pop. 576 – alt. 100 m – ✉ 51170
Northern France and the Paris Region 13 **B2**

Paris 135 – Châlons-en-Champagne 71 – Reims 28 – Soissons 39

La Maison Bleue
46 r. Haute – ✆ 03 26 50 84 63 – maisonbleue@aol.com – Fax 03 26 97 43 92 – Closed 20 December-31 January

6 rm – †€ 78 ††€ 93, ☕ € 6,50 – **Table d'hôte** – Menu € 26 bi

◆ A welcoming residence and grounds pervaded by a restful atmosphere. Individually decorated rooms; the most spacious, on the top floor, give a fine view of the village and the Ardre valley. Straightforward cuisine with homely dishes.

CRUIS – 04 Alpes-de-Haute-Provence – 334 D8 – pop. 551 – alt. 728 m – ✉ 04230
40 **B2**

Paris 732 – Digne-les-Bains 42 – Forcalquier 22 – Manosque 42 – Sisteron 26

Auberge de l'Abbaye
– ✆ 04 92 77 01 93 – auberge-abbaye-cruis@wanadoo.fr – Fax 04 92 77 01 92 – Closed autumn half-term holidays, Christmas and February holidays

9 rm – †€ 55/75 ††€ 55/75, ☕ € 10 – ½ P € 64/74 – **Rest** – *(closed Monday lunch, Tuesday lunch, Wednesday lunch and Thursday lunch in July-August, Tuesday from November to March, Sunday dinner and Wednesday from September to June) (number of covers limited, pre-book)* Menu (€ 24), € 29/49 – Carte € 44/52

◆ A pleasant, family-run hotel in a village in the Montagne de Lure. Simply furnished but well-kept rooms. Home-made bread for breakfast. This rustic restaurant with its shaded terrace is located on the town square. Cuisine with a distinctly regional feel.

CRUSEILLES – 74 Haute-Savoie – 328 J4 – pop. 3 186 – alt. 781 m – ✉ 74350

46 **F1**

Paris 537 – Annecy 19 – Bellegarde-sur-Valserine 44 – Bonneville 37 – Genève 27

Syndicat d'initiative, 46, place de la Mairie ☎ 04 50 44 20 92

L'Ancolie with rm — rest, VISA

au parc des Dronières, Northeast : 1 km via D 15 – ☎ 04 50 44 28 98 – info@lancolie.com – Fax 04 50 44 09 73 – Closed autumn half-term holidays

10 rm – €83/119 €83/119, ☕ €13 – ½ P €85/100 – **Rest** – *(closed Sunday dinner except July-August and Monday)* Menu €29 (weekday lunch), €43/71 – Carte €58/75

♦ Well-equipped modern chalet (quintessentially Savoyard) overlooking a lake. Wood-panelled rooms with balcony (bar one). Classic cuisine, panoramic terrace.

in Avenières 6 km North by D 41 and secondary road – ✉ 74350 Cruseilles

Château des Avenières — Aravis chain, VISA

– ☎ 04 50 44 02 23

– reservation@chateau-des-avenieres.com – Fax 04 50 44 29 09

– Closed autumn half-term holidays, Christmas and February holidays

12 rm – €150/280 €150/280, ☕ €17 – **Rest** – *(closed Monday, Tuesday and lunch except week-ends)* Menu €58/98

♦ A 1907 manor house with a mysterious history. Personalised rooms, a charming butterfly-shaped park and a marvellous view of the Aravis mountain range. Superb classic-baroque dining room with woodwork incorporating antique cameos.

CUBRY – 25 Doubs – 321 I2 – pop. 70 – alt. 340 m – ✉ 25680

17 **C1**

Paris 389 – Belfort 49 – Besançon 53 – Lure 27 – Montbéliard 42 – Vesoul 31

Château de Bournel — VISA

– ☎ 03 81 86 00 10 – info@bournel.com – Fax 03 81 86 01 06

– Open 1st April-1st November

16 rm – €127/140 €195/215, ☕ €15 – 2 suites – ½ P €130/140

Rest ***Le Maugré*** – *☎ 03 81 86 06 60 (closed Tuesday) (dinner only)* Menu €30/55

♦ Hotel in the 18C outbuildings of the château of the Marquis de Moustier, in the heart of an 80h park. Spacious rooms. Formal gardens and 18-hole golf course. Modern cuisine served in a vaulted dining room at Le Maugré. Fast food in the brasserie.

CUCUGNAN – 11 Aude – 344 G5 – pop. 113 – alt. 310 m – ✉ 11350

Languedoc-Roussillon-Tarn Gorges

22 **B3**

Paris 847 – Carcassonne 77 – Limoux 79 – Perpignan 42 – Quillan 51

Circuit of Corbières cathares★★.

La Tourette without rest

4 passage de la Vierge – ☎ 04 68 45 07 39 – coco@latourette.eu

3 rm ☕ – €105 €115

♦ The lady of the house cannot be faulted for her taste; the Prune, Turquoise and Indigo rooms are not only unusual, they are exquisite. Jacuzzi on the patio under an olive tree.

Auberge du Vigneron with rm — rm, rm, VISA

– ☎ 04 68 45 03 00 – auberge.vigneron@ataraxie.fr – Fax 04 68 45 03 08

– Open 16 March-10 November

7 rm – €49 €49/65, ☕ €7 – ½ P €54 – **Rest** – *(closed Sunday dinner off season, Saturday lunch July-August and Monday)* Menu €22 (weekdays)/38 – Carte €35/46

♦ The chef takes great pride in using the finest produce to prepare regional dishes to which he adds his own creative touches. Dining room in the old wine cellar and pretty terrace facing the vineyards.

Auberge de Cucugnan with rm — rm, VISA

2 pl. Fontaine – ☎ 04 68 45 40 84 – contact@auberge-cucugnan.com

– Fax 04 68 45 01 52 – Closed 1st January-1st March

9 rm – €46 €46, ☕ €6,50 – ½ P €49/73 – **Rest** – *(closed Thursday)* Menu €18/44

♦ A country atmosphere pervades this converted barn that lies at the end of a maze of alleys. Generous cuisine with a rural flavour. Perfectly maintained rooms.

CUCURON – 84 Vaucluse – 332 F11 – pop. 1 792 – alt. 350 m – ✉ 84160

Provence 42 **E1**

Paris 739 – Apt 25 – Cavaillon 39 – Digne-les-Bains 109 – Manosque 35

Office de tourisme, rue Léonce Brieugne ✆ 04 90 77 28 37

XX **La Petite Maison** VISA MC AE

pl. Étang – ✆ 04 90 68 21 99 – info@lapetitemaisondecucuron.com – Closed Monday and Tuesday

Rest – Menu € 35 (weekdays)/55

◆ A charming restaurant, splendidly decorated (17C tapestry on the ground floor). Regional cuisine and international and local wines served.

X **L'Horloge** VISA MC AE

55 r. L. Brieugne – ✆ 04 90 77 12 74 – horlog@wanadoo.fr – Fax 04 90 77 29 90 – Closed 30 June-5 July, 18-27 December, 9 February-13 March, Monday 1st September-6 April, Tuesday dinner and Wednesday

Rest – Menu (€ 15 bi), € 18/42 – Carte € 34/52

◆ 14C building in a Luberon village once used as an oil press, now converted into a rustic restaurant decorated in bright colours. Regional dishes.

CUERS – 83 Var – 340 L6 – pop. 8 174 – alt. 140 m – ✉ 83390 41 C3

Paris 834 – Brignoles 25 – Draguignan 59 – Marseille 84 – Toulon 22

Office de tourisme, 18, Place de la Convention ✆ 04 94 48 56 27, Fax 04 94 28 03 56

XX **Le Verger des Kouros** P VISA MC AE

2 km on Solliès-Pont road D 97 – ✆ 04 94 28 50 17 – couros@wanadoo.fr – Fax 04 94 48 69 77 – Closed 15-30 October, 2-15 February, Tuesday dinner off season, Tuesday lunch in season and Wednesday

Rest – Menu € 19 (weekdays lunch), € 34/45

◆ Restaurant set up in a regional building. In spite of its name, you won't see any statues of ephebes, but the three brothers running the place are Greek. Cool dining room and local dishes.

CUISEAUX – 71 Saône-et-Loire – 320 M11 – pop. 1 749 – alt. 280 m – ✉ 71480

Burgundy-Jura 8 **D3**

Paris 395 – Chalon-sur-Saône 60 – Lons-le-Saunier 26 – Mâcon 74 – Tournus 52

Syndicat d'initiative, cours des Princes d'Orange ✆ 03 85 72 76 09

Vuillot AC rest, P VISA MC

36 r. Vuillard – ✆ 03 85 72 71 79 – hotel.vuillot@wanadoo.fr – Fax 03 85 72 54 22 – Closed 13-24 June, 27 December-19 January, Sunday dinner and Monday lunch

15 rm – †€ 40/42 ††€ 52/56, ☕ € 8,50 – ½ P € 47/50 – **Rest** – Menu € 14 (weekdays)/45 – Carte € 21/47

◆ A Burgundy building in lovely local stone, with neat and tidy little rooms. The small town still has vestiges of its old fortifications. Country-type restaurant with restrained decor and a veranda. Specialities from the Bresse and Dombes regions.

CUISERY – 71 Saône-et-Loire – 320 J10 – pop. 1 612 – alt. 211 m – ✉ 71290

Burgundy-Jura 8 **C3**

Paris 367 – Chalon-sur-Saône 35 – Lons-le-Saunier 50 – Mâcon 38 – Tournus 8

Syndicat d'initiative, 32, place d'Armes ✆ 03 85 40 11 70

Hostellerie Bressane AC P VISA MC AE

56, rte de Tournus – ✆ 03 85 32 30 66 – hostellerie.bressane@wanadoo.fr – Fax 03 85 40 14 96 – Closed 29 December-12 February, Wednesday and Thursday

15 rm – †€ 60/90 ††€ 70/120, ☕ € 10 – ½ P € 76/100 – **Rest** – Menu € 26/66 – Carte € 35/55

◆ This family hostelry dating back to 1870 offers carefully renovated, spacious rooms; ask for one to the rear in the former stables. Delightful garden. Traditional local dishes are cheerfully served in a stylish modern setting. Fine plane tree on the terrace.

CULT – 70 Haute-Saône – 321 E3 – pop. 158 – alt. 270 m – ✉ 70150 16 B2

Paris 367 – Besançon 35 – Dole 44 – Vesoul 56

Les Egrignes

rte d'Hugier – ✆ 03 84 31 92 06 – lesegrignes@wanadoo.fr – Fax 03 84 31 92 06 – Closed 17 November-6 January

3 rm – €75 €85 – **Table d'hôte** – *(closed Thursday)* Menu €28 bi

◆ Parkland with centuries-old trees surrounds this fine residence dating back to 1849. The rooms are large and tastefully furnished. Elegant lobby with Art deco furniture. The table d'hôte meals invite guests to discover the region's culinary specialities and wines.

CUQ-TOULZA – 81 Tarn – 338 D9 – pop. 519 – alt. 203 m – ✉ 81470 29 C2

Paris 713 – Toulouse 47 – Albi 72 – Castelnaudary 35 – Castres 33 – Gaillac 54

Cuq en Terrasses

rm, rm, VISA MC AE

south-east: 2.5 km on the D 45 – ✆ 05 63 82 54 00 – info@cuqenterrasses.com – Fax 05 63 82 54 11 – Open 2April-30 October

6 rm – €105/155 €105/155, €14 – 1 suite – ½ P €96/120

Rest – *(closed Wednesday) (dinner only) (residents only)* Menu €36

◆ This charming 18C building with a guesthouse atmosphere is a rare pearl, with an unusual terraced garden, and tastefully and individually decorated rooms. In the evening, a fixed menu is served in the cosy little dining room.

LA CURE – 39 Jura – 321 G8 – see les Rousses

CUREBOURSE (COL) – 15 Cantal – 330 D5 – see Vic-sur-Cère

CURTIL-VERGY – 21 Côte-d'Or – 320 J6 – see Nuits-St-Georges

CURZAY-SUR-VONNE – 86 Vienne – 322 G6 – pop. 426 – alt. 125 m – ✉ 86600 39 C1

Paris 364 – Lusignan 11 – Niort 54 – Parthenay 34 – Poitiers 29 – St-Maixent-l'École 28

Château de Curzay

rm, rm, VISA MC AE

rte Jazeneuil – ✆ 05 49 36 17 00 – info@chateau-curzay.com – Fax 05 49 53 57 69 – Open 16 March-30 November

20 rm – €180/300 €180/300, €25 – 2 suites – ½ P €190/280

Rest ***La Cédraie*** – Menu €32 (weekday lunch), €80/120 – Carte €80/106

Spec. Œuf en croûte au parmesan et asperges. Vol au vent de ris de veau, écrevisses et champignons. Saint-Pierre, houmous et saveurs orientales. **Wines** Vin de Pays de la Vienne, Vin de Pays thouarsais.

◆ Superb castle (1710) at the heart of a 120 ha-estate crossed by a river and housing a stud farm. Aristocratic rooms. Creative cuisine made from the Cédraie's vegetable and herb garden.

CUSSAY – 37 Indre-et-Loire – 317 N6 – pop. 562 – alt. 105 m – ✉ 37240 11 B3

Paris 303 – Orléans 179 – Tours 67 – Joué-lès-Tours 62 – Châtellerault 36

La Ferme Blanche

– ✆ 02 47 91 94 43 – af-bouvier@wanadoo.fr – Closed 21 December-28 February

3 rm – €90/120 €90/120 – **Table d'hôte** – Menu €35 bi

◆ This 18C stone farmhouse stands in a pleasant garden overlooking peaceful countryside. The carefully chosen antiques add character to the individually decorated rooms. Sample traditional dishes inspired by the Tours region at the table d'hôte.

CUSSEY-SUR-L'OGNON – 25 Doubs – 321 F2 – pop. 621 – alt. 227 m – ✉ 25870 16 B2

Paris 412 – Besançon 14 – Gray 37 – Vesoul 45

Château de Moncley★, **Burgundy-Jura**

La Vieille Auberge
1 grande rue – ✆ 03 81 48 51 70 – lavieilleauberge@wanadoo.fr – Fax 03 81 57 62 30 – Closed 25 August-8 September, 22 December-5 January, Friday dinner from November to January, Sunday dinner and Monday
Rest – Menu € 15 (weekday lunch), € 23/45 – Carte € 29/46
◆ Old stone house covered with ivy. Traditional cuisine and regional dishes served in the discreetly rustic dining room.

CUTS – **60 Oise** – **305** J3 – **pop. 858** – **alt. 79 m** – ✉ **60400** 37 **C2**
Paris 115 – Chauny 16 – Compiègne 26 – Noyon 10 – Soissons 30 – St-Quentin 45

Auberge Le Bois Doré with rm
5 r. Ramée, D 934 – ✆ 03 44 09 77 66 – sarl-le-bois-dore@wanadoo.fr – Fax 03 44 09 79 27 – Closed 23 February-10 March, Tuesday dinner, Sunday dinner and Monday
3 rm – €44 €48, ☕ €7 – 2 suites – **Rest** – Menu (€ 13,50), € 16 (weekday lunch), € 19/36 – Carte € 29/41
◆ Building more than a century old enlivened by a red canopy on the facade. The renovated dining room is light and unpretentiously furnished. Spacious banqueting hall on the upper floor. A non-smoking inn with a handful of rooms for guests.

CUVES – **50 Manche** – **303** F7 – **pop. 360** – **alt. 78 m** – ✉ **50670** 32 **A2**
Paris 334 – Avranches 23 – Domfront 42 – Fougères 47 – St-Lô 54 – Vire 25

Le Moulin de Jean
north-east: 2 km on the D 48 – ✆ 02 33 48 39 29 – reservations@lemoulindejean.com – Fax 02 33 48 35 32
Rest – Menu (€ 25), € 32/44 – Carte € 32/40
◆ Situated in a bucolic location, this old mill is a harmonious mix of restored stone, parquet flooring and simple, modern decor. Contemporary-style menu. Non-smoking restaurant.

CUVILLY – **60 Oise** – **305** H3 – **pop. 520** – **alt. 78 m** – ✉ **60490** 36 **B2**
Paris 93 – Compiègne 21 – Amiens 54 – Beauvais 61 – Montdidier 15 – Noyon 32 – Roye 20

L'Auberge Fleurie
64 rte Flandres, D 1017 – ✆ 03 44 85 06 55 – Fax 03 44 85 06 55 – Closed 16 August-4 September, 26-30 December, Sunday dinner, Tuesday dinner, Wednesday dinner, Thursday dinner and Monday
Rest – Menu € 14 (weekdays)/38 – Carte € 40/70
◆ Formerly a post house and then a farmhouse, this creeper-covered restaurant has a rustic dining area set in the old sheepfold and serves traditional meals.

DABISSE – **04 Alpes-de-Haute-Provence** – **334** D9 – ✉ **04190 Les Mees** 40 **B2**
Paris 734 – Digne-les-Bains 34 – Forcalquier 20 – Manosque 27 – Sisteron 30

Le Vieux Colombier
rte d'Oraison, 2 km south on D 4 – ✆ 04 92 34 32 32 – snowak@wanadoo.fr – Fax 04 92 34 34 26 – Closed 1st-15 January, Tuesday dinner October-March, Sunday dinner and Wednesday
Rest – Menu (€ 20), € 30/59 – Carte € 43/59
◆ Dining room in an old farmhouse with exposed beams. Pleasant terrace shaded by two, centuries-old chestnut trees. Traditional cuisine.

DACHSTEIN – **67 Bas-Rhin** – **315** J5 – **pop. 1 271** – **alt. 160 m** – ✉ **67120** 1 **A1**
Paris 477 – Molsheim 6 – Saverne 28 – Sélestat 40 – Strasbourg 23

Auberge de la Bruche
– ✆ 03 88 38 14 90 – info@auberge-bruche.com – Fax 03 88 48 81 12 – Closed 16-31 August, 27 December-6 January, Saturday lunch, Sunday dinner and Wednesday
Rest – Menu € 26/68 bi – Carte € 38/55
◆ Head straight for the old watchtower; at its feet flows the Bruche, and beside it, forming a pretty picture, stands this flower-filled and elegantly furnished hotel.

DAGLAN – 24 Dordogne – 337 D3 – pop. 535 – alt. 101 m – ✉ 24250 4 D2

Paris 558 – Bordeaux 203 – Cahors 51 – Sarlat-la-Canéda 23

Syndicat d'initiative, le Bourg ✆ 05 53 29 88 84, Fax 05 53 29 88 84

Le Petit Paris

au bourg – ✆ 05 53 28 41 10 – Fax 05 53 28 41 10 – Open 7 March-21 December and closed Sunday dinner off season, Saturday lunch and Monday

Rest – *(number of covers limited, pre-book)* Menu (€ 22), € 27/39 – Carte approx. € 40

◆ Two rustic style dining rooms - the finer of the two is on the upper floor. Terrace for summer dining. Carefully prepared cuisine in keeping with current tastes and based on regional produce.

LA DAILLE – 73 Savoie – 333 O5 – see Val-d'Isère

DAMBACH-LA-VILLE – 67 Bas-Rhin – 315 I7 – pop. 1 973 – alt. 210 m – ✉ 67650 Alsace-Lorraine 2 C1

Paris 443 – Obernai 24 – Saverne 61 – Sélestat 8 – Strasbourg 52

Office de tourisme, 11, place du Marché ✆ 03 88 92 61 00, Fax 03 88 92 47 11

Le Vignoble without rest

– ✆ 03 88 92 43 75 – info@hotel-vignoble-alsace.fr – Fax 03 88 92 62 21 – Closed January

7 rm – †€ 55/60 ††€ 60/62, ☕ € 7

◆ Former Alsace-style barn (1765) with a village atmosphere (church bells chime every hour), warm welcome and stylish little rooms.

DAMGAN – 56 Morbihan – 308 P9 – pop. 1 327 – ✉ 56750 9 B3

Paris 469 – Muzillac 10 – Redon 46 – La Roche-Bernard 25 – Vannes 29

Office de tourisme, Place Alexandre Tiffoche ✆ 02 97 41 11 32

De la Plage without rest

38 bd de l'Océan – ✆ 02 97 41 10 07 – contact@hotel-morbihan.com – Fax 02 97 41 12 82 – Closed 11 November-6 February

17 rm – †€ 54/55 ††€ 54/93, ☕ € 10 – 1 suite

◆ The smiling welcome extended by the owners is irresistible. Most of the rooms command a fine view of the Atlantic. Snacks and a wide choice of salads.

Albatros

rest,

1 bd de l'Océan – ✆ 02 97 41 16 85 – albatros56@wanadoo.fr – Fax 02 97 41 21 34 – Open 15 March-3 November

27 rm – †€ 45/54 ††€ 51/67, ☕ € 7,50 – ½ P € 52/59 – **Rest** – Menu (€ 12), € 19/41 – Carte € 29/53

◆ This seafront house in a residential neighbourhood is friendly and lively. Most of the rooms enjoy a sea view; all are very well kept. Restaurant with attractive colourful decor and a pleasant view of the sea. Fish menu.

DAMPIERRE-EN-YVELINES – 78 Yvelines – 311 H3 – 101 31 – see Paris, Area

DAMPRICHARD – 25 Doubs – 321 L3 – pop. 1 768 – alt. 825 m – ✉ 25450 17 C2

Paris 505 – Basel 94 – Belfort 64 – Besançon 82 – Montbéliard 47 – Pontarlier 67

Le Lion d'Or

7 pl. du 3e RTA – ✆ 03 81 44 22 84 – hotel.damprichard@wanadoo.fr – Fax 03 81 44 23 10 – Closed 25 October-7 November, 22-27 February, Sunday dinner and Monday

Rest – Menu (€ 11), € 13,50 (weekday lunch), € 20/50 – Carte € 30/61

◆ In the centre of a village bordering Switzerland, a pleasant restaurant (beams and fireplace) serving classic cuisine made with fresh produce. Good choice of wines by the glass.

DANIZY – 02 Aisne – 306 C5 – pop. 560 – alt. 54 m – ✉ 02800 37 C2

Paris 148 – Amiens 111 – Laon 32 – Saint-Quentin 28 – Soissons 53

Domaine le Parc

r. du Quesny – ✆ 03 23 56 55 23 – contact@domaineleparc.fr

5 rm – €65/85 €65/85 – **Table d'hôte** – Menu €35 bi

◆ Handsome 18C abode of character standing in magnificent wooded grounds. The rooms are softly lit and classically decorated; some enjoy a view of the Oise valley. The lady of the house's tasty home cooking is greatly appreciated.

DANJOUTIN – 90 Territoire de Belfort – 315 F11 – see Belfort

DANNEMARIE – 68 Haut-Rhin – 315 G11 – pop. 1 988 – alt. 320 m – ✉ 68210 1 A3

Paris 447 – Basel 43 – Belfort 25 – Colmar 58 – Mulhouse 25 – Thann 25

Ritter

(opposite the station) – ✆ 03 89 25 04 30 – restaurant.ritter@wanadoo.fr – Fax 03 89 08 02 34 – Closed 8-18 July, 22-31 December, 24 February-12 March, Monday dinner, Thursday dinner and Tuesday

Rest – Menu €13 (weekday lunch), €18/58 bi – Carte €33/57

◆ The interior of this pretty 1900 house - once the village theatre - is typically Alsatian: a collection of beer mugs and farming implements. Fried carp speciality.

Wach

13 pl. H. de Ville – ✆ 03 89 25 00 01 – Fax 03 89 25 00 01 – Closed 4-18 August, 22 December-5 January and Monday

Rest – *(lunch only)* Menu €12,50 (weekdays)/35 – Carte €29/42

◆ The modest façade of this family restaurant is covered in flowers in the summer. The appetising cuisine based on local produce is served with reasonably priced good quality wines.

DAVAYAT – 63 Puy-de-Dôme – 323 F7 – pop. 510 – alt. 369 m – ✉ 63200

Auvergne 5 B2

Paris 402 – Clermont-Ferrand 28 – Cournon-d'Auvergne 29 – Vichy 46

La Maison de la Treille without rest

25 r. de l'Église – ✆ 04 73 63 58 20 – honnorat.la.treille@wanadoo.fr

4 rm – €66/83 €73/90

◆ The architectural style of this 1810 building draws on Italian neo-classicism. The stylish rooms are in the Orangerie, surrounded by an attractive garden. Tapestry courses available.

DAX – 40 Landes – 335 E12 – pop. 19 515 – alt. 12 m – Spa : at St-Paul-lès-Dax : all year – Casinos : La Potinière, and St-Paul-lès-Dax – ✉ 40100

Atlantic Coast 3 B3

Paris 727 – Biarritz 61 – Bordeaux 144 – Mont-de-Marsan 54 – Pau 85

Office de tourisme, 11, cours Foch ✆ 05 58 56 86 86, Fax 05 58 56 86 80

Plan on next page

Grand Hôtel Mercure Splendid rm, rest,

cours Verdun – ✆ 05 58 56 70 70 – h2148@accor-hotels.com – Fax 05 58 74 76 33 – Closed January and February B a

100 rm – €98/115 €110/120, €10 – 6 suites – **Rest** – Carte €32/54

◆ The original Art Deco setting has been preciously preserved in the entrance hall, the bar and in the spacious rooms with old-world charm. Renovated spa centre. A magnificent dining hall that some say is reminiscent of the transatlantic liner, Normandie.

Le Grand Hôtel rm, rest,

r. Source – ✆ 05 58 90 53 00 – grandhotel@thermesadour.com – Fax 05 58 90 52 88 B f

128 rm – €68/99 €75/103, €8 – 8 suites – ½ P €65/77 – **Rest** – *(closed 23 December-6 January)* Menu €18/25

◆ This hotel has had new life breathed into it following careful renovation. Well sound-proofed modern rooms. Integrated thermal baths and numerous special events (tea dances, etc.). A very spacious dining room mainly used by people taking the waters.

DAX

ST-PAUL-LÈS-DAX

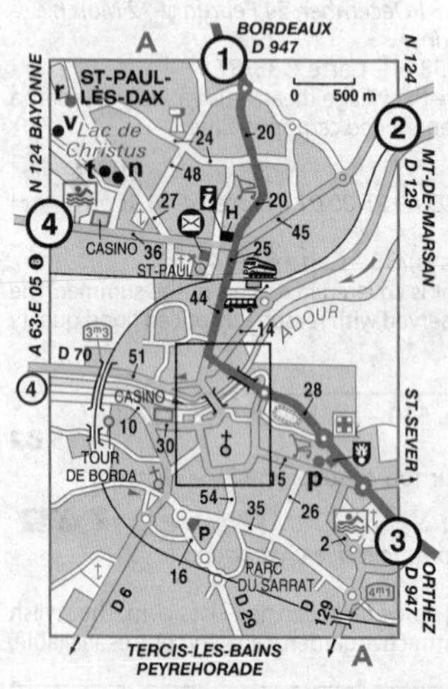

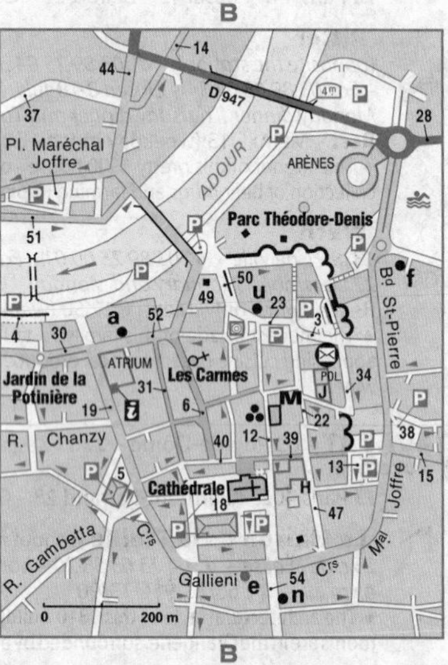

Le Richelieu

13 av. V. Hugo – ✆ 05 58 90 49 49 – hotellerichelieu@wanadoo.fr – Fax 05 58 90 80 86 – Closed 25 December-10 January B **n**

30 rm – €55 €65, □ €6 – ½ P €90/98 – **Rest** – *(closed Saturday lunch, Sunday dinner and Monday)* Menu €23 – Carte €24/44

◆ Renovated functional rooms - ask for one at the back. A tip for spa fans: the annexe houses practical studios equipped with a kitchenette. A dining room with colourful decor right up to the beams, and a patio where tables are laid in fine weather.

Le Vascon without rest

pl. Fontaine Chaude – ✆ 05 58 56 64 60 – hotel-levascon@wanadoo.fr – Fax 05 58 90 85 47 – Open 2 March-29 November B **u**

25 rm – €34/36 €50/52, □ €7

◆ Opposite the warm fountain (64°C!), the main attraction of Dax. Small, stylish, colourful rooms furnished by craftsmen. Friendly welcome.

L'Amphitryon

38 cours Galliéni – ✆ 05 58 74 58 05 – Closed 23 August-5 September, 1st-30 January, Saturday lunch, Sunday dinner and Monday B **e**

Rest – *(number of covers limited, pre-book)* Menu €20 (weekdays)/38 – Carte €37/48

◆ The restaurant has been done up from top to toe: immaculate facade and a pleasant dining room with naval decor. Updated regionally sourced cuisine.

Une Cuisine en Ville (Philippe Lagraula)
11 av. G. Clemenceau – 05 58 90 26 89 – Fax 05 58 90 26 89 – Closed 15 August-7 September, 2-14 January, Sunday dinner, Monday and Tuesday
A **p**

Rest – Menu € 23 (weekday lunch), € 35/60 – Carte € 57/63
Spec. Foie gras poché à la sangria (summer). Saint-Jacques, potimarron et chanterelles (October to January). Le "Russe" de Dax. **Wines** Jurançon.
◆ Inventiveness and originality throughout – as much in the decor which combines old stone walls and modern ornamentaion as in the savoury cuisine with a personal touch.

St-Paul-lès-Dax – pop. 10 226 – alt. 21 m – 40990

Office de tourisme, 68, avenue de la Résistance 05 58 91 60 01, Fax 05 58 91 97 44

Calicéo
rm, rest, rest,
355 r. du Centre Aéré, on Lake Christus –
05 58 90 66 00 – caliceo@thermesadour.com – Fax 05 58 90 66 64 A **n**
47 rm – €76/89 €89/101, € 9,50 – 148 suites – € 107/118
Rest – Menu € 19/28 – Carte € 20/39
◆ A recently built complex with rooms decorated in a 1940s style. An aquatic fitness centre and small spa. The restaurant has a terrace facing Christus lake. Traditional cuisine and a choice of light meals.

Du Lac
rest, rest,
allée de Christus – 05 58 90 60 00 – hoteldulac@thermesadour.com – Fax 05 58 91 34 88 – Open 2 March-23 November A **t**
209 rm – €59/65 €65/73, € 10 – ½ P € 59/63
Rest ***L'Arc-en-Ciel*** – *05 58 90 63 00* – Menu € 14,50/23 – Carte € 20/32
◆ A hotel and spa complex with a good location near the Lac de Christus. Functional rooms, some of which have a loggia. The Arc-en-Ciel has modern decor and a view of the lake. Menus are traditional and light meals are available for dieting guests.

Les Jardins du Lac
rest, rest,
au lac de Christus – 05 58 91 43 43 – jardinsdulac@wanadoo.fr – Fax 05 58 91 34 24 A **v**
30 rm – €72/93 €72/93, € 9,50 – 20 suites – **Rest** – *(closed Friday, Saturday and Sunday except August) (dinner only)* Menu € 16/23 – Carte € 26/30
◆ Modern building between the lake and the forest. Spacious studio-type accommodation with restrained decor and modern comforts. Separate lounge and kitchenette. Small, light modern dining room (for non-smokers only) opening onto the swimming-pool.

Le Moulin de Poustagnacq
– 05 58 91 31 03 – moulindepoustagnacq@orange.fr – Fax 05 58 91 37 97 – Closed autumn half-term holidays, 20-30 December, February holidays, Tuesday lunch, Sunday dinner and Monday A **r**
Rest – Menu € 29/69 – Carte € 65/73
◆ Successfully renovated former mill on the edge of a wood. Original decoration in the dining room and a terrace beside a pond. Cuisine with a contemporary touch and regional dishes.

DEAUVILLE – **14 Calvados** – **303** M3 – **pop. 4 364** – **alt. 2 m** – **Casino AZ** – 14800 **Normandy** 32 **A3**

Paris 202 – Caen 50 – Évreux 101 – Le Havre 44 – Lisieux 30 – Rouen 90
Deauville-St-Gatien: 02 31 65 65 65, by ②: 8 km BY.
Office de tourisme, place de la Mairie 02 31 14 40 00, Fax 02 31 88 78 88
New Golf de Deauville, South: 3 km by D 278, 02 31 14 24 24 ;
de l'Amirauté Tourgéville Route Départementale 278, South: 4 km by D 278, 02 31 14 42 00 ;
de Saint-Gatien Saint-Gatien-des-Bois Le Mont Saint Jean, East: 10 km by D 74, 02 31 65 19 99.
Mont Canisy★ 5 km by ④ then 20 mn.
La corniche normande★★ - La côte fleurie★★

Plan on next page

DEAUVILLE

Blanc (R. E.) . . . . AZ 4
Colas (R. E.) . . . . AZ 5
Fossorier (R. R.) . . . . ABZ 8
Fracasse (R. A.) . . . . AZ
Gambetta (R.) . . . . BY 9
Gaulle (Av. Gén.-de) . . . . AZ 10
Gontaut-Biron (R.) . . . . AYZ 13
Hoche (R.) . . . . AYZ 20
Le-Hoc (R. D.) . . . . BZ 24
Laplace (R.) . . . . AZ 23
Le Marois (R.) . . . . AZ 25
Mirabeau (R.) . . . . BY 26
Morny (Pl. de) . . . . BZ 28
République (Av. de la) . . . . ABZ

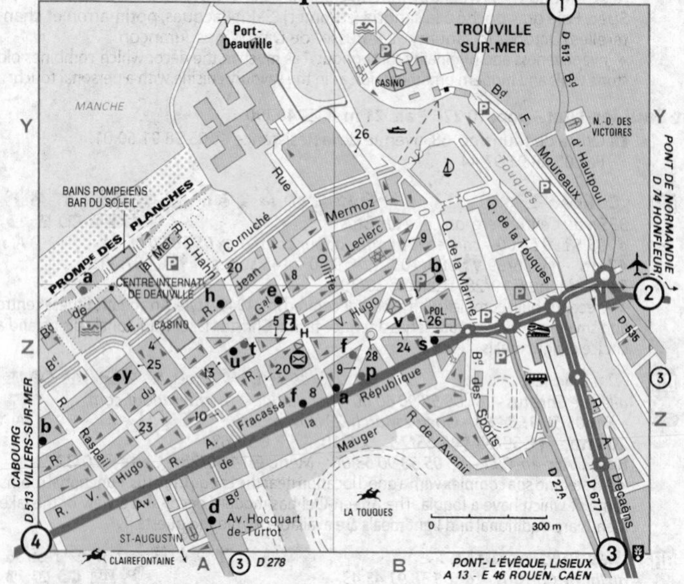

Normandy-Barrière
rm, rest,

38 r. J. Mermoz – ✆ 02 31 98 66 22 – normandy@lucienbarriere.com – Fax 02 31 98 66 23
VISA AE
AZ **h**

259 rm – €292/726 €292/726, €24 – 31 suites

Rest *La Belle Époque* – Menu €48/64 bi – Carte €62/84

◆ The Anglo-Norman manor appearance of this luxury hotel designed in 1912 has become a symbol of the resort. Spacious, well-kept rooms and an excellent fitness centre. A Belle Époque style restaurant and tables laid in the pleasant Normandy courtyard in summer.

Royal-Barrière
rm, rest,

bd E. Cornuché – ✆ 02 31 98 66 33 – royal@lucienbarriere.com – Fax 02 31 98 66 34 – Open March-October
P VISA AE
AZ **y**

236 rm – €255/890 €255/890, €24 – 16 suites

Rest *L'Etrier* – *(dinner only except Saturday and Sunday)* Menu €62/92 – Carte €79/125

Rest *Côté Royal* – *(dinner only except Saturday, Sunday and public holidays)* Menu €50 – Carte €55/93

Spec. Lisette roulée cuite dans un bouillon et petit sauté de cuisse de grenouilles. Bar sauvage à la peau croustillante, tapenade de tomate et rhubarbe. Millefeuille gourmand.

◆ Imposing 1900 building popular with the jet set and film stars. Luxuriously appointed rooms, some with a view of the English Channel. The Étrier provides a cosy atmosphere and delicious modern cuisine. Luxury hotel atmosphere at the Côté Royal.

L'Augeval without rest
VISA AE

15 av. Hocquart de Turtot – ✆ 02 31 81 13 18 – info@augeval.com – Fax 02 31 81 00 40
AZ **d**

40 rm – €68/242 €95/242, €13 – 2 suites

◆ This attractively restored manor house is near the race course and stud farms. Quiet atmosphere and restrained decor in the rooms.

Le Trophée without rest
81 r. Gén. Leclerc – ☎ 02 31 88 45 86 – information@letrophee.com – Fax 02 31 88 07 94 AZ **u**
35 rm – †€ 59/99 ††€ 64/144, ☕ € 11
◆ All the rooms in this hotel have been carefully renovated. Some have a balneotherapy bathtub, others a balcony. Here and there one finds colonial-type furnishings. Small sauna and Turkish baths.

Continental without rest
1 r. Désiré Le Hoc – ☎ 02 31 88 21 06 – info@hotel-continental-deauville.com – Fax 02 31 98 93 67 – Closed 12 November-19 December BZ **s**
42 rm – †€ 57/84 ††€ 57/96, ☕ € 8,50
◆ This hotel right in the centre of the resort has been renovated from top to toe. The rooms are spacious, fresh and simply furnished. Welcoming lounge and breakfast room.

Mercure Deauville Hôtel du Yacht Club without rest
2 r. Breney – ☎ 02 31 87 30 00 – h2876@accor.com – Fax 02 31 87 05 80 – Closed 6 January-6 February BY **b**
53 rm – †€ 84/166 ††€ 90/172, ☕ € 14
◆ A recently built hotel with freshly renovated functional rooms. Their balconies either overlook the sailing boats moored in the marina or the public gardens. Hearty breakfasts.

Marie-Anne without rest
142 av. République – ☎ 02 31 88 35 32 – info@hotelmarieanne.com – Fax 02 31 81 46 31 AZ **f**
25 rm – †€ 100/250 ††€ 100/250, ☕ € 11
◆ A pretty villa popular for its central location close to all the facilities in the resort. In 2006, half the rooms were renovated and a new garden created.

Villa Joséphine without rest
23 r. Villas – ☎ 02 31 14 18 00 – villajosephine@wanadoo.fr – Fax 02 31 14 18 10 – Closed 5-15 January AZ **b**
9 rm ☕ – †€ 130/165 ††€ 155/380
◆ Charming listed Norman villa (19C) set in a beautiful garden. Everything here is cosy and delicate (pastel colours, period furniture, drapes, family portraits...).

Le Chantilly without rest
120 av. République – ☎ 02 31 88 79 75 – hchantilly@orange.fr – Fax 02 31 88 41 29 – Closed 3-20 January BZ **a**
17 rm – †€ 62/95 ††€ 82/115, ☕ € 8,50
◆ The hotel is a stone's throw from the Touques race course. The spruce colourful rooms have all been refurbished, and the quieter ones give onto the patio.

Hélios without rest
10 r. Fossorier – ☎ 02 31 14 46 46 – hotelhelios@wanadoo.fr – Fax 02 31 88 53 87 – Closed 9-22 January AZ **e**
43 rm – †€ 65/80 ††€ 76/80, ☕ € 8 – 1 suite
◆ A convenient location in the centre of the renowned seaside resort on the Côte Fleurie. Discreet rooms, recently redecorated with split level accommodation. Small swimming pool.

XXX **Ciro's**
prom. Planches – ☎ 02 31 14 31 31 – rpapoz@lucienbarriere.com – Fax 02 31 88 32 02 – Closed February and Sunday dinner-Friday lunch except school holidays AZ **a**
Rest – Menu € 39 (weekdays)/85 – Carte € 48/98
◆ Pavilion overlooking the famous boardwalk. Quiet atmosphere in the dining room facing the English Channel and serving seafood; a chic venue popular with the famous.

XX **Le Spinnaker**
52 r. Mirabeau – ☎ 02 31 88 24 40 – Fax 02 31 88 43 58 – Closed 23-30 June, 17-29 November, January, Monday and Tuesday BZ **v**
Rest – Menu € 32/47 – Carte € 51/80
◆ This is one spinnaker that won't win you the regatta but it will take you into a pretty contemporary setting where seafood dishes and spit-roast meat are served.

La Flambée

81 r. Général Leclerc – ✆ 02 31 88 28 46 – restaurant.laflambee@wanadoo.fr – Fax 02 31 87 50 27 – Closed 1 - 15 Jan. AZ **t**

Rest – Menu € 26/48 – Carte € 39/72

◆ A cheerful fire in the large fireplace where grills are prepared in front of you. Other choices include traditional dishes and lobster from the tank. Brasserie decor.

Le Garage

118 bis av. République – ✆ 02 31 87 25 25 – Fax 02 31 87 38 37 – Closed 22 December-12 January BZ **p**

Rest – Menu € 18/29 – Carte € 24/59

◆ The former garage still has a car fresco. Brasserie-style restaurant decorated with photographs of stars. The menu is based on seafood.

in Touques **2,5 km by ③ – pop. 3 500 – alt. 10 m – ✉ 14800**

Office de tourisme, place Lemercier ✆ 02 31 88 70 93

Les Landiers

90 r. Louvel et Brière – ✆ 02 31 87 41 08 – nycgerard@hotmail.com – Fax 02 31 81 90 31 – Closed 14-18 April, 6-17 October, 9-13 February, Thursday lunch, Sunday dinner and Wednesday

Rest – Menu € 20/45

◆ Behind the typical Normandy-style timbered façade are two charming dining rooms where exposed beams and a fireplace add a pleasant rural touch. Modern cuisine.

L'Orangeraie

12 quai Monrival – ✆ 02 31 81 47 81 – isabelle.camillieri@wanadoo.fr – Closed 17-30 November, 6-15 February, Thursday during term time and Wednesday

Rest – Menu € 26/39 – Carte € 38/104

◆ The rustic atmosphere provided by the whitewashed walls and half-timbers combines well with the elegant table settings. Modern cuisine. Exotic wood terrace.

in Canapville **6 km by ③ – pop. 222 – alt. 10 m – ✉ 14800**

Le Mont d'Auge without rest

by D 279 and secondary road, St-Gatien road – ✆ 02 31 64 95 17 – zeniewski@hotmail.com

4 rm – †€ 90/130 ††€ 110/130

◆ This fine Normandy mansion is bathed in the peace of the Deauville countryside. Rustic-style rooms; the largest one, with living room and mini terrace, is ideal for family accommodation.

Auberge du Vieux Tour

on D 677 – ✆ 02 31 65 21 80 – le.vieux.tour@free.fr – Fax 02 31 65 03 75 – Closed 1st-9 July, Christmas holidays, February holidays, Sunday dinner, Monday dinner, Tuesday dinner and Wednesday except 14 July-31 August

Rest – Menu € 23 (weekdays)/57 – Carte € 33/75

◆ This thatched-roof inn stands beside the main road but the stylish dining room (with rafters, salmon-tinted walls, paintings, red floor tiles) and the terrace on the garden side are peaceful.

in New Golf **3 km South by D 278** - BAZ – ✉ **14800 Deauville**

Du Golf-Barrière ≤ Deauville countryside, rm, rest,

– ✆ 02 31 14 24 00 – hoteldugolfdeauville@lucienbarriere.com – Fax 02 31 14 24 01 – Closed from mid November-end December

178 rm – †€ 172/545 ††€ 172/545, € 22 – 9 suites

Rest *Le Lassay* – *(dinner only)* Menu € 30 (weekdays), € 38/55 – Carte € 51/68

Rest *Le Club House* – *✆ 02 31 14 24 23 (lunch only)* Menu (€ 20), € 25 – Carte € 28/60

◆ Art Deco hotel on Mount Canisy with a view over the sea and countryside, surrounded by a golf course. Spacious rooms that are gradually being renovated. Elegant Thirties decor and classic cuisine at the Pommeraie. Buffet-style meals are served at the Club House.

South 6 km by D 278 and chemin de l'Orgueil – ✉ 14800 Deauville

Hostellerie de Tourgéville
– ✆ 02 31 14 48 68
– *info@hostellerie-de-tourgeville.fr – Fax 02 31 14 48 69*
– *Closed 8 February-2 March and lunch except Sunday and public holidays*
20 rm – †€ 130/185 ††€ 130/185, ☐ € 16 – 6 suites – ½ P € 115/143
Rest – Menu (€ 29), € 39/56 – Carte € 48/70
♦ A delightful Norman manor house in the heart of the Auge woodland. The split or triple-level rooms are named after film stars and each has its own decoration theme (golf, horses, etc.). The delightful country-style dining room gives onto an attractive patio.

at golf de l'Amirauté 7 km South by D 278 – ✉ 14800 Deauville

Les Chaumes
– ✆ *02 31 14 42 00 – golf@amiraute.com – Fax 02 31 88 32 00*
Rest – *(lunch only)* Menu € 19/39 – Carte € 41/61
♦ Once a stud farm, now a club house restaurant with a modern setting. Panoramic views of the 27-hole golf course decorated with modern sculptures.

DECAZEVILLE – 12 Aveyron – 338 F3 – pop. 6 805 – alt. 230 m – ✉ 12300

Languedoc-Roussillon-Tarn Gorges 29 **C1**

Paris 605 – Aurillac 64 – Figeac 27 – Rodez 39 – Villefranche-de-Rouergue 39

Office de tourisme, square Jean Segalat ✆ 05 65 43 18 36, Fax 05 65 43 19 89

Moderne et Malpel
16 av. A. Bos, (behind the church) – ✆ 05 65 43 04 33 – Fax 05 65 43 17 17
24 rm – †€ 42/47 ††€ 47/60, ☐ € 6,50 – ½ P € 54 – **Rest** – *(closed Saturday, Sunday and public holidays)* Menu € 14,50/28 – Carte € 29/41
♦ Opposite the post office, practical for an overnight stay along the pilgrim trail. Family atmosphere and plainly decorated rooms. Light, half-modern, half-rustic dining room serving robust, regional cuisine.

DECIZE – 58 Nièvre – 319 D11 – pop. 6 456 – alt. 197 m – ✉ 58300

Burgundy-Jura 7 **B3**

Paris 270 – Châtillon-en-Bazois 34 – Luzy 44 – Moulins 35 – Nevers 34

Office de tourisme, place du Champ de Foire ✆ 03 86 25 27 23, Fax 03 86 77 16 58

Le Charolais
33 bis rte Moulins – ✆ 03 86 25 22 27 – frank.rapiau@wanadoo.fr
– Fax 03 86 25 52 52 – Closed 1st-7 January, February holidays, Tuesday 15 November-15 April, Sunday dinner and Monday
Rest – Menu € 17/55 – Carte € 48/73
♦ The chef of this contemporary-styled restaurant rustles up dishes in keeping with modern tastes. In fine weather, grilled and plancha dishes are served on the terrace.

LA DÉFENSE – 92 Hauts-de-Seine – 311 J2 – 101 14 – see Paris, Area

DELME – 57 Moselle – 307 J5 – pop. 728 – alt. 220 m – ✉ 57590 27 C2

Paris 364 – Château-Salins 12 – Metz 33 – Nancy 36 – Pont-à-Mousson 27 – St-Avold 43

Syndicat d'initiative, 33, rue Raymond Poincaré ✆ 03 87 01 37 19, Fax 03 87 01 43 14

A la XIIe Borne rest,
6 pl. République – ✆ 03 87 01 30 18 – XIIborne@wanadoo.fr – Fax 03 87 01 38 39
– Closed Sunday dinner and Monday
15 rm – †€ 53/70 ††€ 53/70, ☐ € 7,50 – ½ P € 54 – **Rest** – Menu € 20 (weekdays)/46 – Carte € 44/67
♦ This long building with its pastel-tinted facade and white shutters overlooking the main square is run by four brothers. The rooms are functional and very effectively soundproofed. Traditional cuisine served in a modern setting with restrained decor; calf's head is one of the specialities.

DERCHIGNY – 76 Seine-Maritime – 304 H2 – pop. 416 – alt. 100 m – ✉ 76370
33 **D1**

Paris 206 – Barentin 64 – Dieppe 10 – Rouen 74

Manoir de Graincourt

10 pl. Ludovic Panel – ✆ 02 35 84 12 88 – contact@manoir-de-graincourt.fr – Fax 02 35 84 12 88

5 rm – €78/100 €78/119 – **Table d'hôte** – Menu €32 bi

◆ This distinctive 19C manor and its annexe, once a convent, are adjacent to the church. Stylish rooms open onto a well-kept cloister-type garden. Reading room and a billiard room. Table d'hôte in the attractive kitchen (reservation required).

DESCARTES – 37 Indre-et-Loire – 317 N7 – pop. 4 019 – alt. 50 m – ✉ 37160
Châteaux of the Loire 11 **B3**

Paris 292 – Châteauroux 94 – Châtellerault 24 – Chinon 51 – Loches 32 – Tours 59

Office de tourisme, place Blaise Pascal ✆ 02 47 92 42 20, Fax 02 47 59 72 20

Moderne with rm

15 r. Descartes – ✆ 02 47 59 72 11 – hotel.moderne.ft@wanadoo.fr – Fax 02 47 92 44 90 – Closed Monday lunch mid April-October, Friday lunch and Saturday lunch November-mid April and Sunday dinner

11 rm – €39 €45, €6,50 – ½ P €42 – **Rest** – Menu €15/34 – Carte €33/43

◆ A rustic style restaurant near the house where René Descartes was born, which is now a museum. In summer, tables are laid out on the terrace in the small garden. Traditional dishes.

Auberge de Lilette

21 r. Robert-Lecomte, west: 3 km on D 58 and D5 – ✆ 02 47 59 72 22 – auberge.lilette@wanadoo.fr – Fax 02 47 92 93 93 – Closed Sunday dinner off season and Friday dinner

Rest – Menu €10,50 bi (weekday lunch), €16/35 – Carte €28/40

◆ A simple dining area accessible from the village bar-tobacconist. Serves mostly regional dishes at well spaced out tables.

DESVRES – 62 Pas-de-Calais – 301 E3 – pop. 5 205 – alt. 98 m – ✉ 62240

Paris 263 – Calais 40 – Arras 98 – Boulogne 19 30 **A2**

Syndicat d'initiative, 25, rue des Potiers ✆ 03 21 92 09 09

Ferme du Moulin aux Draps without rest

rte Crémarest, 1.5 km by D 254[E] – ✆ 03 21 10 69 59 – moulinauxdraps@orange.fr – Fax 03 21 87 14 56 – Closed 29 December-19 January

20 rm – €75 €85/115, €12

◆ This appealing hotel, nestling between the forest and the meadows, has been rebuilt on the same lines as the old family farmhouse. Pleasant rooms and covered pool in the inner courtyard.

LES DEUX-ALPES (Alpes de Mont-de-Lans et de Vénosc) – 38 Isère – 333 J7 – Winter sports : 1 650/3 600 m 7 49 – ✉ 38860 French Alps

Paris 640 – Le Bourg-d'Oisans 26 – Grenoble 78 45 **C2**

Office de tourisme, 4, place Deux-Alpes ✆ 04 76 79 22 00, Fax 04 76 79 01 38

des Deux-Alpes Rue des Vikings, East: 2 km, ✆ 04 76 80 52 89.

Viewpoints: de la Croix★, des Cîmes★ - Croisière Blanche★★★.

Plan on next page

Chalet Mounier

– ✆ 04 76 80 56 90 – doc@chalet-mounier.com – Fax 04 76 79 56 51 – Open from mid June to beg. September, from December to beg. May n

42 rm – €85/174 €120/250, €13 – 4 suites – ½ P €87/160

Rest – *(dinner only) (residents only)*

Rest *Le P'tit Polyte* – *(dinner only except Sunday and public holidays)* Menu (€36), €49/59

◆ This alpine chalet from 1879 sports a distinctive contemporary look: super cosy interior of wood and warm colours in the sitting room and (gradually redone) rooms. Wellness centre. Inventive food is served in the attractive dining room overlooking the mountain.

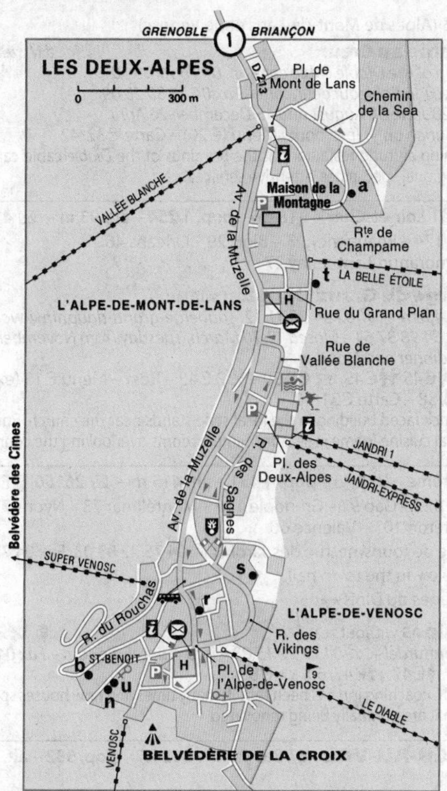

Souleil'Or

10 r. Grand Plan – ✆ 04 76 79 24 69 – hotel.le.souleil.or@wanadoo.fr – Fax 04 76 79 20 64 – Open 17 June-31 August and 2 December-20 April **t**

42 rm – †€ 103/122 ††€ 134/176, ☕ € 14 – ½ P € 88/135 – **Rest** – *(dinner only)* Menu € 33

◆ Chalet style hotel with a wooden façade. Gradually renovated rooms with balconies. Comfortable and impeccably looked after establishment. Sauna and steam bath. A restaurant with a terrace by the pool. Traditional dishes and Dauphinois specialities.

Les Mélèzes

– ✆ 04 76 80 50 50 – reservation@hotelmelezes.com – Fax 04 76 79 20 70 – Open 15 December-26 April **s**

34 rm – †€ 61/70 ††€ 95/120, ☕ € 10 – 3 suites – ½ P € 78/111 – **Rest** – *(open 20 December-26 April)* Menu € 33/74

◆ At the foot of the ski slopes, a pretty, welcoming hotel, gradually being redone in a cosy chalet style. Most rooms are south facing. Pleasant sitting rooms, fitness centre, sauna and Jacuzzi. Quite simple food at lunchtime and a set menu in the evening (mountain menu on Tuesdays).

Serre-Palas without rest

13 pl. de l'Alpe de Venosc – ✆ 04 76 80 56 33 – limounier@wanadoo.fr – Fax 04 76 79 04 36 – Open mid June-end August, 24 October-3 November and December-April **u**

24 rm ☕ – †€ 28/67 ††€ 40/140

◆ Fifty metres from the Venosc ski lift. Unpretentious rooms (except one, prettily redone in a chalet style), some of which have balconies with views over the Écrins national park.

Le Diable au Cœur La Muzelle, VISA

at the top of the Diable cable car – 04 76 79 99 50 – contact@lediableaucoeur.com – Fax 04 76 80 23 09 – Open 28 June-30 August and 15 December-26 April

Rest – *(lunch only) (pre-book)* Menu (€ 20) – Carte € 32/42

◆ Charming altitude restaurant at the terminus of the *Diable* cable car (2400m). Wood decor, regional specialities, attentive service.

DHUIZON – 41 Loir-et-Cher – 318 G6 – pop. 1 254 – alt. 93 m – ✉ 41220

Paris 174 – Beaugency 23 – Blois 29 – Orléans 46 – Romorantin-Lanthenay 27 12 **C2**

Auberge du Grand Dauphin with rm P VISA

17 pl. St.-Pierre – 02 54 98 31 12 – auberge-grand-dauphin@wanadoo.fr – Fax 02 54 98 37 64 – Closed 1st-20 March, Tuesday from November to March, Sunday dinner and Monday

9 rm – €45 €45, ☕ €7,50 – ½ P €45 – **Rest** – Menu €15 (except Sunday)/38 – Carte €31/50

◆ This brick faced building in the local style stands near the church. Rustic dining room, traditional cuisine (game in season). Simple rooms overlooking the courtyard.

DIE – 26 Drôme – 332 F5 – pop. 4 451 – alt. 415 m – ✉ 26150 French Alps

Paris 623 – Gap 92 – Grenoble 110 – Montélimar 73 – Nyons 77 – Sisteron 103 – Valence 66 44 **B3**

Office de tourisme, rue des Jardins 04 75 22 03 03, Fax 04 75 22 40 46

Mosaic★ in the town hall.

Paysages du Diois★★.

Des Alpes without rest VISA AE

87 r. C. Buffardel – 04 75 22 15 83 – info@hotel-die.com – Fax 04 75 22 09 39

24 rm – €47 €47/60, ☕ €8

◆ This 14C coaching inn has been rebuilt many times and now houses spacious, well-kept rooms that are gradually being renovated.

DIEFFENBACH-AU-VAL – 67 Bas-Rhin – 315 H7 – pop. 582 – alt. 350 m – ✉ 67220 2 **C1**

Paris 538 – Colmar 33 – Lahr 65 – Strasbourg 53

La Romance without rest AC P

17 r. de Neuve-Église – 03 88 85 67 09 – corinne@la-romance.net – Fax 03 88 57 61 58

6 rm ☕ – €83/93 €88/98

◆ This regional-style residence in the upper part of the town offers quiet, colourfully furnished rooms. Two of the rooms have a terrace with views of the valley.

La Maison Fleurie without rest P

19 r. de Neuve-Église – 03 88 85 60 48 – engel-thierry@wanadoo.fr – Fax 03 88 85 60 48

4 rm ☕ – €45 €56/72

◆ The neat, comfortable rooms in this hillside property command fine views. Breakfast, composed of kouglof, homemade jams and honey, is a real feast.

DIEFFENTHAL – 67 Bas-Rhin – 315 I7 – pop. 226 – alt. 185 m – ✉ 67650 2 **C1**

Paris 441 – Lunéville 100 – St-Dié 45 – Sélestat 7 – Strasbourg 54

Le Verger des Châteaux rm, P VISA

2 rte Romaine – 03 88 92 49 13 – verger-des-chateaux@villes-et-vignoble.com – Fax 03 88 92 40 99

32 rm – €58/64 €58/64, ☕ €8 – ½ P €58 – **Rest** – *(closed Monday lunch)* Menu €20/30 – Carte €30/52

◆ This imposing building stands by the edge of the famous Alsace vineyards. The somewhat bare rooms are large, with modern furniture. Spacious dining room with restrained decor and a pleasant view overlooking the countryside; traditional food. Winstub with colourful decor.

DIEFMATTEN – 68 Haut-Rhin – 315 G10 – pop. 251 – alt. 300 m – ✉ 68780

Paris 450 – Belfort 25 – Colmar 48 – Mulhouse 21 – Thann 15 1 **A3**

XXX **Auberge du Cheval Blanc** with rm rest, P VISA MC AE
17 r. Hecken – ☎ 03 89 26 91 08 – patrick@auchevalblanc.fr – Fax 03 89 26 92 28
8 rm – †€ 54/80 ††€ 54/120, ☕ € 8 – ½ P € 85
Rest – *(closed 15-31 July, 5-15 January, Monday and Tuesday except holidays)*
Menu € 23 bi (weekday lunch), € 28/72 – Carte € 47/69
♦ 19C Alsatian house, redone in a contemporary spirit but without losing its authentic country soul. Splendid view of the park from the rear terrace. Five brand new pleasant apartments; the rooms are older.

DIENNE – 15 Cantal – 330 E4 – pop. 293 – alt. 1 053 m – ✉ 15300

Auvergne 5 **B3**

Paris 529 – Allanche 21 – Aurillac 54 – Condat 30 – Mauriac 52 – Murat 10 – St-Flour 34

<★★ du Pas de Peyrol.

X **Poste** with rm < P VISA MC
– ☎ 04 71 20 80 40 – Fax 04 71 20 82 75 – Closed 15 November-1st February
10 rm – †€ 42/45 ††€ 42/45, ☕ € 8 – ½ P € 43/45
Rest – *(dinner only)* Menu € 18/20
♦ This stone-built former post house has been extending a warm welcome in the Auvergne spirit since 1916; homegrown garden produce and small terrace.

DIEPPE – 76 Seine-Maritime – 304 G2 – pop. 34 653 – alt. 6 m – Casino Municipal AY – ✉ 76200 Normandy 33 **D1**

Paris 197 – Abbeville 68 – Caen 176 – Le Havre 111 – Rouen 66

Syndicat d'initiative, pont Jehan Ango ☎ 02 32 14 40 60, Fax 02 32 14 40 61

de Dieppe-Pourville Route de Pourville, West: 2 km by D 74, ☎ 02 35 84 25 05.

St-Jacques church ★ - N.-D.-de-Bon-Secours chapel <★ - Château ★ museum (Dieppe ivory★).

Plan on next page

Aguado without rest < VISA MC AE
30 bd Verdun – ☎ 02 35 84 27 00 – chris.bert@tiscali.fr – Fax 02 35 06 17 61
56 rm – †€ 55/95 ††€ 60/115, ☕ € 10 BY **s**
♦ The building is on a street leading to the seafront. The rooms on the promenade side or overlooking the town and harbour have efficient soundproofing.

De l'Europe without rest < VISA MC
63 bd Verdun – ☎ 02 32 90 19 19 – chris.bert@tiscali.fr – Fax 02 32 90 19 00
60 rm – †€ 55/88 ††€ 65/106, ☕ € 9 BY **t**
♦ The hotel facade is in wood and concrete. Bright, spacious rooms furnished in wickerwork and facing towards the English Channel. Quiet atmosphere in the bar popular with the locals.

La Présidence < rest, VISA MC AE
1 bd Verdun – ☎ 02 35 84 31 31 – contact@hotel-la-presidence.com – Fax 02 35 84 86 70 AY **v**
89 rm – †€ 65/90 ††€ 70/140, ☕ € 11 – ½ P € 70/80 – **Rest** – Menu € 24/46 – Carte € 30/53
♦ Reserve a renovated room in this 1970s hotel ideally located close to the beach and the castle museum. The large bay windows on this top-floor restaurant provide a spectacular view of the English Channel.

La Villa Florida without rest P
24 chemin du Golf, via D 75 – ☎ 02 35 84 40 37 – adn@lavillaflorida.com – Fax 01 72 74 33 76
4 rm ☕ – †€ 70/78 ††€ 70/78
♦ This Bed & Breakfast with an oriental atmosphere is a successful conversion of a fine modern architect's house in the residential area. Pleasant garden giving onto the golf course.

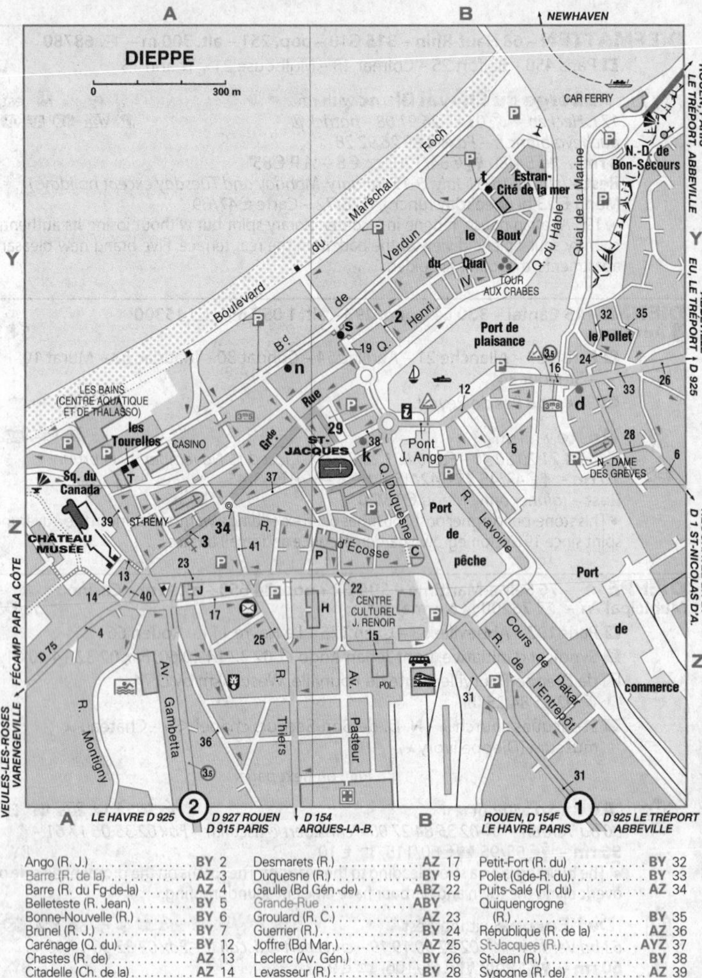

Ango (R. J.)	BY	2	Desmarets (R.)	AZ	17	Petit-Fort (R. du)	BY	32
Barre (R. de la)	AZ	3	Duquesne (R.)	BY	19	Polet (Gde-R. du)	BY	33
Barre (R. du Fg-de-la)	AZ	4	Gaulle (Bd Gén.-de)	ABZ	22	Puits-Salé (Pl. du)	AZ	34
Belleteste (R. Jean)	BY	5	Grande-Rue	ABY		Quiquengrogne (R.)	BY	35
Bonne-Nouvelle (R.)	BY	6	Groulard (R. C.)	AZ	23	République (R. de la)	AZ	36
Brunel (R. J.)	BY	7	Guerrier (R.)	BY	24	St-Jacques (R.)	AYZ	37
Carénage (Q. du)	BY	12	Joffre (Bd Mar.)	AZ	25	St-Jean (R.)	BY	38
Chastes (R. de)	AZ	13	Leclerc (Av. Gén.)	BY	26	Sygogne (R. de)	AZ	39
Citadelle (Ch. de la)	AZ	14	Levasseur (R.)	BY	28	Toustain (R.)	AZ	40
Clemenceau (Bd G.)	BZ	15	Nationale (Pl.)	BY	29	Victor-Hugo (R.)	AZ	41
Colbert (Pont)	BY	16	Normandie-Sussex (Av.)	BZ	31			

Villa des Capucins without rest

11 r. des Capucins – ✆ 02 35 82 16 52 – villa.des.capucins@wanadoo.fr – Fax 02 32 90 97 52

5 rm – €60 €70

◆ This stylish guesthouse in the Pollet district makes good use of the old priory's outbuildings. Attractive rooms overlooking an enclosed garden. Dining room-kitchen in the old style.

Les Voiles d'Or

2 chemin de la Falaise, near the N.-D.-de-Bon-Secours chapel – ✆ 02 35 84 16 84 – Closed 17 November-3 December, Sunday dinner, Monday and Tuesday

Rest – *(number of covers limited, pre-book)* Menu € 30 bi (weekday lunch)/48 – Carte € 50/58

◆ Restaurant perched on the Pollet cliff side, not far from the chapel of Notre-Dame de Bon-Secours and the signal station. Welcoming, colourful interior with designer furnishings. Cuisine in keeping with current taste.

XX **La Marmite Dieppoise** VISA MC

8 r. St-Jean – ✆ 02 35 84 24 26 – Fax 02 35 84 31 12 – Closed 20 June-3 July, 21 November-8 December, 15-28 February, Thursday dinner from September to June, Sunday dinner and Monday BY **k**

Rest – Menu € 30/46 – Carte € 31/56

♦ Restaurant near the fishing port where the famous "marmite dieppoise" dish takes pride of place. The decor is more distinctive on the upper floor than on the lower. Dining by candlelight on Fridays and Saturdays.

X **Bistrot du Pollet** VISA MC

23 r. Tête de Boeuf – ✆ 02 35 84 68 57 – Closed 20-29 April, 17 August-1st September-8 January, Sunday and Monday BY **e**

Rest – *(number of covers limited, pre-book)* Carte € 25/39

♦ This bistro on Pollet port island is famous for its convivial atmosphere, hearty cuisine based on freshly-caught fish, and its naval decor with old-world charm.

in Vertus **3.5 km by ② and D 927 – ✉ 76550 St-Aubin-sur-Scie**

XXX **La Bucherie** P VISA MC

– ✆ 02 35 84 83 10 – Fax 02 35 84 83 10 – Closed Sunday dinner, Tuesday dinner and Monday

Rest – Menu € 19 (weekdays)/51 – Carte € 44/69

♦ Regional-style building near the main road with a garden planted with trees. Two colourful, modern dining rooms, one with an open fireplace. Choice of traditional dishes and a set menu.

in Offranville **6 km by ②, D 927 and D 54 – pop. 3 470 – alt. 80 m – ✉ 76550**

XX **Le Colombier** VISA MC

r. Loucheur, parc du Colombier – ✆ 02 35 85 48 50 – lecourski@wanadoo.fr – Fax 02 35 83 76 87 – Closed 20 October-5 November, 23 February-11 March, Tuesday dinner except from 2 July to 27 August, Sunday dinner and Wednesday

Rest – Menu € 25/61

♦ This venerable Normandy building dating back to 1509 is said to be the oldest in the town. The dining room has yellow walls, restored beams, a fine open fireplace and an old-fashioned spit-turning mechanism. Cuisine in keeping with current taste.

in Pourville-sur-Mer **5 km West by D 75** AZ **– ✉ 76550 Hautot-sur-Mer**

XX **Le Trou Normand** VISA MC

128 r. des Verts Bois – ✆ 02 35 84 59 84 – Fax 02 35 40 29 41 – Closed 16 August-4 September, 22 December-7 January, Sunday except lunch Easter-September and Wednesday

Rest – Menu € 23/35 – Carte € 39/53

♦ The inn is near the beach where in 1942 the Canadians landed in Operation Jubilee. Rustic decor and menus varying according to the season, based on seafood and local produce.

DIEULEFIT – 26 Drôme – 332 D6 – pop. 3 096 – alt. 366 m – ✉ 26220

Lyon - Rhone Valley 44 **B3**

Paris 614 – Crest 30 – Montélimar 29 – Nyons 30 – Orange 58 – Valence 57

Office de tourisme, 1, place Abbé Magnet ✆ 04 75 46 42 49, Fax 04 75 46 36 48

XX **Le Relais du Serre** with rm P VISA MC AE

rte de Nyons , 3 km on D 538 – ✆ 04 75 46 43 45 – le-relais-du-serre@orange.fr – Fax 04 75 46 40 98 – Closed 5-20 January, Sunday dinner and Monday from September to May

7 rm – †€ 40/60 ††€ 50/70, ☕ € 8 – ½ P € 60/70

Rest – Menu € 13 (weekday lunch), € 22/36 – Carte € 31/52

♦ Pleasant building with a renovated facade on the road to the Lez valley. Colourful dining room embellished by flowers and paintings. Traditional cuisine and game in season.

in Poët-Laval 5 km West by D 540 – pop. 809 – alt. 311 m – ✉ 26160

Site★.

Les Hospitaliers

– ✆ 04 75 46 22 32 – contact@hotel-les-hospitaliers.com – Fax 04 75 46 49 99
– Open 15 March-9 November

20 rm – €75/140 €75/160, ☕ €15

Rest – *(closed Mon. and Tues. out of season)* Menu (€26), €39/53
– Carte €59/75

◆ Rooms in drystone buildings in the old village, and a swimming pool overlooking the valley. Difficult for these Hospitallers to set out on a crusade again! Cuisine with a contemporary touch served in a dining room full of character or on the terrace commanding a panoramic view.

North 9 km by D 538, D 110 and D 245 - ✉ 26460 Truinas

La Bergerie de Féline

*Les Charles – ✆ 04 75 49 12 78 – welcome@labergeriedefeline.com
– Fax 04 75 49 12 78*

5 rm ☕ – €110/200 €110/200 – **Table d'hôte** – Menu €30 bi

◆ This delightful 18C former sheepfold is now home to contemporary rooms. The perfect spot to enjoy the lovely Vercors countryside. Splendid pool, cabin and hammock in the garden. Regional dishes at the table d'hôte in setting which blends authenticity and designer-style.

DIGNE-LES-BAINS

DIGNE-LES-BAINS P – 04 Alpes-de-Haute-Provence – **334** F8 – **pop. 16 064**
– **alt. 608 m – Spa : early March-early Dec.** – ✉ **04000** French Alps 41 **C2**

Paris 744 – Aix-en-Provence 109 – Avignon 167 – Cannes 135 – Gap 89

Office de tourisme, place du Tampinet ✆ 04 92 36 62 62, Fax 04 92 32 27 24

de Digne-les-Bains 57 route du Chaffaut, by Nice road and D 12: 7 km, ✆ 04 92 30 58 00.

Musée départemental★ B M² - N.D.-du-Bourg cathedral ★ - Giant ammonite slabs★ North: 1 km by D 900^A.

≤★ of the television relay station.

Plan on next page

Le Grand Paris

*19 bd Thiers – ✆ 04 92 31 11 15 – info@hotel-grand-paris.com
– Fax 04 92 32 32 82 – Open 1st March-30 November* A **a**

16 rm – €75/105 €88/137, ☕ €17 – 4 suites – ½ P €85/120

Rest – *(closed Monday lunchtime, Tuesday lunchtime and Wednesday lunchtime in low season)* Menu (€26), €32/67 – Carte €60/92

◆ The atmosphere of old France prevails in this former convent dating back to the 17C. Some rooms have been renovated with the inclusion of modern bathrooms. Attractive, colourful dining room and shaded terrace. Traditional cuisine with an excellent choice of Côtes-du-Rhône wines.

Le Coin Fleuri

*9 bd V. Hugo – ✆ 04 92 31 04 51 – lecoinfleuri9@orange.fr
– Fax 04 92 32 55 75* B **v**

13 rm – €40/45 €43/53, ☕ €6,50 – ½ P €60/68

Rest – *(closed Sunday evening, Tuesday evening and Monday)* Menu (€13), €21/27 – Carte approx. €34

◆ The rooms in this establishment, popular with people taking the spa waters, are simple, practical and well soundproofed. Guesthouse-style restaurant with restrained Provençal decor and a large shady terrace where buffet-style meals are served in the summer.

Central without rest

*26 bd Gassendi – ✆ 04 92 31 31 91 – webmaster@lhotel-central.com
– Fax 04 92 31 49 78* A **t**

20 rm – €31 €49, ☕ €6

◆ The scrupulously kept rooms of this little hotel in the capital of the "Lavender Alps" are discreetly decorated in the style of Provence.

DIGNE-LES-BAINS

Ancienne Mairie (R. de l') .... B 8
Arès (Cours des) .... B 2
Capitoul (R.) .... B 3
Dr-Romieu (R. du) .... B 4
Gassendi (Bd) .... AB
Gaulle (Pl. Ch.-de) .... B 6
Hubac (R. de l') .... A 7
Mitan (Pl. du) .... B 10
Payan (R. du Col.) .... A 12
Pied-de-Ville (R.) .... A 13
Saint-Charles (Montée) ...... A 14
Tribunal (Cours du) .... B 15
11-Novembre 1918 (Rd-Pt du) .... A 17

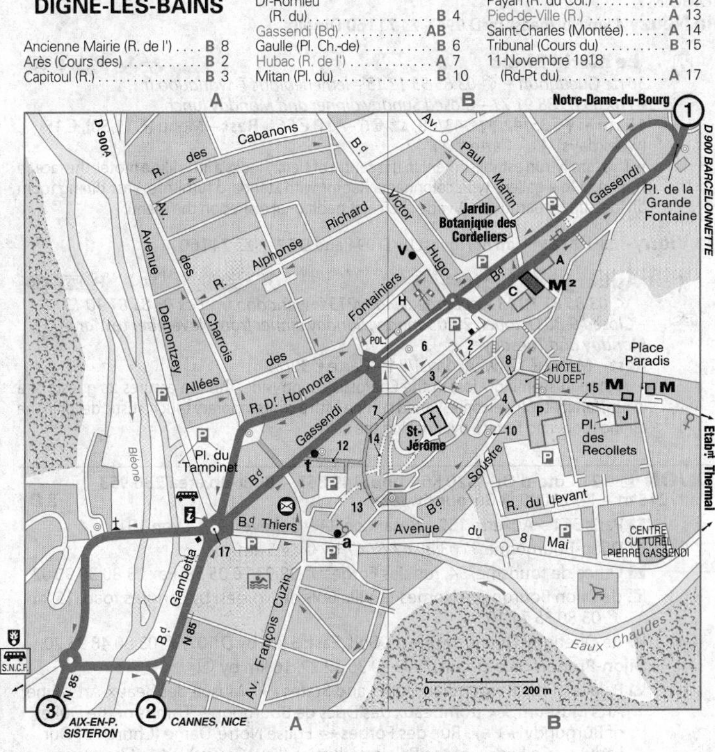

Nice road 2 km by ② and N 85 – ✉ 04000 Digne-les-Bains

Villa Gaïa rm, P VISA MC

24 rte de Nice – ☎ 04 92 31 21 60 – hotel.gaia@wanadoo.fr – Fax 04 92 31 20 12 – Open 15 April-21 October

10 rm – †€ 65/95 ††€ 95/102, ☕ € 9 – ½ P € 76/82 – **Rest** – *(closed 1st-11 July and Wednesday except 11 July-26 August) (dinner only) (resident only)* Menu € 26

◆ A friendly atmosphere in this charming mansion set amid the trees of the surrounding gardens. With lounges, library, stylish furniture and personalised rooms.

DIGOIN – 71 Saône-et-Loire – **320** D11 – **pop. 8 947** – **alt. 232 m** – ✉ **71160**

Burgundy-Jura 7 **B3**

Paris 337 – Autun 69 – Charolles 26 – Moulins 57 – Roanne 57 – Vichy 69

Office de tourisme, 8, rue Guilleminot ☎ 03 85 53 00 81, Fax 03 85 53 27 54

De la Gare with rm AC rest, P VISA MC

79 av. Gén. de Gaulle – ☎ 03 85 53 03 04 – jean-pierre.mathieu@worldonline.fr – Fax 03 85 53 14 70 – Closed 1 week in June, 5 January-6 February, Sunday dinner and Wednesday except July-August

13 rm – †€ 38/45 ††€ 46/60, ☕ € 10 – ½ P € 60/65 – **Rest** – Menu € 18 (weekdays)/62 – Carte € 37/56

◆ Traditional type menus with a touch of classicism. The decor is a blend of the Louis XIII style and that of the 1970s. Orange coloured armchairs in the lobby, and rooms with an original combination of antique furnishings.

in Neuzy 4 km Northeast by D 994 – ✉ 71160 Digoin

Le Merle Blanc

36 rte Gueugnon – ✆ 03 85 53 17 13 – lemerleblanc@wanadoo.fr – Fax 03 85 88 91 71 – Closed Sunday dinner and Monday lunch

15 rm – †€ 35/42 ††€ 43/48, ☕ € 6 – ½ P € 56 – **Rest** – Menu (€ 11,50), € 15 (weekdays)/41 – Carte € 24/42

◆ This family-run establishment in the centre of Neuzy looks a little like a motel; the facade is framed in a gallery-type colonnade. Rooms with standard furniture. Vast dining room divided up by partitions. A wide choice of traditional dishes on the menu.

in Vigny-les-Paray 9 km northeast by D 994 and D 52 – ✉ 71160

Auberge de Vigny

– ✆ 03 85 81 10 13 – aubergedevigny213@wanadoo.fr – Fax 03 85 81 10 13 – Closed 9-30 October, 2-20 January, Sunday dinner from November to March, Monday and Tuesday

Rest – Menu € 17 (weekdays)/34 – Carte € 30/37

◆ Although seemingly lost in the Charolais countryside, this inn assures its guests of a warm, family-type welcome. Varied cuisine with a contemporary touch, rustic decor in the dining room and terrace overlooking the fields.

DIJON Ⓟ – 21 Côte-d'Or – 320 K6 – pop. 149 867 – Built-up area 236 953 – alt. 245 m – ✉ 21000 Burgundy-Jura 8 **D1**

Paris 311 – Auxerre 152 – Besançon 94 – Genève 192 – Lyon 191

Dijon-Bourgogne ✆ 03 80 67 67 67 by ⑤: 4,5 km.

Office de tourisme, 34, rue des Forges ✆ 08 92 70 05 58, Fax 03 80 30 90 02

de Dijon Bourgogne Norges-la-Ville Bois de Norges, by Langres road: 15 km, ✆ 03 80 35 71 10 ;

de Quetigny Quetigny Rue du Golf, East: 5 km by D 107, ✆ 03 80 48 95 20.

Dijon-Prenois race circuit ✆ 03 80 35 32 22, 16 km by ⑧

Palace of the Burgundian Dukes and States★★ : Musée des Beaux-Arts (Fine Arts Museum)★★ (tombeaux des Ducs de Bourgogne [Tombs of the Dukes of Burgundy]★★★) - Rue des Forges★ - Eglise Notre-Dame (Church of Our Lady)★ - Ceilings★ of the Palais de Justice (Law Courts) DY **J** - Chartreuse de Champmol★ : Puits de Moïse★★★, Portail de la Chapelle★ A - Église St-Michel (St Michael's Church)★ - Jardin de l'Arquebuse★ CY - Rotonda★★ in the Cathédrale St-Bénigne (St Bénigne's Cathedral) - Musée de la Vie bourguignonne (Museum of Burgundian Life)★ DZ **M**[7] - Musée Archéologique (Museum of Archaeology)★ CY **M**[2] - Musée Magnin (Magnin Museum)★ DY **M**[5] - Jardin des Sciences (Science Garden)★ CY **M**[8].

Plans on following pages

Sofitel La Cloche rm, CY **f**

14 pl. Darcy – ✆ 03 80 30 12 32 – h1202@accor.com – Fax 03 80 30 04 15

64 rm – †€ 170/275 ††€ 200/300, ☕ € 20 – 4 suites

Rest *Les Jardins de la Cloche* – Menu € 33/43 bi – Carte € 54/82

◆ The current building only dates back to the 19C but La Cloche actually opened in 1424. Modern, partly refurbished rooms. Piano bar, internet access. At the Jardins de la Cloche the pleasantly decorated dining room has a glass roof, and there is an attractive terrace. Cuisine with a contemporary touch.

Hostellerie du Chapeau Rouge (William Frachot) CY **a**

5 r. Michelet – ✆ 03 80 50 88 88 – chapeaurouge@bourgogne.net – Fax 03 80 50 88 89

30 rm – †€ 132/150 ††€ 143/159, ☕ € 16 – 2 suites

Rest – *(closed 2-16 January)* Menu € 40 (lunch), € 48/100 – Carte € 66/83

Spec. Langue de veau et langoustine. Le thon rouge. Cochon noir de Bigorre.
Wines Chablis, Pernand Vergelesses.

◆ This elegant hostelry opened in 1863. Pleasant, individually decorated rooms and a winter garden-style lounge with a glass roof. Recently renovated restaurant serving creative cuisine. Good selection of wines.

DIJON

Rue	Carré	N°
Aiguillottes (Bd des)	A	2
Albert-1er (Av.)	A	
Allobroges (Bd des)	A	3
Auxonne (R. d')	B	
Bachelard (Bd Gaston)	A	4
Bellevue (R. de)	A	5
Bertin (Av. J.B.)	B	6
Bourroches (Bd des)	A	
Briand (Av. A.)	B	8
Camus (Av. Albert)	B	12
Castel (Bd du)	A	13
Champollion (Av.)	B	15
Chanoine-Bardy (Imp.)	B	16
Chanoine-Kir (Bd)	A	17
Chateaubriand (R. de)	B	19
Chevreul (R.)	AB	
Chèvre-Morte (Bd de)	A	20
Chicago (Bd de)	B	
Churchill (Bd W.)	B	24
Clomiers (Bd des)	A	26
Concorde (Av. de la)	B	28
Cracovie (R. de)	B	
Dijon (R. de)	A	
Dr-Petitjean (Bd du)	B	
Doumer (Bd Paul)	B	
Drapeau (Av. du)	B	
Dumont (R. Ch.)	AB	
Eiffel (Av. G.)	A	
Einstein (Av. Albert)	A	36
Europe (Bd de l')	B	38
Europe (Rd-Pt de l')	B	40
Faubourg-St-Martin (R. du)	A	
Fauconnet (R. Gén.)	AB	42
Fontaine-des-Suisses (Bd)	B	44
Fontaine-lès-Dijon (R.)	A	43
France-Libre (Pl. de la)	AB	45
Gabriel (Bd)	B	46
Gallieni (Bd Mar.)	AB	48
Gaulle (Crs Gén.-de)	B	50
Gorgets (Bd des)	A	52
Gray (R. de)	B	
Jeanne-d'Arc (Bd)	B	55
Jean-Jaurès (Av.)	A	
Joffre (Bd Mar.)	B	
Jouvence (R. de)	A	
Kennedy (Bd J.)	A	56
Langres (Av. de)	B	
Longvic (R. de)	B	
Magenta (R.)	B	58
Maillard (Bd)	A	60
Malines (R. de)	B	
Mansard (Bd)	B	62
Mayence (R. de)	B	
Mirande (R. de)	B	
Mont-Blanc (Av. du)	B	65
Moulins (R. des)	A	
Moulin (R. Jean)	B	63
Nation (Rd-Pt de la)	B	66
Orfèvres (R. des)	A	68
Ouest (Bd de l')	A	69
Parc (Cours du)	B	70
Pascal (Bd)	B	
Poincaré (Av. R.)	B	71
Pompidou (Rd-Pt Georges)	B	72
Pompidou (Voie Georges)	B	
Pompon (Bd F.)	A	73
Prat (Av. du Colonel)	B	75
Rembrandt (Bd)	B	78
Rolin (Q. Nicolas)	A	79
Roosevelt (Av. F. D.)	B	80
Saint-Exupéry (Pl.)	B	85
Salengro (Pl. R.)	B	
Schuman (Bd Robert)	B	88
Stalingrad (Av. de)	B	
Stearinerie (R. de la)	A	
Strasbourg (Bd de)	B	90
Sully (R.)	B	
Talant (R. de)	A	
Trimolet (Bd)	B	91
Troyes (Bd de)	A	
Université (Bd de l')	B	
Valendons (Bd des)	A	
Valendons (R. des)	A	
Victor-Hugo (Av.)	A	
1er-Consul (Av. du)	A	
8-Mai-1945 (Rd-Pt du)	B	96
26e-Dragons (R. du)	B	98

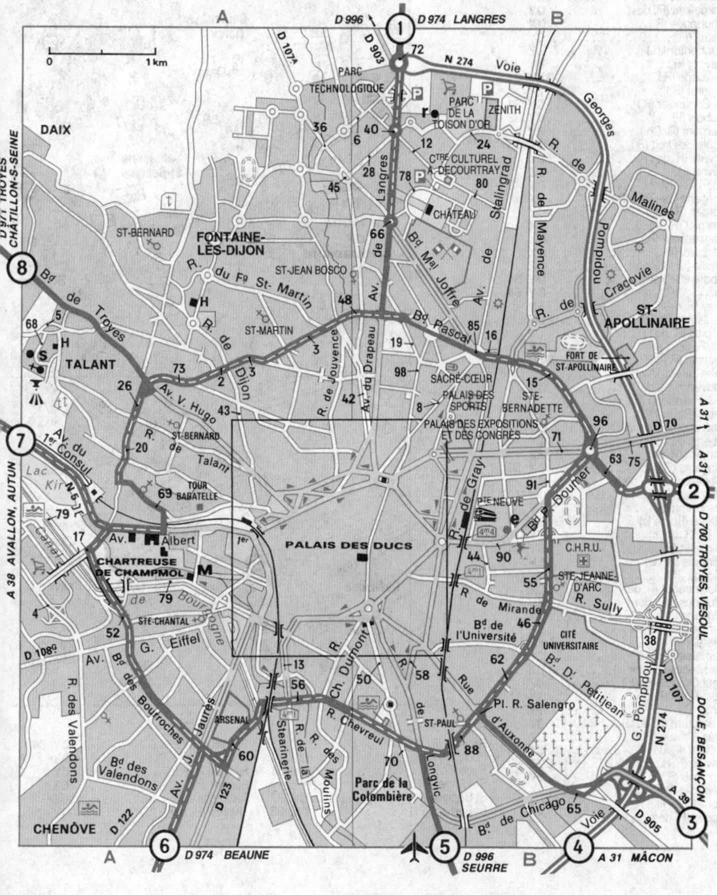

DIJON

Adler (Pl. E.) EZ
Albert-1er (Av.) CY
Arquebuse (R. de l') CY
Audra (R.) CY
Auxonne (R. d') EZ
Barabant (Pl. Henri) DZ
Baudin (R. J.-B.) EYZ
Berbisey (R.) CYZ
Berlier (R.) DEY
Bordot (R.) DZ
Bossuet (R. et Pl.) CDY
Bouhey (Pl. J.) EX
Bourg (R. du) DY
Briand (Av. A.) EX 8
Brosses (Bd de) CY 9
Buffon (R.) DY
Cabet (R. P.) EY
Carnot (Bd) DEY
Castell (Bd du) CZ
Cellerier (R. J.) CX
Chabot-Charny (R.) DYZ
Champagne (Bd de) EX 14
Charrue (R.) DY 18
Chouette (R. de la) DY 21
Clemenceau (Bd G.) EX
Colmar (R. de) EX
Comte (R. A.) DY 27
Condorcet (R.) CY
Cordeliers (Pl. des) DY
Courtépée (R.) DX
Darcy (Pl.) CY
Daubenton (R.) CZ
Davout (R.) EY
Devosge (R.) CDXY
Diderot (R.) EY
Dr-Chaussier (R.) CY 32
Dubois (Pl. A.) CY 33
Dumont (R. Ch.) DZ
École-de-Droit (R.) DY 35
Égalité (R. de l') CX
Févret (R.) DZ
Foch (Av. Mar.) CY 43
Fontaine-lès-Dijon (R.) CX
Forges (R. des) DY
Fremiet (R. A.) DX
Gagnereaux (R.) DX
Garibaldi (Av.) DX
Gaulle (Crs Général-de) DZ
Godrans (R. des) DY 51
Grangier (Pl.) DY 54
Gray (R. de) EY
Guillaume-Tell (R.) CY
Hôpital (R. de l') CZ
Ille (R. de l') CZ
Jeannin (R.) DEY
Jean-Jaurès (Av.) CZ
Jouvence (R. de) DX
J.-J.-Rousseau (R.) DY
Ledru-Rollin (R.) EXY
Libération (Pl. de la) DY 57
Liberté (R. de la) CY
Longvic (R. de) DEZ
Magenta (R.) EZ 58
Manutention (R. de la) CZ
Marceau (R.) DX
Mariotte (R.) CY
Marne (Bd de la) EX
Metz (R. de) EY
Michelet (R.) CY 64
Mirande (R. de) EY
Monge (R.) CY
Montchapet (R. de) CX
Mulhouse (R. de) EXY
Musette (R.) DY
Parmentier (R.) EX
Pasteur (R.) DYZ
Perrières (R. des) CY
Perspective (Pl. de la) CZ
Petit-Cîteaux (R. du) CZ
Petit-Potet (R. du) DY 71
Piron (R.) DY
Préfecture (R. de la) DY
Prés.-Wilson (Pl.) DZ
Prévert (Pl. J.) CZ
Raines (R. du Fg) CYZ
Rameau (R.) DY 77
République (Pl. de la) DX
Rolin (Quai N.) CZ
Roses (R. des) CX

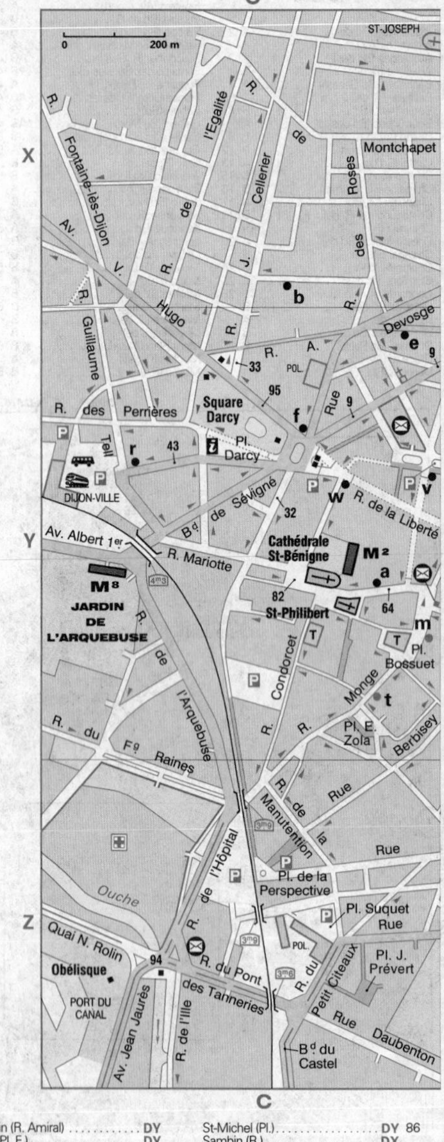

Roussin (R. Amiral) DY
Rude (Pl. F.) DY
Rude (R. F.) DY 81
Ste-Anne (R.) DYZ
St-Bénigne (Pl.) CY 82
St-Bernard (Pl.) DY 83
St-Michel (Pl.) DY 86
Sambin (R.) DX
Sévigné (Bd de) CY
Suquet (Pl.) CZ
Tanneries (Rd-Pt des) CZ
Théâtre (Pl. du) DY

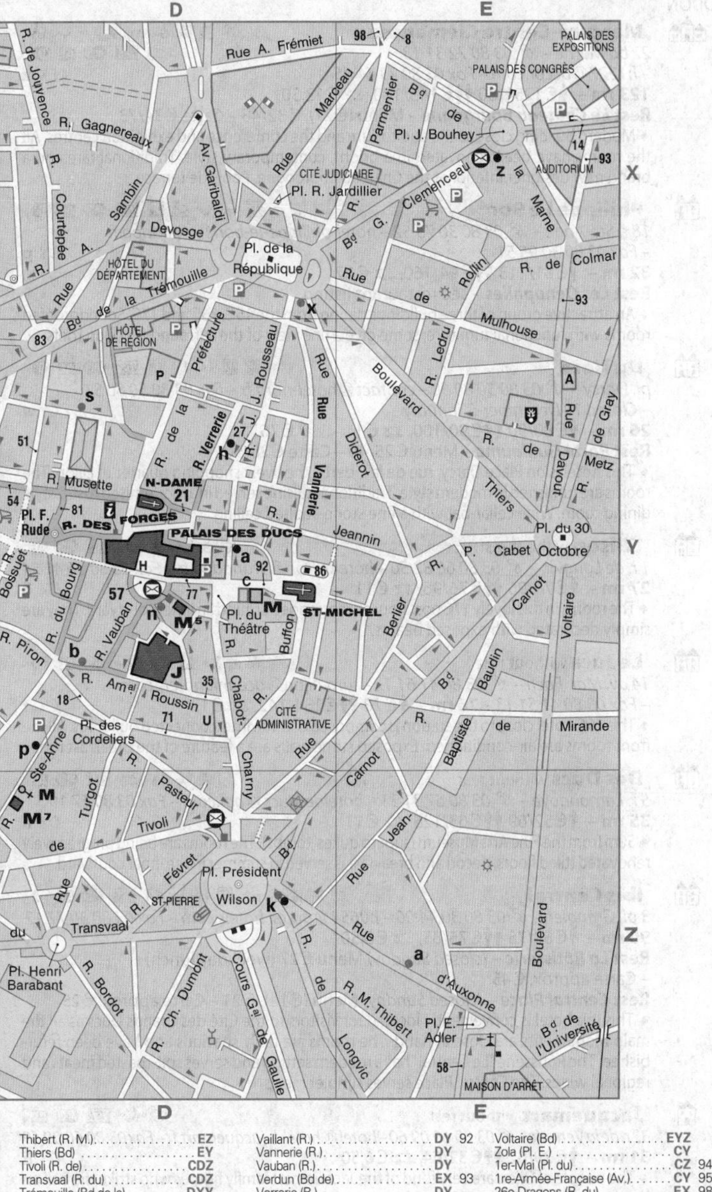
D
E
X
Y
Z
Rue A. Frémiet
R. de Jouvence
R. Gagnereaux
Av. Garibaldi
Rue Marceau
Parmentier
Bd de la Marne
PALAIS DES EXPOSITIONS
PALAIS DES CONGRÈS
Pl. J. Bouhey
AUDITORIUM
CITÉ JUDICIAIRE
Pl. R. Jardillier
Bd G. Clemenceau
R. Courtépée
R. A. Sambin
Devosge
HÔTEL DU DÉPARTEMENT
Pl. de la République
Rue de Mulhouse
R. de Colmar
Rollin
Bd de la Trémouille
HÔTEL DE RÉGION
Préfecture
R. de la Préfecture
R. J. J. Rousseau
Rue Diderot
Boulevard Thiers
R. Ledru
R. Verrerie
R. Musette
N-DAME
Pl. F. Rude
R. DES FORGES
PALAIS DES DUCS
Rue Vannerie
R. Jeannin
R. de Metz
Rue Davout
R. de Gray
Pl. du 30 Octobre
P. Cabet
R. Bossuet
R. du Bourg
ST-MICHEL
Pl. du Théâtre
R. Buffon
R. Berlier
R. Carnot
Rue Voltaire
R. Vauban
R. Piron
R. Amal Roussin
R. Chabot-Charny
CITÉ ADMINISTRATIVE
Bd Carnot
Baudin
R. Baptiste
R. de Mirande
Pl. des Cordeliers
R. Ste-Anne
R. Turgot
R. Pasteur
Rue de Tivoli
R. Févret
Pl. Président Wilson
ST-PIERRE
Rue du Transvaal
Pl. Henri Barabant
R. Bordot
R. Ch. Dumont
Cours Gal de Gaulle
Rue Jean-Jaurès
Rue d'Auxonne
R. de Longvic
R. M. Thibert
Pl. E. Adler
Bd de l'Université
Boulevard Voltaire
MAISON D'ARRÊT

Mercure-Centre Clemenceau
22 bd Marne – ✆ 03 80 72 31 13 – h1227@accor.com – Fax 03 80 73 61 45 EX **z**
123 rm – €125/180 €145/180, ☕ €13,50
Rest *Le Château Bourgogne* – Menu (€27), €32/48 – Carte €34/73
♦ Modern building close to the auditorium and the conference and exhibition centres. All the rooms have been renovated in a bright, contemporary style. Traditional fare and a brand new designer interior at the Château Bourgogne. Poolside terrace.

Philippe Le Bon
18 r. Ste-Anne – ✆ 03 80 30 73 52 – hotel-philippe-le-bon@wanadoo.fr – Fax 03 80 30 95 51 DY **p**
32 rm – €81/113 €94/160, ☕ €12
Rest *Les Oenophiles* – see restaurant listing
♦ An attractive group of three buildings dating from the 15C, 16C and 17C. Soundproofed rooms with functional furniture; some give a fine view of the surrounding Dijon roofs.

Du Nord
pl. Darcy – ✆ 03 80 50 80 50 – contact@hotel-nord.fr – Fax 03 80 50 80 51 – Closed 19 December-5 January CY **w**
26 rm – €80/90 €90/100, ☕ €11 – ½ P €76
Rest *Porte Guillaume* – Menu €25/40 – Carte €28/50
♦ This hotel is on Place Darcy, rue de la Liberté, the lively shopping quarter of Dijon. The rooms are furnished in modern style. Traditional cuisine served in a modernised rustic-style dining room. Wine cellar-bar with a fine stone-vaulted ceiling.

Wilson without rest
1 r. de Longvic – ✆ 03 80 66 82 50 – hotelwilson@wanadoo.fr – Fax 03 80 36 41 54
27 rm – €76/96 €76/96, ☕ €11 DZ **k**
♦ The rooms in this lovely 17C post house are arranged around an inner courtyard. They are simply decorated with exposed beams.

Le Jura without rest
14 av. Mar. Foch – ✆ 03 80 41 61 12 – jura.dijon@oceaniahotels.com – Fax 03 80 41 51 13 – **76 rm** – €78 €134/142, ☕ €12 CY **r**
♦ This 19C hotel close to the station is composed of three interconnected buildings. All the front rooms are air-conditioned. Exposed stone walls are a feature of the breakfast room.

Des Ducs without rest
5 r. Lamonnoye – ✆ 03 80 67 31 31 – hoteldesducs@aol.com – Fax 03 80 67 19 51
35 rm – €52/69 €63/125, ☕ €11 DY **a**
♦ 50m from the Fine Arts Museum (superb dukes' tombs). The rooms are being progressively renovated (tiled floors, decor) and breakfast is served in summer in the inner courtyard.

Ibis Central
3 pl. Grangier – ✆ 03 80 30 44 00 – h0654@accor-hotels.com – Fax 03 80 30 77 12
90 rm – €68/75 €75/85, ☕ €8,50 CY **v**
Rest *La Rôtisserie* – *(closed Sunday)* Menu €27 (weekday lunch) – Carte approx. €45
Rest *Central Place* – *(closed Sunday)* Menu (€14), €21 – Carte approx. €25
♦ This Ibis hotel is conveniently located for visitors to the Cité des Grands Ducs as all the main monuments are close at hand. The rooms are fairly spacious and have been refurbished. The Rôtisserie "Le Central" has a modern setting and serves spit-roasted meats and regional wines. The Central Place serves simpler meals.

Jacquemart without rest
32 r. de la Verrerie – ✆ 03 80 60 09 60 – hotel@hotel-lejacquemart.fr – Fax 03 80 60 09 69
31 rm – €29/62 €32/64, ☕ €6,50 DY **h**
♦ The people of Dijon are very fond of the Jacquemart family figures who strike the bell on the Notre-Dame clock. 17C building, comfortable rooms and the sumptuous private residences of the town just a short distance away.

Victor Hugo without rest
23 r. Fleurs – ✆ 03 80 43 63 45 – hotel.victor.hugo@wanadoo.fr – Fax 03 80 42 13 01
23 rm – €39 €49, ☕ €6,50 CX **b**
♦ The friendly welcome, the scrupulousness and the charming garage make up for the somewhat weak soundproofing and the no-nonsense decor in the rooms.

Montigny without rest

8 r. Montigny – ✆ 03 80 30 96 86 – hotel.montigny@wanadoo.fr – Fax 03 80 49 90 36 – Closed 21 December-4 January CY **e**

28 rm – 🚹€ 50/52 🚹🚹€ 55/57, ☕ € 7,50

◆ Hotel conveniently located near the town centre, with a private car park. Functional, well soundproofed and faultlessly kept rooms. Courtesy is a hallmark of the service.

XXX ✿ **Stéphane Derbord**

10 pl. Wilson – ✆ 03 80 67 74 64 – contactderbord@aol.com – Fax 03 80 63 87 72 – Closed 30 July-16 August, 2-7 January, Monday lunch, Tuesday lunch and Sunday

Rest – Menu € 25 (weekday lunch), € 48/88 – Carte € 65/79 DZ **k**

Spec. Foie gras de canard à la chapelure de truffe de Bourgogne. Sandre de Saône rôti, mousseline à l'estragon. Pigeon aux grains de cassis. **Wines** Saint-Aubin, Marsannay.

◆ An elegant, modern setting. Inventive cuisine, a blend of exotic flavours and local dishes, with an extensive wine list. A vital port of call in the city of the "Great Dukes".

XXX **Les Oenophiles** – Hôtel Philippe Le Bon

18 r. Ste-Anne – ✆ 03 80 30 73 52 – hotel-philippe-le-bon@wanadoo.fr – Fax 03 80 30 95 51 – Closed lunch 11-24 August and Sunday except holidays

Rest – Menu € 25 (weekdays)/55 – Carte € 55/70 DY **p**

◆ Dining-rooms with lots of character in a 15C private mansion. Wine museum and collection of figurines relating to the history of the Duchy of Burgundy.

XXX ✿ **Le Pré aux Clercs** (Jean-Pierre et Alexis Billoux)

13 pl. Libération – ✆ 03 80 38 05 05 – billoux@club-internet.fr – Fax 03 80 38 16 16 – Closed 17-29 August, 23 February-7 March, Sunday dinner and Monday

Rest – Menu € 36 bi (weekday lunch), € 50/95 – Carte € 64/111 DY **n**

Spec. Oeufs cocotte aux truffes fraîches de Bourgogne (season). Paillasson de langoustines au vinaigre de Xérès. Carré de veau fermier, jus chicorée, gnocchi de pommes de terre aux truffes. **Wines** Marsannay blanc, Saint-Romain rouge.

◆ Enjoy fine views of the square designed by Hardouin-Mansart from the bay windows of this elegant restaurant. Designer decor and exposed beams provide the backdrop for delicious classical cuisine.

XX **La Dame d'Aquitaine**

23 pl. Bossuet – ✆ 03 80 30 45 65 – dame.aquitaine@wanadoo.fr – Fax 03 80 49 90 41 – Closed Monday lunch and Sunday CY **m**

Rest – Menu € 22 (weekday lunch), € 29/45 – Carte € 35/70

◆ A restaurant with an unusual location in a 13C vaulted crypt. Modern furnishings and dramatic lighting provide the backdrop for a cuisine which blends the flavours of Gascony and Burgundy.

XX **Ma Bourgogne**

1 bd P. Doumer – ✆ 03 80 65 48 06 – Fax 03 80 67 82 65 – Closed 26 July-21 August, 15-23 February, Sunday dinner and Saturday B **e**

Rest – Menu € 22/34 – Carte € 34/51

◆ Bow to custom by drinking a kir – the aperitif of a renowned, but somewhat truculent, local churchman; then embark upon the discovery of regional specialities. Landscaped terrace.

XX **Petit Vatel**

73 r. Auxonne – ✆ 03 80 65 80 64 – Fax 03 80 31 69 92 – Closed 28 July-20 August, Saturday lunch and Sunday except holidays EZ **a**

Rest – Menu (€ 21), € 27/40 – Carte € 50/59

◆ Pleasant local restaurant with two small, simply-decorated dining rooms. Traditional cuisine. Warm welcome.

X **Bistrot des Halles**

10 r. Bannelier – ✆ 03 80 49 94 15 – Fax 03 80 38 16 16 – Closed 25 December-2 January, Sunday and Monday DY **s**

Rest – Menu € 17 (weekday lunch) – Carte € 29/32

◆ Restaurant facing the attractively restored covered market. Its straightforward dishes, rotisserie, and 1900s bistro decor with a slightly theatrical atmosphere make this place a convivial haunt for local clients.

Les Deux Fontaines

16 pl. République – ☎ 03 80 60 86 45 – Fax 03 80 28 54 80 – Closed 4-25 August, Sunday and Monday DX x

Rest – Menu € 27 – Carte € 22/39

◆ Successful reconstruction of an old time bistro (whitewashed walls, old-fashioned bench seating, wooden tables). The cuisine is traditional and interestingly reinterpreted.

at Toison d'Or Park 5 km north by D 974 – ✉ 21000 Dijon

Holiday Inn

1 pl. Marie de Bourgogne – ☎ 03 80 60 46 00 – holiday-inn.dijonfrance@wanadoo.fr – Fax 03 80 72 32 72 B r

100 rm – †€ 95/110 ††€ 105/135, ☕ € 15 – **Rest** – *(Closed Saturday lunch, Sunday lunch and lunch bank holidays)* Menu € 19, € 25/40 – Carte € 30/68

◆ This modern building in the Toison d'Or area is adjacent to the shopping centre and aquatic park. The rooms are identical and functional. Traditional dishes are served in the spacious, modern dining hall.

in Chevigny 9 km by ⑤ and D 996 – ✉ 21600 Fenay

Le Relais de la Sans Fond

33 rte Dijon – ☎ 03 80 36 61 35 – sansfond@aol.com – Fax 03 80 36 94 89 – Closed 22 December-1st January – **17 rm** – †€ 52/57 ††€ 62/67, ☕ € 8 – ½ P € 72/77 – **Rest** – *(closed Sunday dinner and Bank Holiday dinner)* Menu € 16 (weekday lunch), € 27/49 – Carte € 33/53

◆ This is a small, simple, well-kept family-run hotel. The rooms are light, with laminated wood furniture. The modern dining room has an open fireplace and there is a pleasant garden terrace. Traditional cuisine.

in Chenôve 6 km by ⑥ – pop. 16 257 – alt. 263 m – ✉ 21300

Quality Hôtel l'Escargotière

120 av. Roland-Carraz – ☎ 03 80 54 04 04 – contact@hotel-escargotiere.fr – Fax 03 80 54 04 05 – Closed 19 December-4 January

41 rm – †€ 62/74 ††€ 62/100, ☕ € 10 – ½ P € 56/60

Rest *La Véranda* – Menu (€ 16), € 20 – Carte € 24/36

◆ The hotel is set along a busy road, but the rooms – renovated or functional – are efficiently soundproofed. Buffet breakfast. A winter-garden atmosphere. Grilled food and spit-roast dishes are offered at La Véranda.

Le Clos du Roy

35 av. 14-Juillet – ☎ 03 80 51 33 66 – clos.du.roy@wanadoo.fr – Fax 03 80 51 36 66 – Closed August, Wednesday dinner, Sunday dinner and Monday

Rest – Menu € 17 (weekday lunch), € 24/56 – Carte € 51/61

◆ This restaurant with its modern decor is an ideal stopover on the way to the vineyards. Cuisine in keeping with current taste enhanced by regional touches, and a fine choice of Burgundy wines.

in Marsannay-la-Côte 8 km by ⑥ – pop. 5 211 – alt. 275 m – ✉ 21160

ℹ Office de tourisme, 41, rue de Mazy ☎ 03 80 52 27 73, Fax 03 80 52 30 23

Les Gourmets

8 r. Puits de Têt, (near church) – ☎ 03 80 52 16 32 – romainetagnesdetot.lesgourmets@orange.fr – Fax 03 80 52 03 01 – Closed 4-19 August, 20 January-12 February, Tuesday lunch, Sunday dinner and Monday

Rest – Menu € 25/82 – Carte € 57/87

◆ A superb wine list, contemporary cuisine with a personal touch, and a stylish dining room opening onto a terrace in summer. Gourmets are in their element here!

in Talant 4 km – pop. 12 176 – alt. 354 m – ✉ 21240

Viewpoint indicator ≤★.

La Bonbonnière without rest

24 r. Orfèvres, (In the old village) – ☎ 03 80 57 31 95 – labonbonniere@wanadoo.fr – Fax 03 80 57 23 92 – Closed 28 July-15 August and 22 December-4 January A s

20 rm – †€ 65/75 ††€ 70/95, ☕ € 10

◆ Near the artificial lake (water sports) created by Canon Kir, a small family-run hotel with well-kept facilities. Spacious, fresh rooms and a pleasant garden.

in Prenois 12 km by ⑧ by D 971 and D 104 – pop. 310 – alt. 485 m – ✉ 21370

Auberge de la Charme (David Zuddas) VISA

12 r. de la Charme – ✆ 03 80 35 32 84 – davidlacharme@aol.com – Fax 03 80 35 34 48 – Closed 4-14 August, 23 February-5 March, Tuesday lunch, Thursday lunch, Sunday dinner and Monday

Rest – *(pre-book)* Menu (€ 18 bi), € 25 (weekdays)/80 – Carte € 61/75

Spec. Escargots, galette de chèvre au pain trempé, jus de persil. Saint-Jacques juste saisies, citronnelle, mélisse et ipomée au lait de coco (autumn-winter). Carré de chevreuil rôti, champignons sauvages, jus au cacao (autumn-winter). **Wines** Chablis, Saint-Aubin.

♦ The nearby racetrack was once used for Formula 1 racing but the village's claim to fame nowadays is this stylishly converted old forge. Inventive cuisine.

Troyes road 4 km by ⑧ – ✉ 21121 Daix

Castel Burgond without rest VISA

3 rte Troyes, (D 971) – ✆ 03 80 56 59 72 – castel.burgond@wanadoo.fr – Fax 03 80 57 69 48 – Closed 25 December-4 January

46 rm – €64 €70, ☕ €8,50

♦ A modern building in a residential area with a few small rooms; those on the top floor are more recent, the others are simple and functional.

Les Trois Ducs VISA

5 rte de Troyes – ✆ 03 80 56 59 75 – eric-briones@wanadoo.fr – Fax 03 80 56 00 16 – Closed 4-24 August, Saturday lunch, Sunday dinner and Monday

Rest – Menu € 21 (weekdays), € 30/100 bi – Carte € 51/72

♦ Comfortable restaurant with a spruce new decor enhanced by modern paintings. Cuisine with a contemporary touch. Terrace dining in fine weather.

in Hauteville-lès-Dijon 6 km by ⑧ and D 107F – pop. 1 023 – alt. 402 m – ✉ 21121

La Musarde with rm VISA

7 r. des Riottes – ✆ 03 80 56 22 82 – hotel.rest.lamusarde@wanadoo.fr – Fax 03 80 56 64 40 – Closed 21 December-6 January

12 rm – €49/57 €57/67, ☕ €9,50 – ½ P €63/65 – **Rest** – *(closed Tuesday lunchtime, Sunday evening and Monday)* Menu (€ 20), € 24 (weekday lunch), € 30/61 – Carte € 47/66

♦ This 19C farmhouse has been converted into a restful hotel-restaurant surrounded by greenery. Quiet atmosphere in the dining-room, a fine summer terrace, and cuisine with a contemporary touch. A relaxing and comfortable stay is assured.

DINAN – 22 Côtes-d'Armor – 309 J4 – pop. 10 907 – alt. 92 m – ✉ 22100

Brittany 10 **C2**

- Paris 400 – Rennes 54 – St-Brieuc 61 – St-Malo 32 – Vannes 120
- Office de tourisme, 9, rue du Château ✆ 02 96 87 69 76, Fax 02 96 87 69 77
- La Corbinais Golf Club Saint-Michel-de-Plélan La Corbinais, West: 15 km, ✆ 02 96 27 64 81 ;
- de Saint-Malo Le TronchetDol-de-Bretagne road: 19 km, ✆ 02 99 58 96 69 ;
- de Tréméreuc Tréméreuc 14 rue de Dinan, by Dinard road: 11 km, ✆ 02 96 27 10 40.
- Old town ★★: Tour de l'Horloge ✻★★ R, English garden ≤★★, place des Merciers★ BZ, rue du Jerzual★ BY, - Promenade de la Duchesse-Anne ≤★, Tour du Gouverneur ≤★★, Tour Ste-Catherine ≤★★ - Château★: ✻★.

Plan on next page

Jerzual

26 quai Talards, (at the harbour) – ✆ 02 96 87 02 02 – reservation@bestwesterndinan.fr – Fax 02 96 87 02 03 BY **b**

55 rm – €82/118 €89/140, ☕ €14 – ½ P €74/104 – **Rest** – Menu € 15 (weekday lunch), € 19/34 – Carte € 31/55

♦ This new hotel, reminiscent of Breton-style cloisters, melds in well with its surroundings in the port area. The rooms are spacious and modern. Attractive patio with a swimming-pool. The restaurant-grill room with its light-coloured wood panelling extends onto a terrace on the Rance side.

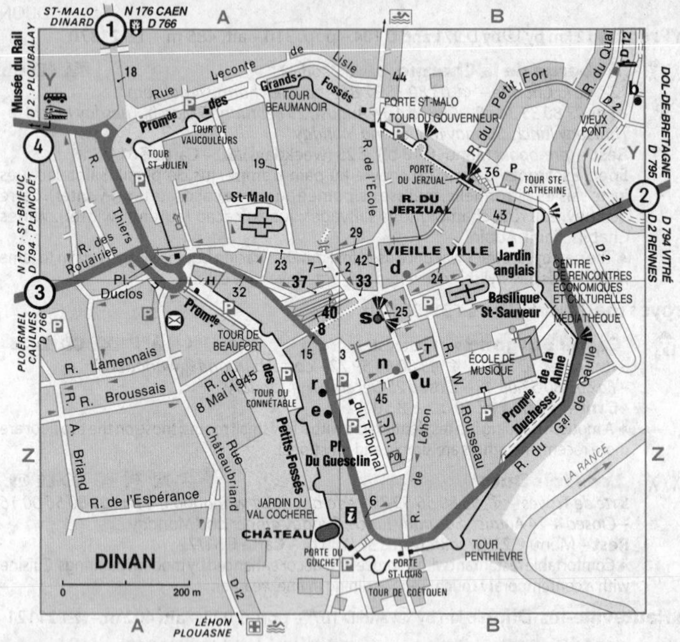

Apport (R. de l')	ABY	2	Garaye (R. Comte de la)	AY	19	Michel (R.)	BY	36
Champ Clos (Pl. du)	ABZ	3	Grande-R.	AY	23	Mittrie (R. de la)	AZ	37
Château (R. du)	BZ	6	Haute-Voie (R.)	BY	24	Petit-Pain (R. du)	AZ	40
Cordeliers (Pl. des)	AY	7	Horloge (R. de l')	BZ	25	Poissonnerie (R. de la)	BY	42
Cordonnerie (R. de la)	AZ	8	Lainerie (R. de la)	BY	29	Rempart (R. du)	BY	43
Ferronerie (R. de la)	AZ	15	Marchix (R. du)	AYZ	32	Ste-Claire (R.)	BZ	45
Gambetta (R.)	AY	18	Merciers (Pl. des)	BYZ	33	St-Malo (R.)	BY	44

Le d'Avaugour without rest — VISA

1 pl. Champ – ☎ 02 96 39 07 49 – contact@avaugourhotel.com
– Fax 02 96 85 43 04 – Open from March to October AZ **r**

24 rm – †€ 80/180 ††€ 80/190, ☐ € 12,50

◆ This fine building in local stone has a backdrop of ramparts. The rooms are classical and give a view of the square or the attractive garden where tables are set up for breakfast in summer.

Challonge without rest — VISA

29 pl. Duguesclin – ☎ 02 96 87 16 30 – lechallonge@wanadoo.fr
– Fax 02 96 87 16 31 AZ **e**

18 rm – †€ 53/64 ††€ 64/130, ☐ € 8

◆ This building with its long classical facade stands alongside the old fairground, guarded by the statue of Du Guesclin. Comfortable rooms with a British atmosphere. Friendly welcome.

Ibis without rest — VISA

1 pl. Duclos – ☎ 02 96 39 46 15 – h5977@accor.com – Fax 02 96 85 44 03

62 rm – †€ 48/95 ††€ 48/95, ☐ € 7,50

◆ This hotel in the town centre has been freshly refurbished. The rooms are spacious and air-conditioned and fully comply with the chain's latest standards as to quality and comfort.

Arvor without rest — VISA

5 r. Pavie – ☎ 02 96 39 21 22 – hotel-arvor@wanadoo.fr – Fax 02 96 39 83 09
– Closed 5-25 January BZ **u**

24 rm – †€ 45/70 ††€ 59/114, ☐ € 6,50

◆ A carved Renaissance portal leads into this 18C building on the site of an old convent. A modern, functional interior; spacious rooms.

L'Auberge du Pélican

3 r. Haute Voie – ✆ 02 96 39 47 05 – Fax 02 96 87 53 30 – Closed 10 January-10 February, Monday except dinner July-August, Thursday dinner September-June and Saturday lunch BY **d**

Rest – Menu € 19/58 – Carte € 32/84

◆ Pleasant restaurant in the old quarter of Dinan. The dining room has been redecorated in modern style and there is a lovely terrace for summer dining. Traditional cuisine and seafood.

Le Cantorbery

6 r. Ste-Claire – ✆ 02 96 39 02 52 – Closed 15 November-4 December, 15 January-3 February and Sunday 15 November-15 March BZ **n**

Rest – Menu (€ 12,50), € 16 (weekday lunch), € 25/38 – Carte € 34/56

◆ In this 17C townhouse restaurant, the grills are cooked over the stone fireplace on the ground floor. Old wood panelling in the dining room on the first floor.

DINARD – 35 Ille-et-Vilaine – 309 J3 – pop. 10 430 – alt. 25 m – Casino BY – ✉ 35800 Brittany 10 C1

- Paris 408 – Dinan 22 – Dol-de-Bretagne 31 – Rennes 73 – St-Malo 10
- Dinard-Pleurtuit-St-Malo ✆ 02 99 46 18 46, by ①: 5 km.
- Office de tourisme, 2, boulevard Féart ✆ 02 99 46 94 12, Fax 02 99 88 21 07
- Dinard Golf Saint-Briac-sur-Mer Boulevard de la Houle, West: 7 km, ✆ 02 99 88 32 07 ;
- de Tréméreuc Tréméreuc 14 rue de Dinan, by Dinan road: 6 km, ✆ 02 96 27 10 40.
- Pointe du Moulinet ≤★★ - Grande Plage or Plage de l'Écluse★ - Promenade du Clair de Lune★ - Pointe de la Vicomté★★ - La Rance★★ by boat - St-Lunaire: pointe du Décollé ≤★★ and grotte des Sirènes★ 4,5 km by ② - Usine marémotrice de la Rance (wave-powered plant): dike ≤★ Southeast: 4 km.
- Pointe de la Garde Guérin★: ✻★★ by ②: 6 km then 15 mn.

Plan on following page

Grand Hôtel Barrière de Dinard

≤ rm, P VISA MC AE

46 av. George V – ✆ 02 99 88 26 26 – grandhoteldinard@lucien barriere.com – Fax 02 99 88 26 27 – Open 14 March-22 November BY **v**

90 rm – †€ 180/450 ††€ 180/450, ☕ € 21

Rest *Le Blue B* – *(dinner only)* Menu € 39/55 – Carte € 29/62

Rest *333 Café* – *(lunch only)* Menu (€ 20) – Carte € 30/45

◆ This 19C luxury hotel, on the Clair de Lune seaside promenade, welcomes movie stars during the British Film Festival. Restrained, sophisticated rooms. A lovely sea view from the Blue B. In summertime, the 333 Café serves light snacks on the terrace.

Novotel Thalassa

≤ sea, rm, rest, P VISA MC AE

1 av. Château Hébert – ✆ 02 99 16 78 10 – H1114@accor.com – Fax 02 99 16 78 29 – Closed 2-25 December AY **r**

106 rm – †€ 130/176 ††€ 130/176, ☕ € 13 – ½ P € 103/124

Rest – Menu € 28/48 (week-end) – Carte € 24/51

◆ A modern complex in a unique setting on St-Énogat's Point. A thalassotherapy centre, beauty parlour and modern rooms with a sea view. Panoramic view over the English Channel, modern decor and diet dishes.

Villa Reine Hortense without rest

≤ sea and St-Malo, P VISA MC AE

19 r. Malouine – ✆ 02 99 46 54 31 – reine.hortense@wanadoo.fr – Fax 02 99 88 15 88 – Open from end February to end September

7 rm – †€ 150/245 ††€ 150/245, ☕ € 16 – 1 suite BY **e**

◆ The Belle Époque comes alive again in the decor of this villa, typical of the 'Pearl' of the Emerald Coast. Luxurious, individually decorated rooms, three of which overlook the private beach.

Crystal without rest

≤ VISA MC AE

15 r. Malouine – ✆ 02 99 46 66 71 – hcrystal@club-internet.fr – Fax 02 99 88 17 73

24 rm – †€ 79/135 ††€ 79/135, ☕ € 11 – 2 suites BY **n**

◆ This hotel dating back to the 1970s has spacious, well-kept rooms; those on the street side have been renovated while the others command a view of the beach and the Malouine headland.

DINARD

Abbé-Langevin (R.) . . . . AY 2
Albert-1er (Bd) . . . . BY 3
Anciens Combattants
(R. des) . . . . AZ 5
Barbine (R. de) . . . . AZ 7
Boutin (Pl. J.) . . . . BY 9
Clemenceau (R. G.) . . . . BY 10
Coppinger (R.) . . . . BY 12
Corbinais (R. de la) . . . . AZ 13
Croix-Guillaume (R.) . . . . AZ 15
Douet-Fourche (R. du) . . . . . AZ 17
Dunant (R. H.) . . . . AY 19
Féart (Bd) . . . . BYZ
Français-Libres (R.) . . . . . . ABZ 22
Gaulle (Pl. du Gén.-de) . . . . . BZ 25
Giraud (Av. du Gén.) . . . . BZ 26
Leclerc (R. Mar.) . . . . BYZ 28
Levasseur (R.) . . . . BY 29
Lhotelier (Bd) . . . . AY 31
Libération (Bd de la) . . . . AZ 32
Malouine (R. de la) . . . . BY 34
Mettrie (R. de la) . . . . BZ 35
Pionnière (R. de la) . . . . . . ABY 38
Prés.-Wilson
(Bd) . . . . BY 40
Renan (R. E.) . . . . AY 43
République (Pl. de la) . . . . . . BY 44
St-Lunaire (R. de) . . . . AY 48
Vallée (R. de la) . . . . BYZ 50
Verney (R. Y.) . . . . BY 52

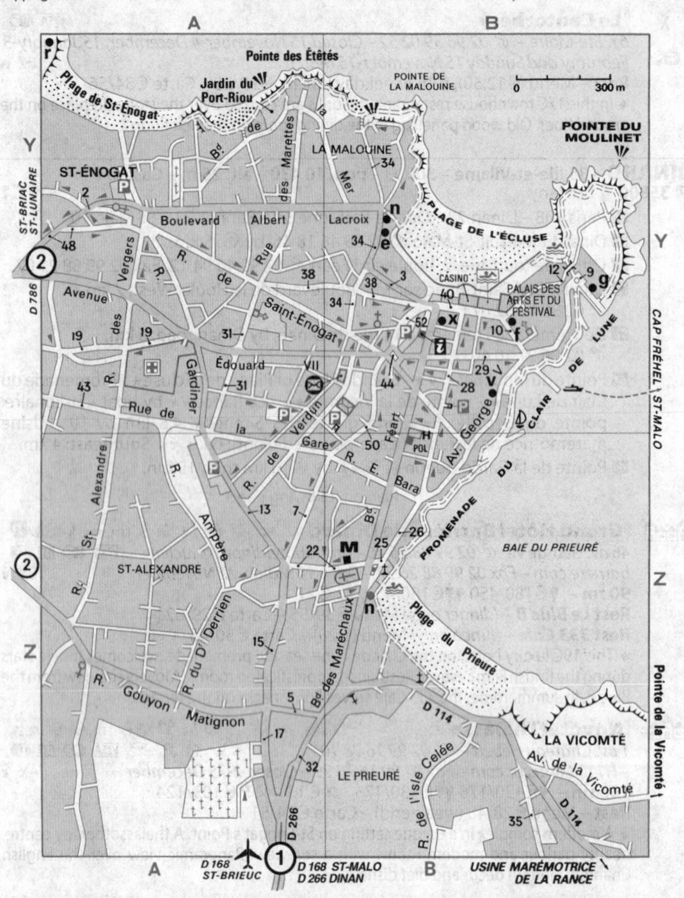

La Vallée rm, VISA

6 av. George-V – ✆ 02 99 46 94 00 – hdlv@wanadoo.fr – Fax 02 99 88 22 47 – Closed January BY **g**

24 rm – €60/150 €60/150, €12

Rest – *(closed Sunday dinner and Monday)* Carte €36/50

◆ Seashore construction built on a former landing stage. Handsome contemporary rooms, decorated in a different colour (rust, turquoise and bright green) depending on the floor. Two modern rooms, one in a loft style overlooking the bay. Bistro and seafood menu.

Roche Corneille rm, VISA MC AE DC

4 r. G. Clemenceau – ✆ 02 99 46 14 47 – roche.corneille@wanadoo.fr – Fax 02 99 46 40 80 BY **f**

28 rm – †€ 60/95 ††€ 90/165, ☕ € 13 – ½ P € 85/123 – **Rest** *(closed 15 November-31 March except fêtes, lunch and Monday)* Menu € 29/35 – Carte € 46/63

◆ Late 19C seaside resort type villa. The interior combines charm and comfort with high quality fixtures and fittings plus wifi access. Seasonal market "surf and turf" cuisine.

La Plage without rest VISA MC AE

3 bd Féart – ✆ 02 99 46 14 87 – hotel-de-la-plage@wanadoo.fr – Fax 02 99 46 55 52 – Closed Sunday from 15 November to 1st March except school holidays BY **x**

18 rm – †€ 55/67 ††€ 59/93, ☕ € 9,50

◆ This pleasant hotel promises breakfast on the terrace overlooking Écluse beach and a peaceful night in an attractively-renovated room.

Didier Méril with rm ≤ Baie du Prieuré, AC VISA MC AE DC

1 pl. Gén. de Gaulle – ✆ 02 99 46 95 74 – didiermeril@wanadoo.fr – Fax 02 99 16 07 75 – Closed 17 November-14 December and Wednesday October-March BZ **n**

8 rm – †€ 65/85 ††€ 90/160, ☕ € 10 – ½ P € 85/115 – **Rest** – Menu (€ 22), € 29 (weekdays)/75 – Carte € 54/74

◆ Oranges and greys, a glazed cellar, designer furniture and, above all, a splendid view of the Prieuré bay: a splendid combination of a modern interior with traditional fare. Small, tastefully decorated rooms.

in St-Lunaire 5 km by ② by D786 – pop. 2 250 – alt. 20 m – ✉ 35800

Office de tourisme, 72, boulevard du Général-de-Gaulle ✆ 02 99 46 31 09, Fax 02 99 46 31 09

Le Décollé ≤ sea and coastline, VISA MC

1 Pointe du Décollé – ✆ 02 99 46 01 70 – Fax 02 99 46 01 70 – Closed 12 November-31 January, Tuesday except July-August and Monday

Rest – *(pre-book)* Menu (€ 19), € 29/39 – Carte € 44/69

◆ The menu here has a steadfast focus on fish and seafood. The restrained decor enhances the magnificent view of the Emerald Coast. Idyllic summer terrace.

DIOU – 36 Indre – 323 I4 – see Issoudun

DISNEYLAND RESORT PARIS – 77 Seine-et-Marne – 312 F2 – 106 22 – see Paris, Area (Marne-la-Vallée)

DISSAY – 86 Vienne – 322 I4 – pop. 2 634 – alt. 69 m – ✉ 86130
Atlantic Coast 39 **C1**

Paris 320 – Châtellerault 19 – Poitiers 16

Office de tourisme, place du 8 Mai 1945 ✆ 05 49 52 34 56, Fax 05 49 62 58 72

Wall paintings★ in the château's chapel.

Le Binjamin with rm AC rest, P VISA MC AE

D 910 – ✆ 05 49 52 42 37 – binjamin1@aol.com – Fax 05 49 62 59 06 – ClosedSaturday lunch, Sunday dinner and Monday

9 rm – †€ 43/48 ††€ 43/51, ☕ € 7 – ½ P € 60/80 – **Rest** – Menu (€ 30), € 37/56

◆ A local craftsman made the pretty plates that adorn the tables of this family restaurant. Neo-rustic decor and well-thought out modern menu. Countrified rooms.

DIVES-SUR-MER – 14 Calvados – 303 L4 – see Cabourg

DIVONNE-LES-BAINS – 01 Ain – 328 J2 – pop. 6 171 – alt. 486 m – Spa : mid March-mid Nov. – Casino – ✉ 01220 Burgundy-Jura 46 **F1**

Paris 488 – Bourg-en-Bresse 129 – Genève 18 – Gex 9 – Nyon 9 – Thonon-les-Bains 51

Office de tourisme, rue des Bains ✆ 04 50 20 01 22, Fax 04 50 20 00 40

de Divonne-les-Bains Route de Gex, West: 2 km, ✆ 04 50 40 34 11 ;

de Maison-Blanche ÉchenevexSouthwest: 11 km, ✆ 04 50 42 44 42.

Le Grand Hôtel
av. des Thermes – ☎ 04 50 40 34 34 – info@domaine-de-divonne.com – Fax 04 50 40 34 24
130 rm – €230/290 €230/290, €25 – 4 suites
Rest *La Terrasse* – *☎ 04 50 40 35 39 (closed 1st January-7 February, Sunday dinner, Monday and Tuesday)* Menu (€35 bi), €39/65 – Carte €45/58
Rest *Le Léman* – *☎ 04 50 40 34 18 (closed Wednesday, Thursday, Friday and Saturday)* Menu €24 (weekday lunch), €35 € (dinner)/45 – Carte €31/44
◆ Built in 1931, this luxury hotel stands in a well-tended park. Elegant, spacious rooms in three styles: bourgeois, Art Deco or contemporary. Casino and golf course. Summer restaurant in the garden and a conservatory-style room. Lovely 1930s-style restaurant overlooking Lake Geneva.

Château de Divonne lake Geneva and Mont-Blanc, rest, rest,
115 r. des Bains – ☎ 04 50 20 00 32 – divonne@grandesetapes.fr – Fax 04 50 20 03 73
28 rm – €95/135 €110/155, €22 – 6 suites – **Rest** – *(closed Monday lunchtime, Tuesday lunchtime and Wednesday lunchtime in January-February)* Menu (€28), €55 (weekday lunch), €56/96 – Carte €65/93
◆ A 19C building, constructed on the ruins of an 11C fortified house, surrounded by a splendid park planted with trees. Rooms with personal touches reached via a monumental staircase. Elegant dining room, a panoramic terrace, and cuisine in keeping with current tastes.

La Villa du Lac rm, rm,
93 chemin du Chatelard – ☎ 04 50 20 90 00 – info@lavilladulac.com – Fax 04 50 99 40 00
90 rm – €135/180 €135/180, €11 – **Rest** – Menu (€19), €22 – Carte €26/36
◆ A brand new complex in a quiet location between lake and town. Contemporary style bedrooms with balconies. Hi-tech meeting rooms and a fully equipped spa. Traditional cuisine served in a contemporary-style dining room or on the terrace overlooking the lake.

Le Jura without rest
54 r. d'Arbère – ☎ 04 50 20 05 95 – reservation@hotellejura.com – Fax 04 50 20 21 21
29 rm – €62/98 €69/104, €9,50
◆ Family-run hotel with well-kept rooms. Those in the wing are new (modern furniture) and have terraces. Breakfast served on a veranda overlooking the garden.

Le Rectiligne lake,
2981 rte du Lac – ☎ 04 50 20 06 13 – lerectiligne@residencedulac.fr – Fax 04 50 20 53 81 – Closed Sunday from September to May and Monday from June to August
Rest – Menu €23 (lunch), €40/65 – Carte €48/67
◆ Modern white construction with dining-room and terrace overlooking the lake. Streamlined interior (pastel tones, water-wall) and tasty modern cuisine.

Le Pavillon du Golf
av. des Thermes – ☎ 04 50 40 34 13 – restauration@domaine-de-divonne.com – Fax 04 50 40 34 24 – Closed 20 December-6 February, Monday and Tuesday off season
Rest – Menu €24 (weekday lunch), €40/55 – Carte €40/52
◆ An old farmhouse next to a golf course. The refurbished dining room is bright and quiet (large fireplace). Charming terrace. Appetising, traditional menu.

DIZY – 51 Marne – 306 F8 – see Épernay

DOLANCOURT – 10 Aube – 313 H4 – pop. 145 – alt. 112 m – ✉ 10200 13 B3

Paris 229 – Châlons-en-Champagne 92 – Saint-Dizier 63 – Troyes 45

Moulin du Landion
5 r. St-Léger – ☎ 03 25 27 92 17 – contact@moulindulandion.com – Fax 03 25 27 94 44 – Closed 17-29 December
16 rm – €72/88 €72/88, €10 – ½ P €73/79 – **Rest** – Menu €23/56 – Carte €29/51
◆ Here, an entire family will bend over backwards to please you! The rooms have been renovated, with new bathrooms, and have balconies facing either the Landion river or the park. The restaurant has been set up in the old mill dating back to 1872. Traditional menus.

DOLE ⟨SP⟩ – 39 Jura – 321 C4 – pop. 24 949 – alt. 220 m – ✉ 39100 Burgundy-Jura

Paris 363 – Beaune 65 – Besançon 55 – Dijon 50 – Lons-le-Saunier 57

Office de tourisme, 6, place Grévy ☎ 03 84 72 11 22, Fax 03 84 82 49 27

Public du Val d'Amour Parcey Chemin du Camping, South: 9 km by D 405 and N 5, ☎ 03 84 71 04 23.

Old Dole★★ BZ : Notre-Dame collegiate church ★ - Wrought-iron★ railings of St-Jean-l'Evangéliste church AZ - Le musée des Beaux-Arts★.

Fôret de Chaux★. 16 **B2**

La Cloche without rest

1 pl. Grévy – ☎ 03 84 82 06 06 – lacloche.hotel@wanadoo.fr – Fax 03 84 72 73 82 – Closed 24 December-2 January BY **v**

28 rm – †€ 60 ††€ 70, ☐ € 8,50

◆ Stendhal is said to have stayed in this old house near the Cours St-Mauris. The rooms are spacious and are gradually being redecorated. Sauna.

DOLE

Arènes (R. des) .... ABZ
Besançon (R. de) .... BYZ
Béthouart (R. du Gén.) ..... BZ 2
Boyvin (R.) .... BZ 4
Chifflot (R. L.) .... AZ 5
Duhamel (Av. J) .... AZ 6
Gouvernement (R. du) .... BY 9
Grande-Rue .... BZ 10
Jean-Jaurès (Av.) .... BY 13
Juin (Av. du Mar.) .... BZ 14
Lattre de Tassigny (Av. du Mar.de) .... BY 15
Messageries (R. des) .... AY 16
Nationale, Charles-de-Gaulle (Pl.) .... BZ 17
Parlement (R. du) .... BZ 18
Rockefeller (R. J.) .... BY 21
Sous-Préfecture (R. de la) .... BY 22

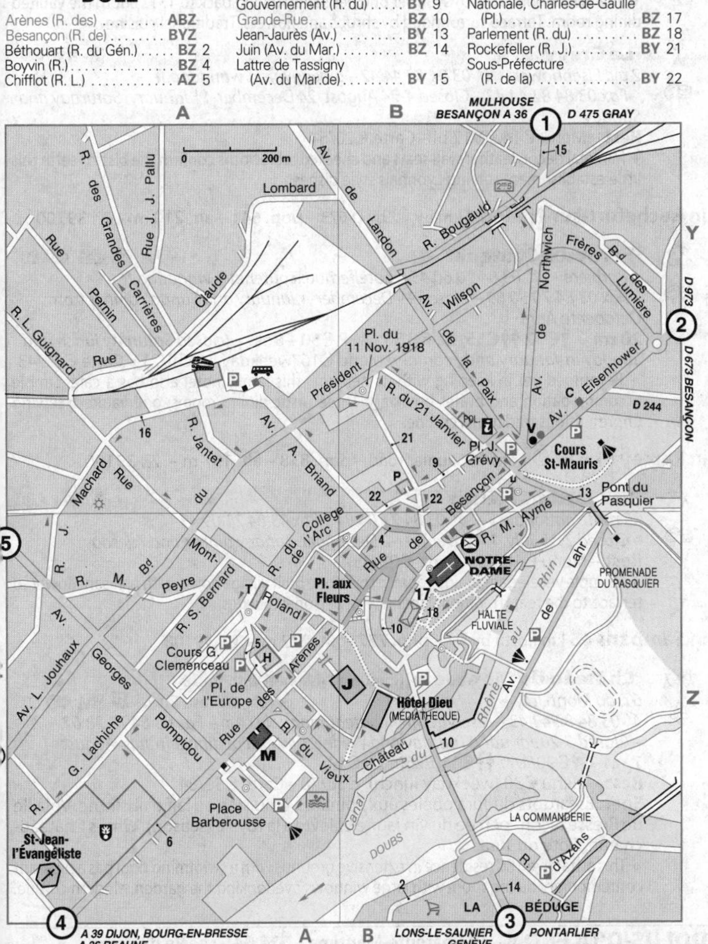

XXX **La Chaumière** (Joël Césari) with rm VISA AE
346 av. Mar. Juin – ✆ 03 84 70 72 40 – lachaumiere.dole@wanadoo.fr – Fax 03 84 79 25 60 – Closed 24 August-1st September (except hotel), 24 December-5 January, Sunday (except hotel July-August), Monday lunch and Saturday lunch
19 rm – €68/120 €77/120, €14
Rest – Menu (€19 bi), €32 (weekdays)/75 – Carte €54/63
Spec. Dos de sandre du Val de Saône, jus à l'infusion de baies de genièvre. Rouelles de poularde aux morilles et vin jaune. Dégustation de crèmes brûlées aux saveurs du Jura.
◆ The interior of this cottage is a subtle blend of modernity and local traditions. Inventive recipes made with regional sourced produce and fine selection of local wines.

XX **La Romanée** VISA
13 r. Vieilles Boucheries – ✆ 03 84 79 19 05 – la-romanee.franchini@wanadoo.fr – Fax 03 84 79 26 97 – Closed Sunday evening and Wednesday except July-August BZ **n**
Rest – Menu (€12 bi), €18/50 – Carte €33/56
◆ The meat hooks from this former butcher's shop dating back to 1717 adorn the vaulted dining room. Terrace surrounded by shrubs and flowers. Traditional cuisine.

X **Le Grévy** VISA
2 av. Eisenhower – ✆ 03 84 82 44 42 – gibeauvais@wanadoo.fr – Fax 03 84 82 44 42 – Closed 4-24 August, 24 December-1st January, Saturday and Sunday BY **v**
Rest – Menu €14,50/17 bi – Carte €20/54
◆ Minimal decor, leather wall seats and checked tablecloths confirm the bistro feel in this little establishment serving Lyonnais style dishes.

in Rochefort-sur-Nenon 7 km by ② by D 673 – pop. 641 – alt. 210 m – ✉ 39700

Fernoux-Coutenet VISA AE
r. Barbière – ✆ 03 84 70 60 45 – hotelfernouxcoutenet@wanadoo.fr – Fax 03 84 70 50 89 – Closed 19 December-4 January and Sunday dinner from October to April
20 rm – €52 €55, €8,50 – ½ P €50 – **Rest** – *(closed Saturday lunch and Sunday in January and February)* Menu €16 (weekday lunch)/21 – Carte €22/43
◆ Revamped yet in keeping with its heritage, this family hotel also has a café. Simple accommodation and buffet breakfast. Three rustic dining rooms, one vaulted, serving unpretentious traditional cuisine.

in Parcey 8 km by ③ Lons-le-Saunier road – pop. 838 – alt. 197 m – ✉ 39100

XX **Les Jardins Fleuris** VISA
35 route nationale 5 – ✆ 03 84 71 04 84 – Fax 03 84 71 09 43 – Closed 2-15 July, 11 November-2 December, Sunday dinner and Tuesday
Rest – Menu €16/43 – Carte €29/45
◆ A simple yet elegant dining room in this stone built village house with pleasant flowered terrace to the rear. Traditional menu with personal touches.

in Sampans 6.5 km north by ① – pop. 777 – alt. 222 m – ✉ 39100

XXX **Château du Mont Joly** (Romuald Fassenet) with rm
6 r. du Mont-Joly – rest, AC rest, P VISA AE
✆ 03 84 82 43 43 – reservation@chateaumontjoly.com – Fax 03 84 79 28 07 – Closed 5-20 January, Tuesday and Wednesday except dinner in July-August
7 rm – €90/140 €110/250, €14
Rest – Menu €30 (weekday lunch), €38/78 – Carte €56/84
Spec. Escargots du Jura poêlés aux épinards, émulsion au lait d'absinthe. Volaille de Bresse façon "percée du vin jaune". Lièvre à la royale (season). **Wines** Château-chalon, Côte du Jura.
◆ This attractive 18C residence in extensive grounds with a swimming pool has a pleasant contemporary dining room with large windows overlooking the garden. Modern cuisine.

DOLUS-D'OLERON – 17 Charente-Maritime – **324** C4 – see île d'Oléron

DOMFRONT-EN-CHAMPAGNE – 72 Sarthe – 310 J6 – pop. 936 – alt. 131 m – ✉ 72240 35 C1

Paris 216 – Alençon 54 – Laval 77 – Le Mans 20 – Mayenne 55

XX **Midi**

33 r. du Mans, D 304 – ☎ 02 43 20 52 04 – jeanluc-haudry@orange.fr – Fax 02 43 20 56 03 – Closed 15-31 August, 15 February-15 March, Monday and dinner except Friday and Saturday

Rest – Menu € 13 (weekday lunch), € 19/35 – Carte approx. € 31

◆ Small village hotel with a colourful dining room, furnished in modern style. The well-spaced out tables create an environment of intimacy. Cuisine in keeping with current taste.

DOMMARTEMONT – 54 Meurthe-et-Moselle – 307 I6 – see Nancy

DOMME – 24 Dordogne – 329 I7 – pop. 987 – alt. 250 m – ✉ 24250

Dordogne-Berry-Limousin 4 D1

Paris 538 – Sarlat-la-Canéda 12 – Cahors 51 – Fumel 50 – Gourdon 20 – Périgueux 76

Office de tourisme, place de la Halle ☎ 05 53 31 71 00, Fax 05 53 31 71 09

La bastide★: ✳★★★.

L'Esplanade

2 r. Pontcarral – ☎ 05 53 28 31 41 – esplanade.domme@wanadoo.fr – Fax 05 53 28 49 92 – Open 14 March-2 November

15 rm – †€ 77/84 ††€ 77/148, ☕ € 13 – ½ P € 98/136 – **Rest** – *(closed Saturday lunch March-April, Monday except dinner May-September and Wednesday lunch)* Menu € 40 (weekdays)/100 – Carte € 38/90

◆ Périgord-style dwelling next to the walled town, overlooking the Dordogne Valley. Elegant rooms, some of which have lovely views. An elegant dining room offering a lovely panoramic view and hearty traditional dishes.

DOMPAIRE – 88 Vosges – 314 F3 – pop. 919 – alt. 300 m – ✉ 88270 26 B3

Paris 366 – Épinal 21 – Luxeuil-les-Bains 61 – Nancy 64 – Neufchâteau 56 – Vittel 24

XX **Le Commerce** with rm

pl. Gén. Leclerc – ☎ 03 29 36 50 28 – Fax 03 29 36 66 12 – Closed 22 December-12 January, Sunday dinner except hotel and Monday

7 rm – †€ 38 ††€ 40/44, ☕ € 6 – ½ P € 35/38 – **Rest** – Menu € 13 (weekday lunch)/32 – Carte € 20/35

◆ Modern dining room, whose large bay window overlooks the garden. Traditional cuisine with a regional twist. Simple, spacious rooms.

DOMPIERRE-SUR-BESBRE – 03 Allier – 326 J3 – pop. 3 477 – alt. 234 m – ✉ 03290 6 C1

Paris 324 – Bourbon-Lancy 19 – Decize 46 – Digoin 27 – Lapalisse 36 – Moulins 31

Office de tourisme, 145, Grande Rue ☎ 04 70 34 61 31, Fax 04 70 34 27 16

XX **Auberge de l'Olive** with rm — ♿ rm, rest,

av. de la Gare – ☎ 04 70 34 51 87 – contact@auberge-olive.fr – Fax 04 70 34 61 68 – Closed 20-28 September, Sunday dinner from November to March and Friday except July-August

17 rm – †€ 49 ††€ 55, ☕ € 7 – ½ P € 54 – **Rest** – Menu € 19 (Except Sunday lunchtime)/58 – Carte € 32/51

◆ Two dining areas, one country-style, the other modern with a veranda. Traditional recipes with a contemporary touch. Just two turns of the Ferris wheel away from the Pal amusement park, this inn offers refurbished, rustic-style rooms; those in the annexe are more modern.

DOMPIERRE-SUR-VEYLE – 01 Ain – 328 E4 – pop. 968 – alt. 285 m – ✉ 01240 44 B1

Paris 439 – Belley 70 – Bourg-en-Bresse 18 – Lyon 58 – Mâcon 54 – Nantua 47

L'Auberge de Dompierre

7 r. des Ecoles – ✆ 04 74 30 31 19 – aubergededompierresurveyle@orange.fr – Closed 26 August-15 September, 23-30 December, 11-18 February, Sunday dinner, Tuesday dinner and Wednesday

Rest – *(pre-book)* Menu € 12 bi (weekday lunch), € 21/36

♦ Village restaurant on the church square. Tastefully refurbished dining room serving Dombes specialities. The daily special is available in the bar.

DONNAZAC – 81 Tarn – 338 D6 – pop. 85 – alt. 291 m – ✉ 81170 29 C2

Paris 654 – Albi 22 – Montauban 66 – Toulouse 75

Les Vents Bleus without rest

rte de Caussade – ✆ 05 63 56 86 11 – lesventsbleus@orange.fr – Fax 05 63 56 86 11 – Open 20 March-28 October

5 rm ☕ – †€ 80/100 ††€ 80/140

♦ This fine 18C white stone building stands in the heart of the Gaillac vineyard, flanked by a dovecote. Each room is individually and tastefully decorated. Garden and swimming-pool.

DONON (COL) – 67 Bas-Rhin – 315 G5 – see Col du Donon

DONZENAC – 19 Corrèze – 329 K4 – pop. 2 147 – alt. 204 m – ✉ 19270

Dordogne-Berry-Limousin 24 B3

Paris 469 – Brive-la-Gaillarde 11 – Limoges 81 – Tulle 27 – Uzerche 26

Office de tourisme, place de la Liberté ✆ 05 55 85 65 35, Fax 05 55 85 72 30

Les Pans de Travassac★.

Northeast On D 920, near exit 47 A20, dir. Sadroc

Relais du Bas Limousin

at 6 km – ✆ 05 55 84 52 06 – relais-du-bas-limousin@wanadoo.fr – Fax 05 55 84 51 41 – Closed 26 October-6 November, school holidays February, Sunday dinner except July-August and Monday lunch

22 rm – †€ 46 ††€ 61, ☕ € 8,50 – ½ P € 55/64 – **Rest** – Menu (€ 16), € 26/54 – Carte € 34/52

♦ This regional style inn is set back from the main road. Individually styled rooms. Truly charming welcome. A rustic dining area and veranda, overlooking the garden and pool. Traditional fare.

DONZY – 58 Nièvre – 319 B7 – pop. 1 659 – alt. 188 m – ✉ 58220

Burgundy-Jura 7 A2

Paris 203 – Auxerre 66 – Bourges 73 – Clamecy 39 – Cosne-sur-Loire 19 – Nevers 50

Office de tourisme, 18, rue du Gal Leclerc ✆ 03 86 39 45 29

Le Grand Monarque

10 r. de l'Etape, (near the church) – ✆ 03 86 39 35 44 – monarque.jacquet@laposte.net – Fax 03 86 39 37 09 – Closed 2 January-14 February, Sunday dinner and Monday from October to Easter

11 rm – †€ 49 ††€ 58/74, ☕ € 8,50 – ½ P € 55 – **Rest** – Menu € 14 (weekday lunch), € 23/38 – Carte € 31/39

♦ Small family-run hotel in a peaceful village. A fine 16C spiral staircase leads to the guestrooms, some of which are delightful (king size beds). An attractive, original 19C kitchen. Unpretentious, traditional menu.

LE DORAT – 87 Haute-Vienne – 325 D3 – pop. 1 963 – alt. 209 m – ✉ 87210

Dordogne-Berry-Limousin 24 B1

Paris 369 – Bellac 13 – Le Blanc 49 – Guéret 68 – Limoges 58 – Poitiers 77

Office de tourisme, 17, place de la Collégiale ✆ 05 55 60 76 81, Fax 05 55 60 76 81

St-Pierre collegiate church ★★.

La Marmite

29 av. de la Gare – ✆ 05 55 60 66 94 – Fax 05 55 60 66 94 – Closed 24 June-2 July, 8-24 September, 23 February-2 March, Wednesday except dinner July-August and Tuesday

Rest – Menu € 12 (weekdays)/36 – Carte € 24/32

◆ The chef prepares hearty traditional meals, while the landlady runs the show in the wood panelled dining room. Children's play area in the garden.

DORMANS – 51 Marne – 306 D8 – pop. 3 126 – alt. 70 m – ✉ 51700 Champagne

Paris 118 – Château-Thierry 24 – Épernay 25 – Meaux 71 – Reims 41 – Soissons 46 13 **B2**

Office de tourisme, parc du Château ✆ 03 26 53 35 86, Fax 03 26 53 35 87

La Table Sourdet

6 r. Docteur Moret – ✆ 03 26 58 20 57 – Fax 03 26 58 88 82

Rest – Menu € 37/64 – Carte € 46/72

Rest *La Petite Table* – *(lunch only)* Menu € 17/32

◆ At the Table Sourdet, culinary art has been handed down from father to son for six generations! This large establishment has a comfortable dining room where one can enjoy traditional dishes. La Petite Table offers veranda dining; simple menus at reasonable prices.

DORRES – 66 Pyrénées-Orientales – 344 C8 – pop. 219 – alt. 1 458 m – ✉ 66760 Languedoc-Roussillon-Tarn Gorges 22 A3

Paris 849 – Ax-les-Thermes 47 – Font-Romeu-Odeillo-Via 15 – Perpignan 104

Marty

3 carrer Major – ✆ 04 68 30 07 52 – info@hotelmarty.com – Fax 04 68 30 08 12 – Closed 15 October-20 December

21 rm – €46 €53, €9 – ½ P €45/47 – **Rest** – Menu €16/31 – Carte €20/47

◆ Family guesthouse in the Cerdagne hills close to a sulphurous spring and its small lake. Slightly faded rooms, some with loggias. Panoramic restaurant decorated with farm tools and hunting trophies. Generous portions of Catalan cuisine.

DOUAI – 59 Nord – 302 G5 – pop. 42 796 – Built-up area 518 727 – alt. 31 m – ✉ 59500 Northern France and the Paris Region 31 C2

Paris 194 – Arras 26 – Lille 42 – Tournai 39 – Valenciennes 47

Office de tourisme, 70, place d'Armes ✆ 03 27 88 26 79, Fax 03 27 99 38 78

de Thumeries ThumeriesNorth: 15 km by D 8, ✆ 03 20 86 58 98.

Belfry★ BY **D** - Musée de la Chartreuse★★.

Historical centre of the Lewarde mining area★★ Southeast: 8 km by ②.

Plan on next page

La Terrasse AC rest, P VISA

36 terrasse St-Pierre – ✆ 03 27 88 70 04 – contact@laterrasse.fr – Fax 03 27 88 36 05

24 rm – €55 €80, €10,50 – ½ P €60 – **Rest** – Menu (€19), €23 bi/79 – Carte €43/63 BY **a**

◆ A welcoming hotel tucked away in a small street next to the collegiate Church of St. Peter. The rooms are modest in size and decorated in a 1980s style. Generous classic cuisine, prepared simply but skilfully and an especially good wine list (900 appellations).

Ibis without rest

pl. St-Amé – ✆ 03 27 87 27 27 – h0956@accor.com – Fax 03 27 98 31 64

42 rm – €55/65 €55/65, €7,50 AY **e**

◆ An Ibis hotel standards in an historic setting. These 16C and 18C houses have practical rooms of various sizes; exposed beams in the 3rd floor attic rooms.

Au Turbotin AC VISA

9 r. Massue – ✆ 03 27 87 04 16 – g.coussement@wanadoo.fr – Closed 1st-21 August, Saturday lunch, Sunday dinner and Monday AY **s**

Rest – Menu € 21 (weekdays)/72 bi – Carte € 45/55

◆ The lobster tank is displayed as if it were a work of art in this restaurant, revamped in a pleasantly contemporary spirit. Updated recipes that continue to uphold regional traditions.

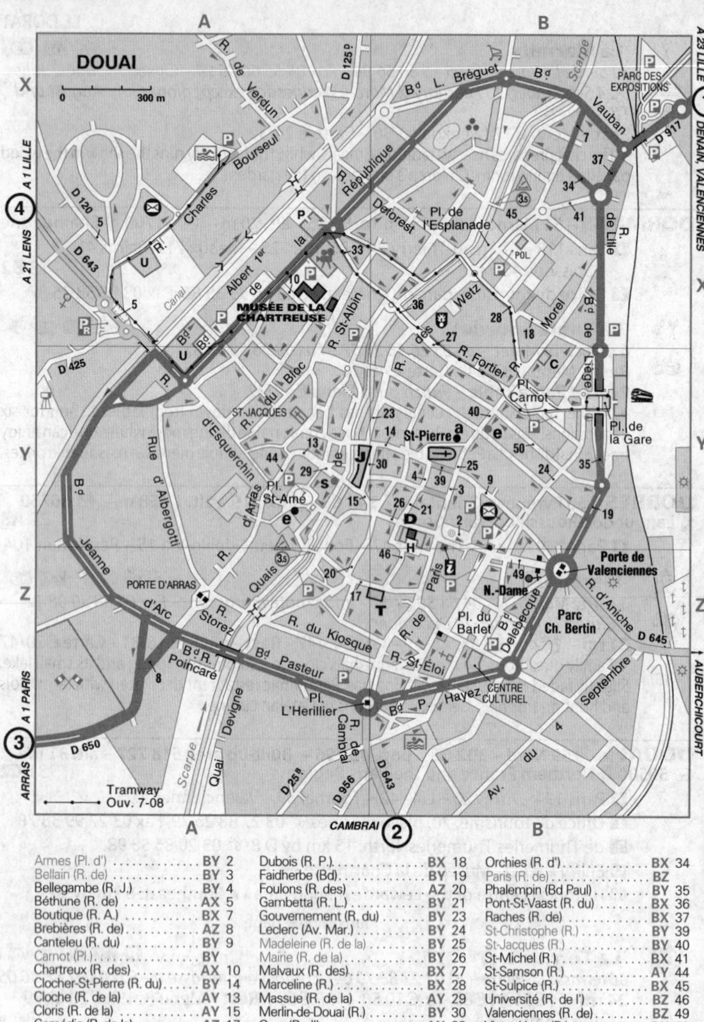

Armes (Pl. d')	BY	2	Dubois (R. P.)	BX	18	Orchies (R. d')	BX	34
Bellain (R. de)	BY	3	Faidherbe (Bd)	BY	19	Paris (R. de)	BZ	
Bellegambe (R. J.)	BY	4	Foulons (R. des)	AZ	20	Phalempin (Bd Paul)	BY	35
Béthune (R. de)	AX	5	Gambetta (R. L.)	BY	21	Pont-St-Vaast (R. du)	BX	36
Boutique (R. A.)	BX	7	Gouvernement (R. du)	BY	23	Raches (R. de)	BX	37
Brebières (R. de)	AZ	8	Leclerc (Av. Mar.)	BY	24	St-Christophe (R.)	BY	39
Canteleu (R. du)	BY	9	Madeleine (R. de la)	BY	25	St-Jacques (R.)	BY	40
Carnot (Pl.)	BY		Mairie (R. de la)	BY	26	St-Michel (R.)	BX	41
Chartreux (R. des)	AX	10	Malvaux (R. des)	BX	27	St-Samson (R.)	AY	44
Clocher-St-Pierre (R. du)	BY	14	Marceline (R.)	BX	28	St-Sulpice (R.)	BX	45
Cloche (R. de la)	AY	13	Massue (R. de la)	AY	29	Université (R. de l')	BZ	46
Cloris (R. de la)	AY	15	Merlin-de-Douai (R.)	BY	30	Valenciennes (R. de)	BZ	49
Comédie (R. de la)	AZ	17	Ocre (R. d')	AX	33	Victor-Hugo (R.)	BY	50

X

Le P'tit Gouverneur

76 r. St-Jean – ✆ 03 27 88 90 04
– leptitgouverneur@voila.fr
– Closed 1st-15 August, 1st-8 January, Sunday and Monday BY **e**

Rest – Menu € 18 (weekday lunch), € 24/46 – Carte € 36/51

◆ This smart bistro on a street corner is adorned with statues of animals, adding a touch of fantasy to the neighbourhood. Market sourced cuisine and a 'main dish and beer' formula for those in a hurry.

in Roost-Warendin 10 km by ①, D 917 and D 8 – pop. 5 744 – alt. 22 m – ✉ 59286

Syndicat d'initiative, 270, rue Brossolette ☎ 03 27 95 90 00, Fax 03 27 95 90 01

XX **Le Chat Botté**

Château de Bernicourt – ☎ 03 27 80 24 44 – contact@restaurantlechatbotte.com – Fax 03 27 80 35 81 – Closed 1st-15 August, Sunday dinner and Monday

Rest – Menu (€ 20), € 32/65 – Carte € 50/65

◆ The pretty 18C Bernicourt Castle is surrounded by parkland and has pastel colours, cane furniture and green plants in the outhouses. Classical cuisine and impressive wine list.

in Brebières 7 km by ③ – pop. 4 424 – alt. 48 m – ✉ 62117

XXX **Air Accueil**

D 950 – ☎ 03 21 50 01 02 – Fax 03 21 50 84 17 – Closed 18-31 August, Sunday dinner and Monday

Rest – Menu € 29/60

◆ A long brick building near an aerodrome. A Louis XIII-style dining room with bright floral fabrics and a luxuriant terrace. Wine-tasting in one of the lounges.

DOUAINS – 27 Eure – 304 I7 – see Vernon

DOUARNENEZ – 29 Finistère – 308 F6 – pop. 15 827 – alt. 25 m – ✉ 29100 Brittany

Paris 585 – Brest 76 – Lorient 88 – Quimper 23 – Vannes 141 9 **A2**

Office de tourisme, 2, rue Docteur Mével ☎ 02 98 92 13 35, Fax 02 98 92 70 47

Boulevard Jean-Richepin and new harbour★ ≤★ Y - Port du Rosmeur★ - Musée à flot★★ - collection★ in the boat museum - Ploaré: church ★ tower South: 1 km - Pointe de Leydé★ ≤★ Northwest: 5 km.

DOUARNENEZ

Street	Grid	No.
Anatole-France (R.)	Y	2
Baigneurs (R. des)	Y	5
Barré (R. J.)	YZ	7
Berthelot (R.)	Z	8
Centre (R. du)	Y	10
Croas-Talud (R.)	Z	14
Duguay-Trouin (R.)	YZ	15
Enfer (Pl. de l')	YZ	16
Grand-Port (Quai du)	Y	19
Grand-Port (R. du)	Y	20
Jaurès (R. Jean)	YZ	
Jean-Bart (R.)	Y	24
Kerivel (R. E.)	YZ	21
Laënnec (R.)	Z	25
Lamennais (R.)	Z	27
Marine (R. de la)	Y	32
Michel (R. L.)	Y	36
Monte-au-Ciel (R.)	Z	37
Péri (Pl. Gabriel)	Y	42
Petit-Port (Quai du)	Y	43
Plomarc'h (R. des)	YZ	44
Stalingrad (Pl.)	Z	65
Vaillant (Pl. E.)	Y	59
Victor-Hugo (R.)	Z	60
Voltaire (R.)	Y	62

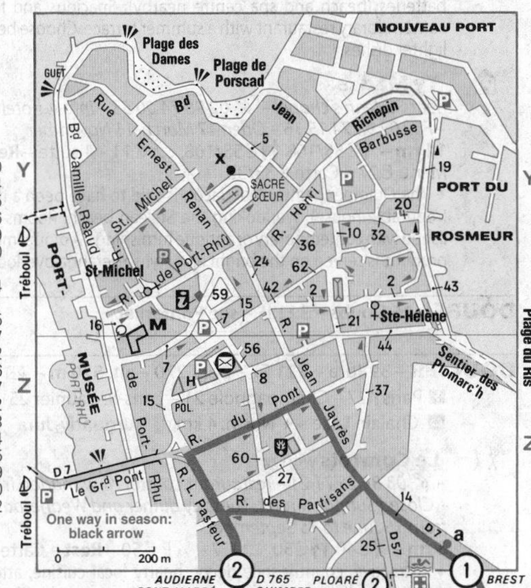

Le Clos de Vallombreuse

7 r. d'Estienne-d'Orves – ☎ 02 98 92 63 64 – clos.vallombreuse@wanadoo.fr – Fax 02 98 92 84 98 Y **x**

25 rm – †€ 46/122 ††€ 52/122, ☕ € 11 – ½ P € 56/91 – **Rest** – Menu € 19 (weekdays)/55 – Carte € 38/58

◆ This early-20C mansion, built by a canning magnate, overlooks the bay. Individually decorated rooms in the lodge and wing; walled garden and pool with a view of the port. An elegant decor and seafood explain the restaurant's appeal.

Le Kériolet with rm rm, VISA MC

29 r. Croas-Talud – ✆ 02 98 92 16 89 – keriolet2@wanadoo.fr – Fax 02 98 92 62 94 – Closed 9-22 February and Monday lunch off season Z **a**

8 rm – †€ 50/60 ††€ 50/60, ☕ € 6,50 – ½ P € 58 – **Rest** – Menu € 13,50 (weekday lunch), € 20/38 – Carte € 26/52

◆ The chef prepares traditional dishes that do full justice to local country and seafood produce. The dining room, decorated in a tasteful unobtrusive nautical style, overlooks a small garden. Simple but well renovated rooms.

Quimper road 4 km – ✉ 29100 Douarnenez

Auberge de Kerveoc'h rest, P VISA MC

42, rte de Kerveoc'h, via D 765 – ✆ 02 98 92 07 58 – contact@auberge-kerveoch.com – Fax 02 98 92 03 58

14 rm – †€ 47/56 ††€ 47/75, ☕ € 8 – ½ P € 54/68 – **Rest** – *(closed Sunday dinner October-May) (dinner only)* Menu € 24

◆ The rooms in the farmhouse have been tastefully refurbished; those in the small manor house are older but remain pleasant and attractive. Enjoy the peace and quiet in the pretty garden. Short set menu devised depending on the season and a distinctly countrified decoration.

in Tréboul 3 km Northwest – ✉29100 Douarnenez

Thalasstonic rm, rest, P VISA MC AE

r. des Professeurs Curie – ✆ 02 98 74 45 45 – info-hotel-dz@thalasso.com – Fax 02 98 74 36 07

46 rm – †€ 51/72 ††€ 75/110, ☕ € 11 – 4 suites – ½ P € 74/116

Rest – Menu (€ 18), € 25/95 – Carte € 34/75

◆ This non-smoking hotel by the sea enjoys the ideal location in which to recharge your batteries (beach and spa centre nearby). Spacious and functional guestrooms. Huge contemporary restaurant with a summer terrace. Choose between traditional cuisine and lighter dishes.

Ty Mad P VISA MC

near St. Jean's chapel – ✆ 02 98 74 00 53 – info@hoteltymad.fr – Fax 02 98 74 15 16 – Open 17 March-11 November

14 rm – †€ 55/168 ††€ 55/168, ☕ € 11 – 1 suite – **Rest** – *(dinner only)* Menu € 27 – Carte € 33/35

◆ The Quimper painter Max Jacob is said to have been a frequent visitor to this ty mad (reputable house) overlooking the St-Jean beach. Rooms are personalised and embellished with contemporary or antique furnishings. A dinner menu based on seasonal market produce is served on the bright and stylish veranda overlooking the garden.

DOUBS – 25 Doubs – 321 I5 – see Pontarlier

DOUCIER – 39 Jura – 321 E7 – pop. 270 – alt. 526 m – ✉ 39130 16 B3

Paris 427 – Champagnole 21 – Lons-le-Saunier 25

Chalain Lake ★★ North: 4 km, **Burgundy-Jura**

Le Comtois with rm VISA MC AE

– ✆ 03 84 25 71 21 – restaurant.comtois@wanadoo.fr – Fax 03 84 25 71 21 – Closed Sunday dinner, Tuesday dinner and Wednesday dinner except from 15 June to 15 September

8 rm – †€ 40 ††€ 50, ☕ € 7 – ½ P € 50 – **Rest** – Carte € 30/37

◆ Attractive, country-style decor, hearty local cuisine, attentive service and a friendly welcome – all this and a fine selection of Jura wines in this stylish inn!

DOUÉ-LA-FONTAINE – 49 Maine-et-Loire – 317 H5 – pop. 7 450 – alt. 75 m – ✉ 49700 Châteaux of the Loire 35 C2

Paris 322 – Angers 40 – Châtellerault 86 – Cholet 50 – Saumur 19 – Thouars 30

Office de tourisme, 30, place des Fontaines ✆ 02 41 59 20 49, Fax 02 41 59 93 85

Zoo de Doué★★.

La Saulaie without rest

2 km on Montreuil-Bellay road – ✆ 02 41 59 96 10 – hoteldelasaulaie@wanadoo.fr – Fax 02 41 59 96 11 – Closed 19 December-4 January

44 rm – €40/52 €48/90, €7,50

◆ After a visit to the "cave dwellings" in the vicinity, return to natural light in this recently built establishment with modern, colourful and fairly spacious rooms.

Auberge Bienvenue with rm

104 rte de Cholet, (opposite the zoo) – ✆ 02 41 59 22 44 – info@aubergebienvenue.com – Fax 02 41 59 93 49 – Closed 22 December-14 January

10 rm – €47/62 €47/62, €8,50 – ½ P €65/85 – **Rest** – *(closed Sunday dinner and Monday)* Menu €23 (weekdays)/52 – Carte €39/56

◆ This inn serves tasty, traditional dishes in a warm, welcoming atmosphere. Flower-decked terrace. Spacious modern rooms.

De France with rm

19 pl. Champ de Foire – ✆ 02 41 59 12 27 – jarnot@hoteldefrance-doue.com – Fax 02 41 59 76 00 – Closed 20 December-20 January, Sunday dinner and Monday

17 rm – €42 €44, €7 – ½ P €48/55 – **Rest** – Menu (€17), €21/38 – Carte €28/41

◆ A restaurant in the city of the rose with mellow decor: Louis XVI chairs and walls and ceilings hung with drapes. Simple rooms, being progressively renovated.

DOURDAN – 91 Essonne – 312 B4 – pop. 9 555 – alt. 100 m – ✉ 91410

Northern France and the Paris Region 18 **B2**

Paris 54 – Chartres 48 – Étampes 18 – Évry 44 – Orléans 81 – Rambouillet 22 – Versailles 51

Office de tourisme, place du Général-de-Gaulle ✆ 01 64 59 86 97, Fax 01 60 81 05 69

Rochefort Chisan Country Club Rochefort-en-Yvelines Château de Rochefort/Yvelines, North: 8 km by D 836 and D 149, ✆ 01 30 41 31 81 ;

de Forges-les-Bains Forges-les-Bains Route du Général Leclerc, North: 14 km by D 838, ✆ 01 64 91 48 18.

Place du Marché aux grains★ - Virgin with parrot★ in the museum.

Host. Blanche de Castille

pl. Marché aux Herbes – ✆ 01 60 81 19 10 – info@residourdan.fr – Fax 01 60 81 19 11

33 rm – €90 €90, €8 – 12 suites – **Rest** – *(closed 1st-15 August, Saturday lunch and Sunday)* Menu €16/27

◆ In the heart of old Dourdan, an old house opposite the place des Halles. Comfortable rooms (12 for families). Half of them have views over the church with its three steeples. The dining room is both elegant and rustic (hearth, chandeliers and beams). Traditional menu.

Auberge de l'Angélus

4 pl. Chariot – ✆ 01 64 59 83 72 – Fax 01 64 59 83 72 – Closed 30 July-20 August, 24-30 December, 21 February-4 March, Monday dinner, Tuesday dinner and Wednesday

Rest – Menu €22/42 – Carte €68/78

◆ Just off the picturesque historical centre, 18C posthouse with three recently renovated dining rooms. Pretty courtyard terrace.

DOURGNE – 81 Tarn – 338 E10 – pop. 1 186 – alt. 250 m – ✉ 81110

29 **C2**

Paris 742 – Toulouse 67 – Carcassonne 52 – Castelnaudary 35 – Castres 19 – Gaillac 64

Office de tourisme, 1, avenue du maquis ✆ 05 63 74 27 19, Fax 05 63 74 27 19

Hostellerie de la Montagne Noire with rm

15 pl. Promenades – ✆ 05 63 50 31 12 rest,

– hotel.restaurant.montagne.noire@wanadoo.fr – Fax 05 63 50 13 55 – Closed 1st-7 September, 2 weeks in November-18 February-2 March

9 rm – €46 €49, €8,50 – ½ P €31 – **Rest** – *(closed Sunday evening and Monday)* Menu €15 (weekday lunch), €22/44 – Carte €29/41

◆ This village residence has two dining rooms - one is modern, the other decorated in an elegant country style. The terrace is shaded by plane trees and the cuisine is traditional.

North 4 km by D 85 and D 14 – ✉ 81110 St-Avit

XX **Les Saveurs de St-Avit**

– ✆ 05 63 50 11 45 – simonscott6@aol.com – Fax 05 63 50 11 45 – Closed 15-30 November, 1st-15 January, Tuesday lunch, Wednesday lunch and Thursday lunch from mid October to mid April, Saturday lunch, Sunday dinner and Monday

Rest – *(number of covers limited, pre-book)* Menu € 28/82 bi – Carte € 58/82

◆ This restaurant in a converted farmhouse has a charming dining room that skilfully blends rustic and modern styles. Fine cuisine in keeping with current taste and based on local produce.

DOURLERS – 59 Nord – 302 L6 – pop. 568 – alt. 171 m – ✉ 59440 31 D3

Paris 245 – Avesnes-sur-Helpe 10 – Lille 94 – Maubeuge 13 – Le Quesnoy 27 – St-Quentin 75

XX **Auberge du Châtelet**

rte d'Avesnes-sur-Helpe, on the N 2 : 1 km ✉ 59440 Avesnes-sur-Helpe – ✆ 03 27 61 06 70 – carlierchatelet@aol.com – Fax 03 27 61 20 02 – Closed Sunday evening and evenings on public holidays

Rest – Menu (€ 23 bi), € 25/55 bi – Carte € 36/67

◆ The same family has been running this pretty long cottage since 1971. A rustic interior, quiet terrace, traditional menu and magnificent wine list (excellent vintages).

DOURNAZAC – 87 Haute-Vienne – 325 C7 – pop. 728 – alt. 368 m – ✉ 87230

Dordogne-Berry-Limousin 24 B2

Paris 436 – Limoges 42 – Panazol 47 – Saint-Junien 41

Château de Montbrun without rest

at Montbrun, 2 km northwest by D 64 – ✆ 05 55 78 65 26 – Montbrun@Montbrun.com – Fax 05 55 78 65 34

6 rm – †€ 175/200 ††€ 175/200

◆ Several of the rooms in this chateau are furnished in the style of the 15C. Wide choice of leisure activities available, including billiards, fishing, hunting, crossbow shooting and horse riding.

DOUSSARD – 74 Haute-Savoie – 328 K6 – pop. 2 781 – alt. 456 m – ✉ 74210

Paris 555 – Albertville 27 – Annecy 20 – Megève 42 46 F1

Arcalod rm, rest,

– ✆ 04 50 44 30 22 – info@hotelarcalod.fr – Fax 04 50 44 85 03 – Open 10 May-30 September

33 rm – †€ 58/67 ††€ 62/85, € 10 – ½ P € 59/76 – **Rest** – Menu € 20 (weekday lunch), € 26/31 – Carte € 26/33

◆ The numerous free leisure activities (bicycling, hiking, archery, etc.) are the great bonus of this family chalet. Small, well kept rooms and large tree lined garden. Spacious, modern dining room serving Savoyard inspired guesthouse cuisine.

DOUVAINE – 74 Haute-Savoie – 328 K3 – pop. 3 859 – alt. 428 m – ✉ 74140 46 F1

Paris 555 – Annecy 63 – Chamonix-Mont-Blanc 87 – Genève 18 – Thonon-les-Bains 16

Office de tourisme, place de l'Hôtel de Ville ✆ 04 50 94 10 55, Fax 04 50 94 36 13

XXX **Ô Flaveurs** (Jérôme Mamet)

Château de Chilly, 2 km south-east via rte de Crépy – ✆ 04 50 35 46 55 – restaurantoflaveurs@wanadoo.fr – Fax 04 50 35 41 31 – Closed Tuesday and Wednesday

Rest – Menu € 29 (weekday lunch), € 45/75 – Carte € 68/115

Spec. Foie gras de canard des Landes confit. Suprême de volaille fermière parfumé au pin. Millefeuille chocolat, crème praliné.

◆ Modern inventive cuisine is to the fore in this refined restaurant occupying a small 15C château which has retained its authentic feel (stone, exposed beams, fireplace).

La Couronne

– ✆ 04 50 85 10 20 – *la.couronne2@freesbee.fr* – *Fax 04 50 85 10 40*
– *Closed 26 July-17 August, 22 December-7 January, Sunday dinner and Monday*
Rest – Menu € 13 bi (weekday lunch), € 32/36 – Carte € 37/54
◆ Dating from 1780, this inn has a warm dining room (exposed beams, sunny shades) opening onto a small shaded courtyard. Up-to-date cuisine.

DOUVRES-LA-DÉLIVRANDE – 14 Calvados – 303 J4 – pop. 4 809 – alt. 19 m – ✉ 14440 Normandy 32 B2

Paris 246 – Bayeux 26 – Caen 15 – Deauville 48

Syndicat d'initiative, 41, rue Général-de-Gaulle ✆ 02 31 37 93 10, Fax 02 31 37 93 10

in Cresserons 2 km East by D 35 – pop. 1 202 – alt. 9 m – ✉ 14440

La Valise Gourmande

7 rte de Lion sur Mer – ✆ *02 31 37 39 10* – *contact@lavalisegourmande-caen.com* – *Fax 02 31 37 59 13* – *Closed Sunday dinner, Tuesday lunch and Monday*
Rest – Menu € 28/52 – Carte € 45/75
◆ 18C priory and walled garden. Three small, elegantly decorated rooms with a country feel, one including a fireplace. Traditional cuisine.

DRACY-LE-FORT – 71 Saône-et-Loire – 320 I9 – see Chalon-sur-Saône

DRAGUIGNAN – 83 Var – 340 N4 – pop. 32 829 – alt. 178 m – ✉ 83300 French Riviera 41 C3

Paris 862 – Fréjus 30 – Marseille 124 – Nice 89 – Toulon 79

Office de tourisme, 2, avenue Lazard Carnot ✆ 04 98 10 51 05, Fax 04 98 10 51 10

de Saint Endréol La Motte Route de Bagnols en Forêt, by Le Muy road and D 47: 15 km, ✆ 04 94 51 89 89.

Musée des Arts et Traditions populaires de moyenne Provence★ M².

Site★ of Trans-en-Provence South: 5 km.

Plan on next page

Mercure without rest

11 bd G. Clemenceau – ✆ *04 94 50 95 09* – *h2969@accor.com* – *Fax 04 94 68 23 49* Z n
38 rm – †€ 88/119 ††€ 98/129, ☕ € 12
◆ Modern hotel complex in the centre of town, near the museums. Spacious, well-equipped and soundproofed rooms, some of which have been refurbished.

Lou Galoubet

23 bd J. Jaurès – ✆ *04 94 68 08 50* – *lougaloubet@orange.fr* – *Fax 04 94 68 08 50* – *Closed 17 July-6 August, Sunday dinner, Tuesday dinner and Wednesday* Z e
Rest – Menu € 24 (weekday lunch), € 29/45 – Carte € 39/51
◆ Red leatherette chairs and benches add colour and give this town centre restaurant a brasserie feel. Open kitchens. Classic cuisine.

Flayosc road 4 km by ③ and D 557 – ✉ 83300 Draguignan

Les Oliviers without rest

– ✆ *04 94 68 25 74* – *hotel-les-oliviers@club-internet.fr* – *Fax 04 94 68 57 54* – *Closed 10-20 January*
12 rm – †€ 49/58 ††€ 51/58, ☕ € 8
◆ This unpretentious hotel has undergone constant renovation and offers well-kept, ground floor rooms opening onto a flower garden where one can breakfast in summertime.

DRAGUIGNAN

Cisson (R.) .... YZ 3
Clemenceau (Bd) .... Z
Clément (R. P.) .... Z 4
Droits-de-l'Homme (Parvis des) .... Z 5
Gay (Pl. C.) .... Y 6
Grasse (Av. de) .... Y 8
Joffre (Bd. Mar.) .... Z 9
Juiverie (R. de la) .... Y 12
Kennedy (Bd J.) .... Z 13
Leclerc (Bd Gén.) .... Z 14
Marchands (R. des) .... Y 15
Marché (Pl. du) .... Y 16
Martyrs-de-la-Résistance (Bd des) .... Z 17
Marx-Dormoy (Bd) .... Z 18
Mireur (R. F.) .... Y 19
Observance (R. de l') .... Y 20
République (R. de la) .... Z 23
Rosso (Av. P.) .... Z 24

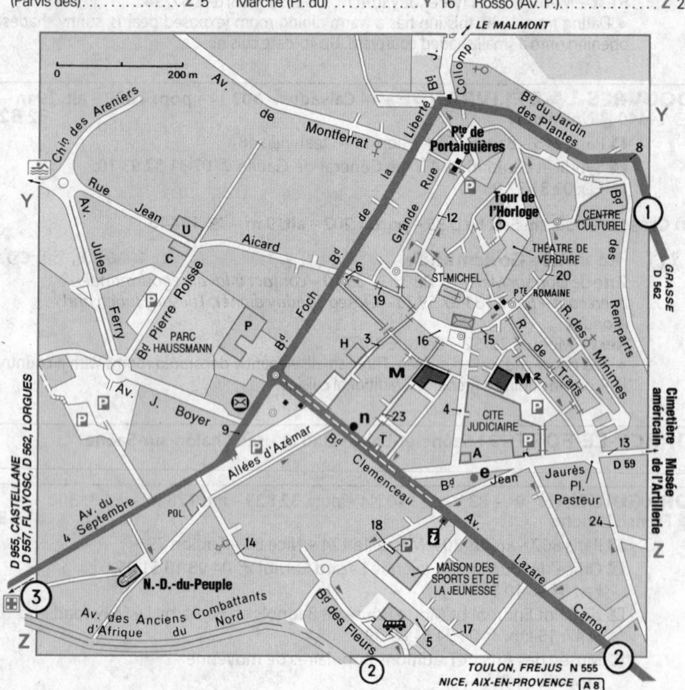

in Flayosc 7 km by ③ and D 557 – pop. 3 924 – alt. 310 m – ✉ 83780

Office de tourisme, place Pied Bari ✆ 04 94 70 41 31, Fax 04 94 70 47 91

L'Oustaou

au village – ✆ 04 94 70 42 69 – lymal74@aol.com – Fax 04 94 84 64 92 – Closed Sunday dinner and Wednesday from October to April, Tuesday lunch and Friday lunch from May to September and Monday

Rest – Menu (€ 20), € 26/40 – Carte € 34/59

◆ The cuisine here is regional, with a contemporary touch, and takes full advantage of local produce. Attentive service and rustic atmosphere in what was once a post house with a name that means small farmhouse.

La Salle à Manger

9 pl. République – ✆ 04 94 84 66 04 – ronald-abbink@wanadoo.fr – Fax 04 94 85 30 59 – Closed 27 October-6 November, 23 December-3 January, Sunday dinner November-March, Tuesday lunch April-October and Monday

Rest – Menu € 25/43 – Carte € 42/66

◆ Welcoming establishment run by a Batavian couple. A neo-rustic setting (exposed beams, stone or whitewashed walls) where cuisine with a contemporary touch is served at tables with linen cloths.

DRAIN – 49 Maine-et-Loire – 317 B4 – pop. 1 668 – alt. 53 m – ✉ 49530 34 B2

Paris 359 – Cholet 60 – Nantes 41 – Saint-Herblain 48

Le Mésangeau

5 km south on the D 154 – ✆ 02 40 98 21 57 – le.mesangeau@wanadoo.fr – Fax 02 40 98 28 62

5 rm – €80/100 €90/110 – ½ P €76/85 – **Table d'hôte** – Menu €35 bi

◆ This spacious 1830 residence has a relaxing atmosphere, with extensive gardens, a small lake, golf course and collection of early 20C motor cars. Renovated guestrooms decorated in the style of the region.

LE DRAMONT – 83 Var – 340 Q5 – see St-Raphaël

DRAVEIL – 91 Essonne – 312 D3 – 101 36 – see Paris, Area

DREUX – 28 Eure-et-Loir – 311 E3 – pop. 31 849 – alt. 82 m – ✉ 28100

Normandy 11 B1

Paris 78 – Chartres 36 – Évreux 44 – Mantes-la-Jolie 43

Office de tourisme, 6, rue des Embûches ✆ 02 37 46 01 73, Fax 02 37 46 19 27

Belfry ★ AY B - Painted mirrors★★ of the royale St-Louis chapel AY.

Plan on next page

Le Beffroi without rest

12 pl. Métézeau – ✆ 02 37 50 02 03 – hotel.beffroi@club-internet.fr – Fax 02 37 42 07 69 – Closed 24 July-15 August AZ e

15 rm – €65 €65, €7

◆ The rooms give a view of the River Blaise or St-Pierre Church. The decor features a variety of objects selected by the owner, a former international reporter. Fine mosaics in the bathrooms.

Le St-Pierre

19 r. Sénarmont – ✆ 02 37 46 47 00 – contact@lesaint-pierre.com – Fax 02 37 64 26 37 – Closed 14-30 July, 2-10 March, Thursday dinner, Sunday dinner and Monday

Rest – Menu (€14), €16 (weekdays)/29 – Carte €26/36 BY r

◆ This restaurant tucked away in a tiny side street near St-Pierre Church has three small colourful dining rooms furnished in bistro sytle. Tasty traditional cuisine.

in Cherisy 4,5 km by ② – pop. 1 768 – alt. 88 m – ✉ 28500

Le Vallon de Chérisy

12 rte de Paris – ✆ 02 37 43 70 08 – Fax 02 37 43 86 00 – Closed in July, Sunday dinner, Tuesday dinner and Wednesday

Rest – Menu €28/57 – Carte €28/57

◆ Half-timbered building offering a choice of two settings: dining room with exposed beams and Louis Philippe furniture, or veranda with picture windows and cane chairs. Cuisine in keeping with current taste.

in Ste-Gemme-Moronval 6 km by ②, N 12, D 912 and D 308[1] – pop. 691 – alt. 79 m – ✉ 28500

L'Escapade

pl. du Dr Jouve – ✆ 02 37 43 72 05 – Fax 02 37 43 86 96 – Closed 4-27 August, 6-20 February, Sunday dinner, Monday dinner and Tuesday

Rest – Menu €35 – Carte €57/92

◆ Prepare for a culinary adventure in this welcoming country type inn that offers traditional recipes. Restful terrace and stylish dining hall embellished by attractive woodwork.

in Vernouillet-centre 2 km South by D 311 AZ – pop. 11 496 – alt. 97 m – ✉ 28500

Auberge de la Vallée Verte with rm

6 r. Lucien Dupuis, (near the church) – ✆ 02 37 46 04 04 – aubergevallee@wanadoo.fr – Fax 02 37 42 91 17 – Closed 3-27 August, 21 December-6 January, Monday except hotel and Sunday

16 rm – €70/90 €70/90, €10 – **Rest** – Menu €30/55 bi – Carte €40/60

◆ Religiously preserved, age-old rafters and red floor tiles create the rural atmosphere of this old Vernouillet restaurant. Traditional menus. Recently opened rooms in the annexe with a garden.

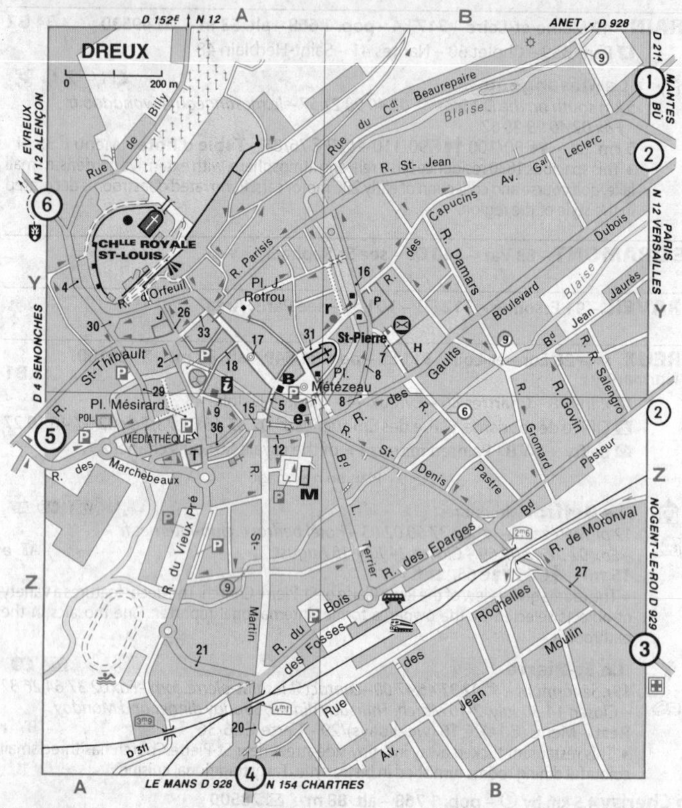

in Vert-en-Drouais 8 km west by N 12 and D 314 – pop. 1 049 – alt. 92 m – ✉ 28500

Château de Marsalin

– ✆ 02 37 82 85 06 – marsalin@chateau-de-marsalin.com – Fax 02 37 82 85 06 – *Closed February holidays*

5 rm – 🚹€ 145/260 🚹🚹€ 145/260, ☕ € 28 – 1 suite – **Table d'hôte** – Menu € 70

◆ Château rebuilt in 1850 (vestiges of two 16C towers) with French style gardens. Refined atmosphere, period costume evenings and prestige meals in the sumptuous dining-room. *Grands crus* and cooking classes.

DRUSENHEIM – 67 Bas-Rhin – 315 L4 – pop. 4 723 – alt. 122 m – ✉ 67410

1 **B1**

Paris 499 – Haguenau 17 – Saverne 61 – Strasbourg 33 – Wissembourg 48

Auberge du Gourmet with rm

rte Strasbourg, Southwest : 1 km – ✆ *03 88 53 30 60* – *info@auberge-gourmet.com* – *Fax 03 88 53 31 39* – *Closed 18 August-10 September and 18 February-5 March*

11 rm – 🚹€ 37/43 🚹🚹€ 45/51, ☕ € 6 – ½ P € 49 – **Rest** – *(closed Saturday lunchtime, Tuesday evening and Wednesday)* Menu € 24/50 – Carte € 26/59

◆ The hotel at the entrance to this pleasant village has a welcoming dining room with a coffered ceiling. Alsace cuisine and dishes based on fresh market produce. Stylish rooms.

DRUYES-LES-BELLES-FONTAINES – 89 Yonne – 319 D6 – pop. 288 – alt. 168 m – ✉ 89560 7 **B2**

Paris 183 – Auxerre 34 – Clamecy 17 – Gien 75 – Montargis 98

L'Auberge des Sources

– ✆ 03 86 41 55 14 – *aubergedessources@wanadoo.fr – Closed January and February*

8 rm – €60/70 €60/70, €9 – ½ P €70 – **Rest** – *(closed Monday and Tuesday from September to May)* Menu €27/33 – Carte €28/55

◆ Former post house in a quiet Burgundy village. Ask for one of the recently refurbished rooms in the main wing. Get an overview of regional specialities in the countrified dining room or on the patio terrace.

DUCEY – 50 Manche – 303 E8 – pop. 2 174 – alt. 15 m – ✉ 50220 Normandy

Paris 348 – Avranches 11 – Fougères 41 – Rennes 80 – St-Hilaire-du-Harcouët 16 – St-Lô 68 32 **A3**

Office de tourisme, 4, rue du Génie ✆ 02 33 60 21 53, Fax 02 33 60 54 07

Moulin de Ducey without rest

1 Grande Rue – ✆ 02 33 60 25 25 – info@moulindeducey.com – Fax 02 33 60 26 76 – Closed 19 December-4 January

28 rm – €46/100 €61/110, €10,50

◆ Between the watercourse and the Sélune, the old mill seems to be sitting on a green islet. English-style rooms and breakfast room overlooking the river (salmon fishing).

Auberge de la Sélune

2 r. Saint-Germain – ✆ 02 33 48 53 62 – info@selune.com – Fax 02 33 48 90 30 – Closed 23 November-15 December, 18 January-9 February and Monday October-March

20 rm – €60 €64, €8,50 – ½ P €65 – **Rest** – Menu €17 (weekdays)/40 – Carte €23/39

◆ This handsome stone house is home to progressively renovated rooms, some of which enjoy a view of the pretty garden with a picturesque shelter on the banks of the Sélune. Pleasant dining rooms, including one overlooking the greenery.

DUINGT – 74 Haute-Savoie – 328 K6 – pop. 797 – alt. 450 m – ✉ 74410 French Alps 46 **F1**

Paris 548 – Albertville 34 – Annecy 12 – Megève 48 – St-Jorioz 3

Office de tourisme, rue du Vieux Village ✆ 04 50 77 64 75

Le Clos Marcel

rest,

410 allée de la Plage – ✆ 04 50 68 67 47 – lionel@clos-marcel.com – Fax 04 50 68 61 11 – Open 19 April-27 September

15 rm – €40/86 €40/86, €8,50 – ½ P €53/76 – **Rest** – *(closed Tuesday except July-August)* Menu (€20), €26 – Carte €35/50

◆ All rooms overlook the lake and the peaks on the opposite bank; pleasant lakeside garden and private jetty. Panoramic restaurant and enchanting tree-lined terrace.

Auberge du Roselet with rm

– ✆ 04 50 68 67 19 – nicolas.falquet@wanadoo.fr – Fax 04 50 68 64 80

14 rm – €80/104 €80/110, €10 – ½ P €80 – **Rest** – Menu €22 (weekdays)/55 – Carte €34/63

◆ Fish fresh from the lake (caught by the owner's cousin) served on the waterside terrace or in one of two dining rooms (one classical, the other more nautical). The rooms are a tad old fashioned; small private beach.

DUNES – 82 Tarn-et-Garonne – 337 A7 – pop. 893 – alt. 120 m – ✉ 82340

Paris 655 – Agen 21 – Auvillar 13 – Miradoux 12 – Moissac 32 28 **B2**

Les Templiers

1 pl. Martyrs – ✆ 05 63 39 86 21 – lestempliers4@wanadoo.fr – Fax 05 63 39 86 21 – Closed 5-15 March, autumn half-term holidays, Tuesday dinner, Saturday lunch, Sunday dinner and Monday

Rest – Menu €22 (weekdays)/47

◆ This 16C building makes the most of its rustic charm. Bright decor (yellow tones, stonework, bricks and flowers) and a terrace under the arches. Contemporary cuisine.

DUNIÈRES – 43 Haute-Loire – 331 I2 – pop. 2 949 – alt. 760 m – ✉ 43220

▶ Paris 549 – Le Puy-en-Velay 52 – St-Agrève 30 – St-Étienne 37 6 **D3**

XX **La Tour** with rm

7 ter r. Fraisse, (D 61) – ✆ 04 71 66 86 66 – la.tour-hotel-restaurant@wanadoo.fr – Fax 04 71 66 82 32 – Closed 1st-9 March, 23 August-5 September, 1er-5 January, 2-28 February

11 rm – 🚹€ 53/58 🚹🚹€ 53/58, ☕ € 8 – ½ P € 54/58 – **Rest** – *(closed Friday dinner October-May, Sunday dinner and Monday lunch)* Menu € 15 (weekday lunch), € 21/56 – Carte € 45/67

◆ A modern building overlooking the village of Dunières. Tasteful, modern dining room, flower-decked terrace and well prepared traditional dishes. Practical rooms.

DUNKERQUE – 59 Nord – 302 C1 – pop. 70 850 – Built-up area 191 173 – alt. 4 m – Casino : Malo-les-Bains – ✉ 59140 ▮ Northern France and the Paris Region

▶ Paris 288 – Amiens 205 – Calais 47 – Ieper 56 – Lille 73 – Oostende 57

ℹ Office de tourisme, rue de l'Amiral Ronarc'h ✆ 03 28 66 79 21, Fax 03 28 63 38 34

⛳ de Dunkerque Coudekerque Fort Vallières, Southeast: 1 km by D 72, ✆ 03 28 61 07 43. 30 **B1**

👁 Harbour★★ - Musée d'Art contemporain★: jardin des sculptures (sculpture garden) ★ CDY - Musée des Beaux-Arts★ CDZ **M²** - Musée portuaire★ CZ **M³**.

DUNKERQUE

Banc Vert (R. du) . . . . **AX** 8
Berteaux (Av. M.). . . . . **AX** 10
Cambon (Bd P.). . . . . **BX** 17
Darses (Chaussée des) . . . . . **AX** 25
Jean-Jaurès (R.). . . . . **BX** 39
Lille (R. de) . . . . **BX** 45
Malo (R. Célestin). . . . . **BX** 50
Mendès-France (Bd) . . . . . . **BX** 52
Pasteur (R.). . . . . **BX** 56
République (R. de la) . . . . . . **AX** 61
Waldeck-Rousseau (R.). . . . . **BX** 73

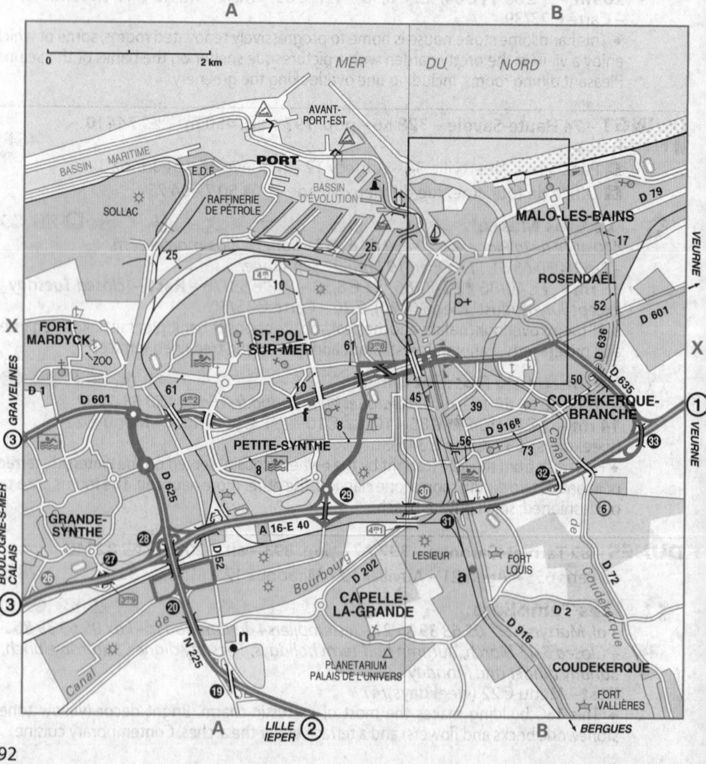

DUNKERQUE

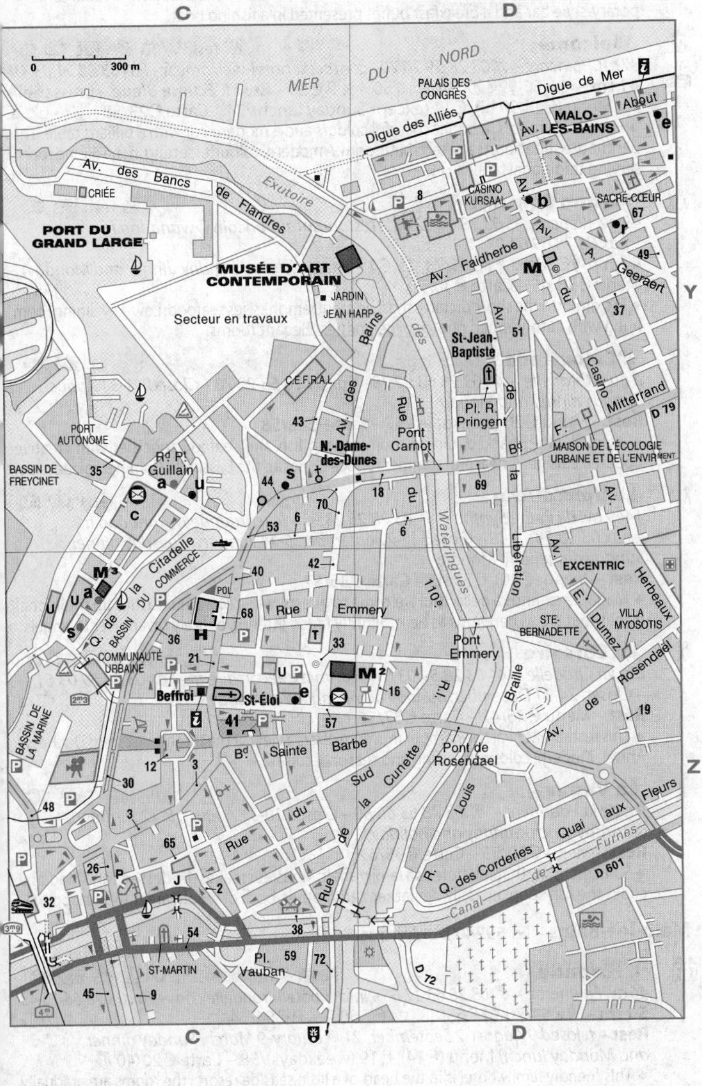

Borel without rest VISA

6 r. L'Hermite – 03 28 66 51 80 – borel@hotelborel.fr – Fax 03 28 59 33 82
48 rm – €72 €78/110, €10 CY **u**
◆ Brick building near the marina. Well-equipped, well-kept rooms. Agreeable muted sitting room. Buffet breakfast.

Ibis without rest VISA

13 r. Leughenaer – 03 28 66 29 07 – h6546@accor.com – Fax 03 28 63 67 87
110 rm – €66/69 €66/69, €8 CY **s**
◆ This fully renovated 1970s hotel offers comfortable rooms, a shopping arcade, contemporary-style bar and a breakfast buffet presented in a fishing boat.

Welcome rm, rest, VISA

37 r. R. Poincaré – 03 28 59 20 70 – contact@hotel-welcome.fr – Fax 03 28 21 03 49
41 rm – €66 €77, €10,50 – ½ P €58 – **Rest *L'Écume Bleue*** – brasserie – – Menu (€14,50 bi), €17 (except Sunday lunch)/24 – Carte €23/38 CZ **e**
◆ Functional rooms in bright cheerful colours and a modern bar with a billiard table. The penthouse suite boasts a hi-tech bathroom. A modern, colourful setting in the dining room, serving traditional fare.

Au Bon Coin with rm rest, VISA

49 av. Kléber – 03 28 69 12 63 – restaurantauboncoin@wanadoo.fr – Fax 03 28 69 64 03
4 rm – €58/63 €63/73, €7 – **Rest** – *(closed Sunday dinner and Monday)* Menu €28/45 – Carte €30/70
◆ Proximity to the shore dictates that the menu emphasises seafood. Low-key dining room hung with autographed photos of celebrities. Elegant rooms.

L'Estouffade VISA

2 quai Citadelle – 03 28 63 92 78 – Fax 03 28 63 92 78 – Closed 11-31 August, Sunday dinner and Monday CZ **s**
Rest – Menu €26 (weekdays)/37 – Carte €43/58
◆ A small, often packed, dining room serving fish and seafood together with creative updated cuisine. A peaceful summer terrace opposite the Bassin du Commerce quayside.

Le Vent d'Ange VISA

1449 av. de Petite Synthe – 03 28 25 28 98 – leventdange@wanadoo.fr – Fax 03 28 58 12 88 – Closed 1st-7 September, 5-11 January, Tuesday dinner, Sunday dinner and Monday AX **f**
Rest – Menu (€20), €25/45 – Carte €35/57
◆ Madame extends a delightful welcome to guests, while Monsieur rustles up traditional dishes that are as generous as he is. Slightly faded interior, entirely given over to angels.

Le Corsaire VISA

6 quai Citadelle – 03 28 59 03 61 – contact@lecorsaire.fr – Fax 03 28 59 03 61 – Closed 24-31 December, Sunday dinner and Wednesday CZ **a**
Rest – Menu €26/42 – Carte €37/56
◆ This restaurant near the harbour museum offers a view of the three-mast ship "Duchesse Anne". Modern, colourful setting and seasonal cuisine.

La Vague VISA

9 r. de la Poudrière – 03 28 63 68 80 – Closed 10-31 August, 5-12 January, Saturday lunch, Sunday and holidays CY **a**
Rest – Menu €30/55 – Carte €35/62
◆ Suffice it to say that this hotel is a family affair: Monsieur makes the desserts and Madame cooks the fish supplied daily her father and brother, both of whom are trawler skippers.

in Malo-les-Bains – ✉ 59240 Dunkerque

L'Hirondelle rm, rm, VISA

46 av. Faidherbe – 03 28 63 17 65 – info@hotelhirondelle.com – Fax 03 28 66 15 43
50 rm – €54/70 €65/88, €7,50 – ½ P €54/64 DY **r**
Rest – *(closed 9 August-2 September, 21 February-9 March, Sunday dinner and Monday lunch)* Menu (€14), €19 (weekdays)/58 – Carte €20/40
◆ This friendly family hotel is in the heart of a little seaside resort ; the rooms are gradually being made over in a pleasant understated contemporary spirit; those in the annexe are new. Seafood dishes complement a largely classic menu; wines from Languedoc-Roussillon.

Victoria Hôtel rm, VISA MC

5 av. de la Mer – ✆ 03 28 28 28 11 – zanzibar.victoria@wanadoo.fr – Fax 03 28 28 77 29 DY **b**

11 rm – †€ 65 ††€ 65, ☐ € 7,50 – 1 suite

Rest *Zanzibar* – *(closed Saturday lunch and Sunday dinner)* Menu € 17 (weekday lunch), € 25/45 bi – Carte € 23/47

◆ Exotic wood, four-poster beds and African furniture: the decor of the modern, comfortable rooms is reminiscent of a continent dear to the hearts of the hotel's owners. Ethnic decor and African and Creole specialities, but also a few traditional French dishes.

Au Côté Sud VISA MC

19 av du Casino – ✆ 03 28 63 55 12 – contact@aucotesud.com – Fax 03 28 61 54 49 – Closed 24 December-8 January DY **e**

10 rm – †€ 43/45 ††€ 56/58, ☐ € 7 – ½ P € 48/49

Rest – *(dinner only)* Menu € 13/22

◆ Practical, well-soundproofed rooms and a continental breakfast: a handy fully renovated establishment two minutes from the Palais des Congrès. This inviting restaurant is the backdrop to a subtle mixture of northern and southern cuisine.

in Téteghem 6 km southeast by D 601 BX – **pop. 7 237 – alt. 1 m – ✉ 59229**

La Meunerie with rm VISA MC AE

au Galghouck, 2 km south-east on D 4 – ✆ 03 28 26 14 30 – contact@lameunerie.fr – Fax 03 28 26 17 32 – Closed 20 July-10 August and 12-18 February

9 rm – †€ 90/218 ††€ 90/218, ☐ € 12,50 – ½ P € 110

Rest – *(closed 15 July-1st August, 8-16 February, Sunday dinner and Monday) (dinner only except Sunday)* Menu € 28/61

◆ Divided into several comfortable, bourgeois dining rooms opening onto the garden, this restaurant is set in an old steam mill. Traditional cuisine that changes with the seasons.

in Coudekerque-Branche – pop. 24 152 – alt. 1 m – ✉ 59210

Syndicat d'initiative, 4, rue de la Convention ✆ 03 28 64 60 00

Le Soubise P VISA MC AE

49 rte Bergues – ✆ 03 28 64 66 00 – restaurant.soubise@wanadoo.fr – Fax 03 28 25 12 19 – Closed 10-22 April, 24 July-19 August, 18 December-6 January, Saturday and Sunday BX **a**

Rest – Menu € 27/48 – Carte € 46/62

◆ This 18C posthouse bordering the canal now houses an extremely friendly restaurant. Traditional, well-prepared and generously portioned dishes.

in Cappelle-la-Grande 5 km South On D 916 – pop. 8 613 – ✉ 59180

Syndicat d'initiative, Mairie ✆ 03 28 64 94 41, Fax 03 28 60 25 31

Fleur de Sel P VISA MC AE

48 rte Bergues – ✆ 03 28 64 21 80 – laurentbraem@wanadoo.fr – Fax 03 28 61 22 00 – Closed Sunday dinner and Monday BX **a**

Rest – Menu € 25 (weekdays)/45 – Carte € 34/66

◆ Find a faultless welcome and tasty traditional cuisine in a cosy, modern interior of bare stonework, shades of grey and contemporary art and furniture.

in Armbouts-Cappel by ② N 225 exit 19a – pop. 2 677 – ✉ 59380

Du Lac rm, P VISA MC AE

2 bordure du Lac – ✆ 03 28 60 70 60 – contact@hoteldulacdk.com – Fax 03 28 61 06 39 AX **n**

66 rm – †€ 57 ††€ 74, ☐ € 9,50 – **Rest** – *(closed Saturday lunch)* Menu (€ 13), € 16 (weekdays), € 18/24 – Carte € 27/39

◆ The hotel is located in a verdant setting on the shores of Lake Armbouts. Comfortable rooms; choose one overlooking the lake for the view, or the car park for more space. This contemporary dining room opens onto a terrace, garden, lake and the Flemish countryside.

DUN LE PALESTEL – 23 Creuse – 325 G3 – pop. 1 106 – alt. 370 m – ✉ 23800

25 **C1**

Paris 349 – Limoges 83 – Guéret 29 – La Souterraine 18 – Argenton-sur-Creuse 47

Office de tourisme, 81, Grande Rue ✆ 05 55 89 24 61, Fax 05 55 89 95 11

Joly

3 r. Bazenerye – 05 55 89 00 23 – hoteljoly@wanadoo.fr – Fax 05 55 89 15 89 – Closed 3-8 March, 29 September-6 October, Sunday dinner and Monday lunch except holidays

27 rm – €40 €44/55, €9 – ½ P €40 – **Rest** – Menu €19/36 – Carte €35/49

◆ In the centre of the village. The individually furnished rooms in the main building have been completely renovated; those in the annexe are simpler in style. Fresh produce is key to the carefully prepared, traditional dishes served in this rustic restaurant.

DURAS – 47 Lot-et-Garonne – 336 D1 – pop. 1 214 – alt. 122 m – ✉ 47120

Atlantic Coast 4 **C2**

Paris 577 – Agen 90 – Marmande 23 – Périgueux 88 – Ste-Foy-la-Grande 22

Office de tourisme, 2, boulevard Jean Brisseau 05 53 83 63 06, Fax 05 53 76 04 36

Hostellerie des Ducs with rm

bd. J. Brisseau – 05 53 83 74 58 – hostellerie.des.ducs@wanadoo.fr – Fax 05 53 83 75 03 – Closed Monday except dinner from July to September, Sunday dinner from October to June and Saturday lunch

15 rm – €57 €70/107, €9 – ½ P €71/87 – **Rest** – Menu (€17), €29/68

◆ This former presbytery adjacent to the chateau offers traditional cuisine, served in the Louis XIII style dining hall or on the veranda. Modern rooms.

DURY – 80 Somme – 301 G8 – see Amiens

EAUX-PUISEAUX – 10 Aube – 313 D5 – pop. 194 – alt. 220 m – ✉ 10130

Paris 161 – Auxerre 53 – Sens 63 – Troyes 32 13 **B3**

L'Étape du P'tit Sim without rest

6 Gde-Rue – 03 25 42 02 21 – etapeduptitsim@wanadoo.fr – Fax 03 25 42 03 30 – Closed Sunday dinner

19 rm – €49 €49, €7

◆ The hotel opposite the restaurant has modern rooms and offers buffet-type breakfasts. There is a private car park.

EBERSMUNSTER – 67 Bas-Rhin – 315 J7 – pop. 435 – alt. 165 m – ✉ 67600

Paris 508 – Strasbourg 40 – Obernai 23 – Saint-Dié-des-Vosges 55 – Sélestat 9 2 **C1**

Des Deux Clefs

72 r. Gén. Leclerc – 03 88 85 71 55 – Fax 03 88 85 71 55 – Closed 9-21 July, 24 December-17 January, Monday and Thursday

Rest – Menu €17 (weekday lunch), €30/60 – Carte €30/46

◆ Restaurant opposite an abbey church well-known for its baroque interior. The restaurant decor is more restrained but just as stylish. Specialities include matelote fish stew, fried fish and eel.

ECCICA-SUARELLA – 2A Corse-du-Sud – 345 C8 – see Corse

LES ÉCHELLES – 73 Savoie – 333 H5 – pop. 1 248 – alt. 386 m – ✉ 73360 Les Echelles

French Alps 45 **C2**

Paris 552 – Chambéry 24 – Grenoble 40 – Lyon 92 – Valence 106

Office de tourisme, rue Stendhal 04 79 36 56 24, Fax 04 79 36 53 12

in Chailles 5 km North – ✉ 73360 St-Franc

Auberge du Morge with rm

D 1006, Gorges de Chailles – 04 79 36 62 76 – contact@aubergedumorge.com – Fax 04 79 36 51 65 – Closed 11 November-20 January, Thursday lunch and Wednesday

8 rm – €48/54 €48/54, €9 – ½ P €60/63 – **Rest** – Carte €26/44

◆ Local building at the entrance to the Chailles gorges, between the road and a river that is popular with fishermen. Warm country restaurant. Renovated rooms.

in St-Christophe-la-Grotte **5 km northeast by D 1006 and secondary road – pop. 442 – alt. 425 m – ✉ 73360**

La Ferme Bonne de la Grotte VISA

– ✆ 04 79 36 59 05 – info@ferme-bonne.com – Fax 04 79 36 59 31 – Closed January

6 rm – **†**€ 63/77 **††**€ 71/89 – ½ P € 63 – **Table d'hôte** – Menu € 28 bi

◆ This 18C farmhouse backed up against a cliff is an ideal starting point for a walking tour to the splendid St Christophe cave. Stylish, welcoming rooms. Regional fare served in a charming decor enhanced by authentic Savoyard furniture.

ECHENEVEX – 01 Ain – 328 J3 – see Gex

LES ÉCHETS – 01 Ain – 328 C5 – alt. 276 m – ✉ 01700 MIRIBEL

43 **E1**

Paris 454 – L'Arbresle 28 – Bourg-en-Bresse 47 – Lyon 20 – Villefranche-sur-Saône 30

Christophe Marguin with rm rest, VISA AE

916 rte de Strasbourg – ✆ 04 78 91 80 04 – contact@christophe-marguin.com – Fax 04 78 91 06 83 – Closed 1st-20 August, 20 December-5 January, Saturday lunch, Sunday dinner and Monday

7 rm – **†**€ 65 **††**€ 95, € 12 – **Rest** – Menu € 28 (except Sunday)/70 – Carte € 53/82

◆ Photographs of 'ancestors', woodcarvings, library... a pleasant home from home. Semi-classic, semi-regional cuisine and fine list of Bordeaux and Burgundy wines.

ÉCHIROLLES – 38 Isère – 333 H7 – see Grenoble

ÉCULLY – 69 Rhône – 327 H5 – see Lyon

EFFIAT – 63 Puy-de-Dôme – 326 G6 – pop. 744 – alt. 350 m – ✉ 63260 Auvergne

Paris 392 – Clermont-Ferrand 38 – Gannat 11 – Riom 22 – Thiers 39 – Vichy 18

Château★.

5 **B2**

Cinq Mars VISA

r. Cinq-Mars , (D 984) – ✆ 04 73 63 64 16 – Fax 04 73 63 64 16 – Closed 9-31 August, 14-27 February and dinner in week

Rest – Menu € 11 (weekday lunch)/18

◆ An 1876 village café near the castle of the Marquis de Cinq Mars. The owner-chef prepares traditional dishes served in a welcoming, countrified dining room.

ÉGLETONS – 19 Corrèze – 329 N3 – pop. 4 087 – alt. 650 m – ✉ 19300

25 **C3**

Paris 499 – Aubusson 75 – Aurillac 97 – Limoges 112 – Mauriac 46 – Tulle 31 – Ussel 29

Office de tourisme, rue Joseph Vialaneix ✆ 05 55 93 04 34, Fax 05 55 93 00 09

Ibis rm, VISA AE

Ussel road by D 1089: 1.5 km – ✆ 05 55 93 25 16 – h0816@accor.com – Fax 05 55 93 37 54

41 rm – **†**€ 47/62 **††**€ 47/62, € 8 – **Rest** – *(dinner only)* Menu (€ 13), € 16

◆ The slightly larger than usual rooms and contemporary furnishings make this Ibis an attractive choice, close to a lake in the rural setting of the upper Correze. The dining area includes a lounge with open fireplace. Traditional menu.

EGUISHEIM – 68 Haut-Rhin – 315 H8 – pop. 1 548 – alt. 210 m – ✉ 68420 Alsace-Lorraine

2 **C2**

Paris 452 – Belfort 68 – Colmar 7 – Gérardmer 52 – Guebwiller 21 – Mulhouse 42

Office de tourisme, 22a, Grand'Rue ✆ 03 89 23 40 33, Fax 03 89 41 86 20

Ramparts circuit★ - Cinq Châteaux (five castles) road ★ Southwest: 3 km.

Hostellerie du Château without rest

2 r. Château – ✆ 03 89 23 72 00 – info@hostellerieduchateau.com – Fax 03 89 41 63 93

11 rm – 🛉€ 68/98 🛉🛉€ 79/125, ☕ € 11

◆ A hotel full of character standing on a pretty square in this small town. Behind the half-timbered façade, guests can enjoy bright, contemporary rooms furnished with a personal touch. Good breakfast.

Hostellerie du Pape

10 Grand'Rue – ✆ 03 89 41 41 21 – info@hostellerie-pape.com – Fax 03 89 41 41 31 – Closed 5 January-9 February

33 rm – 🛉€ 68 🛉🛉€ 80, ☕ € 10 – ½ P € 78 – **Rest** – *(closed Mon. and Tues.)* Menu € 18/39 – Carte € 27/47

◆ The name of this former winery refers to Pope Leo IX, whose château is close by. Functional guestrooms which have been modernised in traditional style. Regional dishes are served in the welcoming dining room.

St-Hubert without rest

6 r. Trois Pierres – ✆ 03 89 41 40 50 – hotel.st.hubert@wanadoo.fr – Fax 03 89 41 46 88 – Closed 13-27 November, 18 January-28 February

13 rm – 🛉€ 85 🛉🛉€ 109, ☕ € 11 – 2 suites

◆ This hotel on the outskirts of the village has a pleasant bed & breakfast ambience. Functional bedrooms basking in the tranquillity of the vineyards. Small terraces and an indoor swimming pool.

Hostellerie des Comtes

2 r. des Trois Châteaux – ✆ 03 89 41 16 99 – aubergedescomtes@wanadoo.fr – Fax 03 89 24 97 10 – Closed 5-25 January

14 rm – 🛉€ 49/55 🛉🛉€ 49/65, ☕ € 8 – ½ P € 68/76 – **Rest** – *(closed Friday lunch and Thursday)* Menu € 12 (weekdays)/39 – Carte € 23/39

◆ A family-run auberge with well-maintained, unpretentious bedrooms, some with a small terrace. Traditional cuisine is the order of the day in this rustic restaurant. Outdoor dining on warm, summer days.

Auberge des Trois Châteaux

26 Grand'Rue – ✆ 03 89 23 11 22 – contact@auberge-3-chateaux.com – Fax 03 89 23 72 88 – Closed 1st-14 January

12 rm – 🛉€ 49 🛉🛉€ 54/66, ☕ € 8 – ½ P € 58/64 – **Rest** – *(closed 1st-9 July, 12-19 November, Tuesday dinner and Wednesday)* Menu € 17/32 – Carte € 25/49

◆ The three 17C houses that make up this auberge offer typical Alsatian rustic charm with flowers galore on display in spring and summer. The clean, functional guestrooms have all been recently renovated. The menu in this bright and attractive restaurant is centred on local dishes.

Caveau d'Eguisheim (Jean-Christophe Perrin)

3 pl. Château St-Léon – ✆ 03 89 41 08 89 – Fax 03 89 23 79 99 – Closed 23-27 December, end January to mid March, Monday and Tuesday

Rest – Menu € 29 bi (weekday lunch), € 37/59 – Carte € 47/86

Spec. Ravioles de carpe au bouillon de vin blanc safrané. Epaule de cochon de lait sur un lit de foin. Trésor du gourmet. **Wines** Pinot gris, Pinot noir.

◆ Authentic winegrower's home: all wood dining room, tasty traditional cuisine, pork specialities and very reasonably priced lunchtime menu.

Au Vieux Porche

16 r. des Trois Châteaux – ✆ 03 89 24 01 90 – vieux.porche@wanadoo.fr – Fax 03 89 23 91 25 – Closed June, February holidays, Tuesday and Wednesday

Rest – Menu € 23/60 bi – Carte € 30/53

◆ Exposed beams, stained glass and wood panelling provide a refined backdrop in this wine-grower's property dating from 1707. Good traditional cuisine and an impressive selection of wines from the estate and beyond.

La Grangelière

59 r. Rempart Sud – ✆ 03 89 23 00 30 – lagrangeliere@wanadoo.fr – Fax 03 89 23 61 62 – Closed mid January-mid February, Sunday dinner November-April and Thursday

Rest – Menu € 23 bi (weekdays)/67 bi – Carte € 42/62

◆ Behind the lovely, half-timbered façade of this typical Alsace property is a friendly ground-floor brasserie and a more refined gastronomic restaurant on the first floor.

Le Pavillon Gourmand

101 r. Rempart Sud – ✆ 03 89 24 36 88 – pavillon.schubnel@wanadoo.fr – Fax 03 89 23 93 94 – Closed end June-beg. July, mid January-mid February, Tuesday and Wednesday

Rest – Menu € 16/60 bi – Carte € 26/60

◆ This family-run restaurant in a picturesque street serves appetising Alsace dishes based on the freshest of produce. Rustic decor with views of the kitchens.

EICHHOFFEN – 67 Bas-Rhin – 315 I6 – pop. 410 – alt. 200 m – ✉ 67140 2 C1

Paris 497 – Strasbourg 38 – Colmar 43 – Offenburg 50 – Lahr 65

Les Feuilles d'Or without rest

52 r. du Vignoble – ✆ 03 88 08 49 80 – kuss.francis@libertysurf.fr – Fax 03 88 08 49 80 – **5 rm** – €65 €75

◆ On the wine route between vineyards and villages. A warm welcome is assured in the classical-rustic setting. Breakfast beneath the pergola in summer.

ÉLOISE – 74 Haute-Savoie – 328 I4 – see Bellegarde-sur-Valserine

EMBRUN – 05 Hautes-Alpes – 334 G5 – pop. 6 152 – alt. 871 m – ✉ 05200

French Alps 41 C1

Paris 706 – Barcelonnette 55 – Briançon 48 – Digne-les-Bains 97 – Gap 41 – Guillestre 21

Office de tourisme, place Général-Dosse ✆ 04 92 43 72 72, Fax 04 92 43 54 06

N.-D. du Réal cathedral ★: treasure-house★, portal★ - Wall paintings★ in the Cordeliers chapel - Rue de la Liberté and Rue Clovis-Huques★.

Mairie

rest, VISA AE

pl. Barthelon – ✆ 04 92 43 20 65 – courrier@hoteldelamairie.com – Fax 04 92 43 47 02 – Closed October and November

24 rm – €47/50 €50/53, € 7,50 – ½ P € 48/55 – **Rest** – *(closed Sunday dinner and Monday from December to May, Monday lunch in June and September)* Menu € 19/26 – Carte € 26/42

◆ A lovely old residence in the heart of the old town, on a picturesque square redolent of Provence. Pre-1940s style bar. Simple rooms with pinewood furnishings. A traditional restaurant with terrace where one dines to the accompaniment of a softly splashing fountain.

Gap road 3 km Southwest by N 94 – ✉ 05200 Embrun

Les Bartavelles

rest, P VISA AE

– ✆ 04 92 43 20 69 – info@bartavelles.com – Fax 04 92 43 11 92 – Closed 4-19 January, Sunday dinner and Monday lunch October-April

42 rm – €48/88 €78/125, € 10 – 1 suite – ½ P € 68/88 – **Rest** – *(closed Sunday evening and Monday lunchtime from October to April)* Menu € 18 (weekday lunch), € 20/48 – Carte € 32/63

◆ Rooms and duplex apartments occupying the main house and 3 bungalows, plus an interesting decor of rosettes carved in larchwood. Garden, sauna, hammam and jacuzzi. Classical dishes served in a rotunda-type room supported by a Guillestre column. In summer, grilled specialities are served on the terrace overlooking the swimming pool.

ÉMERINGES – 69 Rhône – 327 H2 – pop. 215 – alt. 353 m – ✉ 69840 43 E1

Paris 408 – Bourg-en-Bresse 56 – Lyon 65 – Mâcon 20 – Villefranche-sur-Saône 33

L'Auberge des Vignerons-La Tassée

VISA

Les Chavannes – ✆ 04 74 04 45 72 – Fax 04 74 04 45 72 – Closed 23-30 December, February holidays, Sunday dinner, Monday dinner and Tuesday

Rest – Menu € 12 bi (weekday lunch), € 22/38 – Carte € 33/45

◆ This restaurant, run by a Franco-Japanese couple, has a lovely view of the Beaujolais vineyards. The interior is decorated with wood panelling, check tablecloths and rustic furniture. Traditional cuisine.

EMMERIN – 59 Nord – 302 F4 – see Lille

ENGHIEN-LES-BAINS – 95 Val-d'Oise – 305 E7 – 101 5 – see Paris, Area

ENNORDRES – 18 Cher – 323 K2 – pop. 249 – alt. 166 m – ✉ 18380 12 C2

Paris 191 – Orléans 102 – Bourges 44 – Vierzon 38 – Gien 37

Les Chatelains

– ✆ 02 48 58 40 37 – contact@leschatelains.com – Fax 02 48 58 40 37

5 rm – €69 €75/105 – **Table d'hôte** – Menu €28 bi

♦ Charming restored farm furnished with antiques and flea-market finds. Warm welcome and country style *table d'hôte* serving traditional dishes.

ENSISHEIM – 68 Haut-Rhin – 315 I9 – pop. 6 640 – alt. 217 m – ✉ 68190 1 A3

Paris 487 – Strasbourg 100 – Colmar 27 – Freiburg im Breisgau 68 – Basel 44

Le Domaine du Moulin

44 r. 1ère Armée – ✆ 03 89 83 42 39
– reservation@domainedumoulin.com – Fax 03 89 66 21 40

65 rm – €76/105 €82/115, €12 – ½ P €66/82

Rest ***La Villa du Meunier*** – *✆ 03 89 81 15 10 (closed Saturday lunch)* Menu €20 (weekdays), €25/52 – Carte €33/60

♦ Large modern building with Alsatian charm, opening onto garden with pond. Spacious, practical rooms. Good swimming pool, sauna, hammam and Jacuzzi. Occupying a former mill and dedicated to the local culinary tradition.

ENTRAYGUES-SUR-TRUYÈRE – 12 Aveyron – 338 H3 – pop. 1 267 – alt. 236 m – ✉ 12140 Languedoc-Roussillon-Tarn Gorges 29 C1

Paris 600 – Aurillac 45 – Figeac 58 – Rodez 43 – St-Flour 83

Syndicat d'initiative, place de la République ✆ 05 65 44 56 10, Fax 05 65 44 50 85

Old Quarter: Rue Basse★ - Gothic bridge★.

Vallée du Lot★★.

La Rivière

60 av. du Pont-de-Truyère – ✆ 05 65 66 16 83 – info@hotellariviere.com
– Fax 05 65 66 24 98 – Closed 9 February-2 March

31 rm – €55/70 €75/90, €10 – ½ P €70/82 – **Rest** – *(closed Tuesday and Wednesday 15 October-1st April)* Menu €28/42 – Carte €37/48

♦ This hotel on the banks of the Truyère has enjoyed a recent facelift. The result: a full range of modern comforts and a contemporary decor (harmonious tones, quality materials). Contemporary cuisine in a bright and airy dining room overlooking the river.

Les Deux Vallées

av. du Pont de Truyère – ✆ 05 65 44 52 15 – hotel.2vallees@wanadoo.fr
– Fax 05 65 44 54 47 – Closed February, November, Christmas holidays, Sunday dinner, Friday dinner and Saturday October-April

20 rm – €42 €42, €7,50 – ½ P €45/48

Rest – *(closed 5 - 22 Nov. and 24 - 31 Dec.)* Menu €16/35 – Carte €23/32

♦ The Lot and Truyère river valleys meet in Entraygues. The well-soundproofed rooms have all been renovated with an eye to practicality rather than aesthetics. Country inn-style restaurant opening onto a small courtyard-terrace.

Le Clos St Georges

19 côteaux St Georges – ✆ 05 65 48 68 22 – catherine.rethore@hotmail.fr
– Closed 15 December-15 January

4 rm – €47 €57 – ½ P €47 – **Table d'hôte** – *(closed Sunday15 June-15 September)* Menu €18 bi

♦ In the upper part of the village, this former wine-grower's house (1637) has pretty rooms, an attractive lounge, paved courtyard and flower garden overlooking a meadow. Meals and breakfasts are served in a former kitchen graced by a fine fireplace.

in Fel 10 km West by D 107 and D 573 – pop. 146 – alt. 530 m – ✉ 12140

Auberge du Fel

– ✆ 05 65 44 52 30 – info@auberge-du-fel.com – Fax 05 65 48 64 96
– Open 23 March-2 November

10 rm – €54/65 €54/65, €8 – ½ P €49/59 – **Rest** – *(closed lunch except Saturday and Sunday off season)* Menu €20 (weekdays)/40 – Carte €24/42

♦ A vine-covered shingle-roofed house in a picturesque hamlet overlooking the Lot River. The personalised contemporary rooms are simple and faultlessly kept. Pounti, truffade and cabécou washed down with Fel wine in the restaurant.

ENTRECHAUX – 84 Vaucluse – 332 D8 – see Vaison-la-Romaine

ENTZHEIM – 67 Bas-Rhin – 315 J5 – see Strasbourg

ÉPAIGNES – 27 Eure – 304 C6 – pop. 1 158 – alt. 159 m – ✉ 27260 32 A3

Paris 175 – Le Grand-Quevilly 63 – Le Havre 50 – Rouen 69

L'Auberge du Beau Carré with rm

1 rte des Anglais – ✆ 02 32 41 52 42 – aubergedubeaucarre@wanadoo.fr – Fax 02 32 41 48 60

7 rm – €45 €60, €6 – ½ P €48 – **Rest** – *(closed Sunday dinner and Monday)* Menu (€18), €25/55

◆ Family-run restaurant in a smart redbrick house. Appetising classic repertoire using quality produce. Comfortable rooms.

ÉPENOUX – 70 Haute-Saône – 314 E7 – see Vesoul

ÉPERNAY – 51 Marne – 306 F8 – pop. 25 844 – alt. 75 m – ✉ 51200

Northern France and the Paris Region 13 B2

Paris 143 – Châlons-en-Champagne 35 – Château-Thierry 57 – Reims 28

Office de tourisme, 7, avenue de Champagne ✆ 03 26 53 33 00, Fax 03 26 51 95 22

Caves de Champagne (cellars) ★★ - Archeological collection ★ at the municipal museum.

Plan on next page

La Villa Eugène without rest

82 av. de Champagne, 1 km via ② – ✆ 03 26 32 44 76 – info@villa-eugene.com – Fax 03 26 32 44 98

15 rm – €100/300 €100/300, €14

◆ Imposing restored house once the home of a famous Champagne producer. Colonial or Louis XVI style bedrooms, a bar devoted to bubbly and breakfast in the conservatory.

Clos Raymi without rest

3 r. Joseph de Venoge – ✆ 03 26 51 00 58 – closraymi@wanadoo.fr – Fax 03 26 51 18 98 – Closed 24 December-2 January BZ **a**

7 rm – €100/160 €100/160, €14

◆ This pretty redbrick family mansion was owned by the Chandon family. Refined, individually decorated rooms. Pleasant breakfast room overlooking the garden.

Les Berceaux (Patrick Michelon) rest,

13 r. Berceaux – ✆ 03 26 55 28 84 – les.berceaux@wanadoo.fr – Fax 03 26 55 10 36

28 rm – €95/115 €95/115, €11 – 1 suite AZ **a**

Rest – *(closed 15-31 August, February holidays, Monday and Tuesday)* Menu (€24), €33/69 – Carte €60/82

Rest *Bistrot le 7* – *(closed Wednesday and Thursday)* Menu (€17,50), €24 – Carte €33/56

Spec. Millefeuille de homard bleu et artichaut croustillant. Ris de veau braisé sur matignon de légumes. Soufflé glacé aux deux chocolats.

◆ An elegant restaurant in the heart of the city serving delicious, traditional cuisine. Modern bistro with a warm ambiance (wines by the glass). Renovated rooms in the hotel.

Les Cépages

16 r. Fauvette – ✆ 03 26 55 16 93 – lescepages@wanadoo.fr – Fax 03 26 54 51 30 – Closed Wednesday and Sunday except public holidays AY **n**

Rest – Menu (€15), €18 (weekdays)/69 – Carte €46/61

◆ This restaurant in the town centre features exhibitions of work by local artists. Modern cuisine and a fine choice of champagnes.

Théâtre

8 pl. P. Mendès-France – ✆ 03 26 58 88 19 – Fax 03 26 58 88 38 – Closed 15 July-31 July, 21-28 December, 20 February-10 March, Sunday dinner, Tuesday dinner and Wednesday BY **f**

Rest – Menu (€16), €24/46 – Carte €41/55

◆ Cane chairs and warm colours bring a "colonial" touch to this large and elegant restaurant in an early 20C building.

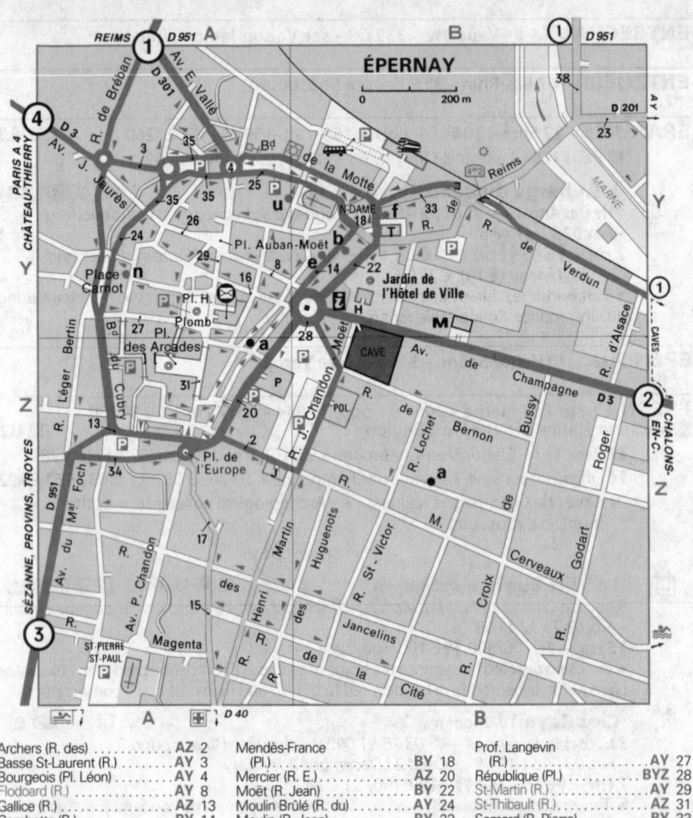

Archers (R. des)	AZ 2	Mendès-France (Pl.)	BY 18	Prof. Langevin (R.)	AY 27
Basse St-Laurent (R.)	AY 3	Mercier (R. E.)	AZ 20	République (Pl.)	BYZ 28
Bourgeois (Pl. Léon)	AY 4	Moët (R. Jean)	BY 22	St-Martin (R.)	AY 29
Flodoard (R.)	AY 8	Moulin Brûlé (R. du)	AY 24	St-Thibault (R.)	AZ 31
Gallice (R.)	AZ 13	Moulin (R. Jean)	BY 23	Semard (R. Pierre)	BY 33
Gambetta (R.)	BY 14	Perrier (Rempart)	AY 25	Sézanne (R. de)	AZ 34
Hôpital Auban-Moët (R.)	AZ 15	Plomb (Pl. Hugues)	AY	Tanneurs (R. des)	AY 35
Leclerc (R. Gén.)	AY 16	Porte Lucas (R.)	AY 26	Thévenet (Av.)	BY 38
Louis (R. Charles)	AZ 17				

La Table Kobus

3 r. Dr Rousseau – 03 26 51 53 53 – Fax 03 26 58 42 68 – Closed 14-24 April, 28 July-15 August, 22 December-6 January, Thursday dinner, Sunday dinner and Monday ABY **u**

Rest – Menu (€ 20), € 27/47 – Carte € 42/60

◆ Pleasant 1900 bistro where you can sip your own champagne without paying corkage! Popular with the locals.

La Cave à Champagne

16 r. Gambetta – 03 26 55 50 70 – cave.champagne@wanadoo.fr – Fax 03 26 51 07 24 – Closed Tuesday and Wednesday BY **b**

Rest – *(number of covers limited, pre-book)* Menu € 17/32 – Carte € 24/37

◆ A small cellar with regional wines on display. Reasonably-priced Champagne meals. Traditional cuisine.

La Table de Tristan

21 r. Gambetta – 03 26 51 11 44 – magalie.dauvissat@wanadoo.fr – Closed 15-22 August, 18-26 January, Sunday and Monday BY

Rest – Menu € 16 (lunch)/27 – Carte € 38/50

◆ Tiny restaurant whose bright, well cared for interior features stone walls, a fresco and wrought iron furniture. Tasty traditional fare; midday menu chalked up on a blackboard.

in Dizy 3 km by ① – pop. 1 832 – alt. 77 m – ✉ 51530

Les Grains d'Argent rest, rest, VISA

1 allée du Petit Bois – ✆ 03 26 55 76 28 – hotel.lesgrainsdargent@wanadoo.fr – Fax 03 26 55 75 96 – Closed 26 December-6 January

21 rm – €80 €88, €11 – ½ P €98 – **Rest** – *(closed Saturday lunch, Sunday dinner and Monday)* Menu €25 (weekday lunch), €32 € bi/66 – Carte €71/94

◆ The rooms of this newly constructed hotel bordering vineyards have fine, eclectic decor (painted or ceruse wood, ethnic furnishings); Champagne bar. Bright and spacious dining room where guests can enjoy modern dishes which reflect the changing seasons.

in Champillon 6 km by ① – pop. 528 – alt. 210 m – ✉ 51160

Royal Champagne < Épernay, vineyard and Marne valley, rm, rest, rest, VISA AE

D 201 – ✆ 03 26 52 87 11 – royalchampagne@relaischateaux.com – Fax 03 26 52 89 69 – Closed 29 December-2 February

21 rm – €205/355 €205/355, €29 – 4 suites – **Rest** – *(closed Monday lunch and Tuesday lunch)* Menu €65/110 – Carte €84/113

◆ Overlooking Épernay, this old coaching inn has well-appointed, luxurious guestrooms. The elegant dining room boasts fine views of the Champagne vineyards and the Marne Valley.

Reims road 8 km by ① – ✉ 51160 St-Imoges

Maison du Vigneron VISA AE

N 51 – ✆ 03 26 52 88 00 – Fax 03 26 52 86 03 – Closed Sun. evening and Wed.

Rest – Menu €22 (weekdays)/50 – Carte €55/63

◆ The atmosphere of the forest pervades this inn adjacent to the N 51 road. Exposed beams, wrought iron lamps and a fireplace create a delightful setting for the traditional cuisine.

in Vinay 6 km by ③ – pop. 463 – alt. 102 m – ✉ 51530

Hostellerie La Briqueterie rm, rest, VISA AE

4 rte Sézanne – ✆ 03 26 59 99 99 – briqueterie@relaischateaux.com – Fax 03 26 59 92 10 – Closed 16 December-11 January and Saturday lunch

42 rm – €170/290 €200/320, €22 – ½ P €230/300

Rest – Menu €34 (weekday lunch), €78/95 – Carte €78/88

Spec. Daurade en deux visions, émincé de chou en salade, écrevisses et agrumes. Blanc de turbot braisé, poireaux fondants sauce champagne. Pigeonneau farci aux cerises et vinaigre de Reims, jus au ratafia. **Wines** Coteaux champenois blanc et rouge.

◆ Hotel surrounded by a graceful garden with attractively-renovated rooms. Fitness centre. Try the house champagne at the bar. Beams, shades of cream, and linen drapes set the elegant scene for the tasty cuisine.

ÉPINAL P – 88 Vosges – 314 G3 – pop. 35 794 – alt. 324 m – ✉ 88000

Alsace-Lorraine 27 **C3**

Paris 385 – Belfort 96 – Colmar 88 – Mulhouse 106 – Nancy 72 – Vesoul 90

Office de tourisme, 6, place Saint-Goëry ✆ 03 29 82 53 32, Fax 03 29 82 88 22

des Images d'Épinalby St-Dié-des-Vosges road: 3 km, ✆ 03 29 31 37 52.

Old town★: Basilica★ - Château park★ - Musée départemental d'art ancien et contemporain★ - Imagerie d'Épinal.

Plan on next page

Le Manoir VISA AE

5 av. Provence – ✆ 03 29 29 55 55 – Fax 03 29 29 55 56 BZ **n**

12 rm – €100 €100/149, €14

Rest ***Ducs de Lorraine*** – see restaurant listing

◆ An attractive large residence dating from 1876. The rooms here are spacious and well-equipped (high-speed Internet access, video game console and fax) with personal touches. Fitness centre.

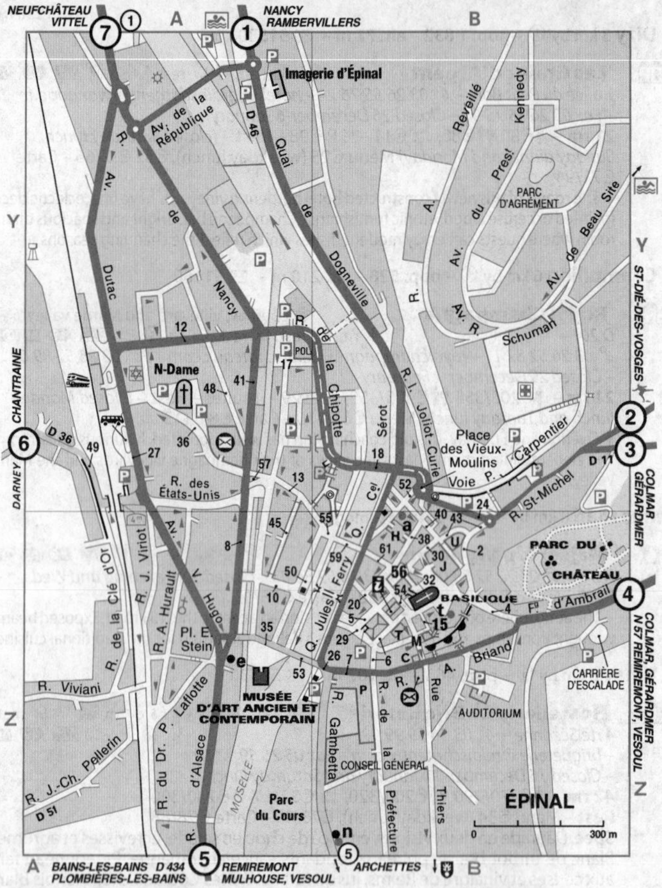

ÉPINAL

Mercure

13 pl. E. Stein – ✆ 03 29 29 12 91 – h0831@accor.com – Fax 03 29 29 12 92 AZ **e**

54 rm – €65/135 €75/170, ☕ €14 – **Rest** – *(dinner only)* Menu €25 – Carte €28/34

◆ A 19C hotel near the Classic and Modern Art Museum. Most of the rooms have been renovated and equipped with a wifi system. The rooms at the back are quieter. A pleasant, modern restaurant with a terrace facing the canal. 'Mercure' menu of traditional inspiration.

Ducs de Lorraine (Claudy Obriot et Stéphane Ringer) – Hôtel Le Manoir
5 av. Provence – ☎ 03 29 29 56 00 – obriot.ringer@wanadoo.fr
– Fax 03 29 29 56 01 – Closed 10-25 August, 2-5 January and Sunday BZ **n**
Rest – Menu € 35 (weekday lunch), € 45/76 – Carte € 75/105
Spec. Carpaccio de Saint-Jacques à la truffe fraîche (November-January).Tournedos de pigeon fourré au foie blond. Soufflé à la mirabelle, sorbet et coulis. **Wines** Côtes de Toul gris, Riesling.
◆ Fine-looking late-19C villa. Elegant dining room with mouldings and Louis XV-style furniture. Tasty cuisine with a contemporary touch, and select wines.

La Voûte
7 pl. de l'Atre – ☎ 03 29 35 47 25 – thomas.hd88@neuf.fr – Closed 15-23 March, 2-9 November, 11-18 January, Wednesday dinner and Sunday BZ **t**
Rest – *(number of covers limited, pre-book)* Menu (€ 13) – Carte € 23/41
◆ Friendly welcome at this unpretentious restaurant with its vaulted dining room (*voûte* in French). Market-inspired cuisine.

Le Petit Robinson
24 r. R. Poincaré – ☎ 03 29 34 23 51 – lepetitrobinson@free.fr – Fax 03 29 31 27 17 – Closed 1st-4 May, 18 July-17 August, 1st-4 January, Saturday lunch and Sunday
Rest – Menu (€ 14,50 bi), € 20/38 – Carte € 36/59 BZ **a**
◆ Family-run restaurant with a colourful facade, between the old town and the River Moselle. Slightly antiquated dining room. Traditional dishes.

via ① 3 km – ✉ 88000 Épinal

La Fayette rm, rm,
3 r. Bazaine (Le-saut-le-Cerf) – ☎ 03 29 81 15 15 – hotel.lafayette.epinal@wanadoo.fr – Fax 03 29 31 07 08
58 rm – €85 €99, € 12 – 1 suite – ½ P € 92
Rest – Menu € 19 (weekdays)/43 – Carte € 39/48
◆ Hotel complex on the doorstep of Épinal. Spacious, functional rooms; ask for one of the new, modern ones. Wellness centre: counter current pool, sauna, Jacuzzi tub. Unpretentious classic and regional cuisine served in a glazed dining room.

in Chaumousey **10 km by ⑥ and D 460 – pop. 784 – alt. 360 m – ✉ 88390**

Calmosien
37 r. d'Epinal – ☎ 03 29 66 80 77 – lecalmosien@wanadoo.fr – Fax 03 29 66 89 41 – Closed 5-21st July, Sunday dinner and Monday
Rest – Menu € 22/62 – Carte € 37/49
◆ Spruce, early-20C building near the church. Elegant dining room in pastel shades with paintings and well-laid tables. Cuisine in keeping with current taste.

in Golbey **4 km north by ⑦ – pop. 7 924 – alt. 320 m – ✉ 88190**

Atrium without rest
89 r. de Lorraine – ☎ 03 29 81 15 20 – info@hotel-atrium.fr – Fax 03 29 29 09 06 – Closed 24 December-4 January – **22 rm** – €52 €58, € 7
◆ A major renovation has given a new spark to this hotel, built around a flower filled patio. Spacious rooms with beams, comfortable beds and flat-screen TVs.

L'ÉPINE – 51 Marne – 306 I9 – see Châlons-en-Champagne

L'ÉPINE – 85 Vendée – 316 C6 – see Île de Noirmoutier

ÉPINEAU-LES-VOVES – 89 Yonne – 319 D4 – see Joigny

ÉPINOUZE – 26 Drôme – 332 C2 – pop. 1 096 – alt. 208 m – ✉ 26210 43 E2

Paris 523 – Grenoble 79 – Lyon 68 – St-Étienne 86 – Valence 62

Galliffet rm,
au village – ☎ 04 75 31 72 98 – aubergevalloire@tiscali.fr – Fax 04 75 03 58 20
18 rm – €45 €50, € 5 – **Rest** – *(closed Saturday) (dinner for resident only)*
Menu € 10 (weekday lunch)/30
◆ Two buildings enclosing a well-shaded garden; the more recent of the two has small, simple and practical rooms with a balcony or terrace where guests can enjoy the restful atmosphere.

ÉQUEURDREVILLE-HAINNEVILLE – 50 Manche – 303 C2 – see Cherbourg-Octeville

see Cherbourg-Octeville

ERBALUNGA – 2B Haute-Corse – 345 F3 – see Corse

ERMENONVILLE – 60 Oise – 305 H6 – pop. 830 – alt. 92 m – ✉ 60950

Northern France and the Paris Region 36 **B3**

- Paris 51 – Beauvais 70 – Compiègne 42 – Meaux 25 – Senlis 14 – Villers-Cotterêts 38
- Syndicat d'initiative, rue René de Girardin ✆ 03 44 54 01 58, Fax 03 44 54 04 96
- Mer de Sable★ - Ermenonville forest ★ - Chaalis abbey★★ North: 3 km.

Le Prieuré without rest

6 pl. de l'Église – ✆ 03 44 63 66 70 – reception@hotel-leprieure.com – Fax 03 44 63 95 01 – Closed Christmas holidays and Sunday

9 rm – €85/165 €85/165, ☕ €12

◆ A guesthouse atmosphere is to be found in this wonderful 18C residence surrounded by a pretty English garden next to a church. Elegant rooms with hand-picked furniture.

XX **Le Relais de la Croix d'Or** with rm rest, VISA AE

2 r. Prince Radziwill – ✆ 03 44 54 00 04 – relaisor@wanadoo.fr – Fax 03 44 54 99 16 – Closed 4-18 August, Sunday dinner and Monday

8 rm – €67/72 €76/86, ☕ €6 – **Rest** – Menu €20 (weekday lunch), €33/65 – Carte €48/72

◆ Enjoy traditional cuisine in the wooden-beamed dining room with exposed stone walls, in a vaulted cellar or, in summer, on the terrace overlooking the water and gardens. Functional rooms.

ERMITAGE-DU-FRÈRE-JOSEPH – 88 Vosges – 314 J5 – see Ventron

see Ventron

ERNÉE – 53 Mayenne – 310 D5 – pop. 5 703 – alt. 120 m – ✉ 53500

Normandy 34 **B1**

- Paris 304 – Domfront 47 – Fougères 22 – Laval 31 – Mayenne 25 – Vitré 30
- Syndicat d'initiative, place de l'Hôtel de Ville ✆ 02 43 08 71 10

XX **Le Grand Cerf** VISA AE

19 r. A.-Briand – ✆ 02 43 05 13 09 – infos@legrandcerf.net – Fax 02 43 05 02 90 – Closed 15-31 January, Sunday dinner and Monday

Rest – Menu €23/32 – Carte €43/50

◆ The dining room is embellished with sculptures and its decor combines bare stone with modern features. A spruce setting for well-prepared cuisine based on local dishes.

in La Coutancière 9 km East on N 12 – ✉ 53500 Vautorte

X **La Coutancière** VISA

– ✆ 02 43 00 56 27 – Fax 02 43 00 66 09 – Closed Sunday dinner, Tuesday dinner and Wednesday

Rest – Menu (€11), €24/38 – Carte €23/42

◆ A welcoming hotel on the edge of the Mayenne forest in the heart of the region described by Balzac in his novel Les Chouans. Traditional cuisine and attentive service.

ERQUY – 22 Côtes-d'Armor – 309 H3 – pop. 3 760 – alt. 12 m – ✉ 22430

Brittany 10 **C1**

- Paris 451 – Dinan 46 – Dinard 39 – Lamballe 21 – Rennes 102 – St-Brieuc 33
- Office de tourisme, 3, rue du 19 Mars 1962 ✆ 02 96 72 30 12, Fax 02 96 72 02 88
- Cap d'Erquy ★ Northwest: 3.5 km puis 30 mn.

Beauséjour

21 r. Corniche – ✆ 02 96 72 30 39 – hotel.beausejour@wanadoo.fr – Fax 02 96 72 16 30 – Open 15 March-15 November and closed Monday

15 rm – †€ 53/55 ††€ 57/68, ☕ € 8,50 – ½ P € 58/69 – **Rest** – Menu € 20/36 – Carte € 23/41

◆ Family-run hotel-restaurant, only 100 m from the beach, with well-kept rooms enlivened by colourful floral fabrics; half of the rooms have a view of the fishing port. Seafood dishes and views of the sea from the large dining room windows.

L'Escurial

bd de la Mer – ✆ 02 96 72 31 56 – contact@lescurial.com – Fax 02 96 63 57 92 – Closed 5 January-3 February, Sunday dinner except July-August, Thursday dinner off season and Monday

Rest – Menu € 35/59 – Carte € 46/112

◆ Elegant contemporary restaurant overlooking the seafront. Updated culinary specialties, fish dishes and, in season, the famous Saint-Jacques scallops.

in St-Aubin 3 km southeast by secondary road – ✉ 22430 Erquy

Relais St-Aubin

– ✆ 02 96 72 13 22 – gilbert.josset@wanadoo.fr – Fax 02 96 63 54 31 – Closed 6-14 October, 20-29 December, 7-25 February, Wednesday 15 November-18 March, Tuesday off season and Monday

Rest – Menu € 17 (weekday lunch), € 23/57 – Carte € 28/60

◆ This 17C country residence built in local stone has a lovely rustic-style dining room. In fine weather one can enjoy the terrace and the delightful flower-filled garden.

ERSTEIN – 67 Bas-Rhin – 315 J6 – pop. 9 664 – alt. 150 m – ✉ 67150 1 B2

Paris 514 – Colmar 49 – Molsheim 24 – St-Dié 69 – Sélestat 27 – Strasbourg 28

Office de tourisme, 16, rue du Général-de-Gaulle ✆ 03 88 98 14 33, Fax 03 88 98 12 32

Crystal

41-43 av. de la Gare – ✆ 03 88 64 81 00 – baumert@hotelcrystal.info – Fax 03 88 98 11 29 – Closed 1st-10 August

71 rm – †€ 59/72 ††€ 68/98, ☕ € 13 – 3 suites – ½ P € 59/74

Rest – *(closed 25 July-17 August, 19 December-1st January, Friday dinner, Saturday lunch, Sunday and holidays)* Menu € 22 (weekdays)/41 – Carte € 26/54

◆ A modern hotel near the main road, with functional, well-arranged rooms. The largest are on the third floor and have sloping ceilings. The dining room, with light colours and modern paintings, is both sober and pleasant.

Jean-Victor Kalt

41 av. de la Gare – ✆ 03 88 98 09 54 – jean-victor.kalt@wanadoo.fr – Fax 03 88 98 83 01 – Closed 21 July-14 August, 2-8 January, Sunday dinner and Monday

Rest – Menu € 22 (weekday lunch), € 30/62 – Carte € 45/73

◆ Appealing wood-panelled dining room with Weisbuch paintings and well-spaced out tables. Traditional fare and a fine choice of Asace and Rhône Valley wines.

ERVAUVILLE – 45 Loiret – 318 O3 – see Courtenay

ESCATALENS – 82 Tarn-et-Garonne – 337 D8 – pop. 689 – alt. 60 m – ✉ 82700 28 B2

Paris 649 – Colomiers 58 – Montauban 16 – Toulouse 53

Maison des Chevaliers

pl. de la Mairie – ✆ 05 63 68 71 23 – claude.choux@wanadoo.fr – Fax 05 63 30 25 90

5 rm ☕ – †€ 60 ††€ 75 – **Table d'hôte** – Menu € 22 bi

◆ This brick-built residence has very large rooms, richly and carefully furnished with antiques, travel souvenirs, and washbasins and faience from Portugal. Kitchenette and games room for the use of guests. Regional cuisine.

ESCOIRE – 24 Dordogne – 329 G4 – pop. 429 – alt. 100 m – ✉ 24420 4 C1

Paris 485 – Bordeaux 147 – Périgueux 13 – Sarlat-la-Canéda 72 – Coulounieix-Chamiers 18

Château d'Escoire without rest

– *05 53 05 99 80 – sylvie.kordalov@wanadoo.fr – Fax 05 53 05 99 80 – Open 1st April-31 October*

4 rm – €60 €75/80

◆ This romantic 18C abode dominating the village is surrounded by parkland and a formal French style garden. Majestic breakfast room and spacious bedrooms.

ESPALION – 12 Aveyron – 338 I3 – pop. 4 360 – alt. 342 m – ✉ 12500

Languedoc-Roussillon-Tarn Gorges 29 D1

Paris 592 – Aurillac 72 – Figeac 93 – Mende 101 – Millau 81 – Rodez 31 – St-Flour 80

Office de tourisme, 2, rue Saint-Antoine 05 65 44 10 63, Fax 05 65 44 10 39

Perse church ★ Southeast: 1 km.

De France without rest

36 bd J. Poulenc – 05 65 44 06 13 – Fax 05 65 44 76 26

9 rm – €42 €47, €7

◆ This small, centrally located hotel is close to several museums. Provides clean bright rooms with light wooden furniture. Soundproofing, good service and reasonable prices.

Moderne et rest. l'Eau Vive rest,

27 bd Guizard – 05 65 44 05 11 – hotelmoderne12@aol.com – Fax 05 65 48 06 94 – Closed 5 November-10 December and 4-20 January

28 rm – €43 €58, €7 – ½ P €43/50 – **Rest** – *(closed Sunday evening and Monday except July-August)* Menu €12 (weekdays)/45 – Carte €34/52

◆ Half-timbered house that maintains the tradition of welcoming pilgrims. Two generations of ageing rooms; the oldest have the advantage of the courtyard. The angler/chef offers freshwater fish specialities in a bright setting.

Le Méjane

r. Méjane – 05 65 48 22 37 – lemejane@wanadoo.fr – Fax 05 65 48 13 00 – Closed 3-28 March, 26-30 June, Monday except dinner September-June, Wednesday except July-August and Sunday dinner

Rest – Menu (€18), €24/56 – Carte €37/51

◆ The presence of mirrors gives an impression of space in this small dining room. The modern decor is as well thought out as the contemporary cuisine.

ESPALY-ST-MARCEL – 43 Haute-Loire – 331 F3 – alt. 650 m – see le Puy-en-Velay

ESPELETTE – 64 Pyrénées-Atlantiques – 342 D2 – pop. 1 879 – alt. 77 m – ✉ 64250 3 A3

Paris 775 – Bordeaux 215 – Pau 134 – Donostia-San Sebastián 78 – Irun 59

Office de tourisme, 145, route Karrika Nagusia 05 59 93 95 02

Euzkadi rest, rm,

285 Karrika Nagusia – 05 59 93 91 88 – hotel.euzkadi@wanadoo.fr – Fax 05 59 93 90 19 – Closed 1st November-24 December, Tuesday off season and Monday

27 rm – €44/48 €54/68, €8 – ½ P €53/62 – **Rest** – Menu €18/35 – Carte €26/42

◆ Hotel with a typically Basque-style façade, in the centre of the chilli pepper capital. The completely refurbished first floor rooms are more comfortable than those in the annexe. Swimming pool. Copious and authentic traditional cuisine served in a rustic-style dining room.

Irazabala without rest

155 Mendiko Bidéa – 05 59 93 93 02 – irazabala@wanadoo.fr

4 rm – €54/60 €65/80

◆ A charming residence built in the style of the region using traditional materials. Elegant guestrooms, rustic lounge, peaceful surroundings and the mountains as a backdrop.

ESQUIÈZE-SÈRE – 65 Hautes-Pyrénées – 342 L7 – see Luz-St-Sauveur

ESQUIULE – 64 Pyrénées-Atlantiques – 342 H3 – pop. 500 – alt. 277 m – ✉ 64400

3 **B3**

Paris 813 – Pau 43 – Lourdes 69 – Orthez 44 – Saint-Jean-Pied-de-Port 62

Chez Château

– ✆ 05 59 39 23 03 – jb.hourcourigaray@wanadoo.fr – Fax 05 59 39 81 97 – Closed 15 February-15 March, Wednesday dinner, Sunday dinner and Monday

Rest – Menu € 19/60 – Carte € 33/56

◆ A bar, grocer's and restaurant live happily together in this old farmhouse which adjoins the hamlet's pelota court. Pleasant, rustic dining rooms and regional cuisine.

ESTAING – 12 Aveyron – 338 I3 – pop. 612 – alt. 313 m – ✉ 12190

Languedoc-Roussillon-Tarn Gorges

29 **D1**

Paris 602 – Aurillac 63 – Conques 33 – Espalion 10 – Figeac 74 – Rodez 35

Syndicat d'initiative, 24, rue François d'Estaing ✆ 05 65 44 03 22, Fax 05 65 44 03 22

L'Auberge St-Fleuret

opposite the town hall – ✆ 05 65 44 01 44 – auberge-st-fleuret@wanadoo.fr – Fax 05 65 44 72 19 – Open mid March-mid November and closed Sunday dinner and Monday off season, Monday lunch July-August

14 rm – €46/53 €46/53, € 8 – ½ P € 47/54

Rest – Menu € 19 (weekdays)/59 – Carte € 45/58

◆ This 19C coaching inn offers modern rooms, either overlooking the garden or the old village dominated by its château. Two dining rooms: one rustic, the other neat and bright. Regional specialities including the famous *aligot* potato and cheese dish. Poolside terrace.

Aux Armes d'Estaing

1 quai Lot – ✆ 05 65 44 70 02 – remi.catusse@estaing.net – Fax 05 65 44 74 54 – Open 16 March-2 November and closed Sunday dinner and Monday

30 rm – €45/60 €45/60, € 8 – ½ P € 43/51

Rest – Menu € 16 (weekdays)/50

◆ Opposite the Gothic bridge spanning the River Lot at the foot of the castle once owned by the d'Estaing family. Plain, bright rooms. Warm welcome. This restaurant specialises in updated regional specialities.

ESTAING – 65 Hautes-Pyrénées – 342 K7 – pop. 67 – alt. 970 m – ✉ 65400

Atlantic Coast

28 **A3**

Paris 874 – Argelès-Gazost 12 – Arrens 7 – Laruns 43 – Lourdes 24 – Pau 69 – Tarbes 43

d'Estaing Lake ★ South: 4 km.

Lac d'Estaing with rm

au lac, South : 4 km – ✆ 05 62 97 06 25 – Fax 05 62 97 06 25 – Open 15 May-15 October

8 rm – €40 €48, € 8 – ½ P € 49 – **Rest** – Menu € 20/42 – Carte € 30/50

◆ Appealing though modest hotel standing on a superb site between the lake and the mountains. Appetising traditional cuisine. Large shady terrace. Small, well-renovated rooms.

ESTÉRENÇUBY – 64 Pyrénées-Atlantiques – 342 E6 – see St-Jean-Pied-de-Port

ESTISSAC – 10 Aube – 313 C4 – pop. 1 724 – alt. 133 m – ✉ 10190

13 **B3**

Paris 158 – Châlons-en-Champagne 105 – Sens 44 – Troyes 23

Syndicat d'initiative, Mairie ✆ 03 25 40 42 42

Moulin d'Eguebaude

– ✆ 03 25 40 42 18 – eguebaude@aol.com – Fax 03 25 40 40 92

8 rm – €42/50 €49/71 – **Table d'hôte** – Menu € 21 bi

◆ 1789 mill overlooking a vast fish farming estate; the best of the fresh simple rooms are in the annexe. Boutique selling local Aube products. Trout has pride of place on this restaurant's menu, which varies according to market availability.

Domaine du Voirloup

3 pl. Betty Dié – ✆ 03 25 43 14 27 – le.voirloup@free.fr

3 rm – †€ 60 ††€ 60/80 – ½ P € 85 – **Table d'hôte** – Menu € 19/25 bi

◆ This large, elegant 1904 residence is in an extensive park complete with a stream, waterfall and canals; the tastefully colourful rooms are called Orient, Occident and Midi. The menus change according to market availability; home-made cakes and jams at breakfast time.

ESTIVAREILLES – 03 Allier – 326 C4 – pop. 1 033 – alt. 90 m – ✉ 03190 5 B1

Paris 317 – Bourbon-l'Archambault 45 – Montluçon 12 – Montmarault 36 – Moulins 80

Le Lion d'Or with rm

D 2144 – ✆ 04 70 06 00 35 – rmliondor@orange.fr – Fax 04 70 06 09 78 – Closed 28 July-11 August, 16 February-2 March, Sunday dinner and Monday

5 rm – †€ 38/45 ††€ 38/45, ☕ € 7 – ½ P € 44/48 – **Rest** – Menu (€ 15), € 19 (weekdays)/48 – Carte € 34/54

◆ Age-old building by the side of the main road. Fine beams give the dining room a certain charm. The terrace overlooks a wooded park with a lake. Comfortable, recently refurbished guestrooms, some with a view of the lake.

ESTRABLIN – 38 Isère – 333 C4 – see Vienne

ESTRÉES-ST-DENIS – 60 Oise – 305 G4 – pop. 3 542 – alt. 70 m – ✉ 60190

Paris 81 – Beauvais 46 – Clermont 21 – Compiègne 17 – Senlis 34

du Château d'Humières Monchy Humières Rue de Gournay, Northeast: 11 km, ✆ 03 44 86 48 22. 36 B2

Moulin Brûlé

70 r. Flandres – ✆ 03 44 41 97 10 – lemoulinbrule@wanadoo.fr – Fax 03 44 51 87 96 – Closed 9-17 April, 6 August-4 September, 1st-6 January, Sunday dinner, Monday and Tuesday

Rest – *(pre-book)* Menu (€ 17), € 22/50 – Carte € 39/57

◆ Dressed-stone building on the main road through the village. Country-style interior with old beams, pastel shades and a fireplace. Small, peaceful terrace. Cuisine with a contemporary touch.

ÉTAIN – 55 Meuse – 307 E3 – pop. 3 709 – alt. 210 m – ✉ 55400

Alsace-Lorraine 26 B1

Paris 285 – Briey 26 – Longwy 43 – Metz 66

Office de tourisme, 31, rue Raymond Poincaré ✆ 03 29 87 20 80, Fax 03 29 87 20 80

La Sirène

r. Prud'homme-Havette, (rte de Metz) – ✆ 03 29 87 10 32 – hotel.sirene@free.fr – Fax 03 29 87 17 65 – Closed 22 December-31 January, Sunday dinner and Monday

21 rm – †€ 47/60 ††€ 47/70, ☕ € 7 – ½ P € 41/48 – **Rest** – Menu (€ 12), € 14 (weekdays)/40 – Carte € 24/43

◆ This place remains deaf to the call of fashion but resounds to the tumult of history: Napoleon III is said to have dropped in here - perhaps by accident - after the battle of Gravelotte. Renovated rooms. Traditional cuisine served in the dining room or on the veranda embellished by the works of local artists.

ÉTAMPES – 91 Essonne – 312 B5 – pop. 21 839 – alt. 80 m – ✉ 91150

Northern France and the Paris Region 18 B3

Paris 51 – Chartres 59 – Évry 35 – Fontainebleau 45 – Melun 49 – Orléans 76 – Versailles 58

Office de tourisme, place de l'Hôtel de Ville ✆ 01 69 92 69 00, Fax 01 69 92 69 28

de Belesbat Boutigny-sur-Essonne Domaine de Belesbat, East: 17 km by D 837 and D 153, ✆ 01 69 23 19 10.

Notre-Dame collegiate church ★.

XX **Auberge de la Tour St-Martin** VISA MC AE

97 r. St-Martin – ✆ 01 69 78 26 19 – tourpenchee@aliceadsl.fr – Fax 01 69 78 26 07 – Closed 11-25 August, Sunday dinner and Monday

Rest – Menu (€ 27), € 34 – Carte € 38/42

◆ With ceiling beams, stonework and fireplace, this dining area has a very rustic feel. Traditional meals prepared with choice produce.

in Ormoy-la-Rivière **5 km South by D 49 and secondary road – pop. 943 – alt. 81 m – ✉ 91150**

X **Le Vieux Chaudron** VISA MC

45 Grande Rue – ✆ 01 64 94 39 46 – guillaume.giblin@wanadoo.fr – Fax 01 64 94 39 46 – Closed 4-25 August, 22 December-5 January, Thursday dinner, Sunday dinner and Monday

Rest – Menu € 32/44 – Carte € 32/44

◆ A small, centrally located inn opposite the church. A country-style interior warmed by its fireplace in winter. Summer dining outdoors. Contemporary dishes.

ÉTANG-DE-HANAU – 57 Moselle – 307 Q4 – see Philippsbourg

LES ÉTANGS-DES-MOINES – 59 Nord – 302 M7 – see Fourmies

ÉTAPLES – 62 Pas-de-Calais – 301 C4 – pop. 11 177 – alt. 10 m – ✉ 62630

Northern France and the Paris Region 30 **A2**

Paris 228 – Calais 67 – Abbeville 55 – Arras 101 – Boulogne-sur-Mer 28 – Le Touquet-Paris-Plage 6

Office de tourisme, boulevard Bigot Descelers ✆ 03 21 09 56 94, Fax 03 21 09 76 96

X **Aux Pêcheurs d'Étaples** VISA MC AE

quai Canche – ✆ 03 21 94 06 90 – rptetaples@cmeop.com – Fax 03 21 89 74 54 – Closed 1st-23 January and Sunday dinner October-March

Rest – Menu € 14 (weekdays)/35 – Carte € 27/56

◆ Bright restaurant on the first floor of a large fishmonger's on the banks of the Canche. Extremely fresh seafood dishes. View of Le Touquet aerodrome.

ÉTEL – 56 Morbihan – 308 L9 – pop. 2 165 – alt. 20 m – ✉ 56410 Brittany

9 **B2**

Paris 494 – Lorient 26 – Quiberon 24 – Vannes 37

Syndicat d'initiative, place des Thoniers ✆ 02 97 55 23 80

Trianon P VISA MC

14 r. Gén. Leclerc – ✆ 02 97 55 32 41 – hotel.letrianon@wanadoo.fr – Fax 02 97 55 44 71 – Closed January

24 rm – †€ 50/68 ††€ 55/100, ☕ € 10 – ½ P € 55/79

Rest – *(open 1st April-31 October) (dinner only) (residents only)*

◆ Near the fishing port are faultlessly kept, candy box-style rooms in a 1960s style; choose one in the wing. A lounge with fireplace and peaceful little garden. Well-kept rustic-style dining room serving traditional cuisine.

ÉTOILE-SUR-RHÔNE – 26 Drôme – 332 C4 – pop. 4 054 – alt. 170 m – ✉ 26800

44 **B3**

Paris 569 – Crest 17 – Privas 34 – Valence 12

Office de tourisme, 45, Grande Rue ✆ 04 75 60 75 14, Fax 04 75 60 70 12

XX **Le Vieux Four** AC VISA MC

1 pl. Léon Lérisse – ✆ 04 75 60 72 21 – levieuxfour@9online.fr – Fax 04 75 62 02 24 – Closed 18 August-11 September, 1st-15 January, Sunday dinner, Monday and Tuesday off season

Rest – Menu € 36/69 bi

◆ Fine stone house, near a stately home, whose regional-style exterior contrasts with the modern interior. Cuisine combining local produce and modern recipes.

ÉTOUY – 60 Oise – 305 F4 – see Clermont

L'ÉTRAT – Loire – **327** F7 – see St-Étienne

ÉTRÉAUPONT – 02 Aisne – **306** F3 – **pop. 933** – **alt. 127 m** – ✉ **02580** 37 **D1**

Paris 184 – Avesnes-sur-Helpe 24 – Hirson 16 – Laon 44 – St-Quentin 51

Clos du Montvinage rm, VISA AE

8 r. Albert Ledant – ✆ 03 23 97 91 10 – contact@clos-du-montvinage.fr – Fax 03 23 97 48 92 – Closed 10-18 August, 26 December-5 January, Monday lunch and Sunday dinner

20 rm – €55/85 €67/110, € 10 – ½ P € 55/85

Rest *Auberge du Val de l'Oise* – ✆ *03 23 97 40 18* – Menu (€ 17), € 23/40 bi – Carte € 28/42

◆ A welcoming 19C family mansion with individually decorated (mountain, bourgeois, etc.) rooms. The leisure facilities include billiards, tennis courts, bicycles and croquet in the park. Don't miss the chance to sample the local delicacy: tourte au maroilles (cheese pie).

ÉTRETAT – 76 Seine-Maritime – **304** B3 – **pop. 1 615** – **alt. 8 m** – **Casino** A – ✉ **76790** Normandy 33 **C1**

Paris 206 – Bolbec 30 – Fécamp 16 – Le Havre 29 – Rouen 90

Office de tourisme, place Maurice Guillard ✆ 02 35 27 05 21, Fax 03 35 28 87 20

d'Étretat Route du Havre, ✆ 02 35 27 04 89.

Le Clos Lupin★ - Falaise d'Aval★★★ - Falaise d'Amont★★.

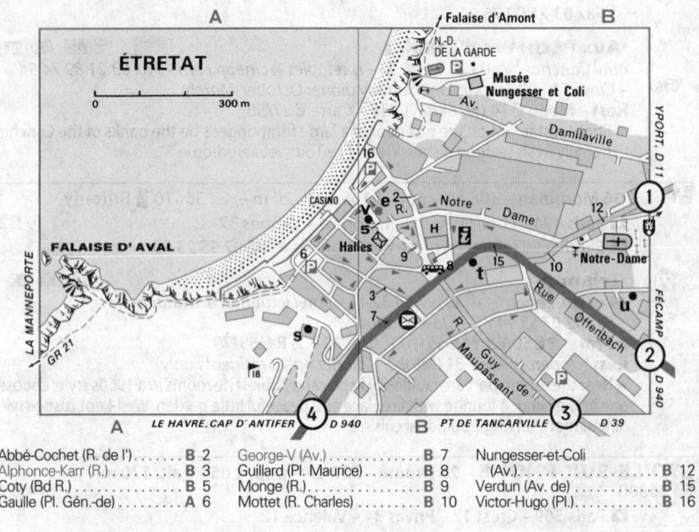

Abbé-Cochet (R. de l') . . . . . . B 2	George-V (Av.) . . . . . . B 7	Nungesser-et-Coli (Av.) . . . . . . B 12
Alphonce-Karr (R.) . . . . . . B 3	Guillard (Pl. Maurice) . . . . . . B 8	Verdun (Av. de) . . . . . . B 15
Coty (Bd R.) . . . . . . B 5	Monge (R.) . . . . . . B 9	Victor-Hugo (Pl.) . . . . . . B 16
Gaulle (Pl. Gén.-de) . . . . . . A 6	Mottet (R. Charles) . . . . . . B 10	

Dormy House ← cliffs and sea, rm, rest, VISA AE

rte du Havre – ✆ *02 35 27 07 88 – dormy.house@wanadoo.fr – Fax 02 35 29 86 19* A **s**

60 rm – €65/185 €65/185, € 15 – 1 suite – ½ P € 88/139

Rest – Menu € 32 (weekday lunch), € 40/70 – Carte approx. € 55

◆ This peaceful 1870 manor house and its outbuildings stand in a park near the golf course. They overlook the resort and face the cliffs of Amont. The rooms are in various styles, from traditional to cosy to more simple. The restaurant, bar and terrace offer a fine view of the coastline.

Domaine Saint-Clair rest,
chemin de St-Clair – ✆ 02 35 27 08 23 – info@hoteletretat.com – Fax 0235 29 92 24 B **u**
21 rm – †€ 62/192 ††€ 62/352, ☕ € 14 – **Rest** – *(closed lunch and Monday)* Menu € 60/85 – Carte € 92/111
◆ Ideal for a relaxing break, this 19C Anglo-Norman château and fine Belle Époque villa are set on the heights of Étretat. The cosy sitting rooms and bedrooms are adorned with choice fabrics. Contemporary cuisine made with garden produce served in a cosy setting.

Ambassadeur without rest
10 av. Verdun – ✆ 02 35 27 00 89 – hotel-ambassadeur@wanadoo.fr – Fax 02 35 28 63 69 B **t**
20 rm – †€ 45/79 ††€ 69/135, ☕ € 8
◆ Attractive, century-old villa near the Clos Lupin, the museum residence of the renowned 'Gentleman Burglar'. Individually decorated rooms in three buildings looking onto a courtyard.

Des Falaises without rest
1 bd R. Coty – ✆ 02 35 27 02 77 – Fax 02 35 28 87 59 B **v**
24 rm – †€ 29/49 ††€ 48/69, ☕ € 7
◆ This small building is located close to the shingle beach that stretches between the Aval and Amont cliffs. The rooms are not very large but functional and sparingly decorated.

Villa sans Souci without rest
27ter r. Guy de Maupassant – ✆ 02 35 28 60 14 – villa-sans-souci@wanadoo.fr – Fax 02 35 28 60 14
4 rm ☕ – †€ 75/85 ††€ 105/140
◆ A 1903 villa with a restful atmosphere and individually decorated rooms. The breakfast room decor focuses on cinema and automobiles. Pretty reading room and shady garden.

Le Galion
bd R. Coty – ✆ 02 35 29 48 74 – Fax 02 35 29 74 48 – Closed 17 December-20 January, Tuesday and Wednesday except school holidays B **e**
Rest – Menu € 23/39 – Carte € 40/52
◆ The treasure of this galleon is not found at the bottom of the hold but on the ceiling: the forest of carved beams dates back to the 14C and comes from a house in Lisieux.

Du Golf beach and cliffs,
rte du Havre – ✆ 02 35 27 04 56 – Fax 02 35 10 89 12 – Closed Tuesday from 1st October to 1st April
Rest – Menu € 19/24
◆ Superb coastal views from the bay windows of this golf course clubhouse perched above the Aval cliffs. The contemporary menu is highlighted on a slate board.

ÉTUPES – 25 Doubs – 321 L1 – see Sochaux

EU – 76 Seine-Maritime – 304 I1 – pop. 8 081 – alt. 19 m – ✉ 76260 Normandy
Paris 176 – Abbeville 34 – Amiens 88 – Dieppe 33 – Rouen 102 – Le Tréport 5
Office de tourisme, 41, rue Paul Bignon ✆ 02 35 86 04 68, Fax 02 35 50 16 03
Notre-Dame and St-Laurent collegiate church ★ - Collège chapel ★. 33 **D1**

Maine rm,
20 av. de la Gare – ✆ 02 35 86 16 64 – info@hotel-maine.com – Fax 02 35 50 86 25 – Closed Sunday dinner except July-August and holidays
19 rm – †€ 44/62 ††€ 54/76, ☕ € 8 – ½ P € 74/92 – **Rest** – Menu € 16 (weekday lunch), € 25/42
◆ Attractive mansion dating back to 1897 with small unassumingly appointed rooms with modern furniture. Stylish decor in the dining room reminiscent of the Belle Époque. Traditional menus and a fine choice of fish dishes.

Manoir de Beaumont without rest
rte de Beaumont, via D 49 – ✆ 02 35 50 91 91 – catherine@demarquet.eu – Fax 02 35 50 19 45
3 rm ☕ – †€ 36 ††€ 48/56
◆ Former hunting lodge, a stone's throw from Eu forest and five minutes from the beach. Louis XVI breakfast room. Lovely park.

EUGÉNIE-LES-BAINS – 40 Landes – 335 I12 – pop. 507 – alt. 65 m – Spa : mid Feb.-early Dec. – ✉ 40320 Atlantic Coast 3 B3

Paris 731 – Aire-sur-l'Adour 12 – Dax 71 – Mont-de-Marsan 26 – Orthez 52 – Pau 56

Office de tourisme, 147, rue René Vielle ✆ 05 58 51 13 16, Fax 05 58 51 12 02

Les Greens d'Eugénie Bahus-Soubiran Golf du Tursan, South: 4 km by D 11 and D 62, ✆ 05 58 51 11 63.

Les Prés d'Eugénie (Michel Guérard)

pl. de l'Impératrice – ✆ 05 58 05 06 07 – guerard@relaischateaux.com – Fax 05 58 51 10 10 – Closed 4 January-20 March

25 rm – €270/310 €300/360, €30 – 7 suites

Rest – Menu €55 (diet menu for residents only)

Rest ***rest. Michel Guérard*** – *(closed lunch weekdays except holidays and 8 July-26 August and Monday dinner) (number of covers limited, pre-book)* Menu €150/195 – Carte €135/162

Spec. Homard ivre des pêcheurs de lune. Petits rougets poêlés à vif sous une dentelle de pain beurré. Pêche blanche brûlée au sucre candi en melba de fruits rouges. **Wines** Tursan blanc, Vin de Pays des Terroirs Landais.

◆ Truly splendid, elegantly decorated 19C mansion with a park and spa "farm". A pleasant combination of townhouse and country house, luxury and healthy living. At Michel Guérard's garden-village, the food is inspired by Mother Nature.

Le Couvent des Herbes

– Closed 4 January-12 February

4 rm – €340/420 €340/420, €30 – 4 suites – €420/540

◆ Napoleon III had this pretty 18C convent with its pinnacle turret lovingly restored for Empress Eugénie. The delightful rooms are surrounded by a heavenly garden.

La Maison Rose rm, rest,

– ✆ 05 58 05 06 07 – reservation@michelguerard.com – Fax 05 58 51 10 10 – Closed 3 December-6 February

26 rm – €120/145 €140/180, €20 – 5 suites – **Rest** – *(residents only)*

◆ A highly refined "guesthouse" ambiance with relaxing pastel colours, white cane furniture, fresh flowers and a cosy sitting room.

La Ferme aux Grives with rm

– ✆ 05 58 05 05 06 – guerard@relaischateaux.com – Fax 05 58 51 10 10 – Closed 4 January-12 February

4 suites – €420/540, €25 – **Rest** – *(closed Tuesday dinner and Wednesday except 12 July-25 August and except public holidays)* Menu €46

◆ Old village inn that has had new life breathed into it. Vegetable garden, old beams and floor tiles serve to enhance the reinvigorated country cuisine. Exquisite suites and rooms for a peaceful night's sleep.

ÉVIAN-LES-BAINS – 74 Haute-Savoie – 328 M2 – pop. 7 273 – alt. 370 m – Spa : Feb.-early Nov. – Casino B – ✉ 74500 French Alps 46 F1

Paris 577 – Genève 44 – Montreux 40 – Thonon-les-Bains 10

Office de tourisme, place d'Allinges ✆ 04 50 75 04 26, Fax 04 50 75 61 08

Évian Masters Golf Club Rive Sud du Lac de Genève, by Thonon road: 1 km, ✆ 04 50 75 46 66.

Lake Geneva ★★★ - Boat trip ★★★ - Main staircase ★ of the town hall.

Falaises ★★.

Royal rest,

– ✆ 04 50 26 85 00 – royalpalace@evianroyalresort.com – Fax 04 50 75 38 40 C z

132 rm – €195/870 €300/870, €30 – 21 suites – ½ P €255/530

Rest ***Fresques Royales*** – *(closed Sunday and Monday except school holidays) (dinner only)* Menu €70/150 – Carte €90/126 – **Rest** ***La Véranda*** – rôtisserie Menu €60 – Carte approx. €88 – **Rest** ***Le Jardin des Lys*** – health-food rest. *(lunch only)* Menu €60/70– **Rest** ***Café Sud*** – *(dinner only)* Menu €60 – Carte €35/78

◆ Beautiful Art Deco architecture in this luxurious hotel built in 1907. Majestic gardens, superb fitness centre and spacious rooms with period furnishings. At the Fresques Royales, the paintings embellishing the splendid Belle Époque-style decor are the work of Gustave Jaulmes. Terrace with superb lake views. Well-balanced gastronomic cuisine. Buffet and grills at La Véranda. Slimmers' cuisine at Le Jardin des Lys. Southern cuisine in the relaxed atmosphere of Café Sud.

ÉVIAN-LES-BAINS

A B C

Ermitage – lake and mountains, rest,
– ✆ 04 50 26 85 00 – ermitage@evianroyal resort.com – Fax 04 50 75 29 37 – rest, VISA AE C a
91 rm – †€ 130/455 ††€ 200/670, ☕ € 33 – 3 suites – ½ P € 140/375
Rest *Le Gourmandin* – ✆ 04 50 26 85 54 (dinner only except weekends)
Menu € 60/80 – Carte € 63/90
Rest *La Toscane* – (lunch only) Menu € 55 – Carte € 51/65
◆ Early-20C luxury hotel in a magnificent park, perfect for a relaxing stay. 16C-style vegetable garden, lovely spa and children's play area. Le Gourmandin has refined decor, a superb terrace and serves regional dishes. La Toscane serves Italian cuisine and salads.

Hilton VISA AE
53 quai Paul Léger – ✆ 04 50 84 60 00 – info.hiltonevianlesbains@hilton.com – Fax 04 50 84 60 50 C b
173 rm – †€ 99/530 ††€ 124/555, ☕ € 32 – 3 suites – ½ P € 110/325
Rest *Cannelle* – Menu € 35/75 – Carte € 34/53
◆ A modern, uncluttered hotel. Most of the bedrooms (with their own balcony), command a view of the lake. Relax by the pool or in the wellness centre. A modern restaurant where the cuisine mirrors the contemporary decor. Large terrace facing the garden.

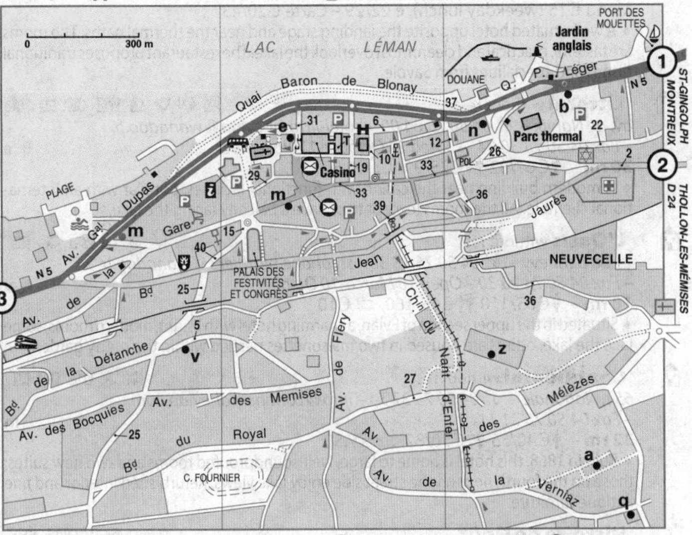

La Verniaz et ses Chalets VISA AE
rte d'Abondance – ✆ 04 50 75 04 90 – verniaz@ relaischateaux.com – Fax 04 50 70 78 92 – Open 7 February-11 November
33 rm – †€ 105/210 ††€ 128/280, ☕ € 16 – 6 suites – ½ P € 131/207
Rest – Menu € 39/72 – Carte € 50/65 C q
◆ A lovely complex of buildings and chalets in a superb park filled with flowers in season. Large, slightly outdated rooms. View over the lake. Classic cuisine, specialities of grills and fish from Lake Leman served in the rustic restaurant.

Alizé rm,

2 av. J. Léger – ✆ 04 50 75 49 49 – alize.hotel@wanadoo.fr – Fax 04 50 75 50 40 – Closed 15 November-31 January C **n**

22 rm – €69/96 €77/107, €8,50 – ½ P €66/81

Rest – *(closed 6 December-30 January, Monday and Tuesday except July-August)* Menu €15 (weekday lunch), €22/29 – Carte €20/45

◆ A well situated hotel opposite the landing stage and near the thermal baths. The rooms are tasteful, practical and clean: most overlook the lake. The restaurant proposes traditional dishes and specialities from Savoie.

Littoral without rest

av. de Narvik – ✆ 04 50 75 64 00 – hotel-littoral-evian@wanadoo.fr – Fax 04 50 75 30 04 – Closed 24 October-11 November B **e**

30 rm – €67/82 €75/99, €8,50

◆ A modern building near the casino with functional facilities, popular with an international clientele. All the rooms (except two) have a balcony facing the lake.

L'Oasis without rest

11 bd Bennevy – ✆ 04 50 75 13 38 – stephane.berthier3@wanadoo.fr – Fax 04 50 74 90 30 – Open 10 March-10 October A **v**

18 rm – €65/110 €65/160, €10

◆ Situated in the upper section of Évian, a charming hotel with bright, modern rooms; some face the lake, others are housed in two maisonettes nestled within the pretty garden.

Continental without rest

65 r. Nationale – ✆ 04 50 75 37 54 – info@continental-evian.com – Fax 04 50 75 31 11 B **m**

32 rm – €40/55 €50/82, €7,50

◆ Built in 1868, this hotel is home to large, well-soundproofed rooms and two new suites; those on the fourth floor on the street side enjoy lake views. Refurbished interior and fine antique furniture.

Histoire de Goût

1 av. gén. Dupas – ✆ 04 50 70 09 98 – froissart.dominique@wanadoo.fr – Fax 04 50 70 10 69 – Closed 4-15 January and Monday A **m**

Rest – Menu (€18 bi), €24/39 – Carte €35/50

◆ With wine racks lining the walls and an attractive pine bar in one dining room, and an arched ceiling and wrought-iron chandelier in the other, this restaurant focuses on contemporary cuisine.

ÉVISA – 2A Corse-du-Sud – 345 B6 – see Corse

ÉVOSGES – 01 Ain – 328 F5 – pop. 109 – alt. 750 m – ✉ 01230 45 C1

Paris 481 – Aix-les-Bains 69 – Belley 37 – Bourg-en-Bresse 57 – Lyon 79 – Nantua 32

L'Auberge Campagnarde

– ✆ 04 74 38 55 55 – auberge-campagnarde@wanadoo.fr – Fax 04 74 38 55 62 – Closed 1st-8 September, 16-30 November, January, Sunday dinner, Monday dinner off season, Tuesday dinner and Wednesday

15 rm – €44/85 €44/85, €10 – ½ P €52/65 – **Rest** – Menu €23 (weekdays)/60

◆ The same family has run this inn, popular with nature lovers, for five generations. Welcoming staff, simple but faultless rooms, crazy golf and pool. Countrified dining room (old utensils) and flower-decked terrace; cuisine with regional touches.

ÉVREUX P – 27 Eure – 304 G7 – pop. 51 198 – alt. 64 m – ✉ 27000

Normandy 33 D2

Paris 100 – Alençon 119 – Caen 135 – Chartres 78 – Rouen 56

Office de tourisme, 1 ter, place de Gaulle ✆ 02 32 24 04 43, Fax 02 32 31 28 45

d'Évreux Chemin du Valème, by Lisieux road: 3 km, ✆ 02 32 39 66 22.

Notre-Dame cathedral★★ - Shrine★★ in St-Taurin church - Museum ★★ M.

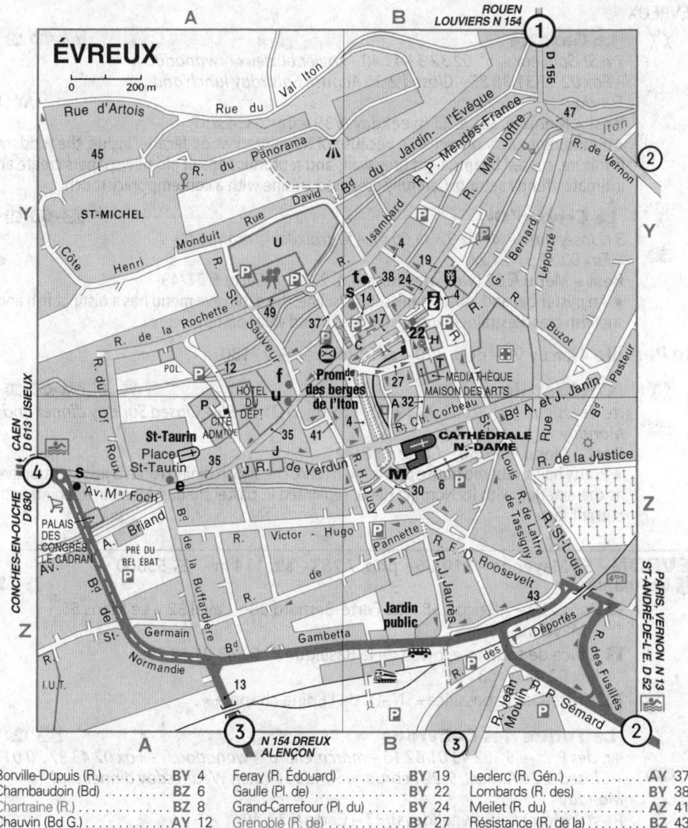

Borville-Dupuis (R.)	BY	4	Feray (R. Édouard)	BY	19	Leclerc (R. Gén.)	AY	37
Chambaudoin (Bd)	BZ	6	Gaulle (Pl. de)	BY	22	Lombards (R. des)	BY	38
Chartraine (R.)	BZ	8	Grand-Carrefour (Pl. du)	BY	24	Meilet (R. du)	AZ	41
Chauvin (Bd G.)	AY	12	Grenoble (R. de)	BY	27	Résistance (R. de la)	BZ	43
Cités Unies (Bd des)	AZ	13	Harpe (R. de la)	BZ	30	St-Michel (R. de)	AY	45
Clemenceau (Pl.)	BY	14	Horloge (R. de l')	BZ	32	Vigor (R.)	BY	47
Dr-Oursel (R.)	BY	17	Joséphine (R.)	AZ	35	7e-Chasseurs (R. du)	AY	49

Mercure
bd Normandie – ✆ 02 32 38 77 77 – h1575@accor.com – Fax 02 32 39 04 53 AZ **s**
60 rm – €72/98 €77/106, ☕ €11 – **Rest** – Menu €20/29 – Carte €29/42
◆ Modern building at a major road intersection, with well-equipped and well-soundproofed rooms. Figured wood, warm colours and good lighting create a pleasant ambience in the dining room.

L'Orme without rest
13 r. Lombards – ✆ 02 32 39 34 12 – patrick.lechevrel@orange.fr – Fax 02 32 33 62 48
39 rm – €55 €72, ☕ €9 BY **t**
◆ This town-centre establishment is convenient for visitors passing through. Sparingly decorated, functional rooms, some with bamboo furniture.

La Vieille Gabelle
3 r. Vieille Gabelle – ✆ 02 32 39 77 13 – Fax 02 32 39 77 13 – Closed 1st-21 August, 23 December-1st January, Saturday lunch, Sunday dinner and Monday
Rest – Menu €17 (weekday lunch)/28 – Carte €38/47 BY **s**
◆ The typically Norman half-timbered facade is particularly welcoming. Two country-style dining rooms with exposed beams, one with a lovely stone fireplace.

XX **La Gazette** VISA MC AE

7 r. St-Sauveur – ✆ 02 32 33 43 40 – xavier.buzieux@wanadoo.fr – Fax 02 32 31 38 87 – Closed 2-26 August, Saturday lunch and Sunday AY **f**

Rest – Menu (€ 20), € 23 (weekdays)/39 – Carte € 43/57

◆ Restaurant easily discernable because of its painted wood facade. Inside, the modern furniture, coated beams, light grey walls and reproductions of old newspapers create an intimate, trendy setting. Carefully prepared cuisine with a contemporary touch.

X **La Croix d'Or** VISA MC AE

3 r. Joséphine – ✆ 02 32 33 06 07 – la.croixdor@orange.fr – Fax 02 32 31 14 27 AZ **e**

Rest – Menu € 12 (weekday lunch), € 22/32 – Carte € 27/43

◆ An oyster bar and lobster tank set the scene: the extensive menu has a distinct fish and shellfish bias. Restrained, rustic-style decor and veranda-terrace.

in Parville **4 km by ④ – pop. 320 – alt. 130 m – ✉ 27180**

XX **Côté Jardin** AC P VISA MC AE

rte de Lisieux – ✆ 02 32 39 19 19 – Fax 02 32 31 21 85 – Closed Sunday dinner and Monday

Rest – Menu € 18/50 – Carte € 18/32

◆ Pretty half-timbered house by the main road. The stylish dining room is just as attractive as the exterior, with its Norman decor repainted in pastel shades. Menu in keeping with current taste.

ÉVRON – 53 Mayenne – 310 G6 – pop. 7 283 – alt. 114 m – ✉ 53600

Normandy 35 **C1**

Paris 250 – Alençon 58 – La Ferté-Bernard 98 – Laval 32 – Le Mans 55 – Mayenne 25

Office de tourisme, place de la Basilique ✆ 02 43 01 63 75, Fax 02 43 01 63 75

Notre-Dame bassilica★: N.-D.-de l'Épine chapel★★.

X **La Toque des Coëvrons** VISA MC

4 r. des Prés – ✆ 02 43 01 62 16 – marcmenard@wanadoo.fr – Fax 02 43 37 20 01 – Closed 4-24 August, 9-22 February, Sunday dinner, Wednesday dinner and Monday

Rest – Menu € 18 (weekdays)/33 – Carte € 27/40

◆ The chef of this friendly restaurant is wild about traditional recipes and lovingly prepares tasty dishes. The pretty, rustic-style dining room has recently been refurbished.

Mayenne road **6 km by D 7 – ✉ 53600 Mézangers**

Relais du Gué de Selle rm, P VISA MC

rte de Mayenne , (D 7) – ✆ 02 43 91 20 00 – relaisduguedeselle@wanadoo.fr – Fax 02 43 91 20 10 – Closed 22 December-8 January, 15 February-4 March, Friday dinner, Sunday dinner and Monday October-May

30 rm – †€ 59/113 ††€ 74/171, ☕ € 10 – ½ P € 81/104

Rest – *(closed Monday lunch from June to September)* Menu (€ 17 bi), € 24 (weekdays)/52 – Carte € 48/56

◆ An old restored farmhouse and garden on the shore of a lake. Some of the pleasant rooms have a lake view. A waterside promenade has been laid out, and there are bikes, fishing etc. Stylish, welcoming dining room decor complete with fireplace.

ÉVRY – 91 Essonne – 312 D4 – 101 37 – see Paris, Area

EYBENS – 38 Isère – 333 H7 – see Grenoble

EYGALIÈRES – 13 Bouches-du-Rhône – 340 E3 – pop. 1 851 – alt. 134 m – ✉ 13810 Provence

42 **E1**

Paris 701 – Avignon 28 – Cavaillon 14 – Marseille 83 – St-Rémy-de-Provence 12

La Bastide d'Eygalières rm, VISA
Route Orgon (D24^B) and Chemin de Pestelade – 04 90 95 90 06 – contact@labastide.com.fr – Fax 04 90 95 99 77
14 rm – €63/85 €78/125, €13 – ½P €70/97 – **Rest** – *(closed lunch October-March) (dinner for resident only in winter)* Menu €20 (dinner)/36 – Carte €25/37
◆ Charming Provençal farmhouse with blue shutters. The delicate interior sports off white walls, well-worn furniture and old floor tiles. Spacious, refurbished rooms. Organic produce use in the lunchtime salads and the evening traditional menu.

Mas dou Pastré VISA
1.5 kmon Orgon road (D 24^B) – 04 90 95 92 61 – contact@masdupastre.com – Fax 04 90 90 61 75 – Closed 15 November-15 December
15 rm – €125/180 €125/180, €14 – 2 suites – **Rest** – *(closed Sunday)* Menu €39
◆ This family-run sheep farm has a charm of its own. Find a guesthouse atmosphere, an Olde Provence décor with antiques and ornaments, and a garden and three authentic gypsy caravans. Seasonal cuisine served in an attractive setting.

Maison Roumanille VISA
au village – 04 90 95 92 61 – Fax 04 90 90 61 75 – Closed 15 November-15 December
4 rm – €105/120 €105/120, €10 – 2 suites
◆ Attractive farmhouse in the centre of the village, decorated in the same style as the main residence. All the individually decorated, cheerful rooms except one have a terrace. Breakfast veranda.

L'Oliviera Eygalières, VISA
chemin des Jaisses, 1 km on the D 74^a – 04 90 90 65 28 – contact@loliviera.fr – Fax 04 90 90 66 40 – Open 15 March-15 November
4 rm – €90/100 €90/100, €11 – **Table d'hôte** – Menu €32 bi
◆ Nestling amid olive groves, this welcoming Provençal farmhouse is a haven of peace and quiet. Spruce, prettily decorated rooms. Splendid view of the Alpilles from the terrace. The chef lavishly employs local produce and the house olive oil in his menus.

Bistrot d'Eygalières "Chez Bru" (Wout Bru) with rm
r. de la République – 04 90 90 60 34 – sbru@club-internet.fr – Fax 04 90 90 60 37 – Open 1st May-3 November and closed 2-7 August, Sunday dinner in October, Tuesday lunch from May to September and Monday VISA AE
2 rm – €130/150 €130/150, €20 – 2 suites – €180
Rest – *(number of covers limited, pre-book)* Menu €95/115 – Carte €103/132
Spec. Ris de veau en salade, glace parmesan. Homard grillé aux jeunes oignons anisés, glace au foie gras. Croustillant de cochon de lait au porto et champignons.
Wines Vin de Pays des Bouches du Rhône, Coteaux d'Aix-en-Provence-les-Baux.
◆ Tasty updated Provençal cuisine served in a stylish bistro. Dine in the room decorated in creams and browns with paintings and sculpture or on an attractive patio terrace.

Sous Les Micocouliers VISA
Traverse de Montfort – 04 90 95 94 53 – contact@souslesmicocouliers.com – Fax 04 90 95 94 53 – Closed 1st-15 December, 1st-15 February, Tuesday from 11 November to 1st March and Wednesday
Rest – Menu (€20), €28 – Carte €39/57
◆ This colourful dining room with a handsome fireplace and terrace shaded by lime trees pays homage to a modern gourmet menu, which has not forgotten its Provençal roots.

EYGUIÈRES – 13 Bouches-du-Rhône – 340 F3 – pop. 5 392 – alt. 75 m – 13430

Provence 42 **E1**

Paris 715 – Aix-en-Provence 49 – Arles 45 – Avignon 40 – Istres 27 – Marseille 66

Office de tourisme, place de l'ancien Hôtel de Ville 04 90 59 82 44, Fax 04 90 59 89 07

Le Relais du Coche VISA
pl. Monier – 04 90 59 86 70 – Fax 04 90 45 09 78 – Closed 1st-15 July, 2-15 January, Saturday lunch, Sunday dinner and Monday
Rest – Menu €16 (weekday lunch), €28/34 – Carte €30/48
◆ This restaurant is located in the converted stables of an old 18C coaching inn. A pleasant patio terrace covered with Virginia creeper. Regional menu.

EYMET – 24 Dordogne – 329 D8 – pop. 2 552 – alt. 54 m – ✉ 24500

Dordogne-Berry-Limousin 4 **C2**

Paris 560 – Arcachon 72 – Bayonne 239 – Bordeaux 101 – Dax 188 – Périgueux 74

Office de tourisme, place de la Bastide ✆ 05 53 23 74 95, Fax 05 53 23 74 95

Les Vieilles Pierres

La Gillette – ✆ 05 53 23 75 99 – les.vieilles.pierres@wanadoo.fr – Fax 05 53 27 87 14 – Closed 27 October-17 November and 16 February-9 March

9 rm – €43 €49/59, €6,50 – ½ P €41/45 – **Rest** – *(closed Saturday lunch from November to Easter and Sunday dinner except July-August)* Menu €11 (weekdays)/35 – Carte €20/45

◆ Simple rooms housed in three buildings arranged around a walnut-shaded patio. This converted barn is now a fittingly rustic dining room serving classic cuisine. A glazed summer restaurant overlooks the children's play area.

La Cour d'Eymet with rm

rest, VISA

32 bd National – ✆ 05 53 22 72 83 – Closed 30 June-10 July, 15 February-15 March, Thursday lunch, Saturday lunch from March to October, Sunday dinner, Monday, Tuesday from November to February and Wednesday

3 rm – €60/80 €80/100 – **Rest** – *(number of covers limited, pre-book)* Menu €25 (weekday lunch), €38/48 – Carte €34/66

◆ Restaurant in a fine comfortable building. Discreet, elegant interior and pretty courtyard-terrace. Traditional cuisine and short wine list, rich in local wines. Restaurant in a fine comfortable building. Discreet, elegant interior and pretty courtyard-terrace. Traditional cuisine and short wine list, rich in local wines.

EYSINES – 33 Gironde – 335 H5 – see Bordeaux

LES EYZIES-DE-TAYAC – 24 Dordogne – 329 H6 – pop. 909 – alt. 70 m – ✉ 24620

Dordogne-Berry-Limousin 4 **C3**

Paris 536 – Brive-la-Gaillarde 62 – Fumel 62 – Périgueux 47 – Sarlat-la-Canéda 21

Office de tourisme, 19, av. de la Préhistoire ✆ 05 53 06 97 05, Fax 05 53 06 90 79

Musée national de Préhistoire★ - Grotte du Grand Roc★★ : ≤★ - Grotte de Font-de-Gaume★★.

Du Centenaire without rest

2 av. du Cingle – ✆ 05 53 06 68 68 – hotel.centenaire@wanadoo.fr – Fax 05 53 06 92 41 – Open April-beg. November

14 rm – €100/138 €100/230, €17 – 5 suites

◆ This residence nestling in a quiet enclosed garden with a delightful swimming pool offers its guests a choice of pleasant, cosy rooms. Breakfast beneath an attractive glass canopy.

Les Glycines

rte Périgueux – ✆ 05 53 06 97 07 – les-glycines-aux-eyzies@wanadoo.fr – Fax 05 53 06 92 19 – Open Easter to 1st November

27 rm – €85/235 €85/235, €14 – ½ P €92/178 – **Rest** – *(closed Wednesday lunch, Monday and Tuesday except July-August)* Menu €37 – Carte €48/72

◆ Former post house (1862) in a verdant setting near the Vézère. Impressive grounds and wisteria-clad arbour. Renovated guestrooms, with four at garden level. Restaurant with views of the hotel grounds, a pleasant, tranquil terrace and up-to-date cuisine.

Hostellerie du Passeur

pl. de la Mairie – ✆ 05 53 06 97 13 – hostellerie-du-passeur@perigord.com – Fax 05 53 06 91 63 – Open Easter to 1st November

19 rm – €76/120 €76/120, €9 – ½ P €72/92 – **Rest** – *(closed Tuesday lunch and Saturday lunch except July-August)* Menu €19 (lunch), €34/46

◆ The hall, bar and most of the rooms in this characterful hotel on the village square have been renovated. Carefully laid tables in the two elegant dining rooms and shaded terrace. Traditional offerings in the evening, with bistro menus at lunchtime.

Moulin de la Beune
– 05 53 06 94 33 – contact@moulindelabeune.com – Fax 05 53 06 98 06
– Open 2 April-31 October
20 rm – €50 €59/68, €7 – ½ P €69
Rest *Au Vieux Moulin* – *(closed Tuesday lunchtime, Wednesday lunchtime and Saturday lunchtime)* Menu €30/42 bi – Carte €42/63
◆ Spacious rooms, antique furniture and tasteful decoration in these two old mills in a peaceful garden with the Beune running through it. Pleasant lounge with an attractive fireplace. A rustic restaurant with views of the mill's paddle wheel. Riverside terrace. Cuisine with a regional flavour.

Des Roches without rest
rte de Sarlat – 05 53 06 96 59 – hotel@roches-les-eyzies.com
– Fax 05 53 06 95 54 – Open 11 April-31 October
40 rm – €70/76 €76/90, €9,50
◆ Local-style construction at the foot of cliffs crowned by oak trees. Classic decor in the guestrooms. Restful garden by the river; swimming pool.

Le Cro Magnon
54 av. Préhistoire – 05 53 06 97 06 – hotel.cro.magnon.les-eyzies@wanadoo.fr
– Fax 05 53 06 95 45 – Open 1st March-30 November
15 rm – €65 €70/130, €10 – ½ P €64/74 – **Rest** – Menu (€17), €23/43 – Carte €30/42
◆ This welcoming hotel built against the cliff-face offers large, individually furnished rooms. Pleasant lounge warmed by an open fire. Swimming pool. Enjoy traditional cuisine either on the veranda or the courtyard terrace. Breakfast is served in the cosy winter dining room.

East 7 km by Sarlat road – ✉ 24620 Les Eyzies-de-Tayac

La Métairie
on D 47 – 05 53 29 65 32 – bourgeade@wanadoo.fr – Fax 05 53 29 65 30
– Open from March to November and closed Sunday dinner except July-August, Wednesday lunch and Monday
Rest – Menu €16 (weekday lunch), €27/31
◆ The former farm of the Château de Beyssac stands at the foot of the cliff. The feeding troughs in the rustic dining room testify to the building's initial vocation. Regional cuisine.

East 8 km by Sarlat road, C 3 dir. Meyrals and secondary road – ✉ 24220 Meyrals

Ferme Lamy without rest
– 05 53 29 62 46 – ferme-lamy@wanadoo.fr – Fax 05 53 59 61 41
12 rm – €95/165 €105/175, €15
◆ A farm with a cosy feel and lovely garden. Quiet guestrooms attractively decorated with antique furniture. Truffle evenings in season and hot-air ballooning.

ÈZE – 06 Alpes-Maritimes – 341 F5 – pop. 2 509 – alt. 390 m – ✉ 06360

French Riviera 42 **E2**

Paris 938 – Cap d'Ail 6 – Menton 17 – Monaco 8 – Monte-Carlo 8 – Nice 12

Office de tourisme, place du Général-de-Gaulle 04 93 41 26 00, Fax 04 93 41 04 80

Site★★ - Sentier Frédéric Nietzsche★ - Old village★ - Exotic garden ★★★.

"Belvédère" d'Èze (Viewpoint) West : 4 km.

Château de la Chèvre d'Or coast and peninsula, rest,
r. Barri, (pedestrian access) –
04 92 10 66 66 – reservation@chevredor.com – Fax 04 93 41 06 72
– Open 14 March-1st December
31 rm – €270/830 €270/830, €45 – 4 suites
Rest – *(closed Wednesday in March, Monday and Tuesday in November)* *(pre-book)* Menu €65 (weekday lunch), €210/340 – Carte €145/350
Spec. Coquillages et crustacés interprétés au fil des saisons. Homard bleu en deux services. Filet d'agneau des Pyrénées ou de l'Aveyron. **Wines** Côtes de Provence, Bellet.
◆ Picturesque building overlooking the sea, a real eagle's nest with hanging gardens clinging to the rock. This enchanting residence promises an unforgettable stay. The restaurant serves delicious food and commands splendid views of the countryside.

Château Eza — coast and peninsula, rest,
r. Pise, (pedestrian access) – ☎ 04 93 41 12 24
– reception@chateaueza.com – Fax 04 93 41 16 64
– Closed 1st November-15 December
9 rm – †€ 180/795 ††€ 180/795, ☕ € 25 – 1 suite
Rest – *(closed Monday and Tuesday from November to March)* Menu € 39 (weekday lunch), € 80/100 – Carte € 59/97
Spec. Filets de rouget et jeunes pousses de mesclun. Saint-Pierre poché dans un bouillon corsé. Carré d'agneau mariné et rôti, pressé de légumes. **Wines** Bellet.
◆ This opulent 14C abode perched between sky and sea commands a breathtaking view of the coast. Elegant, personalised rooms with terrace, balcony or private Jacuzzi tub. Medieval-inspired decor, sliding roof, magnificent view and subtle, up-to-date menu.

Les Terrasses d'Eze — sea, rest,
La Turbie road on D 6007 and D 45: 1.5 km –
☎ 04 92 41 55 55 – info@hotel-eze.com – Fax 04 92 41 55 10
81 rm – †€ 160/390 ††€ 160/390, ☕ € 20 – 6 suites
Rest – Menu € 40 – Carte € 41/62
◆ Contemporary architecture perched on the hillside. Spacious rooms (with a terrace), some of which have been refurbished, and the lovely overflow swimming pool enjoys a sea view. Regionally inspired cuisine, and a snack menu in summertime.

Troubadour
r. du Brec, (pedestrian access) – ☎ 04 93 41 19 03 – troubadoureze@wanadoo.fr
– Closed 2-10 March, 29 June-8 July, 12 November-18 December, Sunday and Monday
Rest – *(pre-book)* Menu € 35/48 – Carte € 45/62
◆ In the heart of the old village, three small and intimate dining areas serving traditional cuisine prepared with market produce. Some Provençal specialities.

at Col d'Èze 3 km Northwest – ✉ 06360 Eze – pop. 2 509 – alt. 390 m

La Bastide aux Camélias without rest
23c rte de l'Adret – ☎ 04 93 41 13 68
– sylviane.mathieu@libertysurf.fr – Fax 04 93 41 13 68
4 rm ☕ – †€ 100/150 ††€ 100/150
◆ The rooms in this splendid villa surrounded by greenery are personalised and stylishly furnished (antique and ethnic furniture); there is a swimming-pool and fitness centre.

ÈZE-BORD-DE-MER – 06 Alpes-Maritimes – 341 F5 – ✉ 06360 Eze

French Riviera 42 **E2**

Paris 959 – Monaco 8 – Nice 14 – Menton 22

Cap Estel — sea,
1312 av. Raymond Poincaré – ☎ 04 93 76 29 29
– contact@capestel.com – Fax 04 93 01 55 20 – Open 4 January-26 September
8 rm – †€ 350/1350 ††€ 350/1350, ☕ € 25 – 12 suites – ††€ 680/12900
Rest – Menu € 55 (weekday lunch), € 75/95 – Carte € 95/107
◆ This haven of peace and tranquillity, built on the peninsula by a Russian prince at the end of the 19C, has regained all its former splendour. Luxurious bedrooms, sumptuous suites, plus a private beach. An elegant restaurant facing the sea where the cuisine is distinctly contemporary.

FAGNON – 08 Ardennes – 306 J4 – see Charleville-Mézières

FALAISE – 14 Calvados – 303 K6 – pop. 8 434 – alt. 132 m – ✉ 14700

Normandy 32 **B2**

Paris 264 – Argentan 23 – Caen 36 – Flers 37 – Lisieux 45 – St-Lô 107

Office de tourisme, boulevard de la Libération ☎ 02 31 90 17 26, Fax 02 31 90 98 70

Château Guillaume-Le-Conquérant (William the Conqueror's castle) ★ - la Trinité church ★.

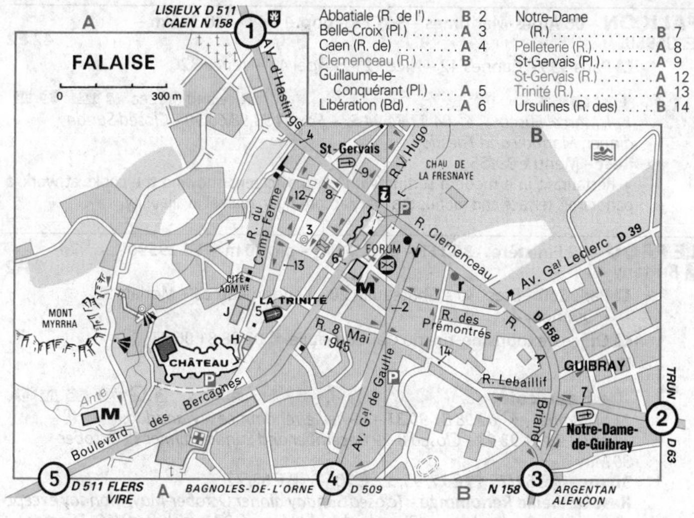

De la Poste

38 r. G. Clemenceau – ✆ 02 31 90 13 14 – hotel.delaposte@wanadoo.fr – Fax 02 31 90 01 81 – Closed 1st-23 January, Sunday dinner, Friday dinner and Monday October-April — B v

17 rm – †€ 53 ††€ 53/76, ☕ € 8 – **Rest** – *(closed Friday lunch from May to September)* Menu € 16 (weekdays)/50 – Carte € 28/61

◆ The rooms in this post-war building are discreet and well kept; those at the rear are quieter. A dining room in pastel colours serving traditional dishes.

La Fine Fourchette

52 r. G. Clemenceau – ✆ 02 31 90 08 59 – Fax 02 31 90 00 83 – Closed 18 February-8 March and Tuesday dinner off season — B r

Rest – Menu € 16/54 – Carte € 36/54

◆ This stone building from the 1950s is home to a restaurant serving modern cuisine in two refurbished dining rooms. Attractively presented dishes.

L'Attache

rte de Caen, by ①: 1.5 km – ✆ 02 31 90 05 38 – sarlhastain@orange.fr – Fax 02 31 90 57 19 – Closed 22 September-9 October, Tuesday and Wednesday

Rest – *(number of covers limited, pre-book)* Menu € 19/60 – Carte € 39/61

◆ A former coaching inn with a charming façade and attractive, classic interior. Focus on local cuisine with the occasional heirloom variety of herbs and vegetables.

LE FALGOUX – 15 Cantal – 330 D4 – pop. 193 – alt. 930 m – Winter sports : 1 050 m 1 – ✉ 15380 — 5 B3

Paris 533 – Aurillac 57 – Mauriac 29 – Murat 34 – Salers 15

Falgoux Valley ★.

Cirque du Falgoux★★ Southeast: 6 km - Puy Mary ✻★★★: 1 h return journey from Pas de Peyrol★★ Southeast: 12 km, **G. Auvergne-Rhone Valley.**

Des Voyageurs

– ✆ 04 71 69 51 59 – Fax 04 71 69 48 05 – Closed 5 November-20 January and Wednesday dinner off season

14 rm – †€ 44 ††€ 44, ☕ € 7 – ½ P € 42 – **Rest** – Menu (€ 15), € 18 (weekdays)/27 – Carte € 18/30

◆ A typical Auvergne-style inn with a large fireplace (lined with benches) in the bar. Friendly service, redecorated well-kept rooms with rustic furniture. The restaurant commands a fine view of the Cantal mountain landscape. Regional menu.

FALICON – 06 Alpes-Maritimes – 341 E5 – pop. 1 644 – alt. 396 m – ✉ 06950

42 **E2**

▶ Paris 935 – Cannes 42 – Nice 12 – Sospel 41 – Vence 32

Parcours ← Nice and the sea, AC VISA MC AE

1 pl. Marcel Eusebi – ✆ 04 93 84 94 57 – Fax 04 93 98 66 90 – Closed Sunday dinner, Monday and Tuesday

Rest – Menu € 39/55

◆ Restaurant in a modern setting with plasma screens showing the cooks at work, a panoramic terrace and menus that vary according to market availability.

LE FAOU – 29 Finistère – 308 F5 – pop. 1 571 – alt. 10 m – ✉ 29590

Brittany

9 **A2**

▶ Paris 560 – Brest 30 – Châteaulin 20 – Landerneau 23 – Morlaix 52 – Quimper 43

ℹ Office de tourisme, rue du Gal-de-Gaulle ✆ 02 98 81 06 85

◉ Site★.

De Beauvoir VISA MC AE

11 pl. Mairie – ✆ 02 98 81 90 31 – la-vieille-renommee@wanadoo.fr – Fax 02 98 81 92 93 – Closed 8-29 December and Sunday dinner 1st October-30 May

30 rm – †€ 52/75 ††€ 77/95, ☕ € 10 – ½ P € 62/72

Rest *La Vieille Renommée* – *(closed Sunday dinner October-May, Monday except dinner June-September and Tuesday lunch)* Menu € 27 (weekdays)/60 – Carte € 35/61

◆ Large building in the centre of an typically Breton village nestling at the end of the Faou Estuary. Ask for one of the recently refurbished rooms. The Vieille Renommée dining room has neat table settings and serves traditional cuisine. Good wine list.

FARGES-ALLICHAMPS – 18 Cher – 323 K6 – pop. 216 – alt. 194 m – ✉ 18200

12 **C3**

▶ Paris 290 – Orléans 164 – Bourges 38 – Montluçon 67 – Issoudun 47

Château de la Commanderie VISA MC

– ✆ 02 48 61 04 19 – chateaudelacommanderie@wanadoo.fr – Fax 02 48 61 01 84

5 rm ☕ – †€ 135 ††€ 160/250 – **Table d'hôte** – Menu € 85 bi

◆ The charming owners of this former Templars commandery have preserved its original decor. Refined rooms in a peaceful 10 ha park. Romantic meals (upon reservation) in the superb dining room.

FARROU – 12 Aveyron – 338 E4 – see Villefranche-de-Rouergue

LA FAUCILLE (COL) – 01 Ain – 328 J2 – see Col de la Faucille

FAULQUEMONT – 57 Moselle – 307 K4 – pop. 5 478 – alt. 275 m – ✉ 57380

27 **C1**

▶ Paris 367 – Metz 38 – Château-Salins 29 – Pont-à-Mousson 46 – St-Avold 15

Le Chatelain without rest VISA MC AE

1 pl. Monroë, (near the church) – ✆ 03 87 90 70 80 – hotel-lechatelain.com@wanadoo.fr – Fax 03 87 90 74 78

25 rm – †€ 49/64 ††€ 49/64, ☕ € 7

◆ This old farmhouse located on a quiet square beside an ancient church has been converted into comfortable accommodation with attractively furnished rooms; greenery flourishes on the pleasant patio.

FAVERGES – 74 Haute-Savoie – 328 K6 – pop. 6 310 – alt. 507 m – ✉ 74210

French Alps

45 **C1**

▶ Paris 562 – Albertville 20 – Annecy 27 – Megève 35

ℹ Office de tourisme, place Marcel Piquand ✆ 04 50 44 60 24, Fax 04 50 44 45 96

Florimont
rte d'Albertville, 2,5 km – ✆ 04 50 44 50 05 – info@hotelflorimont.com – Fax 04 50 44 43 20 – Closed 20 December-5 January
27 rm – †€ 66/80 ††€ 75/120, ☕ € 12 – ½ P € 72/100
Rest – *(closed 13 December-5 January, Sunday dinner and Saturday)*
Menu € 26/62 – Carte € 52/75
◆ Friendly hotel complex ideally located near a golf course and overlooking Mont Blanc. Brightly decorated, well kept rooms. Two dining rooms, one classic and the other Savoyard in style, together with a green terrace.

De Genève without rest
34 r. République – ✆ 04 50 32 46 90 – hotel-de-geneve@wanadoo.fr – Fax 04 50 44 48 09 – Closed 18 April-4 May, 19 December-4 January
30 rm – †€ 46/70 ††€ 55/78, ☕ € 8
◆ Easily recognisable by its painted façade, this centrally located hotel is very handy. Practical rooms, well soundproofed on the road side. Exhibitions in the bar (snacks).

in Tertenoz 4 km Southeast by D 12 and secondary road – ✉ 74210 Seythenex

Au Gay Séjour with rm
– *✆ 04 50 44 52 52 – hotel-gay-sejour@wanadoo.fr – Fax 04 50 44 49 52 – Closed Sunday dinner and Monday except holidays and except July-August*
11 rm – †€ 70/75 ††€ 85/100, ☕ € 13 – ½ P € 88/98 – **Rest** – Menu (€ 23), € 33/82 – Carte € 43/62
◆ An imposing 17C farmhouse tucked away in a mountain hamlet with a view of the valley. Traditional cuisine and brightly coloured modern dining room. Simple bedrooms.

LA FAVIÈRE – 83 Var – 340 N7 – see Bormes-les-Mimosas

FAVIÈRES – 80 Somme – 301 C6 – pop. 405 – alt. 1 m – ✉ 80120 36 A1

Paris 212 – Abbeville 22 – Amiens 77 – Berck-Plage 27 – Le Crotoy 5
Le Crotoy: Butte du Moulin ≤★ Southwest: 5 km,
Northern France and the Paris Region.

Les Saules without rest
1075 r. Forges – ✆ 03 22 27 04 20 – hotellessaules@wanadoo.fr – Fax 03 22 27 00 38
13 rm – †€ 60/65 ††€ 65/80, ☕ € 10
◆ Tranquillity is ensured in this modern house near the Marquenterre Bird Park. Functional rooms overlooking a garden or the surrounding countryside.

La Clé des Champs
– *✆ 03 22 27 88 00 – Fax 03 22 27 79 36 – Closed 25 August-2 September, 5-20 January, 23 February-10 March, Monday and Tuesday except public holidays*
Rest – Menu € 15 (weekdays)/40
◆ This old Picardy farmhouse has been sympathetically restored. The decor remains classic and simple, embellished with paintings by local artists. Seasonal menu.

FAVONE – 2A Corse-du-Sud – 345 F9 – see Corse

FAYENCE – 83 Var – 340 P4 – pop. 4 253 – alt. 350 m – ✉ 83440 French Riviera

Paris 884 – Castellane 55 – Draguignan 30 – Fréjus 36 – Grasse 26 – St-Raphaël 37 41 C3
Office de tourisme, place Léon Roux ✆ 04 94 76 20 08, Fax 04 94 39 15 96
≤★ from the church terrace.

Les Oliviers without rest
quartier La Ferrage , Grasse road – ✆ 04 94 76 13 12 – hotel.oliviers.fayen@free.fr – Fax 04 94 76 08 05
22 rm ☕ – †€ 73/78 ††€ 86/96
◆ Small building overlooking the Plaine du Gué and its large gliding centre. Sports enthusiasts and lazybones alike will enjoy the practical rooms at the Oliviers.

La Farigoulette
pl. Château – 04 94 84 10 49 – la-farigoulette@wanadoo.fr – Fax 04 94 84 10 49 – Closed 4-10 December, 15-29 January, 21 February-12 March, Tuesday and Wednesday
Rest – Menu € 20 bi (weekday lunch)/36 – Carte € 54/61
◆ Skilful reconstruction has turned this old stable into a shaded terrace and two small rooms where open stonework and traditional furnishings combine ideally with a Provençal décor; the cuisine is regional.

Le Temps des Cerises
pl. République – 04 94 76 01 19 – louis.schroder@tiscali.fr – Fax 04 94 76 92 50 – Closed 1st-27 December and Tuesday
Rest – *(dinner only except Sunday)* Menu € 39 – Carte € 42/54
◆ This attractive Fayence residence has been converted into a restaurant that offers diners the choice between its ochre-red dining hall (non smokers) and its shady open-air terrace. The cuisine is traditional.

La Table d'Yves
1357 rte de Fréjus, on the D563: 2 km – 04 94 76 08 44 – contact@latabledyves.com – Fax 04 94 76 19 32 – Closed Nov. school holidays, from February, Thursday except evenings in high season and Wednesday
Rest – Menu € 28/60 bi – Carte € 34/55
◆ The lovely terrace gives a splendid view of the village perched on a hillside. The dining rooms are enhanced by a pleasant, sunny décor, and the savoury cuisine is based on market-fresh products – all good reasons to dine at Yves'!

West **by Seillans road (D 19) and secondary road – ✉ 83440 Fayence**

Moulin de la Camandoule
at 2 km – 04 94 76 00 84 – moulin.camandoule@wanadoo.fr – Fax 04 94 76 10 40
12 rm – €51/118 €72/190, € 12 – ½P € 87/125 – **Rest** – *(closed 3-19 January, Thursday except dinner in season and Wednesday)* Menu € 30/45 – Carte € 41/61
◆ At the centre of a park traversed by a Roman aqueduct, this 17C oil mill today houses pleasant, Provençal country style rooms. Fine terrace giving onto a charming orchard garden. Regional cuisine in the restaurant.

Le Castellaras (Alain Carro)
461 chemin Peymeyan, 4 km away – 04 94 76 13 80 – contact@restaurant-castellaras.com – Fax 04 94 84 17 50 – Closed 6 January-6 February, Tuesday except July-August and Monday
Rest – Menu € 45 (weekdays)/100 bi – Carte € 50/75
Spec. Carpaccio de queues de langoustines (July to September). Carpaccio de filet de bœuf et foie gras (September to November). Déclinaison autour de l'asperge (April to June). **Wines** Côtes de Provence.
◆ This attractively reconstructed stone villa is perched on a hillside and overlooks Fayence and the valley – a splendid location that vies with the palatable pleasures of the restaurant's Provençal-style cuisine.

LE FAYET – 74 Haute-Savoie – 074 08 – see St-Gervais-les-Bains

---

FÉCAMP – 76 Seine-Maritime – 304 C3 – pop. 21 027 – alt. 15 m – Casino AZ – ✉ 76400 Normandy 33 C1

Paris 201 – Amiens 165 – Caen 113 – Dieppe 66 – Le Havre 43 – Rouen 74

Office de tourisme, quai Sadi Carnot 02 35 28 51 01, Fax 02 35 27 07 77

La Trinité abbey church ★ - Palais Bénédictine★★ - Musée des Terres-Neuvas et de la Pêche★ M3 - N.-D.-du-Salut chapel ✻★★ North: 2 km by D 79 BY.

Plan on next page

Le Grand Pavois without rest
15 quai Vicomté – 02 35 10 01 01 – le.grandpavois@wanadoo.fr – Fax 02 35 29 31 67 AY **r**
32 rm – €84/139 €84/139, € 12,50 – 3 suites
◆ On the quayside, built on the site of a canning factory. The hall has a marine decor and the large rooms are furnished with contemporary furniture; some overlook the harbour.

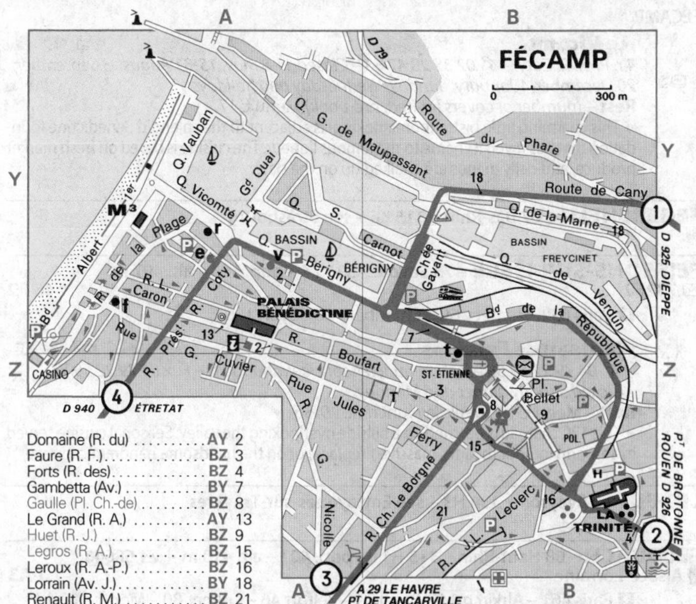

Domaine (R. du)	AY	2
Faure (R. F.)	BZ	3
Forts (R. des)	BZ	4
Gambetta (Av.)	BY	7
Gaulle (Pl. Ch.-de)	BZ	8
Le Grand (R. A.)	AY	13
Huet (R. J.)	BZ	9
Legros (R. A.)	BZ	15
Leroux (R. A.-P.)	BZ	16
Lorrain (Av. J.)	BY	18
Renault (R. M.)	BZ	21

La Ferme de la Chapelle rm, VISA

2 km by ①, rte du Phare and D 79 – ✆ 02 35 10 12 12 – fermedelachapelle@wanadoo.fr – Fax 02 35 10 12 13 – Closed 15-22 November

22 rm – €82/90 €82/90, €11 – **Rest** – *(closed Mon. lunchtime)* Menu €26/32 – Carte €33/37

◆ On a cliff overlooking the town, the converted farm buildings adjoin the old seamen's chapel. Neatly furnished rooms around a sqaure courtyard. The restaurant is both simple and welcoming, serving traditional meals.

De la Plage without rest VISA

87 r. de la Plage – ✆ 02 35 29 76 51 – hoteldelaplagefecamp@wanadoo.fr – Fax 02 35 28 68 30 AY **f**

22 rm – €40/66 €40/66, €6,50

◆ The rooms in this modern hotel near the seaside are small but fresh and practical. Breakfast room decorated with a maritime theme.

Vent d'Ouest without rest VISA

3 av. Gambetta – ✆ 02 35 28 04 04 – hotel@hotelventdouest.tm.fr – Fax 02 35 28 75 96

15 rm – €34/40 €40/48, €5 BY **t**

◆ This unpretentious family hotel, entirely renovated, is suitable for tight budgets. The rooms are painted in yellow and well equipped. A charming breakfast room.

Auberge de la Rouge with rm VISA

rte du Havre, 2 km via ③ – ✆ 02 35 28 07 59 – auberge.rouge@wanadoo.fr – Fax 02 35 28 70 55

8 rm – €60 €60, €7 – **Rest** – *(closed Saturday lunchtime, Sunday evening and Monday)* Menu €19/59 – Carte €59/68

◆ A country-style dining room with beams and fireplace and a veranda looking onto the flower garden: two renovated settings for traditional cuisine. Rustic garden-floor rooms.

La Marée VISA

77 quai Bérigny, (1st floor) – ✆ 02 35 29 39 15 – Fax 02 35 29 73 27 – Closed Thursday dinner, Sunday dinner and Monday off season AY **v**

Rest – Menu €19 (weekday lunch), €26/36 – Carte €34/55

◆ Fish recipes predominate on this restaurant's menus; the décor is soberly modern and certain tables give a view of the seaport. The small terrace faces due south.

Le Vicomté
4 r. Prés. R. Coty – ✆ 02 35 28 47 63 – Closed 1st-8 May, 15-31 August-3 September, 20 December-4 January, Sunday, Wednesday and holidays AY **e**
Rest – *(number of covers limited, pre-book)* Menu € 17
◆ This charming little bistro (non-smoking) is adjacent to the splendid Benedictine foundation that has given its name to the famous liqueur. The cuisine is based on fresh market produce, and daily menus are chalked up on the slate.

FEGERSHEIM – 67 Bas-Rhin – 315 K6 – see Strasbourg

FEISSONS-SUR-ISÈRE – 73 Savoie – 333 L4 – pop. 505 – alt. 407 m – ✉ 73260

46 **F2**

Paris 632 – Annecy 60 – Chambéry 66 – Lyon 166

Château de Feissons
– ✆ 04 79 22 59 59 – lechateaudefeissons@wanadoo.fr – Fax 04 79 22 59 76 – Closed Sunday dinner and Monday
Rest – Menu € 19 (weekday lunch), € 29/56
◆ This 12C château is perched on a hillside overlooking the valley. Seasonal cuisine served in an warm interior (beams, massive fireplace) or on the handsome panoramic terrace.

LE FEL – 12 Aveyron – 338 H3 – see Entraygues-sur-Truyères

FELDBACH – 68 Haut-Rhin – 315 H11 – pop. 401 – alt. 410 m – ✉ 68640

Alsace-Lorraine 1 **A3**

Paris 461 – Altkirch 14 – Basel 34 – Belfort 46 – Colmar 80 – Montbéliard 41 – Mulhouse 32

Cheval Blanc
1 r. Bisel – ✆ 03 89 25 81 86 – Fax 03 89 07 72 88 – Closed 23 June-8 July, 26 January-10 February, Monday and Tuesday
Rest – Menu € 11 (weekday lunch), € 15/36 – Carte € 22/49
◆ A few contemporary dishes enhance the semi-traditional, semi-regional menu of this traditional Sundgau property (non smoking). Fine wine list

FELICETO – 2B Haute-Corse – 345 C4 – see Corse

FENEYROLS – 82 Tarn-et-Garonne – 337 G7 – pop. 166 – alt. 124 m – ✉ 82140

29 **C2**

Paris 632 – Cahors 63 – Limoges 245 – Lyon 424 – Montpellier 251 – Toulouse 642

Hostellerie Les Jardins des Thermes with rm
Le bourg – ✆ 05 63 30 65 49 – hostellerie@jardinsdesthermes.com – Fax 05 63 30 60 17 – Open 1st March-15 November rm,
5 rm – †€ 42/46 ††€ 42/46, ☕ € 7,50 – 2 suites – ½ P € 47/49 – **Rest** – *(closed Wednesday and Thursday except July-August)* Menu (€ 14,50) – Carte € 39/46
◆ On the banks of the Aveyron, this old spa hotel is in a park near the remains of Roman baths. Modern rooms and nicely decorated restaurant.

FERAYOLA – 2B Haute-Corse – 345 B5 – see Corse (Galéria)

FÈRE-EN-TARDENOIS – 02 Aisne – 306 D7 – pop. 3 356 – alt. 180 m – ✉ 02130

Northern France and the Paris Region 37 **C3**

Paris 111 – Château-Thierry 23 – Laon 55 – Reims 50 – Soissons 27

Office de tourisme, 18, rue Etienne-Moreau-Nelaton ✆ 03 23 82 31 57, Fax 03 23 82 28 19

de Champagne Villers-Agron-Aiguizy Moulin de Neuville, East: 17 km by D 2, ✆ 03 23 71 62 08.

Château de Fère★: Bridge-gallery★★ North: 3 km.

Château de Fère ⅋ ≤ rm, VISA MC AE
rte de Fismes, 3 km north on D 967 – ✆ 03 23 82 21 13 – chateau.fere@wanadoo.fr – Fax 03 23 82 37 81 – Closed 2 January-1st February
19 rm – €150/170 €180/360, ☕ €22 – 7 suites
Rest – *(closed Tuesday lunch and Monday from November to March)*
Menu €36 (weekdays)/90 – Carte €77/110
♦ With the ruins of the château of Anne de Montmorency and its famous bridge in the background, this fine 16C mansion has sumptuous decor. Vast grounds. The two dining rooms exude elegance (with a fresco depicting the glory of La Fontaine and lovely wood panelling).

FERNEY-VOLTAIRE – 01 Ain – 328 J3 – pop. 7 083 – alt. 430 m – ✉ 01210

Burgundy-Jura 46 **F1**

- Paris 499 – Bellegarde-sur-Valserine 37 – Genève 10 – Gex 10 – Thonon-les-Bains 43
- Genève-Cointrin ✆ (00 41 22) 717 71 11, South: 4 km.
- Office de tourisme, 26, Grand'Rue ✆ 04 50 28 09 16, Fax 04 50 40 78 99
- de Gonville Saint-Jean-de-GonvilleSouthwest: 14 km by D 35 and D 984, ✆ 04 50 56 40 92.
- Château★.
- Genève★★★.

Novotel rm, VISA MC AE
via D 35 – ✆ 04 50 40 85 23 – h0422@accor.com – Fax 04 50 40 76 33
80 rm – €95 €175, ☕ €13,50 – **Rest** – Menu €22 – Carte €24/41
♦ This Novotel, conveniently located near the Swiss border, has been treated to a make-over. Contemporary rooms in keeping with the chain's latest design: light wood and Japanese influence. Elegant dining room and terrace. Traditional dishes and regional specialities.

XX **De France** with rm VISA MC AE
1 r. de Genève – ✆ 04 50 40 63 87 – hotelfranceferney@wanadoo.fr – Fax 04 50 40 47 27 – Closed 19-28 April, 26 July-4 August, 25 October-3 November, 20 December-8 January
14 rm – €66/100 €84/115, ☕ €9 – ½ P €72/88 – **Rest** – *(closed Saturday lunch, Sunday and Monday)* Menu (€20), €23 (weekdays), €43/66 – Carte €38/60
♦ This house built in 1742 has been masterfully taken over: modernised dining room, cosy bar, veranda extended by a terrace lined by lime trees, and an updated menu.

XX **Le Pirate** VISA MC AE
chemin de la Brunette – ✆ 04 50 40 63 52 – contact@lepirate.fr – Fax 04 50 40 64 50 – Closed 1st-21 August, 2-10 January, Sunday and Monday except holidays
Rest – Menu (€24), €28 (weekday lunch), €36/61 – Carte €45/69
♦ An establishment devoted to seafood. Elegant dining rooms decorated in warm colours and dotted with plants. A veranda enlivened by a fountain in warm weather.

X **Le Chanteclair** VISA MC
13 r. Versoix – ✆ 04 50 40 79 55 – Fax 04 50 40 93 04 – Closed 27 July-26 August, 28 December-6 January, Sunday and Monday
Rest – Menu €27 (weekdays)/55 – Carte €42/54
♦ The cuisine is in tune with the seasons in this pleasant, predominantly blue and yellow, contemporary style restaurant. Unusual façade covered in 'graffiti'.

FERRETTE – 68 Haut-Rhin – 315 H12 – pop. 1 020 – alt. 470 m – ✉ 68480

Alsace-Lorraine 1 **A3**

- Paris 467 – Altkirch 20 – Basel 28 – Belfort 52 – Colmar 85 – Montbéliard 48 – Mulhouse 38
- Office de tourisme, route de Lucelle ✆ 03 89 08 23 88, Fax 03 89 40 33 84
- de la Largue Seppois-le-Bas Rue du Golf, West: 10 km by D 473 and D 24, ✆ 03 89 07 67 67.
- Site★ - Château ruins ≤★.

in Ligsdorf 4 km South by D 432 – pop. 297 – alt. 520 m – ✉ 68480

Le Moulin Bas et rest. La Mezzanine with rm

1 r. Raedersdorf – ✆ 03 89 40 31 25 – info@le-moulin-bas.fr

8 rm – €65/75 €85/95, ☕ €9,50 – ½ P €69/98

Rest – *(Closed Tuesday)* Menu €12,50 (weekday lunch), €34/62 – Carte €26/64

Rest *Stuba* – *(Closed Tuesday)* Menu €34/62 – Carte €26/64

◆ This 1796 mill on the banks of the Ill is home to an elegant dining room, serving regional dishes and grilled meats in season. The winstub-style Stuba displays old machinery; regional cuisine and tartes flambées. Peaceful and practical rooms.

in Moernach 5 km West by D 473 – pop. 536 – alt. 470 m – ✉ 68480

Aux Deux Clefs with rm

– ✆ 03 89 40 80 56 – auxdeuxclefs@wanadoo.fr – Fax 03 89 08 10 47

– Closed 20 July-5 August, autumn half-term holidays and February holidays

7 rm – €36 €47, ☕ €7,50 – ½ P €55 – **Rest** – *(closed Wednesday dinner and Thursday)* Menu €21/46 – Carte €31/55

◆ Pretty half-timbered house typical of the Sundgau. An opulent dining room with paintings; traditional cuisine. Welcoming rooms with parquet floors in a neighbouring annexe.

in Lutter 8 km Southeast by D 23 – pop. 297 – alt. 428 m – ✉ 68480

L'Auberge Paysanne with rm

1 r. de Wolschwiller – ✆ 03 89 40 71 67 – aubergepaysanne2@wanadoo.fr

– Fax 03 89 07 33 38 – Closed 30 June-14 July, 3 weeks in January, Tuesday lunch and Monday

7 rm – €39 €50, ☕ €8 – ½ P €49 – **Rest** – Menu €11,50 (weekday lunch), €23/40 – Carte €23/49

◆ Family run establishment near the Swiss border. Among the several dining rooms, the winstub has the most charm. Regional and Mediterranean cuisine. Modern bedrooms.

Hostellerie Paysanne

8 r. de Wolschwiller – ✆ 03 89 40 71 67 – aubergepaysanne2@wanadoo.fr

– Fax 03 89 07 33 38

9 rm – €48 €62/70, ☕ €8 – ½ P €55/59

◆ This Alsatian farm dating from 1618 was dismantled and rebuilt in this village. Rooms with period furniture. A warm welcome at the Auberge Paysanne.

LA FERRIÈRE-AUX-ÉTANGS – 61 Orne – 310 F3 – see Flers

FERRIÈRES-EN-GÂTINAIS – 45 Loiret – 318 N3 – pop. 3 049 – alt. 96 m –

✉ 45210 Burgundy-Jura 12 **D2**

Paris 99 – Auxerre 81 – Fontainebleau 40 – Montargis 12 – Nemours 26 – Orléans 86

Office de tourisme, place des Églises ✆ 02 38 96 58 86, Fax 02 38 96 60 39

Transept crossing★ of St-Pierre and St-Paul church.

L'Abbaye

– ✆ 02 38 96 53 12 – info@hotel-abbaye.fr – Fax 02 38 96 57 63

30 rm – €63/89 €63/89, ☕ €8,50 – ½ P €58 – **Rest** – Menu (€14), €23/55

◆ The name refers to the former abbey of St Peter and St Paul around which the village was built. Choose one of the new, spacious, well-equipped rooms. Large restaurant serving traditional cuisine; terrace popular in summer.

FERRIÈRES-LES-VERRERIES – 34 Hérault – 339 H5 – pop. 38 – alt. 320 m –

✉ 34190 23 **C2**

Paris 747 – Montpellier 41 – Alès 47 – Florac 86 – Millau 102

La Cour-Mas de Baumes with rm

4 km east on the D 107[E4] – ✆ 04 66 80 88 80

– info@oustaldebaumes.com – Fax 04 66 80 88 82

– Closed Tuesday and Wednesday 1st November-15 March, Sunday dinner, Monday and hotel closed weekdays off season

6 rm – €58/80 €70/98, ☕ €9 – ½ P €70/84 – **Rest** – Menu (€25), €38/65 – Carte €48/59

◆ Ex-smallholding and glass works isolated in the middle of the countryside where you can enjoy original food in an elegant setting combining old and new. Pretty, contemporary rooms.

FERTE-BEAUHARNAIS – 41 Loir-et-Cher – 318 I6 – pop. 510 – alt. 101 m – ✉ 41210 Châteaux of the Loire 12 C2

▶ Paris 183 – Orléans 45 – Blois 46 – Vierzon 56 – Fleury-les-Aubrais 63

Château de la Ferté Beauharnais without rest

172 r. du Prince-Eugène – ☎ 02 54 83 72 18 – Fax 02 54 83 72 18

3 rm – †€ 135/145 ††€ 135/145

♦ This château was once the home of the Beauharnais family, notably Josephine, first wife of Napoleon. Stylish rooms with parquet floors, decorative mouldings and fireplace.

LA FERTÉ-BERNARD – 72 Sarthe – 310 M5 – pop. 9 239 – alt. 90 m – ✉ 72400 Châteaux of the Loire 35 D1

▶ Paris 164 – Alençon 56 – Chartres 79 – Châteaudun 65 – Le Mans 54

Office de tourisme, 15, place de la Lice ☎ 02 43 71 21 21, Fax 02 43 93 25 85

du Perche Souancé-au-Perche La Vallée des Aulnes, Northeast: 21 km by D 923 and D137, ☎ 02 37 29 17 33.

N.-D.-des Marais church ★★.

XXX **La Perdrix** with rm — rest, VISA

2 r. de Paris – ☎ 02 43 93 00 44 – restaurantlaperdrix@hotmail.com – Fax 02 43 93 74 95 – Closed February, Monday evening and Tuesday

7 rm – †€ 47 ††€ 54/59, ☕ € 7 – **Rest** – Menu € 18 (weekdays)/38 – Carte € 39/45

♦ An imposing building bordering the main road. Two dining rooms redecorated in bourgeois style with mouldings throughout, and blue and white decor in one room and red and beige in the other.

XX **Le Dauphin** — VISA

3 r. d'Huisne , (pedestrian access) – ☎ 02 43 93 00 39 – Fax 02 43 71 26 65 – Closed 20-26 April, 10-23 August, Sunday dinner and Monday

Rest – Menu € 17 (weekdays)/41 – Carte € 40/55

♦ This building in the old town dates from the 16C. With a beautiful period fireplace and terrace overlooking the pedestrian street.

LA FERTÉ-HAUTERIVE – 03 Allier – 326 H5 – see Varennes-sur-Allier

LA FERTÉ-IMBAULT – 41 Loir-et-Cher – 318 I7 – pop. 1 035 – alt. 99 m – ✉ 41300

▶ Paris 191 – Bourges 66 – Orléans 68 – Romorantin-Lanthenay 19 – Vierzon 23 12 C2

Syndicat d'initiative, 31, route Nationale ☎ 02 54 96 34 83, Fax 02 54 96 34 83

Auberge À la Tête de Lard — rest, rm, VISA AE

13 pl. des Tilleuls – ☎ 02 54 96 22 32 – Fax 02 54 96 06 22 – Closed 12-25 September, 20 January-13 February, Sunday dinner, Tuesday lunch and Monday

11 rm – †€ 50 ††€ 76, ☕ € 8 – ½ P € 59 – **Rest** – Menu (€ 19), € 26 (weekdays), € 44/51 – Carte € 32/70

♦ Modern, tasteful rooms in this pleasant little Sologne inn, a former post house. Wide choice of leisure activities: rambling and mountain biking. Rustic dining room in a pretty countrified spirit. Regional cuisine and game in season.

LA FERTÉ-MACÉ – 61 Orne – 310 G3 – pop. 6 679 – alt. 250 m – ✉ 61600 Normandy 32 B3

▶ Paris 227 – Alençon 46 – Argentan 33 – Domfront 23 – Falaise 41 – Flers 26

Syndicat d'initiative, 11, rue de la Victoire ☎ 02 33 37 10 97, Fax 02 33 37 10 97

Plan on following page

Auberge d'Andaines — VISA AE

rte Bagnoles-de-l'Orne, via ③: 2 km – ☎ 02 33 37 20 28 – resa@aubergeandaines.com – Fax 02 33 37 25 05 – Closed 20 January-10 February and Friday from 15 October to 1st April

15 rm – †€ 40/70 ††€ 40/70, ☕ € 9,50 – ½ P € 45/55 – **Rest** – Menu € 16/40

♦ Family guesthouse on the edge of the Andaines Forest. Simple, well-kept rooms; choose those facing the garden. A delightful, welcoming restaurant in a slightly retro style. Traditional cuisine.

LA FERTÉ-MACÉ

Armand-Macé (R.) . . . . B 2
Barre (R. de la) . . . . B 4
Chauvière (R.) . . . . B 7
Clouet (R. du) . . . . A 8
De-Contades (Bd Gérard) . . . . A 10
Fossés Nicole (R. des) . . . . B 12
Hautvie (R. d') . . . . B
Leclerc (Pl. du Gén.) . . . . B 15
Le-Meunier-de-la-Raillère (Av.) . . . . B 13
République (Pl. de la) . . . . . . B 16
Teinture (R. de la) . . . . B 18
Val Vert (R. du) . . . . A 19
4-Roues (R. des) . . . . B 21

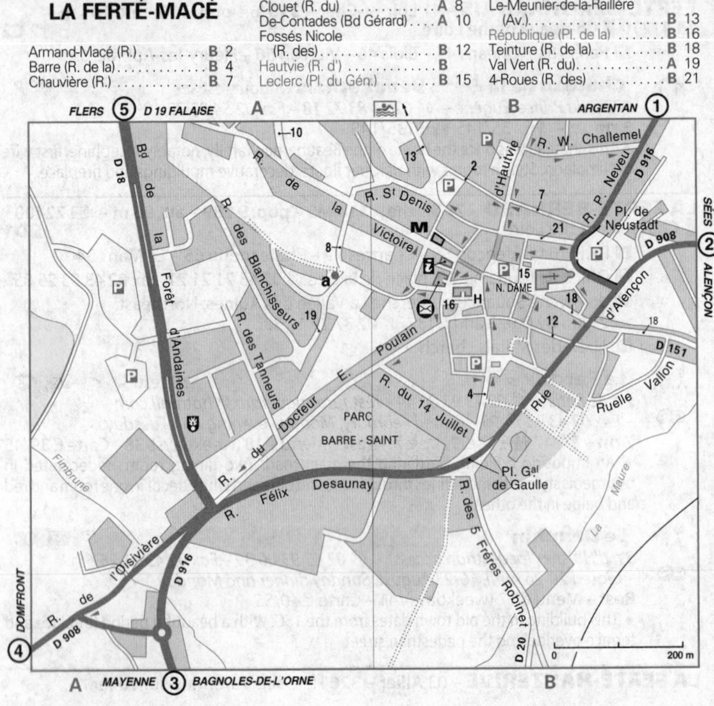

Auberge de Clouet with rm rm, VISA

Le Clouet – ✆ 02 33 37 18 22 – Fax 02 33 38 28 52 – Closed 1st-17 November, Sunday dinner and Monday October-Easter A **a**

6 rm – †€ 46 ††€ 67, ☕ € 8,50 – ½ P € 72

Rest – *(closed Monday October-Easter and Sunday dinner)* Menu (€ 17), € 22/75 – Carte € 28/68

◆ Local fare served in the rustic interior of this old farmhouse in the Normandy woodland or on the flower-decked terrace. A few modest rooms.

LA FERTÉ-ST-AUBIN – 45 Loiret – 318 I5 – pop. 6 783 – alt. 114 m – ✉ 45240

Châteaux of the Loire 12 **C2**

Paris 153 – Blois 62 – Orléans 23 – Romorantin-Lanthenay 45 – Salbris 34

Office de tourisme, rue des Jardins ✆ 02 38 64 67 93, Fax 02 38 64 61 39

des Aisses Domaine des Aisses, Southeast: 3 km by N 20, ✆ 02 38 64 80 87 ;

de Sologne Route de Jouy-le-Potier, Northwest: 5 km, ✆ 02 38 76 57 33.

Château★.

L'Orée des Chênes VISA AE

north-east: 3.5 km via rte Marcilly – ✆ 02 38 64 84 00 – info@loreedeschenes.com – Fax 02 38 64 84 20

26 rm – †€ 100/130 ††€ 110/150, ☕ € 15 – ½ P € 110/140

Rest – Menu € 30 (weekdays)/50 – Carte € 55/86

◆ The silhouette of this recent hotel complex is in keeping with Sologne architecture. Quiet rooms. Large park with a lake offering fishing and hunting. Rustic dining room (exposed beams and terracotta tiles) offering well-prepared and presented food.

La Ferme de la Lande

Northeast : 3 km via rte Marcilly – ✆ 02 38 76 64 37 – solognote@fermedelalande.com – Fax 02 38 64 68 87 – Closed 24 September-6 October, 14 January-3 February, Sunday dinner and Monday

Rest – Menu € 37/59 – Carte € 61/74

♦ A restaurant in a converted farmhouse whose authenticity has been skilfully preserved (brick and timber-frame walls). Cooking suited to current tastes. A park for a walk before dinner.

Auberge de l'Écu de France

6 r. Gén.-Leclerc, (N 20) – ✆ 02 38 64 69 22 – Fax 02 38 64 09 54 – Closed Monday dinner, Sunday dinner and Friday

Rest – Menu (€ 12), € 16 (weekday lunch), € 23/42 – Carte € 35/51

♦ Small, 17C regional-style house, a stone's throw from the majestic château. Charming country-style interior with half-timbering. Traditional cuisine.

in Menestreau en Villette 7 km East by D 17 – pop. 1 384 – alt. 122 m – ✉ 45240

Le Relais de Sologne

63 pl. 8 Mai 1945 – ✆ 02 38 76 97 40 – lerelaisdesologne@wanadoo.fr – Fax 02 38 49 60 43 – Closed 1st-10 March, 21 July-6 August, 22-28 December, Tuesday dinner, Sunday dinner and Wednesday

Rest – Menu € 17 (weekday lunch), € 27/55

♦ Appealing rustic dining room in the heart of the village. Traditional dishes. Don't miss visiting the Ciran estate (Sologne animal reserve), only 2km away.

LA FERTÉ-ST-CYR – 41 Loir-et-Cher – 318 H6 – pop. 894 – alt. 82 m – ✉ 41220

Paris 170 – Orléans 37 – Blois 32 – Romorantin-Lanthenay 35 12 **C2**

Saint-Cyr without rest

15 r. de Bretagne – ✆ 02 54 87 90 51 – hotel-st-cyr@tiscali.fr – Fax 02 54 87 94 64

20 rm – †€ 45/60 ††€ 48/65, ☕ € 8

♦ Small, colourful rooms decorated with wrought iron furniture and woven banana leaves. Guesthouse atmosphere, shop selling regional produce, cycle hire.

LA FERTÉ-SOUS-JOUARRE – 77 Seine-et-Marne – 312 H2 – pop. 8 584 – alt. 58 m – ✉ 77260

19 **D1**

Paris 67 – Melun 70 – Reims 83 – Troyes 116

Office de tourisme, 34, rue des Pelletiers ✆ 01 60 01 87 99, Fax 01 60 22 99 82

Château des Bondons

2 km east on D 70, Montménard road – ✆ 01 60 22 00 98 – castel@chateaudesbondons.com – Fax 01 60 22 97 01

11 rm – †€ 100/120 ††€ 100/160, ☕ € 20 – 3 suites

Rest – *(closed 2-30 January, Monday and Tuesday)* Menu € 20 (weekdays)/49 – Carte € 53/117

♦ This 18th century residence was once owned by the novelist G. Ohnet and used as headquarters by the French army during the phoney war; rooms are personalised and vary in size. Woodwork, a fresco of Marseille and a fireplace with ceramic decor adorn the restaurant.

in Jouarre 3 km South by D 402 – pop. 3 415 – alt. 141 m – ✉ 77640

Office de tourisme, rue de la Tour ✆ 01 60 22 64 54, Fax 01 60 22 65 15

Crypt★ of the abbey, **Northern France and the Paris Region**

Le Plat d'Étain

6 pl. A. Tinchant – ✆ 01 60 22 06 07 – infos@le-plat-d-etain.com – Fax 01 60 22 35 63

18 rm – †€ 55/62 ††€ 62, ☕ € 7 – ½ P € 44/54 – **Rest** – *(closed Friday dinner, Sunday dinner and Bank Holiday dinner)* Menu € 18 (weekdays)/46 – Carte € 39/71

♦ Guesthouse built in 1840 just by the abbey and its Carolingian crypts. The rooms are modern. A pewter plate, evoking the name of the place, decorates a wall of the recently refurbished neo-rustic dining room.

FEURS – 42 Loire – 327 E5 – pop. 7 669 – alt. 343 m – ✉ 42110

Lyon - Rhone Valley 44 **A2**

Paris 433 – Lyon 69 – Montbrison 24 – Roanne 38 – St-Étienne 47 – Thiers 68 – Vienne 93

Office de tourisme, place du Forum ✆ 04 77 26 05 27, Fax 04 77 26 00 55

Etésia without rest

rte de Roanne – ✆ 04 77 27 07 77 – contact@hotel-etesia.fr – Fax 04 77 27 03 33 – Closed 25 December-1st January

15 rm – €50/56 €50/56, €7

◆ This completely renovated hotel offers attractively furnished garden-floor rooms enlivened by bright colours. There is a pleasant wooded garden; buffet-style breakfasting is an original feature.

La Boule d'Or

42 r. R. Cassin, (Lyon road) – ✆ 04 77 26 20 68 – labouledorfeurs@wanadoo.fr – Fax 04 77 26 56 84 – Closed 27 July-17 August, 18 January-3 February, Sunday dinner, Wednesday dinner and Monday

Rest – Menu € 20 (weekdays)/58 – Carte € 34/62

◆ In summertime meals are served beneath a chestnut tree over fifty years old. Inside, the huge rustic dining room is made up of three areas. Traditional, well-prepared cuisine.

in Salt-en-Donzy 5 km Lyon road – pop. 393 – alt. 337 m – ✉ 42110

L'Assiette Saltoise

au bourg – ✆ 04 77 26 04 29 – info-et-reservation@assiette-saltoise.com – Fax 04 77 28 52 58 – Closed 1st-7 January, Tuesday and Wednesday

Rest – Menu € 11,50 (weekday lunch), € 16/31

◆ Wholesome traditional fare such as saucisson lyonnais and bavette d'aloyau set the scene for this friendly unpretentious inn. Terrace shaded by lime trees is for the summer.

in Naconne 3 km Northwest by N 89 and D 112 – ✉ 42110

Brin de Laurier with rm

– ✆ 04 77 26 07 50 – info@brindelaurier.com – Fax 04 77 26 07 50 – Closed 1st-8 May, 1st-17 September, 22 December -5 January, Saturday lunch, Sunday dinner and Monday

3 rm – €68 €68 – **Rest** – Menu € 15 bi, € 28/45

◆ A pleasant, non-smoking restaurant situated in the hamlet. The chef takes inspiration from his many travels to create a fusion-style cuisine using regional produce. Attractive summer terrace.

FEYTIAT – 87 Haute-Vienne – 325 E6 – pop. 5 634 – alt. 365 m – ✉ 87220

Paris 398 – Limoges 9 – Saint-Junien 41 – Panazol 5 – Isle 13 24 **B2**

Prieuré du Puy Marot

allée du Puy-Marot, 2 km north-east on St-Just-le-Martel road (D 98) – ✆ 05 55 48 33 97 – gerardchatagner@wanadoo.fr – Fax 05 55 30 31 86

3 rm – €58 €68 – **Table d'hôte** – Menu € 28 bi

◆ Guaranteed calm in this 16-17C priory, surrounded by a walled garden overlooking the Valoisse valley. Comfortable rooms furnished with antiques and traditional dishes prepared by the *patronne*.

FIGEAC – 46 Lot – 337 I4 – pop. 9 606 – alt. 214 m – ✉ 46100

Dordogne-Berry-Limousin 29 **C1**

Paris 578 – Aurillac 64 – Rodez 66 – Villefranche-de-Rouergue 36

Office de tourisme, place Vival ✆ 05 65 34 06 25, Fax 05 65 50 04 58

Old Figeac★★: hôtel de la Monnaie★ M¹, musée Champollion★ M² near place aux Ecritures★ - N.D.-de-Pitié chapel ★ in St-Sauveur church.

Plan on next page

Le Pont d'Or without rest

2 av. J. Jaurès – ✆ 05 65 50 95 00 – contact@hotelpontdor.com – Fax 05 65 50 95 39

35 rm – €55/102 €55/102, €12 x

◆ A functional hotel on the banks of the Célé, opposite the old town. Elegant, well-equipped bedrooms – ask for one facing the river. Small brasserie.

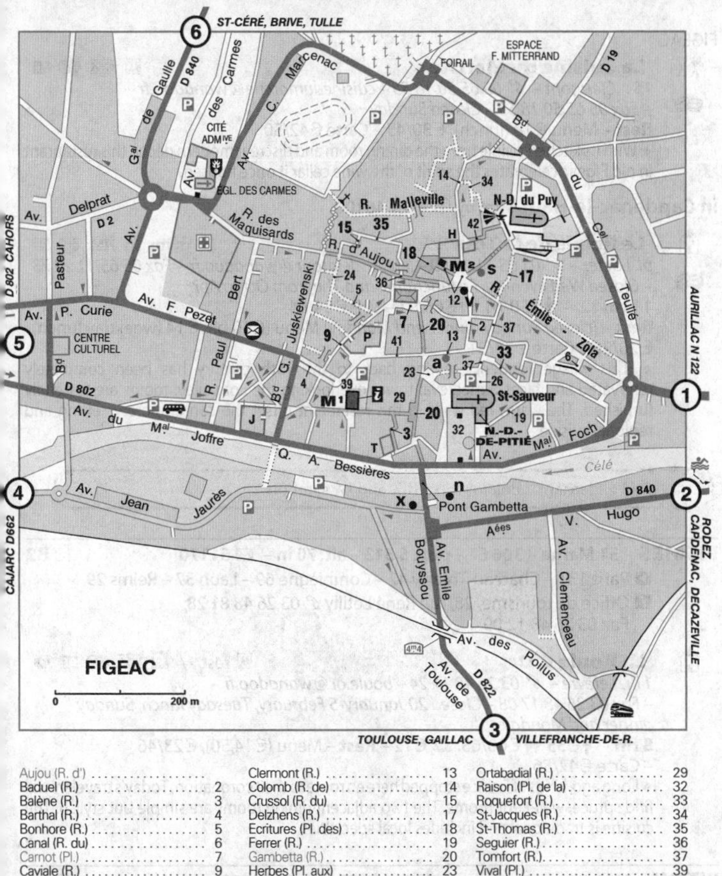

Aujou (R. d')		Clermont (R.)	13	Ortabadial (R.)	29
Baduel (R.)	2	Colomb (R. de)	14	Raison (Pl. de la)	32
Balène (R.)	3	Crussol (R. du)	15	Roquefort (R.)	33
Barthal (R.)	4	Delzhens (R.)	17	St-Jacques (R.)	34
Bonhore (R.)	5	Ecritures (Pl. des)	18	St-Thomas (R.)	35
Canal (R. du)	6	Ferrer (R.)	19	Seguier (R.)	36
Carnot (Pl.)	7	Gambetta (R.)	20	Tomfort (R.)	37
Caviale (R.)	9	Herbes (Pl. aux)	23	Vival (Pl.)	39
Champollion (Pl. et R. des Frères)	12	Laurière (R.)	24	11-Novembre (R. du)	41
		Michelet (Pl. E.)	26	16-Mai (R. du)	42

Le Champollion without rest
3 pl. Champollion – ✆ 05 65 34 04 37 – Fax 05 65 34 61 69 **v**
10 rm – €44 €50, €6,50
◆ Medieval house in the heart of the old quarter, opposite the Musée Champollion. Homely atmosphere and functional guestrooms with a modern black and white decor.

Des Bains without rest
1 r. Griffoul – ✆ 05 65 34 10 89 – figeac@hoteldesbains.fr – Fax 05 65 14 00 45 – Closed 19 December-5 January and week-end 2 November-27 February
19 rm – €45/55 €45/70, €7,50 **n**
◆ These former public baths on the left bank of the Célé were turned into a hotel in the 1970s. Well-kept rooms and bar with terrace on the water's edge.

La Dînée du Viguier
r. Boutaric – ✆ 05 65 50 08 08 – Fax 05 65 50 09 09 – Closed 24-30 November, 26 January-8 February, Sunday dinner off season, Monday except dinner from May to September and Saturday lunch **s**
Rest – Menu (€ 20), € 29/75 – Carte € 55/69
◆ A few medieval features give the dining room character: a majestic fireplace with a sculpted mantelpiece, painted beams, etc... All that's missing is the old magistrate (viguier)!

La Cuisine du Marché AC VISA MC AE

15 r. Clermont – ✆ 05 65 50 18 55 – cuisinedumarche@wanadoo.fr – Fax 05 65 50 18 55 – Closed Sunday a

Rest – Menu € 18 (lunch), € 30/45 – Carte € 42/50

◆ With its kitchen visible from the dining room and discreet modern décor, this restaurant in old Figeac celebrates the spirit of the wine cellar it once housed.

in Capdenac-le-Haut **5 km by** ② – ✉ **46100**

Le Relais de la Tour & rm, VISA MC AE

pl. Lucter – ✆ 05 65 11 06 99 – lerelaisdelatour@wanadoo.fr – Fax 05 65 11 20 73 – Closed Wed evening, Fri lunchtime and Thu from Oct to Apr

11 rm – €50/61 €65/91 – ½ P €54/64

Rest – *(closed Sunday dinner and Monday)* Menu (€ 10 bi), € 14 (weekday lunch), € 20/26 – Carte € 23/31

◆ This village residence dating back to the 15th century has been completely renovated and faces a medieval tower overlooking the Lot valley; rooms are tastefully furnished. The warm red walls in this restaurant offset the contemporary setting and regional cuisine.

Red = Pleasant. Look for the red and symbols.

FISMES – **51 Marne** – **306** E7 – **pop. 5 313** – **alt. 70 m** – ✉ **51170** 13 **B2**

Paris 131 – Château-Thierry 42 – Compiègne 69 – Laon 37 – Reims 29

Office de tourisme, 28, rue René Letilly ✆ 03 26 48 81 28, Fax 03 26 48 12 09

La Boule d'Or AC rest, P VISA MC AE

11 r. Lefèvre – ✆ 03 26 48 11 24 – boule.or@wanadoo.fr – Fax 03 26 48 17 08 – Closed 20 January-5 February, Tuesday lunch, Sunday dinner and Monday

8 rm – €55 €60/65, € 12 – **Rest** – Menu (€ 14,50), € 23/46 – Carte € 42/56

◆ Long ago, kings of France stopped here en route to their coronation. Today's travelers will find spruce, well-kept rooms. The two adjacent dining rooms are simple but stylish. The cuisine is traditional and includes local specialties.

FITOU – **11 Aude** – **344** I5 – **pop. 676** – **alt. 38 m** – ✉ **11510** 22 **B3**

Paris 823 – Carcassonne 90 – Narbonne 40 – Perpignan 29

Fort de Salses★★ Southwest: 11 km, Languedoc-Roussillon-Tarn Gorges

La Cave d'Agnès P VISA MC

29 r. Gilbert-Salamo – ✆ 04 68 45 75 91 – restocavedagnes@orange.fr – Fax 04 68 45 75 91 – Open 1st April-12 November and closed Wednesday

Rest – *(number of covers limited, pre-book)* Menu € 16 (weekday lunch), € 23/38 – Carte € 26/51

◆ This former barn in the upper part of the village has lost none of its rustic character: fireplace, beams, stonework, bare wood and exhibition s of work by local artists. Tasty regional cuisine.

FLACEY – **28 Eure-et-Loir** – **311** E7 – **see Châteaudun**

FLAGEY-ÉCHEZEAUX – **21 Côte-d'Or** – **320** J7 – **see Vougeot**

FLAMANVILLE – **50 Manche** – **303** A2 – **pop. 1 683** – **alt. 74 m** – ✉ **50340** 32 **A1**

Paris 371 – Barneville-Carteret 23 – Cherbourg 27 – Valognes 36

Syndicat d'initiative, ✆ 02 33 52 61 23

Bel Air without rest

2 r. du Château – ✆ 02 33 04 48 00 – hotelbelair@aol.com – Fax 02 33 04 49 56 – Closed December-January

11 rm – €59/68 €65/99, €10,50

◆ Once the house occupied by the château's farm manager, this establishment has a peaceful atmosphere. Predominantly rustic-style rooms, each with a different decor.

Le Sémaphore sea, Channel Islands, VISA

Chasse de la Houe – ✆ 02 33 52 18 98 – lesemaphore2@wanadoo.fr – Fax 02 33 52 36 39 – Closed 7 December-7 February, Sunday dinner, Tuesday except July-August and Monday

Rest – Menu €20/37 – Carte €28/46

◆ Old clifftop signal station commanding a panoramic view of the Channel and the Channel Islands. Traditional cuisine and dishes with a southwest flavour.

FLAVIGNY-SUR-MOSELLE – 54 Meurthe-et-Moselle – 307 I7 – see Nancy

FLAYOSC – 83 Var – 340 N4 – see Draguignan

LA FLÈCHE – 72 Sarthe – 310 I8 – pop. 15 241 – alt. 33 m – ✉ 72200

Châteaux of the Loire 35 **C2**

- Paris 244 – Angers 52 – Laval 70 – Le Mans 44 – Tours 71
- Office de tourisme, boulevard de Montréal ✆ 02 43 94 02 53, Fax 02 43 94 43 15
- Military academy★ - Panelling★ of N.-D.-des-Vertus chapel - Parc zoologique du Tertre Rouge (zoo)★ 5 km by ② then D 104.
- Bazouges-sur-le-Loir: bridge ≤★, 7 km by ④.

Plan on next page

Le Relais Cicero without rest

18 bd Alger – ✆ 02 43 94 14 14 – hotel.cicero@wanadoo.fr – Fax 02 43 45 98 96 – Closed 1st-15 August and 23 December-6 January Y **a**

21 rm – €75 €115, €11

◆ A 17C convent with an attractive interior decor and period furniture; well-preserved authenticity in this haven of peace with a garden separating it from the rest of the world.

Le Vert Galant without rest

70 Grande Rue – ✆ 02 43 94 00 51 – contact@vghotel.com – Fax 02 43 45 11 24 Y **r**

21 rm – €59/77 €84/88, €10,50

◆ Not far from the Prytanée in the town centre, this former, 18th century post house has been completely renovated; furnishings and fittings are modern and state of the art (Internet, wi-fi); breakfast can be served on the veranda.

Le Moulin des Quatre Saisons

r. Gallieni – ✆ 02 43 45 12 12 – contacts@moulindesquatresaisons.com – Fax 02 43 45 10 31 – Closed autumn half-term holidays, February holidays, Sunday dinner, Wednesday dinner and Monday except July-August Z **e**

Rest – Menu €25 (weekdays)/37 – Carte €41/70

◆ A 17C mill on the banks of the Loire with traditional Mediterranean-inspired dishes, wines from all over the world and an Austrian decor: a decidedly eclectic establishment!

La Fesse d'Ange

pl. 8 Mai 1945 – ✆ 02 43 94 73 60 – fdange@tele2.fr – Fax 02 43 45 97 33 – Closed Sunday dinner, Tuesday lunch and Monday Y **b**

Rest – Menu €17 (weekdays)/40 – Carte €40/57

◆ Let there be no equivocation! In plain language the cuisine here is traditional and served in generous portions; the restaurant's décor is stylish and enhanced by paintings that are the work of the owner himself.

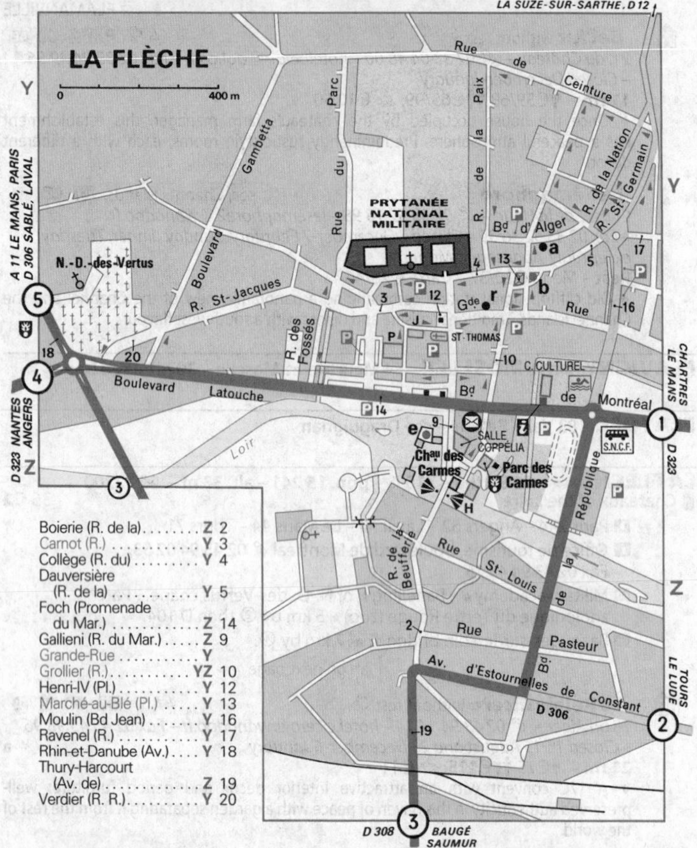

FLÉCHIN – 62 Pas-de-Calais – 301 G4 – pop. 512 – alt. 96 m – ✉ 62960 30 B2

▶ Paris 246 – Lille 72 – Arras 63 – Lens 55 – Liévin 50

La Maison VISA

20 r. Haute – ✆ 03 21 12 69 33 – berthelemy.laurent@wanadoo.fr – Fax 03 21 12 69 33 – Closed 4-14 August, 16-20 February, Saturday lunch, Wednesday and Monday

Rest – *(number of covers limited, pre-book)* Menu € 16 (weekday lunch)/46 – Carte € 37/58

◆ 1900s building with an attractive dining room (original parquet flooring, antiques). The cuisine here is regional with an emphasis on organic ingredients and heirloom vegetable varieties.

FLÉRÉ-LA-RIVIÈRE – 36 Indre – 323 C4 – pop. 594 – alt. 95 m – ✉ 36700

▶ Paris 277 – Le Blanc 50 – Châtellerault 60 – Châtillon-sur-Indre 7 – Loches 17 – Tours 61 11 B3

Le Relais du Berry VISA MC

2 rte de Tours – ✆ 02 54 39 32 57 – Closed January, Sunday dinner, Monday and Tuesday

Rest – *(number of covers limited, pre-book)* Menu € 14 (weekdays)/38 – Carte € 36/46

◆ Former post house with its flowering garden and rustic setting at the entrance to the village. Authentically traditional menus enriched according to season with home-grown vegetables and fruits.

FLERS – 61 Orne – 310 F2 – pop. 16 947 – alt. 270 m – ✉ 61100

Normandy 32 **B2**

Paris 234 – Alençon 73 – Argentan 42 – Caen 60 – Laval 86 – Vire 31

Office de tourisme, place du Docteur Vayssières ✆ 02 33 65 06 75, Fax 02 33 65 09 84

du Houlme La Selle-la-Forge Le Bourg, by Bagnoles-de-l'Orne road: 4 km, ✆ 02 33 64 42 83.

FLERS

Boule (R. de la) . . . . **AY**
Charleston (Pl.) . . . . **AYZ** 3
Delaunay (R.) . . . . **AY** 4
Dr-Vayssières (Pl. du) . . . . . . **AY** 6
Domfront (R. de) . . . . **AZ**
Duhalde (Pl. P.) . . . . **AZ**
Gaulle (Pl. Ch.-de) . . . . **AY** 9
Géroudière (R. de la) . . . . **BZ** 10
Gévelot (R. J.) . . . . **AY** 12
Messei (R. de) . . . . **AZ**
Moulin (R. du) . . . . **ABY** 14
Paris (R. de) . . . . **BY**
Pont Feron (R. du) . . . . **BZ** 15
République (R. de la) . . . . . **AYZ** 16
St-Gilles (R.) . . . . **BYZ** 18
Salles (R. J.) . . . . **AY** 19
Schnetz (R.) . . . . **AYZ**
6-Juin (R. du) . . . . **AY**

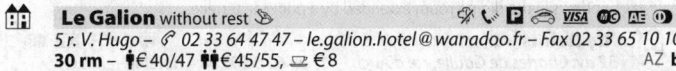

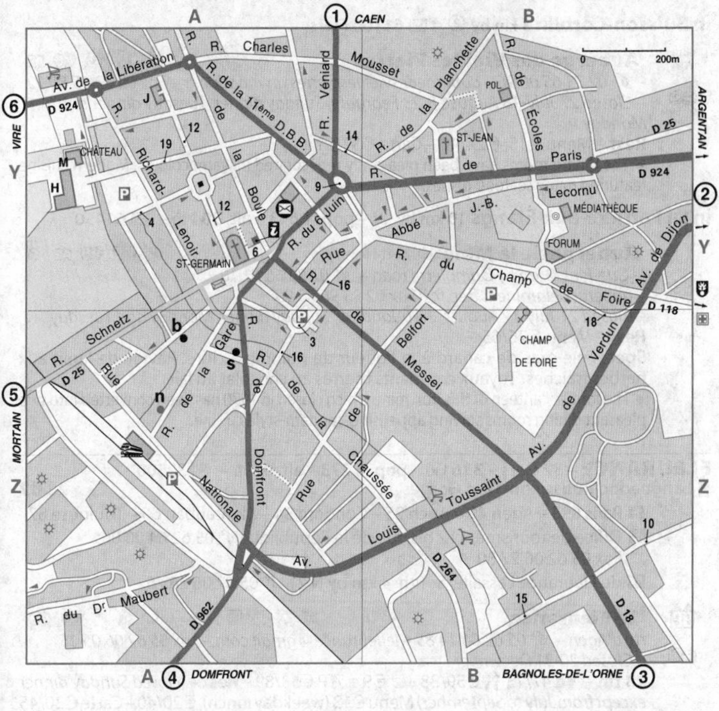

Le Galion without rest

5 r. V. Hugo – ✆ 02 33 64 47 47 – le.galion.hotel@wanadoo.fr – Fax 02 33 65 10 10

30 rm – †€ 40/47 ††€ 45/55, ☕ € 8 AZ **b**

◆ A quiet hotel in the town centre with good soundproofing. A programme of refurbishment is underway in the spacious guestrooms.

Beverl'inn rm,

9 r. Chaussée – ✆ 02 33 96 79 79 – beverlinn@beverlinn.com – Fax 02 33 65 94 89 – Closed 22 December-5 January AZ **s**

16 rm – †€ 38/41 ††€ 44/47, ☕ € 5 – ½ P € 37 – **Rest** – grill *(closed Saturday lunch and Sunday)* Menu (€ 9 bi), € 13/27 – Carte € 18/34

◆ This hotel is located close to the château museum. Rooms with pine furniture that are gradually being redecorated in a somewhat sober style. A cosy restaurant decorated in tones of red and yellow serving traditional recipes and dishes grilled on a wood fire.

Au Bout de la Rue

60 r. de la Gare – ✆ 02 33 65 31 53 – yoann.lelaizant@orange.fr – Fax 02 33 65 46 81 – Closed 4-11 May, 3-24 August, 1st-11 January, Wednesday dinner, Saturday lunch, Sunday and holidays AZ **n**

Rest – Menu (€ 17), € 22/29 – Carte € 32/41

◆ Old posters and photographs line the walls of this (non-smoking) 1940s-style bistro where you can see all the activity in the kitchens. Sitting room for smokers.

Auberge du Relais Fleuri

115 r. Schnetz – ✆ 02 33 65 23 89 – aubergedurelaisfleuri@orange.fr – Closed Sunday dinner and Monday

Rest – Menu (€ 15), € 24/37 – Carte € 30/46

◆ The façade is a little sad but the interior, with its bare stone walls and exposed beams, is quite smart. Regional cuisine and fine wine list.

in Buisson-Corblin 3 km by ② – ✉ 61100 Flers

Auberge des Vieilles Pierres

– ✆ 02 33 65 06 96 – aubergedesvieillespierres@wanadoo.fr – Fax 02 33 65 80 72 – Closed 27 July-18 August, 8-23 February, Sunday dinner, Tuesday dinner and Monday

Rest – Menu € 15, € 24/40 – Carte € 37/51

◆ The dining rooms have been pleasantly redecorated in warm colours. Modern cuisine featuring many seafood dishes.

in La Ferrière-aux-Étangs 10 km by ③ – pop. 1 643 – alt. 304 m – ✉ 61450

Auberge de la Mine (Hubert Nobis)

le Gué-Plat, 2 km by Dompierre road – ✆ 02 33 66 91 10 – aubergedelamine@free.fr – Fax 02 33 96 73 90 – Closed 21 July-12 August, 2-20 January, Sunday dinner, Monday and Tuesday

Rest – Menu € 26/65

Spec. Foie gras de canard à la liqueur de pomme à cidre. Ravioli de lapin aux herbes fraîches. Tuyaux croquants fourrés au chocolat au lait.

◆ The former canteen of this iron mine which closed in 1970 has been converted into two pleasant dining rooms serving appetising, modern-style cuisine.

FLEURANCE – 32 Gers – 336 G6 – pop. 6 273 – alt. 97 m – ✉ 32500

Languedoc-Roussillon-Tarn Gorges 28 **B2**

Paris 693 – Agen 49 – Auch 25 – Condom 34 – Montauban 66 – Toulouse 87

Office de tourisme, 112 bis, rue de la République ✆ 05 62 64 00 00, Fax 05 62 06 27 80

de Fleurance Lassalle, South: 4 km by N 21, ✆ 05 62 06 26 26.

Le Fleurance rest,

rte d'Agen – ✆ 05 62 06 14 85 – lefleurance@gmail.com – Fax 05 62 06 05 15 – Closed 20-31 December

23 rm – †€ 47/73 ††€ 59/88, ☕ € 9 – ½ P € 53/89 – **Rest** – *(closed Sunday dinner except from July to September)* Menu € 13 (weekday lunch), € 20/40 – Carte € 30/45

◆ Convenient base in the heart of the Lomagne area. Practical rooms, some opening onto the garden or with balcony. Shades of yellow and orange, rattan furniture, and huge bay windows in the dining room extended by a poolside terrace.

Le Relais without rest

32 av. Charles de Gaulle, rte d'Auch – ✆ 05 62 06 05 08 – hotel-le-relais@wanadoo.fr – Fax 05 62 06 03 84

20 rm – †€ 43/55 ††€ 50/62, ☕ € 8

◆ Small hotel at the gates of the 13th century walled town with its geometrical map and covered market. Offers well soundproofed rooms, gradually being refurbished. Pleasant service.

FLEURIE – 69 Rhône – 327 H2 – pop. 1 190 – alt. 320 m – ✉ 69820

Lyon - Rhone Valley 43 **E1**

Paris 410 – Bourg-en-Bresse 46 – Lyon 58 – Mâcon 22 – Villefranche-sur-Saône 27

Des Grands Vins without rest

1 km south on the D 119ᴱ – 04 74 69 81 43 – despres@hoteldesgrandsvins.com – Fax 04 74 69 86 10 – Closed 30 November-8 February

20 rm – €70/79 €70/84, €10

◆ A family establishment with a garden on the edge of a vineyard. Simple, well-kept rooms; a vast dining room. Wines produced in the village are on display and can be purchased.

Domaine du Clos des Garands without rest — Fleurie and vineyard,

1 km east on the D 32 – 04 74 69 80 01 – contact@closdesgarands.fr – Fax 04 74 69 82 05 – Closed January

4 rm – €86/106 €86/106

◆ This wine-producing estate proposes rooms all opening onto Fleurie and the hills of the Beaujolais. Elegant decor. Tastings of the estate wines.

Le Cep (Chantal Chagny)

pl. de l'Église – 04 74 04 10 77 – Fax 04 74 04 10 28 – Closed 29 June-7 July, December, January, Sunday and Monday

Rest – *(pre-book)* Menu €45/95 – Carte €58/82

Spec. Cuissots de grenouilles saisis au beurre, en persillade. Pigeonneau de grain, jus simple au poivre concassé. Cassis de Lancié en sorbet, pulpe acidulée et glace vanille. **Wines** Beaujolais blanc, Fleurie.

◆ This worthy Beaujolais restaurant has renounced luxury, serving authentic tasty regional cuisine in a simple atmosphere.

FLEURVILLE – 71 Saône-et-Loire – 320 J11 – pop. 471 – alt. 174 m – ✉ 71260

8 **C3**

Paris 375 – Cluny 26 – Mâcon 18 – Pont-de-Vaux 8 – St-Amour 43 – Tournus 16

Château de Fleurville

– 03 85 27 91 30 – chateaufleurville@free.fr – Fax 03 85 27 91 29 – Open 7 February-2 November

15 rm – €90/170 €90/170, €16 – 1 suite – ½ P €131/145

Rest – *(closed lunch except Sunday)* Menu €38/78 – Carte €68/82

◆ This elegant castle built with golden stones (17th century) is modern as well as genuine. The rooms have been refurbished with antique furniture. Rustic dining room with a fireplace and pleasant terrace opening onto the park. Traditional cuisine.

in Mirande 3 km Northwest – ✉ 71260 Montbellet

La Marande with rm — rest,

Lugny road – 03 85 33 10 24 – restaurant-la-marande@wanadoo.fr – Fax 03 85 33 95 06 – Closed 17 November-2 December, 12 January-4 February, Monday and Tuesday

5 rm – €58/65 €58/65, €7 – **Rest** – Menu €27/65 – Carte €41/50

◆ This pleasant hundred-year-old house has two dining rooms: one opening onto the terrace, the other rustic. Classical cuisine. Small clean rooms.

FLEURY-LA-FORÊT – 27 Eure – 304 J5 – pop. 269 – alt. 161 m – ✉ 27480

33 **D2**

Paris 108 – Rouen 42 – Évreux 99 – Beauvais 49 – Mantes-la-Jolie 69

Château de Fleury la Forêt without rest

1.5 km south-west on D 14 – 02 32 49 63 91 – info@chateau-fleury-la-foret.com – Fax 02 32 49 71 67

3 rm – €65 €72

◆ The rooms of this splendid 16C and 18C château are furnished with genuine period pieces. Breakfast is served in the characteristic Normandy kitchen. Collection of antique dolls and objects.

FLEURY-SUR-ORNE – 14 Calvados – 303 J5 – see Caen

FLORAC – 48 Lozère – 330 J9 – pop. 1 996 – alt. 542 m – ✉ 48400
Languedoc-Roussillon-Tarn Gorges 23 **C1**

Paris 622 – Alès 65 – Mende 38 – Millau 84 – Rodez 123 – Le Vigan 72

Office de tourisme, 33, avenue J. Monestier ✆ 04 66 45 01 14, Fax 04 66 45 25 80

Corniche des Cévennes★.

Des Gorges du Tarn

48 r. Pêcher – ✆ 04 66 45 00 63 – gorges-du-tarn.adonis@wanadoo.fr – Fax 04 66 45 10 56 – Open from Easter to 1 November and closed Wednesday except July-August

30 rm – †€ 46/70 ††€ 46/70, ☕ € 8,50 – ½ P € 43/55

Rest *L'Adonis* – Menu € 17 (weekdays)/55 – Carte € 37/46

◆ At the entrance (or exit) to the Tarn Gorges. Renovated rooms in the main building; those in the wing are not as spruce but are bigger. The restaurant proposes regional Cévennes dishes in a modern wood panelled decor.

in Cocurès 5.5 km northeast by D 806 and D 998 – pop. 175 – alt. 600 m – ✉ 48400

La Lozerette

rm, rest,

– ✆ 04 66 45 06 04 – lalozerette@wanadoo.fr – Fax 04 66 45 12 93 – Open from 16 March to autumn half-term holidays

21 rm – †€ 53/75 ††€ 55/82, ☕ € 8 – ½ P € 53/70

Rest – *(closed Tuesday dinner off season except residents, Tuesday lunch and Wednesday lunch)* Menu € 19 (weekdays), € 26/49 – Carte € 33/46

◆ In a hamlet on the edge of the Cévennes National Park, this old house has spruce, individually decorated rooms. Smart restaurant with exposed beams. Traditional cuisine and a good wine list.

LA FLOTTE – 17 Charente-Maritime – 324 C2 – see Île de Ré

FLOURE – 11 Aude – 344 F3 – see Carcassonne

FLUMET – 73 Savoie – 333 M3 – pop. 769 – alt. 920 m – Winter sports : 1 000/ 2 030 m 11 – ✉ 73590 French Alps 46 **F1**

Paris 582 – Albertville 22 – Annecy 51 – Chamonix-Mont-Blanc 43 – Megève 10

Syndicat d'initiative, avenue de Savoie ✆ 04 79 31 61 08, Fax 04 79 31 84 67

Hostellerie le Parc des Cèdres without rest

– ✆ 04 79 31 72 37 – Fax 04 79 31 61 66 – Open from end June to mid September and 24 December-5 January

20 rm – †€ 50/55 ††€ 58/72, ☕ € 9

◆ The hotel grounds have 35 different species of trees. Rooms with balconies or terraces overlooking the Aravis mountains.

in St-Nicolas-la-Chapelle 1.2 km southwest by D 1212 – pop. 418 – alt. 950 m – ✉ 73590

Du Vivier

D 1212 – ✆ 04 79 31 73 79 – contact@hotelduvivier.fr – Fax 04 79 31 60 70 – Closed 30 March-22 April, 12 October-8 December, Sunday dinner and Monday off season

20 rm – †€ 50 ††€ 50, ☕ € 6,50 – ½ P € 47/51

Rest – *(closed 30 March-29 April, 28 September-16 December, Sunday dinner and Monday off season)* Menu € 13,50/20 – Carte € 21/32

◆ This chalet has a lovely location in the Arly Valley, offers a warm welcome and plain but well kept rooms. Traditional, family-style meals served in the dining area or on the small terrace.

FOIX 🅿 – 09 Ariège – 343 H7 – pop. 9 109 – alt. 375 m – ✉ 09000

Languedoc-Roussillon-Tarn Gorges 29 **C3**

Paris 762 – Andorra-la-Vella 102 – Carcassonne 89 – St-Girons 45

Office de tourisme, 29, rue Delcassé ✆ 05 61 65 12 12, Fax 05 61 65 64 63

de l'Ariège La Bastide-de-Sérou Unjat, by St-Girons road: 15 km, ✆ 05 61 64 56 78.

Site★ - ☀★ of the château tower - Route Verte★★ West by D17 A.

Underground river of Labouiche★ Northwest: 6,5 km by D1.

FOIX

Alsace-Lorraine (Bd) .... B 2
Bayle (R.) .... B
Chapeliers (R. des) .... A 3
Delcassé (R. Th.) .... B 4
Delpech (R. Lt P.) .... A 5
Duthil (Pl.) .... B 6
Fauré (Cours G.) .... AB 7
Labistour (R. de) .... B 8
Lazéma (R.) .... A 9
Lérida (Av. de) .... A 10
Lespinet (R. de) .... A 13
Marchands (R. des) .... B 12
Préfecture (R. de la) .... A 14
Rocher (R. du) .... A 20
St-Jammes (R.) .... A 22
St-Volusien (Pl.) .... A 23
Salenques (R. des) .... A 24

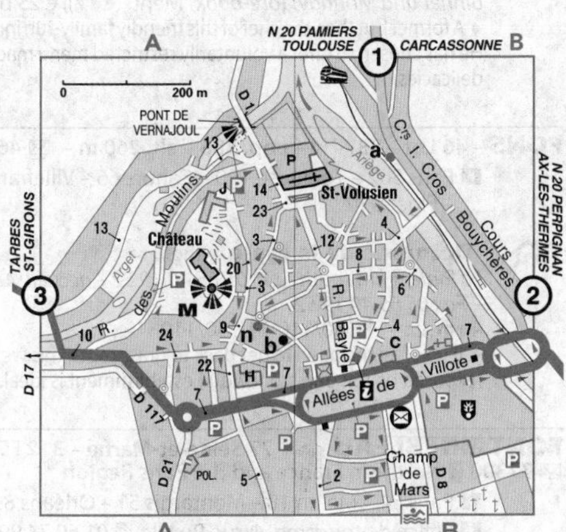

Du Lac rm, rm, rest, VISA AE

rte de Toulouse, 3 km via ① – ✆ 05 61 65 17 17 – hotel.du.lac.foix@free.fr – Fax 05 61 02 94 24

35 rm – †€ 58/75 ††€ 58/75, ☕ € 8,50 – ½ P € 50/65

Rest – *(closed 21 December-2 January and Sunday dinner from October-June)* Menu (€ 29), € 36

◆ The new, comfortable guestrooms in this old sheep barn (1599) benefit from the peace and quiet of the park and lake. Numerous water sports on offer, as well as air-conditioned bungalows for rent. The decor in the restaurant is resolutely rustic (exposed beams and stonework, fireplace etc).

Eychenne without rest VISA AE

11 r. N. Peyrevidal – ✆ 05 61 65 00 04 – hotel.eychenne@orange.fr – Fax 05 61 65 56 63 A **b**

16 rm – †€ 45/50 ††€ 52/58, ☕ € 6

◆ Easily recognisable because of its wooden tower and English pub-style bar, this simple but modernised hotel is a practical and well-located choice for visiting Foix.

Le Ste-Marthe VISA AE

21 r. N. Peyrevidal – ✆ 05 61 02 87 87 – restaurant@le-saintemarthe.fr – Fax 05 61 02 87 87 – Closed 15-31 January, Tuesday dinner and Wednesday except July-August A **n**

Rest – Menu € 23/40 – Carte € 26/60

◆ This rustic-style restaurant is perfect for those keen on trying local specialities (cassoulet, foie gras etc). Attractive table settings with white tablecloths.

Phoebus VISA

3 cours Irénée Cros – ✆ 05 61 65 10 42 – Fax 05 61 65 10 42 – Closed 20 July-21 August, 15-25 February, Saturday lunch, Sunday dinner and Monday

Rest – Menu (€ 19), € 29/85 – Carte € 33/68 B **a**

◆ Traditional cuisine served in a dining room overlooking the Ariège with an attractive view of Gaston Phoebus' château. Braille menu for the visually impaired. Attentive service.

FONDAMENTE – 12 Aveyron – 338 K7 – pop. 303 – alt. 430 m – ✉ 12540 29 D2

Paris 679 – Albi 109 – Millau 43 – Montpellier 98 – Rodez 111 – St-Affrique 28

Baldy with rm rm, VISA MC AE

– ✆ *05 65 99 37 38 – Fax 05 65 99 92 84 – Hotel: Open from Easter to September and closed Sunday evening and Monday evening*

9 rm – †€ 44/48 ††€ 44/48, ☕ € 10 – ½ P € 52/54

Rest – *(open Easter-November and closed dinner from October-November, Sunday dinner and Monday) (pre-book)* Menu (€ 17), € 25 bi (weekday lunch), € 30/42

♦ A former butcher, the chef of this friendly family-run inn works with only quality produce. He has chosen to offer a voluntarily restricted menu made up of mouth-watering regional delicacies.

FONS – 46 Lot – 337 H4 – pop. 386 – alt. 260 m – ✉ 46100 29 C1

Paris 562 – Toulouse 190 – Cahors 66 – Villefranche-de-Rouergue 47 – Figeac 12

Domaine de la Piale without rest P

La Piale, 1 km south – ✆ 05 65 40 19 52 – accueil@domainedelapiale.com – Fax 05 65 40 19 52

4 rm ☕ – †€ 50/110 ††€ 50/110

♦ If you feel the need to get back to grass roots, this welcoming, pleasantly country-style (exposed beams and stonework) establishment is ideal. Rooms in a converted barn.

FONTAINEBLEAU – 77 Seine-et-Marne – 312 F5 – pop. 15 942 – alt. 75 m – ✉ 77300 Northern France and the Paris Region 19 C3

Paris 64 – Melun 18 – Montargis 51 – Orléans 89 – Sens 54

Office de tourisme, 4, rue Royale ✆ 01 60 74 99 99, Fax 01 60 74 80 22

U.C.P.A. Bois-le-Roi Bois-le-Roi Base de loisirs, by Melun road: 10 km, ✆ 01 64 81 33 31.

Palace★★★: Grand apartments★★★ (Galerie François 1er★★★, Salle de Bal★★★) - Gardens★ - Musée napoléonien d'Art et d'Histoire militaire: collection of sabres and swords★ M1 - Forest★★★ - Gorges de Franchard★★ 5 km by ⑥.

Plan on next page

Grand Hôtel de l'Aigle Noir without rest VISA MC AE

27 pl. Napoléon Bonaparte – ✆ 01 60 74 60 00 – hotel.aigle.noir@wanadoo.fr – Fax 01 60 74 60 01 – Closed 1st-23 August and 18 December-2 January AZ **a**

15 rm – †€ 100/160 ††€ 110/170, ☕ € 15 – 3 suites

♦ Old private mansion (15th century) next to the castle. Elegant atmosphere and rooms with a personal touch, stylish furnishings. Health and relaxation area.

Mercure rm, P VISA MC AE

41 r. Royale – ✆ 01 64 69 34 34 – h1627@accor.com – Fax 01 64 69 34 39

97 rm – †€ 130/140 ††€ 135/185, ☕ € 15

Rest – *(closed 31 July-24 August and 21 December-2 January)* Carte € 27/49 AZ **d**

♦ A comfortable high-quality establishment offering functional rooms. In the evening, relax in front of the fireplace in the lounge or enjoy the snug bar. Contemporary dining room with terrace overlooking the park.

Napoléon VISA MC AE

9 r. Grande – ✆ 01 60 39 50 50 – resa@naposite.com – Fax 01 64 22 20 87 BZ **n**

57 rm – †€ 100/160 ††€ 100/160, ☕ € 15 – ½ P € 180

Rest *La Table des Maréchaux* – Menu (€ 32 bi), € 40/55 – Carte € 47/60

♦ Just 100m from the castle where Napoleon made his final appearance in front of the Imperial Guard in 1814. Former post house with Empire-style rooms opening onto an inner courtyard. The elegant Table des Maréchaux, a reference to Malmaison, borders a pleasant patio-terrace.

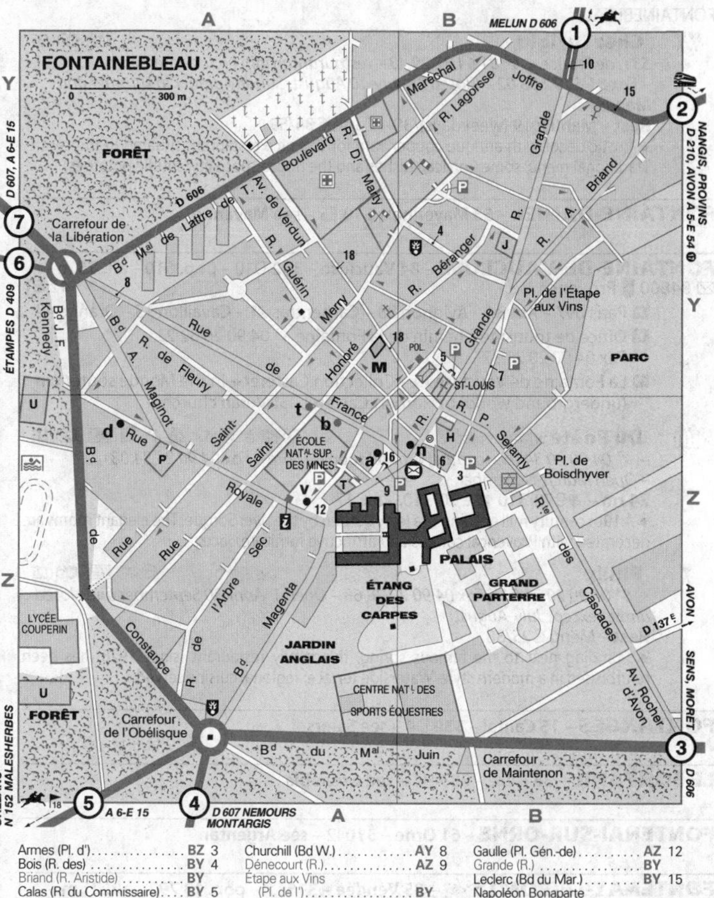

Armes (Pl. d') . . . . . BZ 3
Bois (R. des) . . . . . BY 4
Briand (R. Aristide) . . . . . BY
Calas (R. du Commissaire) . . . . BY 5
Chancellerie (R. de la) . . . . . BZ 6
Château (R. du) . . . . . BY 7
Churchill (Bd W.) . . . . . AY 8
Dénecourt (R.) . . . . . AZ 9
Étape aux Vins (Pl. de l') . . . . . BY
Foch (Bd du Mar.) . . . . . BY 10
France (R. de) . . . . . AYZ
Gaulle (Pl. Gén.-de) . . . . . AZ 12
Grande (R.) . . . . . BY
Leclerc (Bd du Mar.) . . . . . BY 15
Napoléon Bonaparte (Pl.) . . . . . AZ 16
Paroisse (R. de la) . . . . . AY 18

De Londres without rest

1 pl. Gén. de Gaulle – ✆ 01 64 22 20 21
– hdelondres1850@aol.com
– Fax 01 60 72 39 16
– Closed 12-18 August and 23 December-7 January AZ **v**

15 rm – €90/150 €120/180, €11

◆ Facing the castle, this 19th century building has large and soundproofed rooms that are elegantly decorated with fine fabrics, rustic furniture and hunting prints.

Croquembouche

43 r. de France – ✆ 01 64 22 01 57
– info@restaurant-croquembouche.com
– Fax 01 60 72 08 73
– Closed 1st-15 August, 24 December-2 January, Saturday lunch, Monday lunch and Sunday except holidays AZ **b**

Rest – Menu €18 (lunch)/45 – Carte €39/70

◆ In a shopping street in the town centre, a restaurant with numerous attractions: traditional cuisine with fresh products, pastel colours and a warm welcome.

Chez Arrighi

53 r. de France – 01 64 22 29 43 – restaurantarrighi@club-internet.fr – Fax 01 60 72 68 02 – Closed 28 July-10 August, Sunday dinner in summer and Monday AZ **t**

Rest – Menu € 19 (weekdays)/38 – Carte € 34/59

♦ Rustic décor with antique copperware for this nice restaurant situated in the centre. Traditional menu, some Corsican dishes and the house speciality: soufflé potatoes.

FONTAINE-DANIEL – 53 Mayenne – 310 E5 – see Mayenne

FONTAINE-DE-VAUCLUSE – 84 Vaucluse – 332 D10 – pop. 610 – alt. 75 m – 84800 Provence 42 E1

Paris 697 – Apt 34 – Avignon 33 – Carpentras 21 – Cavaillon 15 – Orange 42

Office de tourisme, chemin de la Fontaine 04 90 20 32 22, Fax 04 90 20 21 37

La Fontaine de Vaucluse★★ - Collection Casteret★ in the Monde souterrain (underground world) of Norbert Casteret - St-Véran church ★.

Du Poète without rest

– 04 90 20 34 05 – contact@hoteldupoete.com – Fax 04 90 20 34 08 – Open March-November

24 rm – †€ 70/310 ††€ 70/310, ☕ € 17

♦ A 19th century mill nestling in a leafy garden by the river Sorgue. The elegant rooms are decorated with Provençal colours and attractive furniture. Jacuzzi.

Philip

– 04 90 20 31 81 – Fax 04 90 20 28 63 – Open 1st April-30 September and closed dinner except July-August

Rest – Menu € 25/38

♦ Standing next to the famous spring, this family restaurant (since 1926) has been refurbished in a modern style. Waterside terrace; regional cuisine served.

FONTANGES – 15 Cantal – 330 D4 – see Salers

LE FONTANIL – 38 Isère – 333 H6 – see Grenoble

FONTENAI-SUR-ORNE – 61 Orne – 310 I2 – see Argentan

FONTENAY-LE-COMTE – 85 Vendée – 316 L9 – pop. 13 792 – alt. 21 m – 85200 Atlantic Coast 34 B3

Paris 442 – Cholet 103 – La Rochelle 51 – La Roche-sur-Yon 64

Office de tourisme, 8, rue de Grimouard 02 51 69 44 99, Fax 02 51 50 00 90

Steeple ★ of N.-Dame church **B** - Interior ★ of château de Terre-Neuve.

Plan on next page

Le Rabelais

19 r. Ouillette – 02 51 69 86 20 – hotel-lerabelais@wanadoo.fr – Fax 02 51 69 80 45 BZ **a**

54 rm – †€ 74/82 ††€ 86/96, ☕ € 10 – ½ P € 68/72 – **Rest** – Menu (€ 13,50), € 18/32 – Carte approx. € 30

♦ The name refers to the writer who stayed for three years in the town. Most of the functional but pleasantly renovated rooms overlook a flower-decked garden. This restaurant has a terrace by the pool and a large buffet of starters and desserts.

Le Logis de la Clef de Bois without rest

5 r. du Département – 02 51 69 03 49 – clef_de_bois@hotmail.com – Fax 02 51 69 03 49 AY **b**

4 rm – †€ 80/95 ††€ 80/115, ☕ € 10

♦ This mansion offers beautifully coloured rooms, each named after a famous writer. The Rabelais suite, with a decor evoking the commedia dell'arte, is the most outstanding.

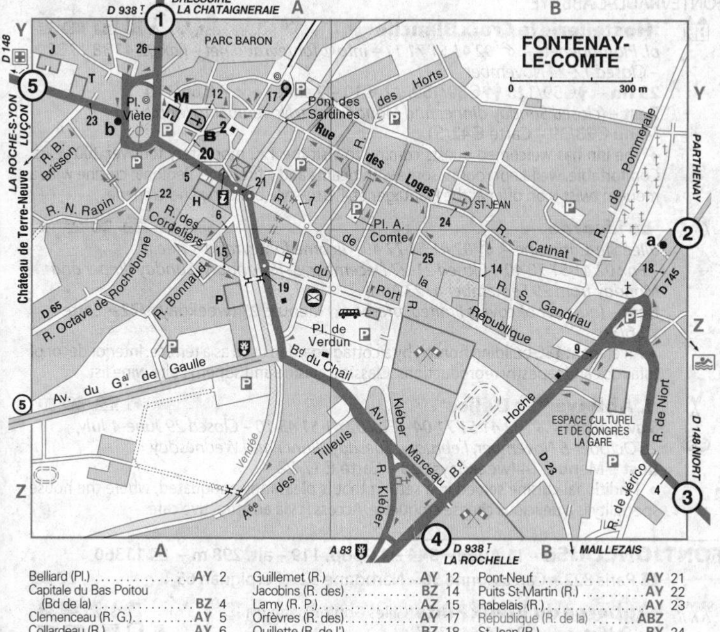

Belliard (Pl.)	AY	2	Guillemet (R.)	AY	12	Pont-Neuf	AY	21
Capitale du Bas Poitou (Bd de la)	BZ	4	Jacobins (R. des)	BZ	14	Puits St-Martin (R.)	AY	22
Clemenceau (R. G.)	AY	5	Lamy (R. P.)	AZ	15	Rabelais (R.)	AY	23
Collardeau (R.)	AY	6	Orfèvres (R. des)	AY	17	République (R. de la)	ABZ	
Dr-Audé (R. du)	AY	7	Ouillette (R. de l')	BZ	18	St-Jean (R.)	BY	24
Du Guesclin (Bd)	BZ	9	Poey d'Avant (Quai)	AZ	19	St-Nicolas (R.)	BZ	25
			Pont aux Chèvres (R.)	AY	20	Tiraqueau (R.)	AY	26

in Velluire 11 km by ④, D 938 ter and D 68 – pop. 508 – alt. 9 m – ✉ 85770

XXX **Auberge de la Rivière** with rm — VISA MC AE

r. du Port de la Fouarne – ✆ 02 51 52 32 15 – auberge.delariviere@wanadoo.fr – Fax 02 51 52 37 42 – Closed 19 January-22 February, Sunday dinner and Wednesday lunch except July-August and Monday

11 rm – 🛉€ 50/94 🛉🛉€ 50/94, ☕ € 11 – ½ P € 62/85 – **Rest** – Menu € 26/50 – Carte € 36/60

◆ Stylish inn on the banks of the Vendée serving regional cuisine with a contemporary touch. Rustic dining room. Spacious, well-kept rooms.

FONTETTE – 89 Yonne – 319 F7 – see Vézelay

FONTEVRAUD-L'ABBAYE – 49 Maine-et-Loire – 317 J5 – pop. 1 189 – alt. 75 m – ✉ 49590 Châteaux of the Loire

35 **C2**

▶ Paris 296 – Angers 78 – Chinon 21 – Loudun 22 – Poitiers 78 – Saumur 15 – Thouars 38

ℹ Office de tourisme, place Saint-Michel ✆ 02 41 51 79 45, Fax 02 41 51 79 01

◉ Abbey★★ - St-Michel church ★.

Prieuré St-Lazare — P VISA MC AE

(In the royal abbey) – ✆ 02 41 51 73 16 – contact@hotelfp-fontevraud.com – Fax 02 41 51 75 50 – Open 15 March-15 November

52 rm – 🛉€ 53/99 🛉🛉€ 53/99, ☕ € 11 – ½ P € 62/85 – **Rest** – Menu € 38 (weekdays)/80 bi – Carte € 40/54

◆ A haven of peace and tranquillity set amid the gardens of Fontevraud Abbey, the former priory of St Lazare. Small, modern and soberly decorated rooms. The cloister is today the setting for the restaurant. The chapel is used for banquets. Modern cuisine.

Hostellerie la Croix Blanche rest, VISA AE

pl. Plantagenets – ☎ 02 41 51 71 11 – info@fontevraud.net – Fax 02 41 38 15 38 – Closed 17-24 November

23 rm – †€ 59/125 ††€ 59/159, ☕ € 10 – 2 suites – ½ P € 66/110

Rest – *(closed Sunday dinner and Monday from November to March)*

Menu € 23/39 – Carte € 42/51

♦ The inn has welcomed guests coming to visit the 12C monastery for over 300 years. Comfortable, well-kept rooms, some with beams and a fireplace. Regional cuisine with a modern twist is on offer at the Plantagenêt. Retro-style brasserie and crêperie.

La Licorne VISA AE

allée Ste-Catherine – ☎ 02 41 51 72 49 – licorne.fontevraud@free.fr – Fax 02 41 51 70 40 – Closed 21-27 December, 5-19 January, Sunday dinner and Monday from 29 September to 23 April

Rest – *(number of covers limited, pre-book)* Menu € 27 (weekdays)/72 – Carte € 56/86

♦ An elegant 18C building fronted by a cottage garden used as a terrace. Interior decor of tufa rock and tapestry reproductions. Classical cuisine and superb Loire wine list.

L'Abbaye "Le Délice" VISA AE

8 av. Roches – ☎ 02 41 51 71 04 – Fax 02 41 51 43 10 – Closed 29 June-4 July, 26 October-5 November, February, Tuesday dinner and Wednesday

Rest – Menu € 14 (weekdays)/28 – Carte € 17/28

♦ Traditional cuisine served in a setting that is pleasantly antiquated, where the house speciality is a delicious cheese croquette. Access is via an attractive café.

FONTJONCOUSE – 11 Aude – 344 H4 – pop. 119 – alt. 298 m – ✉ 11360

Paris 822 – Carcassonne 56 – Narbonne 32 – Perpignan 65 22 **B3**

Auberge du Vieux Puits (Gilles Goujon) with rm VISA AE

av. St Victor – ☎ 04 68 44 07 37 – aubergeduvieuxpuits@wanadoo.fr – Fax 04 68 44 08 31 – Closed 2 January-5 March, Sunday dinner, Monday and Tuesday from 15 September to 15 June

8 rm – †€ 150/230 ††€ 150/230, ☕ € 17 – ½ P € 180/237

Rest – Menu € 55 (weekday lunch), € 93/110 – Carte € 100/144

Spec. Couteaux raidis à la plancha au beurre d'ail (July to September). Filet de rouget barbet, pomme bonne bouche fourrée d'une brandade à la cèbe en "bullinada". Sablé feuille à feuille au chocolat, surprise de framboise sauce choc o' thé, sorbet framboise. **Wines** Corbières blanc et rouge.

♦ Elegant contemporary dining room, excellent wine list and fine, creative cuisine with regional touches. Modern minimalist guestrooms.

La Maison des Chefs VISA AE

(at 300 m in the village) – ☎ 04 68 44 07 37 – aubergeduvieuxpuits@wanadoo.fr – Fax 04 68 44 08 31

6 rm – †€ 105/115 ††€ 105/115, ☕ € 17

♦ The decor of the rooms pays tribute to great chefs with culinary utensils and jackets signed by Bocuse, Troisgros, etc. The establishment is entirely non-smoking.

FONT-ROMEU – 66 Pyrénées-Orientales – 344 D7 – pop. 2 003 – alt. 1 800 m – Winter sports : 1 900/2 250 m 1 28 – Casino – ✉ 66120

Languedoc-Roussillon-Tarn Gorges 22 **A3**

Paris 858 – Andorra la Vella 73 – Ax-les-Thermes 56 – Bourg-Madame 18

Office de tourisme, 38, avenue Emmanuel Brousse ☎ 04 68 30 68 30, Fax 04 68 30 29 70

de Font-Romeu Espace Sportif Colette Besson, North: 1 km, ☎ 04 68 30 10 78.

Camaril★★★, altar-piece★ and chapelle★ de l'Ermitage - ★★ Calvary.

Plan on next page

Le Grand Tétras without rest VISA AE

av. E. Brousse – ☎ 04 68 30 01 20 – infos@hotelgrandtetras.fr – Fax 04 68 30 35 67

36 rm – †€ 60/92 ††€ 60/92, ☕ € 9 AX **r**

♦ Mountain-style renovated decor. Balcony and panoramic view of the Pyrenees from rooms on the south side. Spa and covered pool on the roof. Wi-fi.

FONT-ROMEU

Allard (R. Henri) . . . . **BX** 2
Brousse (Av. Emmanuel) . . . **BX** 3
Calvet (R.) . . . . **BX** 5
Capelle (R. du Docteur) . . . . **AX** 6
Cytises (R. des) . . . . **AX** 8
Ecureuils (R. des) . . . . **AX** 9
Espagne (Av. d') . . . . **AX**
Genêts d'Or (R. des) . . . . **BY** 12
Liberté (R. de la) . . . . **AY** 13
Maillol (R.) . . . . **BX** 15
République (R. de la) . . . . **AY** 16
Saules (R. des) . . . . **AY** 18
Trombe (R. Professeur) . . . . **AY** 19

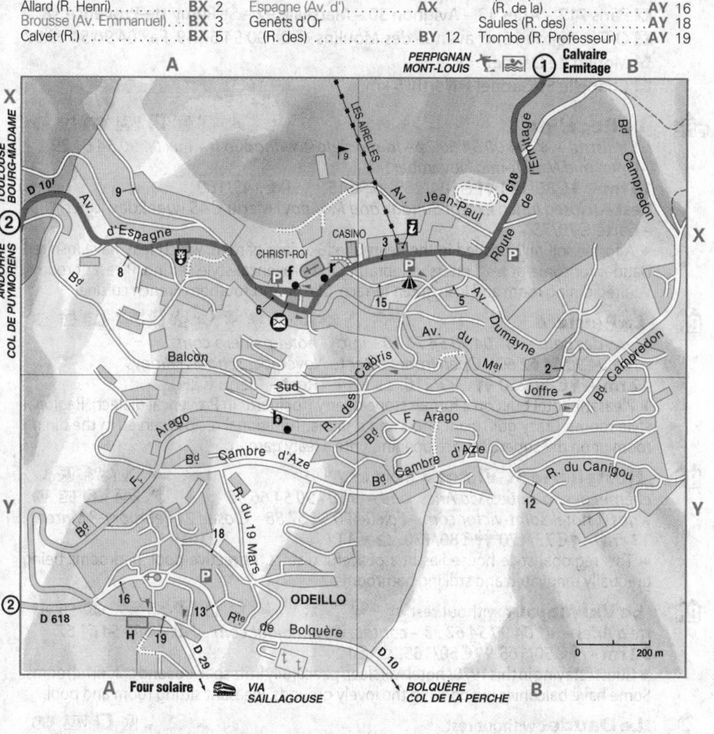

Sun Valley

rest, VISA

3 av. Espagne – ✆ *04 68 30 21 21* – *contact@hotelsunvalley.fr*
– *Fax 04 68 30 30 38* – *Closed 14 October-2 December* AX **f**

41 rm – **†**€ 75/95 **††**€ 88/116, ☕ € 11 – ½ P € 72/92 – **Rest** – *(resident only)* Menu € 21

◆ The rooms, in the process of an alpine-inspired renovation, all have sunny south-facing balconies. Splendid fitness facilities on the top floor. Simple, generous meals.

Clair Soleil

VISA

29 av. François Arago, Odeillo road: 1 km – ✆ *04 68 30 13 65* – *Fax 04 68 30 08 27*
– *Closed 13 April-17 May and 25 October-19 December* AY **b**

29 rm – **†**€ 50/59 **††**€ 50/59, ☕ € 7,50 – ½ P € 51/59

Rest – *(closed lunch Monday-Thursday off season, Tuesday lunch and Wednesday lunch)* Menu € 22, € 34 – Carte approx. € 39

◆ This pleasant well-located family guesthouse (non-smoking) faces the Odeillo solar furnace. Modest rooms with balcony or terrace. A dining room and veranda offering regional cuisine and attentive service.

in Via 5 km South by D 29 AY – ✉ **66210 Font Romeu Odeillo Via**

L'Oustalet

rest, VISA

– ✆ *04 68 30 11 32* – *hotelloustalet@wanadoo.fr* – *Fax 04 68 30 31 89*
– *Closed 15 April-8 May and 15 October-15 November*

25 rm – **†**€ 45/60 **††**€ 45/60, ☕ € 7 – ½ P € 44/51

Rest – snack *(dinner only) (resident only)* Menu € 16

◆ This establishment is popular with CNRS research staff. A few rooms furnished in Catalan style; most of the rooms have balconies. Country-style dining room.

FONTVIEILLE – 13 Bouches-du-Rhône – 340 D3 – pop. 3 456 – alt. 20 m – ✉ 13990 Provence 42 E1

Paris 712 – Arles 12 – Avignon 30 – Marseille 92 – St-Rémy-de-Provence 18

Office de tourisme, avenue des Moulins ✆ 04 90 54 67 49, Fax 04 90 54 69 82

Moulin de Daudet ⩽★.

Chapelle St-Gabriel★ North: 5 km.

La Regalido

r. F. Mistral – ✆ 04 90 54 60 22 – la-regalido@wanadoo.fr – Fax 04 90 54 64 29 – Open mid March-mid November

15 rm – †€ 80/104 ††€ 104/265, ☕ € 15 – ½ P € 145/160

Rest – *(closed lunch except Sunday and Monday)* Menu € 45 (weekday lunch)/55 – Carte € 70/75

◆ A former oil mill, nestled in the heart of a luxuriant garden, which may have inspired Daudet for some of his 'Letters' celebrating the Provençal-style setting. Pleasant rooms. Vaulted dining room and lush green terrace. Classic and southern French cuisine.

La Peiriero

rm, VISA AE

36 av. des Baux – ✆ 04 90 54 76 10 – info@hotel-peiriero.com – Fax 04 90 54 62 60 – Open from Easter to November school holidays

42 rm – †€ 89/210 ††€ 89/210, ☕ € 14 – **Rest** – Menu € 28

◆ Pleasant hotel built on a former stone quarry ("peiriero" in Provençal dialect). Regional style rooms. Crazy golf, giant chess and a sauna. Traditional recipes served in the dining room or on the superb terrace opening onto a leafy garden.

Hostellerie St-Victor without rest

chemin des Fourques, via Arles road – ✆ 04 90 54 66 00 – aps@hotel-saint-victor.com – Fax 04 90 54 67 88 – Closed 21 February-8 March

13 rm – †€ 75/170 ††€ 80/170, ☕ € 11

◆ This regional-style house lies in a peaceful district. Attractive pool, bedrooms being gradually renovated and striking bathrooms.

Le Val Majour without rest

rte d'Arles – ✆ 04 90 54 62 33 – contact@valmajour.com – Fax 04 90 54 61 67

32 rm – †€ 50/165 ††€ 50/165, ☕ € 12

◆ Guests staying in this 1970s hotel will sleep peacefully in its spacious and colourful rooms. Some have balconies overlooking the lovely grounds. Pleasant sitting room and pool.

Le Daudet without rest

7 av. Montmajour – ✆ 04 90 54 76 06 – contact@hotelledaudet.com – Fax 04 90 54 76 95 – Open end March-beg. November

14 rm – †€ 60/70 ††€ 60/70, ☕ € 8,50

◆ The attractive rooms of this peaceful hotel are spread around a courtyard complete with fountain. The bijou terraces, inviting pool and reasonable prices are added bonuses!

Hostellerie de la Tour

3 r. Plumelets, Arles road – ✆ 04 90 54 72 21 – bounoir@wanadoo.fr – Fax 04 90 54 86 26 – Open 16 March-24 October

10 rm – †€ 51 ††€ 58, ☕ € 9,50 – ½ P € 54/62 – **Rest** – *(dinner only)* Menu € 25 (single menu)

◆ Warm, attentive service in this small inn, popular with regulars for its high standards; small, simple rooms and pleasant garden-pool. Good home cooking served in a room that mingles old stonework with contemporary features.

La Table du Meunier

42 cours Hyacinthe Bellon – ✆ 04 90 54 61 05 – Fax 04 90 54 77 24 – Closed November school holidays, February school holidays, 20-29 December, Tuesday except July-August and Wednesday

Rest – *(number of covers limited, pre-book)* Menu (€ 20), € 26/34 – Carte approx. € 37

◆ While Madame prepares tasty regional cuisine, Monsieur is very attentive to your comfort in the rustic dining room or on the terrace, adorned with a henhouse dating from 1765.

Le Patio

117 rte du Nord – ✆ 04 90 54 73 10 – Closed February school holidays, Tuesday dinner and Wednesday

Rest – *(number of covers limited, pre-book)* Menu € 26/31 – Carte € 44/52

◆ This 18C sheepfold features a country-chic interior and an attractive patio shaded by acacias, palm and magnolia trees. Updated Provençal menu.

Tarascon road 5 km Northwest by D 33 – ✉ 13150 Tarascon

Les Mazets des Roches

rte de Fonvieille – ℘ 04 90 91 34 89 – mazets-roches@wanadoo.fr – Fax 04 90 43 53 29 – Open from Easter-mid October

37 rm – †€ 60/125 ††€ 69/153, ☕ € 12 – 1 suite – **Rest** – *(Closed Thursday lunch and Saturday lunch except July-August)* Menu € 25 (weekdays)/38 – Carte € 36/57

◆ Ideal establishment for a quiet country break with 13ha of wooded parkland and a 25m pool. Functional, comfortable rooms adorned with bright fabrics. Welcoming dining room-veranda with bamboo furniture, house plants and floral designs.

FORBACH – **57 Moselle** – **307** M3 – **pop. 22 807** – **Built-up area 104 074** – **alt. 222 m** – ✉ **57600** Alsace-Lorraine 27 **C1**

Paris 385 – Metz 59 – St-Avold 23 – Sarreguemines 21 – Saarbrücken 13

Office de tourisme, 174, rue nationale ℘ 03 87 85 02 43, Fax 03 87 85 17 15

FORBACH

Street	Square	No.
Alliés (R. des)	B	2
Arras (R. d')	A	3
Briand (Pl. A.)	A	6
Chapelle (R. de la)	A	7
Couturier (R.)	B	9
Église (R. de l')	B	10
Gare (R. de la)	B	12
Jardins (R. des)	A	13
Moulins (R. des)	A	15
Nationale (R.)	AB	
Ney (R. P.)	A	17
Parc (R. du)	B	18
Remsing (R. de)	A	20
République (Pl. de la)	B	21
St-Remy (Av.)	AB	
Schlossberg (R. du)	A	23
Schuman (Pl. R.)	B	24
Tuilerie (R. de la)	A	26
22-Novembre (R. du)	B	27

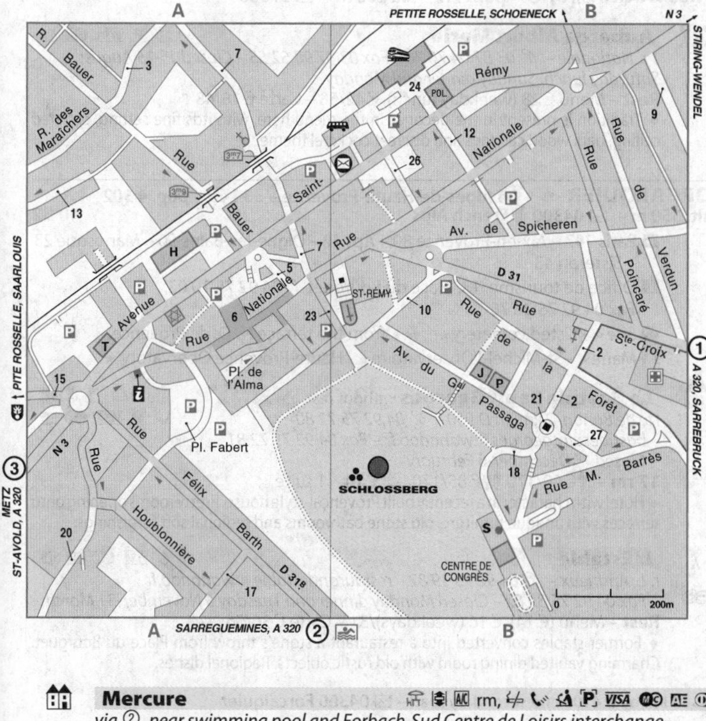

Mercure rm,

via ②, near swimming pool and Forbach-Sud Centre de Loisirs interchange – ℘ 03 87 87 06 06 – h1976@accor.com – Fax 03 87 84 04 23

67 rm – †€ 65/95 ††€ 75/95, ☕ € 12,50 – **Rest** – Menu € 20 (weekdays)/55 – Carte € 22/44

◆ Located between the highway and a sport complex, the Mercure provides rooms in two categories ("standard" and "comfortable"). Facilities for conferences. A modern dining room with a veranda.

XX **Le Schlossberg**

13 r. Parc – ✆ 03 87 87 88 26 – Fax 03 87 87 83 86 – Closed 24 July-10 August, 1st-12 January, Sunday dinner, Tuesday dinner and merc B s

Rest – Menu € 20 (weekdays)/49 – Carte € 37/53

◆ Built of local stone, this restaurant stands by the Schlossberg park. Dining room with beautiful inlaid ceiling and bright painted panelling. Terrace under the lime trees.

in Stiring-Wendel 3 km northeast by D 603 – pop. 13 129 – alt. 240 m – ✉ 57350

Syndicat d'initiative, 1, place de Wendel ✆ 03 87 87 07 65, Fax 03 87 87 69 98

XXX **La Bonne Auberge** (Lydia Egloff)

15 r. Nationale – ✆ 03 87 87 52 78 – Fax 03 87 87 18 19 – Closed 21-28 April, 18 August-4 September, 29 December-6 January, Saturday lunch, Sunday dinner and Monday except public holidays

Rest – Menu € 40 (weekday lunch), € 50/95 – Carte € 66/94

Spec. Turbot au verjus de fenouil et d'aneth à l'ouzo. Foie d'oie confit au melon-miel-sauge, "comme un calisson". Lady "Mirabelle". **Wines** Côtes de Toul.

◆ Elegant dining room set around a winter garden. Inventive cuisine, great wine list: la Bonne Auberge lives up to its name!

in Rosbrück 6 km by ③ – pop. 912 – alt. 200 m – ✉ 57800

XXX **Auberge Albert Marie**

1 r. Nationale – ✆ 03 87 04 70 76 – Fax 03 87 90 52 55 – Closed 1st-15 August, Saturday lunch, Sunday dinner and Monday

Rest – Menu € 28 (weekday lunch), € 42/58 – Carte € 18/48

◆ Tradition is present in the décor as in the menu here, with itds fine setting, coffered ceiling, dark wood carvings and discreet cockerel theme.

FORCALQUIER – 04 Alpes-de-Haute-Provence – 334 C9 – pop. 4 302 – alt. 550 m – ✉ 04300 French Alps 40 B2

Paris 747 – Aix-en-Provence 80 – Apt 42 – Digne-les-Bains 50 – Manosque 23 – Sisteron 43

Office de tourisme, 13, place du Bourguet ✆ 04 92 75 10 02, Fax 04 92 75 26 76

Site★ - Listed cemetery★ - ✳★ from the terrace N.-D. de Provence.

Mane★ - St-Michel-l'Observatoire★ - Haute-Provence Obervatory ★.

La Bastide Saint Georges without rest

rte de Banon, 2 km on D 950 – ✆ 04 92 75 72 80 – bastidesaintgeorges@wanadoo.fr – Fax 04 92 75 72 81 – Closed 1st December-6 February

17 rm – €60/170 €85/170, € 14 – 1 suite

◆ Hotel with character in a recently built Provençal-style house. Pretty rooms opening onto terraces with antique furniture, old stone bathrooms and regional soft furnishings.

X **L'Establé**

r. L. Andrieux – ✆ 04 92 75 39 82 – restaurantlestable@wanadoo.fr – Fax 04 92 75 39 82 – Closed Monday dinner and Tuesday 5 November-31 March

Rest – Menu (€ 14), € 16 (weekdays)/31 – Carte € 36/56

◆ Former stables converted into a restaurant a stone's throw from Place du Bourguet. Charming vaulted dining room with old rustic objects. Regional dishes.

East 4 km by D 4100 and secondary road – ✉ 04300 Forcalquier

Auberge Charembeau without rest

– ✆ 04 92 70 91 70 – contact@charembeau.com – Fax 04 92 70 91 83 – Open 1st March-15 November

24 rm – €59/78 €59/120, € 9

◆ An 18th century farmhouse in a charming park. The lovely surroundings and the Provençal-style decoration in the vast rooms offer peace and quiet to the visitor.

South 4 km by D 16 and secondary road – ✉ 04300 Forcalquier

Le Colombier
– ✆ 04 92 75 03 71 – lecolombier@wanadoo.fr – Fax 04 92 75 14 30
14 rm – †€ 63/74 ††€ 68/108, ☕ € 11 – ½ P € 63/90 – **Rest** – *(closed Tuesday)* Menu € 14 (weekday lunch), € 27/32
◆ This prettily restored 18C house was once home to Louis XV's royal guard. Tastefully decorated rooms, opening onto an immense Mediterranean garden. Regional cuisine offered in a rustic dining room, especially cool in the summer.

in Mane 4 km south by D 4100 – pop. 1 169 – alt. 500 m – ✉ 04300

Mas du Pont Roman without rest
chemin de Châteauneuf, (Apt road) – ✆ 04 92 75 49 46 – info@pontroman.com – Fax 04 92 75 36 73
9 rm – †€ 55 ††€ 75/115, ☕ € 8
◆ Warm welcome in this former farmhouse set back from the N 100 road, near an old medieval bridge. Charming lounge and quiet rooms with Provençal furniture.

LA FORÊT-FOUESNANT – 29 Finistère – 308 H7 – pop. 2 809 – alt. 19 m – ✉ 29940 Brittany

9 **B2**

Paris 552 – Concarneau 8 – Pont-l'Abbé 22 – Quimper 16 – Quimperlé 36
Office de tourisme, 2, rue du Port ✆ 02 98 51 42 07, Fax 02 98 51 44 52

Beauséjour
pl. de la Baie – ✆ 02 98 56 97 18 – beausejourhotel@wanadoo.fr – Fax 02 98 51 40 77 – *Open 1st April-15 October*
17 rm – †€ 44/56 ††€ 46/62, ☕ € 7 – ½ P € 57/62 – **Rest** – *(open 1st April-30 September and closed Sunday dinner and Monday)* Menu € 16/39 – Carte € 30/43
◆ At the end of a cove in the bay of La Forêt, this simple family hotel is well kept. The rooms are bright and spacious for the most part; some are redecorated. Rustic dining room with fireplace and covered terrace just a few metres from the waterside.

Auberge St-Laurent
2 km Concarneau road along the coast – ✆ 02 98 56 98 07 – Fax 02 98 56 98 07 – *Closed autumn half-term holidays, February holidays, Monday dinner, Tuesday dinner off season and Wednesday*
Rest – Menu € 15 (weekday lunch), € 21/39 – Carte € 25/43
◆ Pleasant guesthouse on the Concarneau coastal road. One of the two rustic dining rooms, with a fireplace and beams, overlooks the garden and the summer terrace.

FORGES-LES-EAUX – 76 Seine-Maritime – 304 J4 – pop. 3 465 – alt. 161 m – Casino – ✉ 76440 Normandy

33 **D1**

Paris 117 – Rouen 44 – Abbeville 73 – Amiens 72 – Beauvais 52 – Le Havre 123
Office de tourisme, rue Albert Bochet ✆ 02 35 90 52 10, Fax 02 35 90 34 80

Le Continental without rest
av. des Sources, (Dieppe road) – ✆ 02 32 89 50 50 – casinoforges@wanadoo.fr – Fax 02 35 90 26 14
44 rm – †€ 59/73 ††€ 69/73, ☕ € 10
◆ A small, regional style house featuring spacious rooms refurbished with a modern touch. Pleasant lounge and delightful breakfast room.

Auberge du Beau Lieu with rm
rte de Gournay, 2 km via D 915 – ✆ 02 35 90 50 36 – aubeaulieu@aol.com – *Closed 12 January-6 February, Monday and Tuesday except July-August*
3 rm – †€ 40 ††€ 60, ☕ € 11 – **Rest** – Menu € 28/58 – Carte € 35/64
◆ Country-style guesthouse in the Bray country. In winter, it is a pleasure to relax near the hearth in the cosy restaurant. Summer terrace. Ground-floor rooms.

La Paix with rm
15 r. de Neufchâtel – ✆ 02 35 90 51 22 – contact@hotellapaix.fr – Fax 02 35 09 83 62 – *Closed 22 December-15 January, Sunday dinner off season and Monday lunch*
18 rm – †€ 57 ††€ 57, ☕ € 6,50 – ½ P € 53 – **Rest** – Menu (€ 14), € 20/35 – Carte € 23/45
◆ This spacious country-style dining room has plenty of character with its earthenware, antique copperware, fireplace and exposed beams. Traditional cuisine. Simple rooms.

FORT-MAHON-PLAGE – 80 Somme – 301 C5 – pop. 1 140 – alt. 2 m – Casino – ✉ 80120 Northern France and the Paris Region 36 A1

Paris 225 – Abbeville 41 – Amiens 90 – Berck-sur-Mer 19 – Calais 94 – Étaples 30

Office de tourisme, 1000, avenue de la Plage ✆ 03 22 23 36 00, Fax 03 22 23 93 40

de Belle-Dune Promenade du Marquenterre, (near Aquaclub), ✆ 03 22 23 45 50.

Marquenterre Ornithological Park ★★ South: 15 km.

Auberge Le Fiacre

rm, rm, VISA

à Routhiauville, 2 km south-east on Rue road ✉ 80120 Quend – ✆ 03 22 23 47 30 – lefiacre@wanadoo.fr – Fax 03 22 27 19 80 – Closed 15-26 December, 7 January-3 February

11 rm – €70/95 €70/95, €11 – 3 suites – ½ P €120/130

Rest – *(closed lunch except week-ends)* Menu (€25), €32/45 – Carte €43/60

◆ The perfect spot for a relaxing country break, this old Marquenterre farm enjoys an attractive rural setting. Cosy atmosphere in the guestrooms, enlivened with individual touches. Classical cuisine served in an elegant dining room or on the terrace overlooking the garden.

La Terrasse

rest, rest, rm, VISA AE

– ✆ 03 22 23 37 77 – info@hotellaterrasse.com – Fax 03 22 23 36 74 – Closed 8-25 January

56 rm – €40/93 €40/93, €10 – ½ P €38/65 – **Rest** – Menu €14/55 bi – Carte €21/46

◆ Family-run seafront hotel with comfortable rooms, some with a sea view, the quietest overlooking the courtyard. Panoramic view and nautical decor; seafood menu and terrace on the restaurant side; brasserie section.

LA FOSSETTE (PLAGE) – 83 Var – 340 N7 – see le Lavandou

FOS-SUR-MER – 13 Bouches-du-Rhône – 340 E5 – pop. 13 922 – alt. 11 m – ✉ 13270 Provence 40 A3

Paris 750 – Aix-en-Provence 55 – Arles 42 – Marseille 51 – Martigues 12

Syndicat d'initiative, avenue René Cassin ✆ 04 42 47 71 96, Fax 04 42 05 27 55

Village ★.

Ariane Fos

rm, VISA AE

Istres road: 3 km – ✆ 04 42 05 00 57 – contact@arianefoshotel.com – Fax 04 42 05 51 00

72 rm – €81/99 €105/136, €10,50 – **Rest** – Menu €27/33 – Carte €35/44

◆ Near the Estomac lagoon, a hotel with spacious, soundproofed, modern rooms (a third with balconies). Good leisure and conference facilities. Recently renovated restaurant serving traditional cuisine.

FOUCHÈRES – 10 Aube – 313 F5 – pop. 450 – alt. 138 m – ✉ 10260 13 B3

Paris 189 – Troyes 25 – Bar-sur-Aube 42 – Bar-sur-Seine 11

Auberge de la Seine

VISA AE

1 fg de Bourgogne – ✆ 03 25 40 71 11 – contact@aubergedelaseine.com – Fax 03 25 40 84 09 – Closed 23 February-8 March, Sunday dinner, Monday dinner and Wednesday

Rest – Menu €19 (weekdays)/65 bi – Carte €40/59

◆ 18C post house extended by a lovely terrace overlooking the river Seine. Traditional cuisine served in the modern, simple and cosy dining room.

FOUDAY – 67 Bas-Rhin – 315 H6 – pop. 303 – ✉ 67130 Alsace-Lorraine

Paris 412 – St-Dié 34 – Saverne 55 – Sélestat 37 – Strasbourg 61 1 A2

Julien

rm, rest, VISA AE

D 1420 – ✆ 03 88 97 30 09 – hoteljulien@wanadoo.fr – Fax 03 88 97 36 73 – Closed 5-25 January

37 rm – €89/115 €89/115, €15 – 10 suites – ½ P €85/106

Rest – *(closed Tuesday)* Menu €15 (weekday lunch), €25/38 – Carte €33/49

◆ This country house offers attractive, elegant rooms in a combination of wood and red tones. Extensive wellness centre and theme stays. Generous portions of simple, classic cuisine served in stylish dining rooms.

FOUESNANT – 29 Finistère – 308 G7 – pop. 8 076 – alt. 30 m – ✉ 29170

Brittany 9 **B2**

Paris 555 – Carhaix-Plouguer 69 – Concarneau 11 – Quimper 16 – Quimperlé 39

Office de tourisme, Espace Kernevelech ✆ 02 98 51 18 88, Fax 02 98 56 64 02

de Cornouaille La Forêt-Fouesnant Manoir du Mesmeur, East: 4 km by D 44, ✆ 02 98 56 97 09.

L'Orée du Bois without rest

4 r. Kergoadig – ✆ 02 98 56 00 06 – hotel.loreedubois@wanadoo.fr – Fax 02 98 56 14 17

15 rm – €30 €57, €6,50

♦ Guests to this stone house with small, simple rooms are met with an unpretentious family welcome. Depending on the season, breakfast is served in the garden or in a nautically inspired room.

in Cap Coz 2,5 km Southeast by secondary road – ✉ 29170 Fouesnant

Mona Lisa

plage du Cap Coz – ✆ 02 98 51 18 10 – resa-capcoz@monalisahotels.com – Fax 02 98 56 03 40 – Open mid March-October

49 rm – €67/128 €67/128, €11 – ½ P €65/95 – **Rest** – Menu €23 – Carte €19/53

♦ Renovated building by the beach with cheerful rooms, some providing balconies with a panoramic view (2nd floor). The communal areas are modern and bright. A dining room with a veranda opening onto the foreshore.

De la Pointe du Cap Coz sea and port, rest, rest,

153 av. de la Pointe – ✆ 02 98 56 01 63 – bienvenue@hotel-capcoz.com – Fax 02 98 56 53 20 – Closed 24-29 November, 1st January-12 February and Sunday dinner 1st October-15 March

16 rm – €57/60 €66/95, €9,50 – ½ P €71/86

Rest – *(closed Sunday dinner and Monday lunch from 15 September to 15 June and Wednesday)* Menu €25/47 – Carte €45/79

♦ This hotel sits on the sandy coast of Cap Coz. The functional rooms enjoy views over the harbour or the sea. Good-quality fish and seafood with a contemporary twist served in the pleasant restaurant.

Belle-Vue

30 descente Belle-Vue – ✆ 02 98 56 00 33 – hotel-belle-vue@wanadoo.fr – Fax 02 98 51 60 85 – Open 1st March-31 October

16 rm – €52/62 €60/90, €8,50 – ½ P €57/66 – **Rest** – *(open 15 March-31 October and closed Monday)* Menu €22/40 – Carte €29/45

♦ Family guesthouse overlooking the bay of La Forêt. Small rooms, most with views of the ocean. Simple decor and unpretentious cuisine in the restaurant. In summer, panoramic terrace.

in la Pointe de Mousterlin 6 km Southwest by D 145 and D 134 – ✉ 29170 Fouesnant

De la Pointe de Mousterlin rest, rest,

108 rte de la Pointe – ✆ 02 98 56 04 12 – hoteldelapointe@wanadoo.fr – Fax 02 98 56 61 02 – Closed 10 February-3 March, Tuesday lunch, Sunday dinner and Monday October-15 April

48 rm – €55/76 €74/142, €11 – ½ P €74/93 – **Rest** – Menu €22/37 – Carte €46/59

♦ A seaside complex at the end of the headland. Practical, spacious rooms in three buildings facing the garden. Good leisure facilities. Two dining rooms, one a veranda. Regional and seafood cuisine.

FOUGÈRES – 35 Ille-et-Vilaine – 309 O4 – pop. 21 779 – alt. 115 m – ✉ 35300

Brittany 10 **D2**

Paris 326 – Avranches 44 – Laval 53 – Le Mans 132 – Rennes 52 – St-Malo 80

Office de tourisme, 2, rue Nationale ✆ 02 99 94 12 20, Fax 02 99 94 77 30

Château ★★ - St-Sulpice church ★ - Public garden ★: ★ - Stained-glass windows ★ of St-Léonard church - Rue Nationale ★.

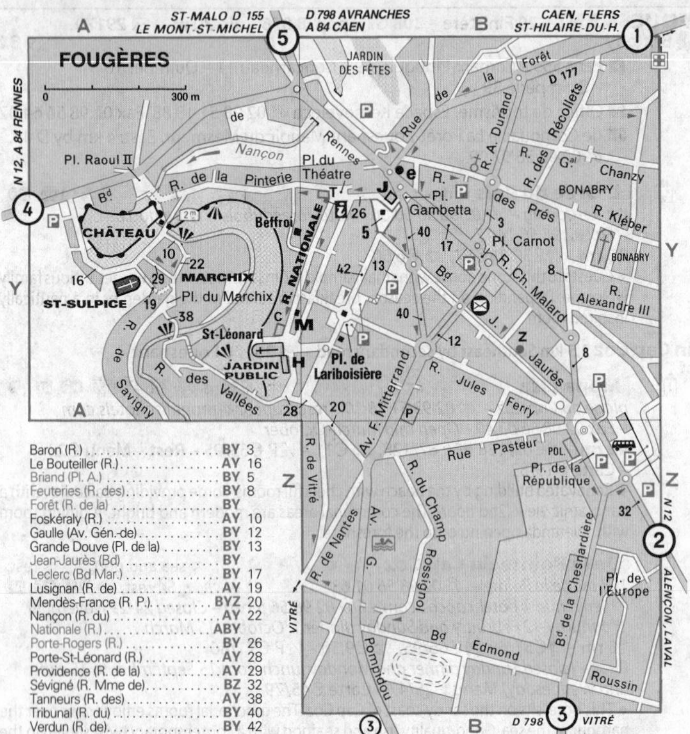

Les Voyageurs without rest

– ✆ 02 99 99 08 20 – hotel-voyageurs-fougeres@wanadoo.fr – Fax 02 99 99 99 04
– Closed 23 December-5 January and Saturday in January BY **e**

37 rm – 🛉€ 43/56 🛉🛉€ 52/58, ☕ € 9

◆ A century-old hotel in the heart of the upper town. Most of the refurbished rooms sport a bright, colourful and personal touch.

Haute Sève

37 bd J. Jaurès – ✆ 02 99 94 23 39 – Closed 20 July-20 August, February holidays, Sunday dinner and Monday BY **z**

Rest – Menu € 20 bi, € 25/43

◆ Beyond the attractive half-timbered facade is a dining room recently refurbished in a contemporary spirit. Updated regional cuisine with market produce.

FOUGEROLLES – 70 Haute-Saône – 314 G5 – pop. 3 967 – alt. 311 m – ✉ 70220

Burgundy-Jura 17 **C1**

Paris 374 – Épinal 49 – Luxeuil-les-Bains 10 – Remiremont 25 – Vesoul 43

Office de tourisme, 1, rue de la Gare ✆ 03 84 49 12 91, Fax 03 84 49 12 91

Ecomusée du Pays de la Cerise et de la Distillation (Cherry and distillation museum of man and the environment)★.

Au Père Rota

8 Grande Rue – ✆ 03 84 49 12 11 – jean-pierre-kuentz@wanadoo.fr
– Fax 03 84 49 14 51 – Closed 1st-5 September, 5-29 January, Sunday dinner, Tuesday dinner and Monday

Rest – Menu (€ 20), € 25 (weekdays)/67 – Carte € 43/78

◆ Set up in the capital of kirsch, this elegant and quiet restaurant offers delicious traditional cuisine. A good wine list with numerous vintage wines.

LA FOUILLOUSE – 42 Loire – **327** E7 – see St-Étienne

FOULBEC – 27 Eure – **304** C5 – see Conteville

FOURAS – 17 Charente-Maritime – **324** D4 – pop. 3 835 – alt. 5 m – Casino – ✉ 17450 Atlantic Coast 38 **A2**

Paris 485 – Châtelaillon-Plage 18 – Rochefort 15 – La Rochelle 34

Office de tourisme, avenue du Bois Vert ✆ 05 46 84 60 69, Fax 05 46 84 28 04

Keep ✳★.

Grand Hôtel des Bains without rest VISA

15 r. Gén. Bruncher – ✆ 05 46 84 03 44 – hoteldesbains@wanadoo.fr – Fax 05 46 84 58 26 – Open 15 March-31 October

31 rm – €43/67 €45/72, €7

◆ The sea view from room N° 1 is undoubtedly the star feature of this old post house. The others overlook the road (double-glazing) or flowered patio, where breakfast is served in summer.

FOURCÈS – 32 Gers – **336** D6 – pop. 277 – alt. 76 m – ✉ 32250 Languedoc-Roussillon-Tarn Gorges 28 **A2**

Paris 728 – Agen 53 – Tonneins 57 – Toulouse 130

Syndicat d'initiative, le Village ✆ 05 62 29 50 96, Fax 05 62 29 50 96

Château de Fourcès rest, VISA

– ✆ 05 62 29 49 53 – contact@chateau-fources.com – Fax 05 62 29 50 59 – Open 1st March-30 November

18 rm – €100/210 €135/250, €14 – ½ P €100/195

Rest – *(closed Thursday March-June, Wednesday and lunch except Sunday)* Menu €29/47 – Carte €37/54

◆ Located in one of the most beautiful villages in France, this medieval castle has nice rooms housed in towers, all with a personal touch. Small cosy lounges. Park and river. Warm and elegant dining room, local cuisine served with a modern touch.

FOURGES – 27 Eure – **304** J7 – pop. 772 – alt. 14 m – ✉ 27630 33 **D2**

Paris 74 – Les Andelys 26 – Évreux 47 – Mantes-la-Jolie 23 – Rouen 75 – Vernon 14

Le Moulin de Fourges VISA

– ✆ 02 32 52 12 12 – info@moulin-de-fourges.com – Fax 02 32 52 92 56 – Open 1st April-31 October and closed Sunday dinner and Monday

Rest – Menu €32/55 – Carte €42/75

◆ Old mill by the Epte which Monet would undoubtedly have liked when he visited from neighbouring Giverny; no white water lilies but a pleasant country setting. Traditional fare.

FOURMIES – 59 Nord – **302** M7 – pop. 13 867 – alt. 200 m – ✉ 59610 Northern France and the Paris Region 31 **D3**

Paris 214 – Avesnes-sur-Helpe 16 – Charleroi 60 – Hirson 14 – Lille 115 – St-Quentin 65

Office de tourisme, 20, rue Jean Jaurès ✆ 03 27 59 69 97, Fax 03 27 57 30 44

Musée du textile et de la vie sociale★.

in Étangs-des-Moines 2 km East by D 964 and secondary road – ✉ 59610 Fourmies

Ibis without rest VISA

– ✆ 03 27 60 21 54 – hotelibisfourmies@orange.fr – Fax 03 27 57 40 44

31 rm – €50/58 €50/58, €7,50

◆ Modern hotel on the edge of a beautiful forest of oaks, perfect for making the most of the quiet, bucolic watery setting. Practical well-kept rooms.

Auberge des Étangs des Moines VISA

– ✆ 03 27 60 02 62 – Fax 03 27 60 10 25 – Closed 1st-21 August, February holidays, Saturday lunch, Sunday dinner and Monday except holidays

Rest – Menu €18 (weekdays)/38 – Carte €32/51

◆ This former lakeside open-air café is a delight with its friendly atmosphere, terrace, and pleasant rustic dining room complete with revamped veranda. Traditional dishes.

LA FOUX D'ALLOS – 04 Alpes-de-Haute-Provence – 334 H7 – see Allos

FRANCESCAS – 47 Lot-et-Garonne – 336 E5 – pop. 714 – alt. 109 m – ✉ 47600

Paris 720 – Agen 28 – Condom 18 – Nérac 14 – Toulouse 134 4 **C2**

Le Relais de la Hire

11 r. Porte-Neuve – ✆ 05 53 65 41 59 – la.hire@wanadoo.fr – Closed 27 October-4 November, Sunday dinner, Wednesday dinner and Monday

Rest – *(pre-book)* Menu (€ 14,50 bi), € 20/56 – Carte € 45/56

◆ A comfortable classical decor (sky blue ceiling), summer terrace and intelligently personalised regional fare are what set this attractive 18C abode apart.

FRANCUEIL – 37 Indre-et-Loire – 317 P5 – pop. 1 214 – alt. 90 m – ✉ 37150

11 **A1**

Paris 249 – Orléans 124 – Tours 38 – Blois 58 – Joué-lès-Tours 37

Le Moulin de Francueil

28 r. du Moulin-Neuf, Loches road – ✆ 02 47 23 93 44 – moulinfrancueil@aol.com

5 rm – †€ 102 ††€ 110/130 – **Table d'hôte** – Menu € 25 bi

◆ A few minutes from Chenonceau, the bucolic setting of this tasteful 19C house is ideal for relaxation. Classic style rooms with personal touches.

FRANQUEVILLE-ST-PIERRE – 76 Seine-Maritime – 304 H5 – see Rouen

FRÉHEL – 22 Côtes-d'Armor – 309 H3 – pop. 2 047 – alt. 72 m – Casino – ✉ 22240

10 **C1**

Paris 433 – Dinan 38 – Lamballe 28 – St-Brieuc 40 – St-Cast-le-Guildo 15 – St-Malo 36

Office de tourisme, place de Chambly ✆ 02 96 41 53 81, Fax 02 96 41 59 46

✻★★★.

Fort La Latte★★: site★★, ✻★★ Southeast: 5 km.

Le Victorine

pl. Chambly – ✆ 02 96 41 55 55 – Fax 02 96 41 55 55 – Closed 28 October-12 November, 10-22 February, Sunday dinner and Monday except 14 July-30 August

Rest – Menu € 15 (weekday lunch)/29 – Carte € 23/37

◆ A family restaurant located on the village square. Traditional cuisine using fresh market produce is served in the simply decorated dining area or on the terrace.

LA FREISSINOUSE – 05 Hautes-Alpes – 334 E5 – see Gap

FRÉJUS – 83 Var – 340 P5 – pop. 46 801 – alt. 20 m – ✉ 83600 French Riviera

Paris 868 – Cannes 40 – Draguignan 31 – Hyères 90 – Nice 66 41 **C3**

✆ 3635 (0,34 €/mn)

Office de tourisme, 325, rue Jean Jaurès ✆ 04 94 51 83 83, Fax 04 94 51 00 26

de Roquebrune Roquebrune-sur-Argens Quartier des Planes, West: 6 km by D 8, ✆ 04 94 19 60 35 ;

de Valescure Saint-Raphaël Route des golfs, Northeast: 8 km, ✆ 04 94 82 40 46.

Groupe épiscopal★★ : baptistry★★, cloister★, cathedral★ - Roman town★ A : amphitheatre★ - Parc zoologique (zoo)★ North: 5 km by ③.

Plans on next page

L'Aréna

rm, rm,

145 r. Gén. de Gaulle – ✆ 04 94 17 09 40 – info@arena-hotel.com – Fax 04 94 52 01 52 – Closed 1st December-5 January C **r**

36 rm – †€ 70/100 ††€ 90/160, € 14 – ½ P € 80/120 – **Rest** – *(closed Saturday lunch and Monday)* Menu € 26 (weekday lunch)/59 – Carte € 48/76

◆ Napoleon stayed in this charming Provençal house on his way back from Egypt. Rooms open onto a patio and herb garden. Pleasant swimming-pool and friendly service. Sunny decor and Provençal menu.

FRÉJUS

Agachon (Av. de l') . . . . **A** 2
Alger (Bd) . . . . **B** 5
Brosset (Av. du Gén.) . . . . . **AB** 13
Carrara (R. Jean) . . . . **A** 16
Decuers (Bd S.) . . . . **A** 23
Donnadieu (R.) . . . . **B** 24
Einaudi (R. Albert) . . . . **A** 25
Europe (Av. de l') . . . . **A** 26
Fabre (Av. Hippolyte) . . . . **B** 27
Garros (R. Roland) . . . . **B** 32
Libération (Bd de la) . . . . **B** 40
Papin (R. Denis) . . . . **B** 46
Triberg (R. de) . . . . **A** 53
Verdun (Av. de) . . . . **A** 56
Victor-Hugo (Av.) . . . . **B** 60
XVe-Corps (Av. du) . . . . **A** 62

ST-RAPHAËL

Coty (Promenade René) . . . . **B** 20
Gaulle (Av. du Gén.-de) . . . . . **B** 33
Leclerc (Av. Mar.) . . . . **B** 39
Mimosas (Bd des) . . . . **B** 43
Myrtes (Av. des) . . . . **B** 45
Poincaré (Av. Raymond) . . . . **B** 47
Rivière (Av. Théodore) . . . . . . **B** 51
Valescure (Av. de) . . . . **B** 54

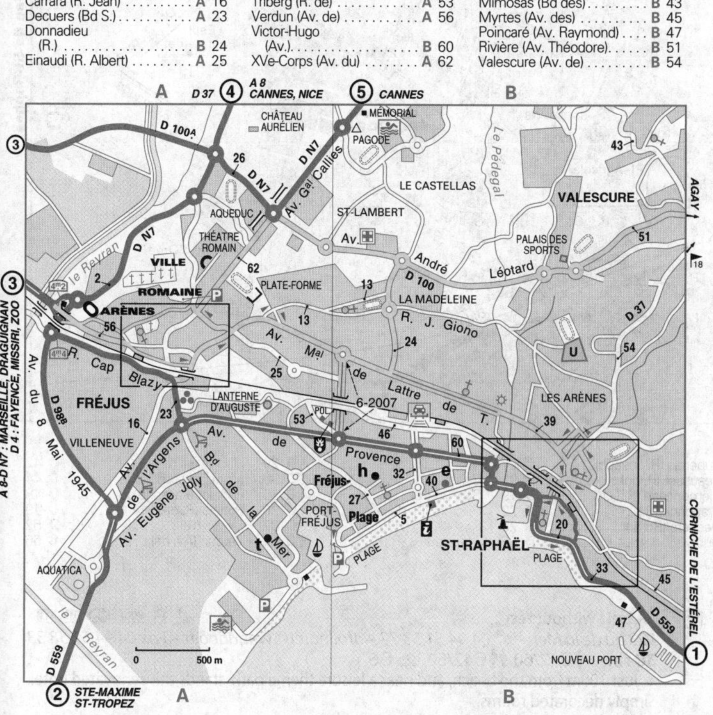

L'Amandier

19 r. Marc-Antoine Desaugiers – ✆ 04 94 53 48 77
– Closed 26 October-12 November, 1st-14 January, Monday lunch, Wednesday lunch and Sunday
Rest – Menu (€ 19), € 23/36 – Carte € 29/43 — D **v**
◆ Restaurant situated on a pedestrianised street near the town hall. Charming service and good, well-prepared modern cuisine at reasonable prices.

Les Potiers

135 r. Potiers – ✆ 04 94 51 33 74
– Closed 1st-21 December, lunch in July-August, Wednesday lunch and Tuesday from September to June — C **s**
Rest – *(number of covers limited, pre-book)* Menu € 24/36
◆ Pleasant rustic atmosphere at this small restaurant, where they don't work with clay, but rather prepare delicious modern cuisine with Provençal touches.

in Fréjus-Plage AB – ✉ 83600 Fréjus

L'Oasis without rest

imp. Charcot – ✆ 04 94 51 50 44 – info@hotel-oasis.net – Fax 04 94 53 01 04
– Open 1st February-12 November — B **h**
27 rm – € 38/55 € 48/68, € 7
◆ Built in the 1950s, this hotel stands back from the promenade, nestling in a quiet street in a wealthy neighbourhood. Family atmosphere. Most of the rooms refurbished. Pergola in the middle of the pine trees.

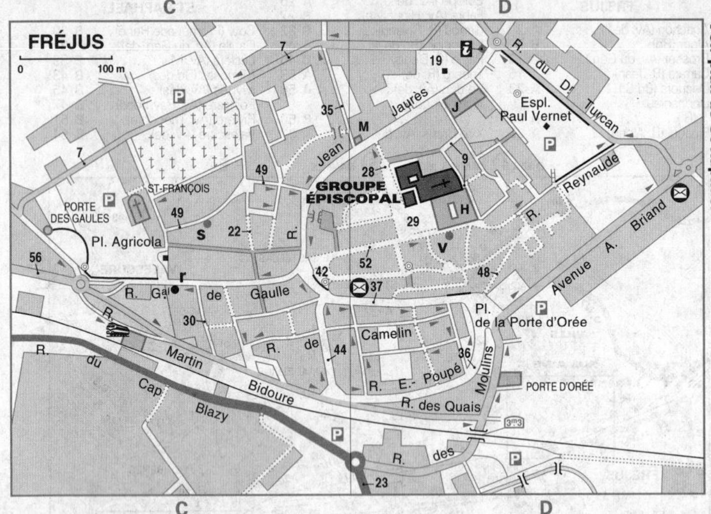

Atoll without rest — A/C, P, VISA, MC, AE, DC

923 bd de la Mer – ✆ 04 94 51 53 77 – atollhotel@wanadoo.fr – Fax 04 94 51 58 33

30 rm – †€ 42/60 ††€ 42/60, ☕ € 6 — A **t**

◆ Just 100m from the beach, and near a leisure theme park, stands this renovated hotel. Simply decorated rooms.

Le Mérou Ardent — terrace, A/C, VISA, MC

157 bd la Libération – ✆ 04 94 17 30 58 – patrickdelpierre@wanadoo.fr – Fax 04 94 17 33 79 – Closed 4-12 June, 19 November-18 December, Saturday lunch, Monday lunch and Thursday lunch in season, Wednesday and Thursday off season

Rest – Menu € 16/36 – Carte € 21/46 — B **e**

◆ A small restaurant with a nautical decor, located on the beachfront boulevard. Excellent service, fish specialities.

FREMIFONTAINE – 88 Vosges – 314 I3 – see Grandvillers

LE FRENEY-D'OISANS – 38 Isère – 333 J7 – pop. 221 – alt. 926 m – ✉ 38142

Paris 626 – Bourg-d'Oisans 12 – La Grave 16 – Grenoble 64 — 45 **C2**

Syndicat d'initiative, Le Village ✆ 04 76 80 05 82, Fax 04 76 80 05 82

Barrage du Chambon★★ Southeast: 2 km - Gorges de l'Infernet★ Southwest: 2 km, **French Alps.**

in Mizoën Northeast: 4 km by N 91 and D 1091 – pop. 163 – alt. 1 100 m – ✉ 38142

Panoramique — mountain and valley, P, VISA, MC, AE, DC

rte des Aymes – ✆ 04 76 80 06 25 – info@hotel-panoramique.com – Fax 04 76 80 25 12 – Open 2 May-21 September and 20 December-31 March

9 rm – †€ 55/65 ††€ 65/95, ☕ € 10 – ½ P € 55/85 – **Rest** – *(dinner only except weekend and holidays)* Menu (€ 17), € 23/27 – Carte € 24/30

◆ Apart from its lovely surroundings, this flower-decked chalet (for non-smokers only) offers a charming welcome, is extremely well kept and has amenities such as a south-facing solarium and sauna. Panoramic dining room and pleasant summer terrace facing the peaks.

LE FRENZ – 68 Haut-Rhin – 315 F9 – see Kruth

FRESNAY-EN-RETZ – 44 Loire-Atlantique – 316 E5 – pop. 855 – alt. 15 m – ✉ 44580 34 **A2**

▶ Paris 425 – Nantes 40 – La Roche-sur-Yon 64 – Saint-Nazaire 51

Le Colvert

– ✆ 02 40 21 46 79 – Fax 02 40 21 95 99 – *Closed 10 August-6 September, Sunday dinner, Tuesday dinner, Wednesday dinner and Monday*

Rest – Menu (€ 14), € 17 (weekday lunch), € 26/40 – Carte € 41/63

◆ A rustic, original dining room with exposed timbers and a lobster tank. Modern cuisine is served in this old house in the heart of the village.

FRESNICOURT – 62 Pas-de-Calais – 301 I5 – pop. 880 – alt. 114 m – ✉ 62150 30 **B2**

▶ Paris 218 – Lille 62 – Arras 24 – Villeneuve-d'Ascq 61 – Douai 46

Auberge du Donjon

28 r. Léo-Lagrange – ✆ 03 21 27 93 76 – *contact@auberge-donjon.com* – *Fax 03 21 26 20 71* – *Closed 30 July-26 August, 18-24 February, Sunday dinner, Monday and Tuesday*

Rest – Menu (€ 18), € 23/56 – Carte € 36/50

◆ Hearty portions of delicious cuisine served in a neo-rustic, Flemish-style restaurant. Bruegelesque wall paintings in the dining rooms. Meat barbecued in the open fireplace.

LE FRET – 29 Finistère – 308 D5 – see Crozon

FRICHEMESNIL – 76 Seine-Maritime – 304 G4 – see Clères

FROENINGEN – 68 Haut-Rhin – 315 H10 – see Mulhouse

FROIDETERRE – 70 Haute-Saône – 314 H6 – see Lure

FRONCLES-BUXIERES – 52 Haute-Marne – 313 K4 – pop. 1 760 – alt. 226 m – ✉ 52320 14 **C3**

▶ Paris 282 – Bar-sur-Aube 41 – Chaumont 28 – Neufchâteau 52 – Saint-Dizier 52

Au Château

Parc d'Activités – ✆ 03 25 02 93 84 – *didier.pougeoise@wanadoo.fr* – *Closed Christmas holidays, Saturday lunch and Sunday dinner*

Rest – Menu € 13 (weekday lunch), € 27/42 – Carte € 33/49

◆ Large, elegant house with small lounges used as dining rooms and a vast covered terrace overlooking the park. Modern, well-presented food.

FRONTIGNAN – 34 Hérault – 339 H8 – pop. 19 145 – alt. 2 m – ✉ 34110 Languedoc-Roussillon-Tarn Gorges 23 **C2**

▶ Paris 775 – Lodève 59 – Montpellier 26 – Sète 10

Montpellier road 4 km northeast on D 612– ✉ 34110 Frontignan

Hôtellerie de Balajan rest,

41 rte de Montpellier – ✆ 04 67 48 13 99 – *hotel.balajan@wanadoo.fr* – *Fax 04 67 43 06 62* – *Closed 24 December-4 January, February and Sunday dinner from November to March*

18 rm – †€ 68/70 ††€ 70/103, ☐ € 10 – ½ P € 60/71 – **Rest** – *(closed Sunday dinner off season, Saturday lunch and Monday lunch)* Menu (€ 17), € 27/53 – Carte € 34/63

◆ Vineyards producing the famous Muscat surround the hotel. Discreet but recently decorated rooms. The Gardiole mountains serve as a backdrop. Flower-decked tables add a friendly feel to this restaurant. Mediterranean inspired cuisine is served and there is a cosy sitting room.

FRONTIGNAN-DE-COMMINGES – 31 Haute-Garonne – pop. 73 – alt. 450 m – ✉ 31510
28 **B3**

Paris 796 – Toulouse 120 – Saint-Gaudens 31 – Bagnères-de-Bigorre 70 – Saint-Girons 77

Le Relais des Frontignes

au village, via D 33^A – ✆ 05 61 79 61 67 – yann.debruycker@wanadoo.fr – Fax 05 61 79 61 67

5 rm – €50 €60 – **Table d'hôte** – Menu €20

◆ The owner of this 19C house is more than happy to take guests up into the mountains. Attractive themed bedrooms (Asia, Europe, Africa) and large park with mountain stream.

FRONTONAS – 38 Isère – 333 E4 – pop. 1 714 – alt. 260 m – ✉ 38290
44 **B2**

Paris 495 – Ambérieu-en-Bugey 44 – Lyon 34 – La Tour-du-Pin 26 – Vienne 35

Auberge du Ru

VISA

Le Bergeron-Les-Quatre-Vies – ✆ 04 74 94 25 71 – info@aubergeduru.fr – Fax 04 74 94 25 71 – Closed 18 February-4 March, 14 July-5 August, Sunday dinner, Monday and Tuesday

Rest – Menu €26/34

◆ Country guesthouse in the heart of a hamlet. Smart dining room decorated with farm implements. Modern cuisine, menu according to daily market produce.

FUISSÉ – 71 Saône-et-Loire – 320 I12 – pop. 317 – alt. 290 m – ✉ 71960

Burgundy-Jura
8 **C3**

Paris 401 – Charolles 54 – Chauffailles 52 – Mâcon 9 – Villefranche-sur-Saône 48

Au Pouilly Fuissé

VISA AE

– ✆ 03 85 35 60 68 – Fax 03 85 35 60 68 – Closed Monday dinner, Tuesday dinner and Wednesday from October to March and Sunday dinner

Rest – Menu €20 (weekday lunch), €27/47 – Carte €33/50

◆ Family guesthouse named after the local wine, served to accompany the traditional cuisine. Veranda/dining room and shaded terrace.

LA FUSTE – 04 Alpes-de-Haute-Provence – 334 D10 – see Manosque

FUTEAU – 55 Meuse – 307 B4 – see Ste-Menehould (51 Marne)

FUVEAU – 13 Bouches-du-Rhône – 340 I5 – pop. 7 509 – alt. 283 m – ✉ 13710
40 **B3**

Paris 765 – Marseille 36 – Brignoles 53 – Manosque 73

Office de tourisme, cours Victor Leydet ✆ 04 42 50 49 77

Mona Lisa

rm, VISA AE

D 6, (opposite the Château l'Arc Golf Course) – ✆ 04 42 68 19 19 – heb-ste-victoire@monalisahotels.com – Fax 04 42 68 19 18

81 rm – €125 €125, €11 – ½ P €110 – **Rest** – Menu €26 bi (weekdays), €37 € bi/90 bi – Carte approx. €29

◆ A modern style building next to a golf course. Beige monochromes and painted wood furniture in the relaxing and well-designed rooms. High speed internet connection. Sauna and gym. Bright restaurant with bay windows opening onto a terrace and swimming pool.

GABRIAC – 12 Aveyron – 338 I4 – pop. 446 – alt. 580 m – ✉ 12340
29 **D1**

Paris 605 – Espalion 13 – Mende 88 – Rodez 27 – Sévérac-le-Château 35

Bouloc with rm

VISA

– ✆ 05 65 44 92 89 – franckbouloc@wanadoo.fr – Fax 05 65 48 86 74 – Closed 5-19 March, 25 June-2 July, 1st-22 October, Wednesday except dinner in July-August and Tuesday dinner from September to June

11 rm – €40/44 €49/53, €7 – ½ P €49/50 – **Rest** – Menu (€12 bi), €17 (weekdays)/36 – Carte €26/36

◆ This regional house has been in the same family for six generations. Serves many Rouergue specialities. New dining room/veranda. Rooms have yet to be renovated.

GAGNY – 93 Seine-Saint-Denis – 305 G7 – 101 18 – see Paris, Area

GAILLAC – 81 Tarn – 338 D7 – pop. 11 073 – alt. 143 m – ✉ 81600
Languedoc-Roussillon-Tarn Gorges 29 **C2**

Paris 672 – Albi 26 – Cahors 89 – Castres 52 – Montauban 50 – Toulouse 58

Syndicat d'initiative, Abbaye Saint-Michel ☎ 05 63 57 14 65, Fax 05 63 57 61 37

La Verrerie
rm, rest, rest, VISA

r. Égalité – ☎ 05 63 57 32 77 – contact@la-verrerie.com – Fax 05 63 57 32 27 – Closed 16-22 February and 24-31 December

14 rm – €55/70 €55/85, €11 – **Rest** – *(closed Saturday lunch, Sunday dinner and Friday)* Menu €15 bi (weekday lunch), €25/32 – Carte €38/59

◆ A small museum tells the past of this 200-year-old building that was once a glassmaker's then a pasta factory. Modern functional rooms; chose one overlooking the park (with a beautiful bamboo grove). Bright dining room extended by a pleasant terrace overlooking the greenery.

Les Sarments
VISA

27 r. Cabrol, behind St. Michel abbey – ☎ 05 63 57 62 61 – sarments.les2@orange.fr – Fax 05 63 57 62 61 – Closed 21 December-11 January, 23 February-7 March, Tuesday dinner October-February, Sunday dinner, Wednesday dinner and Monday

Rest – *(number of covers limited, pre-book)* Menu €25 (weekdays)/35 – Carte approx. €39

◆ Explore Gaillac wines at this medieval wine and spirits house next to the Maison des Vins. Pretty vaulted restaurant and nice paintings. Modern menu and excellent wines served.

La Table du Sommelier
VISA

34 pl.du Griffoul – ☎ 05 63 81 20 10 – Fax 05 63 81 20 10 – Closed Sunday and Monday

Rest – Menu €13/35 bi

◆ With such a name, there is no doubt that Bacchus is the guest star of this bistro-shop. Great wine list served by the glass or bottle. Market cuisine served.

GAILLAN-EN-MÉDOC – 33 Gironde – 335 F3 – see Lesparre-Médoc

GAILLON – 27 Eure – 304 I7 – pop. 6 861 – alt. 15 m – ✉ 27600 Normandy

Paris 94 – Les Andelys 13 – Rouen 48 – Évreux 25 – Vernon 15 33 **D2**

Office de tourisme, 4, place Aristide Briand ☎ 02 32 53 08 25

de Gaillon Les Artaignes, East: 1 km by D 515, ☎ 02 32 53 89 40.

in Vieux-Villez West: 4 km by D 6015 – pop. 160 – alt. 125 m – ✉ 27600

Château Corneille
VISA

– ☎ 02 32 77 44 77 – chateau-corneille@wanadoo.fr – Fax 02 32 77 48 79

20 rm – €84 €100/120, €12 – ½ P €128

Rest *Closerie* – *☎ 02 32 77 42 97 (closed 15-31 August, Saturday lunch, Sunday dinner and Monday)* Menu €20 (weekday lunch), €32/45 – Carte €26/58

◆ This welcoming building, nestling in a small park, has comfortable, recently redecorated rooms. Wrought-iron chairs, beams, bricks and a fireplace form the decor for this restaurant in a converted sheepfold.

GALÉRIA – 2B Haute-Corse – 345 A5 – see Corse

GALLARGUES-LE-MONTUEUX – 30 Gard – 339 J6 – pop. 2 957 – alt. 55 m – ✉ 30660
23 **C2**

Paris 735 – Montpellier 36 – Nîmes 26 – Arles 51 – Alès 68

Orchidéa
VISA

9 pl. Coudoulié – ☎ 04 66 73 34 07 – orchidea30@orange.fr – Closed Sunday

Rest – Menu €18 bi (lunch)/36

◆ Restaurant with a *table d'hôte* feel, friendly and casual, with *Pays Basque, Camargue* and *Réunion* influenced cuisine. Original decor.

GAMBAIS – 78 Yvelines – 311 G3 – pop. 2 064 – alt. 119 m – ✉ 78950 18 A2

Paris 55 – Dreux 27 – Mantes-la-Jolie 32 – Rambouillet 22 – Versailles 38

XX **Auberge du Clos St-Pierre**

2 bis r. Goupigny – ✆ 01 34 87 10 55 – clossaintpierre@wanadoo.fr – Fax 01 34 87 03 88 – Closed 3-26 August, Sunday dinner, Tuesday dinner and Monday

Rest – Menu € 37/55 – Carte € 53/78

◆ A guesthouse with a red façade serving traditional cuisine in a modern dining area or on the terrace, shaded by a linden tree.

GAN – 64 Pyrénées-Atlantiques – 342 J5 – pop. 4 971 – alt. 210 m – ✉ 64290 3 B3

Paris 786 – Pau 10 – Arudy 17 – Lourdes 39 – Oloron-Ste-Marie 26

XX **Hostellerie L'Horizon** with rm

chemin Mesplet – ✆ 05 59 21 58 93 – eytpierre-hotelresto@wanadoo.fr – Fax 05 59 21 71 80 – Closed 2 January-13 February

10 rm – €55/90 €65/90, €8 – ½ P €80/100 – **Rest** – *(closed Sunday evening and Monday)* Menu € 15, € 28/68 bi – Carte € 47/57

◆ The veranda-dining room and fine terrace overlook a pleasant garden with palm trees; view of the Pyrenees in the distance in fine weather. Stylish rooms.

GANNAT – Allier – 326 G6 – pop. 5 838 – alt. 345 m – ✉ 03800

Auvergne 5 B1

Paris 383 – Clermont-Ferrand 49 – Montluçon 78 – Moulins 58 – Vichy 20

Office de tourisme, 11, place Hennequin ✆ 04 70 90 17 78, Fax 04 70 90 19 45

Gospel book★ au musée municipal (château) [at the town museum (castle)].

XX **Le Frégénie**

4 r. des Frères-Bruneau – ✆ 04 70 90 04 65 – Fax 04 70 90 04 65 – Closed 18 August-7 September, 26 December-4 January, Sunday dinner and Monday dinner

Rest – Menu € 23/43 – Carte € 32/52

◆ Situated in a quiet road, this impressive restaurant has two dining rooms decorated in crisp, classical style. Friendly service and contemporary cuisine.

GAP Ⓟ – 05 Hautes-Alpes – 334 E5 – pop. 36 262 – alt. 735 m – ✉ 05000

French Alps 41 C1

Paris 665 – Avignon 209 – Grenoble 103 – Sisteron 52 – Valence 158

Office de tourisme, 2a, cours Frédéric Mistral ✆ 04 92 52 56 56, Fax 04 92 52 56 57

Alpes Provence Gap Bayard Station Gap Bayard, by Grenoble road: 7 km, ✆ 04 92 50 16 83.

Old town ★ - Musée départemental★.

Plan on next page

Le Clos

via ① Grenoble road and private path – ✆ 04 92 51 37 04 – leclos@voila.fr – Fax 04 92 52 41 06 – Closed 20 October-24 November, Monday (except hotel) and Sunday dinner except July-August

28 rm – €47 €51/54, €8,50 – ½ P €49 – **Rest** – Menu € 18/31

◆ This hotel on the outskirts of Gap has functional rooms, half with balconies. Trees in the garden and games for children. Large, non-smoking, rustic dining room with a veranda and a summer terrace.

Kyriad without rest

via ③: 2.5 km (near the swimming pool), rte Sisteron – ✆ 04 92 51 57 82 – kyriad.gap@wanadoo.fr – Fax 04 92 51 56 52

26 rm – €59/70 €59/70, €7,50

◆ At the entrance to Gap, on the Route Napoléon, a hotel with fresh, spacious rooms laid out around a garden where breakfast is served in fine weather.

GAP

Balmens (R.) . . . . **Z** 3	Euzières (Pl. Frédéric) . . . . **Z** 7	Mazel (R. du) . . . . **Z** 15
Carnot (R.) . . . . **Z** 4	Eymar (R. Jean) . . . . **Y** 8	Moreau (R. E.) . . . . **Z** 16
Curie (Bd P. et M.) . . . . **Y** 5	Faure-du-Serre (R.) . . . . **Y** 9	Révelly (Pl. du) . . . . **Y** 17
Dumont (Av. du Cdt) . . . . **Y** 6	France (R. de) . . . . **Y** 10	Roux (R. Colonel) . . . . **Z** 19
	Jean-Jaurès (Av.) . . . . **Z** 12	St-Arnoux (Pl.) . . . . **Z** 20
	Ladoucette (Cours) . . . . **Y** 13	Valserres (R. de) . . . . **Z** 23
	Libération (Bd de) . . . . **Y** 14	

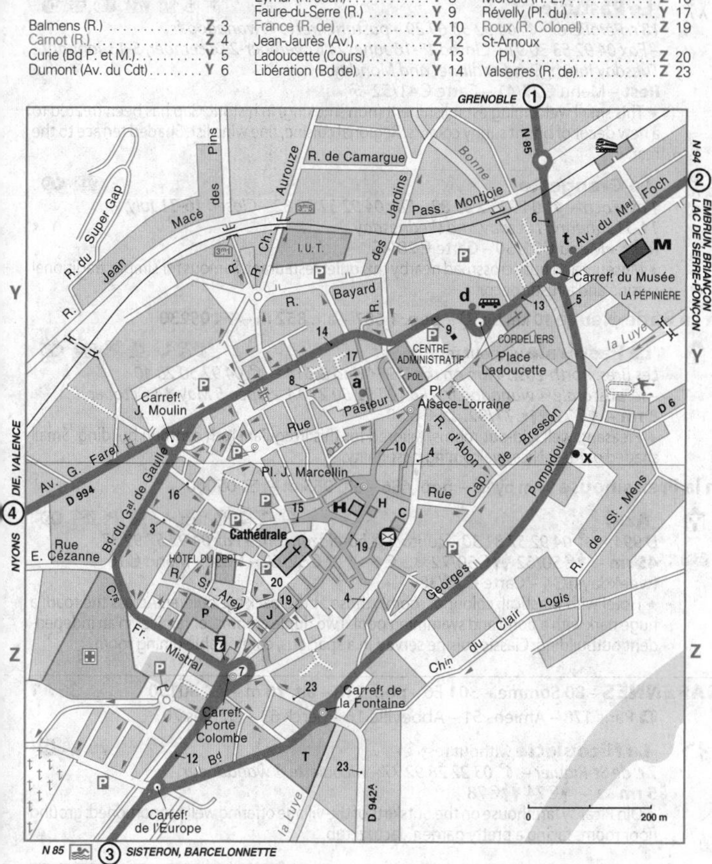

Ibis
rm, VISA AE

5 bd G. Pompidou – ✆ 04 92 53 57 57 – ibisgap@wanadoo.fr
– Fax 04 92 53 38 15 Y **x**

61 rm – †€ 49/71 ††€ 49/71, ☕ € 8
Rest – Menu € 10/17
◆ All the usual features offered by the chain in evidence here, including effective double-glazing. Good seminar area. This Ibis restaurant is well kept, and guests receive a warm welcome. Pastel coloured decor.

XXX Patalain
VISA AE

2 pl. Ladoucette – ✆ 04 92 52 30 83
– sarl-le-patalain@wanadoo.fr – Fax 04 92 52 30 83
– Closed 25 December-15 January, and Sunday Y **d**

Rest – Menu € 36/41
Rest *Bistro du Patalain* – Menu (€ 16), € 19/23
◆ Fine mansion (1890) with a garden and a terrace shaded by wisteria. The traditional cuisine is served in a comfortable, classically designed dining room. A genuine bistro atmosphere with daily specials and regional cuisine displayed on a blackboard.

XX **Le Pasturier**

18 r. Pérolière – ✆ 04 92 53 69 29 – pasturier.resto@wanadoo.fr – Fax 04 92 53 30 91 – Closed 1st-16 June, 24 November-2 December, 5-13 January, Tuesday lunch, Sunday dinner and Monday Y **a**

Rest – Menu € 27/41 – Carte € 41/52

◆ This small welcoming establishment (non smoking) in historic Gap has been treated to a new decor of bright sunny colours. Regional cuisine, fine wine list. Shaded terrace to the rear.

X **La Grangette**

1 av. Foch – ✆ 04 92 52 39 82 – Fax 04 92 52 39 82 – Closed 16-31 July, 14-31 January, Tuesday and Wednesday Y **t**

Rest – Menu € 21/30 – Carte € 28/45

◆ Museum and busy crossroad nearby this quiet restaurant. Famous for simple, traditional cuisine and a rustic decor.

in La Bâtie-Neuve 10 km by ② – pop. 1 687 – alt. 852 m – ✉ 05230

La Pastorale without rest

Les Brès, north-east: 4 Km on the D 214 and D 614 – ✆ 04 92 50 28 40 – la-pastorale@wanadoo.fr – Fax 04 92 50 21 14 – Open 5 May-14 October

8 rm – †€ 77 ††€ 77/92, ☕ € 8,50

◆ Pleasant, well laid-out rooms, tailored for this irregular (16th century) building. Small shaded garden. Nice, welcoming hospitality.

in la Freissinouse 9 km by ④ – pop. 456 – alt. 965 m – ✉ 05000

Azur rest,

D 994 – ✆ 04 92 57 81 30 – contact@hotelazur.com – Fax 04 92 57 92 37

45 rm – †€ 50/62 ††€ 50/72, ☕ € 6 – ½ P € 52/62 – **Rest** – Menu € 16 (weekdays)/34 – Carte € 25/38

◆ Hotel with practical, colourful rooms; those at the back are quieter. Across the road, a huge park with a pond and swimming pool. Two duplex rooms for families in an independent outbuilding. Classic cuisine served in a spacious, comfortable dining room.

GAPENNES – **80 Somme – 301** E6 – **pop. 218 – alt. 76 m – ✉ 80150** 36 **A1**

Paris 178 – Amiens 51 – Abbeville 16 – Berck 63 – Étaples 70

La Nicoulette without rest

7 r. de St-Riquier – ✆ 03 22 28 92 77 – nicoulette@wanadoo.fr

5 rm ☕ – †€ 74 ††€ 78

◆ Old Picardy farmhouse on the outskirts of the village offering well proportioned, ground floor rooms facing a pretty garden. Jacuzzi tub.

GARABIT (VIADUC) – **15 Cantal – 330** H5 – **see Viaduc de Garabit**

LA GARDE – **04 Alpes-de-Haute-Provence – 334** H10 – **see Castellane**

LA GARDE – **48 Lozère – 330** H5 – **see St-Chély-d'Apcher**

LA GARDE-ADHÉMAR – **26 Drôme – 332** B7 – **pop. 1 075 – alt. 178 m – ✉ 26700** Lyon - Rhone Valley 44 **B3**

Paris 624 – Montélimar 24 – Nyons 42 – Pierrelatte 7

Syndicat d'initiative, le village ✆ 04 75 04 40 10

Church ★ - ≤★ from the terrace.

Le Logis de l'Escalin rm, rm, rm,

north: 1 km on the D 572 – ✆ 04 75 04 41 32 – info@lescalin.com – Fax 04 75 04 40 05 – Closed 10-26 January

14 rm – †€ 65/70 ††€ 68/90, ☕ € 12 – ½ P € 71/77 – **Rest** – *(closed Sunday dinner and Monday)* Menu € 25 (weekdays)/61 – Carte € 45/69

◆ Escalin, Baron de la Garde, Ambassador of Francis 1 might have been born in this farm. Rooms have every comfort and a pleasant, colourful decor. A Provençal dining room, warmed by an open fireplace, with a pleasant terrace in the shade of the plane trees.

LA GARDE-GUÉRIN – 48 Lozère – 330 L8 – ✉ 48800
Languedoc-Roussillon-Tarn Gorges 23 **C1**

Paris 610 – Alès 59 – Aubenas 69 – Florac 71 – Langogne 37 – Mende 55

Keep ★ - Belvédère du Chassezac (viewpoint) ★★.

Auberge Régordane

– *04 66 46 82 88 – aubergeregordane@orange.fr – Fax 04 66 46 90 29 – Open 12 April-12 October*

16 rm – €55 €55/66, €8 – ½ P €53/61 – **Rest** – Menu €20/37 – Carte €33/48

◆ Attractive interior with great character in this 16th century house. Located in the heart of a fortified medieval village on the ancient Voie Regordane running between Auvergne and Languedoc. Granite vaults, spruce rustic decor and a pretty terrace lend the restaurant charm.

LA GARENNE-COLOMBES – 92 Hauts-de-Seine – 311 J2 – 101 – see Paris, Area

LA GARETTE – 79 Deux-Sèvres – 322 C7 – ✉ 79270 Sansais Atlantic Coast

Paris 419 – Fontenay-le Comte 28 – Niort 12 – La Rochelle 60 – St-Jean-d'Angély 59 38 **B2**

Les Mangeux de Lumas

78 r. des Gravées, pedestrian access – 05 49 35 93 42 – Fax 05 49 35 82 89 – Closed 24-30 November, 5-23 January, Monday dinner, Wednesday dinner and Tuesday except July-August

Rest – Menu €18/43 – Carte €38/59

◆ Typical of the Poitiers Marais, the double entrance to the house leads you onto the terraces: street side or conch side. Small snails or "lumas" specialities. Summer grill.

GARIDECH – 31 Haute-Garonne – 343 H2 – pop. 954 – alt. 180 m – ✉ 31380 29 **C2**

Paris 687 – Toulouse 21 – Albi 58 – Auch 96

Le Club

rte d'Albi – 05 61 84 20 23 – rest-leclub@wanadoo.fr – Fax 05 61 84 43 21 – Closed 18 August-1st September, 16-22 February, Saturday lunch, Sunday dinner and Monday

Rest – Menu €17 (weekday lunch), €27/42 – Carte €42/53

◆ Family house in a garden set back from the main road. Charming rustic dining room. Terrace and veranda overlooking the countryside. Traditional menu.

GARNACHE – 85 Vendée – 316 F6 – see Challans

GARONS – 30 Gard – 339 L6 – see Nîmes

GARREVAQUES – 81 Tarn – 338 D10 – pop. 252 – alt. 192 m – ✉ 81700

Paris 727 – Carcassonne 53 – Castres 31 – Toulouse 52 29 **C2**

Le Pavillon du Château rest,

Château de Garrevaques – 05 63 75 04 54 – m.c.combes@wanadoo.fr – Fax 05 63 70 26 44

15 rm – €150/180 €180/220, €15 – ½ P €110/130 – **Rest** – *(number of covers limited, pre-book)* Menu €15 (weekday lunch), €25/35 – Carte €25/55

◆ This hotel is located in the outbuildings of a chateau, and is home to fine rooms with period or old-style furnishings. Superb spa with modern facilities. Modern cuisine served in a vaulted cellar.

Le Château de Garrevaques

– *05 63 75 04 54 – m.c.combes@wanadoo.fr – Fax 05 63 70 26 44*

5 rm – €150/180 €180/220, €15 – ½ P €110/130

◆ Refined, plush rooms available in this 16th century chateau, renovated in the 19th century. Pleasant, lovely park.

GASNY – 27 Eure – 304 J7 – pop. 2 941 – alt. 36 m – ✉ 27620 33 **D2**

Paris 77 – Évreux 43 – Mantes-la-Jolie 20 – Rouen 71 – Vernon 10 – Versailles 67

de Villarceaux Chaussy Château du Couvent, North: 11 km by D 37, ☎ 01 34 67 73 83.

Auberge du Prieuré Normand

1 pl. République – ☎ 02 32 52 10 01 – prieure.normand@wanadoo.fr – Closed 4-25 August, Tuesday dinner and Wednesday

Rest – Menu (€ 19), € 25/43 – Carte € 39/52

◆ From Roche-Guyon, the road winds through rocky chalkland to this pleasant village inn serving well-prepared, traditional cuisine.

GASPARETS – 11 Aude – 344 H4 – ✉ 11200 Boutenac 22 **B3**

Paris 815 – Béziers 55 – Montpellier 114 – Perpignan 73

La Bastide de Gasparets without rest

2 r. de l'Église – ☎ 04 68 48 66 43 – labastide.degasparets@wanadoo.fr

3 rm – †€ 85/150 ††€ 85/150

◆ Beautiful mansion offering discreet and luxurious bedrooms, with antique, family furniture and heirlooms. Pleasant French garden.

GASSIN – 83 Var – 340 O6 – pop. 2 710 – alt. 200 m – ✉ 83580 French Riviera

Paris 872 – Fréjus 34 – Le Lavandou 31 – St-Tropez 9 – Ste-Maxime 14 – Toulon 69 41 **C3**

Gassin Golf Country Club Route de Ramatuelle, ☎ 04 94 55 13 44.

Terrasse des Barri ≤★.

Moulins de Paillas ✻★★ Southeast: 3,5 km.

Auberge la Verdoyante

866 chemin vicinal Coste Brigade – ☎ 04 94 56 16 23 – la.verdoyante@wanadoo.fr – Fax 04 94 56 43 10 – Open mid February-mid November and closed Monday-Thursday in February and March, Monday lunch and Wednesday April-mid November

Rest – Menu € 27/49 – Carte € 42/52

◆ Guesthouse nestling in a green setting. Appetizing regional cuisine served on the terrace overlooking the bay of St Tropez or in the charming Provençal dining room with fireplace.

GAURIAC – 33 Gironde – 335 H4 – pop. 826 – alt. 50 m – ✉ 33710 3 **B1**

Paris 551 – Blaye 11 – Bordeaux 42 – Jonzac 57 – Libourne 38

La Filadière

West: 2 km on D 669E1 – ☎ 05 57 64 94 05 – la-filadiere@wanadoo.fr – Fax 05 57 64 94 06 – Closed Tuesday and Wednesday

Rest – Menu € 29/32 – Carte € 34/50

◆ The terrace on the banks of the Gironde estuary is a major plus point for this restaurant located in what was once an oil storage complex. Meals can be served in the lounge.

GAVARNIE – 65 Hautes-Pyrénées – 342 L8 – pop. 164 – alt. 1 350 m – Winter sports : 1 350/2 400 m 11 – ✉ 65120 Languedoc-Roussillon-Tarn Gorges

Paris 901 – Lourdes 52 – Luz-St-Sauveur 20 – Pau 96 – Tarbes 71 28 **A3**

Office de tourisme, le village ☎ 05 62 92 48 05, Fax 05 62 92 42 47

Village★ - Cirque de Gavarnie★★★ South: 3 h 30.

Vignemale without rest

– ☎ 05 62 92 40 00 – hotel.vignemale@orange.fr – Fax 05 62 92 40 08 – Open 15 May-30 September

24 rm – †€ 130 ††€ 150, € 15

◆ Massive stone building (1902) overlooking the cirque of Gavarnie. Functional bedrooms. Pine trees and horses on the estate.

Le Marboré

– ✆ 05 62 92 40 40 – contacts@lemarbore.com – Fax 05 62 92 40 30 – Closed 15 November-20 December

24 rm – €65 €100, ☕ €12 – ½ P €62 – **Rest** – Menu €26 – Carte €25/47

♦ This 19th century Mansard style building is located just near the circus. Friendly atmosphere, simple clean rooms, some with a view of the mountain. British pub-style bar. Traditional cuisine served in a bistro-style dining room, on the veranda or the terrace.

GAZERAN – **78 Yvelines** – **311** G4 – **see Rambouillet**

GÉMENOS – **13 Bouches-du-Rhône** – **340** I6 – **pop. 5 485** – **alt. 150 m** – ✉ **13420**

Provence 40 **B3**

Paris 788 – Aix-en-Provence 39 – Brignoles 48 – Marseille 25 – Toulon 50

Syndicat d'initiative, cours Pasteur ✆ 04 42 32 18 44, Fax 04 42 32 15 49

Parc de St-Pons★ East: 3 km.

Relais de la Magdeleine

rm, rest,

rd-pt de la Madeleine, N 396 – ✆ 04 42 32 20 16 – contact@relais-magdeleine.com – Fax 04 42 32 02 26 – Open 15 March-15 November

28 rm – €100/110 €110/185, ☕ €14 – ½ P €105/142

Rest – *(closed Monday lunch and Wednesday lunch)* Menu €30 (weekday lunch), €43/57 – Carte €49/69

♦ Provence can be felt throughout this stylish 18C house with its antique furniture, floor tiles, paintings, drapes... right down to the cicadas chirping in the garden! Classic food and refined decor characterise the restaurant.

Bed & Suites without rest

au parc d'activités de Gémenos, Sud : 2 km, (250 av.Chateau de Jouques) – ✆ 04 42 32 72 73 – bedandsuites@voila.fr – Fax 04 42 32 72 74

29 rm – €85 €140, ☕ €12

♦ New hotel with an ochre façade. Modern and simple Provençal and nautical inspired rooms; some have balconies and terraces. Front rooms quieter.

Du Parc

Vallée St-Pons, on the D 2: 1 km – ✆ 04 42 32 20 38 – hotel.parc.gemenos@wanadoo.fr – Fax 04 42 32 10 26

13 rm – €49/55 €56/89, ☕ €8 – ½ P €56/71 – **Rest** – Menu €17, €25/35 – Carte €30/50

♦ Not far from St Pons park, in a garden set back from the road, this pleasant, lively establishment has colourful rooms. Regional specialities served in a spacious restaurant or on the shaded terrace.

GENAS – **69 Rhône** – **327** J5 – **pop. 11 140** – **alt. 218 m** – **see Lyon**

GÉNÉRARGUES – **30 Gard** – **339** I4 – **see Anduze**

GENESTON – **44 Loire-Atlantique** – **316** G5 – **pop. 2 217** – **alt. 28 m** – ✉ **44140** 34 **B2**

Paris 398 – Cholet 60 – Nantes 20 – La Roche-sur-Yon 47

Le Pélican

13 pl. G. Gaudet – ✆ 02 40 04 77 88 – Fax 02 40 04 77 88 – Closed 4-29 August, 18-28 February, Sunday dinner, Monday and Tuesday

Rest – Menu €20/30

♦ Behind the smart painted wood façade are two small dining rooms, renovated in shades of blue and yellow. Updated cuisine of regional inspiration.

GENEUILLE – **25 Doubs** – **321** F3 – **see Besançon**

GENILLÉ – 37 Indre-et-Loire – 317 P5 – pop. 1 425 – alt. 88 m – ✉ 37460

Châteaux of the Loire 11 **B3**

Paris 239 – Tours 48 – Blois 57 – Châtellerault 67 – Loches 12

Syndicat d'initiative, 17, place Agnès Sorel ☎ 02 47 59 57 85, Fax 02 47 59 57 85

Agnès Sorel with rm VISA

6 pl. Agnès Sorel – ☎ 02 47 59 50 17 – agnessorel@wanadoo.fr – Fax 02 47 59 59 50 – Closed 6-17 October, 2 January-6 February, Sunday dinner October-June, Tuesday October-February, Tuesday lunch March-June and Monday

3 rm – €45 €59, €8 – ½ P €70 – **Rest** – Menu €17 (weekday lunch), €38/54

◆ A local-style house with two pleasant dining rooms, serving tasty up-to-date cuisine.

GÉNIN (LAC) – 01 Ain – 328 H3 – see Oyonnax

GENNES – 49 Maine-et-Loire – 317 H4 – pop. 1 946 – alt. 28 m – ✉ 49350

Châteaux of the Loire 35 **C2**

Paris 305 – Angers 33 – Bressuire 65 – Cholet 68 – La Flèche 46 – Saumur 20

Office de tourisme, square de l'Europe ☎ 02 41 51 84 14

Church ★★ of Cunault Southeast: 2.5 km - Church ★ of Trèves-Cunault Southeast: 3 km.

Les Naulets d'Anjou rest, VISA

18 r. Croix de Mission – ☎ 02 41 51 81 88 – lesnauletsdanjou@wanadoo.fr – Fax 02 41 38 00 78 – Closed 23 December-31 January

19 rm – €50/56 €50/56, €8 – ½ P €47/51 – **Rest** – *(closed Wednesday from 15 October to 15 April) (dinner only)* Menu (€17), €21/38

◆ A 1970s building in the upper part of the village, an ideal stopover between Anjou and Saumurois. Bright modern restaurant with a balcony-terrace overlooking the pool and garden. Simple, traditional cuisine.

GENSAC – 33 Gironde – 335 L6 – pop. 800 – alt. 78 m – ✉ 33890 4 C1

Paris 554 – Bergerac 39 – Bordeaux 63 – Libourne 33 – La Réole 34

Office de tourisme, 5, place de l'Hôtel de Ville ☎ 05 57 47 46 67, Fax 05 57 47 46 63

Remparts with rm rm, VISA

16 r. Château – ☎ 05 57 47 43 46 – info@lesremparts.net – Fax 05 57 47 46 76 – Closed 1st January-4 March

7 rm – €60/85 €60/85, €8,50 – ½ P €64/76 – **Rest** – *(closed Sunday dinner, Monday and lunch except Sunday)* Menu €25/30

◆ An English chef runs this characteristic restaurant near the church. Traditional fare in a pleasant understated dining room, furnished with rustic chairs. Great view of the valley. Pleasant rooms housed in a medieval presbytery in the shadow of a bell tower. Well-tended garden.

North 2 km by D16 and D130 (Juillac road) – ✉ 33890 Juillac

Le Belvédère VISA

– ☎ 05 57 47 40 33 – le-belvedere@wanadoo.fr – Fax 05 57 47 48 07 – Closed October, Tuesday except at lunchtime in July-August and Wednesday

Rest – Menu €19 bi (weekday lunch), €28/58 – Carte €31/61

◆ This immense chalet overlooks a meander in the Dordogne. Welcoming restaurant with a distinctly rustic feel and pleasant viewpoint terrace. Regional-inspired fare.

Southwest 2 km by D18 and D15E1 – ✉ 33350 Ste-Radegonde

Château de Sanse rest, VISA

– ☎ 05 57 56 41 10 – contact@chateaudesanse.com – Fax 05 57 56 41 29 – Closed 1st January-28 February

16 rm – €100/135 €100/195, €12 – ½ P €85/128

Rest – *(closed Tuesday, Wednesday and lunch except weekends from October to April)* Menu (€18), €32 – Carte €34/66

◆ This noble 18C building built of white stone enjoys views of the surrounding countryside and vineyards. Attractive grounds and swimming pool. Modern, spacious and quiet bedrooms full of character. Up-to-date cuisine served in a pleasant veranda or on a high-perched terrace.

GÉRARDMER – 88 Vosges – 314 J4 – pop. 8 845 – alt. 669 m – Winter sports : 660/1 350 m 31 – Casino AZ – ✉ 88400 Alsace-Lorraine 27 C3

Paris 425 – Belfort 78 – Colmar 52 – Épinal 40 – St-Dié 27 – Thann 50

Office de tourisme, 4, place des Déportés ✆ 03 29 27 27 27, Fax 03 29 27 23 25

Gerardmer lake ★ - Longemer lake ★ - Saut des Cuves★ East: 3 km by ①.

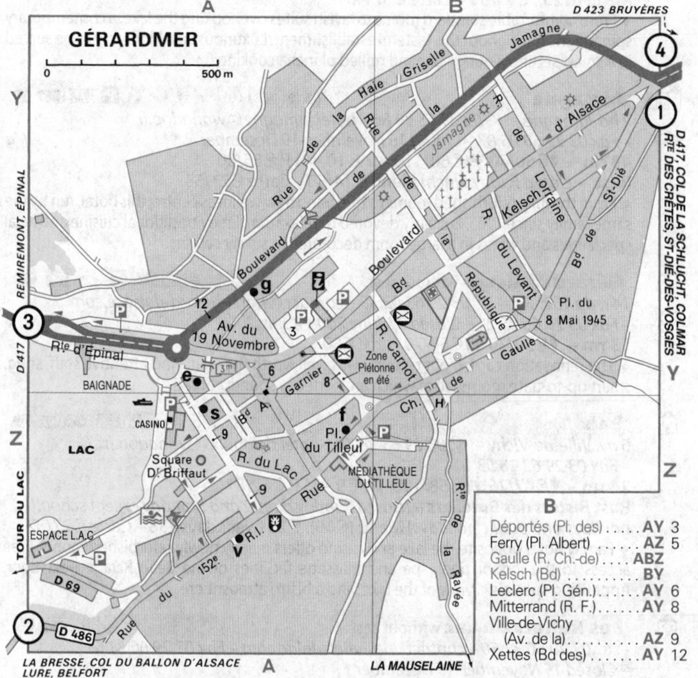

Le Grand Hôtel

pl. du Tilleul – ✆ 03 29 63 06 31 – contact@grandhotel-gerardmer.com – Fax 03 29 63 46 81 AZ **f**

58 rm – €78/130 €98/195, €14 – 14 suites – ½ P €77/125

Rest *Le Pavillon Pétrus* – *(dinner only except Sunday and holidays)* Menu €46/88 – Carte €53/70

Rest *L'Assiette du Coq à l'Âne* – Menu (€15 bi), €18 bi (weekdays)/26 – Carte €29/40

Rest *Le Grand Cerf* – *(dinner only except Sunday and holidays)* Menu €26

◆ An impressive, renovated 19C home in a tree lined garden. The rooms sport a cosy mixture of English and Alpine styles. A chalet offers two beautiful suites. An elegant setting and modern dishes. Pretty, regional decor and local specialities on offer at l'Assiette du Coq à l'Âne. Classic food on offer at the Grand Cerf.

Le Manoir au Lac

lake, rm, rest,

chemin de la Droite du Lac, Épinal road 1 km via ③ – ✆ 03 29 27 10 20 – contact@manoir-au-lac.com – Fax 03 29 27 10 27

12 rm – €150/290 €150/380, €20 – ½ P €125/195

Rest – *(Closed Sunday and Monday) (dinner only) (residents only)* Menu €30

◆ Typical Vosges chalet from 1830 in a park, where Maupassant used to stay. Guesthouse atmosphere, piano, fine furniture, stylish rooms and superb view of the lake. Tearoom.

Beau Rivage lake, VISA

esplanade du Lac – ✆ 03 29 63 22 28 – hotel-beau-rivage@wanadoo.fr – Fax 03 29 63 29 83 AY **e**

51 rm – €75/92 €94/198, €13 – 1 suite – ½ P €89/141

Rest *Côté Lac* – *(closed Saturday lunch and Friday off season, school holidays and holidays)* Menu €23 (weekday lunch), €38/75 – Carte €54/63

Rest *Le Toit du Lac* – *(closed Wednesday off season, school holidays and holidays)* Menu (€25), €35/55 – Carte €37/46

◆ From comfortable standard rooms to lavish suites overlooking the lake, a contemporary spirit reigns throughout this tasteful establishment. Luxurious spa. Modern cuisine served in a smart setting. Lounge bar and grilled plancha cooking.

Jamagne rest, VISA

2 bd Jamagne – ✆ 03 29 63 36 86 – hotel.jamagne@wanadoo.fr – Fax 03 29 60 05 87 – Closed 16 November-19 December AY **g**

48 rm – €50/70 €60/110, €10 – ½ P €55/80

Rest – *(closed Friday lunch)* Menu €14/50 – Carte €21/53

◆ From the fully refurbished rooms to the brand new wellness centre, this hotel, run by the same family since 1905, is clearly devoted to relaxation. Enjoy traditional cuisine and local specialities and wines in a large room decorated in sunny colours.

Gérard d'Alsace without rest VISA

14 r. du 152º R.I. – ✆ 03 29 63 02 38 – contact@hotel-gerard-dalsace.com – Fax 03 29 60 85 21 – Closed 27 June 2008-4 July 2008 AZ **v**

13 rm – €50/70 €50/70, €7,50

◆ The renovation carried out recently was well worth the wait. Find attentive staff, snug, smart up-to-date rooms, all of which are perfectly soundproofed.

Paix rest, VISA

6 av. Ville-de-Vichy – ✆ 03 29 63 38 78 – hotel.delapaix@wanadoo.fr – Fax 03 29 63 18 53 AZ **s**

24 rm – €47/76 €58/108, €9 – ½ P €62/87

Rest *Bistrot des Bateliers* – *(closed Sunday dinner and Monday except school holidays and public holidays)* Menu (€19), €26 (weekdays)/38 – Carte €27/37

◆ Family hotel opposite the lake and casino offers mainly newly refurbished rooms. Free access to the indoor pool, spa and massage facilities of the Beau Rivage next door. Appetising specials, a view of the lake, and a bistro atmosphere.

Les Reflets du Lac without rest VISA

– ✆ 03 29 60 31 50 – contact@lesrefletsdulac.com – Fax 03 29 60 31 51 – Closed 15 November-15 December

14 rm – €49/57 €49/57, €6,50

◆ The restful view of the lake from most of the rooms is undoubtedly the highpoint of the establishment. The rooms are decorated simply, faultlessly kept and quite comfortable.

in Xonrupt-Longemer 4 km by ① – pop. 1 489 – alt. 714 m – ✉ 88400

Les Jardins de Sophie - Domaine de la Moineaudière VISA

rte du Valtin, 4 km north-west on D23 and secondary road – ✆ 03 29 63 37 11 – jardinsdesophie@gmail.com – Fax 03 29 63 17 63

32 rm – €95/200 €115/220, €15 – 1 suite – ½ P €108/160

Rest – *(closed Tuesday dinner and Wednesday off season and outside holiday)* Menu €25 (weekday lunch), €38/58 – Carte €59/65

◆ Nestling amongst spruce trees, this fully revamped luxury hotel is both sophisticated and cosy. Tasteful blend of Alpine and designer-inspired decor. A warm wood interior highlights the minimalist elegance of the restaurant's tables. Updated cuisine.

La Devinière without rest

318 montée des Broches – ✆ 03 29 63 23 89 – feltzsylvie@hotmail.com – Fax 03 29 63 15 22 – Closed 30 March-11 April, 15 June-4 July and 12-26 October

5 rm – €58/82 €62/88

◆ This restored farm is known for its peacefulness, the view of the forest, and its wellness centre (Finnish sauna). Five large rooms, including one for families.

in Bas-Rupts 4 km by ② – ✉ 88400 Gérardmer

Les Bas-Rupts (Michel Philippe) rest, rest, VISA AE
– ✆ *03 29 63 09 25*
– basrupts@relaischateaux.com – Fax 03 29 63 00 40
21 rm – †€ 140/170 ††€ 140/200, ☕ € 22 – 4 suites – ½ P € 150/220
Rest – *(pre-book Sat - Sun)* Menu € 32 (weekday lunch), € 50/95 – Carte € 59/101
Spec. Carpaccio de tête de veau et queues de langoustines rôties. Poulette de Bresse rôtie, sauce au vin jaune et morilles. Tripes au riesling à la crème et moutarde. **Wines** Muscat d'Alsace, Pinot gris.
◆ The wood façade, fine Austrian-style rustic decor, pleasant rooms with personal touches, indoor pool, sauna and steam bath, endow this hotel with a lavish blend of comfort and style. Smart country restaurant that features regional produce with an inventive twist.

Cap Sud VISA
144 rte de la Bresse – ✆ 03 29 63 06 83 – contact@capsud-bellemaree.fr
– Fax 03 29 63 20 76 – Closed Tuesday lunch and Monday except school holidays
Rest – Menu (€ 15), € 25/38 – Carte € 26/51
◆ A port of call in the Vosges: portholes and mahogany liner fittings in the dining room, view of the mountains from the veranda, and Mediterranean inspired cuisine.

GERBEROY – 60 Oise – 305 C3 – pop. 111 – alt. 180 m – ✉ 60380 36 A2

Paris 110 – Aumale 30 – Beauvais 22 – Breteuil 37 – Compiègne 82 – Rouen 62

Hostellerie du Vieux Logis VISA AE
25 r. Logis du Roy – ✆ 03 44 82 71 66 – levieuxlogis@worldonline.fr
– Fax 03 44 82 61 65 – Closed Christmas and February school holidays, dinner except Saturday from November to March, Tuesday dinner, Sunday dinner and Wednesday
Rest – Menu € 25/46 – Carte € 42/55
◆ House at the entrance to the old fortified village now invaded by flowers, painters and tourists. Fireplace and exposed beams brighten the restaurant.

GESTEL – 56 Morbihan – 308 K8 – pop. 2 227 – alt. 47 m – ✉ 56530 9 B2

Paris 510 – Rennes 158 – Vannes 65 – Lorient 13 – Lanester 13

Piscine et Golf without rest
6 allée Kerguestenen, 3 km south-east on D 163 and secondary road –
✆ 02 97 05 15 03 – ng.gwen@tiscali.fr – Fax 02 97 05 15 03
– Closed 7-23 February
4 rm ☕ – †€ 59/74 ††€ 59/74
◆ This peaceful house in a residential estate is home to pleasant, theme-decorated rooms (Roses, Angels) overlooking the golf course. Small heated pool (30°C) with counter current.

GÉTIGNÉ – 44 Loire-Atlantique – 316 I5 – see Clisson

LES GETS – 74 Haute-Savoie – 328 N4 – pop. 1 352 – alt. 1 170 m – Winter sports : 1 170/2 000 m 5 47 – ✉ 74260 French Alps 46 F1

Paris 579 – Annecy 77 – Bonneville 33 – Cluses 19 – Morzine 7 – Thonon-les-Bains 36

Office de tourisme, place Mairie ✆ 04 50 75 80 80, Fax 04 50 79 76 90
des Gets Les Chavannes, East: 3 km, ✆ 04 50 75 87 63.
Mont Chéry ✱★★.

Le Labrador rest, VISA AE
rte de La Turche – ✆ 04 50 75 80 00
– info@labrador-hotel.com – Fax 04 50 79 87 03
– Open 21 June-7 July and 20 December-13 April
23 rm – †€ 80/180 ††€ 110/240, ☕ € 15 – ½ P € 110/170
Rest *Le St-Laurent* – *(dinner only except summer)* Menu € 28 (lunch), € 40/90 – Carte € 48/63
◆ This chalet with a pretty garden offers numerous services and leisure opportunities. Richly decorated lounge and rooms with balconies, often with a mountain view. Modern cuisine and grills prepared before your very eyes in the Savoy-style dining room.

La Marmotte rest, VISA

– ✆ 04 50 75 80 33 – info@hotel-marmotte.com – Fax 04 50 75 83 26
– Open 5 July-31 August and 20 December-12 April

48 rm – †€ 155/279 ††€ 255/372, ☐ € 12 – ½ P € 139/225 – **Rest** – *(dinner only) (resident only)* Menu € 28/50

◆ After a day's skiing relax near the fireplace before treating yourself to the superb spa (750sq.m). Recently refurbished and cosy rooms featuring woodwork. Restaurant looking out onto the ski slopes.

Mont Chéry without rest VISA

– ✆ 04 50 75 80 75 – hotelmontchery@orange.fr – Fax 04 50 79 70 13
– Open 19 December-15 April

27 rm ☐ – †€ 110/190 ††€ 160/340

◆ At the foot of the ski lifts, spruce rooms with chic Alpine decor. Those in the chalet category look out over the ski slopes. Panoramic jacuzzi and pool, sauna.

Alpina rest, VISA

55 imp. de la Grange-Neuve – ✆ 04 50 75 80 22 – resa@hotelalpina.fr
– Fax 04 50 75 83 48 – Open 27 May-23 September and 16 December-14 April

33 rm – †€ 64/84 ††€ 85/145, ☐ € 8,50 – 1 suite – ½ P € 73/112

Rest – Menu € 20 (weekday lunch), € 22/36 – Carte € 26/43

◆ This chalet-hotel which dominates the town offers mainly large rooms, redecorated in a gay, modern Savoy style. A pleasant garden in the summer. A welcoming decor in warm colours awaits you in the two dining rooms. Cuisine with a local flavour.

Crychar VISA

136 impasse de la Grange-Neuve, via rte La Turche – ✆ 04 50 75 80 50
– info@crychar.com – Fax 04 50 79 83 12
– Open 1st July-14 September and 21 December-18 April

15 rm – †€ 55/165 ††€ 65/220, ☐ € 12 – ½ P € 72/160 – **Rest** – *(dinner only)* Menu € 35

◆ With the snow in winter and green Alps in the summer, this little building has simple rooms with balconies in surroundings that are popular with sporty types.

Bellevue rm, VISA

125 rte du Front de Neige – ✆ 04 50 75 80 95 – info@hotelbellevue-lesgets.com
– Fax 04 50 79 81 81 – Open 1st July-31 August and 20 December-15 April

16 rm – †€ 55/115 ††€ 65/165, ☐ € 9 – ½ P € 65/94 – **Rest** – Menu € 17 (lunch), € 20/24 – Carte € 23/37

◆ This chalet situated next to the ski school has been entirely redecorated. The rooms are not large but are well kept and have balconies; the most pleasant face due south. The bar-brasserie serves daily specialities. The restaurant has a view over the ski slopes and offers a regional menu.

Régina rest, VISA

– ✆ 04 50 75 80 44 – hotelpla@wanadoo.fr – Fax 04 50 79 87 29
– Open 29 June-5 September and 21 December-12 April

21 rm – †€ 58/80 ††€ 65/105, ☐ € 9 – ½ P € 62/92 – **Rest** – *(closed Tuesday lunch and Wednesday lunch)* Menu (€ 14,50 bi), € 17/36 – Carte € 29/42

◆ One of the first hotels opened in the resort and run by the same family since 1937; the current owner is also an alpine guide. Simple rooms and a warm friendly ambience. An all wood decor and fireplace in the restaurant; classic dishes and local specialities.

Bel'Alpe VISA

r. du Centre – ✆ 04 50 79 74 11 – info@hotel-belalpe.com – Fax 04 50 79 80 99
– Open 16 June-12 September and 18 December-11 April

34 rm – †€ 74/95 ††€ 74/95, ☐ € 7 – ½ P € 59/81 – **Rest** – Menu € 17/19 – Carte € 38/58

◆ A traditional chalet equipped to meet the needs of a family clientele. Simple rooms, some with balconies. In the kitchen the chef prepares inventive dishes which could almost outdo the regional specialities.

GEVREY-CHAMBERTIN – 21 Côte-d'Or – 320 J6 – pop. 3 258 – alt. 275 m –

✉ **21220** ▌ **Burgundy-Jura** 8 **D1**

Paris 315 – Beaune 33 – Dijon 13 – Dole 61

Office de tourisme, 1, rue Gaston Roupnel ✆ 03 80 34 38 40, Fax 03 80 34 15 49

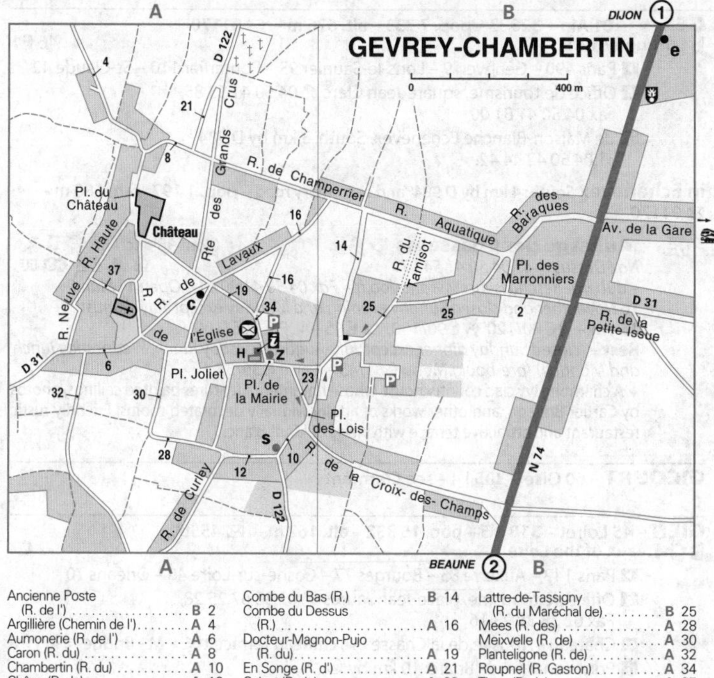

Arts et Terroirs without rest — VISA

28 rte de Dijon – ✆ 03 80 34 30 76 – arts-et-terroirs@wanadoo.fr – Fax 03 80 34 11 79 — B **e**

20 rm – €58/86 €66/86, €10

◆ Most of the snug, appealing rooms overlook a peaceful garden to the rear, only three face the road but are well-soundproofed. Chesterfield sitting room with piano.

Grands Crus without rest — VISA

r. de Lavaux – ✆ 03 80 34 34 15 – hotel.lesgrandscrus@nerim.net – Fax 03 80 51 89 07 – Open from March to November — A **c**

24 rm – €75/85 €75/85, €12

◆ The vineyards of the great vintages are just next to this warm village house surrounded by a pretty flower garden. Comfortable rooms and a salon with plenty of character.

Rôtisserie du Chambertin — VISA

r. du Chambertin – ✆ 03 80 34 33 20 – rotisserieduchambertin-bonbistrot@wanadoo.fr – Closed 27 July-12 August, February holidays, Sunday dinner, Tuesday lunch and Monday — A **s**

Rest – Menu €34/72 – Carte €45/71 – **Rest *Le Bonbistrot*** – Carte €26/33

◆ Going up the stairs from the vaulted dining room is sometimes trying, as the selection of Chambertins on the wine list is amazing. Small barrel-making museum. The Bonbistrot is situated in a converted barn. Traditional and local menu with Chicken in Wine in pride of place.

Chez Guy — VISA

3 pl. de la Mairie – ✆ 03 80 58 51 51 – chez-guy@hotel-bourgogne.com – Fax 03 80 58 50 39 — A **z**

Rest – Menu (€25), €28/59

◆ Elegant modern furnishings, warm tones and colourful paintings on a culinary theme make up the décor of this renovated restaurant serving modern cuisine and regional wines.

GEX – 01 Ain – 328 J3 – pop. 7 733 – alt. 626 m – ✉ 01170
Burgundy-Jura 46 **F1**

Paris 490 – Genève 19 – Lons-le-Saunier 93 – Pontarlier 110 – St-Claude 42

Office de tourisme, square Jean Clerc ✆ 04 50 41 53 85, Fax 04 50 41 81 00

de Maison-Blanche Échenevex, South: 3 km by D 984, ✆ 04 50 42 44 42.

in Echenevex **South: 4 km by D 984ᶜ and secondary road – pop. 1 197 – alt. 580 m –** ✉ **01170**

Auberge des Chasseurs ≤ Mont-Blanc,
Naz Dessus – ✆ 04 50 41 54 07
– aubergedeschasseurs@wanadoo.fr – Fax 04 50 41 90 61 – Open 1st March-16 November and closed Sunday evening and Monday except July-August
15 rm – €80/120 €90/150, €15 – ½ P €105/160
Rest – *(closed Sunday dinner except July-August, Tuesday lunch, Wednesday lunch and Monday) (pre-book)* Menu €31/45 – Carte €36/53
◆ A charming ivy clad country house whose fine interior features painted ceilings, photos by Cartier Bresson, and other works of art. Individually decorated rooms. Friendly rustic restaurant and attractive terrace with views of Mont Blanc.

GICOURT – 60 Oise – 305 F4 – see Clermont

GIEN – 45 Loiret – 318 M5 – pop. 15 332 – alt. 162 m – ✉ 45500
Châteaux of the Loire 12 **C2**

Paris 149 – Auxerre 85 – Bourges 77 – Cosne-sur-Loire 46 – Orléans 70

Office de tourisme, place Jean Jaurès ✆ 02 38 67 25 28, Fax 02 38 38 23 16

Château★: musée de la Chasse★★, château terrace t ≤★ **M** - Bridge ≤★.

Pont-canal★★ de Briare: 10 km by ②.

GIEN

Street	Square	No.
Anne-de-Beaujeu (R.)	Z	2
Bildstein (R. du Lt.)	Y	3
Briqueteries (R. des)	Y	
Château (Pl. du)	Z	
Clemenceau (R. G.)	Z	5
Curie (Pl.)	Y	
Gambetta (R.)	Z	6
Hôtel-de-Ville (R. de l')	Z	7
Jeanne-d'Arc (R.)	YZ	
Jean-Jaurès (Pl.)	Z	9
Joffre (Q. du Mar.)	Z	
Leclerc (Av. du Mar.)	Z	12
Lenoir (Quai)	Z	
Louis-Blanc (R.)	Z	13
Marienne (R. de l'Adj.-Chef)	Z	15
Montbricon (R. de)	YZ	
Noé (R. de)	Y	
Paris (R. de)	YZ	
Paul-Bert (R.)	Z	16
Président-Wilson (Av.)	Y	17
République (Av. de la)	Y	19
Thiers (R.)	Z	23
Verdun (R. de)	Y	
Victor-Hugo (R.)	Z	24
Vieille Boucherie (R.)	Z	25
Villejean (R. J.)	Y	

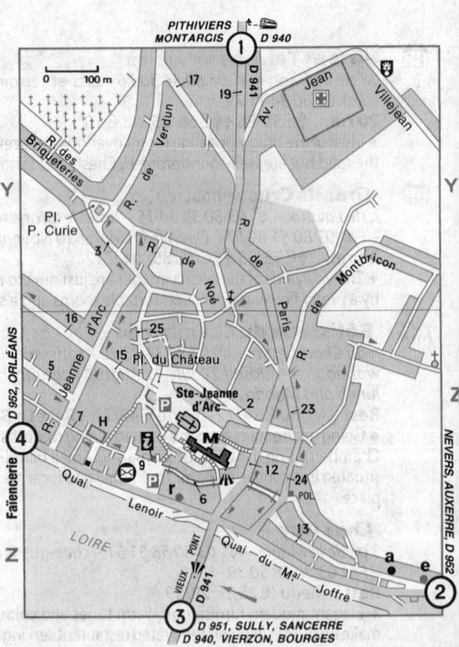

Rivage without rest
1 quai Nice – ✆ 02 38 37 79 00 – Fax 02 38 38 10 21 – Closed Christmas holidays Z **a**
16 rm – €55/90 €65/110, €8,50 – 3 suites
◆ Some of the rooms in this hotel overlook the Loire and its picturesque old bridge; nearly half of them have been recently decorated. Comfortable bar and lounge.

Axotel without rest
14 r. de la Bosserie, 3 km on ① – ✆ 02 38 67 11 99 – axotelgien.com@wanadoo.fr – Fax 02 38 38 16 61
48 rm – €55/60 €60/70, €7
◆ Modern hotel at the northern entrance to the town. Comfortable, cheerfully-decorated lounges and spacious rooms, adorned with limed wood furniture and colourful drapes.

Anne de Beaujeu without rest
10 rte de Bourges, via ③ – ✆ 02 38 29 39 39 – hotel.a.beaujeu@wanadoo.fr – Fax 02 38 38 27 29
30 rm – €44 €49, €8
◆ This left-bank establishment is named after the famous Countess of Gien. Functional rooms. Choose one at the back.

Sanotel without rest
21 quai Sully, via ③: 0.5 km – ✆ 02 38 67 61 46 – sanotel-gien@wanadoo.fr – Fax 02 38 67 13 01
60 rm – €35/45 €35/45, €6,50
◆ This modern building set on the banks of the Loire offers practical rooms, many with a view of the chateau and the river.

La Poularde with rm rest,
13 quai Nice – ✆ 02 38 67 36 05 – lapoularde2@wanadoo.fr – Fax 02 38 38 18 78 – Closed 1st-12 January Sunday dinner and Monday lunch Z **e**
9 rm – €53/60 €60/69, €10 – ½ P €58 – **Rest** – Menu €20 (weekdays)/65 – Carte €57/74
◆ Traditional cuisine served in an elegant riverside dining room embellished with paintings, antique tapestries, Gien crockery and silverware. Well-maintained guestrooms.

Côté Jardin
14 rte Bourges, via ③ – ✆ 02 38 38 24 67 – cote-jardin45@orange.fr – Fax 02 38 38 24 67 – Closed 21 December-8 January, Tuesday and Wednesday
Rest – *(number of covers limited, pre-book)* Menu €28 (weekday lunch)/50 – Carte €43/54
◆ Pleasant restaurant on the left bank of the Loire with a revitalised decor of classic furnishings and attractive Gien ceramics. Contemporary cuisine.

Le P'tit Bouchon
66 r. B. Palissy, via r. Hôtel de Ville Z – ✆ 02 38 67 84 40 – Fax 02 38 67 84 40 – Closed 15-31 July, Saturday lunch and Sunday
Rest – Menu (€16), €23
◆ Typical bistro dishes such as calf's head, rabbit terrine and Morteau sausage are chalked up on the blackboard. Attractive small dining room furnished with bentwood chairs.

La Loire
18 quai Lenoir – ✆ 02 38 67 00 75 – trambu67@yahoo.it – Fax 02 38 38 01 49 – Closed 23 December-15 January and Monday Z **r**
Rest – Menu €19 (weekday lunch), €24/34 – Carte €29/46
◆ This restaurant on the quayside serves modern cuisine in a redecorated dining area overlooking the Loire. Works of art regularly exhibited.

South by ③, D 940 and secondary road: 3 km – ✉ 45500 Poilly-lez-Gien

Villa Hôtel rm,
– ✆ 02 38 27 03 30 – Fax 02 38 27 03 43
24 rm – €36 €36, €6 – ½ P €39 – **Rest** – *(closed 2-5 March, 14-24 July, 22 December-1st January, Friday, Saturday and Sunday) (dinner only) (resident only)* Menu €12/15
◆ Expect a warm, friendly welcome at this modern, simple hotel. The well-kept rooms are another advantage. Restaurant decorated with attractive pieces of Gien earthenware. A single dish of the day; buffets for starters and desserts.

GIENS – 83 Var – **340** L7 – ✉ **83400 Hyères** **French Riviera** 41 **C3**

Paris 860 – Carqueiranne 10 – Draguignan 87 – Hyères 9 – Toulon 27

Ruins of the château des Pontevès ✻★★.

See plan of Giens to Hyères.

Le Provençal rest, VISA

Place Saint Pierre – ✆ 04 98 04 54 54 – leprovencal@wanadoo.fr – Fax 04 98 04 54 50 – Open 12 April-19 October X s

41 rm – €82/120 €110/150, €14 – ½ P €92/120 – **Rest** – Menu €28/53 – Carte €49/75

◆ The hotel is built on a hillside and has a shaded flower garden that descends in terraces to the water. Provence-style rooms. The view this restaurant commands perhaps inspired the poet Saint-John Perse, a famous resident of this peninsula.

LA GIETTAZ – 73 Savoie – **333** L2 – **pop. 488** – **alt. 1 120 m** – ✉ **73590** 46 **F1**

Paris 575 – Albertville 29 – Chambéry 80 – Chamonix-Mont-Blanc 49 – Megève 16

Office de tourisme, Chef-lieu ✆ 04 79 32 91 90, Fax 04 79 32 93 28

Flor'Alpes rest, VISA

– ✆ 04 79 32 90 88 – mary-anne.schouppe@wanadoo.fr – Closed 10 April-15 May and 10 October-10 December

11 rm – €40/46 €45/51, €7 – ½ P €42/48 – **Rest** – *(closed lunch April-October)* Menu (€15), €18 (weekdays)/35 – Carte €20/44

◆ Enjoy authentic Savoyard hospitality in this pleasant, beautifully maintained little guesthouse, next to the church. Balconies full of flowers, and attentive service. The bay windows in the rustic dining room open onto the garden. Service with a smile.

GIFFAUMONT-CHAMPAUBERT – 51 Marne – **306** K11 – **pop. 234** – **alt. 130 m** – ✉ **51290** **Northern France and the Paris Region** 14 **C2**

Paris 208 – Bar-le-Duc 53 – Chaumont 75 – St-Dizier 25 – Vitry-le-François 28

Office de tourisme, Maison du Lac ✆ 03 26 72 62 80, Fax 03 26 72 64 69

Der-chantecoq Lake ★★.

Le Cheval Blanc rm, VISA

21 r. du Lac – ✆ 03 26 72 62 65 – lechevalblanc7@aol.com – Fax 03 26 73 96 97 – Closed 7-25 September, 4-22 January, Tuesday lunch, Sunday dinner and Monday

14 rm – €60 €65, €8 – ½ P €65 – **Rest** – Menu €24/55 – Carte €35/55

◆ Almost a mile from the largest man-made lake in Europe, this hotel is perfect for guests in search of a "green" holiday. Comfortable lounge and bright, modern bedrooms. Ochre colours prevail in the restaurant, summer terrace to the rear. Classic dishes.

GIF-SUR-YVETTE – 91 Essonne – **312** B3 – **pop. 21 364** – **alt. 61 m** – ✉ **91190** 20 **A3**

Paris 34 – Évry 37 – Boulogne-Billancourt 23 – Montreuil 41 – Argenteuil 42

Les Saveurs Sauvages A/C VISA

4 r. Croix Grignon – ✆ 01 69 07 01 16 – les-saveurs-sauvages@wanadoo.fr – Fax 01 69 07 20 84 – Closed 5-25 August, 25 December-2 January, Sunday and Monday

Rest – Menu (€18), €24 – Carte €36/44

◆ A concise seasonal menu which changes daily. Bright dining room-veranda in this non-smoking restaurant opposite the RER train station.

GIGARO – 83 Var – **340** O6 – see La Croix-Valmer

GIGNAC – 34 Hérault – **339** G7 – **pop. 3 955** – **alt. 53 m** – ✉ **34150** 23 **C2**

Paris 719 – Béziers 58 – Lodève 25 – Montpellier 30 – Sète 57

Office de tourisme, place du Gen Claparède ✆ 04 67 57 58 83, Fax 04 67 57 67 95

XX **De Lauzun**

3 bd de l'Esplanade – ✆ 04 67 57 50 83 – restaurantlauzun@aol.com – Fax 04 67 57 93 70 – Closed March, Thursday lunch and Wednesday
Rest – Menu (€ 20), € 38/80 – Carte € 39/61
◆ This elegantly decorated restaurant, with its changing art exhibitions and sandstone fireplace, is located opposite an attractive shaded esplanade. Contemporary cuisine.

GIGONDAS – 84 Vaucluse – 332 D9 – pop. 648 – alt. 313 m – ✉ 84190

Provence 42 **E1**

Paris 662 – Avignon 40 – Nyons 31 – Orange 20 – Vaison-la-Romaine 16
Office de tourisme, rue du Portail ✆ 04 90 65 85 46, Fax 04 90 65 88 42

Les Florets

2 km east on minor road – ✆ 04 90 65 85 01 – accueil@hotel-lesflorets.com – Fax 04 90 65 83 80 – Closed 1st January-15 March, Monday dinner, Tuesday and Wednesday in November December
15 rm – †€ 98 ††€ 98/125, ☕ € 13,50 – ½ P € 94/112 – **Rest** – *(closed Wednesday) (number of covers limited, pre-book)* Menu (€ 21), € 28/42 – Carte € 54/68
◆ This hotel offers delightful and colourful rooms in a secluded area of the countryside at the foot of the Montmirail Dentelles. Tasty local cuisine and wines are served amidst typical Provencal décor or on the pleasant, shady terrace.

XX **L'Oustalet**

pl. Gabrielle Andéol – ✆ 04 90 65 85 30 – cyril-glemot@meffre.com – Fax 04 90 12 30 03 – Closed 21 December-18 January, Monday dinner, Tuesday dinner, Wednesday dinner, Sunday dinner and Thursday 3 April-31 March
Rest – Menu (€ 20), € 29/56 – Carte € 36/59
◆ This restaurant has an impressive façade that conceals an elegant, rustic dining area, serving modern cuisine with Provençal influences, and a good selection of regional wines.

GILETTE – 06 Alpes-Maritimes – 341 D4 – pop. 1 254 – alt. 420 m – ✉ 06830

French Riviera 41 **D2**

Paris 946 – Antibes 43 – Nice 36 – St-Martin-Vésubie 45
Syndicat d'initiative, place du Dr Morani ✆ 04 92 08 98 08, Fax 04 93 08 55 24
☼★★ of the château ruins.

in Vescous by Rosquesteron road (D 17): 9 km – ✉ 06830 Toudon

X **La Capeline**

– ✆ 04 93 08 58 06 – Fax 04 93 08 58 06 – Open March-October, les weekends from November to March and closed Wednesday
Rest – *(closed dinner except Friday and Saturday in season) (pre-book)* Menu € 20 (weekdays)/30 bi
◆ A small and remote roadside restaurant in the Esteron valley. The tasty menu, based on local produce, is announced orally at each table. Pleasant shaded terrace.

GILLY-LÈS-CÎTEAUX – 21 Côte-d'Or – 320 J6 – see Vougeot

GIMBELHOF – 67 Bas-Rhin – 315 K2 – see Lembach

GIMEL-LES-CASCADES – 19 Corrèze – 329 M4 – pop. 630 – alt. 375 m – ✉ 19800

Paris 493 – Limoges 104 – Tulle 13 – Brive-la-Gaillarde 40 – Ussel 56
Office de tourisme, le Bourg ✆ 05 55 21 44 32 25 **C3**

Hostellerie de la Vallée

au bourg – ✆ 05 55 21 40 60 – hostellerie_de_la_vallée@hotmail.com – Fax 05 55 21 38 74 – Closed 20 December-5 January, Sunday dinner, Monday lunch, Friday and Saturday from 1st October to 31 March
9 rm – †€ 53/57 ††€ 53/57, ☕ € 11,50 – ½ P € 45/47 – **Rest** – Menu € 23/35 – Carte € 35/43
◆ At the heart of a village renowned for its waterfalls, this renovated country house offers guests comfortable bedrooms, three of which face the valley. Panoramic dining room where the traditional cuisine is prepared by a mother and daughter team.

LA GIMOND – 42 Loire – 327 F6 – pop. 217 – alt. 625 m – ✉ 42140 44 A2

Paris 485 – Saint-Étienne 18 – Annonay 67 – Lyon 58 – Montbrison 37 – Vienne 64

Le Vallon du Moulin

– *04 77 30 97 06 – Fax 04 77 30 97 06 – Closed 28 July- 14 August, 1st-11 January, 18-29 February and Sunday dinner*

Rest – Menu € 26/45

◆ Refurbished in a contemporary style, this restaurant in the heart of a small village, offers an up-to-date menu that varies with the seasons.

GIMONT – 32 Gers – 336 H8 – pop. 2 734 – alt. 180 m – ✉ 32200

Languedoc-Roussillon-Tarn Gorges 28 B2

Paris 701 – Colomiers 40 – Toulouse 51 – Tournefeuille 40

Office de tourisme, 83, rue Nationale 05 62 67 77 87, Fax 05 62 67 93 61

Château de Larroque

rest,

rte de Toulouse – 05 62 67 77 44 – chateaularroque@free.fr – Fax 05 62 67 88 90 – Closed 2-22 January, Sunday dinner and Monday from October to April

17 rm – €85/99 €105/200, € 14 – 1 suite – ½ P € 103/140

Rest – *(closed Monday except dinner May-September and Tuesday lunch)* Menu € 25/58 – Carte € 30/70

◆ This chateau built in 1805 is set in a peaceful park, with comfortable and refined interiors, pleasant personalised rooms and fine lounges. Traditional cuisine served in an elegant dining area or on the shaded terrace.

GINASSERVIS – 83 Var – 340 K3 – pop. 984 – alt. 407 m – ✉ 83560 40 B3

Paris 781 – Aix-en-Provence 53 – Avignon 111 – Manosque 23 – Marseille 82 – Toulon 91

Chez Marceau with rm

pl. Jean Jaurès – 04 94 80 11 21 – chezmarceau@wanadoo.fr – Fax 04 94 80 16 82 – Closed 22-26 December, 12-30 January, Tuesday dinner except July-August and merc

6 rm – €45 €45, € 6 – ½ P € 50 – **Rest** – Menu € 15 bi (weekdays)/40 – Carte € 24/77

◆ Set between the Durance and Verdon rivers, this welcoming village centre inn with terrace stands on the square. It is typically Provençal and serves regional cuisine.

GINCLA – 11 Aude – 344 E6 – pop. 43 – alt. 570 m – ✉ 11140 22 B3

Paris 821 – Carcassonne 77 – Foix 88 – Perpignan 67 – Quillan 25

Hostellerie du Grand Duc

2 rte de Boucheville – 04 68 20 55 02 – hotelgranduc@wanadoo.fr – Fax 04 68 20 61 22 – Open 1st April-1st November

12 rm – €60 €72/78, € 11 – ½ P € 75/80 – **Rest** – *(closed Wednesday lunch)* Menu € 32/62 – Carte € 41/68

◆ Exposed stonework, wood panelling and antique furniture give character to the rooms of this 18C country house in the land of the Cathars. Walled wooded garden. Smart, rustic dining room, terrace and giant helpings of traditional fare.

GIRMONT-VAL-D'AJOL – 88 Vosges – 314 H5 – see Remiremont

GISORS – 27 Eure – 304 K6 – pop. 10 882 – alt. 60 m – ✉ 27140 Normandy

Paris 73 – Beauvais 33 – Évreux 66 – Mantes-la-Jolie 40 – Pontoise 38 – Rouen 59 33 D2

Office de tourisme, 4, rue du Général-de-Gaulle 02 32 27 60 63, Fax 02 32 27 60 75

de Chaumont-en-Vexin Chaumont-en-Vexin Château de Bertichères, East: 8 km by D 982, 03 44 49 00 81 ;

de Rebetz Chaumont-en-Vexin Route de Noailles, East: 12 km by D 981, 03 44 49 15 54.

Fortified castle ★★ - St-Gervais and St-Protais church ★.

Moderne

1 pl. de la Gare – ✆ 02 32 55 23 51 – hotel.moderne@free.fr – Fax 02 32 55 08 75 – Closed 10-18 August

31 rm – ♦€ 50/65 ♦♦€ 50/65, ☕ € 9 – ½ P € 60/84 – **Rest** – *(closed 26 July-18 August, 20 December-5 January, Saturday and Sunday)* Menu € 14/27 – Carte € 29/36

◆ This family hotel opposite the station is suitable for an overnight stay. The discreetly-decorated rooms are well kept. A rustic dining area, serving traditional cuisine and a cheery "table d'hôte" menu.

Le Cappeville

17 r. Cappeville, (transfer arranged) – ✆ 02 32 55 11 08 – pierre.potel@worldonline.fr – Fax 02 32 55 93 92

Rest – Menu € 26/55 – Carte € 48/62

◆ This restaurant, in the capital of the Norman Vexin region, is decorated with bright colours and has kept its laminated beams and fireplace. Regional cuisine served.

in Bazincourt-sur-Epte North: 6 km by D 14 – pop. 578 – alt. 55 m – ✉ 27140

Château de la Rapée

2 km west on secondary road – ✆ 02 32 55 11 61 – infos@hotel-la-rapee.com – Fax 02 32 55 95 65 – Closed 17 August-1st September and 28 January-1st March

16 rm – ♦€ 89 ♦♦€ 120/145, ☕ € 12 – ½ P € 82/96 – **Rest** – *(closed Wednesday)* Menu € 35/50 – Carte € 64/96

◆ The Epte Valley is popular with painters and is the background for this lovely Anglo-Norman manor standing in a park of trees. Spacious rooms with antique furniture. The dining room has a comfortable and welcoming decor, with attractive wood panelling.

in St-Denis-le-Ferment Northwest: 7 km by secondary road and D 17 – pop. 456 – alt. 70 m – ✉ 27140

Auberge de l'Atelier

55 r. Guérard – ✆ 02 32 55 24 00 – Fax 02 32 55 10 20 – Closed 15-30 September, Sunday dinner, Tuesday dinner and Monday

Rest – Menu € 27/53 – Carte € 46/59

◆ Relax in this pastel-coloured dining room with its abundance of floral decoration, cane chairs, period furniture and traditional cuisine.

GIVERNY – 27 Eure – 304 I6 – pop. 524 – alt. 17 m – ✉ 27620 — 33 D2

Paris 75 – Cergy 47 – Évreux 37 – Rouen 65

La Réserve without rest

1.5 km north on r. Blanche-Hochedé-Monet (after the church) – ✆ 02 32 21 99 09 – mlreserve@gmail.com – Fax 02 32 21 99 09

5 rm ☕ – ♦€ 85/100 ♦♦€ 130/160

◆ A garden and orchard serve as the setting for this family hotel with a soft yellow façade, located on the heights of Giverny. Nice hospitality. Charming rooms with a personal touch.

GIVET – 08 Ardennes – 306 K2 – pop. 7 372 – alt. 103 m – ✉ 08600

Northern France and the Paris Region — 14 C1

Paris 287 – Charleville-Mézières 58 – Fumay 23 – Rocroi 41

Office de tourisme, 10, quai des Fours ✆ 08 10 81 09 75, Fax 03 24 42 92 41

<★ from Charlemont fort ★.

Les Reflets Jaunes without rest

2 r. du Gén. de Gaulle – ✆ 03 24 42 85 85 – reflets.jaunes@wanadoo.fr – Fax 03 24 42 85 86

17 rm – ♦€ 54/89 ♦♦€ 60/115, ☕ € 7,50

◆ This building from 1685, converted into a hotel in the late 20th century, blends blue and yellow tones in the rooms and open spaces. Some rooms come with a video player and Jacuzzi.

Le Val St-Hilaire without rest

7 quai des Fours – ✆ 03 24 42 38 50 – hotel.val.saint.hilaire@wanadoo.fr – Fax 03 24 42 07 36

20 rm – ♦€ 55 ♦♦€ 65, ☕ € 8

◆ This regional-style building set on the left bank of the Meuse has identical rooms with good soundproofing. A fine view of the river from the rooms at the front.

Le Roosevelt without rest

14 quai Remparts – ☎ 03 24 42 14 14 – Fax 03 24 42 15 15 – Closed 22 December-4 January

8 rm – 🚹€ 49 🚹🚹€ 64, ☕ € 8

◆ This old stone house on the banks of the Meuse has small, recently renovated guestrooms. The breakfast room is also a tea room and tavern. No smoking establishment.

Auberge de la Tour

6 quai des Fours – ☎ 03 24 40 41 71 – info@auberge-de-la-tour.net – Fax 03 24 56 90 78 – Closed 15 December-14 January and Monday October-March

Rest – Menu (€ 13), € 16 (weekday lunch), € 26/39 – Carte € 25/57

◆ Typical Ardennes atmosphere serving classic traditional cuisine in a refined, rustic dining area with old brick and stone walls.

GLAINE-MONTAIGUT – 63 Puy-de-Dôme – 326 H8 – pop. 482 – alt. 350 m – ✉ 63160 6 C2

▶ Paris 440 – Clermont-Ferrand 31 – Issoire 37 – Thiers 21

Auberge de la Forge with rm

– ☎ 04 73 73 41 80 – a.delaforge@wanadoo.fr – Fax 04 73 73 33 83 – Closed 1st-20 September

4 rm – 🚹€ 30/40 🚹🚹€ 30/40, ☕ € 6 – ½ P € 38/48 – **Rest** – *(closed Sunday evening, Monday and Tuesday)* Menu (€ 13 bi), € 16/34 – Carte € 21/33

◆ Opposite the beautiful Romanesque church, a pleasant inn refitted in the old style (adobe walls) with a reconstruction of the village forge (fire, bellows, anvil).

GLUIRAS – 07 Ardèche – 331 J4 – pop. 349 – alt. 800 m – ✉ 07190 44 B3

▶ Paris 606 – Le Cheylard 20 – Lamastre 40 – Privas 33 – Valence 48

Le Relais de Sully with rm

pl. centrale – ☎ 04 75 66 63 41 – lerelaisdesully@orange.fr – Fax 04 75 64 69 88 – Closed 20-27 December, 1st February-15 March, Sunday dinner, Wednesday dinner and Monday except July-August

4 rm – 🚹€ 34 🚹🚹€ 34, ☕ € 6 – **Rest** – Menu € 16 (weekdays)/36

◆ This stone building in the centre of a mountain village is thought to have been a monastery. Local country cuisine served in a smart dining room veranda and on the terrace.

GOLBEY – 88 Vosges – 314 G3 – see Épinal

GOLFE DE SANTA-GIULIA – 2A Corse-du-Sud – 345 E10 – see Corse (Porto-Vecchio)

LE GOLFE-JUAN – 06 Alpes-Maritimes – 341 D6 – ✉ 06220 Vallauris

French Riviera 42 E2

▶ Paris 905 – Antibes 5 – Cannes 6 – Grasse 23 – Nice 29

ℹ Office de tourisme, boulevard des Frères Roustan ☎ 04 93 63 73 12, Fax 04 93 63 21 07

for Vallauris see plan of Cannes

Beau Soleil without rest

6 impasse Beau-Soleil, via D6007 (towards Antibes) – ☎ 04 93 63 63 63 – contact@hotel-beau-soleil.com – Fax 04 93 63 02 89 – Open 7 March-31 October

30 rm – 🚹€ 54/79 🚹🚹€ 67/134, ☕ € 9

◆ This modern hotel, located in a cul-de-sac 500m from the Midi beach and Théâtre de la Mer, has colourful, well-kept rooms, some with balconies.

De la Mer without rest

226 av. Liberté, (D 6007) – ☎ 04 93 63 80 83 – hotel.de.la.mer@wanadoo.fr – Fax 04 93 63 10 83 – Closed 3 November-3 December

33 rm – 🚹€ 49/102 🚹🚹€ 59/115, ☕ € 8

◆ The rooms have good soundproofing and face the back to make up for the nearness to the N 7. Some of those facing the pool have a balcony.

XX **Tétou** ≤ Lérins islands,

à la plage – ✆ 04 93 63 71 16 – Fax 04 93 63 16 77 – Open 2 March-30 October and closed Wednesday

Rest – Carte € 100/181

◆ This local institution, founded in 1920, retains the atmosphere of a luxury seaside resort restaurant. Bouillabaisse always appears on the short regional seafood menu.

XX **Nounou** ≤ Lérins islands, VISA AE

à la plage – ✆ 04 93 63 71 73 – Fax 04 93 63 46 91 – Closed 12 November-25 December, Sunday dinner and Monday except July-August

Rest – Menu € 44/66 – Carte € 44/91

◆ A beach restaurant with bay windows overlooking the coast. Fish and seafood dishes together with a few Provençal specialities complete the seaside atmosphere.

in Vallauris Northwest: 2,5 km by D 135 – pop. 25 773 – alt. 120 m – ✉ 06220

Office de tourisme, 84, avenue de la Liberté ✆ 04 93 63 18 38, Fax 04 93 63 95 01

Musée national la Guerre et la Paix (château) - Musée de l'Automobile★ Northwest: 4 km.

Le Mas Samarcande without rest

138 Grand-Boulevard de Super-Cannes – ✆ 04 93 63 97 73 – mireille.diot@wanadoo.fr – Fax 04 93 63 97 73 – Closed 18-28 December

5 rm – †€ 125/130 ††€ 125/130

◆ This charming villa provides refined, distinctive rooms combining Provençal and exotic styles, with a terrace affording a superb view.

GORDES – 84 Vaucluse – 332 E10 – pop. 2 092 – alt. 372 m – ✉ 84220

Provence 42 **E1**

Paris 712 – Apt 19 – Avignon 38 – Carpentras 26 – Cavaillon 18 – Sault 35

Office de tourisme, le Château ✆ 04 90 72 02 75, Fax 04 90 72 02 26

Site★ - Village★ - Château: fireplace★ - Village des Bories★★ Southwest: 2 km by D 15 then 15 mn - Sénanque abbey ★★ Northwest: 4 km - Press★ in the musée des Moulins de Bouillons South: 5 km.

La Bastide de Gordes & Spa ≤ le Luberon, rm, rest, VISA AE

le village – ✆ 04 90 72 12 12 – mail@bastide-de-gordes.com – Fax 04 90 72 05 20 – Closed 2 January-7 February

40 rm – †€ 170/446 ††€ 180/490, € 27 – 5 suites – ½ P € 173/328

Rest – Menu € 39 (lunch), € 64/94 – Carte € 88/109

◆ This 16C residence boasts Provençal style rooms overlooking the valley or the village. Excellent spa. Mediterranean-style food and a fine selection of regional wines served in an elegant setting. Veranda facing a hanging garden and a panoramic terrace with magnificent views of the Lubéron and the Alpilles.

Les Bories ≤ The Lubéron, rest, VISA AE

rte de Sénanque, 2 km – ✆ 04 90 72 00 51 – lesbories@wanadoo.fr – Fax 04 90 72 01 22 – Closed 4 January-13 February

27 rm – †€ 195/410 ††€ 195/410, € 23 – 2 suites – ½ P € 180/287

Rest – *(closed Sunday dinner and Monday from 3 November to 30 April and lunch Monday-Thursday in July-August) (pre-book)* Menu € 55/88 – Carte € 83/96

Spec. Tomates anciennes en déclinaison (season). Saint-Pierre poêlé aux courgettes et olives noires de Nyons. Profiteroles revisitées.

◆ These luxurious "bories" seem lost in the garrigue, amidst the lavender and olive trees. Stylish rooms. Superb pool and spa. A restaurant occupying an old sheepfold with an attractive shaded terrace and herb garden. Mediterranean cooking and local wines.

Le Gordos without rest VISA AE

1.5 km via rte de Cavaillon – ✆ 04 90 72 00 75 – mail@hotel-le-gordos.com – Fax 04 90 72 07 00 – Open 15 March-2 November

19 rm – †€ 95/126 ††€ 120/205, € 15

◆ This recent stone farmhouse stands at the entrance to the village. Some rooms on a level with the Italian garden of aromatic plants.

Le Mas des Romarins without rest – village
rte de Sénanque – 04 90 72 12 13 – info@masromarins.com – Fax 04 90 72 13 13 – Closed 16 November-19 December, 6 January-28 February
13 rm – €88/112 €99/188
◆ Breakfast with the sunrise on the terrace of this 100-year-old farm overlooking Gordes. Neat and tidy rooms with individualised furnishings. Non-smoking.

Mas de la Beaume without rest
rte de Cavaillon – 04 90 72 02 96 – la.beaume@wanadoo.fr – Fax 04 90 72 06 89
5 rm – €105/175 €105/175
◆ A former barn in a garden of olive trees is now a hotel with a seawater swimming pool and Jacuzzi. The rooms (non-smoking) are decorated in Provençal style. Library.

Apt road East: by D 2 – 84220 Gordes

Auberge de Carcarille – rm,
rte d'Apt, on the D2: 4 km – 04 90 72 02 63 – carcaril@club-internet.fr – Fax 04 90 72 05 74 – Closed 11 November-26 January
20 rm – €68/105 €68/105, €11 – ½ P €77/101 – **Rest** – *(closed Friday except dinner from April to September)* Menu €20/47 – Carte €26/55
◆ Just below the village, this pleasant dry-stone building has rooms redecorated in Provençal style, with a balcony or terrace. Bright white walls in the restaurant with its colourful chairs and floral curtains.

La Ferme de la Huppe – rm,
5 km on D156 Goult road – 04 90 72 12 25 – gerald.konings@wanadoo.fr – Fax 04 90 72 01 83 – Open 1st April-30 October
9 rm – €90/125 €90/170, €10 – ½ P €85/125
Rest – *(closed Wednesday) (dinner only except Sunday)* Menu €45
◆ Pretty 18C farmhouse of dry stone with cosy and fresh rooms arranged around the well. Rustic "borie"-style dining room decorated with a collection of agricultural tools. Terrace under an awning with wrought-iron furniture.

des Imberts road Southwest: 4 km by D 2 – 84220 Gordes

Mas de la Senancole
(Hamlet of Les Imberts) – 04 90 76 76 55 – gordes@mas-de-la-senancole.com – Fax 04 90 76 70 44
21 rm – €98/140 €98/229, €13
Rest L'Estellan – see restaurant listing
◆ The Sénancole runs just by this modern hotel. Soundproofed rooms with painted furniture; some have a private terrace.

Le Moulin des Sources
Hameau des Gros – 04 90 72 11 69 – contact@le-moulin-des-sources.com
4 rm – €90/145 €90/145 – 1 suite – **Table d'hôte** – Menu €35 bi
◆ A peaceful stay guaranteed in this establishment as you wander from the lounge-library to the garden and swimming pool. Cosy guestrooms. A vaulted, partly troglodyte dining room is the setting for cuisine based on fresh, local produce.

Le Mas Tourteron
Chemin de St-Blaise – 04 90 72 00 16 – elisabeth.bourgeois@wanadoo.fr – Fax 04 90 72 09 81 – Open 1st March-31 October and closed Sunday dinner in October and March, and Tuesday
Rest – *(dinner only except Sunday)* Menu €62
◆ A small country farmhouse hidden behind a high wall, with a charming rustic dining area and terrace under the linden trees. Provençal dishes.

L'Estellan – Hôtel Mas de la Senancole
– 04 90 72 04 90 – Fax 04 90 72 04 90
Rest – Menu €26 (weekday lunch)/55 – Carte €46/60
◆ Attractive bistro occupying an old stone farmhouse. Daudet and Mistral quotations adorn the ochre dining room walls. Fine terrace. Regional cuisine.

GORGES DE LA RESTONICA – 2B Haute-Corse – 345 D6 – see Corse (Corte)

GORZE – 57 Moselle – 307 H4 – pop. 1 392 – alt. 300 m – ✉ 57680 Alsace-Lorraine

Paris 324 – Jarny 17 – Metz 20 – Pont-à-Mousson 22 – St-Mihiel 43 – Verdun 54 26 **B1**

Office de tourisme, 22, rue de l'Église ✆ 03 87 52 04 57, Fax 03 87 52 04 57

Hostellerie du Lion d'Or with rm
105 r. Commerce – ✆ 03 87 52 00 90 – h.r.liondor@wanadoo.fr – Fax 03 87 52 09 62 – Closed Sun. evening and Mon.
15 rm – €49 €55/60, €8 – **Rest** – Menu (€22 bi), €30/40 – Carte €42/52
◆ This 19th century post house has carefully preserved its original beams, stonework and fireplace. Regional cuisine served.

GOSNAY – 62 Pas-de-Calais – 301 I4 – see Béthune

LA GOUESNIÈRE – 35 Ille-et-Vilaine – 309 K3 – pop. 1 068 – alt. 22 m – ✉ 35350

Paris 390 – Dinan 25 – Dol-de-Bretagne 13 – Lamballe 65 – Rennes 64 – St-Malo 13 10 **D1**

Maison Tirel-Guérin (Jean-Luc Guérin)
at the station (rte Cancale): 1.5 km D 76 – ✆ 02 99 89 10 46 – info@tirel-guerin.com – Fax 02 99 89 12 62 – Closed 22 December-1st February
46 rm – €65 €82/138, €12 – 10 suites – ½ P €105/238
Rest – *(closed Sunday dinner October-March and Monday lunch except public holidays) (pre-book Sat - Sun)* Menu €27 (weekdays)/105 – Carte €50/100
Spec. Salade de cailles poêlées, truffe et foie gras. Homard bleu grillé "Jean-Luc". Soufflé au Grand Marnier.
◆ A family establishment, opposite a country station, with many assets: flower garden, spacious and well-kept rooms, jacuzzi and faultless service. Delicious personalised cuisine served in a dining room infused with a pleasant, country-style atmosphere.

Château de Bonaban
r. Alfred de Folliny – ✆ 02 99 58 24 50 – chateau.bonaban@wanadoo.fr – Fax 02 99 58 28 41
34 rm – €100/210 €100/300, €15 – **Rest** – *(closed Sunday dinner except May-September, Wednesday except dinner May-September, Tuesday lunch May-September and Monday lunch)* Menu €30 (weekdays)/50 – Carte €44/54
◆ This 18th century chateau has retained its original marble staircase and wood panelling. A range of rooms available, with a view of the park. Simpler accommodation in the second wing. Slightly aristocratic atmosphere in the dining rooms.

GOULT – 84 Vaucluse – 332 E10 – pop. 1 285 – alt. 258 m – ✉ 84220 42 **E1**

Paris 714 – Apt 14 – Avignon 41 – Bonnieux 8 – Carpentras 35 – Cavaillon 19 – Sault 38

La Bartavelle
r. Cheval Blanc – ✆ 04 90 72 33 72 – Fax 04 90 72 33 72 – Open from beg. March-mid November and closed Tuesday and Wednesday
Rest – *(dinner only)* Menu €39
◆ 'Petit Marcel' and his hunter father would have appreciated this vaulted dining room with its floor tiles as red as a rock partridge! Small restaurant serving regional dishes.

GOUMOIS – 25 Doubs – 321 L3 – pop. 196 – alt. 490 m – ✉ 25470 17 **C2**

Paris 513 – Besançon 92 – Bienne 486 – Montbéliard 55 – Morteau 47
Corniche de Goumois★★, Burgundy-Jura

Taillard < Doubs valley, rm,
3 rte de la Corniche – ✆ 03 81 44 20 75 – hotel.taillard@wanadoo.fr – Fax 03 81 44 26 15 – Open 16 March-14 November
21 rm – €75/82 €75/145, €12 – ½ P €72/105
Rest – *(closed Wednesday dinner October-March, Monday lunch and Wednesday lunch)* Menu €23 (lunch), €33/70 – Carte €41/68
◆ Family hotel (1875) set in gardens in the Corniche de Gourmois offering pleasant rooms with individual touches. Plainer rooms in the annexe. Classic cuisine and fine list of local wines in the restaurant with pleasant views of the valley.

Le Moulin du Plain

– ✆ *03 81 44 41 99 – moulinduplain@orange.fr – Fax 03 81 44 45 70 – Open 25 February-31 October*

22 rm – ♦€ 42 ♦♦€ 57/64, ☕ € 7 – ½ P € 50 – **Rest** – Menu € 17 (weekdays)/35 – Carte € 19/41

◆ This hotel on the banks of the Doubs is surrounded by woodland. Some rooms have a view of the river. Paradise for anglers. Trout, morel and other local produce take pride of place at the table.

GOUPILLIÈRES – 14 Calvados – 303 J5 – pop. 150 – alt. 162 m – ✉ 14210

32 **B2**

▶ Paris 255 – Caen 24 – Condé-sur-Noireau 27 – Falaise 34 – Saint-Lô 63

Auberge du Pont de Brie

Halte de Grimbosq, east: 1.5 km – ✆ 02 31 79 37 84 – contact@pontdebrie.com – Closed 30 June-9 July, 22 December-22 January, 16-25 February, November and December except weekends, Sunday dinner October-April, Tuesday except July-August and Monday

Rest – Menu € 21/44 – Carte € 28/51

◆ Small family inn tucked away in the Orne valley. The bright veranda dining room is recently renovated and there is a summer terrace. Traditional fare.

GOURDON – 46 Lot – 337 E3 – pop. 4 882 – alt. 250 m – ✉ 46300

Dordogne-Berry-Limousin

28 **B1**

▶ Paris 543 – Sarlat-la-Canéda 26 – Bergerac 91 – Brive-la-Gaillarde 66 – Cahors 44 – Figeac 63

ℹ Office de tourisme, 24, rue du Majou ✆ 05 65 27 52 50, Fax 05 65 27 52 52

◉ Rue du Majou★ - Font★ in the Cordeliers church - Esplanade ✻★.

◉ Grottes de Cougnac★ Northwest: 3 km.

Hostellerie de la Bouriane

rest,

pl. du Foirail – ✆ 05 65 41 16 37 – hostellerie-la-bouriane@wanadoo.fr – Fax 05 65 41 04 92 – Closed 12-21 October, 23 January-10 March, Sunday dinner and Monday from 12 October to 30 April

20 rm – ♦€ 72/109 ♦♦€ 72/109, ☕ € 12 – ½ P € 75/79

Rest – *(closed Sunday dinner and Monday from 12 October to 30 April and lunch except Sunday)* Menu € 25/49 – Carte € 45/82

◆ This century-old hotel has retained its tradition of hospitality. Rustic, elegant rooms, with attic ceilings on the top floor. Pleasant garden. Reproductions of Aubusson tapestries and paintings in the dining area. Tasty, traditional cuisine.

in Vigan 5 km East by D 801 – pop. 1 189 – alt. 224 m – ✉ 46300

Auberge Chez Louise

in the village – ✆ 05 65 32 64 88 – Closed 15 December-15 February, Sunday dinner, Friday dinner and Saturday lunch

Rest – Menu € 19 (weekday lunch), € 23/34

◆ This village restaurant has retained its original rustic charm, with its old bar counter, beams and stone work. Traditional cuisine in a very friendly atmosphere.

GOURDON – 06 Alpes-Maritimes – 341 C5 – pop. 379 – alt. 800 m – ✉ 06620

French Riviera

42 **E2**

▶ Paris 921 – Cannes 27 – Castellane 62 – Grasse 15 – Nice 39 – Vence 25

ℹ Office de tourisme, place Victoria ✆ 04 93 09 68 25

◉ Site★★ - ≤★★ of the church apse - Château : musée des Arts décoratifs et de la modernité.

Au Vieux Four

r. Basse – ✆ 04 93 09 68 60 – Closed dinner October-June except Friday and Saturday, Wednesday dinner June-October and Thursday

Rest – *(number of covers limited, pre-book)* Menu (€ 20), € 32 – Carte € 40/44

◆ An charming old house tucked away in the village. Warm welcome; the menu of the day, which reveals a marked southern accent and perfume, is marked up on a blackboard.

GOURETTE – 64 Pyrénées-Atlantiques – **342** K7 – alt. 1 400 m – Winter sports : 1 400/2 400 m 1 18 – ✉ 64440 Eaux Bonnes Atlantic Coast 3 **B3**

Paris 829 – Argelès-Gazost 35 – Eaux-Bonnes 9 – Laruns 14 – Lourdes 47 – Pau 52

Office de tourisme, burreau d'accueil d'Eaux-Bonnes ✆ 05 59 05 33 08, Fax 05 59 05 32 58

Col d'Aubisque ✳★★ North: 4 km.

Boule de Neige

– ✆ 05 59 05 10 05 – bouledeneige@wanadoo.fr – Fax 05 59 05 11 81 – Open from beg. July to end August and end November to 15 April

22 rm – €60/100 €70/150, €10 – ½ P €62/72 – **Rest** – Menu €20/30 – Carte €22/49

♦ A 1970s building at the foot of the ski runs, facing the Pyrenean peaks. Functional rooms, some with bunk beds for children. Family restaurant and busy terrace. Traditional cuisine; snacks at lunchtime.

L'Amoulat with rm

– ✆ 05 59 05 12 06 – chalet.hotel.amoulat@wanadoo.fr – Fax 05 59 05 13 45 – Open 16 June-14 September and 21 December-29 March

12 rm – €58 €72, €9 – ½ P €64 – **Rest** – *(closed lunch winter)* Menu €18/24 – Carte €17/33

♦ A chalet situated on the Aubisque Pass, a famous stretch in the Tour de France cycle race. Rustic dining room and veranda. Regional dishes and up-to-date cuisine. Simple rooms.

GOURNAY-EN-BRAY – 76 Seine-Maritime – **304** K5 – pop. 6 275 – alt. 94 m – ✉ 76220 Normandy 33 **D2**

Paris 97 – Amiens 78 – Les Andelys 38 – Beauvais 31 – Dieppe 76 – Gisors 25 – Rouen 50

Office de tourisme, 9, place d'Armes ✆ 02 35 90 28 34, Fax 02 35 09 62 07

Le Saint Aubin

Dieppe road 3 km on D 915 – ✆ 02 35 09 70 97 – hotel.le.saint.aubin@wanadoo.fr – Fax 02 35 09 30 93

60 rm – €70/85 €72/120, €8 – ½ P €93 – **Rest** – *(closed Sunday dinner and Saturday)* Menu €25 (weekdays), €30/45 – Carte €30/52

♦ This modern building, slightly set back from the road, has functional rooms, suitable for an overnight stay. The restaurant in the hotel basement serves unpretentious, traditional cuisine. Simple decor.

Le Cygne without rest

20 r. Notre Dame – ✆ 02 35 90 27 80 – hotel.le.cygne@orange.fr – Fax 02 35 90 59 00

29 rm – €46 €57, €6,50

♦ The hotel is located in the centre of this small town in the Bray region. Simple, well-kept rooms; those facing the back are quieter at night.

GOUVIEUX – 60 Oise – **305** F5 – see Chantilly

GOUY-ST-ANDRÉ – 62 Pas-de-Calais – **301** E5 – see Hesdin

GRAMAT – 46 Lot – **337** G3 – pop. 3 545 – alt. 305 m – ✉ 46500 Dordogne-Berry-Limousin 29 **C1**

Paris 534 – Brive-la-Gaillarde 57 – Cahors 58 – Figeac 36 – Gourdon 38 – St-Céré 22

Office de tourisme, place de la République ✆ 05 65 38 73 60, Fax 05 65 33 46 38

Lion d'Or

pl. de la République – ✆ 05 65 38 73 18 – liondorhotel@wanadoo.fr – Fax 05 65 38 84 50 – Closed January

15 rm – €44/82 €55/88, €10 – ½ P €92/110 – **Rest** – *(closed Fri. lunch and Sat. lunch from 11 Nov. to end - Mar.)* Menu €17 (weekday lunch), €26/39 – Carte €42/62

♦ Local house with character in the centre of town just 200m from a park. Soundproofed, tastefully decorated rooms. Regional and classic dishes are served in the chic dining room or on the pleasant, shaded and flower-decked terrace.

Le Relais des Gourmands VISA

(at the station) – ✆ 05 65 38 83 92 – relais-des-gourmands@orange.fr – Fax 05 65 38 70 99 – Closed one week in October, 9-22 February, Sunday dinner and Monday except July-August
16 rm – €56/62 €56/62, €8,50 – ½ P €57/70 – **Rest** – *(closed Sunday dinner and Monday)* Menu (€15), €17 (weekdays)/40 – Carte €26/51
◆ Attentive service in this establishment with modern rooms opposite the station. Lovely swimming pool surrounded by a garden. Bright modern restaurant with yellow colours. Regional menu.

Hostellerie du Causse VISA AE

2 km on Cahors road – ✆ 05 65 10 60 60 – contact@hostellerieducausse.com – Fax 05 65 10 60 61 – Closed 16 November-12 February and Sunday dinner
28 rm – €48/59 €60/75, €9 – ½ P €57/60 – **Rest** – Menu (€14 bi), €18 (weekdays)/57 – Carte €34/60
◆ Located outside the town centre, this modern, local-style building offers spacious and well-kept rooms. Swimming pool. Generous traditional cuisine, enriched by local specialities, served in an attractive dining room or on the summer terrace.

Du Centre rm, rest, VISA AE

pl. de la République – ✆ 05 65 38 73 37 – le.centre@wanadoo.fr – Fax 05 65 38 73 66
18 rm – €46/55 €55, €7,50 – ½ P €54 – **Rest** – Menu (€11), €13 (weekday lunch)/32 – Carte €22/39
◆ Functional guestrooms in the centre of a town hosting regular agricultural shows. Traditional, Breton-influenced cuisine served in a bright dining room or on the terrace in fine weather.

Moulin de Fresquet

1 km via rte de Figeac – ✆ 05 65 38 70 60 – info@moulindefresquet.com – Fax 05 65 33 60 13 – Open April-October
5 rm – €64 €110 – **Table d'hôte** – *(closed Thurs.)* Menu €25 bi
◆ This mill, with elements from the 14C to 19C, is set in a garden with a mill race and an amazing assortment of ducks. The rooms are decorated with antique furniture and paintings; some also come with a terrace. The restaurant serves appetising regional cuisine.

in Lavergne Northeast: 4 km by D 677 – pop. 410 – alt. 320 m – ✉ 46500

Le Limargue with rm VISA

– ✆ 05 65 38 76 02 – lelimargue@wanadoo.fr – Fax 05 65 38 76 02 – Open 3 March-10 November and closed 6-17 October, Tuesday and Wednesday except July-August
3 rm – €44 €44, €5,50 – ½ P €46 – **Rest** – Menu €15/25 – Carte €21/39
◆ Stop at this pleasant freestone building, while crossing the Gramat plateau, to savour the Quercy cuisine. Rooms with attractive personal touches.

Brive road : 4,5 km by N 140 and secondary road – ✉ 46500 Gramat

Château de Roumégouse < Causse de Gramat, VISA AE

– ✆ 05 65 33 63 81 – chateau.de.roumegouse@wanadoo.fr – Fax 05 65 33 71 18 – Open 1st May-31 December
15 rm – €80 €110/320, €16 – **Rest** – *(closed Tuesday dinner except July-August) (dinner only except Sunday)* Menu €42 bi (lunch)/55 (dinner) – Carte €52/68
◆ The round tower with its library-bar, the antique furniture, and the "bories" in the park make this 19C castle - honoured by a visit from General de Gaulle - a unique place. Elegant dining rooms with a veranda and flower-decked terrace; regional menu.

LE GRAND-BORNAND – **74 Haute-Savoie** – **328** L5 – **pop. 2 115** – **alt. 934 m** – **Winter sports : 1 000/2 100 m 2 37** – ✉ **74450** French Alps 46 **F1**

Paris 564 – Albertville 47 – Annecy 31 – Bonneville 23 – Chamonix-Mont-Blanc 76

Office de tourisme, place de l'Église ✆ 04 50 02 78 00, Fax 04 50 02 78 01

Vermont without rest
rte du Bouchet – ✆ 04 50 02 36 22 – hotel.vermont@wanadoo.fr – Fax 04 50 02 39 36 – Open mid June-mid September and mid December-mid April
23 rm – ♦€ 75/98 ♦♦€ 89/130
♦ Close to the La Joyère cable car, a regional construction with plenty of space for relaxation and revitalisation (jacuzzi and sauna). Panelled rooms, often with balconies.

Delta without rest
L'Envers de Villeneuve – ✆ 04 50 02 26 25 – info@hotel-delta74.com – Fax 04 50 02 32 71 – Open mid June-mid September and mid December-mid April
15 rm – ♦€ 39/69 ♦♦€ 44/69, € 7
♦ A small recently built chalet on the outskirts of the village, containing a sports shop (ski hire) and a hotel with reasonably-sized, wood-panelled rooms. Library, billiard table and games for children.

Croix St-Maurice rest,
(opposite the church) – ✆ 04 50 02 20 05 – info@hotel-lacroixstmaurice.com – Fax 04 50 02 35 37 – Closed 1st-20 October
21 rm – ♦€ 49/83 ♦♦€ 49/83, € 7,50 – ½ P € 47/72 – **Rest** – Menu € 18/27 – Carte € 26/37
♦ Traditional chalet in the heart of the town famous for its Reblochon cheese. The rooms, many of which have balconies, have been renovated in regional style. Traditional cuisine and Savoyard specialities. Lovely view of the church and Aravis mountain range from the dining room.

XX **L'Hysope**
Le Pont de Suize, (Bouchet road) – ✆ 04 50 02 29 87 – Fax 04 50 02 29 87 – Closed 6-26 October, Wednesday and Thursday off season
Rest – Menu € 29/69 – Carte € 43/73
♦ This bright, convivial dining room is very different from a typical mountain restaurant. Comprehensive wine list (about 40 wines) and contemporary, personalised cuisine. Meals served on the terrace in summer.

X **Le Traîneau d'Angeline**
Le Pont de Suize – ✆ 04 50 63 27 64 – Fax 04 50 63 27 64 – Closed June, 15 November-15 December, Monday and Tuesday except school holidays and Wednesday off season
Rest – Menu (€ 13,50) – Carte € 28/40
♦ Pleasant, rustic restaurant with a exhibition of contemporary art. Local specialities and meat grilled in the fireplace in front of guests.

in Chinaillon **North: 5,5 km by D 4 – ✉ 74450 Le Grand-Bornand**

Les Cimes without rest
– ✆ 04 50 27 00 38 – info@hotel-les-cimes.com – Fax 04 50 27 08 46 – Open 13 June-6 September and 25 October-25 April
10 rm – ♦€ 70/110 ♦♦€ 75/155, € 11
♦ A little chalet with pretty rooms in the centre of the Grand Bo sporting hamlet; contemporary mountain-style décor, antique furniture, trinkets, etc. A real find!

Crémaillère
Le Chinaillon – ✆ 04 50 27 02 33 – cremaill@wanadoo.fr – Fax 04 50 27 07 91 – Open 15 June-15 September and 20 December-20 April
15 rm – ♦€ 59/95 ♦♦€ 59/95, € 7,50 – ½ P € 56/74 – **Rest** – *(closed Tues. lunchtime and Mon.)* Menu € 19 (lunch), € 24/34 – Carte € 20/43
♦ All rooms in this small family-run hotel have balconies and face south towards the ski slopes. Very well-maintained. Cosy lounge with a fireplace. Savoyard cuisine served in the rustic, light wood decor of the dining room.

in la Vallée du Bouchet – ✉ 74450

Le Chalet des Troncs
3.5 km east – ✆ 04 50 02 28 50 – contact@chaletdestroncs.com – Fax 04 50 63 25 28
4 rm – ♦€ 132/158 ♦♦€ 148/216, € 15 – ½ P € 116/158
Table d'hôte – *(open 22 December-23 April and July-August)* Menu € 35/52
♦ The rooms of this old farmhouse deep in the countryside are little alpine gems. Panoramic hammam and magnificent indoor pool fed by spring water. Family cooking made with home-grown produce served by the fireside.

GRANDCAMP-MAISY – 14 Calvados – 303 F3 – pop. 1 831 – alt. 5 m – ✉ 14450 Normandy 32 B2

Paris 297 – Caen 63 – Cherbourg 73 – St-Lô 40

Office de tourisme, 118, rue Aristide-Briand ✆ 02 31 22 62 44, Fax 02 31 22 62 44

La Faisanderie without rest
– ✆ 02 31 22 70 06
3 rm – €45 €50
◆ A welcoming house covered in vines, located on an estate with a stud farm. Charming rooms with a personal touch. Breakfast served in a warm dining area with a fine fireplace.

La Marée VISA AE
5 quai Henri Cheron – ✆ 02 31 21 41 00 – restolamaree@wanadoo.fr – Fax 02 31 21 44 55 – Closed 1st January-12 February
Rest – Menu (€ 16), € 25/40 – Carte € 34/49
◆ Sailing ambience and naval decor opposite the fish market; the dining room has a veranda and serves fresh seafood caught in the Channel or from the ocean.

GRAND'COMBE-CHÂTELEU – 25 Doubs – 321 J4 – see Morteau

LA GRANDE-MOTTE – 34 Hérault – 339 J7 – pop. 6 458 – alt. 1 m – Casino – ✉ 34280 Languedoc-Roussillon-Tarn Gorges 23 C2

Paris 747 – Aigues-Mortes 12 – Lunel 16 – Montpellier 28 – Nîmes 45 – Sète 47

Office de tourisme, allée des Parcs ✆ 04 67 56 42 00, Fax 04 67 29 91 42

de La Grande-Motte Avenue du Golf, North: 2 km, ✆ 04 67 56 05 00.

Les Corallines the coast, rest, VISA AE
615 allée de la Plage, (Le Point Zéro) – ✆ 04 67 29 13 13 – info@thalasso-grandemotte.com – Fax 04 67 29 14 74 – Closed 22 December-29 January
39 rm – €96/142 €120/178, € 13 – 3 suites – ½ P € 104/133
Rest – Menu (€ 23), € 25/30 – Carte € 30/51
◆ Just outside the centre, by the sea, a recent hotel complex with a thalassotherapy centre. Rooms with a balcony. Fine pool and panoramic terrace. In the restaurant, modern setting and furnishings and a Mediterranean ambiance.

Mercure the coast, rm, VISA AE
140 r. du port – ✆ 04 67 56 90 81 – h1230@accor.com – Fax 04 67 56 92 29
99 rm – €120/170 €140/200, € 13 – 18 suites – ½ P € 80/120
Rest – Carte € 28/38
◆ This hotel's tower dominates the harbour, in the busy centre of the resort. The rooms all have balconies. Simple cuisine based on salads and grills served in a contemporary dining room or terrace shaded by plane trees.

Novotel VISA AE
1641 av. du Golf – ✆ 04 67 29 88 88 – h2190@accor.com – Fax 04 67 29 17 01
81 rm – €90/150 €90/150, € 12,50 – **Rest** – Menu (€ 18) – Carte € 21/37
◆ An establishment at the entrance to the golf course which greets guests with a fine glass-domed hallway. Spacious and functional rooms in keeping with the chain's usual standards. Brasserie-style fare in a contemporary dining room with a terrace.

Golf Hôtel without rest VISA AE
1920 av. du Golf – ✆ 04 67 29 72 00 – golfhotel.montpellier@hotelbestwestern.fr – Fax 04 67 56 12 44
45 rm – €83/197 €87/197, € 14
◆ Recent building with renovated rooms in a contemporary style, all with loggias overlooking the golf course or Ponant lake. Pleasant garden with pool.

Azur Bord de Mer without rest VISA AE
pl. Justin – ✆ 04 67 56 56 00 – hotelazur34@aol.com – Fax 04 67 29 81 26
20 rm – €75/185 €80/185, € 12
◆ Located on the jetty on the south side of the port and commanding a splendid sea view; well-kept rooms with classic or modern decoration. Verdant surroundings.

Europe without rest
allée des Parcs – ✆ 04 67 56 62 60 – hoteleurope@wanadoo.fr – Fax 04 67 56 93 07 – Open from March to October
34 rm – †€ 64/115 ††€ 64/115, ☕ € 9,50
◆ A cheerful family hotel located behind the conference centre. Practical rooms, a pool and solarium on the terrace.

De la Plage
rm, rest,
allée du Levant, (towards Grau-du-Roi) – ✆ 04 67 29 93 00 – contact@hp-lagrandemotte.fr – Fax 04 67 56 00 07 – Open 1st March-30 October
39 rm – †€ 80/113 ††€ 85/117, ☕ € 13,50 – ½ P € 71/85
Rest – *(open 1st April-30 September and closed Sunday and Monday off season) (dinner only)* Menu € 22
◆ This establishment is in a residential area facing the beach. Spacious and bright rooms, with loggia for those overlooking the sea. Chairs and tablecloths in sunny colours set the scene for a simple meal with the emphasis on fish.

Alexandre
esplanade Maurice Justin – ✆ 04 67 56 63 63 – michel@alexandre-restaurant.com – Fax 04 67 29 74 69 – Closed 24 October-8 November, 2 January-2 February, Sunday dinner except July-August, Monday and Tuesday October-March
Rest – Menu € 48/75 – Carte € 42/109
Rest *Bistrot d'Alexandre* – *(open 23 June-2 September)* Menu € 20
◆ This restaurant provides a view of the port and the sea. Modern décor and elegant presentation. Classic meals and seafood dishes with a good selection of wines from the Languedoc region. The Bistrot offers a relaxed atmosphere and a menu featuring grilled meat and fish dishes.

GRAND-FOUGERAY – 35 Ille-et-Vilaine – 309 L8 – pop. 1 970 – alt. 40 m – ✉ 35390

10 **D2**

Paris 392 – Rennes 49 – Cesson-Sévigné 52 – Bruz 41 – Châteaubriant 34

Les Palis
15 pl. de l'Église – ✆ 02 99 08 30 80 – contact@restaurantlespalis.fr – Fax 02 99 08 45 20 – Closed 8-16 February
13 rm – †€ 70 ††€ 70, ☕ € 9,50 – ½ P € 65
Rest – *(closed Sunday dinner and Monday lunch)* Menu (€ 15), € 20 (weekdays)/37 – Carte € 37/45
◆ Entirely renovated hotel on the main square of the village. Contemporary rooms in grey and white tones, with light coloured wooden furniture. Traditional dishes served under a Bacchus fresco and beamed ceiling.

LE GRAND VILLAGE PLAGE – 17 Charente-Maritime – 324 C4 – see Île d'Oléron

GRANDVILLERS – 88 Vosges – 314 I3 – pop. 712 – alt. 365 m – ✉ 88600

Paris 404 – Épinal 22 – Lunéville 48 – Gérardmer 29 – Remiremont 38 – St-Dié 28

27 **C3**

Europe et Commerce
rm,
3 et 4 rte de Bruyères – ✆ 03 29 65 71 17 – hotel.bastien.europe@wanadoo.fr – Fax 03 29 65 85 23
21 rm – †€ 46/56 ††€ 56/66, ☕ € 8 – ½ P € 44
Rest – *(closed Friday dinner and Sunday dinner)* Menu € 13 (weekdays)/38 – Carte € 21/45
◆ The oldest building houses a few rooms; those in the wing are quieter and overlook the garden. Light, stylish dining room where you can enjoy tasty, classic cuisine.

in Frémifontaine 5 km north by D 48 and D 70 – pop. 365 – alt. 343 m – ✉ 88600

Les Chambres du Bois Collé
1 B le Petit-Pierrepont – ✆ 03 29 65 90 68 – jean-marie.ferreira@wanadoo.fr – Fax 03 29 65 88 90
4 rm ☕ – †€ 45 ††€ 60 – ½ P € 55 – **Table d'hôte** – Menu € 20 bi
◆ This tastefully restored old farmhouse is ideal for forest lovers. Each of the four rooms, decorated in a different colour, sports a distinctly cocooning atmosphere.

GRANGES-LÈS-BEAUMONT – 26 Drôme – 332 C3 – see Romans-sur-Isère

LES GRANGES-STE-MARIE – 25 Doubs – 321 H6 – see Malbuisson

GRANS – 13 Bouches-du-Rhône – 340 F4 – pop. 3 753 – alt. 52 m – ✉ 13450

Paris 729 – Arles 43 – Marseille 50 – Martigues 29 – Salon-de-Provence 7

Syndicat d'initiative, boulevard Victor Jauffret ✆ 04 90 55 88 92, Fax 04 90 55 86 27 40 **B3**

X **Le Planet** VISA

pl. J. Jaurès – ✆ 04 90 55 83 66 – Fax 04 90 55 83 66 – Closed 21 September-8 October, autumn half-term holidays, February holidays, Sunday dinner November-February, Monday and Tuesday

Rest – Menu € 18 (weekday lunch), € 25/40 – Carte € 30/50

◆ This old oil mill now houses a little vaulted restaurant with roughcast walls. Pleasant terrace under the plane trees. Friendly service, regional cuisine.

GRANVILLE – 50 Manche – 303 C6 – pop. 12 687 – alt. 10 m – Casino Z, and St-Pair-sur-Mer – ✉ 50400 Normandy 32 **A2**

Paris 342 – Avranches 27 – Cherbourg 105 – St-Lô 57 – St-Malo 93

Office de tourisme, 4, cours Jonville ✆ 02 33 91 30 03, Fax 02 33 91 30 19

de Granville Bréville-sur-Mer Pavillon du Golf, by Coutances road: 5 km, ✆ 02 33 50 23 06.

Tour of the ramparts★: place de l'Isthme ≤★ Z - Pointe du Roc: site★.

Plan on next page

Mercure le Grand Large without rest VISA AE

5 r. Falaise – ✆ 02 33 91 19 19 – infos@mercure-granville.com – Fax 02 33 91 19 00 Z **r**

51 rm – †€ 65/125 ††€ 65/160, ☐ € 10

◆ Looking down over the beach from the clifftop, this hotel associated with a thalassotherapy centre offers duplex or studio accommodation, mostly with sea views.

Michelet without rest P VISA

5 r. J. Michelet – ✆ 02 33 50 06 55 – contact@hotel-michelet-granville.com – Fax 02 33 50 12 25 Z **u**

19 rm – †€ 38/53 ††€ 38/53, ☐ € 7

◆ This hotel was named after one of the resort's famous visitors. Simple rooms that make the most of the peaceful setting; some offer a glimpse of the Channel. Warm hospitality.

XX **La Citadelle** AC VISA

34 r. Port – ✆ 02 33 50 34 10 – citadell@club-internet.fr – Fax 02 33 50 15 36 – Closed 12 November-11 December, Tuesday October-March and Wednesday

Rest – Menu € 19/33 – Carte € 27/46 Y **d**

◆ Taste the Chausey lobster and other seafood in a marine decor or on the sheltered terrace overlooking the harbour. It was from here that privateers and Newfoundland fishermen used to set sail.

via ① 4,5 km Coutances road – ✉ 50290 Bréville-sur-Mer

Villa Beaumonderie rm, P VISA AE

20 rte de Coutances – ✆ 02 33 50 36 36 – la-beaumonderie@wanadoo.fr – Fax 02 33 50 36 45

15 rm – †€ 70/180 ††€ 70/190, ☐ € 12 – 1 suite – ½ P € 50/125

Rest – *(closed 1st- 6 January)* Menu (€ 18), € 21 (weekday lunch)/27 – Carte € 28/48

◆ This 1920s house was the HQ of Eisenhower during the Normandy landings. Personalised rooms, an English lounge-bar, French billiards, squash and a pleasant park. The attractive rotunda restaurant serves traditional cuisine influenced by its seaside setting.

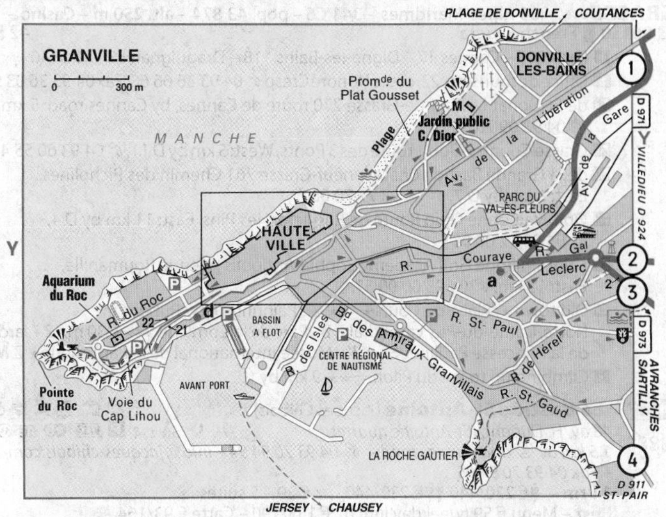

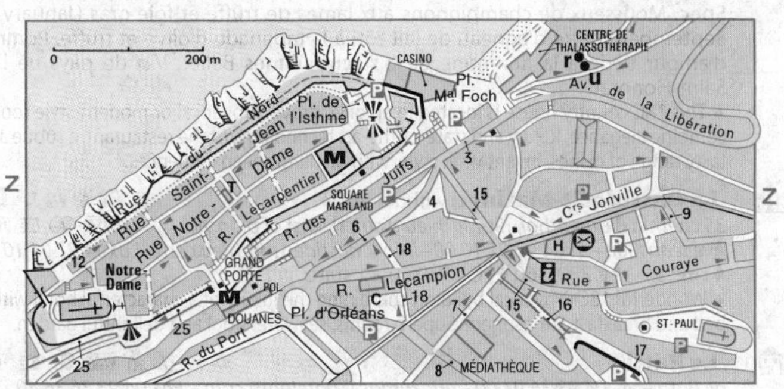

Briand (Av. A.) . . . . **Y** 2
Clemenceau (R. G.) . . . . **Z** 3
Corsaires (Pl. des) . . . . **Z** 4
Corsaires (R. des) . . . . **Z** 6
Couraye (R.) . . . . **Z**
Desmaisons (R. C.) . . . . **Z** 7
Granvillais (Bd des Amiraux) . . . . **Z** 8
Hauteserve (Bd d') . . . . **Z** 9
Juifs (R. des) . . . . **Z**
Lecampion (R.) . . . . **Z**
Leclerc (Av. Gén.) . . . . **Y**
Parvis-Notre-Dame (Montée du) . . . . **Z** 12
Poirier (R. Paul) . . . . **Z** 15
Ste-Geneviève (R.) . . . . **Z** 17
Saintonge (R.) . . . . **Z** 18
St-Sauveur (R.) . . . . **Z** 16
Terreneuviers (Bd des) . . . . . . **Y** 21
Vaufleury (Bd) . . . . **Y** 22
2e-et-202e-de-Ligne (Bd du) . . . . **Z** 25

in St-Pair-sur-Mer 4 km by ④ – pop. 3 616 – alt. 30 m – ✉ 50380

Office de tourisme, 3, rue Charles Mathurin
✆ 02 33 50 52 77

Au Pied de Cheval

au Casino – ✆ 02 33 91 34 01 – Fax 02 33 50 26 27 – Closed 16-22 June, 1st-21 October, 1st22 January, Sunday dinner off season, Monday and Tuesday

Rest – Menu € 19/26 – Carte € 25/46

◆ Restaurant near the casino and beach overlooking Granville. A large brasserie style low-key dining room serving French and Italian cuisine.

GRASSE – 06 Alpes-Maritimes – 341 C6 – pop. 43 874 – alt. 250 m – Casino – ✉ 06130 French Riviera 42 E2

Paris 905 – Cannes 17 – Digne-les-Bains 118 – Draguignan 53 – Nice 40

Office de tourisme, 22, cours Honoré Cresp ✆ 04 93 36 66 66, Fax 04 93 36 03 56

de St-Donat Le Plan-de-Grasse 270 route de Cannes, by Cannes road: 5 km, ✆ 04 93 09 76 60 ;

Grasse Country Club 1 route des 3 Ponts, West: 5 km by D 11, ✆ 04 93 60 55 44 ;

de la Grande Bastide Châteauneuf-Grasse 761 Chemin des Picholines, East: 6 km by D 7, ✆ 04 93 77 70 08 ;

Opio Valbonne Opio Route de Roquefort les Pins, East: 11 km by D 4, ✆ 04 93 12 00 08 ;

Saint-Philippe Golf Academy Sophia-Antipolis Avenue Roumanille, East: 12 km, ✆ 04 93 00 00 57.

Old town★: Place du Cours★ ≤★ Z - Paintings★ by Rubens in Notre-Dame-du-Puy cathedral Z **B** - Parc de la Corniche ❋★★ 30 mn Z - Jardin de la Princesse Pauline ≤★ X **K** - Musée international de la Parfumerie★ Z **M³**.

Climbing up to col du Pilon ≤★★ 9 km by ④.

La Bastide St-Antoine (Jacques Chibois)

48 av. H. Dunant, (St-Antoine quarter), 1,5 km by ② and Cannes road – ✆ 04 93 70 94 94 – info@jacques-chibois.com – Fax 04 93 70 94 95

11 rm – ♦€ 220/440 ♦♦€ 230/440, ☕ € 29 – 5 suites

Rest – Menu € 59 (weekday lunch), € 155/190 – Carte € 93/164

Spec. Mousseux de champignons aux lames de truffe et foie gras (January to September). Carré d'agneau de lait rôti à la tapenade d'olive et truffe. Pomme d'amour tiède à la florentine de pistache. **Wines** Bellet, Vin de pays de l'Ile Saint-Honorat.

◆ This 18C country house is located in an olive grove. Provençal or modern-style rooms combine elegance, luxury and state-of-the-art technology. At the restaurant, a subtle and tasty range of dishes, inventive in style, with Mediterranean influences.

La Bastide St-Mathieu without rest

35 chemin Blumenthal, (St-Mathieu district), east of plan via Ave Jean XXIII – ✆ 04 97 01 10 00 – info@bastidestmathieu.com – Fax 04 97 01 10 09

4 rm ☕ – ♦€ 330/360 ♦♦€ 330/360 – 1 suite

◆ Wonderful 18C Provençal building combining the luxury of a characterful hotel with a bed and breakfast atmosphere. Superb rooms, seawater pool and delightful garden.

Le Patti

pl. Patti – ✆ 04 93 36 01 00 – eric.ramos@hotelpatti.com – Fax 04 93 36 36 40

73 rm – ♦€ 54/79 ♦♦€ 69/115, ☕ € 8 – ½ P € 53/76 – **Rest** – *(closed January and Sunday)* Menu € 19/36 – Carte € 26/55 Y **a**

◆ The rooms in this hotel near the international centre have Provencal or modern decor. Shop selling products from southeastern France in the vestibule. Modern dining room and terrace looking onto a small square. Traditional cuisine with a regional bias.

Moulin St-François without rest

60 av. Maupassant, 2 km west on St-Cézaire road – ✆ 04 93 42 14 35 – contact@moulin-saint-francois.com – Fax 04 93 42 13 53

3 rm ☕ – ♦€ 220/250 ♦♦€ 220/350

◆ Savour the delightful peace and quiet of this mill (1760) surrounded by a park of olive groves whilst relishing the luxury and refinement of its superb rooms. Non-smoking establishment.

Southeast 5 km by D 4 – ✉ 06130 Grasse

Lou Fassum "La Tourmaline" (Emmanuel Ruz)

381 rte de Plascassier – ≤ Plain of Grasse,

✆ 04 93 60 14 44 – contact@loufassum.com – Fax 04 93 60 07 92 – Closed November, Tuesday, Wednesday except dinner July-August and Monday in season

Rest – *(number of covers limited, pre-book)* Menu (€ 22 bi), € 36/56 – Carte € 63/92

Spec. Le fassum et son mesclun. Foie gras de canard, confit de pétales de rose. Crème brûlée à la lavande.

◆ The terrace shaded by lime trees commands a magnificent view of Cannes and the sea. Rustic interior and tasty Provençal cooking.

GRASSE

Barri (Pl. du) . . . . Z 4
Bellevue (Bd) . . . . X 5
Charabot (Bd) . . . . XY 6
Conte (R. D.) . . . . Y 7
Cresp (Cours H.) . . . . Z 8
Crouët (Bd Jacques) . . . X 10
Droite (R.) . . . . Y 12
Duval (Av. M.) . . . . X 14
Évêché (R. de l') . . . . Z 15
Fontette (R. de) . . . . Y 16
Foux (Pl. de la) . . . . Y 17
Fragonard (Bd) . . . . Z 18
Gaulle (Av. Gén.-de) . . . . X 20
Gazan (R.) . . . . Z 22
Herbes (Pl. aux) . . . . Y 23
Jeu-de-Ballon (Bd) . . . . YZ
Journet (R. M.) . . . . YZ 26
Juin (Av. Mar.) . . . . Y 27
Lattre-de-Tassigny (Av. Mar.-de) . . . . X 28
Leclerc (Bd Mar.) . . . . X 30
Libération (Av.) . . . . X 32
Mougins-Roquefort (R.) . Z 33
Moulin-des-Paroirs (R.) . . X 34
Oratoire (R. de l') . . . . Y 35
Ossola (R. Jean) . . . . Z 38
Petit-Puy (Pl. du) . . . . Z 42
Poissonnerie (Pl.) . . . . . . Z 43
Prés.-Kennedy (Bd) . . . . . X 45
Reine-Jeanne (Bd) . . . . . . X 48
Rothschild (Bd de) . . . . . . X 49
St-Martin (Traverse) . . . . Z 50
Sémard (Av. P.) . . . . X 53
Thiers (Av.) . . . . Y
Touts-Petits (Trav.) . . . . . Z 55
Tracastel (R.) . . . . Z 57
Victoria (Av.) . . . . X 60
Victor-Hugo (Bd) . . . . . . X, Z 59
11-Novembre (Av. du) X, Y 63

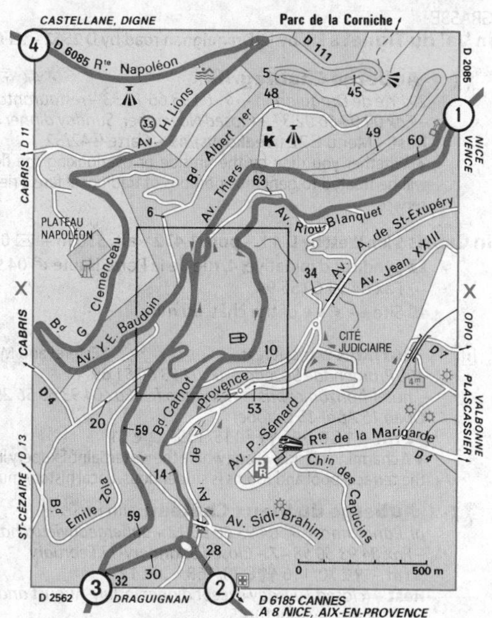

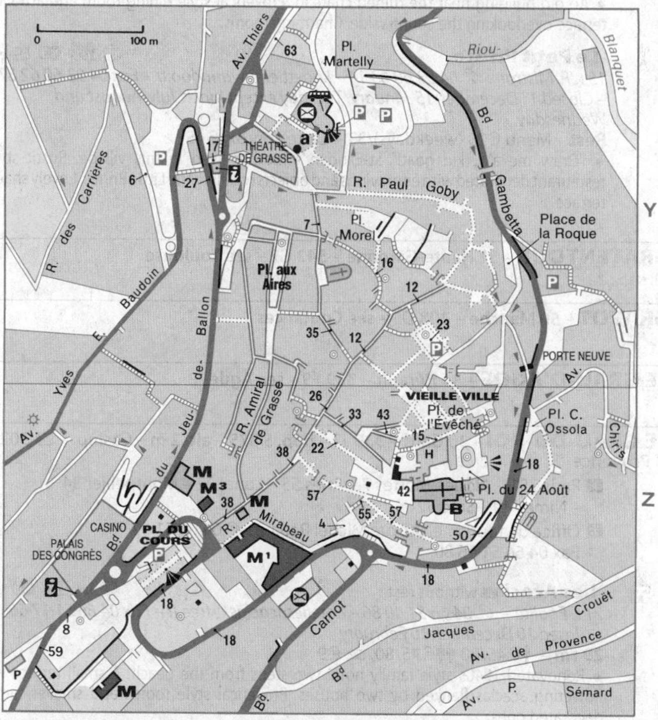

0 100 m
Av. Thiers
Pl. Martelly
Riou- Blanquet
THÉATRE DE GRASSE
R. Paul Goby
Bd Gambetta
Place de la Roque
Pl. Morel
Pl. aux Aires
R. des Carrières
Yves E. Baudoin
Bd du Jeu-de-Ballon
PORTE NEUVE
Av. Chiris
VIEILLE VILLE
Pl. de l'Évêché
Pl. C. Ossola
R. Amiral de Grasse
Pl. du 24 Août
R. Mirabeau
CASINO
PALAIS DES CONGRÈS
PL. DU COURS
Bd Carnot
Bd Jacques Crouët
Av. de Provence
Av. P. Sémard

in Val du Tignet 8 km by ③ Draguignan road by D 2562 – ✉ 06530 Peymeinade

XX **Auberge Chantegrill**

291 rte de Draguignan – ✆ 04 93 66 12 33 – restaurantchantegrill@wanadoo.fr – Fax 04 93 66 02 31 – Closed November, Sunday dinner and Monday off season

Rest – Menu € 22 (weekdays)/49 – Carte € 42/52

◆ Whether you dine by the fireside or overlooking the flowered garden-terrace, you will be treated to generous portions of traditional fare. Friendly welcome and attentive service.

in Cabris 5 km West by D 4 X – pop. 1 472 – alt. 550 m – ✉ 06530

Syndicat d'initiative, 4, rue de la Porte Haute ✆ 04 93 60 55 63, Fax 04 93 60 55 94

Site★ - ≤★★ of the château ruins.

Horizon without rest ≤ Esterel and Maures massifs,

100 Promenade St-Jean – ✆ 04 93 60 51 69 – hotel-horizon.cabris@wanadoo.fr – Fax 04 93 60 56 29

Open 15 April-15 October

22 rm – †€ 85/95 ††€ 115/135, ☕ € 11

◆ A charming hillside village where the writer Saint-Exupéry lived for a while. The view from the terrace, pool and rooms is stupendous. Local history museum.

XX **Auberge du Vieux Château** with rm

pl. Panorama – ✆ 04 93 60 50 12 – aubergeduvieuxchateau@wanadoo.fr – Fax 04 93 60 58 47 – Closed 5 January-11 February

5 rm – †€ 70/116 ††€ 70/168, ☕ € 12

Rest – *(closed Tuesday except dinner in July-August and Monday)* Menu (€ 26), € 39 (weekday lunch)/45

◆ An old building near the ruined château. Provençal-style dining room and attractive terrace overlooking the countryside. Charming rooms.

X **Le Petit Prince**

15 r. F. Mistral – ✆ 04 93 60 63 14 – knoettler@wanadoo.fr – Fax 04 93 60 62 87 – Closed 1st December-15 January, Tuesday except lunch July-August and Wednesday

Rest – Menu € 23 (weekdays)/33 – Carte approx. € 45

◆ "Draw me a ... kid goat!" St-Exupéry's mother lived in this village. Rustic-styled restaurant decorated with engravings and objects recalling the Little Prince. Lovely shaded terrace.

GRATENTOUR – 31 Haute-Garonne – **343** G2 – see Toulouse

GRATOT – 50 Manche – **303** D5 – see Coutances

LE GRAU-D'AGDE – 34 Hérault – **339** F9 – see Agde

LE GRAU-DU-ROI – 30 Gard – 339 J7 – pop. 5 875 – alt. 2 m – Casino – ✉ 30240

Provence 23 **C2**

Paris 751 – Aigues-Mortes 7 – Arles 55 – Lunel 22 – Montpellier 34 – Nîmes 49 – Sète 52

Office de tourisme, 30, rue Michel Rédarès ✆ 04 66 51 67 70, Fax 04 66 51 06 80

Les Acacias without rest

21 r. Egalité – ✆ 04 66 51 40 86 – hotellesacacias@free.fr – Fax 04 66 51 17 66 – Closed 10 December-10 February

29 rm – †€ 45/80 ††€ 45/80, ☕ € 9

◆ Renovated 1940s style family hotel two steps from the beach. A small terrace with flowering acacias flanked by two houses. Provençal style rooms and smaller, simply decorated ones.

in Port Camargue South: 3 km by D 62^{B} – ✉ 30240 Le Grau-du-Roi

Spinaker
pointe de la Presqu'île – ✆ 04 66 53 36 37 – spinaker@wanadoo.fr – Fax 04 66 53 17 47 – Closed 22-28 December, and Sunday to Wednesday from 11 November to 14 February
16 rm – €80/149 €80/149, ☕ €12 – 5 suites
Rest ***Carré des Gourmets*** – *(closed 11 November-14 February, Monday and Tuesday except July-August)* Menu €61/91 – Carte €63/105
◆ Hotel by the marina quayside at the end of the peninsula. Attractive, personalised, ground floor rooms (Provence, Africa and Morocco) opening onto the garden and pool, lined with palm trees. Contemporary restaurant and terrace overlooking the marina; inventive food.

Mercure
rm, rest,
rte Marines – ✆ 04 66 73 60 60 – h1947@accor.com – Fax 04 66 73 60 50 – Closed 7-27 December
89 rm – €97/147 €97/147, ☕ €12 – **Rest** – Menu (€20), €26 – Carte €29/39
◆ Hotel complex with a thalassotherapy centre opposite the dunes and the sea. Refurbished, comfortable and modern rooms with balcony. This restaurant situated on the sixth floor, offers a choice between traditional and diet dishes.

L'Oustau Camarguen
rm, rest,
3 rte Marines – ✆ 04 66 51 51 65 – oustaucamarguen@wanadoo.fr – Fax 04 66 53 06 65 – Open 14 March-5 November
39 rm – €81/103 €81/103, ☕ €11 – 8 suites – ½ P €75/86 – **Rest** – *(open 1st May-end September and closed Wednesday dinner except July-August) (dinner only except weekend from May to September)* Menu €27/33 – Carte €32/46
◆ Small Camargue farmhouse decorated in the Provence style (wrought iron, terracotta, polished wood). Spacious rooms with private gardens or terraces. Pleasant wellness centre. Classic cuisine served in a rustic dining area or outside by the pool.

L'Amarette
centre commercial Camargue 2000 – ✆ 04 66 51 47 63 – lamarette2@wanadoo.fr – Fax 04 66 51 47 63 – Closed end November-mid January
Rest – Menu €23 (weekday lunch), €36/60 – Carte €40/74
◆ A well-kept interior and pleasant terrace on the first floor of a shopping centre, near the North beach. Fresh fish and seafood cuisine.

GRAUFTHAL – 67 Bas-Rhin – 315 H4 – see La Petite-Pierre

GRAULHET – 81 Tarn – 338 D8 – pop. 12 663 – alt. 166 m – ✉ 81300 29 C2

Paris 694 – Albi 39 – Castres 31 – Toulouse 63
Office de tourisme, square Maréchal Foch ✆ 05 63 34 75 09, Fax 05 63 34 75 09

La Rigaudié
rte de St-Julien-du-Puy – ✆ 05 63 34 49 54 – poser.stephane@wanadoo.fr – Fax 05 63 34 78 91 – Closed 1st-9 May, 1st-15 September, 2-7 January, Saturday lunch, Sunday dinner and Monday
Rest – Menu (€12), €15 bi (weekday lunch), €24/65 – Carte €26/52
◆ A fine 19th century manor set in a large park, with a warm and refined dining area, and a terrace under the plane trees. Serving well-prepared modern cuisine.

LA GRAVE – 05 Hautes-Alpes – 334 F2 – pop. 511 – alt. 1 526 m – Winter sports : 1 450/3 250 m 2 2 – ✉ 05320 French Alps 41 C1

Paris 642 – Briançon 38 – Gap 126 – Grenoble 80 – Col du Lautaret 11
Office de tourisme, route nationale 91 ✆ 04 76 79 90 05, Fax 04 76 79 91 65
Glacier de la Meije★★★ (by cable car) - ★★★.
Oratoire du Chazelet★★★ Northwest: 6 km.

Les Chalets de la Meije without rest ← Meije and glacier,
– 04 76 79 97 97 – contact@chalet-meije.com – Fax 04 76 79 97 98 – Closed 19 April-23 May and 12 October-20 December
18 rm – €50/76 €62/81, €9,50 – 9 suites
◆ A hotel and residential complex on a superb site facing Écrins park. Pretty rooms (wood panels, wrought iron, exotic furniture) located in several different chalets.

La Meijette ← rest, VISA
– 04 76 79 90 34 – hotel.lameijette.juge@wanadoo.fr – Fax 04 76 79 94 76 – Open 2 June-19 September
18 rm – €58 €86, €8,50 – ½ P €60/80 – **Rest** – Menu €20/33 – Carte €29/53
◆ Two buildings opposite the grandiose Meije mountain range, separated by a road. Rooms are furnished in pine, well kept and often spacious. Superb view of the glaciers from the restaurant, particularly from the ideally situated panoramic terrace.

GRAVELINES – 59 Nord – 302 A2 – pop. 12 430 – ✉ 59820

Northern France and the Paris Region 30 **A1**

Paris 287 – Calais 26 – Cassel 38 – Dunkerque 21 – Lille 89 – St-Omer 36

Office de tourisme, 11, rue de la République 03 28 51 94 00, Fax 03 28 65 58 19

Hostellerie du Beffroi rm, rm, VISA
2 pl. Ch. Valentin – 03 28 23 24 25 – contact.hoteldubeffroi@wanadoo.fr – Fax 03 28 65 59 71
40 rm – €68 €74, €9,50 – ½ P €98 – **Rest** – *(closed Saturday lunch and Sunday dinner)* Menu €16 (weekdays)/35 – Carte €23/38
◆ A modern brick-built building at the foot of the belfry inside the Vauban town wall. Functional, well-kept rooms available. Modern dining room with a terrace facing the square. Traditional unpretentious cuisine.

GRAVESON – 13 Bouches-du-Rhône – 340 D2 – pop. 3 188 – alt. 14 m – ✉ 13690

Provence 42 **E1**

Paris 696 – Avignon 14 – Carpentras 40 – Cavaillon 30 – Marseille 102 – Nîmes 38

Office de tourisme, cours National 04 90 95 88 44, Fax 04 90 95 81 75

Musée Auguste-chabaud★.

Moulin d'Aure rest, VISA
rte de St-Rémy-de-Provence, 1 km via D 5 – 04 90 95 84 05 – reception@hotel-moulindaure.com – Fax 04 90 95 73 84
19 rm – €60/200 €60/200, €14 – **Rest** – *(open March-15 November and closed Monday lunch except in July-August)* Menu €38 – Carte €46/74
◆ This recent southern-style house set in a large olive grove has attractive Provençal-style rooms (wrought iron, terracotta tile floors), some with a terrace. Bright, welcoming dining room with exposed rafters, overlooking the pool.

Le Mas des Amandiers rm, rest, VISA
rte d'Avignon, 1.5 km – 04 90 95 81 76 – contact@hotel-des-amandiers.com – Fax 04 90 95 85 18 – Open 16 March-14 October
28 rm – €58 €61, €9 – ½ P €58/61 – **Rest** – Menu €15 bi (weekday lunch), €19/36 – Carte €23/53
◆ Rooms in sunny colours with painted rustic furniture are grouped around the swimming pool. Botanical trail, as well as bicycles and scooters for hire. Modern dining room decorated with a hint of Provence; classic, regional menu.

Le Cadran Solaire without rest VISA
r. Cabaret-Neuf – 04 90 95 71 79 – cadransolaire@wanadoo.fr – Fax 04 90 90 55 04 – Open from March to November
12 rm – €60 €60/82, €9
◆ The façade of this charming 16C coaching inn, tucked away in a pretty garden, is decorated with a sundial. Delightfully cosy rooms (no TV) and a delicious terrace.

Le Clos des Cyprès

rte de Châteaurenard – ☎ 04 90 90 53 44 – Closed Tuesday dinner and Thursday dinner off season, Wednesday dinner, Sunday dinner and Monday

Rest – *(pre-book)* Menu € 27/34

♦ Set in parkland, a Provençal villa with plush dining room (ochre tones) and canopied terrace. Attentive staff and up-to-date gourmet menu chalked up on the blackboard.

GRAY – 70 Haute-Saône – 314 B8 – pop. 6 773 – alt. 220 m – ✉ 70100

Burgundy-Jura 16 **B2**

Paris 336 – Besançon 45 – Dijon 50 – Dole 46 – Langres 56 – Vesoul 58

Office de tourisme, Ile Sauzay ☎ 03 84 65 14 24, Fax 03 84 65 46 26

Town hall★ - Collection of pastels and drawings★ by Prud'hon at the musée Baron-Martin★ M[1].

in Rigny by ① D 70 and D 2: 5 km – pop. 586 – alt. 196 m – ✉ 70100

Château de Rigny

rm, rest,

– ☎ 03 84 65 25 01

– info@chateau-de-rigny.com – Fax 03 84 65 44 45

28 rm – € 75/120 € 110/210, € 12 – ½ P € 105/150

Rest – Menu € 32/45 – Carte € 43/57

♦ The paths through the park attached to this 17th century hotel wind down to the Saône. The rooms include old-style furnishings. Choose one in the silk farm. Comfortable dining room or pleasant terrace. The cuisine is largely classic.

in Nantilly by ① and D 2: 5 km – pop. 452 – alt. 200 m – ✉ 70100

Château de Nantilly

rm,

1 r. Millerand – ☎ 03 84 67 78 00 – chateau.nantilly@wanadoo.fr – Fax 03 84 67 78 01 – Closed 2 January-mid February

39 rm – € 70/110 € 110/150, € 13 – 2 suites – ½ P € 120/160

Rest – *(closed Sunday dinner, Monday, Tuesday and lunch except Sunday)* Menu € 35/63 – Carte € 50/63

♦ Pretty vine covered family mansion set in a park crossed by a river. The rooms in the main building have more charm than those in the annexes. Very refined restaurant with bright tones, mouldings, frescos and silverware. Regional cuisine.

GRENADE-SUR-L'ADOUR – 40 Landes – 335 I12 – pop. 2 265 – alt. 55 m – ✉ 40270

3 **B2**

Paris 720 – Aire-sur-l'Adour 18 – Mont-de-Marsan 15 – Orthez 53 – St-Sever 14 – Tartas 33

Office de tourisme, 1, place des Déportés ☎ 05 58 45 45 98, Fax 05 58 45 45 55

Pain Adour et Fantaisie (Philippe Garret) with rm

rm,

14 pl. des Tilleuls – ☎ 05 58 45 18 80

– pain.adour.fantaisie@wanadoo.fr – Fax 05 58 45 16 57

– Closed Sunday and Monday mid December-Easter

11 rm – € 70/164 € 70/164, € 15

Rest – *(closed Monday except dinner from 14 July to 31 August, Sunday dinner from September to mid July and Wednesday lunch)* Menu € 38/95 bi – Carte € 54/81

Spec. Foie gras de canard confit au jurançon. Rouget grillé, purée de carotte à la réglisse, jus au safran. Milk-shake à la fraise épicée, sucettes glacées à la rhubarbe.

Wines Vin de Pays des Côtes de Gascogne, Madiran.

♦ The name of this 17C hotel evokes the Neo-realist cinema of Italy. It features an elegant dining area and an attractive terrace on the banks of the Adour. Inventive cuisine.

Southeast 7,5 km by Larrivière and D 352 - ✉ 40270 Renung

Domaine de Benauge without rest

– ☎ 05 58 71 77 30 – benauge@tiscali.fr

5 rm – € 50/95 € 50/95

♦ This commander's residence dating from the 15C has retained traces of its original fortifications. Attractive contemporary-style guestrooms, plus a garden overlooking the surrounding countryside.

GRENOBLE 🅿 – 38 Isère – 333 H6 – pop. 153 317 – Built-up area 419 334 – alt. 213 m – ✉ 38000 French Alps 45 **C2**

- Paris 566 – Chambéry 55 – Genève 143 – Lyon 105 – Torino 235
- Grenoble-Isère ☎ 04 76 65 48 48, by ⑥: 45 km.
- Office de tourisme, 14, rue de la République ☎ 04 76 42 41 41, Fax 04 76 00 18 98
- de Seyssins Seyssins 29 rue du Plâtre, ☎ 04 76 70 12 63 ;
- de Grenoble Bresson Route de Montavie, South: 6 km by D 269, ☎ 04 76 73 65 00.
- Site★★★ - St Laurent's Church-museum★★ : crypte St-Oyand (St Oyrand's crypt)★★ FY - Fort de la Bastille (Bastille Fort) ※★★ by cable car EY - Vieille ville (Old Town)★ EY : Palais de Justice (Law Courts)★ (panelling★) - staircase★ of the hôtel d'Ornacieux EY **J** - Museums: de Grenoble★★★ FY, de la Résistance et de la Déportation (Resistance and Deportation)★ F , de l'ancien Evêché-Patrimoines de l'Isère(Former Bishop's Palace – Heritage of Isère)★★ - Musée dauphinois (Museum of the Dauphin)★ : chapel★★, themed exhibition★★ EY.

Plans on following pages

Park Hôtel
rest, VISA AE

10 pl. Paul Mistral – ☎ 04 76 85 81 23 – resa@park-hotel-grenoble.fr – Fax 04 76 46 49 88 – Closed 25 July-25 August and 21 December-2 January
50 rm – €135 €245, ☕ €16 – 16 suites FZ **w**
Rest ***Le Parc*** – *(closed Sunday lunch, Saturday and lunch holidays)* Menu €29/54 – Carte €35/66

◆ The spacious guestrooms exude a certain antiquated charm in this cosy hotel which brings to mind the atmosphere of an English gentlemen's club. Brick walls, a stone fireplace, exposed beams and stained glass provide the rustic decor in this traditional restaurant.

Novotel Centre
rm, VISA AE

à Europole, pl. R. Schuman – ☎ 04 76 70 84 84 – h1624@accor.com – Fax 04 76 70 24 93 AV **r**
116 rm – €125/145 €125/145, ☕ €13,50 – 2 suites – **Rest** – Menu €24/29 – Carte €23/41

◆ Opposite the station, contemporary style hotel adjoining the WTC and a conference centre. Spacious rooms with Japanese-inspired décor; impressive modern fitness centre. Traditional recipes and grilled dishes feature on the menu of this contemporary restaurant.

Grand Hôtel Mercure Président
rm, rest, VISA AE

11 r. Gén. Mangin ✉ 38100 – ☎ 04 76 56 26 56 – h2947@accor.com – Fax 04 76 56 26 82 AX **y**
105 rm – €112/169 €124/181, ☕ €15 – 3 suites
Rest – *(closed 10-23 August, 20 December-4 January, Sunday lunch and Saturday)* Menu (€20) – Carte €32/40

◆ Successful renovation for this pleasant Mercure. Facilities include comfortable guestrooms, an exotic bar and lobby, meeting and fitness facilities, sauna, Jacuzzi and terrace-garden. African-inspired decor and international dishes at the restaurant.

Mercure Centre Alpotel
rm, VISA AE

12 bd Mar. Joffre – ☎ 04 76 87 88 41 – h0652@accor.com – Fax 04 76 47 58 52
88 rm – €119/139 €129/149, ☕ €13,50
Rest – *(closed 2-24 August, 20 December-1st January, Saturday, Sunday and holidays)* Menu (€14) – Carte €23/30 EZ **d**

◆ Built for the 1968 Olympics and a symbol of the "concrete" trend of the time, this hotel is now a listed building. Uniform, modern and well-appointed rooms. The Café Pourpre's designer decor is the backdrop for a menu of traditional and straightforward cuisine.

Europole
VISA AE

29 r. Pierre Sémard – ☎ 04 76 49 51 52 – resa@hoteleuropole.com – Fax 04 76 21 99 00 – **71 rm** – €86 €86, ☕ €12 – 3 suites AV **a**
Rest – brasserie Menu (€16), €21/28 – Carte €26/59

◆ An imposing hotel in the Europole district with a loyal business clientele. Functional air-conditioned guestrooms, generally quieter at the rear. A typical Alsatian brasserie with stylised decor and seafood specialities.

Lesdiguières rm,
122 cours de la Libération – ✆ 04 38 70 19 50 – hotellesdiguieres@gastronomie.com – Fax 04 38 70 19 69 – Closed school holidays, Friday, Saturday and Sunday AX **b**
23 rm – 🛉€ 56 🛉🛉€ 61, ☕ € 7,50 – 1 suite – **Rest** – Menu € 21/49
◆ A veritable Grenoble institution, home to a renowned hotel school since 1917. Comfortable guestrooms with those facing the park generally quieter. Attractive menus focusing on Dauphiné regional produce.

Terminus without rest
10 pl. de la Gare – ✆ 04 76 87 24 33 – terminush@aol.com – Fax 04 76 50 38 28 DY **t**
39 rm – 🛉€ 68/99 🛉🛉€ 84/149, ☕ € 12
◆ As its name suggests, this family-run hotel is located opposite the railway station. Views of the Moucherotte and Vercors range from the upper floors, breakfast served beneath a glass roof.

Quality Hotel without rest
116 cours de la Libération – ✆ 04 76 21 26 63 – qualityhotel@wanadoo.fr – Fax 04 76 48 01 07 AX **n**
56 rm – 🛉€ 85 🛉🛉€ 95, ☕ € 12
◆ Tile-covered façade for this hotel located on a major road. Well-maintained, modern rooms with good sound-proofing. Small bar-lounge refurbished in chocolate tones.

Angleterre without rest
5 pl. Victor-Hugo – ✆ 04 76 87 37 21 – reservations@hotel-angleterre-grenoble.com – Fax 04 76 50 94 10 EZ **z**
62 rm – 🛉€ 105/180 🛉🛉€ 105/180, ☕ € 13
◆ Well-located in front of a park, this hotel offers functional rooms adorned with cane and wood furniture, some with sloping ceilings, others with Jacuzzis.

Splendid without rest
22 r. Thiers – ✆ 04 76 46 33 12 – info@splendid-hotel.com – Fax 04 76 46 35 24 DZ **q**
45 rm – 🛉€ 57/89 🛉🛉€ 71/95, ☕ € 6,50
◆ The guestrooms (some adorned with original frescoes) in this hotel close to the Musée des Rêves Mécaniques are gradually being renovated. Buffet breakfast.

Le Gambetta
59 bd Gambetta – ✆ 04 76 87 22 25 – hotelgambetta@wanadoo.fr – Fax 04 76 87 40 94 – Closed 21 July-10 August EZ **a**
45 rm – 🛉€ 54 🛉🛉€ 59, ☕ € 7 – ½ P € 47/52 – **Rest** – *(Closed Friday dinner, Saturday and Sunday)* Menu (€ 13), € 16 – Carte € 19/35
◆ After restoration, the façade of this hotel founded in 1924 has regained its original style. Practical rooms with double glazing. Traditional cuisine served in a bright and spacious dining room.

Europe without rest
22 pl. Grenette – ✆ 04 76 46 16 94 – hotel.europe.gre@wanadoo.fr – Fax 04 76 43 13 65 EY **t**
45 rm – 🛉€ 39/55 🛉🛉€ 60/78, ☕ € 7,50
◆ Located at the heart of Grenoble's historic quarter, the Europe was the first hotel to be built in the city. Refurbished guestrooms in a sober, contemporary style.

Gallia without rest
7 bd Mar. Joffre – ✆ 04 76 87 39 21 – gallia-hotel@wanadoo.fr – Fax 04 76 87 65 76 – Closed 26 July-25 August EZ **s**
35 rm – 🛉€ 50/53 🛉🛉€ 54/57, ☕ € 7
◆ Most of the guestrooms in this family-run hotel have been brightly refurbished in Provençal tones. Pleasant lobby-lounge.

Institut without rest
10 r. L. Barbillon – ✆ 04 76 46 36 44 – contact@institut-hotel.fr – Fax 04 76 47 73 09 DY **h**
48 rm – 🛉€ 52 🛉🛉€ 55, ☕ € 7,50
◆ The main selling-points of this functional hotel are its friendly welcome, well-maintained facilities and reasonable prices. Brightly decorated, well-appointed guestrooms.

CORENC

Eygala (Av. de l') ... BCV
Grésivaudan (Av. du) ... BCV

EYBENS

Innsbruck (Av. d') ... BX 38
Jean-Jaurès (Av.) ... BX
Mendès-France (R.) ... BX
Poisat (Av. de) ... BX 47

ÉCHIROLLES

Etats-Généraux (Av. des) ... AX 30
Grugliasco (Av. de) ... AX
Jean-Jaurès (Crs) ... AX
Kimberley (Av. de) ... ABX

FONTAINE

Briand (Av. A.) ... AV
Joliot-Curie (Bd) ... AV
Vercors (Av. du) ... AV

GRENOBLE

Alliés (R. des) ... AX
Alsace-Lorraine (Av.) ... DYZ 3
Ampère (R.) ... AV
Augereau (R.) ... DZ
Barnavel (R.) ... EFY 5
Bayard (R.) ... FY 6
Belgique (Av. Albert-1er de) ... EFZ 7
Belgrade (R. de) ... EY 9
Bernard (Q. Cl.) ... DY
Berriat (Crs) ... AV, DZ
Berthelot (Av. M.) ... BX
Bistesi (R.) ... FZ 10
Bizanet (R.) ... FGY
Blanchard (R. P.) ... EYZ
Blum (Av. Léon) ... AX
Boissieux (R. B.-de) ... EZ
Bonne (R. de) ... EZ 12
Brenier (R. C.) ... DY 13
Briand (Pl. A.) ... DY
Brocherie (R.) ... EY 15
Casimir-Périer (R.) ... EZ 16
Champollion (R.) ... FZ 17
Champon (Av. Gén.) ... FZ
Chanrion (R. J.) ... FYZ
Chenoise (R.) ... EFY 18
Claudel (R. P.) ... BX 20
Clemenceau (Bd) ... FGZ
Clot-Bey (R.) ... EYZ 21
Condillac (R.) ... EZ
Condorcet (R.) ... DZ
Créqui (Q.) ... DEY
Diables-Bleus (Bd des) ... FZ 24
Diderot (R.) ... AV 25
Dr-Girard (Pl.) ... FY 26
Driant (Bd Col.) ... FZ 27
Dubedout (Pl. H.) ... DY 28
Esclangon (R. F.) ... AV 29
Esmonin (Av. E.) ... AX
l'Europe (Av. de) ... BX 31
Fantin-Latour (R.) ... FZ 32
Faure (R. E.) ... FZ
La Fayette (R.) ... EY 39
Flandrin (R. J.) ... GZ 33
Foch (Bd Mar.) ... DEZ
La Fontaine (Crs) ... EZ
Fourier (R.) ... FZ 34
France (Q. de) ... DEY
Gambetta (Bd) ... DEZ
Graille (Q. de la) ... DY
Grande-Rue ... EY 37
Grenette (Pl.) ... EY
Gueymard (R. E.) ... DY
Haxo (R.) ... FZ
Hébert (R.) ... FYZ
L'Herminier (R. Cdt) ... FY 41
Hoche (R.) ... EZ
Jay (Q. S.) ... EY
Jeanne-d'Arc (Av.) ... GZ
Jean-Jaurès (Crs) ... DYZ
Joffre (Bd Mar.) ... DEZ
Jongking (Q.) ... FY
Jouhaux (R. L.) ... BX, GZ
Jouvin (Q. X.) ... FY
Lakanal (R.) ... EZ
Lavalette (Pl.) ... FY 40
Leclerc (Av. Mar.) ... FY
Lesdiguières (R.) ... EZ
Libération et du Gén.-de Gaulle (Crs de la) ... AX
Lyautey (Bd Mar.) ... EZ 42
Lyon (Rte de) ... DY
Malakoff (R.) ... FGZ
Mallifaud (R.) ... EFZ 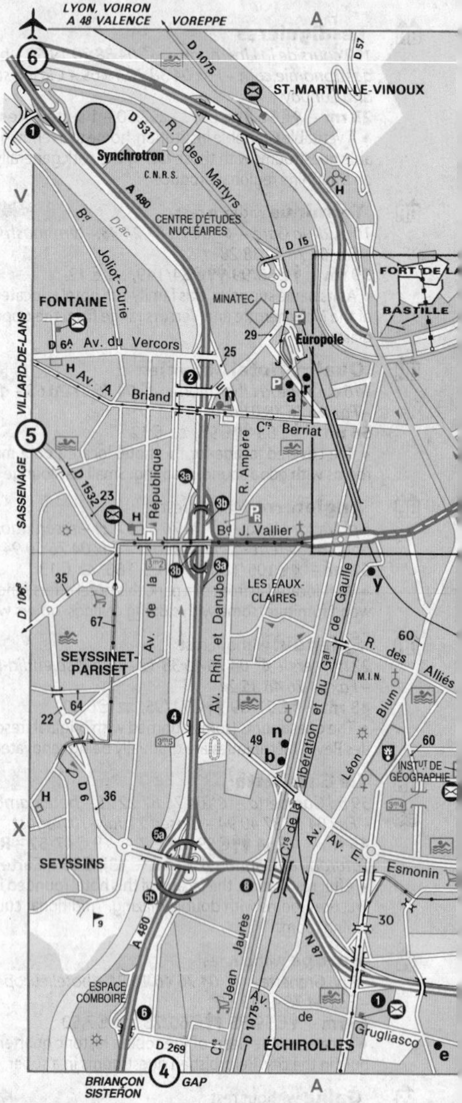
Martyrs (R. des) ... AV
Mistral (Pl. P.) ... FZ
Montorge (R.) ... EY 43
Mortillet (R. de) ... FGY
Moyrand (R.) ... FGZ
Notre-Dame (Pl.) ... FY
Pain (Bd J.) ... FZ
Palanka (R.) ... EY 44
Pasteur (Pl.) ... FZ 45
Perrière (Q.) ... EY 46
Perrot (Av. J.) ... BX, FZ
Poulat (R. F.) ... EY 48
Prévost (R. J.) ... DZ
Randon (Av. Mar.) ... FY
Reynier (R. A.) ... AX 49
Reynoard (Av. M.) ... BX 50
Rey (Bd Ed.) ... EY
Rhin-et-Danube (Av.) ... AX
Rivet (Pl. G.) ... EZ 53
Rousseau (R. J.-J.) ... EY 55
Sablon (Pont du) ... GY
Ste-Claire (Pl.) ... EY 57
St-André (Pl.) ... EY 56
Sembat (Bd A.) ... EZ
Servan (R.) ... FY 59
Stalingrad (R. de) ... AX 60
Strasbourg (R. de) ... EFZ 62
Thiers (R.) ... DZ
Très-Cloîtres (R.) ... FY 63
Turenne (R.) ... DZ

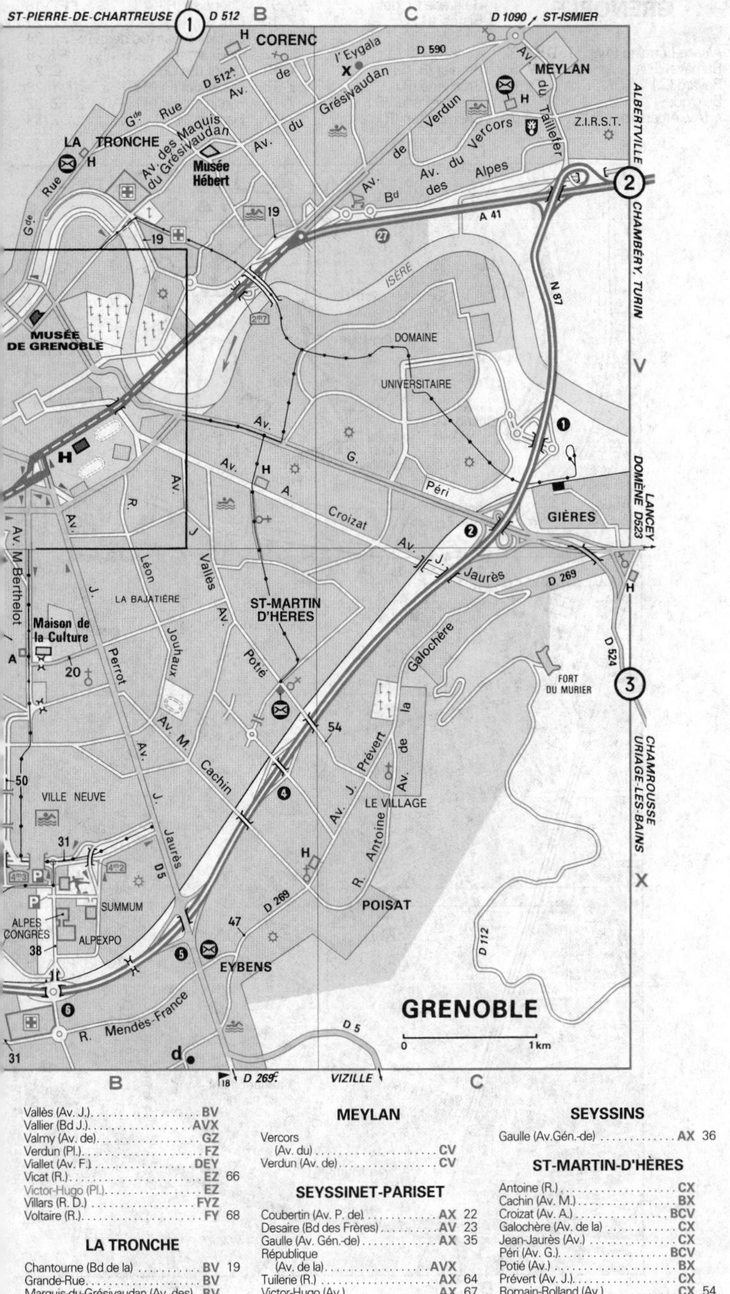
ST-PIERRE-DE-CHARTREUSE
D 512
D 1090
ST-ISMIER
CORENC
MEYLAN
LA TRONCHE
Musée Hébert
MUSÉE DE GRENOBLE
DOMAINE UNIVERSITAIRE
GIÈRES
ST-MARTIN D'HÈRES
LA BAJATIÈRE
Maison de la Culture
VILLE NEUVE
SUMMUM
ALPES CONGRÈS
ALPEXPO
EYBENS
POISAT
LE VILLAGE
FORT DU MURIER
ALBERTVILLE
CHAMBÉRY, TURIN
LANCEY
DOMÈNE D523
CHAMROUSSE
URIAGE-LES-BAINS
VIZILLE
D 269
GRENOBLE
0
1 km

GRENOBLE

Alsace-Lorraine (Av.) . . . . DYZ 3
Barnavel (R.) . . . . EFY 5
Bayard (R.) . . . . FY 6
Belgique (Av. Albert-1er-de) . . . . . EFZ 7
Belgrade (R. de) . . . . EY 9
Bistesi (R.) . . . . FZ 10
Blanchard (R. P.) . . . . EYZ
Bonne (R. de) . . . . EZ 12
Brenier (R. C.) . . . . DY 13
Brocherie (R.) . . . . EY 15
Casimir-Périer (R.) . . . . EZ 16
Champollion (R.) . . . . FZ 17
Chenoise (R.) . . . . EFY 18
Clot-Bey (R.) . . . . EYZ 21
Diables-Bleus (Bd des) . . . . FZ 24
Dr-Girard (Pl.) . . . . FY 26
Driant (Bd Col.) . . . . FZ 27
Dubedout (Pl. H.) . . . . DY 28
Fantin-Latour (R.) . . . . FZ 32
Flandrin (R. J.) . . . . GZ 33

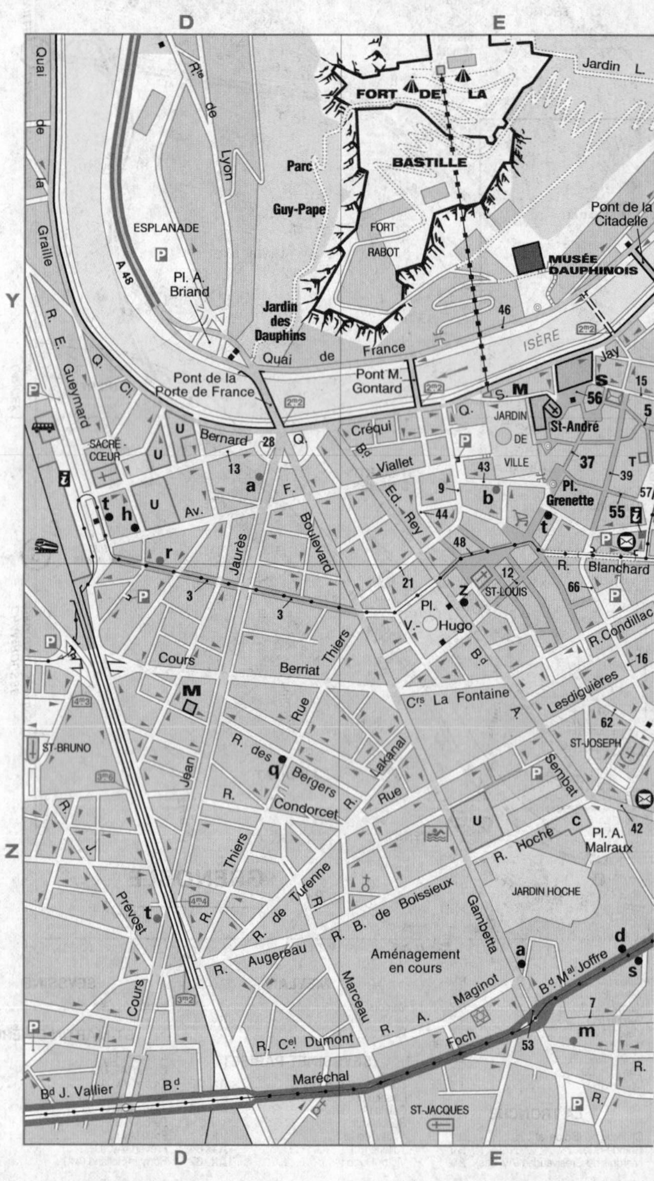

XXX **Le Fantin Latour**

1 r. Gén. Beylié – ✆ 04 76 01 00 97 – fantin.latour@hotmail.fr – Fax 04 76 01 02 41 – Closed 3-24 August FZ **a**

Rest – *(closed Sunday, Monday and lunch except Saturday)* Menu € 59/95

Rest *Le 18.36* – 5 r. Abbé de la Salle *(closed Saturday and Sunday) (lunch only)* Menu (€ 19 bi), € 26 bi

◆ New chef (who trained under Marc Veyrat) and inventive cuisine based around mountain plants at this 19th century manor, once home to a museum devoted to the artist Fantin Latour. Named after the year in which the artist was born. Concise brasserie *carte* and daily set menu.

XXX **Auberge Napoléon**

7 r. Montorge – ✆ 04 76 87 53 64 – Fcaby@wanadoo.fr – Closed 4-31 August and Sunday EY **b**

Rest – *(dinner only) (number of covers limited, pre-book)* Menu € 47/87 – Carte € 59/77

◆ Restaurant dedicated to the memory of Napoleon Bonaparte, its most famous guest. Personalised, inventive cuisine served in the Empire-style dining room.

XX **A Ma Table**

92 cours J. Jaurès – ✆ 04 76 96 77 04 – Fax 04 76 96 77 04 – Closed August, Saturday lunch, Sunday and Monday DZ **t**

Rest – *(number of covers limited, pre-book)* Carte € 39/57

◆ A tiny, welcoming restaurant which makes you feel very much at home. Generous and flavoursome classical cuisine.

XX **Marie Margaux**

12 r. Marcel Porte ✉ 38100 – ✆ 04 76 46 46 46 – lemariemargaux@orange.fr – Fax 04 76 46 46 46 – Closed 7-28 July, Sunday dinner and Monday EZ **m**

Rest – Menu € 15 (weekday lunch), € 25/46 – Carte € 29/53

◆ A welcoming family establishment (named after the two grandmothers) with a Provençal decor and a straightforward repertoire of traditionally-cooked fish.

XX **Chasse-Spleen**

6 pl. Lavalette – ✆ 04 38 37 03 52 – Fax 04 76 63 01 58 – Closed Saturday and Sunday FY **e**

Rest – Menu € 21/32 – Carte € 31/49

◆ Hommage to Charles Baudelaire who named this wine during a stay at Moulis-en-Médoc. Poems by the author on the walls, as food for thought. Dauphiné dishes.

X **Grill Parisien**

34 bd Alsace-Lorraine – ✆ 04 76 46 10 16 – Closed Easter holidays, 19 July-19 August, Saturday, Sunday and holidays DYZ **r**

Rest – Menu (€ 19), € 36 – Carte € 40/54

◆ Regulars to this bistro enjoy traditional Mediterranean cuisine either sitting at the kitchen table or beneath the wooden beams in the dining room.

X **Le Coup de Torchon**

8 r. Dominique Villars – ✆ 04 76 63 20 58 – Closed Wednesday dinner, Sunday and Monday FY **a**

Rest – Menu (€ 12,50), € 16/22 – Carte € 29/34

◆ Close to the city's antique shops, this restaurant serves well-prepared, reasonably priced modern cuisine based around seasonal market produce. Attractive setting.

X **La Glycine**

168 cours Berriat – ✆ 04 76 21 95 33 – Fax 04 76 96 31 60 – Closed 3-17 August and Sunday AV **n**

Rest – *(pre-book)* Menu (€ 17), € 30/39

◆ Rustic dining rooms, decorated with old plates and posters. In summer, a meal beneath the superb wisteria (glycine), a listed monument, is a must. Mediterranean-inspired cuisine.

X **L'Exception**

4 cours Jean-Jaurès – ✆ 04 76 47 03 12 – contact@lexception.com – Closed 19 July-3 August, 3-11 January, Saturday and Sunday DY **a**

Rest – Menu € 25/52 – Carte € 47/69

◆ This small unpretentious restaurant is always busy. Abundant creative cuisine drawing inspiration from the local area, and reasonable prices.

X **Le Village**

20 r. de Strasbourg – ✆ 04 76 87 88 44 – Closed 5-28 July, 21 December-5 January, Sunday and Monday except holidays FZ **b**

Rest – Menu (€ 14), € 25/38 – Carte € 31/44

◆ This simply furnished restaurant in a village-like district in the centre of town is often full, testimony to the friendly atmosphere and fine modern cuisine.

in Corenc – pop. 3 856 – alt. 450 m – ✉ 38700

XX **Corne d' Or**

159 rte Chartreuse, par ① : 3,5 km sur D 512 – ✆ 04 38 86 62 36 – info@cornedor.fr – Fax 04 38 86 62 37 – Closed 12 August-5 September, 2-17 January, Sunday dinner, Tuesday dinner and Wednesday

Rest – Menu € 25 (weekday lunch), € 38/78 – Carte € 48/74

◆ The window tables and the terrace allow pleasant views of Grenoble and the Belledonne mountains. Contemporary menu inspired by some of the country's leading chefs.

XX **Le Provence**

28 av. du Grésivaudan – ✆ 04 76 90 03 38 – contact@leprovence.fr – Fax 04 76 90 46 13 – Closed 3-25 August, Monday lunch, Saturday lunch and Sunday dinner CV **x**

Rest – Menu (€ 20), € 25 (weekday lunch), € 28/55 – Carte € 38/58

◆ Fish, simply grilled with olive oil in Provençal style is the speciality here. Sunlit dining room and terrace for the summer months.

in Meylan : 3 km by D 1090 – **pop. 18 741 – alt. 331 m – ✉ 38240**

Le Mas du Bruchet without rest

Chemin du Bruchet, above the Clos des Capucins – ✆ 04 76 90 18 30 – amferguson38@aol.com – Fax 04 76 41 92 36 – Closed 15 August-1st September

4 rm – € 55/65 € 60/70

◆ At the foot of Mont St Eynard, this small 18th century wine producing estate now provides charming rooms, two duplexes, set up in the old barn. Warm welcome. Wine tasting.

in Eybens : 5 km – **pop. 9 471 – alt. 230 m – ✉ 38320**

Château de la Commanderie

17 av. d'Échirolles – ✆ 04 76 25 34 58 – resa@commanderie.fr – Fax 04 76 24 07 31 – Closed 21 December-5 January BX **d**

28 rm – € 92/164 € 102/180, € 15 – ½ P € 111/119

Rest – *(closed autumn half-term holidays and Christmas, Saturday lunch, Sunday and Monday)* Menu (€ 27 bi), € 40/71 – Carte € 57/89

◆ A little castle - former command post of the Templar Knights - in a tree-lined garden. Ancestral furniture, family portraits and Aubusson tapestries. A place steeped in history. Modernised classic cuisine in a plush setting or on the summer terrace.

in Bresson South via Avenue J. Jaurès: 8 km by D 269c – **pop. 739 – alt. 300 m – ✉ 38320**

XXX **Chavant** with rm

– ✆ 04 76 25 25 38 – chavant@wanadoo.fr – Fax 04 76 62 06 55 – Closed 9-18 August and 24-31 December, Saturday lunch, Sunday dinner and Monday

5 rm – € 115/160 € 115/160, € 13 – 2 suites – **Rest** – *(closed Sat. lunchtime, Sun. evening and Mon.)* Menu € 35 (lunch), € 48/115 (dinner) – Carte € 58/87

◆ A country inn with a wood-panelled dining room and a terrace overlooking the garden. Cellar offering tastings and wines for purchase. Spacious, somewhat old-fashioned guestrooms.

in Échirolles : 4 km – **pop. 32 806 – alt. 237 m – ✉ 38130**

Dauphitel

16 av. Kimberley – ✆ 04 76 33 60 60 – info@dauphitel.fr – Fax 04 76 33 60 00 AX **e**

68 rm – € 90/105 € 100/115, € 10 – **Rest** – *(closed 2-24 August, 20 December-4 January, Saturday, Sunday and holidays)* Menu (€ 19), € 27/32 – Carte € 23/45

◆ A modern hotel offering guests comfortable, functional and sound-proofed rooms, a full range of conference facilities, and a swimming pool adjoining the garden. Large, bright dining room, summer terrace and traditional cuisine.

via exit ⑥ :

in Fontanil : 8 km by A 48, exit 14 and D 1075 – pop. 2 454 – alt. 210 m – ✉ 38120

XX **La Queue de Cochon**

rte de Lyon – ✆ 04 76 75 65 54 – qcochon@wanadoo.fr – Fax 04 76 75 76 85 – Closed 27 October-10 November, 26-30 December, Saturday lunch, Sunday dinner and

Rest – buffet Menu (€ 20), € 28/42 – Carte € 28/51

◆ This establishment is as popular for its buffets and grills as for its immense terrace surrounded by greenery. Modern decor with lobster tank; pig theme on the tableware.

near A 48 interchange exit nº 12/13: 12 km – ✉ 38340 Voreppe

Novotel rm,

1625 rte de Veurey – ✆ 04 76 50 55 55 – h0423@accor.com – Fax 04 76 56 76 26

114 rm – †€ 69/125 ††€ 69/125, ☕ € 12,50 – **Rest** – Menu (€ 19), € 23 – Carte € 23/38

◆ Near the motorway yet surrounded by fields, this hotel offers spacious, comfortable rooms, some refurbished in line with the chain's latest standards. Novotel Café. Spruced up dining room; terrace overlooking the garden. Grill-type meals.

GRÉOUX-LES-BAINS – 04 Alpes-de-Haute-Provence – 334 D10 – pop. 1 921 – alt. 386 m – Spa : early March-mid Dec. – Casino – ✉ 04800

French Alps 40 **B2**

Paris 783 – Aix-en-Provence 55 – Brignoles 52 – Digne-les-Bains 69 – Manosque 14

Office de tourisme, 5, avenue des Marronniers ✆ 04 92 78 01 08, Fax 04 92 78 13 00

La Crémaillère rm, rest,

rte de Riez – ✆ 04 92 70 40 04 – lacremaillere@chainethermale.fr – Fax 04 92 78 19 80 – Open 16 March-20 December

51 rm – †€ 84/105 ††€ 84/105, ☕ € 14 – ½ P € 73/110

Rest – Menu (€ 18), € 26/48 – Carte € 42/54

◆ The rooms with balcony or loggia feature a bright and colourful contemporary décor for a pleasant stay, not far from the troglodyte thermal baths. Provençal-style cuisine and bright décor in this restaurant.

Villa Borghèse rest,

av. des Thermes – ✆ 04 92 78 00 91 – villa.borghese@wanadoo.fr – Fax 04 92 78 09 55 – Open 16 March-7 December

67 rm – †€ 58/150 ††€ 78/150, ☕ € 11,50 – ½ P € 76/115

Rest – Menu € 31 (weekdays)/42 – Carte € 41/49

◆ No art collections in this Villa Borghese decorated with ampelopsis vines, but spacious rooms often with loggias and a sauna, beauty salon and bridge club. A restaurant with warm, contemporary décor serving tasty classic cuisine.

La Chêneraie

Les Hautes Plaines, via av. Thermes – ✆ 04 92 78 03 23 – contact@la-cheneraie.com – Fax 04 92 78 11 72 – Open mid March-mid November

20 rm – †€ 58/78 ††€ 66/85, ☕ € 11 – ½ P € 53/70

Rest – Menu (€ 15), € 20/32 – Carte € 29/52

◆ Modern building on a hill in this resort, in a quiet residential area. Functional rooms of a good size. Well-lit dining room thanks to the wide bay windows overlooking the pool, old village and castle.

Le Verdon rest, rest,

rte de Riez – ✆ 04 92 70 40 03 – leverdon@chainethermale.fr – Fax 04 92 70 43 99 – Open 9 March-29 November

64 rm – †€ 63/76 ††€ 63/76, ☕ € 12 – ½ P € 64/72

Rest – Menu € 23 – Carte approx. € 32

◆ This renovated hotel has clean, practical rooms with balconies overlooking the village or the scrubland. Pleasant garden with a pétanque playing area. Pleasant, modern dining room and shaded terrace overlooking the countryside.

Les Alpes

av. des Alpes – ✆ 04 92 74 24 24 – hoteldesalpes.greoux@wanadoo.fr – Fax 04 92 74 24 26 – Closed December and January

30 rm – €60/120 €80/135 – ½ P €55/83 – **Rest** – Menu €23 – Carte approx. €28

♦ This small family hotel, in a renovated building at the foot of the Knights Templars' castle, provides practical, soundproofed rooms. The Alps are mentioned in the restaurant's name, but it is mainly Provence that comes through, both in the menu and in the decor. Pleasantly shaded terrace.

GRESSE-EN-VERCORS – 38 Isère – 333 G8 – pop. 299 – alt. 1 205 m – Winter sports : 1 300/1 700 m 16 – ✉ 38650 French Alps 45 C2

Paris 610 – Clelles 22 – Grenoble 48 – Monestier-de-Clermont 14 – Vizille 43

Office de tourisme, le Faubourg ✆ 04 76 34 33 40, Fax 04 76 34 31 26

Col de l'Allimas ≤★ South: 2 km.

Le Chalet

– ✆ 04 76 34 32 08 – lechalet@free.fr – Fax 04 76 34 31 06 – Closed 9 March-3 May, 12 October-20 December and Wednesday lunch except school holidays

25 rm – €46/56 €83, €10 – ½ P €64/82

Rest – Menu €20/51 – Carte €31/48

♦ This is a Dauphinois-style house, rather than a chalet, which looks after its guests well. Large rooms, which are being gradually renovated. Some have a loggia. Generous, traditional cuisine served in an elegant dining room or on a pleasant summer terrace.

GRESSY – 77 Seine-et-Marne – 312 F2 – 101 10 – see Paris, Area

GRÉSY-SUR-ISÈRE – 73 Savoie – 333 K4 – pop. 1 043 – alt. 350 m – ✉ 73460

Paris 595 – Aiguebelle 12 – Albertville 18 – Chambéry 35 – St-Jean-de-Maurienne 48 46 F2

Site★★ - Château de Miolans ≤★: Tour St-Pierre ≤★★, underground defence network★ Alpes du Nord

La Tour de Pacoret with rm ≤ valley and mountains,

North-east: 1.5 km on D 201 – ✆ 04 79 37 91 59 rest,

– info@hotel-pacoret-savoie.com – Fax 04 79 37 93 84 – Open 9 May-19 October

10 rm – €65 €70/110, €12 – 1 suite – ½ P €67/110

Rest – *(closed Wednesday lunch except July-August, Monday in October and Tuesday)* Menu (€15), €19 (weekdays)/50 – Carte €37/58

♦ This watchtower built in 1283 still guards the Savoy Combe. A bright dining area with pleasant terrace affording views of the mountains. Traditional cuisine.

GREZ-EN-BOUÈRE – 53 Mayenne – 310 F7 – pop. 981 – alt. 85 m – ✉ 53290

Paris 276 – Nantes 143 – Laval 35 – Angers 66 – La Flèche 43 35 C1

Château de Chanay

4 km west on D 28 – ✆ 02 43 70 98 81 – info@chateau-de-chanay.com

3 rm – €70/100 €80/110 – **Table d'hôte** – Menu €27 bi

♦ Set in wooded parkland in the heart of the countryside, this abode has lost none of its original style. Personalised, comfortable rooms, stylish sitting room-library. The table d'hôte serves home cooking in a classic dining room.

GRÈZES – 46 Lot – 337 G4 – pop. 133 – alt. 312 m – ✉ 46320 29 C1

Paris 562 – Aurillac 84 – Cahors 50 – Figeac 21 – Rocamadour 37

Le Grézalide

rest,

– ✆ 05 65 11 20 40 – chateaugrezes@wanadoo.fr – Fax 05 65 11 20 41 – Open 20 March-15 November

19 rm – €77/97 €77/97, €10 – ½ P €70/80 – **Rest** – *(closed Tuesday and Wednesday October-April) (dinner only)* Menu €25/28

♦ This establishment, in the heart of a Quercy village, takes you on a journey of art through its rooms devoted to artists (Dali, Rodin, etc.) and its exhibition centre. Regionally inspired cuisine served in an attractive, vaulted dining room.

LA GRIÈRE – 85 Vendée – 316 H9 – see La Tranche-sur-Mer

GRIGNAN – 26 Drôme – 332 C7 – pop. 1 353 – alt. 198 m – ✉ 26230
Provence 44 **B3**

Paris 629 – Crest 46 – Montélimar 25 – Nyons 25 – Orange 52 – Pont-St-Esprit 38

Office de tourisme, place du jeu de Ballon ✆ 04 75 46 56 75, Fax 04 75 46 55 89

Château★★ - St-Sauveur church ✻★.

Manoir de la Roseraie rm, rest,
chemin des Grands Prés, (Valréas road) –
✆ 04 75 46 58 15 – roseraie.hotel@wanadoo.fr – Fax 04 75 46 91 55
– Open beg. February-beg. November and closed Tuesday, Wednesday off season
21 rm – €152/380 €152/380, €20
Rest – *(closed Tuesday and Wednesday off season and lunch weekdays July-August) (pre-book)* Menu €28 (weekday lunch), €35/60 – Carte €54/69
◆ "Exquisite" may well have been how the Marchioness would have described this elegant 19C manor at the foot of the castle. Spacious rooms, a rose garden and attractive swimming pool. The elegant rotunda dining room has a conservatory giving onto a pretty wooded park.

Le Clair de la Plume without rest
pl. du Mail – ✆ 04 75 91 81 30 – plume2@wanadoo.fr – Fax 04 75 91 81 31
15 rm – €98/170 €98/170, €13
◆ This fine 17th century building is full of charm, providing Provençal-style rooms set around a flower garden. Boutique and tea room. Excellent service.

La Bastide de Grignan without rest
1 km on D 541 Montélimar road –
✆ 04 75 90 67 09 – info@labastidedegrignan.com – Fax 04 75 46 10 62
16 rm – €60/80 €60/80, €15
◆ This brand new establishment, attached to the nearby Relais de Grignan and built on former truffle-producing land, offers smart rooms with modern, Provençal decor.

La Table des Délices
1 km on D 541 Montélimar road – ✆ 04 75 46 57 22 – Fax 04 75 46 92 96
– Closed Tuesday dinner off season, Sunday dinner and Monday
Rest – Menu €24 (weekday lunch)/48 – Carte €46/59
◆ On the road to the grotto of Madame de Sévigné, traditional cuisine served in modern surroundings or under foliage on the terrace. In winter, truffles are a speciality.

Le Probus
at the village miniature – ✆ 04 75 46 13 34 – Fax 04 75 46 13 34
– Closed 30 June-6 July, 27 October-6 November, 22-30 December, Thursday from October to May and Wednesday
Rest – *(number of covers limited, pre-book)* Menu €18 (weekdays), €28/46 bi – Carte €24/40
◆ This restaurant is inspired by ancient Rome, both in its name (that of an emperor) and decor (frescos and columns). Appetising modern food.

Le Poème de Grignan
r. St-Louis – ✆ 04 75 91 10 90 – Fax 04 75 91 10 90
– Closed 24-30 March, 17-30 November and Wednesday
Rest – Menu €22 (weekday lunch), €30/39
◆ Mini-restaurant with a Provençal decor, on a pedestrian street in the old town. Seasonally-inspired cuisine with a Mediterranean accent.

Montélimar road – 26230 Grignan

La Maison du Moulin
– ✆ 04 75 46 56 94 – maisondumoulin@wanadoo.fr
5 rm – €68/100 €75/130 – ½ P €65/92 – **Table d'hôte** – Menu €30 bi/45 bi
◆ An 18C mill on the banks of a peaceful river. Charming rooms with antique furnishings, bright dining room, flower-decked garden and pool. Regional cuisine and cookery classes.

GRIMAUD – 83 Var – 340 O6 – pop. 3 780 – alt. 105 m – ✉ 83310
French Riviera 41 **C3**

Paris 861 – Fréjus 32 – Le Lavandou 32 – St-Tropez 12 – Ste-Maxime 12 – Toulon 64

Office de tourisme, 1, boulevard des Aliziers ☎ 04 94 55 43 83, Fax 04 94 55 72 20

Château ≤★.

Port Grimaud★: ≤★ 5 km.

La Boulangerie without rest

2 km west via rte de Collobrières D14 – ☎ 04 94 43 23 16 – hotelboulangerie@orange.fr – Fax 04 94 43 38 27 – Open Easter-9 November

10 rm – †€ 100/115 ††€ 110/135, ☕ € 11 – 2 suites

◆ Relaxation and wellbeing in this little farmhouse hidden away in a green park; rooms with simple Provence décor, friendly atmosphere.

Athénopolis

rm, rest,

3.5 km north-west on D 558, La Garde-Freinet road – ☎ 04 98 12 66 44 – hotel@athenopolis.com – Fax 04 98 12 66 40 – Open 2 April-31 October

11 rm – †€ 89/115 ††€ 89/115, ☕ € 10 – ½ P € 73/80

Rest – *(closed Wednesday except July-August)* Menu (€ 18), € 23/33 – Carte € 30/94

◆ In the Mediterranean – almost Greek – countryside of the Maures mountain range, stands a house with blue shutters and colourful rooms with a loggia or private terrace.

Hostellerie du Coteau Fleuri

pl. des Pénitents – ☎ 04 94 43 20 17 – coteaufleuri@wanadoo.fr – Fax 04 94 43 33 42 – Closed 1st November-20 December

14 rm – †€ 46/115 ††€ 46/115, ☕ € 8 – ½ P € 58/93 – **Rest** – *(closed lunch in July-August, Monday lunch, Friday lunch and Tuesday)* Menu € 30 bi (weekday lunch), € 45/68 bi – Carte € 55/72

◆ Former silk farm situated on the old village square. The simply styled rooms are gradually being renovated. Pleasant rustic dining room with large fireplace and a terrace-balcony overlooking the Maures mountain range. Classic cuisine served.

Les Santons (Claude Girard)

rte Nationale – ☎ 04 94 43 21 02 – lessantons@wanadoo.fr – Fax 04 94 43 24 92 – Closed 12 November-15 December, Thursday lunch in season, Wednesday except dinner in winter, Monday and Tuesday off season

Rest – Menu € 35 bi (lunch)/55 – Carte € 74/143

Spec. Risotto crémeux de homard. Petite bourride des Santons. Selle d'agneau de Sisteron rôtie au thym sauvage. **Wines** Côtes de Provence.

◆ An inn with character, along the main road through the village, with an excellent local reputation. Elegant Provençal setting, with antiques, ornamental figures, copperware and flowers. Classic cuisine.

La Bretonnière

pl. des Pénitents – ☎ 04 94 43 25 26 – Fax 04 94 43 25 26 – Open from mid March to mid November and closed Sunday dinner off season and Monday

Rest – Menu € 18 (lunch), € 28/35 – Carte € 39/53

◆ In a street in the medieval town, this restaurant has a very comprehensive menu. Pretty decor, with a mixture of dark wood (Louis Philippe furniture) and shades of blue.

Le Murier

1,5 km south-east via D 14 – ☎ 04 94 43 34 94 – dubourglemurier@wanadoo.fr – Fax 04 94 43 32 65 – Closed 10 January-10 February, Sunday dinner from 15 October to Easter, Saturday lunch from Easter to 15 October, Monday and Tuesday

Rest – Menu (€ 32), € 42/62 – Carte € 57/64

◆ Pleasant beige-toned décor in this cosy restaurant housing a large dining area and veranda facing the garden. Inventive cuisine and nice selection of wines.

Auberge La Cousteline

2.5 km south-east via D 14 – ☎ 04 94 43 29 47 – aubergelacousteline@wanadoo.fr – Fax 04 94 44 83 19 – Closed Tuesday in Winter, lunch in July-August and Wednesday lunch

Rest – Menu € 22 (weekday lunch), € 33/60 – Carte € 37/77

◆ Old isolated farm, lost in the greenery. The Provence-style interior and pretty terrace are clearly popular in the peak season. Country cooking.

LA GRIVE – 38 Isère – 333 E4 – see Bourgoin-Jallieu

GROFFLIERS – 62 Pas-de-Calais – 301 C5 – see Berck-sur-Mer

GROISY – 74 Haute-Savoie – 328 K4 – pop. 2 605 – alt. 690 m – ✉ 74570

46 **F1**

Paris 534 – Annecy 17 – Bellegarde-sur-Valserine 40 – Bonneville 29 – Genève 37

Auberge de Groisy VISA

– ✆ 04 50 68 09 54 – Fax 04 50 68 09 54 – *Closed 30 June-15 July, 2-21 January, Sunday dinner, Monday and Tuesday*

Rest – *(number of covers limited, pre-book)* Menu € 28/65 – Carte € 46/67

◆ Next to the church, this 19C farm is well restored (exposed beams and stonework); a pleasantly rustic spot offering thoughtful modern cuisine.

GROIX (ÎLE) – 56 Morbihan – 308 K9 – see Île de Groix

GRUFFY – 74 Haute-Savoie – 328 J6 – pop. 1 157 – alt. 570 m – ✉ 74540

46 **F1**

Paris 545 – Aix-les-Bains 19 – Annecy 17 – Chambéry 36 – Genève 62

Aux Gorges du Chéran rest, P VISA

au Pont de l'Abîme – ✆ 04 50 52 51 13 – savary.marc@wanadoo.fr – Fax 04 50 52 57 33 – *Open 15 March-15 November*

8 rm – €65/85 €65/85, € 9 – ½ P € 62/70 – **Rest** – Menu € 18/28 – Carte € 24/44

◆ Quiet rooms with wood panelling in an establishment with a remarkable backdrop: the spectacular metallic bridge (1887) spanning the gorges. Generous traditional cuisine drawing on local inspiration plus snack menu. Fine panoramic terrace.

GRUISSAN – 11 Aude – 344 J4 – pop. 3 061 – alt. 2 m – Casino – ✉ 11430

Languedoc-Roussillon-Tarn Gorges

22 **B3**

Paris 796 – Carcassonne 73 – Narbonne 15 – Perpignan 76

Office de tourisme, 1, boulevard du Pech-Maynaud ✆ 04 68 49 09 00, Fax 04 68 49 33 12

Le Phoebus rm, rm, P VISA

bd Sagne, (at the casino) – ✆ 04 68 49 03 05 – hotel.lephoebus@casinos-sfc.com – Fax 04 68 49 07 67

50 rm – € 30/81 € 30/91, € 9,50 – **Rest** – Menu € 26/45 bi – Carte € 21/43

◆ Motel-style comfortable rooms in the casino complex, decorated according to themes, such as The South, The Sea, Fishermen or Customs and Traditions. Small gardens on the ground floor. A restaurant in a modern setting with a grill menu in the summer by the swimming pool.

Du Port rest, P VISA

bd Corderie – ✆ 04 68 49 07 33 – info@gruissan-hotel-du-port.com – Fax 04 68 49 52 41 – *Open Easter-beg. October*

48 rm – € 52/65 € 52/65, € 8 – **Rest** – *(dinner only)* Menu € 20

◆ Rather austere cuboid exterior contrasting with the new interior layout which is welcoming. Painted wood furniture and Mediterranean hues, small practical bedrooms. Spirit of the south in the restaurant (wrought iron, sunny colours), an attractive terrace shaded by vines.

Accueil de la Plage without rest P VISA

r. Bernard l'Hermite, At Chalands beach – ✆ 04 68 49 00 75 – lconsonni@hotmail.fr – Fax 04 68 49 00 75 – *Open Easter-1st November*

17 rm – € 50/58 € 60/64

◆ In a quiet alley, two minutes from the stilt houses immortalised in the film "Betty Blue" are these bright well-kept rooms, some with a balcony. Pleasant welcome.

L'Estagnol

12 av. Narbonne – ✆ 04 68 49 01 27 – Fax 04 68 32 23 38 – Open end April-end September and closed Sunday dinner except July-August, Tuesday lunch from September to June and Monday

Rest – Menu € 16 (weekday lunch), € 25/31 – Carte € 22/56

◆ An authentic former fisherman's house: Provençal decor, small terrace overlooking the lake and good simple regional cuisine with the emphasis on fish.

Le Lamparo

au village – ✆ 04 68 49 93 65 – restaurant.lelamparo@wanadoo.fr – Fax 04 68 49 93 65 – Closed Christmas holidays, Monday and Tuesday except July-August

Rest – Menu € 23/39

◆ On the semicircular quayside of this old town, a spacious, discreet restaurant with a central winter garden. Cuisine with an emphasis on fish and seafood.

LE GUA – 17 Charente-Maritime – 324 E5 – pop. 1 856 – alt. 3 m – ✉ 17600

Paris 493 – Bordeaux 126 – Rochefort 26 – La Rochelle 63 – Royan 16

Syndicat d'initiative, 28, rue Saint-Laurent ✆ 05 46 23 17 28, Fax 05 46 23 17 28 — 38 **B3**

Le Moulin de Châlons with rm

à Châlons, West : 1 km rte de Royan – ✆ 05 46 22 82 72 – moulin-de-chalons@wanadoo.fr – Fax 05 46 22 91 07

10 rm – †€ 95/140 ††€ 95/160, ☕ € 13 – ½ P € 89/121 – **Rest** – Menu (€ 20), € 25/45 – Carte € 37/64

◆ An appetising up-to-date menu and welcoming rustic-bourgeois decor (exposed stonework and beams) distinguish this authentic 18C tide mill. Rooms, six of which have been attractively renovated, all overlooking the park.

GUEBERSCHWIHR – 68 Haut-Rhin – 315 H8 – pop. 816 – alt. 260 m – ✉ 68420

Alsace-Lorraine — 1 **A2**

Paris 487 – Colmar 12 – Guebwiller 18 – Mulhouse 36 – Strasbourg 92

Relais du Vignoble

33 r. Forgerons – ✆ 03 89 49 22 22 – relaisduvignoble@wanadoo.fr – Fax 03 89 49 27 82 – Closed 1st February-1st March

30 rm – †€ 48/60 ††€ 63/95, ☕ € 9 – ½ P € 62/75

Rest *Belle Vue* – *✆ 03 89 49 31 09 (closed Thursday lunch and Wednesday)* Menu € 18 (weekdays)/38 – Carte € 33/47

◆ A "spiritual"stop on la Route des Vins: the new building is next to the family cellar and most of the old fashioned but well-kept rooms are facing the vineyards. Seminary facilities. Traditional dishes and local wines to be sampled on the panoramic terrace in fine weather.

GUEBWILLER – 68 Haut-Rhin – 315 H9 – pop. 11 525 – alt. 300 m – ✉ 68500

Alsace-Lorraine — 1 **A3**

Paris 474 – Belfort 52 – Colmar 27 – Épinal 96 – Mulhouse 24 – Strasbourg 107

Office de tourisme, 73, rue de la République ✆ 03 89 76 10 63, Fax 03 89 76 52 72

St-Léger church ★: west front★★ - Interior★★ of N.-Dame church ★: High altar★★ - Town hall★ - Musée du Florival★.

Guebwiller Valley★★ Northwest.

Domaine du Lac

244 r. de la République, towards Buhl – ✆ 03 89 76 15 00 – contact@domainedulac-alsace.com – Fax 03 89 74 14 63

35 rm – †€ 41/70 ††€ 41/70, ☕ € 8,50 – ½ P € 70/99

Rest *Les Terrasses* – *✆ 03 89 76 15 76 (closed Saturday lunch)* Menu (€ 17), € 20 (weekday lunch), € 26/45 – Carte € 28/41

◆ Well-appointed, reasonably-priced establishment. Minimalist graphic style in the rooms overlooking the lake or a stream to the rear. Designer inspired restaurant and panoramic terrace. Regional specialities take pride of place on the contemporary menu.

L'Ange

4 r. de la Gare – ✆ 03 89 76 22 11 – hoteldelange@wanadoo.fr – Fax 03 89 76 50 08

36 rm – †€ 39/50 ††€ 65/70, ☕ € 8 – ½ P € 65 – **Rest** – *(closed Saturday lunchtime)* Menu € 9,50 (weekday lunch), € 17/35 – Carte € 20/44

◆ The name – unless it's a coincidence – and an elevator used as a lift show that the hotel was indeed once a maternity hospital. Functional rooms set around a well of light. Italian and Alsatian cuisine influences the menu here; pretty shaded terrace.

in Murbach 5 km Northwest by D 40[II] – pop. 136 – alt. 420 m – ✉ 68530

Church ★★.

Hostellerie St-Barnabé

– ✆ 03 89 62 14 14 – hostellerie.st.barnabe@wanadoo.fr – Fax 03 89 62 14 15 – Closed 24-26 December and 6-30 January

27 rm – †€ 57/76 ††€ 183, ☕ € 16 – ½ P € 70/124 – **Rest** – Menu € 13 (weekday lunch), € 20/65 – Carte € 28/59

◆ An old Alsatian house and garden sitting brightly in the scenic Murbach Valley. Some rooms renovated in a modern and colourful style. Comfortable lounge. Cooking suited to current tastes and discreetly medieval atmosphere in this elegant dining room.

Le Schaeferhof

6 r. de Guebwiller – ✆ 03 89 74 98 98 – maisondhotes@schaeferhof.fr – Fax 03 89 74 98 99 – Closed 15-25 October and 15-30 January

4 rm ☕ – †€ 110 ††€ 130/150 – **Table d'hôte** – Menu € 40 (weekdays)/110

◆ This former tenanted 18C farm is now a hotel with well-designed rooms (sitting rooms, flat screens and power showers): no detail has been forgotten. Modern Alsatian cuisine, and a fine choice of wines. Home-made breakfasts.

in Rimbach-près-Guebwiller 11 km West by D 5[I] – pop. 244 – alt. 550 m – ✉ 68500

L'Aigle d'Or with rm

5 r. Principale – ✆ 03 89 76 89 90 – hotelmarck@aol.com – Fax 03 89 74 32 41 – Closed mid February-mid March

15 rm – †€ 34 ††€ 44, ☕ € 7 – ½ P € 36/49 – **Rest** – *(closed Monday except mid July-mid September)* Menu (€ 9,50), € 16/35 – Carte € 21/50

◆ A simple family inn, ideal for a peaceful meal in an authentic environment, serving regional style cuisine around the fireplace. Simple well-kept rooms.

GUÉCÉLARD – 72 Sarthe – 310 J7 – pop. 2 594 – alt. 45 m – ✉ 72230 — 35 C1

Paris 219 – Château-du-Loir 38 – La Flèche 26 – Le Grand-Lucé 38 – Le Mans 19

La Botte d'Asperges

49 r. Nationale – ✆ 02 43 87 29 61 – Fax 02 43 87 29 61 – Closed 2-17 March, 3-25 August, Sunday dinner and Monday except holidays

Rest – Menu € 17/50 – Carte € 30/60

◆ Former posthouse on the main road. Frescoes and paintings with floral motifs decorate the dining room with its carefully laid tables. Traditional menu.

GUENROUËT – 44 Loire-Atlantique – 316 E2 – pop. 2 408 – alt. 30 m – ✉ 44530 — 34 A2

Paris 430 – Nantes 56 – Redon 21 – St-Nazaire 41 – Vannes 72

Relais St-Clair

31 r. de l'Isac, (Nozay road) – ✆ 02 40 87 66 11 – g.todesco@wanadoo.fr – Fax 02 40 87 71 01 – Closed Tuesday dinner, Wednesday dinner 15 September-15 June and Monday

Rest – Menu € 30/68 – Carte € 47/75

Rest *Le Jardin de l'Isac* – buffet *(closed Tuesday dinner, Wednesday dinner and Monday 15 September-15 June)* Menu € 13 (weekday lunch)/19 – Carte € 22/41

◆ A flower-decked building near the Nantes-Brest canal and a small outdoor leisure complex. Traditional cuisine and fine Loire wine list. A buffet of starters, grilled dishes and desserts are served at the Jardin d'Isaac.

XX **Le Paradis des Pêcheurs**

au Cougou, 5 km northwest by D 102 – ✆ 02 40 87 64 10 – leparadisdespecheurs@wanadoo.fr – Fax 02 40 87 64 10 – Closed autumn half-term holidays, from February, Monday dinner, Tuesday dinner, Thursday dinner and Wednesday

Rest – Menu € 20 (weekdays)/34 – Carte € 35/42

◆ A 1930s house, surrounded by pine and chestnut trees, in a peaceful Argoat hamlet. Old wood panelling in the bar and dining room. Traditional dishes.

GUÉRANDE – 44 Loire-Atlantique – 316 B4 – pop. 13 603 – alt. 54 m – ✉ 44350

Brittany 34 **A2**

Paris 450 – La Baule 6 – Nantes 77 – St-Nazaire 20 – Vannes 69

Office de tourisme, 1, place du Marché au Bois ✆ 02 40 24 96 71, Fax 02 40 62 04 24

St-Aubin collegiate church ★.

Les Voyageurs

pl. du 8 Mai 1945 – ✆ 02 40 24 90 13 – Fax 02 40 62 06 64 – Closed 23 December-23 January

12 rm – †€ 50 ††€ 56, ☕ € 7 – ½ P € 54 – **Rest** – *(closed Sunday dinner and Monday except July-August)* Menu € 21/34 – Carte € 29/48

◆ This old house was built outside the town walls facing the ramparts. Charming 1940s style interior. Well-maintained rooms with recent bedding. Find four countrified dining rooms and simple, classic dishes here.

La Guérandière without rest

5 r. Vannetaise – ✆ 02 40 62 17 15 – contact@guerandiere.com

6 rm – †€ 58/88 ††€ 58/118, ☕ € 10

◆ This charming 19C hotel at the foot of the battlements provides cosy rooms with colourful decor, all with a fireplace. Breakfasts are served in the garden or in the conservatory in summer.

X **Les Remparts** with rm

bd Nord – ✆ 02 40 24 90 69 – Fax 02 40 62 17 99 – hotel open 16 February-14 November and closed Sunday and Monday except August ; restaurant: closed 1st December-15 January, 17-21 February, dinner 16-31 January, Sunday dinner and Monday except August

8 rm – †€ 45/47 ††€ 45/47, ☕ € 6,50 – ½ P € 52/65 – **Rest** – Menu (€ 15), € 18/38

◆ This restaurant faces the ramparts. Traditional and fish dishes, sprinkled with Guérande salt, naturally. Small, very simple, somewhat antiquated but quiet rooms.

X **Le Vieux Logis**

pl. Psalette , (within the town itself) – ✆ 02 40 62 09 73 – Closed 16 November-20 December, Tuesday dinner except July-August and Wednesday except holidays

Rest – Menu (€ 17), € 25/30 – Carte € 26/40

◆ The residence of the Provost of Guérande, then a notary's office and finally a restaurant, this attractive 17C stone building has retained its original character. Charcoal grill specialities.

X **Le Balzac**

2 pl. du Vieux Marché – ✆ 02 40 42 97 46 – Fax 02 51 76 92 71 – Closed 5-25 November, Sunday dinner, Wednesday dinner and Thursday

Rest – Menu € 17/30 – Carte € 22/43

◆ On a small square behind the collegiate church, this traditional Breton house with red shutters is a restaurant with an attractive décor; modern cuisine with traditional touches.

LA GUERCHE-DE-BRETAGNE – 35 Ille-et-Vilaine – 309 O7 – pop. 4 095 – alt. 77 m – ✉ 35130 Brittany 10 D2

Paris 324 – Châteaubriant 30 – Laval 53 – Redon 84 – Rennes 55 – Vitré 22

Office de tourisme, 30, rue Du Guesclin ✆ 02 99 96 30 78, Fax 02 99 96 41 43

XX **Calèche** with rm

16 av. Gén. Leclerc – ✆ 02 99 96 21 63 – contact@lacaleche.com – Fax 02 99 96 49 52 – Closed 1st-21 August, 23-31 December, Monday except hotel, Friday dinner and Sunday dinner

13 rm – †€ 47 ††€ 57, ☕ € 10 – ½ P € 65 – **Rest** – Menu (€ 12), € 14 (weekdays)/34 – Carte € 29/46

◆ Tasteful dining room, extended by a veranda and small bistro area, serving generous local cuisine. Practical rooms.

GUÉRET 🅿 – 23 Creuse – 325 I3 – pop. 14 123 – alt. 457 m – ✉ 23000

Dordogne-Berry-Limousin 25 **C1**

Paris 351 – Châteauroux 90 – Limoges 93 – Montluçon 66

Office de tourisme, 1, rue Eugène France ✆ 05 55 52 14 29, Fax 05 55 41 19 38

Champlevé enamels★ of the musée d'art et d'archéologie de la Sénatorerie (art and archeology museum).

Le Coq en Pâte

2 r. de Pommeil – ✆ 05 55 41 43 43 – Fax 05 55 41 43 42 – Closed 20 October-8 November, 17 February-6 March, Sunday dinner off season and Monday dinner

Rest – Menu € 17 (weekdays)/54 – Carte € 43/68

Z **m**

◆ A sympathetically restored 19C house with a terrace overlooking a pleasant wooded garden. Generous and refined modern cuisine.

in Ste-Feyre 7 km East – pop. 2 250 – alt. 450 m – ✉ 23000

Les Touristes-Michel Roux

1 pl. de la mairie – ✆ 05 55 80 00 07 – Fax 05 55 81 11 04 – Closed January, Wednesday evening, Sunday evening and Monday

Rest – Menu € 18/48

◆ A regional building in the heart of the village, featuring a dining area with colourful and floral décor and a nice herb cupboard. Market cuisine served.

GUÉRY (LAC) – 63 Puy-de-Dôme – 326 D9 – see le Mont-Dore

GUÉTHARY – 64 Pyrénées-Atlantiques – 342 C4 – pop. 1 284 – alt. 15 m – ✉ 64210

Atlantic Coast 3 **A3**

Paris 780 – Bayonne 19 – Biarritz 9 – Pau 125 – St-Jean-de-Luz 7

Office de tourisme, 74, rue du Comte de Swiecinski ✆ 05 59 26 56 60, Fax 05 59 54 92 67

Villa Catarie without rest

415 av. Gén. de Gaulle – ✆ 05 59 47 59 00 – hotel@villa-catarie.com – Fax 05 59 47 59 02 – Closed from November to mid-December and from January to mid-February

14 rm – †€ 125/175 ††€ 125/175, ☕ € 12 – 2 suites

◆ Delightful Basque house built in 1830 with elegant, cosy rooms in pastel shades. Fine antique furniture and charming breakfast room.

Brikéténia without rest

r. Empereur – ✆ 05 59 26 51 34 – guethary@briketenia.com – Fax 05 59 54 71 55

17 rm – †€ 70/95 ††€ 75/95, ☕ € 8

◆ A 17C building in the typical style of the region with views of the mountains and sea. Convivial breakfast room and spacious guestrooms, some with antique furniture.

Villa Janénéa

352 av. du Gén. de Gaulle – ✆ 05 59 26 50 69 – gaellethibon@aol.com – Fax 05 59 54 94 67 – Closed 23-29 June, January, Wednesday and Thursday except school holidays and holidays

Rest – Menu (€ 20), € 35 – Carte € 36/52

◆ A tasteful, contemporary-style dining area with a roadside and garden terrace. Modern cuisine with a personal touch.

LE GUÉTIN – 18 Cher – 323 O5 – ✉ 18150 12 **D3**

Paris 252 – Bourges 58 – La Guerche-sur-l'Aubois 11 – Nevers 13 – St-Pierre-le-Moutier 29

Auberge du Pont-Canal

37 r.des Ecluses – ✆ 02 48 80 40 76 – Fax 02 48 80 45 11 – Closed 1st-8 January, Sunday dinner from 30 October-30 April and Monday

Rest – Menu € 12 (weekday lunch)/35 – Carte € 15/40

◆ This family guesthouse next to the picturesque canal bridge across the Allier has several dining rooms, including a veranda overlooking the countryside.

GUEUGNON – 71 Saône-et-Loire – 320 E10 – pop. 8 563 – alt. 243 m – ✉ 71130

Paris 335 – Bourbon-Lancy 27 – Mâcon 87 – Montceau-les-Mines 29 – Moulins 63 7 **B3**

Du Centre rest, VISA

34 r. de la Liberté – ✆ 03 85 85 21 01 – Fax 03 85 85 02 67

18 rm – €40/46 €44/50, €6 – **Rest** – Menu €13/38 – Carte €24/44

◆ This family hotel on the main road through the village of Forgerons offers practical rooms, gradually being restored. Plush rustic-style dining areas, serving classic cuisine in a pleasing 'Old France' atmosphere.

GUEWENHEIM – 68 Haut-Rhin – 315 G10 – pop. 1 176 – alt. 323 m – ✉ 68116

Paris 458 – Altkirch 23 – Belfort 36 – Mulhouse 21 – Thann 9 1 **A3**

De la Gare VISA

2 r. Soppe – ✆ 03 89 82 51 29 – Fax 03 89 82 84 62 – Closed 24 July-13 August, 23 February-6 March, Tuesday dinner and Wednesday

Rest – Menu €10 (weekday lunch), €27/70 – Carte €29/59

◆ Once a village café, this pleasant restaurant has been run by the same family for four generations; traditional and local dishes. The superb wine list is worth the trip alone!

GUIGNIÈRE – 37 Indre-et-Loire – 317 M4 – see Tours

GUILHERAND-GRANGES – 07 Ardèche – 331 L4 – see Valence (26 Drôme)

GUILLESTRE – 05 Hautes-Alpes – 334 H5 – pop. 2 211 – alt. 1 000 m – ✉ 05600

French Alps 41 **C1**

Paris 715 – Barcelonnette 51 – Briançon 36 – Digne-les-Bains 114 – Gap 61

Office de tourisme, place Salva ✆ 04 92 45 04 37, Fax 04 95 45 19 09

Porch★ of the church - Pied-la-Viste ≤★ East: 2 km - Peyre-Haute ≤★ South: 4 km then 15 mn.

Combe du Queyras★★ Northeast: 5,5 km.

Dedans Dehors

ruelle Sani – ✆ 04 92 44 29 07 – albancointe@yahoo.fr – Open May-September

Rest – Carte €25/40

◆ This vaulted cellar is located in a medieval street, serving salads, regional plancha dishes and toasted meals to satisfy your appetite in an eclectic and charming bistro-style atmosphere.

in Mont-Dauphin gare 4 km Northwest by D 902^{A} and N 94 – pop. 87 – alt. 1 050 m – ✉ 05600

Office de tourisme, rue Rouget de Lisle ✆ 04 92 45 17 80

Framework★ of Rochambeau barracks.

Lacour et rest. Gare rest, VISA

– ✆ 04 92 45 03 08 – renseignement@hotel-lacour.com – Fax 04 92 45 40 09 – Closed Saturday from 20 April to 30 June and from 1st September to 26 December

46 rm – €34/35 €54/67, €7,50 – ½ P €48/56 – **Rest** – Menu €16/38 – Carte €17/41

◆ Just below the fortifications of Mont-Dauphin, this entirely restored family hotel offers simple rooms, quieter on the garden side. A modern-style restaurant located in a separate building with a sundial on the façade.

GUILLIERS – 56 Morbihan – 308 Q6 – pop. 1 216 – alt. 86 m – ✉ 56490 10 **C2**

Paris 418 – Dinan 66 – Lorient 91 – Ploërmel 13 – Rennes 69 – Vannes 59

Au Relais du Porhoët VISA

11 pl. de l'Église – ✆ 02 97 74 40 17 – relais.du.porhoet@wanadoo.fr – Fax 02 97 74 45 65 – Closed 14-22 April, 30 June-8 July, 29 September-7 October and 2-16 January

12 rm – €38/49 €43/60, €9 – ½ P €45

Rest – *(closed Monday except dinner in July-August and Sunday dinner)*

Menu (€11), €14 (weekdays)/40 – Carte €22/34

◆ This hotel has an attractive seasonal floral facade. Pleasant, soundproofed rooms for non-smokers only. A grand fireplace warms one of the dining rooms in the restaurant where tasty, regional cuisine is served.

GUINGAMP – 22 Côtes-d'Armor – 309 D3 – pop. 8 008 – alt. 81 m – ✉ 22200

Brittany 9 **B1**

Paris 484 – Carhaix-Plouguer 49 – Lannion 32 – Morlaix 53 – St-Brieuc 32

Office de tourisme, place Champ au Roy ✆ 02 96 43 73 89, Fax 02 96 40 01 95

de Bégard Bégard Krec'h An Onn, by Lannion road: 13 km, ✆ 02 96 45 32 64.

N.D.-de-Bon-Secours basilica★ B.

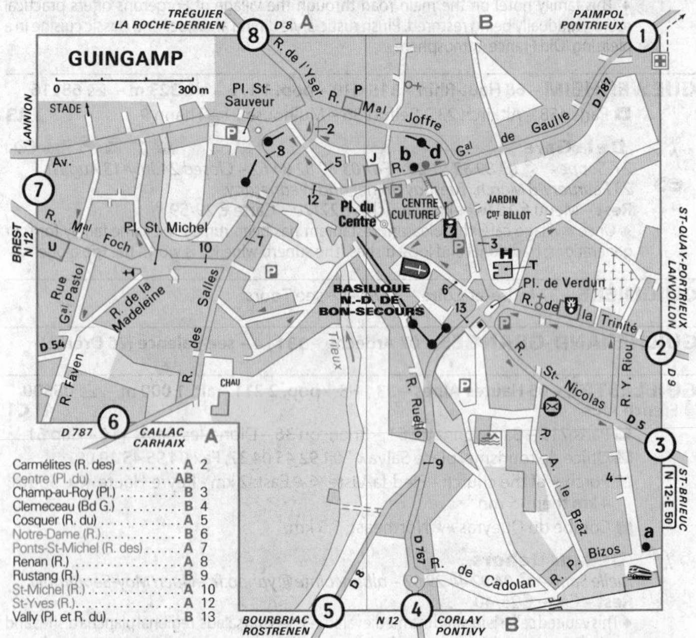

De l'Arrivée without rest

19 bd Clemenceau, (opposite the station) – ✆ 02 96 40 04 57 – hoteldelarrivee.guingamp@wanadoo.fr B **a**

27 rm – €42/46 €56/62, €7,50 – 1 suite

◆ The sign evokes the nearby railway station. This is a handy hotel for travellers to and from Guingamp, with small but well-renovated rooms.

La Demeure without rest

5 r. Gén.de Gaulle – ✆ 02 96 44 28 53 – contact-demeure@wanadoo.fr – Fax 02 96 44 45 54 – Closed January B **b**

7 rm – €66/139 €81/139, €9

◆ In the town centre, this 18th century mansion provides large rooms with period furnishings. Breakfast is served on the veranda overlooking the garden.

La Boissière

r. Yser, 1 km via ⑧ – ✆ 02 96 21 06 35 – Fax 02 96 21 13 38 – Closed 15-30 July, 16-28 February, Saturday lunch, Sunday dinner and Monday

Rest – Menu (€13), €16 (weekday lunch), €23/60 – Carte €35/58

◆ A large century-old house nestling in a park. Traditional cuisine, changing according to the season, is served in two pleasant and comfortable dining rooms.

Le Clos de la Fontaine

9 r. Gén. de Gaulle – ✆ 02 96 21 33 63 – Fax 02 96 21 29 78 – Closed 1st-4 March, 15-31 July, Sunday dinner and Monday B **d**

Rest – Menu (€12,50), €14,50 (weekday lunch), €28/42 – Carte €36/53

◆ This restaurant serves updated traditional cuisine in one of two classically decorated dining areas with parquet and exposed stone work, or on the patio terrace.

GUISSENY – 29 Finistère – 308 E3 – pop. 1 783 – alt. 18 m – ✉ 29880 9 A1

Paris 591 – Brest 35 – Landerneau 27 – Morlaix 56 – Quimper 91

Office de tourisme, place Saint Sezny ✆ 02 98 25 67 99, Fax 02 98 25 69 69

Auberge de Keralloret

South: 3 km on D 10 and secondary road – ✆ 02 98 25 60 37 – auberge@keralloret.com – Fax 02 98 25 69 88 – Closed 4-15 October and 5-31 January
11 rm – €49/58 €57/76, €9 – ½ P €57/67 – **Rest** – *(closed Wednesday except from June to September)* Menu €20 (weekdays)/35 – Carte €28/43

◆ Enjoy the charm and tranquillity of this old Breton farmhouse that has been prettily renovated. Contemporary-style rooms in several granite houses that reflect local architectural styles. The restaurant serves traditional fare in a warm rustic atmosphere.

GUJAN-MESTRAS – 33 Gironde – 335 E7 – pop. 14 958 – alt. 5 m – ✉ 33470

Atlantic Coast 3 B2

Paris 638 – Andernos-les-Bains 26 – Arcachon 10 – Bordeaux 56

Office de tourisme, 19, avenue de Lattre-de-Tassigny ✆ 05 56 66 12 65, Fax 05 56 22 01 41

de Gujan-Mestras Route de Sanguinet, South: 5 km by D 1250 and D 65, ✆ 05 57 52 73 73.

Parc ornithologique du Teich (Ornithological park) ★ East: 5 km.

La Guérinière

18 cours de Verdun, at Gujan – ✆ 05 56 66 08 78 – lagueriniere@wanadoo.fr – Fax 05 56 66 13 39
23 rm – €95/170 €95/170, €11 – 2 suites – ½ P €110/145
Rest – *(closed Sunday dinner in winter and Saturday lunch)* Menu €42 bi/110 – Carte €63/190

Spec. Tempura de langoustines, royale de crustacés, crème de lentilles vertes du Puy. Cochon de lait, andouillette de pied de porc, épinards, pommes soufflées (except summer). Assiette potagère sucrée, crème glacée à l'olive mentholée. **Wines** Entre-deux-Mers, Graves.

◆ A modern building in the centre of the main oyster farming area of the Arcachon Basin. Spacious rooms with tasteful, restrained decor. Contemporary, fragrant cuisine served in an elegant, modern setting or overlooking the swimming pool.

GUNDERSHOFFEN – 67 Bas-Rhin – 315 J3 – pop. 3 490 – alt. 180 m – ✉ 67110

Paris 466 – Haguenau 16 – Sarreguemines 61 – Strasbourg 45 – Wissembourg 33 1 B1

Le Moulin without rest

r. Moulin – ✆ 03 88 07 33 30 – hotel.le.moulin@wanadoo.fr – Fax 03 88 72 83 97 – Closed 4-24 August, 5-12 January and 16 February-3 March
6 rm – €90 €110/200, €17

◆ This former mill is surrounded by a parkland and stream. The rooms have a personal touch, in modern or country-chic styles. Charming, peaceful and sophisticated.

Au Cygne (François Paul)

35 Gd'Rue – ✆ 03 88 72 96 43 – sarl.lecygne@wanadoo.fr – Fax 03 88 72 86 47 – Closed 4-25 August, 5-12 January, 16 February-2 March, Sunday and Monday
Rest – Menu €45 (weekdays)/95 – Carte €78/93

Spec. Morilles farcies dans leur velouté (April to June). Tartare de langoustines marinées au piment d'Espelette. Gibier (October to April). **Wines** Pinot gris, Riesling.

◆ This fine half-timbered building houses an elegant, recently refurbished dining room offering creative and sophisticated cuisine.

Le Soufflet

13 r. de la Gare – ✆ 03 88 72 91 20 – lesoufflet@free.fr – Fax 03 88 72 91 20 – Closed February half-term holidays, Saturday lunch, Monday dinner and Wednesday dinner
Rest – Menu €26/66 bi – Carte €41/53
Rest *Bahnstub* – Menu €12 – Carte €25/43

◆ Flower-decked restaurant opposite the railway station serving classic fare in an interior that sports stuffed animals. Pleasant pergola-terrace. Informal atmosphere: dishes of the day and a small menu of Alsatian specialities.

GY – 70 Haute-Saône – 314 C8 – pop. 1 018 – alt. 237 m – ✉ 70700 Burgundy-Jura

Paris 356 – Besançon 32 – Dijon 69 – Dôle 50 – Gray 20 – Langres 75 – Vesoul 39

Office de tourisme, 15, grande rue ☎ 03 84 32 93 93, Fax 03 84 32 86 87

Château★. 16 **B2**

Pinocchio without rest

– ☎ 03 84 32 95 95 – Fax 03 84 32 95 75 – Closed 25 December-1st January

14 rm – €49 €64, €7

◆ This attractive house, typical of the region, has been restored in contemporary style. It has personalised rooms and an interior decor based on the famous puppet.

GYE-SUR-SEINE – 10 Aube – 313 G5 – pop. 513 – alt. 172 m – ✉ 10250

Paris 209 – Troyes 45 – Châtillon-sur-Seine 26 – Tonnerre 45 13 **B3**

Des Voyageurs

6 r. de la Nation – ☎ 03 25 38 20 09 – hotel-voyageurs-gye@wanadoo.fr – Fax 03 25 38 25 37 – Closed 22-30 August, February holidays, Sunday dinner and Wednesday

7 rm – €48 €48, €6 – ½ P €65 – **Rest** – Menu €15 (weekdays)/22 – Carte €28/45

◆ This late-19C coaching inn, with an attractive stone façade, offers spruce and colourful rooms. Restaurant with modern decor, cane furniture and a traditional menu.

HABÈRE-POCHE – 74 Haute-Savoie – 328 L3 – pop. 729 – alt. 945 m – Winter sports : 930/1 600 m 9 – ✉ 74420 46 **F1**

Paris 564 – Annecy 63 – Bonneville 33 – Genève 37 – Thonon-les-Bains 19

Office de tourisme, Chef-Lieu ☎ 04 50 39 54 46, Fax 04 50 39 56 62

Col de Cou★ Northwest: 4 km, G. French Alps.

Tiennolet

– ☎ 04 50 39 51 01 – pierre.bonnet008@.orangefr – Fax 04 50 39 58 15 – Closed 2-28 June, 13 October-14 November, Sunday dinner, Tuesday dinner and Wednesday except school holidays

Rest – Menu €15 (weekday lunch), €26/36 – Carte €36/40

◆ In the centre of the village, above the family-run pastry shop, a restaurant with a cosy Alpine atmosphere. Classic and regional cuisine. South-facing terrace.

L'HABITARELLE – 48 Lozère – 330 K7 – ✉ 48170 Châteauneuf-de-Randon

Paris 587 – Langogne 19 – Mende 27 – Le Puy-en-Velay 62 23 **C1**

Poste rm,

– ☎ 04 66 47 90 05 – contact@hoteldelaposte48.com – Fax 04 66 47 91 41 – Closed 29 June-4 July, 3-12 November, 19 December-31 January, Sunday dinner and Monday except July-August

16 rm – €46/53 €46/53, €7,50 – ½ P €46 – **Rest** – *(closed Fri. evening, Sat. lunch and Sun. evening except July Aug.)* Menu €16/35 – Carte €22/32

◆ This quaint 18C post-house is situated near the temple erected in honour of Bertrand Du Guesclin, who died from drinking water that was too icy. A restaurant in a converted hay-barn with stone walls and pinewood beams. Regional dishes.

HAGENTHAL-LE-HAUT – 68 Haut-Rhin – 315 I11 – pop. 410 – alt. 400 m – ✉ 68220

Paris 483 – Altkirch 26 – Basel 13 – Colmar 76 – Mulhouse 41 1 **B3**

A l'Ancienne Forge

52 r. Principale – ☎ 03 89 68 56 10 – baumannyves@aol.com – Fax 03 89 68 17 38 – Closed Sunday dinner, Monday and Tuesday

Rest – Menu €28 (weekdays)/48 – Carte €27/52

◆ In a peaceful village, a house with half-timbering surrounded by greenery. Carefully prepared cuisine in keeping with modern taste served in a dining room with attractive painted beams or on the veranda.

HAGETMAU – 40 Landes – 335 H13 – pop. 4 403 – alt. 96 m – ✉ 40700 Atlantic Coast 3 **B3**

Paris 737 – Aire-sur-l'Adour 34 – Dax 45 – Mont-de-Marsan 29 – Orthez 25 – Pau 56

Office de tourisme, place de la République ☎ 05 58 79 38 26, Fax 05 58 79 47 27

Capitals★ in the St-Girons crypt.

Les Lacs d'Halco 🐚 — rest,
3 km southwest on Cazalis road –
✆ 05 58 79 30 79 – contact@hotel-des-lacsdhalco.fr – Fax 05 58 79 36 15
24 rm – 🛉€ 70/98 🛉🛉€ 70/98, ☕ € 12 – ½ P € 70/100 – **Rest** – Menu (€ 20), € 30/60
◆ Steel, glass, wood and stone create the minimalist look of this amazing example of modern architecture overlooking lakes and forest. Attractive contemporary rooms. Boating, crazy golf, etc. The dining room is in a pleasant waterside rotunda overlooking the countryside.

Le Jambon 🐚 — rest,
r. Carnot – ✆ 05 58 79 32 02 – Fax 05 58 79 34 78 – Closed January, Sunday dinner and Monday
9 rm – 🛉€ 50 🛉🛉€ 60/80, ☕ € 7 – **Rest** – Menu € 15 (weekdays)/45
◆ This large hotel in the centre of town has modern, spacious rooms all overlooking the courtyard/swimming pool area. Good soundproofing. The plush, stylish restaurant serves generous portions of traditional and regional cuisine.

HAGUENAU – 67 Bas-Rhin – 315 K4 – pop. 32 242 – alt. 150 m – ✉ 67500
Alsace-Lorraine 1 **B1**

Paris 478 – Baden-Baden 41 – Sarreguemines 93 – Strasbourg 33

Office de tourisme, place de la Gare ✆ 03 88 93 70 00, Fax 03 88 93 69 89

Soufflenheim Baden-Baden Soufflenheim Allée du Golf, East: 14 km by D 1063, ✆ 03 88 05 77 00.

Musée historique★ BZ **M²** - Altar-piece★ in St-Georges church - Panelling★ in St-Nicolas church.

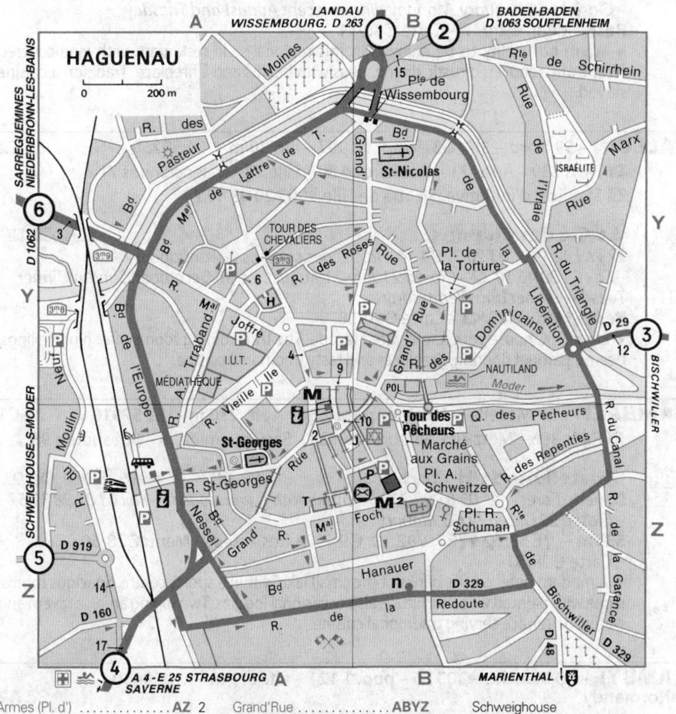

XXX **Le Jardin**

16 r. Redoute – ✆ 03 88 93 29 39 – Fax 03 88 93 29 39 – Closed 29 July-13 August, 6-13 October, 17 February-4 March, Tuesday and Wednesday BZ **n**

Rest – Menu € 17 (weekday lunch), € 36/60 bi

◆ Attractive Hagenau facade revamped in a Renaissance style and a fine interior decoration of warm wood panelling adorned with painted motifs. Classic cuisine with personal touches.

Southeast 3 km by D 329 and secondary road – ✉ 67500 Haguenau

Champ'Alsace rm, rest,

12 r. St-Exupéry – ✆ 03 88 93 30 13 – champalsace@aol.com – Fax 03 88 73 90 04

40 rm – € 60 € 60, € 7,50 – ½ P € 77

Rest – *(Closed Saturday and Sunday)* Menu € 18/32 – Carte € 14/40

◆ Modern hotel complex in an industrial zone. Spacious rooms, furnished with uniform furniture. Two simple dining rooms, brightened with frescos representing regional landscapes and a distillery.

LA HAIE-FOUASSIÈRE – 44 Loire-Atlantique – 316 H5 – see Nantes

LA HAIE-TONDUE – 14 Calvados – 303 M4 – ✉ 14950 32 A3

Paris 198 – Caen 41 – Deauville 15 – Le Havre 53 – Lisieux 20 – Pont-l'Évêque 8

XX **La Haie Tondue**

– ✆ 02 31 64 85 00 – la-haie-tondue@wanadoo.fr – Fax 02 31 64 78 35 – Closed 5-23 January, Monday dinner except August and Tuesday

Rest – Menu € 24/47 – Carte € 30/41

◆ Warm hospitality to be enjoyed in this regional-style restaurant with vine-covered façade and renovated rustic dining areas with beams and a fireplace. Traditional cuisine served.

HALLUIN – 59 Nord – 302 G3 – pop. 18 997 – alt. 30 m – ✉ 59250 31 C2

Paris 239 – Arras 71 – Dunkerque 80 – Lille 22 – Valenciennes 71

Syndicat d'initiative, 58, rue de Lille ✆ 03 20 03 49 24

XX **La Clé des Champs**

273 r. Lille – ✆ 03 20 37 34 34 – la.clef.des.champs@wanadoo.fr – Fax 03 20 46 10 32 – Closed 21 July-21 August, 24-30 December, Sunday dinner, Tuesday dinner and Wednesday

Rest – Menu € 29/43 – Carte € 40/58

◆ Large 19C house with a renovated facade. The three dining rooms offer high ceilings, beams, parquet flooring, fireplaces and tasty traditional cuisine.

HAMBACH – 57 Moselle – 307 N4 – pop. 2 501 – alt. 230 m – ✉ 57910 27 C1

Paris 396 – Metz 70 – Saarbrücken 23 – Sarreguemines 8 – Strasbourg 98

Hostellerie St-Hubert

La Verte Forêt – ✆ 03 87 98 39 55 – annie.roth@wanadoo.fr – Fax 03 87 98 39 57 – Closed 22 December-3 January

53 rm – € 59/62 € 79/82, € 9 – 3 suites – **Rest** – Menu € 28/60 – Carte € 29/51

◆ A modern hotel on the banks of the small lake within a sports centre. Spacious rooms, some with painted wood furniture, also occasional loggias. Two dining areas, a tavern and waterside terrace serving traditional cuisine.

HAMBYE – 50 Manche – 303 E6 – pop. 1 121 – alt. 111 m – ✉ 50450

Normandy 32 A2

Paris 316 – Coutances 20 – Granville 30 – St-Lô 25 – Villedieu-les-Poêles 17

Abbey church ★★.

to the Abbey **3,5 km South by D 51 – ✉ 50450 Hambye**

XXX **Auberge de l'Abbaye** with rm

5 rte de l'Abbaye – ✆ 02 33 61 42 19 – aubergedelabbaye@wanadoo.fr – Fax 02 33 61 00 85 – Closed 1st-15 October, 15-28 February, Sunday dinner and Monday

7 rm – †€ 44 ††€ 54, ☕ € 8 – ½ P € 56 – **Rest** – Menu (€ 22), € 26/65 – Carte € 25/45

♦ A large freestone house near the ruins of the abbey. Summer terrace in a small garden. Smart-rustic dining room; traditional cuisine.

HANVEC – **29 Finistère** – **308** G5 – **pop. 1 605** – **alt. 103 m** – ✉ **29460** 9 **A-B2**

▶ Paris 568 – Rennes 216 – Quimper 48 – Brest 35 – Morlaix 47

Les Chaumières de Kerguan without rest

Kerguan, 2 km on Sizun road – ✆ 02 98 21 97 75 et06 01 96 8753 – kerguan@neuf.fr – Fax 02 98 21 97 75

4 rm – †€ 29/30 ††€ 38/42, ☕ € 5

♦ A typical, thatch-roofed longère in a quiet hamlet of restored agricultural buildings. Charming, reasonably priced rooms.

For a pleasant stay in a charming hotel, look for the red ... symbols.

HARDELOT-PLAGE – **62 Pas-de-Calais** – **301** C4 – ✉ **62152 Neufchâtel-Hardelot** **Northern France and the Paris Region** 30 **A2**

▶ Paris 254 – Arras 114 – Boulogne-sur-Mer 15 – Calais 51 – Le Touquet-Paris-Plage 23

ℹ Office de tourisme, 476, avenue Francois-1er ✆ 03 21 83 51 02, Fax 03 21 91 84 60

⛳ d'Hardelot Neufchâtel-Hardelot 3 avenue du Golf, East: 1 km, ✆ 03 21 83 73 10.

Du Parc

111 av. Francois 1er – ✆ 03 21 33 22 11 – parc.hotel@najeti.com – Fax 03 21 83 29 71

106 rm – †€ 105/140 ††€ 115/160, ☕ € 14 – 1 suite – ½ P € 83/113

Rest – Menu (€ 22 bi), € 27/45 – Carte € 44/66

♦ A recent hotel and sports complex in a woodland environment. Spacious, cosy rooms (painted furniture) looking onto the park. Seafood aromas and tastes abound in this bright restaurant, whose walls are covered in wainscoting and woodwork.

Régina

185 av. François 1er – ✆ 03 21 83 81 88 – leregina.hotel@wanadoo.fr – Fax 03 21 87 44 01 – Closed 30 November-28 February

42 rm – †€ 67/71 ††€ 67/71, ☕ € 9 – ½ P € 59

Rest – *(closed Sunday dinner and Monday except dinner in July-August)* Menu (€ 20), € 24/37 – Carte € 21/46

♦ A modern building on the edge of the pine forest which stretches to the entrance of this elegant Côte d'Opale resort. Rooms gradually being refurbished. Fish and seafood are served in the restaurant with a modern decor. Pleasant terrace for dining in fine weather.

HASPARREN – **64 Pyrénées-Atlantiques** – **342** E4 – **pop. 5 477** – **alt. 50 m** – ✉ **64240** **Atlantic Coast** 3 **AB3**

▶ Paris 783 – Bayonne 24 – Biarritz 34 – Cambo-les-Bains 9 – Pau 106

ℹ Office de tourisme, 2, place Saint-Jean ✆ 05 59 29 62 02, Fax 05 59 29 13 80

◎ Grottoes of Oxocelhaya and Isturits★★ Southeast: 11 km.

Les Tilleuls

pl. Verdun – ✆ 05 59 29 62 20 – hotel.lestilleuls@wanadoo.fr – Fax 05 59 29 13 58 – Closed 15 February-10 March, Sunday dinner and Saturday 13 September-7 July

25 rm – †€ 45/52 ††€ 54/60, ☐ € 6,50 – ½ P € 46/50 – **Rest** – Menu € 16 (weekdays)/30 – Carte € 23/43

◆ The former home of writer Francis Jammes is a stone's throw from this Basque-style construction with well-renovated rooms. Delightful rustic restaurant serving regional dishes.

South 6km by D152 and secondary road - ✉ 64240 Hasparren

Ferme Hégia (Arnaud Daguin)

chemin Curutxeta , (Zelai district) – ✆ 05 59 29 67 86 – info@hegia.com

5 rm ☐ – †€ 415 ††€ 480 – ½ P € 325

Table d'hôte – *(set menu only) (residents only)*

Spec. Menu du marché.

◆ An old farmhouse built in 1746 surrounded by mountains. The interior, superbly renovated in contemporary style, is embellished with high-quality materials. The chef prepares his dishes in front of his guests. Cuisine inspired by the market.

HASPRES – 59 Nord – 302 I6 – pop. 2 753 – alt. 44 m – ✉ 59198 31 C3

Paris 197 – Avesnes-sur-Helpe 49 – Cambrai 18 – Lille 66 – Valenciennes 16

Auberge St-Hubert

62 r. A. Brunet, rte Denain 1km D 955 – ✆ 03 27 25 70 97 – auberge.st.hubert.haspres@wanadoo.fr – Fax 03 27 25 76 21 – Closed August, 3-13 January, Tuesday dinner and Monday except holidays

Rest – Menu € 22/49 – Carte € 35/50

◆ This spruce inn, situated in the Selle valley, is popular for its small garden, rustic-style dining rooms and traditional cuisine (game in season).

HAUTEFORT – 24 Dordogne – 329 H4 – pop. 1 135 – alt. 160 m – ✉ 24390

Dordogne-Berry-Limousin 4 D1

Paris 466 – Bordeaux 189 – Périgueux 59 – Brive-la-Gaillarde 57 – Tulle 92

Office de tourisme, place du Marquis J. F. de Hautefort ✆ 05 53 50 40 27

Au Périgord Noir without rest

La Genèbre – ✆ 05 53 50 40 30 – hotel@auperigordnoir.com – Fax 05 53 51 86 70

29 rm – †€ 40/46 ††€ 43/49, ☐ € 7

◆ Modern construction opposite the château. Practical, calm and well-kept rooms. Panoramic breakfast room.

HAUTE-GOULAINE – 44 Loire-Atlantique – 316 H4 – see Nantes

HAUTE-INDRE – 44 Loire-Atlantique – 316 F4 – see Nantes

HAUTELUCE – 73 Savoie – 333 M3 – pop. 800 – alt. 1 150 m – ✉ 73620

French Alps 45 D1

Paris 606 – Albertville 24 – Annecy 62 – Chambéry 77 – Megève 31

Office de tourisme, 316, Avenue des Jeux Olympiques ✆ 04 79 38 90 30, Fax 04 79 38 96 29

La Ferme du Chozal rm, rest,

– ✆ 04 79 38 18 18 – informations@lafermeduchozal.com – Fax 04 79 38 87 20 – Open 5 June-11 October and 5 December-12 April

11 rm – †€ 100/225 ††€ 100/225, ☐ € 15 – ½ P € 90/153

Rest – *(closed Monday lunch, Tuesday lunch and Wednesday lunch in July-August, Monday dinner and Sunday in June and in September-October)*

Menu € 28 (lunch), € 35/65 – Carte € 46/63

◆ Traditional restored farm that enjoys the quiet of a Beaufortain village. Personalised rooms with modern comfort. Lounge with fireplace. Mountain-style setting and pretty faïence stove in the dining room. Modern food in the evening; more simple at lunchtime.

HAUTERIVES – 26 Drôme – 332 D2 – pop. 1 333 – alt. 299 m – ✉ 26390
Lyon - Rhone Valley 43 **E2**

Paris 540 – Grenoble 77 – Lyon 85 – Valence 46 – Vienne 42

Office de tourisme, rue du Palais Idéal ✆ 04 75 68 86 82, Fax 04 75 68 92 96

Le Palais Idéal★★.

Le Relais

pl. Gén.-de-Miribel – ✆ 04 75 68 81 12 – Fax 04 75 68 92 42
– Closed 15 January-1st March, Sunday dinner except July-August and Monday
16 rm – †€ 55 ††€ 60, ☐ € 8,50 – ½ P € 55 – **Rest** – Menu € 17/34 – Carte € 26/34

◆ Visitors to the Ideal Palace built by Cheval will appreciate this hotel with a façade featuring rolled pebble ornaments. Simple, well-kept rooms. Small, traditional dishes served in the rustic dining area or on the terrace.

LES HAUTES-RIVIÈRES – 08 Ardennes – 306 L3 – pop. 1 949 – alt. 175 m – ✉ 08800 Northern France and the Paris Region 14 **C1**

Paris 254 – Châlons-en-Champagne 150 – Charleville-Mézières 22 – Sedan 29 – Dinant 56

Croix d'Enfer (Hell's Cross) ≤★ South: 1.5 km by D 13 then 30 mn - Vallon de Linchamps★ North: 4 km.

Auberge en Ardenne

15 r. Hôtel de Ville – ✆ 03 24 53 41 93 – auberge.ardenne@orange.fr
– Fax 03 24 53 60 10 – Closed 23 December-15 January
14 rm – †€ 54 ††€ 54/78, ☐ € 7 – ½ P € 55 – **Rest** – *(closed Saturday lunch and Sunday dinner off season)* Menu € 12,50 (weekdays)/35 – Carte € 22/65

◆ A cheerful family restaurant located on both sides of the road through the charming village. Providing neat and tidy rooms with suggestions for walks. Traditional meals served in a rustic Ardennes-style dining area or on the riverside terrace.

Les Saisons

5 Grande Rue – ✆ 03 24 53 40 94 – Fax 03 24 54 57 51
– Closed 16 August-2 September, 1st-9 March, Sunday dinner, Wednesday dinner and Monday except holidays
Rest – Menu € 19/40 – Carte € 24/42

◆ This restaurant, in a small town in the Semoy valley, has several renovated, rustic dining rooms; one of them is simpler and serves daily specials.

HAUTEVILLE-LÈS-DIJON – 21 Côte-d'Or – 320 J5 – see Dijon

LE HAVRE – 76 Seine-Maritime – 304 A5 – pop. 190 905 – Built-up area 248 547 – alt. 4 m – Casino HZ – ✉ 76600 Normandy 33 **C2**

Paris 198 – Amiens 184 – Caen 90 – Lille 318 – Nantes 382 – Rouen 87

Havre-Octeville: ✆ 02 35 54 65 00 A.

Office de tourisme, 186, boulevard Clemenceau ✆ 02 32 74 04 04, Fax 02 35 42 38 39

18 du Havre Octeville-sur-Mer Hameau Saint Supplix, by Etretat road: 10 km, ✆ 02 35 46 36 50.

Harbour★★ EZ - Modern quarter ★ EFYZ : interior★★ of St-Joseph church ★ EZ, pl. de l'Hôtel-de-Ville★ FY47, Av. Foch★ EFY - Musée des Beaux-Arts André-Malraux★ EZ.

Ste-Adresse★: circuit★.

Plans on following pages

Pasino

rm,

pl. Jules Ferry, (At the Casino) – ✆ 02 35 26 00 00 – reservation-lehavre@g-partouche.fr – Fax 02 35 25 62 18 FZ **b**
45 rm – †€ 130/260 ††€ 130/365, ☐ € 18
Rest *Le Havre des Sens* – *(closed August, Saturday lunch, Sunday and Monday)* Menu € 30/60 – **Rest *La Brasserie*** – Menu € 25 – Carte € 19/46
Rest *Le Pas* – *(closed Sunday and Monday)* Carte approx. € 15

◆ Rooms, junior suites and a spa in this ultra-trendy hotel-casino. Contemporary decor and cuisine are the hallmarks of Le Havre des Sens. Modern brasserie with a waterfront terrace. A selection of internationally inspired food, such as tapas and sushi, in this restaurant which stays open late.

HARFLEUR

Doumer (R. Paul) . . . . **D** 30
Verdun (Av. de) . . . . **D** 90
104 (R. des) . . . . **D** 98

LE HAVRE

Abbaye (R. de l') . . . . **C** 2
Aplemont (Av. d') . . . . **C** 7
Churchill (Bd W.) . . . . **B** 24
Hermann-du-Pasquier (Quai) . **B** 44
Joannès-Couvert (Quai) . . . . **B** 52
Mouchez (Bd Amiral) . . . . **B** 68
Octeville (Rte d') . . . . **A** 74
Picasso (Av. Pablo) . . . . **C** 77
Rouelles (R. de) . . . . **C** 82
Sakharov (R. Andrei) . . . . **C** 84

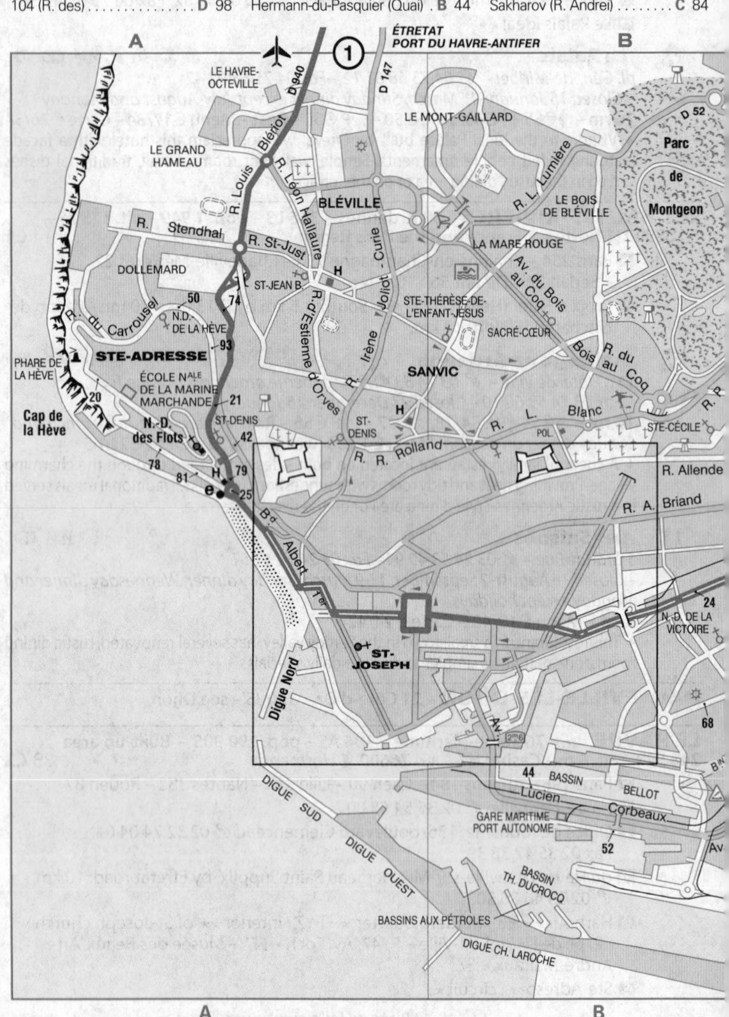

Novotel rest, *VISA*

20 cours Lafayette – ☎ 02 35 19 23 23
– h5650@accor.com
– Fax 02 35 19 23 25 HZ **a**

134 rm – †€ 95/130 ††€ 95/160, ☕ € 13
Rest – Menu (€ 22), € 28 – Carte € 26/45

◆ A modern-style hotel on the banks of Vauban lake, not far from the station. Providing spacious and well-equipped rooms. This restaurant has a designer décor and bay windows opening onto the inner garden. Traditional cuisine.

Val-aux-Corneilles (Av.) . . . . . . C 88

SAINTE-ADRESSE

Cap (Rte du) . . . . A 20
Cavell (R. E.) . . . . A 21
Clemenceau (Pl.) . . . . A 25
Gaulle (R. Gén.-de) . . . . A 42
Ignauval (R. d') . . . . A 50
Prés.-F.-Faure (Bd). . . . . A 78
Reine-Élisabeth (R.) . . . . A 79
Roi-Albert (R. du). . . . . A 81
Vitantal (R. de) . . . . A 93

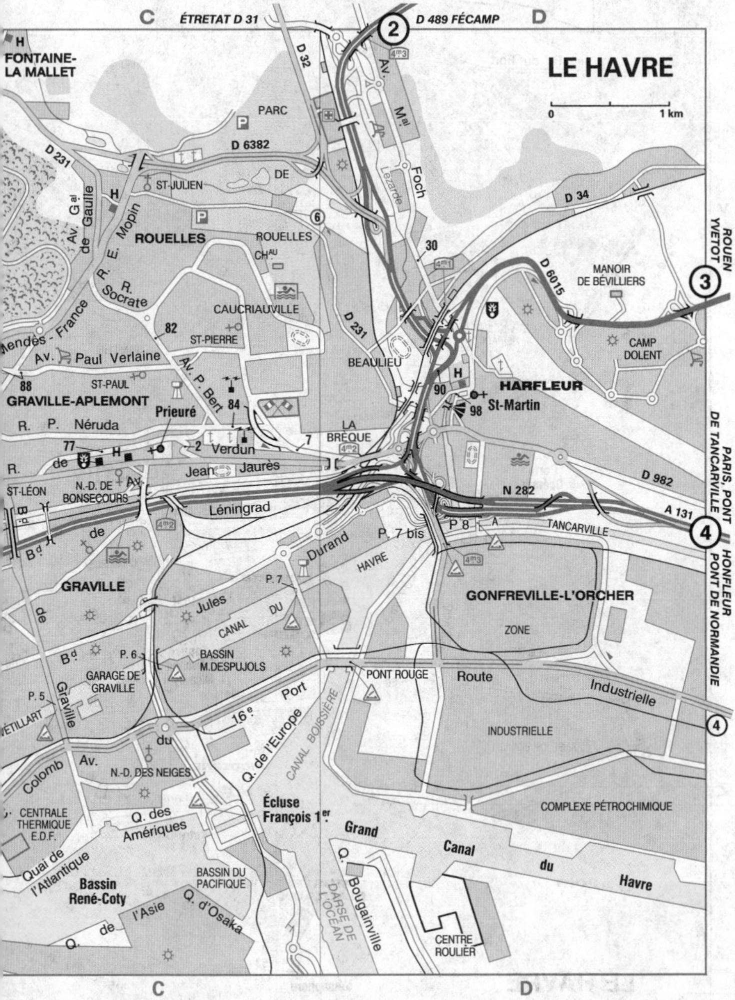

LE HAVRE

Vent d'Ouest without rest

4 r. Caligny
– ✆ 02 35 42 50 69
– contact@ventdouest.fr
– Fax 02 35 42 58 00 EZ **a**

34 rm – 🚹€ 98 🚹🚹€ 98/144, ☕ € 12

◆ This Le Havre hotel has been successfully renovated, providing rooms with attractive décor themes such as Seaside, Captain and Mountain, and with a pleasant lounge and library.

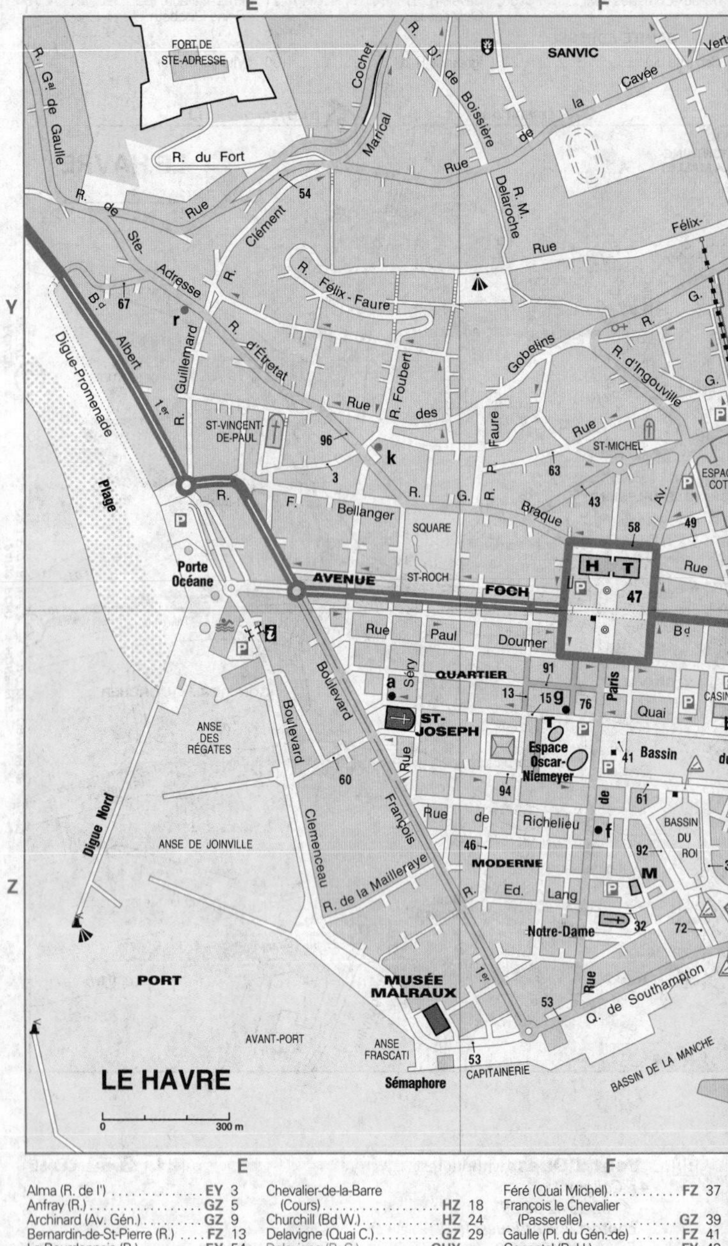

LE HAVRE
0
300 m
E
F
Y
Z
FORT DE STE-ADRESSE
SANVIC
R. Gal de Gaulle
R. du Fort
Rue de la Cavée Verte
R. Dr de Boissière
Cochet
Marical
R. M. Delaroche
Rue Félix-
R. de Ste-Adresse
Rue
R. Clément
R. Félix-Faure
Bd Albert 1er
Digue-Promenade
Plage
R. Guillemard
R. d'Étretat
Rue des Gobelins
R. Foubert
R. d'Ingouville
ST-VINCENT-DE-PAUL
ST-MICHEL
R. Faure
R. G. Braque
R. F. Bellanger
SQUARE ST-ROCH
Porte Océane
AVENUE FOCH
Rue Paul Doumer
Bd
QUARTIER ST-JOSEPH
Séry
Boulevard François 1er
Boulevard Clemenceau
Rue de Paris
Quai
Bassin du
CASIN
Espace Oscar-Niemeyer
ANSE DES RÉGATES
Digue Nord
ANSE DE JOINVILLE
Rue de Richelieu
BASSIN DU ROI
MODERNE
R. Ed. Lang
R. de la Mailleraye
Notre-Dame
PORT
MUSÉE MALRAUX
Q. de Southampton
AVANT-PORT
ANSE FRASCATI
CAPITAINERIE
Sémaphore
BASSIN DE LA MANCHE
ESPAC COT

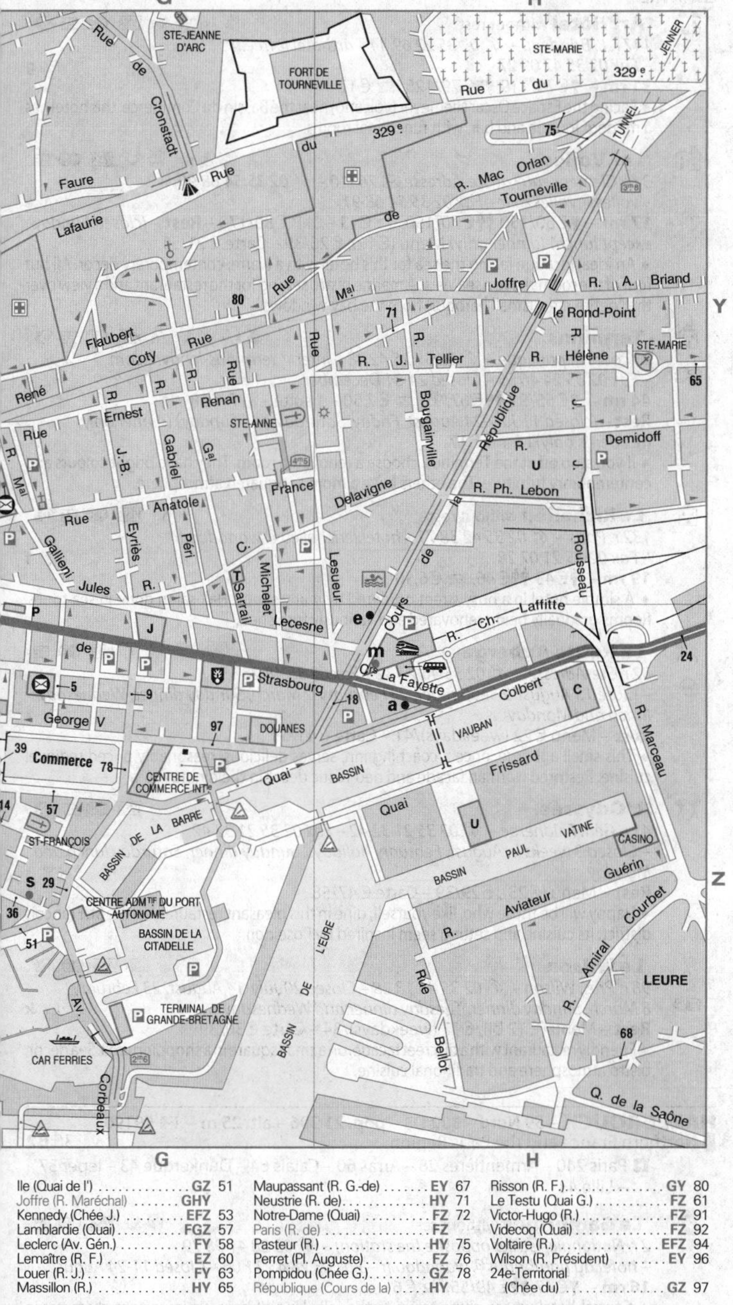
G
H
Y
Z
STE-JEANNE D'ARC
FORT DE TOURNEVILLE
STE-MARIE
JENNER
329 e
Rue du 329 e
Rue de Cronstadt
Faure
Rue
Lafaurie
TUNNEL
75
R. Mac Orlan
Tourneville
de
Rue
Joffre
R. A. Briand
80
Mal
71
le Rond-Point
Flaubert
Rue
Coty
R. J. Tellier
R. Hélène
STE-MARIE
65
René
Ernest
Renan
STE-ANNE
Bougainville
République
Demidoff
U
R. Ph. Lebon
France
Delavigne
Gabriel
Gal
J.-B.
Eyriès
Anatole
Péri
Michelet
Lesueur
Gallieni
Jules
Sarrail
Cours de la
Rousseau
Lecesne
R. Ch. Laffitte
J
de
Strasbourg
Crs La Fayette
24
5
9
George V
18
Colbert
C
97
DOUANES
VAUBAN
R. Marceau
39
Commerce
78
CENTRE DE COMMERCE INTle
Quai
BASSIN
Frissard
14
57
BASSIN DE LA BARRE
Quai
U
VATINE
CASINO
ST-FRANÇOIS
PAUL
BASSIN
Guérin
29
CENTRE ADMTIF DU PORT AUTONOME
Aviateur
Courbet
36
51
BASSIN DE LA CITADELLE
R.
Amiral
LEURE
L'EURE
DE
Rue
BASSIN
TERMINAL DE GRANDE-BRETAGNE
Av.
CAR FERRIES
Bellot
68
Q. de la Saône
Corbeaux
G
H

Art Hôtel without rest
147 r. L. Brindeau – 02 35 22 69 44 – arthotel@free.fr – Fax 02 35 42 09 27 FZ **g**
31 rm – €79/119 €79/125, €12
◆ Facing the Espace Oscar Niemeyer (volcano) near the Bassin du Commerce, this hotel has a modern lounge and bar, with functional rooms.

Les Voiles rm,
3 pl. Clemenceau, at Ste-Adresse 76310 – 02 35 54 68 90 – voiles@voiles76.fr – Fax 02 35 54 68 91 A **e**
17 rm – €60/150 €70/150, €11 – ½ P €80/170 – **Rest** – *(closed Sunday except lunch) (dinner only)* Menu (€12), €26/39 – Carte €21/51
◆ An ideal location facing the sea for this hotel with a warm, contemporary decor. All but four of the rooms have a sea view. A marine bistro setting for the restaurant and a view over the "petite rade"(small harbour) from the bay windows.

Terminus
23 cours République – 02 35 25 42 48 – inter@terminus-lehavre.com – Fax 02 35 24 46 55 – Closed 24-31 December HZ **e**
44 rm – €55/91 €67/95, €7,50 – 1 suite – ½ P €58
Rest – *(closed 11 July-24 August, Friday, Saturday and Sunday) (dinner only) (residents only)* Menu €17
◆ If you stop off at the Terminus, choose a renovated room. They have bright colours and contemporary furniture. The others have a more antiquated atmosphere.

Le Richelieu without rest
132 r. Paris – 02 35 42 38 71 – hotel.lerichelieu@wanadoo.fr – Fax 02 35 21 07 28 FZ **f**
19 rm – €43 €46, €6,50
◆ A simple hotel in a busy street bordered by many shops. Hall-salon done in sea tones. Rooms gradually being renovated and variously furnished.

La Petite Auberge
32 r. Ste-Adresse – 02 35 46 27 32 – Fax 02 35 48 26 15 – Closed 5 August-2 September, 23 February-2 March, Sunday dinner, Wednesday lunch and Monday EY **r**
Rest – Menu €22 (weekdays)/41 – Carte €41/53
◆ This small auberge, once a coaching inn, serves delicious, reasonably priced regional cuisine. Restored Norman façade and neo-rustic decor in the dining room.

L'Odyssée
41 r. Gén. Faidherbe – 02 35 21 32 42 – Fax 02 35 21 32 42 – Closed 3 weeks in August, February holidays, Sunday dinner, Saturday lunch and Monday GZ **s**
Rest – Menu (€23), €29/39 – Carte €47/58
◆ Happy will be those who, like yourself, dine in this pleasant restaurant in the St. François district. Its cuisine and setting seem inspired by Poseidon.

Le Wilson
98 r. Prés. Wilson – 02 35 41 18 28 – Closed 20 July-14 August, 23 February-8 March, Sunday dinner, Tuesday dinner and Wednesday EY **k**
Rest – Menu (€12 bi), €17 (weekdays)/34 – Carte €30/39
◆ Friendly restaurant with a discreet facade, on a small square in a shopping area. Sea decor, bistro atmosphere and traditional cuisine.

HAZEBROUCK – 59 Nord – 302 D3 – pop. 21 396 – alt. 25 m – 59190

Northern France and the Paris Region 30 **B2**

Paris 240 – Armentières 28 – Arras 60 – Calais 64 – Dunkerque 43 – Ieper 37 – Lille 43

Le Gambrinus without rest
2 r. Nationale, (street opposite the station) – 03 28 41 98 79 – hotel.du.gambrinus@wanadoo.fr – Fax 03 28 43 11 06 – Closed 11-24 August
16 rm – €47 €49/55, €6
◆ Central hotel whose name refers to the jolly king of beer, an important character in Flanders. Small simple well-kept rooms, each different; some have been renovated.

XX **Auberge St-Éloi**

60 r. de l'Église – ✆ 03 28 40 70 23 – yannickchever@wanadoo.fr – Fax 03 28 40 70 44 – Closed 22 July-19 August, Monday and dinner except Friday and Saturday

Rest – Menu € 20/42 – Carte € 34/48

♦ At the foot of St Eloi Church, this bright restaurant has friendly service and traditional cuisine. Rotisserie menu available.

in la Motte-au-Bois 6 km southeast by D 946 – ✉ 59190 Morbecque

XXX **Auberge de la Forêt** with rm

– ✆ 03 28 48 08 78 – auberge-delaforet@wanadoo.fr – Fax 03 28 40 77 76 – Closed 20 December-10 January and Sunday dinner October-March

12 rm – †€ 52/55 ††€ 58/62, ☐ € 7,50 – ½ P € 55 – **Rest** – *(closed Friday lunch, Saturday lunch, Sunday dinner and Monday lunch)* Menu (€ 14), € 19 (weekdays)/40

♦ In a village at the heart of the Nieppe forest; vast dining room with a fireplace and Louis XIII chairs serving an inventive cuisine based on plants and spices.

HÉDÉ – 35 Ille-et-Vilaine – 309 L5 – pop. 1 822 – alt. 90 m – ✉ 35630

Brittany 10 **D2**

Paris 372 – Avranches 71 – Dinan 33 – Dol-de-Bretagne 31 – Fougères 70 – Rennes 25

Office de tourisme, Mairie ✆ 02 99 45 46 18, Fax 02 99 45 50 48

Château de Montmuran★ and église des Iffs★ West: 8 km.

XX **La Vieille Auberge**

rte de Tinténiac – ✆ 02 99 45 46 25 – contact@lavieilleauberge35.fr – Fax 02 99 45 51 35 – Closed 21 August-4 September, 9 February-4 March, Sunday dinner and Monday

Rest – Menu € 18 (weekday lunch), € 27/72 – Carte € 43/81

♦ A 17C mill of pastoral charm with a delightful, leafy pondside terrace and a pretty little flower-decked garden. Informal ambience and delicious classic cuisine.

HENDAYE – 64 Pyrénées-Atlantiques – 342 B4 – pop. 12 596 – alt. 30 m – Casino AX – ✉ 64700

Atlantic Coast 3 **A3**

Paris 799 – Biarritz 31 – Pau 143 – St-Jean-de-Luz 12 – San Sebastián 21

Office de tourisme, 67, boulevard de la Mer ✆ 05 59 20 00 34, Fax 05 59 20 79 17

Large crucifix★ in St-Vincent church - Château of Antoine-Abbadie★★ (lounge★) 3 km by ①.

in Hendaye Plage

Serge Blanco rm, rm,

bd de la Mer – ✆ 05 59 51 35 35 – info@thalassoblanco.com – Fax 05 59 51 36 00 – Closed 8-30 December

90 rm – †€ 87/150 ††€ 132/214, ☐ € 14 – ½ P € 108/149 – **Rest** – Menu (€ 37) – Carte € 43/52

♦ The famous rugby player is the owner of this hotel and its thalassotherapy centre, between the beach and marina. Contemporary-style rooms. Some have been renovated. A choice of three types of meals: diet dishes, gastronomic cuisine and grilled food in summer.

in Biriatou 4 km southeast by D 811 – pop. 831 – alt. 60 m – ✉ 64700

Les Jardins de Bakéa

– ✆ 05 59 20 02 01 – contact@bakea.fr – Fax 05 59 20 58 21 – Closed 24 November-10 December and 19 January-4 February

25 rm – †€ 43/120 ††€ 53/120, ☐ € 10 – ½ P € 71/104 – **Rest** – *(closed Monday and Tuesday except dinner April-October)* Menu € 45/65 – Carte € 43/72

♦ This early-20C residence built in regional architectural style is currently being renovated. Once it is finished, it will offer eight comfortable rooms, four of which will be in the attic.

HÉNIN-BEAUMONT – 62 Pas-de-Calais – 301 K5 – pop. 25 178 – alt. 30 m – ✉ 62110 Northern France and the Paris Region

31 **C2**

Paris 194 – Arras 25 – Béthune 30 – Douai 13 – Lens 11 – Lille 34

Novotel

av. de la République , near junction of A1 motorway, via D943 ✉ 62950 – ✆ 03 21 08 58 08 – h0426@accor.com – Fax 03 21 08 58 00

81 rm – €79/129 €79/129, ☐ €13,50 – **Rest** – Menu (€15), €19/39 bi – Carte €21/39

◆ In a shopping centre near a motorway interchange in an oasis of greenery. Rooms being refurbished in stages; choose one facing the patio-terrace. Modern dining room and tables by the swimming pool, weather permitting.

HENNEBONT – 56 Morbihan – 308 L8 – pop. 13 412 – alt. 15 m – ✉ 56700 Brittany

9 **B2**

Paris 492 – Concarneau 57 – Lorient 13 – Pontivy 51 – Quimperlé 26 – Vannes 50

Office de tourisme, 9, place Maréchal-Foch ✆ 02 97 36 24 52, Fax 02 97 36 21 91

Clock tower★ of N.-D.-de-Paradis basilica.

Port-Louis: citadel★★ (musée de la Compagnie des Indes★★, musée de l'Arsenal★) South: 13 km.

Port-Louis road 4 km South by D 781 – ✉ 56700 Hennebont

Château de Locguénolé

rest,

– ✆ 02 97 76 76 76

– locguenole@relaischateaux.com – Fax 02 97 76 82 35

– Closed 4 January-13 February

18 rm – €112/295 €112/295, ☐ €24 – 4 suites – ½ P €143/245

Rest – *(closed Monday from 1st September to 10 July and lunch except Sunday)* Menu €49/94 – Carte €72/119

Spec. Sardines marinées à l'huile de basilic (July-August). Langoustines royales, courgette jaune comme un tian (July to September). Aiguillette de Saint-Pierre en piccata.

◆ Two historical houses in a 120-ha park sloping down to the Blavet ria. Spacious, elegant rooms with personal touches. Pleasant dining room serving a mixture of seafood and vegetable dishes; good wine selection.

Chaumières de Kerniaven

3 km – ✆ 02 97 76 91 90 – locguenole@relaischateaux.com – Fax 02 97 76 82 35 – Open 1st May-28 September

9 rm – €68/112 €68/112, ☐ €18

◆ After checking in at the reception of Château de Locguénolé, you will be taken to these two 17C cottages, deep in the countryside and ideal for relaxing and recuperating.

L'HERBAUDIÈRE – 85 Vendée – 316 C5 – see Île de Noirmoutier

HERBAULT – 41 Loir-et-Cher – 318 D6 – pop. 1 050 – alt. 138 m – ✉ 41190

Paris 196 – Blois 17 – Château-Renault 18 – Montrichard 38 – Tours 47 – Vendôme 26

11 **A1**

Auberge des Trois Marchands

34 pl. de l'Hôtel-de-Ville – ✆ 02 54 46 12 18 – Fax 02 54 46 12 18

Rest – Menu €13 bi (weekday lunch), €17/40 – Carte €19/39

◆ Situated on the main square in the village, this simple auberge serves traditional cuisine in a bright, country style dining room.

LES HERBIERS – 85 Vendée – 316 J6 – pop. 13 932 – alt. 110 m – ✉ 85500 Atlantic Coast

34 **B3**

Paris 381 – Bressuire 48 – Chantonnay 25 – Cholet 26 – Clisson 35 – La Roche-sur-Yon 40

Office de tourisme, 2, rue Saint-Blaise ✆ 02 51 92 92 92, Fax 02 51 92 93 70

Mont des Alouettes★: windmill ≤★★ North: 2 km - Chemin de fer de la Vendée (railway) ★.

Route des Moulins★.

Chez Camille rest, VISA

2 r. Mgr Massé – ✆ 02 51 91 07 57 – chez.camille@online.fr – Fax 02 51 67 19 28
13 rm – €46/59 €50/63, €7,50 – ½ P €46/52 – **Rest** – *(closed Sunday dinner, Friday dinner and Saturday off season)* Menu (€12), €15/29 – Carte €22/34
◆ Near the old Ardelay keep, an establishment with a pleasantly provincial atmosphere (the bar is the HQ of the local football club). Standard rooms. The restaurant's friendly, easy-going ambience can be traced to its unpretentious cuisine.

HERBIGNAC – 44 Loire-Atlantique – 316 C3 – pop. 4 353 – alt. 18 m – ✉ 44410

Paris 446 – Nantes 72 – La Baule 24 – Redon 37 – St Nazaire 28 34 **A2**
Syndicat d'initiative, 2, rue Pasteur ✆ 02 40 19 90 01

South 6 km Guérande road by D774 – ✉ 44410 Herbignac

La Chaumière des Marais VISA

– ✆ 02 40 91 32 36 – lachaumieredesmarais@wanadoo.fr – Fax 02 40 91 33 87 – Closed mid October-mid November, February holidays, Monday except July-August and Tuesday
Rest – Menu €18 (weekday lunch), €28/62 bi – Carte approx. €49
◆ Pretty flower-decked cottage with terrace and vegetable garden. Charming countrified dining room with a huge fireplace and modern cuisine enriched with herbs and spices.

HERMANVILLE-SUR-MER – 14 Calvados – 303 K4 – see Ouistreham

LES HERMAUX – 48 Lozère – 330 G7 – pop. 111 – alt. 1 045 m – ✉ 48340

Paris 594 – Espalion 56 – Florac 73 – Mende 50 – Millau 67 – Rodez 75 – St-Flour 90 22 **B1**

Vergnet

– ✆ 04 66 32 60 78 – vergnet.christophe@wanadoo.fr – Fax 04 66 32 68 13 – Closed Sunday dinner off season
12 rm – €40 €40, €6 – ½ P €40
Rest – *(closed Sun. evening)* Menu €14/23
◆ Family hotel set in a picturesque Aubrac hamlet. Some of the rustic-style rooms could do with a fresh coat of paint. The somewhat outmoded dining room, decorated with stuffed animals, serves unfussy cuisine such as aligot and sausages.

HÉROUVILLE – 95 Val-d'Oise – 305 D6 – 106 6 – see Paris, Area (Cergy-Pontoise)

HÉROUVILLE-ST-CLAIR – 14 Calvados – 303 J4 – see Caen

HESDIN – 62 Pas-de-Calais – 301 F5 – pop. 2 686 – alt. 27 m – ✉ 62140

Northern France and the Paris Region 30 **A2**

Paris 210 – Abbeville 36 – Arras 58 – Boulogne-sur-Mer 65 – Calais 89 – Lille 89
Office de tourisme, place d' Armes ✆ 03 21 86 19 19, Fax 03 21 86 04 05

Trois Fontaines rm, VISA

16 rte d' Abbeville – ✆ 03 21 86 81 65 – hotel.3fontaines@wanadoo.fr – Fax 03 21 86 33 34 – Closed 22 December-5 January, Monday lunch and Saturday lunch
16 rm – €51/63 €57/71, €7 – ½ P €47/50 – **Rest** – Menu (€16), €18 (weekdays)/34
◆ The hotel is made up of two buildings, with small, redecorated, ground floor rooms opening onto the garden. Choose one in the recent Scandinavian style extension. Reasonably-priced food served in a pleasant dining room with a fireplace.

L'Écurie VISA

17 r. Jacquemont – ✆ 03 21 86 86 86 – lecurie846@orange.fr – Fax 03 21 86 86 86 – Closed Sunday dinner, Monday and Tuesday
Rest – Menu (€18), €22 (weekdays)/29
◆ Pleasant restaurant with equine theme (sculptures, signage) situated a short walk from the beautiful town hall. Bright dining area decorated with pottery. Traditional cooking.

in Gouy-St-André 14 km west by N 39 and D 137 – pop. 613 – alt. 100 m – ✉ 62870

XX **Le Clos de la Prairie**

17 r. de St Rémy – ☎ 03 21 90 39 58 – leclosdelaprairie@orange.fr – Closed 1st-7 June, 23-30 December, Thursday except dinner June-August and Wednesday

Rest – Menu € 17 (weekday lunch), € 29/30 – Carte € 29/50

◆ Warm restaurant set in an old farmhouse in a pleasant little village. Its terrace looks out over the countryside. Tasty, modern cuisine using market produce.

HESDIN-L'ABBÉ – **62 Pas-de-Calais** – **301** D3 – **see Boulogne-sur-Mer**

HÉSINGUE – **68 Haut-Rhin** – **315** J11 – **see St-Louis**

HEUDICOURT-SOUS-LES-CÔTES – **55 Meuse** – **307** F5 – **see St-Mihiel**

HEYRIEUX – **38 Isère** – **333** D4 – **pop. 4 163** – **alt. 220 m** – ✉ **38540** 44 **B2**

Paris 487 – Lyon 30 – Pont-de-Chéruy 22 – La Tour-du-Pin 35 – Vienne 25

XXX **L'Alouette**

rte de St-Jean-de-Bournay, at 3 km ✉ 38090 – ☎ 04 78 40 06 08 – alouette@jcmarlhins.com – Fax 04 78 40 54 74 – Closed 21-28 April, 26 July-13 August, 21-29 December, Saturday lunch, Sunday dinner and Monday

Rest – Menu € 21 (weekday lunch), € 31/115 bi – Carte € 39/62

◆ Restaurant in three parts with exposed beams, decorated with paintings and sculptures by a regional artist. Pleasant table settings and traditional cuisine.

HIERES-SUR-AMBY – **38 Isère** – **333** E3 – **pop. 998** – **alt. 216 m** – ✉ **38118** 44 **B1**

Paris 489 – Lyon 61 – Grenoble 107 – Bourg-en-Bresse 57 – Villeurbanne 48

X **Le Val d'Amby** with rm

rest, rm

pl. de la République – ☎ 04 74 82 42 67 – carlona527@wanadoo.fr – Fax 04 74 82 42 68 – Closed 14-20 April, 11-24 August, 16-22 February, Sunday dinner and Wednesday

13 rm – †€ 42 ††€ 50, ☕ € 7 – ½ P € 55 – **Rest** – Menu € 13,50 bi (weekday lunch), € 30/51 – Carte € 33/46

◆ Fine stone construction on the village square. Daily menu served in the café, traditional dishes in the more comfortable dining room. Terrace. Simple and well-kept guestrooms.

HINSINGEN – **67 Bas-Rhin** – **315** F3 – **pop. 72** – **alt. 220 m** – ✉ **67260** 1 **A1**

Paris 405 – St-Avold 35 – Sarrebourg 37 – Sarreguemines 22 – Strasbourg 92

X **Grange du Paysan**

– ☎ 03 88 00 91 83 – Fax 03 88 00 93 23 – Closed Mon.

Rest – Menu € 10 (weekdays)/52 – Carte € 17/41

◆ Old rafters, halters and other farming objects endow this restaurant with a rustic feel. Serves good, local cuisine using produce from the family farm.

HIRMENTAZ – **74 Haute-Savoie** – **328** M3 – **see Bellevaux**

HIRTZBACH – **68 Haut-Rhin** – **315** H11 – **pop. 1 183** – **alt. 308 m** – ✉ **68118**

Paris 462 – Mulhouse 24 – Altkirch 5 – Belfort 31 – Colmar 71 1 **A3**

XX **Hostellerie de l'Illberg**

17 r. Mar. de Lattre de Tassigny – ☎ 03 89 40 93 22 – hostelillberg@tiscali.fr – Fax 03 89 08 85 19 – Closed Sunday dinner and Monday

Rest – Menu € 23 (weekdays)/90 – Carte € 52/57

Rest *Bistrot d'Arthur* – Menu (€ 11), € 20 – Carte € 26/42

◆ Works by local artists adorn the dining room of this attractive house. Classic cuisine with an innovative twist and an emphasis on regional produce. This extremely friendly bistro features a choice of appetising dishes or daily specials.

HOERDT – 67 Bas-Rhin – **315** K4 – **pop. 4 123** – **alt. 135 m** – ✉ **67720** 1 **B1**

Paris 483 – Haguenau 21 – Molsheim 44 – Saverne 46 – Strasbourg 18

À la Charrue

30 r. République – ✆ 03 88 51 31 11 – lacharrue@wanadoo.fr – Fax 03 88 51 32 55 – Closed 5-25 August, 24 December-2 January, dinner except Friday and Saturday and Monday except holidays

Rest – Menu (€ 9), € 14, € 29/36 – Carte € 27/45

◆ The main speciality is asparagus (in season). And so the whole region - including members of the Council of Europe - come here to celebrate.

HOHRODBERG – 68 Haut-Rhin – **315** G8 – **alt. 750 m** – ✉ **68140** Alsace-Lorraine

Paris 462 – Colmar 26 – Gérardmer 37 – Guebwiller 47 – Munster 8 – Le Thillot 57

★★. 1 **A2**

Panorama les Hautes Vosges, rm,

3 rte de Linge – ✆ 03 89 77 36 53 – info@hotel-panorama-alsace.com – Fax 03 89 77 03 93 – Closed 12 November-3 December and 5 January-6 February

30 rm – € 44/71 € 44/71, € 10 – ½ P € 48/67

Rest – Menu € 17 (weekdays)/38 – Carte € 25/46

◆ An old building and modern wing facing the Munster valley. Comfortable rooms, some with a view of the Vosges, decorated with frescoes with a regional theme. Magnificent panoramic view from the restaurant, which serves specialities such as the sea Presskopf.

LE HOHWALD – 67 Bas-Rhin – **315** H6 – **pop. 386** – **alt. 570 m** – **Winter sports : 600/1 100 m** 1 – ✉ **67140** Alsace-Lorraine 2 **C1**

Paris 430 – Lunéville 89 – Molsheim 33 – St-Dié 46 – Sélestat 26 – Strasbourg 51

Office de tourisme, square Kuntz ✆ 03 88 08 33 92, Fax 03 88 08 30 14

Le Neuntelstein★★ ★★ North: 6 km then 30 mn.

La Forestière

10 A chemin du Eck – ✆ 03 88 08 31 08 – catherine.marchal15@orange.fr – Fax 03 88 08 32 96 – Closed 5-13 April and 24 August-1st September

5 rm – € 70/80 € 85/95 – ½ P € 71 – **Table d'hôte** – Menu € 25 bi/35 bi

◆ In the upper village, close to the forest, modern construction offering spacious rooms with Alsatian-style wooden furniture. Regional specialities and game at the *table d'hôte*.

La Petite Auberge

6 r. Principale – ✆ 03 88 08 33 05 – hrpetiteauberge@aol.com – Fax 03 88 08 34 62 – Closed 2-14 March, 30 June-9 July, 12-21 November and 6 January -9 February

Rest – *(closed Tuesday dinner and Wednesday)* Menu € 16/29 – Carte € 23/50

◆ A welcoming restaurant in the heart of a small village. Local cuisine served in a bright dining room with a country-style atmosphere.

Hôtel Petite Auberge

7 rm – € 55 € 64, € 8,50 – ½ P € 60

◆ This wood covered construction offers well-equipped, split-level rooms with small terraces. Breakfast made with regional produce.

HOLNON – 02 Aisne – **306** B3 – see St-Quentin

LE HÔME – 14 Calvados – **303** L4 – see Cabourg

L'HOMME D'ARMES – 26 Drôme – **332** B6 – see Montélimar

HONDSCHOOTE – 59 Nord – **302** D2 – **pop. 3 815** – **alt. 5 m** – ✉ **59122**

Paris 286 – Lille 63 – Dunkerque 22 – Oostende 52 – Roeselare 51 30 **B1**

Office de tourisme, 2, rue des Moëres ✆ 03 28 62 53 00, Fax 03 28 68 30 99

Les Jardins de l'Haezepoël

1151 r. de Looweg – ✆ 03 28 62 50 50 – Fax 03 28 68 31 01 – Closed Monday dinner and Tuesday

Rest – grill Menu (€ 12), € 15/35 – Carte € 23/36

◆ A handsome brick house that is also home to a cabaret. In a countrified setting, you will be served meat grilled in front of you and regional specialities (potjevleech).

HONFLEUR – 14 Calvados – 303 N3 – pop. 8 178 – alt. 5 m – ✉ 14600 Normandy

Paris 195 – Caen 69 – Le Havre 27 – Lisieux 38 – Rouen 83 32 **A3**

Office de tourisme, quai Lepaulmier ✆ 02 31 89 23 30, Fax 02 31 89 31 82

Old Honfleur★★: Old basin★★ AZ, Ste-Catherine church ★★ AY and steeple ★ AY **B** - Côte de Grâce★★AY: calvary★★.

Pont de Normandie★★ by ①: 4 km (toll).

Plan on next page

La Ferme St-Siméon

r. A. Marais, via ③ – ✆ 02 31 81 78 00 – accueil@fermesaintsimeon.fr – Fax 02 31 89 48 48

30 rm – €220/450 €220/450, €27 – 4 suites – ½ P €261/576

Rest – *(closed 12 November-7 December, 14 January-8 February, Tuesday lunch, Thursday lunch and Wednesday)* Menu €129 – Carte €109/151

Spec. Turbot, moutarde et tomates. Agneau de pré-salé, blettes et truffe noire. Pommes, pommes, pommes.

◆ A major site in the history of painting, this former inn, now a magnificent hotel complex with a park overlooking the estuary was frequented by Impressionist artists. Excellent relaxation and fitness facilities. Refined restaurant with a terrace looking out onto the sea, fine selection of calvados and good, classic cuisine.

Le Manoir du Butin

r. A. Marais , via ③ – ✆ 02 31 81 63 00 – accueil@hotel-lemanoir.fr – Fax 02 31 89 59 23 – Closed 2-21December and 20 January-8 February

10 rm – €120/350 €120/350, €15 – ½ P €138/238

Rest – *(closed Monday lunch, Friday lunch and Thursday)* Menu €35/48 – Carte €50/65

◆ Painted timbers, latticed windows, an uneven roof and a park: an 18C manor steeped in charm. Cosy rooms. A discreet elegance reigns in the well-lit dining room; modern menu.

Les Maisons de Léa without rest

pl. Ste-Catherine – ✆ 02 31 14 49 49 – contact@lesmaisonsdelea.com – Fax 02 31 89 28 61

27 rm – €90/195 €90/195, €12 – 3 suites AY **a**

◆ Three old fishing houses from the 16th century and a former salt granary make up this charming hotel near the curious wooden bell tower of St Catherine. Thematic décor throughout the hotel, including country style, romance, Baltimore, and captain. Charming rooms and cosy lounge areas, including one with a nice library.

L'Écrin without rest

19 r. E. Boudin – ✆ 02 31 14 43 45 – hotel.ecrin@honfleur.com – Fax 02 31 89 24 41 AZ **k**

27 rm – €100/180 €100/180, €16 – 2 suites

◆ A museum-like hotel providing rooms and lounges with objets d'art and antiques spread over five different period buildings. The main building from the 18th century is the most sumptuous. Breakfast served in a veranda overlooking the garden.

La Maison de Lucie without rest

44 r. Capucins – ✆ 02 31 14 40 40 – info@lamaisondelucie.com – Fax 02 31 14 40 41 – Closed 25 November-22 December and 6-18 January

12 rm – €150 €150, €18 – 2 suites AY **f**

◆ Recent renovation has allowed this old hotel located in the old centre of Honfleur to retain its charm. Providing attractive and comfortable rooms, one with an attic ceiling, which feature a range of different furnishings.

La Diligence et la Résidence without rest

53 r. République – ✆ 02 31 14 47 47 – hotel.diligence@honfleur.com – Fax 02 31 98 83 87 AZ**m**

31 rm – €70/235 €85/235, €15

◆ The Diligence offers simple rooms spread over several Norman-style buildings set around a courtyard. The Résidence, formerly the home of a nobleman, provides more refined rooms with high ceilings and period furnishings.

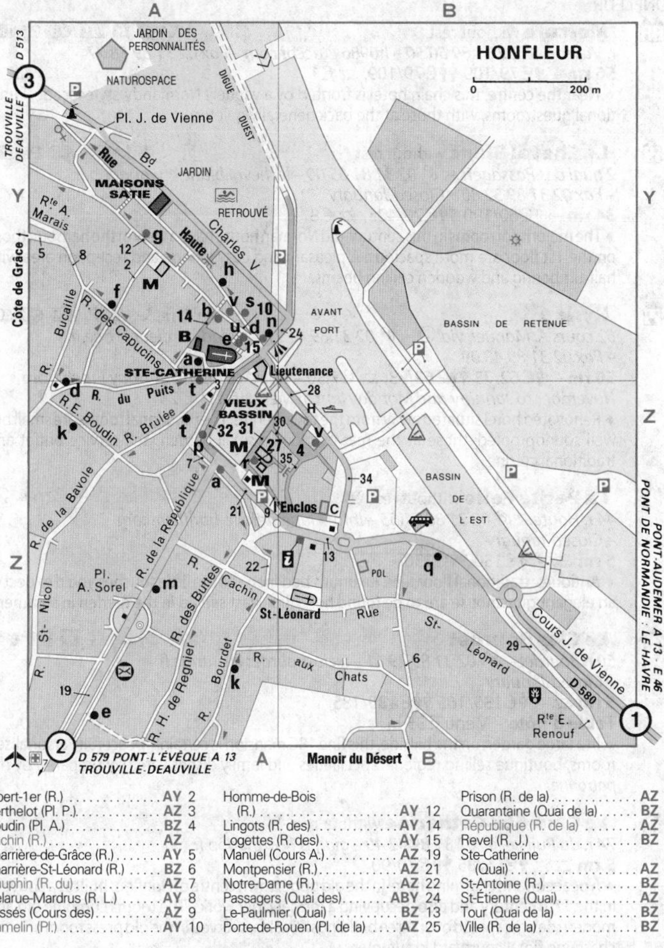

HONFLEUR

Street	Grid	No.
Albert-1er (R.)	AY	2
Berthelot (Pl. P.)	AZ	3
Boudin (Pl. A.)	BZ	4
Cachin (R.)	AZ	
Charrière-de-Grâce (R.)	AY	5
Charrière-St-Léonard (R.)	BZ	6
Dauphin (R. du)	AZ	7
Delarue-Mardrus (R. L.)	AY	8
Fossés (Cours des)	AZ	9
Hamelin (Pl.)	AY	10
Homme-de-Bois (R.)	AY	12
Lingots (R. des)	AY	14
Logettes (R. des)	AY	15
Manuel (Cours A.)	AZ	19
Montpensier (R.)	AZ	21
Notre-Dame (R.)	AZ	22
Passagers (Quai des)	ABY	24
Le-Paulmier (Quai)	BZ	13
Porte-de-Rouen (Pl. de la)	AZ	25
Prison (R. de la)	AZ	27
Quarantaine (Quai de la)	BZ	28
République (R. de la)	AZ	
Revel (R. J.)	BZ	29
Ste-Catherine (Quai)	AZ	32
St-Antoine (R.)	BZ	30
St-Étienne (Quai)	AZ	31
Tour (Quai de la)	BZ	34
Ville (R. de la)	BZ	35

Des Loges without rest

18 r. Brûlée – 02 31 89 38 26 – info@hoteldesloges.com – Fax 02 31 89 42 79 – Closed 5-25 January AZ **t**

14 rm – € 105/130 € 105/130, € 11

◆ This hotel and boutique is made up of three old buildings nicely renovated to provide a contemporary and refined atmosphere in the communal areas and rooms, where a relaxed feeling prevails. Some of the décor can be bought. Non-smoking throughout the hotel.

Castel Albertine without rest

19 cours A. Manuel – 02 31 98 85 56 – info@honfleurhotels.com – Fax 02 31 98 83 18 – Closed January AZ **e**

27 rm – € 75/150 € 75/150, € 10

◆ This lovely 19th century family mansion belonged to the diplomat historian, Albert Sorel, a native of Honfleur. Personalised rooms, a charming lounge and veranda planted with tropical plants and a park with grand old trees.

Mercure without rest
r. Vases – ✆ 02 31 89 50 50 – h0986@accor.com – Fax 02 31 89 58 77
56 rm – €79/109 €79/109, €11 BZ **q**
◆ Near the centre, this chain hotel is fronted by a vaguely Normandy-style façade. Functional guestrooms, with those at the back generally quieter.

Le Cheval Blanc without rest
2 quai des Passagers – ✆ 02 31 81 65 00 – lecheval.blanc@wanadoo.fr – Fax 02 31 89 52 80 – Closed January AY **n**
34 rm – €60/190 €70/425, €8
◆ The majority of rooms in this century-old Norman house have a view of the harbour; those on the 1st floor are more spacious. A pleasant and cosy lounge and reception area with half-timbering and wooden ceiling beams.

Kyriad
62 cours A. Manuel, via ② – ✆ 02 31 89 41 77 – kyriad.honfleur@free.fr – Fax 02 31 89 48 09
50 rm – €62/73 €62/73, €7,50 – **Rest** – *(closed Saturday lunch from November to January and Monday lunch)* Menu (€17), €23
◆ Renovated hotel situated away from the town centre. The functional rooms are small but well soundproofed; those at the rear overlook a small garden. Self-service buffet and traditional cuisine.

La Petite Folie without rest
44 r. Haute – ✆ 02 31 88 71 55 – info@lapetitefolie-honfleur.com – Closed January AY **h**
5 rm – €130 €130
◆ Antiques, traditional floor tiles, luxurious bedlinen - all the little touches you'd expect of an elegant guesthouse are to be found here. Breakfast served in the garden in summer.

Le Clos Bourdet
50 r. Bourdet – ✆ 02 31 89 49 11 – leclosbourdet@orange.fr – Closed January
5 rm – €135/165 €135/185
Table d'hôte – Menu €35 bi AZ **k**
◆ In a large garden on the hillside, this fine 18C mansion is certainly peaceful! Personalised rooms, boutique selling regional specialities and family dishes carefully prepared by the *patronne*.

La Cour Ste-Catherine without rest
74 r. du Puits – ✆ 02 31 89 42 40 – giaglis@wanadoo.fr AYZ **d**
5 rm – €65/85 €70/90
◆ A peaceful and charming hotel in the old upper town centre of Honfleur built as a convent in the 17th century and also occupying a former cider works. The rooms combine old and modern design, spread over three buildings. Breakfast served in the old press room or in the charming floral courtyard in summer.

L'Absinthe with rm
10 quai Quarantaine – ✆ 02 31 89 39 00 – reservation@absinthe.fr – Fax 02 31 89 53 60 – Closed 15 November-15 December BZ **v**
6 rm – €115 €145, €12 – 1 suite
Rest – Menu €33/65 – Carte €64/99
◆ Located in front of the fishing harbour, this restaurant serves modern cuisine in a resolutely rustic decor (15C and 17C) or on the front terrace. A nearby former presbytery enables diners to prolong their stay in welcoming rooms.

La Terrasse et l'Assiette (Gérard Bonnefoy)
8 pl. Ste-Catherine – ✆ 02 31 89 31 33 – Fax 02 31 89 90 17
Closed 5 January-5 February, Tuesday except July-August and Monday AY **e**
Rest – Menu €30/50 – Carte €66/93
Spec. Gaspacho de homard au piment d'Espelette (summer). Noix de ris de veau en aigre-doux. Petit gâteau chaud chocolat-pistache.
◆ Half-timbering and brickwork give this restaurant a distinctive atmosphere. Outdoor dining area overlooking the astonishing church built out of wood. Tasty traditional cuisine.

Entre Terre et Mer
12 pl. Hamelin – ✆ 02 31 89 70 60 – info@entreterreetmer-honfleur.com – Fax 02 31 89 40 55 – Closed 15 January-5 February and Wednesday from 15 November to 1st April AY **d**

Rest – Menu (€ 20), € 26/51 – Carte € 49/70

◆ Two pleasant, modern dining areas. One is rustic with wooden beams and rush flooring, the other has tiled floors and is decorated with photographs of Normandy. Modern cuisine including both meat and seafood dishes.

Le Bréard
7 r. du Puits – ✆ 02 31 89 53 40 – lebreard@wanadoo.fr – Fax 02 31 88 60 37 – Closed 1st-26 December, 2-9 February, Tuesday lunch, Thursday lunch and Wednesday from 1st September to 13 July AY **t**

Rest – Menu (€ 18), € 26/34 – Carte € 52/64

◆ Located in a cobbled lane near St Catherine's church, this establishment has a distinctive green façade. An inner terrace, heated in winter, separates two bright dining areas. Tasty modern cuisine.

La Fleur de Sel
17 r. Haute – ✆ 02 31 89 01 92 – info@lafleurdesel-honfleur.com – Fax 02 31 89 01 92 – Closed January, Tuesday and Wednesday AY **v**

Rest – Menu € 26/36 – Carte € 40/58

◆ This pleasant restaurant serves modern cuisine in two small dining areas with refined modern rustic décor, including tiled flooring, wooden beams and culinary photos on display.

Sa. Qua. Na (Alexandre Bourdas)
22 pl. Hamelin – ✆ 02 31 89 40 80 – saquana@alexandre-bourdas.com – Closed from mid January to end February, Wednesday, Thursday and weekday lunch AY **u**

Rest – *(number of covers limited, pre-book)* Menu € 40/80

Spec. Homard poché au citron vert, feuilles de céleri et coriandre. Carré de veau rôti, bouillon de navets, petits pois, noisettes. Galette soufflée au sarrasin et grains de maïs.

◆ Flavour, quality, nature and fish (sakana in Japanese) are all key ingredients here. Inventive cuisine in a modern, minimalist setting close to the old port.

Auberge du Vieux Clocher
9 r. de l'Homme-de-Bois – ✆ 02 31 89 12 06 – Fax 02 31 89 44 75 – Closed 24-30 November, 12-30 January, Tuesday and Wednesday AY **b**

Rest – Menu (€ 14), € 20/25 – Carte € 30/50

◆ In a street in the picturesque Ste-Catherine district, this restaurant has small dining rooms in pastel colours and a pretty collection of antique plates. Serves traditional meals.

Au Vieux Honfleur
13 quai St-Étienne – ✆ 02 31 89 15 31 – contact@auxvieuxhonfleur.com – Fax 02 31 89 92 04 – Closed January AZ **r**

Rest – Menu € 31/52 – Carte € 49/63

◆ On the ground floor and upstairs, the main attraction of this restaurant is the fascinating view over the Vieux Bassin. Serving seafood and home-made tripe specialities. Plate collection on display.

Au P'tit Mareyeur
4 r. Haute – ✆ 02 31 98 84 23 – auptitmareyeur@free.fr – Fax 02 31 89 99 32 – Closed 5 January-3 February, Monday and Tuesday AY **s**

Rest – *(number of covers limited, pre-book)* Menu € 25/49 – Carte € 38/51

◆ Half-timbered walls, beams, draped chairs and a discreet nautical theme lend this restaurant an intimate character. Fish and seafood dominate the menu.

L'Ecailleur
1 r. de la République – ✆ 02 31 89 93 34 – lecailleur@wanadoo.fr – Fax 02 31 89 53 73 – Closed 17 June-4 July, Wednesday and Thursday off season AZ **a**

Rest – Menu € 25/37 – Carte € 33/46

◆ Fresh, modern cuisine served in a warm décor inspired by the old steam liners, with wooden panelling, ropes and porthole windows. A large bay window offers a fine view of the port.

La Tortue
36 r. de l'Homme de Bois – ✆ 02 31 81 24 60 AY **g**
Rest – Menu (€ 12), € 18/33 – Carte € 21/46
◆ Tucked behind the half-timbered façade is this welcoming restaurant decorated in an elegant maritime style, with bright colours, driftwood and cane furniture. The classic menu pays due reverence to the sea.

in la Rivière-St-Sauveur **2 km by ① – pop. 1 578 – alt. 1 m – ✉ 14600**

Antarès without rest
– ✆ 02 31 89 10 10 – info@antares-honfleur.com – Fax 02 31 89 58 57
78 rm – 🛉€ 65/102 🛉🛉€ 72/145, ☕ € 12
◆ Modern hotel complex with practical facilities, providing small rooms. Some of them, as well as the breakfast room, overlook the Normandy bridge. Well-designed family duplexes. Heated indoor pool.

Les Bleuets without rest
– ✆ 02 31 81 63 90 – contact@motel-les-bleuets.com – Fax 02 31 89 92 12
– Closed 17-27 December, 8-30 January and Sunday dinner off season
18 rm ☕ – 🛉€ 74/94 🛉🛉€ 84/102
◆ A neat and tidy hotel with a holiday village feel. Sky blue and white walls, flower beds, and a relaxation area. Simple, well-kept rooms, most of which have a small terrace or balcony.

via ③ 3 km Trouville road – ✉ 14600 Vasouy

La Chaumière
rte du Littoral, Vasouy – ✆ 02 31 81 63 20 – informations@la-chaumiere.com
– Fax 02 31 89 59 23 – Closed 12 November-7 December and 7 January-1st February
9 rm – 🛉€ 150/450 🛉🛉€ 150/450, ☕ € 15 – ½ P € 150/300
Rest – *(closed Wednesday lunch, Thursday lunch and Tuesday) (number of covers limited, pre-book)* Menu € 40/60 – Carte € 55/70
◆ This pretty Norman farm (17C) stands opposite the Seine estuary in a park that reaches down to the sea. Cosy rooms with fine antique furniture. Beams worn smooth and an attractive fireplace add to the atmosphere of the restaurant.

in Pennedepie **5 km by ③ – pop. 310 – alt. 20 m – ✉ 14600**

Au Moulin St-Georges
rte de la Mer – ✆ 02 31 81 48 48 – Closed mid-February to mid-March, Tuesday evening and Wednesday
Rest – Menu € 16/24 – Carte € 26/45
◆ Access to this restaurant on the coastal road is through the bar-tabac, then via... the kitchen, with an old coal fire. Simple surroundings, copious meals.

via ③ 8 km Trouville road and secondary road – ✉ 14600 Honfleur

Le Romantica
chemin Petit Paris – ✆ 02 31 81 14 00 – hotelromantica@free.fr
– Fax 02 31 81 54 78
27 rm – 🛉€ 55 🛉🛉€ 65, ☕ € 9 – 9 suites – ½ P € 65
Rest – *(closed Thursday lunchtime and Wednesday except high season)*
Menu (€ 16), € 26/37 – Carte € 25/47
◆ Set above the village, this regional-style building provides quiet and comfortable rooms in rustic style. Also featuring a pleasant indoor pool. A beautiful glimpse of the English Channel and the countryside from the bay windows in the restaurant.

in Cricqueboeuf **9 km by ③ and Trouville road – pop. 182 – alt. 25 m – ✉ 14113**

Manoir de la Poterie
– ✆ 02 31 88 10 40 – info@honfleur-hotel.com
– Fax 02 31 88 10 90
23 rm – 🛉€ 116/230 🛉🛉€ 116/230, ☕ € 15 – 1 suite – **Rest** – *(closed lunch week)*
Menu € 32/65 – Carte € 49/74
◆ This modern manor (non-smoking) overlooks the English Channel. Beautiful Louis XVI or Directoire rooms with a view of the sea or the countryside. Spa centre. Restaurant with a cosy atmosphere serving modern cuisine in a recently redecorated room.

in Villerville **10 km by ③, Trouville road – pop. 676 – alt. 10 m – ✉ 14113**

Office de tourisme, rue Général Leclerc ✆ 02 31 87 21 49, Fax 02 31 98 30 65

Le Bellevue rm, **P** VISA MC AE

rte d'Honfleur – ✆ 02 31 87 20 22 – resa@bellevue-hotel.fr – Fax 02 31 87 20 56 – Closed 24 November-18 December and 12 January-12 February

28 rm – €75/90 €85/115, €12 – 2 suites – ½ P €75/115

Rest – *(closed Tuesday lunch, Wednesday lunch and Thursday lunch)* Menu €25/44 – Carte €35/52

◆ This house overlooking the sea was the summer residence of a Paris Opera director in the late 19th century. Rustic rooms; a modern setting and private terraces in the annexe. Choose one of the rooms with panoramic views from the balcony. The charming veranda-dining area offers a pretty view of the garden and coastline.

HORBOURG – **68 Haut-Rhin** – **315** I8 – **see Colmar**

L'HORME – **42 Loire** – **327** G7 – **see St-Chamond**

HOSSEGOR – 40 Landes – 335 C13 – alt. 4 m – Casino – ✉ 40150

Atlantic Coast 3 **A3**

Paris 752 – Bayonne 25 – Biarritz 32 – Bordeaux 170 – Dax 40 – Mont-de-Marsan 93

Office de tourisme, place des Halles ✆ 05 58 41 79 00, Fax 05 58 41 79 09

18 d'Hossegor 333 avenue du Golf, Southeast: 0.5 km, ✆ 05 58 43 56 99 ;

18 de Seignosse Seignosse Avenue du Belvédère, North: 5 km by D 152, ✆ 05 58 41 68 30 ;

9 de Pinsolle Soustons Port d'Albret Sud, North: 10 km by D 4, ✆ 05 58 48 03 92.

The lake ★ - Basque-Landes style villas★.

Les Hortensias du Lac without rest **P** VISA MC AE

av. du Tour du Lac – ✆ 05 58 43 99 00 – reception@hortensias-du-lac.com – Fax 05 58 43 42 81 – Open mid March-beg. November

20 rm – €125/215 €125/215, €20 – 4 suites – €265/425

◆ Three lovely 1930s houses surrounded by a pine forest on the lakeside make up this hotel providing tastefully decorated rooms with balcony or terrace. Lounge with great views.

Pavillon Bleu **P** VISA MC AE

av. Touring Club de France – ✆ 05 58 41 99 50 – pavillon.bleu@wanadoo.fr – Fax 05 58 41 99 59

21 rm – €70/145 €70/145, €10 – ½ P €75/108

Rest – *(closed 26 December-20 January and Monday 15 September-15 April)* Menu €23 bi (weekday lunch), €31/68 – Carte €44/82

◆ A brand new establishment where, if you book a room with a balcony overlooking the lake, you can watch the sailing dinghies and wind-surfers. The restaurant has a contemporary interior, an attractive waterside terrace and modern cuisine.

Mercédès without rest VISA MC AE

av. du Tour du Lac – ✆ 05 58 41 98 00 – hotel.mercedes@wanadoo.fr – Fax 05 58 41 98 10 – Open 2 April-30 October

40 rm – €70/90 €90/130, €10

◆ A seaside building near a marine lake is home to rooms both simple in style and pleasant, all with balcony. Breakfast served around the pool in summer.

Le Cottage **P** VISA MC AE

av. J.-Moulin, Route Seignosse, beside lake (D79) – ✆ 05 58 43 31 39 – restaurant-lecottage@wanadoo.fr – Fax 05 58 43 31 39 – Open from March to October

Rest – Menu €19/39 – Carte €28/48

◆ A fresh dining room brightened with Basque table linen, a charming terrace with the fragrant smell of the pinewoods and "surf and turf" dishes: a much appreciated cottage!

Le Reva VISA MC AE

– ✆ 05 58 43 10 65 – hotel.le-reva@wanadoo.fr – Fax 05 58 43 10 13

5 rm – €55/98 €55/98, €9

◆ A building located next to the restaurant is home to rooms with exotic furnishings and featuring a small terrace. Hairdressing salon.

HOUAT (ÎLE) – 56 Morbihan – 308 N10 – see Île d'Houat

LA HOUBE – 57 Moselle – 307 O7 – ✉ 57850 Dabo 27 **D2**

Paris 453 – Lunéville 86 – Phalsbourg 18 – Sarrebourg 27 – Saverne 17 – Strasbourg 45

Des Vosges with rm

41 r. de la Forêt Brulée ✉ 57850 La Hoube Dabo – ☎ 03 87 08 80 44 – info@hotel-restaurant-vosges.com – Fax 03 87 08 85 96 – Closed 24 September-8 October, 5 February-5 March, Tuesday dinner and Wednesday

9 rm – €32 €47, €7 – ½ P €43 – **Rest** – Menu €19/25 – Carte €21/41

◆ This restaurant is located at the end of the village, serving tasty regional cuisine. Dining area overlooking the Vosges forest, the Dabo rock and the chapel. Simple, well-kept rooms and a quiet relaxing garden.

LES HOUCHES – 74 Haute-Savoie – 328 N5 – pop. 2 706 – alt. 1 004 m – Winter sports : 1 010/1 900 m 2 16 – ✉ 74310 French Alps 46 **F1**

Paris 602 – Annecy 89 – Bonneville 47 – Chamonix-Mont-Blanc 9 – Megève 26

Office de tourisme, place de la Mairie ☎ 04 50 55 50 62, Fax 04 50 55 53 16

Le Prarion★★.

Du Bois

rest,

La Griaz – ☎ 04 50 54 50 35 – reception@hotel-du-bois.com – Fax 04 50 55 50 87 – Closed 3-30 November

51 rm – €50/114 €50/124, €9 – ½ P €58/95 – **Rest** – *(closed 14 April-11 May and 6 October-8 December) (dinner only)* Menu (€19), €24 – Carte €18/35

◆ A large timber chalet providing regional-styled rooms, most with balcony; those facing Mont Blanc are quieter. Handsome indoor pool and sauna. Attractive Savoy-style dining room decorated with farming implements. Updated cuisine.

Auberge Beau Site

(near the church) – ☎ 04 50 55 51 16 – hotelbeausite@netgdi.com – Fax 04 50 54 53 11 – Open 21 May-1st October and 22 December-19 April

18 rm – €73/90 €83/110, €9 – **Rest *Le Pèle*** – *(closed Wednesday except July-August) (dinner only except July-August and Sunday in winter)* Menu €22/45

◆ Pretty family house at the foot of the bell tower in the little resort made famous by Lord Kandahar. Practical rooms of a good size with bright red and green fabrics. Warm restaurant; wooden blocks standing near the fireplace with its copper utensils.

Auberge Le Montagny without rest

Le Pont – ☎ 04 50 54 57 37 – hotel.montagny@wanadoo.fr – Fax 04 50 54 52 97 – Open 15 June-28 September and 20 December-14 April

8 rm – €70 €78, €8,50

◆ Wood predominates throughout in this charming little chalet which incorporates the door and some beams of an 1876 farmhouse; mountain style rooms.

Chris-Tal

242 av. des Alpages – ☎ 04 50 54 50 55 – info@chris-tal.com – Fax 04 50 54 45 77 – Open 25 May-1st October and 21 December-11 April

23 rm – €95/120 €95/130, €10 – ½ P €80/92 – **Rest** – Menu €19/36 – Carte €26/54

◆ In the centre of the little resort, spacious functional rooms (non-smoking); most overlook the famous Kandahar ski slope. A mixture of traditional and local cuisine is on offer in the warm and welcoming dining room.

in Prarion by télécabine – ✉ 74310 Les Houches

★★ 30 mn.

Le Prarion

summits, glaciers and valleys,

rm,

alt.1 860 – ☎ 04 50 54 40 07 – info@prarion.com – Fax 04 50 54 40 03 – Open 21 June-6 September and 20 December to end April

12 rm – €50 €100, €9 – ½ P €75/110 – **Rest** – self Carte €14/28

◆ This hotel enjoys superb vistas of the snow-capped peaks of the Mont-Blanc and Aravis ranges and the Chamonix and Sallanches valleys. Small, simply furnished bedrooms. Traditional meals at lunch (buffet style in winter), set menu in the evening.

HOUDAN – 78 Yvelines – 311 F3 – pop. 3 112 – alt. 104 m – ✉ 78550

Northern France and the Paris Region 18 **A2**

Paris 60 – Chartres 55 – Dreux 20 – Évreux 52 – Mantes-la-Jolie 28 – Versailles 42

Office de tourisme, 4, place de la Tour ✆ 01 30 59 53 86, Fax 01 30 59 66 84

de la Vaucouleurs Civry-la-Forêt Rue de l'Eglise, North: 11 km by D 983, ✆ 01 34 87 62 29 ;

des Yvelines La Queue-les-Yvelines Château de la Couharde, East: 12 km by N 12, ✆ 01 34 86 48 89.

Crépuscule without rest — P VISA

rte des Longs Champs – ✆ 01 30 46 96 96 – crepuscule.hotel@wanadoo.fr – Fax 01 30 46 96 97

21 rm – €60/90 €60/90, €7 – ½ P €75/95

♦ This modern hotel just outside the town centre has spacious rooms in pink or blue tones. Serving simple meals during the week.

XXX **La Poularde** — P VISA AE

24 av. République, (rte Maulette D 912) – ✆ 01 30 59 60 50 – contact@alapoularde.com – Fax 01 30 59 79 71 – Closed 10-18 March, 11-26 August, 24 November-2 December, 19-27 January, Sunday dinner, Monday and Tuesday

Rest – Menu (€ 24), € 36 (weekdays)/60 – Carte € 44/58

♦ In the garden of this lovely house, the famous Houdan chickens cluck - soon to be placed in your plate! Elegant comfortable room, traditional menu.

XX **Donjon** — AC VISA AE

14 r. Epernon, (near the church) – ✆ 01 30 59 79 14 – eric.deserville@wanadoo.fr – Closed 10-25 August, 1 week in March, Sunday dinner, Thursday dinner and Monday

Rest – Menu € 29/43

♦ All that remains of the medieval castle is its keep, close to this restaurant named after it. Classic cuisine served in a pretty and colourful contemporary setting.

HOUDELAINCOURT – 55 Meuse – 307 D7 – pop. 346 – alt. 285 m – ✉ 55130

Paris 270 – Metz 119 – Bar-le-Duc 41 – Saint-Dizier 57 – Toul 51 26 **A2**

XXX **Auberge du Père Louis** with rm — P VISA

– ✆ 03 29 89 64 14 – aubergeperelouis@free.fr – Fax 03 29 89 78 84 – Closed 1st-21 September, Sunday dinner and Monday

7 rm – €50 €50, € 10 – ½ P € 75 – **Rest** – Menu € 19 (weekdays)/80 – Carte € 53/75

♦ For three generations this establishment has been recognised as Lorraine's truffle centre. Shop and museum. Comfortable personalised rooms along a variety of themes.

HOUDEMONT – 54 Meurthe-et-Moselle – 307 H7 – see Nancy

HOULGATE – 14 Calvados – 303 L4 – pop. 1 832 – alt. 11 m – Casino – ✉ 14510

Normandy 32 **B2**

Paris 214 – Caen 29 – Deauville 14 – Lisieux 33 – Pont-l'Évêque 25

Office de tourisme, 10, boulevard des Belges ✆ 02 31 24 34 79, Fax 02 31 24 42 27

d'Houlgate Gonneville-sur-Mer, East: 3 km by D 513, ✆ 02 31 24 80 49.

Vaches Noires cliff★ Northeast.

1900 — AC rest, VISA AE

17 r. des Bains – ✆ 02 31 28 77 77 – hotellenormand@aol.com – Fax 02 31 28 08 07 – Closed 15 November-7 December and 7-31 January

12 rm – €55/85 €55/85, €9 – ½ P €54/70 – **Rest** – Menu € 20/46 – Carte € 21/67

♦ The hotel is on the main street of this charming resort on the Floral Coast. The rooms have been renovated in a Belle Époque style. A charming brasserie in 1900s style with parquet, mirrors, columns, an old bar counter and leather seating. Look out for the cherubs painted on the ceiling.

Hostellerie Normande

11 r. Emile Deschanel – ✆ 02 31 24 85 50 – info@hotel-houlgate.com – Fax 02 31 28 53 61

11 rm – †€ 42/77 ††€ 42/77, ☕ € 8 – ½ P € 67/102 – **Rest** – *(closed Monday and Tuesday October-March)* Menu € 17/30 – Carte € 23/43

◆ This 19C house covered in vines has small but neat and tidy rooms. With a pleasant courtyard terrace in summer. This restaurant has a very country-style atmosphere with rustic chairs, chequered tablecloths, and an old manger.

L'Eden

7 r. Henri Fouchard – ✆ 02 31 24 84 37 – nicolas.tougard@wanadoo.fr – Fax 02 31 28 32 34 – Closed 29 September-7 October, 2 January-4 February, Monday and Tuesday except July-August

Rest – Menu € 19 (weekdays)/39 – Carte € 35/49

◆ Tucked away in a small road in the centre, this charming house in regional style is home to a restaurant serving tasty traditional cuisine. Simple, countrified décor, friendly hospitality and service.

HUEZ – 38 Isère – 333 J7 – see Alpe d'Huez

HUNINGUE – 68 Haut-Rhin – 315 J11 – see St-Louis

HURIGNY – 71 Saône-et-Loire – 320 I12 – see Mâcon

HUSSEREN-LES-CHÂTEAUX – 68 Haut-Rhin – 315 H8 – pop. 397 – alt. 380 m – ✉ 68420 Alsace-Lorraine 2 C2

Paris 455 – Belfort 69 – Colmar 10 – Gérardmer 55 – Guebwiller 22 – Mulhouse 40

Husseren-les-Châteaux

r. Schlossberg – ✆ 03 89 49 22 93 – mail@hotel-husseren-les-chateaux.com – Fax 03 89 49 24 84

36 rm – †€ 88/103 ††€ 115/138, ☕ € 12,50 – 2 suites – ½ P € 106

Rest – Menu (€ 11,50), € 21/60 – Carte € 23/48

◆ Standing in the foothills of the Vosges mountains, this modern building has large functional bedrooms, some of which are split-level. Indoor swimming pool and a tennis court. Enjoy fine views over the Rhine valley from this bright restaurant serving traditional cuisine.

HYÈRES – 83 Var – 340 L7 – pop. 51 417 – alt. 40 m – Casino : des Palmiers Z – ✉ 83400 French Riviera 41 C3

Paris 851 – Aix-en-Provence 102 – Cannes 123 – Draguignan 78 – Toulon 19

Toulon-Hyères: ✆ 0 825 01 83 87, Southeast: 4 km V.

Syndicat d'initiative, 3, avenue Ambroise Thomas ✆ 04 94 01 84 50, Fax 04 94 01 84 51

≤★ from place St-Paul Y **49** - ≤★ from St-Bernard park Y - ≤★ from the N.-D. de Consolation chapel esplananade V **B** - ✻★ from the Château des aires ruins - Presqu'île de Giens (peninsula) ★★.

Plan on next page

Mercure

19 av. A. Thomas – ✆ 04 94 65 03 04 – h1055@accor.com – Fax 04 94 35 58 20

84 rm – †€ 94/179 ††€ 106/191, ☕ € 13 – ½ P € 71/114 – **Rest** – grill Carte € 24/42 V **x**

◆ Modern hotel which forms part of a business centre situated alongside the Olbia highway. Comfortable, contemporary rooms renovated in the Mercure style. Restaurant decorated with a seaside theme, opening onto the terrace and swimming pool; regionally-inspired recipes.

L'Europe without rest

45 av. E. Cavell – ✆ 04 94 00 67 77 – contact@hotel-europe-hyeres.com – Fax 04 94 00 68 48 V **r**

25 rm – †€ 45/87 ††€ 52/96, ☕ € 7,50

◆ If you are looking for a hotel near the station, this fully-renovated, 19C building has light, functional, well-soundproofed rooms.

HYÈRES-GIENS

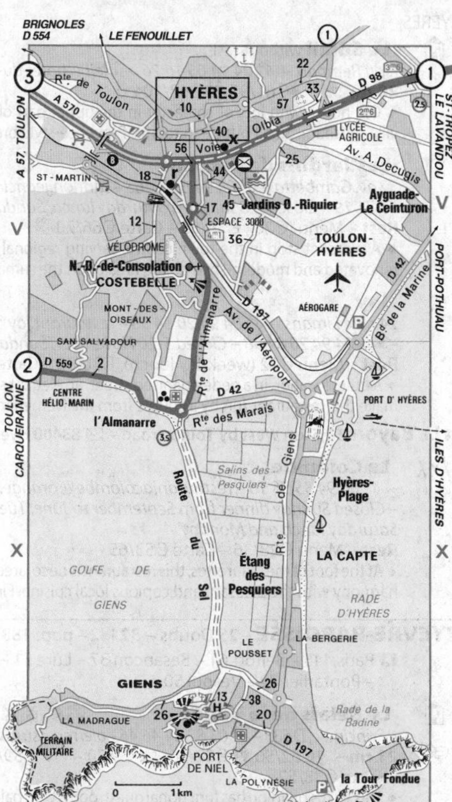

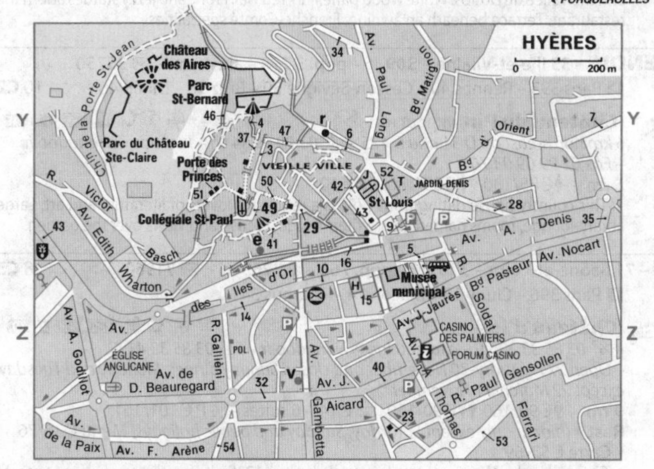

Le Soleil without rest
r. du Rempart – ✆ 04 94 65 16 26 – soleil@hotel-du-soleil.fr – Fax 04 94 35 46 00
20 rm – €61/95 €68/104 Y **r**
◆ Old house with lots of character in the upper part of the old town, near the Noailles villa-museum. Small but clean rooms; Provence-style breakfast room.

Les Jardins de Bacchus
32 av. Gambetta – ✆ 04 94 65 77 63 – santionijeanclaude@wanadoo.fr – Fax 04 94 65 71 19 – Closed 2-8 January, Saturday lunch, Sunday dinner and Monday
Rest – Menu (€ 26), € 34/55 – Carte € 66/70 Z **v**
◆ A pleasant stop in the town centre, serving regional wines and local style meals in a renovated and modern-style dining area or on the summer terrace.

Joy
24 r. de Limans – ✆ 04 94 20 84 98 – restaurant.joy@orange.fr – Fax 04 94 20 84 98 – Closed 5-20 November, Sunday and Monday off season
Rest – Menu € 22 (weekday lunch), € 30/52 – Carte € 40/51 Y **a**
◆ A quiet location in a pedestrianised street, an elegant setting and contemporary cuisine make this restaurant run by a couple from the Netherlands a popular choice.

in La Bayorre **2,5 km West by Toulon road – ✉ 83400 Hyères**

La Colombe
– ✆ 04 94 35 35 16 – restauranlacolombe@orange.fr – Fax 04 94 35 37 68 – Closed Sunday dinner from September to June, Tuesday lunch in July-August, Saturday lunch and Monday
Rest – Menu € 28/36 – Carte € 53/65
◆ At the foot of the Maurettes, this restaurant is decorated in colours of the South in perfect harmony with the pleasant and copious local cuisine. Fine summer terrace at the back.

HYÈVRE-PAROISSE – 25 Doubs – 321 I2 – pop. 188 – alt. 288 m – ✉ 25110

Paris 445 – Belfort 61 – Besançon 37 – Lure 51 – Montbéliard 44 – Pontarlier 72 – Vesoul 50 17 **C2**

Le Relais de la Vallée rest,
r. Principale, D 683 – ✆ 03 81 84 46 46 – pierrecossu@wanadoo.fr – Fax 03 81 84 37 52
21 rm – €52/56 €52/56, € 9,50 – ½ P € 59/73 – **Rest** – Menu € 14,50/37 – Carte € 38/52
◆ This 1970s building has functional guestrooms with balconies overlooking the main road and the Vallée du Doubs. White wood panelling, red wall fabric and jazzy statues adorn the restaurant. Terrace beneath an awning. Franche-Comté specialities.

IFFENDIC – 35 Ille-et-Vilaine – 309 J6 – pop. 3 778 – alt. 48 m – ✉ 35750

Paris 393 – Rennes 40 – Cesson-Sévigné 50 – Bruz 36 – Dinan 46 10 **C2**

Château du Pin without rest
6 km north-east on D 31 and D 125 – ✆ 02 99 09 34 05 – luc.ruan@wanadoo.fr – Fax 02 99 09 03 76
5 rm – €85/130 €85/130, € 10
◆ This country house dating from 1795 is a refuge for lovers of literature and art. Large library-lounge, rooms named after writers (Hugo, Proust) and views over the garden.

IGÉ – 71 Saône-et-Loire – 320 I11 – pop. 768 – alt. 265 m – ✉ 71960 8 **C3**

Paris 396 – Cluny 13 – Mâcon 14 – Tournus 34

Château d'Igé
– ✆ 03 85 33 33 99 – chateau.ige@wanadoo.fr – Fax 03 85 33 41 41 – Open 27 February-30 November and closed Sunday dinner, Monday and Tuesday except 22 March-11 November
9 rm – €90/160 €90/160, € 14 – 6 suites – ½ P € 101/161
Rest – *(dinner only except Saturday, Sunday and public holidays)* Menu € 36/76 – Carte € 52/69
◆ Situated in the Mâcon region, this castle built in 1235 offers a choice of elegant rooms with individual touches (tapestries, four-poster beds, vaulted ceilings etc). Apartments available in the towers. Modern cuisine served in a medieval-style dining area. Rose garden and terrace next to a stream.

ILAY – 39 Jura – 321 F7 – ✉ 39150 Chaux-du-Dombief ▮ Burgundy-Jura

▶ Paris 439 – Champagnole 19 – Lons-le-Saunier 36 – Morez 22 – St-Claude 39

◉ Cascades du Hérisson★★★. 16 **B3**

Auberge du Hérisson

carrefour D 75-D 39 – ✆ 03 84 25 58 18 – auberge@herisson.com – Fax 03 84 25 51 11 – Open February-October

16 rm – †€ 35 ††€ 55, ☕ € 7,50 – ½ P € 42/50 – **Rest** – Menu € 17 (weekdays)/40 – Carte € 22/56

◆ This small family inn is perched above the picturesque waterfalls of the Hérisson, close to Lac d'Ilay. Renovated bedrooms in the main wing; more modest accommodation in the older section. Franche-Comté cuisine, frogs' legs in season and local wines.

ÎLE-AUX-MOINES – 56 Morbihan – 308 N9 – pop. 610 – alt. 16 m – ✉ 56780 ▮ Brittany 9 **A3**

▶ Paris 474 – Auray 15 – Quiberon 46 – Vannes 15

Les Embruns

r. Commerce – ✆ 02 97 26 30 86 – lesembruns.iam@wanadoo.fr – Fax 02 97 26 31 94 – Closed 1st-15 October, January, February and Wednesday except July-August

Rest – Menu € 19/26 – Carte € 24/36

◆ This friendly, unpretentious bar-restaurant, serves simple cuisine influenced by market availability. Splendid shellfish platter.

L'ÎLE BOUCHARD – 37 Indre-et-Loire – 317 L6 – pop. 1 764 – alt. 41 m – ✉ 37220 ▮ Châteaux of the Loire 11 **A3**

▶ Paris 284 – Châteauroux 118 – Chinon 16 – Châtellerault 49 – Saumur 42 – Tours 45

ℹ Office de tourisme, 16, place Bouchard ✆ 02 47 58 67 75, Fax 02 47 58 67 75

◉ Capitals/I★ and throne chair ★ in St-Léonard priory.

◉ Champigny-sur-Veude: stained-glass windows★★ of the Ste-Chapelle★ Southwest: 10.5 km.

Auberge de l'Ile

3 pl. Bouchard – ✆ 02 47 58 51 07 – aubergedelile@wanadoo.fr – Fax 02 47 58 51 07 – Closed 1st-15 December, 19 February-12 March, Tuesday and Wednesday except holidays

Rest – Menu € 19 (weekdays)/31

◆ On an island that once belonged to Richelieu, this inn is much appreciated by lovers of fine produce. Up-to-date cuisine served in a modern decor (art and table settings).

in Sazilly 7 km west by D 760 – 317 L6 – ✉ 37220

Auberge du Val de Vienne

30 rte de Chinon – ✆ 02 47 95 26 49 – valdevienne@wanadoo.fr – Fax 02 47 95 25 97 – Closed 23-30 June, January, Tuesday dinner from 1st October to 14 April, Sunday dinner and Monday

Rest – Menu € 14,50 (weekday lunch), € 33/43

◆ Treat yourself to a gourmet stop-over in this 1870 coaching inn surrounded by the Chinon vineyards. Warm decor in perfect harmony with the contemporary cuisine.

ÎLE-D'AIX ★ – 17 Charente-Maritime – 324 C3 – pop. 186 – alt. 10 m – ✉ 17123 ▮ Atlantic Coast 38 **A2**

Access by sea transport

- from **Pointe de la Fumée** (2.5 km north-west of Fouras) - Crossing 25 mn - Information and prices from Société Fouras-Aix ✆ 0 820 160 017 (0.12 €/mn), Fax 05 46 41 16 96.
- from **La Rochelle** - Seasonal service (April-Oct.)- Crossing 1h 15 mn - Information: Croisières Inter Iles, ✆ 0 825 135 500 (0.15 €/mn) (La Rochelle)
- from **Boyardville** (Ile d'Oléron) - Seasonal service - Crossing 30 mn - Information Inter Iles ✆ 0 825 135 500 (0.15 €/mn),(Boyardville)
- from **Sablanceaux** (Ile de Ré) - Seasonal service - Inter Iles agencies in Sablonceaux - Information and prices ✆ 0 825 135 500
- from **Fouras** (Sté Fouras-Aix) - Permanent service - Crossing 30 mn - Information and prices ✆ 0 820 160 017 (0.12 €/mn), Fax 05 46 41 16 96.

ÎLE-D'ARZ – 56 Morbihan – 308 O9 – pop. 231 – alt. 25 m – ✉ 56840
Brittany 9 **A3**

Access by sea transport.

from **Barrarach and Conleau** - Crossing 20 mn - Information: Compagnie du Golfe ✆ 02 97 01 22 80, Fax 02 97 47 01 60, www.lactm.com

from **Vannes** from April to September - Crossing 30 mn - Information: Navix S.A. Gare Maritime (Vannes) ✆ 0825 162 100.

ÎLE-DE-BATZ – 29 Finistère – 308 G2 – pop. 575 – alt. 30 m – ✉ 29253
Brittany 9 **B1**

Access by sea transport.

from **Roscoff** - Crossing 15 mn - Information and prices: CFTM BP 10 - 29253 Île de Batz ✆ 02 98 61 78 87 - Armein ✆ 02 98 61 77 75 - Armor Excursion ✆ 02 98 61 79 66.

Syndicat d'initiative, lieu-dit le Débarcadère ✆ 02 98 61 75 70
Syndicat d'initiative, Mairie ✆ 02 98 61 75 70, Fax 02 98 61 75 85

Ti Va Zadou without rest

au bourg – ✆ 02 98 61 76 91 – Fax 02 98 61 76 91 – Open 7 February-10 November

4 rm – €40 €60

◆ Smart, nautical rooms, including a family room, await you in this typical regional-style house whose blue shutters are immediately noticeable on reaching the island. Bike hire.

ÎLE-DE-BRÉHAT ★ – 22 Côtes-d'Armor – 309 D1 – pop. 421 – alt. 7 m –
✉ 22870 Brittany 10 **C1**

Access by sea transport, for **Port-Clos.**

from **Pointe de l'Arcouest** - Crossing 10 mn - Information and prices: Vedettes de Bréhat ✆ 02 96 55 79 50, Fax 02 96 55 79 55.

from **St-Quay-Portrieux** - Seasonal service - Crossing 1 h 15 mn - Information and prices: Vedettes de Bréhat (see above).

from **Binic** - Seasonal service - Crossing 1 h 30 mn - Information and prices: Vedettes de Bréhat (see above).

from **Erquy** - Seasonal service - Crossing 1 h 15 mn - Information and prices: Vedettes de Bréhat (see above).

Syndicat d'initiative, le Bourg ✆ 02 96 20 04 15, Fax 02 96 20 06 94

Tour of the island★★ - Phare du Paon (lighthouse) ★ - Maudez Cross ≤★ - St-Michel chapel ✳★★ - Bois de la citadelle ≤★.

La Vieille Auberge VISA MC

au bourg – ✆ 02 96 20 00 24 – vieille-auberge.brehat@wanadoo.fr – Fax 02 96 20 05 12 – Open 11 April-2 November

14 rm – €75/107 €75/107, €9,50 – ½ P €68 – **Rest** – Carte €27/42

◆ Access to this old privateer's house in the town is on foot; the island's exceptional ecological heritage is worth leaving your car behind for! Functional bedrooms. Fish and seafood served in a dining room decorated with fishing nets or in the flower-decked courtyard.

ÎLE DE GROIX ★ – 56 Morbihan – 308 K9 – ✉ 56590 Brittany 9 **B2**

Access by sea transport for **Port-Tudy** (in summer **booking recommended** for vehicles).

from **Lorient** - Crossing 45 mn - Information about prices: S.M.N., r. G. Gahinet ✆ 0 820 056 000, Fax 02 97 64 77 69, www.smn-navigation.fr.

Site★ of Port-Lay - Trou de l'Enfer (Hell's Hole) ★.

Hôtel de la Marine VISA MC

7 r. Gén. de Gaulle, in the town – ✆ 02 97 86 80 05 – hotel.dela.marine@wanadoo.fr – Fax 02 97 86 56 37 – Closed 23 November-8 December, 4 January-5 February, Sunday dinner and Monday October-March except school holidays

22 rm – €38/45 €44/94, €9,50 – ½ P €48/76 – **Rest** – Menu €17/25 – Carte €27/47

◆ A warm welcome in this house offering various room categories. The bar with a nautical atmosphere is popular with the islanders. Attractive rustic dining room (lovely old dresser) and marine menu, including the famous sardines à la groisillonne.

La Jetée without rest

1 quai Port-Tudy – ✆ 02 97 86 80 82 – laurence.tonnerre@wanadoo.fr – Fax 02 97 86 56 11 – Closed 5 January-15 March

8 rm – †€ 53 ††€ 64/79, ☕ € 7,50

◆ This modest white house makes the most of its splendid location and eight of its pretty rooms overlook the wharf or the Gripp coast, as do the breakfast terraces.

ÎLE DE JERSEY ★★ – JSY Jersey – 309 J1 – pop. 85 150 Normandy

Access by sea transport for **St-Helier (compulsory booking).**

from **St-Malo** (compulsory booking). by **Hydroglisseur** (Condor Ferries) - Crossing 1 h 15 mn - Information and prices : gare maritime de la bourse (St-Malo) Terminal Ferry du Naye ✆ 0 825 135 135 (0.15 €/mn).
from **Carteret :** Catamaran – seasonal service (crossing 50 mn -Gorey) by Manche Iles Express ✆ 0 825 133 050 (0.15 €/mn).

from **Granville** - Fast catamaran - crossing 60 mn (St-Helier) by Manche Iles Express: ✆ 0 825 133 050 (0.15 €/mn) - from **Carteret** - Catamaran - seasonal service - crossing 50 mn (Gorey) by Manche Iles Express: ✆ 0 825 133 050 (0.15 €/mn).

Hotels see Michelin Guide : **Great Britain and Ireland**

ÎLE DE NOIRMOUTIER – 85 Vendée – 316 C6 – alt. 8 m

Atlantic Coast — 34 **A2**

Access - by road bridge from Fromentine: free passage.
- via Gois**: 4.5 km.
- during the first or last moon quarter in fine weather (high winds) an hour-and-a-half before low tide, to about an hour-and-a-half after low tide.
- during full or new moon in normal weather: two hours before low tide, to two hours after low tide.
- in all seasons during bad weather (low winds) do not stray from low tide time. See on-site display boards, before access to Gois.

L'ÉPINE – 85 Vendée – pop. 1 685 – alt. 2 m – ✉ 85740 — 34 **A2**

Paris 463 – Cholet 134 – Nantes 79 – Noirmoutier-en-l'Ile 4 – La Roche-sur-Yon 85

Punta Lara — The ocean, rm,

2 km south by D 95 and secondary road ✉ 85680 – ✆ 02 51 39 11 58 – puntalara@leshotelsparticuliers.com – Fax 02 51 39 69 12 – Open May-September

62 rm – †€ 112/195 ††€ 112/260, ☕ € 15 – ½ P € 101/143

Rest – Menu € 32/52 – Carte € 41/57

◆ Vendée-style bungalows, in a pine forest between the ocean and salt marshes. Well looked after bedrooms, all of which have a balcony or terrace facing the Atlantic. Vast dining room with timber ceiling, opening onto the circular swimming pool.

L'HERBAUDIÈRE – 85 Vendée – ✉ 85330 Noirmoutier-en-l'Île — 34 **A2**

Paris 469 – Cholet 140 – Nantes 85 – La Roche-sur-Yon 91

La Marine (Alexandre Couillon)

(at the port) – ✆ 02 51 39 23 09 – Fax 02 51 39 23 09 – Closed March, 1st-22 October, 6-21 January, Sunday dinner, Tuesday dinner and Wednesday

Rest – Menu € 40/60 – Carte € 60/70

Spec. "Crackers" de sardines marinées (May to September). Œuf de pomme de terre iodé aux huîtres creuses (February to September). Pigeonneau à la choucroute de navets longs. **Wines** Vin de pays de Vendée, Fiefs Vendéens.

◆ A regional house on the fishing port. Characteristic maritime decor and terrace overlooking the garden. Inventive menu made from market fresh produce, fish and seafood.

NOIRMOUTIER-EN-L'ÎLE – 85 Vendée – pop. 5 001 – alt. 8 m – ✉ 85330 — 34 **A2**

Paris 464 – Cholet 135 – Nantes 80 – La Roche-sur-Yon 86

Office de tourisme, rue du Général Passaga ✆ 02 51 39 12 42

Collection of English earthenware★ in the château.

Fleur de Sel rest,

r. des Saulniers – ☎ 02 51 39 09 07 – contact@fleurdesel.fr – Fax 02 51 39 09 76 – Open 14 March-2 November

35 rm – †€ 79/148 ††€ 89/175, ☐ € 12,50 – ½ P € 82/130

Rest – *(closed Monday lunch and Tuesday lunch except July-August and public holidays)* Menu (€ 21), € 28 (weekdays)/49 – Carte € 35/62

◆ A peaceful green setting, golf practice range, terrace, pretty sitting rooms and attractive bedrooms (cosily decorated or in nautical style): above all, calm, comfortable and relaxing. A sea-inspired decorative theme in the restaurant and a menu suited to current tastes.

Général d'Elbée without rest

pl. Château – ☎ 02 51 39 10 29 – elbee@leshotelsparticuliers.com – Fax 02 51 39 08 23 – Open May-September

27 rm – †€ 97/122 ††€ 172/237, ☐ € 15

◆ A historical 18C property full of bygone charm (period furniture and beams). Some of the rooms overlook the château that is lit up at night.

Les Douves without rest

11 r. Douves, (opposite the château) – ☎ 02 51 39 02 72 – hotel-les-douves@wanadoo.fr – Fax 02 51 39 73 09 – Closed 6 January-6 February

22 rm – †€ 46/73 ††€ 56/93, ☐ € 8

◆ Light and practical, if small and simply furnished bedrooms, within easy reach of the Place d'Armes, port and château. Swimming pool at the rear of the house.

La Maison de Marine without rest

3 r. Parmentier – ☎ 02 28 10 27 21 – lamaisondemarine@hotmail.fr

5 rm ☐ – †€ 98/130 ††€ 110/130

◆ Lovely personalised rooms, flower-decked terraces overlooking the patio-pool, sitting room with fireplace, spa, aromatic garden: a heavenly property devoted to guests' well-being.

Le Grand Four

1 r. Cure, (behind the château) – ☎ 02 51 39 61 97 – renee.vetele@wanadoo.fr – Fax 02 51 39 61 97 – Closed 1st December-31 January, Sunday dinner and Monday except July-August

Rest – Menu € 19 bi (weekdays), € 25/59 – Carte € 53/63

◆ A Virginia creeper-clad building. Two dining rooms, one of which is embellished by paintings and trinkets; the other has a less exuberant maritime theme. Seafood dishes.

L'Étier

rte de L'Épine, 1 km southwest – ☎ 02 51 39 10 28 – restaurant.etier@wanadoo.fr – Fax 02 51 39 23 00 – Closed December-January, Tuesday except July-August and Monday

Rest – Menu € 18/37 – Carte € 33/52

◆ This low-built old cottage is typical of the island's architecture. Rustic interior, plus a terrace-veranda overlooking the Arceau. Fish from the local catch.

Côté Jardin

1 bis r. Grand Four, (behind the castle) – ☎ 02 51 39 03 02 – Fax 02 51 54 64 58 – Closed 16 October-20 December, 5 January-6 February, Sunday dinner, Wednesday, dinner Thursday except July-August and Monday

Rest – Menu € 18/40 – Carte € 35/43

◆ This restaurant owes its popularity to its traditional cuisine with local produce taking pride of place. Patio-terrace next-door to an old chapel; exhibition of work by local artist.

at Bois de la Chaize 2 km East – ✉ 85330 Noirmoutier-en-l'Île

Wood★.

Les Prateaux rm, rm,

allée du Tambourin – ☎ 02 51 39 12 52 – contact@lesprateaux.com – Fax 02 51 39 46 28 – Open 16 February-30 October

18 rm – †€ 95/120 ††€ 95/160, ☐ € 14 – 1 suite – ½ P € 89/126

Rest – *(closed Wednesday lunchtime and Tuesday)* Menu € 20/62 – Carte € 25/63

◆ Among this hotel's features are its proximity to Dames beach, the calm of a pinewood setting and a flower-decked garden. Spacious, mainly ground-floor, rooms with period furnishings. Bright blue and white dining room; sea produce takes pride of place on the menu.

St-Paul

15 av. Mar.-Foch – ✆ 02 51 39 05 63 – contact@hotel-saint-paul.net – Fax 02 51 39 73 98 – Open 16 February-30 October
41 rm – €84/171 €84/171, €13 – ½ P €112/130
Rest – *(closed Sunday dinner and Monday off season)* Menu €27/68 – Carte €49/65
♦ This property stands in a handsome flowered park surrounded by woodland. Cosy bedrooms (rustic or period furniture) and welcoming sitting room-bar. Traditional dishes, fish and seafood served in an elegant dining room.

Château du Pélavé

9 allée de Chaillot – ✆ 02 51 39 01 94 – chateau-du-pelave@wanadoo.fr – Fax 02 51 39 70 42
18 rm – €61/177 €61/177, €12,50 – ½ P €71/133
Rest – *(closed 12 November-25 December, 11 January-13 February, Wednesday lunch, Sunday dinner, Monday and Tuesday February-March and October-November except holidays)* Menu (€17 bi), €26/56 bi – Carte €38/59
♦ This late-19C château nestled in delighted wooded grounds with abundant floral displays is the perfect base for a quiet, relaxing stay. Personalised guestrooms in a range of styles. Local produce and an impressive choice of domain-bottled wines take pride of place here. Terrace.

Les Capucines

rm,

38 av. de la Victoire – ✆ 02 51 39 06 82 – capucineshotel@aol.com – Fax 02 51 39 33 10 – Open 13 February-1st November and closed Wednesday and Thursday off season
21 rm – €52/85 €52/95, €8 – ½ P €52/83 – **Rest** – Menu (€16), €26/36 – Carte €26/41
♦ Two buildings set on either side of the pool. Simple but practical rooms; larger in the annexe and quieter overlooking the garden. Friendly welcome. Sober, modern dining room and terrace in good weather.

ÎLE DE PORQUEROLLES – 83 Var – 340 M7 – ✉ 83400 41 C3

Access by sea transport.

from **La Tour Fondue** (presqu'île de Giens) (peninsula) - Crossing 20 mn - Information and prices : T.L.V. et T.V.M. ✆ 04 94 58 21 81, (La Tour Fondue) - from **Cavalaire** - seasonal service - Crossing 1 h 40 mn ou **Le Lavandou** - seasonal service - Crossing 50 mn. Vedettes Îles d'Or 15 quai Gabriel-Péri ✆ 04 94 71 01 02 (Le Lavandou), Fax 04 94 01 06 13

from **Toulon** - seasonal service - Crossing 1 h - Information and prices : Information at the Toulon Tourist Office ✆ 04 94 18 53 00.

Le Mas du Langoustier

3.5 km west of the port – ✆ 04 94 58 30 09 – langoustier@wanadoo.fr – Fax 04 94 58 36 02 – Open end April-beg. October
45 rm (½ board only) – 4 suites – ½ P €152/212
Rest – Menu €55/91 – Carte €66/131
Spec. Filets de rougets poêlés et brouillade d'œufs à la rouille. Ravioli ouvert aux artichauts et pistou. Filet de Saint-Pierre rôti au beurre de gingembre et coriandre.
Wines Ile de Porquerolles, Côtes de Provence.
♦ Bright, spacious rooms in a wild setting overlooking the sea, near Grand Langoustier point. Possibility of transport by helicopter from the mainland. Sun-kissed cuisine with a bright modern touch and the great blue sea as far as the eye can see.

Villa Sainte Anne

rm, rm,

pl. Armes – ✆ 04 98 04 63 00 – courrier@sainteanne.com – Fax 04 94 58 32 26 – Closed 5 November-27 December and 2 January-20 February
25 rm (½ board only) – ½ P €74/124
Rest – Menu €18 (lunch)/25 – Carte €30/46
♦ Welcoming house on the lively village square. Renovated rooms in the old section and new, larger rooms in the wing. Cosy dining room and pleasant shaded terrace. Traditional cuisine and seafood and fish dishes.

ÎLE DE PORT-CROS ★★★ – 83 Var – 340 N7 – ✉ 83400
French Riviera 41 **C3**

Access by sea transport

- from **Le Lavandou** -Crossing 35 mn – Information and prices: Vedettes Îles d'Or 15 quai Gabriel-Péri ✆ 04 94 71 01 02 (Le Lavandou), Fax 04 94 01 06 13
- from **Cavalaire** - Crossing 45 mn - Information and prices: see above
- from **La Tour Fondue** - Crossing 1 h - Information and prices: T.L.V. - T.V.M. ✆ 04 94 58 21 81.

Le Manoir — rm, VISA MC

– ✆ 04 94 05 90 52 – lemanoir.portcros@wanadoo.fr – Fax 04 94 05 90 89 – Open 27 April-5 October

22 rm (½ board only) – ½ P € 150/238 – **Rest** – Menu € 45 (weekdays)/55

◆ This attractive 19C house surrounded by a park enjoys an idyllic location on an unspoilt island. Perfect for nature-lovers. The restaurant and terrace command a view of the yachts anchored in the Rade de Port-Cros. Regional cuisine.

ÎLE DE RÉ ★ – 17 Charente-Maritime – 324 B2 Atlantic Coast 38 **A2**

Access by road bridge (see La Rochelle).

Ars-en-Ré – 17 Charente-Maritime – pop. 1 294 – alt. 4 m – ✉ 17590 38 **A2**

Paris 506 – Fontenay-le-Comte 85 – Luçon 75 – La Rochelle 34

Office de tourisme, 26, place Carnot ✆ 05 46 29 46 09, Fax 05 46 29 68 30

Le Sénéchal without rest — VISA MC

6 r. Gambetta – ✆ 05 46 29 40 42 – hotel.le.senechal@wanadoo.fr – Fax 05 46 29 21 25 – Closed beg. January-beg. February

22 rm – †€ 50/200 ††€ 50/200, ☕ € 11 – 2 suites

◆ A guesthouse feel, with tasteful interiors combining old stonework and stylish decoration. Breakfast served on a flower-decked patio. Charm and character combined.

Le Parasol without rest — AC rest, P VISA MC

1 km northwest by Le phare des Baleines road – ✆ 05 46 29 46 17 – contact@leparasol.com – Fax 05 46 29 05 09 – Closed January, February and March

30 rm – †€ 67/99 ††€ 67/99, ☕ € 10

◆ Five small buildings in a green setting; neo-rustic rooms and studios. Faultless upkeep and welcome. Outdoor Jacuzzi and play area.

Le Bistrot de Bernard — VISA MC

1 quai Criée – ✆ 05 46 29 40 26 – bistrot.de.bernard@wanadoo.fr – Fax 05 46 29 28 99 – Closed 1st December-15 February, Monday and Tuesday off season

Rest – Menu (€ 21), € 25 – Carte € 34/63

◆ The flowered courtyard lends a colonial air to this restaurant occupying one of the island's old houses. Bronze sculptures and mosaic frames decorate the dining room.

La Cabane du Fier — P VISA MC AE

Le Martray, 3 km east by D 735 – ✆ 05 46 29 64 84 – cabanedufier@free.fr – Fax 05 46 29 64 84 – Open 16 March-14 November and closed Tuesday dinner and Wednesday except July-August

Rest – Carte € 25/40

◆ A wooden building adjoining an oyster farmer's cabin. A delightful nautical bistro and terrace facing the Fier d'Ars. Daily seafood specials chalked up on a blackboard.

Le Bois-Plage-en-Ré – 17 Charente-Maritime – pop. 2 235 – alt. 5 m – ✉ 17580 38 **A2**

Paris 494 – Fontenay-le-Comte 74 – Luçon 64 – La Rochelle 23

Office de tourisme, 87, rue des Barjottes ✆ 05 46 09 23 26, Fax 05 46 09 13 15

Les Bois Flottais without rest — P VISA MC AE

chemin des Mouettes – ✆ 05 46 09 27 00 – lesboisflottais@wanadoo.fr – Fax 05 46 09 28 00 – Closed 20 November-1st February

17 rm – †€ 81/125 ††€ 81/125, ☕ € 14

◆ A beige and chocolate colour scheme, tiled floors, stained wood and nautical trinkets create the delightful decor of the comfortable rooms. All the rooms are level with the patio-pool.

L'Océan

172 r. St-Martin – ☎ 05 46 09 23 07 – info@re-hotel-ocean.com – Fax 05 46 09 05 40 – Closed 7 January-7 February

29 rm – †€ 72/120 ††€ 72/180, ☕ € 10 – ½ P € 68/122

Rest – *(closed Wednesday except evenings from April to September)* Menu (€ 18), € 23/32 – Carte € 28/55

♦ Houses with whitewashed walls, whose light wood, counterpanes and embroidered fabrics recreate the charm of Isle of Ré homes. Stylish rooms, seven of which are more modern. Pretty Ile de Ré style dining room opening onto a courtyard-terrace. Bar lounge.

Les Gollandières

av. des Gollandières – ☎ 05 46 09 23 99 – hotel-les-gollandieres@wanadoo.fr – Fax 05 46 09 09 84 – Open 15 March-8 November

34 rm – †€ 93/113 ††€ 93/113, ☕ € 11 – ½ P € 92/111 – **Rest** – Menu € 28 (weekday lunch), € 39/74 – Carte € 42/67

♦ Behind the dunes, this hotel has small, simple rooms laid out around two patios. Pleasant swimming pool. This restaurant serves traditional cuisine made with high-quality local produce. Pleasant summer terrace.

La Villa Passagère without rest

25 av. du Pas des Bœufs – ☎ 05 46 00 26 70 – reception@lavillapassagere.net – Fax 05 46 00 26 84 – Open 2 February-14 November

13 rm – †€ 60/105 ††€ 60/105, ☕ € 7,50

♦ A new hotel made up of small regional style houses laid out around a herb garden and swimming pool. Simple, light ground floor rooms.

La Couarde-sur-Mer – 17 Charente-Maritime – pop. 1 179 – alt. 1 m – ✉ 17670

Paris 497 – Fontenay-le-Comte 76 – Luçon 66 – La Rochelle 26 38 **A2**

Syndicat d'initiative, rue Pasteur ☎ 05 46 29 82 93, Fax 05 46 29 63 02

Le Vieux Gréement without rest

13 pl. Carnot – ☎ 05 46 29 82 18 – hotelvieuxgreement@wanadoo.fr – Fax 05 46 29 50 79 – Open 31 March-13 November

17 rm – †€ 50/75 ††€ 65/115, ☕ € 12 – 2 suites

♦ On the village square, a family establishment of character. Smart rooms, pretty patio, terrace shaded by a linden tree and oysters and gourmet open sandwiches served at the bar.

La Flotte – 17 Charente-Maritime – pop. 2 737 – alt. 4 m – ✉ 17630 38 A2

Paris 489 – Fontenay-le-Comte 68 – Luçon 58 – La Rochelle 17

Office de tourisme, quai de Sénac ☎ 05 46 09 60 38, Fax 05 46 09 64 88

Richelieu

av. de la Plage – ☎ 05 46 09 60 70 – info@hotel-le-richelieu.com – Fax 05 46 09 50 59 – Closed January

37 rm – †€ 140/580 ††€ 140/580, ☕ € 20 – 3 suites – ½ P € 125/340

Rest – Menu € 50 (lunch), € 55/65 – Carte € 66/80

Spec. Langoustines côtières marinées et grillées. Bar de ligne et casserons, gelée chaude de soupe de poissons. Feuilleté de pommes "crumble", glace caramel.

Wines Vin de pays de la Vienne, Fiefs Vendéens.

♦ Luxurious, personalised rooms with period furniture. The most pleasant have a vast terrace overlooking the sea. Thalassotherapy centre. Restaurant with views the garden and the Atlantic. Refined original cuisine.

L'Écailler

3 quai Sénac – ☎ 05 46 09 56 40 – flosenac@orange.fr – Open 2 March-10 November and closed Tuesday in March, October, November and Monday

Rest – Menu € 34/55 – Carte € 45/102

♦ Terrace overlooking the harbour, tasteful interior (wainscoting, fireplace and old parquet floors) and recipes that focus on the local catch: this 1652 shipowner's house is full of charm.

Chai nous comme Chai vous

– ☎ 05 46 09 49 85 – Closed 5 January-8 February, Friday lunch and Saturday lunch in school holidays, Wednesday and Thursday except school holidays

Rest – *(number of covers limited, pre-book)* Menu (€ 32), € 37

♦ There's a relaxed feel to this sober restaurant, run by a couple. On the menu are seafood, creativity and special attention. Good choice of wines.

LES PORTES-EN-RÉ – 17 Charente-Maritime – pop. 661 – alt. 4 m – ✉ 17880

Paris 514 – Fontenay-le-Comte 93 – Luçon 83 – La Rochelle 43 38 **A2**

Office de tourisme, 52, rue de Trousse-Chemise ✆ 05 46 29 52 71, Fax 05 46 29 52 81

de Trousse-Chemise Route de la Levée Verte, South: 3 km by D 101, ✆ 05 46 29 69 37.

Le Chasse-Marée

1 r. J. David – ✆ 05 46 29 52 03 – restaurant.le.chasse-maree@wanadoo.fr – Fax 05 46 28 00 91 – Open April-December and closed Sunday dinner and Monday 1st September-15 June

Rest – Menu € 26 (weekdays)/40 – Carte € 44/51

◆ Welcoming regional house in the village centre. The up-to-date bistro interior is as pleasant as the summer terrace at the front. Seafood menu.

RIVEDOUX-PLAGE – 17 Charente-Maritime – pop. 1 754 – alt. 2 m – ✉ 17940

Paris 483 – Fontenay-le-Comte 63 – Luçon 53 – La Rochelle 12 38 **A2**

Syndicat d'initiative, place de la République ✆ 05 46 09 80 62, Fax 05 46 09 80 62

De la Marée

321 av. A. Sarrault, (St-Martin road) – ✆ 05 46 09 80 02 – contact@hoteldelamaree.com – Fax 05 46 09 88 25

26 rm – €78/168 €78/168, € 14 – 3 suites – ½ P € 77/152

Rest – Menu € 20/30 – Carte € 29/35

◆ Painted furniture adorn the rooms; the most pleasant have terraces giving onto the rose garden and swimming pool; countless sitting rooms, nooks and crannies. Charming welcome.

ST-CLÉMENT-DES-BALEINES – 17 Charente-Maritime – pop. 728 – alt. 2 m – ✉ 17590

38 **A2**

Paris 509 – Fontenay-le-Comte 89 – Luçon 79 – La Rochelle 38

Office de tourisme, 200, rue du Centre ✆ 05 46 29 24 19, Fax 05 46 29 08 14

L'Arche de Noé (amusement park): Naturama★ (collection of stuffed animals) - Phare des Baleines (lighthouse) ❋★ North: 2.5 km.

Le Chat Botté without rest

2 pl. de l'Église – ✆ 05 46 29 21 93 – hotelchatbotte@wanadoo.fr – Fax 05 46 29 29 97

20 rm – €55/58 €62/152, € 13,50 – 3 suites

◆ A cosy interior (pastel shades, wood and antique furniture), adorable garden where breakfasts are served and a beauty centre: ideal to relax and be pampered!

Le Chat Botté

r. de la Mairie – ✆ 05 46 29 42 09 – restaurant-lechatbotte@wanadoo.fr – Fax 05 46 29 29 77 – Closed December-January, Sunday dinner October-March and Monday

Rest – Menu € 22 (weekdays)/70 – Carte € 41/67

◆ The restaurant's name is derived from Chabot, one of the village's five hamlets. A comfortable dining room with nautical decor, overlooking a pleasant garden.

ST-MARTIN-DE-RÉ – 17 Charente-Maritime – pop. 2 637 – alt. 14 m – ✉ 17410

Paris 493 – Fontenay-le-Comte 72 – Luçon 62 – La Rochelle 22 38 **A2**

Syndicat d'initiative, 2, quai Nicolas Baudin ✆ 05 46 09 20 06, Fax 05 46 09 06 18

Fortifications★.

De Toiras

1 quai Job Foran – ✆ 05 46 35 40 32 – contact@hotel-de-toiras.com – Fax 05 46 35 64 59

18 rm – €135/580 €165/610, € 19 – 2 suites – ½ P € 173/490

Rest – *(Closed Tuesday and Wednesday) (dinner only)* Carte € 70/90

◆ A tasteful interior decoration, both luxurious and simple, very welcoming rooms and delightully attentive service: this 17C shipowner's home is a rare gem. Meals are served in an attractive dining room or on the terrace in fine weather.

Le Clos St-Martin without rest
8 cours Pasteur – 05 46 01 10 62
– hotelclos.saintmartin@wanadoo.fr – Fax 05 46 01 99 89
32 rm – €95/300 €95/300, €15
◆ This recent house and pretty walled park are only a short distance from the harbour. Simple but pleasant rooms, some on the same level as the patio-pool.

La Jetée without rest
quai G. Clemenceau – 05 46 09 36 36 – info@hotel-lajetee.com
– Fax 05 46 09 36 06
24 rm – €95/180 €95/180, €12 – 7 suites
◆ A harbour hotel renovated in a warm contemporary style: trendy colour scheme and minimalist furnishings in the rooms, arranged round a patio (where breakfast is served in summer).

Le Galion without rest
allée Guyane – 05 46 09 03 19 – hotel.le.galion@wanadoo.fr
– Fax 05 46 09 13 26
29 rm – €70/110 €75/115, €9
◆ Vauban's ramparts protect the hotel from the pounding of the ocean. Modern, well-kept rooms, almost all of them facing the sea or the patio. Asian-inspired sitting room.

La Maison Douce without rest
25 r. Mérindot – 05 46 09 20 20 – lamaisondouce@wanadoo.fr
– Fax 05 46 09 90 90 – Closed 15 November-25 December and 7 January-15 February
11 rm – €110/165 €110/185, €15
◆ A 19C establishment typical of the island. Low-key interior, delightful rooms with retro bathrooms; courtyard garden where breakfast is served in summer.

Du Port without rest
29 quai Poithevinière – 05 46 09 21 21 – iledere-hot.port@wanadoo.fr
– Fax 05 46 09 06 85 – Closed 6-30 January
35 rm – €65/95 €65/95, €10
◆ This is the lively district of St-Martin-de-Ré. A hotel with simply-furnished, colourful rooms, some with a harbour view.

Les Colonnes
19 quai Job-Foran – 05 46 09 21 58 – info@hotellescolonnes.com
– Fax 05 46 09 21 49 – Closed 15 December-1st February
30 rm – €72/99 €72/99, €9 – ½ P €79/85 – **Rest** – *(Closed Wednesday)* Menu (€22), €28 (weekdays), €31/40 – Carte €34/51
◆ This regional-style house is fronted by a vast terrace popular with fishermen and locals: friendly and informal! Neat, well-kept rooms, overlooking the harbour or the courtyard. Dining room-veranda with extensive view of the waterfront; traditional cuisine.

Domaine de la Baronnie
21 r. Baron de Chantal – 05 46 09 21 29 – info@domainedelabaronnie.com
– Fax 05 46 09 95 29 – Open March-mid November
5 rm – €150/210 €150/210, €15 – **Table d'hôte** – Menu €24/29
◆ This 18C mansion has been restored in the fashion of a country home, with individually furnished rooms. Those in the tower overlook the garden and the rooftops of the town. Market-fresh cuisine prepared from produce grown on the island.

Le Corps de Garde – La Maison du Port without rest
3 quai Clemenceau – 05 46 09 10 50
– info@lamaisonduport.fr – Fax 05 46 09 76 99
5 rm – €175/200 €175/200, €12
◆ Old furniture and ornaments, splendid old-fashioned bathrooms and rooms overlooking the lock or the harbour. This 17C former guardpost oozes with charm.

La Coursive St-Martin without rest
13 cours Déchézeaux – 05 46 09 22 87 – mail@lacoursine.com
– Fax 05 46 09 22 87 – Closed December and January
4 rm – €75/100 €80/160, €10
◆ Immense 18C mansion, full of history, surrounded by high walls and a beautiful flower garden. Personalised rooms.

Bô
20 cours Vauban – ✆ 05 46 07 04 04 – le-bo@wanadoo.fr – Fax 05 46 29 08 20 – Closed 12 November-16 December, 3 January-4 February and Wednesday except July-August
Rest – Menu € 29/39 – Carte € 33/52
◆ Seductive contemporary atmosphere (candles, plants, comfortable armchairs) a stone's throw from the port. Up-to-date cuisine with seafood to the fore. Luxuriant terrace.

La Baleine Bleue
sur L'Îlot – ✆ 05 46 09 03 30 – info@baleinebleue.com – Fax 05 46 09 30 86 – Closed 12 November-19 December, 5 January-5 February, Tuesday October-March and Monday except July-August
Rest – Menu (€ 24), € 32/45 – Carte € 42/66
◆ A cheerful restaurant and vast terrace facing the port. A warm interior with a 1930s zinc counter, serving updated cuisine featuring many seafood dishes.

STE-MARIE-DE-RÉ – 17 Charente-Maritime – pop. 2 655 – alt. 9 m – ✉ 17740

Paris 486 – Fontenay-le-Comte 66 – Luçon 55 – La Rochelle 15 38 **A2**
Office de tourisme, place d'Antioche ✆ 05 46 30 22 92, Fax 05 46 30 01 68

Atalante
rest, rest,
r. Port Notre-Dame – ✆ 05 46 30 22 44 – iledere@relaisthalasso.com – Fax 05 46 30 13 49 – Closed 6-20 January
107 rm – €83/119 €114/250, € 12 – ½ P € 92/160
Rest – Menu € 24/34 – Carte € 44/64
◆ This hotel facing the sea has modern rooms in acid shades. Those in the modern wing are larger and more comfortable. Direct access to the thalassotherapy centre The veranda-dining room is a veritable window onto the Atlantic.

Les Vignes de la Chapelle without rest
5 r. de la Manne – ✆ 05 46 30 20 30 – hotel@lesvignesdelachapelle.com – Fax 05 46 30 20 31 – Open 19 March-11 November
2 rm – €78/183 €78/183, € 16 – 17 suites – €93/218
◆ Opposite the vineyards and sea, this brand new hotel was built along ecological lines (materials, heating). Contemporary ground floor suites with terrace.

ÎLE-DE-SEIN – 29 Finistère – 308 B6 – pop. 242 – alt. 14 m – ✉ 29990

Brittany 9 **A2**

Pedestrians only
from **Brest** (Sun. in Jul.-Aug.) - Crossing 1 h 30 mn - Information and prices: Cie Maritime Penn Ar Bed (Brest) ✆ 02 98 80 80 80 - from **Audierne** (all year) Crossing 1 h - Information and prices: see above.
from **Camaret** (Sun. in Jul.-Aug.) Crossing 1 h - Information and prices: see above.

Ar Men
rte Phare – ✆ 02 98 70 90 77 – hotel.armen@wanadoo.fr – Fax 02 98 70 93 25 – Closed 28 September-23 October and 4 January-6 February
10 rm – €43 €53, € 7 – ½ P € 50 – **Rest** – *(closed Wednesday from April to September and Sunday dinner)* Menu € 19
◆ A charming family-run island hotel, easy to spot from its pink exterior on the road to the lighthouse near the church. Ocean colours in the rooms that overlook the sea. The local catch takes pride of place in the tasteful dining room. Lobster stew by reservation.

ÎLE-D'HOUAT – 56 Morbihan – 308 N10 – pop. 335 – alt. 31 m – ✉ 56170

Brittany 10 **C3**

Access by sea transport
from **Quiberon** - Crossing 40 mn - Information and prices : SMN ✆ 0 820 056 000 (0.12 €/mn)(Quiberon) www.smn-navigation.fr
from **La Trinité-sur-Mer** (July-August) Crossing 1 h - Navix : cours des quais ✆ 0 825 132 150 (0.15 €/mn) www.navix.fr.
Le Bourg ≤★.

La Sirène
rm, VISA MC AE

rte du Port – ✆ 02 97 30 66 73 – la-sirene-houat@wanadoo.fr – Fax 02 97 30 66 94 – Open from Easter to end October

20 rm – €100/120 €100/130, €12 – ½ P €77/98 – **Rest** – Menu €22/34 – Carte €29/57

♦ Family run hotel in the heart of a small town. Friendly service. The practical and soundproofed rooms, including nine new ones, promise a pleasant stay. Restaurant with nautical decor leading onto a terrace serving traditional and seafood dishes.

ÎLE D'OLÉRON ★ – 17 Charente-Maritime – 324 C4 Atlantic Coast 38 A2

Access by viaduct bridge: no toll.

BOYARDVILLE – 17 Charente-Maritime – ✉ 17190 St-Georges-d'Oléron 38 **A2**

Paris 517 – Marennes 24 – Rochefort 45 – La Rochelle 82 – Saintes 65

Office de tourisme, 14, avenue de l'Océan ✆ 05 46 47 04 76

d'Oléron Saint-Pierre-d'Oléron La Vieille Perrotine, South: 2 km by D 126, ✆ 05 46 47 11 59.

Des Bains
VISA MC AE

1 r. des Quais, (at the port) – ✆ 05 46 47 01 02 – info@hoteldesbains-oleron.com – Fax 05 46 47 16 90 – Open 31 May-21 September and closed Wednesday except dinner 9 July-21 September

Rest – Menu €21/37 – Carte €35/53

♦ Beams, stonework, copperware and rustic furniture endow this canalside family restaurant with the feel of an old inn. Traditional culinary repertoire.

LE CHÂTEAU-D'OLÉRON – 17 Charente-Maritime – pop. 3 552 – alt. 9 m – ✉ 17480

Paris 524 – Poitiers 190 – La Rochelle 72 – Saintes 54 – Rochefort 35 38 **A2**

Les Jardins d'Aliénor with rm
rm, VISA MC AE

11 r. Mar. Foch – ✆ 05 46 76 48 30 – lesjardinsdalienor@wanadoo – Fax 05 46 76 58 47 – Closed 1st-21 March, 1st-14 December and Monday

4 rm – €77/97 €77/97

Rest – *(dinner only in July-August)* Menu €25 (lunch)/39 – Carte €42/49

♦ An interior that mixes old and new and a patio-terrace with a wall of plants: the decor is baroque and full of character, as is the chef's cuisine. Attractive rooms, one of which has a private terrace.

LA COTINIÈRE – 17 Charente-Maritime – ✉ 17310 St-Pierre-d'Oléron 38 **A2**

Paris 522 – Marennes 22 – Rochefort 44 – La Rochelle 80 – Royan 54 – Saintes 63

Face aux Flots
rm, rest, VISA MC AE

24 r. du Four – ✆ 05 46 47 10 05 – face.aux.flots@wanadoo.fr – Fax 05 46 47 45 95 – Open 10 February-11 November and Christmas holidays

21 rm – €45/90 €49/90, €8 – ½ P €52/78 – **Rest** – *(dinner only) (resident only)*

♦ The rooms of this appealing family hotel have been refurbished; they are now modern, colourful and nearly all overlook the sea (four have a small balcony). Bright contemporary restaurant with a view of the sea; traditional repertoire.

Île de Lumière without rest
VISA MC

av. des Pins – ✆ 05 46 47 10 80 – ile.de.lumiere@wanadoo.fr – Fax 05 46 47 30 87 – Open from end March to September

45 rm – €74/93 €74/130

♦ In an unspoilt site, subdued ground floor rooms, many of which have terraces with a view of the ocean, dunes or swimming pool. Some are more modern in style.

in la Ménounière 2 km North by secondary road ✉ 17310 St-Pierre-d'Oléron

Saveurs des Îles
VISA MC

18 r. de la Plage – ✆ 05 46 75 86 68 – osaveursdesiles@wanadoo.fr – Fax 05 46 75 86 68 – Closed beg. January-end March, Monday except dinner July-August, Tuesday lunch except July-August, Wednesday lunch July-August, Tuesday dinner and Wednesday November-December

Rest – Menu €24/36 – Carte €38/52

♦ The owners built this Asian-inspired restaurant themselves, decorating it with Indonesian furniture. Garden-terrace. Creative menu enhanced by exotic spices and flavours.

LE GRAND VILLAGE PLAGE – 17 Charente-Maritime – pop. 898 – alt. 6 m – ✉ 17370

Paris 525 – Poitiers 191 – La Rochelle 73 – Rochefort 36 – Royan 44 38 **A2**

Le Relais des Salines

Port des Salines – ✆ 05 46 75 82 42 – james.robert@hotmail.fr – Fax 05 46 75 16 70 – Open from beg. March to end November and closed Monday except school holidays

Rest – Menu € 17 (weekday lunch)– Carte € 33/39

◆ Relaxed atmosphere, trendy nautical-inspired bistro decor, terrace overlooking the salt marshes and an impressive choice of seafood on the slate menu: this old oyster farmer's cabin is a gem!

ST-PIERRE-D'OLÉRON – 17 Charente-Maritime – pop. 5 944 – alt. 8 m – ✉ 17310

Paris 522 – Marennes 22 – Rochefort 44 – La Rochelle 80 – Royan 54 – Saintes 63

Office de tourisme, place Gambetta ✆ 05 46 47 11 39, Fax 05 46 47 10 41

Church ✻★. 38 **A2**

Habitation Léonie without rest

5 r.du Moulin, au bois fleury, 2 km north on D 734 and secondary road – ✆ 05 46 36 88 42 – jean-jacques-mazoyer@wanadoo.fr – Fax 05 46 36 88 42 – Closed 2-25 March

5 rm – †€ 60/95 ††€ 75/115

◆ Situated in a hamlet, an 18C mansion and gardens with guestrooms occupying a single-storey outbuilding. Quiet rooms, with a maritime-inspired decor, antique furnishings and private terrace.

Les Alizés

4 r. Dubois-Aubry – ✆ 05 46 47 20 20 – Fax 05 46 47 20 20 – Open from beg. March to beg. December and closed Tuesday and Wednesday except mid July-mid September and public holidays

Rest – Menu € 19/34 – Carte € 23/54

◆ This restaurant has a dining area with wooden panelling and a marine décor theme. In fine weather, enjoy a meal outside on the pleasant patio. Seafood served.

ST-TROJAN-LES-BAINS – 17 Charente-Maritime – pop. 1 624 – alt. 5 m – ✉ 17370

Paris 509 – Marennes 16 – Rochefort 38 – La Rochelle 74 – Royan 47 – Saintes 57 38 **A2**

Office de tourisme, carrefour du Port ✆ 05 46 76 00 86, Fax 05 46 76 17 64

Novotel

rm, rm, rest,

plage de Gatseau, South : 2.5 km – ✆ 05 46 76 02 46 – h0417@accor.com – Fax 05 46 76 09 33 – Closed 30 November-20 December

109 rm – †€ 94/188 ††€ 117/205, € 15 – ½ P € 90/132 – **Rest** – Menu € 30 – Carte € 26/56

◆ Relax in this hotel opposite the beach which boasts its own thalassotherapy centre. Ask for one of the renovated or recently created more contemporary rooms. Enjoy the sea view while watching your figure (partially "diet" conscious menu).

Hostellerie Les Cleunes

25 bd.Plage – ✆ 05 46 76 03 08 – hotellescleunes@aol.com – Fax 05 46 76 08 95 – Open 21 March-31 December

40 rm – †€ 83/245 ††€ 83/245, € 12 – ½ P € 78/165 – **Rest** – *(closed Monday lunch)* Menu € 28/58 – Carte € 42/160

◆ A seashore family establishment that has been renovated from top to toe: comfortable, welcoming rooms, cosy sitting room with billiards table, and a lovely patio-swimming pool. A menu that features a modern repertoire with input from the ocean beyond.

Mer et Forêt

rest,

16 bd P. Wiehn – ✆ 05 46 76 00 15 – laforet.oleron@wanadoo.fr – Fax 05 46 76 14 67 – Open 21 March-2 November

43 rm – †€ 54/118 ††€ 54/118, € 9 – ½ P € 54/92 – **Rest** – Menu € 18/36 – Carte € 25/41

◆ Hotel in a quiet residential neighbourhood. Practical, modern rooms with a view over the pine forest or the ocean; pleasant pool. Panoramic views of the viaduct-bridge and the mainland from the restaurant and terrace.

L'Albatros rm, rest, VISA AE

11 bd Dr Pineau – 05 46 76 00 08 – allooleron@free.fr – Fax 05 46 76 03 58 – Open 7 February-2 November

13 rm – €64/110 €64/110, €9,50 – ½ P €70/100 – **Rest** – Menu €28 – Carte €29/65

◆ To make the most of this fantastic waterfront location, book one of the five rooms that have been treated to a pleasant contemporary-style makeover. Local seafood features prominently on the menu; brasserie decor and panoramic sea view terrace.

Le Homard Bleu VISA AE

10 bd Félix Faure – 05 46 76 00 22 – homard.bleu@wanadoo.fr – Fax 05 46 76 14 95 – Open beg. February-beg. November

20 rm – €71/86 €71/86 – ½ P €57/86 – **Rest** – *(closed Tuesday except April-September)* Menu €20/61 – Carte €37/58

◆ Family establishment providing well-equipped functional rooms with soundproofing; half enjoy a sea view. Brightly coloured dining room-veranda with a view of the harbour and the mainland. Traditional cuisine with a distinct seafood slant.

ÎLE D'OUESSANT – 29 Finistère – 308 A4 – 29242 Brittany 9 A1

Pedestrians only - from **Brest** - Crossing 2 h 15 mn - Information and prices: Cie Maritime Penn Ar Bed (Brest) 02 98 80 80 80

from **Le Conquet** - Crossing 1 h - Information and prices: see above

from **Camaret** (mid-July to mid-August only) - Crossing 1 h 15 mn - Information and prices: see above.

Ti Jan Ar C' Hafé without rest VISA

Kernigou – 02 98 48 82 64 – hoteltijan@wanadoo.fr – Fax 02 98 48 88 15 – Closed 11 November-23 December and 4 January-7 February

8 rm – €78/88 €78/88, €9

◆ This charming small hotel between the port and the town extends a warm welcome to its guests. Cosy lounge, bright dining room, wooden terrace and cosy bedrooms.

Le Roc'h Ar Mor rm, VISA

au bourg de Lampaul – 02 98 48 80 19 – roch.armor@wanadoo.fr – Fax 02 98 48 87 51 – Closed 15 November-15 December, 3 January-10 February

15 rm – €55/87 €55/87, €9,50 – ½ P €52/67 – **Rest** – *(Closed Sunday dinner and Monday)* Menu €23/43 – Carte €27/54

◆ This hotel sits on France's westernmost point. Plain rooms, some with a view of Lampaul Bay. Unpretentious ambience. A bar/brasserie with a panoramic terrace and low-key dining room. Single menu for residents only.

Ty Korn VISA

au bourg de Lampaul – 02 98 48 87 33 – Fax 02 98 48 87 33 – Closed 1st-9 June, 23 November-8 December, 4-26 January, Sunday dinner and Monday except holidays

Rest – *(number of covers limited, pre-book)* Menu €29 – Carte €25/57

◆ A popular pub-restaurant near the church. Fish and seafood are on offer in the small dining room with the Atlantic as a backdrop.

ÎLE D'YEU ★★ – 85 Vendée – 361 BC7 – pop. 4 941 Atlantic Coast 34 A3

Access by sea transport for **Port-Joinville.**

from Fromentine : Crossing from 30 to 70 mn - Information to Cie Yeu Continent BP 16-85550 La Barre-de-Monts 0 825 853 000 (0,15 €/mn), www.compagnie-yeu-continent.fr.

from Fromentine (all year) - Crossing from 30 to 45 mn - Information and prices : Cie Yeu Continent (to Fromentine) 0 825 853 000 (0,15 €/mn), www.compagnie-yeu-continent.fr - from Barbâtre : Cie V.I.I.V. 02 51 39 00 00 - from St-Gilles-Croix-de-Vie and from Les Sables d'Olonne (Quai Bénatier) (April to Sept.) : Cie Vendéenne 0 825 139 085 (0,15 €/mn), www.compagnievendeenne.com Seasonal service (April to Sept.).

Office de tourisme, 1, place du Marché 02 51 58 32 58, Fax 02 51 58 40 48

PORT-DE-LA-MEULE – **85 Vendée** – ✉ **85350 L'Ile-d'Yeu** 34 **A3**

Paris 460 – Nantes 72 – La Roche-sur-Yon 73 – Challans 29 – Saint-Hilaire-de-Riez 36

Côte Sauvage★★: ≤★★ East and West - Pointe de la Tranche★ Southeast.

PORT-JOINVILLE – **85 Vendée** – **pop. 4 807** – ✉ **85350 L'Ile-d'Yeu** 34 **A3**

Paris 457 – Nantes 69 – La Roche-sur-Yon 70 – Challans 26 – Pornic 43

Old château ★: ≤★★ Southwest: 3,5 km - Grand Phare ≤★ Southwest: 3 km.

Atlantic Hôtel without rest VISA MC AE

quai Carnot – ✆ 02 51 58 38 80 – atlantic-hotel-yeu@club-internet.fr – Fax 02 51 58 35 92 – Closed 8 January-4 February

18 rm – €43/92 €43/92, €7,50

◆ This hotel opposite the wharf has bright guestrooms and a breakfast room overlooking the sea and the fishing village with its allotments. Tranquil location.

L'Escale without rest VISA MC

r. de La Croix de Port – ✆ 02 51 58 50 28 – yeu.escale@voila.fr – Fax 02 51 59 33 55 – Closed 15 November-15 December

29 rm – €52/72 €52/72, €7,50

◆ Set just behind the port, this hotel has a white exterior with coloured shutters. Simple, well-kept rooms, some of which have air-conditioning. Breakfast room with marine decor.

Port Baron VISA MC

9 r. Georgette – ✆ 02 51 26 01 61 – baron-michel@hotmail.com – Fax 02 51 26 01 61 – Closed January, February, Tuesday lunch and Monday

Rest – Menu € 19 (weekday lunch), € 33/40

◆ A retro-style bistro decorated with old posters, banquettes, photos, old records and other mementoes. The menu is based around seasonal produce and the day's catch.

L'ILE-ROUSSE – **2B Haute-Corse** – **345** C4 – **see Corse**

ÎLE STE-MARGUERITE ★★ – **06 Alpes-Maritimes** – **341** D6 – ✉ **06400 Cannes** **French Riviera** 42 **E2**

Access by sea transport.

from **Cannes** Crossing 15 mn by Cie Esterel Chanteclair-Gare Maritime des Iles ✆ 04 93 38 66 33, Fax 04 92 98 80 32.

Forest★★ - ≤★ of the Fort-Royal terrace.

ÎLES CHAUSEY – **50 Manche** – **303** B6 – ✉ **50400** **Normandy** 32 **A2**

Access by sea transport.

from **Granville** - Crossing 50 mn - Information: Vedette "Jolie France II" Gare Maritime ✆ 02 33 50 31 81 (Granville), Fax 02 33 50 39 90, Compagnie Corsaire : ✆ 0 825 138 050 (0,15 €/mn), Fax 02 33 50 87 80, www.compagniecorsaire.com

from **St-Malo** - Crossing 1 h 10 mn - Compagnie Corsaire : ✆ 0 825 138 035 (0.15 €/mn), Fax 02 23 18 02 97.

Grande Ile★.

Fort et des Îles with rm ≤ archipelago, rm, VISA MC

– ✆ 02 33 50 25 02 – Fax 02 33 50 25 02 – Open 12 April-28 September and closed Monday except holidays

8 rm (½ board only) – ½ P € 64/69 – **Rest** – *(pre-book in high season)* Menu € 22/80 – Carte € 26/47

◆ Lobster, crab, oysters and fish: seafood cuisine based on the day's catch and superb view over the archipelago. A great place to revitalise far from the turbulence of the mainland. Very basic rooms without television to better enjoy the island's tranquillity.

LAS ILLAS – **66 Pyrénées-Orientales** – **344** H8 – **see Maureillas-las-Illas**

ILLHAEUSERN – **68 Haut-Rhin** – **315** I7 – **pop. 646** – **alt. 173 m** – ✉ **68970** 2 **C2**

Paris 452 – Artzenheim 15 – Colmar 19 – St-Dié 55 – Sélestat 15 – Strasbourg 69

La Clairière without rest

rte de Guémar – ☎ 03 89 71 80 80 – hotel.la.clairiere@orange.fr – Fax 03 89 71 86 22 – Closed January and February

25 rm – €78/90 €98/286, €12

♦ On the edge of the Ill forest, a vast building with Alsatian-style architecture. Quiet, spacious, personalised rooms, some of which overlook the Vosges mountains.

Les Hirondelles without rest

au village – ☎ 03 89 71 83 76 – hotelleshirondelles@wanadoo.fr – Fax 03 89 71 86 40 – Closed 1st-14 March and 12-21 November

19 rm – €66/70 €76/82

♦ A warm welcome awaits you in the rustic decor of this old farmstead. Well-equipped rooms, laid out around a pretty courtyard and splendid heated swimming pool.

Auberge de l'Ill (Marc et Paul Haeberlin) ← flowering gardens,

2 r. de Collonges – ☎ 03 89 71 89 00 – aubergedelill@aubergedelill.com – Fax 03 89 71 82 83 – Closed 4 February-6 March, Monday and Tuesday

Rest – *(pre-book)* Menu €95 (weekday lunch), €145/225 bi – Carte €104/235

Spec. Salade de tripes aux fèves et au foie d'oie. Mousseline de grenouilles "Paul Haeberlin". Carré d'agneau allaiton d'Aveyron, beignets d'artichaut farcis. **Wines** Riesling, Pinot blanc.

♦ Designer decor by P. Jouin, excellent service, magical views of the Ill, superb Alsatian-inspired classical cuisine and splendid choice of wines: a truly luxurious dining experience.

Hôtel des Berges

– ☎ 03 89 71 87 87 – hotel-des-berges@wanadoo.fr – Fax 03 89 71 87 88 – Closed 1st-8 January, 4 February-5 March, Monday and Tuesday

13 rm – €300 €520, €28

♦ An original reconstruction of a tobacco drier from the Ried marshlands, at the bottom of the Auberge de l'Ill's garden. Extremely refined rooms, an outside jacuzzi and breakfast served on a wooden boat!

ILLKIRCH-GRAFFENSTADEN – 67 Bas-Rhin – 315 K5 – see Strasbourg

INGERSHEIM – 68 Haut-Rhin – 315 H8 – see Colmar

INNENHEIM – 67 Bas-Rhin – 315 J6 – pop. 1 015 – alt. 150 m – ✉ 67880 1 B2

Paris 487 – Molsheim 12 – Obernai 10 – Sélestat 34 – Strasbourg 23

Au Cep de Vigne

5 r. Barr – ☎ 03 88 95 75 45 – resa@aucepdevigne.com – Fax 03 88 95 79 73 – Closed 16-28 February and Sunday dinner

37 rm – €48/62 €53/70, €8,50 – ½ P €60 – **Rest** – *(closed Sunday evening and Monday)* Menu (€15), €23/42 – Carte €30/48

♦ A typical Alsatian inn, with a half-timbered facade, housing comfortable rooms. Those overlooking the garden are quieter. The regional food served in this restaurant goes well with the local wines (vineyards just a step away).

INXENT – 62 Pas-de-Calais – 301 D4 – see Montreuil

ISBERGUES – 62 Pas-de-Calais – 301 H4 – see Aire-sur-la-Lys

ISIGNY-SUR-MER – 14 Calvados – 303 F4 – pop. 2 920 – alt. 4 m – ✉ 14230

Normandy 32 A2

Paris 298 – Bayeux 35 – Caen 64 – Carentan 14 – Cherbourg 63 – St-Lô 29

Office de tourisme, 16, rue Émile Demagny ☎ 02 31 21 46 00, Fax 02 31 22 90 21

De France

13 r. E. Demagny – ☎ 02 31 22 00 33 – hotel.france.isigny@wanadoo.fr – Fax 02 31 22 79 19 – Closed 20 December-13 January, Friday dinner, Saturday lunch and Sunday dinner from October to March

18 rm – €50/58 €58, €8 – **Rest** – Menu €15/28

♦ On the main street of this small town specialising in dairy produce, an old hotel built around an inner courtyard. Simple bedrooms, some on the ground floor. Traditional dishes, fish and seafood (including local oysters) served in two neat dining rooms.

L'ISLE-ADAM – 95 Val-d'Oise – 305 E6 – pop. 11 163 – alt. 28 m – ✉ 95290
Northern France and the Paris Region 18 **B1**

Paris 41 – Beauvais 49 – Chantilly 24 – Compiègne 66 – Pontoise 13 – Taverny 16

Office de tourisme, 46, Grande Rue ✆ 01 34 69 41 99, Fax 01 34 08 09 79

de l'Isle-Adam 1 chemin des Vanneaux, Northeast: 5 km, ✆ 01 34 08 11 11 ;

Les Golfs de Mont Griffon Luzarches Route Départementale 909, Northeast: 5 km, ✆ 01 34 68 10 10 ;

Paris International Golf Club Baillet-en-France 18 route du Golf, Southeast by D 301: 15 km, ✆ 01 34 69 90 00.

Pulpit★ of St-Martin church.

Maison Delaleu without rest
131 av. Foch, at Parmain, 2km west – ✆ 01 34 73 02 92 – chambresdhotes.parmain@wanadoo.fr – Fax 01 34 08 80 76
4 rm – €42 €53
◆ Ideally situated to discover the Vexin region, this hotel is part of a farm estate still in operation. Spacious, low-key rooms; lively breakfasts around a large table.

Le Gai Rivage VISA
11 r. de Conti – ✆ 01 34 69 01 09 – contact@legairivage.com – Closed 25 August-9 September, 25 December-6 January, 15 February-3 March, Sunday dinner, Tuesday dinner and Monday
Rest – Menu € 34 (weekdays)/38 (weekend) – Carte € 47/75
◆ The restaurant is located on an island. Its bay windows and charming terrace offer a view of the passing boats on the Oise. Traditional cuisine.

Le Relais Fleuri VISA
61 bis r. St-Lazare – ✆ 01 34 69 01 85 – Closed 4-29 August, Sunday dinner, Monday dinner, Wednesday dinner and Tuesday
Rest – Menu (€ 23), € 28 – Carte € 44/52
◆ This family inn sports three styles: rustic dining room, Regency sitting room and a veranda in a more modern style. Classic repertoire served under lime trees in fine weather.

L'ISLE-D'ABEAU – 38 Isère – 333 E4 – pop. 12 034 – alt. 265 m – ✉ 38080
44 **B2**

Paris 499 – Bourgoin-Jallieu 6 – Grenoble 72 – Lyon 38 – La Tour du Pin 21

Le Relais du Çatey with rm VISA AE
10 r. Didier, (Le Bourg) – ✆ 04 74 18 26 50 – relaiscatey@aol.com – Fax 04 74 18 26 59 – Closed 2-26 August, 28 December-5 January and Sunday
7 rm – €57/66 €57/66, € 7 – ½ P € 50/54 – **Rest** – *(closed Sunday and Monday)* Menu € 22 (weekday lunch), € 30/53 – Carte € 34/50
◆ The contemporary decor and lighting emphasise the preserved character of this Dauphinois house built in 1774. Lush green terrace. Modern cuisine. Pretty rooms.

in l'Isle-d'Abeau-Ville-Nouvelle West: 4 km by N 6 – ✉ 38080 L'Isle-d'Abeau – pop. 38 769

Mercure rm, VISA AE
20 r. Condorcet – ✆ 04 74 96 80 00 – H1132@accor.com – Fax 04 74 96 80 99
159 rm – €115/125 €125/135, € 11 – 30 suites
Rest *La Belle Époque* – *(closed 19 July-25 August, Saturday and Sunday from May to August)* Menu (€ 19), € 24 – Carte € 29/44
Rest *New Sunset* – brasserie *(closed Saturday and Sunday except from May to August)* Menu (€ 12,50), € 17 – Carte € 21/35
◆ This Mercure hotel was built according to Feng Shui principles to ensure the well being and tranquillity of its guests. It has a fitness centre and a full range of sports facilities. Refurbished rooms. Traditional cuisine is to be found at La Belle Époque. Brasserie menu at the New Sunset piano bar.

L'ISLE-JOURDAIN – 32 Gers – 336 I8 – pop. 5 560 – alt. 116 m – ✉ 32600
Languedoc-Roussillon-Tarn Gorges 28 **B2**

Paris 682 – Toulouse 37 – Auch 45 – Montauban 58

Office de tourisme, route de Mauvezin ✆ 05 62 07 25 57, Fax 05 62 07 24 81

Las Martines Route de Saint Livrade, North: 4 km, ✆ 05 62 07 27 12 ;

du Château de Barbet Lombez Route de Boulogne, Southwest by D 634: 25 km, ✆ 05 62 62 08 54.

Centre-musée européen d'art campanaire (European Bell-making Museum and Centre)-★.

in Pujaudran East: 8 km by N 124 – pop. 898 – alt. 302 m – ✉ 32600

Le Puits St-Jacques (Bernard Bach)
– ✆ 05 62 07 41 11 – lepuitsstjacques@free.fr – Fax 05 62 07 44 09 – Closed 10-29 August, 1st-23 January, Tuesday except dinner in November, Sunday dinner and Monday
Rest – *(pre-book Sat - Sun)* Menu € 22 (weekday lunch), € 35/105 bi – Carte € 74/101
Spec. Tronçons de lobe de foie gras panés au pain d'épice. Pièce de filet de boeuf "limousin", confits d'échalote et moelle de bœuf. Véritable chocolat liégeois.
Wines Vin de pays des Côtes de Gascogne, Pacherenc du Vic-Bilh.
◆ This typical Gers-style house, a former staging-post on the road to Compostelle, is now home to an elegant restaurant and a patio with a Mediterranean feel. Delicate modern cuisine, inspired by the region.

L'ISLE-JOURDAIN – 86 Vienne – 322 K7 – pop. 1 287 – alt. 142 m – ✉ 86150
Atlantic Coast 39 **C2**

Paris 375 – Confolens 29 – Niort 104 – Poitiers 53

Syndicat d'initiative, place de l'Ancienne Gare ✆ 05 49 48 80 36, Fax 05 49 48 80 36

in Port de Salles South: 7 km by D 8 and secondary road – ✉ 86150

Val de Vienne without rest
– ✆ 05 49 48 27 27 – info@hotel-valdevienne.com – Fax 05 49 48 47 47 – Closed 20 December-5 January
20 rm – †€ 65/78 ††€ 65/130, ☕ € 12 – 1 suite
◆ Deep in the countryside, on the banks of the Vienne, this hotel provides quiet and functional rooms with terraces. Pleasant lounge bar on the veranda overlooking the pool.

L'ISLE-SUR-LA-SORGUE – 84 Vaucluse – 332 D10 – pop. 16 971 – alt. 57 m – ✉ 84800
Provence 42 **E1**

Paris 693 – Apt 34 – Avignon 23 – Carpentras 18 – Cavaillon 11 – Orange 35

Office de tourisme, place de la Liberté ✆ 04 90 38 04 78, Fax 04 90 38 35 43

Decoration★ of Notre-Dame des Anges collegiate church.

★ du Thor church West: 5 km.

Les Névons without rest
chemin des Névons , (behind the mail) – ✆ 04 90 20 72 00 – info@hotel-les-nevons.com – Fax 04 90 20 56 20 – Closed 17 December-22 January
44 rm – †€ 51/77 ††€ 51/77, ☕ € 8,50
◆ This modern hotel has functional rooms. Those in the second building are more spacious and have a balcony overlooking the river. Solarium and swimming pool on the roof.

La Prévôté with rm
4 bis r. J.-J.-Rousseau , (behind the church) – ✆ 04 90 38 57 29 – contact@la-prevote.fr – Fax 04 90 38 57 29 – Closed 1st-13 March, 17 November-5 December, Wednesday except July-August and Tuesday
5 rm ☕ – †€ 80/160 ††€ 90/170 – **Rest** – Menu (€ 20), € 26 (weekday lunch), € 43/68 – Carte approx. € 61
◆ Set in a former convent, this restaurant has a rustic dining area with bay windows that open out onto the Sorgue river. Serving modern meals. Individualised rooms also available.

L'Oustau de l'Isle

147 Chemin du Bosquet, 1 km via rte d'Apt – ✆ 04 90 20 81 36 – contact@restaurant-oustau.com – Fax 04 90 38 50 07 – Closed 12 November-5 December, 12-30 January, Wednesday except dinner mid June-mid September and Tuesday

Rest – Menu (€ 19), € 28/50 – Carte € 37/54

◆ This farmhouse is home to a restaurant with an attractive, shaded terrace and two refined dining areas with large-scale Modigliani reproductions. Regional cuisine served.

Le Vivier (Patrick Fischnaller)

800 cours F. Peyre (rte Carpentras) – ✆ 04 90 38 52 80 – info.levivier@wanadoo.fr – Closed 28 August-4 September, 2-8 January, 24 February-17 March, Thursday lunch in July-August, Sunday dinner from September to June, Friday lunch, Saturday lunch and Monday

Rest – Menu € 25 (weekday lunch), € 38/58 – Carte € 38/58

Spec. Assiette façon tapas. Baron et côtelette d'agneau de Provence, croûte de noisette. Interprétation de la pêche melba.

◆ Very modern, delicate cuisine is the order of the day in this designer-style restaurant with bright colour scheme and windows overlooking the Sorgue. Charming service.

Café Fleurs

9 r. T.-Aubanel – ✆ 04 90 20 66 94 – contact@cafefleurs.com – Closed 1st-26 December, Tuesday and Wednesday

Rest – Menu (€ 21), € 23 (weekday lunch), € 38/49 – Carte € 34/46

◆ Charming modern restaurant with two cosy, Provence-style dining rooms (exhibitions by local artists). Delightful shaded terrace at the water's edge.

Le Jardin du Quai

91 av. J. Guigue, (near the station) – ✆ 04 90 20 14 98 – contact@danielhebet.com – Fax 04 90 20 31 92

Rest – Menu € 30 (weekday lunch)/40

◆ This bistro, opposite the station, displays all the charm of bygone Provence. Market-inspired cuisine which lets the produce speak for itself.

North by D 938 and secondary road – ✉ 84740 Velleron

Hostellerie La Grangette

6 km – ✆ 04 90 20 00 77 – hostellerie-la-grangette@club-internet.fr – Fax 04 90 20 07 06 – Open 13 February-10 November

16 rm – **€ 89/218 €** 89/218 – ½ P € 97/161 – **Rest** – *(closed lunch and Tuesday except June-September) (number of covers limited, pre-book)* Menu € 47/71

◆ A Provençal farmhouse with a lively but refined atmosphere. Rooms with stylish décor and fine bed linen. Non-smokers only. Cuisine redolent of the south.

Apt road Southeast: 6 km by D 900 – ✉ 84800 L'Isle-sur-la-Sorgue

Le Mas des Grès

– ✆ 04 90 20 32 85 – info@masdesgres.com – Fax 04 90 20 21 45 – Open 8 March-11 November

15 rm – € 89/169 € 89/250, € 11 – ½ P € 88/138 – **Rest** – *(dinner only except July-August) (pre-book)* Menu € 20 (lunch)/35

◆ Not just a hotel, but also a house with character. Everything here speaks of summer: the welcome, the peace and quiet, simple rooms, garden and swimming pool. A pleasant restaurant with tables set up under the arbour and the plane trees. Market cuisine.

Southwest 4 km by D 938 (Cavaillon road) and secondary road – ✉ 84800 L'Isle-sur-la-Sorgue

Mas de Cure Bourse

120 chemin de serre – ✆ 04 90 38 16 58 – masdecurebourse@wanadoo.fr – Fax 04 90 38 52 31

13 rm – € 80/120 € 80/120, € 12 – ½ P € 86/106

Rest – *(closed 1st-8 January, Monday from November to February)* Menu € 26 (weekday lunch), € 40/55 – Carte € 37/50

◆ 18C house hidden among the orchards. Rustic interior, impeccable rooms (with Souleïado fabrics), swimming pool and a shaded garden provide relaxation and a sense of well-being. Southern cuisine in the Provençal dining room or under the ancient trees on the terrace.

L'ISLE-SUR-SEREIN – 89 Yonne – 319 H6 – pop. 716 – alt. 190 m – ✉ 89440 7 **B2**

Paris 209 – Auxerre 50 – Avallon 17 – Montbard 36 – Tonnerre 36

XX **Auberge du Pot d'Étain** with rm

24 r. Bouchardat – ✆ 03 86 33 88 10 – potdetain@ipoint.fr – Fax 03 86 33 90 93 – Closed 13-27 October, 2 February-2 March, Sunday dinner and Tuesday lunch except July-August and Monday

9 rm – €56/75 €56/75, ☕ €9 – ½ P €75

Rest – Menu €26/52 – Carte €41/56

♦ Regional cuisine, fine choice of Burgundy wines and elegant stylish rooms. A delightful country inn in the peaceful Serein valley, easily accessible from the A6 motorway.

ISPE – 40 Landes – 335 D8 – see Biscarrosse

LES ISSAMBRES – 83 Var – 340 P5 – ✉ 83380 French Riviera 41 **C3**

Paris 877 – Draguignan 40 – Fréjus 11 – St-Raphaël 14 – Ste-Maxime 9 – Toulon 99

Office de tourisme, place San-Peire ✆ 04 94 19 89 89, Fax 04 94 49 66 55

in San-Peire-sur-Mer – ✉ 83520

Le Provençal rm, VISA AE

D 559 – ✆ 04 94 55 32 33 – hotel-le-provencal@wanadoo.fr – Fax 04 94 55 32 34 – Open 11 February-14 October

27 rm – €63/120 €69/120, ☕ €11 – ½ P €75/100

Rest ***Les Mûriers*** – Menu €28/58 – Carte €38/75

♦ This U-shaped ochre building in the Golfe de St-Tropez overlooks the beach. Renovated bedrooms, some with sea-facing balconies. Mediterranean cuisine served in a dining room adorned with Provençal landscapes or in the shade of the terrace's mulberry trees.

at parc des Issambres – ✉ 83380 Les Issambres

La Quiétude rm, VISA AE

D 559 – ✆ 04 94 96 94 34 – laquietude@hotmail.com – Fax 04 94 49 67 82 – Open 10 March-8 November

20 rm – €48/73 €55/95, ☕ €9,50 – ½ P €56/77 – **Rest** – *(dinner only except Sunday)* Menu €27/36 – Carte €36/46

♦ 1960s house set in a small garden. Functional and colourful bedrooms; a few have views of the open sea. Enjoy a quiet meal looking out onto the sea from the restaurant terrace. Dishes full of maritime flavours.

in la calanque des Issambres – ✉ 83380 Les Issambres

Les Calanques VISA

– ✆ 04 98 11 36 36 – contact@french-riviera-hotel.com – Fax 04 98 11 36 37 – Open 16 March-14 October

12 rm – €58/95 €84/136, ☕ €12 – ½ P €58/97 – **Rest** – *(closed Sunday and Monday) (dinner only)* Menu €23/32 – Carte €31/42

♦ A recent building in regional style with direct access to the beach. Provençal rooms with a theme; those on the 2nd floor have a terrace with a sea view. Snacks and wine by the glass in this modern, colourful bistro setting.

XX **Chante-Mer** VISA

in the village – ✆ 04 94 96 93 23 – Fax 04 94 96 88 49 – Closed 15 December-31 January, Sunday dinner from October to Easter, Tuesday lunch and Monday

Rest – Menu €24/45 – Carte €36/68

♦ A small but welcoming dining area with light wooden wainscoting. Attractively presented tables, mouth-watering traditional menu. Summer dining outdoors.

ISSOIRE – 63 Puy-de-Dôme – 326 G9 – pop. 13 773 – alt. 400 m – ✉ 63500 Auvergne 5 **B2**

Paris 446 – Clermont-Ferrand 36 – Le Puy-en-Velay 94 – Thiers 56

Office de tourisme, place Charles de Gaulle ✆ 04 73 89 15 90, Fax 04 73 89 96 13

Former St-Austremoine abbey church ★★ Z.

ISSOIRE

Altaroche (Pl.) . . . . Z 2
Ambert (R. d') . . . . Y
Ancienne Caserne (R. de l') . . Z 3
Berbiziale (R. de la) . . . . Y
Buisson (Bd A.) . . . . Y
Cerf Volant (R. du) . . . . Y 4
Châteaudun (R. de) . . . . Z 5
Cibrand (Bd J.) . . . . Y
Dr-Sauvat (R.) . . . . Z
Duprat (Pl. Ch.) . . . . Y
Espagnon (R. d') . . . . Z
Foirail (Pl. du) . . . . Y
Fours (R. des) . . . . Z
Gambetta (R.) . . . . Z 6
Gare (Av. de la) . . . . Z 9
Gaulle (Pl. du Gén.-de) . . . . . . Y
Gauttier (R. Eugène) . . . . Y
Haïnl (Bd G.) . . . . Z
Hauterive (R. E. d') . . . . Z
Libération (Av. de la) . . . . Z 10
Manlière (Bd de la) . . . . Z
Mas (R. du) . . . . Y
Montagne (Pl. de la) . . . . Y
Notre-Dame des Filles (R.) . . . Z 12
Palais (R. du) . . . . Y
Pomel (Pl. N.) . . . . Z 13
Ponteil (R. du) . . . . Y 16
Pont (R. du) . . . . Z 14
Postillon (R. du) . . . . Z
République (Pl. de la) . . . . Z
St-Avit (Pl.) . . . . Y 22
Sous-Préfecture (Bd de la) . . . Z
Terraille (R. de la) . . . . Z 24
Triozon-Bayle (Bd) . . . . YZ 25
Verdun (Pl. de) . . . . Z 26
8 Mai (Av. du) . . . . Y 30

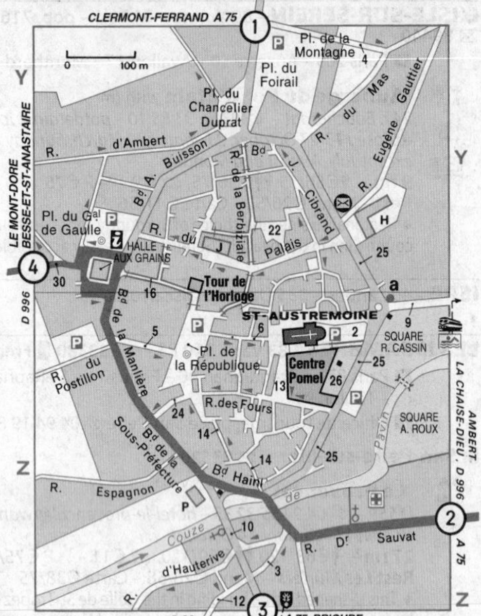

Le Pariou

18 av. Kennedy, 1 km via ① – ✆ 04 73 55 90 37 – info@hotel-pariou.com – Fax 04 73 55 96 16 – Closed 19 December-4 January
54 rm – 🚹€ 67/68 🚹🚹€ 70/72, ☕ € 11 – ½ P € 64
Rest *Le Jardin* – *(closed Saturday lunch 15 August-15 June, Sunday and Monday)* Menu (€ 13,50), € 20 (weekdays)/38 – Carte € 30/43
♦ 1950s building with guestrooms that that are gradually being renovated. Modern furniture, with rooms in the new wing offering more space. Two dining rooms, one painted in southern colours and overlooking the garden. Modern food.

Le Relais with rm

1 av. de la Gare – ✆ 04 73 89 16 61 – lerelais-issoire@laposte.net – Fax 04 73 89 55 62 – Closed 19-31 October, 2-15 February YZ **a**
6 rm – 🚹€ 36/48 🚹🚹€ 36/48, ☕ € 6 – ½ P € 42/45 – **Rest** – *(closed Sunday dinner and Monday)* Menu € 11/35 – Carte € 17/33
♦ Former post house, a stone's throw from St. Austremoine abbey church. Spacious and colourful dining room. Traditional cuisine and regional specialities. Small rooms.

in Varennes-sur-Usson 5 km by ② and D 996 – pop. 161 – alt. 315 m – ✉ 63500

Les Baudarts without rest

– ✆ 04 73 89 05 51 – Open 1st May-30 September
4 rm ☕ – 🚹€ 65/70 🚹🚹€ 80/85
♦ This impressive manor set in a park proudly displays artwork throughout the house. Rooms in three themes – Africa, Teddy Bear and Lace, and Loft.

in St-Rémy-de-Chargnat 7 km by ② and D 999 – pop. 461 – alt. 400 m – ✉ 63500

Château de la Vernède without rest

– ✆ 04 73 71 07 03 – chateauvernede@aol.com – Fax 04 73 71 07 03
5 rm ☕ – 🚹€ 68 🚹🚹€ 75/100
♦ This former hunting lodge (1850) once owned by Queen Margot is now home to guestrooms adorned with antique furnishings and fresh flowers. Leisure activities include billiards and trout fishing.

in Sarpoil 10 km by ② and D 999 – ✉ 63490 St-Jean-en-Val

XX **La Bergerie**

– ✆ 04 73 71 02 54 – Fax 04 73 71 01 99 – *Closed 15-23 June, 14-22 September, 6-29 January, Sunday dinner from September to June and Monday*

Rest – *(number of covers limited, pre-book)* Menu € 16 (weekdays)/62 – Carte € 40/64

◆ Catch an enticing glimpse of the kitchens and rotisserie as you enter this restaurant. Classic dining room with an open fire in winter and a menu focusing on contemporary dishes.

in Perrier 5 km by ④ and D 996 – pop. 775 – alt. 415 m – ✉ 63500

XX **La Cour Carrée** with rm

av. Tramot – ✆ 04 73 55 15 55 – *contact@cour-carree.com* – *Fax 04 73 55 98 26* – *Closed 22 December-11 January, Wednesday lunch, Saturday lunch, Sunday dinner and Monday 15 September-15 June and lunch except Sunday 15 June-15 September*

3 rm – †€ 70/90 ††€ 70/90, ☕ € 10 – ½ P € 73/83 – **Rest** – *(number of covers limited, pre-book)* Menu € 28/40

◆ The vaulted vat room of a winegrower's house dating from 1830 has been converted into a restaurant. Terrace in the square courtyard shaded by a horse chestnut tree. Non-smoking.

ISSONCOURT – 55 Meuse – 307 C5 – pop. 119 – alt. 260 m – ✉ 55220 Les Trois Domaines

26 **A2**

▶ Paris 265 – Bar-le-Duc 28 – St-Mihiel 28 – Verdun 28

XX **Relais de la Voie Sacrée** with rm

1, Voie Sacrée – ✆ 03 29 70 70 46 – *christian-caillet@wanadoo.fr* – *Fax 03 29 70 75 75* – *Closed January, February, Sunday dinner (except hotel) from October to May and Monday*

7 rm – †€ 58 ††€ 58, ☕ € 9 – ½ P € 72 – **Rest** – Menu € 18/58 – Carte € 33/65

◆ An inn on the famous Holy Way, which changed the outcome of the Battle of Verdun. A rustic-bourgeois dining room, shaded terrace and enticing wine list.

ISSOUDUN – 36 Indre – 323 H5 – pop. 13 685 – alt. 130 m – ✉ 36100

Dordogne-Berry-Limousin

12 **C3**

▶ Paris 244 – Bourges 37 – Châteauroux 29 – Tours 127 – Vierzon 35

Syndicat d'initiative, place Saint-Cyr ✆ 02 54 21 74 02, Fax 02 54 03 03 36

des Sarrays Les Sarrays, Southwest: 12 km by D 151 and secondary road, ✆ 02 54 49 54 49.

Musée de l'hospice St-Roch★: Jesse tree ★ in the chapel and apothecary's ★ AB.

Plan on next page

Hôtel La Cognette

r. des Minimes – ✆ 02 54 03 59 59 – *lacognettehotel@wanadoo.fr* – *Fax 02 54 03 13 03* A **e**

13 rm – †€ 75/125 ††€ 75/125, ☕ € 15 – 3 suites – ½ P € 85/125

Rest ***La Cognette*** – see restaurant listing

◆ Air-conditioned rooms with period furniture, named after famous people. Most of them are on the level of the small garden where breakfast is served in summer.

XXX **Rest. La Cognette** (Alain Nonnet et Jean-Jacques Daumy)

bd Stalingrad – ✆ 02 54 03 59 59 – *lacognette@wanadoo.fr* – *Fax 02 54 03 13 03* – *Closed January, Sunday dinner, Tuesday lunch and Monday from October to May* A **z**

Rest – *(pre-book)* Menu (€ 28), € 31/70 – Carte € 48/70

Spec. Crème de lentilles vertes du Berry aux truffes. Cannelloni d'huîtres, jus de cresson et gingembre. Massepain d'Issoudun à la fleur d'oranger. **Wines** Reuilly, Quincy.

◆ This inn was the inspiration for Balzac's La Rabouilleuse and boasts a rich, refined decor, typical of the 19th century. Generous cuisine.

Avenier (R. de l')	B	2	Estienne-d'Orves (R. d')	B	13	Poterie (R. de la)	A	20
Bons-Enfants (R. des)	B	5	Fossés-de-Villatte (R. des)	B	14	Quatre-Vents (R. des)	B	21
Capucins (R. des)	B	6	Gaulle (Av. Ch. de)	B	15	République (R. de la)	AB	22
Casanova (R. D.)	A	7	Hospices St-Roch (R.)	B	16	Roosevelt (Bd Prés.)	B	24
Chinault (Av. de)	A	8	Minimes (R. des)	A	17	St-Martin (R.)	B	25
Croix-de-Pierre (Pl. de la)	B	9	Père-Jules-Chevalier (R. du)	B	18	Semard (R. P.)	A	27
Dormoy (Bd M.)	A	10	Ponts (R. des)	A	19	Stalingrad (Bd de)	A	28
Entrée-de-Villatte (R.)	B	12				10-Juin (Pl. du)	A	32

in Diou by ①: 12 km on D 918 – pop. 235 – alt. 130 m – ✉ 36260

XX **L'Aubergeade**

rte d'Issoudun – ✆ 02 54 49 22 28 – jacky.patron@wanadoo.fr – Fax 02 54 49 27 48 – Closed Sunday dinner and Wednesday dinner

Rest – Menu € 20 (weekdays)/36 – Carte € 42/53

◆ A friendly inn in a pretty flower-decked village on the River Théols. Simple, fresh dining room, terrace overlooking the garden, cuisine in keeping with current tastes.

ISSY-LES-MOULINEAUX – 92 Hauts-de-Seine – 311 J3 – 101 25 – see Paris, Area

ISTRES – 13 Bouches-du-Rhône – 340 E5 – pop. 38 993 – alt. 32 m – ✉ 13800

Provence 40 **A3**

Paris 745 – Arles 46 – Marseille 55 – Martigues 14 – Salon-de-Provence 25

Office de tourisme, 30, allées Jean Jaurés ✆ 04 42 81 76 00, Fax 04 42 81 76 15

Plan on next page

Le Castellan without rest

pl. Ste-Catherine – ✆ 04 42 55 13 09 – renseignements@hotel-lecastellan.com – Fax 04 42 56 91 36 AX **a**

17 rm – †€ 49 ††€ 58, ☕ € 6,50

◆ Close to the Greco-Ligurian Place du Castellan. Rooms are spacious and airy, some decorated in Provençal style. A friendly welcome at this impeccably well-kept hotel.

XX **La Table de Sébastien**

7 av. H. Boucher – ✆ 04 42 55 16 01 – contact@latabledesebastien.fr – Fax 04 42 55 95 02 – Closed 6-13 April, 18-31 August, 22 December-3 January, Sunday dinner and Monday AX **n**

Rest – Menu € 28/83 – Carte € 60/77

◆ Deliciously inventive cuisine prepared by a young chef and complemented by a fine selection of regional wines. Choose between the renovated dining room or the shaded courtyard terrace.

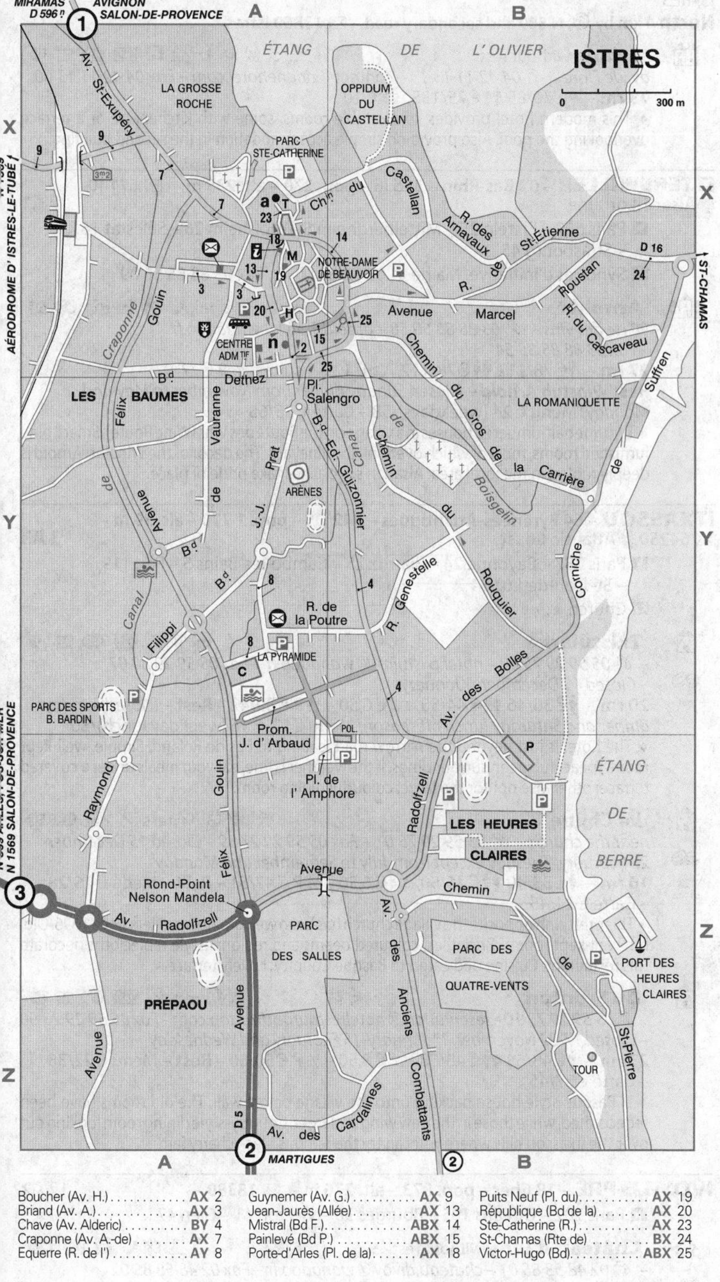

Boucher (Av. H.)	**AX** 2	Guynemer (Av. G.)	**AX** 9	Puits Neuf (Pl. du)	**AX** 19
Briand (Av. A.)	**AX** 3	Jean-Jaurès (Allée)	**AX** 13	République (Bd de la)	**AX** 20
Chave (Av. Alderic)	**BY** 4	Mistral (Bd F.)	**ABX** 14	Ste-Catherine (R.)	**AX** 23
Craponne (Av. A.-de)	**AX** 7	Painlevé (Bd P.)	**ABX** 15	St-Chamas (Rte de)	**BX** 24
Equerre (R. de l')	**AY** 8	Porte-d'Arles (Pl. de la)	**AX** 18	Victor-Hugo (Bd)	**ABX** 25

North **4 km by ③, N 569 and secondary road – ✉ 13800 Istres**

Ariane without rest

av. de Flore – ✆ 04 42 11 13 13 – contact@arianehotel.com – Fax 04 42 11 13 00

73 rm – †€ 70/85 ††€ 75/135, ☕ € 10

◆ This modern hotel provides comfortable rooms, some with kitchenette or a terrace overlooking the pool. Also providing simple accommodation in the second building.

ITTERSWILLER – 67 Bas-Rhin – 315 I6 – pop. 270 – alt. 235 m – ✉ 67140

Alsace-Lorraine 2 **C1**

Paris 502 – Erstein 25 – Mittelbergheim 5 – Molsheim 26 – Sélestat 16 – Strasbourg 45

Syndicat d'initiative, Mairie ✆ 03 88 85 50 12, Fax 03 88 85 56 09

Arnold

98 rte des vins – ✆ 03 88 85 50 58 – arnold-hotel@wanadoo.fr – Fax 03 88 85 55 54

27 rm – †€ 78/112 ††€ 78/112, ☕ € 12 – 1 suite – ½ P € 77/97

Rest *Winstub Arnold* – *(closed Sunday dinner from November to May and Monday)* Menu € 24 (weekdays)/58 – Carte € 35/65

◆ Two fine half-timbered houses in a village on the Route des Vins (Wine Route). Smart, pine furnished rooms, most of which overlook the vineyard. The decor of the Winstub Arnold is deeply rooted in the local area. Alsatian specialities take pride of place.

ITXASSOU – 64 Pyrénées-Atlantiques – 342 D5 – pop. 1 770 – alt. 39 m – ✉ 64250

Atlantic Coast 3 **A3**

Paris 787 – Bayonne 24 – Biarritz 25 – Cambo-les-Bains 5 – Pau 119 – St-Jean-de-Luz 34

Church ★.

Txistulari

– ✆ 05 59 29 75 09 – hotel.txistulari@wanadoo.fr – Fax 05 59 29 80 07 – Closed 15 December-6 January

20 rm – †€ 36/46 ††€ 44/50, ☕ € 6,50 – ½ P € 39/42 – **Rest** – *(closed Sunday dinner and Saturday lunch off season)* Menu € 12, € 16 (weekday lunch)/30

◆ The hotel is just beyond the narrow road leading to Pas de Roland. Simple, well-kept rooms; peaceful green surroundings. If the weather is fine, eat your meals under a covered terrace; otherwise opt for the large, colourful dining room.

Le Chêne

near the church – ✆ 05 59 29 75 01 – Fax 05 59 29 27 39 – Closed 15 December-28 February, Tuesday except from July to September and Monday

16 rm – †€ 35/40 ††€ 46/50, ☕ € 6,50 – ½ P € 47/51 – **Rest** – Menu € 16/28 – Carte € 24/45

◆ This pretty inn opposite the village church has been welcoming travellers since 1696. Old, but well-kept rooms. Brick tiles, coloured beams and regional-style tablecloths decorate this restaurant. Cuisine dedicated to Basque Country. Lovely terrace.

Du Fronton

– ✆ 05 59 29 75 10 – reservation@hotelrestaurantfronton.com – Fax 05 59 29 23 50 – Closed 17-22 November, 1st January-15 February and Wednesday

23 rm – †€ 48/68 ††€ 48/68, ☕ € 8,50 – ½ P € 50/60 – **Rest** – Menu € 22/38 – Carte € 37/45

◆ A Basque-style house backing onto the village pelota wall. The old rooms have been redecorated, while those in the new wing are larger. Country-style dining room looking out over the Itxassou hills where you can try the famous black cherry jam.

IVOY-LE-PRÉ – 18 Cher – pop. 873 – alt. 276 m – ✉ 18380 12 **C2**

Paris 202 – Orléans 105 – Bourges 38 – Vierzon 41 – Gien 47

Château d'Ivoy without rest

– ✆ 02 48 58 85 01 – chateau.divoy@wanadoo.fr – Fax 02 48 58 85 02

5 rm ☕ – †€ 140 ††€ 160/195

◆ This 16-17C château in a fine estate has quite a history, hosting Henry IV and, rather more recently, the shooting of the film *Le Grand Meaulnes*. Country house atmosphere.

IVRY-LA-BATAILLE – 27 Eure – 304 I8 – pop. 2 639 – alt. 54 m – ✉ 27540
Normandy 33 **D2**

Paris 75 – Anet 6 – Dreux 21 – Évreux 36 – Mantes-la-Jolie 25 – Pacy-sur-Eure 17

de La Chaussée d'Ivry La Chaussée-d'Ivry, North: 2 km, ✆ 02 37 63 06 30.

Moulin d'Ivry VISA
10 r. Henri IV – ✆ 02 32 36 40 51 – Fax 02 32 26 05 15 – Closed 7-21 October, 9 February-3 March, Monday and Tuesday except holidays
Rest – Menu € 30/50 – Carte € 48/79
◆ An old mill with several small country-style rooms, with a deliberately antiquated charm. A garden and terrace pleasantly situated on the banks of the River Eure. Classic dishes.

JANVRY – 91 Essonne – 101 33 – see Paris, Area

JARNAC – 16 Charente – 324 I5 – pop. 4 659 – alt. 26 m – ✉ 16200
Atlantic Coast 38 **B3**

Paris 475 – Angoulême 31 – Barbezieux 30 – Bordeaux 113 – Cognac 15 – Jonzac 41

Office de tourisme, place du Château ✆ 05 45 81 09 30, Fax 05 45 36 52 45

Donation François-Mitterrand - Courvoisier House - Louis-Royer House.

Château St-Martial without rest VISA
56 r. des Chabannes – ✆ 05 45 83 38 64 – brigitte.cariou@wanadoo.fr – Fax 05 45 83 38 38 – Closed 25 October-5 November, 27 December-4 January and 21 February-8 March
5 rm – €70/110 €85/130
◆ The Bisquit family, famous for its cognac, lived in this splendid 19C chateau. Paintings, period furniture, spacious comfortable rooms and pleasant wooded park.

Du Château VISA AE
15 pl. du Château – ✆ 05 45 81 07 17 – contact@restaurant-du-chateau.com – Fax 05 45 35 35 71 – Closed Sunday dinner and Monday
Rest – Menu € 26/64 bi – Carte € 56/63
◆ Friendly restaurant next-door to the storehouse of the Maison Courvoisier. The local-born chef selects excellent regional produce for his high-quality cuisine. Non-smoking.

in Bourg-Charente West: 6 km by N 141 and secondary road – pop. 753 – alt. 14 m – ✉ 16200

La Ribaudière (Thierry Verrat) VISA AE
2 pl. du port – ✆ 05 45 81 30 54 – la.ribaudiere@wanadoo.fr – Fax 05 45 81 28 05 – Closed 20 October-7 November, February school holidays, Sunday dinner, Tuesday lunch and Monday
Rest – Menu € 38/74 – Carte € 65/88
Spec. Soupe de cèpes et foie gras de canard poêlé (1st September to 15 February.). Pièce de bœuf limousin légèrement fumé aux sarments de vigne. Ravioles d'ananas à la noix de coco. **Wines** Vin de pays Charentais.
◆ A popular, excellent address on the Left Bank of the Charente: distinctly designer-inspired decor, fine brandy list, tasty fashionable menus and a riverside terrace.

in Bassac Southeast: 7 km by N 141 and D 22 – pop. 461 – alt. 20 m – ✉ 16120

L'Essille VISA AE
r. de Condé – ✆ 05 45 81 94 13 – l.essille@wanadoo.fr – Fax 05 45 81 97 26 – Closed 1st-8 January
14 rm – €50 €50, € 9 – ½ P € 58 – **Rest** – *(closed Saturday lunch and Sunday dinner)* Menu € 16 (weekday lunch), € 25/45 – Carte € 43/49
◆ Family run hotel with a charming welcome, a stone's throw from the abbey. Spacious revamped rooms with period furniture. Dining room-veranda overlooking the park; traditional cuisine and fine cognac list (over 100 choices).

JARVILLE-LA-MALGRANGE – 54 Meurthe-et-Moselle – 307 I6 – see Nancy

JAUJAC – 07 Ardèche – **331** H6 – **pop. 1 065** – **alt. 450 m** – ✉ **07380**
Lyon - Rhone Valley 44 **A3**

Paris 616 – Lyon 185 – Montélimar 59 – Pierrelatte 71

Syndicat d'initiative, place du Champ de Mars ✆ 04 75 93 28 54, Fax 04 75 93 28 54

Le Rucher des Roudils without rest

Les Roudils, 4 km north-west – ✆ 04 75 93 21 11 – le-rucher-des-roudils@wanadoo.fr – Open 2 April-14 November

3 rm – €60 €60

◆ This hotel overlooks the Tanargue mountains, with charming rooms and a lounge with a Cevennes-style fireplace.

JAUSIERS – **04 Alpes-de-Haute-Provence** – **334** I6 – **see Barcelonnette**

JERSEY (ÎLE) – **JSY Jersey** – **309** J1 – **see Île de Jersey**

JOIGNY – **89 Yonne** – **319** D4 – **pop. 10 032** – **alt. 79 m** – ✉ **89300**
Burgundy-Jura 7 **B1**

Paris 144 – Auxerre 28 – Gien 74 – Montargis 59 – Sens 33 – Troyes 76

Office de tourisme, 4, quai Ragobert ✆ 03 86 62 11 05, Fax 03 86 91 76 38

18 du Roncemay Chassy Château du Roncemay, by Montargis road: 18 km, ✆ 03 86 73 50 50.

Smiling Virgin ★ in St-Thibault church A **E** - Côte St-Jacques★ ★ 1,5 km by D 20 A.

La Côte St-Jacques (Jean-Michel Lorain)

14 fg de Paris – rm, VISA AE

✆ 03 86 62 09 70 – lorain@relaischateaux.com – Fax 03 86 91 49 70 – Closed 5-29 January, Monday lunch and Tuesday lunch A **r**

31 rm – €150/460 €150/460, €32 – 1 suite – ½ P €235/300

Rest – *(closed Mon lunchtime and Tues lunchtime from Nov to Apr except public holidays) (pre-book Sat - Sun)* Menu €85 bi (weekday lunch), €135/165 – Carte €101/212

Spec. Genèse d'un plat sur le thème de l'huître. Bar légèrement fumé au caviar osciètre. Noix de ris de veau au gingembre, petits oignons, rhubarbe et radis roses. **Wines** Bourgogne blanc, Irancy.

◆ A luxury hotel facing the Yonne with stylish rooms. Pool, spa, private boat (river trips) and shop. The prestigious restaurant is renowned for its creative cuisine made with only the finest produce. Sumptuous wine list.

Rive Gauche rm, rest, VISA AE

r. Port-au-Bois – ✆ 03 86 91 46 66 – contact@hotel-le-rive-gauche.fr – Fax 03 86 91 46 93 A **s**

42 rm – €70/110 €70/110, €9,50 – ½ P €68

Rest – *(closed Sunday dinner from November to Easter)* Menu (€16 bi), €19 (weekday lunch), €28/35 – Carte €34/49

◆ Well located on the left bank of the Yonne. Spacious, practical and light rooms. Pleasant park with ornamental lake and helicopter landing pad. The veranda/dining room and terrace both overlook the river.

in Épineau-les-Voves 7.5 km by ② – **pop. 665** – **alt. 92 m** – ✉ **89400**

L'Orée des Champs VISA

(D 606) – ✆ 03 86 91 20 39 – Fax 03 86 91 24 92 – Closed 15-31 August, February holidays, Thursday dinner, Sunday dinner, Monday dinner, Tuesday dinner and Wednesday

Rest – Menu (€18), €23 (weekdays)/40 – Carte €33/47

◆ The appealing dining room attractively combines red and ochre, as well as serving traditional cuisine. Pleasant shaded terrace and garden with a children's playground.

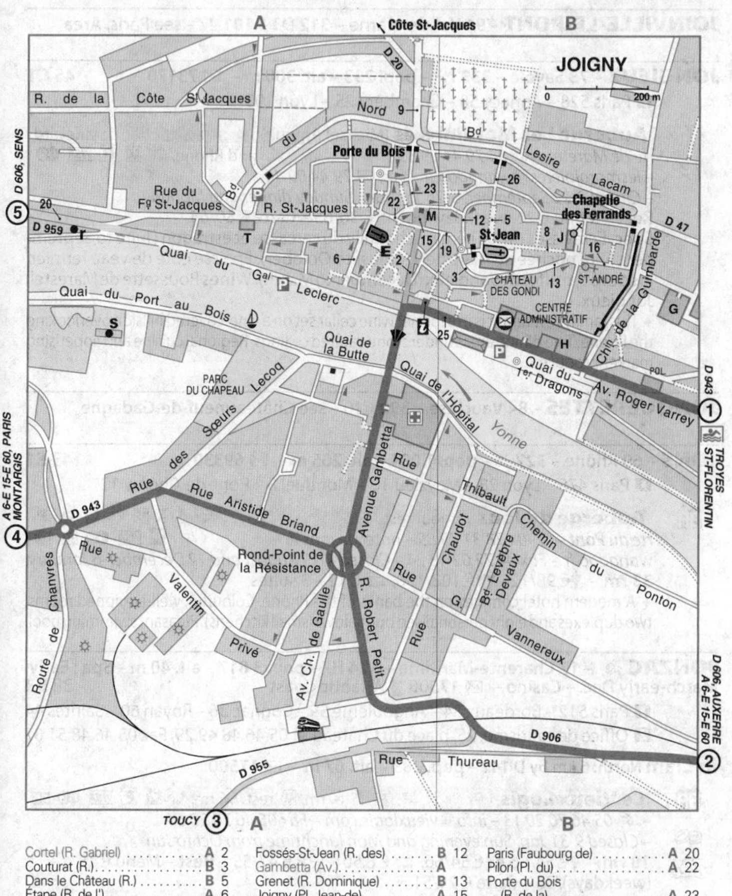

Street			Street			Street		
Cortel (R. Gabriel)	A	2	Fossés-St-Jean (R. des)	B	12	Paris (Faubourg de)	A	20
Couturat (R.)	B	3	Gambetta (Av.)	A		Pilori (Pl. du)	A	22
Dans le Château (R.)	B	5	Grenet (R. Dominique)	B	13	Porte du Bois (R. de la)	A	23
Étape (R. de l')	A	6	Joigny (Pl. Jean-de)	A	15	Ragobert (Quai Henri)	AB	25
Ferrand (R. Jacques)	B	8	Moines (R. des)	B	16	Tour Carrée (R. de la)	B	26
Forêt d'Othe (Av. de la)	A	9	Montant au Palais (R.)	B	19			

JOINVILLE – 52 Haute-Marne – 313 K3 – pop. 4 380 – alt. 195 m – ✉ 52300

Northern France and the Paris Region 14 **C2**

Paris 244 – Bar-le-Duc 54 – Bar-sur-Aube 47 – Chaumont 44 – St-Dizier 32

Syndicat d'initiative, place Saunoise ✆ 03 25 94 17 90, Fax 03 25 94 68 93

Château du Grand Jardin★.

Le Soleil d'Or

rest, VISA MC AE

9 r. des Capucins – ✆ 03 25 94 15 66 – info@hotellesoleildor.com – Fax 03 25 94 39 02 – Closed 15-28 February

23 rm – †€ 55/100 ††€ 65/130, ☕ € 10 – ½ P € 75/90

Rest – *(closed 18-31 August, 16-28 February, Sunday dinner, Tuesday lunch and Monday)* Menu € 20 (weekdays)/50 – Carte € 48/62

◆ Warm house dating back to the 17C, in the birthplace of the De Guise family. Rooms undergoing renovation in stages; plain decor that is tasteful in the most recent rooms. Neo-gothic restaurant with medieval sculpture and contemporary paintings.

JOINVILLE-LE-PONT – 94 Val-de-Marne – 312 D3 – 101 27 – see Paris, Area

JONGIEUX – 73 Savoie – 333 H3 – pop. 233 – alt. 300 m – ✉ 73170 45 C1

Paris 528 – Annecy 58 – Chambéry 25 – Lyon 103

Auberge Les Morainières (Michaël Arnoult) ← vineyard and Rhône, VISA
rte de Marétel – ☎ 04 79 44 09 39 – lesmorainieres@wanadoo.fr – Fax 04 79 44 09 46 – Closed 8-22 September, 5-26 January, Sunday dinner and Monday
Rest – Menu € 26 (weekday lunch), € 36/65 – Carte € 50/64
Spec. Écrevisses du lac Léman, chantilly de carcasse et estragon (June to September). Féra pochée au marestel (August to October). Épaisse côte de veau fermier, jus de rôti, truffes de Jongieux (December to March). **Wines** Roussette de Marestel, Jongieux.

◆ This family restaurant is in a former wine cellar set on a vine-covered hillside overlooking the Rhone. Two dining areas under stone vaulted ceilings. Regional cuisine and appetising market produce.

JONQUERETTES – 84 Vaucluse – 332 C10 – see Châteauneuf-de-Gadagne

JONS – 69 Rhône – 327 J5 – pop. 1 094 – alt. 205 m – ✉ 69330 43 E1

Paris 476 – Lyon 28 – Meyzieu 10 – Montluel 8 – Pont-de-Chéruy 12

Auberge de Jons without rest
rte du Pont – ☎ 04 78 31 29 85 – hotel.de.jons@wanadoo.fr – Fax 04 72 02 48 24 – Closed 4-19 August and 22 December-6 January
33 rm – €98/125 €108/130, € 12 – 3 suites

◆ A modern hotel complex on the banks of the Rhône. Colourful, well-equipped rooms, two duplexes and eight personalised bungalows (small kitchens). Pleasant swimming pool.

JONZAC – 17 Charente-Maritime – 324 H7 – pop. 3 817 – alt. 40 m – Spa : Early March-early Dec. – Casino – ✉ 17500 Atlantic Coast 38 B3

Paris 512 – Bordeaux 84 – Angoulême 59 – Cognac 36 – Royan 60 – Saintes 44

Office de tourisme, 25, place du Château ☎ 05 46 48 49 29, Fax 05 46 48 51 07

in Clam North: 6 km by D 142 – pop. 283 – alt. 67 m – ✉ 17500

Le Vieux Logis rm, rest, rm, VISA
– ☎ 05 46 70 20 13 – info@vieuxlogis.com – Fax 05 46 70 20 64 – Closed 9-31 Jan, Sun evening and Mon lunchtime from Oct to Jun
10 rm – €54/66 €54/66, € 8,50 – ½ P € 47/55 – **Rest** – Menu € 15 (weekdays)/38 – Carte € 25/51

◆ Hotel in the heart of the Jonzac region. Photographs by the owner on display. Contemporary, well kept, ground floor rooms with terrace. The chef's regional cuisine is served in one of three neo-rustic dining rooms.

JOUARRE – 77 Seine-et-Marne – 312 H2 – see La Ferté-sous-Jouarre

JOUCAS – 84 Vaucluse – 332 E10 – pop. 317 – alt. 263 m – ✉ 84220 42 E1

Paris 716 – Apt 14 – Avignon 42 – Carpentras 32 – Cavaillon 22

Le Mas des Herbes Blanches ← le Luberon, VISA
rte Murs: 2.5 km – ☎ 04 90 05 79 79 – reservation@herbesblanches.com – Fax 04 90 05 71 96 – Closed 2 January-6 March
19 rm – €149/350 €149/350, € 23 – 2 suites
Rest – *(closed Tuesday and Wednesday from 15 October to 16 April)* Menu € 49 (weekday lunch), € 55/105 – Carte € 97/122
Spec. Pressé de foie gras de canard, fine gelée à l'arabica. Rouget de roche et mosaïque de jambon cru. Pommes de ris de veau laquées, jus mixé d' anchois, câpres et crème de chou fleur. **Wines** Côtes du Lubéron, Côtes du Ventoux.

◆ This superb establishment, set against the Vaucluse plateau and overlooking the Apt plain, houses individually decorated rooms which have either a balcony or private garden. Chic restaurant and terrace offering an unforgettable view over Mount Lubéron. Excellent modern cuisine.

Hostellerie Le Phébus (Xavier Mathieu) ≤ le Lubéron,
rte de Murs – *04 90 05 78 83* rm, rm, VISA
– phebus@relaischateaux.com – Fax 04 90 05 73 61 – Open 15 March-15 October
16 rm – €245/300 €245/300, €20 – 8 suites – ½ P €185/205
Rest *Restaurant Xavier Mathieu* – *(closed Tuesday lunchtime, Wednesday lunchtime and Thursday lunchtime)* Menu €60/110 – Carte €86/125
Rest *Le Café de la Fontaine* – *(open June-September) (lunch only)* Menu €45/65 – Carte €49/76
Spec. Pied d'agneau truffé, brouillade aux truffes (spring). Dos de loup rôti à l'huile d'argan vanillée (spring-summer). Agneau confit à l'os, effiloché puis roulé dans sa croûte (spring-summer). **Wines** Côtes du Ventoux, Côtes du Lubéron.
♦ This contemporary hotel stands alone in the Garrigue region. Lovely Provençal-style rooms, some with a private swimming pool. Refined decor and covered terrace, from which there is a splendid view over the Lubéron; creative cuisine.

Le Mas du Loriot ≤ le Lubéron, rm, VISA
rte de Murs, 4 km – 04 90 72 62 62 – mas.du.loriot@wanadoo.fr
– Fax 04 90 72 62 54 – Open 15 March-15 November
8 rm – €52/130 €52/130, €12 – ½ P €77/102 – **Rest** – *(closed Tuesday, Thursday, Saturday and Sunday) (dinner only)* Menu €30
♦ Family house hidden away in the garrigue, with the Lubéron as a backdrop. Small, up-to-the-minute rooms on the garden level. Pleasant swimming pool perfumed by lavender.

JOUÉ-LÈS-TOURS – 37 Indre-et-Loire – 317 M4 – see Tours

JOUGNE – 25 Doubs – 321 I6 – pop. 1 198 – alt. 1 001 m – Winter sports : to Métabief 880/1 450 m 22 – ✉ 25370 Burgundy-Jura 17 C3

Paris 464 – Besançon 79 – Champagnole 50 – Lausanne 48 – Morez 49 – Pontarlier 20

La Couronne VISA
6 r. de l'Église – 03 81 49 10 50 – lacouronnejougne@wanadoo.fr
– Fax 03 81 49 19 77 – Closed November, Sunday dinner and Monday dinner except in season and school holidays
10 rm – €48 €62/64, €6,50 – ½ P €54/62 – **Rest** – Menu €18 (weekdays)/46 – Carte €34/55
♦ Near the church, this beautiful 18C house has been almost entirely renovated. Comfortable rooms, including some with views of the Monts du Jura. Warm setting in the restaurant and generous regional cuisine.

JOUILLAT – 23 Creuse – pop. 402 – alt. 396 m – ✉ 23220 25 C1

Paris 345 – Limoges 102 – Guéret 14 – La Souterraine 49 – La Châtre 42

La Maison Verte
2 Lombarteix , 2 km north on D 940 and secondary road – 05 55 51 93 34
– info@lamaisonvertecreuse.com
4 rm – €50 €70 – **Table d'hôte** – Menu €20 bi
♦ Perfectly preserved, peaceful 19C farm with vegetable garden and swimming pool. Traditional meals, prepared by the *patronne*, served in an updated rustic dining-room.

JOYEUSE – 07 Ardèche – 331 H7 – pop. 1 483 – alt. 180 m – ✉ 07260 Lyon - Rhone Valley 44 A3

Paris 650 – Alès 54 – Mende 97 – Privas 55

Office de tourisme, montée de la Chastellane 04 75 89 80 92, Fax 04 75 89 80 95

Corniche du Vivarais Cévenol★★ West.

Les Cèdres rm, rm, VISA
– 04 75 39 40 60 – hotelcedres@wanadoo.fr – Fax 04 75 39 90 16
– Open 15 April-15 October
44 rm – €52 €61, €7,50 – ½ P €58 – **Rest** – Menu €15/30 – Carte €20/38
♦ This hotel is in a former textile factory overlooking the Beaume. Small, well-kept rooms. Archery, canoeing, heated pool and theme evenings. Half-rustic, half-Provençal dining room; starter buffet and classic food.

JUAN-LES-PINS – 06 Alpes-Maritimes – 341 D6 – alt. 2 m – Casino : Eden Beach

FZ – ✉ 06160 French Riviera 42 **E2**

Paris 910 – Aix-en-Provence 161 – Cannes 10 – Nice 22

Office de tourisme, 51, boulevard Guillaumont ✆ 04 92 90 53 05, Fax 04 93 61 55 13

Massif de l'Esterel★★★ - Massif de Tanneron★.

JUAN-LES-PINS

Ardisson (Bd B.) . . . . . FZ 5
Courbet (Av. Amiral) . . . . . EZ 18
Docteur-Dautheville (Av.) . . . . . FZ 22
Docteur-Hochet (Av. du) . . . . . FZ 23
Gallet (Av. Louis) . . . . . EZ 27
Gallice (Av. G.) . . . . . FZ 29
Hôtel-des-Postes (R. de l') . . . . . EZ 44
Iles (R. des) . . . . . EZ 46
Joffre (Av. du Maréchal) . . . . . EFZ 47
Lauriers (Av. des) . . . . . FZ 48
Maupassant (Av. Guy-de) . . . . . EFZ 53
Oratoire (R. de l') . . . . . FZ 56
Palmiers (Av. des) . . . . . FZ 59
Paul (R. M.) . . . . . EZ 60
Printemps (R. du) . . . . . FZ 63
Ste-Marguerite (R.) . . . . . EZ 74
St-Honorat (R.) . . . . . EZ 71
Vilmorin (Av.) . . . . . EZ 88

Access and exits: see Antibes

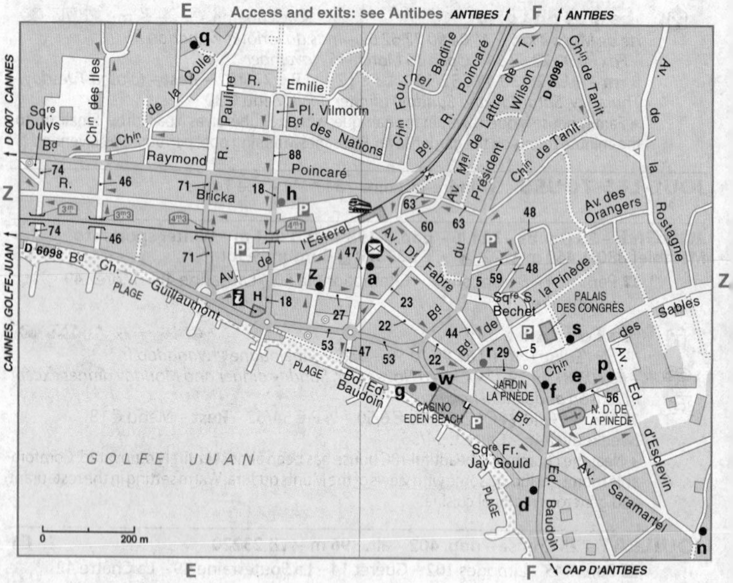

Juana – rest, VISA

la Pinède, av. G. Gallice – ✆ 04 93 61 08 70 – reservation@hotel-juana.com – Fax 04 93 61 76 60 – Closed 26 October-26 December FZ **f**

37 rm – †€ 220/665 ††€ 220/665, ☐ € 23 – 3 suites – **Rest** – *(dinner only)* Carte € 49/75

◆ A luxurious 1930s hotel, with a real tradition of hospitality. Elegant, renovated Art Deco-style rooms with high-quality facilities. Attractive swimming pool. Veranda restaurant and lounge full of natural light. Pleasant terrace facing the pine forest.

Belles Rives – ≤ sea and Massif de l'Estérel, rest, VISA

33 bd E. Baudoin – ✆ 04 93 61 02 79 – info@brj-hotels.com – Fax 04 93 67 43 51 – Closed 2 January-3 February FZ **d**

38 rm – †€ 145/740 ††€ 145/740, ☐ € 25 – 5 suites

Rest *La Passagère* – *(closed Monday and Tuesday off season) (dinner only from April to October)* Menu € 45 (weekday lunch), € 70/95 – Carte € 78/107

Rest *Plage Belles Rives* – *(Open April-October) (lunch only)* Carte € 50/87

◆ This little Art Deco gem right on the edge of the sea seems to await the return of F. Scott Fitzgerald. Private beach and pontoon. The 'Passenger' serves fine modern cuisine in a dining area with a 1930s steam liner décor. Tables with sea views at the Plage Belle Rives.

Méridien Garden Beach rm, VISA MC AE
15 bd E. Baudoin – ✆ 04 92 93 57 57
– contact.juanlespins@lemeridien.com – Fax 04 92 93 57 58
– Closed 7-28 December FZ **w**
175 rm – †€ 110/320 ††€ 110/320, ☕ € 30 – 17 suites
Rest ***Brasserie de la Plage*** – Carte € 40/75
◆ A glass and concrete building next to the casino with views over the sea. Spacious, comfortable rooms; choose one overlooking the sea. Sports facilities. Mediterranean cuisine, salads and grilled dishes served at the Brasserie de la Plage.

Ambassadeur VISA MC AE
50 chemin des Sables – ✆ 04 92 93 74 10 – manager@hotel-ambassadeur.com
– Fax 04 93 67 79 85 – Closed December FZ **s**
225 rm – †€ 150/207 ††€ 180/242, ☕ € 22
Rest ***Le Gauguin*** – *✆ 04 92 93 74 52 (closed July-August)* Carte € 38/52
Rest ***La Terrasse*** – *(open July-August) (dinner only)* Carte € 38/52
◆ This vast hotel complex behind the convention centre caters for seminars and holiday guests. Southern colours in the rooms. Pretty swimming pool surrounded with palm trees. Provençal decor and regional cuisine. Summer dining at La Terrasse.

Ste-Valérie without rest P VISA MC AE
r. Oratoire – ✆ 04 93 61 07 15 – saintevalerie@juanlespins.net
– Fax 04 93 61 47 52 – Open 29 April-14 October FZ **p**
24 rm – †€ 175/230 ††€ 265/400, ☕ € 23 – 6 suites
◆ A hotel set against a swathe of greenery and flowers. Well-presented rooms decorated in southern style; those overlooking the garden and pool are quieter. Charming welcome.

La Villa without rest P VISA MC AE
av. Saramartel – ✆ 04 92 93 48 00 – resa@hotel-la-villa.fr – Fax 04 93 61 86 78
– Open from March to end November FZ **n**
26 rm – †€ 165/325 ††€ 165/325, ☕ € 17
◆ The garden and swimming pool add charm to this peaceful, recently refurbished villa. Colonial-style lounge-bar, and modern, simply furnished rooms with wenge wood. Delicious welcome.

Astoria without rest P VISA MC AE
15 av. Mar. Joffre – ✆ 04 93 61 23 65 – reservation@hotellastoria.com
– Fax 04 93 67 10 40 FZ **a**
49 rm – †€ 79/139 ††€ 85/253, ☕ € 10
◆ A small, entirely refurbished building close to the station and two minutes from the beach. The rooms at the back are quieter. Attractive breakfast room.

Des Mimosas without rest P VISA MC AE
r. Pauline – ✆ 04 93 61 04 16 – hotel.mimosas@wanadoo.fr – Fax 04 92 93 06 46
– Open 23 April-30 September EZ **q**
34 rm – †€ 95 ††€ 140, ☕ € 10
◆ The immaculate façade of this hotel rises in the centre of a park with palm trees. Renovated rooms; those on the garden level or with a balcony overlooking the pool are the most pleasant.

Juan Beach rm, VISA MC AE
5 r. Oratoire – ✆ 04 93 61 02 89 – info@hoteljuanbeach.com – Fax 04 93 61 16 63
– Open 5 April-18 October FZ **e**
24 rm – †€ 77/143 ††€ 93/165, ☕ € 9 – 2 suites – **Rest** – *(lunch only) (resident only)* Menu (€ 13) – Carte € 18/35
◆ A warm atmosphere can be enjoyed in this all-renovated white and blue villa providing Provençal-style rooms, also featuring a bar & lounge with marine-style décor looking onto the pool.

Eden Hôtel without rest VISA MC
16 av. L. Gallet – ✆ 04 93 61 05 20 – edenhoteljuan@wanadoo.fr
– Fax 04 92 93 05 31 – Open from March to October EZ **z**
17 rm – †€ 51/65 ††€ 62/88, ☕ € 6
◆ The plus points of this 1930s hotel: breakfast on the terrace, the beach close by and a friendly atmosphere. Simple rooms, some with a glimpse of the sea.

XX **Bijou Plage** ← Lérins islands,

bd du Littoral – ✆ 04 93 61 39 07 – bijou.plage@free.fr – Fax 04 93 67 81 78

Rest – Menu € 21 (weekday lunch)/49 – Carte € 53/70 *see map of Antibes* AU **d**

◆ A beach restaurant redecorated in a pleasant low-key lounge style (beiges and a large fish tank) and extended by a veranda. Lovely sandy terrace; Mediterranean sourced produce.

XX **L'Amiral**

7 av. Amiral Courbet – ✆ 04 93 67 34 61 – restaurant.amiral@wanadoo.fr – Closed 4-14 April, 30 June-15 July, 1st-31 December, Tuesday except dinner May-September, Sunday dinner October-April and Monday EZ **h**

Rest – Menu € 25/35 – Carte € 34/54

◆ This pleasant family restaurant serves traditional and fish/seafood dishes in an intimate dining room adorned with paintings.

XX **Le Perroquet**

La Pinède, av. G. Gallice – ✆ 04 93 61 02 20 – Fax 04 93 61 02 20 – Closed 31 October-26 December and lunch July-August FZ **r**

Rest – Menu € 30/34 – Carte € 36/80

◆ Opposite the pinewoods where regular festivals are held. Ornaments, coffee grinders and flowers adorn the pretty Provençal dining room. Traditional cuisine.

XX **Le Paradis** ←

13 bd Beaudouin – ✆ 04 93 61 22 30 – resto.paradis@voila.fr – Fax 04 93 67 46 60 – Closed November, Sunday dinner and Monday 1st November-1st March

Rest – Menu € 33 (weekday lunch), € 38/48 – Carte € 45/93 FZ **g**

◆ A designer-influenced dining room with ethnic touches, splendid sea views and an appetising up-to-date menu. Accessible via a passageway beneath a building near the casino.

JULIÉNAS – 69 Rhône – 327 H2 – pop. 792 – alt. 276 m – ✉ 69840

Lyon - Rhone Valley 43 **E1**

Paris 403 – Bourg-en-Bresse 51 – Lyon 63 – Mâcon 15 – Villefranche-sur-Saône 32

Les Vignes without rest

0.5 km from St-Amour road – ✆ 04 74 04 43 70 – contact@hoteldesvignes.com – Fax 04 74 04 41 95 – Closed 20 December-5 January

22 rm – †€ 51/71 ††€ 56/71, ☐ € 9

◆ On a hillside surrounded by vineyards, a hotel with bedrooms that are neat, tidy and well-soundproofed. Choice of cold meats from the Beaujolais for breakfast.

XX **Chez la Rose** with rm

pl. du Marché – ✆ 04 74 04 41 20 – info@chez-la-rose.fr – Fax 04 74 04 49 29 – Open 9 March-9 December

8 rm – †€ 46/65 ††€ 46/65, ☐ € 10 – 5 suites – ½ P € 60/96

Rest – *(closed Tuesday lunch, Thursday lunch, Friday lunch and Monday except public holidays)* Menu € 28/51 – Carte € 40/60

◆ Good local cuisine served in a rustic decor or on the floral terrace outside. Rooms of varying sizes fitted with antique or rustic furniture. Modern breakfast room.

X **Le Coq à Juliénas**

pl. du Marché – ✆ 04 74 04 41 98 – reservation@leondelyon.com – Fax 04 74 04 41 44 – Closed 15 December-17 January, Sunday dinner, Tuesday dinner and Wednesday

Rest – Menu € 23

◆ Lavender-blue shutters, a distinct retro interior with cockerel ornaments, Bacchic frescoes and popular summer terrace: a stylish chef's bistro.

JULLIÉ – 69 Rhône – 327 H2 – pop. 384 – alt. 370 m – ✉ 69840 43 E1

Paris 415 – Bourg-en-Bresse 55 – Lyon 67 – Mâcon 20

Domaine de la Chapelle de Vâtre without rest

Le Bourbon, ← Juliénas and the Saône plain,

2 km south on the D 68 – ✆ 04 74 04 43 57 – vatre@wanadoo.fr – Fax 04 74 04 40 27

4 rm ☐ – †€ 60/80 ††€ 70/130

◆ This wine-growing estate set on the top of a hill boasts an exceptional view of the Saone plain. Rooms with superb, contemporary décor.

JUMIÈGES – 76 Seine-Maritime – 304 E5 – pop. 1 714 – alt. 25 m – ✉ 76480
Normandy 33 C2

Paris 160 – Caudebec-en-Caux 16 – Rouen 28

Office de tourisme, rue Guillaume le Conquérant ☎ 02 35 37 28 97, Fax 02 35 37 07 07

Abbey ruins★★★.

Le Clos des Fontaines without rest VISA MC AE

191 r. des Fontaines – ☎ 02 35 33 96 96 – hotel@leclosdesfontaines.com – Fax 02 35 33 96 97

18 rm – €90/190 €90/190, €16

◆ At the end of a country lane, this modern, hotel built in regional style is located close to the ruins of the abbey. Cosy bedrooms in two small houses. Attractive swimming pool in the garden.

L'Auberge des Ruines VISA MC AE

17 pl. de la Mairie – ☎ 02 35 37 24 05 – loic.henry9@wanadoo.fr – Closed 20 August-3 September, 20 December-7 January, 21 February-1st March, Monday dinner and Thursday dinner 1st November-28 February, Sunday dinner, Tuesday and Wednesday

Rest – Menu €35/70 – Carte €64/70

◆ Enjoyable stop opposite the ruins of the Benedictine abbey. A terrace and veranda serve as extensions of the main room. Modern decor which preserves some older fittings.

JUNGHOLTZ – 68 Haut-Rhin – 315 H9 – pop. 658 – alt. 332 m – ✉ 68500 1 A3

Paris 475 – Mulhouse 23 – Belfort 62 – Colmar 32 – Guebwiller 6

Les Violettes without rest AC rest, VISA MC AE

westward: 1 km – ☎ 03 89 76 91 19 – reservation@lesviolettes.com – Fax 03 89 74 29 12

22 rm – €150/300 €150/300, €11 – 3 suites

◆ Near Thierenbach Basilica, this former hunting lodge is home to superb, authentically Alsatian rooms and suites. Comfortable but less plush at the Gentilhommière.

JURANÇON – 64 Pyrénées-Atlantiques – 342 J5 – see Pau

JUVIGNAC – 34 Hérault – 339 H7 – see Montpellier

JUVIGNY-SOUS-ANDAINE – 61 Orne – 310 F3 – pop. 1 055 – alt. 200 m – ✉ 61140 32 B3

Paris 239 – Alençon 51 – Argentan 47 – Domfront 12 – Mayenne 33

Au Bon Accueil with rm AC rest, VISA MC

– ☎ 02 33 38 10 04 – hotel.aubonaccueil@wanadoo.fr – Fax 02 33 37 44 92 – Closed 15 February-15 March, Sunday dinner and Monday

8 rm – €52 €52/67, €9 – ½ P €57 – **Rest** – Menu €14,50 (weekday lunch), €18/42 – Carte €37/50

◆ In the centre of a picturesque village, a welcoming house serving generous portions. One of the two dining rooms has a glass roof and a small winter garden.

JUZET-DE-LUCHON – 31 Haute-Garonne – 343 B8 – see Bagnères-de-Luchon

KATZENTHAL – 68 Haut-Rhin – 315 H8 – pop. 497 – alt. 280 m – ✉ 68230 2 C2

Paris 445 – Colmar 8 – Gérardmer 53 – Munster 18 – St-Dié 48

À l'Agneau with rm P VISA MC AE

16 Grand'Rue – ☎ 03 89 80 90 25 – contact@agneau-katzenthal.com – Fax 03 89 27 59 58 – Closed 30 June-11 July, 12-20 November, 12-29 January, 23 February-12 March

12 rm – €43/55 €43/55, €9,50 – 1 suite – ½ P €49/60

Rest – *(closed Thursday except dinner from July to September and Wednesday)* Menu €19 (weekdays)/50 – Carte €27/47

◆ Regional-style house, adjacent to the family-run winery, with two smart, typically Alsatian dining rooms. Cuisine based on local and market produce, wines from the estate.

KAYSERSBERG – 68 Haut-Rhin – 315 H8 – pop. 2 676 – alt. 242 m – ✉ 68240

Alsace-Lorraine 2 C2

Paris 438 – Colmar 12 – Gérardmer 46 – Guebwiller 35 – Munster 22 – St-Dié 41 – Sélestat 24

Office de tourisme, 39, rue du Gal-de-Gaulle ✆ 03 89 78 22 78, Fax 03 89 78 27 44

Ste-Croix church ★: altar-piece★★ - Town hall★ - Old houses★ - Fortified bridge★ - Maison Brief★.

Chambard (Olivier Nasti) rm, VISA MC AE

r. Gén.-de-Gaulle – ✆ 03 89 47 10 17 – info@lechambard.fr – Fax 03 89 47 35 03

20 rm – €104 €122/225, ☕ €21 – 3 suites – ½ P €127/156

Rest – *(closed 5 January-9 February, Tuesday lunch, Wednesday lunch and Monday)* Menu €30 (weekday lunch), €48/78 – Carte €68/83

Rest *Winstub* – Menu (€17), €24 – Carte €29/44

Spec. Escargots à l'alsacienne façon "nouvelle mode". Bar de ligne et homard en carcasse. Carré d'agneau du Limousin aux gnocchi à la truffe. **Wines** Riesling, Pinot gris.

♦ A large hotel at the entrance to the town. Comfortable rooms and three magnificent modern suites. Elegant restaurant, attractive terrace, fine wine list and tasty, inventive dishes. Alsatian setting at the Winstub.

Les Remparts without rest VISA MC AE

4 r. Flieh – ✆ 03 89 47 12 12 – hotel@lesremparts.com – Fax 03 89 47 37 24

28 rm – €54/69 €69/79, ☕ €8

♦ Hotel in a quiet residential area on the town's outskirts. Practical rooms with large terraces that are decked with flowers in summer.

Les Terrasses without rest VISA MC AE

15 rm – €54/69 €69/86, ☕ €8

♦ Neo-Alsatian architecture, a quiet environment and comfortable rooms characterise the annexe of the hotel where you can find the reception, shared by both establishments.

Constantin without rest VISA MC AE

10 r. Père Kohlman – ✆ 03 89 47 19 90 – reservation@hotel-constantin.com – Fax 03 89 47 37 82

20 rm – €50/55 €62/72, ☕ €7,50

♦ This old wine-grower's house now provides comfortable rooms, some on two levels. Breakfast room with glass ceiling and attractive earthenware stove.

À l'Arbre Vert VISA MC AE

1 r. Haute du Rempart – ✆ 03 89 47 11 51 – arbrevertbellepromenade@wanadoo.fr – Fax 03 89 78 13 40 – Closed 8 January-12 February

19 rm – €59/61 €65/75, ☕ €9 – ½ P €70 – **Rest** – *(closed Mon.)* Menu €23/35 – Carte €24/52

♦ Regional-style building, facing the Docteur Schweitzer Museum, with an appealing floral façade. Rustic rooms. Dining room with warm wood panelling, serving traditional Alsatian cuisine.

La Vieille Forge AC VISA MC

1 r. des Écoles – ✆ 03 89 47 17 51 – Fax 03 89 78 13 53 – Closed 27 June-11 July, 4-21 January, Wednesday and Thursday

Rest – Menu €20/33 – Carte €30/42

♦ A family restaurant hidden behind a charming half-timbered 16C façade. Regional menu supplemented by seasonal suggestions.

Au Lion d'Or VISA MC AE

66 r. Gén. de Gaulle – ✆ 03 89 47 11 16 – auliond.or@wanadoo.fr – Fax 03 89 47 19 02 – Closed 3-10 July, 26 January-12 March, Tuesday except lunch de May-October and Wednesday

Rest – Menu €16/38 – Carte €21/56

♦ A house built in 1521 and run by the same family since 1764! Period dining rooms, one with an authentic fireplace, that can seat up to 180 guests!

in Kientzheim **East: 3 km by D 28 – pop. 827 – alt. 225 m – ✉ 68240**

Tombstones★ in the church.

L'Abbaye d'Alspach without rest

2 r. Foch – ☎ 03 89 47 16 00 – hotel@abbayealspach.com – Fax 03 89 78 29 73 – Closed 7 January-15 March

28 rm – €65/81 €71/109, €10,50 – 5 suites

◆ A hotel located in the outhouses of a 13C convent. Five superb suites; attractive courtyard; delicious breakfasts (kougelhopf and home-made jams).

Hostellerie Schwendi

2 pl. Schwendi – ☎ 03 89 47 30 50 – hotel@schwendi.fr – Fax 03 89 49 04 49 – Closed 5 January-1st March

29 rm – €66 €78/102, €11 – ½ P €77/89 – **Rest** – *(closed 24 December-10 March, Thursday lunch and Wednesday)* Menu €22/59 – Carte €29/58

◆ This house with a beautiful half-timbered façade stands on a small cobbled square. Partly rustic, partly stylish interior. Pretty personalised rooms, even more comfortable in the annexe. Regional menu and wines from the estate served on the terrace overlooking a fountain in summer.

KEMBS-LOÉCHLÉ – 68 Haut-Rhin – 315 J11 – alt. 245 m – ✉ 68680 1 B3

Paris 493 – Altkirch 26 – Basel 16 – Belfort 70 – Colmar 60 – Mulhouse 25

Les Écluses

8 r. Rosenau – ☎ 03 89 48 37 77 – restaurantlesecluses@orange.fr – Fax 03 89 48 49 31 – Closed autumn half-term holidays, February half-term holidays, Wednesday dinner from October to April, Sunday dinner and Monday

Rest – Menu €16/40 – Carte €27/44

◆ Near the Huningue Canal and the Alsatian Petite Camargue, this friendly establishment offers fish specialities in a contemporary-style dining room.

KIENTZHEIM – 68 Haut-Rhin – 315 H8 – see Kaysersberg

KILSTETT – 67 Bas-Rhin – 315 L4 – pop. 1 923 – alt. 130 m – ✉ 67840 1 B1

Paris 489 – Haguenau 23 – Saverne 51 – Strasbourg 14 – Wissembourg 60

Oberlé

11 rte Nationale – ☎ 03 88 96 21 17 – hroberle@wanadoo.fr – Fax 03 88 96 62 29 – Closed 18-31 August and 23 February-7 March

30 rm – €40 €51/60, €6 – ½ P €39/43 – **Rest** – *(closed Friday lunch and Thursday)* Menu €10, €22/37 – Carte €21/45

◆ This family-run establishment offers several types of rather comfortable and modern rooms. The largest have been carefully renovated. Cheerful restaurant serving regionally inspired cuisine.

Au Cheval Noir

1 r. du Sous-Lieutenant-Maussire – ☎ 03 88 96 22 01 – Fax 03 88 96 61 30 – Closed 16 July-10 August, 10-25 January, Monday and Tuesday

Rest – Menu €14 (weekdays), €25/48 – Carte €42

◆ The same family has run the restaurant for five generations in this fine, 18C, half-timbered house. A welcoming interior with a hunting scene mural and traditional menu.

KOENIGSMACKER – 57 Moselle – 307 I2 – pop. 1 893 – alt. 150 m – ✉ 57970

Paris 349 – Luxembourg 50 – Metz 39 – Völklingen 69 26 B1

Syndicat d'initiative, 1, square du Père Scheil ☎ 03 82 83 75 54, Fax 03 82 83 75 54

Moulin de Méwinckel without rest

– ☎ 03 82 55 03 28

5 rm – €47/60 €55/70

◆ Peaceful yet eye-catching rooms located in the former stables of this farmhouse and mill, which are still operational. Warm hospitality and a country setting, where the wheel of the mill still turns.

LE KREMLIN-BICÊTRE – 94 Val-de-Marne – 312 D3 – 101 26 – see Paris, Area

KRUTH – 68 Haut-Rhin – 315 F9 – pop. 1 010 – alt. 498 m – ✉ 68820
Alsace Lorraine 1 **A3**

Paris 453 – Colmar 63 – Épinal 68 – Gérardmer 31 – Mulhouse 40 – Thann 20 – Le Thillot 29

Cascade St-Nicolas★ Southwest: 3 km by D 13b[1] - Musée du textile et des costumes de Haute-Alsace à Husseren-Wesserling Southeast: 6 km.

in Frenz West: 5 km by D 13bis – ✉68820 Kruth – pop. 1 010 – alt. 498 m

Les Quatre Saisons Vosges Massif, P VISA MC AE

r. Frentz – *03 89 82 28 61* – *hotel4saisons@wanadoo.fr* – *Fax 03 89 82 21 42* – *Closed 1st-6 April*

10 rm – €45/65 €45/65, €8 – ½ P €44/53 – **Rest** – *(Tuesday and Wednesday)* Menu €18/36 – Carte €26/41

◆ Retaining its mountain roots yet prettily modernised, this family chalet has pleasant accommodation, cosy reading room and home-made breakfasts. Updated regional dishes and good selection of wines. Attractive dining room with view of the Vosges.

LABAROCHE – 68 Haut-Rhin – 315 H8 – pop. 1 985 – alt. 750 m – ✉ 68910 2 **C2**

Paris 441 – Colmar 17 – Gérardmer 49 – Munster 25 – St-Dié 44

Office de tourisme, 2, impasse Prés. Poincaré 03 89 49 80 56, Fax 03 89 49 80 68

La Rochette P VISA MC

500 lieu-dit La Rochette – *03 89 49 80 40* – *hotel.la.rochette@wanadoo.fr* – *Fax 03 89 78 94 82* – *Closed 12-23 November and 20 February-15 March*

7 rm – €52/55 €55/65, €9 – ½ P €60/65 – **Rest** – *(closed Monday dinner and Tuesday)* Menu €18/48 – Carte €32/47

◆ Enjoy a drink before dinner in the lush green garden that surrounds this family home. Stylish, bright rooms that are well soundproofed. Attractive predominantly yellow and green dining room; regionally focused menu.

XX **Blanche Neige** P VISA MC AE

692 Les Evaux, 6 km south-east along the D 11 and secondary road – *03 89 78 94 71* – *info@auberge-blanche-neige.fr* – *Closed Thursday lunch, Tuesday and Wednesday*

Rest – Menu €25 (weekday lunch), €39/100 bi – Carte €52/64

◆ At an altitude of 700m, a delightful inn overlooking the Vosges. The tasteful blend of old and new inside is extremely effective. Splendid terrace and creative menu.

LABARTHE-SUR-LÈZE – 31 Haute-Garonne – 343 G4 – pop. 4 632 – alt. 162 m – ✉ 31860 28 **B2**

Paris 694 – Auch 91 – Pamiers 45 – St-Gaudens 81 – Toulouse 21

18 de Toulouse VieillevigneNorth: 10 km by D 4, 05 61 73 45 48.

XX **Le Poêlon** VISA MC AE

19 pl. V. Auriol – *05 61 08 68 49* – *Fax 05 61 08 78 48* – *Closed 5-25 August, 23 December-7 January, Sunday and Monday*

Rest – Menu €22 (weekdays)/41 – Carte €35/55

◆ A plush bourgeois home that is popular with the regulars for its traditional cuisine and a fine wine list (over 600 choices). Exhibition-sale of art, shaded terrace.

XX **La Rose des Vents** P VISA MC AE

crossroads D 19-D 4 – *05 61 08 67 01* – *Fax 05 61 08 85 84* – *Closed 15 August-6 September, February holidays, Sunday dinner, Monday and Tuesday*

Rest – Menu €17 (weekday lunch), €25/43 – Carte €29/53

◆ A comfortable regional-style house shielded from the noise of the road by its surrounding greenery. Take a seat by the fireside or on the veranda covered by a Virginia creeper.

LABASTIDE-BEAUVOIR – 31 Haute-Garonne – 343 I4 – pop. 664 – alt. 260 m – ✉ 31450 29 **C2**

Paris 701 – Toulouse 25 – Albi 97 – Castelnaudary 35 – Foix 76

L' Oustal du Lauragais

– ✆ 05 34 66 16 16 – contact@oustal-lauragais.fr – Fax 05 34 66 16 26 – Closed 23 December-3 January

14 rm – €65 €65, ☕ €7 – ½ P €56 – **Rest** – *(closed 4-24 August and 23 December-3 January)* Menu €16/25 – Carte €22/30

◆ This former farmhouse has been restored and converted into a peaceful hotel providing simply furnished rooms with fine bathroom facilities. Traditional food served in the modern-style dining room.

LABASTIDE DE VIRAC – 07 Ardèche – pop. 218 – alt. 207 m – ✉ 07150 44 **A3**

Paris 675 – Lyon 213 – Privas 73 – Alès 42 – Montélimar 67

Le Mas Rêvé

3 km east on D 217 and secondary road – ✆ 04 75 38 69 13 – info@lemasreve.com – Open mid April-September

5 rm ☕ – €90/145 €90/145 – **Table d'hôte** – Menu €32 bi

◆ Admire the pretty rooms of this old Ardèche farmhouse, tastefully restored by Marie Rose et Guido Goossens. Lovely garden and pool.

LABASTIDE-MURAT – 46 Lot – 337 F4 – pop. 690 – alt. 447 m – ✉ 46240 29 **C1**

Dordogne-Berry-Limousin

Paris 543 – Brive-la-Gaillarde 66 – Cahors 32 – Figeac 45 – Gourdon 26 – Sarlat-la-Canéda 50

Office de tourisme, Grand'Rue ✆ 05 65 21 11 39, Fax 05 65 24 57 66

La Garissade

pl. de la Mairie – ✆ 05 65 21 18 80 – garissade@wanadoo.fr – Fax 05 65 21 10 97 – Open April-October

19 rm – €59/65 €65/70, ☕ €7,50 – ½ P €55/60 – **Rest** – *(closed Monday lunch)* Menu €13,50 (weekday lunch)/25

◆ An informal atmosphere depicts this 13C village house. Low-key rooms with painted wood furniture, made by a local craftsman. A menu designed to meet with the approval of regional produce lovers. Quiet summer terrace.

LABATUT – 40 Landes – 335 F13 – pop. 1 102 – alt. 45 m – ✉ 40300 3 **B3**

Paris 759 – Anglet 58 – Bayonne 53 – Bordeaux 173

Le Bousquet

37 bd de l'Océan – ✆ 05 58 98 11 01 – aubergedubousquet@yahoo.fr – Fax 05 58 98 11 63 – Closed Wednesday and Saturday

Rest – Menu €25/45 – Carte €45/53

◆ This charming 18C house is home to a restaurant in a country setting, with wooden beams and rustic furniture. Serving modern cuisine. Herb garden.

LABÈGE – 31 Haute-Garonne – 343 H3 – see Toulouse

LABOURSE – 62 Pas-de-Calais – 301 J5 – see Béthune

LACABARÈDE – 81 Tarn – 338 H10 – pop. 304 – alt. 325 m – ✉ 81240 29 **C2**

Paris 754 – Béziers 71 – Carcassonne 53 – Castres 36 – Mazamet 19 – Narbonne 62

Demeure de Flore

106 Grand'rue – ✆ 05 63 98 32 32 – contact@demeuredeflore.com – Fax 05 63 98 47 56 – Closed 2-30 January and Monday off season

11 rm – €70/100 €100/190, ☕ €10 – ½ P €93/98

Rest – Menu €27 (weekday lunch)/35

◆ The Roman goddess gave this 19C family house a beautiful green setting facing the Montagne Noire (Black Mountain). A stylish interior, antique furnishings and an attentive welcome. Market cuisine with a Provençal touch or Italian influences, served in a modern, refined atmosphere.

LACAPELLE-MARIVAL – 46 Lot – 337 H3 – pop. 1 247 – alt. 375 m – ✉ 46120

Dordogne-Berry-Limousin 29 **C1**

Paris 555 – Aurillac 66 – Cahors 64 – Figeac 21 – Gramat 22 – Rocamadour 32 – Tulle 75

Office de tourisme, place de la Halle ✆ 05 65 40 81 11, Fax 05 65 40 81 11

La Terrasse with rm

rest, VISA

near the château – ✆ 05 65 40 80 07 – hotel-restaurant-la-terrasse@wanadoo.fr – Fax 05 65 40 99 45 – Closed 1st January-5 March and Sunday dinner off season

13 rm – €45/47 €50/70, €7 – ½ P €50/60 – **Rest** – *(closed Sunday dinner, Monday dinner and Tuesday lunch October-June and Monday lunch)* Menu €14 (weekday lunch), €25/55 – Carte €42/73

◆ Appetising modern food to be enjoyed in a bright, renovated dining room. Hotel near the château's huge square keep. Functional, well-kept rooms. Some have been renovated. Pleasant garden bordered by a stream.

LACAPELLE-VIESCAMP – 15 Cantal – 330 B5 – pop. 434 – alt. 550 m – ✉ 15150

Paris 547 – Aurillac 19 – Figeac 57 – Laroquebrou 12 – St-Céré 48 5 **A3**

Du Lac

rm, rest, VISA AE

– ✆ 04 71 46 31 57 – info@hoteldulac-cantal.com – Fax 04 71 46 31 64 – Closed 20 December-10 January, Friday dinner and Sunday dinner from 1st November to Easter

23 rm – €45/55 €50/60, €12 – ½ P €55/65 – **Rest** – Menu €20 (weekdays)/35 – Carte €24/43

◆ This 1950s establishment is full of appeal: peace and quiet, close to St Etienne Cantalès Lake, which is good for fishing, perfectly kept rooms and a convivial welcome. The restaurant, overlooking the surrounding countryside, serves traditional fare and regional wines.

LACAUNE – 81 Tarn – 338 I8 – pop. 2 914 – alt. 793 m – Casino – ✉ 81230

Languedoc-Roussillon-Tarn Gorges 29 **D2**

Paris 708 – Albi 67 – Béziers 89 – Castres 48 – Lodève 73 – Millau 69 – Montpellier 131

Office de tourisme, place Général-de-Gaulle ✆ 05 63 37 04 98, Fax 05 63 37 03 01

Calas with rm

VISA AE

pl. Vierge – ✆ 05 63 37 03 28 – hotelcalas@wanadoo.fr – Fax 05 63 37 09 19 – Closed 15 December-15 January

16 rm – €38/50 €43/60, €7 – ½ P €43/45 – **Rest** – *(closed Sunday dinner, Friday dinner and Saturday lunch from October to April)* Menu €15 (weekdays)/36 – Carte €31/50

◆ Four generations of the same family have been running this restaurant serving good regional cuisine. Featuring works by local artists. Rooms with lively décor.

LACAVE – 46 Lot – 337 F2 – pop. 293 – alt. 130 m – ✉ 46200

Dordogne-Berry-Limousin 29 **C1**

Paris 528 – Brive-La-Gaillarde 51 – Cahors 58 – Gourdon 26 – Sarlat-La-Canéda 41

Grottoes★★.

Château de la Treyne

VISA AE

west: 3 km on the D 23, D 43 and private road – ✆ 05 65 27 60 60 – treyne@relaischateaux.com – Fax 05 65 27 60 70 – Open 22 March-15 November and 21 December-3 January

14 rm – €180/380 €180/380, €22 – 2 suites – ½ P €290/490

Rest – *(closed lunch Tuesday-Friday)* Menu €48 (lunch), €88/128 – Carte €112/137

Spec. Pot-au-feu de foie de canard aux cocos de Paimpol (end August to end October). Potage meringué au lait de poule truffé, brioche gratinée, crème renversée aux truffes. Côtelettes et noisettes d'agneau du Quercy à la moutarde de thym. **Wines** Bergerac, Cahors.

◆ A 17C château overlooking the Dordogne in a park with a formal garden and Romanesque chapel (exhibitions, concerts). An idyllic setting and sumptuous guest rooms. Fine wooden panelling and coffered ceiling in the restaurant serving modern cuisine.

Pont de l'Ouysse (Daniel Chambon) rm,
– *℘ 05 65 37 87 04 – pont.ouysse@wanadoo.fr – Fax 05 65 32 77 41 – Open beg. March-11 November and closed Monday except dinner in season and Tuesday lunch*
14 rm – €140/150 €140/185, € 16 – ½ P € 150/160
Rest – Menu € 50/130 – Carte € 71/128
Spec. Foie de canard "Bonne Maman". Queues de langoustines aux truffes. Daube de pied de porc truffé, aligot au lard paysan. **Wines** Cahors, Vin de Pays du Lot.
◆ This delightful 19C house built into the cliff boasts an attractive dining room, shady terrace, and a pathway along the banks of the Ouysse. Inventive cuisine inspired by the south-west.

LAC CHAMBON ★★ – 63 Puy-de-Dôme – 326 E9 – alt. 877 m – Winter sports : 1 150/1 760 m 9 – ✉ 63790 Chambon-sur-Lac Auvergne 5 **B2**

Paris 456 – Clermont-Ferrand 37 – Condat 39 – Issoire 32 – Le Mont-Dore 18

Le Grillon rest,
– *℘ 04 73 88 60 66 – info@hotel-grillon.com – Fax 04 73 88 65 55 – Open 7 February-11 November*
22 rm – €40 €40/48, € 8 – ½ P € 44/52 – **Rest** – *(closed Monday lunch except 15 June-15 September)* Menu (€ 15), € 18 (except Sunday)/38 – Carte € 30/44
◆ A well-run family establishment. The stylish, colourful rooms all bear witness to the lady of the house's decorative talents. Traditional and regional dishes served in the dining room or on the terrace overlooking the lake.

Beau Site
– *℘ 04 73 88 61 29 – info@beau-site.com – Fax 04 73 88 66 73 – Open 1st February-30 October*
17 rm – €40/45 €45/52, € 8 – ½ P € 45/52 – **Rest** – *(open February holidays-30 October and closed lunch March and October except weekends)* Menu € 15 (weekdays)/28 – Carte € 24/36
◆ A hillside hotel overlooking the lake. Rooms of varying sizes facing the water and beach. Terrace and modern dining rooms whose bay windows overlook the lake. Regional food.

LAC DE GUÉRY – 63 Puy-de-Dôme – 326 D9 – see le Mont-Dore

LAC DE LA LIEZ – 52 Haute-Marne – 313 M6 – see Langres

LAC DE PONT – 21 Côte-d'Or – 320 G5 – see Semur-en-Auxois

LAC DE VASSIVIÈRE – 23 Creuse – 325 I6 – see Peyrat-le-Château (87 H.-Vienne)

LAC GÉNIN – 01 Ain – 328 H3 – see Oyonnax

LACHASSAGNE – 69 Rhône – 327 H4 – pop. 769 – alt. 368 m – ✉ 69480 43 **E1**

Paris 445 – Lyon 30 – Villeurbanne 39 – Vénissieux 43 – Caluire-et-Cuire 34

Au Goutillon Beaujolais
850 rte de la colline – ℘ 04 74 67 14 99 – au-goutillon-beaujolais@wanadoo.fr – Fax 04 74 67 14 99 – Closed dinner and Saturday 15 September-30 June, Sunday dinner 1st July-14 September
Rest – Menu (€ 13), € 19/39 – Carte approx. € 50
◆ Modern cuisine with exotic touches served in this establishment located among vineyards. The terrace overlooking the Saône valley is especially charming.

LACROIX-FALGARDE – 31 Haute-Garonne – 343 G3 – see Toulouse

LADOIX-SERRIGNY – 21 Côte-d'Or – 320 J7 – see Beaune

LAFARE – 84 Vaucluse – 332 D9 – pop. 97 – alt. 220 m – ✉ 84190 42 E1

Paris 670 – Avignon 37 – Carpentras 13 – Nyons 34 – Orange 26

Le Grand Jardin ← vineyards and Dentelles de Montmirail,
– ✆ 04 90 62 97 93 – bonnin-noel@ rm, VISA MC AE
wanadoo.fr – Fax 04 90 65 03 74 – Open 4 March-2 November and closed Tuesday lunch and Monday
8 rm – †€ 70/75 ††€ 80/95, ☕ € 12 – ½ P € 70/80 – **Rest** – Menu € 23 (weekday lunch), € 31/42 – Carte € 45/51
◆ A new building surrounded by Côtes-du-Rhône vines. Rooms decorated in Provençal style. Warm welcome. Contemplate the Dentelles de Montmirail from the flower-decked terrace, in the shade of the cane screens.

LAGARDE-ENVAL – 19 Corrèze – 329 L4 – pop. 748 – alt. 480 m – ✉ 19150 25 C3

Paris 488 – Aurillac 71 – Brive-la-Gaillarde 35 – Mauriac 66 – St-Céré 48 – Tulle 14

Le Central with rm rest, VISA MC
– ✆ 05 55 27 16 12 – hotelmestre19@orange.fr – Fax 05 55 27 48 00 – Closed September
7 rm – †€ 45 ††€ 45, ☕ € 5,50 – **Rest** – *(closed Saturday and Sunday)* Menu € 13 (lunch), € 22/30
◆ Friendly family-run hotel also home to the village bar. Rustic dining room serving typical Corrèze meals. Modest guest rooms.

LAGARRIGUE – 81 Tarn – 338 F9 – see Castres

LAGRASSE – 11 Aude – 344 G4 – pop. 615 – alt. 108 m – ✉ 11220
Languedoc-Roussillon-Tarn Gorges 22 B3

Paris 819 – Montpellier 133 – Carcassonne 51 – Perpignan 97 – Narbonne 43
Syndicat d'initiative, 6, boulevard de la Promenade ✆ 04 68 43 11 56, Fax 04 68 43 16 34

Hostellerie des Corbières rm, VISA MC
9 bd de la Promenade – ✆ 04 68 43 15 22 – hostelleriecorbieres@free.fr – Fax 04 68 43 16 56 – Closed 5 January-5 February
6 rm – †€ 70 ††€ 70/90, ☕ € 11 – ½ P € 70 – **Rest** – *(closed Thursday)* Menu € 15 bi (weekday lunch), € 20/35 – Carte € 40
◆ The character of this small renovated mansion on the outskirts of the village has been carefully preserved. Louis Philippe style furniture in the rooms; collection of Asian art in the lounge. The shaded terrace of the restaurant commands a view of the Corbières vineyards.

LAGUÉPIE – 82 Tarn-et-Garonne – 337 H7 – pop. 720 – alt. 149 m – ✉ 82250 29 C2

Paris 649 – Albi 38 – Montauban 71 – Rodez 70 – Villefranche-de-Rouergue 34
Office de tourisme, place de Foirail ✆ 05 63 30 20 34, Fax 05 63 30 20 34

Les Deux Rivières rm, VISA MC AE
– ✆ 05 63 31 41 41 – les2rivieres.laguepie@wanadoo.fr – Fax 05 63 30 20 91 – Closed February half-term holidays, Saturday lunch, Sunday dinner and Friday
8 rm – †€ 34 ††€ 38, ☕ € 8 – ½ P € 38 – **Rest** – Menu € 20/33 – Carte € 21/33
◆ At the confluence of the Aveyron and the Viaur, a small welcoming hotel with modest but well-maintained rooms. Lunchtime service in the bar. Evening meals are served in a functional dining room.

LAGUIOLE – 12 Aveyron – 338 J2 – pop. 1 248 – alt. 1 004 m – Winter sports : 1 100/1 400 m 12 – ✉ 12210 Languedoc-Roussillon-Tarn Gorges 29 D1

Paris 571 – Aurillac 79 – Espalion 22 – Mende 83 – Rodez 52 – St-Flour 59
Office de tourisme, place de la Mairie ✆ 05 65 44 35 94, Fax 05 65 44 35 76
de Mezeyrac Soulages, West: 12 km by D 541, ✆ 05 65 44 41 41.

Grand Hôtel Auguy (Isabelle Muylaert-Auguy)
2 allée de l'Amicale – ✆ 05 65 44 31 11
– contact@hotel-auguy.fr – Fax 05 65 51 50 81
– Open 2 April-4 November and closed Monday except July-August
20 rm – €75/105 €75/105, €12 – ½ P €70/100
Rest – *(closed Monday except dinner in July-August, Tuesday lunch and Thursday lunch except July-August, Friday lunch in July-August and Wednesday lunch) (number of covers limited, pre-book)* Menu €35 (weekday lunch)/54 – Carte €64/68
Spec. Tronçon de lotte rôti et capuccino de girolles de pays (June-July). Côte de bœuf Aubrac grillée et os à moelle avec aligot de montagne. Transparent d'aubergine à la crème de fenouil, glace au thym-citron (May to September). **Wines** Vin de table de l'Aveyron, Marcillac.

◆ This fine hotel perpetuates its tradition of hospitality, offering colourful, well-maintained guestrooms and a peaceful garden. A pleasant restaurant serving specialities from the Aubrac region.

Le Relais de Laguiole
espace Les Cayres – ✆ 05 65 54 19 66 – relais.de.laguiole@wanadoo.fr
– Fax 05 65 54 19 49 – Open 11 April-1st November
33 rm – €74/168 €74/168, €11 – ½ P €65/99 – **Rest** – *(dinner only)*
Menu €19/33 – Carte €31/52

◆ A modern building with a slate roof, large functional rooms and a beautiful indoor swimming pool. Copious breakfast buffet. Ideal for groups. This bright restaurant is decorated with modern chandeliers and white curtains and furniture.

Régis without rest
– ✆ 05 65 44 30 05 – hotel.regis@wanadoo.fr – Fax 05 65 48 46 44
– Open 10 February-10 November
22 rm – €37/47 €42/99, €6,70

◆ A 19C coaching inn, tucked away in the centre of this small Aveyron town. The largest, particularly comfortable rooms are on the second floor. Pleasant swimming pool to the rear.

La Ferme de Moulhac without rest
2.5 km north-eastward by secondary road – ✆ 05 65 44 33 25 – Fax 05 65 44 33 25
– Closed 26-29 May and 14-17 September
6 rm – €52/55 €62/95

◆ A peaceful, relaxing atmosphere and fresh air are guaranteed at this family farm. Attractive rooms, simply furnished in a mix of old and modern styles. Generous home-made breakfast, and a small kitchen available for guests.

East 6 km by L'Aubrac road (D 15) – ✉ **12210 Laguiole**

Bras (Michel et Sébastien Bras) ← the Aubrac countryside,
– ✆ 05 65 51 18 20 rm, rest,
– info@michel-bras.fr – Fax 05 65 48 47 02
– Open from beg. of April to end of October and closed Monday except July-August
15 rm – €230/550 €230/550, €26
Rest – *(closed Tuesday lunch and Wednesday lunch except July-August and Monday) (number of covers limited, pre-book)* Menu €110/175 – Carte €118/165
Spec. "Gargouillou" de jeunes légumes. Pièce de bœuf Aubrac rôtie à la braise. Biscuit tiède de chocolat coulant. **Wines** Gaillac, Marcillac.

◆ This futuristic Construction seems lost among the harsh landscapes of the Aubrac. Large rooms with a refined contemporary decor overlooking the countryside and superb botanical gardens. Highly inspired cuisine using local produce served in an ultra-modern, panoramic restaurant.

at the Golf 12 km West by D541, D213 and secondary road

Domaine de Mezeyrac rm, rm, rm,
– ✆ 05 65 44 41 41 – golfhotel-mezeyrac@wanadoo.fr
– Fax 05 65 44 46 90 – Open 1st April-5 November
15 rm – €59/140 €59/140, €9 – **Rest** – *(dinner for resident only)*
Menu €15/18

◆ An old farm converted into hostelry and complex devoted to golf. Peace and quiet guaranteed, comfortable rooms and a view of the golf course. Restaurant in a converted barn.

LAILLY-EN-VAL – **45 Loiret** – **318** H5 – **pop. 2 367** – **alt. 86 m** – ✉ **45740**

Paris 160 – Orléans 36 – Blois 42 – Chartres 104 – Eury 147 12 **C2**

Domaine de Montizeau

– *02 38 45 34 74 – abeille@domaine-montizeau.com*

4 rm – €70 €70 – **Table d'hôte** – Menu €28 bi

◆ Relaxation is the order of the day at this regional construction, set in a flower-filled park. Cosy rooms with various themes (hunting, Italy etc.). Contemporary cuisine.

LAJOUX – **39 Jura** – **321** F8 – **see Lamoura**

LALACELLE – **61 Orne** – **310** I4 – **pop. 268** – **alt. 300 m** – ✉ **61320** 32 **B3**

Paris 208 – Alençon 20 – Argentan 34 – Domfront 42 – Falaise 57 – Mayenne 41

Château de Carrouges★★ North: 11 km, **G. Normandy.**

La Lentillère with rm VISA AE

Alençon road : 1.5 km on the N 12 – 02 33 27 38 48 – gentil.jeanmichel@wanadoo.fr – Fax 02 33 27 38 30 – Closed 24-30 November, 8 January-6 February, Friday dinner, Sunday dinner and Monday lunch from September to March

8 rm – €45/57 €45/57, €7 – ½ P €49/54 – **Rest** – Menu €10,50 bi/39 – Carte €31/46

◆ This inn is easily accessible from the main road. Aperitifs in the garden, dinner served in a country-style dining area with old-fashioned charm.

LALINDE – **24 Dordogne** – **329** F6 – **pop. 2 966** – **alt. 46 m** – ✉ **24150** 4 **C1**

Paris 537 – Bergerac 23 – Brive-La-Gaillarde 103 – Périgueux 49 – Villeneuve-sur-Lot 61

Office de tourisme, Jardin Public 05 53 61 08 55, Fax 05 53 61 00 64

in St-Capraise-de-Lalinde West, Bergerac road: 7 km – pop. 531 – alt. 42 m – ✉ 24150

Relais St-Jacques with rm rest, VISA AE

pl. de l'Église – 05 53 63 47 54 – patrick.rossignol12@wanadoo.fr – Fax 05 53 73 33 52 – Closed Wednesday

7 rm – €49 €55/75, €9,50 – ½ P €47/62 – **Rest** – Menu €18 (lunch)/45 – Carte €30/49

◆ This former post house near a church on the pilgrim route to Compostela is believed to date back to the 13C. Rustic decor, warm hospitality and regional dishes.

LALLEYRIAT – **01 Ain** – **328** E4 – **see Bourg-en-Bresse**

LAMAGDELAINE – **46 Lot** – **337** E5 – **see Cahors**

LAMALOU-LES-BAINS – **34 Hérault** – **339** D7 – **pop. 2 156** – **alt. 200 m** – **Spa : mid Feb.-mid Dec.** – **Casino** – ✉ **34240** Languedoc-Roussillon-Tarn Gorges

Paris 732 – Béziers 39 – Lodève 38 – Montpellier 79 – St-Pons-de-Thomières 38 22 **B2**

Office de tourisme, 1, avenue Capus 04 67 95 70 91, Fax 04 67 95 64 52

de Lamalou-les-Bains Route de Saint-Pons, Southeast: 2 km by D 908, 04 67 95 08 47.

St-Pierre-de-Rhèdes church ★ Southwest: 1,5 km.

St-Pierre-de-Rhèdes★ Southwest: 1,5 km.

L'Arbousier VISA AE

18 r. Alphonse Daudet – 04 67 95 63 11 – arbousier.hotel@wanadoo.fr – Fax 04 67 95 67 64 – Closed 21 January-1st February

31 rm – €49/61 €49/85, €8 – ½ P €54/62 – **Rest** – Menu €23/36 – Carte €30/59

◆ A charming early 20C establishment, near the baths and popular with people taking a cure. Light and functional rooms of various sizes. A colourful fresco adorns the walls of the restaurant. Terrace shaded by century-old plane trees.

Du Square without rest

11 av. Mal.-Foch – ☎ 04 67 23 09 93 – contact@hoteldusquare.com – Fax 04 67 23 04 27

14 rm – †€ 48/50 ††€ 48/53, ☕ € 7

◆ Motel-type construction with practical ground-floor rooms, calmer at the rear, some with terrace.

Les Marronniers

8 av. Capus, (D 22) – ☎ 04 67 95 76 00 – restolesmarronniers@free.fr – Fax 04 67 95 29 75 – Closed 26 January-8 February, Wednesday dinner off season, Sunday dinner and Monday

Rest – Menu € 13/59 bi – Carte approx. € 36

◆ An invigorating stopover after healthy excursions in the Caroux or on the Bédarieux-Mons scenic railway. Classic cuisine with Mediterranean touches and a choice of regional wines.

LAMARCHE-SUR-SAÔNE – 21 Côte-d'Or – 320 M6 – see Auxonne

LAMASTRE – 07 Ardèche – 331 J4 – pop. 2 467 – alt. 375 m – ✉ 07270

Lyon - Rhone Valley 44 **B2**

Paris 577 – Privas 55 – Le Puy-en-Velay 72 – St-Étienne 90 – Valence 38 – Vienne 92

Office de tourisme, place Montgolfier ☎ 04 75 06 48 99, Fax 04 75 06 37 53

Château d'Urbilhac ⟨ mountains,

2 km south-east on Vernoux-en-Vivarais road – ☎ 04 75 06 42 11 – info@chateaudurbilhac.fr – Fax 04 75 06 52 75

6 rm – †€ 130 ††€ 130, ☕ € 15 – ½ P € 110 – **Table d'hôte** – Menu € 38

◆ A small 19C neo-Renaissance château in the heart of a 30ha park overlooking the Doux valley. Antique charm in the rooms; panoramic swimming pool.

Midi (Bernard Perrier)

pl. Seignobos – ☎ 04 75 06 41 50 – Fax 04 75 06 49 75 – Closed from end December to end January, 23-29 June, Friday dinner, Sunday dinner and Monday

Rest – Menu € 38/84

Spec. Salade tiède de foie gras de canard. Poularde de Bresse en vessie. Soufflé glacé aux marrons de l'Ardèche. **Wines** Saint-Péray, Saint-Joseph.

◆ This restaurant in the heart of the village has retained its original charm, with a comfortable dining area and well-prepared classic cuisine.

LAMBALLE – 22 Côtes-d'Armor – 309 G4 – pop. 10 563 – alt. 55 m – ✉ 22400

Brittany 10 **C2**

Paris 431 – Dinan 42 – Rennes 81 – St-Brieuc 21 – St-Malo 50 – Vannes 130

Office de tourisme, place du Champ de Foire ☎ 02 96 31 05 38, Fax 02 96 50 88 54

Haras national★.

Plan on next page

Kyriad without rest

29 bd Jobert – ☎ 02 96 31 00 16 – kyriad.lamballe@wanadoo.fr – Fax 02 96 31 91 54 B **a**

27 rm – †€ 58/78 ††€ 58/78, ☕ € 8,50

◆ This hotel just opposite the station has renovated, well-soundproofed rooms. Friendly welcome, comfortable lounge-library.

Lion d'Or without rest

3 r. du Lion d'Or – ☎ 02 96 31 20 36 – leliondorhotel@wanadoo.fr – Fax 02 96 31 93 79 – Closed 23 December-6 January A **d**

17 rm – †€ 48/51 ††€ 50/53, ☕ € 8

◆ This family-run hotel in a quiet street in the town centre has been entirely renovated, with well-kept, light rooms featuring floral fabrics. Buffet menu available for breakfast.

LAMBALLE

Street	Grid	No.
Augustins (R. des)	A	2
Bario (R.)	A	3
Blois (R. Ch. de)	B	5
Boucouets (R. des)	B	7
Cartel (R. Ch.)	A	8
Charpentier (R. Y.)	B	14
Dr-A.-Calmette (R. du)	A	15
Dr-Lavergne (R. du)	A	16
Foch (R. Mar.)	B	19
Gesle (Ch. de la)	A	23
Grand Bd (R. du)	A	24
Hurel (R. du Bg)	B	25
Jeu-de-Paume (R. du)	A	26
Leclerc (R. Gén.)	B	29
Marché (Pl. du)	A	30
Martray (Pl. du)	A	
Mouëxigné (R.)	B	31
Poincaré (R.)	B	34
Préville (R.)	B	35
St-Jean (R.)	A	37
St-Lazare (R.)	A	38
Tery (R. G.)	A	39
Tour-aux-Chouettes (R.)	B	42
Val (R. du)	AB	
Villedeneu (R.)	A	45

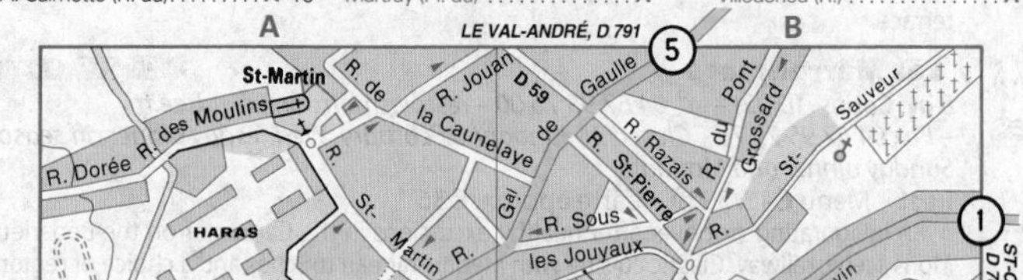

La Tour des Arc' hants
rest, VISA

2 r. Dr Lavergne – 02 96 31 01 37 – latourdesarchants@wanadoo.fr – Fax 02 96 31 37 59 A **b**

16 rm – €47/66 €52/66, €6 – ½ P €47/58 – **Rest** – Menu €18/34 – Carte €22/42

♦ This 14C hotel with a timbered façade is located in the centre of town. Providing simple, well-kept rustic rooms in modern style. Hanging on the walls of one dining room are works by local artists. The other has an impressive fireplace. Traditional cuisine served.

in la Poterie East: 3,5 km – ✉ 22400 Lamballe

Manoir des Portes
VISA

– 02 96 31 13 62 – contact@manoirdesportes.com – Fax 02 96 31 20 53 – Closed 22 December-2 January, 16 February-3 March

13 rm – €49/56 €58/99, €7,50 – ½ P €51/74 – **Rest** – *(closed Saturday lunch, Sunday lunch and Monday lunch)* Menu €23

♦ A 16C manor, close to a horse-riding centre, with both a flower and a vegetable garden, as well as an orchard. Peaceful and colourful rooms. Pleasant dining room, with beams and a fireplace, offering seasonal cuisine.

LAMOTTE-BEUVRON – 41 Loir-et-Cher – 318 J6 – pop. 4 251 – alt. 114 m – ✉ 41600
12 **C2**

Paris 171 – Blois 59 – Gien 58 – Orléans 36 – Romorantin-Lanthenay 39 – Salbris 21

Office de tourisme, 1, rue de l'Allée verte 02 54 83 01 73, Fax 02 54 83 00 94

Tatin

(opposite the station) – ✆ 02 54 88 00 03 – hotel-tatin@wanadoo.fr – Fax 02 54 88 96 73 – Closed 25 March-6 April, 27 July-13 August, 21 December-6 January, Monday and Tuesday

14 rm – †€ 56 ††€ 78, ☕ € 8,50 – **Rest** – Menu € 31 (weekday lunch), € 37/55 – Carte € 43/62

♦ This comfortable, family-run hotel provides contemporary, well-equipped rooms. Pleasant garden and terrace. It was here that the Tatin sisters invented their famous caramelised apple tart (the original stove can be seen in the bar). The tradition lives on!

LAMOTTE-WARFUSEE – 80 Somme – 301 I8 – pop. 513 – alt. 90 m – ✉ 80800

36 **B2**

▶ Paris 141 – Abbeville 72 – Amiens 22 – Cambrai 68 – Saint-Quentin 53

Le Saint-Pierre

3 r. Delambre – ✆ 03 22 42 26 66 – lacry.capart@neuf.fr – Fax 03 22 42 26 16 – Closed Sunday dinner and Monday

Rest – Menu (€ 13), € 16 (weekdays)/25 – Carte € 28/55

♦ Smart, brick-faced house in a village near the Somme canal, with two light and modern dining rooms. Family service and generous, classic cuisine.

Look out for red symbols, indicating particularly pleasant establishments.

LAMOURA – 39 Jura – 321 F8 – pop. 436 – alt. 1 156 m – Winter sports : see "aux Rousses" – ✉ 39310

16 **B3**

▶ Paris 477 – Genève 47 – Gex 29 – Lons-le-Saunier 74 – St-Claude 16

ℹ Office de tourisme, Grande Rue ✆ 03 84 41 27 01, Fax 03 84 41 25 59

La Spatule

Grande'rue – ✆ 03 84 41 20 23 – laspatule.hotel.restaurant@wanadoo.fr – Fax 03 84 41 24 16 – Closed 19 April-5 May, 20 October-15 December and Monday off season

26 rm – †€ 38/41 ††€ 52/62, ☕ € 7,50 – ½ P € 49/56 – **Rest** – Menu € 18/30 – Carte € 24/42

♦ At the foot of the slopes, a non-smoking chalet offering functional rooms with firwood furnishings (choose rooms with mountain view). Regional fare and interesting cheeses. Dish of the day available in adjoining café.

in Lajoux 6 km south by D 292 – ✉ 39310 – pop. 256 – alt. 1 180 m

De la Haute Montagne

– ✆ 03 84 41 20 47 – hotel-haute-montagne@wanadoo.fr – Fax 03 84 41 24 20 – Closed 29 March-21 April and 4 October-15 December

20 rm – †€ 36 ††€ 52, ☕ € 7,50 – ½ P € 47/52 – **Rest** – Menu € 14,50 (weekdays)/33

♦ A family-run hotel founded by a former cross country skiing champion in the heart of the Haut Jura nature park. Modest, well-kept rooms. Garden. Rustic dining room serving regional recipes or dish of the day. Brasserie menu in the café next door.

LAMPAUL PLOUARZEL – 29 Finistère – 308 C4 – pop. 1 766 – alt. 34 m – ✉ 29810

9 **A1**

▶ Paris 615 – Rennes 263 – Quimper 98 – Brest 24 – Landerneau 46

ℹ Office de tourisme, 7, rue de la Mairie ✆ 02 98 84 04 74

Auberge du Vieux Puits

pl. de l'Église – ✆ 02 98 84 09 13 – Fax 02 98 84 09 13 – Closed 4-20 March, 23 September-15 October, Sunday dinner and Monday

Rest – Menu € 22 (weekday lunch), € 34/51

♦ Typical old granite building in the village centre. Traditional cuisine served in a rustic dining room or on the south-facing terrace, where the old well that gives its name to the restaurant can be seen.

LAMURE-SUR-AZERGUES – 69 Rhône – 327 F3 – pop. 871 – alt. 383 m – ✉ 69870 44 **B1**

Paris 446 – Lyon 50 – Mâcon 51 – Roanne 49 – Tarare 36 – Villefranche-sur-Saône 29

Office de tourisme, rue du Vieux Pont ✆ 04 74 03 13 26, Fax 04 74 03 13 26

Château de Pramenoux

2 km to the west – ✆ 04 74 03 16 43 – pramenoux@aol.com

4 rm – €125 €125 – **Table d'hôte** – Menu €33 bi

◆ This château features a large entrance hall with a magnificent staircase and quiet rooms furnished with antiques. The Royal room also features a four-poster bed. Candlelit dinner accompanied by fine music.

LANARCE – 07 Ardèche – 331 G5 – pop. 199 – alt. 1 180 m – ✉ 07660 44 **A3**

Paris 579 – Aubenas 44 – Langogne 18 – Privas 72 – Le Puy-en-Velay 48

Le Provence

rm, VISA

N 102 – ✆ 04 66 69 46 06 – reservation@hotel-le-provence.com – Fax 04 66 69 41 56 – Open 15 March-15 November

19 rm – €38/55 €42/55, €8 – ½ P €43/54

Rest – Menu (€13,50), €18/34 – Carte €21/32

◆ All the rooms in this modern building, on a busy thoroughfare, are soundproofed and overlook the rear. Choose those that have just been renovated. Appetising local cuisine served in the dining room or on the peaceful terrace.

LANCIEUX – 22 Côtes-d'Armor – 309 J3 – see St-Briac-sur-Mer

LANCRANS – 01 Ain – 328 I4 – see Bellegarde-sur-Valserine

LANDÉAN – 35 Ille-et-Vilaine – 309 P4 – see Fougères

LANDES-LE-GAULOIS – 41 Loir-et-Cher – 318 E6 – pop. 582 – alt. 105 m – ✉ 41190 11 **B2**

Paris 195 – Blois 17 – Château-Renault 25 – Tours 54 – Vendôme 21

Château de Moulins without rest

VISA

north-east: 2 km on the D 26 – ✆ 02 54 20 17 93 – Fax 02 54 20 17 99

23 rm – €158 €183, €11 – 2 suites

◆ In the heart of a wooded estate with a lake, this elegant château, built between the 12C and 17C has large rooms, many of which are furnished with antiques. Heliport.

LANDONVILLERS – 57 Moselle – 307 J4 – ✉ 57530 Courcelles Chaussy 27 **C1**

Paris 348 – Metz 21 – Saarbrücken 55 – Völklingen 52

Le Moulin without rest

Allée du Moulin – ✆ 03 87 64 24 81 – weber.c2@orange.fr – Fax 03 87 64 24 81 – Closed January

4 rm – €60/72 €60/72

◆ On the banks of a river, a former mill with the look of a manor and surrounding park popular with birds; personalised, original rooms combining old and new elements.

LANDSER – 68 Haut-Rhin – 315 I10 – see Mulhouse

LANDUDEC – 29 Finistère – 308 E6 – pop. 1 154 – alt. 105 m – ✉ 29710 9 **A2**

Paris 584 – Rennes 232 – Quimper 20 – Brest 92 – Concarneau 45

Château du Guilguiffin without rest

VISA

rte de Quimper – ✆ 02 98 91 52 11 – chateau@guilguiffin.com – Fax 02 98 91 52 52 – Closed 15 November-20 December and 5 January-1st February

4 rm – €135/160 €135/170

◆ Founded in the 12C and remodelled six centuries later, this château full of history has been home to the same family for five generations. Delightful grounds, period furniture and king-size bedrooms.

LANGEAC – 43 Haute-Loire – 331 C3 – pop. 4 070 – alt. 505 m – ✉ 43300
Auvergne 6 **C3**

Paris 508 – Brioude 31 – Mende 92 – Le Puy-en-Velay 45 – St-Flour 54

Office de tourisme, place Aristide Briand ☎ 04 71 77 05 41, Fax 04 71 77 19 93

in Reilhac North: 3 km by D 585 – ✉ 43300 Mazeyrat-d'Allier

Val d'Allier rest, rest, VISA

– ☎ 04 71 77 02 11 – Fax 04 71 77 19 20
– Open 1st April-31 October and closed Sunday dinner and Monday off season
22 rm – €45/50 €55/60, €9 – ½ P €50/56
Rest – *(dinner only) (pre-book)* Menu (€20), €23/37

◆ This comfortable hotel in a typical village in the Gorges de l'Allier is particularly popular with hikers and sports' enthusiasts. Traditional, regional cuisine served in a modern dining room.

LANGEAIS – 37 Indre-et-Loire – 317 L5 – pop. 3 865 – alt. 41 m – ✉ 37130
Châteaux of the Loire 11 **A2**

Paris 259 – Angers 101 – Château-la-Vallière 28 – Chinon 26 – Saumur 41 – Tours 24

Office de tourisme, place du 14 Juillet ☎ 02 47 96 58 22, Fax 02 47 96 83 41

Château★★: apartments★★★.

Park ★ du château de Cinq-Mars-la-Pile Northeast: 5 km by N 152.

Errard VISA AE

2 r. Gambetta – ☎ 02 47 96 82 12 – info@errard.com – Fax 02 47 96 56 72
– Closed 7 December-13 February, Sunday dinner and Monday 1st October-14 May
Rest – *(dinner only from 15 May to 30 September)* Menu €29/53 bi – Carte €52/67

◆ Former post house (1653) in a tasteful rustic setting near the château. Classic family cooking featuring Touraine flavours.

in St-Patrice West: 10 km by Bourgueil road – pop. 639 – alt. 39 m – ✉ 37130

Château de Rochecotte rest, VISA AE

43 r. Dorothée de Dino – ☎ 02 47 96 16 16
– chateau.rochecotte@wanadoo.fr – Fax 02 47 96 90 59
– Closed 14 January-12 February
32 rm – €126/230 €126/230, €17 – 3 suites – ½ P €115
Rest – Menu €40 – Carte €66/87

◆ Aristocratic residence frequented by the Prince de Talleyrand. Period furnishings in the bedrooms and pleasant terrace with pergola overlooking the gardens. The dining rooms sport an elegant 18C style. Updated cuisine.

LANGON – 33 Gironde – 335 J7 – pop. 6 168 – alt. 10 m – ✉ 33210
Atlantic Coast 3 **B2**

Paris 624 – Bergerac 83 – Bordeaux 49 – Libourne 54 – Marmande 47 – Mont-de-Marsan 86

Office de tourisme, 11, allées Jean-Jaurès ☎ 05 56 63 68 00, Fax 05 56 63 68 09

des Graves et Sauternais Lac de Seguin, East: 5 km by D 116, ☎ 05 56 62 25 43.

Château de Roquetaillade★★ South: 7 km.

Claude Darroze with rm VISA AE

95 cours Gén. Leclerc – ☎ 05 56 63 00 48
– restaurant.darroze@wanadoo.fr – Fax 05 56 63 41 15
– Closed 14 October-7 November, 5-22 January, Sunday dinner and Monday lunch
16 rm – €50/60 €65/110, €12 – ½ P €95/115
Rest – Menu €42/80 – Carte €70/101

Spec. Lamproie à la bordelaise aux blancs de poireaux (January to April). Noix de ris de veau braisée au jus, saveur andalouse. Gibier (October to January). **Wines** Côtes de Bordeaux-Saint Macaire, Graves.

◆ Savoury classic cuisine and good Bordeaux wine list (600 appellations): this traditional establishment invites you to enjoy your meal. Terrace under the plane trees.

Chez Cyril

62 cours Fossés – ✆ 05 56 76 25 66 – sarlles3c@orange.fr – Fax 05 56 63 25 21 – Closed Monday dinner
Rest – Menu € 21/28 – Carte € 27/55
◆ Pleasant welcome in a warm contemporary dining room (teak furnishings) or on the courtyard terrace with fountain. Traditional cuisine.

in St-Macaire North: 2 km – pop. 1 541 – alt. 15 m – ✉ 33490

Verdelais: calvary ⩽★ North: 3 km - Château de Malromé★ North: 6 km - Ste-Croix-du-Mont: ⩽★, grottoes★ Northwest: 5 km.

Abricotier with rm

RN 113 – ✆ 05 56 76 83 63 – restaurant.abricotier@wanadoo.fr – Fax 05 56 76 28 51 – Closed 12 November-10 December, 2-10 March, Tuesday dinner and Monday
3 rm – †€ 55 ††€ 58, ☕ € 6,50 – **Rest** – Menu € 20 (weekdays)/45 – Carte € 34/52
◆ A regional building near the medieval city. Welcoming modern decor, shaded terrace garden and appetising traditional cuisine.

LANGRES – 52 Haute-Marne – 313 L6 – pop. 9 586 – alt. 466 m – ✉ 52200

Northern France and the Paris Region 14 **C3**

Paris 285 – Chaumont 35 – Dijon 79 – Nancy 142 – Vesoul 76

Office de tourisme, square Olivier Lahalle ✆ 03 25 87 67 67, Fax 03 25 87 73 33

Site★★ - Ramparts walkway★★ - St-Mammès cathedral★ Y - Gallo-Roman Section ★ in the musée d'art et d'histoire Y **M**[1].

LANGRES

Aubert (R.) . . . Y
Barbier-d'Aucourt (R.) . . . Y 3
Beligné (R. Ch.) . . . Y 4
Belle-Allée (La) . . . Y 5
Boillot (R.) . . . Y 6
Boulière (Porte) . . . Y
Boulière (R.) . . . Y 7
Canon (R.) . . . Y 8
Centenaire (Pl. du) . . . Y 10
Chambrûlard (R.) . . . X 12
Chavannes (R. des) . . . Z 13
Crémaillière (R. de la) . . . Y 14
Croc (R. du) . . . Y 15
Denfert-Rochereau (R.) . . . Z 16
Diderot (Pl.) . . . Y
Diderot (R.) . . . YZ
Durand (R. Pierre) . . . Y 17
Duvet (Pl. J.) . . . Y
États-Unis (Pl. des) . . . Z
Gambetta (R.) . . . Y 18
Grand-Bie (R. du) . . . Y 19
Grand-Cloître (R. du) . . . Y 20
Grouchy (Pl. Col.-de) . . . Z 21
Hôtel-de-Ville (Porte de l') . . . Y
Jenson (Pl.) . . . Z
Lambert-Payen (R.) . . . Y 24
Lattre-de-Tassigny (Bd Mar.-de) . . . YZ
Leclerc (R. Général) . . . Y 25
Lescornel (R.) . . . Y 26
Longe-Porte (Porte de) . . . X
Longe-Porte (R. de) . . . X 27
Mance (Square J.) . . . Y 28
Minot (R.) . . . Z 31
Morlot (R. Card.) . . . Y 32
Roger (R.) . . . Y 33
Roussat (R. Jean) . . . Y 35
St-Didier (R.) . . . Y 36
Tassel (R.) . . . X
Terreaux (R. des) . . . Y 37
Tournelle (R. de la) . . . Y 39
Turenne (R. de) . . . Y 41
Ursulines (R. des) . . . Y 43
Verdun (Pl. de) . . . X
Walferdin (R.) . . . Y 44
Ziegler (Pl.) . . . Y 45

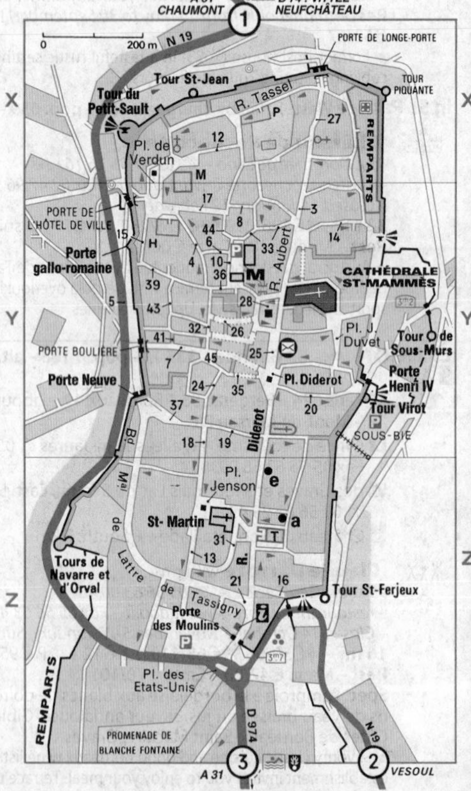

Le Cheval Blanc rm, VISA AE

4 r. de l'Estres – ✆ 03 25 87 07 00 – info@hotel-langres.com – Fax 03 25 87 23 13 – Closed 2-30 November Z **a**

22 rm – 🚹€ 68/95 🚹🚹€ 68/95, ☕ € 9 – ½ P € 78/115 – **Rest** – *(closed Wednesday lunch)* Menu € 20 (weekday lunch), € 34/52 – Carte € 52/81

◆ Bishop Bossuet received the sub-deacons at this historic church which became an inn during the Revolution. Characterful rooms, more functional in the annexe. Dining room decorated with work by local artists. Quiet terrace. Modern menu.

Grand Hôtel de L'Europe P VISA

23 r. Diderot – ✆ 03 25 87 10 88 – hotel-europe.langres@wanadoo.fr – Fax 03 25 87 60 65 – Closed Sunday dinner from 1st November to 31 May

26 rm – 🚹€ 55/75 🚹🚹€ 63/80, ☕ € 9 – ½ P € 55/64 – **Rest** – Menu € 17 (weekdays)/46 – Carte € 21/58 Z **e**

◆ Inside the ramparts, a former posthouse along a main road in the old town. Spacious rooms, quieter at the back. Light wood, parquet flooring and country furniture in this dining room adjoining the hotel bar.

at Lac de la Liez by ②, N 19 and D 284: 6 km – ✉ 52200 Langres

Auberge des Voiliers with rm P VISA

au bord du Lac – ✆ 03 25 87 05 74 – auberge.voiliers@wanadoo.fr – Fax 03 25 87 24 22 – Open 10 March-15 December and closed Sunday dinner and Monday dinner except July -August

10 rm – 🚹€ 50/100 🚹🚹€ 50/120, ☕ € 8 – ½ P € 58/83 – **Rest** – *(closed Sunday dinner and Monday)* Menu € 20/45 – Carte € 22/46

◆ An inn ideally situated next to the lake. Restaurant dining room decorated with frescos; views from the veranda. Small, air-conditioned rooms on a nautical theme.

LANGUIMBERG – 57 Moselle – 307 M6 – pop. 175 – alt. 290 m – ✉ 57810 27 C2

Paris 411 – Lunéville 43 – Metz 79 – Nancy 65 – Sarrebourg 21 – Saverne 48

Chez Michèle VISA AE

– ✆ 03 87 03 92 25 – contact@chezmichele.fr – Fax 03 87 03 93 47 – Closed 23 December-10 January, Tuesday except lunch from May to August and Wednesday

Rest – Menu € 17 (weekday lunch), € 27/68 – Carte € 42/58

◆ The old village café is now a gourmet inn. Dine on delicious modern cuisine in the former tavern or on the veranda surrounded by greenery. Collection of coffee pots.

LANNILIS – Finistère – 308 D3 – pop. 4 473 – alt. 48 m – ✉ 29870 9 A1

Paris 599 – Brest 23 – Landerneau 29 – Morlaix 63 – Quimper 89

Office de tourisme, 1, place de l'Église ✆ 02 98 04 05 43

Auberge des Abers VISA

5 pl. Gén. Leclerc, (near the church) – ✆ 02 98 04 00 29 – anne-laure.brouzet@wanadoo.fr

Rest – *(open dinner Wednesday-Saturday and Sunday lunch) (number of covers limited, pre-book)* Menu € 45/120 bi

Rest *Côté Bistrot* – *(open lunch Tuesday-Saturday)* Menu (€ 17), € 22 – Carte € 26/32

◆ Fine and light gastronomic cuisine with the focus on fish and seafood. Elegant decor (display of menus from prestigious restaurants where the chef has eaten). Cookery class on Tuesday evenings. Traditional home cooking takes pride of place on the Côté Bistrot's menu.

LANNION – 22 Côtes-d'Armor – 309 B2 – pop. 18 368 – alt. 12 m – ✉ 22300 Brittany 9 B1

Paris 516 – Brest 96 – Morlaix 42 – St-Brieuc 65

Lannion: ✆ 02 96 05 82 00, North by ①: 2 km.

Office de tourisme, 2, quai d'Aiguillon ✆ 02 96 46 41 00, Fax 02 96 37 19 64

Old houses★ (pl.Général Leclerc Y17) - Brélévenez church ★: burial★ Y.

Perros-Guirec road by ① D 788: 5 km – ✉ 22300 Lannion

Arcadia without rest
– ✆ 02 96 48 45 65 – hotel-arcadia@wanadoo.fr – Fax 02 96 48 15 68
– Closed 19 December-11 January
23 rm – €47/62 €50/62, €7
◆ Not far from the Telecom centre, this modern-looking hotel provides neat and tidy rooms and some duplexes. Those at the back are quieter. Snooker bar and swimming pool.

in La Ville-Blanche by ②, Tréguier road: 5 km on D 786 – ✉ 22300 Rospez

La Ville Blanche (Jean-Yves Jaguin)
– ✆ 02 96 37 04 28 – jaguin@la-ville-blanche.com – Fax 02 96 46 57 82
– Closed 30 June-7 July, 22 December-30 January, Sunday dinner and Wednesday except July-August and Monday
Rest – (pre-book Sat - Sun) Menu (€ 24), € 32 (weekdays)/77 – Carte € 64/81
Spec. Homard rôti au beurre salé, pinces en ragoût (April to October). Saint-Jacques des Côtes d'Armor (October to March). Parfait glacé à la menthe et au chocolat.
◆ An elegant dining room and kitchen garden where herbs are gathered to give subtle flavour to the highly individual, delicious cuisine in this "family home".

LANS-EN-VERCORS

LANS-EN-VERCORS – 38 Isère – 333 G7 – pop. 2 026 – alt. 1 120 m – Winter sports : 1 020/1 980 m 16 – ✉ 38250 45 **C2**

Paris 576 – Grenoble 27 – Villard-de-Lans 8 – Voiron 37
Office de tourisme, 246, avenue Léopold Fabre ✆ 08 11 46 00 38, Fax 04 76 95 47 99

Le Val Fleuri rest,
730 av. L. Fabre – ✆ 04 76 95 41 09 – hotel.levalfleuri@orange.fr
– Fax 04 76 94 34 69 – Open 3 May-22 October, 21 December-29 March and closed Sunday dinner and Monday in September and October
14 rm – €38/67 €38/67, €9 – ½ P €52/66 – **Rest** – Menu €25 (weekdays)/48
◆ Time seems to have stood still in this attractive residence from 1928, with a perfectly preserved pre-1940s character. Extremely well-kept rooms, sometimes adorned with Art Deco furniture and lamps. Lovely 1930s dining room, terrace under the lime trees and traditional recipes.

at col de la Croix-Perrin Southwest: 4 km by D 106 – ✉ 38250 Lans-en-Vercors

Auberge de la Croix Perrin with rm
Croix-Perrin pass – ✆ 04 76 95 40 02 – frederic.joly10@wanadoo.fr
– Fax 04 76 94 33 10 – Closed from April to beg. May and 3-20 November
8 rm – €41/45 €48/55, €7,50 – ½ P €46/50
Rest – (closed Wednesday and weekday dinner except school holidays)
Menu €16 (weekday lunch), €22/41 – Carte €22/37
◆ The dining room of this old forest house, surrounded by fir trees, offers a clear view. Local lunchtime dishes and more inventive cuisine in the evening. Charming rooms.

LANSLEBOURG-MONT-CENIS

LANSLEBOURG-MONT-CENIS – 73 Savoie – 333 O6 – pop. 640 – alt. 1 399 m – Winter sports : 1 400/2 800 m 1 21 – ✉ 73480 French Alps 45 **D2**

Paris 685 – Albertville 112 – Chambéry 125 – St-Jean-de-Maurienne 53 – Torino 94
Office de tourisme, Grande Rue ✆ 04 79 05 23 66, Fax 04 79 05 82 17

La Vieille Poste
– ✆ 04 79 05 93 47 – info@lavieilleposte.com – Fax 04 79 05 86 85
19 rm – €43/59 €49/70, €7,50 – ½ P €50/70 – **Rest** – Menu €13,50 (weekday lunch), €20/30 – Carte €22/34
◆ A friendly, recently renovated family pension in the centre of this resort in the Haute Maurienne. Small, up-to-the-minute, impeccably maintained rooms. Rustic Savoyard decor in the dining room.

Le Relais des Deux Cols

66 r. Mont-Cenis – ✆ 04 79 05 92 83 – hotel@relais-des-2-cols.fr – Fax 04 79 05 83 74 – Closed 2 November-19 December and 21-30 April

28 rm – †€ 42/52 ††€ 48/60, ☕ € 8 – ½ P € 48/65 – **Rest** – Menu € 18/35 – Carte € 29/43

♦ This overnight hotel on the road leading through the Mont Cenis and Iseran passes provides all different and renovated rooms. The bay windows of the bright family-run establishment overlook the countryside; distinctive regional cuisine.

LANSLEVILLARD – **73 Savoie** – **333** O6 – **pop. 431** – **alt. 1 500 m** – **Winter sports : (see Lanslebourg-Mont-Cenis)** – ✉ **73480** ▮ **French Alps** 45 **D2**

▶ Paris 689 – Albertville 116 – Briançon 87 – Chambéry 129 – Val-d'Isère 51

ℹ Office de tourisme, rue Sous Église ✆ 04 79 05 99 15

◎ Wall paintings★ in St-Sébastien chapel.

Les Mélèzes

– ✆ 04 79 05 93 82 – Fax 04 79 05 93 82 – Open 23 June-5 September and 20 December-20 April

11 rm – †€ 51/60 ††€ 66/70, ☕ € 8 – 2 suites – ½ P € 54/74 – **Rest** – *(Closed dinner in winter)* Menu € 16 (weekdays)/24 – Carte € 18/32

♦ A 1980s-style building ideally located at the foot of the ski slopes. Wood-panelled rooms, most of which face the Dent Parrachée. Guided hikes. The restaurant is run by the owner's son. Serving crepes and Savoy dishes in winter.

LANTOSQUE – **06 Alpes-Maritimes** – **341** E4 – **pop. 1 019** – **alt. 550 m** – ✉ **06450** 41 **D2**

▶ Paris 883 – Nice 51 – Puget-Théniers 53 – St-Martin-Vésubie 16 – Sospel 42

ℹ Syndicat d'initiative, Mairie ✆ 04 93 03 00 02, Fax 04 93 03 03 12

Hostellerie de l'Ancienne Gendarmerie

– ✆ 04 93 03 00 65 – faivre.mireille@wanadoo.fr – Fax 04 93 03 06 31 – Open 1st March-1st November

8 rm – †€ 70/115 ††€ 70/115, ☕ € 10 – ½ P € 65/95 – **Rest** – *(closed lunch 15 July-20 August, Sunday dinner and Monday)* Menu € 30 (weekdays)/36

♦ This 19C building, a former Gendarmerie, offers welcoming and updated rooms. Cells not available! A snug, rustic restaurant facing the garden, which slopes down to the Vésubie. Traditional menu chalked up on a blackboard.

La Source

Montée des casernes, D 373 – ✆ 04 93 O3 05 44 – lasource11@wanadoo.fr – Closed 1st-18 January, Sunday dinner and Monday

Rest – *(number of covers limited, pre-book)* Menu (€ 18), € 25

♦ A small Provençal inn with rustic charm and a lively atmosphere. The owner, who is passionate about cooking, offers one simply prepared but delicious menu.

LANVOLLON – **22 Côtes-d'Armor** – **309** E3 – **pop. 1 388** – **alt. 90 m** – ✉ **22290**

▶ Paris 475 – Guingamp 17 – Lannion 51 – Paimpol 19 – St-Brieuc 27

ℹ Office de tourisme, 8, place du marché au blé ✆ 02 96 70 12 47, Fax 02 96 70 27 34 10 **C1**

Lucotel

rm, rest,

rte de St-Quay-Portrieux via D 9 : 1 km – ✆ 02 96 70 01 17 – lucotel@wanadoo.fr – Fax 02 96 70 08 84 – Closed 13 October-2 November and 16-25 February

30 rm – †€ 51/65 ††€ 59/65, ☕ € 7,50 – ½ P € 61/66 – **Rest** – *(closed Sunday dinner and Saturday October-May)* Menu € 15 (weekday lunch), € 21/35 – Carte € 29/51

♦ The rooms in this new hotel just outside the village are simple, but functional and well maintained, some having been recently renovated. A simple dining area in lively yellow tones. Serving simple, traditional cuisine.

If breakfast is included the ☕ symbol appears after the number of rooms.

LAON P – 02 Aisne – 306 D5 – pop. 26 265 – alt. 181 m – ✉ 02000

Northern France and the Paris Region 37 **D2**

- Paris 141 – Reims 62 – St-Quentin 48 – Soissons 38
- Office de tourisme, place du Parvis Gautier de Mortagne ✆ 03 23 20 28 62, Fax 03 23 20 68 11
- de l'Ailette Cerny-en-LaonnoisSouth: 16 km by D 967, ✆ 03 23 24 83 99.
- Site★★ - Notre-Dame cathedral ★★: nave★★★ - Rempart du Midi and porte d'Ardon★ CZ - St-Martin abbey ★ BZ - Porte de Soissons★ ABZ - Rue Thibesard ≤★ BZ - Museum ★ and Templiers church ★ CZ.

La Bannière de France

11 r. F. Roosevelt – ✆ 03 23 23 21 44 – hotel.banniere.de.france@wanadoo.fr – Fax 03 23 23 31 56 – Closed 19 December-18 January BCZ **t**

18 rm – †€ 50/65 ††€ 63/75, ☕ € 9 – ½ P € 59/65 – **Rest** – *(closed lunch July-August)* Menu (€ 18), € 25/56 – Carte € 26/62

◆ This post house in the upper part of town was built in 1685, but in the 1920s it was home to the town's first cinema. Spruce rooms. The classicism of the long narrow dining room is full of the charm of provincial France.

LAON

Arquebuse (R. de l') .... **CZ** 2	Bossus (R. de l'Abbé) ..... **DY** 6	Cloître (R. du) .... **CZ** 15
Aubry (Pl.) .... **CZ** 3	Bourg (R. du) .... **BCZ** 8	Combattants d'Afrique du Nord (Pl. des) .... **DZ** 16
Berthelot (R. Marcelin) ..... **AZ** 5	Carnot (Av.) .... **CY**	Cordeliers (R. des) .... **CZ** 18
	Change (R. du) .... **CZ** 9	Doumer (R. Paul) .... **CZ** 19
	Charles de Gaulle (Av.) ..... **DY** 12	Ermant (R. Georges) .... **CZ** 21
	Châtelaine (R.) .... **CZ** 13	

Hostellerie St-Vincent

av. Ch. de Gaulle , via ② – ✆ 03 23 23 42 43 – hotel.st.vincent@wanadoo.fr – Fax 03 23 79 22 55 – Closed Christmas holidays

47 rm – 🚹€ 58 🚹🚹€ 58, ☕ € 7,50 – ½ P € 50 – **Rest** – *(closed Sunday)* Menu (€ 13), € 18 – Carte € 16/33

◆ A modern motel-style establishment built below the old Carolingian capital perched on its rock. Functional rooms. Spacious dining room in a restaurant where Alsatian gastronomy is given pride of place.

La Petite Auberge

45 bd Brossolette – ✆ 03 23 23 02 38 – palaon@orange.fr – Fax 03 23 23 31 01 – Closed Easter holidays, 5-20 August, February half-term holidays, Saturday lunch, Monday dinner and Sunday except public holidays CY **a**

Rest – Menu (€ 18), € 25/33 – Carte € 38/78

Rest *Bistrot St-Amour* – ✆ *03 23 23 31 01* – Menu (€ 11), € 14/17 – Carte € 29/33

◆ A restaurant in the lower part of the town, featuring soft colours, with painted beams, tapestries and Louis XIII furniture. Inventive modern menu and speedy service in a simple bistro.

Hurée (R. de la) . . . . **DY** 23
Jur (Prom. Barthélémy de) . . **CZ** 24
Leduc (R. Eugène) . . . . **DY**
Libération (R. de la) . . . . . . **ABZ** 25
Marquette (R. Père) . . . . **BZ** 27
Martinot (Allée Jean) . . . . . . **DZ** 28
Mortagne (Pl. Gautier de) . . . **CZ** 29
Rabin (Promenade Yitzhak) . . **CZ** 30
Roosevelt (R. Franklin) . . . . . **CZ** 31
St-Jean (R.) . . . . **BZ** 33
St-Martin (R.) . . . . **BZ** 34
Signier (R. de) . . . . **CZ** 36
Thuillart (R. Fernand) . . . . . . **DY** 37
Victor-Hugo (Pl.) . . . . **DY** 39
Vinchon (R.) . . . . **CZ** 40

in Samoussy by ② and D 977: 13 km – pop. 376 – alt. 84 m – ✉ 02840

XXX **Le Relais Charlemagne**

4 rte de Laon – ☎ 03 23 22 21 50 – relais.charlemagne@wanadoo.fr – Fax 03 23 22 18 75 – Closed 1st-16 August, February holidays, Wednesday dinner, Sunday dinner and Monday

Rest – Menu € 25 (weekdays)/58 – Carte € 50/64

◆ Berthe, the mother of Charlemagne, was originally from this village. The restaurant has two elegant dining areas, one overlooking the garden. Classic cuisine.

in Chamouille by D 967 DZ : 13 km – pop. 204 – alt. 112 m – ✉ 02860

Mercure ≤ rm, rest,

parc nautique de l'Ailette, 0.5 km south by D 967 – ☎ 03 23 24 84 85 – hotel-mercure@ailette.fr – Fax 03 23 24 81 20

58 rm – †€ 92 ††€ 102, ☕ € 13

Rest – Menu (€ 19), € 24 – Carte € 21/37

◆ A modern building standing alone on the banks of a huge stretch of water with water sports facilities. Spacious rooms with loggias. Golf. A modern dining room and terrace by the swimming pool, on the banks of the Ailette water park.

LAPALISSE – 03 Allier – 326 I5 – pop. 3 332 – alt. 280 m – ✉ 03120

Auvergne 6 **C1**

Paris 346 – Digoin 45 – Mâcon 122 – Moulins 50 – Roanne 49 – St-Pourçain-sur-Sioule 30

Office de tourisme, 26, rue Winston Churchill ☎ 04 70 99 08 39, Fax 04 70 99 28 09

Château★★.

XX **Galland** with rm

20 pl. de la République – ☎ 04 70 99 07 21 – Fax 04 70 99 34 64 – Closed 24 November-9 December, 19 January-10 February, Sunday dinner off season, Tuesday lunch and Monday

8 rm – †€ 50 ††€ 50, ☕ € 7,50 – **Rest** – *(pre-book Sat - Sun)* Menu € 28 (weekdays)/55 – Carte € 42/50

◆ Elegant, contemporary dining room in pastel shades serving modern dishes; comfortable, well-kept rooms.

LAPOUTROIE – 68 Haut-Rhin – 315 H8 – pop. 2 104 – alt. 420 m – ✉ 68650

Alsace-Lorraine 1 **A2**

Paris 430 – Colmar 21 – Munster 31 – Ribeauvillé 20 – St-Dié 33 – Sélestat 33

Du Faudé

28 r. Gén. Dufieux – ☎ 03 89 47 50 35 – info@faude.com – Fax 03 89 47 24 82 – Closed 17 February-8 March, 2-22 November

30 rm – †€ 43/93 ††€ 43/93, ☕ € 13 – 2 suites – ½ P € 70/104

Rest *Faudé Gourmet* – *(Closed Tuesday and Wednesday)* Menu € 32/75 – Carte € 54/60

Rest *Au Grenier Welche* – *(Closed Tuesday and Wednesday)* Menu € 20/28 – Carte € 30/46

◆ Regional buildings with comfortable rooms, larger and renovated in the wing (all non-smoking). Pleasant riverside garden. The Faudé Gourmet is modern in style and cuisine; rich wine list. Country fare served in local costume at the Grenier Welche.

XX **Les Alisiers** with rm ≤ valley, rm, rm,

3 km southwest by secondary road – ☎ 03 89 47 52 82 – hotel@alisiers.com – Fax 03 89 47 22 38 – Closed 28 June-4 July, 21-25 December, 5-31 January, Monday, Tuesday and Wednesday off season

16 rm – †€ 50/180 ††€ 50/180, ☕ € 11 – **Rest** – *(closed Wednesday off season, Monday and Tuesday except residents) (pre-book Sat - Sun)* Menu € 25/55 – Carte € 33/49

◆ This 1819 farmhouse is now a pretty non-smoking inn providing country-style rooms and a restaurant overlooking the valley. Regional dishes.

LAQUEUILLE – 63 Puy-de-Dôme – 326 D9 – pop. 384 – alt. 1 000 m – ✉ 63820 5 **B2**

Paris 455 – Aubusson 74 – Clermont-Ferrand 40 – Mauriac 73 – Le Mont-Dore 15 – Ussel 43

Northeast : 2 km by D 922 and secondary road – ✉ 63820 Laqueuille

Auberge de Fondain

Fondain – ✆ 04 73 22 01 35 – auberge.de.fondain@wanadoo.fr – Fax 04 73 22 06 13 – Closed 9-19 March and 6 November-11 December

6 rm – €45/50 €66/72, ☕ €9 – ½ P €53/56

Rest – *(pre-book)* Menu (€12 bi), €15/23 – Carte €22/26

◆ A large old house lost in the countryside, individual rooms with flower themes, mountain biking, a fitness centre, etc. A lovely green setting! Rustic interior serving classic fare: Auvergne specialities chalked up on a slate.

LARAGNE-MONTÉGLIN – 05 Hautes-Alpes – 334 C7 – pop. 3 296 – alt. 571 m – ✉ 05300 40 **B2**

Paris 687 – Digne-les-Bains 58 – Gap 40 – Sault 60 – Serres 17 – Sisteron 18

Office de tourisme, place des Aires ✆ 04 92 65 09 38, Fax 04 92 65 28 41

Chrisma without rest

VISA

rte de Grenoble – ✆ 04 92 65 09 36 – Fax 04 92 65 08 12 – Closed 29 September-6 October and 15 December-2 January

13 rm – €40/42 €42/50, ☕ €6

◆ The pleasant garden and terrace are the main assets of this hotel at the foot of the Chabre mountain, famous for hang-gliding. The rooms are spacious and well-renovated.

Les Terrasses

rest, VISA

av. de Provence , (D 1075) – ✆ 04 92 65 08 54 – hotellesterrasses@wanadoo.fr – Fax 04 92 65 21 08 – Open 1st April-1st November

15 rm – €28/52 €52, ☕ €7,50 – ½ P €50 – **Rest** – *(open 1er May-1st October) (dinner only)* Menu (€17), €22/27 – Carte €23/33

◆ A traditional family guesthouse with simple, pleasant rooms; those on the garden side have a terrace with an attractive view of the village and Chabre mountain. Traditional meals served in a sunny dining area, or under the vine-covered pergola with panoramic views in the summer.

L'Araignée Gourmande

VISA

8 r. de la Paix – ✆ 04 92 65 13 39

Rest – *(closed 15-30 November, 23-26 December, February holidays, Sunday dinner October-April, Tuesday dinner and Wednesday)* Menu €14 (weekday lunch), €23/44 – Carte €32/48

◆ This family-run eatery with fairly modest decor has all the qualities of a successful restaurant - simple, delicious traditional cuisine, friendly service and reasonable prices.

LARÇAY – 37 Indre-et-Loire – 317 N4 – pop. 2 037 – alt. 82 m – ✉ 37270 11 **B2**

Paris 243 – Angers 134 – Blois 55 – Poitiers 103 – Tours 10 – Vierzon 113

Manoir de Clairbois without rest

VISA

2 imp. du Cher – ✆ 02 47 50 59 75 – info@manoirdeclairbois.com – Fax 02 47 50 59 76

3 rm ☕ – €115 €115/140

◆ This 19C manor stands in a park along the Cher river. Offering large, bright rooms with fine decor and bed linen. The communal areas are furnished with period pieces.

Les Chandelles Gourmandes

VISA

44 r. Nationale – ✆ 02 47 50 50 02 – charret@chandelles-gourmandes.fr – Fax 02 47 50 55 94 – Closed 25 July-5 August, 25 August-5 September, Sunday dinner and Monday

Rest – Menu €29/65 – Carte €41/63

◆ Beams, tufa, and a fireplace embellish this former post house near the banks of the Cher. Regional cuisine, fried fish and other Loire river specialities.

LE LARDIN-ST-LAZARE – 24 Dordogne – **329** I5 – **pop. 1 846** – **alt. 86 m** – ✉ **24570** 4 **D1**

Paris 503 – Brive-la-Gaillarde 28 – Lanouaille 38 – Périgueux 47 – Sarlat-la-Canéda 31

South : **4 km by D 704, D 62 and secondary road** – ✉ **24570 Condat-sur-Vézère**

Château de la Fleunie
– ☎ *05 53 51 32 74 – lafleunie@free.fr*
– Fax 05 53 50 58 98 – Closed 30 November-1st March
33 rm – €70/110 €70/190, €15 – ½ P €75/135 – **Rest** – Menu €30/60
◆ This medieval castle, surrounded by a 100-ha park with an animal enclosure, houses rooms with character, sometimes adorned with beams. Other rooms available in a more recent building. Classic food to enjoy in a "château" dining room with a noble air.

in Coly Southeast: 6 km by D 74 and D 62 – **pop. 230** – **alt. 113 m** – ✉ **24120**

Church ★★ of St-Amand-de-Coly Southwest: 3 km, **Dordogne-Berry-Limousin**

Manoir d'Hautegente
– ☎ *05 53 51 68 03 – hotel@manoir-hautegente.com – Fax 05 53 50 38 52*
– Open 2 April-31 October
17 rm – €100 €126/265, €16 – ½ P €100/195 – **Rest** – Menu €50/100 bi – Carte approx. €60
◆ In a riverside park, this 14C Virginia creeper-clad mill is now an elegant hotel. Cosy interior with antique furniture. Succession of charming vaulted dining rooms and pretty riverside terrace.

LARDY – 91 Essonne – **312** C4 – **pop. 4 375** – **alt. 70 m** – ✉ **91510** 18 **B2**

Paris 46 – Évry 29 – Boulogne-Billancourt 49 – Montreuil 47 – Argenteuil 63

Auberge de l'Espérance
80 Grande-Rue – ☎ 01 69 27 40 82 – Fax 01 60 82 71 01 – Closed 7-31 August, February school holidays, Wednesday dinner, Sunday dinner and Monday
Rest – Menu €29 – Carte approx. €40
◆ Smart tables, Lois XVI-style chairs and large central buffet. The fine contemporary cuisine is served in a gayly floral country-style room.

LARGENTIÈRE – 07 Ardèche – **331** H6 – **pop. 1 942** – **alt. 240 m** – ✉ **07110** **Lyon - Rhone Valley** 44 **A3**

Paris 645 – Alès 66 – Aubenas 18 – Privas 49

Office de tourisme, 8, rue Camille Vielfaure ☎ 04 75 39 14 28, Fax 04 75 39 23 66

Old Largentière★.

in Rocher North: 4 km by D 5 – **pop. 227** – **alt. 353 m** – ✉ **07110**

Le Chêne Vert
– ☎ *04 75 88 34 02 – contact@hotellechenevert.com – Fax 04 75 88 33 85*
– Open 1st April-31 October and closed Monday lunch and Tuesday lunch
25 rm – €56/77 €56/77, €9 – ½ P €51/67 – **Rest** – Menu €19/39 – Carte €31/47
◆ On the border between Vivarais and Cévennes, a convivial place with practical guest rooms, some of which have a balcony and a view over the attractive swimming pool. Traditional dishes and regional recipes served in a discreet, modern setting.

in Sanilhac South: 7 km by D 312 – **pop. 346** – **alt. 420 m** – ✉ **07110**

Auberge de la Tour de Brison ≤ the Alps, Monts Lozère and Mont Ventoux, rm, rm,
at la Chapelette – ☎ 04 75 39 29 00 – belin.c@wanadoo.fr – Fax 04 75 39 19 56
– Open 1st April-31 October and closed Wednesday except from June to August
14 rm – €56/66 €56/66, €9,50 – ½ P €57/66
Rest – *(pre-book)* Menu €29 – Carte €27/36
◆ This friendly inn is built on a hillside, and commands a view of the valley and the Coiron plateau. Modern rooms, garden and overflow pool. Warm and welcoming restaurant, panoramic terrace and tasty regional cuisine.

LARMOR-BADEN – 56 Morbihan – 308 N9 – pop. 954 – alt. 10 m – ✉ 56870 9 A3

▶ Paris 474 – Auray 15 – Lorient 59 – Pontivy 66 – Vannes 15

ℹ Office de tourisme, 24, rue Pen Lannic ✆ 02 97 58 01 26

◉ Cairn ★★ of Gavrinis island: 15 mn by boat.

Auberge du Parc Fétan

rest, rest, P VISA MC

17 r. Berder – ✆ 02 97 57 04 38 – contact@hotel-parcfetan.com – Fax 02 97 57 21 55 – Open 8 February-12 November

20 rm – €45/120 €45/120, ☕ €8 – ½ P €53/90 – **Rest** – *(closed Sunday dinner except 6 July-31 August) (dinner only) (resident only)* Menu €22

◆ This hotel, situated a stone's throw from Morbihan bay, has been given a successful overhaul. Small but bright rooms with new fittings.

LARMOR-PLAGE – 56 Morbihan – 308 K8 – pop. 8 470 – alt. 4 m – ✉ 56260 Brittany 9 B2

▶ Paris 510 – Lorient 7 – Quimper 74 – Vannes 66

◉ ≤★ of St-Maurice bridge.

Les Rives du Ter

P VISA MC AE

bd Jean-Monnet – ✆ 02 97 35 33 50 – info@lesrivesduter.com – Fax 02 97 35 39 02

58 rm – €91/108 €99/226, ☕ €12,50 – ½ P €83/88 – **Rest** – Menu €23/41 – Carte €27/30

◆ Quietly located near a bridge, this large, modern hotel provides refined and warm rooms with balconies overlooking the Ter lake. Restaurant with a concise, modern menu, contemporary decor and a lake view.

Les Mouettes

P VISA MC AE

Anse de Kerguélen, 1.5 km west – ✆ 02 97 65 50 30 – info@lesmouettes.com – Fax 02 97 33 65 33

21 rm – €74 €81, ☕ €10,50 – ½ P €82 – **Rest** – Menu €23 (weekdays)/60 – Carte €45/75

◆ Peace and quiet (out of season), barely interrupted by the cries of the seagulls, in this modern seaside hotel in Kerguelen cove. Gradually renovated rooms. Stunning view of the sea and the isle of Groix from the terrace or dining room.

LARNAC – 30 Gard – 339 K3 – see St-Ambroix

LAROQUE DES ALBERES – 66 Pyrénées-Orientales – 344 I7 – pop. 1 909 – alt. 100 m – ✉ 66740 22 B3

▶ Paris 883 – Montpellier 187 – Perpignan 39 – Figueres 50 – Banyoles 90

ℹ Office de tourisme, 20, rue Carbonneil ✆ 04 68 95 49 97, Fax 04 68 95 42 58

Les Palmiers

VISA MC

33 av. Louis et Michel Soler – ✆ 04 68 89 73 61 – contact@lespalmiers.eu – Fax 04 68 81 08 76 – Closed 7-18 March, November, Sunday dinner and Tuesday October-May, Saturday lunch and Monday

Rest – Menu €22, €36/75 – Carte €60/82

◆ Les Palmiers is known for its friendly staff and carefully prepared modern cuisine. Mediterranean fish and seafood washed down with a good choice of Roussillon wines.

LARRAU – 64 Pyrénées-Atlantiques – 342 G6 – pop. 214 – alt. 636 m – ✉ 64560

▶ Paris 832 – Oloron-Ste-Marie 42 – Pau 75 – St-Jean-Pied-de-Port 64 3 B3

Etchemaïté

rm, P VISA MC

– ✆ 05 59 28 61 45 – hotel.etchemaite@wanadoo.fr – Fax 05 59 28 72 71 – Closed 6 January-12 February, Sunday dinner and Monday except from 23 March to 11 November

16 rm – €42/48 €42/64, ☕ €8 – ½ P €44/56

Rest – *(closed Sunday dinner and Monday from 11 November to 31 May)* Menu €18 (weekdays)/34 – Carte €43/56

◆ Simplicity and a family atmosphere in this mountain inn situated in a hamlet in picturesque High Soule. Cosy rooms. Welcoming dining room with exposed stonework and beams, Basque tablecloths, fireplace and view over the valley. Local dishes.

LASCABANES – **46 Lot** – **337** D5 – **pop. 167** – **alt. 180 m** – ✉ **46800** 28 **B1**

Paris 598 – Montauban 69 – Toulouse 120 – Villeneuve-sur-Lot 61

Le Domaine de Saint-Géry rest, VISA

– ✆ *05 65 31 82 51 – info@saint-gery.com – Fax 05 65 22 92 89*
– Open 16 May-30 September
5 rm – €186/364 €186/515, €25 – **Table d'hôte** – Menu €96

♦ This estate includes a truffle and general agricultural farm, with pleasant walking paths. The hotel provides five rooms in different buildings. The décor combines a mixture of old and modern styles. The restaurant serves regional cuisine and roast meat dishes.

LASCELLE – **15 Cantal** – **330** D4 – **pop. 317** – **alt. 760 m** – ✉ **15590** 5 **B3**

Paris 555 – Aurillac 16 – Bort-les-Orgues 84 – Brioude 94 – Murat 36

Lac des Graves rm, VISA

Jaulhac – ✆ 04 71 47 94 06 – hotel.lac.graves@wanadoo.fr – Fax 04 71 47 96 55
– Closed November
23 rm – €59/69 €59/69, €7 – **Rest** – Menu €18/38 – Carte €31/47

♦ A large park by a popular fishing lake. Unusual lakeside wooden chalets; a few family rooms. The large dining room and panoramic terrace overlook beautiful countryside.

LASSEUBE – **64 Pyrénées-Atlantiques** – **342** J3 – **pop. 1 526** – **alt. 188 m** – ✉ **64290** 3 **B3**

Paris 797 – Bordeaux 219 – Pau 19 – Tarbes 60

La Ferme Dagué without rest

chemin Croix de Dagué – ✆ 05 59 04 27 11 – famille.maumus@wanadoo.fr
– Fax 05 59 04 27 11 – Open 28 April-30 October
5 rm – €42/62 €51/62

♦ This 18C regional-style farm has retained its superb courtyard with outdoor gallery. Providing charming rooms located in the old loft. Copious breakfast served.

LASTOURS – **11 Aude** – **344** F3 – ✉ **11600** 22 **B2**

Paris 782 – Toulouse 107 – Carcassonne 19 – Castres 52 – Narbonne 18

Le Puits du Trésor (Jean-Marc Boyer) VISA

21 rte Quatre Châteaux – ✆ 04 68 77 50 24
– contact@lepuitsdutresor.com – Fax 04 68 77 50 24
– Closed 5-18 January, 15 February-7 March, Sunday dinner, Monday and Tuesday
Rest – *(number of covers limited, pre-book)* Menu €39/75 – Carte €52/77
Spec. Foie gras de canard et anguille fumée (spring). Agneau de lait rôti à l'origan, navets confits (winter). Timbale de macaroni et ris de veau financière à la truffe du Cabardès (December to February.). **Wines** Limoux, Minervois.

♦ Village at the foot of the ruined Lastours château. Modern restaurant serving creative dishes. Simpler bistro area for lunchtime specials only.

LATOUR-DE-CAROL – **66 Pyrénées-Orientales** – **344** C8 – **pop. 367** – **alt. 1 260 m** – ✉ **66760** 22 **A3**

Paris 839 – Ax-les-Thermes 37 – Font-Romeu-Odeillo-Via 21 – Perpignan 110

Auberge Catalane VISA

10 av. Puymorens – ✆ 04 68 04 80 66 – auberge-catalane@club-internet.fr
– Fax 04 68 04 95 25 – Closed 6-14 April, 11 November-20 December, Sunday dinner and Monday except school holidays
10 rm – €40/44 €48/52, €6 – ½ P €41/46 – **Rest** – Menu €16 (weekday lunch), €22/34 – Carte €25/38

♦ At the heart of the Cerdagne plateau, a 100% Catalan inn run by the same family since it was founded in 1929. Stylish well renovated rooms. Spruce rustic dining room, veranda or terrace serving regional recipes.

LATTES – **34 Hérault** – **339** I7 – **see Montpellier**

LAUTARET (COL) – **05 Hautes-Alpes** – **334** G2 – **see Col du Lautaret**

LAUTERBOURG – 67 Bas-Rhin – 315 N3 – pop. 2 269 – alt. 115 m – ✉ 67630

Paris 519 – Haguenau 40 – Karlsruhe 22 – Strasbourg 63 – Wissembourg 20

Office de tourisme, 21, rue de la 1re Armée ✆ 03 88 94 66 10, Fax 03 88 54 61 33 — 1 **B1**

XXX **La Poêle d'Or**

35 r. Gén. Mittelhauser – ✆ 03 88 94 84 16 – info@poeledor.com – Fax 03 88 54 62 30 – Closed 25 July-10 August, 5-26 January, Wednesday and Thursday

Rest – Menu € 26 (weekday lunch), € 40/74 – Carte € 37/66

◆ A half-timbered house with an elegant dining room (Louis XIII-style furniture), veranda and terrace. Classical cuisine and a tempting dessert trolley for those with a sweet tooth.

LAUZERTE – 82 Tarn-et-Garonne – 337 C6 – pop. 1 487 – alt. 224 m – ✉ 82110

Paris 614 – Agen 53 – Auch 98 – Cahors 39 – Montauban 38 — 28 **B1**

Office de tourisme, place des Cornières ✆ 05 63 94 61 94, Fax 05 63 94 61 93

des Roucous SauveterreEast: 16 km by D 34, ✆ 05 63 95 83 70.

X **Du Quercy** with rm

fg d'Auriac – ✆ 05 63 94 66 36 – hotel.du.quercy@wanadoo.fr – Fax 05 63 39 06 56 – Closed 27 October-3 November, 9-16 February, Sunday dinner, Tuesday dinner except July-August and Monday

10 rm – †€ 40 ††€ 42/50, ☕ € 7 – ½ P € 55 – **Rest** – Menu € 11 (weekday lunch), € 27/36 – Carte € 30/59

◆ In the heart of the town known as the "Toledo of Quercy," this 19C country-style house is home to a charming restaurant featuring a light bistro-style dining area with views of the surrounding hills and valleys. Regional cuisine served. Some rooms affording views of the valley.

LAVAL Ⓟ – 53 Mayenne – 310 E6 – pop. 50 947 – alt. 65 m – ✉ 53000 Normandy

Paris 280 – Angers 79 – Le Mans 86 – Rennes 76 – St-Nazaire 153 — 35 **C1**

Office de tourisme, 1, allée du Vieux Saint-Louis ✆ 02 43 49 46 46, Fax 02 43 49 46 21

de Laval Changé Le Jariel, North: 8 km by D 104, ✆ 02 43 53 16 03.

Old château★ Z : framework★★ of the keep, musée d'Art naïf★, ≤★ from the ramparts - Old town★ YZ: - Embankments★ ≤★ - Jardin de la Perrine★ Z - Apse★ of N.-D. d'Avesnières basilica X - N.-D. des Cordeliers church ★: altar-pieces★★ X - Lactopôle★★.

Plan on next page

De Paris without rest

22 r. de la Paix – ✆ 02 43 53 76 20 – hoteldeparislaval@wanadoo.fr – Fax 02 43 56 91 83 – Closed 21 December-3 January — Y **a**

50 rm – †€ 63/155 ††€ 68/165, ☕ € 9

◆ Fully renovated building, constructed in 1954, in the heart of a shopping area. Modern, functional rooms, well looked after and quieter at the rear.

Marin'Hôtel without rest

102 av. R. Buron – ✆ 02 43 53 09 68 – contact@marin-hotel.fr – Fax 02 43 56 95 35 — X **d**

25 rm – †€ 38/52 ††€ 46/57, ☕ € 6,50

◆ The grotesque figures on the façade reflect the age of the building but the rooms are modern and practical. Those to the rear are quieter. Continental breakfasts.

XXX **Bistro de Paris** (Guy Lemercier)

67 r. Val de Mayenne – ✆ 02 43 56 98 29 – bistro.de.paris@wanadoo.fr – Fax 02 43 56 52 85 – Closed 1st-25 August, Saturday lunch, Sunday dinner and Monday — Y **k**

Rest – Menu € 27/48 – Carte approx. € 45

Spec. Frivolité de bar, pistache et bigorneaux, crème brûlée aux cèpes. Sifflet de sole au jus de homard. Filet de bœuf, foie gras, poivres, pommes fondantes à l'échalote. **Wines** Savennières, Anjou-Villages.

◆ In an old house, this elegant bistro is decorated in a very welcoming Art Nouveau style. Delicious contemporary cuisine.

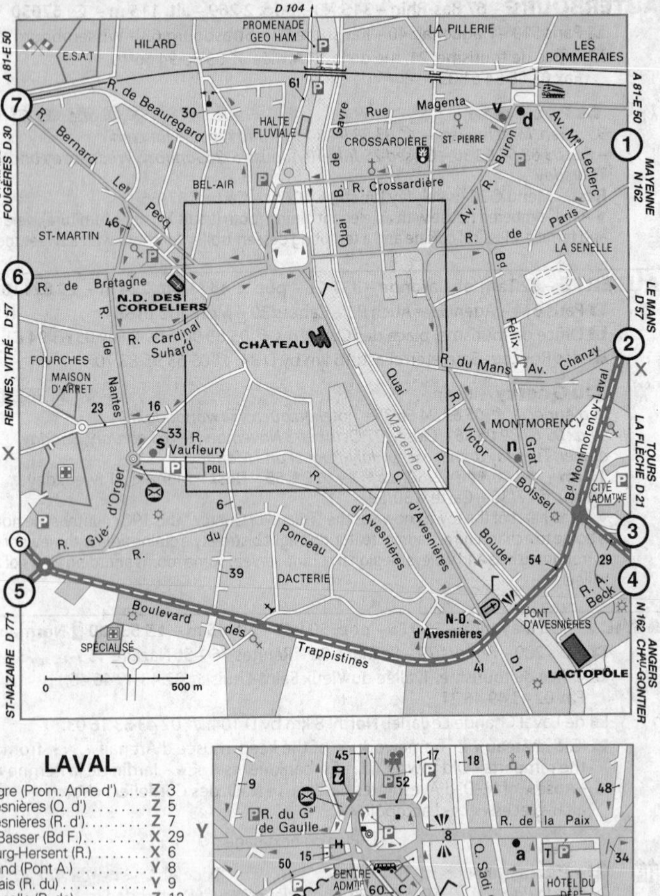

D 104
PROMENADE GEO HAM
LA PILLERIE
HILARD
E.S.A.T
LES POMMERAIES
A 81-E 50
R. de Beauregard
61
30
HALTE FLUVIALE
Rue Magenta
B. de Gavre
CROSSARDIÈRE
ST-PIERRE
R. Buron
Av. Mal Leclerc
MAYENNE N 162
R. Bernard Le Pecq
BEL-AIR
R. Crossardière
ST-MALO FOUGÈRES D 30
46
ST-MARTIN
Quai
Av. R. de Paris
LA SENELLE
R. de Bretagne
N.D. DES CORDELIERS
Bd Félix
LE MANS D 57
R. Cardinal Suhard
CHÂTEAU
R. de Nantes
FOURCHES
MAISON D'ARRET
R. du Mans
Av. Chanzy
RENNES, VITRÉ D 57
23
16
Quai Mayenne
R. Victor Boissel
MONTMORENCY
Bd Montmorency-Laval
33
R. Vaufleury
POL.
R. Grat
P.
Q. d'Avesnières
TOURS LA FLÈCHE D 21
R. Gué-d'Orger
CITÉ ADMTIVE
6
R. d'Avesnières
R. du Ponceau
Boudet
29
54
R. A. Beck
39
DACTERIE
Boulevard des Trappistines
N.-D. d'Avesnières
PONT D'AVESNIÈRES
ST-NAZAIRE D 771
SPÉCIALISÉ
41
D 1
LACTOPÔLE
ANGERS CHau-GONTIER N 162
0
500 m

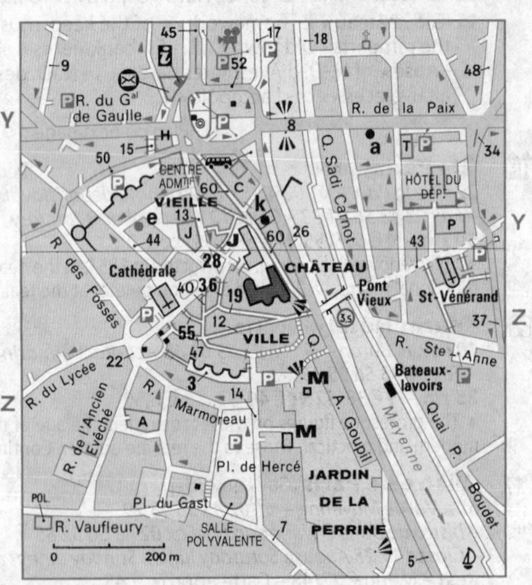

LAVAL

Alègre (Prom. Anne d') .... Z 3
Avesnières (Q. d') .... Z 5
Avesnières (R. d') .... Z 7
Le Basser (Bd F.) .... X 29
Bourg-Hersent (R.) .... X 6
Briand (Pont A.) .... Y 8
Britais (R. du) .... Y 9
Chapelle (R. de) .... Z 12
Déportés (R. des) .... Y 13
Douanier-Rousseau (R.) .... Z 14
Droits de l'homme (Parvis des) .... Y 15
Étaux (R. des) .... X 16
Gambetta (Quai) .... Y 17
Gaulle (R. Gén.-de) .... Y
Gavre (Q. B.-de) .... Y 18
Grande-Rue .... Z 19
Hardy-de-Lévaré (Pl.) ...... Z 22
Haut-Rocher (R.) .... X 23
Jean-Fouquet (Q.) .... Y 26
Macé (R. J.) .... X 30
Messager (R.) .... X 33
Moulin (Pl. J.) .... Y 34
Orfèvres (R. des) .... Z 36
Paix (R. de la) .... Y
Paradis (R. de) .... Z 37
Picardie (R. de) .... X 39
Pin-Doré (R. du) .... Z 40
Pont-d'Avesnières (Bd du) . X 41
Pont-de-Mayenne (R. du) .. Z 43
Renaise (R.) .... Y 44
Résistance (Crs de la) ..... Y 45
St-Martin (R.) .... X 46
Serruriers (R. des) .... Z 47

45
17
18
9
52
48
R. du Gal de Gaulle
8
R. de la Paix
Y
a
34
15
H
50
CENTRE ADMTIF
60
C
Q. Sadi Carnot
HÔTEL DU DÉP.
VIEILLE
k
e
13
J
J
60
26
43
Y
44
R. des Fossés
28
Cathédrale
CHÂTEAU
Pont Vieux
St-Vénérand
40
36
19
12
VILLE
37
Z
55
R. Ste-Anne
47
22
3
M
Bateaux-lavoirs
Z
R. du Lycée
R. de l'Ancien Évêché
R. Marmoreau
14
Q. A. Goupil
Quai P. Boudet
Mayenne
A
M
Pl. de Hercé
JARDIN DE LA PERRINE
POL.
Pl. du Gast
R. Vaufleury
SALLE POLYVALENTE
7
0
200 m
5

Solférino (R.) .... Y 48
Souchu-Servinière (R.) .... Y 50
Strasbourg (R. de) .... Y 52
Tisserands (Bd des) .... X 54

Trémoille (Pl. de la) .... Z 28
Trinité (R. de la) .... Z 55
Val-de-Mayenne (R. du) .... YZ 60
Vieux-St-Louis (R. du) ...... X 61

Le Capucin Gourmand
66 r. Vaufleury – ✆ 02 43 66 02 02 – capucingourmand@free.fr – Fax 02 43 66 13 50 – Closed 4-26 August, 6-13 February, Sunday dinner, Tuesday lunch and Monday X **s**
Rest – Menu (€ 18 bi), € 22 (weekdays)/47 – Carte € 40/50
◆ Behind a Virginia clad façade, this restaurant is home to smart, welcoming dining rooms. Contemporary cuisine served on the quiet terrace in fine weather.

La Gerbe de Blé with rm
83 r. V.-Boissel – ✆ 02 43 53 14 10 – gerbedeble@wanadoo.fr – Fax 02 43 49 02 84 – Closed 1st-5 May, 28 July-20 August, 1st-4 November, 9-15 February, Saturday lunch and Sunday X **n**
8 rm – †€ 74/105 ††€ 90/125, ☕ € 12 – ½ P € 70/95 – **Rest** – Menu (€ 19), € 27/36
◆ Traditional cuisine made with seasonal, local produce served in an up-to-date, welcoming dining room (cream tones, carefully lit). Functional rooms.

Hostellerie à la Bonne Auberge with rm
170 r. de Bretagne by ⑥ – ✆ 02 43 69 07 81 – contact@alabonneauberge.com – Fax 02 43 91 15 02 – Closed 2-30 August, 24 December-5 January, Friday dinner, Sunday dinner, Saturday and dinners holidays
12 rm – †€ 65/72 ††€ 75/82, ☕ € 9 – **Rest** – Menu € 18 (weekdays)/42 – Carte € 39/55
◆ Away from the town centre, a regional-style building, covered with Virginia creeper. The dining room, enlarged by a veranda, is bright and modern. Tasty traditional cuisine.

L'Antiquaire
5 r. Béliers – ✆ 02 43 53 66 76 – Fax 02 43 56 92 18 – Closed 1st-22 July, 6-27 January, Saturday lunch, Sunday dinner and Monday Y **e**
Rest – Menu (€ 16), € 22/47 – Carte € 30/48
◆ This restaurant located in the heart of the old town centre has a pleasant dining area serving generous classic cuisine with modern touches.

Edelweiss
99 av. R. Buron – ✆ 02 43 53 11 00 – restau.edelweiss@wanadoo.fr – Closed 15 July-12 August, 16-22 February, Sunday dinner, dinners holidays and Monday
Rest – Menu (€ 12), € 14 (weekdays)/25 – Carte approx. € 28 X **v**
◆ Restaurant, next to the railway station, with a dining room redecorated in a modern style (pastel shades). Enjoy traditional dishes here in a friendly atmosphere without ceremony.

LAVALADE – 24 Dordogne – 329 G7 – pop. 97 – alt. 190 m – ✉ 24540 4 C2

Paris 580 – Bordeaux 144 – Périgueux 94 – Bergerac 46 – Villeneuve-sur-Lot 48

Le Grand Cèdre without rest
– ✆ 05 53 22 57 70 – legrandcedre.j@wanadoo.fr – Open Easter-11 November
5 rm ☕ – †€ 55 ††€ 65/75
◆ A sympathetic renovation has preserved the original character of this establishment. Well-kept, spacious (save one) rooms, furnished with antiques.

LE LAVANCHER – 74 Haute-Savoie – 328 O5 – see Chamonix

LE LAVANDOU – 83 Var – 340 N7 – pop. 5 449 – alt. 1 m – ✉ 83980 French Riviera

Paris 873 – Cannes 102 – Draguignan 75 – Fréjus 61 – Toulon 41 41 C3
Office de tourisme, quai Gabriel-Péri, ✆ 04 94 00 40 50, Fax 04 94 00 40 59
Ile d'Hyères★★★.

Plan on next page

La Petite Bohème
av. F.-Roosevelt – ✆ 04 94 71 10 30 – hotelpetiteboheme@wanadoo.fr – Fax 04 94 64 73 92 B **f**
17 rm – †€ 45/65 ††€ 55/95, ☕ € 8,50 – ½ P € 60/83
Rest – *(closed 11 November-1st February, lunch Monday-Thursday 15 June-15 September, Tuesday and Wednesday off season)* Menu € 25/33 – Carte € 28/44
◆ Have a lie-in in a simple Provençal-style room, then a siesta on a sun lounger under the arbour between aperitifs: a real Bohemian lifestyle! Mediterranean-style dining room and shaded terrace beside the garden.

LE LAVANDOU

Bois-Notre-Dame (R. du) . . . . . A 2
Bouvet (Bd Gén.-G) . . . . A 3
Cazin (R. Charles) . . . . A 4
Gaulle (Av. Gén.-de) . . . . AB
Lattre-de-Tassigny (Bd de) . . . A 7
Martyrs-de-la-Résistance (Av. des) . . . . A 8
Patron Ravello (R.) . . . . B 10
Péri (Quai Gabriel) . . . . B 12
Port Cros (R.) . . . . A 15
Port (R. du) . . . . B 13
Vincent-Auriol (Av. Prés.) . . . . A 16

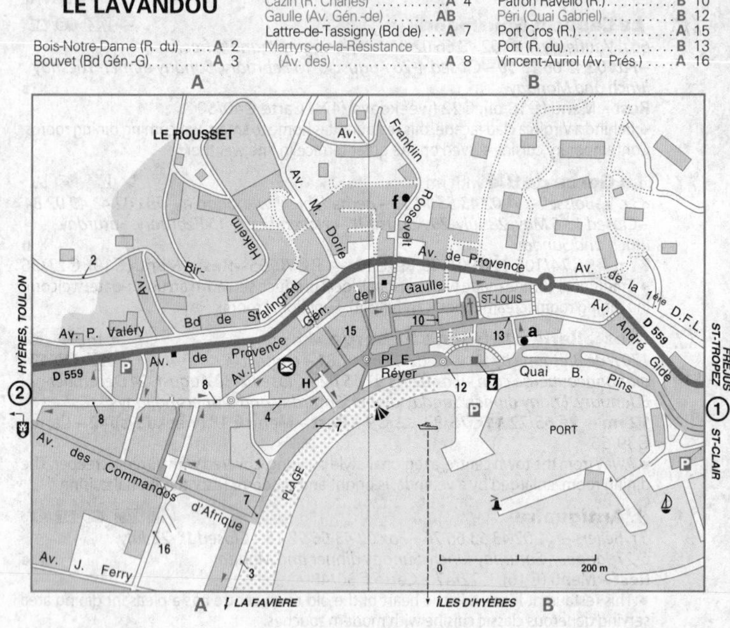

Le Rabelais without rest VISA
opposite the old port – ☎ 04 94 71 00 56 – hotel.lerabelais@wanadoo.fr – Fax 04 94 71 82 55 – Closed 11 November-1st January B a
21 rm – †€ 52/105 ††€ 52/115, ☕ € 5,50
♦ Well-located on the seafront, this hotel has small yet cool and colourful rooms. In summer, breakfast is served on the terrace facing the harbour.

in St-Clair by ①: 2 km – ✉ 83980 Le Lavandou

Roc Hôtel without rest VISA
r. des Dryades – ☎ 04 94 01 33 66 – roc-hotel@wanadoo.fr – Fax 04 94 01 33 67 – Open mid March-mid October
29 rm – †€ 72/154 ††€ 72/240, ☕ € 9
♦ A modern hotel built on rocks washed by the waves. Bright rooms with terrace. Choose one overlooking the sea. A refreshing break guaranteed.

Méditerranée rest, VISA
– ☎ 04 94 01 47 70 – hotel.med@wanadoo.fr – Fax 04 94 01 47 71 – Open 17 March-20 October
20 rm – †€ 76/84 ††€ 84/120, ☕ € 8,50 – ½ P € 68/90
Rest – *(closed Wednesday) (dinner only) (resident only)* Menu € 25
♦ This hotel is built near a sandy and very sunny Mediterranean beach. Small, practical rooms and a shaded terrace. A pleasant shaded terrace. Serving traditional cuisine.

Belle Vue rm, VISA
– ☎ 04 94 00 45 00 – hotelbellevue@wanadoo.fr – Fax 04 94 00 45 25 – Open April-October
19 rm – †€ 80/90 ††€ 90/230, ☕ € 15 – ½ P € 90/150
Rest – *(open June-September and closed Sunday)* Menu € 34/36 – Carte € 41/54
♦ Away from the busy seaside, a pleasant villa on the flower-decked outskirts overlooking the bay of St.Clair. Rustic rooms, some of which enjoy a lovely view. Beautiful views from the dining room of this hotel (stunning sunsets over the coast).

La Bastide without rest

pl. des Pins Penchés – ✆ 04 94 01 57 00 – contact@hotel-la-bastide.fr – Fax 04 94 01 57 13 – Open 1st April-10 November

18 rm – €60/118 €60/153, ☕ €9

◆ Only 50m from the riverbank, this 1920s house sports immaculate walls, colourful shutters and Roman tiles. Simple rooms with terrace or balcony.

in la Plage de La Fossette by ①: 3 km – ✉ 83980 Le Lavandou

83 Hôtel ≤ coast and sea,

– ✆ 04 94 71 20 15 – hotel83@wanadoo.fr – Fax 04 94 71 63 42 – Open from Easter to end September

30 rm – €100/120 €120/270, ☕ €15 – ½ P €110/364

Rest *Jardin de la Fossette* – *(dinner only)* Menu €40/65 – Carte €45/63

◆ The Var coast takes on the appearance of a Pacific island here. Save yourself travelling thousands of kilometres by staying in this hotel designed purely for pleasure. Spacious rooms. Restaurant with a veranda dining area and pleasant terrace with fine views. Traditional cuisine served.

in Aiguebelle by ①: 4,5 km – ✉ 83980 Le Lavandou

Les Roches ≤ sea and the islands,

1 av. des Trois-Dauphins – ✆ 04 94 71 05 07 – resa@hotellesroches.com – Fax 04 94 71 08 40 – Open 18 March-31 October

33 rm – €160/210 €190/320, ☕ €28 – 6 suites

Rest Mathias Dandine – see restaurant listing

◆ The opulent rooms with terraces rising up the slope by the creek make this hotel a little seaside paradise.

Les Alcyons without rest

av. des Trois-Dauphins – ✆ 04 94 05 84 18 – hotellesalcyons@free.fr – Fax 04 94 05 70 89 – Open April-mid October – **24 rm** – €60/106, ☕ €7

◆ The meeting of the Halcyons is a sign of peace and tranquillity. The attentive welcome and good housekeeping in this establishment tend to support the legend.

Hydra without rest

av. du Levant – ✆ 04 94 71 65 46 – hydra.hotel@wanadoo.fr – Fax 04 94 15 08 07

30 rm – €75/94 €88/230, ☕ €13

◆ This hotel has inherited the brightness and spartan nature of its interior decor from the Greek island which gave it its name. An underground passage leads directly to the sea.

Beau Soleil rm,

– ✆ 04 94 05 84 55 – beausoleil@hotel-lavandou.com – Fax 04 94 22 27 05 – Open beg. April-beg. October

15 rm – €54/119 €69/125, ☕ €6,50 – ½ P €57/94 – **Rest** – snack *(open beg. May-beg. October)* Menu €25/34 – Carte €36/46

◆ The 'beautiful sunshine' is the perfect place to spend your holidays, with renovated rooms featuring balconies. A revamped dining room, plus a terrace under the shade of a plane tree. Light lunches; menus in the evening.

Mathias Dandine – Hôtel Les Roches ≤ sea and the islands,

1 av. des Trois-Dauphins – ✆ 04 94 71 15 53 – restaurant@mathiasdandine.com – Fax 04 94 71 66 66 – Closed Tuesday from 1st November to 1st March

Rest – Menu €45 (lunch), €70/115 – Carte €86/130

Spec. Bouillabaisse d'œuf de la ferme poché (October to March). Oursins de pays aux aromates (October to February). Chapon de Méditerranée farci façon ménagère provençale (July-August). **Wines** Côtes de Provence.

◆ Creative cuisine served in this panoramic restaurant which rules the waves.

Le Sud (Christophe Pétra)

av. des Trois-Dauphins – ✆ 04 94 05 76 98 – Closed lunch in July-August except Sunday

Rest – Menu €65 (set menu)

Spec. Capuccino de cèpes et truffes. Pigeon en croûte, foie gras, choux et truffes. Lapin confit de quatre heures, polenta aux pignons. **Wines** Côtes de Provence, Coteaux Varois.

◆ An elegant Provençal-style dining area with antique objects, providing a pleasant atmosphere for dining on the tasty, copious cuisine. Ask the chef for the daily special.

LAVANNES – 51 Marne – 306 H7 – pop. 446 – alt. 100 m – ✉ 51110 13 B2

Paris 161 – Châlons-en-Champagne 56 – Épernay 43 – Reims 14

La Closerie des Sacres without rest

7 r. Chefossez – ✆ 03 26 02 05 05 – closerie-des-sacres@wanadoo.fr – Fax 03 26 08 06 73

3 rm – †€ 74 ††€ 88/115

◆ The stables of this old farm have been tastefully reconverted into a guesthouse providing rooms with wrought-iron furnishings and fine fabrics. Breakfast is served around the great stone fireplace.

LAVARDIN – 41 Loir-et-Cher – 318 C5 – see Montoire-sur-le-Loir

LAVAUDIEU – 43 Haute-Loire – 331 C2 – pop. 225 – alt. 465 m – ✉ 43100

Auvergne 6 C3

Paris 488 – Brioude 11 – Clermont-Ferrand 78 – Le Puy-en-Velay 56 – St-Flour 63

Frescoes★ of the abbey church - Cloister★ - Carrefour du vitrail (stained-glass window centre)★.

Le Colombier without rest

rte des Fontannes – ✆ 04 71 76 09 86 – colombier.chambredhote@wanadoo.fr – Open mid October-mid April

4 rm – †€ 60 ††€ 70

◆ A modern stone house in which the bedrooms are individually themed – Velay, Africa (bamboo four-poster bed), Morocco (wrought-iron bed). Old dovecote, plus attractive views of the surrounding countryside.

Auberge de l'Abbaye

– ✆ 04 71 76 44 44 – Fax 04 71 76 41 08 – Closed 15 December-15 January, Sunday dinner and Thursday except July-August

Rest – Menu (€ 16), € 21/29 – Carte € 28/37

◆ A rustic dining room, with exposed beams and a fireplace, in the centre of the village, near the abbey with its beautiful frescoes. Regional cuisine.

Court La Vigne

– ✆ 04 71 76 45 79 – Fax 04 71 76 45 79 – Closed December, January, Tuesday and Wednesday

Rest – *(number of covers limited, pre-book)* Menu € 18 (weekdays)/28

◆ Charming 15C sheepfold next door to medieval cloisters. Tastefully furnished, bar with open fire, art gallery and a pleasant courtyard. Good regional cooking made with fresh produce.

LES LAVAULTS – 89 Yonne – 319 H8 – see Quarré-les-Tombes

LAVAUR – 24 Dordogne – 329 H8 – pop. 88 – alt. 250 m – ✉ 24550 4 D2

Paris 622 – Bordeaux 213 – Périgueux 87 – Villeneuve-sur-Lot 45 – Cahors 49

Auberge de Bayle Viel with rm rest,

– ✆ 05 53 28 16 89 – aubergebayle@wanadoo.fr – Fax 05 53 28 16 89

3 rm – †€ 69 ††€ 75, € 8,50 – ½ P € 70 – **Rest** – *(number of covers limited, pre-book)* Menu € 24/42 – Carte € 31/40

◆ This former barn with beams, stone walls, terracotta tiles, and oak and chestnut furniture is the perfect setting for regional food prepared with home-grown vegetables. Bright, welcoming bedrooms, one with sitting room and terrace.

LAVAUR – 81 Tarn – 338 C8 – pop. 8 537 – alt. 140 m – ✉ 81500

Languedoc-Roussillon-Tarn Gorges 29 C2

Paris 682 – Albi 51 – Castelnaudary 56 – Castres 40 – Montauban 58 – Toulouse 44

Office de tourisme, Tour des Rondes ✆ 05 63 58 02 00, Fax 05 63 41 42 89

des Étangs de Fiac Fiac Brazis, East: 11 km by D 112, ✆ 05 63 70 64 70.

St-Alain cathedral★.

Ibis without rest
1 av. G. Pompidou – ✆ 05 63 83 08 08 – loic.borie@accor.com – Fax 05 63 83 01 05
58 rm – †€ 52/69 ††€ 52/69, ☕ € 7,50
◆ In a residential area, this entirely renovated hotel provides light and functional rooms with air conditioning. Also featuring a small garden, floral terrace and a fountain.

LAVELANET – 09 Ariège – 343 J7 – pop. 6 872 – alt. 512 m – ✉ 09300 29 C3

Paris 784 – Carcassonne 71 – Castelnaudary 53 – Foix 28 – Limoux 47 – Pamiers 42

Office de tourisme, place Henri-Dunant ✆ 05 61 01 22 20, Fax 05 61 03 06 39

in Nalzen West: 6 km on D 117 – pop. 141 – alt. 632 m – ✉ 09300

Les Sapins
– ✆ 05 61 03 03 85 – Fax 05 61 65 58 45 – Closed Wednesday dinner, Sunday dinner and Monday except public holidays
Rest – Menu € 14 bi (weekday lunch), € 22/46 – Carte € 31/57
◆ Traditional chalet nestling at the foot of a forest of fir trees. Good wholesome cooking served in a simple countrified interior.

in Montségur South: 13 km by D 109 and D 9 – pop. 117 – alt. 900 m – ✉ 09300

Syndicat d'initiative, Village ✆ 05 61 03 03 03

Costes with rm
– ✆ 05 61 01 10 24 – info@chez-costes.com – Fax 05 61 03 06 28
13 rm – †€ 37/115 ††€ 37/115, ☕ € 8 – ½ P € 49/90 – **Rest** – Menu € 15 (weekday lunch), € 21/31 – Carte € 21/39
◆ A friendly inn with a decor dominated by stone and wood. Seasonal local cuisine (stews, confits, magret etc) prepared using organic produce from mountain farms. Simple rooms.

LAVENTIE – 62 Pas-de-Calais – 301 J4 – pop. 4 383 – alt. 18 m – ✉ 62840 30 B2

Paris 229 – Armentières 13 – Arras 45 – Béthune 18 – Lille 29 – Dunkerque 63 – Ieper 30

Le Cerisier (Eric Delerue)
3 r. de la Gare – ✆ 03 21 27 60 59 – contact@lecerisier.com – Fax 03 21 27 60 87 – Closed 5-13 April, August, Sunday dinner, Saturday lunch and Monday
Rest – Menu € 29 (lunch)/68 (dinner) – Carte € 71/86
Spec. Ravioles d'huîtres de Marennes juste pochées. Saint-Pierre rôti au thym, poêlée de girolles. Cœur de ris de veau, galettes de pomme de terre fumée et truffe d'été.
◆ An elegant red-brick building, which has been recently refurbished. Delicious modern cuisine served in two dining rooms with a contemporary decor.

LAVERGNE – 46 Lot – 337 G3 – see Gramat

LAVOUX – 86 Vienne – 322 J5 – see Poitiers

LAYE – 05 Hautes-Alpes – 334 E5 – see Col Bayard

LA LÉCHÈRE – 73 Savoie – 333 L4 – pop. 1 936 – alt. 461 m – Spa : early April-late Oct. – ✉ 73260 French Alps 46 F2

Paris 602 – Albertville 21 – Celliers 16 – Chambéry 70 – Moûtiers 6

Office de tourisme, les Eaux-Claires ✆ 04 79 22 51 60, Fax 04 79 22 57 10

Radiana ⚘ rm, rest, rest, VISA

– ✆ 04 79 22 61 61 – *hotels-residences@lalechere.com* – *Fax 04 79 22 65 25*
– Closed 26 October-26 December

86 rm – €67/113 €83/129, ☕ €9,50 – ½ P €66/90 – **Rest** – rest. diététique *(closed 26 October-7 February)* Menu €20/39 – Carte €26/35

♦ Beautiful 1930s construction with direct access to the spa. Functional rooms partially overlook the spa and park. A renovated Art Deco-style lounge. A long dining room for those using the spa and hotel guests. Special-diet meals during the main season.

LES LECQUES – 83 Var – 340 J6 – see St-Cyr-sur-Mer

LECTOURE – 32 Gers – 336 F6 – pop. 3 933 – alt. 155 m – ✉ 32700

Languedoc-Roussillon-Tarn Gorges 28 **B2**

Paris 708 – Agen 39 – Auch 35 – Condom 26 – Montauban 84 – Toulouse 114

Syndicat d'initiative, place du Général-de-Gaulle ✆ 05 62 68 76 98, Fax 05 62 68 79 30

Site★ - Promenade du bastion ≤★ - Musée municipal★.

De Bastard ⚘ VISA

r. Lagrange – ✆ *05 62 68 82 44* – *hoteldebastard@wanadoo.fr*
– Fax 05 62 68 76 81 – Closed 21 December-1st February

28 rm – €46/78 €46/78, ☕ €11 – 2 suites – ½ P €55/75 – **Rest** – *(closed Sunday dinner, Tuesday lunch and Monday)* Menu €18 (weekday lunch), €27/50 – Carte €53/68

♦ In the heart of Gers, this fine 18C hotel has stylishly renovated rooms. Those on the 2nd floor have attic ceilings. A comfortable bar and smoking lounge. Three fine lounges with Louis 16th furnishings, and a pleasant summer terrace. Serving tasty regional cuisine.

LEMBACH – 67 Bas-Rhin – 315 K2 – pop. 1 689 – alt. 190 m – ✉ 67510

Alsace-Lorraine 1 **B1**

Paris 470 – Bitche 32 – Haguenau 25 – Strasbourg 58 – Wissembourg 15

Syndicat d'initiative, 23, route de Bitche ✆ 03 88 94 43 16, Fax 03 88 94 20 04

Château de Fleckenstein★ Northwest: 7 km.

Heimbach without rest VISA

15 rte de Wissembourg – ✆ *03 88 94 43 46* – *contact@hotel-au-heimbach.fr*
– Fax 03 88 94 20 85

18 rm – €45/55 €55/107, ☕ €9

♦ A regional-style, half-timbered building with rustic rooms, in the heart of a small, typically Alsatian town. Generous breakfasts.

Auberge du Cheval Blanc (Fernand Mischler) with rm rm, rm, VISA

4 rte Wissembourg – ✆ *03 88 94 41 86*
– info@au-cheval-blanc.fr – Fax 03 88 94 20 74
– Closed 6-25 July and 12 January-6 February

1 rm – €107 €107, ☕ €12 – 5 suites – €138/199

Rest – *(closed Friday lunch, Monday and Tuesday)* Menu €45/92 – Carte €72/81

Rest *D'Rössel Stub* – Menu €26 – Carte €27/46

Spec. Langoustines, Saint-Jacques et huîtres pressées à l'eau de mer, cappuccino de homard. Bar en croûte de sel, jus iodé, fondue et salade de fenouil, petite soupe d'huîtres. Noisettes de dos de chevreuil aux girolles "Fleckenstein" (except April).
Wines Riesling, Pinot gris.

♦ The large dining room of this elegant 18C post house is set behind an attractive paved courtyard. Coffered ceiling, antique furniture and Alsatian cuisine with personal touches. The D'Rössel Stub is a charming bistro located in a former farm, which has been restored with taste. Personalised rooms.

in Gimbelhof North: 10 km by D 3, D 925 and forest road – ✉ 67510 Lembach

Gimbelhof with rm

– ✆ 03 88 94 43 58 – info@gimbelhof.com – Fax 03 88 94 23 30 – Closed 17 November-26 December

8 rm – †€ 39 ††€ 44/61, ☕ € 7 – ½ P € 46/53 – **Rest** – *(closed Mon. and Tues.)* Menu € 11,50 (weekdays)/30 bi – Carte € 11,50/37

◆ This forest inn isolated in the Vosges massif in "three frontiers country" will charm nature lovers. Very simple guest rooms and dining room.

LEMPDES – 63 Puy-de-Dôme – **326** G8 – **pop. 8 401** – **alt. 330 m** – ✉ 63370 5 **B2**

Paris 420 – Clermont-Ferrand 11 – Issoire 36 – Thiers 36 – Vichy 51

Sébastien Perrier

6 r. Caire – ✆ 04 73 61 74 71 – Fax 04 73 61 74 71 – Closed August, 2-7 January, Sunday dinner and Monday

Rest – Menu € 17 (weekday lunch), € 26/45 – Carte € 39/50

◆ The town scales were once situated on the village square opposite this friendly restaurant specialising in Mediterranean-influenced cuisine. Traditional decor and a contemporary-style mezzanine.

Good food and accommodation at moderate prices?
Look for the Bib symbols: red Bib Gourmand for food,
blue Bib Hotel for hotels.

LENCLOITRE – 86 Vienne – **322** H4 – **pop. 2 253** – **alt. 71 m** – ✉ 86140
Atlantic Coast 39 **C1**

Paris 319 – Châtellerault 18 – Mirebeau 12 – Poitiers 30 – Richelieu 24

Office de tourisme, place du Champ de Foire ✆ 05 49 19 70 75, Fax 05 49 19 70 76

in Savigny-sous-Faye 10 km North by D 757, D 14 and D 72 – **pop. 298** – **alt. 120 m** – ✉ 86140

Château Hôtel de Savigny

– ✆ *05 49 20 41 14 – chateau-hotel-savigny@chsfrance.com – Fax 05 49 86 76 38 – Closed 1st November-29 February*

10 rm – †€ 180/290 ††€ 180/290, ☕ € 20

Rest – *(closed lunch except week-ends and public holidays)* Menu € 39/85 – Carte € 48/133

◆ This elegant Renaissance-inspired chateau looks like something out of a fairytale. With refined and personalised rooms affording views of the park. Modern cuisine served in the restaurant with two elegant dining areas, one featuring a grand fireplace.

LENS – 62 Pas-de-Calais – **301** J5 – **pop. 36 206** – **Built-up area 323 174** – **alt. 38 m** – ✉ 62300 Northern France and the Paris Region 30 **B2**

Paris 199 – Arras 18 – Béthune 19 – Douai 24 – Lille 37 – St-Omer 69

Office de tourisme, 26, rue de la Paix ✆ 03 21 67 66 66, Fax 03 21 67 65 66

Plan on next page

Lensotel

centre commercial Lens 2, 4 km by ⑤ ✉ 62880 – ✆ 03 21 79 36 36 – lensotel@wanadoo.fr – Fax 03 21 79 36 00

70 rm – †€ 70 ††€ 77, ☕ € 10,50 – ½ P € 67 – **Rest** – Menu € 20/35 – Carte € 28/52

◆ Provençal-style hotel complex in the heart of a shopping area. Pleasant modern rooms, all on the ground floor. Choose a room on the garden side. Brickwork dining room, with a fireplace and veranda facing the swimming pool.

LENS

Anatole-France (R.) . . . . . . BXY 2
Basly (Bd Émile). . . . . ABY
Berthelot (R. Marcelin) . . . . . BY 3
Combes (R. Émile) . . . . CX 4
Decrombecque (R. Guilsain) . . . . BXY 6
Diderot (R. Denis). . . . . CY 7
Faidherbe (R. Louis) . . . . BY 8
Flament (R. Étienne) . . . . . . BX 10
Freycinet (R. Louis-de) . . . . . CX 12
Gare (R. de la) . . . . BCY
Gauthier (R. François). . . . . . BY 13
Havre (R. du) . . . . BY 14
Hospice (R. de l') . . . . CY 15
Huleux (R. François) . . . . . . BXY 16
Jean-Jaurès (Pl.) . . . . BY 18
Jean-Moulin (R.) . . . . BX 19
Lamendin (R. Arthur). . . . . CXY 20
Lanoy (R. René) . . . . BXY 21
Leclerc (R. du Mar.) . . . . BY 22
Paix (R. de la) . . . . BY 23
Paris (R. de) . . . . BY 24
Pasteur (R. Louis) . . . . BX 25
Pourquoi Pas (R. du) . . . . . ABX 26
Pressense (R. Francis-de) . . CX 27
République (Pl. de la) . . . . . . BY 28
Reumaux (Av. Elie) . . . . . . ABX 29
Sorriaux (R. Uriane) . . . . . . BCX 30
Varsovie (Av. de) . . . . CY 31
Wetz (R. du) . . . . BX 32
8-Mai-1945 (R.) . . . . CY 33
11-Novembre (R. du) . . . . ABX 36

L'Arcadie II

XX ⊕ VISA MC AE

13 r. Decrombecque – ✆ 03 21 70 32 22 – arcadie.2@wanadoo.fr – Fax 03 21 70 32 22 – Closed 15-24 August, Saturday lunch and dinner Sunday-Wednesday BY **r**

Rest – Menu € 17 (weekday lunch), € 26/45 – Carte approx. € 52

◆ Elegant restaurant in the town centre (colourful pictures and large silver chandeliers) welcomes gourmets who enjoy well-prepared, modern cuisine.

LÉON – 40 Landes – 335 D11 – pop. 1 453 – alt. 9 m – ✉ 40550 3 B2

Paris 724 – Castets 14 – Dax 30 – Mont-de-Marsan 75

Syndicat d'initiative, 65, place Jean Baptiste Courtiau ✆ 05 58 48 76 03, Fax 05 58 48 70 38

de Moliets Moliets-et-Maa Côte d'Argent - Club House, Southwest: 8 km by D 652 then D 117, ✆ 05 58 48 54 65.

Courant d'Huchet★ by barge Northwest: 1.5 km, **G. Atlantic Coast.**

Hôtel du Lac without rest

2 r. des Berges du Lac – ✆ 05 58 48 73 11 – contact@hoteldulac-leon.com – Fax 05 58 49 27 79 – Open 1st April-15 October

14 rm – †€ 47/60 ††€ 47/60, ☕ € 6,50

◆ Hotel providing simple but well-kept rooms, most overlooking the lake. Breakfast served on the veranda or summer terrace on the waterside.

LÉRAN – 09 Ariège – 343 J7 – pop. 539 – alt. 395 m – ✉ 09600 29 C3

Paris 781 – Carcassonne 67 – Pamiers 38 – Toulouse 104

Office de tourisme, rue de la Mairie ✆ 05 61 01 34 93, Fax 05 61 01 11 73

L'Impasse du Temple

1 imp. du Temple – ✆ 05 61 01 50 02 – john.furness@wanadoo.fr – Fax 05 61 01 50 02

5 rm – †€ 53/58 ††€ 65/70 – **Table d'hôte** – Menu € 22

◆ An old house with spacious guestrooms with a blue and white colour scheme, antique furniture and top-of-the-range bedding. This restaurant serves cuisine from Australia, the owners' country of origin.

LÉRÉ – 18 Cher – 323 N2 – pop. 1 296 – alt. 145 m – ✉ 18240

Dordogne-Berry-Limousin 12 D2

Paris 185 – Auxerre 78 – Bourges 65 – Cosne-sur-Loire 10 – Nevers 68 – Vierzon 74

Syndicat d'initiative, rue Achille Laforge ✆ 02 48 72 54 32

Lion d'Or

10 r. de la Judelle – ✆ 02 48 72 60 12 – hoteliondor@aol.com – Fax 02 48 72 56 18 – Closed Monday

Rest – Menu € 24/33 – Carte € 39/80

◆ This 18C post house has had a face-lift and now offers yellow walls, prettily-laid tables and colourful furniture. Appetising, up-dated traditional food and selected wines.

LESCAR – 64 Pyrénées-Atlantiques – 342 J5 – see Pau

LÉSIGNY – 77 Seine-et-Marne – 312 E3 – 101 29 – see Paris, Area

LESPARRE-MÉDOC – 33 Gironde – 335 F3 – pop. 4 855 – alt. 12 m – ✉ 33340 3 B1

Paris 541 – Bordeaux 68 – Soulac-sur-Mer 31

Office de tourisme, 37, cours du Maréchal de Tassigny ✆ 05 56 41 21 96, Fax 05 56 41 21 96

in Gaillan-en-Médoc Northwest: 2 km by D 1215 – pop. 1 915 – alt. 9 m – ✉ 33340

Château Beau Jardin with rm

Verdon road: 3 km – ✆ 05 56 41 26 83 – book@chateaubeaujardin.com – Fax 05 56 41 19 52

7 rm – †€ 80/120 ††€ 100/140, € 12 – ½ P € 100/110

Rest – *(closed January)* Menu € 20/55 – Carte € 24/59

◆ An elegant 19C property with a garden in the heart of the Médoc vineyards. Classic cuisine and wines from the vineyard (tours of the storehouses). Comfortable guest rooms.

La Table d'Olivier

La Mare aux Grenouilles, 53 rte Lesparre – ✆ 05 56 41 13 32 – Fax 05 56 41 17 57 – Closed 16-23 February, Saturday lunch, Sunday dinner and Monday except July-August

Rest – Menu (€ 17 bi), € 26 bi, € 38/69 – Carte € 61/70

◆ A pleasant restaurant by a small lake with frogs. Sober modern interior with wooden tables, wrought-iron chairs and paintings. Seasonal cuisine.

LESPIGNAN – 34 Hérault – 339 E9 – pop. 2 568 – alt. 61 m – ✉ 34710 22 B2

Paris 769 – Béziers 11 – Capestang 20 – Montpellier 78 – Narbonne 20

Hostellerie du Château

4 r. Figuiers – ✆ 04 67 37 67 71 – hostellerie-du-chateau-lespignan@wanadoo.fr – Fax 04 67 76 46 23 – Closed Sunday dinner and Wednesday from September to May

Rest – Menu (€ 15), € 19 (weekdays), € 27/46 – Carte € 35/47

◆ This former château perched above the village houses a dining room with paintings depicting traditional French fables. Fine views of the region from the terrace.

LESPONNE – 65 Hautes-Pyrénées – **342** M4 – see Bagnères-de-Bigorre

LESTELLE-BÉTHARRAM – 64 Pyrénées-Atlantiques – **342** K6 – **pop. 786** – **alt. 299 m** – ✉ **64800** Atlantic Coast 3 **B3**

Paris 801 – Laruns 35 – Lourdes 17 – Nay 8 – Oloron-Ste-Marie 42 – Pau 28

Office de tourisme, Mairie ☎ 05 59 71 96 35

Grottoes★ of Bétharram South: 5 km.

Le Vieux Logis rm, VISA MC AE

2 km Grottes de Bétharram road – ☎ 05 59 71 94 87 – contact@hotel-levieuxlogis.com – Fax 05 59 71 96 75 – Closed 31 October-6 November, 22 December-4 January, 16 February-1st March, Sunday dinner and Monday off season

35 rm – €55/58 €70/75, €10,50 – ½ P €70/72 – **Rest** – Menu €25/40 – Carte €35/56

◆ The old farmhouse (restaurant) is next to the new wing (functional rooms) in huge grounds (five amusing chalets) near the Bétharram caves. Warm, rustic dining rooms, regional food and attentive service.

LESTIAC-SUR-GARONNE – 33 Gironde – **335** I6 – **pop. 586** – **alt. 80 m** – ✉ **33550** 3 **B2**

Paris 604 – Bordeaux 28 – Mérignac 40 – Pessac 34

Les Logis de Lestiac

71 rte de Bordeaux – ☎ 05 56 72 17 90 – philippe@logisdelestiac.com

5 rm – €80/95 €80/95 – **Table d'hôte** – Menu €25 bi/30 bi

◆ The owner's passion for decoration is evident in this superbly restored 18C mansion, featuring rooms on the first floor with a seasonal theme and a duplex on the ground floor. The restaurant serves tasty sweet and savoury dishes.

LEUCATE – 11 Aude – **344** J5 – **pop. 2 732** – **alt. 21 m** – ✉ **11370** Languedoc-Roussillon-Tarn Gorges 22 **B3**

Paris 821 – Carcassonne 88 – Narbonne 38 – Perpignan 35 – Port-la-Nouvelle 18

Office de tourisme, Espace Culturel ☎ 04 68 40 91 31, Fax 04 68 40 24 76

★ from the the Cap semaphore East: 2 km.

Jardin des Filoche VISA MC

64 av. J.-Jaurès – ☎ 04 68 40 01 12 – Fax 04 68 40 74 80 – Closed January, February, lunch except Sunday, Tuesday from 1st October to 31 March and Monday

Rest – Menu €27 (weekdays)/31

◆ Pleasant restaurant surrounded by a walled garden and shaded terrace that isolates it from the urban hustle and bustle. Classic cuisine and view of the kitchen.

Le Village AC VISA MC

129 av. J.-Jaurès – ☎ 04 68 40 06 91 – Fax 04 68 40 06 91 – Closed Sunday dinner, Tuesday and Wednesday

Rest – Menu €17/22 – Carte €25/32

◆ The walls are covered with posters, photos and nautical paraphernalia while the blue tablecloths reinforce the marine character of this old farm building. Traditional fare.

in Port-Leucate South: 7 km by D 627 – ✉ **11370 Leucate**

Syndicat d'initiative, rue Dour ☎ 04 68 40 91 31

Des Deux Golfs without rest VISA MC AE

on the harbour – ☎ 04 68 40 99 42 – contact@hoteldes2golfs.com – Fax 04 68 40 79 79 – Open 15 March-15 November

30 rm – €35/47 €47/63, €5

◆ In the marina built between the lake and the sea is this new building with small, functional rooms. Most have private loggias looking out over the yachts.

LEUTENHEIM – 67 Bas-Rhin – 315 M3 – pop. 788 – alt. 119 m – ✉ 67480 1 B1

Paris 501 – Haguenau 22 – Karlsruhe 46 – Strasbourg 45

Auberge Au Vieux Couvent

à Koenigsbruck – ✆ 03 88 86 39 86 – hirschel.vieux-couvent@wanadoo.fr – Fax 03 88 05 28 78 – Closed 25 August-7 September, 27 December-7 January, 23 February-8 March, Monday and Tuesday

Rest – Menu € 11,50 (weekday lunch), € 27/36 – Carte € 27/46

◆ Spruce, half-timbered, late 17C Alsatian-style residence. Gothic proverbs adorn the walls of the rustic dining room. Well-prepared modern cuisine.

LEVALLOIS-PERRET – 92 Hauts-de-Seine – 311 J2 – 101 15 – see Paris, Area

LEVENS – 06 Alpes-Maritimes – 341 E4 – pop. 3 700 – alt. 600 m – ✉ 06670

French Riviera 41 D2

Paris 946 – Antibes 43 – Cannes 53 – Nice 25 – Puget-Théniers 50 – St-Martin-Vésubie 39

Office de tourisme, 3, placette Paul Olivier ✆ 04 93 79 71 00, Fax 04 93 79 75 64

≤★ - Saut des Français★★ North: 8 km.

La Vigneraie

1.5 km St-Blaise road – ✆ 04 93 79 77 60 – Fax 04 93 79 82 35 – Open 17 February-5 October

18 rm – †€ 38 ††€ 45/51, ☕ € 6 – ½ P € 46/54 – **Rest** – *(dinner for resident only)* Menu € 18/25

◆ A family atmosphere and generous cuisine in this house in a green setting. Rustic guest rooms, some with balconies. Wide bay windows in the dining room.

LEVERNOIS – 21 Côte-d'Or – 320 J8 – see Beaune

LEVIE – 2A Corse-du-Sud – 345 D9 – see Corse

LEYNES – 71 Saône-et-Loire – 320 I12 – pop. 503 – alt. 340 m – ✉ 71570 8 C3

Paris 402 – Mâcon 15 – Bourg-en-Bresse 51 – Charolles 58 – Villefranche-sur-Saône 36

Le Fin Bec

pl. de la Mairie – ✆ 03 85 35 11 77 – Fax 03 85 35 13 71 – Closed 21 July-6 August, 17-26 November, 1st-7 January, Thursday dinner except July-August, Sunday dinner and Monday except holidays

Rest – Menu € 16 (weekdays)/41 – Carte € 25/37

◆ This restaurant provides a warm welcome in a pleasant rustic dining area featuring ceramic paintings depicting Beaujolais wine themes. Copious regional cuisine served.

LÉZIGNAN-CORBIÈRES – 11 Aude – 344 H3 – pop. 8 266 – alt. 51 m – ✉ 11200 22 B3

Paris 804 – Carcassonne 39 – Narbonne 22 – Perpignan 85 – Prades 129

Office de tourisme, 9, cours de la République ✆ 04 68 27 05 42, Fax 04 68 27 05 42

Le Mas de Gaujac

r. Gustave Eiffel, Gaujac Industrial Estate towards A61 access – ✆ 04 68 58 16 90 – masdegaujac@free.fr – Fax 04 68 58 16 91 – Closed 19 December-4 January, Saturday and Sunday October-May

21 rm – †€ 75/98 ††€ 75/98, ☕ € 10 – **Rest** – Menu € 16 – Carte € 25/60

◆ Recent red-ochre coloured building situated near a shopping area. The rooms are simple, fresh and above all practical and handy for a stopover. Contemporary dining room in warm tones; traditional, unpretentious food.

Rest. Le Tournedos et H. Le Tassigny with rm

rd-pt de Lattre-de-Tassigny – ✆ 04 68 27 11 51 – tournedos@wanadoo.fr – Fax 04 68 27 67 31 – Closed Sunday dinner

19 rm – €40 €45/47, ☕ €7,50 – ½ P €45/49

Rest – *(closed 30 June-3 July, Sunday dinner and Monday)* Menu (€12 bi), €14,50 bi (weekday lunch)/44 bi – Carte €25/59

◆ Grills and tournedos - the house specialities - are served in a well-lit pale yellow dining room. The rooms, in the same style, have been partially made over.

LEZOUX – 63 Puy-de-Dôme – 326 H8 – pop. 4 957 – alt. 340 m – ✉ 63190

Auvergne 6 **C2**

Paris 434 – Clermont-Ferrand 33 – Issoire 43 – Riom 38 – Thiers 16 – Vichy 43

Syndicat d'initiative, rue Pasteur ✆ 04 73 73 01 00, Fax 04 73 73 04 48

Les Voyageurs with rm

pl. de la Mairie – ✆ 04 73 73 10 49 – Fax 04 73 73 92 60 – Closed 16 August-7 September, 3-15 January, Friday dinner, Sunday dinner and Saturday

10 rm – €36/38 €46/48, ☕ €6,50 – ½ P €42/44 – **Rest** – Menu (€12), €14, €22/38 – Carte €27/48

◆ This 1960s building opposite the town hall serves traditional cuisine in a spacious dining room, adorned with an old rubber plant. Well-kept rooms.

in Bort-l'Étang 8 km Southeast by D 223 and D 309 – pop. 445 – alt. 420 m – ✉ 63190

✻★ from the château terrace ★ to Ravel West: 5 km.

Château de Codignat rm,

west: 1 km – ✆ 04 73 68 43 03 – codignat@relaischateaux.com – Fax 04 73 68 93 54 – Open 20 March-2 November

15 rm (½ board only) – 4 suites – ½ P €185/350

Rest – *(closed at lunchtime from Monday to Friday except public holidays) (number of covers limited, pre-book)* Menu €55/100 – Carte €90/101

Spec. Emietté de chair de tourteau. Homard bleu rôti au melon caramélisé (July-August). Grosse madeleine, mousseline vanille, fraises des bois et framboises (season). **Wines** Saint-Pourçain, Côtes d'Auvergne.

◆ A charming 15C chateau in a superb park, with refined rooms, most named after and decorated on the theme of a famous person, including many kings of France. Fine, personalised cuisine served in the medieval keep, around the impressive fireplace.

West 5 km by N 89 ✉63190 Seychalles

Chante Bise

à Courcourt – ✆ 04 73 62 91 41 – restaurant.chantebise@wanadoo.fr – Fax 04 73 68 29 53 – Closed 16 August-6 September, 15 February-6 March, Sunday dinner, Wednesday dinner and Monday except holidays

Rest – Menu €11,50 bi (weekday lunch), €19/36 – Carte €26/42

◆ A friendly atmosphere in this family restaurant featuring exposed stone and wood work. Traditional cuisine changing over the seasons. Shaded terrace area.

LIBOURNE – 33 Gironde – 335 J5 – pop. 21 761 – alt. 7 m – ✉ 33500

Atlantic Coast 3 **B1**

Paris 576 – Agen 129 – Bergerac 64 – Bordeaux 30 – Périgueux 100

Office de tourisme, 45, allée Robert Boulin ✆ 05 57 51 15 04, Fax 05 57 25 00 58

de Teynac Beychac-et-Caillau Domaine de Teynac, by Bordeaux road and D 1089: 15 km, ✆ 05 56 72 85 62 ;

de Bordeaux Cameyrac Saint-Sulpice-et-Cameyrac by Bordeaux road and D 1089: 16 km, ✆ 05 56 72 96 79.

LIBOURNE

Amade (Q. du Gén.-d') . . . . AZ 4
Clemenceau (Av. G.). . . . . . BY 5
Decazes (Pl.) . . . . BY 6
Ferry (R. J.) . . . . AZ 7
Foch (Av. du Mar.). . . . . BY 8
Gambetta (R.) . . . . ABY
Jean-Jaurès (R.) . . . . ABZ
J.-J.-Rousseau (R.). . . . . . . ABZ 10
Lattre-de-Tassigny (Pl. du Mar.-de) . . . . AZ 14
Montaigne (R. M.) . . . . BZ 21
Montesquieu (R.) . . . . BY 23
Prés.-Carnot (R. du) . . . . . . ABY
Prés.-Doumer (R. du) . . . . ABY 28
Prés.-Wilson (R. du) . . . . BY 29
Princeteau (Pl.). . . . . ABY 30
Salinières (Quai des) . . . . . . AY 35
Surchamp (Pl. A.) . . . . AZ
Thiers (R.) . . . . AZ
Waldeck-Rousseau (R.). . . . . AY 45

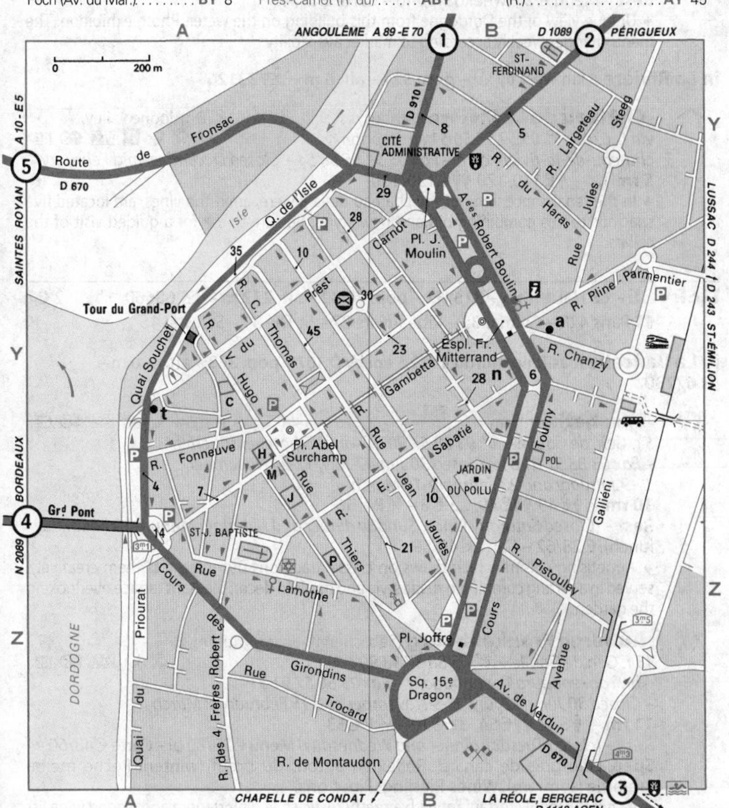

Mercure

rest,

3 quai Souchet – ✆ 05 57 25 64 18 – H6238@accor.com – Fax 05 57 25 64 19
81 rm – †€ 92/112 ††€ 102/122, ☕ € 13 – 3 suites – **Rest** – bar à vins *(dinner only)* Carte approx. € 20

◆ On the quays of the Dordogne, recent construction with contemporary decor and standardised bedrooms. Three suites. Seminar facilities. Wine bar serving a traditional menu displayed on blackboards (dinner only). Terrace.

De France without rest

7 r. Chanzy – ✆ 05 57 51 01 66 – hoteldefrance33@tiscali.fr – Fax 05 57 25 34 04
19 rm – †€ 50/145 ††€ 55/145, ☕ € 11 BY **a**

◆ The décor of this fully renovated post house is a mix of traditional and modern: warm tones, modern, Eastern-style and designer furnishings. Comfortable rooms.

Chez Servais

14 pl. Decazes – ✆ 05 57 51 83 97 – Fax 05 57 51 83 97
– Closed 1st-7 May, 14-28 August, Sunday evening and Monday BY **n**
Rest – Menu (€ 18), € 25/46

◆ Warm hospitality, a relaxed atmosphere, contemporary cuisine and bright interior at this restaurant in the heart of the fortified town.

XX **Bord d'Eau** < P VISA MC

via ⑤: 1,5 km – ✆ 05 57 51 99 91 – Fax 05 57 25 11 56 – Closed 15-22 September, 17 November-1st December, 16 February – 2 March, Wednesday dinner, Sunday dinner and Monday

Rest – Menu € 20 (weekdays)/46 – Carte € 37/45

◆ Unique view of the Dordogne from this building on the water. Photo exhibition. The menu changes weekly according to market availability.

in La Rivière **6 km West by ⑤ – pop. 321 – alt. 6 m – ✉ 33126**

Château de La Rivière without rest < Dordogne valley,

via D 670 – ✆ 05 57 55 56 51 – reception@chateau-de-la-riviere.com – Fax 05 57 55 56 54 – Closed December-mid February

5 rm – €110/170 €130/190

◆ In the renaissance wing of the chateau de la Rivière, amid the vines, are located five spacious rooms combining old and new styles. Be sure to ask for a guided visit of the cellars.

LIÈPVRE – 68 Haut-Rhin – 315 H7 – pop. 1 632 – alt. 272 m – ✉ 68660 2 C1

Paris 428 – Colmar 35 – Ribeauvillé 27 – St-Dié 31 – Sélestat 15

in La Vancelle **(Bas-Rhin) Northeast: 2,5 km by D 167 – pop. 373 – alt. 400 m – ✉ 67730**

XX **Elisabeth** with rm rest, P VISA MC AE

5 r. Gén. de Gaulle – ✆ 03 88 57 90 61 – info@hotel-elisabeth.fr – Fax 03 88 57 91 51 – Closed 30 June-7 July, 17-24 November, 1st-9 January and 23 February-10 March

10 rm – €49 €49, € 8 – ½ P € 56

Rest – *(Closed Saturday lunch, Sunday dinner and Monday)* Menu € 10 (weekday lunch), € 28/62 – Carte € 40/59

◆ Appetising cuisine which draws on classic traditions but interprets them creatively, served in a setting combining rustic style and modern decor; pleasant terrace overlooking the garden.

XX **Auberge Frankenbourg** (Sébastien Buecher) with rm

13 r. Gén.de Gaulle – ✆ 03 88 57 93 90 – hr.frankenbourg@wanadoo.fr – Fax 03 88 57 91 31 – Closed 30 June-12 July, 1st-9 November and 15 February-8 March VISA MC AE

11 rm – €48 €54, € 10 – ½ P € 53

Rest – *(closed Tuesday dinner and Wednesday)* Menu € 28/80 bi – Carte € 48/60

Spec. Foie gras de canard. Réflexion autour du bœuf (winter). Pêche melba fantaisie (summer). **Wines** Riesling, Pinot gris.

◆ A cheerful family restaurant with a pretty rustic-style dining room and a good wine list serving delicious and inventive cuisine at unbeatable prices.

LIESSIES – 59 Nord – 302 M7 – pop. 501 – alt. 165 m – ✉ 59740

Northern France and the Paris Region 31 D3

Paris 223 – Avesnes-sur-Helpe 14 – Charleroi 48 – Hirson 24 – Maubeuge 23 – St-Quentin 74

Syndicat d'initiative, 20, rue du Maréchal Foch ✆ 03 27 57 91 11, Fax 03 27 57 91 11

Parc départemental du Val Joly★ East: 5 km.

Château de la Motte P VISA MC AE

South: 1 km by secondary road – ✆ 03 27 61 81 94 – contact@chateaudelamotte.fr – Fax 03 27 61 83 57 – Closed 19 December-9 February, Sunday dinner and Monday lunch off season

9 rm – €57 €67, € 8,50 – ½ P € 66 – **Rest** – Menu € 22 (weekdays)/65 – Carte € 35/61

◆ Once a retreat for the monks from the neighbouring abbey, this brick building surrounded by fine parkland provides well-equipped accommodation. A dining room of character, terrace overlooking the countryside and traditional and regional dishes.

La Forge de l'Abbaye without rest
13 r. de la Forge – ✆ 03 27 60 74 27 – Fax 03 27 60 74 27
– Closed 2 January-9 February
4 rm – €52 €59
◆ A delightful country ambience reigns in this old forge full of character. Attractive rooms, kitchen available for the use of guests and a view of the country and a pond. Non-smoking.

Le Carillon
opposite the church – ✆ 03 27 61 80 21 – contact@le-carillon.com
– Fax 03 27 61 82 34 – Closed 20-27 August, 18 November-3 December, 18 February-11 March, Monday dinner, Tuesday dinner, Thursday dinner, Sunday dinner and Wednesday
Rest – *(number of covers limited, pre-book)* Menu € 17 (weekdays)/42
◆ A house of some charm; terrace shaded by plane trees and a dining room featuring beams and bricks. Traditional recipes based on local market produce. Gourmet shop.

LA LIEZ (LAC) – **52 Haute-Marne** – **313** M6 – **see Langres**

LIGNY-EN-CAMBRÉSIS – **59 Nord** – **302** I7 – **pop. 1 658** – **alt. 127 m** – ✉ **59191**
31 **C3**

Paris 193 – Arras 51 – Cambrai 17 – Valenciennes 42 – St-Quentin 35

Château de Ligny rm,
2 r. Curie – ✆ 03 27 85 25 84
– contact@chateau-de-ligny.fr – Fax 03 27 85 79 79
– Closed 3-17 August, February, Sunday dinner, Monday and Tuesday
21 rm – €120 €170, € 20 – 5 suites – ½ P € 128/317
Rest – Menu € 48/82 – Carte € 69/95
Spec. Tarte friande de rouget barbet au romarin. Sole et petits crustacés mijotés dans une bisque de crevettes grises. Soufflé à la chicorée.
◆ This lovely medieval manor has personalised rooms; those in the beautifully designed "Résidence" are larger. Excellent wellness facilities. The former armoury room and library-lounge give the restaurant an aristocratic touch.

LIGSDORF – **68 Haut-Rhin** – **315** H12 – **see Ferrette**

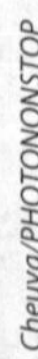

Chamber of commerce: belfry

LILLE

P **Department:** 59 Nord
Michelin LOCAL map: n° **302** G4
Paris 223 – Bruxelles 114 – Gent 75 – Luxembourg 310 – Strasbourg 530

Population: 184 657 31 **C2**
Pop. built-up area: 1 000 900
Altitude: 10 m – **Postal Code:** ✉ 59000
Northern France and the Paris Region

USEFUL INFORMATION

TOURIST OFFICE

place Rihour ✆ 08 91 56 20 04, Fax 03 59 57 94 14

TRANSPORT

Auto-train ✆ 3635 et tapez 42 (0,34 €/mn)

AIRPORT

Lille-Lesquin: ✆ 0 891 67 32 10 (0,23 €/mn), by A1: 8 km HT

A FEW GOLF COURSES

18 Lille Métropole Ronchin Rond Point des Acacias, ✆ 03 20 47 42 42 ;
9 du Sart Villeneuve-d'Ascq 5 rue Jean Jaurès, by D 656: 7 km, ✆ 03 20 72 02 51 ;
18 des Flandres Marcq-en-Barœul 159 boulevard Clémenceau, by D 670: 4.5 km, ✆ 03 20 72 20 74 ;
36 de Brigode Villeneuve-d'Ascq 36 avenue du Golf, by D 146: 9 km, ✆ 03 20 91 17 86.

TO BE SEEN

AROUND CITY HALL BELFRY

Quartier St-Sauveur FZ : porte de Paris★, ≤★ du beffroi - Palais des Beaux-Arts ★★★ EZ

AROUND CHAMBER OF COMMERCE BELFRY

Le Vieux Lille★★ EY: Vieille Bourse★★, House of Gilles de la Boé★ (29 place Louise-de-Bettignies) - rue de la Monnaie★ - Hospice Comtesse★ - House where General de Gaulle was born EY - St-Maurice church ★ EFY, The Citadel ★ BV

LIVELY DISTRICTS

Place du Général de Gaulle (Grand'Place)★ EY - Place Rihour EY - Rue de Béthune (cinemas) EYZ - Euralille (Crédit Lyonnais Tower★)

- and around Lille-Flandres railway station FY

... AND SURROUNDING AREA

Villeneuve d'Ascq: musée d'Art moderne (Modern Art Museum)★★ HS **M**

- Bondues: château du Vert-Bois★ HR
- Bouvines: church stained-glass windows and evocation of the battle JT

L'Hermitage Gantois
224 r. de Paris – ☎ 03 20 85 30 30 – contact@hotelhermitagegantois.com – Fax 03 20 42 31 31 p. 3 EZ **b**
67 rm – †€ 205/260 ††€ 205/260, ☐ € 18
Rest – Menu (€ 33), € 43
Rest *L'Estaminet* – brasserie *(closed Sat. lunchtime and Sun.)* Menu (€ 13), € 19
◆ Delightful personalized rooms, beautiful bathrooms, massage salon: luxury, history, comfort and modern design are tastefully combined in this 14C hospice. Restaurant with red and gold vaults offering a seasonal menu. The Estaminet has a brasserie atmosphere and serves generous portions of Flemish dishes.

Crowne Plaza rm, VISA
335 bd Leeds – ☎ 03 20 42 46 46 – contact@lille-crowneplaza.com – Fax 03 20 40 13 14 p. 8 FY **n**
121 rm – †€ 190/225 ††€ 190/225, ☐ € 21 – 1 suite – **Rest** – Menu (€ 19), € 26 – Carte € 37/55
◆ A modern hotel opposite the TGV railway station. Large, modern, well-equipped rooms with a 'Zen' influence; some with a splendid view of Lille and its belfry. A designer restaurant (furniture by Starck), up-to-date menu and buffets.

Alliance rm, rm, VISA
17 quai du Wault ✉ 59800 – ☎ 03 20 30 62 62 – alliancelille@alliance-hospitality.com – Fax 03 20 42 94 25 p. 6 BV **d**
83 rm – †€ 215/225 ††€ 215/225, ☐ € 18 – 8 suites – **Rest** – *(closed Monday 15 July-20 August)* Menu (€ 29), € 38 bi
◆ A 17C red brick convent located between old Lille and the Citadel. Contemporary decor in the bedrooms, set around an interior garden. A huge, pyramid-shaped glass roof covers the cloister where this restaurant is situated. Piano bar.

Novotel Centre Grand Place rm, rm, VISA
116 r. de L'Hôpital-Militaire – ☎ 03 28 38 53 53 – h0918@accor.com – Fax 03 28 38 53 54 p. 8 EY **k**
104 rm – †€ 99/169 ††€ 99/169, ☐ € 13,50 – **Rest** – Menu € 24 bi/30 bi – Carte € 25/43
◆ Completely refurbished hotel in line with Novotel's latest concept: large contemporary bedrooms, designed for both work and leisure (modular furniture) and modern bathrooms. Traditional dishes with the emphasis on healthy eating in the restaurant. Service all day long.

Grand Hôtel Bellevue without rest VISA
5 r. J. Roisin – ☎ 03 20 57 45 64 – contact@grandhotelbellevue.com – Fax 03 20 40 07 93 p. 8 EY **a**
60 rm – †€ 95/135 ††€ 95/135, ☐ € 12
◆ The rooms, graced with Directoire-style furniture and marble bathrooms, are unabashedly elegant; the most sought-after overlook the Grand'Place.

Novotel Lille Gares rm, VISA
49 r. Tournai ✉ 59800 – ☎ 03 28 38 67 00 – h3165@accor.com – Fax 03 28 38 67 10 p. 8 FZ **u**
86 rm – †€ 99/175 ††€ 109/185, ☐ € 14,50 – 5 suites – **Rest** – Carte € 27/40
◆ The hotel, next to the Lille-Flandres station, is gradually renovating its rooms to meet the chain's latest standards: space, comfort, modern fittings and a minimalist decor. Meals served at the bar or in the trendy dining room (simple menu and daily suggestions).

Mercure Opéra without rest VISA
2 bd Carnot ✉ 59800 – ☎ 03 20 14 71 47 – h0802@accor.com – Fax 03 20 14 71 48
101 rm – †€ 80/160 ††€ 90/265, ☐ € 14 p. 8 EY **h**
◆ Beams and bricks,? in the reception area and the lounges reflect the charm of this century-old, freestone building. Modern, carefully renovated rooms.

Art Déco Romarin without rest VISA
110 Rue de la République in La Madeleine – ☎ 03 20 14 81 81 – hotel-art-decoromarin@wanadoo.fr – Fax 03 20 14 81 80 p. 8 FY **t**
56 rm – †€ 89/130 ††€ 110/150, ☐ € 12
◆ This modern hotel is located on a busy avenue but with good soundproofing. Art Deco interiors, and spacious rooms. Also has a plush lounge and bar.

HAUBOURDIN

Carnot (R. Sadi) .... GT 22
Vanderhaghen (R. A.) .... GT 157

HELLEMMES-LILLE

Salengro (R. Roger) .... HS 142

HEM

Clemenceau (Bd G.) .... JS 28
Croix (R. de) .... JS 40
Gaulle (Av. Ch.-de) .... JS 64

LAMBERSART

Hippodrome (Av. de l') .... GS 76

LANNOY

Leclerc (R. du Gén.) .... JS 97
Tournai (R. de) .... JS 153

LA MADELEINE

Gambetta (R.) .... GS 63
Gaulle (R. du Gén.-de) .... HS 69
Lalau (R.) .... HS 87

LILLE

Arras (R. du Fg d') .... GT 4
Postes (R. du Fg des) .... GST 129

LOMME

Dunkerque (Av. de) .... GS 52

LOOS

Doumer (R. Paul) .... GT 49
Foch (R. du Mar.) .... GST 58
Potié (R. Georges) .... GT 130

LYS-LEZ-LANNOY

Guesde (R. Jules) .... JS 75
Lebas (R. J.-B.) .... JS 94

MARCQ-EN-BARŒUL

Clemenceau (Bd) .... HS 30
Couture (R. de la) .... HS 39
Foch (Av. Mar.) .... HS 57
Nationale (R.) .... HS 122

MARQUETTE-LEZ-LILLE

Lille (R. de) .... GS 103
Menin (R. de) .... HS 117

MONS-EN-BARŒUL

Gaulle (R. du Gén.-de) .... HS 70

MOUVAUX

Carnot (Bd) .... HR 21

ST-ANDRÉ-LEZ-LILLE

Lattre-de-Tassigny (Av. du Mar.-de) .... GS 91
Leclerc (R. du Gén.) .... GS 99

TOUFFLERS

Déportés (R. des) .... JS 48

TOURCOING

Yser (R. de l') .... JR 165
3-Pierres (R. des) .... JR 166

VILLENEUVE-D'ASCQ

Ouest (Bd de l') .... HS 124
Ronsse (R. Ch.) .... JT 136
Tournai (Bd de) .... JT 151

WAMBRECHIES

Marquette (R. de) .... GZ 108

WATTIGNIES

Clemenceau (R.) .... GT 31
Gaulle (R. du Gén.-de) .... GT 72
Victor-Hugo (R.) .... GT 160

WATTRELOS

Carnot (R.) .... JRS 24
Jean-Jaurès (R.) .... JR 82
Lebas (R. J.-B.) .... JR 96
Mont-à-Leux (R. du) .... JR 121

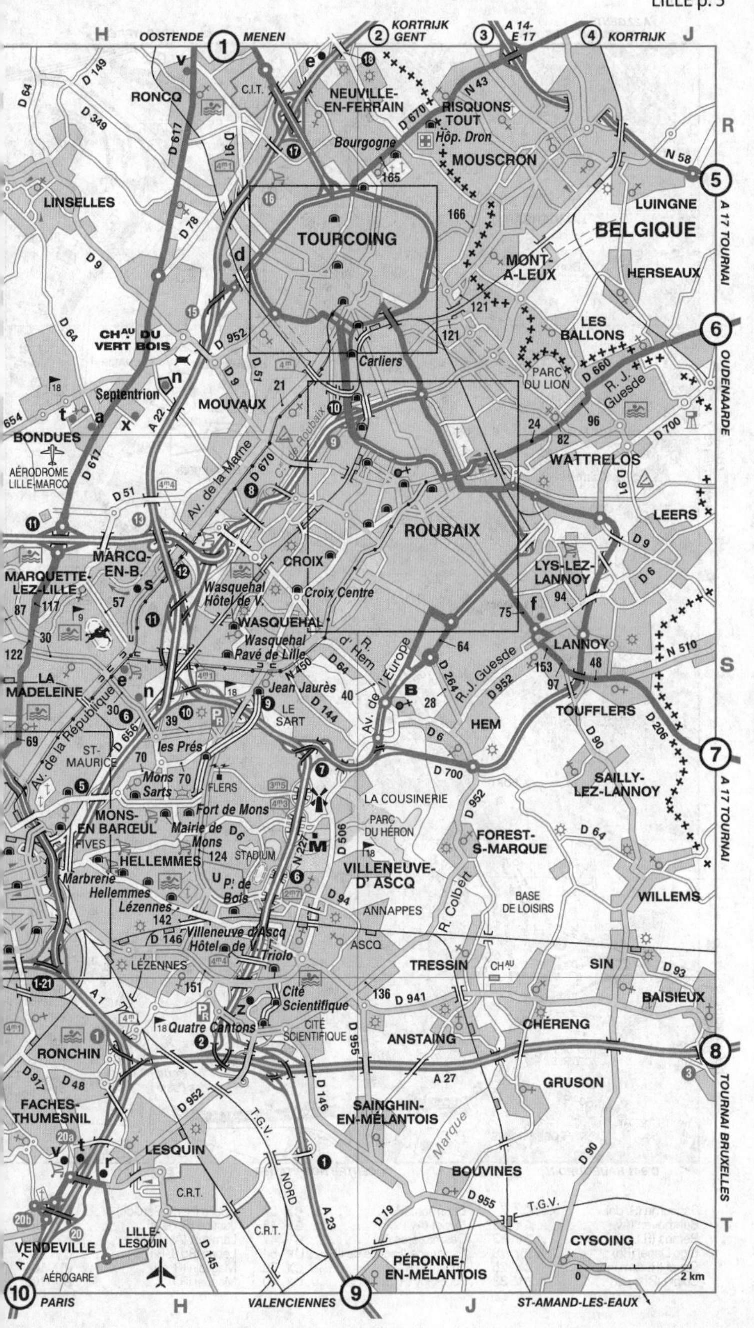
OOSTENDE
MENEN
KORTRIJK GENT
A 14-E 17
KORTRIJK
RONCQ
NEUVILLE-EN-FERRAIN
RISQUONS TOUT
Hôp. Dron
MOUSCRON
Bourgogne
LINSELLES
TOURCOING
LUINGNE
BELGIQUE
MONT-A-LEUX
HERSEAUX
CHAU DU VERT BOIS
LES BALLONS
Carliers
PARC DU LION
Septentrion
MOUVAUX
BONDUES
AÉRODROME LILLE-MARCQ
WATTRELOS
Av. de la Marne
ROUBAIX
LEERS
MARCQ-EN-B.
MARQUETTE-LEZ-LILLE
CROIX
LYS-LEZ-LANNOY
Wasquehal Hôtel de V.
Croix Centre
WASQUEHAL
Wasquehal Pavé de Lille
LANNOY
LA MADELEINE
Jean Jaurès
LE SART
TOUFFLERS
Av. de l'Europe
R. J. Guesde
HEM
Av. de la République
ST-MAURICE
les Prés
Mons Sarts
FLERS
LA COUSINERIE
SAILLY-LEZ-LANNOY
MONS-EN BARŒUL
Fort de Mons
Mairie de Mons
PARC DU HÉRON
FIVES
HELLEMMES
STADIUM
FOREST-S-MARQUE
Marbrerie
Hellemmes
Pt de Bois
VILLENEUVE-D'ASCQ
Lézennes
ANNAPPES
R. Colbert
BASE DE LOISIRS
WILLEMS
Villeneuve d'Ascq Hôtel de V.
Triolo
ASCQ
LÉZENNES
TRESSIN
CHAU
SIN
Cité Scientifique
BAISIEUX
Quatre Cantons
CITÉ SCIENTIFIQUE
ANSTAING
CHÉRENG
RONCHIN
GRUSON
FACHES-THUMESNIL
SAINGHIN-EN-MÉLANTOIS
Marque
LESQUIN
BOUVINES
C.R.T.
T.G.V.
NORD
LILLE-LESQUIN
VENDEVILLE
CYSOING
AÉROGARE
PÉRONNE-EN-MÉLANTOIS
0
2 km
PARIS
VALENCIENNES
ST-AMAND-LES-EAUX
A 17 TOURNAI
OUDENAARDE
A 17 TOURNAI
TOURNAI BRUXELLES

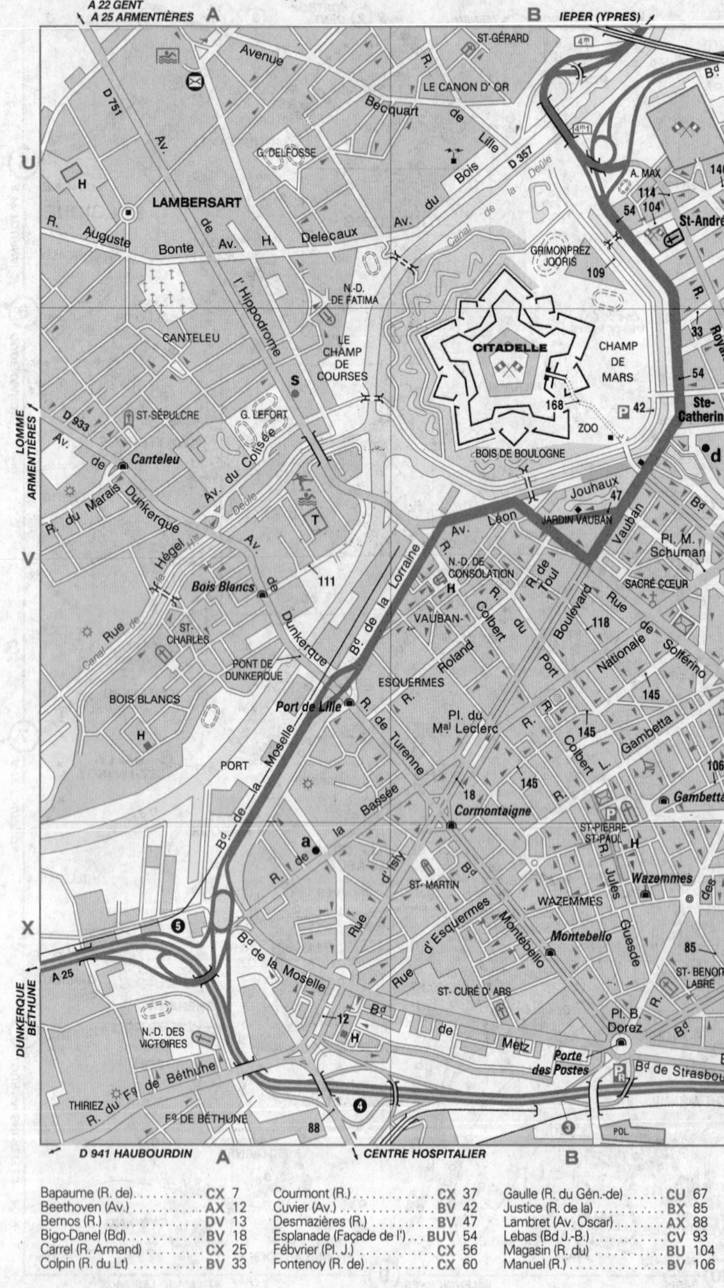
A 22 GENT
A 25 ARMENTIÈRES
A
B
IEPER (YPRES)
ST-GÉRARD
Avenue
Becquart
R. de Lille
LE CANON D' OR
D 751
Av.
G. DELFOSSE
Bois
du
Av.
D 357
U
H
A. MAX
140
114
104
54
St-André
LAMBERSART
R. Auguste Bonte
de
Av. H. Delecaux
Canal de la Deûle
GRIMONPREZ JOORIS
109
N.-D. DE FATIMA
l'Hippodrome
CANTELEU
LE CHAMP DE COURSES
CITADELLE
CHAMP DE MARS
R. Royale
33
54
S
ST-SÉPULCRE
G. LEFORT
D 933
Av. du Colisée
168
ZOO
42
Ste-Catherine
d
LOMME ARMENTIÈRES
Av. de Dunkerque
Canteleu
BOIS DE BOULOGNE
Jouhaux
47
JARDIN VAUBAN
R. du Marais
T
Av. Léon
Vauban
Bd
Pl. M. Schuman
V
Hégel
R. de la Hte Deûle
Bois Blancs
111
Bd de la Lorraine
N.-D. DE CONSOLATION
H
R. de Toul
SACRÉ CŒUR
Rue
Boulevard
ST-CHARLES
Canal
VAUBAN
R. Colbert
du Port
118
de Solférino
Rue de
PONT DE DUNKERQUE
Nationale
ESQUERMES
R. Roland
145
BOIS BLANCS
Port de Lille
R. de Turenne
Pl. du Mal Leclerc
R. Colbert
Gambetta
H
PORT
Bd de la Moselle
Bassée
18
145
106
Cormontaigne
Gambetta
a
R. de la
ST-PIERRE ST-PAUL
H
R. Jules Guesde
Wazemmes
R. d'Isly
ST-MARTIN
Bd
WAZEMMES
des
5
Rue
Rue d'Esquermes
Montebello
X
Montebello
85
A 25
Bd de la Moselle
ST- BENOIT LABRE
DUNKERQUE BÉTHUNE
ST- CURÉ D'ARS
12
Bd de Metz
Pl. B. Dorez
N.-D. DES VICTOIRES
H
Porte des Postes
Bd de Strasbourg
R. du Fg de Béthune
THIRIEZ
Fg DE BÉTHUNE
88
4
3
POL
D 941 HAUBOURDIN
CENTRE HOSPITALIER

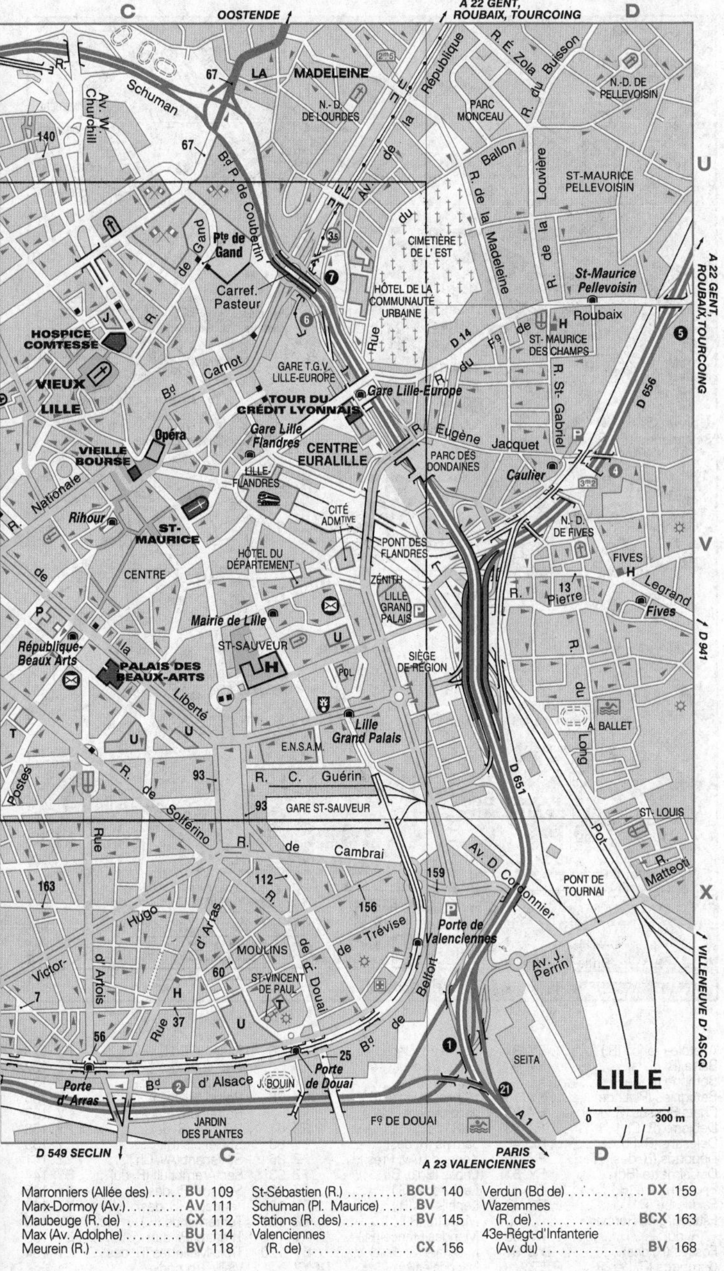

Marronniers (Allée des) . . . . **BU** 109
Marx-Dormoy (Av.) . . . . **AV** 111
Maubeuge (R. de) . . . . **CX** 112
Max (Av. Adolphe) . . . . **BU** 114
Meurein (R.) . . . . **BV** 118
St-Sébastien (R.) . . . . **BCU** 140
Schuman (Pl. Maurice) . . . . . **BV**
Stations (R. des) . . . . **BV** 145
Valenciennes
(R. de) . . . . **CX** 156
Verdun (Bd de) . . . . **DX** 159
Wazemmes
(R. de) . . . . **BCX** 163
43e-Régt-d'Infanterie
(Av. du) . . . . **BV** 168

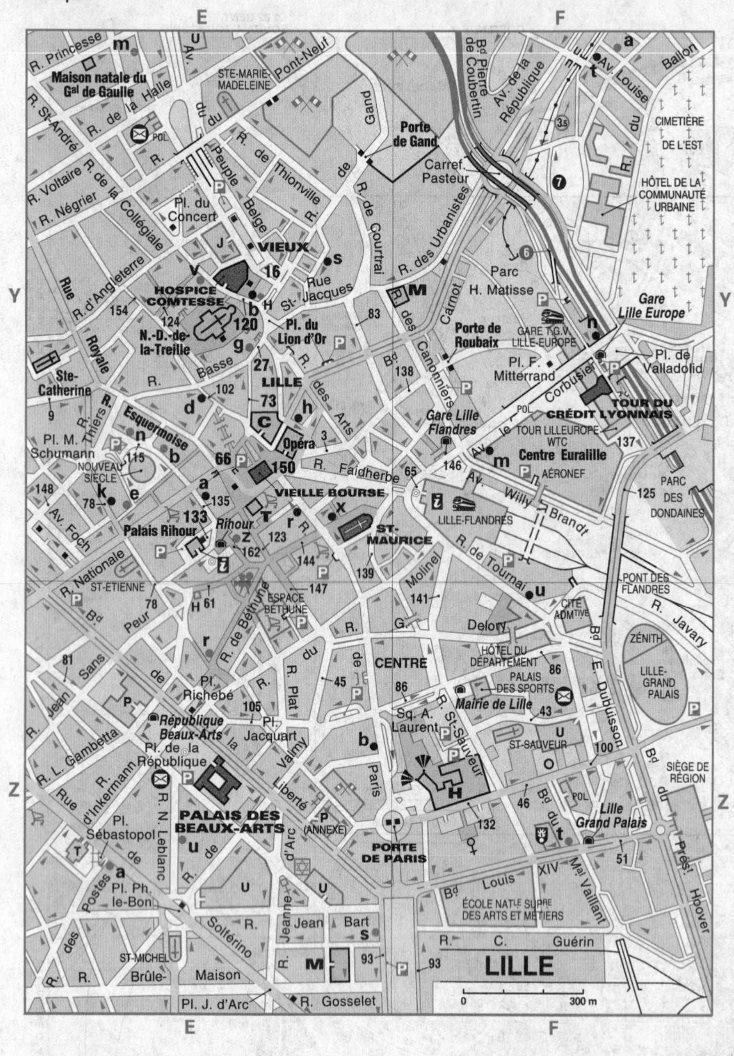

Anatole-France (R.)	EY	3
Barre (R. de la)	EY	9
Béthune (R. de)	EYZ	
Bettignies (Pl. L. de)	EY	16
Chats-Bossus (R. des)	EY	27
Debierre (R. Ch.)	FZ	43
Delesalle (R. E.)	EZ	45
Déportés (R. des)	FY	46
Dr-Calmette (Bd)	FY	51
Esquermoise (R.)	EY	
Faidherbe (R.)	EY	
Faubourg-de-Roubaix (R. du)	FY	55
Fosses (R. des)	EYZ	61
Gambetta (R. Léon)	DEZ	
Gare (Pl. de la)	FY	65
Gaulle (Pl. Gén.-de)	EY	66
Grande-Chaussée (R. de la)	EY	73
Hôpital-Militaire (R.)	EY	78
Jacquemars-Giélée (R.)	EZ	81
Jardins (R. des)	EY	83
Kennedy (Av. Prés.)	FZ	86
Lebas (Bd J. B.)	FZ	93
Lefèvre (R. G.)	FZ	100
Lepelletier (R.)	EY	102
Maillotte (R.)	EZ	105
Mendès-France (Pl.)	EY	115
Monnaie (R. de la)	EY	120
Nationale (R.)	DEYZ	
Neuve (R.)	EY	123
Pasteur (Bd L.)	FY	125
Réduit (R. du)	FZ	132
Rihour (Pl.)	EY	133
Roisin (R. Jean)	EY	135
Rotterdam (Parvis de)	FY	137
Roubaix (R. de)	EFY	138
St-Génois (R.)	EY	139
St-Venant (Av. Ch.)	FYZ	141
Sec-Arembault (R. du)	EY	144
Suisses (Pl. des)	FY	146
Tanneurs (R. des)	EYZ	147
Tenremonde (R.)	EY	148
Théâtre (Pl. du)	EY	150
Trois-Mollettes (R. des)	EY	154
Vieille-Comédie (R. de la)	EY	162

De la Paix without rest

46 bis r. de Paris – ✆ 03 20 54 63 93 – hotelpaixlille@aol.com – Fax 03 20 63 98 97
36 rm – †€ 80/88 ††€ 88/110, ☕ € 9 *p. 8* EY **r**
◆ A hotel built in 1782. The art-loving landlord displays reproductions of paintings and the mural in the breakfast room is all her own work. Snug rooms.

Des Tours without rest

27 r. des Tours – ✆ 03 59 57 47 00 – contact@hotel-des-tours.com – Fax 03 59 57 47 99 *p. 8* EY **s**
64 rm – †€ 110/120 ††€ 115/130, ☕ € 14
◆ A pleasant hotel superbly located in the heart of Old Lille, with a guarded garage and a hall and lounge adorned with contemporary paintings. Modern, practical rooms.

Brueghel without rest

parvis St-Maurice – ✆ 03 20 06 06 69 – hotel.brueghel@nordnet.fr – Fax 03 20 63 25 27 *p. 8* EY **x**
65 rm – †€ 76 ††€ 88/95, ☕ € 8
◆ Typically Flemish façade, retro charm in the hallway and lift, small fresh personalised rooms and central location.

Lille Europe without rest

av. Le Corbusier – ✆ 03 28 36 76 76 – infos@hotel-lille-europe.com – Fax 03 28 36 77 77 *p. 8* FY **m**
97 rm – †€ 73/88 ††€ 73/88, ☕ € 8,50
◆ A modern building between the two railway stations, part of the Euralille centre (shops and restaurants). Functional, well-soundproofed rooms. Breakfast room with a panoramic view.

De La Treille without rest

7/9 pl. Louise de Bettignies – ✆ 03 20 55 45 46 – hoteldelatreille@free.fr – Fax 03 20 51 51 69 *p. 8* EY **b**
42 rm – †€ 70/130 ††€ 70/130, ☕ € 12
◆ With slightly-cramped yet fresh and well-appointed rooms, this hotel is perfectly located for exploring the old town. Generous buffet breakfast.

Ibis Opéra without rest

21 r. Lepelletier – ✆ 03 20 06 21 95 – h0902@accor.com – Fax 03 20 74 91 30
59 rm – †€ 60/89 ††€ 60/89, ☕ € 7 *p. 8* EY **d**
◆ A smart traditional façade and new rooms in line with the chain's standards (modern furniture, desk space): an excellent base camp to visit the historic city centre.

La Maison Carrée rest,

29 r. Bonte Pollet – ✆ 03 20 93 60 42 – reservation@lamaisoncarree.fr *p. 6* AX **a**
5 rm ☕ – †€ 140/200 ††€ 150/230 – **Table d'hôte** – Menu € 30/60 bi
◆ Magnificent early 20C private mansion, run by contemporary art and home decoration enthusiasts. The quintessence of peacefulness, sophistication and comfort.

À L'Huîtrière

3 r. Chats Bossus ✉ 59800 – ✆ 03 20 55 43 41 – contact@huitriere.fr – Fax 03 20 55 23 10 – Closed 27 July-25 August, Sunday dinner and dinner on public holidays
Rest – Menu € 45 (weekday lunch)/140 – Carte € 72/124 *p. 8* EY **g**
Spec. Vinaigrette tiède d'anguille fumée et foie gras chaud (September to May). Gros turbot rôti, toast à la moelle (March to November). Fraises, tomates et olives confites, huile d'olive et basilic, granité rhubarbe (May to September).
◆ The decorative tiles of this former fishmongers are well worth seeing to whet your appetite. Interior houses three luxurious, elegant dining rooms. One of Lille's gourmet high spots.

La Laiterie (Benoit Bernard)

138 r. de l'Hippodrome, at Lambersart ✉ 59130 – ✆ 03 20 92 79 73 – Fax 03 20 22 16 19 – Closed 3-25 August, Sunday and Monday *p. 6* AV **s**
Rest – Menu (€ 38 bi), € 41/80 – Carte € 57/117
Spec. Thon aux cinq épices chinoises. Turbot rôti en tronçon, os à moelle aux petits gris. Déclinaison d'agneau de lait des Pyrénées (spring).
◆ Restaurant on the outskirts of Lille. The attractive modern interior is discreet to do full justice to the chef's delicious, creative cuisine full of flavours.

XXX **Le Sébastopol** (Jean-Luc Germond)

1 pl. Sébastopol – ✆ 03 20 57 05 05 – n.germond@restaurant-sebastopol.fr – Closed 3-25 August, Sunday dinner, Saturday lunch and Monday lunch p. 8 EZ **a**

Rest – Menu € 52 bi/68 – Carte € 66/79

Spec. Saint-Jacques d'Étaples. Filets de sole aux jets de houblon (spring). Notre raison d'aimer la chicorée du Nord (dessert).

◆ A curtain of greenery and an unusual glass canopy adorn the façade of this warm establishment. Traditional cuisine with a good wine list.

XXX **Champlain**

13 r. N. Leblanc – ✆ 03 20 54 01 38 – le.champlain@wanadoo.fr – Fax 03 20 40 07 28 – Closed August, Saturday lunch, Sunday dinner and Monday dinner p. 8 EZ **u**

Rest – Menu € 25 bi (weekday lunch), € 30/45

◆ Take a seat in the plush dining room or in the peaceful inner courtyard of this 19C abode to sample the first-rate cuisine which does full justice to the excellence of its produce.

XX **Baan Thaï**

22 bd J.-B. Lebas – ✆ 03 20 86 06 01 – gtbi@wanadoo.fr – Fax 03 20 86 72 94 – Closed Sunday evening and Saturday lunchtime p. 8 EZ **s**

Rest – Menu € 23 (weekday lunch), € 41/51 – Carte € 27/53

◆ This restaurant on the first floor of a bourgeois house is a veritable invitation to take a trip to the land of Siam: elegant exotic decor and traditional Thai food.

XX **Clément Marot**

16 r. Pas ✉ 59800 – ✆ 03 20 57 01 10 – clmarot@nordnet.fr – Fax 03 20 57 39 69 – Closed Sunday evening p. 8 EY **n**

Rest – Menu (€ 18), € 34/43 bi – Carte € 41/83

◆ A small brick house run by the descendants of Clément Marot, a poet from Cahors. Modern decor, walls hung with pictures and a friendly atmosphere.

XX **Le Colysée**

201 av. Colisée ✉ 59130 Lambersart – ✆ 03 20 45 90 00 – contact@le-colysee.com – Fax 03 20 45 90 70 – Closed 11 August-2 September, Saturday lunch, Monday dinner and Sunday p. 6 AV

Rest – Menu (€ 18), € 27/59 bi – Carte € 38/56

◆ The ground floor of the Colysée is home to this muted restaurant decorated in an avant-garde style (films projected onto the ceiling) in keeping with the innovative characterful cuisine.

XX **L'Écume des Mers**

10 r. Pas – ✆ 03 20 54 95 40 – aproye@nordnet.com – Fax 03 20 54 96 66 – Closed Sunday dinner – **Rest** – brasserie Menu (€ 15), € 20 – Carte € 29/56 p. 8 EY **n**

◆ A lively atmosphere, fish caught the same day, a good oyster bar and some meat dishes for those who prefer meat: a vast brasserie with the wind in its sails!

XX **Brasserie de la Paix**

25 pl. Rihour – ✆ 03 20 54 70 41 – contactpaix@restaurantsdelille.com – Fax 03 20 40 15 52 – Closed Sun p. 8 EY **z**

Rest – brasserie Menu € 18/26 – Carte € 26/55

◆ Ceramics, woodwork, benches and tightly packed tables set the Art Deco scene of this pleasant brasserie situated near the Palais Rihour (Tourist Office). Most friendly.

XX **Le Bistrot Tourangeau**

61 bd Louis XIV ✉ 59800 – ✆ 03 20 52 74 64 – hhochart@laposte.net – Fax 03 20 85 06 39 – Closed 3-24 August, 26 December-4 January, Monday dinner, Tuesday dinner, Wednesday dinner, Saturday lunch and Sunday p. 8 FZ **t**

Rest – Carte € 31/56

◆ A charming red façade hides a long dining room, separated from the kitchens by a pane of glass. Updated traditional repertoire, regional dishes from Tours, wine from the Loire.

XX **Le Why Not**

9 r. Maracci – ✆ 03 20 74 14 14 – lewhynot@nordnet.fr – Fax 03 20 74 14 15 – Closed 28 July-17 August, 1st-6 January, Monday dinner, Tuesday dinner, Saturday lunch and Sunday p. 8 EY **m**

Rest – Menu (€ 22), € 26/31

◆ In the heart of historic Lille, this trendy-yet-friendly restaurant is set in a designer-decorated cellar. Tasty, up-to-date cooking by a globe-trotting chef.

L'Assiette du Marché
61 r. Monnaie – ✆ 03 20 06 83 61 – contact@assiettedumarche.com – Fax 03 20 14 03 75 – Closed 3-25 August and Sunday p. 8 EY **v**
Rest – Menu (€ 16), € 20 – Carte € 25/40
◆ The happy blend of old and new decoration and the glass roof covering the interior courtyard enhance this 18C Hôtel des Monnaies (Mint). Dishes with seasonal market produce.

La Coquille
60 r. St-Étienne ✉ 59800 – ✆ 03 20 54 29 82 – dadeleval@nordet.fr – Fax 03 20 54 29 82 – Closed 1st-15 August and Sunday p. 8 EY **e**
Rest – *(pre-book)* Menu (€ 18), € 27/37 bi – Carte € 32/50
◆ Stone, beams, tightly packed tables and checkered tablecloths: a countrified ambiance that sets you at ease. The menu chalked up on a slate varies with the seasons.

Le Bistrot de Pierrot
6 pl. Béthune – ✆ 03 20 57 14 09 – Fax 03 20 30 93 13 – Closed 10-25 August, 4-12 January, Sunday and Monday p. 8 EZ **r**
Rest – bistrot Carte € 29/46
◆ The new owners have preserved the soul and character of this authentic bistro. On the menu: a fine choice of "old-fashioned" dishes and a lighter selection for the diet conscious.

in Bondues – pop. 10 680 – alt. 37 m – ✉ 59910

Syndicat d'initiative, 266, domaine de la vigne ✆ 03 20 25 94 94

Auberge de l'Harmonie
pl. Abbé Bonpain – ✆ 03 20 23 17 02 – contact@aubergeharmonie.fr – Fax 03 20 23 05 99 – Closed 15 July-10 August, Sunday dinner, Tuesday dinner, Thursday dinner and Monday p. 5 HR **t**
Rest – Menu (€ 28 bi), € 37 bi/88 bi – Carte € 45/67
◆ Colourful and warm with rustic furniture, exposed beams, lush green terrace and seasonally varied dishes. A good blend of decor and cuisine.

Val d'Auge (Christophe Hagnerelle)
805 av. Gén. de Gaulle – ✆ 03 20 46 26 87 – valdauge@numericable.fr – Fax 03 20 37 43 78 – Closed Easter holidays, 28 July-17 August, 24-30 December, Sunday dinner, Monday dinner, Wednesday and holidays p. 5 HR **a**
Rest – Menu (€ 44 bi), € 55 bi – Carte € 64/84
Spec. Œuf cocotte aux champignons de saison. Pièce de veau cuite à basse température. Soufflé au chocolat grand cru.
◆ A restaurant on the main road. Modern, pleasantly bright interior. The cuisine features a subtle blend of flavours and aromas.

in La Madeleine – pop. 22 399 – alt. 48 m – ✉ 59110

Syndicat d'initiative, 177, rue du Général-de-Gaulle ✆ 03 20 74 32 35, Fax 03 20 74 32 35

L'Atelier "La Cour des Grands"
15 r. François de Badts à la Madeleine – ✆ 03 20 74 26 33 – Fax 03 20 55 89 66 – Closed 1st-21 August, February holidays, Sunday, Monday and holidays
Rest – Menu € 22 (lunch), € 37/51 – Carte € 37/51 p. 8 FY **a**
◆ Industrial loft decor, artwork and photography, an inventive minimalist cuisine and good choice of wines by the glass: this former garage has become the in-place of Lille.

in Marcq-en-Baroeul – pop. 37 177 – alt. 15 m – ✉ 59700

Office de tourisme, 111, avenue Foch ✆ 03 20 72 60 87, Fax 03 20 72 56 65

Mercure
157 av. Marne, via D 670: 5 km – ✆ 03 28 33 12 12 – h1099@accor.com – Fax 03 28 33 12 24 p. 5 HS **s**
125 rm – † € 55/160 †† € 65/170, ☕ € 13,50 – 1 suite
Rest ***L'Europe*** – *✆ 03 28 33 12 68* – Menu (€ 18), € 23 – Carte € 31/50
◆ A 1970s building surrounded by greenery near a motorway interchange. Stylish, contemporary renovated rooms. Snug sitting room and pleasant piano bar. Daily specials chalked up on the blackboard, classic menu and oyster bar.

XXX **Le Septentrion**

parc du château Vert-Bois, by D 617: 9 km – ✆ 03 20 46 26 98 – contact-septentrion@nordnet.fr – Fax 03 20 46 38 33 – Closed 19 July-13 August, 19-26 February, Tuesday dinner, Wednesday dinner, Thursday dinner and Monday

Rest – Menu € 38/70 – Carte € 53/69 *p. 5* HR **n**

◆ Within the Prouvost-Septentrion Foundation, this former outbuilding of the Vert-Bois château commands a pastoral view of the park. Tasty updated cuisine.

XX **Auberge de la Garenne**

17 chemin de Ghesles – ✆ 03 20 46 20 20 – contact@aubergegarenne.fr – Fax 03 20 46 32 33 – Closed 1st-23 August, Sunday dinner, Monday and Tuesday

Rest – Menu € 32 bi (weekday lunch), € 52 € bi/90 bi – Carte € 42/69 *p. 5* HR **x**

◆ In the heart of unspoilt countryside, this pleasant country inn boasts a lovely garden and terrace! A repertoire which upholds regional cooking traditions.

X **La Table de Marcq**

944 av. de la République – ✆ 03 20 72 43 55 – Closed 29 July-28 August, Sunday dinner and Monday *p. 4* HS **e**

Rest – Menu (€ 17), € 22/32 – Carte € 32/42

◆ Formerly a café, this restaurant has been decorated in a modern vein, without however forgoing the lovely old counter. Friendly atmosphere and market-inspired menu.

in Villeneuve d'Ascq – pop. 65 042 – alt. 26 m – ✉ 59491

Office de tourisme, chemin du Chat Botté ✆ 03 20 43 55 75, Fax 03 20 91 28 28

Ascotel

av. P. Langevin-Cité Scientifique – ✆ 03 20 67 34 34 – ascotel@club.fr – Fax 03 20 91 39 28 *p. 5* HT **z**

83 rm – †€ 59/85 ††€ 67/89, ☐ € 14 – 2 suites – ½ P € 85/114 – **Rest** – *(Closed Saturday and Sunday)* Menu € 17/23 – Carte € 29/34

◆ In the centre of the science park, a hotel complex for business trips - vast conference room, large lecture hall and functional rooms undergoing renovation. A modern dining room and traditional buffet-style dishes.

to Lille-Lesquin Airport – ✉ 59810 Lesquin

Mercure Aéroport

– ✆ 03 20 87 46 46 – h1098@accor.com – Fax 03 20 87 46 47 *p. 5* HT **r**

215 rm – †€ 55/160 ††€ 60/170, ☐ € 13,50

Rest ***La Flamme*** – Menu € 23 bi (weekday lunch), € 29/45 – Carte € 25/49

◆ Contemporary architecture; spacious, comfortable rooms. Avoid rooms overlooking the motorway. Shuttle service to nearby airport. A friendly atmosphere, regional dishes and spit-roast meats on view at the Flamme.

Novotel Aéroport

55 rte de Douai – ✆ 03 20 62 53 53 – h0427@accor.com – Fax 03 20 97 36 12

92 rm – †€ 54/133 ††€ 54/133, ☐ € 12,50 – **Rest** – Carte € 19/39 *p. 5* HT **t**

◆ This low building is the chain's oldest hotel (1967). Functional rooms gradually being refurbished in the latest Novotel style. Traditional dishes and diet recipes rub shoulders in the fully redecorated restaurant.

Agena without rest

451 av du Gén.-Leclerc ✉ 59155 – ✆ 03 20 60 13 14 – hotelagena@nordnet.fr – Fax 03 20 97 31 79 *p. 5* HT **v**

40 rm – †€ 64 ††€ 69, ☐ € 10,50

◆ The rooms in this semi-circular building are on garden level; the quieter ones face the patio. A discreet setting, roughcast walls, simple furniture and faultless upkeep.

in Wattignies – pop. 14 440 – alt. 39 m – ✉ 59139

X **Le Cheval Blanc**

110 r. Gén-.de Gaulle – ✆ 03 20 97 34 62 – le-cheval-blanc3@wanadoo.fr – Fax 03 20 97 34 62 – Closed Sunday dinner *p. 4* GT **x**

Rest – Menu € 25 bi (weekday lunch)/43 – Carte € 48/69

◆ A warm welcome and decor (light colours, modern art, handsome wooden bar) and an appetising repertoire that focuses on market fresh and locally sourced produce.

in Emmerin – **pop. 3 029 – alt. 24 m – ✉ 59320**

La Howarderie
1 r. Fusillés – ✆ 03 20 10 31 00 – contact@lahowarderie.com – Fax 03 20 10 31 09 – Closed 4-25 August, 22 December-5 January and Sunday dinner p. 4 GT **e**
7 rm – €95/135 €135/220, ☕ €17
Rest – Menu €26/58 – Carte €40/69
♦ One wing of this old brick farmhouse opposite the church offers a choice of elegant rooms with an individual touch and antique or period furnishings. Tasty contemporary cuisine in intimate dining rooms.

in Capinghem – **pop. 1 524 – alt. 50 m – ✉ 59160**

La Marmite de Pierrot
93 r. Poincaré – ✆ 03 20 92 12 41 – pierrot@marmite-de-pierrot.com – Fax 03 20 92 72 51 – Closed Sunday dinner, Tuesday dinner, Wednesday dinner, Thursday dinner and Monday p. 4 GS **v**
Rest – Menu €24/32
♦ Rustic-style bistro specialising in pork products and tripe. Informal ambience and interior decorated with halters and other farming implements.

in St-André-Lez-Lille – **pop. 10 113 – alt. 20 m – ✉ 59350**

Office de tourisme, 89, rue du Général Leclerc ✆ 03 20 51 79 05, Fax 03 20 63 07 60

La Quintinie
501 av. Mal-de-Lattre-de-Tassigny , (D 57) – ✆ 03 20 40 78 88 – anita@alaquintinie.com – Fax 03 20 40 62 77 – Closed 15 July-15 August, Sunday dinner, Tuesday dinner, Wednesday dinner and Monday p. 4 GS **t**
Rest – Menu (€26), €32/40 – Carte €47/80
♦ Brick house in a pretty garden with a vegetable patch. Elegant, contemporary decor inside with faïence paintings; classic cuisine.

LIMAY – 78 Yvelines – 311 G2 – pop. 15 709 – alt. 16 m – ✉ 78520 18 A1

Paris 56 – Argenteuil 50 – Boulogne-Billancourt 52 – Saint-Denis 60

Au Vieux Pêcheur
5 quai Albert 1er – ✆ 01 30 92 77 78 – Fax 01 34 77 34 62 – Closed 10-20 May, 28 July-28 August, Wednesday dinner, Sunday dinner and
Rest – Menu €30 – Carte €34/59
♦ This restaurant on the banks of the Seine serves good traditional cuisine in a refined and rustic dining area. Set menu at midday served in a simpler room.

LIMERAY – 37 Indre-et-Loire – 317 P4 – see Amboise

LIMOGES Ⓟ – 87 Haute-Vienne – 325 E6 – pop. 133 968 – Built-up area 173 299 – alt. 300 m – ✉ 87000 Dordogne-Berry-Limousin 24 B2

Paris 391 – Angoulême 105 – Brive-la-Gaillarde 92 – Châteauroux 126

Limoges: ✆ 05 55 43 30 30, by ⑦: 10 km.

Office de tourisme, 12, boulevard de Fleurus ✆ 05 55 34 46 87, Fax 05 55 34 19 12

de la Porcelaine Panazol Celicroux, by Clermont-Ferrand road: 9 km, ✆ 05 55 31 10 69 ;

de Limoges Avenue du Golf, by St-Yriex road: 3 km, ✆ 05 55 30 21 02.

Cathédrale St-Etienne (St Etienne Cathedral)★ - Église St-Michel-des-Lions (St Michel des Lions Church)★ - Cour du temple (Temple courtyard)★ CZ 115 - Jardins de l'évêché (Bishop's Palace gardens)★ - Musée national de la porcelaine Adrien Dubouché (Adrien Dubouché National Porcelaine Museum)★★ (porcelaines) BY - Rue de Boucherie★ - Musée de l'évêché (Bishop's Palace Museum)★ : enamels★ - Chapelle St-Aurélien (Chapel of St Aurelien)★ - Gare des Bénédictins★.

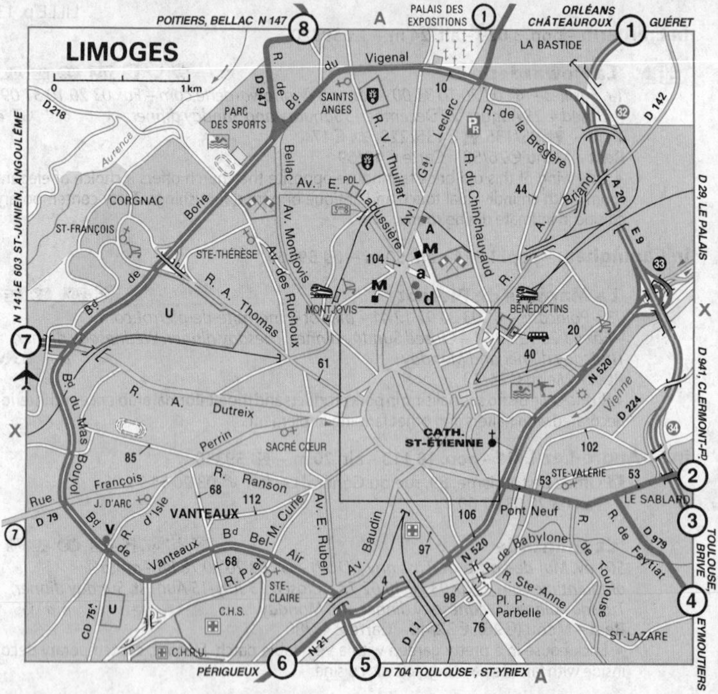

LIMOGES

Street	Grid	No.	Street	Grid	No.	Street	Grid	No.
Allende (Quai Salvador)	AX	4	Lattre-de-Tassigny (Av. Mar. de)	AX	53	Révolution (Av. de la)	AX	97
Arcades (Bd des)	AX	10	Mauvendière (R. de la)	AX	61	Révolution (Pont de la)	AX	98
Casseaux (Av. des)	AX	20	Naugeat (Av. de)	AX	68	Sablard (Av. du)	AX	102
Gagnant (Av. J.)	AX	40	Pompidou (Av. G.)	AX	76	Sadi-Carnot (Pl.)	AX	104
Grand-Treuil (R. du)	AX	44	Puy-Las-Rodas (R. du)	AX	85	Ste-Claire (R.)	AX	112
Labussière (Av. E.)	AX	51				St-Martial (Quai)	AX	106

Mercure Royal Limousin without rest
1 pl. République – ✆ 05 55 34 65 30 – h5955@accor.com – Fax 05 55 34 55 21 CY **u**
78 rm – ♦€ 88/115 ♦♦€ 98/125, ☐ € 12,50
◆ A tasteful blend of light wood and pastel colours characterises this hotel standing on a huge square. Three categories of rooms depending on your wish, from simple to comfortable.

Atrium without rest
22 allée de Seto - Parc du Ciel – ✆ 05 55 10 75 75 – ha8703@inter-hotel.com – Fax 05 55 10 75 76 DY **a**
70 rm – ♦€ 85/140 ♦♦€ 90/145, ☐ € 10
◆ A former customs warehouse converted into a hotel offering pleasant rooms, some of which overlook the superb railway station of Limoges. Those overlooking the courtyard are quieter.

Domaine de Faugeras
allée Faugeras, 3 km northwest by Rue A-Briand and D 142 – ✆ 05 55 34 66 22 – infos@domainedefaugeras.fr – Fax 05 55 34 18 05 AY **e**
9 rm – ♦€ 95 ♦♦€ 200, ☐ € 14 – 2 suites
Rest *White Owl* – *(closed Sunday dinner and Monday)* Menu € 24 (weekday lunch), € 42/70 – Carte € 30/63
◆ This 18C château overlooking Limoges is an interesting blend of history and modern comfort. Extremely well-appointed bedrooms, fireside lounge, wine-tasting cellar, and spa. "Lounge" ambience and plate-glass windows at The White Owl.

LIMOGES

Aine (Pl. d') . . . . **BZ** 2
Allois (R. des) . . . . **DZ** 6
Amphithéâtre (R. de l') . . . . **BY** 8
Barreyrrette (Pl. de la) . . . . **CZ** 12
Bénédictins (Av. des) . . . . . **DY** 14
Betoulle (Pl. L.) . . . . **CZ** 16
Boucherie (R. de la) . . . . . . **CZ** 18
Cathédrale (R. de la) . . . . . . **DZ** 23
Clocher (R. du) . . . . **CZ** 25
Collège (R. du) . . . . **CZ** 26
Consulat (R. du) . . . . **CZ**
Coopérateurs (R. des) . . . . **BY** 27
Dupuytren (R.) . . . . **CZ** 30
Ferrerie (R.) . . . . **CZ** 33
Fonderie (R. de la) . . . . **BY** 35
Fontaine-des-Barres (Pl.) . . . **CY** 37
Gambetta (Bd) . . . . **BCZ**
Giraudoux (Square Jean) . . . **CY** 42
Haute-Cité (R.) . . . . **DZ** 46
Jacobins (Pl. des) . . . . **CZ** 49
Jean-Jaurès (R.) . . . . **CYZ**
Louis-Blanc (Bd) . . . . **CZ**
Louvrier-de-Lajolais (R.) . . . **BY** 55
Manigne (Pl.) . . . . **CZ** 57
Maupas (R. du) . . . . **DY** 59
Michels (R. Charles) . . . . . . **CZ** 63
Motte (Pl. de la) . . . . **CZ** 66
Périn (Bd G.) . . . . **CY** 71
Préfecture (R. de la) . . . . . . **CY** 83
Raspail (R.) . . . . **DZ** 89
Réforme (R. de la) . . . . **CY** 91
République (Pl. de la) . . . . . **CY** 95
St-Martial (R.) . . . . **CY** 107
St-Maurice (Bd) . . . . **DZ** 109
St-Pierre (Pl.) . . . . **CZ** 110
Stalingrad (Pl.) . . . . **CY** 113
Temple (Cour du) . . . . **CZ** 115
Temple (R. du) . . . . **CZ** 116
Tourny (Carrefour) . . . . **CY** 118
Victor-Hugo (Bd) . . . . **BY** 120
Vigne-de-Fer (R.) . . . . **CZ** 122
71e-Mobile (R. du) . . . . **DZ** 125

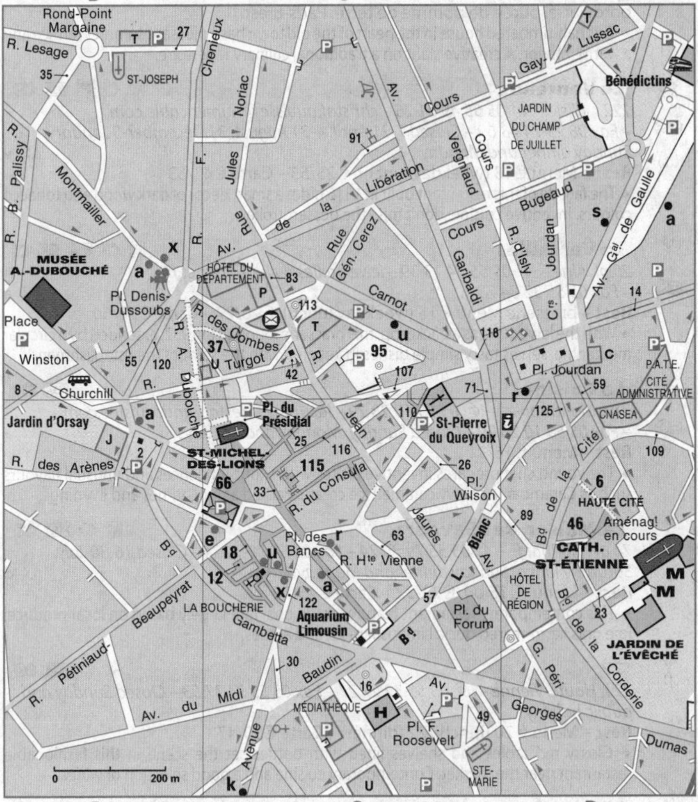

Richelieu without rest

40 av. Baudin – ☎ 05 55 34 22 82 – info@hotel-richelieu.com – Fax 05 55 34 35 36

40 rm – †€ 81/99 ††€ 91/109, ☕ € 12 – 2 suites CZ **k**

◆ Close to the Town Hall and the Media Library, this hotel combines modern comforts with a discreet classical decor of 1930s inspiration. Ideal for business travellers.

Jeanne-d'Arc without rest

17 av. Gén. de Gaulle – ☎ 05 55 77 67 77 – hoteljeannedarc.limoges@wanadoo.fr – Fax 05 55 79 86 75 – Closed 21 December-8 January DY **s**

50 rm – †€ 62/79 ††€ 74/92, ☕ € 7,50

◆ This former 19C post-house, not far from the station, features a delightfully outdated provincial atmosphere. Well-kept rooms and pleasant breakfast room.

De la Paix without rest
25 pl. Jourdan – 05 55 34 36 00 – Fax 05 55 32 37 06 DY **r**
31 rm – €41 €56/68, €7
◆ This late 19C building features lounges decorated with an impressive collection of phonographs worthy of a museum. Simple rooms (WC on the landing for eight rooms).

Amphitryon (Richard Lequet)
26 r. Boucherie – 05 55 33 36 39 – amphitryon87000@aol.com – Fax 05 55 32 98 50 – Closed 5-12 May, 25 August-8 September, 5-12 January, Sunday and Monday CZ **u**
Rest – Menu (€19), €24 (weekday lunch), €36/69 – Carte €64/95
Spec. Les trois foies gras. Filet de bœuf limousin à la moelle, réduction de bordelaise, purée de pomme de terre. Paris-Brest.
◆ This half-timbered house in the heart of the old town has a pleasant summer terrace and a warm interior. A creative slant on a traditional culinary repertoire.

Le Vanteaux
122 r. d'Isle – 05 55 49 01 26 – christof.aubisse@numericable.com – Fax 08 25 74 43 69 – Closed 7-21 April, 4-31 August, 31 December-5 January, Sunday dinner and Monday AX **v**
Rest – Menu €18 (weekday lunch), €25/53 – Carte €43/53
◆ The façade of this restaurant built in 1815 hides a smart decor of dark wood and tobacco colours. Inventive cuisine; don't miss the dessert trolley.

Le Versailles
20 pl. Aine – 05 55 34 13 39 – le.versailles@club-internet.fr – Fax 05 55 32 84 73 BZ **a**
Rest – brasserie Menu €15 (weekday lunch), €20/27 – Carte €21/60
◆ With the law courts as a backdrop, this brasserie founded in 1932, extended by a circular mezzanine, serves tasty simple dishes in keeping with the spirit of the establishment.

La Cuisine
21 r. Montmailler – 05 55 10 28 29 – lacuisine@restaurantlacuisine.com – Fax 05 55 10 28 29 – Closed Sunday, Monday and holidays BY **a**
Rest – Menu €16/31
◆ The young chef prepares inventive dishes with exotic influences and unusual flavours such as Carambar (a chewy caramel) ice cream. Packed at lunchtimes and evenings.

La Maison des Saveurs
74 av. Garibaldi – 05 55 79 30 74 – Fax 05 55 79 30 74 – Closed 16-30 July, Saturday lunch, Sunday dinner and Monday AX **d**
Rest – Menu (€15 bi), €22/52 – Carte €45/58
◆ This contemporary restaurant features traditional fare largely based on local produce: foie gras, farm-reared duck, Limousin meat and apples.

27
27 r. Haute-Vienne – 05 55 32 27 27 – Fax 05 55 34 37 53 – Closed Sunday and public holidays CZ **a**
Rest – Menu €20 (lunch)/22 (dinner) – Carte €30/47
◆ Glossy red tables and shelves lined with bottles set the scene in this fashionable restaurant near the market. Contemporary cuisine and a good selection of wines.

L'Épicurien
18 r. Montmailler – 05 55 77 71 95 – manson.laurent@wanadoo.fr – Fax 05 55 77 71 95 – Closed 3-25 August, 1st-8 January, Sunday and Monday
Rest – Menu (€15 bi), €30/34 BY **x**
◆ This modest establishment, an alternative to the many local Japanese restaurants, features up-to-date bistro-style cuisine in a modern setting.

Les Petits Ventres
20 r. Boucherie – 05 55 34 22 90 – emavic-sarl@wanadoo.fr – Fax 05 55 32 41 04 – Closed 6-20 April, 6-23 September, 17 February-2 March, Sunday and Monday CZ **u**
Rest – Menu (€14,50), €22/36 – Carte €27/54
◆ An impressive choice of menus (tripe is the house speciality) is on offer in this rustic-style restaurant. Half-timbered decor, with colourful paintings hanging from the walls.

Le Bouche à Oreille

72 bis av. Garibaldi – ☎ 05 55 10 09 57 – david.daudon@wanadoo.fr – Fax 05 55 10 09 57 – Closed 11-25 August, 1st-12 January, 22-28 February, Tuesday dinner from 15 September to 15 June, Sunday except lunch from 15 September to 15 June and Monday AX **a**

Rest – bistrot Menu € 23 (weekdays)/40 – Carte approx. € 46

◆ A friendly town centre bistro with a clientele of regulars. Market fresh cuisine served in a non-smoking dining room decorated in bright reds and yellows.

Chez Alphonse

5 pl. Motte – ☎ 05 55 34 34 14 – bistrot.alphonse@wanadoo.fr – Fax 05 55 34 34 14 – Closed Sunday and public holidays CZ **e**

Rest – bistrot Menu € 12,50 bi (weekday lunch) – Carte € 20/46

◆ In keeping with tradition, the chef of this lively bistro pays a daily visit to the market next door for produce with which to concoct his authentic repertoire.

La Table de Jean

5 r. Boucherie – ☎ 05 55 32 77 91 – Closed 1st-15 August, 24 December-5 January, 23-28 February, Sunday, Monday and holidays CZ **x**

Rest – *(number of covers limited, pre-book)* Menu (€ 17) – Carte € 29/52

◆ A fine restaurant in the historic district. Pleasant service and a minimalist decor. Tasty market fresh cooking with a choice of wines from independent winegrowers.

via ① and A 20 – ✉ 87280 Limoges

Novotel rm,

2 av. d'Uzurat, ZI Nord exit, Lac d'Uzurat : 5 km – ☎ 05 44 20 20 00 – h0431@accor.com – Fax 05 44 20 20 10

90 rm – 🚹€ 104/114 🚹🚹€ 115/125, ☕ € 13 – **Rest** – Carte € 23/41

◆ On an industrial estate, a hotel with a 1970s overlooking Uzurat Lake in the centre of a 3ha park. Jogging track for clients eager to stay fit or relax. Modern dining room, terrace overlooking expanses of water; classic fare.

in St-Martin-du-Fault by ⑦, N 141, D 941 and D 20: 13 km – ✉ 87510 Nieul

Chapelle St-Martin (Gilles Dudognon)

– ☎ 05 55 75 80 17 – chapelle@relaischateaux.fr – Fax 05 55 75 89 50 – Closed 1st January-8 February

10 rm – 🚹€ 80/220 🚹🚹€ 80/220, ☕ € 16 – 3 suites – ½ P € 116/214

Rest – *(closed Sunday dinner from November to March, Tuesday lunch, Wednesday lunch and Monday) (number of covers limited, pre-book)* Menu € 30 (lunch), € 58/90 – Carte € 60/95

Spec. Duo de foie gras de canard. Carré de veau fermier du Limousin, cèpes et ris de veau. Le monde autour des pommes.

◆ A plush elegant manor house in a park on the edge of a wood; rooms which sport colourful fabrics, sophisticated furniture and wall hangings. Well-prepared regional products feature in the cuisine.

LIMONEST – 69 Rhône – 327 H4 – see Lyon

LIMOUX – 11 Aude – 344 E4 – pop. 9 411 – alt. 172 m – ✉ 11300

Languedoc-Roussillon-Tarn Gorges 22 **B3**

Paris 769 – Carcassonne 25 – Foix 70 – Perpignan 104 – Toulouse 94

Syndicat d'initiative, promenade du Tivoli ☎ 04 68 31 11 82, Fax 04 68 31 87 14

Grand Hôtel Moderne et Pigeon rm,

1 pl. Gén.-Leclerc, (near the post office) – ☎ 04 68 31 00 25 – hotelmodernepigeon@wanadoo.fr – Fax 04 68 31 12 43 – Closed 15 December-26 January and Sunday dinner from 15 October to 30 April

11 rm – 🚹€ 82/86 🚹🚹€ 98/102, ☕ € 14,50 – 3 suites – ½ P € 92/94

Rest – *(closed Sunday dinner except July-August, Tuesday lunch, Saturday lunch and Monday)* Menu € 27 (weekday lunch), € 43/88 – Carte € 49/84

◆ This 17C mansion has been restored from top to toe. The spacious rooms are tastefully personalised and the magnificent staircase has murals and stained glass. Attractive 1900s style dining rooms and a verdant patio-terrace; classic bourgeois cuisine.

La Maison de la Blanquette
46 bis promenade du Tivoli – ✆ 04 68 31 01 63 – Fax 04 68 31 28 37 – Closed Wednesday
Rest – Menu € 18 bi (weekday lunch), € 27 € bi/55 bi
◆ This restaurant serves generous portions of local dishes to accompany the famous Blanquette de Limoux and other local wines. Wine shop. Wine is included in the price.

LINGOLSHEIM – 67 Bas-Rhin – 315 K5 – see Strasbourg

LINIÈRES-BOUTON – 49 Maine-et-Loire – 317 J4 – pop. 96 – alt. 53 m – ✉ 49490

35 **C2**

Paris 293 – Nantes 155 – Angers 67 – Tours 58 – Joué-lès-Tours 85

Château de Boissimon without rest
– ✆ 02 41 82 30 86 – contact@chateaudeboissimon.com
– Closed 1 November-31 March
5 rm – €130/150 €150/190
◆ This château, set in quiet wooded parkland, offers meticulously renovated rooms decorated with a host of refined details. Ideal for a romantic break.

LE LIOUQUET – 13 Bouches-du-Rhône – 340 I6 – see La Ciotat

LIPSHEIM – 67 Bas-Rhin – 315 J6 – see Strasbourg

LISIEUX – 14 Calvados – 303 N5 – pop. 23 166 – alt. 51 m – Pilgrimage (end September) – ✉ 14100 Normandy

33 **C2**

Paris 179 – Alençon 94 – Caen 64 – Évreux 73 – Le Havre 60 – Rouen 93

Office de tourisme, 11, rue d'Alençon ✆ 02 31 48 18 10, Fax 02 31 48 18 11

St-Pierre cathedral ★ BY.

★ of St-Germain-de-Livet 7 km by ④.

Plan on next page

Mercure rm,
via ②: 2.5 km (rte de Paris) – ✆ 02 31 61 17 17 – h1725@accor.com
– Fax 02 31 32 33 43
69 rm – €76/97 €87/100, € 12 – **Rest** – Menu (€ 17), € 21/23 – Carte € 22/40
◆ On the outskirts, a hotel with contemporary architecture. Small but well-designed, soundproofed rooms with sloping ceilings on the top floor. A restaurant with a modern setting overlooking the swimming pool with a nearby terrace for the summer.

Azur without rest
15 r. au Char – ✆ 02 31 62 09 14 – resa@azur-hotel.com – Fax 02 31 62 16 06
15 rm – €60/70 €80/90, € 9 BYZ **b**
◆ A renovated hotel in a 50-year old building. Spring-like, comfortable guest rooms. Winter garden breakfast room.

De la Place without rest
67 r. H. Chéron – ✆ 02 31 48 27 27 – hoteldelaplacebw@wanadoo.fr
– Fax 02 31 48 27 20 – Closed 1st December-3 January ABY **a**
33 rm – €46/69 €59/79, € 9,50
◆ The size of the bedrooms varies a great deal, but all have just been renovated, which has made them cheerful and up-to-date. Generous breakfast buffet.

L'Espérance
16 bd Ste-Anne – ✆ 02 31 62 17 53 – booking@lisieux-hotel.com
– Fax 02 31 62 34 00 – Open mid April-mid October BZ **e**
100 rm – €69/99 €79/107, € 9 – ½ P € 66/91 – **Rest** – *(open beg. May-mid October)* Menu € 19/32 – Carte € 37/53
◆ On the main boulevard, this large Norman-style hotel built in 1930 has spacious and light rooms with modern bed linen. A large country fresco covers the walls of this grand dining area. Serving up-dated traditional meals.

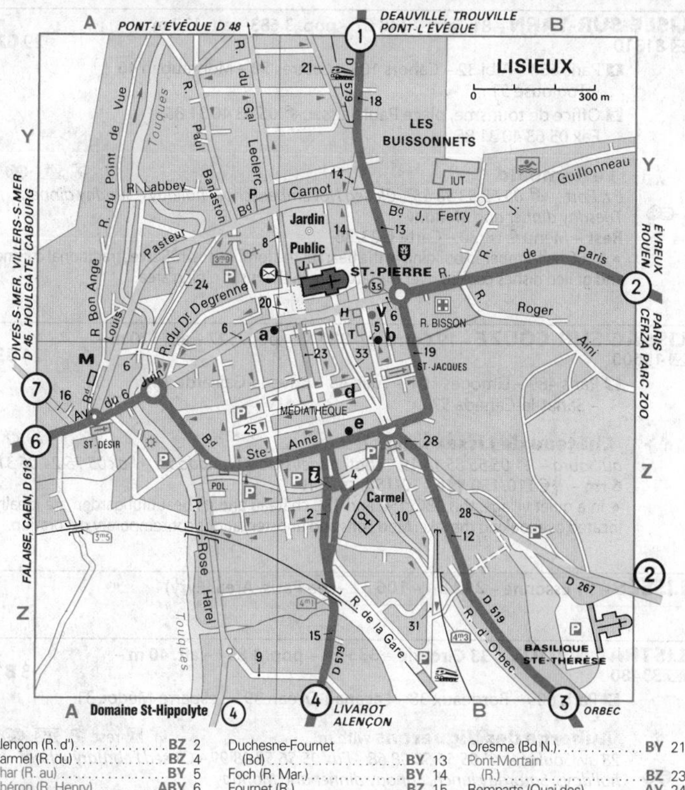

Alençon (R. d') BZ 2
Carmel (R. du) BZ 4
Char (R. au) BY 5
Chéron (R. Henry) ABY 6
Condorcet (R.) AY 8
Creton (R.) ABZ 9
Dr-Lesigne (R.) BZ 10
Dr-Ouvry (R.) BZ 12
Duchesne-Fournet (Bd) BY 13
Foch (R. Mar.) BY 14
Fournet (R.) BZ 15
Guizot (R.) AZ 16
Herbet-Fournet (Bd) BY 18
Jeanne-d'Arc (Bd) BZ 19
Mitterrand (Pl. F.) ABY 20
Oresme (Bd N.) BY 21
Pont-Mortain (R.) BZ 23
Remparts (Quai des) AY 24
République (Pl. de la) ABZ 25
Ste-Thérèse (Av.) BZ 28
Verdun (R. de) BZ 31
Victor-Hugo (Av.) BZ 33

Aux Acacias

VISA MC

13 r. Résistance – ✆ 02 31 62 10 95 – Fax 02 31 32 59 06 – Closed Sunday dinner and Monday except holidays BZ **d**

Rest – Menu € 17 (weekdays)/45 – Carte € 37/54

◆ Pastel-coloured tablecloths and curtains with painted wooden furniture in a tasteful setting where traditional cuisine, based on local produce, is served.

Le France

VISA MC AE

5 r. au Char – ✆ 02 31 62 03 37 – lefrancerestaurant@wanadoo.fr – Fax 02 31 62 03 37 – Closed 17-23 November, 5-26 January, Sunday dinner except July-August and Monday – **Rest** – Menu € 18/32 – Carte € 30/51 BY **v**

◆ Located near the cathedral, this restaurant featuring up-dated traditional cuisine has a rustic and interesting décor, with an old wine press, fireplace, wooden beams, copperware and old phonographs.

in Ouilly-du-Houley by ②, D 510 and D 262: 10 km – pop. 193 – alt. 55 m – ✉ 14590

De la Paquine

P VISA MC

rte de Moyaux – ✆ 02 31 63 63 80 – championlapaquine@orange.fr – Fax 02 31 63 63 80 – Closed 10-19 March, 2-10 September, 11-28 November, Sunday dinner, Tuesday dinner and Wednesday

Rest – *(pre-book)* Menu € 33 – Carte € 49/69

◆ Set just outside the village, this small restaurant surrounded by a floral garden serves seasonal produce in a rustic and warm atmosphere.

LISLE-SUR-TARN – 81 Tarn – 338 C7 – pop. 3 683 – alt. 127 m – ✉ 81310 29 C2

Paris 668 – Albi 32 – Cahors 105 – Castres 58 – Montauban 46 – Toulouse 51

Office de tourisme, place Paul Saissac ✆ 05 63 40 31 85, Fax 05 63 40 31 85

Le Romuald

6 r. Port – ✆ 05 63 33 38 85 – Closed November school holidays, Sunday dinner, Tuesday dinner and Monday
Rest – Menu € 18/30 – Carte € 23/36
◆ A 16C half-timbered building in the heart of the fortified town. Serves traditional cuisine and grilled dishes cooked over the large fire in the rustic dining area.

LISSAC-SUR-COUZE – 19 Corrèze – 329 J5 – pop. 527 – alt. 170 m – ✉ 19600 24 B3

Paris 489 – Limoges 101 – Tulle 45 – Brive-la-Gaillarde 14 – Sarlat-la-Canéda 57

Château de Lissac without rest

au bourg – ✆ 05 55 85 14 19 – chateaudelissac@wanadoo.fr – Fax 05 75 24 06 31
6 rm – †€ 110/150 ††€ 110/150, ☕ € 10
◆ In a quiet village, this 13C, 15C and 18C château and its beautiful garden are ideally located overlooking the lake. Mod cons and unostentatious contemporary decoration.

LISSES – 91 Essonne – 312 D4 – 106 32 – see Paris, Area (Évry)

LISTRAC MEDOC – 33 Gironde – 335 G4 – pop. 1 854 – alt. 40 m – ✉ 33480 3 B1

Paris 609 – Bordeaux 38 – Lacanau-Océan 39 – Lesparre-Médoc 31

Auberge des Vignerons with rm

28 av. Soulac – ✆ 05 56 58 08 68 – Fax 05 56 58 08 99 – Closed February school holidays, Saturday lunch, Sunday dinner and Monday
7 rm – †€ 40 ††€ 40, ☕ € 7 – ½ P € 60 – **Rest** – Menu (€ 11), € 14, € 26/47 – Carte € 36/41
◆ Inn next to the Maison des Vins (Wine House). Traditional cuisine, wine list topped by Listrac vintages and view of the storeroom where the wine is matured. Terrace facing the vineyards.

LIVRY-GARGAN – 93 Seine-Saint-Denis – 305 G7 – 101 18 – see Paris, Area

LA LLAGONNE – 66 Pyrénées-Orientales – 344 D7 – see Mont-Louis

LLO – 66 Pyrénées-Orientales – 344 D8 – see Saillagouse

LOCHES – 37 Indre-et-Loire – 317 O6 – pop. 6 328 – alt. 80 m – ✉ 37600 11 B3

Châteaux of the Loire

Paris 261 – Blois 68 – Châteauroux 72 – Châtellerault 56 – Tours 42

Office de tourisme, place de la Marne ✆ 02 47 91 82 82, Fax 02 47 91 61 50

de Loches-Verneuil Verneuil-sur-Indre La Capitainerie, by D 943: 10 km, ✆ 02 47 94 79 48.

Medieval town★★: keep★★, St-Ours church ★, Porte Royale★, porte des cordeliers★, town hall★ Y H - Chateaux★★: recumbent statue of Agnès Sorel★, triptych★ - troglodytic quarries Vignemont★.

Portal ★ of Chartreuse du Liget East: 10 km by ②.

LOCHES

Anciens A.F.N. (Pl. des) . . . . . . Z
Auguste (Bd Ph.) . . . . Z
Balzac (R.) . . . . YZ
Bas-Clos (Av. des) . . . . Y 2
Blé (Pl. au) . . . . Y 3
Château (R. du) . . . . YZ 5
Cordeliers (Pl. des) . . . . Y
Descartes (R.) . . . . Y 7
Donjon (Mail du) . . . . Z
Droulin (Mail) . . . . Z
Filature (Q. de la) . . . . Y 8
Foulques-Nerra (R.) . . . . Z 9
Gare (Av. de la) . . . . Y
Gaulle (Av. Gén.-de) . . . . Y 10
Grande-Rue . . . . Y 13
Grand Mail (Pl. du) . . . . Y 12
Lansyer (R.) . . . . Z 14
Marne (Pl. de la) . . . . Y
Mazerolles (Pl.) . . . . Y 15
Moulins (R. des) . . . . Y 16
Pactius (R. T.) . . . . Z 17
Picois (R.) . . . . Y
Ponts (R. des) . . . . Y 18
Porte-Poitevine (R. de la) . . . . . Z 19
Poterie (Mail de la) . . . . Z
Quintefol (R.) . . . . YZ
République (R. de la) . . . . Y
Ruisseaux (R. des) . . . . Z 20
St-Antoine (R.) . . . . Y 21
St-Ours (R.) . . . . Z 22
Tours (R. de) . . . . Y
Verdun (Pl. de) . . . . Y
Victor-Hugo (R.) . . . . Y
Vigny (R. A.-de) . . . . Y
Wermelskirchen (Pl. de) . . . . . Y 29

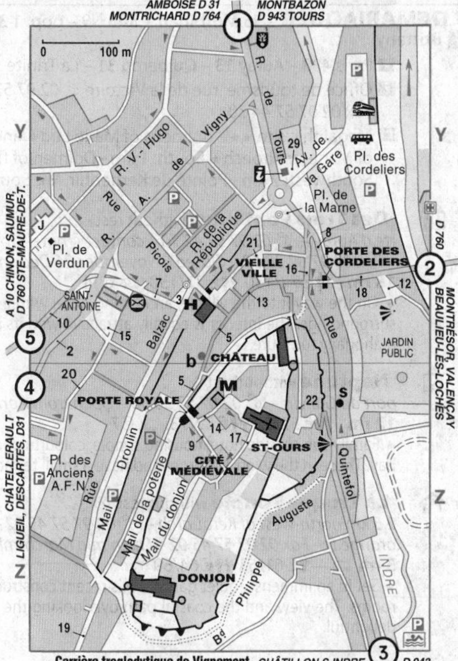

Le George Sand

39 r. Quintefol – 02 47 59 39 74
– contactgs@hotelrestaurant-georgesand.com
– Fax 02 47 91 55 75 Z **s**

19 rm – €40/125 €40/125, €9 – ½ P €62

Rest – *(closed 1 week February, 1 week October, Sunday dinner and Monday lunch except June-September)* Menu €21 (weekdays)/47

◆ A 15C house on the banks of the Indre with the feel of a family inn. Rustic bedrooms, half of which overlook the river. Impressive stone spiral staircase. Pleasant restaurant with exposed beams and a fireplace, plus a delightful covered terrace with bucolic views.

Luccotel

12 r. Lézards, 1 km by ⑤ – 02 47 91 30 30
– luccotel@wanadoo.fr – Fax 02 47 91 30 35
– Closed 8 December-5 January

69 rm – €46/74 €46/74, €8 – ½ P €43/54

Rest – *(closed Saturday lunch)* Menu €18 (weekday lunch), €25/42 – Carte €33/45

◆ This new hotel, flanked by two annexes, overlooks the medieval town and château, which are visible from some of the rather functional rooms. The modern dining room and terrace offer a pleasant view of the town.

L'Entracte

4 r. Château – 02 47 94 05 70 – Fax 02 47 91 55 75
– Closed Sunday dinner and Monday dinner from 15 October to 15 April Y **b**

Rest – Menu €18/24

◆ This restaurant situated in a picturesque little street near the castle offers a Lyon-style atmosphere; appetising dishes chalked up on large boards.

LOCMARIAQUER – 56 Morbihan – 308 N9 – pop. 1 367 – alt. 5 m – ✉ 56740
Brittany 9 **A3**

Paris 488 – Auray 13 – Quiberon 31 – La Trinité-sur-Mer 10 – Vannes 31

Office de tourisme, rue de la Victoire ✆ 02 97 57 33 05, Fax 02 97 57 44 30

Megalithic site ★★ - dolmens of Mané Lud★ and Mané Rethual★ - Tumulus of Mané-er-Hroech★ South: 1 km - Dolmen of the Pierres Plates★ Southwest: 2 km - Pointe de Kerpenhir ≤★ Southeast: 2 km.

Des Trois Fontaines without rest

rte d'Auray – ✆ 02 97 57 42 70 – contact@hotel-troisfontaines.com – Fax 02 97 57 30 59 – Closed 6 November-26 December and 6 January-7 February

18 rm – †€ 72/130 ††€ 72/130, ☕ € 11

◆ On the way into the village, an inviting hotel with a well-shaped façade and flowery surroundings. The interior is equally attractive with its pleasant lounge and rooms with mahogany furniture.

Neptune without rest

port du Guilvin – ✆ 02 97 57 30 56 – Open from April to September

12 rm – †€ 52/73 ††€ 52/73, ☕ € 7

◆ Family-run seaside hotel housing simple, colourful rooms, some of which overlook the bay. Those in the wing are larger and have a small terrace.

La Troque Toupie without rest

2.5 km north-west of Kerouarch – ✆ 02 97 57 45 02 – chambredhotetroque@orange.fr – Fax 02 97 57 45 02 – Open mid March-mid November

5 rm ☕ – †€ 61/63 ††€ 64/69

◆ Set in an immense, quiet garden, this recent construction offers comfortable, elegant rooms. The view and the coastal path overlooking the islands of the Morbihan gulf are delightful.

LOCMINÉ – 56 Morbihan – 308 N7 – pop. 3 430 – alt. 108 m – ✉ 56500
Brittany 10 **C2**

Paris 453 – Lorient 52 – Pontivy 24 – Quimper 114 – Rennes 104 – Vannes 29

Syndicat d'initiative, place Anne de Bretagne ✆ 02 97 60 00 37, Fax 02 97 44 24 64

in Bignan East: 5 km by D 1 – pop. 2 546 – alt. 148 m – ✉ 56500

Auberge La Chouannière

– ✆ 02 97 60 00 96 – Fax 02 97 44 24 58 – Closed 3-19 March, 1st-11 July, 1st-16 October, Sunday dinner, Tuesday dinner, Wednesday dinner and Monday

Rest – Menu € 22/72 bi

◆ The inn sign refers to Pierre Guillemot, Cadoudal's fierce lieutenant, born in this village. A discreet decor, Louis XVI-style chairs and classic cuisine.

LOCQUIREC – 29 Finistère – 308 J2 – pop. 1 293 – alt. 15 m – ✉ 29241
Brittany 9 **B1**

Paris 534 – Brest 81 – Guingamp 52 – Lannion 22 – Morlaix 26

Office de tourisme, place du Port ✆ 02 98 67 40 83, Fax 02 98 79 32 50

Church★ - Pointe de Locquirec★ 30 mn - Viewpoint indicator of Marc'h Sammet ≤★ West: 3 km.

Le Grand Hôtel des Bains ≤ the bay,

15 bis r. de l'Église – ✆ 02 98 67 41 02 – reception@grand-hotel-des-bains.com – Fax 02 98 67 44 60

36 rm – †€ 203 ††€ 227, ☕ € 14 – **Rest** – *(dinner only)* Menu € 27 (weekdays)/36 – Carte € 42/68

◆ The famous French film, "Hôtel de la Plage" was made here. Salt-water swimming pool, waterside flower garden, massage room and contemporary "seaside" style rooms. Smart restaurant with pastel panelling and seafood cuisine.

LOCRONAN – 29 Finistère – 308 F6 – pop. 799 – alt. 105 m – ✉ 29180

Brittany 9 **A2**

Paris 576 – Brest 66 – Briec 22 – Châteaulin 18 – Crozon 33 – Douarnenez 11 – Quimper 16

Office de tourisme, place de la Mairie ✆ 02 98 91 70 14, Fax 02 98 51 83 64

Square★★ - St-Ronan church and Le Pénity chapel ★★ - Montagne de Locronan ✵★ East: 2 km.

Le Prieuré rm, VISA AE

11 r. Prieuré – ✆ 02 98 91 70 89 – leprieure1@aol.com – Fax 02 98 91 77 60 – hotel: Open 16 March-10 November, Restaurant: closed 11 November-3 December, 10 February-3 March and Sunday dinner November-March

15 rm – €51/56 €60/70, €8 – ½ P €56/62 – **Rest** – Menu (€13), €18/47 – Carte €20/55

♦ A small family run hotel on the edge of a famous and picturesque Breton village. The rooms overlooking the garden are quieter as are those in the older wing. Traditional cuisine in a welcoming dining room embellished with exposed beams, stonework, a fireplace and furniture from the local area.

Northwest : 3 km by secondary road – ✉ 29550 Plonévez-Porzay

Manoir de Moëllien rm, VISA AE

– ✆ 02 98 92 50 40 – manmoel@aol.com – Fax 02 98 92 55 21 – Closed beg. January-20 March

18 rm – €72 €72/145, €12 – ½ P €74/107 – **Rest** – *(closed Wednesday mid September-mid June) (dinner only) (resident only)* Menu €30

♦ A fine 17C manor with extensive parkland in open country. The rooms, in separate buildings, are very quiet. Impressive fireplaces in the restaurant.

LOCTUDY – 29 Finistère – 308 F8 – pop. 3 659 – alt. 8 m – ✉ 29750

Brittany 9 **A2**

Paris 587 – Rennes 236 – Quimper 26 – Concarneau 40 – Douarnenez 40

Office de tourisme, place des Anciens Combattants ✆ 02 98 87 53 78, Fax 02 98 87 57 07

Auberge Pen Ar Vir VISA

r. Cdt. Carfort – ✆ 02 98 87 57 09 – auberge.pen.arvir@wanadoo.fr – Fax 02 98 87 57 62 – Closed autumn half-term holidays and 5-25 January, Tuesday, Wednesday mid September-mid April, Sunday dinner except 14 July-15 August and Monday

Rest – Menu €29 (weekdays)/70

♦ A recent villa set in a pretty garden (where drinks are served) by the seaside; fashionable modern interior; short menu with a strong focus on market produce and local fish.

LOCUNOLE – 29 Finistère – 308 K7 – pop. 869 – alt. 109 m – ✉ 29310 9 **B2**

Paris 530 – Rennes 179 – Quimper 61 – Lorient 34 – Lanester 34

Ster Wen without rest

Le Pouldu – ✆ 02 98 71 31 63 – ster.wen@free.fr

4 rm – €47 €52

♦ This old house (1790) in a quiet setting surrounded by greenery offers guests a choice of bedrooms with soothing colour schemes. Typical Breton breakfast by the fire and an old dresser.

LODÈVE – 34 Hérault – 339 E6 – pop. 6 900 – alt. 165 m – ✉ 34700

Languedoc-Roussillon-Tarn Gorges 23 **C2**

Paris 695 – Alès 98 – Béziers 63 – Millau 60 – Montpellier 55 – Pézenas 39

Office de tourisme, 7, place de la République ✆ 04 67 88 86 44, Fax 04 67 44 07 56

Former St-Fulcran cathedral ★ - Musée de Lodève★- Cirque du Bout du Monde★.

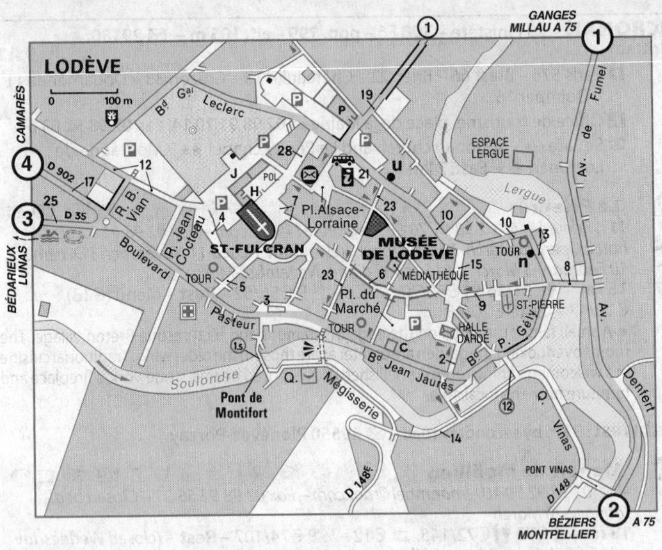

Baudin (R.) 2
Bouquerie (Bd et Pl. de la) 3
Galtier (R. J.) 4
Gambetta (Bd) 5
Grand'Rue 6
Hôtel-de-Ville (Pl. et R. de l') 7
Lergue (Pont de) 8
Lergue (R. de) 9
Liberté (Bd de la) 10
Maury (Bd J.) 12
Montalangue (Bd) 13
Montbrun (R.) 14
Neuve des Marchés (R.) 15
Railhac (Bd J.) 17
République (Av. de la) 19
République (Pl.) 21
République (R.) 23
Vallot (Av. J.) 25
4-Septembre (R. du) 28

Paix

11 bd Montalangue – ☎ 04 67 44 07 46 – hotel-de-la-paix@wanadoo.fr – Fax 04 67 44 30 47 – Closed 11-27 November, 4 February-6 March, Sunday dinner and Monday d October-April except school holidays **n**

23 rm – €45 €60, €7,50 – 1 suite – ½ P €57 – **Rest** – Menu €18/37 – Carte €28/37

◆ On the edge of the Grands Causses, an old post house with rooms gradually being renovated in a colourful Provençal style. The patio-terrace (grills in summer) has a Moorish charm reminiscent of Andalusia, with ochre walls, mosaics, tiled floor, palm trees and swimming pool.

Du Nord without rest

18 bd Liberté – ☎ 04 67 44 10 08 – hoteldunord.lodeve@wanadoo.fr – Fax 04 67 44 92 78 – Open from June to October **u**

24 rm – €39/45 €44/51, €6 – 1 suite

◆ Georges Auric, the composer, was born in this old town-centre residence in 1899. It is now a fully-renovated hotel with discreet and soundproofed rooms.

Domaine du Canalet without rest

av. Joseph Vallot, via ③ – ☎ 04 67 44 29 33 – domaineducanalet@wanadoo.fr – Fax 04 67 44 29 33

4 rm – €185/250 €185/250, €15

◆ More than just a guesthouse, this establishment also features an art gallery with works for sale. Personalised rooms celebrate local artists. Park featuring sequoias and a stream.

in Poujols North: 6.5 km by D 609 and D 149 – pop. 125 – alt. 250 m – ✉ 34700

Le Temps de Vivre

rte de Pegairolles – ☎ 04 67 44 03 78 – Fax 04 67 44 03 78 – Closed December, January, Wednesday off season, Sunday dinner and Monday

Rest – Menu (€19), €29/48 – Carte €42/68

◆ Clinging to a hillside overlooking the Escalette valley, this restaurant has two dining rooms, one a veranda opening onto the countryside. Personalised dishes and regional wines.

LODS – 25 Doubs – 321 H4 – pop. 271 – alt. 361 m – ✉ 25930

Burgundy-Jura 17 **C2**

Paris 440 – Baume-les-Dames 50 – Besançon 37 – Levier 22 – Pontarlier 25 – Vuillafans 5

Truite d'Or

– ✆ 03 81 60 95 48 – la-truite-dor@wanadoo.fr – Fax 03 81 60 95 73
– *Closed 15 December-1st February, Sunday dinner and Monday October-June*

11 rm – †€ 47 ††€ 47, ☕ € 6,50 – ½ P € 51 – **Rest** – Menu (€ 12,50), € 18/44 – Carte € 27/48

◆ On the edge of this picturesque village on the banks of the Loue. Once a stonemason's house, it will delight fishermen. Modest rooms. Trout takes pride of place in this regional repertoire.

LOGELHEIM – 68 Haut-Rhin – 315 I8 – see Colmar

LES LOGES-EN-JOSAS – 78 Yvelines – 311 I3 – 101 23 – see Paris, Area

LOGNES – 77 Seine-et-Marne – 312 E2 – 101]29 – see Paris, Area (Marne-la-Vallée)

LOGONNA-DAOULAS – 29 Finistère – 308 F5 – pop. 1 579 – alt. 45 m – ✉ 29460

9 **A2**

Paris 579 – Rennes 227 – Quimper 59 – Brest 26 – Morlaix 75

Le Domaine de Moulin Mer

34 rte de Moulin Mer, 1 km on D 333 – ✆ *02 98 07 24 45* – *info@domaine-moulin-mer.com*

5 rm ☕ – †€ 65/80 ††€ 80/110 – **Table d'hôte** – Menu € 40 bi

◆ On the coast road, in a garden planted with palms, early 20C residence with a sympathetically renovated interior. Charming rooms, sitting room-library. Menu which changes according to the market and the owner's inspiration.

LOIRÉ – 49 Maine-et-Loire – 317 D3 – pop. 754 – alt. 39 m – ✉ 49440 34 B2

Paris 322 – Ancenis 35 – Angers 45 – Châteaubriant 34 – Laval 66 – Nantes 69 – Rennes 84

Auberge de la Diligence (Michel Cudraz)

4 r. de la Libération – ✆ *02 41 94 10 04* – *info@diligence.fr* – *Fax 02 41 94 10 04*
– *Closed 12-19 April, 2-24 August, 1st-8 January, Saturday lunch, Sunday dinner and Monday*

Rest – *(number of covers limited, pre-book)* Menu € 23/69 – Carte € 38/62

Spec. Salade de légumes croquants, poularde saisie à la plancha. Émincé de magret d'oie rôti, semoule de blé aux fruits secs. Nage de pamplemousse au granité de gin.

◆ This 18C restaurant features a rustic dining area with a large fireplace, and serves generous personalised cuisine accompanied by an excellent selection of regional wines.

LOMENER – 56 Morbihan – 308 K8 – see Ploemeur

LA LONDE-LES-MAURES – 83 Var – 340 M7 – pop. 10 034 – alt. 24 m – ✉ 83250

41 **C3**

Paris 868 – Marseille 93 – Toulon 29 – La Seyne-sur-Mer 35 – Hyères 10

Office de tourisme, avenue Albert Roux ✆ 04 94 01 53 10, Fax 04 94 01 53 19

Cédric Gola "Le Bistrot à l'Ail"

22 av. Georges-Clemenceau – ✆ *04 94 66 97 93* – *cedric.gola@wanadoo.fr*
– *Closed 23 November-23 December, Wednesday lunch, Monday and Tuesday*

Rest – *(dinner only in July-August) (number of covers limited, pre-book)* Menu € 32

◆ Flavourful classical cuisine at the Bistrot à l'Ail. The interesting menu changes every month and the restaurant also offers a "truffle menu". Warm atmosphere in the dining room. Terrace.

LONDINIÈRES – 76 Seine-Maritime – **304** I3 – **pop. 1 158** – **alt. 78 m** – ✉ **76660** 33 **D1**

Paris 147 – Amiens 78 – Dieppe 27 – Neufchâtel-en-Bray 14 – Le Tréport 31

Syndicat d'initiative, Mairie ☎ 02 35 94 90 69, Fax 02 35 94 90 69

Auberge du Pont VISA MC AE

14 r. du Pont de Pierre – ☎ 02 35 93 80 47 – Fax 02 32 97 00 57 – Closed 1st-15 February and Monday

Rest – Menu € 14/36 – Carte € 16/38

◆ A small Norman-style restaurant located on the banks of the Eaulne river, serving regional cuisine in a small, rustic dining area.

LA LONGEVILLE – 25 Doubs – **321** I4 – see Montbenoît

LONGJUMEAU – 91 Essonne – **312** C3 – **101** 35 – see Paris, Area

LONGUES – 63 Puy-de-Dôme – **326** G9 – see Vic-le-Comte

LONGUEVILLE-SUR-SCIE – 76 Seine-Maritime – **304** G3 – **pop. 936** – **alt. 61 m** – ✉ **76590** 33 **D1**

Paris 183 – Dieppe 20 – Le Havre 97 – Rouen 52

Le Cheval Blanc VISA MC

3 r. Guynemer – ☎ 02 35 83 30 03 – Fax 02 35 83 30 03 – Closed 10-31 August, 15-24 February, Sunday dinner, Monday dinner and Wednesday

Rest – Menu (€ 13), € 24 (weekdays)/50 – Carte € 47/56

◆ Pleasant guesthouse in the village centre. Traditional cuisine served under the beams of a rustic dining room with fresh and bright colours.

LONGUYON – 54 Meurthe-et-Moselle – **307** E2 – **pop. 5 876** – **alt. 213 m** – ✉ **54260** 26 **B1**

Paris 314 – Metz 79 – Nancy 133 – Sedan 69 – Thionville 56 – Verdun 48

Office de tourisme, place S. Allende ☎ 03 82 39 21 21, Fax 03 82 26 44 37

in Rouvrois-sur-Othain (Meuse) South: 7.5 km by D 618 – pop. 190 – alt. 223 m – ✉ 55230

La Marmite AC VISA MC AE

11 rte Nationale – ☎ 03 29 85 90 79 – gerardsilvestre55@orange.fr – Fax 03 29 85 99 23 – Closed 2 weeks in August, February holidays, Sunday dinner, Monday and Tuesday except holidays

Rest – Menu € 15 (weekdays)/55 – Carte € 32/62

◆ Find generous portions of authentic, local dishes at this former village café. In summertime, admire the flower-decked façade.

LONGVILLERS – 14 Calvados – **303** I5 – see Villers-Bocage

LONGWY – 54 Meurthe-et-Moselle – **307** F1 – **pop. 14 521** – **alt. 262 m** – ✉ **54400** Alsace-Lorraine 26 **B1**

Paris 328 – Luxembourg 38 – Metz 64 – Thionville 41

Office de tourisme, place Darche ☎ 03 82 24 94 54, Fax 03 82 24 77 75

Musée municipal: collection of irons ★ M.

in Méxy South: 3 km by ② (N 52) – pop. 1 997 – alt. 369 m – ✉ 54135

Ibis rm, AC rm, P VISA MC AE

r. Château d'Eau – ☎ 03 82 23 14 19 – h2051@accor.com – Fax 03 82 25 61 06

62 rm – †€ 57/62 ††€ 57/62, ☕ € 7,50 – **Rest** – Menu € 10/25 – Carte € 19/33

◆ Hotel near a busy thoroughfare. Spacious interior, excellent fixtures and fittings and contemporary furnishings. Modern rooms. Gourmet dishes and a buffet, in a classic dining area or on the terrace.

LONS-LE-SAUNIER Ⓟ – 39 Jura – 321 D6 – pop. 18 483 – alt. 255 m – Spa : early April-late Oct. – Casino – ✉ 39000 Burgundy-Jura 16 **B3**

- Paris 408 – Besançon 84 – Bourg-en-Bresse 73 – Chalon-sur-Saône 61
- Office de tourisme, place du 11 Novembre ✆ 03 84 24 65 01, Fax 03 84 43 22 59
- du Val de Sorne Vernantois, South: 6 km by D 117 and D 41, ✆ 03 84 43 04 80.
- Rue du Commerce★ - Theatre★ - Pharmacie★ de l'Hôtel-Dieu (chemist's).

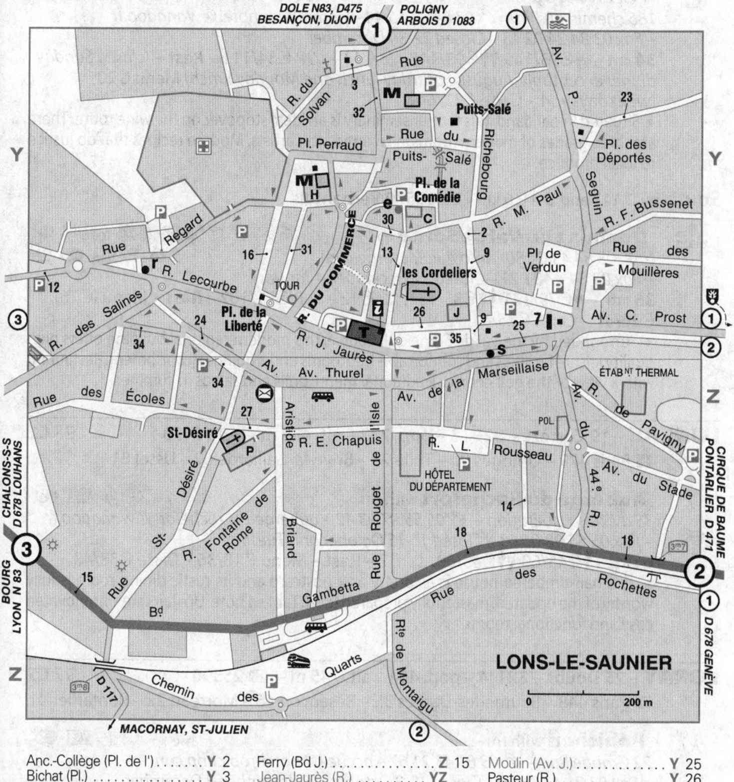

Anc.-Collège (Pl. de l') . . . . . . Y 2
Bichat (Pl.) . . . . Y 3
Chevalerie (Prom. de la) . . . . . V 7
Chevalerie (R. de la) . . . . Y 9
Colbert (Cours) . . . . Y 12
Commerce (R. du) . . . . Y
Cordeliers (R. des) . . . . Y 13
Curé-Marion (R. du) . . . . Z 14
Ferry (Bd J.) . . . . Z 15
Jean-Jaurès (R.) . . . . YZ
Lafayette (R.) . . . . Y 16
Lattre-de-T. (Bd Mar. De) . . . . Z 18
Lecourbe (R.) . . . . Y
Liberté (Pl. de la) . . . . Y
Mendès-France (Av. P.) . . . . . . Y 23
Monot (R. E.) . . . . Y 24
Moulin (Av. J.) . . . . Y 25
Pasteur (R.) . . . . Y 26
Préfecture (R. de la) . . . . Z 27
Sébile (R.) . . . . Y 30
Tamisier (R.) . . . . Y 31
Trouillot (R. G.) . . . . Y 32
Vallière (R. de) . . . . YZ 34
11-Novembre (Pl. du) . . . . Y 35

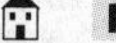

Parc rest, VISA

9 av. J. Moulin – ✆ 03 84 86 10 20 – Fax 03 84 24 97 28 Y **s**

16 rm – €51 €55, €7 – ½ P €65 – **Rest** – *(closed Sunday dinner)*
Menu €11 (weekday lunch), €17/26 – Carte €22/35

◆ Two minutes from the thermal baths, this hotel (a centre for reinsertion) offers simple, functional rooms adorned with stained wooden furniture. Plain dining room and simple cuisine using regional produce.

Nouvel Hôtel without rest
50 r. Lecourbe – ☎ 03 84 47 20 67 – nouvel.hotel39@wanadoo.fr
– Fax 03 84 43 27 49 – Closed 20 December-4 January and Sunday from end September to end February Y r
26 rm – €39 €45/54, €7,50
◆ The owner's model ships adorn the lobby of this central hotel. The practical rooms are well kept; warm welcome and moderate prices.

in Chille by ① Besançon roadand D 157: 3 km – pop. 254 – alt. 330 m – ✉ 39570

Parenthèse rm, VISA MC AE
186 chemin du Pin – ☎ 03 84 47 55 44 – parenthese.hotel@wanadoo.fr
– Fax 03 84 24 92 13 – Closed 22-30 December
34 rm – €93/145 €93/145, €11 – ½ P €84/111 – **Rest** – *(closed Sunday dinner except July-August, Saturday lunch and Monday lunch)* Menu €20 (weekdays)/54 – Carte €33/64
◆ Situated in parkland, this former seminary is an ideal stopover on the wine route. There are three grades of modern rooms, all named after artists. Modern recipes that do justice to local produce.

South by D 117 and D 41: 6 km – ✉ 39570 Vernantois

Domaine du Val de Sorne rest, VISA MC AE
– ☎ 03 84 43 04 80 – info@valdesorne.com
– Fax 03 84 47 31 21 – Closed 22 December-4 January
36 rm – €79/121 €85/131, €12 – ½ P €71/102 – **Rest** – Menu (€16), €26/31 – Carte €25/41
◆ Surrounded by the Val de Sorne golf course, this modern regional building offers high quality leisure facilities and comfortable bedrooms undergoing refurbishment. Restaurant with a view of the golf course. Traditional menu; grills and salads in summer.

LONZAC – 19 Corrèze – 329 L3 – pop. 772 – alt. 450 m – ✉ 19470 25 C2

Paris 479 – Limoges 90 – Tulle 29 – Brive-la-Gaillarde 62 – Ussel 81

Auberge du Rochefort with rm VISA MC
35 av. de la Libération – ☎ 05 55 97 93 42 – auberge-du-rochefort@wanadoo.fr
– Fax 05 55 98 06 63 – Closed 1st-15 October and Tuesday
6 rm – €45/60 €45/60, €7 – **Rest** – Menu €18/36 – Carte €33/48
◆ This half-timbered house is as pretty as a postcard and its rustic dining room is fully worthy of the updated, masterfully prepared food. Table d'hôte. Upstairs are six renovated cosy and functional rooms.

LORAY – 25 Doubs – 321 I4 – pop. 404 – alt. 745 m – ✉ 25390 17 C2

Paris 448 – Baume-les-Dames 35 – Besançon 46 – Morteau 22 – Pontarlier 41

Robichon with rm VISA MC
22 Grande Rue – ☎ 03 81 43 21 67 – accueil@hotel-robichon.com
– Fax 03 81 43 26 10 – Closed 1st-8 October, 25 November-2 December, 15-30 January, Sunday dinner and MondayMonday
11 rm – €44 €57, €8,50 – ½ P €57
Rest – Menu €13 (weekday lunch), €26/48 – Carte €27/61
Rest *P'tit Bichon* – *(closed Saturday lunch, Sunday dinner and Monday)*
Carte €22/38
◆ Sturdy regional house situated in the centre of the village. Modern dining room decorated with green plants and claustras. Traditional cooking. Practical stopover point. The P'tit Bichon offers Franche-Comté chalet-style decor, regional dishes, grilled food and a daily set menu.

Your opinions are important to us:
please write and let us know about your discoveries
and experiences – good and bad!

LORGUES – 83 Var – 340 N5 – pop. 7 319 – alt. 200 m – ✉ 83510
French Riviera 41 **C3**

Paris 841 – Brignoles 34 – Draguignan 12 – Fréjus 37 – St-Raphaël 41 – Toulon 72

Office de tourisme, place Trussy ✆ 04 94 73 92 37, Fax 04 94 84 34 09

La Bastide du Pin
rm, VISA

1017 rte de Salernes, 1 km on D10 – ✆ 04 94 73 90 38 – bastidedupin@wanadoo.fr – Fax 04 94 73 63 01

5 rm – €80/115 €90/120 – **Table d'hôte** – *(open from March to October)* Menu €28

◆ A former 18C olive and wine producing estate, now a hotel providing Provençal style rooms. Pool. Breakfasts served outdoors in summertime. Mediterranean inspired dishes.

XXX Bruno with rm
rm, VISA

Campagne Mariette, 3 km southeast by Les Arcs road – ✆ 04 94 85 93 93 – chezbruno@wanadoo.fr – Fax 04 94 85 93 99 – Closed Sunday dinner and Monday from 15 September to 15 June

6 rm – €100/306 €200/306, €15 – **Rest** – *(pre-book)* Menu €60/130

Spec. Pomme de terre cuite en robe des champs, crème de truffe. Truffe tuber aestivum bardée de lard et foie gras en feuilleté. Épaule d'agneau de lait confite et garniture de légumes. **Wines** Côtes de Provence.

◆ A colourful chef with a passion for truffles runs this farmhouse restaurant surrounded by vineyards. Rustic Provençal decor, serving a single set menu with truffles in winter and summer. Pretty rooms at garden level.

XX Le Chrissandier
VISA

18 cours de la République – ✆ 04 94 67 67 15 – christophe.chabredier@wanadoo.fr – Fax 04 94 67 67 15 – Closed 24-30 June, January, Tuesday and Wednesday from October to June

Rest – Menu €29 (weekday lunch)/58 – Carte €54/72

◆ This restaurant has a rustic dining room with exposed beams and a fireplace, plus an attractive summer terrace in an inner courtyard. Traditional, seasonal cuisine.

Northwest by Salernes road, D 10 and secondary road: 8 km – ✉ 83510

Château de Berne
rm, VISA

– ✆ 04 94 60 48 88 – auberge@chateauberne.com – Fax 04 94 60 48 89 – Open 14 February-1st November

18 rm – €195/360 €250/440 – 1 suite – **Rest** – Menu €19 (lunch), €49 € (dinner)/69 – Carte €49/75

◆ Situated in the centre of a wine-growing estate, this château offers attractive Provençal style rooms, exhibitions, concerts, and a fitness centre, as well as wine, cookery and watercolour classes. Elegant restaurant and terrace under an arbour: market and organic garden produce. Simpler fare at lunchtime (grilled meats).

LORIENT – 56 Morbihan – 308 K8 – pop. 59 189 – Built-up area 116 174 – alt. 4 m – ✉ 56100 Brittany
9 **B2**

Paris 503 – Quimper 69 – St-Brieuc 116 – St-Nazaire 146 – Vannes 60

Lorient-Bretagne Sud: ✆ 02 97 87 21 50, by D 162: 8 km AZ.

Office de tourisme, quai de Rohan ✆ 02 97 21 07 84, Fax 02 97 21 99 44

de Valqueven Quéven Lieu dit Kerruisseau, North: 8 km by D 765, ✆ 02 97 05 17 96.

Submarine base★ AZ - Interior★ of N.-D.-de-Victoire church BY **E.**

Plan on next page

Mercure without rest
VISA

31 pl. J. Ferry – ✆ 02 97 21 35 73 – h0873@accor.com – Fax 02 97 64 48 62

58 rm – €90/92 €98/100, €12,50 BZ **m**

◆ Shops, a conference centre and harbour moorings are conveniently located nearby. The lounge-bar and room decor discreetly recall the East India Company.

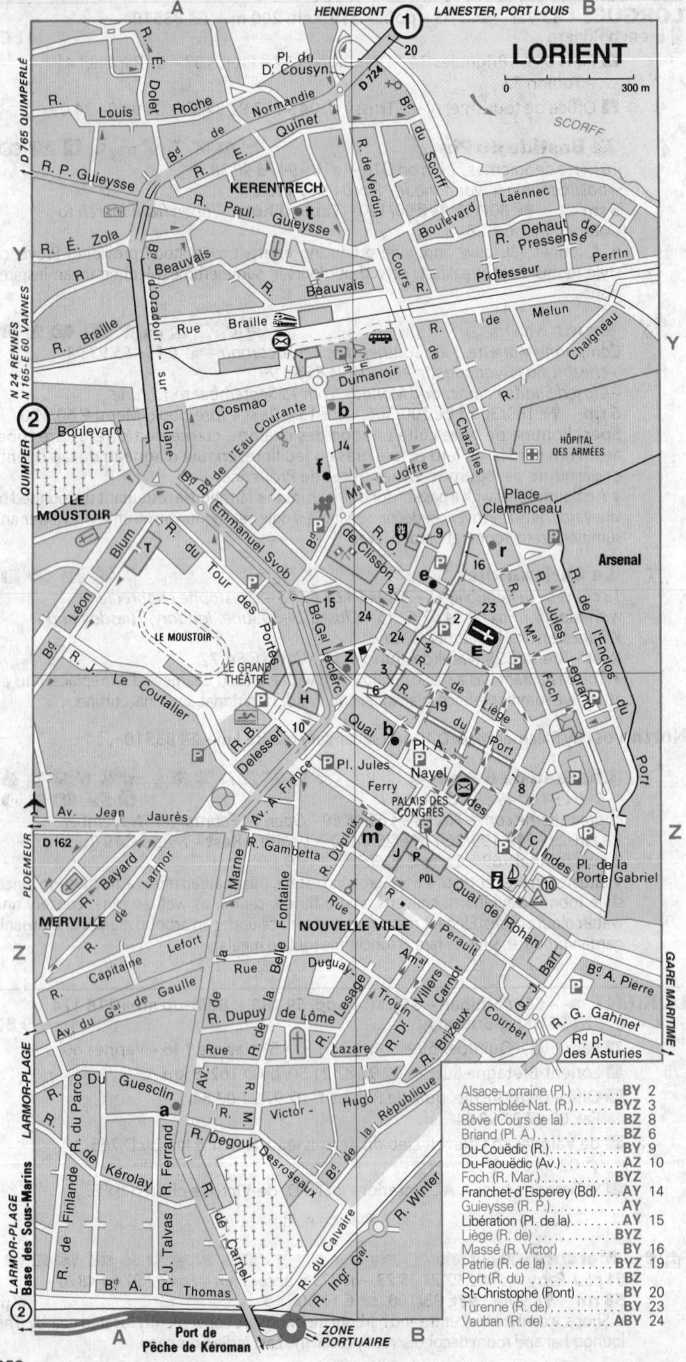

LORIENT
0
300 m
HENNEBONT
LANESTER, PORT LOUIS
D 765 QUIMPERLÉ
N 24 RENNES
N 165-E 60 VANNES
QUIMPER
PLOEMEUR
LARMOR-PLAGE
LARMOR-PLAGE
Base des Sous-Marins
GARE MARITIME
ZONE PORTUAIRE
Port de Pêche de Kéroman
SCORFF
KERENTRECH
LE MOUSTOIR
MERVILLE
NOUVELLE VILLE
Arsenal
HÔPITAL DES ARMÉES
LE GRAND THÉATRE
PALAIS DES CONGRÈS
Pl. du Dr Cousyn
D 724
Bd du Scorff
R. É. Dolet
R. Louis Roche
Bd de Normandie
R. E. Quinet
R. de Verdun
R. P. Guieysse
R. Paul Guieysse
R. É. Zola
R. Beauvais
Bd d'Oradour-sur-Glane
Rue Braille
R. Braille
Boulevard Laënnec
R. Dehaut de Pressensé
R. Professeur Perrin
Cours de Chazelles
R. de Melun
R. Chaigneau
Dumanoir
Boulevard Cosmao Dumanoir
Bd de l'Eau Courante
Bd Franchet-d'Esperey
R. Ml Joffre
Place Clemenceau
Bd Emmanuel Svob
R. Blum
R. du Tour des Portes
R. Léon Blum
R. J. Le Coutaller
Bd Gal Leclerc
R. O. de Clisson
R. Ml Foch
R. Jules Legrand
R. de l'Enclos du Port
R. de Liège
R. du Port
Quai des Indes
Pl. A. Briand
Pl. Jules Ferry
Nayel
R. B. Delessert
Av. A. France
Av. Jean Jaurès
D 162
R. Bayard
R. de Larmor
R. Capitaine Lefort
Av. du Gal de Gaulle
R. Gambetta
R. Dupleix
Rue de la Marne
R. Fontaine
Rue Belle Fontaine
Rue Duguay-Trouin
R. Dupuy de Lôme
R. de la Belle
R. Lesage
R. Lazare
R. Perault
R. Amal Villers
R. Dr. Carnot
R. Brizeux
Quai de Rohan
Q. J. Bart
Bd A. Pierre
R. G. Gahinet
Courbet
Rd pt des Asturies
Pl. de la Porte Gabriel
R. Du Guesclin
R. du Parco
R. de Finlande
R. de Kérolay
R. Ferrand
R. J. Talvas
Bd A. Thomas
R. M. Victor-Hugo
R. Degoul
R. Desroseaux
Bd de la République
R. de Carnel
R. du Calvaire
R. Ingr Gal
R. Winter
POL
Alsace-Lorraine (Pl.) . . . . BY 2
Assemblée-Nat. (R.) . . . . BYZ 3
Bôve (Cours de la) . . . . BZ 8
Briand (Pl. A.) . . . . BZ 6
Du-Couëdic (R.) . . . . BY 9
Du-Faouëdic (Av.) . . . . AZ 10
Foch (R. Mar.) . . . . BYZ
Franchet-d'Esperey (Bd) . . . . AY 14
Guieysse (R. P.) . . . . AY
Libération (Pl. de la) . . . . AY 15
Liège (R. de) . . . . BYZ
Massé (R. Victor) . . . . BY 16
Patrie (R. de la) . . . . BYZ 19
Port (R. du) . . . . BZ
St-Christophe (Pont) . . . . BY 20
Turenne (R. de) . . . . BY 23
Vauban (R. de) . . . . ABY 24

Cléria without rest
27 bd Mar. Franchet d'Esperey – ✆ 02 97 21 04 59 – info@hotel-cleria.com – Fax 02 97 64 19 10 AY **f**
33 rm – †€ 54/62 ††€ 60/89, ☕ € 9,50
◆ The rooms of this central hotel are gradually being spruced up; those overlooking the flower-decked courtyard (where breakfast is served in summer) are quieter.

Astoria without rest
3 r. Clisson – ✆ 02 97 21 10 23 – hotelastoria.lorient@wanadoo.fr – Fax 02 97 21 03 55 – Closed 20 December-9 January BY **e**
35 rm – †€ 60/80 ††€ 60/90, ☕ € 8
◆ A pleasant establishment for many reasons: warm, friendly welcome, simple, but individually decorated rooms and art exhibitions in the breakfast room.

Central Hôtel without rest
1 r. Cambry – ✆ 02 97 21 16 52 – centralhotel.lorient@orange.fr – Fax 02 97 84 88 94 – Closed Christmas holidays BZ **b**
21 rm – †€ 50/75 ††€ 62/82, ☕ € 7,50
◆ Town-centre hotel, as the name suggests, whose rooms have been successfully renovated with new materials, cheerful colours and good soundproofing.

Le Jardin Gourmand
46 r. J. Simon – ✆ 02 97 64 17 24 – jardingourmandlorient@yahoo.fr – Fax 02 97 64 15 75 – Closed 5-14 May, 25 August-10 September, school holidays February, Sunday dinner, Monday and Tuesday AY **t**
Rest – Menu (€ 22), € 28 (weekday lunch), € 40/54 – Carte € 28/38
◆ The owner-chef gives Breton produce pride of place in her inventive recipes, escorted by a fine choice of wines, whiskies and brandies. Attractive, modern interior.

Le Quai des Arômes
1 r. Maître Esvelin – ✆ 02 97 21 60 40 – Fax 02 97 35 29 04 – Closed 17 August-1st September, 8-16 February and Sunday BZ
Rest – Menu € 17/23 – Carte € 24/33
◆ A new and contemporary feel for this traditional restaurant, opposite the Palais de Justice. Grey/white colour scheme, old photos, paintings and modern furniture. Covered terrace.

Henri et Joseph (Philippe Le Lay)
4 r. Léo Le Bourgo – ✆ 02 97 84 72 12 – Closed Saturday lunch in July-August, Sunday, Monday and dinner from Tuesday to Thursday AY **z**
Rest – *(pre-book)* Menu (€ 32), € 48
Spec. Menu du marché
◆ An original concept for this trendy bistro with a choice of a 'masculine' or 'feminine' dish of the day. Set menu in the evening. Friendly and hospitable.

Le Pécharmant
5 r. Carnel – ✆ 02 97 21 33 86 – Fax 02 97 35 11 01 – Closed 20 April-28 April, 6-21 July, 26 October-3 November, 1st-7 January, Sunday and Monday AZ **a**
Rest – Menu € 17 (weekdays)/69 – Carte € 42/62
◆ The orange façade decorated with copper pans does not go unnoticed. Yet it is the generous, subtle cuisine served in this small restaurant that makes it so popular.

Le Pic
2 bd Mar. Franchet d'Esperey – ✆ 02 97 21 18 29 – restaurant.lepic@wanadoo.fr – Fax 02 97 21 92 64 – Closed Wednesday dinner, Saturday lunch and Sunday
Rest – Menu (€ 15), € 19/38 – Carte € 29/48 AY **b**
◆ Bright red façade, smart 1940s decor (stained glass, mirrors and bar), bistro ambience, traditional menu and fresh fish daily: what more could you want!

L'Ocre Marine
8 r. Mar.-Foch – ✆ 02 97 84 05 77 – contact@creperie-locremarine.com – Closed 1st-15 January, Saturday lunch except school holidays, Wednesday dinner and Sunday BY **r**
Rest – crêperie Menu (€ 13) – Carte approx. € 21
◆ Family photos adorn this all wood, hospitable restaurant. The lady of the house's sweet and savoury pancakes are not to be missed: organic, home-grown produce only.

Northwest : 3,5 km by D 765 AY – ✉ 56100 Lorient

XXX ✿✿ **L'Amphitryon** (Jean-Paul Abadie) VISA AE

127 r. Col. Müller – ✆ 02 97 83 34 04 – amphitryon-abadie@wanadoo.fr – Fax 02 97 37 25 02 – Closed 18 May-9 June, Sunday and Monday

Rest – Menu € 60 (weekdays)/122 – Carte € 87/139

Spec. Jeunes ormeaux laqués et palourdes en sabayon de muscat de Rivesaltes. Barbue saisie, croustillant aux morilles. Chouquettes au chocolat et cerise, gelée à l'eucalyptus, glace aux éclats de nougat (summer).

◆ A masterful, almost playfully inventive cuisine; superb choice of little known vintages; service that is as professional as it is friendly; and a handsome modern decor.

LORMONT – 33 Gironde – 335 H5 – see Bordeaux

LORRIS – 45 Loiret – 318 M4 – pop. 2 674 – alt. 126 m – ✉ 45260

Châteaux of the Loire 12 **C2**

Paris 132 – Gien 27 – Montargis 23 – Orléans 55 – Pithiviers 45 – Sully-sur-Loire 19

Office de tourisme, 2, rue des Halles ✆ 02 38 94 81 42, Fax 02 38 94 88 00

N.-Dame church ★.

XX **Guillaume de Lorris** VISA AE

8 Grande Rue – ✆ 02 38 94 83 55 – vanoverberghe.christophe@aliceadsl.fr – Fax 02 38 94 83 55 – Closed 7-20 April, 21 December-4 January, 23 February-1st March, Sunday dinner, Monday and Tuesday

Rest – *(number of covers limited, pre-book)* Menu € 28/34 – Carte € 32/40

◆ The restaurant is named after the poet author of the "Roman de la Rose" who was born in Lorris. A fireplace, beams and stonework add to the pleasant rustic with dishes in keeping with current taste.

LOUBRESSAC – 46 Lot – 337 G2 – pop. 432 – alt. 320 m – ✉ 46130

Dordogne-Berry-Limousin 29 **C1**

Paris 531 – Brive-la-Gaillarde 47 – Cahors 73 – Figeac 44 – Gramat 16 – St-Céré 10

Office de tourisme, le bourg ✆ 05 65 10 82 18

Site★ from the château.

Le Relais de Castelnau ← Dordogne valley, rm, rest, VISA

rte de Padirac – ✆ 05 65 10 80 90 – rdc46@wanadoo.fr – Fax 05 65 38 22 02 – Open April-end October and closed Sunday dinner April-October

40 rm – †€ 55/105 ††€ 55/150, ☕ € 9 – ½ P € 65/85 – **Rest** – *(closed lunch except Sunday and public holidays)* Menu € 18/45 – Carte € 35/51

◆ This modern building stands opposite the château of Castelnau-Bretenoux, which dominates the valley. Colourful, practical rooms. Panoramic views of the Bave and Dordogne valleys from the terrace and dining room.

LOUDÉAC – 22 Côtes-d'Armor – 309 F5 – pop. 9 371 – alt. 155 m – ✉ 22600

Brittany 10 **C2**

Paris 438 – Carhaix-Plouguer 69 – Dinan 76 – Pontivy 24 – Rennes 88 – St-Brieuc 41

Syndicat d'initiative, 1, rue Saint-Joseph ✆ 02 96 28 25 17, Fax 02 96 28 25 33

Voyageurs rest, VISA AE

10 r. Cadélac – ✆ 02 96 28 00 47 – hoteldesvoyageurs@wanadoo.fr – Fax 02 96 28 22 30

30 rm – †€ 45/65 ††€ 49/75, ☕ € 9 – ½ P € 49/59

Rest – *(closed 22 December-3 January, Sunday dinner and Saturday)* Menu € 15 (weekdays)/40 – Carte € 23/41

◆ This hotel provides modern rooms at affordable prices. The double-glazing keeps the busy street noise to a minimum. A chic bistro-style restaurant with a spacious dining area and modern atmosphere. Traditional cuisine served.

LOUDUN – 86 Vienne – 322 G2 – pop. 7 704 – alt. 120 m – ✉ 86200

Atlantic Coast 39 **C1**

Paris 311 – Angers 79 – Châtellerault 47 – Poitiers 55 – Tours 72

Syndicat d'initiative, 2 rue des Marchands ☎ 05 49 98 15 96, Fax 05 49 98 69 49

de Loudun Roiffé Domaine de Saint Hilaire, North: 18 km by D 147, ☎ 05 49 98 78 06.

Tour carrée ❊★ AY.

L'Aumônerie without rest

3 bd Mar. Leclerc – ☎ 05 49 22 63 86 – chris.lharidon@wanadoo.fr AY **t**

4 rm – ♦€ 40 ♦♦€ 46/50

◆ The owner of this handsome 13C lodge cannot be faulted for her gracious welcome. Personalised rooms with antiques and bright colours and a breakfast veranda facing the garden.

LOUÉ – 72 Sarthe – 310 I7 – pop. 2 042 – alt. 112 m – ✉ 72540 35 C1

Paris 230 – Laval 59 – Le Mans 30 – Rennes 127 – Sillé-le-Guillaume 26

Ricordeau with rm

rm, VISA AE

13 r. de la Libération – ☎ 02 43 88 40 03 – hotel-ricordeau@wanadoo.fr – Fax 02 43 88 62 08 – Closed Sunday dinner from October to April

10 rm – ♦€ 85/170 ♦♦€ 85/300, € 15 – 3 suites

Rest – *(closed Sunday dinner and Tuesday from September to May and Monday)* Menu € 27 (weekdays)/88 – Carte € 65/90

Rest *Le Coq Hardi* – *(closed Wednesday dinner, Thursday dinner and Sunday)* Menu € 13 bi (weekday lunch)/20

◆ In fine weather, dine on the charming terrace of this former post house in grounds along the banks of the Vègre. Modern cuisine. Auberge atmosphere and regional cuisine at Le Coq Hardi.

LOUHANS – 71 Saône-et-Loire – 320 L10 – pop. 6 237 – alt. 179 m – ✉ 71500

Burgundy-Jura 8 **D3**

Paris 373 – Bourg-en-Bresse 61 – Chalon-sur-Saône 38 – Dijon 85 – Dole 76 – Tournus 31

Office de tourisme, 1, Arcade Saint-Jean ☎ 03 85 75 05 02, Fax 03 85 75 48 70

Grande-Rue★.

Le Moulin de Bourgchâteau

VISA

r. Guidon, Chalon road – ☎ 03 85 75 37 12 – bourgchateau@netcourrier.com – Fax 03 85 75 45 11 – Closed 1 - 23 Jan.

19 rm – ♦€ 46 ♦♦€ 57/105, € 9 – ½ P € 65/85 – **Rest** – *(closed 2-26 November, Monday except dinner June-September and Tuesday lunch June-September) (number of covers limited, pre-book)* Menu € 29 (weekdays)/75 – Carte € 40/53

◆ This mill built in 1778 on the banks of the Seille is now a hotel-restaurant with rustic-style guestrooms. Lounge arranged around the old mill machinery. This restaurant has an original décor including a millstone, wooden beams and old stonework. Serving traditional cuisine with Italian influences due to the owners' origins.

Host. du Cheval Rouge et La Buge

rm, rest, VISA

5 r. d'Alsace – ☎ 03 85 75 21 42 – hotel-chevalrouge@wanadoo.fr – Fax 03 85 75 44 48 – Closed 16-26 June, 22 December-19 January, Sunday dinner from December to March and Monday

20 rm – ♦€ 32/42 ♦♦€ 39/61, € 8 – ½ P € 57 – **Rest** – *(closed Tuesday lunch and Monday April-November)* Menu € 19/42 – Carte € 26/48

◆ A former post house located in a side street is now home to neat and tidy rooms at affordable prices. Those in the building nearby provide the best level of comfort and quiet. Traditional cuisine and regional meals served in a provincial-style atmosphere.

Barbier des Bois

rm, rm, VISA AE

rte de Cuiseaux, South-East: 3.5 km on D996 – ☎ 03 85 75 55 65 – Fax 03 85 75 70 56

10 rm – ♦€ 56/61 ♦♦€ 67/72, € 10 – ½ P € 85/105 – **Rest** – *(closed Sunday dinner off season)* Menu € 14 (weekday lunch), € 18/56 – Carte € 38/55

◆ This country motel provides practical rooms with a terrace overlooking the greenery. Each room decorated in a different colour. Featuring a pleasant bar on the top floor. Modern cuisine served in contemporary atmosphere, with open veranda featuring teak furnishings.

LOURDES – 65 Hautes-Pyrénées – **342** L6 – **pop. 15 203** – **alt. 420 m** – **Major pilgrimage site** – ✉ **65100** Languedoc-Roussillon-Tarn Gorges 28 **A3**

Paris 850 – Bayonne 147 – Pau 45 – St-Gaudens 86 – Tarbes 19
Tarbes-Lourdes-Pyrénées: ✆ 05 62 32 92 22, by ①: 12 km.
Office de tourisme, place Peyramale ✆ 05 62 42 77 40, Fax 05 62 94 60 95
Lourdes Golf Club Chemin du Lac, by Pau road: 3 km, ✆ 05 62 42 02 06.
Château fort★ DZ - Musée de Cire de Lourdes (Lourdes Wax Museum)★ DZ **M**[1] - Basilique souterraine St-Pie X (St Pie X underground basilica) CZ - Pic du Jer★.

Éliseo

rm, rm, VISA

4 r. Reine Astrid – ✆ 05 62 41 41 41 – eliseo@cometolourdes.com CZ **p**
– Fax 05 62 41 41 50 – Open 1st January-15 December – **197 rm** – †€ 86/108 ††€ 114/178, ☕ € 15 – 7 suites – ½ P € 94/116 – **Rest** – Menu € 28/43 – Carte € 36/70

◆ Near the cave, a brand-new establishment with large, modern, very well-equipped rooms. A souvenir shop; rooftop terraces with a panoramic view. Several spacious dining rooms decorated in an elegant contemporary style.

Padoue

VISA

1 r. Reine-Astrid – ✆ 05 62 53 07 00 – reservation@hotelpadoue.fr CZ **a**
– Fax 05 62 53 07 01 – Open 14 March-27 October – **155 rm** – †€ 70/82 ††€ 80/92, ☕ € 12 – ½ P € 70/76 – **Rest** – Menu (€ 12), € 16/18 – Carte € 19/39

◆ 150m from the cave, brand new hotel with all the modern comforts. Spacious rooms, seminar facilities, souvenir shop and tea room. Simple traditional cuisine served in a vast contemporary restaurant.

Grand Hôtel de la Grotte

VISA

66 r. de la Grotte – ✆ 05 62 94 58 87 – booking@hoteldelagrotte.com
– Fax 05 62 94 20 50 – Open 12 February-25 October DZ **y**
82 rm – †€ 71/139 ††€ 80/165, ☕ € 14 – 6 suites – ½ P € 70/113
Rest – Menu € 24/28 – Carte € 42/62 – **Rest *Brasserie*** – *✆ 05 62 42 39 34 (open 26 April-25 October)* Menu (€ 16), € 20/26 – Carte € 32/54

◆ A traditional hotel situated at the foot of the castle. Louis XVI-style rooms, some with views of the basilica. Master suite. Hushed dining rooms, with buffet menus in summer. A brasserie offering contemporary decor and a terrace under the chestnut trees.

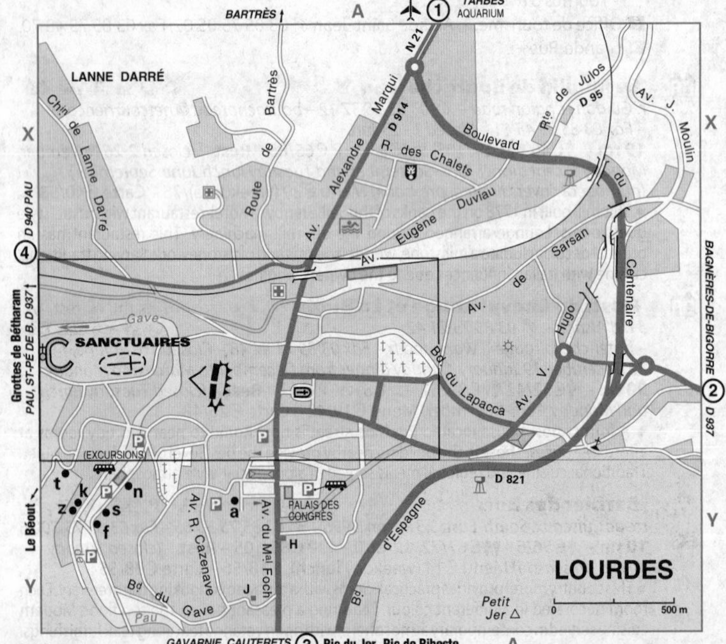

Gallia et Londres

26 av. B. Soubirous – ☎ 05 62 94 35 44 – contact@hotelgallialondres.com – Fax 05 62 42 24 64 – Open 23 March-18 October CZ **c**

87 rm – †€ 93/118 ††€ 120/170, ☕ € 20 – 3 suites – ½ P € 80/140
Rest – Menu € 22/28 – Carte € 38/57

◆ An entrancing *Vieille France* atmosphere in this fine hotel near the sanctuaries. Comfortable rooms, furnished in Louis XVI style. A dining room with pleasant wood-panelling, crystal chandeliers and a fresco of Venice.

Alba

27 av. Paradis – ☎ 05 62 42 70 70 – hotelalba@aol.com – Fax 05 62 94 54 52 – Open 15 March-30 October AY **f**

237 rm – †€ 74 ††€ 93, ☕ € 8 – ½ P € 66/71 – **Rest** – Menu € 16 – Carte € 21/37

◆ A vast modern building situated at the edge of the Pau mountain stream. Practical bedrooms, spacious lounges and a small chapel. Large modern dining rooms welcome groups of pilgrims from all over the world. Comfortable bar and shop.

Paradis

15 av. Paradis – ☎ 05 62 42 14 14 – info@hotelparadislourdes.com – Fax 05 62 94 64 04 – Open 15 March-1st November AY **n**

300 rm – †€ 110 ††€ 120, ☕ € 15 – ½ P € 85 – **Rest** – *(residents only)* Menu € 28

◆ This hotel, which opened in 1992 on the banks of a mountain stream, has functional rooms, practical furnishings and good sound insulation. A large and simply decorated dining area, with refined lounges and bar featuring comfortable leather armchairs.

Mercure Impérial

3 av. Paradis – ☎ 05 62 94 06 30 – hotel.mercure.imperial@wanadoo.fr – Fax 05 62 94 48 04 – Closed 15 December-5 February CZ **u**

93 rm – †€ 63/132 ††€ 69/145, ☕ € 12 – **Rest** – Carte € 31/45

◆ At the foot of the château, overlooking the mountain stream, a 1930s hotel with rooms renovated in a retro style. Panoramic roof terrace. A lovely staircase leads up to the classic style dining area and lounge with stained glass window.

Méditerranée

23 av. Paradis – ☎ 05 62 94 72 15 – hotelmed@aol.com – Fax 05 62 94 10 54 – Open 13 March-5 November AY **s**

171 rm – †€ 63/74 ††€ 79/93, ☕ € 8 – ½ P € 59/69 – **Rest** – Menu € 17/26 – Carte € 19/32

◆ The establishment has been refurbished and has well-designed bedrooms, a small solarium and a chapel. This immense, modern dining room overlooks the Pau river. The bar is more intimate.

Christ-Roi

9 r. Mgr Rodhain – ☎ 05 62 94 24 98 – hotelchristroi@wanadoo.fr – Fax 05 62 94 17 65 – Open Easter-15 October AY **t**

180 rm – †€ 56/59 ††€ 69/73, ☕ € 6,50 – ½ P € 58/60 – **Rest** – Menu € 19

◆ Pilgrims can take a lift situated a stone's throw from the hotel to reach the religious area. Modern bedrooms in a recent building. English bar. A vast contemporary dining room, mainly used by hotel residents.

Beauséjour

16 av. de la Gare – ☎ 05 62 94 38 18 – beausejour.p.martin@wanadoo.fr – Fax 05 62 94 96 20 EZ **s**

45 rm – †€ 68/92 ††€ 78/165, ☕ € 10 – ½ P € 64/108
Rest *Le Parc* – ☎ 05 62 94 73 48 – Menu (€ 14), € 17 – Carte € 26/40

◆ This small hotel adjoining the station is quite charming with an attractive century-old façade, garden, lounge, redecorated rooms and shop. A restaurant-veranda and terrace overlooking greenery serving traditional dishes.

Solitude

3 passage St-Louis – ☎ 05 62 42 71 71 – contact@hotelsolitude.com – Fax 05 62 94 40 65 – Open 10 April-6 November CZ **s**

293 rm – †€ 61/78 ††€ 72/102, ☕ € 15 – 4 suites – ½ P € 60/70
Rest – Menu (€ 12), € 16/25

◆ This building bordering the Pau river has pleasant up-to-date rooms. A panoramic view from the small rooftop swimming pool. A rotunda dining room with a terrace overlooking the river.

LOURDES

Street	Grid	No.
Basse (R.)	DZ	5
Bourg (Chaussée du)	DZ	8
Capdevielle (R. Louis)	EZ	12
Carrières Peyramale (R. des)	CZ	15
Fontaine (R. de la)	DZ	20
Fort (R. du)	DZ	22
Grotte (Bd de la)	DZ	30
Jeanne-d'Arc (Pl.)	DZ	35
Latour-de-Brie (R. de)	DZ	40
Marcadal (Pl. du)	DZ	45
Martyrs-de-la-Déportation (R. des)	EZ	47
Paradis (Espl. du)	CZ	50
Petits Fossés (R. des)	DZ	53
Peyramale (Av.)	CZ	55
Peyramale (Pl.)	DZ	56
Pont-Vieux	CZ	57
Pyrénées (R. des)	DZ	59
Reine-Astrid (R. de la)	CZ	60
Ste-Marie (R.)	CZ	68
St-Frai (R. Marie)	CZ	65
St-Michel (Pont)	DZ	66
St-Pierre (R.)	DZ	67
Schœpfer (Av. Mgr)	CZ	71
Soubirous (Av. Bernadette)	CZ	73
Soubirous (R. Bernadette)	DZ	74

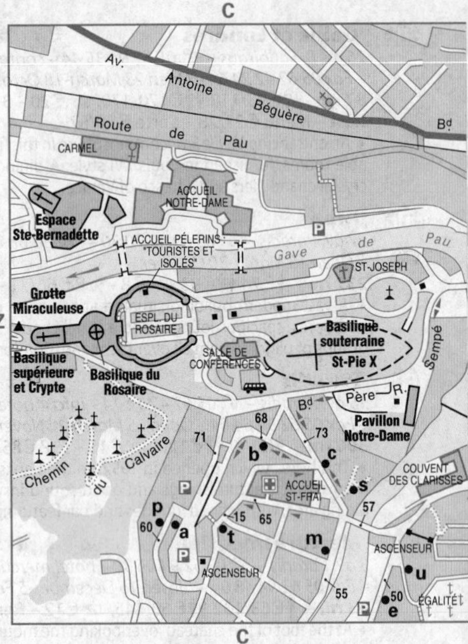

Espagne
rest, VISA AE

9 av. Paradis – 05 62 94 50 02 – hoteldespagne@wanadoo.fr
– Fax 05 62 94 58 15 – Open 15 March-25oct. CZ **e**

129 rm – €62/71 €76/87, €8 – ½ P €54/59

Rest – Menu €18/19 – Carte €24/45

◆ The name and the discreet décor of the Spanish-Moorish lounge remind you how close Spain is. Simple, functional rooms available. Choose one with a terrace. A vaulted ceiling in this restaurant with arches, exposed beams and a fireplace.

Christina
VISA AE

42 av. Peyramale – 05 62 94 26 11 – hotel.christina@orange.fr
– Fax 05 62 94 97 09 – Open 20 March-1st November AY **z**

199 rm – €60/81 €78/114, €7 – ½ P €57/62

Rest – Menu €13/20 bi – Carte €20/34

◆ This large, white hotel is home to neat and tidy rooms, the most pleasant overlooking the Pyrenees. Rooftop terrace and rock garden also featured. A spacious dining area decorated with a nautical theme, serving traditional cuisine.

Excelsior
rest, VISA AE

83 bd de la Grotte – 05 62 94 02 05 – hotel.excelsior@wanadoo.fr
– Fax 05 62 94 82 88 – Open 20 March-31 October DZ **h**

67 rm – €59/62 €80/107, €7,50 – ½ P €58/62

Rest – Menu €19/31 – Carte €21/48

◆ Pilgrims can choose between several types of rooms, all of which have been renovated. Some have a view of the basilica, and others overlook the castle. A lounge and comfortable bar on the ground floor; panoramic dining room upstairs.

Florida
rm, rm, rest, VISA AE

3 r. Carrières Peyramale – 05 62 94 51 15 – flo_aca_mira_hotels@hotmail.com
– Fax 05 62 94 69 49 – Open 14 March-30 October CZ **t**

115 rm – €48/52 €65/70, €6 – 2 suites – ½ P €48/52

Rest – Menu €13

◆ This hotel provides comfortable rooms, some ideal for families. Note that the hotel has good facilities for the disabled. A discreet decor in the dining room and an awe-inspiring view of the town and Pyrenees from the rooftop terrace.

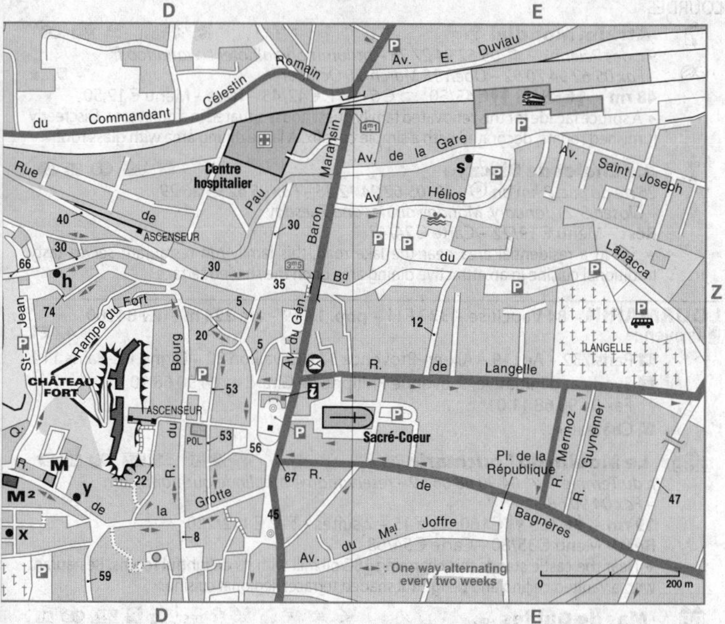

Notre Dame de France

rm, rest, VISA

8 av. Peyramale – ✆ 05 62 94 91 45 – contact@hotelnd-france.fr
– Fax 05 62 94 57 21 – Open 21 March-31 October CZ **m**

76 rm – €50/60 €64/80, ☕ €7 – ½ P €55/79 – **Rest** – Menu €10/18 – Carte €17/26

◆ A hotel run by the same family for several generations on the River Pau. The rooms have just been given a facelift (furniture, fitted carpet, linen). The redecorated restaurant has a friendly atmosphere.

St-Sauveur

rm, rm, VISA

9 r. Ste-Marie – ✆ 05 62 94 25 03 – contact@hotelsaintsauveur.com
– Fax 05 62 94 36 52 – Closed 10 Dec.-31 Jan. CZ **b**

174 rm – €61/78 €72/102, ☕ €15 – ½ P €60/70 – **Rest** – Menu (€12), €16/25 – Carte €16/28

◆ Modern hotel near the sanctuaries. You reach the bedrooms, which are pleasant and well sound-proofed, via a bright and colourful hallway. A choice of pizzas, salads and light snacks, served beneath the glass roof or traditional cuisine served in the vast dining room.

Beau Site

rm, rest, VISA

36 av. Peyramale – ✆ 05 62 94 04 08 – hotelbeausite@aol.com
– Fax 05 62 94 06 59 – Open 13 March-5 November AY **k**

63 rm – €59/70 €72/86, ☕ €8 – ½ P €56/66 – **Rest** – Menu €17/26 – Carte €19/32

◆ This modern building, which has just been renovated, has functional bedrooms, some with views of the mountain stream and surrounding relief. The restaurant on the first floor of the hotel has a view of the Pyrenees.

Cazaux without rest

VISA

2 chemin des Rochers – ✆ 05 62 94 22 65 – hotelcazaux@yahoo.fr
– Fax 05 62 94 48 32 – Open from Easter-mid October AY **a**

20 rm – €34 €39/54, ☕ €5,50

◆ Friendly hospitality and well-kept rooms at reasonable prices at this small, family run hotel near the food market. Fresh, simple rooms.

Atrium Mondial
9 r. des Pélerins – ✆ 05 62 94 27 28 – atriummondialhotel@wanadoo.fr
– Fax 05 62 94 70 92 – Open 15 March-20 October DZ x
48 rm – €38/43 €45/50, €6 – ½ P €42/45 – **Rest** – Menu €12,50
◆ A spruce façade for this renovated family guest house situated in a quiet area. Discreetly furnished rooms, decorated with a simple crucifix. A large dining area with glass roof.

Le Chalet de Biscaye
26 rte du Lac, 2 km on ④ – ✆ 05 62 94 12 26 – Fax 05 62 94 26 29
– Closed 5-21 January, Monday dinner and Tuesday
Rest – Menu €19/22 – Carte €24/47
◆ Set in a residential area near the lake road, this family-run restaurant serves tasty traditional cuisine in an attractive dining area or on the shaded terrace.

LOURMARIN – 84 Vaucluse – **332** F11 – **pop. 1 119** – **alt. 224 m** – ✉ 84160
Provence 42 **E1**

Paris 732 – Apt 19 – Aix-en-Provence 37 – Cavaillon 32 – Digne-les-Bains 114

Syndicat d'initiative, 9, avenue Philippe de Girard ✆ 04 90 68 10 77, Fax 04 90 68 11 01

Château★.

Le Moulin de Lourmarin
r. du Temple – ✆ 04 90 68 06 69 – reservation@moulindelourmarin.com
– Fax 04 90 68 31 76
19 rm – €160 €160, €15 – 2 suites – ½ P €112/220
Rest – Menu €35/80 – Carte €54/68
◆ Near the castle stands this charming 18C oil mill with its delightful rooms. Restaurant with a vaulted ceiling and delightful shaded terrace. Regional cuisine.

Mas de Guilles rest,
Vaugines road : 2 km – ✆ 04 90 68 30 55 – hotel@guilles.com – Fax 04 90 68 37 41
– Open beg. April-beg. November
28 rm – €68/85 €90/200, €14 – ½ P €93/159 – **Rest** – *(dinner only)*
Menu €50 – Carte approx. €56
◆ A bumpy path leads to this attractive Provençal house set amidst the orchards and vineyards. Pleasant individually styled bedrooms, featuring beautiful old wardrobes. A small restaurant with a vaulted dining area and terrace with wrought-iron furnishings.

La Bastide de Lourmarin
rte de Cucuron – ✆ 04 90 07 00 70 – info@hotel-bastide.com – Fax 04 90 68 89 48
– Closed 3 January-3 February
19 rm – €90/125 €90/125, €12 – **Rest** – *(closed 2 January-15 February and Monday)* Carte €29/54
◆ Recent farmhouse with local charm; fine suites and themed accommodation. Contemporary furniture, ethnic touches and the latest technology. Provençal cuisine served on the poolside terrace in summer.

Auberge La Fenière (Reine Sammut) with rm Durance plain,
– ✆ 04 90 68 11 79 rm,
– reine@wanadoo.fr – Fax 04 90 68 18 60
– Closed 17 November-4 December and January
18 rm – €140/190 €180/210, €25 – 6 suites – ½ P €185/210
Rest – *(closed Tuesday lunch and Monday)* Menu €48 (weekday lunch), €80/120 – Carte €91/111
Spec. Saint-Pierre rôti, croquette de patate douce et jus de veau corsé. Poitrine de pigeonneau en cocotte, chou farci des cuisses, rôtie de foie. Calissons glacés, coulis d'abricot à l'amande amère. **Wines** Côtes du Lubéron, Coteaux d'Aix.
◆ A salutory refuge for lovers of fine cuisine, facing the Grand Lubéron. Attractive dining room; decoration of the elegant rooms inspired by traditional trades. Or stay in a Gypsy caravan!

L'Antiquaire
9 r. Grand Pré – ✆ 04 90 68 17 29 – Fax 04 90 68 17 29 – Closed 17-30 November, 5-25 January, Sunday dinner from October to April, Tuesday lunch and Monday
Rest – Menu €20 (weekday lunch), €30/42 – Carte approx. €40
◆ This restaurant is housed in an old stone building, named after the work by Henri Bosco, one of the eulogists of Lourmarin. Upstairs dining area in Provençal style.

LOUVIERS – 27 Eure – 304 H6 – pop. 18 328 – alt. 15 m – ✉ 27400 Normandy

Paris 104 – Les Andelys 22 – Lisieux 75 – Mantes-la-Jolie 51 – Rouen 33

Syndicat d'initiative, 10, rue du Maréchal Foch ✆ 02 32 40 04 41, Fax 02 32 61 28 85 33 **D2**

du Vaudreuil Le Vaudreuilby Rouen road: 6 km, ✆ 02 32 59 02 60.

N.-Dame church ★: works of art★, porch★ BY.

Vironvay ⩽★.

LOUVIERS

Anc.-Combattants-d'Afrique-du-N. (R.) **BY** 2	Dr-Postel (Bd du) **BZ** 6	Mendès-France (R. P.) **ABY** 15
Beaulieu (R. de) **AZ** 3	Flavigny (R.) **AZ** 7	Pénitents (R. des) **BY** 16
Coq (R. au) **ABY** 5	Foch (R. Mar.) **BZ** 8	Poste (R. de la) **BY** 18
	Gaulle (R. Gén.-de) **AZ** 9	Quai (R. du) **BY**
	Halle-aux-Drapiers (Pl.) **AZ** 10	Quatre-Moulins (R. des) **BY** 21
	Huet (R. J.) **AZ** 12	Thorel (Pl. E.) **AY** 22
	Matrey (R. du) **AZ** 14	Vexin (Chaussée du) **BY** 24

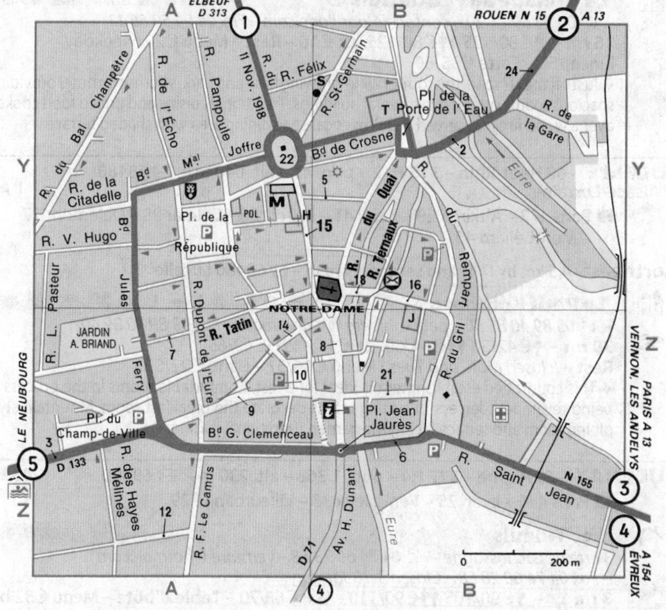

Le Pré-St-Germain

rm, VISA AE

7 r. St-Germain – ✆ 02 32 40 48 48 – le.pre.saint.germain@wanadoo.fr – Fax 02 32 50 75 60 BY **s**

30 rm – €73 €89, ☕ €10 – ½ P €75 – **Rest** – *(closed Friday dinner, Saturday and Sunday)* Menu €15/28 – Carte €22/49

◆ Centrally-located but quiet, an imposing residence with modern rooms and functional facilities. Cuisine in keeping with modern taste served in a contemporary dining room with a terrace. Speedy meals at the bar.

in Vironvay by ③: 5 km – pop. 275 – alt. 119 m – ✉ 27400

Church★.

La Suite et Hôtel Les Saisons with rm

rest, VISA AE

492 rte des Saisons – ✆ 02 32 40 02 56 – les-saisons@wanadoo.fr – Fax 02 32 25 05 26 – Closed 4-31 August, 24-31 December, Sunday dinner, Monday dinner, Tuesday dinner and Saturday lunch

4 rm – €130/150 €130/150, ☕ €15 – 1 suite – **Rest** – Menu (€28), €40 bi – Carte €25/62

◆ An elegantly decorated brasserie serving traditional dishes and daily specials highlighted on a blackboard. Pleasant terrace overlooking the garden. Cosy guestrooms.

LE LUC – 83 Var – 340 M5 – pop. 7 282 – alt. 160 m – ✉ 83340 French Riviera

Paris 836 – Cannes 75 – Draguignan 29 – Fréjus 41 – St-Raphaël 45 – Toulon 52 41 **C3**

Office de tourisme, 3, place de la Liberté ✆ 04 94 60 74 51

Le Gourmandin

pl. L. Brunet – ✆ 04 94 60 85 92 – gourmandin@wanadoo.fr – Fax 04 94 47 91 10 – Closed 25 August-21 September, 25 February-10 March, Sunday dinner, Thursday dinner and Monday

Rest – *(pre-book Sat - Sun)* Menu € 25/45

◆ This welcoming restaurant in the heart of the village serves traditional cuisine with southern touches in a rustic Provençal atmosphere.

West : 4 km by D N7 – ✉ 83340 Le Luc

La Grillade au Feu de Bois

– ✆ 04 94 69 71 20 – contact@lagrillade.com – Fax 04 94 59 66 11

16 rm – €80/125 €80/125, € 10 – **Rest** – Menu € 20 (weekday lunch)/50 – Carte € 35/60

◆ Just off the N7 road, this former wine-growing farm and park is home to a hotel providing spacious rooms spread over several buildings. Traditional cuisine and grilled food cooked over a wood fire and served in a Provençal-style dining area with shaded terrace.

LUCELLE – 68 Haut-Rhin – 315 H12 – pop. 47 – alt. 640 m – ✉ 68480 Alsace-Lorraine 1 **A3**

Paris 472 – Altkirch 29 – Basel 41 – Belfort 56 – Colmar 98 – Delémont 17 – Montbéliard 46

Northeast : 4,5 km by D 41 and secondary road – ✉ 68480 Lucelle

Le Petit Kohlberg

– ✆ 03 89 40 85 30 – petitkohlberg@wanadoo.fr – Fax 03 89 40 89 40

30 rm – €42/50 €54/60, € 11 – ½ P € 60/65

Rest – *(closed Mon. and Tues.)* Menu € 16/57 – Carte € 22/52

◆ This countrified establishment is ideal for a rest. Comfortable rooms in the process of being revamped. Jerseys of cycling teams decorate the breakfast room. Mountain-style dining room and terrace facing the garden. Traditional cuisine.

LUCENAY – 69 Rhône – 327 H4 – pop. 1 368 – alt. 230 m – ✉ 69480 43 **E1**

Paris 446 – Lyon 25 – Vénissieux 38 – Villeurbanne 29

Les Tilleuls

31 rte de Lachassagne – ✆ 04 74 60 28 58 – vermare@hotmail.com – Fax 04 74 60 28 58 – Closed 3-18 January

3 rm – €90/105 €90/110 – ½ P € 68/70 – **Table d'hôte** – Menu € 32 bi

◆ Located opposite a church, this former wine estate dates back to the 17C, now featuring light rooms decorated with travel souvenirs collected by the owner. Tasty regional dishes served in a pretty dining room.

LUCEY – 54 Meurthe-et-Moselle – 307 G6 – see Toul

LUCHÉ-PRINGÉ – 72 Sarthe – 310 J8 – pop. 1 531 – alt. 34 m – ✉ 72800 Châteaux of the Loire 35 **C2**

Paris 242 – Angers 68 – La Flèche 14 – Le Lude 10 – Le Mans 39

Syndicat d'initiative, 4, rue Paul Doumer ✆ 02 43 45 44 50, Fax 02 43 45 75 71

Auberge du Port des Roches with rm

au Port des Roches, 2.5 km east on D 13 and D 214 – ✆ 02 43 45 44 48 – Fax 02 43 45 39 61 – Closed 26 January-15 March, 26 October-5 November, Sunday dinner, Tuesday lunch and Monday

12 rm – €48/58 €48/58, € 7 – ½ P € 52/58

Rest – Menu € 24/48 – Carte € 38/48

◆ Terrace and garden by the water's edge, pleasant and comfortable dining room, fresh and colourful rooms. A cosy inn on the banks of the Loire to brighten your day!

LUCHON – 31 H.-Gar. – 343 B8 – see Bagnères-de-Luchon

LUCINGES – 74 Haute-Savoie – 328 k3 – pop. 1 211 – alt. 700 m – ✉ 74380

Paris 559 – Annecy 49 – Thonon-les-Bains 33 – Bonneville 18 – Dingy-en-Vuache 39 46 **F1**

Le Bonheur dans Le Pré

rest, rest, rm,

2011 rte Bellevue – ☎ 04 50 43 37 77 – lebonheurdanslepre.lucinges@wanadoo.fr – Fax 04 50 43 38 57 – Closed autumn half-term holidays and 1st-15 January

8 rm – €60 €70/100, €7,50 – ½ P €55 – **Rest** – *(closed Sunday and Monday) (dinner only) (pre-book)* Menu €26

♦ A name that holds true for this old farm, set at the foot of the village out in the countryside: garden, assured peace and quiet and pleasantly personalised rooms. Rustic dining room and wine cellar. Only one set menu focusing on local produce and depending on the market.

LUÇON – 85 Vendée – 316 I9 – pop. 9 311 – alt. 8 m – ✉ 85400 Atlantic Coast

Paris 438 – Cholet 89 – Fontenay-le-Comte 30 – La Rochelle 43 – La Roche-sur-Yon 33 34 **B3**

Office de tourisme, square Édouard Herriot ☎ 02 51 56 36 52, Fax 02 51 56 03 56

Notre-Dame cathedral★ - Dumaine garden★.

La Mirabelle

89 bis r. de Gaulle, des Sables d'Olonne road – ☎ 02 51 56 93 02 – b.hermouet@wanadoo.fr – Fax 02 51 56 35 92 – Closed Tuesday except dinner 15 July-26 August, Sunday dinner and Monday dinner

Rest – Menu (€18), €25/65 – Carte €46/70

♦ A welcoming restaurant near the cathedral where Richelieu was made a bishop in 1608. Modern dining room and flower-decked terrace. Tasty regional cooking.

Au Fil des Saisons with rm

55 rte de la Roche-sur-Yon – ☎ 02 51 56 11 32 – hotel-restaurant-aufildessaisons@orange.fr – Fax 02 51 56 98 25 – Closed 18-31 August, 21 February-6 March, Saturday lunch, Sunday dinner and Monday

4 rm – €44 €50, €6 – **Rest** – Menu (€18), €24/39

♦ Choose between the dining room adorned with paintings and a veranda overlooking the garden in this regional-style auberge. Contemporary cuisine. Simple, bright guestrooms.

LUC-SUR-MER – 14 Calvados – 303 J4 – pop. 3 036 – Casino – ✉ 14530

Normandy 32 **B2**

Paris 249 – Arromanches-les-Bains 23 – Bayeux 29 – Cabourg 28 – Caen 18

Office de tourisme, rue du Docteur Charcot ☎ 02 31 97 33 25, Fax 02 31 96 65 09

Municipal park★.

Des Thermes et du Casino

rm, rest,

– ☎ 02 31 97 32 37 – hotelresto@hotelresto-lesthermes.com – Fax 02 31 96 72 57 – Open 15 March-2 November

48 rm – €78/114 €78/114, €10 – ½ P €69/87

Rest – Menu €26/56 – Carte €42/92

♦ A stimulating hotel on the seafront promenade near the spa baths and casino. The rooms with balconies have a sea view. The restaurant overlooks the English channel on one side with a flower garden and apple trees on the other.

LE LUDE – 72 Sarthe – 310 J9 – pop. 4 201 – alt. 48 m – ✉ 72800

Châteaux of the Loire 35 **D2**

Paris 244 – Angers 63 – Chinon 63 – La Flèche 20 – Le Mans 45 – Saumur 51 – Tours 51

Office de tourisme, place François de Nicolay ☎ 02 43 94 62 20, Fax 02 43 94 62 20

Château★★.

XX **La Renaissance** with rm — rm, rest,

2 av. Libération – ✆ 02 43 94 63 10 – lelude.renaissance@wanadoo.fr – Fax 02 43 94 21 05 – Closed 5-10 August, 27 October-10 November and Sunday dinner

8 rm – †€ 47/57 ††€ 47/57, ☐ € 8,50 – ½ P € 60 – **Rest** – *(closed Monday)* Menu € 15 (weekdays)/37 – Carte approx. € 44

◆ This restaurant is located just near the chateau, serving modern cuisine in a contemporary-style dining area with a summer terrace on the inner courtyard.

LUDES – 51 Marne – 306 G8 – pop. 628 – alt. 140 m – ✉ 51500 13 B2

Paris 157 – Châlons-en-Champagne 52 – Reims 15 – Épernay 22 – Tinqueux 20

Domaine Ployez-Jacquemart

8 r. Astoin – ✆ 03 26 61 11 87 – contact@ployez-jacquemart.fr – Fax 03 26 61 12 20 – Closed 23 December-14 January

5 rm ☐ – †€ 84/103 ††€ 96/115 – **Table d'hôte** – *(closed 12-28 April, August, September and 25 October-6 November)* Menu € 136 bi

◆ This mansion in the middle of a champagne vineyard celebrates the French art of living. Comfortable and refined rooms based on various themes. Table d'hôte serving a house champagne dinner (on reservation).

LUMBRES – 62 Pas-de-Calais – 301 F3 – pop. 3 873 – alt. 45 m – ✉ 62380

Paris 261 – Arras 81 – Boulogne-sur-Mer 43 – Calais 44 – Dunkerque 51 – St-Omer 11 30 A2

Office de tourisme, rue François Cousin ✆ 03 21 93 45 46, Fax 03 21 12 15 87

Moulin de Mombreux — rm, rest,

2 km west on Boulogne road, D 225 and secondary road – ✆ 03 21 39 13 13 – contact@moulindemombreux.com – Fax 03 21 93 61 34 – Closed January, Monday lunch and Saturday lunch from 1st October to 21 March

24 rm – †€ 113/129 ††€ 113/129, ☐ € 18

Rest – Menu (€ 29), € 37/45 – Carte € 43/54

◆ Comfortable nights at this 18C windmill on the banks of the Bléquin with the murmur of a waterfall to send you to sleep. Recently renovated to enhance the old style refinement. Exposed beams and rustic furniture grace the upstairs dining room.

LUNEL – 34 Hérault – 339 J6 – pop. 22 352 – alt. 6 m – ✉ 34400

Languedoc-Roussillon-Tarn Gorges 23 C2

Paris 733 – Aigues-Mortes 16 – Alès 58 – Arles 56 – Montpellier 30 – Nîmes 31

Office de tourisme, 16, cours Gabriel Péri ✆ 04 67 71 01 37, Fax 04 67 71 26 67

XX **Chodoreille**

140 r. Lakanal – ✆ 04 67 71 55 77 – chodoreille@wanadoo.fr – Fax 04 67 83 19 97 – Closed 15 August-1st September, 2-19 January, Sunday and Monday

Rest – Menu € 22 (weekdays)/53 – Carte € 44/64

◆ At this establishment they prepare classic dishes with a modern touch, served in the contemporary dining room or shaded terrace. Camargue beef a speciality.

LUNÉVILLE – 54 Meurthe-et-Moselle – 307 J7 – pop. 20 200 – alt. 224 m – ✉ 54300

Alsace-Lorraine 27 C2

Paris 347 – Épinal 69 – Metz 95 – Nancy 36 – St-Dié 56 – Strasbourg 132

Office de tourisme, aile sud du Château ✆ 03 83 74 06 55, Fax 03 83 73 57 95

Château★ A - Les Bosquets park ★ AB - Panelling★ of St-Jacques church A.

Plan on next page

Les Pages — rm,

5 quai des Petits-Bosquets – ✆ 03 83 74 11 42 – hotel-les-pages@9business.fr – Fax 03 83 73 46 63 A u

37 rm – †€ 55/65 ††€ 65/95, ☐ € 8,50 – ½ P € 54

Rest *Le Petit Comptoir* – *✆ 03 83 73 14 55 (closed 1st-12 August, 21-24 December, Saturday lunch and Sunday dinner)* Menu € 17 (weekdays)/28 – Carte € 28/41

◆ This large group of buildings stands opposite the château. The renovated bedrooms have quite an original modern style which makes up for them being slightly on the small side. The restaurant is laid out in bistro style. Simple appetising cuisine.

LUNÉVILLE

Banaudon (R.) . . . . A 2
Basset (R. R.) . . . . B 3
Bosquets (R. des) . . . . B 4
Brèche (R. de la) . . . . A 5
Carnot (R.) . . . . B 7
Castara (R.) . . . . A 9
Chanzy (R.) . . . . A 10
Charier (R. G.) . . . . A 13
Charité (R. de la) . . . . A 15
Château (R. du) . . . . A 16
Erckmann (R.) . . . . B 18
Gaillardot (R.) . . . . A 20
Gambetta (R.) . . . . B 21
Haxo (R.) . . . . B 23
Lebrun (R.) . . . . B 25
Leclerc (R. Gén.) . . . . A 27
Léopold (Pl.) . . . . AB 28
République (R.) . . . . A 30
Ste-Marie (R.) . . . . A 37
St-Jacques (Pl.) . . . . A 32
St-Rémy (Pl.) . . . . A 36
Sarrebourg (R. de) . . . . A 39
Templiers (R. des) . . . . A 41
Thiers (R.) . . . . A 43
Viller (R. de) . . . . A 48
2e-Div.-de-Cavalerie (Pl. de la) A 50

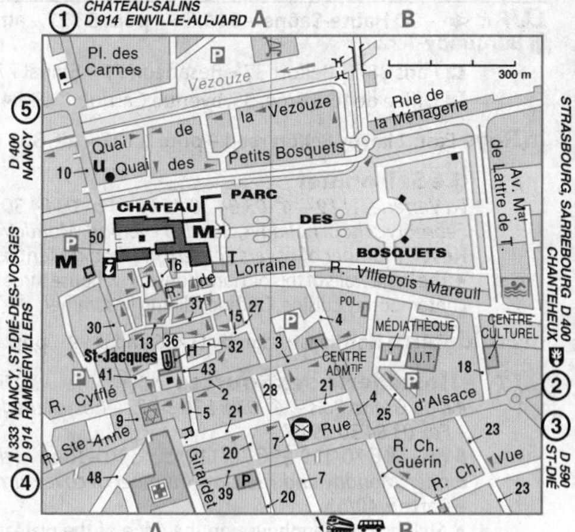

in Moncel-lès-Lunéville St-Dié road by ③: 3 km – pop. 391 – alt. 234 m – ✉ 54300

Relais St-Jean

22 av. de l'Europe, on N 59 – ✆ 03 83 74 08 65 – Fax 03 83 75 33 16 – Closed 1st-21 August, Sunday dinner, Wednesday dinner and Monday
Rest – Menu € 12,50 (weekdays)/35 – Carte € 23/47
◆ The main dining room in this restaurant in the Meurthe valley is welcoming, furnished with wrought iron. Classic cuisine.

South by ④ then Avenue G. Pompidou and cités Ste-Anne: 5 km – ✉ 54300 Lunéville

Château d'Adoménil

– ✆ 03 83 74 04 81 – adomenil@relaischateaux.com – Fax 03 83 74 21 78 – Closed 5-29 January, 16-27 February, Sunday dinner from 1st November to 15 April and Monday
9 rm – €170/210 €170/210, ☕ € 20 – 5 suites – ½ P € 185/225
Rest – *(closed Sunday dinner from 1st November-15 April, Tuesday lunch, Friday lunch and Monday)* Menu € 47 (weekdays)/90 – Carte € 81/111
Rest *Version A* – *(open Wednesday lunch, Thursday lunch and Friday lunch)* Menu € 29 – Carte € 32/49
Spec. Saint-Jacques émincées crues, cristalline de beurre demi-sel, mascarpone, anis vert (November to March). Cabillaud de petite pêche et œuf poché dans bouillon de crevettes grises. Cornets craquants de pavot bleu et mirabelles de Lorraine (20 August to 20 September). **Wines** Côtes de Toul blanc et rouge.
◆ A beautiful 18C residence situated in an attractive park. Traditional bedrooms in the château, or Provençal-style in the outbuildings. Up-to-date cuisine in the restaurant, and a contemporary, Baroque-style decor combining dark tones with touches of colour. At lunch, a bistro with large windows overlooking an English-style garden.

LURBE-ST-CHRISTAU – 64 Pyrénées-Atlantiques – 342 I6 – pop. 235 – alt. 260 m – Spa : closed, opening date unknown at present – ✉ 64660 3 B3

Paris 820 – Laruns 32 – Lourdes 61 – Oloron-Ste-Marie 10 – Pau 44 – Tardets-Sorholus 29

Au Bon Coin

rte des Thermes – ✆ 05 59 34 40 12 – thierrylassala@wanadoo.fr – Fax 05 59 34 46 40 – Closed 1 week in February and Sunday dinner 20 September-20 June
18 rm – €56/88 €56/88, ☕ € 10 – ½ P € 58/70 – **Rest** – *(closed Monday except dinner 21 June-19 September, Sunday dinner 20 September-20 June and Tuesday lunch)* Menu € 22 bi (weekday lunch), € 42/60 – Carte € 42/53
◆ Friendly family-run hotel on the edge of the forest. Comfortable and practical rooms. Those at the back are quieter. Regional, updated cuisine and Madiran wines to be enjoyed in a dining room with exposed beams and stonework, or on the veranda.

LURE – 70 Haute-Saône – 314 G6 – pop. 8 727 – alt. 290 m – ✉ 70200
Burgundy-Jura 17 **C1**

Paris 387 – Belfort 37 – Besançon 77 – Épinal 77 – Montbéliard 35 – Vesoul 30

Office de tourisme, 35, avenue Carnot ✆ 03 84 62 80 52, Fax 03 84 62 74 61

in Roye East: 2 km by Belfort road – pop. 1 127 – alt. 301 m – ✉ 70200

Le Saisonnier
La Verrerie , N 19 – ✆ 03 84 30 46 00 – Fax 03 84 30 46 00 – Closed 1st-15 August, February school holidays, Sunday evening, Monday evening and Wednesday
Rest – *(number of covers limited, pre-book)* Menu € 22/56 – Carte € 37/50
◆ The large walls of this old farmhouse now house three country-style dining areas serving contemporary cuisine. Outdoor dining in summer.

in Froideterre Northeast: 3 km by D 486 and D 99 – pop. 311 – alt. 306 m – ✉ 70200

Hostellerie des Sources with rm
4 r. du Grand Bois – ✆ 03 84 30 34 72 – hostelleriedessources@wanadoo.fr – Fax 03 84 30 29 87
5 rm – €70/119 €70/119, € 10 – **Rest** – *(closed 3 weeks January, Sunday dinner, Monday and Tuesday) (number of covers limited, pre-book)* Menu € 25/80 – Carte € 40/55
◆ Stylish stone farmhouse on the edge of the plateau des Mille Étangs. Elegant rustic interior. Up-to-date cuisine and good wine list (wine tasting in cellar). A hotel comprising five new villas (three with their own spa) in a variety of styles (exotic, classic etc).

LURS – 04 Alpes-de-Haute-Provence – 334 D9 – pop. 347 – alt. 600 m – ✉ 04700
French Alps 40 **B2**

Paris 737 – Digne-les-Bains 40 – Forcalquier 11 – Manosque 22 – Sisteron 33

Office de tourisme, place de la Fontaine ✆ 04 92 79 10 20, Fax 04 92 79 10 20

Site★.

Le Séminaire
– ✆ 04 92 79 94 19 – info@hotel-leseminaire.com – Fax 04 92 79 11 18 – Closed 1st December-1st February – **16 rm** – €89 €119, € 13 – ½ P € 85 –
Rest – Menu € 20 (weekday lunch), € 26/59
◆ Non-smoking establishment occupying the ex-seminary of the Bishops of Sisteron's summer residence. Plain, practical rooms; panoramic garden. Vaulted dining room and beautiful view from the attractive, shaded terrace. Regional cooking.

LUSSAC-LES-CHÂTEAUX – 86 Vienne – 322 K6 – pop. 2 532 – alt. 104 m –
✉ 86320 Atlantic Coast 39 **D2**

Paris 355 – Bellac 42 – Châtellerault 52 – Montmorillon 12 – Poitiers 39 – Ruffec 51

Office de tourisme, place du 11 novembre 1918 ✆ 05 49 84 57 73, Fax 05 49 84 57 73

Merovingian necropolis★ of Civaux Northwest: 6 km on D 749.

Les Orangeries
12 av. du Dr Dupont – ✆ 05 49 84 07 07 – contact@lesorangeries.fr – Fax 05 49 84 98 82 – Closed 15-30 November
7 rm – €75/115 €75/115, € 13 – 4 suites – ½ P € 80/103
Rest – *(closed Sun.-Mon. except residents)* Menu € 30
◆ A characterful interior, snug inviting rooms, a superb 35m-long pool, a collection of old toys and an irresistible garden are just a few of the reasons to book a room in this 18C house. Regional menu of generous home cooking.

LUTTER – 68 Haut-Rhin – 315 I12 – see Ferrette

LUTZELBOURG – 57 Moselle – 307 O6 – pop. 695 – alt. 212 m – ✉ 57820
Alsace-Lorraine 27 **D2**

Paris 438 – Metz 113 – Obernai 49 – Sarrebourg 20 – Sarreguemines 53 – Strasbourg 62

Syndicat d'initiative, 147, r. A.J. Konzett ✆ 03 87 25 30 19, Fax 03 87 25 33 76

Plan-incliné (slope) ★ of St-Louis-Arzviller Southwest: 3.5 km.

Des Vosges with rm

2 r. Ackermann – ✆ 03 87 25 30 09 – info@hotelvosges.com – Fax 03 87 25 42 22
10 rm – †€ 55 ††€ 55, ☕ € 7,50 – ½ P € 65 – **Rest** – *(closed Sunday evening and Wednesday)* Menu € 20/32 – Carte € 27/45

◆ This restaurant features a terrace overlooking the Marne - Rhine canal. The dining area has maintained its wooden panelling and original parquet floors. Serves regional cuisine and truite au bleu (trout poached in court bouillon).

LUX – **71 Saône-et-Loire** – **320** J9 – **see Chalon-sur-Saône**

LUXÉ – **16 Charente** – **324** K4 – **see Mansle**

LUYNES – **37 Indre-et-Loire** – **317** M4 – **pop. 4 501** – **alt. 60 m** – ✉ **37230**
Châteaux of the Loire 11 **B2**

Paris 247 – Angers 115 – Chinon 41 – Langeais 15 – Saumur 56 – Tours 11

Office de tourisme, 9, r. Alfred Baugé ✆ 02 47 55 77 14, Fax 02 47 55 77 14

Church★ in the Vieux-Bourg (old town) of St-Etienne de Chigny West: 3 km.

Domaine de Beauvois rest, rest,

4 km northwest by D 49 – ✆ 02 47 55 50 11
– beauvois@grandesetapes.fr – Fax 02 47 55 59 62
36 rm – †€ 190/300 ††€ 190/300, ☕ € 22 – **Rest** – Menu € 32 (lunch), € 48/66 – Carte € 51/87

◆ Huge 16C and 17C manor house, nestling in a park planted with trees with a small lake. Superb rooms with individual touches in a country house style. Elegant dining room and intimate lounges offering modern food (dinner and on Sundays) or local dishes (at lunchtime).

LUZ-ST-SAUVEUR – **65 Hautes-Pyrénées** – **342** L7 – **pop. 1 098** – **alt. 710 m** – **Winter sports : 1 800/2 450 m 14** – **Spa : early April-late Oct.** – ✉ **65120**
Languedoc-Roussillon-Tarn Gorges 28 **A3**

Paris 882 – Argelès-Gazost 19 – Cauterets 24 – Lourdes 32 – Pau 77 – Tarbes 51

Office de tourisme, 20, place du 8 mai ✆ 05 62 92 30 30, Fax 05 62 92 87 19

Fortified church★.

in Esquièze-Sère **North** – **pop. 464** – **alt. 710 m** – ✉ **65120**

Le Montaigu rest,

rte de Vizos – ✆ 05 62 92 81 71 – hotel.montaigu@wanadoo.fr
– Fax 05 62 92 94 11 – Closed October and November
42 rm – †€ 60/80 ††€ 60/80, ☕ € 8 – ½ P € 53/63
Rest – *(dinner only)* Menu € 15/25 – Carte € 27/40

◆ A recent establishment situated at the foot of a ruined château. Spacious, functional rooms, seven of which are brand new; some with a balcony overlooking the mountains. Traditional menu in the restaurant and bright lounge-bar area facing the garden.

Terminus without rest

– ✆ 05 62 92 80 17 – Fax 05 62 92 32 89 – Closed November
16 rm – †€ 42 ††€ 48, ☕ € 6,50

◆ Large village house, providing all-renovated and colourful rooms. Enjoy your breakfast in the garden on fine mornings.

LUZY – **58 Nièvre** – **319** G11 – **pop. 2 077** – **alt. 275 m** – ✉ **58170** Burgundy

Paris 319 – Dijon 122 – Nevers 81 – Le Creusot 47 – Montceau-les-Mines 40

Syndicat d'initiative, place Chanzy ✆ 03 86 30 02 65 7 **B3**

Le Morvan

73 av. Dr-Dollet – ✆ 03 86 30 00 66 – hotel.morvan@wanadoo.fr
– Fax 03 86 30 04 92 – Closed 27 August-4 September, 4-10 January, 23 February-7 March, Sunday dinner from November to March, Saturday lunch and Wednesday
Rest – Menu € 13 (weekday lunch), € 20/68 – Carte € 40/63

◆ The setting of this old inn oozes with charm, however it is the mouth-watering inventive cuisine of the owner/chef and pretty countrified dining room that make it so popular!

LYAS – **07 Ardèche** – **331** J5 – **see Privas**

T. Deschamps/PHOTONONSTOP

Le quai de Saône et Notre-Dame de Fourvière

LYON

P **Department:** 69 Rhône
Michelin LOCAL map: n° **327** I5
▶ Paris 458 – Genève 151 – Grenoble 106 – Marseille 314 – St-Étienne 61
Population: 445 452

Pop. built-up area: 1 348 832 43 **E1**
Altitude: 175 m – **Postal Code:** ✉ 69000
Lyon - Rhone Valley

USEFUL INFORMATION

TOURIST OFFICE

place Bellecour ✆ 04 72 77 69 69, Fax 04 78 42 04 32

TRANSPORT

Auto-train ✆ 3635 et tapez 42 (0,34 €/mn)

AIRPORT

Lyon Saint-Exupéry ✆ 0 826 800 826 (0.15 €/mn), by ④: 27 km

CASINO

at the Tour de Salvagny
le Pharaon (quai Charles-de-Gaulle in Lyon) GV

A FEW GOLF COURSES

18 de Lyon Chassieu Chassieu Route de Lyon, ✆ 04 78 90 84 77 ;
18 de Salvagny La Tour-de-Salvagny 100 rue des Granges, by Roanne road: 20 km, ✆ 04 78 48 88 48 ;
9 public de Miribel Jonage Vaulx-en-Velin Chemin de la Bletta, Northeast: 9 km, ✆ 04 78 80 56 20 ;
18 de Mionnay-la-Dombes Mionnay Domaine de Beau Logis, North: 23 km by D 1083, ✆ 04 78 91 84 84 ;
36 de Lyon Villette-d'AnthonEast: 25 km by D 517, D6 and D 55, ✆ 04 78 31 11 33.

TO BE SEEN

SITE

⋞★★★ of Notre-Dame de Fourvière basilica EX

- Up Garillan★ EX
- ⋞★ on the Saône and peninsula from Place Rouville EV

ROMAN AND GALLO-ROMAN LYON

Roman and Odéon theatresEY - Roman aqueducts EY - Musée de la civilisation gallo-romaine (Gallo-Roman Civilization Museum) ★★ : table claudienne (Claudian table)★★★ EY M10

OLD LYON

Districts of St-Jean, St-Paul and St-Georges★★★ EFXY - Rue St-Jean: Courtyard★★ at nº 28 and courtyard★of the hôtel du Gouvernement at nº 2 – Vaulted corridor★ at nº 18 rue Lainerie - Gallery★★ of hôtel Bullioud at nº 8 rue Juiverie - Hôtel Gadagne★ FX M4 : musée historique de Lyon (Lyon History Museum)★, musée lapidaire (Lapidary Museum)★, musée international de la Marionnette (International Puppet Museum)★ - Primitiale St-Jean★ (Choir★★) EFY - Maison du Crible★ at nº 16 rue du Boeuf - Theatre " FX T

THE PRESQU'ÎLE

Place Bellecour FY - Fountain★ of place des Terreaux FX - Palais St-Pierre★ FX M9 Musée des Beaux-Arts (Fine Arts Museum)★★★ FX M9 - Musée historique des tissus (Cloth History Museum) ★★★ FY M17 - Musée de l'imprimerie (Printing Museum)★★ FX M16 - Musée des Arts décoratifs (Decorative Arts Museum) ★★ FY M7

LA CROIX ROUSSE

Origins of the Lyon silk industry

- Mur des Canuts (Silk Worker's Wall) FV R - Maison des Canuts (Silk Workers' House) FV M5 - Ateliers de Soierie vivante (Living Silk Workshops)★ FV E

LEFT BANK OF THE RHÔNE

Districts: les Brotteaux, la Guillotière, Gerland, la Part-Dieu

- Tête d'Or Park ★ : Rose garden ★ GHV - Musée d'Histoire naturelle Natural History Museum)★★ GV M20 - Centre d'Histoire de la Résistance et de la Déportation (Resistance and Deportation History Centre)★ FZ M1
- Musée d'Art contemporain (Modern Art Museum)★ GU - Musée urbain Tony-Garnier (Tony Garnier Urban Museum) CQ - Halle Tony-Garnier BQR - Château Lumière CQ M2

SURROUNDING AREA

Musée de l'automobile Henri-Malartre (car museum)★★ to Rochetaillée-sur-Saône : 12 km by ⑪

City Centre (Bellecour-Terreaux)

Sofitel
20 quai Gailleton ✉ 69002 Ⓜ Bellecour – ✆ 04 72 41 20 20 – h0553@accor.com – Fax 04 72 40 05 50 p. 8 FY **p**

164 rm – †€ 205/350 ††€ 230/375, ☕ € 26 – 29 suites

Rest Les Trois Dômes – see restaurant listing

Rest *Sofishop* – *✆ 04 72 41 20 80* – Menu € 28 (weekdays)/40 – Carte € 31/52

◆ The cuboid exterior contrasts with the luxurious interior: contemporary rooms in good taste, modern conference facilities, smart shops and a hair-dressing salon. Brasserie atmosphere and fare at the Sofishop (oyster bar).

Le Royal Lyon without rest
20 pl. Bellecour ✉ 69002 Ⓜ Bellecour – ✆ 04 78 37 57 31 – h2952@accor.com – Fax 04 78 37 01 36 p. 8 FY **g**

77 rm – †€ 210/450 ††€ 290/450, ☕ € 22 – 3 suites

◆ After renovation, this 19C hotel run by the Paul Bocuse Institute has regained its former splendour. Magnificent rooms. The breakfast room is decorated in the manner of a kitchen.

Carlton without rest
4 r. Jussieu ✉ 69002 Ⓜ Cordeliers – ✆ 04 78 42 56 51 – h2950@accor.com – Fax 04 78 42 10 71 p. 8 FX **b**

83 rm – †€ 89/199 ††€ 99/209, ☕ € 14

◆ Purple and gold prevail in this traditional hotel, decorated in the manner of an old-fashioned luxury hotel. The period lift cage has a charm of its own. Comfortable rooms.

Globe et Cécil without rest
21 r. Gasparin ✉ 69002 Ⓜ Bellecour – ✆ 04 78 42 58 95 – accueil@globeetcecilhotel.com – Fax 04 72 41 99 06 p. 8 FY **b**

60 rm ☕ – †€ 130/135 ††€ 160/165

◆ One of the last silk-merchants of the town decorated the conference room of this hotel. Antique and modern furniture adorns the tastefully decorated rooms. Irresistible welcome.

Mercure Lyon Beaux-Arts without rest
75 r. Prés. E. Herriot ✉ 69002 Ⓜ Cordeliers – ✆ 04 78 38 09 50 – h2949@accor.com – Fax 04 78 42 19 19 p. 8 FX **t**

75 rm – †€ 109/179 ††€ 119/189, ☕ € 14 – 4 suites

◆ Beautiful building from 1900, most of the bedrooms are furnished in Art Deco style. Four are more unusual and are decorated by contemporary artists.

Mercure Plaza République without rest
5 r. Stella ✉ 69002 Ⓜ Cordeliers – ✆ 04 78 37 50 50 – h2951@accor.com – Fax 04 78 42 33 34 p. 8 FY **k**

78 rm – †€ 109/169 ††€ 119/179, ☕ € 14

◆ 19C architecture, central location, modern interior, full range of comforts and conference facilities: a hotel especially popular with its business clientele.

Grand Hôtel des Terreaux without rest
16 r. Lanterne ✉ 69001 Ⓜ Hôtel de ville – ✆ 04 78 27 04 10 – ght@hotel-lyon.fr – Fax 04 78 27 97 75 p. 6 FX **u**

53 rm – †€ 85/105 ††€ 115/164, ☕ € 12

◆ Personalised, tastefully decorated rooms, a pretty indoor pool and attentive service ensure that guests can relax to the full in this former 19C post house.

Des Artistes without rest
8 r. G. André ✉ 69002 Ⓜ Cordeliers – ✆ 04 78 42 04 88 – hartiste@club-internet.fr – Fax 04 78 42 93 76 p. 8 FY **r**

45 rm – †€ 78/130 ††€ 90/140, ☕ € 10

◆ The hotel is named after the "artistes" of the neighbouring Célestins theatre. Stylish rooms; a Cocteau style fresco adorns the breakfast room.

La Résidence without rest
18 r. V. Hugo ✉ 69002 Ⓜ Bellecour – ✆ 04 78 42 63 28 – hotel-la-residence@wanadoo.fr – Fax 04 78 42 85 76 p. 8 FY **s**

67 rm – †€ 78 ††€ 78, ☕ € 7

◆ In a pedestrian street near Bellecour square, this hotel provides rooms and a lounge in a 1970s style. A few rooms are more elegant and graced with wainscoting.

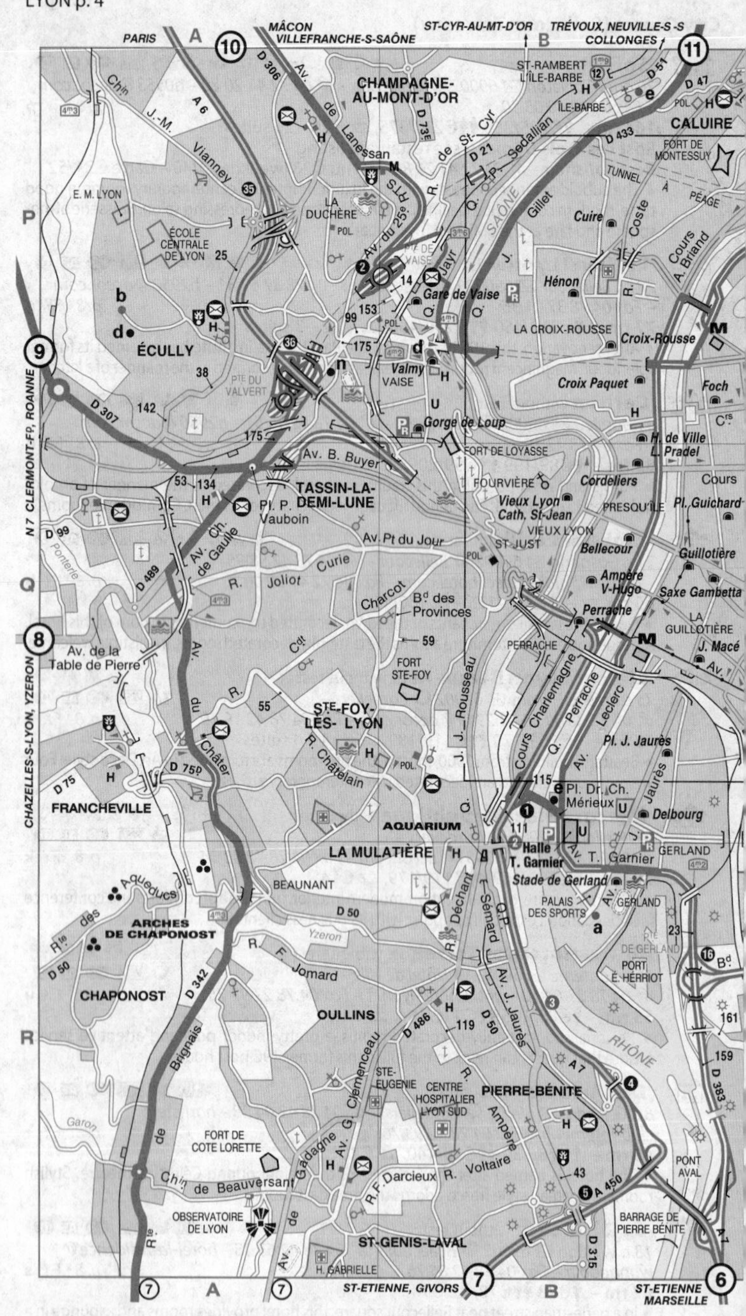

PARIS
MÂCON
VILLEFRANCHE-S-SAÔNE
ST-CYR-AU-MT-D'OR
TRÉVOUX, NEUVILLE-S-S
COLLONGES
CHAMPAGNE-
AU-MONT-D'OR
ST-RAMBERT
L'ÎLE-BARBE
ÎLE-BARBE
CALUIRE
FORT DE
MONTESSUY
TUNNEL
À
PÉAGE
E. M. LYON
ÉCOLE
CENTRALE
DE LYON
LA
DUCHÈRE
Gare de Vaise
Hénon
Cuire
LA CROIX-ROUSSE
Croix-Rousse
ÉCULLY
Valmy
VAISE
Croix Paquet
Foch
Gorge de Loup
FORT DE LOYASSE
H. de Ville
L. Pradel
TASSIN-LA-
DEMI-LUNE
FOURVIÈRE
Cordeliers
Vieux Lyon
Cath. St-Jean
PRESQU'ÎLE
Pl. Guichard
VIEUX LYON
ST-JUST
Bellecour
Guillotière
Ampère
V-Hugo
Saxe Gambetta
Perrache
LA
GUILLOTIÈRE
J. Macé
PERRACHE
FORT
STE-FOY
STE-FOY-
LES- LYON
Pl. J. Jaurès
FRANCHEVILLE
Pl. Dr. Ch.
Mérieux
Delbourg
AQUARIUM
Halle
T. Garnier
GERLAND
LA MULATIÈRE
Stade de Gerland
BEAUNANT
PALAIS
DES SPORTS
ARCHES
DE CHAPONOST
PORT
É. HERRIOT
CHAPONOST
OULLINS
RHÔNE
STE-
EUGÉNIE
CENTRE
HOSPITALIER
LYON SUD
PIERRE-BÉNITE
FORT DE
COTE LORETTE
PONT
AVAL
OBSERVATOIRE
DE LYON
BARRAGE DE
PIERRE BÉNITE
ST-GENIS-LAVAL
H. GABRIELLE
ST-ETIENNE, GIVORS
ST-ETIENNE
MARSEILLE
N 7 CLERMONT-FD, ROANNE
CHAZELLES-S-LYON, YZERON

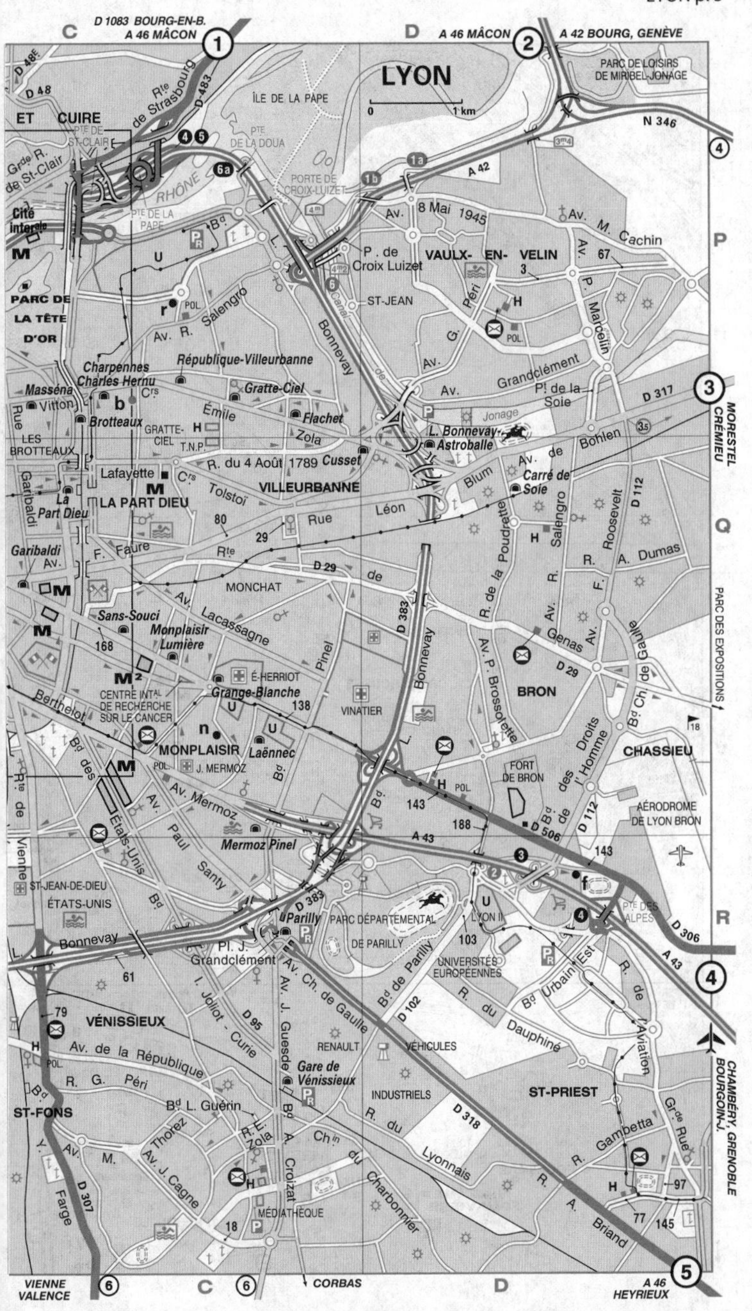

LYON
D 1083 BOURG-EN-B.
A 46 MÂCON
A 46 MÂCON
A 42 BOURG, GENÈVE
PARC DE LOISIRS DE MIRIBEL-JONAGE
ÎLE DE LA PAPE
N 346
VAULX-EN-VELIN
VILLEURBANNE
LA PART DIEU
MONCHAT
BRON
CHASSIEU
MONPLAISIR
VÉNISSIEUX
ST-FONS
ST-PRIEST
PARC DE LA TÊTE D'OR
PARC DÉPARTEMENTAL DE PARILLY
AÉRODROME DE LYON BRON
PARC DES EXPOSITIONS
MORESTEL CRÉMIEU
CHAMBÉRY, GRENOBLE BOURGOIN-J.
A 46 HEYRIEUX
CORBAS
VIENNE VALENCE

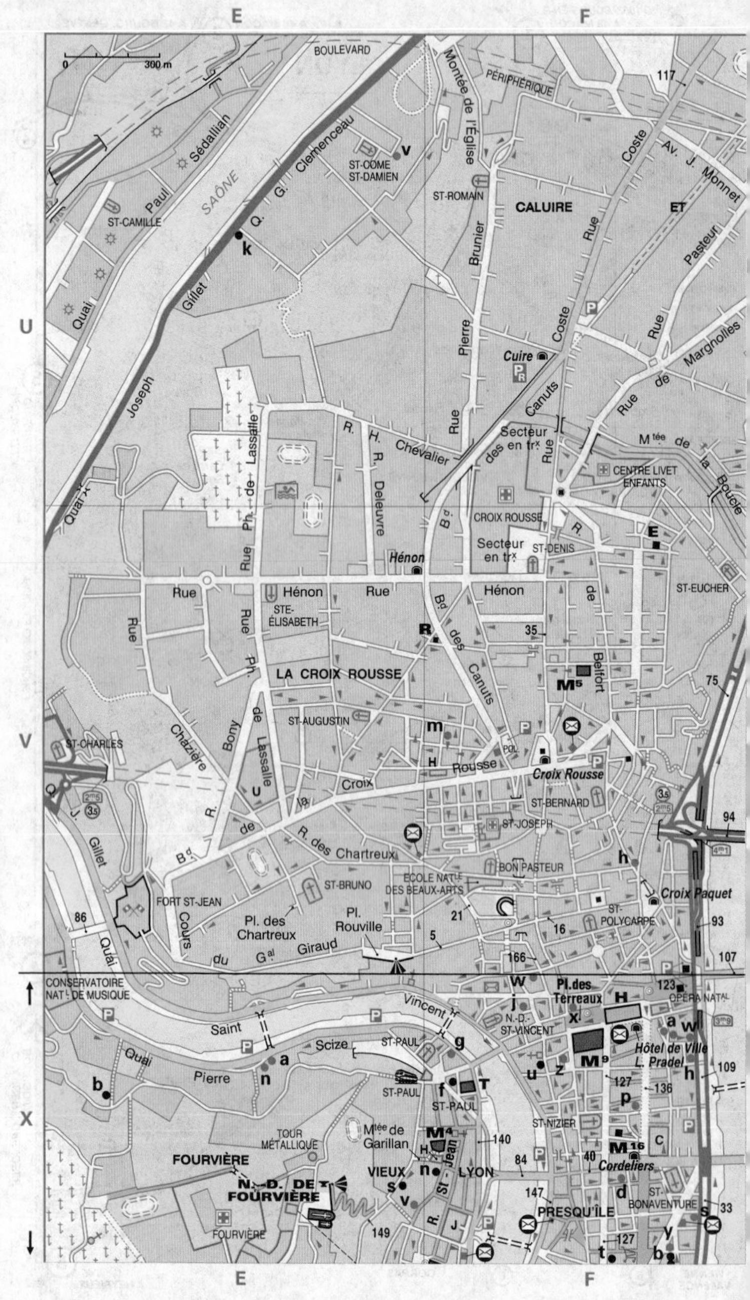

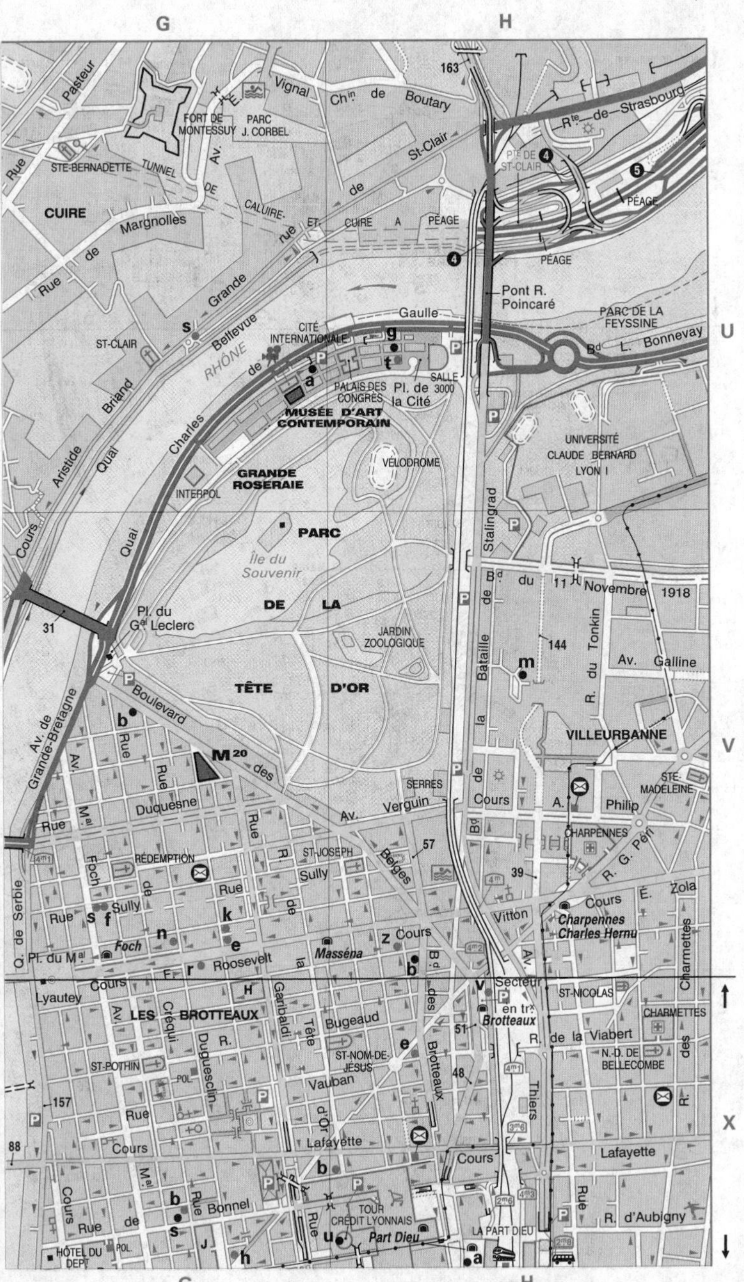
G
H
U
V
X
CUIRE
FORT DE MONTESSUY
PARC J. CORBEL
STE-BERNADETTE
TUNNEL DE CALUIRE-ET-CUIRE A PÉAGE
Rue Pasteur
Vignal
Chin de Boutary
Rte de Strasbourg
Pte DE ST-CLAIR
PÉAGE
Pont R. Poincaré
PARC DE LA FEYSSINE
Bd L. Bonnevay
Rue de Margnolles
Grande rue de St-Clair
ST-CLAIR
RHÔNE
Quai Charles de Gaulle
Quai Aristide Briand
Cours Bellevue
CITÉ INTERNATIONALE
PALAIS DES CONGRÈS
Pl. de la Cité
SALLE 3000
MUSÉE D'ART CONTEMPORAIN
GRANDE ROSERAIE
INTERPOL
VÉLODROME
PARC DE LA TÊTE D'OR
Île du Souvenir
JARDIN ZOOLOGIQUE
UNIVERSITÉ CLAUDE BERNARD LYON I
Bd de la Bataille de Stalingrad
Bd du 11 Novembre 1918
Av. Galline
R. du Tonkin
VILLEURBANNE
Pl. du Gal Leclerc
Av. de Grande-Bretagne
Boulevard des Belges
M20
SERRES
Av. Verguin
Cours A. Philip
STE-MADELEINE
CHARPENNES
R. G. Péri
Cours É. Zola
Charpennes Charles Hernu
Vitton
Rue Duquesne
Av. Mal Foch
RÉDEMPTION
ST-JOSEPH
Rue Sully
Rue de Créqui
Foch
Q. de Serbie
Pl. du Mal Lyautey
Cours F. Roosevelt
Masséna
Bd des Brotteaux
Secteur en trx
Brotteaux
ST-NICOLAS
CHARMETTES
R. des Charmettes
R. de la Viabert
N.-D. DE BELLECOMBE
LES BROTTEAUX
Rue Garibaldi
Rue Tête d'Or
Bugeaud
ST-NOM-DE-JÉSUS
Vauban
ST-POTHIN
R. Duguesclin
POL.
Rue Thiers
Cours Lafayette
Lafayette
R. d'Aubigny
Rue Bonnel
Cours Rue de Mal
TOUR CRÉDIT LYONNAIS
Part Dieu
LA PART DIEU
HÔTEL DU DEPT
163
31
144
57
39
51
48
157
88
4m1
4m2
4m3
3m6
2m6
2m8

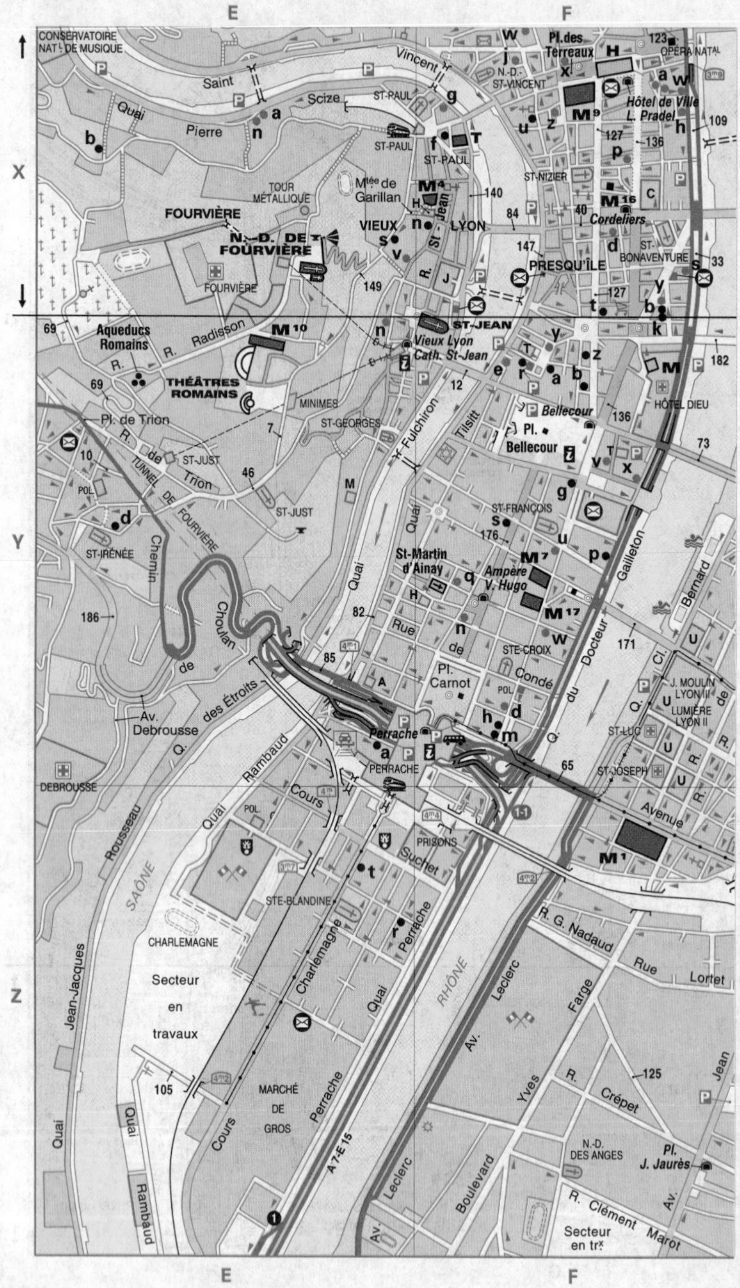
E
F
X
Y
Z
CONSERVATOIRE NAT. DE MUSIQUE
Quai Saint Pierre Scize
Vincent
ST-PAUL
N.-D.-ST-VINCENT
Pl. des Terreaux
OPÉRA NATAL
Hôtel de Ville L. Pradel
ST-NIZIER
Cordeliers
ST-BONAVENTURE
PRESQU'ÎLE
TOUR MÉTALLIQUE
Mtée de Garillan
FOURVIÈRE
N.-D. DE FOURVIÈRE
VIEUX LYON
R. St-Jean
ST-JEAN
Vieux Lyon Cath. St-Jean
Aqueducs Romains
R. Radisson
THÉÂTRES ROMAINS
MINIMES
ST-GEORGES
Pl. de Trion
R. de Trion
ST-JUST
TUNNEL DE FOURVIÈRE
ST-IRÉNÉE
Chemin de Choulan
Quai Fulchiron
Tilsitt
Pl. Bellecour
Bellecour
HÔTEL DIEU
ST-FRANÇOIS
St-Martin d'Ainay
Ampère V. Hugo
Rue de Condé
STE-CROIX
Pl. Carnot
Quai du Docteur Gailleton
Bernard
J. MOULIN LYON III
LUMIÈRE LYON II
ST-LUC
ST-JOSEPH
Avenue
Av. Debrousse
Q. des Étroits
DEBROUSSE
Perrache
PERRACHE
Quai Rambaud
Cours Suchet
PRISONS
STE-BLANDINE
SAÔNE
CHARLEMAGNE
Secteur en travaux
Cours Charlemagne
Quai Perrache
MARCHÉ DE GROS
A7-E15
RHÔNE
Av. Leclerc
R. G. Nadaud
Rue Lortet
Yves Farge
R. Crépet
Boulevard
N.-D. DES ANGES
Pl. J. Jaurès
R. Clément Marot
Secteur en trx
Av. Jean
Quai Jean-Jacques Rousseau
Quai Rambaud

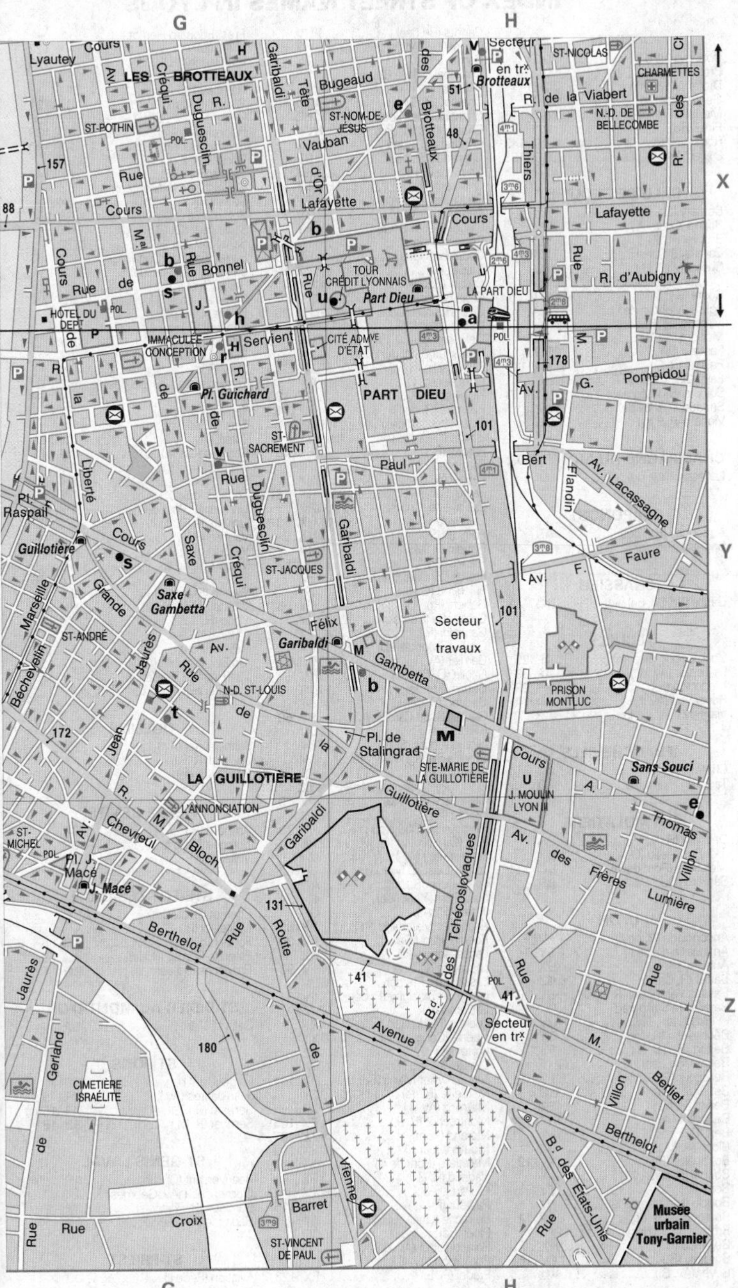

G
H
X
Y
Z
LES BROTTEAUX
Brotteaux
ST-POTHIN
ST-NOM-DE-JÉSUS
ST-NICOLAS
CHARMETTES
N.-D. DE BELLECOMBE
TOUR CRÉDIT LYONNAIS
Part Dieu
LA PART DIEU
HÔTEL DU DÉPT
IMMACULÉE CONCEPTION
CITÉ ADMVE D'ÉTAT
PART DIEU
Pl. Guichard
ST-SACREMENT
Pl. Raspail
Guillotière
Saxe Gambetta
ST-JACQUES
Secteur en travaux
ST-ANDRÉ
Garibaldi
N-D. ST-LOUIS
PRISON MONTLUC
Pl. de Stalingrad
STE-MARIE DE LA GUILLOTIÈRE
LA GUILLOTIÈRE
Sans Souci
J. MOULIN LYON III
L'ANNONCIATION
ST-MICHEL
Pl. J. Macé
J. Macé
Secteur en trx
CIMETIÈRE ISRAÉLITE
ST-VINCENT DE PAUL
Musée urbain Tony-Garnier
Cours Lafayette
Cours Gambetta
Rue Garibaldi
Rue Duguesclin
Rue Bugeaud
Rue Vauban
Rue Servient
Av. Lacassagne
Av. F. Faure
Av. G. Pompidou
Av. des Frères Lumière
Av. Berthelot
Rue de Marseille
Rue Béchevelin
Grande Rue de la Guillotière
Av. Jean Jaurès
Route de Vienne
Bd des Tchécoslovaques
Bd des États-Unis
Rue M. Berliet
Rue de Gerland
Rue Croix Barret
Cours Albert Thomas
Villon
R. de la Viabert
R. d'Aubigny
Rue Thiers
Rue Paul Bert
Flandin
R. M. Bloch
Chevreul
Saxe
Créqui
Rue de Bonnel
Cours de la Liberté
Lyautey
157
88
51
48
178
101
172
131
41
180

INDEX OF STREET NAMES IN LYONS

BRON

CALUIRE ET CUIRE

CHAMPAGNE-AU-MONT-D'OR

CHAPONOST

CHASSIEU

ÉCULLY

FRANCHEVILLE

LA MULATIÈRE

LYON

OULLINS

PIERRE-BÉNITE

STE-FOY-LÈS-LYON

ST-DIDIER-AU-MONT-D'OR

ST-FONS

ST-GÉNIS-LAVAL

ST-PRIEST

ALPHABETICAL LIST OF HOTELS AND RESTAURANTS

A

B

C

D

E

Célestins without rest
4 r. Archers ✉ 69002 Ⓜ Guillotière – ☎ 04 72 56 08 98 – info@hotelcelestins.com – Fax 04 72 56 08 65 p. 8 FY **a**
25 rm – €62/90 €68/100, ☕ €8
♦ Hotel occupying several floors in a residential building. Bright rooms with simple furnishings; those at the front have a view over the Fourvière hillside.

Élysée Hôtel without rest
92 r. Prés. E. Herriot ✉ 69002 Ⓜ Cordeliers – ☎ 04 78 42 03 15 – accueil@hotel-elysee.fr – Fax 04 78 37 76 49 p. 8 FY **z**
29 rm – €50/69 €69/82, ☕ €8
♦ Recently renovated, functional rooms, a central location, continental breakfasts and reasonable prices: this family establishment is popular with a business clientele.

Perrache

Grand Hôtel Mercure Château Perrache
12 cours Verdun ✉ 69002 Ⓜ Perrache – ☎ 04 72 77 15 00 – h1292@accor.com – Fax 04 78 37 06 56 p. 8 EY **a**
111 rm – €145/195 €145/195, ☕ €14 – 2 suites
Rest *Les Belles Saisons* – *(closed 25 July-25 August, weekends and holidays)* Menu (€16 bi) – Carte €25/35
♦ This hotel built in 1900 has partially conserved its Art Nouveau setting: intricate wood carving in the lobby and period furniture in some of the rooms and suites. The full effect of the Majorelle style is reflected in this superb restaurant.

Charlemagne
23 cours Charlemagne ✉ 69002 Ⓜ Perrache – ☎ 04 72 77 70 00 – charlemagne@hotel-lyon.fr – Fax 04 78 42 94 84 p. 8 EZ **t**
116 rm – €80/155 €85/170, ☕ €10 – ½ P €100/128
Rest – *(closed Saturday and Sunday)* Menu €22 – Carte €24/31
♦ Two buildings home to renovated, comfortable and tastefully appointed rooms; a business centre; winter-garden style breakfast room. Modern restaurant with a pleasant terrace in summer and unpretentious, standard fare.

Axotel
12 r. Marc-Antoine Petit ✉ 69002 Ⓜ Perrache – ☎ 04 72 77 70 70 – axotel.perrache@hotel-lyon.fr – Fax 04 72 40 00 65 p. 8 EZ **r**
126 rm – €71/75 €76/90, ☕ €9 – ½ P €90/98
Rest *Le Chalut* – *(closed 28 July-24 August, 22 December-1st January, Friday dinner, Saturday lunch and Sunday)* Menu €25 – Carte €33/46
♦ A business clientele appreciates this establishment's extensive seminar facilities. The rooms vary in size and style. As well as excellent fish dishes, there are also some meat dishes on the menu.

Verdun without rest
82 r. de la Charité ✉ 69002 Ⓜ Perrache – ☎ 04 78 37 34 71 – reservation@hoteldeverdun.com – Fax 04 78 37 45 35 p. 8 FY**m**
28 rm – €75/130 €95/140, ☕ €11
♦ Near the railway station, well-kept brightly coloured rooms, copious breakfast buffet. Entirely non-smoking.

Des Savoies without rest
80 r. de la Charité ✉ 69002 Ⓜ Perrache – ☎ 04 78 37 66 94 – hotel.des.savoies@wanadoo.fr – Fax 04 72 40 27 84 p. 8 FY **h**
46 rm – €52/72 €58/76, ☕ €6
♦ A façade embellished with Savoyard coats of arms. Small, functional and recently refurbished rooms. Good value for money. Convenient garage.

Vieux-Lyon

Villa Florentine ≤ Lyon,
25 montée St-Barthélémy ✉ 69005 Ⓜ Fourvière – ☎ 04 72 56 56 56 – florentine@relaischateaux.com – Fax 04 72 40 90 56
20 rm – €160/410 €160/410, ☕ €24 – 8 suites p. 6 EX **s**
Rest *Les Terrasses de Lyon* – see restaurant listing
♦ On the Fourvière hill, this Renaissance-inspired abode commands a matchless view of the town. The interior sports an elegant blend of old and new.

Cour des Loges rest, VISA

6 r. Boeuf ✉ 69005 Ⓜ Vieux Lyon Cathédrale Saint-Jean – ☎ 04 72 77 44 44 – contact@courdesloges.com – Fax 04 72 40 93 61 *p. 6* FX **n**

58 rm – €240/290 €240/290, ☕ €27 – 4 suites

Rest *Les Loges* – *(closed July, August, Sunday and Monday) (dinner only)* Menu €55/80 – Carte €69/82

Rest *Café-Épicerie* – *(closed Tuesday and Wednesday except July-August)* Menu (€17) – Carte €37/47

◆ An exceptional group of 14C-18C houses set around a splendid galleried courtyard have been decorated by contemporary designers and artists. Creative cuisine and decor with a personal touch. Tempting lunchtime menu at the Café-Épicerie.

Collège without rest VISA

5 pl. St Paul ✉ 69005 Ⓜ Vieux Lyon Cathédrale St-Jean – ☎ 04 72 10 05 05 – contact@college-hotel.com – Fax 04 78 27 98 84 *p. 6* FX **f**

39 rm – €105/125 €125/140, ☕ €12

◆ Take a trip down memory lane: old-fashioned school desks, a pommel horse and geography maps. The rooms are white, resolutely modern, with a balcony or terrace.

Du Greillon without rest VISA

12 montée du Greillon ✉ 69009 – ☎ 06 08 22 26 33 – contact@legreillon.com – Fax 04 72 29 10 97 – Closed 1st-12 August and 18-24 February *p. 8* EX **b**

5 rm ☕ – €78/92 €85/100

◆ The former property of sculptor J. Chinard has been turned into a guesthouse. Pretty rooms, old furniture and ornaments, gorgeous garden and superb view of the Saône and Croix-Rousse.

La Grange de Fourvière without rest P VISA

86 r. des Macchabées ✉ 69005 Ⓜ St-Just – ☎ 04 72 33 74 45 – catherine@grangedefourviere.com – Fax 04 72 33 74 45 *p. 8* EY **d**

4 rm ☕ – €55/70 €65/80

◆ In the "village" of St-Irénée, this 19C barn and stables have been fully converted. Pleasant rooms, sitting room-library and small kitchen for the use of guests.

La Croix-Rousse (banks of the Saône)

Lyon Métropole rm, P VISA

85 quai J. Gillet ✉ 69004 – ☎ 04 72 10 44 44 – metropole@lyonmetropole.com – Fax 04 72 10 44 42 *p. 6* EU **k**

118 rm – €170/250 €170/250, ☕ €18

Rest *Brasserie Lyon Plage* – ☎ *04 72 10 44 30* – Menu (€22), €27 – Carte €34/53

◆ This 1980s hotel, reflected in the Olympic swimming pool, offers a superb spa, fitness facilities, tennis and squash courts, as well as golf practice areas. Modern rooms. Seafood takes pride of place on the menu of the Brasserie Lyon Plage.

Cité Internationale

Hilton rm, VISA

70 quai Ch. de Gaulle ✉ 69006 – ☎ 04 78 17 50 50 – reservations.lyon@hilton.com – Fax 04 78 17 52 52 *p. 7* GU **a**

200 rm – €148/365 €148/530, ☕ €24

Rest *Blue Elephant* – ☎ *04 78 17 50 00 (closed 21 July-18 August, Saturday lunch and Sunday)* Menu €28 (weekday lunch), €43/55 – Carte €30/51

Rest *Brasserie* – ☎ *04 78 17 51 00* – Menu (€19), €23 (lunch) – Carte €31/56

◆ This impressive modern hotel built in brick and glass is equipped with a comprehensive business centre. Fully equipped bedrooms and apartments facing the Tête d'Or park or the Rhône. Thai specialities and decor at the Blue Elephant. Traditional food is to be found at the Brasserie.

De la Cité rest, VISA

22 quai Ch.-de-Gaulle ✉ 69006 – ☎ 04 78 17 86 86 – hoteldelacite@concorde-hotel.com – Fax 04 78 17 86 99 *p. 6* HU **g**

159 rm – €95/320 €95/320, ☕ €22 – 5 suites

Rest – Menu (€20), €23/36 – Carte €42/67

◆ This modern building designed by Renzo Piano stands between the Tête d'Or park and the Rhône. Bright rooms decorated in a contemporary vein. Traditional meals (buffet lunch). Terrace overlooking the patio of the Cité Internationale. Cocktail bar.

Les Brotteaux

Du Parc without rest
16 bd des Brotteaux ✉ 69006 Ⓜ Brotteaux – ☎ 04 72 83 12 20 – accueil@hotelduparc-lyon.com – Fax 04 78 52 14 32 – Closed 1st-15 August p. 7 HV **b**
23 rm – €86/116 €96/126, €10,50
◆ Hotel situated between the Brotteaux train station and the Tête d'Or park. The rooms, quieter at the back, have a welcoming decor and modern fittings.

La Part-Dieu

Radisson SAS Lyon and Rhône valley, rest,
129 r. Servient (32th Floor) ✉ 69003 Ⓜ Part Dieu – ☎ 04 78 63 55 00 – info.lyon@radissonsas.com – Fax 04 78 63 55 20 p. 7 GX **u**
245 rm – €120/300 €120/300, €20
Rest *L'Arc-en-Ciel* – *(closed 15 July-25 August, Saturday lunch and Sunday)* Menu €42/90 – Carte €62/96
Rest *Bistrot de la Tour* – *(closed Saturday and Sunday) (lunch only)* Menu (€16), €19 – Carte €24/43
◆ At the top of the "pencil" (100m high), interior layout inspired by the houses of old Lyons: interior courtyards and superimposed galleries. Exceptional view from some rooms. The Arc-en-Ciel is on the 32nd floor of the tower. Packed at lunchtime.

Novotel La Part-Dieu rm,
47 bd Vivier-Merle ✉ 69003 Ⓜ Part Dieu – ☎ 04 72 13 51 51 – h0735@accor.com – Fax 04 72 13 51 99 p. 9 HX **a**
124 rm – €118/153 €126/161, €13,50 – **Rest** – Menu (€19), €24 – Carte €24/43
◆ Two minutes from the railway station. The rooms are being progressively revamped in line with latest Novotel standards. Lounge-bar with an Internet area. This Novotel restaurant is practical for business travellers with a train to catch or between meetings.

Créqui Part-Dieu rm,
37 r. Bonnel ✉ 69003 Ⓜ Place Guichard – ☎ 04 78 60 20 47 – inforesa@hotel-crequi.com – Fax 04 78 62 21 12 – Closed August, Saturday and Sunday p. 7 GX **s**
46 rm – €71/150 €71/160, €12 – 3 suites
Rest *Le Magistère* – Menu (€15), €18/30 – Carte €26/41
◆ The establishment is located opposite the law courts district. The renovated rooms are decorated in warm tones; those in the new wing are particularly modern in style.

La Guillotière

De Noailles without rest
30 cours Gambetta ✉ 69007 Ⓜ Guillotière – ☎ 04 78 72 40 72 – hotel-de-noailles@wanadoo.fr – Fax 04 72 71 09 10 – Closed 1st-25 August
24 rm – €79/99 €86/115, €14 p. 9 GY **s**
◆ The well-kept rooms open onto the inner courtyard or the garden. The garage and nearby underground station make this a handy spot.

Gerland

Novotel Gerland rm,
70 av. Leclerc ✉ 69007 – ☎ 04 72 71 11 11 – h0736@accor.com – Fax 04 72 71 11 00 p. 4 BQ **e**
186 rm – €85/168 €95/178, €14 – **Rest** – Menu (€20), €24 – Carte €26/42
◆ Near Tony Garnier market and the football stadium, this Novotel has been renovated from top to toe: attractive modern rooms, hi-tech bar lounge and spacious seminar facilities. Pleasant rendering of the chain's latest style; traditional menu.

Montchat-Monplaisir

Mercure Lumière rm,
69 cours A. Thomas ✉ 69003 Ⓜ Sans Souci – ☎ 04 78 53 76 76 – h1535@accor.com – Fax 04 72 36 97 65 p. 9 HZ **e**
78 rm – €68/170 €69/190, €13,50 – **Rest** – *(closed 8-16 August, Saturday, Sunday and holidays)* Menu €25 – Carte €24/40
◆ Located near the Lumière film studios, this Mercure has been decorated in a fashion inspired by the cinema. The practical rooms are all identical. Photos recalling the history of film adorn the contemporary dining room.

in Villeurbanne – **pop. 124 215** – **alt. 168 m** – ✉ **69100**

Congrès rest, VISA AE
pl. Cdt Rivière – ✆ 04 72 69 16 16 – reservation@hoteldescongres.com – Fax 04 78 94 64 86 – Closed 1st-24 August and 24 December-4 January p. 7 HV **m**
134 rm – †€ 113/134 ††€ 124/145, ☕ € 15 – ½ P € 102/113
Rest – *(closed Friday dinner, Saturday and Sunday)* Menu (€ 19), € 26/29 bi – Carte € 27/35
◆ Concrete architecture near the Tête d'Or park. Standard 1980s decor. The Prestige rooms are more spacious and well cared for. Traditional fare in the restaurant.

Holiday Inn Garden Court rm, rest, VISA AE
130 bd du 11 Nov. 1918 – ✆ 04 78 89 95 95 – higcvilleurbanne@alliance-hospitality.com – Fax 04 72 43 91 55 p. 5 CP **r**
79 rm – †€ 64/200 ††€ 64/200, ☕ € 13
Rest – *(closed Saturday lunch and Sunday lunch)* Menu € 20/27 – Carte € 23/37
◆ The comfortable, well-appointed rooms, modular conference areas and practical location make this hotel popular with a business clientele. Bright sunny dining room and traditional menu.

in Bron – **pop. 37 369** – **alt. 204 m** – ✉ **69500**

Novotel Bron rm, VISA AE
260 av. J. Monnet – ✆ 04 72 15 65 65 – h0436@accor.com – Fax 04 72 15 09 09 p. 5 DR **f**
190 rm – †€ 87/180 ††€ 94/187, ☕ € 14
Rest – Menu € 23 – Carte € 25/44
◆ Well equipped for seminars, this handy hotel now sports a decor and level of comfort in keeping with the new Novotel standards. Contemporary restaurant and traditional menu, conveniently located just outside Lyons.

Restaurants

Paul Bocuse VISA AE
✿✿✿
au pont de Collonges, 12 km north along the Saône (D 433, D 51) ✉ 69660 – ✆ 04 72 42 90 90 – paul.bocuse@bocuse.fr – Fax 04 72 27 85 87 p. 4 BP
Rest – Menu € 125/200 – Carte € 102/183
Spec. Soupe aux truffes noires VGE. Loup en croûte feuilletée. Volaille de Bresse en vessie "Mère Fillioux". **Wines** Pouilly-Fuissé, Moulin-à-Vent.
◆ The culinary world beats a path to the colourful, elegant inn of "Monsieur Paul". His celebrated dishes in the dining room, murals of great chefs in the courtyard.

Pierre Orsi VISA AE
✿
3 pl. Kléber ✉ 69006 Ⓜ Masséna – ✆ 04 78 89 57 68 – orsi@relaischateaux.com – Fax 04 72 44 93 34 – Closed Sunday and Monday except public holidays p. 7 GV **e**
Rest – Menu € 60 (weekday lunch), € 85/115 – Carte € 70/155
Spec. Ravioles de foie gras de canard au jus de porto et truffes. Homard acadien en carapace. Pigeonneau en cocotte aux gousses d'ail confites. **Wines** Mâcon-Villages, Saint-Joseph.
◆ This old house is home to elegant dining rooms and a rose garden terrace. Fine up-to-date cuisine and good wine list.

Les Terrasses de Lyon – Hôtel Villa Florentine ≤ Lyon, VISA AE
✿
25 montée St-Barthélémy ✉ 69005 Ⓜ Fourvière – ✆ 04 72 56 56 56 – lesterrassesdelyon@villaflorentine.com – Fax 04 72 40 90 56 – Closed Sunday and Monday p. 6 EX **s**
Rest – Menu € 48 (weekday lunch except July-August)/104 – Carte € 84/127
Spec. Homard en fine gelée, tartine de guacamole et barigoule de légumes. Darne de turbot rôti à la fève de cacao, pommes soufflées. Filet de bœuf de Salers cuit au sautoir, jus corsé au vieux vinaigre de vin. **Wines** Condrieu, Saint-Joseph.
◆ Breathtaking view of Lyon from the terrace. The interior and conservatory are stylish and the modern cuisine subtly enhances excellent produce.

XXX **Nicolas Le Bec**

✿✿ *14 r. Grolée ✉ 69002 Ⓜ Cordeliers – ☎ 04 78 42 15 00 – restaurant@nicolaslebec.com – Fax 04 72 40 98 97 – Closed 3-24 August, 1st-11 January, Sunday, Monday and public holidays* p. 6 FX **y**

Rest – Menu € 58 (weekday lunch), € 98/148 – Carte € 75/100

Spec. Foie gras, anguille fumée et asperges vertes au bouillon de poule. Homard breton poché minute. Tartelette au caramel mou. **Wines** Moulin-à-Vent, Viognier.

◆ Restaurant with a modern welcoming feel, serving food that is as refined as it is subtle. Wine list rejoicing in the nation's diversity; smoking lounge.

XXX **Christian Têtedoie**

✿ *54 quai Pierre Scize ✉ 69005 – ☎ 04 78 29 40 10 – restaurant@tetedoie.com – Fax 04 72 07 05 65 – Closed 4-24 August, 16-22 February, Saturday lunch, Monday lunch and Sunday* p. 6 EX **n**

Rest – Menu € 48 (weekdays)/80 – Carte € 64/76

Spec. Fraîcheur de concombre aux agrumes, coquillages et homard (spring-summer). Pastilla de pigeonneau rôti aux agrumes et fleur d'oranger. Carpaccio de figues au vinaigre de Banyuls. **Wines** Brouilly, Coteaux du Tricastin.

◆ On the banks of the Saône, this smart cosy restaurant sports a happy mix of old and new. Contemporary cuisine and a magnificent wine list with over 700 appellations.

XXX **Les Trois Dômes** – Hôtel Sofitel — Lyon,

✿ *20 quai Gailleton , (8th Floor) ✉ 69002 Ⓜ Bellecour – ☎ 04 72 41 20 97 – reservation@les-3-domes.com – Fax 04 72 40 05 50 – Closed 27 July-28 August, 24 February-4 March, Sunday and Monday* p. 8 FY **p**

Rest – Menu € 53 (weekday lunch), € 75/143 bi – Carte € 92/121

Spec. Quenelle de brochet soufflée, écrevisses, coques et palourdes. Saint-Jacques au thé vert et parfum de truffe (end December to mid February). Agneau de lait au pistou, poupeton d'aubergine et fèves (end January to mid May). **Wines** Condrieu, Côte-Rôtie.

◆ Admire the matchless panorama from the top floor of the Sofitel hotel, where you can also enjoy delicious cuisine in keeping with current tastes. Flawless wine list.

XXX **Auberge de Fond Rose** (Gérard Vignat)

✿ *23 quai G. Clemenceau ✉ 69300 Caluire-et-Cuire – ☎ 04 78 29 34 61 – contact@aubergedefondrose.com – Fax 04 72 00 28 67 – Closed 18 February-5 March, Tuesday lunch October-April, Sunday dinner and Monday except public holidays*

Rest – Menu € 38 bi (weekday lunch), € 51/78 – Carte € 75/80 p. 6 EU **v**

Spec. Mesclun de langoustines aux céréales et citron confit. Féra du lac Léman au caviar d'aubergine. Pigeonneau cuit dans la rôtissoire, jus aux olives. **Wines** Côte-Rôtie, Cornas.

◆ This handsome 1920s house features an idyllic terrace leading into the garden planted with ancient trees. Fine up-to-date menu and interesting wine list.

XXX **Mathieu Viannay**

✿ *47 av. Foch ✉ 69006 Ⓜ Foch – ☎ 04 78 89 55 19 – Fax 04 78 89 08 39 – Closed 2-31 August, 14-22 February, Saturday and Sunday* p. 7 GV **s**

Rest – Menu (€ 30), € 35 (lunch), € 53/90 – Carte € 66/91

Spec. Pâté en croûte de volaille de Bresse et foie gras. Tombée d'ormeaux et pignons de pin aux champignons des bois (October to June). Fricassée de homard et ris de veau de lait à l'émulsion de carapace (winter and spring). **Wines** Beaujolais blanc, Côte-Rôtie.

◆ Resolutely modern dining room with parquet flooring, colourful chairs and an original candelabra created by the Lyon designer, Alain Vavro. Delicious contemporary cuisine.

XX **Auberge de l'Île** (Jean-Christophe Ansanay-Alex) (dinner)

✿✿ *On Barbe Island ✉ 69009 – ☎ 04 78 83 99 49 – info@aubergedelile.com – Fax 04 78 47 80 46 – Closed Sunday and Monday*

Rest – Menu € 60 (weekday lunch), € 90/120 p. 4 BP **e**

Spec. Salade tiède exotique de homard breton. Saint-Jacques à la feuille d'or, beurre de truffe noire (winter). Crème glacée à la réglisse, cornet de pain d'épice. **Wines** Condrieu, Côte-Rôtie.

◆ Situated on Ile Barbe, this charming 17C inn is known for its fine cuisine made from local, seasonal produce. The chef himself comes to your table to announce his legendary dish of the day.

XX **L'Alexandrin** (Laurent Rigal)
✿
83 r. Moncey ✉ 69003 Ⓜ Place Guichard – ✆ 04 72 61 15 69 – lalexandrin@lalexandrin.com – Fax 04 78 62 75 57 – Closed 3-25 August, 21 December-5 January, Sunday and Monday *p. 7* GX **h**
Rest – Menu € 38 (weekday lunch), € 60/115 – Carte € 62/80
Spec. Mousseline de brochet au crémeux d'écrevisse. Filet de bar rôti en croûte d'épices (June to August). Cocotte de légumes aux châtaignes (October to December). **Wines** Saint-Péray, Crozes-Hermitage.
◆ New management and new decor at this popular restaurant. Impressive choice of Côtes-du-Rhône, and regional dishes prepared with an original flair. Terrace.

XX **Le Gourmet de Sèze** (Bernard Mariller)
✿
129 r. Sèze ✉ 69006 Ⓜ Masséna – ✆ 04 78 24 23 42 – legourmetdeseze@wanadoo.fr – Fax 04 78 24 66 81 – Closed 8-12 May, 18 July-19 August, 15-23 February, Sunday, Monday and public holidays *p. 7* HV **z**
Rest – *(number of covers limited, pre-book)* Menu (€ 30), € 38 (lunch), € 47/72
Spec. Croustillants de pieds de cochon. Ravioles de langoustines de Loctudy (April to September). Grand dessert. **Wines** Pouilly-Fuissé, Saint-Joseph.
◆ A brand new brown and white look for this restaurant. The classic recipes are cleverly modernised and have universal appeal.

XX **Cazenove**
75 r. Boileau ✉ 69006 Ⓜ Masséna – ✆ 04 78 89 82 92 – orsi@relaischateaux.com – Fax 04 72 44 93 34 – Closed August, Saturday and Sunday *p. 7* GV **k**
Rest – Menu € 35/45 – Carte € 42/107
◆ Low-key ambiance and a fine Belle Époque-inspired interior: upholstered banquettes, mirrors, old-fashioned wall lighting and bronze statues. Traditional, sometimes inventive, cooking.

XX **Le Passage**
8 r. Plâtre ✉ 69001 Ⓜ Hôtel de ville – ✆ 04 78 28 11 16 – restaurant@le-passage.com – Fax 04 72 00 84 34 – Closed August, Sunday, Monday and holidays *p. 8* FX **r**
Rest – Menu € 40/90 – Carte € 47/80
◆ Theatre seats and trompe-l'oeil backdrop in the bistro, more restrained decor in the main room and a courtyard-terrace adorned with frescoes. Reinterpreted classic repertoire.

XX **Fleur de Sel**
3 r. Remparts d'Ainay ✉ 69002 Ⓜ Ampère Victor Hugo – ✆ 04 78 37 40 37 – Fax 04 78 37 26 37 – Closed August, Sunday and Monday *p. 8* FY **q**
Rest – Menu (€ 15), € 19/29 – Carte € 22/43
◆ The light gently filters through the green and yellow curtains of this vast plush dining room. Personalised up-to-date cooking, inspired by spices from near and afar.

XX **J.-C. Pequet**
59 pl. Voltaire ✉ 69003 Ⓜ Saxe Lafayette – ✆ 04 78 95 49 70 – Fax 04 78 62 85 26 – Closed August, 24 December-2 January, Saturday and Sunday *p. 9* GY **v**
Rest – Menu € 34/50
◆ Decor without eccentricity and thoughtful classical cooking based on market produce: a reliable establishment with a regular clientele.

XX **Alex**
44 bd des Brotteaux ✉ 69006 Ⓜ Brotteaux – ✆ 04 78 52 30 11 – chez.alex@club-internet.fr – Fax 04 78 52 34 16 – Closed August, Sunday and Monday
Rest – Menu € 20 (weekday lunch), € 44/59 *p. 8* HX **e**
◆ Restaurant whose smart, refined setting boldly allies colour, designer furniture and contemporary artworks. Menu concocted by the owner-chef from market produce.

XX **La Brunoise**
4 r. A. Boutin ✉ 69100 Villeurbanne Ⓜ Charpennes – ✆ 04 78 52 07 77 – info@labrunoise.fr – Fax 04 72 83 54 96 – Closed 29 July-28 August, Sunday dinner, Monday dinner, Tuesday and Wednesday *p. 5* CP **b**
Rest – Menu € 20 (weekday lunch), € 25/43 – Carte € 24/47
◆ The house specialities decorate the façade. Bright dining room. Modern menu inspired by classic dishes.

XX **La Tassée**

20 r. Charité ✉ 69002 Ⓜ Bellecour – ✆ 04 72 77 79 00 – jpborgeot@latassee.fr – Fax 04 72 40 05 91 – Closed Sun p. 8 FY **u**

Rest – Menu (€ 23), € 26 (lunch), € 29/70 – Carte € 34/57

◆ Celebrities pin their portraits on the walls of this local institution, also adorned with a Bacchic fresco painted in the 1950s. Bistro ambiance and Lyons cooking.

XX **Brasserie Georges**

30 cours Verdun ✉ 69002 Ⓜ Perrache – ✆ 04 72 56 54 54 – brasserie.georges@wanadoo.fr – Fax 04 78 42 51 65 p. 8 FZ **b**

Rest – Menu € 20/22 – Carte € 24/45

◆ Good beer and good cheer since 1836, an Art Deco setting meticulously preserved since 1925 and relaxed ambiance: this listed brasserie is one of the landmarks of Lyons. Non-smoking.

XX **La Voûte - Chez Léa**

11 pl. A. Gourju ✉ 69002 Ⓜ Bellecour – ✆ 04 78 42 01 33 – Fax 04 78 37 36 41 – Closed Sun. p. 8 FY **e**

Rest – Menu € 19 (weekday lunch), € 28/40 – Carte € 29/48

◆ One of the oldest restaurants in Lyons, it continues to brilliantly uphold the region's gastronomic traditions. Welcoming ambiance and decor. Game menu in autumn.

XX **Olivier Degand**

90 r. Duguesclin ✉ 69006 Ⓜ Foch – ✆ 04 78 89 12 21 – contact@olivier-degand.com – Fax 04 78 89 12 21 – Closed August, Sunday, Monday and holidays p. 7 GV **n**

Rest – Menu € 18 (weekday lunch), € 31/42 – Carte € 46/56

◆ Contemporary decor in saffron tones, frequently changed art exhibitions and carefully laid tables. Creative menu that varies with the seasons.

XX **Le Potiquet**

27 r. de l'Arbre Sec ✉ 69001 Ⓜ Hotel de ville – ✆ 04 78 30 65 44 – lepotiquet@free.fr – Closed August, Saturday lunch, Sunday and Monday p. 6 FX **w**

Rest – Menu € 28/34 – Carte € 32/46

◆ Elegance and sobriety set the scene for this pleasant family restaurant that serves updated cuisine, often summery in flavour, always well prepared and sometimes surprising.

X **Argenson Gerland**

40 allée P.-de-Coubertin, at Gerland ✉ 69007 Ⓜ Stade de Gerland – ✆ 04 72 73 72 73 – argenson2@wanadoo.fr – Fax 04 72 73 72 74 p. 4 BR **a**

Rest – Menu € 23 (weekdays)/28 – Carte € 32/57

◆ One of the brasseries opened by Paul Bocuse, near the Gerland stadium. Stylish interior and pleasant shaded terrace. Traditional menu with a distinct southern flavour.

X **Le Nord**

18 r. Neuve ✉ 69002 Ⓜ Hôtel de ville – ✆ 04 72 10 69 69 – commercial@brasseries-bocuse.com – Fax 04 72 10 69 68 p. 8 FX **p**

Rest – Menu (€ 21), € 23 (weekdays)/28 (weekend) – Carte € 26/55

◆ Authentic 1900s decor in the first of Bocuse's brasseries: banquettes, colourful tiled floor, wood panelling and spherical lamps. Traditional cuisine.

X **L'Est**

14 pl. J. Ferry, (Brotteaux station) ✉ 69006 Ⓜ Brotteaux – ✆ 04 37 24 25 26 – Fax 04 37 24 25 25 p. 7 HX **v**

Rest – Menu (€ 21), € 23 (weekdays)/28 (weekend) – Carte € 31/57

◆ Trendy brasserie popular with the locals. The kitchens can be seen from the dining room, miniature trains chug round above diners' heads and world cooking is on the menu.

X **L'Ouest**

1 quai Commerce, North via the banks of the Saône (D 51) ✉ 69009 – ✆ 04 37 64 64 64 – commercial@brasseries-bocuse.com – Fax 04 37 64 64 65

Rest – Menu (€ 21), € 23 (weekdays)/28 (weekend) – Carte € 31/56

◆ A distinctive modern building of wood, concrete and metal. Bar, giant screens, open kitchen, river facing terrace and exotic dishes. Bocuse is on a western course!

33 Cité

33 quai Charles de Gaulle ✉ 69006 – ✆ 04 37 45 45 45 – 33cite.restaurant@free.fr – Fax 04 37 45 45 46

Rest – Menu (€ 19), € 23 (weekdays)/27 – Carte € 29/52 *p. 7* HU **t**

◆ Contemporary designer setting opposite the Salle 3000 at the Cité Internationale. View of the Parc de la Tête d'Or through the large windows. Choice of modern and classic dishes.

Le Sud

11 pl. Antonin Poncet ✉ 69002 Ⓜ Bellecour – ✆ 04 72 77 80 00 – Fax 04 72 77 80 01

Rest – Menu (€ 21), € 23 (weekdays)/28 (weekend) – Carte € 30/48 *p. 8* FY **x**

◆ "Le Sud" is another of chef Paul Bocuse's creations, with Mediterranean cuisine and decor. Delightful summer terrace overlooking the square.

Le Contretête

55 quai Pierre Scize ✉ 69005 – ✆ 04 78 29 41 29 – restaurant@tetedoie.com – Fax 04 72 07 05 65 – Closed 4-24 August, Saturday lunch and Sunday *p. 6* EX **a**

Rest – Menu (€ 17) – Carte € 27/32

◆ This bistro, run by the restaurateur Christian Têtedoie, focuses on authentic home cooking. An interior decor strewn with old objects and utensils.

Le Gabion

13 bd E. Deruelle ✉ 69003 Ⓜ Part Dieu – ✆ 04 72 60 81 57 – legabion@wanadoo.fr – Fax 04 78 60 83 18 – Closed 2-24 August, Monday dinner, Sunday and holidays *p. 7* HX **b**

Rest – Menu (€ 16), € 19 (lunch)/25 – Carte € 26/45

◆ Unusual modern decor with a wall of pebbles in steel mesh by the architect Chaduc. Seafood and fish dishes, sometimes with a sprinkling of Eastern spices.

Les Comédiens

2 pl. Célestins ✉ 69002 Ⓜ Bellecour – ✆ 04 78 42 08 26 – lescomedienslyon@aol.com – Fax 04 72 40 04 51 – Closed 1st-21 August, Sunday and Monday

Rest – Menu € 22 (weekday lunch), € 28/58 – Carte € 22/55 *p. 8* FY **y**

◆ This restaurant is located near the Célestins theatre. A fashionable colour scheme of cream and chocolate tones. Traditional menu and a few regional dishes.

Francotte

8 pl. Célestins ✉ 69002 Ⓜ Bellecour – ✆ 04 78 37 38 64 – infos@francotte.fr – Fax 04 78 38 20 35 – Closed 1st-20 August, Sunday and Monday *p. 8* FY **r**

Rest – Menu € 23/33 – Carte € 28/43

◆ Brasserie-style cuisine in a bistro/bouchon-inspired setting adorned with photos of matriarchs and famous chefs from the region. Breakfasts served in the morning; tea room in the afternoon.

La Machonnerie

36 r. Tramassac ✉ 69005 Ⓜ Ampère Victor Hugo – ✆ 04 78 42 24 62 – felix@lamachonnerie.com – Fax 04 72 40 23 32 – Closed 15-30 July, 2 weeks in January, Sunday and lunch except Saturday *p. 8* EY **n**

Rest – *(pre-book)* Menu € 20/43 bi – Carte € 25/47

◆ The traditions of informal service, a friendly atmosphere and authentic regional cuisine are perpetuated in this typical neighbourhood *mâchon*. Attractive lounge devoted to jazz.

La Terrasse St-Clair

2 Grande Rue St-Clair ✉ 69300 Caluire-et-Cuire – ✆ 04 72 27 37 37 – Fax 04 72 27 37 38 – Closed 5-22 August, 23 December-15 January, Sunday and Monday *p. 7* GU **s**

Rest – Menu € 24

◆ There is a slight air of an open-air dance hall about the restaurant and especially the terrace shaded by plane trees. Pétanque pitch.

Les Adrets

30 r. Boeuf ✉ 69005 Ⓜ Vieux Lyon Cathédrale Saint Jean – ✆ 04 78 38 24 30 – Fax 04 78 42 79 52 – Closed 1st-10 May, August, Christmas holidays, Saturday and Sunday *p. 6* EX **v**

Rest – Menu € 14 bi (lunch), € 22/42 – Carte € 32/51

◆ A venerable establishment in Vieux Lyons. Rustic interior with exposed beams, tiled floor and a partial view of the kitchens. Hearty traditional dishes.

L'Étage

4 pl. Terreaux, (2nd floor) ✉ 69001 Ⓜ Hôtel de ville – ✆ 04 78 28 19 59 – Fax 04 78 28 19 59 – Closed 21 July-21 August, Sunday and Monday *p. 8* FX **x**

Rest – *(pre-book)* Menu € 22 (lunch)/55 – Carte € 38/64

◆ Located on the building's second floor (no lift), this refitted silk worker's studio has a stylish up-to-date setting and is popular with Lyon folk. Appetising, creative menu.

Les Oliviers

20 r. Sully ✉ 69006 Ⓜ Foch – ✆ 04 78 89 07 09 – Fax 04 78 89 08 39 – Closed 2-24 August, 9-15 February, Saturday and Sunday *p. 7* GV **f**

Rest – Menu (€ 16), € 23/31 – Carte € 26/39

◆ A tiny corner of Provence hidden in Paris' 6th district: intimate, low key dining room in warm colours and a tasty, sun-drenched cuisine, including bouillabaisse.

Le Comptoir des Marronniers

8 r. Marronniers ✉ 69002 Ⓜ Bellecour – ✆ 04 72 77 10 00 – reservation@leondelyon.com – Fax 04 72 77 10 01 – Closed 2-25 August, Monday lunch and Sunday

Rest – Menu € 24 *p. 8* FY **v**

◆ In a pedestrian street near Bellecour square, a "chef's bistro", seemingly haphazardly decorated with a profusion of objects and posters relating to cooking. Modern reasonably priced cuisine.

Cuisine & Dépendances

46 r. Ferrandière ✉ 69002 Ⓜ Cordeliers – ✆ 04 78 37 44 84 – restaurant@cuisineetdependances.com – Fax 04 78 38 33 28 – Closed 1st-20 August and Sunday and Monday *p. 8* FX **s**

Rest – Menu (€ 15), € 20 (lunch), € 25/49 – Carte € 37/54

◆ Elongated little dining room, designer decor and welcoming lounge ambiance, serving inventive cuisine with a strong fish focus: already a firm favourite with the locals.

Cuisine & Dépendances Acte II

68 r. de la Charité ✉ 69002 Ⓜ Perrache – ✆ 04 78 37 45 02 – cuisineetdependancesacte2@hotmail.fr – Fax 04 78 37 52 46 – Closed 3-18 August, Sunday and Monday

Rest – Menu (€ 15), € 25/49 – Carte € 38/54 *p. 8* FY **d**

◆ Hot on the heels of the first venture, Act II has taken over the renowned former bistro of "la mère Brazier". Signature fish and seafood in a modernised setting.

Maison Villemanzy

< Lyon,

25 montée St-Sébastien ✉ 69001 Ⓜ Croix Paquet – ✆ 04 72 98 21 21 – reservation@leondelyon.com – Fax 04 72 98 21 22 – Closed 22 December-16 January, Monday lunch and Sunday *p. 6* FV **h**

Rest – *(pre-book)* Menu € 24

◆ Clinging to the slopes of the Croix Rousse this terraced house commands a splendid view of the town. Home cooking, a specials menu and a 1940s bistro-style interior.

Le Bistrot du Palais

220 r. Duguesclin ✉ 69003 Ⓜ Place Guichard – ✆ 04 78 14 21 21 – reservation@leondelyon.com – Fax 04 78 14 21 22 – Closed 2-25 August, Monday dinner and Sunday

Rest – Menu € 24 *p. 9* GY **r**

◆ Attractive bistro located opposite the courthouse offering welcoming decor, pleasant enclosed terrace and traditional cooking varying in accordance with market availability.

Bernachon Passion

42 cours Franklin-Roosevelt ✉ 69006 Ⓜ Foch – ✆ 04 78 52 23 65 – bernachon.chocolats@free.fr – Fax 04 78 52 67 77 – Closed 27 July-26 August, Sunday, Monday and holidays *p. 7* GV **r**

Rest – *(lunch only) (number of covers limited, pre-book)* Menu € 26 – Carte € 31/44

◆ This restaurant is run by Paul Bocuse's daughter and her husband, owner of the renowned chocolate shop next door. Classic menu; dish of the day at lunchtime. Tea room.

Magali et Martin

11 r. des Augustins ✉ 69001 Ⓜ Place des Terreaux – ✆ 04 72 00 88 01 – Closed 4-24 August, 24 December-14 January, Saturday and Sunday *p. 6* FX **j**

Rest – Menu € 19 (lunch), € 28/50 – Carte € 27/36

◆ Magali is in charge of welcoming guests and advising them on their choice of wine. Martin for his part is responsible for the tasty cuisine inspired by local market produce. A winning duet!

Le Saint Florent

106 cours Gambetta ✉ 69007 Ⓜ Garibaldi – ✆ 04 78 72 32 68 – Fax 04 78 72 32 68 – Closed 5-10 May, 28 July-16 August, Saturday lunch, Monday lunch and Sunday *p. 9* HY **b**

Rest – Menu € 15 (weekday lunch), € 21/35 – Carte € 25/50

◆ In Lyons, the Bresse embassy is at 106 rue Gambetta: from the floor to the ceiling, and the starter to the dessert, this pleasant restaurant celebrates poultry in all its forms.

Thomas

6 r. Laurencin ✉ 69002 Ⓜ Bellecour – ✆ 04 72 56 04 76 – info@restaurant-thomas.com – Fax 04 72 56 04 76 – Closed 1st-15 May, 7-21 August, 24 December-2, Saturday and Sunday *p. 8* FY **w**

Rest – Menu € 18 (lunch)/39 – Carte approx. € 37

◆ The enthusiastic young chef proposes a theme dinner (Nice, Pork, Morocco) once a month in his inviting bistro. Take away service of cooked dishes.

Le Verre et l'Assiette

20 Grande Rue de Vaise ✉ 69009 – ✆ 04 78 83 32 25 – leverreetlassiette@free.fr – Closed 26 July-19 August, 7-16 February, dinner except Thursday and Friday, Saturday, Sunday and public holidays *p. 4* BP **d**

Rest – Menu (€ 18 bi), € 28/39

◆ The talented chef reinvents and personalises traditional Lyon specialities as well as a few French classics. Stone and wood prevail in the modern decor. Smiling service.

Le Bistrot de St-Paul

2 quai de Bondy ✉ 69005 Ⓜ Vieux Lyon Cathédrale St-Jean – ✆ 04 78 28 63 19 – jplabaste@orange.fr – Fax 04 78 28 63 19 – Closed 1st-7 May, 1st-23 August, Saturday lunch from 15 May to 15 September and Sunday *p. 6* FX **g**

Rest – Menu € 13,50 (weekday lunch), € 20/31 – Carte € 32/57

◆ Cassoulet, duck breast, Bordeaux and Cahors wines, etc.: the essence of south-west France in this friendly bistro on an embankment of the Saône.

La Famille

18 r. Duviard ✉ 69004 Ⓜ Croix Rousse – ✆ 04 72 98 83 90 – lafamille.croixrousse@yahoo.fr – Closed 12-26 August, 1st-14 January, Sunday and Monday

Rest – Menu € 18 (lunch), € 21/25 – Carte € 21/32 *p. 6* FV **m**

◆ Old family photos adorn the walls of this relaxed restaurant. A slate lists the daily specials of traditional dishes that vary according to market availability.

BOUCHONS : *regional food and wines in a typical Lyonnais ambiance*

Daniel et Denise

156 r. Créqui ✉ 69003 Ⓜ Place Guichard – ✆ 04 78 60 66 53 – Fax 04 78 60 66 53 – Closed August, 23 December-3 January, Saturday, Sunday and public holidays *p. 7* GX **b**

Rest – bistrot Carte € 28/41

◆ Attractive well-worn setting and a relaxed informal atmosphere in this welcoming bistro, that serves traditionally prepared tasty Lyon specialities.

Le Garet

7 r. Garet ✉ 69001 Ⓜ Hôtel de ville – ✆ 04 78 28 16 94 – legaret@wanadoo.fr – Fax 04 72 00 06 84 – Closed 25 July-25 August, 14-22 February, Saturday and Sunday *p. 6* FX **a**

Rest – *(pre-book)* Menu € 18 (lunch)/23 – Carte € 20/35

◆ This institution in Lyon is well-known to lovers of good cooking: calf's head, tripe, quenelles and andouillettes served in a relaxed characteristic setting.

Café des Fédérations

8 r. Major Martin ✉ 69001 Ⓜ Hôtel de ville – ✆ 04 78 28 26 00 – yr@lesfedeslyon.com – Fax 04 72 07 74 52 – Closed 22 December-2 January and Sunday

Rest – *(pre-book)* Menu € 20 (lunch)/24 (dinner) *p. 6* FX **z**

◆ Checked tablecloths, tightly packed tables, giant sausages hanging from the ceiling and a relaxed informal atmosphere: a genuine "bouchon" for sure!

Le Jura

25 r. Tupin ✉ 69002 Ⓜ Cordeliers – ✆ 04 78 42 20 57 – Closed August, Monday from September to April, Saturday from May to September and Sunday p. 8 FX d

Rest – *(pre-book)* Menu € 20 – Carte € 25/38

◆ This authentic "bouchon", in existence since 1864, has scrupulously preserved a stylish 1930s decor. Traditional tasty dishes of Lyons.

SURROUNDING AREA

in Rillieux-la-Pape 7 km by ① D 483 and D 484 – pop. 28 367 – alt. 269 m – ✉ 69140

Larivoire (Bernard Constantin)

chemin des Iles – ✆ 04 78 88 50 92 – bernard.constantin@larivoire.com – Fax 04 78 88 35 22 – Closed 16-30 August, Sunday dinner, Monday dinner and Tuesday

Rest – Menu € 35 (weekday lunch), € 49/87 – Carte € 72/90

Spec. Savarin de saumon d'Écosse et poêlée de crevettes. Royale de foies blonds aux écrevisses. Ris de veau braisé à la réduction de béarnaise. **Wines** Côte Roannaise, Beaujolais.

◆ Three generations of the same family have been running this attractive house built in the early 20C. Refined interior, popular summer terrace and updated classic cuisine.

in Meyzieu 14 km by ③ and D 517 – pop. 28 009 – alt. 201 m – ✉ 69330

de Lyon Villette-d'AnthonNortheast: 12 km by D 6, ✆ 04 78 31 11 33.

La Petite Auberge du Pont d'Herbens

32 r. V. Hugo – ✆ 04 78 31 41 09 – direction@petite-auberge-pont-dherbens.com – Fax 04 78 04 34 93 – Closed March, Sunday dinner and Monday except lunch on public holidays

Rest – Menu (€ 22), € 26 (weekday lunch)/56 – Carte € 32/56

◆ Not far from the Grand Large Lake, this pleasant inn boasts a plush dining room and a VIP area (terrace and sitting room). Traditional repertoire and fine wine list.

in Genas 12 km east by Genas road (D 29) - DQ – pop. 11 140 – alt. 218 m – ✉ 69740

Syndicat d'initiative, 55, rue de la République ✆ 04 72 79 05 31, Fax 04 72 79 05 31

Ambassadeur

36 r. Antoine-Pinay – ✆ 04 78 40 02 02 – contact@ambassadeur-hotel.fr – Fax 04 78 90 23 53 – Closed 25 December-1st January

84 rm – € 110/130 € 110/130, € 12 – 6 suites

Rest – *(closed 25 July-24 August, Saturday and Sunday)* Menu € 24 – Carte € 32/45

◆ A new hotel popular with business travellers for its relatively spacious, well-appointed, restful and contemporary-style bedrooms (wenge furniture). A minimalist-style restaurant serving contemporary cuisine. Japanese garden.

in Tassin-la-Demi-Lune 5 km west (A6, exit 36) - APQ – pop. 15 977 – alt. 220 m – ✉ 69160

Novotel Tassin

13D av. V. Hugo – ✆ 04 78 64 68 69 – h1201@accor.com – Fax 04 78 64 61 11

103 rm – € 101/138 € 111/148, € 13,50 – **Rest** – Menu € 27/50 – Carte € 19/39 p. 4 AP n

◆ This modern hotel, near a large intersection not far from the Fourvière tunnel, provides good, standard Novotel-style rooms. Restaurant overlooking a pleasant pool in the hotel. Service until midnight at the Novotel Café.

in Ecully 7 km west (A6, exit 36) - AP – pop. 18 011 – alt. 240 m – ✉ 69130

Les Hautes Bruyères without rest

5 chemin des Hautes Bruyères – ✆ 04 78 35 52 38 – htesbruyeres@wanadoo.fr – Fax 04 78 35 52 38 p. 4 AP d

5 rm – € 120/140 € 130/180

◆ Once belonging to a nearby chateau and surrounded by parkland, this former 19C gardener's house offers an authentic atmosphere and elegant surroundings.

XXX **Saisons**

Château du Vivier, 8 chemin Trouillat – ✆ 04 72 18 02 20 – Fax 04 78 43 33 51 – Closed 4-25 August, 19 December-5 January, Wednesday dinner, Saturday and Sunday

Rest – Menu € 26 (lunch)/48 *p. 4* AP **b**

◆ A 19C château and grounds, home to an international catering school founded in 1990 under the leadership of Paul Bocuse. Students prepare and serve dishes.

in Charbonnières-les-Bains **8 km by ⑨ and N 7 – pop. 4 377 – alt. 233 m – ✉ 69260**

Lacroix Laval Park: château de la Poupée★.

Le Pavillon de la Rotonde

3 av. du Casino – ✆ 04 78 87 79 79 – contact@pavillon-rotonde.com – Fax 04 78 87 79 78 – Closed 20 July-20 August

16 rm – †€ 295 ††€ 325/525, ☕ € 24 – **Rest *La Rotonde*** – see restaurant listing

◆ A stone's throw from the casino, a luxurious hotel with contemporary decor and discreet Art Deco touches. Spacious rooms with terrace giving onto the gardens. Heated indoor swimming pool and spa.

Mercure Charbonnières rest,

78 bis rte de Paris, (D 307) – ✆ 04 78 34 72 79 – h0345@accor.com – Fax 04 78 34 88 94

60 rm – †€ 58/130 ††€ 63/140, ☕ € 12,50 – **Rest** – *(closed 9-24 August, 24 December-4 January, Saturday, Sunday and holidays)* Menu (€ 20), € 26

◆ The hotel is in a strategic position, a stone's throw from the regional council. The rooms have undergone a facelift in shimmering colours. Designer restaurant lit by a large liner-style window. Menu in keeping with current taste.

Le Beaulieu without rest

19 av. Gén. de Gaulle – ✆ 04 78 87 12 04 – Fax 04 78 87 00 62

44 rm – †€ 62/68 ††€ 65/110, ☕ € 8

◆ Popular with locals, the same family has been running this town centre hotel for thirty years. Recently renovated, practical rooms.

XXXX **La Rotonde**

at casino Le Lyon Vert ✉ 69890 La Tour de Salvagny – ✆ 04 78 87 00 97 – restaurant-rotonde@g-partouche.fr – Fax 04 78 87 81 39 – Closed 1st-12 May, 20 July-22 August, Sunday and Monday

Rest – Menu € 43 (weekday lunch), € 95/150 – Carte € 98/169

Spec. Grosse morille "jumbo" farcie de cuisses de grenouilles et queues d'écrevisses. Canard étouffé de Challans cuit à la broche rosé. Cannelloni de chocolat amer à la glace crème brûlée. **Wines** Condrieu, Côte-Rôtie.

◆ A renowned gourmet restaurant on the first floor of the casino. Elegant Art Deco-style dining room opening onto the gardens and park, subtle cuisine and fine wine list.

XX **L'Orangerie de Sébastien**

domaine de Lacroix Laval ✉ 69280 Marcy l'Etoile – ✆ 04 78 87 45 95 – info@orangeriedesebastien.fr – Fax 04 78 87 45 96 – Closed 9-22 February, Monday and Tuesday

Rest – Menu € 25 (weekdays)/40 – Carte € 34/51

◆ The 17C castle orangery houses an elegant restaurant serving modern cuisine. Lovely terrace overlooking the gardens. Countless activities on offer on the estate.

Porte de Lyon **10 km by ⑩ (A 6-N 6 junction) – ✉ 69570 Dardilly**

Novotel Lyon Nord rm,

– ✆ 04 72 17 29 29 – h0437@accor.com – Fax 04 78 35 08 45

107 rm – †€ 88/115 ††€ 95/147, ☕ € 13,50 – **Rest** – Menu € 22 – Carte € 22/36

◆ 1970s Novotel in the business park of Dardilly in the process of being brought up to the highest standards of the chain: contemporary comfort and decor. Traditional dishes served in a dining room facing the landscaped garden.

in Limonest **13 km by ⑩, A 6 and D 42 – pop. 2 733 – alt. 390 m – ✉ 69760**

XX **Laurent Bouvier**

25 rte du Puy d'Or, crossroads of D 306 and D 42 – ✆ 04 78 35 12 20 – contact@restaurant-puydor.com – Fax 04 78 64 55 15 – Closed 26 July-25 August, Sunday and Monday

Rest – Menu (€ 22), € 28/76 – Carte € 53/73

◆ A family-run inn entirely refurbished by Alain Vavro in a contemporary style. Creative, classic cuisine in tune with the seasons.

in St-Cyr-au-Mont-d'Or **10 km north by St-Cyr road - BP – pop. 5 392 – alt. 320 m – ✉ 69450**

L'Ermitage ← Lyon and Monts d'Or,
chemin de l'Ermitage, 2.5 km at Sommet du Mont Cindre
– *✆ 04 72 19 69 69 – contact@ermitage-college-hotel.com – Fax 04 72 19 69 71*
28 rm – €135 €135, ☕ €12 – 1 suite – **Rest** – Menu €30
♦ The concept of this new hotel is to combine the extraordinary views of Lyon and the Monts-d'Or with a contemporary decor (picture windows, recycled objects). Peace and quiet guaranteed! Lyonnaise specialities served in the kitchen-cum-dining room; panoramic terrace.

in Collonges-au-Mont-d'Or **12 km north along the Saône (D 433, D 51) - BP – pop. 3 420 – alt. 176 m – ✉ 69660**

see XXXXX ✿✿✿ Paul Bocuse à Lyon

LYONS-LA-FORÊT – **27 Eure** – **304** I5 – **pop. 795** – **alt. 88 m** – **✉ 27480**
Normandy 33 **D2**

Paris 104 – Beauvais 57 – Mantes-la-Jolie 66 – Rouen 35

Office de tourisme, 20, rue de l'Hôtel de Ville ✆ 02 32 49 31 65, Fax 02 32 48 10 60

Les Lions de Beauclerc
7 r. Hôtel de ville – ✆ 02 32 49 18 90 – leslionsdebeauclerc@free.fr – Fax 02 32 48 27 80
6 rm – €59 €62/67, ☕ €9 – ½ P €58/66
Rest – *(closed Tuesday)* Menu €15/28 – Carte €17/33
♦ In the heart of a pretty Norman town, this large brick house is home to enchanting rooms decorated with old furniture and knick-knacks. Breakfast on the terrace in fine weather.

La Licorne rm, rest,
pl. de la Halle – ✆ 02 32 48 24 24 – contact@hotel-licorne.com – Fax 02 32 49 80 09
15 rm – €70/175 €70/175, ☕ €10 – 5 suites – ½ P €75/115
Rest – *(closed Sunday dinner, Tuesday lunch and Monday)* Menu €19/25 – Carte €32/46
♦ A regional-style hotel in the heart of a charming village surrounded by beech trees. Featuring regional furnishings and traditional, individually decorated rooms.

LYS-LEZ-LANNOY – **59 Nord** – **302** H3 – **pop. 13 018** – **alt. 28 m** – **see Roubaix**

LYS-ST-GEORGES – **36 Indre** – **323** G7 – **pop. 213** – **alt. 200 m** – **✉ 36230**

Paris 287 – Argenton-sur-Creuse 29 – Bourges 80 – Châteauroux 29 – La Châtre 22 12 **C3**

XX **Auberge la Forge**
7 r. du Château – ✆ 02 54 30 81 68 – contacts@restaurantlaforge.com – Fax 02 54 30 81 68 – Closed 1st July-6 July, 24 September-10 October, 2-January, Sunday dinner, Tuesday from September to June and Monday
Rest – Menu €18/50 – Carte €29/50
♦ Small village inn covered in ampelopsis. Beams, hexagonal tiles, a fireplace and paintings; rustic decor in harmony with the regional cooking. Pretty verdant terrace.

MACÉ – **61 Orne** – **310** J3 – **see Sées**

MACHILLY – **74 Haute-Savoie** – **328** K3 – **pop. 862** – **alt. 525 m** – **✉ 74140**

Paris 548 – Annemasse 11 – Genève 21 – Thonon-les-Bains 20 46 **F1**

XXX **Le Refuge des Gourmets**
90 rte des Framboises – ✆ 04 50 43 53 87 – chanove@refugedesgourmets.com – Fax 04 50 43 53 76 – Closed 28 July-20 August, 16-25 February, Sunday dinner and Monday
Rest – Menu €30 bi (weekday lunch)/66 – Carte €59/72
♦ Wine-bar entrance hall and elegant Belle Époque-inspired setting inside this "refuge" where gourmets can appreciate the creative, seasonal cuisine.

LA MACHINE (COL) – **26 Drôme** – **332** F4 – **see St-Jean-en-Royans**

MACINAGGIO – 2B Haute-Corse – **345** F2 – see Corse

MÂCON P – 71 Saône-et-Loire – **320** I12 – pop. 34 469 – alt. 175 m – ✉ 71000
Burgundy-Jura 8 **C3**

- Paris 391 – Bourg-en-Bresse 38 – Chalon-sur-Saône 59 – Lyon 71 – Roanne 96
- Office de tourisme, 1, place Saint-Pierre ✆ 03 85 21 07 07, Fax 03 85 40 96 00
- de la Commanderie Crottet L'Aumusse, by Bourg-en-Bresse road: 7 km, ✆ 03 85 30 44 12 ;
- de Mâcon La Salle La Salleby Tournus road: 14 km, ✆ 03 85 36 09 71.
- Musée des Ursulines★ BY M[1] - Musée Lamartine BZ M[2] - Apothicary's ★ of the Hôtel-Dieu BY - ≤★ of Pont St-Laurent.
- Roche de Solutré★★ West: 9 km - Steeple★ of St-André de Bagé church East: 8,5 km.

MÂCON

Barre (Pl. de la)	AYZ	2
Barre (R. de la)	BZ	3
Dombey (R.)	BZ	5
Dufour (R.)	BZ	6
Gaulle (Av. Gén.-de)	BY	7
Laguiche (R. Ph.)	BZ	8
Lamartine (R.)	BYZ	9
Paix (Square de la)	BY	10
Perrier (R.)	AY	12
Poissonnière (Pl.)	BZ	13
Pont (R. du)	BZ	14
Préfecture (R. de la)	BY	15
St-Étienne (Pl.)	BY	17
St-Nizier (R.)	BZ	18
Sigorgne (R.)	BZ	19
Strasbourg (R. de)	BY	20
Ursulines (R. des)	BY	21
11-Nov.-1918 (R. du)	ABY	22
28-Juin-1944 (R.)	BY	24

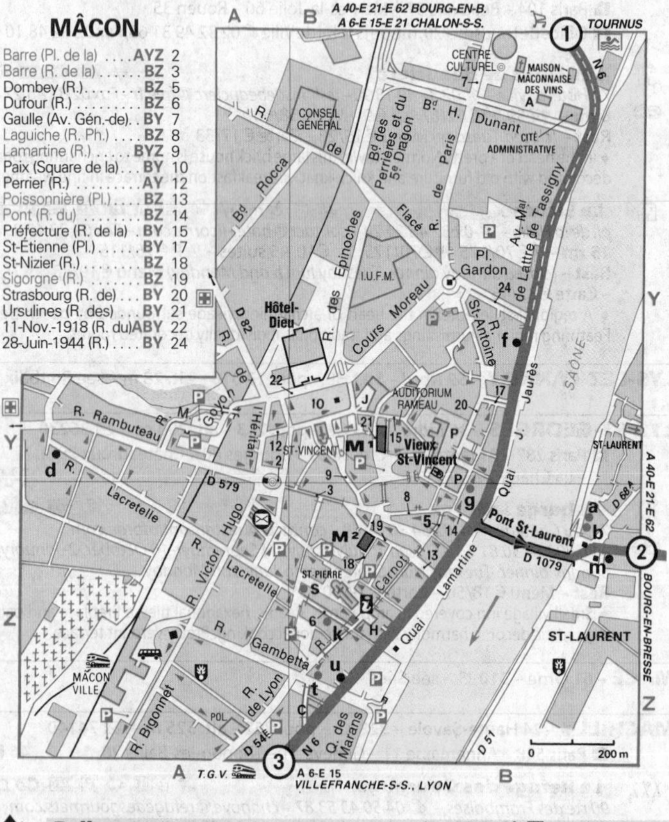

A 40-E 21-E 62 BOURG-EN-B.
A 6-E 15-E 21 CHALON-S-S.
TOURNUS
A 40-E 21-E 62 BOURG-EN-BRESSE
A 6-E 15 VILLEFRANCHE-S-S., LYON

Bellevue without rest
416 quai Lamartine – ✆ 03 85 21 04 04 – bellevue.macon@wanadoo.fr – Fax 03 85 21 04 02 – Closed 30 April-14 May and mid December-beg. January BZ **u**
24 rm – †€ 88/162 ††€ 88/162, ☕ € 12
◆ Traditional hotel on the banks of the Saône, alongside the N 6. An attractive spiral staircase leads to quiet, elegant bedrooms.

Park Inn

26 r. Pierre de Coubertin, via ①: 0.5 km – ✆ 03 85 21 93 93 – info.macon@rezidorparkinn.com – Fax 03 85 39 11 45

64 rm – †€ 80/120 ††€ 85/130, ☕ € 13 – ½ P € 65/95 – **Rest** – *(closed Friday lunch, Saturday lunch and Sunday lunch)* Menu € 20/30 – Carte € 32/48

♦ A peaceful chain-type hotel, in green surroundings, with the advantage that most rooms enjoy a view of the River Saône. Renovated contemporary dining room and bar. Poolside terrace for fine weather dining.

D'Europe et d'Angleterre without rest

92 quai J. Jaurès – ✆ 03 85 38 27 94 – info@hotel-europeangleterre-macon.com – Fax 03 85 39 22 54 – Closed Sunday from January to March BY **f**

29 rm – †€ 45/60 ††€ 50/70, ☕ € 8

♦ This early 19C hotel was popular in the 1930s, recently renovated, but still maintains its former charm. Providing spacious rooms with old-style furnishings.

Concorde without rest

73 r. Lacretelle – ✆ 03 85 34 21 47 – hotel.concorde.71@wanadoo.fr – Fax 03 85 29 21 79 – Closed 5 January-31 February, and Sunday 15 October-15 April AY **d**

14 rm – †€ 45/59 ††€ 52/59, ☕ € 8

♦ Bedrooms which are basic but well kept - choose those looking over the floral garden - and breakfast served inside or on the terrace: an attractive family hotel.

Pierre (Christian Gaulin)

7 r. Dufour – ✆ 03 85 38 14 23 – contact@restaurant-pierre.com – Fax 03 85 39 84 04 – Closed 7-28 July, February school holidays, Sunday dinner, Tuesday lunch and Monday BZ **k**

Rest – Menu (€ 22), € 29 (weekdays)/74 – Carte € 51/69

Spec. Foie gras de canard poêlé, sauce au cassis de Bourgogne. Tournedos charolais et foie gras poêlé sauce bourguignonne. Soufflé chaud aux griottines et kirsch. **Wines** Viré-Clessé, Mâcon blanc.

♦ This restaurant features a décor including stone and wooden beams, a fireplace and a modern rustic feel. Regional and modern cuisine.

L'Amandier

74 r. Dufour – ✆ 03 85 39 82 00 – Fax 03 85 38 92 21 – Closed 11-24 August, February holidays, Saturday lunch, Sunday dinner and Monday BZ **s**

Rest – Menu € 26/55 – Carte € 32/67

♦ This regional-style restaurant in the centre of town has an elegant dining area and serves modern cuisine. Also featuring a shaded terrace on the pedestrian street.

Le Poisson d'Or

port de plaisance, via ① and beside the Saône – ✆ 03 85 38 00 88 – contact@lepoissondor.com – Fax 03 85 38 82 55 – Closed 24 March-2 April, 19 October-12 November, Sunday dinner, Tuesday dinner and Wednesday

Rest – Menu € 24 (weekdays)/65 – Carte € 54/68

♦ The Sâone flows alongside the garden of this restaurant near the port. A refined dining area overlooks the river, with a waterside terrace. Serving fricassé of frogs' legs all year round and fried fish dishes in summer.

Au P'tit Pierre

10 r. Gambetta – ✆ 03 85 39 48 84 – laurechant@hotmail.fr – Fax 03 85 22 73 78 – Closed 27 July-18 August, 1st-4 January, Sunday dinner, Tuesday dinner and Wednesday from September to June, Sunday and Monday in July-August BZ **t**

Rest – Menu (€ 14,50), € 17 (weekdays)/32 – Carte € 26/34

♦ This bistro-style restaurant with a regular local clientele has a lively decor and nice table presentation, serving good traditional dishes.

Le Matisco

45 r. Franche – ✆ 03 85 38 79 84 – Fax 03 85 38 79 84 – Closed August, Monday dinner, Tuesday dinner and Sunday BZ **g**

Rest – Menu (€ 11,50), € 21 – Carte € 24/36

♦ This small bistro in the old town centre has an authentic Italian feel, with red benches, frescos of Venice, and serving antipasti and risotto. La dolce vita!

in St-Laurent-sur-Saône (01Ain) – pop. 1 655 – alt. 176 m – ✉ 01750

Du Beaujolais without rest
88 pl. de la République – ✆ 03 85 38 42 06 – hotel.beaujolais@wanadoo.fr – Fax 03 85 38 78 02 – Closed 31 December-15 January BZ **m**
17 rm – †€ 40 ††€ 45/57, ☕ € 6
◆ On the left bank of the Saône, opposite the bridge of St-Laurent, a basic comfortable hotel where most of the refitted rooms have a pretty view of the town.

L'Autre Rive
143 quai Bouchacourt – ✆ 03 85 39 01 02 – lechef@lautrerive.fr – Fax 03 85 38 16 92 – Closed 24-30 December, Sunday dinner and Monday
Rest – Menu € 21 (weekdays)/39 – Carte € 34/50 BZ **a**
◆ This restaurant on the river bank facing Mâcon has everything: an attractive veranda-dining room, a pleasant terrace overlooking the Saône and generous regional dishes featuring seafood.

Le Saint-Laurent
1 quai Bouchacourt – ✆ 03 85 39 29 19 – saintlaurent@georgesblanc.com – Fax 03 85 38 29 77 BZ **b**
Rest – Menu € 20 (weekday lunch), € 24/45 – Carte € 34/48
◆ A terrace with a view over Mâcon, and stew dishes. Cross the bridge of St-Laurent to reach this "retro" bistro which became famous after Mitterrand and Gorbatchev dined here.

to A6-N6 Mâcon-Nord interchange 7 km by ① – ✉ 71000 Mâcon

Novotel
A6 motorway Mâcon North toll station Exit 28 – ✆ 03 85 20 40 00 – h0438@accor.com – Fax 03 85 20 40 33
114 rm – †€ 102/152 ††€ 102/152, ☕ € 12,50 – **Rest** – Carte € 23/38
◆ A standard-looking hotel in the popular hotel district in Macon north. Choose one of the more modern rooms. A games area for the children. Functional dining room with kitchen-grill visible to all, terrace by the side of the swimming pool.

North 3 km by ① on N 6 – ✉ 71000 Mâcon

La Vieille Ferme
– ✆ 03 85 21 95 15 – vieil.ferme@wanadoo.fr – Fax 03 85 21 95 16 – Closed 20 December-10 January
24 rm – †€ 50 ††€ 50, ☕ € 7 – **Rest** – Menu € 12/29 – Carte € 18/34
◆ A rural stop in a park by the side of the Saône. The bedrooms are in a new motel-type building. This "old farmhouse" is home to a rustic restaurant with exposed beams, stonework and a fireplace, also featuring a charming terrace.

in Sennecé-lès-Mâcon 7,5 km by ① – ✉ 71000 Mâcon

Auberge de la Tour
604 r. Vrémontoise – ✆ 03 85 36 02 70 – aubergedelatour@wanadoo.fr – Fax 03 85 36 03 47 – Closed 22 October-10 November, 9-25 February, Sunday dinner, Tuesday lunch and Monday
24 rm – †€ 46/52 ††€ 55/77, ☕ € 9 – ½ P € 58/65 – **Rest** – Menu (€ 13,50), € 19 (weekday lunch), € 24/48 – Carte € 23/46
◆ This hotel is located next to the village lookout tower, a local curiosity. Providing rooms in various sizes and styles. Traditional cuisine served in a rustic atmosphere with paintings of vineyards. Featuring a fine selection of Macon wines.

via ② Bourg-en-Bresse road – ✉ 01750 Replonges

La Huchette
4.5 km, near exit n°3 of the A40 – ✆ 03 85 31 03 55 – lahuchette@wanadoo.fr – Fax 03 85 31 10 24 – Closed 1st-10 November
14 rm – †€ 85/105 ††€ 100/230, ☕ € 13 – ½ P € 90/100
Rest – *(closed 1st- 17 November Tuesday lunch and Monday)* Menu € 32/55 – Carte € 35/69
◆ This hotel is located in an attractive park, featuring rooms with 1970s-style décor, overlooking the garden. Rustic dining room with exposed beams, fireplace and frescos with a rural theme.

in Crèches-sur-Saône 8 km South by ③ and N 6 – pop. 2 753 – alt. 180 m – ✉ 71680

Syndicat d'initiative, 466, route nationale 6 ☎ 03 85 37 48 32, Fax 03 85 36 57 91

Hostellerie du Château de la Barge

rte des Bergers, 1 km northwest by D89 – ☎ 03 85 23 93 23 – hotelchateaudelabarge@wanadoo.fr – Fax 03 85 23 93 39 – Closed 20 December-5 January

21 rm – €90 €95, ☐ €12 – 4 suites – **Rest** – Menu €19 bi (weekday lunch), €25/67 bi – Carte €36/67

♦ This lovely residence, hidden in a 4-ha park, dates back to the 17C. Large, plush rooms in the château; modern, renovated decor in the recent extension. Heated pool. Exposed beams, a fireplace and rustic furniture characterise this attractive dining room.

in Charnay-lès-Mâcon 2.5 km West – pop. 6 739 – alt. 217 m – ✉ 71850

Syndicat d'initiative, 27, route de Davayé ☎ 03 85 20 53 90, Fax 03 85 20 53 91

Moulin du Gastronome with rm

D 17, Cluny road – ☎ 03 85 34 16 68 – moulindugastronome@wanadoo.fr – Fax 03 85 34 37 25 – Closed 21 July-4 August, 16 February-2 March, Sunday dinner and Monday

7 rm – €60 €72/76, ☐ €10 – 1 suite – ½ P €70 – **Rest** – Menu €24 (weekdays)/58 – Carte €36/64

♦ This restaurant has a façade of lavender blue shutters, giving it a southern feel. A neoclassic dining area and garden terrace. Serving fine wines from the region and from Bordeaux.

in Hurigny 5.5 km Northeast by D 82 AY and secondary road – pop. 1 474 – alt. 275 m – ✉ 71870

Château des Poccards without rest

120 rte des Poccards – ☎ 03 85 32 08 27 – chateau.des.poccards@wanadoo.fr – Fax 03 85 32 08 19 – Open mid March-mid December

6 rm ☐ – €75/125 €100/140

♦ A chateau built in 1805, set in landscaped gardens. The original furnishings add individual touches to the superb rooms. Fine lounge areas, one in Art Deco style.

LA MADELAINE-SOUS-MONTREUIL – 62 Pas-de-Calais – 301 D5 – see Montreuil

MADIÈRES – 34 Hérault – 339 G5 – ✉ 34190 St-Maurice-Navacelles 23 C2

Paris 705 – Lodève 30 – Montpellier 62 – Nîmes 79 – Le Vigan 20

Château de Madières

Hamlet of Madières on the D 25 – ☎ 04 67 73 84 03 – madieres@wanadoo.fr – Fax 04 67 73 55 71 – Open 7 April-October

12 rm – €150/233 €150/233, ☐ €17 – **Rest** – *(closed Thursday)* Menu €49/55 – Carte €46/62

♦ In the heart of a park scaling the plateau, this fine 12C chateau, enlarged during the Renaissance, overlooks the Vis gorges. A grandiose, authentic setting... yet cosy. Dining room with attractive stone vaulting and pleasant terrace. Sunny cuisine.

MADIRAN – 65 Hautes-Pyrénées – 342 L1 – pop. 536 – alt. 125 m – ✉ 65700 28 A2

Paris 753 – Pau 51 – Tarbes 41 – Toulouse 154

Le Prieuré

4 r. de l'Eglise – ☎ 05 62 31 44 52 – restaurantleprieure@cegetel.net – Closed 5-11 January, 8-15 February, Sunday dinner, Monday and Tuesday

Rest – Menu €13 (weekday lunch), €18/25 – Carte €35/44

♦ This restaurant is set in a former monastery, also home to the Madiran wine producers. Featuring a rustic and modern décor, and serving modern cuisine with a fine selection of locally made wines.

MAFFLIERS – 95 Val-d'Oise – **305** E6 – **pop. 1 370** – **alt. 145 m** – ✉ **95560** 18 **B1**

Paris 29 – Beaumont-sur-Oise 10 – Beauvais 53 – Compiègne 73 – Senlis 45

Novotel rm, rest, VISA AE
allée des Marronniers – ✆ 01 34 08 35 35 – h0383@accor.com – Fax 01 34 08 35 00
99 rm – €90/250 €90/250, €13 – **Rest** – Carte €24/41
◆ Admirably quiet and peaceful! On the way into the park, this modern wing houses rooms refurbished according to the chain's standards. A restaurant in a late-19C abode serving classic fare. Summer terrace overlooking the park and forest.

MAGALAS – 34 Hérault – **339** E8 – **pop. 2 489** – **alt. 115 m** – ✉ **34480** 22 **B2**

Paris 755 – Montpellier 82 – Béziers 17 – Narbonne 54 – Sète 71
Office de tourisme, Z.A.E l'Audacieuse ✆ 04 67 36 67 13, Fax 04 67 36 07 54

Ô. Bontemps VISA
pl. de l'Église – ✆ 04 67 36 20 82 – contact@o-bontemps.com – Closed 9-17 March, 11-26 May, 7-15 September, 21 December-5 January, Sunday and Monday
Rest – Menu (€18), €23 (lunch), €28/55 – Carte €32/44
◆ Opposite the church, contemporary address decorated in light tones (mauve, aniseed). Fine creative cuisine.

MAGESCQ – 40 Landes – **335** D12 – **pop. 1 378** – **alt. 28 m** – ✉ **40140** 3 **B2**

Paris 722 – Bayonne 45 – Biarritz 52 – Castets 13 – Dax 16 – Mont-de-Marsan 71
Office de tourisme, 1, place de l'Église ✆ 05 58 47 76 24, Fax 05 58 47 75 81

Relais de la Poste (Jean Coussau) rm, VISA AE
24 av. de Maremne – ✆ 05 58 47 70 25 – poste@relaischateaux.com – Fax 05 58 47 76 17 – Closed 12 November-20 December, Tuesday except evenings from May to September, Thursday lunchtime from May to September and Monday
16 rm – €135/365 €150/380, €17 – 1 suite – ½ P €160/260
Rest – *(pre-book Sat - Sun)* Menu €57 (weekday lunch), €77/105 – Carte €80/126
Spec. Foie gras de canard en trois cuissons. Saumon de l'Adour simplement grillé, sauce béarnaise (15 March to 30 June). Gibier (season). **Wines** Jurançon, Tursan.
◆ This small château is surrounded by a large park, offering warm hospitality with individually decorated rooms with balconies. Also featuring a sauna, steam room and Jacuzzi. An elegant restaurant and terrace overlooking the pine forest. Excellent regional cuisine and a fine wine selection.

MAGLAND – 74 Haute-Savoie – **328** M4 – **pop. 2 801** – **alt. 513 m** – ✉ **74300**

Paris 583 – Annecy 68 – Genève 49 – Lyon 192 46 **F1**

Le Relais du Mont Blanc VISA AE
1 km south on D 1205 – ✆ 04 50 21 00 85 – lerelaisdumontblanc@wanadoo.fr – Fax 04 50 34 31 83 – Closed 1st-11 May, 1st-24 August, 24 October-2 November, 27 December-2 January
16 rm – €65 €75, €9 – **Rest** – *(closed Friday dinner, Saturday lunch and Sunday dinner)* Menu €18 (weekdays)/40 – Carte €35/51
◆ This attractive mountain chalet just 20 minutes from Mont Blanc provides renovated rooms with much wooden décor. This rustic restaurant serves tasty regional cuisine in modern style.

MAGNAC-BOURG – 87 Haute-Vienne – **325** F7 – **pop. 795** – **alt. 444 m** – ✉ **87380** 24 **B2**

Paris 419 – Limoges 31 – St-Yrieix-la-Perche 28 – Uzerche 28
Office de tourisme, 2, place de la Bascule ✆ 05 55 00 89 91, Fax 05 55 00 78 38

 **Auberge de l'Étang**

– ✆ 05 55 00 81 37 – *ml.hermann@wanadoo.fr* – *Fax 05 55 48 70 74*
– *Closed 9 November-8 December, 22 February-9 March, Sunday dinner and Monday except July-August*
14 rm – †€ 45/48 ††€ 42/53, ☕ € 8 – **Rest** – *(closed Sunday dinner, Monday from September to June and Wednesday lunch in July-August)* Menu € 14 (weekdays)/42 – Carte € 30/55

♦ This welcoming family inn overlooking a pond stands at the entrance to the village. Recently refurbished rooms; some enjoy a view of the swimming pool and pond. Generous helpings of traditional cuisine and a pleasant summer terrace.

MAGNY-COURS – **58 Nièvre** – **319** B10 – **see Nevers**

MAGNY-LE-HONGRE – **77 Seine-et-Marne** – **312** F2 – **106** 22 – **see Paris, Area (Marne-la-Vallée)**

MAÎCHE – **25 Doubs** – **321** K3 – **pop. 3 978** – **alt. 777 m** – ✉ **25120** **Burgundy-Jura**

Paris 498 – Besançon 75 – Belfort 60 – Montbéliard 42 – Pontarlier 61 17 **C2**

Syndicat d'initiative, place de la Mairie ✆ 03 81 64 11 88, Fax 03 81 64 02 30

in Mancenans Lizerne **2.5 km East by D 464 and D 272** – **pop. 152** – **alt. 720 m** – ✉ **25120**

Au Coin du Bois

r. sous le rang, La Lizerne – ✆ *03 81 64 00 55* – *Fax 03 81 64 21 98* – *Closed 30 July-5 August, 4-11 February, Sunday dinner, Monday dinner and Wednesday dinner*
Rest – Menu € 14 (weekday lunch), € 22/52 – Carte € 27/63

♦ Attractive chalet, surrounded by pine trees. Discreet rustic dining room and pleasant terrace serving traditional cuisine and local country dishes.

MAILLANE – **13 Bouches-du-Rhône** – **340** D3 – **see St-Rémy-de-Provence**

MAILLEZAIS – **85 Vendée** – **316** L9 – **pop. 934** – **alt. 6 m** – ✉ **85420**
Atlantic Coast 35 **C3**

Paris 443 – Nantes 129 – La Roche-sur-Yon 76 – La Rochelle 50 – Niort 33

Office de tourisme, rue du Dr Daroux ✆ 02 51 87 23 01, Fax 02 51 00 72 51

Madame Bonnet without rest

69 r. Abbaye – ✆ *02 51 87 23 00* – *liliane.bonnet@wanadoo.fr* – *Fax 02 51 00 72 44*
5 rm ☕ – †€ 55/58 ††€ 65/68

♦ Elegant bedrooms, a decor full of history, breakfast by the fire, garden and vegetable plot, and charming hosts. What more can you ask of a bed & breakfast?

MAISONNEUVE – **15 Cantal** – **330** F6 – **see Chaudes-Aigues**

MAISONS-ALFORT – **94 Val-de-Marne** – **312** D3 – **101** 27 – **see Paris, Area**

MAISONS-DU-BOIS – **25 Doubs** – **321** I5 – **see Montbenoit**

MAISONS-LAFFITTE – **78 Yvelines** – **311** I2 – **101** 13 – **see Paris, Area**

MAISONS-LÈS-CHAOURCE – **10 Aube** – **313** F5 – **see Chaource**

MALAUCÈNE – **84 Vaucluse** – **332** D8 – **pop. 2 538** – **alt. 333 m** – ✉ **84340**
Provence 40 **B2**

Paris 673 – Avignon 45 – Carpentras 18 – Vaison-la-Romaine 10

Office de tourisme, place de la Mairie ✆ 04 90 65 22 59, Fax 04 90 65 22 59

Le Domaine des Tilleuls without rest VISA
rte du Mont-Ventoux – ✆ 04 90 65 22 31 – info@hotel-domainedestilleuls.com – Fax 04 90 65 16 77 – Open from March to October
20 rm – †€ 79 ††€ 89, ☕ € 10
♦ This 18C silkworm farm is now home to a charming hotel renovated in the Provencal style. Favour the rooms facing the pleasant park planted with sycamores and limetrees

MALAY-LE-PETIT – 89 Yonne – **319** D2 – **see Sens**

MALBUISSON – 25 Doubs – 321 H6 – pop. 400 – alt. 900 m – ✉ 25160
Burgundy-Jura 17 **C3**

Paris 456 – Besançon 74 – Champagnole 42 – Pontarlier 16 – St-Claude 72
Office de tourisme, 69, Grande Rue ✆ 03 81 69 31 21, Fax 03 81 69 71 94
St-Point Lake★.

Le Lac rest, VISA
– ✆ 03 81 69 34 80 – hotellelac@wanadoo.fr – Fax 03 81 69 35 44 – Closed 12 November-18 December
51 rm – †€ 39/57 ††€ 43/87, ☕ € 9 – 3 suites – ½ P € 47/69
Rest – Menu € 18 (weekdays)/45 – Carte € 31/64
Rest *du Fromage* – Menu € 18/21 – Carte € 15/33
♦ Old house along the main village street and facing the lake on the garden side. Opulent retro interior and some modernised rooms. Generous breakfasts with home made pastries in the tea room. Regional cuisine served at le Lac. Tarts, fondues, raclette at the Restaurant du Fromage.

Beau Site VISA
– ✆ 03 81 69 70 70 – Fax 03 81 69 35 44 – Closed 12 November-18 December
17 rm – †€ 29 ††€ 35, ☕ € 9 – ½ P € 43
♦ Early 19C building with an entrance flanked by columns. Functional rooms. Reception at the Hôtel du Lac.

De la Poste VISA
– ✆ 03 81 69 79 34 – hotellelac@wanadoo.fr – Fax 03 81 69 35 44 – Closed 12 November-18 December
10 rm – †€ 35 ††€ 47, ☕ € 9 – ½ P € 44 – **Rest** – *(closed Tuesday dinner and Monday except July-August)* Menu (€ 7,50), € 10 (weekday lunch), € 12/19 – Carte € 14/40
♦ This small renovated hotel has rooms adorned with colourful furniture. Choose a quieter room facing the lake. You can expect traditional cuisine and specialities cooked on hot stone in a prettily rustic setting.

Le Bon Accueil (Marc Faivre) with rm VISA AE
Grande Rue – ✆ 03 81 69 30 58 – marcfaivre@le-bon-accueil.fr – Fax 03 81 69 37 60 – Closed 14-23 April, 27 October-5 November, 15 December-14 January, Sunday dinner 1st September-14 July, Tuesday lunch and Monday
12 rm – †€ 68 ††€ 68/98, ☕ € 10 – ½ P € 67/86
Rest – Menu (€ 22 bi), € 30/55 – Carte € 47/75
Spec. Gaudes façon gnocchi au vieux comté (20 September to 31 March). Poissons à l'absinthe de Pontarlier (15 June to 15 September). Croustillant glacé au pain d'épice de Mouthe, banane flambée (20 September to 15 December). **Wines** Arbois-Chardonnay, Côtes du Jura.
♦ A charming restaurant with owners providing attentive service. Excellent modern cuisine; spacious and comfortable rooms.

Jean-Michel Tannières with rm VISA
17 Grande Rue – ✆ 03 81 69 30 89 – contact@restaurant-tannieres.com – Fax 03 81 69 39 16 – Closed 18-25 April, 7-16 November, 2-18 January, Sunday dinner, Wednesday lunch, Thursday lunch, Friday lunch, Monday and Tuesday
4 rm – †€ 50/100 ††€ 50/100, ☕ € 8 – ½ P € 50/100
Rest – Menu € 38/45
Rest *Le Bistrot d'Angèle* – *(closed Monday, Tuesday and Sunday dinner during term time)* Menu (€ 15), € 22 bi
♦ Classical cooking accompanied by a large choice of wines. The tasteful dining room overlooks a garden with a babbling brook. Warm hospitality. At the Bistrot d'Angèle, the decor is country style. Traditional dishes.

in Granges-Ste-Marie 2 km Southwest– ✉25160 Labergement-Ste-Marie

Auberge du Coude
– ✆ *03 81 69 31 57 – Fax 03 81 69 33 90 – Closed 8 November-16 December*
11 rm – †€ 52 ††€ 52, ☕ € 8 – ½ P € 52
Rest – *(closed Sunday dinner)* Menu € 18/46
◆ Located between the lakes of Saint Point and Remoray Boujeons, this house dating from 1826 has a warm atmosphere. Charming bedrooms. Garden with lake. Rustic dining room with wood panelling and Louis XIII furniture. Regional cuisine.

LA MALÈNE – 48 Lozère – 330 H9 – pop. 171 – alt. 450 m – ✉ 48210

Languedoc-Roussillon-Tarn Gorges 23 **C1**

Paris 609 – Florac 41 – Mende 41 – Millau 44 – Sévérac-le-Château 33 – Le Vigan 77

Office de tourisme, ✆ 04 66 48 50 77

West: les Détroits★★ and cirque des Baumes★★ (by boat).

Manoir de Montesquiou
– ✆ *04 66 48 51 12 – montesquiou@demeures-de-lozere.com*
– Fax 04 66 48 50 47 – Open end March to end October
10 rm – †€ 70/142 ††€ 70/142, ☕ € 14 – 2 suites – ½ P € 110/114
Rest – Menu € 25/45 – Carte € 31/64
◆ This 15C stone manor is rich in appeal: friendly welcome, personalised rooms (four-poster beds, period furniture) and a lovely rose garden. Regionally sourced dishes served on a pleasant terrace in fine weather.

Northeast 5,5 km on D 907bis – ✉ 48210 Ste-Énimie

Château de la Caze rm,
– ✆ *04 66 48 51 01 – chateau.de.la.caze@wanadoo.fr – Fax 04 66 48 55 75*
– Open 30 March-11 November and closed Thursday in October
7 rm †€ 112/166 ††€ 112/166, ☕ € 14 – 9 suites – ††€ 166/276 – ½ P € 104/131
Rest – *(closed Thursday except dinner from November to September and Wednesday except July-August)* Menu € 34/82 – Carte approx. € 38
◆ Majestic 15C chateau in a park beside the Tarn. Exquisite, individualised bedrooms (those in the annexe are also very comfortable, but less characterful). Particularly pleasant welcome. Restaurant in an old chapel serving flavoursome modern dishes based on local produce.

MALESHERBES – 45 Loiret – 318 L2 – pop. 5 989 – alt. 108 m – ✉ 45330

Châteaux of the Loire 12 **C1**

Paris 75 – Étampes 26 – Fontainebleau 27 – Montargis 62 – Orléans 62 – Pithiviers 19

Office de tourisme, 19-21, place du Martroi ✆ 02 38 34 81 94, Fax 02 38 34 81 94

du Château d'Augerville Augerville-la-Rivière Place du Château, South: 8 km by D 410, ✆ 02 38 32 12 07.

Écu de France
10 pl. Martroi – ✆ 02 38 34 87 25 – ecudefrance@wanadoo.fr – Fax 02 38 34 68 99
16 rm – †€ 54/68 ††€ 54/68, ☕ € 6,50 – ½ P € 58/65
Rest – *(closed 1st-17 August, Thursday dinner and Sunday dinner)* Menu € 24/50 – Carte € 24/56
Rest *Brasserie de l'Écu* – *(closed 1st-17 August, Thursday dinner and Sunday dinner)* Menu (€ 13) – Carte € 18/43
◆ This former post house, a short distance from the Château de Malesherbes, has stylish, very well kept rooms. Old beams and fireplace give this restaurant a certain cachet. Terrace in the courtyard. Fast meals in the brasserie area.

La Lilandière without rest
7 chemin de la Messe, (Hamlet of Trézan) – ✆ 02 38 34 84 51 – la-lilandiere@wanadoo.fr – **5 rm** ☕ – †€ 56 ††€ 60
◆ A successful mix of stone, beams and modern furniture at this tastefully renovated former farm. Keen anglers and canoeists will appreciate the river at the bottom of the garden.

MALICORNE-SUR-SARTHE – 72 Sarthe – 310 I8 – pop. 1 686 – alt. 39 m – ✉ 72270 Châteaux of the Loire 35 **C2**

Paris 236 – Château-Gontier 52 – La Flèche 16 – Le Mans 32

Office de tourisme, 5, place Du Guesclin ✆ 02 43 94 74 45, Fax 02 43 94 59 61

XX **La Petite Auberge** VISA MC

5 pl. Duguesclin – ✆ 02 43 94 80 52 – contact@petite-auberge-malicorne.fr – Fax 02 43 94 31 37 – Closed 22 December-28 February, dinner except Saturday September-April, Sunday dinner and Tuesday dinner May-August and Monday

Rest – Menu € 17 (weekday lunch), € 24/50 – Carte € 33/40

◆ Summer dining on the terrace by the waterside. In winter, enjoy a meal around the 13C fireplace. Serving fine, traditional meals.

MALLING – 57 Moselle – 307 I2 – pop. 512 – alt. 158 m – ✉ 57480 26 **B1**

Paris 352 – Luxembourg 35 – Metz 43 – Trier 63

in Petite Hettange 1 km east on D 654 – ✉ 57480

XX **Olmi** VISA MC AE

11 rte Nationale – ✆ 03 82 50 10 65 – relais3frontieres@wanadoo.fr – Fax 03 82 83 61 01 – Closed 28 July-11 August, 9-16 January, Tuesday dinner, Wednesday dinner and Monday

Rest – Menu € 32/70 – Carte € 52/63

◆ Located close to the border, former truck stop which has been refurbished in pastel tones. Good, traditional cuisine.

MALO-LES-BAINS – 59 Nord – 302 C1 – see Dunkerque

LE MALZIEU-VILLE – 48 Lozère – 330 I5 – pop. 970 – alt. 860 m – ✉ 48140 23 **C1**

Paris 541 – Mende 51 – Millau 107 – Le Puy-en-Velay 74 – Rodez 125 – St-Flour 38

Office de tourisme, tour de Bodon ✆ 04 66 31 82 73

Voyageurs rm, rm, P VISA MC AE

rte Saugues – ✆ 04 66 31 70 08 – pagesc@wanadoo.fr – Fax 04 66 31 80 36 – Closed 15 December-28 February

19 rm – †€ 55 ††€ 55, ☐ € 9 – ½ P € 52/70 – **Rest** – *(closed Sunday dinner and Saturday except July-August)* Menu (€ 9), € 15/25 – Carte € 23/43

◆ In a pretty village of the Margeride, a 1970s building with functional bedrooms. A practical base from which to explore the region. Traditional and local dishes are served in this countrified dining room.

MAMERS – 72 Sarthe – 310 L4 – pop. 6 084 – alt. 128 m – ✉ 72600 Normandy 35 **D1**

Paris 185 – Alençon 25 – Le Mans 51 – Mortagne-au-Perche 25 – Nogent-le-Rotrou 40

Office de tourisme, 29, place Carnot ✆ 02 43 97 60 63, Fax 02 43 97 42 87

in Pérou (61 Orne) 7 km East by Bellême road – ✉ 61360 Chemilly

X **La Petite Auberge** P VISA MC AE

– ✆ 02 33 73 11 34 – la.petite.auberge.@free.fr – Closed Monday dinner and Tuesday

Rest – Menu € 12,50 (weekday lunch), € 17/35 – Carte € 20/46

◆ A "small" roadside inn off the beaten path. Sit in the rustic dining room near the warmth of the fireplace or on the terrace giving onto a flower garden.

MANCENANS LIZERNE – 25 Doubs – 321 K3 – see Maîche

L'Ermitage du Riou
av. H. Clews – ✆ 04 93 49 95 56 – hotel@ermitage-du-riou.fr – Fax 04 92 97 69 05
41 rm – €126/192 €126/301, €16 – 4 suites – ½ P €97/185
Rest – Menu €25/80 – Carte €63/132 Z **e**
◆ This old ochre and brick Provençal abode has comfortable bedrooms overlooking the ocean or the golf course. A dining room-veranda facing the port in which traditional dishes, seafood and wines from the estate take pride of place.

Villa Parisiana without rest
5 r. Argentière – ✆ 04 93 49 93 02 – villa.parisiana@wanadoo.fr – Fax 04 93 49 62 32 – Closed 24 November-28 December Z **d**
13 rm – €40/67 €40/67, €7
◆ This 1900 villa exudes charm: well renovated inviting rooms, some with sunny balconies and a summer terrace under the vines. Non-smoking.

La Corniche d'Or without rest
pl. de la Fontaine – ✆ 04 93 49 92 51 – info@cornichedor.com – Fax 04 93 49 71 95 – Closed 29 November-8 December – **12 rm** – €43/59 €43/79, €8 Z **s**
◆ This hotel offers simple spruce rooms (all have balcony) with pine furnishings, new bed linen and air-conditioning (on request). Pleasant terrace and friendly staff.

L'Oasis (Stéphane, Antoine et François Raimbault)
r. J. H. Carle – ✆ 04 93 49 95 52 (dinner)
– oasis@relaischateaux.com – Fax 04 93 49 64 13
– Closed from mid December to mid January, Sunday and Monday Z **r**
Rest – Menu €56 (lunch), €155/195 – Carte €116/196
Spec. Soleil levant de poisson cru retour du marché Forville. Poissons de pêche locale ou de Méditerranée rôtis entiers en tian de petits légumes. Caravane de tartes, gâteaux et entremets. **Wines** Bellet, Les Baux-de-Provence.
◆ A lush patio, elegant setting and delicious southern cuisine with an oriental touch, a "caravan" of desserts: this caravanserai for gourmet nomads is not a mirage!

La Pomme d'Amour
209 av. 23 Août – ✆ 04 93 49 95 19 – Fax 04 93 49 95 24
– Closed 17 November-8 December, Tuesday lunch and Monday Z **u**
Rest – Menu €32/55 – Carte €44/74
◆ Discreet culinary venue in the centre of La Napoule, right next to the station. A pleasant, cosy dining room with neat table settings. Traditional and local cuisine.

Les Bartavelles
1 pl. Château – ✆ 04 93 49 95 15 – Closed 5-28 January, Sunday dinner and Wednesday October-April – **Rest** – Menu (€20 bi), €28/39 – Carte €35/53 Z **f**
◆ This friendly informal house makes a point of serving generous traditional dishes. Dining room-veranda extended by a terrace shaded by plane trees in summer.

La Palméa
198 av. Henri Clews – ✆ 04 92 19 22 50 – info@lapalmea.com – Fax 04 92 19 22 51
– Closed Sunday dinner and Monday except July-August Z **c**
Rest – Menu €33 – Carte €35/69
◆ The southern-inspired menu of this harbour-side restaurant focuses on seafood. The veranda overlooks the marina and the dining room has an ethnic feel to it.

Le Bistrot du Port
At the port – ✆ 04 93 49 80 60 – bistrotduport@wanadoo.fr – Fax 04 93 49 69 76
– Closed 25 November-15 December, Wednesday off-season and school holidays
Rest – Menu €26/32 – Carte €37/64 Z **b**
◆ To enjoy a unique view of the boats, drop anchor in this harbour bistro. Welcoming nautical interior, a veranda extended by a terrace in fine weather and excellent seafood.

MANDEREN – **57 Moselle** – **307** J2 – **see Sierck-les-Bains**

MANE – **04 Alpes-de-Haute-Provence** – **334** C9 – **see Forcalquier**

MANIGOD – **74 Haute-Savoie** – **328** L5 – **pop. 789** – **alt. 950 m** – ✉ **74230**
Paris 558 – Albertville 39 – Annecy 25 – Chamonix-Mont-Blanc 67 – Thônes 6
Office de tourisme, Chef-lieu ✆ 04 50 44 92 44, Fax 04 50 44 94 68
Manigod Valley ★★, French Alps 46 **F1**

col de la Croix-Fry road : 5 ,5 km - ✉ 74230 Manigod

Chalet Hôtel Croix-Fry

mountains,
– ✆ 04 50 44 90 16 – hotelcroixfry@wanadoo.fr
– Fax 04 50 44 94 87 – Open mid June-mid September and mid December-mid April
10 rm – €145/165 €260/420, €18 – ½ P €130/205
Rest – *(closed Tuesday lunch, Wednesday lunch and Monday)* Menu €26 (weekday lunch), €46/76 – Carte €57/82

◆ Idyllically located in alpine meadows, this lovely chalet has been run by the same family for decades. Cosy mountain decor and adorably snug bedrooms. Friendly table d'hôte in the restaurant; panoramic terrace facing the Aravis peaks.

MANOSQUE – 04 Alpes-de-Haute-Provence – 334 C10 – pop. 19 603 – alt. 387 m – ✉ 04100 French Alps 40 B2

Paris 758 – Aix-en-Provence 57 – Avignon 91 – Digne-les-Bains 61

Office de tourisme, place du Docteur Joubert ✆ 04 92 72 16 00, Fax 04 92 72 58 98

du Lubéron Pierrevert La Grande Gardette, by la Bastide-des-Jourdans road: 7 km, ✆ 04 92 72 17 19.

Old Manosque★: Porte Saunerie★, façade★ of the town hall - Sarcophagus★ and Black Virgin★ in N.-D. de Romigier church - Carzou Foundation★ M - ≤★ du Mont d'Or Northeast: 1.5 km.

Pré St-Michel without rest

1.5 km north on bd M. Bret and Dauphin road – ✆ 04 92 72 14 27 – pre.st.michel@wanadoo.fr – Fax 04 92 72 53 04 – **24 rm** – €56/100 €56/100, €9

◆ A modern, regional-style hotel with spacious rooms decorated in Provençal style, some with a private terrace. Featuring a charming view over the town.

Le Sud

rm,
bd Charles de Gaulle – ✆ 04 92 87 78 58 – hotelbestwesternlesud@orange.fr
– Fax 04 92 72 66 60 – **36 rm** – €80/96 €85/102, €10 – ½ P €60/65
Rest – Menu (€16), €19/35 – Carte €25/47

◆ Just outside the old town centre of Manosque, this practical hotel provides rooms and lounges with a warm atmosphere decorated in Provençal style. The spirit of the South is omnipresent in this restaurant (painted woodwork and sunny colours).

Le Luberon

21 bis pl. Terreau – ✆ 04 92 72 03 09 – Fax 04 92 72 03 09 – Closed 13-27 October, Sunday dinner and Monday **m**
Rest – Menu (€14), €19/55 – Carte €34/59

◆ A small restaurant in the centre of town with a rustic dining area decorated in sunny tones. Verdant terrace providing welcome shade in summer. Southern French cuisine.

MANOSQUE

Arthur-Robert (R.) 2
Aubette (R. d') 3
Bret (Bd M.) 5
Chacundier (R.) 6
Cougourdelles (Bd des) 7
Dauphine (R.) 8
Giono (Av. J.) 9
Grande (R.) 10
Guilhempierre (R.) 12
Hôtel-de-Ville (Pl. de l') 13
Jean-Jacques-Rousseau (R.) 14
Marchands (R. des) 15
Mirabeau (Bd) 16
Mont-d'Or (R. du) 17
Observantins (Pl. des) 19
Ormeaux (Pl. des) 20
Paul-Martin Nalin (Bd) 21
Pelloutier (Bd C.) 22
Plaine (Bd de la) 23
République (R. de la) 26
St-Lazare (Av.) 28
Saunerie (R. de la) 30
Soubeyran (R.) 32
Tanneurs (R. des) 33
Tourelles (R. des) 34
Voland (R.) 35
Vraies-Richesses (Montée des) 36

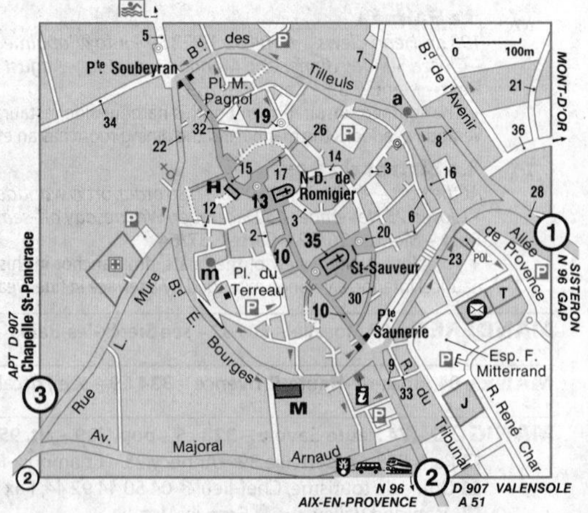

in La Fuste **6,5 km Southeast by Valensole road – ✉ 04210 Valensole**

Hostellerie de la Fuste rest, P VISA MC AE
lieu dit la Fuste – ☎ 04 92 72 05 95 – lafuste@aol.com
– Fax 04 92 72 92 93 – Open 20 March-30 September and 20 December-3 January
14 rm – € 100/190 € 100/190, € 15 – ½ P € 160/250
Rest – *(closed Tuesday lunch, Sunday dinner and Monday) (number of covers limited, pre-book)* Menu € 47/58 – Carte € 80/118
◆ Elegant country hostelry in a floral park with an excellent vegetable garden. Comfortable rooms and utter peace, barely disturbed by the sound of the crickets. A restaurant with view of the garden and an attractive terrace shaded by fine plane trees.

to A51 interchange **4 km by ② - ✉ 04100 Manosque**

Ibis VISA MC AE
– ☎ 04 92 71 18 00 – h5611@accor.com – Fax 04 92 72 00 45
47 rm – € 55/72 € 55/72, € 8 – **Rest** – Menu € 17
◆ This modern hotel has a distinctive yellow façade, providing functional well-planned rooms in line with the hotel chain's standards. Bright dining room offering traditional food.

LE MANS P – **72 Sarthe** – **310** K6 – **pop. 146 105** – **Built-up area 194 825**
– alt. 80 m – ✉ **72000** Châteaux of the Loire 35 **D1**

Paris 206 – Angers 97 – Le Havre 213 – Nantes 184 – Rennes 154 – Tours 85
Office de tourisme, rue de l'Étoile ☎ 02 43 28 17 22, Fax 02 43 28 12 14
de Sargé-lès-le-Mans, by Bonnétable road: 6 km, ☎ 02 43 76 25 07 ;
des 24 Heures-Le Mans Mulsanne, by Tours road: 11 km, ☎ 02 43 42 00 36.
24-hour race circuit and Bugatti circuit ☎ 02 43 40 24 24: 5 km by ④.
St-Julien cathedral ★★: apse★★★ - Old Le Mans★★: House of Queen Bérengère★, Gallo-Roman wall★ DV **M²** - La Couture church★: Virgin★★ - Ste-Jeanne-d'Arc church ★ - Musée de Tessé★ - Épau abbey★ BZ , 4 km by D 152 - Musée de l'Automobile★★: 5 km by ④.

Mercure Centre without rest P VISA MC AE
19 r. Chanzy – ☎ 02 43 40 22 40 – h5641@accor.com – Fax 02 43 40 22 31
73 rm – € 105 € 115, € 14 – 5 suites DX **p**
◆ Hotel located in a listed building that formerly housed the Mutuelles du Mans (friendly society). Modern, practical rooms with good soundproofing.

Novotel rm, P VISA MC AE
bd R. Schuman, (Sablons development area) – ☎ 02 43 85 26 80
– h0440@accor.com – Fax 02 43 75 31 76 BZ **a**
94 rm – € 106/150 € 106/150, € 13 – **Rest** – Carte € 25/38
◆ Humdrum external 1970s architecture but pleasant contemporary interior. Functional bedrooms, quieter at the back, on the garden and river side. Pleasant modern dining room and terrace facing the garden; "Novotel" menu.

Chantecler without rest P VISA MC AE
50 r. Pelouse – ☎ 02 43 14 40 00 – hotel.chantecler@wanadoo.fr – Fax 02 43 77 16 28
– Closed 3-17 August – **32 rm** – € 69 € 69/86, € 8,50 – 3 suites CY **f**
◆ Rattan furniture and greenery adorn the breakfast room, a real winter garden under the veranda. Restful pastel colours in the bedrooms.

Mercure Batignolles rm, P VISA MC AE
17 r. Pointe – ☎ 02 43 72 27 20 – h0344@accor.com – Fax 02 43 85 96 06 AZ
68 rm – € 45/90 € 55/100, € 9 – **Rest** – *(closed 21 December-2 January, Saturday, Sunday from September to May, Monday lunch)* Menu € 20 – Carte approx. € 25
◆ A 1970s building housing practical and well-kept rooms; those to the rear are quieter. Modern, spacious accommodation in the recent annexe. Garden with minigolf. Dining room decorated with photographs recalling the legendary Le Mans 24-hour race.

Émeraude without rest VISA MC AE
18 r. Gastelier – ☎ 02 43 24 87 46 – emeraudehotel@wanadoo.fr – Fax 02 43 24 60 64
33 rm – € 52/68 € 68/75, € 12 CY **z**
◆ A warm welcome in this hotel near the station. Rooms in pastel tones. Breakfast served in the inner courtyard on fine days.

LE MANS

Ambroise Paré (R.) . . . . AZ 4	Flore (R. de) . . . . BZ 31	Négrier (Bd du Gén.) . . . . BZ 58
Ballon (R. de) . . . . AZ 6	Gaulle (R. du Gén.-de) . . . . ABZ 36	Néruda (R. Pablo) . . . . BZ 60
Bertinière (R. de la) . . . . BZ 10	Géneslay (Av. F.) . . . . ABZ 37	Pied-Sec (R. de) . . . . AZ 63
Brosselette (Bd P.) . . . . AZ 15	Grande-Maison (R. de la) . . . . AZ 39	Pointe (R. de la) . . . . AZ 64
Carnot (Bd) . . . . AZ 16	Heuzé (Av. O.) . . . . AZ 42	Prémartine (Rte de) . . . . BZ 67
Churchill (Bd W.) . . . . BZ 17	Jean-Jaurès (Av.) . . . . BZ 43	Riffaudières (Bd des) . . . . AZ 73
Clemenceau (Bd G.) . . . . BZ 18	Lefeuvre (Av. H.) . . . . AZ 44	Rondeau (R. J.) . . . . AZ 74
Douce-Amie (R. de) . . . . BZ 22	Maillets (R. des) . . . . BZ 46	Rubillard (Av.) . . . . AZ 78
Durand (Av. G.) . . . . BZ 26	Mare (CH. de la) . . . . BZ 49	Schuman (Bd R.) . . . . BZ 80
Esterel (R. de l') . . . . BZ 30	Mariette (R. de la) . . . . BZ 51	Victimes du Nazisme (R. des) . . . . BZ 82
	Monthéard (Av. de) . . . . BZ 55	Yvré-Levêque (Ch. d') . . . . BZ 87
	Moulin (Av. J.) . . . . BZ 57	

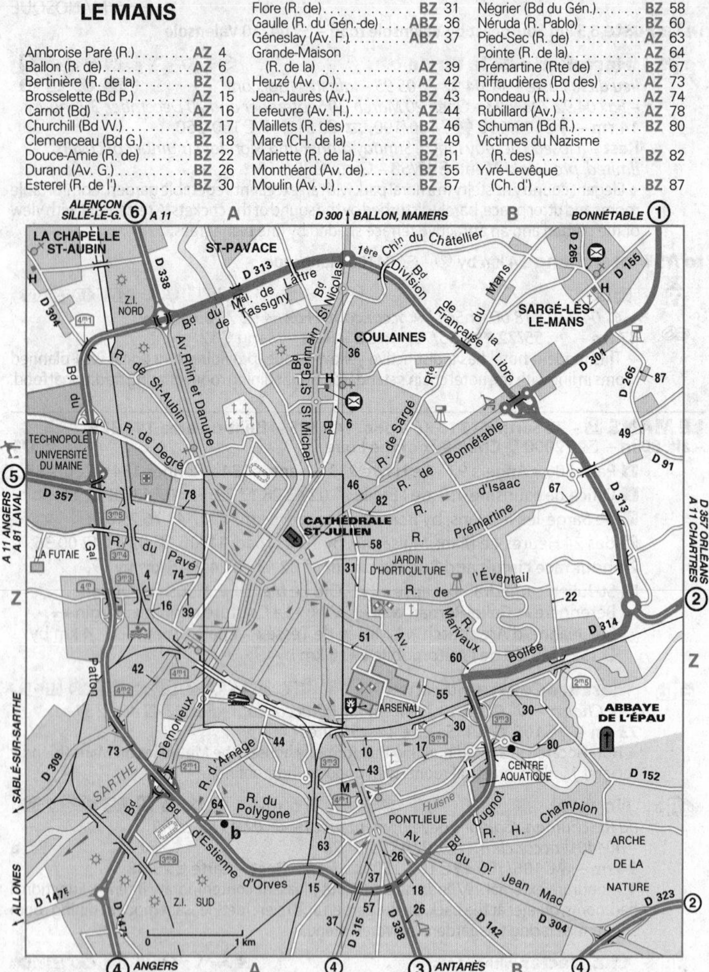

Du Commerce without rest

41 bd de la Gare – ☎ 02 43 83 20 20 – commerce.hotel@wanadoo.fr
– Fax 02 43 83 20 21 – **31 rm** *– †€ 52/62 ††€ 56/62, ☕ € 10* CY **d**

◆ This hotel located near the station has excellent sound insulation, providing renovated and functional rooms, all very well kept.

Beaulieu (Olivier Boussard)

pl. des Ifs – ☎ 02 43 87 78 37 – Fax 02 43 87 78 27
– Closed August, 16-22 February, Saturday and Sunday DX **h**

Rest – Menu € 29 (lunch), € 40/101 – Carte € 69/117

Spec. Déclinaison "terre et mer" (spring-summer). Cuisse de poularde en pot-au-feu et blanc rôti à la truffe (autumn). Lièvre à la royale (winter). **Wines** Jasnières, Bourgueil.

◆ This restaurant features a range of styles, including modern, designer and baroque, nicely blended to provide a pleasant atmosphere. Tasty modern cuisine.

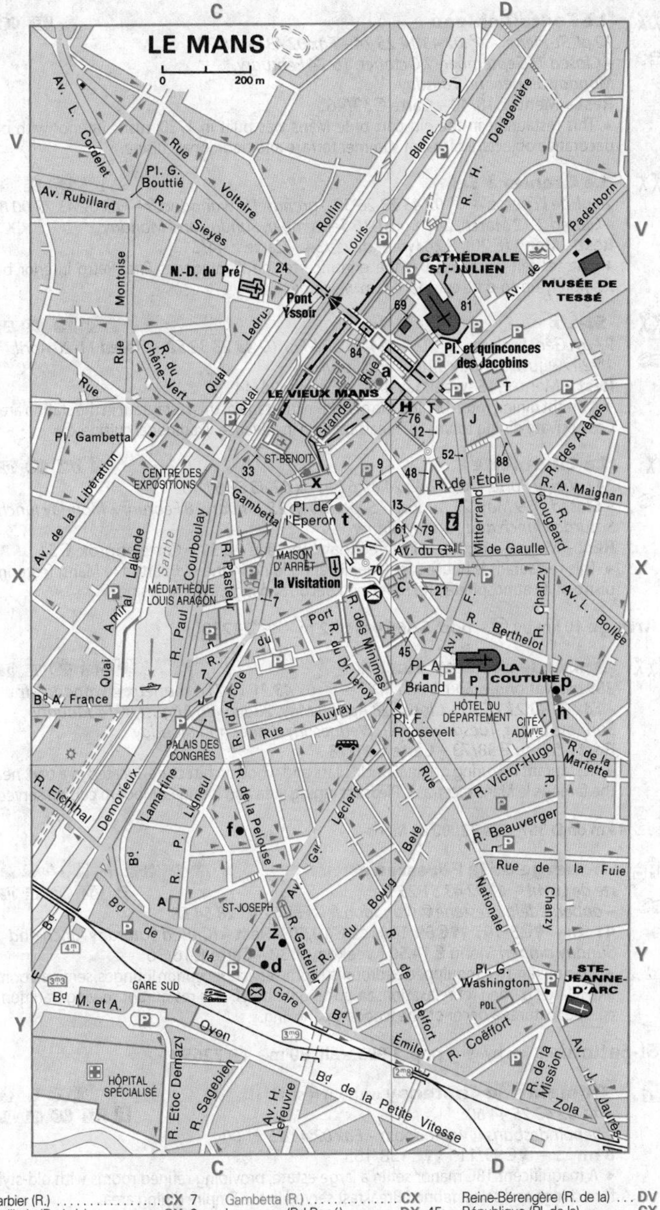

C
D
LE MANS
0
200 m
V
X
Y
Av. L. Cordelet
Rue Voltaire
Pl. G. Bouttié
Av. Rubillard
R. Sieyès
Rollin
Louis Blanc
R. H. Delagenière
Av. de Paderborn
CATHÉDRALE ST-JULIEN
MUSÉE DE TESSÉ
Montoise
N.-D. du Pré
24
Pont Yssoir
69
81
Pl. et quinconces des Jacobins
Rue
R. du Chêne-Vert
Quai Ledru-
84
Grande Rue
a
LE VIEUX MANS
H
T
J
Quai
76
12
Pl. Gambetta
52
88
R. des Arènes
33
ST-BENOIT
9
48
R. de l'Étoile
R. A. Maignan
CENTRE DES EXPOSITIONS
x
Av. de la Libération
Gambetta
Pl. de l'Eperon
t
13
Mitterrand
R. Gougeard
61
79
Lalande
Sarthe
Courboulay
R. Pasteur
MAISON D'ARRET
la Visitation
Av. du Gal de Gaulle
70
C
21
R. Chanzy
Av. L. Bollée
MÉDIATHÈQUE LOUIS ARAGON
7
Port
R. des Minimes
R. du Dr Leroy
Av. F.
R. Berthelot
Amiral
R. Paul
du
45
Quai
R.
7
Pl. A. Briand
LA COUTURE
p
Bd A. France
R. d'Arcole
Auvray
HÔTEL DU DÉPARTEMENT
CITÉ ADMIVE
h
Pl. F. Roosevelt
Rue
PALAIS DES CONGRÈS
R. de la Mariette
R. Victor-Hugo
R. Eichthal
Demorieux
Lamartine
Ligneul
R. de la Pelouse
Leclerc
Rue Bele
R.
f
R. Beauverger
Bd
R. P.
Rue de la Fuie
Av. Gal
Bourg
Nationale
Chanzy
A
Bd
ST-JOSEPH
R. Gastelier
du
R. de
de
z
v
d
la
Pl. G. Washington
STE-JEANNE-D'ARC
GARE SUD
Gare
POL
Bd M. et A.
Oyon
Bd
Belfort
Émile
R. Coëffort
HÔPITAL SPÉCIALISÉ
R. Etoc Demazy
R. Sagebien
Av. H. Lefeuvre
Bd de la Petite Vitesse
R. de la Mission
Zola
Av. J. Jaurès

Le Fontainebleau

12 pl. St-Pierre – ✆ 02 43 14 25 74 – Fax 02 43 14 25 74 – Closed 15 September- 7 October, 16-24 February, Monday dinner and Tuesday CV **a**

Rest – Menu € 18/40 – Carte € 39/46

◆ This restaurant in the old part of le Mans was built in 1720; rustic interior with old decorative objects, a pleasant summer terrace and traditional cuisine.

Le Grenier à Sel

26 pl. de l'Eperon – ✆ 02 43 23 26 30 – grenasel@wanadoo.fr – Fax 02 43 77 00 80 – Closed 2-12 March, 24 August-16 September, Sunday and Monday CX **t**

Rest – Menu (€ 20), € 24 (weekdays)/34 – Carte € 44/51

◆ Former salt warehouse at the entrance to the Plantagenet *Cité*. Retro interior but resolutely up-to-date cuisine. Warm welcome.

St-Lô

97 av. Gén. Leclerc – ✆ 02 43 24 71 85 – Fax 02 43 23 32 52 – Closed 11-20 April, 1st-24 August, Sunday dinner and Saturday CY **v**

Rest – Menu € 15 (weekdays)/30 – Carte € 26/44

◆ A bright dining room behind the glazed-in frontage of this restaurant in the station area. Cosy private dining rooms for meals booked in advance. Traditional cuisine.

La Ciboulette

14 r. Vieille Porte – ✆ 02 43 24 65 67 – Fax 02 43 87 51 18 – Closed 1st-9 May, 25 August-7 September, 25 January- 8 February, Monday lunch, Saturday lunch and Sunday dinner CX **x**

Rest – Menu (€ 12,50), € 17 (weekday lunch), € 22/31 – Carte approx. € 51

◆ This restaurant is housed in a medieval building in the old part of le Mans, featuring bistro-style atmosphere and red-toned décor. Serving modern cuisine.

in Arnage 10 km by ④ – pop. 5 565 – alt. 42 m – ✉ 72230

Auberge des Matfeux

289 av. Nationale, South on D 147 – ✆ 02 43 21 10 71 – matfeux@wanadoo.fr – Fax 02 43 21 25 23 – Closed 28 April-8 May, 28 July-26 August, 2-14 January, Sunday dinner, Tuesday dinner, Wednesday dinner and Monday

Rest – Menu € 38/73 – Carte € 41/78

◆ Restaurant featuring original brick, glass and wood architecture, located in a park near the famous le Mans racetrack. Pleasant dining area and lounges. Modern cuisine served.

via ⑤ 4 km on D 357 – ✉ 72000 Le Mans

Auberge de la Foresterie

rm,

rte de Laval – ✆ 02 43 51 25 12 – aubergedelaforesterie@wanadoo.fr – Fax 02 43 28 54 58

41 rm – †€ 59/95 ††€ 69/110, ☕ € 10,50 – **Rest** – *(Closed Saturday lunch and Sunday dinner)* Menu € 14,50 (weekdays)/30 – Carte € 16/36

◆ Spacious and well equipped bedrooms, room-service, reception lounges, seminar rooms and a large garden for relaxation: an up-to-date hotel. This restaurant serving traditional cuisine features a décor of fine wooden-panelling.

in St-Saturnin 8 km by ⑥ – pop. 1 995 – alt. 80 m – ✉ 72650

Domaine de Chatenay without rest

– ✆ 02 43 25 44 60 – benoit.desbans@wanadoo.fr – Fax 02 43 25 21 00

8 rm ☕ – †€ 99/115 ††€ 138/165

◆ A magnificent 18C manor set in a large estate, providing refined rooms with old-style furnishings and select fabrics. Breakfast served in the Empire dining area.

MANSLE – 16 Charente – 324 L4 – pop. 1 597 – alt. 65 m – ✉ 16230 39 C2

Paris 421 – Angoulême 26 – Cognac 53 – Limoges 93 – Poitiers 88 – St-Jean-d'Angély 62

Office de tourisme, place du Gardoire ✆ 05 45 20 39 91, Fax 05 45 20 39 91

Beau Rivage

pl. Gardoire – ✆ 05 45 20 31 26 – hotel.beau.rivage.16@orange.fr – Fax 05 45 22 24 24 – Closed 16 February-10 March, 24 November-15 December, Sunday dinner and Monday lunch October-April

30 rm – 🚹€ 53/55 🚻€ 53/55, ☕ € 8,50 – ½ P € 49 – **Rest** – Menu € 13,50 (weekday lunch), € 18/32 – Carte € 28/50

◆ Behind a slightly austere façade, this hotel has elegant rooms, some of which have been tastefully renovated. Garden on the banks of the Charente (canoe hire). A large dining area and terrace with a view of the river. Traditional cuisine.

in Luxé **6 km West by D 739 – pop. 756 – alt. 70 m –** ✉ **16230**

Auberge du Cheval Blanc

à la gare – ✆ 05 45 22 23 62 – restaurantlechevalblanc@wanadoo.fr – Fax 05 45 39 94 75 – Closed 1st-10 September, February, Sunday dinner, Tuesday dinner and Monday

Rest – Menu € 16 bi (weekday lunch), € 28/38 – Carte € 34/40

◆ This century-old building with an attractive façade has a pleasant rustic dining area with floral designs and serves fine regional cuisine.

MANTES-LA-JOLIE – 78 Yvelines – 311 G2 – pop. 43 672 – alt. 34 m –

✉ **78200** **Northern France and the Paris Region** 18 **A1**

Paris 56 – Beauvais 69 – Chartres 78 – Évreux 46 – Rouen 80 – Versailles 47

Office de tourisme, 8 bis, rue Marie et Robert Dubois ✆ 01 34 77 10 30.

de Guerville Guerville La Plagne, by Houdan road: 6 km, ✆ 01 30 92 45 45 ;

de Moisson-Mousseaux Moisson Base de Loisir de Moisson, by Vernon road and secondary road: 14 km, ✆ 01 34 79 39 00 ;

de Villarceaux Chaussy Château du Couvent, North: 20 km by D 147, ✆ 01 34 67 73 83.

Notre-Dame collegiate church ★★ B **B.**

Rive Gauche

1 r. du Fort – ✆ 01 30 92 30 16 – rivegauche.mantes@wanadoo.fr – Fax 01 30 92 30 16 – Closed 3 August-1st September, Saturday lunch, Sunday and Monday B **a**

Rest – Carte € 42/51

◆ Not far from the Notre Dame church, this nice little restaurant serves modern cuisine in a charming décor combining old and new styles, including stone and wooden beams.

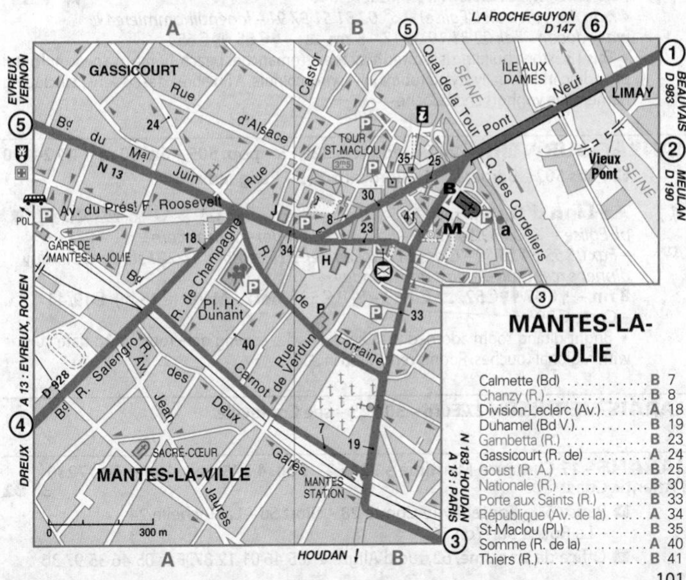

in Mantes-la-Ville 2 km by ③ – **pop. 19 231 – alt. 36 m –** ✉ **78711**

XXX **Le Moulin de la Reillère**

171 rte Houdan – ✆ 01 30 92 22 00 – le-moulin.reillere@wanadoo.fr – Fax 01 34 97 82 85 – Closed 10 August-1st September, Saturday lunch, Sunday dinner and Monday

Rest – Menu € 25 (weekdays), € 32/48 – Carte € 39/60

◆ Pleasant, refined restaurant located in an old mill with exposed beams. The terrace opens onto an attractive flower garden. Classic cuisine and a nice selection of cheeses.

in Rosay 10 km by ③ – **pop. 364 – alt. 98 m –** ✉ **78790**

XX **Auberge de la Truite**

1 r. Boinvilliers – ✆ 01 34 76 30 52 – aubergedelatruite@wanadoo.fr – Fax 01 34 76 30 65 – Closed 25 August-9 September, 1st-13 January, Tuesday lunch, Sunday dinner and Monday

Rest – Menu € 30 (weekdays)/53

◆ A charming interior and terrace giving onto the Mantes countryside: this spruce stone inn is a charming rural establishment. Classic dishes and selected wines.

MANTES-LA-VILLE – 78 Yvelines – 311 G2 – see Mantes-la-Jolie

MANTHELAN – 37 Indre-et-Loire – 317 N6 – alt. 102 m – ✉ 37240 11 B3

Paris 291 – Orléans 166 – Tours 55 – Joué-lès-Tours 49 – Châtellerault 53

Le Vieux Tilleul

8 r. Nationale – ✆ 02 47 92 24 32 – le-vieux-tilleul@wanadoo.fr

4 rm – €60 €70/85 – **Table d'hôte** – Menu € 22 bi

◆ Charming house run by a Belgian couple, beautifully decorated with a successful coupling of classic and modern. Relaxing garden; painting classes. The owner concocts traditional family cuisine in the restaurant.

MANVIEUX – 14 Calvados – 303 I3 – pop. 107 – alt. 53 m – ✉ 14117 32 B2

Paris 273 – Caen 39 – Hérouville-Saint-Clair 41 – Saint-Lô 47

La Gentilhommière without rest

4 r. du Port, (lieu dit L'Eglise) – ✆ 02 31 51 97 91 – lagentilhommiere4@wanadoo.fr – Fax 02 31 10 03 17 – **5 rm** – €65 €65

◆ This 18C stone building is located near the Arromanches beach, home to a peaceful hotel providing individually styled rooms in varying colours. A fine breakfast is served including homemade yoghurt and brioche.

MANZAC-SUR-VERN – 24 Dordogne – 329 E5 – pop. 505 – alt. 80 m – ✉ 24110

Paris 502 – Bergerac 34 – Bordeaux 112 – Périgueux 20 4 **C1**

XX **Le Lion d'Or** with rm

pl. Eglise – ✆ 05 53 54 28 09 – lion-dor@lion-dor-manzac.com – Fax 05 53 54 25 50 – Closed 17 November-2 December, 1st-22 February, Sunday dinner except July-August and Monday

8 rm – €47 €52, € 7,50 – ½ P € 52 – **Rest** – Menu (€ 15 bi), € 19/44 – Carte € 28/45

◆ Bright dining room adorned with knick-knacks, serving generous, up-to-date cuisine with regional touches. Rooms renovated in 2004.

MARAIS-VERNIER – 27 Eure – 304 C5 – see Conteville

MARANS – 17 Charente-Maritime – 324 E2 – pop. 4 375 – alt. 1 m – ✉ 17230

Atlantic Coast 38 **B2**

Paris 461 – Fontenay-le-Comte 28 – Niort 56 – La Rochelle 24 – La Roche-sur-Yon 60

Office de tourisme, 62, rue d'Aligre ✆ 05 46 01 12 87, Fax 05 46 35 97 36

La Porte Verte with rm
20 quai Foch – ✆ 05 46 01 09 45 – laporteverte@aol.com
5 rm – €52 €52 – **Rest** – *(open March-October and closed Wednesday) (number of covers limited, pre-book)* Menu €16/32 – Carte €25/46
◆ This charming 19C building on the banks of the canal near the ocean port is a rustic restaurant serving regional cuisine, also providing well-kept guest rooms.

MARAUSSAN – **34 Hérault** – **339** D8 – **see Béziers**

MARÇAY – **37 Indre-et-Loire** – **317** K6 – **see Chinon**

MARCILLAC-LA-CROISILLE – **19 Corrèze** – **329** N4 – **pop. 778** – **alt. 550 m** – ✉ **19320** Dordogne-Berry-Limousin 25 **C3**

Paris 498 – Argentat 26 – Aurillac 80 – Égletons 17 – Mauriac 40 – Tulle 27

at Pont du Chambon 15 km Southeast, by D 978 (dir. Mauriac), D 60 and D 13
✉ **19320 St-Merd-de-Lapleau**

Fabry (Au Rendez-vous des Pêcheurs) with rm
– ✆ 05 55 27 88 39 – contact@rest-fabry.com – Fax 05 55 27 83 19 – Open 13 February-12 November and closed Sunday dinner and Monday off season
8 rm €44 €44/49, €7 – ½ P €44/46 – **Rest** – Menu €16/37 – Carte €29/46
◆ A verdant backdrop to this house standing alone on the banks of the Dordogne, which for three generations has provided regional cooking, light bedrooms and friendly hospitality.

MARCILLY-EN-VILLETTE – **45 Loiret** – **318** J5 – **pop. 1 900** – **alt. 124 m** – ✉ **45240** 12 **C2**

Paris 153 – Blois 83 – Orléans 23 – Romorantin-Lanthenay 55 – Salbris 40

La Ferme des Foucault without rest
6 km south-east on the D 64 (rte de Sennely) – ✆ 02 38 76 94 41 – rbeau@wanadoo.fr – Fax 02 38 76 94 41 – **4 rm** – €70/80 €75/85
◆ This old half-timbered farmhouse is located in the heart of the Sologne forest, providing charming and spacious rooms with rustic furnishings, one of which also features a terrace.

MARCQ-EN-BARŒUL – **59 Nord** – **302** G3 – **see Lille**

MAREUIL-CAUBERT – **80 Somme** – **301** D7 – **see Abbeville**

MARGAUX – **33 Gironde** – **335** G4 – **pop. 1 338** – **alt. 16 m** – ✉ **33460** 3 **B1**

Paris 599 – Bordeaux 29 – Lesparre-Médoc 42

de Margaux 5 route de l'Ile Vincent, North: 1 km, ✆ 05 57 88 87 40.

Relais de Margaux
5 route de l'Ile Vincent, 2.5 km north-westward – ✆ 05 57 88 38 30 – relais-margaux@relais-margaux.fr – Fax 05 57 88 31 73
92 rm – €159/319 €159/319, €25 – 8 suites
Rest *L'Ile Vincent* – chemin de l'Ile Vincent *(closed 1st December-30 March, lunch except Sunday from September-June, Monday and Tuesday)* Menu €46/84 – Carte €57/106
Rest *Brasserie du Lac* – chemin de l'Ile Vincent – Menu €21 (lunch) – Carte €37/55
◆ Former winegrower's estate between the estuary and vineyards. Golf in the park, hi-tech spa and comfortable rooms. Smart interior, lovely terrace, modern menu and selection of local vintages. A trendy brasserie with its culinary roots in the soil. In summer, enjoy outdoor dining on the attractive terrace.

Le Pavillon de Margaux
3 r. G. Mandel – ✆ 05 57 88 77 54 – le-pavillon-margaux@wanadoo.fr – Fax 05 57 88 77 73 – Closed 22 December-3 January
14 rm – €70/120 €70/120, €12 – ½ P €153/205
Rest – *(closed Tuesday and Wednesday 1st November-1st April)* Menu €14 (weekday lunch), €28/51 – Carte €33/36
◆ Handsome 19C abode surrounded by vineyards. Attractive plush sitting room and pleasant bedrooms decorated on the theme of the Médoc estates. Smart dining room and veranda facing the prestigious Margaux vineyard. Traditional menu.

XX **Le Savoie**

1 pl. Trémoille – ✆ 05 57 88 31 76 – Fax 05 57 88 31 76 – Closed 22-28 December, Monday dinner except from June to September and Sunday dinner
Rest – Menu (€ 15), € 27/88 – Carte € 36/59
◆ This 19C house has a pleasant interior and a patio terrace with a glass ceiling. Tasty cuisine prepared in a coal-fired oven, plus a good selection of Bordeaux wines.

in Arcins 6 km Northwest On D 2 – **pop. 304** – **alt. 10 m** – ✉ 33460

X **Le Lion d'Or**

✆ 05 56 58 96 79 – Closed July, 24 December-2 January, Sunday, Monday and holidays
Rest – *(number of covers limited, pre-book)* Menu € 14 bi (weekdays) – Carte € 22/52
◆ Attractive rustic bistro with light wood panelling and wine rack decor. Generous, country-style cuisine. A warm and friendly ambience guaranteed.

MARGÈS – 26 Drôme – 332 D3 – pop. 723 – alt. 282 m – ✉ 26260 43 E2

Paris 551 – Grenoble 92 – Hauterives 14 – Romans-sur-Isère 13 – Valence 36

Auberge Le Pont du Chalon

2 km south on D 538 – ✆ 04 75 45 62 13 – pontduchalon@wanadoo.fr – Fax 04 75 45 60 19 – Closed 18 August-4 September, 22-30 December, 16 February-4 March, Sunday dinner and Monday
9 rm – †€ 39/44 ††€ 39/54, ☕ € 6 – ½ P € 44/46 – **Rest** – *(closed Wednesday dinner from September to May, Sunday dinner, Monday and Tuesday)* Menu € 18/32 – Carte € 23/33
◆ This inn built in 1900 is nestled behind a curtain of plane trees, providing a warm and refined atmosphere with modern and colourful décor. A "rustic chic" restaurant with terrace and a French bowls pitch for a game before or after your meal.

MARGUERITTES – 30 Gard – 339 L5 – see Nîmes

MARIENTHAL – 67 Bas-Rhin – 315 K4 – ✉ 67500 1 B1

Paris 479 – Haguenau 5 – Saverne 42 – Strasbourg 30

XX **Le Relais Princesse Maria Leczinska**

1 r. Rothbach – ✆ 03 88 93 43 48 – Closed Saturday lunch, Sunday dinner and Wednesday – **Rest** – *(number of covers limited, pre-book)* Menu € 16 (weekday lunch), € 34/48 – Carte € 36/41
◆ Traditional setting (beams, stained glass, enamelled stove) for a concise modern menu, rich in flavour.

MARIGNANE – 13 Bouches-du-Rhône – 340 G5 – pop. 34 006 – alt. 10 m – ✉ 13700 Provence 40 B3

Paris 753 – Aix-en-Provence 24 – Marseille 26 – Martigues 16 – Salon-de-Provence 33
Marseille-Provence: ✆ 04 42 14 14 14.
Office de tourisme, 4, bld Frédéric Mistral ✆ 04 42 77 04 90, Fax 04 42 31 49 39
Rove underground canal ★ Southeast: 3 km.

to Marseille-Provence Airport North – ✉ 13700

Pullman

– ✆ 04 42 78 42 78 – h0541@accor.com – Fax 04 42 78 42 70
177 rm – †€ 185/295 ††€ 185/315, ☕ € 23 – 1 suite
Rest – *✆ 04 42 78 42 83* – Menu € 45/65
◆ This 1970s hotel is in the process of a makeover: renovated rooms, some in an elegant Provençal style, others with a more low-key contemporary look. Fitness facilities. This in vogue restaurant is decorated in a minimalist style and has modern fusion cuisine to match.

Best Western

✉ 13127 Vitrolles – ✆ 04 42 15 54 00 – info@bwmrs.com – Fax 04 42 89 69 18
120 rm †€ 104/145 ††€ 104/145, ☕ € 11,50 – **Rest** Menu € 29 bi – Carte € 30/43
◆ This recent building hides an unexpectedly classic interior. Louis XVI furniture in the bedrooms and crystal chandelier in the hall. Modern dining room with wood panelling. Teak terrace by the swimming pool.

Z.I. Les Estroublans **4 km Northeast by D 9 (Vitrolles road) – ✉ 13127 Vitrolles**

Novotel
24 r. de Madrid – ☎ 04 42 89 90 44 – h0442@accor.com – Fax 04 42 79 07 04
117 rm – €100/150 €100/150, ☕ €14
Rest – Menu (€21), €24 – Carte €24/41
◆ Spacious and soundproofed rooms, gradually being redone in the latest style of this chain hotel. Pretty rose garden and swimming pool. Restaurant serving traditional cuisine. Novotel café with snacks and trendy decor.

MARIGNY-ST-MARCEL – 74 Haute-Savoie – 328 I6 – pop. 629 – alt. 404 m – ✉ 74150

46 **F1**

Paris 536 – Aix-les-Bains 22 – Annecy 19 – Bellegarde-sur-Valserine 43 – Rumilly 6

Blanc with rm
– ☎ 04 50 01 09 50 – hotelblanc@wanadoo.fr – Fax 04 50 64 58 05
– Closed 26 December-2 January
16 rm – €55/120 €55/120, ☕ €11 – 1 suite – ½ P €65/85
Rest – *(closed Sunday dinner and Saturday except July-August)* Menu (€16), €24/86 – Carte €41/66
◆ Family-run inn with two neat dining rooms (one for winter, one for summer); classic menu. Shaded terrace giving onto the garden and pool. Pleasant rooms.

MARINGUES – 63 Puy-de-Dôme – 326 G7 – pop. 2 504 – alt. 315 m – ✉ 63350

Auvergne

6 **C2**

Paris 409 – Clermont-Ferrand 32 – Lezoux 16 – Riom 22 – Thiers 23 – Vichy 29

Le Clos Fleuri with rm
rte de Clermont – ☎ 04 73 68 70 46 – closfleuri63@wanadoo.fr
– Fax 04 73 68 75 58 – Closed 16 February-14 March, Monday except dinner July-August, Friday dinner and Sunday dinner September-June
14 rm – €44/48 €49/54, ☕ €7 – ½ P €52 – **Rest** – Menu (€17), €23/40 – Carte €27/47
◆ Run by the same family for three generations, the rustic dining rooms of this house on the way out of the village, overlook the lovely garden. Regional-classic fare.

MARLENHEIM – 67 Bas-Rhin – 315 I5 – pop. 3 365 – alt. 195 m – ✉ 67520

Alsace-Lorraine

1 **A1**

Paris 468 – Haguenau 50 – Molsheim 13 – Saverne 18 – Strasbourg 21

Office de tourisme, place du Kaufhus ☎ 03 88 87 75 80, Fax 03 88 87 75 80

Le Cerf (Michel Husser)
30 r. Gén. de Gaulle – ☎ 03 88 87 73 73 – info@lecerf.com – Fax 03 88 87 68 08
– Closed 2-8 January
13 rm – €90 €140/200, ☕ €15 – ½ P €98/147
Rest – *(closed Tuesday and Wednesday)* Menu €39 (weekday lunch), €85/125 – Carte €56/104
Spec. Tartare de daurade sauvage, garniture aigre-douce. Chevreuil des chasses du Geissweg poêlé aux griottes (May to January). Baba à l'alsacienne. **Wines** Riesling, Pinot noir.
◆ An old posthouse transformed into an elegant hostelry. Stylish bedrooms. Pretty flower-decked courtyard. Alsace takes pride of place in this restaurant decorated with wood panelling and regional paintings. Inventive cuisine focused on the produce and the region.

Hostellerie Reeb
– ☎ 03 88 87 52 70 – hostellerie-reeb@wanadoo.fr – Fax 03 88 87 69 73
Closed 7-21 January, Sunday dinner and Monday
26 rm – €50 €50, ☕ €8 – ½ P €50 – **Rest** – *(lunch only)* Menu €35/46
Rest *La Crémaillère* – Menu €11,50 (weekday lunch), €35/38 – Carte €25/47
◆ A half-timbered building on the doorstep of the village where the wine route starts. Comfortable, light rooms furnished in a rustic spirit (family heirlooms and local fabrics). Classic menu in tune with the plush interior. At the Crémaillère find an all-wood decor and regional fare.

MARLY-LE-ROI – 78 Yvelines – **312** B2 – **101** 12 – **see Paris, Area**

MARMANDE – 47 Lot-et-Garonne – **336** C2 – **pop. 17 199** – **alt. 30 m** – ✉ **47200** Atlantic Coast 4 **C2**

Paris 666 – Agen 67 – Bergerac 57 – Bordeaux 90 – Libourne 65

Office de tourisme, boulevard Gambetta ✆ 05 53 64 44 44, Fax 05 53 20 17 19

Le Capricorne rm, VISA

Agen road, 2 km on D 813 – ✆ 05 53 64 16 14 – contact@lecapricorne-hotel.com – Fax 05 53 20 80 18 – Closed 19 December-4 January

34 rm – €62 €72, €8 – ½ P €64/90

Rest ***Le Trianon*** *– ✆ 05 53 20 80 94 (closed Sunday except dinner June-October and Saturday)* Menu (€16), €20 (weekdays)/45 – Carte €23/48

◆ Built in the 1970s, this hotel is regularly spruced up: functional, well-kept, soundproofed rooms. Brand new bathrooms. Excellent value for money. Traditional cuisine and Marmandais wines await you at the Trianon. Small summer terrace.

to A 62 interchange 9 km South by D 933 – ✉ **47430 Ste-Marthe**

Les Rives de l'Avance without rest VISA

Moulin de Trivail – ✆ 05 53 20 60 22 – Fax 05 53 20 98 76

16 rm – €38/48 €43/52, €6

◆ This hotel adjoining a water mill makes an unexpected peaceful and green haven so close to the motorway. Functional and colourful rooms. Lounge with a piano.

at Pont-des-Sables 5 km south by D 933 – ✉ **47200**

Syndicat d'initiative, Val de Garonne-Pont des Sables ✆ 05 53 89 25 59, Fax 05 53 93 28 03

Auberge de l'Escale VISA

– ✆ 05 53 93 60 11 – restaurant.escale@wanadoo.fr – Fax 05 53 83 09 15 – Closed 1st-15 September, 2-12 January, Sunday dinner and Monday

Rest – Menu €19 (weekday lunch), €23/63 bi – Carte €30/62

◆ This Landes house is popular with boaters on the canal. Attractive interior with fireplace (grilled meats) and summer terrace. Traditional and seasonal cuisine.

MARMANHAC – 15 Cantal – **330** C4 – **pop. 706** – **alt. 650 m** – ✉ **15250** 5 **B3**

Paris 566 – Clermont-Ferrand 154 – Aurillac 17 – Saint-Flour 69 – Arpajon-sur-Cère 19

Château de Sédaiges without rest VISA

– ✆ 04 71 47 30 01 – bdvarax@netcourrier.com – Open 1st May-30 September

5 rm – €110/120 €110/120

◆ This family château, typical of the Troubadour style (12C-19C), is surrounded by parkland. Charming rooms adorned with antiques and tapestries. Tasty country breakfast.

MARNE-LA-VALLÉE – Île-de-France – **312** E2 – **101** 19 – **see Paris, Area**

MARQUAY – 24 Dordogne – **329** H6 – **pop. 477** – **alt. 175 m** – ✉ **24620** Dordogne-Berry-Limousin 4 **D3**

Paris 530 – Brive-la-Gaillarde 55 – Périgueux 60 – Sarlat-la-Canéda 12

La Condamine rm, VISA

Meyrals road: 1 km – ✆ 05 53 29 64 08 – hotel.lacondamine@wanadoo.fr – Fax 05 53 28 81 59 – Open from Easter to Nov. school holidays

22 rm – €40/58 €40/58, €8 – ½ P €47/57

Rest – *(dinner only)* Menu €16/35 – Carte €16/36

◆ A traditional-style building overlooking the Périgord countryside. A few rooms have balconies with a view of the countryside. Simple rustic decor. Miniature golf, and boules pitch. Family guesthouse-style restaurant and terrace opening onto the garden and swimming pool.

MARQUISE – 62 Pas-de-Calais – 301 D3 – pop. 4 580 – alt. 57 m – ✉ 62250

Northern France and the Paris Region 30 **A1**

Paris 264 – Calais 24 – Arras 113 – Boulogne-sur-Mer 13 – Saint-Omer 355

Office de tourisme, 13, place Louis le Sénéchal ✆ 08 20 20 76 00, Fax 03 21 85 39 64

XX **Le Grand Cerf**

34 av. Ferber – ✆ 03 21 87 55 05 – s.pruvot@legrandcerf.com – Fax 03 21 33 61 09 – Closed Sunday dinner, Thursday dinner and Monday

Rest – Menu (€ 24), € 28/59 – Carte € 45/65

◆ This former post house dating from 1795 has been renovated, and diners will enjoy its appetising up-to-date cuisine in the smart dining room.

MARSAC-SUR-DON – 44 Loire-Atlantique – 316 F2 – pop. 1 327 – alt. 50 m – ✉ 44170

34 **B2**

Paris 408 – Nantes 50 – Saint-Herblain 53 – Rezé 59 – St-Sébastien-sur-Loire 59

La Mérais without rest

1,3 km south on D44 – ✆ 02 40 79 50 78 – lamerais@wanadoo.fr

3 rm – €42 €55

◆ This low lying, blue schist cottage set in grounds near the village is full of the charm of a country home. Warm, welcoming rooms. Breakfast served on the terrace in fine weather.

MARSANNAY-LA-CÔTE – 21 Côte-d'Or – 320 J6 – see Dijon

MARSANNE – 26 Drôme – 332 C6 – pop. 998 – alt. 250 m – ✉ 26740

Lyon - Rhone Valley 44 **B3**

Paris 611 – Lyon 149 – Romans-sur-Isère 69 – Valence 48

Office de tourisme, Place Emile Loubet ✆ 04 75 90 31 59, Fax 04 75 90 31 40

Le Mas du Chatelas rm,

La Plaine – ✆ 04 75 52 97 31 – philippe@lemasduchatelas.com – Fax 04 75 53 14 48

5 rm – €75/90 €85/135 – ½ P € 255/300

Table d'hôte – Menu € 20/35 bi

◆ This 18C farmhouse provides rooms with a refined country-style décor, and romantic candle-lit dinners; terrace dining also possible.

MARSEILLAN – 34 Hérault – 339 G8 – pop. 6 199 – alt. 3 m – ✉ 34340

Languedoc-Roussillon-Tarn Gorges 23 **C2**

Paris 754 – Agde 7 – Béziers 31 – Montpellier 49 – Pézenas 20 – Sète 24

Office de tourisme, avenue de la Méditerranée ✆ 04 67 21 82 43, Fax 04 67 21 82 58

XX **La Table d'Émilie**

8 pl. Couverte – ✆ 04 67 77 63 59 – Fax 04 67 01 72 02 – Closed 5-30 November, 15-28 February, Monday lunch and Thursday lunch 1st July-30 September, Sunday dinner, Monday and Wednesday 1st October-1st July

Rest – Menu € 19 (weekday lunch), € 28/50 – Carte € 45/55

◆ Enjoy a lovely dinner in this small 12C house and its dining room with exposed stonework, ogive vaults and verdant patio. Cuisine based on ingredients of the day.

XX **Le Château du Port**

9 quai de la Résistance – ✆ 04 67 77 31 67 – lechateauduport@wanadoo.fr – Fax 04 67 77 11 30 – Open March-October

Rest – Menu € 26/32 – Carte € 35/65

◆ A contemporary bistro housed in a fine 19C residence, serving seafood and regional modern cuisine; pleasant terrace overlooking the canal.

X **Chez Philippe**

20 r. Suffren – ✆ 04 67 01 70 62 – chezphilippe@club-internet.fr – Fax 04 67 01 70 62 – Closed 18 November-16 February, Tuesday except from 15 June to 15 September and Monday

Rest – *(pre-book)* Menu € 28

◆ An attractive restaurant with a southern-French atmosphere near the Thau basin, serving Mediterranean cuisine in a colourful dining area or on the summer terrace.

G. Gsell/PHOTONONSTOP

Le vieux port et Notre-Dame de la Garde

MARSEILLE

P **Department:** 13 Bouches-du-Rhône
Michelin LOCAL map: n° **340** H6 **114** 28
Paris 769 – Lyon 314 – Nice 189 – Torino 373 – Toulon 64 – Toulouse 405

Population: 798 430 **B3**
Pop. built-up area: 1 349 772
Postal Code: ✉ 13000
Provence

USEFUL INFORMATION

TOURIST OFFICES

Annexe Gare Saint-Charles ☎ 04 91 50 59 18
Office de tourisme, 4, la Canebière ☎ 04 91 13 89 00, Fax 04 91 13 89 20

TRANSPORT

Auto-train ☎ 3635 et tapez 42 (0,34 €/mn)
Tunnel Prado-Carénage : péage 2007, tarif normal : 2,50 €

SEA TRANSPORT

For Château d'If: Frioul If Express boats ☎ 04 91 46 54 65
For Corsica: SNCM 61 bd des Dames (2e) ☎ 0 825 888 088 (0.15 €/mn), Fax 04 91 56 35 86 - CMN 4 quai d'Arenc (2e) ☎ 0 810 201 320, Fax 04 91 99 45 95

AIRPORT

Marseille-Provence ☎ 04 42 14 14 14, by ①: 28 km

A FEW GOLF COURSES

18 de Marseille-La Salette 65, impasse des Vaudrans, East: 10 km at La Valentine, ☎ 04 91 27 12 16 ;
9 d'Allauch Allauch Domaine de Fontvieille, Northeast: 14 km by Allauch road, ☎ 04 91 07 28 22.

TO BE SEEN

AROUND OLD HARBOUR

Le vieux port★★ - Quai des Belges (fish market) ET 5 - Musée d'Histoire de Marseille★ ET M3 - Musée du Vieux Marseille DET M7 - Musée des Docks romains★ DT M6 - ⋞★ from the St-Laurent viewpoint DT D - Musée Cantini★ FU M2

QUARTIER DU PANIER

Vieille Charité Centre ★★: Musée d'archéologie méditerranéenne, Musée d'Arts africains, océaniens, amérindiens MAAOA★★ DS E - Former Major Cathedral★ DS B

NOTRE-DAME-DE-LA-GARDE

⋞★★★ of the N.-D.-de -la-Garde basilica square EV

- St-Victor basilica★ (crypte★★) DU

LA CANEBIÈRE

from rue Longue-des-Capucins to cours Julien: place du Marché-des-Capucins, rue du Musée, rue Rodolph-Pollack, rue d'Aubagne, rue St-Ferréol.

QUARTIER LONGCHAMP

Musée Grobet-Labadié★★ GS M8 - Palais Longchamp★ GS: musée des Beaux-Arts★ and musée d'Histoire naturelle★

SOUTHERN DISTRICTS

Corniche Président-J.-F.-Kennedy★★ AYZ - Parc du Pharo DU

AROUND MARSEILLE

Visit of the harbour★ - Château d'If★★: ✻★★★ off Marseille - Massif des Calanques★★ - Musée de la faïence★

Sofitel Vieux Port ← old port, rm, VISA AE
36 bd Ch.-Livon ✉ 13007 – ✆ 04 91 15 59 00
– h0542@accor.com – Fax 04 91 15 59 50 *p. 6* DU **n**
131 rm – †€ 149/410 ††€ 159/425, ☐ € 22 – 3 suites
Rest *Les Trois Forts* – *✆ 04 91 15 59 56* – Menu (€ 44), € 57/87
– Carte € 88/110
◆ This fine hotel, overlooking the Vieux Port and its historic forts, provides spacious Provençal or contemporary rooms; some have a terrace and a sea view. Restaurant serving modern cuisine, featuring panoramic views.

Radisson SAS rest, VISA AE
38 quai Rive-Neuve ✉ 13007 – ✆ 04 88 92 19 50
– info.marseille@radissonsas.com – Fax 04 88 92 19 51 *p. 6* DU **d**
189 rm – †€ 165/495 ††€ 175/495, ☐ € 22 – 12 suites
Rest – *(closed Saturday lunch and Sunday)* Menu € 35 (weekdays)/105 bi
– Carte € 39/78
◆ Imposing modern designer building overlooking the old port. Provençal or African influences in the hi-tech rooms. Some command picture postcard views. Softly lit trendy restaurant with Mediterranean inspired menu.

Villa Massalia ← VISA AE
17 pl. Louis-Bonnefon ✉ 13007 – ✆ 04 91 72 90 00
– villamassalia@concorde-hotels.com – Fax 04 91 72 90 01 *p. 5* BZ
136 rm – †€ 325 ††€ 325, ☐ € 18 – 4 suites
Rest *Yin Yang* – Menu (€ 22), € 38 – Carte € 44/51
◆ Recent construction on the edge of Borély Park, with contemporary style, comfortable and well-equipped rooms, ideal for a business clientele. At Ying Yang, the Asian inspired décor is in harmony with the fusion cuisine. Terrace opposite the race track.

Pullman Palm Beach ← Prado bay, VISA AE
200 Corniche J.-F.-Kennedy ✉ 13007 – ✆ 04 91 16 19 00
– h3485@accor.com – Fax 04 91 16 19 39 *p. 4* AZ **b**
150 rm – †€ 160/325 ††€ 180/350, ☐ € 23 – 10 suites
Rest *La Réserve* – *✆ 04 91 16 19 21* – Menu (€ 38 bi), € 45 bi
– Carte € 49/63
◆ Nautical in design and spirit, this huge modern vessel is anchored opposite the famous Château d'If island. Comfortable, well-equipped rooms, well being centre and extensive conference facilities. La Réserve features a very modern setting and updated Mediterranean food.

Le Petit Nice (Gérald Passédat) ← sea, rest, VISA AE
anse de Maldormé, 160 Corniche J.-F.-Kennedy
✉ 13007 – ✆ 04 91 59 25 92 – passedat@relaischateaux.com
– Fax 04 91 59 28 08 – Closed 1st-15 January *p. 4* AZ **d**
13 rm – †€ 230/700 ††€ 230/700, ☐ € 30 – 3 suites
Rest – *(closed Sunday except dinner mid June-August and Monday except dinner May-September)* Menu € 65 (weekday lunch), € 110/200
– Carte € 119/200
Spec. Menu "Découverte de la mer". Anémones de mer en onctueux iodé puis en beignets légers, lait mousseux au caviar. Bouille-Abaisse comme un menu. **Wines** Vins de pays des Bouches-du-Rhône, Bandol.
◆ These two superbly located villas dating from 1910 ooze with unostentatious luxury. Informal atmosphere, modern decor and enchanting views. Remarkable, retired and inventive cuisine.

New Hôtel of Marseille rm, VISA AE
71 bd Ch.-Livon ✉ 13007 – ✆ 04 91 31 53 15
– info@newhotelofmarseille – Fax 04 91 31 20 00 *p. 6* DU **v**
92 rm – †€ 195/235 ††€ 215/260, ☐ € 16 – 8 suites
Rest – Menu € 25 bi (lunch)/40 – Carte € 38/53
◆ Brand new hotel incorporating a 19C building. Low key, modern, well-equipped bedrooms, some of which command splendid views of the old port. The trendy restaurant serves food of southern and further flung inspiration.

MARSEILLE

Street	Grid	No.
Aix (R. d')	BY	
Anthoine (R. d')	AX	
Baille (Bd)	BCY	
Belsunce (Cours)	BY	
Blancarde (Bd de la)	CY	
Bompard (Bd)	AYZ	
Briançon (Bd de)	BX	13
Canebière (La)	BY	
Cantini (Av. Jules)	BCZ	
Capelette (Av. de la)	CYZ	
Castellane (Pl.)	BY	
Catalans (R. des)	AY	16
Chartreux (Av. des)	CY	17
Chave (Bd)	BCY	
Chutes Lavie (Av.)	CX	
Dunkerque (Bd de)	AX	
Duparc (Bd Françoise)	CXY	
Endoume (R. d')	AY	
Estrangin (Bd G.)	ABZ	
Fleming (Bd Alexander)	CX	
Foch (Av. Mar.)	CY	
Guesde (Pl. Jules)	BY	35
Guibal (R.)	BX	
Guigou (Bd)	BX	36
Jeanne-d'Arc (Bd)	CY	
Jean-Jaurès (Pl.)	BY	
Lazaret (Quai du)	AX	
Leclerc (Av. Gén.)	BY	
Lesseps (Bd Ferdinand de)	AX	40
Lieutaud (Cours)	BY	
Livon (Bd Charles)	AY	
Mazargues (Av. de)	BZ	
Mermoz (R. Jean)	BZ	
Michelet (Bd)	BCZ	
Moulin (Bd Jean)	CY	47
National (Bd)	BX	
Notre-Dame (Bd)	BY	
Paradis (R.)	BYZ	
Paris (Bd de)	ABX	
Pelletan (Av. C.)	BXY	
Périer (Bd)	BZ	
Plombières (Bd de)	BX	
Pologne (Pl. de)	CY	51
Pompidou (Prom. Georges)	BZ	52
Prado (Av. du)	BYZ	
Président-J.-F.-Kennedy (Corniche)	AYZ	
Pyat (R. Félix)	BX	
Rabatau (Bd)	BCZ	
République (R. de la)	ABY	
Roches (Av. des)	AZ	
Rolland (Bd Romain)	CZ	
Rolland (R. du Cdt)	BZ	
Rome (R. de)	BY	
Roucas Blanc (Chemin du)	AZ	
Rouet (R. du)	BYZ	
Ste-Marguerite (Bd)	CZ	
Ste-Marthe (Ch. de)	BX	
St-Just (Av. de)	CX	
St-Pierre (R.)	BCY	
Sakakini (Bd)	CY	
Salengro (Av. Roger)	BX	
Sartre (Av. Jean-Paul)	CX	59
Schlœsing (Bd)	CZ	
Sébastopol (Pl.)	CY	
Strasbourg (Bd)	BX	61
Teisseire (Bd R.)	CZ	
Tellène (Bd)	AY	
Timone (Av. de la)	CY	
Toulon (Av. de)	BCY	
Vallon l'Oriol (Chemin)	AZ	
Vauban (Bd)	BY	
Verdun (R. de)	CY	70

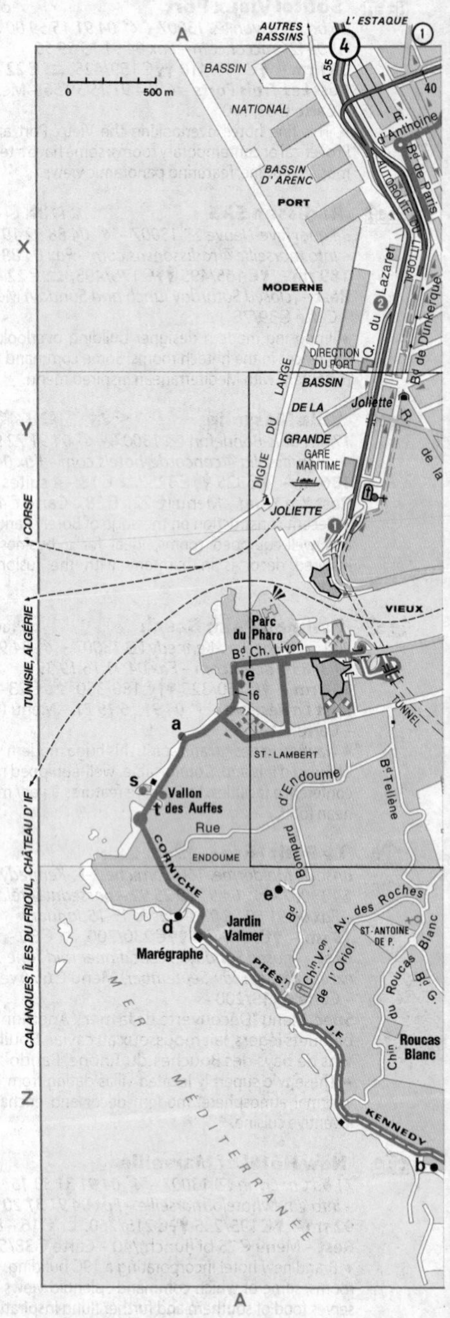

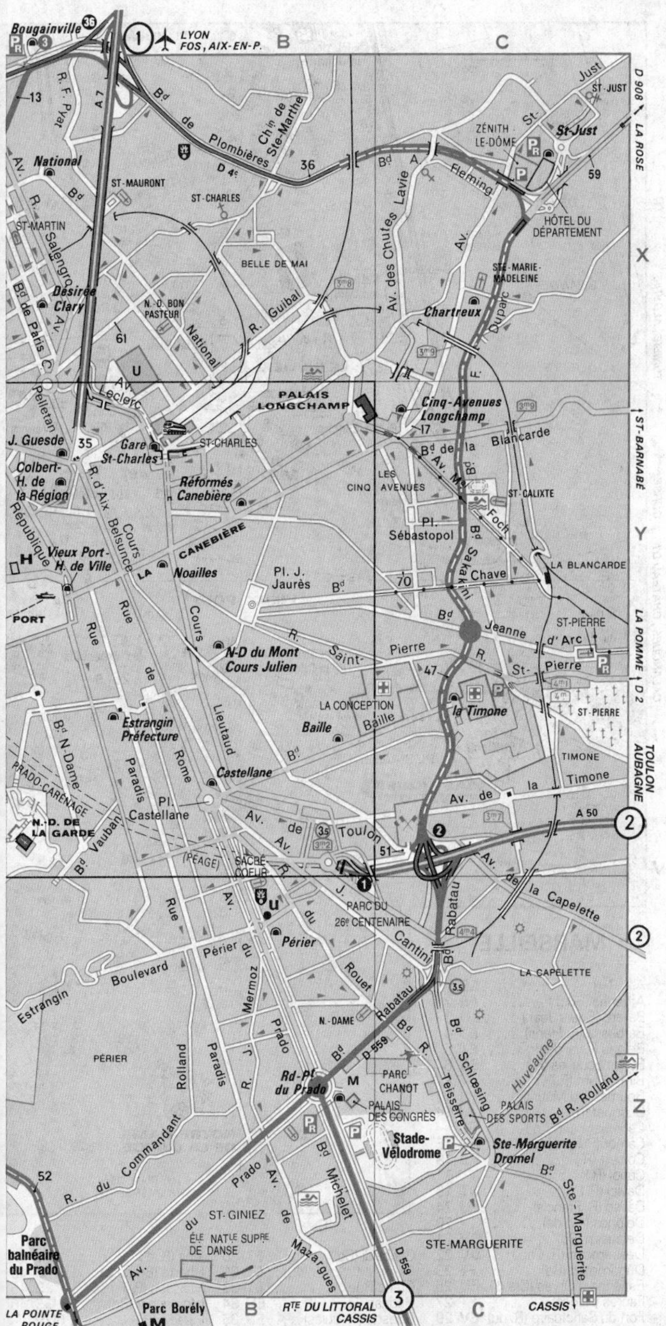

LYON
FOS, AIX-EN-P.
Bougainville
B
C
X
Y
Z
D 908 LA ROSE
ST-BARNABÉ
LA POMME D 2
TOULON AUBAGNE
A 50
St-Just
ZÉNITH LE-DÔME
HÔTEL DU DÉPARTEMENT
Bd de Plombières
National
ST-MAURONT
ST-CHARLES
ST-MARTIN
BELLE DE MAI
Désirée Clary
N.-D. BON PASTEUR
Chartreux
STE-MARIE-MADELEINE
PALAIS LONGCHAMP
Cinq-Avenues Longchamp
Gare St-Charles
J. Guesde
Colbert-H. de la Région
Réformés Canebière
LES CINQ AVENUES
ST-CALIXTE
Pl. Sébastopol
LA BLANCARDE
Vieux Port-H. de Ville
PORT
LA CANEBIÈRE
Noailles
Pl. J. Jaurès
ST-PIERRE
N-D du Mont Cours Julien
LA CONCEPTION
la Timone
Baille
Estrangin Préfecture
Castellane
Pl. Castellane
TIMONE
PRADO-CARENAGE
N.-D. DE LA GARDE
SACRÉ-CŒUR
PARC DU 26e CENTENAIRE
Périer
LA CAPELETTE
N.-DAME
PÉRIER
Rd-Pt du Prado
PARC CHANOT
PALAIS DES CONGRÈS
PALAIS DES SPORTS
Stade-Vélodrome
Ste-Marguerite Dromel
ST-GINIEZ
ÉLE NATLE SUPRE DE DANSE
STE-MARGUERITE
Parc balnéaire du Prado
LA POINTE ROUGE
Parc Borély
RTE DU LITTORAL CASSIS
CASSIS

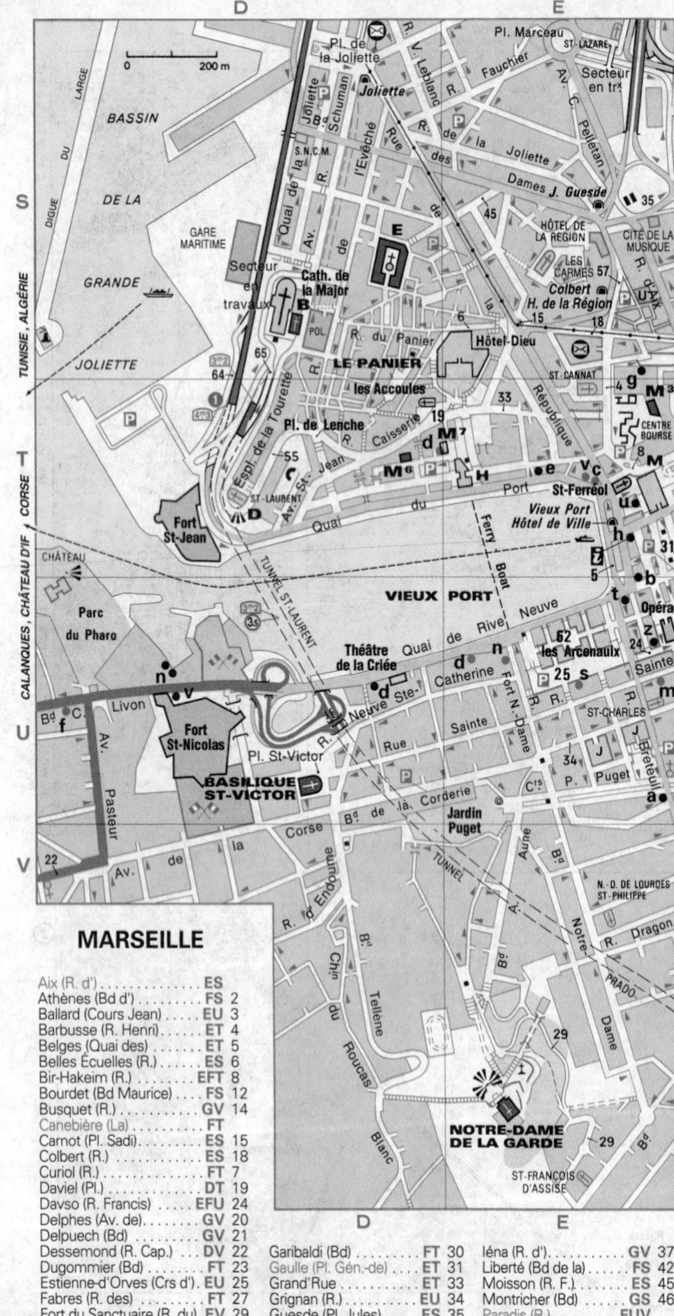

Aix (R. d') . . . . ES
Athènes (Bd d') . . . . FS 2
Ballard (Cours Jean) . . . . . EU 3
Barbusse (R. Henri) . . . . . . ET 4
Belges (Quai des) . . . . ET 5
Belles Écuelles (R.) . . . . . . ES 6
Bir-Hakeim (R.) . . . . EFT 8
Bourdet (Bd Maurice) . . . . FS 12
Busquet (R.) . . . . GV 14
Canebière (La) . . . . FT
Carnot (Pl. Sadi) . . . . ES 15
Colbert (R.) . . . . ES 18
Curiol (R.) . . . . FT 7
Daviel (Pl.) . . . . DT 19
Davso (R. Francis) . . . . . EFU 24
Delphes (Av. de) . . . . GV 20
Delpuech (Bd) . . . . GV 21
Dessemond (R. Cap.) . . . DV 22
Dugommier (Bd) . . . . FT 23
Estienne-d'Orves (Crs d') . EU 25
Fabres (R. des) . . . . FT 27
Fort du Sanctuaire (R. du) EV 29
Garibaldi (Bd) . . . . FT 30
Gaulle (Pl. Gén.-de) . . . . . ET 31
Grand'Rue . . . . ET 33
Grignan (R.) . . . . EU 34
Guesde (Pl. Jules) . . . . . ES 35
Iéna (R. d') . . . . GV 37
Liberté (Bd de la) . . . . . . FS 42
Moisson (R. F.) . . . . ES 45
Montricher (Bd) . . . . GS 46
Paradis (R.) . . . . FUV

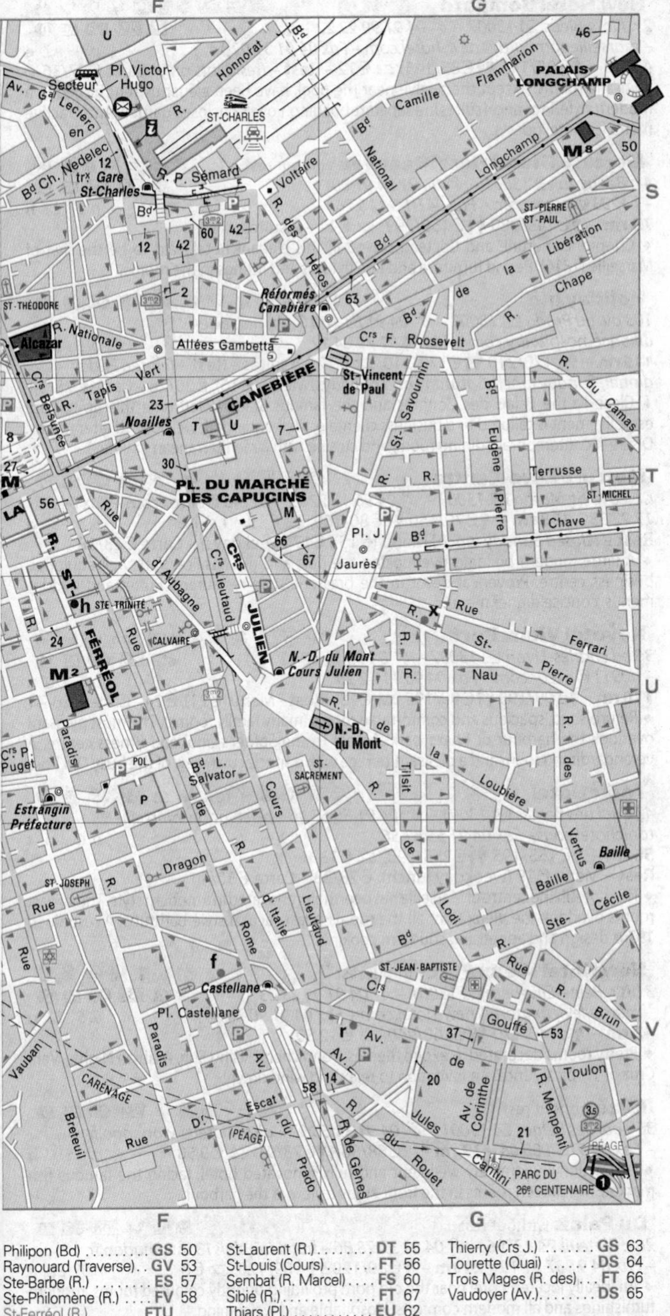
F
G
S
T
U
V
PALAIS LONGCHAMP
Pl. Victor-Hugo
Secteur
Av. Gal Leclerc
en
Bd Ch. Nedelec
trx Gare St-Charles
R. Honnorat
Bd
ST-CHARLES
R. P. Sémard
Voltaire
R. des Héros
Bd National
Camille
Flammarion
Longchamp
M8
ST-PIERRE ST-PAUL
Bd de la Libération
R. Chape
Réformés Canebière
ST-THÉODORE
Alcazar
R. Nationale
Allées Gambetta
Crs F. Roosevelt
Crs Belsunce
R. Tapis Vert
CANEBIÈRE
St-Vincent de Paul
R. St-Savournin
Bd Eugène Pierre
R. du Camas
Noailles
PL. DU MARCHÉ DES CAPUCINS
Terrusse
ST-MICHEL
Chave
Pl. J. Jaurès
Rue d'Aubagne
R. St-Férréol
STE-TRINITÉ
CALVAIRE
Crs Lieutaud
CRS JULIEN
N.-D. du Mont Cours Julien
R. Ferrari
Rue St-Pierre
R. Nau
R. de la Loubière
N.-D. du Mont
M2
Paradis
Crs P. Puget
POL
Bd L. Salvator
ST-SACREMENT
R. de Tilsit
R. des Vertus
Estrangin Préfecture
Cours Lieutaud
R. de Rome
R. d'Italie
Dragon
ST-JOSEPH
Baille
Ste-Cécile
Bd Baille
Lodi
Castellane
Pl. Castellane
ST-JEAN-BAPTISTE
Rue Brun
Crs Gouffé
Av. de Toulon
Av. de Corinthe
R. Menpenti
Vauban
CARÉNAGE
Breteuil
Rue
Escat
Av. du Prado
(PÉAGE)
R. de Gênes
R. Jules
du Rouet
Cantini
PARC DU 26e CENTENAIRE
PÉAGE

New Hôtel Bompard
2 r. Flots-Bleus ✉ 13007 – ✆ 04 91 99 22 22
– marseillebompard@new-hotel.com – Fax 04 91 31 02 14 p. 4 AZ **e**
49 rm – €85/145 €85/145, € 12 – **Rest** – *(residents only)* Carte € 27/36
◆ All the rooms, except the twelve near the pool, have been elegantly refurbished in a modern style. Provençal suites in a separate building. Lovely enclosed garden. An attractive menu for hotel guests.

Mercure Grand Hôtel Beauvau without rest
4 r. Beauvau ✉ 13001 – ✆ 04 91 54 91 00
– h1293@accor.com – Fax 04 91 54 15 76 p. 6 ET **h**
73 rm – €149/289 €159/299, € 17 – 2 suites
◆ Chopin, Lamartine and Cocteau stayed in this elegant hotel, said to be the first of Marseille (1816). Period furniture and fine fixtures and fittings in the rooms.

Holiday Inn
103 av. du Prado ✉ 13008 – ✆ 04 91 83 10 10 – himarseille@alliance-hospitality.com – Fax 04 91 79 84 12 p. 5 BZ **u**
115 rm – €170/210 €170/210, € 17 – 4 suites – **Rest** – *(closed Friday dinner, Sunday lunch, Saturday and holidays)* Menu (€ 16), € 20/26 – Carte € 25/34
◆ Close to the Palais des Congrès and the famous Stade Vélodrome this up-to-date establishment is tailored to a business clientele. Well-equipped, well looked after rooms. Discreet contemporary dining room, and cuisine with a Mediterranean flavour.

Mercure Euro-Centre
r. Neuve-St-Martin ✉ 13001 – ✆ 04 96 17 22 22 – h1148@accor.com – Fax 04 96 17 22 33 – **198 rm** – €70/150 €80/160, € 13 – 1 suite p. 6 EST **g**
Rest – *(closed Sunday lunch)* Menu (€ 15), € 17 (weekdays) – Carte € 23/38
◆ A large modern building overlooking the port and the basilica. Very well equipped business centre. Provençal decor in the brasserie-style restaurant. Buffet and midday menus; concise dinner menu.

Novotel Vieux Port
rm, rm,
36 bd charles-Livon ✉ 13007 – ✆ 04 96 11 42 11
– h0911@accor.com – Fax 04 96 11 42 20 p. 6 DU **n**
110 rm – €99/195 €99/195, € 15 – **Rest** – Menu (€ 21), € 24 – Carte € 26/41
◆ Refurbished, spacious and comfortable rooms (many family rooms). The most pleasant overlook the harbour or Pharo park. Access to the Sofitel's pool and fitness centre. A veranda/dining room and a pleasant terrace with a spectacular view of the busy Old Port.

Tonic Hôtel
rest,
43 quai des Belges ✉ 13001 – ✆ 04 91 55 67 46 – reservation-marseille@tonichotel.com – Fax 04 91 55 67 56 p. 6 EU **t**
56 rm – €155/195 €255/295, € 13
Rest – Menu € 19 (weekday lunch), € 28/38 – Carte € 30/46
◆ This hotel in the centre of Marseille has been fully renovated in a modern style. The largest rooms overlook the Vieux Port; all the rooms boast Jacuzzi style bathtubs. A restrained 1970s design and appetising southern cooking.

New Hôtel Vieux Port without rest
3 bis r. Reine-Élisabeth ✉ 13001 – ✆ 04 91 99 23 23
– marseillevieux-port@new-hotel.com – Fax 04 91 90 76 24 p. 6 ET **u**
42 rm – €140/170 €160/240, € 12,50
◆ Pretty rooms decorated in exotic themes: Pondichery, Rising Sun, Arabian Nights, Vera Cruz or Tropical Africa. An invitation to relax and wind down!

Alizé without rest
35 quai des Belges ✉ 13001 – ✆ 04 91 33 66 97 – alize-hotel@wanadoo.fr – Fax 04 91 54 80 06 – **39 rm** – €68/86 €73/91, € 9,50 p. 6 ETU **b**
◆ A functional, extremely well kept and fully renovated hotel, facing the famous fish market. The sixteen rooms in the front enjoy a view of the harbour.

Du Palais without rest
26 r. Breteuil ✉ 13006 – ✆ 04 91 37 78 86 – hoteldupalais13@wanadoo.fr – Fax 04 91 37 91 19 – **21 rm** – €89/120 €89/120, € 8 p. 7 EU **a**
◆ An ideally located hotel near the old port: providing brightly coloured rooms, modern furnishings and all modern comforts. Hospitable and welcoming.

Hermès without rest
2 r. Bonneterie ✉ 13002 – ✆ 04 96 11 63 63 – hermes@hotelmarseille.com
– Fax 04 96 11 63 64 p. 6 ET **e**
28 rm – †€ 50/98 ††€ 68/98, ☕ € 9
◆ Unpretentious, centrally located hotel with small well-kept rooms; those on the fifth floor have a terrace overlooking the quayside. Panoramic rooftop sun deck.

Une Table au Sud (Lionel Lévy)
2 quai du Port, (1st floor) ✉ 13002 – ✆ 04 91 90 63 53 – unetableausud@wanadoo.fr
– Fax 04 91 90 63 86 – Closed 1st-28 August, 3-11 January, Sunday and Monday
Rest – Menu € 37 (weekday lunch), € 52/105 bi p. 6 ET **c**
Spec. Milkshake de Bouille-Abaisse. Crumble de loup au gingembre et agrumes. Calisson de foie gras au coing et cardamome. **Wines** Côteaux d'Aix-en-Provence, Vin de pays des Bouches du Rhône.
◆ This colourful restaurant delights both the eye and the taste buds, thanks to its inventive cuisine with delicious southern accents, as well as views of the forts and hilltop basilica.

Miramar
12 quai du Port ✉ 13002 – ✆ 04 91 91 10 40 – contact@bouillabaisse.com
– Fax 04 91 56 64 31 – Closed Sunday and Monday p. 6 ET **v**
Rest – Carte € 56/95
◆ This restaurant serving bouillabaisse and other fish specialities on the Vieux Port has a very 1960s style with varnished wood and red armchairs.

L'Épuisette ← Iles du Frioul and Château d'If,
Vallon des Auffes ✉ 13007 – ✆ 04 91 52 17 82 – contact@l-epuisette.com
– Fax 04 91 59 18 80 – Closed 5 August-5 September, Sunday and Monday p. 4 AY **s**
Rest – Menu € 50/110 – Carte € 85/100
Spec. Dôme de cabillaud en carpaccio, paccheri d'œufs brouillés à la truffe. Filets de rouget, sanguins au vinaigre balsamique (autumn). Morue "Lomos", artichauts barigoule. **Wines** Coteaux d'Aix-en-Provence.
◆ Set near the rocks in the picturesque Auffes valley, this restaurant takes you on a pleasant culinary voyage in a light, warm and refined atmosphere. Attentive staff.

Péron ← archipelago of Frioul and château d'If,
56 Corniche J.-F.-Kennedy ✉ 13007 – ✆ 04 91 52 15 22 – info@restaurant-peron.com
– Fax 04 91 52 17 29 – Closed Sunday dinner and Monday from 1st November to 15 April
Rest – Menu € 56/68 p. 4 AY **a**
Spec. Gambas poêlées au tandoori, guacamole, chips de radis noir. Chipirons farcis aux petits légumes, crumble de fenouil. Noisettes d'agneau en croûte de tapenade, poêlée d'artichauts poivrades.
◆ The dining room's elegant contemporary setting and works by local artists complement the superb panoramic sea view. Fine modern cuisine with regional touches.

Chez Fonfon
140 Vallon des Auffes ✉ 13007 – ✆ 04 91 52 14 38 – chezfonfon@aol.com
Fax 04 91 52 14 16 – Closed 2-17 January, Monday lunch and Sunday p. 4 AY **t**
Rest – Menu € 42/55 – Carte € 46/55
◆ A family-run establishment (1952) that is as popular for its decor as for its menu of fresh fish, bought straight off the little boats you can see bobbing down in the harbour.

Charles Livon
89 bd Charles-Livon ✉ 13007 – ✆ 04 91 52 22 41 – info@charleslivon.fr
– Fax 04 91 31 41 63 – Closed August, Christmas holidays, Saturday lunch, Monday lunch and Sunday p. 6 DU **f**
Rest – *(number of covers limited, pre-book)* Menu (€ 19), € 33/68 – Carte € 49/61
◆ Opposite the Palais du Pharo this restaurant has a minimalist decor adorned with orchids. Reinterpreted regional cuisine; fine selection of Provence and Rhône wines.

Des Mets de Provence "Chez Maurice Brun"
18 quai de Rive-Neuve, (2nd Floor) ✉ 13007 – ✆ 04 91 33 35 38
– lesmets.deprovence@orange.fr – Fax 04 91 33 05 69 – Closed 9-25 August, Monday lunch, Saturday lunch and Sunday p. 6 EU **d**
Rest – Menu € 40 bi (lunch only)/60
◆ Reminiscent of Pagnol's Provence, this converted attic of a religious convent is located in the old port. Locally sourced menu served in a decor worthy of a museum!

XX **Michel-Brasserie des Catalans**

6 r. des Catalans ✉ 13007 – ✆ 04 91 52 30 63 – Fax 04 91 59 23 05 – Fermé 15 February-1st March p. 4 AY **e**

Rest – Carte € 58/89

◆ A renovated Marseille restaurant specialising in bouillabaisse, situated opposite the Catalans beach. Locals also enjoy the fish of the day on display.

XX **Les Arcenaulx**

25 cours d'Estienne-d'Orves ✉ 13001 – ✆ 04 91 59 80 30 – restaurant@les-arcenaulx.com – Fax 04 91 54 76 33 – Closed 11-17 August and Sunday p. 6 EU **s**

Rest – Menu € 34/54 – Carte € 40/71

◆ This original establishment, located in a 17C galley ship warehouse, includes a bookshop, publishing company, tea room and restaurant serving Mediterranean style food.

XX **Cyprien**

56 av. de Toulon ✉ 13006 – ✆ 04 91 25 50 00 – faure.lequien@hotmail.fr – Fax 04 91 25 50 00 – Closed 31 July-2 September, 24 December-2 January, Monday dinner, Saturday lunch, Sunday and holidays p. 7 GV **t**

Rest – Menu € 25/60 – Carte € 30/65

◆ This restaurant near the Place Castellane offers classic tasty cuisine and a decor to match. Interior adorned with floral touches and paintings.

X **La Table du Fort**

8 r. Fort-Notre-Dame ✉ 13007 – ✆ 04 91 33 97 65 – mathieulajoinie13@hotmail.fr – Closed 10-25 August, lunch and Sunday p. 6 EU **n**

Rest – Menu € 29 – Carte € 30/55

◆ Popular with locals, this quayside restaurant has a trendy feel with designer lamps, modern art and a host of colourful details. Innovative cuisine.

X **Le Café des Épices**

4 r. Lacydon ✉ 13002 – ✆ 04 91 91 22 69 – cafedesepices@yahoo.fr p. 6 DT **d**

Rest – *(number of covers limited, pre-book)* Menu € 25 bi, € 30 € bi (lunch)/40 bi

◆ This tiny restaurant seats only 20, but the esplanade terrace and its olive grove in the background are delightful. Inventive well-prepared food.

X **Axis**

8 r. Ste-Victoire ✉ 13006 – ✆ 04 91 57 14 70 – axis_restaurant@yahoo.fr – Fax 04 91 57 14 70 – Closed 3-31 August, 24-30 December, Saturday lunch, Monday dinner and Sunday p. 7 VF **f**

Rest – Menu (€ 14), € 17 (weekday lunch), € 28/35 – Carte € 32/43

◆ The seasonal, contemporary-style cuisine makes this establishment worth a detour. Modern decor, with views of the chefs in action and charming welcome.

X **Ca Blanca**

53 r. St-Pierre ✉ 13005 – ✆ 04 91 48 68 23 – contact@restaurant-cablanca.com – Closed Sunday and Monday p. 7 GU **x**

Rest – *(dinner only) (number of covers limited, pre-book)* Menu € 30

◆ Jovial and friendly: patio terrace, candles, tealights, sketches on white walls and jazz. The Spanish influenced southern French cuisine is equally daring.

X **Le Ventre de l'Architecte - Le Corbusier**

280 bd Michelet, (Cité Radieuse, 3rd floor), via ③ ✉ 13008 – ✆ 04 91 16 78 00 – alban.gerardin@club-internet.fr – Fax 04 91 16 78 28 – Closed 5-20 August, 5-15 January, Sunday and Monday p. 5 BCZ

Rest – Carte € 46/56

◆ The rooftop terrace of the 'maison du fada' is home to an unusual restaurant. It overlooks Marseilles and the sea in the distance. Deliciously inventive menu.

in Plan-de-Cuques **10 km Northeast by La Rose and D 908 – pop. 10 503 – alt. 70 m – ✉ 13380**

Caesar

av. G. Pompidou – ✆ 04 91 07 25 25 – contact@lecesar.fr – Fax 04 91 05 37 16

30 rm – †€ 98 ††€ 110/160, ☕ € 10 – ½ P € 95

Rest – Menu € 18 (weekday lunch), € 26/45 – Carte € 32/54

◆ Mediterranean serenity, ochre colour theme, Provencal-styled bedrooms, fitness centre and colonnaded pool: an overwhelming invitation to relax! Regional menu; light airy dining room and pleasant terrace.

MARSOLAN – 32 Gers – 336 F6 – pop. 388 – alt. 171 m – ✉ 32700 28 **B2**

Paris 721 – Toulouse 115 – Auch 43 – Agen 49 – Moissac 67

Lous Grits

au village – ✆ 05 62 28 37 10 – contact@hotel-lousgrits.com – Fax 05 62 28 37 59
4 rm – †€ 200/240 ††€ 200/280, ☕ € 20 – **Rest** – *(dinner only) (resident only)* Menu € 30

◆ Feel right at home at this welcoming establishment which tastefully recreates the Gascon lifestyle (antique furniture, ornaments, local pottery and mosaics, paintings). No-choice set dinner for residents only, served at the fireside.

MARTAINVILLE-EPREVILLE – 76 Seine-Maritime – 304 H5 – pop. 611 – alt. 152 m – ✉ 76116 33 **D2**

Paris 115 – Rouen 18 – Saint-Étienne-du-Rouvray 23 – Sotteville-lès-Rouen 19

Sweet Home

534 r. des Marronniers, access via the Coquetier cul-de-sac – ✆ 02 35 23 76 05 – jean-yves.aucreterre@libertysurf.fr – Fax 02 35 23 76 05
4 rm ☕ – †€ 46/86 ††€ 50/90 – **Table d'hôte** – Menu € 15 bi

◆ A small villa located at the end of a cul-de-sac, providing charming and romantic rooms, each in a different colour. Excellent breakfast and warm hospitality.

MARTEL – 46 Lot – 337 F2 – pop. 1 467 – alt. 225 m – ✉ 46600

Dordogne-Berry-Limousin 29 **C1**

Paris 510 – Brive-la-Gaillarde 33 – Cahors 79 – Figeac 59 – St-Céré 30

Office de tourisme, place des Consuls ✆ 05 65 37 43 44, Fax 05 65 37 37 27

Place des Consuls★ - Façade★ of the Hotel de la Raymondie★.

Relais Ste-Anne

r. Pourtanel – ✆ 05 65 37 40 56 – relais.sainteanne@wanadoo.fr – Fax 05 65 37 42 82 – Hotel: Open 1st March-15 November
16 rm – †€ 40/45 ††€ 70/135, ☕ € 15 – 5 suites – **Rest *Le Patio Ste-Anne*** – *✆ 05 65 37 19 10 (Open mid March-mid November and closed Tuesday except dinner mid June-mid September and Friday lunch)* Menu (€ 22), € 35/54 – Carte € 57/65

◆ A former girls' boarding school surrounded by a garden. Old chapel, elegant lounge and rooms with personal touches. A charming little restaurant, just opposite the hotel, serving contemporary cuisine in a modern dining room. Small patio-terrace.

Auberge des Sept Tours with rm

– ✆ 05 65 37 30 16 – auberge7tours@wanadoo.fr – Fax 05 65 37 41 69 – Closed February holidays – **8 rm** – †€ 40/49 ††€ 40/49, ☕ € 7,50 – ½ P € 57
Rest *(closed Sunday dinner and Monday dinner 28 August-12 July, Monday lunch and Saturday lunch)* Menu € 13,50 bi (weekday lunch), € 25/32 – Carte € 30/52

◆ Attractive veranda-dining room overlooking the countryside. Traditional menu, duck specialities and a mainly regional wine list. Rustic rooms.

MARTIEL – 12 Aveyron – 338 D4 – pop. 823 – alt. 400 m – ✉ 12200 29 **C1**

Paris 613 – Toulouse 134 – Rodez 63 – Cahors 49 – Villefranche-de-Rouergue 11

Les Fontaines without rest

Pleyjean, via Villeneuve road, D 76 – ✆ 05 65 29 46 70 – andreacam@wanadoo.fr – Fax 05 65 29 46 70 – **3 rm** ☕ – †€ 50/70 ††€ 60/80

◆ Old house renovated by an English couple in a rural hamlet near the Aveyron Valley. Attractive lounge, welcoming guestrooms and rustic dining room. Copious breakfast.

MARTIGNÉ-BRIAND – 49 Maine-et-Loire – 317 G5 – pop. 1 847 – alt. 75 m – ✉ 49540

Paris 324 – Nantes 113 – Angers 33 – Cholet 46 – Saumur 33 35 **C2**

Château des Noyers

5 km west on D 208 – ✆ 02 41 54 09 60 – webmaster@chateaudesnoyers.com – Fax 02 41 44 32 63 – Open 1st April-15 November – **5 rm** ☕ – †€ 130/190 ††€ 130/190 – 2 suites – ½ P € 175/235 – **Table d'hôte** – Menu € 45 bi (weekday dinner), € 50 € bi/100 bi

◆ Listed as an historic monument, 16-17C château surrounded by a wine estate. Prestigious setting with period furniture (Louis XV and XVI, Empire). Swimming pool, tennis court. Richelieu fireplace and dressers in the dining room. Gaol converted into a wine cellar with tastings available.

MARTIGUES – 13 Bouches-du-Rhône – 340 F5 – pop. 43 493 – alt. 1 m –
✉ 13500 Provence 40 **B3**

- Paris 769 – Aix-en-Provence 45 – Arles 53 – Marseille 40
- Syndicat d'initiative, rond point de l'Hôtel de Ville ☎ 04 42 42 31 10, Fax 04 42 42 31 11
- Miroir aux oiseaux★ - Étang de Berre★ Z.
- ≤★ of N.D.-des-Marins chapel, 3.5 km by ④.

MARTIGUES

Allende (Bd S.) . . . . **Y** 2
Belges (Esplanade des) . . . . . . **Z** 3
Brescon (Quai) . . . . **Z** 4
Cachin (Bd Marcel) . . . . **Z** 5
Combes (R. L.) . . . . **Z** 7
Denfert-Rochereau (R. Colonel P.) . . . . **Y** 8
Dr-Flemming (Av. du) . . . . **Y** 9
Gambetta (R. L.) . . . . **Z** 12
Girondins (Quai des) . . . . **Y** 13
Lamartine (Pl.) . . . . **Z** 15
Libération (Pl. de la) . . . . **Z** 16
Lorto (Av. P.-di) . . . . **Z** 17
Marceau (Quai F.) . . . . **Z** 18
Martyrs (Pl. des) . . . . **Z** 19
Richaud (Bd) . . . . **Z** 22
Roques (R. Jean) . . . . **Y** 24
Tessé (Quai Maurice) . . . . **Y** 25
4-Septembre (Cours du) . . . . **Z** 27

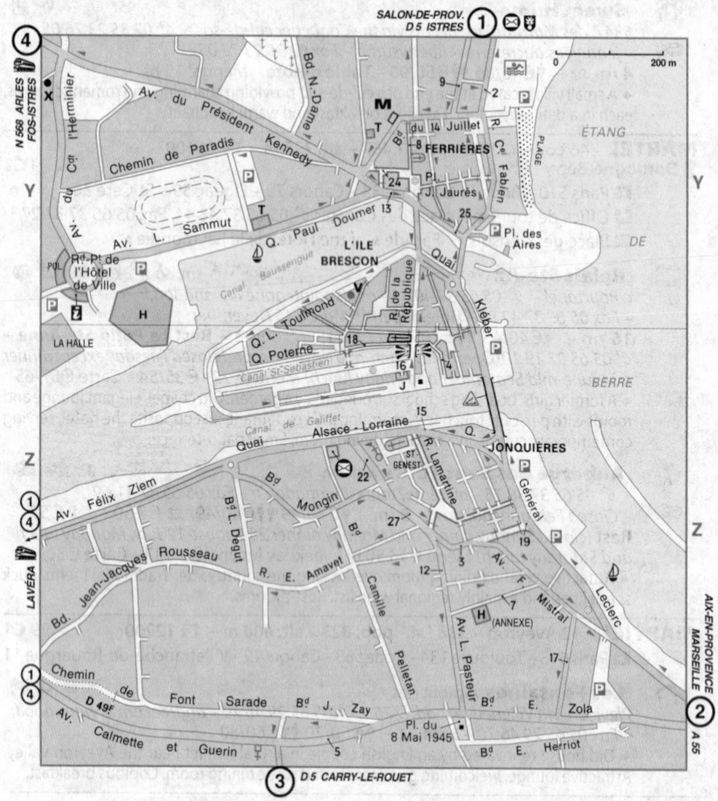

St-Roch

av. G. Braque – ☎ 04 42 42 36 36 – hotel-st-roch@wanadoo.fr
Fax 04 42 80 01 80
63 rm – ♦€ 97 ♦♦€ 114 – ½ P € 70
Rest – *(closed 25 December-1st January)* Menu € 21 – Carte € 28/51 Y **x**

◆ This hotel in the upper reaches of Provençal Venice is gradually being refurbished: modern lobby-sitting room, and warm red colour scheme in the modern rooms. A lovely terrace with a view of a 1516 tower (remains of an old mill). Classic cuisine.

XX **Le Bouchon à la Mer**

19 quai L. Toulmond – ✆ 04 42 49 41 41 – lebouchonalamer@wanadoo.fr – Fax 04 42 42 14 40 – Closed Easter holidays, autumn and February school holidays, Tuesday lunch, Sunday dinner and Monday Y **v**

Rest – Menu (€ 22), € 30/40

♦ Located near the Miroir aux Oiseaux, a popular painter's spot, this restaurant serves classic cuisine in a charming dining area with cream and chocolate toned décor. Canal-side terrace.

MARTILLAC – 33 Gironde – 335 H6 – see Bordeaux

MARTIN-ÉGLISE – 76 Seine-Maritime – 304 G2 – pop. 1 331 – alt. 11 m – ✉ 76370

Paris 199 – Dieppe 6 – Mont-Saint-Aignan 60 – Rouen 67 33 **D1**

XX **Auberge du Clos Normand** with rm

22 r. Henri IV – ✆ 02 35 40 40 40 – leclosnormand2@wanadoo.fr – Fax 02 35 40 40 42 – Closed 19 November-10 December and 19 February-5 March

7 rm – €65 €65, ☕ €7 – **Rest** – *(closed Monday, Tuesday and Wednesday except evenings in July-August)* Menu € 20/30 – Carte € 32/46

♦ This stylish 17C Norman inn, located in a park alongside a river, now houses a restaurant serving traditional meals in a typical rustic atmosphere. Quiet rooms, recently renovated in the wing on the garden side.

LA MARTRE – 83 Var – 340 O3 – pop. 133 – alt. 984 m – ✉ 83840 41 C2

Paris 808 – Castellane 19 – Digne-les-Bains 73 – Draguignan 50 – Grasse 50

Château de Taulane rm,

(Le Logis du Pin), at the golf club, northeast: 4 km via D6085 – ✆ 04 93 40 60 80 – resahotel@chateau-taulane.com – Fax 04 93 60 37 48 – Open 1st April-5 November

45 rm – € 129/199 € 149/319, ☕ € 18 – ½ P € 140/225

Rest – Menu (€ 28), € 35 (lunch) – Carte € 51/65 dinner

♦ An 18C chateau surrounded by four dovecotes, located near a 340-hectare golf course and park. Home to well-equipped, standard rooms, and simpler rooms in the secondary building. A charming restaurant and clubhouse with a snack bar. Terrace overlooking the greens.

MARVEJOLS – 48 Lozère – 330 H7 – pop. 5 501 – alt. 650 m – ✉ 48100

Languedoc-Roussillon-Tarn Gorges 23 **C1**

Paris 580 – Montpellier 178 – Mende 28 – Espalion 83 – Saint-Chély-d'Apcher 34

Office de tourisme, place Henri IV ✆ 04 66 32 02 14, Fax 04 66 32 02 14

XX **L'Auberge Domaine de Carrière**

2 km east via D1 – ✆ 04 66 32 47 05 – ramon.carmona@wanadoo.fr – Closed January, autumn half-term holidays, Wednesday dinner and Sunday dinner except July-August and Monday

Rest – Menu € 18/32

♦ Old stables converted into a plush, contemporary-style restaurant with white-washed beams, modern chairs in black leather, and an open fireplace. Pleasant wines from the Languedoc.

MARVILLE – 55 Meuse – 307 D2 – pop. 532 – alt. 216 m – ✉ 55600 26 A1

Paris 302 – Bar-le-Duc 96 – Longuyon 13 – Metz 92 – Verdun 40

Auberge de Marville rm,

(near the church) – ✆ 03 29 88 10 10 – jcctm55@gmail.com – Fax 03 29 88 14 60 – Closed 22-28 December and 2-13 January

11 rm – €38 €43/57, ☕ €5,50 – ½ P €57/64

Rest – Menu € 25 (weekdays)/60

♦ Fully-renovated former barn at the foot of St. Nicolas church (16C organ loft balustrade). Functional rooms. A pleasant decor in the restaurant, where one can enjoy traditional cuisine and Lorraine dishes.

MASEVAUX – 68 Haut-Rhin – **315** F10 – **pop. 3 329 – alt. 425 m** – ✉ **68290**
Alsace-Lorraine 1 **A3**

Paris 440 – Altkirch 32 – Belfort 24 – Colmar 57 – Mulhouse 30 – Thann 15 – Le Thillot 38

Office de tourisme, 1, place Gayardon ✆ 03 89 82 41 99, Fax 03 89 82 49 44

Descent of the Hundsrück Pass ≤★★ Northeast: 13 km.

L'Hostellerie Alsacienne with rm rm,
r. Mar. Foch – ✆ 03 89 82 45 25 – philippe.battman@wanadoo.fr – Fax 03 89 82 45 25 – Closed 20 October-10 November and 24 December-2 January
8 rm – €45 €55, €8 – ½ P €45 – **Rest** – *(closed Sunday dinner and Monday)* Menu (€ 10), € 12,50 (weekday lunch), € 24/43 – Carte € 37/56
◆ Independent local growers and organic produce take pride of place on the menu, which features regional recipes inspired by local traditions. Alsace decor and partly refurbished rooms.

MASSERET – 19 Corrèze – **329** K2 – **pop. 608 – alt. 380 m** – ✉ **19510** 24 **B2**

Paris 432 – Limoges 45 – Guéret 132 – Tulle 48 – Ussel 101

Syndicat d'initiative, le Bourg ✆ 05 55 98 24 79, Fax 05 55 73 49 69

De la Tour rest,
7 pl. Marcel Champeix – ✆ 05 55 73 40 12 – hoteldelatour19@aol.com – Fax 05 55 73 49 41 – Closed Sunday dinner except July-August
15 rm – €43 €43, €6,50 – ½ P €55 – **Rest** – Menu € 19/50
◆ On the quiet heights of this Limousin town is a family-run hostelry with well-kept, refurbished, simple rooms. Spacious dining room extended by a terrace from which you can admire the 'tower', a water tower - medieval in appearance only.

MASSIAC – 15 Cantal – **330** H3 – **pop. 1 857 – alt. 534 m** – ✉ **15500** Auvergne
Paris 484 – Aurillac 84 – Brioude 23 – Issoire 38 – Murat 37 – St-Flour 30 5 **B3**

Office de tourisme, 24, rue du Dr Mallet ✆ 04 71 23 07 76, Fax 04 71 23 08 50

North: Gorges de l'Alagnon★ - Site of Ste-Madeleine chapel ★ North: 2 km.

Grand Hôtel de la Poste rest,
26 av. Ch. de Gaulle – ✆ 04 71 23 02 01 – hotel.massiac@wanadoo.fr – Fax 04 71 23 09 23 – Closed 15 November-22 December, Tuesday dinner and Wednesday from January to Easter
33 rm – €44/56 €44/56, €7 – ½ P €47/54
Rest – Menu € 15 (weekdays), € 35/40 – Carte € 23/39
◆ Imposing building, just outside town and near the A75 exit. Comfortable rooms and a wealth of leisure activities (fitness centre, Jacuzzi, squash court). A non-smoking dining room with a fireplace serving Auvergne-inspired cuisine.

La Colombière without rest
rte de Grenier Montgon, 1 km north on D 909 – ✆ 04 71 23 18 50 – contact@hotel-lacolombiere.com – Fax 04 71 23 18 58 – Closed 15 January-15 February
30 rm – €37 €45, €6
◆ Recently built hotel ideally located on the road to the Gorges de l'Alagnon. Spacious functional rooms (new furniture, well-equipped bathrooms, faultless upkeep).

MASSY – 91 Essonne – **312** C3 – **101** 25 – see Paris, Area

MATOUR – 71 Saône-et-Loire – **320** G12 – **pop. 998 – alt. 500 m** – ✉ **71520**
Burgundy-Jura 8 **C3**

Paris 405 – Charolles 28 – Cluny 24 – Lapalisse 82 – Lyon 102 – Mâcon 36 – Roanne 57

Office de tourisme, ✆ 03 85 59 72 24, Fax 03 85 59 72 24

Christophe Clément
pl. de l'Église – ✆ 03 85 59 74 80 – Fax 03 85 59 75 77 – Closed 22 December-15 January, dinner except Saturday October-May, Sunday dinner and Monday
Rest – Menu € 12 (weekday lunch), € 18/36 – Carte € 26/40
◆ This restaurant located on the church square has an attractive façade and a distinctive sign of a rooster's head. Serving copious, traditional cuisine and an unusual house special in a rustic, country-style atmosphere.

MAUBEUGE – 59 Nord – 302 L6 – pop. 33 546 – Built-up area 117 470 – alt. 134 m – ✉ 59600 Northern France and the Paris Region 31 D2

Paris 242 – Mons 21 – St-Quentin 114 – Valenciennes 39

Office de tourisme, place Vauban ✆ 03 27 62 11 93, Fax 03 27 64 10 23

South by Avesnes-sur-Helpe road– ✉ 59330 Beaufort

Auberge de l'Hermitage

at 6 km on N 2 – ✆ 03 27 67 89 59 – Fax 03 27 39 84 52 – Closed 28 July-2 August, 1st-14 September, 26 – 31 December, Sunday dinner, Tuesday dinner, Thursday dinner and Monday

Rest – Menu (€ 20), € 25 (weekdays)/70 – Carte € 41/76

◆ A welcoming brick building near the main road on the edge of the Avesnois Nature Park. Well-appointed dining room and traditional cuisine in the land of the Maroilles cheese.

Le Relais de Beaufort

8 km away on N 2 – ✆ 03 27 63 50 36 – relaisdebeaufort@worldonline.fr – Fax 03 27 67 85 11 – Closed 18 August-8 September, February holidays, Sunday dinner and Monday

Rest – Menu € 33/41 – Carte € 28/54

◆ Two dining rooms: one marine in style with a splendid olive tree, the other rustic and full of light. Terrace overlooking a pretty garden. Traditional menu.

MAULÉON – 79 Deux-Sèvres – 322 B3 – pop. 7 327 – alt. 180 m – ✉ 79700 Atlantic Coast 38 B1

Paris 376 – Cholet 22 – Nantes 80 – Niort 82 – Parthenay 56 – La Roche-sur-Yon 65

Office de tourisme, 27, Grand' Rue ✆ 05 49 65 10 27, Fax 05 49 80 41 49

Terrasse

7 pl. Terrasse – ✆ 05 49 81 47 24 – laterrasse.mauleon@wanadoo.fr – Fax 05 49 81 65 04 – Closed 10-18 August and 21-29 December

14 rm – †€ 45/49 ††€ 50/54, ☕ € 6,50 – ½ P € 66/71

Rest – *(closed Sunday and Monday)* Menu € 13,50/31 – Carte € 19/32

◆ This old coaching house set below the small town is a well-located stopover for a visit to Puy-du-Fou. Functional, partially-panelled rooms. An appealing, recently redecorated dining area, and a pleasant shaded terrace.

MAULÉVRIER – 49 Maine-et-Loire – 317 E6 – see Cholet

MAUREILLAS-LAS-ILLAS – 66 Pyrénées-Orientales – 344 H8 – pop. 2 281 – alt. 130 m – ✉ 66480 Languedoc-Roussillon-Tarn Gorges 22 B3

Paris 873 – Gerona 71 – Perpignan 31 – Port-Vendres 31 – Prades 69

Syndicat d'initiative, avenue Mal Joffre ✆ 04 68 83 48 00

in Las Illas 11 km Southwest by D 13 – ✉ 66480

Hostal dels Trabucayres with rm

– ✆ 04 68 83 07 56 – Fax 04 68 83 07 56 – Closed 25-30 October, 6 January-15 March, Tuesday and Wednesday off season

5 rm – †€ 31/35 ††€ 31/35, ☕ € 5,50 – ½ P € 36

Rest – Menu € 12,50 bi (weekdays)/50 bi – Carte € 21/32

◆ An old, simple inn along the GR10 footpath at the heart of a forest. Original rustic interior where the menu is based on Catalan dishes. Peace and quiet guaranteed. Basic bedrooms and two modern gîtes.

MAUREPAS – 78 Yvelines – 311 H3 – 101 21 – see Paris, Area

MAURIAC – 15 Cantal – 330 B3 – pop. 4 019 – alt. 722 m – ✉ 15200 Auvergne

Paris 490 – Aurillac 53 – Le Mont-Dore 77 – Clermont-Ferrand 113 – Tulle 73

Office de tourisme, 1, rue Chappe d'Auteroche ✆ 04 71 67 30 26, Fax 04 71 68 25 08 5 A3

Val-Saint-JeanWest: 2 km, ✆ 06 07 74 22 29.

Notre-Dame-des-Miracles basilica ★ - Le Vigean: shrine★ in the church Northeast: 2 km.

Barrage de l'Aigle★★: 11 km by D 678 and D105, Dordogne-Berry-Limousin

Des Voyageurs

pl. de la Poste – 04 71 68 01 01 – auberge.des.voyageurs@wanadoo.fr – Fax 04 71 68 01 56 – Closed 14 December-5 January, Sunday dinner and Saturday off season

19 rm – €35 €40/58, €8

Rest ***La Bonne Auberge*** – Menu €12/35 – Carte €21/39

◆ An unpretentious town centre establishment for weary travellers. Well-kept, above all practical bedrooms. The restaurant La Bonne Auberge has preserved its 1980s "look". Regional and family cooking.

Serre without rest

4 r. du 11 Novembre – 04 71 68 19 10 – Fax 04 71 68 17 77 – Closed 1st-8 March and 2-15 January

13 rm – €36/38 €43/52, €6,50

◆ Near the Norman church N.-D.-des-Miracles. Air-conditioning, functional fixtures and fittings, good quality rustic furniture. One non-smoking bedroom. Warm hospitality.

MAUROUX – 46 Lot – 337 C5 – see Puy-l'Évêque

MAURY – 66 Pyrénées-Orientales – 344 G6 – pop. 901 – alt. 200 m – 66460

Paris 876 – Montpellier 179 – Perpignan 35 – Carcassonne 142 – Canet-en-Roussillon 45 22 **B3**

Syndicat d'initiative, Mairie 04 68 59 15 24, Fax 04 68 59 08 74

Pascal Borrell

la Maison du Terroir av. Jean Jaurès – 04 68 86 28 28 – pascalborrell@wanadoo.fr – Closed Sunday dinner and Monday from November to March

Rest – Menu (€19 bi), €25 bi (weekdays)/58 – Carte €49/65

Spec. Grosses crevettes cuites en tempura, cappuccino de petits pois à la menthe sauvage. Civet de lotte au vieux maury, risotto au parmesan. Chocolat Cao Grande Bio et crémeux sur sablé à la fève tonka.

◆ Contemporary restaurant decorated in typical Catalan colours, specialising in regional cuisine with an innovative twist. Shop selling wine and regional products to whet your appetite.

MAUSSAC – 19 Corrèze – 329 N3 – see Meymac

MAUSSANE-LES-ALPILLES – 13 Bouches-du-Rhône – 340 D3 – pop. 1 968 – alt. 32 m – 13520 42 **E1**

Paris 712 – Arles 20 – Avignon 30 – Marseille 81 – Martigues 44 – St-Rémy-de-Provence 10

Office de tourisme, place Laugier de Monblan 04 90 54 52 04, Fax 04 90 54 39 44

Le Pré des Baux without rest

r. Vieux Moulin – 04 90 54 40 40 – info@lepredesbaux.com – Fax 04 90 54 53 07 – Open 14 March-27 October

10 rm – €90/120 €90/120, €12

◆ The rooms are situated around a Mediterranean garden away from prying glances and noise and open directly onto private, ground-level terraces where breakfast is served.

Castillon des Baux without rest

10 bis av. de la Vallée des Baux – 04 90 54 31 93 – castillondesbaux@orange.fr – Fax 04 90 54 51 31 – Closed January and February

15 rm – €81/123 €81/125, €11,50

◆ This red ochre construction stands in a garden with olive trees and an attractive pool. Most of the spacious, pastel-decorated rooms have a balcony or a terrace.

Aurelia without rest

124 av. de la Valléee des Baux – 04 90 54 22 54 – resa-maussane@monalisahotels.com – Fax 04 90 54 20 75 – 15 Mar. - 15 Nov.

39 rm – €90/125 €90/125, €11

◆ Sun drenched decor in this regionally-inspired construction. The unfussy, well-equipped rooms are more pleasant by the pool, with views of the countryside.

Val Baussenc rm, rm, rest, VISA AE

122 av. de la Vallée des Baux – 04 90 54 38 90 – information@valbaussenc.com – Fax 04 90 54 33 36 – Open 1st March-31 October

21 rm – €69/96 €81/118, €11 – 1 suite – ½ P €70/89

Rest – *(closed Wednesday) (dinner only)* Menu €27/35 – Carte approx. €48

◆ Provençal-style construction built with limestone from Les Baux. The bedrooms, nearly all of which have a terrace or balcony, offer views of the countryside. Small, colourful dining room and pleasant terrace under a trellis.

Ou Ravi Provençau VISA

34 av. de la Vallée des Baux – 04 90 54 31 11 – infos@ouravi.net – Fax 04 90 54 41 03 – Closed 15 November-15 December, Tuesday and Wednesday

Rest – Menu €34 – Carte €40/67

◆ Authentic, generous and tasty: it's almost as if the food served in this attractive southern house came straight out of the "Reboul", the bible of Provençal cooking.

La Place VISA AE

65 av. de la Vallée des Baux – 04 90 54 23 31 – Closed January and Tuesday

Rest – Menu (€21), €32 – Carte €36/44

◆ Savour the intimate, trendy atmosphere of this restaurant serving tasty southern inspired cuisine in two cosy sitting rooms and a shaded terrace.

in Paradou 2 km West by D 17, Arles road – pop. 1 167 – alt. 21 m – ✉ 13520

Le Hameau des Baux rm, VISA AE

chemin de Bourgeac – 04 90 54 10 30 – reservation@hameaudesbaux.com – Fax 04 90 54 45 30 – Closed January-mid February

10 rm – €190/265 €190/300, €18 – 5 suites – **Rest** – *(closed Wednesday) (number of covers limited, pre-book)* Menu €40 (lunch)/48

◆ Superbly reconstituted Provençal hamlet surrounded by cypress and olive trees, offering extreme refinement and quiet in rooms with a personal touch; an address for the aesthetically-minded. The contemporary cuisine influenced by southern flavours enhances the magical appeal of the spot.

Du Côté des Olivades rm, rm, VISA AE

lieu dit de Bourgeac – 04 90 54 56 78 – ducotedesolivades@wanadoo.fr – Fax 04 90 54 56 79

10 rm – €90/147 €120/186, €16 – ½ P €130/156 – **Rest** – *(number of covers limited, pre-book)* Menu €32/52 – Carte €44/67

◆ This restful modern villa, tucked away among olive groves, offers a warm welcome: smart Mediterranean decor, guesthouse atmosphere and pleasant pool. Savour regionally inspired food that varies according to the season in a Provençal setting.

La Maison du Paradou VISA AE

2 rte de St-Roch – 04 90 54 65 46 – reservations@maisonduparadou.com – Fax 04 90 54 85 83 – **5 rm** – €270/285 €270/285, €20

Table d'hôte – 04 90 54 65 46 – Menu €35 bi (lunch)/75 bi

◆ An old staging post (1699) run by a British couple. Comfortable guestrooms featuring myriad individual touches and high-tech gadgetry. Library-lounge, Provençal garden and swimming pool. A table d'hôte (reservation required) beneath a shady pergola with the Alpilles as a backdrop.

Bistrot de la Petite France VISA

av. de la Vallée des Baux – 04 90 54 41 91 – Fax 04 90 54 52 50 Closed 1st-30 November, one week in February, Thursday except dinner in July-August and Wednesday

Rest – Menu €28

◆ Attractive interior with stonework, beams and modern paintings. Tasty cuisine made with market produce, displayed on a blackboard, and rich wine list. Collection of Michelin Guides.

Le Bistrot du Paradou "Chez Jean-Louis" VISA

– 04 90 54 32 70 – Fax 04 90 54 32 70 – Closed autumn half-term holidays, 20 January-15 February, Sunday, Monday and dinner from 1st October to 15 June except Friday

Rest – *(pre-book)* Menu €42 bi (lunch)/49 bi

◆ This blue shuttered Provençal house is a local institution. Tasty regional fare served in a friendly decor adorned with a vast collection (2,400) of beer bottles.

MAYENNE – 53 Mayenne – 310 F5 – pop. 13 724 – alt. 124 m – ✉ 53100

Normandy 35 C1

Paris 283 – Alençon 61 – Flers 56 – Fougères 47 – Laval 30 – Le Mans 89

Office de tourisme, quai de Waiblingen ✆ 02 43 04 19 37, Fax 02 43 00 01 99

Former château ≤★.

Le Grand Hôtel

2 r. Ambroise de Loré – ✆ 02 43 00 96 00 – grandhotelmayenne@wanadoo.fr – Fax 02 43 00 69 20 – Closed 3-17 August, 19 December-4 January, Saturday dinner from November to April

22 rm – €67/91 €80/116, €10 – ½ P €76/93 – **Rest** – *(closed Sunday from November to April and Saturday except dinner from May to October)* Menu (€17), €20, €31/36 – Carte €37/80

◆ This traditional-looking hotel located in the town centre near the Mayenne bridge has been renovated, providing modern, soundproofed rooms, a comfortable lounge and whisky bar, and a practical car park. This restaurant also features a veranda dining area. Standard cuisine.

La Croix Couverte with rm

Alençon road: 2 km on N 12 – ✆ 02 43 04 32 48 – la-croixcouverte@wanadoo.fr – Fax 02 43 04 43 69 – Closed 4-18 August, 24 December-7 January, Sunday dinner and dinners holidays

11 rm – €48 €54, €8,50 – ½ P €54 – **Rest** – Menu (€15), €19 (weekdays)/38 – Carte €41/55

◆ Hundred-year-old house by the main road with "vintage" style dining room opening onto a pleasant terrace and garden. Unpretentious rooms, quieter to the rear.

at Fontaine-Daniel 6 km southwest by D 104 – ✉ 53100

La Forge

au bourg – ✆ 02 43 00 34 85 – restaurant-laforge@wanadoo.fr – Fax 02 43 00 38 57 – Closed 1st-15 January, Tuesday except dinner June-September, Sunday dinner and Monday

Rest – Menu €32/44 – Carte €32/41

◆ On the village square, former blacksmith's converted into a contemporary-style restaurant. Visually striking inventive cuisine and original wine list.

Laval road South by N 162 – ✉ 53100 Mayenne

La Marjolaine with rm

6.5 km on, at the Domaine du Bas-Mont – ✆ 02 43 00 48 42 – lamarjolaine@wanadoo.fr – Fax 02 43 08 10 58 – Closed 4-10 August, 9-21 February and Sunday dinner from 1st October to 30 April

23 rm – €51/120 €51/120, €10 – ½ P €68/80

Rest – *(closed Friday dinner January-April and Saturday lunch 15 October-30 April)* Menu €19 (weekdays)/42 – Carte €48/55

Rest *Le Bistrot de La Marjolaine* – *(closed Saturday, Sunday and holidays) (lunch only)* Menu (€16), €17 – Carte €33/36

◆ Old restored farm on a wooded estate near a river. Pleasant dining room with a terrace facing the park, serving up-to-date cuisine with a good wine list. Pleasant rooms. The Bistrot has wall coverings depicting peacocks, fast service and well-presented dishes.

Beau Rivage with rm

4 km away – ✆ 02 43 00 49 13 – fbeaurivage@9online.fr – Fax 02 43 00 49 26 – Closed Sunday dinner, public holiday dinner and Monday

8 rm – €52 €66, €8 – ½ P €55/66 – **Rest** – rôtisserie Menu (€14), €17 (weekdays)/36 – Carte €26/48

◆ Delightful and stylish open-air café atmosphere in this house with a fine shaded terrace on the banks of the Mayenne. Dishes cooked on a roasting spit. Cheerful rooms.

MAYET – 72 Sarthe – 310 K8 – pop. 2 915 – alt. 74 m – ✉ 72360 35 D2

Paris 226 – Château-la-Vallière 26 – La Flèche 32 – Le Mans 31 – Tours 58 – Vendôme 70

Office de tourisme, espace Lichtenau ✆ 02 43 46 33 72

Forêt de Bercé★ East: 6 km, G. Châteaux of the Loire

Auberge des Tilleuls
pl. H. de Ville – ✆ 02 43 46 60 12 – Fax 02 43 46 60 12 – Closed 1er-15 February, Sunday dinner, Monday dinner, Tuesday dinner and Wednesday
Rest – Menu € 9,50/25 – Carte € 14/23
◆ This old restaurant has retained all its original charm, with a country-style dining area that communicates with the village café. Serves traditional meals.

LE MAYET-DE-MONTAGNE – **03 Allier** – **326** J6 – **pop. 1 598** – **alt. 535 m** – ✉ **03250** **Auvergne** 6 **C2**

Paris 369 – Clermont-Ferrand 81 – Lapalisse 23 – Moulins 73 – Thiers 44 – Vichy 27

Office de tourisme, rue Roger Degoulange ✆ 04 70 59 38 40, Fax 04 70 59 37 24

Le Relais du Lac with rm
rte de Laprugne, 0.5 km south by D 7 – ✆ 04 70 59 70 23 – renécazals@orange.fr – Closed Monday and Tuesday
6 rm – †€ 46 ††€ 46/55, ☕ € 8 – ½ P € 53 – **Rest** – Menu € 12,50 (weekday lunch), € 22/40 – Carte € 21/49
◆ In the heart of the Bourbonnais mountains next to a lake, this restaurant has a local flavour, with rural decor, and regional specialities. Neat and tidy rooms available.

MAZAMET – **81 Tarn** – **338** G10 – **pop. 10 544** – **alt. 241 m** – ✉ **81200**
Languedoc-Roussillon-Tarn Gorges 29 **C2**

Paris 739 – Albi 64 – Carcassonne 50 – Castres 21 – Toulouse 92

Castres-Mazamet: ✆ 05 63 70 34 77, West: 14 km.

Office de tourisme, rue des Casernes ✆ 05 63 61 27 07, Fax 05 63 61 31 35

de Mazamet-la-Barouge Pont de l'Arn, North: 3 km, ✆ 05 63 61 06 72.

≤★ of the gorges de l'Arnette South: 4 km.

Mets et Plaisirs rest,
7 av. A. Rouvière – ✆ 05 63 61 56 93 – contact@metsetplaisir.com – Fax 05 63 61 83 38 – Closed 4-24 August, 2-13 January and Sunday dinner
11 rm – †€ 44 ††€ 50, ☕ € 7 – ½ P € 56 – **Rest** – *(closed Monday)* Menu € 16 (weekday lunch)/25 – Carte € 25/70
◆ This early 20C manor, located in the town centre opposite the post office, has well-equipped rooms that are being gradually refurbished. Elegant atmosphere in this restaurant, which was once an aristocratic home. Contemporary cuisine.

in Bout-du-Pont-de-Larn **2 km east by D 612 and D 54** – **pop. 1 070** – **alt. 280 m** – ✉ **81660**

La Métairie Neuve
Bout du Pont de Larn – ✆ 05 63 97 73 50 – metairieneuve@wanadoo.fr – Fax 05 63 61 94 75 – Closed 15 December-20 January
14 rm – †€ 62/80 ††€ 71/89, ☕ € 10 – ½ P € 64/73 – **Rest** – *(closed Wednesday from 1st June to 30 September, Saturday and Sunday from 1st October to 31 May) (dinner only) (residents only)* Menu € 23
◆ An 18C country seat renovated with taste. Paved courtyard, a pretty lounge in the corner by the fire and bedrooms bearing the names of Bordeaux great wines. Smart, rustic dining room and terrace under an old barn, opposite a pretty flower garden with a swimming pool.

MAZAN – **84 Vaucluse** – **332** D9 – **see Carpentras**

MAZAYE – **63 Puy-de-Dôme** – **326** E8 – **pop. 560** – **alt. 760 m** – ✉ **63230** 5 **B2**

Paris 441 – Clermont-Fd 23 – Le Mont-Dore 32 – Pontaumur 27 – Pontgibaud 7

Auberge de Mazayes rm,
à Mazayes-Basses – ✆ 04 73 88 93 30 – Fax 04 73 88 93 80 Closed 15 December-22 January, Monday from October to March and Tuesday lunch
15 rm – †€ 51 ††€ 62/74, ☕ € 8,50 – ½ P € 62
Rest – Menu € 17 (weekdays), € 26/36 – Carte € 25/40
◆ This former farmhouse makes an ideal pied-à-terre for discovering the Auvergne countryside: the rural beauty of the site is only equalled by its facilities. Pretty, country-style restaurant; tasty regional dishes; lovely selection of Bordeaux and local wines.

MÉAUDRE – 38 Isère – **333** G7 – see Autrans

MEAULNE – 03 Allier – **326** C3 – **pop. 759 – alt. 185 m** – ✉ **03360**
Auvergne 5 **B1**

Paris 307 – Clermont-Ferrand 126 – Moulins 96 – Montluçon 31 – Saint-Amand-Montrond 19

Au Cœur de Meaulne rest, VISA
20 pl. de l'Eglise – ✆ 04 70 06 20 30 – info@aucoeurdemeaulne.com – Fax 04 70 06 92 58 – Closed 13-19 October and January
8 rm – €51/70 €51/70, €8 – ½ P €53/62
Rest – *(closed Tuesday except dinner July-August and Wednesday)* Menu € 15 bi (weekday lunch), € 21/35 – Carte € 34/47
♦ This renovated auberge has fresh, clean rooms, where old tree trunks from the Forêt du Tronçais take the place of bedside tables! Contemporary cuisine served in a smart dining room or, in summer, in the shade of an old horse chestnut tree.

MEAUX – 77 Seine-et-Marne – **312** G2 – **pop. 49 421 – alt. 51 m** – ✉ **77100**
Northern France and the Paris Region 19 **C1**

Paris 54 – Compiègne 68 – Melun 56 – Reims 98

Office de tourisme, 1, place Doumer ✆ 01 64 33 02 26, Fax 01 64 33 24 86

de Meaux Boutigny Boutignyby A 140 and D 228: 11km, ✆ 01 60 25 63 98 ;

de la Brie Crécy-la-Chapelle Ferme de Montpichet, by A 140 and Melun road: 16 km, ✆ 01 64 75 34 44 ;

Disneyland Paris Magny-le-Hongre Allée de la Mare Houleuse, South: 16 km by D5, ✆ 01 60 45 68 90.

Episcopal Centre ★ ABY : cathedral★ B, ≤★ from ramparts terrace.

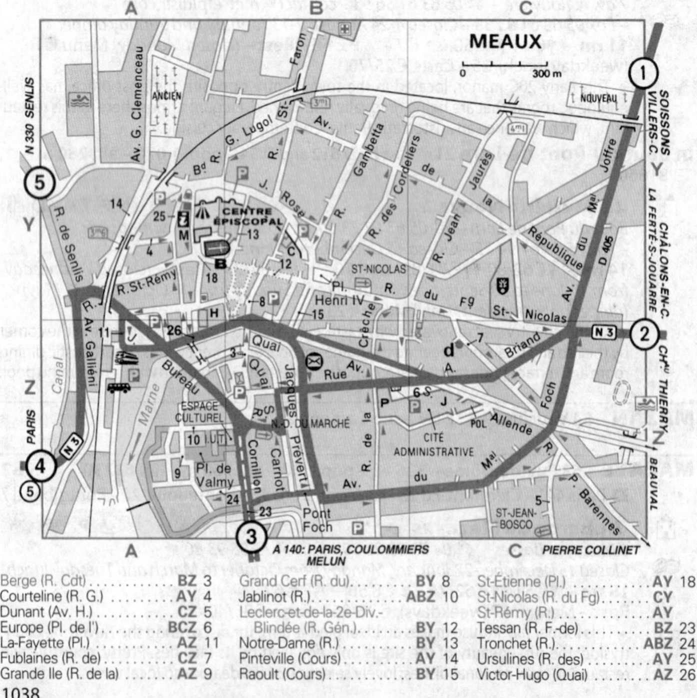

Berge (R. Cdt)	**BZ** 3	Grand Cerf (R. du)	**BY** 8	St-Étienne (Pl.)	**AY** 18
Courteline (R. G.)	**AY** 4	Jablinot (R.)	**ABZ** 10	St-Nicolas (R. du Fg)	**CY**
Dunant (Av. H.)	**CZ** 5	Leclerc-et-de-la-2e-Div.-		St-Rémy (R.)	**AY**
Europe (Pl. de l')	**BCZ** 6	Blindée (R. Gén.)	**BY** 12	Tessan (R. F.-de)	**BZ** 23
La-Fayette (Pl.)	**AZ** 11	Notre-Dame (R.)	**BY** 13	Tronchet (R.)	**ABZ** 24
Fublaines (R. de)	**CZ** 7	Pinteville (Cours)	**AY** 14	Ursulines (R. des)	**AY** 25
Grande Ile (R. de la)	**AZ** 9	Raoult (Cours)	**BY** 15	Victor-Hugo (Quai)	**AZ** 26

La Grignotière
36 r. Sablonnière – ☎ 01 64 34 21 48 – Fax 01 64 33 93 93 – Closed August, Saturday lunch, Tuesday and Wednesday CZ **d**
Rest – Menu € 29 (weekday lunch)/42 – Carte € 49/66
◆ La Grignotière is easily recognised by its wrought-iron sign. Pleasant rustic interior, friendly atmosphere and appealing traditional cuisine.

in Poincy 5 km by ② and D 17A – pop. 694 – alt. 53 m – ✉ 77470

Le Moulin de Poincy
r. du Moulin – ☎ 01 60 23 06 80 – Fax 01 60 23 12 56 – Closed 1st-25 September, 2-24 January, Monday dinner, Tuesday and Wednesday
Rest – Menu € 30/60 – Carte € 48/71
◆ Pretty mill from the 17C and garden beside the Marne. Classy interior: wood panelling, exposed beams, weathered furniture, flea market items and a coffee pot collection.

in Trilbardou 7 km by ④ and D 27 – pop. 517 – alt. 47 m – ✉ 77450

M. et Mme Cantin without rest
2 r. de l'Église – ☎ 01 60 61 08 75 – cantin.evelyne@voila.fr
3 rm – €50 €58
◆ This 19C building is located on the banks of the canal de l'Ourcq. Some travellers even arrive via the bike track all the way from Paris. Rooms with refined décor.

MEAUZAC – 82 Tarn-et-Garonne – 337 D7 – pop. 890 – alt. 76 m – ✉ 82290 28 **B2**

Paris 628 – Cahors 57 – Montauban 16 – Toulouse 67

Manoir des Chanterelles
Bernon-Boutounelle, 2 km north on the D 45 – ☎ 05 63 24 60 70 – nathalie@manoirdeschanterelles.com – Fax 05 63 24 60 71
5 rm – €60/70 €70/120 – ½ P €65/85
Table d'hôte – Menu € 25 bi/35 bi
◆ An apple orchard and a pleasant park surround this charming turreted manor. Each floor features rooms of a different style, including Savannah, Louis XVI, Oriental, Romantic and Zen. The restaurant, located on the ground floor, serves traditional cuisine.

MEGÈVE – 74 Haute-Savoie – 328 M5 – pop. 4 509 – alt. 1 113 m – Winter sports : 1 113/2 350 m 9 70 – Casino AY – ✉ 74120 French Alps 46 **F1**

Paris 598 – Albertville 32 – Annecy 60 – Chamonix-Mont-Blanc 33

Altiport Megève ☎ 04 50 21 33 67, Southeast: 7 km BZ

Office de tourisme, maison des Frères ☎ 04 50 21 27 28, Fax 04 50 93 03 09

du Mont-d'Arbois 3001 route Edmond de Rotschild, East: 2 km, ☎ 04 50 21 29 79.

Mont d'Arbois★★.

Les Fermes de Marie
chemin de Riante Colline via ② – ☎ 04 50 93 03 10 – contact@fermesdemarie.com – Fax 04 50 93 09 84 – Open 28 June-2 September and 20 December-14 April
64 rm – €260/945 €260/945, € 27 – 7 suites – ½ P € 198/710
Rest – Carte € 62/73
Rest *Restaurant Alpin* – *(dinner only)* Carte € 48/82
◆ This hamlet of authentic Savoy farms, carefully reconstructed, is a great success. Cosy rooms, superb spa. Luxurious and unique. Splendid alpine setting and up-to-date cuisine. Regional recipes in the restaurant specialising in cheese.

Lodge Park
100 r. Arly – ☎ 04 50 93 05 03 – contact@lodgepark.com – Fax 04 50 93 09 52 – Open 21 December-31 March AY **s**
39 rm – €220/390 €220/390, € 25 – 11 suites – ½ P € 190/563
Rest – Carte € 55/75
◆ The nicely done decor in the bedrooms is on the theme of the Canadian lakes and gold prospectors: logs, waterfalls, hunting trophies, stone hearths ... A new take on the Adirondacks, but in a fashionable Megève style! Inventive cuisine.

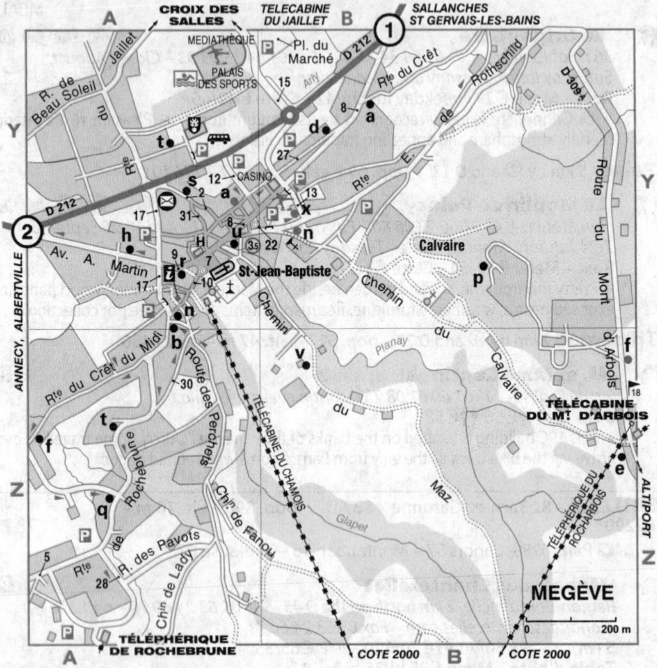

Arly (R. d') . . . . AY 2
Bouchet (Rte du). . . . . AZ 5
Église (Pl. de l') . . . . AY 7
Feige (R. Ch.) . . . . ABY 8
Martin (R. A.) . . . . AY 9
Monseigneur-Conseil (R.). . . . . AY 10
Muffat-de-St-Amour (R. du Gén.) . . . . AY 12
Oberstdorf (R.) . . . . BY 13
Palais des Sports (Rte du). . . . . ABY 15
Poste (R. de la) . . . . AY 17
Résistance (Pl. de la). . . . . AY 22
St-François (R.) . . . . ABY 27
Téléphérique (Rte du) . . . . AZ 28
Verte (Allée). . . . . AZ 30
5-Rues (Passage des). . . . . AY 31

Le Fer à Cheval rest, rest, VISA

36 rte Crêt d'Arbois – ☎ 04 50 21 30 39
– fer-a-cheval@wanadoo.fr – Fax 04 50 93 07 60
– Closed beg. September-mid December and Monday dinner during low season BY **a**

42 rm (½ board only) – 14 suites – ½ P € 281/581
Rest – *(closed Monday off season and lunch in Winter)* Menu € 60 – Carte € 57/65
Rest *L'Alpage* – *(Open from mid December to beg. of April)* Carte € 50/60

◆ The chalet, built in 1938 by the village blacksmith, boasts a superb Alpine-style interior. Cosy lounges and rooms (regional furniture), luxurious bathrooms. Dinner by candlelight near the fireplace in an intimate dining room. Regional cuisine at l'Alpage.

Mont-Blanc VISA

pl. de l'Église – ☎ 04 50 21 20 02
contact@hotelmontblanc.com – Fax 04 50 21 45 28
Closed 20 April-7 June AY **r**

40 rm – †€ 250/370 ††€ 420/570, ☕ € 25
Rest *Les Enfants Terribles* – Carte € 43/107

◆ Legendary doyen of Mégève hotels: "21st arrondissement of Paris" according to Cocteau, theatre of Les Liaisons Dangereuses in the Vadim version ... Very pretty individual bedrooms. Champagne bar and brasserie-style restaurant.

Chalet du Mont d'Arbois
447 chemin de la Rocaille, via Edmond de Rothschild road – 04 50 21 25 03 – montarbois@relaischateaux.fr – Fax 04 50 21 24 79 – Open from mid June to mid October and from mid December to mid April BY **p**
23 rm – €307/794 €329/994, €28 – 1 suite
Rest – *(closed at lunchtime on weekdays and Mon. except school holidays)* Menu €60/230 – Carte €88/149
◆ Remote chalets on the Mont d'Arbois plateau with superb views of the surrounding peaks. Hunting trophies, wood panelling and attractive furniture create a warm and welcoming setting. Minimalist spa. Elegant restaurant, busy summer terrace, carefully-prepared food and superb wine list.

Chalet de Noémie
5 suites – €959/4000, €28
◆ The five luxury apartments of the Chalet de Noémie make up a lovely, wonderfully-equipped annexe.

Chalet d'Alice
7 rm – €484/1500 €484/1500, €28 – 1 suite
◆ Enchanting rooms, a cosy sitting room and a rare collection of pipes and canes belonging to the Rothschilds await in this lovely old chalet.

Chalet St-Georges rm, rest,
159 r. Mgr Conseil – 04 50 93 07 15 – chalet-st-georges@wanadoo.fr – Fax 04 50 21 51 18 – Open 28 June-13 September and 21 December-9 April AY **n**
21 rm – €140/220 €150/380, €18 – 3 suites – ½ P €150/280
Rest *La Table du Pêcheur* – *(open 21 December-31 march) (dinner only)* Carte €34/60
Rest *La Table du Trappeur* – *04 50 21 15 73 (open 28 June-13 September, 25 October-9 April and closed Monday, Tuesday and Wednesday 12 November-20 December)* Carte €31/55
◆ A real "doll's house" whose small bedrooms and wood-covered sitting rooms are adorned with trinkets, books, Savoy furniture and coloured fabrics. Seafood and regional specialities at the fisherman's table. Roast meats and good wine list at the trapper's table.

Le Manège rest,
rte Crêt du Midi, (Rochebrune roundabout) – 04 50 21 41 09 – reservation@hotel-le-manege.com – Fax 04 50 21 44 76 – Open 25 June-1st September and 15 December-5 April AYZ **b**
14 rm – €215/290 €295/395, €15 – 19 suites – €475/605
Rest – Menu (€22), €39 – Carte €32/40
◆ New building a stone's throw from the resort. Cosy interior with wood and mostly red and green colour schemes. Pretty rooms with balconies, including some split-level rooms. Italian and Savoy flavours mingle in the panelled restaurant.

Au Coin du Feu
252 rte Rochebrune – 04 50 21 04 94 – contact@coindufeu.com – Fax 04 50 21 20 15 – Open 15 December-4 April AZ **t**
23 rm – €205/265 €205/360, €17 – ½ P €150/229
Rest *Le Saint Nicolas* – *04 50 21 20 15 (dinner only)* Menu €48
◆ Named after its welcoming fireplace, this hotel provides comfortable, well-decorated rooms. Larger rooms with a small lounge area are available. Traditional cuisine and cheese specialities in a setting reminiscent of a mountain inn.

La Grange d'Arly rm,
10 r. Allobroges – 04 50 58 77 88 – contact@grange-darly.com – Fax 04 50 93 07 13 – Open from end June to mid September and from mid December to end March AY **t**
25 rm – €135/179 €155/215, €7 – ½ P €111/141 – **Rest** – *(dinner only)* Menu €18/33
◆ A chalet surrounded by greenery not far from a river. Charming decor mingling light wood and colourful fabrics. The sloped-ceiling bedrooms are the prettiest. Smart dining room - light panelling and bright southern fabrics – regional fare.

Ferme Duvillard without rest
3048 rte Edmond-de-Rothschild – ☏ 04 50 21 14 62 – ferme.duvillard@wanadoo.fr – Fax 04 50 21 42 82 – Open mid June-mid October and mid December-mid April BZ **e**
19 rm – †€ 137/232 ††€ 184/339, ☕ € 13
◆ Old farm converted into a hotel at the foot of the cable-car of Mont d'Arbois. Practical wood panelled bedrooms quieter on the valley side.

La Chaumine without rest
36 chemin des Bouleaux, via chemin du Maz – ☏ 04 50 21 37 05 – lachauminemegeve@orange.fr – Fax 04 50 21 37 21 – Open 29 June-30 August and 20 December-30 March BZ **v**
11 rm – †€ 66/81 ††€ 84/110, ☕ € 8,50
◆ 300m from the village and the Chamois cable car, a farm attractively restored in typical Alpine style. Smart rooms and evening snack service (local dishes).

Au Cœur de Megève rest, VISA MC AE
44 av. Ch. Feige – ☏ 04 50 21 25 30 – info@hotel-megeve.com – Fax 04 50 91 91 27
36 rm – †€ 90/200 ††€ 140/380, ☕ € 12 – 7 suites
Rest – *(closed Wednesday and Thursday off season)* Menu € 22/25 – Carte € 26/58
Rest *St-Jean* – *(open December-April) (dinner only)* Carte € 30/50 AY **u**
◆ Elegant renovated rooms in typical Savoyard style, some of which have a view of the peaks, others of the river. In the restaurant: traditional and regional recipes, salon de thé and summer terrace. The Saint Jean offers cheese specialities.

Au Vieux Moulin without rest
188 r. A. Martin – ☏ 04 50 21 22 29 – vieuxmoulin@compuserve.com – Fax 04 50 93 07 91 – Open beg. June-mid September and mid December-mid April
38 rm – †€ 145/240 ††€ 145/390, ☕ € 15 AY **h**
◆ Two chalets with rooms renovated in a subdued pleasant alpine style. The sauna, swimming pool and beauty centre further enhance the experience.

La Prairie without rest
407 r. Ch. Feige – ☏ 04 50 21 48 55 – contact@hotellaprairie.com – Fax 04 50 21 42 13 – Open June-September and December-April BY **d**
39 rm – †€ 80/320 ††€ 80/320, ☕ € 10
◆ At the entrance to the resort, functional bedrooms with balconies. Those in the annexe are more modern. Snack menu (regional dishes) available day and night.

Le Gai Soleil
rte Crêt du Midi – ☏ 04 50 21 00 70 – info@le-gai-soleil.fr – Fax 04 50 21 57 63 – Open 11 June-14 September and 16 December-14 April AZ **f**
21 rm – †€ 70/94 ††€ 78/127, ☕ € 10 – ½ P € 77/98 – **Rest** – Menu € 20 (lunch), € 25/35
◆ This 1920s chalet has a regular clientele due to its stylishness and the beneficial effects of its small fitness centre. Bedrooms quieter at the back. Friendly rustic restaurant with regional dishes and Savoyard menus on Mondays and Thursdays.

Alp'Hôtel rest, VISA MC
434 rte de Rochebrune – ☏ 04 50 21 07 58 – alp.hotel@wanadoo.fr – Fax 04 50 21 13 82 – Open 1st July-20 September and 20 December-15 April
18 rm – †€ 45/87 ††€ 57/87, ☕ € 8 – ½ P € 57/73
Rest – *(closed lunch winter)* Menu € 21/30 AZ **q**
◆ Halfway between the centre of the village and the Rochebrune ring road, this impeccably maintained, traditional chalet offers simple rustic decor and a friendly welcome. Well-prepared family-style cuisine and local specialities.

Le Chalet de l'Ancolie
1295 rte de Sallanches, (in Demi-Quartier), 2,5 km via ① – ☏ 04 50 21 21 37 – contact@chalet-ancolie.com – Fax 04 50 58 95 06 – Closed 14-29 April, 13-23 May, 23-26 June and 22 October-5 December
10 rm – †€ 62/110 ††€ 69/118, ☕ € 9 – ½ P € 60/90 – **Rest** – *(closed Wednesday lunch except Christmas holidays and February)* Menu (€ 25), € 33 – Carte € 34/39
◆ Pleasant little hotel on the road to the resort. The inside has been entirely renovated in alpine style, with minimalist, bright panelled rooms, quieter at the back. In the restaurant, traditional menu with some regional specialities.

Les Oyats without rest

771 chemin de Lady, south – ✆ 04 50 21 11 56 – lesoyats3@wanadoo.fr – Closed mid April-mid May

4 rm – €74 €84

◆ This atypical family farm has everything going for it: wood-inspired decor; home-made, solid furniture; rooms with terraces with views of the hamlet, a kitchen opening onto the stables with donkeys...

Flocons de Sel (Emmanuel Renaut) VISA

75 r. St-François – ✆ 04 50 21 49 99 – flocons.de.sels@wanadoo.fr – Fax 04 50 21 68 22 – Closed May, June, November, Tuesday and Wednesday off season, Tuesday lunch and Wednesday lunch in season and Monday lunch AY **a**

Rest – Menu €35 (weekday lunch)/115 – Carte €65/110

Spec. Millefeuille de légumes, herbes du jardin et champignons sauvages (spring-summer). Omble chevalier avec un beurre fermier, pomme de terre en poterie et sabayon thé vert. Tarte chartreuse. **Wines** Roussette de Savoie, Mondeuse d'Arbin.

◆ This 19C farmhouse at the heart of the resort has two rustic dining rooms nicely decorated with numerous objects. Deliciously creative cuisine.

Taverne du Mont d'Arbois VISA AE

2811 rte Edmond de Rothschild – ✆ 04 50 21 03 53 – taverne-sehtma@sfhm.fr – Fax 04 50 58 93 02 – Closed May, November, Tuesday and Wednesday except school holidays BZ **f**

Rest – *(dinner only)* Menu €38/55 bi – Carte €48/88

Rest *L'Atelier* – *(closed May, October, November, Monday and Tuesday except school holidays) (dinner only)* Menu €40/55

◆ A pleasant Alpine atmosphere in this fashionable chalet: a cosy setting and modern takes on traditional recipes. The dishes are roasted in the fireplace before your very eyes. Trendy setting, rustic and contemporary. Inventive menu presented on the boards.

Le Puck VISA

31 r. Oberstdorf – ✆ 04 50 21 06 61 – Fax 04 50 21 68 22 – Closed May and Monday except school holidays BY **x**

Rest – Menu €29 – Carte €30/52

◆ The Puck, set in the main ice rink, is ideal for ice hockey enthusiasts. Modern decoration with shades of grey, well-placed terrace and brasserie cuisine.

Le Vieux Megève VISA

58 pl. de la Résistance – ✆ 04 50 21 16 44 – vieux-megeve@py-internet.com – Fax 04 50 93 06 69 – Open 11 July-30 September and 16 December-31 March BY **n**

Rest – Menu €23 (lunch)/25 (lunch) – Carte €22/54

◆ This (1880) chalet is reminiscent of Megève as it used to be: high-quality service, gleaming woodwork, a large fireplace, old-fashioned bed linen and regional specialities.

Le Crystobald VISA

489 rte Nationale, via ① – ✆ 04 50 21 26 82 – lecrystobald@orange.fr – Closed 16 June-4 July, 24 November-18 December, Monday dinner, Tuesday and Wednesday off season

Rest – Menu (€16), €20 (weekday lunch), €32/45 – Carte €25/54

◆ This family-run chalet has a pleasant rustic atmosphere. Good contemporary cuisine in a dining room decorated in light wood or on the terrace. Friendly service.

at the top of Mont d'Arbois by cable car from Mont d'Arbois or cable car from La Princesse – ✉ 74170 St-Gervais

L'Igloo ← Mont Blanc chain, VISA AE

3120 rte des Crêtes – ✆ 04 50 93 05 84 – igloo2@wanadoo.fr – Fax 04 50 21 02 74 – Open 25 June-10 September and 17 December-20 April

12 rm (½ board only) – ½ P €130/210 – **Rest** – Menu €40/60 – Carte €47/72

◆ At the meeting point of three cable-cars, a stunning view over the Mont-Blanc Massif. Well-chosen furniture, Jacuzzi and sauna add to the fittings of this place. The panorama from the restaurant terrace is amazing! Also, self-service for skiers.

X **L'idéal** < from the Aravis range to Mont-Blanc, VISA MC AE
– 04 50 21 31 26 – *ideal-sehtma@efhm.fr – Fax 04 50 93 02 63 – Open mid December-mid April*
Rest – *(lunch only)* Carte € 37/70
◆ Old mountain farm which is now a chic high-altitude restaurant. Impressive landscape; huge terrace and mountain cuisine.

in la Côte 2000 **8 km Southeast by Edmond de Rothschild road** - BZ – ✉ **74120 Megève**

X **Côte 2000** < (dinner) VISA MC AE
3461 rte de la Cote 2000 – 04 50 21 31 84 – c2000-sehtma@sfhm.fr – Fax 04 50 21 59 25 – Open 2 July-9 September and 16 December-30 April
Rest – Menu € 47 (lunch), € 62/70 – Carte € 47/72
◆ This superb Austrian chalet (a Rothschild property) was dismantled and rebuilt here in the 1960s. Large panoramic terrace and regional menu.

in Leutaz **4 km Southwest by Le Bouchet road** AZ – ✉ **74120 Megève**

XX **La Sauvageonne** < (dinner) VISA MC AE
– 04 50 91 90 81 – *Fax 04 50 58 75 44 – Open 12 July-14 September and 4 December-16 April*
Rest – Menu (€ 23) – Carte € 58/77
◆ 1907 farm whose smart interior is adorned with paintings on sculpted wood representing alpine landscapes. Superb lounge with cigar box. "Showbiz" clientele.

X **Le Refuge** < P VISA MC
– 04 50 21 23 04 – *franck@refuge-megeve.com – Fax 04 50 91 99 76 – Closed 10 June-10 July, 15 October-15 November and Wednesday except school holidays*
Rest – Menu (€ 22), € 27 (lunch) – Carte € 41/57
◆ Charming "refuge" located above the resort. Mountain influences in the decor and on the plate. Simple, tasty cuisine. Large panoramic terrace.

MEILLARD – 03 Allier – 326 G4 – pop. 280 – alt. 340 m – ✉ 03500 5 B1

Paris 319 – Clermont-Fd 86 – Mâcon 149 – Montluçon 68 – Moulins 27 – Nevers 82

X **L'Auberge Gourmande** VISA MC
au bourg – 04 70 42 06 09 – auberge.gourmande@wanadoo.fr – Closed 1st-15 July, Christmas holidays, February holidays, Sunday dinner, Monday, Tuesday and Wednesday
Rest – *(pre-book)* Menu € 30/54 – Carte € 44/59
◆ This old regional establishement has a rather ordinary countrified interior. The outside dining area offers a view of the village's unusual church. Small, up-to-date menu. Children's play area.

MEILLONNAS – 01 Ain – 328 F3 – pop. 1 204 – alt. 271 m – ✉ 01370 44 B1

Paris 432 – Bourg-en-Bresse 12 – Mâcon 47 – Nantua 37 – Oyonnax 46

X **Auberge Au Vieux Meillonnas** P VISA MC AE
– 04 74 51 34 46 – *auvieuxmeillonas@orange.fr – Fax 04 74 51 34 46 – Closed 23 August-3 September, 30 October-5 November, 11-18 February, Tuesday dinner, Sunday dinner and Wednesday*
Rest – Menu € 16 (weekdays)/34 – Carte € 24/54
◆ A refreshingly unaffected inn known for its friendly atmosphere. Regional menu served in a rustic dining room, opening onto a shaded terrace and garden.

MEISENTHAL – 57 Moselle – 307 P5 – pop. 766 – alt. 380 m – ✉ 57960 27 D2

Paris 440 – Haguenau 47 – Sarreguemines 38 – Saverne 40 – Strasbourg 62

Auberge des Mésanges P VISA MC AE
r. des Vergers – 03 87 96 92 28 – hotel-restaurant.auberge-mesanges@wanadoo.fr – Fax 03 87 96 99 14 – Closed 22 December-1st January, 8-23 February
20 rm – †€ 35/41 ††€ 41/48, □ € 7 – ½ P € 46/48
Rest – *(closed Sunday dinner and Monday)* Menu € 11 (weekday lunch), € 18/25 – Carte € 26/38
◆ A family inn located in a century-old house on the edge of a forest in the North Vosges natural park. Well-kept rooms. Traditional cuisine. The Flammekueche (an onion and bacon tart) on the evening menu is particularly recommended.

MÉJANNES-LÈS-ALÈS – 30 Gard – 339 J4 – see Alès

MÉLISEY – 70 Haute-Saône – 314 H6 – pop. 1 794 – alt. 330 m – ✉ 70270
Burgundy-Jura 17 **C1**

Paris 397 – Belfort 33 – Besançon 92 – Épinal 63 – Lure 13 – Luxeuil-les-Bains 22

Office de tourisme, place de la Gare ✆ 03 84 63 22 80, Fax 03 84 63 26 94

XX **La Bergeraine** AC P VISA

27 rte des Vosges – ✆ 03 84 20 82 52 – Fax 03 84 20 04 47 – Closed Sunday dinner, Tuesday dinner and Wednesday except public holidays

Rest – Menu € 15 (weekday lunch), € 24/85 – Carte € 38/70

◆ On the road just outside the village located on the Mille Etang plateau, this charming little restaurant surrounded by flowers and shaded by lime trees serves carefully prepared modern dishes.

MELLE – 79 Deux-Sèvres – 322 F7 – pop. 3 851 – alt. 138 m – ✉ 79500 39 **C2**

Paris 394 – Niort 30 – Poitiers 60 – St-Jean-d'Angély 45

Office de tourisme, 3, rue Émilien Traver ✆ 05 49 29 15 10, Fax 05 49 29 19 83

L'Argentière rm, AC rest, P VISA AE

at St-Martin, on Niort road: 2 km – ✆ 05 49 29 13 22 – hotel-restaurant.largentiere@wanadoo.fr – Fax 05 49 29 06 63 – Closed 15 November-15 March

25 rm – †€ 45/49 ††€ 47/53, ☕ € 7 – ½ P € 58/62 – **Rest** – *(closed Friday dinner from November to April, Sunday dinner and Monday lunch)* Menu € 16 (weekdays)/48 – Carte € 42/53

◆ The name recalls the former local silver mines. The pavilions feature antique-style columns, and have small, colourful rooms (quieter at the rear). Modern dining area and terrace under an arbour.

XX **Les Glycines** with rm AC VISA AE

5 pl. R. Groussard – ✆ 05 49 27 01 11 – contact@hotel-lesglycines.com – Fax 05 49 27 93 45 – Closed 3-8 November and 5-18 January, Sunday dinner 15 September-30 June and Monday 15 September-31 March

7 rm – †€ 42/55 ††€ 49/63, ☕ € 7,50 – ½ P € 53/62 – **Rest** – Menu € 25/43 – Carte € 38/56

◆ This restaurant has a charming wrought-iron veranda, and features a refined dining area with spring-time décor, and a small brasserie area. Traditional cuisine served. Rooms available.

MELUN P – 77 Seine-et-Marne – 312 E4 – pop. 35 695 – Built-up area 107 705 – alt. 43 m – ✉ 77000 Northern France and the Paris Region 19 **C2**

Paris 47 – Fontainebleau 18 – Orléans 104 – Troyes 128

Office de tourisme, 18, rue Paul Doumer ✆ 01 64 52 64 52, Fax 01 60 56 54 31

U.C.P.A. Bois-le-Roi Bois-le-Roi Base de loisirs, by Fontainebleau road: 8 km, ✆ 01 64 81 33 31 ;

de Greenparc Saint-Pierre-du-Perray Route de Villepècle, by Cesson road: 15 km, ✆ 01 60 75 40 60 ;

Blue Green Golf de Villeray Saint-Pierre-du-Perrayby Corbeil road: 21 km, ✆ 01 60 75 17 47.

Portal★ of St-Aspais church.

Vaux-le-Vicomte: chateau★★ and gardens★★★ 6 km by ②.

Plans on next page

XX **Le Mariette** AC VISA

31 r. St-Ambroise – ✆ 01 64 37 06 06 – restaurant@lemariette.fr – Fax 01 64 37 00 47 – Closed August, Monday dinner, Saturday lunch and Sunday AZ **a**

Rest – Menu € 28 bi (weekday lunch), € 36/60 – Carte € 55/75

◆ Façade, walls, carpeting and lobster aquarium. Blue dominates the elegant decor of this restaurant with up-to-date cuisine featuring seafood and truffles.

LE MÉE-SUR-SEINE

Courtilleraies (Av. des)	X	10
Dauvergne (Av. M.)	X	12

MELUN

Alsace-Lorraine (Q.)	BZ	2
Carnot (R.)	AY	3
Chartrettes (Rte de)	X	6
Chasse (R. de la)	X	7
Corbeil (Av. de)	X	8
Courtille (R. de la)	BZ	9
Doumer (R. Paul)	BY	13
Europe (Rd-Pt de l')	X	14
Gallieni (Pl.)	X	17
Gaulle (Av. du Gén. de)	X	18
Godin (Av. E.)	AZ	19
Jean-Jaurès (Av.)	X	20
Leclerc (Av. Gén.)	X	22
Libération (Av. de la)	X	23
Miroir (R. du)	AY	25
Montagne-du-Mée (R. de la)	AY	26
Pompidou (Av. G.)	X	33
Pouteau (R. René)	BY	34
Prés.-Despatys (R.)	AY	35
Rossignol (Q. H.)	X	39
St-Ambroise (R.)	AZ	
St-Aspais (R.)	BY	41
St-Étienne (R.)	AZ	43
Thiers (Av.)	AZ, X	46
Vaux (R. de)	X	49
Voisenon (Rte de)	X	53
13e-Dragons (Av.)	X	60
31e-d'Inf. (Av. du)	X	65

La Melunoise

5 r. Gâtinais – ✆ 01 64 39 68 27 – Fax 01 64 39 81 81
– Closed August, February school holidays, Sunday dinner, Monday and Tuesday X b

Rest – Menu € 28, € 32/50 – Carte € 39/54

◆ Discreet house away from the traffic. Two simple, rustic dining areas, separated by a small reception featuring stonework. Traditional meals served.

in Crisenoy 10 km by ② – pop. 604 – alt. 89 m – ✉ 77390

Auberge de Crisenoy

r. Grande – ✆ 01 64 38 83 06 – Fax 01 64 38 89 06
– Closed 28 July-18 August, 22-31 December, 23 February-2 March, Sunday dinner, Wednesday dinner and Monday

Rest – Menu € 24 (weekday lunch), € 32/49 – Carte € 42/52

◆ Pleasant inn setting in the heart of a small village, including bare stone, beams, a fireplace and rustic furnishings. Modern cooking served.

in Vaux-le-Pénil 3 km Southeast – pop. 10 688 – alt. 60 m – ✉ 77000

La Table St-Just (Fabrice Vitu)

r. de la Libération, (near the château) – ✆ 01 64 52 09 09
– latablesaintjust@free.fr – Fax 01 64 52 09 09
– Closed 27 April-6 May, 10 August-2 September, 24 December-7 January, Sunday, Monday and public holidays X s

Rest – Menu € 43/95 – Carte € 62/94

Spec. Salade de homard à l'orange. Terrine de cèpes aux gambas (autumn). Soufflé au Grand Marnier, glace aux zestes d'orange.

◆ An old farm formerly part of the chateau of Vaux le Pénil. Today it is a tastefully designed restaurant beneath a high oak framed ceiling. Updated cuisine.

MENDE P – 48 Lozère – 330 J7 – pop. 11 804 – alt. 731 m – ✉ 48000

Languedoc-Roussillon-Tarn Gorges 23 **C1**

Paris 584 – Alès 102 – Aurillac 150 – Gap 305 – Issoire 139 – Millau 96

Office de tourisme, Place du Foirail ✆ 04 66 94 00 23, Fax 04 66 94 21 10

Cathedral★ - Pont N.-Dame★.

MENDE

Aigues-Passes (R. d') 2
Ange (R. de l') 3
Angiran (R. d') 4
Arjal (R. de l') 5
Beurre (Pl. au) 6
Blé (Pl. au) 7
Britexte (Bd) 8
Capucins (Bd des) 9
Carmes (R. des) 10
Chanteronne (R. de) 12
Chaptal (R.) 13
Chastel (R. du) 14
Collège (R. du) 18
Droite (R.) 19
Écoles (R. des) 20
Épine (R. de l') 21
Estoup (Pl. René) 22
Gaulle (Pl. Ch.-de) 23
Montbel (R. du Fg) 24
Piencourt (Allée) 25
Planche (Pont de la) 26
Pont N.-Dame (R. du) 27
République (Pl. et R.) 30
Roussel (Pl. Th.) 32
Soubeyran (Bd du) 33
Soubeyran (R.) 34
Soupirs (Allée des) 36
Urbain V (Pl.) 37

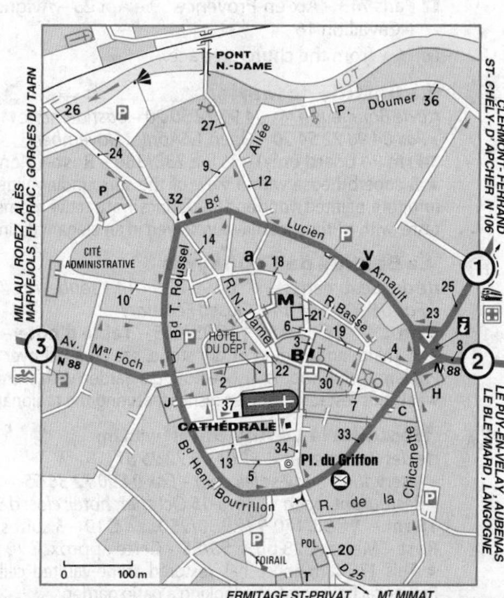

De France VISA

9 bd L. Arnault – 04 66 65 00 04 – contact@hoteldefrance-mende.com – Fax 04 66 49 30 47 – Closed 27 December-14 January **v**

24 rm – €58/100 €58/100, €8,50 – 3 suites – ½ P €60/80

Rest – *(closed Saturday lunch and Monday lunch)* Menu (€22), €26/34 – Carte €30/37

♦ A handsome wrought-iron gateway leads to this attractively renovated old coaching inn, which has welcomed guests since 1856. Modern dining room and charming guestrooms. Traditional cuisine served in an attractive, refurbished dining room or in the courtyard in summer.

Du Pont Roupt rest, VISA

av. 11-Novembre, via ③ – 04 66 65 01 43 – hotel-pont-roupt@wanadoo.fr – Fax 04 66 65 22 96 – Closed 22-30 December

26 rm – €68/120 €68/120, €11 – ½ P €78/98 – **Rest** – *(closed Sunday except dinner 1st November-1st April and Saturday)* Menu €26/55 bi – Carte €34/48

♦ Family-run hotel on the banks of the Lot. Modern fireplace and stylish armchairs in the sitting room, smart bedrooms, splendid indoor pool and illuminated well. Tasty regional dishes prepared by the same family for four generations.

Le Mazel VISA

25 r. Collège – 04 66 65 05 33 – Fax 04 66 65 05 33 – Open 1st April-5 November and closed Monday dinner and Tuesday **a**

Rest – Menu €16/28 – Carte €22/36

♦ A mural in clay moss by Loul Combes, a well-known artist, adorns one of the walls of this restaurant. Traditional family recipes.

in Chabrits 5 km Northwest by ③ and D 42 – ✉ 48000 Mende

La Safranière VISA

– 04 66 49 31 54 – Fax 04 66 49 31 54 – Closed 1st-17 March, 15-22 September, 16-28 February, Wednesday lunch except July-August, Sunday dinner and Monday

Rest – *(pre-book)* Menu €23 (weekdays)/47

♦ Occupying old stable buildings in the foothills of the Gévaudan, this restaurant serves contemporary cuisine in a modern, attractive setting. Good choice of wines and regional cheeses.

MÉNERBES – 84 Vaucluse – 332 E11 – pop. 995 – alt. 224 m – ✉ 84560 Provence

Paris 713 – Aix-en-Provence 59 – Apt 23 – Avignon 40 – Carpentras 34 – Cavaillon 16 42 **E1**

≤★ from the church terrace.

La Bastide de Marie rm, VISA

rte de Bonnieux – 04 90 72 30 20 – bastidemarie@c-h-m.com – Fax 04 90 72 54 20 – Open 17 April-3 November

14 rm (½ board only) – ½ P €238/380 – **Rest** – Menu €78 bi – Carte €35/60

♦ A superb house with a view of the surrounding vineyards. A subtle mix of antique furniture, painted wood and fine fabrics in attractive rooms. Cuisine in keeping with current taste, with a Provençal flavour, served in an elegant dining room.

La Bastide de Soubeyras

rte des Beaumettes – 04 90 72 94 14 – soubeyras@wanadoo.fr – Fax 04 90 72 94 14 – Closed February

6 rm – €85/155 €95/165 – **Table d'hôte** – Menu €35 bi

♦ A charming building of dry stone, set on a hill over the village, this hotel provides Provençal-style rooms, also featuring a garden with swimming pool. Open three nights a week, this restaurant serves dishes featuring the regional flavours of the Luberon.

Hostellerie Le Roy Soleil with rm rm, rest, VISA

rte des Beaumettes – 04 90 72 25 61 – reservation@roy-soleil.com – Fax 04 90 72 36 55 – Restaurant: open 1st April-15 October, hotel: closed 5 January-1st March

18 rm – €90/170 €130/250, €19 – 3 suites – ½ P €139/199

Rest – Menu (€28 bi), €55/85 – Carte approx. €70

♦ This 17C farmhouse has restored stone-vaulted ceilings in its smart dining room. Provençal bedrooms overlooking a patio garden.

MÉNESQUEVILLE – 27 Eure – **304** I5 – **pop. 349** – **alt. 65 m** – ✉ **27850**
Normandy 33 **D2**

Paris 100 – Les Andelys 16 – Évreux 53 – Gournay-en-Bray 33 – Lyons-la-Forêt 8 – Rouen 29

Le Relais de la Lieure rm, VISA AE
1 r. Gén. de Gaulle – ✆ 02 32 49 06 21 – relais.lieure@orange.fr – Fax 02 32 49 53 87 – Closed 19-31 March and 22-31 October
14 rm – †€ 54/66 ††€ 54/66, ☕ € 7,50 – ½ P € 56/65 – **Rest** – *(closed Sunday dinner, Monday lunch and Friday)* Menu € 16 (weekdays)/42 – Carte € 28/47
♦ Family stop in a hamlet located alongside the magnificent forest of Lyons. Large enough bedrooms, furnished simply and well kept. Traditional meals served in a country-style dining area.

MENESTEROL – **24 Dordogne** – **329** B5 – **see Montpon-Ménestérol**

MENESTREAU-EN-VILLETTE – **45 Loiret** – **318** J5 – **see La Ferté-St-Aubin**

LE MÉNIL – **88 Vosges** – **314** I5 – **see le Thillot**

LA MÉNITRÉ – **49 Maine-et-Loire** – **317** H4 – **pop. 1 899** – **alt. 21 m** – ✉ **49250** 35 **C2**

Paris 301 – Angers 27 – Baugé 23 – Saumur 26
Syndicat d'initiative, place Léon Faye ✆ 02 41 45 67 51

Auberge de l'Abbaye VISA AE
port St-Maur – ✆ 02 41 45 64 67 – aubergedelabbaye@hotmail.com – Fax 02 41 57 69 75 – Closed 18 August-3 September, 22-31 December, 17 February-4 March, Sunday dinner, Monday and Tuesday
Rest – Menu (€ 15), € 19 (weekdays)/64 – Carte € 40/55
♦ A pleasant, contemporary-style dining room in this house on an embankment overlooking the Loire. Focus on regional produce (fish from the river and fresh vegetables).

LA MÉNOUNIÈRE – **17 Charente-Maritime** – **324** B4 – **see île d'Oléron**

MENTHON-ST-BERNARD – **74 Haute-Savoie** – **328** K5 – **pop. 1 659** – **alt. 482 m** – ✉ **74290** French Alps 46 **F1**

Paris 548 – Albertville 37 – Annecy 10 – Bonneville 50 – Megève 52 – Talloires 4 – Thônes 14
Office de tourisme, Chef-lieu ✆ 04 50 60 14 30, Fax 04 50 60 22 19
Château of Menthon★: ≤★ East: 2 km.

Palace de Menthon ≤ lake and castle, rm, AC rest, rest, VISA AE
665 rte des Bains – ✆ 04 50 64 83 00 – reception@palacedementhon.com – Fax 04 54 64 83 81 – Open 15 April-15 October
63 rm – †€ 85/99 ††€ 180/255, ☕ € 15 – 2 suites
Rest – *(open 15 October-15 May)* Menu (€ 30), € 38
Rest *Palace Beach* – *(closed 15 October-15 May)* Menu (€ 30), € 38
♦ Hotel dating from 1911, recently renovated and boasting a superb view of the lake and château. Large park and comfortable bedrooms with period or Art Deco furniture. Contemporary cuisine in an elegant setting at the restaurant. Moorish decor and terrace overlooking the water at the Palace Beach.

Beau Séjour without rest
161 allée Tennis – ✆ 04 50 60 12 04 – h.beau-sejour@laposte.net – Fax 04 50 60 05 56 – Open 15 April-end-September
18 rm – †€ 67 ††€ 75, ☕ € 8
♦ Peaceful villa, surrounded by a flower garden, 100m from the lake and full of retro charm. Countrified rooms, gradually being spruced up, varied furnishings and several balconies.

La Vallombreuse without rest

534 rte Moulins, 700 m east on Col de Bluffy road – ✆ 04 50 60 16 33 – contact@la-vallombreuse.com – Fax 04 50 64 88 87 – **5 rm** ☕ – 🚹€ 60/114 🚹🚹€ 75/130

◆ In a quiet garden, this handsome 15C fortified house is home to immense rooms furnished with antique, Savoyard or period pieces. Art exhibitions in the sitting rooms.

MENTON – 06 Alpes-Maritimes – 341 F5 – pop. 28 812 – Casino : du Soleil AZ – ✉ 06500 French Riviera 42 E2

Paris 956 – Cannes 63 – Cuneo 102 – Monaco 11 – Nice 30

Office de tourisme, 8, avenue Boyer ✆ 04 92 41 76 76, Fax 04 92 41 76 78

Site★★ - Old town ★★: Parvis St-Michel★★, Façade★ of the La Conception chapel BY **B** - ⩽★ of the English cemetery BX **D** - Promenade du Soleil★★, ⩽★ of the Impératrice-Eugénie pier BV - Jardin de Menton★: le Val Rameh★ BV **E** - Salle des mariages (wedding room)★ of the town hall BY **H** - Musée des Beaux-Arts★ (palais Carnolès) AX **M¹**.

Jardin Hanbury★★ Vintimille, West: 2 km.

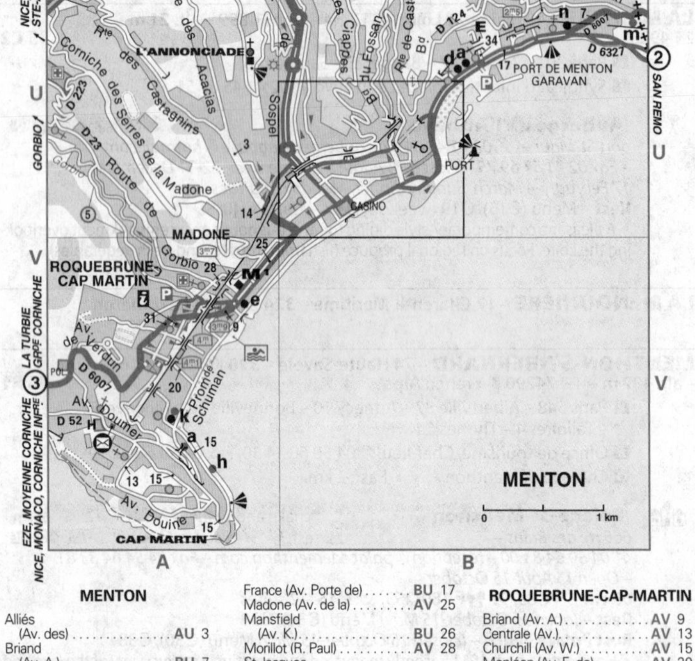

MENTON		
Alliés (Av. des)	AU	3
Briand (Av. A.)	BU	7
Coty (Cours René)	AU	14
France (Av. Porte de)	BU	17
Madone (Av. de la)	AV	25
Mansfield (Av. K.)	BU	26
Morillot (R. Paul)	AV	28
St-Jacques (Ch.)	BU	34

ROQUEBRUNE-CAP-MARTIN		
Briand (Av. A.)	AV	9
Centrale (Av.)	AV	13
Churchill (Av. W.)	AV	15
Monléon (Av. F. de)	AV	20
Pasteur (Av. L.)	AV	31

Grand Hôtel des Ambassadeurs without rest

3 r. Partouneaux – ✆ 04 93 28 75 75 – info@ambassadeurs-menton.com – Fax 04 93 35 62 32 – Closed 9 November-7 December CY **k**

31 rm ☕ – 🚹€ 150/230 🚹🚹€ 170/350 – 1 suite

◆ This hotel features a different theme on each floor: poetry, music, cinema and art. The rooms are adorned with original objects (manuscripts and lithographs). Superb relaxation and beauty centre.

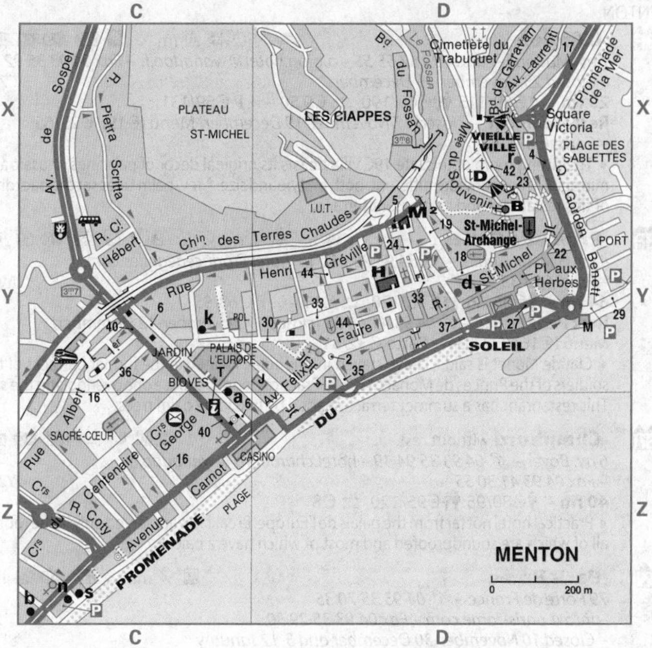

Adémar de Lantagnac (R. d') . . . . DY 2
Bonaparte (Quai) . . . . DX 4
Bosano (R. Lt) . . . . DY 5
Boyer (Av.) . . . . CYZ 6
Édouard-VII (Av.) . . . . CYZ 16
Félix-Faure (Av.) . . . . CDY
Gallieni (R. Gén.) . . . . DY 18
Guyau (R.) . . . . DY 19
Logettes (R. des) . . . . DY 22
Longue (R.) . . . . DX 23
Lorédan-Larchey (R.) . . . . DY 24
Monléon (Quai de) . . . . DY 27
Napoléon-III (Quai) . . . . DY 29
Partouneaux (R.) . . . . DY 30
République (R. de la) . . . . DY 33
St-Michel (R.) . . . . DY
St-Roch (R.) . . . . DY 35
Thiers (Av.) . . . . CY 36
Trenca (R.) . . . . DY 37
Verdun (Av. de) . . . . CYZ 40
Vieux-Château (R.) . . . . DX 42
Villarey (R.) . . . . DY 44

Riva without rest

600 promenade du Soleil – ☎ 04 92 10 92 10 – contact@rivahotel.com – Fax 04 93 28 87 87 CZ **n**

40 rm – €88/119 €88/119, ☕ €11

◆ On the seafront a new spa hotel with sun deck, Jacuzzi and summer restaurant on the roof. All the rooms have been renovated; some have sea-view balconies.

Napoléon

29 Porte de France – ☎ 04 93 35 89 50 – info@napoleon-menton.com – Fax 04 93 35 49 22 BU **a**

43 rm – €84/139 €94/139, ☕ €11 – 1 suite

Rest – *(closed 15 November-15 December, Sunday dinner and Monday off season)* Menu €29 – Carte €40/59

◆ Elegant contemporary décor in the rooms named after famous people who have stayed in Menton (Cocteau, Sutherland, etc.). Those with sea views also have lovely teak terraces. This beach restaurant serves grilled and barbecued fish; mouthwatering ice cream menu.

Princess et Richmond

617 promenade du Soleil – ☎ 04 93 35 80 20 – princess.hotel@wanadoo.fr – Fax 04 93 57 40 20 – Closed 2 November-12 December CZ **s**

46 rm – €82/129 €82/215, ☕ €10 – **Rest** – *(due to open in march)*

◆ A pebble beach right outside the door, ocean liner-style lounge, and a panoramic rooftop solarium and Jacuzzi are the main attractions of this hotel. Comfortable guestrooms, some with a sea view.

L'Aiglon rm, VISA AE
7 av. Madone – ✆ 04 93 57 55 55 – aiglon.hotel@wanadoo.fr – Fax 04 93 35 92 39 – Closed 23 November-19 December CZ **b**
29 rm – †€ 69/115 ††€ 69/190, ☕ € 9,50 – ½ P € 69/131
Rest *Riaumont* – *(closed 17 November-19 December)* Menu (€ 19), € 25/65 – Carte € 33/66
◆ The sitting room of this late 19C villa boasts its original decor of paintings, mosaic and mirrors. All the rooms are different, both in style and size. A few palm trees set the backdrop of this restaurant and its pleasant terrace.

Prince de Galles rm, VISA AE
4 av. Gén. de Gaulle – ✆ 04 93 28 21 21 – hotel@princedegalles.com – Fax 04 93 35 92 91 AV **e**
64 rm – †€ 66/86 ††€ 78/128, ☕ € 11 – ½ P € 68/95
Rest *Petit Prince* – *✆ 04 93 41 66 05 (closed 17 November-12 December)* Menu (€ 16), € 22/34 – Carte € 32/51
◆ Claude Monet is said to have stayed in this hotel, located in the former barracks of the soldiers of the Princes de Monaco (1860). Practical rooms, choose one overlooking the sea. This restaurant has a summer terrace shaded by two large palm trees.

Chambord without rest VISA AE
6 av. Boyer – ✆ 04 93 35 94 19 – hotel.chambord@wanadoo.fr – Fax 04 93 41 30 55 CYZ **a**
40 rm – †€ 80/95 ††€ 95/120, ☕ € 8
◆ Practical hotel not far from the palais de l'Europe. Breakfasts are served only in the rooms, all of which are soundproofed and most of which have a balcony.

Paris Rome rm, VISA AE
79 Porte de France – ✆ 04 93 35 70 35 – info@paris-rome.com – Fax 04 93 35 29 30 – Closed 10 November-30 December and 5-12 January BU **n**
22 rm – †€ 47/57 ††€ 60/115, ☕ € 11 – 1 suite
Rest – *(closed Tuesday lunch and Monday) (number of covers limited, pre-book)* Menu (€ 30), € 44/90 (dinner)
Spec. Foie gras de canard rôti et confit. Poissons sauvages du pays cuits dans l'argile de Vallauris, barigoule de légumes au citron de Menton (15 June to 15 September). Moelleux pur chocolat. **Wines** Bellet.
◆ A pleasant little family home near Garavan harbour. Pretty Provençal rooms. Theme holidays (culture, fishing, etc.). The new Mediterranean-inspired sophisticated decor (stonework, wrought iron, painted beams) does full justice to the creative menu.

Mirazur (Mauro Colagreco) < sea and Menton old town, VISA AE
30 av. Aristide Briand – ✆ 04 92 41 86 86 – info@mirazur.fr – Fax 04 92 41 86 87 – Closed 17 November-9 December, lunch 15 July-31 August except weekends, Tuesday 1st September-14 July and Monday BU **m**
Rest – *(number of covers limited, pre-book)* Menu € 35, € 55/90 – Carte € 65/81
Spec. Gamberoni de San Remo, mousseline de pignons de pin. Poissons sauvages de Méditerranée, sauce fumée. Pigeon cuit à basse température. **Wines** Bellet, Côtes de Provence.
◆ The contemporary architecture and streamlined decor enhance the 360° sea view and the fine, contemporary cuisine prepared by the Argentinean-born chef.

A Braijade Méridiounale VISA AE
66 r. Longue – ✆ 04 93 35 65 65 – contact@abraijade.com – Fax 04 93 35 65 65 – Closed 15 November-7 December and Wednesday DX **r**
Rest – Menu € 29 bi/34 bi – Carte € 28/45
◆ This pleasant establishment in a side street in the old town is worth a detour for its generous southern French cuisine (grills cooked in the dining room) and extremely warm welcome.

La Cantinella VISA
8 r. Trenca – ✆ 04 93 41 34 20 – puccio.francesco@free.fr – Closed January, lunch in August and Tuesday DY **d**
Rest – *(number of covers limited, pre-book)* Menu € 20 – Carte € 25/44
◆ Nothing is too much trouble for the Sicilian-born owner, who rustles up tasty southern-inspired (Nice meets Italy) dishes with fresh market produce. Delightfully friendly.

in Monti 5 km North by Sospel road – ✉ 06500 Menton

XX **Pierrot-Pierrette** with rm — rest, P VISA MC

pl. de l'Église – ☎ 04 93 35 79 76 – pierrotpierrette@hotmail.fr – Fax 04 93 35 79 76 – Closed 3 December-12 January and Monday except holidays

7 rm – †€ 68/77 ††€ 68/77, ☕ € 8 – ½ P € 70/86

Rest – Menu € 28 (weekdays)/40 – Carte € 32/70

♦ A family inn in the hills where the hospitality is as abundant as the local cuisine. Attractive interior, renovated rooms and a loyal band of regulars.

LES MENUIRES – 73 Savoie – **333** M6 – **alt. 1 400 m – Winter sports : 1 400/3 200 m** 8 36 – ✉ **73440 St-Martin-de-Belleville** French Alps 46 **F2**

Paris 632 – Albertville 51 – Chambéry 101 – Moûtiers 27

Office de tourisme, immeuble Belledonne ☎ 04 79 00 73 00, Fax 04 79 00 75 06

Kaya — mountains, P VISA MC AE

à Reberty – ☎ 04 79 41 42 00 – info@hotel-kaya.com – Fax 04 79 41 42 01 – Open 15 December-19 April

40 rm ☕ – †€ 183 ††€ 183 – 4 suites

Rest ***Le K*** – Menu € 36 (lunch)/60 – Carte € 36/44

♦ Hotel decorated in a spare, modern style, from the peaceful lounges (billiards, fireplace) to the comfortable bedrooms, all warmed by a touch of wood. Sauna and steam bath. Light lunches and specialities from the Savoie served in the evening.

L'Ours Blanc — mountains, rm, P VISA MC AE

at Reberty 2000 – ☎ 04 79 00 61 66 – info@hotel-ours-blanc.com – Fax 04 79 00 63 67 – Open 5 December-16 April

49 rm – †€ 85/117 ††€ 115/255, ☕ € 15 – ½ P € 75/99 – **Rest** – Menu € 23/80 – Carte € 37/64

♦ Overlooking the ski resort, this large mountain-style chalet provides airy rooms with balconies, and a lounge with a central fireplace. Good fitness facilities. Warm all wood restaurant overlooking the Masse range. Regional recipes.

MERCATEL – 62 Pas-de-Calais – **301** J6 – see Arras

MERCUÈS – 46 Lot – **337** E5 – see Cahors

MERCUREY – 71 Saône-et-Loire – **320** I8 – **pop. 1 269 – alt. 269 m** – ✉ **71640** 8 **C3**

Paris 344 – Autun 39 – Beaune 26 – Chagny 11 – Chalon-sur-Saône 13 – Mâcon 73

Hôtellerie du Val d'Or — P VISA MC AE

Grande-Rue – ☎ 03 85 45 13 70 – contact@le-valdor.com – Fax 03 85 45 18 45 – Closed 15 December-17 January, Tuesday lunch and Monday

12 rm – †€ 77/98 ††€ 77/98, ☕ € 11 – ½ P € 87

Rest – Menu (€ 21), € 24 bi (lunch), € 39/71 (dinner) – Carte € 58/102

Spec. Etuvée de morilles, pois frais et asperges vertes (April to June). Canard chalandais au jus d'olive (July to September). Soufflé glacé au marc de Bourgogne et coulis de cassis. **Wines** Mercurey, Givry.

♦ Old posthouse in a winegrowers' village on the Chalons Côte. Smart bedrooms. A charming, rustic restaurant featuring a fireplace with columns and exposed wooden beams. Tasty traditional cuisine.

MÉRÉVILLE – 54 Meurthe-et-Moselle – **307** H7 – see Nancy

MÉRIBEL – 73 Savoie – **333** M5 – **Winter sports : 1 450/2 950 m** 16 45 – ✉ **73550** French Alps 46 **F2**

Paris 621 – Albertville 41 – Annecy 85 – Chambéry 90 – Moûtiers 15

Office de tourisme, ☎ 04 79 08 60 01, Fax 04 79 00 59 61

Méribel B.P. 54, Northeast: 4 km, ☎ 04 79 00 52 67.

☀★★★ la Saulire, ☀★★ Mont du Vallon, ☀★★ Roc des Trois marches, ☀★★ Tougnète.

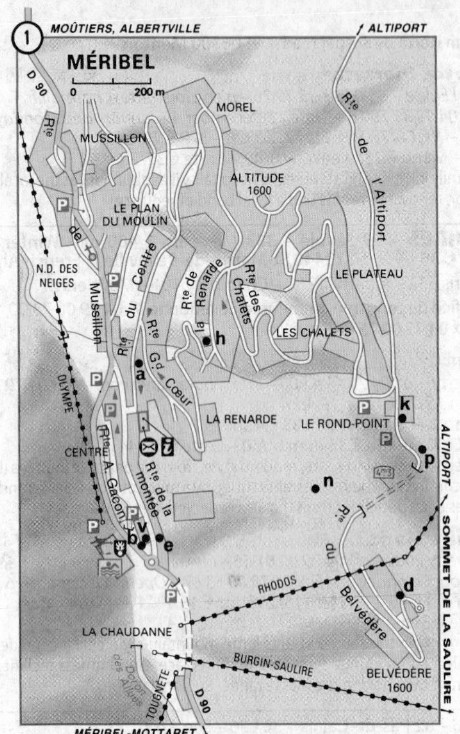

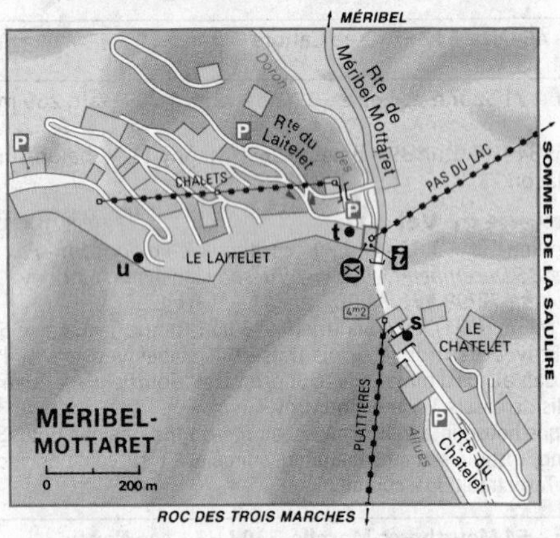

 **Le Grand Cœur & Spa**

– ✆ 04 79 08 60 03 – grandcoeur@relaischateaux.com – Fax 04 79 08 58 38
– *Open 13 December-6 April* **a**

35 rm – †€ 210/430 ††€ 205/440, ☕ € 20 – 5 suites – ½ P € 180/348

Rest – Menu € 45 (lunch), € 60/85 – Carte € 80/141

◆ The omnipresent light wood, pretty bedrooms and cosy piano-bar give this hotel - one of the oldest in the resort - a romantic feel. New spa. Arcades and light-wood panelling in the warm restaurant; modern cooking.

Allodis mountains, rm,

au Belvédère – 04 79 00 56 00
– allodis@wanadoo.fr – Fax 04 79 00 59 28
– Open July-August and mid December to mid April **d**
44 rm – €87/319 €156/488, €17 – ½ P €102/334
Rest – Menu (€33), €47/73 – Carte €60/85
◆ This chalet overlooking the resort opens onto the ski slopes. Spacious comfortable rooms with balcony. Pleasant pool, sauna and steam bath. In the evening, traditional cuisine served in a refined setting.

Le Yéti rm,

rd-pt des Pistes – 04 79 00 51 15 – welcome@hotel-yeti.com
– Fax 04 79 00 51 73 – Open 5 July-31 August and 15 December-20 April **p**
28 rm – €118 €252, €18 – ½ P €103/205
Rest – Menu (€28), €30/45 (dinner) – Carte €40/51
◆ Cosy furniture, polished wood panelling, kilim rugs, Austrian-style beds, a sauna, and a lounge with an open fire provide the welcoming decor in this mountain hotel. Terrace with view of the slopes for lunch; tables prettily laid in the dining room for dinner.

Marie-Blanche rm, rest,

rte Renarde – 04 79 08 65 55 – info@marie-blanche.com – Fax 04 79 08 57 07
– Open 7 July-26 August and 13 December-20 April **h**
21 rm – €77/218 €90/302, €16 – ½ P €65/204
Rest – Menu €42 (dinner) – Carte €50/65
◆ This attractive chalet houses you in smart Savoy bedrooms, all fitted with a balcony. Welcoming lounge-bar with a central fireplace and view over the mountain. Small cosy dining room lit by bay windows. Family clientele.

L'Éterlou rm, rest,

rte de la Montée – 04 79 08 89 00 – infos@chaudanne.com
– Fax 04 79 08 57 75 – Open end November-end April and June-September **b**
42 rm – €140/294 €140/294, €19 – 1 suite – ½ P €132/209
Rest *La Grange* – *04 79 08 53 19* – Carte €50/70
Rest *Kouisena* – *04 79 08 89 23 (dinner only)* Carte €50/70
◆ A centrally located hotel with a warm atmosphere. Featuring fitness facilities and pool, and a piano bar for a fun, relaxing time. Regional cuisine. The Kouisena serves Savoyard cuisine.

L'Orée du Bois

rd-pt des Pistes – 04 79 00 50 30 – contact@meribel-oree.com
– Fax 04 79 08 57 52 – Open July-August and December-Easter **k**
35 rm – €113/200 €123/200, €17 – ½ P €88/165
Rest – Menu €35 (lunch), €44/48
◆ The rooms in this chic family chalet are wood-panelled and equipped with balconies. Nice blazing flames are crackling in the lounge fireplace, with chess tables nearby. Bright dining room, panoramic terrace and traditional and regional specialities.

Le Tremplin without rest

– 04 79 08 89 17 – infos@chaudanne.com – Fax 04 79 08 57 75
– Open mid June-September and beg. December-April **v**
41 rm – €140/294 €140/294, €19
◆ Hiding behind this wood and stone facade are pleasant, alpine-style bedrooms - opt for those facing the road or skating area. A good "springboard" for a successful stay in the Trois Vallées.

La Chaudanne rest,

rte de la Montée – 04 79 08 61 76 – infos@chaudanne.com
– Fax 04 79 08 57 75 – Open June-September and 1st December-30 April **e**
73 rm – €140/294 €140/294, €19 – 7 suites – ½ P €62
Rest – *(dinner only) (residents only)* Menu €43
◆ Hotel complex at the foot of the cable car line offering both relaxation and fitness facilities: comfortable rooms, access to health spa, heated outdoor pool.

Adray Télébar ≤ mountains and pistes, VISA MC AE
on the pistes (pedestrian access) – ☎ 04 79 08 60 26 – welcome@ telebar-hotel.com – Fax 04 79 08 53 85 – Open 15 December-15 April n
24 rm (½ board only) – ½ P € 130/170 – **Rest** – Menu € 33 – Carte € 35/45
◆ The friendly welcome - they come to meet you - and the site help you forget the somewhat antiquated decor. Well-maintained rooms, some with balneotherapy baths. A family atmosphere in the restaurant, serving home-style cuisine. Terrace with panoramic views.

Le Blanchot ≤ P VISA MC AE
3.5 km by L'Altiport road – ☎ 04 79 00 55 78 – le-blanchot@wanadoo.fr – Fax 04 79 00 53 20 – Open 26 June-9 September, 16 December-19 April and closed Sunday dinner and Monday dinner
Rest – *(closed Sun. evening and Mon. evening)* Carte € 37/80
◆ This nicely-situated chalet, featuring golf in summer and Nordic ski slopes in winter, provides a cosy atmosphere and a terrace facing a forest of pines. Contemporary and Savoyard dishes.

in l'altiport **Northeast: 4,5 km – ✉ 73550 Méribel-les-Allues**

Altiport Hôtel ≤ mountains, rest, VISA MC AE
– ☎ 04 79 00 52 32 – message@altiporhotel.com – Fax 04 79 08 57 54 – Open mid December-mid April
33 rm (½ board only) – 8 suites – ½ P € 175/215 – **Rest** – Menu € 55 (dinner) – Carte € 55/90
◆ Chalet adjacent to the altiport (flights over Mont Blanc) and golf in the summer. Wood-panelled and well-soundproofed rooms. Shopping mall on the ground floor. Attractive mountain restaurant and sunny terrace. Good traditional menu.

in Méribel-Mottaret **6 km – ✉ 73550 Méribel les Allues**

Alpen Ruitor ≤ rest, VISA MC AE
– ☎ 04 79 00 48 48 – info@alpenruitor.com – Fax 04 79 00 48 31 – Open 12 December-6 April t
44 rm – †€ 220/335 ††€ 310/430, ☕ € 15 – 1 suite
Rest – Menu € 35 – Carte € 41/49
◆ Nicely arranged rooms, all with a balcony with a view of the slopes (south) or the valley (north). Friendly, Tyrolean-style bar lounge. Good service. Enjoy dining here in a room attractively decorated with frescos.

Mont Vallon ≤ rest, P VISA MC AE
– ☎ 04 79 00 44 00 – info@hotel-montvallon.com – Fax 04 79 00 46 93 – Open mid December-mid April s
90 rm (½ board only) – 2 suites – ½ P € 225/490
Rest ***Le Chalet*** – *(dinner only)* Menu € 68
Rest ***Brasserie Le Schuss*** – Menu € 30 (lunch)/55
◆ Warm wood and bed covers create a cosy atmosphere in the rooms of this large chalet at the foot of the ski slopes. Sauna, hammam and squash courts. Wooden decor in the Chalet restaurant. Fast food in the brasserie at lunch; Savoyard specialities at night.

Les Arolles ≤ rest, VISA MC
– ☎ 04 79 00 40 40 – info@arolles.com – Fax 04 79 00 45 50 – Open 21 December-30 April u
56 rm – †€ 150/200 ††€ 180/260, ☕ € 16 – ½ P € 125/195
Rest – Menu (€ 23), € 30/45 (dinner) – Carte € 24/32
◆ Direct access to the slopes, also near the pine tree forest. This large chalet provides functional rooms with balcony; well-equipped games and recreation area. Non-smoking rooms. Discreetly decorated restaurant and large terrace; regional food.

in Allues **North: 7 km by D 915A – pop. 1 869 – alt. 1 125 m – ✉ 73550**

La Croix Jean-Claude VISA MC
– ☎ 04 79 08 61 05 – lacroixjeanclaude@wanadoo.fr – Fax 04 79 00 32 72 – Closed 1st May-1st June
16 rm – †€ 74/87 ††€ 74/87, ☕ € 8,50 – ½ P € 67/98 – **Rest** – *(closed 1st May-1st June, 25 September-25 October, Tuesday dinner and Monday off season)* Carte € 34/69
◆ This establishment from the year 1860 is said to be one of the first hotels in the Trois Vallées. Comfy alpine-style rooms, pleasant lounge (with an amazing collection of cockerels) and friendly bar. Restaurant with pleasant Savoyard interior. Locally inspired cooking.

Prenez le temps d'aller vite

MÉRIGNAC – 33 Gironde – 335 H5 – see Bordeaux

MERKWILLER-PECHELBRONN – 67 Bas-Rhin – 315 K3 – pop. 828 – alt. 160 m – ✉ 67250 Alsace-Lorraine

1 **B1**

Paris 496 – Haguenau 17 – Strasbourg 51 – Wissembourg 18

Syndicat d'initiative, 1, route de Lobsann ✆ 03 88 80 72 36, Fax 03 88 80 63 33

XX Auberge Baechel-Brunn with rm

3 rte de Soultz – ✆ 03 88 80 78 61 – baechel-brunn@wanadoo.fr – Fax 03 88 80 75 20 – Closed 11 August-4 September, 19-31 January, Sunday dinner, Monday dinner and Tuesday

5 rm – €40 €50/65 – **Rest** – Menu (€15), €26 (weekday lunch), €38/50 – Carte €40/57

◆ Old barn with a cosy, modern, well-kept interior. Classic and contemporary cuisine, blending the culinary talents of the chef-owner and his son. The oil has dried up since 1970 but lots of ideas remain. This inn, located in Alsatian black-gold country, offers a stylish contemporary interior and well-prepared modern cooking.

X Auberge du Puits VI

– ✆ 03 88 80 76 58 – Fax 03 88 80 75 91 – Closed January, Wednesday lunchtime, Monday and Tuesday

Rest – Menu €34/60 – Carte €39/53

◆ The cafeteria for the nº VI oil well has become a charming restaurant adorned with miners' lamps and the landlord's paintings. Modern cuisine and wine from the family estate.

MERLETTE – 05 Hautes-Alpes – 334 F4 – see Orcières

MERRY-SUR-YONNE – 89 Yonne – 319 E6 – pop. 216 – alt. 150 m – ✉ 89660

Paris 203 – Dijon 139 – Auxerre 44 – Avallon 32 – Migennes 56 7 **B2**

Le Charme Merry

30 rte de Compostelle – ✆ 03 86 81 08 46 – olivia.peron@wanadoo.fr – Fax 03 86 81 08 46 – Closed 1st January-15 March

4 rm – €120 €120 – **Table d'hôte** – Menu €35 bi

◆ This establishment boasts superb contemporary style rooms (photos by the owner, designer bathrooms, quality materials, local stone). Garden, swimming pool. Updated dishes served beneath the dining room's exposed rafters (open-plan kitchen).

MÉRU – 60 Oise – 305 D5 – pop. 12 712 – alt. 110 m – ✉ 60110 Northern France and the Paris Region

36 **B3**

Paris 60 – Beauvais 27 – Compiègne 74 – Mantes-la-Jolie 62 – Pontoise 22

18 des Templiers Ivry-le-Temple, West: 9 km by D 121 and D 105, ✆ 03 44 08 73 72.

X Les Trois Toques

21 r. P. Curie – ✆ 03 44 52 01 15 – Fax 03 44 52 01 15 – Closed Sunday dinner and Wednesday

Rest – Menu €18 (weekdays)/48 – Carte €38/53

◆ Updated menu prepared by the chef-patron and served in a spruced-up dining room enhanced with rustic touches.

MERVILLE FRANCEVILLE-PLAGE – 14 Calvados – 303 K4 – pop. 1 521 – alt. 2 m – ✉ 14810

32 **B2**

Paris 225 – Caen 20 – Beuvron-en-Auge 20 – Cabourg 7 – Lisieux 41

Office de tourisme, place de la Plage ✆ 02 31 24 23 57, Fax 02 31 24 17 49

Le Vauban without rest

8 rte de Cabourg – ✆ 02 31 24 23 37 – res-hot-le-vauban@wanadoo.fr – Fax 02 31 24 54 40 – Closed 28 September-8 October, 1st-17 December, Wednesday except July-August

15 rm – €57 €57, €9

◆ A family establishment near the beach and the Batteries museum, located in a blockhouse. Rooms are discreetly decorated; those at the rear are quieter.

MÉRY-SUR-OISE – 95 Val-d'Oise – **305** E6 – **101** 4 – **see Paris, Area (Cergy-Pontoise)**

MESCHERS-SUR-GIRONDE – **17 Charente-Maritime** – **324** E6 – **pop. 2 234** – **alt. 5 m** – ✉ **17132** Atlantic Coast 38 **B3**

Paris 511 – Blaye 78 – La Rochelle 87 – Royan 12 – Saintes 45

Office de tourisme, 3, place de Verdun ✆ 05 46 02 70 39, Fax 05 46 02 51 65

La Forêt

1 bd Marais – ✆ 05 46 02 79 87 – laforet-resto@wanadoo.fr – Fax 05 46 02 61 45 – Closed 22 September-3 October, 21 December-9 January, 2-13 March, Tuesday except dinner in July-August and Monday

Rest – Menu € 26/35 – Carte € 30/64

◆ On the edge of the woods, not far from the Gironde beaches; vast dining room serving fresh seafood, notably the house speciality, mouclade (mussels). Countrified decor.

MESNIÈRES-EN-BRAY – **76 Seine-Maritime** – **304** I3 – **see Neufchâtel-en-Bray**

LE MESNIL-AMELOT – **77 Seine-et-Marne** – **312** E1 – **see Paris, Area**

MESNIL-ST-PÈRE – **10 Aube** – **313** G4 – **pop. 331** – **alt. 131 m** – ✉ **10140** Northern France and the Paris Region 13 **B3**

Paris 200 – Bar-sur-Aube 32 – Châtillon-sur-Seine 55 – St-Dizier 74 – Troyes 22

Regional Natural Park of the Forêt d'Orient★★.

Auberge du Lac - Au Vieux Pressoir with rm

– ✆ 03 25 41 27 16 – auberge.lac.p.gublin@wanadoo.fr – Fax 03 25 41 57 59 – Closed 16 December-18 January, Sunday dinner from 15 October to 15 March, Monday lunch and Tuesday lunch

21 rm – †€ 66 ††€ 70/120, ☕ € 11 – ½ P € 81/110 – **Rest** – Menu € 28, € 37/77

◆ A half-timbered house typical of the Champagne region. Bright neo-rustic interior and summer terrace. Contemporary cuisine.

LE MESNIL-SUR-OGER – **51 Marne** – **306** G9 – **pop. 1 077** – **alt. 119 m** – ✉ **51190** Northern France and the Paris Region 13 **B2**

Paris 158 – Châlons-en-Champagne 31 – Épernay 16 – Reims 43 – Vertus 6

Musée de la vigne et du vin (Launois House).

Le Mesnil

2 r. Pasteur – ✆ 03 26 57 95 57 – contact@restaurantlemesnil.com – Fax 03 26 57 78 57 – Closed 20 August-10 September, 20 February-5 March, Monday dinner, Tuesday dinner and Wednesday

Rest – Menu € 34/45 – Carte € 41/59

◆ An old house with character in the centre of a wine-growing town. Classic cooking served in the discreetly-decorated dining room; Good, eclectic wine list

MESNIL-VAL – **76 Seine-Maritime** – **304** H1 – ✉ **76910** 33 **D1**

Paris 184 – Amiens 96 – Dieppe 28 – Le Tréport 6

Royal Albion without rest

1 r. de la Mer – ✆ 02 35 86 21 42 – evergreen2@wanadoo.fr – Fax 02 35 86 78 51 – Closed 21-27 December

20 rm – †€ 64/72 ††€ 69/133, ☕ € 9

◆ The architecture and well-designed decor of this establishment perched on a cliff indeed recall Albion (almost a neighbour) and its White Cliffs. Park with trees.

MESQUER – **44 Loire-Atlantique** – **316** B3 – **pop. 1 467** – **alt. 6 m** – ✉ **44420** 34 **A2**

Paris 460 – La Baule 16 – Nantes 86 – St-Nazaire 29 – Vannes 58

Office de tourisme, place du Marché - Quimiac ✆ 02 40 42 64 37, Fax 02 40 42 50 89

La Vieille Forge
– *02 40 42 62 68 – keumsun@orange.fr – Fax 02 51 73 91 52*
– Closed 16-25 June, 21 September-3 October, February, Monday, Tuesday and Wednesday off season
Rest – *(dinner only in July-August except Saturday-Sunday)* Menu € 25/48 – Carte € 43/64
◆ This former forge, from 1711, houses two dining rooms: one has a furnace and bellows while the other is modern and opens onto the garden terrace. Updated cuisine with Asian touches.

in St-Molf **3.5 km southeast by D 33, D 52 and D 252 – pop. 1 501 – alt. 10 m – ✉ 44350**

Office de tourisme, 10, rue Duchesse Anne 02 40 62 58 99, Fax 02 40 62 58 74

Kervenel without rest
– *02 40 42 50 38 – ybrasselet@aol.com – Fax 02 40 42 50 38*
– Open from March to September
3 rm – **€ 50 €60**
◆ Distinctive restored Breton cottage in a quiet setting. The old wheat barn houses three rooms opening onto the garden in varying styles: Louis Philippe, Louis XV and Contemporary.

MESSANGES – 40 Landes – 335 C12 – pop. 647 – alt. 8 m – ✉ 40660 3 A2

Paris 717 – Bordeaux 157 – Mont-de-Marsan 92 – Bayonne 46 – Anglet 49

Office de tourisme, route des Lacs 05 58 48 93 10

La Maison de la Prade without rest
rte de la Plage – 05 58 48 38 96
– lamaisondelaprade@orange.fr – Fax 05 58 49 26 75 – Open from March to November
16 rm – **€ 87/112 € 118/210,** € 10 – 2 suites
◆ Close to a secluded beach, surrounded by pines, Art Deco construction converted into a contemporary hotel. Bright, spacious guestrooms. Terrace next to the pool.

MESSERY – 74 Haute-Savoie – 328 K2 – pop. 1 434 – alt. 428 m – ✉ 74140 46 F1

Paris 560 – Annecy 68 – Thonon-les-Bains 17 – Annemasse 23 – Cluses 52

Office de tourisme, 5, rue des Écoles 04 50 94 75 55, Fax 04 50 94 75 55

Atelier des Saveurs
7 chemin sous les Près – 04 50 94 73 40 – daillouxfamille@aol.com
– Closed 3-13 March, 4-15 July, 1st-13 November, Sunday and Monday
Rest – Menu € 24/60 – Carte € 44/54
◆ A pleasant establishment combining a restaurant (modern decoration and small terrace) with a wine bar. Tasty traditional cuisine accompanied by fine wine.

MÉTABIEF – 25 Doubs – 321 I6 – pop. 691 – alt. 960 m – Winter sports : 1000/1423 m 20 – ✉ 25370 Burgundy-Jura 17 C3

Paris 466 – Besançon 78 – Champagnole 45 – Morez 49 – Pontarlier 18

Étoile des Neiges
4 r. Village – 03 81 49 11 21 – contact@hoteletoiledesneiges.fr
– Fax 03 81 49 26 91
23 rm – **€ 54 € 54,** € 6 – ½ P € 48/50 – **Rest** – *(closed Thursday dinner and Sunday dinner off season)* Menu € 16/25 – Carte € 18/36
◆ A totally-renovated family hotel in a busy resort, popular both in summer and winter with mountain bikers, walkers and skiers. Pretty, wood-panelled rooms with flowered balconies. Regional food to be enjoyed in a welcoming dining room decorated with wood.

METZ 🅿 – 57 Moselle – **307** I4 – **pop. 123 776** – **Built-up area 322 526** – **alt. 173 m** – ✉ **57000** Alsace-Lorraine 26 **B1**

Paris 330 – Luxembourg 62 – Nancy 57 – Saarbrücken 69 – Strasbourg 163

Metz-Nancy-Lorraine: ✆ 03 87 56 70 00, by ③: 23 km.

✆ 3635 (0,34 €/mn)

Office de tourisme, place d'Armes ✆ 03 87 55 53 76, Fax 03 87 36 59 43

de la Grange-aux-Ormes Marly Rue de la Grange aux Ormes, South: 3 km by D 5, ✆ 03 87 63 10 62 ;

du Technopôle Metz 1 rue Félix Savart, by D 955: 5 km, ✆ 03 87 39 95 95 ;

de Metz Chérisey Verny Château de Cherisey, by D 913 and D 67: 14 km, ✆ 03 87 52 70 18.

St-Etienne cathedral ★★★ CDV - Porte des Allemands★ DV - Esplanade★ CV: St-Pierre-aux-Nonnains church ★ CX **V** - Place St-Louis★ DVX - St-Maximin church ★ DVX - Narthex★ of St-Martin church DX - ≤★ du Moyen Pont CV - Musée de la Cour d'Or★★ (archeological section ★★★) **M**[1] - Place du Général de Gaulle★.

Plans on following pages

La Citadelle (Christophe Dufossé)

5 av. Ney – ✆ *03 87 17 17 17*
– contact@citadelle-metz.com – Fax 03 87 17 17 18 CX **y**

79 rm – €185/245 €205/375, ☕ €20

Rest ***Le Magasin aux Vivres*** – *(closed 1st-18 August, 9-22 February, Sunday dinner and Monday)* Menu €40 (weekday lunch), €60/110 – Carte €85/93

Spec. Les cassolettes gourmandes. Bar en croûte de sel, algues iodées. Déclinaison autour de la mirabelle de Lorraine (August-September). **Wines** Vins de Moselle.

◆ This former military establishment located in the centre of town dates back to the 16C; now a hotel with spacious contemporary-style rooms. The restaurant serves inventive, high-quality cuisine in a modern atmosphere that contrasts with the old-style building.

Mercure Centre rest,

29 pl. St-Thiébault – ✆ *03 87 38 50 50* – *h1233@accor.com*
– Fax 03 87 75 48 18 DX **d**

112 rm – €134 €139, ☕ €14 – 5 suites

Rest – Menu €22/34 – Carte €28/39

◆ A modern building not far from the historic centre and pedestrianised streets. Rooms are regularly renovated and have good soundproofing. A dining room decorated according to the "seasons" of the painter Giuseppe Arcimboldo.

Novotel Centre rm,

pl. Paraiges – ✆ *03 87 37 38 39* – *h0589@accor.com* – *Fax 03 87 36 10 00*

120 rm – €69/165 €69/165, ☕ €13,50

Rest – Carte €21/43 DV **t**

◆ This 1970s style building is located next to a shopping centre. Functional and rather spacious rooms. Restaurant with a small terrace on the poolside serving traditional meals.

De la Cathédrale without rest

25 pl. Chambre – ✆ *03 87 75 00 02* – *hotelcathedrale-metz@wanadoo.fr*
– Fax 03 87 75 40 75 CV **v**

30 rm – €68/95 €68/105, ☕ €11

◆ At the foot of the St. Etienne cathedral, this 17C hotel once provided accommodation for Mme de Staël and Chateaubriand. Elegant rooms with individual furnishings and fine fabrics.

Du Théâtre

3 r. du Pont St-Marcel – ✆ *03 87 31 10 10* – *reception@hoteldutheatre-metz.com*
– Fax 03 87 30 04 66 CV **b**

65 rm – €85/150 €95/180, ☕ €12 – ½ P €79/130

Rest – Menu €15/29 – Carte €25/43

◆ An ideally located hotel in the historic town centre, providing freshly renovated rooms, more peaceful on the Moselle side. Fine regional furnishings in the reception area. This restaurant displays regional wall paintings and serves traditional cuisine. Waiters in traditional dress.

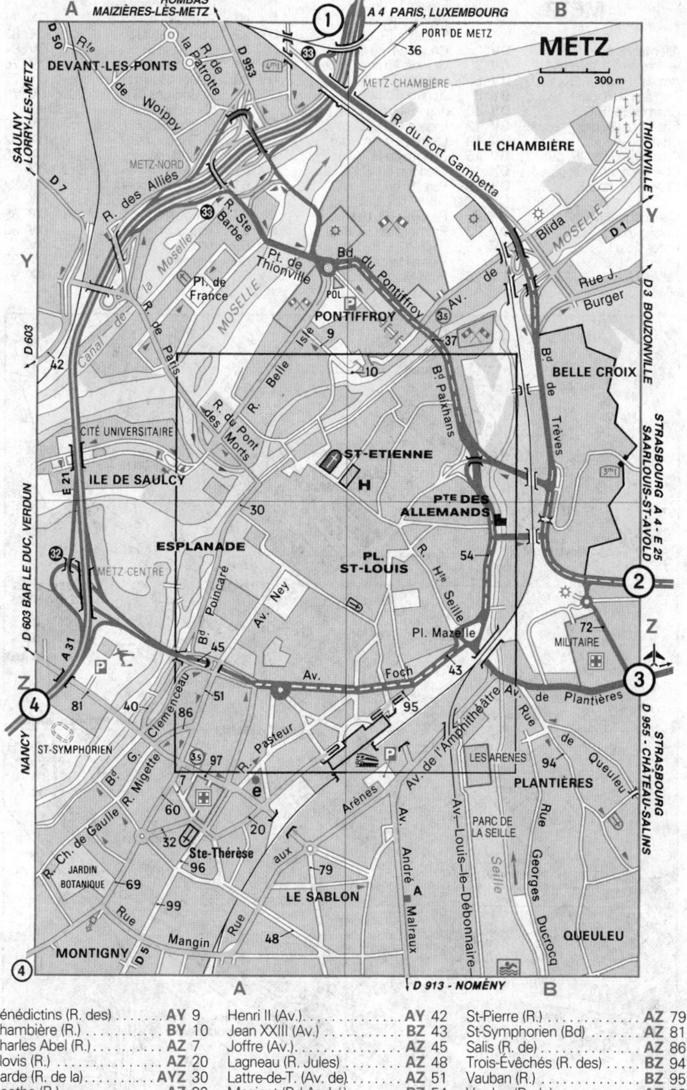

Bénédictins (R. des)	AY	9	Henri II (Av.)	AY	42	St-Pierre (R.)	AZ	79
Chambière (R.)	BY	10	Jean XXIII (Av.)	BZ	43	St-Symphorien (Bd)	AZ	81
Charles Abel (R.)	AZ	7	Joffre (Av.)	AZ	45	Salis (R. de)	AZ	86
Clovis (R.)	AZ	20	Lagneau (R. Jules)	AZ	48	Trois-Évêchés (R. des)	BZ	94
Garde (R. de la)	AYZ	30	Lattre-de-T. (Av. de)	AZ	51	Vauban (R.)	BZ	95
Goethe (R.)	AZ	32	Maginot (Bd André)	BZ	54	Verdun (R. de)	AZ	96
Grange-aux-Dames (R.)	BY	36	Nancy (Av. de)	AZ	60	Verlaine (R.)	AZ	97
Grilles (Pont des)	BY	37	Pont-à-Mousson (R. de)	AZ	69	20e-Corps-Américain (R. du)	AZ	99
Hegly (Allée V.)	AZ	40	Pont-Rouge (R. du)	BZ	72			

Métropole without rest

5 pl. Gén. de Gaulle – ✆ 03 87 66 26 22 – contact@hotelmetropole.com – Fax 03 87 66 29 91 DX **q**

72 rm – €45/59 €54/63, €8

◆ This hotel is housed in a nice freestone building opposite the station, providing rooms with warm tones, modern furnishings and a welcoming atmosphere.

METZ

Allemands (R. des) . . . . DV 2
Ambroise-Thomas (R.) . . . . . CV 3
Armes (Pl. d') . . . . DV 5
Augustins (R. des) . . . . DX 6
Chambière (R.) . . . . DV 10
Chambre (Pl. de) . . . . CV 12
Champé (R. du) . . . . DV 13
Chanoine-Collin (R. du) . . . . DV 15
Charlemagne (R.) . . . . CX 17
Chèvre (R. de la) . . . . DX 19
Clercs (R. des) CV
Coëtlosquet (R. du) . . . . CX 22
Coislin (R.) . . . . DX 23
Enfer (R. d') . . . . DV 25
En Fournirue . . . . DV
Fabert (R.) . . . . CV 26
Faisan (R. du) . . . . CV 27
La-Fayette (R.) . . . . CX 47
Fontaine (R. de la) . . . . DX 29
Gaulle (Pl. du Gén.-de) . . . . . DX 31
Grande-Armée (R. de la) . . . . DV 34
Hache (R. de la) . . . . DV 39
Jardins (R. des) . . . . DV
Juge-Pierre-Michel (R. du) . . CV 46
Lasalle (R.) . . . . DX 49
Lattre-de-T. (Av. de) . . . . CX 51
Leclerc-de-H. (Av.) . . . . CX 52
Mondon (Pl. R.) . . . . CX 57
Paix (R. de la) . . . . CV 61
Palais (R. du) . . . . CV 62
Paraiges (Pl. des) . . . . DV 63
Parmentiers (R. des) . . . . . . DX 64
Petit-Paris (R. du) . . . . CV 65
Pierre-Hardie (R. de la) . . . . . CV 66
Pont-Moreau (R. du) . . . . . CDV 70
Prés.-Kennedy (Av. J.-F.) . . . . CX 73
République (Pl. de la) . . . . . . CX 75
Ste-Croix (Pl.) . . . . DV 83
Ste-Marie (R.) . . . . CV 84
St-Eucaire (R.) . . . . DV 76
St-Gengoulf (R.) . . . . CX 77
St-Georges (R.) . . . . CV 78
St-Louis (Pl.) . . . . DVX
St-Simplice (Pl.) . . . . DV 80
St-Thiébault (Pl.) . . . . DX 82
Salis (R. de) . . . . CX 86
Schuman (Av. R.) CX
Sérot (Bd Robert) . . . . CV 87
Serpenoise (R.) CV
Taison (R.) . . . . DV 88
Tanneurs (R. des) . . . . DV 90
Tête d'Or (R. de la) . . . . DV
Trinitaires (R. des) . . . . DV 93
Verlaine (R.) . . . . CX 97

Escurial without rest

18 r. Pasteur – ✆ 03 87 66 40 96 – hotelescurial.metz@wanadoo.fr
– Fax 03 87 63 43 61 – Closed 29 December-1st January CX **d**

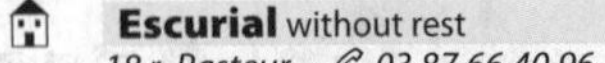

36 rm – €50/72 €68/80, ☕ €11

◆ This hotel in the imperial district has recently had a facelift. Providing modern and practical rooms, a breakfast area and large lounge with a warm and colourful atmosphere.

Cécil' without rest

14 r. Pasteur – ✆ 03 87 66 66 13 – info@cecilhotel-metz.com – Fax 03 87 56 96 02 – Closed 27 December-7 January CX **x**

39 rm – †€ 56 ††€ 62, ☕ € 7,50

◆ An English-built hotel dating from 1920. Rooms are impeccably well kept, discreetly colourful with subdued furniture. Billiard table.

Au Pampre d'Or (Jean-Claude Lamaze)

31 pl. Chambre – ✆ 03 87 74 12 46 – Fax 03 87 36 96 92 – Closed 5-11 January, Sunday dinner, Monday lunch and Tuesday lunch CV **a**

Rest – Menu (€ 28), € 38 bi/65 – Carte € 55/90

Spec. Cassolette de cuisses de grenouilles. Truffes melanosporum (November to March). Escalope de foie gras d'oie poêlé aux pommes caramélisées. **Wines** Gris de Toul, Rouge de Toul.

◆ This former 17C private mansion is named after the vineyard that once grew here. Original interiors with yellow tones, and tasty classic cuisine served.

Maire

1 r. Pont des Morts – ✆ 03 87 32 43 12 – restaurant.maire@wanadoo.fr – Fax 03 87 31 16 75 – Closed Wednesday lunchtime and Tuesday CV **f**

Rest – Menu € 40/61 – Carte € 45/64

◆ This restaurant features a dining area that overlooks the Moselle, with a waterside terrace also affording panoramic views of the town. Standard cuisine served.

L'Écluse (Eric Maire)

45 pl. Chambre – ✆ 03 87 75 42 38 – Fax 03 87 37 30 11 – Closed 1st - 15 August, Saturday lunch, Sunday dinner and Monday CV **r**

Rest – Menu (€ 24), € 35/65 – Carte € 60/79

Spec. Carpaccio de Saint-Jacques aux truffes (15 November to 15 February). Agape de poissons crus marinés à l'huile d'argan. Ravioles de foie gras de canard au bouillon truffé (15 November to 15 February).

◆ This restaurant has been recently redone in a modern minimalist style enhanced by contemporary artwork and bare tables. Well-prepared contemporary cuisine.

Georges-A La Ville de Lyon

7 r. Piques – ✆ 03 87 36 07 01 – george-ville-de-lyon@wanadoo.fr – Fax 03 87 74 47 17 – Closed 1st-10 January, Monday except lunch on public holidays and Sunday dinner DV **e**

Rest – Menu (€ 19), € 25 (weekdays)/65 – Carte € 50/57

◆ Restaurant rooms split between outbuildings of the cathedral – one room is set up in a 14C chapel – and the old walls of a coaching house.

Le Chat Noir

30 r. Pasteur – ✆ 03 87 56 99 19 – rest-le-chat@wanadoo.fr – Fax 03 87 66 67 64 – Closed 24 December-5 January, Sunday and Monday AZ **e**

Rest – Menu (€ 20 bi), € 26/45 – Carte € 34/59

◆ Leopard-skin chairs and African masks with warm tones make up the décor in this restaurant serving traditional cuisine. Oyster stall in season.

Thierry "Saveurs et Cuisine"

5 r. Piques, "Maison de la Fleure de Ly" – ✆ 03 87 74 01 23 – lechef@restaurant-thierry.fr – Fax 03 87 77 81 03 – Closed 21 July-10 August, 27 October-2 November, 9-22 February, Wednesday and Sunday DV **a**

Rest – Menu (€ 17), € 23 (weekdays)/34 – Carte € 30/48

◆ Inventive cuisine enhanced by herbs and spices, an attractive brick and wood setting and a summer terrace all contribute to this stylish bistro's popularity.

Le Bistrot des Sommeliers

10 r. Pasteur – ✆ 03 87 63 40 20 – lebistrotdessommeliers@wanadoo.fr – Fax 03 87 63 54 46 – Closed 23 December-4 January, Saturday lunch, Sunday and public holidays CX **a**

Rest – Menu (€ 15) – Carte € 24/42

◆ Colourful facade and decor on a wine theme in this bistro near the station. A good selection of wines by the glass and dishes based on market produce on a blackboard.

via ① and A 31 Maizières-lès-Metz exit: 10 km – ✉ 57280 Maizières-lès-Metz

Novotel-Hauconcourt
– *✆ 03 87 80 18 18 – h0446@accor.com – Fax 03 87 80 36 00*
132 rm – €89/150 €89/150, ☕ €13 – **Rest** – Carte €24/43
◆ Thirty years after it was built, this Novotel has been fully refurbished and is a convenient place to stay near the motorways. Spacious dining room leading onto a terrace by the swimming pool. Non-stop bar meals.

Saarlouis road 13 km by ②, N 233 and D 954 - ✉ 57640 Ste-Barbe

Mazagran
lieu-dit Mazagran – ✆ 03 87 76 62 47 – mele-cass@orange.fr – Fax 03 87 76 79 50 – Closed 25 August-9 September, 3-11 January, Sunday dinner, Monday and Tuesday
Rest – Menu (€21), €26 (weekdays)/51 – Carte €44/68
◆ This farmhouse was built for one of the soldiers who defended the Mazagran fort in Algeria in 1840. Dining rooms adorned with paintings. Garden terrace. Contemporary menu.

in Borny by ③ and Strasbourg road: 3 km – ✉ 57070 Metz

Le Jardin de Bellevue
58 r. Claude Bernard, (near Metz 2000 Technology park) – ✆ 03 87 37 10 27 – lejardindebellevue@wanadoo.fr – Fax 03 87 37 15 45 – Closed 15 July-13 August, 16-28 February, Saturday lunch, Sunday dinner, Tuesday dinner and Monday
Rest – Menu €22 (weekday lunch), €37/61 – Carte €52/67
◆ Chic facade for this century-old house in a residential area. Attractively set tables in a pleasant, yellow dining room. Cuisine in keeping with current taste.

in Technopole 2000 by ③ and Strasbourg road: 5 km – ✉ 57070 Metz

Holiday Inn
1 r. F. Savart – ✆ 03 87 39 94 50 – reception@holidayinn-metz.com – Fax 03 87 39 94 55
90 rm – €80/107 €80/128, ☕ €12 – ½ P €97
Rest ***Les Alizés*** – Menu (€14,50), €20 (weekday lunch) – Carte €19/38
◆ This ultramodern hotel is far from the noise of the town, on the edge of an 18-hole golf course. Practical rooms with contemporary furniture. An elegant setting and traditional cuisine at the Alizés.

in Ancy-sur-Moselle Southeast: 13 km by ④ A 31, D 657, D 11 and D 6 – pop. 1 475 – alt. 172 m – ✉ 57130

Haumalet without rest
2 r. des Quarrés – ✆ 03 87 30 91 54 – haumalet@wanadoo.fr – Fax 03 87 30 91 54 – Closed 1st-20 March
3 rm ☕ – €45 €65
◆ In a wine-growing village, this refurbished old house (once owned by the Bishop-Prince of Metz) features rooms with a personal touch and antique furniture; small garden and terrace.

in Plappeville via Avenue Henri II - AY : 7 km – pop. 2 341 – alt. 280 m – ✉ 57050

Jardin d'Adam
50 r. Gén. de Gaulle – ✆ 03 87 30 36 68 – le-jardin-d-adam@numericable.fr – Fax 03 87 30 79 01 – Closed 15-31 August, Christmas holidays, Tuesday dinner and Wednesday
Rest – Menu €25/60 – Carte €45/65
◆ In the heart of the village, this old wine-grower's house is now a modern restaurant with a summer terrace, serving modern cuisine and a fine selection of wines.

METZERAL – 68 Haut-Rhin – 315 G8 – pop. 1 065 – alt. 480 m – ✉ 68380

Paris 464 – Colmar 25 – Gérardmer 39 – Guebwiller 41 – Thann 43 1 **A2**

Aux Deux Clefs
12 r. Altenhof – ✆ 03 89 77 61 48 – auxdeuxclefs@free.fr – Fax 03 89 77 63 88 – Closed 1st-15 March and 1st-7 November
14 rm – €38/40 €46/65, ☕ €9 – ½ P €46/55 – **Rest** – *(closed Wednesday)* Menu €12 (weekdays)/46 – Carte €19/60
◆ In the upper reaches of the village, this guesthouse-style hotel is pleasantly peaceful. The rooms have an alpine décor. Elegant dining room (classical cuisine).

MEUCON – 56 Morbihan – **308** O8 – **pop. 1 268 – alt. 80 m** – ✉ **56890** 9 **A3**

Paris 464 – Vannes 8 – Lorient 62 – Ploërmel 49 – Pontivy 45

XX **Le Tournesol** VISA

20 rte de Vannes – ✆ 02 97 44 50 50 – le.tournesol@wanadoo.fr – Fax 02 97 44 65 42 – Closed 30 June-8 July, 15-30 September, 5-13 January, Sunday, Wednesday dinner and Monday

Rest – Menu € 16 (weeday lunch), € 21/55 – Carte € 32/48

◆ The two dining rooms in this building are decorated in pretty, sunflower yellow; one of them offers a view of the wine cellar. Appetising, traditional food.

MEUDON – 92 Hauts-de-Seine – **311** J3 – **101** 24 – **see Paris, Area**

MEURSAULT – 21 Côte-d'Or – **320** I8 – **see Beaune**

LE MEUX – 60 Oise – **305** H4 – **see Compiègne**

MEXIMIEUX – 01 Ain – **328** E5 – **pop. 6 840 – alt. 245 m** – ✉ **01800** 44 **B1**

Paris 458 – Bourg-en-Bresse 37 – Chambéry 120 – Genève 118 – Grenoble 125 – Lyon 38

Office de tourisme, 1, rue de Genève ✆ 04 74 61 11 11, Fax 04 74 61 00 50

XXX **La Cour des Lys** VISA

17 r. de Lyon – ✆ 01 74 61 06 78 – la.cour.des.lys@orange.fr – Fax 01 74 34 75 23 – Closed 31 March-7 April, 15-23 July, Wednesday lunch and Monday

Rest – Menu € 20 (weekdays)/58 – Carte € 44/68

◆ A new chef has taken over at this local institution. Enticing menu based on Dombes culinary traditions, with a touch of modern flair. Decor typical of the region.

at Pont de Chazey-Villieu 3 km east by D 1084 – ✉ **01800 Villieu-Loyes-Mollon**

XX **La Mère Jacquet** with rm rm, rm, VISA

Pont de Chazey – ✆ 04 74 61 94 80 – contact@lamerejacquet.com – Fax 04 74 61 92 07 – Closed 21-27 April, 28 July-10 August, autumn half-term holidays, 22 December-4 January

19 rm – € 54/64 € 63/73, € 8 – **Rest** – *(closed Saturday lunch, Sunday dinner and Monday)* Menu € 24/55 – Carte € 44/67

◆ Inviting dining room and veranda overlooking a pretty garden. Classic cuisine with a regional focus: Mother Jacquet's traditions live on in this establishment.

MÉXY – 54 Meurthe-et-Moselle – **307** F2 – **see Longwy**

MEYLAN – 38 Isère – **333** H6 – **see Grenoble**

MEYMAC – 19 Corrèze – **329** N2 – **pop. 2 627 – alt. 702 m** – ✉ **19250**
Dordogne-Berry-Limousin 25 **C2**

Paris 443 – Aubusson 57 – Limoges 96 – Neuvic 30 – Tulle 49 – Ussel 17

Office de tourisme, 1, place de l'Hôtel de Ville ✆ 05 55 95 18 43, Fax 05 55 95 66 12

Black Virgin★ in the abbey church.

X **Chez Françoise** with rm VISA

24 r. Fontaine du Rat – ✆ 05 55 95 10 63 – Fax 05 55 95 40 22 – Closed January, Sunday dinner and Monday

4 rm – € 60 € 60, € 8 – **Rest** – Menu € 15/50 – Carte € 22/48

◆ Authentic home cooking and a good choice de wines await you in this 16C rustic house flanked by a tower. Regional produce shop next door.

in Maussac **9 km south by D 36 and D 1089 – pop. 385 – alt. 615 m – ✉ 19250**

Europa rm, rest, rm, VISA

on D 1089 – 05 55 94 25 21 – hoteleuropa1@orange.fr – Fax 05 55 94 26 08 – Closed 23 December-2 January

22 rm – €42 €44, ☕ €8 – ½ P €55 – **Rest** – *(closed Sunday off season)* Menu €12 (weekdays)/24 – Carte €12/24

◆ This hotel, easily accessible from the main road, provides functional rooms with king size beds. Rooms at the rear are quieter. Traditional, unpretentious cuisine. Mostly business clientele.

MEYRONNE – 46 Lot – 337 F2 – pop. 269 – alt. 130 m – ✉ 46200 29 C1

Paris 524 – Brive-la-Gaillarde 47 – Cahors 76 – Figeac 54 – Sarlat-la-Canéda 40

La Terrasse rm, VISA

– 05 65 32 21 60 – terrasse.liebus@wanadoo.fr – Fax 05 65 32 26 93 – Open 9 March-11 November

15 rm – €70/80 €70/125, ☕ €12 – 5 suites – ½ P €80/122

Rest – *(closed Tuesday lunch)* Menu €20 (weekday lunch), €28/50 – Carte €50/74

◆ This 11C château and adjoining old stone houses overlook the Dordogne. Rooms adorned with antique furniture. Attractive vaulted winter dining room, a more contemporary area or an idyllic shady terrace with an arbour.

MEYRUEIS – 48 Lozère – 330 I9 – pop. 851 – alt. 698 m – ✉ 48150

Languedoc-Roussillon-Tarn Gorges 23 C1

Paris 643 – Florac 36 – Mende 57 – Millau 43 – Rodez 99 – Le Vigan 56

Office de tourisme, Tour de l'Horloge 04 66 45 60 33, Fax 04 66 45 65 27

Northwest: Gorges de la Jonte★★.

Aven Armand★★★ Northwest: 11 km - Grotte de Dargilan★★ Northwest: 8,5 km.

Château d'Ayres rest, VISA

1.5 km east by D 57 – 04 66 45 60 10 – chateau-d-ayres@wanadoo.fr – Fax 04 66 45 62 26 – Closed 3 January-15 February

22 rm – €96/124 €96/160, ☕ €14 – 7 suites – ½ P €83/132

Rest – Menu €23 (lunch), €31/47 – Carte €40/52

◆ In a 6-ha park, solid 12C walls imbued with Cévennes history. "Châtelaine" bedrooms afford complete peace. Vaulted dining room with a fireplace; terrace shaded by sequoias and regional dishes.

Du Mont Aigoual VISA

34 quai Barrière – 04 66 45 65 61 – hotelmontaigoual@free.fr – Fax 04 66 45 64 25 – Open 23 March-2 November

30 rm – €55/75 €55/75, ☕ €8 – ½ P €55/62

Rest – *(closed Tuesday lunchtime except July-August)* Menu €20/40

◆ At the foot of the picturesque Aigoual range, this village is an ideal base to discover the Grands Causses and the Cévennes. Well kept rooms; lovely pool in the garden. Tasty traditional cuisine served in a charming Provençal-style room.

De l'Europe without rest VISA

2 quai Barrière – 04 66 45 60 05 – frederic-robert-48@wanadoo.fr – Fax 04 66 45 65 31 – Open 21 March-5 November

29 rm – €32/36 €37/41, ☕ €7

◆ An old family guesthouse with simple but faultlessly kept bedrooms. Access to the pool of the hotel (Mont Aigoual) next door.

Family Hôtel rest, VISA

4 r. Barrière – 04 66 45 60 02 – hotel.family@wanadoo.fr – Fax 04 66 45 66 54 – Open 1st April-5 November

48 rm – €38/39 €38/49, ☕ €7,50 – ½ P €48/49 – **Rest** – Menu €12,50 bi (weekday lunch), €18/32 – Carte €15/36

◆ This family-run hotel stands on the banks of the Bétuzon, a tributary of the Jonte. Practical, well kept rooms. Pool and garden on the opposite bank. Stone walls, wainscoting and pastel colours add to the charm of the spruce dining room. Copious Lozère cooking.

Grand Hôtel de France rest, VISA AE

pl. J. Séquier – ☎ 04 66 45 60 07 – grandhoteldefrance@wanadoo.fr – Fax 04 66 45 67 62 – Open 12 April-30 September

45 rm – †€ 40/45 ††€ 45/49, ☕ € 6,50 – ½ P € 46/48

Rest – *(open 30 April-30 September)* Menu € 16/30 – Carte € 23/38

◆ Built out of regional stone, this hotel offers small, colourful bedrooms. At the rear of hotel are a hillside garden and swimming pool. Pleasantly countrified restaurant with a fireplace and rustic furniture. Basic setting, traditional menus.

MEYZIEU – 69 Rhône – 327 J5 – see Lyon

MÈZE – 34 Hérault – 339 G8 – pop. 7 630 – alt. 20 m – ✉ 34140

Languedoc-Roussillon-Tarn Gorges 23 **C2**

Paris 746 – Agde 21 – Béziers 43 – Lodève 52 – Montpellier 36 – Pézenas 19 – Sète 20

Office de tourisme, 8, rue Massaloup ☎ 04 67 43 93 08, Fax 04 67 43 55 61

Gallo-Roman villa ★ of Loupian North: 1,5 km.

in Bouzigues 4 km northeast by D 613 and secondary road – pop. 1 208 – alt. 3 m – ✉ 34140

La Côte Bleue rm, rm, VISA AE

– ☎ 04 67 78 31 42 – lacotebleue0572@orange.fr – Fax 04 67 78 35 49

31 rm – †€ 65/90 ††€ 65/90, ☕ € 9 – **Rest** – ☎ 04 67 78 30 87 *(closed February school holidays and Wednesday off season)* Menu € 29/43 – Carte € 39/70

◆ The Thau pool, Mecca for shellfish growers, is near this modern building with functional bedrooms and balconies. Seafood cooking with pride of place given to the famous Bouzigues oysters; try them in summer on the shady terrace.

À La Voile Blanche rm, rm, VISA AE

1 av. Louis Tudesq – ☎ 04 67 78 35 77 – alavoileblanche@wanadoo.fr – Fax 04 67 74 44 06 – Closed 17-30 November, 12-31 January, Monday and Tuesday from October to February

8 rm – †€ 65/190 ††€ 65/190, ☕ € 8 – ½ P € 95/220

Rest – Menu € 20 (weekday lunch) – Carte € 32/60

◆ A well-designed hotel by the lake, with its oyster beds and small port. Refined, ultra-modern decor. Some bedrooms with terrace.

MÉZIÈRES-EN-BRENNE – 36 Indre – 323 D6 – pop. 1 160 – alt. 88 m – ✉ 36290

Dordogne-Berry-Limousin 11 **B3**

Paris 303 – Le Blanc 28 – Châteauroux 40 – Châtellerault 59 – Poitiers 96 – Tours 87

Office de tourisme, 1, rue du Nord ☎ 02 54 38 12 24, Fax 02 54 38 13 76

Boeuf Couronné with rm rm, VISA

9 pl. du général de Gaulle – ☎ 02 54 38 04 39 – au.boeuf.couronne@hotmail.fr – Fax 02 54 38 02 84 – Closed 23-30 June, 10 December-31 January, Sunday dinner and Monday

8 rm – †€ 42 ††€ 54, ☕ € 6,50 – ½ P € 40 – **Rest** – Menu € 11 (weekday lunch), € 21/43 – Carte € 44/54

◆ A former post house dating back to 1640 in the heart of the regional park of Brenne. Serving fine, traditional meals in a country-style atmosphere.

MÉZOS – 40 Landes – 335 E10 – pop. 817 – alt. 23 m – ✉ 40170 3 **B2**

Paris 684 – Bordeaux 124 – Mont-de-Marsan 107 – Dax 58 – Biscarrosse 44

Office de tourisme, avenue du Born ☎ 05 58 42 64 37, Fax 05 58 42 64 60

La Maison de Mézos without rest VISA

av. de l' Océan – ☎ 05 58 42 61 38 – maisondemezos@orange.fr – Fax 05 58 42 61 38

10 rm – †€ 60/78 ††€ 60/78, ☕ € 8

◆ In a small Landes village, charming establishment with a family feel (rustic interior, antique furniture). More recent villa and piscine in the vast garden.

MEZY MOULINS – 02 Aisne – 306 D8 – pop. 461 – alt. 81 m – ✉ 02650

Paris 103 – Amiens 221 – Laon 92 – Reims 55 – Meaux 56 37 **C3**

Le Moulin Babet with rm
8 r. du Moulin Babet – ☎ 03 23 71 44 72 – lemoulinbabet@orange.fr – Fax 03 23 71 48 11 – Closed 24 December-11 January, Sunday dinner Tuesday and Wednesday
7 rm – €70 €70, €9 – **Rest** – Menu €31/65 – Carte €48/58
◆ In open countryside, this mill's old wheel is still visible from the lobby. Nice contemporary rooms, and restaurant combining rustic and modern.

MIEUSSY – 74 Haute-Savoie – 328 M4 – pop. 1 739 – alt. 636 m – ✉ 74440

French Alps 46 **F1**

Paris 563 – Annecy 62 – Bonneville 21 – Chamonix-Mont-Blanc 59 – Thonon-les-Bains 49

Office de tourisme, Le Pont du Diable ☎ 04 50 43 02 72, Fax 04 50 43 01 87

Accueil Savoyard
– ☎ 04 50 43 01 90 – accueil-savoyard@wanadoo.fr – Fax 04 50 43 09 59 – Closed 5-18 May
8 rm – €45 €52, €7 – ½ P €50 – **Rest** – *(closed Sunday)* Menu €12 (weekday lunch), €19/25 – Carte €29/39
◆ Family guesthouse type hotel in the verdant Giffre valley. Well-kept rooms, some with balcony; ask for one with a view of the mountains. A rustic dining room serving a traditional menu and Savoy specialities.

Maison des Sœurs
pl. de l'Église – ☎ 04 50 43 15 74 – mlm@mieussy.net – Fax 04 50 43 15 74
3 rm – €53/62 €64/95 – **Table d'hôte** – *(closed Monday)* Menu €22 bi
◆ This sturdily built house (1841), easily recognisable by its turquoise shutters, has long been used by nuns and colonies de vacances. Large, attractive bedrooms with personal touches. Open fireplace in the lounge. Kitchen-cum-dining room with an open fireplace where casseroles and grilled poultry are sometimes cooked.

MILLAU – 12 Aveyron – 338 K6 – pop. 21 339 – alt. 372 m – ✉ 12100

Languedoc-Roussillon-Tarn Gorges 29 **D2**

Paris 636 – Albi 106 – Mende 95 – Montpellier 114 – Rodez 67

Office de tourisme, 1, place du Beffroi ☎ 05 65 60 02 42, Fax 05 65 60 95 08

Musée de Millau★ : pottery ★, maison de la Peau et du Gant ★ (1st floor) **M** - Viaduct ★★★.

Canyon de la Dourbie★★ 8 km by ②.

Plan on next page

Mercure
1 pl. de la Tine – ☎ 05 65 59 29 00 – h5614@accor.com – Fax 05 65 59 29 01
57 rm – €89/120 €101/135, €15 – **Rest** – *(closed Saturday and Sunday from 1st January to 15 March)* Menu €16/25 – Carte €24/38 YB **m**
◆ This renovated hotel is located in the village centre, with a modern atmosphere, providing several rooms with a view of the viaduct. This regional-style restaurant serves local cuisine.

Cévenol Hôtel
115 r. Rajol – ☎ 05 65 60 74 44 – contact@cevenol-hotel.fr – Fax 05 65 60 85 99
42 rm – €48/58 €48/58, €7,50 – ½ P €50/57 – **Rest** – Menu €16/35 – Carte €25/44 BY **k**
◆ This 1980s building, separated from the Tarn by a trunk road, houses functional, spacious rooms. The neo-rustic dining room opens on to a summer terrace with small grill. Regional cuisine.

Millau Hôtel Club
via ④ and rte Montpellier – ☎ 05 65 59 71 33 – millauhotelclub@wanadoo.fr – Fax 05 65 59 71 67 – Open 1st March-30 November
37 rm – €66 €66, €9,50 – ½ P €58/78
Rest – grill Menu €21 – Carte €26/32
◆ Contemporary building with up-to-date, practical bedrooms; ask for one overlooking Millau, the Tarn and the viaduct. Pétanque and small fitness room. Grilled food, salads and a good regional wine list on offer in the plain rotunda dining room.

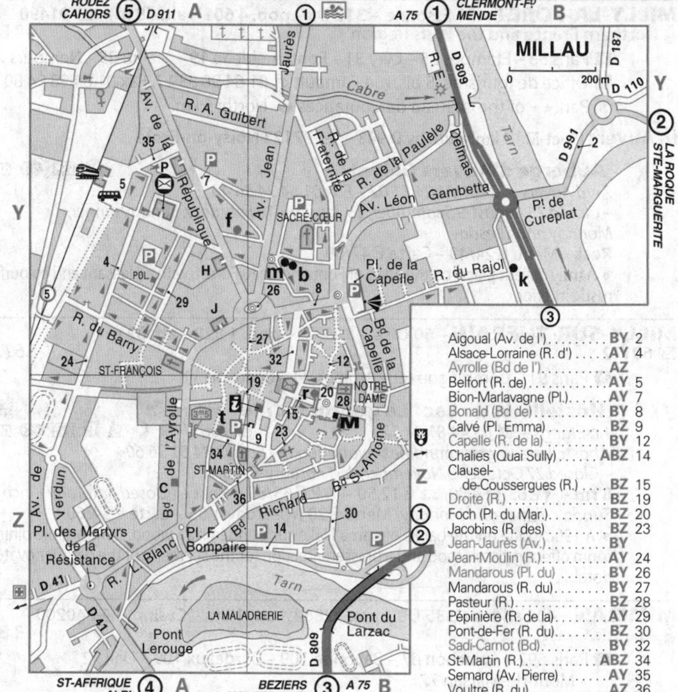

Ibis without rest
r. du Sacré Cœur – ✆ 05 65 59 29 09 – h5613@accor.com – Fax 05 65 59 29 01 YB **b**
46 rm – 🚹€ 71/89 🚹🚹€ 77/97, ☕ € 9
◆ This hotel in the town centre is conveniently located for a walk along the famous viaduct. Spacious, bright and comfortable rooms.

Capion
3 r. J.-F. Alméras – ✆ 05 65 60 00 91 – Fax 05 65 60 42 13 – Closed 1st-16 July, Thursday in August, Tuesday dinner and wednesday AY **f**
Rest – Menu € 13,50 bi (weekday lunch), € 18/36 – Carte € 27/43
◆ Town-centre establishment which is often full. Generous traditional cuisine using local products and a more exotic "menu des îles" set menu.

La Braconne
7 pl. Mar. Foch – ✆ 05 65 60 30 93 – Closed 23-30 June, Sunday dinner and Monday BZ **r**
Rest – Menu € 19/39 – Carte € 31/49
◆ The restaurant is located under "cover" of the columns of this picturesque square in old Millau, in a pretty 13C vaulted room. Family cooking and service.

via ④ 2 km St-Affrique road – ✉ 12100 Millau

Château de Creissels
– ✆ 05 65 60 16 59 – chateau-de-creissels@wanadoo.fr – Fax 05 65 61 24 63 – Closed January, February and Sunday evening from 1st November to 30 March
30 rm – 🚹€ 49 🚹🚹€ 63/96, ☕ € 9 – ½ P € 59/77 – **Rest** – *(closed Sunday dinner and Monday lunch except from June to September)* Menu € 23/50 – Carte € 35/54
◆ This 12C château and its modern extension (1971) offer a choice between charming period and more conventional bedrooms. Stylish sitting room; billiards. Dining room with attractive stone vaulting, panoramic terrace and tasty classical cooking.

MILLY-LA-FORÊT – 91 Essonne – 312 D5 – pop. 4 601 – alt. 68 m – ✉ 91490

Northern France and the Paris Region 18 **B3**

Paris 58 – Étampes 25 – Évry 31 – Fontainebleau 19 – Melun 25 – Nemours 27

Office de tourisme, 8 bis, rue Farnault ✆ 01 64 98 83 17, Fax 01 64 98 94 80

Park★★ of the chateau de Courances★★ North: 5 km.

in Auvers (S.-et-M.) 4 km south by D 948 – ✉ 77123 Noisy-on-Ecole

XX **Auberge d'Auvers Galant** VISA MC AE

7 r. d'Auvers – ✆ 01 64 24 51 02 – Fax 01 64 24 56 40
– Closed 25 August-9 September, 19 January-10 February, Sunday dinner, Monday and Tuesday
Rest – Menu € 24/49 – Carte € 47/69

◆ A truly gallant place; on the edge of Fontainebleau Forest, with a pleasant and colourful rustic interior.

MILLY-SUR-THERAIN – 60 Oise – 305 C3 – pop. 1 520 – alt. 82 m – ✉ 60112

36 **A2**

Paris 91 – Compiègne 69 – Amiens 74 – Beauvais 11

XX **Hostellerie du Lac "La gourmandine"** with rm

1 r. Étangs – ✆ 03 44 81 07 52 rest, P VISA MC AE
– hostellerie-la-gourmandine@wanadoo.fr – Fax 03 44 81 36 60
– Closed 27 October-3 November, 16 February-9 March
8 rm – €65 €80, € 12,50 – ½ P € 65/85 – **Rest** – *(Closed Saturday lunch, Sunday dinner and Monday)* Menu € 20 (weekdays)/55 – Carte € 34/60

◆ A 1900 lodge on the banks of a small lake surrounded by a wood. Comfortable dining room offering classic food and a brasserie section for the set menu of the day. Renovated hotel.

MIMIZAN – 40 Landes – 335 D9 – pop. 6 864 – alt. 13 m – Casino – ✉ 40200

Atlantic Coast 3 **B2**

Paris 692 – Arcachon 67 – Bayonne 109 – Bordeaux 109 – Dax 72 – Mont-de-Marsan 77

Office de tourisme, 38, avenue Maurice Martin ✆ 05 58 09 11 20, Fax 05 58 09 40 31

Sud Beach

L'Émeraude des Bois rest, P VISA MC

66/68 av. Courant – ✆ 05 58 09 05 28 – emeraudedesbois@wanadoo.fr
– Fax 05 58 09 35 73 – Open 1st April-29 September
15 rm – €45/55 €50/62, € 7 – ½ P € 49/53 – **Rest** – *(open 16 April-14 September) (dinner only)* Menu € 17/39 – Carte € 20/58

◆ A pleasant hotel 3 minutes from the beaches of the Côte d'Arget and the large Mimizan forest. Simple rooms and small, renovated bathrooms. (No smoking.) A dining room with veranda and a pleasant shady terrace.

L'Airial without rest P VISA MC AE

6 r. Papeterie – ✆ 05 58 09 46 54 – hotel.airial@tiscali.fr – Fax 05 58 09 32 10
– Closed Sunday dinner off season
16 rm – €43/50 €45/60, € 7,50

◆ Warm hospitality, well-maintained bedrooms furnished in pine, rest lounges, breakfast in the garden; here is an ocean stay to remember.

de France without rest P VISA MC AE

18 av. de la Côte d'Argent – ✆ 05 58 09 09 01 – hoteldefrancemimizan@orange.fr
– Fax 05 58 09 47 16 – Open 1st March-20 October
21 rm – €50/80 €50/150, € 6

◆ Not far from the beach, this small, practical hotel provides renovated rooms with simple furnishings and decorated in pastel tones. Snacks also served in high season.

MINERVE – 34 Hérault – 339 B8 – pop. 111 – alt. 227 m – ✉ 34210

Languedoc-Roussillon-Tarn Gorges 22 **B2**

Paris 812 – Béziers 45 – Carcassonne 44 – Narbonne 33 – St-Pons 30

Syndicat d'initiative, 9, rue des Martyrs ✆ 04 68 91 81 43, Fax 04 68 91 81 43

Site★★.

Relais Chantovent with rm
17 Grand'Rue – ✆ 04 68 91 14 18 – relais.chantovent@orange.fr – Fax 04 68 91 81 99 – Open 1st April-11 November and closed Sunday dinner and Monday
5 rm – €35 €45, ☕ €6 – ½ P €55 – **Rest** – *(open 15 March-15 December and closed Sunday dinner and Monday)* Menu €20/38 – Carte €32/52
◆ In the heart of the Cathar village, an attractive family-run inn serving appetising regional cuisine. A view of the Brian gorges from the terrace. Practical rooms.

MIOMO – 2B Haute-Corse – **345** F3 – see Corse (Bastia)

MIONNAY – 01 Ain – **328** C5 – **pop. 2 109 – alt. 276 m** – ✉ 01390 43 **E1**

Paris 457 – Bourg-en-Bresse 44 – Lyon 23 – Meximieux 26 – Villefranche-sur-Saône 33

de Mionnay-la-Dombes Domaine de Beau Logis, East: 3 km, ✆ 04 78 91 84 84.

Alain Chapel with rm
– ✆ 04 78 91 82 02 – chapel@relaischateaux.com – Fax 04 78 91 82 37 – Closed January, Friday lunch, Monday and Tuesday except public holidays
12 rm – €125/145 €125/145, ☕ €20
Rest – Menu €75 (weekday lunch), €115/157 – Carte €117/175
Spec. Foie gras de canard poêlé à l'amande fraîche, pêche et rhubarbe (summer). Langoustines et tomates groseille sur coulis de fenouil, sauce d'encre aux olives noires (summer). "Comme une tartelette" d'abricots rôtis aux arômes de sauge-ananas sur parfait au caramel. **Wines** Mâcon-Villages, Cerdon.
◆ The three tastefully decorated dining rooms sport a warm, romantic typically Bresse ambience. Classic gourmet cuisine. Spruce rooms and flower-decked garden.

MIRABEL-AUX-BARONNIES – 26 Drôme – **332** D8 – see Nyons

MIRAMAR – 06 Alpes-Maritimes – **341** C7 – see Théoule-sur-Mer

MIRAMBEAU – 17 Charente-Maritime – **324** G7 – **pop. 1 461 – alt. 59 m** – ✉ 17150

Paris 515 – Bordeaux 72 – Angoulême 73 – Cognac 48 – Royan 52

Office de tourisme, 90, avenue de la République ✆ 05 46 49 62 85, Fax 05 46 49 62 85 38 **B3**

Château de Mirambeau
– ✆ 05 46 04 91 20 – mirambeau@relaischateaux.com – Fax 05 46 04 26 72 – Open 5 April-1st November
20 rm – €230/525 €230/525, ☕ €28 – 3 suites
Rest – Menu €40 (lunch)/65 – Carte €67/88
◆ Sumptuous lounges, antique furniture, refined rooms, luxury bathrooms, vast park and beautiful indoor pool: charm and elegance abound in this magnificent 19C château. Three small intimate dining rooms and a terrace overlooking the estate.

MIRANDE – 71 Saône-et-Loire – **320** J11 – see Fleurville

MIRANDOL-BOURGNOUNAC – 81 Tarn – **338** E6 – **pop. 1 081 – alt. 393 m** – ✉ 81190 29 **C2**

Paris 653 – Albi 29 – Rodez 51 – St-Affrique 79 – Villefranche-de-Rouergue 39

Office de tourisme, 2, place de la Liberté ✆ 05 63 76 97 65, Fax 05 63 76 90 11

Hostellerie des Voyageurs with rm
rest, VISA
pl. du Foirail – ✆ 05 63 76 90 10 – Fax 05 63 76 96 01 – Closed dinner 1st October-15 April
8 rm – €33 €42/50, ☕ €6,50 – ½ P €47/53 – **Rest** – Menu €13 (weekdays)/25 – Carte €24/47
◆ This traditional-looking building is also home to the village café. Classic country-style dining area with exposed beams and a flower-decked terrace. Warm hospitality.

MIREBEAU-SUR-BÈZE – 21 Côte-d'Or – 320 L5 – pop. 1 573 – alt. 202 m – ✉ 21310 8 D2

Paris 338 – Châtillon-sur-Seine 107 – Dijon 26 – Dole 49 – Gray 24 – Langres 67

Syndicat d'initiative, 1 bis, rue du Moulin ☎ 03 80 36 76 17, Fax 03 80 36 76 17

in Bèze 9 km North by D 959 – pop. 632 – alt. 217 m – ✉ 21310 Burgundy-Jura

Le Bourguignon

rm, rest, VISA

8 r. Porte de Bessey – ☎ 03 80 75 34 51 – hotel-le-bourguignon@wanadoo.fr – Fax 03 80 75 37 06 – Closed 20 October-10 November

25 rm – €43/60 €57/65, €8 – ½ P €58/65

Rest – Menu €20/40 – Carte €26/56

◆ Contemporary-style rooms in a new, half-timbered building. The rustic dining room, with exposed beams and fireplace occupies a building with a Renaissance facade. Remember to ask for a Kir when it's time for a drink!

MIREBEL – 39 Jura – 321 E6 – pop. 202 – alt. 580 m – ✉ 39570 16 B3

Paris 419 – Champagnole 17 – Lons-le-Saunier 17

Mirabilis

VISA

41 Grande Rue – ☎ 03 84 48 24 36 – lemirabilis@wanadoo.fr – Fax 03 84 48 22 25 – Closed 2-12 January, Tuesday and Wednesday from September to May and Monday

Rest – Menu €13, €20/50 – Carte €27/45

◆ Dating from 1760, this family residence is well equipped with indoor and outdoor activities for children. Elegant dining room overlooking the terrace and garden. Modern, regional cuisine.

MIREPOIX – 09 Ariège – 343 J6 – pop. 3 061 – alt. 308 m – ✉ 09500 Languedoc-Roussillon-Tarn Gorges 29 C3

Paris 753 – Carcassonne 52 – Castelnaudary 34 – Foix 37 – Limoux 33 – Pamiers 25

Office de tourisme, place Maréchal Leclerc ☎ 05 61 68 83 76, Fax 05 61 68 89 48

Place principale★★.

Relais Royal

VISA

8 r. Mar. Clauzel – ☎ 05 61 60 19 19 – relaisroyal@relaischateaux.com – Fax 05 61 60 14 15 – Closed 9-15 November and 5 January-10 February

5 rm – €160/240 €160/240, €20 – 3 suites – ½ P €135/175

Rest – *(closed lunch November-Easter except Sunday, Saturday lunch, Monday and Tuesday)* Menu €35/55 – Carte €70/78

◆ This lovely residence (1742) used to be the home of the mayor. A large staircase leads to the spacious rooms decorated with stylish furniture and modern equipment. Small, plush dining room where you can enjoy appetising, modern recipes.

La Maison des Consuls without rest

VISA

6 pl. du Mar. Leclerc – ☎ 05 61 68 81 81 – hotel@maisondesconsuls.com – Fax 05 61 68 81 15

8 rm – €80/95 €80/150, €15

◆ This old 14C courthouse is now a hotel with personalised rooms (one suite with a terrace) embellished with a mix of medieval- and contemporary-style furniture. Views over the square and a patio.

Les Minotiers

VISA

av. Mar. Foch – ☎ 05 61 69 37 36 – Fax 05 61 69 48 55

27 rm – €45/47 €49/55, €7 – ½ P €57 – **Rest** – *(closed Saturday lunch except July-August)* Menu €16/35 – Carte €29/51

◆ A brand-new hotel within the walls of an old flour mill. Soft tones and modern equipment in the simple but comfortable guestrooms. Unpretentious and reasonably priced traditional cuisine.

Le Comptoir Gourmand

cours Mar. de Mirepoix – ✆ 05 61 68 19 19 – comptoir.gourmand@wanadoo.fr – Fax 05 61 68 19 19 – Closed Sunday dinner, Tuesday dinner and Wednesday except July-August

Rest – Menu (€ 22), € 28/48

◆ The enticing, refined and traditional cuisine served here is based on ingredients and wines sourced from small local producers. Boutique at the entrance to the restaurant. Summer terrace.

MIRMANDE – 26 Drôme – 332 C5 – pop. 503 – alt. 204 m Lyon - Rhone Valley

Paris 603 – Lyon 141 – Valence 42 – Romans-sur-Isère 61 – Montélimar 21

Syndicat d'initiative, place du Champ de Mars ✆ 04 75 63 10 88

La Capitelle

Le Rempart – ✆ 04 75 63 02 72 – capitelle@wanadoo.fr – Fax 04 75 63 02 50 – Closed 15 December-15 February and Tuesday except July-August

11 rm – €82/140 €82/140, € 12 – ½ P € 82/130

Rest – *(closed Wednesday lunch except July-August)* Menu € 25/38 – Carte € 52/60

◆ This former silkworm farm, lit by mullioned windows, was once the home of Cubist André Lhote. Beautiful antique furniture in the rooms. The monumental stone fireplace is the soul of this vaulted dining room. The terrace commands a view of the orchards and hills.

MISSILLAC – 44 Loire-Atlantique – 316 D3 – pop. 3 813 – alt. 44 m – ✉ 44780

Brittany 34 **A2**

Paris 436 – Nantes 62 – Redon 24 – St-Nazaire 37 – Vannes 55

Office de tourisme, la Chinoise ✆ 02 40 88 35 14

Altar-piece★ in the church - Site★ of the château de la Bretesche West: 1 km.

La Bretesche

rm,

Domaine de la Bretesche, la Baule road – ✆ 02 51 76 86 96 – bretesche@relaischateaux.com – Fax 02 40 66 99 47

32 rm – €250/430 €250/430, € 19 – ½ P € 196/286

Rest – *(closed lunch Monday-Friday)* Menu € 52/95 – Carte € 83/101

Rest *Le Club* – brasserie *(closed dinner 15 October-31 March)* Menu (€ 18), € 23 – Carte € 26/49

Spec. Langoustines du Guilvinec aux girolles (season). Bar de pays rôti, camus de Bretagne et cébettes. Pigeonneau de Mesquer à l'émulsion d'ail de Lautrec. **Wines** Savennières, Saint-Nicolas de Bourgueil.

◆ A world of fairytales in the heart of La Brière... Converted outbuildings opposite a crenelated chateau surrounded by moats. Refined restaurant, pleasant courtyard terrace and delicious modern recipes. A modern brasserie spirit at Le Club that caters for hurried diners.

MITTELBERGHEIM – 67 Bas-Rhin – 315 I6 – pop. 617 – alt. 220 m – ✉ 67140

Alsace-Lorraine 2 **C1**

Paris 499 – Barr 2 – Erstein 24 – Molsheim 23 – Sélestat 21 – Strasbourg 41

Syndicat d'initiative, 2, rue Principale ✆ 03 88 08 01 66, Fax 03 88 08 01 66

Am Lindeplatzel

71 r. Principale – ✆ 03 88 08 10 69 – Fax 03 88 08 45 08 – Closed 25 August-3 September, 20-30 November, 9-28 February, Monday lunch, Wednesday dinner and Thursday

Rest – Menu € 25 bi/35 – Carte € 39/56

◆ Located in a beautiful village, this restaurant is popular for its traditional and contemporary dishes, as well as its regional specialities with an up-to-the-minute focus.

Gilg with rm

1 r. Rotland – ✆ 03 88 08 91 37 – info@hotel-gilg.com – Fax 03 88 08 45 17 – Closed 23 June-10 July, 5-28 January, Tuesday and wednesday

19 rm – €52/62 €57/87, € 7,50 – **Rest** – Menu € 26 (weekdays)/75 – Carte € 31/60

◆ Beautiful house in the Low-Rhenish style (1614) in the centre of the village. The original winstub, possibly home to the first pâté vigneron (winegrower's meat pie), has been transformed into a restaurant with an Alsatian setting.

MITTELHAUSBERGEN – 67 Bas-Rhin – 315 K5 – see Strasbourg

MITTELHAUSEN – 67 Bas-Rhin – 315 J4 – pop. 509 – alt. 185 m – ✉ 67170

Paris 478 – Haguenau 21 – Saverne 22 – Strasbourg 24 1 **B1**

À l'Étoile rest, VISA

12 r. La Hey – ☎ 03 88 51 28 44 – hotelrestaurant.etoile@wanadoo.fr – Fax 03 88 51 24 79 – Closed 1st-14 January

24 rm – €46 €52/58, €7 – ½ P €58 – **Rest** – *(closed 13 July-7 August, 1st-14 January, Sunday dinner and Monday)* Menu (€8,50), €11/32 – Carte €22/46

◆ New building with a flower-filled facade and a regional look far from the busy main roads. Functional bedrooms renovated in stages. Warm and welcoming dining rooms decorated with old wood panelling.

MITTELWIHR – 68 Haut-Rhin – 315 H8 – pop. 823 – alt. 210 m – ✉ 68630

Paris 445 – Colmar 10 – Kaysersberg 6 – Ribeauvillé 403 – Sélestat 20 2 **C2**

Le Mandelberg without rest VISA

chemin du Mandelberg – ☎ 03 89 49 09 49 – hotelmandelberg@wanadoo.fr – Fax 03 89 49 09 48 – Closed 5 January-1st February

18 rm – €70/97 €80/110, €10

◆ A neo-Alsatian-style establishment in the heart of the "Midi of Alsace", so named due to its microclimate. Comfortable, spacious rooms, some overlooking the vineyards.

Le Mittelwihr without rest VISA

19 rte du Vin – ☎ 03 89 49 09 90 – hotelmittelwihr@wanadoo.fr – Fax 03 89 86 02 29 – Closed 1st February-20 March

15 rm – €70/97 €80/110, €10

◆ On the wine route, a brand-new, traditionally constructed house where a typically generous local breakfast is served after a comfortable night.

La Table de Mittelwihr VISA

rte du Vin – ☎ 03 89 78 61 40 – latabledemittelwihr@wanaddo.fr – Fax 03 89 86 01 66 – Closed 3-16 November, 23 February-8 March, Tuesday lunch and Monday

Rest – Menu €17 (weekday lunch), €31/45 – Carte €36/48

◆ Enjoy modern local cuisine in the rather original contemporary interior architecture (curved wooden beams) or on the pleasant summer terrace.

MIZOËN – 38 Isère – 333 J7 – see le Freney-d'Oisans

MOËLAN-SUR-MER – 29 Finistère – 308 J8 – pop. 6 592 – alt. 58 m – ✉ 29350

Brittany 9 **B2**

Paris 523 – Carhaix-Plouguer 66 – Concarneau 27 – Lorient 27 – Quimper 50 – Quimperlé 10

Office de tourisme, 20, place de l'Église ☎ 02 98 39 67 28, Fax 02 98 39 63 93

Manoir de Kertalg without rest VISA

Riec-sur-Belon road 3 km westward via the D 24 and private path – ☎ 02 98 39 77 77 – kertalg@free.fr – Fax 02 98 39 72 07 – Open 12 April-12 November

9 rm – €105/198 €105/250, €14

◆ Nestling in a wooded estate, this historic abode appeals to customers fond of art with its painting exhibitions. Plush, well-kept rooms; slightly smaller in the tower.

Les Moulins du Duc rm, VISA

2 km north-westward – ☎ 02 98 96 52 52 – moulin.duc@wanadoo.fr – Fax 02 98 96 52 53 – Open 1st March-30 November

26 rm – €78/189 €78/189, €13 – ½ P €79/131

Rest – *(closed Sunday dinner and Monday in March, Monday lunch and Tuesday lunch)* Menu €37/68 – Carte €41/68

◆ A leafy park with a tranquil lake, a 16C mill, plus guestrooms in attractive small houses by the river. This former mill, with its original workings on display in the lounge, is now home to a restaurant serving traditional cuisine. Riverside veranda.

MOERNACH – 68 Haut-Rhin – 315 H11 – see Ferrette

MOIRAX – 47 Lot-et-Garonne – 336 F5 – see Agen

MOISSAC – 82 Tarn-et-Garonne – 337 C7 – pop. 12 321 – alt. 76 m – ✉ 82200
Languedoc-Roussillon-Tarn Gorges 28 **B2**

Paris 632 – Agen 57 – Auch 87 – Cahors 63 – Montauban 31 – Toulouse 71

Office de tourisme, 6, place Durand de Bredon ✆ 05 63 04 01 85, Fax 05 63 04 27 10

d'Espalais Valence-d'Agen L'Ilôt, by Agen road: 20 km, ✆ 05 63 29 04 56.

St-Pierre church★: south portal ★★★, cloister★★★, christ★.

Boudou ✳★ 7 km by ③.

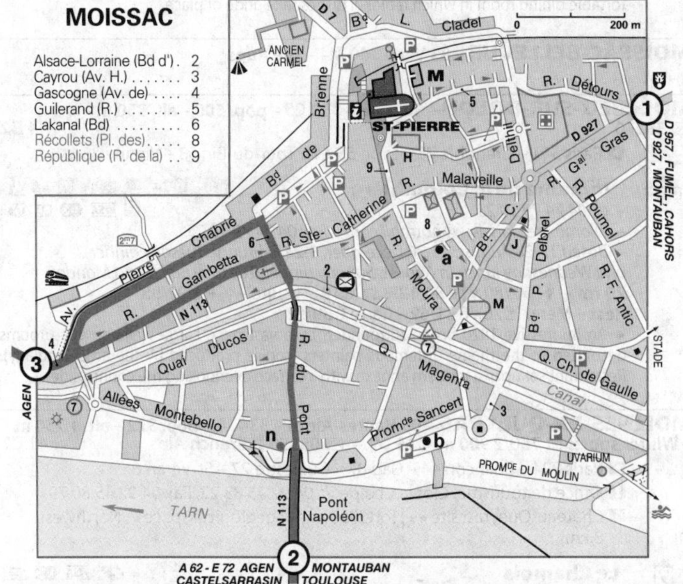

Le Moulin de Moissac
Esplanade du Moulin – ✆ 05 63 32 88 88 – hotel@lemoulindemoissac.com – Fax 05 63 32 02 08 **b**

36 rm – €68/93 €68/140, ☕ €10 – **Rest** – *(closed Saturday lunchtime and Sunday)* Menu €22 (weekday lunch), €28/45 – Carte €32/59

◆ This mill dates back to the 15. It has been transformed many times and now has a pleasantly-decorated interior and pretty, themed rooms (sea, countryside and mountains). Simple and elegant restaurant overlooking the Tarn; traditional menu.

Le Chapon Fin without rest
3 pl. des Récollets – ✆ 05 63 04 04 22 – info@lechaponfin-moissac.com – Fax 05 63 04 58 44 **a**

22 rm – €45/80 €45/80, ☕ €9

◆ Located on the market square, just a stone's throw from the Romanesque abbey. Classically decorated, functional guestrooms and warm welcome.

Le Pont Napoléon-La Table de Nos Fils with rm
2 allées Montebello – ✆ 05 63 04 01 55 – lepontnapoleon@orange.fr – Fax 05 63 04 34 44 – Closed autumn half-term holidays, 10 January-10 February, Monday lunch from October to April, Wednesday lunch and Tuesday **n**

14 rm – €48/52 €52/66, ☕ €12 – ½ P €70/80

Rest – Menu (€28), €37 (weekdays)/45

◆ Located opposite the Pont Napoléon, the multi-choice menu here is based on fresh produce. A decor of grey and deep purple tones, with parquet flooring and paintings on the walls.

North 9 km by D 7 - ✉ 82400 St-Paul-Espis

Le Manoir Saint-Jean rest, **VISA**
à St-Jean-de-Cornac – ✆ 05 63 05 02 34 – info@manoirsaintjean.com – Fax 05 63 05 07 50 – Closed 2-20 November and 2-20 January
1 rm € 100/120 € 100/120, € 13 – 9 suites – € 140/170 – ½ P € 93/105
Rest – *(closed Sunday dinner and Monday from 1st October to 15 May) (pre-book)* Menu € 38/70
◆ This 19C manor house owes much of its character to its many antiques. The rooms-suites are decorated on various themes: Art Deco, marine, etc. Pleasant garden and pool. Comfortable dining room in which regional dishes take pride of place.

MOISSAC-BELLEVUE – 83 Var – 340 M4 – see Aups

MOISSIEU-SUR-DOLON – 38 Isère – 333 C5 – pop. 500 – alt. 350 m – ✉ 38270

44 **B2**

Paris 511 – Grenoble 78 – Lyon 55 – La Tour-du-Pin 53 – Vienne 25

Domaine de la Colombière **VISA**
– ✆ 04 74 79 50 23 – colombieremoissieu@hotmail.com – Fax 04 74 79 50 25 – Closed 17-28 August, 26-30 December, 8-24 February, Tuesday dinner and Wednesday lunch in August, Sunday dinner, Tuesday lunch and Monday
20 rm – € 72/80 € 84/129, € 19 – 1 suite – ½ P € 82/95
Rest – Menu (€ 26), € 31/69 – Carte € 39/58
◆ An impressive 1820 house surrounded by a vast park. Large well-equipped rooms decorated to the theme of famous painters (copies produced by the artist-landlady). Restaurant set up in a modern annexe with a terrace overlooking the countryside.

MOLINES-EN-QUEYRAS – 05 Hautes-Alpes – 334 J4 – pop. 322 – alt. 1 750 m – Winter sports : 1 750/2 900 m 15 – ✉ 05350 French Alps

41 **C1**

Paris 724 – Briançon 44 – Gap 87 – Guillestre 27 – St-Véran 6

Office de tourisme, Clot la Chalpe ✆ 04 92 45 83 22, Fax 04 92 45 80 79

Château-Queyras: site★★, fort Queyras★, geological space★, Northwest: 8 km.

Le Chamois **VISA**
– ✆ 04 92 45 83 71 – contact@hotel-lechamois.com – Fax 04 92 45 80 58 – Open 1st-11 May, 1st June-30 September, 25 October-2 November and 25 December-31 March
17 rm – € 54/61 € 54/61, € 9 – ½ P € 55/59 – **Rest** – *(closed lunch 25 December-30 April and Monday)* Menu € 21/25 – Carte € 26/45
◆ Here everything is reminiscent of the mountain environment: the rustic-style bedrooms (six with balconies) and the warm and simple hospitality. Traditional meals served in a dining area with a view of the mountains.

MOLINEUF – 41 Loir-et-Cher – 318 E6 – see Blois

MOLITG-LES-BAINS – 66 Pyrénées-Orientales – 344 F7 – pop. 207 – alt. 607 m – Spa : early April-late Nov. – ✉ 66500 Languedoc-Roussillon-Tarn Gorges

22 **B3**

Paris 896 – Perpignan 50 – Prades 7 – Quillan 56

Syndicat d'initiative, route des Bains ✆ 04 68 05 03 28

Château de Riell rm, rest, **VISA**
– ✆ 04 68 05 04 40 – riell@relaischateaux.fr – Fax 04 68 05 04 37 – Open 30 March-3 November
16 rm – € 144/304 € 144/304, € 18 – 3 suites – ½ P € 137/261
Rest – *(closed lunch except weekends)* Menu € 46 – Carte € 70/76
◆ Built in wooded parkland and baroque in spirit, this 19C Catalan 'folly' has snug personalised bedrooms. There are seven others in little cottages. A smart bodega atmosphere in the dining room and terrace surrounded by lush vegetation.

Grand Hôtel Thermal

– 04 68 05 00 50 – molitglesbains@chainethermale.fr – Fax 04 68 05 02 91 – Open 30 March-23 November

60 rm – €95/122 €95/122, €13 – 4 suites – ½ P €97/136

Rest – *(closed Saturday lunch and Sunday lunch)* Menu €27

◆ In a lakeside park, this hotel offers colourful rooms refurbished in a tasteful Catalan style. A few spacious and very attractive suites. One of the dining rooms is in an old chocolate factory. Classic menu.

MOLLANS-SUR-OUVÈZE – 26 Drôme – 332 E8 – pop. 840 – alt. 280 m – ✉ 26170 French Alps 44 B3

Paris 676 – Carpentras 30 – Nyons 21 – Vaison-la-Romaine 13

Le St-Marc rest, VISA MC AE

av. de l'Ancienne Gare – 04 75 28 70 01 – le-saint-marc@club-internet.fr – Fax 04 75 28 78 63 – Open 20 March-2 November

31 rm – €60/82 €60/82, €9 – ½ P €62/73 – **Rest** – Menu €25/31

◆ This Provencal-style house, fronted by a garden, lies at the foot of Mont Ventoux. Rooms enlivened by colourful fabrics. A rustic restaurant with an open fireplace, serving southern French cuisine and featuring a pleasant shaded and floral terrace.

MOLLÉGÈS – 13 Bouches-du-Rhône – 340 E3 – pop. 2 171 – alt. 55 m – ✉ 13940

Paris 704 – Avignon 24 – Cavaillon 9 – Marseille 80 – Saint-Rémy-de-Provence 12 42 E1

Mas du Capoun with rm rm, rm, VISA MC

27 av. des Paluds – 04 90 26 07 12 – lemasducapoun@wanadoo.fr – Fax 04 90 26 08 17 – Rest closed 1st-14 November and mid February to mid March hotel: Open mid March to mid October

6 rm – €75/85 €85/95, €7 – **Rest** – *(closed Tuesday dinner, Saturday lunch and Wednesday)* Menu €16/33

◆ Refined farmhouse with bright dining room where you can enjoy modern dishes, served under the exposed beams of the chic, rustic barn. Pretty rooms with private terrace.

MOLLKIRCH – 67 Bas-Rhin – 315 I5 – pop. 765 – alt. 320 m – ✉ 67190 1 A2

Paris 485 – Molsheim 11 – Saverne 35 – Strasbourg 40

Fischhutte VISA MC AE

30 rte de la Fischhutte, rte Grendelbruch: 3,5 km – 03 88 97 42 03 – fischhutte@wanadoo.fr – Fax 03 88 97 51 85 – Closed 25 March-25 April and 28 July-6 August

16 rm – €60/65 €70/115, €10 – ½ P €68/95 – **Rest** – *(closed Monday and Tuesday)* Menu (€13,50), €32 (weekday lunch), €46 € bi/52 – Carte €31/47

◆ A country hotel in the Magel valley. Comfortable rooms with modern decor. Some offer a view of the Vosges forest. Brasserie area flanking a smart dining room. Regional menu and game in season.

MOLSHEIM – 67 Bas-Rhin – 315 I5 – pop. 9 335 – alt. 180 m – ✉ 67120 Alsace-Lorraine 1 A1

Paris 477 – Lunéville 94 – St-Dié 79 – Saverne 28 – Sélestat 37 – Strasbourg 32

Office de tourisme, 19, place de l'Hôtel Ville 03 88 38 11 61, Fax 03 88 49 80 40

La Metzig★ - Jésuites church ★.

Frescoes★ of St-Ulrich chapel North: 3.5 km.

Diana rm, rm, VISA MC AE

pont de la Bruche – 03 88 38 51 59 – info@hotel-diana.com – Fax 03 88 38 87 11

61 rm – €95 €95/185, €10,50 – 1 suite – ½ P €73 – **Rest** – *(closed 22-31 December and Sunday dinner)* Menu (€25), €31/62 bi – Carte €48/54

◆ A 1970s hotel providing pleasant and spacious rooms, and featuring art work on display, an indoor swimming pool, fitness facilities and a garden. Restaurant with a modern menu and beautiful wine cellar.

Le Bugatti without rest

r. Commanderie – ☎ 03 88 49 89 00 – info@hotel-le-bugatti.com – Fax 03 88 38 36 00 – Closed 24 December-1st January

48 rm – †€ 55/70 ††€ 55/70, ☕ € 7 – 3 suites

◆ The contemporary architecture of Bugatti, near the factories of the legendary name, has simple, practical rooms, equipped with laminated-wood furniture.

LES MOLUNES – 39 Jura – 321 F8 – pop. 124 – alt. 1 274 m – ✉ 39310 16 B3

Paris 485 – Genève 49 – Gex 30 – Lons-le-Saunier 74 – St-Claude 16

Le Pré Fillet rm, VISA

rte Moussières – ☎ 03 84 41 62 89 – leprefillet@wanadoo.fr – Fax 03 84 41 64 75 – Closed 28 April-6 May, 20 October-9 December, Sunday dinner and Monday

15 rm – †€ 49 ††€ 49, ☕ € 6,50 – ½ P € 50

Rest – Menu € 13 bi (weekday lunch), € 20/36 – Carte € 15/48

◆ Basic yet pleasant hostelry (non-smoking) in a mountain setting. Well-kept rooms, sauna and Jacuzzi with view over the countryside. Regional fare generously served; good local and Burgundy wine list.

MONACO (PRINCIPALITY) – 341 F5 – 115 27 – see end of guide

MONCÉ-EN-BELIN – 72 Sarthe – 310 K7 – pop. 2 463 – alt. 60 m – ✉ 72230

Paris 214 – La Flèche 33 – Le Grand-Lucé 23 – Le Mans 14 35 D1

Le Belinois VISA

bd Avocats – ☎ 02 43 42 01 18 – Fax 02 43 42 22 16 – Closed Monday and dinner except Saturday

Rest – Menu € 14 (weekday lunch), € 20/45

◆ A pleasant country restaurant nestling in the centre of the village. Serving traditional meals in a refined dining area.

MONCEL-LÈS-LUNÉVILLE – 54 Meurthe-et-Moselle – 307 K7 – see Lunéville

MONCOUTANT – 79 Deux-Sèvres – 322 C4 – pop. 2 985 – alt. 180 m – ✉ 79320 38 B1

Paris 403 – Bressuire 16 – Cholet 49 – Niort 54 – La Roche-sur-Yon 79

Syndicat d'initiative, 18, avenue du Maréchal Juin ☎ 05 49 72 78 83

St-Pierre rm, VISA

rte de Niort – ☎ 05 49 72 88 88 – contact@le-saintpierre.fr – Fax 05 49 72 88 89

30 rm ☕ – †€ 57 ††€ 72 – **Rest** – *(closed Saturday lunch and Sunday dinner)* Menu € 10,50 bi (weekday lunch), € 20/33 – Carte € 30/51

◆ The dining room of this recent construction with wooden facade faces due south. Wood frame ceiling and garden view (small pond). Functional rooms.

MONDEMENT-MONTGIVROUX – 51 Marne – 306 E10 – see Sézanne

MONDOUBLEAU – 41 Loir-et-Cher – 318 C4 – pop. 1 608 – alt. 170 m – ✉ 41170 Châteaux of the Loire 11 B2

Paris 170 – Blois 62 – Chartres 74 – Châteaudun 40 – Le Mans 64 – Orléans 92

Office de tourisme, 2, rue Bizieux ☎ 02 54 80 77 08, Fax 02 54 80 77 08

Le Grand Monarque VISA

pl. du Marché – ☎ 02 54 80 92 10 – legrandmonarque@wanadoo.fr – Fax 02 54 80 77 40 – Closed 15-21 September, 16-28 February, Sunday except lunch from 1st March to 30 November and Monday

13 rm – †€ 52 ††€ 52, ☕ € 8 – ½ P € 58 – **Rest** – Menu € 19 (weekdays)/41 – Carte € 35/48

◆ Alongside a region dear to the Kings of France, an old posthouse to welcome you... in princely style! Cool bedrooms await you. Modern dining room with well laid and well spaced tables. Pleasant terrace under the wisteria. Traditional cooking.

MONDRAGON – 84 Vaucluse – 332 B8 – pop. 3 363 – alt. 40 m – ✉ 84430

▶ Paris 640 – Avignon 45 – Montélimar 40 – Nyons 41 – Orange 17 40 **A2**

XX **La Beaugravière** with rm

N 7 – ☎ 04 90 40 82 54 – labeaugraviere84@wanadoo.fr – Fax 04 90 40 91 01 – Closed 15-30 September, Sunday dinner and Monday

3 rm – †€ 65/100 ††€ 65/100, ☕ € 8 – **Rest** – Menu € 27/100 – Carte € 40/125

◆ This Provençal restaurant has a dining area with a large fireplace and a shaded terrace, serving traditional cuisine with truffle specialties in season, and an excellent wine selection.

MONEIN – 64 Pyrénées-Atlantiques – 342 I3 – pop. 4 183 – alt. 154 m – ✉ 64360 3 B3

▶ Paris 799 – Pau 23 – Navarrenx 20 – Oloron-Sainte-Marie 21 – Orthez 29

X **L'Auberge des Roses**

Quartier Loupien – ☎ 05 59 21 45 63 – auberge.des.roses@clubinternet.fr Fax 05 59 21 32 85 – Closed 7-30 July, 25 February-5 March, Monday and Wednesday

Rest – Menu € 22/34 – Carte € 28/46

◆ This inn with flowered surroundings houses a rustic dining room with a veranda and small, shaded terraces. Appetising, modern food.

MONESTIER-DE-CLERMONT – 38 Isère – 333 G8 – pop. 921 – alt. 825 m – ✉ 38650 French Alps 45 C2

▶ Paris 598 – Grenoble 36 – La Mure 29 – Serres 72 – Sisteron 107

ℹ Office de tourisme, 103 bis, Grand Rue ☎ 04 76 34 15 99, Fax 04 76 34 15 99

Au Sans Souci

at St-Paul-lès- Monestier, 2 km northwest on D 8 - alt. 800 – ☎ 04 76 34 03 60 – au.sans.souci@club-internet.fr – Fax 04 76 34 17 38 – Closed 15 December to end January, Sunday dinner and Monday except July-August

12 rm – †€ 42 ††€ 64, ☕ € 8 – ½ P € 67

Rest – Menu € 19 (weekdays)/48 – Carte € 30/52

◆ Old sawmill covered in virginia creeper with rustic bedrooms. A family-run business since 1934, serving tasty cuisine prepared with market produce.

Piot

7 chemin des Chambons – ☎ 04 76 34 07 35 – hotepiot@club-internet.fr – Fax 04 76 34 12 74 – Open 15 March-15 November and closed Monday and Tuesday except July-August

16 rm – †€ 38/55 ††€ 43/55, ☕ € 8 – ½ P € 55/58 – **Rest** – Menu (€ 15), € 19 (weekdays)/32 – Carte € 24/39

◆ Impressive 1912 villa in a small park planted with century-old pines. Simple, well-kept bedrooms and friendly atmosphere. Spacious, recently decorated dining room, pleasant terrace shaded by conifers and traditional cooking.

LE MONÊTIER-LES-BAINS – 05 Hautes-Alpes – 334 H3 – see Serre-Chevalier

LA MONGIE – 65 Hautes-Pyrénées – 342 N5 – Winter sports : 1 800/2 500 m 3 41 – ✉ 65200 Bagneres de Bigorre Languedoc-Roussillon-Tarn Gorges

▶ Paris 853 – Bagnères-de-Bigorre 25 – Bagnères-de-Luchon 72 – Tarbes 48

ℹ Office de tourisme, place de la Grenouillere ☎ 05 62 91 94 15, Fax 05 62 95 33 13 28 **A3**

Le Taoulet ≤★★ North by cable car - Col du Tourmalet★★: 4 km.

Pic du Midi de Bigorre★★★.

Le Pourteilh rest,

av. Tourmalet – ☎ 05 62 91 93 33 – contact@hotel-pourteilh.com – Fax 05 62 91 90 88 – Open December-March

40 rm – †€ 72/110 ††€ 72/110, ☕ € 9 – ½ P € 60/79 – **Rest** – Menu € 24/32 – Carte € 35/55

◆ This 1970s hotel set at the foot of the slopes is popular with skiers in winter. A friendly tavern and simple guest rooms gradually being renovated. Traditional cuisine served in a country-style dining area with a family guesthouse atmosphere.

Northeast 8 km by D 918 – ✉ 65710 Campan

La Maison d'Hoursentut

– ☎ 05 62 91 89 42 – contact@maison-hoursentut.com
– Fax 05 62 91 88 13
13 rm – †€ 60/85 ††€ 60/85, ☕ € 8 – ½ P € 58/61
Rest – *(number of covers limited, pre-book)* Menu (€ 15), € 20
◆ Contemporary, mountain-style décor and a warm atmosphere in this small hotel providing charming rooms, a lounge with fireplace and a pretty garden with a Norwegian-style bath. The menu is announced by the waiters. Featuring a terrace on the banks of the Adour.

MONHOUDOU – 72 Sarthe – 310 K5 – pop. 192 – alt. 130 m – ✉ 72260

Paris 199 – Alençon 30 – Le Mans 42 – Nantes 223 — 35 **D1**

South 2 km by D 117 and secondary road - ✉72260 Monhoudou

Château de Monhoudou

rest, VISA MC AE

– ☎ 02 43 97 40 05 – info@monhoudou.com – Fax 02 43 33 11 58
5 rm – †€ 100/160 ††€ 100/160, ☕ € 9 – ½ P € 92/122
Table d'hôte – Menu € 42 bi/69 bi
◆ Set in an English-style park with free-roaming animals, this 16C-18C Renaissance chateau has been in the same family for 19 generations. Large, elegant rooms with antique furniture, a lounge with fireplace and a library. Meals served personally by the owner.

MONNAIE – 37 Indre-et-Loire – 317 N4 – pop. 3 302 – alt. 113 m – ✉ 37380

Paris 227 – Château-Renault 15 – Tours 16 – Vouvray 10 — 11 **B2**

Au Soleil Levant

53 r. Nationale – ☎ 02 47 56 10 34 – Fax 02 47 56 19 97
– Closed 2 weeks in September, 3 weeks in January, Sunday dinner and Monday
Rest – Menu € 23/39 – Carte € 37/50
◆ This inn on the way through the town is well known for its tasty updated cooking: a hearty stop on the doorstep of the Angers marsh and woodlands.

MONPAZIER – 24 Dordogne – 329 G7 – pop. 516 – alt. 180 m – ✉ 24540

Dordogne-Berry-Limousin — 4 **C2**

Paris 575 – Bergerac 47 – Périgueux 75 – Sarlat-la-Canéda 50 – Villeneuve-sur-Lot 46

Office de tourisme, place des Cornières ☎ 05 53 22 68 59, Fax 05 53 74 30 08

Place des Cornières★.

Edward 1er

5 r. Saint Pierre – ☎ 05 53 22 44 00 – info@hoteledward1er.com
– Fax 05 53 22 57 99 – Open 7 March-16 November
12 rm – †€ 50/78 ††€ 64/178, ☕ € 12 – 2 suites – ½ P € 68/113
Rest – *(open 21 March-2 November and closed Wednesday except July-August) (dinner only) (pre-book)* Menu € 28/36
◆ This 19C gentleman's house offers a taste of the good life. High ceilings, mouldings, period furniture and wall hangings. Spacious rooms with a view. Every day the chef creates a menu based on Périgord produce (evenings only by reservation).

Bistrot 2

Foirail Nord – ☎ 05 53 22 60 64 – info@bistrot2.fr – Fax 05 53 58 36 27
– Closed 17-30 November, 1st-13 February, Tuesday dinner, Friday dinner from December to March, Sunday dinner and Monday
Rest – Menu (€ 14,50), € 18 (lunch)/29 – Carte € 27/34
◆ Part of the Edward I's team has taken over this new contemporary bistro, offering enticingly reinterpreted regional recipes. Terrace shaded by wisteria.

MONTAGNAT – 01 Ain – 328 E3 – pop. 1 421 – alt. 262 m – ✉ 01250 44 B1

Paris 447 – Lyon 84 – Bourg-en-Bresse 8 – Mâcon 55 – Oyonnax 56

Au Pot de Grès

2013 rte du Village – ✆ 04 74 51 67 05 – franck.provillard@free.fr – Fax 04 74 51 67 05 – Closed Easter holidays, autumn half-term holidays, Sunday dinner, Monday and Tuesday

Rest – Menu € 13 (weekday lunch), € 23/39 – Carte € 33/48

♦ This inviting country home welcomes guests into a dining room lit by an open fire. The chef cleverly reinvents regional dishes using fresh produce.

MONTAGNE – 33 Gironde – 335 K5 – pop. 1 585 – alt. 80 m – ✉ 33570 4 C1

Paris 541 – Agen 129 – Bordeaux 41 – Bergerac 61 – Libourne 11

Castel Saint Joseph

– ✆ 05 57 24 71 08 – patricia.de-cathelineau@wanadoo.fr

4 rm – € 110/140 € 120/140, € 15 – **Table d'hôte** – Menu € 35 bi/55 bi

♦ In a winegrowing village, a large house fronted by a drive and cobbled courtyard for summer dining. The decor mixes family heirlooms, paintings and four-poster or canopied beds. The table d'hôte proposes contemporary cuisine served with regional wines.

Le Vieux Presbytère

pl. de l'Église – ✆ 05 57 74 65 33 – Closed 5-25 January, Tuesday and Wednesday

Rest – Menu (€ 16 bi), € 20 bi/50 bi

♦ A restaurant in a former presbytery at the foot of a Romanesque chapel. Cosy, rustic setting, fine courtyard terrace, traditional cuisine and local wines.

LA MONTAGNE – 21 Côte-d'Or – 320 I7 – see Beaune

MONTAGNE-DU-SEMNOZ – 74 Haute-Savoie – 328 J6 – ✉ 74000 French Alps

Paris 552 – Aix-les-Bains 43 – Albertville 60 – Annecy 17 – Chambéry 59

Crêt de Châtillon ✻★★★ (**access** by D 41: from Annecy 20 km or from Leschaux Pass 14 km, then 15 mn). 46 F1

on D 41 – ✉ 74000 Annecy

Les Rochers Blancs

near the summit, alt. 1650 – ✆ 04 50 01 23 60 – lesrochersblancs@wanadoo.fr – Fax 04 50 01 40 68 – Closed 15 September-15 December and 15 April-10 June

15 rm – € 48 € 60, € 12 – ½ P € 58/62 – **Rest** – *(closed November)* Menu € 18/25 – Carte € 26/40

♦ At an altitude of 1650m, this chalet enjoys an outstanding view and matchless peace and quiet. Somewhat minimalist rooms, gradually being made over in the local style. Restaurant decorated in pure alpine tradition, cuisine in the same vein. Terrace.

MONTAGNY – 42 Loire – 327 E3 – pop. 1 111 – alt. 530 m – ✉ 42840 44 A1

Paris 408 – Lyon 70 – Montbrison 78 – Roanne 15 – St-Étienne 96 – Thizy 7

L'Air du Temps

1 r. de la République – ✆ 04 77 66 11 31 – restaurant.lairdutemps@orange.fr – Fax 04 77 66 15 63 – Closed Sunday dinner and Monday

Rest – Menu € 16 (weekday lunch), € 32/56 – Carte € 34/52

♦ Pastel hues, a contemporary decor and well-spaced round tables in the dining room of this restaurant on the first floor of an old café. Cooking suited to current tastes.

MONTAGNY-LÈS-BEAUNE – 21 Côte-d'Or – 320 J8 – see Beaune

MONTAIGU – 85 Vendée – 316 I6 – pop. 4 708 – alt. 40 m – ✉ 85600 34 B3

Paris 389 – Cholet 36 – Fontenay-le-Comte 88 – Nantes 37 – La Roche-sur-Yon 39

Office de tourisme, 6, rue Georges Clemenceau ✆ 02 51 06 39 17, Fax 02 51 06 39 17

Vendée Memorial ★★: le logis de la Chabotterie★ (historical rooms★★) Southwest: 14 km, le chemin de la Mémoire des Lucs★ Southwest: 24 km Atlantic Coast

at Pont de Sénard 7 km north by N 137 and D 77 – ✉ 85600 St-Hilaire-de-Loulay

Le Pont de Sénard rm, rest, VISA AE
– ✆ 02 51 46 49 50 – hotel.pont.senard@wanadoo.fr – Fax 02 51 94 11 11
– *Closed 4-21 August, 27 October-2 November, 26-31 December, Friday dinner October-April and Sunday dinner*
25 rm – †€ 48 ††€ 66, ☐ € 8 – ½ P € 72 – **Rest** – *(closed Friday dinner October-May)* Menu € 19/50 – Carte € 44/56
♦ This hotel overlooking the River Maine has a loyal following drawn here by the delightful, bucolic location, good seminar facilities, and guestrooms which are gradually being renovated. Veranda-dining room and attractive rustic terrace overlooking the river.

MONTAIGUT-LE-BLANC – 63 Puy-de-Dôme – 326 F9 – see Champeix

MONTAREN-ET-ST-MÉDIERS – 30 Gard – 339 L4 – pop. 1 328 – alt. 115 m – see Uzès

MONTARGIS – 45 Loiret – 318 N4 – pop. 15 030 – alt. 95 m – ✉ 45200

Burgundy-Jura 12 **D2**

Paris 109 – Auxerre 81 – Bourges 117 – Orléans 73 – Sens 50
Office de tourisme, rue du Port ✆ 02 38 98 00 87, Fax 02 38 98 82 01
de Vaugouard Fontenay-sur-Loing Chemin des Bois, by Fontainebleau: road 9 km, ✆ 02 38 89 79 09.
Collection Girodet★ of the museum **M**[1].

Plans on next page

Ibis rm, VISA AE
2 pl. V. Hugo – ✆ 02 38 98 00 68 – h0861@accor.com – Fax 02 38 89 14 37
59 rm – †€ 49/65 ††€ 49/65, ☐ € 7,50 Z **b**
Rest *Brasserie de la Poste* – Menu (€ 12), € 20/27 – Carte € 20/44
♦ The bedrooms in this modern and practical hotel provide the chain's usual services. Those on the third floor are particularly well-suited for families. A pleasant retro-style restaurant with glass roof, elegant lighting and red bench seating. Serves bistro-style meals.

Central without rest VISA AE
2 r. Gudin – ✆ 02 38 85 03 07 – info@hotel-montargis.com – Fax 02 38 98 33 39 – Closed 25 December-1st January Z **a**
12 rm – †€ 48 ††€ 55, ☐ € 6,50
♦ Once a monastery, this fine residence in the town centre was converted into a hotel in the late 20C and renovated in 2004. A carved oak staircase leads to the simple, clean guestrooms.

Dorèle without rest P VISA AE
222 r. Émile Mengin – ✆ 02 38 07 18 18 – les-hotels-dorele@wanadoo.fr – Fax 02 38 07 18 19 Y **t**
50 rm – †€ 43/50 ††€ 49/57, ☐ € 7
♦ A recent cubic-looking construction in the area around the train station. The rather small rooms are well thought out and have good soundproofing. Comfortable lounge.

XXX **La Gloire** (Jean-Claude Martin) with rm rest, VISA AE
74 av. Gén. de Gaulle – ✆ 02 38 85 04 69 – contact@lagloire-montargis.com – Fax 02 38 98 52 32 – Closed 18 August-3 September, 16 February-12 March, Tuesday and Wednesday Y **m**
11 rm – †€ 50 ††€ 64, ☐ € 8,50 – **Rest** – Menu € 30/52 – Carte € 58/95
Spec. Salade de homard. Blanc de turbot moutardé en écailles de tomate. Grenadin de queue de bœuf et escalope de foie gras de canard poêlé. **Wines** Sancerre, Menetou-Salon.
♦ This establishment is indeed the 'glory' of Montargis: subtly updated, generous portions of classical fare served in an elegant dining room. Faultless welcome and service. Comfortable rooms.

XX **L'Agrappe Cœur** P VISA AE
22 r. J. Jaurès – ✆ 02 38 85 22 65 – Closed August, Sunday dinner, Tuesday dinner and Monday Y **a**
Rest – Menu € 19/37 – Carte € 39/54
♦ Enjoy a pleasant bistro atmosphere in the first dining room adorned with a fine 1930s wooden counter. The other three rooms have a more low-key decor.

MONTARGIS

Street	Grid	No.
Anatole-France (Bd)	Y	2
Ancien Palais (R.)	Z	3
Baudin (Bd Paul)	YZ	4
Belles Manières (Bd)	Z	5
Bon-Guillaume (R. du)	Z	6
Carnot (R. Lazare)	Y	8
Cormenin (R.)	Z	12
Decourt (R. E.)	Y	13
Dr-Roux (R. du)	Y	15
Dr-Szigeti (Av. du)	Y	16
Dorée (R.)	Z	
Ferry (Pl. Jules)	Z	20
Fg de la Chaussée (R. du)	YZ	17
Fg d'Orléans (R. du)	YZ	18
Jean-Jaurès (R.)	Y	21
Kléber (R.)	Y	22
Laforge (R. R.)	Z	23
Lamy (R. Jean)	Y	24
Longeard (R. du)	Y	26
Moulin à Tan (R.du)	Z	28
Pêcherie (R. de la)	Z	30
Poterne (R. de la)	Z	32
Pougin-de-la-Maisonneuve (R.)	Z	33
Prés.-Roosevelt (R.)	Y	34
République (Pl. de la)	Z	36
Sédillot (R.)	Y	37
Tellier (R. R.)	Z	39
Vaublanc (R. de)	Z	41
Verdun (Av. de)	Y	42
18-Juin-1940 (Pl. du)	Z	45

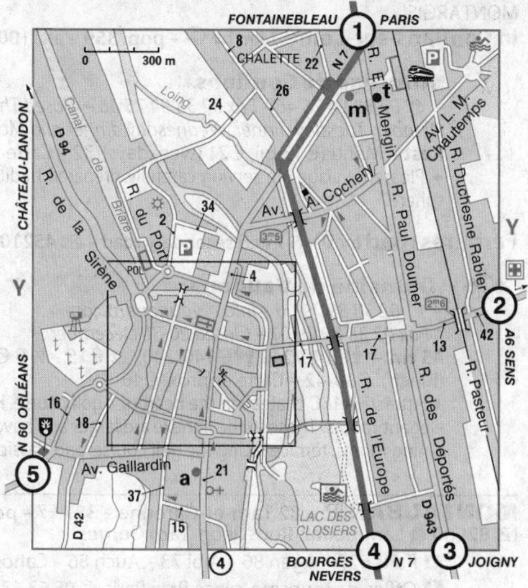

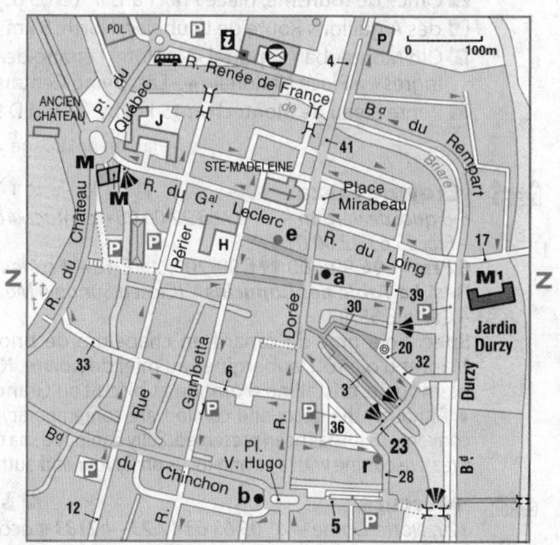

Les Dominicaines

r. du Dévidet – ☎ 02 38 98 10 22 – odile.freddy@wanadoo.fr – Fax 02 38 98 41 41 – Closed 16-31 August, Sunday and public holidays Z e

Rest – *(pre-book)* Menu (€ 13,50), € 29

◆ A nod to the town's history with a stained glass window featuring Dominican nuns. Fish and Provençal specialities.

in Amilly 5 km by ③ – **pop. 11 497 – alt. 110 m – ✉ 45200**

Le Belvédère without rest

– ☎ 02 38 85 41 09 – h.belvedere@wanadoo.fr – Fax 02 38 98 75 63 – Closed 15-28 August and 20 December-4 January

24 rm – €52 €58, ☐ €10

◆ This family-run hotel, fronted by a flower garden, faces the village school. The small, comfortable and peaceful rooms have personal touches.

in Conflans-sur-Loing 7 km by ③ – **pop. 359 – alt. 100 m** – ✉ **45700**

Auberge de Conflans
– ✆ 02 38 94 75 46 – Fax 02 38 94 75 46 – Closed Thursday dinner except in October, Tuesday dinner, Wednesday dinner and Monday
Rest – Menu (€ 13 bi), € 21 (weekdays)/32 – Carte € 38/50
♦ Pleasant village inn serving carefully-prepared traditional dishes in a convivial atmosphere.

Ferrières road by ①, **N 7 and secondary road** – ✉ **45210 Fontenay-sur-Loing**

Domaine de Vaugouard rest,
– ✆ 02 38 89 79 00 – info@vaugouard.com
– Fax 02 38 89 79 01 – Closed 20-30 December
45 rm – €140/240 €140/240, ☕ € 15 – ½ P € 130/180 – **Rest** – Menu € 22 (lunch), € 30/42 – Carte approx. € 46
♦ Attractive 18C chateau in the heart of a golf course. Horse riding centre. Comfortable, elegant rooms. Those in the annexe are larger and have been renovated. Small, opulent dining rooms, terrace facing the golf course, and classic cuisine.

MONTAUBAN Ⓟ – 82 Tarn-et-Garonne – 337 E7 – pop. 51 855 – alt. 98 m –

✉ 82000 Languedoc-Roussillon-Tarn Gorges 28 **B2**

Paris 627 – Agen 86 – Albi 73 – Auch 86 – Cahors 64 – Toulouse 53
Office de tourisme, place Prax Paris ✆ 05 63 63 60 60, Fax 05 63 63 65 12
des Aiguillons Route de Loubejac, North: 8 km by D 959, ✆ 05 63 31 35 40.
Old Montauban★: portal★ of Hôtel Lefranc-de-Pompignan Z **E** - Musée Ingres★ - Place Nationale★ - Last dying Centaur★ (bronze by Bourdelle) **B.**
Pente d'eau de Montech★: 15 km by ③ and D 928.

Plan on next page

Crowne Plaza
6-8 quai de Verdun – ✆ 05 63 22 00 00 – contact@cp-montauban.com
– Fax 05 63 22 00 01 Z **e**
62 rm – €99/200 €99/200, ☕ € 18 – 4 suites
Rest *La Table des Capucins* – *(Closed Sunday)* Menu € 25 (lunch), € 38/70 – Carte € 55/87
Spec. Foie gras de canard en chapelure de brioche, marmelade de piments. Magret d'oie rôti, aubergines au miel de poivre. Nage cardamome, sorbet pamplemousse, cristalline d'orange et biscuit au Grand-Marnier.
♦ Although the decor and comfort are contemporary, the monastic aura of this listed convent (1630) has been preserved. Fully equipped spa to re-energise both body and soul. Creative cuisine with a strong focus on flavour and authenticity.

Mercure rest,
12 r. Notre-Dame – ✆ 05 63 63 17 23 – h2183@accor.com
– Fax 05 63 66 43 66 Z **s**
44 rm – €92 €102, ☕ € 12 – **Rest** – Menu € 15/35 – Carte € 25/41
♦ This 18C private mansion was completely renovated in 1999. The rooms are spacious and contemporary and are well sound-proofed. The dining room furnished in Louis XVI-style is topped by a vast glass roof.

Du Commerce without rest
9 pl. Roosevelt – ✆ 05 63 66 31 32 – info@hotel-commerce-montauban.com
– Fax 05 63 66 31 28 – Closed 22-31 December Z **b**
27 rm – €53/56 €55/78, ☕ € 8,50
♦ A large, 18C hotel near the cathedral with a reception and lounge featuring lovely antique furniture, simple, well-kept rooms and colourfully decorated bathrooms.

Les Saveurs d'Ingres
13 r. Hôtel de Ville, (due to move in spring) – ✆ 05 63 91 26 42 – Fax 05 63 66 28 92 – Closed 27 April-5 May, 17 August-1st September, Sunday and Monday Z **u**
Rest – Menu € 25 (weekday lunch), € 39/75 – Carte € 56/64
♦ This restaurant's name pays tribute to the Montauban artist (Ingres museum nearby). Pleasant vaulted dining room with modern furniture. Local dishes with personal touches.

MONTAUBAN

Abbaye (R. de l') . . . . Z
Alsace-Lorraine (Bd) . . . . . . X 3
Arago (R.) . . . . Z
Banque (R. de la) . . . . Z
Barbazan (R.) . . . . Z
Bourdelle (Pl.) . . . . Z 4
Bourjade (Pl. L.) . . . . Z 6
Briand (Av. A.) . . . . Y 7
Cambon (R.) . . . . Z 9
Carmes (R. des) . . . . Z 10
Chamier (Av.) . . . . Y 12
Cladel (R. L.) X
Comédie (R. de la) . . . . Z 13
Consul-Dupuy (Allée du) . . Z 14
Coq (Pl. du) . . . . Z 16
Dr-Alibert (R.) X
Dr-Lacaze (R. du) . . . . Z 19
Doumerc (Bd B.) X
Foch (Pl. du Mar.) . . . . Z
Fort (R. du) . . . . Z
Gambetta (Av.) . . . . YZ
Garrisson (Bd G.) . . . . YZ
Gaulle (Av. Ch.-de) . . . . Y 25
Grand'Rue Sapiac . . . . Z
Grand'Rue Villenouvelle . . . X 28
Guibert (Pl.) . . . . Z 29
Herriot (Av. É.) . . . . Y 30
Hôtel-de-Ville (R. de l') . . . Z 31
Ingres (R. D.) X
Jourdain (R. A.) . . . . Z
Lacapelle (Fg) . . . . YZ
Lafon (R. du Pasteur L.) . . . Y 34
Lafon (R. Mary) . . . . Z 32
Lagrange (R. L.) . . . . YZ 35
Leclerc (Pl. du Gén.) . . . . . Z
Libération (Pl. de la) X
Lycée (R. du) . . . . Z
Malcousinat (R.) . . . . Z 36
Mandoune (R. de la) . . . . . . Z
Marceau-Hamecher (Av.) . . Y 37
Marre (R. H.) . . . . Z
Martyrs (Carrefour des) . . . Z 46
Marty (Pl. A.) . . . . XY
Mayenne (Av.) . . . . Y 50
Michelet (R.) . . . . Z 51
Midi-Pyrénées (Bd) . . . . Z 52
Monet (R. J.) . . . . Z 53
Montauriol (Bd) . . . . Y
Montmurat (Q. de) . . . . Z 54
Mortarieu (Allées de) . . . . . Z 56
Moustier (Fg du) . . . . Z
Nationale (Pl.) . . . . Z
Notre-Dame (R.) . . . . Z 60
Piquard (Sq Gén.) . . . . Z 62
Pouvillon (R. E.) . . . . Z
Prax-Paris (Pl.) . . . . Z
République (R. de la) . . . . . . Z 63
Résistance (R. de la) . . . . . . Z 64
Roosevelt (Pl. F.) . . . . Z 66
Ste-Claire (R.) . . . . Z
St-Jean (R.) . . . . X 67
Sapiac (Pont de) . . . . YZ 68
Sarrail (R. Gén.) . . . . Y 70
Verdun (Q. de) . . . . Z 71
10e-Dragons (Av. du) X
11e-Rég.-d'Infanterie
(Av. du) . . . . X 73
19-Août-1944 (Av. du) . . . . . X 75
22-Septembre (Pl. du) . . . . . Z 76

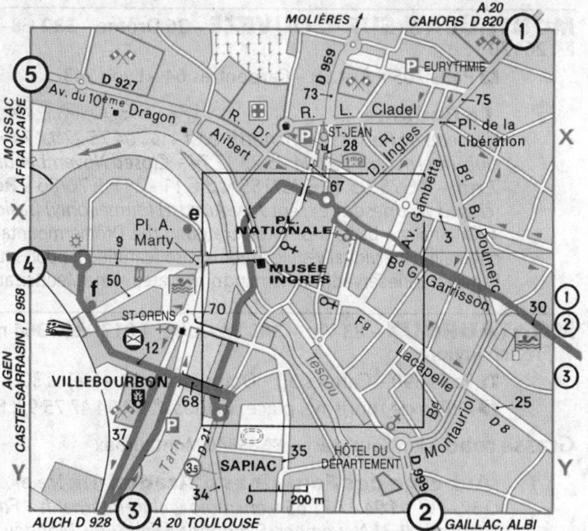

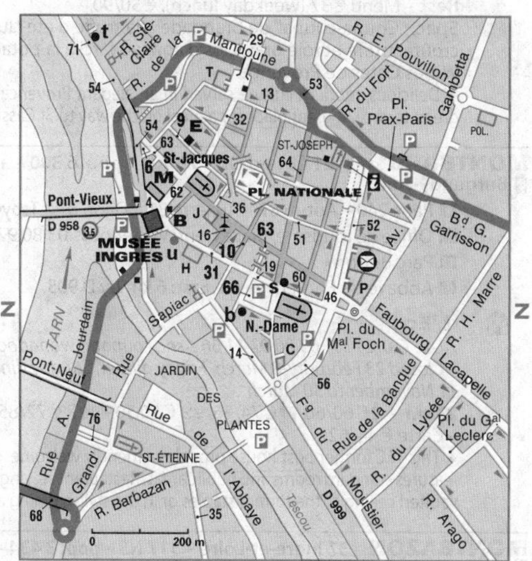

La Cuisine d'Alain

VISA

(opposite the station) – ✆ 05 63 66 06 66 – cuisinedalain@wanadoo.fr – Fax 05 63 66 19 39 – Closed 1st-20 August, 20 December-5 January, Monday lunch, Saturday lunch and Sunday Y f

Rest – Menu € 23 bi/60 – Carte € 47/64

◆ Dining room and lounge adorned with still life paintings, china and flower arrangements. Attractive terrace. Traditional cuisine; extensive choice of desserts.

Au Fil de l'Eau

VISA

14 quai Dr Lafforgue – ✆ 05 63 66 11 85 – aufildeleau82@wanadoo.fr – Fax 05 63 91 97 56 – Closed 10-20 July, Wednesday dinner except July-August, Sunday except lunch from September to June and Monday X e

Rest – Menu € 18 (weekday lunch), € 35/55 – Carte € 44/72

◆ This old-style house in a quiet street is home to a spacious and modern restaurant serving traditional meals and with a good selection of regional wines.

MONTAUBAN-SUR-L'OUVEZE – 26 Drôme – 332 G8 – pop. 85 – alt. 719 m – ✉ 26170 45 C3

▶ Paris 705 – Apt 68 – Carpentras 64 – Lyon 243

La Badiane

Hameau de Ruissas, 3 km north-east – ✆ 04 75 27 17 74 – la-badiane@club-internet.fr – Fax 04 75 27 17 74 – Closed November and December

7 rm – †€ 75/95 ††€ 75/155, ☕ € 11 – ½ P € 76/86 – **Rest** – table d'hôte *(closed Wednesday except July-August) (dinner only) (residents only)*

◆ Originally a barn, this hotel located in the Drôme mountains has been restored with originality. Individually-styled rooms, also featuring a pool, sauna and relaxation facilities. Family cuisine served in a charming dining area with a Mediterranean touch or on the terrace.

MONTAUROUX – 83 Var – 340 P4 – pop. 4 017 – alt. 364 m – ✉ 83440

French Riviera 41 C3

▶ Paris 890 – Cannes 36 – Draguignan 37 – Fréjus 30 – Grasse 21

ℹ Office de tourisme, place du Clos ✆ 04 94 47 75 90, Fax 04 94 47 61 97

Grasse road 3 km Southeast – ✉ 83340 Montauroux

Auberge des Fontaines d'Aragon (Eric Maio)

D 37 – ✆ 04 94 47 71 65 – ericmaio@club-internet.fr – Fax 04 94 47 71 65 – Closed 10-21 November, 5 January-4 February, Monday and Tuesday

Rest – Menu € 37 (weekday lunch), € 50/90

Spec. "Chupa-chupa" de brandade à la truffe d'été (June to August). Pigeon en croûte, truffe et foie gras. Dos d'agneau farci à la potagère (May to September).

Wines Côtes de Provence.

◆ Delicious, modern cuisine served in an elegant Provencal-style dining area or on the green terrace. A great place for a meal on the way to St Cassien lake.

MONTBARD – 21 Côte-d'Or – 320 G4 – pop. 6 300 – alt. 221 m – ✉ 21500

Burgundy-Jura 8 C2

▶ Paris 240 – Autun 87 – Auxerre 81 – Dijon 81 – Troyes 100

ℹ Office de tourisme, place Henri Vincenot ✆ 03 80 92 53 81, Fax 03 80 89 17 38

Parc Buffon★.

Abbaye de Fontenay★★★ East: 6 km by D 905.

L'Écu

7 r. A. Carré – ✆ 03 80 92 11 66 – snc.coupat@wanadoo.fr – Fax 03 80 92 14 13 – Closed 23 February-8 March, Friday dinner, Sunday dinner and Saturday from 11 November to 30 March

23 rm – †€ 60/66 ††€ 74/86, ☕ € 10,50 – ½ P € 72/85 – **Rest** – Menu € 20/52 – Carte € 44/62

◆ This 16C former post house provides a friendly welcome, country-style hospitality and features standard rooms and public areas. Restaurant serving traditional cuisine under the vaulted ceiling of the former stables or in the stylish dining area. Courtyard terrace.

MONTBAZON – 37 Indre-et-Loire – 317 N5 – pop. 3 434 – alt. 59 m – ✉ 37250

Châteaux of the Loire 11 B2

▶ Paris 247 – Châtellerault 59 – Chinon 41 – Loches 33 – Saumur 73 – Tours 15

ℹ Office de tourisme, esplanade du Val de l'Indre ✆ 02 47 26 97 87, Fax 02 47 26 22 42

Château d'Artigny ← Indre valley,

2 km southwest by D 17 – ✆ 02 47 34 30 30 – artigny@grandesetapes.fr – Fax 02 47 34 30 39

58 rm – †€ 160/450 ††€ 160/450, ☕ € 22 – 2 suites – **Rest** – Menu € 55/85 – Carte € 64/84

◆ This château with its wooded grounds and French-style gardens was designed in the 1920s by the perfumer Coty. Pure classical style and omnipresent splendour. Classic cuisine, excellent selection of wines and vintage armagnacs.

Moulin d' Artigny

7 rm – †€ 90 ††€ 90, ☕ € 22

◆ This pretty riverside pavilion, 800m from the château, offers rustic, less luxurious accommodation in a bucolic vein.

Domaine de la Tortinière ≤ the Indre valley,
2 km north on D 910 and D 287 – rm,
02 47 34 35 00 – domaine.tortiniere@wanadoo.fr – Fax 02 47 65 95 70
– Closed 20 December-28 February
25 rm – €150/340 €150/340, €16 – 5 suites – ½ P €140/235
Rest – *(closed Sunday dinner from November to March) (pre-book)* Menu (€32 bi), €39 bi (weekday lunch), €42/72 – Carte €54/61

♦ A Second Empire château in the grounds of a park overlooking the Indre. Elegant bedrooms full of charm. Pleasant swimming pool. The plush panoramic dining room has a pleasant terrace extension. Cooking in line with to current tastes.

Chancelière "Jeu de Cartes"
1 pl. Marronniers – 02 47 26 00 67
– lachanceliere@lachanceliere.fr – Fax 02 47 73 14 82
– Closed 10-27 August, 14 February-11 March, Sunday and Monday except holidays
Rest – Menu €38/43
Spec. Ravioles d'huîtres au champagne (October to May). Tajine de lotte aux fruits secs et aux fèves. Soufflé au Grand Marnier. **Wines** Montlouis, Chinon.

♦ An elegant regional-style building featuring a range of interior styles, including a cosy dining area with colourful décor. Inventive and classic cuisine.

West **5 km by D 910, D 287 and D 87 – ✉ 37250 Montbazon**

Le Moulin Fleuri with rm
– 02 47 26 01 12 – lemoulinfleuri@wanadoo.fr – Fax 02 47 34 04 71
– Closed 17-25 December, 21 January-28 February, Sunday dinner from 12 November to 30 March, Thursday lunch and Monday
9 rm – €75 €75, €13 – 1 suite – ½ P €79 – **Rest** – Menu (€22), €30/50 – Carte approx. €40

♦ This 16C former flourmill was once powered by a branch of the Indre River. Traditional recipes with a local flavour, superb cellar with over 800 wines, and waterside terrace. Classically furnished guestrooms with views of the river or garden.

MONTBÉLIARD – 25 Doubs – 321 K1 – pop. 27 570 – Built-up area 113 059 – alt. 325 m – ✉ 25200 Burgundy-Jura 17 C1

Paris 477 – Belfort 22 – Besançon 76 – Mulhouse 60 – Vesoul 60

Office de tourisme, 1, rue Henri-Mouhot 03 81 94 45 60, Fax 03 81 94 14 04

de Prunevelle Dampierre-sur-le-Doubs Ferme des Petits Bans, by Besançon road: 8 km, 03 81 98 11 77.

Old Montbéliard★: hôtel Beurnier-Rossel★ - Sochaux: Musée de l'aventure Peugeot★★.

Plan on following page

Bristol without rest
2 r. Velotte – 03 81 94 43 17 – hotel.bristol@wanadoo.fr – Fax 03 81 94 15 29
– Closed 26 July-18 August Z **b**
43 rm – €57/65 €60/70, €7

♦ A 1930s hotel in a partly pedestrianised street. Rooms with modern or older style decor. Quieter rooms at the rear. Wine bar.

Aux Relais Verts rm,
le Pied des Gouttes – 03 81 90 10 69
– hotelrelaisvert@wanadoo.fr – Fax 03 81 90 15 18
– Closed 23 December-1st January X **v**
64 rm – €68/88 €68/88, €7,50 – ½ P €89/109
Rest *Le Tire Bouchon* – *(closed Sat. lunchtime and Sun.)* Menu (€16), €29/40 – Carte €44/69

♦ A modern hotel in an urban development zone with small functional rooms that are arranged around a patio, or in a new wing where they are warmer and more spacious. Houseplants and paintings enliven the subdued decor in the dining room.

MONTBÉLIARD

Albert-Thomas (Pl.) .... Z 2
Audincourt (R. d') .... XY 4
Belchamp (R. de) .... Y 5
Besançon (Fg de) .... X 7
Blancheries (R.des) .... Z 8
Chabaud-Latour (Av.) .... X 9
Cuvier (R.) .... Z
Denfert-Rochereau (Pl.) .... Z 10
Dorian (Pl.) .... Z 12
Épinal (R. d') .... Z 13
Febvres (R. des) .... Z 14
Gambetta (Av.) .... X 15
Helvétie (Av. d') .... X 18
Jean-Jaurès (Av.) .... Y 20
Joffre (Av. du Mar.) .... X 22
Lattre-de-Tassigny (Av. du Mar. de) .... Z 23
Leclerc (R. Gén.) .... Z 24
Ludwigsburg (Av. de) .... X 26
Petite-Hollande (R.) .... XY 28
St-Georges (Pl.) .... Z 29
Schiffre (R. de) .... Z 32
Toussain (R. P.) .... X 36
Valentigney (R. de) .... Y 40

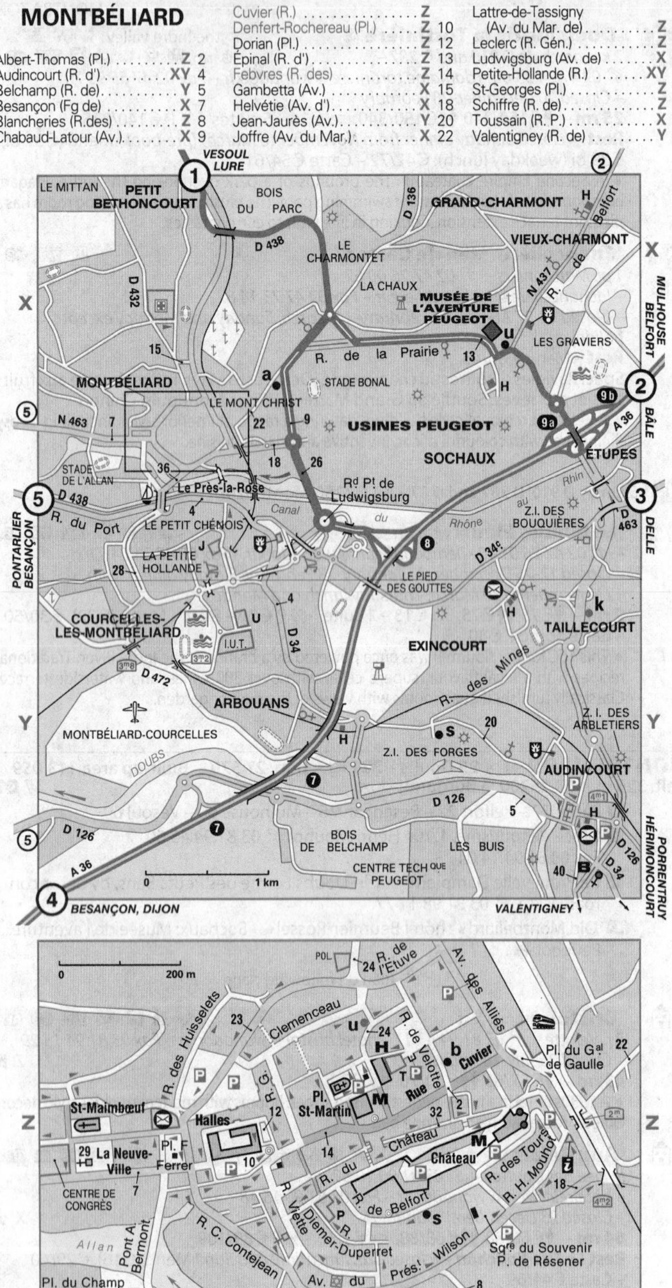

Le St-Martin (Olivier Prevot-Carme)
1 r. Gén. Leclerc – ✆ 03 81 91 18 37 – Fax 03 81 91 18 37 – Closed 1st-24 August, 1st-6 January, Saturday, Sunday and public holidays
Rest – Menu € 29/55 – Carte € 42/56 Z **u**
Spec. Cappuccino de grenouilles et cresson. Côte de veau braisée, purée de pomme de terre à l'huile d'olive. Chariot de desserts.
♦ Old building near Saint Martin Square. Small, intimate and stylish dining rooms. Traditional meals served; one set menu made up of market produce and another with seafood.

MONTBENOÎT – 25 Doubs – 321 I5 – pop. 219 – alt. 804 m – ✉ 25650

Burgundy-Jura 17 **C2**

Paris 464 – Besançon 61 – Morteau 17 – Pontarlier 15

Office de tourisme, 8, rue du Val Saugeais ✆ 03 81 38 10 32, Fax 03 81 38 10 32

Former abbey★: stalls★★, abbey church niche★★.

in La Longeville 5.5 km North by D 131 – pop. 488 – alt. 900 m – ✉ 25650

Le Crêt l'Agneau
Les Auberges – ✆ 03 81 38 12 51 – lecret.lagneau@wanadoo.fr – Closed 5-28 July
5 rm – €69/75 €78/98 – **Table d'hôte** – Menu € 25/28
♦ This 17C farmhouse in the countryside with very well-kept rooms, is run by a dynamic couple. There is a cosy ambiance particular to houses in the region. Local-style cuisine, cooked with care, and homemade bread.

in Maisons-du-Bois 4 km Southwest on D 437 – pop. 494 – alt. 810 m – ✉ 25650

Du Saugeais rm, VISA
– ✆ 03 81 38 14 65 – Fax 03 81 38 11 27 – Closed 20 January-8 February, Sunday dinner and Monday
Rest – Menu € 14,50 (weekday lunch), € 17/35
♦ Family roadside inn serving regional specialities in a country style dining room.

MONTBOUCHER-SUR-JABRON – 26 Drôme – 332 B6 – see Montélimar

MONTBRISON – 42 Loire – 327 D6 – pop. 14 589 – alt. 391 m – ✉ 42600

Lyon - Rhone Valley 44 **A2**

Paris 444 – Lyon 103 – Le Puy-en-Velay 99 – Roanne 68 – St-Étienne 45 – Thiers 68

Office de tourisme, cloître de Cordeliers ✆ 04 77 96 08 69, Fax 04 77 96 20 88

18 de Savigneux-les-Étangs Savigneux GAIA CONCEPT SAVIGNEUX, East: 4 km by D 496, ✆ 04 77 58 70 74 ;

9 Superflu Golf Club Saint-Romain-le-Puy Domaine des Sucs, Southeast: 8 km by D 8, ✆ 04 77 76 93 41.

Interior★ of N.-D.-d'Espérance collegiate church.

La Roseraie VISA
61 av. Alsace-Lorraine, (opposite the station) – ✆ 04 77 58 15 33 – Fax 04 77 58 93 88 – Closed 14-25 April, 18 August-6 September, Sunday dinner, Tuesday dinner and Wednesday
Rest – Menu € 18/56 – Carte € 19/51
♦ Modern fare made with local produce. Enjoy in a colourful dining room on the pleasant veranda or in the shade of a lime tree in summer.

in Savigneux 2 km East by D 496 – pop. 2 565 – alt. 382 m – ✉ 42600

Marytel without rest VISA
95 rte de Lyon – ✆ 04 77 58 72 00 – hm4203@inter-hotel.com – Fax 04 77 58 42 81
45 rm – €48/85 €53/95, € 8
♦ Practical roadside hotel. A new wing, the Relais Alice, offers very modern rooms equipped with the latest hi-tech gadgets. Double-glazing throughout.

XX **Yves Thollot**

93 rte de Lyon – ✆ 04 77 96 10 40 – mail@yves-thollot.com – Fax 04 77 58 31 92 – Closed 4-25 August, 5-12 January, 9-23 February, Sunday dinner, Tuesday dinner and Monday

Rest – Menu € 23/56 – Carte € 35/54

◆ A modern house surrounded by greenery. We recommend tasting the monkfish and tomato salad, scallops, and iced parfait with crystallised fruits.

in St-Romain-le-Puy 8 km Southeast by D8 and D107 – pop. 2 803 – alt. 405 m – ✉ 42610

Sous le Pic-La Pérolière without rest

20 r. Jean-Moulin – ✆ 04 77 76 97 10 – laperoliere@wanadoo.fr – Fax 04 77 76 97 10 – Closed 25 March-5 April, 5-17 September and 28 December-28 February

4 rm – €47/62 €55/70

◆ A haven of peace and quiet at the foot of an 11C priory. Antique and wrought iron furniture adorn this late 19C Forèze farmhouse. Breakfast is served in the conservatory overlooking the garden in summer.

MONTCEAU-LES-MINES – 71 Saône-et-Loire – 320 G9 – pop. 20 634 – alt. 285 m – ✉ 71300 Burgundy-Jura 8 C3

Paris 333 – Autun 47 – Chalon-sur-Saône 46 – Mâcon 69 – Moulins 100

Office de tourisme, 16, rue Carnot ✆ 03 85 69 00 00, Fax 03 85 69 00 01

du Château d'Avoise Montchanin 9 rue de Mâcon, by Chalon-sur-Saône road: 14 km, ✆ 03 85 78 19 19.

Mont-St-Vincent: tower ★★ 12 km by ②.

Plan on next page

Nota Bene

70 quai Jules Chagot – ✆ 03 85 69 10 15 – nota.bene.hotel@wanadoo.fr – Fax 03 85 69 10 20 AZ **b**

46 rm – €39 €62/72, €7

Rest – *(closed 5-20 August and Sunday)* Menu € 9 (weekday lunch), € 17/27 – Carte € 19/36

◆ Set opposite the canal bridge, this renovated hotel has a distinctive light wood façade. Providing simple and functional rooms. The house special is Tavola, a slice of bread garnished and cooked in the oven. The dining area features an Italian fresco.

XXX **Le France** (Jérôme Brochot) with rm rest, rm,

7 pl. Beaubernard – ✆ 03 85 67 95 30 – hotel-restaurant.lefrance@wanadoo.fr – Fax 03 85 67 95 44 – Closed 3-17 March, 28 July-18 August, 2-12 January, Saturday lunch, Sunday dinner and Monday AZ **k**

9 rm – €48 €58, €8 – ½ P €70

Rest – Menu (€ 20), € 38/80 – Carte € 44/88

Spec. Filet de bœuf confit au parmesan, rond de gîte en carpaccio. Sandre de Saône en croustillant de chèvre sec du Charolais (September to December). Filet rosé de pigeon, cuisse confite aux baies de genièvre, fricassée de fèves et girolles au foie gras (March to September). **Wines** Rully, Givry.

◆ This restaurant located on the heights of the town has an elegant, contemporary dining room in beige and white tones. Inventive fine dining and excellent value for money.

in St-Vallier 5 km South – pop. 9 541 – alt. 335 m – ✉ 71230

XX **L'Usine**

15 r. Robespierre – ✆ 03 85 57 67 62 – lusine@montceau-les-mines.com – Closed 19 February-10 March, 28 July-3 August, Sunday dinner, Monday and Tuesday

Rest – Menu € 17/41 – Carte € 27/46

◆ A factory converted into a restaurant. Unusual place with eclectic furnishings: office chairs, round tables, art exhibitions. Modern cuisine. Terrace.

MONTCEAU-LES-MINES

André-Malraux (R.) . . . . AY 3
Barbès (R.) . . . . ABZ
Bel Air (R. de) . . . . BY 4
Carnot (R.) . . . . AZ 6
Champ du Moulin (R. du) . BYZ 7
Chausson (R. Henri) . . . . BZ 9
Emorine (R. Antoine) . . . . . . BZ 10
Gauthey (Quai) . . . . AZ 12
Génelard (R. de) . . . . BZ 13
Guesde (Quai Jules) . . . . AY 14
Hospice (R. de l') . . . . AZ 15
Jean-Jacques-Rousseau (R.) . . . . BZ 16
Jean-Jaurès (R.) . . . . AZ
Lamartine (R.) . . . . AZ 19
Merzet (R. Étienne) . . . . BY 21
Palinges (R. de) . . . . BZ 22
Paul-Bert (R.) . . . . AZ 24
Pépinière (R. de la) . . . . AY 25
République (R. de la) . . . . . . AY 26
Sablière (R. de la) . . . . ABY 27
St-Vallier (R. de) . . . . BZ 28
Semard (R. de) . . . . BZ 30
Strasbourg (R. de) . . . . BZ 31
Tournus (R. de) . . . . BZ 33
8-Mai-1945 (R. du) . . . . BY 34
11-Nov.-1918 (R. du) . . . . AY 36

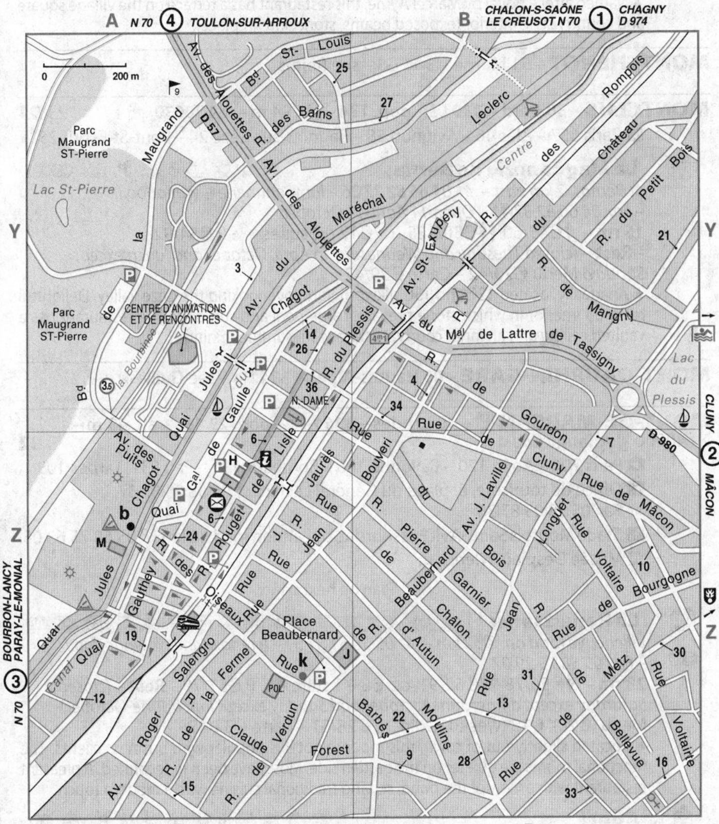

in Galuzot 5 km southwest by ③ and D 974 – ✉ 71230 St-Vallier

Le Moulin

– ✆ 03 85 57 18 85 – thierry.et.emilie@wanadoo.fr
– Closed 20 August-11 September, 20 February-5 March, Sunday dinner, Tuesday dinner and Wednesday
Rest – Menu (€ 16), € 19/28 – Carte approx. € 41
◆ This restaurant on the banks of the attractive Canal du Centre features a country-style dining area, and another room with a more refined and modern atmosphere. Serves traditional meals.

MONTCENIS – 71 Saône-et-Loire – **320** G9 – **see le Creusot**

MONTCHAUVET – 78 Yvelines – 311 F2 – pop. 254 – alt. 100 m – ✉ 78790

Paris 67 – Dreux 33 – Évreux 47 – Mantes-la-Jolie 16 – Rambouillet 39 – Versailles 49 18 **A2**

La Jument Verte

pl. de l'Église – ☎ 01 30 93 43 60 – Fax 01 30 93 49 20 – Closed 2-15 September and 9 February-1st March

Rest – Menu € 28/39 – Carte € 36/51

◆ Named after a novel by Marcel Aymé, this restaurant has a terrace on the village square and country style interior (exposed beams, stone and fireplace).

MONTCHENOT – 51 Marne – 306 G8 – see Reims

MONTCLUS – 30 Gard – 339 L3 – pop. 134 – alt. 94 m – ✉ 30630 23 D1

Paris 657 – Alès 46 – Avignon 58 – Bagnols-sur-Cèze 24 – Pont-St-Esprit 25

La Magnanerie de Bernas

rm, VISA MC AE

at Bernas, 2 km east – ☎ 04 66 82 37 36 – lamagnanerie@wanadoo.fr – Fax 04 66 82 37 41 – Open 11 April-19 October

15 rm – €45/60 €50/125, ☕ €12 – 2 suites – ½ P €54/92

– **Rest** – *(closed Tuesday and Wednesday in April, October and lunch except Sunday)* Menu € 20/42 – Carte € 29/47

◆ An ideally located 12C and 13C silkworm farm overlooking the Cèze valley. Delightful restored interior in which stone prevails. Large pool and sun deck. The restaurant has a vaulted ceiling and an inner courtyard terrace for summer dining.

MONT-DAUPHIN-GARE – 05 Hautes-Alpes – 334 H4 – see Guillestre

MONT-DE-MARSAN P – 40 Landes – 335 H11 – pop. 29 489 – alt. 43 m – ✉ 40000 Atlantic Coast 3 B2

Paris 706 – Agen 120 – Bayonne 106 – Bordeaux 131 – Pau 83 – Tarbes 103

Office de tourisme, 6, place du Général Leclerc ☎ 05 58 05 87 37, Fax 05 58 05 87 36

Stade Montois Saint-Avit Pessourdat, by Langon road: 10 km, ☎ 05 58 75 63 05.

Musée Despiau-Wlérick★.

Plan on next page

Le Renaissance

rm, rm, VISA MC AE

Villeneuve road on ②: 2 km – ☎ 05 58 51 51 51 – lerenaissance@wanadoo.fr – Fax 05 58 75 29 07

28 rm – €56/78 €62/91, ☕ €8 – 1 suite – ½ P €57/79 – **Rest** – *(closed Saturday except dinner June-October and Sunday except lunch June-October)* Menu (€ 20), € 18 (weekday diner), € 28/51 – Carte € 34/45

◆ Located slightly out of town, this modern hotel is popular with business clients. The functional rooms are quieter on the garden side. Most have been redecorated. A pleasant restaurant with a view of the pond, serving traditional cuisine with a modern touch.

Abor

rm, VISA MC

112 chemin de Lubet, Grenade road, 3 km on ④ ✉ 40280 – ☎ 05 58 51 58 00 – contact@aborhotel.com – Fax 05 58 75 78 78

68 rm – €61/72 €68/150, ☕ €12 – ½ P €57/74 – **Rest** – *(closed 22 December-2 January, Saturday lunch and Sunday lunch)* Menu (€ 13), € 22/35 – Carte € 26/47

◆ A modern building on the outskirts of the capital of the Marsan region with small, practical, soundproofed bedrooms. Decor without frills, but careful maintenance. Restaurant with colourful décor, serving traditional cuisine and buffet options.

Richelieu

rest, VISA MC AE

3 r. Wlérick – ☎ 05 58 06 10 20 – le.richelieu@wanadoo.fr – Fax 05 58 06 00 68 BY

33 rm – €47/60 €58/90, ☕ €8,50 – ½ P €50/64

Rest – *(closed 1st-11 January, Friday dinner from 25 July to 12 September, Sunday dinner and Saturday)* Menu (€ 17), € 19 (weekdays), € 27/40 – Carte approx. € 40

◆ A central hotel, near the Despiau Wlérick sculpture museum. The well-kept rooms are plain and modern and are gradually being redecorated. This restaurant is set up like a brasserie.

MONT-DE-MARSAN

Alsace-Lorraine (R. d') . . . AZ 2
Auribeau (Bd d') . . . . AZ 3
Bastiat (R. F.). . . . . ABZ
Bosquet (R. Mar.) . . . . AZ 4
Briand (R. A.). . . . . BY 5
Brouchet (Allées) . . . . BZ 6
Carnot (Av. Sadi) . . . . BZ 7
Delamarre (Bd) . . . . BZ 8
Despiau (R. Ch.) . . . . AZ 9
Farbos (Allées Raymond) . BZ 10
Gambetta (R. L.) . . . . BZ 12
Gaulle (Pl. Ch.-de) . . . . . . BY 13
Gourgues (R. D.-de) . . . . . BY 14
Landes (R. L.-des) . . . . BZ 15
Lasserre (R. Gén.). . . . . AZ 16
Lattre-de-Tassigny (Bd de) BY 17
Leclerc (Pl. du Gén.) . . . . . BZ 18
Lesbazeilles (R. A.) . . . . . . BZ 19
Martinon (R.) . . . . BZ 20
Pancaut (Pl. J.) . . . . AZ 21
Poincaré (Pl. R.). . . . . AY 22
Président-Kennedy (Av. du). . . . . BZ 23
Ruisseau (R. du) . . . . AZ 24
St-Jean-d'Août (R.) . . . . . . AY 25
St-Roch (Pl.). . . . . BZ 26
Victor-Hugo (R.). . . . . BY 27
8-Mai-1945 (R. du) . . . . . . BY 28
34e-d'Inf. (Av. du) . . . . BZ 29

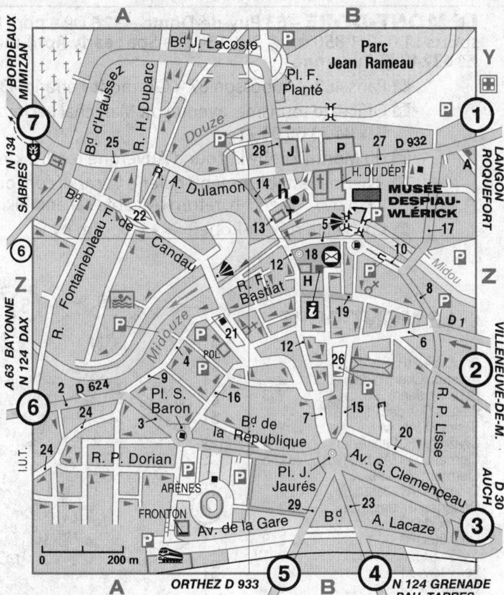

Les Clefs d'Argent

333 av.des Martyrs de la Résistance, via ⑥ – ✆ 05 58 06 16 45 – lesclefsdargent@orange.fr – Closed Christmas holidays and in August, Sunday dinner and Monday

Rest – Menu € 20 bi (weekday lunch), € 40/90 bi – Carte € 50/65

◆ Several cosy dining rooms and fireplace which is glorious in winter; this modest yet charming establishment serves regional fare tweaked with a few external influences.

à Uchacq-et-Parentis by ⑦ : 7 km – pop. 495 – alt. 50 m – ✉ 40090

Didier Garbage

N 134 – ✆ 05 58 75 33 66 – restau.didier.garbage@wanadoo.fr – Fax 05 58 75 22 77 – Closed 2-20 January, Tuesday dinner, Sunday dinner and Monday

Rest – Menu € 25/75 – Carte € 47/74

Rest *Bistrot* – R N 134 – Carte € 22/41

◆ Rustic interior, wooden tables and old knick-knacks. Regulars jostle for tables when baby eels turn up in the day's catch! A simple setting with garlands of peppers hanging from the ceiling. Hearty bistro dishes.

MONTDIDIER – 80 Somme – 301 I10 – pop. 6 328 – alt. 82 m – ✉ 80500

Northern France and the Paris Region 36 **B2**

Paris 108 – Compiègne 36 – Amiens 39 – Beauvais 49 – Péronne 48 – St-Quentin 65

Office de tourisme, 5, place du Général-de-Gaulle ✆ 03 22 78 92 00, Fax 03 22 78 00 88

Dijon

1 pl. 10 Août 1918, (Breteuil road) – ✆ 03 22 78 01 35 – Fax 03 22 78 27 24 – Closed 11-31 August and Sunday dinner

19 rm – †€ 40 ††€ 60, ☐ € 7 – ½ P € 56 – **Rest** – *(closed Sunday dinner and Saturday)* Menu (€ 13,50), € 17/27 – Carte € 25/43

◆ This hotel, near the railway station, offers a carefully-arranged rustic setting. All rooms have been renovated. Those at the front have double-glazing. Charming service. Traditional food in the birthplace of Parmentier, the famous potato promoter.

LE MONT-DORE – 63 Puy-de-Dôme – 326 D9 – pop. 1 682 – alt. 1 050 m – Winter sports : 1 050/1 850 m 2 18 – Spa : early April-mid Oct. – Casino Z – ✉ 63240 Auvergne

5 B2

- Paris 462 – Aubusson 87 – Clermont-Ferrand 43 – Issoire 49 – Ussel 56
- Office de tourisme, avenue du Maréchal Leclerc ☎ 04 73 65 20 21, Fax 04 73 65 05 71
- du Mont-Doreby la Tour d'Auvergne road: 2 km, ☎ 04 73 65 00 79.
- Thermal establishment: galerie César★, concourse ★ - Puy de Sancy ✻★★★ 5 km by ② then 1 h. return by cable car and hiking - Funiculaire du capucin★.
- Col de la Croix-St-Robert ✻★★ 6,5 km by ②.

LE MONT-DORE

Apollinaire (R. S.) .... Y 2
Artistes (Chemin des) .... Z
Banc (R. Jean) .... Y 3
Belges (Av. des) .... Y
Bertrand (Av. M.) .... Y
Chazotte (R. Capitaine) .... Y 4
Clemenceau (Av.) .... Z 5
Clermont (Av. de) .... Y 7
Crouzets (Av. des) .... Y
Déportés (R. des) .... Z 8
Dr-Claude (R.) .... Y
Duchâtel (R.) .... Z 9
Favart (R.) .... Y 12
Ferry (Av. J.) .... YZ
Gaulle (Pl. Ch.-de) .... Y 14
Guyot-Dessaigne (Av.) .... Y 15
Latru (R.) .... Y
Lavialle (R.) .... Y
Leclerc (Av. du Gén.) .... Y
Libération (Av. de la) .... YZ
Melchi-Roze (Chemin) .... Y
Meynadier (R.) .... YZ
Mirabeau (Bd) .... Y
Montlosier (R.) .... Y 19
Moulin (R. Jean) .... Z 20
Panthéon (Pl. du) .... Z 22
Pasteur (R.) .... Y
Ramond (R.) .... Z 24
République (Pl. de la) .... Z 26
Rigny (R.) .... Z 28
Sand (Allée G.) .... YZ 29
Sanistas (R. F.) .... Y
Verrier (R. P.) .... Y
Wilson (Av.) .... Y
19-Mars-1962 (R. du) .... Y 32

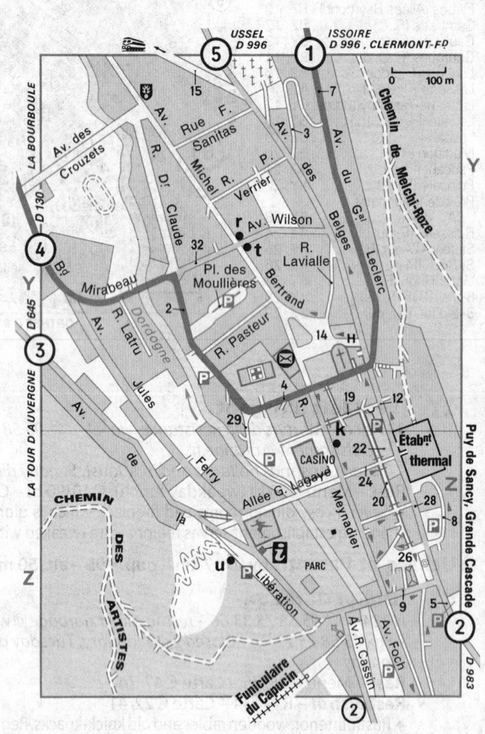

 **Panorama** – rest, P, VISA, MC, AE

av. de la Libération – ☎ 04 73 65 11 12 – contact@hotel-le-panorama.com – Fax 04 73 65 20 80 – Open 1st May-6 October and 22 December-10 March

39 rm – €70/85 €70/85, €14 – ½ P €64/74 – **Rest** – *(dinner only in winter)* Menu (€16), €29/58 – Carte €39/48 Z u

◆ A 1960s building overlooking the railway station, near the "Chemin des Artistes". Wood-panelled, well-kept rooms. Fine panoramic pool. From one of the dining rooms you can see the whole valley. Traditional food.

Le Castelet – rest, P, VISA, MC, AE

av. M. Bertrand – ☎ 04 73 65 05 29 – info@hotel-castelet.com – Fax 04 73 65 27 95 – Open 11 May-27 September, 22 December-30 March Y t

35 rm – €55/65 €59/76, €9 – ½ P €51/65 – **Rest** – Menu €20/24

◆ A 1920s house with a contemporary feel to the lobby-lounge. Soberly decorated bedrooms; those facing the garden are brighter and more cheerful. Two dining rooms, one of which is decorated with an Asian touch. Regional menu.

Parc rest, VISA MC AE

r. Meynadier – ☎ 04 73 65 02 92 – hotelduparc.md@wanadoo.fr – Fax 04 73 65 28 36 – Open 2 May-5 October and 26 December-25 March Z **k**

37 rm – †€ 47/51 ††€ 51/56, ☕ € 6,50 – ½ P € 47/50

Rest – *(residents only)* Menu € 15/17 – Carte € 12,50/28

♦ A century-old building in the centre of the famous thermal spa, where the Gauls used to take the waters. Practical and successfully-renovated rooms. Pretty mouldings, high ceiling, restored parquet and a lovely fireplace characterise this pleasant dining room.

Le Wilson without rest VISA MC

1 av. Wilson – ☎ 04 73 65 00 06 – residencewilson@free.fr – Fax 04 73 65 27 95 – Closed 1st April-15 May and 7 October-20 December Y **r**

16 rm – †€ 49/60 ††€ 49/60, ☕ € 7

♦ A large, early-20C villa, housing functional and well-equipped studio flats, available for one night or longer stays.

Les Charmettes without rest VISA MC AE

30 av. G. Clemenceau, via ② – ☎ 04 73 65 05 49 – charmettes-lemontdore@wanadoo.fr – Fax 04 73 65 20 28 – Closed 14 May-2 June and 3 November-12 December

21 rm – †€ 41/43 ††€ 44/48, ☕ € 8

♦ Hotel facing in the direction of the majestic Puy de Sancy. Small, simple rooms are available here for a faithful hiker clientèle.

La Closerie de Manou without rest

Le Genestoux, 3 km via ⑤ and D 996 – ☎ 04 73 65 26 81 – lacloseriedemanou@club-internet.fr – Fax 04 73 65 58 34 – Open April-mid October

5 rm ☕ – †€ 55/65 ††€ 80/85

♦ This regional style 18C Auvergne building is a real wonder. The spacious cosy rooms all have personal details. Great hospitality.

Le Pitsounet VISA MC AE

3km by ⑤ on D 996 – ☎ 04 73 65 00 67 – aubergelepitsounet@wanadoo.fr – Fax 04 73 65 06 22 – Closed mid October-mid December, Sunday dinner and Monday except July-August and February

Rest – Menu € 18/34 – Carte € 20/38

♦ This chalet at the side of a main road offers a rural atmosphere with two rustic dining rooms, copious regional food and reasonable prices.

at Guéry Lake 8.5 km by ① on D 983 – ✉ 63240 Auvergne

Lake★.

Auberge du Lac de Guéry with rm VISA MC

– ☎ 04 73 65 02 76 – jean.leclerc2@wanadoo.fr – Fax 04 73 65 08 78 – Open 15 January-30 March and 7 April-15 October

10 rm – †€ 48 ††€ 57, ☕ € 8 – ½ P € 59

Rest – *(closed Wednesday lunch except school holidays)* Menu € 18/40 – Carte € 23/37

♦ An inn by a lake in the enchanting Auvergne Regional Volcano Park. Regional cuisine served in a recently redecorated rustic dining room.

at the foot of Puy de Sancy 3 km by ② – ✉ 63240 Le Mont-Dore

Puy Ferrand rest, VISA MC

– ☎ 04 73 65 18 99 – info@hotel-puy-ferrand.com – Fax 04 73 65 28 38 – Closed 31 March-5 April and 3 November-20 December

36 rm – †€ 62/82 ††€ 64/84, ☕ € 8,50 – ½ P € 55/71 – **Rest** – Menu € 15 (weekday lunch)/35 – Carte € 25/43

♦ This imposing chalet built at the foot of the ski slopes offers you a deep breath of fresh air. Panoramic bar, cosy lounge, lovely pool and pleasantly-redecorated rooms. Wood-panelled restaurant with fireplace that creates a pleasant, mountain-style atmosphere.

MONTEAUX – 41 Loir-et-Cher – 318 D7 – pop. 691 – alt. 62 m – ✉ 41150

Paris 210 – Orléans 85 – Blois 25 – Tours 40 – Joué-lès-Tours 51 — 11 **A1**

Le Château du Portail without rest

at Besnerie, 1 km on Mesland road – ✆ 02 54 70 22 88 – chateauduportail@orange.fr – Fax 02 54 70 22 32 – Closed 15 December-15 January

6 rm – €150 €160/250

◆ Ideally located for visiting the chateaux of the Loire, between Blois and Amboise. Luxurious 17C-18C residence with formal garden and rooms with antique furniture.

MONTECH – 82 Tarn-et-Garonne – 337 D8 – pop. 3 491 – alt. 100 m – ✉ 82700

28 **B2**

Paris 643 – Toulouse 50 – Montauban 14 – Colomiers 56 – Tournefeuille 57

La Maison de l'Eclusier

Le Port – ✆ 05 63 65 37 61 – Fax 05 63 67 56 67 – Closed 29 June-8 July, 30 August-6 September, 1st-January, Tuesday lunch in July -August, Sunday dinner from September to June, Saturday lunch and Monday

Rest – Menu (€ 19), € 23 (weekday lunch), € 26/37 – Carte € 26/40

◆ An old lock keeper's house and pretty terrace by the canal side. Tasty traditional fare chalked up on a slate; small but well chosen cellar and fine selection of wines by the glass.

MONTEILS – 82 Tarn-et-Garonne – 337 F6 – see Caussade

MONTÉLIER – 26 Drôme – 332 D4 – pop. 3 120 – alt. 219 m – ✉ 26120

43 **E2**

Paris 567 – Crest 27 – Romans-sur-Isère 13 – Valence 12

La Martinière

ZA La Pimpie, Chabeuil road – ✆ 04 75 59 60 65 – Fax 04 75 59 69 20

30 rm – €47 €57, € 7,50 – ½ P € 50 – **Rest** – Menu € 16 (weekdays)/61 – Carte € 21/64

◆ This hotel is housed in a contemporary building, providing redecorated rooms and a lovely swimming pool. A modern Provençal dining area with covered terrace. Traditional cuisine and a good selection of Bordeaux wines.

MONTÉLIMAR – 26 Drôme – 332 B6 – pop. 31 344 – alt. 90 m – ✉ 26200

Lyon - Rhone Valley — 44 **B3**

Paris 602 – Avignon 83 – Nîmes 108 – Le Puy-en-Velay 132 – Valence 47

Office de tourisme, allées Provençales ✆ 04 75 01 00 20, Fax 04 75 52 33 69

de La Valdaine Montboucher-sur-Jabron Château du Monard, East: 4 km by D 540, ✆ 04 75 00 71 33 ;

de la Drôme provencale Clansayesby N 7 and Nyons road: 21 km, ✆ 04 75 98 57 03.

Allées provençales★ - Musée de la Miniature★ M.

Site★★ du Château de Rochemaure★, 7 km by ④.

Plan on next page

Sphinx without rest

19 bd Desmarais – ✆ 04 75 01 86 64 – reception@sphinx-hotel.fr – Fax 04 75 52 34 21 – Closed 21 December-12 January — Y **b**

24 rm – €49/51 €54/75, € 6,50

◆ The pretty courtyard, warm parquet floors and wood panelling give an undeniable charm to this 17C mansion located opposite the typical Provençal streets. Fairly quiet rooms.

Du Parc without rest

27 av. Ch. de Gaulle – ✆ 04 75 01 00 73 – hotelduparc26@wanadoo.fr – Fax 04 75 51 27 93 – Closed 21-28 December and 8-22 February — Y **a**

16 rm – €40/55 €46/60, € 6,50

◆ A welcoming little hotel located near a park and the centre of town. Providing redecorated rooms, and serving breakfast in a warm and colourful dining area or on the terrace.

MONTÉLIMAR

Adhémar (R.) . . . . Z 2
Aygu (Av.). . . . . Z 4
Baudina (R.) . . . . Y 5
Blanc (Pl. L.) . . . . Z 6
Bourgneuf (R.) . . . . Y 8
Carmes (Pl. des) . . . . Y 9
Chemin Neuf (R. du) . . . . Z 10
Clercs (Pl. des). . . . . Y 12
Corneroche (R.) . . . . Y 14
Cuiraterie (R.) . . . . Z 15
Desmarais (Bd Marre). . . . . Y 17
Dormoy (Pl. M.) . . . . Z 18
Espoulette (Av. d') . . . . Z 19
Europe (Pl. de l') . . . . Z 21
Fust (Pl. du) . . . . Y 23
Gaulle (Bd Gén.-de) . . . . Z 25
Juiverie (R.) . . . . Y 28
Julien (R. Pierre) . . . . YZ
Loubet (Pl. Émile) . . . . Z 29
Loubet (R. Émile) . . . . Z 30
Meyer (R. M.) . . . . Y 32
Monnaie-Vieille (R.) . . . . Y 34
Montant-au-Château (R.) . . . . . Y 35
Planel (Pl. A.) . . . . Z 37
Poitiers (R. Diane de). . . . . Z 38
Porte Neuve (R.) . . . . Z 39
Prado (Pl. du) . . . . Y 41
Puits Neuf (R. du) . . . . Y 42
Rochemaure (Av. de) . . . . Y 47
St-Martin (Montée) . . . . Y 50
St-Pierre (R.). . . . . Y 51
Villeneuve (Av. de). . . . . Y 54

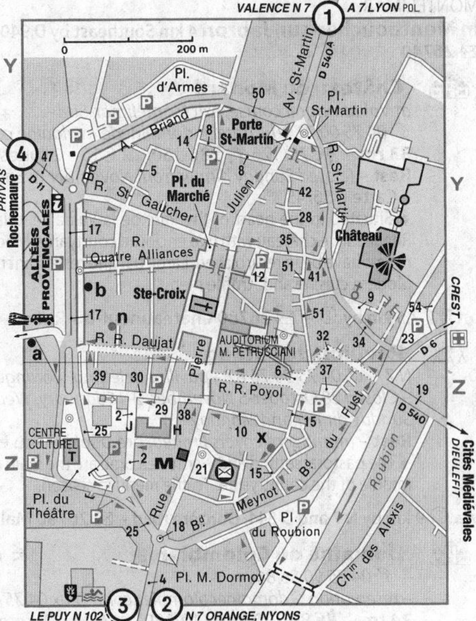

Les Senteurs de Provence

202 rte de Marseille, via ② – ✆ 04 75 01 43 82 – lsdp.restaurant@wanadoo.fr – Fax 04 75 01 21 81 – Closed Sunday dinner, Tuesday dinner and Wednesday

Rest – Menu € 16/34 – Carte € 28/54

◆ New Provençal decoration in yellow and green with wrought-iron furniture in this restaurant serving modern cuisine with a distinct Southern flavour.

Petite France

34 imp. Raymond Daujat – ✆ 04 75 46 07 94 – Closed 13 July-4 August, 21-25 December, Sunday and Monday Y **n**

Rest – Menu (€ 12,50), € 20/28 – Carte € 30/45

◆ This restaurant was named after the old district of Strasbourg. The interior mural depicts an Alsatian village square. Traditional dishes served.

Le Grillon

40 r. Cuiraterie – ✆ 04 75 01 79 02 – Fax 04 75 01 79 02 Z **x**
– Closed 4-28 July, 22-29 December, Thursday dinner, Sunday dinner and Monday

Rest – Menu € 13 (weekday lunch), € 15/30 – Carte € 25/45 ◆ You may not hear any crickets, but you'll certainly taste the flavours of regional cooking (including a "truffle menu" in winter) in the rustic dining area or on the terrace.

in St-Marcel-lès-Sauzet **7 km Northeast by D 6 – pop. 1 104 – alt. 110 m – ✉ 26740**

Le Prieuré

– ✆ 04 75 46 78 68 – restaurant-leprieuré@wanadoo.fr – Fax 04 75 46 10 96 – Closed 1st-15 October, 19-26 February, Sunday dinner, Wednesday dinner and Monday from September to mid July, Monday lunch and Saturday lunch from mid July to end August

Rest – Menu (€ 16), € 29/39 – Carte € 33/63

◆ A large shaded terrace with a colourful dining area feature in this lovely regional stone building. A pleasant place to stop for a traditional, Provencal meal.

in Montboucher-sur-Jabron 4 km Southeast by D 940 – pop. 1 424 – alt. 124 m – ✉ 26740

Château du Monard – rm,
at Valdaine golf course, exit Montélimar-Sud –
✆ 04 75 00 71 30 – hotel@domainedelavaldaine.com – Fax 04 75 00 71 31
33 rm – €75/126 €86/150, € 15 – 2 suites – ½ P € 76/106
Rest – *(closed Sunday dinner from November to Easter)* Menu (€ 20), € 25 bi/45 – Carte € 36/45
◆ Situated in the heart of the Parc de la Valdaine, this group of buildings comprises a Renaissance château with two enclosed courtyards. Modernised interior. Ten of the guestrooms have been refurbished. Large bar and restaurant refurbished in contemporary style. Modern cuisine and "truffle menu".

on N 7 7.5 km by ② – ✉ 26780 Châteauneuf-du-Rhône

Pavillon de l'Étang
N 7 – ✆ 04 75 90 76 82 – pavillondelétang@orange.fr – Fax 04 75 90 72 39 – Closed 28 October-5 November, 2-16 January, Wednesday dinner, Sunday dinner and Monday
Rest – *(number of covers limited, pre-book)* Menu € 26/70 bi – Carte € 35/65
◆ The pastoral setting and warm welcome are the main assets of this house, located in the middle of the countryside. Truffle menu in season.

via ② 9 km by N 7 and D 844, Donzère road – ✉ 26780 Malataverne

Domaine du Colombier rest,
– ✆ 04 75 90 86 86
– reservation@domainecolombier.com – Fax 04 75 90 79 40
24 rm – €80/110 €110/180, € 15 – 2 suites – **Rest** – Menu € 30 (weekday lunch), € 50/83 – Carte € 78/85
◆ Large, completely renovated residence with elegant guestrooms, the most luxurious of which are decorated with period furniture. Attractive swimming pool and flower garden. Contemporary-style dining rooms, one of which has a vaulted ceiling, plus a courtyard terrace surrounded by greenery.

MONTENACH – 57 Moselle – 307 J2 – see Sierck-les-Bains

MONTESQUIOU – 32 Gers – 336 D8 – pop. 586 – alt. 214 m – ✉ 32320 28 A2

Paris 783 – Toulouse 112 – Auch 33 – Tarbes 60 – Aureilhan 57
Office de tourisme, Mairie ✆ 05 62 70 91 18

Maison de la Porte Fortifiée
in the Village – ✆ 05 62 70 97 06 – maison@porte-fortifiee.eu – Fax 05 62 70 97 06 – Closed 6 January-29 February
4 rm – €65/80 €80/110 – ½ P € 69/84 – **Table d'hôte** – Menu € 29/39
◆ Establishment located near the fortified gate (13C) of a peaceful village dominating the valley. Large rooms with fireplace and period furniture. Garden-terrace. Local or more exotic dishes at dinner (reservation required).

MONTEUX – 84 Vaucluse – 332 C9 – see Carpentras

MONTFAUCON – 25 Doubs – 321 G3 – see Besançon

MONTFAVET – 84 Vaucluse – 332 C10 – see Avignon

MONTFORT-EN-CHALOSSE – 40 Landes – 335 F12 – pop. 1 210 – alt. 110 m – ✉ 40380 Atlantic Coast 3 B3

Paris 744 – Aire-sur-l'Adour 57 – Dax 19 – Hagetmau 27 – Mont-de-Marsan 43 – Orthez 29
Office de tourisme, 25, place Foch ✆ 05 58 98 58 50, Fax 05 58 98 58 01
Musée de la Chalosse★.

Aux Tauzins rest, VISA
rte d'Hagetmau – ✆ 05 58 98 60 22 – auxtauzins@wanadoo.com – Fax 05 58 98 45 79 – Closed 1st-15 October, February, Sunday dinner and Monday except July-August
16 rm – €57 €76, €7,50 – ½ P €74 – **Rest** – *(closed Monday lunchtime in July-August)* Menu €22/40 – Carte €27/62
◆ A large building with simple, well-kept rooms, most of them with a balcony and a view of the Chalosse vales. Attractive garden with miniature golf. This restaurant is reserved for non-smokers on Sundays and public holidays. Featuring a country-style dining area and terrace with panoramic views, serving regional specialties.

MONTFORT-L'AMAURY – 78 Yvelines – 311 G3 – pop. 3 137 – alt. 185 m – ✉ 78490 Northern France and the Paris Region 18 A2

Paris 46 – Dreux 36 – Houdan 18 – Mantes-la-Jolie 31 – Rambouillet 19 – Versailles 29

Syndicat d'initiative, 3, rue Amaury ✆ 01 34 86 87 96, Fax 01 34 86 87 96

du Domaine du Tremblay Le Tremblay-sur-Mauldre Place de l'Eglise, East: 8 km, ✆ 01 34 94 25 70.

Church★ - Former cemetery★ - Château ruins ←★.

Saint-Laurent without rest VISA AE
2 pl. Lebreton – ✆ 01 34 57 06 66 – reception@hotelsaint-laurent.com – Fax 01 34 86 12 27 – Closed 3-25 August
15 rm – €88/148 €98/158, €11
◆ This superb 17C manor house has been tastefully renovated, now providing rooms, some with private terrace, others on the top floor with original wooden beams.

MONTGIBAUD – 19 Corrèze – 329 J2 – pop. 241 – alt. 460 m – ✉ 19210 24 B2

Paris 434 – Arnac-Pompadour 15 – Limoges 47 – St-Yrieix-la-Perche 23 – Tulle 21 – Uzerche 25

Le Tilleul de Sully VISA
– ✆ 05 55 98 01 96 – Fax 05 55 98 01 96 – Closed 15 December-5 January, Tuesday dinner from mid November to mid March, Sunday dinner and Monday except holidays
Rest – *(number of covers limited, pre-book)* Menu €17/34 – Carte €30/40
◆ A country restaurant near an old linden tree, serving as a pilgrim stopover on the Santiago de Compostela route. Rustic dining area with fireplace. Traditional fare.

MONTGRÉSIN – 60 Oise – 305 G6 – see Chantilly

LES MONTHAIRONS – 55 Meuse – 307 D4 – see Verdun

MONTHERMÉ – 08 Ardennes – 306 K3 – pop. 2 791 – alt. 180 m – ✉ 08800 Northern France and the Paris Region 14 C1

Paris 247 – Charleville-Mézières 18 – Fumay 21

Office de tourisme, place Jean-Baptiste Clément ✆ 03 24 54 46 73, Fax 03 24 54 87 88

Roche aux Sept Villages ←★★ South: 3 km - Roc de la Tour ←★★ East: 3,5 km then 20 mn - Longue Roche ←★★ Northwest: 2.5 km then 30 mn - Roche à Sept Heures ←★ North: 2 km - Roma rock ←★ South: 4 km - Semoy Valley ★: Croix d'enfer ←★ East.

Roches de Laifour★ Northwest: 6 km.

Franco-Belge rest, VISA AE
2 r. Pasteur – ✆ 03 24 53 01 20 – le.franco.belge@wanadoo.fr – Closed December
15 rm – €44 €49/61, €6,50 – **Rest** – *(closed Friday off season and Sunday dinner)* Menu €13 (weekday lunch), €22/33 – Carte €21/37
◆ A cheerful family-run hotel near the old town centre on the right bank of the Meuse. Modestly styled but well-kept rooms, gradually being renovated. This "pre-1940s style" restaurant has a flower-decked terrace with a climbing vine.

MONTHIEUX – 01 Ain – **328** C5 – **pop. 578 – alt. 295 m** – ✉ **01390** 43 **E1**

Paris 443 – Lyon 31 – Bourg-en-Bresse 38 – Meximieux 26 – Villefranche-sur-Saône 19

Le Gouverneur rm,

(D 6) – ☎ 04 72 26 42 00
– info@golfgouverneur.fr – Fax 04 72 26 42 20 – Closed 21 December-7 January
53 rm – €95/115 €105/160, €11 – ½ P €89/94 – **Rest** – *(closed Sunday off season) (dinner only)* Menu €25/55 – Carte €43/74

◆ Out in the countryside, this former 14C property of the Governor of the Dombes has a new wing housing stylish modern rooms. Nine and 18-hole golf courses and fishing. Attractive, modern dining rooms (one overlooks the golf course); traditional menus.

MONTHION – 73 Savoie – **333** L4 – see Albertville

MONTI – 06 Alpes-Maritimes – **341** F5 – see Menton

MONTIGNAC – 24 Dordogne – **329** H5 – **pop. 3 023 – alt. 77 m** – ✉ **24290**
Dordogne-Berry-Limousin 4 **D1**

Paris 513 – Brive-la-Gaillarde 39 – Limoges 126 – Périgueux 54 – Sarlat-la-Canéda 25

Office de tourisme, place Bertran-de-Born ☎ 05 53 51 82 60, Fax 05 53 50 49 72

Grottes de Lascaux★★ Southeast: 2 km.

Le Thot, Cro-magnon area★ South: 7 km - Église★★ de St-Amand de Coly East: 7 km.

Relais du Soleil d'Or rm,

16 r. 4 Septembre – ☎ 05 53 51 80 22 – soleil-or@wanadoo.fr – Fax 05 53 50 27 54 – Closed 18 February-3 March
32 rm – €66/75 €66/150, €12 – ½ P €70/90
Rest – *(closed Sunday dinner and Monday from 4 November to 16 March)* Menu €25/54 – Carte €44/55
Rest *Le Bistrot* – *(closed Sunday dinner and Monday from 4 November to 16 March)* Menu €12,50 – Carte €16/34

◆ A former coaching inn in the centre of the small Périgord town. In the annexe, the comfortable rooms have discreet modern touches; most of them overlook a peaceful park. Restaurant-veranda offering a traditional menu. Simple meals offered at Le Bistrot.

Hostellerie la Roseraie

11 pl. d'Armes – ☎ 05 53 50 53 92 – hotelroseraie@wanadoo.fr
– Fax 05 53 51 02 23 – Open 23 March-1st November
14 rm – €75/110 €80/240, €12 – ½ P €78/140 – **Rest** – *(closed lunch weekdays off season)* Menu (€19 bi), €22/48 – Carte approx. €38

◆ In the heart of the medieval village, this 19C hotel on the banks of the Vézère provides cosy, personalised rooms and a lovely rose garden. Stylish dining room, pleasant shaded terrace and classical menu.

MONTIGNAT – 23 Creuse – **325** J3 – see Chénérailles

MONTIGNY – 76 Seine-Maritime – **304** F5 – see Rouen

MONTIGNY-LA-RESLE – 89 Yonne – **319** F4 – **pop. 548 – alt. 155 m** – ✉ **89230** 7 **B1**

Paris 170 – Auxerre 14 – St-Florentin 19 – Tonnerre 32

Le Soleil d'Or

N77 – ☎ 03 86 41 81 21 – le-soleil-dor@wanadoo.fr – Fax 03 86 41 86 88
16 rm – €54 €57, €9,50 – ½ P €54 – **Rest** – Menu (€12), €22/48 – Carte €40/62

◆ A former coaching inn on the main road, this hotel provides practical rooms to the rear in the converted outbuildings. Slightly reminiscent of a motel in layout. Traditional fare served in a colourful setting; lovely little wainscoted sitting room.

MONTIGNY-LE-BRETONNEUX – 78 Yvelines – 311 I3 – 101 22 – see Paris, Area (St-Quentin-en-Yvelines)

MONTIGNY-LE-ROI – 52 Haute-Marne – 313 M6 – pop. 2 211 – alt. 404 m – ✉ 52140 14 C3

Paris 296 – Bourbonne-les-Bains 21 – Chaumont 35 – Langres 23 – Neufchâteau 50

Moderne rest, P VISA

– *03 25 90 30 18 – hotel.moderne52@wanadoo.fr – Fax 03 25 90 71 80*
– Closed Friday and Saturday in January, Sunday from October to March
24 rm – €59 €80, €8,50 – ½ P €75/78 – **Rest** – *(closed Sunday dinner October-March and Friday dinner)* Menu €20/42 – Carte €39/49

◆ Building located at a crossroads with well-kept, soundproofed rooms (some renovated), equipped with modern furniture. Family atmosphere. 1980s-style dining room. Large choice of menus, including a small traditional menu.

MONTIGNY-SUR-AVRE – 28 Eure-et-Loir – 311 C3 – pop. 275 – alt. 140 m – ✉ 28270 11 B1

Paris 111 – Alençon 85 – Argentan 86 – Chartres 52 – Dreux 35 – Verneuil-sur-Avre 9

Moulin des Planches rm, P VISA

North-east: 1.5 km along the D 102 – 02 37 48 25 97
– moulin.des.planches@wanadoo.fr
– Closed 29 July-10 August, 25 February-18 March, Sunday dinner and Monday
18 rm – €56/97 €62/113, €9 – ½ P €73
Rest – Menu €30/68 – Carte €30/48

◆ A mill on the Avre, in the heart of the countryside. Bedrooms are equipped with period furniture and mostly have views of the river, while a few overlook the park. The restaurant is full of character, with its tiled floor, patina beams and brick walls. Modern cuisine served.

MONTIPOURET – 36 Indre – 323 H7 – pop. 507 – alt. 200 m – ✉ 36230

Paris 295 – Châteauroux 28 – Issoudun 37 – Orléans 169 12 C3

in La Brande 5 km northeast by D49 and secondary road - ✉36230 Montipouret

Maison Voilà P

– *02 54 31 17 91 – maisonvoila@yahoo.com – Fax 02 54 31 17 91*
4 rm – €40/60 €70/100 – **Table d'hôte** – Menu €25

◆ A 19C farmhouse in the countryside with a fine garden of fruit trees. Attractive interiors, with cosy rooms, many featuring old-style furnishings. Enjoy a meal in the company of the owners around the fireplace or on the terrace in summer. International cuisine served.

MONTJEAN-SUR-LOIRE – 49 Maine-et-Loire – 317 D4 – pop. 2 652 – alt. 44 m – ✉ 49570 Châteaux of the Loire 34 B2

Paris 324 – Angers 28 – Ancenis 30 – Châteaubriant 64 – Château-Gontier 56 – Cholet 43

Office de tourisme, rue d'Anjou 02 41 39 07 10, Fax 02 41 39 03 38

Auberge de la Loire with rm rest, P VISA

2 quai des Mariniers – 02 41 39 80 20 – contacts@aubergedelaloire.com
– Fax 02 41 39 80 20 – Closed 25 August-5 September, autumn half-term holidays, Christmas, Sunday dinner September-March and Wednesday
8 rm – €47 €54, €11 – ½ P €58/82 – **Rest** – Menu €13,50 (weekday lunch), €19/54 – Carte €35/64

◆ A welcoming, family inn on the banks of the Loire. Here you can enjoy delicious, traditional food using fresh products, many from the local fishermen. Simple, well-kept rooms, half of which overlook the river.

MONTLIARD – 45 Loiret – 318 L3 – see Bellegarde

MONTLIOT – 21 Côte-d'Or – 320 H2 – see Châtillon-sur-Seine

MONTLIVAULT – 41 Loir-et-Cher – 318 F6 – pop. 1 337 – alt. 77 m – ✉ 41350

Paris 180 – Blois 13 – Olivet 58 – Orléans 56 11 **B2**

La Maison d'à côté rm, VISA

25 rte de Chambord – ☎ 02 54 20 62 30 – contact@lamaisondacote.fr – Closed December

8 rm – †€ 67 ††€ 67, ☐ € 8 – **Rest** – Menu € 15 (weekday lunch), € 29/36 – Carte € 39/55

♦ This village inn has been well-renovated with a contemporary touch – décor with clean lines, high-tech equipment and air-conditioning. Pleasant upstairs patio. This restaurant combines rustic and modern touches. Serves traditional cuisine.

MONT-LOUIS – 66 Pyrénées-Orientales – 344 D7 – pop. 270 – alt. 1 565 m – ✉ 66210 Languedoc-Roussillon-Tarn Gorges 22 **A3**

Paris 867 – Andorra-la-Vella 90 – Font-Romeu-Odeillo-Via 10 – Perpignan 81

Syndicat d'initiative, 3, rue Lieutenant Pruneta ☎ 04 68 04 21 97

Ramparts★ - Lacs des Bouillouses★.

in la Llagonne 3 km North by D 118 – pop. 263 – alt. 1 600 m – ✉ 66210

Corrieu rest, VISA

– ☎ 04 68 04 22 04 – hotel.corrieu@wanadoo.fr – Fax 04 68 04 16 63 – Open 11 June-19 September, 22 December-5 January and 12 January-15 March

24 rm – †€ 32/74 ††€ 36/80, ☐ € 9 – ½ P € 56/67 – **Rest** – *(closed Thursday lunchtime except during school holidays)* Menu (€ 16), € 23/36 – Carte € 23/40

♦ Run by the same family since 1882, this old coaching inn has peaceful, simply furnished rooms and have views of the Pyrenees. New tennis facilities. Refurbished restaurant with simple, classic fare.

MONTLOUIS – 18 Cher – 323 K4 – pop. 115 – alt. 180 m – ✉ 18160

Domaine de Varennes

– ☎ 02 48 60 11 86 – lumet.varennes@wanadoo.fr

5 rm ☐ – †€ 65/70 ††€ 65/70 – **Table d'hôte** – Menu € 25 bi

♦ Charming establishment set in a superb estate. Warm welcome, romantic décor, comfortable rooms, swimming pool and golf driving range.

MONTLOUIS-SUR-LOIRE – 37 Indre-et-Loire – 317 N4 – pop. 9 657 – alt. 60 m – ✉ 37270 Châteaux of the Loire 11 **B2**

Paris 235 – Amboise 14 – Blois 49 – Château-Renault 32 – Loches 39 – Tours 11

Office de tourisme, place François Mitterrand ☎ 02 47 45 00 16, Fax 02 47 45 87 10

Château de la Bourdaisière without rest VISA

– ☎ 02 47 45 16 31 – contact@chateaulabourdaisiere.com – Fax 02 47 45 09 11 – Open 19 March-2 November

20 rm – †€ 125/225 ††€ 125/225, ☐ € 12

♦ Built by François I for his mistress, the chateau was later home to Gabrielle d'Estrées, the favourite of Henri IV. Individually furnished rooms, park and vegetable garden.

La Tourangelle VISA AE

47 quai Albert Baillet – ☎ 02 47 50 97 35 – Fax 02 47 50 88 57 – Closed 30 June-7 July, 17-24 November, 2-8 March, Sunday dinner and Monday except public holidays

Rest – Menu € 22/60 – Carte € 40/61

♦ House built of tufa, set against the rock, with two bright dining rooms and a pretty, shaded terrace. Modern cuisine and fine choice of Montlouis wines.

MONTLUÇON – 03 Allier – 326 C4 – pop. 41 362 – alt. 220 m – ✉ 03100 Auvergne 5 **B1**

Paris 327 – Bourges 97 – Clermont-Ferrand 112 – Limoges 155 – Moulins 82

Office de tourisme, 67 ter, boulevard de Courtais ☎ 04 70 05 11 44, Fax 04 70 03 89 91

du Val de Cher Nassigny 1 route du Vallon, North: 20 km by D 2144, ☎ 04 70 06 71 15.

Interior ★ of St-Pierre church (Sainte Madeleine★★) CYZ - Château esplanade ★.

MONTLUÇON

Barathon (R.)	CZ	2
Beaulieu (R. de)	AX	4
Blanzat (R. de)	AX	5
Château (R. du)	CZ	6
Châtelet (Pont du)	AX	8
Courtais (Bd de)	BCZ	
Desmoulins (R. C.)	AX	9
Dienat (R. du)	AX	10
Egalité (R. de l')	AX	12
Einstein (R. A.)	AX	13
Faucheroux (R.)	AX	14
Favières (Quai)	BY	15
Fontaine (R. de la)	CZ	16
Forges (R. Porte)	CZ	17
Jean-Jaurès (Pl.)	CZ	18
Menut (R. L.)	CY	22
Nègre (Av. J.)	AX	24
Notre-Dame (Pl.)	CZ	25
Notre-Dame (R.)	CZ	26
Pamparoux (R.)	AX	27
Petit (R. P.)	CY	30
Picasso (R. P.)	CY	31
Piquand (R. E.)	BZ	32
République (Av.)	BY	
St-Pierre (Pl.)	BCZ	35
St-Pierre (R. Fg)	BY	36
St-Roch (R.)	BCZ	38
Semard (R. P.)	AX	40
Serruriers (R.)	BCZ	42
Thomas (Av. A.)	AX	45
Verrerie (R. et Pl. de la)	AX	46
Victor-Hugo (R.)	AX	47
Villon (R. P.)	AX	49
Voltaire (R.)	AX	50
5 Piliers (R. des)	CZ	52

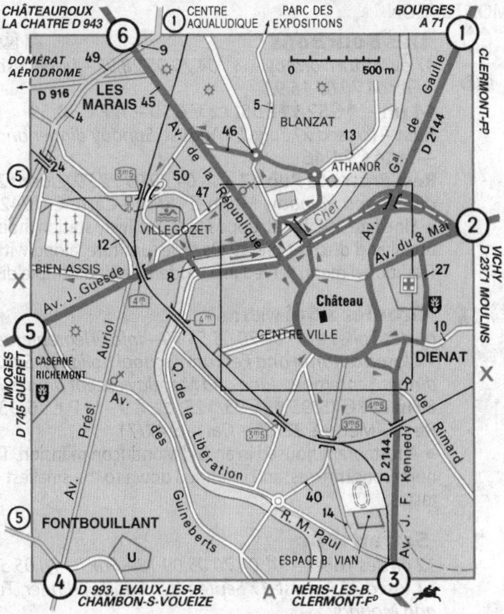

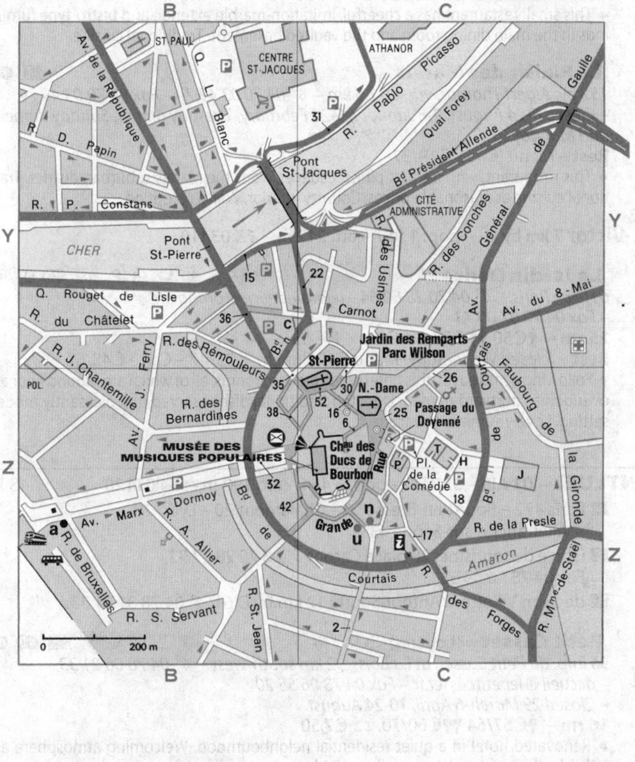

CHÂTEAUROUX LA CHATRE D 943
CENTRE AQUALUDIQUE
PARC DES EXPOSITIONS
BOURGES A 71
CLERMONT-Fᴰ
DOMÉRAT AÉRODROME
LES MARAIS
BLANZAT
ATHANOR
VILLEGOZET
BIEN ASSIS
Château
CENTRE VILLE
DIENAT
VICHY D 2371 MOULINS
LIMOGES D 745 GUÉRET
CASERNE RICHEMONT
FONTBOUILLANT
ESPACE B. VIAN
D 993, EVAUX-LES-B. CHAMBON-S-VOUEIZE
NÉRIS-LES-B. CLERMONT-Fᴰ

CENTRE ST-JACQUES
Pont St-Jacques
CITÉ ADMINISTRATIVE
Pont St-Pierre
CHER
Jardin des Remparts Parc Wilson
St-Pierre
N.-Dame
Passage du Doyenné
MUSÉE DES MUSIQUES POPULAIRES
Chau des Ducs de Bourbon
Pl. de la Comédie
Grande Rue

Des Bourbons rest, VISA MC AE

47 av. Marx Dormoy – ☎ 04 70 05 28 93 – hoteldesbourbons@wanadoo.fr – Fax 04 70 05 16 92 BZ **a**

44 rm – †€ 52 ††€ 55, ☐ € 6,50 – ½ P € 50/59

Rest – *(closed 21 July-19 August, Sunday dinner and Monday)* Menu € 23/40 – Carte € 24/46

Rest *Brasserie Pub 47* – *☎ 04 70 05 22 79 (closed 21 July-19 August, Sunday dinner and Monday)* Menu € 15/18 – Carte € 18/42

◆ Fine late-19C hotel, opposite the railway station, housing renovated rooms with functional and discreet pre-1940s style furniture, along with well-kept, colourful bathrooms. Traditional menu served in a modern setting. Simple dishes served.

XXX **Grenier à Sel** with rm P VISA MC AE

pl. des Toiles – ☎ 04 70 05 53 79 – info@legrenierasel.com – Fax 04 70 05 87 91 – Closed autumn and February school holidays, Saturday lunch in winter, Sunday dinner September-June and Monday except dinner July-August CZ **n**

8 rm – †€ 75/95 ††€ 95/125, ☐ € 9 – ½ P € 76/93

Rest – Menu € 22/66 – Carte € 47/71

◆ A restaurant housed in an Old Montluçon mansion. The dining room is decorated with numerous trinkets, and is refined down to the smallest details. Cooking suited to current tastes.

X **Safran d'Or** VISA MC AE

12 pl. des Toiles – ☎ 04 70 05 09 18 – Fax 04 70 05 55 60 – Closed 25 August-17 September, Sunday dinner, Tuesday dinner and Monday CZ **u**

Rest – Menu (€ 17), € 22/32 – Carte € 39/46

◆ This small restaurant has a cheerful, imitation-marble exterior, and bistro-type furnishings in the main dining room and the vaulted basement. Traditional cuisine.

X **Le Plaisir des Marais** VISA MC

152 av. Albert Thomas, via ⑥: 1.5 km – ☎ 04 70 03 49 74 – Fax 04 70 03 49 74 – Closed 4-24 August, 2-8 January, 5-20 February, Tuesday dinner, Sunday dinner and Monday

Rest – Menu (€ 15), € 19/37

◆ This restaurant, with a smart pink facade, enlivens the Marais suburban district. Traditional cuisine at reasonable prices. Country interior. Warm reception.

in St-Victor 7 km by ① – **pop. 1 957 – alt. 212 m –** ✉ **03410**

Le Jardin Délice P VISA MC AE

6 rte de Paris – ☎ 04 70 28 80 64 – lejardindelice@orange.fr – Fax 04 70 02 00 73

25 rm – †€ 50 ††€ 50, ☐ € 7 – ½ P € 65

Rest – *(closed Wednesday)* Menu € 17 (lunch), € 35/47 – Carte € 48/62

◆ Following a makeover, this hotel offers modern rooms, all of which are ground floor and overlook a courtyard garden. Updated traditional dishes served in a pleasantly modern setting. Lovely summer terrace.

MONTLUEL – 01 Ain – 328 D5 – pop. 6 454 – alt. 190 m – ✉ 01120 43 E1

Paris 472 – Bourg-en-Bresse 59 – Chalamont 20 – Lyon 26 – Villefranche-sur-Saône 43

Office de tourisme, 28 place Carnot ☎ 08 75 28 27 72, Fax 04 78 06 09 53

de Lyon Villette-d'AnthonSouth: 12 km by D 61, ☎ 04 78 31 11 33.

Petit Casset without rest P VISA MC AE

96 imp. du Petit Casset, at La Boisse, 2 km south-west – ☎ 04 78 06 21 33 – accueil@lepetitcasset.fr – Fax 04 78 06 55 20 – Closed 29 March-6 April, 10-24 August

16 rm – †€ 57/64 ††€ 60/70, ☐ € 7,50

◆ Renovated hotel in a quiet residential neighbourhood. Welcoming atmosphere and individually decorated rooms, all overlooking the tree-lined flower garden.

in Ste-Croix 5 km North by D 61 – pop. 468 – alt. 263 m – ✉ 01120

XX **Chez Nous**

– ☎ 04 78 06 61 20 – Fax 04 78 06 63 26 – Closed 18-26 August, 3-10 November, 2-23 January, Tuesday lunch, Sunday dinner and Monday

Rest – Menu € 23/48 – Carte € 39/51

♦ Pleasant dining rooms and a large, plane tree shaded terrace serving regional market fresh cuisine.

Hôtel Chez Nous

– ☎ 04 78 06 60 60

29 rm – †€ 48 ††€ 52, ☕ € 7 – ½ P € 43

♦ New building facing the restaurant, home to small rooms adorned with Louis XVI style furniture. Five refurbished rooms in a wing.

MONTMARAULT – 03 Allier – 326 E5 – pop. 1 663 – alt. 480 m – ✉ 03390

Paris 346 – Gannat 41 – Montluçon 31 – Moulins 47 – St-Pourçain-sur-Sioule 28

5 **B1**

XX **France** with rm

AC rest, P VISA MC

1 r. Marx Dormoy – ☎ 04 70 07 60 26 – hoteldefrance3@wanadoo.fr – Fax 04 70 07 68 45 – Closed 2 March-3 April, 12 November-3 December, Sunday dinner and Monday except public holidays

8 rm – †€ 45 ††€ 45, ☕ € 8,50 – **Rest** – Menu € 19 (weekdays)/44 – Carte € 29/49

♦ Friendly hotel offering rooms furnished in Louis-Philippe style. The chef's son has added a contemporary touch to the traditional cuisine. Special menus on Sundays and holidays.

MONTMÉLARD – 71 Saône-et-Loire – 320 G12 – pop. 333 – alt. 522 m – ✉ 71520

Paris 393 – Mâcon 43 – Paray-le-Monial 34 – Montceau-les-Mines 56 – Roanne 53

8 **C3**

X **Le St-Cyr** with rm

AC rest, P VISA MC

– ☎ 03 85 50 20 76 – lesaintcyr@cegetel.net – Fax 03 85 50 36 98 – Closed 2-9 January, 16-28 February, Wednesday lunch and Friday dinner from October to May and Tuesday lunch

7 rm – †€ 44 ††€ 49/65, ☕ € 6,50 – ½ P € 48

Rest – Menu € 15/40 – Carte € 21/35

♦ Simple hotel on St Cyr mountain with plain rooms named after flowers. Traditional fare plus creole food, evoking the proprietress's roots.

MONTMÉLIAN – 73 Savoie – 333 J4 – pop. 3 926 – alt. 307 m – ✉ 73800

French Alps

46 **F2**

Paris 574 – Albertville 35 – Allevard 22 – Chambéry 14 – Grenoble 49

Syndicat d'initiative, 46, rue du Docteur Veyrat ☎ 04 79 84 42 23, Fax 04 79 84 42 23

du Granier Apremont Apremont Chemin de Fontaine Rouge, West: 8 km by D 201, ☎ 04 79 28 21 26.

☼★★ from the rock.

George

P VISA MC AE

11 quai de l'Isère, (D 1006) – ☎ 04 79 84 05 87 – infos@hotelgeorge.fr – Fax 04 79 84 40 14

11 rm – †€ 32 ††€ 38, ☕ € 5,50 – ½ P € 49 – **Rest** – snack *(closed 1st-15 July and autumn half-term holidays) (dinner only) (residents only)* Menu € 15

♦ A former 18C salt granary on the roadside. Corridors decorated with old tools, leading to soundproofed rooms. Some have been renovated. Unpretentious snacks that are served mainly to residents.

X **L'Arlequin**

P VISA MC AE

D 1006 – ☎ 04 79 84 33 14 – arlequin.abe@wanadoo.fr – Fax 04 79 84 25 77 – Closed 7 July-31 August and Saturday

Rest – *(lunch only)* Menu € 14 (weekdays)/16 – Carte approx. € 31

♦ Just off the road, this restaurant's apprentice chefs prepare traditional cuisine.

MONTMERLE-SUR-SAÔNE – 01 Ain – 328 B4 – pop. 2 830 – alt. 170 m – ✉ 01090
43 **E1**

▶ Paris 419 – Bourg-en-Bresse 44 – Lyon 48 – Mâcon 34 – Villefranche-sur-Saône 13

Emile Job

12 r. du Pont – ✆ 04 74 69 33 92 – contact@hotelemilejob.com – Fax 04 74 69 49 21 – Closed 25 February-9 March, 25 October-16 November, Sunday dinner October-May, Tuesday lunch June-September and Monday

22 rm – †€ 68 ††€ 70, ☕ € 8 – ½ P € 90 – **Rest** – Menu € 21 (weekdays)/55 – Carte € 38/66

◆ Regional style house on the banks of the Saône that has preserved its family atmosphere. Classic or more modern rooms (refurbished and colourful). Plush, elegant restaurant and shaded terrace; classic menu and local specialities.

MONTMIRAIL – 84 Vaucluse – 332 D9 – see Vacqueyras

MONTMORENCY – 95 Val-d'Oise – 305 E7 – 101 5 – see Paris, Area

MONTMORILLON – 86 Vienne – 322 L6 – pop. 6 898 – alt. 100 m – ✉ 86500
Atlantic Coast
39 **D2**

▶ Paris 354 – Bellac 43 – Châtellerault 56 – Limoges 88 – Niort 123 – Poitiers 51

ℹ Office de tourisme, 2, place du Maréchal Leclerc ✆ 05 49 91 11 96, Fax 05 49 91 11 96

Notre-Dame church: frescoes★ in the Ste-Catherine crypt.

Hôtel de France et Lucullus rm,

4 bd de Strasbourg – ✆ 05 49 84 09 09 – lucullus.hoteldefrance@wanadoo.fr – Fax 05 49 84 58 68 – Closed 12 Nov. - 5 Dec.

35 rm – †€ 42/62 ††€ 45/68, ☕ € 8,50 – ½ P € 46

Rest – *(closed 12 November-6 December, Sunday dinner, Monday and Tuesday)* Menu € 20/50 – Carte € 29/43

Rest *Bistrot de Lucullus* – *(closed Sunday except dinner in season and Saturday dinner)* Menu (€ 14,50 bi) – Carte € 19/36

◆ Near the bridge over the Gartempe, a regional building with spacious, practical and brightly coloured rooms. Sunny decor and carefully prepared cuisine that varies with the seasons. Light meals served at the Bistrot de Lucullus for a busy clientele.

MONTNER – 66 Pyrénées-Orientales – 344 H6 – pop. 244 – alt. 127 m – ✉ 66720
22 **B3**

▶ Paris 860 – Perpignan 28 – Amélie-les-Bains-Palalda 60 – Font-Romeu-Odeillo-Via 82 – Prades 37

Auberge du Cellier with rm rest,

1 r. Ste Eugénie – ✆ 04 68 29 09 78 – marinplb@cegetel.net – Fax 04 68 29 10 61 – Closed 17-25 June, 12 November-11 December, Monday from November to March, Tuesday and Wednesday

6 rm – †€ 54 ††€ 61, ☕ € 9 – ½ P € 64 – **Rest** – Menu € 29 (weekday lunch), € 39/85 – Carte € 55/64

◆ A wine inspired restaurant located in a former wine cellar, hence its name. Fine Côtes du Roussillon wine list. Updated regional cuisine.

MONTOIRE-SUR-LE-LOIR – 41 Loir-et-Cher – 318 C5 – pop. 4 275 – alt. 65 m – ✉ 41800
Châteaux of the Loire
11 **B2**

▶ Paris 186 – Blois 52 – La Flèche 81 – Le Mans 70 – Vendôme 19

ℹ Syndicat d'initiative, 16, place Clemenceau ✆ 02 54 85 23 30, Fax 02 54 85 23 87

St-Gilles chapel ★: frescoes★★ - Bridge ≤★.

Du Cheval Rouge with rm

1 pl. Foch – 02 54 85 07 05 – hotel-restaurant-le-cheval-rouge@wanadoo.fr – Fax 02 54 85 17 42 – Closed 16-23 March, 23 November-7 December, 25 January-8 February

13 rm – €50 €55, €7 – ½ P €55/80 – **Rest** – *(closed Friday dinner, Tuesday dinner and Wednesday)* Menu €25/36 – Carte approx. €55

◆ Time seems to have stood still in this former coaching inn, located in the town centre. Dining rooms have a patina setting. Standard cooking.

in Lavardin **2 km Southeast by D 108 – pop. 262 – alt. 78 m – 41800**

Relais d'Antan

– 02 54 86 61 33 – Fax 02 54 85 06 46 – Closed 29 September-21 October, 16 February-10 March, Sunday dinner from 1st October to 15 May, Monday and Tuesday

Rest – Menu €28/38

◆ This rustic inn stands in a picturesque village. One of its dining rooms is adorned with wall paintings inspired by the Middle Ages. Pleasant terrace on the banks of the Loir.

MONTPELLIER P – 34 Hérault – 339 I7 – pop. 225 392 – Built-up area 287 981 – alt. 27 m – 34000 Languedoc-Roussillon-Tarn Gorges 23 C2

Paris 758 – Marseille 173 – Nice 330 – Nîmes 55 – Toulouse 242

Montpellier-Méditerranée 04 67 20 85 00 Southeast by ③: 7 km.

Office de tourisme, 30, allée Jean de Latrre de Tassigny 04 67 60 60 60, Fax 04 67 60 60 61

de Fontcaude Juvignac Route de Lodève, by Lodève road: 8 km, 04 67 45 90 10 ;

de Coulondres Saint-Gély-du-Fesc 72 rue des Erables, by Ganges road: 12 km, 04 67 84 13 75 ;

Montpellier Massane Baillargues Domaine de Massane, by Nîmes road: 13 km, 04 67 87 87 89.

Old Montpellier★★: hôtel de Varennes★ FY **M²**, hôtel des Trésoriers de la Bourse★ FY **Q**, rue de l'Ancien Courrier★ EFY **4** - Promenade du Peyrou★★: ≤★ from the upper terrace - Quartier Antigone★ - Musée Fabre★★ FY - Musée Atger★ (in the faculté de médecine) EX - Musée languedocien★ (in the Hôtel des trésoriers de France) FY **M¹**.

Château de Flaugergues★ East: 3 km - Château de la Mogère★ East: 5 km by D 24 DU.

Plans on following pages

Sofitel Antigone rest,

1 r. Pertuisanes – 04 67 99 72 72 – h1294@accor.com – Fax 04 67 65 17 50

89 rm – €210/250 €210/250, €22 – 1 suite – **Rest** – Menu (€31), €40 – Carte €44/58 CU **v**

◆ This hotel is located in the district designed by Ricardo Bofill. Home to modern, cosy rooms. Rooftop terrace with swimming pool, bar and fitness facilities. The restaurant is located on the eighth floor, serving traditional, Southern-style cuisine.

Holiday Inn Métropole rm,

3 r. Clos René – 04 67 12 32 32 – himontpellier@alliance-hospitality.com – Fax 04 67 92 13 02 FZ **a**

84 rm – €180 €180/210, €17 – **Rest** – *(closed Saturday and Sunday)* Menu €25 – Carte €26/38

◆ This building, dating from 1898, is said to have been the home of Queen Helena of Italy. Functional bedrooms. English bar. Garden-terrace shaded by palm trees. Simple modern décor in this restaurant featuring superb ceiling mouldings.

Mercure Antigone rm,

285 bd aéroport international – 04 67 20 63 63 – h1544-gm@accor.com – Fax 04 67 20 63 64 DU **f**

114 rm – €130 €150, €13 – 9 suites – **Rest** – *(closed 14 July-30 August, 24 December-1st January, Saturday lunch and Sunday)* Menu €30/36 – Carte €43/49

◆ This hotel near the neo-Classical Antigone district provides modern, attractively-renovated rooms, most with king-size beds. This circular restaurant offers pleasant colonial decor. Thematic gourmet evenings.

MONTPELLIER

Anatole-France (R.) . . . . **BU** 3
Arceaux (Bd des) . . . . **AU** 7
Bazille (R. F.) . . . . **BCV** 12
Blum (R. Léon) . . . . **CU** 13
Broussonnet (R. A.) . . . . **AT** 18
Chancel (Av.) . . . . **AT** 25
Citadelle (Allée) . . . . **CU** 26
Clapiès (R.) . . . . **AU** 28
Comte (R. A.) . . . . **AU** 29
Délicieux (R. B.) . . . . **CT** 31
États-du-Languedoc (Av.) . . . . . . **CU** 35
Fabre-de-Morlhon (Bd) . . . . **BV** 36
Fg-Boutonnet (R.) . . . . **BT** 37
Fg-de-Nîmes (R. du) . . . . **CT** 41
Flahault (Av. Ch.) . . . . **AT** 43

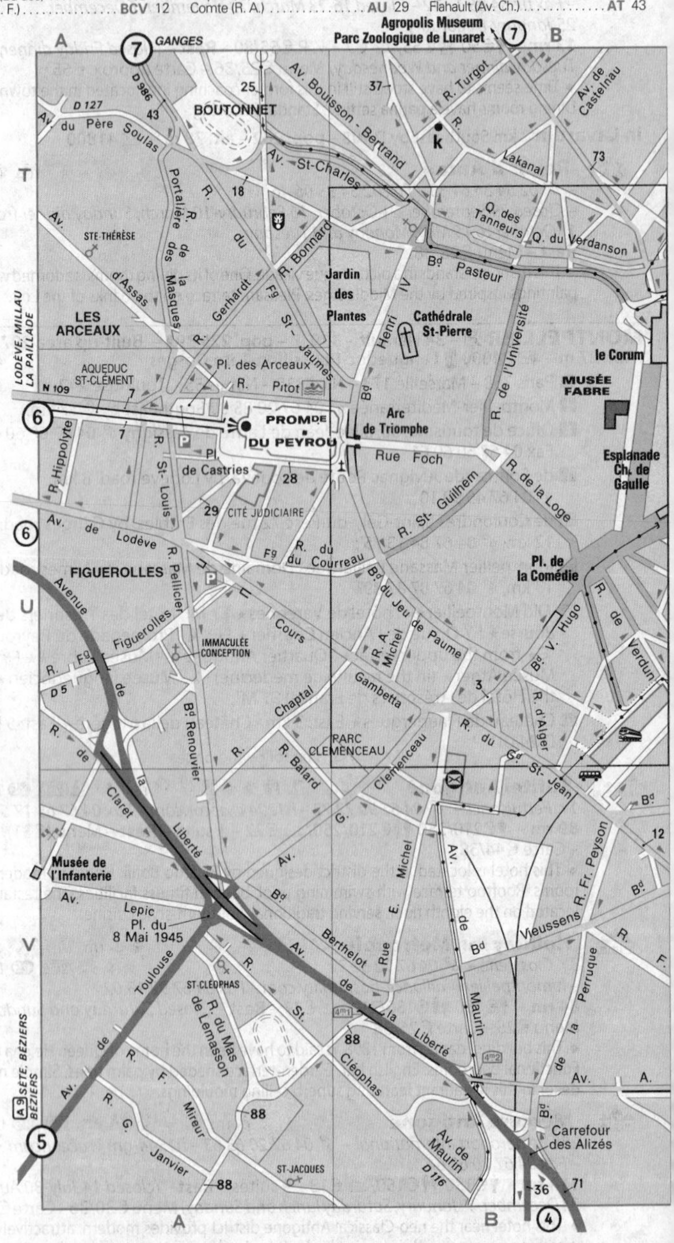

Fontaine-de-Lattes (R.) . . . . CU 44
Henri-II-de-Montmorency (Allée) CU 51
Leclerc (Av. du Mar.). . . . . CV 58
Millénaire (Pl. du) . . . . CU 62
Nombre-d'Or (Pl. du) . . . . CU 64
Ollivier (R. A.). . . . . CU 66
Le Polygone . . . . CU
Pont-de-Lattes (R. du) . . . . CU 69
Pont-Juvénal (Av.) . . . . CDU 70
Près-d'Arènes (Av. des) . . . . BV 71
Prof.-E.-Antonelli (Av.) . . . . CDV 72
Proudhon (R.). . . . . BT 73
René (R. H.). . . . . CV 74
Villeneuve-d'Angoulême (Av.). . . . . ABV 88

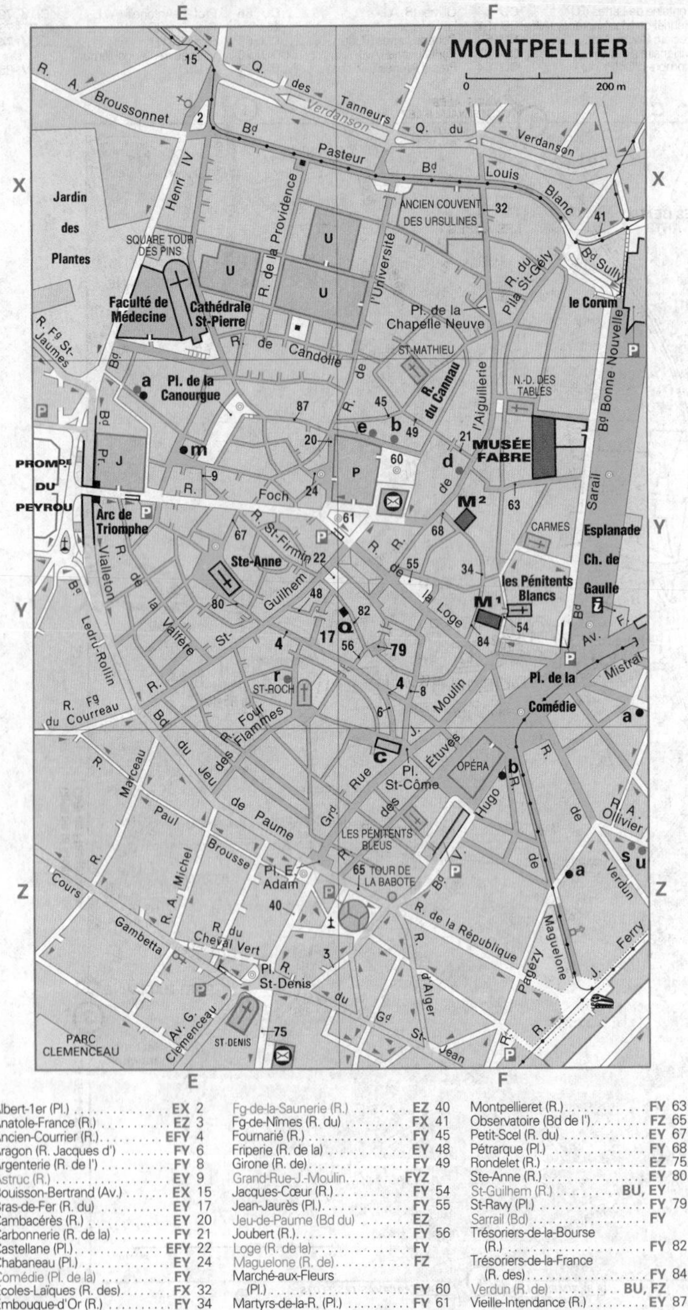

Albert-1er (Pl.) . . . . **EX** 2
Anatole-France (R.) . . . . **EZ** 3
Ancien-Courrier (R.) . . . . **EFY** 4
Aragon (R. Jacques d') . . . . **FY** 6
Argenterie (R. de l') . . . . **FY** 8
Astruc (R.) . . . . **EY** 9
Bouisson-Bertrand (Av.) . . . . **EX** 15
Bras-de-Fer (R. du) . . . . **EY** 17
Cambacérès (R.) . . . . **EY** 20
Carbonnerie (R. de la) . . . . **FY** 21
Castellane (Pl.) . . . . **EFY** 22
Chabaneau (Pl.) . . . . **EY** 24
Comédie (Pl. de la) . . . . **FY**
Écoles-Laïques (R. des) . . . . **FX** 32
Embouque-d'Or (R.) . . . . **FY** 34
Fg-de-la-Saunerie (R.) . . . . **EZ** 40
Fg-de-Nîmes (R. du) . . . . **FX** 41
Fournarié (R.) . . . . **FY** 45
Friperie (R. de la) . . . . **EY** 48
Girone (R. de) . . . . **FY** 49
Grand-Rue-J.-Moulin . . . . **FYZ**
Jacques-Cœur (R.) . . . . **FY** 54
Jean-Jaurès (Pl.) . . . . **FY** 55
Jeu-de-Paume (Bd du) . . . . **EZ**
Joubert (R.) . . . . **FY** 56
Loge (R. de la) . . . . **FY**
Maguelone (R. de) . . . . **FZ**
Marché-aux-Fleurs (Pl.) . . . . **FY** 60
Martyrs-de-la-R. (Pl.) . . . . **FY** 61
Montpellieret (R.) . . . . **FY** 63
Observatoire (Bd de l') . . . . **FZ** 65
Petit-Scel (R. du) . . . . **EY** 67
Pétrarque (Pl.) . . . . **FY** 68
Rondelet (R.) . . . . **EZ** 75
Ste-Anne (R.) . . . . **EY** 80
St-Guilhem (R.) . . . . **BU, EY**
St-Ravy (Pl.) . . . . **FY** 79
Sarrail (Bd) . . . . **FY**
Trésoriers-de-la-Bourse (R.) . . . . **FY** 82
Trésoriers-de-la-France (R. des) . . . . **FY** 84
Verdun (R. de) . . . . **BU, FZ**
Vieille-Intendance (R.) . . . . **EY** 87

Suitehotel without rest
45 av. Pirée – ✆ 04 67 20 57 57 – h6017@accor.com – Fax 04 67 20 58 58 DU **t**
139 rm – €105/115 €105/115, €15
◆ Particularly suited to business clients, this hotel mainly offers suites, with a work space and lounge separate from the bedroom. Practical and spacious.

Mercure Centre rest,
218 r. Bastion Ventadour – ✆ 04 67 99 89 89 – h3043@accor.com – Fax 04 67 99 89 88 CU **q**
120 rm – €85/120 €85/130, €13 – **Rest** – *(closed Saturday and Sunday)* Carte approx. €30
◆ An attractive, resolutely modern interior with art on display and a library for guests. The rooms are a little small, however. A refined, contemporary restaurant serving Mediterranean cuisine and daily specials marked up on the board. Small selection of Languedoc wines.

New Hôtel du Midi without rest
22 bd Victor Hugo – ✆ 04 67 92 69 61 – montpelliermidi@new-hotel.com – Fax 04 67 92 73 63 FZ **b**
44 rm – €135 €155, €12
◆ A fine 20C building in the centre of town, providing comfortable, renovated rooms in modern style with touches of the old.

D'Aragon without rest
10 r. Baudin – ✆ 04 67 10 70 00 – info@hotel-aragon.fr – Fax 04 67 10 70 01 – Closed from 1st-15 January FY **a**
12 rm – €69/72 €99/129, €9,50
◆ This charming building is home to a brand new hotel providing soundproofed rooms designed with taste and providing all modern conveniences.

Le Guilhem without rest
18 r. J.-J. Rousseau – ✆ 04 67 52 90 90 – hotel-le-guilhem@mnet.fr – Fax 04 67 60 67 67 EY **a**
35 rm – €81/150 €91/150, €12
◆ A group of 16C and 17C houses with cosy rooms; those on the top floor have a view of the cathedral. Breakfast served on the balcony and terrace. Non-smoking throughout.

Du Parc without rest
8 r. A. Bège – ✆ 04 67 41 16 49 – hotelduparcmtp@wanadoo.fr – Fax 04 67 54 10 05 BT **k**
19 rm – €45/72 €50/83, €10
◆ A former 18C manor house close to the historic town centre, providing pleasant, individually styled rooms, and a courtyard terrace for breakfast in summer. Friendly service.

Du Palais without rest
3 r. Palais – ✆ 04 67 60 47 38 – hoteldupalais2@wanadoo.fr – Fax 04 67 60 40 23 EY **m**
26 rm – €64 €69/81, €11
◆ A fine, century-old building near the law courts. Attentive touches in the small rooms (fresh flowers, chocolates, etc.). Efficient soundproofing.

Ulysse without rest
338 av. St-Maur – ✆ 04 67 02 02 30 – hotelulysse@free.fr – Fax 04 67 02 16 50 – Closed 28 December-4 January CT **b**
23 rm – €48/58 €58/69, €9
◆ Stylish bedrooms, with wrought-iron furniture in this hotel appreciated by guests for its pleasant atmosphere. A quiet residential district. Extremely well kept.

Les Troënes without rest
17 av. É. Bertin-Sans, via Ave Charles Flahaut and Ganges road, towards Hôpitaux-Faculté (hospitals) ✉ 34090 – ✆ 04 67 04 07 76 – hotel-les-troenes@wanadoo.fr – Fax 04 67 61 04 43
14 rm – €49/51 €56/58, €8
◆ This modest but homely, renovated 1960s-style hotel is linked to the town centre by tram. Pleasant rooms without superfluous equipment. Non-smoking hotel.

XXXX ✿✿ **Le Jardin des Sens** (Jacques et Laurent Pourcel) with rm
11 av. St-Lazare – ✆ 04 99 58 38 38 – contact@jardindessens.com – Fax 04 99 58 38 39 CT **e**
13 rm – †€ 160/270 ††€ 160/270, ☕ € 22 – 2 suites
Rest – *(closed 2-15 January, Monday lunch, Wednesday lunch and Sunday) (number of covers limited, pre-book)* Menu € 50 (weekday lunch), € 80/190 – Carte € 102/164
Spec. Pressé de homard et légumes au jambon de canard, mangue et melon. Queue de petite baudroie de Méditerranée rôtie à la pointe d'ail et olives. Filets de pigeon rôtis, pastilla des abats au curry, jus de cacao. **Wines** Vin de pays du Gard, Vin de pays des Côtes de Thongue.
◆ An unusual, designer-style restaurant providing a view of the garden below. Both the setting and cuisine are extremely pleasant. Modern-style, very luxurious rooms decorated with paintings from the Pourcel brothers' collection. Suite with private swimming pool.

XX **Cellier Morel**
27 r. Aiguillerie, (Maison de la Lozère) – ✆ 04 67 66 46 36 – contact@celliermorel.com – Fax 04 67 66 23 61 – Closed 1st-15 August, Monday lunch, Wednesday lunch, Saturday lunch, Sunday and public holidays FY **d**
Rest – Menu € 36/62 – Carte € 70/88
◆ A vaulted, 13C dining room with fine designer decor, and a delicious courtyard-terrace enclosed by an 18C mansion. Inventive Lozère cuisine.

XX **La Réserve Rimbaud** ≤ le Lez,
820 av. St-Maur – ✆ 04 67 72 52 53 – contact@reserve-rimbaud.com – Fax 04 67 02 02 77 – Closed 5-21 August, Saturday lunch, Sunday dinner and Monday DT **w**
Rest – Menu € 27/45 – Carte € 31/49
◆ Attractive southern cuisine and local wines served with views of the Lez (from dining room and terrace) - a new lease of life for this restaurant created in 1835.

XX **Castel Ronceray**
130 r. Castel Ronceray, via ⑤ – ✆ 04 67 42 46 30 – lecastelronceray@free.fr – Fax 04 67 27 41 96 – Closed 4-26 August, Sunday and Monday
Rest – Menu (€ 27 bi), € 41/62 – Carte € 46/54
◆ A 19C family mansion, an unexpected sight behind the screen of modern buildings. Polished interior, with a marble fireplace and Antique-style statues. Traditional dishes.

XX **Les Vignes**
2 r. Bonnier d'Alco – ✆ 04 67 60 48 42 – cdmogicato@free.fr – Fax 04 67 60 48 42 – Closed 2-27 April, 3-24 August, Wednesday dinner, Saturday lunch and Sunday
Rest – Menu (€ 24), € 39/55 – Carte € 48/64 FY **e**
◆ Walk down the stairs to the elegant dining area with a vaulted ceiling in this small restaurant located behind the Préfecture building. Serving regional cuisine.

XX **Le Petit Jardin**
20 r. J.-J. Rousseau – ✆ 04 67 60 78 78 – contact@petit-jardin.com – Fax 04 67 66 16 79 – Closed January and Monday EY **a**
Rest – Menu (€ 14), € 22/45 – Carte € 38/69
◆ A pleasant restaurant in the heart of old Montpellier. Its picture windows open onto a hidden jewel: a terrace garden planted with rare species of trees. Regional cuisine.

XX **L'Olivier**
12 r. A. Ollivier – ✆ 04 67 92 86 28 – Fax 04 67 92 10 65 – Closed 24 July-29 August, Sunday and Monday FZ **u**
Rest – *(pre-book)* Menu € 36/58 – Carte € 49/62
◆ Restaurant near the railway station housing a narrow dining room lined with mirrors and tables close together, for convivial meals in a slightly retro setting. Classic cuisine served.

XX **Le Séquoïa**
148 r. de Galata, at Port Marianne – ✆ 04 67 65 07 07 – Fax 04 67 64 50 23 – Closed 22 December-1st January, Saturday lunch, Wednesday and Sunday
Rest – Menu € 24/39 – Carte € 44/62 DV **e**
◆ A contemporary setting, a terrace on the side of the yachting harbour, cuisine of various origins – a trendy restaurant in the new quarter springing up on the left bank of the River Lez.

Prouhèze Saveurs

728 av.de la Pompignane – ✆ 04 67 79 43 34 – prouhezesaveurs@wanadoo.fr – Fax 04 67 79 71 94 – Closed 21 July-25 August, Wednesday dinner, Saturday lunch, Sunday, Monday and Tuesday DU **a**

Rest – Menu (€ 23), € 27/31

◆ Restaurant run by the Prouhèze family, featuring typical southern French colours and serving good, simple regional dishes around the fireplace in winter or on the terrace in summer.

La Compagnie des Comptoirs

51 av. Frédéric Delmas – ✆ 04 99 58 39 29 – contact@jardindessens.com – Fax 04 99 58 39 28 – Closed Tuesday lunch, Saturday lunch and Monday

Rest – Menu € 22 (weekday lunch), € 31/50 – Carte approx. € 52 CT **u**

◆ Décor inspired by the French-Indian trading company in this restaurant with a charming terrace. The menu has an Eastern flavour and Southern accents.

Kinoa

6 r. des Sœurs Noires – ✆ 04 67 15 34 38 – restaurantkinoa@yahoo.fr – Fax 04 67 15 34 33 – Closed 10-23 November, Sunday and Monday EY **r**

Rest – Menu (€ 17 bi), € 27/38 – Carte € 43/51

◆ Elegant modern decor and a charming terrace overlooking a small, shaded square next to an old church. Modern cuisine served, including a diet menu (no cream, alcohol or sugar).

Tamarillos

2 pl. Marché aux Fleurs – ✆ 04 67 60 06 00 – Fax 04 67 60 06 01 – Closed 21-27 April, 25-31 August, 29 October-4 November, 25 February-3 March, Monday lunch, Wednesday lunch and Sunday FY **b**

Rest – Menu € 22 (weekday lunch), € 50/90 – Carte € 52/68

◆ Fruit and flowers are the inspiration for both the cuisine and the colourful decor of this unusual restaurant, run by a young chef who was twice winner of the French dessert championship!

Verdi

10 r. A. Ollivier – ✆ 04 67 58 68 55 – gunara1952@libero.it – Fax 04 67 58 28 47 – Closed August and Sunday FZ **s**

Rest – Menu € 19/28 – Carte € 36/50

◆ This small, simple and relaxed Italian restaurant, close to the railway station, is decorated with Verdi and Opera posters. Italian and fish specialities. Wine shop.

in Castelnau-le-Lez 7 km by ① and N 113 – pop. 14 214 – alt. 60 m – ✉ 34170

Domaine de Verchant

1 bd Philippe-Lamour – ✆ 04 67 07 26 00 – reservation@verchant.com – Fax 04 67 07 26 01 – Closed 6 January-3 February

12 rm – 🚹€ 160/450 🚹🚹€ 160/450, ☕ € 25 – 1 suite – **Rest** – *(number of covers limited, pre-book) (residents only)* Menu € 60 – Carte € 48/68

◆ An impressive wine domaine set in parkland. The interior, by the architect of the Murano and Kube in Paris, blends Italian design with high-tech gadgetry. Superb guestrooms. Up-to-date menu accompanied by wines from the estate.

in Baillargues – pop. 5 842 – alt. 23 m – ✉ 34670

Golf Hôtel de Massane

at the Massane Golf Course – ✆ 04 67 87 87 87 – contact@massane.com – Fax 04 67 87 87 90

32 rm – 🚹€ 99/111 🚹🚹€ 117/133, ☕ € 11

Rest – Menu (€ 19), € 25/37 – Carte € 27/46

◆ Vast hotel complex with extensive leisure and relaxation facilities. Featuring spacious, renovated rooms with Camargue-style décor. A contemporary-style restaurant overlooking the golf course, serving modern meals and a good selection of regional wines.

via ② 5 km : A9 exit 29 and D172[E] – ✉ 34000 Montpellier

Le Mas des Brousses

540 r. Mas des Brousses – ✆ 04 67 64 18 91 – lemasdesbrousses@free.fr – Fax 04 67 64 18 89 – Closed lunch from 1st-20 August, Saturday lunch, Sunday dinner and Monday

Rest – Menu (€ 19 bi), € 24 bi, € 45/65 – Carte € 55/72

◆ This restaurant is located in a building dating back to the 18C, with a décor featuring ochre walls, terra cotta tiled flooring and an old grain vat. Serves modernised traditional meals.

near A9-Montpellier-Sud interchange 2 km by ④ – ✉ 34000 Montpellier

Novotel
125 bis av. Palavas – ☎ 04 99 52 34 34 – h0450@accor.com – Fax 04 99 52 34 33
163 rm – €99/142 €99/142, ☕ €13
Rest – Menu (€16), €20 – Carte €23/43
◆ This typical motel, close to an interchange, houses bedrooms in conformity with chain standards. "Cyberespace" available. Plain, modern restaurant with poolside terrace service in summer.

in Lattes 5 km by ④ – pop. 13 768 – alt. 3 m – ✉ 34970

Office de tourisme, 679, avenue de Montpellier ☎ 04 67 22 52 91

Domaine de Soriech
face Z.A.C. Soriech, near the D 189 and D 21 roundabout – ☎ 04 67 15 19 15 – michel.loustau@domaine-de-soriech.fr – Fax 04 67 15 58 21 – Closed 2-15 February, Sunday dinner and Monday
Rest – Menu (€22), €30 (weekday lunch), €42/75 – Carte €58/70
◆ A fine 1970s villa, with designer décor, modern works of art, giant palm and pine trees in a delightful park. Regional cuisine.

Le Mazerand
Mas De Causse CD 172 – ☎ 04 67 64 82 10 – Fax 04 67 20 10 73 – Closed Saturday lunch, Sunday dinner and Monday
Rest – Menu (€21), €29/59 – Carte €41/75
◆ This former vineyard estate, overlooking the Plain of Lattes, includes a renovated, 19C farmhouse, a 16C chapel and pretty, tiered terraces in the shade of plane trees.

Le Bistrot d'Ariane
at Port Ariane – ☎ 04 67 20 01 27 – lebistrotdariane@free.fr – Fax 04 67 15 03 25 – Closed 20 December-4 January and Sunday except public holidays
Rest – Menu €19 (weekday lunch), €28/38 – Carte €31/54
◆ A subtle art-deco style with a brasserie atmosphere in this attractive restaurant popular with the locals. Terrace overlooking the port. Nice menu of regional wines.

in Juvignac 6 km by ⑥, Millau road – pop. 5 592 – alt. 32 m – ✉ 34990

Golf Hôtel
rte de Lodève, at the international golf club – ☎ 04 67 45 90 00 – info@golfhotelmontpellier.com – Fax 04 67 45 90 20
46 rm – €70 €85, ☕ €10 – **Rest** – Menu (€18), €30 – Carte €31/44
◆ This hotel is popular with golfers at the Juvignac course. Most of the functional rooms provide a view of the greens, some also feature a terrace. A pleasant, comfortable restaurant overlooking the golf greens. Quick set menu available at the bar.

MONTPEZAT-DE-QUERCY – 82 Tarn-et-Garonne – 337 E6 – pop. 1 378 – alt. 275 m – ✉ 82270 Dordogne-Berry-Limousin 28 B1

Paris 600 – Cahors 29 – Montauban 39 – Toulouse 91

Office de tourisme, boulevard des Fossés ☎ 05 63 02 05 55, Fax 05 63 02 05 55

Les Trois Terrasses ← countryside,
r. de la Libération – ☎ 05 63 02 66 21 – info@trois-terrasses.com – Fax 05 63 64 01 62 – Open 1st April-26 October
4 rm ☕ – €90 €150 – **Table d'hôte** – Menu €28
◆ Relax and enjoy your stay in this 18C farmhouse that happily marries old and new styles. The rooms and terraced garden command fine views of the countryside. Regional cuisine to be sampled on the summer terrace or in the classic dining room.

Domaine de Lafon
4 km south via rte de Mirabel, D 20 and D 69 – ☎ 05 63 02 05 09 – micheline.perrone@domainedelafon.com – Closed 15 February-15 March and 15-30 November
3 rm ☕ – €60/63 €73/81 – **Table d'hôte** – Menu €25 bi
◆ This 19C building features a 360-degree view of the surrounding valleys. Providing rooms with the owner's work on display, and featuring fine fabrics. A charming library is located in the old pigeon coop. Traditional cuisine served.

MONTPON-MÉNESTÉROL – 24 Dordogne – 329 B5 – pop. 5 385 – alt. 93 m – ✉ 24700

4 **C1**

Paris 532 – Bergerac 40 – Libourne 43 – Périgueux 56 – Ste-Foy-la-Grande 23

Office de tourisme, place Clemenceau ✆ 05 53 82 23 77, Fax 05 53 81 86 74

in Ménestérol 1 km North – ✉ 24700 Montpon-Ménestérol

Auberge de l'Eclade

rte de Coutras – ✆ 05 53 80 28 64 – auberge-de-leclade@wanadoo.fr – Fax 05 53 80 28 64

Rest – Menu € 15 (weekday lunch), € 27/55 – Carte € 40/61

◆ The dining room's rustic ambiance reminds us that this restaurant was once a barn. Pleasant summer terrace overlooking the countryside and traditional cuisine.

MONT-PRÈS-CHAMBORD – 41 Loir-et-Cher – 318 F6 – pop. 3 025 – alt. 108 m – ✉ 41250

11 **B1**

Paris 184 – Blois 12 – Bracieux 8 – Orléans 63 – Romorantin-Lanthenay 35

Le St-Florent without rest

rest,

14 r. Chabardière – ✆ 02 54 70 81 00 – info@hotel-saint-florent.com – Fax 02 54 70 78 53 – Closed 15 November-1st December

19 rm – €56 €56, ☕ €7,50

◆ The village is adjacent to the Boulogne Forest and Chambord Park. This vast house with a family feel has bright bedrooms, with sloping ceilings on the top floor.

Les Délices du St-Florent

14 r. Chabardière – ✆ 02 54 70 73 17 – lesdelicesdusaintflorent@wanadoo.fr – Fax 02 54 70 88 50 – Closed 15-30 November, 15-31 January, Tuesday October-March and Monday

Rest – Menu € 25/48 – Carte € 41/51

◆ Both classic and creative cooking at this restaurant run by an energetic young couple. Bright setting with rustic touches, such as the press now used as the counter.

MONTRÉAL – 32 Gers – 336 D6 – pop. 1 238 – alt. 131 m – ✉ 32250

Languedoc-Roussillon-Tarn Gorges

28 **A2**

Paris 725 – Agen 57 – Auch 59 – Condom 16 – Mont-de-Marsan 65 – Nérac 27

Office de tourisme, place de l'hôtel de ville ✆ 05 62 29 42 85, Fax 05 62 29 42 46

de Guinlet Eauze, South: 12 km by D 29, ✆ 05 62 09 80 84.

Daubin

(opposite the church) – ✆ 05 62 29 44 40 – daubin.bernard@wanadoo.fr – Fax 05 62 29 49 94 – Closed Sunday dinner, Monday and Tuesday

Rest – Menu € 16 (weekday lunch), € 26/56 – Carte € 37/55

◆ This welcoming, family-run village restaurant has been operating for three generations, serving tasty regional cuisine and local wines and featuring a terrace shaded by plane trees.

MONTREDON – 11 Aude – 344 F3 – see Carcassonne

MONTREUIL – 62 Pas-de-Calais – 301 D5 – pop. 2 428 – alt. 54 m – ✉ 62170

Northern France and the Paris Region

30 **A2**

Paris 232 – Abbeville 49 – Arras 86 – Boulogne-sur-Mer 38 – Calais 73 – Lille 116

Office de tourisme, 21, rue Carnot ✆ 03 21 06 04 27, Fax 03 21 06 57 85

Site★ - Citadel★: ≤★★ - Ramparts★ - St-Saulve church ★.

Château de Montreuil (Christian Germain)
4 chaussée des Capucins – ✆ 03 21 81 53 04 – reservations@chateaudemontreuil.com – Fax 03 21 81 36 43 – Closed 14 December-5 February, Tuesday lunch and Monday except July-August and Thursday lunch
12 rm – €195/240 €220/260, € 20 – 4 suites – ½ P € 205
Rest – Menu € 38 (weekday lunch), € 70/90
Spec. Poissons de petits bateaux. Grouse d'Ecosse rôtie (end August to end October). Pigeonneau de Licques et foie gras de canard dans l'esprit hochepot.
◆ This elegant residence is located inside the ramparts. Refined rooms, adorned with period furniture, overlook a landscaped garden. Modern food with exotic and Mediterranean touches enhanced by a fine wine list.

Hermitage
pl. Gambetta – ✆ 03 21 06 74 74 – contact@hermitage-montreuil.com – Fax 03 21 06 74 75
57 rm – €85/160 €85/260, € 17
Rest *Le Jéroboam* – *✆ 03 21 86 65 80 (closed January, Monday except dinner July-August and Sunday)* Menu € 16 (weekday lunch), € 25/31 – Carte € 34/57
◆ A fine, restored building, built under Napoleon III. Low-key bar and large rooms with discreet modern furniture. A modern menu accompanied by wines from small farmers can be found at this very designer restaurant with a wine-bar setting.

Coq Hôtel
2 pl. de la Poissonnerie – ✆ 03 21 81 05 61 – arsene.pousset@wanadoo.fr – Fax 03 21 86 46 73 – Closed 21 December-6 February
19 rm – €115 €115, € 20 – ½ P € 99 – **Rest** – *(closed Sunday) (dinner only)* Menu € 33/47 – Carte € 45/75
◆ This building with a refined façade of red brick is located on a small square in the town centre, providing charming rooms with modern style. This restaurant features two dining areas with parquet, a fireplace, and simple furnishings. Serves traditional cuisine.

Darnétal with rm
pl. de la Poissonnerie – ✆ 03 21 06 04 87 – Fax 03 21 86 64 67 – Closed 23 June-12 July, 22-31 December, Monday and Tuesday
4 rm – €35 €50, € 5 – **Rest** – Menu € 20/36 – Carte € 23/37
◆ This rustic inn on one of the squares of the upper town is decorated with many paintings, old trinkets and copperware. Convivial atmosphere and traditional cooking.

Froggy's Tavern
51 bis pl. du Gén. de Gaulle – ✆ 03 21 86 72 32 – Closed 18 December-3 February
Rest – rôtisserie Menu (€ 18), € 24
◆ Authenticity and conviviality guaranteed at this old granary loft built from wood and stone. Andouillettes and pork loins turn on the spit.

in La Madelaine-sous-Montreuil 3 km West by D 139 and secondary road – pop. 156 – alt. 7 m – ✉ 62170

Auberge de la Grenouillère (Alexandre Gauthier) with rm
– ✆ 03 21 06 07 22 – auberge.de.la.grenouillere@wanadoo.fr – Fax 03 21 86 36 36 – Closed 18 December-5 February, Tuesday and Wednesday except July-August
4 rm – €120/140 €120/140, € 10 – **Rest** – Menu € 33/90 – Carte € 67/82
Spec. Gnocchi de pomme de terre à la truffe d'été (season). Pavé de bar et polenta crémeuse. Panacotta, gelée de fraise et sorbet menthe.
◆ This Picardy-style farmhouse on the banks of the Canche is adorned with old sideboards, copperware and murals depicting frogs having a meal. Modern cuisine with carefully-selected wines.

in Inxent 9 km North On D 127 – pop. 158 – alt. 28 m – ✉ 62170

Auberge d'Inxent with rm
318 r. de la Vallée de la Course – ✆ 03 21 90 71 19 – auberge.inxent@wanadoo.fr – Fax 03 21 86 31 67 – Closed 23 June-5 July, 20 November-5 February, Wednesday except July-August and Tuesday
6 rm – €66 €66, € 9 – ½ P € 58/66 – **Rest** – Menu € 16/39 – Carte € 19/45
◆ This former presbytery converted into a restaurant has fine furniture and a warm family atmosphere. It offers regional cuisine and an extensive list of carefully-selected wines.

MONTREUIL – 93 Seine-Saint-Denis – **311** k2 – **101** 17 – see Paris Environs

MONTREUIL-BELLAY – 49 Maine-et-Loire – **317** I6 – pop. 4 112 – alt. 50 m –

✉ 49260 Châteaux of the Loire 35 **C2**

Paris 335 – Angers 54 – Châtellerault 70 – Chinon 39 – Cholet 61 – Poitiers 80 – Saumur 16

Office de tourisme, place du Concorde ✆ 02 41 52 32 39, Fax 02 41 52 32 35

Château★★ - Site★.

Hostellerie St-Jean

432 r. Nationale – ✆ 02 41 52 30 41 – Fax 02 41 52 89 02 – Closed 25 February-10 March, Wednesday dinner from 15 October to 15 March, Sunday dinner and Monday

Rest – Menu (€ 14), € 18/33 – Carte € 27/40

◆ Located at the centre of the small, fortified, Medieval town; the cosy country-style main dining room is friendly and simple, while the lounge is more modern.

MONTREUIL-L'ARGILLÉ – 27 Eure – **304** C8 – pop. 740 – alt. 170 m –

✉ 27390 33 **C2**

Paris 178 – L'Aigle 26 – Argentan 50 – Bernay 22 – Évreux 56 – Lisieux 33 – Vimoutiers 27

De Courteilles without rest

D 438, rte d'Orbec – ✆ 02 32 47 41 41 – b.borde@hoteldecourteilles.com – Fax 02 32 47 41 51

20 rm – €49 €49, ☕ € 6

◆ An informal atmosphere in this new hotel, built away from the road. Functional bedrooms with varnished wooden furniture.

MONTREVEL-EN-BRESSE – 01 Ain – **328** D2 – pop. 1 994 – alt. 215 m –

✉ 01340 44 **B1**

Paris 395 – Bourg-en-Bresse 18 – Mâcon 25 – Pont-de-Vaux 22 – St-Amour 24 – Tournus 36

Office de tourisme, place de la Grenette ✆ 04 74 25 48 74

Léa (Louis Monnier)

10 rte d'Etrez – ✆ 04 74 30 80 84 – lea.montrevel@free.fr – Fax 04 74 30 85 66 – Closed 26 June-11 July, 22 December-15 January, Monday except July-August, Sunday dinner and Wednesday

Rest – *(number of covers limited, pre-book)* Menu € 25 (weekday lunch), € 35/64 – Carte € 71/101

Spec. Gâteau de foie blonds. Gratin de homard "façon Eugénie Brazier". Poularde de Bresse à la crème et aux morilles. **Wines** Mâcon-Uchizy, Mâcon-Viré-Clessé.

◆ Classic gourmet menu served in a welcoming inn. Plants, paintings and knick-knacks (prevalence of poultry!) lend the dining room a boudoir air.

Le Comptoir

– ✆ 04 74 25 45 53 – lea.montrevel@free.fr – Fax 04 74 30 85 66 – Closed 26 June-10 July, 18 December-8 January, Sunday dinner, Tuesday dinner and Wednesday

Rest – Menu € 18/31 – Carte € 21/35

◆ The Comptoir sports numerous authentic details such as bench seating, posters, mirrors and a mouth-watering bistro menu. Several regional dishes.

Bourg-en-Bresse road 2 km South on D 975 – ✉ 01340 Montrevel-en-Bresse

Pillebois

– ✆ 04 74 25 48 44 – lepillebois@wanadoo.fr – Fax 04 74 25 48 79 – Closed Sunday from October to April

30 rm – €75 €80, ☕ € 8 – 1 suite – ½ P € 65

Rest *L'Aventure* – *(closed Saturday lunchtime and Sunday evening)* Menu € 17 (weekdays)/45 – Carte € 38/47

◆ This hotel has a modern look and Bresse charm with its red brick and wood. Functional, well-kept rooms. The ethnic decor of this restaurant invites you to travel as you sample the interesting menu of reinterpreted regional classics. Poolside terrace.

MONTRICHARD – 41 Loir-et-Cher – 318 E7 – pop. 3 624 – alt. 62 m – ✉ 41400
Châteaux of the Loire 11 **A1**

Paris 220 – Blois 37 – Châteauroux 85 – Châtellerault 95 – Loches 33 – Tours 43 – Vierzon 80

Syndicat d'initiative, 1, rue du Pont ✆ 02 54 32 05 10, Fax 02 54 32 28 80

Keep★: ✻★★.

Le Bellevue
24 quai de la République – ✆ 02 54 32 06 17 – contact@hotel-le-bellevue41.com – Fax 02 54 32 48 06 – Closed Friday, Saturday and Sunday 16 November-14 December

35 rm – €78/88 €78/106, ☕ €11 – 3 suites – ½ P €68/78

Rest – *(closed Sunday dinner, Monday lunch and Friday October-April)* Menu €18 (weekdays)/54 – Carte €34/49

◆ This hotel bears its name well as most of the rooms offer a panoramic view of the Cher. Practical bedrooms. Restaurant with lovely wood panelling, bay windows facing the delightful valley and traditional food.

in Chissay-en-Touraine 4 km West by D 176 – pop. 916 – alt. 63 m – ✉ 41400

Château de Chissay
rest,

– ✆ 02 54 32 32 01 – chissay@leshotelsparticuliers.com – Fax 02 54 32 43 80 – Open March-November

25 rm – €130 €220, ☕ €15 – 5 suites – ½ P €121/166

Rest – Menu €28/62 – Carte €45/77

◆ This 15C château has welcomed some illustrious guests, including Charles VII, Louis XI and de Gaulle. Spacious rooms with character, especially the troglodyte. Elegant restaurant (ribbed vaults, wood panelling and Louis XIII-style furniture) serving modern food.

MONTROND-LES-BAINS – 42 Loire – 327 E6 – pop. 4 031 – alt. 356 m – Spa : late March-late Nov. – Casino – ✉ 42210 Lyon - Rhone Valley 44 **A2**

Paris 447 – Lyon 69 – Montbrison 15 – Roanne 58 – St-Étienne 31 – Thiers 80

Office de tourisme, avenue des Sources ✆ 04 77 94 64 74, Fax 04 77 94 59 59

du Forez Domaine de Presles, South: 12 km by D 1082 and D 16, ✆ 04 77 30 86 85.

Hostellerie La Poularde (Gilles Etéocle)
rm,

2 r. de Saint Etienne – ✆ 04 77 54 40 06 – la-poularde@wanadoo.fr – Fax 04 77 54 53 14 – Closed 3-19 August, 1st-22 January, Tuesday lunch, Sunday dinner and Monday

7 rm – €80 €125, ☕ €20 – 9 suites

Rest – *(pre-book Sat - Sun)* Menu €62/122 – Carte €74/142

Spec. Déclinaison de foie gras de canard. Grosse langoustine croustillante aux herbes, rouget contisé d'amandes grillées, huître noisettine (April to September). Venaison (April to September). **Wines** Condrieu, Saint-Joseph.

◆ A 1732 post house in the thermal spa of Forez. Choose from a personalised bedroom or apartments and duplexes overlooking the pool. Wine shop. A mouth-watering prospect of classical dishes updated with contemporary touches and an excellent wine list to match.

Motel du Forez without rest
37 rte de Roanne – ✆ 04 77 54 42 28 – motelduforez@wanadoo.fr – Fax 04 77 94 66 58 – Closed 10-17 August and 28 December-4 January

18 rm – €41 €51, ☕ €7,50

◆ This Fifties hotel has comfortable, soundproofed bedrooms with pine furniture, well protected from the noise of the road. Extremely well-kept. Family hospitality.

Carré Sud
4 rte Lyon – ✆ 04 77 54 42 71 – carresudfs@orange.fr – Fax 04 77 54 52 85 – Closed Sunday except lunch from September to May, Tuesday dinner except from June to August and Wednesday lunch

Rest – Menu €17 bi (weekday lunch), €30/55 – Carte €40/64

◆ Suggestions on the specials board at lunch, more substantial menu in the evening. Market-inspired cuisine based around spices and Mediterranean flavours. Summer terrace.

MONTROUGE – 92 Hauts-de-Seine – 311 J3 – 101 25 – see Paris, Area

LE MONT-ST-MICHEL – 50 Manche – 303 C8 – pop. 46 – alt. 10 m – ✉ 50170

Normandie Cotentin, Brittany 32 A3

- Paris 359 – Alençon 135 – Avranches 23 – Dinan 58 – Fougères 45 – Rennes 68 – St-Malo 55
- Office de tourisme, boulevard de l'Avancée ✆ 02 33 60 14 30, Fax 02 33 60 06 75
- Abbey★★★: La Merveille★★★, Cloister★★★ - Ramparts★★ - Grande-Rue★ - Abbey gardens★ - Mont-St-Michel Bay ★★.

Auberge St-Pierre

rm, VISA MC AE

– ✆ 02 33 60 14 03 – aubergesaintpierre@wanadoo.fr – Fax 02 33 48 59 82 – Closed 30 Dec - 1 Jan

21 rm – €98/140 €112/160, €13 – ½ P €90/162 – **Rest** – Menu €22/48 – Carte €35/61

◆ This 15C half-timbered inn is home to a restaurant and small well-kept bedrooms. The latter are bigger in an adjacent wing and offer sea views. You have a choice between a brasserie on the road side, a dining room upstairs or the terrace built against the ramparts.

La Mère Poulard with rm

VISA MC AE

Gde Rue – ✆ 02 33 89 68 68 – hotel@merepoulard.com – Fax 02 33 89 68 69

27 rm – €100/280 €100/280, €15 – ½ P €125/215

Rest – Menu €45/65 – Carte €68/90

◆ Mother Poulard's famous omelette rubs shoulders with appetising regional recipes. Inviting rooms, some of which command a panoramic view.

in la Digue 2 km South On D 976 – ✉ 50170 Le Mont-St-Michel

Relais St-Michel

< Mont - St - Michel, rm, P VISA MC AE

– ✆ 02 33 89 32 00 – hotel@relais-saint-michel.com – Fax 02 33 89 32 01

32 rm – €120/250 €120/250, €14 – 7 suites – ½ P €115/195

Rest – Menu (€25), €35 (lunch), €45/65 – Carte €49/70

◆ The abbey in the background and elegant English-style furniture add to this establishment's charm. Large rooms with balcony or terrace. A dining room with a view of the famous Mount. Classic fare.

Mercure

rm, P VISA MC AE

– ✆ 02 33 60 14 18 – contact@hotelmercure-montsaintmichel.com – Fax 02 33 60 39 28 – Open 11 February-10 November

100 rm – €68/111 €74/117, €10

Rest *Le Pré Salé* – Menu €19/48 – Carte €27/61

◆ This hotel complex, along the Couesnon and at the dyke's initial section, offers mostly identical and practical bedrooms with the chain's new design. Taste the renowned salt meadow lamb in the bright, spacious dining room.

De la Digue

< AC rest, rm, P VISA MC AE

– ✆ 02 33 60 14 02 – hotel-de-la-digue@wanadoo.fr – Fax 02 33 60 37 59 – Open from end March to beg. November

35 rm – €60/65 €65/88, €9,50 – ½ P €70/85 – **Rest** – Menu €20/33 – Carte €32/50

◆ Since 1877, the dyke links Mont-St-Michel to the mainland. The long, coastal hotel offers functional bedrooms of various sizes. Sober dining room commanding a view of the Mont St Michel. Traditional cooking, seafood specialities.

Do not confuse X with ✿!
X defines comfort, while stars are awarded for the best cuisine, across all categories of comfort.

MONTSALVY – 15 Cantal – 330 C6 – pop. 896 – alt. 800 m – ✉ 15120
Auvergne 5 **B3**

Paris 586 – Aurillac 31 – Entraygues-sur-Truyère 14 – Figeac 57 – Rodez 56

Office de tourisme, rue du Tour-de-Ville ✆ 04 71 49 21 43, Fax 04 71 49 65 56

Puy-de-l'Arbre ✻★ Northeast: 1.5 km.

L'Auberge Fleurie with rm VISA

– ✆ 04 71 49 20 02 – info@auberge-fleurie.com – Fax 04 71 49 29 65 – Closed 29 September-6 October, 6 January-13 February, Sunday dinner and Monday except July-August

7 rm – ♦€ 46/62 ♦♦€ 46/62, ☕ € 7,50 – ½ P € 50/61

Rest – *(closed Sun evening and Mon from mid - Sept. to mid - Jun)* Menu € 16 (weekday lunch), € 24/43 – Carte € 30/46

◆ The charm of yesteryear happily rubs shoulders with contemporary elegance in this smart inn where the chef rustles up tasty updated country fare. Excellent cellar. Attractive, very calm colonial-style rooms and delicious breakfasts.

MONT-SAXONNEX – 74 Haute-Savoie – 328 L4 – pop. 1 477 – alt. 1 000 m – ✉ 74130
46 **F1**

Paris 572 – Lyon 189 – Annecy 57 – Genève 38 – Vernier 55

Office de tourisme, 294 route de l'Eglise ✆ 04 50 96 97 27, Fax 04 50 96 97 63

Jalouvre P VISA AE

45 rte Gorge du Cé – ✆ 04 50 96 90 67 – lejalouvre@iletait3fois.com – Fax 04 50 96 91 41

15 rm – ♦€ 60 ♦♦€ 75, ☕ € 8 – ½ P € 55 – **Rest** – Menu € 13,50 bi (weekday lunch), € 20/50 – Carte € 28/42

◆ This completely renovated hotel in a quiet, mountain-village location offers comfortable, modern rooms decorated in the style of a contemporary chalet. Modern cuisine served in a wood-dominated decor. Panoramic views, plus a terrace under the shade of a lime tree.

LES MONTS-DE-VAUX – 39 Jura – 321 E6 – see Poligny

MONTSÉGUR – 09 Ariège – 343 I7 – see Lavelanet

MONTSOREAU – 49 Maine-et-Loire – 317 J5 – pop. 544 – alt. 77 m – ✉ 49730
Châteaux of the Loire 35 **C2**

Paris 292 – Angers 75 – Châtellerault 65 – Chinon 18 – Poitiers 82 – Saumur 11 – Tours 56

Office de tourisme, avenue de la Loire ✆ 02 41 51 70 22

✻★★ from the viewpoint.

Candes St-Martin★: Collégiales★.

La Marine de Loire without rest P VISA AE

9 quai de la Loire – ✆ 02 41 50 18 21 – resa@hotel-lamarinedeloire.com – Fax 02 41 50 19 26 – Closed 4-9 January

8 rm – ♦€ 130 ♦♦€ 130/170, ☕ € 15 – 3 suites

◆ This hotel on the banks of the Loire is home to a flower-decked interior garden and delightful rooms. Large Jacuzzi swim tub and massages on request. Sunday brunch.

Le Bussy without rest P VISA AE

4 r. Jehanne d'Arc – ✆ 02 41 38 11 11 – hotel.lebussy@wanadoo.fr – Fax 02 41 38 18 10 – Open mid February-mid November

12 rm – ♦€ 59/78 ♦♦€ 59/78, ☕ € 9

◆ Most of the rooms in this 18C house face the pretty castle of La Dame de Monsoreau, whose lover was Bussy. "Troglodyte" breakfast room.

Diane de Méridor VISA AE

12 quai Ph. de Commines – ✆ 02 41 51 71 76 – dianedemeridor@wanadoo.fr – Fax 02 41 51 17 17 – Closed 17-30 November, 8 January-8 February, Tuesday and Wednesday

Rest – Menu (€ 15), € 28/70 bi – Carte € 57/71

◆ Behind the old tufa façade of this restaurant is a dining room with views of the Loire. The brick-coloured walls are embellished with paintings. Elegant traditional cuisine.

MOOSCH – 68 Haut-Rhin – 315 G9 – pop. 1 912 – alt. 390 m – ✉ 68690 1 A3

Paris 469 – Strasbourg 128 – Colmar 53 – Mulhouse 29 – Belfort 48

Aux Trois Rois

35 r. du Gén. de Gaulle – ✆ 03 89 82 34 66 – contact@aux-trois-rois.com – Fax 03 89 82 39 27 – Closed 2-10 March, 22 June-9 July, 24 December-7 January, Monday and Tuesday

Rest – Menu € 32/48 – Carte € 35/50

♦ A restaurant with a specials board that focuses on fish and seafood. Typically Alsatian-style (wood panelling, stained glass) or more dining rooms. Shaded terrace.

MORANGIS – 91 Essonne – 312 D3 – 101 35 – see Paris, Area

MOREILLES – 85 Vendée – 316 J9 – pop. 219 – alt. 5 m – ✉ 85450 34 B3

Paris 443 – Nantes 103 – La Roche-sur-Yon 50 – La Rochelle 42 – Fontenay-le-Comte 43

Le Château de l'Abbaye

– ✆ 02 51 56 17 56 – daniellerenard@hotmail.com – Fax 02 51 56 30 30

5 rm – †€ 69/109 ††€ 69/159, ☕ € 12 – ½ P € 79/125

Table d'hôte – Menu € 36

♦ A romantic château built on the ruins of an abbey where Richelieu officiated. Elegant rooms (antique furniture and family heirlooms), attractive sitting rooms and attentive service. Table d'hôte ambiance and generous portions of good family cooking.

MORESTEL – 38 Isère – 333 F3 – pop. 3 034 – alt. 220 m – ✉ 38510 45 C2

Paris 506 – Lyon 65 – Vénissieux 63 – Villeurbanne 64

Office de tourisme, 100, place des Halles ✆ 04 74 80 19 59, Fax 04 74 80 56 71

Ferme de Montin without rest

1 km south-west on D 244 and D 19C – ✆ 04 74 80 52 15 – vchomard@aol.com – Fax 04 74 80 52 15

3 rm ☕ – †€ 129/139 ††€ 149/159

♦ This authentic 14C farmhouse is home to a refined decor and luxurious, romantic rooms. Without forgetting the garden, handsome pool or the silence of the countryside.

MORET-SUR-LOING – 77 Seine-et-Marne – 312 F5 – pop. 4 402 – alt. 50 m – ✉ 77250 Northern France and the Paris Region 19 C3

Paris 74 – Fontainebleau 11 – Melun 28 – Nemours 17 – Sens 44

Office de tourisme, 4 bis, place de Samois ✆ 01 60 70 41 66, Fax 01 60 70 82 52

de la Forteresse Thoury-Férottes Domaine de la Forteresse, Southwest: 15 km by D 218 and D 22, ✆ 01 60 96 95 10.

Site★.

Auberge de la Terrasse

40 r. Pêcherie – ✆ 01 60 70 51 03 – aubergedelaterrasse@wanadoo.fr – Fax 01 60 70 51 69 – Closed 15 October-4 November, Friday dinner, Sunday dinner and Monday

17 rm – †€ 39/61 ††€ 53/75, ☕ € 10 – ½ P € 48/59 – **Rest** – Menu € 22 – Carte € 24/39

♦ An old building on the banks of the River Loing. Providing small, well-kept rooms with sound-proofed windows. Rustic-style dining room and terrace overlooking the river often painted by Alfred Sisley. Serving traditional cuisine.

Le Relais de Pont-Loup

14 r. Peintre Sisley – ✆ 01 60 70 43 05 – relaispontloup@wanadoo.fr – Fax 01 60 70 22 54 – Closed Sunday dinner and Monday

Rest – *(pre-book Sat - Sun)* Menu € 28/55 – Carte € 38/63

♦ Bricks, beams, fireplace and roasting spit make up the décor in this restaurant that is reached via the kitchens. Terrace facing the garden that winds down to the Loing.

Hostellerie du Cheval Noir with rm
47 av. J. Jaurès – 01 60 70 80 20 – infos@chevalnoir.fr – Fax 01 60 70 80 21 – Closed 21 July-11 August, 19 January-3 February, Monday lunch and Tuesday lunch
10 rm – €55/110 €65/125, €12 – 1 suite – ½ P €73/102
Rest – Menu €30/90 – Carte €70/104
◆ This 18C post house opposite the gateway to the old fortified town has a dining room hung with paintings. Inventive "sugar and spice" cuisine.

MOREY-ST-DENIS – 21 Côte-d'Or – 320 J6 – pop. 673 – alt. 275 m – ✉ 21220

Paris 318 – Beaune 30 – Dijon 16 8 **D1**

Castel de Très Girard rm,
7 r. de Très Girard – 03 80 34 33 09 – info@castel-tres-girard.com – Fax 03 80 51 81 92 – Closed 16-26 November and 17 February-5 March
9 rm – €79/129 €79/186, €14,50 – ½ P €105/143
Rest – Menu €23/80 – Carte €51/63
◆ Attractive 18C mansion amid the Côte d'Or vineyards. Personalised rooms (four-poster beds and exposed rafters). Fine wine list and up-to-date dishes in a dining room with a modern touch but still in the same rustic style.

MORGAT – 29 Finistère – 308 E5 – ✉ 29160 Crozon Brittany 9 **A2**

Paris 590 – Brest 62 – Châteaulin 38 – Douarnenez 42 – Morlaix 84 – Quimper 52
Large grottoes★.

Le Grand Hôtel de la Mer
av. de la Plage – 02 98 27 02 09 – thierry.regnier@vvf-vacances.fr – Fax 02 98 27 02 39 – Open 6 April-5 October
78 rm – €48/91 €56/125, €14 – **Rest** – *(closed Tuesday lunch, Saturday lunch and Monday except dinner in July-August)* Menu €21/39
◆ A Belle Époque atmosphere pervades in this hotel, which is run by the VVF group. Spacious, simple bedrooms overlooking the sea or the garden planted with palm trees. This hotel has two dining areas: a large room for guests on half-board and a more intimate restaurant. Both rooms overlook Douarnene bay.

Julia rest,
43 r. de Tréflez – 02 98 27 05 89 – contact@hoteljulia.fr – Fax 02 98 27 23 10 – Closed 3 January-28 February
18 rm – €51/140 €51/140, €9 – 1 suite – ½ P €58/102
Rest – *(open 1st April-6 November, 20 December-2 January and closed lunch Tuesday-Friday except July-August and Monday)* Menu €13 (lunch), €19/58 – Carte €27/53
◆ Situated in a quiet residential area, this hotel is gradually being renovated to provide modern levels of comfort (to date, four large, contemporary-style bedrooms and a brand new seminar room). "Boarding house" atmosphere in the circular dining room. Regional recipes.

De la Baie without rest
46 bd Plage – 02 98 27 07 51 – hotel.de.la.baie@presquile-crozon.com – Fax 02 98 26 29 65 – **26 rm** – €35/65 €35/65, €7
◆ A small, simple hotel with practical, well-maintained and slightly old-fashioned bedrooms. Fine sea views from the attractive breakfast room and some of the guestrooms.

MORILLON – 74 Haute-Savoie – 328 N4 – see Samoëns

MORLAÀS – 64 Pyrénées-Atlantiques – 342 K2 – pop. 3 658 – alt. 287 m – ✉ 64160 Atlantic Coast 3 **B3**

Paris 767 – Pau 15 – Tarbes 37
Office de tourisme, place Sainte-Foy 05 59 33 62 25, Fax 05 59 33 62 25
Portal★ of Sainte-Foy church.

Le Bourgneuf with rm
3 r. Bourg Neuf – 05 59 33 44 02 – courbet.daniel@wanadoo.fr – Fax 05 59 33 07 74 – Closed 15 October-8 November, Sunday dinner and Saturday
12 rm – €43 €47/52, €5 – ½ P €42/52
Rest – Menu €14 bi/40 – Carte €21/39
◆ Regional cuisine served in a simple, rustic decor. Dishes of the day also served at the bar. The essentially practical rooms are in a recent building.

MORLAIX – 29 Finistère – **308** H3 – pop. 15 990 – alt. 7 m – ✉ 29600
Brittany

- Paris 538 – Brest 61 – Quimper 78 – St-Brieuc 86
- Office de tourisme, place des Otages ☎ 02 98 62 14 94, Fax 02 98 63 84 87
- de Carantec Carantec Rue de Kergrist, North: 13 km by D73, ☎ 02 98 67 09 14.
- Old Morlaix★: Viaduct★ - Grand'Rue★ - Interior★ of "Reine Anne" (Queen Anne) house - Virgin★ in St-Mathieu church - Rose★ in the musée des Jacobins★.
- Calvaire★★ de Plougonven★ 12 km by D 9.

MORLAIX

- Aiguillon (R. d') ..... BZ 2
- Allende (Pl. S.) ..... BZ 3
- Ange-de-Guernisac (R.) ..... BY 5
- Bouchers (R. des) .. BZ 6
- Brest (R. de) ..... AZ
- Carnot (R.) ..... BZ 7
- Dossen (Pl.du) ..... BZ 8
- Grand'R. ..... BZ
- Jacobins (Pl. des) .. BZ 12
- Mur (R. du) ..... BZ 13
- Otages (Pl. des) ..... AY
- Paris (Rte de) ..... BZ 14
- Paris (R. de) ..... BZ
- Poan-Ben (allée du) . BZ 16
- Son (Venelle au) .... BZ 18
- Traoulen (Pl.) ..... BZ 20

De l'Europe without rest
1 r. Aiguillon – ☎ 02 98 62 11 99 – reservations@hotel-europe-com.fr – Fax 02 98 88 83 38 – Closed 18 December-6 January BZ **a**
60 rm – 🛉€ 76/120 🛉🛉€ 80/250, ☕ € 8
◆ The hall and staircase of this 200-year old building have fine carved 17C wooden-panelling. Choose a refurbished room with prettier decor. Cheerful hospitality.

Du Port without rest
3 quai de Léon – ☎ 02 98 88 07 54 – info@lhotelduport.com – Fax 02 98 88 43 80 – Closed 20 December-10 January AY **r**
25 rm – 🛉€ 58/72 🛉🛉€ 65/80, ☕ € 8,50
◆ A 19C Breton house facing the marina. Practical rooms, which are all modernised and well-soundproofed. Some have a view of the quayside and viaduct.

Les Bruyères without rest
3 km via Plouigneau road, east on the D712 – ☎ 02 98 88 08 68 – hotellesbruyeres@wanadoo.fr – Fax 02 98 88 66 54
32 rm – 🛉€ 47/72 🛉🛉€ 47/75, ☕ € 7,50
◆ A low level, typical 1970s building providing fully refurbished rooms (practical furnishings and lively colours) and welcoming breakfast room.

Manoir de Coat Amour
rte de Paris – ☏ 02 98 88 57 02 – coatamour@wanadoo.fr – Fax 02 98 88 57 02 BZ **r**
6 rm – €72/100 €80/113 – **Table d'hôte** – Menu €32 bi/47 bi
◆ Set above the town, this regional-style 19C manor is surrounded by a floral park. Providing plush and spacious rooms with antique furnishings. Table d'hôte on some evenings during the week.

Brasserie de l'Europe
pl. E. Souvestre – ☏ 02 98 88 81 15 – contact@brasseriedeleurope.com – Fax 02 98 63 47 24 – Closed 4-11 May, 1st-7 January and Sunday BZ **y**
Rest – Menu €15 – Carte €20/35
◆ A wide choice of wines by the bottle, pitcher or glass accompanies the appetising traditional cuisine served in this large brasserie with contemporary decor.

La Marée Bleue
3 rampe St-Mélaine – ☏ 02 98 63 24 21 – la.marée.bleue@wanadoo.fr – Closed 1st-20 October, Sunday dinner and Monday except July-August BY **s**
Rest – Menu €25 – Carte €20/45
◆ Restaurant in one of the oldest houses in the St-Mélaine church district. The interior is rustic, with regional furniture, paintings by local artists and traditional cuisine.

L'Hermine
35 r. Ange de Guernisac – ☏ 02 98 88 10 91 – Closed 13-22 June, 24 November-7 December, 30 December-14 January, Sunday and Wednesday BY **d**
Rest – crêperie Carte €11/21
◆ Beams, waxed wooden tables and country objects form the setting for this pleasant pancake house on a pedestrian street. Fresh seaweed pancakes a speciality.

via ① 4 km by D 76 (right bank) and secondary road - ✉ 29600 Morlaix

Manoir de Roch ar Brini without rest
Ploujean – ☏ 02 98 72 01 44 – contact@brittanyguesthouse.com – Fax 02 98 88 04 49
3 rm – €70/85 €70/85
◆ This manor, built in 1870 and surrounded by a wooded park, has individually furnished rooms (two of them are very large) and features a fine stone staircase. Elegant original dining room.

MORNAC-SUR-SEUDRE – 17 Charente-Maritime – 324 D5 – pop. 652 – alt. 5 m – ✉ 17113 Poitou Charentes Vendée 38 A3

Paris 508 – Poitiers 175 – La Rochelle 66 – Rochefort 36 – Saintes 38

Le Mornac without rest
21 r. des Halles – ☏ 05 46 22 63 20 – le-mornac@orange.fr – Fax 05 46 22 63 20 – Closed 14 January-4 February
5 rm – €55/70 €60/75
◆ Handsome 18C abode converted into a guesthouse by a charming couple of Dutch origin. Cosy rooms in which guests will immediately feel at home. Garden, terrace, swimming pool.

MORNAS – 84 Vaucluse – 332 B8 – pop. 2 209 – alt. 37 m – ✉ 84550 Provence 40 A2

Paris 646 – Avignon 40 – Bollène 12 – Montélimar 47 – Nyons 46 – Orange 12

Le Manoir rest, VISA AE
16 av. Jean Moulin – ☏ 04 90 37 00 79 – info@lemanoir-mornas.fr – Fax 04 90 37 10 34 – Closed 1st January-12 February, Sunday, Monday and Tuesday October-May
24 rm – €52/54 €54/96, €8 – ½ P €62/83
Rest – *(closed Tuesday except dinner June-September, Sunday dinner October-May and Monday)* Menu €27/45 – Carte €33/44
◆ At the foot of a tall cliff and a famous fortress, this refined 18C hotel has rooms with charm and a retro-style environment. Renovated rooms in various styles. Rustic, Provençal dining room and delightfully shaded patio terrace. Traditional cooking.

MORSBRONN-LES-BAINS – 67 Bas-Rhin – 315 K3 – pop. 522 – alt. 200 m – ✉ 67360 1 B1

Paris 489 – Haguenau 11 – Sarreguemines 68 – Strasbourg 44 – Wissembourg 28

Office de tourisme, 1, route de Haguenau ✆ 03 88 05 82 40, Fax 03 88 94 20 04

La Source des Sens

19 rte Haguenau – ✆ 03 88 09 30 53 – info@lasourcedessens.com – Fax 03 88 09 35 65 – Closed 15-31 July, 10-16 November and 15 January-15 February

19 rm – €40/170 €55/190, ☕ €11 – 7 suites – ½ P €60/125

Rest – *(closed Sunday dinner and Monday)* Menu €15/90 bi – Carte €46/57

♦ An in vogue establishment: minimalist design, dark wood, Japanese light fixtures in the rooms and an extensive wellness centre. In the restaurant, a plasma screen broadcasts action live from the kitchens. Modern decor and creative dishes.

MORTAGNE-AU-PERCHE – 61 Orne – 310 M3 – pop. 4 513 – alt. 260 m – ✉ 61400 Normandy 33 C3

Paris 153 – Alençon 39 – Chartres 80 – Lisieux 89 – Le Mans 73 – Verneuil-sur-Avre 40

Office de tourisme, Halle aux Grains ✆ 02 33 85 11 18, Fax 02 33 83 34 37

De Bellême Saint-Martin Bellême Les Sablons, South: 17 km by D 938, ✆ 02 33 73 12 79.

Panelling★ of N.-Dame church.

Du Tribunal

rm,

4 pl. Palais – ✆ 02 33 25 04 77 – hotel.du.tribunal@wanadoo.fr – Fax 02 33 83 60 83

21 rm – €50/100 €50/100, ☕ €9 – ½ P €60/75 – **Rest** – Menu (€13,50), €19/40 – Carte €30/47

♦ This delightful 13C and 18C flower-decked house offers guests a choice of well-maintained, old-style bedrooms decorated in harmonious tones. An elegant dining room where the culinary offerings include black pudding, a speciality of Mortagne. Quiet terrace and courtyard garden.

in Pin-la-Garenne 9 km South by Bellême road on D 938 – pop. 639 – alt. 158 m – ✉ 61400

La Croix d'Or

6 r. de la Herse – ✆ 02 33 83 80 33 – Fax 02 33 83 06 03 – Closed 4 February-2 March, Tuesday dinner and Wednesday

Rest – Menu (€9,50), €17/45 – Carte €26/48

♦ Friendly inn alongside the main road through the village. In Winter, the fireplace warms the recently renovated, rustic dining area. Traditional cooking served.

MORTAGNE-SUR-GIRONDE – 17 Charente-Maritime – 324 F7 – pop. 967 – alt. 51 m – ✉ 17120 Atlantic Coast 38 B3

Paris 509 – Blaye 59 – Jonzac 30 – Pons 26 – La Rochelle 115 – Royan 34 – Saintes 36

Syndicat d'initiative, 1, place des Halles ✆ 05 46 90 52 90, Fax 05 46 90 52 90

Chapel★ of the St-Martial hermitage South : 1,5 km.

La Maison du Meunier without rest

36 quai de l'Estuaire, (at the port) – ✆ 05 46 97 75 10 – info@maisondumeunier.com – Fax 05 46 92 25 54

5 rm ☕ – €55/60 €55/90

♦ Modern art, old photos and even an old motorbike decorate this house that once belonged to a miller. Attractive personalised rooms and delightful welcome.

MORTEAU – 25 Doubs – 321 J4 – pop. 6 375 – alt. 780 m – ✉ 25500 Burgundy-Jura 17 C2

Paris 468 – Basel 121 – Belfort 88 – Besançon 65 – Neuchâtel 42 – Pontarlier 31

Office de tourisme, place de la Halle ✆ 03 81 67 18 53, Fax 03 81 67 62 34

La Guimbarde without rest
10 pl. Carnot – ✆ 03 81 67 14 12 – info@la-guimbarde.com – Fax 03 81 67 48 27
19 rm – €49/100 €54/100, ☕ €7,50
◆ Imposing 19C building with updated rooms; only the breakfast room has kept its rustic appearance. Piano bar in the lounge at weekends.

Auberge de la Roche (Philippe Feuvrier)
at Pont de la Roche, 3 km southwest by D 437 ✉ 25570 – ✆ 03 81 68 80 05 – pfeuvrier@wanadoo.fr – Fax 03 81 68 87 64
– Closed 24 June-5 July, 12-31 January, Tuesday dinner, Sunday dinner and Monday
Rest – Menu €27/78 – Carte €58/81
Spec. Terrine de foie gras d'oie. Filet de sandre rôti, sabayon de trousseau. Brochette de caille désossée. **Wines** Château-Châlon, Côtes du Jura-Trousseau.
◆ A warm welcome and updated Franche Comté cuisine have brought renown to this restaurant in the green Haut Doubs countryside. Aperitifs and coffee are served on the terrace.

in Grand'Combe-Châteleu 5 km Southwest by D 437 and D 47 – pop. 1 266 – alt. 760 m – ✉ 25570

Old farmhouses★.

Faivre
– ✆ 03 81 68 84 63 – Fax 03 81 68 87 80 – Closed Sunday dinner and Monday
Rest – Menu €18 bi (weekday lunch), €25/60 – Carte €22/66
◆ A large Comté house in a picturesque hamlet with attractive old farmhouses. Rustic setting where regulars sample regional dishes, including the renowned Morteau sausage, the 'Jesus'.

in Combes 7 km West by D 48 and secondary road – pop. 598 – alt. 935 m – ✉ 25500

L'Auberge de la Motte
la Motte – ✆ 03 81 67 23 35 – auberge.delamotte@orange.fr – Fax 03 81 67 63 45 – Closed 15-30 November
7 rm – €42/45 €45/48, ☕ €6,50 – ½ P €44/48
Rest – *(closed Sunday dinner and Monday lunch)* Menu €10, €20/29
◆ Restored regional style farmhouse dating from 1808. Wood panelled rooms with modern furniture. Simple regional menu with the emphasis on local produce. Summer terrace.

MORTEMART – 87 Haute-Vienne – 325 C4 – pop. 126 – alt. 300 m – ✉ 87330

Dordogne-Berry-Limousin 24 **A1**

Paris 388 – Bellac 14 – Confolens 31 – Limoges 41 – St-Junien 20

Syndicat d'initiative, Château des Ducs ✆ 05 55 68 98 98

Le Relais with rm
1 pl. Royale – ✆ 05 55 68 12 09 – dominique.pradeau189@wanadoo.fr – Fax 05 55 68 12 09 – Closed February, Tuesday except 15 July-31 August and Monday
5 rm – €45/52 €45/68, ☕ €8 – ½ P €62
Rest – Menu €19/45 – Carte €43/54
◆ A pleasant country restaurant with exposed beams, bare stonework and fireplace. Opposite the lovely food market. Tasty traditional cuisine, and simple but attractive rooms.

MORTHEMER – 86 Vienne – 322 J6 – ✉ 86300

Poitou Charentes Vendée 39 **C2**

Paris 370 – Poitiers 33 – Châtellerault 70 – Buxerolles 35 – Chauvigny 17

La Passerelle
– ✆ 05 49 01 13 33 – Fax 05 49 01 13 33 – Closed 4-11 February, Sunday dinner, Monday and Wednesday
Rest – Menu €11 bi (weekday lunch), €25/45 – Carte €37/41
◆ The majestic chateau of Morthemer dominates this tiny country house reached via a footbridge (hence the name). Rustic interior, traditional fare made from fresh produce.

MORZINE – 74 Haute-Savoie – 328 N3 – pop. 2 948 – alt. 960 m – Winter sports : 1 000/2 100 m 6 61 – ✉ 74110 French Alps 46 F1

Paris 586 – Annecy 84 – Cluses 26 – Genève 58 – Thonon-les-Bains 31

Office de tourisme, 23, Place du Baraty ✆ 04 50 74 72 72, Fax 04 50 79 03 48

Avoriaz Office du Tourisme Avoriaz, East: 12 km by D 338, ✆ 04 50 74 11 07.

Le Pléney★ by cable car, pointe du Nyon★ by cable car - Télésiège de Chamoissière (Chamoissière chairlift)★★.

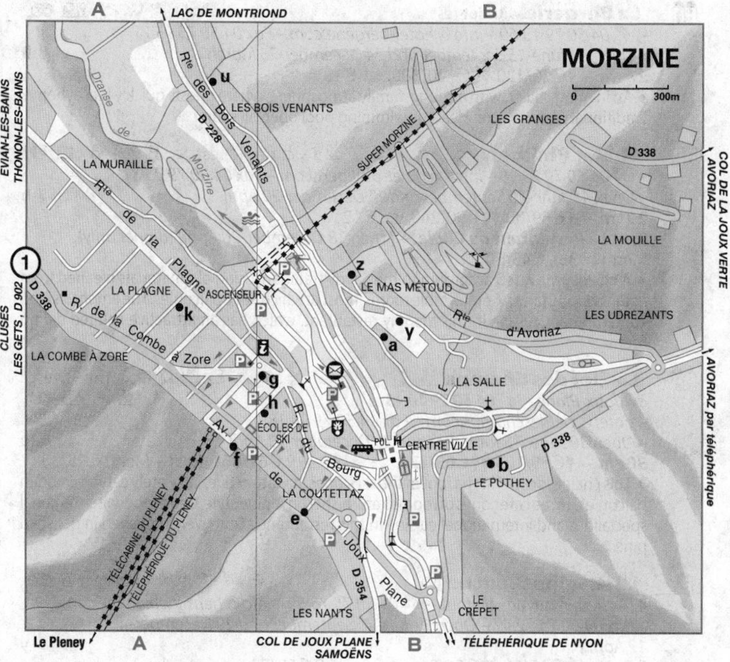

Le Samoyède

– ✆ 04 50 79 00 79 – info@hotel-lesamoyede.com – Fax 04 50 79 07 91
– *Open mid June to mid September and mid December to mid April* B **g**
30 rm – 🚹€ 50/105 🚹🚹€ 147/250, ☕ € 13 – 1 suite – ½ P € 70/180
Rest ***L'Atelier*** – *(closed lunch except Sunday and public holidays)* Menu € 37/66 – Carte € 43/61
Rest ***La Taverne*** – Menu € 21/30 – Carte € 26/43

♦ Most of the spacious guestrooms in this large, centrally located chalet face west, with views of the ski slopes. Personal touches in the rooms. Elegant ambience and innovative cuisine. This restaurant serves regional and bistro-style cuisine. Simple decor.

Le Dahu

293 chemin du Mas Métout – ✆ *04 50 75 92 92*
– *info@dahu.com* – *Fax 04 50 75 92 50*
– *Open 20 June-10 September and 20 December-15 April*
39 rm – 🚹€ 42/130 🚹🚹€ 67/205, ☕ € 13 – 8 suites – ½ P € 67/150
Rest – *(closed lunch in winter except school holidays and Tuesday dinner from 20 December to 15 April)* Menu € 26/55 B **z**

♦ Family hotel dominating the valley on the right bank of the Dranse. Cosy mountain accommodation, often with balcony. A good place to recharge one's batteries. Panoramic restaurant with an original menu.

Champs Fleuris rest, VISA MC AE
– ☎ 04 50 79 14 44 – info@hotel-champsfleuris.fr – Fax 04 50 79 27 75
– *Open 21 June-14 September and 16 December-14 April* A **f**
47 rm – †€ 80/120 ††€ 80/150, ☕ € 12 – 6 suites – ½ P € 90/170
Rest – Menu € 24 bi (lunch), € 28 € bi/35 bi
◆ Ideally situated at the foot of the Le Pléney cable-car. Spacious guestrooms, most of which have been renovated in Alpine style. Lounge with fireplace and a view over the ski slopes. Traditional cuisine served in a semi-contemporary, chalet-style dining room.

La Bergerie without rest VISA MC
– ☎ 04 50 79 13 69 – info@hotel-bergerie.com – Fax 04 50 75 95 71
– *Open 30 June-15 September and 24 December-23 March* B **h**
27 rm – †€ 70/120 ††€ 120/300, ☕ € 12
◆ An inviting chalet, with a young, family atmosphere, where guests quickly feel at home. Traditional Alpine decor. Heated swimming pool open all year.

Chalet Philibert rm, rest, P VISA MC AE
– ☎ 04 50 79 25 18 – info@chalet-philibert.com – Fax 04 50 79 25 81
– *Open 1st June-20 September and 1st December-20 April* B **b**
29 rm – †€ 69/98 ††€ 90/240, ☕ € 12
Rest ***Le Restaurant du Chalet*** – *(open 18 December-20 April) (dinner only)*
Menu (€ 35), € 45/60
◆ A chalet renovated according to the Savoy tradition, using old materials gleaned from neighbouring farms. Comfortable rooms, most of which have balconies. The emphasis is on contemporary cuisine in this friendly restaurant, which has an attractive vaulted dining room

La Clef des Champs rm, rest, P VISA MC
av. Joux-Plane – ☎ 04 50 79 10 13
– *hotel@clefdeschamps.com – Fax 04 50 79 08 18*
– *Open 30 June-2 September and 20 December-10 April* B **e**
30 rm – †€ 55/105 ††€ 65/120, ☕ € 12 – ½ P € 67/86 – **Rest** – Menu € 25/30
◆ This chalet, located at the foot of the ski slopes, has attractive, intricately carved wooden balconies. Three categories of rooms, refurbished in Alpine style. Choose between regional specialities and international cuisine in this restaurant, attractively furnished in polished pine.

L'Hermine Blanche rest, P VISA MC
414 chemin du Mas Metout – ☎ 04 50 75 76 55 – *info@hermineblanche.com*
– *Fax 04 50 74 72 47 – Open 1st July-1st September and 20 December-12 April* B **y**
25 rm – †€ 46/61 ††€ 56/81, ☕ € 8 – ½ P € 58/75
Rest – *(dinner only)* Menu € 20
◆ Near the road to Avoriaz, this attractive chalet offers simple, fresh and welcoming rooms, all with a balcony. A pleasant half-covered swimming pool and jacuzzi face the garden. Residents can choose from a range of international dishes prepared by the Italian chef.

Fleur des Neiges P VISA MC
– ☎ 04 50 79 01 23 – info@chaletfleurdesneiges.com – Fax 04 50 75 95 75
– *Open 1st July-5 September and 20 December-10 April* A **k**
31 rm – †€ 40/78 ††€ 70/120, ☕ € 10 – ½ P € 50/95
Rest – Menu € 15 (weekday lunch), € 20/25
◆ This fully renovated establishment offers cosy rooms with pine furniture and snug duvets. Leisure facilities: fitness centre, sauna, tennis court and pool. A panelled dining room in winter. In summer, service in the garden. Set menu.

Les Côtes P VISA MC
265 Chemin de la Salle – ☎ 04 50 79 09 96 – *info@hotel-lescotes.com*
– *Fax 04 50 75 97 38 – Open 1st July-31 August and 20 December-4 April* B **a**
4 rm – †€ 55/65 ††€ 55/65, ☕ € 8 – 19 suites – ††€ 66/136 – ½ P € 55/81 –
Rest – *(dinner only)* Menu € 20/23
◆ This double chalet, with carved wooden balconies, is well situated on a south-facing slope. Simple but well-kept rooms and studio apartments. Good choice of leisure activities, including an attractive glass-covered swimming pool.

L'Ours Blanc rest,
– 04 50 79 04 02 – info@oursblanc-morzine.com – Fax 04 50 75 97 82
– Open 5 July-7 September and 22 December-10 April A **u**
22 rm – €45 €56/70, €9 – ½ P €55/68
Rest – *(dinner only) (residents only)* Menu €22 (weekdays)/26
♦ Standard south-facing chalet, set away from the centre. Clean, attractive and simply furnished guestrooms, some of which have balconies. Hospitable welcome. This restaurant only serves one menu - fondue and raclette twice a week.

in Avoriaz **14 km East by D 338 – ✉ 74110**

Office de tourisme, place centrale 04 50 74 02 11, Fax 04 50 74 24 29

Les Dromonts VISA AE
pedestrian access – 04 50 74 08 11 – info@christophe-leroy.com
– Fax 04 50 74 02 79 – Open 15 December-28 April
29 rm (½ board only) – 6 suites – ½ P €115/350
Rest *Table du Marché* – Menu (€18), €29/69 – Carte €53/71
♦ Cosy contemporary rooms, intimate lounges, bar and an ultra-modern fireplace. This famous hotel opened in 1965 and remains as popular as ever. Smart bistro interior and a specials board at the Table du Marché.

MOSNAC – **17 Charente-Maritime** – **324** G6 – **see Pons**

MOSNES – **37 Indre-et-Loire** – **317** P4 – **pop. 757** – **alt. 70 m** – ✉ **37530** 11 **A1**

Paris 211 – Orléans 86 – Tours 37 – Blois 26 – Joué-lès-Tours 48

Domaine des Thômeaux rm,
12 r. des Thômeaux – 02 47 30 40 14 – hotel@domainedesthomeaux.fr
– Fax 02 47 30 43 32
27 rm – €75/110 €75/110, €11
Rest – Menu (€9), €17 (lunch) – Carte approx. €24
♦ This brick and tufa stone château offers rooms decorated on the theme of cities around the world. Relaxation and leisure activities in the spa and Fantasy Forest theme park. World cuisine served in a cosy setting or on a large terrace.

LA MOTHE-ACHARD – **85 Vendée** – **316** G8 – **pop. 2 050** – **alt. 20 m** – ✉ **85150**

Paris 446 – Nantes 90 – La Roche-sur-Yon 25 – Challans 40 – Les Sables-d'Olonne 19 34 **B3**

Office de tourisme, 56, rue G. Clémenceau 02 51 05 90 49

Domaine de Brandois VISA AE
La Forêt, Near to the extraordinary garden – 02 51 06 24 24 – contact@domainedebrandois.com – Fax 02 51 06 37 87 – Closed 1st-15 January
38 rm – €65/180 €65/180, €12 – ½ P €80/140 – **Rest** – *(closed Sunday dinner October-March)* Menu (€25), €35
♦ A former agricultural school, this small château (1868) has been converted into a resolutely modern hotel. Guestrooms with a designer or more restrained feel. Spacious grounds plus a swimming pool. The ambience in this restaurant is a successful mix of the old and modern. Traditional cuisine.

LA MOTTE – **83 Var** – **340** O5 – **pop. 2 345** – **alt. 79 m** – ✉ **83920** 41 **C3**

Paris 864 – Cannes 54 – Fréjus 25 – Marseille 118

Office de tourisme, 25, boulevard André Bouis 04 94 84 33 76

Le Mas du Père without rest
280 Chemin du Péré – 04 94 84 33 52 – le.mas.du.pere@club-internet.fr
– Fax 04 94 84 33 52
6 rm – €74 €74/105
♦ Charming Provençal-style rooms with private terrace, communal cooking facilities and a pool set in a floral garden. This hotel provides a pleasant stay.

LA MOTTE-AU-BOIS – **59 Nord** – **302** D3 – **see Hazebrouck**

MOTTEVILLE – 76 Seine-Maritime – 304 F4 – see Yvetot

MOUCHARD – 39 Jura – 321 E5 – pop. 1 018 – alt. 285 m – ✉ 39330 16 B2

Paris 397 – Arbois 10 – Besançon 38 – Dole 35 – Lons-le-Saunier 48 – Salins-les-Bains 9

Chalet Bel'Air with rm rest, VISA

7 pl. Bel Air – ☎ 03 84 37 80 34 – brunogatto@wanadoo.fr – Fax 03 84 73 81 18 – Closed 22-29 June, 21 November-12 December, Sunday dinner and Wednesday except school holidays

9 rm – €53 €53, ☕ €9 – ½ P €86

Rest – Menu (€ 18), € 24 (weekdays)/74 – Carte € 28/67

Rest *Rôtisserie* – Menu € 24/38 (week-end) – Carte € 25/38

◆ 1970s chalet with a kitsch interior offering an accommodating welcome. Classic menu and mouth-watering dessert trolley. At the Rôtisserie, meat is roasted in front of diners in the huge fireplace; terrace overlooking the road.

MOUDEYRES – 43 Haute-Loire – 331 G4 – pop. 104 – alt. 1 177 m – ✉ 43150 6 C3

Paris 565 – Aubenas 64 – Langogne 58 – Le Puy-en-Velay 26

Le Pré Bossu VISA

– ☎ 04 71 05 10 70 – Fax 04 71 05 10 21 – Open 2 May-30 October and closed Monday dinner in May, June and October

6 rm – €100 €100/135, ☕ €17 – ½ P €100/120 – **Rest** – Menu €40/65

◆ Attractive stone cottage at the entrance to a picturesque mountain village. Most of the rooms have a private sitting room; breakfast near the fireplace. Pleasant country restaurant; dishes prepared using home-grown and local produce.

MOUGINS – 06 Alpes-Maritimes – 341 C6 – pop. 16 051 – alt. 260 m – ✉ 06250 42 E2

French Riviera

Paris 902 – Antibes 13 – Cannes 8 – Grasse 12 – Nice 31 – Vallauris 8

Office de tourisme, 15, avenue Jean Charles Mallet ☎ 04 93 75 87 67, Fax 04 92 92 04 03

Royal Mougins Golf Club 424 avenue du Roi, by D 35: 3.5 km, ☎ 04 92 92 49 69 ;

de Cannes Mougins 175 avenue du Golf, Southwest: 8 km, ☎ 04 93 75 79 13.

Site★ - N.-D. de Vie hermitage: site★, ≤★ Southeast: 3.5 km - Musée de l'Automobiliste★ Northwest: 5 km.

Le Mas Candille rm, VISA

bd C. Rebuffel – ☎ 04 92 28 43 43 – candille@relaischateaux.com – Fax 04 92 28 43 40

39 rm – €345/635 €345/635, ☕ €25 – 1 suite

Rest *Le Candille* – *(closed 2-31 January, Tuesday lunch and Monday)* Menu € 58 bi (lunch), € 70/105 – Carte € 110/134

Rest *Pergola* – *(open 1st May-30 September and closed dinner except July-August)* Carte € 74/83

Spec. Tatin de foie gras à l'armagnac. Thon rouge de Méditerranée aux épices tandori (summer). Aiguillette de Saint-Pierre piquée de tomates et citron (summer). **Wines** Vin de Pays des Alpes Maritimes, Côtes de Provence.

◆ A fine 18C farmhouse and its more modern side building, located in the heart of a 4-hectare Mediterranean-style park. Fine rooms with peace and quiet guaranteed. Japanese-style spa. Le Candille boasts a delightful, panoramic terrace and delicious up-to-date food.

De Mougins rm, VISA

205 av. Golf, Antibes road: 2.5 km – ☎ 04 92 92 17 07 – info@hotel-de-mougins.com – Fax 04 92 92 17 08

50 rm – €180/380 €190/393, ☕ €20 – 1 suite – **Rest** – *(closed Sunday and Monday from November to March)* Menu € 43/92 – Carte € 83/123

◆ Hotel with spacious Provençal-style rooms in various houses dotted around the garden of lavender, rosemary and orange trees. Stylish restaurant extended by summer terrace shaded by an old ash tree. Regional recipes.

Le Manoir de l'Étang
66 allée du Manoir, 3 km via rte d'Antibes – ☎ 04 92 28 36 00 – manoir.etang@wanadoo.fr – Fax 04 92 28 36 10 – Open April-October
19 rm – €160/275 €160/275, €20 – 2 suites
Rest – Menu (€29), €39 – Carte €53/64
◆ A 19C building with a nearby pond featuring water lilies in summer, seen from most of the rooms. Nice interiors, a blend of the old and the new. 4-hectare park. Italian cuisine, including antipasti, pasta and Mediterranean fish.

Les Muscadins
18 bd Courteline – ☎ 04 92 28 43 43 – info@lemascandille.com – Fax 04 92 28 43 40 – Open March-October
11 rm – €130/340 €130/460, €17
Rest – *(closed Wednesday lunch and Tuesday)* Menu €18 – Carte €23/52
◆ This charming residence on the outskirts of the village invites you to stay in attractively personalised rooms and to enjoy the spa and swimming pool of Mas Candille. The restaurant has a cosy setting and a modern menu with an Italian slant.

Arc Hôtel
1082 av. Gén. de Gaulle, 2 km Valbonne road – ☎ 04 93 75 77 33 – infos@archotelmougins.com – Fax 04 92 92 20 57 – Closed December and January
46 rm – €60/130 €90/160, €11,50
Rest – *(closed 1stNovember-25 February) (dinner only)* Menu €24
◆ An extremely well kept hotel built in the 1980s. The practical rooms have a balcony or terrace and are quieter on the garden side; some have been renovated. Simple cooking served in an unassuming dining room and on the poolside terrace.

Alain Llorca - Le Moulin de Mougins with rm
at Notre-Dame-de-Vie, 2.5 km southeast by D 3 – ☎ 04 93 75 78 24 – reservation@moulindemougins.com – Fax 04 93 90 18 55
3 rm – €160/230 €210/290, €15 – 4 suites – €300/390
Rest – *(closed Monday from November to April)* Menu €56, €98/170 – Carte €109/201
Spec. Pizza en cubes, poulpe, chorizo, anchois. Rougets du pays piqués aux olives taggiasches, fine ratatouille (summer). Pigeon laqué au vinaigre balsamique, escalopine de foie gras chaud. **Wines** Bellet, Côtes de Provence.
◆ Fine southern cuisine savoured in the romantic, intimate setting of this 16C oil mill. The restaurant overlooks a flower garden, adorned with modern sculptures by famous artists.

La Terrasse Cannes bay,
31 bd Courteline – ☎ 04 92 28 36 20 – laterrasseamougins@voila.fr – Fax 04 92 28 36 21
Rest – *(closed Tuesday lunch and Monday)* Menu (€19), €25 (lunch), €45/65 – Carte €67/94
◆ Both the terrace and the bay windows of the elegant Provençal-style dining area command a unique view of the countryside. Appetising modern cuisine.

Le Clos St-Basile
351 av. St-Basile – ☎ 04 92 92 93 03 – benoit.dargere@orange.fr – Fax 04 92 92 19 34 – Closed Tuesday and Wednesday September-June and lunch Monday-Thursday in July-August
Rest – Menu (€19), €24/37 – Carte €52/77
◆ A spruce Provençal setting and exhibition-sale of modern art and sculpture; this pleasant art gallery-cum-restaurant also has a terrace in the shade of cypress trees.

L'Amandier de Mougins
in the village – ☎ 04 93 90 00 91 – phoue@ics.fr – Fax 04 92 92 89 95
Rest – Menu €25 (lunch), €34/44 – Carte €42/74
◆ A 14C oil press building on the outskirts of the village dear to Picasso and Man Ray. Provençal interior, adorned with mosaics and modern paintings. Regional dishes.

Brasserie de la Méditerranée
in the village – ☎ 04 93 90 03 47 – lamediterrannee2@wanadoo.fr – Fax 04 93 75 72 83 – Closed 7 January-13 February, Sunday dinner and Tuesday off season
Rest – bistrot *(pre-book)* Menu €24 (lunch), €38/48 – Carte €36/65
◆ Pleasant restaurant, with a bistro-type decor, on the picturesque main square. You can savour Mediterranean-inspired up-to-date cuisine.

Le Bistrot de Mougins
pl. du village – ✆ 04 93 75 78 34 – Fax 04 93 75 25 52 – Closed 26 November-27 December, Thursday lunch, Saturday lunch and Wednesday
Rest – *(pre-book)* Menu € 21 (weekday lunch), € 34/47 – Carte € 49/61
◆ This restaurant-bistro, fitted out in a pleasant vaulted cellar, makes a welcome change from the inevitable Mougins terraces. Smart, rustic interior and Provençal cooking.

MOUILLERON-EN-PAREDS – 85 Vendée – 316 K7 – pop. 1 177 – alt. 101 m – ✉ 85390 Atlantic Coast

34 **B3**

Paris 426 – Nantes 95 – La Roche-sur-Yon 53 – Cholet 70 – Bressuire 40

Office de tourisme, 13, place de Lattre de Tassigny ✆ 02 51 00 32 32

La Boisnière without rest
– ✆ 02 51 51 36 39 – laboisniere@wanadoo.fr
5 rm – €60/70 €80/90
◆ Comfort is the key word in this restored farmhouse dominating the Chemin de la colline des Moulins: spruce, recent well-equipped rooms, faultless upkeep and lovely pool.

MOULICENT – 61 Orne – 310 N3 – pop. 266 – alt. 335 m – ✉ 61290

33 **C3**

Paris 148 – Caen 134 – La Ferté-Bernard 51 – Nogent-le-Rotrou 35

Château de la Grande Noë without rest
500 m west on D 289 – ✆ 02 33 73 63 30 – contact@chateaudelagrandenoe.com – Fax 02 33 83 62 92
4 rm – €70/110 €80/120
◆ A family-run hotel located in a large park, providing a fine welcome. Featuring individually furnished rooms in the old style, and a pleasant dining area with 18C wooden panelling.

MOULIHERNE – 49 Maine-et-Loire – 317 J4 – pop. 874 – alt. 80 m – ✉ 49390

Paris 282 – Nantes 150 – Angers 63 – Saumur 31 – La Flèche 33

35 **C2**

Le Cèdre de Monnaie
La Verrie, 4.5 km south on Longué road and Forestière road – ✆ 02 41 67 09 27 – cedredemonnaie@gmail.com – Fax 02 41 67 09 27
5 rm – €45 €55 – ½ P € 59 – **Table d'hôte** – Menu € 19
◆ On the edge of the Monnaie forest, this site is perfect for nature lovers. Authentically rustic rooms in a converted barn and breakfasts in the former cowshed. The table d'hôte is installed in the attractive kitchen with fireplace; home cooking.

MOULIN-DE-MALFOURAT – 24 Dordogne – 329 D7 – see Bergerac

MOULINS – 03 Allier – 326 H3 – pop. 21 892 – alt. 240 m – ✉ 03000 Auvergne

6 **C1**

Paris 294 – Bourges 101 – Clermont-Ferrand 105 – Nevers 56 – Roanne 98

Office de tourisme, 11, rue François Péron ✆ 04 70 44 14 14, Fax 04 70 34 00 21

de Moulins-Les Avenelles Toulon-sur-Allier Les Avenelles, by Vichy road: 7 km, ✆ 04 70 44 02 39.

Notre-Dame cathedral ★: triptych★★★, stained-glass windows★★ - Jacquemart Statue ★ - Mausoleum of the Duke of Montmorency★ (visitation chapel) - Musée d'Art et d'Archéologie★★.

Plan on next page

Le Parc rest,
31 av. Gén Leclerc – ✆ 04 70 44 12 25 – hotelrestaurant.leparc03@wanadoo.fr – Fax 04 70 46 79 35 – Closed 27 July-18 August and 21 December-6 January
BX **a**
26 rm – €42/70 €42/70, € 7,50 – ½ P € 48/52
Rest – *(closed Sunday dinner and Saturday)* Menu € 21/45 – Carte € 35/54
◆ This family establishment is located near a green park and the railway station. The proprietors do their utmost to make your stay a pleasant one. Simple and clean rooms. Attractively decorated dining room where carefully prepared traditional food is served.

MOULINS

Allier (Pl. d')	CDZ	
Allier (R. d')	DYZ	
Alsace-Lorraine (Av. d')	BX	3
Ancien Palais (R.)	DY	4
Bourgogne (R. de)	BV, DY	6
Bréchimbault (R.)	DZ	7
Cerf-Volant (R. du)	BV	8
Clermont-Ferrand (Rte de)	AX	10
Desboutins (R. M.)	BX	16
Fausses Braies (R. des)	DY	19
Flèche (R. de la)	DZ	20
Grenier (R.)	DY	25
Horloge (R. de l')	DZ	26
Hôtel de Ville (Pl. de l')	DY	27
Jeu de Paume (R. du)	BV	28
Leclerc (Av. Général)	BX	30
Libération (Av. de la)	AX	31
Montilly (Rte de)	AX	32
Orfèvres (R. des)	DY	33
Pascal (R. Blaise-)	CZ	34
Péron (R. F.)	DY	35
République (Av. de la)	BX	36
Tanneries (R. des)	BV, DV	38
Tinland (R. M.)	CY	39
Vert Galant (R. du)	CDY	40
4 Septembre (R. du)	DZ	42

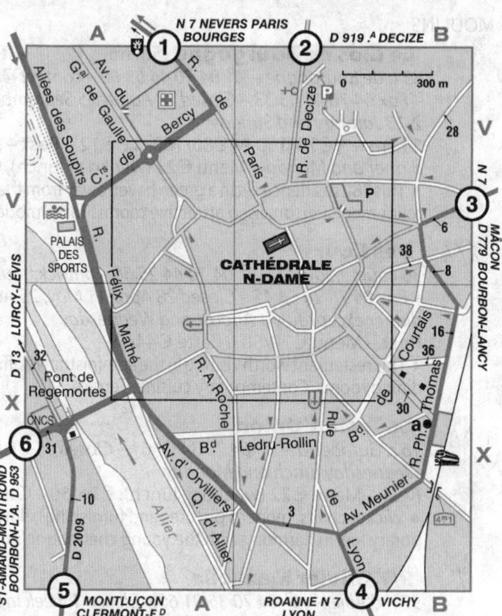

N 7 NEVERS PARIS
BOURGES
D 919 A DECIZE
N 7 MÂCON
D 779 BOURBON-LANCY
ROANNE N 7
LYON
VICHY
MONTLUÇON
CLERMONT-F D
ST-AMAND-MONTROND
BOURBON-L'A. D 953
D 13 LURCY-LÉVIS
CATHÉDRALE
N-DAME
PALAIS
DES
SPORTS
Pont de
Regemortes
Allées des Soupirs
Av. Gal de Gaulle
Crs de Bercy
R. de Paris
R. de Decize
R. Félix Mathé
R. A. Roche
Bd Ledru-Rollin
Rue de Lyon
Av. d'Orvilliers
Q. d'Allier
Av. Meunier
Bd de Courtais
R. Ph. Thomas
Allier
D 2009
300 m

LYCÉE BANVILLE
MAUSOLÉE DU
DUC DE MONTMORENCY
MUSÉE
ANNE DE BEAUJEU
JARDIN
DES BOURBONS
CATHÉDRALE
NOTRE-DAME
Musée
Bourbonnais
JACQUEMART
HÔTEL DU
DÉPARTEMENT
Cours A.
France
Pl. Jean
Moulin
Quartier
des Mariniers
SACRÉ CŒUR
Musée du
Bâtiment
Pl.
Garibaldi
Pl. de
la Liberté
Pl. d'Allier
Pl. Regemortes
ST-PIERRE
POL.
Cours de Bercy
Crs Vincent d'Indy
R. du Lycée
R. Regnaudin
R. de Paris
R. de Decize
Rue des Potiers
R. M. de l'Hospital
Rue Durand
R. Diderot
R. Denain
R. Voltaire
J. Jaurès
Crs J. Jaurès
R. des Pêcheurs
R. de la Fraternité
R. Blanc
R. des Bouchers
R. d'Enghien
R. M. de Dombasle
Rue d'Allier
R. de Pont
R. Datas
R. des Couteliers
R. Gambetta
R. Delorme
R. J.-J. Rousseau
Av. Th. de Banville
Bd de Courtais
R. du Pont Ginguet
Regemortes
R. F Mathé
R. Jean Bart
R. A. Roche
200 m

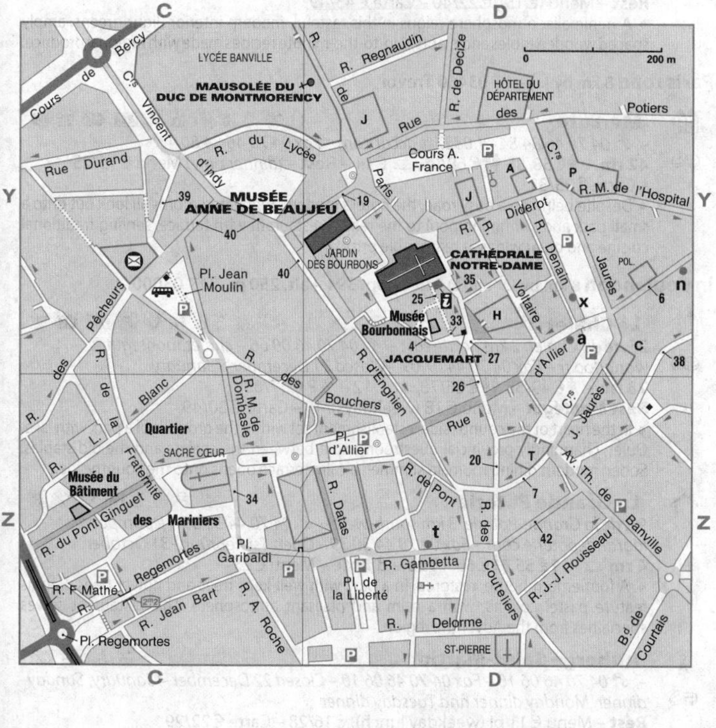

XXX **Le Clos de Bourgogne** with rm

83 r. de Bourgogne – ✆ 04 70 44 03 00 – contact@closdebourgogne.fr – Fax 04 70 44 03 33 – Closed 18 August-5 September, 22-29 December, 2-13 January and Sunday DY **n**

11 rm – †€ 70/150 ††€ 80/160, ☐ € 12 – **Rest** – *(closed Saturday lunch, Sunday dinner and Monday)* Menu € 22 (weekday lunch), € 27/57 – Carte € 48/64

◆ This 18C residence set in a green haven away from the town centre combines charm and refinement. Personalised attractive rooms. Tasty, modern food.

XXX **Des Cours**

36 cours J. Jaurès – ✆ 04 70 44 25 66 – patrick.bourhy@wanadoo.fr – Fax 04 70 20 58 45 – Closed 28 April-11 May, 25 August-7 September, Tuesday dinner except July – August and Wednesday DY **x**

Rest – Menu € 20/50 – Carte € 44/59

◆ This restaurant worth visiting in the administrative office district offers two elegant, plush dining rooms. Contemporary cuisine. Terrace.

XX **Le Trait d'Union**

16 r. Gambetta – ✆ 04 70 34 24 61 – Closed 1st-21 July, 18-26 February, Wednesday lunch and Monday DZ **t**

Rest – Menu € 22 (weekday lunch), € 26/50 – Carte € 48/68

◆ Wicker chairs, modern pictures and furnishings, flowers and well-set tables: a contemporary feel in harmony with the young chef-patron's up-to-date cuisine.

X **9/7 Olivier Mazuelle**

97 r. d'Allier – ✆ 04 70 35 01 60 – Closed 1 week in July, 2 weeks in August, Monday dinner, Saturday dinner and Sunday DY **a**

Rest – Menu (€ 15), € 22/40 – Carte € 43/49

◆ A minimalist atmosphere reigns in this tasteful, modern interior (light greens, amply spaced wooden tables and plants). Up-to-the-minute recipes made with regional produce.

Paris road 8 km by ① – ✉ 03460 Trevol

Mercure

– ✆ 04 70 46 84 84 – h0827@accor.com – Fax 04 70 46 84 80

42 rm – †€ 58/85 ††€ 68/95, ☐ € 11 – **Rest** – *(dinner only)* Menu € 15/25 – Carte € 25/31

◆ Despite being on a busy road, the hotel's modern, renovated rooms all look out onto a small park and swimming pool to the rear. A restaurant with terrace, serving traditional cuisine and great wines at reasonable prices.

in Coulandon 8 km by ⑥ and D 945 – pop. 594 – alt. 250 m – ✉ 03000

Le Chalet

26 rte du Chalet, 2 km north-east – ✆ 04 70 46 00 66 – chalet.montegut@wanadoo.fr – Fax 04 70 44 07 09 – Closed 21 December-7 January

28 rm – †€ 49/55 ††€ 66/78, ☐ € 12 – ½ P € 57/63

Rest *Montégut* – Menu € 18 (weekdays)/45 – Carte € 30/49

◆ In the heart of the countryside, establishment set within the grounds of a park with lake. Quiet, charmingly provincial guestrooms split between the chalets and the old stables. Sober, modern dining room. In summer, a calm terrace opens onto the countryside.

La Grande Poterie

9 r. de la Grande-Poterie, 3 km south-west – ✆ 04 70 44 30 39 – jcpompon@lagrandepoterie.com – Fax 04 70 44 30 39 – Open 1st February-31 October

4 rm ☐ – †€ 55 ††€ 66 – **Table d'hôte** – Menu € 25

◆ A former farmhouse, restored, in a park with well-kept trees and flower beds. Rooms feature pastel colours, with a calm and pleasant atmosphere. This restaurant serves specialties from the Auvergne region.

X **Auberge Saint-Martin**

– ✆ 04 70 46 06 10 – Fax 04 70 46 06 10 – Closed 22 December-4 January, Sunday dinner, Monday dinner and Tuesday dinner

Rest – Menu € 11 bi (weekday lunch), € 16/28 – Carte € 22/29

◆ This inn, also a grocer's-bar-bread depot, is a focal point in the village. Serving no-frills traditional dishes in a country-style dining room.

MOULINS-LA-MARCHE – 61 Orne – 310 L3 – pop. 774 – alt. 257 m – ✉ 61380

33 **C3**

Paris 156 – L'Aigle 19 – Alençon 50 – Argentan 45 – Mortagne-au-Perche 17
Syndicat d'initiative, 1, Grande Rue ✆ 02 33 34 45 98

Le Dauphin

66 Grande Rue – ✆ 02 33 34 50 55 – createur-dinstant@hotel-ledauphin.fr – Fax 02 33 34 25 35 – Closed 17-28 February

7 rm – €55/60 €60/75, €8 – ½ P €75

Rest – *(closed Sunday dinner and Monday except public holidays)* Menu €16 bi (weekday lunch), €21/55 – Carte €28/44

◆ One of the dining room's decorations and various specialities found in the menus lead us towards Alsace: which happens to be the landlord's region of origin !

LE MOULLEAU – 33 Gironde – 335 D7 – see Arcachon

MOURÈZE – 34 Hérault – 339 F7 – pop. 128 – alt. 200 m – ✉ 34800

Languedoc-Roussillon-Tarn Gorges

23 **C2**

Paris 717 – Bédarieux 22 – Clermont-l'Hérault 8 – Montpellier 50
Cirque★★.

Navas "Les Hauts de Mourèze" without rest

Cirque dolomitique – ✆ 04 67 96 04 84 – Fax 04 67 96 25 85 – Open 27 March-31 October

16 rm – €42/45 €52/60, €6

◆ Rustic rooms without TV and telephone for more peace and quiet. Nearby park and a superb Dolomite cirque. A relaxing stay guaranteed.

MOURIÈS – 13 Bouches-du-Rhône – 340 E3 – pop. 2 752 – alt. 13 m – ✉ 13890

42 **E1**

Paris 713 – Avignon 36 – Arles 29 – Marseille 75 – Martigues 38
Office de tourisme, 2, rue du Temple ✆ 04 90 47 56 58, Fax 04 90 47 67 33

Terriciaë without rest

rte de Maussane (D 17) – ✆ 04 90 97 06 70 – terriciaehotel@byprovence.com – Fax 04 90 47 63 85

31 rm – €82/114 €98/130, €12 – 4 suites

◆ In a peaceful setting, this brand new hotel offers Provençal style rooms, some overlooking the pool, others split-level or junior suites. Terrace and garden with olive trees.

Le Vallon du Gayet

rm, rm,

rte Servannes – ✆ 04 90 47 50 63 – wcarre@aol.com – Fax 04 90 47 64 31

24 rm – €84/100 €95/110, €11

Rest – *(closed Monday)* Menu €26/30 – Carte €34/84

◆ All rooms in this farmhouse, nestled at the foot of the Alpilles, have a small garden-level loggia with the exception of the most recent, more spacious rooms. Food grilled on a wood fire in a rustic setting. Terrace shaded by a century-old pine tree.

MOUSSEY – 10 Aube – 313 E4 – see Troyes

MOUSTIERS-STE-MARIE – 04 Alpes-de-Haute-Provence – 334 F9 – pop. 625 – alt. 631 m – ✉ 04360 French Alps

41 **C2**

Paris 783 – Aix-en-Provence 90 – Digne-les-Bains 47 – Draguignan 61 – Manosque 50
Office de tourisme, place de l'Église ✆ 04 92 74 67 84, Fax 04 92 74 60 65
Site★★ - Church ★ - Musée de la Faïence★.
Grand Canyon du Verdon★★★ -Lac de Ste-Croix★★.

Bastide de Moustiers rm, rm,

to the south of the village, via D 952 and secondary road – 04 92 70 47 47 – contact@bastide-moustiers.com – Fax 04 92 70 47 48 – Closed 7-31 January, Tuesday and Wednesday from November to March and Monday from November to February

12 rm – €160/320 €160/335, €20

Rest *(number of covers limited, pre-book)* Menu €48/68 – Carte €49/74 lunch only

Spec. Artichauts violets et fenouil cuisinés en barigoule. Agneau de pays au pèbre d'aï. Petits farcis de légumes tièdes au coulis de tomate (15 July to 30 September).

Wines Côteaux varois, Bandol.

♦ A 17C earthenware maker's country house, converted into an inn. Attractive Provençal rooms, high-tech equipment and a superb park (a deer farm and a vegetable garden). An intimate atmosphere to be enjoyed in the restaurant featuring unusual furnishings and a fine terrace.

Le Colombier without rest

à 500 m. par rte de Castellane Moustiers-Ste-Marie – 04 92 74 66 02 – infos@le-colombier.com – Fax 04 92 74 66 70 – Open March-mid November

22 rm – €62/85 €62/85, €9

♦ This hotel is ideally located at the entrance to the Grand Canyon of Verdon. Providing discreetly decorated rooms, most with a private terrace. Jacuzzi and small pool.

Le Clos des Iris without rest

South of the village, via D 952 and secondary road – 04 92 74 63 46 – closdesiris@wanadoo.fr – Fax 04 92 74 63 59 – Closed December, January and Tuesday from 1st February to 15 March – **9 rm** – €63/69 €63/120, €9,50

♦ Smart Provençal rooms (no TV), private terraces, pleasant Mediterranean garden, charming and friendly welcome – a peaceful hotel with a number of plus points.

La Bonne Auberge

rte de Castellane, (au Village) – 04 92 74 66 18 – labonneauberge@club-internet.fr – Fax 04 92 74 65 11 – Open 1st April-31 October

19 rm – €49/56 €56/80, €8 – ½ P €60/65

Rest – *(closed Sunday dinner and Monday off season, Saturday lunch, Tuesday lunch and Thursday lunch 15 June-15 September)* Menu €19/39 – Carte €36/47

♦ This hotel, just a stone's throw from the Verdon Gorges, has light practical rooms, being renovated in stages, and an infinity pool. Discreetly decorated, rustic-style dining room; traditional food and regional dishes.

La Ferme Rose without rest

to the south of the village, via rte Ste - Croix - du - Verdon – 04 92 75 75 75 – contact@lafermerose.com – Fax 04 92 73 73 73 – Open 29 March-14 November and 29 December-6 January – **12 rm** – €78 €98/148, €9,50

♦ Friendly "guest house" feel to this old farm at the foot of the village. Furniture from here and there, knickknacks and various collections all make it an appealing place.

La Bouscatière rm,

chemin Marcel Provence – 04 92 74 67 67 – bonjour@labouscatiere.com – Fax 04 92 74 65 72

5 rm – €115/190 €115/190, €15 – **Table d'hôte** – Menu €30/120

♦ This fabulous 18C building on a cliff provides luxury, calm and simplicity. Individually furnished rooms, a walled garden, and regional dishes served at the table d'hôte.

Les Santons

pl. de l'Église – 04 92 74 66 48 – les-santons@orange.fr – Fax 04 92 74 63 67 – Open 1st March-5 November and closed Monday except July-August and Tuesday

Rest – *(number of covers limited, pre-book)* Menu €25/34 – Carte €51/69

♦ Dominated by the imposing chalk cliff, this restaurant serves modern dishes in a pleasant, southern-style dining room and on an idyllic terrace on the village side.

La Ferme Ste-Cécile

1.5 km on Castellane road – 04 92 74 64 18 – patcrespin@aol.com – Fax 04 92 74 63 51 – Closed 15 November-28 February, Sunday dinner except July-August and Monday – **Rest** – Menu €25/35

♦ This old farmhouse has retained its original rustic charm, with old stone work and a fireplace in the dining room, and a large terrace. Serving regional dishes and good wines by the glass.

XX **Treille Muscate** VISA AE

pl. de l'Église – 04 92 74 64 31 – la.treille.muscate@wanadoo.fr – Fax 04 92 74 63 75 – Open 11 February-14 November and closed Wednesday except lunch off season and Thursday except July-August

Rest – Menu € 27/36 – Carte € 49/56

♦ Small, attractive Provençal bistro. A vine-covered footbridge links the dining room with the attractive terrace, which is shaded by an old plane tree and overlooks the church square.

MOUTHIER-HAUTE-PIERRE – 25 Doubs – 321 H4 – pop. 343 – alt. 450 m – ✉ 25920 Burgundy-Jura

17 **C2**

Paris 442 – Baume-les-Dames 55 – Besançon 39 – Pontarlier 23 – Salins-les-Bains 42

Belvédère de Mouthier (viewpoint) ≤★★ Southeast: 2.5 km - Gorges de Nouailles★ Southeast: 3.5 km - Belvédère du moine de la vallée (viewpoint)★★.

La Cascade ≤ valley, & rm, P VISA AE

– 03 81 60 95 30 – hotellacascade@wanadoo.fr – Fax 03 81 60 94 55 – Open 21 March-2 November – **16 rm** – †€ 52 ††€ 67, ☐ € 9 – ½ P € 55/63

Rest – *(dinner for residents only)* Menu € 20/47 – Carte € 38/61

♦ Hotel facing the Loue valley housing modern, well-kept rooms, some with a small balcony. At breakfast time: bread, croissants and jam, all home-made. Regional cuisine served in the panoramic dining room.

MOÛTIERS – 73 Savoie – 333 M5 – pop. 4 151 – alt. 480 m – ✉ 73600 French Alps

46 **F2**

Paris 607 – Albertville 26 – Chambéry 76 – St-Jean-de-Maurienne 85

Office de tourisme, place Saint-Pierre 04 79 24 04 23, Fax 04 79 24 56 05

Auberge de Savoie VISA AE

45 square Liberté – 04 79 24 20 15 – aubergedesavoie@wanadoo.fr – Fax 04 79 24 54 65 – Closed May – **20 rm** – †€ 59/104 ††€ 67/149, ☐ € 11

Rest – brasserie Menu (€ 18 bi), € 20 bi – Carte € 25/62

♦ A recently renovated hotel providing smart rooms with wooden panelling. Savoy-style décor in the reception area. Bistro cuisine, including regional and seafood dishes (in season), served in a typical mountain-style atmosphere or on a lovely terrace.

XX **Le Coq Rouge** VISA AE

115 pl. A. Briand – 04 79 24 11 33 – restaurant@lecoqrouge.com – Closed 29 June-29 July, Sunday and Monday – **Rest** – Menu € 29/45 – Carte € 37/59

♦ This restaurant is housed in a building dating from 1735. Modern cuisine in a charming atmosphere with the owner's artwork on display. Sheltered terrace.

X **La Voûte** AC VISA

172 Grande rue – 04 79 24 23 23 – vivet.falcoz.antoine@wanadoo.fr – Fax 04 79 06 04 75 – Closed 21 April-5 May, 29 September-13 October, 5-12 January, Sunday dinner and Monday

Rest – Menu € 18 (lunch), € 25/46 bi – Carte € 29/54

♦ In the pedestrian centre of town, just 50m from the cathedral, this rustic-style restaurant with modern furnishings and a distinctive glass façade serves modern cuisine.

MOUZON – 08 Ardennes – 306 M5 – pop. 2 616 – alt. 160 m – ✉ 08210 Northern France and the Paris Region

14 **C1**

Paris 261 – Carignan 8 – Charleville-Mézières 41 – Longwy 62 – Sedan 17 – Verdun 64

Syndicat d'initiative, place du Colombier 03 24 26 56 11

Notre-Dame church★.

XX **Les Échevins** VISA

33 r. Ch. de Gaulle – 03 24 26 10 90 – lesechevins@orange.fr – Fax 03 24 29 05 95 – Closed Sunday dinner and Monday

Rest – Menu (€ 19), € 25/39 – Carte approx. € 42

♦ A welcoming dining area with rustic decor, on the first floor of a 17C half-timbered building. A relaxed atmosphere and contemporary cuisine.

MUHLBACH-SUR-MUNSTER – 68 Haut-Rhin – 315 G8 – pop. 725 – alt. 460 m – ✉ 68380 Alsace-Lorraine 1 A2

Paris 462 – Colmar 24 – Gérardmer 37 – Guebwiller 45

Perle des Vosges

22 rte Gaschney – ✆ 03 89 77 61 34 – perledesvoges@wanadoo.fr – Fax 03 89 77 74 40 – Closed 2 January-2 February

45 rm – †€ 40/73 ††€ 40/117, ☕ € 9 – ½ P € 45/62 – **Rest** – Menu € 19/65 – Carte € 33/49

◆ At the foot of the Hohneck, this hotel boasts a panoramic fitness centre. Modern rooms, some in Alsatian style, most of which overlook the Vosges. The dining room with a summer terrace extension has a slightly solemn air.

MUIDES-SUR-LOIRE – 41 Loir-et-Cher – 318 G5 – pop. 1 157 – alt. 82 m – ✉ 41500

Paris 169 – Orléans 48 – Blois 20 – Châteauroux 109 11 B2

Syndicat d'initiative, place de la Libération ✆ 02 54 87 58 36, Fax 02 54 87 58 36

Château de Colliers without rest

rte de Blois, RD 951 – ✆ 02 54 87 50 75 – contact@chateau-colliers.com – Fax 02 54 87 03 64

5 rm ☕ – †€ 118 ††€ 129/169 – 1 suite

◆ The most beautiful chateaux in France are to be found on the banks of the Loire. This one enchants its guests with its antique paintings and period furnishings.

Auberge du Bon Terroir

20 r. 8-Mai – ✆ 02 54 87 59 24 – Fax 02 54 87 59 19 – *Closed 20 November-5 December, 1st-15 January, Sunday dinner October-April, Wednesday lunch, Monday and Tuesday except dinner in season*

Rest – Menu € 24 (weekday lunch), € 34/58 – Carte € 47/62

◆ Traditional menus and Loire Valley specialities in one of the dining rooms or on the terrace in the shade of a lime tree.

MULHOUSE – 68 Haut-Rhin – 315 I10 – pop. 110 359 – Built-up area 234 445 – alt. 240 m – ✉ 68100 Alsace-Lorraine 1 A3

Paris 465 – Basel 34 – Belfort 43 – Freiburg-im-Breisgau 59 – Strasbourg 122

Basel Mulhouse Freiburg (Euro-Airport) by ③: 27 km, ✆ 03 89 90 31 11, ✆ 061 325 3111 from Switzerland, ✆ 0761 1200 3111 from Germany.

✆ 3635 (0,34 €/mn)

Office de tourisme, 9, avenue du Maréchal Foch ✆ 03 89 35 48 48, Fax 03 89 45 66 16

Parc zoologique et botanique (zoo and botanic parc) ★★ - Town hall★★ FY H1, musée historique (history museum) ★★ - Stained glass windows★ of St-Étienne temple - Musée de l'automobile- Schlumpf collection ★★★ BU - Musée français du chemin de fer★★★ AV - Musée de l'Impression sur étoffes★ FZ M6 - Electropolis: musée de l'énergie électrique (electric power museum)★ AV M2.

Musée du Papier peint (Wallpaper Museum)★: collection★★ at Rixheim East: 6 km DV M7.

Plans on following pages

Bristol without rest

18 av. de Colmar – ✆ 03 89 42 12 31 – hbristol@club-internet.fr – Fax 03 89 42 50 57

85 rm – †€ 60/120 ††€ 70/160, ☕ € 13,50 – 5 suites FY e

◆ Hotel close to the historic town centre, offering large, modern rooms; some have been renovated, personalised and equipped with lavish bathrooms (Versace tiles).

Mercure Centre

4 pl. Gén. de Gaulle – ✆ 03 89 36 29 39 – h1264@accor.com – Fax 03 89 36 29 49

96 rm – †€ 109/165 ††€ 119/175, ☕ € 13,50 – **Rest** – Carte € 19/30 FZ b

◆ A 1970s hotel near the Fabric print museum. Practical well-kept rooms, a cosy bar and Japanese inspired small garden-terrace. Traditional menu, completed by dishes of the day and Alsatian specialities.

Kyriad Centre without rest
15 r. Lambert – 03 89 66 44 77 – kyriad@hotel-mulhouse.com – Fax 03 89 46 30 66 – **60 rm** – €55/90 €55/90, €8,50 FY **a**
◆ Smart practical bedrooms renovated in contemporary style; particularly spacious and comfortable in the business category. Breakfast on the terrace in summer.

Il Cortile (Stefano D'Onghia)
11 r. Franciscains – 03 89 66 39 79 – Fax 03 89 36 07 97 – Closed 18 August-1st September, 12-26 January, Sunday and Monday EY **a**
Rest – Menu €26 (weekday lunch), €39/70 – Carte €52/64
Spec. "Palette de l'artiste", composition de hors d'œuvre typiques italiens. Risotto à la truffe noire. Taglioni à la truffe blanche (season).
◆ The essence of Italy: contemporary interior (Murano glass) and deliciously simple and creative cuisine using only high quality produce. Stunning courtyard-terrace.

Poincaré II
6 porte Bâle – 03 89 46 00 24 – Fax 03 89 56 33 15 – Closed 27 July-10 August, Saturday and Sunday FY **m**
Rest – bistrot Menu (€19), €26/54 – Carte €28/81
◆ A pleasant dining room with a view of the chefs conjuring up traditional cuisine. Extensive cellar of Bordeaux and Loire wines.

Oscar
1 av. Maréchal Joffre – 03 89 45 25 09 – bistrot.oscar@wanadoo.fr – Fax 03 89 45 23 65 – Closed 2-17 August, 20 December-4 January, Saturday and Sunday
Rest – bistrot Menu (€22 bi), €26 bi/35 – Carte €33/58 FZ **x**
◆ Appetising bistro cuisine, daily specials listed on a blackboard, served in a cosy brasserie. Busy atmosphere and friendly service. Fine list of estate wines.

La Table de Michèle
16 r. Metz – 03 89 45 37 82 – michele.brouet@wanadoo.fr – Fax 03 89 45 37 82 – Closed 1 week in April, 1st-21 August, 22 December-4 January, Saturday lunch, Sunday and Monday – **Rest** – bistrot Menu (€17) – Carte €39/53 FY **t**
◆ Michèle concocts classic and seasonal dishes; dining room has rugged wood, soft lighting.

L'Estérel
83 av. de la 1ère Division Blindée – 03 89 44 23 24 – esterel.weber@hotmail.fr – Fax 03 89 64 05 63 – Closed 7-13 April, 15-31 August, autumn and February school holidays, Sunday dinner, Wednesday dinner and Monday V **t**
Rest – Menu €23/48 – Carte €40/63
◆ Near the zoo, a small rustic restaurant with a veranda extension; the shaded terrace is extremely popular in fine weather. Traditional menu with a southern slant.

in Sausheim

Mercure
D 442 – 03 89 61 87 87 – h0556@accor.com – Fax 03 89 61 88 40 DU **r**
100 rm – €65/138 €68/350, €14 – **Rest** – Carte €23/41
◆ In a shopping area readily accessed from the major roads, this hotel built in the 1970s has large practical, well-kept rooms. This restaurant's features include a terrace and traditional menu comprising Alsatian specialities.

Novotel
r. Ile Napoléon – 03 89 61 84 84 – h0452@accor.com – Fax 03 89 61 77 99
77 rm – €119/165 €126/165, €12,50 – **Rest** – Menu (€16) – Carte €23/38 DU **s**
◆ The location and convenience of this hotel make it very handy. The rooms are consistent with the chain's standards. Restaurant appreciated for its non-stop service from 6 a.m. to midnight and friendly terrace.

in Baldersheim **8 km by ① – pop. 2 206 – alt. 226 m – ✉ 68390**

Au Cheval Blanc rm,
27 r. Principale – 03 89 45 45 44 – cheval-blanc@wanadoo.fr – Fax 03 89 56 28 93 – Closed 23 December-4 January
82 rm – €58/77 €67/106, €10 – ½ P €61/67 – **Rest** – *(closed Sunday dinner)* Menu (€11,50), €17/50 – Carte €21/58
◆ Alsatian-style hotel passed down from father to son for over a century. Comfortable, good quality rooms with rustic furnishings. Inn-type dining room, reached via the village café. Wide choice, including a great selection of regional dishes and game in season.

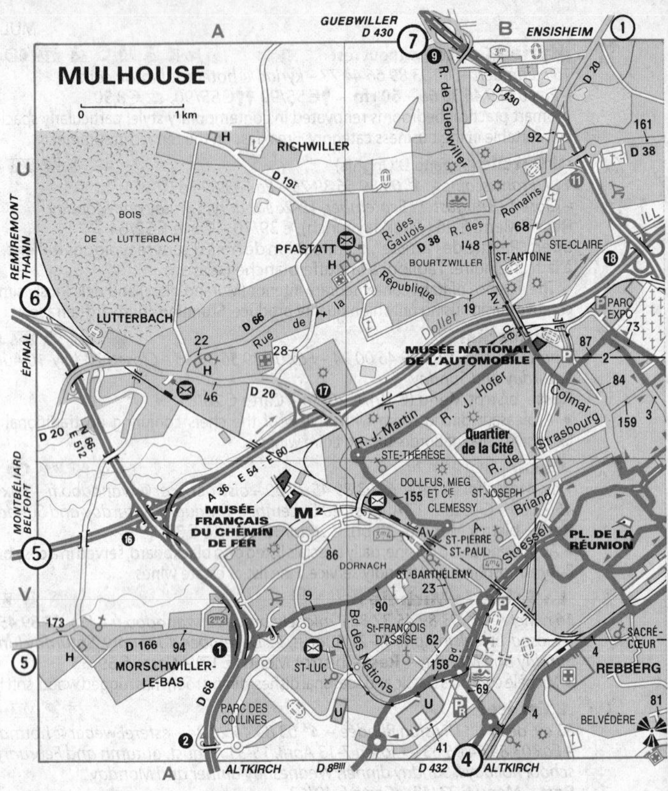

Agen (R. d') . . . . BU 2
Alliés (Bd des) . . . . BCU 3
Altkrich (Av.) . . . . BV 4
Bâle (Rte de) . . . . CU 7
Bartholdi (R.) . . . . CV 8
Belfort (R. de) . . . . AV 9
Belgique (Av. de) . . . . CU 12
Bourtz (R. Sébastien) . . . . . BU 19
Briand (R. Aristide) . . . . . . AU 22
Brunstatt (R. de) . . . . BV 23
Dollfus (Av. Gustave) . . . . . . CV 27
Dornach (R. de) . . . . AU 28
Fabrique (R. de la) . . . . CU 36
Frères-Lumière (R. des) . . . BV 41
Gambetta (Bd Léon) . . . . . . CV 42
Gaulle (R. du Gén.-de) . . . . AU 46
Hardt (R. de la) . . . . CV 51
Hollande (Av. de) . . . . CU 57
Ile Napoléon (R. de l') . . . . . CU 58
Illberg (R. de l') . . . . BV 62
Ilot (R. de l') . . . . DU 63
Jardin-Zoologique (R. du) . . . CV 64
Juin (R. A.) . . . . CU 66
Katz (Allée Nathan) . . . . CU 67
Kingersheim (R. de) . . . . . . BU 68
Lagrange (R. Léo) . . . . BV 69
Lefèbvre (R.) . . . . BU 73

Au Vieux Marronnier 🏨 ♿ AC ✆ P VISA MC AE

300 m. further on – ✆ 03 89 36 87 60 – vieux-marronnier@wanadoo.fr – Fax 03 89 56 28 93

8 rm – †€ 88 ††€ 88, ☕ € 10 – 6 suites – ††€ 96

◆ Recent building offering practical studios and apartments for long stays or passing families: space, well-equipped kitchenettes and modern rooms.

in Rixheim southeast by D 66 – pop. 12 608 – alt. 240 m – ✉ 68170

⌂ **Le Clos du Mûrier** without rest ✆ P VISA MC D

42 Grand'Rue – ✆ 03 89 54 14 81 – rosa.volpatti@orange.fr – Fax 03 89 64 47 08 D y

5 rm – †€ 66 ††€ 66, ☕ € 8

◆ This well-restored 16C half-timbered house is protected by a high wall, also enclosing a floral garden. Quite spacious rooms with original exposed wooden beams. Small kitchen, ironing and washing facilities, as well as bikes available.

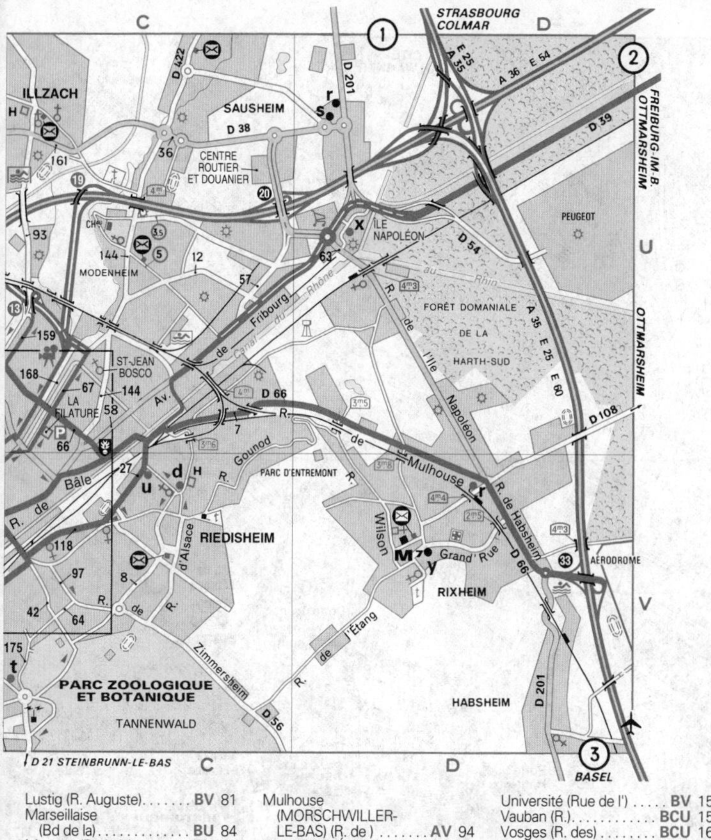

Lustig (R. Auguste) . . . . **BV** 81
Marseillaise (Bd de la) . . . . **BU** 84
Mertzau (R. de la) . . . . **BU** 87
Mer-Rouge (R. de la) . . . . . **AV** 86
Mitterrand (Av. F.) . . . . **BV** 90
Mulhouse (Fg de) . . . . **BU** 92
Mulhouse (ILLZACH) (R. de) . . . . **CU** 93
Mulhouse (MORSCHWILLER-LE-BAS) (R. de) . . . . **AV** 94
Noetling (R. Émilio) . . . . **CV** 97
Nordfeld (R. du) . . . . **CV** 98
Riedisheim (Av. de) . . . . . . **CV** 118
Sausheim (R. de) . . . . **CU** 144
Soultz (R. de) . . . . **BU** 148
Thann (R. de) . . . . **BV** 155
Université (Rue de l') . . . . . **BV** 158
Vauban (R.) . . . . **BCU** 159
Vosges (R. des) . . . . **BCU** 161
Wyler (Allée William) . . . . . **CU** 168
1ère-Armée-Française (R.) . . . . **AV** 173
9e-Div.-d'Infanterie-Col. (R.) . . . . **CV** 175

Le Manoir (Eric Runser)

65 av. Gén. de Gaulle – ✆ 03 89 31 88 88 – info@runser.fr – Fax 03 89 31 88 89 – Closed Sunday except public holidays DV **r**

Rest – Menu (€ 20), € 25/75 – Carte € 32/76

Spec. Ballotine de foie gras d'oie. Loup en croûte de sel de Guérande. Pigeon farci à l'ancienne en croûte de pain. **Wines** Riesling, Pinot noir.

◆ A lovely 1900 house in a walled garden. Contemporary interior (immense abstract paintings) serving regional dishes with modern touches and produce of the season.

Le Petit Prince

100 r. de l'Aérodrome – ✆ 03 89 64 24 85 – Fax 03 89 64 05 21 – Closed 20 August-4 September, 23 December-7 January, Sunday and Monday

Rest – *(pre-book)* Menu € 35 – Carte € 51/61

◆ A tasty tour of world flavours awaits in this unassuming blue "cabin" whose interior is inspired by the Little Prince. Terrace with a view of the runway.

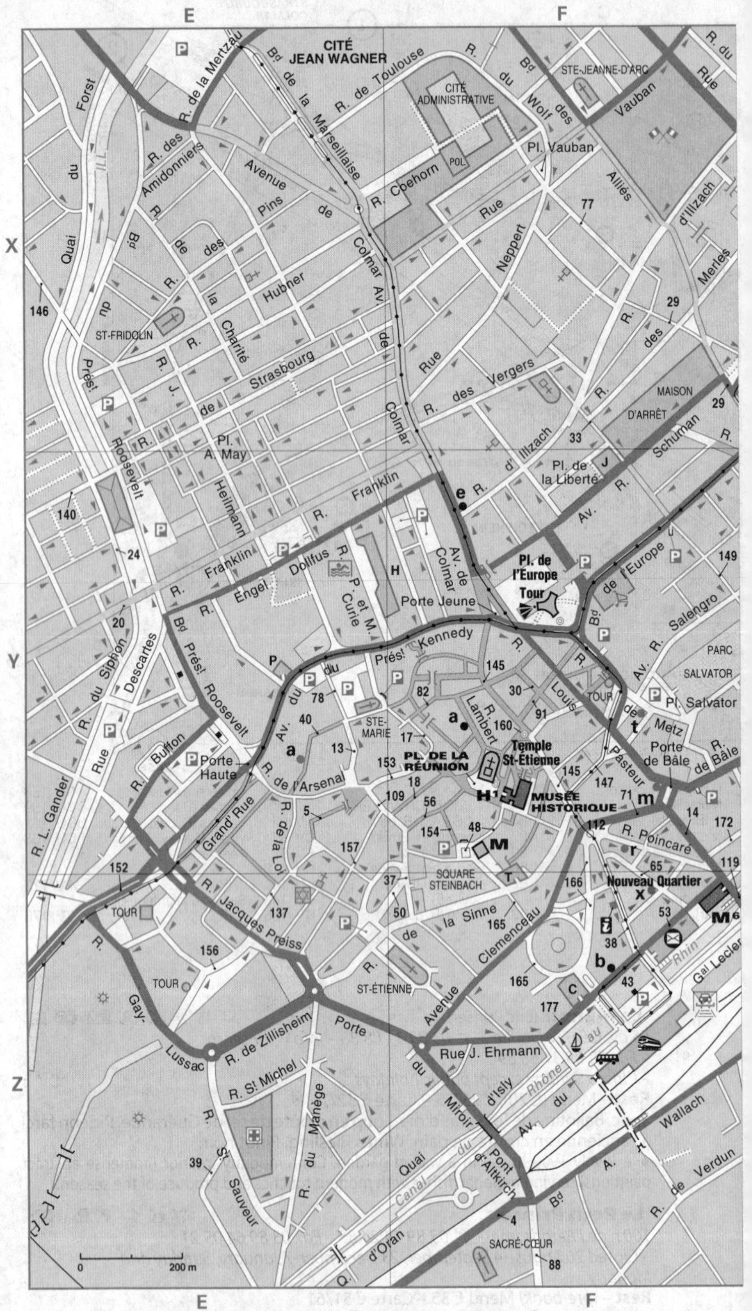
CITÉ JEAN WAGNER
CITÉ ADMINISTRATIVE
STE-JEANNE-D'ARC
MAISON D'ARRÊT
ST-FRIDOLIN
Pl. A. May
Pl. de la Liberté
Pl. de l'Europe
Tour
Porte Jeune
Porte Haute
STE-MARIE
PL. DE LA RÉUNION
Temple St-Étienne
MUSÉE HISTORIQUE
Nouveau Quartier
SQUARE STEINBACH
ST-ÉTIENNE
PARC SALVATOR
Pl. Salvator
Porte de Bâle
SACRÉ-CŒUR
Canal du Rhône au Rhin
0 200 m

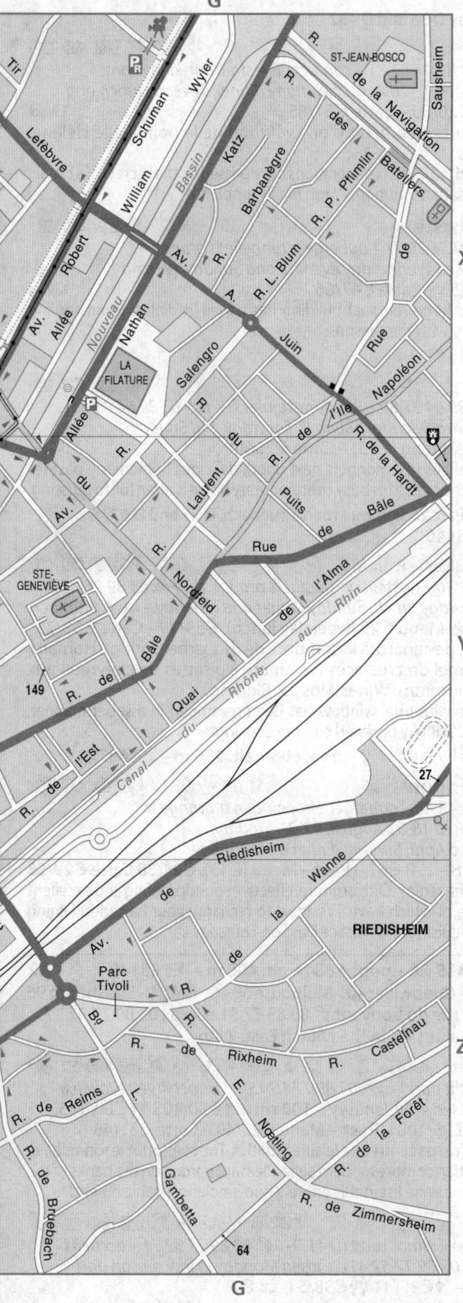

MULHOUSE

Altkrich (Av. d') . . . . FZ 4
Augustins (Passage des) . . EY 5
Bonbonnière (R.) . . . . EY 13
Bonnes-Gens (R. des) . . . . FY 14
Bons-Enfants (R. des) . . . . FY 17
Boulangers (R. des) . . . . . . FY 18
Briand (Av. Aristide) . . . . . . EY 20
Cloche (Quai de la) . . . . . . EY 24
Colmar (Av. de) . . . . EFXY
Dollfus (Av. Gustave) . . . . GY 27
Dreyfus (R. du Capit.) . . . . FX 29
Engelmann (R.) . . . . FY 30
Ensisheim (R. d') . . . . FX 33
Fleurs (R. des) . . . . FYZ 37
Foch (Av. du Mar.) . . . . FZ 38
Fonderie (R. de la) . . . . EZ 39
Franciscains (R. des) . . . . . EY 40
Gaulle (Pl. du Gén.-de) . . . . FZ 43
Guillaume-Tell (Pl. et R.) . . FY 48
Halles (R. des) . . . . FZ 50
Henner (R. J.-J.) . . . . FZ 53
Henriette (R.) . . . . FY 56
Jardin-Zoologique (R. du) . . GZ 64
Joffre (Av. du Mar.) . . . . . . FYZ 65
Lambert (R.) . . . . FY
Lattre-de-Tassigny (Av. Mar.-de) . . . . FY 71
Loisy (R. du Lt de) . . . . FX 77
Lorraine (R. de la) . . . . EY 78
Maréchaux (R. des) . . . . FY 82
Montagne (R. de la) . . . . FZ 88
Moselle (R. de la) . . . . FY 91
Président-Kennedy (Av. du) . . . . EFY
Raisin (R. du) . . . . EFY 109
République (Pl. de la) . . . . . FY 112
Riedisheim (Pont de) . . . . . . FZ 119
Ste-Claire (R.) . . . . EZ 137
Ste-Thérèse (R.) . . . . EY 140
Sauvage (R. du) . . . . FY 145
Schoen (R. Anna) . . . . EX 146
Somme (R. de la) . . . . FY 147
Stalingrad (R. de) . . . . FY 149
Stoessel (Bd Charles) . . . . EYZ 152
Tanneurs (R. des) . . . . EFY 153
Teutonique (Passage) . . . . . FY 154
Tour-du-Diable (R.) . . . . EZ 156
Trois-Rois (R. des) . . . . EY 157
Victoires (Pl. des) . . . . FY 160
Wicky (Av. Auguste) . . . . . . FZ 165
Wilson (R.) . . . . FYZ 166
Zuber (R.) . . . . FY 172
17-Novembre (R. du) . . . . . . FZ 177

in Riedisheim **2 km Southeast by D 56 and D 432**

XXX **La Poste** (Jean-Marc Kieny)
7 r. Gén. de Gaulle – ✆ 03 89 44 07 71 – contacts@restaurant-kieny.com – Fax 03 89 64 32 79 – Closed 1st-20 August, Sunday dinner, Tuesday lunch and Monday – **Rest** – Menu € 26/80 – Carte € 57/85 CV **d**
Spec. Tapas alsaciens. Turbot en habit d'or. Evolution de la poire Belle Hélène. **Wines** Riesling, Pinot gris.
◆ A coaching inn established in 1850. Six generations have passed on the secrets of a classic repertoire, blended with Alsatian tradition. Warm family ambience.

XX **Auberge de la Tonnelle**
61 r. Mar.-Joffre – ✆ 03 89 54 25 77 – auberge.latonnelle@orange.fr – Fax 03 89 64 29 85 – Closed Wednesday evening and Sunday evening
Rest – Menu (€ 25), € 27/53 – Carte € 47/66 CV **u**
◆ In a residential area, this large regional building has a well-lit dining room serving traditional dishes which vary with the seasons.

in Zimmersheim **5 km by D 56**

X **Jules**
5 r. de Mulhouse – ✆ 03 89 64 37 80 – info@restojules.fr – Fax 03 89 64 03 86 – Closed 4-17 August, February school holidays, Saturday and Sunday
Rest – *(booking advisable)* Menu (€ 15) – Carte € 26/49
◆ Meat and seafood specialities (fishmongers next door), delicious homemade pastries and wide choice of wine by the glass: this busy contemporary bistro is often full to bursting.

in Landser **11 km Southeast by Parc zoologique road, Bruebach, D 21 and D 6 BIS – pop. 1 687 – alt. 230 m – ✉ 68440**

XXX **Hostellerie Paulus** (Hervé Paulus)
4 pl. Paix – ✆ 03 89 81 33 30 – hostellerie-paulus@orange.fr – Fax 03 89 26 81 85 – Closed 3-18 August, Saturday lunch, Sunday dinner and Monday – **Rest** *(number of covers limited, pre-book)* Menu € 29 (weekday lunch), € 59/79 – Carte € 58/75
Spec. Terrine de foie gras de canard à la compote de rhubarbe (spring). Homard, wok de légumes et caramel de crustacés (summer). Noisettes de chevreuil aux champignons des bois (autumn). **Wines** Muscat, Riesling.
◆ This half-timbered house with oriel window has been revamped in a sober manner, retaining its original charm. Skilfully updated country cooking.

in Froeningen **9 km Southwest by D 8BIII** - BV – **pop. 606 – alt. 256 m – ✉ 68720**

Auberge de Froeningen
2 rte Illfurth – ✆ 03 89 25 48 48 – aubergedefroeningen@orange.fr – Fax 03 89 25 57 33 – Closed 18-31 August, 12-31 January, Tuesday from November to April, Sunday dinner and Monday
7 rm € 58 € 68, € 8 – ½ P € 67 – **Rest** – Menu (€ 13), € 24/58 Carte € 29/58
◆ An inviting inn typical of the region. Old furniture, effective soundproofing and excellent upkeep of the rooms, none of which have TVs. Ideal to recharge your batteries! Dining rooms with character, local cuisine and "Alsace Day" on Thursdays.

MUNSTER – 68 Haut-Rhin – 315 G8 – pop. 4 884 – alt. 400 m – ✉ 68140 1 A2

Paris 458 – Colmar 19 – Guebwiller 40 – Mulhouse 60 – St-Dié 54 – Strasbourg 96
Office de tourisme, 1, rue du Couvent ✆ 03 89 77 31 80, Fax 03 89 77 07 17
Soultzbach-les-Bains: altars★★ in the church East: 7 km.

Verte Vallée
10 r. A. Hartmann, (La Fecht park) – ✆ 03 89 77 15 15 – contact@vertevallee.fr – Fax 03 89 77 17 40 – Closed 4-29 January – **100 rm** – € 80/105 € 80/145, € 14 – 8 suites – ½ P € 76/108 – **Rest** – Menu € 23/49 – Carte € 31/48
◆ A large, modern hotel with a spa centre and leisure facilities. The comfortable rooms have been refurbished in an Alsatian or more modern style. Pleasant garden on the banks of the Fecht. Classic cuisine and fine wine list in this entirely non-smoking establishment.

Deybach without rest
4 r. du Badischhof, 1 km on Colmar road (D 417) – ✆ 03 89 77 32 71 – accueil@hotel-deybach.com – Fax 03 89 77 52 41 – Closed Monday in low season and Sunday evening – **16 rm** – € 35/41 € 38/54, € 7
◆ The friendly reception and warm atmosphere set this roadside family hotel apart. Practical and extremely well-kept rooms. Small bar and garden (deck chairs).

Nouvelle Auberge

Colmar road, on D 417, east: 6 km – 03 89 71 07 70 – Fax 03 89 71 07 70 – Closed 1st-15 July, autumn half-term holidays, February holidays, Sunday dinner, Monday and Tuesday

Rest – Menu € 10 (weekday lunch), € 30/58

◆ This post house serves traditional cuisine in the ground floor winstub or a gourmet menu in an attractive interior upstairs.

À l'Agneau d'Or

2 r. St-Grégoire – 03 89 77 34 08 – info@martinfache.com – Fax 03 89 77 34 08 – Closed 1st-14 July, Monday and Tuesday

Rest – *(number of covers limited, pre-book)* Menu € 35/45 – Carte € 42/48

◆ A regional-style building in the heart of the village, home to a restaurant serving a blend of traditional and regional cuisine. Game served in season. A cheerful atmosphere.

MURAT – 15 Cantal – 330 F4 – pop. 2 153 – alt. 930 m – 15300 Auvergne

Paris 520 – Aurillac 48 – Brioude 59 – Issoire 74 – Le Puy-en-Velay 121 – St-Flour 23 5 **B3**

Office de tourisme, 2, rue du fauboug Notre-Dame 04 71 20 09 47, Fax 04 71 20 21 94

Site★★ - Church ★ of Albepierre-Bredons South: 2 km.

Hostellerie Les Breuils without rest

34 av. Dr Mallet – 04 71 20 01 25 – info@hostellerie-les-breuils.com – Fax 04 71 20 33 20 – Open end May-10 October

10 rm – €66 €69/87, €8

◆ The bedrooms of this hundred-year-old abode are spacious on the first floor (Louis XVI-style furniture), more recent on the second floor and family-sized upstairs.

East 4 km by N 122, Clermont-Ferrand road – 15300 Murat

Le Jarrousset

– 04 71 20 10 69 – info@restaurant-le-jarrousset.com – Fax 04 71 20 15 26 – Closed December-January, Monday and Tuesday except July-August

Rest – Menu (€ 16), € 22/45 – Carte € 43/52

◆ This stylish stone inn offers a contemporary dining room, and a more intimate room facing the countryside. Appetising up-to-date menu made with regional produce.

LA MURAZ – 74 Haute-Savoie – 328 K4 – pop. 700 – alt. 630 m – 74560

Paris 545 – Annecy 33 – Annemasse 11 – Thonon-les-Bains 41 46 **F1**

L'Angélick

– 04 50 94 51 97 – info@angelick.com – Fax 04 50 94 59 05 – Closed 10-20 August, 22 December-6 January, Sunday dinner, Monday and Tuesday

Rest – Menu € 33/80 bi – Carte € 51/61

◆ Colourful restaurant with wrought-iron and leather seating, well-set tables and a terrace with an unusual fountain, serving inventive cuisine.

MURBACH – 68 Haut-Rhin – 315 G9 – see Guebwiller

MUR-DE-BARREZ – 12 Aveyron – 338 H1 – pop. 880 – alt. 790 m – 12600 Languedoc-Roussillon-Tarn Gorges 29 **D1**

Paris 567 – Aurillac 38 – Rodez 73 – St-Flour 56

Office de tourisme, 12, Grand' Rue 05 65 66 10 16, Fax 05 65 66 31 90

Auberge du Barrez rm, rest,

av. du Carladez – 05 65 66 00 76 – auberge.du.barrez@wanadoo.fr – Fax 05 65 66 07 98 – Closed 4 January-12 February

18 rm – €40/56 €56/79, €8 – ½ P €55/71 – **Rest** – *(closed Monday)* Menu € 14 (weekdays)/39 – Carte € 26/43

◆ This large house provides rooms of varying sizes, all contemporary and practical; flower garden. Pleasant modern dining area with some tables offering a view of the countryside. Generous portions of tasty fare.

MÛR-DE-BRETAGNE – **22 Côtes-d'Armor** – **309** E5 – **pop. 2 090** – **alt. 225 m** – ✉ **22530** Brittany 10 **C2**

Paris 457 – Guingamp 47 – Loudéac 20 – Pontivy 17 – St-Brieuc 44

Office de tourisme, place de l'Église ✆ 02 96 28 51 41, Fax 02 96 26 35 31

Rond-Point du lac ≤★ - Guerlédan lake ★★ West: 2 km.

XXX **Auberge Grand'Maison** with rm VISA MC AE

1 r. Léon le Cerf – ✆ 02 96 28 51 10 – auberge-grand-maison@wanadoo.fr – Fax 02 96 28 52 30 – Closed 6-21 October, 2-13 January, 16-28 February, Sunday dinner and Tuesday lunch off season and Monday

9 rm – †€ 48/98 ††€ 48/98, ☕ € 11 – ½ P € 101/153 – **Rest** – Menu € 27 (weekday lunch), € 36/90 – Carte € 60/107

◆ This grand restaurant features a warm welcome and a rustic yet refined atmosphere. Serving traditional and modern cuisine. Also providing a range of guest rooms.

LES MUREAUX **78 Yvelines** – **311** H2 – **pop. 31 739** – **alt. 28 m** – ✉ **78130** 18 **A1**

Paris 41 – Mantes-la-Jolie 19 – Pontoise 24 – Rambouillet 57 – Versailles 32

La Chaumière & rm, P VISA MC AE

quartier Grand Ouest, (near the A 13 junction), by Bouafle road – ✆ 01 34 74 72 50 – lachaumiere.lesmureaux@tiscali.fr – Fax 01 30 99 39 04

41 rm – †€ 61/65 ††€ 61/65, ☕ € 8 – ½ P € 50 – **Rest** – *(closed 1st- 24 August, 23 December-2 January, Saturday and Sunday)* Menu € 14/22 – Carte € 21/29

◆ A 1980s building close to a shopping centre. Bedrooms still have their original furniture. Bright restaurant, terrace service in summer and traditional, unpretentious menu.

MURON – **17 Charente-Maritime** – **324** F3 – **pop. 996** – **alt. 19 m** – ✉ **17430**

Paris 455 – Poitiers 122 – La Rochelle 45 – Niort 47 – Rochefort 20 38 **B2**

X **Le Puits Fleuri** VISA MC

7 r. du Prieuré, near the church – ✆ 05 46 27 71 15 – Fax 05 46 27 71 15 – Closed 1st-10 September, Sunday dinner from November to April and Tuesday

Rest – Menu € 17 (weekday lunch), € 25/40 – Carte € 30/37

◆ Smart rustic interior, personalised cuisine full of character and flavour, delightful welcome and very reasonable prices: this establishment in the heart of the village is on a roll.

MUS – **30 Gard** – **339** K6 – **pop. 1 049** – **alt. 53 m** – ✉ **30121** Provence 23 **C2**

Paris 737 – Arles 52 – Montpellier 37 – Nîmes 26

La Paillère P

26 av. du Puits Vieux – ✆ 04 66 35 55 93 – welcome@paillere.com

5 rm ☕ – †€ 70/80 ††€ 70/80 – **Table d'hôte** – Menu € 25

◆ Relax in style in this charming 17C home that wears its age with grace. Provençal or Eastern inspired furnishings and plush sitting rooms. Tree-lined patio terrace. A copious breakfast served. Mediterranean dishes made for guests by reservation.

MUSSIDAN – **24 Dordogne** – **329** D5 – **pop. 2 843** – **alt. 50 m** – ✉ **24400** Dordogne-Berry-Limousin 4 **C1**

Paris 526 – Angoulême 84 – Bergerac 26 – Libourne 59 – Périgueux 39

Office de tourisme, place de la République ✆ 05 53 81 73 87, Fax 05 53 81 73 87

XX **Relais de Gabillou** P VISA MC

Périgueux road: 1.5 km – ✆ 05 53 81 01 42 – relaisdegabillou@hotmail.com – Fax 05 53 81 01 42 – Closed 23-30 June, 17 November-16 December, dinner 4 January-1st February, Sunday dinner off season and Monday

Rest – Menu (€ 13), € 15/40 – Carte € 27/49

◆ The atmosphere of this roadside hotel is rustic; the dining hall is enhanced by a huge stone fireplace and a shaded terrace invites relaxation. Regional cuisine.

XX **Le Clos Joli** P VISA MC

7 km west on D 6089 and secondary road – ✆ 05 53 81 00 24 – le-clos-joli@wanadoo.fr – Fax 05 53 81 00 24 – Closed 30 June-11 July, 2-15 January, 17-25 February, Tuesday and Wednesday

Rest – Menu € 28/60 – Carte € 39/56

◆ In open country, this charming old presbytery has a pretty dining room and shaded terrace. Southern menu which is regularly varied.

in Sourzac 4 km east by D 6089 – pop. 1 032 – alt. 50 m – ✉ 24400

Le Chaufourg en Périgord
– ✆ 05 53 81 01 56 – info@lechaufourg.com – Fax 05 53 82 94 87
– *Closed 7 January-10 February* – **5 rm** – †€ 175/285 ††€ 175/285, ☕ € 17
4 suites – **Rest** – *(dinner only) (residents only)* Carte € 41/61
◆ This 17C residence, with incredible romantic charm, takes great care over its decor. Discreetly luxurious bedrooms, guesthouse atmosphere and timeless garden.

MUTIGNY – 51 Marne – 306 G8 – pop. 188 – alt. 221 m – ✉ 51160 13 B2

Paris 150 – Châlons-en-Champagne 33 – Épernay 9 – Reims 32

North 2 km by D 271 – ✉ 51160 Mutigny

Manoir de Montflambert without rest
– ✆ 03 26 52 33 21 – contact@manoirdemontflambert.fr – Fax 03 26 59 71 08
5 rm ☕ – †€ 90/100 ††€ 95/105
◆ This large 17C manor is located in the heart of the Champagne region, providing individually furnished rooms and featuring a nice French garden and an ornamental lake.

MUTZIG 67 Bas-Rhin – 315 I5 – pop. 5 584 – alt. 190 m – ✉ 67190 Alsace-Lorraine

Paris 479 – Obernai 11 – Saverne 30 – Sélestat 38 – Strasbourg 32 1 A1

L'Ours de Mutzig rm,
pl. Fontaine – ✆ 03 88 47 85 55 – hotel@loursdemutzig.com – Fax 03 88 47 85 56
47 rm – †€ 49/85 ††€ 49/85, ☕ € 9 – ½ P € 50/68 – **Rest** – *(closed Thursday)*
Menu € 16/28 – Carte € 27/42
◆ Built in 1900, this brasserie with a blue façade once belonged to Mutzig brewery. Now a hotel providing some recently built rooms in a pleasant modern style. Traditional menu and light dining room in the restaurant. Dotted here and there are... teddy bears.

NACONNE – 42 Loire – 327 E5 – see Feurs

NAINVILLE-LES-ROCHES – 91 Essonne – 312 D4 – pop. 457 – alt. 77 m – ✉ 91750

Paris 49 – Boulogne-Billancourt 49 – Montreuil 50 – Saint-Denis 62 19 C2

Le Clos des Fontaines without rest
3 r. de l'Église – ✆ 01 64 98 40 56 – soton@closdesfontaines.com – Fax 01 64 98 40 56 – **5 rm** ☕ – †€ 70/90 ††€ 88/105
◆ Located in a large park, this former presbytery now provides peaceful rooms, all individually furnished. Deluxe breakfast served in a modern dining area.

NAJAC – 12 Aveyron – 338 D5 – pop. 744 – alt. 315 m – ✉ 12270
Languedoc-Roussillon-Tarn Gorges 29 C1

Paris 629 – Albi 51 – Cahors 85 – Gaillac 51 – Rodez 71 – Villefranche-de-Rouergue 20
Office de tourisme, place du Faubourg ✆ 05 65 29 72 05, Fax 05 65 29 72 29
The Fortress★: ≤★.

Les Demeures de Longcol
6 km north-east on D 39 and D 638 – ✆ 05 65 29 63 36 – longcol@wanadoo.fr
– Fax 05 65 29 64 28 – *Closed January*
18 rm – †€ 120/160 ††€ 120/160, ☕ € 15 – ½ P € 110/130
Rest – *(dinner only) (number of covers limited, pre-book)* Menu € 35
◆ A property with a medieval ambience in a bucolic setting on the banks of the Aveyron. Rustic guestrooms with a hint of the Orient, well-tended garden and infinity swimming pool with a view. A set menu which varies according to the season, with an emphasis on organic ingredients and exotic flavours.

Le Belle Rive rest,
3 km northwest by D 39 – ✆ 05 65 29 73 90 – hotel.bellerive.najac@wanadoo.fr
– Fax 05 65 29 76 88 – *Open 1st April-31 October and closed Sunday evening in October*
22 rm – †€ 54/58 ††€ 54/58, ☕ € 9 – ½ P € 58 – **Rest** – *(closed Sunday dinner in October and Monday lunch in April and October)* Menu (€ 11), € 20/39 – Carte € 34/45
◆ Run by the same family for five generations, this hotel is pleasantly located on the banks of the River Aveyron. Regularly redecorated rooms. Cuisine with a regional flavour is served in the restaurant, on the veranda or on the large, shaded terrace in fine weather.

L' Oustal del Barry with rm rm,
pl. du Bourg – 05 65 29 74 32 – oustaldelbarry@wanadoo.fr – Fax 05 65 29 75 32 – Open 15 March-11 November
18 rm – €45/48 €54/75, €9 – ½ P €58/70 – **Rest** – *(closed Tuesday lunch and Monday except from mid June to mid September)* Menu (€17), €19 (weekday lunch), €23/49 bi – Carte €41/63
♦ A welcoming hotel in a lovely hillside village. Comfortable country-chic dining room. Delicious modern cuisine. Ask for one of the renovated rooms.

NALZEN – **09 Ariège** – **343** I7 – **see Lavelanet**

NANCY – **54 Meurthe-et-Moselle** – **307** I6 – **pop. 103 605** – **Built-up area 331 363** – **alt. 206 m** – **54000** Alsace-Lorraine 26 **B2**

Paris 314 – Dijon 216 – Metz 57 – Reims 209 – Strasbourg 154
Metz-Nancy-Lorraine: 03 87 56 70 00, by ⑥: 43 km.
3635 (0,34 €/mn)
Office de tourisme, place Stanislas 03 83 35 22 41, Fax 03 83 35 90 10
de Nancy Pulnoy Pulnoy 10 rue du Golf, by Château-Salins road and D 83: 7 km, 03 83 18 10 18 ;
de Nancy Liverdun Aingeray, Northwest: 17 km by D 90, 03 83 24 53 87.
Place Stanislas★★★, Arc de Triomphe★ BY **B** - Place de la Carrière★ and Palais du Gouverneur★ BX **R** - Palais ducal★★: musée historique lorrain★★★ - Les Cordeliers church and convent ★: recumbent figure of Philippe de Gueldre★★ - Porte de la Craffe★ - N.-D.-de-Bon-Secours church ★ EX - Front★ of St-Sébastien church - Museums: Beaux-Arts★★ BY **M**[3], Ecole de Nancy★★ DX **M**[4], tropical aquarium★ of the museum-aquarium CY **M**[8] - Jardin botanique du Montet★ DY.
Basilica ★★ of St-Nicolas-de-Port by ②: 12 km.

Plans on following pages

Grand Hôtel de la Reine rm,
2 pl. Stanislas – 03 83 35 03 01 – nancy@concorde-hotels.com – Fax 03 83 32 86 04 BY **d**
42 rm – €145/295 €145/295, €19 – 7 suites
Rest *Stanislas* – *(closed Monday except May-September, Sunday except lunch 1st April-31 October and Saturday lunch)* Menu (€27 bi), €34 (weekdays)/64 – Carte €70/82
♦ Marie-Antoinette stayed in this 18C pavilion with attractive bedrooms furnished in Louis XV style. High ceilings, Baccarat crystal chandeliers, gilded stuccoes and painted panelling in sumptuous restaurant giving onto Place Stanislas.

Park Inn
11 r. Raymond Poincaré – 03 83 39 75 75 – info.nancy@rezidorparkinn.com – Fax 03 83 32 78 17 – **192 rm** – €114/149 €114/149, €15 AY **r**
Rest *Le Rendez Vous* – *(closed 10-25 August, 15-31 December, Saturday, dinner holidays) (lunch only)* Menu €24/30 – Carte €25/40
♦ This hotel is ideally located in the heart of the business district near the historic centre of town. Providing spacious rooms with all modern conveniences. Discreet, modern dining room with wide bay windows giving a soft, diffused light.

D'Haussonville without rest
9 r. Mgr Trouillet – 03 83 35 85 84 – direction@hotel-haussonville.fr – Fax 03 83 32 78 96 – Closed 3-25 August and 1st-18 January AX **g**
3 rm – €140 €160, €16 – 4 suites – €190/230
♦ A grand, refined 16C townhouse, home to a hotel providing plush rooms with original fireplaces and parquet flooring. Magnificent breakfast dining area.

Mercure Centre Stanislas without rest
5 r. Carmes – 03 83 30 92 60 – h1068@accor.com – Fax 03 83 30 92 92 – **80 rm** – €109/169 €119/179, €14,50 BY **m**
♦ Ideally situated in the town centre shopping area, this hotel has complete, well-kept facilities. Rooms have furniture in an Art Nouveau style.

Crystal without rest
5 r. Chanzy – ☎ 03 83 17 54 00 – hotelcrystal.nancy@wanadoo.fr
– Fax 03 83 17 54 30 – Closed 24 December-2 January AY **a**
58 rm – †€ 85/110 ††€ 85/125, ☐ € 11
◆ A recently fully-renovated building, offering very neat, spacious and colourful bedrooms with modern furniture. Cosy lounge-bar.

Des Prélats without rest
56 pl. Mgr Ruch – ☎ 03 83 30 20 20 – contact@hoteldesprelats.com
– Fax 03 83 30 20 21 – Closed 24 December-4 January CY **r**
42 rm – †€ 78/86 ††€ 98/106, ☐ € 12
◆ This 17C building attached to the cathedral has been wonderfully restored with spacious, individually styled rooms and a pleasant veranda opening onto the inner courtyard. Non-smoking establishment.

Albert 1er-Astoria without rest
3 r. Armée Patton – ☎ 03 83 40 31 24 – albert.astoria@wanadoo.fr
– Fax 03 83 28 47 78 – Closed 27 December-2 January AY **e**
83 rm – †€ 55/71 ††€ 55/71, ☐ € 8,50
◆ This hotel near the station has simple, practical rooms which, like the breakfast room, overlook a peaceful courtyard in the shade of a weeping willow.

Le Capucin Gourmand
31 r. Gambetta – ☎ 03 83 35 26 98 – info@lecapu.com – Fax 03 83 35 99 29
Closed Sunday except lunch from September to June, Saturday lunch and Monday
Rest – Menu € 28 (weekday lunch), € 38/48 – Carte € 73/81 BY **m**
◆ A new decor for this local institution: beige tones (wood panelling, Louis XV-style tablecloths and chairs), attractive parquet flooring and carved mouldings. Up-to-date cuisine.

Le Grenier à Sel (Patrick Frechin)
28 r. Gustave Simon – ☎ 03 83 32 31 98 – patrick.frechin@free.fr
– Fax 03 83 35 32 88 – Closed 21 July-13 August, Sunday and Monday
Rest – Menu € 32 (weekday lunch), € 45/65 – Carte € 93/114 BY **x**
Spec. Pigeonneau poché aux griottines de Fougerolles. Tartelette aux truffes (winter). Sushi de riz au lait et fruits de saison. **Wines** Côtes de Toul.
◆ Restaurant on the first floor of one of the town's oldest houses. Dining room renovated in a discreet yet warm contemporary style. Inventive cuisine.

La Mignardise
28 r. Stanislas – ☎ 03 83 32 20 22 – didier.metzelard@wanadoo.fr
– Fax 03 83 32 19 20 – Closed 28 July-3 August and Sunday dinner BY **n**
Rest – Menu € 25/45 – Carte € 51/62
◆ Brick-coloured walls, discreet modern furniture and carefully created lighting make up the refined, elegant contemporary decor by a designer from Nancy. Inventive cuisine with an emphasis on spices.

Les Agaves
2 r. Carmes – ☎ 03 83 32 14 14 – les-agaves.durand-gilles@wanadoo.fr
Closed 17-25 August, 16-22 February, Monday dinner, Wednesday dinner and Sunday
Rest – Carte € 35/51 BY **u**
◆ Two rooms, different atmospheres: one modern and cosy and the other Provençal, decorated with photos from the 1950s. Blend of Italian inspiration and southern flavours. Varied wines.

Les Petits Gobelins
18 r. Primatiale – ☎ 03 83 35 49 03 – Fax 03 83 37 41 49
– Closed 1st-21 August, Sunday and Monday CY **z**
Rest – Menu € 23/60 – Carte € 41/50
◆ A charming restaurant housed in an 18C building on the pedestrian street. Featuring fine modern décor in the dining area and lounge. Good wine selection available.

La Toque Blanche
1 r. Mgr Trouillet – ☎ 03 83 30 17 20 – restaurant@latoqueblanche.fr
– Fax 03 83 32 60 24 – Closed Easter holidays, 28 July-18 August, February holidays, Sunday dinner, Wednesday lunch and Monday ABY **z**
Rest – Menu € 25/65 – Carte € 60/79
◆ A family restaurant in the heart of the Old Town with two dining rooms offering an intimate atmosphere, one with a mural of Harlequin.

JARVILLE-LA-MALGRANGE

République (R. de la) ...... EX 76

LAXOU

Europe (Av. de l') .... DX 32
Poincaré (R. R.)........... DX 71
Résistance (Av. de la)...... CV 78
Rhin (Av. du) .... CV 79

NANCY

Adam (R. Sigisbert) .... BX 2
Albert-1er (Bd) .... DV 3
Anatole-France (Av.)....... DV 6
Armée-Patton (R.) .... DV 7
Auxonne (R. d') .... DV 8
Barrès (R. Maurice)........ CY 10
Bazin (R. H.) .... CY 13
Benit (R.) .... BY 14
Blandan (R. du Sergent).... DX 15
Braconnot (R.)............. BX 19
Carmes (R. des) .... BY 20
Chanoine-Jacob (R.)........ AX 23
Chanzy (R.) .... AY 24
Cheval-Blanc (R. du) ...... BY 25
Clemenceau (Bd G.)......... EX 26
Craffe (R. de la).......... AX 27
Croix de Bourgogne (Espl.) . AZ 28
Dominicains (R. des) ...... BY 29
Erignac (R. C.) .... BY 31
La-Fayette (Pl. de)........ BY 47
Foch (Av.) .... DV 34
Gambetta (R.) .... BY 36
Gaulle (Pl. Gén.-de)....... BX 37
Grande-Rue .... BXY
Haussonville (Bd d') ...... DX 38
Haut-Bourgeois (R.) .... AX 39
Héré (R.) .... BY 40
Ile de Corse (R. de l') ... CY 41
Jeanne-d'Arc (R.).......... DEX 44
Jean-Jaurès (Bd)........... EX 43
Keller (R. Ch.)............ AX 46
Linnois (R.) .... EX 49
Louis (R. Baron)........... AXY 50
Loups (R. des) .... AX 51
Majorelle (R. Louis) ...... DX 52
Mazagran (R.) .... AY 54
Mengin (Pl. Henri)......... BY 55
Mgr-Ruch (Pl.)............. CY 63
Molitor (R.)............... CZ 60
Monnaie (R. de la) .... BY 62
Mon-Désert (R. de) .... ABZ 61
Mouja (R. du Pont)......... BY 64
Nabécor (R. de)............ EX 65
Oudinot (R. Maréchal) ..... EX 68
Poincaré (R. H.) .... AY 69
Poincaré (R. R.) .... AY 70
Point-Central .... BY 72
Ponts (R. des)............. BYZ 73
Primatiale (R. de la)...... CY 74

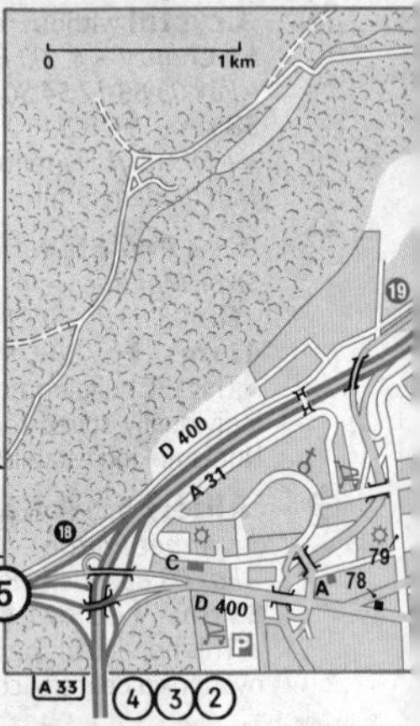

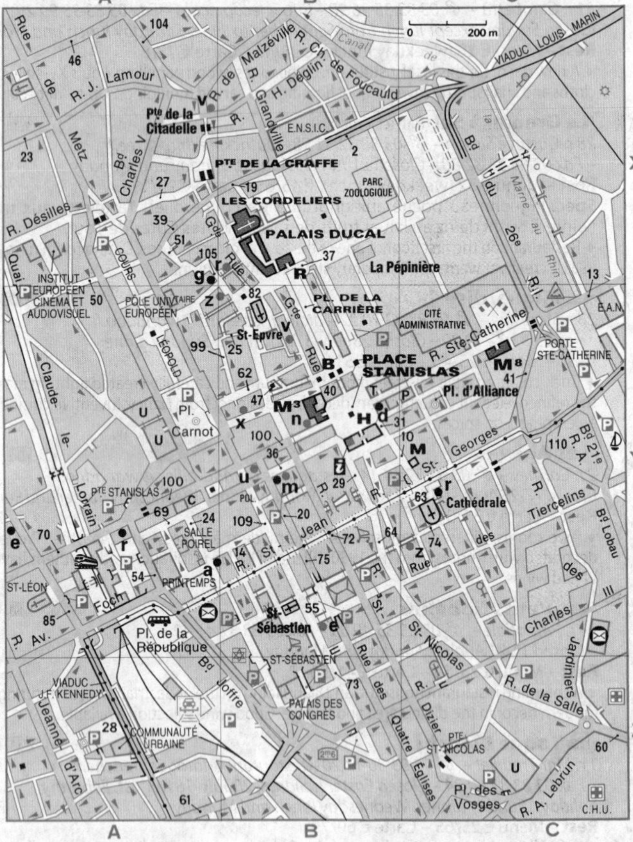

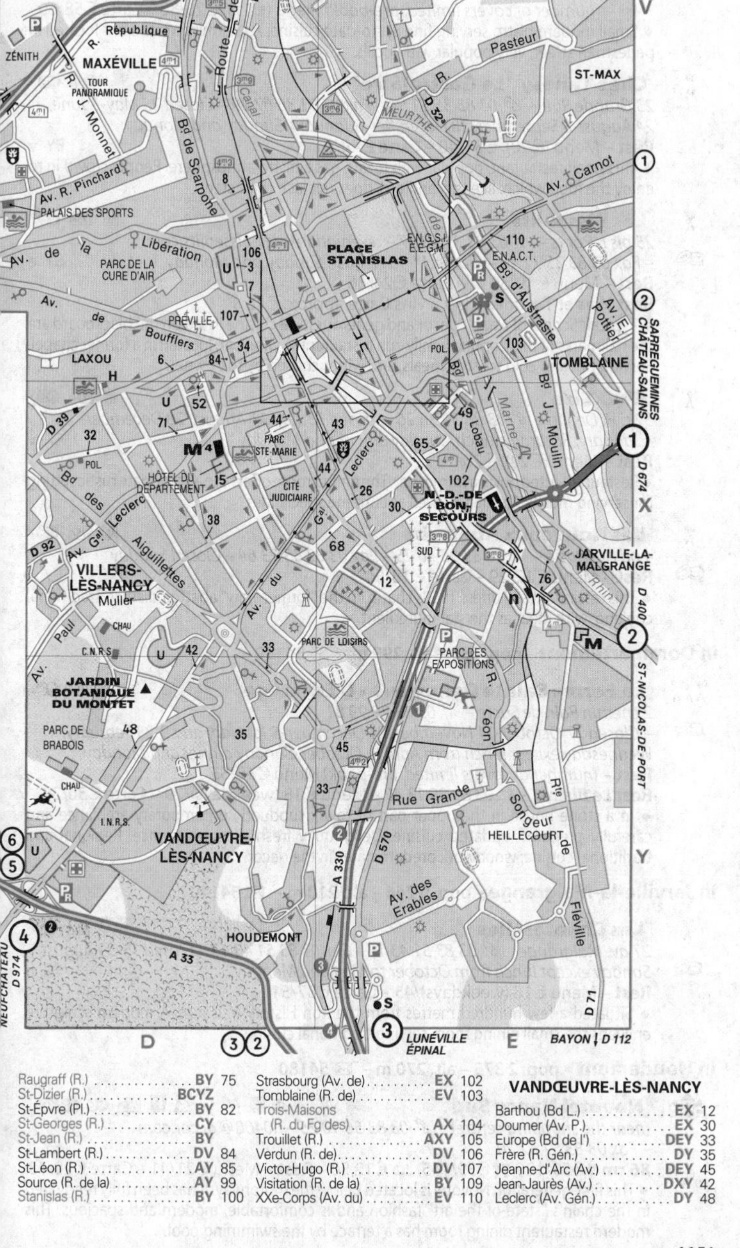

Raugraff (R.) . . . . . BY 75
St-Dizier (R.) . . . . . BCYZ
St-Épvre (Pl.) . . . . . BY 82
St-Georges (R.) . . . . . CY
St-Jean (R.) . . . . . BY
St-Lambert (R.) . . . . . DV 84
St-Léon (R.) . . . . . AY 85
Source (R. de la) . . . . . AY 99
Stanislas (R.) . . . . . BY 100
Strasbourg (Av. de) . . . . . EX 102
Tomblaine (R. de) . . . . . EV 103
Trois-Maisons (R. du Fg des) . . . . . AX 104
Trouillet (R.) . . . . . AXY 105
Verdun (R. de) . . . . . DV 106
Victor-Hugo (R.) . . . . . DV 107
Visitation (R. de la) . . . . . BY 109
XXe-Corps (Av. du) . . . . . EV 110

VANDŒUVRE-LÈS-NANCY

Barthou (Bd L.) . . . . . EX 12
Doumer (Av. P.) . . . . . EX 30
Europe (Bd de l') . . . . . DEY 33
Frère (R. Gén.) . . . . . DY 35
Jeanne-d'Arc (Av.) . . . . . DEY 45
Jean-Jaurès (Av.) . . . . . DXY 42
Leclerc (Av. Gén.) . . . . . DY 48

V Four
10 r. St-Michel – ✆ 03 83 32 49 48 – bruno.faonio@numericable.fr – Fax 03 83 32 49 48 – Closed 14-24 September, 1st-10 February, Sunday dinner and Monday BX **r**
Rest – *(number of covers limited, pre-book)* Menu (€ 17), € 26/38 – Carte € 58/69
◆ Small modern bistro serving fine up-to-date cuisine. A charming restaurant located in pedestrian street, very popular with locals.

Chez Tanésy "Le Gastrolâtre"
23 Grande Rue – ✆ 03 83 35 51 94 – Fax 03 83 36 67 29 – Closed 25 May-3 June, 24 August-8 September, 28 December-6 January, Sunday and Monday
Rest – Menu (€ 20), € 35/40 – Carte € 44/61 BY **v**
◆ This small restaurant, popular with locals, has a bistro atmosphere. People crowd in to enjoy the food which, like the landlord, does not lack character.

Les Pissenlits
25 bis r. Ponts – ✆ 03 83 37 43 97 – reservation@les-pissenlits.com – Fax 03 83 35 72 49 – Closed 1st-15 August, Sunday and Monday BY **e**
Rest – Menu € 19/50 bi – Carte € 24/36
Rest *Vins et Tartines* – bar à vins Carte approx. € 18
◆ Typical "School of Nancy" decor and generous local cuisine listed on the blackboard are the hallmarks of this popular family-run restaurant. A wine bar, located in a former chapel. Serving hot and cold toasted meals, and wines chosen by the owner.

Chez Lize
52 r. H. Déglin – ✆ 03 83 30 36 26 – Closed 13 July-11 August, 28 December-4 January, Saturday lunch, Sunday dinner and Monday AX **v**
Rest – Menu (€ 22), € 26/29
◆ Restaurant fitted out in a former bar. The dining room offers the appropriate rustic setting for serving mostly Alsatian, as well as Lorraine specialities.

Les Nouveaux Abattoirs
4 bd Austrasie – ✆ 03 83 35 46 25 – Fax 03 83 35 13 64 – Closed Sunday
Rest – Menu € 17/29 – Carte € 18/54 EV **s**
◆ This restaurant still offers 1960s charm, in the "former-new" abattoir district. Traditional cooking, with meat as the star ingredient.

in Dommartemont – pop. 630 – alt. 299 m – ✉ 54130

La Ferme Sainte Geneviève - L'Ermitage
2 chemin Pain de Sucre – ✆ 03 83 29 99 81 – Closed 27 October-11 November, 21 December-5 January and 9-23 February, Wednesday except lunch from April to October, Sunday dinner and Monday
Rest – *(number of covers limited, pre-book)* Menu € 40/55
Rest *Le Bistrot* – ✆ 03 83 29 13 49 – Menu € 18 (weekdays)/29 – Carte € 30/38
◆ In a stone house in the upper part of town; subdued contemporary ambiance and carefully prepared updated cuisine. Delightfully fresh summer terrace. Regional and traditional cuisine; woodwork predominates in the decor.

in Jarville-la-Malgrange – pop. 9 746 – alt. 210 m – ✉ 54140

Les Chanterelles
27 av. Malgrange – ✆ 03 83 51 43 17 – Fax 03 83 51 43 17 – Closed 15-31 August, Sunday except lunch from October to May and Monday EX **n**
Rest – Menu € 18 (weekdays)/45 – Carte € 37/51
◆ Situated a few hundred metres from the Iron History Museum. A modern sculpture enlivens the small dining room serving traditional cuisine.

in Houdemont – pop. 2 375 – alt. 270 m – ✉ 54180

Novotel Nancy Sud
(near the shopping centre) – ✆ 03 83 56 10 25 – h0408@accor.com – Fax 03 83 57 62 20 EY **s**
86 rm †€ 59/126 ††€ 59/145, ☕ € 12,50 – **Rest** – Menu € 21/41 – Carte € 20/43
◆ This first-generation Novotel is located below the motorway. It has been fully renovated in the chain's "state-of-the art" fashion and is comfortable, modern and spacious. This modern restaurant dining room has a terrace by the swimming pool.

in Flavigny-sur-Moselle 16 km by ③ and A 330 – pop. 1 636 – alt. 240 m – ✉ 54630

XXX **Le Prieuré** with rm

– ✆ 03 83 26 70 45 – rjoelroy@aol.com – Fax 03 83 26 75 51 – *Closed 1st-8 May, 25 August-7 September, 30 December-6 January, 16-28 February, Sunday dinner, Wednesday dinner and Monday* – **4 rm** – †€ 117 ††€ 117, ☕ € 13
Rest – *(number of covers limited, pre-book)* Menu € 61 – Carte € 73/89
◆ A grand dining room behind the modest façade, where Lorraine furniture, pewterware and a fireplace create an intimate setting. Spacious rooms. Modern cuisine.

in Vandœuvre-lès-Nancy – pop. 32 048 – alt. 300 m – ✉ 54500

Cottage-Hôtel AC rest,

4 allée de Bourgogne – ✆ 03 83 44 69 00 – reservation@cottagenancy.com – Fax 03 83 44 06 14 – *Closed 1st-15 August, 24-31 December*
55 rm – †€ 47/55 ††€ 47/55, ☕ € 7,50 – ½ P € 42/46
Rest – *(Closed Sunday dinner)* Menu € 14/23 – Carte € 24/35
◆ Close to the racecourse, these modern buildings offer practical accommodation. Refined colonial feel to the bar and lounge. Tasty and generous simple traditional fare served in a pretty veranda dining room.

in Méréville 16 km by ③, A 330, D 570 and D 115 – pop. 1 349 – alt. 250 m – ✉ 54850

La Maison Carrée

12 r. du Bac – ✆ 03 83 47 09 23 – hotel@maisoncarree.com – Fax 03 83 47 50 75 – *Closed 22 December-5 January and Sunday dinner from November to March*
22 rm – †€ 65/70 ††€ 78/86, ☕ € 9,50 – ½ P € 70/74 **Rest** – *(closed 26-30 December, Sunday dinner and Monday)* Menu € 22 (weekdays)/60 – Carte € 28/56
◆ The rooms of this hotel, refurbished in 2006, overlook the pool, garden or Moselle. Those on the first floor have a balcony; pleasantly Breton furnished breakfast room. Restaurant situated 100m away in a converted ferryman's cottage with a waterside terrace.

in Neuves-Maisons 14 km by ④ – pop. 6 849 – alt. 230 m – ✉ 54230

XX **L'Union**

1 imp. A. Briand – ✆ 03 83 47 30 46 – Fax 03 83 47 33 42 – *Closed 1st-15 August, Monday and dinner except Friday and Saturday*
Rest – Menu € 26/36 – Carte € 33/45
◆ A restaurant in a pretty, colourful house, once the village café. The two dining rooms, one a covered terrace, are pleasantly simple.

NANS-LES-PINS – 83 Var – 340 J5 – pop. 3 159 – alt. 380 m – ✉ 83860

Paris 794 – Aix-en-Provence 44 – Brignoles 26 – Marseille 42 – Toulon 71

Office de tourisme, 2, cours Général-de-Gaulle ✆ 04 94 78 95 91, Fax 04 94 78 60 07 — 40 **B3**

de la Sainte-Baume "La Mouchouane", North: 4 km by D 80, ✆ 04 94 78 60 12.

Domaine de Châteauneuf rm, AC rm, rest,

3 km north on D 560
– ✆ 04 94 78 90 06 – chateauneuf@relaischateaux.com – Fax 04 94 78 63 30 – *Open 4 April-1st November*
29 rm – †€ 133/256 ††€ 166/390, ☕ € 19 – 1 suite
Rest *(closed at lunchtime on weekdays)* Menu € 49 (lunch), € 52/60 – Carte € 54/72
◆ Napoleon I is believed to have stayed in this 18C residence, surrounded by a park with a golf course. Tastefully decorated period bedrooms. Frescoes in one of the salons. Elegant classical decor in the restaurant and terrace under foliage.

XX **Château de Nans** with rm

on the D 560 at 3 km (Auriol road) – ✆ 04 94 78 92 06 – info@chateau-de-nans.com – Fax 04 94 78 60 46 – *Hotel open 1st April-30 September, Restaurant: closed 24-30 November, mid February-mid March, Tuesday except July-August and Monday*
5 rm ☕ – †€ 106 ††€ 122/138 – **Rest** – Menu € 48/59 – Carte approx. € 49
◆ Provençal cuisine, dishes with southern accents and a pretty veranda-dining room. An attractively restored 19C mansion overlooking the Ste-Baume golf course. Comfortably personalised rooms, original in the tower. Pétanque.

NANTERRE – 92 Hauts-de-Seine – 311 J2 – 101 14 – see Paris, Area

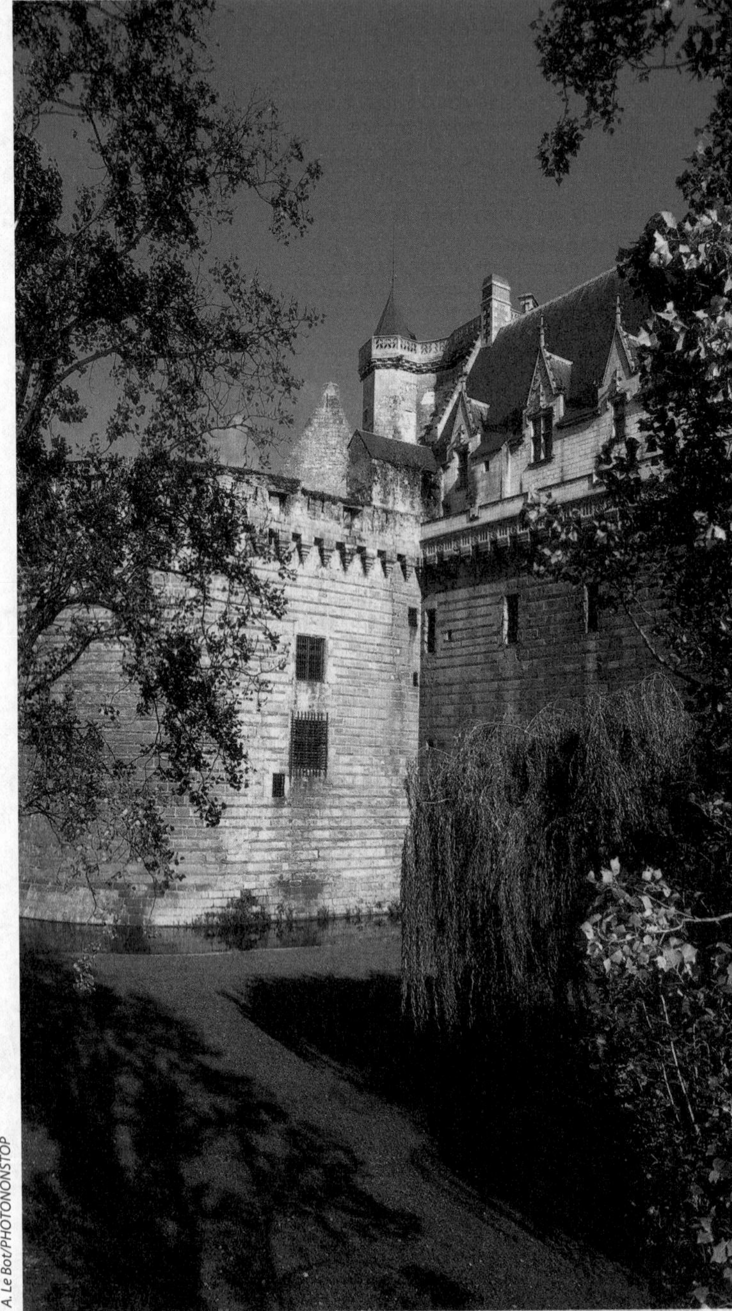

A. Le Bot/PHOTONONSTOP

The château des Ducs

NANTES

Department: 44 Loire-Atlantique
Michelin LOCAL map: n° **316** G4
Paris 381 – Angers 88 – Bordeaux 325 – Quimper 233 – Rennes 109

Population: 270 251 34 **B2**
Pop. built-up area: 544 932
Altitude: 8 m – Postal Code: 44000
Brittany

USEFUL INFORMATION

TOURIST OFFICE

7, rue de Valmy ✆ 08 92 46 40 44, Fax 02 40 89 11 99

TRANSPORT

Auto-train ✆ 3635 et tapez 42 (0,34 €/mn)

AIRPORT

International Nantes-Atlantique ✆ 02 40 84 80 00, by D 85: 8,5 km BX

A FEW GOLF COURSES

de Nantes Erdre Chemin du Bout des Landes, North: 6 km by D 69, ✆ 02 40 59 21 21 ;
de Carquefou Carquefou Boulevard de l'Epinay, North: 9 km by D 337, ✆ 02 40 52 73 74 ;
de Nantes Vigneux-de-Bretagne RD 81, Northwest: by D965 and D 81: 16 km, ✆ 02 40 63 25 82.

TO BE SEEN

MEMORIES OF THE DUKES OF BRITANNY

Château★★: tour de la Couronne d'Or (Golden Crown Tower)★★, well★★ HY - Interior★★ of Cathedral St-Pierre-et-St-Paul: tomb of François II★★, cenotaph of Lamoricière★ HY

18C NANTES S.

Former Ile Feydeau★ GZ

19C TOWN S.

Passage Pommeraye★ GZ 150 - Quartier Graslin★ FZ - Cours Cambronne★ FZ - Jardin des Plantes★ HY

MUSEUMS

Musée des Beaux-Arts★★ HY - Muséum d'histoire naturelle★★ FZ M4 - Musée Dobrée★ FZ - Musée archéologique★ M3 - Musée Jules-Verne★ BX M1

Grand Hôtel Mercure rm, VISA AE

4 r. Couëdic – ✆ 02 51 82 10 00 – H1985@accor.com – Fax 02 51 82 10 10

152 rm – €100/200 €110/210, ☕ €12 – 10 suites *p. 7* GZ **m**

Rest – *(closed Sun)* Menu (€13,50 bi), €30

♦ Attractive 19C façade, glass roofed hall and cosy piano bar. Rooms with Art Deco style furniture and travel photographs. Restaurant decorated in a modern, bistro style. Spontaneous cuisine and a selection of wines by the glass.

Novotel Cité des Congrès rm, rm, VISA AE

3 r. Valmy – ✆ 02 51 82 00 00 – h1571@accor.com – Fax 02 51 82 07 40 *p. 7* HZ **t**

103 rm – €118/145 €118/145, ☕ €13,50 – 2 suites – **Rest** – Carte €22/38

♦ The hotel is next to the Cité des Congrès, providing large renovated rooms, some with a pleasant view of the St-Félix canal. Children's play area. Grill area for all to see, "Novotel" menu and daily specials.

Mercure Île de Nantes P VISA AE

15 bd A. Millerand ✉ 44200 – ✆ 02 40 95 95 95 – H0555@accor.com – Fax 02 40 48 23 83 *p. 5* CX **a**

100 rm – €140/150 €150/200, ☕ €14 – **Rest** – *(closed Christmas holidays, Friday dinner, Saturday and Sunday)* Menu (€18) – Carte €24/27

♦ A 1970s hotel with a Jules Vernes themed decor. Spacious rooms, typical of the chain, many of them with views of the Loire. Simple setting and menu. Grilled meat in the restaurant; wine bar.

Holiday Inn Garden Court rm, rest, VISA AE

1 bd Martyrs Nantais ✉ 44200 – ✆ 02 40 47 77 77 – holiday.inn.nantes@wanadoo.fr – Fax 02 40 47 36 52 *p. 7* HZ **v**

108 rm – €65/160 €65/200, ☕ €13 – **Rest** – *(closed 24 December-6 January, Saturday lunch and Sunday lunch)* Menu (€18), €21 – Carte approx. €29

♦ A chain hotel on the Ile de Nantes, near the tramway. Some of the rooms overlook the Loire; all are spacious and have king size beds. Comfortable modern dining room. Pergola shaded service in summer.

L'Hôtel without rest VISA AE

6 r. Henri IV – ✆ 02 40 29 30 31 – lhotel@mageos.com – Fax 02 40 29 00 95 – Closed 24 December-2January *p. 7* HY **z**

31 rm – €72/140 €79/140, ☕ €9

♦ A contemporary style lobby provides a stylish entrance to this hotel. The clean lines continue in the bedrooms facing the château or overlooking the garden.

Jules Verne without rest VISA AE

3 r. Couëdic – ✆ 02 40 35 74 50 – hoteljulesverne@wanadoo.fr – Fax 02 40 20 09 35 *p. 7* GZ **h**

65 rm – €55/115 €60/125, ☕ €11

♦ Close to Place Royale, a recent hotel with contemporary, discreet, well-cared-for rooms; those on the top floor have a view over the Nantes rooftops.

Graslin without rest VISA AE

1 r. Piron – ✆ 02 40 69 72 91 – info@hotel-graslin.com – Fax 02 40 69 04 44

47 rm – €59/102 €59/102, ☕ €9 *p. 6* FZ **v**

♦ This hotel is currently being renovated and has two types of rooms. Choose those which are redecorated, streamlined and Art deco in style. The others have pine furnishings.

Pommeraye without rest VISA AE

2 r. Boileau – ✆ 02 40 48 78 79 – info@hotel-pommeraye.com – Fax 02 40 47 63 75 *p. 7* GZ **t**

50 rm – €54/89 €59/114, ☕ €9

♦ Hotel located a stone's throw from the famous Passage Pommeraye and Rue Crébillon shops. Well kept, colourful rooms with a refined contemporary decor.

Des Colonies without rest VISA AE

5 r. Chapeau Rouge – ✆ 02 40 48 79 76 – hoteldescolonies@free.fr – Fax 02 40 12 49 25 *p. 7* GZ **e**

38 rm – €54/66 €61/73, ☕ €8

♦ This hotel located in a small side street has a reception area that features art on display. Contemporary rooms in bright colours (good linen).

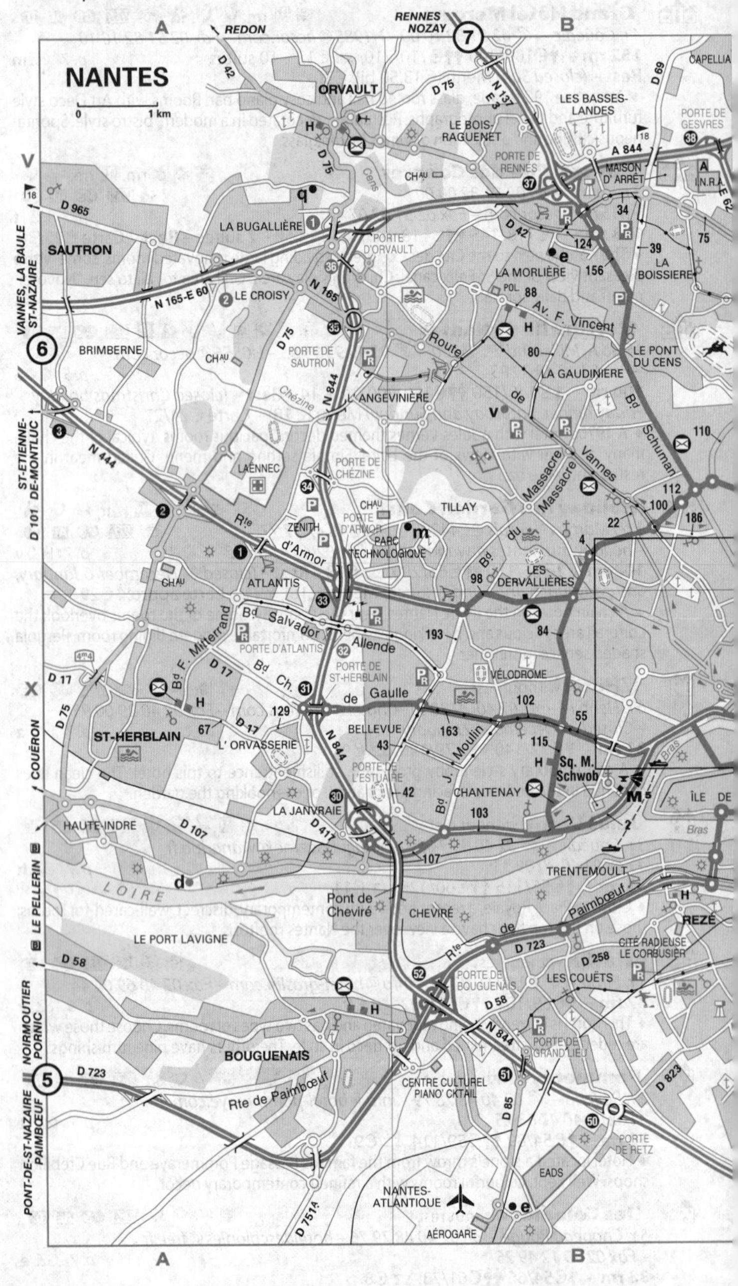
NANTES
REDON
RENNES
NOZAY
ORVAULT
LE BOIS-RAGUENET
LES BASSES-LANDES
PORTE DE GESVRES
PORTE DE RENNES
MAISON D' ARRÊT
I.N.R.A.
A 844
LA BUGALLIÈRE
PORTE D'ORVAULT
SAUTRON
LE CROISY
N 165-E 60
N 165
LA MORLIÈRE
LA BOISSIERE
Av. F. Vincent
LE PONT DU CENS
BRIMBERNE
PORTE DE SAUTRON
LA GAUDINIERE
L'ANGEVINIÈRE
Route de Vannes
Bd Schuman
N 444
LAËNNEC
PORTE DE CHÉZINE
ZENITH
PORTE D'ARMOR
PARC TECHNOLOGIQUE
TILLAY
Rte d'Armor
ATLANTIS
LES DERVALLIÈRES
Bd du Massacre
Bd Salvador Allende
PORTE D'ATLANTIS
PORTE DE ST-HERBLAIN
Bd F. Mitterrand
Bd Ch. de Gaulle
VÉLODROME
ST-HERBLAIN
L' ORVASSERIE
BELLEVUE
Bd J. Moulin
Sq. M. Schwob
PORTE DE L'ESTUAIRE
CHANTENAY
LA JANVRAIE
HAUTE-INDRE
ÎLE DE
LOIRE
TRENTEMOULT
Pont de Cheviré
CHEVIRÉ
Rte de Paimbœuf
REZÉ
LE PORT LAVIGNE
CITÉ RADIEUSE LE CORBUSIER
PORTE DE BOUGUENAIS
LES COUËTS
PORTE DE GRAND LIEU
BOUGUENAIS
CENTRE CULTUREL PIANO' CKTAIL
Rte de Paimbœuf
PORTE DE RETZ
EADS
NANTES-ATLANTIQUE
AÉROGARE
VANNES, LA BAULE ST-NAZAIRE
ST-ETIENNE-DE-MONTLUC
COUËRON
LE PELLERIN
NOIRMOUTIER PORNIC
PONT-DE-ST-NAZAIRE PAIMBŒUF

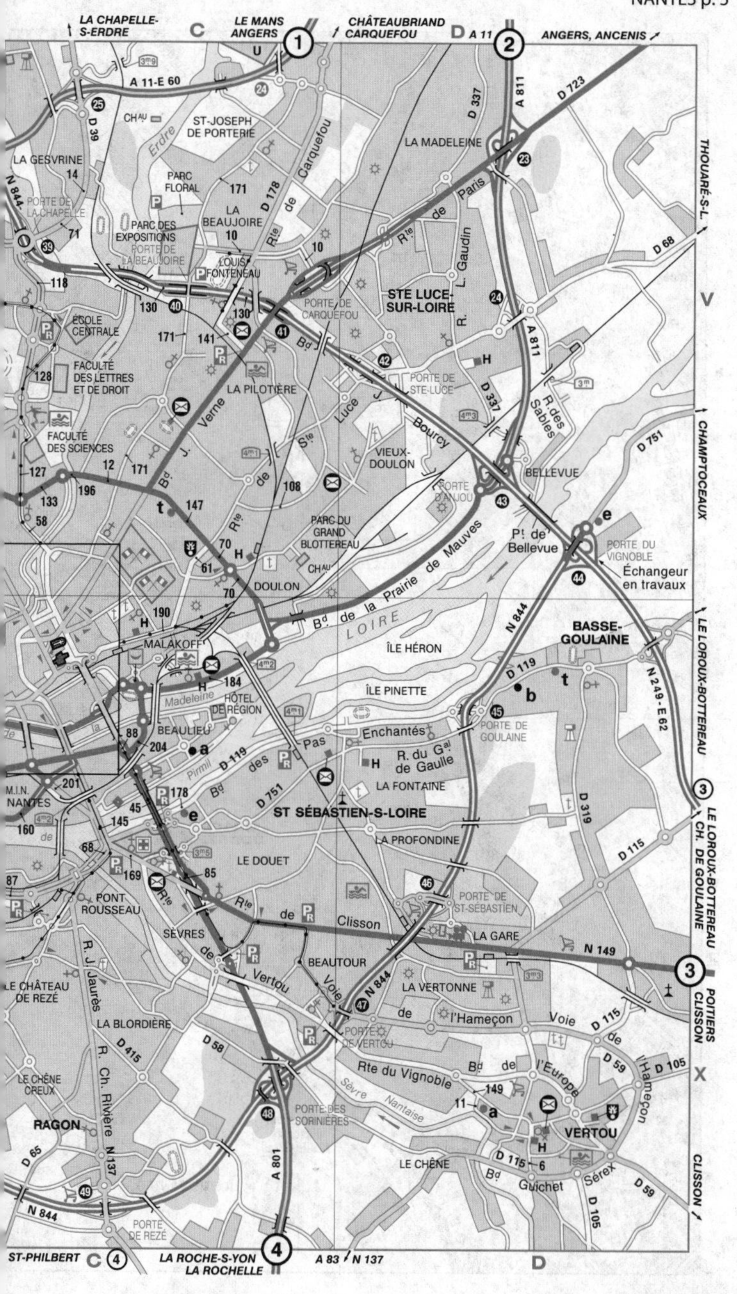

LA CHAPELLE-S-ERDRE
LE MANS ANGERS
CHÂTEAUBRIAND CARQUEFOU
ANGERS, ANCENIS
THOUARÉ-S-L.
CHAMPTOCEAUX
LE LOROUX-BOTTEREAU
LE LOROUX-BOTTEREAU CH. DE GOULAINE
POITIERS CLISSON
CLISSON
ST-PHILBERT
LA ROCHE-S-YON LA ROCHELLE
A 83 N 137
ST-JOSEPH DE PORTERIE
LA MADELEINE
LA GESVRINE
PARC FLORAL
LA BEAUJOIRE
PARC DES EXPOSITIONS
LOUIS FONTENEAU
STE LUCE-SUR-LOIRE
ÉCOLE CENTRALE
FACULTÉ DES LETTRES ET DE DROIT
FACULTÉ DES SCIENCES
LA PILOTIÈRE
VIEUX-DOULON
BELLEVUE
PARC DU GRAND BLOTTEREAU
DOULON
Pt de Bellevue
Échangeur en travaux
LOIRE
ÎLE HÉRON
BASSE-GOULAINE
MALAKOFF
ÎLE PINETTE
HÔTEL DE RÉGION
BEAULIEU
M.I.N. NANTES
LA FONTAINE
ST SÉBASTIEN-S-LOIRE
LA PROFONDINE
LE DOUET
PONT ROUSSEAU
SÈVRES
LA GARE
BEAUTOUR
LA VERTONNE
LE CHÂTEAU DE REZÉ
LA BLORDIÈRE
LE CHÊNE CREUX
RAGON
VERTOU
LE CHÊNE
PORTE DE REZÉ
PORTE DES SORINIÈRES
PORTE DE VERTOU
PORTE DE ST-SÉBASTIEN
PORTE DE GOULAINE
PORTE DU VIGNOBLE
PORTE D'ANJOU
PORTE DE STE-LUCE
PORTE DE CARQUEFOU
PORTE DE LA BEAUJOIRE
PORTE DE LA CHAPELLE
A 11-E 60
N 844
A 811
D 723
D 751
N 249-E 62
D 319
D 115
N 149
D 105
D 59
A 801
N 137
Rte de Paris
Rte de Carquefou
Bd J. Verne
Rte de Ste Luce
Bd de la Prairie de Mauves
Rte de Clisson
Rte de Vertou
Rte du Vignoble
Bd de l'Europe
Voie de l'Hameçon
Sèvre Nantaise
R. J. Jaurès
R. Ch. Rivière
R. du Gal de Gaulle
Bd des Pas Enchantés
Bd Guichet Sérex

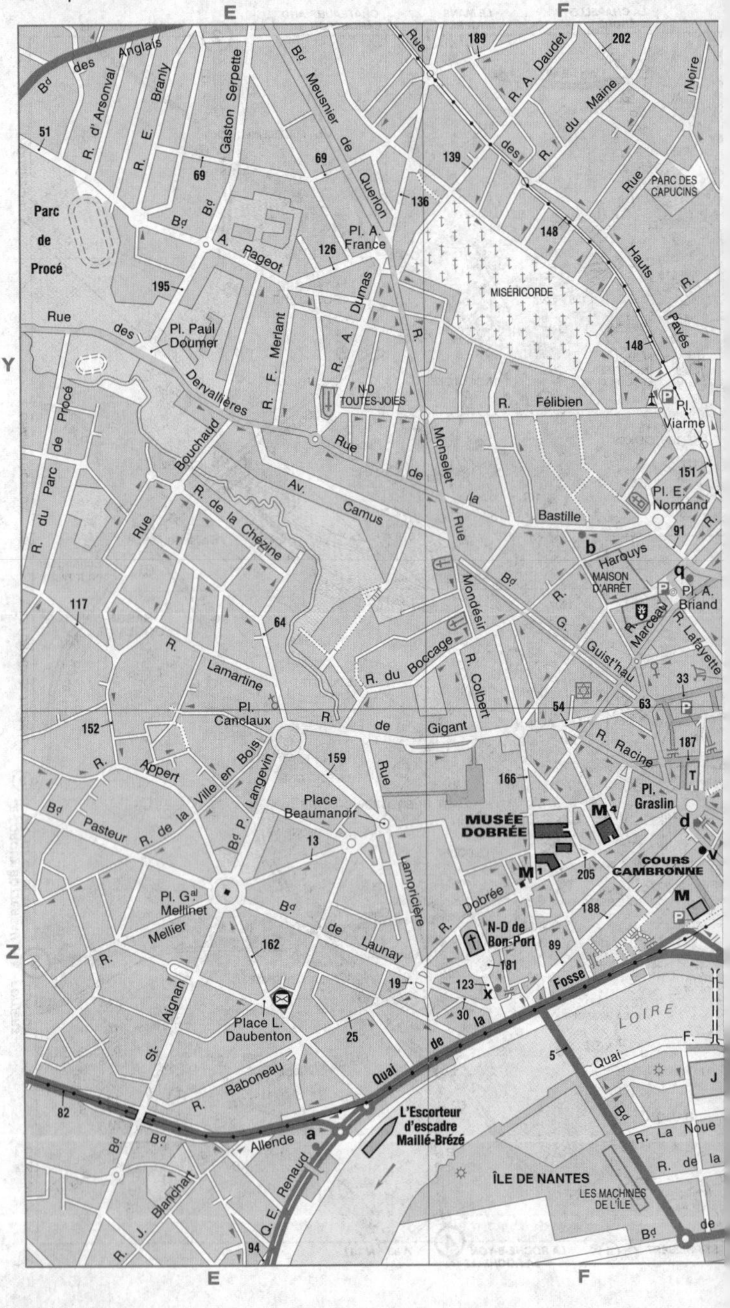

E
F
Y
Z
Bd des Anglais
R. d'Arsonval
R. E. Branly
Gaston Serpette
Bd Meusnier de Querlon
Rue
189
202
R. A. Daudet
R. du Maine
Noire
51
69
139
des
Rue
PARC DES CAPUCINS
Parc de Procé
Bd
136
148
Hauts
A. Pageot
Pl. A. France
126
R.
195
R. A. Dumas
MISÉRICORDE
Pavés
Rue des Dervallières
Pl. Paul Doumer
R. F. Merlant
R.
148
N-D TOUTES-JOIES
R. Félibien
Pl. Viarme
R. du Parc de Procé
Bouchaud
Rue de la Bastille
Monselet
151
Av. Camus
Pl. E. Normand
R. de la Chézine
Rue
91
b
Harouys
q
MAISON D'ARRÊT
Pl. A. Briand
Bd G. Guist'hau
R. Marceau
117
Mondésir
R. Lafayette
64
R. Lamartine
R. du Boccage
R. Colbert
33
Pl. Canclaux
54
63
152
R. de Gigant
R. Racine
R. Appert
187
R. de la Ville en Bois
159
Rue
166
Bd P. Langevin
Place Beaumanoir
Pl. Graslin
M4
MUSÉE DOBRÉE
d
Bd Pasteur
13
Lamoricière
COURS CAMBRONNE
v
M1
205
Pl. Gal Mellinet
R. Dobrée
M
188
Mellier
Bd de Launay
N-D de Bon-Port
162
89
R. St-Aignan
181
Fosse
19
123
x
30
LOIRE
Place L. Daubenton
25
Quai de la
F.
5
Quai
R. Baboneau
J
82
L'Escorteur d'escadre Maillé-Brézé
Bd
R. La Noue
Bd Allende
a
R. de la
Q. E. Renaud
ÎLE DE NANTES
R. J. Blanchart
LES MACHINES DE L'ÎLE
de
Bd
94
R.
E
F

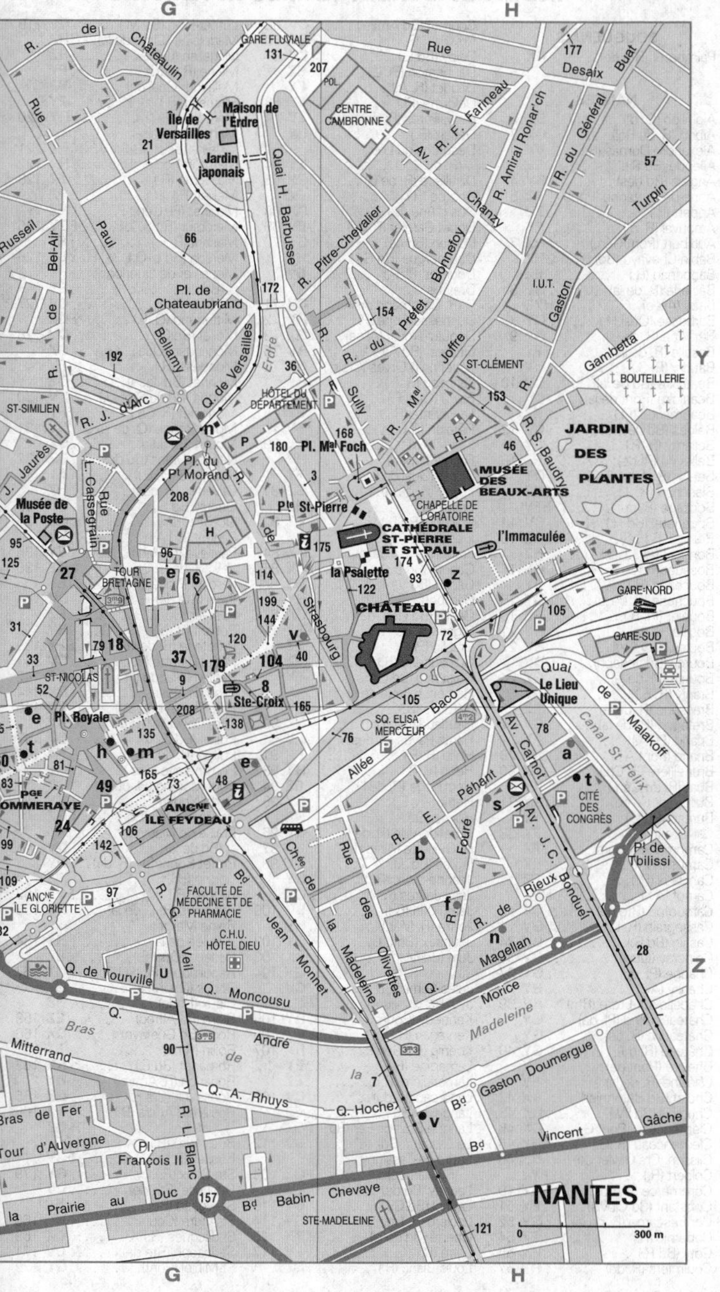
G
H
Y
Z
GARE FLUVIALE
CENTRE CAMBRONNE
POL
Île de Versailles
Maison de l'Erdre
Jardin japonais
Rue Desaix
R. Amiral Ronar'ch
R. du Général Buat
Av. R. F. Farineau
Chanzy
Turpin
Quai H. Barbusse
R. Pitre-Chevalier
Bonnefoy
R. du Préfet
Joffre
I.U.T.
Gaston
Gambetta
ST-CLÉMENT
BOUTEILLERIE
JARDIN DES PLANTES
R. S. Baudry
MUSÉE DES BEAUX-ARTS
CHAPELLE DE L'ORATOIRE
l'Immaculée
Pl. de Chateaubriand
Q. de Versailles
Erdre
HÔTEL DU DÉPARTEMENT
Sully
Pl. Mal Foch
Pte St-Pierre
CATHÉDRALE ST-PIERRE ET ST-PAUL
la Psalette
CHÂTEAU
GARE-NORD
GARE-SUD
Quai de Malakoff
Canal St Félix
Le Lieu Unique
ST-SIMILIEN
R. J. d'Arc
J. Jaurès
L. Cassegrain
Musée de la Poste
Pl. du Pt Morand
TOUR BRETAGNE
ST-NICOLAS
Pl. Royale
Ste-Croix
Strasbourg
Baco
SQ. ELISA MERCŒUR
Allée
PGE POMMERAYE
ANCNE ÎLE FEYDEAU
ANCNE ÎLE GLORIETTE
Av. Carnot
Péhant
CITÉ DES CONGRÈS
Pl. de Tbilissi
R. E. Fouré
Rue des Olivettes
Chée de la Madeleine
Bd Jean Monnet
R. G. Veil
FACULTÉ DE MÉDECINE ET DE PHARMACIE
C.H.U. HÔTEL DIEU
Av. J. C. Bonduel
R. de Rieux
R. Magellan
Q. de Tourville
Q. Moncousu
Q. André
Q. Magellan
Morice
Madeleine
Bras de la
Mitterrand
Q. A. Rhuys
Q. Hoche
Gaston Doumergue
Bd Vincent Gâche
Bras de Fer
Tour d'Auvergne
Pl. François II
R. L. Blanc
la Prairie au Duc
Bd Babin-Chevaye
STE-MADELEINE
Rue de Châteaulin
Rue Paul Bellamy
R. Russeil
R. de Bel-Air
NANTES
0
300 m

INDEX OF STREET NAMES IN NANTES

St-Pierre (Cours) .... **HY** 174
St-Pierre (Pl.) .... **GY** 175
St-Rogatien (R.) .... **HY** 177
St-Sébastien (Côte) ...... **CX** 178
Salengro (Pl. R.) .... **GY** 180
Sanitat (Pl. du) .... **FZ** 181
Santeuil (R.) .... **GY** 183
Sarrebrück (Bd de) .... **CX** 184
Say (R. L.) .... **BV** 186
Schuman (Bd R.) .... **BV**
Scribe (R.) .... **FZ** 187
Serpette (Bd G.) .... **EY**
Sibille (R. M.) .... **FZ** 188
Simon (R. Jules) .... **EY** 189
Stalingrad (Bd de) .... **CX** 190
Strasbourg (R. de) .... **GY**
Sully (R.) .... **HY**
Talensac (R.) .... **GY** 192
Tbilissi (Pt de) .... **ZH**
Tertre (Bd du) .... **BX** 193
Thomas (Bd A.) .... **EY** 195
Tortière (Pont de la) .... **CV** 196
Tourville (Quai de) .... **GZ**
Turpin (R. Gaston) .... **HY**
Vannes (Rte de) .... **BV**
Veil (R. G.) .... **GZ**
Verdun (R. de) .... **GY** 199
Versailles (Quai de) .... **GY**
Vertou (Rte de) .... **CX**
Viarme (Pl.) .... **FY**
Victor-Hugo (Bd) .... **CX** 201
Villebois-Mareuil (R.) .... **FY** 202
Ville-en-Bois (R. de la) .... **EZ**
Viviani (R. René) .... **CX** 204
Voltaire (R.) .... **FZ** 205
Waldeck-Rousseau (Pl.) . **GHY** 207
50-Otages (Crs des) .... **GYZ** 208

ORVAULT

Ferrière (Av. de la) .... **BV** 80
Goupil (Av. A.) .... **BV** 88
Mendès-France (Bd) .... **BV** 124
Rennes (Rte de) .... **BV** 156
Vannes (Rte de) .... **BV**
Vincent (Av. F.) .... **BV**

REZÉ

Gaulle (Bd Gén.-de) .... **CX** 87
Jean-Jaurès (R.) .... **CX**
Rivière (R. Ch.) .... **CX**

STE-LUCE-SUR-LOIRE

Bellevue (Pont de) .... **DV**
Gaudin (R. L.) .... **DV**
Sables (R. des) .... **DV**

ST-HERBLAIN

Allende (Bd S.) .... **ABX**
Armor (Rte d') .... **AV**
Dr-Boubée (R. du) .... **AX** 67
Gaulle (Av. Ch.-de) .... **AX**
Massacre (Bd du) .... **BV**
Mitterrand (Bd F.) .... **AX**
Monnet (R. J.) .... **AX** 125

ST-SÉBASTIEN-SUR-LOIRE

Clisson (Rte de) .... **CDX**
Gaulle (R. du Gén.-de) .... **CDX**
Pas-Enchantés (Bd des) . **CDX**

VERTOU

Arnaud (R. A.) .... **DX** 6
Beauséjour (R.) .... **DX** 11
Europe (Bd de l') .... **DX**
Guichet Sérex (Bd) .... **DX**
Pont de l'Arche (R. du) .... **DX** 149
Vignoble (Rte du) .... **DX**

L'Atlantide (Jean-Yves Guého)
the Loire and Nantes, AC VISA MC AE

16 quai E. Renaud ✉ 44100 – ✆ 02 40 73 23 23 – jygueho@club-internet.fr – Fax 02 40 73 76 46 – Closed 1st-4 May, 26 July-25 August, 23 December-1st January, Saturday lunch, Sunday and public holidays p. 6 EZ **a**

Rest – Menu € 30 (lunch), € 40/95 – Carte € 68/80

Spec. "Mollets" de grenouilles meunière et brandade d'anguille fumée (March to September). Saint-Jacques poêlées et foie gras d'oie en paupiette de chou (December to March). Poitrine de pigeonneau rôtie à la broche, homard en tronçon (April to September). **Wines** Muscadet de Sèvre-et-Maine, Anjou blanc.

◆ This contemporary restaurant at the top of a modern building offers a splendid view of the town and river. Original cuisine and good Loire wine list.

L'Océanide
AC VISA MC

2 r. P. Bellamy – ✆ 02 40 20 32 28 – Fax 02 40 48 08 55 – Closed 21 July-18 August, Sunday and Monday p. 7 GY **n**

Rest – Menu € 20/61 – Carte € 34/64

◆ Restaurant with an attractive counter, wood panelling, banquettes and paintings. Seafood dishes and a fine wine list.

La Poissonnerie
AC VISA MC AE

4 r. Léon Maître – ✆ 02 40 47 79 50 – lestroisas@orange.fr – Closed 4-26 August, 21 December-7 January, Saturday lunch, Sunday and Monday p. 7 GZ **e**

Rest – Menu (€ 14), € 43 – Carte € 37/60

◆ The name says it all: the sea is an integral part of this restaurant, both in its decor with shades of blue and nautical objects, and in the fish and seafood cuisine. Good choice of Muscadet wine.

L'Abélia
P VISA MC AE

125 bd des Poilus – ✆ 02 40 35 40 00 – Fax 02 40 93 27 26 – Closed August, 22 December-5 January, Sunday and Monday p. 5 CV **t**

Rest – Menu (€ 25), € 30/49

◆ Friendly welcome at this fine house dating from 1900. Modern food served in the warm coloured dining rooms, featuring parquet and tiled flooring and exposed stone.

Félix
AC VISA MC

1 r. Lefèvre Utile – ✆ 02 40 34 15 93 – contact@felixbrasserie.com – Fax 02 40 34 46 23 p. 7 HZ **a**

Rest – Menu (€ 15) – Carte € 31/46

◆ This brasserie is popular with the locals, with a contemporary atmosphere, a terrace overlooking the St Félix canal and serving tempting brasserie cuisine.

XX **La Cigale**

4 pl. Graslin – ✆ 02 51 84 94 94 – lacigale@lacigale.com – Fax 02 51 84 94 95

Rest – Menu € 17/27 – Carte € 22/46 *p. 6* FZ **d**

◆ Inaugurated in 1895, this famous brasserie has had a multitude of celebrated customers. The superb setting (mosaics, wood panelling, etc.) is the epitome of Modern Style ornamentation.

XX **Christophe Bonnet**

6 r. Mazagran – ✆ 02 40 69 03 39 – info@christophebonnet.com – Closed 27 July-1st September, 1st-5 January, Sunday and Monday *p. 6* FZ **x**

Rest – Menu € 30 bi (weekday lunch), € 38/120 bi

◆ The chef's inventive cuisine is the inspiration behind the redecorated rooms at this apple green former workers' restaurant.

XX **Le Rive Gauche**

10 côte St-Sébastien ✉ 44200 – ✆ 02 40 34 38 52 – rive.gauche@wanadoo.fr – Fax 02 40 33 21 20 – Closed 14-20 April, 26 July-18 August, 24 December-4 January, Saturday lunch, Sunday dinner and Monday *p. 5* CX **e**

Rest – Menu € 22 (weekday lunch), € 31/63 – Carte € 49/63

◆ Long, low house with a veranda overlooking the quayside, the Loire and Beaulieu island. Modern setting and carefully laid tables offering up-to-date food.

XX **La Courtine**

15 r. Strasbourg – ✆ 02 40 48 13 30 – contact@la-courtine.com – Fax 02 40 48 13 30 – Closed Wednesday dinner, Sunday dinner and Monday *p. 5* GY **v**

Rest – Menu € 12 (weekdays)/40 – Carte € 26/51

◆ This contemporary restaurant near the château has beige, grey, black and white decoration and offers cleverly updated traditional cuisine.

X **Maison Baron Lefèvre**

33 r. de Rieux – ✆ 02 40 89 20 20 – baron.lefevre@wanadoo.fr – Fax 02 40 89 20 22 – Closed 1st-20 August, Sunday and Monday *p. 7* HZ **n**

Rest – Menu (€ 15), € 18 (weekday lunch)/25 – Carte € 39/55

◆ New style brasserie and fine foods deli (hams, wine and other produce) set in a warehouse that was formerly a market gardener's shop. Refined decor, mezzanine.

X **Les Temps Changent**

1 pl. A. Briand – ✆ 02 51 72 18 01 – les.temps.changent@wanadoo.fr – Fax 02 51 88 91 82 – Closed Easter holidays, 1st-20 August, 1st-7 January, Saturday and Sunday *p. 6* FY **q**

Rest – Menu € 19 (weekday lunch), € 25/46 – Carte approx. € 42

◆ This restaurant's name describes the seasonal suggestions in one of the set menus of this chic bistro, where the atmosphere gets cosier in the evening. Two hundred wines available.

X **L'Embellie**

14 r. Armand Brossard – ✆ 02 40 48 20 02 – francoisproquin@yahoo.co.uk – Fax 02 72 01 72 25 – Closed 1st-21 August, Sun. and Monday *p. 7* GY **e**

Rest – Menu € 16 (lunch)/52 – Carte € 35/51

◆ Sensible prices, modern recipes prepared with care, a small selection of well-selected wines and a warm, modern interior: L'Embellie is the place to be!

X **Le Gressin**

40 bis r. Fouré – ✆ 02 40 48 26 24 – legressin@wanadoo.fr – Fax 02 40 48 26 24 – Closed 5-20 August, Monday dinner and Sunday *p. 7* HZ **f**

Rest – Menu € 14/25

◆ Little local restaurant with exposed walls, rustic furnishings and art on display. Traditional set menus that change with the seasons.

X **À Ma Table**

11 r. Fouré – ✆ 02 40 47 01 18 – amatable@aliceadsl.fr – Fax 02 51 83 86 74 – Closed 1st au 20 August, February holidays, Saturday and Sunday *p. 7* HZ **s**

Rest – bistrot Menu € 15 (weekdays)/24

◆ Fans of petit beurre Nantais will enjoy this bistro, located next to the old Lu biscuit factory. Old photos of the area, retro posters and seasonal cuisine. Simple and good quality.

X **Les Capucines**

11 bis r. Bastille – ✆ 02 40 20 41 58 – Fax 02 51 72 02 96 – Closed 3-25 August, Saturday lunch, Monday dinner and Sunday p. 6 FY **b**

Rest – Menu € 11,50 (weekday lunch), € 16/32 – Carte € 30/40

♦ Informal restaurant with three retro bistro style dining rooms (two of which open onto a patio). Traditional seasonal dishes and specialities from southwest France.

SURROUNDING AREA

on the banks of the Erdre **11 km by D 178 or exit n° 24 of A 11 motorway and La Chantrerie road-** CV

XXX **Manoir de la Régate**

155 rte Gachet ✉ 44300 Nantes – ✆ 02 40 18 02 97 – info@manoir-regate.com – Fax 02 40 25 23 36 – Closed 26-30 December, Sunday dinner and Monday

Rest – Menu € 19 (weekday lunch), € 26/67 – Carte € 54/71

♦ Fine 19C residence with comfortable, contemporary atmosphere. Meals served in one of the dining rooms or on the pleasant terrace overlooking the gardens. Modern menu.

XX **Auberge du Vieux Gachet**

rte Gachet ✉ 44470 Carquefou – ✆ 02 40 25 10 92 – Fax 02 40 18 03 92 – Closed Sunday dinner and Monday

Rest – Menu € 16 (weekday lunch), € 35/65 – Carte € 58/87

♦ An old farm which gives you the impression of being in the country, although it is very close to town. Old beams, rustic atmosphere and a terrace on the banks of the Erdre.

Angers road **on N 23 or exit n° 23 of motorway A 11-** DV **– ✉ 44470 Carquefou**

Novotel Carquefou

rm, rest,

4, allée des sapins, 11 km: Belle Etoile roundabout – ✆ 02 28 09 44 44 – H0410@accor.com – Fax 02 28 09 44 54

79 rm – †€ 62/99 ††€ 62/99, ☕ € 13 – **Rest** – Carte € 17/39

♦ This 1970s hotel is close to major roads and has simple, functional rooms. Half of which have been refurbished to the chain's latest standards. The modern dining room opens onto the terrace and pool.

Bords de Loire road **on D 751** DV**, exit 44 Porte du Vignoble**

XXX **Villa Mon Rêve**

9 km ✉ 44115 Basse-Goulaine – ✆ 02 40 03 55 50 – contact@villa-mon-reve.com – Fax 02 40 06 05 41 – Closed 17-30 November, February holidays, Sunday dinner and Tuesday DV **e**

Rest – Menu (€ 23), € 27 (weekdays)/86 – Carte € 44/76

♦ This 1900 establishment with shady tables to the front is between the Loire and the market gardens. Timeless atmosphere, regional cuisine, nice selection of Muscadets.

XX **Auberge Nantaise**

at 13 km, at the Bout des Ponts ✉ 44450 St-Julien-de-Concelles – ✆ 02 40 54 10 73 – Fax 02 40 36 83 28 – Closed 10-26 July, Sunday dinner and Monday

Rest – Menu (€ 13 bi), € 17 bi/50 – Carte € 46/56

♦ Modern upstairs dining room whose picture windows overlook the Loire. Ground floor with a colourful setting. Regional menu including frogs, fish in light butter sauce, etc.

XX **La Divate**

at 11 km, at Boire-Courant ✉ 44450 St-Julien-de-Concelles – ✆ 02 40 54 19 66 – Fax 02 40 36 58 39 – Closed 20 August-7 September, February half-term holidays, Sunday dinner, Monday dinner, Tuesday dinner and Wednesday

Rest – Menu (€ 12,50), € 14,50 (weekday lunch), € 18/46 – Carte € 45/53

♦ Loire Valley specialities are served in this small country house set on the riverbank. Stonework and wood create an attractive rustic setting.

X **Clémence**

at 15 km, at la Chebuette ✉ 44450 St-Julien-de-Concelles – ✆ 02 40 36 03 18 – contact@restaurantclemence.fr – Fax 02 40 36 03 22 – Closed 4-26 August, Thursday dinner, Sunday dinner and Monday

Rest – Menu € 20 (weekday lunch), € 26/45 – Carte € 40/56

♦ Refurbished house in a refined setting. It is here that the chef Clémence Lefeuvre (1860-1932) created the famous beurre blanc, still present in the inventive regional cuisine.

in Basse-Goulaine 10 km by D 119 – pop. 7 499 – alt. 22 m – ✉ 44115

L'Orangerie du Parc without rest
195 r. Grignon, (D 119) – ✆ 02 40 54 91 30 – lorangerieduparc@voila.fr – Fax 02 40 54 91 30 p. 5 DX b
5 rm – €60/65 €72/78
◆ The orangery of a residence formerly owned by a minister under Napoleon III. With five charming rooms on the ground floor (four with separate sleeping area).

Du Pont
147 r. Grignon – ✆ 02 40 03 58 62 – Fax 02 40 06 20 80 – Closed 1st July-26 August, February holidays, Tuesday dinner, Wednesday dinner, Sunday dinner and Monday
Rest – Menu € 17, € 25/39 – Carte € 33/37 p. 5 DX t
◆ Restaurant with a leafy facade housing a brightly coloured dining room and another in more muted shades. Appetising half-traditional, half-regional cooking.

in Haute-Goulaine 14 km by ③ and D 119 – pop. 4 925 – alt. 41 m – ✉ 44115

Manoir de la Boulaie (Laurent Saudeau)
33 r. Chapelle St Martin – ✆ 02 40 06 15 91 – reservation@manoir-de-la-boulaie.fr – Fax 02 40 54 56 83 – Closed 28 July-22 August, 22 December-16 January, Sunday dinner, Monday and Wednesday
Rest – Menu € 35 (weekday lunch), € 65 € (dinner)/120 – Carte € 90/102
Spec. Yaourt aux champignons et foie gras (autumn-winter). Tronçon de rouget aux huîtres, compotée de chorizo, écume noisette. Cataplana d'agneau cuisiné dans un bouquet de thym et romarin. **Vins** Muscadet de Sèvre-et-Maine, Savennières.
◆ This fine, large 1920s residence, surrounded by a park and vineyards, is popular with people from Nantes due to its delicious, inventive cuisine. Good selection of Muscadet wine.

in La Haie-Fouassière 15 km by ③, D 149 and D 74 – pop. 3 337 – alt. 25 m – ✉ 44690

Château du Breil without rest
– ✆ 02 40 36 71 55 – lebreil@wanadoo.fr – Fax 02 40 36 71 58 – Closed December and January
4 rm – €100/120 €120/140
◆ This Nantes folly built in 1863 is set in the centre of a vineyard estate with wooded park, pool and lounge-library. Comfortable rooms with period furniture.

Le Cep de Vigne
at the north station: 1 km on the D 74 – ✆ 02 40 36 93 90 – Fax 02 51 71 60 69 – Closed Sunday dinner, Monday dinner, Tuesday dinner and Wednesday
Rest – Menu (€ 15), € 23 bi (weekdays)/50 – Carte € 47/69
◆ The facade of this restaurant is decorated with a vine theme. Two of the three dining rooms have been refurbished, one has a veranda. Rustic lounge. Choice of Muscadet wines.

in Vertou 10 km by D 59 exit porte de Vertou – pop. 20 268 – alt. 32 m – ✉ 44120

Office de tourisme, place du Beau Verger ✆ 02 40 34 12 22, Fax 02 40 34 06 86

Monte-Cristo
Chaussée des Moines – ✆ 02 40 34 40 36 – restel3@wanadoo.fr – Fax 02 40 03 26 20 – Closed 26 December-9 January, Wednesday dinner, Sunday dinner and Monday p. 5 DX a
Rest – Menu € 23/48 – Carte € 41/87
◆ The first lines of the Count of Monte Cristo were written on these premises. Rustic dining room, simple veranda and terrace with broad views of the Sèvre. Modern cooking.

in Château-Thébaud 18 km by ③ , D 149, D74 and D63 – pop. 2 484 – alt. 58 m – ✉ 44690

Auberge la Gaillotière
– ✆ 02 28 21 31 16 – benoit.debailly@wanadoo.fr – Fax 02 28 21 31 17 – Closed mid February-mid March, 27 July-13 August, Tuesday dinner and Wednesday
Rest – Menu € 13 (weekday lunch), € 18/25
◆ An inn isolated in the middle of the vineyards of the Nantes area. Traditional, seasonal market dishes and local wine served in a simple rustic setting.

La Roche-sur-Yon road 12 km by ④ and D 178 – ✉ 44840 Les Sorinières

Abbaye de Villeneuve rest,
– ✆ 02 40 04 40 25
– villeneuve@leshotelsparticuliers.com – Fax 02 40 31 28 45
21 rm – €87 €175, €15 – ½ P €94/138
Rest – Menu €38/72 – Carte €41/74
◆ An 18C residence built on the remains of a medieval abbey. Some tombstones decorate the lobby. Very traditional rooms; smaller rustic rooms on the second floor. Guests pass through cloisters to reach this restaurant. The dining room opens onto the park.

in Pont-St-Martin 12 km South by D 65 – pop. 4 754 – alt. 10 m – ✉ 44860

Château du Plessis-Atlantique without rest
– ✆ 02 40 26 81 72 – chateauduplessis@wanadoo.fr – Fax 02 40 32 76 67
3 rm – €90/110 €120/175
◆ Fine, floral gardens surround this listed chateau, remodelled in the 15C and 17C. The rooms each have their own history, style and ornaments. Breakfast fit for the lord of the manor.

to Nantes-Atlantique International Airport exit 51 porte de Grandlieu-Bouguenais – ✉ 44340 Bouguenais

Océania
– ✆ 02 40 05 05 66 – oceania.nantes@oceaniahotels.com
– Fax 02 40 05 12 03 p. 4 BX **e**
87 rm – €129 €129, €13,50 – 2 suites
Rest – *(closed Saturday lunchtime and Sunday lunchtime)* Menu €20/28 – Carte €30/46
◆ Imposing contemporary facade lined with pilasters. Practical rooms refurbished in a clean modern style. Shuttle linking the hotel to the airport. Pleasant lounge with fireplace, large dining room and terrace by the swimming pool.

in Bouaye 15 km by D 751A - AX – pop. 5 251 – alt. 16 m – ✉ 44830
Office de tourisme, 2, place du Bois Jacques ✆ 02 40 65 53 55

Kyriad
rte de Nantes – ✆ 02 40 65 43 50 – info@champsdavaux.com
– Fax 02 40 32 64 83 – Closed 24 December-4 January
44 rm – €68/70 €68/70, €10,50 – ½ P €63/65
Rest *Les Champs d'Avaux* – *(closed Sunday dinner)* Menu (€17), €20 (weekdays)/58 – Carte €32/64
◆ All the rooms in this modern building have double-glazing; some give onto the garden. French bowls pitch and a children's play area. Pleasant restaurant opening onto a garden. Traditional and regional dishes.

in Haute-Indre 10 km West by D 107, exit porte de l'Estuaire – ✉ 44610 Indre

Belle Rive
8 pl. Jean Saillant – ✆ 02 40 86 01 07 – Fax 02 40 86 01 07
– Closed 21 July-24 August, 22-25 December, Saturday lunch, Sunday dinner, Monday dinner, Tuesday dinner and Wednesday p. 4 AX **d**
Rest – Menu €15 (weekday lunch), €23/31
◆ Restaurant near the small port of Haute Indre located on the Loire. Chocolate coloured dining room with matching tablecloths and chairs where market inspired food is served.

in Coueron 15 km by D 107, exit porte de l'Estuaire – pop. 17 808 – alt. 13 m – ✉ 44220

François II
5 pl. Aristide Briand – ✆ 02 40 38 32 32 – Fax 02 40 38 32 32
– Closed 1st-8 May, 29 July-22 August, 2-8 January, 16-24 February, Sunday dinner, Tuesday dinner, Thursday dinner and Monday
Rest – Menu (€12), €14,50 (weekday lunch), €20/41 – Carte €31/45
◆ The name pays tribute to the Duke of Brittany, father of Anne, who died in Couëron. Rustic style decor (exposed stonework, carpets and tapestries). Copious traditional food.

in St-Herblain 8 km West – pop. 43 726 – alt. 8 m – ✉ 44800

La Marine
esplanade de la Bégraisière – ✆ 02 40 95 26 66 – hotelmarine@wanadoo.fr – Fax 02 40 46 85 70 p. 4 BV **m**
24 rm – €48/69 €54/75, ☕ €9 – ½ P €51/61 – **Rest** – *(closed Saturday lunch and Sunday)* Menu €14 (weekday lunch), €18/32 – Carte €26/36
◆ Guests are assured a warm welcome in this hotel set in the heart of a large, peaceful garden. The spacious rooms are classically furnished and all identical. Dining room-veranda opening onto greenery; traditional food.

Les Caudalies
229 rte de Vannes – ✆ 02 40 94 35 35 – restaurant.les-caudalies@wanadoo.fr – Fax 02 40 40 89 90 – Closed 26 July-26 August, 7-17 February, Sunday dinner, Monday and Wednesday p. 4 BV **v**
Rest – Menu €19 (weekdays)/40 – Carte approx. €31
◆ A 1980s roadside villa with two small, discreet dining rooms. Cuisine based on market produce draws on specialities from all the regions of France.

in Orvault 6 km by N 137 exit porte de Rennes – pop. 23 554 – alt. 45 m – ✉ 44700

Le Domaine d'Orvault rest,
24 chemin des Marais-du-Cens – ✆ 02 40 76 84 02 – contact@domaine-orvault.com – Fax 02 40 76 04 21 p. 4 BV **e**
40 rm – €86/114 €98/114, ☕ €20 – ½ P €78
Rest – *(closed Saturday lunch and Sunday)* Menu (€24), €28/48
◆ Despite its appearance, this villa tucked away in a green setting dates from the 1970s. Large rooms furnished in various styles; choose one of the more modern. Contemporary restaurant with terrace shaded by lime trees. Modern 'deconstructe' cuisine.

Du Parc without rest
92 r. de la Garenne – ✆ 02 40 63 04 79 – parc.hotel@wanadoo.fr – Fax 02 40 63 62 99 – Closed 6-26 August and 23 December-1st January p. 4 AV **q**
30 rm – €50/64 €50/64, ☕ €7
◆ Discreet modern decor, new bedding, effective soundproofing and impeccable housekeeping characterise the rooms of this 1970s building, which is surrounded by pretty undergrowth.

NANTILLY – 70 Haute-Saône – 314 B8 – see Gray

NANTUA – 01 Ain – 328 G4 – pop. 3 902 – alt. 479 m – ✉ 01130
Burgundy-Jura 45 **C1**

Paris 476 – Aix-les-Bains 79 – Annecy 67 – Bourg-en-Bresse 52 – Genève 67 – Lyon 93

Office de tourisme, place de la Déportation ✆ 04 74 75 00 05, Fax 04 74 75 06 83

St-Michel church★ : Martyre de St-Sébastien★★ by E. Delacroix - Lake★.

La cuivrerie★ de Cerdon.

L'Embarcadère rm,
av. Lac – ✆ 04 74 75 22 88 – contact@hotelembarcadere.com – Fax 04 74 75 22 25 – Closed 20 December-5 January
49 rm – €58/72 €58/72, ☕ €9,50 – ½ P €64/71 – **Rest** *(closed 20 December-16 January)* Menu €25 (weekdays)/63 – Carte €43/73
◆ Half the rooms overlook the lake and they have all been treated to a tasteful makeover in warm colours. The attractive panoramic view over the lake and the delicious regional cuisine are the main appeals of the restaurant, reached by a covered walkway.

in Brion Northwest: 5 km by D 1084 and D 979 – pop. 559 – alt. 475 m – ✉ 01460

Bernard Charpy
1 r. Croix-Chalon – ✆ 04 74 76 24 15 – Fax 04 74 76 22 36 – Closed 27 April-5 May, 3 August-1st September, 16 December-5 January, Saturday lunch, Sunday and Monday
Rest – Menu €20 (weekday lunch), €25/40 – Carte €40/55
◆ The recently revamped contemporary dining room with timber ceiling serves enticing traditional fare, including a splendid selection of fresh fish.

in La Cluse **Northwest: 3.5 km by D 1084– ✉ 01460 Montréal-la-Cluse**

Lac Hôtel without rest

22 av. Bresse – ✆ 04 74 76 29 68 – alblanc@club-internet.fr – Fax 04 74 76 13 70 – Closed 1stNovember-31 December

28 rm – †€ 35/41 ††€ 36/42, ☕ € 6

◆ Well kept, practical rooms with good soundproofing at unbeatable prices. An attractive location within easy reach of the main road. Internet access available.

LA NAPOULE – **06 Alpes-Maritimes** – **341** C6 – **see Mandelieu**

NARBONNE – 11 Aude – 344 J3 – pop. 46 510 – alt. 13 m – ✉ 11100

Languedoc-Roussillon-Tarn Gorges 22 **B3**

Paris 787 – Béziers 28 – Carcassonne 61 – Montpellier 96 – Perpignan 64

✆ 3635 (0,34 €/mn)

Office de tourisme, place Roger Salengro ✆ 04 68 65 15 60, Fax 04 68 65 59 12

St-Just-et-St-Pasteur cathedral★★ (Treasure-house: tapestry portraying the Creation★★) - Donjon Gilles Aycelin★ ✳★ **H** - Choir★ of St-Paul basilica - Palais des Archevêques★ BY : musée d'Art et d'Histoire★ - Musée archéologique★ - Musée lapidaire★ BZ - Pont des marchands★.

Plan on following page

Novotel rm, rm,

Plaisance Industrial Estate 3 km via ③, Perpignan road – ✆ 04 68 42 72 00 – H0412@accor.com – Fax 04 68 42 72 10

96 rm – †€ 69/140 ††€ 69/140, ☕ € 13 – **Rest** – Carte € 20/37

◆ This chain hotel is regularly renovated, providing a practical stop-off on the way to Spain. Comfortable rooms provided. Modern restaurant with a pergola shaded terrace and garden planted with yew and pine trees. Regional wines.

La Résidence without rest

6 r. du 1er Mai – ✆ 04 68 32 19 41 – hotellaresidence@free.fr – Fax 04 68 65 51 82 – Closed 20 January-15 February AY **r**

26 rm – †€ 56/90 ††€ 62/97, ☕ € 8,50

◆ Jean Marais, Louis de Funès, Georges Brassens, Michel Serrault: a prestigious visitors' book in this traditional hotel in a 19C residence.

De France without rest

6 r. Rossini – ✆ 04 68 32 09 75 – accueil@hotelnarbonne.com – Fax 04 68 65 50 30 – Closed 15 February-15 March BZ **s**

15 rm – †€ 32/66 ††€ 34/69, ☕ € 7

◆ Functional, well kept rooms on either side of a small inner courtyard. The archaeology museum, with a collection of Roman paintings, is 500m away.

La Table St-Crescent (Lionel Giraud)

68 av. Gén. Leclerc, at the Palais du Vin via ③ – ✆ 04 68 41 37 37 – saint-crescent@wanadoo.fr – Fax 04 68 41 01 22 – Closed Saturday lunch, Sunday dinner and Monday

Rest – Menu (€ 20 bi), € 40/79 bi – Carte € 53/83

Spec. Foie gras de canard des Landes mi-cuit. Œuf mollet en kadaïf. Pigeon rôti en cocotte, jus relevé à l'anchois de Collioure. **Wines** Vin de pays de l'Aude, Vin de pays de l'Hérault.

◆ Elegant, designer décor in this medieval oratory, with vine-covered terrace. Tasty, inventive cuisine and Languedoc-Roussillon wine.

Le Petit Comptoir

4 bd Mar. Joffre – ✆ 04 68 42 30 35 – lepetitcomptoir@aol.com – Fax 04 68 41 52 71 – Closed 27 July-11 August, 1st-7 January, Sunday and Monday AY **b**

Rest – Menu € 18 (weekday lunch), € 25/35 – Carte € 33/60

◆ Traditional recipes with a southern flavour and efficient attentive service: this pleasant 1930s bistro-style restaurant is often fully booked.

NARBONNE

Anatole-France (Av.) .... AYZ 2
Ancienne Porte de Béziers (R. de l') .... BY 4
Ancien Courrier (R. de l') .... BY 3
Blum (Sq. Th.-Léon) .... BY 6
Cabirol (R.) .... AZ 7
Chennebier (R.) .... AY 9
Concorde (Pont de la) .... AY 10
Condorcet (Bd) .... BY 12
Courier (R. P.-L.) .... BZ 13
Crémieux (R. B.) .... BZ 15
Deymes (R. du Lt-Col.) .... BY 16
Droite (R.) .... BY
Escoute (Pont de l') .... AY 17
Fabre (R. Gustave) .... AY 18
Foch (Av. Mar.) .... BY 19
Garibaldi (R.) .... BY 20
Gaulle (Bd Gén.-de) .... BY 21
Gauthier (R. Armand) .... BY 22
Hôtel de Ville (Pl. de l') .... BYZ
Jacobins (R. des) .... BZ 23
Jean-Jaurès (R.) .... AY 24
Joffre (Bd Mar.) .... AYZ 25
Liberté (Pont de la) .... BZ 27
Lion d'Or (R. du) .... AY 28
Louis-Blanc (R.) .... BY 29
Luxembourg (R. du) .... AZ 30
Major (R. de la) .... BZ 31
Maraussan (R.) .... AZ 32
Marchands (Pont des) .... BZ 36
Michelet (R.) .... BY 33
Mirabeau (Cours) .... BZ 35
Pyrénées (Av. des) .... AY 37
Pyrénées (Pl. des) .... AZ 39
Rabelais (R.) .... AZ 40
République (Crs de la) .... BZ 41
Salengro (Pl. R.) .... BY 43
Sermet (Av. E.) .... BY 44
Toulouse (Av. de) .... AZ 45
Voltaire (Pont) .... AY 47

L'Estagnol

5 bis cours Mirabeau – 04 68 65 09 27
– fabricemeynadier@wanadoo.fr
– Fax 04 68 32 23 38
– Closed Monday evening and Sunday

BZ **t**

Rest – Menu (€ 12), € 18/30 – Carte € 19/42

◆ A modernised brasserie serving cuisine with a regional flavour made with produce from the next-door covered market. Pretty view of the canal from the first floor.

Le 26

8 bd Dr-Lacroix – ✆ 04 68 41 46 69 – restole26@free.fr
– Closed Sunday dinner and Monday AZ **a**
Rest – Menu € 20/30 – Carte € 40/47
◆ Traditional fare prepared by the owner is served in the sober dining room (parquet flooring and stone walls) of this friendly and welcoming restaurant.

in Coursan 7 km by ① – **pop. 5 241 – alt. 6 m – ✉ 11110**

Syndicat d'initiative, 10 bis, avenue Jean-Jaurès ✆ 04 68 33 60 86

L'Os à Table

88 av. Jean Jaurès, Salles d'Aude road – ✆ 04 68 33 55 72
– losatable-coursan@wanadoo.fr – Fax 04 68 33 35 39 – Closed 15-29 September, Wednesday dinner except July-August, Sunday dinner and Monday
Rest – Menu € 25/46 – Carte € 29/50
◆ This restaurant is housed in a small mansion on the edge of the village near the Aude river. Well-lit dining areas decorated in pastel tones, serving traditional cuisine, fine choice of wines.

in l'Hospitalet 10 km by ② **Narbonne-Plage road (D 168) – ✉ 11100**

Château l'Hospitalet

rest,

– ✆ 04 68 45 28 50 – hotel@gerard-bertrand.com – Fax 04 68 45 28 78
38 rm – €125 €125/250, € 12 – **Rest** – *(closed Sunday dinner and Monday)* Menu € 26 bi – Carte € 23/41
◆ A hotel linked to a wine estate, including several craft museums and workshops. Fine interior decoration. Regional menu and estate wines served in this former sheepfold.

in Bages 8 km by ③, **D 6009 and D 105 – pop. 755 – alt. 30 m – ✉ 11100**

Syndicat d'initiative, 8, rue des Remparts ✆ 04 68 42 81 76, Fax 04 68 42 81 76

Les Palombières d'Estarac

Estarac, to the south-west – ✆ 04 68 42 45 56 – estarac@wanadoo.fr
– Fax 04 68 42 45 56
4 rm – €58/120 €68/130 – **Table d'hôte** – Menu € 25 bi
◆ This restored farmhouse surrounded by scrubland is home to cheerful, fresh personalised rooms: "Ocean", "Soleillad" and "Olivine". Serving Mediterranean dishes, this restaurant has a dining area overlooking parkland; roaring fire in winter.

Le Portanel

Bages lake,

La Placette – ✆ 04 68 42 81 66 – jean-christophe.rousseau4@wanadoo.fr
– Fax 04 68 41 75 93 – Closed Sunday dinner from September to June and Monday
Rest – Menu (€ 20 bi), € 25/35 – Carte € 32/63
◆ Mediterranean inspired cuisine using fresh local produce and distinctive flavours served in a former fisherman's house. Exhibition-sale of art and veranda with a view of the harbour.

in Ornaisons 14 km by ④, **D 6113 and D 24 – pop. 951 – alt. 34 m – ✉ 11200**

Le Relais du Val d'Orbieu

on D 24 – ✆ 04 68 27 10 27 – contact@relaisdurvaldorbieu.com
– Fax 04 68 27 52 44 – Closed 15 November-1st February and Sunday in November and February
18 rm – €85/105 €110/170, € 20 – 2 suites – ½ P € 135/165
Rest – *(open March-October) (dinner only)* Menu (€ 32), € 40/65
– Carte approx. € 70
◆ This former windmill, standing in the middle of the Corbières vineyards, features attractive bedrooms laid out around the fine patio. Good leisure facilities. Traditional cooking and regional wine selection served under a pretty pergola in summer.

LA NARTELLE – 83 Var – 340 O6 – **see Ste-Maxime**

NASBINALS – 48 Lozère – 330 G7 – **pop. 504 – alt. 1 180 m – Winter sports : 1 240/1 320 m** 1 – ✉ **48260** Languedoc-Roussillon-Tarn Gorges 22 **B1**

Paris 573 – Aurillac 105 – Aumont-Aubrac 24 – Mende 57 – Rodez 64 – St-Flour 53

Office de tourisme, Village ✆ 04 66 32 55 73, Fax 04 66 32 55 73

Relais de l'Aubrac

au Pont de Gournier, (D 12 - D 112 crossroads), north : 4 km along the D 12 – ✆ 04 66 32 52 06 – relais-aubrac@wanadoo.fr – Fax 04 66 32 56 58 – Open beg. March-mid November

27 rm – †€ 49/61 ††€ 49/61, ☕ € 8 – ½ P € 49/59 – **Rest** – *(closed Sunday dinner and Thursday except school holidays)* Menu € 18/36 – Carte € 18/37

◆ This large house, popular with walkers and anglers, is next to a bridge over the Bès. Informal atmosphere, practical rooms and breakfast on the veranda. Regional cuisine (aligot) served in a rustic interior or on the terrace. Friendly service.

NATZWILLER – 67 Bas-Rhin – 315 H6 – pop. 624 – alt. 500 m – ✉ 67130 2 C1

Paris 422 – Barr 25 – Molsheim 31 – St-Dié 43 – Strasbourg 59

Auberge Metzger with rm

55 r. Principale – ✆ 03 88 97 02 42 – auberge.metzger@wanadoo.fr – Fax 03 88 97 93 59 – Closed 24 June-8 July, 22-25 December, 6-26 January, Sunday and Monday except July-August

16 rm – †€ 55 ††€ 65/76, ☕ € 10 – ½ P € 73/83

Rest – Menu € 13,50 (weekday lunch), € 19/56 – Carte € 28/47

◆ The flower-decked façade gives on to a pleasant family inn, well known for its tasty regional cuisine. Paved courtyard with terrace. Comfortable rooms.

NAVARRENX – 64 Pyrénées-Atlantiques – 342 H5 – pop. 1 133 – alt. 125 m – ✉ 64190

Paris 787 – Pau 43 – Mourenx 15 – Oloron-Ste-Marie 23 – Orthez 22 – Peyrehorade 44 3 B3

Office de tourisme, place des Casernes ✆ 05 59 66 54 80, Fax 05 59 66 54 80

Du Commerce

pl. des Casernes – ✆ 05 59 66 50 16 – hotel.du.commerce@wanadoo.fr – Fax 05 59 66 52 67

24 rm – †€ 48/57 ††€ 56/65, ☕ € 8 – ½ P € 45/51 – **Rest** – Menu € 11, € 18/32 – Carte € 30/48

◆ A regional-style hotel in the heart of a small, walled town founded in 1316. Choose the most recent building for its renovated and comfortable rooms; the others are slightly older. The dining room is done in a country style with bright colours. Regional cuisine.

NAZELLES-NÉGRON – 37 Indre-et-Loire – 317 O4 – see Amboise

NEAUPHLE-LE-CHÂTEAU – 78 Yvelines – 311 H3 – pop. 2 771 – alt. 185 m – ✉ 78640 Northern France and the Paris Region 18 A2

Paris 38 – Dreux 42 – Mantes-la-Jolie 32 – Rambouillet 24 – Versailles 21

Syndicat d'initiative, 14, place du Marché ✆ 01 34 89 78 00, Fax 01 34 89 78 00

Domaine du Verbois

38 av. de la République – ✆ 01 34 89 11 78 – verbois@hotelverbois.com – Fax 01 34 89 57 33 – Closed 10-22 August and 21-28 December

22 rm – †€ 98 ††€ 110/180, ☕ € 12 – ½ P € 144 – **Rest** – *(closed Sunday dinner)* Menu € 36/49

◆ This stylish home dating from the late 19C is surrounded by a park. It offers delightful, customized bedrooms, furnished in various 18C styles. Elegant dining room, with a marble fireplace and gilded mirrors, and shaded terrace.

Le Clos Saint-Nicolas without rest

33 r. St-Nicolas – ✆ 01 34 89 76 10 – mariefrance.drouelle@wanadoo.fr – Fax 01 34 89 76 10

3 rm ☕ – †€ 90 ††€ 90

◆ A peaceful atmosphere pervades this 19C hotel and garden. Large rooms with refined décor, and delicious breakfasts served on the veranda under the lemon and orange trees.

La Griotte

58 av. de la République – ✆ 01 34 89 19 98 – restaurantlagriotte@free.fr – Fax 01 34 89 68 86 – Closed 1st-21 August, Sunday and Monday

Rest – Menu (€ 23), € 28 – Carte € 28/52

◆ An old-style restaurant with pastel-tone décor, overlooking a charming garden with a pergola for outdoor dining in summer. Personalised cuisine served.

NÉGREVILLE – 50 Manche – **303** C3 – **pop. 734** – **alt. 70 m** – ✉ **50260** 32 **A1**

Paris 342 – Caen 108 – Saint-Lô 72 – Cherbourg 22 – Équeurdreville-Hainneville 28

Northeast, 5 km by D 146 and D 62 – ✉ **50260 Négreville**

Château de Pont Rilly without rest
– *℘ 02 33 40 47 50 – chateau-pont-rilly@wanadoo.fr* – **5 rm** ☕ €150 €150
◆ A perfectly preserved 18C château surrounded by formal, French-style gardens. Antique furniture and a rustic ambience add to the charm. Beautiful guestrooms with a fireplace.

NÉRIS-LES-BAINS – 03 Allier – **326** C5 – **pop. 2 708** – **alt. 364 m** – **Spa : early April-late Oct.** – **Casino** – ✉ **03310** **Auvergne** 5 **B1**

Paris 336 – Clermont-Ferrand 86 – Montluçon 9 – Moulins 73
Office de tourisme, carrefour des Arènes ℘ 04 70 03 11 03, Fax 04 70 09 05 29
de Sainte-Agathe Villebret, by Montluçon road: 4 km, ℘ 04 70 03 21 77.

NÉRIS-LES-BAINS

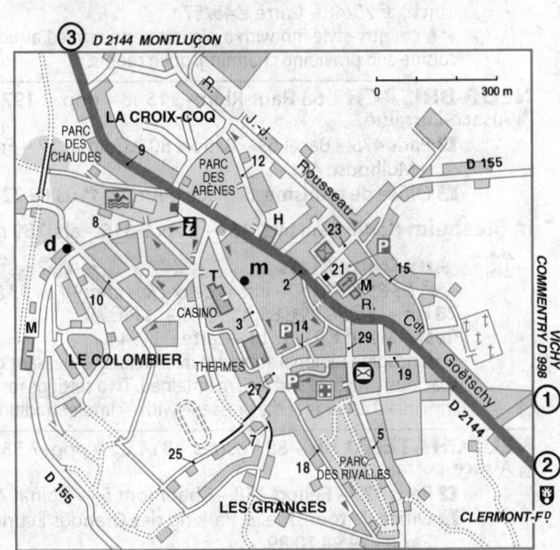

Mona Lisa rm,
40 r. Boisrot-Desserviers – ℘ 04 70 08 79 80 – resa-neris@monalisahotels.com – Fax 04 70 08 79 81 – Closed lunch in week except holidays **m**
59 rm €69/85 €69/116, ☕ €11 – **Rest** – Menu €22/35 – Carte approx. €38
◆ Behind the Belle Époque facade of this hotel located opposite the casino lie air-conditioned comfort, contemporary style, and the latest technology. A restaurant with soberly dressed tables and designer furniture in keeping with the chef's modern cuisine.

Le Garden rm,
12 av. Marx Dormoy – ℘ 04 70 03 21 16 – hotel.le.garden@wanadoo.fr – Fax 04 70 03 10 67 – Closed 26-31 December, 28 January-8 March **d**
19 rm – €46/62 €46/62, ☕ €6,50 – ½ P €48/53
Rest – *(closed Sunday dinner and Monday from November to March)*
Menu €16 (weekdays)/39 – Carte €24/66
◆ This villa, in a garden in bloom, was converted into a hotel, and lies near the centre of the resort. Modern and regularly redecorated bedrooms. This stylish dining room, appreciated for its brightness and cheerfulness, serves simple cuisine.

NÉRONDES – 18 Cher – **323** M5 – **pop. 1 618** – **alt. 200 m** – ✉ 18350 12 **D3**

Paris 240 – Bourges 37 – Montluçon 84 – Nevers 33 – St-Amand-Montrond 44
la Vallée de Germigny Saint-Hilaire-de-Gondilly Domaine de Villefranche, Northeast: 9 km by D 6, ℘ 02 48 80 23 43.

Le Lion d'Or with rm — rest, VISA
pl. de la Mairie – ✆ 02 48 74 87 81 – Fax 02 48 74 92 63
– Closed 1st-9 March, 27 August-3 September, 22-29, Sunday dinner and Wednesday
10 rm – €42/50 €46/54, €8 – ½ P €50/54 – **Rest** – Menu €20/40 – Carte €47/62
◆ Family-run, town centre inn, offering a stylish, rustic dining room, serving traditional cuisine. Renovated rooms, with the quietest ones at the back.

NESTIER – **65 Hautes-Pyrénées** – **342** O6 – **pop. 165** – **alt. 500 m** – ✉ **65150**
Paris 789 – Auch 74 – Bagnères-de-Luchon 45 – Lannemezan 14 – St-Gaudens 24 28 **A3**

Relais du Castéra with rm — rm, VISA
– ✆ 05 62 39 77 37 – Fax 05 62 39 77 29 – Closed 2-10 June, 13-20 October, 2-31 January, Sunday dinner, Tuesday dinner and Monday
6 rm – €50/70 €50/70, €8 – ½ P €52/70 – **Rest** – Menu €18 (weekday lunch), €25/48 – Carte €45/57
◆ A country-style inn with a pleasant and refined atmosphere. Serving locally inspired cuisine and providing charming, quiet rooms.

NEUF-BRISACH – **68 Haut-Rhin** – **315** J8 – **pop. 2 197** – **alt. 197 m** – ✉ **68600**
Alsace-Lorraine 2 **C2**
Paris 475 – Basel 63 – Belfort 80 – Colmar 17 – Freiburg-im-Breisgau 35 – Mulhouse 40
Office de tourisme, 6, place d'Armes ✆ 03 89 72 56 66, Fax 03 89 72 91 73

in Biesheim **North: 3 km by D 468** – **pop. 2 315** – **alt. 189 m** – ✉ **68600**

Aux Deux Clefs — rest, rest, VISA
– ✆ 03 89 30 30 60 – info@deux-clefs.com – Fax 03 89 72 92 94
28 rm – €58 €85, €10 – ½ P €75
Rest – Menu €21/32 bi – Carte €29/44
◆ Handsome regional structure overlooking a pleasant garden. The rooms are relatively spacious, practical and well maintained. Two settings for your meal. A plush dining room with inlaid ceilings and a brasserie with a simpler traditional menu.

NEUFCHÂTEAU – **88 Vosges** – **314** C2 – **pop. 7 533** – **alt. 300 m** – ✉ **88300**
Alsace-Lorraine 26 **B3**
Paris 321 – Belfort 158 – Chaumont 57 – Épinal 75 – Langres 78 – Verdun 106
Office de tourisme, 3, Parking des Grandes Ecuries ✆ 03 29 94 10 95, Fax 03 29 94 10 89
Town hall★ staircase **H** - Stone group★ in St-Nicolas church **K.**

L'Eden — rm, rm, VISA
r. 1ère Armée Française – ✆ 03 29 95 61 30 – hotel-eden@wanadoo.fr
– Fax 03 29 94 03 42 – **27 rm** – €55/80 €60/85, €10 – ½ P €35/45
Rest – *(closed 2-15 January, Sunday dinner and Monday lunch)* Menu €25/46 – Carte €31/51
◆ A recent hotel with comfortable, colourful rooms of various sizes. The rooms on the top floor boast Jacuzzi bathtubs. A plush dining room, decorated mainly in blue and ochre. Up-to-the-minute menu.

Romain — VISA
rte de Chaumont – ✆ 03 29 06 18 80 – Fax 03 29 06 18 80
– Closed 18 February-3 March and Monday
Rest – Menu €12,50 (weekday lunch), €17/34 – Carte €22/42
◆ A roadside restaurant, with a vast, bright and modern dining room. Traditional, country menu with a few regional specialities and seafood.

NEUFCHÂTEL-EN-BRAY – **76 Seine-Maritime** – **304** I3 – **pop. 5 103** – **alt. 99 m** – ✉ **76270** Normandy 33 **D1**
Paris 133 – Rouen 50 – Abbeville 57 – Amiens 72 – Dieppe 40 – Gournay-en-Bray 37
Office de tourisme, 6, place Notre-Dame ✆ 02 35 93 22 96, Fax 02 32 97 00 62
de Saint-Saëns Saint-Saëns Domaine du Vaudichon, Southwest: 17 km by D 6028 and D 929, ✆ 02 35 34 25 24.
Forêt d'Eawy★★ 10 km Southwest.

XX **Les Airelles** with rm

2 passage Michu, (near the church) – ✆ 02 35 93 14 60 – les-airelles-sarl@wanadoo.fr – Fax 02 35 93 89 03 – Closed autumn half-term holidays, February, Sunday dinner September-June, Tuesday lunch and Monday except July-August and except hotel

14 rm – †€ 45/67 ††€ 45/67, ☐ € 7 – ½ P € 51/62 –
Rest – Menu € 16 (weekdays)/35 – Carte € 32/53

◆ An attractive, traditional-style building in the centre of town is home to this restaurant with two simple, modern dining areas and a summer terrace in the small garden.

in Mesnières-en-Bray Northwest: 5.5 km by D 1 – pop. 706 – alt. 65 m – ✉ 76270

Château★.

XX **Auberge du Bec Fin**

1 r. du Château – ✆ 02 35 94 15 15 – Fax 02 35 94 42 14 – Closed Sunday dinner, Tuesday dinner and Wednesday

Rest – Menu (€ 13), € 24/43 – Carte € 37/54

◆ Traditional cuisine is to the fore in the welcoming, low-ceilinged dining room of this rustic restaurant. Dinner by candlelight.

NEUFCHÂTEL-SUR-AISNE – 02 Aisne – 306 G6 – pop. 492 – alt. 59 m – ✉ 02190

Paris 163 – Laon 46 – Reims 22 – Rethel 33 – Soissons 60 — 37 **D2**

de Menneville Menneville La Haie Migaut, Southwest: 3 km, ✆ 03 23 79 79 88.

XX **Le Jardin**

22 r. Principale – ✆ 03 23 23 82 00 – lejardint@wanadoo.fr – Fax 03 23 23 84 05 – Closed 3-17 September, 13 January-5 February, Sunday dinner, Monday and Tuesday

Rest – Menu (€ 16), € 25/53 – Carte € 44/59

◆ A "lawned" floor, flowered walls, green plants, a veranda facing flower beds - the restaurant lives up to its name. Menus are chosen according to the market produce available.

NEUILLÉ-LE-LIERRE – 37 Indre-et-Loire – 317 O3 – pop. 582 – alt. 92 m – ✉ 37380

11 **B2**

Paris 217 – Amboise 16 – Château-Renault 10 – Montrichard 34 – Reugny 5 – Tours 27

XX **Auberge de la Brenne** with rm

19 r. de la République – ✆ 02 47 52 95 05 – hotel.brenne@wanadoo.fr – Fax 02 47 52 29 43 – Closed 24 November-3 December, 22 January-4 February and 16 February-15 March

5 rm – †€ 59 ††€ 77/85, ☐ € 13 – ½ P € 77 – **Rest** – *(closed Sunday dinner 15 September-15 June, Tuesday and Wednesday) (pre-book Sat - Sun)* Menu (€ 21), € 25/46 – Carte € 38/67

◆ The owners of this inviting village inn gracefully welcome diners into an attractive dining room. Traditional dishes. Comfortable rooms in a 1900 house 50m away.

NEUILLY-LE-RÉAL – 03 Allier – 326 H4 – pop. 1 303 – alt. 260 m – ✉ 03340

Paris 313 – Mâcon 128 – Moulins 16 – Roanne 82 – Vichy 48 — 6 **C1**

XX **Logis Henri IV**

13 r. du 14 Juillet – ✆ 04 70 43 87 64 – Closed Sunday dinner and Monday except holidays

Rest – Menu € 21 (weekday lunch), € 31/50

◆ This 16C, former hunting lodge is adorned with floor-tiles and a timber frame that give it lots of character. Traditional cooking.

NEUILLY-SUR-SEINE – 92 Hauts-de-Seine – 311 J2 – 101 15 – see Paris, Area

---

NEUVÉGLISE – 15 Cantal – 330 F5 – pop. 1 022 – alt. 938 m – ✉ 15260 — 5 **B3**

Paris 528 – Aurillac 78 – Espalion 66 – St-Chély-d'Apcher 42 – St-Flour 17

Office de tourisme, le Bourg ✆ 04 71 23 85 43, Fax 04 71 23 86 40

Château d'Alleuze★★: site★★ Northeast: 14 km, **Auvergne-Rhone Valley**

in Cordesse East: 1,5 km on D 921 – ✉ 15260 Neuvéglise

Relais de la Poste with rm
– ✆ 04 71 23 82 32 – relais.poste@wanadoo.fr – Fax 04 71 23 86 23
– *Open 1st April-5 November* –
9 rm – †€ 50/65 ††€ 55/70, ☕ € 10 – ½ P € 56/65
Rest – Menu (€ 12), € 16, € 25/45 – Carte € 22/51
◆ A recent establishment with rustic decor including fireplace and attractive wood panelling. Children's play area. Generous and simple regional fare.

NEUVES-MAISONS – 54 Meurthe-et-Moselle – 307 H7 – see Nancy

NEUVILLE-DE-POITOU – 86 Vienne – 322 H4 – pop. 4 058 – alt. 116 m – ✉ 86170

Paris 335 – Châtellerault 36 – Parthenay 41 – Poitiers 16 – Saumur 82 – Thouars 51 39 **C1**

Office de tourisme, 28, place Joffre ✆ 05 49 54 47 80

La Roseraie
78 r. A. Caillard – ✆ 05 49 54 16 72 – info@laroseraiefrance.fr
6 rm ☕ – †€ 53/70 ††€ 58/135 – **Table d'hôte** – Menu € 23 bi/28 bi
◆ Mid-19C manor house set in a rose garden and vineyard (small quantity of Pineau de Charentes produced). Personalised guestrooms. International cuisine (the owners hail from Zimbabwe and Britain) served on the terrace or in an elegant dining room.

St-Fortunat
4 r. Bangoura-Moridé – ✆ 05 49 54 56 74 – fabien.dupont@voila.fr
– Fax 05 49 53 18 02 – Closed 13-26 August, Sunday dinner and Monday
Rest – Menu € 19/33
◆ This former farmhouse has been tastefully refurbished with a modern and rustic dining area and courtyard veranda. Also with shaded terrace. Serving contemporary cuisine.

NEUVILLE-ST-AMAND – 02 Aisne – 306 B4 – see St-Quentin

NEUZY – 71 Saône-et-Loire – 320 E11 – see Digoin

NÉVACHE – 05 Hautes-Alpes – 334 H2 – pop. 290 – alt. 1 640 m – ✉ 05100

Paris 693 – Briançon 21 – Le Monêtier-les-Bains 35 – Montgenèvre 25

Office de tourisme, Ville Haute ✆ 04 92 20 02 20 41 **C1**

Le Chalet d'en Hô rm, rest,
hameau des Chazals – ✆ 04 92 20 12 29 – chaletdenho@orange.fr
– Fax 04 92 20 59 70 – Open 1st June-13 September, 25 October-1st November and 20 December-12 April
14 rm – †€ 63 ††€ 99/127, ☕ € 13 – ½ P € 82 – **Rest** – *(dinner only)* Menu € 26
◆ The wood panelling, Provencal quilting, cushions and photos create a cosy atmosphere at this chalet set in a peaceful and attractive landscape. The charming decor of the dining room is based on mountain activities of times past. Traditional cuisine.

NEVERS Ⓟ – 58 Nièvre – 319 B10 – pop. 40 932 – Built-up area 100 556 – alt. 194 m – St Bernadette's pilgrimage from April to October : St Gildard's convent – ✉ 58000 Burgundy-Jura 7 **A2**

Paris 236 – Bourges 70 – Clermont-Ferrand 161 – Orléans 167

Office de tourisme, rue Sabatier, Palais Ducal ✆ 03 86 68 46 00, Fax 03 86 68 45 98

du Nivernais Magny-Cours Le Bardonnay, East: 2 km by D 200, ✆ 03 86 58 18 30.

Circuit Automobile permanent to Magny-Cours ✆ 03 86 21 80 00, by ④ : 12 km.

St-Cyr and Ste-Juliette cathedral ★★ - Palais ducal★ - St-Étienne church ★ - Façade★ of Ste-Marie chapel - Porte du Croux★ - Nevers earthenware ★ of the musée municipal Frédéric Blandin M¹.

Circuit de Nevers-Magny-Cours: musée Ligier F1★.

Plan on following page

Mercure Pont de Loire rm, VISA AE
quai Médine – 03 86 93 93 86 – h3480@accor.com – Fax 03 86 59 43 29
59 rm – €87 €98, €11 – **Rest** – Menu €22/31 – Carte €28/40 Z **a**
◆ Pleasantly located on the banks of the Loire. Comfortable bar with piano. Attractive rooms, some of which offer a delightful view of the river. Panoramic dining room and huge terrace. Regionally inspired cuisine and wine list.

De Diane VISA AE
– 03 86 57 28 10 – diane.nevers@wanadoo.fr – Fax 03 86 59 45 08 – Closed 20 December-4 January – **30 rm** – €74/96 €86/104, €10,50 Z **b**
Rest – *(closed Friday lunchtime and Sunday)* Menu €18/28
◆ This former residence near the station houses sizeable, renovated rooms, furnished with care. The breakfast room is in a 14C tower. The restaurant offers classic food, a discreet setting.

Ibis rm, rm, VISA AE
rte de Moulins, via ④ – 03 86 37 56 00 – h0947@accor.com – Fax 03 86 37 64 48
56 rm – €57/68 €57/73, €7,50 – **Rest** – *(dinner only)* Menu €17
◆ This hotel is located on the left bank, near the Loire bridge. The recently refurbished rooms are quieter on the car park side. Light, pretty dining room with cane seats, wrought-iron lamps and bright colours.

Molière without rest VISA
25 r. Molière – 03 86 57 29 96 – contact@hotel-moliere-nevers.com – Fax 03 86 36 00 13 – **18 rm** – €45 €49, €6 V **k**
◆ A warm welcome at this clean and simple hotel situated in a residential area. You can choose between rustic or modern bedrooms.

Jean-Michel Couron VISA
21 r. St-Étienne – 03 86 61 19 28 – info@jm-couron.com – Fax 03 86 36 02 96 – Closed 2-10 March, 14 July-5 August, 5-13 January, Sunday dinner, Tuesday lunch and Monday Y **r**
Rest *(number of covers limited, pre-book)* Menu €20 (weekdays)/49 – Carte €52/65
Spec. Tarte de tomate et chèvre frais fermier. Pièce de bœuf charolais rôtie. Soupe au chocolat. **Wines** Pouilly-Fumé, Sancerre.
◆ In the old quarter of Nevers. One of the three tiny dining rooms is under the 14C vaults of the former St. Etienne church cloister. Fine, inventive cuisine.

La Botte de Nevers VISA
r. Petit Château – 03 86 61 16 93 – labottedenevers@wanadoo.fr – Fax 03 86 36 42 22 – Closed 4-25 August, Sunday dinner, Tuesday lunch and Monday
Rest – Menu €21/50 – Carte €45/67 Y **n**
◆ The attractive wrought-iron sign, a medieval-style setting and swords decorating the staircase echo the reference to the Duke of Never's famous final sword thrust.

L'Assiette VISA
7 bis r. F. Gambon – 03 86 36 24 99 – Fax 03 86 36 24 99 – Closed Easter holidays, 18 August-7 September, 1st-10 January and Sunday Y **d**
Rest – Menu (€13,50) – Carte €24/35
◆ An original concept for this delightful establishment: theme dishes (starter, main dish, cheese) made from fresh produce. Modern blue and chocolate decor.

Orléans road by ① – ✉ 58640 Varennes-Vauzelles

Le Bengy VISA AE
at 4.5 km on D 907 – 03 86 38 02 84 – lebengyrestaurant@wanadoo.fr – Fax 03 86 38 29 00 – Closed 27 July-19 August, 1st-5 January, 22 February-10 March, Sunday and Monday – **Rest** – Menu €19/32 – Carte €27/45
◆ A fashionable colour scheme, contemporary lines, leather, wrought iron and potted plants create the soothing Japanese inspired setting of this often fully booked restaurant. Modern menu.

in Sauvigny-les-Bois 10 km by ③ D 978 and D 18 – pop. 1 527 – alt. 210 m – ✉ 58160

Moulin de l'Étang VISA
64 rte de l'Etang – 03 86 37 10 17 – Fax 03 86 37 12 06 – Closed 1st-20 August, February school holidays, Sunday dinner, Wednesday dinner and Monday
Rest – Menu €23/50
◆ Former dairy on the outskirts of the village, near a lake. Rustic dining room with exposed beams, an old clock and art exhibitions. Modern cuisine.

NEVERS

Rue		
Ardilliers (R. des)	Y	2
Banlay (R. du)	V	3
Barre (R. de la)	Y	4
Bourgeois (R. Mlle)	V	5
Champ-de-Foire (R. du)	Z	6
Charnier (R. du)	Y	7
Chauvelles (R. des)	V	8
Cloître-St-Cyr (R. du)	Z	9
Colbert (Av.)	Y	10
Coquille (Pl. G.)	Y	12
Docks (R. des)	V	13
Fer (R. du)	Y	47
Fonmorigny (R.)	Y	48
Francs-Bourgeois (R. des)	Y	14
Gaulle (Av. Gén.-de)	YZ	
Gautron-du-Coudray (Bd)	Y	15
Jacobins (R. des)	Z	16
Lattre-de-Tassigny (Bd Mar.-de)	V	17
Mancini (Pl.)	Y	50
Mantoue (Quai de)	Z	18
Marceau (Av.)	Y	19
Midi (R. du)	Z	20
Mirangron (R.)	Y	49
Mitterrand (R. F.)	YZ	
Nièvre (R. de)	Y	21
Ouches (R. des)	YZ	22
Pelleterie (R. de la)	Y	24
Petit-Mouësse (R. du)	X	26
Porte-du-Croux (R. de la)	Z	51
Préfecture (R. de la)	Y	27
Récollets (R. des)	Z	52
Remigny (R. de)	Y	28
Renardats (R. des)	V	30
République (Bd de la)	X	32
République (Pl. de la)	Z	34
Roy (R. C.)	Y	36
St-Martin (R.)	Y	38
St-Sébastien (Pl.)	Y	39
Tillier (R. C.)	Z	40
Vaillant-Couturier (R. Paul)	V	42
14-Juillet (R. du)	Z	45

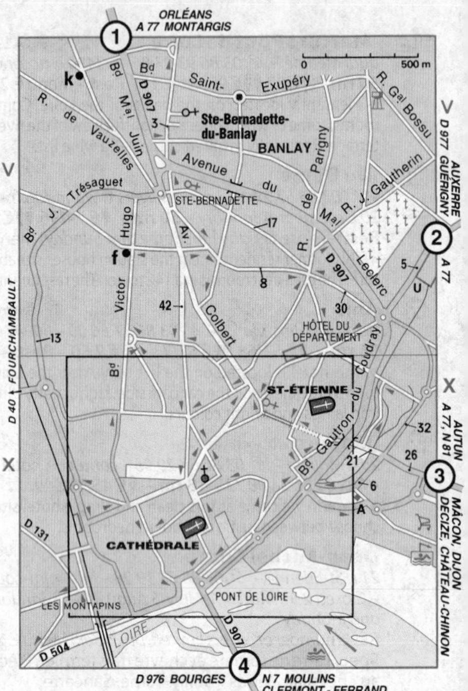

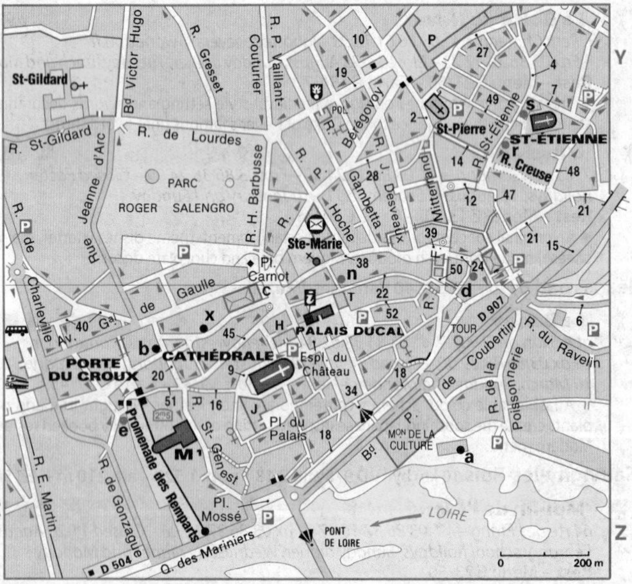

Moulins road 3 km by ④, on N 7 – ✉ 58000 Challuy

XX **La Gabare**
171 rte de Lyon – ✆ 03 86 37 54 23 – la-gabare58000@yahoo.fr – Fax 03 86 37 64 49 – Closed 14 July-12 August, Sunday dinner and Monday
Rest – Menu € 19/27 – Carte € 28/50
◆ A finely-restored old farmhouse offering two rustic dining rooms with exposed beams, colourful walls and a large fireplace. Terrace with flowers for a meal outside in fine weather.

in Magny-Cours 12 km by ④, Moulins road – pop. 1 486 – alt. 205 m – ✉ 58470

Holiday Inn
Ferme du domaine de Bardonnay – ✆ 03 86 21 22 33 – himagnycours@alliance-hospitality.com – Fax 03 86 21 22 03 – **70 rm** – 🛉€ 96/215 🛉🛉€ 96/215, ☕ € 17
Rest – Menu (€ 12), € 17/28 – Carte € 24/53
◆ Located near a motor-racing circuit and golf course. The original farmhouse has been extended with a modern bedroom wing. Some rooms overlook the swimming pool or greens. Bright dining room opening onto a vast terrace. Traditional cuisine.

NÉVEZ – 29 Finistère – 308 I8 – pop. 2 466 – alt. 40 m – ✉ 29920 9 B2

▶ Paris 547 – Rennes 196 – Quimper 40 – Lorient 51 – Lanester 51
ℹ Office de tourisme, place de l' Église ✆ 02 98 06 87 90, Fax 02 98 06 73 09

Ar Men Du ← ocean,
à Raguenès-Plage, 4 km south on secondary road – ✆ 02 98 06 84 22 – contact@men-du.com – Fax 02 98 06 76 69 – Closed 1st-14 March, 12 November-21 December and 2 January-1st March
15 rm – 🛉€ 80/110 🛉🛉€ 100/125, ☕ € 13 – 1 suite – **Rest** – *(closed Wednesday lunch and Tuesday) (pre-book)* Menu € 35/72 – Carte € 37/74
◆ In a conservation area overlooking the ocean, this 1970s neo-Breton house has a distinctly maritime feel. Guestrooms decorated in nautical style, sea views and peaceful surroundings. Fish and seafood specialities, with views of Île Raguénez in the distance. Good choice of wines by the glass.

X **Le Bistrot de l'Écailler**
au port de Kerdruc, 3 km east par D 77 and secondary road – ✆ 02 98 06 78 60 – Open April-end September and closed Tuesday and Wednesday except dinner July-August – **Rest** – Menu € 45 – Carte € 33/53
◆ An attractive bistro specialising in fish and seafood with a terrace overlooking the port and the Aven. Superb seafood platters, daily suggestions, lobster and chips, and an imaginative wine list.

NEXON – 87 Haute-Vienne – 325 E6 – pop. 2 325 – alt. 359 m – ✉ 87800

▶ Paris 416 – Limoges 27 – Saint-Junien 56 – Panazol 27 – Isle 27 24 B2
ℹ Office de tourisme, Conciergerie du Château ✆ 05 55 58 28 44

XX **Les Chaumières** with rm
Domaine des Landes, at 2 km along the D 11 – ✆ 05 55 58 25 26 – jfcane@les-chaumieres.com – Fax 05 55 58 25 25
3 rm – 🛉€ 65 🛉🛉€ 65, ☕ € 8 – **Rest** – *(closed Sunday dinner, Monday and Tuesday) (pre-book)* Menu € 32/39
◆ Pretty thatched cottage in a garden with old trees. Warm, elegant interior, friendly welcome and contemporary cuisine which varies with the seasons.

NEYRAC-LES-BAINS – 07 Ardèche – 331 H5 – ✉ 07380 44 A3

▶ Paris 606 – Aubenas 16 – Montélimar 56 – Privas 45 – Le Puy-en-Velay 75

XX **Du Levant**
– ✆ 04 75 36 41 07 – info@hotel-levant.com – Fax 04 75 36 48 09 – Open 30 April-20 November and closed Wednesday from December to March, Monday, Tuesday and Sunday dinner
Rest – Menu (€ 18 bi), € 24/55
◆ In the same family since 1885, this inn specialises in appetising regional dishes with a modern slant and a fine wine list. Panoramic half-rustic, half-designer room, terrace.

NÉZIGNAN-L'ÉVÈQUE – 34 Hérault – 339 F8 – see Pézenas

H. Le Gac/ MICHELIN

Old Nice

NICE

P **Department:** 06 Alpes-Maritimes
Michelin LOCAL map: n° **341** E5 **115**]26]27
Paris 927 – Cannes 33 – Genova 192 – Lyon 471 – Marseille 189 – Torino 210

Population: 342 738 — 42 **E2**
Pop. built-up area: 888 784
Altitude: 6 m – **Postal Code:** ✉ 06000
French Riviera

USEFUL INFORMATION

TOURIST OFFICES

5, promenade des Anglais ✆ 08 92 70 74 07
Office de tourisme, avenue Thiers ✆ 08 92 70 74 07
Office de tourisme, Aéroport ✆ 08 92 70 74 07

TRANSPORT

Auto-train ✆ 3635 et tapez 42 (0,34 €/mn)

SEA TRANSPORT

For Corsica: SNCM - Ferryterranée quai du Commerce ✆ 0 825 888 088 (0.15 €/mn) JZ
CORSICA FERRIES Port de Commerce ✆ 04 92 00 42 93, Fax 04 92 00 42 94

AIRPORT

Nice-Côte-d'Azur ✆ 0820 423 333 (0,12 €/mn), 7 km AU

CASINO

Ruhl, 1 promenade des Anglais FZ
Le Palais de la Méditerannée, 15 promenade des Anglais FZ

TO BE SEEN

SEAFRONT AND OLD NICE

Site★★ - Promenade des Anglais★★ - ⋞★★ of the château - Interior★ of St-Martin church - St-Augustin HY - St-Jacques church ★ HZ - Monumental staircase ★ of the palais Lascaris HZ V - Interior ★ of Ste-Réparate cathedral HZ - decorations★ of the Annonciation chapel HZ B - Altar-pieces★ of the Miséricorde chapel ★ HZ D

CIMIEZ

Musée Marc-Chagall★★ GX - Musée Matisse★★ HV M4 - Franciscan monastery★: primitive Niçois paintings★★ in the church HV K - Gallo-Roman archeological site★

WESTERN DISTRICTS

Musée des beaux-Arts (Jules Chéret)★★ DZ - Musée d'Art naïf A.Jakovsky★ AU M10 - Giant greenhouse★ of the Phoenix Park ★ AU - Musée des Arts asiatiques★★

PROMENADE DU PAILLON

Musée d'Art moderne et d'Art contemporain★★ HY M2 - Palais des Arts, du Tourisme et des Congrès (Arts, Tourism and Congress Centre) (Acropolis)★ HJX

OTHER SIGHTS

St-Nicolas Russian Orthodox Cathedral ★ EXY - Mosaic★ by Chagall in the Law Faculty DZ U - Musée Masséna★ FZ M3

Negresco

37 promenade des Anglais – ✆ 04 93 16 64 00 – direction@hotel-negresco.com – Fax 04 93 88 35 68 p. 6 FZ **k**

128 rm – €285/570 €285/570, €28 – 9 suites

Rest *Chantecler* – see restaurant listing

Rest *La Rotonde* – Menu (€29), €34 – Carte €29/58

◆ In 1913, Henri Negresco, son of a Romanian hotel keeper, built this palace, or rather, this mythical and majestic museum hotel brimming with works of art and grandeur. The Rotonde: an unusual brasserie with a merry-go-round decor, wooden horses and automatons.

Palais de la Méditerranée rm, rest,

13 promenade des Anglais – ✆ 04 92 14 77 00 – reservation@lepalaisdelamediterranee.com – Fax 04 92 14 77 14 p. 6 FZ **g**

181 rm – €295/830 €280/830, €26 – 7 suites

Rest *Le Padouk* – *(closed 15-31 January, Sunday and Monday except July-August)* Menu €35 (lunch), €49/75 – Carte €58/80

Rest *Pingala Bar* – *(lunch only)* Carte approx. €35

◆ This famous building with a listed Art Deco façade now houses a new hotel offering soberly modern, spacious and luxurious rooms. The Padouk offers Asian and southern-inspired food. The Pingala Bar offers simple Niçoise dishes in a chic setting.

Radisson SAS rm,

223 promenade des Anglais – ✆ 04 97 17 71 77 – info.nice@radissonsas.com – Fax 04 93 71 21 71 p. 4 AU **n**

318 rm – €140/220 €140/220, €25 – 13 suites

Rest – Carte €49/70

◆ Hotel in the spirit of the times, with modern architecture, large stylish bedrooms (Urban, Chilli and Ocean themes), designer bar, fitness suite and rooftop terrace pool. Comfortable dining room decorated in blue and lemon tones; local cuisine.

Méridien rest,

1 promenade des Anglais – ✆ 04 97 03 44 44 – reservation.nice@lemeridien.com – Fax 04 97 03 44 45 p. 6 FZ **d**

318 rm – €265/325 €265/325, €23 – 2 suites

Rest *Le Colonial Café* – ✆ 04 97 03 40 36 – Carte €42/61

Rest *La Terrasse du Colonial* – ✆ 04 97 03 40 37 – Carte €42/61

◆ On offer at this luxury hotel: the heated rooftop pool overlooking the Baie des Anges, attractive rooms in southern colours, beauty salon and high-tech meeting rooms. A restaurant with an ethnic decor and dishes from around the world at the Colonial Café. A superb sea view at the Terrasse.

Élysée Palace rm, rest,

59 promenade des Anglais – ✆ 04 93 97 90 90 – restauration@elyseepalace.com – Fax 04 93 44 50 40 p. 6 EZ **d**

141 rm – €123/480 €135/480, €19 – 2 suites

Rest *Le Caprice* – Menu (€22), €29 (weekday lunch), €49/180 – Carte €30/68

◆ The highlight of this futuristic architecture is a giant bronze Venus. An Art Deco-style decor, extremely comfortable amenities, excellent soundproofing and a rooftop pool. Appetising regional menu served on the terrace in summer.

Boscolo Hôtel Plaza rest,

12 av. de Verdun – ✆ 04 93 16 75 75 – reservation@nice.boscolo.com – Fax 04 93 88 61 11 p. 7 GZ **u**

171 rm – €255/470 €285/525, €22 – 5 suites

Rest – *(closed Sunday and Monday from November to March)* Menu (€17), €34 – Carte €45/57

◆ An imposing hotel, adjacent to the Albert I garden. Spacious bedrooms. Roof terrace offering a fine view of the Mediterranean. Fully equipped for seminars. A dining room in warm colours and large panoramic terrace with town views.

INDEX OF STREET NAMES IN NICE

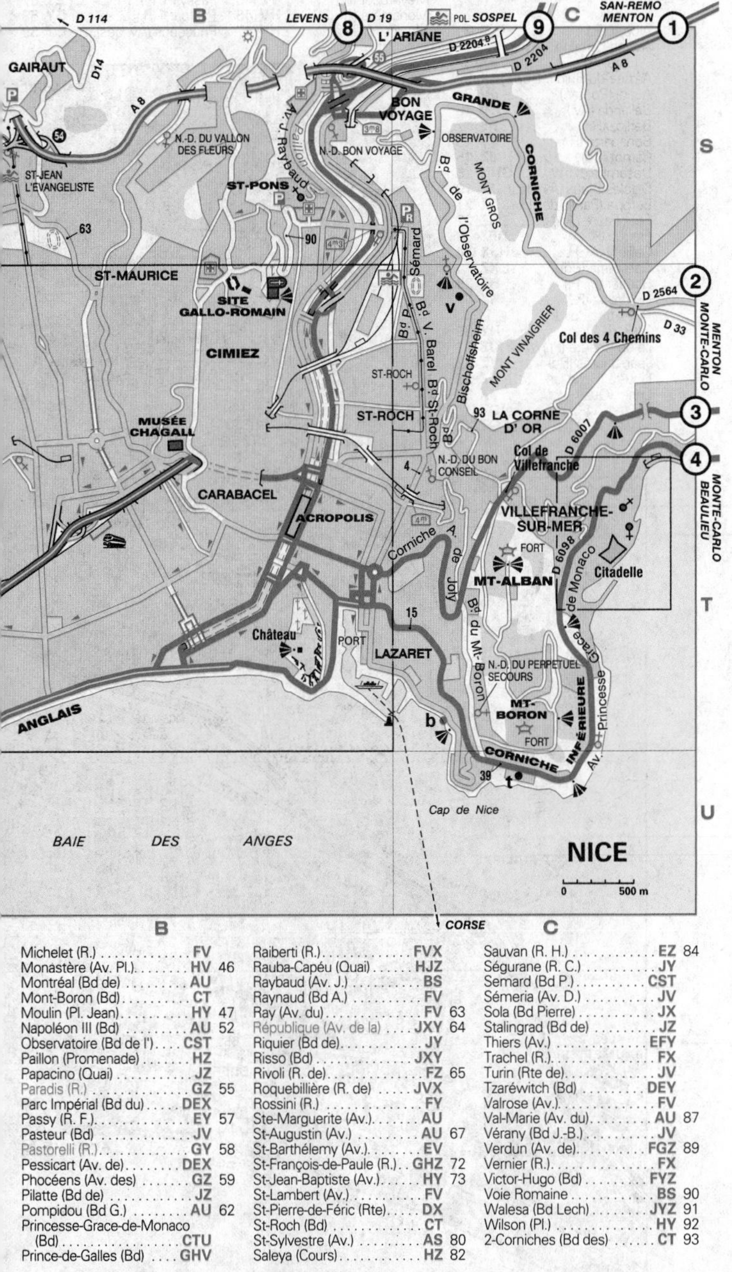

Michelet (R.) . . . . **FV**
Monastère (Av. Pl.) . . . . **HV** 46
Montréal (Bd de) . . . . **AU**
Mont-Boron (Bd) . . . . **CT**
Moulin (Pl. Jean) . . . . **HY** 47
Napoléon III (Bd) . . . . **AU** 52
Observatoire (Bd de l') . . . . **CST**
Paillon (Promenade) . . . . **HZ**
Papacino (Quai) . . . . **JZ**
Paradis (R.) . . . . **GZ** 55
Parc Impérial (Bd du) . . . . **DEX**
Passy (R. F.) . . . . **EY** 57
Pasteur (Bd) . . . . **JV**
Pastorelli (R.) . . . . **GY** 58
Pessicart (Av. de) . . . . **DEX**
Phocéens (Av. des) . . . . **GZ** 59
Pilatte (Bd de) . . . . **JZ**
Pompidou (Bd G.) . . . . **AU** 62
Princesse-Grace-de-Monaco
(Bd) . . . . **CTU**
Prince-de-Galles (Bd) . . . . **GHV**

Raiberti (R.) . . . . **FVX**
Rauba-Capéu (Quai) . . . . . . **HJZ**
Raybaud (Av. J.) . . . . **BS**
Raynaud (Bd A.) . . . . **FV**
Ray (Av. du) . . . . **FV** 63
République (Av. de la) . . . . **JXY** 64
Riquier (Bd de) . . . . **JY**
Risso (Bd) . . . . **JXY**
Rivoli (R. de) . . . . **FZ** 65
Roquebillière (R. de) . . . . . **JVX**
Rossini (R.) . . . . **FY**
Ste-Marguerite (Av.) . . . . **AU**
St-Augustin (Av.) . . . . **AU** 67
St-Barthélemy (Av.) . . . . **EV**
St-François-de-Paule (R.) . . **GHZ** 72
St-Jean-Baptiste (Av.) . . . . . **HY** 73
St-Lambert (Av.) . . . . **FV**
St-Pierre-de-Féric (Rte) . . . . **DX**
St-Roch (Bd) . . . . **CT**
St-Sylvestre (Av.) . . . . **AS** 80
Saleya (Cours) . . . . **HZ** 82

Sauvan (R. H.) . . . . **EZ** 84
Ségurane (R. C.) . . . . **JY**
Semard (Bd P.) . . . . **CST**
Séméria (Av. D.) . . . . **JV**
Sola (Bd Pierre) . . . . **JX**
Stalingrad (Bd de) . . . . **JZ**
Thiers (Av.) . . . . **EFY**
Trachel (R.) . . . . **FX**
Turin (Rte de) . . . . **JV**
Tzaréwitch (Bd) . . . . **DEY**
Valrose (Av.) . . . . **FV**
Val-Marie (Av. du) . . . . **AU** 87
Vérany (Bd J.-B.) . . . . **JV**
Verdun (Av. de) . . . . **FGZ** 89
Vernier (R.) . . . . **FX**
Victor-Hugo (Bd) . . . . **FYZ**
Voie Romaine . . . . **BS** 90
Walesa (Bd Lech) . . . . **JYZ** 91
Wilson (Pl.) . . . . **HY** 92
2-Corniches (Bd des) . . . . . . **CT** 93

NICE

Alberti (R.) . . . . GHY 2
Alsace-Lorraine (Jardin d') . . . . EZ 3
Armée-du-Rhin (Pl. de l') JX 5
Auriol (Pont V.). . . . . JV 7
Bellanda (Av.) . . . . HV 10
Berlioz (R.) . . . . FY 12
Bonaparte (R.) . . . . JY 13
Carnot (Bd). . . . . JZ 15
Desambrois (Av.). . . . GHX 18
Diables-Bleus (Av. des). JX 19
Europe (Parvis de l') . . . JX 21
Félix-Faure (Av.). . . . . . GZ 22
France (R. de) . . . . DFZ
Gallieni (Av.) . . . . HJX 24
Gambetta (Bd) . . . . . . EXZ
Gautier (Pl. P.) . . . . HZ 25
Gioffredo (R.) . . . . HY
Hôtel-des-Postes (R. de l') . . . . HY 30
Ile-de-Beauté (Pl.) . . . . . JZ 31
Jean-Jaurès (Bd) . . . . HYZ 32
Liberté (R. de la) . . . . . . GZ 35
Lunel (Quai) . . . . JZ 37
Masséna (Pl. et Espace) GZ
Masséna (R.) . . . . FGZ 43
Médecin (Av. J.). . . . . FGY 44
Meyerbeer (R.) . . . . FZ 45
Monastère (Av. Pl.). . . . HV 46
Moulin (Pl. J.) . . . . HY 47
Paradis (R.) . . . . GZ 55
Passy (R. F.). . . . . EY 57
Pastorelli (R.). . . . . GY 58
Phocéens (Av. des). . . . GZ 59

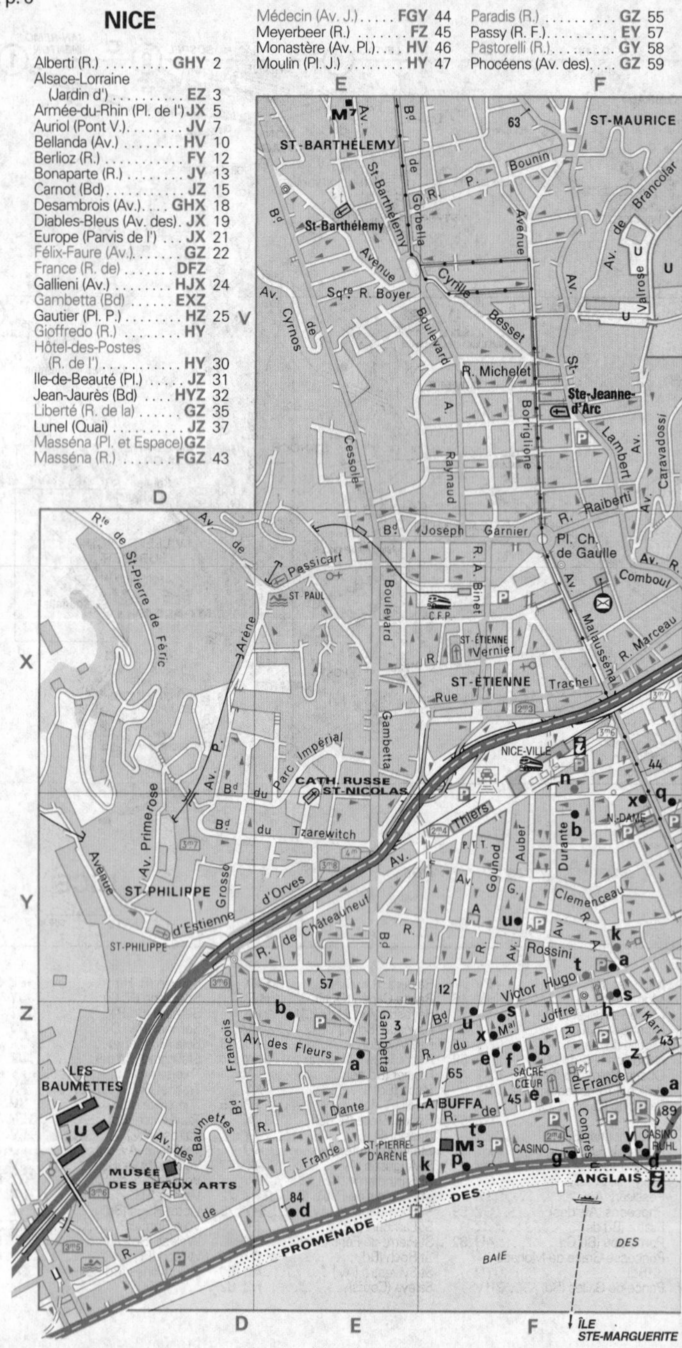

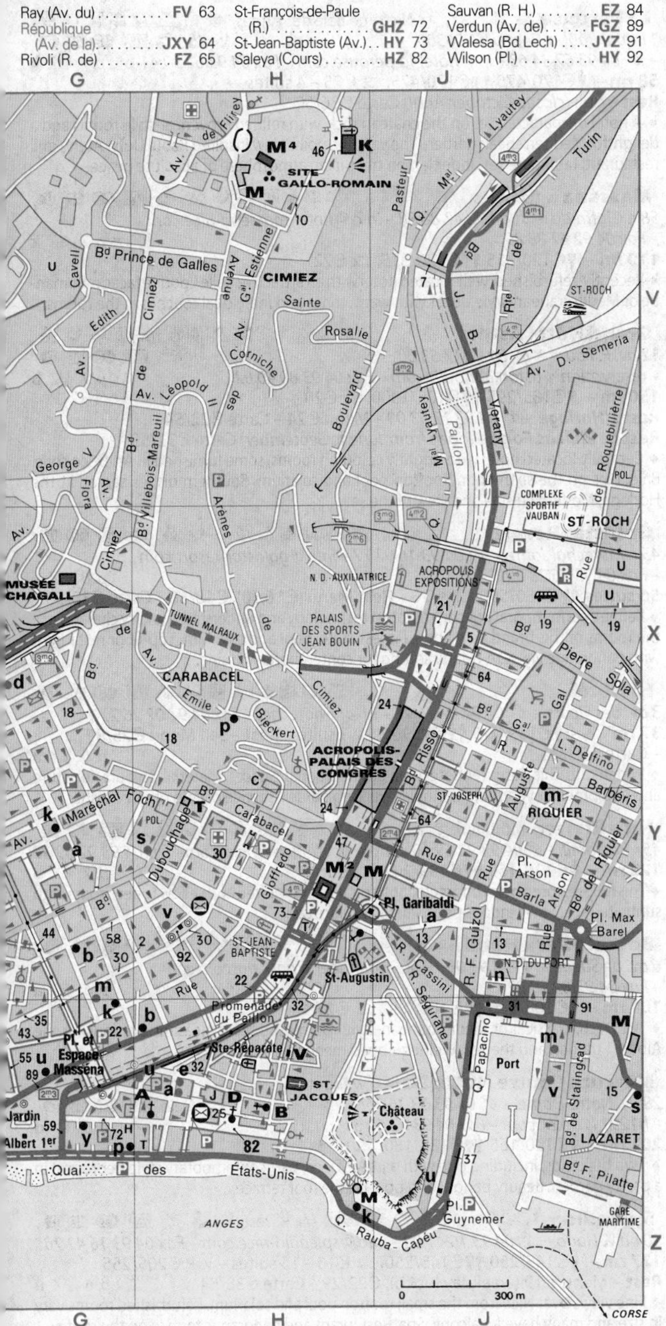

CIMIEZ
SITE GALLO-ROMAIN
MUSÉE CHAGALL
TUNNEL MALRAUX
CARABACEL
ACROPOLIS-PALAIS DES CONGRÈS
ACROPOLIS EXPOSITIONS
PALAIS DES SPORTS JEAN BOUIN
N. D. AUXILIATRICE
COMPLEXE SPORTIF VAUBAN
ST-ROCH
RIQUIER
Pl. Garibaldi
St-Augustin
Ste-Réparate
ST-JACQUES
Château
Port
LAZARET
GARE MARITIME
Pl. et Espace Masséna
Jardin Albert 1er
Quai des États-Unis
Q. Rauba-Capéu
Pl. Guynemer
ANGES
CORSE
300 m

La Pérouse ⋖ Nice and Baie des Anges,

11 quai Rauba-Capéu ✉ 06300
– ☎ 04 93 62 34 63 – lp@hotel-la-perouse.com – Fax 04 93 62 59 41 p. 7 HZ **k**
58 rm – †€ 170/475 ††€ 170/475, ☕ € 25 – 4 suites
Rest – grill *(closed October-April)* Carte € 36/52
♦ A hotel of character, set on the château rock, with refined Provençal-style rooms and a delightful Mediterranean garden. The vantage point view inspired Raoul Dufy. At the grill restaurant, tables are set under lemon trees in an atmosphere of absolute peace.

Masséna without rest

58 r. Gioffredo – ☎ 04 92 47 88 88 – info@hotel-massena-nice.com
– Fax 04 92 47 88 89 p. 7 GZ **k**
110 rm – †€ 120/315 ††€ 120/315, ☕ € 22
♦ Recently-refurbished, well-located hotel with an attractive Belle Époque façade. Romantic or Mediterranean-style décor with warm tones and individual touches in the rooms.

Grand Hôtel Aston ⋖ rm,

12 av. F. Faure – ☎ 04 92 17 53 00
– reservation@aston.3ahotels.com – Fax 04 93 80 40 02 p. 7 HZ **b**
150 rm – †€ 185/295 ††€ 185/1000, ☕ € 20
Rest *L'Horloge* – ☎ 04 92 17 53 09 – Menu € 24 – Carte € 22/54
Rest *Le Phileas Fogg* – *(open from June to September)* Carte € 32/55
♦ Centrally located hotel with brightly coloured rooms, some furnished in Art Deco style. Balconies on the sixth floor. Rooftop pool and solarium. Southern dishes served at the Horloge. Modern cuisine and view of the sea.

Goldstar Resort

45 r. Maréchal Joffre – ☎ 04 93 16 92 77 – info@goldstar-resort.com
– Fax 04 93 76 23 30 p. 6 FZ **e**
56 suites ††€ 180/550, ☕ € 20 – **Rest** Menu (€ 16,50), € 18/38 – Carte € 33/53
♦ Refined contemporary decor, the latest technology and understated luxury characterise the rooms of this brand new hotel. Fitness suite, pool and solarium. Top-floor restaurant with panoramic views. A trendy setting for contemporary cuisine.

Hi Hôtel rm,

3 av. des Fleurs – ☎ 04 97 07 26 26 – hi@hi-hotel.net – Fax 04 97 07 26 27
37 rm ☕ – †€ 159/415 ††€ 159/435 – 1 suite – **Rest** – self Menu € 25/99
– Carte € 23/31 p. 6 EZ **a**
♦ Watch out! This designer hotel is all but traditional. Spaces, material, colours, furniture and equipment; everything is innovative. Original self-service of cold organic dishes.

Nice Riviera without rest

45 r. Pastorelli – ☎ 04 93 92 69 60 – info@hotel-nice-riviera.com – Fax 04 93 92 69 22
122 rm – †€ 129/169 ††€ 159/209, ☕ € 15 p. 7 GY **b**
♦ This fully restored hotel offers elegant, colourful rooms (red and yellow tones), some with sunny terrace. Small indoor pool, sauna and Jacuzzi.

Boscolo Park Hôtel without rest ⋖

6 av. de Suède – ☎ 04 97 03 19 00 – manager@park.boscolo.com
– Fax 04 93 82 29 27 p. 6 FZ **a**
104 rm – †€ 108/510 ††€ 108/760, ☕ € 25
♦ Art Deco, classical or Mediterranean-style rooms, the most pleasant overlooking the Albert 1 garden and the sea. Well-equipped meeting rooms.

Mercure Centre Notre Dame without rest

28 av. Notre-Dame – ☎ 04 93 13 36 36
– h1291@accor.com – Fax 04 93 62 61 69 p. 6 FXY **q**
201 rm – †€ 120/165 ††€ 135/180, ☕ € 15
♦ Two buildings, including one with part Art Deco, part contemporary style bedrooms in a pretty garden. Beauty parlour and pool on the roof terrace.

Splendid rest,

50 bd V. Hugo – ☎ 04 93 16 41 00 – info@splendid-nice.com – Fax 04 93 16 42 70
127 rm – †€ 145/250 ††€ 145/250, ☕ € 16 – 15 suites – ½ P € 205/255
Rest – Menu € 19 (weekday lunch), € 22/29 – Carte € 38/54 p. 6 FZ **u**
♦ Fine views over Nice from the small rooftop pool and solarium. Refurbished rooms vary in size and many have a balcony. Spa. Restaurant and panoramic terrace on the roof.

Le Grimaldi without rest
15 r. Grimaldi – ✆ 04 93 16 00 24 – zedde@le-grimaldi.com – Fax 04 93 87 00 24
46 rm – †€ 85/160 ††€ 95/205, ☕ € 20 *p. 6* FY **s**
◆ Provençal furniture, wrought iron and beautiful Pierre Frey fabrics add a personal touch to the rooms with small terraces on the top floor. Cosy hall-bar-lounge.

Villa Victoria without rest
33 bd V. Hugo – ✆ 04 93 88 39 60 – contact@villa-victoria.com – Fax 04 93 88 07 98 – Closed 20-28 December *p. 6* FZ **s**
38 rm – †€ 75/160 ††€ 90/160, ☕ € 15
◆ A beautiful old building with a southern feel. Choose a room with a balcony overlooking the attractive Mediterranean garden. Those on the road side are well soundproofed.

Windsor rest,
11 r. Dalpozzo – ✆ 04 93 88 59 35 – contact@hotelwindsornice.com – Fax 04 93 88 94 57 *p. 6* FZ **f**
57 rm – †€ 90/175 ††€ 90/175, ☕ € 12 – **Rest** – *(closed Sunday) (dinner only)* Menu € 29 – Carte € 31/42
◆ This hotel has a particular attraction: 25 'artists' rooms' with paintings by contemporary artists including one by the Nice artist, Ben. Exotic garden and well being centre (steam bath, massages, sauna). Snacks served in the bar and, in summer, amid the palm trees and bougainvilleas.

Mercure Promenade des Anglais without rest
2 r. Halévy – ✆ 04 93 82 30 88 – H0360@accor.com – Fax 04 93 82 18 20 *p. 6* FZ **q**
122 rm – †€ 81/205 ††€ 91/325, ☕ € 15
◆ Hotel set in the Ruhl casino building. Comfortable, refurbished rooms decorated in gaming-inspired style. Breakfast room with view over the Promenade des Anglais.

Petit Palais without rest ≤ Nice and the sea,
17 av. E. Bieckert – ✆ 04 93 62 19 11 – reservation@petitpalaisnice.com – Fax 04 93 62 53 60 *p. 7* HX **p**
25 rm – †€ 80/140 ††€ 90/170, ☕ € 13
◆ Sacha Guitry lived in this 1900s villa, perched on the Cimiez Hill. Most of the bedrooms have a view looking down on the rooftops of the old quarter of Nice and the Baie des Anges.

Brice rm, rest,
44 r. Mar. Joffre – ✆ 04 93 88 14 44 – info@nice-hotel-brice.com – Fax 04 93 87 38 54 *p. 6* FZ **x**
58 rm – †€ 80/118 ††€ 100/139, ☕ € 12 – ½ P € 75/100 – **Rest** – *(open June to September and closed Monday) (dinner only)* Menu € 25/30 – Carte € 30/45
◆ This hotel's functional and well-kept rooms are protected from traffic noise by a flower-decked garden-terrace. Asian-influenced decor in the bar and Internet connection. Unpretentious family cooking served outside in fine weather.

Alba without rest
41 av. Jean Médecin – ✆ 04 93 88 02 88 – reservation@hotellalba.com – Fax 04 93 88 55 03 *p. 6* FXY **x**
35 rm – †€ 95/120 ††€ 110/270, ☕ € 13
◆ This town-centre hotel has been successfully renovated with its very well-equipped and soundproofed rooms now sporting trendy decor (grey and brown tones).

Aria without rest
15 av. Auber – ✆ 04 93 88 30 69 – reservation@aria-nice.com – Fax 04 93 88 11 35
30 rm – †€ 84/94 ††€ 94/124, ☕ € 13 – 4 suites *p. 6* FY **u**
◆ In the heart of the musicians' district, good-sized rooms, well-soundproofed and with classic or Provençal-style furnishings; choose one overlooking the little square.

De Flore without rest
2 r. Maccarani – ✆ 04 92 14 40 20 – info@hoteldeflore-nice.fr – Fax 04 92 14 40 21
61 rm – †€ 80/145 ††€ 90/160, ☕ € 12 – 3 suites *p. 6* FZ **z**
◆ Wrought-iron furniture, wicker chairs and colours of the south in the cheery, functional rooms. A patio for breakfast in a typical Mediterranean setting.

Anis Hôtel
50 av. Lanterne ✉ 06200 – ✆ 04 93 18 29 00 – info@hotel-anis.com – Fax 04 93 83 31 16 p. 5 AU **a**
42 rm – †€ 79/99 ††€ 90/110, ☕ € 9
Rest – *(closed Sunday dinner and Monday)* Menu € 17 (weekday lunch), € 27/35 – Carte € 26/53
◆ Hidden in a quiet residential area, this establishment has plenty going for it: renovated, well-soundproofed rooms, a pleasant pool and reasonable prices. Enjoy regional cuisine on the terrace or in a dining room in southern colours.

Durante without rest
16 av. Durante – ✆ 04 93 88 84 40 – info@hotel-durante.com – Fax 04 93 87 77 76 – Closed January p. 6 FY **b**
28 rm – †€ 70/150 ††€ 70/150, ☕ € 10
◆ The calm of this cul-de-sac lets guests sleep with windows open, in rooms that face a sweet-smelling orange-tree garden. Non-smoking throughout.

Nautica without rest
38 r. Barbéris – ✆ 04 92 00 21 21 – reservation@hotelnautica.com – Fax 04 92 00 21 22 p. 7 JXY **m**
87 rm – †€ 75/115 ††€ 90/130, ☕ € 10
◆ This fully renovated hotel is located near the harbour and has chosen a nautical decor. Practical, well-soundproofed rooms, impeccably kept.

Les Cigales without rest
16 r. Dalpozzo – ✆ 04 97 03 10 70 – infos@hotel-lescigales.com – Fax 04 97 03 10 71 p. 6 FZ **b**
19 rm – †€ 75/110 ††€ 80/129, ☕ € 12
◆ This former mansion, with a pretty, finely worked façade has a pleasant little courtyard terrace. Functional and colourful rooms, with sloping ceilings on the top floor.

Mercure Marché aux Fleurs without rest
91 quai des Etats-Unis – ✆ 04 93 85 74 19 – H0962@accor.com – Fax 04 93 13 90 94 p. 6 GZ **p**
49 rm – †€ 92/267 ††€ 102/277, ☕ € 13,50
◆ Polished furniture and beige and chocolate tones in the warm, well-equipped rooms, six of which have sea views. Friendly, efficient welcome.

Armenonville without rest
20 av. Fleurs – ✆ 04 93 96 86 00 – nice@hotel-armenonville.com – Fax 04 93 44 66 53 p. 6 EZ **b**
12 rm – †€ 62/98 ††€ 62/98, ☕ € 10
◆ This 1900s villa and its pretty garden stand in a cul-de-sac in the old Russian émigrés district. Furnishings from the Negresco Hotel personalise the rooms which are being gradually updated.

De la Fontaine without rest
49 r. France – ✆ 04 93 88 30 38 – hotel-fontaine@webstore.fr Fax 04 93 88 98 11
29 rm – †€ 87/105 ††€ 97/125, ☕ € 9,50 p. 6 FZ **t**
◆ Hotel standing in a busy shopping street. For peace and quiet, choose a room on the small patio with fountain, where breakfast is served in season.

Star Hôtel without rest
14 r. Biscarra – ✆ 04 93 85 19 03 – info@hotel-star.com – Fax 04 93 13 04 23 – Closed 12 November-25 December p. 7 GY **k**
24 rm – †€ 45/60 ††€ 55/80, ☕ € 6
◆ Small, plain but clean rooms, some with balcony. Quite a simple establishment, but benefiting from a central location and reasonable prices.

Villa la Lézardière ≤ Nice and the Alps,
87 bd de l'Observatoire ✉ 06300 – ✆ 04 93 56 22 86 – rpaauw@free.fr – Fax 04 93 56 22 86 p. 5 CT **v**
5 rm ☕ – †€ 80 ††€ 90/170 – **Table d'hôte** – Menu € 39 bi
◆ This Provençal-style villa on the Grande Corniche has magnificent views over the town and Alps. Personalised rooms, pool and large enclosed garden. Traditional or Thai cuisine.

XXXX **Chantecler** – Hôtel Negresco

37 promenade des Anglais – ✆ 04 93 16 64 00 – chantecler@hotel-negresco.com – Fax 04 93 88 35 68 – Closed 4 January-4 February, Monday and Tuesday except public holidays p. 6 FZ **k**

Rest – Menu € 55 bi (lunch), € 90/130 – Carte € 83/166

Spec. Langoustines rôties au piment d'Espelette, croustillant de tête de veau. Dos de loup sauvage en croûte d'herbes, émulsion de coquillages. Carré d'agneau rôti en spirale d'herbes, fleur de courgette en tempura. **Wines** Vins de pays des Alpes Maritimes.

◆ A French Regency-style setting enhanced by wood panelling, Aubusson tapestries, masterpieces and damask or lampas silk curtains. Up-to-date cuisine with personal touches.

XXX **L'Âne Rouge**

7 quai Deux-Emmanuel ✉ 06300 – ✆ 04 93 89 49 63 – anerouge@free.fr – Fax 04 93 26 51 42 – Closed February holidays, Thursday lunch and Wednesday

Rest – Menu (€ 26), € 35 (weekday lunch), € 55/85 – Carte € 63/81 p. 7 JZ **m**

◆ This restaurant, facing the marina and château, offers tasty surf'n'turf dishes in a warm and recently redecorated dining room.

XXX **Les Viviers**

22 r. A. Karr – ✆ 04 93 16 00 48 – viviers.bretons@wanadoo.fr – Fax 04 93 16 04 06 – Closed 21 July-18 August, Saturday lunch and Sunday

Rest – Menu € 38 (weekday lunch)/85 – Carte € 39/90 p. 6 FY **k**

◆ An elegant dining room with light wood panelling or a 1900s-style bistro: two decors but the same cuisine, based on fish, seafood and dishes of the day.

XX **L'Univers-Christian Plumail**

54 bd J. Jaurès ✉ 06300 – ✆ 04 93 62 32 22 – plumailunivers@aol.com – Fax 04 93 62 55 69 – Closed Saturday lunch, Monday lunch and Sunday

Rest – *(pre-book)* Menu (€ 22), € 44/70 – Carte € 46/95 p. 7 HZ **u**

Spec. Langoustines rôties à la pancetta. Daurade royale rôtie aux herbes de la garrigue. Soufflé aux citrons du pays. **Wines** Vin de pays des Alpes Maritimes, Bellet.

◆ Canvasses and modern sculptures embellish this much frequented restaurant in Nice; here one can enjoy personalised local cuisine but booking is often advisable.

XX **Jouni "Atelier du Goût"** (Jouni Tormanen) ← The Bay of Angels,

60 bd. F.Pilatte, (1st floor) – ✆ 04 97 08 14 80 – contact@jouni.fr – Closed 9 November-1st December, Sunday and Monday except from May to September p. 5 CT **b**

Rest – Menu € 65 (weekday lunch)/100 – Carte € 88/128

Rest *Bistrot de la Réserve* – Menu (€ 35) – Carte € 61/73

Spec. Velouté de crabes verts, gnocchi à la ricotta. Pêche du jour, barigoule d'artichaut aux olives vertes du Maroc. Duo pistache et figue, sorbet framboise.

◆ A 19C abode with a stunning view of the sea. Art Deco fixtures, ground floor bistro, gourmet first floor dining room and rooftop terrace. Fine modern cuisine.

XX **Keisuke Matsushima**

22 ter r. de France – ✆ 04 93 82 26 06 – info@keisukematsushima.com – Fax 04 92 00 08 49 – Closed 10-31 January, Saturday lunch, Monday lunch and Sunday p. 6 FZ **e**

Rest – Menu € 35 (weekday lunch), € 65/130 – Carte € 85/117

Spec. Langoustines à la plancha, jus de têtes. Filet de Saint-Pierre aux haricots cocos et vongole. Millefeuille de bœuf simmental au wasabi. **Wines** Côtes de Provence, Bellet.

◆ Formerly Kei's Passion, the restaurant may have grown in size and has a different decor (fashionable, minimalist) but the cuisine is just as creative and the service faultless. Table d'hôte by reservation.

XX **Aphrodite**

10 bd Dubouchage – ✆ 04 93 85 63 53 – reception@restaurant-aphrodite.com – Fax 04 93 80 10 41 – Closed 2-20 January, Sunday and Monday p. 7 HY **s**

Rest – Menu € 23 (lunch), € 35/85 – Carte € 52/73

◆ Clean designer lines, wood, red leather and alcove tables: chic, cosy and contemporary decor match the chef's individual cooking style.

XX **Les Épicuriens**

6 pl. Wilson – ✆ 04 93 80 85 00 – Fax 04 93 85 65 00 – Closed August, Saturday lunch and Sunday – **Rest** – Carte € 30/51 *p. 7* HY **v**

◆ Regional menu and tasty blackboard specials attract a loyal clientele to this warm, panelled restaurant. Terrace on the square.

XX **L'Allegro**

6 pl. Guynemer ✉ 06300 – ✆ 04 93 56 62 06 – sarl.divin@orange.fr – Fax 04 93 56 38 28 – Closed 1st-6 January, lunch in August, Saturday lunch and Sunday *p. 7* JZ **u**

Rest – Menu € 19 (weekday lunch), € 45/54 – Carte € 29/56

◆ Freshly prepared pasta and ravioli dishes from the open kitchen, served in an exuberant decor of fresco trompe-l'oeils showing "Commedia dell'arte" characters.

XX **Brasserie Flo** (dinner)

4 r. S. Guitry – ✆ 04 93 13 38 38 – Fax 04 93 13 38 39 *p. 7* GYZ **m**

Rest – brasserie Menu (€ 23), € 30 bi (lunch)/55 – Carte € 32/67

◆ A parterre of tables and troop of waiters at the ready: the bell rings and the deep-red curtain goes up on the kitchens of this brasserie housed in a 1930 theatre.

XX **Stéphane Viano**

26 bd. Victor Hugo – ✆ 04 93 82 48 63 – vianostephane@wanadoo.fr – Closed Sunday – **Rest** – Menu € 32/58 – Carte € 42/58 *p. 6* FY **t**

◆ Easily recognisable by its long veranda furnished with Provençal-blue chairs, this fashionable restaurant also has a dining room with a vaulted ceiling and black and white decor. Typical Nice dishes given a modern twist.

XX **Les Pêcheurs**

18 quai des Docks – ✆ 04 93 89 59 61 – lespecheurs@aliceadsl.fr – Fax 04 93 55 47 50 – Closed 15 January-15 February, Monday and Tuesday in winter, Thursday lunch and Wednesday in summer – **Rest** – Menu € 26/36 – Carte € 32/71 *p. 7* JZ **v**

◆ Enjoy local and more exotic fish and seafood dishes on the summer terrace with views of the port, or in the dining room refurbished by the new owners.

X **Luc Salsedo**

14 r. Maccarani – ✆ 04 93 82 24 12 – contact@restaurant-salsedo.com – Fax 04 93 82 93 68 – Closed 1st-20 January, Thursday lunch, Saturday lunch and Wednesday

Rest – Menu € 42 – Carte € 42/62 *p. 6* FY **h**

◆ Mediterranean shades, a colourful abstract mural and Asian furniture give this small dining room particular appeal. Modern cuisine with Provençal touches.

X **Bông-Laï**

14 r. Alsace-Lorraine – ✆ 04 93 88 75 36 *p. 6* FX **n**

Rest – Menu € 29/39 – Carte € 26/44

◆ A long dining room, unsurprisingly Oriental decorations yet an intimate atmosphere. Vietnamese family cooking, accompanied by a few Chinese dishes.

X **Mireille**

19 bd Raimbaldi – ✆ 04 93 85 27 23 – Closed 2-10 June, 28 July-20 August, 31 December-8 January, Monday and Tuesday – **Rest** – Carte approx. € 32 *p. 7* GX **d**

◆ Restaurant with Spanish decor and a Provençal name, in the heart of the Italian "Nissa"! The paella (only main dish available) is presented on copper crockery.

X **Lou Pistou**

4 r. Raoul Bosio ✉ 06300 – ✆ 04 93 62 21 82 – Closed Saturday and Sunday

Rest – taverne Carte € 23/37 *p. 7* HZ **a**

◆ Located next to the Palace of Justice, this lawyers' "canteen" serves simple regional dishes, in a rather small dining room. Friendly reception.

X **La Casbah**

3 r. Dr Balestre – ✆ 04 93 85 58 81 – Closed July, August, Sunday dinner and Monday

Rest – Carte € 18/31 *p. 7* GY **a**

◆ Small family restaurant offering a choice of homemade mainly couscous dishes and lamb specialities. North African pastries for dessert.

X **La Merenda**

4 r. Raoul Bosio – Closed 4-17 August, Saturday and Sunday *p. 7* HZ **a**

Rest – *(limited number of settings)* – Carte € 27/33

◆ Uncomfortable stools, no telephone and credit cards are not accepted. Despite all of this, crowds flock to La Merenda every day to sample its authentic Niçois cuisine!

in l'Aire St-Michel North: 9 km by Boulevard de Cimiez – ✉ 06100 Nice

Au Rendez-vous des Amis
176 av. Rimiez ✉ 06100 – ✆ 04 93 84 49 66 – contact@rdvdesamis.fr – Fax 04 93 52 62 09 – Closed 27 October-27 November, 23 February-12 March, Tuesday except July-August and Wednesday
Rest – Menu (€ 18), € 24/30 – Carte € 28/38
◆ The warm reception and ambiance of this restaurant confirm the promise in its name! Tasty, typically local dishes with menus purposely limited. Delightful shaded terrace.

to Nice-Côte-d'Azur Airport 7 km – ✉ 06200 Nice

Park Inn Nice rm, VISA
179 bd René Cassin – ✆ 04 93 18 34 00 – reservations.nice@rezidorparkinn.com – Fax 04 93 71 40 63 *p. 4* AU **d**
151 rm – €110/155 €120/200, € 16 – ½ P € 106/146 – **Rest** – Menu € 25 – Carte € 28/32
◆ This hotel near the airport has pleasant, contemporary rooms, repainted in various colours depending on the floor (red, green, blue or yellow). Modern restaurant (traditional menu) and poolside snack bar in summer.

Novotel Arenas rm, VISA
455 promenade des Anglais – ✆ 04 93 21 22 50 – h0478@accor.com – Fax 04 93 21 63 50 *p. 4* AU **e**
131 rm – €90/140 €90/140, € 13 – **Rest** – Carte € 20/41
◆ Rooms progressively updated in a trendy style: modern furniture in grey and chocolate tones. Good soundproofing and numerous conference rooms. An unusually intimate dining room serving traditional cuisine.

in St-Isidore by ⑦: 13 km – ✉ 06200

Servotel VISA
30 av. A. Verola – ✆ 04 93 29 99 00 – info@servotel-nice.fr – Fax 04 93 29 99 01
84 rm – €68/145 €78/175, € 12 – **Rest** – *(closed Sunday lunch, holidays lunch and Saturday)* Menu € 22/33 – Carte € 40/64
◆ New hotel near a shopping centre. Well-equipped functional rooms, ideal for business travellers. Lounge with fireplace and seminar facilities. A modern dining room with southern shades, serving simple traditional cuisine.

NIEDERBRONN-LES-BAINS – 67 Bas-Rhin – 315 J3 – pop. 4 319 – alt. 190 m – Spa : early April-late Nov. – Casino – ✉ 67110 Alsace-Lorraine 1 B1

Paris 460 – Haguenau 23 – Sarreguemines 55 – Saverne 40 – Strasbourg 52

Office de tourisme, 6, place de l'Hôtel de Ville ✆ 03 88 80 89 70, Fax 03 88 80 37 01

Mercure without rest VISA
av. Foch – ✆ 03 88 80 84 48 – h5548@accor.com – Fax 03 88 80 84 40
59 rm – €62/88 €68/96, € 11 – 5 suites
◆ This establishment houses large, refined, renovated rooms and suites. Good soundproofing. Modern-style bar-lounge. Pleasant peaceful garden planted with trees.

Muller rm, rest, rest, VISA
av. de la Libération – ✆ 03 88 63 38 38 – hotel.muller@wanadoo.fr – Fax 03 88 63 38 39
43 rm – €50/63 €60/74, € 9 – ½ P € 48/58 – **Rest** – *(closed Sunday dinner and Monday dinner) (pre-book Sat - Sun)* Menu € 9,50 (weekdays)/37 – Carte € 18/40
◆ The hotel section of this well-kept establishment has a modern, solid wood and soft lights setting. Wainscoted dining room and modern veranda. Classic food and a few bistro-type dishes.

Le Bristol rest, VISA
pl. de l'Hôtel-de-Ville – ✆ 03 88 09 61 44 – hotel.lebristol@wanadoo.fr – Fax 03 88 09 01 20 – Closed 15 January-15 February
29 rm – €45/53 €53/90, € 8 – ½ P € 55/62 – **Rest** – Menu € 9 (weekday lunch), € 15/39 – Carte € 25/48
◆ This family hotel is in the centre of the spa resort: most of the rooms have been refurbished (wood furniture and bright colours) and well soundproofed. Traditional cooking served in a plush dining room overflowing onto the veranda on busy days.

Cully rm, VISA

r. de la République – 03 88 09 01 42 – hotel-cully@wanadoo.fr – Fax 03 88 09 05 80 – Closed 26 December-7 January, 6-28 February

34 rm – €46 €60/65, €8,50 – ½ P €49/51 – **Rest** – *(closed Sunday dinner and Monday)* Menu €11 (weekday lunch), €20/35 – Carte €23/48

◆ A hotel comprising two buildings in a busy street. Simple, functional and well-kept rooms which are being gradually renovated. Traditional cuisine served in an Alsace-style dining area or under the trees in fine weather.

L'Atelier du Sommelier VISA

35 r. des Acacias, 2 km on towards the sports complex – 03 88 09 06 25 – stephane.knecht@wanadoo.fr – Closed 11-26 August, 23 February-10 March, Monday and Tuesday

Rest – Menu €21 (weekday lunch), €27/50 – Carte €32/51

◆ Pleasant rustic setting dedicated to the glory of Bacchus. Light-coloured wooden furniture, stained glass, wine cases (boutique). Unfussy, focused dishes and fine wine list.

NIEDERSCHAEFFOLSHEIM – 67 Bas-Rhin – 315 K4 – pop. 1 268 – alt. 185 m – 67500 1 B1

Paris 473 – Haguenau 7 – Saverne 35 – Strasbourg 28

Au Bœuf Rouge with rm rest, VISA

39 r. du Gén. de Gaulle – 03 88 73 81 00 – auboeufrouge@wanadoo.fr – Fax 03 88 73 89 71 – Closed 15 July-4 August and 23 February-9 March

13 rm – €66 €70, €9 – ½ P €66/70 – **Rest** – *(Closed Sunday dinner, Tuesday lunch and Monday)* Menu €28/69 – Carte €56/65

◆ The same family has been welcoming guests to this renowned Alsatian restaurant since 1880. Elegant, classic-style dining room with wooden panelling. Classical cuisine with a modern twist.

NIEDERSTEINBACH – 67 Bas-Rhin – 315 K2 – pop. 155 – alt. 225 m – 67510 Alsace-Lorraine 1 B1

Paris 460 – Bitche 24 – Haguenau 33 – Lembach 8 – Strasbourg 66 – Wissembourg 23

Cheval Blanc rest, rest, VISA

11 r. Principale – 03 88 09 55 31 – contact@hotel-cheval-blanc.fr – Fax 03 88 09 50 24 – Closed 18 June-3 July, 24 November-4 December and 28 January – 6 March

25 rm – €47 €64, €9,50 – 1 suite – ½ P €55

Rest – *(closed Thurs.)* Menu €18 (weekdays)/55 – Carte €29/64

◆ Beautiful, traditional inn, housing stylish and perfectly-kept rooms. Choose those away from the road. In the restaurant, you can savour hearty, regional cooking in a rustic Alsatian setting in wooden "stubes".

in Wengelsbach Northwest: 5 km by D 190 – 67510

Au Wasigenstein VISA

32 r. Principale – 03 88 09 50 54 – wasigenstein@wanadoo.fr – Fax 03 88 09 50 54 – Closed mid January-end-February, Monday and Tuesday except holidays

Rest – Menu €12, €21/30 – Carte €16/35

◆ Small family business in a peaceful and charming village. One of the dining rooms, with a pleasant country-style decor, is adorned with an earthenware stove. Fine terrace.

NIEUIL – 16 Charente – 324 N4 – pop. 907 – alt. 150 m – 16270 39 C2

Paris 434 – Angoulême 42 – Confolens 24 – Limoges 66 – Nontron 58 – Ruffec 34

East by D 739 and secondary road: 2 km – 16270 Nieuil

Château de Nieuil without rest VISA

– 05 45 71 36 38 – chateaunieuilhotel@wanadoo.fr – Fax 05 45 71 46 45 – Open March-November

12 rm – €113/238 €125/265, €16 – 3 suites – €245/400

◆ A Renaissance château, once a hunting lodge used by Francis I, in a vast wooded park. Handsome Empire, Art deco, classical, etc. rooms.

La Grange aux Oies

in the grounds of the château – ✆ 05 45 71 81 24 – info@grange-aux-oies.com – Fax 05 45 71 81 25 – Closed 25 March-4 April and 2 November-12 December
Rest – Menu (€ 26 bi), € 45 bi/60 bi – Carte € 38/53
♦ Pleasant dining room combining modern decor with stone features in the former stables of the Château de Nieuil. Updated cuisine in keeping with the spirit of the place.

NIEUL – 87 Haute-Vienne – 325 E5 – pop. 1 350 – alt. 396 m – ✉ 87510 24 B2

Paris 391 – Limoges 16 – Bellac 27 – Guéret 86

Les Justices with rm

3 km south-east on Limoges road – ✆ 05 55 75 84 54 – Closed Sunday dinner, Monday and public holiday dinner
3 rm – €45 €45, € 7,50 – **Rest** – *(number of covers limited, pre-book)* Menu € 26/32 – Carte € 26/41
♦ With its collections of porcelain, brightly dressed costume dolls, engraved glass and exotic plants, the decor in this restaurant is homely, if a little twee. Traditional cuisine. Clean, retro-style guestrooms with fake-fur blankets on the beds.

NIEULLE-SUR-SEUDRE – 17 Charente-Maritime – 324 D5 – pop. 643 – alt. 3 m – ✉ 17600 38 A2

Paris 503 – Poitiers 170 – La Rochelle 60 – Rochefort 30 – Saintes 32

Le Logis de Port Paradis

12 r. de Port Paradis – ✆ 05 46 85 37 38 – logis.portparadis@wanadoo.fr
5 rm – €56/66 €60/90 – **Table d'hôte** – Menu € 28 bi
♦ The delightful rooms of this house typical of the Charentes region feature bedheads made out of old wood or slate salvaged from oyster farming sheds. Dine with the owners on regional dishes and hearty 100% homemade breakfasts.

NÎMES P – 30 Gard – 339 L5 – pop. 133 424 – Built-up area 148 889 – alt. 39 m – ✉ 30000 Provence 23 C3

Paris 706 – Lyon 251 – Marseille 123 – Montpellier 58

Nîmes-Arles-Camargue: ✆ 04 66 70 49 49, by ⑤: 8 km.

Office de tourisme, 6, rue Auguste ✆ 04 66 58 38 00, Fax 04 66 58 38 01

de Nimes Vacquerolles 1075 chemin du Golf, by D 999: 6 km, ✆ 04 66 23 33 33 ;

de Nimes Campagne Route de Saint Gilles, by Airport road: 11 km, ✆ 04 66 70 17 37.

Amphitheatre★★★ - Maison Carrée★★★ - Jardin de la Fontaine★★: Tour Magne★, ≤★ - Interior★ of the Jesuits chapel DU B - Carré d'Art★ - Musée d'Archéologie★ M1 - Musée du Vieux Nîmes M3 - Musée des Beaux-Arts★ M2.

Plans on following pages

Jardins Secrets without rest

3 r. Gaston-Maruejols – ✆ 04 66 84 82 64 – contact@jardinssecrets.net – Fax 04 66 84 27 47 BY m
12 rm – €195/220 €195/350, € 20 – 3 suites
♦ An 18C interior tastefully updated and modernised. Magnificent poolside garden planted with fragrant Mediterranean varieties and a splendid spa. A rare find in the town centre!

Imperator Concorde

quai de la Fontaine – ✆ 04 66 21 90 30 – hotel.imperator@wanadoo.fr – Fax 04 66 67 70 25 AX g
60 rm – €145/230 €160/250 – 3 suites – ½ P € 103/155
Rest – Menu € 30 bi/65 – Carte € 49/62
♦ This 1929 abode is laid out around a pretty Florentine patio with a fountain. Gradually renovated interior: spruced up rooms and a sitting room full of the opulence of yesteryear. Elegant restaurant, arranged as a gallery around the charming courtyard. Classic food.

NÎMES

Briçonnet (R.) . . . . **BY** 8
Cirque Romain (R. du) . . . . **AY** 13
Fontaine (Quai de la) . . . . **AX** 20
Gambetta (Bd) . . . . **ABX**
Gamel (Av. P.) . . . . **BZ** 22
Générac (R. de) . . . . **AYZ** 23
Mallarmé (R. Stéphane) . . . . . . **AX** 34
Martyrs de la Résistance (Pl. des) . . . . **AZ** 36
Mendès-France (Av. Pierre) . . . **BZ** 39
République (R. de la) . . . . **AYZ**
Ste-Anne (R.) . . . . **AY** 46
Verdun (R. de) . . . . **AY** 47

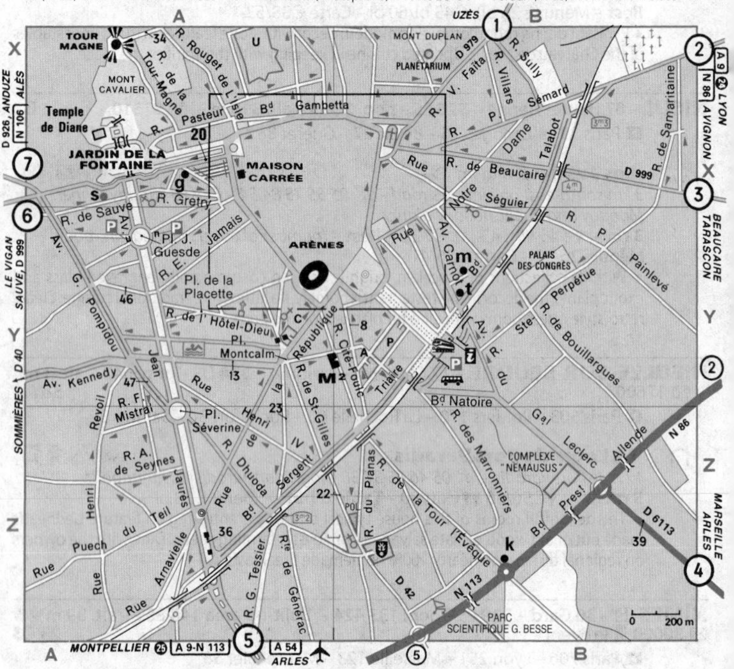

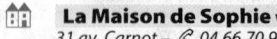

Vatel rest,

140 r. Vatel – ✆ 04 66 62 57 57 – hotel@vatel.fr – Fax 04 66 62 57 50

46 rm – 🛉€ 120/130 🛉🛉€ 130/140, ☕ € 12

Rest *Les Palmiers* – *(closed August, Sunday dinner, Monday and lunch except Sunday)* Menu € 30 (weekdays)/110 – Carte € 52/75

Rest *Le Provençal* – Menu (€ 20), € 25/58

◆ Students from the Ecole Hotelière work hard for your wellbeing. Rooms are spacious and comfortable with marble bathrooms. Classic, Southern-style food and a lovely view of the town can be found at Les Palmiers. Bountiful Provençal-inspired buffets.

Novotel Atria Nîmes Centre

5 bd de Prague – ✆ 04 66 76 56 56 – h0985@accor.com – Fax 04 66 76 56 59 DV **f**

119 rm – 🛉€ 100/185 🛉🛉€ 100/185, ☕ € 13 – 7 suites

Rest – Menu € 22/24 – Carte € 19/38

◆ The rooms of this hotel, refurbished from top to toe, are greatly appreciated by business guests, as is its conference centre. Modern interior and fine view of Nîmes from the top floor. Breakfast served on the patio. Restaurant in line with the chain's requirements.

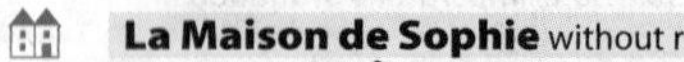

La Maison de Sophie without rest

31 av. Carnot – ✆ 04 66 70 96 10 – lamaisondesophie@orange.fr – Fax 04 66 36 00 47 BY **t**

8 rm – 🛉€ 130/232 🛉🛉€ 130/290, ☕ € 15

◆ Marble lobby, fine staircase, period stained glass, cosy sitting rooms and bookcases: a pleasant homeliness pervades Sophie's plush 1900s-style property.

NÎMES

Arènes (Bd des) . . . . **CV** 2
Aspic (R. de l') . . . . **CUV**
Auguste (R.) . . . . **CU** 4
Bernis (R. de) . . . . **CV** 6
Chapitre (R. du) . . . . **CU** 12
Courbet (Bd Amiral) . . . . . **DUV** 14
Crémieux (R.) . . . . **DU** 16
Curaterie (R.) . . . . **DU** 17
Daudet (Bd Alphonse) . . . . . **CU** 18
Fontaine (Quai de la) . . . . . . **CU** 20
Gambetta (Bd) . . . . **CDU**
Grand'Rue . . . . **DU** 24
Guizot (R.) . . . . **CU** 26
Halles (R. des) . . . . **CU** 27
Horloge (R. de l') . . . . **CU** 28
Libération (Bd de la) . . . . . . **DV** 30
Madeleine (R. de la) . . . . . . **CU** 32
Maison Carrée (Pl. de la) . . . . **CU** 33
Marchands (R. des) . . . . **CU** 35
Nationale (R.) . . . . **CDU**
Perrier (R. Gén.) . . . . **CU**
Prague (Bd de) . . . . **DV** 42
République (R. de la) . . . . . . **CV** 43
Saintenac (Bd E.) . . . . **DU** 45
Victor-Hugo (Bd) . . . . **CUV**
Violettes (R.) . . . . **CV** 49

New Hôtel la Baume without rest
21 r. Nationale – 04 66 76 28 42 – nimeslabaume@new-hotel.com – Fax 04 66 76 28 45 DU **b**
34 rm – €105 €135, €10
◆ This pleasant private mansion is embellished with a charming open-air square courtyard, a vaulted breakfast room and warm, tastefully renovated guestrooms.

L'Orangerie rm,
755 r. Tour-de-l'Évêque – 04 66 84 50 57 – hr-orang@wanadoo.fr – Fax 04 66 29 44 55 BZ **k**
37 rm – €75/99 €79/129, €10 – ½ P €65/69
Rest – *(closed Sat. lunchtime)* Menu (€17), €23 – Carte €31/39
◆ Built in the style of an old farmhouse. Pretty Provençal decorated rooms (some have terraces and others Jacuzzis), six are brand new. Traditional menu rich in regional produce.

Kyriad without rest
10 r. Roussy – 04 66 76 16 20 – contact@hotel-kyriad-nimes.com – Fax 04 66 67 65 99 DU **n**
28 rm – €60/71 €69/71, €9,50
◆ A pleasant town centre hotel: practical garage, small, cheerful, well-soundproofed rooms (two with a terrace and view over the Nîmes rooftops), endearing welcome.

Le Lisita (Olivier Douet)

2 bd des Arènes – ✆ 04 66 67 29 15 – restaurant@lelisita.com – Fax 04 66 67 25 32 – Closed Sunday and Monday CV **h**

Rest – Menu € 35 (lunch), € 54/78 – Carte € 84/117

Spec. Fleurs de courgette farcies à la brandade. Pigeon aux pois gourmands et girolles. Abricots rôtis, amandes fraîches, sorbet verveine. **Wines** Costières de Nîmes, Vin de pays du Duché d'Uzès.

◆ An enviable location near the arenas. Gourmet dishes with a southern twist are served in the tasteful, modern interior of the stone built dining room or on the terrace beneath plane trees.

Aux Plaisirs des Halles

4 r. Littré – ✆ 04 66 36 01 02 – Fax 04 66 36 08 00 – Closed autumn and February school holidays, Sunday and Monday CU **r**

Rest – Menu € 20 (weekday lunch), € 25/55 – Carte € 46/64

◆ A handsome modern dining room (woodwork, designer furniture) and a pleasant flower-decked patio for summer dining. Generous tasty cuisine; fine list of regional wines.

Le Bouchon et L'Assiette

5 bis r. de Sauve – ✆ 04 66 62 02 93 – Fax 04 66 62 03 57 – Closed14 July-15 August, 2-17 January, Tuesday and Wednesday AX **s**

Rest – Menu € 17 (weekday lunch), € 27/45 – Carte € 34/41

◆ This restaurant has a particularly well-designed décor with paintings and antique objects, as well as a very friendly reception. You'll find tasty seasonal cooking at the table.

Le Magister

5 r. Nationale – ✆ 04 66 76 11 00 – le.magister@wanadoo.fr – Fax 04 66 67 21 05 – Closed Saturday lunch and Sunday DU **q**

Rest – Menu € 21 (lunch), € 26/35 – Carte € 33/49

◆ Art exhibitions adorn the well worn, wood panelled walls of this welcoming chalet type restaurant. Appetising regional fare.

Shogun

38 bd Victor-Hugo – ✆ 04 66 27 59 88 – restaurant.shogun@wanadoo.fr – Fax 04 66 64 23 92 – Closed 4-12 May, 3-21 August, 12-15 September, 12-19 January, Sunday and Monday CV **v**

Rest – Menu € 14 (weekday lunch), € 38/48 – Carte € 44/65

◆ People come from far and near to sample the talented creations of the chef and the Sushi master. Find the inimitable art of hospitality in this feng shui restaurant.

Le Darling

40 r. Madeleine – ✆ 04 66 67 04 99 – restaurantledarling@wanadoo.fr – Fax 04 66 67 04 99 – Closed 1st-23 July, 31 December-10 January, lunch except Sunday October-May and Wednesday CU **d**

Rest – *(number of covers limited, pre-book)* Menu € 42/45 – Carte € 50/70

◆ Smart contemporary interior for this in vogue establishment: stone vaults, gold leaf embellished fresco, and creative cuisine with successfully unusual combinations.

L'Exaequo

11 r. Bigot – ✆ 04 66 21 71 96 – l.exaequo@wanadoo.fr – Fax 04 66 21 77 96 – Closed 15-25 August, 24 December-2 January, Saturday lunch and Sunday CV **a**

Rest – Menu (€ 15), € 19 (weekday lunch), € 37/75 bi – Carte approx. € 45

◆ Near the arenas, a distinctive lounge ambience in reds and oranges (background music and designer furniture), delightful patio with water sprays, and current cuisine.

Le Marché sur la Table

10 r. Littré – ✆ 04 66 67 22 50 – Fax 04 66 76 19 78 – Closed Monday and Tuesday CU **d**

Rest – Menu € 33 – Carte approx. € 40

◆ A friendly little restaurant offering bistro cuisine based on fresh ingredients, sourced by the owner every morning in the local market.

in Marguerittes by ② and D 981: 8 km – pop. 8 181 – alt. 60 m – ✉ 30320

L'Hacienda rm, rest,
Le Mas de Brignon, south-east: 2 km on minor road – ✆ 04 66 75 02 25 – contact@hotel-hacienda-nimes.fr – Fax 04 66 75 45 58 – Open mid March-end November
12 rm – †€ 72/142 ††€ 82/162, ☕ € 15 – ½ P € 92/132 – **Rest** – *(dinner only)* Menu € 33 (weekdays)/44 – Carte € 50/63
◆ Tucked away in the countryside, this secluded house offers quiet, spacious rooms furnished in a charming Provençal style. The two dining rooms, one for winter and one for summer, command a direct view of the kitchen and pool. Tasty, updated traditional fare.

in Garons by ⑤, D 42 and D 442: 9 km – pop. 3 692 – alt. 90 m – ✉ 30128

Alexandre (Michel Kayser)
2 r. X.-Tronc – ✆ 04 66 70 08 99 – restaurant.alexandre@wanadoo.fr – Fax 04 66 70 01 75 – Closed 24 August-9 September, 5-13 January, 16 February-3 March, Tuesday September-June, Sunday except lunch September-June and Monday
Rest – Menu € 44 bi (weekday lunch), € 62/107 – Carte € 89/142
Spec. Ile flottante aux truffes sur velouté de cèpes (September to April). Filet de rouget de petit bateau, raviole de picholine. Calisson de pied, langue et ris d'agneau, aligot. **Wines** Costières de Nîmes blanc et rouge.
◆ Tasty Provençal cooking available in elegant and resolutely modern dining rooms, opening onto a magnificent garden. Good choice of Languedoc-Roussillon wines.

NIORT – 79 Deux-Sèvres – **322** D7 – pop. 56 663 – **Built-up area 125 594** – alt. 24 m – ✉ 79000 **Atlantic Coast** 38 **B2**

Paris 408 – Bordeaux 184 – Nantes 142 – Poitiers 76 – La Rochelle 65

Office de tourisme, 16, rue du Petit Saint-Jean ✆ 05 49 24 18 79, Fax 05 49 24 98 90

de Niort Chemin du Grand Ormeau, South: 3 km near hippodrome, ✆ 05 49 09 01 41.

Keep★: salle de la chamoiserie et de la ganterie (shammy leather and glove room)★ - Le Pilori★.

Le Marais Poitevin★★.

Plan on following page

Mercure rm, rm,
80 bis av. de Paris – ✆ 05 49 24 29 29 – hotel.mercure@mercure-niort.fr – Fax 05 49 28 00 90 BY **a**
79 rm – †€ 85/153 ††€ 99/175, ☕ € 12,50 – ½ P € 88/110 – **Rest** – Menu (€ 20), € 26/29 – Carte € 30/42
◆ Modern building in a green environment. Large, well-equipped rooms that are being gradually renovated. Those in the new wing have modern-style furnishings. Elegant dining room in a veranda with a glass roof and terrace service in fine weather.

Niort Grand Hôtel without rest
32 av. de Paris – ✆ 05 49 24 22 21 – grandhotel-niort@wanadoo.fr – Fax 05 49 24 42 41 – Closed 24 December-1st January BY **v**
39 rm – †€ 56/68 ††€ 58/75, ☕ € 9
◆ A 1960s building with functional rooms which are gradually being renovated. Pleasant lounge; breakfast served in a conservatory or on a terrace surrounded by greenery.

Ambassadeur without rest
82 r. de la Gare – ✆ 05 49 24 00 38 – info@ambassadeur-hotel.com – Fax 05 49 24 94 38 – Closed 21 December-2 January BZ **b**
32 rm – †€ 52/62 ††€ 52/62, ☕ € 7
◆ Modern furnishings, warm colours and good soundproofing. The rooms in this hotel near the station have been renovated. Bistro-style breakfast room.

Sandrina without rest
43 av. St-Jean d'Angély, via ④ 200 m – ✆ 05 49 79 28 42 – hotelsandrina@wanadoo.fr – Fax 05 49 73 10 85 – Closed 24 December-4 January
18 rm – †€ 49 ††€ 51, ☕ € 6,50
◆ Hotel, between the railway station and hospital, fully redecorated in bright and modern shades. Perfectly well-kept, simple but stylish rooms. Closed car park.

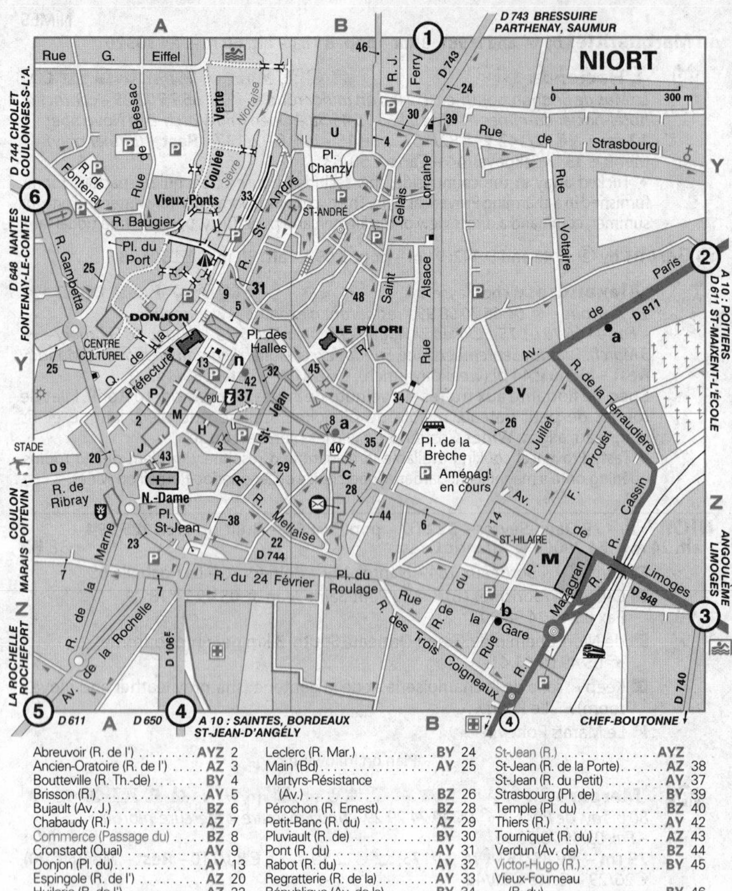

- Abreuvoir (R. de l') .... **AYZ** 2
- Ancien-Oratoire (R. de l') ..... **AZ** 3
- Boutteville (R. Th.-de) .... **BY** 4
- Brisson (R.) .... **AY** 5
- Bujault (Av. J.) .... **BZ** 6
- Chabaudy (R.) .... **AZ** 7
- Commerce (Passage du) ..... **BZ** 8
- Cronstadt (Quai) .... **AY** 9
- Donjon (Pl. du) .... **AY** 13
- Espingole (R. de l') .... **AZ** 20
- Huilerie (R. de l') .... **AZ** 22
- Largeau (R. Gén.) .... **AZ** 23
- Leclerc (R. Mar.) .... **BY** 24
- Main (Bd) .... **AY** 25
- Martyrs-Résistance (Av.) .... **BZ** 26
- Pérochon (R. Ernest) .... **BZ** 28
- Petit-Banc (R. du) .... **AZ** 29
- Pluviault (R. de) .... **BY** 30
- Pont (R. du) .... **AY** 31
- Rabot (R. du) .... **AY** 32
- Regratterie (R. de la) .... **AY** 33
- République (Av. de la) .... **BY** 34
- Ricard (R.) .... **BZ** 35
- St-Jean (R.) .... **AYZ**
- St-Jean (R. de la Porte) .... **AZ** 38
- St-Jean (R. du Petit) .... **AY** 37
- Strasbourg (Pl. de) .... **BY** 39
- Temple (Pl. du) .... **BZ** 40
- Thiers (R.) .... **AY** 42
- Tourniquet (R. du) .... **AZ** 43
- Verdun (Av. de) .... **BZ** 44
- Victor-Hugo (R.) .... **BY** 45
- Vieux-Fourneau (R. du) .... **BY** 46
- Yvers (R.) .... **BY** 48

XXX **La Belle Étoile** P VISA AE

115 quai M. Métayer, near western ring road -AY- West: 2.5 km – ✆ 05 49 73 31 29 – info@la-belle-etoile.fr – Fax 05 49 09 05 59 – Closed 4-25 August, Sunday dinner, Wednesday dinner and Monday

Rest – Menu (€ 22), € 29/79 bi – Carte € 48/72

◆ Along the Sèvre, house isolated from the ring road by a screen of greenery. Elegant dining room, decorated in the Directoire style. Old wine bottles in the window.

X **La Table des Saveurs** A/C VISA AE

9 r. Thiers – ✆ 05 49 77 44 35 – tablesaveurniort@wanadoo.fr – Fax 05 49 16 06 29 – Closed Sunday except holidays AY **n**

Rest – Menu € 17 (weekdays)/40 – Carte € 34/87

◆ This spacious restaurant, formerly a fabrics store, has been revived with modern, refined decor in varying shades of brown and white. Chocolate takes pride of place on the impressive dessert menu.

Mélane
1 pl. du Temple – 05 49 04 00 40 – contact@lemelane.com – Fax 05 49 79 25 61 – Closed Sunday and Monday BZ **a**
Rest – Menu (€ 15), € 23/49 – Carte € 30/48
◆ This restaurant, well known to Niort's inhabitants, offers a menu that combines traditional and up-to-date dishes. Modern decor, adorned with photos and model boats.

La Rochelle road 4.5 km by ⑤ on D 611 – 79000 Niort

Tuilerie (Coq'corico)
– 05 49 09 12 45 – tuilerie@tuilerie.com – Fax 05 49 09 16 22 – Closed 23 February-7 March, Sunday dinner and Monday
Rest – Menu (€ 14), € 19/34 – Carte € 22/44
◆ A former farmhouse, converted into a restaurant, where poultry reigns both in your plate and on decorations. Who made both the chicken and the egg? The chef, of course!

in St-Liguaire 4,5 km West by D9 and secondary road – 79000 Niort

La Magnolière without rest
16 imp. de l'Abbaye, (near the church) – 05 49 35 36 06 – a.marchadier@lamagnoliere.fr – Fax 05 49 79 14 28 – Closed 22 December-1st January
3 rm – €76 €80
◆ Elegant, attractive house, overlooking the Sèvre Niortaise, where the scent of a magnificent magnolia fills the garden in springtime. Bijou-type rooms and cosy lounge, adorned with paintings.

NISSAN-LEZ-ENSERUNE – 34 Hérault – 339 D9 – pop. 2 907 – alt. 21 m – 34440 Languedoc-Roussillon-Tarn Gorges 22 B2

Paris 774 – Béziers 12 – Capestang 9 – Montpellier 82 – Narbonne 17
Office de tourisme, square Rene Dez 04 67 37 14 12
Oppidum d'Ensérune★: museum★, ≤★ Northwest: 5 km.

Résidence
35 av. Cave – 04 67 37 00 63 – contact@hotel-residence.com – Fax 04 67 37 68 63 – Closed 21 December-27 January
18 rm – €62/72 €65/75, € 10 – ½ P € 69/79 – **Rest** – Menu (€ 16), € 21, € 26/48 – Carte € 34/49
◆ Fine residence at the heart of a small village. Many rooms are furnished with antiques. Those in the wing (a former 19C wine-grower's house) are larger. In fine weather, enjoy a meal on the pleasant shaded terrace opposite the pool.

Le Plô without rest
7 av. de la Cave – 04 67 37 38 21 – patry.c@wanadoo.fr – Fax 04 67 37 38 21 – Open April-December
4 rm – €45/60 €45/80, € 9,50
◆ In the village centre, this impressive manor house is a hotel providing spacious rooms with a calm atmosphere and plenty of light. Pleasant hospitality provided.

NITRY – 89 Yonne – 319 G5 – pop. 371 – alt. 240 m – 89310 7 B1

Paris 195 – Auxerre 36 – Avallon 23 – Vézelay 31

Auberge la Beursaudière
9 chemin de Ronde – 03 86 33 69 69 – message@beursaudiere.com – Fax 03 86 33 69 60 – Closed 5-23 January
11 rm – €75/115 €75/115, € 10 – **Rest** – Menu (€ 19), € 25/38 – Carte € 26/61
◆ Rooms with character, breakfast rooms with vaulted ceilings and a medieval pigeon loft: the conversion of this old priory outbuilding has been particularly successful. Carefully-laid tables and country-style decor with waiters/waitresses in regional costume. Regional food and well-stocked cellar.

NOAILHAC – 81 Tarn – 338 G9 – pop. 712 – alt. 222 m – ✉ 81490 29 C2

Paris 730 – Toulouse 90 – Albi 55 – Béziers 99 – Carcassonne 61 – Castres 12

Hostellerie d'Oc

av. Charles Tailhades – ✆ 05 63 50 50 37 – Fax 05 63 50 50 37 – Closed 1st-15 September, January, Wednesday dinner and Monday

Rest – Menu € 11/32 – Carte € 23/43

◆ Former coaching inn converted into a restaurant, housing rustic dining rooms. Regional cooking mainly using local products.

NOAILLY – 42 Loire – 327 D3 – pop. 719 – alt. 240 m – ✉ 42640 44 A1

Paris 395 – Lyon 98 – Roanne 13 – Vichy 68

Château de la Motte

rest, VISA

La Motte Nord, 1,5 km – ✆ 04 77 66 64 60 – chateaudelamotte@wanadoo.fr – Fax 04 77 66 68 10 – Closed 12-19 March and 1st-7 October

6 rm – €68/100 €77/108, € 8 – ½ P € 65/81 – **Table d'hôte** – *(closed Sunday dinner)* Menu € 27 bi

◆ This 18-19C château nestles in sumptuous parkland. The bedrooms, decorated with period furniture, are named after famous authors. Lamartine, the most unusual room has a round bathtub in the tower. Homegrown produce takes pride of place on the traditional menu. Theme stays.

NOCÉ – 61 Orne – 310 N4 – see Bellême

NOEUX-LES-MINES – 62 Pas-de-Calais – 301 I5 – pop. 11 966 – alt. 29 m – ✉ 62290 Northern France and the Paris Region 30 B2

Paris 208 – Arras 28 – Béthune 5 – Bully-les-Mines 8 – Doullens 49 – Lens 17 – Lille 38

d'Olhain Houdain Parc départemental de Nature, South: 11 km by D 65 and D 301, ✆ 03 21 02 17 03.

Carrefour des Saveurs

VISA AE

94 rte Nationale – ✆ 03 21 26 74 74 – david.wojtkowiak@wanadoo.fr – Fax 03 21 27 12 14 – Closed 1st-21 August, 1st-10 January, Wednesday dinner, Sunday dinner and Monday

Rest – Menu (€ 17), € 21 (weekdays)/58 – Carte € 44/65

◆ This restaurant has a convivial dining room with stone and brick walls. Serving a range of appetising modern meals.

NOGARO – 32 Gers – 336 B7 – pop. 1 881 – alt. 98 m – ✉ 32110 28 A2

Paris 729 – Agen 88 – Auch 63 – Mont-de-Marsan 45 – Pau 72 – Tarbes 69

Office de tourisme, 81, rue Nationale ✆ 05 62 09 13 30, Fax 05 62 08 88 21

Solenca

rest, rest, VISA AE

– ✆ 05 62 09 09 08 – info@solenca.com – Fax 05 62 09 09 07

47 rm – €57/62 €62/67, € 8 – ½ P € 54/80

Rest – Menu € 11,50, € 14,50/32 – Carte € 30/51

◆ This hotel provides well-kept and well-furnished rooms with wifi connections, and a garden featuring a pool. Restaurant with exposed roof beams and a terrace facing the greenery. Regionally-inspired cuisine.

in Manciet Northeast: 9 km by N 124 – pop. 764 – alt. 131 m – ✉ 32370

La Bonne Auberge with rm

VISA AE

– ✆ 05 62 08 50 04 – labonneauberge32@orange.fr – Fax 05 62 08 58 84 Closed 2-16 January, Sunday evening and Monday

14 rm – €42 €52, € 8 – ½ P € 58

Rest – Menu € 15 bi/50 – Carte € 35/58

◆ This century-old building is home to a restaurant with two comfortable dining areas, one on the veranda and the other with a fireplace, wooden panelling and a collection of armagnac on display.

NOGENT – 52 Haute-Marne – 313 M5 – pop. 4 343 – alt. 410 m – ✉ 52800
Northern France and the Paris Region 14 **C3**

Paris 289 – Bourbonne-les-Bains 35 – Chaumont 24 – Langres 25 – Neufchâteau 53

Syndicat d'initiative, place du Général de Gaulle ✆ 03 25 03 69 18, Fax 03 25 03 69 18

Musée de la coutellerie de l'espace Pelletier - Musée du patrimoine coutelier.

Le Commerce

pl. Gén. de Gaulle – ✆ 03 25 31 81 14 – hotelcommerce.nogent@wanadoo.fr – Fax 03 25 31 74 00 – Closed 22 December-4 January and Sunday

19 rm – €38 €68, ☕ €8,50 – ½ P €55 – **Rest** – Menu €10,50 (lunch)/30 – Carte €27/46

♦ A good overnight stop opposite the town hall and near the Musée de la Coutellerie. Recently renovated rooms furnished in Louis Philippe style. Regional cuisine served to a choice of backdrop: the traditional restaurant or the more relaxed brasserie.

NOGENT-LE-ROI – 28 Eure-et-Loir – 311 F4 – pop. 4 142 – alt. 93 m – ✉ 28210
Northern France and the Paris Region 11 **B1**

Paris 77 – Ablis 35 – Chartres 28 – Dreux 19 – Maintenon 10 – Rambouillet 26

Syndicat d'initiative, Mairie ✆ 02 37 51 23 20

du Château de Maintenon Maintenon 1 route de Gallardon, Southeast: 8 km by D 983, ✆ 02 37 27 18 09.

Relais des Remparts

2 pl. Marché aux Légumes – ✆ 02 37 51 40 47 – Fax 02 37 51 40 47 Closed 7-28 August, 18 February-4 March, Monday dinner from November to February, Sunday dinner, Tuesday dinner and Wednesday

Rest – Menu €19 (weekdays)/38 – Carte €26/48

♦ The keys to this restaurant's success are tasty traditional cuisine, pleasant, efficient service and a harmoniously decorated and comfortable dining room.

Capucin Gourmand

1 r. Volaille – ✆ 02 37 51 96 00 – capucin-gourmand@wanadoo.fr – Fax 02 37 31 90 31 – Closed 24 August-2 September, Sunday dinner, Thursday dinner and Monday

Rest – Menu (€15), €21 (weekday lunch), €27/35 – Carte €33/48

♦ Stylish dining room occupying a narrow, 15C half-timbered house. Blue and yellow decor, adorned with paintings by local artists. Traditional repertoire.

NOGENT-LE-ROTROU – 28 Eure-et-Loir – 311 A6 – pop. 11 524 – alt. 116 m – ✉ 28400 Normandy 11 **B1**

Paris 146 – Alençon 65 – Chartres 54 – Châteaudun 55 – Le Mans 76

Office de tourisme, 44, rue Villette-Gaté ✆ 02 37 29 68 86, Fax 02 37 29 68 86

Plan on following page

Brit Hôtel du Perche without rest

r. de la Bruyère by ⑤ – ✆ 02 37 53 43 60 – hotelduperche@brithotel.fr – Fax 02 37 53 43 69

40 rm – €48/55 €55/66, ☕ €6,50

♦ A modern, colourful building on the outskirts of the town with bright, cosy bedrooms furnished in a characteristic Provençal spirit. Welcoming breakfast area.

Sully without rest

51 r. Viennes – ✆ 02 37 52 15 14 – hotel.sully@wanadoo.fr – Fax 02 37 52 15 20 – Closed 22 December-2 January Y **s**

40 rm – €55/59 €59/68, ☕ €7

♦ The Duke of Sully's tomb is located in the Hôtel-Dieu. The rooms in this modern building in a quiet area of Nogent are discreet and functional.

NOGENT-LE-ROTROU

Bouchers (R. des) . . . . Z 2
Bourg-le-Comte (R.) . . . . Z 3
Bretonnerie (R.) . . . . Z
Château-St-Jean (R.) . . . . Z
Croix-la-Comtesse (R.) . . . . . . Y
Deschanel (R.). . . . . YZ
Dr-Desplantes (R.) . . . . Z 8
Foch (Av. Mar.). . . . . Y 9
Fuye (R. de la). . . . . YZ 10
Giroust (R.). . . . . Y 12
Gouverneur (R.) . . . . YZ 13
Marches-St-Jean (R. des) . . . . Z 14
Paty (R. du). . . . . Z 15
Poupardières (R. des) . . . . . . Z 16
Prés (Av. des). . . . . Y
République (Pl. de la). . . . . . . Z 17
Rhône (R. de). . . . . Z 18
St-Hilaire (R.) . . . . Y
St-Laurent (R.) . . . . Z 20
St-Martin (R.). . . . . Y
Sully (R. de) . . . . YZ 23
Villette-Gaté (R.). . . . . Y 25

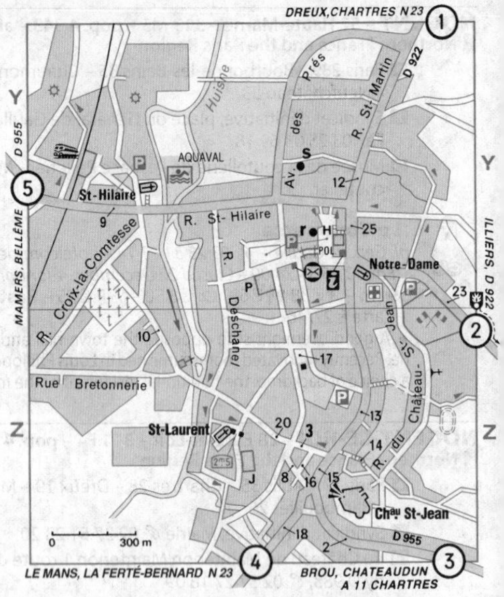

Au Lion d'Or without rest

28 pl. St-Pol – ☎ 02 37 52 01 60 – hotelauliondor@wanadoo.fr – Fax 02 37 52 23 82 – Closed 3-28 August, 31 October-5 November and 26 December-4 January

18 rm – †€ 46/56 ††€ 55/56, ☕ € 6,50 p. 4 Y **r**

◆ A small, practical town-centre hotel with fully-renovated rooms (cerused furniture, colourful fabrics) and equipped with brand new bathrooms.

L' Alambic

20 av. de Paris, at Margon 1.5 km via ① – ☎ 02 37 52 19 03 – joel.tremeaux@wanadoo.fr – Closed 4-25 August, 22-30 September, 18-28 February, Wednesday dinner, Sunday dinner and Monday

Rest – Menu € 15 (weekdays)/39 – Carte € 38/55

◆ This former "roadside café" is now a smart restaurant housing dining rooms in bright shades of red, green and yellow. Traditional cuisine, including a speciality: calf's head.

in L'Ambition 10 km by ③ and D 955 – ✉ 28480 Vichères

Les Vallées du Perche rm,

– ☎ 02 37 29 47 58 – lesvalleesduperche@tiscali.fr – Fax 02 37 29 91 55 – Closed 2-23 January

14 rm – †€ 38 ††€ 45/50, ☕ € 6 – ½ P € 42

Rest – *(closed Sunday dinner, Monday lunch and Tuesday lunch)* Menu € 11,50/30 – Carte € 20/48

◆ The rooms are in the annex of this small country inn. Some are new, while the others remain functional, simple and pleasant. Good soundproofing. Restaurant dining room with a country setting and traditional cuisine.

NOGENT-SUR-MARNE – 94 Val-de-Marne – 312 D2 – 101 27 – see Paris, Area

Luxury pad or humble abode?
X and 🏠 denote categories of comfort.

NOGENT-SUR-SEINE – 10 Aube – 313 B3 – pop. 5 963 – alt. 67 m – ✉ 10400 Northern France and the Paris Region 13 A2

Paris 105 – Épernay 83 – Fontainebleau 66 – Provins 19 – Sens 47 – Troyes 56

Domaine des Graviers rm, rest,

30 r. des Graviers – ☎ 03 25 21 81 90 VISA MC AE
– info@domaine-des-graviers.com – Fax 03 25 21 81 91
– Closed 27 July-17 August and 21 December-4 January
26 rm – €69/114 €69/114, ☕ €11 – **Rest** – *(Closed Saturday and Sunday) (dinner only) (resident only)* Menu €25/28

◆ This fine 1899 residence and its outbuildings lie in a 17-ha park. Elegant lounge and pleasant rooms furnished diversely. Crazy golf. Fine view of the estate's venerable trees; traditional fare.

Beau Rivage with rm rm, VISA MC AE

r. Villiers-aux-Choux – ☎ 03 25 39 84 22 – aubeaurivage@wanadoo.fr
– Fax 03 25 39 18 32 – Closed 18 August-2 September, 16 February-10 March, Sunday evening and Monday
10 rm – €58 €68, ☕ €9 – ½ P €70 – **Rest** – Menu €22/43 – Carte €45/62

◆ Modern dining room, bucolic terrace on the banks of the Seine, fine cooking and spruce rooms - four good reasons for stopping over at the Beau Rivage.

Auberge du Cygne de la Croix VISA MC

22 r. Ponts – ☎ 03 25 39 91 26 – cygnedelacroix@wanadoo.fr – Fax 03 25 39 81 79
– Closed 24 December-5 January, 23 February-2 March, Sunday dinner, Tuesday dinner and Monday except lunch April-September and Wednesday October-March
Rest – Menu €20 (weekday lunch), €25/50 – Carte €32/63

◆ A former 16C coaching inn, where two countrified dining rooms (the one at the rear is lighter) a peaceful courtyard-terrace and traditional recipes await.

NOIRLAC – 18 Cher – 323 K6 – see St-Amand-Montrond

NOIRMOUTIER (ÎLE) – 85 Vendée – 316 C6 – see Île de Noirmoutier

NOISY-LE-GRAND – 93 Seine-Saint-Denis – 305 G7 – 101 18 – see Paris, Area

NOIZAY – 37 Indre-et-Loire – 317 O4 – pop. 1 155 – alt. 56 m – ✉ 37210 11 B2

Paris 230 – Amboise 11 – Blois 44 – Tours 21 – Vendôme 49

Château de Noizay VISA MC AE

rte de Chançay – ☎ 02 47 52 11 01 – noizay@relaischateaux.com
– Fax 02 47 52 04 64 – Closed 16 January-14 March
19 rm – €145/285 €145/285, ☕ €20 – ½ P €158/228
Rest – *(closed Wednesday lunch, Thursday lunch and Tuesday)* Menu €38 (weekday lunch), €51/76 – Carte €62/70

◆ This 16C château is nestled in a park, dominating the village and its vineyards. Large rooms with personal touches and fine furniture. Those in the outbuilding are more modern. The restaurant is comprised of elegant plush rooms serving up-to-date cuisine and Loire Valley wines.

NOLAY – 21 Côte-d'Or – 320 H8 – pop. 1 547 – alt. 299 m – ✉ 21340 Burgundy-Jura

Paris 316 – Autun 30 – Beaune 20 – Chalon-sur-Saône 34 – Dijon 64 7 A3

Office de tourisme, 24, rue de la République ☎ 03 80 21 80 73, Fax 03 80 21 80 73

site★ of the Château de la Rochepot East: 5 km - Site★ of the Cirque du Bout-du-Monde Northeast: 5 km.

Du Parc rest, VISA MC

3 pl. Hôtel-de-Ville – ☎ 03 80 21 78 88 – Fax 03 80 21 86 39
– Open 15 March-30 November
14 rm – €61/64 €64/96, ☕ €10 – ½ P €59/72 – **Rest** – *(open 1st April-30 November)* Menu €14 (weekday lunch), €18/39 – Carte €24/45

◆ A former 16C coaching inn. It offers small, fresh and well-soundproofed bedrooms, with simple furniture. Exposed framework in the second-floor rooms. A small rustic dining room with beams and a fireplace. Pleasant terrace courtyard

De la Halle without rest VISA MC
pl. des Halles – ☎ 03 80 21 76 37 – noelle.pocheron@wanadoo.fr – Fax 03 80 21 76 37
14 rm – †€ 46/54 ††€ 46/54, ☕ € 8
◆ The two main buildings, set on either side of an interior courtyard decked with flowers, face the 14C covered market. Rather modest, but well-kept bedrooms, which are bigger at the back.

LES NONIÈRES – **26 Drôme** – **332** G5 – **alt. 282 m** – ✉ **26410** 45 **C3**
Paris 648 – Die 25 – Gap 84 – Grenoble 73 – Valence 91

Le Mont-Barral VISA MC
– ☎ 04 75 21 12 21 – mtbarral@aol.com – Fax 04 75 21 12 70 – Closed 15 November-20 February, Tuesday dinner and Wednesday except school holidays
21 rm – †€ 50/52 ††€ 50/56, ☕ € 10 – ½ P € 51/57 – **Rest** – Menu € 15 (weekdays)/40 – Carte € 23/34
◆ A mountain stopping place for Upper Drôme hikers. Bedrooms fitted out in the newly-built extension are bigger. Modest rustic-style restaurant. Traditional dishes and a "country" menu.

NONTRON – **24 Dordogne** – **329** E2 – **pop. 3 500** – **alt. 260 m** – ✉ **24300**
Dordogne-Berry-Limousin 4 **C1**
Paris 454 – Angoulême 45 – Libourne 135 – Limoges 68 – Périgueux 50 – Rochechouart 42
Office de tourisme, 3, avenue du Général Leclerc ☎ 05 53 56 25 50, Fax 05 53 60 34 13

Grand Hôtel P VISA MC
3 pl. A. Agard – ☎ 05 53 56 11 22 – grand-hotel-pelisson@wanadoo.fr – Fax 05 53 56 59 94 – Closed Sunday dinner October-June
23 rm – †€ 50 ††€ 61, ☕ € 7 – ½ P € 60 – **Rest** – Menu € 22 (weekdays)/52 – Carte € 29/55
◆ This former coaching inn, with an "Old France" atmosphere, is located in the town famous for its boxwood knives. Regularly-maintained, country-style bedrooms. Regional dishes served in a rustic dining room or on the terrace overlooking the garden.

NONZA – **2B Haute-Corse** – **345** F3 – **see Corse**

NOTRE-DAME-DE-BELLECOMBE – **73 Savoie** – **333** M3 – **pop. 510** – **alt. 1 150 m** – **Winter sports : 1 150/2 070** 19 – ✉ **73590** **French Alps** 46 **F1**
Paris 585 – Albertville 25 – Annecy 54 – Chambéry 76 – Chamonix-Mt-Blanc 43
Office de tourisme, Chef Lieu ☎ 04 79 31 61 40, Fax 04 79 31 67 09

Ferme de Victorine P VISA MC AE D
Le Planay, 3 km east by Les Saisies road – ☎ 04 79 31 63 46 – Fax 04 79 31 79 91 – Closed 20 June-3 July, 10 November-16 December, Sunday dinner and Monday from April to June and from September to November
Rest – Menu € 21 (weekday lunch), € 26/48 – Carte € 31/60
◆ The farmhouse of Victorine, the grandmother, has been successfully converted into a fine bar overlooking the stable and the milking stalls. Appealing country atmosphere in the dining room serving tasty traditional and local cuisine.

NOTRE-DAME-DE-BONDEVILLE – **76 Seine-Maritime** – **304** G5 – **see Rouen**

NOTRE-DAME-DE-GRAVENCHON – **76 Seine-Maritime** – **304** D5 – **pop. 8 618** – **alt. 35 m** – ✉ **76330** **Normandy** 33 **C2**
Paris 176 – Bolbec 14 – Le Havre 40 – Rouen 51 – Yvetot 25

Pascal Saunier rest, P VISA MC AE
1 r. Amiral Grasset – ☎ 02 35 38 60 67 – info@hotelpascalsaunier.com – Fax 02 35 38 30 64 – Closed 29 July-9 August and 21 December-3 January
29 rm – †€ 68 ††€ 74, ☕ € 10 – ½ P € 80 – **Rest** – *(closed August, 21 December-3 January, Friday dinner, Saturday and Sunday)* Carte € 37/57
◆ A big half-timbered residence (1930), surrounded by a garden, with large, bright and simply furnished rooms. Breakfast buffet. The restaurant's picture windows offer a view of the Port-Jérôme complex.

NOTRE-DAME-DE-LIVAYE – 14 Calvados – 303 M5 – pop. 130 – alt. 27 m – ✉ 14340 33 C2

Paris 185 – Caen 36 – Le Havre 86 – Lisieux 16 – Hérouville-Saint-Clair 39

Aux Pommiers de Livaye

– ☎ 02 31 63 01 28 – bandb-normandy@wanadoo.fr – Fax 02 31 63 73 63 – Closed mid November-beg. February

5 rm – €75 €89 – **Table d'hôte** – Menu €25/35

◆ Half-timbered Norman farm (1720) and barns with personalised rooms (floral décor, four-poster beds, antique or reproduction furniture). Apple orchard and pretty garden. Regional dishes served in a rustic dining room; home-produced cider.

NOTRE-DAME-DE-MONTS – 85 Vendée – 316 D6 – pop. 1 528 – alt. 6 m – ✉ 85690 34 A3

Paris 457 – Challans 22 – Nantes 72 – Noirmoutier-en-l'Ile 26 – La Roche-sur-Yon 66

Office de tourisme, 6, rue de la Barre ☎ 02 51 58 84 97, Fax 02 51 58 15 56

La Barre-de-Monts: Centre de découverte du Marais breton-vendéen North: 6 km

L'Orée du Bois

rm, VISA

14 r. Frisot – ☎ 02 51 58 84 04 – hoteloreedubois@aol.com – Fax 02 51 58 81 78 – Open 1st April-30 September

30 rm – €50/65 €50/70, €7,50 – ½ P €49/55 – **Rest** – Menu €19/29

◆ Bright, practical accommodation occupying three buildings around a swimming pool, in a residential district. Those on the ground floor have a terrace.

NOTRE-DAME D'ORSAN – 18 Cher – 323 J6 – see le Châtelet

NOTRE-DAME-DU-GUILDO – 22 Côtes-d'Armor – 309 I3 – pop. 3 187 – alt. 52 m – ✉ 22380 10 C1

Paris 427 – Rennes 94 – Saint-Brieuc 49 – Saint-Malo 32

Château du Val d'Arguenon without rest

VISA

1 km east on D 786 ✉ 22380 St-Cast – ☎ 02 96 41 07 03 – chateau@chateauduval.com – Fax 02 96 41 02 67 – Open Easter-All Saints'

5 rm – €90/140 €90/150

◆ This fine family-run residence (16C-18C) nestles in a park that runs down to the sea. Stylish interior with period furniture in the lounge and rooms.

NOTRE-DAME-DU-HAMEL – 27 Eure – 304 D8 – pop. 194 – alt. 200 m – ✉ 27390 33 C2

Paris 158 – L'Aigle 21 – Argentan 48 – Bernay 28 – Évreux 55 – Lisieux 40 – Vimoutiers 28

Le Moulin de la Marigotière

VISA

D 45 – ☎ 02 32 44 58 11 – contact@moulin-marigotiere.com – Fax 02 32 44 40 12 – Closed 17 February-2 March, Monday dinner except July-August, Sunday dinner, Tuesday and Wednesday

Rest – Menu €30 (weekday lunch), €39/68 – Carte €48/85

◆ Former mill converted into a restaurant, where you can enjoy traditional meals in a stylish atmosphere. Pretty park where the Charentonne flows in the background.

NOTRE-DAME-DU-PÉ – 72 Sarthe – 310 H8 – pop. 313 – alt. 73 m – ✉ 72300

Paris 262 – Angers 51 – La Flèche 28 – Nantes 140 35 C2

La Reboursière

rm,

1 km south on the D 134 and minor road – ☎ 02 43 92 92 41 – gilles-chappuy@wanadoo.fr – Fax 02 43 92 92 41

4 rm – €55 €65 – ½ P €56 – **Table d'hôte** – Menu €23 bi

◆ A former, restored farmhouse (mid-19C), surrounded by a park, which guarantees peaceful nights for guests in its large rooms, furnished with antiques. Traditional cuisine, served with a smile, in an authentic rustic setting.

NOUAN-LE-FUZELIER – 41 Loir-et-Cher – 318 J6 – pop. 2 319 – alt. 113 m – ✉ 41600

12 **C2**

Paris 177 – Blois 59 – Cosne-sur-Loire 74 – Gien 56 – Lamotte-Beuvron 8 – Orléans 44

Syndicat d'initiative, place de la Gare ✆ 02 54 88 76 75

Les Charmilles without rest

D 122-rte Pierrefitte-sur-Sauldre – ✆ 02 54 88 73 55 – hotel.lescharmilles@tele2.fr – Fax 02 54 88 74 55 – Closed February

12 rm – **†**€ 41/44 **††**€ 48/54, ☕ € 7 – 1 suite

◆ A tasteful, early-20C residence nestled in a park with a pond. You'll sleep in rustic-style rooms, which are spacious and well kept. Home-made pastries.

Le Dahu

14 r. H. Chapron – ✆ 02 54 88 72 88 – ledahu.restaurant@wanadoo.fr – Fax 02 54 88 21 28 – Closed 26 March-18 April, 13 November-4 December, 2 January-9 February, Tuesday dinner from 15 November-15 April, Wednesday and Thursday

Rest – Menu € 29/41 – Carte € 47/56

◆ In the middle of a lush garden (summer terrace), an old shepherd's dwelling converted into a restaurant. Sitting under the exposed framework of the rustic dining room, you'll really feel in the country!

NOUILHAN – 65 Hautes-Pyrénées – 342 M4 – pop. 175 – alt. 196 m – ✉ 65500

Paris 771 – Pau 47 – Tarbes 24 – Toulouse 144

28 **A2**

Les 3 B with rm

8 rte des Pyrénées, D 935 – ✆ 05 62 96 79 78 – restaurantdes3b@wanadoo.fr

7 rm – **†**€ 40/45 **††**€ 40/45, ☕ € 5 – ½ P € 45

Rest – *(closed Wednesday)* Menu € 18/37 – Carte approx. € 37

◆ Former family farmhouse converted into a restaurant. Enjoy generous traditional cuisine, prepared with fresh produce, in a simple and warm setting. The brand new rooms are pleasant and practical.

LE NOUVION-EN-THIÉRACHE – 02 Aisne – 306 E2 – pop. 2 917 – alt. 185 m – ✉ 02170

37 **D1**

Paris 198 – Avesnes-sur-Helpe 20 – Guise 21 – Hirson 25 – St-Quentin 49 – Vervins 27

Syndicat d'initiative, Hôtel de Ville ✆ 03 23 97 98 06, Fax 03 23 97 98 04

Paix

37 r. J. Vimont-Vicary – ✆ 03 23 97 04 55 – la.paix.pierrart@wanadoo.fr – Fax 03 23 98 98 39 – Closed 18 August-5 September, 26 December-2 January, 13 February-9 March and Sunday dinner

15 rm – **†**€ 55 **††**€ 55/71, ☕ € 10 – ½ P € 53/62

Rest – *(closed Saturday lunch, Sunday dinner and Monday)*
Menu (€ 15), € 20 (weekdays)/50 – Carte € 27/52

◆ A well-kept hotel, whose various bedrooms are fitted out differently. Some have been redecorated in a more modern style. Hospitable welcome. Bricks, mirrors, pastel tones and ornaments make up the attractive decor of the dining room. Classic menu.

NOUZERINES – 23 Creuse – 325 J2 – see Boussac

NOVALAISE – 73 Savoie – 333 H4 – see Aiguebelette-le-Lac

NOVES – 13 Bouches-du-Rhône – 340 E2 – pop. 4 440 – alt. 97 m – ✉ 13550

Provence

42 **E1**

Paris 688 – Arles 38 – Avignon 14 – Carpentras 33 – Cavaillon 17 – Marseille 86 – Orange 36

Syndicat d'initiative, place Jean Jaurès ✆ 04 90 92 90 43, Fax 04 90 92 90 43

Auberge de Noves (Robert Lalleman)
rte de Châteaurenard, 2 km via D 28 –
04 90 24 28 28 – resa@aubergedenoves.com – Fax 04 90 24 28 00
– Closed from end October to mid December
19 rm – €150/325 €150/325, €22 – 2 suites – ½ P €172/257
Rest – *(closed Sunday dinner, Monday off season and Saturday lunch)*
Menu €45 (weekday lunch), €80/115 – Carte €82/122
Spec. Marbré de foie de canard au sanqué d'échalote. Baron d'agneau fourré ail et romarin. Tarte au citron meringuée. **Wines** Lirac blanc, Coteaux d'Aix-en-Provence.
◆ This noble 19C residence, nestling in an extensive park, houses spacious rooms with varied decor (including one in the old chapel). Elegant restaurant with a charming terrace. Modern recipes with Provencal flavours; at lunchtime, the menu is less extensive.

NOYAL-MUZILLAC – 56 Morbihan – 308 Q9 – pop. 1 920 – alt. 52 m – ✉ 56190

Paris 456 – La Baule 44 – St-Nazaire 52 – Vannes 30 10 **C3**

Manoir de Bodrevan rest,
to the north-east: 2 km on the D 153 and minor road – 02 97 45 62 26
– contact@manoir-bodrevan.com
6 rm – €107/149 €107/149, €14 – **Rest** – *(closed Tuesday) (dinner only) (pre-book)* Menu €35
◆ A former hunting lodge converted into a charming hotel in a rural setting. Warm welcome, relaxed atmosphere and comfortable, elegant rooms with a personal touch.

NOYALO – 56 Morbihan – 308 O9 – pop. 666 – ✉ 56450 9 **A3**

Paris 468 – Rennes 116 – Vannes 15 – La Baule 75

L'Hortensia with rm rest, rm,
18 r. Ste-Brigitte – 02 97 43 02 00 – lhortensia@orange.fr – Fax 02 97 43 67 25
– Closed Monday except July-August
5 rm – €62/76 €62/76, €8 – ½ P €63/70
Rest – Menu €23 (weekday lunch), €29/100 bi – Carte €50/90
◆ 19C stone farmhouse converted into a restaurant. Up-to-the-minute dishes served to a background of modern art with a view of the well-stocked wine cellar. Spacious rooms decorated on the theme of hydrangeas.

NOYAL-SUR-VILAINE – 35 Ille-et-Vilaine – 309 M6 – see Rennes

NOYANT-DE-TOURAINE – 37 Indre-et-Loire – 317 M6 – see Ste-Maure-de-Touraine

NOYANT-LA-GRAVOYÈRE – 49 Maine-et-Loire – 317 D2 – pop. 1 761 – alt. 95 m – ✉ 49520 34 **B2**

Paris 321 – Angers 51 – Laval 52 – Nantes 81

Le Petit Manoir
Le Prieuré de St-Blaise – 02 41 61 20 70 – lepetitmanoir49@hotmail.com
– Closed 15-30 July, 15-28 February, Monday and Wednesday except lunch October-May, Saturday lunch, Sunday dinner and Tuesday
Rest – *(number of covers limited, pre-book)* Menu (€18), €23/65 – Carte €37/53
◆ An Anglo-French couple run this restaurant in a building that was first a priory (13C), and then a manor house (17C) and farm. Modern cuisine in a rustic setting.

NOYELLES-SUR-MER – 80 Somme – 301 D6 – see St- Valéry-sur-Somme

NOYON – 60 Oise – 305 J3 – pop. 14 471 – alt. 52 m – ✉ 60400

Northern France and the Paris Region 37 **C2**

Paris 108 – Amiens 67 – Compiègne 29 – Laon 53 – St-Quentin 47 – Soissons 40

Office de tourisme, place Bertrand Labarre 03 44 44 21 88, Fax 03 44 93 08 53

Notre-Dame cathedral ★★ - Ourscamps abbey ★ 5 km by N 32.

Le Cèdre without rest
8 r. de l'Évêché – ☎ 03 44 44 23 24 – reservation@hotel-lecedre.com – Fax 03 44 09 53 79 – **35 rm** – 🛉€ 66 🛉🛉€ 77, ☕ € 8
◆ Modern red brick hotel, in keeping with the style of the town, offering warm and successfully-renovated rooms. Most of them offer a view of the cathedral.

Saint Eloi with rm
81 bd Carnot – ☎ 03 44 44 01 49 – reception@hotelsainteloi.fr – Fax 03 44 09 20 90 – Closed 1st-15 August, Saturday lunch and Sunday dinner
23 rm 🛉€ 55 🛉🛉€ 70, ☕ € 8 – ½ P € 72 – **Rest** – Menu € 34/100 – Carte € 55/67
◆ Restaurant with an elegant decor in a lovely 19C manor. Mouldings, warm lighting and comfortable Louis XV-style chairs in the dining room. Guest rooms in an annex.

Dame Journe
2 bd Mony – ☎ 03 44 44 01 33 – Fax 03 44 09 59 68 – Closed 1st-14 July, 4-12 January, Sunday dinner, Tuesday dinner, Wednesday dinner, Thursday dinner and Monday
Rest – Menu € 22 (weekdays)/45 – Carte € 29/67
◆ This restaurant with a regular clientele has a warm, well-cared-for setting: Louis XVI-style armchairs and wood panelling. Good choice of menus offering traditional cuisine.

NUAILLÉ – 49 Maine-et-Loire – 317 E6 – see Cholet

NUEIL-LES-AUBIERS – 79 Deux-Sèvres – 316 M6 – pop. 2 116 – alt. 120 m – ✉ 79250

38 **B1**

Paris 364 – Bressuire 15 – Cholet 29 – Poitiers 100

Le Moulin de la Sorinière
southwest: 2 km by D 33, Cerizay road and C 3 – ☎ 05 49 72 39 20 – moulin-soriniere@wanadoo.fr – Fax 05 49 72 90 78 – Closed 7-21 April
8 rm – 🛉€ 45/48 🛉🛉€ 50/53, ☕ € 7,50 – ½ P € 49 – **Rest** – *(closed Sunday dinner and Monday)* Menu (€ 12), € 15/32 – Carte € 28/37
◆ The vegetable garden and the River Argent that crosses the garden are part of the bucolic charm of this restored 19C mill. Rustic rooms. Bigger and modern rooms in the wing. Up-to-date cuisine served by the fireplace or on the summer terrace.

NUITS-ST-GEORGES – 21 Côte-d'Or – 320 J7 – pop. 5 573 – alt. 243 m – ✉ 21700 Burgundy-Jura

8 **D1**

Paris 320 – Beaune 22 – Chalon-sur-Saône 45 – Dijon 22 – Dole 67
Office de tourisme, 3, rue Sonoys ☎ 03 80 62 11 17, Fax 03 80 61 30 98

La Gentilhommière
Meuilley road, west: 1.5 km – ☎ 03 80 61 12 06 – contact@lagentilhommiere.fr – Fax 03 80 61 30 33 – Closed mid December-end January
41 rm – 🛉€ 90 🛉🛉€ 90/200, ☕ € 13,50
Rest *Le Chef Coq* – *(closed Wednesday lunchtime, Saturday lunchtime and Tuesday)* Menu € 23 (weekday lunch), € 47/60 – Carte € 54/65
◆ Former 16C hunting lodge with rustic rooms or rooms with personal touches ("African", "Nature", "Oriental", etc.). Some overlook the park with a river flowing through it. The restaurant offers modern food and a fine Burgundy wine list (old vintages).

Hostellerie St-Vincent
r. Gén. de Gaulle – ☎ 03 80 61 14 91 – hostellerie.st.vincent@club-internet.fr Fax 03 80 61 24 65 – Closed Christmas holidays and Sunday from December to March
23 rm – 🛉€ 74 🛉🛉€ 76, ☕ € 11
Rest *L'Alambic* – *☎ 03 80 61 35 00 (closed Sunday dinner off season and Monday lunch)* Menu € 22/45 – Carte € 27/57
◆ A recent building with practical, well-soundproofed rooms. A restaurant, with a superb still, is in a cellar built with stones from the old Beaune prison! Good selection of local wines.

La Cabotte
24 Grand Rue – ☎ 03 80 61 20 77 – Closed Monday lunch, Saturday lunch and Sunday
Rest – *(number of covers limited, pre-book)* Menu € 27/47 – Carte € 39/45
◆ The dining room, with exposed beams and stonework, modern lighting and rustic furniture, has a view of the kitchen. Modern dishes inspired by local produce.

in Curtil-Vergy **Northwest: 7 km by D 25, D 35 and secondary road – pop. 85 – alt. 350 m –** ✉ **21220**

Manassès without rest

r. Guillaume de Tavanes – ✆ 03 80 61 43 81 – hotel.manasses@freesurf.fr – Fax 03 80 61 42 79 – Open from March to November – **12 rm** – €75/100 €75/100, ☕ €12

♦ This beautiful regional residence with its collection of rustic furniture is also home to a vine museum and is able to boast The Price of Wales himself as one of its guests!

NYONS – **26 Drôme – 332** D7 – **pop. 6 723 – alt. 271 m** – ✉ **26110** Provence

Paris 653 – Alès 109 – Gap 106 – Orange 43 – Sisteron 99 – Valence 98

Office de tourisme, place de la Libération ✆ 04 75 26 10 35, Fax 04 75 26 01 57

Old Nyons★: Rue des Grands Forts★ - Pont Roman (old bridge)★. 44 **B3**

La Caravelle without rest

8 r. Antignans, by the walkway along the Dyke – ✆ 04 75 26 07 44 – Fax 04 75 26 07 40 – Open 1st April-31 October – **11 rm** – €79/99 €79/99, ☕ €8,50

♦ 1900 villa with interesting architecture and garden planted with catalpas. Well-kept (non-smoking) rooms, some with portholes taken from an old warship.

La Picholine rest, rm,

promenade de la Perrière – ✆ 04 75 26 06 21 – picholine26@wanadoo.fr – Fax 04 75 26 40 72 – Closed 13 October-4 November and 4-26 February

16 rm – €58/74 €58/74, ☕ €10 – ½ P €60/70 – **Rest** – *(closed Monday from October to April and Tuesday)* Menu €26/40 – Carte €32/49

♦ A pleasant place above Nyons in a residential area among the olive trees. The rooms are colourful, some with balconies. The wide picture windows open onto the garden and terrace.

Le Petit Caveau

9 r. V. Hugo – ✆ 04 75 26 20 21 – Fax 04 75 26 07 28 – Closed 23 December-23 January, Wednesday dinner off season, Sunday dinner and Monday

Rest – *(number of covers limited, pre-book)* Menu €25/50 – Carte €49/65

♦ Charming vaulted dining room, a stone's throw from the main square, with an intimate and refined atmosphere. Modern cuisine with southern touches. Good choice of wines by the glass.

NYONS

Autiero (Pl.) 2
Chapelle (R. de la) 3
Digue (Promenade de la) 4
Liberté (R. de la) 6
Maupas (R.) 8
Petits Forts (R. des) 10
Randonne (R.) 12
Résistance (R.de la) 14

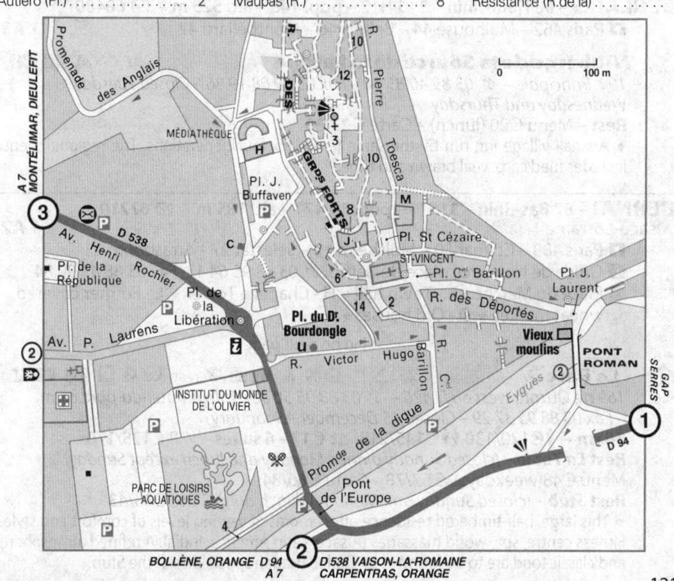

in Pilles by ①: 6 km on D94 – pop. 226 – alt. 303 m – ✉ 26110

XX **La Fleur de Thym**

Le village – ✆ *04 75 27 77 91* – *fleur.thym@orange.fr* – *Closed Thursday lunch, Sunday dinner and Monday* – **Rest** – Menu € 38/75 bi – Carte € 63/70

◆ Two smart dining rooms with Provençal colours and a mini-terrace make up the welcoming setting of this restaurant. Modern food and a good selection of Côtes du Rhône wines.

Gap road by ①: 7 km on D 94 – ✉ 26110 Nyons

X **La Charrette Bleue**

– ✆ *04 75 27 72 33* – *Fax 04 75 27 76 14* – *Closed 15 December-31 January, Sunday dinner from October to March, Tuesday from September to June and Wednesday*

Rest – Menu € 19 (weekday lunch), € 25/39 – Carte € 30/57

◆ The sign at this old chalk-stone farmhouse evokes the autobiography of René Barjavel, a native of the region. Pretty rustic surroundings, regional cuisine and selected wines.

Orange road by ③ On D 94 – ✉ 26110 Nyons

La Bastide des Monges without rest

4 km – ✆ *04 75 26 99 69* – *lesmonges@wanadoo.fr* – *Fax 04 75 26 99 70* – **9 rm** – †€ 72/115 ††€ 72/115, ☕ € 10

◆ Major restoration work has converted this former farmhouse into a charming hotel. Delightful welcome, refined rooms overlooking the vineyards and stylish garden.

OBERHASLACH – 67 Bas-Rhin – 315 H5 – pop. 1 505 – alt. 270 m – ✉ 67280

Alsace-Lorraine 1 **A1**

Paris 482 – Molsheim 16 – Saverne 32 – St-Dié 57 – Strasbourg 45

Syndicat d'initiative, 22, rue du Nideck ✆ 03 88 50 90 15, Fax 03 88 48 75 24

Hostellerie St-Florent rm, rm,

– ✆ *03 88 50 94 10* – *hotel.stflorent@wanadoo.fr* – *Fax 03 88 50 99 61* – *Closed January, Sunday dinner and Monday*

20 rm – †€ 44 ††€ 50, ☕ € 7 – ½ P € 52 – **Rest** – Menu (€ 12), € 18 (weekdays)/45 – Carte € 26/68

◆ Alsatian residence offering bright rooms on the third floor with sloping ceilings and Louis-Philippe-style furniture. Elegant Rhenish-style dining room with its coffered ceiling and wooden panelling.

OBERLARG – 68 Haut-Rhin – 315 H12 – pop. 143 – alt. 525 m – ✉ 68480

Paris 462 – Mulhouse 44 – Belfort 46 – Montbéliard 42 1 **A3**

X **Auberge de la Source de la Largue**

19 r. Principale – ✆ *03 89 40 85 10* – *Fax 03 89 08 19 86* – *Closed Tuesday, Wednesday and Thursday*

Rest – Menu € 20 (lunch) – Carte € 23/36

◆ A small village inn run by the same family for four generations. The regional menu includes fried carp, veal brawn and tripe.

OBERNAI – 67 Bas-Rhin – 315 I6 – pop. 10 471 – alt. 185 m – ✉ 67210

Alsace-Lorraine 1 **A2**

Paris 488 – Colmar 50 – Molsheim 12 – Sélestat 27 – Strasbourg 31

Office de tourisme, place du Beffroi ✆ 03 88 95 64 13, Fax 03 88 49 90 84

Place du Marché★★ - Town hall★ **H** - Chapelle Tower ★ **L** - Former covered wheat market ★ **D** - Old houses★.

Plan on next page

Le Parc rm, rest,

169 rte Ottrott, west on D 426 – ✆ *03 88 95 50 08* – *info@hotel-du-parc.com* – *Fax 03 88 95 37 29* – *Closed 15 December-15 January*

56 rm – †€ 120/130 ††€ 145/215, ☕ € 17 – 6 suites – ½ P € 125/170

Rest *La Table* – *(closed Sunday dinner, Monday and lunch except Sunday)* Menu € 48(weekdays), € 57/78 – Carte € 66/84

Rest *Stub* – *(closed Sunday and Monday) (lunch only)* Carte € 33/43

◆ This large, half-timbered residence offers rooms of varying levels of comfort and style. Fitness centre, spa, world massages (Alsace, Latin America, India). A refined atmosphere and classic food are to be found at La Table. Alsatian specialities at the Stub.

OBERNAI

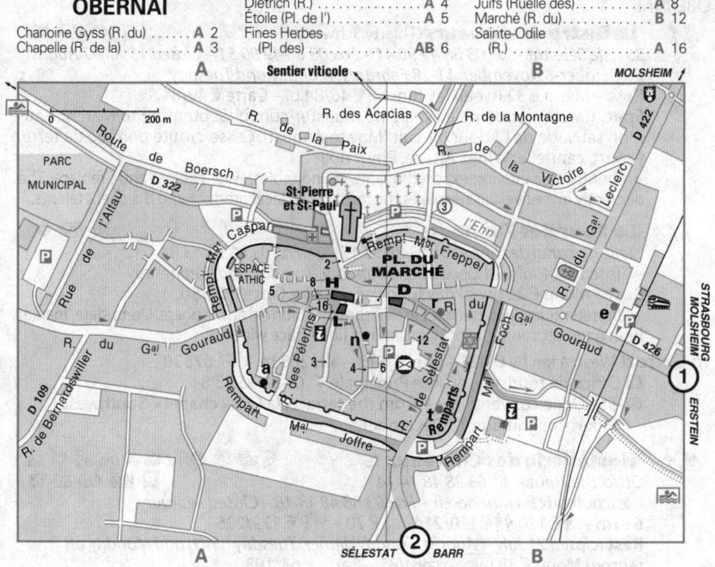

A la Cour d'Alsace

3 r. Gail – ✆ 03 88 95 07 00 – info@cour-alsace.com – Fax 03 88 95 19 21 – Closed 24 December-27 January A a

43 rm – †€ 99/138 ††€ 122/289, ☐ € 16 – ½ P € 110/130

Rest *Jardin des Remparts* – *(closed 28 July-1st September and 24 December-4 March, Thursday lunch, Saturday lunch, Sunday dinner, Monday, Tuesday and Wednesday)* Menu € 48/68 bi – Carte € 52/83

Rest *Caveau de Gail* – *(closed Thursday dinner)* Menu € 31/44 bi – Carte € 35/54

◆ Former property of the Barons of Gail with a central courtyard. Comfortable, variously dimensioned rooms in a soothing monochrome beige colour scheme. Stylish dining room and reinvented up-to-date cuisine. Regional dishes at the Caveau de Gail.

Le Colombier without rest

6 r. Dietrich – ✆ 03 88 47 63 33 – info@hotel-colombier.com – Fax 03 88 47 63 39

36 rm – †€ 84/110 ††€ 84/110, ☐ € 11 – 8 suites A n

◆ The regional style façade of this house in the heart of the historic town hides a distinctly contemporary look. Some rooms have balconies.

Les Jardins d'Adalric without rest

19 r. Mar. Koenig, via ① – ✆ 03 88 47 64 47 – jardins.adalric@wanadoo.fr – Fax 03 88 49 91 80

46 rm – †€ 75/90 ††€ 85/170, ☐ € 12

◆ Modern building, away from the town centre, with well-kept rooms. Plush breakfast room with bay window, extended by a poolside terrace and garden.

La Fourchette des Ducs (Nicolas Stamm) with rm

6 r. de la Gare – ✆ 03 88 48 33 38 – Fax 03 88 95 44 39 – Closed 28 July-12 August, 1st-8 January, 23 February-8 March, Sunday dinner, Monday and lunch except Sunday – **4 rm** ☐ – †€ 100 ††€ 160 B e

Rest – *(number of covers limited, pre-book)* Menu € 85/115 – Carte € 99/137

Spec. Duo de langoustines en tartare et gelée, mousse de chou-fleur au caviar. Raviole de purée de potimarron, truffe et beurre noisette (September to March). Pigeonneau d'Alsace, suprêmes et cuisses, réduction au chocolat. **Wines** Riesling, Pinot gris.

◆ Contemporary gourmet cuisine served in two small rooms with marquetry by Charles Spindler and lighting by René Lalique, both commissioned by Etore Bugatti. Faultless service.

Le Bistro des Saveurs (Thierry Schwartz)
35 r. de Sélestat – 03 88 49 90 41 – Fax 03 88 49 90 51 – Closed 15 July-7 August, 21 October-8 November, 11-28 February, Monday and Tuesday B **t**
Rest – Menu € 32 (weekday lunch), € 46/84 bi – Carte € 49/84
Spec. Carotte fondante au caillé de munster-cumin (September to March). Saumon sauvage de l'Adour mi-cuit (May to August). Casse-croûte pomme de terre, yaourt, cannelle. **Wines** Alsace, Pinot noir.
◆ Country chic interior: exposed beams, round tables, wine cabinet and fireplace. The discreetly inventive cuisine makes the most of the local produce and the chef's talents.

La Cour des Tanneurs
ruelle du canal de l'Ehn – 03 88 95 15 70 – Fax 03 88 95 43 84 – Closed 3-14 July, 24 December-2 January, Tuesday and Wednesday B **r**
Rest – Menu € 20 (weekday lunch), € 25/35 – Carte € 22/50
◆ Unpretentious, well cared for establishment. Informal atmosphere. Up-to-date, market fresh gourmet cuisine, accompanied by a fine Alsace wine list.

in Ottrott **West: 4 km by D 426 – pop. 1 513 – alt. 268 m – ✉ 67530**
Office de tourisme, 46, rue Principale 03 88 95 83 84
Ste-Odile convent: ★★ from the terrace, la Croix chapel★ Southwest: 11 km - pilgrimage 13 December.

Hostellerie des Châteaux
Ottrott-le-Haut – 03 88 48 14 14 – leschateaux@wanadoo.fr – Fax 03 88 48 14 18 – Closed February
61 rm – €120 €120/214, € 20 – ½ P € 129/206
Rest *(closed 21 July-4 August, Sunday dinner, Tuesday lunch and Monday off season)* Menu € 38 (weekdays)/85 – Carte € 63/103
◆ This hostelry is ideal for those in need of a little pampering: spa and beauty centre, stunning indoor pool. All wood, Alsace inspired rooms. Classic fare served in a restaurant made up of three low-key, snug dining rooms.

Beau Site
Ottrott-le-Haut – 03 88 48 14 30 – lebeausiteott@wanadoo.fr – Fax 03 88 48 14 18 – Closed February
18 rm – €98 €98/168, € 16 – ½ P € 95/130 – **Rest** – *(closed 26 June-10 July, Wednesday and Thursday off season)* Menu € 23/54 – Carte € 35/68
◆ Large half-timbered house with an oriel window. Comfortable rooms, some with balconies. Those on the top floor are spacious and individually decorated. This luxury winstub, adorned by works by Spindler, focuses on regional delicacies.

Le Clos des Délices
17 rte Klingenthal, north-west: 1 km on the D 426 – 03 88 95 81 00 – contact@leclosdesdelices.com – Fax 03 88 95 97 71
21 rm – €93/100 €100/180, € 16 – 1 suite – **Rest** – *(closed Sunday dinner)* Menu € 26 (weekday lunch), € 39/59 – Carte € 45/72
◆ A haven of peace and quiet in the heart of superb grounds. This magnificent, ivy clad inn/spa boasts hi-tech, tastefully decorated rooms. A light, well-dimensioned restaurant overlooking woodland, and a discreetly creative classic menu.

À l'Ami Fritz
Ottrott-le-Haut – 03 88 95 80 81 – ami-fritz@wanadoo.fr – Fax 03 88 95 84 85 – Closed 12-31 January
21 rm – €75/107 €75/128, € 12,50 – 1 suite – ½ P € 75/97
Rest – *(closed 30 June-10 July, 12-31 January and Wednesday)* Menu € 24 (weekdays)/62 – Carte € 35/54
◆ Regional style house offering comfortable rooms with personal touches. The establishment's name recalls Erckmann Chatrian's novel, as well as the owners' name. Tastefully decorated restaurant; regional dishes accompanied by a red Ottrott wine from the family vineyards.

Aux Chants des Oiseaux without rest
Ottrott-le-Haut – 03 88 95 87 39 – ami-fritz@wanadoo.fr – Fax 03 88 95 84 85 – Closed 30 June-10 July and 7 January-6 February
16 rm – €74/95 €74/106, € 12,50
◆ Regional style house in the middle of the countryside. Pleasant colourful rooms. Wainscoted, timber-roofed breakfast room and poolside terrace.

Domaine Le Moulin rm, rest,
Klingenthal road, north-west: 1 km on D 426 –
03 88 95 87 33 – domaine.le.moulin@wanadoo.fr – Fax 03 88 95 98 03
– Closed 23 December-20 January
23 rm – €58 €70, €13 – 3 suites – ½ P €67/76 – **Rest** – *(closed Saturday lunch, Sunday dinner and Monday lunch)* Menu €16 (weekday lunch), €23/55 – Carte €25/55
◆ The Wine Route passes by this hotel, behind which lies an immense park with a river and small lake. Snug rooms and, in the wing, spacious more modern duplex apartments. Regional menu in the restaurant and terrace facing the forest.

OBERSTEIGEN – 67 Bas-Rhin – 315 H5 – ✉ 67710 Alsace-Lorraine 1 A1

Paris 466 – Molsheim 27 – Sarrebourg 32 – Saverne 16 – Strasbourg 39 – Wasselonne 13

Mossig Valley ★ East: 2 km.

Hostellerie Belle Vue rest, rest,
16 rte de Dabo – 03 88 87 32 39
– hostellerie.belle-vue@wanadoo.fr – Fax 03 88 87 37 77
– Open 13 April-1st January and closed Sunday dinner and Monday off season except holidays
25 rm – €70/80 €70/80, €10 – 2 suites – ½ P €70/75
Rest – Menu €25/40 – Carte €30/54
◆ This hostelry, in the heart of Saverne forest, offers a magnificent view of the valley. Comfortable rooms with period furnishings. Wellness centre, garden and pool. Large, regional style dining room and flower-decked summer terrace. Reinterpreted regional dishes.

OBERSTEINBACH – 67 Bas-Rhin – 315 K2 – pop. 184 – alt. 239 m – ✉ 67510 Alsace-Lorraine 1 B1

Paris 458 – Bitche 22 – Haguenau 35 – Strasbourg 68 – Wissembourg 25

Anthon with rm
40 r. Principale – 03 88 09 55 01 – info@restaurant-anthon.fr
– Fax 03 88 09 50 52 – Closed January, Tuesday and Wednesday except July-August
8 rm – €48/62 €62/98, €10 – ½ P €75
Rest – Menu €25/65 – Carte €42/59
◆ A half-timbered house (1860) with an elegant, round dining room, facing the garden. Local cuisine. Redecorated rooms, including two that have beds set into wooden alcoves.

OBJAT – 19 Corrèze – 329 J4 – pop. 3 372 – alt. 131 m – ✉ 19130 24 B3

Paris 467 – Brive-la-Gaillarde 21 – Limoges 79 – Tulle 45 – Uzerche 30

Office de tourisme, place Charles de Gaulle 05 55 25 96 73, Fax 05 55 25 97 45

De France rest,
av. G. Clemenceau, (towards the station) – 05 55 25 80 38
– hoteldefrance.objat@wanadoo.fr – Fax 05 55 25 91 87
– Closed 15 September-5 October, 23 December-2 January and Saturday
27 rm – €35 €45, €9 – ½ P €42/52 – **Rest** – *(closed Sunday dinner and Saturday)* Menu €14 (weekdays)/42 – Carte €32/52
◆ Charming welcome in this family hotel near the station. The rooms are simple and functional and are progressively being equipped with air-conditioning. Renovated restaurant opening onto an inner courtyard. Regional specialities on the menu.

La Tête de L'Art
53 av. J. Lascaux – 05 55 25 50 42 – latetedelart@wanadoo.fr – Closed 26 June-10 July, 30 October-5 November, 2-7 January, Tuesday except lunch in July-August and Wednesday
Rest – Menu €10 (weekday lunch), €28/40
◆ Art meets gastronomy at this family restaurant which organises exhibitions of paintings and sculptures by local artists. Traditional dishes.

ODENAS – 69 Rhône – **327** G3 – **pop. 735** – **alt. 300 m** – ✉ **69460** 43 **E1**

Paris 427 – Bourg-en-Bresse 54 – Lyon 47 – Mâcon 33 – Villefranche-sur-Saône 15

Christian Mabeau

261 r. du Beaujolais – ✆ 04 74 03 41 79 – chrisvie@hotmail.fr – Fax 04 74 03 49 40 – Closed 27 August-16 September, Sunday dinner and Monday except lunch public holidays – **Rest** – Menu € 32/63 – Carte € 54/58

◆ This simple façade conceals a charming restaurant that combines rustic and contemporary styles. In summer, enjoy the terrace bordering the vineyards.

OFFRANVILLE – 76 Seine-Maritime – **304** G2 – **see Dieppe**

OGNES – 02 Aisne – **306** B5 – **see Chauny**

L'OIE – 85 Vendée – **316** J7 – **pop. 835** – **alt. 102 m** – ✉ **85140** 34 **B3**

Paris 394 – Cholet 40 – Nantes 62 – Niort 94 – La Roche-sur-Yon 29

Le Grand Turc rest, rest,

33 r. Nationale – ✆ 02 51 66 08 74 – legrandturc@wanadoo.fr – Fax 02 51 66 14 13 – Closed 24 December-6 January

19 rm – †€ 53 ††€ 66, ☕ € 7,50 – ½ P € 58 – **Rest** – *(closed Saturday dinner off season and Sunday)* Menu € 19/48 – Carte € 25/38

◆ The sign depicts Mameluke Amakuc, chief guard of Napoleon I when the latter visited the inn. The rooms behind are functional and well kept. One room is devoted to traditional fare, while the other features a buffet and dish of the day.

OINVILLE-SOUS-AUNEAU – 28 Eure-et-Loir – **311** G5 – **pop. 279** – **alt. 150 m** – ✉ 28700 12 **C1**

Paris 77 – Chartres 20 – Montigny-le-Bretonneux 50 – Orléans 88

Caroline Lethuillier without rest

2 r. Prunus, in Cherville, 2 km west – ✆ 02 37 31 72 80 – info@cherville.com – Fax 02 37 31 38 56

4 rm ☕ – †€ 47/53 ††€ 56/60

◆ The charming rooms in the former farmhouse lofts have red floor-tiles, beams, themed decoration and family furniture. Delicious home-made breakfasts.

OISLY – 41 Loir-et-Cher – **318** F7 – **pop. 310** – **alt. 120 m** – ✉ **41700** 11 **A1**

Paris 208 – Tours 61 – Blois 27 – Châteauroux 80 – Romorantin-Lanthenay 32

St-Vincent

– ✆ 02 54 79 50 04 – Fax 02 54 79 50 04 – Closed 15 December-15 January, Monday dinner, Tuesday and Wednesday

Rest – Menu € 25/54 – Carte € 44/60

◆ The delicately spiced contemporary cuisine attracts gourmets to this country-style restaurant with its sign depicting the patron saint of winegrowers. Tasting of local wines.

OIZON – 18 Cher – **323** L2 – **pop. 752** – **alt. 230 m** – ✉ 18700 12 **C2**

Paris 179 – Bourges 54 – Cosne-sur-Loire 35 – Gien 29 – Orléans 66 – Salbris 38 – Vierzon 50

Les Rives de l'Oizenotte

at Nohant lake, east: 1 km – ✆ 02 48 58 06 20 – oizenotte.g@infonie.fr – Fax 02 48 58 28 97 – Closed 21 December-17 January, Monday and Tuesday

Rest – *(number of covers limited, pre-book)* Menu € 19 (weekdays)/28

◆ A pastoral atmosphere in this friendly lakeside restaurant. An amusing decor based on a fishing theme. Simple food.

OLEMPS – 12 Aveyron – **338** H4 – **see Rodez**

OLÉRON (ÎLE) – 17 Charente-Maritime – **324** C4 – **see île d'Oléron**

OLIVET – 45 Loiret – 318 I4 – see Orléans

LES OLLIÈRES-SUR-EYRIEUX – 07 Ardèche – 331 J5 – pop. 797 – alt. 200 m – ✉ 07360 44 B3

Paris 593 – Le Cheylard 28 – Lamastre 33 – Montélimar 53 – Privas 19 – Valence 34

Office de tourisme, le pont ✆ 04 75 66 30 21, Fax 04 75 66 20 31

Le Truffolier

D 120 – ✆ 04 75 66 20 32 – letruffolier@wanadoo.fr – Fax 04 75 66 20 63 – Closed 2-10 June, 29 September-14 October, 10 November-16 March, Monday except lunch in July-August and Sunday dinner except holidays

Rest – Menu € 15/36 – Carte € 24/47

◆ A rustic dining room serving traditional, unpretentious cuisine; simple hospitality in this family inn in the Eyrieux valley.

OLLIOULES – 83 Var – 340 K7 – pop. 12 198 – alt. 52 m – ✉ 83190 French Riviera

Paris 829 – Aix-en-Provence 80 – Marseille 59 – Toulon 8 40 B3

Office de tourisme, 116, avenue Philippe de Hauteclocque ✆ 04 94 63 11 74, Fax 04 94 63 33 72

Gorges d'Ollioules★.

L'Assiette Gourmande

2 pl. Victor Clément, (square in front of the church) – ✆ 04 94 63 04 61 – Closed Tuesday and Wednesday from September to June and lunch in July-August

Rest – *(number of covers limited, pre-book)* Menu € 24/34 – Carte € 30/56

◆ Enjoy this establishment's distinctive cuisine on the terrace, weather permitting, or in the small, colourful Provençal-style dining room with mezzanine.

OLMETO – 2A Corse-du-Sud – 345 C9 – see Corse

OLMETO PLAGE – 2A Corse-du-Sud – 345 C9 – see Olmeto

OLORON-STE-MARIE – 64 Pyrénées-Atlantiques – 342 I5 – pop. 10 992 – alt. 224 m – ✉ 64400 Atlantic Coast 3 B3

Paris 809 – Bayonne 105 – Mont-de-Marsan 101 – Pau 34

Office de tourisme, allée du Comte de Tréville ✆ 05 59 39 98 00, Fax 05 59 39 43 97

Portal★★ of Ste-Marie church.

OLORON-STE-MARIE

Barthou (R. Louis) . . . . B
Bellevue (Promenade) . . . . B 2
Biscondau (R. du) . . . . B 3
Bordelongue (R. A.) . . . . B 4
Camou (R.) . . . . B
Casamayor-Dufaur (R.) . . . . A 5
Cathédrale (R. de la) . . . . . . A 6
Dalmais (R.) . . . . B 7
Derême (Av. Tristan) . . . . . . A 8
Despourrins (R.) . . . . A 9
Gabe (Pl. Amédée) . . . . B 10
Gambetta (Pl.) . . . . B 12
Jaca (Pl.) . . . . A 13
Jeliote (R.) . . . . B 14
Lattre-de-Tassigny (Av. du Mar.de) . . . . A 23
Mendiondou (Pl. Léon) . . . . B 15
Moureu (Av. Charles et Henri) . . . A 16
Oustalots (Pl. des) . . . . A 18
Pyrénées (Bd des) . . . . A 19
Résistance (Pl. de la) . . . . . . B 20
St-Grat (R.) . . . . A 22
Toulet (R. Paul-Jean) . . . . . . A 24
Vigny (Av. Alfred de) . . . . . . A 26
4-Septembre (Av. du) . . . . . . A 28
14-Juillet (Av. du) . . . . A 30

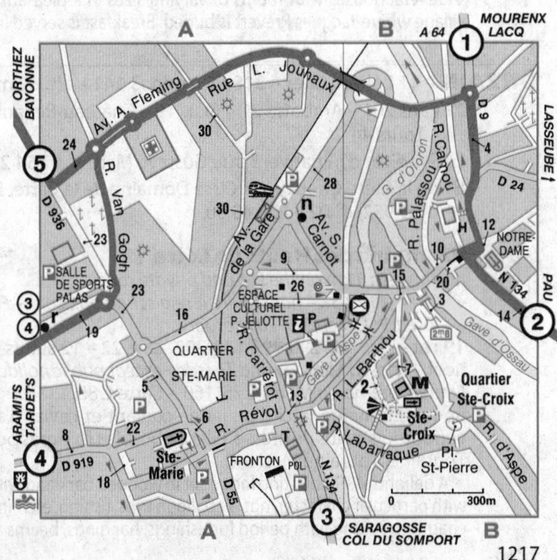

Alysson

bd des Pyrénées ✉ 64400 – ✆ 05 59 39 70 70 – alysson.hotel@wanadoo.fr – Fax 05 59 39 24 47 A r

47 rm – †€ 72/90 ††€ 80/110, ☕ € 10,50 – 1 suite – ½ P € 65/80

Rest – *(closed 19 December-3 January, 14-28 February, Friday dinner October-April, Saturday except dinner May-September)* Menu € 22 (weekday lunch), € 27/42 – Carte € 47/66

◆ A modern hotel with spacious, functional rooms (some with hydromassage baths) and well-equipped conference rooms. Light wood and contemporary furniture in the vast dining room opening onto a garden.

La Paix without rest

24 av. Sadi-Carnot – ✆ 05 59 39 02 63 – hoteloloron@aliceadsl.fr – Fax 05 59 39 98 20 A n

24 rm – †€ 44/49 ††€ 44/53, ☕ € 7

◆ This family-run establishment, in the railway station area, has been renovated. Cheerful, colourful and very well-kept rooms.

OMIÉCOURT – 80 Somme – 301 K9 – pop. 235 – alt. 85 m – ✉ 80320 37 B2

Paris 128 – Amiens 64 – Saint-Quentin 39 – Compiègne 53 – Tergnier 63

Château d'Omiécourt without rest

4 r. du Bosquet – ✆ 03 22 83 01 75 – thezy@terre-net.fr – Fax 03 22 83 09 56

5 rm ☕ – †€ 65/80 ††€ 80/95

◆ Guests are welcomed by the sixth generation of owners of this family château. Personalised rooms furnished with antiques. Driving range in the grounds and counter-current pool.

OMONVILLE-LA-PETITE – 50 Manche – 303 A1 – pop. 132 – alt. 33 m – ✉ 50440 32 A1

Paris 380 – Barneville-Carteret 45 – Cherbourg 25 – Nez de Jobourg 7 – St-Lô 101

La Fossardière without rest

in the hamlet of La Fosse – ✆ 02 33 52 19 83 – Fax 02 33 52 73 49 – Open 15 March-15 November

10 rm – †€ 41 ††€ 65, ☕ € 9

◆ Several houses with rooms of varying sizes in a pleasant hamlet near Omonville, the village where Jacques Prévert is buried. Breakfast is served in the old bakery.

ONZAIN – 41 Loir-et-Cher – 318 E6 – pop. 3 141 – alt. 69 m – ✉ 41150 11 A1

Paris 201 – Amboise 21 – Blois 19 – Château-Renault 24 – Montrichard 23 – Tours 44

Syndicat d'initiative, 3, rue Gustave Marc ✆ 02 54 20 78 52

de la Carte Chouzy-sur-Cisse Domaine de la Carte, Southwest: 6 km by D 952, ✆ 02 54 20 49 00.

Domaine des Hauts de Loire rm,

north-west: 3 km on the D 1 and private road – ✆ 02 54 20 72 57 – hauts-loire@relaischateaux.com – Fax 02 54 20 77 32 – Closed 1st December-20 February

19 rm – †€ 130/290 ††€ 130/290, ☕ € 22 – 12 suites – ½ P € 200/245

Rest – *(closed Monday and Tuesday except public holidays) (number of covers limited, pre-book)* Menu € 75/160 – Carte € 88/137

Spec. Œuf neige farci d'un jaune coulant et caviar d'aquitaine. Pigeonneau du vendomois au jus de presse. Filet de bœuf et foie gras pochés au Montlouis. **Wines** Touraine, Touraine Mesland.

◆ A delightful 19C hunting lodge set in wooded parkland with a lake. Personalised rooms with particular character, hot-air balloon trips, fishing, etc. Fine modern cuisine served in a charming setting with period furnishings, hangings, beams and fireplace.

Château des Tertres without rest

– ✆ 02 54 20 83 88 – contact@chateau-tertres.fr – Fax 02 54 20 89 21
– Open 20 March-26 October

18 rm – †€ 68 ††€ 122, ☕ € 10

♦ A Second Empire country seat in a magnificent 5-ha park. Rooms are either Napoleon III or Louis-Philippe in style; those in a nearby cottage are original and contemporary in design.

OPIO – 06 Alpes-Maritimes – 341 C5 – pop. 1 922 – alt. 300 m – ✉ 06650 42 E2

Paris 911 – Cannes 17 – Digne-les-Bains 125 – Draguignan 74 – Grasse 9 – Nice 31

Syndicat d'initiative, route Village ✆ 04 93 77 23 18

Le Mas des Géraniums

1 km at San Peyre, east on D 7 – ✆ 04 93 77 23 23 – info@le-mas-des-geraniums.com – Fax 04 93 77 76 05 – Closed 15 November-20 December, Tuesday and Wednesday

Rest – Menu € 18 (weekday lunch), € 35/40 – Carte € 39/67

♦ Traditional cuisine served in a cosy, rustic dining room or on the shady, flower-decked terrace with a view of the old village. Arbour, tall palm tree and olive trees in the garden.

ORADOUR-SUR-GLANE – 87 Haute-Vienne – 325 D5 – pop. 2 025 – alt. 275 m – ✉ 87520 Dordogne-Berry-Limousin 24 B2

Paris 408 – Angoulême 85 – Bellac 26 – Confolens 33 – Limoges 25 – Nontron 66

Office de tourisme, place du Champ de Foire ✆ 05 55 03 13 73, Fax 05 55 03 13 73

"Martyred village "whose inhabitants were slaughtered in June 1944.

La Glane

8 pl. Gén. de Gaulle – ✆ 05 55 03 10 43 – Fax 05 55 03 15 42

10 rm – †€ 44 ††€ 46, ☕ € 8 – ½ P € 46 – **Rest** – *(closed 15 December-28 February and Saturday)* Menu € 14,50/25 – Carte € 20/34

♦ In the busy central square of the rebuilt village, hotel offering small, modest but well kept rooms. Guests eat shoulder to shoulder in this rustic restaurant offering starter and dessert buffets and simple grill-based main courses.

Le Milord

10 av. du 10-Juin – ✆ 05 55 03 10 35 – Fax 05 55 03 21 76 – Closed Sunday dinner and Wednesday dinner – **Rest** – Menu € 13/39 – Carte € 18/38

♦ The brasserie-style dining room has beige velvet banquettes and simply decorated tables set close together. Simple but generous traditional cuisine.

ORADOUR-SUR-VAYRES – 87 Haute-Vienne – 325 C6 – pop. 1 636 – alt. 322 m – ✉ 87150 24 A2

Paris 433 – Limoges 40 – Saint-Junien 23 – Panazol 45 – Isle 36

Office de tourisme, 3, avenue du 8 Mai 1945 ✆ 05 55 78 22 21

La Bergerie des Chapelles

– ✆ 05 55 78 29 91 – info@domainedeschapelles.com – Fax 05 55 71 70 19 – Closed in November and in January

7 rm – †€ 50/55 ††€ 65/90, ☕ € 9 – ½ P € 65/70 – **Rest** – *(closed Sunday dinner and Monday off season)* Menu € 18 (weekday lunch), € 26/38 bi

♦ This renovated sheep barn has recently been converted into quiet and cosy accommodation with impressive bathrooms and terraces overlooking the park. Contemporary cuisine served to a modernised rustic backdrop of dark walls adorned with large paintings.

ORANGE – 84 Vaucluse – 332 B9 – pop. 27 989 – alt. 97 m – ✉ 84100 Provence 42 E1

Paris 655 – Alès 84 – Avignon 31 – Carpentras 24 – Nîmes 56

Office de tourisme, 5, cours Aristide Briand ✆ 04 90 34 70 88, Fax 04 90 34 99 62

d'Orange Route de Camaret, by Mt-Ventoux road: 4 km, ✆ 04 90 34 34 04.

Théatre antique★★★ - Arc de Triomphe★★ - Colline St-Eutrope ≤★.

ORANGE

Arc de Triomphe (Av. de l') **AY**
Artaud (Av. A.) . . . . **ABY**
Blanc (R. A.). . . . . **BZ**
Briand (Crs A.) . . . . **AYZ**
Caristie (R.) . . . . **BY** 2
Châteauneuf (R. de) . . . . . **BZ** 3
Clemenceau (Pl. G.) . . . . . **BY** 4
Concorde (R. de la) . . . . . . **BY**
Contrescarpe (R. de la) . . . **BY**
Daladier (Bd E.) . . . . **ABY**
Fabre (Av. H.). . . . . **BY**
Frères-Mounet (Pl. des) . . **BY** 5
Guillaume-le-Taciturne (Av.) . . . . **BY**
Herbes (Pl. aux). . . . . **BY** 7
Lacour (R.). . . . . **AY**
Leclerc (Av. Gén.) . . . . **BZ**
Levade (R. de la) . . . . **BY**
Mistral (Av. F.). . . . . **BY** 9
Noble (R. du) . . . . **ABY**
Pourtoules (Cours) . . . . . . **BZ**
Pourtoules (R.) . . . . **BZ** 12
Princes d'Orange-Nassau (Mtée des). . . . . **AZ**
République (Pl. de la) . . . . **BY** 14
République (R. de la) . . . . **BY** 16
Roch (R. Madeleine). . . . . . **BZ** 18
St-Clement (R.) . . . . **AZ**
St-Florent (R.) . . . . **BY** 20
St-Jean (R.) . . . . **AY**
St-Martin (R.) . . . . **AY** 22
Tanneurs (R. des) . . . . **AY** 24
Thermes (Av. des). . . . . . . **AZ**
Tourre (R. de). . . . . **AZ** 26
Victor-Hugo (R.) . . . . **AY**

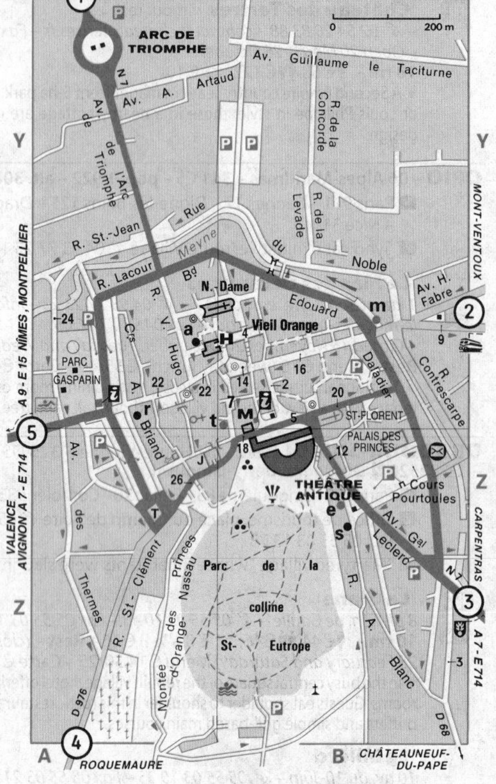

Park Inn rm,
rte Caderousse, via ⑤ – ✆ 04 90 34 24 10 – info.orange@rezidorparkinn.com – Fax 04 90 34 85 48
99 rm – †€ 75/125 ††€ 85/135, ☐ € 12 – ½ P € 62/75
Rest – *(closed Saturday lunch and Sunday lunch from November to February)* Menu € 21/26 – Carte € 26/41
◆ Elegant Provençal decor in the rooms, cheerful lounge and excellent service that will appeal to both business people and tourists. The dining room opens onto the hotel pool, beside which meals may be enjoyed in the summer.

Arène rm, rest,
pl. Langes – ✆ 04 90 11 40 40 – reservation@hotel-arene.fr – Fax 04 90 11 40 45
35 rm – †€ 56/120 ††€ 74/170, ☐ € 8 – ½ P € 65/98 AY **a**
Rest – *(closed dinner except Wednesday and Sunday)* Menu € 12,50 (lunch)/28
◆ These two large houses from the 1800s are situated on a pedestrian square shaded by plane trees. The completely renovated building offers a choice of Provençal or executive guestrooms. Two restaurants, one offering local cuisine, the other, Italian specialities.

Le Glacier without rest
46 cours A. Briand – ✆ 04 90 34 02 01 – info@le-glacier.com – Fax 04 90 51 13 80 – Closed 20 December-5 January, Friday, Saturday and Sunday from November to February AY **r**
28 rm – †€ 49/68 ††€ 49/80, ☐ € 7,50
◆ A strong family atmosphere is evident in this hotel passed down from father to son for the past three generations. Small air-conditioned bedrooms (except three) gradually being renovated in Provençal style.

St-Jean without rest
1 cours Pourtoules – ✆ 04 90 51 15 16 – hotel.saint-jean@wanadoo.fr – Fax 04 90 11 05 45 – Closed 20-27 December BZ **s**
22 rm – †€ 45/90 ††€ 45/90, ☕ € 7
◆ Former post house backing onto St-Eutrope Hill, and neighbour to the old theatre. Original lounge hewn into the rock and bedrooms of varying size, all furnished differently.

XX **Le Parvis**
55 cours Pourtoules – ✆ 04 90 34 82 00 – le-parvis2@wanadoo.fr – Fax 04 90 51 18 19 – Closed 9 November-1st December, 11 January-2 February, Sunday and Monday – **Rest** – Menu (€ 14), € 19/45 BZ **e**
◆ Polished parquet floors and contemporary paintings create an elegant atmosphere in this restaurant. Contemporary cuisine with a Provençal note.

X **Le Monteverdi**
443 bd E. Daladier – ✆ 04 90 29 53 77 – Fax 04 90 29 53 77 BY **m**
Rest – Menu € 25 – Carte € 30/45
◆ Cosy yet trendy decor (earthy tones, communal tables, lounge area); tasty cuisine matching the ambiance.

X **Le Forum**
3 r. de Mazeau – ✆ 04 90 34 01 09 – Fax 04 90 34 01 09 – Closed 25 August-10 September, 23 February-10 March, Saturday lunch, Sunday dinner and Monday
Rest – Menu € 18 (weekday lunch), € 21/38 – Carte € 29/52 BY **t**
◆ Small restaurant hidden in a tiny, narrow street, a stone's throw from the antique theatre. Elegant Provençal-style decor. Traditional cuisine prepared with fresh produce.

via ① N 7 and secondary road: 4 km – ✉ 84100 Orange

XX **Le Mas des Aigras** with rm
Chemin des Aigras – ✆ 04 90 34 81 01 – masdesaigras@free.fr – Fax 04 90 34 05 66 – Closed 23 Oct.-9 Nov., 18 Dec.-11 Jan, Monday evening, Tuesday and Wed. from Oct. to March
12 rm – †€ 70/75 ††€ 70/75, ☕ € 12 – ½ P € 75/95 – **Rest** – *(closed Monday lunch, Wednesday lunch and Saturday lunch from May to September except public holidays) (number of covers limited, pre-book)* Menu € 20, € 28/52 – Carte € 39/58
◆ Guestrooms decorated in Provençal colours. An attractive stone farmhouse surrounded by fields and vineyards. Cosy dining room and attractive terrace. Delicious organic-based cuisine prepared in full view of diners.

in Sérignan-du-Comtat by ①, **N 7 and D 976: 8 km – pop. 2 254 – alt. 80 m – ✉ 84830**

XXX **Le Pré du Moulin** (Pascal Alonso) with rm
rte Ste-Cécile les Vignes – ✆ 04 90 70 14 55 – info@predumoulin.com – Fax 04 90 70 05 62 – Closed Sunday dinner and Monday from mid September to May and Monday lunch from May to mid September
11 rm ☕ – †€ 100/150 ††€ 110/230 – ½ P € 99/153
Rest – Menu € 35/100 bi – Carte € 69/94
Spec. Raviole ouverte de truffes du Tricastin et artichauts sautés (December to March). Pigeon farci au chou et foie gras. Soufflé au Grand Marnier. **Wines** Gigondas, Côtes du Rhône.
◆ Delicious dishes made with fresh market produce are served in this former village schoolhouse. Elegant dining room and shaded terrace. Rooms of various sizes and decoration. Some have a balcony or terrace.

ORBEC – 14 Calvados – 303 O5 – pop. 2 564 – alt. 110 m – ✉ 14290 Normandy

Paris 173 – L'Aigle 38 – Alençon 80 – Argentan 53 – Bernay 18 – Caen 85 – Lisieux 21 33 **C2**

Office de tourisme, 6, rue Grande ✆ 02 31 32 56 68, Fax 02 31 32 04 37

Old manor ★.

XXX **Au Caneton**
32 r. Grande – ✆ 02 31 32 73 32 – Fax 02 31 62 48 91 – Closed 1st-16 September, 5-19 January, Tuesday dinner except July-August, Sunday dinner and Monday
Rest – *(number of covers limited, pre-book)* Menu € 20/75 – Carte € 54/114
◆ A 17C house in the centre of the village with two low-key dining rooms decorated with copperware and a collection of antique plates. Classic cuisine.

L'Orbecquoise
60 r. Grande – ✆ 02 31 62 44 99 – herve.doual@wanadoo.fr – Fax 02 31 62 44 99 – Closed 25 June-12 July, Wednesday except lunch 15 July-15 September and Thursday
Rest – Menu € 17/30 – Carte € 34/40
◆ Rustic inn occupying a 17C residence. Old photos of the town decorate the dining room walls. Regional cuisine.

ORBEY – **68 Haut-Rhin** – **315** G8 – **pop. 3 548** – **alt. 550 m** – **Winter sports : see "Le Bonhomme"** – ✉ **68370** **Alsace-Lorraine** 1 **A2**

Paris 434 – Colmar 23 – Gérardmer 42 – Munster 21 – St-Dié 37 – Sélestat 35

Office de tourisme, 48, rue du Général-de-Gaulle ✆ 03 89 71 30 11, Fax 03 89 71 34 11

Bois Le Sire et son Motel
20 r. Ch. de Gaulle – ✆ 03 89 71 25 25 – boislesire@bois-le-sire.fr – Fax 03 89 71 30 75 – Closed 4 January-6 February
35 rm – †€ 52/80 ††€ 52/80, ☕ € 10 – 1 suite – ½ P € 58/72
Rest – *(closed Monday except July-August)* Menu € 9,50 (weekday lunch), € 16/48 – Carte € 20/51
◆ This hotel is made up of two buildings with practical rooms. Choose the motel rooms, which are quieter and more spacious. Fitness area, sauna, Jacuzzi. Stylish wainscoting and furniture in the restaurant, which serves simple, traditional fare.

Aux Bruyères rm,
35 r. Ch. de Gaulle – ✆ 03 89 71 20 36 – info@auxbruyeres.com – Fax 03 89 71 35 30 – Open 20 March-26 October and 15-31 December
29 rm – †€ 42 ††€ 42/65, ☕ € 8 – ½ P € 41/55 – **Rest** – *(closed Wednesday lunch and Thursday lunch in season)* Menu (€ 11), € 13,50/28 – Carte € 21/38
◆ In the centre of the village, this hotel has functional rooms. Those on the garden side are quieter and more spacious. Lovely family suite under the eaves. Tea room. Muted dining room, summer terrace and regional food.

in Basses-Huttes South: 4 km by D 48 – ✉ **68370 Orbey**

Wetterer rm,
– ✆ 03 89 71 20 28 – info@hotel-wetterer.com – Fax 03 89 71 36 50 – Closed 10-14 March, 31 March-13 April, 5-28 November and Wednesday from 28 November to 24 December and from 5 January to 8 February
15 rm – †€ 36/46 ††€ 45/62, ☕ € 7,50 – ½ P € 44/47
Rest – *(closed Monday, Tuesday and Wednesday from 28 November to 24 December and from 5 January to 8 February)* Menu (€ 14), € 16/30 – Carte € 18/36
◆ Built in the heart of superb forest and mountain scenery, this 1960s hotel offers practical, well-kept rooms. Peace and quiet guaranteed! Rustic-chic dining room with rafters, fire-place and silverware. Classic repertory.

in Pairis 3 km southwest by D 48ᴵᴵ – ✉ **68370 Orbey**

Lac Noir (Black Lake) ★: ≤★ 30 mn West: 5 km.

Le Domaine de Pairis
233 Pairis – ✆ 03 89 71 20 15 – info@pairis.fr – Fax 03 89 71 39 90 – Closed 5-15 November, 10-25 January and Tuesday dinner
14 rm – †€ 55 ††€ 65/95, ☕ € 9,50 – ½ P € 64/71
Rest – *(closed lunch except Sunday)* Menu € 19/33 – Carte € 26/55
◆ Simply and tastefully decorated rooms: minimalist, ecru coloured furniture offset by paintings and colourful rugs. Organic farm produce and home-made jams. Regional menu and concise wine list.

Bon Repos
– ✆ 03 89 71 21 92 – au-bon-repos@wanadoo.fr – Fax 03 89 71 24 51 – Open 8 February-19 October, 19 December-3 January and closed Wednesday
17 rm – †€ 43/48 ††€ 43/48, ☕ € 8 – ½ P € 47/52
Rest – *(dinner only except Sunday)* Menu € 16/34 – Carte € 19/41
◆ On the lake road, a small family inn giving onto a peaceful garden. Simple, practical rooms; those in the annexe are more peaceful, overlooking a forest of fir trees. Welcoming rustic style dining room offering regional cooking.

ORCHIES – 59 Nord – **302** H5 – **pop. 7 472** – **alt. 40 m** – ✉ **59310** 31 **C2**

Paris 219 – Denain 28 – Douai 20 – Lille 29 – Tournai 20 – Valenciennes 30

Syndicat d'initiative, 42, rue Jules Roch ☎ 03 20 64 86 32, Fax 03 20 64 86 32

Le Manoir

rm, VISA

Hameau de Manneville, D 549: west via route Seclin – ☎ 03 20 64 68 68 – contact@manoir.net – Fax 03 20 64 68 69 – Closed 2-29 August

34 rm – €70/115 €70/115, €12 – ½ P €66/86

Rest – *(closed 22-31 December, Friday dinner, Saturday lunch, Sunday dinner and dinner on public holidays)* Menu (€18), €24/48 – Carte €27/60

♦ This hotel, located between a busy road and the motorway, offers modern rooms with good sound insulation. Linked to the hotel by a covered passage, the Manoir restaurant includes a cosy bar and three intimate, rustic-style dining rooms.

La Chaumière

VISA

south 3 km on D 957, Marchiennes road – ☎ 03 20 71 86 38 – Fax 03 20 61 65 91 – Closed 1st-15 September, February, Sunday dinner and Monday

Rest – Menu (€14), €30/79 bi – Carte €40/59

♦ Horses feature prominently among the animal ornaments, adding to the rustic feel of this restaurant. Classic fare, fine cheese platter and excellent choice of Bordeaux.

ORCIÈRES – 05 Hautes-Alpes – **334** F4 – **pop. 810** – **alt. 1 446 m** – **Winter sports : to Orcières-Merlette 1 850/2 650 m** 2 26 – ✉ **05170**

French Alps 41 **C1**

Paris 676 – Briançon 109 – Gap 32 – Grenoble 113 – La Mure 73

Office de tourisme, maison du Tourisme ☎ 04 92 55 89 89, Fax 04 92 55 89 64

Vallée du Drac Blanc★★ Northwest: 14 km.

in Merlette **North: 5 km by D 76** – ✉ **05170 Orcières**

Les Gardettes with rm

rm, VISA

– ☎ 04 92 55 71 11 – info@gardettes.com – Fax 04 92 55 77 26 – Open 1st December-24 April and 15 June-10 September

15 rm – €48/95 €48/95, €7,50 – ½ P €42/70 – **Rest** – *(closed 1 - 15 Dec)* Menu €23/33 – Carte €23/41

♦ A family-run restaurant in a converted cattle shed. Pretty, typically Alpine decoration and regional dishes with a personal touch. Small rooms.

ORCINES – 63 Puy-de-Dôme – **326** F8 – **see Clermont-Ferrand**

ORCIVAL – 63 Puy-de-Dôme – **326** E8 – **pop. 244** – **alt. 840 m** – ✉ **63210** Auvergne

Paris 441 – Aubusson 82 – Clermont-Ferrand 27 – Le Mont-Dore 17 – Ussel 55

Office de tourisme, le bourg ☎ 04 73 65 89 77, Fax 04 73 65 89 78

Notre-Dame basilica ★★. 5 **B2**

Roche without rest

VISA

– ☎ 04 73 65 82 31 – Fax 04 73 65 94 15 – Closed 11 November-25 December and Monday off season – **8 rm** – €35 €45, €9

♦ This establishment facing the basilica houses small, simple and well-kept rooms that are gradually being redecorated. Small garden at the back.

ORGELET – 39 Jura – **321** D7 – **pop. 1 686** – **alt. 500 m** – ✉ **39270** 16 **B3**

Paris 434 – Besançon 104 – Lons-le-Saunier 20 – Bourg-en-Bresse 68 – Oyonnax 42

La Valouse

VISA

(opposite the church) – ☎ 03 84 25 54 80 – lavalouse@wanadoo.fr – Fax 03 84 25 54 70 – Closed 24 December-20 January and Sunday dinner

14 rm – €53 €73, €7,50 – ½ P €68

Rest – Menu €16 bi/48 bi – Carte €28/46

♦ This non-smoking family hotel has just been fully renovated. The simple and well-soundproofed rooms are modern and colourful. Updated local cuisine, or dish of the day available in adjoining café.

ORGEVAL – 78 Yvelines – 311 H2 – 101 11 – see Paris, Area

ORGON – 13 Bouches-du-Rhône – 340 F3 – pop. 2 642 – alt. 90 m – ✉ 13660
Provence 42 **E1**

Paris 712 – Aix-en-Provence 58 – Avignon 29 – Marseille 72

Office de tourisme, place de la Liberté ☎ 04 90 73 09 54, Fax 04 90 73 09 54

Le Mas de la Rose rm,
4 km south-westward along the D 24b – ☎ 04 90 73 08 91 – contact@mas-rose.com – Fax 04 90 73 31 03 – Closed 5 January-1st March
8 rm – €150/320 €150/320, €15 – 1 suite – ½ P €135/220
Rest – *(closed 5 January-13 April, 6 November-20 December, Tuesday, Wednesday and Thursday from 14 April to 31 May and from 1st October to 5 November, Sunday and Monday) (dinner only) (pre-book) (residents only)* Menu €45 (set menu)
◆ In a bucolic setting, these old 17C sheep barns have been tastefully converted. Provençal style rooms with individual touches. Superb landscaped garden with a pool. Elegant, rustic-contemporary decor and seasonal cuisine.

Domaine de Saint-Véran without rest
1.5 km north on the D 26 – ☎ 04 90 73 32 86 – d1jour@wanadoo.fr – Fax 04 90 73 39 57 – Closed January and February
5 rm – €70 €80/100
◆ Fine house, nestling in a large park planted with umbrella pine and cypress trees. Tastefully decorated interior, well-kept rooms, cosy lounge, pool, etc.

Auberge du Parc
rte de la Gare – ☎ 04 90 73 35 85 – info@aubergeduparc.net – Fax 04 90 73 39 60 – Closed 1st-31 November, Sunday dinner and Monday
Rest – *(number of covers limited, pre-book)* Menu (€20), €38/48
◆ At the bottom of rocky cliffs in the foothills of the Alpilles, this large warm residence surrounded by greenery has a colourful dining room and small terrace. Modern cuisine.

ORLÉANS P – 45 Loiret – 318 I4 – pop. 113 126 – Built-up area 263 292 – alt. 100 m – ✉ 45000 Châteaux of the Loire
12 **C2**

Paris 132 – Caen 311 – Clermont-Ferrand 295 – Le Mans 143 – Tours 118

Office de tourisme, 2, place de l'Étape ☎ 02 38 24 05 05, Fax 02 38 54 49 84

de Limère Ardon 1411 allée de la Pomme de Pin, South: 9 km by D 326, ☎ 02 38 63 89 40 ;

d'Orléans Donnery Donnery Domaine de la Touche, East:17 km by N 460, ☎ 02 38 59 25 15 ;

de Sologne La Ferté-Saint-Aubin Route de Jouy-le-Potier, South: 24 km by N 20 and D 18, ☎ 02 38 76 57 33 ;

de Marcilly Marcilly-en-Villette Domaine de la Plaine, Southeast by D 14 and D 108: 18 km, ☎ 02 38 76 11 73.

Ste-Croix cathedral ★★: panelling★★ - Maison de Jeanne d'Arc (Joan of Arc's House)★ V - Quai Fort-des-Tourelles ≤★ EZ **60** - Musée des Beaux-Arts★★ **M**[1] - Musée Historique et Archéologique★ **M**[2] - Muséum★.

Olivet: La Source floral park ★★ Southeast: 8 km CZ.

Plans on following pages

Mercure rm, rm,
44 quai Barentin – ☎ 02 38 62 17 39 – h0581@accor.com – Fax 02 38 53 95 34
112 rm – €80/130 €95/195, €14,50 DZ **t**
Rest – *(closed Saturday lunch and Sunday lunch)* Menu €16/21 – Carte €23/38
◆ The spacious, soundproofed rooms of this hotel now sport the latest design of the Mercure chain (modern furniture); those on the top floor command a view of the Loire. Boat-styled decor for this restaurant; collection of plates on a boating theme.

D'Arc without rest
– ☎ 02 38 53 10 94 – hotel.darc@wanadoo.fr – Fax 02 38 81 77 47 EY **g**
35 rm – €82/120 €96/155, €11
◆ Hotel with an original facade (Art Nouveau-inspired arch), housing redecorated rooms with Louis Philippe-style furniture. The period lift is museum-quality.

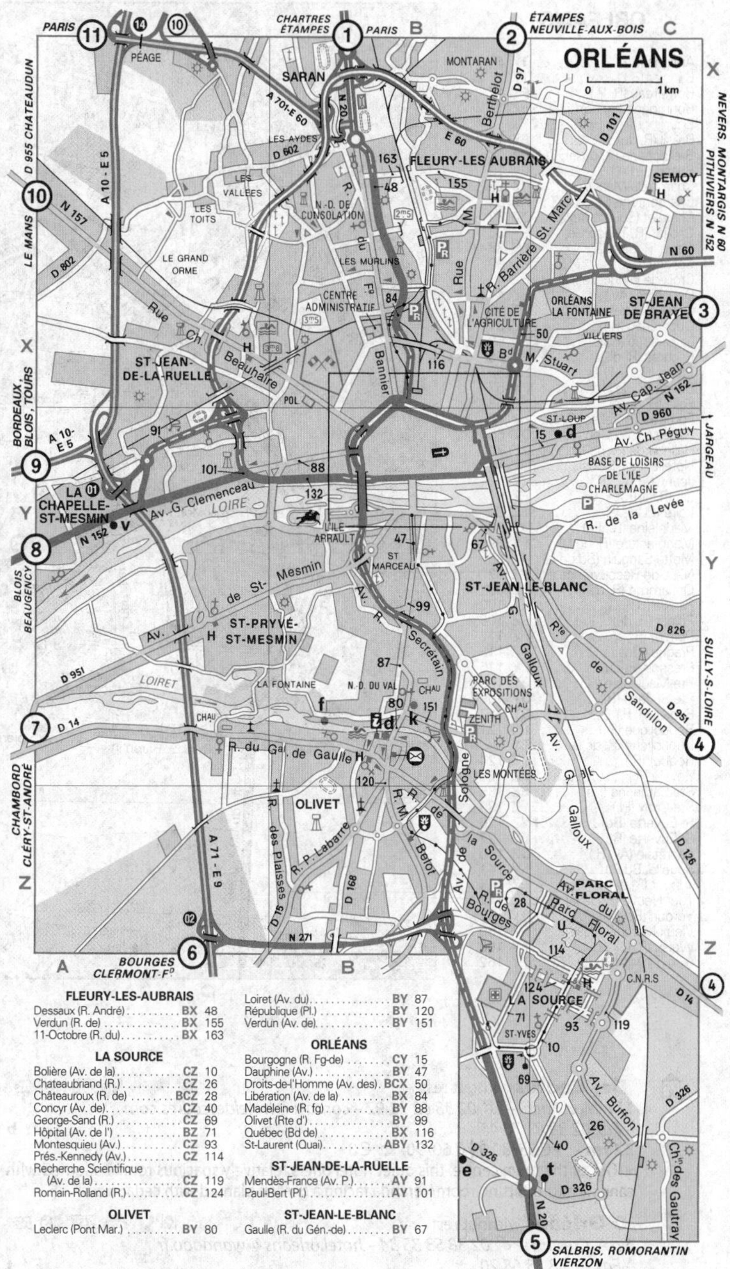

FLEURY-LES-AUBRAIS

Dessaux (R. André) . . . . **BX** 48
Verdun (R. de) . . . . **BX** 155
11-Octobre (R. du) . . . . **BX** 163

LA SOURCE

Bolière (Av. de la) . . . . **CZ** 10
Chateaubriand (R.) . . . . **CZ** 26
Châteauroux (R. de) . . . . **BCZ** 28
Concyr (Av. de) . . . . **CZ** 40
George-Sand (R.) . . . . **CZ** 69
Hôpital (Av. de l') . . . . **BZ** 71
Montesquieu (Av.) . . . . **CZ** 93
Prés.-Kennedy (Av.) . . . . **CZ** 114
Recherche Scientifique (Av. de la) . . . . **CZ** 119
Romain-Rolland (R.) . . . . **CZ** 124

OLIVET

Leclerc (Pont Mar.) . . . . **BY** 80
Loiret (Av. du) . . . . **BY** 87
République (Pl.) . . . . **BY** 120
Verdun (Av. de) . . . . **BY** 151

ORLÉANS

Bourgogne (R. Fg-de) . . . . **CY** 15
Dauphine (Av.) . . . . **BY** 47
Droits-de-l'Homme (Av. des) . **BCX** 50
Libération (Av. de la) . . . . **BX** 84
Madeleine (R. fg) . . . . **BY** 88
Olivet (Rte d') . . . . **BY** 99
Québec (Bd de) . . . . **BX** 116
St-Laurent (Quai) . . . . **ABY** 132

ST-JEAN-DE-LA-RUELLE

Mendès-France (Av. P.) . . . . **AY** 91
Paul-Bert (Pl.) . . . . **AY** 101

ST-JEAN-LE-BLANC

Gaulle (R. du Gén.-de) . . . . **BY** 67

ORLÉANS

Antigna (R.) . . . . DY 4
Bannier (R.) . . . . DY
Bothereau (R. R.). . . . . FY 14
Bourgogne (Fg de) . . . . . . FZ 15
Bourgogne (R. de). . . . . . EFZ
Brésil (R. du) . . . . FY 16
Bretonnerie (R. de la) . . . DEY 17
Briand (Bd A.) . . . . FY 19
Champ-de-Mars (Av.) . . . . DZ 25
Charpenterie (R. de la) . . . EZ 34
Châtelet (Square du) . . . . . EZ 32
Chollet (R. Théophile) . . . . EY 36
Claye (R. de la). . . . . FY 38
Coligny (R.). . . . . FZ 39
Croix-de-la-Pucelle (R.) . . . EZ 43
Dauphine (Av.). . . . . EZ 47
Dolet (R. Étienne) . . . . EZ 49
Ducerceau (R.). . . . . EZ 51
Dupanloup (R.) . . . . EFY 53
Escures (R. d') . . . . EY 55
Étape (Pl. de l') . . . . EY 56
Ételon (R. de l') . . . . FY 57
Folie (R. de la) . . . . FZ 58
Fort-des-Tourelles (Q.). . . . EZ 60
Gaulle (Pl. du Gén.-de) . . . DZ 65
Hallebarde (R. de la) . . . . . DY 70
Hôtelleries (R. des) . . . . . . EZ 71
Jeanne d'Arc (R.) . . . . EY
Lin (R. au). . . . . EZ 81
Loire (Pl. de la) . . . . EZ 85
Madeleine (R. Fg) . . . . . . DZ 88
Manufacture (R. de la) . . . FY 89
Motte-Sanguin (Bd de la) . FZ 95
N.-D.-de-Recouvrance (R.) DZ 97
Oriflamme (R. de l') . . . . . . FZ 98
Parisie (R.) . . . . EZ 100
Poirier (R. du). . . . . EZ 106
Pothier (R.). . . . . EZ 112
Prague (Quai) . . . . DZ 113
Pressoir (R. du). . . . . FY 115
Pte-Madeleine (R.) . . . . . . DY 108
Pte-St-Jean (R.). . . . . DY 109
Rabier (R. F.) . . . . EY 117
République (Pl.) . . . . EZ 121
République (R. de la). . . . . EY
Roquet (R.) . . . . EZ 124
Royale (R.) . . . . EZ 125
Ste-Catherine (R.) . . . . EZ 135
Ste-Croix (Pl.) . . . . EYZ 139
St-Euverte (Bd) . . . . FYZ 126
St-Euverte (R.). . . . . FY 127
Secrétain (Av. R.) . . . . DZ 140
Segellé (Bd P.). . . . . FY 141
Tabour (R. du) . . . . EZ 145
Tour Neuve (R. de la). . . . . FZ 147
Verdun (Bd de). . . . . DY 152
Vieux-Marché (Pl.). . . . . . . DZ 159
Weiss (R. L.) . . . . FY 160
6-Juin 1944 (Pl. du) . . . . . . FY 162

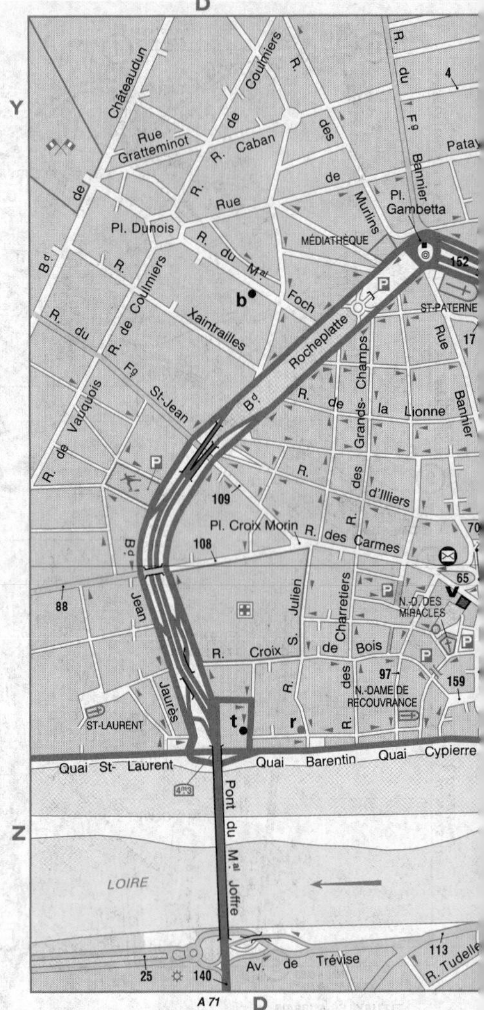

Des Cèdres without rest

17 r. Mar. Foch – ☎ 02 38 62 22 92 – contact@hoteldescedres.com – Fax 02 38 81 76 46 DY **b**

32 rm – 🚹€ 55/80 🚹🚹€ 60/90, ☕ € 8

◆ Out of the town centre, this quiet hotel offers relatively spacious rooms adorned with cane furniture. Sitting room/veranda facing a garden planted with cedar trees.

D'Orléans without rest

6 r. A. Crespin – ☎ 02 38 53 35 34 – hotel.orleans@wanadoo.fr – Fax 02 38 53 68 20 EY **t**

18 rm – 🚹€ 55/68 🚹🚹€ 65/80, ☕ € 7,50

◆ Two buildings set around a courtyard and linked together by the breakfast room. The rooms (new bedding) and interior are gradually being renovated.

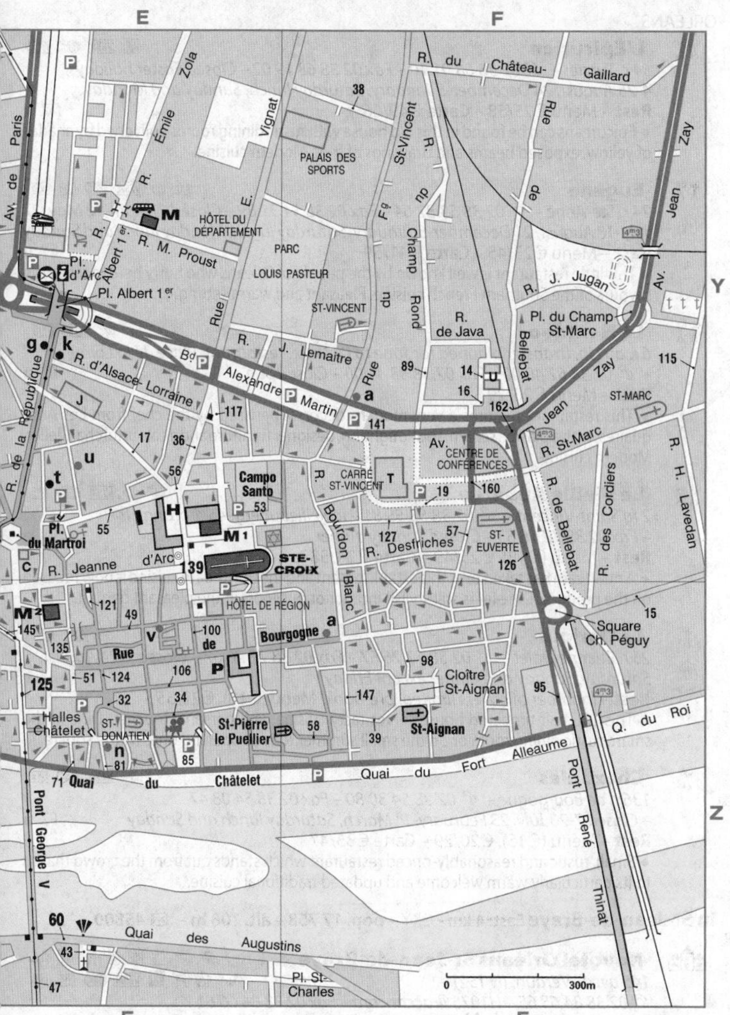

Marguerite without rest

14 pl. du Vieux Marché – ✆ 02 38 53 74 32 – hotel.marguerite@wanadoo.fr – Fax 02 38 53 31 56 DZ **f**

25 rm – †€ 51/62 ††€ 60/74, ☕ € 7

◆ This hotel is being progressively enhanced: tastefully refurbished interior and rooms (contemporary furnishings, flatscreen TV, wifi) with faultless soundproofing.

De l'Abeille without rest

64 r. d'Alsace-Lorraine – ✆ 02 38 53 54 87 – hoteldelabeille@wanadoo.fr – Fax 02 38 62 65 84 EY **k**

31 rm – †€ 47/79 ††€ 62/89, ☕ € 11

◆ This town-centre hotel offers small and stylish rooms; the majority have been redecorated. Personalised decoration with a choice of colours and hand-picked old furniture.

XX **L'Épicurien** AC VISA MC AE

54 r. Turcies – ✆ 02 38 68 01 10 – Fax 02 38 68 19 02 – Closed Easter holidays, 4-25 August, 24 December-5 January, Saturday lunch, Sunday and Monday
Rest – Menu € 25/58 – Carte € 49/66 DZ **r**

◆ Epicureans can be found in this old house with rustic dining rooms enlivened by shades of yellow, exposed beams and drawings of fruit. Modern cuisine.

XX **Eugène** AC VISA MC AE

24 r. Ste-Anne – ✆ 02 38 53 82 64 – Fax 02 38 54 31 89 – Closed 27 April-12 May, 27 July-18 August, 21 December-5 January, Saturday lunch, Monday lunch and Sunday
Rest – Menu € 23/45 – Carte € 41/59 EY **u**

◆ This little restaurant is well known by the people of Orleans who hurry here to relish the savours of the Southern French cuisine. Pleasant and warm setting.

XX **Le Nextdoor** AC VISA MC

6 r. au Lin, (transfer planned for June to Le Nexxt restaurant, Place de la Loire) – ✆ 02 38 62 40 00 – Fax 02 38 53 41 00 – Closed Sun EZ **n**
Rest – Menu € 20/29

◆ This restaurant features a very modern décor, supervised by the chef from Les Antiquaires, with a plasma screen, subtle lighting, designer furniture and a colourful chandelier. Modern cuisine.

XX **La Vieille Auberge** VISA MC AE

2 fg Saint-Vincent – ✆ 02 38 53 55 81 – lavieilleauberge45@orange.fr – Fax 02 38 77 16 63 – Closed Sunday dinner FY **a**
Rest – Menu (€ 18), € 25/49 – Carte € 34/58

◆ A new team has taken over this establishment and the up-to-date cuisine is now focused on the produce. Dine in its still stylish interior or outdoors in the pleasant garden.

X **La Dariole** VISA MC

25 r. Etienne Dolet – ✆ 02 38 77 26 67 – Fax 02 38 77 26 67 – Closed 2-24 August, Saturday, Sunday and dinner except Friday EZ **v**
Rest – *(number of covers limited, pre-book)* Menu (€ 18), € 22/35

◆ This 15C half-timbered house serves tasty cuisine with personal touches. Dine in the smart, rustic dining room or on the small summer terrace opening onto a little square.

X **Chez Jules** VISA MC AE

136 r. de Bourgogne – ✆ 02 38 54 30 80 – Fax 02 38 54 08 47 – Closed 7-20 July, 23 February-1st March, Saturday lunch and Sunday FZ **a**
Rest – Menu (€ 15), € 20/29 – Carte € 35/47

◆ Small, rustic and reasonably-priced restaurant which stands out from the crowd thanks to its particularly warm welcome and updated traditional cuisine.

in St-Jean-de-Braye East: 4 km - CXY – pop. 17 758 – alt. 108 m – ✉ 45800

Novotel Orléans St-Jean-de-Braye rm, AC P P VISA MC AE

145 av. de Verdun, (N 152) – ✆ 02 38 84 65 65 – H1075@accor.com – Fax 02 38 84 66 61
107 rm – †€ 70/140 ††€ 70/140, ☕ € 12,50 – **Rest** – Carte € 21/38

◆ Latest generation of Novotel rooms, garden and pool, children's play area and a location on the edge of a forest: such are a few of the pleasant features of this Novotel. Restaurant serving traditional cuisine.

Promotel without rest P VISA MC

117 fg Bourgogne – ✆ 02 38 53 64 09 – Fax 02 38 53 13 22 – Closed 2-31 August and 27 December-5 January CY **d**
83 rm – †€ 54/58 ††€ 58/72, ☕ € 8

◆ The most modern of these two buildings, well soundproofed, lies on a busy road; the other offers a shaded garden. Rooms are spacious and practical.

XX **Les Toqués** VISA MC

71 chemin du Halage – ✆ 02 38 86 50 20 – lestoques@noos.fr – Fax 02 38 84 30 96 – Closed August, Sunday and Monday
Rest – Menu € 19 (weekday lunch)/29

◆ On the banks of the Loire, tastefully converted former inn. Modern style interior, delightful summer terrace and appetising menu.

in La Source Southeast: 11 km- BCZ – ✉ 45100 Orléans

Novotel Orléans La Source
2 r. H. de Balzac, (crossroads N20-D326, Concyr road)
– ✆ 02 38 63 04 28 – h0419@accor.com – Fax 02 38 69 24 04 CZ **t**
119 rm – €85/129 €85/129, ☕ €12,50 – **Rest** – Carte €22/39
◆ The modern rooms (modular furniture) of this Novotel have been renovated in keeping with the chain's latest concept. Children's play area. The stylish restaurant offers a pleasant view of the pool and garden. Minimalist cuisine and diet recipes.

at Limère Park Southeast: 13 km by N 20 and D 326 – ✉ 45160 Ardon

Domaine des Portes de Sologne
200 allée des 4 vents – ✆ 02 38 49 99 99 rm,
– resa@portes-de-sologne.com – Fax 02 38 49 99 00 BZ **e**
117 rm – €106 €118, ☕ €11 – 14 suites – ½ P €95
Rest – Menu (€18), €25/42 – Carte €46/64
◆ Hotel complex, in the middle of the countryside, near a golf course and balneotherapy centre. Simply decorated rooms, charming cottages (two-floor family accommodation) and conference facilities. Modern and opulent restaurant serving updated cuisine; summer terrace.

in Olivet South: 5 km via Avenue Loiret and banks of the Loiret – pop. 19 195 – alt. 100 m – ✉ 45160 Châteaux of the Loire

Office de tourisme, 236, rue Paul Genain ✆ 02 38 63 49 68, Fax 02 38 63 50 45

Le Rivage with rm
635 r. Reine Blanche – ✆ 02 38 66 02 93 – hotel-le-rivage.jpb@wanadoo.fr
– Fax 02 38 56 31 11 – Closed 25 December-20 January BY **f**
17 rm – €80/95 €80/95, ☕ €13 – ½ P €87/102
Rest – *(closed Saturday lunch and Sunday dinner from November to Easter)*
Menu €28/58 – Carte €47/93
◆ Handsome villas and old mills: take full advantage of the pastoral scene on the banks of the Loiret from the bright veranda/dining room or the waterside terrace.

Laurendière
68 av. Loiret – ✆ 02 38 51 06 78 – lalaurendiere@wanadoo.fr – Fax 02 38 56 36 20
– Closed 7-17 July, 23 February-4 March, Monday dinner, Tuesday dinner and Wednesday BY **k**
Rest – Menu €23/49 – Carte €36/57
◆ Traditional cuisine and a fine choice of wines (many from the Loire) await you in this colourful restaurant located in an old, regional style house.

L'Eldorado
10 r. M.-Belot – ✆ 02 38 64 29 74 – eldorado45@wanadoo.fr – Fax 02 38 69 14 33
– Closed 1st-16 August, February school holidays, Monday and Tuesday
Rest – Menu €24 (weekday lunch), €36/50 – Carte €46/58 BY **d**
◆ The charming terrace by the banks of the Loiret and the pretty garden running down to the river are the two main assets of this former open-air café. Simply decorated dining rooms.

in la Chapelle-St-Mesmin West: 4 km - AY – pop. 8 967 – alt. 101 m – ✉ 45380

Orléans Parc Hôtel without rest
55 rte d'Orléans – ✆ 02 38 43 26 26 – lucmar@aol.com – Fax 02 38 72 00 99
– Closed 20 December-5 January – **33 rm** – €59 €75/92, ☕ €10
AY **v**
◆ Simply decorated, comfortable rooms (choose one overlooking the Loire), a welcoming lounge and breakfast room. The attractive, shady riverside park is ideal for a pleasant stroll.

Ciel de Loire
55 rte Orléans – ✆ 02 38 72 29 51 – Fax 02 38 72 29 67 – Closed Sunday dinner, Saturday lunch and Monday – **Rest** – Menu €26/45 – Carte €39/56 AY **v**
◆ Lovely 19C residence surrounded by gardens with opulent bedrooms and lounges (period furniture and beautiful Gien earthenware crockery). Modern cuisine.

ORLY (Aéroports de Paris) – 91 Essonne – 312 D3 – 101 26 – see Paris, Area

ORMOY-LA-RIVIÈRE – 91 Essonne – 312 B5 – see Étampes

ORNAISONS – 11 Aude – 344 I3 – see Narbonne

ORNANS – 25 Doubs – 321 G4 – pop. 4 037 – alt. 355 m – ✉ 25290

Burgundy-Jura 16 **B2**

Paris 428 – Baume-les-Dames 42 – Besançon 26 – Morteau 48 – Pontarlier 37

Office de tourisme, 7, rue Pierre Vernier ✆ 03 81 62 21 50, Fax 03 81 62 02 63

Grand Pont ≤★ - West: Vallée de la Loue (Loue Valley)★★ - Le Château (Castle) ≤★ North: 2.5 km.

De France

r. P. Vernier – ✆ 03 81 62 24 44 – contact@hoteldefrance-ornans.com – Fax 03 81 62 12 03 – Closed 10-23 November, 21 December-26 January, Friday dinner and Sunday dinner from November to April

26 rm – †€ 60/65 ††€ 85/90, ☕ € 9 – 1 suite – ½ P € 80/85

Rest – *(closed Friday dinner, Saturday lunch, Sunday dinner from November to April and Monday lunch)* Menu (€ 14), € 19/43 – Carte € 41/59

◆ A traditional hotel in a village known as the Pearl of the Loue. Rooms of varying sizes gradually being renovated, and fine suites. Private, world-renowned fly fishing course. A pleasant restaurant in an elegant rustic setting facing the Great Bridge over the Loue.

Le Jardin de Gustave

28 r. Édouard Bastide – ✆ 03 81 62 21 47 – info@lejardindegustave.fr Fax 03 81 62 21 47 – **3 rm** ☕ – †€ 60/78 ††€ 60/78 – **Table d'hôte** – Menu € 25 bi

◆ Charming house on the banks of the Loue with a most pleasant welcome. The names of the rooms (Champêtre, Gustavienne, Jungle) indicate the decor within. Homemade jam at breakfast; cuisine with local flavours served in the garden in summer.

Courbet

34 r. P. Vernier – ✆ 03 81 62 10 15 – restaurantlecourbet@wanadoo.fr – Fax 03 81 62 13 34 – Closed Christmas holidays, 16 February-15 March, Sunday dinner and Tuesday except July-August and Monday

Rest – Menu € 18/38 – Carte € 32/40

◆ A few feet from the house where Courbet was born, the dining room where delicious modern cuisine is served, pays homage to the painter with reproductions. Terrace on the Loue.

in Saules 6 km northeast by D 492 – pop. 191 – alt. 585 m – ✉ 25580

La Griotte

27 b Grande Rue – ✆ 03 81 57 17 71 – Closed 1st-10 September, 16 February-11 March, Tuesday from September to April, Sunday dinner and Wednesday

Rest – *(number of covers limited, pre-book)* Menu € 14/29 – Carte € 24/40

◆ Successful, recently opened restaurant set in an old staging post. Friendly welcome, simple decor and well-priced regional cuisine.

OROUET – 85 Vendée – 316 E7 – see St-Jean-de-Monts – ✉ 85160

ORPIERRE – 05 Hautes-Alpes – 334 C7 – pop. 256 – alt. 682 m – ✉ 05700

French Alps 40 **B2**

Paris 689 – Château-Arnoux 47 – Digne-les-Bains 72 – Gap 55 – Serres 20 – Sisteron 33

Office de tourisme, le Village ✆ 04 92 66 30 45, Fax 04 92 66 32 52

in Bégües Southwest: 4,5 km – ✉ 05700 Orpierre

Le Céans

rest,

rte des Princes d'Orange – ✆ 04 92 66 24 22 – le.ceans@gmail.com – Fax 04 92 66 28 29 – Open 15 March-1st November and closed Wednesday from October to 15 April – **23 rm** – †€ 42/48 ††€ 42/88, ☕ € 8 – ½ P € 41/55

Rest – Menu € 16/37 – Carte € 22/39

◆ In the centre of a hamlet in the Massif des Baronnies, small renovated rooms and family lodges dotted around a country park that stretches down to the river. A restaurant with a guesthouse atmosphere, and family cooking based on regional specialities. Street-facing terrace.

ORSCHWILLER – 67 Bas-Rhin – 315 I7 – pop. 535 – alt. 240 m – ✉ 67600

Paris 441 – Colmar 22 – St-Dié 44 – Sélestat 7 – Strasbourg 61 2 **C1**

Le Fief du Château

– ✆ 03 88 82 56 25 – fiefduchateau@evc.net – Fax 03 88 82 26 24 – Closed 3-10 March, 30 June-5 July, 27 October-3 November – **8 rm** € 45 € 47, € 7,50 – ½ P € 47 – **Rest** – *(closed Wednesday)* Menu € 19/30 – Carte € 33/40

◆ A late-19C, regional style house with a pretty, flower-decked facade in a typical village on the Alsace wine route. Simple, refurbished rooms. Restaurant with a rustic feel, a friendly welcome and Alsatian cuisine.

ORTHEZ – 64 Pyrénées-Atlantiques – 342 H4 – pop. 10 121 – alt. 55 m – ✉ 64300

Atlantic Coast 3 **B3**

Paris 765 – Bayonne 74 – Dax 39 – Mont-de-Marsan 57 – Pau 47

Office de tourisme, rue Bourg-Vieux ✆ 05 59 38 32 84, Fax 05 59 69 12 00

de Salies-de-Béarn Quartier Hélios, by Bayonne road: 17 km, ✆ 05 59 38 37 59.

Pont Vieux★.

Au Temps de la Reine Jeanne

44 r. Bourg-Vieux – ✆ 05 59 67 00 76 – reine.jeanne.orthez@wanadoo.fr – Fax 05 59 69 09 63

30 rm – € 57/78 € 63/98, € 8,50 – ½ P € 60/71

Rest – *(closed 23-29 December, 17 February-9 March, Sunday dinner and Monday from 15 October to 15 March)* Menu € 23/39 – Carte € 41/52

◆ Former 18C and 19C residences housing small rooms set around a covered patio. The neighbouring building offers modern, larger and more comfortable rooms. Pleasant, rustic restaurant. Traditional menu and jazz evenings with dinner in the season.

ORVAULT – 44 Loire-Atlantique – 316 G4 – see Nantes

OSNY – 95 Val-d'Oise – 305 D6 – 106 5 – 101 2 – see Paris, Area (Cergy-Pontoise)

OSTHOUSE – 67 Bas-Rhin – 315 J6 – pop. 946 – alt. 155 m – ✉ 67150 1 **B2**

Paris 502 – Obernai 17 – Offenburg 35 – Sélestat 23 – Strasbourg 32

À la Ferme without rest

10 r. du Château – ✆ 03 90 29 92 50 – hotelalaferme@wanadoo.fr – Fax 03 90 29 92 51 – **7 rm** – € 83/86 € 86/135, € 14

◆ Former 18C farmhouse and stables, offering peaceful, smart and spacious rooms with a personal touch. Attentive service too.

A l'Aigle d'Or

– ✆ 03 88 98 06 82 – hotelalaferme@wanadoo.fr – Fax 03 88 98 81 75 – Closed 3 weeks in August, Christmas holidays, February school holidays, Monday and Tuesday – **Rest** – Menu € 33 (weekdays)/70 – Carte € 52/64

Rest *Winstub* – Menu (€ 10) – Carte € 20/40

◆ The family goes to great lengths to welcome you in this warm, elegant and refined restaurant (wood panelling and attractive painted coffered ceiling). Classic cuisine. The Winstub offers a relaxed atmosphere and fairly plush decor serving Alsatian specialities.

OSTWALD – 67 Bas-Rhin – 315 K5 – see Strasbourg

OTTROTT – 67 Bas-Rhin – 315 I6 – see Obernai

OUCHAMPS – 41 Loir-et-Cher – 318 E7 – pop. 803 – alt. 92 m – ✉ 41120 11 **A1**

Paris 199 – Blois 18 – Montrichard 19 – Romorantin-Lanthenay 40 – Tours 57

Château de Fougères-sur-Bièvre★ Northwest: 5 km, Châteaux of the Loire

Relais des Landes

1.5 km north on D 7 – ✆ 02 54 44 40 40 – info@relaisdeslandes.com – Fax 02 54 44 03 89 – Open 7 March-30 November

28 rm – € 103/124 € 103/154, € 14,50 – ½ P € 113/139

Rest – Menu € 40/47 – Carte € 46/57

◆ This fine 17C manor house stands in extensive grounds with an ornamental lake. Quite large, country smart rooms; private terrace for the duplex. Cosy, countrified lounge-bar. Beautiful rustic dining room (fireplace, fresco) and veranda facing the garden.

OUCQUES – 41 Loir-et-Cher – 318 E5 – pop. 1 313 – alt. 127 m – ✉ 41290 11 B2

Paris 160 – Beaugency 30 – Blois 27 – Châteaudun 30 – Orléans 62 – Vendôme 21

Syndicat d'initiative, Mairie ✆ 02 54 23 11 00, Fax 02 54 23 11 04

Du Commerce with rm

9 r. de Beaugency – ✆ 02 54 23 20 41 – hotelrestaurantcommerce@wanadoo.fr – Fax 02 54 23 02 88 – Closed 20 December-5 January, 5-13 March, Sunday dinner and Monday except July -August

11 rm – €61 €66, ☕ €9 – ½ P €64 – **Rest** – *(pre-book Sat - Sun)* Menu €21/60 – Carte €45/68

◆ A 1970s-style dining room with attentive service, serving well-prepared up-to-date cuisine. Colourful and well-kept rooms.

OUESSANT (ÎLE) – 29 Finistère – 308 A4 – see Île d' Ouessant

OUHANS – 25 Doubs – 321 H5 – pop. 334 – alt. 600 m – ✉ 25520 17 C2

Paris 450 – Besançon 48 – Pontarlier 18 – Salins-les-Bains 40

Source of the Loue ★★★ North: 2.5 km then 30 mn - Belvédère du Moine de la Vallée (viewpoint) ★★ Northwest: 5 km - Belvédère de Renédale (viewpoint) ≤★ Northwest: 4 km then 15 mn, **Burgundy-Jura**

Les Sources de la Loue

in the village – ✆ 03 81 69 90 06 – hotel.des.sources@free.fr – Fax 03 81 69 93 17 – Closed 15 November-31 March, Friday dinner and Sunday off season

14 rm – €45 €47/54, ☕ €7,50 – ½ P €50/54 – **Rest** – *(closed 22 December-1st February, 20-30 March, 20-30 September, Friday dinner and Saturday lunch off season)* Menu €13 (weekday lunch), €24/32 – Carte €20/45

◆ A large square house, in the centre of the village, with rather large, simply furnished and well-maintained rooms with double-glazing. Restaurant with a country-style decor; summer terrace and Franche-Comté dishes.

OUILLY-DU-HOULEY – 14 Calvados – 303 N4 – see Lisieux

OUISTREHAM – 14 Calvados – 303 K4 – pop. 8 679 – Casino : Riva Bella – ✉ 14150 Normandy 32 B2

Paris 234 – Arromanches-les-Bains 33 – Bayeux 44 – Cabourg 20 – Caen 16

Office de tourisme, esplanade Lofi ✆ 02 31 97 18 63, Fax 02 31 96 87 33

St-Samson church ★.

Du Phare

10 pl. Gén. de Gaulle – ✆ 02 31 97 13 13 – hotelduphare@wanadoo.fr – Fax 02 31 97 14 57 – Closed 24 December-3 January

19 rm – €52/61 €52/61, ☕ €6 – **Rest** – *(closed dinner October-May and Wednesday September-May)* Menu €21 – Carte €12/25

◆ A hotel that is strategically located near the locks and opposite the ferry terminal, offering identical, modernised rooms, at reasonable rates. Simple, brasserie-type food served on a veranda that is turned into a terrace in summer.

Le Normandie with rm

71 av. M. Cabieu, au port d'Ouistreham – ✆ 02 31 97 19 57 – hotel@lenormandie.com – Fax 02 31 97 20 07 – Closed 23 December-31 January, Sunday dinner and Monday from November to March

22 rm – €65/75 €65/75, ☕ €10 – ½ P €70 – **Rest** – Menu €19, €22/73 – Carte €36/99

◆ Restaurant in a regional-style house near the harbour. Choose your table in the bright and colourful dining room or on the elegant veranda.

La Mare Ô Poissons

68 r. E.-Herbline – ✆ 02 31 37 53 05 – info@lamareopoissons.fr – Fax 02 31 37 49 61

Rest – *(closed Saturday lunch and Monday)* Menu €38 – Carte €41/61

◆ A contemporary restaurant at the end of a courtyard accessed via a delicatessen. Two elegantly uncluttered dining rooms. Modern cuisine with an individual touch, fish and seafood.

in Riva-Bella – ✉ **14150 Ouistreham**

Riva Bella rest, VISA AE

av. Cdt Kieffer – ✆ 02 31 96 40 40 – ouistreham@thalazur.fr – Fax 02 31 96 45 45 – Closed 7-26 December

89 rm – €110 €145/160, ☕ €12,50 – ½ P €87/112

Rest – Menu (€16), €29/49 – Carte €26/52

◆ Large beachside hotel complex housing a thalassotherapy centre. Spacious, simply furnished rooms, some of which have a sea view. Pool free of charge after 5pm. The panoramic restaurant offers set buffets, special menus for guests taking the waters and low-calorie dishes.

Mercure rm, VISA AE

37 r. des Dunes – ✆ 02 31 96 20 20 – h1967@accor.com – Fax 02 31 97 10 10

49 rm – €75/80 €85/90, ☕ €10 – ½ P €60/65 – **Rest** – Menu (€12), €16/22 – Carte €18/49

◆ Cruise-ship cabins were the inspiration for the decor in the rooms in this modern building a stone's throw from the harbour. The restaurant has colourful walls, adorned with photos of ships, and offers traditional cuisine.

De la Plage without rest VISA AE

39 av. Pasteur – ✆ 02 31 96 85 16 – info-hoteldelaplage@wanadoo.fr – Fax 02 31 97 37 46 – Closed 2-31 January

16 rm – €55/59 €59/72, ☕ €9

◆ A late-19C, Anglo-Norman villa in a quiet street near the beach. Stylish bedrooms, the more spacious ones more suitable for families. Refurbished lounge and attractive garden.

in Hermanville-sur-Mer **5 km West by D35^A and D 35 – pop. 2 661 – alt. 13 m –** ✉ **14880**

Syndicat d'initiative, place du Cuirassé Courbet ✆ 02 31 36 18 00

Le Canada without rest VISA

183 r. Amiral Wietzel – ✆ 02 31 97 23 48 – contact@hotellecanada.com – Fax 02 31 08 00 19 – Closed January

20 rm – €40/75 €45/80, ☕ €7,50

◆ The hotel has a half-timbered façade and offers simple, comfortable and well-kept rooms renovated in bright colours. Choose those at the back, as none enjoy a sea view.

LES OURSINIÈRES – 83 Var – 340 L7 – see le Pradet

OUSSON-SUR-LOIRE – 45 Loiret – 318 N6 – pop. 758 – alt. 158 m – ✉ 45250

12 **D2**

Paris 165 – Orléans 96 – Gien 19 – Montargis 51 – Châlette-sur-Loing 52

Le Clos du Vigneron rm, rm, VISA

18 rte Nationale 7 – ✆ 02 38 31 43 11 – leclosduvigneron@orange.fr – Fax 02 38 31 14 84 – Closed 23 December-4 February, Sunday dinner, Tuesday dinner and Wednesday

8 rm – €56 €56, ☕ €7,50 – ½ P €55 – **Rest** – Menu €17 (weekday lunch), €28/47 – Carte €37/48

◆ Totally renovated regional construction with comfortable rooms (those in the extension are at garden level). Contemporary cuisine served in a soberly-decorated dining room.

OUZOUER-SUR-LOIRE – 45 Loiret – 318 L5 – pop. 2 524 – alt. 140 m – ✉ 45570

Paris 151 – Gien 16 – Montargis 45 – Orléans 54 – Pithiviers 55 – Sully-sur-Loire 9

12 **C2**

L'Abricotier VISA AE

106 r. Gien – ✆ 02 38 35 07 11 – Fax 02 38 35 07 11 – Closed 27 July-12 August, 4-12 January, Sunday dinner, Wednesday dinner and Monday

Rest – *(number of covers limited, pre-book)* Menu (€19), €24/38 – Carte €43/49

◆ A courteous welcome, cosy provincial atmosphere and tasty traditional dishes inspired by market produce are the plus points of this inn situated in the centre of the village.

OYONNAX – 01 Ain – **328** G3 – **pop. 24 162** – **alt. 540 m** – ✉ **01100** Burgundy-Jura

Paris 484 – Bourg-en-Bresse 60 – Nantua 19 45 **C1**

Syndicat d'initiative, 1, rue Bichat ✆ 04 74 77 94 46, Fax 04 74 77 68 27

XX **La Toque Blanche** VISA

11 pl. Émile Zola – ✆ 04 74 73 42 63 – la.toqueblanche@club-internet.fr – Fax 04 74 73 76 48 – Closed 27 July-20 August, 2-10 January, Saturday lunch, Sunday dinner and Monday

Rest – Menu € 19/70 – Carte € 40/59

◆ A restaurant with an attractive decor brightened up with warm colours. Its cuisine blends elements from the Bresse, Jura and Lyon regions.

at Genin Lake Southeast: 10 km by D 13 – ✉ **01130 Charix**

Site★ of the lake.

X **Auberge du Lac Genin** with rm rm, VISA

– ✆ 04 74 75 52 50 – lacgenin@wanadoo.fr – Fax 04 74 75 51 15 – Closed 13 October-27 November, Sunday dinner and Monday

3 rm – €48 €58, € 5,50 – **Rest** – Menu € 12/20 – Carte € 19/34

◆ This lakeside inn is surrounded by peace and quiet. Smart dining room with fireplace and frequently packed terrace. Rooms refurbished in a modern alpine spirit.

OZOIR-LA-FERRIÈRE – 77 Seine-et-Marne – **312** F3 – **106** 33 – **101** 30 – see Paris, Area

PACY-SUR-EURE – 27 Eure – **304** I7 – **pop. 4 751** – **alt. 40 m** – ✉ **27120** Normandy

Paris 81 – Dreux 38 – Évreux 20 – Louviers 33 – Mantes-la-Jolie 28 – Rouen 62 – Vernon 14 33 **D2**

Office de tourisme, place Dufay ✆ 02 32 26 18 21, Fax 02 32 36 96 67

Altina rm, VISA

rte de Paris – ✆ 02 32 36 13 18 – altinasa@aol.com – Fax 02 32 26 05 11

29 rm – €55/63 €58/66, € 8

Rest – Menu € 13 (weekday lunch), € 21/32 – Carte € 26/45

◆ Located in a business district, this establishment has large, simple and contemporary rooms. A lounge bar decked in flowers and cacti. This recently refurbished restaurant offers guests a friendly welcome and simple, reasonably priced menus.

L'Etape de la Vallée VISA

1 r. Edouard Isambard – ✆ 02 32 36 12 77 – etapedelavallee@wanadoo.fr – Fax 02 32 36 22 74

15 rm – €52/74 €62/82, € 10 – ½ P € 62/71 – **Rest** – *(closed Sunday dinner and Monday)* Menu € 19 (weekday lunch), € 28/49 – Carte € 30/66

◆ A large, attractive and fine riverside villa. Two kinds of rooms available: cosy with personal touches at the front, or more functional and all the same at the back. Traditional restaurant with a warm setting; picture windows overlooking the River Eure.

in Cocherel Northwest: 6,5 km by D 836 – ✉ **27120 Houlbec-Cocherel**

XXX **La Ferme de Cocherel** with rm VISA

8 r. Aristide Briand – ✆ 02 32 36 68 27 – info@lafermedecocherel.fr – Fax 02 32 26 28 18 – Closed 2-24 September, 5-22 January, Tuesday and Wednesday except holidays

3 rm – €119 €119/143, € 12 – ½ P € 112/124

Rest – *(number of covers limited, pre-book)* Menu € 40/58 – Carte € 84/121

◆ Cosy dining room with fireplace or a pleasant rotunda opening onto the flower-decked garden. Classic fare and fine cheese platter. Non-smoking establishment.

PADIRAC – 46 Lot – **337** G2 – **pop. 168** – **alt. 360 m** – ✉ **46500** 29 **C1**

Paris 531 – Brive-la-Gaillarde 50 – Cahors 68 – Figeac 41 – Gramat 10 – St-Céré 17

Syndicat d'initiative, village ✆ 05 65 33 47 17, Fax 05 65 33 47 17

Gouffre de Padirac★★ North: 2,5 km, **Dordogne-Berry-Limousin**

L'Auberge de Mathieu rm, VISA

rte du gouffre, 2 km – ✆ 05 65 33 64 68 – cathy.pinquie@wanadoo.fr – Fax 05 65 33 64 68 – Open 1st April-15 November
6 rm – €52 €52/64, €7 – ½ P €55 – **Rest** – Menu (€17), €26/37 – Carte €37/55
◆ Located just a couple of hundred metres from the entrance to the Gouffre de Padirac, this auberge offers guests unpretentious service and accommodation that is basic but functional. Regional dishes speedily served in the pastel-coloured dining room or on the shady terrace.

PAILHEROLS – 15 Cantal – 330 E5 – pop. 153 – alt. 1 000 m – ✉ 15800 5 B3

Paris 558 – Aurillac 32 – Entraygues-sur-Truyère 45 – Murat 39 – Vic-sur-Cère 14

Auberge des Montagnes rm, VISA

– ✆ 04 71 47 57 01 – aubdesmont@aol.com – Fax 04 71 49 63 83 – Closed 11 November-20 December
23 rm – €55/68 €55/68, €7,50 – ½ P €47/55
Rest *(closed 7 October-20 December and Tuesday)* Menu €20/35 – Carte €22/33
◆ This prettily restored farmhouse offers numerous leisure activities (Turkish bath, climbing wall, etc.). Attractive wood-panelled rooms; those in the annex are more spacious. Welcoming dining rooms, one on a veranda; well-prepared, generous portions of Auvergne cuisine.

PAIMPOL – 22 Côtes-d'Armor – 309 D2 – pop. 7 932 – alt. 15 m – ✉ 22500 Brittany

Paris 494 – Guingamp 29 – Lannion 33 – St-Brieuc 46 10 C1

Office de tourisme, 19, rue du Général Leclerc ✆ 02 96 20 83 16, Fax 02 96 55 11 12

Beauport abbey★ 2 km by D 786 - Tour de Kerroc'h ←★ 3 km by D 789 then 15 mn.

Pointe de Minard★★ 11 km by D 786.

K'Loys without rest VISA

21 quai Morand – ✆ 02 96 20 40 01 – hotelkloys@orange.fr – Fax 02 96 20 72 68
17 rm – €85 €85/200, €8
◆ Former ship owner's residence facing the harbour. Reception area enhanced with period or Breton furniture. Cosy lounge, rooms with classical decor and breakfast in the conservatory.

Goëlo without rest VISA

quai Duguay-Trouin – ✆ 02 96 20 82 74 – contact@legoelo.com – Fax 02 96 20 58 93 – Closed 23 May-1st June and 30 November-2 December
32 rm – €45/50 €51/75, €7
◆ A recent building set on the marina quayside. Nearly all the small but comfortable rooms have been renovated (warm tones and new furniture).

De la Marne with rm rest, rm, VISA

30 r. de la Marne – ✆ 02 96 20 82 16 – hotel.marne22.restaurant@wanadoo.fr – Fax 02 96 20 92 07 – Closed 5-21 October, 9-23 February, Tuesday from October to March, Sunday dinner and Monday
10 rm – €58 €58/78, €9 – ½ P €68 – **Rest** – Menu €29/60
◆ Stone house not far from the railway station. Friendly welcome. Dining room in sunny colours, modern cuisine with more than a pinch of personality, and neo-rustic rooms.

La Vieille Tour VISA

13 r. de l'Église – ✆ 02 96 20 83 18 – restaurant.lavieilletour.paimpol@orange.fr – Fax 02 96 20 90 41 – Closed 23-30 June, Sunday dinner and Wednesday except July-August and Monday – **Rest** – Menu (€16), €29/70 – Carte €40/68
◆ Welcoming, rustic 16C inn, at the heart of the old town. Dining rooms on several floors, individual table settings and seasonal traditional cuisine.

La Cotriade ← VISA

16 quai Armand Dayot – ✆ 02 96 20 81 08 – natalietvincent@yahoo.fr – Closed 1st-4 July, 17 November-1st December, 2-16 February, Wednesday dinner off season, Monday except dinner in season, Wednesday lunch in season and Saturday lunch
Rest – Menu €25 – Carte €41/64
◆ Luminous dining room with seascapes, a terrace on the harbourside, a charming welcome and tasty fish/seafood cuisine with dishes based on the daily catch.

in Ploubazlanec 3.5 km north by D 789 – **309** D2 – **pop. 3 321** – **alt. 60 m** – ✉ **22620**

Les Agapanthes without rest
1 r. Adrien Rebours – ✆ 02 96 55 89 06 – contact@hotel-les-agapanthes.com – Fax 02 96 55 79 79 – Closed 1st-14 January
9 rm – €40/68 €40/68, €7
◆ This small renovated hotel at the heart of the village occupies a distinctive house looking onto a garden, with a terrace facing the bay. Pleasant rooms and a friendly welcome.

in la Pointe de l'Arcouest North: 6 km – ✉ **22620 Ploubazlanec**
★★.

Le Barbu   Ile de Bréhat, rm,
– ✆ 02 96 55 86 98 – hotel.lebarbu@wanadoo.fr – Fax 02 96 55 73 87
21 rm – €62/112 €62/112, €12 – **Rest** – Menu €19 (lunch), €29/55 – Carte €33/74
◆ An imposing house next to the landing stage for "the island of flowers and pirates". Rooms overlooking the sea or at garden level. Fish and seafood while you admire the magnificent view of the bay of Bréhat.

Look out for red symbols, indicating particularly pleasant establishments.

PAIMPONT – **35 Ille-et-Vilaine** – **309** I6 – **pop. 1 395** – **alt. 159 m** – ✉ **35380** 10 **C2**
Brittany

Paris 393 – Bruz 37 – Cesson-Sévigné 54 – Rennes 42
Syndicat d'initiative, 5, esplanade de Brocéliande ✆ 02 99 07 84 23, Fax 02 99 07 84 24

La Corne de Cerf without rest
Le Cannée, 2 km south – ✆ 02 99 07 84 19 – Fax 02 99 07 84 19 – Closed January
3 rm – €47 €55
◆ The legendary Brocéliande Forest is only a stone's throw from this long house, decorated like an artist's home. Cheerful rooms. Homemade organic bread and jams at breakfast.

PAIRIS – **68 Haut-Rhin** – **315** G8 – **see Orbey**

LE PALAIS – **56 Morbihan** – **308** M10 – **see Belle-Ile-en-Mer**

PALAVAS-LES-FLOTS – **34 Hérault** – **339** I7 – **pop. 5 421** – **alt. 1 m** – **Casino** – ✉ **34250** Languedoc-Roussillon-Tarn Gorges 23 **C2**

Paris 763 – Aigues-Mortes 26 – Montpellier 17 – Nîmes 60 – Sète 33
Office de tourisme, Phare de la Méditerranée ✆ 04 67 07 73 34, Fax 04 67 07 73 58
Former★ aguelone cathedral Southwest: 4 km.

Amérique Hôtel without rest
av. F. Fabrège – ✆ 04 67 68 04 39 – hotel.amerique@wanadoo.fr – Fax 04 67 68 07 83
49 rm – €51/80 €51/80, €9
◆ A hotel, opened in the 1970s, comprising two buildings separated by an avenue leading to the sea. The original style of the rooms has been maintained. Swimming pool and Jacuzzi.

Brasilia without rest
9 bd Joffre – ✆ 04 67 68 00 68 – hotel@brasilia-palavas.com – Fax 04 67 68 40 41 – Closed 1st December-2 January
22 rm – €49/101 €49/101, €7
◆ This seafront hotel has simple rooms, we suggest choosing one with a balcony looking out to sea or to the lighthouse.

L'Escale

5 bd Sarrail, (left bank) – 04 67 68 24 17 – rizzotti@club-internet.fr – Fax 04 67 68 24 17 – Closed Wednesday September-June except public holidays, Wednesday lunch and Thursday lunch in July-August
Rest – Menu € 19 (weekday lunch), € 28/65 – Carte € 42/80
♦ The elegant dining hall and veranda offer a fine prospect of the beach and waterfront. Appetising up-to-date cuisine largely inspired by the nearby sea.

PALEYRAC – **24 Dordogne** – **329** G7 – **see Buisson-de-Cadouin**

LE PALLET – **44 Loire-Atlantique** – **316** H5 – **see Clissson**

LA PALMYRE – 17 Charente-Maritime – 324 C5 – ✉ 17570 38 A3

Paris 519 – La Rochelle 80 – Royan 16
Office de tourisme, 2, avenue de Royan 05 46 22 41 07, Fax 05 46 22 52 69

Palmyr'hotel

– 05 46 23 65 65 – resa-palmyre@monalisahotels.com – Fax 05 46 22 44 13 – Open 22 March-10 November
46 rm – €65/115 €65/115, € 11 – **Rest** – Menu (€ 23), € 29/44 – Carte € 35/43
♦ Not far from the zoo, forest and beaches, this hotel complex offers functional rooms, almost all of which have a balcony. A few duplex rooms. Contemporary low-key decor and a terrace that is teeming in fine weather.

LA PALUD-SUR-VERDON – 04 Alpes-de-Haute-Provence – 334 G10 – pop. 297 – alt. 930 m – ✉ 04120 French Alps 41 C2

Paris 796 – Castellane 25 – Digne-les-Bains 65 – Draguignan 60 – Manosque 68
Syndicat d'initiative, le Château 04 92 77 32 02, Fax 04 92 77 32 02
Viewpoints: Trescaïre★★, 5 km, Escalès★★★, 7 km by D 952 then D 23 - Point Sublime★★★, ≤ on the Grand Canyon du Verdon Northeast: 7.5 km then 15 mn.

Des Gorges du Verdon

rte de la Maline South : 1 km – 04 92 77 38 26 – bog@worldonline.fr – Fax 04 92 77 35 00 – Open 11 April-20 October
27 rm – €105/190 €110/190 – 3 suites – ½ P € 80/170 – **Rest** – Menu € 33
♦ On a hillside near the village, the hotel is a favourite with hikers. Rooms enlivened by colourful fabrics; duplex family rooms and lovely suites. The menu is inspired by the region and served in a setting that also reflects local traditions.

Auberge des Crêtes

rest,

East : 1 km on D 952 – 04 92 77 38 47 – aubergedescretes@orange.fr – Fax 04 92 77 30 40 – Open 1st April-15 October
12 rm – €55/74 €64/86, € 9 – ½ P € 54/63 – **Rest** – Menu € 27
♦ Rock climbers love this stopover where they can unwind in simple and well-maintained rooms, under the eaves on the upper floor.

PAMIERS – 09 Ariège – 343 H6 – pop. 13 417 – alt. 280 m – ✉ 09100 Languedoc-Roussillon-Tarn Gorges 29 C3

Paris 745 – Auch 147 – Carcassonne 76 – Castres 106 – Foix 20 – Toulouse 70
Office de tourisme, boulevard Delcassé 05 61 67 52 52, Fax 05 34 01 00 39

De France

rm, rest,

5 cours J Rambaud – 05 61 60 20 88 – contact@hoteldefrancepamiers.com – Fax 05 61 67 29 48
31 rm – €45/55 €50/60, € 8 – ½ P € 45/50
Rest – *(closed 21 December-5 January, Monday lunch, Saturday lunch and Sunday)* Menu € 18 (weekdays)/70 – Carte € 46/66
♦ Located close to the town centre, the Hotel de France has benefited from a welcome makeover. Rooms gradually being upgraded in a contemporary style with wood furniture. The dining room has retained its exposed beams and whitewashed walls. Tasty cuisine with a personal touch.

De la Paix AC rest, P VISA MC AE
4 pl. A. Tournier – ☎ 05 61 67 12 71 – Fax 05 61 60 61 02 – Closed 24 December-8 January
14 rm – †€ 50/55 ††€ 53/60, ☕ € 7 – ½ P € 60 – **Rest** – *(closed Sunday dinner)* Menu € 20/32 – Carte € 37/55
◆ Colourful rooms, furnished rustically or practically in this former post house. The warm atmosphere of bygone days pervades the dining room crowned by its superb (and original) moulded ceiling dating from 1760.

PANAZOL – 87 Haute-Vienne – **325** E5 – **pop. 9 731** – **alt. 302 m** – ✉ 87350 24 **B2**
Paris 395 – Limoges 5 – Saint-Junien 39 – Isle 9 – Saint-Yrieix-la-Perche 43

Domaine du Forest without rest P
5 km north-east on N 141 and Golf de la Porcelaine road – ☎ 05 55 31 33 68 – domainedeforest@wanadoo.fr – Fax 05 55 31 85 08
5 rm ☕ – †€ 95 ††€ 105
◆ A lovely drive leads up to this peaceful 18C manor. Plush sitting rooms and comfortable, meticulously decorated bedrooms. Tennis courts, fitness, sauna, Jacuzzi.

PANISSIÈRES – 42 Loire – **327** F5 – **pop. 2 860** – **alt. 641 m** – ✉ 42360 44 **A1**
Paris 448 – Lyon 62 – Saint-Étienne 65 – Villeurbanne 66
Office de tourisme, 1, rue de la République ☎ 04 77 28 67 70, Fax 04 77 28 82 18

La Ferme des Roses P
Le Clair – ☎ 04 77 28 63 63 – jednostka.arabians@free.fr – Fax 04 77 28 63 63
5 rm ☕ – †€ 42 ††€ 52/57 – **Table d'hôte** – Menu € 16 bi
◆ This former farmhouse (1813) is well known for its friendly atmosphere, as well as the landlord's twin passions: Arab thoroughbreds, that he trains, and roses. Very well-equipped modern rooms. Local cuisine washed down with Forez wines.

LE PARADOU – 13 Bouches-du-Rhône – **340** D3 – see Maussane-les-Alpilles

---

PARAMÉ – 35 Ille-et-Vilaine – **309** J3 – see St-Malo

PARAY-LE-MONIAL – 71 Saône-et-Loire – **320** E11 – **pop. 9 191** – **alt. 245 m** – ✉ 71600 Burgundy-Jura 7 **B3**
Paris 360 – Mâcon 67 – Montceau-les-Mines 37 – Moulins 67 – Roanne 55
Office de tourisme, 25, av. Jean-Paul II ☎ 03 85 81 10 92, Fax 03 85 81 36 61
Sacré-Cœur basilica ★★ - Town hall★ **H.**

Plan on next page

Le Parada without rest AC P VISA MC
Z.A.C. Champ Bossu, via ①, Montceau road – ☎ 03 85 81 91 71 – leparada@wanadoo.fr – Fax 03 85 81 91 70
30 rm – †€ 45/53 ††€ 54/68, ☕ € 7
◆ A new hotel surrounded by walled grounds, just outside town. Spacious and well-soundproofed rooms, equipped with a widescreen TV. Breakfast in a tinted glass veranda. Automatic payment and key delivery terminal in the evening.

Terminus P VISA MC AE
27 av. de la Gare – ☎ 03 85 81 59 31 – hotel.terminus@club-internet.fr – Fax 03 85 81 38 31 – Closed November school holidays and Sunday s
16 rm – †€ 48 ††€ 62, ☕ € 7,50 – ½ P € 49 – **Rest** – *(dinner only)* Menu € 17/21 – Carte € 27/42
◆ A typical, well-renovated, Belle époque railway station, easily recognisable by its candy-pink and turquoise facade. Period hall and good rooms with futuristic single-unit bathrooms. Restaurant serving simple, traditional cuisine.

Grand Hôtel de la Basilique AC rest, VISA MC AE
18 r. de la Visitation – ☎ 03 85 81 11 13 – resa@hotelbasilique.com – Fax 03 85 88 83 70 – Open 15 April-30 October a
54 rm – †€ 34/48 ††€ 40/55, ☕ € 7 – ½ P € 38/45 – **Rest** – Menu (€ 13,50), € 15/40 – Carte € 17/35
◆ Five generations of the same family have managed this hotel, offering rooms that are being gradually renovated. Many overlook the basilica. Meals are served in a flower-filled dining room reflecting the countryside and local tradition.

PARAY-LE-MONIAL

Alsace-Lorraine (Pl.) 2
Billet (R.) 3
Chapelains (Allée des) 5
Charolles (Av. de) 6
Commerce (Quai du) 7
Dauphin-Louis (Bd) 8
Desrichard (R. Louis) 9
Deux ponts (R.) 12
Dr-Griveaud (R.) 13
Four (R. du) 14
Gaulle (Av. Ch.-de) 15
Guignault (Pl.) 17
Industrie (Quai de l') 18
Jean-Jaurès (Cours) 20
Lamartine (Pl.) 21
Paix (R. de la) 23
Regnier (Bd H.-de) 26
République (R.) 27
St-Vincent (R.) 28
Victor-Hugo (R.) 29
Visitation (R.) 30

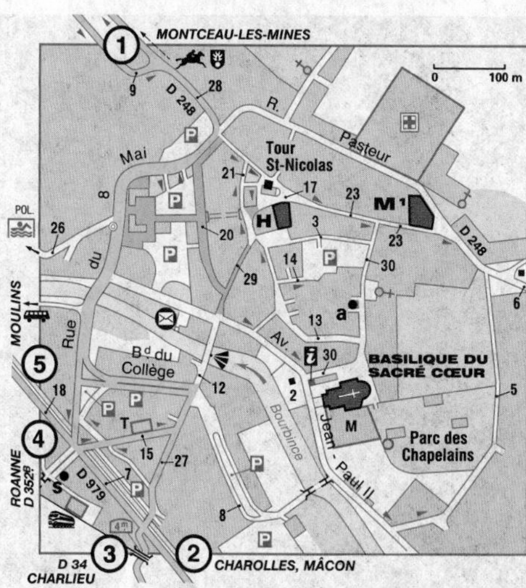

in Sermaize-du-Bas **12,5 km by ③ by D 34 then D 458 to Poisson dir. St -Julien-de-Civry – ✉ 71600 Poisson**

M. Mathieu without rest 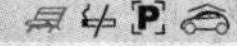
– ✆ *03 85 81 06 10 – mp.mathieu@laposte.net – Fax 03 85 81 06 10*
– Open 15 March-11 November
5 rm ☕ – 🚹€ 45 🚹🚹€ 60
◆ A former rustic hunting lodge, in yellow stonework, offering spruce rooms with different antique furniture in each room and served by a spiral staircase in a round tower.

in Poisson **8 km by ③ On D 34 – pop. 590 – alt. 300 m – ✉ 71600**

XX **La Poste et Hôtel La Reconce** with rm – ✆ *03 85 81 10 72 – la.reconce@wanadoo.fr – Fax 03 85 81 64 34 – Closed 28 September-15 October, 1st February-6 March, Monday and Tuesday except dinner July-August*
rm, A/C rest, P VISA MC
7 rm – 🚹€ 58 🚹🚹€ 68, ☕ € 11 – 1 suite
Rest – Menu € 28/84 bi – Carte € 29/59
◆ Old Charolais residence in which to sample traditional, updated cuisine of predominantly local produce. Fish menu on Fridays. Terrace shaded by plane trees. Attractively decorated and peaceful rooms located in a separate house, with a bar-tabac in between.

via ⑤ 4 km on N 79 – ✉ 71600 Paray-le-Monial

Le Charollais P VISA MC
– ✆ *03 85 81 03 35 – candussol@aol.com – Fax 03 85 81 50 31*
20 rm – 🚹€ 45/49 🚹🚹€ 51/55, ☕ € 7 – **Rest** – grill Menu (€ 16), € 20 – Carte € 16/46
◆ A roadside grill-restaurant at the front of a building offering fresh, clean and variously-arranged rooms that overlook a park with a children's play area. Charolais meat and pizzas are cooked on a wood fire in the timbered dining room. Veranda and terrace.

PARC du FUTUROSCOPE – 86 Vienne – 322 I4 – **see Poitiers**

PARCEY – 39 Jura – 321 C4 – **see Dole**

H. Le Gac/MICHELIN

La place de la Concorde

PARIS and OUTSKIRTS

Department: 75 Ville-de-Paris
Population: 2 125 246
Pop. built-up area: 9 644 507
Altitude: 30 m – **Postal Code:** ✉ 75000

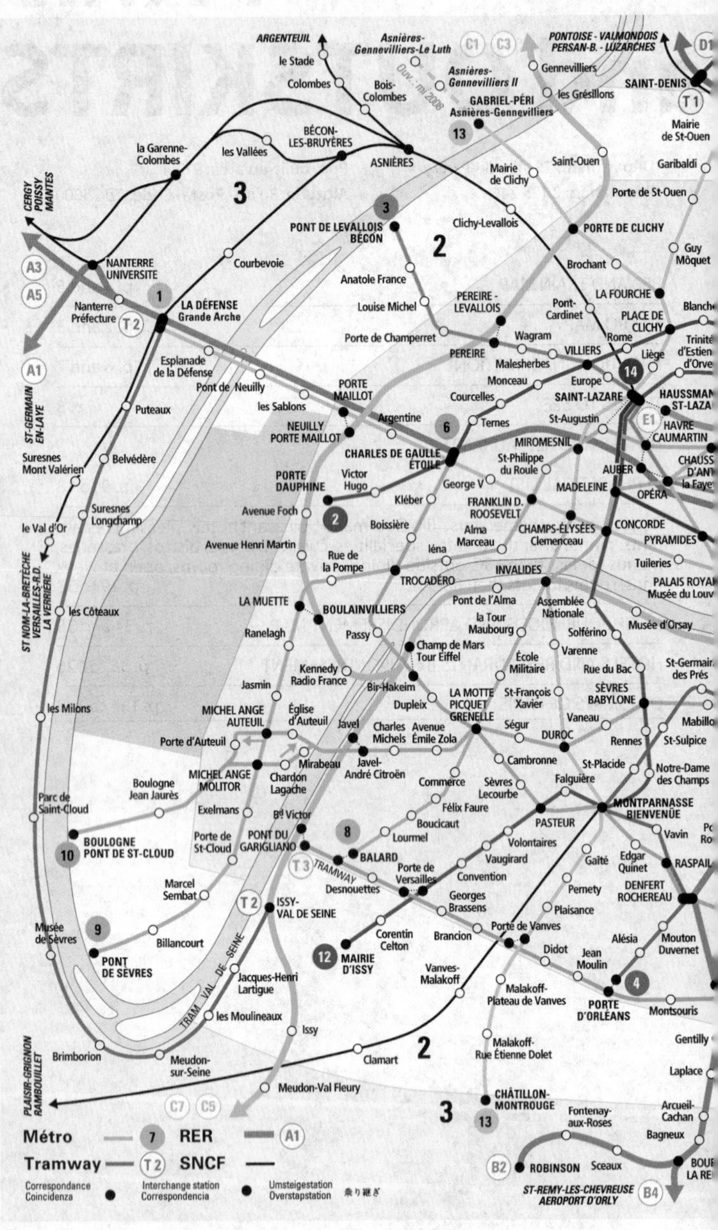

ARGENTEUIL
Asnières-Gennevilliers-Le Luth
Asnières-Gennevilliers II
Ouv. : mi 2008
PONTOISE - VALMONDOIS
PERSAN-B. - LUZARCHES
le Stade
Colombes
Bois-Colombes
GABRIEL-PÉRI
Asnières-Gennevilliers
Gennevilliers
les Grésillons
SAINT-DENIS
Mairie de St-Ouen
BÉCON-LES-BRUYÈRES
la Garenne-Colombes
les Vallées
ASNIÈRES
Mairie de Clichy
Saint-Ouen
Garibaldi
Porte de St-Ouen
CERGY POISSY MANTES
PONT DE LEVALLOIS BÉCON
Clichy-Levallois
PORTE DE CLICHY
Guy Môquet
NANTERRE UNIVERSITE
Courbevoie
Brochant
Anatole France
LA FOURCHE
Nanterre Préfecture
LA DÉFENSE Grande Arche
Louise Michel
PEREIRE - LEVALLOIS
Pont-Cardinet
PLACE DE CLICHY
Blanche
Porte de Champerret
Wagram
Rome
Trinité d'Estienne d'Orves
Esplanade de la Défense
PEREIRE
Malesherbes
VILLIERS
Liège
Pont de Neuilly
Monceau
Europe
ST-GERMAIN EN-LAYE
Puteaux
les Sablons
PORTE MAILLOT
Courcelles
SAINT-LAZARE
HAUSSMANN ST-LAZARE
NEUILLY PORTE MAILLOT
Argentine
Ternes
St-Augustin
HAVRE CAUMARTIN
MIROMESNIL
CHARLES DE GAULLE ÉTOILE
Suresnes Mont Valérien
Belvédère
PORTE DAUPHINE
Victor Hugo
St-Philippe du Roule
AUBER
George V
Kléber
MADELEINE
OPÉRA
Avenue Foch
FRANKLIN D. ROOSEVELT
Suresnes Longchamp
le Val d'Or
Boissière
Alma Marceau
CHAMPS-ÉLYSÉES Clemenceau
CONCORDE
PYRAMIDES
Avenue Henri Martin
Iéna
Tuileries
Rue de la Pompe
TROCADÉRO
INVALIDES
PALAIS ROYAL Musée du Louvre
ST NOM-LA-BRETÈCHE VERSAILLES-R.D. LA VERRIÈRE
les Côteaux
LA MUETTE
BOULAINVILLIERS
Pont de l'Alma
Assemblée Nationale
la Tour Maubourg
Musée d'Orsay
Ranelagh
Passy
Champ de Mars Tour Eiffel
Solférino
Varenne
Kennedy Radio France
École Militaire
Rue du Bac
St-Germain des Prés
Jasmin
Bir-Hakeim
SÈVRES BABYLONE
les Milons
MICHEL ANGE AUTEUIL
Église d'Auteuil
Dupleix
LA MOTTE PICQUET GRENELLE
St-François Xavier
Javel
Charles Michels
Avenue Émile Zola
Ségur
Vaneau
Mabillon
Porte d'Auteuil
DUROC
Rennes
St-Sulpice
Mirabeau
Javel-André Citroën
Cambronne
St-Placide
Notre-Dame des Champs
Boulogne Jean Jaurès
MICHEL ANGE MOLITOR
Chardon Lagache
Commerce
Sèvres Lecourbe
Falguière
Parc de Saint-Cloud
Exelmans
Félix Faure
MONTPARNASSE BIENVENÜE
Bd Victor
Boucicaut
PASTEUR
BOULOGNE PONT DE ST-CLOUD
Porte de St-Cloud
PONT DU GARIGLIANO
Lourmel
Volontaires
Vavin
BALARD
Vaugirard
Gaîté
Edgar Quinet
RASPAIL
TRAMWAY
Porte de Versailles
Convention
Marcel Sembat
Desnouettes
Pernety
DENFERT ROCHEREAU
ISSY-VAL DE SEINE
Georges Brassens
Plaisance
Musée de Sèvres
Corentin Celton
Brancion
Porte de Vanves
Alésia
Mouton Duvernet
Billancourt
PONT DE SÈVRES
MAIRIE D'ISSY
Didot
Jean Moulin
Vanves-Malakoff
Jacques-Henri Lartigue
TRAM VAL DE SEINE
Malakoff-Plateau de Vanves
PORTE D'ORLÉANS
Montsouris
les Moulineaux
Issy
Gentilly
Brimborion
Malakoff-Rue Étienne Dolet
Meudon-sur-Seine
Clamart
Laplace
PLAISIR-GRIGNON RAMBOUILLET
Meudon-Val Fleury
CHÂTILLON-MONTROUGE
Fontenay-aux-Roses
Arcueil-Cachan
Bagneux
ROBINSON
Sceaux
ST-REMY-LES-CHEVREUSE AEROPORT D'ORLY
Métro
RER
Tramway
SNCF
Correspondance Coincidenza
Interchange station Correspondencia
Umsteigestation Overstapstation
乗り継ぎ

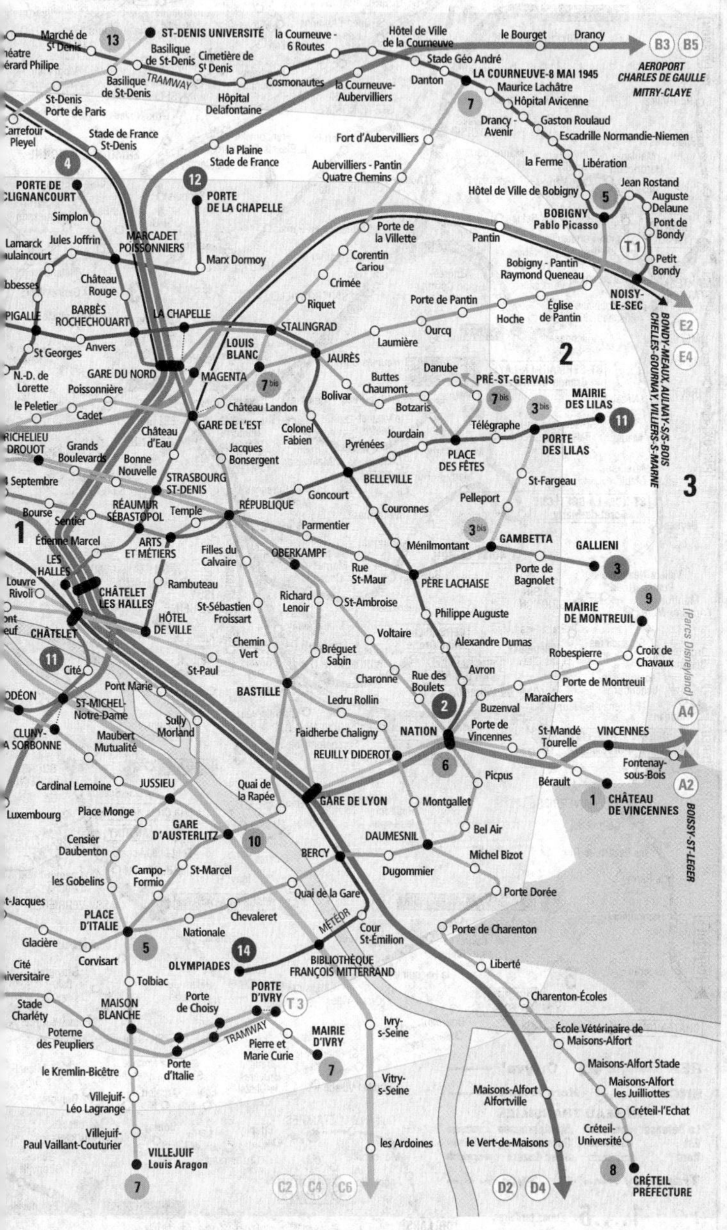

ST-DENIS UNIVERSITÉ
Basilique de St-Denis
Cimetière de St Denis
la Courneuve - 6 Routes
Hôtel de Ville de la Courneuve
le Bourget
Drancy
AEROPORT CHARLES DE GAULLE
MITRY-CLAYE
Stade Géo André
LA COURNEUVE-8 MAI 1945
Danton
Maurice Lachâtre
Hôpital Avicenne
Drancy - Avenir
Gaston Roulaud
Escadrille Normandie-Niemen
la Ferme
Libération
Jean Rostand
Auguste Delaune
Hôtel de Ville de Bobigny
BOBIGNY Pablo Picasso
Pont de Bondy
Petit Bondy
NOISY-LE-SEC
Cosmonautes
la Courneuve-Aubervilliers
Hôpital Delafontaine
TRAMWAY
St-Denis Porte de Paris
Stade de France St-Denis
la Plaine Stade de France
Fort d'Aubervilliers
Aubervilliers - Pantin Quatre Chemins
PORTE DE CLIGNANCOURT
PORTE DE LA CHAPELLE
Simplon
MARCADET POISSONNIERS
Jules Joffrin
Lamarck
Marx Dormoy
Porte de la Villette
Pantin
Corentin Cariou
Bobigny - Pantin Raymond Queneau
Crimée
Château Rouge
BARBÈS ROCHECHOUART
LA CHAPELLE
Riquet
Porte de Pantin
Église de Pantin
Hoche
STALINGRAD
Ourcq
Laumière
Anvers
St Georges
LOUIS BLANC
JAURÈS
BONDY-MEAUX, AULNAY-S/S-BOIS
CHELLES-GOURNAY, VILLIERS-S-MARNE
N.-D. de Lorette
GARE DU NORD
MAGENTA
Danube
PRÉ-ST-GERVAIS
Buttes Chaumont
Bolivar
Poissonnière
Botzaris
MAIRIE DES LILAS
le Peletier
Cadet
Château Landon
GARE DE L'EST
Colonel Fabien
Télégraphe
Jourdain
PORTE DES LILAS
RICHELIEU DROUOT
Grands Boulevards
Château d'Eau
Pyrénées
PLACE DES FÊTES
Bonne Nouvelle
Jacques Bonsergent
Septembre
STRASBOURG ST-DENIS
BELLEVILLE
St-Fargeau
Goncourt
Pelleport
Bourse
Sentier
RÉAUMUR SÉBASTOPOL
Temple
RÉPUBLIQUE
Couronnes
Parmentier
GAMBETTA
GALLIENI
Étienne Marcel
ARTS ET MÉTIERS
Ménilmontant
LES HALLES
Filles du Calvaire
OBERKAMPF
Rue St-Maur
Porte de Bagnolet
PÈRE LACHAISE
Louvre Rivoli
Rambuteau
CHÂTELET LES HALLES
Richard Lenoir
St-Ambroise
St-Sébastien Froissart
MAIRIE DE MONTREUIL
Philippe Auguste
CHÂTELET
HÔTEL DE VILLE
Chemin Vert
Voltaire
Alexandre Dumas
[Parcs Disneyland]
Cité
Bréguet Sabin
Robespierre
Croix de Chavaux
St-Paul
Avron
Charonne
Rue des Boulets
Porte de Montreuil
Pont Marie
BASTILLE
Maraîchers
ODÉON
ST-MICHEL-Notre-Dame
Ledru Rollin
Buzenval
Sully Morland
Porte de Vincennes
St-Mandé Tourelle
VINCENNES
CLUNY-LA SORBONNE
Maubert Mutualité
Faidherbe Chaligny
NATION
REUILLY DIDEROT
Fontenay-sous-Bois
Picpus
Bérault
Cardinal Lemoine
JUSSIEU
Quai de la Rapée
GARE DE LYON
Montgallet
CHÂTEAU DE VINCENNES
BOISSY-ST-LEGER
Luxembourg
Place Monge
GARE D'AUSTERLITZ
Bel Air
Censier Daubenton
DAUMESNIL
Michel Bizot
BERCY
Campo-Formio
St-Marcel
Dugommier
les Gobelins
Porte Dorée
Quai de la Gare
St-Jacques
PLACE D'ITALIE
Chevaleret
MÉTÉOR
Cour St-Émilion
Porte de Charenton
Glacière
Nationale
Corvisart
OLYMPIADES
BIBLIOTHÈQUE FRANÇOIS MITTERRAND
Liberté
Cité Universitaire
Tolbiac
Stade Charléty
MAISON BLANCHE
Porte de Choisy
PORTE D'IVRY
Charenton-Écoles
Ivry-s-Seine
Poterne des Peupliers
Pierre et Marie Curie
MAIRIE D'IVRY
École Vétérinaire de Maisons-Alfort
le Kremlin-Bicêtre
Porte d'Italie
Maisons-Alfort Stade
Vitry-s-Seine
Maisons-Alfort les Juilliottes
Villejuif-Léo Lagrange
Maisons-Alfort Alfortville
Créteil-l'Echat
Villejuif-Paul Vaillant-Couturier
les Ardoines
le Vert-de-Maisons
Créteil-Université
VILLEJUIF Louis Aragon
CRÉTEIL PRÉFECTURE

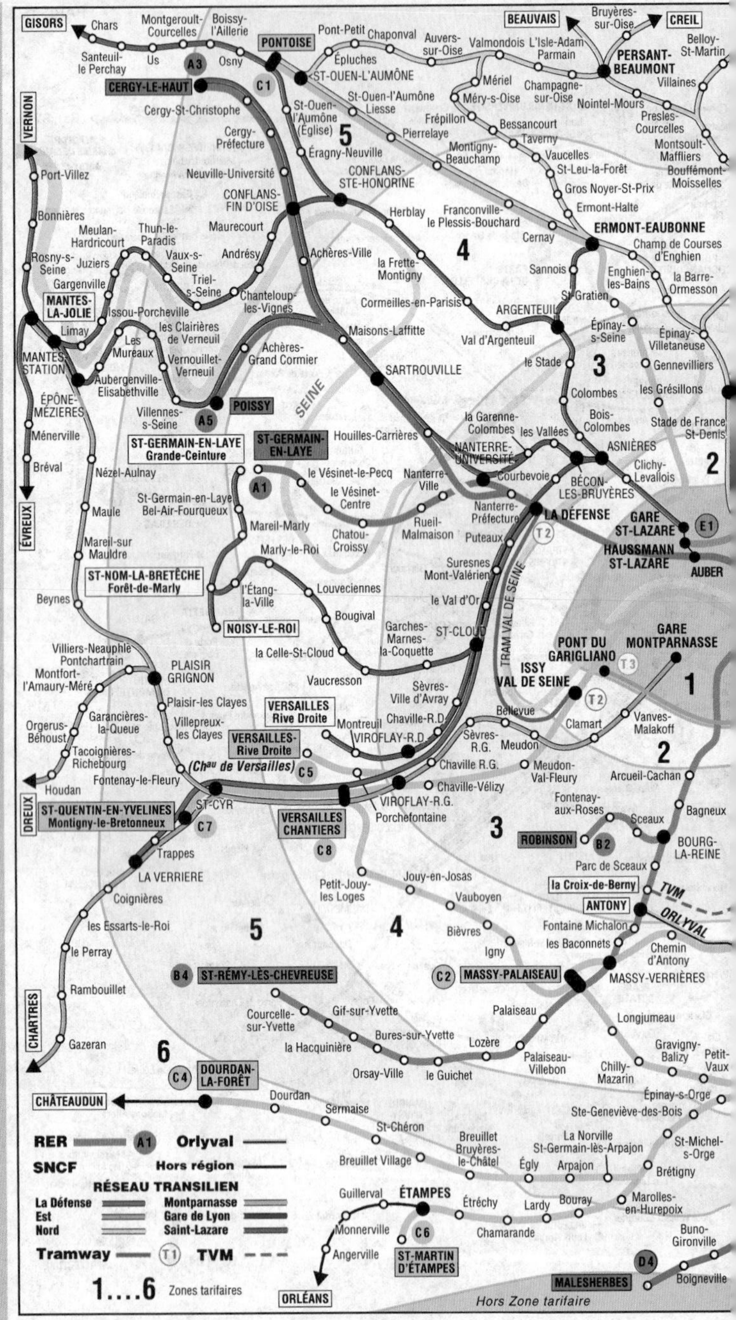
GISORS
Chars
Montgeroult-Courcelles
Boissy-l'Aillerie
Santeuil-le Perchay
Us
Osny
A3
PONTOISE
C1
CERGY-LE-HAUT
Cergy-St-Christophe
Cergy-Préfecture
Neuville-Université
CONFLANS-FIN D'OISE
Maurecourt
Andrésy
Chanteloup-les-Vignes
Achères-Ville
Pont-Petit
Chaponval
Auvers-sur-Oise
Valmondois
L'Isle-Adam Parmain
BEAUVAIS
Bruyères-sur-Oise
CREIL
Belloy-St-Martin
PERSANT-BEAUMONT
Villaines
Épluches
ST-OUEN-L'AUMÔNE
St-Ouen-l'Aumône (Église)
St-Ouen-l'Aumône Liesse
Mériel
Méry-s-Oise
Champagne-sur-Oise
Nointel-Mours
Presles-Courcelles
Montsoult-Maffliers
Bouffémont-Moisselles
Frépillon
Bessancourt
Taverny
Vaucelles
St-Leu-la-Forêt
Gros Noyer-St-Prix
Ermont-Halte
Pierrelaye
Montigny-Beauchamp
Éragny-Neuville
CONFLANS-STE-HONORINE
5
Herblay
Franconville-le Plessis-Bouchard
Cernay
ERMONT-EAUBONNE
Champ de Courses d'Enghien
la Frette-Montigny
4
Sannois
Enghien-les-Bains
la Barre-Ormesson
St-Gratien
Cormeilles-en-Parisis
ARGENTEUIL
Épinay-s-Seine
Épinay-Villetaneuse
Val d'Argenteuil
Maisons-Laffitte
le Stade
3
Gennevilliers
Colombes
les Grésillons
SARTROUVILLE
Bois-Colombes
Stade de France St-Denis
Houilles-Carrières
la Garenne-Colombes
les Vallées
ASNIÈRES
Clichy-Levallois
2
NANTERRE-UNIVERSITÉ
Courbevoie
BÉCON-LES-BRUYÈRES
Nanterre-Ville
LA DÉFENSE
GARE ST-LAZARE
E1
HAUSSMANN ST-LAZARE
AUBER
Nanterre-Préfecture
Puteaux
T2
Suresnes Mont-Valérien
le Val d'Or
TRAM VAL DE SEINE
ST-CLOUD
GARE MONTPARNASSE
PONT DU GARIGLIANO
T3
ISSY VAL DE SEINE
1
VERNON
Port-Villez
Bonnières
Meulan-Hardricourt
Thun-le-Paradis
Vaux-s-Seine
Triel-s-Seine
Rosny-s-Seine
Juziers
Gargenville
MANTES-LA-JOLIE
Issou-Porcheville
Limay
MANTES-STATION
Les Mureaux
les Clairières de Verneuil
Vernouillet-Verneuil
Achères-Grand Cormier
Aubergenville-Elisabethville
POISSY
A5
SEINE
ÉPÔNE-MÉZIERES
Villennes-s-Seine
Ménerville
Bréval
ST-GERMAIN-EN-LAYE Grande-Ceinture
ST-GERMAIN-EN-LAYE
A1
le Vésinet-le-Pecq
le Vésinet-Centre
Nézel-Aulnay
St-Germain-en-Laye Bel-Air-Fourqueux
Maule
Mareil-Marly
Rueil-Malmaison
Chatou-Croissy
ÉVREUX
Mareil-sur Mauldre
Marly-le-Roi
ST-NOM-LA-BRETÊCHE Forêt-de-Marly
l'Étang-la-Ville
Louveciennes
Beynes
Bougival
NOISY-LE-ROI
Garches-Marnes-la-Coquette
la Celle-St-Cloud
Villiers-Neauphle Pontchartrain
PLAISIR GRIGNON
Vaucresson
Montfort-l'Amaury-Méré
Sèvres-Ville d'Avray
Plaisir-les Clayes
VERSAILLES Rive Droite
Garancières-la-Queue
Villepreux-les Clayes
Chaville-R.D.
Bellevue
Clamart
Vanves-Malakoff
Orgerus-Béhoust
Montreuil
VIROFLAY-R.D.
Sèvres-R.G.
Meudon
VERSAILLES-Rive Droite
Tacoignières-Richebourg
C5
(Chau de Versailles)
Chaville R.G.
Meudon-Val-Fleury
2
Arcueil-Cachan
Houdan
Fontenay-le-Fleury
Chaville-Vélizy
DREUX
ST-CYR
ST-QUENTIN-EN-YVELINES Montigny-le-Bretonneux
VIROFLAY-R.G.
Fontenay-aux-Roses
Bagneux
C7
Porchefontaine
VERSAILLES CHANTIERS
3
Sceaux
ROBINSON
B2
BOURG-LA-REINE
Trappes
C8
Parc de Sceaux
LA VERRIERE
Petit-Jouy-les Loges
Jouy-en-Josas
la Croix-de-Berny
TVM
Coignières
Vauboyen
ANTONY
ORLYVAL
les Essarts-le-Roi
5
4
Bièvres
Fontaine Michalon
le Perray
Igny
les Baconnets
Chemin d'Antony
B4
ST-RÉMY-LÈS-CHEVREUSE
C2
MASSY-PALAISEAU
MASSY-VERRIÈRES
Rambouillet
CHARTRES
Courcelle-sur-Yvette
Gif-sur-Yvette
Palaiseau
Longjumeau
Bures-sur-Yvette
Lozère
la Hacquinière
Gravigny-Balizy
Petit-Vaux
Gazeran
6
Orsay-Ville
le Guichet
Palaiseau-Villebon
Chilly-Mazarin
C4
DOURDAN-LA-FORÊT
Épinay-s-Orge
CHÂTEAUDUN
Dourdan
Sermaise
Ste-Geneviève-des-Bois
St-Chéron
Breuillet Bruyères-le-Châtel
La Norville St-Germain-lès-Arpajon
St-Michel-s-Orge
Breuillet Village
Égly
Arpajon
Brétigny
Guillerval
ÉTAMPES
Étréchy
Lardy
Bouray
Marolles-en-Hurepoix
Monnerville
C6
Chamarande
Angerville
ST-MARTIN D'ÉTAMPES
Buno-Gironville
D4
MALESHERBES
Boigneville
ORLÉANS
Hors Zone tarifaire
RER
A1
Orlyval
SNCF
Hors région
RÉSEAU TRANSILIEN
La Défense
Montparnasse
Est
Gare de Lyon
Nord
Saint-Lazare
Tramway
T1
TVM
1....6
Zones tarifaires

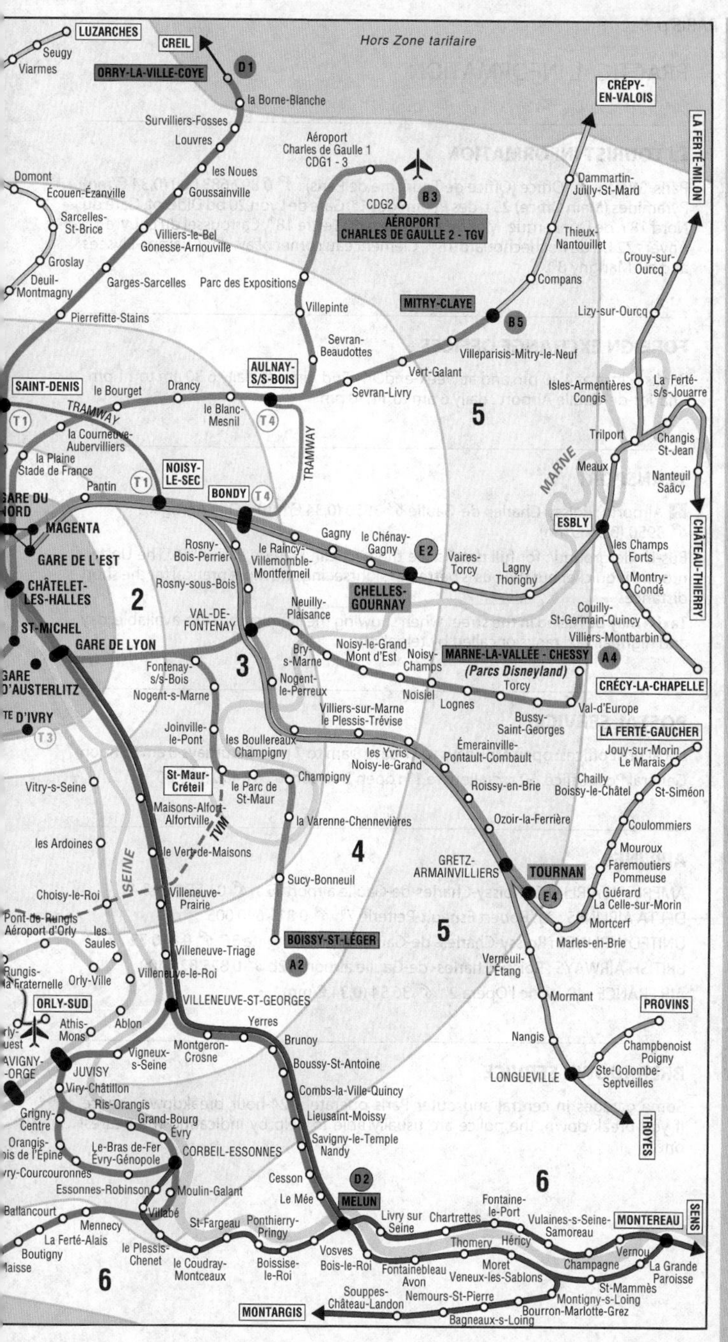

Hors Zone tarifaire
LUZARCHES
CREIL
ORRY-LA-VILLE-COYE
CRÉPY-EN-VALOIS
LA FERTÉ-MILON
AÉROPORT CHARLES DE GAULLE 2 - TGV
MITRY-CLAYE
AULNAY-S/S-BOIS
SAINT-DENIS
NOISY-LE-SEC
BONDY
GARE DU NORD
MAGENTA
GARE DE L'EST
CHÂTELET-LES-HALLES
ST-MICHEL
GARE DE LYON
GARE D'AUSTERLITZ
CHELLES-GOURNAY
MARNE-LA-VALLÉE - CHESSY
(Parcs Disneyland)
ESBLY
CHÂTEAU-THIERRY
CRÉCY-LA-CHAPELLE
LA FERTÉ-GAUCHER
TOURNAN
BOISSY-ST-LÉGER
St-Maur-Créteil
ORLY-SUD
VILLENEUVE-ST-GEORGES
CORBEIL-ESSONNES
MELUN
PROVINS
LONGUEVILLE
TROYES
MONTEREAU
SENS
MONTARGIS
TRAMWAY
MARNE
SEINE
TVM

PRACTICAL INFORMATION

TOURIST INFORMATION

Paris "Welcome" Office (Office de Tourisme de Paris) : ✆ 0 892 683 000 (0,34 €/mn) Pyramides (Main Office) 25 r. des Pyramides 1st, Gare de Lyon 20 bd Diderot, Gare du Nord 18 r. de Dunkerque, Montmartre place du Tertre 18th, Carroussel du Louvre 1st, Anvers 72 bd de Rochechouard 18 th, Clemenceau corner of av. des Champs-Elysées and av. Marigny 8th.

FOREIGN EXCHANGE OFFICES

Banks : close at 4.30 pm and at week-endOrly Sud Airport : daily 6.30 am to 11 pm Charles-de-Gaulle Airport : daily 6 am to 11.30 pm

TRANSPORT

Airports : Roissy-Charles-de-Gaulle ✆ 3950 (0,34 €/mn) – Orly Aérogare ✆ 3950 (0,34 €/mn)

Bus-Underground : for full details see the Michelin Plan de Paris n°56. The Underground is quicker but the bus is better for sightseeing and more pratical for the short distances

Taxis : may be hailed in the street when showing the illuminated sign-available, day and night all taxi ranks or called by telephone

POSTAL SERVICE

Local post offices: open Mondays to Fridays 8 am to 7 pm - Saturdays 8 am to noon

General Post Office, 52 r. du Louvre 1st : open 24 hours ✆ 01 40 28 76 00

AIRLINES

AMERICAN AIRLINES : Roissy-Charles-de-Gaulle airport T2a ✆ 01 55 17 43 41

DELTA AIRLINES : 2 r. Robert Esnault-Pelterie 7th ✆ 0 811 640 005

UNITED AIRLINES : Roissy-Charles- de-Gaulle airport, T1 gate 36 ✆ 0 810 72 72 72

BRITISH AIRWAYS : Roissy-Charles- de-Gaulle airport, T2b ✆ 0 825 825 400

AIR FRANCE : 49 av. de l'Opéra 2nd ✆ 36 54 (0,34 €/mn)

BREAKDOWN SERVICE

Some garages in central and outer Paris operate a 24-hour breakdown service. If you break down, the police are usually able to help by indicating the nearest one.

TIPPING

In France, in addition to the usual people who are tipped (the barber or ladies'hairdresser, hat-check girl, taxi-driver, doorman, porter, et al.), the ushers in Paris theaters ans cinemas, as well as the custodians of the ";men's"; and ";ladies"; in all kinds of establishments, expect a small gratuity
In restaurants, the tip (";service";) is always included in the bill to the tune of 15%. However you may choose to leave in addition the small change in your plate, especially if it is a place you would like to come back to, but there is no obligation to do so

---

MICHELIN in Paris

Services de Tourisme (Tourist Services)

46 Av. de Breteuil - 75324 PARIS CEDEX 07 - ✆ 01 45 66 12 34, Fax 01 45 66 11 63. Open Monday to Friday from 08:45 to 16:30 (16:00 on Friday)

Michelin on-line shop: www.michelin.fr tab: "voyage et déplacements" (travel and business trips), heading: Cartes et Guides (Maps and Guides), and Espace Michelin (Michelin Area) on the 1st floor of BHV Rivoli, Rue de Rivoli, 75004 PARIS (métro station: Hôtel de Ville)

THINGS TO SEE

FAMOUS VIEWS AND PARIS SEEN FROM THE SKY

⩽★★★ from the Obelisk of the place de la Concorde : Champs-Élysées, Arc-de-Triomphe, Grande Arche de la Défense. - ⩽★★ from the Obelisk of the place de la Concorde : La Madeleine, Assemblée Nationale. - ⩽★★★ from the Palais de Chaillot terrace: Tour Eiffel, École Militaire, Trocadéro. - ⩽★★ from Allexandre III Bridge: Invalides, Grand and Petit Palais – Eiffel Tower★★★ - Montparnasse Tower ★★★ - Notre-Dame Tower ★★★ - Sacré-Cœur dome★★★ - Arc-de-Triomphe terrace★★★

A FEW HISTORICAL BUILDINGS

The Louvre★★★ (cour carrée, Perrault colonnade, pyramid) - Eiffel Tower ★★★ - Notre-Dame★★★ - Sainte-Chapelle★★★ - Arc de Triomphe★★★ - Invalides★★★ (Tombeau de Napoléon) - Palais-Royal★★ - Opéra★★ - Conciergerie★★ - Panthéon★★ - Luxembourg★★ (Palace and gardens)

Churches :
Notre-Dame★★★ - La Madeleine★★ - Sacré-Cœur★★ - St-Germain-des-Prés★★ - St-Étienne-du-Mont★★ - St-Germain-l'Auxerrois★★

In the Marais district:
Place des Vosges★★★ - Hôtel Lamoignon★★ - Hôtel Guénégaud★★ - Palais Soubise★★

A FEW MUSEUMS

Le Louvre★★★ - Orsay★★★ (mid-19C to early 20C s.) - Art moderne★★★ (in the Centre Pompidou) - Armée★★★ (in the Invalides) - Arts décoratifs★★ (107 r. de Rivoli) - Musée National du Moyen Âge et Thermes de Cluny★★ - Rodin★★ (Hôtel de Biron) - Carnavalet★★ (Histoire de Paris) - Picasso★★ - Cité des Sciences et de l'Industrie★★ (La Villette) - Marmottan★★ (collection of Impressionist painters) - Orangerie★★ (Impressionists to 1930) - Jacquemart-André★★ - Musée des Arts et Métiers ★★- Musée national des Arts asiatiques - Guimet★★★

MODERN BUILDINGS

La Défense★★ (C.N.I.T., la Grande Arche) - Centre Georges-Pompidou★★★ - Institut du Monde Arabe★ - Opéra Bastille - Bercy★ (palais Omnisports, Ministère des Finances) - Bibliothèque Nationale de France - Site François Mitterrand★

PICTURESQUE DISTRICTS

Montmartre★★★ - Le Marais★★★ - Île St-Louis★★ - Les Quais★★★ (Between Pont des Arts and Pont de Sully) - St-Germain-des-Prés★★ - Quartier St-Séverin★★

SHOPPING

Department stores:
Printemps, Galeries Lafayette (bd Haussmann), B.H.V. (r. de Rivoli), Bon Marché (r. de Sèvres).

Luxury goods shops:
Faubourg St-Honoré (fashion), Rue de la Paix and place Vendôme (jewelry), Rue Royale (earthenware and crystal), Avenue Montaigne (fashion).

Secondhand goods and antiques:
Marché aux Puces (Flea market)★ (Porte de Clignancourt), Village Suisse (av. de la Motte-Picquet), Louvre des Antiquaires.

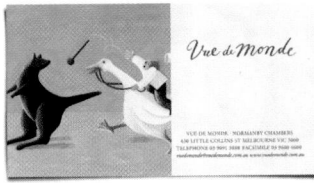

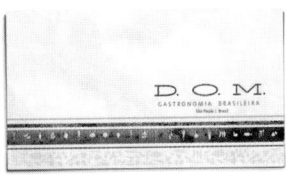

ALPHABETICAL OF HOTELS AND RESTAURANTS

A

B

C

D

E

F

G

H

I

J

K

L

M

N

O

P

Q

R

S

T

U – V

W

Y - Z

STARRED ESTABLISHMENTS

✿✿✿ 2008

			Page
	Alain Ducasse au Plaza Athénée - 8e	XXXXX	78
	Ledoyen - 8e	XXXXX	79
	Le Meurice (Rest.) - 1er	XXXXX	39
	L'Ambroisie *(Bernard Pacaud)* - 4e	XXXX	48
	Guy Savoy - 17e	XXXX	120
	Pierre Gagnaire - 8e	XXXX	80
	Pré Catelan - 16e	XXXX	117
	Arpège *(Alain Passard)* - 7e	XXX	65
	Astrance *(Pascal Barbot)* - 16e	XXX	114

✿✿ 2008

In red the 2008 Rising Stars for ✿✿✿

	Les Ambassadeurs - 8e	XXXXX	78
	Apicius - 8e	XXXXX	79
	Le Bristol - 8e	XXXXX	79
	Le "Cinq" - 8e	XXXXX	78
	Lasserre - 8e	XXXXX	79
	Taillevent - 8e	XXXXX	79
	Carré des Feuillants - 1er	XXXX	39
	Le Grand Véfour - 1er	XXXX	39
	Michel Rostang - 17e	XXXX	120
	Les Élysées - 8e	XXX	80
	Hélène Darroze-La Salle à Manger - 6e	XXX	59
	Relais Louis XIII - 6e	XXX	59
	Senderens - 8e	XXX	80
	La Table de Joël Robuchon - 16e	XXX	114
N	**L'Atelier de Joël Robuchon** - 7e	X	67

✿ 2008

In red the 2008 Rising Stars for ✿✿

L'Espadon - 1er	XXXXX	39
La Tour d'Argent - 5e	XXXXX	52
Goumard - 1er	XXXX	39
La Grande Cascade - 16e	XXXX	118
Hiramatsu - 16e	XXXX	114
Laurent - 8e	XXXX	79
Montparnasse'25 - 14e	XXXX	103
Auberge des Saints Pères Aulnay-sous-Bois	XXX	128
Auberge du Château "Table des Blot" Dampierre-en-Yvelines	XXX	139
La Belle Époque Châteaufort	XXX	136
La Bretèche St-Maur-des-Fossés	XXX	160
Le Camélia Bougival	XXX	130
Le Céladon - 2e	XXX	44
Le Chiberta - 8e	XXX	81
Au Comte de Gascogne Boulogne-Billancourt	XXX	131
Copenhague - 8e	XXX	81
Gérard Besson - 1er	XXX	39
Jacques Cagna - 6e	XXX	59
Le Divellec - 7e	XXX	65
Les Magnolias Le Perreux-sur-Marne	XXX	153
Paris - 6e	XXX	59

BIBS GOURMANDS

Outskirts

PLEASANT HÔTELS

Outskirts

PLEASANT RESTAURANTS

Outskirts

TRADITIONAL DISHES

Andouillette

Boudin

Bouillabaisse

Cassoulet

Cheese

Restaurant	Comfort	Page
Montparnasse'25 - 14e	XXXX	103

Choucroute

Restaurant	Comfort	Page
Ballon des Ternes - 17e	XX	121
Bofinger - 4e	XX	48
La Coupole - 14e	XX	103
Terminus Nord - 10e	XX	93
Mon Vieil Ami - 4e	X	48

Confit

Restaurant	Comfort	Page
Cazaudehore St-Germain-en-Laye	XXX	158
Au Clair de la Lune - 18e	XX	125
La Bastide Villeparisis	XX	170
Canal Evry	XX	141
Chez Jacky - 13e	XX	100
D'Chez Eux - 7e	XX	67
La Petite Marmite Livry-Gargan	XX	145
Le Sarladais - 8e	XX	82
St-Pierre Longjumeau	XX	145
La Table d'Antan Ste-Geneviève-des-Bois	XX	162
L' A.O.C. - 5e	X	53
Au Bascou - 3e	X	46
Auberge Etchegorry - 13e	X	100
Chez René - 5e	X	53
Fontaine de Mars - 7e	X	69
Joséphine "Chez Dumonet" - 6e	X	61
Lescure - 1er	X	42
Louis Vins - 5e	X	53
Pierrot - 2e	X	44

Coq au vin

Restaurant	Comfort	Page
Bourgogne Maisons-Alfort	XX	145
Le Coq de la Maison Blanche St-Ouen	XX	161
Allard - 6e	X	61
Au Moulin à Vent - 5e	X	53
La Biche au Bois - 12e	X	99
Chez René - 5e	X	53
Moissonnier - 5e	X	53
Quincy - 12e	X	98

Escargots

Restaurant	Comfort	Page
Au Petit Riche - 9e	XX	90
Ballon des Ternes - 17e	XX	121
Benoit - 4e	XX	48
Bourgogne Maisons-Alfort	XX	145
Gallopin - 2e	XX	44
Les Lauriers Le Perreux-sur-Marne	XX	153
La Petite Marmite Livry-Gargan	XX	145
Vaudeville - 2e	XX	44
Allard - 6e	X	61
Au Moulin à Vent - 5e	X	53
Bistrot St-Honoré - 1er	X	41
Au Pouilly Reuilly Le Pré-St-Gervais	X	154

Grills

Restaurant	Comfort	Page
Au Pied de Cochon - 1er	XX	40
Bofinger - 4e	XX	48
Le Coq de la Maison Blanche St-Ouen	XX	161
La Coupole - 14e	XX	103
Fermette Marbeuf 10000 - 8e	XX	83
Gallopin - 2e	XX	44
Terminus Nord - 10e	XX	93
L' A.O.C. - 5e	X	53
Bistrot St-Honoré - 1er	X	41
Joséphine "Chez Dumonet" - 6e	X	61
La Maison de L'Aubrac - 8e	X	85
Rôtisserie d'en Face - 6e	X	61

Seafood

Restaurant	Comfort	Page
Goumard - 1er	XXXX	000
Le Divellec - 7e	XXX	65
Le Dôme - 14e	XXX	103
Le Duc - 14e	XXX	103
Pétrus - 17e	XXX	120
Port Alma - 16e	XXX	115
Prunier - 16e	XXX	115
Au Pied de Cochon - 1er	XX	40
Ballon des Ternes - 17e	XX	121
Bofinger - 4e	XX	48
La Coupole - 14e	XX	103
Dessirier - 17e	XX	121
Gallopin - 2e	XX	44
Jarrasse L'Ecailler de Paris Neuilly-sur-Seine	XX	151
La Luna - 8e	XX	82
La Marée de Versailles Versailles	XX	168
Marius et Janette - 8e	XX	83
Marty - 5e	XX	52
Méditerranée - 6e	XX	60
Terminus Nord - 10e	XX	93
Vin et Marée - 7e	XX	67
Vin et Marée - 11e	XX	95
Vin et Marée - 14e	XX	103
Le Bistrot de Marius - 8e	X	86
Bistrot du Dôme - 4e	X	49
Bistrot du Dôme - 14e	X	104
L'Ecaille de la Fontaine - 2e	X	45
L'Espadon Bleu - 6e	X	61
Les Fables de La Fontaine - 7e	X	61
L'Huîtrier - 17e	X	123
La Rotonde - 6e	X	60
35 ° Ouest - 7e	X	69

Soufflés

Tête de veau

Tripe

CUISINE BY TYPE

Antilles, Réunion, Seychelles

Page

Belgian

Chinese, Thai and Vietnamese

Greek

Indian

Italian

Japonese

Korean

Lebanese

North African

Portuguese

Russian

Scandinavian

Spanish

Tibetan

Turkish

BISTROS

Outskirts

BRASSERIES

Outskirts

OUTDOOR DINING

		Page
La Grande Cascade – 16e	XXXX	000
Laurent – 8e	XXXX	79
Pré Catelan – 16e	XXXX	117
Palais Royal – 1er	XX	40
Pavillon Montsouris – 14e	XX	

Outskirts

Auberge de la Poularde – Vaucresson	XXX	103
Cazaudehore – St-Germain-en-Laye	XXX	158
L'Écu de France – Chennevières-sur-Marne	XXX	136
Tastevin – Maisons-Laffitte	XXX	146
Van Gogh – Asnières-sur-Seine	XXX	128
Moulin de la Renardière – Cergy-Pontoise	XX	132

DINNER AFTER THE THEATRE

		Page
Le Dôme - 14e (0 h30)	XXX	103
Drouant - 2e (0 h)	XXX	44
Fouquet's - 8e (0 h)	XXX	80
Al Ajami - 8e (0 h)	XX	84
Alcazar - 6e (0 h)	XX	60
Au Petit Riche - 9e (0 h15)	XX	90
Au Pied de Cochon - 1er (jour et nuit)	XX	40
Bofinger - 4e (0 h30)	XX	48
La Coupole - 14e (1 h)	XX	103
L'Esplanade - 7e (2 h)	XX	67
Gallopin - 2e (0 h)	XX	44
Il Vino d'Enrico Bernardo - 7e (0 h)	XX	66
Pierre au Palais Royal - 1er (0 h)	XX	40
Terminus Nord - 10e (0 h30)	XX	93
Vaudeville - 2e (1 h)	XX	44
Village d'Ung et Li Lam - 8e (0 h)	XX	84
L'Atelier de Joël Robuchon - 7e (0 h)	X	67
Chez Michel - 10e (0 h)	X	93
Dell Orto - 9e (0 h)	X	91
Devez - 8e (0 h30)	X	85
Fontaine de Mars - 7e (0 h)	X	69
La Maison de L'Aubrac - 8e (jour et nuit)	X	85
Les Oudayas - 5e (1 h)	X	54
La Rotonde - 6e (0 h000)	X	60

OPEN AT WEEK ENDS

Outskirts

PRIVATE DINING ROOMS

Outskirts

MENU FOR LESS THAN € 33

Outskirts

ROOMS FOR LESS THAN € 88

Outskirts

NEIGHBOURHOODS AND ARRONDISSEMENTS

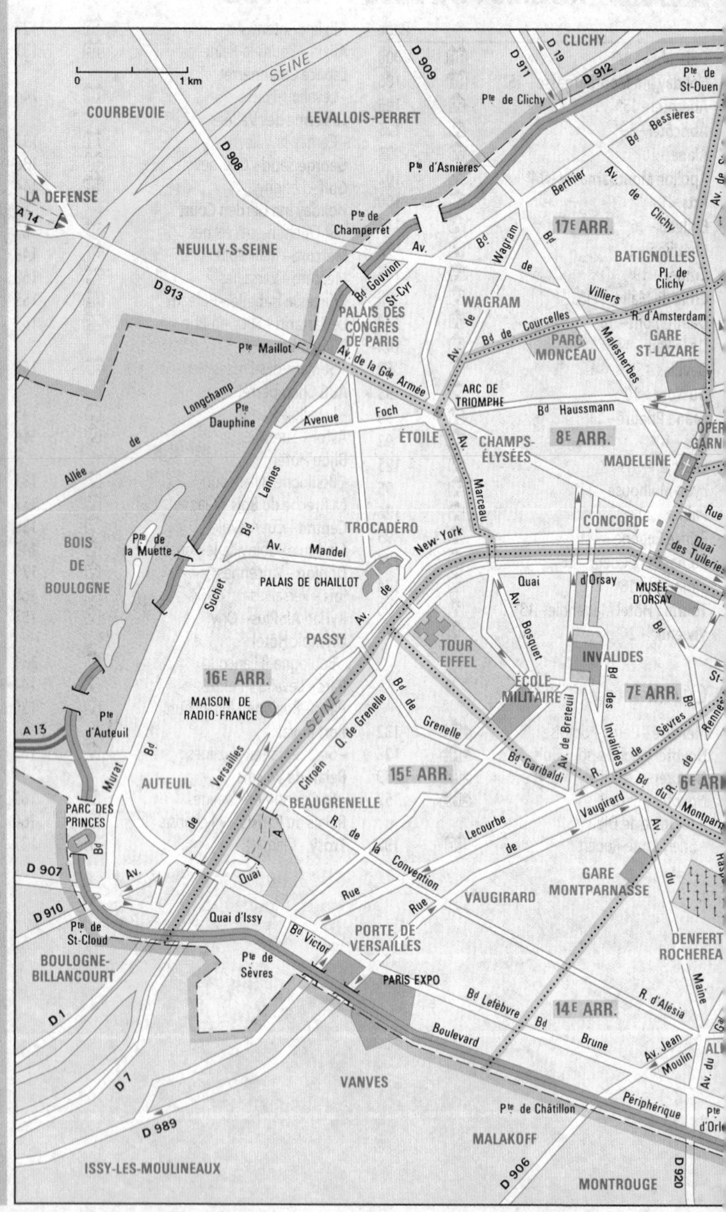

G12 : These co-ordinates refer to **Michelin maps Paris n° 54, Paris with index n° 55, Paris North to South n° 56**, and **Paris by Arrondissement n° 57**

In these publications you will also find the closest car parks to the selected establishment.

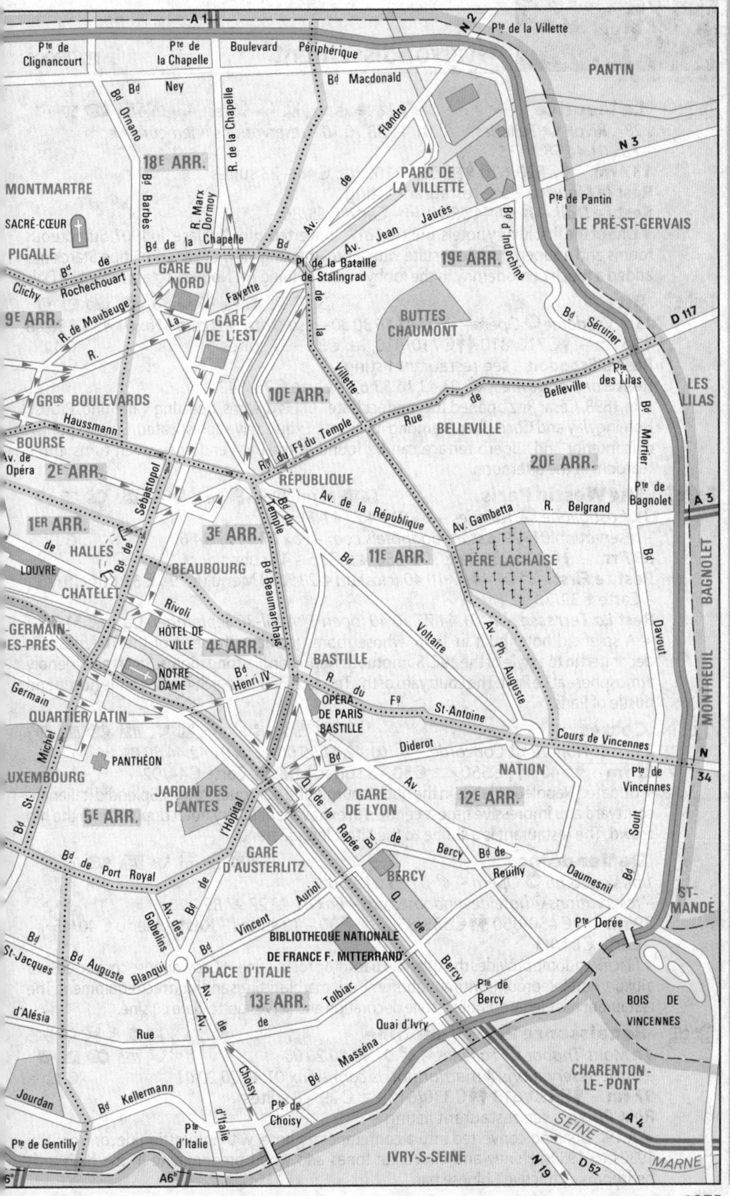

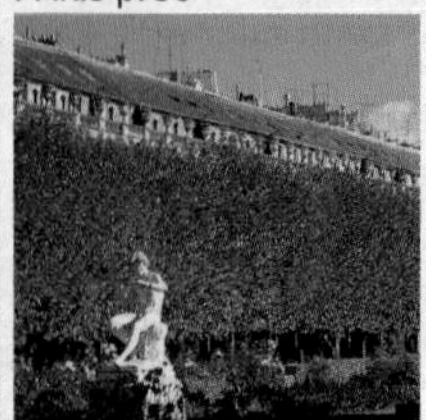
S. Sauvignier/MICHELIN

Palais-Royal, Louvre-Tuileries, Châtelet

1st arrondissement ✉ 75001

Le Meurice Spa rm, A/C rest, VISA MC AE
228 r. Rivoli Ⓜ Tuileries – ✆ 01 44 58 10 10 – reservations@lemeurice.com – Fax 01 44 58 10 15 G 12
137 rm – €520/620 €680/2100, €48 – 23 suites
Rest *le Meurice* – see restaurant listing
Rest *Le Dali* – *✆ 01 44 58 10 44* – Carte €65/86
◆ One of the first luxury hotels, built in 1817, converted into a "palace" in 1907. Sumptuous rooms and a superb top floor suite with a breathtaking view of Paris. Philippe Starck has added a touch of modernity in the lobby area. Stunning Art Nouveau glass roof at Le Dali.

Ritz Spa A/C VISA MC AE
15 pl. Vendôme Ⓜ Opéra – ✆ 01 43 16 30 30 – resa@ritzparis.com – Fax 01 43 16 36 68
124 rm – €710/810 €710/810, €36 – 37 suites G 12
Rest *L'Espadon* – see restaurant listing
Rest *Bar Vendôme* – *✆ 01 43 16 33 63* – Carte €75/142
◆ In 1898, César Ritz opened the 'perfect hotel' of his dreams, boasting Valentino, Proust, Hemingway and Coco Chanel among its guests. Exquisitely sophisticated. Superb pool. A chic interior and superb terrace can be found at the Bar Vendôme, which turns into a tearoom in the afternoon.

The Westin Paris rm, A/C rest, VISA MC AE
3 r. Castiglione Ⓜ Tuileries – ✆ 01 44 77 11 11 – reservation.01729@starwoodhotels.com – Fax 01 44 77 14 60 G 12
397 rm – €300/850 €300/850, €35 – 41 suites
Rest *Le First* – *✆ 01 44 77 10 40 (closed 14-28 July)* Menu (€29), €32 (lunch)/75 – Carte €32/73
Rest *La Terrasse* – *✆ 01 44 77 10 40 (open 1st April-30 September)* Carte €31/69
◆ A splendid hotel built in 1878, whose rooms (some with views of the Tuileries) are decorated in the style of the 19C. Sumptuous Napoleon III sitting rooms. Smart and friendly atmosphere at Le First. The courtyard of the Terrasse Fleurie is secluded from the hustle and bustle of Paris.

Costes rm, A/C VISA MC AE
239 r. St-Honoré Ⓜ Concorde – ✆ 01 42 44 50 00 – Fax 01 42 44 50 01
82 rm – €400 €550, €30 – 3 suites – **Rest** – Carte €44/92 G 12
◆ Updated Napoleon III style in the hotel's purple and gold guestrooms. Splendid Italianate courtyard and impressive fitness centre. An extravagant luxury hotel popular with the hip crowd. The restaurant is a shrine to the latest lounge trend.

De Vendôme A/C rm, VISA MC AE
1 pl. Vendôme Ⓜ Opéra – ✆ 01 55 04 55 00 – reservations@hoteldevendome.com – Fax 01 49 27 97 89 G 12
29 rm – €450/660 €535/855, €30 – 10 suites – **Rest** – Menu €40/45 – Carte €61/83
◆ Place Vendôme provides the splendid backdrop for this fine 18C townhouse converted into a luxury hotel. Bedrooms with antique furniture, marble fittings and high tech equipment. The restaurant has elegant, English-style decoration and serves up-to-date cuisine.

Renaissance Paris Vendôme A/C
4 r. Mont-Thabor Ⓜ Tuileries – ✆ 01 40 20 20 00 VISA MC AE
– francereservations@marriotthotels.com – Fax 01 40 20 20 01 G 12
97 rm – €330/610 €330/610, €29 – 8 suites
Rest *Pinxo* – see restaurant listing
◆ A 19C building converted into a contemporary hotel with interesting decor from the 1930s to 1950s. Honey and chocolate tones and wood predominate in the high-tech bedrooms. Attractive Chinese bar.

Castille Paris
33 r. Cambon Ⓜ *Madeleine – ✆ 01 44 58 44 58 – reservations@castille.com – Fax 01 44 58 44 00* G 12
86 rm – †€ 380/780 ††€ 380/780, ☕ € 28 – 21 suites
Rest *Il Cortile* – 37 r. Cambon, *✆ 01 44 58 45 67 (closed August, 24-30 December, Saturday and Sunday)* Menu (€ 38), € 48/95 – Carte € 53/80
♦ Delightful Venetian-inspired decor in the Opéra wing, with black and white chic in the Rivoli wing (in reverence to nearby fashion house Chanel). Il Cortile serves Italian cuisine in a Villa d'Este-style dining room. Attractive patio-terrace.

Louvre
pl. A. Malraux Ⓜ *Palais Royal Musée du Louvre – ✆ 01 44 58 38 38 – hoteldulouvre@hoteldulouvre.com – Fax 01 44 58 38 01* H 13
132 rm – †€ 220/600 ††€ 220/600, ☕ € 27 – 45 suites
Rest *Brasserie Le Louvre* – , *✆ 01 42 96 27 98* – Menu € 40 (lunch) – Carte € 45/73
♦ One of the first great Parisian hotels, where the painter Pissarro stayed. Some rooms offer a unique view of the Avenue de l'Opéra and the 'Palais Garnier' (Paris Opera House). The Brasserie Le Louvre is traditional both in its 1900s decor and in its cuisine.

Regina
2 pl. des Pyramides Ⓜ *Tuileries – ✆ 01 42 60 31 10 – reservation@regina-hotel.com – Fax 01 40 15 95 16* H 13
120 rm – †€ 360/430 ††€ 430/495, ☕ € 31 – 8 suites – **Rest** – Menu (€ 28) – Carte € 32/53
♦ The superb Art Nouveau reception of this 1900 hotel has been preserved. The rooms, rich in antique furniture, are quieter on the patio side; some offer views of the Eiffel Tower. Dining room with a pretty Majorelle fireplace and a courtyard-terrace that is very popular in summer.

Cambon without rest
3 r. Cambon Ⓜ *Concorde – ✆ 01 44 58 93 93 – info@hotelcambon.com – Fax 01 42 60 30 59* G 12
40 rm – †€ 250/280 ††€ 320/360, ☕ € 18 – 2 suites
♦ Between the gardens of the Tuileries and Rue St-Honoré, pleasant rooms combining contemporary furniture, attractive engravings and old paintings. Regular clientele.

Royal St-Honoré without rest
221 r. St-Honoré Ⓜ *Tuileries – ✆ 01 42 60 32 79 – rsh@hroy.com – Fax 01 42 60 47 44* G 12
72 rm – †€ 330/380 ††€ 380/590, ☕ € 22
♦ An opulent-looking 19C building on the site of the former Hôtel de Noailles. Elegant and refined guestrooms, with Louis XVI decor in the breakfast room. Cosy bar.

Meliá Vendôme without rest
8 r. Cambon Ⓜ *Concorde – ✆ 01 44 77 54 00 – melia.vendome@solmelia.com – Fax 01 44 77 54 01* G 12
83 rm – †€ 347/407 ††€ 347/407, ☕ € 27 – 4 suites
♦ Smart, restrained decor in tones of red and gold. Bedrooms with period furniture, elegant lounge with a Belle Époque glass roof, chic bar and attractive breakfast area.

Washington Opéra without rest
50 r. Richelieu Ⓜ *Palais Royal – ✆ 01 42 96 68 06 – hotel@washingtonopera.com – Fax 01 40 15 01 12* G 13
36 rm – †€ 195/245 ††€ 215/275, ☕ € 15
♦ Former townhouse of the Marquise de Pompadour. Directoire or 'Gustavian'-style rooms. The 6th floor terrace offers beautiful views over the gardens of the Palais-Royal.

Mansart without rest
5 r. des Capucines Ⓜ *Opéra – ✆ 01 42 61 50 28 – mansart@espritfrance.com – Fax 01 49 27 97 44* G 12
57 rm – †€ 155/335 ††€ 155/335, ☕ € 12
♦ Close to Place Vendôme, this hotel pays homage to Mansart, architect to Louis XIV. Classic rooms furnished in Empire or Directoire style. A more modern lobby-lounge.

Opéra Richepanse without rest
14 r. Chevalier de St-George Ⓜ *Madeleine – ✆ 01 42 60 36 00 – hotel@richepanse.com – Fax 01 42 60 13 03* G 12
35 rm – †€ 240/432 ††€ 240/432, ☐ € 17 – 3 suites
◆ The hotel has been fully renovated and furnished in Art Deco style. Harmonious, well-appointed bedrooms, some with views of the Madeleine. Vaulted breakfast room in the basement.

Novotel Les Halles
8 pl. M.-de-Navarre Ⓜ *Châtelet – ✆ 01 42 21 31 31 – h0785@accor.com – Fax 01 40 26 05 79* – **280 rm** – †€ 190/300 ††€ 210/320, ☐ € 17 – 5 suites H 14
Rest – *(closed Sunday lunch and Saturday)* Carte € 22/46
◆ A central location near the St Eustache church and Forum des Halles, meeting facilities and renovated minimalist-style rooms are the main selling points at this modern hotel. Palm trees add a zest of exoticism to this restaurant beneath an immense glass roof.

Britannique without rest
20 av. Victoria Ⓜ *Châtelet – ✆ 01 42 33 74 59 – mailbox@hotel-britannique.fr – Fax 01 42 33 82 65* – **39 rm** – †€ 124/155 ††€ 172/215, ☐ € 16 J 14
◆ Founded by an English family during the reign of Queen Victoria, this hotel has retained its elegantly British Imperial charm and refined exotic feel. Charming lounge.

Thérèse without rest
5 r. Thérèse Ⓜ *Pyramides – ✆ 01 42 96 10 01 – info@hoteltherese.com – Fax 01 42 96 15 22* – **43 rm** – †€ 150/298 ††€ 150/311, ☐ € 13 G 13
◆ The charm of this hotel lies in its refined contemporary decor of paintings, attractive fabrics and pastel shades. Vaulted breakfast room occupying the former cellars.

Relais St-Honoré without rest
308 r. St Honoré Ⓜ *Tuileries – ✆ 01 42 96 06 06 – relaissainthonore@wanadoo.fr – Fax 01 42 96 17 50* – **15 rm** – †€ 203 ††€ 203/340, ☐ € 13 G 12
◆ This 17C building is home to quiet, antique furnished rooms with exposed beams (except first floor). Breakfasts in the rooms only.

Molière without rest
21 r. Molière Ⓜ *Palais Royal Musée du Louvre – ✆ 01 42 96 22 01 – info@hotel-moliere.fr – Fax 01 42 60 48 68* – **32 rm** – †€ 140/165 ††€ 165/300, ☐ € 14 G 13
◆ The hotel is named after the famous playwright, said to have been born in this street in 1622 (hence the statues adorning the lounge). Cosy and reasonably spacious guestrooms with period furniture.

Relais du Louvre without rest
19 r. Prêtres-St-Germain-l'Auxerrois Ⓜ *Louvre Rivoli – ✆ 01 40 41 96 42 – contact@relaisdulouvre.com – Fax 01 40 41 96 44* H 14
18 rm – †€ 108/135 ††€ 165/220, ☐ € 13 – 1 suite
◆ A stylish, quiet and well-maintained hotel behind a narrow 18C façade. Colourful yet refined guestrooms offering modern comfort. Attractive suite on the top floor.

Place du Louvre without rest
21 r. Prêtres-St-Germain-L'Auxerrois Ⓜ *Louvre Rivoli – ✆ 01 42 33 78 68 – hpl@espritdefrance.com – Fax 01 42 33 09 95* H 14
20 rm – †€ 118 ††€ 156/177, ☐ € 13
◆ Stylish rooms, each bearing the name of a painter, in the shadow of the St-Germain-l'Auxerrois church. Breakfast is served in a 14C vaulted cellar which was once connected to the Louvre.

Aux Ducs de Bourgogne without rest
19 r. Pont-Neuf Ⓜ *Châtelet – ✆ 01 42 33 95 64 – bourgogne@paris-hotel-capital.com – Fax 01 40 39 01 25* H 14
50 rm – †€ 195 ††€ 230, ☐ € 13
◆ Situated in a 19C building, the well-soundproofed rooms are graced with period furniture. Recent, functional bathrooms. Plush sitting room.

Louvre Ste-Anne without rest
32 r. Ste-Anne Ⓜ *Pyramides – ✆ 01 40 20 02 35 – contact@louvre-ste-anne.fr – Fax 01 40 15 91 13* – **20 rm** – †€ 116/130 ††€ 135/190, ☐ € 12 G 13
◆ In a street lined with Japanese restaurants, this hotel has small but well-equipped rooms decorated in pastel shades. Vaulted breakfast room.

XXXXX ✿✿✿ **le Meurice** – Hôtel Le Meurice
228 r. Rivoli Ⓜ *Tuileries – ✆ 01 44 58 10 55*
– restaurant@lemeurice.com – Fax 01 44 58 10 76
– Closed 26 July-24 August, 14 February-1st March, Saturday and Sunday
Rest – Menu € 90 (lunch)/220 – Carte € 164/292 G 12
Spec. Jaunes d'œuf de poule au caviar "golden oscietre". Selle d'agneau parfumée à la fleur d'oranger en cours de cuisson (June to October). Palet fondant au chocolat.
◆ The dining room in this hotel has clearly drawn its inspiration from the state apartments of Versailles. Talented, updated cuisine much appreciated by gourmets.

XXXXX ✿ **L'Espadon** – Hôtel Ritz
15 pl. Vendôme Ⓜ *Opéra – ✆ 01 43 16 30 80 – espadon@ritzparis.com*
– Fax 01 43 16 33 75 G 12
Rest – Menu € 75 (lunch), € 170/305 bi – Carte € 134/217
Spec. Belons au sabayon gratiné et mousseline d' épinards. Tronçon de turbot rôti à la fleur de sel, gnocchi au parmesan. Noix de ris de veau doré, jus perlé et pommes soufflées.
◆ The restaurant area is weighted in gold and drapery, a dazzling decor reminiscent of its famous guests. Pleasant terrace in a flower garden. A ritzy extravaganza!

XXXX ✿✿ **Le Grand Véfour**
17 r. Beaujolais Ⓜ *Palais Royal – ✆ 01 42 96 56 27*
– grand.vefour@wanadoo.fr – Fax 01 42 86 80 71
– Closed 28 April-4 May, 28 July-25 August, 24 December-1st January, Friday dinner, Saturday and Sunday G 13
Rest – Menu € 88/268 – Carte € 194/235
Spec. Ravioles de foie gras crème foisonnée truffée. Pigeon Prince Rainier III. Palet noisette et chocolat au lait, glace caramel brun.
◆ Many famous personalities have dined in the elegant Directoire-style *salons* of this luxurious restaurant, located in the gardens of the Palais-Royal. Innovative cuisine created by an inspired chef.

XXXX ✿✿ **Carré des Feuillants** (Alain Dutournier)
14 r. Castiglione Ⓜ *Tuileries – ✆ 01 42 86 82 82*
– carrédesfeuillants@orange.fr – Fax 01 42 86 07 71
– Closed August, Saturday and Sunday G 12
Rest – Menu € 65/165 (dinner) – Carte € 127/159
Spec. Cuisses de grenouilles épicées, blé cassé, écume de roquette et cresson, girolles en tempura (summer-autumn). Tronçons de Saint-Pierre ficelés de pommes de terre et caviar (winter). Envie de vacherin, grosses framboises, meringue légère au yuzu, crème fermière mascavo (summer).
◆ A modern restaurant on the site of the former Feuillants convent. The cuisine shows distinct Gascon influences and there is a superb choice of wines.

XXXX ✿ **Goumard**
9 r. Duphot Ⓜ *Madeleine – ✆ 01 42 60 36 07 – goumard.philippe@wanadoo.fr*
– Fax 01 42 60 04 54 G 12
Rest – Menu € 46 (lunch)/60 bi (lunch) – Carte € 75/127
Spec. Fleur de courgette farcie de chair de tourteau, jus à l' orange sanguine (May to October). Bar de ligne rôti, poêlée d'artichaut poivrade et crevettes grises (May to October). Homard bleu rôti, cocotte de blettes et tronçons de macaroni.
◆ Small intimate dining rooms whose Art Deco style is enhanced by seascapes. Don't miss the toilets, where the original decor by Majorelle can still be seen. Fine seafood menu.

XXX ✿ **Gérard Besson**
5 r. Coq Héron Ⓜ *Louvre Rivoli – ✆ 01 42 33 14 74*
– gerard.besson4@libertysurf.fr – Fax 01 42 33 85 71
– Closed 26 July-18 August, Monday lunch, Saturday lunch and Sunday H 14
Rest – Menu (€ 48), € 120/125 – Carte € 113/157
Spec. Homard bleu en fricasssée "Georges Garin", macaroni à la duxelles. Gibier (season). Fenouil confit aux épices, glace vanille de Tahiti.
◆ Elegant restaurant near Les Halles decorated in beige tones with still life paintings and Jouy wall hangings. Subtly reinterpreted classic cuisine, game in season.

XXX Macéo

15 r. Petits-Champs Ⓜ Bourse – ✆ 01 42 97 53 85 – info@maceorestaurant.com – Fax 01 47 03 36 93 – Closed 2-17 August, Saturday lunch and Sunday

Rest – Menu (€ 27), € 30/49 – Carte € 52/76 G 13

◆ A daring marriage of French Second Empire decor and modern furnishings. Updated cuisine, a vegetarian menu and international wine list. Friendly lounge-bar.

XX Palais Royal

110 Galerie de Valois - Jardin du Palais Royal Ⓜ Bourse – ✆ 01 40 20 00 27 – palaisrest@aol.com – Fax 01 40 20 00 82 – Closed 21 December-1st January and Sunday G 13

Rest – Carte € 45/76

◆ Beneath the windows of Colette's apartment, an Art Deco-style restaurant with an idyllic terrace, opening onto the Palais-Royal garden.

XX Pierre au Palais Royal

10 r. Richelieu Ⓜ Palais Royal – ✆ 01 42 96 09 17 – pierreaupalaisroyal@wanadoo.fr – Fax 01 42 96 26 40 – Closed August, Saturday lunch and Sunday H 13

Rest – Menu (€ 33), € 39

◆ Discreet and pleasant decor in aubergine shades with prints of the neighbouring Palais Royal. Contemporary cuisine based on seasonal market produce.

XX Au Pied de Cochon

6 r. Coquillière Ⓜ Châtelet-Les Halles – ✆ 01 40 13 77 00 – pieddecochon@blanc.net – Fax 01 40 13 77 09 H 14

Rest – Menu (€ 20), € 24 – Carte € 28/75

◆ This brasserie, founded in 1946 and renowned for its pigs' trotters, stays open late into the night. Original period frescoes and fruit themed chandeliers.

XX Le Soufflé

36 r. Mont-Thabor Ⓜ Tuileries – ✆ 01 42 60 27 19 – c_rigaud@club-internet.fr – Fax 01 42 60 54 98 – Closed 3-24 August, 15 February-1st March, Sunday and public holidays G 12

Rest – Menu (€ 24 bi), € 30/40 – Carte € 36/58

◆ This welcoming small restaurant near the Tuileries has devoted itself to soufflés. Find a savoury and sweet menu totally dedicated to this culinary creation.

XX Delizie d'Uggiano

18 r. Duphot Ⓜ Madeleine – ✆ 01 40 15 06 69 – losapiog@wanadoo.fr

Rest – Menu € 89 bi – Carte € 49/102– *Fax 01 40 15 03 90 – Closed 5-20 August, Saturday lunch and Sunday* G 12

◆ Main dining room on the first floor with attractive Tuscany-inspired decor. Wine bar and delicatessen on the ground floor. All is dedicated to Italian cuisine.

XX Au Gourmand

17 r. Molière Ⓜ Pyramides – ✆ 01 42 96 22 19 – Fax 01 42 96 05 72 – Closed August, Saturday lunch, Monday lunch, Sunday and public holidays G 13

Rest – Menu € 30 (weekday lunch)/36

◆ Traditional cuisine with a contemporary twist (including a menu based on Joël Thiébault's famous vegetables) prepared by a self-taught chef. Knowledgeable sommelier and friendly, welcoming ambience.

XX Saudade

34 r. Bourdonnais Ⓜ Pont Neuf – ✆ 01 42 36 30 71 – Fax 01 42 36 30 71 – Closed Sunday H 14

Rest – Menu € 22 – Carte € 28/49

◆ Enjoy an authentic Portuguese meal in the heart of Paris, in this restaurant decorated with azulejos tiles. Sample typical dishes and Lusitanian wines to the sound of fados.

XX Pinxo – Hôtel Renaissance Paris Vendôme

9 r. d'Alger Ⓜ Tuileries – ✆ 01 40 20 72 00 – Fax 01 40 20 72 02 – Closed 5-25 August G 12

Rest – Menu (€ 32 bi) – Carte € 38/57

◆ A restaurant with minimalist furniture, black and white shades, an open kitchen and understated but stylish decoration, serving simple, tasty dishes à la Dutournier.

XX **Kinugawa** (dinner) VISA

9 r. Mont Thabor Ⓜ *Tuileries – ✆ 01 42 60 65 07 – higashiuchi.kinugawa@free.fr – Fax 01 42 60 45 21 – Closed 24 December-6 January and Sunday* G 12

Rest – Menu € 30 (weekday lunch), € 75/125 – Carte € 31/83

◆ Japanese cuisine served on the first floor dining room with a contemporary, Japanese look: paintings, refined lines and discreet colours. Sushi bar on the ground floor.

X **L'Atelier Berger** VISA

49 r. Berger Ⓜ *Louvre Rivoli – ✆ 01 40 28 00 00 – atelierberger@wanadoo.fr – Fax 01 40 28 10 65 – Closed Saturday lunchtime and Sunday* H 14

Rest – Menu € 36/65 – Carte € 36/47

◆ Opposite the Jardin des Halles, the modern first floor dining room is popular with locals who come here to enjoy the contemporary menu. Ground floor bar and smoking area.

X **Willi's Wine Bar** VISA

13 r. Petits-Champs Ⓜ *Bourse – ✆ 01 42 61 05 09 – info@williswinebar.com – Fax 01 47 03 36 93 – Closed 9-24 August and Sunday* G 13

Rest – Menu (€ 20), € 25 (lunch)/34 – Carte approx. € 35

◆ A friendly wine bar made up of a long oak counter and a small room adorned with old beams and posters. Simple fare and carefully selected vintage wines.

X **Pharamond** VISA

1 r. de la Grande-Truanderie Ⓜ *Châtelet-Les -Halles – ✆ 01 40 28 45 18 – Closed 5-25 August, February school holidays, Sunday and Monday* H 15

Rest – Carte € 42/87

◆ An historic bistro dating back to the heyday of Les Halles, the Pharamond held a star for many years. Traditional dishes (tripe and offal a speciality) and authentic 1900s decor.

X **Bistrot St-Honoré** VISA

10 r. Gomboust Ⓜ *Pyramides – ✆ 01 42 61 77 78 – bistrotsthonore@orange.fr – Fax 01 42 61 74 10 – Closed 24 December-2 January and Sunday* G 13

Rest – Menu € 28 – Carte € 30/70

◆ This small bistro showcases the gastronomic traditions and wines of Burgundy, the owner's home country, in a lively and relaxed ambience.

X **Kaï** VISA

18 r. du Louvre Ⓜ *Louvre Rivoli – ✆ 01 40 15 01 99 – Closed 31 March-7 April, 4-25 August, Sunday lunch and Monday* H 14

Rest – Menu € 38 (lunch), € 65/110 – Carte € 45/73

◆ Simple, minimalist decor in traditional Japanese style in this restaurant specialising in dishes from Tokyo (fish and charcoal-grilled meats). Desserts by Pierre Hermé.

X **Baan Boran** VISA

43 r. Montpensier Ⓜ *Palais Royal – ✆ 01 40 15 90 45 – baan.boran@orange.fr – Fax 01 40 15 90 45 – Closed Saturday lunchtime and Sunday* G 13

Rest – Menu € 14,50 (lunch)/45 (dinner) – Carte € 26/40

◆ An Asian venue opposite the Palais-Royal, with a modern setting enlivened by numerous orchids and serving Thai wok specialities.

X **Chez La Vieille "Adrienne"** VISA

1 r. Bailleul Ⓜ *Louvre Rivoli – ✆ 01 42 60 15 78 – Fax 01 42 33 85 71 – Closed 1st-21 August, Saturday and Sunday* H 14

Rest – *(pre-book)* Menu € 25 – Carte € 37/52

◆ This well-worn bistro with bar, beams and old photos is located in a 16C house. Generous traditional fare: calf's kidney and liver specialities. Laid back atmosphere.

X **Cristina's Tapas by Mavrommatis** VISA

18 r. Duphot Ⓜ *Madeleine – ✆ 01 42 97 53 04 – Fax 01 42 97 52 37 – Closed Monday dinner, Tuesday dinner, Wednesday dinner and Sunday* G 12

Rest – Menu € 21/29 – Carte € 33/47

◆ Experience the flavour of the Mediterranean in this tapas bar with specialities from Greece, Italy, Spain, North Africa and Provence. Restaurant upstairs, delicatessen (Iberian ham tasting) and wine shop.

Lescure

7 r. Mondovi Ⓜ Concorde – ✆ 01 42 60 18 91 – Closed August, Christmas holidays, Saturday and Sunday G 11

Rest – Menu € 23 – Carte € 21/29

◆ A rustic inn near Place de la Concorde. Closely packed diners enjoy generous portions of specialities from Limousin, as well as bistro cuisine at a common table.

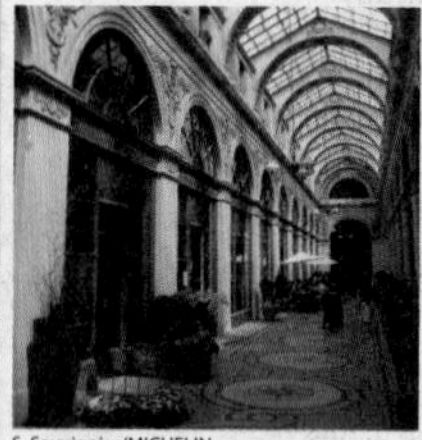
S. Sauvignier/MICHELIN

Bourse

2e arrondissement ✉ 75002

Park Hyatt VISA

5 r. de la Paix Ⓜ Opéra – ✆ 01 58 71 12 34 – vendome@hyattintl.com – Fax 01 58 71 12 35 G 12

167 rm – †€ 600/810 ††€ 600/810, ☕ € 40 – 22 suites

Rest Le Pur' Grill – see restaurant listing

Rest *Les Orchidées* – *✆ 01 58 71 10 61 (lunch only)* Carte € 61/123

◆ This group of five Haussmannian buildings has been converted into an ultra-modern luxury hotel with contemporary decor by Ed Tuttle. Collection of modern art, a spa and high-tech equipment throughout. Cuisine in keeping with current tastes, served to diners beneath a glass roof.

Westminster VISA

13 r. de la Paix Ⓜ Opéra – ✆ 01 42 61 57 46 – resa.westminster@warwickhotels.com – Fax 01 42 60 30 66 G 12

101 rm – †€ 280/630 ††€ 280/630, ☕ € 28 – 21 suites

Rest *Le Céladon* – see restaurant listing

Rest *Le Petit Céladon* – *✆ 01 47 03 40 42 (closed August and Monday to Friday)* Menu € 51 bi

◆ In was in 1846 that this elegant hotel took the name of its most loyal guest, the Duke of Westminster. Sumptuous rooms, luxurious apartments. The hall is redecorated every season. The Céladon becomes the Petit Céladon at the weekend, with a simplified menu and more relaxed service.

Édouard VII VISA

39 av. Opéra Ⓜ Opéra – ✆ 01 42 61 56 90 – info@edouard7hotel.com – Fax 01 42 61 47 73 G 13

71 rm – †€ 345/445 ††€ 405/595, ☕ € 23 – 5 suites

Rest *Angl' Opéra* – see restaurant listing

◆ Edward VII, Prince of Wales liked to stay here on his trips through Paris. Spacious, luxurious rooms. Dark wood panelling and stained glass decorate the bar.

Mercure Stendhal without rest VISA

22 r. D. Casanova Ⓜ Opéra – ✆ 01 44 58 52 52 – h1610@accor.com – Fax 01 44 58 52 00 G 12

20 rm – †€ 225/330 ††€ 235/340, ☕ € 17

◆ On the trail of the famous writer, stay in the "Red and Black" suite of this stylish residence. Smart, personalised rooms and snug lounge-bar with fireplace.

L'Horset Opéra without rest VISA

18 r. d'Antin Ⓜ Opéra – ✆ 01 44 71 87 00 – reservation@hotelhorsetopera.com – Fax 01 42 66 55 54 G 13

54 rm ☕ – †€ 180/255 ††€ 195/285

◆ Colourful wall hangings, warm wood panelling and fine furnishings add style to the rooms of this traditional hotel a short distance from the Opera House. Cosy atmosphere in the lounge.

Noailles without rest

9 r. Michodière Ⓜ *Quatre Septembre* – ✆ *01 47 42 92 90 – goldentulip.denoailles@wanadoo.fr – Fax 01 49 24 92 71* G 13

59 rm – †€ 180/255 ††€ 200/345, ☕ € 15 – 2 suites

◆ Staunch contemporary elegance behind a pretty old façade. Minimalist decor in the rooms, most of which open onto a patio-terrace. Fashionable lounge (jazz on Thursdays).

États-Unis Opéra without rest

16 r. d'Antin Ⓜ *Opéra* – ✆ *01 42 65 05 05 – us-opera@wanadoo.fr – Fax 01 42 65 93 70* G 13

45 rm – †€ 100/215 ††€ 130/330, ☕ € 12

◆ This hotel in a 1930s building offers modern, comfortable, recently renovated rooms. Breakfast is served in the inviting English-style bar.

Victoires Opéra without rest

56 r. Montorgueil Ⓜ *Etienne Marcel* – ✆ *01 42 36 41 08 – hotel@victoiresopera.com – Fax 01 45 08 08 79* G 14

24 rm – †€ 180/244 ††€ 192/335, ☕ € 12

◆ In a lively and fashionable pedestrian shopping street this establishment offers tasteful and elegant contemporary rooms (marble bathrooms). Delightful welcome.

Malte Opéra without rest

63 r. Richelieu Ⓜ *Quatre Septembre* – ✆ *01 44 58 94 94 – hotel.malte@astotel.com – Fax 01 42 86 88 19* G 13

64 rm – †€ 176/240 ††€ 176/240, ☕ € 14

◆ Facing the National Library, rooms of varying size with Louis XV-style furniture and a few large duplex suites with exercise bicycles. Elegant lounge opening onto a flowerd patio.

Favart without rest

5 r. Marivaux Ⓜ *Richelieu Drouot* – ✆ *01 42 97 59 83 – favart.hotel@wanadoo.fr – Fax 01 40 15 95 58* F 13

37 rm ☕ – †€ 95/114 ††€ 120/145

◆ The artist Goya stayed in this charming hotel of timeless appeal. The rooms to the front, facing the Opéra-Comique, are the most pleasant.

Baudelaire Opéra without rest

61 r. Ste-Anne Ⓜ *Quatre Septembre* – ✆ *01 42 97 50 62 – resa@hotel-baudelaire.com – Fax 01 42 86 85 85* G 13

29 rm – †€ 141 ††€ 172/203, ☕ € 10

◆ In the 'Japanese street' of Paris, this establishment offers smart, well equipped and well soundproofed rooms (balconies on the top floors).

Vivienne without rest

40 r. Vivienne Ⓜ *Grands Boulevards* – ✆ *01 42 33 13 26 – paris@hotel-vivienne.com – Fax 01 40 41 98 19* F 14

45 rm – †€ 60/115 ††€ 75/115, ☕ € 12

◆ The spacious rooms are simply practical or equipped with period furniture. Some have a balcony, others a terrace, but only one has a view of the rooftops of Paris.

Le Pur' Grill – Hôtel Park Hyatt

5 r. de la Paix Ⓜ *Opéra* – ✆ *01 58 71 10 60 – Closed August* G 12

Rest – *(dinner only)* Menu € 125/300 bi – Carte € 92/225

Spec. Vapeur d'escargots petits gris, radis rouge et raifort. Déclinaison d'agneau allaiton, haricots coco cuisinés au chorizo."Choco Tag", chutney banane/galanga et épine vinette.

◆ Simplicity and refinement best describe the modern dinner menu served in the chic and contemporary rotunda-shaped dining room (kitchen in full view). Attractive summer terrace.

La Fontaine Gaillon

pl. Gaillon Ⓜ *Quatre Septembre* – ✆ *01 47 42 63 22 – Fax 01 47 42 82 84 – Closed 9 August-1st September, Saturday and Sunday* G 13

Rest – Menu € 41 – Carte € 48/64

◆ Seafood dishes and wine selection supervised by the actor Gérard Depardieu in an elegant, 17C townhouse dining room. Terrace with central fountain.

XXX **Le Céladon** – Hôtel Westminster
15 r. Daunou Ⓜ Opéra – ✆ 01 47 03 40 42 – christophemoisand@leceladon.com – Fax 01 42 61 33 78 – Closed August, Saturday and Sunday G 12
Rest – Menu € 48 (lunch), € 72 € bi/110 – Carte € 82/111
Spec. Langoustines bretonnes en carpaccio. Lapin du Poitou farci de ses abats. Chocolat de Tanzanie sur sablé breton.
◆ Sophisticated decor that combines Regency-style furniture, green walls and a collection of Chinese porcelain. Cuisine in line with current tastes.

XXX **Drouant**
16 pl. Gaillon Ⓜ Quatre Septembre – ✆ 01 42 65 15 16 – reservations@drouant.com – Fax 01 49 24 02 15 G 13
Rest – Menu € 42/67 – Carte € 40/87
◆ Small Art Deco dining rooms set around a splendid Ruhlmann staircase. The Louis XVI sitting room upstairs is where the Goncourt (literary prize) jury has met since 31 October 1914.

XX **Gallopin**
40 r. N.-D.-des-Victoires Ⓜ Bourse – ✆ 01 42 36 45 38 – administration@brasseriegallopin.com – Fax 01 42 36 10 32 G 14
Rest – Menu (€ 20), € 28/34 bi – Carte € 28/76
◆ Arletty, Raimu and the plush Victorian decor have brought fame to this brasserie situated opposite the Palais Brongniart. Lovely conservatory in the rear room.

XX **Vaudeville**
29 r. Vivienne Ⓜ Bourse – ✆ 01 40 20 04 62 – Fax 01 40 20 14 35 G 14
Rest – Menu (€ 21), € 24 (weekdays)/31 – Carte € 33/69
◆ This large brasserie with its sparkling Art Deco details has become the 'canteen' of numerous journalists. It is especially lively after theatre performances.

XX **Le Versance**
16 r. Feydeau Ⓜ Bourse – ✆ 01 45 08 00 08 – contact@leversance.fr – Fax 01 45 08 47 99 – Closed August, 24 December-2 January, Saturday lunch, Sunday and Monday F 14
Rest – Menu (€ 32 bi), € 38 bi – Carte € 46/68
◆ A tasteful combination of elegant modern (white/grey tones, designer furniture) and period decor (exposed beams, stained glass). Contemporary cuisine from a globetrotting chef.

X **Chez Georges**
1 r. du Mail Ⓜ Bourse – ✆ 01 42 60 07 11 – Closed August, 24 December-2 January, Saturday, Sunday and public holidays G 14
Rest – Carte € 42/66
◆ This authentic Parisian bistro has conserved its original 1900s decor: bar, seats, stucco and mirrors. A neighbourhood institution.

X **Aux Lyonnais**
32 r. St-Marc Ⓜ Richelieu Drouot – ✆ 01 42 96 65 04 – auxlyonnais@online.fr – Fax 01 42 97 42 95 – Closed 20 July-18 August, Saturday lunch, Sunday and Monday F 13
Rest – *(pre-book)* Menu € 30 – Carte € 38/55
◆ This bistro founded in 1890 proposes delicious, intelligently updated Lyonnais recipes. A delightfully retro setting with bar counter, banquettes, bevelled mirrors and mouldings.

X **Le Mesturet**
77 r. de Richelieu Ⓜ Bourse – ✆ 01 42 97 40 68 – lemesturet@wanadoo.fr – Fax 01 42 97 40 68 G 13
Rest – Menu (€ 20), € 26 – Carte € 27/38
◆ Authentic regional produce, generous traditional dishes, fine choice of wines and friendly welcome: this old-fashioned style bistro is often completely full.

X **Pierrot**
18 r. Étienne Marcel Ⓜ Etienne Marcel – ✆ 01 45 08 00 10 – Fax 01 42 77 35 92 – Closed 30 July-22 August and Sunday H 15
Rest – Menu (€ 28), € 50 bi – Carte € 34/50
◆ In the lively Sentier district, this bistro offers a discovery tour of the flavours and produce of the Aveyron. Summer pavement terrace.

Angl' Opéra – Hôtel Edouard VII VISA MC AE
39 av. Opéra Ⓜ Opéra – ✆ 01 42 61 86 25 – resto@anglopera.com – Fax 01 42 61 47 73 – Closed 11-24 August, Saturday and Sunday G 13
Rest – Menu € 29 (lunch) – Carte € 48/58
◆ The warm contemporary decor of the Angl' Opéra is as pleasant as its unusual fusion food.

L'Ecaille de la Fontaine VISA MC AE
15 r. Gaillon Ⓜ Quatre Septembre – ✆ 01 47 42 02 99 – Fax 01 47 42 82 84 – Closed 9 August-1st September, Saturday and Sunday G 13
Rest – *(number of covers limited, pre-book)* Carte approx. € 35
◆ Oysters and seafood to take away or sample in the delightful little room, decorated with souvenir photos of actor Gérard Depardieu, the owner.

Le Saint Amour VISA AE
8 r. Port Mahon Ⓜ Quatre Septembre – ✆ 01 47 42 63 82 – hervbrun@hotmail.fr – Fax 01 47 42 63 82 – Closed 1st-15 August, Saturday and Sunday G 13
Rest – Menu (€ 25), € 34/46
◆ Banquettes and tables in exotic wood, or warm provincial style: two distinct settings for a generous traditional cuisine (fish direct from the ports of Brittany).

H. Le Gac/MICHELIN

Le Marais, Beaubourg

3e arrondissement ✉ 75003

Pavillon de la Reine without rest VISA MC AE
28 pl. des Vosges Ⓜ Bastille – ✆ 01 40 29 19 19 – contact@pavillon-de-la-reine.com – Fax 01 40 29 19 20 J 17
41 rm – †€ 370/460 ††€ 430/460, ☕ € 25 – 15 suites
◆ Behind one of the 36 brick houses lining the Place des Vosges stand two buildings, one of which is 17C, housing elegant rooms on the courtyard or (private) garden side.

Murano VISA MC AE
13 bd du Temple Ⓜ Filles du Calvaire – ✆ 01 42 71 20 00 – paris@muranoresort.com – Fax 01 42 71 21 01 H 17
49 rm – †€ 360/650 ††€ 440/1850, ☕ € 32 – 2 suites – **Rest** – Menu (€ 21), € 55 bi (weekday lunch), € 85 € bi/130 bi – Carte € 41/145
◆ The Murano is a trendy hotel that stands out from the crowd with its immaculate designer decor, play of colours, high-tech equipment and pop-art bar (150 types of vodka). The restaurant has a colourful contemporary style, international food and a D.J. at the decks.

Villa Beaumarchais without rest VISA MC AE
5 r. Arquebusiers Ⓜ Chemin Vert – ✆ 01 40 29 14 00 – beaumarchais@leshotelsdeparis.com – Fax 01 40 29 14 01 H 17
50 rm – †€ 380/480 ††€ 380/680, ☕ € 19 – 4 suites
◆ Set back from the hustle and bustle of the boulevard Beaumarchais. Refined rooms graced with gold-leafed furniture; all rooms overlook a pretty winter garden.

Du Petit Moulin without rest VISA MC AE
29 r. du Poitou Ⓜ St-Sébastien Froissart – ✆ 01 42 74 10 10 – contact@hoteldupetitmoulin.com – Fax 01 42 74 10 97 H 16
17 rm – †€ 190/350 ††€ 190/350, ☕ € 15
◆ For this hotel in the Marais, Christian Lacroix has designed a unique and refined decor, playing on the contrasts between traditional and modern. Each room has a different design. Cosy bar.

Little Palace rm,

4 r. Salomon de Caus Ⓜ *Réaumur Sébastopol* – *01 42 72 08 15 – info@littlepalacehotel.com – Fax 01 42 72 45 81* G 15

49 rm – €155/220 €175/255, €13 – 4 suites – **Rest** – *(closed 2 August-1st September, Friday, Saturday and Sunday)* Carte €28/44

◆ A charming address with decor combining Belle Époque and contemporary styles. Attractive guestrooms; those on the 5th and 6th have a balcony with views of Paris. Lovely brown, sculpted wood panelling, light tones and minimalist furniture can be found in the restaurant.

Meslay République without rest

3 r. Meslay Ⓜ *République* – *01 42 72 79 79 – hotel.meslay@wanadoo.fr – Fax 01 42 72 76 94* G 16

39 rm – €91/120 €96/145, €9,50

◆ Near Place de la République, a fine, ornamented and listed façade (1840). Rooms have modern facilities and are well soundproofed. Breakfast is served in the arched cellar.

Des Archives without rest

87 r. des Archives Ⓜ *Temple* – *01 44 78 08 00 – contact@hoteldesarchives.com – Fax 01 44 78 08 10* H 16

19 rm – €150/180 €150/180, €12 – 4 suites

◆ Charming hotel near the National Archives with small yet prettily decorated and contemporary rooms. Modern lobby enlivened by red furnishings.

Austin's without rest

6 r. Montgolfier Ⓜ *Arts et Métiers* – *01 42 77 17 61 – austins.amhotel@wanadoo.fr – Fax 01 42 77 55 43* G 16

29 rm – €104/110 €140/145, €8

◆ In a quiet street facing the Arts et Métiers museum. All rooms have been renovated and are warm and bright. Some have original exposed beams.

Ambassade d'Auvergne

22 r. Grenier St-Lazare Ⓜ *Rambuteau* – *01 42 72 31 22 – info@ambassade-auvergne.com – Fax 01 42 78 85 47* H 15

Rest – Menu (€20 bi), €28 – Carte €30/46

◆ True ambassadors of a province rich in flavours and traditions; Auvergne-style furniture and setting offering products, recipes and wines of the region.

Au Bascou

38 r. Réaumur Ⓜ *Arts et Métiers* – *01 42 72 69 25 – Fax 01 55 90 99 77 – Closed August, 24 December to 2 January, Saturday and Sunday* G 16

Rest – Menu (€18) – Carte €33/42

◆ Discover the warm flavours of Basque cuisine in this bistro with its attractive patina-finish walls. Produce comes directly from the region, and a friendly welcome awaits you.

Le Carré des Vosges

15 r. St-Gilles Ⓜ *Chemin Vert* – *01 42 71 22 21 – lecarredesvosges@yahoo.fr – Fax 01 41 17 09 33 – Closed 5-25 August, 23-30 December, Monday lunch and Sunday* G 17

Rest – Menu (€21), €27 (lunch) – Carte €34/60

◆ A stone's throw from the Rue des Francs-Bourgeois and its trendy shops, friendly bistro with a contemporary interior. Up-to-date dishes.

Auberge Chez Rosito

4 r. Pas de la Mule Ⓜ *Bastille* – *01 42 76 04 44 – Fax 01 42 76 98 52 – Closed 8-23 August, Saturday lunch and Sunday* J 17

Rest – Menu (€15) – Carte €32/54

◆ Behind the discreet façade is a restaurant with the look of a simple and friendly country inn. Corsican wines in keeping with the cuisine, which focuses on pork.

404

69 r. des Gravilliers Ⓜ *Arts et Métiers* – *01 42 74 57 81 – 404resto@wanadoo.fr – Fax 01 42 74 03 41* H 16

Rest – Menu (€17), €30 (lunch), €50/80 – Carte €30/50

◆ Renowned for its tajines and couscous dishes, this trendy restaurant sports a typical Moroccan decor of low tables, sofas, lanterns and a patio terrace.

S. Sauvignier/MICHELIN

Île de la Cité, Île St-Louis, Hôtel de Ville, St-Paul

4e arrondissement ✉ 75004

Jeu de Paume without rest
54 r. St-Louis-en-l'Ile Ⓜ Pont Marie – ✆ 01 43 26 14 18 – info@jeudepaumehotel.com – Fax 01 40 46 02 76 – Closed 4-18 August K 16
30 rm – †€ 165/255 ††€ 275/900, ☕ € 18
◆ This 17C building at the heart of the Ile St-Louis was once the venue for real tennis. Nowadays it is a unique hotel with plenty of character and a clever use of space.

Bourg Tibourg without rest
19 r. Bourg Tibourg Ⓜ Hôtel de Ville – ✆ 01 42 78 47 39 – hotel@bourgtibourg.com – Fax 01 40 29 07 00 J 16
30 rm – †€ 180 ††€ 230/360, ☕ € 16
◆ The pleasant rooms in this charming hotel are decorated in a variety of styles (neo-Gothic, Baroque or Oriental). A little gem at the heart of the Marais quarter.

Villa Mazarin without rest
6 r. des Archives Ⓜ Hôtel de Ville – ✆ 01 53 01 90 90 – paris@villamazarin.com – Fax 01 53 01 90 91 J 15
29 rm – †€ 130/400 ††€ 130/400, ☕ € 12
◆ With its high tech equipment (wifi, flat screen TVs) and mix of modern and period furniture, this comfortable hotel near the Hôtel de Ville combines tradition and modernity.

Caron de Beaumarchais without rest
12 r. Vieille-du-Temple Ⓜ Hôtel de Ville – ✆ 01 42 72 34 12 – hotel@carondebeaumarchais.com – Fax 01 42 72 34 63 J 16
19 rm – †€ 125/162 ††€ 125/162, ☕ € 12
◆ Figaro's creator lived on this historic Marais street, and the stylish decoration in this charming hotel pays a faithful tribute to him. Small, comfortable rooms.

Duo without rest
11 r. Temple Ⓜ Hôtel de Ville – ✆ 01 42 72 72 22 – contact@duoparis.com – Fax 01 42 72 03 53 J 15
56 rm – †€ 130/340 ††€ 200/340, ☕ € 15 – 2 suites
◆ The trendily refurbished second wing with its warm and vivid tones has given new life to this hotel full of character, run by the same family for three generations. Fitness room.

Bretonnerie without rest
22 r. Ste-Croix-de-la-Bretonnerie Ⓜ Hôtel de Ville – ✆ 01 48 87 77 63 – hotel@bretonnerie.com – Fax 01 42 77 26 78 J 16
29 rm – †€ 120/180 ††€ 120/180, ☕ € 9,50
◆ Some of the rooms in this elegant 17C mansion in the Marais include four-poster beds and exposed beams. Vaulted ceiling in the breakfast room.

Beaubourg without rest
11 r. S. Le Franc Ⓜ Rambuteau – ✆ 01 42 74 34 24 – htlbeaubourg@hotellerie.net – Fax 01 42 78 68 11 H 15
28 rm – †€ 120/140 ††€ 125/140, ☕ € 9
◆ Nestled in a tiny street behind the Georges-Pompidou Centre. Some of the friendly, well-soundproofed rooms have exposed stone walls and wooden beams.

Lutèce without rest
65 r. St-Louis-en-l'Ile Ⓜ Pont Marie – ✆ 01 43 26 23 52 – hotel.lutece@free.fr – Fax 01 43 29 60 25 K 16
23 rm – †€ 160 ††€ 195, ☕ € 12
◆ The rustic charm of this mansion on the Ile St-Louis is particularly popular with American visitors. Modernised guestrooms with a country feel, plus attractive old woodwork in the lounge.

Deux Iles without rest
59 r. St-Louis-en-l'Ile Ⓜ Pont Marie – ✆ 01 43 26 13 35 – hotel.2iles@free.fr – Fax 01 43 29 60 25 K 16
17 rm – †€ 159 ††€ 189, ☕ € 12
♦ A few yards from the most popular ice-cream parlour in the city, comfortable, cane furnished, peaceful rooms, cosy lounges (one of which is vaulted and one with a fireplace).

Castex without rest
5 r. Castex Ⓜ Bastille – ✆ 01 42 72 31 52 – info@castexhotel.com – Fax 01 42 72 57 91
30 rm – †€ 120 ††€ 120/220, ☕ € 10 K 17
♦ Very Grand Siècle setting in this residence renovated from top to toe: toile de Jouy prints, traditional red tiles and Louis XIII furniture make you forget that the rooms are small.

Nice without rest
42 bis r. de Rivoli Ⓜ Hôtel de Ville – ✆ 01 42 78 55 29 – contact@hoteldenice.com – Fax 01 42 78 36 07 J 16
23 rm – †€ 60/80 ††€ 90/110, ☕ € 8
♦ Ornaments, prints, Kilim carpets and antique furniture in both the rooms and lounges: a special atmosphere completed by good soundproofing.

L'Ambroisie (Bernard Pacaud)
9 pl. des Vosges Ⓜ St-Paul – ✆ 01 42 78 51 45 – Closed August, 23 February-11 March, Sunday and Monday J 17
Rest – Carte € 196/252
Spec. Feuillantine de langoustines aux graines de sésame. Escalopines de bar à l'émincé d'artichaut, caviar osciètre gold. Tarte fine sablée au chocolat, glace vanille.
♦ Under the arcades of the Place des Vosges, royal decor and subtle cuisine, close to perfection. The name is most appropriate: ambrosia was the food of the gods of Antiquity.

Benoit
20 r. St-Martin Ⓜ Châtelet-Les Halles – ✆ 01 42 72 25 76 – restaurant.benoit@wanadoo.fr – Fax 01 42 72 45 68 – Closed 26 July-25 August and 25 February-2 March
Rest – Menu € 38 – Carte € 55/88 J 15
Spec. Escargots en coquille, beurre d'ail, fines herbes. Filet de sole nantua, épinards à peine crémés. Tête de veau traditionnelle sauce ravigote.
♦ Venture into this smart, lively bistro run by Alain Ducasse and sample its authentic, carefully prepared cuisine.

L'Orangerie
28 r. St-Louis-en-L'lle Ⓜ Pont-Marie – ✆ 01 46 33 93 98 – lorangerie75@orange.fr – Fax 01 43 29 25 52 – Closed 3-24 August, Wednesday lunch and Tuesday
Rest – Menu € 35 (weekday lunch), € 75/130 – Carte € 80/102 K 16
♦ An experienced team runs this new restaurant on the Ile Saint-Louis. Long and narrow dining room, elegant table settings and lively, inventive cuisine.

Bofinger (dinner)
5 r. Bastille Ⓜ Bastille – ✆ 01 42 72 87 82 – ebern@groupeflo.fr – Fax 01 42 72 97 68
Rest – Menu (€ 24), € 32 – Carte € 32/79 J 17
♦ The famous clients and remarkable decor have bestowed enduring renown on this brasserie created in 1864. The interior boasts a finely worked cupola, and a room on the first floor decorated by Hansi.

Le Dôme du Marais
53 bis r. Francs-Bourgeois Ⓜ Rambuteau – ✆ 01 42 74 54 17 – ledomedumarais@hotmail.com – Fax 01 42 77 78 17 – Closed 10 August-4 September, Sunday and Monday H 16-J 16
Rest – Menu € 36/48 – Carte € 50/70
♦ Tables are arranged under the pretty dome in the old sales room of the Crédit Municipal, and in a second dining room that resembles a winter garden. Modern cuisine.

Mon Vieil Ami
69 r. St-Louis-en-l'Ile Ⓜ Pont Marie – ✆ 01 40 46 01 35 – mon.vieil.ami@wanadoo.fr – Fax 01 40 46 01 35 – Closed 1st-20 August, 1st-20 January, Monday and Tuesday K 16
Rest – Menu € 41
♦ In this old house with a refurbished interior on Ile St Louis, sample tasty, traditional recipes infused with modern touches and Alsatian culinary influences.

Le Fin Gourmet
VISA MC AE

42 r. Saint-Louis en l'Ile ✉ 75004 Ⓜ Pont-Marie – ☎ 01 43 26 79 27 – contact@lefingourmet.fr – Fax 01 43 26 96 08 – Closed 1st-15 August, 5-20 January, Tuesday lunch and Monday K 16

Rest – Menu € 20 (weekday lunch), € 27/35 – Carte € 45/49

◆ Enjoy to the full the charm of this semi-historic, semi-contemporary restaurant run by a young and enthusiastic team. Elegant setting for up-to-date cuisine.

Bistrot du Dôme
AC VISA MC AE

2 r. Bastille Ⓜ Bastille – ☎ 01 48 04 88 44 – Fax 01 48 04 00 59 – Closed 1st-21 August J 17

Rest – Carte € 30/45

◆ Seafood served in a Slavic décor. The ground floor is lit by bunches of grapes in a trellis design.

L'Enoteca
VISA MC AE

25 r. Charles V Ⓜ St-Paul – ☎ 01 42 78 91 44 – enoteca@enoteca.fr – Fax 01 44 59 31 72 – Closed 9-18 August and lunch in August J 16

Rest – *(pre-book)* Menu (€ 14 bi), € 30/45 bi – Carte € 30/45

◆ A 16C building housing a restaurant whose superb wine list of about 500 Italian wines is its main asset. Italian dishes and very lively atmosphere.

L'Osteria
AC VISA MC

10 r. Sévigné ✉ 75004 Ⓜ St-Paul – ☎ 01 42 71 37 08 – osteria@noos.fr – Closed August, Monday lunch, Saturday lunch and Sunday J 16

Rest – *(pre-book)* Carte € 33/102

◆ No name or menu appears on the façade of this trattoria frequented by a faithful band of regulars and celebrities (if the autographs and drawings on the walls are anything to go by!).

Isami
AC VISA

4 quai d'Orléans Ⓜ Pont-Marie – ☎ 01 40 46 06 97 – Closed 5-25 August, 22 December-6 January, Sunday and Monday K 16

Rest – *(number of covers limited, pre-book)* Menu (€ 30) – Carte € 42/75

◆ A hitherto unheralded Japanese restaurant which probably serves some of the best raw fish in Paris. Sushi and chirashi specialities. A few calligraphies enhance the decor.

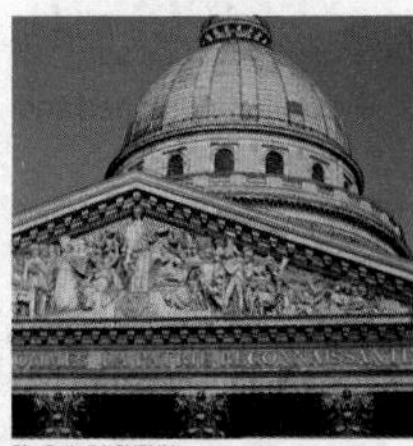

Ph. Gajic/MICHELIN

Panthéon, Jardin des plantes, Mouffetard

5e arrondissement ✉ 75005

Villa Panthéon without rest
AC VISA MC AE

41 r. des Écoles Ⓜ Maubert Mutualité – ☎ 01 53 10 95 95 – pantheon@leshotelsdeparis.com – Fax 01 53 10 95 96 K 14

59 rm – † € 160/350 †† € 160/350, ☕ € 18

◆ The reception, rooms and bar (good selection of whiskies) have a British feel, with parquet floors, colourful hangings, exotic wood furniture and Liberty-style lights.

Les Rives de Notre-Dame without rest
AC VISA MC AE

15 quai St-Michel Ⓜ St-Michel – ☎ 01 43 54 81 16 – hotel@rivesdenotredame.com – Fax 01 43 26 27 09 J 14

10 rm – † € 195/255 †† € 195/550, ☕ € 14

◆ Splendidly preserved 16C residence with spacious Provençal-style rooms all overlooking the Seine and Notre-Dame. Penthouse.

Royal St-Michel without rest

3 bd St-Michel Ⓜ St-Michel – ☎ 01 44 07 06 06 – hotelroyalsaintmichel@wanadoo.fr – Fax 01 44 07 36 25 K 14

39 rm – †€ 180/240 ††€ 195/290, ☕ € 18

◆ On the Boulevard St Michel, opposite the fountain of the same name, this hotel enjoys an excellent location in the heart of the lively Latin Quarter. Attractive, modern rooms.

Panthéon without rest

19 pl. Panthéon Ⓜ Luxembourg – ☎ 01 43 54 32 95 – reservation@hoteldupantheon.com – Fax 01 43 26 64 65 L 14

36 rm – †€ 130/250 ††€ 160/270, ☕ € 12

◆ The cosy or Louis XVI-style rooms offer a view of the Temple de la Renommée dome. Attractive sitting room and vaulted breakfast room.

Grands Hommes without rest

17 pl. Panthéon Ⓜ Luxembourg – ☎ 01 46 34 19 60 – reservation@hoteldesgrandshommes.com – Fax 01 43 26 67 32 L 14

31 rm – †€ 80/310 ††€ 90/430, ☕ € 12

◆ Facing the Panthéon, pleasant hotel decorated in Directoire style (antique furnishings). Over half the rooms overlook the final resting place of some of France's most eminent citizens.

Tour Notre-Dame without rest

20 r. Sommerard Ⓜ Cluny la Sorbonne – ☎ 01 43 54 47 60 – tour-notre-dame@magic.fr – Fax 01 43 26 42 34 K 14

48 rm – †€ 129/176 ††€ 139/190, ☕ € 12

◆ This hotel is very well situated, almost adjoining the Cluny museum. Comfortable, recently-renovated rooms. Those at the back are quieter.

Grand Hôtel St-Michel without rest

19 r. Cujas Ⓜ Luxembourg – ☎ 01 46 33 33 02 – grand.hotel.st.michel@wanadoo.fr – Fax 01 40 46 96 33 K 14

40 rm – †€ 140/170 ††€ 170/220, ☕ € 14 – 5 suites

◆ Hotel in a Haussmannian building offering comfortable rooms adorned with painted furniture. Napoleon III-style lounge. Breakfast served beneath a vaulted ceiling.

Notre Dame without rest

1 quai St-Michel Ⓜ St-Michel – ☎ 01 43 54 20 43 – hotel.denotredame@libertysurf.fr – Fax 01 43 26 61 75 K 14

26 rm – †€ 150 ††€ 199, ☕ € 7

◆ The cosy little rooms in this hotel have all been refurbished and are air-conditioned and well appointed. Most rooms have a view over Notre-Dame cathedral.

Relais St-Jacques without rest

3 r. Abbé de l'Épée Ⓜ Luxembourg – ☎ 01 53 73 26 00 – hotel-relais@wanadoo.fr – Fax 01 43 26 17 81 L 14

22 rm – †€ 179/320 ††€ 179/499, ☕ € 17

◆ Rooms of various styles (Directoire, Louis Philippe, etc.), a glass-roofed breakfast room, Louis XV lounge and 1920s bar, make this a stylish hotchpotch hotel!

St-Christophe without rest

17 r. Lacépède Ⓜ Place Monge – ☎ 01 43 31 81 54 – saintchristophe@wanadoo.fr – Fax 01 43 31 12 54 L 15

31 rm – †€ 97/120 ††€ 107/132, ☕ € 8

◆ The naturalist Lacépède gave his name to this street, a reminder of the proximity of the Jardin des Plantes. Small, rustic-style rooms; all are non-smoking.

Sully St-Germain without rest

31 r. des Écoles Ⓜ Maubert Mutualité – ☎ 01 43 26 56 02 – sully@sequanahotels.com – Fax 01 43 29 74 42 K 15

61 rm – †€ 100/155 ††€ 110/165, ☕ € 12

◆ Perhaps it is the proximity of the Middle Ages museum that inspires the medieval decor in this establishment. Glass-roofed sitting room.

Jardin de Cluny without rest
9 r. Sommerard Ⓜ Maubert Mutualité – ✆ 01 43 54 22 66 – reservation@hoteljardindecluny.com – Fax 01 40 51 03 36 K 14
40 rm – †€ 139/169 ††€ 169/239, ☕ € 14
◆ Functional rooms, equipped with cane furniture. Vaulted breakfast room, adorned with a "Dame à la Licorne" (the original tapestry is just nearby in the Cluny museum).

Select without rest
1 pl. Sorbonne Ⓜ Cluny la Sorbonne – ✆ 01 46 34 14 80 – info@selecthotel.fr – Fax 01 46 34 51 79 K 14
67 rm ☕ – †€ 169/225 ††€ 179/225
◆ Staunchly contemporary hotel in the heart of the student quarter of Paris. Bar and lounges disposed around a patio with a cactus garden. Some rooms offer views over the rooftops.

Du Levant without rest
18 r. Harpe Ⓜ St-Michel – ✆ 01 46 34 11 00 – hlevant@club-internet.fr – Fax 01 46 34 25 87 K 14
47 rm – †€ 73/100 ††€ 118/160, ☕ € 8
◆ Pleasant guestrooms in this hotel built in 1875 in the heart of the Latin Quarter. Admire photos from the 1920s in the corridors, as well as the mural in the breakfast room.

Albe without rest
1 r. Harpe Ⓜ St-Michel – ✆ 01 46 34 09 70 – albehotel@wanadoo.fr – Fax 01 40 46 85 70 K 14
45 rm – †€ 140/160 ††€ 165/250, ☕ € 13
◆ Attractive, modern hotel with smallish, yet nicely-arranged and cheerful rooms. With the Latin quarter and the Île de la Cité close by, Paris is at your doorstep!

Agora St-Germain without rest
42 r. Bernardins Ⓜ Maubert Mutualité – ✆ 01 46 34 13 00 – resa@agora-paris-hotel.com – Fax 01 46 34 75 05 K 15
39 rm – †€ 99/189 ††€ 120/195, ☕ € 11
◆ This hotel near the St-Nicolas-du-Chardonnet church has benefited from a recent facelift. Cosy bedrooms, with those facing the courtyard generally quieter. Charming stone-walled breakfast room.

Dacia-Luxembourg without rest
41 bd St-Michel Ⓜ Cluny la Sorbonne – ✆ 01 53 10 27 77 – info@hoteldacia.com – Fax 01 44 07 10 33 K 14
38 rm – †€ 96/135 ††€ 111/156, ☕ € 10
◆ A large number of improvements have been made in this friendly Latin quarter establishment. Attractive white quilted bedspreads in the well-equipped rooms (two with four-poster beds).

Henri IV without rest
9 r. St-Jacques Ⓜ St-Michel – ✆ 01 46 33 20 20 – info@hotel-henri4.com – Fax 01 46 33 90 90 K 14
23 rm – †€ 167 ††€ 185, ☕ € 12
◆ Almost all the attractive guestrooms in this hotel overlook the chevet of St Séverin church. Traditional floor tiles, antique furniture and a fireplace grace the charming lounge.

Minerve without rest
13 r. des Écoles Ⓜ Maubert Mutualité – ✆ 01 43 26 26 04 – resa@parishotelminerve.com – Fax 01 44 07 01 96 L 15
54 rm – †€ 90/156 ††€ 104/156, ☕ € 8
◆ This building, from 1864, offers a pleasant entrance hall (exposed stone and period furniture) and small, well-kept and rooms full of character.

Pierre Nicole without rest
39 r. Pierre Nicole Ⓜ Port Royal – ✆ 01 43 54 76 86 – hotelpierre-nicole@voila.fr – Fax 01 43 54 22 45 – Closed 28 July-27 August M 13
33 rm – †€ 80 ††€ 90/100, ☕ € 7
◆ The name pays tribute to the Port-Royal moralist. Small but well-kept and reasonably-priced, practical rooms. The Luxembourg gardens are nearby.

St-Jacques without rest
35 r. des Écoles Ⓜ Maubert Mutualité – ✆ 01 44 07 45 45 – hotelsaintjacques@wanadoo.fr – Fax 01 43 25 65 50 K 15
38 rm – †€ 61/92 ††€ 105/137, ☕ € 9,50
◆ Modern comfort allies with old-style charm in the rooms of this hotel. Library with 18C and 19C works. Breakfast room with Roaring Twenties cabaret-style decor.

Familia without rest
11 r. des Écoles Ⓜ Cardinal Lemoine – ✆ 01 43 54 55 27 – hotelfamilia@wanadoo.fr – Fax 01 43 29 61 77 K 15-L 15
30 rm – †€ 78/81 ††€ 89/121, ☕ € 6,50
◆ Notre-Dame and the Collège des Bernardins provide the backdrop for the Familia, with its rustic bedrooms adorned with frescoes and sepia photos highlighting the monuments of Paris. Family-style breakfast room.

Devillas without rest
4 bd St-Marcel Ⓜ St-Marcel – ✆ 01 43 31 37 50 – info@hoteldevillas.com – Fax 01 43 31 96 03 M 16
39 rm – †€ 79/89 ††€ 83/170, ☕ € 10
◆ Renovated and well-equipped rooms in this hotel situated in a street near La Pitié-Salpêtrière hospital. For more quiet, reserve at the back.

La Tour d'Argent ← Notre - Dame,
15 quai Tournelle Ⓜ Maubert Mutualité – ✆ 01 43 54 23 31 – resa@latourdargent.com – Fax 01 44 07 12 04 – Closed August and Monday
Rest – Menu € 70 (lunch) – Carte € 140/487 K 16
Spec. Quenelles de brochet "André Terrail". Noisette d'agneau des Tournelles. Gâteau au chocolat "Vasco de Gama".
◆ The 'skyline' dining room offers a magnificent view of Notre Dame Cathedral. Exceptional wine list, famous Challans duck and a celebrity clientele since the 16C. An institution!

La Truffière
4 r. Blainville Ⓜ Place Monge – ✆ 01 46 33 29 82 – restaurant.latruffiere@wanadoo.fr – Fax 01 46 33 64 74 – Closed 20-26 December, Sunday and Monday
Rest – Menu € 24 (weekday lunch), € 105/180 – Carte € 71/164 L 15
◆ A 17C house with two dining rooms. One is rustic with exposed beams and the other is vaulted. Traditional cuisine from southwest France and a fine wine list.

Mavrommatis
42 r. Daubenton Ⓜ Censier Daubenton – ✆ 01 43 31 17 17 – info@mavrommatis.fr – Fax 01 43 36 13 08 – Closed 15 August-15 September, Sunday and Monday
Rest – Menu (€ 28), € 37/60 – Carte € 49/70 M 15
◆ The ambassador of Greek cuisine in Paris. Nothing mythical; just sober elegance and comfortable surroundings enhanced by soft lighting and a gracious welcome. Summer terrace.

Marty
20 av. Gobelins Ⓜ Les Gobelins – ✆ 01 43 31 39 51 – restaurant.marty@wanadoo.fr – Fax 01 43 37 63 70 M 15
Rest – Menu € 34 – Carte € 36/54
◆ This restaurant has pleasant 1930s decor including mahogany wood panelling, hand-picked antique furniture and paintings. Traditional menu and seafood dishes.

Atelier Maître Albert
1 r. Maître Albert Ⓜ Maubert Mutualité – ✆ 01 56 81 30 01 – ateliermaitrealbert@guysavoy.com – Fax 01 53 10 83 23 – Closed 5-25 August, Christmas holidays, Saturday lunch and Sunday lunch K 15
Rest – Menu € 24 (weekday lunch), € 40/50 – Carte approx. € 44
◆ Guy Savoy and his team propose carefully prepared dishes in a modern designer setting that also features a huge medieval fireplace, a spit for roasted meat and exposed beams.

L'Équitable
47bis r. Poliveau Ⓜ St-Marcel – ✆ 01 43 31 69 20 – equitable.restaurant@wanadoo.fr – Fax 01 43 37 85 52 – Closed Easter holidays, 5-25 August, Tuesday lunch and Monday M16
Rest – Menu € 21/32
◆ This restaurant retains the pleasant atmosphere of a provincial inn, via its rustic decor (exposed stonework and beams) and generous traditional cuisine.

Toustem
AC (dinner) VISA MC AE

12 rue de l'Hôtel Colbert Ⓜ Maubert Mutualité – ✆ 01 40 51 99 87 – toustem@helenedarroze.com – Closed Monday lunch, Saturday lunch and Sunday

Rest – Menu (€ 24), € 32 (lunch) – Carte € 45/49 K 15

◆ With "Toustem" (always in the Landes dialect), Hélène Darroze has moved firmly into the (south-western cuisine) bistro segment. 13C setting with designer touches and intimate cellars.

Les Délices d'Aphrodite
AC VISA MC AE

4 r. Candolle Ⓜ Censier Daubenton – ✆ 01 43 31 40 39 – info@mavrommatis.fr – Fax 01 43 36 13 08 M 15

Rest – Menu (€ 20) – Carte € 31/44

◆ Convivial bistro with a holiday atmosphere: photos of Greek scenery, ivy covered ceiling and the flavour of olive oil in the Greek cuisine.

La Table de Fabrice
AC VISA MC

13 quai de la Tournelle Ⓜ Pont-Marie – ✆ 01 44 07 17 57 – latabledefabrice@orange.fr – Fax 01 43 25 37 55 – Closed 5-25 August, Saturday lunch and Sunday

Rest – Menu € 40 – Carte € 51/79 K 16

◆ A charming small restaurant in a 17C building. Provincial atmosphere and views of the banks of the Seine from the first floor. A single menu and seasonal specials on a blackboard.

Chez René
(dinner) VISA MC

14 bd St-Germain Ⓜ Maubert Mutualité – ✆ 01 43 54 30 23 – Fax 01 43 54 33 57 – Closed August, 24 December-2 January, Sunday and Monday K 15

Rest – Carte € 24/65

◆ Friendly atmosphere and a loyal team at this neighbourhood institution. Authentic bistro décor: banquettes, mirrors, brass... Summer terrace.

Moissonnier
VISA MC

28 r. Fossés-St-Bernard Ⓜ Jussieu – ✆ 01 43 29 87 65 – Fax 01 43 29 87 65 – Closed August, Sunday and Monday K 15

Rest – Menu € 24 – Carte € 29/51

◆ The typical decor of this bistro has not been altered for years: gleaming bar, patina on the walls and bench seats. Jugs of Beaujolais and a definite flavour of Lyons in the cuisine.

Au Moulin à Vent
VISA MC

20 r. Fossés-St-Bernard Ⓜ Jussieu – ✆ 01 43 54 99 37 – alexandra.damas@au-moulinavent.fr – Fax 01 40 46 92 23 – Closed 2-26 August, 31 December-8 January, Saturday lunch, Sunday and Monday K 15

Rest – Carte € 46/61

◆ Nothing has changed in this Parisian bistro since 1948. Although the decor has developed a well-worn sheen over the years, and meat specialities have been added to the traditional menu.

Buisson Ardent
AC VISA MC

25 r. Jussieu Ⓜ Jussieu – ✆ 01 43 54 93 02 – jtlopez@noos.fr – Closed August, Saturday lunch and Sunday L 15

Rest – Menu € 31/45

◆ An informal atmosphere in this small, local restaurant packed at lunchtime with students from Jussieu University. Bistro cuisine. Original 1923 frescoes.

Louis Vins
AC

9 r. Montagne-Ste-Geneviève Ⓜ Maubert Mutualité – ✆ 01 43 29 12 12

Rest – Menu (€ 24), € 27 K 15

◆ A warm Belle époque-style decor (walnut counter, mirrors, murals), in which you can enjoy generous bistro-type dishes and a fine wine list.

L' A.O.C.
VISA MC

14 r. des Fossés St-Bernard Ⓜ Maubert Mutualité – ✆ 01 43 54 22 52 – aocrestaurant@wanadoo.fr – Closed August, Sunday and Monday

Rest – Carte € 28/57 K 16

◆ An address for carnivores with top-quality meats, matured by the owner. Rotisserie at the entrance and back-to-basics bistro feel.

Ribouldingue

10 r. St-Julien le Pauvre Ⓜ Maubert Mutualité – ✆ 01 46 33 98 80 – Fax 01 43 54 09 34 – Closed 1st-24 August, Sunday and Monday K 14

Rest – Menu € 27

◆ This pleasant bistro has an unusual theme: it specialises in offal (brain, tongue, tripe etc), but also serves classical dishes. Charming service.

Petit Pontoise

9 r. Pontoise Ⓜ Maubert Mutualité – ✆ 01 43 29 25 20 K 15

Rest – Carte € 31/52

◆ A stone's throw from the Quays of the Seine and Notre-Dame, local bistro decorated in the style of the 1950's. Menu suggestions chalked on the slate. Regular clientele.

Les Oudayas

34 Bd St-Germain Ⓜ Maubert Mutualité – ✆ 01 43 29 97 38 – oudayas@oudayas.com K 15

Rest – Menu (€ 15), € 23/29 – Carte € 31/44

◆ A stone's throw from the Institut du Monde Arabe, restaurant named after the casbah of Rabat. Moroccan ambiance, refined cuisine and tea room.

Papilles

30 r. Gay Lussac Ⓜ Luxembourg – ✆ 01 43 25 20 79 – lespapilles@hotmail.fr – Fax 01 43 25 24 35 – Closed Easter holidays, 1st-21 August, 1st-8 January, Sunday and Monday L 14

Rest – Menu € 31 – Carte € 36/43

◆ Bistro, cellar and grocer's: on one side are wine racks, on the other shelves with jars of southwest specialities and in the middle...you can enjoy market-inspired food!

Christophe

8 r. Descartes Ⓜ Maubert Mutualité – ✆ 01 43 26 72 49 – Closed 5 August-5 September, Sunday and Monday L 15

Rest – Menu (€ 12), € 19 – Carte € 37/56

◆ This simply furnished bistro (black furniture, photos of Paris) serves excellent cuisine with individual touches. Fish and pork figure prominently on the menu.

Coco de Mer

34 bd St-Marcel Ⓜ St-Marcel – ✆ 01 47 07 06 64 – contact@cocodemer.fr – Fax 01 43 31 45 75 – Closed Saturday lunch and Sunday lunch M 16

Rest – Menu (€ 23), € 28

◆ Fed up with the weather? Take a trip to the Seychelles: ti-punch in bare feet on the fine sand of the veranda, and typical dishes of the Isles with fresh fish delivered weekly.

Lhassa

13 r. Montagne Ste-Geneviève Ⓜ Maubert Mutualité – ✆ 01 43 26 22 19 – Fax 01 42 17 00 08 – Closed Mon. K 15

Rest – Menu € 11 (weekday lunch), € 15/21 – Carte € 17/25

◆ As the name suggests, this little restaurant is entirely devoted to Tibet: coloured fabrics, crafts, photos of the Dalai Lama and Tibetan specialities.

S. Sauvignier/MICHELIN

St-Germain-des-Prés, Quartier Latin, Luxembourg

6e arrondissement ✉ 75006

Lutetia
45 bd Raspail Ⓜ Sèvres Babylone – ✆ 01 49 54 46 46
– lutetia-paris@lutetia-paris.com – Fax 01 49 54 46 00 K 12
231 rm – †€ 250/950 ††€ 250/950, ☐ € 27 – 11 suites
Rest *Paris* – see restaurant listing
Rest *Brasserie Lutetia* – ✆ 01 49 54 46 76 – Menu (€ 38), € 45 – Carte € 59/72
◆ Built in 1910, this luxury hotel on the Left Bank has lost none of its sparkle. It happily blends Art Deco fixtures with contemporary details (sculptures by César, Arman, etc). Refurbished rooms. Popular with well-heeled Parisians, Brasserie Lutetia is famous for its seafood menu.

Victoria Palace without rest
6 r. Blaise-Desgoffe Ⓜ St-Placide – ✆ 01 45 49 70 00 – info@victoriapalace.com
– Fax 01 45 49 23 75 L 11
62 rm – †€ 332/390 ††€ 332/620, ☐ € 18
◆ Small luxury hotel with undeniable charm: toiles de Jouy, Louis XVI-style furniture and marble bathrooms in the rooms. Paintings, red velvet and porcelain in the lounges.

D'Aubusson without rest
33 r. Dauphine Ⓜ Odéon – ✆ 01 43 29 43 43
– reservations@hoteldaubusson.com – Fax 01 43 29 12 62 J 13
49 rm – †€ 310/470 ††€ 310/470, ☐ € 23
◆ A 17C townhouse with character, offering elegant rooms with Versailles parquet, Aubusson tapestries and jazz evenings at the Café Laurent on weekends.

Relais Christine without rest
3 r. Christine Ⓜ St-Michel – ✆ 01 40 51 60 80 – contact@relais-christine.com
– Fax 01 40 51 60 81 J 14
51 rm – †€ 370/540 ††€ 415/780, ☐ € 25
◆ Townhouse built on the site of a medieval convent (the vaulted breakfast room is 13C). Handsome cobbled courtyard, small garden, rooms with a personal touch.

Relais St-Germain
9 carr. de l'Odéon Ⓜ Odéon – ✆ 01 43 29 12 05 – hotelrsg@wanadoo.fr
– Fax 01 46 33 45 30 K 13
22 rm ☐ – †€ 165/220 ††€ 205/440
Rest *Le Comptoir* – see restaurant listing
◆ Elegant hotel comprising three 17C buildings. Polished beams, shimmering fabrics and antique furniture.

Bel Ami St-Germain des Prés without rest
7 r. St-Benoit Ⓜ St-Germain des Prés –
✆ 01 42 61 53 53 – contact@hotel-bel-ami.com – Fax 01 49 27 09 33
115 rm – †€ 270/540 ††€ 270/600, ☐ € 25 J 13
◆ This attractive building may well be 19C in origin but the era of Maupassant is long gone! Resolutely modern interior where minimalist luxury rubs shoulders with hi-tech gadgets and a relaxed ambience.

Buci without rest
22 r. Buci Ⓜ Mabillon – ✆ 01 55 42 74 74 – hotelbuci@wanadoo.fr
– Fax 01 55 42 74 44 J 13
21 rm – †€ 185/215 ††€ 215/400, ☐ € 18 – 3 suites
◆ A stylish midnight blue façade gives an idea of the style of this small hotel. Classy bedrooms (canopies on the beds, English period furniture), others sport a more contemporary finish.

L'Abbaye without rest

10 r. Cassette Ⓜ *St-Sulpice – ✆ 01 45 44 38 11 – hotel.abbaye@wanadoo.fr – Fax 01 45 48 07 86* K 12

40 rm ☕ – 🚹€ 215/251 🚹🚹€ 215/251 – 4 suites

◆ Hotel in a former 18C convent combining old-world charm with modern comfort. Pleasant veranda, duplex apartment with a terrace, and stylish rooms. Some overlook a delightful patio.

Littré without rest

9 r. Littré Ⓜ *Montparnasse Bienvenüe – ✆ 01 53 63 07 07 – hotellittre@hotellittreparis.com – Fax 01 45 44 88 13* L 11

79 rm – 🚹€ 275/315 🚹🚹€ 315/350, ☕ € 20 – 11 suites

◆ Classic building, halfway between Saint Germain des Prés and Montparnasse. The stylish rooms are all very comfortable. Magnificent view from the top floor.

L'Hôtel

13 r. des Beaux-Arts Ⓜ *St-Germain-des-Prés – ✆ 01 44 41 99 00 – stay@l-hotel.com – Fax 01 43 25 64 81* J 13

16 rm – 🚹€ 255/640 🚹🚹€ 280/640, ☕ € 18 – 4 suites

Rest Le Restaurant – see restaurant listing

◆ This hotel is where Oscar Wilde passed away, leaving an unpaid bill behind him. It sports a vertiginous well of light and an extravagant decor by Garcia (Baroque, French Empire and Oriental).

Esprit Saint-Germain without rest

22 r. St-Sulpice Ⓜ *Mabillon – ✆ 01 53 10 55 55 – contact@espritsaintgermain.com – Fax 01 53 10 55 56* K 13

28 rm – 🚹€ 310/550 🚹🚹€ 310/550, ☕ € 26 – 5 suites

◆ Elegant and contemporary rooms pleasantly combining red, chocolate and beige colours with modern paintings and furniture; bathrooms with slate walls.

Pas de Calais without rest

59 r. des Saints-Pères Ⓜ *St-Germain-des-Prés – ✆ 01 45 48 78 74 – infos@hotelpasdecalais.com – Fax 01 45 44 94 57* J 12

38 rm – 🚹€ 145/300 🚹🚹€ 160/300, ☕ € 15

◆ The hotel lobby is lit by a glass ceiling and has a beautiful vertical garden made up of orchids. Lovely rooms with individual touches; exposed beams on the top floor.

Madison without rest

143 bd St-Germain Ⓜ *St-Germain des Prés – ✆ 01 40 51 60 00 – resa@hotel-madison.com – Fax 01 40 51 60 01* J 13

54 rm – 🚹€ 150/345 🚹🚹€ 157/385, ☕ € 15 – 1 suite

◆ This hotel was popular with Albert Camus. Some of its elegant rooms offer views of the church of St-Germain-des Prés. Attractive Louis Philippe lounge.

Left Bank St-Germain without rest

9 r. de l'Ancienne Comédie Ⓜ *Odéon – ✆ 01 43 54 01 70 – reservation@hotelleftbank.com – Fax 01 43 26 17 14* K 13

31 rm ☕ – 🚹€ 140/250 🚹🚹€ 150/370

◆ Wainscoting, damask, Jouy drapes, Louis XIII style furniture and half-timbered walls set the scene. Some rooms command views of Notre Dame.

La Villa d'Estrées et Résidence des Arts without rest

17 r. Gît le Coeur Ⓜ *Saint-Michel – ✆ 01 55 42 71 11 – resa@villadestrees.com – Fax 01 55 42 71 00* J 14

21 rm – 🚹€ 175/295 🚹🚹€ 175/355, ☕ € 10

◆ These two buildings are decorated in Napoleon III style, updated with modern details by a protegé of the designer Garcia. Cosy, well-appointed bedrooms and apartments.

La Villa without rest

29 r. Jacob Ⓜ *St-Germain des Prés – ✆ 01 43 26 60 00 – hotel@villa-saintgermain.com – Fax 01 46 34 63 63* J 13

31 rm – 🚹€ 225/285 🚹🚹€ 225/445, ☕ € 25

◆ The façade is 19C but the interior is staunchly smart and contemporary: wenge furniture, rich fabrics and soft lighting set the scene.

Sénat without rest
10 r. Vaugirard Ⓜ Luxembourg – ✆ 01 43 54 54 54 – reservations@hotelsenat.com – Fax 01 43 54 54 55 K 14
47 rm – †€ 190/265 ††€ 285/315, ☕ € 16 – 6 suites
♦ The stylish black façade, and immense grey vases topped with clusters of mistletoe, set the scene in this contemporary smart establishment. Very pleasant rooms.

Ste-Beuve without rest
9 r. Ste-Beuve Ⓜ Notre-Dame des Champs – ✆ 01 45 48 20 07 – saintebeuve@wanadoo.fr – Fax 01 45 48 67 52 L 12
22 rm – †€ 145/345 ††€ 145/345, ☕ € 15
♦ The intimate atmosphere of this establishment makes its feel like a private house. The rooms have been renovated in a tasteful modern style; bathrooms in black and white.

Millésime without rest
15 r. Jacob Ⓜ St-Germain des Prés – ✆ 01 44 07 97 97 – reservation@millesimehotel.com – Fax 01 46 34 55 97 J 13
22 rm – †€ 190/220 ††€ 190/380, ☕ € 16
♦ Colours of the south and select furniture and fabrics create a warm atmosphere in the splendid rooms at this hotel. Superb 17C staircase, patio and fine vaulted dining room.

Des Académies et des Arts without rest
15 r. de la Grande-Chaumière Ⓜ Vavin – ✆ 01 43 26 66 44 – reservation@hoteldesacademies.com – Fax 01 40 46 86 85 L 12
20 rm – †€ 220/285 ††€ 220/285, ☕ € 16
♦ The walls of this creative and artistic hotel are adorned with white figures painted by Jérôme Mesnager and sculptures by Sophie de Watrigant. Elegant, well-appointed guestrooms.

Relais Médicis without rest
23 r. Racine Ⓜ Odéon – ✆ 01 43 26 00 60 – reservation@relaismedicis.com – Fax 01 40 46 83 39 K 13
16 rm ☕ – †€ 142/172 ††€ 172/258
♦ A hint of Provence enhances the rooms of this hotel near the Odeon theatre; those overlooking the patio are quieter. Interesting antique furniture.

Au Manoir St-Germain-des-Prés without rest
153 bd St-Germain Ⓜ St-Germain des Prés – ✆ 01 42 22 21 65 – reservation@hotelaumanoir.com – Fax 01 45 48 22 25 J 12
32 rm ☕ – †€ 150/330 ††€ 150/330
♦ Elegant hotel, opposite the Flore and Deux Magots (famous St Germain des Prés cafés) with period furniture, murals, wood panelling and toile de Jouy prints.

St-Grégoire without rest
43 r. Abbé-Grégoire Ⓜ St-Placide – ✆ 01 45 48 23 23 – hotel@saintgregoire.com – Fax 01 45 48 33 95 L 12
20 rm – †€ 195/250 ††€ 250/300, ☕ € 14
♦ Elegant and welcoming decor at this establishment. Two of the rooms have small leafy terraces. Attractive vaulted breakfast room.

Villa des Artistes without rest
9 r. Grande-Chaumière Ⓜ Vavin – ✆ 01 43 26 60 86 – hotel@villa-artistes.com – Fax 01 43 54 73 70 L 12
55 rm – †€ 158/190 ††€ 158/190, ☕ € 15
♦ The name pays tribute to the artists who embellished the history of the Montpa rnasse district. Pleasant rooms, most overlooking the courtyard. Glass-roofed breakfast room.

Artus without rest
34 r. de Buci Ⓜ Mabillon – ✆ 01 43 29 07 20 – info@artushotel.com – Fax 01 43 29 67 44 J 13
27 rm – †€ 240/285 ††€ 250/300, ☕ € 15
♦ Contemporary yet intimate, with modern bedrooms ornamented with antiques, an attractive vaulted cellar, designer bar, and paintings from nearby galleries on display.

Relais St-Sulpice without rest

3 r. Garancière Ⓜ *St-Sulpice – ✆ 01 46 33 99 00 – relaisstsulpice@wanadoo.fr – Fax 01 46 33 00 10* K 13

26 rm – †€ 176/215 ††€ 177/216, ☕ € 12

◆ Appealing hotel not far from the Sénat and the Luxembourg gardens housing spacious, well-decorated rooms. Those at the back are very quiet.

De Fleurie without rest

32 r. Grégoire de Tours Ⓜ *Odéon – ✆ 01 53 73 70 00 – bonjour@hotel-de-fleurie.fr – Fax 01 53 73 70 20* K 13

29 rm – †€ 160/180 ††€ 210/240, ☕ € 14

◆ Spruce 18C facade adorned with statues in niches. Elegant rooms with soft tones, enhanced by woodwork. Choose the quieter rooms overlooking the courtyard.

Prince de Conti without rest

8 r. Guénégaud Ⓜ *Odéon – ✆ 01 44 07 30 40 – princedeconti@wanadoo.fr – Fax 01 44 07 36 34* J 13

26 rm – †€ 166/281 ††€ 167/282, ☕ € 13

◆ This 18C building adjoining the Hotel de la Monnaie has a charming lounge full of interesting features; refined bedrooms; and a bright duplex decorated with precious objects.

Clos Médicis without rest

56 r. Monsieur Le Prince Ⓜ *Odéon – ✆ 01 43 29 10 80 – message@closmedicis.com – Fax 01 43 54 26 90* K 14

38 rm – †€ 141/300 ††€ 175/300, ☕ € 13 – 1 suite

◆ Hotel dating from 1773 a few feet from the Marie de Médicis garden. The modern interior, warm tones, soft lighting and attention to detail makes it ideal for a relaxing stay.

Odéon without rest

3 r. Odéon Ⓜ *Odéon – ✆ 01 43 25 90 67 – odeon@odeonhotel.fr – Fax 01 43 25 55 98*

33 rm – †€ 130/180 ††€ 180/270, ☕ € 12 K 13

◆ The façade, stone walls and exposed beams bear witness to the age of this building (17C). Personalised guestrooms, some with views of the Eiffel Tower.

Odéon St-Germain without rest

13 r. St-Sulpice Ⓜ *Odéon – ✆ 01 43 25 70 11 – reservation@paris-hotel-odeon.com – Fax 01 43 29 97 34* K 13

32 rm – †€ 150/250 ††€ 175/360, ☕ € 14

◆ The interior of this 16C house is varied to say the least: old brass or four-poster beds, bric-a-brac from antique markets, etc. Tiny lush garden.

Prince de Condé without rest

39 r. de Seine Ⓜ *Mabillon – ✆ 01 43 26 71 56 – princedeconde@wanadoo.fr – Fax 01 46 34 27 95* J 13

11 rm – †€ 196/281 ††€ 197/282, ☕ € 13

◆ An intimate hotel close to numerous art galleries. Cosy rooms with stone walls, fine vaulted cellar and lounge-library.

Régent without rest

61 r. Dauphine Ⓜ *Odéon – ✆ 01 46 34 59 80 – hotel.leregent@wanadoo.fr – Fax 01 40 51 05 07* J 13

24 rm – †€ 170 ††€ 250, ☕ € 14

◆ Tall façade dating from 1769. The rooms are cosy and well equipped. The charming breakfast room with exposed stone walls is located in the basement.

Bréa without rest

14 r. Bréa Ⓜ *Vavin – ✆ 01 43 25 44 41 – brea.hotel@wanadoo.fr – Fax 01 44 07 19 25*

23 rm – †€ 120/185 ††€ 130/210, ☕ € 14 L 12

◆ Two buildings joined by an attractive glass-roofed winter garden room. Mediterranean feel to the spacious, well-equipped rooms.

Le Clément without rest

6 r. Clément Ⓜ *Mabillon – ✆ 01 43 26 53 60 – info@hotel-clement.fr – Fax 01 44 07 06 83* K 13

28 rm – †€ 120/155 ††€ 120/155, ☕ € 10

◆ Opposite the St Germain market, this hotel with an elegant grey facade has been in the same family for three generations. Reasonably priced, well-kept rooms.

De Sèvres without rest
22 r. Abbé-Grégoire Ⓜ St-Placide – ✆ 01 45 48 84 07 – info@hoteldesevres.com – Fax 01 42 84 01 55 K 11-12
31 rm – †€ 95/150 ††€ 110/150, ☕ € 10
◆ This peaceful hotel near the Bon Marché has been fully refurbished and offers modern rooms. The breakfast room overlooks a tiny courtyard decked with flowers.

Paris – Hôtel Lutetia
45 bd Raspail Ⓜ Sèvres Babylone – ✆ 01 49 54 46 90 – lutetia-paris@lutetia-paris.com – Fax 01 49 54 46 00 – Closed August, Saturday, Sunday and public holidays K 12
Rest – Menu € 60 bi (lunch), € 80/130 – Carte € 98/130
Spec. Araignée de mer au pamplemousse, jus parfumé de colombo au pollen grillé. Homard à la vanille, avocat à la tomate au citron vert. Saint-Honoré aux fruits rouges.
◆ In keeping with the style of the hotel, the Sonia Rykiel Art Deco dining room is a recreation of one of the lounges from the Normandie ocean liner. Inspired traditional cuisine.

Jacques Cagna (dinner)
14 r. Grands Augustins Ⓜ St-Michel – ✆ 01 43 26 49 39 – jacquescagna@hotmail.com – Fax 01 43 54 54 48 – Closed 27 July-24 August, Monday lunch, Saturday lunch and Sunday J 14
Rest – Menu € 48 (lunch)/100 – Carte € 87/153
Spec. Foie gras de canard poêlé aux fruits de saison caramélisés. Noix de ris de veau en croûte de sel au romarin. Gibier (season).
◆ Located in one of the oldest buildings in Paris, the comfortable dining hall is embellished with massive rafters, 16C woodwork and Flemish paintings. Refined cuisine.

Relais Louis XIII (Manuel Martinez)
8 r. Grands Augustins Ⓜ Odéon – ✆ 01 43 26 75 96 – contact@relaislouis13.com – Fax 01 44 07 07 80 – Closed August, 22 December-3 January, Sunday and Monday J 14
Rest – Menu € 50 (lunch), € 80/110 – Carte € 115/133
Spec. Ravioli de homard, foie gras et crème de cèpes. Caneton challandais rôti entier aux épices, cuisse confite en parmentier. Millefeuille, crème légère à la vanille bourbon.
◆ The building dates from the 16C and there are three Louis XIII-style dining rooms with balustrades, tapestries and open stonework. The cuisine is subtle and up-to-date.

Hélène Darroze-La Salle à Manger
4 r. d'Assas Ⓜ Sèvres Babylone – ✆ 01 42 22 00 11 – reservation@helenedarroze.com – Fax 01 42 22 25 40 K 12
Rest – *(1st floor) (closed lunch 19 July-30 August, Monday except dinner 19 July-30 August and Sunday)* Menu € 72 (lunch), € 175/280 – Carte € 111/189
Rest *Le Salon* – *(closed 19 July-30 August, Sunday and Monday)* Menu (€ 35), € 45 (lunch)/88 – Carte € 64/141
Rest *Le Boudoir* – *(closed 19 July-30 August, Sunday and Monday)* Menu € 45 (lunch)/88 – Carte € 70/141
Spec. Riz carnaroli acquarello noir et crémeux, chipirons au chorizo et tomates confites, jus au persil, émulsion de parmesan. Grosses langoustines bretonnes rôties aux épices tandoori, mousseline de carottes aux agrumes. Pigeonneau fermier de Racan flambé au capucin et foie gras de canard des Landes grillé au feu de bois.
◆ Close to the Bon Marché store, the decor is modern, low key and softly lit in aubergine and orange. Delicious cuisine and wines from southwest France. On the ground floor, Hélène Darroze presides over the Salon and serves tapas and small dishes with a rustic flavour of the Landes. Intimate decor at the Boudoir and cuisine with "feeling".

Le Restaurant – Hôtel L'Hôtel
13 r. des Beaux-Arts Ⓜ St-Germain-des-Prés – ✆ 01 44 41 99 01 J 13
Rest – *(closed August, 21-29 December, Sunday and Monday)* Menu (€ 38), € 75/125 bi – Carte € 74/83
Spec. Le Saint Pierre. Le Cochon de Lait. Le Chocolat.
◆ Part of "L'Hôtel", the equally simply named "Le Restaurant" boasts decor by Jacques Garcia and a small inner courtyard. Refined, contemporary cuisine.

XX **Sensing**

19 r. Bréa, (Paris 06) Ⓜ Vavin – ✆ 01 43 27 08 80 – sensing@orange.fr – Fax 01 43 26 99 27 – Closed August, Monday lunch and Sunday L 12

Rest – Menu (€ 25), € 55 (weekday lunch), € 95/140 – Carte € 60/73

◆ A short menu with refined, contemporary dishes prepared using excellent produce and served in an uncluttered, ultra-stylish setting. Run by the famous chef, Guy Martin.

XX **Bastide Odéon** (dinner)

7 r. Corneille Ⓜ Odéon – ✆ 01 43 26 03 65 – reservation@bastide-odeon.com – Fax 01 44 07 28 93 – Closed 3-25 August, Sunday and Monday K 13

Rest – Menu € 26 (lunch)/40

◆ Near the Luxembourg Gardens, a pleasant, comfortable restaurant with decor reminiscent of a Provençal farm. Private room upstairs. Mediterranean specialities.

XX **Méditerranée**

2 pl. Odéon Ⓜ Odéon – ✆ 01 43 26 02 30 – la.mediterranee@wanadoo.fr – Fax 01 43 26 18 44 – Closed 22-28 December K 13

Rest – Menu (€ 27), € 32 – Carte € 38/64

◆ Mediterranean cuisine is served in two dining rooms decorated with frescos depicting the sea, as well as a veranda facing the Théâtre de l'Europe.

XX **Yugaraj**

14 r. Dauphine Ⓜ Odéon – ✆ 01 43 26 44 91 – contact@yugaraj.com – Fax 01 46 33 50 77 – Closed 1st-4 May, 5-27 August, 1st-4 January, Thursday lunch and Monday J 14

Rest – Menu € 31/46 – Carte € 36/60

◆ New look but the same refinement at this highly acclaimed Indian restaurant with its museum-like decor (wood panelling, silks and antiques). Comprehensive menu.

XX **Alcazar**

62 r. Mazarine Ⓜ Odéon – ✆ 01 53 10 19 99 – contact@alcazar.fr – Fax 01 53 10 23 23 J 13

Rest – Menu € 20 bi (weekday lunch)/40 – Carte € 37/60

◆ The famous cabaret has been transformed into a huge, trendy designer restaurant. The cooking hobs are visible from the tables, and the cuisine is contemporary.

XX **Les Bouquinistes**

53 quai Grands Augustins Ⓜ St-Michel – ✆ 01 43 25 45 94 – bouquinistes@guysavoy.com – Fax 01 43 25 23 07 – Closed 5-23 August, 23 December-5 January, Saturday lunch and Sunday J 14

Rest – Menu € 25 (weekday lunch)/75 – Carte € 50/62

◆ Opposite the second hand bookstalls of the embankments, enjoy original cuisine in no less original surroundings: designer furnishings, coloured lamps and abstract artwork.

X **Yen**

22 r. St-Benoît Ⓜ St-Germain des Prés – ✆ 01 45 44 11 18 – restau.yen@wanadoo.fr – Fax 01 45 44 19 48 – Closed Sunday J 13

Rest – Menu (€ 31), € 55 (dinner) – Carte € 31/64

◆ Two dining rooms with highly refined Japanese decor, the one on the first floor is slightly warmer in style. Pride of place on the menu for the chef's speciality: soba (buckwheat noodles).

X **La Rotonde**

105 bd Montparnasse Ⓜ Vavin – ✆ 01 43 26 68 84 – Fax 01 46 34 52 40 L 12

Rest – Menu (€ 17 bi), € 35 – Carte € 36/69

◆ The history of this typical Parisian brasserie is printed on the back of the menu. It has served many famous people since 1903. An ideal place for a meal after an evening out at the theatre.

X **La Marlotte**

55 r. du Cherche-Midi Ⓜ St-Placide – ✆ 01 45 48 86 79 – Fax 01 44 07 28 93 – Closed 3-24 August, Sunday and holidays K 12

Rest – Menu (€ 23), € 40/50 – Carte € 32/64

◆ Near the Bon Marché, a pleasant local restaurant where you may rub shoulders with publishers and politicians. Long dining room, rustic decor and traditional cuisine.

L'Épi Dupin

11 r. Dupin Ⓜ Sèvres Babylone – ✆ 01 42 22 64 56 – lepidupin@wanadoo.fr – Fax 01 42 22 30 42 – Closed 1st-24 August, Monday lunch, Saturday and Sunday

Rest – *(number of covers limited, pre-book)* Menu (€ 25 bi), € 34 K 12

◆ Beams and stonework for character, closely-packed tables for conviviality and delicious cuisine to delight the palate; this pocket-handkerchief-sized restaurant has captivated the clientele in the Bon Marché area.

L'Espadon Bleu

(dinner)

25 r. Grands Augustins Ⓜ St-Michel – ✆ 01 46 33 00 85 – jacquescagna@hotmail.com – Fax 01 43 54 54 48 – Closed August, Monday lunch, Saturday lunch and Sunday J 14

Rest – Menu (€ 25), € 33 – Carte € 39/74

◆ Pleasant restaurant specialising in fish and seafood dishes. Swordfish adorn the walls painted in southern shades. Mosaic tables.

Joséphine "Chez Dumonet"

117 r. du Cherche-Midi Ⓜ Duroc – ✆ 01 45 48 52 40 – Fax 01 42 84 06 83 – Closed Saturday and Sunday L 11

Rest – Carte € 40/80

◆ An authentic Twenties-style establishment with its counter, bench seating and gleaming bistro decor. A good wine list and traditional cuisine.

Ze Kitchen Galerie (William Ledeuil)

4 r. Grands Augustins Ⓜ St-Michel – ✆ 01 44 32 00 32 – zekitchen.galerie@wanadoo.fr – Fax 01 44 32 00 33 – Closed Saturday lunchtime and Sunday

Rest – Menu € 36 – Carte € 55/59 J 14

Spec. Légumes marinés et grillés, tomates, girolles, émulsion parmesan. Joue de veau, jus thaï, marmelade de tomate, gingembre. Chocolat gianduja, sésame, cacahuète, glace coco.

◆ Ze Kitchen is 'ze' hip place to be on the Left Bank. Minimalist decor, contemporary works of art, designer furniture and in vogue cuisine prepared in front of your eyes.

Allard

1 r. l'Eperon Ⓜ St-Michel – ✆ 01 43 26 48 23 – Fax 01 46 33 04 02 – Closed 3-25 August – **Rest** – Menu (€ 25), € 34 – Carte € 35/66 J 14

◆ This 1900 bistro offers home-made-type dishes, a friendly atmosphere, a period bar, engravings and paintings depicting scenes of everyday life in Burgundy.

Le Comptoir – Hôtel Relais-St-Germain

9 carr. de l'Odéon Ⓜ Odéon – ✆ 01 44 27 07 97 – hotelrsg@wanadoo.fr – Fax 01 46 33 45 30 K 13

Rest – *(number of covers limited, pre-book)* Menu € 45 (dinner) – Carte € 35/55 (lunch)

◆ In this pleasant little bistro, Yves Camdeborde offers tasty, generous traditional cuisine, including specialities from Southwest France. Authentic 1930s decor.

Rôtisserie d'en Face

2 r. Christine Ⓜ Odéon – ✆ 01 43 26 40 98 – la-rotisserie@orange.fr – Closed Saturday lunchtime and Sunday J 14

Rest – Menu (€ 25), € 29 (weekday lunch) – Carte € 39/63

◆ Pleasant Jacques Cagna bistro across the street from his eponymous restaurant. Relaxed atmosphere and discreetly elegant decor in varying shades of ochre.

Fish La Boissonnerie

69 r. de Seine Ⓜ Odéon – ✆ 01 43 54 34 69 – Closed one week in August, one week in December and Monday C 1

Rest – Menu € 22/34 (dinner)

◆ Former fish shop with mosaic facade, now a fully fledged authentic gastropub. Bistro cuisine with a menu that changes monthly (market produce); good wine list.

Azabu

3 r. A. Mazet Ⓜ Odéon – ✆ 01 46 33 72 05 – Closed 20 April-5 May, 27-30 July, 26-29 October, Sunday dinner and Monday J 13

Rest – Menu € 19 (weekday lunch), € 33/59 – Carte € 36/50

◆ Modern Japanese cuisine served in a small, simple, contemporary dining room, or at the bar opposite the teppanyaki (cooking hob).

La Table de Fès

5 r. Ste-Beuve Ⓜ Notre Dame des Champs – ✆ 01 45 48 07 22 – digitalmedia@orange.fr – Fax 01 45 49 47 88 – Closed 24 July-30 August and Sunday

Rest – *(dinner only)* Carte € 44/61 L 12

◆ A discreet façade hides two small carefully decorated dining rooms, adorned with craftwork from Morocco. Authentic North African cuisine.

Le Bistrot de L'Alycastre

2 r. Clément Ⓜ Mabillon – ✆ 01 43 25 77 66 – jmlemmery@hotmail.com – Fax 01 43 25 77 66 – Closed 12-27 August and Monday lunch K 13

Rest – Menu € 50/65 – Carte € 41/62

◆ An enthusiastic chef has taken over this chic bistro opposite the St Germain market. Simple, modern and tasty cuisine with quality service. Popular terrace.

La Table d'Erica

6 r. Mabillon Ⓜ Mabillon – ✆ 01 43 54 87 61 – table-erica@proximedia.fr – Closed August, Sunday and Monday K 13

Rest – Menu € 13/29 – Carte € 25/49

◆ Cross the footbridge to La Table d'Erica for a taste of the exotic! A concise, typically Creole menu, with fish from the Caribbean, spicy chicken and curried specialities.

S. Sauvignier/MICHELIN

Tour Eiffel, École Militaire, Invalides

7e arrondissement ✉ 75007

Pont Royal without rest

7 r. Montalembert Ⓜ Rue du Bac – ✆ 01 42 84 70 00 – hpr@hotel-pont-royal.com – Fax 01 42 84 71 00 J 12

65 rm – †€ 395/455 ††€ 395/455, ☕ € 27 – 10 suites

◆ Bold colours and mahogany walls adorn the bedrooms; the romance of the salad days of St-Germain-des-Prés with all the comfort of an elegant "literary hotel"!

Duc de St-Simon without rest

14 r. St-Simon Ⓜ Rue du Bac – ✆ 01 44 39 20 20 – duc.de.saint.simon@wanadoo.fr – Fax 01 45 48 68 25 J 11

34 rm – †€ 225/290 ††€ 225/395, ☕ € 15

◆ Cheerful colours, wood panelling, antique furniture and objects. The atmosphere here is that of a beautiful house of olden times, with the additional appeal of a friendly welcome and peaceful surroundings.

Montalembert

3 r. Montalembert Ⓜ Rue du Bac – ✆ 01 45 49 68 68 – welcome@montalembert.com – Fax 01 45 49 69 49 J 12

56 rm – †€ 380/500 ††€ 380/500, ☕ € 24 – 7 suites – **Rest** – Carte € 39/85

◆ Dark wood, leather, glass and steel, with tobacco, plum and lilac-coloured decor. The rooms combine all the components of contemporary style. Designer dining room, terrace protected by a boxwood partition, and cuisine for appetites large and small!

K+K Hotel Cayré without rest

4 bd Raspail Ⓜ Rue du Bac – ✆ 01 45 44 38 88 – reservations@kkhotels.fr – Fax 01 45 44 98 13 J 12

125 rm – †€ 320/412 ††€ 348/680, ☕ € 25

◆ The discreet Haussmann façade contrasts with the elegant designer rooms within. Fitness centre (with sauna), elegant lounge and bar serving simple bistro-style dishes.

Saint Vincent without rest
5 r. Pré aux Clercs Ⓜ *Rue du Bac – ☎ 01 42 61 01 51*
– reservation@hotel-st-vincent.com
– Fax 01 42 61 01 54 J 12
22 rm – †€ 190/210 ††€ 220/240, ☕ € 12 – 2 suites
◆ A delightful luxury hotel in the heart of the Left Bank. This 18C private mansion is home to warm, spacious rooms appointed in a Napoleon III spirit.

Le Bellechasse without rest
8 r. de Bellechasse Ⓜ *Musée d'Orsay – ☎ 01 45 50 22 31 – info@lebellechasse.com – Fax 01 45 51 52 36* H 11
34 rm – †€ 290/440 ††€ 320/490, ☕ € 25
◆ Top couturier Christian Lacroix designed the rooms of this hotel. He has joyfully mixed colour with antique and modern details to create an almost dreamlike but distinctly fashionable setting.

Bourgogne et Montana without rest
3 r. de Bourgogne Ⓜ *Assemblée Nationale – ☎ 01 45 51 20 22*
– bmontana@bourgogne-montana.com
– Fax 01 45 56 11 98 H 11
28 rm ☕ – †€ 160/180 ††€ 180/340 – 4 suites
◆ Elegance and beauty fill every room of this discreet 18C hotel. The top floor rooms offer superb views over the "Palais-Bourbon" (French Parliament buildings).

Le Walt without rest
37 av. de La Motte Picquet Ⓜ *Ecole Militaire – ☎ 01 45 51 55 83 – lewalt@inwoodhotel.com – Fax 01 47 05 77 59* J 9
25 rm – †€ 275/325 ††€ 295/345, ☕ € 19
◆ The imposing reproductions of classical masterpieces and "panther" or "zebra" bedspreads add originality to the comfortable, contemporary rooms.

Le Tourville without rest
16 av. Tourville Ⓜ *Ecole Militaire – ☎ 01 47 05 62 62 – hotel@tourville.com*
– Fax 01 47 05 43 90 J 9
30 rm – †€ 150/180 ††€ 195/450, ☕ € 15
◆ A pleasing mix of primary and pastel tones, of modern and period furniture sets the scene in this cosy hotel. Four bedrooms with terrace, breakfast in a vaulted cellar.

Verneuil without rest
8 r. Verneuil Ⓜ *Rue du Bac – ☎ 01 42 60 82 14 – info@hotelverneuil.com*
– Fax 01 42 61 40 38 J 12
26 rm – †€ 140 ††€ 170/215, ☕ € 13
◆ This old building on the Left Bank is decorated in the style of a private house. Elegant rooms adorned with 18C prints. Serge Gainsbourg lived opposite.

Lenox St-Germain without rest
9 r. de l'Université Ⓜ *St-Germain des Prés – ☎ 01 42 96 10 95 – hotel@lenoxsaintgermain.com – Fax 01 42 61 52 83* J 12
32 rm – †€ 130/175 ††€ 130/200, ☕ € 14 – 2 suites
◆ A discreetly luxurious Art Deco style depicts this hotel. Rooms are a little on the small side but attractively decorated. "Egyptian" frescoes adorn the breakfast room. Pleasant bar.

D'Orsay without rest
93 r. Lille Ⓜ *Solférino – ☎ 01 47 05 85 54 – orsay@espritfrance.com*
– Fax 01 45 55 51 16 H 11
41 rm – †€ 150/210 ††€ 170/360, ☕ € 13
◆ The hotel occupies two handsome, late-18C buildings. Attractive classical style rooms and welcoming lounge overlooking a small leafy patio.

De Suède Saint Germain without rest
31 r. Vaneau Ⓜ *Rue du Bac – ☎ 01 47 05 00 08 – hoteldesuede@aol.com*
– Fax 01 47 05 69 27 J 11
39 rm – †€ 129/230 ††€ 129/300, ☕ € 12
◆ Flanked by ministries, this family-run 18C hotel offers Louis XVI-style rooms. Some command a view of the gardens of the prime minister's Matignon residence.

Muguet without rest
11 r. Chevert Ⓜ Ecole Militaire – ✆ 01 47 05 05 93 – muguet@wanadoo.fr – Fax 01 45 50 25 37 J 9
43 rm – †€ 103 ††€ 135/190, ☕ € 9,50
♦ Hotel spruced up in a classic spirit.Sitting room furnished in Louis Philippe style, well-appointed rooms (7 overlook the Eiffel Tower or the Invalides), veranda and small garden.

Eiffel Park Hôtel without rest
17bis r. Amélie Ⓜ La Tour Maubourg – ✆ 01 45 55 10 01 – reservation@eiffelpark.com – Fax 01 47 05 28 68 J 9
36 rm – †€ 160/215 ††€ 160/240, ☕ € 12
♦ From the Indian and Chinese artefacts to the ethnic fabrics, exoticism reigns throughout this elegant hotel. Even more unusual, it boasts a rooftop summer terrace complete with beehives.

Relais Bosquet without rest
19 r. Champ-de-Mars Ⓜ Ecole Militaire – ✆ 01 47 05 25 45 – hotel@relaisbosquet.com – Fax 01 45 55 08 24 J 9
40 rm – †€ 135/180 ††€ 135/195, ☕ € 15
♦ This discreet hotel has a prettily furnished Directoire style interior. The classic style rooms feature the same attention to detail with thoughtful little touches.

Splendid Tour Eiffel without rest
29 av. Tourville Ⓜ Ecole Militaire – ✆ 01 45 51 29 29 – reservation@hotel-splendid-paris.com – Fax 01 44 18 94 60 J 9
45 rm – †€ 145/195 ††€ 165/235, ☕ € 13
♦ Haussmannian building, housing elegant rooms adorned with contemporary furnishings. Most of them offer a splendid view, some a glimpse of the Eiffel Tower. Cosy lounge-bar.

Londres Eiffel without rest
1 r. Augereau Ⓜ Ecole Militaire – ✆ 01 45 51 63 02 – info@londres-eiffel.com – Fax 01 47 05 28 96 J 8
30 rm – †€ 130/150 ††€ 135/205, ☕ € 12
♦ Cosy hotel done up in warm colours near the leafy paths of the Champ-de-Mars. The second building, reached through a small courtyard, has quieter rooms.

Du Cadran without rest
10 r. du Champ-de-Mars Ⓜ Ecole Militaire – ✆ 01 40 62 67 00 – info@cadranhotel.com – Fax 01 40 62 67 13 J 9
42 rm – †€ 129/165 ††€ 142/178, ☕ € 13
♦ A stone's throw from the lively rue Cler market. The modern rooms are enhanced by a number of Louis XVI-style touches. Fine 17C fireplace in the lounge-cum-library.

St-Germain without rest
88 r. du Bac Ⓜ Rue du Bac – ✆ 01 49 54 70 00 – info@hotel-saint-germain.fr – Fax 01 45 48 26 89 J 11
29 rm – †€ 150/220 ††€ 150/240, ☕ € 12
♦ Empire, Louis-Philippe, high-tech design, antique objects, contemporary paintings - the charm of variety. Comfortable library, patio pleasant in summer.

De Varenne without rest
44 r. Bourgogne Ⓜ Varenne – ✆ 01 45 51 45 55 – info@hoteldevarenne.com – Fax 01 45 51 86 63 J 10
25 rm – †€ 115/167 ††€ 115/197, ☕ € 10
♦ A quietly located hotel adorned with French Empire and Louis XVI style furniture. In summer, breakfast is served in a small, leafy courtyard.

Champ-de-Mars without rest
7 r. du Champ-de-Mars Ⓜ Ecole Militaire – ✆ 01 45 51 52 30 – reservation@hotelduchampdemars.com – Fax 01 45 51 64 36 J 9
25 rm – †€ 84/90 ††€ 90/94, ☕ € 8
♦ Small hotel with an English atmosphere, between the Champ-de-Mars and the Invalides. Dark green façade, cosy rooms (soon to be renovated) and neat "Liberty" style decor.

Bersoly's without rest
28 r. de Lille Ⓜ Musée d'Orsay – ✆ 01 42 60 73 79 – hotelbersolys@wanadoo.fr – Fax 01 49 27 05 55 J 13
16 rm – €100/106 €120/150, €10
◆ Impressionist nights in this 17C building in which each room honours an artist whose works are displayed in the nearby Musée d'Orsay (Renoir, Gauguin, etc.).

Grand Hôtel Lévêque without rest
29 r. Cler Ⓜ Ecole Militaire – ✆ 01 47 05 49 15 – info@hotel-leveque.com – Fax 01 45 50 49 36 J 9
50 rm – €60 €90/115, €9
◆ In a busy pedestrian street, this small establishment is ideal for exploring traditional Paris. New management and gradual renovation underway. Street side rooms are lighter.

France without rest
102 bd de la Tour Maubourg Ⓜ Ecole Militaire – ✆ 01 47 05 40 49 – hoteldefrance@wanadoo.fr – Fax 01 45 56 96 78 J 9
60 rm – €88/140 €110/140, €10
◆ Two buildings with a guesthouse feel. The rooms, in pastel colours, are discreetly Provençal. The street side overlooks the Hôtel des Invalides; the courtyard side is quieter.

Arpège (Alain Passard)
84 r. de Varenne Ⓜ Varenne – ✆ 01 45 51 47 33 – arpege.passard@wanadoo.fr – Fax 01 44 18 98 39 – Closed Saturday and Sunday J 10
Rest – Menu €130 (lunch)/340 (dinner) – Carte €188/247
Spec. Couleur, saveur, parfum et dessin du jardin cueillette éphémère. Aiguillettes de homard des îles Chausey au savagnin. Avocat soufflé au chocolat noir, pointe de pistache.
◆ Choose the elegant modern dining room, with rare wood and glass decorations by Lalique, rather than the basement. Savour dazzling vegetable garden-based cuisine by a master chef and poet of the land.

Le Jules Verne ≤ Paris,
2nd floor Eiffel Tower, private lift, South pillar Ⓜ Bir-Hakeim – ✆ 01 45 55 61 44 – Fax 01 47 05 29 41 J 7
Rest – Menu €75 (lunch), €155/450 – Carte €132/195
◆ Although the views of Paris remain the same, the decor in this famous restaurant in the Eiffel Tower has been modernised. For a truly memorable experience, book a window table.

Le Divellec (Jacques Le Divellec)
107 r. Université Ⓜ Invalides – ✆ 01 45 51 91 96 – ledivellec@noos.fr – Fax 01 45 51 31 75 – Closed 25 July-25 August, 25 December-2 January, Saturday and Sunday
Rest – Menu €55 (lunch)/70 (lunch) – Carte €105/205 H 10
Spec. Carpaccio de turbot et truffe, citronnelle et huile d'olive. Homard bleu à la presse avec son corail. Harmonie d'huitres chaudes et froides.
◆ A chic nautical interior: frosted glass, lobster tank and blue and white colour scheme. Outstanding seafood menu direct from the Atlantic ocean.

Pétrossian
144 r. de l'Université Ⓜ Invalides – ✆ 01 44 11 32 32 – Fax 01 44 11 32 35 – Closed August, Sunday and Monday H 10
Rest – Menu €35 (weekday lunch), €45/100 – Carte €56/98
◆ The Petrossians have treated Parisians to caviar from the Caspian sea since 1920. Above the boutique, inventive cuisine is served in a comfortable, elegant dining room.

La Maison des Polytechniciens
12 r. Poitiers Ⓜ Solférino – ✆ 01 49 54 74 54 – le.club@maisondesx.com – Fax 01 49 54 74 84 – Closed 27 July-27 August, 23 December-3 January, Saturday, Sunday and public holidays H 12
Rest – *(number of covers limited, pre-book)* Menu €36 – Carte €39/59
◆ Even though Polytechnic students enjoy coming here, you don't have to be a "techie" to eat in the dining room of the hôtel de Poulpry (1703), near the musée d'Orsay.

Le Violon d'Ingres (Christian Constant and Stéphane Schmidt)
135 r. St-Dominique Ⓜ *Ecole Militaire –*
01 45 55 15 05 – violondingres@wanadoo.fr – Fax 01 45 55 48 42
– Closed in August, Sunday and Monday J 8
Rest – Menu € 48/65 – Carte € 50/67
Spec. Millefeuille de langue et foie gras façon Lucullus. Cassoulet montalbanais. Soufflé vanille, sauce caramel au beurre salé.
◆ Wood-furnishings enliven the atmosphere of this dining room which is an elegant meeting point for gourmets attracted by the very individual cuisine of the master chef.

Il Vino d'Enrico Bernardo
13 bd La Tour-Maubourg Ⓜ *Invalides – 01 44 11 72 00*
– info@ilvinobyenricobernardo.com – Fax 01 44 11 72 02 H 10
Rest – Menu € 50 bi (lunch), € 100 € bi/1000 bi – Carte € 70/120
Spec. Risotto aux cèpes. Agneau de Sept heures. Dacquoise à la poire.
◆ Pick a wine and leave the food to chance! In his chic designer restaurant, the World's Best Sommelier (2004 vintage) goes the opposite way and associates dishes to your choice of beverage.

Les Ombres Paris,
27 quai Branly Ⓜ *Alma Marceau – 01 47 53 68 00 – ombres.restaurant@elior.com – Fax 01 47 53 68 18* H 8
Rest – Menu € 37/95 – Carte € 61/98
◆ This restaurant enjoys fine views of the Eiffel Tower and its nocturnal illuminations from the roof-terrace of the Musée du Quai Branly. Contemporary dining.

Cigale Récamier
4 r. Récamier Ⓜ *Sèvres Babylone – 01 45 48 86 58 – Closed Sun* K 12
Rest – Carte approx. € 55
◆ A welcoming establishment with a clientele of writers and editors. Classic cuisine and sweet and savoury soufflé specialities, renewed every month. Peaceful terrace.

Vin sur Vin
20 r. de Monttessuy Ⓜ *Pont de l'Alma – 01 47 05 14 20*
– Closed 1st-11 May, 27 July-25 August, 22 December-6 January, Monday except dinner from mid September to end-March, Saturday lunch and Sunday H 8
Rest – *(number of covers limited, pre-book)* Carte € 68/118
Spec. Ravioles de jaune d'œuf aux truffes. Gros turbot sauvage. Ris de veau de lait français.
◆ Warm welcome, elegant decor, delicious traditional dishes and extensive wine list (600 references) – full marks for this restaurant close to the Eiffel Tower!

Tante Marguerite
5 r. Bourgogne Ⓜ *Assemblée Nationale – 01 45 51 79 42 – tante.marguerite@bernard-loiseau.com – Fax 01 47 53 79 56 – Closed August, Saturday and Sunday*
Rest – Menu € 47 H 11
◆ A smart, low key decor, classic cuisine and a great deal of success for this restaurant named after Marguerite de Bourgogne, founder of Tonnerre's hospital.

Chez les Anges
54 bd de la Tour Maubourg Ⓜ *La Tour Maubourg – 01 47 05 89 86*
– mail@chezlesanges.com – Fax 01 47 05 45 56 – Closed Saturday and Sunday
Rest – Menu (€ 25), € 34 – Carte € 44/73 J 10
◆ A trendy atmosphere, minimalist contemporary decor and long counter where you can take a seat to sample the tasty cuisine, half-traditional, half-modern.

New Jawad
12 av. Rapp Ⓜ *Ecole Militaire – 01 47 05 91 37 – Fax 01 45 50 31 27*
Rest – Menu € 16/40 – Carte € 21/42 H 8
◆ Pakistani and Indian specialities, attentive service and a plush, cosy setting characterise this restaurant in the vicinity of the Pont de l'Alma.

Thiou
49 quai d'Orsay Ⓜ *Invalides – 01 40 62 96 50 – Fax 01 40 62 97 30*
– Closed August, Saturday lunch and Sunday – **Rest** – Carte € 46/91 H 9
◆ Thiou is the nickname of the lady chef of this restaurant, often mentioned in the press, whose regular customers include celebrities. Thai dishes served in a discreetly exotic, comfortable dining room.

XX **La Cuisine** AC VISA MC AE DC
14 bd La Tour-Maubourg Ⓜ Invalides – ✆ 01 44 18 36 32 – lacuisine@lesrestos.com – Fax 01 44 18 30 42 – Closed Saturday lunch H 10
Rest – Menu (€ 28), € 35 (weekday lunch)/42 – Carte € 53/75
◆ A charming decor of sunny colours, paintings, mirrors, banquettes and upholstered chairs provides a warm setting for the chef's tasty dishes.

XX ✿ **Auguste** (Gaël Orieux) AC MC AE DC
54 r. Bourgogne Ⓜ Varenne – ✆ 01 45 51 61 09 – Fax 01 45 51 27 34 – Closed 3-24 August, Saturday and Sunday J 10
Rest – Menu € 35 – Carte € 58/76
Spec. Foie gras de canard poêlé, supions et enokis. Noix de ris de veau croustillante aux cacahuètes caramelisées. Soufflé au chocolat pur Caraïbe.
◆ The pleasant colourful decor of this up-to-date establishment is the setting for a cuisine that is as flavourful as it is inventive. A fine tribute to Auguste Escoffier.

XX **Le Clarisse** AC VISA MC
29 r. Surcouf Ⓜ La Tour Maubourg – ✆ 01 45 50 11 10 – contact@leclarisse.fr – Fax 01 45 50 11 14 – Closed August, Saturday lunch and Sunday H 9
Rest – Menu (€ 32), € 39 (lunch)/56
◆ Near the Invalides, this contemporary restaurant sports a predominantly black and white interior. Cosy private dining room upstairs. Contemporary, seasonally-changing menu.

XX **Le Bamboche** AC VISA MC AE
15 r. Babylone Ⓜ Sèvres Babylone – ✆ 01 45 49 14 40 – lebamboche@aol.com – Fax 01 45 49 14 44 – Closed 27 July-10 August and Sunday lunch K 11
Rest – Menu (€ 28), € 35 – Carte € 60/71
◆ A discreet and seductive address a stone's throw from the Bon Marché. The contemporary decor of the dining room is the setting for creative food. Attentive service.

XX **D'Chez Eux** AC VISA MC DC
2 av. Lowendal Ⓜ Ecole Militaire – ✆ 01 47 05 52 55 – contact@chezeux.com – Fax 01 45 55 60 74 – Closed 1st-18 August and Sunday J 9
Rest – Menu (€ 35), € 40 (lunch) – Carte € 46/77
◆ For 40 years customers have been seduced by this restaurant where hearty dishes from Auvergne and southwest France are served by waiters in smocks in a "provincial inn" atmosphere.

XX **L'Esplanade** AC VISA MC AE
52 r. Fabert Ⓜ La Tour Maubourg – ✆ 01 47 05 38 80 – Fax 01 47 05 23 75 J 9
Rest – Carte € 39/83
◆ This Costes establishment is ideally located opposite the Invalides. Unusual ball-and-canon décor, very Napoleon III. Trendy fusion brasserie menu.

XX **Vin et Marée** AC VISA MC AE
71 av. Suffren Ⓜ La Motte Picquet Grenelle – ✆ 01 47 83 27 12 – vmsuffren@vin-et-maree.com – Fax 01 53 86 98 26 K 8
Rest – Menu (€ 21) – Carte € 32/58
◆ A modern brasserie style (bench seating, mirrors and copperware) in seaside colours. The blackboard menu offers fish and seafood only.

X ✿✿ **L'Atelier de Joël Robuchon** AC VISA MC
5 r. Montalembert Ⓜ Rue du Bac – ✆ 01 42 22 56 56 – latelierdejoelrobuchon@wanadoo.fr – Fax 01 42 22 97 91 – Open from 11.30 am to 3.30 pm and from 6.30 pm to midnight. Reservations only for certain services : please enquire J 12
Rest – Menu € 110 – Carte € 53/100 ✿
Spec. La langoustine en ravioli à l'étuvée de chou vert. Le ris de veau clouté de laurier frais à la feuille de romaine farcie. La Chartreuse en soufflé chaud et sa crème glacée à la pistache.
◆ An original concept in a chic decor designed by Rochon. No tables, just high stools in a row facing the counter where you can sample a selection of fine, modern dishes, served tapas style. Car parking service.

Gaya Rive Gauche par Pierre Gagnaire

44 r. Bac Ⓜ Rue du Bac – ✆ 01 45 44 73 73 – p.gagnaire@wanadoo.fr – Fax 01 45 44 73 73 – Closed 3-24 August, 23 December-4 January, Sunday and public holidays J 12

Rest – Menu (€ 35) – Carte € 63/102

Spec. Croque-monsieur noir. Langoustines. Gâteau au chocolat.

◆ Popular with a well-heeled left bank clientele, seafood takes pride of place in this restaurant. Tasteful marine decor and chinaware designed by Jean Cocteau.

Au Bon Accueil

14 r. Monttessuy Ⓜ Pont de l'Alma – ✆ 01 47 05 46 11 – Fax 01 45 56 15 80 – Closed 7-20 August, Saturday and Sunday H 8

Rest – Menu € 27/31 – Carte € 50/75

◆ Beneath the shadow of the Eiffel Tower, this modern restaurant and small adjacent room offer delicious up-to-date dishes pleasantly reflecting the changing seasons.

Les Fables de La Fontaine (Sébastien Gravé)

131 r. Saint-Dominique Ⓜ Ecole Militaire – ✆ 01 44 18 37 55 – Fax 01 44 18 37 57 – Closed 23-28 December J 8

Rest – Menu (€ 35) – Carte approx. € 50

Spec. Saint-Jacques à la plancha, velouté de topinambour à la truffe noire (December to March). Merlu de Saint-Jean de Luz rôti au lard, caviar d'aubergine fumé, velouté de cèpes (September to December). Gâteau Basque.

◆ Restaurant dedicated to seafood set in a small low-key dining room (brown tones, velvet benches). Short, intelligent menu and good wine list.

L 'Agassin

8 r. Malard Ⓜ La Tour Maubourg – ✆ 01 47 05 18 18 – Fax 01 45 55 64 41 – Closed August, Sunday and Monday H 9

Rest – Menu € 23 (lunch)/34

◆ The Agassin, the lowest bud on a vine branch, sets the tone of this new, minimalist, contemporary bistro (dark wood and light walls) serving up-to-date cuisine.

Nabuchodonosor

6 av. Bosquet Ⓜ Alma Marceau – ✆ 01 45 56 97 26 – rousseau.e@wanadoo.fr – Fax 01 45 56 98 44 – Closed 2-25 August, Saturday lunch and Sunday

Rest – Menu € 28, € 32/50 bi (dinner) – Carte € 37/66 H 9

◆ The sign honours the largest champagne bottle. Walls adorned with Sienna earthenware, oak panels and nebuchadnezzars add decorative effect. Market cuisine.

Bistrot de Paris

(dinner)

33 r. Lille Ⓜ Musée d'Orsay – ✆ 01 42 61 16 83 – Fax 01 49 27 06 09 – Closed August, 24 December-1st January, Sunday and Monday J 12

Rest – Carte € 22/68

◆ André Gide was once a regular of this former "soup kitchen". The 1900 decor, revised by Slavik, shimmers with copperware and mirrors. Bistro ambiance and cuisine.

Les Olivades

41 av. Ségur Ⓜ Ségur – ✆ 01 47 83 70 09 – Fax 01 42 73 04 75 – Closed August, Saturday lunch, Monday lunch, Sunday and public holidays K 9

Rest – Menu (€ 20), € 25 (lunch) – Carte € 40/53

◆ A restaurant where olive oil flows freely with appetising up-to-date dishes based on fresh produce. Attractive photos enhance the contemporary decor.

Clos des Gourmets

16 av. Rapp Ⓜ Alma Marceau – ✆ 01 45 51 75 61 – closdesgourmets@wanadoo.fr – Fax 01 47 05 74 20 – Closed 10-25 August, Sunday and Monday

Rest – Menu (€ 25), € 29 (weekday lunch)/35 H 8

◆ Many regulars love this discreet restaurant decorated in warm colours. The tempting menu varies according to the availability of market produce.

Le Perron

6 r. Perronet Ⓜ St-Germain des Prés – ✆ 01 45 44 71 51 – Fax 01 45 44 71 51 – Closed in August and Sunday J 12

Rest – Carte € 36/46

◆ Discreet trattoria in the heart of Saint Germain des Prés. Rustic setting with exposed stonework and beams. Italian, mainly Sardinian and Venetian, cuisine.

Florimond
19 av. La Motte-Picquet Ⓜ *Ecole Militaire – ✆ 01 45 55 40 38 – Fax 01 45 55 40 38 – Closed 28 April-4 May, 28 July-17 August, 22 December-4 January, Saturday lunch and Sunday* J 9
Rest – Menu € 21 (weekday lunch)/36 – Carte € 38/54
◆ Pocket-sized restaurant named after Monet's gardener in Giverny. Bistro decor, popular with locals for its tasty traditional cooking.

Pasco
74 bd La Tour Maubourg Ⓜ *La Tour Maubourg – ✆ 01 44 18 33 26 – restaurant.pasco@wanadoo.fr – Fax 01 44 18 34 06 – Closed Mon.* J 9
Rest – Menu (€ 21), € 26 – Carte approx. € 38
◆ Mainly Mediterranean cuisine with market produce served in a relaxed atmosphere and a setting of brick walls and ochre shades.

Fontaine de Mars
129 r. St-Dominique Ⓜ *Ecole Militaire – ✆ 01 47 05 46 44 – lafontainedemars@orange.fr – Fax 01 47 05 11 13 –* **Rest** – Carte € 35/68 J 9
◆ This name of this perfectly restored 1930s bistro recalls the nearby fountain dedicated to the warrior god. Terrace under the arcades; traditional and southwestern cuisine.

Café de l'Alma
5 av. Rapp Ⓜ *Alma Marceau – ✆ 01 45 51 56 74 – cafedelalma@wanadoo.fr – Fax 01 45 51 10 08 –* **Rest** – Carte € 35/70 H 8
◆ A stylish, resolutely contemporary dining room by François Champsaur, the new idol of the interior decoration world. Up-to-date dishes and elegant cuisine.

35 ° Ouest
35 r. Verneuil Ⓜ *Rue du Bac – ✆ 01 42 86 98 88 – 35degresouest@orange.fr – Fax 01 42 86 00 65 – Closed 3-25 August, Sunday and Monday* J 12
Rest – Menu (€ 30 bi) – Carte € 31/94
◆ This smart, faultlessly designed fish restaurant is decorated in a tasteful mix of greys of greens and sports a handsome lightwood bar. Inventive seafood cuisine.

Le Soleil
153 r. Grenelle Ⓜ *La Tour Maubourg – ✆ 01 45 51 54 12 – Closed August, Monday lunch and Sunday* J 9
Rest – Menu € 28/66 bi
◆ The sun and the sea come together at this welcoming address whose decor pays due reverence to the Mediterranean. Traditional dishes with a southern accent.

Aida (Koji Aida)
1 r. Pierre Leroux Ⓜ *Vaneau – ✆ 01 43 06 14 18 – Fax 01 43 06 14 18 – Closed 5-25 August, February school holidays, Tuesday lunch, Saturday lunch, Sunday lunch and Monday*
Rest – *(dinner only) (number of covers limited, pre-book)* Menu € 90/160 – Carte € 87/200 K 11
Spec. Huîtres sautées au beurre d'algues sur lit de cresson. Chateaubriant cuit au teppanyaki. Menu omakase.
◆ A minimalist feel to this Japanese restaurant with softly lit counter and private dining room. Choice of teppanyaki menus and fine Burgundies chosen by the wine buff chef.

P'tit Troquet
28 r. Exposition Ⓜ *Ecole Militaire – ✆ 01 47 05 80 39 – Fax 01 47 05 80 39 – Closed 1st-24 August, Saturday lunch, Monday lunch and Sunday* J 9
Rest – *(number of covers limited, pre-book)* Menu (€ 20), € 28 (weekday lunch)/32 – Carte approx. € 40
◆ This bistro is certainly as small as its name suggests! But it has so much going for it: a charming setting enlivened by old advertisements, friendly atmosphere and tasty market fresh cuisine.

L'Affriolé
17 r. Malar Ⓜ *Invalides – ✆ 01 44 18 31 33 – Closed 3 weeks in August, Sunday and Monday* H 9
Rest – Menu (€ 23), € 29 (lunch)/34
◆ This bistro's chef prepares seasonal dishes with fresh market produce, which are announced as daily specials on the blackboard or in a set menu that changes every month.

Chez l'Ami Jean

27 r. Malar Ⓜ La Tour Maubourg – ✆ 01 47 05 86 89 – Fax 01 45 55 41 82 – Closed August, 23 December-2 January, Sunday and Monday H 9

Rest – Menu € 32

◆ Chez l'Ami Jean offers tasty, copious dishes, with market produce, and from Southwest France (game specialities in season) in a warm, Basque Country setting.

Oudino

17 r. Oudinot Ⓜ Vaneau – ✆ 01 45 66 05 09 – Fax 01 45 66 53 35 – Closed 9-19 August, 25 December-2 January, Saturday lunch and Sunday K 11

Rest – Menu € 16 (weekday lunch) – Carte € 26/43

◆ Take a pleasant gourmet break near French government ministry buildings. Dining room with slight Art Deco touches and bistro-type dishes displayed on a blackboard.

Al Dente

38 r. Varenne Ⓜ Rue du Bac – ✆ 01 45 48 79 64 – Closed 20 July-20 August, 25 December-1st January, Sunday and Monday J 11

Rest – Carte € 29/48

◆ A modern trattoria with red benches and subdued wood furnishings serving simple, light and al dente Italian cuisine from every part of the country.

Léo Le Lion

23 r. Duvivier Ⓜ Ecole Militaire – ✆ 01 45 51 41 77 – restaurantleolelion@hotmail.com – Fax 01 45 51 41 77 – Closed August, 25 December-1st January, Sunday and Monday J 9

Rest – Carte € 40/50

◆ A 1930's bistro with a charcoal grill. Fish dishes claim the lion's share of the menu all year round; but in season game too evokes a murmur of sheer delight!

Maupertu

94 bd de la Tour-Maubourg Ⓜ École Militaire – ✆ 01 45 51 37 96 – info@restaurant-maupertu-paris.com – Fax 01 53 59 94 83 – Closed 5-25 August and Sunday J 10

Rest – Menu (€ 23), € 32

◆ Overlooking the Esplanade des Invalides, this Provençal inspired establishment sports a rejuvenated bistro style (plum colours, paintings). Enjoy the view from the terrace.

Sa Mi In

74 av. Breteuil Ⓜ Sèvres-Lecourbe – ✆ 01 47 34 58 96 – han@samiin.com – Fax 01 47 34 58 96 – Closed Saturday lunch and Sunday lunch K 10

Rest – Menu € 15 (weekday lunch), € 30/50 – Carte € 32/91

◆ This small, authentic Korean restaurant offers tasty, exotic flavours in a refined and intimate setting. Vegetarian menu.

Café Constant

139 r. Saint-Dominique Ⓜ Ecole Militaire – ✆ 01 47 53 73 34 – Fax 01 45 55 48 42 – Closed 2 weeks in August, Sunday and Monday J 8

Rest – Menu (€ 16), € 31/35

◆ Convivial simplicity is the order of the day in this café annexe developed by Christian Constant. Tasty, good value market cuisine showing the chef's obvious hallmark.

Les Cocottes

135 r. St Dominique Ⓜ Ecole Militaire – violondingres@wanadoo.fr – Fax 01 45 55 00 91 – Closed Sunday J 8

Rest – Carte € 24/34

◆ The concept of this friendly establishment, more bar (high counter) than restaurant, lies in its reinvented bistro cuisine, served in cast-iron casserole dishes. No booking.

Miyako

121 r. Université Ⓜ Invalides – ✆ 01 47 05 41 83 – Fax 01 45 55 13 18 – Closed 1st August-1st September, Saturday lunch and Sunday H 9

Rest – Menu € 14 (weekday lunch), € 18/30 – Carte € 26/43

◆ This establishment in the Gros-Caillou area takes you on a culinary journey to the land of the Rising Sun – to sample kebabs cooked over wood and, of course, extremely popular sushi dishes.

S. Sauvignier/MICHELIN

Champ-Elysées, Concorde, Madeleine

8e arrondissement ✉ 75008

Plaza Athénée

25 av. Montaigne Ⓜ *Alma Marceau – ✆ 01 53 67 66 65 – reservations@plaza-athenee-paris.com – Fax 01 53 67 66 66* G 9

146 rm – 🚹€ 720/740 🚹🚹€ 820/840, ☕ € 48 – 45 suites

Rest *Alain Ducasse au Plaza Athénée* et ***Le Relais Plaza*** – see restaurant listing

Rest *La Cour Jardin* – rest.-terrasse – *✆ 01 53 67 66 02 (open mid May-mid September)* Carte € 82/118

◆ Enjoy true luxury in this hotel with its comfortable, Classic or Art Deco-style rooms, afternoon teas with music in the Gobelins gallery and a stunning designer bar. The charming, greenery-filled terrace of La Cour Jardin opens when the weather turns fine.

Four Seasons George V

31 av. George-V Ⓜ *George V – ✆ 01 49 52 70 00 – par.lecinq@fourseasons.com – Fax 01 49 52 70 10* F 8

197 rm – 🚹€ 700/1350 🚹🚹€ 730/1350, ☕ € 38 – 48 suites

Rest *Le Cinq* – see restaurant listing – **Rest *La Galerie*** – Carte € 72/130

◆ Completely renovated in an 18C style, the George V has luxurious bedrooms, which are extremely spacious by Paris standards. Beautiful collections of artwork and a superb spa. In summer, the tables in the restaurant are set out in the delightful interior courtyard.

Le Bristol

112 r. Fg St-Honoré Ⓜ *Miromesnil – ✆ 01 53 43 43 00 – resa@lebristolparis.com – Fax 01 53 43 43 01* F 10

124 rm – 🚹€ 610/630 🚹🚹€ 710/1160, ☕ € 53 – 38 suites

Rest *Le Bristol* – see restaurant listing

◆ 1925 luxury hotel set around a magnificent garden. Sumptuous rooms, mainly Louis XV or Louis XVI-style with an exceptional "boat" swimming pool on the top floor.

Crillon

10 pl. de la Concorde Ⓜ *Concorde – ✆ 01 44 71 15 00 – crillon@crillon.com – Fax 01 44 71 15 02* G 11

119 rm – 🚹€ 695/750 🚹🚹€ 765/830, ☕ € 47 – 28 suites

Rest *Les Ambassadeurs* – see restaurant listing

Rest *L'Obélisque* – *✆ 01 44 71 15 15* – Menu € 54/94 bi – Carte € 59/114

◆ This 18C townhouse has kept its sumptuous, decorative features. The bedrooms, decorated with wood-furnishings, are magnificent. A French style luxury hotel through-and-through.

Prince de Galles

33 av. George-V Ⓜ *George V – ✆ 01 53 23 77 77 – hotel.prince.de.galles@luxurycollection.com – Fax 01 53 23 78 78* G 8

138 rm – 🚹€ 350/650 🚹🚹€ 480/770, ☕ € 42 – 30 suites

Rest *Jardin des Cygnes* – *✆ 01 53 23 78 50* – Menu € 51 (lunch), € 59/95

◆ One discovers the inter-war Art Deco style of this luxurious hotel once inside, echoing the patio and its mosaics. Rooms decorated with confident taste. At the Swan Garden, dining room with an aristocratic atmosphere (lovely fountain) and a beautiful courtyard-terrace.

Fouquet's Barrière

46 av. George-V Ⓜ *George V – ✆ 01 40 69 60 00 – hotelfouquets@lucienbarriere.com – Fax 01 40 69 60 05* F 8

67 rm – 🚹€ 690/910 🚹🚹€ 690/910, ☕ € 35 – 40 suites– **Rest *Fouquet's*** – see restaurant listing – **Rest *Le Diane*** – *(closed 19 July-18 August, 3-12 January, Sunday and Monday)* Menu € 60 (weekday lunch), € 90/135 – Carte € 96/188

◆ A hushed ambience at Le Diane with its brightly-lit niches adorned with flowers. Contemporary cuisine.

Hilton Arc de Triomphe

51 r. de Courcelles Ⓜ Courcelles
– ✆ 01 58 36 67 00 – reservation.adt@hilton.com
– Fax 01 58 36 67 84 E 9

438 rm – **†€ 290/680 ††€ 290/730, ☕ € 30 – 25 suites**
Rest *Safran* – ✆ 01 58 36 67 96 – Menu € 49 (dinner) – Carte € 46/69

◆ This new hotel, inspired by the liners of the 1930s, has successfully created their luxurious and refined atmosphere. Elegant Art Deco rooms designed by Jacques Garcia, patio with a fountain, fitness centre etc. At Safran, contemporary cuisine influenced by the flavours and scents of Asia.

Lancaster

7 r. Berri Ⓜ George V – ✆ 01 40 76 40 76
– reservations@hotel-lancaster.fr – Fax 01 40 76 40 00 F 9

46 rm – **†€ 320 ††€ 490, ☕ € 37 – 11 suites**
Rest *La Table du Lancaster* – see restaurant listing

◆ Boris Pastoukhoff paid for his lodging in this hotel with paintings, thus adding richly to this old townhouse's elegant decor, so beloved by Marlène Dietrich.

Vernet

25 r. Vernet Ⓜ Charles de Gaulle-Etoile – ✆ 01 44 31 98 00
– reservations@hotelvernet.com
– Fax 01 44 31 85 69 F 8

42 rm – **†€ 320/340 ††€ 370/450, ☕ € 35 – 9 suites**
Rest *Les Elysées* – see restaurant listing

◆ A fine building dating from the 1920s, with a dressed-stone façade and wrought-iron balconies. Empire- or Louis XVI-style rooms. Fashionable bar and grill.

Napoléon

40 av. Friedland Ⓜ Charles de Gaulle-Etoile – ✆ 01 56 68 43 21
– napoleon@hotelnapoleon.com – Fax 01 47 66 82 33 F 8

101 rm – **†€ 440/630 ††€ 440/690, ☕ € 26**
Rest – *(closed dinner, Saturday and Sunday)* Menu € 45 bi (weekday lunch), € 85/120

◆ A stone's throw from Place de l'Étoile, this hotel-museum honours the emperor's memory via autographs, figurines and paintings from the period. Directoire or Empire style bedrooms. A traditional menu served in the restrained, cosy, wainscoted restaurant.

Balzac without rest

6 r. Balzac Ⓜ George V – ✆ 01 44 35 18 00 – reservation-balzac@jjwhotels.com
– Fax 01 44 35 18 05 F 8

69 rm – **†€ 420/470 ††€ 470/550, ☕ € 38 – 13 suites**

◆ Hotel completely refurbished in luxury style, with neo-Classical décor, a vibrant colour scheme and references to the writer Balzac. Period furniture and high-tech facilities in the guestrooms.

Astor Saint Honoré

11 r. d'Astorg Ⓜ St-Augustin – ✆ 01 53 05 05 05
– reservation@astor.3ahotels.com – Fax 01 53 05 05 30 F 11

128 rm – **†€ 290/520 ††€ 290/520, ☕ € 25 – 4 suites**
Rest *L'Astor* – ✆ 01 53 05 05 20 *(closed August, Saturday lunch, Sunday and Monday)* Menu (€ 38), € 48/76 – Carte € 53/71

◆ A successful marriage of Regency and Art Deco styles endows this cosy hotel with its unique appearance. A handful of small terraces. The light coloured elegant oval dining room is furnished in a dark wood Directoire style.

San Régis

12 r. J. Goujon Ⓜ Champs-Elysées Clemenceau – ✆ 01 44 95 16 16
– message@hotel-sanregis.fr – Fax 01 45 61 05 48 G 9

41 rm – **†€ 340 ††€ 450/725, ☕ € 34 – 3 suites**
Rest – *(closed August and Sunday)* Menu € 35 (lunch) – Carte € 46/61

◆ This 1857 townhouse has been remodelled with taste. A fine staircase adorned with stained glass and statues leads to delightful guestrooms furnished with a diverse range of furniture. The hotel's exquisitely appointed restaurant occupies a subdued but luxurious lounge-library.

Sofitel Arc de Triomphe rm, rest,
14 r. Beaujon Ⓜ *Charles de Gaulle-Etoile* VISA
– *℘ 01 53 89 50 50 – h1296@accor.com – Fax 01 53 89 50 51* F 8
134 rm – †€ 510/590 ††€ 580/620, ☕ € 29 – 1 suite
Rest *Le Clovis* – *℘ 01 53 89 50 53 (closed 26 July-24 August, 20-30 December, Saturday, Sunday and holidays)* Menu € 35 – Carte € 48/90
◆ Typical late-19C Parisian building, with 18C-inspired decoration but fitted up to 21C standards. Elegant rooms. Try and book the amazing "Concept Room". Le Clovis is renowned for its contemporary decor and cuisine and attentive service.

Hyatt Regency rm, VISA
24 bd Malhesherbes Ⓜ *Madeleine – ℘ 01 55 27 12 34*
– *madeleine@hyattintl.com – Fax 01 55 27 12 35* F 11
86 rm – †€ 330/520 ††€ 330/1005, ☕ € 28
Rest *Café M* – *(closed Sunday dinner)* Menu € 54 – Carte € 46/75
◆ Near the Madeleine, the discreet façade hides a distinctly contemporary interior that is both restrained and warm. Spacious personalised guestrooms. The Café M is popular for its delicious modern cuisine and its tempting weekend brunches.

De Vigny rm, VISA
9 r. Balzac Ⓜ *George V – ℘ 01 42 99 80 80*
– *reservation@hoteldevigny.com*
– *Fax 01 42 99 80 40* F 8
26 rm – †€ 305/395 ††€ 320/440, ☕ € 29 – 11 suites
Rest *Baretto* – *(closed 15-24 August)* Menu € 60 bi/95 bi
– Carte € 54/84
◆ A discreet hotel close to the Champs-Elysées with refined bedrooms with personalised touches including four-poster beds. Cosy lounge with attractive fireplace. The Baretto serves traditional cuisine in a stylish, low-key atmosphere and Art Deco setting.

Champs-Élysées Plaza without rest
35 r. de Berri Ⓜ *George V – ℘ 01 53 53 20 20* VISA
– *info@champselyseesplaza.com – Fax 01 53 53 20 21* F 9
35 rm – †€ 490/690 ††€ 490/690, ☕ € 24 – 10 suites
◆ The spacious and elegant rooms of this opulent (and completely non-smoking) hotel near the Champs-Élysées all have fireplaces and Art Deco-style bathrooms.

Marriott rm, VISA
70 av. des Champs-Élysées Ⓜ *Franklin D. Roosevelt – ℘ 01 53 93 55 00*
– *mhrs.pardt.ays@marriotthotels.com – Fax 01 53 93 55 01* F 9
174 rm – †€ 365/650 ††€ 365/650, ☕ € 29 – 18 suites
Rest *Sur les Champs* – *℘ 01 53 93 55 44* – Menu (€ 42) – Carte € 39/71
◆ Enjoy American efficiency and cocoon-like comfort in this smart hotel. Most of the bedrooms overlook the Champs-Élysées. The fanciful decor of lampposts and frescoes in this restaurant plays to a clichéd image of Paris in bygone days.

California VISA
16 r. Berri Ⓜ *George V – ℘ 01 43 59 93 00 – cal@hroy.com*
– *Fax 01 45 61 03 62* F 9
158 rm – †€ 415/440 ††€ 415/495, ☕ € 30 – 16 suites
Rest – *(closed August, Saturday and Sunday) (lunch only)* Menu € 35/45
◆ Several thousand paintings adorn the walls of this old luxury hotel dating from the 1920s. The collection of 200 whiskies in the piano-bar is equally impressive! The restaurant room has a stunning patio-terrace extension (fountain, mosaics, and greenery).

La Trémoille rm, VISA
14 r. Trémoille Ⓜ *Alma Marceau – ℘ 01 56 52 14 00*
– *reservation@hotel-tremoille.com – Fax 01 40 70 01 08* G 9
90 rm – †€ 350/475 ††€ 400/560, ☕ € 28 – 3 suites
Rest *Louis2* – *(closed Saturday lunch, Sunday and public holidays)* Menu (€ 35)
– Carte € 48/72
◆ The hotel has been successfully refurbished with contemporary decor combining the old and the ultra-modern, the latest high-tech equipment, and marble bathrooms with Portuguese tiles. An elegant dining room with a low key atmosphere; contemporary cuisine.

Claridge Bellman without rest
37 r. François 1er Ⓜ *Franklin Roosevelt – ✆ 01 47 23 54 42*
– resa@claridgebellman.com – Fax 01 47 23 08 84 G 9
42 rm – €235/620 €255/620, ☕ €22 – 1 suite
◆ A mix of opulent refinement and modern luxury are the hallmarks of this charmingly classical hotel. Spacious, personalised bedrooms embellished with tapestries, wood panelling, furniture of varying provenance and four-poster beds.

Bedford rm, rest, VISA AE
17 r. de l'Arcade Ⓜ *Madeleine – ✆ 01 44 94 77 77*
– reservation@hotel-bedford.com – Fax 01 44 94 77 97 F 11
135 rm – €168 €222, ☕ €18 – 10 suites
Rest – *(closed 28 July-24 August, Saturday and Sunday) (lunch only)* Menu (€33), €42 – Carte €58/74
◆ This hotel, built in 1860 in the elegant Madeleine district, offers guests tastefully decorated rooms of varying size. 1900s-style decor with an abundance of decorative, stucco motifs and a lovely cupola. The restaurant room is the Bedford's real jewel.

De Sers rm, VISA AE
41 av. Pierre 1er de Serbie Ⓜ *George V – ✆ 01 53 23 75 75*
– contact@hoteldesers.com – Fax 01 53 23 75 76 G 8
49 rm – €480/550 €550/900, ☕ €29 – 3 suites
Rest – *(closed August and Sunday)* Menu (€29) – Carte €34/180
◆ Successfully refurbished late-19C townhouse. While the hall has kept its original character, the rooms are thoroughly modern. The food reflects current tastes and is served in a designer dining room or, in summer, on the pleasant terrace.

François 1er without rest VISA AE
7 r. Magellan Ⓜ *George V – ✆ 01 47 23 44 04 – hotel@hotel-francois1er.fr*
– Fax 01 47 23 93 43 F 8
40 rm – €300/780 €350/1000, ☕ €22 – 2 suites
◆ Mexican marble, mouldings, curios, antique furniture and a plethora of paintings make up the luxurious decor created by French architect Pierre Yves Rochon. Substantial buffet breakfasts.

Sofitel le Faubourg VISA AE
15 r. Boissy d'Anglas Ⓜ *Concorde – ✆ 01 44 94 14 14 – h1295@accor.com*
– Fax 01 44 94 14 28 G 11
163 rm – €460/560 €560/850, ☕ €30 – 10 suites
Rest *Café Faubourg* – *(closed August, Saturday lunch, Sunday lunch)* Carte €53/73
◆ This Sofitel is housed in two buildings, one 18C, the other 19C. Rooms with high-tech facilities; a 1930s bar; plus a lounge with a glass roof. Trendy decor, relaxing interior garden and modern cuisine at the Café Faubourg.

Montaigne without rest VISA AE
6 av. Montaigne Ⓜ *Alma Marceau – ✆ 01 47 20 30 50*
– contact@hotel-montaigne.com – Fax 01 47 20 94 12 G 9
29 rm – €200/300 €300/450, ☕ €20
◆ The wrought-iron grilles, beautiful flower-decked façade and graciously cosy interior all contribute to the Hotel Montaigne's appeal. The avenue is lined by haute couture fashion designers.

Daniel rm, VISA AE
8 r. Frédéric Bastiat Ⓜ *St-Philippe du Roule – ✆ 01 42 56 17 00*
– danielparis@relaischateaux.com – Fax 01 42 56 17 01 F 9
22 rm – €350/490 €410/490, ☕ €32 – 4 suites
Rest *(closed 26 July-25 August, Saturday, Sunday)* Menu (€40), €80 – Carte €59/86
◆ This hotel likes travel! Furniture and objects brought back from all over the world combined with toile de Jouy create a refined and welcoming decor for Parisian globetrotters.

Bradford Élysées without rest VISA AE
10 r. St-Philippe-du-Roule Ⓜ *St-Philippe du Roule – ✆ 01 45 63 20 20*
– hotel.bradford@astotel.com – Fax 01 45 63 20 07 F 9
50 rm – €257/350 €257/350, ☕ €22
◆ Marble fireplaces, mouldings, brass beds, retro decor and a hundred-year-old lift - this hotel has preserved Paris' irresistible charm of old and combined it with modern features (LCD screens).

Royal without rest
33 av. Friedland Ⓜ *Charles de Gaulle-Etoile* – ✆ *01 43 59 08 14*
– rh@royal-hotel.com – Fax 01 45 63 69 92 F 8
58 rm – 🚹€ 250 🚹🚹€ 330/360, ☕ € 22
◆ The partially renovated rooms sport a low key, updated, classic decor and have excellent soundproofing; some command a view of the Arc de Triomphe.

Sofitel Champs-Élysées rm,
8 r. J. Goujon Ⓜ *Champs-Elysees Clemenceau*
– ✆ *01 40 74 64 64 – h1184-re@accor.com – Fax 01 40 74 79 66* G 9
40 rm – 🚹€ 395/560 🚹🚹€ 395/560, ☕ € 27 – 2 suites
Rest *Les Signatures* – , ✆ *01 40 74 64 94 (closed 27 July-17 August, 25 December-4 January, Saturday, Sunday and public holidays) (lunch only)*
Menu (€ 35), € 48 – Carte € 52/64
◆ A Second Empire building shared with the Press Club de France. The rooms have a contemporary new look and are equipped with state-of-the-art facilities. Business centre. Simple decor and a lovely terrace. A restaurant popular with journalists.

Radisson SAS Champs-Élysées rm,
78 av. Marceau Ⓜ *Charles de Gaulle-Etoile –*
✆ *01 53 23 43 43 – reservations.paris@radissonsas.com*
– Fax 01 53 23 43 44 F 8
46 rm – 🚹€ 250/550 🚹🚹€ 250/650, ☕ € 26
Rest *La Place* – *(closed August, Christmas holidays, Saturday and Sunday)*
Carte € 57/79
◆ A new hotel occupying the former headquarters of Louis Vuitton. Restful, contemporary rooms, high-tech equipment (plasma TVs) and excellent soundproofing. Take a seat at the bar or on the summer terrace; concise Provençal-styled menu.

Powers without rest
52 r. François 1er Ⓜ *Franklin D. Roosevelt* – ✆ *01 47 23 91 05*
– contact@hotel-powers.com – Fax 01 49 52 04 63 G 9
50 rm – 🚹€ 260/520 🚹🚹€ 260/600, ☕ € 25
◆ The well-equipped rooms have an elegant feel, with mouldings, fireplaces, bronze clocks, pendant chandeliers, etc. Cosy lounges and an English club-style bar.

Franklin Roosevelt without rest
18 r. Clément-Marot Ⓜ *Franklin D. Roosevelt* – ✆ *01 53 57 49 50*
– hotel@hroosevelt.com – Fax 01 53 57 49 59 G 9
47 rm – 🚹€ 295 🚹🚹€ 295/440, ☕ € 23 – 1 suite
◆ This hotel with Victorian charm cuts a fine figure. Refined decor including an abundance of rare wood, chintz, leather and marble. Pleasant bar.

Chateaubriand without rest
6 r. Chateaubriand Ⓜ *George V* – ✆ *01 40 76 00 50*
– welcome@hotelchateaubriand.com – Fax 01 40 76 09 22 F 9
28 rm – 🚹€ 210/410 🚹🚹€ 210/450, ☕ € 22
◆ Original paintings, furniture from around the world and marble bathrooms adorn the guestrooms, each with their own individual charm. Breakfasts facing the interior courtyard.

Relais Monceau without rest
85 r. Rocher Ⓜ *Villiers* – ✆ *01 45 22 75 11 – relaismonceau@wanadoo.fr*
– Fax 01 45 22 30 88 E 11
51 rm – 🚹€ 171 🚹🚹€ 172/197, ☕ € 11
◆ A modern hotel between the Parc Monceau and the Gare St Lazare. Contemporary rooms endowed with rustic charm. Lounge-library, plus a bar which opens onto an attractive small patio.

Marignan
12 r. Marignan Ⓜ *Franklin D. Roosevelt* – ✆ *01 40 76 34 56*
– contact@hotelmarignan.fr – Fax 01 40 76 34 34 G 9
73 rm – 🚹€ 420/470 🚹🚹€ 470/850, ☕ € 25 – **Rest** – *(lunch only)* Carte € 30/50
◆ Located a stone's throw from the Champs-Élysées. Charming bedrooms with Directoire period furnishings, and comfortable duplexes with work areas designed with business visitors in mind.

Pershing Hall rm, VISA

49 r. P. Charon Ⓜ *George V – ✆ 01 58 36 58 00 – info@pershinghall.com – Fax 01 58 36 58 01* G 9

26 rm – †€ 312/420 ††€ 420/500, ☕ € 26 – 6 suites

Rest – Carte € 57/91

◆ Once the home of General Pershing, then a veterans club and finally a charming hotel designed by Andrée Putman. Chic interior, original and enchanting hanging garden. Behind the curtain of glass beads, the decor is trendy and the cuisine fashionable. Lounge evenings.

Chambiges Élysées without rest VISA AE

8 r. Chambiges Ⓜ *Alma Marceau – ✆ 01 44 31 83 83 – reservation@hotelchambiges.com – Fax 01 40 70 95 51* G 9

32 rm ☕ – †€ 270/310 ††€ 270/390 – 2 suites

◆ Wood panelling, select drapes and fabrics, period furniture; a romantic, cosy atmosphere reigns in this fully renovated hotel. Comfortable rooms and a pretty interior garden.

Le A without rest VISA AE

4 r. d' Artois Ⓜ *St-Philippe du Roule – ✆ 01 42 56 99 99 – hotel-le-a@wanadoo.fr – Fax 01 42 56 99 90* F 9

16 rm – †€ 355/485 ††€ 355/485, ☕ € 23 – 10 suites

◆ F. Hybert, a visual artist, and F. Méchiche, an interior designer, masterminded this trendy hotel (or museum, perhaps?) in black and white. Relaxing lounge-library and bar-lounge.

De l'Arcade without rest VISA AE

9 r. Arcade Ⓜ *Madeleine – ✆ 01 53 30 60 00 – reservation@hotel-arcade.com – Fax 01 40 07 03 07* F 11

41 rm – †€ 160/194 ††€ 194/240, ☕ € 12

◆ The marble and wood panels in the hall and lounges, and the soft colours and carefully-chosen furniture in the rooms, all contribute to the charm of this elegant and discreet hotel near the Madeleine.

Monna Lisa VISA AE

97 r. La Boétie Ⓜ *St-Philippe du Roule – ✆ 01 56 43 38 38 – contact@hotelmonnalisa.com – Fax 01 45 62 39 90* F 9

22 rm – †€ 220/235 ††€ 245/265, ☕ € 17

Rest *Caffe Ristretto* – *(closed 3-24 August, 20-28 December, Saturday and Sunday)* Menu (€ 26) – Carte € 48/66

◆ This fine hotel built in 1860 is a showpiece for audacious Italian design. Larger rooms on the street side. The Caffe Ristretto offers a delicious journey through the specialities of the Italian peninsula in a wonderfully modern setting.

Le 123 without rest VISA AE

123 r. du Faubourg St Honoré Ⓜ *St-Philippe du Roule – ✆ 01 53 89 01 23 – hotel.le123@astotel.com – Fax 01 45 61 09 07* F 9

41 rm – †€ 269/420 ††€ 309/450, ☕ € 24

◆ Contemporary decor and a mix of styles, materials and colours. The personalised rooms, which are decorated with fashion sketches, are both appealing and unusual.

Le Lavoisier without rest VISA AE

21 r. Lavoisier Ⓜ *St-Augustin – ✆ 01 53 30 06 06 – info@hotellavoisier.com – Fax 01 53 30 23 00* F 11

27 rm – †€ 179/270 ††€ 179/270, ☕ € 14 – 3 suites

◆ Contemporary rooms, cosy little library-cum-lounge also serving as a bar, and a vaulted breakfast room are the hallmarks of this hotel in the St-Augustin district.

Élysées Mermoz without rest VISA AE

30 r. J. Mermoz Ⓜ *Franklin D. Roosevelt – ✆ 01 42 25 75 30 – hotel@emhotel.com – Fax 01 45 62 87 10* F 10

22 rm – †€ 107/195 ††€ 119/221, ☕ € 12 – 5 suites

◆ This cosy hotel has rooms with sunny colours or shades of grey; varnished wood panelling and blue stone in the bathrooms, as well as a lounge with cane furniture and a glass roof.

Queen Mary without rest
9 r. Greffulhe Ⓜ Madeleine – ✆ 01 42 66 40 50 – reservations@hotelqueenmary.com – Fax 01 42 66 94 92 F 12
36 rm – †€ 175/230 ††€ 199/254, ☕ € 19
◆ A refined establishment with a "British" feel to it, where a welcome gift of a carafe of sherry awaits you. Attentive service, pleasant patio, charming breakfast room and hushed bedrooms.

Le Vignon "8" without rest
23 r. Vignon Ⓜ Madeleine – ✆ 01 47 42 93 00 – reservation@hotelvignon.com – Fax 01 47 42 04 60 F 12
28 rm – †€ 195/390 ††€ 195/390, ☕ € 20
◆ A friendly, discreet hotel just a few steps away from Place de la Madeleine. Cosy rooms – those on the top floor have just been refurbished in a distinctly contemporary style.

Mercure Opéra Garnier without rest
4 r. de l'Isly Ⓜ St Lazare – ✆ 01 43 87 35 50 – h1913@accor.com – Fax 01 43 87 03 29 F 12
140 rm – †€ 170/300 ††€ 170/300, ☕ € 15
◆ Practically located between St Lazare train station and the big department stores. Practical rooms and buffet breakfast served in a small inner garden in summertime.

Champs-Élysées Friedland without rest
177 r. Faubourg-St-Honoré Ⓜ Charles de Gaulle-Etoile – ✆ 01 45 63 64 65 – friedland@my-paris-hotel.com – Fax 01 45 63 88 96 F 9
40 rm – †€ 149/279 ††€ 159/319, ☕ € 20
◆ Close to the salle Pleyel and being gradually renovated. Small, elegant rooms that are soundproofed and equipped with modern conveniences (LCD screens).

St-Augustin without rest
9 r. Roy Ⓜ George V – ✆ 01 42 93 32 17 – hotel.staugustin@astotel.com – Fax 01 42 93 19 34 F 11
63 rm – †€ 210/290 ††€ 210/290, ☕ € 14
◆ This renovated hotel in a quiet district has a modern, attractive interior decor. Pleasant contemporary-style guestrooms furnished with dark wood and bright colours.

Élysées Céramic without rest
34 av. Wagram Ⓜ Ternes – ✆ 01 42 27 20 30 – info@elysees-ceramic.com – Fax 01 46 22 95 83 E 8
57 rm – †€ 175/195 ††€ 210/230, ☕ € 12
◆ The Art Nouveau glazed stoneware façade (1904) is an architectural gem. The interior lives up to the same standard with furniture and decor in the same spirit.

Atlantic without rest
44 r. de Londres Ⓜ St-Lazare – ✆ 01 43 87 45 40 – contact@atlanticparis.fr – Fax 01 42 93 06 26 E 12
82 rm – †€ 105/200 ††€ 155/200, ☕ € 16
◆ Wavy lines, paintings and boat models... A few discreet touches of the sea enliven this hotel's contemporary decor. Vast glassed-in lounge and bar.

Astoria Opéra without rest
42 r. de Moscou Ⓜ Rome – ✆ 01 42 93 63 53 – hotel.astoria@astotel.com – Fax 01 42 93 30 30 D 11
86 rm – †€ 124/220 ††€ 165/220, ☕ € 14
◆ This hotel in the Europe quarter seems particularly popular with a business clientele. Lounge embellished with modern paintings. Breakfast room with a glass roof.

La Flèche d'Or without rest
29 r. d'Amsterdam Ⓜ St-Lazare – ✆ 01 48 74 06 86 – info@hotelflechedor.com – Fax 01 48 74 06 04 E 12
61 rm – †€ 95/545 ††€ 99/559, ☕ € 10
◆ The sign for this hotel near St Lazare railway station refers to a famous luxury train. Well-kept, recently redecorated rooms and lounge as comfortable as a Flèche d'Or Pullman carriage!

Mayflower without rest
3 r. Chateaubriand Ⓜ George V – ✆ 01 45 62 57 46 – mayflower@escapade-paris.com – Fax 01 42 56 32 38 F 9
24 rm – †€ 140/150 ††€ 175/210, ☕ € 12
◆ Simple, comfortable rooms, some of which have marble bathrooms. The breakfast room is brightened with a mural depicting the voyage of the Pilgrim Fathers.

West-End without rest
7 r. Clément-Marot Ⓜ Alma Marceau – ✆ 01 47 20 30 78 – contact@hotel-west-end.com – Fax 01 47 20 34 42 G 9
49 rm ☕ – †€ 285/460 ††€ 285/460
◆ Old lithographs, original paintings and modern fittings await you in the simple, chic rooms of this peaceful hotel. Some offer a glimpse of the Eiffel Tower.

Cordélia without rest
11 r. Greffulhe Ⓜ Madeleine – ✆ 01 42 65 42 40 – hotelcordelia@wanadoo.fr – Fax 01 42 65 11 81 F 12
30 rm – †€ 135/165 ††€ 150/185, ☕ € 14
◆ Hotel with warm, welcoming rooms of various sizes, a nice vaulted room for breakfast and a lounge with fireplace and wood panelling.

Alison without rest
21 r. de Surène Ⓜ Madeleine – ✆ 01 42 65 54 00 – hotel.alison@orange.fr – Fax 01 42 65 08 17 F 11
34 rm – †€ 82/165 ††€ 115/165, ☕ € 9
◆ A family hotel in a quiet street near the Théâtre de la Madeleine with an entrance hall decorated with modern paintings. Neat and tidy, functional bedrooms, with attic-style rooms on the 6th floor.

Newton Opéra without rest
11 bis r. de l'Arcade Ⓜ Madeleine – ✆ 01 42 65 32 13 – newtonopera@easynet.fr – Fax 01 42 65 30 90 F 11
31 rm – †€ 165 ††€ 170/205, ☕ € 15
◆ Little rooms brightened with lively colours, pleasant reading-room and personalised welcome including a carafe of Imperial Mandarine on arrival.

Le "Cinq" – Hôtel Four Seasons George V
31 av. George V Ⓜ George V – ✆ 01 49 52 71 54 – par.lecinq@fourseasons.com – Fax 01 49 52 71 81 F 8
Rest – Menu € 75 (lunch), € 135/210 – Carte € 136/360
Spec. Tarialini à la fonduta et à la truffe d'Alba (beg. October-mid December). Poireau cuit à la ficelle aux saveurs d'hiver et à la truffe noire (beg. December-mid March). Poularde de Bresse et homard Georges V en cocotte lutée.
◆ The superb dining room, a majestic evocation of the Grand Trianon, opens onto a delightful interior garden. A refined atmosphere and masterful classic cuisine.

Les Ambassadeurs – Hôtel Crillon
10 pl. Concorde Ⓜ Concorde – ✆ 01 44 71 16 16 – restaurants@crillon.com – Fax 01 44 71 15 02 – Closed August, 1st-8 January, Sunday and Monday
Rest – Menu € 75 (weekday lunch)/200 – Carte € 156/275 G 11
Spec. Blanc à manger d'œuf, truffe noire (January to March). Pigeonneau désossé, foie gras, jus à l'olive. "Paquet gâteau" à manger, chocolat, banane.
◆ This splendid dining room was once the ballroom of an 18C mansion. Sophisticated, inventive cuisine and a superb wine list.

Alain Ducasse au Plaza Athénée – Hôtel Plaza Athénée
25 av. Montaigne Ⓜ Alma Marceau – ✆ 01 53 67 65 00 – adpa@alain-ducasse.com – Fax 01 53 67 65 12 – Closed 18 July-25 August, 19-30 December, Monday lunch, Tuesday lunch, Wednesday lunch, Saturday and Sunday
Rest – Menu € 240/340 – Carte € 180/330 G 9
Spec. Caviar osciètre d'Iran, langoustines rafraîchies, nage réduite, bouillon parfumé. Volaille de Bresse, sauce albuféra aux truffes d'Alba (15 October to 31 December). Fraises des bois en coupe glacée, sablé coco.
◆ The sumptuous regency decor has been redone with a "design and organza" look; creative menus from a talented team overseen by Alain Ducasse. 1001 selected wines available!

Le Bristol – Hôtel Bristol
112 r. Fg St-Honoré Ⓜ *Miromesnil* – ✆ *01 53 43 43 00 – resa@lebristolparis.com – Fax 01 53 43 43 01* F 10
Rest – Menu € 95 (lunch)/210 – Carte € 118/222
Spec. Macaroni farcis, truffe noire, artichaut et foie gras de canard, gratinés au parmesan. Merlan de ligne en croûte de pain aux amandes, tétragone mi-cuite, huile de péquillos. Poularde de Bresse cuite en vessie aux écrevisses, royale d'abats et morilles.
◆ With its splendid wood panelling, the winter dining room resembles a small theatre. The summer dining room overlooks the hotel's charming garden.

Ledoyen
carré Champs-Élysées Ⓜ *Champs Elysées Clemenceau* – ✆ *01 53 05 10 01 – pavillon.ledoyen@ledoyen.com – Fax 01 47 42 55 01 – Closed 2-24 August, Monday lunch, Saturday and Sunday* G 10
Rest – Menu € 88 (lunch), € 198/284 bi – Carte € 149/227
Spec. Grosses langoustines bretonnes croustillantes, émulsion d'agrumes à l'huile d'olive. Blanc de turbot de ligne braisé, pommes rattes truffées. Noix de ris de veau en brochette de bois de citronnelle, jus d'herbes.
◆ A neo-Classical lodge built on the Champs Élysées in 1848. Magnificent Napoleon III style decor, view of the gardens designed by Hittorff and delicious cuisine.

Taillevent
15 r. Lamennais Ⓜ *Charles de Gaulle-Etoile* – ✆ *01 44 95 15 01 – mail@taillevent.com – Fax 01 42 25 95 18 – Closed 26 July-25 August, Saturday, Sunday and public holidays* F 9
Rest – *(number of covers limited, pre-book)* Menu € 70 (lunch), € 140/190 – Carte € 116/204
Spec. Rémoulade de tourteau à l'aneth, sauce fleurette citronnée. Foie gras de canard au banyuls, fruits et légumes caramélisés. Trilogie gourmande.
◆ Wainscoting and works of art adorn this 19C townhouse, once home to the duke of Morny, and now a guardian of French haute cuisine. Exquisite preparations and magnificent wine list.

Apicius (Jean-Pierre Vigato)
20 r. d'Artois Ⓜ *St-Philippe du Roule* – ✆ *01 43 80 19 66 – restaurant-apicius@wanadoo.fr – Fax 01 44 40 09 57 – Closed August, Saturday, Sunday and holidays* F 9
Rest – Menu € 150 (lunch), € 160/180 – Carte € 89/166
Spec. Déclinaison sur le thème de la langoustine. Saint-Pierre grillé sur la peau, pâtes en risotto d'anchois. Grand dessert "tout caramel".
◆ This elegant restaurant, in a townhouse, is adorned with 19C Flemish paintings and 17C Indian sculptures. Up-to-date cuisine and superb wine list.

Lasserre
17 av. F.-D.-Roosevelt Ⓜ *Franklin D. Roosevelt* – ✆ *01 43 59 53 43 – lasserre@lasserre.fr – Fax 01 45 63 72 23 – Closed August, Saturday lunch, Monday lunch, Tuesday lunch, Wednesday lunch and Sunday* G 10
Rest – Menu € 75 (lunch)/185 – Carte € 125/233
Spec. Macaroni fourrés aux truffes et foie gras. Turbot aux cèpes et échalotes, palourdes gratinées (September-October). Pigeon André Malraux.
◆ Considered an institution by Parisian gourmets, the neo-Classical dining room features an amazing retractable roof decorated with a fresco of dancers. Superb wine list.

Laurent
41 av. Gabriel Ⓜ *Champs Elysées Clemenceau* – ✆ *01 42 25 00 39 – info@le-laurent.com – Fax 01 45 62 45 21 – Closed 25 December-2 January, Saturday lunch, Sunday and public holidays*
Rest – Menu € 80/160 – Carte € 130/216 G 10
Spec. Araignée de mer dans ses sucs en gelée, crème de fenouil. Foie gras de canard grillé, posé sur une "cracotte". Flanchet de veau de lait braisé, blettes à la moelle et au jus.
◆ This lodge built by Hittorff has elegant, shaded terraces and cuisine that continues to uphold culinary traditions: a little corner of paradise in the Champs Élysées gardens.

Pierre Gagnaire

6 r. Balzac Ⓜ *George V – ✆ 01 58 36 12 50*
– p.gagnaire@wanadoo.fr – Fax 01 58 36 12 51
– Closed 2-22 August, 22 December-4 January, Sunday lunch and Saturday F 8

Rest – Menu € 95 (weekday lunch), € 250/350 – Carte € 230/449

Spec. Langoustines de trois façons. Canard Pékin rôti entier. Grand dessert Pierre Gagnaire.

◆ The low key, chic, contemporary decor (light wood panelling, modern art) provides the setting for this temple of modern French cuisine. Unbridled creativity, akin to free-form jazz. Music maestro !

Les Élysées – Hôtel Vernet

25 r. Vernet Ⓜ *Charles de Gaulle-Etoile*
– ✆ 01 44 31 98 98 – elysees@hotelvernet.com – Fax 01 44 31 85 69
– Closed 26 July-25 August, Monday lunch, Saturday and Sunday F 8

Rest – Menu € 64 (lunch), € 105/140 – Carte € 102/159

Spec. Langoustines bretonnes dorées au curry, galettes de pois chiches aux légumes croquants. Pithiviers de perdreau, grouse et poule faisane au miel de châtaignier (season). Vrai baba au vieux rhum agricole, sorbet ananas.

◆ Sample masterfully inventive cuisine based on classic culinary principles beneath Eiffel's splendid Belle Époque glass dome that bathes the dining room in a soft light.

La Table du Lancaster – Hôtel Lancaster

7 r. Berri Ⓜ *George V – ✆ 01 40 76 40 18*
– restaurant@hotel-lancaster.fr
– Fax 01 40 76 40 00 F 9

Rest – *(closed Saturday lunch)* Menu € 52 (weekday lunch)/120 – Carte € 73/132

Spec. Cuisses de grenouilles au tamarin, chou-fleur en copeaux. Pièce de thon au ponzu, sur un riz "koshi hikari". Soufflé au citron vert et sirop au miel d'acacia.

◆ Inventive food supervised by Michel Troisgros, and a pleasant, contemporary setting (Chinese prints) opening onto the garden. A fitting restaurant for the Lancaster.

Maison Blanche

15 av. Montaigne Ⓜ *Alma Marceau – ✆ 01 47 23 55 99*
– info@maison-blanche.fr – Fax 01 47 20 09 56
– Closed Saturday lunch and Sunday lunch G 9

Rest – Menu (€ 30), € 55 bi (lunch)/65 bi (lunch) – Carte € 77/139

◆ On top of the Théâtre des Champs Élysées, whose loft-duplex design features a huge glass roof facing the golden dome of Les Invalides. Languedoc-inspired cuisine.

Fouquet's

99 av. Champs Élysées Ⓜ *George V – ✆ 01 40 69 60 50*
– fouquets@lucienbarriere.com – Fax 01 40 69 60 35 F 8

Rest – Menu € 78 – Carte € 60/142

◆ A listed dining room, updated by J. Garcia, a terrace that is popular come summer or winter and brasserie cuisine: Fouquet's has been catering to the jet set since 1889.

Senderens

9 pl. de la Madeleine Ⓜ *Madeleine – ✆ 01 42 65 22 90*
– restaurant@senderens.fr – Fax 01 42 65 06 23
– Closed 3-25 August G 11

Rest – Carte € 72/91

Rest *Bar le Passage* – ✆ 01 42 65 56 66 – Carte approx. € 35

Spec. Langoustines croustillantes, chou pak-choï, coriandre et livèche. Agneau de lait de Castille, péquillos et cocos. Tarte tatin aux coings, glace séchouan et orange (autumn-winter).

◆ Designer furnishings and Art Nouveau wood panels by Majorelle combine well in this elegant, lively brasserie. Innovative cuisine with a fine choice of accompanying wines. The Bar Le Passage has a lounge atmosphere and eclectic menu offering various spirits, tapas, sushis, etc.

XXX ✿ **Copenhague**

142 av. des Champs-Élysées Ⓜ George V – ☎ 01 44 13 86 26 – reservation.copenhague@blanc.net – Fax 01 58 05 44 98 – Closed 2-24 August, Saturday, Sunday and public holidays F 8

Rest – *(1st floor)* Menu € 50 (lunch), € 69/109 – Carte € 74/115

Rest *Flora Danica* – Menu € 43 – Carte € 40/78

Spec. Foie gras poché à la bière. Cabillaud rôti et braisé au fumet de palourdes, émulsion aux coquillages. Renne légèrement fumé et rôti, champignons, légumes et fruits de saison.

◆ This restaurant within the Maison du Danemark offers Scandinavian cuisine, elegant Danish design, a view of the Champs Elysées. and a terrace facing a lovely garden. At the Flora Danica, salmon is given pride of place in the shop and on the menu.

XXX ✿ **Le Chiberta**

3 r. Arsène-Houssaye Ⓜ Charles de Gaulle-Etoile – ☎ 01 53 53 42 00 – chiberta@guysavoy.com – Fax 01 45 62 85 08 – Closed 2-24 August, Saturday lunch and Sunday F 8

Rest – Menu € 60/100 – Carte € 73/120

Spec. Crème de langoustines et carottes, citronnelle-gingembre. Côte de bœuf Hereford rôtie, sabayon ciboulette. Moelleux guanaja au pralin feuilleté.

◆ The Chiberta is off to a new start in the J.M. Wilmotte designed restaurant (dark colours and unusual wine bottle walls). The inventive cuisine is supervised by Guy Savoy.

XXX **El Mansour**

7 r. Trémoille Ⓜ Alma Marceau – ☎ 01 47 23 88 18 – Fax 01 40 70 13 53 – Closed Monday lunch and Sunday G 9

Rest – Carte € 43/69

◆ This quiet Moroccan restaurant located in the heart of the Triangle d'Or quarter is lined with warm wood panels and brightened with Eastern touches.

XXX **Le Marcande**

52 r. Miromesnil Ⓜ Miromesnil – ☎ 01 42 65 19 14 – info@marcande.com – Fax 01 42 65 76 85 – Closed 11-25 August, 24 December-5 January, Friday dinner from October to April, Saturday except dinner from May to September and Sunday F 10

Rest – Menu € 35/41 – Carte € 54/83

◆ Discreet restaurant frequented by a business clientele. Contemporary dining room, facing a pleasant patio terrace that is often overflowing in summertime.

XXX ✿ **Stella Maris** (Tateru Yoshino)

4 r. Arsène Houssaye Ⓜ Charles de Gaulle-Etoile – ☎ 01 42 89 16 22 – stella.maris.paris@wanadoo.fr – Fax 01 42 89 16 01 – Closed 10-24 August, Saturday lunch, Sunday and public holidays lunch F 8

Rest – Menu € 49 (lunch), € 99/130 – Carte € 112/156

Spec. Terrine de chou au foie gras et truffes (winter). Lièvre à la royale (autumn). Saumon mi-cuit à l'émulsion de citron confit.

◆ A pleasant restaurant with a refined decor and warm welcome near the Arc de Triomphe. Classic French cuisine with a modern touch by a skilful Japanese chef.

XXX **Indra**

10 r. Cdt-Rivière Ⓜ St-Philippe du Roule – ☎ 01 43 59 46 40 – toutounat@wanadoo.fr – Fax 01 42 25 70 32 – Closed Saturday lunchtime and Sunday F 9

Rest – Menu € 40 (lunch), € 44/65 – Carte € 40/59

◆ Delightful decor of patchwork walls and finely carved wood panels: a charming decor for an extensive menu of Indian specialities.

XX **Le Relais Plaza** – Hôtel Plaza Athénée

25 av. Montaigne Ⓜ Alma Marceau – ☎ 01 53 67 64 00 – reservation@plaza-athenee-paris.com – Fax 01 53 67 66 66 – Closed August G 9

Rest – Menu € 50 – Carte € 76/148

◆ The chic, intimate "local" for the nearby fashion houses. Timeless atmosphere and beautiful 1930s decor inspired by the Normandie cruise ship. Classic, refined cuisine.

XX **Spoon**
12 r. Marignan Ⓜ Franklin D. Roosevelt – ✆ 01 40 76 34 44 – spoonfood@hotelmarignan.fr – Fax 01 40 76 34 37 – Closed 2 August-1st September, 25 December-5 January, Saturday and Sunday G 9
Rest – Menu € 47 (lunch)/89 – Carte € 57/84
◆ Designer furniture, exotic wood and an open kitchen: a decor that mingles contemporary and Zen influences. Unusual, modular menu and wines from around the globe.

XX **La Luna**
69 r. Rocher Ⓜ Villiers – ✆ 01 42 93 77 61 – laluna75008@yahoo.fr – Fax 01 40 08 02 44 – Closed 30 July-26 August and Sunday E 11
Rest – Carte € 68/105
◆ A restrained Art Deco setting and fine cuisine based on fish and seafood delivered fresh from the Atlantic. Don't miss the rum baba...

XX **Tante Louise**
41 r. Boissy-d'Anglas Ⓜ Madeleine – ✆ 01 42 65 06 85 – tantelouise@bernard-loiseau.com – Fax 01 42 65 28 19 – Closed August, Saturday, Sunday and public holidays F 11
Rest – Menu € 36/40 – Carte € 47/67
◆ The name refers to the former owner of this restaurant, which serves traditional cuisine alongside typical Burgundy specialities. Discreet Art Deco decor.

XX **Citrus Étoile**
6 r. Arsène-Houssaye Ⓜ Charles de Gaulle-Étoile – ✆ 01 42 89 15 51 – info@citrusetoile.fr – Fax 01 42 89 28 67 – Closed 8-19 August, 21 December-3 January, Saturday, Sunday and public holidays F 8
Rest – Menu € 39/90 – Carte € 77/91
◆ Chef Gilles Épié creates dishes full of interesting flavours inspired by his travels in California and Japan. Elegant, simple decor and a delicious welcome.

XX **Les Saveurs de Flora**
36 av. George V Ⓜ George V – ✆ 01 40 70 10 49 – Fax 01 47 20 52 87 – Closed August, February half-term holidays, Saturday lunch and Sunday G 8
Rest – Menu (€ 28), € 38/68
◆ Flora, the proprietress of this smart understated restaurant, prepares dishes full of Mediterranean flavour: olive oil, preserved lemons, parmesan, etc.

XX **Chez Catherine**
3 r. Berryer Ⓜ George V – ✆ 01 40 76 01 40 – Fax 01 40 76 03 96 – Closed Saturday, Sunday and public holidays F 9
Rest – Menu (€ 43), € 49
◆ Elegant modern dining room, opening onto the kitchens and partly crowned by a glass roof. A stylish, low key restaurant serving updated cuisine.

XX **1728**
8 r. d'Anjou Ⓜ Madeleine – ✆ 01 40 17 04 77 – restaurant1728@wanadoo.fr – Fax 01 42 65 53 87 – Closed 5-25 August, Sunday and public holidays G 11
Rest – Menu (€ 35) – Carte € 55/110
◆ An 18C town house where La Fayette lived from 1827 until his death. Modern cuisine with an Asian accent served in elegant rooms adorned with wainscoting and period furniture.

XX **La Table d'Hédiard**
21 pl. Madeleine Ⓜ Madeleine – ✆ 01 43 12 88 99 – latablehediard@hediard.fr – Fax 01 43 12 88 98 – Closed August and Sunday F 11
Rest – Carte € 47/71
◆ A touch of exoticism in the decor and cuisine with a thousand spices; it's an invitation to a culinary "safari" – but have a peek at the appetising aisles in the famous luxury food shop first.

XX **Le Sarladais**
2 r. Vienne Ⓜ St-Augustin – ✆ 01 45 22 23 62 – Fax 01 45 22 23 62 – Closed 30 April-12 May, August, 24-31 December, Saturday except dinner from 20 September to 30 April, Sunday and public holidays E 11
Rest – Menu € 38/64 – Carte € 48/124
◆ Wainscoting, warm colour scheme, paintings and freshly cut flowers characterise this comfortable dining room that serves filling specialities from the Périgord region.

XX **Fermette Marbeuf 1900** A/C VISA MC AE

5 r. Marbeuf Ⓜ Alma Marceau – ✆ 01 53 23 08 00 – fermettemarbeuf@blanc.net – Fax 01 53 23 08 09 G 9

Rest – Menu (€ 24), € 32 – Carte € 35/63

◆ One must reserve a table to enjoy the Art Nouveau decor of this glass dining hall dating back to 1898 and discovered by chance in the course of renovation. Classic cuisine.

XX **Marius et Janette** A/C VISA MC AE

4 av. George V Ⓜ Alma Marceau – ✆ 01 47 23 41 88 – Fax 01 47 23 07 19 – Closed 27 July-5 August G 8

Rest – Menu € 46 (lunch)/100 bi – Carte € 88/168

◆ The name of this restaurant recalls Robert Guédiguian's films and Marseille's Estaque quarter. Elegant nautical deco, a pleasant street terrace and seafood fare.

XX **Sens par la Compagnie des Comptoirs** A/C

23 r. de Ponthieu Ⓜ Franklin D. Roosevelt (dinner) VISA MC AE

– ✆ 01 42 25 95 00 – resacdcparis@wanadoo.fr – Fax 01 42 25 95 02 – Closed 1st-21 August, Saturday lunch, Sunday and Monday F 9

Rest – Menu € 45 (weekday lunch), € 75 € bi/90 bi – Carte € 36/72

◆ The Pourcel brothers' Parisian restaurant occupies a large dining room crowned by a glass roof. Mezzanine with bar and billiards table. Refreshing cuisine in a modern, grey-toned decor.

XX **Hanawa** A/C VISA MC AE

26 r. Bayard Ⓜ Franklin D. Roosevelt – ✆ 01 56 62 70 70 – hanawa2007@free.fr – Fax 01 56 62 70 71 – Closed Sunday G 9

Rest – Menu € 34 (lunch)/125 – Carte € 34/89

◆ Covering 1,100m², this sober, refined restaurant (wood, fresh flowers) offers a choice of Japanese (first floor) and French (basement) cuisine, with teppanyaki tables and a sushi bar.

XX **Ratn** VISA MC AE

9 r. de la Trémoille Ⓜ Alma Marceau – ✆ 01 40 70 01 09 – contact@restaurantratn.com – Fax 01 40 70 01 22 G 9

Rest – Menu (€ 21), € 39 – Carte € 39/50

◆ A genuine Indian restaurant serving delicately spiced cuisine. Traditional and elegant decor with gold-coloured fabrics and carved wooden panelling. Friendly service.

XX **Le Stresa** A/C VISA MC AE

7 r. Chambiges Ⓜ Alma Marceau – ✆ 01 47 23 51 62 – Closed 1st-8 May, August, 21 December-3 January, Saturday and Sunday G 9

Rest – *(pre-book)* Carte € 57/105

◆ Golden Triangle trattoria frequented by a very jet-set clientele. Paintings by Buffet and compressed sculptural art by César – artists also appreciate the Italian cuisine here.

XX **Bistrot du Sommelier** A/C VISA MC AE

97 bd Haussmann Ⓜ St-Augustin – ✆ 01 42 65 24 85 – bistrot-du-sommelier@noos.fr – Fax 01 53 75 23 23 – Closed 25 July-24 August, 24 December-5 January, Saturday and Sunday F 11

Rest – Menu (€ 32), € 39 (lunch), € 60 € bi/100 bi – Carte € 47/56

◆ This bistro of free-flowing Bacchanalian pleasure belongs to Philippe Faure-Brac, elected World's Best Cellarman in 1992.

XX **Rue Balzac** A/C VISA MC AE

8 r. Lord Byron Ⓜ George V – ✆ 01 53 89 90 91 – ruebalzac@wanadoo.fr – Fax 01 53 89 90 94 – Closed 1st-20 August, Saturday lunch and Sunday lunch F 8

Rest – Carte € 32/80

◆ The decor of this immense bourgeois-inspired dining room is said to be styled on New York's Cirque 2000. The establishment's in vogue status is borne out by a sprinkling of star guests.

XX ✿ **L'Angle du Faubourg**

195 r. Fg St-Honoré Ⓜ *Ternes – ✆ 01 40 74 20 20 – anglefaubourg@cavestaillevent.com – Fax 01 40 74 20 21 – Closed 26 July-25 August, Saturday, Sunday and public holidays* E 9

Rest – Menu € 35/70 (dinner) – Carte € 45/71

Spec. Sablé de thon aux épices. Râble de lapin rôti à la marjolaine. Cannelloni au citron, sorbet basilic.

◆ On the corner of Rue du Faubourg-St-Honoré and Rue Balzac. This modern bistrot serves skilfully updated classic cuisine to suit current tastes. Simple decor.

XX **Market**

15 av. Matignon Ⓜ *Franklin D. Roosevelt – ✆ 01 56 43 40 90 – prmarketsa@aol.com – Fax 01 43 59 10 87* F 10

Rest – Menu € 34 (lunch) – Carte € 49/87

◆ A trendy establishment with a prestigious location. Wood and marble decor, including African masks in niches. Mixed cuisine (French, Italian and Asian).

XX **Maxan**

37 r. Miromesnil Ⓜ *Miromesnil – ✆ 01 42 65 78 60 – rest.maxan@wanadoo.fr – Fax 01 49 24 96 17 – Closed 5-28 August, 24 December-2 January, Monday dinner, Saturday lunch and Sunday* F 10

Rest – Menu (€ 30), € 38 (lunch)/45 (dinner) – Carte € 48/75

◆ Simple modern décor, designed by Pierre Pozzi, whose restrained tones seem to highlight and enhance the updated authentic cuisine.

XX **Village d'Ung et Li Lam**

10 r. J. Mermoz Ⓜ *Franklin D. Roosevelt – ✆ 01 42 25 99 79 – Fax 01 42 25 12 06 – Closed Saturday lunchtime and Sunday lunchtime* F 10

Rest – Menu € 19/35 – Carte € 25/40

◆ Ung and Li welcome you into a very original Asian setting: suspended aquariums and a flooring of glass-and-sand tiles. Chinese-Thai cuisine.

XX **Al Ajami**

58 r. François 1er Ⓜ *George V – ✆ 01 42 25 38 44 – ajami@free.fr – Fax 01 42 25 38 39* G 9

Rest – Menu (€ 19), € 25 (weekday)/46 – Carte € 36/61

◆ This temple of traditional Lebanese cuisine has been run by the same family since 1920. Near East decor, family atmosphere and a faithful band of regulars.

X ✿ **Dominique Bouchet**

11 r. Treilhard Ⓜ *Miromesnil – ✆ 01 45 61 09 46 – dominiquebouchet@yahoo.fr – Fax 01 42 89 11 14 – Closed in August, Saturday and Sunday* E 10

Rest – *(pre-book)* Menu (€ 46), € 55/87 – Carte € 55/75

Spec. Charlotte de crabe et tomate, chiffonnade de laitue, mangue fraîche et basilic (April to September). Gros macaroni de homard sur purée de champignons, noyé de sa bisque. Gigot d'agneau de sept heures, sauce parfumée au cacao torréfié, pomme purée.

◆ Tasteful contemporary decor, a friendly atmosphere and delicious, traditionally-based cuisine using market produce are the hallmarks of this small, successful and trendy bistro.

X **L'Arôme**

3 r. St-Philippe-du-Roule Ⓜ *St-Philippe-du-Roule – ✆ 01 42 25 55 98 – contact@larome.fr – Fax 01 42 25 55 97 – Closed August, 22-29 December, Saturday and Sunday* F 9

Rest – Menu (€ 27), € 34 (lunch), € 45/60 – Carte € 45/59

◆ A chic "neo-bistro" run by Eric Martins (in the dining room) and Thomas Boullault (in the kitchen). Decor in shades of coral-pink and taupe. Updated traditional cuisine.

X **Bistro de l'Olivier**

13 r. Quentin Bauchart Ⓜ *George V – ✆ 01 47 20 78 63 – Fax 01 47 20 74 58 – Closed August, Saturday lunch and Sunday* G 8

Rest – *(number of covers limited, pre-book)* Menu (€ 28), € 35 – Carte € 68/82

◆ Provençal fabrics and paintings recalling southern France brighten the very warm dining room in this restaurant near Avenue George V. Mediterranean cuisine.

Chez Cécile la Ferme des Mathurins

17 r. Vignon Ⓜ Madeleine – ✆ 01 42 66 46 39 – cecile@chezcecile.com – Closed Saturday lunch and Sunday F 12

Rest – bistrot Menu € 34 (lunch)/37

◆ Generous portions of fine, traditional cuisine are served in this authentic Parisian bistro, which has a loyal clientele. Lively atmosphere and often fully booked.

Le Cou de la Girafe

7 r. Paul Baudry Ⓜ St-Philippe du Roule – ✆ 01 56 88 29 55 – nicolas-richard@wanadoo.fr – Fax 01 42 25 28 82 – Closed 1st-20 August, Saturday lunch and Sunday F 9

Rest – Menu (€ 24), € 30/50 – Carte € 34/55

◆ Restrained modern decor by PierreYves Rochon and flavourful cuisine in keeping with current tastes. To celebrate his arrival in Paris, Grégory Coutanceau has left nothing to chance.

Café Lenôtre - Pavillon Elysée

10 av. Champs-Elysées Ⓜ Champs Elysées Clemenceau – ✆ 01 42 65 85 10 – Fax 01 42 65 76 23 – Closed 3 weeks in August, 1 week in February, Monday dinner from November to February and Sunday dinner G 10

Rest – Carte € 44/64

◆ This elegant pavilion built for the 1900 World Fair has been treated to a make over. It houses a boutique, a catering school and a distinctly modern restaurant.

L'Appart'

9 r. Colisée Ⓜ Franklin D. Roosevelt – ✆ 01 53 75 42 00 – boris.terdjman@blanc.net – Fax 01 53 75 42 09 F 9

Rest – Menu € 23 (lunch), € 30/55 (dinner) – Carte € 29/58

◆ Living room, library or kitchen? Choose a room in this re-created "flat" and sample its up-to-date cuisine. Sunday brunch and warm welcome.

Toi

(dinner)

27 r. Colisée Ⓜ Franklin D. Roosevelt – ✆ 01 42 56 56 58 – restaurant.toi@wanadoo.fr – Fax 01 42 56 09 60 F 9

Rest – Menu (€ 17), € 24/69 bi – Carte € 35/79

◆ Bright reds, oranges and designer furniture depict the 1970s style decor at this trendy, friendly restaurant-bar serving up-to-date and creative cuisine.

Devez

5 pl. de l'Alma Ⓜ Alma Marceau – ✆ 01 53 67 97 53 – contact@devezparis.com – Fax 01 47 23 09 48 G 8

Rest – Carte € 33/67

◆ The landlord, also a cattle breeder, clearly loves his region; up-to-date cuisine based on tasty Aubrac meat. Fine modern interior and table d'hôte.

L'Atelier des Compères

56 r. Galilée Ⓜ George V – ✆ 01 47 20 75 56 – contact@atelierdescomperes.com – Closed August, Christmas holidays, Saturday, Sunday and public holidays F 8

Rest – *(number of covers limited, pre-book)* Menu (€ 40), € 50/65

◆ A chic café-style address in a paved courtyard with a roof that opens in summer. Appetising daily specials based around market availability.

La Maison de L'Aubrac

37 r. Marbeuf Ⓜ Franklin D. Roosevelt – ✆ 01 43 59 05 14 – ldurot.aubrac@wanadoo.fr – Fax 01 42 25 29 87 G9

Rest – Menu (€ 30), € 55 – Carte € 34/54

◆ Aveyron farmhouse-style decor, generous portions of rustic cuisine (with an emphasis on Aubrac beef) and an excellent wine list: a piece of Aubrac just a stone's throw from the Champs-Élysées.

SYDR
6 r. de Tilsitt Ⓜ Charles de Gaulle-Etoile – ✆ 01 45 72 41 32 – sydrerie@orange.fr – Fax 01 45 72 41 79 – Closed August, Sunday and Monday F 8
Rest – Menu € 27 (lunch)/39 bi – Carte € 33/53
◆ This post-modern cider bar created by Alain Dutournier and Philippe Sella is extremely minimalist in style. Regional cuisine with a modern twist, plus a bar offering tapas and cider tastings.

Bocconi
10 bis r. Artois Ⓜ St-Philippe du Roule – ✆ 01 53 76 44 44 – bocconi@wanadoo.fr – Fax 01 45 61 10 08 – Closed Saturday lunchtime and Sunday F 9
Rest – Carte € 41/55
◆ A trattoria with a restrained, contemporary-style dining room and a pleasant summer terrace. The menu features a selection of typically Italian recipes.

Le Boucoléon
10 r. Constantinople Ⓜ Europe – ✆ 01 42 93 73 33 – Fax 01 42 93 95 44 – Closed 10-25 August, Saturday lunch, Sunday and public holidays E 11
Rest – *(number of covers limited, pre-book)* Menu (€ 24) – Carte € 34/44
◆ This friendly neighbourhood bistro is a resounding success thanks to its wholesome market fresh menu and reasonable prices. Blackboard menu.

Le Bistrot de Marius
6 av. George V Ⓜ Alma Marceau – ✆ 01 40 70 11 76 – Fax 01 40 70 17 08 G 8
Rest – Menu (€ 28), € 32 (weekday lunch) – Carte € 32/63
◆ This pleasant annex of 'Marius et Janette' sports a brightly coloured Provençal decor. Tightly packed and simply laid tables. Seafood menu.

Daru
(dinner)
19 r. Daru Ⓜ Courcelles – ✆ 01 42 27 23 60 – restaurant.daru@orange.fr – Fax 01 47 54 08 14 – Closed August and Sunday E 9
Rest – Menu (€ 29) – Carte € 40/70
◆ Founded in 1918, Daru was the first Russian grocery store in Paris. Today it still offers customers a choice of zakouskis, blinis and caviar in its renowned red and black interior.

Shin Jung
7 r. Clapeyron Ⓜ Rome – ✆ 01 45 22 21 06 – printemp0706@aol.fr – Fax 01 42 94 10 96 – Closed Sunday lunchtime and lunchtime public holidays D 11
Rest – Menu € 9 (lunch), € 15/36 (dinner) – Carte € 19/37
◆ The minimalist decor in this restaurant includes calligraphy paintings on the walls. The focus here is on South Korean cuisine and raw fish. Friendly welcome.

S. Sauvignier/MICHELIN

Opéra, Grands Boulevards

9e arrondissement ✉ 75009

Intercontinental Le Grand
2 r. Scribe Ⓜ Opéra – ✆ 01 40 07 32 32 – legrand@ihg.com – Fax 01 42 66 12 51 F 12
442 rm – †€ 650/830 ††€ 650/830, ☕ € 38 – 28 suites
Rest *Café de la Paix* – see restaurant listing
◆ This famous luxury hotel, a fixture since 1862, reopened after full renovations in 2003. It offers modern comforts, but its French Second Empire spirit has been judiciously preserved.

Scribe

1 r. Scribe Ⓜ Opéra – ✆ *01 44 71 24 24* – *h0663@accor.com*
– *Fax 01 42 65 39 97* F 12

213 rm – †€ 555/1150 ††€ 555/1150, ☕ € 28 – 5 suites

Rest *Café Lumière* – ✆ *01 44 71 24 19* – Carte € 41/67

♦ Discreet luxury is the main feature of this fully refurbished hotel housed in a grand Haussmann-style building. The world première of the Lumière brothers' first film screening was held here in 1895. English style decor and brasserie style cuisine at the Jardin des Muses, located in the basement of the Scribe.

Millennium Opéra

12 bd Haussmann Ⓜ Richelieu Drouot
– ✆ *01 49 49 16 00* – *opera@mill-cop.com*
– *Fax 01 49 49 17 00* F 13

157 rm – †€ 400/450 ††€ 500/550, ☕ € 25 – 6 suites

Rest *Brasserie Haussmann* – ✆ *01 49 49 16 64* – Menu (€ 19 bi)
– Carte € 28/61

♦ This 1927 hotel has lost none of its period lustre. Tastefully appointed rooms with Art Deco furniture. Modern facilities. Carefully renovated with modern decor, and typical brasserie fare at the Brasserie Haussman.

Ambassador

16 bd Haussmann Ⓜ Richelieu Drouot – ✆ *01 44 83 40 40*
– *ambass@concorde-hotels.com* – *Fax 01 44 83 40 57* F 13

274 rm – †€ 500 ††€ 500, ☕ € 26 – 20 suites

Rest *16 Haussmann* – ✆ *01 48 00 06 38* – Menu (€ 32), € 44 (lunch), € 37 € (dinner)/52 – Carte € 48/59

♦ Painted panels, crystal chandeliers and antiques adorn this elegant hotel dating from the 1920s. The renovated rooms are decorated in simple, contemporary style; the others somewhat more traditional. At 16 Haussmann, the royal blue and gold colour scheme is enhanced by light-coloured wood, red Starck chairs and views of the lively boulevard through the large windows.

Pavillon de Paris without rest

7 r. Parme Ⓜ Liège – ✆ *01 55 31 60 00* – *mail@pavillondeparis.com*
– *Fax 01 55 31 60 01* D 12

30 rm – †€ 215/240 ††€ 270/296, ☕ € 16

♦ Contemporary-style hotel in a quiet street. The rooms are on the small side, but have a sober, luxurious decor and a pleasant intimate atmosphere. Japanese garden in the mini-courtyard.

Villa Opéra Drouot without rest

2 r. Geoffroy Marie Ⓜ Grands Boulevards
– ✆ *01 48 00 08 08*
– *drouot@leshotelsdeparis.com*
– *Fax 01 48 00 80 60* F 14

29 rm – †€ 139/370 ††€ 149/380, ☕ € 20

♦ A surprising and subtle blend of Baroque decor and the latest in elegant comfort in these rooms embellished with wall hangings, velvets, silks and wood panelling.

Jules without rest

49 r. La Fayette Ⓜ Le Peletier – ✆ *01 42 85 05 44*
– *info@hoteljules.com*
– *Fax 01 49 95 06 60* F 14

101 rm – †€ 128/260 ††€ 128/260, ☕ € 14

♦ This hotel has embraced contemporary design without sacrificing any of its inherent elegance with the emphasis on refined decor in the refurbished bedrooms. Winter garden-style breakfast room. Wellness centre.

Astra Opéra without rest

29 r. Caumartin Ⓜ Havre Caumartin – ✆ *01 42 66 15 15*
– *hotel.astra@astotel.com* – *Fax 01 42 66 98 05* F 12

82 rm – †€ 225/270 ††€ 255/320, ☕ € 22

♦ Haussmann-style building with large, comfortable rooms. Bright lounge with a glass roof and contemporary art on the walls. Welcoming breakfast room.

St-Pétersbourg without rest
33 r. Caumartin Ⓜ Havre Caumartin – ✆ 01 42 66 60 38 – info@hotelpeters.com – Fax 01 42 66 53 54 F 12
100 rm – €151/189 €193/250
◆ A large, traditional, family-run hotel. Elegant entrance with chandeliers and a marble floor, numerous lounges and meeting rooms. Spacious guestrooms.

Lorette Opéra without rest
36 r. Notre-Dame de Lorette Ⓜ St-Georges – ✆ 01 42 85 18 81 – hotel.lorette@astotel.com – Fax 01 42 81 32 19 E 13
84 rm – €136/240 €136/240, €14
◆ The decor in this completely renovated hotel is a harmonious mix of bare stone and designer style. Pleasant, contemporary rooms; breakfast is served in the cellar with its vaulted ceiling.

Villathéna without rest
23 r. d'Athènes Ⓜ St-Lazare – ✆ 01 44 63 07 07 – reservation@villathena.com – Fax 01 44 63 07 60 E 12
43 rm – €185/215 €185/215, €17
◆ Housed in the former Social Security offices, this brand-new hotel has a resolutely contemporary feel. Lobby decorated in red, white and black; well-appointed guestrooms with light wood furniture.

Richmond Opéra without rest
11 r. Helder Ⓜ Chaussée d'Antin – ✆ 01 47 70 53 20 – paris@richmond-hotel.com – Fax 01 48 00 02 10 F 13
59 rm – €134/149 €154/225, €10
◆ The spacious, elegant rooms almost all give onto the courtyard. The lounge is rather grandly decorated in the Empire style.

Opéra Franklin without rest
19 r. Buffault Ⓜ Cadet – ✆ 01 42 80 27 27 – info@operafranklin.com – Fax 01 48 78 13 04 E 14
67 rm – €139/163 €152/216, €13
◆ Located in a quiet street, this business hotel is built around a central courtyard. Large lobby with a glass roof and bar. Functional, simply decorated rooms.

ATN without rest
21 r. d'Athènes Ⓜ St-Lazare – ✆ 01 48 74 00 55 – atn@atnhotel.fr – Fax 01 42 81 04 75 E 12
36 rm – €139/350 €139/399, €11
◆ Situated a stone's throw from St-Lazare station, completely refurbished hotel in a trendy, contemporary style. Quality materials and attention to detail add to the appeal.

9HOTEL without rest
14 r. Papillon Ⓜ Cadet – ✆ 01 47 70 78 34 – info@le9hotel.com – Fax 01 40 22 91 00 E 14
35 rm – €140/220 €150/230, €15
◆ Renovated in sober designer style, this hotel has a pleasant lounge with art books and international press. Rooms are fairly small but functional, with contemporary furniture and mood lighting.

Caumartin Opéra without rest
27 r. Caumartin Ⓜ Havre Caumartin – ✆ 01 47 42 95 95 – hotel.caumartin@astotel.com – Fax 01 47 42 88 19 F 12
40 rm – €155/240 €165/240, €14
◆ This small hotel in the Grand Magasins district has had a complete face-lift. Contemporary-style guestrooms with immaculate white bathrooms.

Grand Hôtel Haussmann without rest
6 r. Helder Ⓜ Opéra – ✆ 01 48 24 76 10 – ghh@club-internet.fr – Fax 01 48 00 97 18 F 13
59 rm – €135/185 €150/225, €14
◆ Hiding behind this discreet facade are cosy rooms of different sizes with a personal touch; all look out to the back and are gradually being renovated.

Anjou Lafayette without rest
4 r. Riboutté Ⓜ Cadet – ✆ 01 42 46 83 44
– hotel.anjou.lafayette@wanadoo.fr
– Fax 01 48 00 08 97 E 14
39 rm – †€ 98/170 ††€ 118/190, ☕ € 12
◆ Near the leafy Square Montholon, with its Second Empire wrought-iron gates, this hotel offers guests comfortable, soundproofed rooms decorated in warm tones.

Trois Poussins without rest
15 r. Clauzel Ⓜ St-Georges – ✆ 01 53 32 81 81 – h3p@les3poussins.com
– Fax 01 53 32 81 82 E 13
40 rm – †€ 110/140 ††€ 119/156, ☕ € 10
◆ Elegant rooms offering several levels of comfort. View of Paris from the top floors. Prettily vaulted breakfast room. Small courtyard-terrace.

Opéra d'Antin without rest
75 r. de Provence Ⓜ Chaussée d'Antin – ✆ 01 48 74 12 99
– operadantin@paris-hotel-capital.com – Fax 01 48 74 16 14 F 12
29 rm – †€ 195 ††€ 195, ☕ € 13
◆ A restored hotel near the famous Galeries Lafayette. A breakfast room with a glass roof and pleasant rooms in an Art deco style.

Langlois without rest
63 r. St-Lazare Ⓜ Trinité – ✆ 01 48 74 78 24 – info@hotel-langlois.com
– Fax 01 49 95 04 43 E 12
24 rm – †€ 105/120 ††€ 120/140, ☕ € 12 – 3 suites
◆ Built in 1870, the building first housed a bank and then a hotel from 1896 on. Art nouveau, Art deco or Fifties-style rooms – all with a character of their own.

Mercure Monty without rest
5 r. Montyon Ⓜ Grands Boulevards – ✆ 01 47 70 26 10 – hotel@
mercuremonty.com – Fax 01 42 46 55 10 F 14
69 rm – †€ 75/215 ††€ 90/230, ☕ € 15
◆ Beautiful façade dating from the 1930s, Art Deco setting at the front desk, and the hotel chain's standard equipment characterise this Mercure located in view of the Folies Bergère.

Acadia without rest
4 r. Geoffroy Marie Ⓜ Grands Boulevards – ✆ 01 40 22 99 99
– hotel.acadia@astotel.com – Fax 01 40 22 01 82 F 14
36 rm – †€ 124/220 ††€ 165/220, ☕ € 14
◆ In a lively district which is busy day and night, this spotless small hotel has well-equipped rooms with double-glazing.

Peyris without rest
10 r. Conservatoire Ⓜ Poissonnière – ✆ 01 47 70 50 83 – info@hotel-peyris.com
– Fax 01 40 22 95 91 F 14
50 rm – †€ 110 ††€ 145, ☕ € 13
◆ The functional rooms are decorated in yellow and blue colours. Lounge decorated with Napoleon III-style furniture. Pleasant welcome.

Villa Opéra Lamartine without rest
39 r. Lamartine Ⓜ Notre-Dame-de-Lorette – ✆ 01 48 78 78 58
– lamartineopera@wanadoo.fr
– Fax 01 48 74 65 15 E 14
28 rm – †€ 90/110 ††€ 140/180, ☕ € 12
◆ This hotel, a stones' throw from Notre-Dame-de-Lorette church, elegantly evokes the Romantic authors of Paris. Tasteful rooms and breakfast served under a fine vaulted stone ceiling.

du Pré without rest
10 r. P. Sémard Ⓜ Poissonnière – ✆ 01 42 81 37 11 – hotel@duprehotels.com
– Fax 01 40 23 98 28 E 15
40 rm ☕ – †€ 98/100 ††€ 118/130
◆ Functional, attractively coloured rooms, a lounge furnished with Chesterfield sofas, plus a breakfast room and bistro-style bar.

Monterosa without rest

30 r. La Bruyère Ⓜ *St-Georges – ✆ 01 48 74 87 90 – hotel.monterosa@wanadoo.fr – Fax 01 42 81 01 12 – Closed 19-26 December* E 13

36 rm – †€ 115 ††€ 140, ☕ € 8

◆ Intimate hotel in the Nouvelle Athènes neighbourhood, decorated in warm red and yellow tones and wood panelling. Pleasant lounge bar.

Café de la Paix – Hôtel Intercontinental Le Grand

12 bd Capucines Ⓜ *Opéra – ✆ 01 40 07 36 36 – reservation@cafedelapaix.fr – Fax 01 40 07 36 13* F 12

Rest – Menu (€ 35), € 45 (lunch)/85 – Carte € 51/118

◆ Fine murals, gold wainscoting and French Second Empire-inspired furniture: this famous luxury brasserie, open from 7am to midnight, is the meeting place for "Tout-Paris".

Jean

8 r. St-Lazare Ⓜ *Notre-Dame-de-Lorette – ✆ 01 48 78 62 73 – chezjean@wanadoo.fr – Fax 01 48 78 66 04 – Closed 28 July-25 August, 25 February-3 March, Saturday and Sunday* E 12

Rest – Menu (€ 38), € 46 (lunch), € 60/75 – Carte € 63/71

Spec. Jus tremblotant de crevettes grises, herbes parfumées. Noix de veau, yaourt à l'anchois et jus de prune à l' orchidée. Dacquoise à la fleur d'oranger, chasselas, sorbet bière blanche.

◆ A recent makeover for this restaurant serving up-to-the-minute cuisine: beige tones, stained woodwork, light fabrics, banquette seating and an Oriental-style lounge upstairs.

Romain

40 r. St-Georges Ⓜ *St-Georges – ✆ 01 48 24 58 94 – restaurant_romain@yahoo.fr – Fax 01 42 47 09 75* E 13

Rest – *(closed August, Sunday and Monday)* Menu € 33 – Carte € 36/67

◆ This restaurant nestled behind Notre-Dame-de-Lorette offers a concise Italian menu, including excellent charcuterie and home-made pasta, accompanied by wines from the various regions.

Bistrot Papillon

6 r. Papillon Ⓜ *Cadet – ✆ 01 47 70 90 03 – Fax 01 48 24 05 59 – Closed 1st-12 May, 6-31 August, Saturday except dinner from October to April and Sunday*

Rest – Menu € 29 – Carte € 36/48 E 15

◆ A provincial atmosphere in this restaurant where the walls are covered in wood panelling or hung with fabric. Classic menu completed with market-based specials.

Au Petit Riche

25 r. Le Peletier Ⓜ *Richelieu Drouot – ✆ 01 47 70 68 68 – aupetitriche@wanadoo.fr – Fax 01 48 24 10 79 – Closed Saturday from 14 July to 20 August and Sunday* F 13

Rest – Menu (€ 24), € 27/36 – Carte € 30/62

◆ A favourite haunt of Maurice Chevalier and Mistinguett, the gracious sitting-dining rooms, decorated in a late 19C style, are adorned with mirrors and hat stands.

Carte Blanche

6 r. Lamartine Ⓜ *Cadet – ✆ 01 48 78 12 20 – rest.carteblanche@free.fr – Fax 01 48 78 12 21 – Closed 1st-20 August, Saturday lunch and Sunday*

Rest – Menu € 26/40 – Carte approx. € 43 E 14

◆ The owners of this restaurant are great travellers: photos and souvenirs from their trips around the world can be seen in the dining room. Exotic tableware and cuisine that shows French and international influence.

Casa Olympe

48 r. St Georges Ⓜ *St-Georges – ✆ 01 42 85 26 01 – Fax 01 45 26 49 33 – Closed 1st-12 May, 1st-25 August, 23 December-3 January, Saturday and Sunday*

Rest – *(number of covers limited, pre-book)* Menu (€ 29), € 38/60 E 13

◆ Traditional dishes that Olympe, actually Dominique Versini - cuisine icon of the 1980s - interprets as 'à sa sauce'. Served in two small ochre coloured rooms with tightly packed tables.

Dell Orto
VISA MC AE

45 r. St-Georges Ⓜ *St-Georges – ✆ 01 48 78 40 30 – Closed August, Christmas holidays, Sunday and Monday* E 13

Rest – *(dinner only)* Carte € 32/64

♦ A pleasant "chic trattoria" decor, warm atmosphere and, at the stoves, an Italian chef who delicately enhances the dishes of his native land with flavours from elsewhere.

La Petite Sirène de Copenhague
VISA MC AE

47 r. N.-D. de Lorette Ⓜ *St-Georges – ✆ 01 45 26 66 66 – Closed 2-25 August, 23 December-5 January, Saturday lunch, Sunday and Monday* E 13

Rest – *(pre-book)* Menu € 29 (lunch)/34 – Carte € 43/71

♦ A tasteful dining room, colour washed walls and soft Danish lighting set the scene for recipes from Andersen's homeland. Attentive service.

L'Œnothèque
AC VISA MC AE D

20 r. St-Lazare Ⓜ *Notre-Dame-de-Lorette – ✆ 01 48 78 08 76 – Fax 01 40 16 10 27 – Closed 1st-8 May, 2 weeks in August, 24 December-1st January, Saturday and Sunday* E 13

Rest – Carte € 25/53

♦ Neighbourhood establishment combining a simple restaurant with a wine shop. Fine selection of wines to accompany the market fresh fare presented on the chalkboard.

Villa Victoria
AC VISA MC AE

52 r. Lamartine Ⓜ *Notre-Dame-de-Lorette – ✆ 01 48 78 60 05 – victoria52@orange.fr – Fax 01 48 78 60 05 – Closed August and Sunday* E 13

Rest – Menu (€ 24), € 32 – Carte approx. € 40

♦ This cosy bistro with bare stone walls, tightly-packed tables, wines and menus on a black board offers a new twist on traditional dishes. Great homemade bread.

I Golosi
AC VISA MC

6 r. Grange Batelière Ⓜ *Richelieu Drouot – ✆ 01 48 24 18 63 – i.golosi@wanadoo.fr – Fax 01 45 23 18 96 – Closed 5-20 August, Saturday dinner and Sunday* F 14

Rest – Carte € 25/41

♦ On the 1st floor, Italian designer decor with a minimalism made up for by the joviality of the service. Café, shop and little spot for tasting things on the ground floor. Italian cuisine.

Le Pré Cadet
AC VISA MC AE D

10 r. Saulnier Ⓜ *Cadet – ✆ 01 48 24 99 64 – Fax 01 47 70 55 96 – Closed 1st-8 May, 3-21 August, 24 December-1st January, Saturday lunch and Sunday* F 14

Rest – *(number of covers limited, pre-book)* Menu € 30/45 – Carte € 39/52

♦ This friendly, unpretentious restaurant in the vicinity of the 'Folies' is renowned for its specials, such as veal brawn - its pride and joy. Very good coffee list.

Sizin
VISA MC

47 r. St-Georges Ⓜ *St-Georges – ✆ 01 44 63 02 28 – ekilic@free.fr – Closed August and Sunday* E 13

Rest – Carte € 20/30

♦ This welcoming restaurant, decorated with old prints and Izmir earthenware, offers a variety of rich Turkish dishes.

Georgette
VISA MC AE

29 r. St-Georges Ⓜ *Notre-Dame-de-Lorette – ✆ 01 42 80 39 13 – Closed Easter holidays, August, autumn half-term holidays, Saturday, Sunday and Monday* E 13

Rest – Carte € 27/44

♦ With its multicoloured formica tables and vinyl-covered chairs, this restaurant has a pleasant retro air. Bistro cuisine with excellent vegetables to the fore.

Spring
28 r. Tour d'Auvergne Ⓜ Cadet – ✆ 01 45 96 05 72 – freshsnail@free.fr – Closed two weeks in August, Christmas holidays, Tuesday lunch, Wednesday lunch, Saturday, Sunday and Monday E 14
Rest – *(number of covers limited, pre-book)* Menu € 32 (lunch), € 35/39
◆ Friendly neighbourhood feel, set menu changed daily according to the market and the chef's inspiration, and a careful selection of wines from small producers: a *table d'hôte* in the city.

L'Office
3 r. Richer Ⓜ Poissonnière – ✆ 01 47 70 67 31 – Fax 01 47 70 67 31 – Closed 3-25 August, Saturday lunch, Sunday and Monday F 15
Rest – *(number of covers limited, pre-book)* Menu (€ 13,50), € 16 (weekday lunch)/26
◆ Modish new restaurant with simple, sober decor. The self-taught chef offers a well-structured and attractively priced menu based around market produce.

Radis Roses
68 r. Rodier Ⓜ Anvers – ✆ 01 48 78 03 20 – radisroses@tele2.fr – Closed 5-20 August, Sunday and Monday E 14
Rest – *(pre-book)* Menu (€ 27), € 34
◆ Smart small restaurant offering a creative take on specialities from the Drôme region. Charming welcome and contemporary decor.

Momoka
5 r. Jean-Baptiste Pigalle Ⓜ Trinité d'Estienne d'Orves – ✆ 01 40 16 19 09 – masayohashimoto@aol.com – Fax 01 40 16 19 09 – Closed August, Saturday lunch, Sunday, Monday and public holidays E 13
Rest – Menu (€ 25), € 35 (lunch), € 48/68
◆ Book ahead for this tiny restaurant run by a Franco-Japanese couple, where Masayo creates delicious Japanese dishes which change daily. Authentic setting and homely atmosphere.

Ph. Gagic/MICHELIN

Gare de l'Est, Gare du Nord, Canal St-Martin

10e arrondissement ✉ 75010

Mercure Terminus Nord without rest
12 bd Denain Ⓜ Gare du Nord – ✆ 01 42 80 20 00 – h2761@accor.com – Fax 01 42 80 63 89 E 16
236 rm – †€ 148/288 ††€ 168/368, ☐ € 16
◆ A sympathetic renovation has restored this 19C hotel to its former glory. Art Nouveau stained glass, "British" decor and a cosy atmosphere give it the air of an elegant Victorian mansion.

Holiday Inn Paris Opéra
38 r. Échiquier Ⓜ Bonne Nouvelle – ✆ 01 42 46 92 75 – information@hi-parisopera.com – Fax 01 42 47 03 97 F 15
92 rm – †€ 159/219 ††€ 259/319, ☐ € 20 – **Rest** – *(closed Saturday lunch and Sunday)* Menu (€ 25), € 35/39 bi – Carte approx. € 40
◆ A step away from the Grands Boulevards and their string of theatres and brasseries. This hotel offers large rooms decorated in the style of the Belle Époque. The dining room is an authentic gem from the year 1900: mosaics, glass roof, woodwork and fine Art Nouveau furniture.

Paris-Est without rest
4 r. du 8 Mai 1945 Ⓜ Gare de l'Est – ✆ 01 44 89 27 00 – hotelparisest.bestwestern@autogrill.net – Fax 01 44 89 27 49 E 16
45 rm – †€ 114/150 ††€ 114/150, ☕ € 13
◆ Although just next to the train station, this establishment offers quiet rooms, facing the back courtyard, which have been renovated and soundproofed.

Albert 1er without rest
162 r. Lafayette Ⓜ Gare du Nord – ✆ 01 40 36 82 40 – paris@albert1erhotel.com – Fax 01 40 35 72 52 E 16
55 rm – †€ 105/120 ††€ 125/140, ☕ € 15
◆ Hotel where the well-designed modern rooms are equipped with double glazing and have the advantage of being continually redone. Convivial atmosphere.

Du Nord without rest
47 r. Albert Thomas Ⓜ Jacques Bonsergent – ✆ 01 42 01 66 00 – contact@hoteldunord-leparivelo.com – Fax 01 42 01 92 10 F 16
24 rm – †€ 68/79 ††€ 68/79, ☕ € 7,50
◆ Rustic charm at this hotel on a quiet street. Small but individually decorated guestrooms and attractive vaulted breakfast room. Bicycles available for loan.

Alane without rest
72 bd Magenta Ⓜ Gare de l'Est – ✆ 01 40 35 83 30 – alanehotel@wanadoo.fr – Fax 01 46 07 44 03 F 16
32 rm – †€ 65/119 ††€ 70/125, ☕ € 7,50
◆ Conveniently located hotel opposite the Gare de l'Est. Small, well-kept rooms with simple decor; those on the top floor with sloping ceilings. Attractive lounge with cane furnishings.

Ibis without rest
197 r. Lafayette Ⓜ Château Landon – ✆ 01 44 65 70 00 – h1823@accor.com – Fax 01 44 65 70 07 E 17
165 rm – †€ 85/91 ††€ 85/91, ☕ € 8
◆ The advantages of this hotel chain are the space and the modern facilities. The top floor rooms facing the street command views of the Sacré Coeur.

Café Panique
12 r. des Messageries Ⓜ Poissonnière – ✆ 01 47 70 06 84 E 15
Rest – Menu (€ 20 bi), € 27 bi/32
◆ This former textiles workshop now hosts a discreet and pleasant contemporary restaurant. Loft-style decor with skylights, mezzanine, temporary art shows and an open kitchen.

Terminus Nord
23 r. Dunkerque Ⓜ Gare du Nord – ✆ 01 42 85 05 15 – Fax 01 40 16 13 98
Rest – Menu (€ 24), € 31 – Carte € 32/80 E 16
◆ High ceilings, frescoes, posters and sculptures are reflected in the mirrors of this brasserie that successfully mixes Art Deco and Art Nouveau. Cosmopolitan clientele.

Chez Michel
10 r. Belzunce Ⓜ Gare du Nord – ✆ 01 44 53 06 20 – Closed 29 July-20 August, Monday lunch, Saturday and Sunday E 15
Rest – Menu € 30 – Carte € 45/65
◆ Unpretentious and popular retro-style bistro proposing delicious traditional dishes, with a slight Breton slant (the chef's origins and name!) Excellent game in season.

Chez Casimir
6 r. Belzunce Ⓜ Gare du Nord – ✆ 01 48 78 28 80 – Closed Saturday and Sunday
Rest – Menu (€ 22), € 29 E 15
◆ Bistro style, simple and clean-cut cooking with a matching decor: wood, copperware and checked napkins set the tone for this casual address.

Urbane
12 r. Arthur-Groussier Ⓜ Goncourt – ✆ 01 42 40 74 75 – urbane.resto@gmail.com – Closed 3 weeks in August, Saturday lunch, Sunday dinner and Monday
Rest – Menu (€ 15), € 19 (weekday lunch)/29 F 18
◆ A trendy, yet simply decorated restaurant (white walls, bistro-style furniture, imitation leather banquettes and industrial lamps). Modern dishes with an emphasis on quality ingredients.

Et dans mon cœur il y a...
56 r. Lancry Ⓜ Jacques Bonsergent – ✆ 01 42 38 07 37 – reservation@etdansmoncoeur.com – Fax 01 42 02 52 60 – Closed 25 December-1st January, Saturday lunch and Sunday F 17
Rest – Menu (€ 16 bi), € 20 bi (lunch) – Carte € 37/49
◆ This stylish restaurant decorated with bookshelves has a cosy atmosphere, with comfortable armchairs and an attractive Belle Époque bar. Contemporary cuisine.

Mme Shawn
34 r. Y. Toudic Ⓜ Jacques Bonsergent – ✆ 01 42 08 05 07 – reservation@mmeshawn.com – Fax 01 42 02 25 60 – Closed 24 December-2 January
Rest – Menu (€ 12 bi), € 17 bi (lunch) – Carte € 25/33 F 17
◆ The dining room sports stone murals representing Buddha, bamboo screens and soft lighting. A contemporary Thai address.

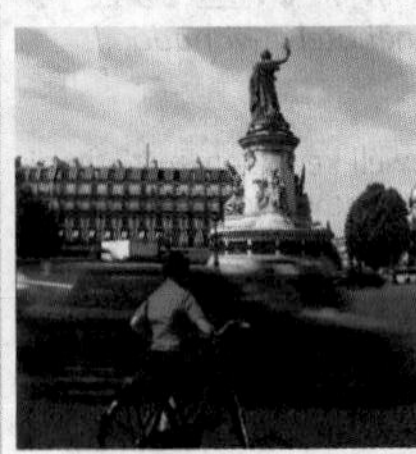
H. Le Gac/MICHELIN

Nation, Voltaire, République

11e arrondissement ✉ 75011

Les Jardins du Marais rm, VISA
74 r. Amelot Ⓜ St-Sébastien Froissart – ✆ 01 40 21 20 00 – resabastille@homeplazza.com – Fax 01 47 00 82 40 H 17
201 rm – †€ 350 ††€ 370, ☕ € 32 – 64 suites
Rest – *(closed Sunday)* Menu (€ 20) – Carte € 27/47
◆ A quiet night's sleep is guaranteed in this hotel made up of several buildings overlooking a large interior garden. Designer entrance hall and bar, and comfortable Art Deco-style bedrooms.

Le Général without rest VISA
5 r. Rampon Ⓜ République – ✆ 01 47 00 41 57 – info@legeneralhotel.com – Fax 01 47 00 21 56 G17
46 rm – †€ 145/165 ††€ 175/235, ☕ € 16 – 3 suites
◆ An appealing hotel near Place de la République, with elegant decoration and modern-style furniture. Wifi connections, small business centre and pleasant fitness room.

Marais Bastille without rest VISA
36 bd Richard Lenoir Ⓜ Bréguet Sabin – ✆ 01 48 05 75 00 – maraisbastille@wanadoo.fr – Fax 01 43 57 42 85 J 18
36 rm – †€ 145 ††€ 145, ☕ € 10
◆ The hotel runs along the boulevard which has covered the Canal St-Martin since 1860. Comfortable, spacious and modern bedrooms embellished with oak and cherry wood furniture.

Le Patio St-Antoine without rest VISA
289bis r. Fg St-Antoine Ⓜ Nation – ✆ 01 40 09 40 00 – resanation@homeplazza.com – Fax 01 40 09 11 55 K 20
89 rm – †€ 150/250 ††€ 150/250, ☕ € 18
◆ Contemporary, renovated rooms, most of which overlook two quiet patio-gardens. Good buffet breakfast served in a room decorated in warm tones.

Le Standard Design without rest
29 r. des Taillandiers Ⓜ Bastille – ✆ 01 48 05 30 97 – reservation@standard-hotel.com – Fax 01 47 00 29 26 J 18
34 rm – †€ 95/140 ††€ 130/195, ☕ € 12
♦ A resolutely contemporary interior in black and white, with touches of colour in the bedrooms. A trendy and unique hotel embellished with numerous designer objects.

Croix de Malte without rest
5 r. Malte Ⓜ Oberkampf – ✆ 01 48 05 09 36 – hotelcroixdemalte@orange.fr – Fax 01 43 57 02 54 H 17
29 rm – †€ 75/95 ††€ 80/100, ☕ € 10
♦ The Croix de Malte has something of a tropical ambience with its colourful furniture, (false) parrot and a breakfast room conceived as a winter garden. Mezzanine bathrooms on the top floor.

Grand Hôtel Français without rest
223 bd Voltaire Ⓜ Nation – ✆ 01 43 71 27 57 – grand-hotel-francais@wanadoo.fr – Fax 01 43 48 40 05 K 20
36 rm – †€ 115/130 ††€ 115/145, ☕ € 10
♦ Corner building in the Haussmann style in a typically Parisian district. Comfortable, quite plush, well-renovated rooms.

Lyon Mulhouse without rest
8 bd Beaumarchais Ⓜ Bastille – ✆ 01 47 00 91 50 – hotelyonmulhouse@wanadoo.fr – Fax 01 47 00 06 31 J 17
40 rm – †€ 65/140 ††€ 78/140, ☕ € 7
♦ This former coaching inn, a hotel since 1920, has been sympathetically renovated. Cosy, well-maintained bedrooms (three with wonderful views of Paris), plus paintings by local artists on display.

Prince Eugène without rest
247 bd Voltaire Ⓜ Nation – ✆ 01 43 71 22 81 – hotelprinceeugene@wanadoo.fr – Fax 01 43 71 24 71 K 21
35 rm – †€ 66/71 ††€ 73/84, ☕ € 8
♦ The sign honours Napoleon I's adopted son. Up-to-date rooms, with efficient double glazing; those on the 6th floor, with sloping ceilings, are larger.

Nord et Est without rest
49 r. Malte Ⓜ Oberkampf – ✆ 01 47 00 71 70 – info@hotel-nord-est.com – Fax 01 43 57 51 16 G 17
45 rm – †€ 80 ††€ 95, ☕ € 8 – 1 suite
♦ The warm family atmosphere draws regulars to this hotel near Place de la République. The recently-renovated rooms are pleasant; the others remain well-kept.

Grand Prieuré without rest
20 r. Grand Prieuré Ⓜ Oberkampf – ✆ 01 47 00 74 14 – gprieure@yahoo.fr – Fax 01 49 23 06 64 G 17
32 rm – †€ 68/80 ††€ 75/95, ☕ € 5,50
♦ You will spend a peaceful night in this quiet street near the Canal St Martin. Friendly welcome, slightly antiquated but spacious and well-kept rooms.

Vin et Marée
276 bd Voltaire Ⓜ Nation – ✆ 01 43 72 31 23 – vmvoltaire@vin-et-maree.com – Fax 01 40 24 00 23 K 21
Rest – Menu (€ 21) – Carte € 32/58
♦ As in the other restaurants of the chain, the seafood specials are chalked up on the board daily. Rear dining room with marine decor and a view of the kitchen.

Mansouria
11 r. Faidherbe Ⓜ Faidherbe Chaligny – ✆ 01 43 71 00 16 – lollisoraya@yahoo.fr – Fax 01 40 24 21 97 – Closed 10-18 August, Monday lunch, Tuesday lunch and Sunday K 19
Rest – Menu € 30/46 bi – Carte € 30/49
♦ Run by a former ethnologist, well-known in Paris in the field of Moroccan cuisine. The delicate, aromatic dishes are prepared by a female team and served in a Moorish decor.

Le Chateaubriand
VISA MC AE

129 av. Parmentier Ⓜ *Goncourt – ✆ 01 43 57 45 95*
– Closed Saturday lunch, Sunday and Monday J19/F17

Rest – Menu (€ 14), € 19 (lunch)/40 (dinner) – Carte € 28/36

◆ A bistro with a retro ambience in which reasonably simple cuisine is served at lunchtime, with more elaborate and equally successful fare in the evening, An emphasis on high-quality, fresh produce.

Au Petit Monsieur
VISA MC AE

50 r. Amelot Ⓜ *Chemin Vert – ✆ 01 43 55 54 04*
– aupetitmonsieur@wanadoo.fr
– Fax 01 43 14 77 03
– Closed August, Saturday lunch, Sunday and Monday H 17

Rest – Menu (€ 19), € 26/35 – Carte € 36/57

◆ A set menu in this charming bistro packed with regulars. Knick-knacks adorn the dining room with a large table d'hôte. Friendly and informal.

Le Temps au Temps
VISA MC AE

13 r. Paul Bert Ⓜ *Faidherbe Chaligny*
– ✆ 01 43 79 63 40 – Fax 01 43 79 63 40
– Closed August, 24 December-1st January, Sunday and Monday K19/K20

Rest – Menu (€ 18), € 30/38

◆ The basic decor and tables packed closely together are quickly forgotten as guests enjoy the creative gourmet cuisine produced by the young owner-chef.

Repaire de Cartouche
VISA MC

99 r. Amelot Ⓜ *St-Sébastien Froissart*
– ✆ 01 47 00 25 86 – Fax 01 43 38 85 91
– Closed 1st-8 May, August, Sunday and Monday H 17

Rest – Menu (€ 14), € 26 (weekday lunch) – Carte € 35/48

◆ Cartouche, the impetuous yet honourable bandit, took refuge here in 1713 after deserting from the army; the restaurant murals recall his epic life. Attractive wine list.

Auberge Pyrénées Cévennes
A/C VISA MC AE

106 r. Folie-Méricourt Ⓜ *République – ✆ 01 43 57 33 78*
– Closed 30 July-20 August, Saturday lunch, Sunday and public holidays

Rest – Menu € 29 – Carte € 28/69 G 17

◆ Hams and sausages hung from the ceiling, chequered tablecloths, tightly packed tables, rough-and-ready cuisine with specialities from Lyon, and a warm ambiance - grouches, stay away!

Astier
VISA MC

44 r. J.-P. Timbaud Ⓜ *Parmentier – ✆ 01 43 57 16 35*
– restaurant.astier@wanadoo.fr G 18

Rest – *(pre-book)* Menu (€ 20), € 26 (lunch)/30

◆ A characteristic French bistro with a friendly but noisy atmosphere and busy service. Daily specials chalked on a board. Extensive wine list.

Villaret
VISA MC AE

13 r. Ternaux Ⓜ *Parmentier – ✆ 01 43 57 75 56*
– Closed August, 24 December-2 January, Saturday lunch and Sunday

Rest – Menu (€ 22), € 27/50 (dinner) – Carte € 33/49 H 18

◆ This simple bistro has hit on a winning formula - a friendly atmosphere, creative dishes, and a fine selection of Burgundy and Côtes du Rhône wines.

S. Sauvignier/MICHELIN

Bastille, Bercy, Gare de Lyon

12e arrondissement

✉ **75012**

Paris Bercy Pullman

rm, VISA

1 r. Libourne Ⓜ *Cour St-Emilion – ✆ 01 44 67 34 00 – h2192@accor.com – Fax 01 44 67 34 01* NP 20

386 rm – 🚹€ 230/460 🚹🚹€ 230/460, ☕ € 26 – 10 suites

Rest *Café Ké* – *(closed 4-25 August, 22-29 December, Saturday and Sunday)* Menu (€ 29), € 36 – Carte € 49/81

♦ A beautiful glass façade, contemporary interior in shades of brown, beige and blue, and modern facilities. Some of the rooms enjoy views across Paris. The stylish Café Ké is a pleasant option in the Bercy village; modern cuisine.

Novotel Gare de Lyon

rm, VISA AE

2 r. Hector Malot Ⓜ *Gare de Lyon – ✆ 01 44 67 60 00 – h1735@accor.com – Fax 01 44 67 60 60* L 18

253 rm – 🚹€ 140/250 🚹🚹€ 150/260, ☕ € 16

Rest – Carte € 20/43

♦ This modern hotel overlooking a tranquil square offers comfortable, typical Novotel-style guestrooms; those on the sixth floor have a terrace. 24-hour swimming pool and well-designed children's area. Brasserie style restaurant (modern decor, benches, bay windows) and traditional fare.

Novotel Bercy

rm, VISA AE

85 r. Bercy Ⓜ *Bercy – ✆ 01 43 42 30 00 – h0935@accor.com – Fax 01 43 45 30 60* M 19

151 rm – 🚹€ 135/250 🚹🚹€ 135/270, ☕ € 15

Rest – Carte € 24/45

♦ The bright rooms in this Novotel are decorated in the chain's new "Novation" style. The nearby Parc de Bercy occupies the site of an old wine depot. Dining room/veranda and popular outdoor terrace in summertime.

Mercure Gare de Lyon without rest

VISA AE

2 pl. Louis Armand Ⓜ *Gare de Lyon – ✆ 01 43 44 84 84 – h2217@accor.com – Fax 01 43 47 41 94* L 18

315 rm – 🚹€ 89/250 🚹🚹€ 99/265, ☕ € 15

♦ The modern architecture of this hotel contrasts with the nearby belfry of the Gare de Lyon. The bedrooms are furnished in ceruse wood and have the benefit of good sound-proofing. Wine bar.

Paris Bastille without rest

VISA AE

67 r. Lyon Ⓜ *Bastille – ✆ 01 40 01 07 17 – infosbastille@wanadoo.fr – Fax 01 40 01 07 27* K 18

37 rm – 🚹€ 165/240 🚹🚹€ 175/240, ☕ € 12

♦ Up-to-date comfort, modern furnishings and carefully chosen colour schemes characterise the rooms in this hotel facing the Opéra.

Claret

rest, VISA AE

44 bd Bercy Ⓜ *Bercy – ✆ 01 46 28 41 31 – reservation@hotel-claret.com – Fax 01 49 28 09 29* M 19

52 rm – 🚹€ 95/115 🚹🚹€ 105/149, ☕ € 10 – ½ P € 93/115

Rest – Menu (€ 12), € 19/26 – Carte € 22/38

♦ This former coaching inn is one of the vestiges of Bercy in the olden days. The cosy rooms have retained their exposed beams. Dining room in pretty ochre and terracotta colours, serving bistro dishes and Lyon specialities.

Terminus Lyon without rest
19 bd Diderot Ⓜ Gare de Lyon – ✆ 01 56 95 00 00 – info@hotelterminuslyon.com – Fax 01 43 44 09 00 L 18
60 rm – †€ 82/124 ††€ 114/124, ☕ € 10
◆ Opposite the Gare de Lyon, this well maintained hotel has plainly furnished rooms. Larger rooms overlooking the road and quieter ones overlook the courtyard. Room service possible.

Pavillon Bercy Gare de Lyon without rest
209 r. Charenton Ⓜ Dugommier – ✆ 01 43 40 80 30 – bercy@leshotelsdeparis.com – Fax 01 43 40 81 30 M 20
48 rm – †€ 220 ††€ 230, ☕ € 9
◆ This modern corner building stands next to the métro, a stone's throw from the town hall of the 12th arrondissement. Small, bright and functional rooms with light wood furniture.

L'Oulette
15 pl. Lachambeaudie Ⓜ Cour St-Emilion – ✆ 01 40 02 02 12 – info@l-oulette.com – Fax 01 40 02 04 77 – Closed Saturday and Sunday N 20
Rest – Menu € 45/90 bi – Carte € 52/79
◆ In the revived Bercy quarter, this firmly contemporary restaurant offers an inventive cuisine with southwestern touches. Sheltered terrace behind the thuya trees.

Au Trou Gascon
40 r. Taine Ⓜ Daumesnil – ✆ 01 43 44 34 26 – trougascon@orange.fr – Fax 01 43 07 80 55 – Closed August, Saturday and Sunday M 21
Rest – Menu € 36 (lunch)/50 (dinner) – Carte € 52/60
Spec. Chipirons cuits à la plaque (summer). Lièvre à la mode d'Aquitaine (autumn). Poire pochée au miel d'arbousier, baba punché.
◆ The decor of this old 1900 bistro combines period mouldings, designer furniture and grey hues. On the menu: Landes and Chalosse produce and seafood southwestern wines.

Le Janissaire
22 allée Vivaldi Ⓜ Daumesnil – ✆ 01 43 40 37 37 – karamanmus@hotmail.com – Fax 01 43 40 38 39 – Closed Saturday lunchtime and Sunday M 20
Rest – Menu (€ 13), € 23/42 – Carte € 21/40
◆ Turkish ambience and cuisine, as the sign indicates, showing an elite soldier of the Ottoman infantry. Pass the threshold of the Sublime Porte!

Ô Rebelle
24 r. Traversière Ⓜ Gare de Lyon – ✆ 01 43 40 88 98 – info@o-rebelle.fr – Fax 01 43 40 88 99 – Closed 4-26 August, 24 December-1st January, Saturday lunch and Sunday L 18
Rest – Menu € 24 (lunch)/57 – Carte € 42/62
◆ Inventive cuisine with an original combination of flavours, international wine list and a colourful Australian style decor: more globetrotter than rebel perhaps!

Jean-Pierre Frelet
25 r. Montgallet Ⓜ Montgallet – ✆ 01 43 43 76 65 – marie_rene.frelet@club-internet.fr – Closed 28-26 August, Saturday lunch and Sunday L 20
Rest – Menu (€ 19), € 27 (dinner) – Carte € 39/46
◆ This small neighbourhood restaurant has a friendly, authentic atmosphere. Minimalist decor, tightly packed tables; generous portions of seasonal cuisine.

Pataquès
40 bd Bercy Ⓜ Bercy – ✆ 01 43 07 37 75 – pataquesbercy@aol.com – Fax 01 43 07 36 64 M 19
Rest – Menu € 30 – Carte € 33/47
◆ This bistro is the Ministry of Finance's 'canteen'. Mediterranean dishes and a colourful setting take the mind off countless economic reforms.

Quincy
28 av. Ledru-Rollin Ⓜ Gare de Lyon – ✆ 01 46 28 46 76 – Fax 01 46 28 46 76 – Closed 15 August-15 September, Saturday, Sunday and Monday L 17
Rest – Carte € 44/76
◆ A warm atmosphere in this rustic bistrot serving hearty cusine which, like "Bobosse" the jovial owner, has plenty of character.

La Biche au Bois VISA MC

45 av. Ledru-Rollin Ⓜ *Gare de Lyon – ✆ 01 43 43 34 38 – Closed 20 July-20 August, 23 December-2 January, Monday lunch, Saturday and Sunday* K 18

Rest – Menu € 25 – Carte approx. € 30

◆ An unpretentious decor in the noisy and smoke-filled dining room, but the service is attentive and the traditional cuisine generously served. Game in season.

Le Lys d'Or A/C VISA MC AE

5 pl. Col-Bourgoin Ⓜ *Reuilly Diderot – ✆ 01 44 68 98 88 – Fax 01 44 68 98 80* L 19

Rest – Menu (€ 12 bi), € 22/26 – Carte € 21/40

◆ Enjoy traditional Chinese cuisine from four different regions (Szechuan, Shangai, Canton and Beijing) in this attractive restaurant. Interior garden with small streams and fountains.

La Gazzetta VISA MC AE

29 r. de Cotte Ⓜ *Ledru Rollin – ✆ 01 43 47 47 05 – team@lagazzetta.fr – Fax 01 43 47 47 17 – Closed August, Sunday and Monday* K 19

Rest – Menu (€ 14), € 19 (lunch), € 34/45 – Carte € 37/58

◆ A trendy all-in-one restaurant (restaurant, wine bar and café with foreign newspapers available) with a Mediterranean ambience. Fine southern cuisine.

L'Auberge Aveyronnaise A/C VISA MC AE

40 r. Lamé Ⓜ *Cour St-Emilion – ✆ 01 43 40 12 24 – lesaubergistes@hotmail.fr – Fax 01 43 40 12 15 – Closed 1st-15 August* N 20

Rest – Menu (€ 19), € 25 – Carte € 29/39

◆ Red and white gingham tablecloths and simply laid tables depict this modern bistro-cum-brasserie. As the name suggests, specialities from Aveyron feature prominently.

Jodhpur Palace VISA MC

42 allée Vivaldi Ⓜ *Daumesnil – ✆ 01 43 40 72 46 – jodhpur-palace@yahoo.fr – Fax 01 43 40 17 02* M 20

Rest – Menu € 16 bi (weekday lunch), € 25 € bi/36 bi – Carte € 23/45

◆ Simple, fresh and exotic decor in this Indian restaurant with friendly service and reasonably priced cuisine. Quiet terrace.

S. Sauvignier/MICHELIN

Place d'Italie, Gare d'Austerlitz, Bibliothèque Nationale de France

13e arrondissement ✉ 75013

Holiday Inn Bibliothèque de France without rest A/C VISA MC AE

21 r. Tolbiac Ⓜ *Bibliothèque F. Mitterrand – ✆ 01 45 84 61 61 – hibdf@wanadoo.fr – Fax 01 45 84 43 38* P 18

71 rm – †€ 97/187 ††€ 97/187, ☕ € 14

◆ In a busy street 20m from the métro station, this hotel offers comfortable, well-kept rooms with double glazing. Simple dishes available in the evening.

Mercure Place d'Italie without rest A/C VISA MC AE

25 bd Blanqui Ⓜ *Place d'Italie – ✆ 01 45 80 82 23 – h1191@accor.com – Fax 01 45 81 45 84* P 15

50 rm – †€ 155/215 ††€ 160/240, ☕ € 14

◆ This hotel, near the Manufacture des Gobelins tapestry museum, offers warm, well-soundproofed and functional rooms.

Demeure without rest
51 bd St-Marcel Ⓜ Les Gobelins – ✆ 01 43 37 81 25 – la_demeure@netcourrier.com – Fax 01 45 87 05 03 M 16
37 rm – †€ 165 ††€ 203, ☕ € 13 – 6 suites
◆ An attentive welcome awaits guests at this family-run establishment. Modern rooms, cosy sitting room and appetising breakfast buffet. Lovely collection of old Paris photos.

Résidence Vert Galant without rest
43 r. Croulebarbe Ⓜ Les Gobelins – ✆ 01 44 08 83 50 – hotel.vert.galant@gmail.com – Fax 01 44 08 83 69 N 15
15 rm – †€ 90/170 ††€ 90/170, ☕ € 8
◆ In a quiet setting, a welcoming residence with charming rooms, all looking out onto a private garden planted with vines, where breakfast is served in summer.

La Manufacture without rest
8 r. Philippe-de-Champagne Ⓜ Place d'Italie – ✆ 01 45 35 45 25 – reservation@hotel-la-manufacture.com – Fax 01 45 35 45 40 N 16
56 rm – †€ 145/165 ††€ 145/230, ☕ € 13
◆ Friendly service and elegant decor are the main features of this well-maintained hotel. Guestrooms somewhat on the small side. Breakfast room with a Provençal atmosphere.

Touring Hôtel Magendie without rest
2 r. Magendie Ⓜ Corvisart – ✆ 01 43 36 13 61 – magendie@vvf-vacances.fr – Fax 01 43 36 47 48 N 14
112 rm – †€ 68/77 ††€ 80/88, ☕ € 7
◆ Situated in a quiet residential street, this hotel has small, well-soundproofed and functional rooms. The modern decor is minimalist in style.

Arts without rest
8 r. Coypel Ⓜ Place d'Italie – ✆ 01 47 07 76 32 – arts@escapade-paris.com – Fax 01 43 31 18 09 N 16
37 rm – †€ 54/80 ††€ 64/90, ☕ € 7
◆ Situated in the Gobelins district, this popular hotel is conveniently located between Place d'Italie and Rue Mouffetard. Renovated rooms, reasonably priced by Paris standards.

XX **Chez Jacky**
109 r. du Dessous-des-Berges Ⓜ Bibliothèque F. Mitterrand – ✆ 01 45 83 71 55 – contact@chezjacky.fr – Fax 01 45 86 57 73 – Closed August, 24 December-5 January, Saturday, Sunday and public holidays P 18
Rest – Menu € 43 bi – Carte € 47/79
◆ Near the Mitterrand Library, this restaurant affirms its status as a very French provincial tavern. Traditional cuisine served graciously.

XX **Petit Marguery**
9 bd Port-Royal Ⓜ Les Gobelins – ✆ 01 43 31 58 59 – marguery@wanadoo.fr – Fax 01 43 36 73 34 – Closed Sunday and Monday M 15
Rest – Menu € 23 (lunch), € 30/35
◆ This restaurant, with a friendly atmosphere, offers pleasant 1940s-style dining rooms. The typical bistro type dishes are popular with a wide following of regulars.

X **L'Avant Goût**
26 r. Bobillot Ⓜ Place d'Italie – ✆ 01 53 80 24 00 – Fax 01 53 80 00 77 – Closed 3-26 August, Sunday and Monday P 15
Rest – *(number of covers limited, pre-book)* Menu € 31/41 – Carte € 36/48
◆ This modern bistro is often crowded. The reasons for its success? How about dishes made from market produce, a good wine list and a relaxed atmosphere.

X **Auberge Etchegorry**
41 r. Croulebarbe Ⓜ Les Gobelins – ✆ 01 44 08 83 51 – Fax 01 44 08 83 69 – Closed Sunday and Monday N 15
Rest – Menu € 22 bi (lunch)/55 bi – Carte € 36/58
◆ Read all about the history of this friendly Basque restaurant and its district in the restaurant brochure. Sausages, hams, Espelette peppers and garlic hang from the ceiling.

L'Ourcine
92 r. Broca Ⓜ Les Gobelins – ☎ 01 47 07 13 65 – Fax 01 47 07 18 48 – Closed Sunday and Monday N14
Rest – Menu (€ 22), € 30
◆ Simple, modern decor in this restaurant with a friendly atmosphere. Inspired, seasonal cuisine chalked up on a blackboard.

Sukhothaï
12 r. Père Guérin Ⓜ Place d'Italie – ☎ 01 45 81 55 88 – Closed 4-24 August, Monday lunch and Sunday P 15
Rest – Menu (€ 11,50 bi), € 21/25 – Carte € 20/30
◆ The name is a reminder of the former capital of a 13-14C Thai kingdom. Chinese and Thai food served under the watchful eye of Buddha (handmade sculptures).

J.-P. Clapham/MICEHLIN

Montparnasse, Denfert-Rochereau

14e arrondissement ✉ 75014

Méridien Montparnasse rm, rest,
19 r. Cdt Mouchotte Ⓜ Montparnasse Bienvenüe – ☎ 01 44 36 44 36 – meridien.montparnasse@lemeridien.com – Fax 01 44 36 49 00 M 11
918 rm – €145/329 €145/329, ☕ € 26 – 35 suites
Rest *Montparnasse'25* – see restaurant listing
Rest *Justine* – ☎ *01 44 36 44 00* – Menu € 42/46 – Carte € 38/49
◆ The spacious rooms in this glass and concrete building have been redone in a modern spirit with Art Deco details. Beautiful view of the capital from the top floors. At Justine's, winter garden decor, green terrace and buffet menus.

Concorde Montparnasse rm,
40 r. Cdt Mouchotte Ⓜ Gaîté – ☎ 01 56 54 84 00 – montparnasse@concorde-hotels.com – Fax 01 56 54 84 84 M 11
354 rm – €140/350 €140/350, ☕ € 20
Rest – buffet Menu € 34 – Carte € 35/43
◆ This hotel, on Place de Catalogne, was treated to a facelift recently. Calm and refined rooms, interior garden, fitness centre and bar. This restaurant, with exotic wood and coloured fabrics, offers buffets and à la carte dishes.

Aiglon without rest
232 bd Raspail Ⓜ Raspail – ☎ 01 43 20 82 42 – aiglon@espritfrance.com – Fax 01 43 20 98 72 M 12
36 rm – €124/189 €124/189, ☕ € 11 – 10 suites
◆ This one time home to Giacometti and Bunuel is gradually being modernised. Bright colours and stylish details (mosaic bathrooms, photos) set the scene for the new decor.

Villa Royale Montsouris without rest
144 r. Tombe-Issoire Ⓜ Porte d'Orléans – ☎ 01 56 53 89 89 – montsouris@leshotelsdeparis.com – Fax 01 56 53 89 80 R 12
36 rm – €85/230 €95/370, ☕ € 18
◆ A change of atmosphere is guaranteed for guests in this hotel, astutely decorated in Andalusian and Moorish style. Rooms are small but very cosy, named after Moroccan towns.

Lenox Montparnasse without rest
15 r. Delambre Ⓜ *Vavin – ✆ 01 43 35 34 50 – hotel@lenoxmontparnasse.com – Fax 01 43 20 46 64* M 12
52 rm – €165/310 €165/310, ☕ €16
◆ Establishment noted for its elegance: plush, low-key bar and sitting rooms, personalised stylish rooms, pleasant suites on the sixth floor.

Nouvel Orléans without rest
25 av. Gén. Leclerc Ⓜ *Mouton Duvernet – ✆ 01 43 27 80 20 – nouvelorleans@aol.com – Fax 01 43 35 36 57* P 12
46 rm – €90/155 €90/190, ☕ €10
◆ The name comes from the Porte d'Orléans, 800m away. In this entirely renovated hotel, modern furniture and warm colourful materials decorate the rooms.

Mercure Raspail Montparnasse without rest
207 bd Raspail Ⓜ *Vavin – ✆ 01 43 20 62 94 – h0351@accor.com – Fax 01 43 27 39 69* M 12
63 rm – €150/210 €155/210, ☕ €14
◆ Enjoy an overnight stay in this Haussmann building near the famous Montparnasse brasseries. Modern rooms with contemporary, light wood furniture, nearly all refurbished.

Delambre without rest
35 r. Delambre Ⓜ *Edgar Quinet – ✆ 01 43 20 66 31 – delambre@club-internet.fr – Fax 01 45 38 91 76* M 12
30 rm – €85/115 €85/160, ☕ €9
◆ André Breton stayed in this hotel located in a quiet street close to Montparnasse railway station. The decor is modern, the rooms simple but bright, and many are spacious.

Midi without rest
4 av. René Coty Ⓜ *Denfert Rochereau – ✆ 01 43 27 23 25 – info@midi-hotel-paris.com – Fax 01 43 21 24 58* N 13
45 rm – €80/98 €98/158, ☕ €12
◆ Near Place Denfert Rochereau find soundproofed rooms, some with hydromassage baths, and organic breakfasts: what more could you want!

Châtillon without rest
11 square Châtillon Ⓜ *Porte d'Orléans – ✆ 01 45 42 31 17 – chatillon.hotel@wanadoo.fr – Fax 01 45 42 72 09* P 11
31 rm – €75 €85/130, ☕ €7
◆ A place frequented by regulars who appreciate its peace and quiet. Spacious well-maintained guestrooms overlooking a square at the end of a cul-de-sac. Friendly atmosphere.

De la Paix without rest
225 bd Raspail Ⓜ *Raspail – ✆ 01 43 20 35 82 – resa@hoteldelapaix.com – Fax 01 43 35 32 63* M 12
39 rm – €76/102 €81/114, ☕ €8,50
◆ The hotel is furnished in a 1970s style offering comfortable, well-kept rooms, progressively redecorated in a modern style. Delightful welcome.

Apollon Montparnasse without rest
91 r. Ouest Ⓜ *Pernety – ✆ 01 43 95 62 00 – apollonm@wanadoo.fr – Fax 01 43 95 62 10* N 10-11
33 rm – €75/89 €86/109, ☕ €8,50
◆ Gradually renovated family hotel near the station. Tastefully decorated rooms, a smiling welcome, and a quiet location in a side street.

Cécil without rest
47 r. Beaunier Ⓜ *Porte d'Orléans – ✆ 01 45 40 93 53 – cecil-hotel@wanadoo.fr – Fax 01 45 40 43 26* R 12
25 rm – €76 €98, ☕ €9
◆ A hotel full of charm in a quiet street near Montsouris park. Furniture and hand picked objects lend each room its own personality. Lounge-library and small garden.

Montparnasse'25 – Hôtel Méridien Montparnasse
19 r. Cdt Mouchotte Ⓜ Montparnasse Bienvenüe – ✆ 01 44 36 44 25 – meridien.montparnasse@lemeridien.com – Fax 01 44 36 49 03 – Closed 28 April-4 May, 14 July-31 August, 22 December-6 January, Saturday, Sunday and public holidays M 25
Rest – Menu € 49 (lunch)/110 (dinner) – Carte € 93/109
Spec. Saint-Jaques dorées à la plancha (season). Saint-Pierre à l'huile de truffe aux blanc de poireaux. Canard laqué aux fruits tamarin.
◆ The modern setting based around black lacquer may surprise but this restaurant turns out to be comfortable and warm. Contemporary cuisine, superb cheese boards.

Le Dôme
108 bd Montparnasse Ⓜ Vavin – ✆ 01 43 35 25 81 – Fax 01 42 79 01 19 – Closed Sunday and Monday in July-August LM 12
Rest – Carte € 52/123
◆ A temple of literary and artistic bohemian life in the Twenties has been turned into a stylish and trendy Left-Bank brasserie, with its Art Deco style intact. Fish and seafood.

Le Duc
243 bd Raspail Ⓜ Raspail – ✆ 01 43 20 96 30 – Fax 01 43 20 46 73 – Closed 1st-10 March, 2-24 August, 24 December-2 January, Saturday lunch, Sunday and Monday M 12
Rest – Menu € 46 (lunch) – Carte € 48/144
◆ Fish and seafood served amid a yacht cabin decor of mahogany panelling, wall lights with a marine theme and gleaming copperware.

Pavillon Montsouris
20 r. Gazan Ⓜ Cité Universitaire – ✆ 01 43 13 29 00 – Fax 01 43 13 29 02 – Closed February half-term holidays and Sunday dinner from mid September to Easter
Rest – Menu € 40 – Carte € 56/87 R 14
◆ This Belle Époque lodge in Montsouris Park offers a calm country atmosphere in the centre of Paris. Pretty glass roof, colonial type decoration and lush green terrace.

Maison Courtine (Yves Charles)
157 av. du Maine Ⓜ Mouton Duvernet – ✆ 01 45 43 08 04 – yves.charles@wanadoo.fr – Fax 01 45 45 91 35 – Closed 2 August-1st September, 23 December-2 January, Monday lunch, Saturday lunch and Sunday N 11
Rest – Menu € 39/44
Spec. Crémeux froid d'araignée de mer et croûtons au cumin. Petites escalopes de foie gras de canard poêlées aux raisins. Médaillon de veau de lait et lentilles blondes de la Planèze.
◆ Here one can enjoy a culinary Tour de France; the brightly-coloured interiors are modern and the furnishing is in the Louis-Philippe style. An assiduously frequented establishment.

La Coupole
102 bd Montparnasse Ⓜ Vavin – ✆ 01 43 20 14 20 – jtosi@groupeflo.fr – Fax 01 43 35 46 14 L 12
Rest – Menu € 31 – Carte € 32/130
◆ The spirit of Montparnasse lives on in this immense Art Deco brasserie, first opened in 1927. The 32 pillars were decorated by artists of the period. A lively atmosphere.

Vin et Marée
108 av. Maine Ⓜ Gaîté – ✆ 01 43 20 29 50 – vmmaine@vin-et-maree.com – Fax 01 43 27 84 11 N 11
Rest – Menu (€ 21) – Carte € 32/58
◆ Fish and seafood, the restaurant's specialities, are chalked up every day on the slate, depending on Neptune's humour. Dining rooms decorated in nautical style.

Monsieur Lapin
11 r. R. Losserand Ⓜ Gaîté – ✆ 01 43 20 21 39 – franck.enee@wanadoo.fr – Fax 01 43 21 84 86 – Closed August, Saturday lunch, Sunday lunch and Monday N 11
Rest – *(number of covers limited, pre-book)* Menu € 35/45 – Carte € 47/65
◆ Just like the March Hare in Alice in Wonderland, Mr. Rabbit is everywhere: in the decor of the dining room and on a menu which makes good use of a wide choice of sauces.

Les Vendanges

40 r. Friant Ⓜ Porte d'Orléans – ✆ 01 45 39 59 98 – guy.tardif@wanadoo.fr – Fax 01 45 39 74 13 – Closed 4-31 August, 23 December-1st January, Saturday except dinner from November to January and Sunday R 11

Rest – Menu (€ 25), € 35

◆ The façade, decorated with clusters of grapes, hints at what is to come - a superb wine cellar (vintage clarets). Updated cuisine redolent of southwest France.

Millésimes 62

13 pl. Catalogne Ⓜ Gaîté – ✆ 01 43 35 34 35 – millesime62@wanadoo.fr – Fax 01 43 20 26 21 – Closed 2-18 August, Saturday lunch and Sunday M 11

Rest – Menu (€ 20), € 25/28

◆ Appealing restaurant with modern decor, near the great hotels and theatres of the Montparnasse area. Enjoy its tasty dishes, made with market produce, and at friendly prices.

La Régalade

49 av. J. Moulin Ⓜ Porte d'Orléans – ✆ 01 45 45 68 58 – la_regalade@yahoo.fr – Fax 01 45 40 96 74 – Closed 25 July-20 August, 1st-10 January, Monday lunch, Saturday and Sunday R 11

Rest – *(pre-book)* Menu € 32

◆ A welcoming smile, tasty country cuisine and a simple decor are the assets of this small bistro near the Porte de Châtillon.

La Cerisaie

70 bd E. Quinet Ⓜ Edgar Quinet – ✆ 01 43 20 98 98 – Fax 01 43 20 98 98 – Closed 1st-11 May, 28 July-25 August, 20 December – 4 January, Saturday and Sunday N 13

Rest – *(pre-book)* Menu (€ 23), € 32/39

◆ A tiny restaurant in the heart of the Breton quarter. Every day, the owner chalks up the carefully prepared dishes of the southwest on a blackboard.

Les Petites Sorcières

12 r. Liancourt Ⓜ Denfert Rochereau – ✆ 01 43 21 95 68 – Fax 01 43 21 95 68 – Closed 12 July-16 August and Sunday N 12

Rest – *(dinner only)* Carte € 32/39

◆ A "bewitching" bistro full of gourmet charms. Prepare to be enchanted!

À La Bonne Table

42 r. Friant Ⓜ Porte d'Orléans – ✆ 01 45 39 74 91 – Fax 01 45 43 66 92 – Closed 13 July-3 August, 21 December-4 January, Saturday lunch and Sunday R 11

Rest – Menu € 26 (lunch)/30 – Carte € 29/46

◆ The chef, originally from Japan, prepares traditional French cuisine enhanced with Japanese flair. Comfortable, long dining room in a 1940s style.

L'Amuse Bouche

186 r. Château Ⓜ Mouton Duvernet – ✆ 01 43 35 31 61 – Closed 1st-20 August, Sunday and Monday N 11

Rest – Menu (€ 21 bi), € 32

◆ This redecorated restaurant (orange and green walls, rustic furniture) has a friendly, lively atmosphere. Up-to-date cuisine using market fresh produce.

Bistrot du Dôme

1 r. Delambre Ⓜ Vavin – ✆ 01 43 35 32 00 – Closed August, Sunday and Monday M 12

Rest – Carte € 39/51

◆ The wing of the Dôme also specialises in fish and seafood. A relaxed atmosphere in the large dining room, the ceiling of which is decorated with vine leaves.

L'Ordonnance

51 r. Hallé Ⓜ Mouton Duvernet – ✆ 01 43 27 55 85 – lestrapade2@wanadoo.fr – Fax 01 43 20 64 72 – Closed August, Christmas holidays, Saturday except dinner in Winter and Sunday P 12

Rest – Menu (€ 24), € 30

◆ A stone's throw from Place Michel Audiard, this warm, modern establishment serves tasty traditional cuisine in a good-humoured atmosphere.

L'Atelier d'Antan
9 r. L.-Robert Ⓜ *Denfert-Rochereau – ✆ 01 43 21 36 19 – Closed August, Saturday lunch and Sunday* N12
Rest – Menu (€ 15), € 18 (weekday lunch) – Carte € 32/51
◆ The bistro style, smiling staff and friendly atmosphere are well suited to the tasty traditional cuisine. A particularly pleasant establishment.

Severo
8 r. Plantes Ⓜ *Mouton Duvernet – ✆ 01 45 40 40 91 – Closed 27 April-4 May, 26 July-24 August, 20-28 December, Saturday and Sunday* N 11
Rest – Carte € 27/54
◆ Products from Auvergne (meat, charcuterie) take centre stage on the daily slate menu of this friendly bistro. The wine list is enticingly eclectic.

H. Le Gac/MICHELIN

Porte de Versailles, Vaugirard, Beaugrenelle

15e arrondissement ✉ 75015

Pullman Rive Gauche rm, rest,
8 r. L. Armand Ⓜ *Balard – ✆ 01 40 60 30 30 – h0572@accor.com – Fax 01 40 60 30 00* N 5
606 rm – €320/390 €320/390, € 25 – 12 suites
Rest *Brasserie* – *✆ 01 40 60 33 77* – Menu (€ 22), € 27 (weekday lunch) – Carte € 37/69
◆ Opposite the heliport, this hotel offers soundproofed rooms, some of which have been refurbished in an elegantly modern style. The upper floors have a lovely view over western Paris. Brasserie with a setting from the Roaring Twenties: Mosaics, cupola, benches, etc..

Novotel Tour Eiffel rm,
61 quai de Grenelle Ⓜ *Charles Michels – ✆ 01 40 58 20 00 – h3546@accor.com – Fax 01 40 58 24 44* K 6
752 rm – €260/450 €290/450, € 20 – 12 suites
Rest *Benkay* – see restaurant listing
Rest *Tour Eiffel Café* – *✆ 01 40 58 20 75* – Menu (€ 25), € 33/42 bi – Carte € 29/46
◆ A hotel overlooking the Seine with comfortable modern rooms (wood, light shades), most of which have views of the river. High-tech conference centre. A pleasant, minimalist decor, modern cuisine and a delicatessen area at the Café Lenôtre.

Mercure Suffren Tour Eiffel rm, rm,
20 r. Jean Rey Ⓜ *Bir-Hakeim – ✆ 01 45 78 50 00 – h2175@accor.com – Fax 01 45 78 91 42* J 7
405 rm – €150/310 €160/310, € 19 – **Rest** – Carte € 27/43
◆ A thorough, careful renovation has been carried out in this perfectly soundproofed hotel, whose new decor sports a 'nature and garden' theme. Some rooms offer a view of the Eiffel Tower. The dining room opens onto a pleasant terrace surrounded by trees and greenery.

Novotel Vaugirard rm,
257 r. Vaugirard Ⓜ *Vaugirard – ✆ 01 40 45 10 00 – h1978@accor.com – Fax 01 40 45 10 10* M 9
187 rm – €145/220 €145/220, € 15 – **Rest** – Menu € 20/25 – Carte € 24/46
◆ A huge hotel in the heart of the city's 15th arrondissement with large, modern and double-glazed rooms. The Novotel Café is characterised by contemporary decor, a summer terrace surrounded by greenery, non-stop service and daily grilled specials.

Océania without rest

52 r. Oradour sur Glane Ⓜ *Porte de Versailles – ✆ 01 56 09 09 09 – oceania.paris@oceaniahotels.com – Fax 01 56 09 09 19* 15 P 6

232 rm – †€ 160/270 ††€ 175/285, ☕ € 15 – 18 suites

♦ Modern comfort in an elegant, contemporary setting. This new hotel offers well-equipped bedrooms, a relaxation centre and an exotic terrace-garden.

Mercure Porte de Versailles without rest

69 bd Victor Ⓜ *Porte de Versailles – ✆ 01 44 19 03 03 – h1131@accor.com – Fax 01 48 28 22 11* N 7

91 rm – †€ 115/300 ††€ 130/315, ☕ € 16 – 7 suites

♦ A hotel in a 1970s building opposite the Parc des Expositions, built on the site of the old Gordini car factory. Simply furnished, functional rooms.

Novotel Gare Montparnasse

17 r. Cotentin Ⓜ *Montparnasse Bienvenüe – ✆ 01 53 91 23 75 – h5060@accor.com – Fax 01 53 91 23 76* M 10

197 rm – †€ 220/280 ††€ 220/280, ☕ € 16 – 2 suites – **Rest** – Menu (€ 21 bi) – Carte € 25/45

♦ A brand-new hotel near the railway station with guestrooms decorated in a minimalist, contemporary style (high-tech facilities and good soundproofing). Generous buffet breakfast.

Holiday Inn Montparnasse without rest

10 r. Gager Gabillot Ⓜ *Vaugirard – ✆ 01 44 19 29 29 – reservations@hiparis-montparnasse.com – Fax 01 44 19 29 39* M 9

60 rm – †€ 72/350 ††€ 72/370, ☕ € 13

♦ A modern building located in a quiet street. Spacious lobby and contemporary lounge with a glass pyramid roof. Identical, functional rooms.

Eiffel Cambronne without rest

46 r. Croix-Nivert Ⓜ *Av. Emile Zola – ✆ 01 56 58 56 78 – hotel@eiffefcambronne.com – Fax 01 56 58 56 79* L 8

31 rm – †€ 119/189 ††€ 119/189, ☕ € 13

♦ Comfy armchairs and an open fire add to the warm ambience of the hotel's lounge-lobby. Average-sized rooms; those to the rear are quieter. Copious breakfast served in the inner courtyard.

Mercure Paris XV without rest

6 r. St-Lambert Ⓜ *Boucicaut – ✆ 01 45 58 61 00 – h0903@accor.com – Fax 01 45 54 10 43* M 7

56 rm – †€ 115/145 ††€ 125/150, ☕ € 12

♦ A hotel located 800m from the Porte de Versailles. The reception, lounges and comfortable, well-kept rooms are in contemporary style.

Alizé Grenelle without rest

87 av. É. Zola Ⓜ *Charles Michels – ✆ 01 45 78 08 22 – info@alizeparis.com – Fax 01 40 59 03 06* L 7

50 rm – †€ 90/134 ††€ 94/135, ☕ € 11,50

♦ Behind the 1930s brick façade is a friendly, well-maintained hotel with practical, soundproofed rooms, all of which follow a similar design.

Beaugrenelle St-Charles without rest

82 r. St-Charles Ⓜ *Charles Michels – ✆ 01 45 78 61 63 – info@beaugrenelleparis.com – Fax 01 45 79 04 38* K 7

49 rm – †€ 82/125 ††€ 89/126, ☕ € 11,50

♦ Hotel near the St-Charles metro station and Beaugrenelle shopping centre with well-maintained, soundproofed rooms, some of which occupy a Tuscan-style villa overlooking an inner courtyard.

Aberotel without rest

24 r. Blomet Ⓜ *Volontaires – ✆ 01 40 61 70 50 – aberotel@wanadoo.fr – Fax 01 40 61 08 31* L 9

28 rm – †€ 60/113 ††€ 70/136, ☕ € 8

♦ A popular hotel with stylish rooms and an inner courtyard for summer breakfasts. It has a pleasant lounge adorned with paintings on wood of playing cards.

XXX **Benkay** – Hôtel Novotel Tour Eiffel
61 quai de Grenelle Ⓜ *Bir-Hakeim – ✆ 01 40 58 21 26 – h3546@accor.com – Fax 01 40 58 21 30* K 6
Rest – Menu € 30 (lunch), € 75/125 – Carte € 42/131
◆ On the top floor of a small building, the restaurant commands a fine view of the Seine. A tasteful decor of marble and wood and a sushi and teppanyaki counter.

XX **Le Quinzième Cuisine Attitude**
14 r. Cauchy Ⓜ *Javel – ✆ 01 45 54 43 43 – resa@lequinzieme.com – Fax 01 45 57 22 96 – Closed 10-20 August, Monday lunch, Saturday lunch and Sunday* L 5
Rest – Menu € 40 (weekday lunch), € 105/150 – Carte € 46/100
◆ A trendy setting, a "chef's table" with a view of the kitchen, and delicious modern cuisine; a seductive recipe from Cyril Lignac, star of the TV cookery show "Oui Chef!".

XX **La Gauloise**
59 av. La Motte-Picquet Ⓜ *La Motte Picquet Grenelle – ✆ 01 47 34 11 64 – Fax 01 40 61 09 70* K 8
Rest – brasserie Menu (€ 25) – Carte € 33/52
◆ This 1900 brasserie must have seen many celebrities pass through, judging from the signed photos on the walls. A pleasant, kerbside terrace.

XX **Thierry Burlot "Le Quinze"**
8 r. Nicolas Charlet Ⓜ *Pasteur – ✆ 01 42 19 08 59 – Fax 01 45 67 09 13 – Closed 15 July-15 August, 22-28 December, Saturday and Sunday* L 10
Rest – Menu (€ 29), € 35/59 – Carte € 40/52
◆ Elegant setting adorned with photographs taken by the chef-patron. Inventive, elegant, and seasonally based cuisine.

XX **Caroubier**
82 bd Lefebvre Ⓜ *Porte de Vanves – ✆ 01 40 43 16 12 – Fax 01 40 43 16 12 – Closed 19 July-25 August and Monday* P 8
Rest – Menu € 19 (weekday lunch)/28 – Carte € 28/47
◆ Modern decor enhanced with touches of the oriental. A family atmosphere and warm welcome presage generous helpings of sun-gorged Moroccan cuisine.

XX **Fontanarosa**
28 bd Garibaldi Ⓜ *Cambronne – ✆ 01 45 66 97 84 – contact@fontanarosa-ristorante.eu – Fax 01 47 83 96 30* L 9
Rest – Menu (€ 17), € 21 (weekday lunch)/30 – Carte € 32/69
◆ This authentic trattoria spirits you far away from the bustle of Paris. Enjoy good Italian cuisine with a focus on Sardinian specialities. Outdoor terrace in summer.

XX **La Dînée**
85 r. Leblanc Ⓜ *Balard – ✆ 01 45 54 20 49 – contact@restaurant-ladinee.com – Fax 01 40 60 73 76 – Closed Saturday and Sunday* M 5
Rest – Menu € 36/39
◆ Up-to-the-minute dining room decorated with contemporary pictures and offering fashionable cuisine. Grill menu served in the adjoining bistro.

XX **L'Épopée**
89 av. É. Zola Ⓜ *Charles Michels – ✆ 01 45 77 71 37 – Fax 01 45 77 71 37 – Closed 26 July-20 August, 24 December-3 January, Saturday lunch and Sunday* L 7
Rest – Menu (€ 29), € 35
◆ Despite the grandeur of its name (The Epic), this is a small, convivial restaurant. Regulars keep coming back for its excellent wine list and traditional cuisine.

XX **Erawan**
76 r. Fédération Ⓜ *La Motte Picquet Grenelle – ✆ 01 47 83 55 67 – Fax 01 47 34 85 98 – Closed 5-25 August and Sunday* K 8
Rest – Menu € 13,50 bi (weekday lunch), € 30/45 – Carte € 20/29
◆ Carved wood, pastel shades and Asian curios set the scene for this restrained restaurant. Delicious Thai cuisine and staff in national costume; delightful welcome.

Stéphane Martin

67 r. Entrepreneurs Ⓜ *Charles Michels – ☎ 01 45 79 03 31 – resto.stephanemartin@free.fr – Fax 01 45 79 44 69 – Closed 3 weeks in August, Christmas and Easter holidays, Sunday and Monday* L 7

Rest – Menu (€ 17), € 22 (weekday lunch)/35 – Carte € 38/49

◆ This inviting restaurant with a library theme (mural of bookshelves), serves up-to-date market fresh cuisine.

Bistro d'Hubert

41 bd Pasteur Ⓜ *Pasteur – ☎ 01 47 34 15 50 – message@bistrodhubert.com – Fax 01 45 67 03 09 – Closed Monday lunch, Saturday lunch, Sunday and public holidays* L 10

Rest – Menu € 34 – Carte € 38/79

◆ Jars and bottles on the shelves, gingham tablecloths, a direct view of the kitchens and gleaming copperware - the decor of this bistro is reminiscent of a Landes farmhouse.

Yanasé

75 r. Vasco-de-Gamma Ⓜ *Lourmel – ☎ 01 42 50 07 20 – yanase@orange.fr – Fax 01 42 50 07 90 – Closed 5-20 August, Saturday lunch and Sunday* N 6

Rest – Menu € 19 bi (weekday lunch), € 38/58

◆ A minimalist interior in Yanasé (Japanese cedar) serving typical Japanese grilled dishes, prepared in front of diners on a charcoal-fired "robata" barbecue.

Afaria

15 r. Desnouettes Ⓜ *Convention – ☎ 01 48 56 15 36 – Fax 01 48 56 15 36 – Closed 24-30 December, 3-24 August, Sunday and Monday lunch*

Rest – Menu (€ 21), € 27 (lunch) – Carte € 30/49

◆ Find tasty, well-prepared cuisine from southwest France in this bistro inspired restaurant (striped tablecloths and large mirrors). Drinks and tapas at the bar.

Beurre Noisette

68 r. Vasco de Gama Ⓜ *Lourmel – ☎ 01 48 56 82 49 – Fax 01 48 28 59 38 – Closed 1st-24 August, 1st-7 January, Sunday and Monday* N 6

Rest – Menu (€ 20), € 24 (weekday lunch)/32 – Carte € 29/36

◆ Two contemporary-style rooms decorated in warm tones serving market-inspired cuisine (dishes chalked on a blackboard). Good choice of wines by the glass.

Le Grand Pan

20 r. Rosenwald Ⓜ *Plaisance – ☎ 01 42 50 02 50 – Fax 01 42 50 02 66 – Closed 1st-24 August, Christmas holidays, Saturday and Sunday* N 9

Rest – Menu (€ 20), € 28/32

◆ Old-fashioned Parisian bistro (copper-topped bar, wood tables and blackboards) decorated in warm shades of brown. Meat specialities (game in season) and soup starter.

Kim Anh

51 av. Emile Zola Ⓜ *Charles Michels – ☎ 01 45 79 40 96 – Fax 01 40 59 49 78 – Closed Easter holidays, 11-25 August and Monday* L 7

Rest – *(dinner only)* Menu € 37 – Carte € 43/71

◆ The restaurant is protected from the avenue by a screen of bushes. Simple setting and aromatic tasty Vietnamese cuisine.

Le Troquet

21 r. François Bonvin Ⓜ *Cambronne – ☎ 01 45 66 89 00 – Fax 01 45 66 89 83 – Closed 2-10 May, 1st-24 August, 24 December-1st January, Sunday and Monday* L 9

Rest – Menu (€ 24), € 28 (weekday lunch), € 30/40

◆ An authentic Parisian "troquet" – single set menu shown on a slate, retro-style dining hall and cuisine redolent of the local market. For locals... and others!

Le Cristal de Sel

13 r. Mademoiselle Ⓜ *Commerce – ☎ 01 42 50 35 29 – Fax 01 42 50 35 29 – Closed August, Christmas holidays, Sunday and Monday* L 8

Rest – Carte € 34/50

◆ Appetising contemporary dishes are listed on blackboards on the walls of this tasteful, bright restaurant. No set menu, but quality cuisine based on fresh produce.

X **Villa Corse** A/C VISA MC AE

164 bd Grenelle Ⓜ La Motte Picquet Grenelle – ✆ 01 53 86 70 81 – lavillacorse@wanadoo.fr – Fax 01 53 86 90 73 – Closed Sunday K 8

Rest – Menu € 25 (lunch)/60 – Carte € 44/58

◆ Each of the three charming dining rooms in this Corsican restaurant has a different atmosphere: library, lounge-bar and terrace. Flavoursome cuisine and wines from the island.

X **Le Mûrier** VISA MC

42 r. Olivier de Serres Ⓜ Convention – ✆ 01 45 32 81 88 – lepimpecmartin@yahoo.fr – Closed 11-17 August, Saturday and Sunday N 8

Rest – Menu € 24/29

◆ Pleasant restaurant near the rue de la Convention shopping area, serving traditional dishes in a dining room decorated with old posters.

X **Le Bélisaire** VISA MC

2 r. Marmontel Ⓜ Vaugirard – ✆ 01 48 28 62 24 – Fax 01 48 28 62 24 – Closed 21-27 April, 4-24 August, 22-28 December, Saturday lunch and Sunday M 8

Rest – Menu (€ 17), € 20 (weekday lunch), € 30/37

◆ This well-presented bistro has built up a strong reputation in the neighbourhood thanks to its excellent contemporary-style cuisine and quality service.

X **Le Dirigeable** VISA MC AE

37 r. d' Alleray Ⓜ Vaugirard – ✆ 01 45 32 01 54 – Closed 1st-24 August, 24-31 December, Sunday and Monday M 9

Rest – Menu (€ 19), € 22 (lunch) – Carte € 30/52

◆ Relaxed atmosphere, unpretentious setting and small traditional dishes at attractive prices: embark now for a cruise on the Dirigeable!

X **Gastroquet** VISA MC AE

10 r. Desnouettes Ⓜ Convention – ✆ 01 48 28 60 91 – Fax 01 45 33 23 70 – Closed August, 1st-10 January, Saturday dinner in summer and Sunday

Rest – Menu € 22/29 – Carte € 49/59 N 7

◆ A family-run bistro, popular with local gourmets and visitors to the Porte de Versailles exhibition centre, serving carefully-prepared traditional dishes.

X **Le Pétel** A/C VISA MC AE

4 r. Pételu Ⓜ Vaugirard – ✆ 01 45 32 58 76 – Fax 01 45 32 58 76 – Closed 25 July-15 August, Sunday and Monday L 8

Rest – Menu (€ 18), € 31

◆ This friendly neighbourhood bistro is invariably packed in the evenings. Traditional market-inspired cuisine chalked up on a blackboard.

X **Banyan** A/C VISA MC AE

24 pl. E. Pernet Ⓜ Félix Faure – ✆ 01 40 60 09 31 – lebanyan@noos.fr – Fax 01 40 60 09 20 – Closed 11-24 August L 7

Rest – Menu (€ 20), € 25 (weekday lunch), € 35/55 – Carte € 33/52

◆ Take your taste buds on holiday to this small Thai restaurant, which prepares subtly-flavoured cuisine. Pleasant modern setting and families welcome.

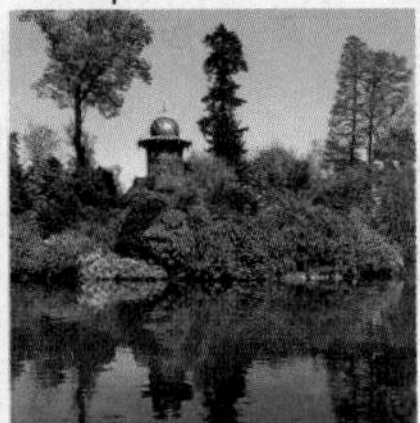
G. Targat/MICHELIN

Étoile, Trocadéro, Passy, Bois de Boulogne, Auteuil

16e arrondissement ✉ 75016 or 75116

Raphael

17 av. Kléber ✉ 75116 Ⓜ Kléber – ✆ 01 53 64 32 00 – reservation@raphael-hotel.com – Fax 01 53 64 32 01 F 7

48 rm – †€ 345/490 ††€ 345/570, ☕ € 38 – 37 suites

Rest *La Salle à Manger* – *(closed August, Saturday and Sunday)* Menu € 50 bi (lunch)/60 bi (dinner) – Carte € 63/85

Rest *Les Jardins Plein Ciel* – rest.-terrasse – ✆ *01 53 64 32 30 (open from May to September and closed Saturday lunch and Sunday)* Menu € 70 (lunch)/90 (dinner)

◆ The Raphael, built in 1925, offers a superb wood-panelled gallery, refined rooms, a rooftop terrace with a panoramic view and a trendy English bar. Superb dining room in Grand Hotel style. A lovely view of Paris and a buffet formula at this 7th floor restaurant.

St-James Paris

43 av. Bugeaud ✉ 75116 Ⓜ Porte Dauphine – ✆ 01 44 05 81 81 – contact@saint-james-paris.com – Fax 01 44 05 81 82 F 5

38 rm – †€ 380/630 ††€ 490/630, ☕ € 28 – 10 suites – **Rest** – *(closed Saturday, Sunday and public holidays) (residents only)* Menu € 50 – Carte € 67/190

◆ Beautiful private townhouse built in 1892 by Mme Thiers, in the heart of a shady garden. Majestic staircase, spacious rooms and a bar-library with the atmosphere of an English club.

Le Parc-Trocadéro

55 av. R. Poincaré ✉ 75116 Ⓜ Victor Hugo – ✆ 01 44 05 66 66 – corinne.leponner@renaissancehotels.com – Fax 01 44 05 66 00 G 6

112 rm – †€ 195/450 ††€ 245/950, ☕ € 27 – 4 suites

Rest *Le Parc* – ✆ *01 44 05 66 10 (closed 3 August-1st September, 21 December-5 January, Saturday lunch, Sunday and Monday)* Menu (€ 45) – Carte € 60/77

◆ The rooms are elegant and pleasingly British in atmosphere. All are well equipped (with wifi) and distributed around a garden terrace. Part of the bar decor is by Arman. The ground floor of this Belle Époque townhouse has a designer interior signed by P Jouin. Classical, seasonal cuisine.

Sofitel Baltimore

88 bis av. Kléber ✉ 75116 Ⓜ Boissière – ✆ 01 44 34 54 54 – h2789@accor.com – Fax 01 44 34 54 44 G 7

103 rm – †€ 420/820 ††€ 420/820, ☕ € 25 – 1 suite

Rest *Table du Baltimore* – see restaurant listing

◆ Simple furniture, trendy fabrics, old photos of the city of Baltimore: the contemporary decor of the rooms contrasts with the architecture of this 19C building.

Costes K. without rest

81 av. Kléber ✉ 75116 Ⓜ Trocadéro – ✆ 01 44 05 75 75 – resak@hotelcostesk.com – Fax 01 44 05 74 74 G 7

83 rm – †€ 300 ††€ 350/500, ☕ € 20

◆ This hotel by Ricardo Bofill is ultra-modern. It invites you to enjoy the discreet calm of its vast rooms with their pure lines, laid out around a Japanese-style patio.

Keppler without rest

10 r. Keppler ✉ 75116 Ⓜ George V – ✆ 01 47 20 65 05 – hotel@keppler.fr – Fax 01 47 23 02 29 F 8

34 rm – †€ 300/350 ††€ 420/490, ☕ € 22 – 5 suites

◆ This luxurious, sophisticated establishment is the work of designer Pierre-Yves Rochon. A magical blend of styles, materials and light sets the tone in the lobby and rooms.

Square rm, rm, VISA

3 r. Boulainvilliers ✉ 75016 Ⓜ Mirabeau – ✆ 01 44 14 91 90 – reservation@hotelsquare.com – Fax 01 44 14 91 99 K 5

20 rm – €300/480 €300/480, ☕ €22 – 2 suites

Rest *Zébra Square* – *✆ 01 44 14 91 91* – Menu (€26 bi), €34 bi – Carte €35/57

◆ A jewel of contemporary architecture across from the Maison de la Radio. Curves, colours, high-tech facilities and abstract paintings: a hymn to modern art! Trendy decor with striped theme in the restaurant, a cellar-library and contemporary cuisine on the menu.

Trocadero Dokhan's without rest VISA

117 r. Lauriston ✉ 75116 Ⓜ Trocadéro – ✆ 01 53 65 66 99 – reservation@dokhans.com – Fax 01 53 65 66 88 G 6

45 rm – €430/460 €430/460, ☕ €27 – 4 suites

◆ Attractive town house (1910) with Palladian architecture and neo-Classical interior decor. 18C celadon wood panelling in the cosy lounges and intimate champagne bar.

Sezz without rest VISA

6 av. Frémiet ✉ 75016 Ⓜ Passy – ✆ 01 56 75 26 26 – mail@hotelsezz.com – Fax 01 56 75 26 16 J6

22 rm – €280/335 €330/460, ☕ €25 – 5 suites

◆ Revamped hotel in a modern style: spacious, minimalist interior (shades of grey, giant vases), hi-tech gadgets and attentive staff. Steam bath and Jacuzzi.

La Villa Maillot without rest VISA

143 av. Malakoff ✉ 75116 Ⓜ Porte Maillot – ✆ 01 53 64 52 52 – resa@lavillamaillot.fr – Fax 01 45 00 60 61 F 6

39 rm – €270/350 €300/400, ☕ €27 – 3 suites

◆ A step away from Porte Maillot. Soft colours, a high level of comfort and good soundproofing in the rooms. Glassed-in space for breakfasts, opening onto the greenery.

Majestic without rest VISA

29 r. Dumont d'Urville ✉ 75116 Ⓜ Kléber – ✆ 01 45 00 83 70 – management@majestic-hotel.com – Fax 01 45 00 29 48 – Closed for refurbishment from April to September F 7

27 rm – €265 €370, ☕ €19 – 3 suites

◆ A step away from the Champs-Elysées, this discreet building dating from the 1960s has quiet rooms, with an 'old-money' comfort, well-proportioned and impeccably well-maintained.

Pergolèse without rest VISA

3 r. Pergolèse ✉ 75116 Ⓜ Argentine – ✆ 01 53 64 04 04 – hotel@pergolese.com – Fax 01 53 64 04 40 E 6

40 rm – €220/380 €264/456, ☕ €18

◆ Restrained 16th arrondissement chic on the outside hides a successful designer interior combining mahogany, glass bricks, chrome and bright colours. Breakfast facing a pleasant patio.

Élysées Régencia without rest VISA

41 av. Marceau ✉ 75116 Ⓜ George V – ✆ 01 47 20 42 65 – info@regencia.com – Fax 01 49 52 03 42 G 8

43 rm – €195/370 €215/550, ☕ €18

◆ Tastefully renovated in a designer style, this hotel offers modern, stylish rooms (blue, fuchsia or aniseed), an elegant sitting room, and a bar/library (red and chocolate coloured wainscoting).

Waldorf Trocadero without rest VISA

97 r. Lauriston ✉ 75116 Ⓜ Boissière – ✆ 01 45 53 83 30 – trocadero@hotelswaldorfparis.com – Fax 01 47 55 92 52 G 7

44 rm – €320/350 €350/410, ☕ €20

◆ This former townhouse between the Arc de Triomphe and Trocadéro offers new facilities and a pretty modern decor. Rooms of various sizes.

Alexander without rest VISA

102 av. V. Hugo ✉ 75116 Ⓜ Victor Hugo – ✆ 01 56 90 61 00 – reservation@hotelalexanderparis.com – Fax 01 56 90 61 01 G 6

61 rm – €315/523 €343/523, ☕ €25 – 2 suites

◆ An elegant building on a chic avenue. The rooms are well proportioned, comfortable and recently refurbished; those to the rear are quieter.

Garden Élysée without rest
12 r. St-Didier ✉ 75116 Ⓜ Boissière – ☎ 01 47 55 01 11 – garden.elysee@wanadoo.fr – Fax 01 47 27 79 24 G 7
46 rm – †€ 180/480 ††€ 180/600, ☕ € 21
◆ Set back from the street, in the calm of a green inner courtyard where breakfast is served in summer, up-to-date rooms and a pretty lounge lined with carved wood panels.

Bassano without rest
15 r. Bassano ✉ 75116 Ⓜ George V – ☎ 01 47 23 78 23 – info@hotel-bassano.com – Fax 01 47 20 41 22 G 8
28 rm – †€ 175/290 ††€ 195/310, ☕ € 18 – 3 suites
◆ Cosy atmosphere, wrought-iron furniture, sunny fabrics – it feels like being at a friend's home in Provence, but is only a few hundred metres from the Champs-Elysées.

Kléber without rest
7 r. Belloy ✉ 75116 Ⓜ Boissière – ☎ 01 47 23 80 22 – kleberhotel@wanadoo.fr – Fax 01 49 52 07 20 G 7
23 rm – †€ 99/299 ††€ 99/299, ☕ € 14 – 1 suite
◆ The sitting rooms of this 1853 hotel have Louis XV style furniture, original frescoes and old paintings. Exposed stonework and parquet floors in the rooms.

Montfleuri without rest
21 av. Grande Armée ✉ 75116 Ⓜ Charles de Gaulle-Etoile – ☎ 01 45 00 33 65 – montfleuri@wanadoo – Fax 01 45 00 06 36 F 7
42 rm – †€ 230/250 ††€ 270/290, ☕ € 13 – 3 suites
◆ Two steps from the Arc de Triomphe, this hotel has been entirely redecorated in a modern style. Peaceful, refined rooms in muted tones, elegantly furnished and adorned with fine fabrics.

Étoile Résidence Impériale without rest
155 av. de Malakoff ✉ 75116 Ⓜ Porte Maillot – ☎ 01 45 00 23 45 – reservation@residenceimperiale.com – Fax 01 45 01 88 82 E 6
37 rm – †€ 170/250 ††€ 170/250, ☕ € 14
◆ Recently-renovated and well-soundproofed hotel, with theme rooms (Africa, Asia, etc.). Some have retained their exposed beams, while others (ground floor) open onto the patio.

Passy Eiffel without rest
10 r. Passy ✉ 75016 Ⓜ Passy – ☎ 01 45 25 55 66 – contact@passyeiffel.com – Fax 01 42 88 89 88 J 6
49 rm – †€ 90/145 ††€ 110/155, ☕ € 11
◆ In a busy street, a family hotel with practical, well-kept rooms that overlook either the street (some enjoy a view of the Eiffel Tower) or a pretty flower-decked patio.

Chambellan Morgane without rest
6 r. Keppler ✉ 75116 Ⓜ George V – ☎ 01 47 20 35 72 – chambellan-morgane@wanadoo.fr – Fax 01 47 20 95 69 GF 8
20 rm – †€ 160/180 ††€ 160/180, ☕ € 13
◆ Small hotel with character, with rooms decorated in Provence colours and all enhanced by the quiet atmosphere. Pleasant Louis XVI lounge decorated with painted wood panels.

Victor Hugo without rest
19 r. Copernic ✉ 75116 Ⓜ Victor Hugo – ☎ 01 45 53 76 01 – paris@victorhugohotel.com – Fax 01 45 53 69 93 G 7
75 rm – †€ 154/250 ††€ 173/390, ☕ € 18
◆ This hotel across from the Passy reservoirs has changed a lot: renovated rooms, period furniture, new bathrooms and, on the top floor, balconies offering unobstructed views.

Floride Étoile without rest
14 r. St-Didier ✉ 75116 Ⓜ Boissière – ☎ 01 47 27 23 36 – floride.etoile@wanadoo.fr – Fax 01 47 27 82 87 G 7
63 rm – †€ 120/235 ††€ 145/235, ☕ € 15
◆ A stone's throw from Trocadéro. The renovated rooms are comfortable; those on the courtyard side are smaller but more tranquil. Stylishly furnished lounge decorated with flowers.

Résidence Foch without rest
10 r. Marbeau ✉ 75116 Ⓜ Porte Maillot – ✆ 01 45 00 46 50 – residence@foch.com – Fax 01 45 01 98 68 F 6
25 rm – †€ 150/160 ††€ 150/250, ☕ € 12
◆ This small family type hotel is not far from the aristocratic Avenue Foch; there is a pleasant breakfast room and practical, well-kept bedrooms.

Du Bois without rest
11 r. Dôme ✉ 75116 Ⓜ Kléber – ✆ 01 45 00 31 96 – reservations@hoteldubois.com – Fax 01 45 00 90 05 F 7
39 rm – †€ 170/220 ††€ 170/245, ☕ € 15
◆ This cosy hotel is in the most Montmartre-type street in the whole 16th district, where Baudelaire passed away. Charming and bright rooms. Georgian-style lounge.

Windsor Home without rest
3 r. Vital ✉ 75016 Ⓜ La Muette – ✆ 01 45 04 49 49 – whparis@wanadoo.fr – Fax 01 45 04 59 50 H 6
8 rm – †€ 120/160 ††€ 130/170, ☕ € 11
◆ This charming, hundred-year-old residence with a garden in front is decorated like a private house: old furniture, mouldings, light colours and contemporary touches.

Gavarni without rest
5 r. Gavarni ✉ 75116 Ⓜ Passy – ✆ 01 45 24 52 82 – reservation@gavarni.com – Fax 01 40 50 16 95 J 6
25 rm – †€ 110/200 ††€ 160/550, ☕ € 15
◆ This red-brick building offers rooms that are small but delightfully snug and well equipped; those on the two top floors are the cosiest.

Queen's without rest
4 r. Bastien Lepage ✉ 75016 Ⓜ Michel Ange Auteuil – ✆ 01 42 88 89 85 – info@hotel-queens-hotel.com – Fax 01 40 50 67 52 K 4
22 rm – †€ 85/99 ††€ 118/142, ☕ € 9
◆ Modern paintings brighten the attractive hall and most of the rooms, which are small but smartly designed.

Nicolo without rest
3 r. Nicolo ✉ 75116 Ⓜ Passy – ✆ 01 42 88 83 40 – hotel.nicolo@wanadoo.fr – Fax 01 42 24 45 41 J 6
28 rm ☕ – †€ 122/146 ††€ 130/209
◆ One reaches this venerable establishment by a peaceful back courtyard. Indonesian or antique furniture and Asian trinkets adorn the rooms, most of which have been renovated.

Marceau Champs Élysées without rest
37 av. Marceau ✉ 75016 Ⓜ George V – ✆ 01 47 20 43 37 – info@hotelmarceau.com – Fax 01 47 20 14 76 G 8
30 rm – †€ 138/168 ††€ 148/198, ☕ € 12
◆ Refurbished rooms with marble bathrooms await behind this classic façade on a busy avenue. Lounge-breakfast room on the 1st floor.

Boileau without rest
81 r. Boileau ✉ 75016 Ⓜ Exelmans – ✆ 01 42 88 83 74 – info@hotel-boileau.com – Fax 01 45 27 62 98 M 3
31 rm – †€ 55/75 ††€ 65/95, ☕ € 9
◆ Brittany and Maghreb figure among the canvasses and antique trinkets; tiny flower-decked patio and rustic furnishings. A welcoming hotel with discreetly personalised rooms.

Le Hameau de Passy without rest
48 r. Passy ✉ 75016 Ⓜ La Muette – ✆ 01 42 88 47 55 – hameau.passy@wanadoo.fr – Fax 01 42 30 83 72 – **32 rm** ☕ – †€ 120/146 ††€ 132/159 J 5-6
◆ An impasse leads to this discreet hamlet with its charming inner courtyard overrun with greenery. Quiet nights ensured in the small rooms which are nevertheless up-to-date and well-maintained.

Au Palais de Chaillot without rest
35 av. R. Poincaré ✉ 75116 Ⓜ Trocadéro – ✆ 01 53 70 09 09 – palaisdechaillot-hotel@magic.fr – Fax 01 53 70 09 08 G 6
28 rm – †€ 114 ††€ 129, ☕ € 9
◆ Beautiful location near Trocadéro for this hotel renovated in the colours of southern France. Rooms are small but fresh and practical. Breakfast-room furnished in cane.

Hiramatsu

(dinner) VISA

52 r. Longchamp ✉ 75116 Ⓜ Trocadéro – ✆ 01 56 81 08 80
– paris@hiramatsu.co.jp – Fax 01 56 81 08 81
– Closed 2-31 August, 29 December-6 January, Saturday and Sunday G 7

Rest – *(number of covers limited, pre-book)* Menu € 48 (lunch), € 95/130 – Carte € 104/140

Spec. Foie gras de canard aux choux frisés, jus de truffe. Feuilleté de homard aux parfums de truffes, jus d'estragon. Gâteau au chocolat "Hiramatsu".

◆ A Japanese name but inventive French cuisine nonetheless, prepared by a talented chef. A gastronomic experience in an elegant setting with beautiful floral displays. Superb wine list.

Relais d'Auteuil (Patrick Pignol)

VISA

31 bd. Murat ✉ 75016 Ⓜ Michel Ange Molitor – ✆ 01 46 51 09 54
– pignol.p@wanadoo.fr – Fax 01 40 71 05 03
– Closed August, Christmas holidays, Monday lunchtime, Saturday lunchtime and Sunday L 3

Rest – Menu € 58 (lunch), € 119/149 – Carte € 116/171

Spec. Amandine de foie gras de canard des Landes et son lobe poêlé. Grosse sole de ligne dorée entière sur l'arête. Gibier (season).

◆ Modern decor and period furniture in this restaurant where the cuisine is both sophisticated and masterful. Take the time to peruse the exceptional wine list.

Astrance (Pascal Barbot)

VISA

4 r. Beethoven ✉ 75016 Ⓜ Passy – ✆ 01 40 50 84 40
– Closed 1st-9 March, August, autumn half-term holidays, Saturday, Sunday and Monday J 7

Rest – *(number of covers limited, pre-book)* Menu € 70 (lunch), € 190/290 bi

Spec. Foie gras mariné au verjus, galette de champignons de Paris, citron confit. Selle d'agneau grillée, aubergine laquée au miso, curry noir. Croustillant chocolat blanc-gingembre, glace thé vert.

◆ The Astrance (from the Latin Aster, a star-like flower) boasts delicious, inventive cuisine, a surprise menu, choice wines and an attractive modern decor.

La Table de Joël Robuchon

VISA

16 av. Bugeaud ✉ 75116 Ⓜ Victor Hugo – ✆ 01 56 28 16 16
– latabledejoelrobuchon@wanadoo.fr – Fax 01 56 28 16 78 F 6

Rest – Menu € 55 bi (lunch)/150 – Carte € 55/145

Spec. La Langoustine en papillotes croustillantes au basilic. La caille au foie gras et caramélisée avec une pomme purée truffée. Le "chocolat sensation" crème onctueuse au chocolat araguani, glace chocolat au biscuit oréo.

◆ In the elegant setting you are sure to enjoy your meal here: sample tapas style snacks and classic dishes subtly updated by Joël Robuchon.

La Table du Baltimore – Hôtel Sofitel Baltimore

VISA

1 r. Léo Delibes ✉ 75016 Ⓜ Boissière –
✆ 01 44 34 54 34 – h2789-fb@accor.com – Fax 01 44 34 54 44
– Closed August, Saturday and Sunday G 7

Rest – Menu € 48 bi (lunch)/50 – Carte € 54/71

Spec. Tourteau assaisonné à la badiane roulé dans une feuille d'algue. Selle d'agneau rôtie en croûte d'herbes, céleri rave mijoté aux sucs. Dos de cabillaud cuit au plat, confit de poireaux au curcuma et thym.

◆ Antique wood panelling, modern furnishings, warm colours and a collection of drawings all combine to create the subtle decor of this restaurant. Fine, up-to-date cuisine.

Le Pergolèse (Stéphane Gaborieau)

VISA

40 r. Pergolèse ✉ 75116 Ⓜ Porte Maillot – ✆ 01 45 00 21 40
– le-pergolese@wanadoo.fr – Fax 01 45 00 81 31
– Closed August, Saturday and Sunday F 6

Rest – Menu € 42 (lunch)/90 – Carte € 73/107

Spec. Ravioli de langoustines, duxelles de champignons, émulsion de crustacés au foie gras. Aiguillette de Saint-Pierre dorée, cannelloni farcis aux multi saveurs, émulsion de verveine. Pigeon fermier au soupçon de gingembre et cannelle.

◆ Yellow wall hangings, pale wood wainscoting and surprising sculptures reflect in the mirrors, forming an elegant decor a step away from select Avenue Foch. Impeccable classic cuisine.

XXX **Prunier**
16 av. Victor-Hugo Ⓜ *Charles de Gaulle-Etoile – ✆ 01 44 17 35 85 – prunier@maison-prunier.fr – Fax 01 44 17 90 10 – Closed August and Sunday* F 7
Rest – Menu € 59/155 – Carte € 68/122
◆ Superb listed Art Deco interior (black marble, mosaics, stained glass) at this institution, created in 1925 by the architect Boileau. Excellent fish and seafood (caviar, salmon etc).

XXX **Les Arts**
9 bis av. d'Iéna ✉ 75116 Ⓜ *Iéna – ✆ 01 40 69 27 53 – restaurant.am@sodexho-prestige.fr – Fax 01 40 69 27 08 – Closed 28 July-28 August, 23 December-2 January, Saturday, Sunday and public holidays* G 7
Rest – Menu € 38 – Carte € 57/79
◆ Hotel in a townhouse built in 1892, "gadzarts" (ENSAM graduates) house since 1925. The dining room (colonnades, mouldings, paintings) and garden-terrace are now open to the public.

XXX **Passiflore** (Roland Durand)
✿ *33 r. Longchamp ✉ 75016* Ⓜ *Trocadéro – ✆ 01 47 04 96 81 – passiflore@club-internet.fr – Fax 01 47 04 32 27 – Closed 20 July-20 August, Saturday lunch and Sunday* G 7
Rest – Menu € 35 (lunch), € 45/54 (dinner) – Carte € 64/100
Spec. Ravioles de homard en mulligatowny. Riz noir et langoustines en saté au citron vert. Quatre sorbets verts pimentés.
◆ An unassumingly elegant decor of ethnic inspiration (yellow tones and wood panelling) and a classic, personalised cuisine combine to rejoice the taste buds of Parisian society.

XXX **Port Alma**
10 av. New York ✉ 75116 Ⓜ *Alma Marceau – ✆ 01 47 23 75 11 – restaurantportalma@wanadoo.fr – Fax 01 47 20 42 92 – Closed Sunday and Monday*
Rest – Menu (€ 25), € 29/39 (dinner) – Carte € 28/90 H 8
◆ On the quays of the Seine, a dining room and veranda with blue beams, where seafood is the star. Market-fresh ingredients and friendly welcome.

XX **Cristal Room Baccarat**
11 pl. des Etats-Unis ✉ 75116 Ⓜ *Boissière – ✆ 01 40 22 11 10 – cristalroom@baccarat.fr – Fax 01 40 22 11 99 – Closed Sunday* G 7
Rest – *(pre-book)* Menu € 59 (lunch), € 92/200 bi – Carte € 90/123
◆ This mansion was used by M-L de Noailles and now belongs to Baccarat. It offers a Starck decor and modern dishes at V.I.P. prices. Beauty can be far from reasonable!

XX **Tsé Yang**
25 av. Pierre 1er de Serbie ✉ 75116 Ⓜ *Iéna – ✆ 01 47 20 70 22 – Fax 01 47 20 75 34*
Rest – Menu € 49/59 – Carte € 35/133 G 8
◆ Interior designers have revamped this chic embassy of traditional Chinese cuisine, with black and gold tones and refined table settings.

XX **Pavillon Noura**
21 av. Marceau ✉ 75116 Ⓜ *Alma Marceau – ✆ 01 47 20 33 33 – noura@noura.fr – Fax 01 47 20 60 31* G 8
Rest – Menu € 36 (weekday lunch), € 56/64 – Carte € 37/54
◆ Elegant room whose walls are adorned with Levantine frescoes. Lebanese influence in evidence, with traditional selection of little hot and cold dishes and glasses of arack.

XX **La Table de Babette**
32 r. Longchamp ✉ 75016 Ⓜ *Trocadéro – ✆ 01 45 53 00 07 – tabledebabette@wanadoo.fr – Fax 01 45 53 00 15 – Closed Saturday lunch, Sunday and public holidays lunch* G 7
Rest – Menu (€ 28), € 38 – Carte € 45/77
◆ Babette invites you to discover her take on Caribbean cuisine, full of finesse and sensitivity. Cosy dining room, musical evenings at week-ends.

XX **Conti**
72 r. Lauriston ✉ 75116 Ⓜ *Boissière – ✆ 01 47 27 74 67 – Fax 01 47 27 37 66 – Closed 4-24 August, 25 December-1st January, Saturday, Sunday and public holidays*
Rest – Menu € 33 – Carte € 41/65 G 7
◆ Red and black predominate in this restaurant's decor, where mirrors and crystal chandeliers glitter. Italian cuisine; wonderful wine list.

XX **Giulio Rebellato** AC VISA MC AE
136 r. Pompe ✉ 75116 Ⓜ Victor Hugo – ✆ 01 47 27 50 26 – Closed August
Rest – Carte € 36/66 G 6
◆ The warm, Venetian-inspired decor by Garcia includes fine fabrics, old prints and glittering mirrors. Northern Italian cuisine.

XX **Tang** AC (dinner) VISA MC
125 r. de la Tour ✉ 75116 Ⓜ Rue de la Pompe – ✆ 01 45 04 35 35 – charlytang16@yahoo.fr – Fax 01 45 04 58 19 – Closed August, 21-29 December, Monday lunch and Sunday H 5
Rest – Menu € 39 (weekday lunch), € 85/108 – Carte € 65/149
◆ A high-ceiling dining room lit by large bay windows and a classic decor with Asian touches. Chinese and Thai specialties.

XX **Chez Géraud** VISA MC
31 r. Vital ✉ 75016 Ⓜ La Muette – ✆ 01 45 20 33 00 – Fax 01 45 20 46 60 – Closed 1st August-1st September, 23 December-5 January, Saturday and Sunday
Rest – Menu € 32 – Carte € 48/71 H 5
◆ The façade and the inside mural, both in Longwy earthenware tiles, are most eye-catching. Stylish bistro setting with a cuisine that highlights game in season.

XX **Roland Garros** (lunch) VISA MC AE
2 bis av. Gordon Bennett ✉ 75016 Ⓜ Porte d'Auteuil – ✆ 01 47 43 49 56 – Fax 01 40 71 83 24 – Closed 31 July-25 August, 24 December-5 January, Saturday and Sunday from October to March and Sunday dinner from April to September L 2
Rest – Menu (€ 42), € 52 – Carte € 51/87
◆ Within the stadium is this haven of greenery which, fortunately, is not reserved to FFT members! Modern menu supervised by Marc Veyrat.

XX **Marius** VISA MC AE
82 bd Murat ✉ 75016 Ⓜ Porte de St-Cloud – ✆ 01 46 51 67 80 – restaurant.marius@orange.fr – Fax 01 40 71 83 75 – Closed August, Saturday lunch and Sunday M 2
Rest – Carte € 43/68
◆ Yellow velvet chairs, bright walls, fabric blinds and large mirrors are the main decorative features in the dining room of this seafood restaurant. Select wine list.

XX **Le Vinci** AC (dinner) VISA MC AE
23 r. P. Valéry ✉ 75116 Ⓜ Victor Hugo – ✆ 01 45 01 68 18 – levinci@wanadoo.fr – Fax 01 45 01 60 37 – Closed 2-24 August, Saturday and Sunday F 7
Rest – Carte € 39/68
◆ Tasty Italian cuisine, pleasant colourful interior and friendly service – a highly-prized establishment a step away from the chic shopping in Avenue Victor-Hugo.

XX **6 New-York** AC VISA MC AE
6 av. New-York ✉ 75016 Ⓜ Alma Marceau – ✆ 01 40 70 03 30 – 6newyork@wanadoo.fr – Fax 01 40 70 04 77 – Closed August, Saturday lunch and Sunday H 8
Rest – Menu (€ 28), € 30 (lunch) – Carte € 48/62
◆ The sign gives you a clue to the address but does not tell you that this stylish bistro prepares dishes perfectly suited to its modern and refined setting.

XX **A et M Restaurant** AC VISA MC AE
136 bd Murat ✉ 75016 Ⓜ Porte de St-Cloud – ✆ 01 45 27 39 60 – am-bistrot-16@wanadoo.fr – Fax 01 45 27 69 71 – Closed August, Saturday lunch and Sunday
Rest – Menu (€ 23), € 30 – Carte € 35/48 M 3
◆ Fashionable contemporary bistro close to the Seine. Tasteful colour scheme of creams and browns, designer lighting and carefully prepared up-to-date cuisine.

XX **L'Acajou** AC VISA MC AE
35bis r. La Fontaine ✉ 75016 Ⓜ Jasmin – ✆ 01 42 88 04 47 – Fax 01 42 88 95 12 – Closed August, Saturday lunch and Sunday K 5
Rest – Menu (€ 28), € 35/40 bi – Carte € 53/68
◆ Up-to-date, well-presented food, modern decor with old wood panelling and pleasant service – the former Fontaine d'Auteuil has had a major facelift.

XX **La Butte Chaillot**

110 bis av. Kléber ✉ 75116 Ⓜ Trocadéro – ✆ 01 47 27 88 88 – buttechaillot@guysavoy.com – Fax 01 47 27 41 46 – Closed 3 weeks in August and Saturday lunch G 7

Rest – Menu € 33/50 – Carte € 37/56

◆ 21C bistro-style restaurant near the Palais de Chaillot with a copper-coloured contemporary decor, modern furniture and fashionable cuisine.

X **Essaouira**

135 r. Ranelagh ✉ 75016 Ⓜ Ranelagh – ✆ 01 45 27 99 93 – Fax 01 45 27 56 36 – Closed August, Monday lunch and Sunday J 4

Rest – Menu (€ 16) – Carte € 32/55

◆ The former Mogador lent its name to this Moroccan restaurant decorated with a mosaic fountain, carpets and craftwork. Couscous, tajine and méchoui, just like back home!

X **La Villa Corse**

141 av. Malakoff Ⓜ Porte Maillot – ✆ 01 40 67 18 44 – lavillacorserivedroite@wanadoo.fr – Fax 01 40 67 18 19 – Closed Sunday E 6

Rest – Menu (€ 25 bi) – Carte € 42/60

◆ The right bank sibling of the "Villa" in the 15th arrondissement. Corsican cuisine served in a large dining room and mezzanine with a relaxed, trendy ambience.

X **Le Petit Pergolèse**

38 r. Pergolèse ✉ 75016 Ⓜ Porte Maillot – ✆ 01 45 00 23 66 – Fax 01 45 00 44 03 – Closed August, Saturday and Sunday F 6

Rest – Carte € 31/59

◆ As the name suggests, this bistro is a daughter establishment of the smart Le Pergolèse. Tightly packed tables and tasty modern dishes.

X **La Table Lauriston**

129 r. Lauriston ✉ 75016 Ⓜ Trocadéro – ✆ 01 47 27 00 07 – Fax 01 47 27 00 07 – Closed 3-24 August, 24 December-2 January, Saturday lunch and Sunday G 6

Rest – Menu (€ 25) – Carte € 40/61

◆ This restaurant in a fashionable district of Paris focuses on simplicity and quality; lovely traditional food to be enjoyed in a modern bistro-style decor.

X **Rosimar**

26 r. Poussin ✉ 75016 Ⓜ Michel Ange Auteuil – ✆ 01 45 27 74 91 – Fax 01 45 20 75 05 – Closed 2 August-2 September, 24-31 December, Saturday, Sunday and public holidays K 3

Rest – *(lunch only except Friday)* Menu € 36 bi – Carte € 36/55

◆ This enlarged dining room contains all the savours of traditional Spain. "Hombre"! A nice little family affair!

X **Oscar**

6 r. Chaillot Ⓜ Iéna – ✆ 01 47 20 26 92 – fredmartinod@orange.fr – Fax 01 47 20 27 93 – Closed 5-20 August, Saturday lunch and Sunday G 8

Rest – Menu € 22 – Carte € 32/47

◆ This bistro, with a discreet façade, tightly packed tables and a blackboard with daily specials, does not need to advertise to attract a clientele from well beyond the area.

at Bois de Boulogne – ✉ 75016

XXXX ✿✿✿ **Pré Catelan**

rte Suresnes ✉ 75016 – ✆ 01 44 14 41 14 – leprecatelan-restaurant@lenotre.fr – Fax 01 45 24 43 25 – Closed 3-25 August, 27 October-3 November, February school holidays, Sunday and Monday H 2

Rest – Menu € 85 (weekday lunch), € 180/230 – Carte € 180/224 ✿

Spec. La Tomate (summer). La langoustine. La Pomme.

◆ Inventive cuisine provides the perfect foil to this elegant Napoleon III pavilion in the woods. New interior by designer Pierre-Yves Rochon.

XXXX ✿ **La Grande Cascade**

allée de Longchamp, (in the Bois de Boulogne) ✉ 75016 – ✆ 01 45 27 33 51 – grandecascade@wanadoo.fr – Fax 01 42 88 99 06 – Closed 20 February-10 March
Rest – Menu € 75/177 – Carte € 130/200
Spec. Grosses langoustines snackées et huître en cromesqui, chou vert croquant et nage réduite au beurre iodé. Thon rouge croustillant poivre et sel, graines de sésame et coriandre en condiment. Pomme de ris de veau cuite lentement, olives, câpres et croutons frits, herbes à tortue comme au Moyen Âge.
♦ A Parisian paradise at the foot of the Grande Cascade (10m!) in the Bois de Boulogne. Delicately distinctive cuisine served in the 1850 pavilion or on the splendid terrace.

S. Sauvignier/MICHELIN

Palais des Congrès, Wagram, Ternes, Batignolles

17e arrondissement ✉ 75017

Méridien Étoile rm, VISA MC AE

81 bd Gouvion St-Cyr Ⓜ Neuilly-Porte Maillot – ✆ 01 40 68 34 34 – guest.etoile@lemeridien.com – Fax 01 40 68 31 31 E 6
1025 rm – †€ 185/504 ††€ 185/504, ☕ € 25 – 17 suites
Rest ***L'Orenoc*** – *✆ 01 40 68 30 40 (closed from end July to end August, 20-28 December, Saturday and Sunday)* Menu (€ 35), € 44 – Carte € 54/73
♦ Facilities at this huge hotel include a jazz club, bar, boutiques and an impressive conference centre. Black granite and shades of beige predominate in the contemporary-style guestrooms. The Orenoc reflects current tastes in food, and has warm, colonial-style decor.

Concorde La Fayette rest, VISA MC AE

3 pl. Gén. Koenig Ⓜ Porte Maillot – ✆ 01 40 68 50 68 – booking@concorde-hotels.com – Fax 01 40 68 50 43 E 6
931 rm – †€ 165/450 ††€ 165/540, ☕ € 27 – 19 suites
Rest ***La Fayette*** – *✆ 01 40 68 51 19* – Menu € 38/70 bi – Carte € 46/72
♦ This 33-floor tower, part of the city's convention centre, offers wonderful views of Paris from most of its spacious and comfortable rooms, as well as from the panoramic bar. Buffet meals are served in the stained glass setting of the La Fayette.

Splendid Étoile rm, rm, VISA MC AE

1bis av. Carnot Ⓜ Charles de Gaulle-Etoile – ✆ 01 45 72 72 00 – hotel@hsplendid.com – Fax 01 45 72 72 01 F 7
50 rm – †€ 295 ††€ 295, ☕ € 23 – 7 suites
Rest ***Le Pré Carré*** – *✆ 01 46 22 57 35 (closed 4-17 August, Saturday lunch and Sunday)* Menu € 34 bi (dinner) – Carte € 35/64
♦ Beautiful classical façade with wrought-iron balconies. Spacious rooms full of character, embellished with Louis XV furnishings; some look out onto the Arc de Triomphe. Two mirrors reflect the infinite elegance of this restaurant's decor, featuring dark wood panelling and subdued orchid lights.

Ampère rm, rest, VISA MC AE

102 av. Villiers Ⓜ Pereire – ✆ 01 44 29 17 17 – resa@hotelampere.com – Fax 01 44 29 16 50 D 8
96 rm – †€ 260/400 ††€ 260/400, ☕ € 20
Rest ***Le Jardin d'Ampère*** – *✆ 01 44 29 16 54 (closed 1st- 21 August and Sunday dinner)* Menu (€ 33), € 36 (weekday lunch) – Carte € 54/69
♦ The main features of this 4-star hotel are the elegant piano bar opening onto a verdant terrace, wi-fi Internet access and comfortable contemporary rooms (some overlooking the interior courtyard). Elegant decor and pleasant terrace at the Jardin d'Ampère; dinner concerts in fine weather.

Balmoral without rest
6 r. Gén. Lanrezac Ⓜ Charles de Gaulle-Etoile – ✆ 01 43 80 30 50 – hotel@hotelbalmoral.fr – Fax 01 43 80 51 56 E 7
57 rm – †€ 128/140 ††€ 148/180, ☕ € 10
◆ A personalised welcome and calm atmosphere characterise this old hotel (1911) a stone's throw from the Étoile. Brightly coloured bedrooms, and elegant wood panelling in the lounge.

Regent's Garden without rest
6 r. P. Demours Ⓜ Ternes – ✆ 01 45 74 07 30 – hotel.regents.garden@wanadoo.fr – Fax 01 40 55 01 42 E 7
40 rm – †€ 109/319 ††€ 109/319, ☕ € 16
◆ Attractive, elegant townhouse commissioned by Napoleon III for his doctor. Vast period rooms, some giving onto the garden, which is very pleasant in summer.

Novotel Porte d'Asnières rm,
34 av. Porte d'Asnières Ⓜ Pereire – ✆ 01 44 40 52 52 – h4987@accor.com – Fax 01 44 40 44 23 C 9
139 rm – †€ 180/200 ††€ 180/200, ☕ € 15 – **Rest** – Carte € 22/40
◆ Modern architecture near the ring road but very well soundproofed. The rooms from the seventh floor upwards command a fine view of Paris' rooftops. A contemporary decor in this restaurant serving brasserie-style meals.

Banville without rest
166 bd Berthier Ⓜ Porte de Champerret – ✆ 01 42 67 70 16 – info@hotelbanville.fr – Fax 01 44 40 42 77 D 8
38 rm – †€ 280/400 ††€ 280/400, ☕ € 18
◆ Tastefully restored building from 1926. Charm pervades throughout from the elegant lobby and lounges to the refined rooms with personal (Provençal) touches. Live music on Tuesday evenings.

Villa Alessandra without rest
9 pl. Boulnois Ⓜ Ternes – ✆ 01 56 33 24 24 – alessandra@leshotelsdeparis.com – Fax 01 56 33 24 30 E 8
49 rm – †€ 310 ††€ 320/385, ☕ € 20
◆ This Ternes quarter hotel is on a delightful quiet little square and is appreciated for its calm. Colours of southern France in the rooms, with wrought-iron beds and painted wood furniture.

Waldorf Arc de Triomphe without rest
36 r. Pierre Demours Ⓜ Ternes – ✆ 01 47 64 67 67 – arc@hotelswaldorfparis.com – Fax 01 40 53 91 34 D 8
44 rm – †€ 340/460 ††€ 370/460, ☕ € 20
◆ Attractively refurbished, elegant contemporary rooms. Good fitness centre, a small pool, sauna and steam bath: ideal after a hard day's work or sightseeing!

Amarante Arc de Triomphe without rest
25 r. Th.-de-Banville Ⓜ Pereire – ✆ 01 47 63 76 69 – amarante-arcdetriomphe@jjwhotels.com – Fax 01 43 80 63 96 D 8
50 rm – †€ 170/250 ††€ 190/300, ☕ € 22
◆ This hotel has Directoire-style rooms which are popular with its business clientele. Attic-type rooms on the top floor, with some rooms opening onto the patio.

Princesse Caroline without rest
1bis r. Troyon Ⓜ Charles de Gaulle-Etoile – ✆ 01 58 05 30 00 – contact@hotelprincessecaroline.fr – Fax 01 42 27 49 53 E 8
53 rm – †€ 158/215 ††€ 158/215, ☕ € 18
◆ In a small street just off the Étoile, this hotel pays homage to Caroline Murat, sister of Napoleon I. Light, cosy and well-appointed rooms with those overlooking the inner courtyard generally quieter.

Champerret Élysées without rest
129 av. Villiers Ⓜ Porte de Champerret – ✆ 01 47 64 44 00 – reservation@champerret-elysees.fr – Fax 01 47 63 10 58 D 7
45 rm – †€ 91 ††€ 140, ☕ € 15
◆ Web surfers will appreciate the colourful rooms (those overlooking the courtyard are quieter) of this "cyberhotel": broadband, wifi, double telephone line and fax available.

Magellan without rest

17 r. J.-B. Dumas Ⓜ Porte de Champerret – ☎ 01 45 72 44 51 – paris@hotelmagellan.com – Fax 01 40 68 90 36 D 7

72 rm – †€ 135/149 ††€ 150/168, ☕ € 13

◆ Large, functional rooms in a beautiful building dating from 1900. The small pavilion at the far end of the garden is used as a breakfast room in summer. Art Deco-style lounge.

Mercure Wagram Arc de Triomphe without rest

3 r. Brey Ⓜ Charles de Gaulle-Etoile – ☎ 01 56 68 00 01 – h2053@accor.com – Fax 01 56 68 00 02 E 8

43 rm – †€ 215/260 ††€ 225/270, ☕ € 14

◆ This new Mercure between Étoile and Ternes offers a warm welcome and cosy little rooms with pale wood panels and pretty fabrics that create a nautical atmosphere.

Tilsitt Étoile without rest

23 r. Brey Ⓜ Charles de Gaulle-Etoile – ☎ 01 43 80 39 71 – info@tilsitt.com – Fax 01 47 66 37 63 E 8

38 rm – †€ 135/150 ††€ 165, ☕ € 12

◆ The hotel is located on a quiet street in the Étoile quarter. Snug, cosy rooms (a few tiny terraces), appealing breakfast room and designer decor lounge bar.

Monceau Élysées without rest

108 r. Courcelles Ⓜ Courcelles – ☎ 01 47 63 33 08 – monceau-elysees@wanadoo.fr – Fax 01 46 22 87 39 E 9

29 rm – †€ 119/189 ††€ 149/239, ☕ € 10

◆ This hotel close to the Parc Monceau offers guests personalised rooms decorated with salmon colours and printed and/or more contemporary fabrics. Stone-vaulted breakfast room.

Guy Savoy

18 r. Troyon Ⓜ Charles de Gaulle-Etoile – ☎ 01 43 80 40 61 – reserv@guysavoy.com – Fax 01 46 22 43 09 – Closed August, 24 December-2 January, Saturday lunchtime, Sunday and Monday E 8

Rest – Menu € 245/295 – Carte € 134/267

Spec. Soupe d'artichaut à la truffe noire, brioche feuilletée aux champignons et truffes. Bar en écailles grillées aux épices douces. Ris de veau rissolés, "petits chaussons" de pommes de terre et truffes.

◆ Glasswork, leather and Wenge, works by great names in contemporary art, African sculpture and inventive cuisine make this 'the inn of the 21C' par excellence.

Michel Rostang

20 r. Rennequin Ⓜ Ternes – ☎ 01 47 63 40 77 – rostang@relaischateaux.com – Fax 01 47 63 82 75 – Closed 3-25 August, Monday lunch, Saturday lunch and Sunday D 8

Rest – Menu € 78 (lunch), € 185/285 – Carte € 125/210

Spec. "Menu truffe" (15 December to 15 March). Grosse sole de ligne "cuisson meunière", marinière de coquillages au curry mauricien. Canette au sang servie saignante en deux services.

◆ Find wainscoting, Robj statuettes, works by Lalique, and Art Deco stained glass in this luxurious and unusual setting. Exquisite cuisine and outstanding wine list.

Sormani

4 r. Gén. Lanrezac Ⓜ Charles de Gaulle-Etoile – ☎ 01 43 80 13 91 – sasormani@wanadoo.fr – Fax 01 40 55 07 37 – Closed 1st-25 August, Saturday, Sunday and holidays E 7

Rest – Carte € 50/114

◆ Latin charm predominates in this restaurant near the Place de l'Etoile, with its new decor (red tones and Murano-glass chandeliers), dolce vita atmosphere and Italian cuisine.

Pétrus

12 pl. Mar. Juin Ⓜ Pereire – ☎ 01 43 80 15 95 – Fax 01 47 66 49 86 – Closed 5-23 August D 8

Rest – Carte € 40/80

◆ A pleasant nautical theme and a profusion of seafood. No one will be surprised to learn that it is known as the kingdom of fish!

La Braisière (Jacques Faussat)
54 r. Cardinet Ⓜ Malesherbes – ✆ 01 47 63 40 37 – labraisiere@free.fr – Fax 01 47 63 04 76 – Closed August, 1st-8 January, Saturday and Sunday
Rest – Menu € 38 (lunch) – Carte € 51/67 D 9
Spec. Gâteau de pommes de terre au foie gras et aux girolles. Pavé de thon rouge laqué au galanga. Gibier (October to January).
◆ Comfortable, modern restaurant in tasteful pastel colours. The menu is influenced by the cuisine of southwest France but also changes with the seasons and the chef's whims.

Dessirier
9 pl. Mar. Juin Ⓜ Pereire – ✆ 01 42 27 82 14 – dessirier@michelrostang.com – Fax 01 47 66 82 07 – Closed 10-17 August, Saturday and Sunday in July-August
Rest – Menu € 38 – Carte € 53/87 D 8
◆ A fun, lively atmosphere, brasserie-style interior with well-padded armchairs and seats, and an impressive seafood menu.

Rech
62 av. des Ternes Ⓜ Ternes – ✆ 01 45 72 29 47 – Fax 01 45 72 41 60 – Closed August, Sunday and Monday E 7
Rest – Menu € 34/53 – Carte € 46/74
◆ Recently renovated, Art Deco-inspired dining rooms (mirrors, stained glass) at this venerable restaurant. Principally fine fish and seafood specialities, but the odd meat dish too.

Timgad
21 r. Brunel Ⓜ Argentine – ✆ 01 45 74 23 70 – contact@timgad.fr – Fax 01 40 68 76 46 E 7
Rest – Menu € 45/60 bi – Carte € 38/71
◆ Delve into the past splendour of the city of Timgad: the elegant Moorish decor of the rooms was carried out by Moroccan stucco-workers. Fragrant North African cuisine.

Graindorge
15 r. Arc de Triomphe Ⓜ Charles de Gaulle-Etoile – ✆ 01 47 54 00 28 – le.graindorge@wanadoo.fr – Closed 1st-15 August, Saturday lunch and Sunday E 7
Rest – Menu (€ 24), € 28 (weekday lunch)/34 – Carte € 42/56
◆ Here you can choose between beer and wine, generous Flemish cuisine and appealing market dishes in an attractive Art Deco setting.

Meating
122 av.de Villiers Ⓜ Pereire – ✆ 01 43 80 10 10 – chezmichelpereire@wanadoo.fr – Fax 01 43 80 31 42 – Closed Sunday and Monday B 2
Rest – Menu € 28/37 – Carte € 48/72
◆ A trendy steakhouse in which the American chef sources the best cuts of meat and cooks them to your exact specifications. Classic dishes also available.

Ballon des Ternes
103 av. Ternes Ⓜ Porte Maillot – ✆ 01 45 74 17 98 – leballondesternes@fr.oleane.com – Fax 01 45 72 18 84 E 6
Rest – Carte € 35/60
◆ No, you have not had a "ballon" (glass of wine) too many! The table set upside down on the ceiling is part of the 1900 decor of this brasserie next to the Palais des Congrès.

Chez Georges
273 bd Péreire Ⓜ Porte Maillot – ✆ 01 45 74 31 00 – chez-georges@hotmail.fr – Fax 01 45 72 18 84 E 6
Rest – bistrot Carte € 40/67
◆ An institution in Paris since 1926, the ambience and decor of this brasserie are perfectly in keeping with its appetising bistro cuisine. Menu and daily suggestions.

Chez Léon
32 r. Legendre Ⓜ Villiers – ✆ 01 42 27 06 82 – chezleon32@wanadoo.fr – Fax 01 46 22 63 67 – Closed 26 July-24 August, 24 December-4 January, Saturday, Sunday and public holidays D 10
Rest – Menu (€ 24), € 32 (lunch)/34 (dinner) – Carte € 42/52
◆ This bistro has been the favourite haunt of a faithful group of regulars for many years. Refined traditional dishes are served in three rooms, one upstairs.

La Maison de Charly

97 bd Gouvion-St-Cyr Ⓜ Porte Maillot – ✆ 01 45 74 34 62 – Fax 01 55 37 90 21 – Closed August and Monday E 6

Rest – Menu € 29 (weekday lunch)/33

◆ An ochre façade, olive trees, elegant Moorish decor and a palm tree beneath the glass ceiling provide the typical decor for this restaurant serving varied couscous, tajine and pastilla dishes.

Bath's

25 r. Bayen Ⓜ Ternes – ✆ 01 45 74 74 74 – contact@baths.fr – Fax 01 45 74 71 15 – Closed 2 August-1st September, 22-28 December, Saturday lunch, Monday lunch, Sunday and public holidays E 7

Rest – Menu € 25 (lunch)/42 – Carte € 50/64

Spec. Pétales de jambon ibérique "bellota". Encornets juste sautés, riz paëlla, sauce chorizo. Filet de bœuf de Salers aux épices douces.

◆ The owner's sculptures and modern paintings set the tone for this contemporary address decorated in orange and black. Delicious market-inspired cuisine.

Caïus

6 r. d'Armaillé Ⓜ Charles de Gaulle-Etoile – ✆ 01 42 27 19 20 – Fax 01 40 55 00 93 – Closed August, Saturday and Sunday E 7

Rest – Menu (€ 23), € 39

◆ Warm wood panelling, bench seating, and coffee and spice themed photos set the scene in this smart bistro devoted to personalised, tasty, market fresh cuisine.

Montefiori

19 r. de l'Etoile Ⓜ Charles de Gaulle-Etoile – ✆ 01 55 37 90 00 – montesiori@wanadoo.fr – Closed 4-23 August, 24 December-2 January, Saturday lunch, Monday dinner and Sunday E 8

Rest – Menu (€ 17), € 22 – Carte € 31/65

◆ This former bakery has been given a new lease of life. High quality Italian specialities accompanied by a fine selection of wines amid a contemporary red and green decor.

La Soupière

154 av. de Wagram Ⓜ Wagram – ✆ 01 42 27 00 73 – cthuillart@yahoo.fr – Fax 01 46 22 27 09 – Closed 1st-24 August, Saturday lunch and Sunday D 9

Rest – Menu € 35/58

◆ The classical menu, mushrooms in season, and highly attentive service, served to a trompe l'œil backdrop, make it well worth heading for this pleasant neighbourhood establishment.

Table des Oliviers

38 r. Laugier Ⓜ Pereire – ✆ 01 47 63 85 51 – latabledesoliviers@wanadoo.fr – Fax 01 47 63 85 81 – Closed in August, Monday lunch, Saturday lunch and Sunday D 7-8

Rest – Menu (€ 22), € 30 – Carte € 49/55

◆ The name of the restaurant 'The Olive Tree Table' says it all: Provençal cuisine flavoured with olive oil, thyme and basil. Only the chirping of the crickets is lacking!

Bistrot Niel

75 av. Niel Ⓜ Pereire – ✆ 01 42 27 88 44 – gensdarmesb@aol.com – Fax 01 42 27 32 12 – Closed Saturday lunch and Sunday D 8

Rest – Menu € 32 (lunch) – Carte € 37/49

◆ The cuisine here is focused on traditional dishes, updated with a hint of spice. A modern bistro that is both chic and welcoming.

Le Café d'Angel

16 r. Brey Ⓜ Charles de Gaulle-Etoile – ✆ 01 47 54 03 33 – Fax 01 47 54 03 33 – Closed 28 July-18 August, 24 December-6 January, Saturday, Sunday and public holidays E 8

Rest – Menu € 25/45 – Carte € 38/45

◆ A small establishment evocative of Parisian bistros of yesteryear: a "retro" setting with leatherette banquettes, pottery on the walls and traditional dishes marked on a black-board.

Le Clou
132 r. Cardinet Ⓜ Malesherbes – ✆ 01 42 27 36 78 – le.clou@wanadoo.fr – Fax 01 42 27 89 96 – Closed 11-24 August and Sunday C 10
Rest – Menu € 22/33 – Carte € 38/50
◆ This neighbourhood bistro is paradise for carnivores. Simply laid tables. Regional produce and daily specials.

Chez Mathilde-Paris XVII
41 r. Guersant Ⓜ Porte Maillot – ✆ 01 45 74 75 27 – Closed 26 July-26 August, 24 December-1st January, Saturday and Sunday D 7
Rest – Carte € 22/31
◆ A modest family run restaurant, far from the Parisian trendy set, offering bistro-type seasonal market dishes, chalked up on a blackboard.

L'Huîtrier
16 r. Saussier-Leroy Ⓜ Ternes – ✆ 01 40 54 83 44 – Fax 01 40 54 83 86 – Closed August, Sunday from May to September and Monday E 8
Rest – Carte € 31/65
◆ As you enter, the oyster bar will make your mouth water. Enjoy the shellfish, elbow to elbow, in a discreetly modern dining room.

L'Entredgeu
83 r. Laugier Ⓜ Porte de Champerret – ✆ 01 40 54 97 24 – Fax 01 40 54 96 62 – Closed 25 April-5 May, 5-25 August, 20-27 December, Sunday and Monday D 7
Rest – Menu € 22 (weekday lunch)/30
◆ Friendly welcome, bistro furniture, menu chalked up on a blackboard, market fresh cuisine and a tongue-twisting name to boot.

Caves Petrissans
30 bis av. Niel Ⓜ Pereire – ✆ 01 42 27 52 03 – cavespetrissans@noos.fr – Fax 01 40 54 87 56 – Closed 1st-11 May, 25 July-25 August, Saturday, Sunday and public holidays D 8
Rest – *(pre-book)* Menu (€ 29), € 35 – Carte € 38/55
◆ Céline, Abel Gance and Roland Dorgelès loved to visit these cellars over a century old, which now double as a wine shop and restaurant. Tasty, bistro-style cooking.

S. Sauvignier/MICHELIN

Montmartre, Pigalle

18e arrondissement ✉ 75018

Terrass'Hôtel
12 r. J. de Maistre Ⓜ Place de Clichy – ✆ 01 46 06 72 85 – reservation@terrass-hotel.com – Fax 01 44 92 34 30 C 13
85 rm – †€ 270/290 ††€ 320/345, ☕ € 18 – 15 suites
Rest *Le Diapason* – *✆ 01 44 92 34 00 (closed Sunday dinner16 September-30 April and Saturday lunch)* Menu (€ 22), € 29 (lunch)/35 bi (dinner) – Carte € 45/63
◆ Situated at the foot of the Sacré-Cœur basilica, this hotel has stunning views of Paris from its upper-floor rooms and top-floor terrace. Elegant interior adorned with ornaments and wood panelling. Attractive Provençal-inspired dining room and rooftop terrace overlooking the capital.

Kube
1 passage Ruelle Ⓜ La Chapelle – ☎ 01 42 05 20 00 – paris@kubehotel.com – Fax 01 42 05 21 01 C 16
41 rm – 🚹€ 250 🚹🚹€ 300/750, ☕ € 25 – **Rest** – Carte € 34/50
◆ The 19C façade belies this hotel's 21C high-tech designer interior. The bar – built entirely from ice (-10°C) – makes for an unusual and unforgettable experience.

Relais Montmartre without rest
6 r. Constance Ⓜ Abbesses – ☎ 01 70 64 25 25 – contact@relaismontmartre.fr – Fax 01 70 64 25 00 D 13
26 rm – 🚹€ 155/195 🚹🚹€ 155/195, ☕ € 13
◆ Discover the unexpected charm of this quiet, country-style residence in a lively district close to Pigalle. Stylish, classical decor and modern facilities.

Holiday Inn Garden Court Montmartre without rest
23 r. Damrémont Ⓜ Lamarck Caulaincourt – ☎ 01 44 92 33 40 – hiparmm@aol.com – Fax 01 44 92 09 30 C 13
54 rm – 🚹€ 90/170 🚹🚹€ 110/190, ☕ € 13
◆ A recently built hotel with renovated, functional rooms on a typically steep Montmartre street. The breakfast room opens onto a small terrace.

Mercure Montmartre without rest
3 r. Caulaincourt Ⓜ Place de Clichy – ☎ 01 44 69 70 70 – h0373@accor.com – Fax 01 44 69 70 71 D 12
305 rm – 🚹€ 143/192 🚹🚹€ 161/202, ☕ € 14
◆ A stone's throw from the famous Moulin Rouge, the hotel lobby is decorated on the theme of Montmartre and its painters. The rooms on the top three floors enjoy lovely views of the rooftops of Paris.

Timhotel without rest
11 r. Ravignan Ⓜ Abbesses – ☎ 01 42 55 74 79 – montmartre.manager@timhotel.fr – Fax 01 42 55 71 01 D 13
59 rm – 🚹€ 75/180 🚹🚹€ 75/180, ☕ € 8,50
◆ Smart, functional hotel on one of the neighbourhood's most charming squares. The rooms on the 4th and 5th floors have been renovated and offer superb views of the capital.

Roma Sacré Cœur without rest
101 r. Caulaincourt Ⓜ Lamarck Caulaincourt – ☎ 01 42 62 02 02 – hotel.roma@wanadoo.fr – Fax 01 42 54 34 92 C 14
57 rm – 🚹€ 75/115 🚹🚹€ 85/140, ☕ € 8
◆ This hotel has a charming location in Montmartre, with a garden to the front, typical flights of steps to the side and Sacré-Cœur above. Attractive, brightly coloured guestrooms.

Damrémont without rest
110 r. Damrémont Ⓜ Jules Joffrin – ☎ 01 42 64 25 75 – hotel.damremont@wanadoo.fr – Fax 01 46 06 74 64 B 13
35 rm – 🚹€ 60/110 🚹🚹€ 65/140, ☕ € 7
◆ Near Montmartre, the functional bedrooms are quieter on the courtyard side; they are not very large but well looked after and appealing. Small sitting room.

A Beauvilliers
52 r. Lamarck Ⓜ Lamarck Caulaincourt – ☎ 01 42 55 05 42 – Closed 10-20 August, Sunday dinner and Monday C 14
Rest – Menu (€ 25), € 35 (lunch), € 45/68 – Carte € 71/83
◆ There is change in the air at this Montmartre institution: delicious contemporary cuisine with a personal touch in an elegant decor. Pleasant terrace for fine weather.

Le Cottage Marcadet
151 bis r. Marcadet Ⓜ Lamarck Caulaincourt – ☎ 01 42 57 71 22 – contact@cottagemarcadet.com – Fax 01 42 57 71 24 – Closed spring holidays, August, Sunday and Monday C 13
Rest – Menu (€ 28), € 35 – Carte € 64/96
◆ An intimate ambience awaits you in this classic dining room with comfortable Louis XVI furnishings. Carefully prepared traditional cuisine.

XX **Le Moulin de la Galette**

83 r. Lepic Ⓜ Abbesses – ✆ 01 46 06 84 77 – moulindelagalette@yahoo.fr – Fax 01 46 06 84 78 C 13

Rest – Menu (€ 17), € 25 (lunch)/42 (dinner) – Carte € 50/78

◆ A windmill in 1622, then a popular dance hall painted by Renoir and Toulouse-Lautrec, this place is now a pleasant restaurant with a charming terrace.

XX **Au Clair de la Lune**

9 r. Poulbot Ⓜ Abbesses – ✆ 01 42 58 97 03 – Fax 01 42 55 64 74 – Closed 18 August-15 September, Monday lunch and Sunday D 14

Rest – Menu € 32 – Carte € 37/69

◆ Situated behind Place du Tertre, this restaurant takes its name from a French nursery rhyme. Classical cuisine served in a friendly atmosphere with frescoes of old Montmartre on the walls.

XX **Au Poulbot Gourmet**

39 r. Lamarck Ⓜ Lamarck Caulaincourt – ✆ 01 46 06 86 00 – renaud1973@hotmail.com – Closed 3-24 August, Sunday and Monday C 14

Rest – Menu (€ 19), € 38 – Carte € 41/55

◆ Named after the street urchins who once inhabited Montmartre, this restaurant retains the bistro style of the period. Simple and concise, market-inspired menu, much appreciated by gourmets.

Ph. Gajic/MICHELIN

La Villette-Cité des Sciences, Buttes Chaumont

19e arrondissement ✉ 75019

Holiday Inn rm,

216 av. J. Jaurès Ⓜ Porte de Pantin – ✆ 01 44 84 18 18 – hilavillette@alliance-hospitality.com – Fax 01 44 84 18 20 C 21

182 rm – †€ 230/600 ††€ 230/600, ☕ € 18 – **Rest** – *(closed Saturday and Sunday)* Menu (€ 21), € 28 (dinner) – Carte € 26/51

◆ Modern construction across from the Cité de la Musique. Spacious and soundproofed rooms, offering modern comfort. Métro station a few metres away. Simple brasserie-style restaurant and small terrace protected from the street by a curtain of plants.

Laumière without rest

4 r. Petit Ⓜ Laumière – ✆ 01 42 06 10 77 – lelaumiere@wanadoo.fr – Fax 01 42 06 72 50 D 19

54 rm – †€ 58/70 ††€ 59/78, ☕ € 8

◆ Yearning for some greenery? This hotel, treated to a new lease of life, will rejuvenate you with its pretty little garden and the nearby Buttes-Chaumont park.

Crimée without rest

188 r. Crimée Ⓜ Crimée – ✆ 01 40 36 75 29 – hotelcrimee19@wanadoo.fr – Fax 01 40 36 29 57 C 18

31 rm – †€ 68/70 ††€ 73, ☕ € 7

◆ Hotel 300m from the Ourcq Canal. The well-soundproofed and air-conditioned rooms have functional furniture and some overlook a small garden.

Abricôtel without rest

15 r. Lally Tollendal Ⓜ Jaurès – ✆ 01 42 08 34 49 – abricotel@wanadoo.fr – Fax 01 42 40 83 95 D 18

39 rm – †€ 55/60 ††€ 60/70, ☕ € 7

◆ This little family business giving onto a busy street offers small simple rooms that are functional and reasonably priced.

XX **Relais des Buttes** VISA MC

86 r. Compans Ⓜ Botzaris – ✆ 01 42 08 24 70 – Fax 01 42 03 20 44 – Closed August, 24 December-3 January, Saturday lunch and Sunday E 20

Rest – Menu € 34 – Carte € 43/57

◆ Close to Buttes Chaumont park. In winter, the up-to-date dining room with fireplace is most welcome, while the peaceful courtyard terrace is ideal in summer. Classic menu.

X **L'Hermès** VISA MC

23 r. Mélingue Ⓜ Pyrénées – ✆ 01 42 39 94 70 – lhermes@wanadoo.fr – Closed Easter holidays, August, February holidays, Wednesday lunch, Sunday and Monday

Rest – Menu € 16 (weekday lunch)/30 – Carte € 33/82 F 20

◆ A charming Provençal ambience of ochre, wood and colourful tableware. Generous, bistro-style dishes highlighted on the daily specials board. A popular local address.

X **La Violette** VISA MC AE

11 av. Corentin Cariou Ⓜ Corentin Cariou – ✆ 01 40 35 20 45 – restolaviolette@free.fr – Closed 9-24 August, 20 December-4 January, Saturday and Sunday

Rest – *(number of covers limited, pre-book)* Carte € 35/47 B 19

◆ A friendly welcome and atmosphere, trendy decor (black and white colour scheme, purple bench, walls covered with bottle racks), and tasty contemporary cuisine.

X **La Cave Gourmande** A/C VISA MC

10 r. Gén. Brunet Ⓜ Botzaris – ✆ 01 40 40 03 30 – lacavegourmande@wanadoo.fr – Fax 01 40 40 03 30 – Closed 1st-24 August, February holidays, Saturday lunch and Sunday E 20

Rest – Menu € 31/36

◆ A friendly ambience, decorative bottle racks, wooden tables and market-inspired dishes are the main features of this pleasant bistro near the Buttes-Chaumont park.

S. Sauvignier/MICHELIN

Père Lachaise, Belleville

20e arrondissement ✉ 75020

Palma without rest A/C VISA MC AE

77 av. Gambetta Ⓜ Gambetta – ✆ 01 46 36 13 65 – hotel.palma@wanadoo.fr – Fax 01 46 36 03 27 G 21

32 rm – †€ 64/69 ††€ 73/79, ☕ € 7

◆ A stone's throw from Place Gambetta and Père-Lachaise cemetery, this hotel offers small, slightly old-fashioned rooms decorated in 1970s style.

XX **Les Allobroges** VISA MC

71 r. Grands-Champs Ⓜ Maraîchers – ✆ 01 43 73 40 00 – Fax 01 40 09 23 22 – Closed 3-27 August, Sunday dinner and Monday K 22

Rest – Menu € 20/34

◆ Step off the beaten track to discover this friendly restaurant close to Porte de Montreuil. Simple, pretty decor and copious modern cuisine prepared by the new chef.

X **Le Bistrot des Soupirs "Chez les On"** VISA MC

49 r. Chine Ⓜ Gambetta – ✆ 01 44 62 93 31 – Fax 01 44 62 77 83 – Closed 1st-10 May, 5-25 August, 25 December-1st January, Sunday and Monday G 21

Rest – Menu € 16 (lunch), € 35/50 – Carte € 28/43

◆ Next to the picturesque Soupirs lane, Auvergne and Lyons specialities take pride of place in this pleasant countrified inn. Resolutely jovial in spirit.

Ph. Gajic/MICHELIN

Environs de Paris

cartes 18-21

"Surrounding area"

ALFORTVILLE – **94 Val-de-Marne** – **312** D3 – **101** 27 – **pop. 36 232** – **alt. 32 m** – ✉ **94140** 21 **C2**

Paris 9 – Créteil 6 – Maisons-Alfort 2 – Melun 40

Chinagora
rm, VISA MC AE

1 pl. du Confluent France-Chine – ✆ 01 43 53 58 88 – hotel@chinagora.fr – Fax 01 49 77 57 17

187 rm – €85 €94, ☕ €10 – 4 suites – **Rest** – Menu €14 (weekday lunch) – Carte €16/119

◆ Where China and France meet, a Manchurian architectural extravaganza and western-style rooms, most of which give onto an exotic garden. Large shopping precinct. Restaurant offering Asian specialities.

ANTONY – **92 Hauts-de-Seine** – **311** J3 – **101** 25 – **pop. 59 855** – **alt. 80 m** – ✉ **92160** 20 **B3**

Paris 13 – Bagneux 6 – Corbeil-Essonnes 28 – Nanterre 23 – Versailles 16

Syndicat d'initiative, place Auguste Mounié ✆ 01 42 37 57 77, Fax 01 46 66 30 80

Sceaux: park★★ and musée de l'Île-de-France★ North: 4 km - Châtenay-Malabry: St-Germain-l'Auxerrois church ★, Chateaubriand House★ Northwest: 4 km, Île de France

Alixia without rest
VISA MC AE

1 r. Providence – ✆ 01 46 74 92 92 – alixia-antony@netgdi.com – Fax 01 46 74 50 55

40 rm – €69/110 €69/116, ☕ €9

◆ A recent hotel situated in a quiet street. The rooms at the rear are very quiet and have air-conditioning; they are all well laid out.

L'Amandier
VISA MC AE

8 r. de l'Église – ✆ 01 46 66 22 02 – colpart.eric@neuf.fr – Closed 5-25 August, 25 December-1st January, Saturday lunch, Sunday dinner and Monday

Rest – Menu €32/60

◆ This restaurant in old Antony houses a spacious and comfortable dining room that is half-classic, half-contemporary. The modern menu is regularly updated.

Les Philosophes
VISA MC AE

53 av. Division Leclerc – ✆ 01 42 37 23 22 – Closed 5-25 August, Saturday lunch, Sunday dinner and Monday

Rest – Carte €25/34

◆ Youthful, dynamic service in this restaurant on the edge of the main road. Up-to-date cuisine, using seasonal market produce, in a minimalist but colourful setting.

La Tour de Marrakech
VISA MC AE

72 av. Division Leclerc – ✆ 01 46 66 00 54 – Fax 01 46 66 12 99 – Closed Aug. and Mon.

Rest – Menu €23 (weekday lunch) – Carte €24/46

◆ All the magic of Morocco is condensed here, from the Moorish decor to the delicately prepared dishes of North Africa. A friendly welcome and attentive service.

ARGENTEUIL – 95 Val-d'Oise – 305 E7 – 101 14 – pop. 93 961 – alt. 33 m – ✉ 95100 Northern France and the Paris Region 20 B1

Paris 16 – Chantilly 38 – Pontoise 20 – St-Germain-en-Laye 19

La Ferme d'Argenteuil

2 bis r. Verte – ✆ 01 39 61 00 62 – lafermedargenteuil@wanadoo.fr – Fax 01 30 76 32 31 – Closed August, Monday dinner, Tuesday dinner, Wednesday dinner and Sunday

Rest – Menu € 36/55 bi – Carte € 57/70

♦ Two sisters run this inn, slightly out of the centre. Amélia welcomes guests into the stylish dining room, while Marie oversees the updated cuisine.

ASNIÈRES-SUR-SEINE – 92 Hauts-de-Seine – 311 J2 – 101 15 – pop. 75 837 – alt. 37 m – ✉ 92600 Northern France and the Paris Region 20 B1

Paris 10 – Argenteuil 6 – Nanterre 8 – Pontoise 26 – St-Denis 8 – St-Germain-en-Laye 20

Van Gogh

2 quai Aulagnier, (access via the Cimetière des Chiens (pet cemetery)) – ✆ 01 47 91 05 10 – levangogh@wanadoo.fr – Fax 01 47 93 00 93 – Closed 11-17 August, Saturday lunch and Sunday dinner

Rest – Menu € 39 – Carte € 45/77

♦ This is where Van Gogh immortalised the La Sirène restaurant. Personal welcome, attentive service, fish direct from the Atlantic and pretty terrace overlooking the Seine.

La Petite Auberge

118 r. Colombes – ✆ 01 47 93 33 94 – lapetite.auberge@orange.fr – Fax 01 47 93 33 94 – Closed 6-21 August, Sunday dinner and Monday

Rest – Menu € 30/40

♦ A small roadside inn with a pleasant atmosphere. Old objects, paintings and a collection of plates decorate the rustic dining room. Traditional cuisine.

AULNAY-SOUS-BOIS – 93 Seine-Saint-Denis – 305 F7 – 101 18 – pop. 80 021 – alt. 46 m – ✉ 93600 21 D1

Paris 19 – Bobigny 9 – Lagny-sur-Marne 23 – Meaux 30 – St-Denis 16 – Senlis 38

Novotel

rm, rest,

carrefour de l'Europe, (N 370) – ✆ 01 58 03 90 90 – h0387@accor.com – Fax 01 58 03 90 99

139 rm – € 55/230 € 55/230, € 13,50 – **Rest** – *(closed Friday dinner, Saturday and Sunday)* Menu (€ 16), € 20 – Carte € 23/38

♦ Classical chain hotel made up of a café (brasserie menu), garden with pool, and a 'cyber terrace'. The rooms have been partly refurbished. Modern dining room; garden dining in fine weather.

Auberge des Saints Pères (Jean-Claude Cahagnet)

212 av. Nonneville – ✆ 01 48 66 62 11 – info@auberge-des-saints-peres.com – Fax 01 48 66 67 44 – Closed 3-9 March, 4-24 August, 10-15 November, Wednesday dinner and Saturday and Sunday

Rest – Menu € 38/60 – Carte € 54/73

Spec. Petites brochettes de maquereau de pêche bretonne fumé au cédrat. "Sandwich" de lotte au foie gras, pomme et andouille. Canard rouennais pressé devant le client.

♦ This house on a corner hides an attractive and subdued interior in a happy contrast to the chef's creative talent, enhanced by herbs fresh from the garden.

AUVERS-SUR-OISE – 95 Val-d'Oise – 305 E6 – 106 6 – 101 3 – pop. 6 820 – alt. 30 m – ✉ 95430 Northern France and the Paris Region 18 B1

Paris 36 – Beauvais 52 – Chantilly 35 – Compiègne 84 – L'Isle-Adam 7 – Pontoise 10

Office de tourisme, rue de la Sansonne ✆ 01 30 36 10 06, Fax 01 34 48 08 47

Van Gogh House★ - Journey-show at the time of the Impressionists★ in the château of Léry.

XXX **Hostellerie du Nord** with rm

6 r. Gén. de Gaulle – ✆ 01 30 36 70 74 – contact@hostelleriedunord.fr – Fax 01 30 36 72 75 – Closed Sunday dinner

8 rm – †€ 98/128 ††€ 128/188, ☕ € 14 – **Rest** – *(closed Saturday lunch and Monday)* Menu € 47 bi (weekday lunch), € 57/77 – Carte € 68/75

◆ Famous painters once stayed in this former post house. The works of art adorning the dining room and bedrooms are a reminder of this rich past. Traditional cuisine.

X **Auberge Ravoux**

– ✆ 01 30 36 60 60 – info@vangoghfrance.com – Fax 01 30 36 60 61 – Open March-end October and closed Wednesday dinner, Thursday dinner, Sunday dinner, Monday and Tuesday

Rest – *(number of covers limited, pre-book)* Menu (€ 28), € 35

◆ A warm atmosphere and the simple cuisine of 19C artists' cafés in the inn where Van Gogh lived towards the end of his life. Visit the painter's little room.

BAGNOLET – **93 Seine-Saint-Denis** – **305** F7 – **101** 17 – **pop. 32 511** – **alt. 96 m** – ✉ **93170** 21 **C2**

▶ Paris 8 – Bobigny 6 – Lagny-sur-Marne 32 – Meaux 39

Novotel Porte de Bagnolet

av. de la République, (Porte de Bagnolet junction) – ✆ 01 49 93 63 00 – h0380@accor.com – Fax 01 49 93 63 93

609 rm – †€ 220/275 ††€ 220/275, ☕ € 14 – 7 suites

Rest – Menu € 23 bi/68 bi – Carte € 22/40

◆ Near the ring road, this hotel, one of the first opened by the chain, has been fully renovated from top to toe. Functional, modern rooms. Business people, groups and tourists from all over the world cross paths at this restaurant, open very late.

BOIS-COLOMBES – **92 Hauts-de-Seine** – **311** J2 – **101** 15 – **pop. 23 885** – **alt. 37 m** – ✉ **92270** 20 **B1**

▶ Paris 12 – Nanterre 6 – Pontoise 25 – St-Denis 11 – St-Germain-en-Laye 19

X **Le Chefson**

17 r. Ch. Chefson – ✆ 01 42 42 12 05 – Fax 01 47 80 51 68 – Closed 1st-28 August, February holidays, Monday dinner, Saturday and Sunday

Rest – bistrot *(number of covers limited, pre-book)* Menu (€ 19), € 25/35

◆ This restaurant is often crowded as the dining room is rather small. A bistro atmosphere and simple, copious traditional cuisine.

BOUGIVAL – **78 Yvelines** – **311** I2 – **101** 13 – **pop. 8 432** – **alt. 40 m** – ✉ **78380**
Northern France and the Paris Region 20 **A2**

▶ Paris 21 – Rueil-Malmaison 5 – St-Germain-en-Laye 6 – Versailles 8 – Le Vésinet 5

Syndicat d'initiative, 7, rue du Général Leclerc ✆ 01 39 69 21 23, Fax 01 39 69 37 65

Holiday Inn

10-12 r. Y. Tourgueneff, (D 113) – ✆ 01 30 08 18 28 – holidayinn.parvb@hotels-res.com – Fax 01 30 08 18 38

181 rm – †€ 110/250 ††€ 110/250, ☕ € 17 – **Rest** – Menu € 25 (lunch)/32 (dinner) – Carte € 32/56

◆ This 1970s building, with its original facade, has had a fully-renovated interior, rearranged around a patio. Spacious rooms, including ten with period furniture that overlook the River Seine. The restaurant has a sunny decor and offers traditional cuisine with southern flavours.

Villa des Impressionnistes without rest

15 quai Rennequin Sualem, (D 113) – ✆ 01 30 08 40 00 – villa.impression@wanadoo.fr – Fax 01 39 18 58 89

50 rm – †€ 100/145 ††€ 125/320, ☕ € 12

◆ Selected objects and furniture, bright colours and reproduction paintings – the charming decor of this recent hotel reflects the Impressionist past of the Bougival quayside.

Le Camélia (Thierry Conte)
7 quai G. Clemenceau – 01 39 18 36 06
– info@lecamelia.com – Fax 01 39 18 00 25
– Closed 20-28 April, 29 July-25 August, 23-31 December, Sunday Monday
Rest – Menu € 42/68 – Carte € 91/109
Spec. Sole française. Lièvre à la royale (season). Millefeuille aux fruits.
◆ A smart façade near Ivan Tourgueniev's Datcha-museum. Classic cuisine served in a modern, warm and colourful setting. Fine French wine selection.

BOULOGNE-BILLANCOURT – **92 Hauts-de-Seine** – **311** J2 – **101** 24 – **pop. 106 360 – alt. 35 m** – **92100** Northern France and the Paris Region 20 **B2**

Paris 10 – Nanterre 9 – Versailles 11
Musée départemental Albert-Kahn ★: gardens ★ - Musée Paul Landowski ★.

Radisson SAS
33 av. E. Vaillant – 01 46 08 85 00 – info.boulogne@radissonsas.com
– Fax 01 46 08 85 01
170 rm – € 150/345 € 150/345, € 22
Rest *A.O.C.* – *(closed 4-25 August and Saturday)* Menu (€ 27), € 34
– Carte € 38/68
◆ This brand new hotel, a stone's throw from the Parc des Princes stadium, offers fine, modern rooms with all the latest equipment. The modern-style and trendy restaurant opens onto a pretty patio-terrace planted with vines. Appetising up-to-date cuisine.

Mercure Porte de St-Cloud rm,
37 pl. René Clair – 01 49 10 49 10
– h6188@accor.com – Fax 01 46 08 26 16
180 rm – € 145/215 € 155/230, € 16 – 4 suites
Rest *Croisette Café* – *01 49 10 49 50 (closed Friday dinner, Saturday, Sunday and holidays)* Menu (€ 21), € 27 (weekday lunch) – Carte € 22/46
◆ Modern glass building housing comfortable rooms. Fully equipped business centre and refined lounge-bar adorned with photos of stars by the Harcourt studio. Murals depicting some 400 famous show business personalities enliven the brasserie.

Acanthe without rest
9 rd-pt Rhin et Danube – 01 46 99 10 40 – hotel-acanthe@akamail.com
– Fax 01 46 99 00 05
69 rm – € 195/215 € 195/240, € 15
◆ Near the Boulogne studios and the unusual gardens of the Albert-Kahn museum, this well-soundproofed hotel has attractive, contemporary rooms. A pleasant flowered patio. Billiards.

Tryp rm, rest,
20 r. Abondances – 01 48 25 80 80 – tryp.paris.boulogne@solmelia.com
– Fax 01 48 25 33 13
75 rm – € 207/247 € 207/247, € 17 – **Rest** – *(closed 1st-25 August, 22 December-2 January, Saturday, Sunday and holidays)* Menu (€ 23), € 28
◆ In a quiet area of the town which nearly became the 21st district of Paris, a hotel with modern rooms, many with balconies. Lounge bar area. Bright contemporary restaurant, decorated with paintings; traditional cuisine.

Sélect Hôtel without rest
66 av. Gén.-Leclerc – 01 46 04 70 47 – reception@select-hotel.fr
– Fax 01 46 04 07 77
62 rm – € 120 € 140, € 10
◆ On the main Paris to Versailles road, a well-soundproofed establishment whose discreet rooms are furnished and decorated in the Art Nouveau style.

Paris without rest
104 bis r. Paris – 01 46 05 13 82 – contact@hotel-paris-boulogne.com
– Fax 01 48 25 10 43
31 rm – € 76 € 84, € 8,50
◆ Situated on a corner, this old brick building has small rooms that are particularly practical and well-soundproofed. A pleasant family welcome and meticulous management.

Bijou Hôtel without rest
15 r. V. Griffuelhes, pl. Marché – ✆ 01 46 21 24 98 – Fax 01 46 21 12 98
50 rm – †€ 64 ††€ 79/84, ☕ € 9
◆ This corner building has a pleasant provincial atmosphere, with clean and well-equipped rooms in a rustic or more modern style.

Olympic Hôtel without rest
69 av. V. Hugo – ✆ 01 46 05 20 69 – olympic.hotel@free.fr – Fax 01 46 04 04 07 – Closed 11 July-11 August
36 rm – †€ 65 ††€ 70/80, ☕ € 7
◆ An early 20C building near the interesting 1930s museum. The rooms are not very spacious but functional. Breakfast is served in a small courtyard in the summer.

Au Comte de Gascogne (Henri Charvet)
89 av. J.-B. Clément – ✆ 01 46 03 47 27 – aucomtedegasc@aol.com – Fax 01 46 04 55 70 – Closed 1st-15 August, Monday dinner, Saturday lunch and Sunday
Rest – Menu € 58 (lunch)/120 – Carte € 89/139
Spec. Grande assiette de tous nos foies gras. Ragoût de homard aux pommes de terre safranées. Suprêmes de pigeon, jus au guanaja.
◆ The conservatory-style décor of this dining room with its mass of lush exotic plants is a veritable oasis of freshness that Lino Ventura would appreciate. Modern cuisine.

L'Auberge
86 av. J.-B. Clément – ✆ 01 46 05 67 19 – legoux.cyrille@9business.fr – Fax 01 46 05 14 24 – Closed 4-25 August, Saturday lunch, Sunday dinner and Monday
Rest – Menu (€ 30), € 36/59
◆ This stylish inn has been redecorated on a fruit and vegetable theme with a profusion of copper utensils. Enjoy its up-to-date cuisine.

Look out for red symbols, indicating particularly pleasant establishments.

LE BOURGET – **93 Seine-Saint-Denis** – **305** F7 – **101** 17 – **pop. 12 110** – **alt. 47 m** – ✉ **93350** **Northern France and the Paris Region** 21 **C1**

Paris 13 – Bobigny 6 – Chantilly 38 – Meaux 41 – St-Denis 8 – Senlis 38

Musée de l'Air et de l'Espace★★.

Novotel rm,
2 r. Perrin, (Pont Yblon au Blanc-Mesnil Industrial Park) ✉ 93150 – ✆ 01 48 67 48 88 – h0388@accor-hotels.com – Fax 01 45 91 08 27
143 rm – †€ 90/170 ††€ 90/170, ☕ € 13,50 – **Rest** – Carte € 21/42
◆ In a business park near the airport, this hotel is nonetheless protected by greenery. The renovated rooms are in keeping with "Novation" standards. Photos illustrating the history of aviation adorn the restaurant. Terrace and pool.

BOURG-LA-REINE – **92 Hauts-de-Seine** – **311** J3 – **101** 25 – **pop. 18 251** – **alt. 56 m** – ✉ **92340** 20 **B2**

Paris 10 – Boulogne-Billancourt 12 – Évry 24 – Versailles 18

Office de tourisme, 1, boulevard Carnot ✆ 01 46 61 36 41, Fax 01 46 61 61 08

L'Hay-les-Roses: rose garden★★ East: 1.5 km, **Northern France and the Paris Region.**

Alixia without rest
82 av. Gén. Leclerc – ✆ 01 46 60 56 56 – alixia-bourglareine@netgdi.com – Fax 01 46 60 57 34
41 rm – †€ 69/92 ††€ 69/98, ☕ € 9
◆ A welcoming façade on the N 20 main road, close to the delightful Sceaux park. Contemporary, well-equipped and soundproofed rooms. Tray meals on request.

BRIE-COMTE-ROBERT – 77 Seine-et-Marne – 312 E3 – 101 39 – pop. 13 397 – alt. 90 m – ✉ 77170 Northern France and the Paris Region 19 C2

Paris 30 – Brunoy 10 – Évry 20 – Melun 18 – Provins 63

Syndicat d'initiative, pl. Jeanne d'Evreux ✆ 01 64 05 30 09, Fax 01 64 05 68 18

Clément Ader Gretz-Armainvilliers Domaine du Château Péreire, Northeast: 12 km by D 216, ✆ 01 64 07 34 10 ;

de Marolles en Brie Marolles-en-Brie Mail de la Justice, Northwest: 6 km, ✆ 01 45 95 18 18 ;

ASPTT Paris Golf des Corbuches Lésigny Ferme des Hyverneaux, North: 6 km by N 104, ✆ 01 60 02 07 26 ;

du Réveillon Lésigny Ferme des Hyverneaux, North: 6 km by N 104, ✆ 01 60 02 17 33.

Window★ of the church apse.

À la Grâce de Dieu VISA

79 r. Gén.-Leclerc, (D 619) – ✆ 01 64 05 00 76 – gracedie@wanadoo.fr – Fax 01 64 05 60 57

16 rm – †€ 45 ††€ 55/70, ☕ € 8,50 – ½ P € 72 – **Rest** – *(closed Sunday evening)* Menu € 22 (weekdays)/38 – Carte € 39/53

◆ In the 17C, this coaching inn was the last stop before possible encounters with highwaymen. It has retained a rather pessimistic name, but now offers modern comfort. This restaurant is reminiscent of an old country inn (Louis XIII furniture, fresco).

BRY-SUR-MARNE – 94 Val-de-Marne – 312 E2 – 101 18 – pop. 15 000 – alt. 40 m – ✉ 94360 21 D2

Paris 16 – Créteil 12 – Joinville-le-Pont 5 – Nogent-sur-Marne 3 – Vincennes 9

Syndicat d'initiative, 2, grande rue ✆ 01 48 82 30 30

L'Auberge du Pont de Bry VISA

3 av. Gén. Leclerc – ✆ 01 48 82 27 70 – Closed August, 1st-15 January, Wednesday evening, Sunday evening and Monday

Rest – Menu € 34 – Carte € 32/52

◆ This discreet is inn home to a comfortable modern dining room in pastel colours with a veranda extension. Tempting up-to-date cuisine made with fresh produce.

CARRIÈRES-SUR-SEINE – 78 Yvelines – 311 J2 – 101 14 – pop. 12 050 – alt. 52 m – ✉ 78420 20 A1

Paris 19 – Argenteuil 8 – Nanterre 7 – Pontoise 28 – St-Germain-en-Laye 7

de l'Île Fleurie Carrières sur Seine, ✆ 01 39 52 61 61.

Le Panoramic de Chine VISA AE

1 r. Fermettes – ✆ 01 39 57 64 58 – Fax 01 39 15 17 68 – Closed August, 24-30 December, Sunday dinner and Monday

Rest – Menu € 12 (weekday lunch), € 15/28 – Carte € 24/58

◆ The pagoda entrance of this 1920s house is an invitation to taste its generous Asian food. Pleasant summer terrace.

CERGY-PONTOISE P – 95 Val-d'Oise – 305 D6 – 106 5 – 101 2 – pop. 178 656 – ✉ 95 Northern France and the Paris Region 18 B1

Paris 35 – Mantes-la-Jolie 40 – Pontoise 3 – Rambouillet 60 – Versailles 33

de Cergy-Pontoise Vauréal 2 allée de l'Obstacle d'Eau, West: 7 km by D 922, ✆ 01 34 21 03 48 ;

d'Ableiges Ableiges Chaussée Jules César, Northwest: 14 km by Ableiges road, ✆ 01 30 27 97 00 ;

de Gadancourt Gadancourtby Rouen road: 20 km, ✆ 01 34 66 12 97.

Cergy – pop. 54 781 – alt. 30 m – ✉ 95000

Mercure without rest VISA AE

3 r. Chênes Émeraude, on bd de l'Oise – ✆ 01 34 24 94 94 – h3452@accor.com – Fax 01 34 24 95 15 Y a

56 rm – †€ 85/112 ††€ 85/262, ☕ € 12,50

◆ Behind the restored façade is a modern hotel with large, extremely well-equipped rooms with period furniture. Choose the quieter rooms at the back.

CERGY-PRÉFECTURE

Arts (Pl. des) . . . . Z 2
Boucle (R. de la) . . . . Y 3
Bourgognes (R. des). . . . . Z 5
Chênes Émeraude . . . . Y 13
Columbia (Square) . . . . Y 14
Diapason (Square du). . . . . Y 17
Écureuil (R. de l') . . . . Y 19
Étoile (Allée de l') . . . . Y 21
Galeries (R. des) . . . . Y 24
Gare (R. de la) . . . . Z 25
Grouettes (Av. des). . . . . Z 33
Herbes (R. aux) . . . . Y 34
Italiens (R. des) . . . . Y 39
Marché Neuf (R. du). . . . . Y 43
Pays de France (R. des) . . . . Y 52
Pergola (Pl. de la) . . . . Z 53
Platanes (Allée des) . . . . Z 59
Préfecture (Parvis de la) . . . . Z 63
Préfecture (R. de la) . . . . Z 64
Prieuré (R. du) . . . . Z 66
Théâtre (Allée du) . . . . Z 71
Traversière (R.) . . . . Y 74
Verger (R. du) . . . . Z 77
Villarceaux (R. de) . . . . Z 81

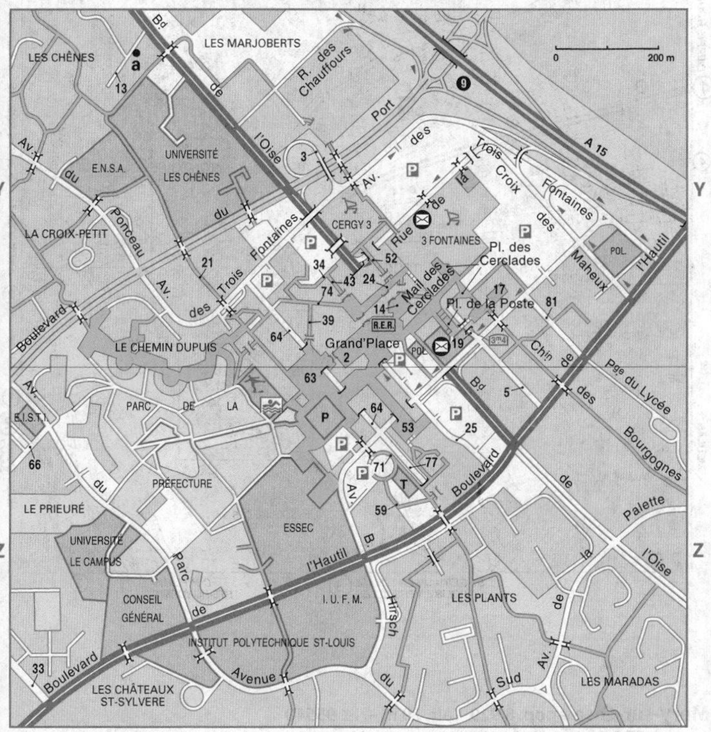

Cormeilles-en-Vexin by ①: 10 km – pop. 863 – alt. 111 m – ✉ 95830

Maison Cagna (Thomas Cagna)

rte de Dieppe – ✆ 01 34 66 61 56 – contact@maison-cagna.fr – Fax 01 34 66 40 31 – Closed 20 July-18 August, 23-27 December, 4-11 January, Sunday and Monday except public holidays

Rest – Menu € 32 (weekday lunch)/65 bi – Carte approx. € 53

Spec. Medley de légumes crus et cuits en tarte fine au parmesan. Saint-Jacques en habit de kadaïf (15 October to 15 March). Panna cotta à la lavande et coulis d'ananas à la badiane.

◆ Today, Mr Cagna's children run the restaurant in this attractive Vexin house. Warm country setting (exposed stonework and beams) enhanced by modern highlights. Refined cuisine.

Hérouville Northeast by D 927: 8 km – pop. 598 – alt. 120 m – ✉ 95300

Les Vignes Rouges

pl. de l'Église – ✆ 01 34 66 54 73 – Fax 01 34 66 20 88 – Closed 1st-10 May, 1st-21 August, 31 December-15 January, Sunday dinner, Monday and Tuesday

Rest – Menu € 38 – Carte € 45/65

◆ A typical Ile de France house named after a painting by Van Gogh. Veranda facing the church. Exhibition of paintings by a local artist. Traditional dishes.

CERGY-PONTOISE

Bougara (Av. Rédouane) . . . **BV** 4
Bouticourt (Bd Ch.). . . . . **BV** 6
Constellation (Av. de la) . . . . **AV** 13
Delarue (Av. du Gén.-G.) . . . **BV** 15
Genottes (Av. des) . . . . **AV** 28
Lavoye (R. Pierre) . . . . **BV** 40
Mendès-France (Mail) . . . . . **AX** 44
Mitterrand (Av. Fr.). . . . . . . **BVX** 45
Moulin à Vent (Bd du) . . . . . **AV** 47
Petit Albi (R. du) . . . . **AV** 55
Verdun (Av. de). . . . . **BX** 76
Viosne (Bd de la) . . . . **BVX** 83

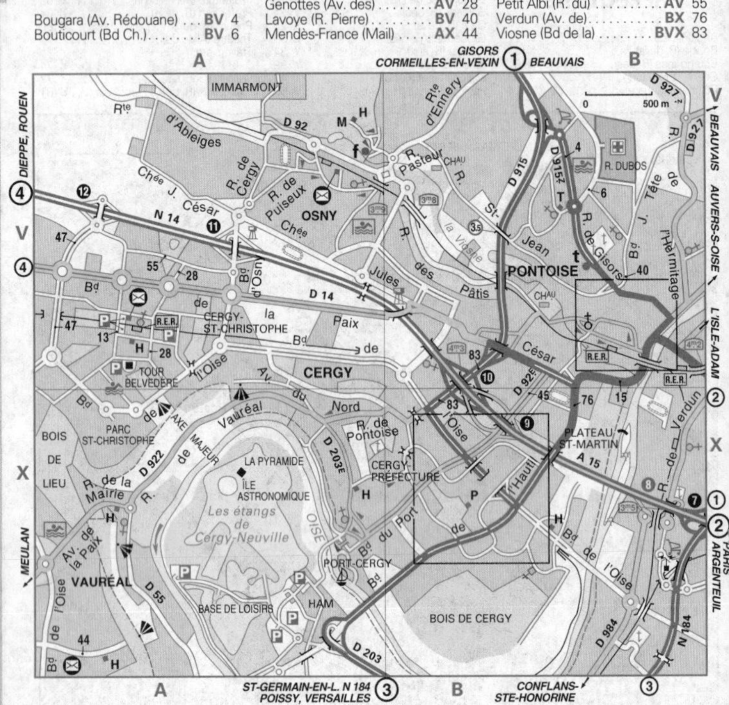

Méry-sur-Oise – pop. 8 929 – alt. 29 m – ✉ 95540

Syndicat d'initiative, 30, avenue Marcel Perrin ✆ 01 34 64 85 15

XXX Le Chiquito

93 r. de l' Oise, (La Bonneville), Pontoise road1 .5 km on D 922 ✉ 95540 – ✆ 01 30 36 40 23 – lechiquito@free.fr – Fax 01 30 36 42 22 – Closed 2-9 January, Saturday lunch, Sunday dinner and Monday

Rest – Menu € 56

♦ An ideal address for a day in the country! Three elegant dining rooms and a pleasant veranda provide the setting for classical cuisine. Attractive garden.

Osny – pop. 14 309 – alt. 37 m – ✉ 95520

XX Moulin de la Renardière

r. Gd Moulin – ✆ 01 30 30 21 13 – severine@e-leos.net – Fax 01 34 25 04 98 – Closed Sunday dinner and Monday AV **f**

Rest – Menu (€ 28 bi), € 35 (weekdays)/60 – Carte € 29/36

♦ An old mill nestling in a park. Choose a table in the Grain Room with its fine fireplace or on the shady, riverside terrace.

Pontoise – pop. 27 494 – alt. 48 m – ✉ 95000

Office de tourisme, 6, place du Petit Martroy ✆ 01 30 38 24 45, Fax 01 30 73 54 84

Syndicat d'initiative, 6, place du Petit Martroy ✆ 01 30 38 24 45, Fax 01 30 73 54 84

PONTOISE

Bretonnerie (R. de la) ...... D 7
Butin (R. Pierre)........... DE 8
Canrobert (Av. du Mar.)..... D 10
Château (R. du) .... E 12
Écluse (Quai de l') .... E 18
Flamel (Pl. Nicolas) .... E 22
Gisors (R. de).............. D 30
Grand Martroy (Pl. du) ..... D 32
Hôtel de Ville (R. de l') ...... E 36
Hôtel Dieu (R. de l') .... E 37
Lavoye (R. Pierre) .... D 40
Leclerc (R. du Gén.)......... E 41
Lecomte (R. A.) .... E 42
Parc aux Charrettes (Pl. du) . D 50
Petit Martroy (Pl. du)........ D 56
Pierre aux Poissons (R. de la) D 57
Pothuis (Quai du)........... E 62
Roche (R. de la) .... E 67
Rouen (R. de) .... D 69
Souvenir (Pl. du) .... D 70
Thiers (R.)................. D 72
Vert Buisson (R. du)......... E 80

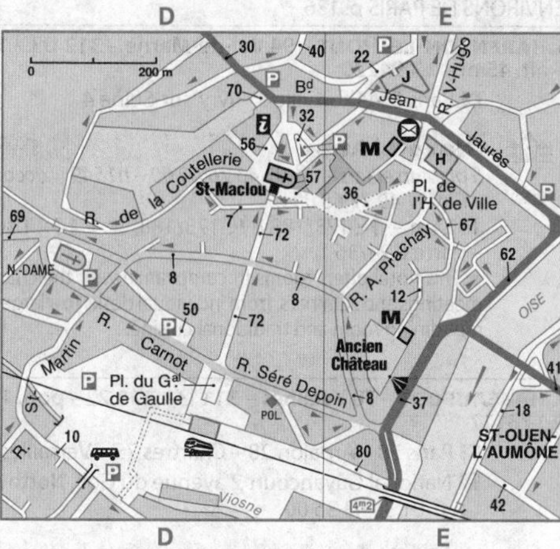

XX **Auberge du Cheval Blanc**

47 r. Gisors – ✆ 01 30 32 25 05 – aubergeduchevalblanc95@wanadoo.fr
– Closed 20 July-21 August, Saturday lunch, Sunday and Monday BV **t**
Rest – Menu € 39 – Carte € 42/70
♦ Contemporary setting with works by local artists on display. Modern cuisine accompanied by a good selection of wines from small producers. Summer terrace.

Cernay-la-Ville – **78 Yvelines** – **311** H3 – **106** 29 – **101** 31 – **pop. 1 727** – **alt. 170 m** – ✉ **78720** 18 **B2**

Paris 45 – Chartres 52 – Longjumeau 31 – Rambouillet 12 – Versailles 25

Abbey ★ of Vaux-de-Cernay West: 2 km, Île de France

Abbaye des Vaux de Cernay rm, rest,

west: 2.5 km on the D 24
– ✆ 01 34 85 23 00 – reception.cernay@leshotelsparticuliers.com
– Fax 01 34 85 11 60
54 rm – €120 €120, € 18 – 3 suites – ½ P € 126/209
Rest – Menu € 32 (weekday lunch), € 50/88 – Carte € 54/83
♦ A 12C Cistercian abbey, restored in the 19C by the Rothschild family. Vast rooms, Gothic remains and contemplative walks in the park. A muted ambiance reigns in this restaurant with a superb vaulted ceiling.

La Ferme des Vallées without rest

west: 3.5 km on the D24 – ✆ 01 30 46 32 42 – vallees@leshotelsparticuliers.com
– Fax 01 30 46 32 23
30 rm – €87/157 €87/247, € 15
♦ This former farmhouse, nestling on the estate of Vaux de Cernay Abbey, now houses variously-furnished rooms with roof windows. There are more simple rooms in the wing, a former sheepfold.

in La Celle-les-Bordes South: 4 km by D 72 – pop. 842 – alt. 125 m – ✉ 78720

X **L'Auberge de l'Élan**

5 r. du Village – ✆ 01 34 85 15 55 – aubergelan@wanadoo.fr – Fax 01 34 85 15 55
– Closed 15-31 August, 28 October-5 November, 1st-7 January, Sunday dinner 15 October-15 March, Tuesday and Wednesday
Rest – Menu € 28 (weekdays)/70 bi
♦ This old village house was renovated but retains its warm rustic feel. Traditional cuisine, highlighting regional produce. Grocer's next door.

CHARENTON-LE-PONT – **94 Val-de-Marne** – **312** D3 – **101** 26 – **pop. 26 582** – **alt. 45 m** – ✉ **94220** 21 **C2**

▶ Paris 8 – Alfortville 3 – Ivry-sur-Seine 4

Novotel Atria VISA

5 pl. Marseillais – ✆ 01 46 76 60 60 – h1549@accor.com – Fax 01 49 77 68 00

132 rm – €173/188 €173/188, € 14 – 1 suite – **Rest** – Menu € 18/24 – Carte € 24/36

◆ This hotel offers rooms in compliance with the chain's style and is fully equipped for meetings and seminars, from individual desks to a large conference room. Modern restaurant dining room and traditional cuisine.

CHÂTEAUFORT – **78 Yvelines** – **311** I3 – **101** 22 – **pop. 1 453** – **alt. 153 m** – ✉ **78117** 20 **A3**

▶ Paris 28 – Arpajon 28 – Chartres 75 – Versailles 15

National Guyancourt 2 avenue du Golf, Northwest: 7 km by D 36, ✆ 01 30 43 36 00.

La Belle Époque (Philippe Delaune) VISA AE

10 pl. Mairie – ✆ 01 39 56 95 48 – Fax 01 39 56 99 93 – Closed 3-25 August, 21 December-4 January, Sunday and Monday

Rest – Menu € 36/56 – Carte € 56/68

Spec. Langoustines rôties au beurre demi-sel. Suprême de pintade fermière farcie, morilles et asperges vertes. Gâteau coulant au chocolat noir.

◆ A charming welcome, elegant Belle Époque-type decor, shaded terrace overlooking the Chevreuse Valley and delicious up-to-date cuisine: enjoy it!

CHATOU – **78 Yvelines** – **311** I2 – **101** 13 – **pop. 28 588** – **alt. 30 m** – ✉ **78400**
Northern France and the Paris Region 20 **A1**

▶ Paris 17 – Maisons-Laffitte 8 – Pontoise 31 – St-Germain-en-Laye 6 – Versailles 13

Office de tourisme, place de la Gare ✆ 01 30 71 30 89

de l'Île Fleurie Carrières sur Seine Carrières sur Seine, ✆ 01 39 52 61 61.

Les Canotiers VISA AE

16 av. Mar. Foch – ✆ 01 30 71 58 69 – didier.focus@wanadoo.fr – Fax 01 47 51 70 09 – Closed August, Christmas holidays, Saturday lunchtime, Sunday evening and Monday

Rest – Menu (€ 18), € 25 – Carte € 29/43

◆ A restaurant, near the island where Renoir painted his masterpiece "Breakfast with Boatmen", offering up-to-date cuisine in a modern dining room adorned with abstract paintings by the landlady-artist.

CHENNEVIÈRES-SUR-MARNE – **94 Val-de-Marne** – **312** E3 – **101** 28 – **pop. 17 837** – **alt. 108 m** – ✉ **94430** 21 **D2**

▶ Paris 18 – Créteil 14 – Melun 35 – Nogent-sur-Marne 8

L'Écu de France VISA

31 r. Champigny – ✆ 01 45 76 00 03 – info@ecudefrance.com – Fax 01 45 93 12 05 – Closed Sunday dinner and Monday

Rest – Menu € 45/75 – Carte € 61/80

◆ This inn, dating from 1717, houses charming rustic dining rooms. Pleasant flower-decked terraces by the River Marne. Traditional menu in tune with the seasons.

CLAMART – **92 Hauts-de-Seine** – **311** J3 – **101** 25 – **pop. 48 572** – **alt. 102 m** – ✉ **92140** 20 **B2**

▶ Paris 10 – Boulogne-Billancourt 7 – Issy-les-Moulineaux 4 – Nanterre 15 – Versailles 13

Syndicat d'initiative, 22, rue Paul Vaillant Couturier ✆ 01 46 42 17 95

La Brèche du Bois without rest
7 pl. J. Hunebelle – ✆ 01 46 42 29 06 – brechebois@aol.com – Fax 01 46 42 00 05
30 rm – †€ 55/59 ††€ 65/70, ☕ € 7
◆ This former open-air café, near the town centre, now offers functional, well-kept rooms, quieter at the rear. Clamart's woodlands are on the hotel's doorstep.

Trosy without rest
41 r. P. Vaillant-Couturier – ✆ 01 47 36 37 37 – hoteltrosy@aol.com – Fax 01 47 36 88 38
40 rm – †€ 56 ††€ 62, ☕ € 7
◆ This modern building features functional well-kept rooms; ask for one overlooking the quieter courtyard side. Courteous welcome and family atmosphere.

CLICHY – 92 Hauts-de-Seine – **311** J2 – **101** 15 – **pop. 50 179** – **alt. 30 m** – ✉ **92110** 20 **B1**

Paris 9 – Argenteuil 8 – Nanterre 9 – Pontoise 26 – St-Germain-en-Laye 21

Office de tourisme, 61, rue Martre ✆ 01 47 15 31 61, Fax 01 47 15 30 45

Holiday Inn
2 r. 8 mai 1945 – ✆ 01 76 68 77 00 – hipclichy@ihg.com – Fax 01 76 68 77 01
270 rm – †€ 300 ††€ 300, ☕ € 18 – **Rest** – *(closed August, Saturday lunch, Sunday and holidays lunch)* Menu (€ 19), € 25 (lunch) – Carte € 24/38
◆ Despite its location close to the ring-road, the rooms in this hotel are quiet, thanks to excellent soundproofing. Modern architecture, harmonious rooms and state-of-the-art facilities.

Europe without rest
52 bd Gén. Leclerc – ✆ 01 47 37 13 10 – europe.hotel@wanadoo.fr – Fax 01 40 87 11 06
83 rm – †€ 130 ††€ 130, ☕ € 10
◆ Renovated brick building (1920) offering comfortable rooms with relaxing and trendy decoration. Fully-equipped, high-quality leisure and fitness area.

Résidence Europe without rest
15 r. Pierre Curie – ✆ 01 47 37 12 13 – europe.hotel@wanadoo.fr – Fax 01 40 87 11 06
28 rm – †€ 130 ††€ 130, ☕ € 10
◆ In a peaceful street, an establishment with recently refurbished rooms, with limed furniture. Nautical decor in the breakfast rooms.

La Romantica
73 bd J. Jaurès – ✆ 01 47 37 29 71 – laromantica@wanadoo.fr – Fax 01 47 37 76 32 – Closed Saturday lunchtime and Sunday
Rest – Menu € 38 (weekday lunch), € 45/80 – Carte € 37/112
◆ The somewhat tired-looking façade hides a pleasant and low-key dining room and garden with a terrace on sunny days. Italian cuisine and superb wine list.

La Barrière de Clichy
1 r. Paris – ✆ 01 47 37 05 18 – labarrieredeclichy@free.fr – Fax 01 47 37 77 05 – Closed 4-31 August, Saturday, Sunday and holidays
Rest – Menu € 33/42 – Carte € 55/81
◆ An elegant, refined restaurant attracting a loyal following. Seasonal dishes with a modern touch; the menu du marché changes daily.

COLOMBES – 92 Hauts-de-Seine – **312** C2 – **101** 14 – **pop. 83 100** – **alt. 38 m** – ✉ **92700**

Paris 19 – Nanterre 9 – Boulogne-Billancourt 19 – Montreuil 23 – Argenteuil 4

Courtyard by Marriott
91 bd Charles de Gaulle – ✆ 01 47 69 59 49 – cy.colombes@courtyard.com – Fax 01 47 69 59 20
150 rm – †€ 89/229 ††€ 89/229, ☕ € 17 – **Rest** – *(closed Sunday lunch and Saturday)* Carte € 27/35
◆ This new building has functional guestrooms and a gym. The lobby, heated by an open fireplace, is home to the Market, serving self-service snacks and refreshments. Seasonal, contemporary cuisine prepared by the chef in full view of diners.

CONFLANS-STE-HONORINE – 78 Yvelines – 311 I2 – 101 3 – pop. 33 327 – alt. 25 m – ✉ 78700 Northern France and the Paris Region 18 B1

Paris 38 – Mantes-la-Jolie 39 – Poissy 10 – Pontoise 8 – Versailles 27

Office de tourisme, 1, rue René Albert ✆ 01 34 90 99 09, Fax 01 39 19 80 77

⋞★ from the château park terrace - Musée de la Batellerie.

Au Bord de l'Eau
15 quai Martyrs-de-la-Résistance – ✆ 01 39 72 86 51 – Closed 8-22 August, 22 December-2 January, dinner except Saturday and Monday
Rest – Menu € 29 (weekday lunch), € 40/54
◆ Boat name plaques and navigation instruments: The interior of this family restaurant on the quays of the Seine renders homage to river craft.

CORBEIL-ESSONNES – 91 Essonne – 312 D4 – 101 37 – pop. 39 378 – alt. 37 m – ✉ 91100 18 B2

Paris 36 – Fontainebleau 37 – Créteil 27 – Évry 6 – Melun 24

Syndicat d'initiative, 36, rue Saint-Spire ✆ 01 64 96 23 97, Fax 01 60 88 05 37

Blue Green Golf de Villeray Saint-Pierre-du-Perray, E : 6 km, ✆ 01 60 75 17 47 ;

de Greenparc Saint-Pierre-du-Perray Route de Villepècle, NE : 6 km par D 947, ✆ 01 60 75 40 60.

in Coudray-Montceaux Southeast: 6 km by N 7 – pop. 2 800 – alt. 81 m – ✉ 91830

Mercure
rte de Milly-la-Forêt – ✆ 01 64 99 00 00 – h0977@accor-hotels.com – Fax 01 64 93 95 55
125 rm – €127 €137, € 13 – **Rest** – Carte € 22/32
◆ Archery, golf and handball, etc., as well as a fine conference centre: this hotel's sports and business facilities are just as appreciated by families as by business guests. Modern dining room/veranda and terrace overlooking the forest and countryside.

COURBEVOIE – 92 Hauts-de-Seine – 311 J2 – 101 15 – pop. 69 694 – alt. 28 m – ✉ 92400 Northern France and the Paris Region 20 B1

Paris 10 – Asnières-sur-Seine 4 – Levallois-Perret 4 – Nanterre 5 – St-Germain-en-Laye 17

George Sand without rest
18 av. Marceau – ✆ 01 43 33 57 04 – george-sand@wanadoo.fr – Fax 01 47 88 59 38
32 rm – €70/130 €80/145, € 12
◆ It is worth staying in this hotel, with a pretty Art Deco facade, for its refined interior reminiscent of the world of George Sand, 19C furniture and romantic lounge where Chopin's music is played.

Central without rest
99 r. Cap. Guynemer – ✆ 01 47 89 25 25 – central-ladefense@wanadoo.fr – Fax 01 46 67 02 21
55 rm – €84 €84/94, € 7
◆ The sound-proofed bedrooms and public areas of this family-run hotel near La Défense have been revamped in a pleasantly modern style.

quartier Charras

Mercure La Défense 5 rm,
18 r. Baudin – ✆ 01 49 04 75 00 – h1546@accor.com – Fax 01 47 68 83 32
507 rm – € 130/215 € 145/230, € 15 – 5 suites
Rest ***Le Bistrot de l'Échanson*** – *✆ 01 49 04 75 85 (closed Friday evening, Sunday lunchtime and Saturday)* Carte € 26/38
◆ Imposing architecture in a circular arc with functional, well-equipped rooms: from the 8th floor up some have a view of Paris or La Défense. The Bistrot de l'Echanson's bar-restaurant offers a warm atmosphere and interesting wine list.

at Bécon Park

Les Trois Marmites
215 bd St-Denis – ✆ 01 43 33 25 35 – Fax 01 43 33 25 35 – Closed August, Saturday, Sunday and public holidays
Rest – *(lunch only)* Menu (€ 32), € 37/65
◆ Popular with a business clientele, this small neighbourhood restaurant near the quays is situated opposite Bécon Park and Roybet Fould Museum (works by Carpeaux). Traditional fare.

CRÉTEIL P – **94 Val-de-Marne** – **312** D3 – **101** 27 – **pop. 82 154** – **alt. 48 m** – ✉ **94000** **Northern France and the Paris Region** 21 **C2**

Paris 14 – Bobigny 22 – Évry 32 – Lagny-sur-Marne 29 – Melun 35

de Marolles-en-Brie Marolles-en-Brie Mail de la Justice, Southeast: 10 km, ✆ 01 45 95 18 18 ;

d'Ormesson Ormesson-sur-Marne Chemin du Belvédère, East: 15 km, ✆ 01 45 76 20 71.

Town hall★: square★.

Novotel
au lac – ✆ 01 56 72 56 72 – h0382@accor.com – Fax 01 56 72 56 73
110 rm – €59/135 €59/135, ☕ € 13,50
Rest – Menu € 22/30
◆ The major attraction of this Novotel is its location overlooking the lake (leisure centre and jogging trail). The rooms have been refurbished according to the chain's charter. A resolutely modern-style restaurant, enlivened by plasma screens. Traditional cuisine.

DAMPIERRE-EN-YVELINES – **78 Yvelines** – **311** H3 – **101** 31 – **pop. 1 051** – **alt. 100 m** – ✉ **78720** 18 **B2**

Paris 38 – Chartres 57 – Longjumeau 32 – Rambouillet 16 – Versailles 21

Office de tourisme, 9, Grande Rue ✆ 01 30 52 57 30, Fax 01 30 52 52 43

de Forges-les-Bains Forges-les-Bains Route du Général Leclerc, Southeast: 14 km, ✆ 01 64 91 48 18.

Château de Dampierre★★, **Northern France and the Paris Region**

Auberge du Château "Table des Blot" (Christophe Blot) with rm
1 Grande rue – ✆ 01 30 47 56 56 – Fax 01 30 47 51 75 – Closed 24-31 August, 24-30 December, 22-28 February, Sunday dinner, Monday and Tuesday
11 rm – €90 €120, ☕ €8
Rest – Menu € 35 (weekday lunch), € 52/60 – Carte € 52/55
Spec. Lobe de foie gras poché au vin rouge (November to March). Rognon de veau en escalopines, pomme macaire, jus de viande dissocié. Savarin tiède au chocolat, glace vanille.
◆ A 17C inn where antique furniture, objets d'art and modern furnishings are harmoniously combined. The cuisine is traditional and personalised.

Les Écuries du Château
au château – ✆ 01 30 52 52 99 – contact@lesecuriesduchateau.com – Fax 01 30 52 59 90 – Closed 31 July-21 August, 16-28 February, Tuesday and Wednesday
Rest – Menu (€ 28), € 42/50 – Carte approx. € 50
◆ These former stables, converted into a restaurant, benefit from the neighbouring Dampierre château. Pleasant dining room, traditional cuisine and game from the estate, in season.

Auberge St-Pierre
1 r. Chevreuse – ✆ 01 30 52 53 53 – Fax 01 30 52 58 57 – Closed August, February school holidays, Sunday evening, Tuesday evening and Monday
Rest – Menu (€ 25), € 30
◆ A half-timbered house almost opposite the chateau. An old pianola features in the hall while the dining room has a sedate country look and is warmed by an open fire.

LA DÉFENSE – 92 Hauts-de-Seine – 311 J2 – 101 14 – ✉ 92400 Paris 20 B1

Paris 10 – Courbevoie 1 – Nanterre 4 – Puteaux 2

District★★: view★ of the square.

Pullman La Défense

11 av. Arche, Défense 6 exit ✉ 92081 – ✆ 01 47 17 50 00 – h3013@accor.com – Fax 01 47 17 56 78

368 rm – €380 €380, ☕ €25 – 16 suites

Rest *Avant Seine* – rôtisserie – *✆ 01 47 17 50 99 (closed 5-20 August, 20-27 December, Friday dinner, Saturday, Sunday and holidays)* Carte approx. €51

◆ Beautiful architecture, resembling a ship's hull, a combination of glass and ochre stonework. Spacious, elegant rooms, lounges and very well-equipped auditorium (with simultaneous translation booths). The Avant Seine offers you quality designer décor and spit-roast dishes.

Renaissance

60 Jardin de Valmy, on the circular road, exit La Défense 7 ✉ 92918 – ✆ 01 41 97 50 50 – rhi.parld.exec.sec@renaissancehotels.com – Fax 01 41 97 51 51

324 rm – €210/450 €210/450, ☕ €25 – 3 suites

Rest – *(closed Saturday lunch, Sunday lunch and holidays lunch)* Menu €31 – Carte €32/59

◆ At the foot of the Carrare marble Grande Arche, this contemporary hotel has well-equipped rooms, with refined decoration. Good fitness facilities. In the restaurant, all-wood features with a "retro" brasserie atmosphere and a view of the gardens of Valmy.

Hilton La Défense

2 pl. de la Défense ✉ 92053 – ✆ 01 46 92 10 10 – parldhirm@hilton.com – Fax 01 46 92 10 50

139 rm – €245/550 €245/550, ☕ €26 – 6 suites

Rest *Coté Parvis* – *✆ 01 46 92 10 30* – Menu €56 bi – Carte €31/65

◆ Hotel situated within the CNIT complex. Some warmly decorated, designer-style rooms ideal for the business traveller. At Côté Parvis, modern cuisine and fine views.

Sofitel Centre

34 cours Michelet, via ring road, La Défense 4 exit ✉ 92060 Puteaux – ✆ 01 47 76 44 43 – h0912@accor.com – Fax 01 47 76 72 10

150 rm – €115/540 €115/540, ☕ €27 – 1 suite

Rest *L'Italian Lounge* – *✆ 01 47 76 72 40* – Carte €40/63

◆ The scalloped façade of this hotel stands out amid the skyscrapers of la Défense. Spacious, well-equipped rooms, which have been refurbished in a more trendy style. A contemporary setting for Mediterranean cuisine and an attractive choice of house wines.

Novotel La Défense

2 bd Neuilly, Défense 1 exit – ✆ 01 41 45 23 23 – h0747@accor.com – Fax 01 41 45 23 24

280 rm – €184/340 €184/420, ☕ €16

Rest – buffet Carte €21/43

◆ Sculpture and architecture: La Défense, a veritable open-air museum, is right at the foot of this hotel. Practical rooms, some overlooking Paris. The bar has a trendy new decor. Contemporary decor in the dining room, which also has a buffet area.

DRAVEIL – 91 Essonne – 312 D3 – 101 36 – pop. 28 093 – alt. 55 m – ✉ 91210 21 C3

Paris 23 – Corbeil Essonnes 11 – Créteil 14 – Versailles 30

Syndicat d'initiative, place de la République ✆ 01 69 03 09 39

Gibraltar

61 av. Libert – ✆ 01 69 42 32 05 – legibraltars@wanadoo.fr – Fax 01 69 52 06 82 – Closed Sunday dinner

Rest – Menu €30 (weekdays)/60 – Carte €44/69

◆ Set sail for Gibraltar... on the banks of the Seine! Pleasant summer terrace overlooking the river and dining room adorned with a fish tank and a ship's cabin mural.

ENGHIEN-LES-BAINS – **95 Val-d'Oise** – **305** E7 – **101** 5 – **pop. 10 368** – **alt. 45 m** – **Spa : all year** – **Casino** – ✉ **95880** Northern France and the Paris Region 20 **B1**

Paris 17 – Argenteuil 7 – Chantilly 34 – Pontoise 22 – St-Denis 7 – St-Germain-en-Laye 25

Office de tourisme, 81, rue du Général-de-Gaulle ✆ 01 34 12 41 15, Fax 01 39 34 05 76

de Domont Montmorency Domont Route de Montmorency, North: 8 km, ✆ 01 39 91 07 50.

Lake ★ - Deuil-la-Barre: historiated capitals★ of Notre-Dame church Northeast: 2 km.

Grand Hôtel Barrière rest,

85 r. Gén. de Gaulle – ✆ 01 39 34 10 00 – grandhotelenghien@lucienbarriere.com – Fax 01 39 34 10 01

37 rm – €224/250 €224/250, €18 – 6 suites

Rest ***L'Aventurine*** – *✆ 01 39 34 10 34 (closed 4-17 August, Wednesday lunch, Thursday lunch, Friday lunch, Sunday dinner, Monday and Tuesday)* Menu €45/95 – Carte €55/77

◆ One of France's largest spa and fitness centres, this hotel has a classic, understated elegance. Stylish, individually decorated rooms. A pleasant restaurant with wood panelling and silk hangings serving up to the minute cuisine. Green terrace.

Du Lac rm,

89 r. Gén. de Gaulle – ✆ 01 39 34 11 00 – hoteldulac@lucienbarriere.com – Fax 01 39 34 11 01

138 rm – €180/205 €180/205, €14 – 3 suites – **Rest** – *(closed Saturday lunch)* Menu (€22), €29/60 bi (weekend) – Carte €41/68

◆ This recent hotel sports a holiday resort feel. Comfortable rooms with a lake view (those on the garden side are quieter). Access to the spa and fitness facilities possible. Cosy restaurant area whose interior sports a 1930s brasserie look. Attractive terrace looking out across the water.

Aux Saveurs d'Alice

32 bd d'Ormesson – ✆ 01 34 12 78 36 – auxsaveursdalice@orange.fr – Fax 01 34 12 22 78 – Closed 5-25 August, Sunday dinner and Monday

Rest – Menu (€22), €28 – Carte €27/45

◆ This town centre restaurant is mainly appreciated for its simple classic cuisine made with fresh produce. Three discreetly rustic dining rooms.

ÉVRY P – **91 Essonne** – **312** D4 – **101** 37 – ✉ **91000** Northern France and the Paris Region 18 **B2**

Paris 32 – Chartres 80 – Créteil 30 – Étampes 36 – Fontainebleau 36 – Melun 23

La Résurrection cathedral ★ - 5 May-Jan. Epiphanies (Exhibition).

All Seasons rm,

52 bd Coquibus, (opposite the cathedral) – ✆ 01 69 47 30 00 – Fax 01 69 47 30 10 – Closed 25 July-17 August and 24 December-1st January

110 rm – €95/118 €105/128 – **Rest** – *(closed Friday dinner, Saturday, Sunday and holidays)* Menu (€17), €26

◆ On a busy boulevard facing the Cathedral of the Resurrection, a hotel with quite spacious, well-soundproofed rooms, equipped with a functional office area. A 'liner' atmosphere in the rotunda dining room and a typical Mercure menu.

in Courcouronnes – **pop. 13 954** – **alt. 80 m** – ✉ **91080**

de Bondoufle Bondoufle Départementale 31, West: 3 km, ✆ 01 60 86 41 71.

Canal

31 r. Pont Amar, (near the hospital) – ✆ 01 60 78 34 72 – Fax 01 60 79 22 70 – Closed August, 25 December-1st January, Saturday and Sunday

Rest – Menu €20/29 – Carte €26/43

◆ Small brasserie, a little old-fashioned. Enjoy the hearty cuisine giving pride of place to pork products (pigs' trotters). Only fresh produce.

in Lisses – pop. 7 206 – alt. 86 m – ✉ **91090**

Espace Léonard de Vinci rest,
av. Parcs – ✆ 01 64 97 66 77 – contact@leonard-de-vinci.com – Fax 01 64 97 59 21
74 rm – €100/110 €100/110, €10 – **Rest** – Menu €29 (lunch)/35 – Carte €29/37
◆ Football pitches, squash courts, pools, steam bath, Jacuzzi tub, fitness facilities and a balneotherapy centre! And practical rooms for a well earned rest after so much activity. Brasserie or plush classical restaurant. Live jazz on Saturday evenings.

GAGNY – **93 Seine-Saint-Denis** – **305** G7 – **101** 18 – **pop. 36 715** – **alt. 70 m** – ✉ **93220** 21 **D1**

Paris 17 – Bobigny 11 – Raincy 3 – St-Denis 18

Syndicat d'initiative, 1, avenue Jean-Jaurès ✆ 01 43 81 49 09

Le Vilgacy
45 av. H. Barbusse – ✆ 01 43 81 23 33 – Vilgacy@wanadoo.fr – Fax 01 43 81 23 33 – Closed 21-29 April, 28 July-21 August, Sunday dinner, Tuesday dinner and Monday except holidays
Rest – Menu (€20), €25 (weekdays)/33 – Carte €45/63
◆ Guests cannot fail to appreciate the modern decor of the two rooms (exhibited paintings for purchase) and, in summer, the garden terrace. Traditional cuisine.

LA GARENNE-COLOMBES – **92 Hauts-de-Seine** – **311** J2 – **101** 14 – **pop. 24 067** – **alt. 40 m** – ✉ **92250** 20 **B1**

Paris 13 – Argenteuil 7 – Asnières-sur-Seine 5 – Courbevoie 2 – Nanterre 4 – Pontoise 27

Syndicat d'initiative, 24, rue d'Estienne-d'Orves ✆ 01 47 85 09 90

L'Instinct
1 r. Voltaire – ✆ 01 56 83 82 82 – Fax 01 47 82 09 53 – Closed 9-26 August, Monday dinner, Saturday lunch and Sunday
Rest – *(pre-book)* Menu €32
◆ Opposite the covered market, a distinctive modern and colourful decor sets the scene in the bright dining room and splendid bar. Up-to-date cuisine.

GRESSY – **77 Seine-et-Marne** – **312** F2 – **101** 10 – **pop. 813** – **alt. 98 m** – ✉ **77410** 19 **C1**

Paris 32 – Meaux 20 – Melun 56 – Senlis 35

Le Manoir de Gressy rm, rest,
– ✆ 01 60 26 68 00 – information@manoirdegressy.com – Fax 01 60 26 45 46
85 rm – €210/230 €210/230, €19 – **Rest** – Menu €46 – Carte €47/57
◆ On the site of an 18C fortified farmstead, this manor house sports an attractive blend of styles. Each bedroom is individually decorated; all overlook the garden and pool. Well-worn walls, parquet flooring and Provence style furniture set the scene for the dining room.

ISSY-LES-MOULINEAUX – **92 Hauts-de-Seine** – **311** J3 – **101** 25 – **pop. 52 647** – **alt. 37 m** – ✉ **92130** **Northern France and the Paris Region** 20 **B2**

Paris 8 – Boulogne-Billancourt 3 – Clamart 4 – Nanterre 11 – Versailles 14

Office de tourisme, esplanade de l'Hôtel de Ville ✆ 01 41 23 87 00, Fax 01 40 95 67 33

Musée de la Carte à jouer★.

La Table des Montquartiers
5 chemin Montquartiers – ✆ 01 46 44 05 45 – contact@crayeres-montquartiers.com – Fax 01 46 45 66 55 – Closed August, 24 December-2 January, Saturday, Sunday and public holidays
Rest – *(lunch only)* Menu €35/45
◆ Apart from its unusual setting; the galleries of a former chalk quarry, and fine up-to-date cuisine, this restaurant also offers an exceptional wine list.

XX **River Café**

Pont d'Issy, 146 quai Stalingrad – ☎ 01 40 93 50 20 – info@lerivercafe.net – Fax 01 41 46 19 45

Rest – Menu € 34/44 – Carte € 42/53

◆ A former barge moored opposite Île St-Germain. Now an unusual restaurant with a colonial-style interior, riverside terrace and car-parking service.

XX **L'Ile**

Parc Ile St-Germain, 170 quai Stalingrad – ☎ 01 41 09 99 99 – v.fresneau@restaurant-lile.com – Fax 01 41 09 99 19

Rest – Menu € 41 bi/55 bi – Carte € 33/59

◆ Enlist at this former barracks sited on an island on the Seine: a trendy restaurant has moved in, immediately taken over by a hip crowd.

XX **Manufacture**

20 espl. Manufacture, (opposite 30 Rue E. Renan) – ☎ 01 40 93 08 98 – Fax 01 40 93 57 22 – Closed 5-20 August, 25 December-1st January, Saturday lunch and Sunday

Rest – Menu € 27/33

◆ This former tobacco factory (1904) has been successfully converted and is now home to flats, shops and this modern designer-inspired restaurant with an attractive terrace. Updated menu.

X **Coquibus**

16 av. de la République – ☎ 01 46 38 75 80 – reservation@coquibus.com – Fax 01 41 08 95 80 – Closed August and Sunday

Rest – Carte € 25/47

◆ Wood-panelling, colourful tables and terracotta cockerels give this town-centre restaurant the appearance of a 1930s brasserie. Traditional cuisine and seafood.

JANVRY – 91 Essonne – **312** B4 – **101** 33 – **pop. 530** – **alt. 160 m** – ✉ **91640** 18 **B2**

▶ Paris 35 – Briis s/s Forges 4 – Dourdan 20 – Palaiseau 19

XX **Bonne Franquette**

1 r. du Marchais – ☎ 01 64 90 72 06 – info@bonnefranquette.fr – Fax 01 64 90 53 63 – Closed 28 April-18 May, 1st-28 September, 22 December-12 January, Saturday lunch, Sunday dinner and Monday

Rest – Menu € 35

◆ Former post house opposite the 17C château of an attractive village in the Paris area. Two large blackboards show daily specials served in a warm rustic setting.

JOINVILLE-LE-PONT – 94 Val-de-Marne – **312** D3 – **101** 27 – **pop. 17 117** – **alt. 49 m** – ✉ **94340** 21 **D2**

▶ Paris 12 – Créteil 7 – Lagny-sur-Marne 22 – Maisons-Alfort 5 – Vincennes 6

ℹ Office de tourisme, 23, rue de Paris ☎ 01 42 83 41 16, Fax 01 49 76 92 98

Kyriad Prestige rm,

16 av. Gén. Gallieni – ☎ 01 48 83 11 99 – joinvillelepont@kyriadprestige.fr – Fax 01 48 89 51 58

89 rm – €98/128 €98/128, € 13

Rest – Menu € 19/26 – Carte € 28/40

◆ Contemporary architecture with spacious, soundproofed rooms equipped with a small sitting room for relaxation or an office for working. Pleasant modern dining room and buffet meals.

Cinépole without rest

8 av. Platanes – ☎ 01 48 89 99 77 – cinepole@wanadoo.fr – Fax 01 48 89 43 92

34 rm – €59/61 €59/61, € 7

◆ The hotel's name conjures up memories of the old Joinville cinema studios. Practical, well-kept rooms. A tiny patio where breakfast is served in the summer.

LE KREMLIN-BICÊTRE – **94 Val-de-Marne** – **312** D3 – **101** 26 – **pop. 23 724** – **alt. 60 m** – ✉ **94270** 21 **C2**

▶ Paris 5 – Boulogne-Billancourt 11 – Évry 28 – Versailles 23

Novotel Porte d'Italie
22 r. Voltaire – ☎ 01 45 21 19 09 – h5586@accor.com – Fax 01 45 21 12 60
168 rm – †€ 137/180 ††€ 147/190, ☕ € 14 – **Rest** – Carte € 23/43
♦ This recently built hotel with a simple, polished granite façade is just five minutes from Place d'Italie and offers rooms that meet the chain's latest standards. Restaurant with a trendy decor. Traditional cuisine.

Express by Holiday Inn without rest
1-3 r. Elisée Reclus – ☎ 01 47 26 26 26 – reservation@porteditalie.hiexpress.com – Fax 01 47 26 16 66
89 rm – †€ 115 ††€ 125, ☕ € 9
♦ Hotel with a simple red brick façade near the French capital's southern districts. Small rooms lined with light wood panelling and colourful fabrics.

LÉSIGNY – **77 Seine-et-Marne** – **312** E3 – **101** 29 – **pop. 7 647** – **alt. 95 m** – ✉ **77150** 19 **C2**

▶ Paris 33 – Brie-Comte-Robert 9 – Évry 29 – Melun 27 – Provins 65

18 du Réveillon Ferme des Hyverneaux, South: 2 km, ☎ 01 60 02 17 33 ;

9 ASPTT Paris Golf des Corbuches Ferme des Hyverneaux, South: 2 km, ☎ 01 60 02 07 26.

at the golf **by secondary road, south: 2 km or by Francilienne: exit 19 – ✉77150 Lésigny**

Golf rm, rest,
ferme des Hyverneaux – ☎ 01 60 02 25 26 – reservation@parisgolfhotel.com – Fax 01 60 02 03 84
48 rm – †€ 75/125 ††€ 75/125, ☕ € 10 – **Rest** – *(closed Friday dinner and Sunday dinner)* Menu € 20 bi
♦ Hotel housed in a former 12C abbey, with a modern extension. Gaily-coloured, modern rooms, either overlooking the interior courtyard or golf course. The restaurant's setting is made up of solid wooden beams, exposed stonework and modern furniture.

LEVALLOIS-PERRET – **92 Hauts-de-Seine** – **311** J2 – **101** 15 – **pop. 54 700** – **alt. 30 m** – ✉ **92300** 20 **B1**

▶ Paris 9 – Argenteuil 8 – Nanterre 8 – Pontoise 27 – St-Germain-en-Laye 20

Evergreen Laurel rm,
8 pl. G. Pompidou – ☎ 01 47 58 88 99 – pardos@evergreen-hotels.com – Fax 01 47 58 88 99
337 rm – †€ 330/480 ††€ 330/480, ☕ € 19 – 1 suite
Rest *Sens* – *☎ 01 46 39 00 72 (closed August, Saturday lunch and Sunday)*
Menu (€ 29), € 37 (lunch) – Carte € 49/88
Rest *Café Galery* – *☎ 01 46 39 00 71* – Menu (€ 19), € 26 – Carte € 28/55
♦ Luxury, elegance and light: a brand new hotel designed with businessmen in mind. The spacious rooms have pleasant rosewood furniture. Traditional dishes served under the immense glass-roof of Café Laurel. Luxury, elegance and light: a brand new hotel designed with businessmen in mind. The spacious rooms have pleasant rosewood furniture.

Espace Champerret without rest
26 r. Louise Michel – ☎ 01 47 57 20 71 – espace.champerret.hotel@wanadoo.fr – Fax 01 47 57 31 39
39 rm – †€ 55/85 ††€ 60/95, ☕ € 7,50
♦ In summer breakfast is served in the courtyard which separates the two buildings of this hotel; the one at the rear is quieter. The refurbished rooms are soundproofed and well kept.

Parc without rest
18 r. Baudin – ☎ 01 47 58 61 60 – hotelparclevallois@wanadoo.fr – Closed 5-25 August and 20-31 December
52 rm – †€ 62/95 ††€ 75/105, ☕ € 8 – 1 suite
♦ An establishment with functional or period style rooms, three of them are on the ground floor with an interior courtyard. Well-maintained rooms and charming welcome.

ABC Champerret without rest
63 r. Danton – ✆ 01 47 57 01 55 – reservation@abcchamphotel.com – Fax 01 47 57 54 23
39 rm – †€ 55/66 ††€ 65/84, ☐ € 8
◆ Practical for businessmen, this hotel has clean rooms with attractive "bamboo" furniture. In summer breakfast is served on the flowered patio.

Les Autodidactes
9 pl, Jean Zay – ✆ 01 47 39 54 02 – autodidactes.restaurant@wanadoo.fr – Fax 01 47 39 59 99 – Closed August, 24 December-1st January, Monday dinner, Wednesday dinner, Saturday, Sunday and holidays
Rest – Menu € 35 – Carte € 43/54
◆ The landlord is also an artist and displays his very colourful paintings in the restaurant dining room. Pleasant shaded terrace and short menu including seasonal market produce.

LIVRY-GARGAN – **93 Seine-Saint-Denis** – **305** G7 – **101** 18 – **pop. 37 288** – **alt. 60 m** – ✉ **93190** 21 **D1**

Paris 19 – Aubervilliers 14 – Aulnay-sous-Bois 4 – Bobigny 8 – Meaux 26 – Senlis 42

Office de tourisme, 5, place François Mitterrand ✆ 01 43 30 61 60, Fax 01 43 30 48 41

La Petite Marmite
8 bd de la République – ✆ 01 43 81 29 15 – Fax 01 43 02 69 59 – Closed August, Sunday dinner and Wednesday
Rest – Menu € 33 – Carte € 40/73
◆ This restaurant serves generous, traditional cuisine in a pleasant, country-style setting. The terrace in the interior courtyard is decorated with frescoes.

LONGJUMEAU – **91 Essonne** – **312** C3 – **101** 35 – **pop. 19 957** – **alt. 78 m** – ✉ **91160** 20 **B3**

Paris 20 – Chartres 70 – Dreux 84 – Évry 15 – Melun 41 – Orléans 113 – Versailles 27

St-Pierre
42 r. F. Mitterrand – ✆ 01 64 48 81 99 – saint-pierre@wanadoo.fr – Fax 01 69 34 25 53 – Closed 28 April-4 May, 27 July-21 August, Monday dinner, Wednesday dinner, Saturday lunch and Sunday
Rest – Menu € 32/46 – Carte € 41/57
◆ This restaurant serves simmering dishes full of the flavour of the southwest, using produce sent directly from the Gers region. A country-style dining room.

MAISONS-ALFORT – **94 Val-de-Marne** – **312** D3 – **101** 27 – **pop. 51 103** – **alt. 37 m** – ✉ **94700** Northern France and the Paris Region 21 **C2**

Paris 10 – Créteil 4 – Évry 34 – Melun 39

La Bourgogne
164 r. J. Jaurès – ✆ 01 43 75 12 75 – restaurant.labourgogne@wanadoo.fr – Fax 01 43 68 05 86 – Closed 8-20 August, 24 December-1st January, Saturday lunch and Sunday
Rest – Menu € 32/49 bi (dinner) – Carte € 35/68
◆ Smiling staff and a provincial country inn atmosphere where modern cuisine is made with market fresh produce. Regional specialities for the regulars.

MAISONS-LAFFITTE – **78 Yvelines** – **311** I2 – **101** 13 – **pop. 21 856** – **alt. 38 m** – ✉ **78600** Northern France and the Paris Region 20 **A1**

Paris 21 – Mantes-la-Jolie 38 – Poissy 9 – Pontoise 17 – St-Germain-en-Laye 8 – Versailles 19

Office de tourisme, 41, avenue de Longueil ✆ 01 39 62 63 64, Fax 01 39 12 02 89

Château★.

Tastevin (Michel Blanchet)
9 av. Eglé – ☎ 01 39 62 11 67 – michel.blanchet5@wanadoo.fr
– Fax 01 39 62 73 09
– Closed 4-28 August, 25 February-10 March, Monday and Tuesday
Rest – Menu € 45 (weekday lunch)/85 – Carte € 78/108
Spec. Poissons. Canard sauvage aux pêches de vigne (September to March). Assiette du maître chocolatier.
◆ An attractive mansion in the "lotissement Laffitte". Attentive service, classic cuisine and a fine wine list are the features of this Manson restaurant.

MARLY-LE-ROI – 78 Yvelines – 312 B2 – 101 12 – pop. 16 759 – alt. 90 m – ✉ 78160

20 **A2**

Paris 24 – Bougival 5 – St-Germain-en-Laye 5 – Versailles 9
Office de tourisme, 2, avenue des Combattants ☎ 01 39 16 16 35

Le Village
3 Grande Rue – ☎ 01 39 16 28 14 – tomohirouido@club-internet.fr
– Fax 01 39 58 62 60 – Closed 1st-24 August, Saturday lunch, Sunday dinner and Monday
Rest – *(number of covers limited, pre-book)* Menu € 38/72 – Carte € 90/146
◆ This appealing restaurant in Old Marly houses a dining room adorned with a mural. The chef, though of Japanese origin, offers tasty French cuisine with personal touches.

MARNE-LA-VALLÉE – Île-de-France – 312 E2 – 101 19 – pop. 246 607 – ✉ 77206

Northern France and the Paris Region

19 **C2**

Paris 27 – Meaux 29 – Melun 40
de Bussy-Saint-Georges Bussy-Saint-Georges Promenade des Golfeurs, ☎ 01 64 66 00 00 ;
de Torcy Torcy Base Régionale de loisirs, North: 5 km, ☎ 01 64 80 80 90 ;
Disneyland Paris Magny-le-Hongre Allée de la Mare Houleuse, ☎ 01 60 45 68 90.

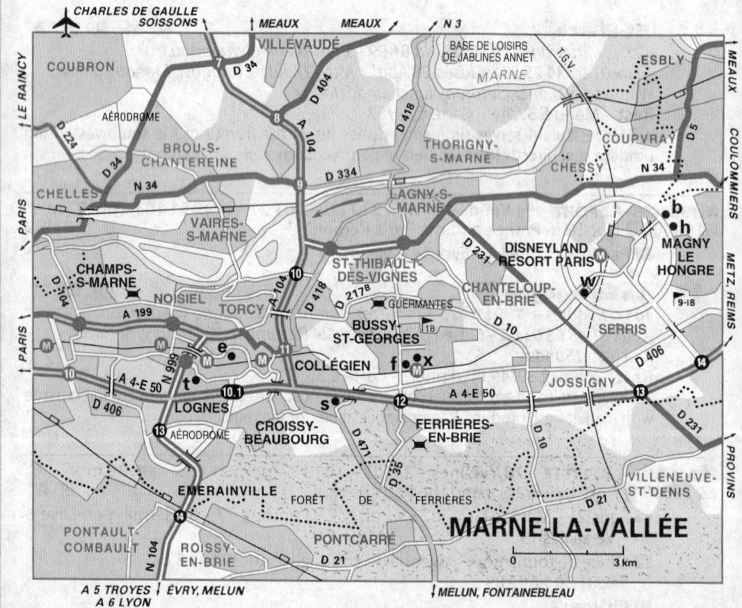

in Bussy-St-Georges – pop. 9 194 – alt. 105 m – ✉ 77600

Marne La Vallée without rest
39 bd Lagny – ✆ 01 64 66 35 65 – reception@cehbussy.com – Fax 01 64 66 03 10 f
120 rm – †€ 160 ††€ 175, ☕ € 15 – 4 suites
◆ On the edge of a wide avenue, spacious rooms impeccably kept with double-glazing. A pleasant bar.

Tulip Inn Marne la Vallée
44 bd A. Giroust – ✆ 01 64 66 11 11 – tulip.reservations@wanadoo.fr – Fax 01 64 66 29 05 x
87 rm – †€ 129 ††€ 129, ☕ € 12 – **Rest** – *(closed Saturday lunch and Sunday)* Carte € 20/25
◆ Part of a large real estate complex opposite the RER station, a hotel with functional, well-soundproofed rooms. The bar is decorated in Louisiana style. The dining room is decorated with frescoes of Italian inspiration. Pasta and pizzas on the menu.

in Collégien – pop. 2 983 – alt. 105 m – ✉ 77090

Novotel
– ✆ 01 64 80 53 53 – h0385@accor.com – Fax 01 64 80 48 37 s
195 rm – †€ 98/115 ††€ 110/130, ☕ € 13 – **Rest** – Menu (€ 21), € 26/34 – Carte € 26/35
◆ This Novotel caters for visitors to Disneyland and business clients. The renovated rooms have an attractive modern decor, with wooden furniture and pretty colours. This restaurant complies with the chain's standards in an attractive designer-inspired decor.

in Disneyland Resort Paris access by A 4 motorway and Disneyland slip road – ✉ 77777

Disneyland Paris ★★★ (see Green Guide of Northern France and the Paris Region)- Hotel booking centre: ✆ (00 33) 08 25 30 60 30 (0.15 €/mn), Fax (00 33) 01 64 74 57 50 - Disneyland Resort Paris hotels offer daily packages including room price and entrance to theme parks - These prices change according to the season - we recommend that you contact the booking centre.

in Lognes – pop. 14 215 – alt. 97 m – ✉ 77185

Suites Inn
57-61 r. Tour d'Auvergne – ✆ 01 60 06 12 12 – direction-lognes@mysuiteapparthotels.com – Fax 01 60 06 12 00 e
63 rm – †€ 105 ††€ 105, ☕ € 12 – 26 suites – **Rest** – Menu € 17/25 – Carte € 27/82
◆ This modern hotel complex offers rather original, modern rooms, all overlooking the lake; some with a balcony. Squash, sauna and hammam. Restaurant serving southern dishes and fine terrace overlooking the lake.

in Magny-le-Hongre – pop. 1 791 – alt. 117 m – ✉ 77700

Holiday Inn
20 av. de la Fosse des Pressoirs – ✆ 01 64 63 37 37 – valdefrance@ichotelsgroup.com – Fax 01 64 63 37 38 h
396 rm – †€ 110/210 ††€ 120/220, ☕ € 15 – 3 suites – **Rest** – *(dinner only)* Menu € 32
◆ This new hotel near Disneyland Paris is decorated in a colourful circus theme. The restaurant has a central ring, columns and murals that are reminiscent of a circus tent.

Dream Castle Hôtel
40 av. Fosse des Pressoirs – ✆ 01 64 17 90 00 – info@dreamcastle-hotel.com – Fax 01 64 17 90 01 b
400 rm ☕ – †€ 104/238 ††€ 104/490 – **Rest** – Menu € 29 (dinner) – Carte € 24/44
◆ This modern hotel pays homage to castles in both its outer and interior decoration. Elegant, spacious rooms. Functional bathrooms. Enjoy themed buffet meals (Asian, Italian, Oriental, etc.) here.

in Serris – pop. 2 320 – alt. 129 m – ✉ 77700

L'Élysée Val d'Europe
7 cours Danube, (opposite the RER station) –
✆ 01 64 63 33 33 – info@hotelelysee.com – Fax 01 64 63 33 30 w
152 rm – ♦€ 120/160 ♦♦€ 130/195, ☕ € 12 – **Rest** – Menu (€ 16), € 21 – Carte € 22/34
♦ Fine Haussman-style building in a new district. Elegant lounge and unusual garden topped by a Baltard-style glass roof. Spacious, well-thought-out rooms. A brasserie with a modern setting serving ad-hoc dishes and grills. A quick set menu at the bar.

MASSY – **91 Essonne** – **312** C3 – **101** 25 – **pop. 37 712** – **alt. 78 m** – ✉ **91300** 20 **B3**
Paris 19 – Arpajon 19 – Évry 20 – Palaiseau 4 – Rambouillet 45

Mercure
21 av. Carnot, (TGV station) – ✆ 01 69 32 80 20 – h1176@accor-hotels.com – Fax 01 69 32 80 25
116 rm – ♦€ 140/155 ♦♦€ 150/165, ☕ € 13 – **Rest** – *(closed August, Christmas holidays, Friday dinner, Saturday and Sunday)* Carte approx. € 29
♦ A resolutely modern hotel ideally located between TGV (high speed trains) and RER (suburban trains) stations. Functional (30 have been redone), well-soundproofed rooms, new bathrooms. A modern dining room serving traditional seasonal cuisine.

MAUREPAS – **78 Yvelines** – **311** H3 – **101** 21 – **pop. 19 586** – **alt. 165 m** –
✉ **78310** 18 **B2**
Paris 40 – Houdan 29 – Palaiseau 35 – Rambouillet 17 – Versailles 21
France Miniature★ Northeast: 3km, **Northern France and the Paris Region**

Mercure
1 Rocade de Camargue, (RN 10) – ✆ 01 30 51 57 27 – h0378@accor.com – Fax 01 30 66 70 14
91 rm – ♦€ 71/155 ♦♦€ 76/170, ☕ € 13 – **Rest** – *(closed 9-24 August, Friday dinner, Saturday and Sunday)* Carte € 21/31
♦ A small road leading off the N 10 leads to this hotel with spacious, well-soundproofed rooms which are gradually being renovated. A wine bar-type restaurant with blackboard-displayed dishes and tapas, as well as wine by the glass.

LE MESNIL-AMELOT – **77 Seine-et-Marne** – **312** E1 – **101** 9 – **pop. 565** – **alt. 80 m** –
✉ **77990** 19 **C1**
Paris 34 – Bobigny 25 – Goussainville 15 – Meaux 28 – Melun 67

Radisson SAS
r. de la Chapelle – ✆ 01 60 03 63 00 – radisson.sas@hotels-res.com – Fax 01 60 03 74 40
240 rm – ♦€ 115/300 ♦♦€ 115/300, ☕ € 18 – ½ P € 150/335
Rest – Menu € 25 (lunch)/59 – Carte € 21/57
♦ A practical stop near Roissy airport. Many leisure and conference facilities, a vast reception, sitting room-bar and modern rooms. Busy ambiance in this large brasserie with modern decor; buffet of starters.

MEUDON – **92 Hauts-de-Seine** – **311** J3 – **101** 24 – **pop. 43 663** – **alt. 100 m** –
✉ **92190** **Northern France and the Paris Region** 20 **B2**
Paris 11 – Boulogne-Billancourt 4 – Clamart 4 – Nanterre 12 – Versailles 10
Terrace★: ❋★ - Meudon forest ★.

L'Escarbille (Régis Douysset)
8 r. Vélizy – ✆ 01 45 34 12 03 – contact@lescarbille.fr – Fax 01 46 89 04 75 – Closed 18 August-1st September, 22 December-2 January, 16 -28 February, Saturday lunch, Sunday dinner and Monday
Rest – Menu € 42/49
Spec. Potage vichyssoise, truffes d'été en rémoulade (May to August).Pigeon en crapaudine, jus lié au foie gras. Turbot rôti, crème légère à la citronnelle.
♦ This establishment located near the station offers meals in tune with today's tastes, respectful of tradition and produce. Charming welcome. Garden terrace.

South to Meudon-la-Forêt – ✉ 92360

Mercure Ermitage de Villebon
rte Col. Moraine – ✆ 01 46 01 46 86 – mercure.meudon@wanadoo.fr – Fax 01 46 01 46 99 – Closed 11-17 August
65 rm – †€ 125 ††€ 133, ☕ € 12 – **Rest** – Carte approx. € 39
◆ On the edge of Meudon forest and the expressway, a well-soundproofed hotel with rooms decorated in Directoire style. Plush dining room in a late 19C building and pleasant terrace surrounded by a curtain of greenery.

MONTMORENCY – 95 Val-d'Oise – **305** E7 – **101** 5 – **pop. 20 599** – **alt. 82 m** – ✉ 95160 Northern France and the Paris Region 18 **B1**

Paris 19 – Enghien-les-Bains 4 – Pontoise 24 – St-Denis 9

Office de tourisme, 1, avenue Foch ✆ 01 39 64 42 94

St-Martin collegiate church ★.

Château d'Écouen★★: musée de la Renaissance★★ (Hanging of David and Bathsheba★★★).

Au Cœur de la Forêt
av. Repos de Diane, and access via forest road – ✆ 01 39 64 99 19 – Fax 01 34 28 17 52 – Closed August, 15-25 February, Thursday dinner, Sunday dinner and Monday
Rest – Menu € 43
◆ A welcoming decor in two rustic rooms, one of which is very spacious with rafters and a fireplace. Shaded summer terrace. Simple, traditional menu in tune with the seasons.

MONTREUIL – 93 Seine-Saint-Denis – **311** K2 – **101** 17 – **pop. 90 674** – **alt. 70 m** – ✉ 93100 Northern France and the Paris Region 21 **C2**

Paris 11 – Bobigny 10 – Boulogne-Billancourt 18 – Argenteuil 28 – Saint-Denis 15

Office de tourisme, 1, rue Kléber ✆ 01 41 58 14 09, Fax 01 41 58 14 13

Villa9Trois
28 r. Colbert – ✆ 01 48 58 17 37 – villa9trois@clubinternet.fr – Closed Sunday dinner
Rest – Menu € 35/40 – Carte € 41/55
◆ A haven of greenery in the middle of the suburbs, the villa offers a relaxed meal in modern surroundings. Large terrace in the garden.

MONTROUGE – 92 Hauts-de-Seine – **311** J3 – **101** 25 – **pop. 37 733** – **alt. 75 m** – ✉ 92120 20 **B2**

Paris 5 – Boulogne-Billancourt 8 – Longjumeau 18 – Nanterre 16 – Versailles 16

Mercure
13 r. F.-Ory – ✆ 01 58 07 11 11 – h0374@accor.com – Fax 01 58 07 11 21
181 rm – †€ 120/165 ††€ 130/175, ☕ € 14 – 7 suites – **Rest** – *(closed Sat. and Sun.)* Menu (€ 18), € 25 – Carte € 26/35
◆ Large building, set slightly away from the ring road, housing functional, well-soundproofed and air-conditioned modern rooms. Modern dining room, enlivened with vegetable themed lithographs (recalling Montrouge's market garden past).

MORANGIS – 91 Essonne – **312** D3 – **101** 35 – **pop. 10 611** – **alt. 85 m** – ✉ 91420 21 **C3**

Paris 21 – Évry 14 – Longjumeau 5 – Versailles 23

Sabayon
15 r. Lavoisier – ✆ 01 69 09 43 80 – von.moos.claude@wanadoo.fr – Fax 01 64 48 27 28 – Closed 1st-29 August, Monday dinner, Tuesday dinner, Wednesday dinner, Saturday lunch and Sunday
Rest – Menu € 30 (lunch), € 43/80
◆ With its ochre walls, yellow-lacquered ceilings, modern canvases, and plants, this restaurant is a ray of sunshine on a somewhat drab industrial estate. Contemporary cuisine.

NANTERRE Ⓟ – **92 Hauts-de-Seine** – **311** J2 – **101** 14 – **pop. 84 281** – **alt. 35 m** – ✉ **92000**

Paris 13 – Beauvais 81 – Rouen 124 – Versailles 15 20 **B1**

Syndicat d'initiative, 4, rue du Marché ✆ 01 47 21 58 02, Fax 01 47 25 99 02

Mercure La Défense Parc rm, VISA MC AE

r. des 3 Fontanot – ✆ 01 46 69 68 00 – h1982@accor.com – Fax 01 47 25 46 24

160 rm – †€ 190/235 ††€ 205/250, ☕ € 20

Rest – *(closed 18 July-21 August, 25 December-2 January, Sunday lunch, Friday dinner Saturday)* Menu € 30/45 bi – Carte € 32/41

◆ A modern building and annex next to the André Malraux park. Modern-style furniture and full facilities. Ask for a renovated room. International cuisine served in a cosy and comfortable dining room boasting a line of modern furniture.

Quality Inn rm, rest, VISA MC AE

2 av. B. Frachon – ✆ 01 46 95 08 08 – shgl@wanadoo.fr – Fax 01 46 95 01 24

85 rm – †€ 138/250 ††€ 158/250, ☕ € 15 – **Rest** – *(closed 1st- 24 August, 25 December-4 January, Friday dinner, Saturday and Sunday)* Menu (€ 22), € 28 – Carte € 29/54

◆ The rooms of this 1922 building are generally spacious with attractive furniture and double-glazing. Warm, welcoming colonial style dining room. Cane chairs, round tables and traditional cuisine.

NEUILLY-SUR-SEINE – **92 Hauts-de-Seine** – **311** J2 – **101** 15 – **pop. 59 848** – **alt. 34 m** – ✉ **92200** **Northern France and the Paris Region** 20 **B1**

Paris 9 – Argenteuil 10 – Nanterre 6 – Pontoise 29 – St-Germain-en-Laye 18 – Versailles 17

Courtyard by Marriott rm, VISA MC AE

58 bd V. Hugo – ✆ 01 55 63 64 65 – cy.parcy.dosm@courtyard.com – Fax 01 55 63 64 66

175 rm – †€ 179/239 ††€ 179/239, ☕ € 19 – 69 suites

Rest – Menu € 25 (weekdays)/34 – Carte € 29/62

◆ A 1970s hotel near the American Hospital with attractively furnished rooms offering every modern comfort. Verdant setting, comfortable lounges, cosy bar and a terrace. A luxurious and convivial bistro-style restaurant serving brasserie cuisine and themed dishes.

Paris Neuilly without rest VISA MC AE

1 av. Madrid – ✆ 01 47 47 14 67 – h0883@accor.com – Fax 01 47 47 97 42

74 rm – †€ 230/245 ††€ 240/255, ☕ € 16 – 6 suites

◆ The rooms are decorated in a variety of styles. Breakfast is served on a covered patio decorated with a fresco representing the Palacio Real in Madrid built by François I in 1528.

Jardin de Neuilly without rest VISA MC AE

5 r. P. Déroulède – ✆ 01 46 24 22 77 – hotel.jardin.de.neuilly@wanadoo.fr – Fax 01 46 37 14 60

29 rm – †€ 150/355 ††€ 150/355, ☕ € 16

◆ A 19C mansion 300m from Porte Maillot. The rooms are individually decorated and furnished with antiques. Some overlook the garden: the countryside on the doorstep of Paris!

De la Jatte without rest VISA MC AE

4 bd Parc – ✆ 01 46 24 32 62 – hoteldelajatte@wanadoo.fr – Fax 01 46 40 77 31

69 rm – †€ 95/143 ††€ 95/168, ☕ € 12 – 2 suites

◆ On the Île de la Jatte, once popular with painters, today there is a trendy hotel. Designer décor (trendy colours, dark wood), pleasant veranda.

Neuilly Park Hôtel without rest VISA MC AE

23 r. M. Michelis – ✆ 01 46 40 11 15 – hotel@neuillypark.com – Fax 01 46 40 14 78

30 rm – †€ 145/165 ††€ 155/175, ☕ € 11

◆ This Sablons district hotel has been fully renovated. Small rooms with Art Nouveau-style furniture and drapes. Charming service.

Foc Ly VISA MC AE

79 av. Ch. de Gaulle – ✆ 01 46 24 43 36 – Fax 01 46 24 70 58 – Closed 3-24 August

Rest – Menu € 18/21 – Carte € 31/67

◆ Two lions frame the entrance to this restaurant with a pagoda-terrace façade. Redecorated modern interior. Chinese and Thai cuisine.

XX **La Truffe Noire** (Patrice Hardy)
2 pl. Parmentier – ✆ 01 46 24 94 14 – patchef.hardy@wanadoo.fr
– Fax 01 46 24 94 60 – Closed 1st-12 May, 1st-24 August, Saturday Sunday
Rest – Menu € 38/130 – Carte € 61/138
Spec. Langoustines sous le grill, jus réduit, mousseux ananas-vanille. Dos de Saint-Pierre cuit en coque d'argile, masqué de truffe (December to May). Lièvre à la royale (October to December).
◆ This attractive, recently-renovated house celebrates this "black gold", but also Parmentier, who grew the first French potatoes in this Sablons district.

XX **Jarrasse L'Écailler de Paris**
4 av. de Madrid – ✆ 01 46 24 07 56 – Fax 01 40 88 35 60
Rest – (pre-book) Menu € 38 – Carte € 43/87
◆ Dining rooms fully redecorated in a modern style: contemporary materials and pastel colours create a relaxed atmosphere. Fish and seafood dishes, and an oyster bar.

X **Les Feuilles Libres**
34 r. Perronet – ✆ 01 46 24 41 41 – nathalie@laporterestaurants.com
– Fax 01 47 38 34 05 – Closed Sunday
Rest – Menu (€ 28), € 48 – Carte € 43/50
◆ Restaurant with a homely atmosphere and a simple but stylish decor. Opulent lounges, wine and cigar cellars. Up-to-date cuisine

X **Le Bistrot d'à Côté Neuilly**
4 r. Boutard – ✆ 01 47 45 34 55 – bistrot@michelrostang.com
– Fax 01 47 45 15 08 – Closed 11-17 August, Saturday lunch and Sunday
Rest – Menu (€ 30), € 43
◆ Relaxed service, wood panelling, collection of old coffee-grinders, daily specials chalked on a blackboard, and wine served "à la ficelle" (you pay for what you drink): a "genuine imitation bistro".

X **À la Coupole**
3 r. Chartres – ✆ 01 46 24 82 90 – pascalroudin@free.fr – Closed August, Saturday, Sunday and public holidays
Rest – Menu € 35/45 – Carte € 30/52
◆ Miniature cars and lorries made in Madagascar from recovered metal decorate the simple dining room of this family-run restaurant. Traditional cuisine and oysters in season.

X **Aux Saveurs du Marché**
4 r. de l' Eglise – ✆ 01 47 45 72 11 – auxsaveursdumarche@wanadoo.fr
– Fax 01 46 37 72 13 – Closed 2-25 August, 23-28 February, Saturday and Sunday
Rest – bistrot Carte € 39/46
◆ Pre-1940s style bistro, near the market, with velvet bench seating and an original wood and mirror ceiling. Blackboard displayed devilishly-tasty dishes. Very busy at lunchtime.

X **Il Punto**
2 r. Gén. H. Bertier – ✆ 01 46 24 21 06 – Fax 01 47 47 46 71
– Closed 14 July-15 August, 25 December-1st January and Saturday lunch
Rest – Carte € 35/55
◆ The 'Giro', as well as a tour of Italian cuisine awaits you here. Neat, comfortable dining room with decoration inspired by Venice and Southern Italy.

NOGENT-SUR-MARNE – **94 Val-de-Marne** – **312** D2 – **101** 27 – **pop. 28 191** – **alt. 59 m** – ✉ **94130** Northern France and the Paris Region 21 **D2**

Paris 14 – Créteil 10 – Montreuil 6 – Vincennes 6

Office de tourisme, 5, avenue de Joinville ✆ 01 48 73 73 97, Fax 01 48 73 75 90

Mercure Nogentel rm, rm,
8 r. du Port – ✆ 01 48 72 70 00 – h1710@accor.com – Fax 01 48 72 86 19
60 rm – €124/139 €140/155, ☕ €15
Rest ***Le Canotier*** – (closed 5-20 August and Sunday dinner) Menu (€ 34), € 39
◆ A hotel on the banks of the Marne with modern rooms. The spirit of Nogent is still present on the river bank ideal for a walk among the flowers. The spacious dining room with nautical decor enjoys a view of the marina. Traditional fare.

NOISY-LE-GRAND – **93 Seine-Saint-Denis** – **305** G7 – **101** 18 – **pop. 58 217** – **alt. 82 m** – ✉ **93160** **Northern France and the Paris Region** 21 **D2**

Paris 19 – Bobigny 17 – Lagny-sur-Marne 14 – Meaux 38

Syndicat d'initiative, 167, rue Pierre Brossolette ✆ 01 43 04 51 55, Fax 01 43 03 79 48

Mercure
2 bd Levant – ✆ 01 45 92 47 47 – h1984@accor.com – Fax 01 45 92 47 10
192 rm – €106/119 €113/125, €12
Rest – *(closed Friday dinner, Saturday, Sunday and holidays)* Carte €23/31
◆ A modern building with a glass façade that reflects the panoramic lifts as they go up and down. Spacious, functional rooms. A brasserie-style restaurant with a wall covered in multicoloured stars. Inner courtyard terrace.

Novotel Atria rest,
2 allée Bienvenue-quartier Horizon – ✆ 01 48 15 60 60 – h1536@accor.com – Fax 01 43 04 78 83
144 rm – €91/159 €101/169, €13,50 – **Rest** – Menu €20/25 – Carte €22/39
◆ Contemporary architecture in a business district. Modern bar, and standard, well-equipped rooms. Spacious dining room serving 'Lenôtre' cuisine. Children's play area in garden.

XX **L'Amphitryon**
56 av. A. Briand – ✆ 01 43 04 68 00 – Fax 01 43 04 68 10 – Closed 5-26 August, February half-term holidays, Saturday lunch and Sunday dinner
Rest – Menu €26 (weekdays)/41 – Carte €46/54
◆ Melon-coloured walls and multi-coloured china set the tone of this elegant restaurant dining room. The food is traditional and served quickly and with a smile.

ORGEVAL – **78 Yvelines** – **311** H2 – **101** 11 – **pop. 4 801** – **alt. 100 m** – ✉ **78630**

Paris 32 – Mantes-la-Jolie 28 – Pontoise 22 – St-Germain-en-Laye 11 – Versailles 22 18 **B1**

de Villennes Villennes-sur-Seine Route d'Orgeval, North: 2 km, ✆ 01 39 08 18 18.

Moulin d'Orgeval
r. de l'Abbaye, south: 1.5 km – ✆ 01 39 75 85 74 – contact@moulindorgeval.com – Fax 01 39 75 48 52
14 rm – €130 €150, €15 – **Rest** – *(closed 20 December-4 January and Sunday dinner)* Menu (€36), €46/68 – Carte €43/65
◆ Former mill, set in a 5-ha park with trees and a pond, offering peace and relaxation. Rooms with personal touches; some with antique furniture. English-style bar. Rustic restaurant dining room and pleasant waterside terrace, offering classical dishes.

ORLY (AÉROPORTS DE PARIS) – **91 Essonne** – **312** D3 – **101** 26 – **pop. 21 646** – **alt. 89 m** – ✉ **94390** 21 **C3**

Paris 16 – Corbeil-Essonnes 24 – Créteil 14 – Longjumeau 15 – Villeneuve-St-Georges 9

Aérogare Sud ✆03 36 68 15 15

Hilton Orly
near Orly Sud airport ✉ 94544 – ✆ 01 45 12 45 12 – rm.orly@hilton.com – Fax 01 45 12 45 00
351 rm – €130/215 €130/230, €19
Rest – brasserie Menu €35 (weekdays) – Carte €22/56
◆ A popular choice for corporate clients, this 1960s hotel has a designer interior, discreet yet elegant bedrooms and state of the art business facilities. Modern, entirely revamped decor and a classic menu.

Mercure rest,
aérogare ✉ 94547 – ✆ 01 49 75 15 50 – h1246@accor.com – Fax 01 49 75 15 51
192 rm – €79/215 €89/225, €13,50
Rest – Menu (€20), €25 – Carte approx. €32
◆ Convenient for travellers between flights. Smiling staff, pleasant verdant setting and above all, well-kept, gradually refurbished rooms. Bar snacks and traditional dishes adapted to the timetables of travellers in transit.

in Orly-ville – **pop. 20 470** – **alt. 71 m** – ✉ **94310**

Kyriad Air Plus rest, P VISA MC AE

58 voie Nouvelle – ✆ 01 41 80 75 75 – airplus@club-internet.fr – Fax 01 41 80 12 12

72 rm – €68/78 €68/78, ☕ €8,50 – **Rest** – *(closed August)* Carte €22/32

◆ Frequented by numerous airline crews on stopovers. English style pub with an aeronautical atmosphere. The nearby Parc Méliès is popular with jogging enthusiasts. Classic repertory served in an interior devoted to aircraft.

See also at **Rungis**

OZOIR-LA-FERRIÈRE – **77 Seine-et-Marne** – **312** F3 – **106** 33 – **101** 30 – **pop. 20 707** – **alt. 110 m** – ✉ **77330** 19 **C2**

Paris 34 – Coulommiers 42 – Lagny-sur-Marne 22 – Melun 29 – Sézanne 84

Syndicat d'initiative, 43, avenue du Général-de-Gaulle ✆ 01 64 40 10 20

XXX **La Gueulardière** P VISA MC AE

66 av. Gén. de Gaulle – ✆ 01 60 02 94 56 – auberge@la-gueulardiere.com – Fax 01 60 02 98 51 – Closed 18 August-3 September and Sunday dinner

Rest – Menu (€28), €38/48 – Carte €48/94

◆ This town-centre inn serves classic cuisine in two elegant dining rooms or under a pergola on the terrace in summer.

LE PERREUX-SUR-MARNE – **94 Val-de-Marne** – **312** E2 – **101** 18 – **pop. 30 080** – **alt. 50 m** – ✉ **94170** 21 **D2**

Paris 16 – Créteil 12 – Lagny-sur-Marne 23 – Villemomble 6 – Vincennes 7

Office de tourisme, 75, avenue Ledru Rollin ✆ 01 43 24 26 58

XXX ✿ **Les Magnolias** (Jean Chauvel) VISA MC AE

48 av. de Bry – ✆ 01 48 72 47 43 – contact@lesmagnolias.com – Fax 01 48 72 22 28 – Closed August, 1st-7 January, Saturday lunchtime, Sunday and Monday

Rest – Menu (€39), €55/90

Spec. Sortie risquée d'escargots en croquettes. Lotte de nos côtes cuite entière sur océan vert de petit pois. Volcan éteint d'une pêche au cassis.

◆ An elegant setting of light wood fixtures adorned with contemporary art and amusing armchairs in which to sample the equally light hearted, inventive cuisine.

XX **Les Lauriers** VISA MC AE

5 av. Neuilly-Plaisance – ✆ 01 48 72 45 75 – garnierisabel@hotmail.com – Fax 01 48 72 45 75 – Closed August, 23 December-1st January, Wednesday dinner, Saturday lunch, Sunday dinner and Monday

Rest – Menu (€26), €35 bi – Carte €56/94

◆ This restaurant is set up in the house of a residential district. Its dining room walls are lined with paintings, prints and drawings. Attractively laid out tables where traditional cuisine is served.

POISSY – **78 Yvelines** – **311** I2 – **101** 12 – **pop. 35 841** – **alt. 27 m** – ✉ **78300**
Northern France and the Paris Region 18 **B1**

Paris 32 – Mantes-la-Jolie 29 – Pontoise 16 – St-Germain-en-Laye 6

Office de tourisme, 132, rue du Général-de-Gaulle ✆ 01 30 74 60 65, Fax 01 39 65 07 00

Bethemont Chisan Country Club 12 rue du Parc de Béthemont, by Orgeval road: 5 km, ✆ 01 39 08 13 70 ;

de Villennes Villennes-sur-Seine Route d'Orgeval, by Vernouillet road: 6 km, ✆ 01 39 08 18 18 ;

de Feucherolles Feucherolles Sainte Gemme, by Plaisir road: 13 km, ✆ 01 30 54 94 94.

Notre-Dame collegiate church ★ - Villa Savoye★.

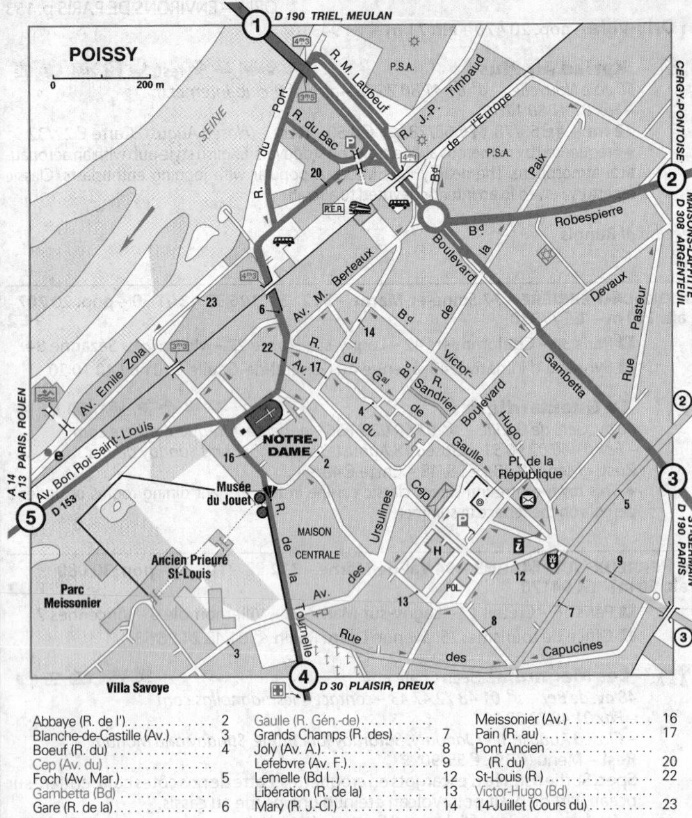

Abbaye (R. de l')	2	Gaulle (R. Gén.-de)		Meissonier (Av.)	16
Blanche-de-Castille (Av.)	3	Grands Champs (R. des)	7	Pain (R. au)	17
Boeuf (R. du)	4	Joly (Av. A.)	8	Pont Ancien (R. du)	20
Cep (Av. du)		Lefebvre (Av. F.)	9	St-Louis (R.)	22
Foch (Av. Mar.)	5	Lemelle (Bd L.)	12	Victor-Hugo (Bd)	
Gambetta (Bd)		Libération (R. de la)	13	14-Juillet (Cours du)	23
Gare (R. de la)	6	Mary (R. J.-Cl.)	14		

XX **Bon Vivant**

30 av. É. Zola – ✆ 01 39 65 02 14 – Fax 01 39 65 28 05
– Closed spring school holidays, 1st-21 August, 25 December-1st January, Sunday dinner and Monday e

Rest – Menu € 37/65 bi – Carte € 49/77

◆ The friendly atmosphere of the 1900 guingette (open-air music café) and its waterfront terrace on the banks of the Seine have been preserved. Rustic setting and traditional menu highlighting fish dishes.

LE PRÉ ST-GERVAIS – 93 Seine-Saint-Denis – **305** F7 – **101** 16 – **pop. 16 377** – **alt. 82 m** – ✉ 93310 21 **C1**

Paris 8 – Bobigny 6 – Lagny-sur-Marne 33 – Meaux 38 – Senlis 47

X **Au Pouilly Reuilly**

68 r. A. Joineau – ✆ 01 48 45 14 59
– Closed Saturday lunchtime and Sunday

Rest – Menu € 29 – Carte € 35/70

◆ A pre-war bistro decor, a cheerful atmosphere and fortifying cuisine, with an emphasis on offal. The Paris smart set tend to congregate here.

PUTEAUX – 92 Hauts-de-Seine – **311** J2 – **101** 14 – **pop. 40 780 – alt. 36 m** – ✉ **92800** 20 **B1**

Paris 11 – Nanterre 4 – Pontoise 30 – St-Germain-en-Laye 17 – Versailles 15

Vivaldi without rest
5 r. Roque de Fillol – ☎ 01 47 76 36 01 – vivaldi@hotelvivaldi.com – Fax 01 47 76 11 45
27 rm – €129 €144, €9
◆ This hotel with a distinguished facade, in a peaceful street near the town hall, houses renovated rooms equipped with functional furniture. Breakfast on the patio.

Princesse Isabelle without rest
72 r. J. Jaurès – ☎ 01 47 78 80 06 – reservation@hotelprincesse.com – Fax 01 47 75 25 20
29 rm – €65/125 €75/265, €16
◆ A hotel offering pleasant modern rooms, some of which have wood panelling. The lobby has a lounge area with a fireplace and a lively bar with music played by a pianola.

La Table d'Alexandre
7 bd Richard Wallace – ☎ 01 45 06 33 63 – latabledalexandre@9business.fr – Fax 01 41 38 27 42 – Closed 2-24 August, Saturday, Sunday and holidays
Rest – Menu €26/35
◆ A few strides from the athletic Île de Puteaux, traditional cuisine is served in a pleasant setting, with ochre tones, well-designed lighting and pretty straw-bottomed chairs.

ROISSY-EN-FRANCE (PARIS AIRPORTS) – 95 Val-d'Oise – **305** G6 – **101** 8 – **pop. 2 367 – alt. 85 m** – ✉ **95700** 19 **C1**

Paris 26 – Chantilly 28 – Meaux 38 – Pontoise 39 – Senlis 28

Charles-de-Gaulle ☎ 03 36 68 15 15.

Office de tourisme, 40, avenue Charles-de-Gaulle ☎ 01 34 29 43 14, Fax 01 34 29 43 33

Z. I. Paris Nord II – ✉ 95912

Hyatt Regency rm, rm,
351 av. Bois de la Pie – ☎ 01 48 17 12 34 – cdg@hyattintl.com – Fax 01 48 17 17 17
376 rm – €550/725 €550/725, €27 – 12 suites
Rest – buffet lunch Menu €46 – Carte €52/72
◆ Spectacular, contemporary architecture in a good location close to the airport. Large, stylish bedrooms equipped with ultra-modern facilities for its predominantly corporate guests. Enjoy buffet cuisine or classic à la carte choices in the Hyatt Regency's glass-ceilinged restaurant.

in l'aérogare nº 2

Sheraton rm,
– ☎ 01 49 19 70 70 – Fax 01 49 19 70 71
254 rm – €199/599 €199/999, €30
Rest *Les Étoiles* – *☎ 01 41 84 64 54 (closed 28 July-31 August, Saturday, Sunday and holidays)* Menu €57 – Carte €67/86
Rest *Les Saisons* – Menu €43/49
◆ Leave your plane or train and take a trip on this "luxury liner" with its futuristic architecture. Decor by Andrée Putman, a view of the runways, absolute quiet and refined rooms. Les Étoiles offers modern cuisine and beautiful contemporary setting. Brasserie dishes at Les Saisons.

in Roissypole

Hilton
– ☎ 01 49 19 77 77 – cdghitwsal@hilton.com – Fax 01 49 19 77 78
385 rm – €159/759 €159/1059, €24
Rest *Les Aviateurs* – *☎ 01 49 19 77 95* – Menu €37/47 – Carte €31/65
◆ Daring architecture, space and light are the main features of this hotel. Its ultra-modern facilities make it an ideal place in which to work and relax. The Aviateurs offers a small choice of brasserie dishes.

Pullman
Zone centrale Ouest – 01 49 19 29 29 – *h0577@accor.com* – *Fax 01 49 19 29 00*
342 rm – €290/345 €320/375, €25 – 8 suites
Rest *L'Escale* – Menu €31/45 – Carte €30/72
◆ A personal welcome, comfortable atmosphere, conference rooms, an elegant bar and well-looked-after rooms are the advantages of this hotel between two airport terminals. A restaurant with a nautical flavour and seafood. A pleasant port of call dedicated to the sea.

in Roissy-Ville

Courtyard by Marriott
allée du Verger – 01 34 38 53 53
– *alexander.krips@courtyard.com* – *Fax 01 34 38 53 54*
300 rm – €169/259 €169/259, €22 – 4 suites – **Rest** – Menu (€27), €35 – Carte €33/58
◆ Behind its colonnaded white façade, this establishment has modern facilities perfectly in tune with the requirements of businessmen transiting through Paris. Themed brasserie menu served in a large and carefully decorated dining room.

Millennium
allée du Verger – 01 34 29 33 33 – *sales.cdg@mill-cop.com* – *Fax 01 34 29 03 05*
239 rm – €380 €380/500, €20 – **Rest** – Menu (€16 bi), €40 – Carte €28/46
◆ Bar, Irish pub, fitness centre, attractive swimming pool, conference rooms, and spacious bedrooms with one floor specially equipped for businessmen: a hotel with good facilities. International cuisine and brasserie buffet or fast food served at the bar.

Novotel Convention et Wellness
allée des Vergers – 01 30 18 20 00
– *h5418@accor.com* – *Fax 01 34 29 95 60*
288 rm – €99/290 €99/290, €18 – 1 suite – **Rest** – Menu (€19), €24/27 – Carte €28/44
◆ The latest arrival in the hotel zone at Roissy offers impressive services: extensive seminar facilities, kids' corner and comprehensive wellness centre. Lenôtre brasserie dishes available twenty-four hours a day at Novotel Café and Côté Jardin.

Mercure
allée des Vergers – 01 34 29 40 00 – *h1245@accor.com* – *Fax 01 34 29 00 18*
203 rm – €89/210 €99/250, €14 – **Rest** – Menu (€19) – Carte €27/44
◆ This hotel has a meticulous decor comprising Provençal style in the hall, old-fashioned zinc in the bar and spacious rooms in light wood. A contemporary menu that changes with the seasons served in the pleasant dining room or on the terrace overlooking the garden.

ROSNY-SOUS-BOIS – **93 Seine-Saint-Denis** – **305** F7 – **101** 17 – **pop. 39 105** – **alt. 80 m** – 93110 21 **D2**

Paris 14 – Bobigny 8 – Le Perreux-sur-Marne 5 – St-Denis 16
AS Golf de Rosny-sous-Bois 12 rue Raspail, 01 48 94 01 81.

Quality Hôtel
4 r. Rome – 01 48 94 33 08 – *qualityhotel.rosny@wanadoo.fr*
– *Fax 01 48 94 30 05*
97 rm – €90/160 €90/350, €11,50 – ½ P €80/95
Rest *Le Vieux Carré* – *(closed August, 25 December-1st January, Friday dinner, Saturday, Sunday and holidays)* Menu €27/30 – Carte €28/46
◆ A hotel on the golf course, with architecture and interior decoration reminiscent of Louisiana. Spacious, comfortable rooms. The sign and the furniture of Le Vieux Carré evoke New Orleans. Terrace facing the golf course.

RUEIL-MALMAISON – **92 Hauts-de-Seine** – **311** J2 – **101** 14 – **pop. 73 469** – **alt. 40 m** – 92500 **Northern France and the Paris Region** 20 **A1**

Paris 16 – Argenteuil 12 – Nanterre 3 – St-Germain-en-Laye 9 – Versailles 12
Office de tourisme, 160, avenue Paul Doumer 01 47 32 35 75
de Rueil-Malmaison 25 Boulevard Marcel Pourtout, 01 47 49 64 67.
Château de Bois-Préau★ - Church ★ organ - Malmaison: château ★★ museum.

Novotel Atria rm, rest, VISA
21 av. Ed. Belin – 01 47 16 60 60 – h1609@accorhotel.com – Fax 01 47 51 09 29
118 rm – €150/270 €150/270, €15 – **Rest** – Menu €29 – Carte €21/45
◆ A modern building in the Rueil 2000 business district near the RER station. Contemporary, well-appointed guestrooms. Conference centre and fitness room. A restaurant with a modern setting and well-balanced, brasserie-style menu.

Cardinal without rest VISA
1 pl. Richelieu – 01 47 08 20 20 – quality-hotel.cardinal@wanadoo.fr – Fax 01 47 08 35 84
64 rm – €155/280 €155/450, €15
◆ A recent building situated close to the châteaux and parks. Modern or rustic-style rooms. Some have a mezzanine for families. Comfortable lounge bar.

Le Bonheur de Chine VISA
6 allée A. Maillol, (opposite 35 Ave J. Jaurès in Suresnes) – 01 47 49 88 88 – bonheurdechine@wanadoo.fr – Fax 01 47 49 48 68 – Closed Monday
Rest – Menu €23 (weekday lunch), €38/59 – Carte €30/70
◆ Furniture and other elements of decoration from the Far East form the authentic setting for this restaurant full of the flavour of Chinese cuisine.

RUNGIS – **94 Val-de-Marne** – **312** D3 – **101** 26 – **pop. 5 424** – **alt. 80 m** – ✉ **94150** 21 **C3**
Paris 14 – Antony 5 – Corbeil-Essonnes 30 – Créteil 13 – Longjumeau 12

in Pondorly **access: from Paris, A6 and Orly slip road; from the provinces, A6 and Rungis exit – ✉ 94150 Rungis**

Holiday Inn VISA
4 av. Ch. Lindbergh – 01 49 78 42 00 – hiorly@alliance-hospitality.com – Fax 01 45 60 91 25
169 rm – €90/270 €90/270, €19 – **Rest** – *(closed school holidays, Friday dinner, Saturday, Sunday and holidays)* Menu (€24), €29 – Carte €29/58
◆ This chain hotel on the motorway offers the usual high levels of comfort in its spacious, sound-proofed and well-appointed rooms decorated in harmonious tones. The up-to-date dining room sports a few discreet Art Deco touches. Traditional dishes.

Novotel VISA
Zone du Delta, 1 r. Pont des Halles – 01 45 12 44 12 – h1628@accor.com – Fax 01 45 12 44 13
181 rm – €79/179 €79/179, €14 – 5 suites
Rest – *(closed Sunday lunch and Saturday)* Menu €19/25 – Carte €24/46
◆ The comfortable rooms in this vast glass building are contemporary in design with the added benefit of double-glazing. Swimming pool with adjoining terrace. The restaurant dining room and the Novotel Café have both adopted the same colourful, designer decor.

SACLAY – **91 Essonne** – **312** C3 – **101** 24 – **pop. 2 883** – **alt. 147 m** – ✉ **91400**
Paris 27 – Antony 14 – Chevreuse 13 – Montlhéry 16 – Versailles 12 20 **A3**

Novotel rm, VISA
r. Charles Thomassin – 01 69 35 66 00 – h0392@accor.com – Fax 01 69 41 01 77
136 rm – €101/145 €101/145, €13 – **Rest** – Menu €28 – Carte €22/41
◆ A 19C manor house and old farmstead comprise the Novotel Saclay. Rooms in keeping with the chain's standards and extensive sports facilities. Attractive restaurant overlooking the pool and century-old woodland.

ST-CLOUD – **92 Hauts-de-Seine** – **311** J2 – **101** 14 – **pop. 28 157** – **alt. 63 m** – ✉ **92210** Northern France and the Paris Region 20 **B2**
Paris 12 – Nanterre 7 – Rueil-Malmaison 6 – St-Germain 16 – Versailles 10
du Paris Country Club 1 rue du Camp Canadien, (Racecourse), 01 47 71 39 22.
Park★★ (Grand fountain★★) - Stella Matutina church ★.

Villa Henri IV
43 bd République – 01 46 02 59 30 – reception@villa-henri4.com – Fax 01 49 11 11 02
36 rm – €85/92 €98/106, €8
Rest ***Le Bourbon*** – *(closed 27 July-28 August, Monday lunch, Sunday dinner and Saturday)* Menu €35 – Carte €45/75
◆ An old-fashioned charm pervades this St. Cloud villa with period furniture in rooms which are all well soundproofed. A cosy provincial inn feel pervades this restaurant whose sign outside recalls St-Cloud's rich past.

Quorum rm, rest,
2 bd République – 01 47 71 22 33 – hotel-quorum@club-internet.fr – Fax 01 46 02 75 64
58 rm – €90/120 €100/180, €10
Rest – *(closed August, Saturday and Sunday)* Carte €32/35
◆ A recent building with renovated, functional rooms fitted with double-glazing, is just two minutes from the beautiful 450-ha Saint-Cloud park. Modern dining room with bamboo furniture. Traditional unpretentious cuisine.

Le Garde-Manger
6 r. Dailly – 01 46 02 03 66 – restaurant@legardemanger.com – Fax 01 46 02 11 55 – Closed Mon on public holidays and Sun
Rest – Carte €29/37
◆ Temporarily housed in a building 400m from its old premises, this restaurant offers a friendly welcome, relaxed service and generous portions. Simple, elegant decor.

ST-DENIS – 93 Seine-Saint-Denis – 305 F7 – 101 16 – pop. 85 832 – alt. 33 m – 93200 Northern France and the Paris Region 21 C1

Paris 11 – Argenteuil 12 – Beauvais 70 – Bobigny 11 – Chantilly 31 – Pontoise 27 – Senlis 44

Office de tourisme, 1, rue de la République 01 55 87 08 70, Fax 01 48 20 24 11

Basilica★★★ - Stade de France★.

ST-GERMAIN-EN-LAYE – 78 Yvelines – 311 I2 – 101 13 – pop. 38 423 – alt. 78 m – 78100 Northern France and the Paris Region 20 A1

Paris 25 – Beauvais 81 – Dreux 66 – Mantes-la-Jolie 36 – Versailles 13

Office de tourisme, Maison Claude Debussy, 38, rue au Pain 01 34 51 05 12, Fax 01 34 51 36 01

de Joyenval Chambourcy Chemin de la Tuilerie, by Mantes road: 6 km by D 160, 01 39 22 27 50.

Terrace★★ - English garden★ - Château★: musée des Antiquités nationales★★ - Musée Maurice Denis★.

Plan on next page

Pavillon Henri IV rest,
21 r. Thiers – 01 39 10 15 15 – reservation@pavillonhenri4.fr – Fax 01 39 73 93 73 BYZ **t**
42 rm – €125/140 €150/350, €16
Rest – *(closed 3-22 August, 20-29 December, Saturday lunch and Sunday dinner)* Carte €58/90
◆ Finished in 1604 under Henry IV, this building was the birthplace of the future king, Louis XIV. A high-class atmosphere and period furniture in the lounges and rooms. A superb panoramic view from the dining room over the River Seine valley and Paris.

Ermitage des Loges rest,
11 av. Loges – 01 39 21 50 90 – hotel@ermitagedesloges.com – Fax 01 39 21 50 91 AY **x**
56 rm – €98/131 €115/148, €13 – ½ P €92/108
Rest – *(closed August)* Menu €22 bi (weekday lunch), €33/52 – Carte €40/53
◆ Hotel near Château de St Germain. Rather classical rooms in the main building; more modern in the annex and with the advantage of the quiet garden. The modern and elegant decor of the restaurant dining room recalls the epic history of aeroplanes.

ST-GERMAIN-EN-LAYE

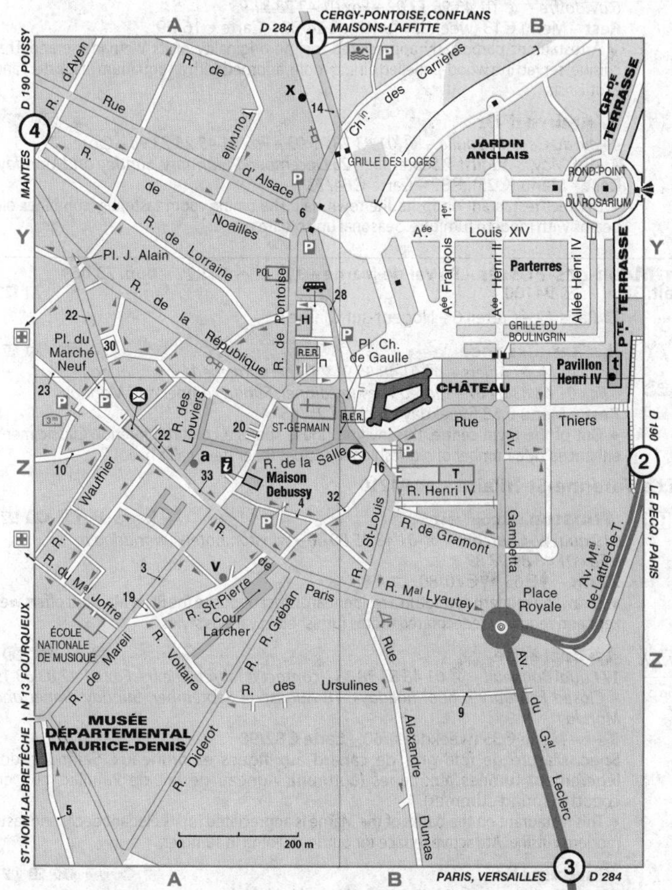

via ① and D 284: 2.5 km – ✉ 78100 St-Germain-en-Laye

La Forestière – rest, VISA

1 av. Prés. Kennedy – ☎ 01 39 10 38 38 – cazaudehore@relaischateaux.com – Fax 01 39 73 73 88

25 rm – †€ 160/175 ††€ 200/210, ☕ € 20 – 5 suites

Rest *Cazaudehore* – see restaurant listing

◆ A captivating house set in a garden on the edge of the forest. The choice of colours and well-made furniture make the rooms more personal and cosy. Jazz evenings.

XXX **Cazaudehore** – Hôtel La Forestière – VISA

1 av. Prés. Kennedy – ☎ 01 30 61 64 64 – cazaudehore@relaischateaux.com – Fax 01 39 73 73 88 – Closed Sunday dinner from November to April and Monday

Rest – Menu € 47 (weekday lunch)/59

◆ The Cazaudehore family have received guests in this attractive residence since 1928. Elegant, welcoming dining room and a delicious terrace shaded by acacias. Fine wine list.

ST-MANDÉ – 94 Val-de-Marne – 312 D2 – 101 27 – pop. 19 697 – alt. 50 m – ✉ 94160 21 C2

Paris 7 – Créteil 10 – Lagny-sur-Marne 29 – Maisons-Alfort 6 – Vincennes 2

L'Ambassade de Pékin

6 av. Joffre – ✆ 01 43 98 13 82 – Fax 01 43 28 31 93

Rest – Menu € 13 (weekday lunch), € 24/32 – Carte € 16/59

◆ A restaurant particularly appreciated for the originality of its Vietnamese and Thai cuisine, served in a wood-panelled dining room, adorned with an aquarium of lobsters and exotic fish.

L'Ambre d'Or

44 av. du Gén. de Gaulle – ✆ 01 43 28 23 93 – Fax 01 43 28 23 93 – Closed 27 April-5 May, 3 August-2 September, 25 December-1st January, Sunday and Monday

Rest – Menu (€ 25), € 32 – Carte € 64/73

◆ Discreet restaurant opposite the town hall. The dining room tastefully combines old beams with modern furniture. Seasonal up-to-date menu.

ST-MAUR-DES-FOSSÉS – 94 Val-de-Marne – 312 D3 – 101 27 – pop. 73 069 – alt. 38 m – ✉ 94100 21 D2

Paris 12 – Créteil 6 – Nogent-sur-Marne 6

La Renaissance

8 pl. des Marronniers – ✆ 01 48 85 91 74 – bernard.ederle@wanadoo.fr – Fax 01 48 83 04 67 – Closed Tuesday dinner, Sunday dinner and Monday

Rest – Menu € 18 (weekday lunch), € 25/45

◆ Out of the town centre, this inviting house sports a colourful interior. Classic menu enhanced by a number of old-fashioned recipes (beef stew, calf's head).

in La Varenne-St-Hilaire – ✉ 94210

Winston without rest

119 quai W. Churchill – ✆ 01 48 85 00 46 – winston.hotel@wanadoo.fr – Fax 01 48 89 98 89

22 rm – †€ 65 ††€ 70/80, ☕ € 8

◆ Sprawling modern cottage in a residential district opposite the River Marne. It offers well kept and regularly redecorated rooms furnished in various styles.

La Bretèche

171 quai Bonneuil – ✆ 01 48 83 38 73 – contact@labreteche.fr – Fax 01 42 83 63 19 – Closed February school holidays, 18 August-1st September, Sunday dinner and Monday

Rest – Menu € 35 (weekdays)/60 – Carte € 82/98

Spec. Marbré de foie gras de canard aux figues et pruneaux. Saint-Jacques légèrement fumées aux cèpes (autumn). Agneau de lait de Pauillac, cuit en cocotte (spring-summer).

◆ This restaurant on the banks of the Marne is appreciated for its elegant decor and tasty modern cuisine. Attractive terrace for outdoor dining in summer.

Gargamelle

23 av. Ch. Péguy – ✆ 01 48 86 04 40 – sarl.la.deviniere@wanadoo.fr – Closed 9-25 August, 14-23 February, Sunday dinner and Monday

Rest – Menu (€ 19), € 29/40 – Carte € 40/44

◆ Simple cuisine, cheerful service, contemporary brown and yellow decor, and a pretty shaded terrace are the assets of this restaurant.

Entre Terre et Mer

15 r. St-Hilaire – ✆ 01 55 97 04 98 – Fax 01 55 96 08 04 – Closed 23 July-22 August, Sunday dinner and Monday – **Rest** – Carte € 36/56

◆ A tiny restaurant worth a stopover to sample its carefully prepared, fresh fish and seafood dishes. Charming colourful decor, adorned with paintings by local artists.

Faim et Soif

28 r. St-Hilaire – ✆ 01 48 86 55 76 – Closed 5-20 August, Sunday and Monday

Rest – Carte € 41/56

◆ A new shamelessly trendy establishment: grey façade, contemporary art, designer furniture and a plasma screen in place of a slate. Updated, minimalist cuisine.

St-Ouen – **93 Seine-Saint-Denis** – **305** F7 – **101** 16 – **pop. 39 722** – **alt. 36 m** – ✉ **93400** 21 **C1**

Paris 9 – Bobigny 12 – Chantilly 46 – Meaux 49 – Pontoise 26 – St-Denis 5

Office de tourisme, 30, avenue Gabriel Péri ✆ 01 40 11 77 36, Fax 01 40 11 01 70

Manhattan

115 av. G. Péri – ✆ 01 41 66 40 00 – reservation@hotel-le-manhattan.com – Fax 01 41 66 40 66

126 rm – €155/190 €165/190, ☕ €14

Rest – *(closed 1st-26 August, Saturday, Sunday and holidays)* Menu (€19) – Carte €30/54

◆ A glass and stone modern building housing bright and practical rooms. Quieter at the back. Dining room-veranda perched on the eighth floor of the hotel, serving traditional dishes.

Le Coq de la Maison Blanche

37 bd J. Jaurès – ✆ 01 40 11 01 23 – coqmaisonblanche@orange.fr – Fax 01 40 11 67 68 – Closed Saturday 14 July-15 August and Sunday

Rest – Menu €32 – Carte €41/85

◆ Authentic 1950s decor, traditional cooking, efficient service and long-standing customers. Just like being in a film of the period.

Le Soleil

109 av. Michelet – ✆ 01 40 10 08 08 – lesoleil2@orange.fr – Fax 01 47 05 44 02

Rest – *(lunch only)* Menu €27/34

◆ A pleasant bistro with an amusing mixture of antique furniture and trinkets, reminding us that the Marché aux Puces (Flea Market) is nearby. Generous traditional dishes.

St-Prix – **95 Val-d'Oise** – **305** E6 – **101** 5 – **pop. 7 214** – **alt. 70 m** – ✉ **95390**

Paris 26 – Cergy 22 18 **B1**

Hostellerie du Prieuré without rest

74 r. A.-Rey – ✆ 01 34 27 51 51 – contact@hostelduprieure.com – Fax 01 39 59 21 12

8 rm – €110/120 €110/120, ☕ €15 – 1 suite

◆ A 17C village bistro. The large bedrooms are an invitation to dream, inspired either by romance or foreign countries... Copious breakfast.

À La Grâce de Dieu

r. de l'Église – ✆ 01 39 59 08 00 – Fax 01 39 59 21 12 – Closed Sunday dinner and Monday lunch

Rest – Menu €28 (weekdays)/42

◆ At the foot of the church, a large construction with three dining rooms, a veranda and a terrace. Up-to-date, regularly changing menu. Good wine selection.

St-Quentin-en-Yvelines – **78 Yvelines** – **311** H3 – **101** 21 – **pop. 116 082**

Northern France and the Paris Region 18 **B2**

Paris 33 – Houdan 33 – Palaiseau 28 – Rambouillet 21 – Versailles 14

Blue Green Golf St-Quentin-en-Yvelines Trappes Base de loisirs, ✆ 01 30 50 86 40 ;

National Guyancourt 2 avenue du Golf, ✆ 01 30 43 36 00.

Montigny-le-Bretonneux – **pop. 35 216** – **alt. 162 m** – ✉ **78180**

Auberge du Manet

61 av. Manet – ✆ 01 30 64 89 00 – mail@aubergedumanet.com – Fax 01 30 64 55 10

53 rm – €115 €130/160, ☕ €13 – ½ P €75

Rest – *(closed Saturday lunch and Sunday dinner)* Carte €38/50

◆ Owned by Port-Royal-des-Champs Abbey in the 17C, a manor farm at the time of the Revolution, and now an inn with a particularly warm atmosphere. Comfortable rooms. A dining room-veranda and a pleasant country terrace by a duck pond.

Holiday Inn Garden Court
r. J.-P. Timbaud, Bois d'Arcy road on D 127 – ✆ 01 30 14 42 00 – higcsaintquentin@alliance-hospitality.com – Fax 01 30 14 42 42
81 rm – €80/157 €80/157, € 14 – **Rest** – *(closed Friday evening, Sunday lunchtime and Saturday)* Menu € 28 – Carte € 30/38
◆ Modern hotel in the Pas-du-Lac district, offering rather small, functional rooms. Pleasant dining room-veranda, summer terrace and up-to-date cuisine.

Mercure
9 pl. Choiseul – ✆ 01 39 30 18 00 – h1983@accor.com – Fax 01 30 57 15 22
74 rm – €140/160 €150/170, € 15 – **Rest** – *(closed 22 December-2 January, Friday dinner, Saturday and Sunday)* Carte € 27/40
◆ Hotel with discreetly elegant rooms included in a real-estate complex. Pleasant low-key bar lounge with a plasma television screen. The restaurant is decorated along an aeronautical theme. Traditional dishes and shaded terrace.

Voisins-le-Bretonneux – pop. 12 153 – alt. 163 m – ✉ 78960

Remains of Port-Royal des Champs abbey ★ Southwest: 4 km.

Novotel St-Quentin Golf National
au Golf National, east: 2 km on the D 36 rm,
✉ 78114 – ✆ 01 30 57 65 65 – h1139@accor.com – Fax 01 30 57 65 00
131 rm – €129/179 €129/179, € 13,50 – **Rest** – Menu € 20/43
◆ This hotel benefits from the peaceful environment of a golf course. It also offers modern rooms and is well equipped for a business clientele. The restaurant, Novotel Café and bar share the same up-to-date menu . Modern decor and terrace.

Port Royal without rest
20 r. H. Boucher – ✆ 01 30 44 16 27 – didiercadoret@wanadoo.fr – Fax 01 30 57 52 11 – Closed 4-17 August and 23 December-3 January – **40 rm** – €72 €78, € 7
◆ This modern hotel, on the edge of the Chevreuse Valley, houses perfectly well-kept and simply-furnished rooms. Pleasant garden planted with trees and flowers.

Relais de Voisins
av. Grand-Pré – ✆ 01 30 44 11 55 – Fax 01 30 44 02 04 – Closed 20 July-20 August, 24 December-7 January
54 rm – €70/79 €70/79, € 6
Rest – *(closed Sunday dinner and Saturday)* Menu € 15/28
◆ Modern hotel, built on the remains of a farmhouse whose 16C outer walls were retained. It offers small and very simply furnished rooms. Functional and colourful restaurant serving traditional food.

STE-GENEVIÈVE-DES-BOIS – 91 Essonne – 312 C4 – 101 35 – pop. 32 125 – alt. 78 m – ✉ 91700 **Northern France and the Paris Region** 18 **B2**

Paris 27 – Arpajon 10 – Corbeil-Essonnes 18 – Étampes 30 – Évry 10 – Longjumeau 9

La Table d'Antan
38 av. Grande Charmille du Parc, (near the Town Hall) – ✆ 01 60 15 71 53 – table-antan@wanadoo.fr – Closed 29 July-25 August, Tuesday dinner, Wednesday dinner, Sunday dinner and Monday
Rest – Menu € 30/48 – Carte € 40/66
◆ This pleasant restaurant in a residential district sports a warm atmosphere and a plush décor. Classic cuisine and specialities of southwest France; list of whiskies.

SÉNART – 312 E4 – 101 39 – pop. 93 069 **Northern France and the Paris Region**

Paris 38 – Boulogne-Billancourt 50 – Montreuil 39 – Argenteuil 67 – Saint-Denis 50 19 **C2**

le Plessis-Picard – ✉ 77550

La Mare au Diable
– ✆ 01 64 10 20 90 – mareaudiable@wanadoo.fr – Fax 01 64 10 20 91 – Closed 28 July-13 August, Tuesday dinner, Sunday dinner and Monday
Rest – Menu € 25 bi (weekdays)/55 – Carte € 41/73
◆ This 15C house covered in ampelopsis was visited by George Sand. The interior, with patinated beams and with a fireplace, does not lack character.

Pouilly-le-Fort – ✉ 77240

Le Pouilly

1 r. de la Fontaine – ✆ 01 64 09 56 64 – contact@lepouilly.fr – Fax 01 64 09 56 64 – Closed 10 August-10 September, 22-28 December, Sunday dinner and Monday

Rest – Menu € 30 bi (weekday lunch), € 47/70 – Carte € 81/87

Spec. Foie gras de canard. Filet de lièvre aux trompettes de la mort (autumn). Velouté de chocolat chaud.

◆ In this old farm, exposed stonework, tapestries and a fireplace make up a decor full of charm, also featuring a garden terrace. Tasty modern cuisine.

St-Pierre-du-Perray – **pop. 5 801** – **alt. 88 m** – ✉ **91280**

de Greenparc route de Villepècle, ✆ 01 60 75 40 60.

Novotel

golf de Greenparc – ✆ 01 69 89 75 75 – h1783-gm@accor.com – Fax 01 69 89 75 50

78 rm – €99/127 €99/127, € 13 – 2 suites – **Rest** – Menu € 20/25 – Carte € 22/40

◆ Modern hotel perfect for a quiet, relaxing stay, with golf course, swimming pool and gym. Half of the "Harmonie"-style rooms overlook the fairways. Some rooms have a balcony. Contemporary-style dining room and lounge overlooking the garden. The menu is traditional and typical of the Novotel chain.

SUCY-EN-BRIE – **94 Val-de-Marne** – **312** E3 – **101** 28 – **pop. 24 812** – **alt. 96 m** – ✉ **94370**

Paris 21 – Créteil 6 – Chennevières-sur-Marne 4 — 21 **D2**

Château de Gros Bois★: furniture★★ South: 5 km, **Northern France and the Paris Region**

Le Clos de Sucy

17 r. Porte – ✆ 01 45 90 29 29 – leclosdesucy@wanadoo.fr – Fax 01 45 90 29 29 – Closed 3-26 August, Saturday lunch, Sunday dinner and Monday

Rest – Menu (€ 23), € 33/43 – Carte € 46/63

◆ A dining room that is both elegant and countrified, with its half-timbered partitions, exposed beams and wine-coloured shades. Traditional cuisine with personal touches.

quartier les Bruyères Southeast: 3 km – ✉ 94370 Sucy-en-Brie

Le Tartarin

carrefour de la Patte d'Oie – ✆ 01 45 90 42 61 – aubergetartarin@gmail.com – Fax 01 45 90 52 55 – Closed August and Sunday dinner

12 rm – €52 €57/135, € 8 – **Rest** – *(closed Thursday dinner, Monday, Tuesday and Wednesday)* Menu € 21/47 – Carte € 34/51

◆ Three generations of the same family have reigned over this former hunting lodge on the outskirts of the forest with a warm, country atmosphere. Swans take pride of place in the dining room (trophies, stuffed animals). Traditional cuisine.

Terrasse Fleurie

1 r. Marolles – ✆ 01 45 90 40 07 – terrasse.fleurie@wanadoo.fr – Fax 01 45 90 40 07 – Closed 27 July-21 August, Sunday dinner, Monday dinner, Tuesday dinner, Thursday dinner and Wednesday

Rest – Menu (€ 19 bi), € 26/39

◆ Situated in a pavilion, this restaurant serves simple, generous food in a country-style dining room or on the pleasant flowered terrace.

SURESNES – **92 Hauts-de-Seine** – **311** J2 – **101** 14 – **pop. 39 706** – **alt. 42 m** – ✉ **92150** **Northern France and the Paris Region** — 20 **B2**

Paris 12 – Nanterre 4 – Pontoise 32 – St-Germain-en-Laye 13 – Versailles 14

Office de tourisme, 50, boulevard Henri Sellier ✆ 01 41 18 18 76, Fax 01 41 18 18 78

Fort du Mont Valérien (Mémorial National de la France combattante).

Novotel

rm,

7 r. Port aux Vins – ✆ 01 40 99 00 00 – h1143@accor.com – Fax 01 45 06 60 06

112 rm – €185/195 €185/195, € 15 – 1 suite – **Rest** – buffet Carte € 21/41

◆ A fully-renovated hotel in a quiet street near the quayside. Rooms with modern decor, in bright, sober and relaxing colours. Traditional cuisine at the restaurant or snack-bar food at the Novotel Café.

Astor without rest
19 bis r. Mt Valérien – ✆ 01 45 06 15 52 – info@hotelastor.fr – Fax 01 42 04 65 29
50 rm – †€ 77 ††€ 79, ☐ € 6
◆ 200 m from Mont Valérien - the French Resistance memorial - a family establishment with small rooms, which are not luxurious but are clean and have efficient double-glazing.

Les Jardins de Camille
70 av. Franklin Roosevelt – ✆ 01 45 06 22 66 – lesjardinsdecamille@free.fr – Fax 01 47 72 42 25 – Closed Sunday evening
Rest – Menu € 40/78 – Carte € 59/78
◆ Magnificent view of Paris and la Défense from the dining room and one of the terraces of this old farm which has been converted into a restaurant. Wonderful Burgundy wine list.

THIAIS – **94 Val-de-Marne** – **312** D3 – **101** 26 – **pop. 28 232** – **alt. 60 m** – ✉ **94320** 21 **C2**

Paris 18 – Créteil 7 – Évry 27 – Melun 37

Ophélie la Cigale Gourmande
82 av. Versailles – ✆ 01 48 92 59 59 – luclamass@aol.com – Fax 01 48 53 91 53 – Closed 4-28 August, 22-31 December, Wednesday dinner, Saturday lunch, Sunday dinner and Monday
Rest – Menu (€ 30), € 35/50
◆ A little corner of Provence at the gates of Paris! Tasty, updated Mediterranean cuisine prepared with fresh produce. Served in a simple but smart and colourful decor.

TREMBLAY-EN-FRANCE – **93 Seine-Saint-Denis** – **305** G7 – **101** 18 – **pop. 33 885** – **alt. 60 m** – ✉ **93290** 21 **D1**

Paris 24 – Aulnay-sous-Bois 7 – Bobigny 13 – Villepinte 4

in Tremblay-Vieux-Pays

Le Cénacle
1 r. de la Mairie – ✆ 01 48 61 32 91 – Fax 01 48 60 43 89 – Closed August, Saturday, Sunday and holidays
Rest – Menu € 38/68 – Carte € 50/68
◆ Behind this cheerful façade with red blinds there are two lovely rooms with painted beams, ochre colour schemes, impressionist paintings, Louis XV–style chairs and a shellfish aquarium. Traditional cuisine.

TRIEL-SUR-SEINE – **78 Yvelines** – **311** I2 – **101** 10 – **pop. 11 097** – **alt. 20 m** – ✉ **78510** **Northern France and the Paris Region** 18 **B1**

Paris 39 – Mantes-la-Jolie 27 – Pontoise 18 – Rambouillet 55 – St-Germain-en-Laye 12

St-Martin church ★.

St-Martin
2 r. Galande, (opposite the post office) – ✆ 01 39 70 32 00 – Closed 3 weeks in August, Christmas holidays, Wednesday and Sunday
Rest – *(number of covers limited, pre-book)* Menu (€ 16), € 30/55 – Carte € 30/55
◆ The restaurant stands next to a truly lovely 13C gothic church; here one can enjoy modernised traditional cooking in a pleasant rustic-style decor.

VANVES – **92 Hauts-de-Seine** – **311** J3 – **101** 25 – **pop. 25 414** – **alt. 61 m** – ✉ **92170** 20 **B2**

Paris 7 – Boulogne-Billancourt 5 – Nanterre 13

Syndicat d'initiative, 2, rue Louis Blanc ✆ 01 47 36 03 26

Mercure Paris Porte de Versailles Expo rm,
36-38 r. Moulin – ✆ 01 46 48 55 55 – h0375@accor.com – Fax 01 46 48 56 56
388 rm – †€ 147/225 ††€ 157/235, ☐ € 14,50 – **Rest** – Carte € 25/42
◆ Facing the Exhibition Centre, a 1980s building with well-soundproofed rooms. They are gradually being renovated in a more modern style. Functional restaurant-atrium, designed for a quick meal (traditional "Mercure" cuisine and oysters).

XXX **Pavillon de la Tourelle**

10 r. Larmeroux – ✆ 01 46 42 15 59 – pavillontourelle@wanadoo.fr – Fax 01 46 42 06 27 – Closed 28 July-27 August, February holidays, Sunday dinner and Monday
Rest – Menu (€ 33), € 39 (lunch), € 49 € bi/92 bi – Carte € 60/71
◆ This house with a small tower, on the edge of the park, is home to an elegant restaurant decorated in pastel tones with Louis XVI-style chairs and attractively-laid tables. Traditional cuisine.

VAUCRESSON – 92 Hauts-de-Seine – **311** I2 – **101** 23 – **pop. 8 141** – **alt. 160 m** – ✉ 92420 20 **A2**

Paris 18 – Mantes-la-Jolie 44 – Nanterre 11 – St-Germain-en-Laye 11 – Versailles 5

Stade Francais 129 av. de la Celle St Cloud, North: 2 km, ✆ 01 47 01 15 04.

Etang de St-Cucufa★ Northeast: 2,5 km - Institut Pasteur - Musée des Applications de la Recherche★ to Marnes-la-Coquette Southwest: 4 km, **Northern France and the Paris Region**

see plan of Versailles

XXX **Auberge de la Poularde**

36 bd Jardy, (near the motorway), D 182 – ✆ 01 47 41 13 47 – auberge.lapoularde@free.fr – Fax 01 47 41 13 47 – Closed August, February school holidays, Sunday evening, Tuesday evening and Wednesday U **a**
Rest – Menu € 30 – Carte € 35/74
◆ A friendly welcome and impeccable service single out this inn with a charming provincial atmosphere. The menu is classic, particularly based on Bresse poultry dishes.

VÉLIZY-VILLACOUBLAY – 78 Yvelines – **311** J3 – **101** 24 – **pop. 20 342** – **alt. 164 m** – ✉ 78140 20 **B2**

Paris 19 – Antony 12 – Chartres 81 – Meudon 8 – Versailles 6

Holiday Inn rm,

av. de l'Europe, (near Vélizy II shopping centre) – ✆ 01 39 46 96 98 – hivelizy@alliance-hospitality.com – Fax 01 34 65 95 21 – Closed Saturday lunch and Sunday lunch
182 rm – 🚹€ 230/490 🚹🚹€ 230/490, ☕ € 19 – **Rest** – Menu € 27/36 – Carte € 30/53
◆ This hotel has spacious, comfortable, well-soundproofed and regularly redecorated rooms. Choose a room away from the motorway. Exposed beams in the comfortable dining room of this Holiday Inn.

VERSAILLES P – 78 Yvelines – **311** I3 – **101** 23 – **pop. 85 726** – **alt. 130 m** – ✉ **78000**
Northern France and the Paris Region 20 **A2**

Paris 22 – Beauvais 94 – Dreux 59 – Évreux 90 – Melun 65 – Orléans 129

Office de tourisme, 2 bis, avenue de Paris ✆ 01 39 24 88 88, Fax 01 39 24 88 89

du Stade Français Vaucresson 129 av. de la Celle St Cloud, by Rueil road: 7 km, ✆ 01 47 01 15 04 ;

de Saint-Aubin Saint-Aubin Route du Golf, by Chevreuse road: 17 km, ✆ 01 69 41 25 19 ;

de Feucherolles Feucherolles Sainte Gemme, by Mantes road (D 307): 17 km, ✆ 01 30 54 94 94 ;

du haras de jardy Marnes-la-Coquette Boulevard de Jardy, Northeast: 9 km, ✆ 01 47 01 35 80.

Château★★★ - Gardens★★★ (Great fountains★★★ and night fairs★★★ in summer) - Ecuries Royales★ - Trianon★★ - Musée Lambinet★ Y **M.**

Jouy-en-Josas: la Diège★ (statue) in the church, 7 km by ③.

Plans on following pages

Trianon Palace rm,

1 bd de la Reine – ✆ 01 30 84 50 00 – reservation.01104@westin.com – Fax 01 30 84 50 01 X **r**
182 rm – 🚹€ 199/830 🚹🚹€ 199/830, ☕ € 30 – 17 suites
Rest – (due to open early 2008)
◆ This classical-style luxury hotel standing on the edge of the château's grounds has been completely renovated. Very comfortable guestrooms with elegant, contemporary furnishings. Excellent spa.

VERSAILLES

- Bellevue (Av. de) . . . . U 2
- Coste (R.) . . . . V 9
- Dr-Schweitzer (Av. du) . . . . . . U 12
- Franchet-d'Esperey (Av. du Mar.) . . . . U 15
- Glatigny (Bd de) . . . . U 19
- Leclerc (Av. du Gén.) . . . . V 22
- Marly-le-Roi (R. de) . . . . U 26
- Mermoz (R. Jean) . . . . V 27
- Moxouris (R.) . . . . U 29
- Napoléon III (Rte) . . . . U 30
- Pelin (R. L.) . . . . U 32
- Porchefontaine (Av.) . . . . V 33
- Pottier (R.) . . . . U 35
- Rocquencourt (Av. de) . . . . U 39
- St-Antoine (Allée) . . . . V 40
- Sports (R. des) . . . . U 43
- Vauban (R.) . . . . V 45

Pullman rm, VISA

2 bis av. de Paris – ✆ 01 39 07 46 46 – h1300@accor.com
– Fax 01 39 07 46 47 Y **a**

146 rm – †€ 150/475 ††€ 150/475, ☕ € 24 – 6 suites – **Rest** – Carte € 46/58

◆ Only the gateway remains of the old artillery riding school. Vast, renovated rooms graced with period furniture and lithographs. A dining room adorned with pelmets hung with Jouy drapes and offering both local and exotic dishes.

VERSAILLES

Carnot (R.) . . . . Y
Chancellerie (R. de la) . . . . . Y 3
Clemenceau (R. Georges) . Y 7
Cotte (R. Robert de) . . . . . . Y 10
États-Généraux (R. des) . . . Z
Europe (Av. de l') . . . . Y 14
Foch (R. du Mar.) . . . . XY
Gambetta (Pl.) . . . . Y 17
Gaulle (Av. du Gén.-de-) . . YZ 18
Hoche (R.) . . . . Y
Indép.-Américaine (R. de l') Y 20
Leclerc (R. du Gén.) . . . . . . Z 24
Mermoz (R. Jean) . . . . Z 27
Nolhac (R. Pierre-de-) . . . . . Y 31
Orangerie (R. de l') . . . . . . YZ
Paroisse (R. de la) . . . . Y
Porte-de-Buc (R. de la) . . . . Z 34
Rockfeller (Av.) . . . . Y 37
Royale (R.) . . . . Z
Satory (R. de) . . . . YZ 42
Vieux-Versailles (R. du) . . . YZ 47

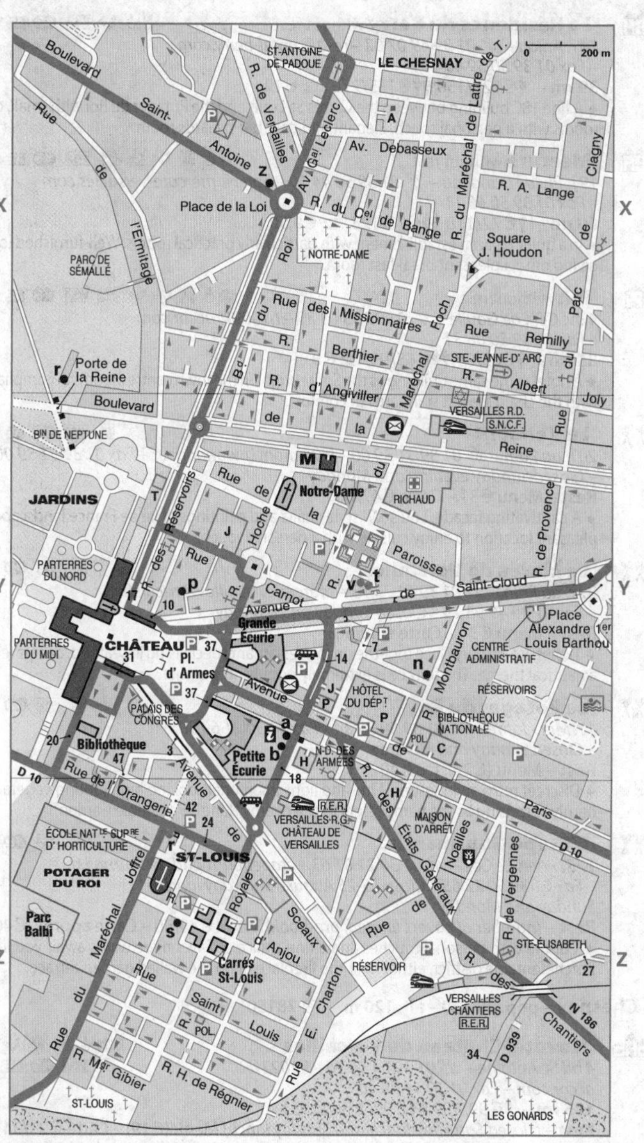

Le Versailles without rest
7 r. Ste-Anne – 01 39 50 64 65 – info@hotel-le-versailles.fr – Fax 01 39 02 37 85 Y **p**
45 rm – €115/148 €125/158, €12
◆ Peaceful, spacious and functional rooms, as well as attentive service explain this pleasant hotel's success with its business guests.

La Résidence du Berry without rest
14 r. Anjou – 01 39 49 07 07 – resa@hotel-berry.com – Fax 01 39 50 59 40 Z **s**
39 rm – €125/150 €135/270, €12
◆ A fine 18C building between the Carrés St-Louis and the Potager du Roi with small, cosy rooms with a personal touch. Elegant and cosy bar-billiards room.

Mercure without rest
19 r. Ph. de Dangeau – 01 39 50 44 10 – hotel@mercure-versailles.com – Fax 01 39 50 65 11 Y **n**
60 rm – €72/118 €72/128, €9,50
◆ In a quiet area, an establishment with particularly practical rooms. Well-furnished lobby giving onto a pleasant breakfast room.

Ibis without rest
4 av. Gén. de Gaulle – 01 39 53 03 30 – h1409@accor.com – Fax 01 39 50 06 31 Y **b**
85 rm – €65/99 €65/99, €8
◆ A hotel in the same building as the Sofitel, right in the town centre. Rooms in compliance with the chain's latest standards of comfort.

Le Valmont
20 r. au Pain – 01 39 51 39 00 – levalmont@wanadoo.fr – Fax 01 39 51 39 00 – Closed Sunday evening and Monday Y **v**
Rest – Menu €31 – Carte €47/68
◆ A captivating façade, Louis XVI style chairs and paintings of Île de France landscapes: a pleasant location to enjoy cuisine with a personal touch.

La Marée de Versailles
22 r. au Pain – 01 30 21 73 73 – mareedeversailles@tiscali.fr – Fax 01 39 49 98 29 – Closed Sunday and Monday Y **t**
Rest – Menu €39 – Carte €48/58
◆ Tables are set very close together in this restaurant specialising in seafood, decorated on a nautical theme. The terrace is extremely popular in summer.

Le Potager du Roy
1 r. Mar.-Joffre – 01 39 50 35 34 – Fax 01 30 21 69 30 – Closed Sunday and Monday Z **r**
Rest – Menu (€26), €33/40
◆ Discreet retro-style setting. Fine and light traditional cooking highlighting vegetables: hardly surprising as the name refers to the nearby "King's Vegetable Garden"!

L'Étape Gourmande
125 r. Yves Le Coz – 01 30 21 01 63 – etapegourmande@hotmail.fr – Fax 01 39 50 22 65 – Closed 5-25 August, Saturday lunch, Sunday and Monday V **n**
Rest – *(number of covers limited, pre-book)* Menu €40/50 – Carte approx. €40
◆ Cuisine with personal touches and a fine choice of Savennière wines await you in the Porchefontaine district, either near the fireplace or on the walled garden terrace.

in Chesnay – pop. 28 530 – alt. 120 m – 78150

Novotel Château de Versailles
4 bd St-Antoine – 01 39 54 96 96 – h1022@accor.com – Fax 01 39 54 94 40 X **z**
105 rm – €99/159 €99/159, €13
Rest – *(closed Saturday lunch and Sunday lunch)* Menu (€19) – Carte €21/34
◆ Hotel at a roundabout. Functional and well-soundproofed rooms lead off an atrium made into a lounge (numerous green plants). Restaurant with modern, bistro-style decor, Novotel chain dishes and non-stop service.

LE VÉSINET – 78 Yvelines – 311 I2 – 101 13 – pop. 15 921 – alt. 44 m – ✉ 78110

Paris 19 – Maisons-Laffitte 9 – Pontoise 23 – St-Germain-en-Laye 4 – Versailles 12 20 **A1**

Syndicat d'initiative, 60, boulevard Carnot, ☎ 01 30 15 47 00

Auberge des Trois Marches rest, VISA AE

15 r. J. Laurent, (pl. de l'église) – ☎ 01 39 76 10 30 – aubergedes3marches@yahoo.fr – Fax 01 39 76 62 58 – Closed 10-27 August

15 rm – €85/100 €95/180, €9,50

Rest – *(closed Sunday evening and Monday lunchtime)* Menu €34/49 (dinner) – Carte €34/50

◆ Quiet guesthouse in an area with a village atmosphere (church, market). Functional rooms which are gradually being renovated. Impeccably maintained and a friendly welcome. A fresco recalling scenes from the 1930s decorates the dining room.

VILLE D'AVRAY – 92 Hauts-de-Seine – 311 J3 – 101 24 – pop. 11 415 – alt. 130 m – ✉ 92410 20 **B2**

Paris 14 – Antony 16 – Boulogne-Billancourt 5 – Neuilly-sur-Seine 10 – Versailles 6

Les Étangs de Corot rm, VISA AE

53 r. de Versailles – ☎ 01 41 15 37 00 – reservation@etangsdecorot.com – Fax 01 41 15 37 99

49 rm – €215/320 €235/320, €20

Rest *Cabassud* – *(pre-book)* Carte €48/60

Rest *Les Paillottes* – *(Open from April to October)* Menu (€28) – Carte €45/57

◆ This delightful hamlet beside a lake inspired the painter Camille Corot. Restored and extended, it now includes a charming hotel and art gallery. Elegant decor and modern menu at the Cabassud. Café feel and typical bistro cuisine at Les Paillottes.

VILLENEUVE-LA-GARENNE – 92 Hauts-de-Seine – 311 J2 – 101 15 – pop. 22 349 – alt. 30 m – ✉ 92390 21 **C1**

Paris 13 – Nanterre 14 – Pontoise 23 – St-Denis 3 – St-Germain-en-Laye 24

Les Chanteraines VISA AE

av. 8 Mai 1945 – ☎ 01 47 99 31 31 – leschanteraines@wanadoo.fr – Fax 01 41 21 31 17 – Closed August, Saturday and Sunday

Rest – Menu €35/53 – Carte €44/66

◆ This restaurant is set in the modern complex next to Chanteraines Park. Up-to-date cuisine, served in a large dining room overlooking the lake.

VILLENEUVE-LE-ROI – 94 Val-de-Marne – 312 D3 – 101 26 – pop. 18 292 – alt. 100 m – ✉ 94290 21 **C3**

Paris 20 – Créteil 9 – Arpajon 29 – Corbeil-Essonnes 21 – Évry 16

Beau Rivage VISA AE

17 quai de Halage – ☎ 01 45 97 16 17 – beaurivage94290@orange.fr – Fax 01 49 61 02 60 – Closed 15 August-4 September, Tuesday evening, Wednesday evening, Sunday evening and Monday

Rest – Menu €38 – Carte approx. €54

◆ As the name indicates, the Beau Rivage is on the riverside; choose a table near the picture windows for a view of the Seine. A modern setting and traditional cuisine.

VILLEPARISIS – 77 Seine-et-Marne – 312 E2 – 101 19 – pop. 21 296 – alt. 72 m – ✉ 77270

Paris 26 – Bobigny 15 – Chelles 10 – Tremblay-en-France 5 19 **C1**

Relais du Parisis without rest VISA AE

2 av. Jean Monnet – ☎ 01 64 27 83 83 – relaisduparisis@wanadoo.fr – Fax 01 64 27 94 49

44 rm – €49/69 €49/69, €8

◆ This hotel in an industrial estate, near a bypass, houses small, functional and simply-furnished rooms.

XX **La Bastide** VISA MC

15 av. J. Jaurès – ✆ 01 60 21 08 99 – la-bastide@cegetel.net – Fax 01 60 21 08 99 – Closed 24 February-2 March, Monday dinner, Saturday lunch and Sunday

Rest – *(pre-book Sat - Sun)* Menu € 28/45 – Carte € 42/63

◆ The atmosphere of this discreet town-centre restaurant is reminiscent of a provincial inn. A country setting with exposed beams and a fireplace. Traditional cuisine.

VINCENNES – **94 Val-de-Marne** – **312** D2 – **101** 17 – **pop. 43 595** – **alt. 51 m** – ✉ **94300** 21 **C2**

Paris 7 – Créteil 11 – Lagny-sur-Marne 26 – Meaux 47 – Melun 45 – Senlis 48

Office de tourisme, 11, avenue de Nogent ✆ 01 48 08 13 00, Fax 01 43 74 81 01

Château★★ - Bois de Vincennes★★: Zoo★★, Parc floral de Paris★★, Musée des Arts d'Afrique et d'Océanie★, **Paris**

St-Louis without rest VISA MC AE

2 bis r. R. Giraudineau – ✆ 01 43 74 16 78 – saint-louis@paris-hotel-capital.com – Fax 01 43 74 16 49

25 rm – †€ 140/190 ††€ 140/190, ☕ € 13

◆ This building near the château houses elegant, period furnished rooms. Some ground floor rooms, which open onto the small garden, have basement bathrooms.

Daumesnil Vincennes without rest VISA MC AE

50 av. Paris – ✆ 01 48 08 44 10 – info@hotel-daumesnil.com – Fax 01 43 65 10 94

50 rm – †€ 82/104 ††€ 97/189, ☕ € 11

◆ A pleasant Provençal-style decor enlivens this hotel, which is situated on a busy avenue. The breakfast room on a veranda opens onto a small patio.

Donjon without rest VISA MC

22 r. Donjon – ✆ 01 43 28 19 17 – info@hotel-donjon-vincennes.fr – Fax 01 49 57 02 04 – Closed 20 July-25 August

25 rm – †€ 62/65 ††€ 65/85, ☕ € 7

◆ A town centre establishment with rather small, spick and span rooms. Pleasantly furnished breakfast and sitting rooms.

X **La Rigadelle** AC VISA MC

23 r. de Montreuil – ✆ 01 43 28 04 23 – Fax 01 43 28 04 23 – Closed 15 July-18 August, 20-28 December, Sunday and Monday

Rest – *(number of covers limited, pre-book)* Menu (€ 24), € 33/51 – Carte € 42/73

◆ The stylish dining room is tiny with mirrors making it appear more spacious. The cuisine is in keeping with modern taste, with the accent on fish.

VIRY-CHÂTILLON – **91 Essonne** – **312** D3 – **101** 36 – **pop. 30 257** – **alt. 34 m** – ✉ **91170** 21 **C3**

Paris 26 – Corbeil-Essonnes 15 – Évry 8 – Longjumeau 10 – Versailles 29

XX **Dariole de Viry** AC VISA MC AE

21 r. Pasteur – ✆ 01 69 44 22 40 – la-dariole-de-viry@wanadoo.fr – Closed Saturday lunch, Sunday dinner and Monday

Rest – Menu € 39/80

◆ Seasonal, traditional cuisine at this restaurant, whose façade is painted in chocolate tones. Recently re-decorated, attractive dining room.

X **Marcigny** AC VISA MC

27 r. D. Casanova – ✆ 01 69 44 04 09 – Closed Saturday lunch, Sunday dinner and Monday

Rest – Menu € 24 (weekday lunch)/34

◆ The Marcigny bears the name of a Burgundy village. Friendly atmosphere, attentive service, traditional French and Burgundian cuisine, accompanied by home-baked bread. A popular restaurant which is often full.

Your opinions are important to us: please write and let us know about your discoveries and experiences – good and bad!

PARVILLE – 27 Eure – **304** G7 – see Évreux

PASSENANS – 39 Jura – **321** D6 – see Poligny

PATRIMONIO – 2B Haute-Corse – **345** F3 – see Corse

PAU P – 64 Pyrénées-Atlantiques – **342** J5 – pop. 78 732 – Built-up area 181 413 – alt. 207 m – Casino – ✉ 64000 Atlantic Coast 3 **B3**

Paris 773 – Bayonne 112 – Bordeaux 198 – Toulouse 198 – Zaragoza 236

Pau-Pyrénées: ✆ 05 59 33 33 00, by ①: 12 km.

Office de tourisme, place Royale ✆ 05 59 27 27 08, Fax 05 59 27 03 21

Pau Golf Club Billère Rue du Golf, ✆ 05 59 13 18 56 ;

de Pau-Artiguelouve Artiguelouve Domaine de Saint-Michel, by Lourdes road: 11 km, ✆ 05 59 83 09 29.

Pau-Arnos race circuit ✆ 05 59 77 11 36, 20 km by ⑦.

Boulevard des Pyrénées ✳★★★ DEZ - Château★★: tapestries★★★ - Musée des Beaux-Arts★ EZ **M.**

Plans on following pages

Parc Beaumont VISA MC AE

1 av. Edouard VII – ✆ 05 59 11 84 00 – manager@hotel-parc-beaumont.com – Fax 05 59 11 85 00 FZ **b**

69 rm – †€ 195/370 ††€ 195/370, ☕ € 20 – 11 suites

Rest ***Le Jeu de Paume*** – Menu (€ 29), € 38/80 – Carte € 56/91

◆ Whether they overlook the town or Beaumont Park, and whatever their size, the designer-decorated rooms are comfortable and stylish. Conference facilities. Pool, Jacuzzi tub and spa. The vast, light dining room enjoys a pretty view of the greenery. South facing terrace.

Villa Navarre VISA MC AE

59 av. Trespoey – ✆ 05 59 14 65 65 – h5677@accor.com – Fax 05 59 14 65 64 BX **a**

26 rm – †€ 152/187 ††€ 172/207, ☕ € 17 – 4 suites – ½ P € 133

Rest – *(Closed Sunday dinner)* Menu (€ 23), € 43/54 bi – Carte € 41/51

◆ A distinctly British atmosphere reigns in this lovely 1865 mansion and its recent extension, hidden in the heart of a 2ha park. Large, well-kept rooms. The sophisticated dining room opens onto the countryside; updated culinary register.

La Palmeraie VISA MC AE

1 passage Europe – ✆ 05 59 14 14 14 – h2103@accor.com – Fax 05 59 14 14 10 BV **f**

36 rm – †€ 83/129 ††€ 91/151, ☕ € 15

Rest – *(closed 3-24 August, 22 December-6 January, Friday dinner, Saturday and Sunday)* Carte € 27/38

◆ Modern hotel in green surroundings, a stone's throw from the Zenith. Spacious, functional rooms, decorated in pastel shades. The tastefully refurbished dining room leads onto a shaded terrace. Traditional cuisine.

Continental rest, VISA MC AE

2 r. Mar. Foch – ✆ 05 59 27 69 31 – hotel@bestwerstern-continental.com – Fax 05 59 27 99 84 EZ **a**

74 rm – †€ 60/92 ††€ 70/115, ☕ € 9 – ½ P € 60/82

Rest – *(closed 28 July-17 August, 25-31 December, Saturday and Sunday)* Menu (€ 12), € 20/25 – Carte € 18/38

◆ Pau's luxury hotel (1912) has retained its period hall and lounges, affording it a certain nostalgia. Refurbished colourful rooms, four of which are circular (in a tower). Dining room brightened with colours and mirrors. Traditional food.

Hôtel de Gramont without rest VISA MC AE

3 pl. Gramont – ✆ 05 59 27 84 04 – hotelgramont@wanadoo.fr – Fax 05 59 27 62 23 – Closed 22 December-5 January DZ **t**

34 rm – †€ 60/68 ††€ 76/104, ☕ € 9,50

◆ This former 17C coaching inn is said to be the oldest hotel in Pau. Tastefully refurbished rooms overlooking the street or the Hédas Valley. Generous breakfast buffet; billiards sitting room.

BILLÈRE

Baron Séguier (Av. du) .... AX 7
Château d'Este (Av. du) ... AX 23
Claverie (R.) .... AX 24
Entrepreneurs (R. des) .... AX 57
Galas (R. de) .... BV 70
Golf (R. du) .... AX 81
J.J. Rousseau (R.) .... AX 145
Lalanne (Av.) .... AVX 91
Lavoir (R. du) .... AX 95
Lons (Av. de) .... ABV 100
Piedmont (R.) .... AX 129
Pilar (R.) .... BV 130
Plaine (R. de la) .... AX 132

BIZANOS

Albert 1er (Av.) .... BCX 2
Clemenceau (R. G.) ...... BX 27
Foch (R. Maréchal) .... BX 64
Larribau (Chemin) .... CX 93
Pic du Midi (R. du) .... CX 127
République (Av. de la) ..... CX 138

GELOS

Barthou (R. L.) .... BX 9
Gélos (Av. de) .... BX 80
Leclerc (Av. du Maréchal) . BX 96
Vallée Heureuse (Av. de la) BX 162

JURANÇON

Cambot (Av. G.) .... AX 17
Corps Franc Pommiès (Av. du) .... AX 36
Espagne (Pont d') .... AX 58
Gaulle (R. Ch.-de) .... AX 77
Ollé-Laprune .... AX 115

LESCAR

Carrérot (Av.) .... AV 19
Coustettes (Chemin des) .. AV 42
Lacau (R.) .... AV 89
Santos-Dumont (Av.) ..... AV 147
Vigné (Côte du) .... AV 168

LONS

Ampère (Av. André-Marie) . AV 3
Ariste (R.) .... AV 6
Château (R. du) .... AV 22
Dassault (Av. Marcel) ..... AX 45
Écoles (R. des) .... AV 51
Église (R. de l') .... AV 53
Frères Farman (Bd des) ... AV 67
Frères Mongolfier (Av. des) AX 68
Mairie (R. de la) .... AV 103
Moulin (Av. du) .... AV 110 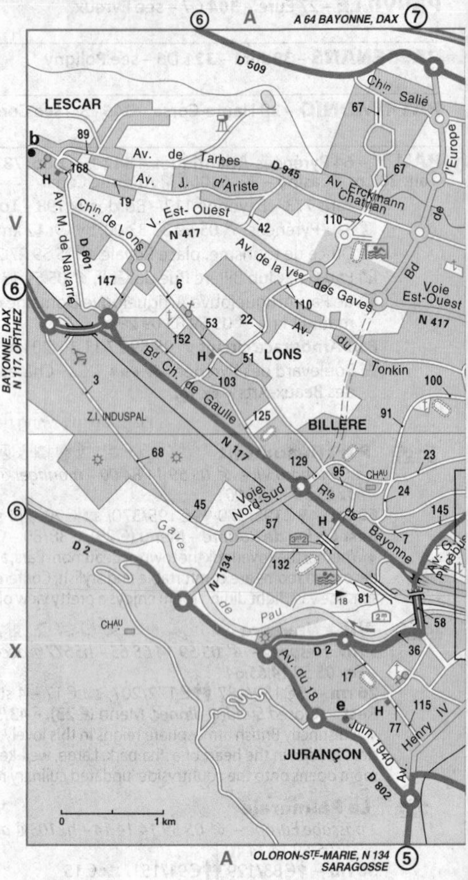
Pau (Av. de) .... AV 125
Souvenir (R. du) .... AV 152

PAU

Bérard (Cours Léon) ...... BV 12

Le Bourbon without rest
12 pl. Clemenceau – ✆ 05 59 27 53 12
– contact@hotel-lebourbon.com
– Fax 05 59 82 90 99 EZ **d**
33 rm – 🚹€ 50/55 🚹🚹€ 60/66, ☕ € 6,50
◆ Hotel in a lively area with many cafés. Most of the gradually renovated rooms overlook the square, as does the brand new breakfast room.

Central without rest
15 r. L. Daran – ✆ 05 59 27 72 75
– contact@hotelcentralpau.com
– Fax 05 59 27 33 28
– Closed 29 December-5 January EZ **t**
26 rm – 🚹€ 49/57 🚹🚹€ 53/82, ☕ € 7
◆ This is indeed a centrally located hotel. The size and decor vary according to the rooms (the oldest are being refurbished) but all are well kept. Some have wireless Internet access.

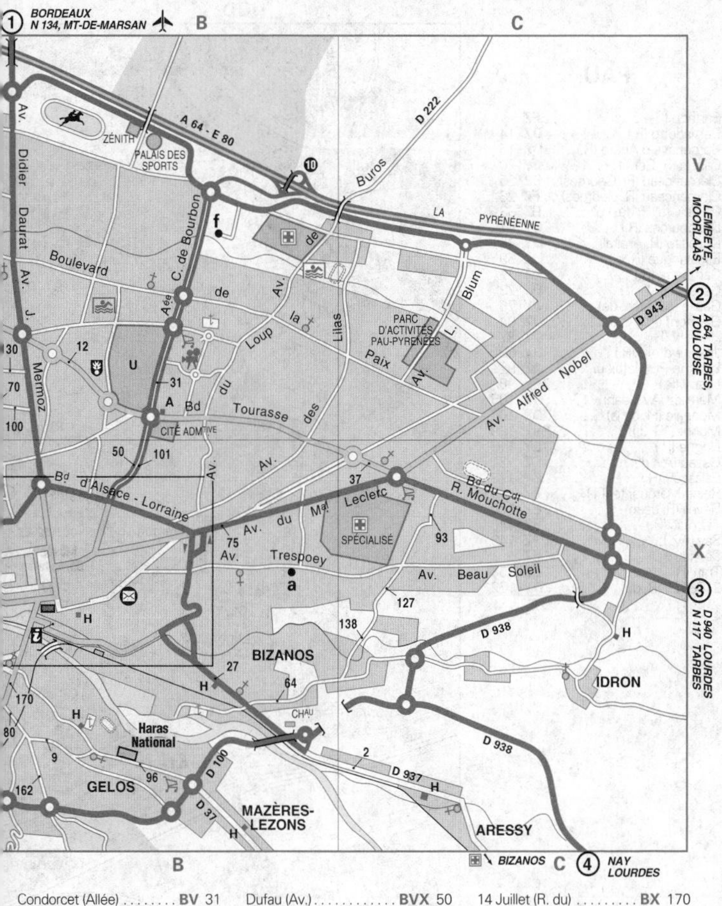

Condorcet (Allée) . . . . **BV** 31
Corps Franc Pommiès et du 49e R.I. (Bd) . . . . . **CX** 37
Dufau (Av.) . . . . **BVX** 50
Gaulle (Av. Gén.-de) . . . . . . **BV** 75
Lyautey (Cours) . . . . **BVX** 101
14 Juillet (R. du) . . . . **BX** 170

XXX **Au Fin Gourmet**

24 av. G. Lacoste, (opposite the station) – ✆ 05 59 27 47 71 – au.fin.gourmet@wanadoo.fr – Fax 05 59 82 96 77 – Closed 25 July-10 August, February holidays, Sunday dinner, Wednesday lunch and Monday EZ **v**

Rest – Menu € 20 (weekday lunch), € 48/76 – Carte € 50/58

◆ A pleasant site at the foot of the funicular. Glass-roofed house resembling a winter garden and an older dining room redecorated in the same vein. Up-to-date cuisine.

XX **Chez Pierre**

16 r. L. Barthou – ✆ 05 59 27 76 86 – restaurant.pierre@wanadoo.fr – Fax 05 59 27 08 14 – Closed 1st-14 August, 1st-14 January, Saturday lunch, Monday lunch and Sunday except holidays EZ **x**

Rest – Menu € 35 – Carte € 46/73

◆ The regulars have been coming here to enjoy Pierre's famous chicken stew for years! British inspired decor on the ground floor, more sober upstairs. Well-prepared classic menu.

PAU

Street	Square	No.
Barthou (R. Louis)	EFZ	
Bernadotte (R.)	DZ	14
Bordenave-d'Abère (R.)	DZ	15
Cassin (R. René)	EY	20
Clemenceau (Pl. Georges)	EZ	25
Clemenceau (R. Georges)	FZ	28
Cordeliers (R. des)	EZ	33
Despourrins (R.)	EY	47
Ducasse (R. Amiral)	DY	48
Espalungue (R. d')	DZ	59
Gambetta (R.)	EZ	72
Gassion (R.)	DZ	73
Gaulle (Av. Gén.-de)	FY	75
Gramont (Pl.)	DZ	84
Henri-IV (R.)	DZ	87
Jeanne-d'Arc (R.)	DY	88
Lalanne (R. Mathieu)	EZ	92
Lespy (R.)	EFY	98
Mermoz (Av. Jean)	DY	105
Monnaie (Pl. de la)	DZ	106
Monnet (R. J.)	EYZ	108
Nogue (R.)	EY	113
Ossau (Av. d')	EZ	121
Palassou (R.)	EY	123
Reine-Marguerite (Pl.)	EZ	135
Réveil (R. Jean)	EY	140
St-Louis (R.)	EZ	146
Say (Av. L.)	EFZ	149
Serviez (R.)	EZ	
Tran (R.)	EZ	158
218e-R.I. (R. du)	DY	172

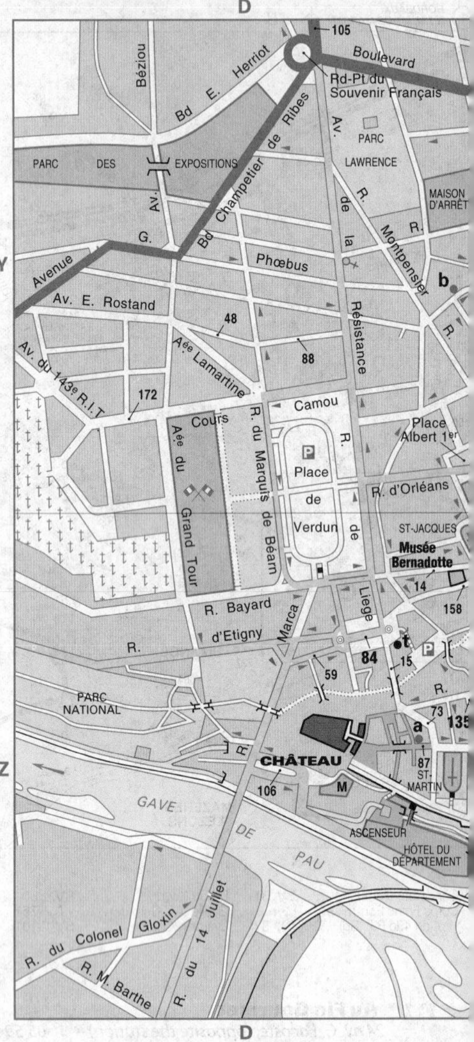

XX La Michodière
VISA MC AE

34 r. Pasteur – ✆ 05 59 27 53 85 – lamichodiere@wanadoo.fr – Fax 05 59 33 60 09 – Closed 28 July-24 August, Sunday and holidays DY **b**

Rest – Menu € 15 (weekday lunch)/27 – Carte € 36/59

◆ Behind the pebbled facade are two dining rooms; the one with wood panelling reveals the chefs at work in the kitchen. Modern setting and dishes made with market produce.

X Henri IV
VISA MC

18 r. Henri IV – ✆ 05 59 27 54 43 – Closed 24 December-7 January, 15 February-15 March, Wednesday lunch, Saturday lunch and Sunday DZ **a**

Rest – Menu € 15 (weekday lunch), € 25/31

◆ Appetising, regional food served in a rustic dining room warmed by a lovely fireplace or on a pleasant terrace on the pedestrian street.

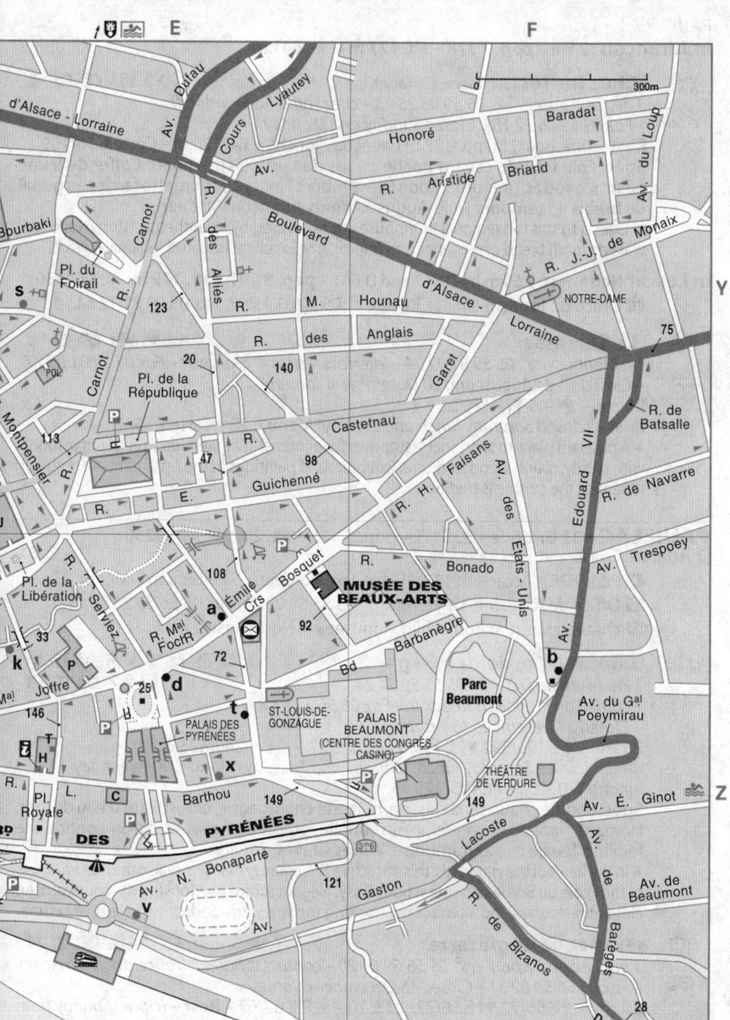

La Planche de Bœuf

30 r. Pasteur – ✆ 05 59 27 62 60 – Fax 05 59 27 62 60 – Closed August, Sunday evening, Wednesday evening and Monday EY **s**

Rest – Menu € 13 bi (weekday lunch), € 26/35 – Carte € 32/43

♦ This inviting old house makes you want to venture inside. The tables near the fireplace are greatly appreciated in winter. Friendly welcome and traditional cuisine.

La Table d'Hôte

1 r. du Hédas – ✆ 05 59 27 56 06 – la-table-dhote@wanadoo.fr – Fax 05 59 27 56 06 – Closed Christmas holidays, Monday except dinners in July-August and Sunday

Rest – Menu (€ 19), € 24/31 EZ **k**

♦ Brick, beams and pebbles give a country atmosphere to this former 17C tannery, nestling in a small medieval street. Pleasant atmosphere. Local cuisine.

in Jurançon : 2 km – **pop. 7 378 – alt. 177 m** – ✉ **64110**

XXX **Chez Ruffet** (Stéphane Carrade)
✿✿ *3 av. Ch. Touzet – ✆ 05 59 06 25 13 – chez.ruffet@wanadoo.fr – Fax 05 59 06 52 18 – Closed Sunday and Monday* AX **e**
Rest – *(pre-book)* Menu € 27 bi (weekday lunch), € 64/120 bi – Carte € 98/109
Spec. Foie frais de canard poché au jus de raisin (September). Coffre de jeune palombe rôti au gras de jambon (November). Fleurs de courgette farcies au greuil de brebis en tempura (July-August). **Wines** Jurançon, Madiran.
♦ Guests to this old regional farmhouse are captivated by its authentic (stonework, well waxed wood) blend of elegance and informality. Excellent updated regional cuisine.

in Lescar Northwest: 7.5 km by D 817 and D 601 – **pop. 8 191 – alt. 179 m** – ✉ **64230**
Office de tourisme, place Royale ✆ 05 59 81 15 98, Fax 05 59 81 12 54

La Terrasse
1 r. Maubec – ✆ 05 59 81 02 34 – laterrasselescar@orange.fr – Fax 05 59 81 08 77 – Closed 1st-24 August and 20 December-4 January
20 rm – € 46 € 50, € 7
Rest – *(closed Saturday lunch and Sunday)* Menu € 28 – Carte € 35/47
♦ A pleasant place to stay (once a stopover for pilgrims) in a quiet side street. Simple rooms with sturdy, rough wood furniture. Exhibitions of paintings in the restaurant are regularly renewed; the cuisine is traditional.

PAUILLAC – 33 Gironde – 335 G3 – pop. 5 175 – alt. 20 m – ✉ 33250
Atlantic Coast 3 **B1**

Paris 625 – Arcachon 113 – Blaye 16 – Bordeaux 54 – Lesparre-Médoc 23
Office de tourisme, La Verrerie ✆ 05 56 59 03 08, Fax 05 56 59 23 38
château Mouton Rothschild★: musée★★ Northwest: 2 km.

Château Cordeillan Bages rm,
✿✿ *1 km south on D 2 – ✆ 05 56 59 24 24 – cordeillan@relaischateaux.fr – Fax 05 56 59 01 89 – Closed 24 December-13 February*
28 rm – € 199/392 € 199/517, € 22 – ½ P € 240/423
Rest – *(closed Saturday lunch, Monday and Tuesday)* Menu € 90 (weekday lunch)/170 – Carte € 105/125
Spec. Soufflé chaud sans cuisson, huître et champagne, croustillant d'eau de mer. Homard, vapeur de verveine citronnelle, pulpe de navet et citron confit. Fine feuille à feuille cacao-framboise. **Wines** Graves, Pauillac.
♦ In the heart of the vineyards, this attractive 17C country mansion is also the headquarters of the École du Bordeaux wine school. Cosy, elegant rooms overlooking the courtyard. An elegant restaurant and a terrace overlooking the vineyards. Seductive, inventive cuisine.

France et Angleterre rest,
3 quai Albert Pichon – ✆ 05 56 59 01 20 – contact@hoteldefrance-angleterre.com – Fax 05 56 59 02 31 – Closed 15 December-6 January
29 rm – € 56/72 € 56/72, € 10 – ½ P € 62/67 – **Rest** – *(closed Sunday from November to February)* Menu € 15 (weekday lunch), € 20/39 – Carte € 33/53
♦ A 19C building, situated on the quayside with practical, well-renovated rooms. Those at the front have an attractive view of the Gironde estuary. A modern dining room and veranda with a menu based on traditional and regional recipes.

Vignoble
3 quai Albert Pichon – Closed 15 December-6 January
20 rm – € 87/100 € 87/103, € 10 – ½ P € 76/80
♦ This modern annex contains functional rooms, decorated on a vineyard theme. Balcony or ground-floor terrace with greenery. Fully-equipped seminar area.

X **Café Lavinal**
à Bages, pl. Desquet – ✆ 05 57 75 00 09 – cafelavinal@bordeauxsaveurs.com – Fax 05 57 75 00 10 – Closed 24 December-3 February and Sunday dinner
Rest – Carte € 27/43
♦ A neo-retro bistro which opened its doors in 2006 in the centre of Pauillac, where the Argentinian chef presides over a predominantly traditional menu. Daily specials and wines from local estates.

PAVILLON (COL) – 69 Rhône – 327 F3 – see Cours

PAYRAC – 46 Lot – 337 E3 – pop. 564 – alt. 320 m – ✉ 46350 28 **B1**

Paris 530 – Brive-la-Gaillarde 53 – Cahors 48 – Figeac 60 – Sarlat-la-Canéda 32

Syndicat d'initiative, avenue de Toulouse ☎ 05 65 37 94 27, Fax 05 65 37 94 27

Hostellerie de la Paix

– ☎ *05 65 37 95 15 – host.la.paix@escalotel.com – Fax 05 65 37 90 37 – Open March-October*

50 rm – €45/86 €51/86, €8 – ½ P €43/50

Rest – Menu €15 (weekdays)/30

◆ This former post house has an attractive stone facade. Most of the renovated rooms face away from the road. Restaurant dining rooms (one of which is non-smoking) and veranda serving recipes from the Quercy region (chicken in verjuice, tourin soup, etc.).

PÉGOMAS – 06 Alpes-Maritimes – 341 C6 – pop. 5 794 – alt. 18 m – ✉ 06580 42 **E2**

Paris 896 – Cannes 12 – Draguignan 59 – Grasse 9 – Nice 41 – St-Raphaël 38

Office de tourisme, 287, avenue de Grasse ☎ 04 92 60 20 70, Fax 04 92 60 20 66

Le Bosquet without rest

chemin des Périssols, Mouans-Sartoux road – ☎ 04 92 60 21 20 – hotel.lebosquet@wanadoo.fr – Fax 04 92 60 21 49 – Closed 15 January-1st February

23 rm – €45/48 €48/70, €7

◆ A warm welcome and a restful environment in a wooded park await in this small, well-kept hotel where you will be treated to home-made jams. Rooms or studios available.

L'Écluse

beside the Siagne – ☎ 04 93 42 22 55 – ecluse@wanadoo.fr – Fax 04 93 40 72 65 – Closed November, weekdays from 30 September to 15 April and Monday from 16 April to 30 September

Rest – Menu (€17), €25/30 – Carte €31/38

◆ A restaurant appreciated for its simplicity, relaxed atmosphere and large waterside terrace reminiscent of an open-air café. Traditional cuisine.

in St-Jean Southeast: 2 km by D 9 – ✉ 06550 La Roquette-sur-Siagne

Les Chasseurs without rest

1175 av. République – ☎ 04 92 19 18 00 – hoteldeschasseurs@wanadoo.fr – Fax 04 92 19 19 61 – Closed 25 October-16 November

17 rm – €30/40 €45/55, €7

◆ Simple rooms, rather old but impeccably well kept; the rooms at the rear are quieter. A reasonably-priced overnight stay not far from Cannes!

PEILLON – 06 Alpes-Maritimes – 341 F5 – pop. 1 227 – alt. 200 m – ✉ 06440
French Riviera 42 **E2**

Paris 947 – Contes 14 – L'Escarène 14 – Menton 38 – Monaco 29 – Nice 20 – Sospel 34

Syndicat d'initiative, 620, avenue de l'Hôtel de Ville ☎ 04 93 91 98 34, Fax 04 93 79 87 65

Village★ - Frescoes★ in the Pénitents Blancs chapel.

Auberge de la Madone (Christian et Thomas Millo)

– ☎ *04 93 79 91 17 – auberge.de.la.madone@wanadoo.fr – Fax 04 93 79 99 36 – Closed 6 November-22 December and Wednesday*

14 rm – €90/180 €95/200, €22 – 3 suites – ½ P €155/165

Rest – Menu (€32), €49 (weekdays)/90 – Carte €67/109

Spec. Filets de rougets juste saisis, haricots cocos confits à la tomate. Pavé de loup de mer cuit en infusion de lait d'amande et verveine (April to October). Agneau des Alpilles en deux cuissons. **Wines** Bellet, Vin de pays des Alpes Maritimes.

◆ Well-kept, quiet rooms are a feature of this characterful hotel surrounded by a flower garden. Fine regionally inspired cuisine is served in an attractive Provençal dining room or on a pleasant terrace facing the delightful village perched on its rocky peak.

Lou Pourtail
welcome to the Auberge de la Madone – ✆ 04 93 79 91 17 – Fax 04 93 79 99 36 – Closed 6 November-22 December, 7-31 January and Wednesday
6 rm – †€ 40/68 ††€ 40/68, ☕ € 14 – **Rest** – *(open May-September) (lunch only)* Menu € 30/35
◆ The charm of an old house with whitewashed walls, vaulted or high ceilings and country furniture - inside the ancient walls of the village. Simple rooms without TV. Small rustic dining room and summer garden terrace serving dishes made with local produce.

PEISEY-NANCROIX – 73 Savoie – 333 N4 – pop. 614 – alt. 1 320 m – ✉ 73210

French Alps 45 **D2**

Paris 635 – Albertville 55 – Bourg-St-Maurice 13

Office de tourisme, place de Roscanvel ✆ 04 79 07 88 67

La Vanoise rm, VISA
at Plan Peisey – ✆ 04 79 07 92 19 – hotel-la-vanoise@wanadoo.fr – Fax 04 79 07 97 48 – Open 1st July-31 August and 18 December-28 April
33 rm – †€ 55/70 ††€ 70/110, ☕ € 11 – ½ P € 65/95
Rest – Menu € 22 – Carte € 26/36
◆ Attractive view of the Bellecôte dome from this establishment with rooms decorated in a regional style (wood and colourful fabrics). The south-facing rooms have a balcony. Warm wood panelling, Savoyard menus, and a lovely open fire - no doubt about it, you're in the mountains!

L'Armoise VISA AE
at Plan-Peisey, west: 4.5 km – ✆ 04 79 07 94 24 – cycomte@wanadoo.fr – Fax 04 79 07 94 24 – Open 7 July-31 August, 15 December-25 April and closed Sunday lunch, Monday lunch, Tuesday lunch 15 December-25 April and Monday dinner July-August
Rest – Menu € 19 (lunch), € 29/50 – Carte € 15/56
◆ A simple, unpretentious restaurant in the heart of the small resort. A traditional menu and dish of the day at lunchtime, a good choice of Savoyard dishes in the evening.

PELVOUX (Commune) – 05 Hautes-Alpes – 334 G3 – pop. 404 – alt. 1 260 m – Winter sports : 1 250/2 300 m 7 – ✉ 05340 French Alps 41 C1

Paris 702 – L'Argentière-la-Bessée 11 – Briançon 22 – Gap 84 – Guillestre 32

Route des Choulières: ≤★★ E.

Ailefroide – alt. 1 510 m – ✉ 05340 Pelvoux

Pré de Madame Carle: landscape★★ Nortwest: 6 km.

Chalet Hôtel d'Ailefroide VISA
– ✆ 04 92 23 32 01 – contact@chalethotel-ailefroide.com – Fax 04 92 23 49 97 – Open 14 June-7 September
24 rm – †€ 37/48 ††€ 42/64, ☕ € 7,50 – ½ P € 38/48 – **Rest** – Menu € 20/23 – Carte € 21/31
◆ A small hotel well known to hikers. Accommodation is in simple, not very large rooms, some with a new mountain-style look. Sauna and jacuzzi. A friendly, invigorating restaurant, whether near the fireplace or in the garden.

PÉNESTIN – 56 Morbihan – 308 Q10 – pop. 1 527 – alt. 20 m – ✉ 56760 10 C3

Paris 458 – La Baule 29 – Nantes 84 – La Roche-Bernard 18 – St-Nazaire 43 – Vannes 48

Office de tourisme, allée du Grand Pré ✆ 02 99 90 37 74, Fax 02 99 90 47 08

Pointe du Bile ≤★ South: 5 km, Brittany

Loscolo VISA
Pointe de Loscolo, south-west: 4 km – ✆ 02 99 90 31 90 – hotelloscolo@neuf.fr – Fax 02 99 90 32 14 – Open 25 April-2 November
14 rm – †€ 49/101 ††€ 57/109, ☕ € 14 – ½ P € 78/104
Rest – *(closed Wednesday) (dinner only)* Menu € 35
◆ You are in the home of the inventor of the oyster-opening machine! Enjoy a peaceful, invigorating stay in discreetly appointed rooms, most of which face the sea. Dining room in soft shades and dishes based on ocean flavours.

PENHORS – 29 Finistère – **308** E7 – see Pouldreuzic

PENNEDEPIE – 14 Calvados – **303** N3 – see Honfleur

PENVÉNAN – 22 Côtes-d'Armor – **309** C2 – pop. 2 434 – alt. 70 m – ✉ 22710

Paris 521 – Guingamp 34 – Lannion 16 – St-Brieuc 70 – Tréguier 8

Syndicat d'initiative, 12, place de l'Église ✆ 02 96 92 81 09 9 **B1**

Le Crustacé VISA MC

2, r de la poste – ✆ 02 96 92 67 46 – Closed 1st-15 November, 1st-15 January, Monday in July-August, Sunday dinner, Tuesday dinner and Wednesday from September to June

Rest – Menu € 17/37 – Carte € 30/58

◆ Small welcoming family-run restaurant, opposite the church, with a simple and well-kept rustic dining room. Traditional cuisine and seafood.

PENVINS – 56 Morbihan – **308** O9 – see Sarzeau

PERI – 2A Corse-du-Sud – **345** C7 – see Corse

PÉRIGNAC – 17 Char.-Mar. – **324** H6 – see Pons

PÉRIGNAC – 16 Charente – **324** K7 – pop. 508 – alt. 164 m – ✉ 16250 39 **C3**

Paris 485 – Poitiers 147 – Angoulême 28 – Cognac 51 – Soyaux 32

Château de Lerse

2 km south by D 10 – ✆ 05 45 60 32 81 – fl.lafargue@wanadoo.fr – Open May-September

3 rm – €80/100 €90/110 – **Table d'hôte** – Menu € 30 bi

◆ This small, fortified 13C château, surrounded by acres of countryside, extends a friendly welcome. Spacious, classically-decorated rooms. Regional cuisine and garden produce served in a period dining room (huge fireplace and family portraits).

PÉRIGNAT-LÈS-SARLIÈVE – 63 Puy-de-Dôme – **326** F8 – see Clermont-Ferrand

PÉRIGNY – 86 Vienne – **322** H5 – see Poitiers

PÉRIGUEUX P – 24 Dordogne – **329** F4 – pop. 30 193 – alt. 86 m – ✉ 24000

Dordogne-Berry-Limousin 4 **C1**

Paris 482 – Agen 138 – Bordeaux 128 – Limoges 96 – Poitiers 198

Office de tourisme, 26, place Francheville ✆ 05 53 53 10 63, Fax 05 53 09 02 50

de Périgueux Marsac-sur-l'Isle Domaine de Saltgourde, by Angoulême road: 5 km, ✆ 05 53 53 02 35.

St-Front cathedral ★★, Saint-Étienne de la Cité church ★ - Quartier St-Front★★★: rue Limogeanne★ BY , Renaissance staircase★ of Hôtel de Lestrade (rue de la sagesse) BY - Galerie Daumesnil★ opposite n° 3 Rue Limogeanne - Musée du Périgord★ CY **M²**.

Plans on following pages

Mercure without rest VISA MC AE

7 pl. Francheville – ✆ 05 53 06 65 00 – h6237@accor.com – Fax 05 53 07 20 33

66 rm – €80/100 €92/112, € 13 BZ **e**

◆ This brand-new hotel with a dressed stone façade enjoys a good location opposite a park and a multiplex cinema. Pleasant, contemporary-style rooms.

Bristol without rest P VISA MC AE

37 r. A. Gadaud – ✆ 05 53 08 75 90 – hotel@bristolfrance.com – Fax 05 53 07 00 49 – Closed 20 December-3 January BY **u**

29 rm – €59/68 €66/76, € 8

◆ This hotel, near the town centre and tourist highlights, is home to gradually refurbished rooms of fine proportions (except no 6) with good soundproofing. Impeccably kept.

PÉRIGUEUX

Abreuvoir (R. de l') . . . . CY 2
Amphithéâtre (R. de l') . . . . AZ 3
Arènes (Bd des) . . . . AZ 6
Aubergerie (R.) . . . . BZ 9
Barbecane (R.) . . . . CY 12
Barbusse (Av. Henri) . . . . . . AY 13
Bride (R. de la) . . . . BZ 15
Bugeaud (Pl.) . . . . BZ
Calvaire (R. du) . . . . BZ 16
Cavaignac (Av.) . . . . AZ 18
Cité (R. de la) . . . . ABZ 23
Clarté (R. de la) . . . . BZ 24
Clautre (Pl. de la) . . . . BZ 26
Clos-Chassaing . . . . BY 27
Coderc (Pl. du) . . . . BYZ 28
Condé (R.) . . . . BZ 29
Constitution (R. de la) . . . . . CY 30
Daumesnil (Av. et Pl.) . . . . BCZ 32
Daumesnil (Galerie) . . . . . BYZ 31
Durand (Rd-Pt Charles) . . . . AZ 34
Eguillerie (R.) . . . . BY 35
Fénelon (Cours) . . . . BZ
Goudeau (Pl. Émile) . . . . CY 36
Hôtel de Ville (Pl. de l') . . . . BZ 37
Lammary (R.) . . . . BY 38
Limogeanne (R.) . . . . BY
Maurois (Pl. André) . . . . BY 39
Miséricorde (R. de la) . . . . . BY 40
Mobiles-de-Coulmiers (R.) . AY 41
Montaigne (Bd M.) . . . . . . BYZ
Montaigne (Cours et Pl. M.) . . . . BYZ
Notre-Dame (R.) . . . . CY 42
Port-de-Graule (R. du) . . . CYZ 44
Port (Allée du) . . . . AY 43
Président-Wilson (R. du) . . . AY
République (R. de la) . . . . BYZ 45
Sagesse (R. de la) . . . . BY 46
Ste-Marthe (R.) . . . . CZ 50
St-Pierre-ès-Liens (R.) . . . ABZ 47
St-Roch (R.) . . . . BZ 48
St-Silain (Pl.) . . . . BY 49
Sully (R.) . . . . BZ 53
Taillefer (R.) . . . . BZ
Talleyrand-Périgord (R.) . . . . CZ 54
Théâtre (Espl. du) . . . . BY 55
Turenne (R. de) . . . . AZ 60
15e-Régt-de-Tirailleurs-Algériens (R. du) . . . . AZ 61
50e-Régt-d'Infanterie (Av. du) . . . . AZ 62

XXX Le Rocher de l'Arsault

15 r. L'Arsault – ✆ 05 53 53 54 06 – rocher.arsault@wanadoo.fr – Fax 05 53 08 32 32 – Closed 14 July-10 August and Sunday dinner CY **s**

Rest – Menu (€ 20), € 27/79 – Carte € 30/104

◆ A long building against the rock. Stylish, colourful dining room with one wall showing exposed stonework. Pleasant private rooms. Regionally sourced cuisine.

XX Le Clos St-Front

5, 7 r. de la Vertu – ✆ 05 53 46 78 58 – leclossaintfront@wanadoo.fr – Fax 05 53 46 78 20 – Closed 28 January-10 February, Sunday dinner and Monday off season CY **r**

Rest – Menu € 26/60 bi – Carte € 36/48

◆ Immense fireplaces and contemporary art adorn this very pleasant restaurant. Terrace shaded by lime trees. The cuisine is an interesting mixture of exotic and regional accents.

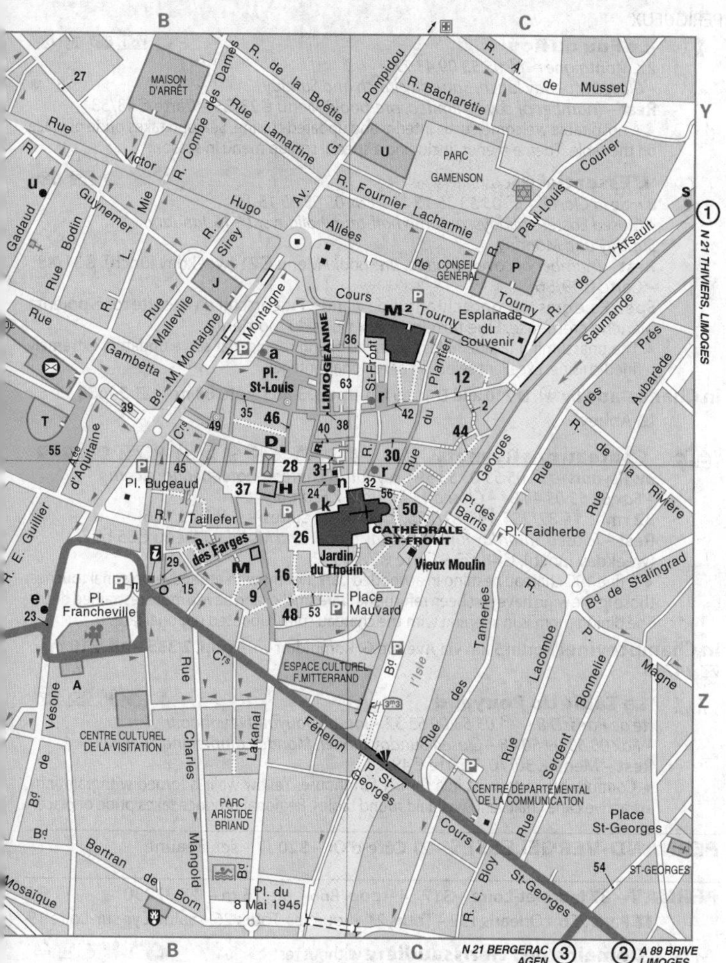

Hercule Poireau

AC VISA MC

2 r. Nation – ✆ 05 53 08 90 76 – Closed 5-18 January, Tuesday dinner in Winter and Wednesday CZ **r**

Rest – Menu € 20/36 – Carte € 39/61

◆ In the rustic 16C dining room (timber and stonework) or old cellar (16C vaulting) you will taste regional recipes reinterpreted and updated by the chef.

La Taula

AC VISA MC

3 r. Denfert-Rochereau – ✆ 05 53 35 40 02 – lataula@laposte.net – Fax 05 53 35 40 02 – Closed 1st-7 July and Monday except 15 July-30 September BZ **k**

Rest – Menu (€ 16), € 27/32 – Carte € 37/43

◆ Welcoming long restaurant serving tasty local cuisine; the name is local dialect for table.

XX **Le Fou du Roy**

2 r. Montaigne – ✆ 05 53 09 43 77
– Closed Monday lunch, Saturday lunch and Sunday BY **a**
Rest – *(number of covers limited, pre-book)* Menu € 23/35 – Carte € 43/53
◆ A hospitable welcome, rustic interior and updated cuisine. Seafood takes pride of place on the table. Theme menus, including a special scallop menu in season.

X **L'Essentiel** (Eric Vidal)

8 r. de la Clarté – ✆ 05 53 35 15 15 – Fax 05 53 35 15 15
– Closed Easter holidays, autumn half-term holidays, 1st-15 January, Sunday and Monday BZ **n**
Rest – *(number of covers limited, pre-book)* Menu € 21 (weekday lunch), € 31/48 – Carte € 49/56
Spec. Foie gras rôti, gnocchi au jus de viande. Pigeon cuit en cocotte rosé, polenta blanche crémeuse. Fine tartelette aux fruits du moment.
◆ The unassuming façade hides two small dining rooms that serve updated, extremely refined cuisine. Excellent selection of regional vintages.

in Chancelade by ⑤, D 710 and D 1: 5.5 km – pop. 3 865 – alt. 88 m – ✉ 24650

Abbey★.

Château des Reynats

av. Reynats – ✆ 05 53 03 53 59 – reynats@chateau-hotel-perigord.com
– Fax 05 53 03 44 84 – Closed 1st January-7 February
32 rm – †€ 82/255 ††€ 82/255, ☕ € 14 – 5 suites – ½ P € 79/166
Rest – *(closed Saturday lunch, Sunday dinner and Monday)* Menu € 35 bi (weekday lunch), € 48/65 – Carte € 78/99
◆ A fine 19C château nestling in a wooded park. Rooms with attractive personal touches; those in the wing have just been refurbished, are smaller and have a more restrained decor. The dining room is in keeping with the chateau spirit. Updated regional fare.

in Champcevinel North: 5 km via Avenue G. Pompidou CY **– pop. 2 335 – alt. 210 m – ✉ 24750**

XXX **La Table du Pouyaud**

rte de Paris, D 8 – ✆ 05 53 09 53 32 – latablepouyaud@yahoo.fr
– Fax 05 53 09 50 48 – Closed Sunday dinner, Monday dinner and Tuesday
Rest – Menu € 30/70 – Carte € 49/77
◆ Comfortable restaurant in a former farmhouse. Yellow walls adorned with paintings, attractive cane chairs and well-laid round tables. Regional produce takes pride of place.

PERNAND-VERGELESSES – 21 Côte-d'Or – 320 J7 – see Beaune

PERNAY – 37 Indre-et-Loire – 317 L4 – pop. 866 – alt. 76 m – ✉ 37230 11 B2

Paris 256 – Orléans 132 – Tours 21 – Joué-lès-Tours 26 – Saint-Cyr-sur-Loire 19

Domaine de l'Hérissaudière without rest

3 km north-east on D 48 – ✆ 02 47 55 95 28
– lherissaudiere@aol.com – Fax 02 47 55 97 45
5 rm ☕ – †€ 130/150 ††€ 140/160
◆ This 17C former hunting estate is surrounded by parkland filled with rare trees. Comfortable lounges; period furnishings in the bedrooms. Copious buffet breakfast (home-made jams).

PERNES-LES-FONTAINES – 84 Vaucluse – 332 D10 – pop. 10 170 – alt. 75 m – ✉ 84210 Provence 42 E1

Paris 685 – Apt 43 – Avignon 23 – Carpentras 6 – Cavaillon 20
Office de tourisme, place Gabriel Moutte ✆ 04 90 61 31 04
Porte Notre-Dame★.

L'Hermitage without rest

614 Grande Rte de Carpentras – ✆ 04 90 66 51 41 – hotel-lhermitage@wanadoo.fr – Fax 04 90 61 36 41 – Open 1st March-15 November
20 rm – †€ 68/79 ††€ 68/79, ☕ € 9,50
◆ A fine residence dating from 1890 in the middle of a park. A colourful Mediterranean atmosphere in the rooms, high-class comfort and period furniture in the lounges.

Au Fil du Temps (Frédéric Robert)
pl. L. Giraud, (opposite the cultural centre) – ✆ 04 90 66 48 61 – fildutemp@wanadoo.fr – Fax 04 90 66 48 61 – Closed 27 October-5 November, 23 December-7 January, 24 February-4 March, Sunday lunch and Saturday lunch July-September, Tuesday October-June and Wednesday
Rest – *(number of covers limited, pre-book)* Menu € 35 (weekday lunch), € 52/72 – Carte € 46/62
Spec. Saumon mariné à la badiane. Potage parmentier aux truffes (winter). Crème brûlée au thym (summer). **Wines** Vacqueyras, Côtes du Ventoux.
◆ This very simple inn situated at the centre of the 'perle du Comtat' houses a distinctly Provençal dining room, where you can sample updated Southern cuisine.

Northeast 4 km by D 1 and secondary road – ✉ 84210 Pernes-les-Fontaines

Mas La Bonoty with rm
chemin de la Bonoty – ✆ 04 90 61 61 09 – infos@bonoty.com – Fax 04 90 61 35 14 – Closed 3 November-7 December and 7 January-10 February
8 rm – †€ 62/95 ††€ 62/95 – ½ P € 66/84 – **Rest** – *(closed Tuesday except evenings from April to September and Monday)* Menu (€ 22), € 41/55 – Carte € 51/64
◆ A 17C shepherd's house full of charm, near the village with its 36 fountains. Stonework and beams in the dining room, a tiled floor and country furniture in the rooms.

PÉRON – 01 Ain – 328 I3 – pop. 1 579 – alt. 524 m – ✉ 01630 45 **C1**
Paris 521 – Annecy 53 – Bellegarde-sur-Valserine 19 – Bourg-en-Bresse 89 – Gex 21

Auberge Communale La Fruitière with rm
39 pl. St-Antoine – ✆ 04 50 56 83 70 – Fax 04 50 56 83 74 – Closed 8-28 August
7 rm – †€ 44 ††€ 46, ☕ € 6 – ½ P € 66 – **Rest** – *(Closed Tuesday and Wednesday)* Menu € 16 (weekday lunch), € 26/46 – Carte € 31/49
◆ Painted milk containers and a large wooden churn recall the past of this converted guestrooms dairy. Smart, modern dining and new rooms. Regional dishes.

PÉRONNAS – 01 Ain – 328 E3 – see Bourg-en-Bresse

PÉRONNE – 80 Somme – 301 K8 – pop. 8 380 – alt. 52 m – ✉ 80200
Northern France and the Paris Region 37 **C1**
Paris 141 – Amiens 58 – Arras 48 – Doullens 54 – St-Quentin 30
Office de tourisme, 1, rue Louis XI ✆ 03 22 84 42 38, Fax 03 22 85 51 25
Historial de la Grande Guerre★★.

St-Claude
42 pl. du Cdt-L.-Daudré – ✆ 03 22 79 49 49 – hotel.saintclaude@wanadoo.fr – Fax 03 22 79 10 57 – **40 rm** – †€ 80 ††€ 105, ☕ € 12 – 2 suites – ½ P € 85
Rest – Menu € 16 (weekday lunch)/30 – Carte € 26/49 **b**
◆ This town centre hotel has been entirely renovated and modernised. Simple and comfortable, well-dimensioned rooms. Traditional regional cooking served in an elegant brick and stone dining room.

in Rancourt by ① and ND 1017: 10 km – pop. 144 – alt. 143 m – ✉ 80360

Le Prieuré
24 rte nationale – ✆ 03 22 85 04 43 – contact@hotel-le-prieure.fr – Fax 03 22 85 06 69 – Closed 24 Dec - 1 Jan – **27 rm** – †€ 64/70 ††€ 67/72, ☕ € 8 – ½ P € 63/69
Rest – Menu € 14 (weekdays)/43 – Carte € 27/57
◆ Moorish-style architecture for this hotel with personalised rooms, the larger ones being located at the rear. A Scottish bar just through an arch. Brick and stone walls add to the elegance of the dining room; regional and traditional fare.

Aire d'Assevillers on A 1 by ②, Amiens road (D 1029) and secondary road: 15 km – ✉ 80200 Péronne

Mercure
– ✆ 03 22 85 78 30 – mercure-peronne@wanadoo.fr – Fax 03 22 85 78 31
79 rm – †€ 70/98 ††€ 85/115, ☕ € 13 – **Rest** – grill Menu € 16/22 – Carte € 23/35
◆ An imposing 1970s building with large functional rooms, gradually being renovated and refitted. Good soundproofing. The restaurant is open from 11am to 11pm. Grilled meats and starter buffet.

PÉROUGES – 01 Ain – 328 E5 – pop. 1 103 – alt. 290 m – ✉ 01800

Lyon - Rhone Valley 44 **B1**

- Paris 460 – Bourg-en-Bresse 39 – Lyon 37 – Villefranche-sur-Saône 58
- Syndicat d'initiative, entrée de la Cité ☎ 04 74 46 70 84, Fax 04 74 46 70 84
- de la Sorelle Villette-sur-Ain Domaine de Gravagneux, North: 12 km by D 984, ☎ 04 74 35 47 27.
- The town★★: place de la Halle★★★.

Ostellerie du Vieux Pérouges

– *☎ 04 74 61 00 88 – thibaut@ostellerie.com – Fax 04 74 34 77 90*
– Closed 9-22 February
13 rm – †€ 125 ††€ 220, ☕ € 15 – 2 suites – ½ P € 150/170
Rest – Menu € 40/62 – Carte € 39/74

◆ Appealing Gothic-Renaissance buildings dotted about the village. Rooms combining antique furniture (some with four-poster beds) with modern comforts. The restaurant's decor ranges from medieval to comfortably plush. Regional dishes including the famous galette.

Le Pavillon
13 rm – †€ 80 ††€ 120, ☕ € 15 – ½ P € 110

◆ A few metres from the Ostellerie, Le Pavillon has practical and more simply furnished rooms. Those in the wing are more comfortable.

PERPIGNAN – 66 Pyrénées-Orientales – 344 I6 – pop. 105 115 – Built-up area 162 678 – alt. 60 m – Casino : at Port-Barcarès – ✉ 66000

Languedoc-Roussillon-Tarn Gorges 22 **B3**

- Paris 848 – Andorra-la-Vella 170 – Béziers 94 – Montpellier 156 – Toulouse 204
- Perpignan-Rivesaltes: ☎ 04 68 52 60 70, by ①: 6 km.
- Office de tourisme, place Armand Lanoux ☎ 04 68 66 30 30, Fax 04 68 66 30 26
- Le Castillet★ - Sea lodge★ BY **K** - Town hall★ BY **H** - St-Jean cathedral ★ - Palais des rois de Majorque★ - Musée numismatique Joseph-Puig★ - Place Arago: maison Julia★.

Plans on following pages

Villa Duflot

rd-pt Albert Donnezan, by ④, towards the motorway : 3 km – ☎ 04 68 56 67 67 – contact@villa-duflot.com – Fax 04 68 56 54 05
24 rm – †€ 120/160 ††€ 120/160, ☕ € 13 – ½ P € 108/128
Rest – Menu (€ 25 bi), € 31 bi (weekday lunch)/40 – Carte € 39/48

◆ A light elegant setting (contemporary statues) and spacious Art Deco furnished rooms overlooking the patio or the park: a haven of greenery, unusually located - in a shopping area! The charm of the south of France in the cuisine and the restaurant faces the pool.

Park Hôtel

18 bd J. Bourrat – ☎ 04 68 35 14 14 – contact@parkhotel-fr.com – Fax 04 68 35 48 18 CY **y**
69 rm – †€ 65/230 ††€ 75/280, ☕ € 10
Rest *Chapon Fin* – *(closed 14-31 August, 1st-27 January, Monday lunch, Friday lunch, Saturday lunch and Sunday)* Menu (€ 22 bi), € 35/70 – Carte € 54/85

◆ Opposite Bir Hakeim square, well-kept rooms with a colourful, Spanish-style decor. Some have attractive Majorcan beds. Fine wood panelling and earthenware create the setting for dining at the Chapon Fin, where meals are prepared with the finest local produce.

Le Mas des Arcades

840 av. d'Espagne, via ④: 2 km on the N 9 ✉ 66100 – ☎ 04 68 85 11 11 – contact@hotel-mas-des-arcades.fr – Fax 04 68 85 21 41
60 rm – †€ 85 ††€ 85/125, ☕ € 12 – 3 suites – **Rest** – *(closed Friday lunch and Saturday lunch)* Menu (€ 20), € 28/60 – Carte € 39/50

◆ Large 1970s building ideal for seminars. Comfortable rooms with balconies; open-air pool and tennis courts. Restaurant leading onto a glass-roofed terrace; traditional dishes and grilled food served in summer.

New Christina rm, rest, VISA
51 cours Lassus – 04 68 35 12 21 – info@hotel-newchristina.com – Fax 04 68 35 67 01 – Closed 20 December-5 January CY **w**
25 rm – €66/76 €72/92, €10 – ½ P €70
Rest – *(closed 1st August-8 September, Saturday, Sunday and holidays) (dinner only)* Menu €21/25 – Carte €24/34
◆ Functional, simple rooms with pebbledashed walls. Leisure facilities include a small rooftop swimming pool, jacuzzi, hammam and bar. A modern bistro-style dining room and traditional dishes on a blackboard.

Ibis rm, VISA AE
16 cours Lazare Escarguel – 04 68 35 62 62 – h1045-gm@accor.com – Fax 04 68 35 13 38 AY **a**
100 rm – €70/72 €70/72, €7,50
Rest – buffet *(closed Saturday lunchtime and Sunday lunchtime)* Menu (€13), €16 – Carte €25/34
◆ Between the old town and the "centre of the world" (according to Salvador Dali). The renovated rooms in this modern hotel are well maintained and soundproofed. Cosy lounge bar. Self-service buffet and simple dishes are served in the hotel's bright, colourful restaurant.

Kyriad without rest VISA AE
8 bd Wilson – 04 68 59 25 94 – kyriad.perpignan@wanadoo.fr – Fax 04 68 61 57 70 BY **t**
38 rm – €69/140 €75/160, €9 – 11 suites
◆ New name for the former Windsor, which has been entirely renovated. Functional rose wood furniture in the bedrooms and a suite decorated in Catalan style. Inner courtyard with fountain.

La Passerelle VISA AE
1 cours Palmarole – 04 68 51 30 65 – Fax 04 68 51 90 58 – Closed 27 April-4 May, 10-17 August, 21 December-4 January, Monday lunch and Sunday BY **z**
Rest – Menu €30/40 – Carte €37/49
◆ Situated on the banks of the River Basse, this restaurant specialises in local fish and seafood dishes. Friendly service amid an attractive maritime-themed decor.

Les Antiquaires VISA AE
pl. Desprès – 04 68 34 06 58 – Fax 04 68 35 04 47 – Closed 24 June-13 July, Sunday dinner and Monday
Rest – Menu €24/43 – Carte €31/54
◆ Pleasant restaurant in old Perpignan decorated with objects found in nearby antique shops. Catalan cuisine.

La Galinette (Christophe Comes) VISA
23 r. Jean Payra – 04 68 35 00 90 – Fax 04 68 35 15 20 – Closed 15 July-15 August, 22 December-5 January, Sunday and Monday BY **e**
Rest – Menu €17 (weekday lunch)/50 – Carte €48/62
Spec. Déclinaison de Saint-Jacques (November to March). Thon rouge de Méditerranée. Dorade royale sauvage aux artichauts violets (February to April). **Wines** Vin de pays des Pyrénées Orientales, Collioure.
◆ Contemporary furniture, mouldings and prettily laid tables create a tasteful decor. Predominantly fish and seafood menu. Fine regional wine list.

via ① near Perpignan-Nord interchange 10 km – ✉ 66600 Rivesaltes

Novotel rm, VISA AE
– 04 68 64 02 22 – h0424@accor.com – Fax 04 68 64 24 27
56 rm – €95/138 €95/138, €11
Rest – Menu (€15) – Carte €22/39
◆ Surrounded by greenery, this Novotel offers relaxation and comfort just off the motorway. The large, functional rooms have been partly renovated to give a contemporary, minimalist look. Catalan-style bar. The restaurant overlooks the pool, with terrace and barbecues in summer.

PERPIGNAN

Alsace-Lorraine (R.) . . . . . BY 2
Anciens-Combattants-d'Indochine (Pl. des) . . BY 3
Ange (R. de l') . . . . BZ 4
Arago (Pl.) . . . . BZ 5
Argenterie (R. de l') . . . . . BY 6
Barre (R. de la) . . . . BY 7
Bartissol (R. E.) . . . . BY 8
Batllo (Quai F.) . . . . BY 9
Castillet (R. du) . . . . BY 21
Clemenceau (Bd G.) . . . . . BY
Cloche d'Or (R. de la) . . BYZ 22
Côte des Carmes (R.) . . CZ 23
Fabriques d'En Nabot (R. des) . . . . BY 24
Fabriques d'En Nadal (R. des) . . . . BY 25
Fontaine-Neuve (R.) . . . . CZ 26
Fontfroide (R.) . . . . BY 27
Gambetta (Pl.) . . . . BY 28
Grande la Monnaie (R.) . . BZ 31
Lattre-de-Tassigny (Quai de) . . . . BZ 32
Loge (R. et Pl. de la) . . . . BY 33
Louis-Blanc (R.) . . . . . . ABY 34
Marchands (R. des) . . . . BY 35
Mermoz (Av. J.) . . . . CZ 36
Mirabeau (R.) . . . . BY 37
Payra (R. J.) . . . . BY 38
Péri (Pl. Gabriel) . . . . BZ 39
Petite la Monnaie (R.) . . . BZ 40
Porte d'Assaut (R.) . . . . . BZ 41
Porte de Canet (R.) . . . . . CZ 42
Remparts la Réal (R. des) BZ 43
République (Pl. de la) . . . BZ 44
Résistance (Pl. de la) . . . BY 45
Révolution Française (R. de la) . . . . CY 46
Rigaud (Pl.) . . . . BZ 47
Sadi-Carnot (Quai) . . . . . . BY 50
St-Jean (R.) . . . . BY 52
Théâtre (R. du) . . . . BZ 55
Trois-Journées (R. des) . . BY 58
Vauban (Quai) . . . . BY 60
Verdun (Pl. de) . . . . BY 64
Victoire (Pl. de la) . . . . BY 67
Vielledent (R. J.) . . . . CZ 69
Waldeck-Rousseau (R.) . CZ 72

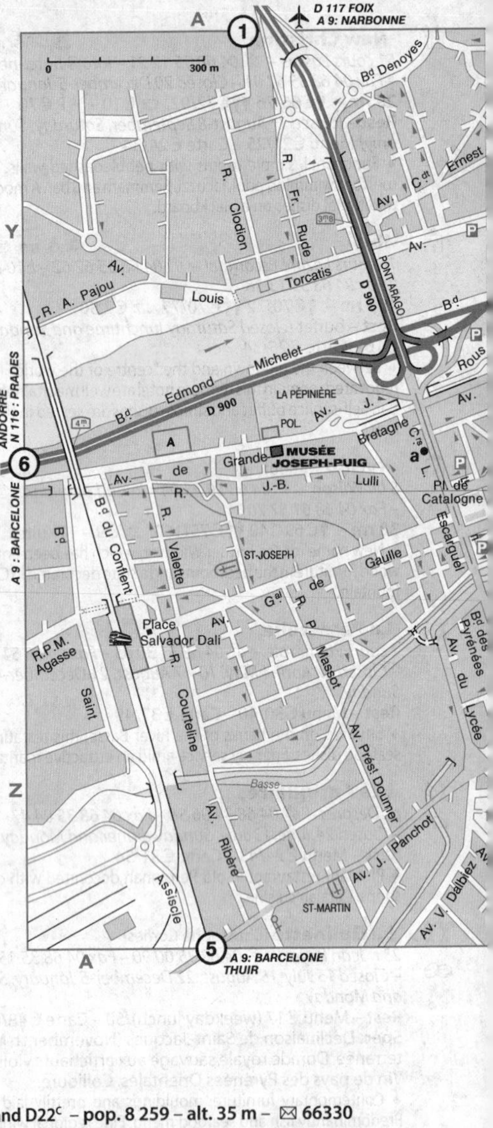

in Cabestany 5 km by ③ and D22^{c} – pop. 8 259 – alt. 35 m – ✉ 66330

Les Deux Mas rm, rest, VISA

1 r. Madeleine Brès, opposite Médipôle
– ✆ 04 68 50 08 08
– contact@hotel-les-2-mas.com
– Fax 04 68 62 32 54
33 rm – †€ 62/85 ††€ 82/106, ☕ € 12 – 1 suite – ½ P € 65/78
Rest – Menu € 18 (weekday lunch), € 24/42 – Carte € 27/61
◆ An unusual hotel: a distinctive mural on the façade depicts a sleeping woman; small colourful bedrooms with Moorish touches surround an Andalusian patio. Simple Catalan dishes served in a sunny setting.

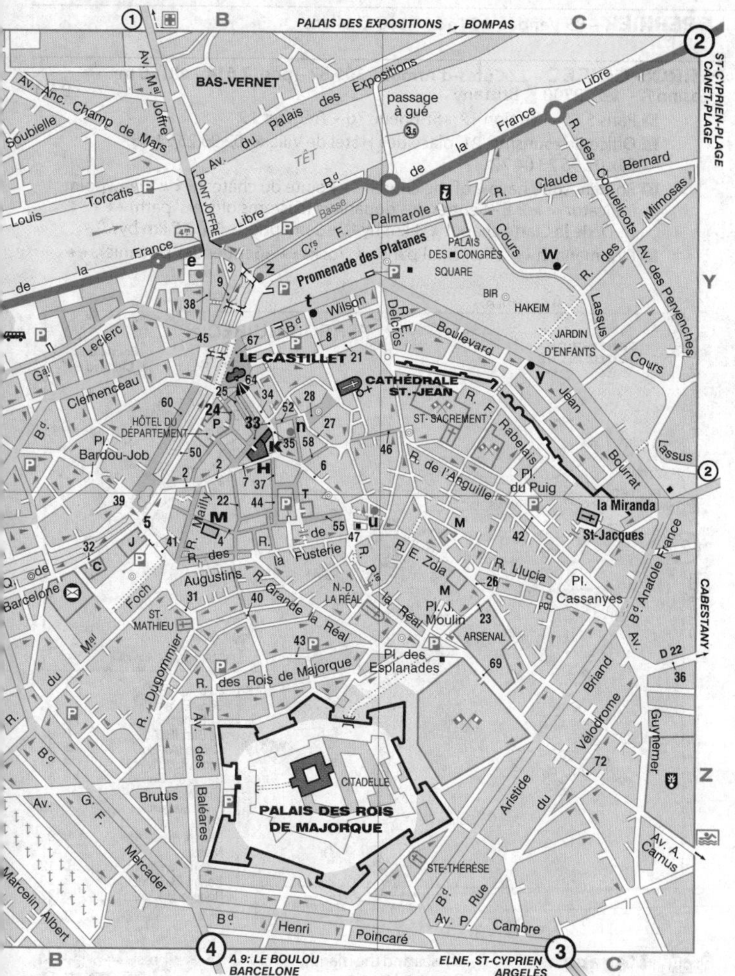

Southeast 5 km by ③ and D 22c – ✉66100 Perpignan

Domaine du Mas Boluix without rest
chemin du Pou de les Colobres – *☎ 04 68 08 17 70 – Fax 04 68 08 17 71*
≤ grapevines and Canigou,
8 rm – †€ 73/82 ††€ 82/91

◆ Each room in this house bears the name of a local artist and displays one of his/ her works. The upstairs rooms offer a superb view of the vineyards and the Pic du Canigou.

LE PERREUX-SUR-MARNE – **94 Val-de-Marne** – **312** E2 – **106** 20 – **101** 18 – **see** **Paris, Area**

PERRIER – **63 Puy-de-Dôme** – **326** G9 – **see Issoire**

LE PERRIER – 85 Vendée – 316 E6 – see Challans

PERROS-GUIREC – 22 Côtes-d'Armor – 309 B2 – pop. 7 614 – alt. 60 m – Casino A – ⊠ 22700 Brittany 9 **B1**

Paris 527 – Lannion 12 – St-Brieuc 76 – Tréguier 19

Office de tourisme, 21, place de l'Hôtel de Ville ✆ 02 96 23 21 15, Fax 02 96 23 04 72

Romanesque nave★ of the church B - Pointe du château ⋜★ - Viewpoint indicator ⋜★ B **E** - Sentier des douaniers (customs officers' path)★★ - N.-D. de la Clarté chapel ★ 3 km by ② - Semaphore ⋜★ 3.5 km by ②.

Ploumanach★★: municipal park ★★, rocks★★ - Sentier des Douaniers★★.

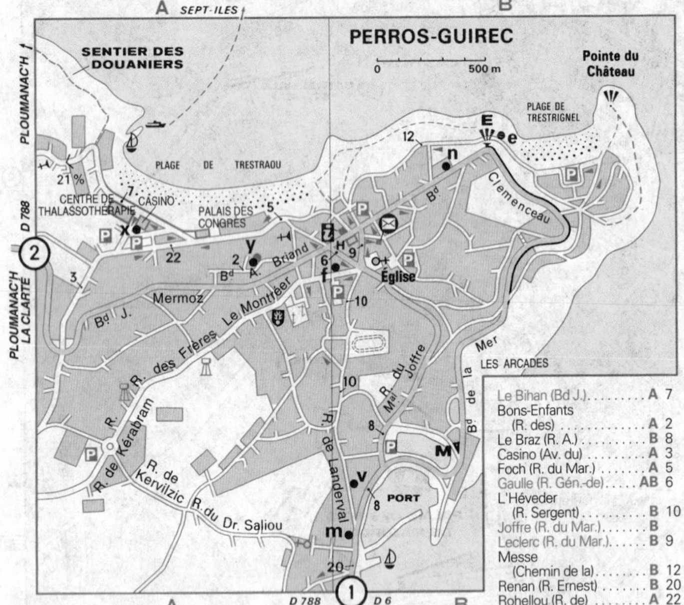

L'Agapa ⋜ sea and the islands, rest, **P** VISA AE
12 r. des Bons Enfants – ✆ 02 96 49 01 10 – hotel@lagapa.com – Fax 02 96 91 16 36 A **y**
47 rm – €160/420 €160/420, ☕ €18 – 1 suite
Rest ***Le Belouga*** *– (closed 3-27 December and 7-31 January)* Menu €28 bi (lunch), €58/80 bi – Carte €51/111

◆ This glass, steel and granite luxury hotel faces the sea and awaits you for a comfortable stay in both a relaxed and high-tech modern-style setting. Rooms are shared between the main building and two villas. Superb spa. Modern cuisine served in a rotunda-belvedere with a trendy decor.

Le Manoir du Sphinx ⋜ sea and the islands, **P** VISA AE
67 chemin de la Messe – ✆ 02 96 23 25 42 – lemanoirdusphinx@wanadoo.fr – Fax 02 96 91 26 13 – Closed 20 November-4 December and 9-21 February
20 rm – €109/113 €117/128, ☕ €10 – ½ P €103/121
Rest – *(closed Sun. evening from Oct. to Mar., Mon. lunch and Fri. lunch except public holidays)* Menu €31/51 – Carte €44/65 B **e**

◆ This delightful Belle Epoque villa overlooks the sea. The British-style rooms have views of the bay and islands. Its charming garden runs down to the rocks. A panoramic veranda-dining room, with a stylish setting, offering a modern, mainly fish and seafood cuisine.

Les Feux des Iles ⇐ rm, P VISA MC AE
53 bd Clemenceau – ✆ 02 96 23 22 94 – feuxdesiles2@wanadoo.fr – Fax 02 96 91 07 30 – Closed 9-15 March, 12-26 November, 22 December-5 January, Sunday dinner and Friday dinner (except hotel) October-May
18 rm – €92/102 €110/135, ☕ €12 – ½ P €90/110 B **n**
Rest – *(dinner only except Sunday)* Menu €24/64 – Carte €36/56
◆ A family-run hotel made up of a stone house and recently-built annex, whose larger and more modern rooms have a sea view. Some have direct access to the garden. Dining room facing the island lights, serving traditional fish and seafood dishes.

Au Bon Accueil AC rest, rm, P VISA MC AE
11 r. Landerval – ✆ 02 96 23 25 77 – au-bon-accueil@wanadoo.fr – Fax 02 96 23 12 66 – Closed 23 December-5 January B **v**
21 rm – €57/65 €57/65, ☕ €8 – ½ P €60/63
Rest – *(closed Sunday dinner and Monday except July-August)* Menu €16 (weekday lunch), €23/43 – Carte €32/52
◆ Establishment split into two sections. The accommodation section overlooks a quiet street and is awaiting renovation. Pleasant welcome. Restaurant with a modern setting, occupying a modern lodge that overlooks the marina. Traditional cuisine.

Mercure without rest VISA MC AE
100 av. du Casino – ✆ 02 96 91 22 11 – H0476@accor.com – Fax 02 96 91 24 78
49 rm – €73/109 €78/114, ☕ €11,50 A **x**
◆ This hotel is situated close to the beach. The rooms are in keeping with the chain's standards with the particularity that the colours change according to the floors. Some have a balcony.

Hermitage rest, P VISA MC AE
20 r. Frères Le Montréer – ✆ 02 96 23 21 22 – hermitage.hotel@wanadoo.fr – Fax 02 96 91 16 56 – Open 1st April-30 September B **f**
23 rm – €42/47 €50/59, ☕ €6,50 – ½ P €51/58
Rest – *(open 8 May-15 September) (dinner only) (resident only)* Menu €22
◆ An old building in the town centre set in a garden. Small, fresh and clean rooms. A pleasant welcome and friendly atmosphere.

Le Levant ⇐ rm, VISA MC AE
91 r. E. Renan, (at the port) – ✆ 02 96 23 20 15 – le-levant@wanadoo.fr – Fax 02 96 23 36 31 – **19 rm** – €55/75 €55/78, ☕ €8 – ½ P €61/71
Rest – *(closed 23 December-3 January, Saturday lunch, Sunday dinner and Friday)* Menu €18/57 – Carte €28/58 B **m**
◆ Modern hotel with renovated, functional rooms and balconies overlooking the harbour. The nautical decor of the dining room blends perfectly with the view over a forest of masts.

La Clarté (Daniel Jaguin) P VISA MC AE
24 r.Gabriel Vicaire, to La Clarté via ② – ✆ 02 96 49 05 96 – laclarte22@aol.com – Fax 02 96 91 41 36 – Closed 30 September-13 October, 30 December-6 February, Sunday dinner except July-August, Wednesday except lunch April-October and Monday
Rest – Menu €25 (weekday lunch), €39/70 – Carte €51/63
Spec. Saint-Jacques des Côtes d'Armor (October to March). Lotte au cidre et aux primeurs du pays (May to October). Fraises de Plougastel et tomate, sorbet framboise et poivron rouge (June to September).
◆ This restaurant in a suburb of Perros-Guirec, on the road to Ploumanach, offers up-to-date cuisine in a warm neo-rustic setting.

in Ploumanach 6 km by ② – ✉ **22700 Perros-Guirec**
Rocks★★ - Municipal park★★.

Castel Beau Site ⇐ sea and beach, P VISA MC
plage St-Guirec – ✆ 02 96 91 40 87 – infos@castelbeausite.com – Fax 02 96 91 66 37 – Closed January
40 rm – €60/125 €60/125, ☕ €11 – ½ P €68/101 – **Rest** – *(closed Sunday dinner from September to June) (dinner only except July-August and Sunday)* Menu €32/48 – Carte €37/56
◆ This 1930s granite building was once used as a barracks for troops. Fully renovated in modern style, it offers a picture-postcard view over the water. Modern rooms. Large, bright and rather exotic dining room, offering modern cuisine.

Parc

174 pl. St-Guirec – ✆ 02 96 91 40 80 – hotel.du.parclacotriade@wanadoo.fr – Fax 02 96 91 60 48 – Open 10 February-11 November, 22 December-6 January and closed Monday, Tuesday and Wednesday in October and March
10 rm – †€ 46/52 ††€ 46/52, ☕ € 7 – ½ P € 52/57 – **Rest** – Menu € 14,50/38 – Carte € 27/54
◆ A pink granite family house in the centre of the village, a stone's throw from the beach and famous rocks, with small, simple and well-kept rooms. Fish and seafood served on the terrace or in the bright dining room.

PERTUIS – 84 Vaucluse – 332 G11 – pop. 17 833 – alt. 246 m – ✉ 84120

Provence 40 **B2**

Paris 747 – Aix-en-Provence 23 – Apt 36 – Avignon 76 – Digne-les-Bains 97 – Manosque 36

Office de tourisme, place Mirabeau ✆ 04 90 79 15 56, Fax 04 90 09 59 06

Sevan

rte de Manosque, east: 1.5 km – ✆ 04 90 79 19 30 – hotel-sevan@orange.fr – Fax 04 90 79 35 77
46 rm – †€ 70/110 ††€ 80/130, ☕ € 11 – ½ P € 70/95
Rest *L'Olivier* – *✆ 04 90 79 08 19 (closed 1st January-7 February, Sunday dinner, Monday dinner and Wednesday)* Menu (€ 19), € 29/50 – Carte € 41/56
Rest *La Paillote* – *✆ 04 90 09 63 67 (closed mid December-mid January and Tuesday)* Carte € 22/40
◆ A 1970s hotel complex at the foot of the Luberon massif. Choose a room that has been refurbished in airy Provencal style or one overlooking the park. The Olivier serves regional cuisine. La Paillotte serves grilled meats and Tex-Mex dishes in a laid back atmosphere. Poolside terrace.

Le Boulevard

50 bd Pecout – ✆ 04 90 09 69 31 – Fax 04 90 09 09 48 – Closed 30 June-12 July, February holidays, Sunday dinner, Tuesday dinner and Wednesday
Rest – *(number of covers limited, pre-book)* Menu € 18/45 – Carte € 33/47
◆ A town-centre restaurant in an attractive old house with blue shutters. A discreetly rustic dining room and carefully laid-out tables.

PESMES – 70 Haute-Saône – 314 B9 – pop. 1 057 – alt. 205 m – ✉ 70140

Burgundy-Jura 16 **B2**

Paris 362 – Besançon 40 – Dijon 51 – Dole 26 – Gray 20

Office de tourisme, 19, rue Jacques Prévost ✆ 06 87 73 13 05, Fax 03 84 31 23 37

La Maison Royale without rest — l'Ognon valley

– ✆ 03 84 31 23 23 – Fax 03 84 31 23 23 – Open 1st April-15 October
5 rm ☕ – †€ 70 ††€ 80
◆ A wonderfully-restored 15C fortified house. The rooms with personal touches, offer a magnificent view of the Ognon Valley. Lounges, library and billiard table.

PETIT-BERSAC – 24 Dordogne – 329 C4 – pop. 177 – alt. 90 m – ✉ 24600

39 **C3**

Paris 501 – Bordeaux 121 – Périgueux 50 – Angoulême 49 – Soyaux 47

Château Le Mas de Montet

– ✆ 05 53 90 08 71 – reception@lemasdemontet.com – Fax 05 53 90 66 92
14 rm – †€ 145/425 ††€ 145/425, ☕ € 25 – ½ P € 125/275 – **Rest** – *(dinner only)* Menu € 50/75
◆ Beautiful surroundings for this superb Renaissance château with flower and vegetable gardens, swimming pool, and terrace. Seductive interior allying romance and sophistication. Traditional cuisine served in the elegant dining room.

PETITE-HETTANGE – 57 Moselle – 307 I2 – see Malling

LA PETITE-PIERRE – 67 Bas-Rhin – 315 H3 – pop. 612 – alt. 340 m – ✉ 67290
Alsace-Lorraine 1 **A1**

Paris 433 – Haguenau 41 – Sarreguemines 48 – Sarre-Union 24 – Strasbourg 57
Office de tourisme, 2a, rue du Château ☏ 03 88 70 42 30, Fax 03 88 70 41 08

La Clairière
rm, rest, VISA
63 rte d'Ingwiller, D 7: 1.5 km – ☏ 03 88 71 75 00 – info@laclairiere.com – Fax 03 88 70 41 05
50 rm – €93 €120/182, €15 – **Rest** – *(closed lunch except week-ends) (dinner only)* Menu €27/52 – Carte €31/49
◆ Tucked away in the forest, this modern hotel is dedicated to well being. Find an outdoor pool overlooking a teak deck, 950m2 spa, and a 'challenge' circuit for conference guests. Spacious guestrooms and a British-style bar. Modern decor, healthy cuisine and organic wines.

Lion d'Or
rest, VISA
– ☏ 03 88 01 47 57 – contact@liondor.com – Fax 03 88 01 47 50 – Closed 30 June-9 July
42 rm – €55/68 €77/103, €11,50 – ½ P €73/86 – **Rest** – Menu €19 (weekdays)/65 – Carte €27/63
◆ Ideal for those in need of a real break. A country hotel complete with an arbrothérapie (tree treatment) centre. The rooms in the old house are very soothing. Regional cuisine served in the dining room overlooking the city and forest.

Des Vosges
rm, rest, rm, VISA
30 r. Principale – ☏ 03 88 70 45 05 – hotel-des-vosges@wanadoo.fr – Fax 03 88 70 41 13 – Closed 21 July-1st August and 18 February-8 March
30 rm – €55 €66/80, €9,50 – ½ P €62/69 – **Rest** – *(closed Tuesday off season)* Menu €24 (weekdays)/54 – Carte €29/55
◆ Snug, well-kept rooms in varying styles (some Alsatian). Pleasant wellness centre. Traditional dishes and a sumptuous wine list of old vintages served in a rustic dining room with a view of the valley.

in Graufthal 11 km Southwest by D 178 and D 122 – ✉ 67320 Eschbourg

Le Cheval Blanc
VISA
19 r. Principale – ☏ 03 88 70 17 11 – restaurant@auchevalblanc.net – Fax 03 88 70 12 37 – Closed 1st-15 September, 1st-21 January, Monday dinner, Wednesday dinner and Tuesday
Rest – Menu (€22), €27/52 – Carte €28/49
◆ This appealing inn, decorated in a somewhat jumbled rustic style, serves regional dishes. Attractive tiled stove in one of the dining rooms.

Au Vieux Moulin with rm
VISA
– ☏ 03 88 70 17 28 – auvieux.moulin@orange.fr – Fax 03 88 70 11 25 – Closed February holidays
14 rm – €40/70 €40/70, €7 – ½ P €47/60 – **Rest** – *(closed Tuesday dinner)* Menu €10 (weekday lunch), €26/32 – Carte €17/44
◆ This establishment offers a warm welcome in a hamlet whose peacefulness was proclaimed by Erckman and Chatrian. Alsatian family cooking served in a light-filled dining room. Small, comfortable rooms in the process of refurbishment.

LE PETIT-PRESSIGNY – 37 Indre-et-Loire – 317 O7 – pop. 366 – alt. 80 m – ✉ 37350
11 **B3**

Paris 290 – Le Blanc 38 – Châtellerault 36 – Châteauroux 68 – Poitiers 73 – Tours 61

La Promenade (Jacky Dallais)
VISA
– ☏ 02 47 94 93 52 – Fax 02 47 91 06 03 – Closed 22 September-7 October, 5 January-4 February, Sunday dinner, Monday and Tuesday
Rest – Menu €38/80 – Carte €48/106
Spec. Tomate cornue des Andes confite, pistou (summer). Géline de Touraine rôtie au citron, beurre d'écrevisses et royale de foies blonds. Lièvre à la royale (October to December). **Wines** Touraine, Touraine-Mesland.
◆ Village inn with surprisingly modern decor, embellished by works of art. Tasty modern cuisine from the Tours area and an appealing wine list.

LE PETIT QUEVILLY – 76 Seine-Maritime – 304 G5 – see Rouen

PETRETO-BICCHISANO – 2A Corse-du-Sud – 345 C9 – see Corse

PEYRAT-LE-CHÂTEAU – 87 Haute-Vienne – 325 H6 – pop. 1 081 – alt. 426 m – ✉ 87470 Dordogne-Berry-Limousin 25 C2

Paris 409 – Aubusson 45 – Guéret 52 – Limoges 53 – Tulle 81 – Ussel 79 – Uzerche 58

Office de tourisme, 1, rue du Lac ✆ 05 55 69 48 75, Fax 05 55 69 47 82

at Vassivière Lake – ✉ 23460 Royère-de-Vassivière

Centre d'art contemporain de l'île de Vassivière (Modern art centre) ★★

Au Golf du Limousin rest, VISA

à Auphelle, (Lake Vassivière) – ✆ 05 55 69 41 34 – hotel-golfdulimousin@wanadoo.fr – Fax 05 55 69 49 16 – Open 16 February-14 November

18 rm – †€ 42/53 ††€ 42/53, ☐ € 10 – ½ P € 43/52 – **Rest** – *(dinner only)* Menu € 22/30

◆ This hotel, perched at an altitude of 650m, enjoys views of the lake. Simple but well-maintained and spacious guestrooms, with attic-style accommodation on the second floor. Traditional cuisine served in an attractive dining room or on the terrace in summer.

PÉZENAS – 34 Hérault – 339 F8 – pop. 7 443 – alt. 15 m – ✉ 34120 Languedoc-Roussillon-Tarn Gorges 23 C2

Paris 734 – Agde 22 – Béziers 24 – Lodève 39 – Montpellier 55 – Sète 38

Office de tourisme, place Gambetta ✆ 04 67 98 36 40, Fax 04 67 98 96 80

Old Pézenas★★: Hôtels of Lacoste★, Alfonce★, Malibran★.

L'Entre Pots AC VISA

8 av. Louis-Montagne – ✆ 04 67 90 00 00 – entre-pots@orange.fr – Fax 04 67 90 17 42 – Closed Monday lunch, Wednesday lunch and Sunday

Rest – Menu (€ 20), € 25 (lunch) – Carte € 19/40 dinner

◆ Fresh seasonal cuisine allying regional tradition and modernity, intimate contemporary interior, peaceful courtyard terrace and cheerful service: let the charm work its wonders...

Le Pré Saint Jean AC VISA AE

18 av. Mar. Leclerc – ✆ 04 67 98 15 31 – leprest.jean@wanadoo.fr – Fax 04 67 98 89 23 – Closed Thursday dinner except July August, Sunday dinner and Monday

Rest – Menu € 25/45 – Carte € 32/64

◆ This discreet busy roadside facade hides a welcoming winter garden-style dining room. Updated regional cuisine and fine local wine list.

in Nézignan-l'Évêque South: 5 km by D 609 and D 13 – pop. 960 – alt. 40 m – ✉ 34120

Hostellerie de St-Alban rm, rest, VISA AE

31 rte Agde – ✆ 04 67 98 11 38 – info@saintalban.com – Fax 04 67 98 91 63 – Open 15 February-12 November

13 rm – †€ 80/123 ††€ 95/195, ☐ € 14 – ½ P € 93/143

Rest – *(closed Thursday lunch and Wednesday except April-October)* Menu € 22 (weekday lunch)/32 – Carte € 40/57

◆ Attractive 19C family mansion, nestling in a charming flower garden. The sometimes original rooms, equipped with wrought-iron furniture, are spacious and colourful. Restaurant with an immaculate decor and modern works of art, serving traditional Mediterranean dishes.

PÉZILLA-LA-RIVIÈRE – 66 Pyrénées-Orientales – 344 H6 – pop. 2 754 – alt. 75 m – ✉ 66370 22 B3

Paris 857 – Argelès-sur-Mer 35 – Le Boulou 25 – Perpignan 12 – Prades 35

L'Aramon Gourmand

127 av. du Canigou, rte Baho, D 614 – ✆ 04 68 92 43 59 – philippe.coste66@wanadoo.fr – Fax 04 68 92 43 59 – Closed 22-31 August, 2-8 January, Sunday dinner, Tuesday dinner and Wednesday

Rest – Menu (€ 13,50 bi), € 27/37

◆ Enjoy the traditional flavours and dishes of the Roussillon in the charming dining room decorated in red and yellow and furnished with solid wood chairs, or outdoors under the shade of the mulberry and plane trees. Wine cellar on view.

PFAFFENHOFFEN – 67 Bas-Rhin – 315 J3 – pop. 2 468 – alt. 170 m – ✉ 67350

Alsace-Lorraine 1 **B1**

Paris 457 – Haguenau 16 – Sarrebourg 55 – Sarre-Union 50 – Saverne 30 – Strasbourg 37

Musée de l'Imagerie peinte et populaire alsacienne★.

De l'Agneau with rm rest, rm, VISA AE

– ✆ 03 88 07 72 38 – anne.ernwein@wanadoo.fr – Fax 03 88 72 20 24 – Closed 3-10 March, 16-23 June, 7-28 September, Sunday dinner, Tuesday except lunch from September to May and Monday

12 rm – †€ 53/59 ††€ 53/70, ☕ € 13 – ½ P € 56/86 – **Rest** – Menu € 27/67 bi – Carte € 42/57

◆ This 1769 inn, now run by the seventh generation, takes you back in time. Tasty, classic dishes with a modern slant and a fine wine list. Stylish rooms.

PFULGRIESHEIM – 67 Bas-Rhin – 315 K5 – see Strasbourg

PHALSBOURG – 57 Moselle – 307 O6 – pop. 4 499 – alt. 365 m – ✉ 57370

Alsace-Lorraine 27 **D2**

Paris 435 – Metz 110 – Sarrebourg 17 – Sarreguemines 50 – Strasbourg 59

Office de tourisme, 30, place d'Armes ✆ 03 87 24 42 42, Fax 03 87 24 42 87

Erckmann-Chatrian rm, rest, VISA

pl. d'Armes – ✆ 03 87 24 31 33 – hotel.rest.e-chatrian@wanadoo.fr – Fax 03 87 24 27 81

16 rm – †€ 66 ††€ 70/89, ☕ € 14 – **Rest** – *(closed Tues. lunchtime and Mon.)* Menu € 15 (weekdays)/49 – Carte € 49/61

◆ Old house with a stylish, flower-decked façade. The good sized rooms sport period furniture and some have a small lounge area. Traditional meals to be enjoyed in a dining room lined with dark wood panelling or in a brasserie atmosphere.

Au Soldat de l'An II (Georges Schmitt) with rm rm, VISA AE

1 rte Saverne – ✆ 03 87 24 16 16 – info@soldatan2.com – Fax 03 87 24 18 18 – Closed 28 July-7 August, 27 October-6 November, 2-12 March, Sunday dinner, Tuesday lunch and Monday

7 rm – †€ 120 ††€ 120/150, ☕ € 18 – ½ P € 145

Rest – Menu € 40 bi (weekday lunch), € 82 € bi/115 bi – Carte € 71/84

Spec. Grenouilles fraîches en tempura. Fruits de mer et crustacés. Gibier (June to February.). **Wines** Gewurztraminer, Alsace.

◆ Trinkets and the soldier guarding the entrance to this former barn are reminiscent of the days of French Revolution patriots and their red, white and blue trousers. Up-to-date cuisine and fine Alsatian wine list. Comfortable rooms in the house next door.

in Bonne-Fontaine East: 4 km by D 604 and secondary road ✉ 57370 Danne-et-Quatre-Vents

Notre-Dame de Bonne Fontaine VISA AE

212 rte Bonne Fontaine – ✆ 03 87 24 34 33 – ndbonnefontaine@aol.com – Fax 03 87 24 24 64 – Closed 11-24 January and 15-22 February

34 rm – †€ 51/61 ††€ 63/76, ☕ € 9 – ½ P € 60/66 – **Rest** – *(closed Sunday dinner in January, February, March and November)* Menu € 17/45 bi – Carte € 19/43

◆ The same family has been running this hotel, nestling in a forest close to a pilgrimage centre, for several generations. Simple rooms. Pretty walks under the pine trees. A veranda-dining room and shaded terrace serving traditional regional dishes.

PHILIPPSBOURG – 57 Moselle – 307 Q5 – pop. 531 – alt. 215 m – ✉ 57230 27 **D1**

Paris 450 – Haguenau 29 – Strasbourg 58 – Wissembourg 42

Office de tourisme, 186, rue de Baerenthal ✆ 03 87 06 56 12, Fax 03 87 06 51 48

Du Tilleul

117 rte de Niederbronn – ✆ 03 87 06 50 10 – au.tilleul.issler@wanadoo.fr – Fax 03 87 06 58 89 – Closed January, Monday dinner, Tuesday dinner and Wednesday

Rest – Menu € 11,50 (weekday lunch)/50 – Carte € 27/51

◆ The entrance to this family inn has a bar where dishes of the day are served, while traditional cuisine is proposed in the rustic-style dining room.

in l'étang de Hanau **Northwest: 5 km by D 662 and secondary road – ✉ 57230 Philippsbourg**

Small lake★, **Alsace-Lorraine-Champagne**

Beau Rivage without rest

– ✆ 03 87 06 50 32 – Fax 03 87 06 57 46 – Closed November and February

22 rm – €40/49 €59/89, €7,50

◆ The rooms of this hotel, isolated in the countryside, look out onto a pond or forest. Some have Alsatian furniture, while others facing the water often have a balcony.

PIANA – 2A Corse-du-Sud – 345 A6 – see Corse

PIERRE-BUFFIERE – 87 Haute-Vienne – 325 F6 – pop. 1 106 – alt. 330 m – ✉ 87260 24 **B2**

Paris 415 – Limoges 22 – Brantôme 84 – Guéret 107 – Tulle 67

Office de tourisme, place du 8 Mai 1945 ✆ 05 55 00 94 33, Fax 05 55 00 94 33

La Providence

pl. Adeline – ✆ 05 55 00 60 16 – laprovidence@hotel-limoges.net – Fax 05 55 00 98 69 – Closed 5 January-2 February, Sunday dinner and Monday lunch 16 November-15 December

14 rm – €54/80 €54/105, €9 – ½ P €70/75 – **Rest** – Menu €19/70 – Carte €36/70

◆ This family run hotel borders the main square of a Limousin village. Comfortable, modern and well-kept rooms. The restaurant offers simple traditional dishes in an unpretentious dining room adorned with rustic furniture.

PIERREFITTE-EN-AUGE – 14 Calvados – 303 N4 – see Pont-L'Évêque

PIERREFITTE-SUR-SAULDRE – 41 Loir-et-Cher – 318 J6 – pop. 851 – alt. 125 m – ✉ 41300 12 **C2**

Paris 185 – Orléans 52 – Aubigny-sur-Nère 23 – Blois 73 – Bourges 55 – Salbris 13

Syndicat d'initiative, 10, place de l'Église ✆ 02 54 88 67 15, Fax 02 54 88 67 15

Le Lion d'Or

1 pl. de l'Église – ✆ 02 54 88 62 14 – liondor41@orange.fr – Fax 02 54 88 62 14 – Closed 1st-24 September, 5-28 January, Wednesday dinner and Thursday dinner off season, Monday and Tuesday except holidays

Rest – Menu € 32/40 – Carte approx. € 52

◆ Timber-framed walls, beams and a collection of old china form an authentic rustic setting for this attractive Sologne house. A pretty garden/terrace. Regional menu.

The sun's out – let's eat alfresco!
Look for a terrace:

PIERREFONDS – 60 Oise – 305 I4 – pop. 1 945 – alt. 81 m – ✉ 60350

Northern France and the Paris Region 37 **C2**

Paris 82 – Beauvais 78 – Compiègne 15 – Soissons 31 – Villers-Cotterêts 18

Office de tourisme, place de l'Hôtel de Ville ✆ 03 44 42 81 44, Fax 03 44 42 86 31

Château★★ - St-Jean-aux-Bois: church ★ West: 6 km.

in Chelles 4.5 km East by D 85 – pop. 384 – alt. 75 m – ✉ 60350

Relais Brunehaut with rm — rest, VISA

3 r. de l'Église – ✆ 03 44 42 85 05 – Fax 03 44 42 83 30

11 rm – €45/50 €52/64, €9 – 1 suite – ½ P €67/70

Rest – *(closed 15 January-13 February, Wednesday lunch and Thursday lunch 16 November-30 April, Monday lunch and Tuesday lunch)* Menu €25 (weekday lunch)/45 bi – Carte €47/63

◆ The watermill with its large wheel and the inn are set around an attractive, flower-decked courtyard. The mill houses pleasant rooms, while the inn offers a rustic dining room.

in St-Jean-aux-Bois : 6 km by D 85 – pop. 349 – alt. 71 m – ✉ 60350

Auberge A la Bonne Idée with rm — rm, VISA

3 r. Meuniers – ✆ 03 44 42 84 09 – a-la-bonne-idee.auberge@wanadoo.fr – Fax 03 44 42 80 45 – Closed 5 January-2 February, Sunday dinner and Monday October-April

23 rm – €75/105 €75/150, €10 – ½ P €80/115

Rest – Menu €30 (weekdays)/75 – Carte €70/76

◆ Restaurant in a charming village. Country interior, with beams, old stonework and a fireplace. Terrace facing a flower garden and classic cuisine.

PIERREFORT – 15 Cantal – 330 F5 – pop. 1 002 – alt. 950 m – ✉ 15230 5 **B3**

Paris 540 – Aurillac 64 – Entraygues-sur-Truyère 55 – Espalion 62 – St-Flour 29

Office de tourisme, 29, avenue Georges Pompidou ✆ 04 71 23 38 04, Fax 04 71 23 94 55

Du Midi — VISA AE

5 av. G. Pompidou – ✆ 04 71 23 30 20 – info@hoteldumidi-pierrefort.com – Fax 04 71 23 39 34 – Closed 22 December-11 January

13 rm – €45/48 €47/52, €7 – ½ P €48/52

Rest – Menu (€11), €14,50 (weekdays)/38 – Carte €28/53

◆ Meeting facilities, children's play area, nursery room: this central establishment is as popular with business travellers as with families: small, spring-like rooms and pleasant atmosphere. Pleasant vaulted dining rooms and excellent regional cuisine.

PIERRELATTE – 26 Drôme – 332 B7 – pop. 11 943 – alt. 50 m – ✉ 26700

Lyon - Rhone Valley 44 **B3**

Paris 624 – Bollène 17 – Montélimar 23 – Nyons 45 – Orange 33 – Pont-St-Esprit 17

Office de tourisme, place du Champ de Mars ✆ 04 75 04 07 98, Fax 04 75 98 40 65

Ferme aux crocodiles (Crocodile farm)★, South: 4 km by N 7 until interchange with D 59.

Du Tricastin without rest — VISA AE

r. Caprais-Favier – ✆ 04 75 04 05 82 – hoteltriscastin@orange.fr – Fax 04 75 04 19 36

13 rm – €39/41 €43/45, €6,50

◆ In a quiet street near the town centre, a spruce façade giving onto well-equipped rooms. Impeccably kept and attentive service.

Du Centre without rest — VISA AE

6 pl. de l'Église – ✆ 04 75 04 28 59 – info@hotelducentre26.com – Fax 04 75 96 97 97 – Closed 22 December-4 January

26 rm – €54/55 €54/55, €9

◆ This former abbey houses simple, good-sized rooms that are gradually being renovated. Pleasant breakfast room. Very friendly welcome.

PIERRE-PERTHUIS – 89 Yonne – 319 F7 – see Vézelay

PIETRANERA – 2B Haute-Corse – 345 F3 – see Corse (Bastia)

LES PILLES – 26 Drôme – 332 E7 – see Nyons

PINEY – 10 Aube – 313 F3 – pop. 1 226 – alt. 116 m – ✉ 10220 13 **B3**

Paris 192 – Troyes 22 – St-Dizier 149 – Sézanne 80

Office de tourisme, Maison du Parc ✆ 03 25 43 38 88

Le Tadorne rm, VISA

1 pl. de la Halle – ✆ 03 25 46 30 35 – le.tadorne@wanadoo.fr – Fax 03 25 46 36 49 – Closed 15 December-10 January, February holidays and Sunday dinner October-Easter

26 rm – †€ 45/52 ††€ 57/62, ☕ € 8 – ½ P € 60

Rest – Menu € 18/49 – Carte € 23/41

◆ Pretty timber-framed houses with beams set around a swimming pool with terrace. Some of the small rooms have a lounge area and some are air-conditioned. Wood dominates the country-style dining room complete with mezzanine floor.

LE PIN-LA-GARENNE – 61 Orne – 310 M4 – see Mortagne-au-Perche

PINSOT – 38 Isère – 333 J5 – see Allevard

PIOGGIOLA – 2B Haute-Corse – 345 C4 – see Corse

PIOLENC – 84 Vaucluse – 332 B8 – pop. 4 296 – alt. 40 m – ✉ 84420 40 **A2**

Paris 659 – Avignon 36 – Marseille 123 – Montélimar 50

Auberge de l'Orangerie with rm rest, VISA

4 r. de l'Ormeau – ✆ 04 90 29 59 88 – orangerie@orangerie.net – Fax 04 90 29 67 74 – Closed 3-12 November, 15-27 December, Monday and Tuesday

5 rm – †€ 44/47 ††€ 58/72, ☕ € 9 – ½ P € 61/72

Rest – Menu € 19 – Carte € 32/50

◆ This former coaching inn behind high walls has a dining room with a magnificent vaulted ceiling. Up-to-date menu, enriched with regional and Guadeloupe specialities. Simple rooms but unusually decorated.

PIRIAC-SUR-MER – 44 Loire-Atlantique – 316 A3 – pop. 1 898 – alt. 7 m – ✉ 44420 Brittany 34 **A2**

Paris 462 – La Baule 17 – Nantes 88 – La Roche-Bernard 33 – St-Nazaire 31

Office de tourisme, 7, rue des Cap-Horniers ✆ 02 40 23 51 42, Fax 02 40 23 51 19

Pointe du Castelli ≤★ Southwest: 1 km.

De la Poste VISA

26 r. de la Plage – ✆ 02 40 23 50 90 – hoteldelaposte.piriac@wanadoo.fr – Fax 02 40 23 68 96 – Open 13 February-2 November

14 rm – †€ 49 ††€ 69, ☕ € 8 – ½ P € 52/62

Rest – *(open 1st April-2 November, Friday, Saturday and Sunday 13 February-31 March and closed Monday lunch off season)*

Menu € 15 (weekdays)/37 – Carte € 29/46

◆ In the centre of a small picturesque fishing port with attractive 17C houses is this 1930s villa. Recently redecorated rooms. Classic dishes to be enjoyed in a warm dining room or on the terrace.

PISCIATELLO – 2A Corse-du-Sud – **345** C8 – see Corse (Ajaccio)

PITHIVIERS – 45 Loiret – **318** K2 – **pop. 9 242** – **alt. 115 m** – ✉ 45300
Châteaux of the Loire 12 **C1**

Paris 82 – Chartres 74 – Fontainebleau 46 – Montargis 46 – Orléans 44

Office de tourisme, 1, mail Ouest ✆ 02 38 30 50 02,
Fax 02 38 30 55 00

Le Relais de la Poste
10 Mail Ouest – ✆ 02 38 30 40 30 – le-relais-de-la-poste@wanadoo.fr – Fax 02 38 30 47 79
41 rm – €50 €55, €8 – ½ P €49
Rest – *(closed Sunday dinner)* Menu € 18/32 – Carte € 32/42
◆ This large building in the town centre was once a post house and offers spacious, wood-panelled rooms decorated with rustic furniture. Light wood panelling and a fireplace make this dining room very welcoming. Traditional food.

Aux Saveurs Lointaines
1 pl. Martroi – ✆ 02 38 30 18 18 – hsnguyen55@gmail.fr – Closed 6 July-4 August, Sunday dinner and Monday
Rest – Menu € 12 (weekday lunch) – Carte € 13/22
◆ Bamboo curtains, woven straw objects and teak and wrought-iron furniture decorate this family restaurant dedicated to Vietnamese food. Exotic fruit specialities.

PIZAY – 69 Rhône – **327** H3 – see Belleville

PLAGE DE CALALONGA – 2A Corse-du-Sud – **345** E11 – see Corse (Bonifacio)

PLAILLY – 60 Oise – **305** G6 – **pop. 1 580** – **alt. 100 m** – ✉ 60128 19 **C2**

Paris 40 – Beauvais 69 – Chantilly 16 – Compiègne 46 – Meaux 36 – Pontoise 48 – Senlis 16

La Gentilhommière
25 r. G. Bouchard, (behind the church) – ✆ 03 44 54 30 20 – Fax 03 44 54 31 27 – Closed 4-25 August, 23 February-9 March, Saturday lunch, Sunday dinner, Monday and Tuesday
Rest – Menu € 24 (weekday lunch), € 33/43 – Carte € 51/60
◆ This restaurant occupies an old house next to the church. A fireplace, beams and copper pots emphasise the rustic style of the dining room. Traditional menu. Non-smoking.

LA PLAINE-SUR-MER – 44 Loire-Atlantique – **316** C5 – **pop. 2 517** – **alt. 26 m** – ✉ 44770
34 **A2**

Paris 438 – Nantes 58 – Pornic 9 – St-Michel-Chef-Chef 7 – St-Nazaire 28

Office de tourisme, square du Fort Gentil ✆ 02 40 21 52 52

Pointe de St-Gildas★ West: 5 km, Atlantic Coast

Anne de Bretagne (Philippe Vételé)
at Port de Gravette, 3 km northwest – ✆ 02 40 21 54 72 – bienvenue@annedebretagne.com – Fax 02 40 21 02 33 – Closed from beg. January to mid February
20 rm – € 125/320 € 135/320, € 17 – ½ P € 143/240
Rest – *(closed Tuesday except dinner in season, Sunday dinner November-March and Monday)* Menu € 35 (weekday lunch), € 53/110
Spec. Déclinaison d'huîtres en température. Pavé de bar basse température, sardines et huîtres en tartare (June to September). Pigeon du pays de Retz désossé et cuit à l'unilatéral. **Wines** Muscadet de Sévre et Maine sur lie, Fiefs Vendéens.
◆ White house on the dunes. Most of the rooms have been spruced up in a minimalist style (lovely furniture and contemporary art). Minimalist modern restaurant whose bay windows command views of the sea. Seafood menu and fine wine list.

PLAISIANS – 26 Drôme – 332 E8 – pop. 175 – alt. 612 m – ✉ 26170 44 B3

Paris 690 – Carpentras 44 – Nyons 33 – Vaison-la-Romaine 27

Auberge de la Clue

pl. de l'Église – ✆ 04 75 28 01 17 – Fax 04 75 28 29 17
– Open 1st April-15 October, weekends and public holidays from November to March except February and closed Sunday dinner except July-August and Monday

Rest – Menu € 25/31 – Carte € 26/43

♦ Regulars of this pleasant restaurant often travel long distances to enjoy the tasty local dishes. Dining room with Provençal colours. Terrace facing the Mont Ventoux.

PLANCOËT – 22 Côtes-d'Armor – 309 I3 – pop. 2 589 – alt. 41 m – ✉ 22130 10 C2

Paris 417 – Dinan 17 – Dinard 20 – St-Brieuc 46 – St-Malo 26

Syndicat d'initiative, 1, rue des Venelles ✆ 02 96 84 00 57

Crouzil et Hôtel L'Ecrin (Maxime et Jean-Pierre Crouzil) with rm

20 les quais – ✆ 02 96 84 10 24 rest, VISA
– jean-pierre.crouzil@wanadoo.fr – Fax 02 96 84 01 93
– Closed 1st-15 October, 10 January-1st February, Sunday dinner except July-August, Tuesday except dinner July-August and Monday

7 rm – €75 €120/160, ☕ €23 – ½ P €130/145

Rest – *(pre-book Sat - Sun)* Menu € 25 (weekday lunch)/120 – Carte approx. € 80

Spec. Saint-Jacques dorées au sautoir, verjus. Homard breton rôti, brûlé au lambic. Turbot en tronçon, légumes primeurs, sucs de cuisson liés de truffe noire.

♦ Plancoët, famous for its mineral water and hostelry since the 19C, boasts an elegant restaurant serving "surf & turf" specialities prepared by talented chefs. Individual-style rooms.

PLAN-D'AUPS – 83 Var – 340 J6 – pop. 764 – alt. 670 m – ✉ 83640 40 B3

Provence

Paris 795 – Aix-en-Provence 46 – Brignoles 37 – Marseille 44 – Toulon 72

Office de tourisme, place de la Mairie ✆ 04 42 62 57 57, Fax 04 42 62 57 57

Lou Pebre d'Aï with rm rm, VISA

– ✆ 04 42 04 50 42 – lou.pebre.dai@wanadoo.fr – Fax 04 42 04 50 71
– Closed 7-17 January, 11-29 February, Tuesday dinner and Wednesday mid September-mid April

11 rm – €50/65 €52/72, ☕ €7 – ½ P €55/65 – **Rest** – Menu (€ 17), € 26/46 – Carte € 31/54

♦ In a village dominated by the steep Ste-Baume incline. A pleasant country decor in the restaurant and terrace leading into a garden. The cuisine is based on local produce.

PLAN-DE-CUQUES – 13 Bouches-du-Rhône – 340 H5 – see Marseille

PLAN-DE-LA-TOUR – 83 Var – 340 O5 – pop. 2 380 – alt. 69 m – ✉ 83120 41 C3

Paris 859 – Cannes 68 – Draguignan 36 – Fréjus 28 – St-Tropez 24 – Ste-Maxime 10

Office de tourisme, 1, rue du 19 mars 1962 ✆ 04 94 43 01 50, Fax 04 94 43 75 08

Mas des Brugassières without rest VISA

1.5 km south on Grimaud road – ✆ 04 94 55 50 55 – mas.brugassieres@free.fr
– Fax 04 94 55 50 51 – Open from March to October

14 rm – €75/90 €80/98, ☕ €9 – 1 suite

♦ Attractive southern farmhouse in the heart of the Maures massif. Most rooms have been tastefully renovated in the Provençal style. Some have a terrace, while others overlook the garden.

in Courruero **South: 3,5 km by Grimaud road – ✉ 83120 Plan-de-la-Tour**

Parasolis without rest

– ✆ *04 94 43 76 05 – hotelparasolis@wanadoo.fr – Fax 04 94 43 77 09 – Open 20 March-30 September*

12 rm – €65/85 €75/110, €10

◆ Small local-style buildings in the middle of the countryside. Rustic lounge bar and simple, ground-floor rooms with private terraces. Fine garden planted with Provençal species.

PLAN-DU-VAR – 06 Alpes-Maritimes – 341 E4 – ✉ 06670 Levens

41 **D2**

Paris 941 – Antibes 38 – Cannes 48 – Nice 32 – Puget-Théniers 35 – Vence 26

Gorges de la Vésubie★★★ Northeast - Chaudan defile★★ North: 2 km.

Bonson: site★, ≤★★ from the church terrace, **French Riviera**

Cassini

231 av. Porte des Alpes, D 6202 – ✆ 04 93 08 91 03 – restaurantcassini@wanadoo.fr – Fax 04 93 08 45 48 – Closed 6-25 November, 10-25 February, Tuesday dinner, Wednesday dinner, Thursday dinner 15 September-15 June, Sunday dinner and Monday

Rest – Menu (€ 19), € 30/50 – Carte € 25/51

◆ The same family has run this roadside inn in the heart of the village for four generations. The dining room has recently been treated to a facelift. Traditional menu.

PLANGUENOUAL – 22 Côtes-d'Armor – 309 G3 – pop. 1 736 – alt. 76 m – ✉ 22400

10 **C2**

Paris 449 – Rennes 96 – Saint-Brieuc 19 – Saint-Malo 89 – Plérin 21

Manoir de la Hazaie without rest

2.5 km south-east on D 59 – ✆ 02 96 32 73 71 – manoir.hazaie@wanadoo.fr – Fax 02 96 32 79 72

5 rm – €130/145 €145/240, €14

◆ This 16C granite manor house and its tree-lined park are ideal for a country break. Period furnished rooms decorated with great attention to detail (spa bath tubs).

PLANPRAZ – 74 Haute-Savoie – 328 O5 – see Chamonix-Mont-Blanc

PLAPPEVILLE – 57 Moselle – 307 H4 – see Metz

PLASCASSIER – 06 Alpes-Maritimes – 341 C6 – see Valbonne

PLATEAU-D'ASSY – 74 Haute-Savoie – 328 N5 – ✉ 74480

French Alps

46 **F1**

Paris 597 – Annecy 83 – Bonneville 41 – Chamonix-Mont-Blanc 23 – Megève 20

Office de tourisme, 1133,av. Jacques Arnaud ✆ 04 50 58 80 52, Fax 04 50 93 83 74

✼★★★ - Church ★: decoration★★ - Pavillon de Charousse ✼★★ West: 2.5 km then 30 mn - Lac Vert (Green Lake)★ Northeast: 5 km - Plaine-Joux ≤★★ Northeast: 5.5 km.

Tourisme without rest

6 r. d'Anterne ✉ 74190 – ✆ 04 50 58 80 54 – hotel.le.tourisme@wanadoo.fr – Fax 04 50 93 82 11 – Closed 15 June-5 July, 20 October-8 November and Wednesday

15 rm – €20 €28/39, €5,50

◆ This PMU (betting office) hotel-bar has basic, well-kept rooms, half of which look out over Mont Blanc. Pleasant terrace with panoramic views where breakfast is served in summer.

Les Métiers d'Art

310 chemin des Parchets, 4 km north-east on D 143 – ✆ 04 50 58 85 01 – Closed 23 November-9 December, Sunday dinner and Monday
Rest – *(number of covers limited, pre-book)* Menu € 30/110 – Carte € 78/138
◆ A creative chef with an artist's soul owns this contemporary chalet. He painted and sculpted the pieces decorating the refined dining room. Terrace with a view of the mountains.

PLAZAC – 24 Dordogne – 329 H5 – pop. 686 – alt. 110 m – ✉ 24580 4 D1

Paris 530 – Bordeaux 170 – Périgueux 38 – Brive-la-Gaillarde 60 – Sarlat-la-Canéda 35

Béchanou

Béchanou, 4 km north by D 6 and secondary road – ✆ 05 53 50 39 52 – info@bechanou.com
5 rm – €70 €80, – **Table d'hôte** – Menu € 25 bi
◆ An old stone manor at the end of a steep path, offering peace and a beautiful view of the valley. Sober rooms in accordance with the spirit of the house. Swimming pool. Inspired homemade cooking, served either in the rustic dining room or on the terrace.

PLÉLO – 22 Côtes-d'Armor – 309 E3 – pop. 2 631 – alt. 110 m – ✉ 22170 10 C1

Paris 470 – Lannion 54 – Rennes 118 – Saint-Brieuc 22

Au Char à Bancs with rm

rm, VISA

1 km north on D 84 – ✆ 02 96 74 13 63 – charabanc@wanadoo.fr – Fax 02 96 74 13 03 – Closed January
5 rm – €59 €66 – **Rest** – *(closed weekdays off season and Tuesday July-August)* Carte € 15/25
◆ A friendly and welcoming auberge which serves dishes prepared using the farm's own produce (including hearty soups cooked over an open fire) at the wooden dining table. Cosy rooms with exposed beams and pretty, retro-style bathrooms.

PLÉNEUF-VAL-ANDRÉ – 22 Côtes-d'Armor – 309 G3 – pop. 3 680 – alt. 52 m – Casino : the Rotonde at Val-André – ✉ 22370 10 C1

Paris 446 – Dinan 43 – Erquy 9 – Lamballe 16 – St-Brieuc 28 – St-Cast 30 – St-Malo 51

Office de tourisme, 1, cours Winston Churchill ✆ 02 96 72 20 55, Fax 02 96 63 00 34

de Pleneuf-Val-André Rue de la plage des Vallées, East: 1 km by D 515, ✆ 02 96 63 01 12.

in Val-André 2 km West – ✉ **22370 Pléneuf-Val-André** Brittany

Pointe de Pléneuf★ North 15 mn - Tour of the Pointe de Pléneuf ≤★★ North 30 mn.

Georges without rest

VISA AE

131 r. Clemenceau – ✆ 02 96 72 23 70 – hotel-georges@g-partouche.fr – Fax 02 96 72 23 72 – Open February-mid November
24 rm – €60,50/71 €77/102, €9
◆ This hotel in the heart of the seaside resort has been entirely renovated in a chic contemporary spirit: dark woodwork, cream tones and modern furniture.

Grand Hôtel du Val André

rm, rest, VISA AE

80 r. Amiral Charner – ✆ 02 96 72 20 56 – accueil@grand-hotel-val-andre.fr – Fax 02 96 63 00 24 – Closed 2 January-5 February
39 rm – €70/81 €84/104, €9,50 – ½ P € 89/101
Rest – *(closed Tuesday lunch, Sunday dinner and Monday)*
Menu (€ 23), € 29 (weekdays)/50 – Carte € 40/63
◆ A hotel built in 1895 on the sea front. The rooms are gradually being renovated and are decorated with bright, glowing fabrics. The rooms at the front have a sea view. Carefully-prepared up-to-date cuisine, highlighting fish dishes, to be enjoyed in a dining room with a panoramic view.

Au Biniou VISA MC

121 r. Clemenceau – ☎ 02 96 72 24 35 – Fax 02 96 63 03 23 – Closed February, Tuesday dinner and Wednesday except July-August

Rest – Menu € 25/32 – Carte € 40/49

◆ Modern façade, fine sea-themed interior with wood panelling and light blue fabrics. Creative, regional-style cuisine. Breton bagpipes par excellence!

LE PLESSIS-PICARD – **77 Seine-et-Marne** – **312** E4 – **see Paris, Area (Sénart)**

PLESTIN-LES-GRÈVES – **22 Côtes-d'Armor** – **309** A3 – **pop. 3 415** – **alt. 45 m** – ✉ **22310** **Brittany** 9 **B1**

Paris 528 – Brest 79 – Guingamp 46 – Lannion 18 – Morlaix 24 – St-Brieuc 77

Syndicat d'initiative, place de la Mairie ☎ 02 96 35 61 93, Fax 02 96 54 12 54

Lieue de Grève★ - Corniche de l'Armorique (cliff road) ★ North: 2 km.

Les Panoramas without rest P VISA MC

rte Corniche Nord: 5.5 km via D 42 – ☎ 02 96 35 63 76 – hotel.les.panoramas@wanadoo.fr – Fax 02 96 35 09 10 – Closed 2 January-15 March

13 rm – †€ 40/45 ††€ 51/58, ☕ € 6

◆ A large renovated building with functional rooms; a view of the bay from the rooms at the front. St-Efflam's beach and coastal pathways nearby.

PLEUDIHEN-SUR-RANCE – **22 Côtes-d'Armor** – **309** K3 – **pop. 2 516** – **alt. 62 m** – ✉ **22690** 10 **D2**

Paris 395 – Rennes 59 – Saint-Brieuc 71 – Saint-Malo 22 – Granville 86

Manoir de St-Meleuc without rest P VISA MC

St-Meleuc – ☎ 02 96 83 34 26 – manoir_de_saint_meleuc@yahoo.fr

4 rm ☕ – †€ 95/120 ††€ 130/205

◆ Carefully renovated small 15C manor, in a 2.5 ha park. Antique styled guestrooms and breakfast served in a vast dining room with bare stones and beams.

PLÉVEN – **22 Côtes-d'Armor** – **309** I4 – **pop. 565** – **alt. 80 m** – ✉ **22130** 10 **C2**

Paris 431 – Dinan 24 – Dinard 28 – St-Brieuc 38 – St-Malo 34

Ruins of the château de la Hunaudaie★ Southwest: 4 km, **Brittany**

Manoir de Vaumadeuc without rest P VISA MC AE

– ☎ 02 96 84 46 17 – manoir@vaumadeuc.com – Fax 02 96 84 40 16 – Open from Easter to 1st November

13 rm – †€ 80/175 ††€ 180/225, ☕ € 12

◆ A 15C manor nestling in a park. Wood panelling, fireplace and period furniture are part of the characterful decor. The second floor rooms are cosy and have sloping ceilings.

PLEYBER-CHRIST – **29 Finistère** – **308** H3 – **pop. 2 790** – **alt. 131 m** – ✉ **29410** **Brittany** 9 **B1**

Paris 548 – Brest 55 – Châteaulin 47 – Morlaix 12 – Quimper 67 – St-Pol-de-Léon 26

De la Gare rm, P VISA MC AE

2 r. Parmentier – ☎ 02 98 78 43 76 – hotelgare@wanadoo.fr – Fax 02 98 78 49 78 – Closed 22 December-14 January and Sunday except July-August

8 rm – †€ 49/52 ††€ 51/55, ☕ € 7 – ½ P € 49/51 – **Rest** – *(closed Saturday lunch and Sunday)* Menu € 13,50 (weekday lunch), € 21/37 – Carte € 20/39

◆ Practical family hotel opposite the station. Functional rooms, which are not spacious but are very well kept, and pleasant little lounge overlooking a garden. Very simple restaurant, serving generous traditional cuisine at a reasonable price.

PLOBSHEIM – **67 Bas-Rhin** – **315** K6 – **see Strasbourg**

PLOEMEUR – 56 Morbihan – 308 K8 – pop. 18 304 – alt. 45 m – ✉ 56270 — 9 B2

Paris 509 – Concarneau 51 – Lorient 6 – Quimper 68 – Vannes 65

Office de tourisme, 25, place de l'Église ✆ 02 97 85 27 88

de Ploemeur-Océan Saint Jude Kerham, West: 8 km by D 162, ✆ 02 97 32 81 82.

in Lomener 4 km South by D 163 – ✉ 56270 Ploemeur

Le Vivier — île de Groix, VISA AE

9 r. de Bergervir – ✆ 02 97 82 99 60 – e-mail.info@levivier-lomener.com – Fax 02 97 82 88 89 – Closed 19 December-5 January, Sunday dinner 23 March-15 September

14 rm – €75 €85, €9 – ½ P €90/98 – **Rest** – *(closed Sunday dinner except July-August)* Menu €26 (weekdays)/48 – Carte €45/72

◆ This hotel, anchored to a rock is dedicated to Neptune. Find a superb view of the sea and the Isle of Groix from modern, welcoming rooms, two of which have a terrace. A restaurant that all but bathes its toes in the water – small wonder seafood is its speciality!

PLOËRMEL – 56 Morbihan – 308 Q7 – pop. 7 525 – alt. 93 m – ✉ 56800 — 10 C2

Paris 417 – Lorient 88 – Loudéac 47 – Rennes 68 – Vannes 46

Office de tourisme, 5, rue du Val ✆ 02 97 74 02 70, Fax 02 97 73 31 82

du Lac-au-Duc Le Clos Hazel, North: 2 km by D 8, ✆ 02 97 73 64 64.

Le Roi Arthur — rm, rest, VISA AE

at Duc lake: 1.5 km by D 8 – ✆ 02 97 73 64 64 – info@hotelroiarthur.com – Fax 02 97 73 64 50 – Closed February holidays

46 rm – €88/93 €102/124, €14 – ½ P €93/138

Rest – Menu €21 (weekday lunch), €32/51 – Carte €45/57

◆ This hotel stands in a park with a lake and golf course. Opt for one of the more comfortable, recently refurbished guestrooms with their new contemporary decor. Take a seat at a round table to enjoy up-to-date dishes, as a tribute to the legend.

PLOGOFF – 29 Finistère – 308 D6 – pop. 1 563 – alt. 70 m – ✉ 29770 — 9 A2

Paris 610 – Audierne 11 – Douarnenez 32 – Pont-l'Abbé 43 – Quimper 48

Ker-Moor — VISA AE

2.5 km Audierne road – ✆ 02 98 70 62 06 – kermoor.h.rest@wanadoo.fr – Fax 02 98 70 32 69 – Closed 7 January-12 February

16 rm – €50 €75/85, €8,50 – ½ P €60/75 – **Rest** – *(closed Sunday dinner and Monday off season)* Menu €19/40 – Carte €22/43

◆ Only the road separates this neo-Breton house from the sea. The furniture and view vary according to the room: some have terraces overlooking the waves. Try the house speciality, lobster cooked in cider, while looking out over Audierne Bay.

PLOMBIÈRES-LES-BAINS – 88 Vosges – 314 G5 – pop. 1 906 – alt. 429 m – Spa : mid March-mid Nov. – Casino – ✉ 88370 Alsace-Lorraine — 27 C3

Paris 378 – Belfort 79 – Épinal 38 – Gérardmer 43 – Vesoul 54 – Vittel 61

Office de tourisme, 1, place Maurice Janot ✆ 03 29 66 01 30, Fax 03 29 66 01 94

La Feuillée Nouvelle ★ 5 km by ② - Semousse Valley ★.

Le Prestige Impérial — rm, VISA

av. des Etats-Unis – ✆ 03 29 30 07 07 – residences.napoleon@plombieres-les-bains.com – Fax 03 29 30 07 33 — a

80 rm – €57/72 €72/102, €14 – 2 suites – ½ P €70/85

Rest – Menu €25/46 – Carte €26/40

◆ A light, glass roofed lobby leads into this fully refurbished Second Empire hotel, directly linked to the thermal spas of the town. Art Deco style rooms. This restaurant has kept its magnificent period setting and offers modern food.

PLOMEUR – 29 Finistère – **308** F7 – **pop. 3 203** – **alt. 33 m** – ✉ **29120** Brittany 9 **A2**

Paris 579 – Douarnenez 39 – Pont-l'Abbé 6 – Quimper 26

Office de tourisme, 1, place de l'Église ✆ 02 98 82 09 05

La Ferme du Relais Bigouden without rest VISA MC

à Pendreff, Guilvinec road: 2.5 km – ✆ 02 98 58 01 32 – Fax 02 98 82 09 62 – Closed in Feb. and week ends from Nov. to Mar.

16 rm – €52 €52/55, €7,50

◆ An old farmhouse in the Bigouden region with discreet, comfortable rooms all overlooking the garden. The breakfast room has its original charm.

PLOMODIERN – 29 Finistère – **308** F5 – **pop. 2 076** – **alt. 60 m** – ✉ **29550** 9 **A2**

Paris 559 – Brest 60 – Châteaulin 12 – Crozon 25 – Douarnenez 18 – Quimper 28

Syndicat d'initiative, place de l'Église ✆ 02 98 81 27 37, Fax 02 98 81 59 91

Altar-pieces★ of Ste-Marie-du-Ménez-Hom chapel North: 3.5 km - Framework★ of St-Côme chapel Northwest: 4.5 km.

Ménez-Hom ✻★★★ North: 7 km by D 47, Brittany

Pors-Morvan VISA MC

3 km eastward by secondary road – ✆ 02 98 81 53 23 – hotel-porsmorvan@wanadoo.fr – Fax 02 98 81 28 61 – Open April-September, autumn half-term holidays and Christmas

12 rm – €50 €50, €6 – **Rest** – crêperie Carte approx. €15

◆ Nature lovers will appreciate this 1830 farmhouse. The outbuildings house small rooms overlooking the quiet countryside. Garden and pond. A crêperie in an old timber-framed barn with a rustic decor and attractive fireplace.

Auberge des Glazicks (Olivier Bellin) VISA MC

7 r. de la Plage – ✆ 02 98 81 52 32 – olivier.bellin@hotmail.fr – Fax 02 98 81 57 18 – Closed 17-31 March, 15 October-30 November, Monday and Tuesday

Rest – Menu €48/150 – Carte €84/120

Spec. Homard étuvé, frite XL, condiment tomate-chorizo. Râble de lapin rôti, scampi sauté, riz pilaf rouge minute. Oeuf végétal, vinaigrette citron vert.

◆ This former blacksmith's has a dramatic view over Douarnenez bay. Inventive cuisine served in a dining room where blue predominates.

PLOUBALAY – 22 Côtes-d'Armor – **309** J3 – **pop. 2 385** – **alt. 32 m** – ✉ **22650** Brittany 10 **C1**

Paris 412 – Dinan 18 – Dol-de-Bretagne 35 – Lamballe 36 – St-Brieuc 56 – St-Malo 15

Water tower ✻★★: 1 km Northeast.

De la Gare VISA MC

4 r. Ormelets – ✆ 02 96 27 25 16 – Fax 02 96 82 63 22 – Closed 23-29 June, 6-12 October, 19-31 January, Monday dinner Tuesday dinner from September to June, Monday lunch and Tuesday lunch in July-August and Wednesday

Rest – Menu €24/52 – Carte €36/51

◆ Two dining rooms; one rustic-style and the other overlooking a small garden, give pride of place to up-to-date Breton land and sea produce. Pleasant welcome and service.

PLOUBAZLANEC – 22 Côtes-d'Armor – **309** D2 – **see Paimpol**

PLOUER-SUR-RANCE – 22 Côtes-d'Armor – **309** J3 – **pop. 2 723** – **alt. 62 m** – ✉ **22490** Brittany 10 **D2**

Paris 397 – Dinan 13 – Dol-de-Bretagne 20 – Lamballe 53 – St-Brieuc 70 – St-Malo 23

Manoir de Rigourdaine without rest VISA MC AE

3 km on Langrolay road and secondary road – ✆ 02 96 86 89 96 – hotel.rigourdaine@wanadoo.fr – Fax 02 96 86 92 46 – Open March-beg. November

19 rm – €62/76 €62/82, €7,50

◆ A well-restored old farmhouse overlooking the Rance estuary whose ancestral beams, large open fireplace and country furniture give the establishment particular character. Very peaceful.

PLOUGASTEL-DAOULAS – 29 Finistère – 308 E4 – pop. 12 248 – alt. 113 m – ✉ 29470 Brittany 9 A2

Paris 596 – Brest 12 – Morlaix 60 – Quimper 64

Office de tourisme, 4 bis, place du Calvaire ✆ 02 98 40 34 98, Fax 02 98 40 68 85

Calvary★★ - Site★ of St-Jean chapel Northeast: 5 km - Kernisi ☀★ Southwest: 4.5 km.

Pointe de Kerdéniel ☀★★ Southwest: 8.5 km then 15 mn.

Le Chevalier de l'Auberlac'h

5 r. Mathurin Thomas – ✆ 02 98 40 54 56 – chevalierauberlach@voila.fr – Fax 02 98 40 65 16 – Closed Monday except lunch July-August and Sunday dinner

Rest – Menu € 16 (weekday lunch), € 22 € bi/38 – Carte € 28/44

◆ Stained glass, wooden beams, an open fireplace, wrought-iron chandelier and armour all combine to create a medieval ambience in this restaurant. Pleasant summer terrace in a small, enclosed garden.

PLOUGONVEN – 29 Finistère – 308 I3 – pop. 3 051 – alt. 176 m – ✉ 29640 Brittany 9 B1

Paris 535 – Lannion 38 – Morlaix 12 – Rennes 183

La Grange de Coatélan

Coatélan, 4 km west on the D 109 – ✆ 02 98 72 60 16 – la-grange-de-coatelan@wanadoo.fr – Fax 02 98 72 60 16 – Closed Christmas holidays

5 rm – †€ 42 ††€ 70 – **Table d'hôte** – *(pre-book)* Menu € 22

◆ This very peaceful 16C Breton farmhouse lies in the middle of the countryside. The personalised bedrooms are located in the outbuildings. Restaurant offering local cuisine (single menu) in the rustic setting of an old barn.

PLOUGOUMELEN – 56 Morbihan – 308 N9 – pop. 1 762 – alt. 27 m – ✉ 56400 9 A3

Paris 475 – Vannes 14 – Auray 10 – Lorient 49

Crêperie de Keroyal

3 imp. Keroyal, 1 km west by secondary road – ✆ 02 97 24 03 81 – creperie-keroyal@wanadoo.fr – Fax 02 97 24 03 81 – Closed 10 March-3 April, 12 November-18 December, Tuesday lunch and Monday off season

Rest – Menu € 13 bi/20 bi – Carte approx. € 20

◆ Crêperie in an old cottage. Here you can enjoy sweet and savoury pancakes mainly made with organic produce. Non-smoking area with a view of le Sal. Children's play area.

PLOUGRESCANT – 22 Côtes-d'Armor – 309 C1 – pop. 1 402 – alt. 53 m – ✉ 22820 Brittany 9 B1

Paris 514 – Guingamp 38 – Lannion 23 – Rennes 162

Manoir de Kergrec'h without rest

– ✆ 02 96 92 59 13 – kergrec.h@wanadoo.fr – Fax 02 96 92 51 27

8 rm – †€ 100 ††€ 110

◆ Former Episcopal manor house (17C) set in a large park that stretches down to the seashore. Stylish lounge, rooms with family furniture and well-prepared breakfast in a pleasant setting.

PLOUHARNEL – 56 Morbihan – 308 M9 – pop. 1 700 – alt. 21 m – ✉ 56340 Brittany 9 B3

Paris 492 – Rennes 141 – Vannes 32 – Lorient 50 – Lanester 44

Office de tourisme, rond-point de l'Océan ✆ 02 97 52 32 93

Carnac Lodge without rest

Kerhueno – ✆ 02 97 58 30 30 – contact@carnaclodge.com – Fax 02 97 58 31 33 – Closed 3 January-10 February

20 rm – †€ 65/110 ††€ 65/145, € 9

◆ Between Carnac and Plouharnel, this hotel, set in a quiet garden, offers rooms whose decoration features a clever blend of 1980s furnishings with modern details.

PLOUIDER – **29 Finistère** – **308** F3 – **pop. 1 751** – **alt. 74 m** – ✉ **29260** 9 **A1**

Paris 582 – Brest 36 – Landerneau 21 – Morlaix 46 – St Pol de Léon 28

La Butte rm, **VISA** **AE**

10 r. de la Mer – ☎ 02 98 25 40 54 – info@labutte.fr – Fax 02 98 25 44 17 – Closed 20 January-14 February

24 rm – †€ 60/104 ††€ 65/108, ☕ € 10 – ½ P € 68/112 – **Rest** – *(closed Sunday evening and Monday)* Menu € 23/65 – Carte € 29/97

◆ This modern building houses spacious, functional and well-kept rooms. Those at the rear overlook a pleasant garden and command a view of the bay of Goulven. The traditional cuisine does full justice to the region's wealth of seafood and country produce.

PLOUIGNEAU – **29 Finistère** – **308** I3 – **pop. 4 138** – **alt. 156 m** – ✉ **29610** 9 **B1**

Paris 530 – Rennes 177 – Quimper 96 – Lannion 32 – Morlaix 14

Manoir de Lanleya without rest

4 km north along the D 64 and secondary road – ☎ 02 98 79 94 15 – manoir.lanleya@wanadoo.fr – Fax 02 98 79 94 15

5 rm ☕ – †€ 66 ††€ 71

◆ This very well-restored 16C manor house (non-smoking) has pretty, antique-furnished rooms, flower-filled courtyard and wonderful riverside garden. Charming welcome.

PLOUMANACH – **22 Côtes-d'Armor** – **309** B2 – **see Perros-Guirec**

LE POËT-LAVAL – **26 Drôme** – **332** D6 – **see Dieulefit**

LE POINÇONNET – **36 Indre** – **323** G6 – **see Châteauroux**

POINCY – **77 Seine-et-Marne** – **312** G2 – **see Meaux**

POINTE DE L'ARCOUEST – **22 Côtes-d'Armor** – **309** D2 – **see Paimpol**

POINTE DE MOUSTERLIN – **29 Finistère** – **308** G7 – **see Fouesnant**

POINTE DE ST-MATHIEU – **29 Finistère** – **308** C5 – **see le Conquet**

POINTE DU GROUIN – **35 Ille-et-Vilaine** – **309** K2 – **see Cancale**

POINTE-DU-RAZ ★★★ – **29 Finistère** – **308** C6 – ✉ **29770 Plogoff**
Brittany 9 **A2**

Paris 614 – Douarnenez 37 – Pont-l'Abbé 48 – Quimper 53

✻★★.

in La Baie des Trépassés by D 784 and secondary road: 3.5 km – ✉ Cleden Cap Sizun

De La Baie des Trépassés rest, **VISA**

– ☎ 02 98 70 61 34 – hoteldelabaie@aol.com – Fax 02 98 70 35 20 – Closed 15 November-15 February

27 rm – †€ 37/72 ††€ 37/72, ☕ € 10 – ½ P € 58/75 – **Rest** – *(closed Monday except school holidays)* Menu € 23/58

◆ A location popular with tourists in the daytime but quiet in the evening. Small partially refurbished rooms; choose one with a sea view. The tightly packed tables of the restaurant have views of the Raz point. Traditional cooking inspired by the sea.

POINT-SUBLIME – 04 Alpes-de-Haute-Provence – 334 G10 – ✉ 04120 ROUGON ▮ French Alps 41 C2

▶ Paris 803 – Castellane 18 – Digne-les-Bains 71 – Draguignan 53 – Manosque 76

◉ ⋞★★★ on Grand Canyon du Verdon 15 mn - Couloir Samson★★ South: 1,5 km - Rougon ⋞★ North: 2,5 km - Clue de Carejuan★ East: 4 km.

◙ Viewpoints Southwest: of Escalès★★★ 9 km, Trescaïre★★ 8 km, Tilleul★★ 10 km, Glacières★★ 11 km, Imbut★★ 13 km.

Auberge du Point Sublime with rm

– ✆ 04 92 83 60 35 – point.sublime@wanadoo.fr – Fax 04 92 83 74 31 – Open Easter-mid October

13 rm – †€ 54 ††€ 58, ☕ € 8 – ½ P € 58 – **Rest** – *(closed Thursday lunch except 14 July-15 August and Wednesday)* Menu (€ 16), € 22/30 – Carte € 30/50

♦ A pleasant family-run inn near a vantage point, where meals (regional cuisine) are served in a pretty rustic setting or on the shaded terrace. Simple rooms.

POISSON – 71 Saône-et-Loire – 320 E11 – see Paray-le-Monial

We try to be as accurate as possible when giving room rates.
But prices are open to change,
so please check rates when booking.

POISSY – 78 Yvelines – 311 I2 – 106 17 – 101 12 – see Paris, Area

POITIERS 🅿 – 86 Vienne – 322 H5 – pop. 83 448 – Built-up area 119 371 – alt. 116 m – ✉ 86000 ▮ Atlantic Coast 39 C1

▶ Paris 335 – Angers 134 – Limoges 126 – Nantes 215 – Niort 76 – Tours 102

✈ Poitiers-Biard-Futuroscope: ✆ 05 49 30 04 40 AV.

ℹ Office de tourisme, 45, place Charles-de-Gaulle ✆ 05 49 41 21 24, Fax 05 49 88 65 84

18 de Poitiers Mignaloux-Beauvoir 635 route de Beauvoir, by Lussac-les-Châteaux road: 8 km, ✆ 05 49 55 10 50 ;

27 du Haut-Poitou Saint-Cyr Parc des Loisirs de Saint Cyr, by Châtellerault road: 22 km, ✆ 05 49 62 53 62.

◉ N.-D.-la-Grande church ★★: front★★★ - St-Hilaire-le-Grand church ★★ - St-Pierre cathedral ★ - Ste-Radegonde church ★ **D** - St-Jean baptistry ★ - Great hall★ of the Palais de Justice (law courts) **J** - Boulevard Coligny ⋞★ - Musée Ste-Croix★★ - Statue of N-D-des-Dunes: ⋞★.

◙ Futuroscope Park ★★★: 12 km by ①.

Plans on following pages

Le Grand Hôtel without rest

28 r. Carnot – ✆ *05 49 60 90 60* – *grandhotelpoitiers@wanadoo.fr* – *Fax 05 49 62 81 89* CZ **k**

42 rm – †€ 67/70 ††€ 77/85, ☕ € 13 – 5 suites

♦ Centrally located but with a peaceful courtyard, the hotel is decorated in a warm Art Deco style. Comfortable rooms and large terrace where breakfast is served in summer.

De l'Europe without rest

39 r. Carnot – ✆ *05 49 88 12 00* – *reservations@hotel-europe-poitiers.com* – *Fax 05 49 88 97 30* – *Closed 19 December-2 January* CZ **n**

88 rm – †€ 52/83 ††€ 58/87, ☕ € 7

♦ Three buildings (the oldest dating from 1810) arranged around an interior courtyard, located close to the pedestrianised area. The rooms are decorated in various styles (contemporary, Louis-Philippe, Oriental etc).

POITIERS

Aérospatiale (R. de l') . . . . . . **AV** 3
Allende (R. Salvador) . . . . . . **BX** 7
Blaiserie (R. de la) . . . . **AV** 9
Ceuille-Mirebalaise (R.) . . . . **AV** 19
Coligny (Bd) . . . . **BX** 23
Demi-Lune (Carr. de la) . . . . **AV** 27
Fg-Ceuille-Mirebalaise (R. du) . . . . **AV** 29
Fg-du-Pont-Neuf (R. du) . . . . **BX** 30
Fg-St-Cyprien (R. du) . . . . . . **AX** 31
Fief-de-Grimoire (R.) . . . . . . **AX** 33
Gibauderie (R. de la) . . . . . . **BX** 39
Guynemer (R.) . . . . **AX** 43
Maillochon (R. de) . . . . **AX** 54
Miletrie (R. de la) . . . . **BX** 57
Montbernage (R. de) . . . . . . **BV** 58
Montmidi (R. de) . . . . **AX** 62
Pierre-Levée (R.) . . . . **BX** 69
Rataudes (R. des) . . . . **AX** 70
Schuman (Av. R.) . . . . **BV** 88
Vasles (Rte de) . . . . **AX** 93

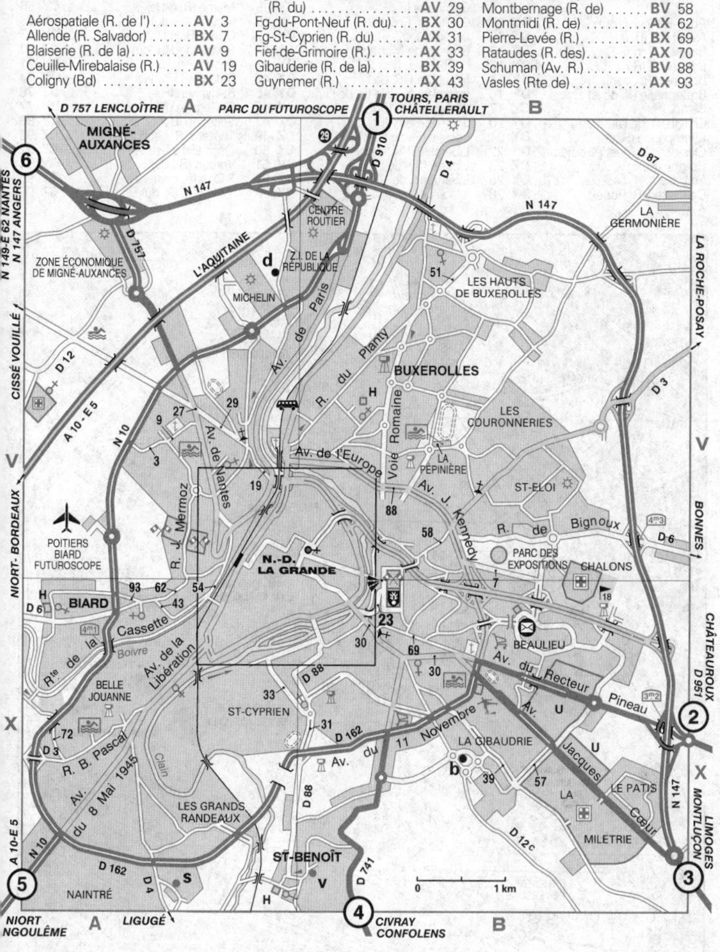

Come Inn

13 r. Albin Haller, (République 2 industrial estate) – ✆ 05 49 88 42 42 – come-inn@wanadoo.fr – Fax 05 49 88 42 44 – Closed 25 July-14 August AV **d**

44 rm – €44 €50, €6,50 – **Rest** – *(closed 25 July-24 August, Saturday and Sunday)* Menu €15

◆ A practical location on a business park near the Aquitaine motorway. Functional bedrooms decorated in restrained style. Restrained contemporary decor provides the backdrop for a traditional menu.

Gibautel without rest

2 r. de la Providence, Nouaillé road – ✆ 05 49 46 16 16 – hotel.gibautel@wanadoo.fr – Fax 05 49 46 85 97 BX **b**

36 rm – €42/48 €52/54, €7

◆ Simple rooms, breakfast buffets and reasonable prices: a useful place to stop in an area away from the centre where several treatment establishments are located.

POITIERS

Abbé-Frémont (Bd) . . . . DY 2
Alexandre (R. J.) . . . . DZ 4
Blossac (R. de) . . . . CZ 10
Boncenne (R.) . . . . CDY 12
Bouchet (R. Jean) . . . . DY 14
Bretonnerie (R. de la) . . . . DY 16
Carnot (R.) . . . . CZ 17
Chaine (R. de la) . . . . DY 20
Champagne (R. de) . . . . DY 21
Clos-des-Carmes (Pl. du) . . . . . DY 22
Coligny (Bd) . . . . DZ 23
Cordeliers (R. des) . . . . DY 25
Descartes (R. René) . . . . DY 28
Fg-du-Pont-Neuf . . . . DZ 30
Gabillet (R. H.) . . . . DY 34
Gambetta (R.) . . . . DY 35
Gaulle (Pl. Ch.-de) . . . . DY 36
Grand-Rue . . . . DY
Grignon-de-Montfort (R.) . . . . DY 40
Hôtel-Dieu (R. de l') . . . . DY 45
Intendant-le-Nain (R. de l') . . . . DY 46
Jeanne-d'Arc (Bd) . . . . DY 48
Jean-de-Berry (Pl.) . . . . DY 47
Leclerc (Pl. du Mar.) . . . . DZ 49
Libération (Av. de la) . . . . CZ 50
Liberté (Av. de la) . . . . BV 51
Liberté (Pl. de la) . . . . DY 52
Macé (R. Jean) . . . . DY 53
Marché-Notre-Dame (R. du) . . . . DYZ 55
Marne (R. de la) . . . . CY 56
Mouton (R. du) . . . . DY 63
Oudin (R. H.) . . . . DY 67
Puygarreau (R. du) . . . . DZ 70
Rat (R. Pierre) . . . . DY 71
Riffault (R.) . . . . DY 74
St-Cyprien (R.) . . . . DZ 76
St-Germain (R.) . . . . DY 77
Solférino (Bd) . . . . CY 89
Thezard (R. Léopold) . . . . CZ 90
Tison (Bd de) . . . . CZ 92
Verdun (Bd de) . . . . CY 94
3-Rois (R. des) . . . . DY 95
125e-R.-I. (R. du) . . . . CZ 97

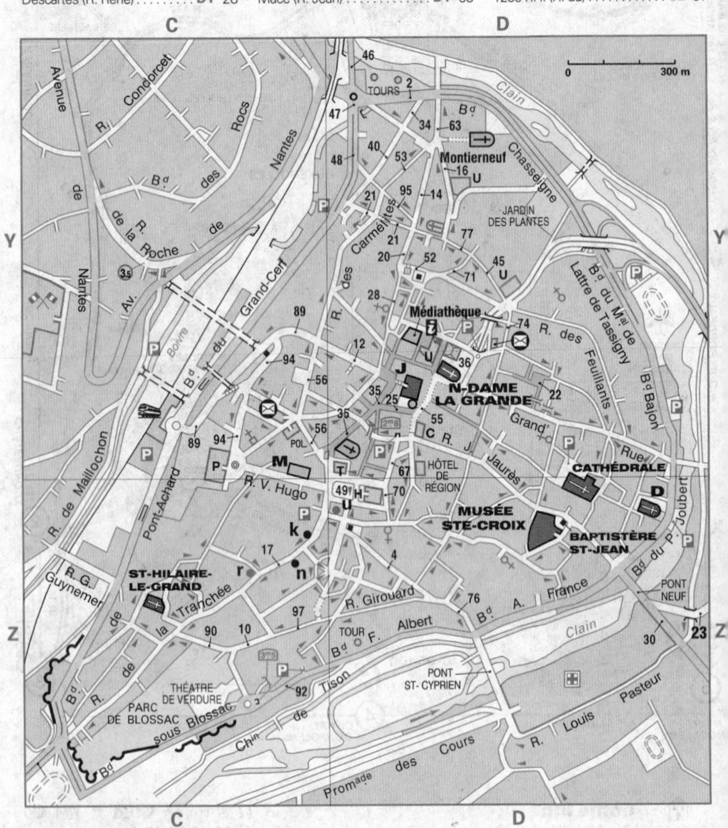

Maxime

4 r. St-Nicolas – ✆ 05 49 41 09 55 – maxime-86@tiscali.fr – Fax 05 49 41 09 55 – Closed 13 July-20 August, Saturday except dinner 1st November-28 January and Sunday

Rest – Menu (€ 16), € 21 (weekdays)/76 bi – Carte € 48/57 DZ **u**

◆ A short distance from the Musée de Chièvres, this colourful restaurant has a hushed atmosphere. Friendly staff and cuisine that is both neo-classical and contemporary.

Le Poitevin

76 r. Carnot – ✆ 05 49 88 35 04 – lepoitevin@poitiers.in – Fax 05 49 52 88 05 – Closed 7-20 April, 7-28 July, 22 December-5 January and Sunday dinner

Rest – Menu (€ 12), € 24/38 – Carte € 39/60 CZ **r**

◆ Restaurant in a shopping street, made up of three small dining rooms with rustic or modern decor. Traditional and regional cuisine.

in Chasseneuil-du-Poitou 9 km by ① – ✉ 86360 Chasseneuil-du-Poitou – pop. 3 845 – alt. 75 m

Office de tourisme, place du Centre ✆ 05 49 52 83 64, Fax 05 49 52 59 31

Château Clos de la Ribaudière rm, rest,

10 r. du Champ de Foire, in the village – ✆ 05 49 52 86 66 – ribaudiere@ribaudiere.com – Fax 05 49 52 86 32

41 rm – €82/125 €102/147, €14 – ½ P €92/100 – **Rest** – Menu €25 (weekday lunch), €30/55 – Carte €42/84

♦ An attractive 19C residence in its own park beside the Clain. Elegant and spacious rooms in the castle and more standard ones in the annexe. The delightful dining room-veranda and terrace overlook the garden with its pond. Modern cuisine.

Mercure Alisée rm,

D 910, 14 r. du Commerce – ✆ 05 49 52 90 41 – h0425@accor.com – Fax 05 49 52 51 72 – Closed 24 December-1st January, Saturday and Sunday from November to January

80 rm – €54/85 €58/99, €12,50

Rest ***Les 3 Garçons*** – *✆ 05 49 37 86 09 (closed Monday dinner, Saturday lunch and Sunday)* Carte €23/35

♦ The corridors, decorated so as to resemble a paved street, lead to large functional rooms, some of which look over the peaceful garden. Changing menus on the boards, friendly brasserie-style setting. Cosy lounge and fine library.

Futuroscope Park 12 km by ① – ✉ 86360 Chasseneuil-du-Poitou

Novotel Futuroscope rm,

Téléport 4 – ✆ 05 49 49 91 91 – contact@novotel-futuroscope.fr – Fax 05 49 49 91 90

128 rm – €95/105 €120/185, €12,50 – **Rest** – Menu (€17), €30 – Carte €25/47

♦ This elegant glass and steel building is in perfect harmony with the futuristic environment of the theme park. Modern functional rooms. The large restaurant overlooking the swimming pool and the piano bar have a decor reminiscent of the cinema.

Plaza Futuroscope rm,

av. du Futuroscope Téléport 1 – ✆ 05 49 49 07 07 – reservation@plaza-futuroscope.com – Fax 05 49 49 55 49

274 rm – €95/250 €105/250, €17 – ½ P €90/120

Rest ***Relais Plaza*** – Menu (€19), €26/32 – Carte €33/49

♦ Equally well-suited to business and tourist guests. A railway feel to the lobby. Comfortable rooms (VIP category is available) and a fitness centre. Traditional cuisine served in a restrained modern decor.

Mercure Aquatis Futuroscope rm,

av. Jean Monnet Téléport 3 ✉ 86962 – ✆ 05 49 49 55 00 – h2773@accor.com – Fax 05 49 49 55 01

140 rm – €64/81 €69/87, €12 – **Rest** – Menu €16 (lunch)/23 – Carte €18/24

♦ A minimalist silhouette contrasts with the strange architecture of Futuroscope. Practical rooms; those in the new wing are more spacious. A huge restaurant with columns, arcades and statues; traditional dishes and small menu featuring roast meats.

Ibis Futuroscope rm,

av. Thomas Edison – ✆ 05 49 49 90 00 – h1193@accor.com – Fax 05 49 49 90 09

140 rm – €50/64 €50/64, €8 – **Rest** – Menu (€13), €17 – Carte €25/33

♦ With its practical rooms, comfortable bar lounge and conference rooms, this Ibis hotel will appeal both to businessmen and to fans of the fourth dimension. In the restaurant there is a boat-style decor and buffet meals featuring seafood.

in Lavoux 15 km by ② and D 1 – pop. 1 008 – alt. 126 m – ✉ 86800

Logis du Château du Bois Dousset

– ✆ 05 49 44 20 26 – Fax 05 49 44 20 26

3 rm – €70/80 €70/80 – **Table d'hôte** – Menu €30 bi

♦ This 400ha family estate includes a château, magnificent formal garden and Louis XIII-style lodge. The latter houses comfortable ground-floor rooms and a luxurious suite. Restaurant serving produce from the vegetable garden and Poitou specialities.

Limoges road 10 km by ③, N 147 and secondary road – ✉ 86550 Mignaloux

Manoir de Beauvoir
635 rte de Beauvoir, at the golf course –
✆ 05 49 55 47 47 – resa-poitiers@monalisahotels.com – Fax 05 49 55 31 95
45 rm – †€ 99 ††€ 99, ☕ € 11 – 4 suites – ½ P € 83 – **Rest** – Menu (€ 17), € 23/37 – Carte € 31/53
◆ The rooms are in the 19C house; the apartments with kitchenettes are in the annexe. A 90ha park and an 18-hole golf course. The Manoir offers diners the choice between a wood-panelled dining room and the more British style in the clubhouse.

à St-Benoît 4 km south of map by D 88 – pop. 7 008 – alt. 77 m – ✉ 86280

Office de tourisme, 18, rue Paul Gauvin ✆ 05 49 88 42 12, Fax 05 49 56 08 82

Passions et Gourmandises (Richard Toix)
6 r. du Square – ✆ 05 49 61 03 99
– info@passionsetgourmandises.com
– Closed 3-17 August, 22-26 December, 2-18 January, Sunday dinner, Wednesday lunch and Monday BX **v**
Rest – Menu (€ 17), € 24/67 – Carte € 82/109
Spec. Gourmandise croustillante de langoustine, vinaigrette de bigorneaux. Tournedos de porc noir cuit en cocotte, légumes de saison. "Pour les fous du chocolat".
◆ Seductive contemporary cuisine in a dazzlingly bright, modern setting. Attractive terrace next to a stream.

Ligugé road 4 km South of map by D 4 – ✉ 86280 St-Benoît

L'Orée des Bois with rm
r. Naintré – ✆ 05 49 57 11 44 – oreedesbois@free.fr – Fax 05 49 43 21 40
– Closed Saturday lunch, Sunday dinner and Monday AX **s**
12 rm – †€ 46 ††€ 52, ☕ € 7,50 – ½ P € 57 – **Rest** – Menu € 17 (weekdays)/47 – Carte € 44/57
◆ A Virginia creeper-clad house at the heart of the Clain Valley. Two rustic-style dining rooms serving traditional cuisine. Renovated, sober and spotless rooms with rustic furniture.

Angoulême road 6 km by ⑤, Hauts-de-Croutelle exit – ✉ 86240 Croutelle

La Chênaie
Les Hauts de Croutelle, Lieu dit La Berlanderie, Rue du Lejat – ✆ 05 49 57 11 52
– restaurantlachenaie@wanadoo.fr – Fax 05 49 57 11 51
– Closed 22 July-6 August, February half-term holidays, Sunday dinner and Monday
Rest – Menu € 20/45 – Carte € 43/65
◆ An old, attractively restored farmhouse standing back from the N 10 road. The smart dining room overlooks a garden with ancient oak trees. Modern cuisine.

Niort road 7 km by ⑤ – ✉ 86240 Ligugé

Le Bois de la Marche
junction of N10 and D611 – ✆ 05 49 53 10 10
– boisdelamarche@wanadoo.fr – Fax 05 49 55 32 25
53 rm – †€ 55/95 ††€ 65/105, ☕ € 10 – ½ P € 63/78 – **Rest** – Menu € 19 (weekdays)/42 – Carte € 25/45
◆ A short drive from the Western world's oldest monastery (Ligugé), the hotel is a large, modern building in a park planted with trees. Rooms are being gradually refurbished. Most of them are furnished in Louis XV style. Traditional and Périgord dishes served on the huge terrace, weather permitting.

in Périgny 17 km by ⑥, N 149 and secondary road – ✉ 86190 Vouillé

Château de Périgny
40 r. des Coteaux – ✆ 05 49 51 80 43 – info@chateau-perigny.com
– Fax 05 49 51 90 09
42 rm – †€ 74/126 ††€ 84/160, ☕ € 16 – 1 suite – ½ P € 91
Rest – Menu (€ 24), € 30/58 – Carte € 44/81
◆ A Renaissance château in a vast park. The pretty rooms have period furniture. Those in the outbuildings are more modern. Restaurant looking out over a delightful patio, where tables are set in summer. Modern recipes.

POLIGNY – 05 Hautes-Alpes – 334 E4 – pop. 230 – alt. 1 062 m – ✉ 05500 41 C1

Paris 658 – Gap 19 – Marseille 199 – Vizille 71

Le Chalet des Alpages

Les Forestons, 1.5 km to the west – ☎ 04 92 23 08 95 – lechaletdesalpages@gmail.com

5 rm – €70/100 €90/120 – ½ P €67/70 – **Table d'hôte** – Menu €22 bi

◆ This 6000 m² property has numerous assets: Alpine-style rooms, some with a balcony, fitness room, hot outdoor tub and clear view of the Noyer Pass, Féraud Barrier and Old Chaillol. Cuisine combining both local and Provençal flavours.

POLIGNY – 39 Jura – 321 E5 – pop. 4 511 – alt. 373 m – ✉ 39800

Burgundy-Jura 16 B3

Paris 397 – Besançon 57 – Dole 45 – Lons-le-Saunier 30 – Pontarlier 63

Office de tourisme, 20, place des Déportés ☎ 03 84 37 24 21, Fax 03 84 37 22 37

Collegiate church ★ - Culée de Vaux★ South: 2 km - Cirque de Ladoye ≤★★ South: 2 km.

in Monts de Vaux Southeast: 4,5 km by Genève road – ✉ 39800 Poligny

≤★.

Hostellerie des Monts de Vaux

rest, VISA AE

– ☎ *03 84 37 12 50 – mtsvaux@hostellerie.com – Fax 03 84 37 09 07 – Closed 27 October-28 December, Tuesday except dinner July-August and Wednesday lunch*

10 rm – €125 € 165/235, €14 – ½ P €160/180 – **Rest** – Menu €30/74 – Carte €50/74

◆ Sitting in parkland overlooking the "reculée de Vaux" (dead-end valley), this old farmhouse has elegant rooms which exude charm. Recently added business meeting facility. Classic and regional cuisine enhanced by a fine selection of regional vintages.

in Passenans Southwest: 11 km by D 1083 and D 57 – pop. 296 – alt. 320 m – ✉ 39230

Revermont

rm, VISA AE

– ☎ *03 84 44 61 02 – schmit-revermont@wanadoo.fr – Fax 03 84 44 64 83 – Closed 22 December-1st March*

28 rm – €64/70 €84/103, €11,50 – ½ P €73/85 – **Rest** – Menu (€16), €22/48 – Carte €27/63

◆ A 1970s building on a hillside overlooking the vineyards. Practical rooms; the best (with balcony or terrace) overlook the pool. A rustic dining room (beams, exposed stonework, fireplace) and updated Franche Comté cuisine.

POLLIAT – 01 Ain – 328 D3 – pop. 2 019 – alt. 260 m – ✉ 01310 44 B1

Paris 415 – Bourg-en-Bresse 12 – Lyon 74 – Mâcon 26 – Villefranche-sur-Saône 53

De la Place with rm

rest, VISA

51 pl. de la Mairie – ☎ 04 74 30 40 19 – Fax 04 74 30 42 34 – Closed 25 July-14 August, 2-13 January, Sunday dinner and Monday

7 rm – €43/49 €46/52, €7,50 – ½ P €49/52 – **Rest** – *(closed Thursday dinner except residents, Sunday dinner and Monday)* Menu €18/55 – Carte €28/46

◆ Bright colours and rustic or wrought iron furniture form the backdrop to tasty Bresse dishes served with a smile. Simple and well-kept rooms.

POLMINHAC – 15 Cantal – 330 D5 – pop. 1 156 – alt. 650 m – ✉ 15800 5 B3

Paris 553 – Aurillac 15 – Murat 34 – Vic-sur-Cère 5

Syndicat d'initiative, rue de la Gare ☎ 04 71 47 48 36, Fax 04 71 47 58 56

Au Bon Accueil

rest, VISA

– ☎ *04 71 47 40 21 – info@hotel-bon-accueil.com – Fax 04 71 47 40 13 – Closed 15 October-1st December, Sunday dinner and Monday except school holidays*

23 rm – €37/47 €42/54, €6 – ½ P €38/44 – **Rest** – Menu €10,50/25

◆ The architecture may be ordinary but the hotel deserves its name: smiles and friendliness are the bywords. Spruce, particularly practical rooms. The restaurant overlooks the Cère valley and its mountainous backdrop; regional food.

LA POMARÈDE – 11 Aude – 344 C2 – pop. 158 – alt. 304 m – ✉ 11400 22 A2

Paris 728 – Auterive 49 – Carcassonne 49 – Castres 38 – Gaillac 72 – Toulouse 57

Hostellerie du Château de la Pomarède (Gérald Garcia) with rm
– ✆ 04 68 60 49 69 rest, VISA AE
– *hostellerie-lapomarede@wanadoo.fr – Fax 04 68 60 49 71*
– *Closed 27 October-27 November*
7 rm – €85/95 €110/195, €15
Rest – *(closed Sunday dinner from December to April, Monday and Tuesday)*
Menu €19 (weekday lunch), €35/95 – Carte €69/91
Spec. Sole en carré de côtes aux passe-pierre, nage d'huître et caviar d'Aquitaine. Pigeonneau en deux cuissons. "Cube et sphère", chocolat pralin anisé. **Wines** Minervois, Corbières.

◆ Elegant dining room with exposed beams, panoramic terrace and spacious modern rooms in the outbuildings of an 11C Cathar château. Inventive cuisine and regional wine list.

POMMERIT-JAUDY – 22 Côtes-d'Armor – 309 C2 – pop. 1 152 – alt. 74 m – ✉ 22450 9 B1

Paris 510 – Rennes 157 – Saint-Brieuc 62 – Lannion 20 – Morlaix 73

Château de Kermezen without rest AE
2 km west on secondary road – ✆ 02 96 91 35 75 – micheldekermel@kermezen.com – Fax 02 96 91 35 75
5 rm – €80/95 €90/104

◆ Authentic family mansion set in vast wooded grounds. Tastefully decorated rooms and magnificent 15C and 16C Breton rustic furniture in the breakfast room.

POMMEUSE – 77 Seine-et-Marne – 312 H3 – see Coulommiers

POMMIERS – 69 Rhône – 327 H4 – pop. 1 804 – alt. 315 m – ✉ 69480 43 E1

Paris 442 – Lyon 32 – Villeurbanne 45 – Vénissieux 45 – Caluire-et-Cuire 36

Les Terrasses de Pommiers < Monts du Lyonnais, VISA
La Buisante – ✆ 04 74 65 05 27 – Fax 04 74 65 05 27
– Closed 20 October-4 November, 25 February-11 March, Monday except lunch March-August and Tuesday
Rest – Menu €19 bi, €26/39 – Carte €35/54

◆ Enjoy fine views of the Saône valley and the Monts du Lyonnais through the windows of the wood-floored, covered terrace, which comes into its own in summer. Modern seasonal menu.

PONS – 17 Charente-Maritime – 324 G6 – pop. 4 427 – alt. 39 m – ✉ 17800
Atlantic Coast 38 B3

Paris 493 – Blaye 64 – Bordeaux 97 – Cognac 24 – La Rochelle 99 – Royan 43 – Saintes 22

Syndicat d'initiative, place de la République ✆ 05 46 96 13 31, Fax 05 46 96 34 52

Keep★ of the former château - Hospice des Pèlerins★ Southwest by D 732 - Panelling★ of the château d'Usson 1 km by D 249.

De Bordeaux rm, VISA
1 av. Gambetta – ✆ 05 46 91 31 12 – info@hotel-de-bordeaux.com
– Fax 05 46 91 22 25 – Closed Christmas holidays, Saturday lunch and Sunday dinner October-March
16 rm – €50 €60, €10 – ½ P €53 – **Rest** – Menu €15/38

◆ In a street in the town centre, this hundred-year-old hotel has been renovated and has small, attractive rooms and an English-style bar. Opening onto a charming patio-terrace, the restaurant's decor is in pleasant harmony with the creative cuisine. Extensive choice of cognacs.

in Pérignac Northeast: 8 km by Cognac road – pop. 966 – alt. 41 m – ✉ 17800

XX **La Gourmandière** VISA

42 av. de Cognac – ✆ 05 46 96 36 01
– lagourmandiere.perignac@wanadoo.fr – Fax 05 46 95 50 71
– Closed 18 November-4 December, 20 January-5 February, Tuesday and Wednesday October-mid June except holidays and Sunday dinner mid June-September
Rest – Menu € 26/43 – Carte € 26/43
◆ A pretty village cottage redecorated by its young owners in a warm modern spirit. Inviting terrace overlooking the garden and up-to-date menu.

in Mosnac South: 11 km by Bordeaux road and D 134 – pop. 448 – alt. 23 m – ✉ 17240

Moulin du Val de Seugne rm, VISA

– ✆ 05 46 70 46 16 – moulin@valdeseugne.com
– Fax 05 46 70 48 14 – Closed 2 January-9 February
14 rm – †€ 99/159 ††€ 99/159, ☕ € 12 – ½ P € 80/110
Rest – Menu € 19 (weekday lunch), € 29/69
– Carte € 39/82
◆ Elegant hostelry on the banks of the River Seugne. Refined rooms, adorned with antique furniture and luxury bathrooms. Lounge opening onto the mill's machinery. Pleasant restaurant and terrace overlooking a river. Regional products on sale in the shop.

PONT (LAC) – 21 Côte-d'Or – **320** G5 – see Semur-en-Auxois

PONTAILLAC – 17 Charente-Maritime – **324** D6 – see Royan

PONT-A-MOUSSON – 54 Meurthe-et-Moselle – **307** H5 – pop. 14 592
– alt. 180 m – ✉ 54700 Alsace-Lorraine 26 **B2**

Paris 325 – Metz 31 – Nancy 30 – Toul 48 – Verdun 66

Office de tourisme, 52, place Duroc ✆ 03 83 81 06 90, Fax 03 83 82 45 84

Place Duroc★ - Former Prémontrés abbey ★.

X **Le Fourneau d'Alain** VISA

64 pl. Duroc, (1st floor) – ✆ 03 83 82 95 09 – Fax 03 83 82 95 09
– Closed 1st-7 May, 1st-15 August, Wednesday dinner, Sunday dinner and Monday
Rest – Menu € 26/51 – Carte € 28/44
◆ A discreetly contemporary restaurant on the main square, on the first floor of one of the 16C arcaded houses. Tables are well laid out and the service unpretentious.

PONTARLIER – 25 Doubs – **321** I5 – pop. 18 360 – alt. 838 m – ✉ 25300
Burgundy-Jura 17 **C2**

Paris 462 – Besançon 60 – Dole 88 – Lausanne 67 – Lons-le-Saunier 82

Office de tourisme, 14 bis, rue de la Gare ✆ 03 81 46 48 33, Fax 03 81 46 83 32

Pontarlier Les Étraches La Grange des Pauvres, East: 8 km by D 47, ✆ 03 81 39 14 44.

Portal★ of the former Annonciades chapel.

Grand Taureau ✻★★ by ②: 11 km.

Plan on next page

XX **L'Alchimie** VISA

1 av. Armée de l'Est – ✆ 03 81 46 65 89 – restau-lalchimie@wanadoo.fr
– Fax 03 81 39 08 75 – Closed 7-17 April, 14 July-4August, 2-8 January, Sunday dinner, Tuesday dinner and Wednesday B **e**
Rest – Menu € 20 (weekday lunch), € 37/50 – Carte € 49/55
◆ The alchemist chef prepares his inventive dishes by 'transmuting' local produce, spices and exotic flavours. Refurbished in a trendy style.

PONTARLIER

Arçon (Pl. d') .... A 2
Augustins (R. des) .... B 3
Bernardines (Pl. des) ...... AB 4
Capucins (R. des) .... A 7
Crétin (Pl.) .... B 8
Écorces (R. des) .... A 12
Gambetta (R.) .... B 13
Halle (R. de la) .... B 15
Industrie (R. de l') .... B 16
Latttre-de-Tassigny (Pl. Mar.-de) .... B 19
Mathez (R. Jules) .... B 26
Mirabeau (R.) .... B 27
Moulin Parnet (R. du) .... A 29
Pagnier (Pl. J.) .... B 30
République (R. de la) .... AB
Ste-Anne (R.) .... AB 35
St-Étienne (R. du Fg) .... B
St-Pierre (Pl.) .... A
Salengro (Pl. R.) .... A 36
Tissot (R.) .... AB 37
Vannolles (R. de) .... B 38
Vieux-Château (R. du) .... A 39
Villingen-Schwenningen (Pl. de) .... A 40

in Doubs by ④: 2 km – pop. 2 266 – alt. 813 m – ✉ 25300

Le Doubs Passage

11 Gde Rue, D 130 – ✆ 03 81 39 72 71
– ledoubspassage@wanadoo.fr
– Fax 03 81 39 72 71
– Closed 20 August-1st September, Sunday dinner, Wednesday dinner and Monday

Rest – Menu € 17/30 – Carte € 23/37

◆ A family inn on the banks of the Doubs. Well decorated dining room with parquet flooring, soft lighting and a profusion of plants and flowers. Traditional cuisine.

The red symbol?
This denotes the very essence of peace –
only the sound of birdsong first thing in the morning...

PONTAUBAULT – 50 Manche – 303 D8 – pop. 445 – alt. 25 m – ✉ 50220

32 **A3**

Paris 345 – Avranches 9 – Dol-de-Bretagne 35 – Fougères 38 – Rennes 78 – St-Malo 60

Les 13 Assiettes

north: 1 km on the D 43^E (former rte d'Avranches) – ✆ 02 33 89 03 03 – 13assiettes@wanadoo.fr – Fax 02 33 89 03 06

39 rm – €50/70 €60/80, ☕ €10 – ½ P €60/65

Rest – Menu €18 (weekdays)/64 – Carte €24/46

◆ The rooms in the bungalows have simple furnishings. Those in the main building are larger with the same level of comfort but more modern (a few family-sized rooms). Bright restaurant giving onto a garden terrace with pool and palm trees. Traditional dishes.

PONTAUBERT – 89 Yonne – 319 G7 – see Avallon

PONT-AUDEMER – 27 Eure – 304 D5 – pop. 8 981 – alt. 15 m – ✉ 27500

Normandy

32 **B3**

Paris 164 – Caen 74 – Évreux 68 – Le Havre 44 – Lisieux 36 – Rouen 52

Office de tourisme, place Maubert ✆ 02 32 41 08 21, Fax 02 32 57 11 12

Stained-glass windows★ of St-Ouen church.

Belle Isle sur Risle

112 rte de Rouen, via ② – ✆ 02 32 56 96 22 – hotelbelle-isle@wanadoo.fr – Fax 02 32 42 88 96 – Open 8 March-11 November

20 rm – €105/125 €110/247, ☕ €15 – ½ P €127/197

Rest – *(closed Monday lunch, Tuesday lunch and Wednesday lunch)* Menu €29 (weekday lunch), €39/63 – Carte €53/78

◆ Attractive ivy clad mansion built in 1856 on an islet of the Risle in a landscaped 2ha park (river fishing). The rooms, of various sizes, have pretty personal touches. This restaurant has a quiet terrace laid out amid trees over two centuries old.

PONT-AUDEMER

Canel (R. Alfred) 2
Carmélites (R. des) 3
Clemencin (R. Paul) 5
Cordeliers (R. des) 6
Delaquaize (R. S.) 7
Déportés (R. des) 8
Épée (R. de l') 9
Félix-Faure (Quai)
Ferry (R. Jules)
Gambetta (R.) 13
Gaulle (Pl. Général-de) 14
Gillain (Pl. Louis) 16
Goulley (Pl. J.)
Jean-Jaurès (R.) 18
Joffre (R. Mar.) 19
Kennedy (Pl.)
Leblanc (Quai R.) 20
Maquis-Surcouf (R.) 21
Maubert (Pl.) 22
Mitterrand (Quai François) 23
N.-D.-du-Pré (R.)
Pasteur (Bd)
Place-de-la-Ville (R.) 24
Pot-d'Étain (Pl. du) 25
Président-Coty (R. du) 26
Président-Pompidou (Av. du)
République (R. de la) 27
Sadi-Carnot (R.)
St-Ouen (Impasse) 29
Seule (R. de la) 30
Thiers (R.) 32
Verdun (Pl. de) 34
Victor-Hugo (Pl.) 35

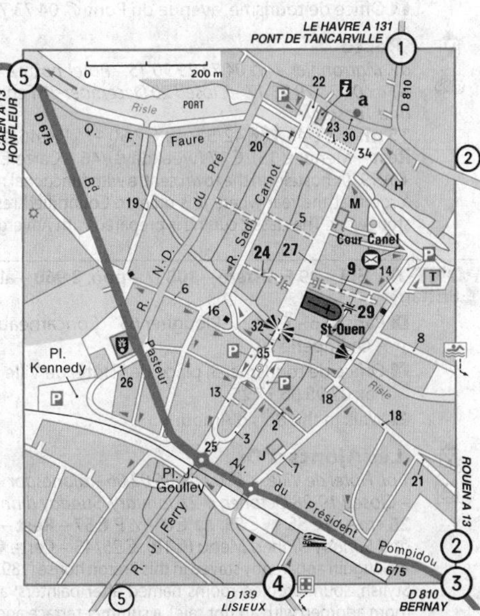

XX **Erawan**

4 r. Sëule – ✆ 02 32 41 12 03 – Closed August and Wednesday a

Rest – Menu € 20/37 – Carte € 25/44

◆ The menu is one hundred percent Thai and the setting seventy-five percent Norman: a surprising contrast and successful blend of cultures in this charming restaurant on the banks of the Risle.

Southeast by ② and D 39: 5 km – ✉ 27500 Pont-Audemer

XXX **Au Jardin d'Eden**

rte Condé-s-Risle – ✆ 02 32 57 01 52 – aujardindeden@wanadoo.fr – Fax 02 32 41 42 01 – Closed 12-30 January, Tuesday dinner October-February, Monday except July-August and Sunday dinner

Rest – Menu (€ 23 bi), € 28 (weekdays)/62 – Carte € 52/78

◆ This fine Norman house, converted into a restaurant, lies on an artificial peninsula in the middle of a big lake. Modern decor and traditional menu.

in Campigny by ③ and D 29: 6 km – pop. 803 – alt. 121 m – ✉ 27500

XXX **Le Petit Coq aux Champs** with rm

– ✆ 02 32 41 04 19 – le.petit.coq.aux.champs@wanadoo.fr – Fax 02 32 56 06 25 – Closed 17-24 November, January, Sunday dinner and Monday 1st November-31 March

12 rm – †€ 137 ††€ 157, ☕ € 12 – ½ P € 124/132

Rest – Menu (€ 29 bi), € 43 bi/68 – Carte € 39/86

◆ A warm welcome and pretty country-style decor at this Normandy cottage. Beautiful terrace giving onto a park with flowers. Classic cuisine and extensive wine list. Comfortable rooms.

PONTAULT-COMBAULT – 77 Seine-et-Marne – 312 E3 – 101 29 – see Paris, Area

PONTAUMUR – 63 Puy-de-Dôme – 326 D7 – pop. 769 – alt. 535 m – ✉ 63380

5 **B2**

Paris 398 – Aubusson 49 – Clermont-Ferrand 42 – Le Mont-Dore 49 – Montluçon 68

Office de tourisme, avenue du Pont ✆ 04 73 79 73 42, Fax 04 73 73 73 36

Poste

AC rest, VISA

av. Marronnier – ✆ 04 73 79 90 15 – hotel-poste2@wanadoo.fr – Fax 04 73 79 73 17 – Closed 20 December-1st February, Sunday dinner, Monday and Tuesday

15 rm – †€ 40 ††€ 42/52, ☕ € 7,50 – ½ P € 46/48

Rest – Menu (€ 15), € 17 (weekdays)/46 – Carte € 29/41

◆ A 1970s hostelry in the town centre with functional rooms of standard comfort. Choose a room at the rear where it is quieter. Countrified restaurant dominated by wood and stonework. The classic cuisine is prepared with Auvergne produce.

PONT-AVEN – 29 Finistère – 308 I7 – pop. 2 960 – alt. 18 m – ✉ 29930

Brittany

9 **B2**

Paris 536 – Carhaix-Plouguer 65 – Concarneau 15 – Quimper 36 – Quimperlé 20

Office de tourisme, 5, place de l'Hôtel de Ville ✆ 02 98 06 04 70, Fax 02 98 06 17 25

Walk in the Bois d'Amour★.

Les Ajoncs d'Or

VISA

1 pl. Hôtel de Ville – ✆ 02 98 06 02 06 – ajoncsdor@aol.com – Fax 02 98 06 18 91 – Closed 19-28 October, 4-27 January, Sunday dinner and Monday October-May

20 rm – †€ 55 ††€ 55, ☕ € 8 – ½ P € 57 – **Rest** – *(closed Monday October-May and Sunday dinner)* Menu (€ 18), € 25/45 – Carte € 27/50

◆ Gauguin apparently stayed in this Breton house (1892) during his last stay in Pont-Aven. Stylish, soundproofed rooms named after painters; a charming welcome. Light dining room adorned with art (for sale), a summer terrace and traditional cuisine.

Moulin de Rosmadec (Frédéric Sebilleau) with rm
near the bridge, town centre – 02 98 06 00 22
– moulinderosmadec@wanadoo.fr – Fax 02 98 06 18 00
– Closed 8-26 October and February holidays
4 rm – €90 €90, €10 – 1 suite
Rest – *(closed Sun. evening out of season and Wed.)* Menu €35/76
– Carte €64/76
Spec. Langoustines croquantes, risotto crémeux tiède. Homard grillé "Rosmadec". Crêpes soufflées au citron.
◆ Copperware, ceramics and Breton furnishings adorn one of the rooms of this astonishing 15C stone and wood mill; the veranda overlooks the garden and the Aven. "Surf and turf" menu.

Concarneau road **West: 4 km by D 783 – ✉ 29930 Pont-Aven**

La Taupinière (Guy Guilloux)
Croissant St André – 02 98 06 03 12
– la.taupiniere@wanadoo.fr – Fax 02 98 06 16 46
– Closed 20 September-15 October, Monday and Tuesday
Rest – Menu €53/85 – Carte €68/92
Spec. Escalope de foie de canard poêlé, queues de langoustines panées au sésame. Gratons de moules de bouchot, crème au curcuma (spring-summer). Millefeuille de crêpes dentelles aux fraises (spring-summer).
◆ This cottage has an elegant dining room enlivened by a view of the kitchers. The cuisine is classical with fish specialities playing a major role. Tempting wine list.

PONTCHARTRAIN – 78 Yvelines – 311 H3 – ✉ 78760 18 A2

Paris 37 – Dreux 42 – Mantes-la-Jolie 32 – Montfort-l'Amaury 10 – Versailles 20
Isabella Plaisir Sainte Appoline, East: 3 km, 01 30 54 10 62.
Domaine de Thoiry★★ Northwest: 12 km,
Northern France and the Paris Region

L'Arpège
41 rte de Paris – 01 34 89 02 45 – Fax 01 34 89 58 24 – Closed 2-31 August
11 rm – €75 €90, €9 – ½ P €120
Rest – *(closed Saturday lunchtime, Sunday and Monday)* Menu €32
– Carte €48/53
◆ This former coaching inn offers either modern and practical or slightly countrified rooms. Cosy lounge and piano-bar with jazz at weekends. Pleasant dining room, low-key atmosphere and cuisine with a contemporary touch.

Bistro Gourmand
7 rte Pontel, (N 12) – 01 34 89 25 36
– bistro.gourmand@free.fr – Fax 08 72 64 48 31
– Closed 10-17 March, 28 July-19 August, Sunday dinner, Wednesday dinner and Monday
Rest – Menu €27/48 – Carte €55/66
◆ In a new decor of electric blue seating and red walls, seafood and seasonal dishes take pride of place on the menu.

in Ste-Apolline **East: 3 km by N 12 and D 134 – ✉ 78370 Plaisir**

La Maison des Bois
av. d'Armorique – 01 30 54 23 17
– maison-des-bois@wanadoo.fr – Fax 01 30 68 92 26
– Closed 4-25 August, Sunday dinner and Thursday
Rest – Menu €36 (weekday lunch) – Carte €47/71
◆ Two refined dining rooms in a rustic-style residence: the largest room, less countrified in style, gives onto the garden. Traditional menu.

PONT-DE-BRIQUES – 62 Pas-de-Calais – 301 C3 – see Boulogne-sur-Mer

PONT-DE-CHAZEY-VILLIEU – 01 Ain – 328 E5 – see Meximieux

PONT-DE-CHERUY – 38 Isère – 333 E3 – pop. 4 540 – alt. 220 m – ✉ 38230

Paris 486 – Belley 57 – Bourgoin-Jallieu 22 – Grenoble 89 – Lyon 35 – Meximieux 22

44 **B1**

Bergeron VISA AE

3 r. Giffard, near the church – ✆ 04 78 32 10 08 – hotel.bergeron@wanadoo.fr – Fax 04 78 32 11 70 – Closed 4-17 August

17 rm – †€ 28/49 ††€ 42/63, ☐ € 7 – ½ P € 40/50 – **Rest** – *(closed Saturday and Sunday) (dinner only) (resident only)* Menu € 11,50

◆ A modest but well-kept hotel. The rustic-style rooms are more spacious in the main house and quieter overlooking the garden. Those in the wing are simpler. In the evening guests sit down in a countrified dining room to sample a set menu.

PONT-DE-DORE – 63 Puy-de-Dôme – 326 H7 – see Thiers

PONT-DE-FILLINGES – 74 Haute-Savoie – 328 L4 – see Bonne

PONT-DE-L'ARCHE – 27 Eure – 304 G6 – pop. 3 499 – alt. 20 m – ✉ 27340

Normandy

33 **D2**

Paris 114 – Les Andelys 30 – Elbeuf 15 – Évreux 36 – Louviers 12 – Rouen 19

De la Tour without rest VISA AE

41 quai Foch – ✆ 02 35 23 00 99 – hotel-de-la-tour@wanadoo.fr – Fax 02 35 23 46 22 – Closed 8-15 August

18 rm – †€ 63 ††€ 63, ☐ € 7

◆ Two spruce semi-detached houses backed up against the ramparts. Well-kept individually decorated rooms with bright colours and period furniture. Family ambience.

La Pomme VISA

Les Damps 1.5 km on the bank of the river Eure – ✆ 02 35 23 00 46 – Fax 02 35 23 52 09 – Closed 28 July-17 August, 29 December-4 January, 1 week in March, Sunday dinner, Tuesday dinner and Wednesday

Rest – Menu € 27 (weekdays)/60 – Carte € 35/62

◆ Restaurant dining room with a cosy and slightly countrified look, in a fine Norman-style thatched cottage on the banks of the Eure. Up-to-date cuisine.

PONT-DE-L'ISÈRE – 26 Drôme – 332 C3 – see Valence

LE PONT-DE-PACÉ – 35 Ille-et-Vilaine – 309 L6 – see Rennes

PONT-DE-POITTE – 39 Jura – 321 E7 – pop. 582 – alt. 450 m – ✉ 39130

Burgundy-Jura

16 **B3**

Paris 423 – Champagnole 34 – Genève 92 – Lons-le-Saunier 17

Ain with rm rest, VISA AE

18 pl. Fontaine – ✆ 03 84 48 30 16 – hoteldelain@wanadoo.fr – Fax 03 84 48 36 95 – Closed 24 December-2 February, Sunday dinner and Friday

9 rm – †€ 38 ††€ 40/45, ☐ € 7,50 – ½ P € 47 – **Rest** – Menu € 13 (weekday lunch), € 18/44 – Carte € 31/49

◆ Stone house surrounded by greenery on the banks of the Ain. Country chic dining room and summer terrace for wholesome regional cooking.

PONT-DE-ROIDE – 25 Doubs – 321 K2 – pop. 4 781 – alt. 351 m – ✉ 25150

Burgundy-Jura

17 **C2**

Paris 478 – Belfort 36 – Besançon 77 – La Chaux-de-Fonds 55 – Porrentruy 29

La Tannerie VISA

1 pl. Gén. de Gaulle – ✆ 03 81 92 48 21 – dominique.autran@wanadoo.fr – Fax 03 81 92 47 79 – Closed 25 June-3 July, 29 October-5 November, 23 December-7 January, Sunday dinner, Thursday dinner and Wednesday

Rest – Menu € 11 (weekday lunch), € 18/24 – Carte € 24/50

◆ This family restaurant serves traditional dishes, trout from the fish tank and blackboard specials in a warm dining room or on a terrace overlooking the river.

PONT-DE-SALARS – 12 Aveyron – 338 I5 – pop. 1 414 – alt. 700 m – ✉ 12290 29 D1

Paris 651 – Albi 86 – Millau 47 – Rodez 25 – St-Affrique 56 – Villefranche-de-Rouergue 71

Office de tourisme, place de la Mairie ✆ 05 65 46 89 90, Fax 05 65 46 81 16

Des Voyageurs rest, P VISA

1 av. Rodez – ✆ 05 65 46 82 08 – hotel-des-voyageurs@wanadoo.fr – Fax 05 65 46 89 99 – Open 2 March-23 October and closed Sunday dinner and Monday from October to June

27 rm – €41/55 €42/60, €7,50 – ½ P €43/55

Rest – *(closed 24 October-14 November, 20 January-1st March, dinner from November to January, Sunday dinner and Monday from October to June)* Menu (€11,50 bi), €15 bi (weekdays)/35 – Carte €21/56

◆ Friendly welcome guaranteed at this hotel in the centre of the village. The light, spacious rooms to the front have been renovated; the others, 1970s in style, await their turn. Two dining rooms: one rustic and one modern in style, serving local dishes.

PONT-DES-SABLES – 47 Lot-et-Garonne – 336 C3 – see Marmande

PONT-DE-VAUX – 01 Ain – 328 C2 – pop. 2 004 – alt. 177 m – ✉ 01190 44 B1

Paris 380 – Bourg-en-Bresse 40 – Lons-le-Saunier 69 – Mâcon 24

Office de tourisme, 2, rue Maréchal de Lattre de Tassigny ✆ 03 85 30 30 02, Fax 03 85 30 68 69

Le Raisin with rm rest, P VISA

2 pl. M.-Poisat – ✆ 03 85 30 30 97 – hotel.leraisin@wanadoo.fr – Fax 03 85 30 67 89 – Closed 5 January-5 February, Sunday dinner except July-August, Tuesday lunch and Monday

18 rm – €55/61 €55/65, €9 – **Rest** – Menu €25/65 – Carte €46/62

◆ A house in the traditional Savoy Bresse style with an elegant, rustic dining room. Tasty regional cuisine. Spacious, quiet rooms at the rear.

Les Platanes with rm rm, P VISA

aux Quatre-Vents – ✆ 03 85 30 32 84 – hotel-des-platanes@wanadoo.fr – Fax 03 85 30 32 15 – Closed 20 February-20 March, Friday lunch and Thursday

8 rm – €48/56 €51/59, €9 – ½ P €65 – **Rest** – Menu €17/48 – Carte €30/49

◆ The rustic-style dining room, attractive terrace beneath plane trees, generous Bresse cuisine and renovated rooms make this inn a most pleasant stopover.

in St-Bénigne Northeast: 2 km on D 2 – pop. 817 – alt. 208 m – ✉ 01190

St-Bénigne P VISA

– ✆ 03 85 30 96 48 – Fax 03 85 30 96 48 – Closed 3-10 November, 15 December-5 January, 9-23 February, Monday and dinner except Saturday

Rest – Menu €12,50 (weekdays)/35 – Carte €22/36

◆ The chef rustles up regional dishes and the house speciality is frogs' legs. Served either in a countrified, or another more stylish dining room.

PONT-D'HÉRAULT – 30 Gard – 339 H5 – see le Vigan

PONT-D'OUILLY – 14 Calvados – 303 J6 – pop. 1 050 – alt. 65 m – ✉ 14690 32 B2

Normandy

Paris 230 – Briouze 24 – Caen 41 – Falaise 20 – Flers 21 – Villers-Bocage 37 – Vire 39

Syndicat d'initiative, boulevard de la Noë ✆ 02 31 69 29 86

Oëtre Rock ★★ South: 6,5 km.

in St-Christophe 2 km North by D 23 – ✉ 14690 Pont-d'Ouilly

XX **Auberge St-Christophe** with rm

– *02 31 69 81 23 – aubergesaintchristophe@wanadoo.fr – Fax 02 31 69 26 58 – Closed 18 August-3 September, 16 February-3 March, Tuesday October-March, Sunday dinner and Monday*

7 rm – €53 €53, €10 – ½ P €58 – **Rest** – Menu €23/51 – Carte €46/61

◆ A pleasant house covered with Virginia creeper in quiet country surroundings. The dining room extends onto a garden terrace. Traditional cuisine and family welcome.

PONT-DU-BOUCHET – 63 Puy-de-Dôme – 326 D7 – ✉ 63770 Les-Ancizes-Comps 5 B2

Paris 390 – Clermont-Ferrand 39 – Pontaumur 13 – Riom 36 – St-Gervais-d'Auvergne 18

Méandre de Queuille★★ Northeast: 11,5 km then 15 mn, **Auvergne-Rhone Valley**

La Crémaillère

Pont du Bouchet – 04 73 86 80 07 – la-cremaillere63@wanadoo.fr – Fax 04 73 86 93 17 – Closed 19 December-26 January, Friday dinner, Sunday dinner and Saturday off season

16 rm – €44 €47, €8 – ½ P €44/49

Rest – Menu €14,50 (weekdays)/40 – Carte €22/44

◆ A welcome breath of fresh air in this family-run lakeside inn. A pleasant welcome and highly attentive staff. Faultless rooms. Rustic style dining room and regional cooking.

PONT-DU-CASSE – 47 Lot-et-Garonne – 336 G4 – see Agen

PONT-DU-CHAMBON – 19 Corrèze – 329 N4 – see Marcillac-la-Croisille

PONT-DU-CHÂTEAU – 63 Puy-de-Dôme – 326 G8 – pop. 8 874 – alt. 365 m – ✉ 63430 Auvergne 5 B2

Paris 418 – Billom 13 – Clermont-Ferrand 16 – Riom 21 – Thiers 37

Syndicat d'initiative, rond-point de Montboissier 04 73 83 37 42, Fax 04 73 83 37 42

L'Estredelle rm,

24 r. Pont – 04 73 83 28 18 – estredelle@wanadoo.fr – Fax 04 73 83 55 23 – Closed 28 July-10 August and 22 December-6 January, Sunday dinner and dinners holidays

44 rm – €43 €45, €6,50 – ½ P €42 – **Rest** – Menu (€12,50), €18/30 – Carte €20/41

◆ A new hotel in the former river craft district. Functional rooms split over three pavilions; eight of them (reservation required) overlook the Allier. The dining room and terrace command a fine view of an 18C bridge.

XX **Auberge du Pont**

70 av. Dr Besserve – 04 73 83 00 36 – info@auberge-du-pont.com – Fax 04 73 83 36 71 – Closed 15 August-3 September, 1st-11 January, Sunday dinner, Tuesday dinner and Wednesday

Rest – Menu €27/75 bi – Carte €36/62

◆ A former canal boat post house (1809) on the banks of the Allier. Coloured brick walls, pale green wood panelling and varnished parquet decorate the dining room. Terrace facing the bridge.

XX **Le Calliope**

6 r. de la Poste – 04 73 83 50 03 – lecalliope@orange.fr – Fax 04 73 83 56 03 – Closed 14-20 April, 27 July-18 August, 21-29 December, 9 16 February, Sunday dinner, Tuesday dinner and Wednesday

Rest – Menu (€20), €27/46 – Carte €37/40

◆ A modern restaurant in the town centre with a distinctive and elegant façade. The menu here is a fusion of the traditional and contemporary.

PONT-DU-GARD – 30 Gard – 339 M5 – ✉ 30210 Vers-Pont-du-Gard
Provence 23 **D2**

Paris 688 – Alès 48 – Arles 40 – Avignon 26 – Nîmes 25 – Orange 38 – Pont-St-Esprit 41

Roman aqueduct bridge★★★.

Colombier VISA MC AE
(right bank), 1 km east on D 981 (right bank) – 04 66 37 05 28 – hotelresto.colombier@free.fr – Fax 04 66 37 35 75
18 rm – €41 €51, €8 – ½ P €47 – **Rest** – Menu €18/27 – Carte €23/37
◆ Hundred-year-old house with attractive gallery-terrace where breakfast is served. The upstairs rooms have just been successfully renovated. Dining room with Provençal decor and traditional, no-frills food.

in Castillon-du-Gard Northeast: 4 km by D 19 and D 228 – pop. 943 – alt. 90 m – ✉ 30210

Le vieux Castillon VISA MC AE
r. Turion Sabatier – 04 66 37 61 61 – vieuxcastillon@relaischateaux.com – Fax 04 66 37 28 17 – Closed 2 January-14 February
29 rm – €211/330 €211/330, €18 – 3 suites – ½ P €187/287
Rest – *(closed Monday lunch and Tuesday lunch)* Menu €51 (weekday lunch), €77/112 – Carte €73/100
Spec. Foie gras de canard poêlé à la rhubarbe. Pavé de bar cuit sur la peau, ravioles de pistou. Selle d'agneau farcie, pomme croquette à l'ail. **Wines** Châteauneuf-du-Pape, Tavel.
◆ Tiered patios and terraces make this a charming hotel in the heart of a medieval hilltop village. Rooms with personal touches. Exposed beams and Provençal colours are the main features of the dining room where you can enjoy delicious, sun-gorged food.

L'Amphitryon VISA MC
pl. 8 Mai 1945 – 04 66 37 05 04 – mario.monterroso@wanadoo.fr – Closed 15-28 February, Tuesday and Wednesday except 15 May-30 September
Rest – Menu €40/55 – Carte €59/70
◆ A vaulted ceiling and rough stonework in these dining rooms in an old sheepfold. An attractive patio for summertime meals. Modernised regional cuisine and a friendly atmosphere.

in Collias West: 7 km by D 981, D 112 and D 3 – pop. 829 – alt. 45 m – ✉ 30210

Hostellerie Le Castellas rm, VISA MC AE
Grand'rue – 04 66 22 88 88 – info@lecastellas.fr – Fax 04 66 22 84 28 – Closed 8-18 December, 5-14 January, 19 January-11 February and 16-4 March
16 rm – €80/130 €90/239, €17 – 1 suite – ½ P €139/214
Rest – *(closed Wednesday from November-April except public holidays)*
Menu (€22), €32 (weekday lunch), €57/104 – Carte €89/116
Spec. Contraste de foie gras en trois versions. Le bœuf race "Aubrac". Risotto de jambonnettes de grenouilles au massalé (October to January). **Wines** Côtes du Rhône Villages, Vin de pays d'Oc.
◆ Gard-style dressed-stone houses around a patio in an imaginative harmony of Art Deco and rustic Provençal style with pebbles and shades of ochre and sepia. Fine vaulted dining rooms opening onto the garden. Tasty inventive cuisine, flavoured with garrigue herbs.

Le Gardon VISA MC AE
Campchestève – 04 66 22 80 54 – auberge-le-gardon@wanadoo.fr – Fax 04 66 22 88 98 – Open 1st March-1st November
14 rm – €65/75 €65/93, €9,50 – ½ P €60/75
Rest – *(closed lunch Monday to Friday)* Menu (€18), €21/31 – Carte €24/40
◆ This recent hotel lined by an olive grove provides a pleasant break amid sweet-scented gorse. Garden, pool and comfortable wrought iron furnished rooms. Market fresh southern French cooking served on the veranda or terrace. Everything is homemade!

PONT-EN-ROYANS – 38 Isère – 333 F7 – pop. 917 – alt. 197 m – ✉ 38680
French Alps 43 **E2**

Paris 604 – Grenoble 63 – Lyon 143 – Valence 45

Office de tourisme, Grande rue 04 76 36 09 10, Fax 04 76 36 09 24

Du Musée de l'Eau
pl. Breuil – ✆ 04 76 36 15 53 – musee.eau@wanadoo.fr – Fax 04 76 36 97 32
31 rm – †€ 36 ††€ 44/48, ☕ € 7 – ½ P € 42/47
Rest – Menu € 16/34 – Carte € 21/36
◆ Big renovated building overlooking the Bourne. Small rooms with modern-style furniture; some have a view of the mountain and perched village. Simple dining room extended by a terrace with sprays. Bottled water bar.

LE PONTET – **84 Vaucluse** – **332** C10 – see Avignon

PONTGIBAUD – **63 Puy-de-Dôme** – **326** E8 – **pop. 776** – **alt. 735 m** – ✉ **63230**
Auvergne 5 **B2**

Paris 432 – Aubusson 68 – Clermont-Ferrand 23 – Le Mont-Dore 37 – Riom 26 – Ussel 68

Office de tourisme, rue du Commerce ✆ 04 73 88 90 99, Fax 04 73 88 90 09

Poste with rm — rest,
pl. de la République – ✆ 04 73 88 70 02 – Fax 04 73 88 79 74
– Closed 2-23 January, 16-28 February, Sunday dinner and Monday October-May
10 rm – †€ 42/49 ††€ 42/49, ☕ € 6 – ½ P € 45
Rest – Menu € 19/37 – Carte € 25/37
◆ This regional-style house in the heart of a quiet country town is over a century old. Well polished parquet flooring, chandeliers, plush table settings and floral paintings.

in La Courteix East: 4 km on D 941^B – ✉ 63230 St-Ours

L'Ours des Roches
– ✆ 04 73 88 92 80 – oursdesroches@wanadoo.fr – Fax 04 73 88 75 07
– Closed 2-24 January, Tuesday October-March, Sunday dinner and Monday except holidays
Rest – Menu € 20 (weekday lunch), € 26/64 – Carte € 34/82
◆ A restaurant under the archways of an old sheepfold. An original decor with an unusual blend of rustic and contemporary styles.

PONTHIERRY – **77 Seine-et-Marne** – **312** E4 – ✉ **77310 St-Fargeau-Ponthierry**

Paris 44 – Corbeil-Essonnes 12 – Étampes 35 – Fontainebleau 20 – Melun 12 19 **C2**

Auberge du Bas Pringy
at Pringy - D 607 – ✆ 01 60 65 57 75 – aubergedubaspringy@orange.fr
– Fax 01 60 65 48 57 – Closed 28 July-28 August, 17-25 February, Sunday dinner, Tuesday and Wednesday
Rest – Menu € 38 – Carte € 55/77
◆ A roadside inn with a country-style dining room. When the weather is fine, a terrace is set up amongst the plants and flowers. Traditional cuisine.

PONTIVY – **56 Morbihan** – **308** N6 – **pop. 13 508** – **alt. 99 m** – ✉ **56300**
Brittany 10 **C2**

Paris 460 – Lorient 59 – Rennes 110 – St-Brieuc 58 – Vannes 53

Syndicat d'initiative, 61, rue du Général de Gaulle ✆ 02 97 25 04 10, Fax 02 97 25 63 69

de Rimaison BieuzySouth: 15 km by D 768, ✆ 02 97 27 74 03.

Old houses ★.

Plan on next page

Rohan without rest
90 r. Nationale – ✆ 02 97 25 02 01 – contact@hotelpontivy.com – Fax 02 97 25 02 85
16 rm – †€ 58/80 ††€ 71/145, ☕ € 10,50 Z **u**
◆ A fine, late-19C residence on the main street of an area built by Napoleon. Rooms tastefully renovated in various styles and based on a number of themes (Oriental, romantic, cinema, comic books etc). Courtyard planted with trees.

PONTIVY

Anne-de-Bretagne (Pl.) . . . . . . Y 2
Caïnain (R.) . . . . Z 3
Couvent (Q. du) . . . . Y 4
Dr-Guépin (R. du) . . . . Y 5
Fil (R. du) . . . . Y 6
Friedland (R. de) . . . . Y 8
Gaulle (R. du Gén.-de) . . . . Y 9
Le Goff (R.) . . . . Z 16
Jean-Jaurès (R.) . . . . Z 10
Lamennais (R. J.-M. de) . . . . . Z 13
Lorois (R.) . . . . Y 17
Marengo (R.) . . . . Z 19
Martray (Pl. du) . . . . Y 20
Mitterrand (R. François) . . . . . Z 24
Nationale (R.) . . . . YZ
Niémen (Q.) . . . . Y 27
Plessis (Q. du) . . . . YZ 29
Pont (R. du) . . . . Y 28
Presbourg (Q.) . . . . Y 32
Récollets (Q. des) . . . . Y 33
Viollard (Bd) . . . . Z 38

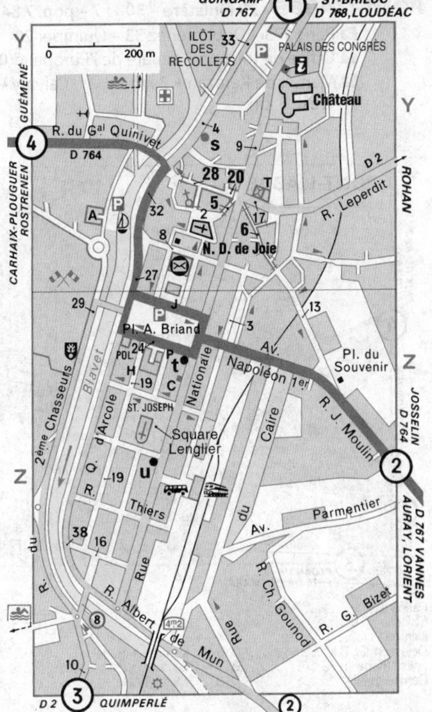

🏨 **L'Europe** without rest

12 r. F. Mitterrand – ✆ 02 97 25 11 14 – hoteleuropepontivy@wanadoo.fr – Fax 02 97 25 48 04 – Closed 25-31 December Z t

18 rm – †€ 62/82 ††€ 65/140, ☕ € 10

◆ Large, pleasant house dating from the reign of Napoleon III. Breakfast is served in the impressive breakfast room, and in summer beneath a glass dome. The guestrooms to the rear are quieter.

XX **Pommeraie** VISA AE

17 quai Couvent – ✆ 02 97 25 60 09 – restaurant.lapommeraie@wanadoo.fr – Fax 02 97 25 75 93 – Closed 20-28 April, 22 August-1st September, 28 December-5 January, Sunday and Monday Y s

Rest – Menu € 19 (weekday lunch), € 26/58 – Carte approx. € 40

◆ A yellow façade and warm colours in the spruce dining room and flower-decked courtyard: this restaurant on the banks of the Blavet is an absolute symphony of colour. Modern dishes.

in Quelven by ③, D 2 and Guern road (D 2B): 10 km – ✉ 56310 Guern

🏠 **Auberge de Quelven** P VISA

à la Chapelle – ✆ 02 97 27 77 50 – Fax 02 97 27 77 50 – Closed Wednesday

8 rm – †€ 50 ††€ 55, ☕ € 6 – **Rest** – Carte € 8/16

◆ Long granite house facing a 15C chapel in a peaceful hamlet. Small, discreet and well-kept rooms. Cheerful reception. The menu of this rustic restaurant and crêperie focuses on Brittany galettes and crêpes.

PONT-L'ABBÉ – 29 Finistère – 308 F7 – pop. 7 849 – alt. 5 m – ✉ 29120 Brittany

Paris 573 – Douarnenez 33 – Quimper 20 9 **A2**

Office de tourisme, square de l'Europe ✆ 02 98 82 37 99, Fax 02 98 66 10 82

Manoir de Kerazan★ 3 km by ② - Calvary★★ of N.-D.-de-Tronoën chapel West: 8 km.

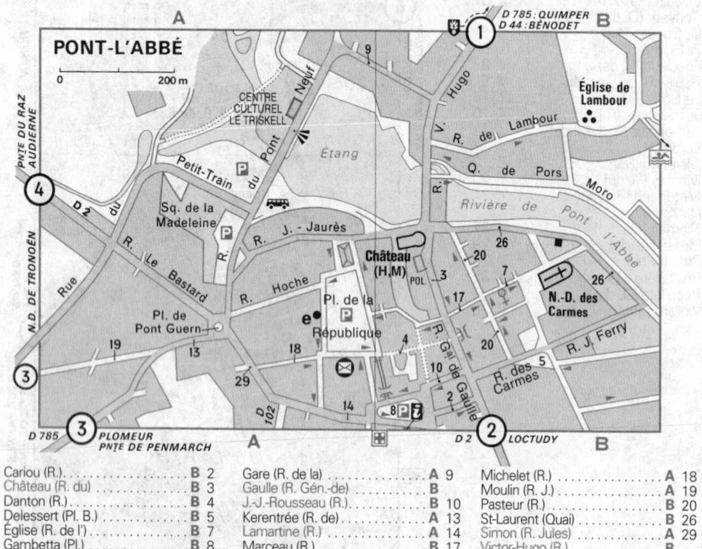

Cariou (R.)	B	2	Gare (R. de la)	A	9	Michelet (R.)	A	18
Château (R. du)	B	3	Gaulle (R. Gén.-de)	B		Moulin (R. J.)	A	19
Danton (R.)	B	4	J.-J.-Rousseau (R.)	B	10	Pasteur (R.)	B	20
Delessert (Pl. B.)	B	5	Kerentrée (R. de)	A	13	St-Laurent (Quai)	B	26
Église (R. de l')	B	7	Lamartine (R.)	A	14	Simon (R. Jules)	A	29
Gambetta (Pl.)	B	8	Marceau (R.)	B	17	Victor-Hugo (R.)	B	

De Bretagne

rm, VISA

24 pl. de la République – ✆ 02 98 87 17 22 – hoteldebretagne29@orange.fr – Fax 02 98 82 39 31 – Closed 13-26 October, 28 January-10 February A **e**

18 rm – €52 €57, ☕ €8 – ½ P €66 – **Rest** – *(closed Monday except dinner July-August, Sunday dinner)* Menu (€13), €16 (weekday lunch), €23/48 – Carte €25/87

♦ This town-centre hotel has small rooms (those at the front are larger) with a fresh appearance and simple furnishings. Seafood takes pride of place in a rustic-style dining room or on the terrace in an inner courtyard.

PONT-L'ÉVÊQUE – 14 Calvados – 303 N4 – pop. 4 133 – alt. 12 m – ✉ 14130 Normandy

32 **A3**

Paris 190 – Caen 49 – Le Havre 43 – Rouen 78 – Trouville-sur-Mer 12

Office de tourisme, 16, rue Saint-Michel ✆ 02 31 64 12 77, Fax 02 31 64 76 96

de Saint-JulienSoutheast: 3 km by D 579, ✆ 02 31 64 30 30.

The belle époque of the motor-car★ South by D 48.

Le Lion d'Or without rest

P VISA

8 pl. Calvaire – ✆ 02 31 65 01 55 – info@leliondorhotel.com – Fax 02 31 64 90 10

25 rm – €60/120 €80/160, ☕ €10

♦ Brand new hotel as you enter the town centre. Both wings house mainly duplex rooms. All have parquet flooring and are well equipped. Billiard and bar lounge where breakfast is served.

Auberge de l'Aigle d'Or

P VISA

68 r. Vaucelles – ✆ 02 31 65 05 25 – thierry.duhamel@alicepro.fr – Fax 02 31 65 12 03 – Closed 17-30 November, Sunday dinner from November to March and Wednesday

Rest – Menu €27(weekdays)/50 – Carte €51/69

♦ This old 16C post house has three small dining rooms with beams and a fireplace creating a cosy atmosphere. The cuisine is adapted to the different seasons.

Auberge de la Touques
pl. de l'Église – ✆ 02 31 64 01 69 – Fax 02 31 64 89 40 – Closed mid December-mid January, Monday and Tuesday except July-August
Rest – Menu € 22/39 – Carte € 31/55
◆ Large, half-timbered inn near St Michel church. Rustic dining room, traditional cuisine and friendly atmosphere.

in St-Martin-aux-Chartrains **3 km by D 677, towards Deauville – pop. 351 – alt. 13 m – ✉ 14130**

Mercure
– ✆ 02 31 64 40 40 – mercurepontleveque@wanadoo.fr – Fax 02 31 64 40 41
53 rm – €63/117 €74/135, € 12 – 14 suites – **Rest** – *(closed Saturday lunch and Sunday lunch except in July-August)* Menu (€ 15), € 20 – Carte € 29/40
◆ Modern hotel set away from the road, in a peaceful 3-ha park, adorned with an ornamental pond. Spacious rooms and junior-suites popular with families. Rooms available for seminars, outdoor pool and tennis courts. Restaurant with brasserie-type food.

Manoir le Mesnil without rest
rte Trouville – ✆ 02 31 64 71 01 – manoirlemesnil@hotmail.fr – Fax 02 31 64 71 01 – Closed 5-20 March and 5-20 November
5 rm – €70 €72/115
◆ Fine late 19C residence overlooking the estate to the rear. Large rooms with personal touches, completed by two studios. Appealing library.

in Pierrefitte-en-Auge **5 km Southeast by D 48 and D 280A – pop. 114 – alt. 59 m – ✉ 14130**

Auberge des Deux Tonneaux ≤ Valley and site,
– ✆ 02 31 64 09 31 – brettetwells@wanadoo.fr – Closed January, Sunday dinner and Monday except from June to August
Rest – Menu € 26 – Carte € 27/46
◆ A delightful Auge cottage overlooking the countryside. Pleasant rustic setting, fuss-free service and menu highlighting local dishes.

PONTLEVOY – 41 Loir-et-Cher – 318 E7 – pop. 1 460 – alt. 99 m – ✉ 41400

Châteaux of the Loire 11 **A1**

Paris 211 – Amboise 25 – Blois 27 – Montrichard 9 – Tours 52
Syndicat d'initiative, 5, rue du Collège ✆ 02 54 32 60 80, Fax 02 54 71 60 71
Former abbey★.

De l'École with rm
12 rte Montrichard – ✆ 02 54 32 50 30 – Fax 02 54 32 33 58 – Closed 17 November-17 December, 16 February-12 March, Sunday dinner and Monday
11 rm – €59 €61, € 12 – ½ P € 66
Rest – *(pre-book Sat - Sun)* Menu € 23/54 – Carte € 28/59
◆ Attractive Loire-region house with two rustic dining rooms, one with a fireplace. Flower garden for summer meals by a fountain. Dishes based on local produce.

PONTMAIN – 53 Mayenne – 310 C4 – pop. 893 – alt. 164 m – ✉ 53220 34 B1

Paris 324 – Domfront 41 – Fougères 18 – Laval 51 – Mayenne 46
Syndicat d'initiative, 5, rue de la Grange ✆ 02 43 05 07 74

Auberge de l'Espérance
9 r. Grange – ✆ 02 43 05 08 10 – pontmain@ladapt.net – Fax 02 43 05 03 19 – Closed 21 December-2 January and 5-11 February
11 rm – €33 €36, € 5 – ½ P € 39 – **Rest** – Menu € 10 (weekdays)/16
◆ A work access centre with functional, well-kept rooms. Special efforts have been made to accommodate the disabled. Dining here when staying overnight is both practical and a gesture of solidarity.

PONTOISE – 95 Val-d'Oise – 305 D6 – 106 5 – 101 3 – see Paris, Area (Cergy-Pontoise)

PONT-RÉAN – 35 Ille-et-Vilaine – 309 L6 – ✉ 35580 Guichen 10 D2

Paris 361 – Châteaubriant 57 – Fougères 67 – Nozay 60 – Rennes 16 – Vitré 56

XX **Auberge de Réan**

– *02 99 42 24 80 – auberge.de.rean@wanadoo.fr – Fax 02 99 42 28 66 – Closed Sunday dinner and Monday*

Rest – Menu (€ 15 bi), € 29/60 – Carte € 32/51

♦ Breton house on the banks of the Vilaine, facing an 18C stone bridge. Pleasant dining room with warm decor and terrace with riverside view.

PONT-ST-PIERRE – 27 Eure – 304 H5 – pop. 935 – alt. 15 m – ✉ 27360 Normandy 33 D2

Paris 106 – Les Andelys 20 – Évreux 47 – Louviers 23 – Pont-de-l'Arche 12 – Rouen 22

Church ★ panelling - Côte des Deux-Amants ≤★★ Southwest: 4.5 km then 15 mn - Ruins of Fontaine-Guérard abbey ★ Northeast: 3 km.

XX **Auberge de l'Andelle**

– *02 32 49 70 18 – Fax 02 32 49 59 43 – Closed 23 December-2 January and Tuesday dinner*

Rest – Menu € 21/59 – Carte € 34/70

♦ A spruce façade, a rustic setting with a stone fireplace and the snug interior with numerous nooks and crannies give this inn a charming atmosphere. Traditional menu.

PONT-STE-MARIE – 10 Aube – 313 E4 – see Troyes

PONT-SCORFF – 56 Morbihan – 308 K8 – pop. 2 623 – alt. 42 m – ✉ 56620 Brittany 9 B2

Paris 503 – Lanester 13 – Lorient 13 – Rennes 152

Syndicat d'initiative, rue de Lorient 02 97 32 50 27, Fax 02 97 32 59 96

XX **Laurent Le Berrigaud**

Le Moulin des Princes – 02 97 32 42 07 – laurent.le-berrigaud@wanadoo.fr – Fax 02 97 32 50 02 – Closed 27 October-3 November, 1st-12 January and Monday

Rest – Menu € 40/75 – Carte € 73/91

♦ This riverside restaurant has a pretty decor combining old stonework, art and flower arrangements. Waterside terrace, tasty, inventive cuisine and a charming welcome.

LES PONTS-NEUFS – 22 Côtes-d'Armor – 309 G3 – ✉ 22400 Morieux

Paris 441 – Dinan 51 – Dinard 52 – Lamballe 9 – St-Brieuc 15 – St-Malo 58 10 C2

XX **La Cascade**

on D 786 – 02 96 32 82 20 – la.cascade.jamme@wanadoo.fr – Fax 02 96 32 70 74 – Closed Tuesday dinner, Wednesday dinner and Thursday dinner 16 September-14 June, Sunday dinner and Monday

Rest – Menu € 19 (weekday lunch), € 29/42

♦ The dining room of this restaurant enjoys views of a small lake. Rustic yet contemporary decor and tempting traditional cuisine.

PORNIC – 44 Loire-Atlantique – 316 D5 – pop. 11 903 – alt. 20 m – Casino : le Môle – ✉ 44210 Atlantic Coast 34 A2

Paris 429 – Nantes 49 – La Roche-s-Yon 89 – Les Sables-d'Olonne 93 – St-Nazaire 30

Office de tourisme, place de la Gare 02 40 82 04 40, Fax 02 40 82 90 12

de Pornic Avenue Scalby Newby, West: 1km, 02 40 82 06 69.

Alliance
Plage de la Source, 1 km south – ☎ 02 40 82 21 21 – info.resa@thalassopornic.com – Fax 02 40 82 80 89 – Closed 1st-15 December
118 rm – †€ 115/220 ††€ 135/290, ☕ € 16 – 2 suites
Rest *La Source* – Menu (€ 23), € 32 – Carte € 43/54
Rest *La Terrasse* – *(booking advisable)* Menu (€ 23), € 32 – Carte € 48/54
◆ Modern hotel and thalassotherapy centre facing the sea. Large rooms (30 of which are brand new) with terraces and deck chairs. Contemporary, rotunda dining room (former casino) commanding a stunning sea view. Classic and diet cuisine. Exclusively fish and seafood menu served in a minimalist decor.

Auberge La Fontaine aux Bretons
chemin des Noëlles, 3 km southeast by La Bernerie road – ☎ 02 51 74 07 07 – auberge@auberge-la-fontaine.com – Fax 02 51 74 15 15 – Closed in January
11 rm – †€ 84/148 ††€ 84/148, ☕ € 12 – 12 suites – ††€ 118/184
Rest – *(closed Sunday dinner and Monday off season except public holidays)* Menu (€ 15), € 20 (weekday lunch), € 27/32 – Carte € 31/36
◆ The Fountain used to refresh Breton pilgrims; today, this inn offers pleasant rooms with balconies, set in an old farm (1867). Vines, vegetable garden and rustic style restaurant. Traditional cuisine.

Beau Soleil without rest
70 quai Leray – ☎ 02 40 82 34 58 – beausoleil@annedebretagne.com – Fax 02 40 82 43 00
17 rm – †€ 53/110 ††€ 53/110, ☕ € 8,50
◆ A modern building opposite the harbour and castle. Rooms are not spacious but functional and well kept. Breakfast served on Pornic pottery tableware.

Relais St-Gilles without rest
7 r. F. de Mun – ☎ 02 40 82 02 25 – Open 21 March-30 September
25 rm – †€ 51/62 ††€ 51/109, ☕ € 7,50
◆ Once owned by the bloodthirsty Gilles de Rais, this 1850 post house is near the port and the castle. Unpretentious, quiet rooms with period furniture.

Les Alizés without rest
44 r. Général de Gaulle – ☎ 02 40 82 00 51 – alizes@brithotel.fr – Fax 02 40 82 87 32
29 rm – †€ 60/75 ††€ 60/75, ☕ € 9,50
◆ Recent hotel with well-equipped, clean rooms, lying in a busy street. Choose one of the rooms at the rear, which are quieter.

Beau Rivage
Birochère beach, 2.5 km southeast – ☎ 02 40 82 03 08 – info@restaurant-beaurivage.com – Fax 02 51 74 04 24 – Closed 15 December-31 January, Tuesday except July-August and Monday
Rest – Menu (€ 26), € 35/80 – Carte € 48/91
◆ Boat models, shellfish and other maritime artefacts adorn this restaurant overlooking the sea. Predominance of fish and seafood, accompanied by a fine selection of Muscadets. Gourmet food shop.

Le Bistrot
pl. Petit Nice – ☎ 02 40 82 51 25 – Fax 02 40 64 94 81 – Closed from mid November to mid December, Wednesday dinner from October to March, Sunday dinner off season and during term time and Thursday
Rest – bistrot Menu (€ 13,50), € 27 – Carte approx. € 31
◆ Inside, there is contemporary, bistro-style decor with nautical touches; outside the terrace faces the castle. Menu offering seafood recipes and traditional dishes.

in Ste-Marie West: 3 km – ✉ 44210 Pornic

Les Sablons
13 r. Sablons – ☎ 02 40 82 09 14 – contact@hotelesablons.com – Fax 02 40 82 04 26
28 rm – †€ 55/70 ††€ 55/90, ☕ € 9 – ½ P € 57/75
Rest – *(closed 15 December-15 January, Sunday dinner, Tuesday lunch and Monday except 1st June-15 September)* Menu € 20/43 – Carte € 30/50
◆ A 1970s hotel midway between the village and the beach. Simply decorated rooms (some with a sea view) in a family guesthouse spirit. Colourful and flower-filled dining room; in summer, tables are pleasantly placed in the garden.

PORNICHET – 44 Loire-Atlantique – 316 B4 – pop. 9 668 – alt. 12 m – Casino – ✉ 44380 Brittany 34 A2

Paris 444 – La Baule 6 – Nantes 70 – St-Nazaire 11

Office de tourisme, 3, boulevard de la République ✆ 02 40 61 33 33, Fax 02 40 11 60 88

Sud Bretagne

42 bd de la République – ✆ 02 40 11 65 00 – contact@hotelsudbretagne.com – Fax 02 40 61 73 70

25 rm – †€ 100/150 ††€ 120/180, ☕ € 13 – 4 suites

Rest – *(closed Sunday off season)* Menu € 45/60 – Carte € 45/80

◆ Hotel run by the same family since 1912. All rooms are attractively decorated along a theme, echoed by the fabrics, furniture and objects. Indoor Jacuzzi pool and massages on request. Stylish dining room, charming terrace, and seafood menu.

Villa Flornoy

7 av. Flornoy, near the Town Hall – ✆ 02 40 11 60 00 – hotflornoy@aol.com – Fax 02 40 61 86 47 – Closed December and January

30 rm – †€ 60/108 ††€ 60/108, ☕ € 9 – ½ P € 54/78

Rest – *(open 1st April-30 September) (dinner only)* Menu € 22 – Carte € 22/30

◆ In a residential district, this large villa is arranged like a cottage and has pastel colours, period furniture and English china. Pretty personalised rooms. Spacious, light dining room; set menu featuring classic dishes.

Ibis

66 bd Océanides – ✆ 02 51 73 13 13 – h1171@accor.com – Fax 02 40 61 74 74

88 rm – †€ 74/119 ††€ 82/165, ☕ € 9 – ½ P € 66/85

Rest *Entre Terre et Mer* – Menu (€ 13), € 15 bi (weekday lunch)/20 – Carte € 21/47

◆ The rooms in this Ibis hotel are clean and simple. Direct access to the thalassotherapy centre next door. An ocean liner atmosphere created by nautical menus, wooden blinds and bay windows. Traditional menus and diet dishes.

Le Régent

150 bd Océanides – ✆ 02 40 61 04 04 – hotel@le-regent.fr – Fax 02 40 61 06 06 – Closed 2-19 January

23 rm – †€ 77/124 ††€ 77/176, ☕ € 10 – ½ P € 74/97

Rest *Grain de Folie* – *(closed Sunday dinner except July-August)* Menu € 24/33 – Carte € 36/49

◆ Early 20C family home with the Atlantic on the horizon. Pleasant, well-kept rooms. A fashionably decorated trendy restaurant, whose predominantly black interior is enhanced by splashes of colour; metal veranda overlooking the sea. Up-to-the-minute menu.

PORQUEROLLES (ÎLE) – 83 Var – 340 M7 – see Île de Porquerolles

PORT-CAMARGUE – 30 Gard – 339 J7 – see Grau-du-Roi

PORT-CROS (ÎLE) – 83 Var – 340 N7 – see Île de Port-Cros

PORT-DE-CARHAIX – 29 Finistère – 308 J5 – see Carhaix

PORT-DE-GAGNAC – 46 Lot – 337 H2 – see Bretenoux

PORT-DE-LA-MEULE – 85 Vendée – 316 B7 – see Île d'Yeu

PORT-DE-LANNE – 40 Landes – 335 D13 – pop. 700 – alt. 28 m – ✉ 40300 3 B3

Paris 747 – Bayonne 29 – Biarritz 37 – Dax 23 – Mont-de-Marsan 77 – Peyrehorade 7

La Vieille Auberge without rest

– ✆ 05 58 89 16 29 – vieille.auberge@wanadoo.fr – Fax 05 58 89 12 89 – Open from beg. May-end September

8 rm – †€ 49/69 ††€ 69/78, ☕ € 8 – 2 suites

◆ This delightful rustic inn houses a small museum dedicated to local traditions. The guestrooms are housed in cottages around the flower garden (pool). Friendly welcome.

PORT-DE-SALLES – **86 Vienne** – **322** J7 – **see l'Isle-Jourdain**

PORT-DE-SECHEX – **74 Haute-Savoie** – **328** L2 – **see Thonon-les-Bains**

PORTEL-DES-CORBIÈRES – **11 Aude** – **344** I4 – **pop. 1 053** – **alt. 32 m** –
✉ **11490** 22 **B3**

Paris 810 – Perpignan 50 – Béziers 50 – Carcassonne 61 – Narbonne 18

Domaine de la Pierre Chaude without rest
Les Campets, rte Durban – ✆ 04 68 48 89 79 – lapierrechaude@yahoo.fr – Fax 04 68 48 89 79 – Closed 4 January-28 February
4 rm – €78/90 €78/90
◆ Old 18C wine and spirit store surrounded by scrubland. Spacious southern-style rooms with wrought iron, mosaics, terra cotta and whitewashed walls. Flower decked terrace, home-made breakfasts.

La Bergerie
au Château de Lastours, 2 km south by secondary road – ✆ 04 68 48 64 77 – pgspringer@yahoo.fr – Closed 1st-15 January, Monday and Tuesday off-season
Rest – Menu €24/31 – Carte approx. €38
◆ An old farm building on the wine estate of Château de Lastours, AOC Corbières. Wines from the estate and up-to-date food served in a handsome vaulted dining room.

PORT-EN-BESSIN – **14 Calvados** – **303** H3 – **pop. 2 139** – **alt. 10 m** –
✉ **14520 Port-en-Bessin-Huppain** **Normandy** 32 **B2**

Paris 275 – Bayeux 10 – Caen 41 – Cherbourg 92 – St-Lô 43

Office de tourisme, quai Baron Gérard ✆ 02 31 22 45 80

La Chenevière
1.5 km south on D 6 – ✆ 02 31 51 25 25 – cheneviere@lacheneviere.fr – Fax 02 31 51 25 20 – Closed 3 January-10 February
29 rm – €202/462 €202/462, €19 – **Rest** – *(dinner only)* Menu €50/110 – Carte €71/107
◆ A noble 19C residence and its outbuilding set in a fine park. Each room has a different decor on a flower theme. Suites are more contemporary. The bourgeois dining room gives the impression of an establishment where they know how to look after their guests. Fish and vegetarian menus.

Mercure
sur le Golf, 2 km west by D 514 – ✆ 02 31 22 44 44 – h1215@accor.com – Fax 02 31 22 36 77 – Closed 17 December-15 January
70 rm – €80/140 €90/175, €12 – ½ P €67/92 – **Rest** – Menu €26/35 – Carte €32/46
◆ An ideally-situated hotel complex on the edge of a golf course. Peaceful nights in renovated, practical, modern rooms. A veranda-dining room serving traditional cuisine and a club house with a small brasserie-type menu.

L'Écailler
2 r. Bayeux, (at the port) – ✆ 02 31 22 92 16 – lecailler@msn.com – Fax 02 31 22 90 38 – Closed 2 January-19 February, Tuesday lunch and Sunday dinner except July-August and Monday
Rest – Menu (€27) – Carte €46/117
◆ Attractive, maritime decor and a menu which focuses on shellfish, seafood and fresh fish. Note: this restaurant is planning to relocate to Caen during 2008.

LES PORTES-EN-RÉ – **17 Charente-Maritime** – **324** B2 – **see Île de Ré**

PORT-GOULPHAR – **56 Morbihan** – **308** L11 – **see Belle-Ile-en-Mer**

PORT-GRIMAUD – **83 Var** – **340** O6 – ✉ **83310 Cogolin** **French Riviera**

Paris 867 – Brignoles 63 – Fréjus 27 – Hyères 47 – St-Tropez 9 – Ste-Maxime 8 – Toulon 66 41 **C3**

≤★ tower of the ecumenical church.

Giraglia ⚓ ← gulf, rest, VISA AE

sur la plage – ✆ 04 94 56 31 33 – message@hotelgiraglia.com – Fax 04 94 56 33 77 – Open beg. May-end September

48 rm – †€ 275/410 ††€ 275/410, ☐ € 20 – 1 suite – **Rest** – Menu € 55 (dinner) – Carte € 47/87

◆ Renovated Provençal-style rooms, either overlooking the golf course or marina, many with a balcony. During the summer use water transport to travel around the resort. The dining room and the flowered terrace command a panoramic view of the sea. Cuisine with a southern flavour and fish dishes.

Suffren without rest VISA AE

16 pl. du Marché – ✆ 04 94 55 15 05 – lesuffren@hotelleriedusoleil.com – Fax 04 94 55 15 06 – Open 21 March-18 October

19 rm ☐ – †€ 95/160 ††€ 95/250

◆ Most of the rooms in this fully renovated hotel overlook the harbour of this lakeside resort. Pleasant interior with polished furniture, enlivened by bright colours. Balconies.

PORTICCIO – 2A Corse-du-Sud – 345 B8 – see Corse

PORTIRAGNES – 34 Hérault – 339 F9 – pop. 2 278 – alt. 10 m – ✉ 34420

23 **C2**

▶ Paris 762 – Montpellier 72 – Agde 13 – Béziers 13 – Narbonne 51

ℹ Office de tourisme, place du Bicentenaire ✆ 04 67 90 92 51, Fax 04 67 90 92 51

Mirador VISA AE

4 bd Front-de-Mer, at Portiragnes-Plage – ✆ 04 67 90 91 33 – hotel_le_mirador@hotmail.com – Fax 04 67 90 88 80 – Open 1st February-31 October

18 rm – †€ 49/69 ††€ 72/108, ☐ € 7 – ½ P € 51/65

Rest *Saveurs du Sud* – *✆ 04 67 90 97 67 (closed Monday lunch, Tuesday lunch, Wednesday lunch and Thursday lunch)* Menu € 20/50 – Carte € 37/83

◆ A fully renovated, waterside, family-run hotel offering functional rooms. Choose those with terraces overlooking the waves. Traditional cuisine with southern touches served in a modern dining room-veranda.

PORTIVY – 56 Morbihan – 308 M9 – see Quiberon

PORT-JOINVILLE – 85 Vendée – 316 B7 – see Île d'Yeu

PORT LA NOUVELLE – 11 Aude – 344 J4 – pop. 4 859 – alt. 2 m – ✉ 11210

Languedoc-Roussillon-Tarn Gorges

22 **B3**

▶ Paris 813 – Montpellier 120 – Carcassonne 81 – Perpignan 49 – Béziers 60

ℹ Syndicat d'initiative, place Paul Valéry ✆ 04 68 48 00 51

Méditerranée rm, VISA AE

bd Front-de-Mer – ✆ 04 68 48 03 08 – hotel.mediterranee@wanadoo.fr – Fax 04 68 48 53 81 – Closed 27 October-13 November and 5-29 January

30 rm – †€ 62/88 ††€ 62/94, ☐ € 8 – ½ P € 46/74 – **Rest** – Menu € 13 (weekdays), € 22/45 – Carte € 22/49

◆ Seaside construction on the promenade facing the beach. Well-proportioned and equipped rooms; ask for one with a balcony overlooking the sea to enjoy the view. Cuisine focused on seafood. Pavement terrace.

PORT-LESNEY – 39 Jura – 321 E4 – pop. 414 – alt. 251 m – ✉ 39330

Burgundy-Jura

16 **B2**

▶ Paris 401 – Arbois 12 – Besançon 36 – Dole 39 – Lons-le-Saunier 51 – Salins-les-Bains 10

Château de Germigney

r. Edgar-Faure – ✆ 03 84 73 85 85
– germigney@relaischateaux.com – Fax 03 84 73 88 88
– Closed 1st January-6 February

20 rm – €130 €180/280, €15 – ½ P €130/225

Rest – *(closed Monday lunch and Tuesday lunch)* Menu €39 (weekday lunch), €60/99 – Carte €60/94

Spec. Foie gras cuit au torchon. Volaille de Bresse cuite en terrine lutée. Moelleux au chocolat et praline. **Wines** Côtes du Jura, Arbois.

◆ Manor house set in fine parkland with "ecological" swimming pool (naturally filtered lake water). Large personalised rooms and low-key lounge. Cuisine combining the best of Provence and the Jura served in a vaulted dining room, in the orangery or on the terrace.

Le Bistrot "Pontarlier"

pl. 8 Mai 1945 – ✆ 03 84 37 83 27 – reservation@chateaudegermigney.com – Fax 03 84 73 88 88 – Closed 1st January-7 February and from Monday to Thursday from October to May

Rest – bistrot Menu €22/25 – Carte €29/37

◆ Bistro-style cuisine in this restaurant on the banks of the Loue. The dining room is decorated with various knick-knacks, including fishing rods. Pleasant terrace shaded by a tulip tree.

PORT-LEUCATE – 11 Aude – 344 J5 – see Leucate

PORT-LOUIS – 56 Morbihan – pop. 2 808 – alt. 5 m – ✉ 56290 9 B2

Paris 505 – Vannes 50 – Lorient 19 – Pontivy 61 – Quimper 84

Office de tourisme, 1, rue de la Citadelle ✆ 02 97 82 52 93

Avel Vor (Patrice Gahinet)

25 r. Locmalo – ✆ 02 97 82 47 59 – Fax 02 97 82 47 59 – Closed 30 June-8 July, 29 September-15 October, 25 January-11 February, Sunday dinner, Monday and Tuesday

Rest – Menu €26 (weekdays)/70 – Carte €65/94

Spec. Pressé d'araignée et topinambour, émulsion de lait de coco aux épices douces (November to April). Tarte croustillante de homard (June to September). Canneloni de légumes, rouget de petit bateau poêlé.

◆ A sea breeze (avel vor in Breton) blows in this restaurant near the port. It offers freshly caught fish, a contemporary decor with nautical touches, and a view of the sea.

PORT-MANECH – 29 Finistère – 308 I8 – ✉ 29920 Nevez Brittany 9 B2

Paris 545 – Carhaix-Plouguer 73 – Concarneau 18 – Quimper 44 – Quimperlé 29

Du Port

30 r. Aven – ✆ 02 98 06 82 17 – hotel.du.port@wanadoo.fr – Fax 02 98 06 62 70 – Open 1st April-1st November

31 rm – €43/65 €45/66, €7 – ½ P €49/58 – **Rest** – *(closed Saturday lunch and Wednesday in July-August) (dinner only except July-August)* Menu €20/50 – Carte €25/87

◆ At the confluence of the Aven and Belon estuaries. The larger of the pleasant and simply furnished rooms are to be found in the annexe. Good home cooking served in a dining room veranda or terrace facing the small port. Shellfish in season.

PORT-MORT – 27 Eure – 304 I6 – pop. 820 – alt. 19 m – ✉ 27940 33 D2

Paris 89 – Les Andelys 11 – Évreux 33 – Rouen 55 – Vernon-sur-Eure 12

Auberge des Pêcheurs

– ✆ 02 32 52 60 43 – auberge-des-pecheurs@wanadoo.fr – Fax 02 32 52 07 62 – Closed 5-20 March, 29 July-23 August, Sunday dinner, Monday dinner and Tuesday

Rest – Menu €15 bi (weekday lunch), €22 € bi/30 bi – Carte approx. €34

◆ The Seine meanders near this inn which has a large, pleasantly-renovated dining room with a veranda facing the garden. Traditional dishes.

PORT NAVALO – 56 Morbihan – 308 N9 – see Arzon

PORTO – 2A Corse-du-Sud – 345 B6 – see Corse

PORTO-POLLO – 2A Corse-du-Sud – 345 B9 – see Corse

PORTO-VECCHIO – 2A Corse-du-Sud – 345 E10 – see Corse

PORTSALL – 29 Finistère – 308 C3 – ✉ 29830 Brittany

Paris 616 – Rennes 263 – Quimper 98 – Brest 29 – Landerneau 46

La Demeure Océane without rest

20 r. Bar Al Lan – ✆ 02 98 48 77 42 – la-demeure-oceane@wanadoo.fr – Fax 02 98 48 04 15 – Open from March to October

7 rm – €55/65 €60/70

◆ An early-20C house located in a quiet district above the port. Attractive lounge-veranda overlooking the garden; bedrooms with sea views; and an English-style dining room.

PORT-SUR-SAÔNE – 70 Haute-Saône – 314 E6 – pop. 2 773 – alt. 228 m – ✉ 70170 16 **B1**

Paris 347 – Besançon 61 – Bourbonne-les-Bains 46 – Épinal 75 – Gray 51 – Vesoul 13

Office de tourisme, rue de la Rézelle ✆ 03 84 78 10 66, Fax 03 84 78 18 09

in Vauchoux South: 3 km by D 6 – pop. 115 – alt. 210 m – ✉ 70170

Château de Vauchoux (Jean-Michel Turin)

Vallée de la Saône road – ✆ 03 84 91 53 55 – Fax 03 84 91 65 38 – Closed 23-28 February, Monday and Tuesday

Rest – *(pre-book)* Menu €70/120

Spec. Foie gras d'oie au torchon. Râble de lapereau "Mère Jeanne". Gourmandise "Plaisir des Gâtines". **Wines** Charcenne, Arbois.

◆ Once a hunting lodge with a striking Louis XV dining room, part of which has rib vaulting. The attractive park is planted with beds of hydrangeas. Well-prepared classical cuisine.

PORT-VENDRES – 66 Pyrénées-Orientales – 344 J7 – pop. 5 881 – alt. 3 m – ✉ 66660 Languedoc-Roussillon-Tarn Gorges 22 **B3**

Paris 881 – Perpignan 32

Office de tourisme, 1, quai François Joly ✆ 04 68 82 07 54, Fax 04 68 82 62 95

Tour Madeloc ✻★★ Southwest: 8 km then 15 mn.

Les Jardins du Cèdre port and sea, rm, rm,

29 rte Banyuls – ✆ 04 68 82 01 05 – contact@lesjardinsducedre.com – Fax 04 68 82 22 13 – Closed 9 November-15 December and 4 January-7 February

19 rm – €58/92 €58/92, €9 – 1 suite – ½ P €64/90

Rest – *(closed Tuesday dinner) (dinner only except Sunday and holidays)* Menu €34/48 – Carte €34/48

◆ The garden of this hotel is very attractive: view of the harbour and sea, palm trees, old cedar of Lebanon and pretty pool. Modern rooms with pleasant colour schemes. Stylish restaurant and charming terrace. A la carte and set menus of local dishes.

Côte Vermeille

quai Fanal, direction la criée – ✆ 04 68 82 05 71 – Fax 04 68 82 05 71 – Closed 1st-8 July, 15 January-15 February, Sunday October-June, Tuesday lunch July-August and Monday

Rest – Menu €25 (weekday lunch), €35/56 – Carte €45/56

◆ Quayside restaurant in the fishing harbour, near the fish market. Nautical decor enhanced by contemporary paintings. Fish and seafood served Catalan style.

LA POTERIE – 22 Côtes-d'Armor – **309** H4 – see Lamballe

POUANÇAY – 86 Vienne – **322** F2 – **pop. 275 – alt. 73 m** 39 **C1**

Paris 348 – Poitiers 75 – Saumur 29 – Bressuire 56 – Thouars 26

Trésor Belge

1 allée du Jardin Secret – 05 49 98 72 25 – info@tresorbelge.com – Closed 1st-7 July, 1st-7 September, January, Monday and Tuesday

Rest – *(number of covers limited, pre-book)* Menu € 23/39 – Carte € 36/49

◆ An outpost of Flemish cuisine serving delicious Belgian specialities to be washed down with traditional Belgian beer (choice of 40!). Friendly relaxed atmosphere.

POUGUES-LES-EAUX – 58 Nièvre – **319** B9 – **pop. 2 493 – alt. 198 m – Casino** – ✉ **58320** Burgundy-Jura 7 **A2**

Paris 225 – Auxerre 123 – Bourges 65 – Nevers 12

Syndicat d'initiative, 42, avenue de Paris 03 86 58 75 69, Fax 03 86 90 96 05

Hôtel des Sources without rest VISA AE

r. Mignarderie – 03 86 90 11 90 – contact@hoteldessources.fr – Fax 03 86 90 11 91

29 rm – €55 €60, €10

◆ Quiet hotel in a residential district a stone's throw from the casino. Spacious and well-equipped rooms. Friendly service provided.

POUILLON – 40 Landes – **335** F13 – **pop. 2 685 – alt. 28 m** – ✉ **40350** 3 **B3**

Paris 742 – Dax 16 – Mont-de-Marsan 69 – Orthez 28 – Peyrehorade 15

Syndicat d'initiative, chemin de Lahitte 05 58 98 38 93, Fax 05 58 98 30 67

L'Auberge du Pas de Vent VISA

– 05 58 98 34 65 – sophiedubern@cegetel.net – Fax 05 58 98 34 65 – Closed 26 October-9 November, 23-26 December, 15 February-2 March, Sunday dinner, Monday dinner, Tuesday dinner and Wednesday

Rest – Menu € 12 (weekday lunch), € 22/37 – Carte € 34/48

◆ The chef of this pleasant country inn uses age-old recipes for his regional dishes. Adjacent ninepins play area.

POUILLY-EN-AUXOIS – 21 Côte-d'Or – **320** H6 – **pop. 1 502 – alt. 390 m** – ✉ **21320** Burgundy-Jura 8 **C2**

Paris 270 – Avallon 66 – Beaune 42 – Dijon 44 – Montbard 59

Office de tourisme, le Colombier 03 80 90 74 24, Fax 03 80 90 74 24

du Château de Chailly Chailly s/Armançon, West: 6 km by D 977, 03 80 90 30 40.

Poste with rm VISA

pl. de la Libération – 03 80 90 86 44 – hoteldelapostepouilly@orange.fr – Fax 03 80 90 75 99 – Closed 11-25 November, Sunday dinner and Monday

6 rm – €49/61 €49/61, €7 – ½ P €60

Rest – Menu € 18/43 – Carte € 23/43

◆ A stone inn set by the main square of this small Burgundy town. Veranda/dining room redecorated in a classical country style. Traditional regionally influenced cuisine. Spacious rooms that have been renovated in a rustic style.

in Créancey 4 km southeast by D 18 – **pop. 482 – alt. 405 m** – ✉ **21320**

Château de Créancey without rest VISA AE

– 03 80 90 57 50 – chateau@creancey.com – Fax 03 80 90 57 51

5 rm – €145/215 €160/230

◆ Experiencing life in a chateau is not an inaccessible dream! Renovated in the spirit of the 17C with high, French style ceilings. Charming, attractive bedrooms.

in Ste-Sabine 8 km southeast by D 981, D 977bis and D 970 – pop. 172 – alt. 365 m – ✉ 21320

Hostellerie du Château Ste-Sabine
– ✆ 03 80 49 22 01 – chateau-ste-sabine@wanadoo.fr – Fax 03 80 49 20 01 – Closed 1st January-17 February
30 rm – †€ 80 ††€ 80/186, ☕ € 10 – ½ P € 75/125 – **Rest** – Menu € 26 (weekday lunch), € 36/66 bi – Carte € 52/68
♦ An elegant 17C château built on the site of an 11C monastery. Rustic-style bedrooms and duplexes in the towers. Park with a lake, where animals are able to roam freely. Enjoy seasonal cuisine in the dining room overlooking the lake or under the vaulted ceiling of the old cloister.

in Chailly-sur-Armançon 6.5 km west by D 977bis – pop. 201 – alt. 387 m – ✉ 21320

Château de Chailly
– ✆ 03 80 90 30 30 – reservation@chailly.com
– Fax 03 80 90 30 00 – Closed 14 December-17 January and 22 February-7 March
37 rm – †€ 215/295 ††€ 260/340, ☕ € 20 – 8 suites
Rest *L'Armançon* – *(closed Monday) (dinner only)* Menu € 60/100
Rest *Le Rubillon* – *(closed dinner except Monday)* Menu € 33 (lunch), € 45/50
♦ One façade has rich Renaissance decoration and the other is a reminder that this was, once, a medieval fortress. The château, adjoining a large park and superb golf course, offers its guests a prestigious setting. L'Armançon offers both a traditional menu and decor. The Rubillon offers a terrace facing the pool, serving buffets and traditional dishes.

POUILLY-LE-FORT – 77 Seine-et-Marne – 312 E4 – see Paris, Area (Sénart)

POUILLY-SOUS-CHARLIEU – 42 Loire – 327 D3 – pop. 2 720 – alt. 264 m – ✉ 42720
44 **A1**

▶ Paris 393 – Charlieu 5 – Digoin 43 – Roanne 15 – Vichy 75

Loire
– ✆ 04 77 60 81 36 – restoloire@yahoo.fr – Fax 04 77 60 76 06
– *Closed 1st-12 September, 5-23 January, 16-26 February, Sunday dinner, Tuesday except dinner July-August and Monday*
Rest – Menu € 22 (except Sunday)/68 – Carte € 31/66
♦ This inn which formerly served simple meals has become an elegant restaurant with a terrace overlooking the garden. Traditional meals served.

POUILLY-SUR-LOIRE – 58 Nièvre – 319 A8 – pop. 1 718 – alt. 168 m – ✉ 58150
Burgundy-Jura
7 **A2**

▶ Paris 200 – Bourges 58 – Clamecy 54 – Cosne-sur-Loire 18 – Nevers 38 – Vierzon 80

ℹ Syndicat d'initiative, 17, quai Jules Pabiot ✆ 03 86 39 54 54, Fax 03 86 39 54 55

Relais de Pouilly
rte de Mesves-sur-Loire, 3 km south on D 28^{A} – ✆ 03 86 39 03 00 – sarl.relais-de-pouilly@wanadoo.fr – Fax 03 86 39 07 47
24 rm – †€ 50/66 ††€ 68/75, ☕ € 9,50 – ½ P € 68/72 – **Rest** – Menu (€ 14,50 bi), € 18/34 – Carte € 22/43
♦ A hotel poised between the wine producing town and a motorway service area (pedestrian access). Rooms are modern, soundproofed and overlook the Loire. Restaurant looking out over the garden, regional menu, buffets, grilled food and a selection of Pouilly wines.

POUJOLS – 34 Hérault – 339 E6 – see Lodève

POULDREUZIC – 29 Finistère – 308 E7 – pop. 1 814 – alt. 51 m – ✉ 29710
9 **A2**

▶ Paris 587 – Audierne 17 – Douarnenez 17 – Pont-l'Abbé 15 – Quimper 25

ℹ Syndicat d'initiative, salle Per Jakez Hélias ✆ 02 98 54 49 90

Ker Ansquer
at Lababan 2 km north-westward along the D 2 – 02 98 54 41 83 – francoise.ansquer@wanadoo.fr – Fax 02 98 54 32 24 – Open 2 June-30 September
10 rm – €65/73 €65/83, €8,50 – 2 suites – ½ P €63/77
Rest – *(closed Saturday dinner except 7 July-30 September) (dinner only) (pre-book)* Menu €23
◆ A granite house in the region of the book and film, The Proud Ones. Regional sculptures, Breton furniture, rustic rooms and guesthouse atmosphere. Fireplace, solid wood tables and furniture painted with naive-style religious scenes: the dining room has a lot of style.

in Penhors west: 4 km by D 40 – ✉ 29710 Pouldreuzic

Breiz Armor
at the beach – 02 98 51 52 53 – breiz-armor@wanadoo.fr – Fax 02 98 51 52 30 – Open end March-beg. October, autumn half-term holidays and Christmas holidays
36 rm – €71/80 €71/128, €9 – ½ P €69/77 – **Rest** – *(closed Monday except dinner July-August)* Menu €15 (weekday lunch), €20/51 – Carte €26/60
◆ A modern, seafront building with well-kept rooms. The delightful museum (shells, birds), billiards table, sundeck, fitness facilities, sauna, bicycles, and laundry are a few of the establishment's attractions. Regional and seafood recipes are served in this restaurant with a breathtaking sea view.

LE POULDU – 29 Finistère – **308** J8 – ✉ 29360 Clohars-Carnoët Brittany

Paris 521 – Concarneau 37 – Lorient 25 – Moëlan-sur-Mer 10 – Quimper 61 – Quimperlé 14 9 **B2**

St-Maurice: site★ and ≤★ of bridge Northeast: 7 km.

Le Panoramique rm, rest,
at Kérou beach – 02 98 39 93 49 – poulduramique@wanadoo.fr – Fax 02 98 96 90 16 – Open 4 April-5 November
25 rm – €45/61 €45/61, €8,50 – **Rest** – crêperie *(open July-August) (dinner only) (residents only)* Carte approx. €12
◆ Clean, functional rooms in this hotel where breakfast is served in a bright sea-facing dining room. Reading/sitting rooms with bar and TV. The basement crêperie is decorated with wood panelling and a mural of the port.

POURVILLE-SUR-MER – 76 Seine-Maritime – **304** G2 – see Dieppe

---

POUZAY – 37 Indre-et-Loire – **317** M6 – see Ste-Maure-de-Touraine

---

LE POUZIN – 07 Ardèche – **331** K5 – pop. 2 668 – alt. 90 m – ✉ 07250 44 **B3**

Paris 590 – Lyon 127 – Privas 16 – Valence 28 – Romans-sur-Isère 48

La Cardinale
– 04 75 41 20 39 – lacardinale@orange.fr – Fax 04 75 41 20 39 – Closed 26 October-6 November and 22 December-2 January
10 rm – €70/90 €130/195, €15 – **Rest** – *(closed Monday, Tuesday, Wednesday October-June, Saturday lunch, Sunday dinner, Monday dinner and Tuesday dinner)* Menu €25/38 – Carte €35/56
◆ This stone house and pool are surrounded by a park planted with rare tree species. The ground floor rooms (superb bathrooms) open onto a terrace. Traditional cuisine served in a cosy, fashionable setting.

PRADES – 66 Pyrénées-Orientales – **344** F7 – pop. 5 800 – alt. 360 m – ✉ 66500 Languedoc-Roussillon-Tarn Gorges 22 **B3**

Paris 892 – Mont-Louis 36 – Olette 16 – Perpignan 46 – Vernet-les-Bains 11

Office de tourisme, 4, rue des Marchands 04 68 05 41 02, Fax 04 68 05 21 79

de Marcevol Arboussols Le Hameau de Marcevol, Northeast: 10 km by D 35, 04 68 96 18 08.

St-Michel-de-Cuxa abbey ★★ South: 3 km - Village of Eus★ Northeast: 7 km.

Pradotel without rest

av. Festival, On the beltway – ✆ 04 68 05 22 66 – pradotel66@orange.fr – Fax 04 68 05 23 22

39 rm – †€ 48/60 ††€ 52/70, ☕ € 8

◆ A contemporary functional building. To the rear, a fine view of the Canigou from the balconies. Terraces for the poolside ground floor rooms are a new feature.

Hexagone ♿ rm, rest, P VISA

rd-pt de Molitg, on the bypass – ✆ 04 68 05 31 31 – hotelhexagone@cegetel.net – Fax 04 68 05 24 89

30 rm – †€ 50/63 ††€ 55/67, ☕ € 7,50 – ½ P € 47/55 – **Rest** – *(closed Saturday and Sunday) (dinner only)* Menu € 17

◆ Identical, simple and well-kept rooms: a practical address in this town renowned for its music festival.

Le Jardin d'Aymeric A/C VISA

3 av. Gén. de Gaulle – ✆ 04 68 96 53 38 – marta.jose@yahoo.fr – Closed 16 June-1st July, February holidays, Wednesday dinner from October to April, Sunday dinner and Monday

Rest – Menu € 21/35 – Carte € 29/55

◆ Contemporary decoration, art exhibitions and flower arrangements make this popular establishment ideal to taste an updated Catalan cuisine. Fine wine list.

in Clara South 5 km by D 35 – ✉ **66500**

Les Loges du Jardin d'Aymeric P VISA

– ✆ 04 68 96 08 72 – jardin.aymeric@wanadoo.fr – Fax 04 68 96 08 72 – Closed January

3 rm ☕ – †€ 55/75 ††€ 65/85 – ½ P € 55/70 – **Table d'hôte** – *(closed Tuesday dinner and Wednesday from October to May)* Menu € 30

◆ Tucked away in a pleasant village at the foot of the Canigou, this establishment has spacious rooms which are sober yet bright. Good pool in the flowered garden. Regional family fare in a charming rustic setting typical of the region.

LE PRADET – 83 Var – 340 L7 – pop. 10 975 – alt. 1 m – ✉ 83220

French Riviera 41 **C3**

Paris 842 – Draguignan 76 – Hyères 11 – Toulon 10

Office de tourisme, place Général-de-Gaulle ✆ 04 94 21 71 69, Fax 04 94 08 56 96

Musée de la mine de Cap Garonne: large room★, 3 km South by D 86.

in Oursinières South: 3 km by D 86 – ✉ 83320 Le Pradet

L'Escapade without rest VISA

– ✆ 04 94 08 39 39 – info@hotel-escapade.com – Open 7 March-5 November

9 rm – †€ 125/165 ††€ 165/215, ☕ € 13 – 1 suite

◆ Small houses 100 m from the sea in a beautiful garden. Rooms decorated in Tyrolean style. The pretty breakfast room looks out on to the swimming pool. Pleasant welcome.

La Chanterelle VISA

– ✆ 04 94 08 52 60 – Closed 3 November-5 December, 5 January-6 March, Monday and Tuesday from September to April

Rest – Menu € 39/49 – Carte € 48/57

◆ The dining room has a carved wood ceiling and coloured stained-glass windows representing still life subjects. A pleasant flower garden. Modern regional cuisine.

PRALOGNAN-LA-VANOISE – 73 Savoie – 333 N5 – pop. 756 – alt. 1 425 m – Winter sports : 1 410/2 360 m 1 13 – ✉ 73710 French Alps 45 D2

Paris 634 – Albertville 53 – Chambéry 103 – Moûtiers 28

Office de tourisme, avenue de Chasseforêt ✆ 04 79 08 79 08, Fax 04 79 08 76 74

Site★ - La Vanoise National Park ★★ - La Chollière★ Southwest: 1.5 km then 30 mn - Mont Bochor ≤★ by cable car.

Les Airelles rest, VISA
les Darbelays, north: 1 km – 04 79 08 70 32 – hotellesairelles@free.fr – Fax 04 79 08 73 51 – Open 8 June-19 September and 21 December-18 April
21 rm – €63/73 €73/93, €8 – ½ P €51/73 – **Rest** – Menu €23/30 – Carte €24/29
◆ An attractive 1980s chalet, located on the edge of Granges Forest. Wood-panelled partially refurbished rooms, whose balconies offer a fine mountain view. A warm regional-style restaurant with cheese specialities (tartiflettes, fondues, gratins, etc.).

Du Grand Bec rest, VISA
– 04 79 08 71 10 – grand_bec@wanadoo.fr – Fax 04 79 08 72 22 – Open 2 June-14 September and 21 December-13 April
39 rm – €55/80 €60/120, €10 – ½ P €52/74 – **Rest** – Menu €20/40 – Carte €21/46
◆ A regional-style hotel, dominated by the Grand Bec mountain, on the outskirts of the resort. Alpine-style rooms with a balcony (12 have a sitting room). Restaurant in warm colours, facing the village and peaks. Traditional menu with Savoy dishes.

De la Vanoise rm, VISA
– 04 79 08 70 34 – hotel@la-vanoise.com – Fax 04 79 08 75 79 – Open mid June-mid September and 20 December-20 April
32 rm – €45/86 €70/108, €9 – ½ P €55/93 – **Rest** – Menu €18 (lunch)/22 (dinner) – Carte €17/37
◆ Big building with character at the centre of the resort and near the ski lifts. All the wood-panelled rooms have a balcony. Family atmosphere. Traditional, Savoy or vegetarian dishes in a dining room lined with light-wood panelling and floral fabrics.

PRA-LOUP – **04 Alpes-de-Haute-Provence** – **334** H6 – **see Barcelonnette**

LE PRARION – **74 Haute-Savoie** – **328** N5 – **see les Houches**

PRATS-DE-MOLLO-LA-PRESTE – 66 Pyrénées-Orientales – 344 F8 – pop. 1 080 – alt. 740 m – ✉ 66230 Languedoc-Roussillon-Tarn Gorges 22 B3

Paris 905 – Céret 32 – Perpignan 64

Office de tourisme, place du Foiral 04 68 39 70 83, Fax 04 68 39 74 51

High town★.

Bellevue rest, VISA
pl. le Foiral – 04 68 39 72 48 – lebellevue@.fr.st – Fax 04 68 39 78 04 – Closed 1st December-14 February, Tuesday and Wednesday except 1st April-30 November
17 rm – €41/50 €48/60, €7,50 – ½ P €41/52 – **Rest** – Menu €21/50 – Carte €33/50
◆ Situated on the market square, this regional-style hotel has simply furnished rooms, some of which have been refurbished. Views of the mountain and the ramparts of the medieval town. Menu offering appetising Catalan recipes in a dining room decorated in pastel shades.

in La Preste : 8 km – ✉ 66230 Prats-de-Mollo-la-Preste – Spa : beg. April-mid Nov.

Ribes Tech valley, rest, VISA
– 04 68 39 71 04 – info@hotel-ribes.com – Fax 04 68 39 78 02 – Open 1st April-20 October
19 rm – €30/52 €45/59, €6 – ½ P €39/43 – **Rest** – Menu (€11 bi), €16 (weekdays)/28 – Carte €27/37
◆ This farmhouse surrounded by meadows is now a pleasant, family-run hotel. The modest, well-maintained rooms have been gradually renovated. This panoramic restaurant overlooking the valley serves traditional Catalan cuisine based on produce from the family farm.

Le Val du Tech VISA
– 04 68 39 71 12 – val.du.tech@wanadoo.fr – Fax 04 68 39 78 07 – Open end April-end November
25 rm – €33/36 €48/54, €7 – ½ P €47/50 – **Rest** – Menu (€12), €16/25
◆ This small hotel situated on the hillside near the spa is popular with hikers and spa visitors alike. Very simple guestrooms, some of which have no shower or WC. Traditional cuisine served in a large dining room with a discreetly rustic, Catalan-style setting.

LE PRAZ – 73 Savoie – **333** M5 – see Courchevel

LES PRAZ-DE-CHAMONIX – 74 Haute-Savoie – **328** O5 – see Chamonix-Mont-Blanc

PRAZ-SUR-ARLY – 74 Haute-Savoie – **328** M5 – pop. 1 081 – alt. 1 036 m – Winter sports : 1 036/2 070 m 12 – ✉ 74120 46 **F1**

Paris 602 – Albertville 28 – Chambéry 79 – Chamonix-Mont-Blanc 37 – Megève 5

Office de tourisme, ✆ 04 50 21 90 57, Fax 04 50 21 98 08

La Griyotire

rte La Tonnaz – ✆ 04 50 21 86 36 – hotel@griyotire.com – Fax 04 50 21 86 34 – Open 7 June-30 September and 21 December-6 April

17 rm – €85/110 €85/110, €10 – ½ P €88/93

Rest – *(dinner only)* Menu €28 – Carte €32/47

◆ An elegant Savoy-style chalet, which is quiet despite its central location. Attractive, cosy bedrooms and a comfortable lounge with open fireplace. Hammam, sauna and massage available. Attractive mountain interior, classic and regional cuisine, cheese specialities.

For a pleasant stay in a charming hotel, look for the red ... symbols.

PRÉCY-SUR-OISE – 60 Oise – **305** F5 – pop. 3 120 – alt. 33 m – ✉ 60460 36 **B3**

Paris 56 – Beauvais 36 – Chantilly 10 – Compiègne 47 – Creil 12 – Pontoise 37 – Senlis 18

Church ★ of St-Leu-d'Esserent Northeast: 3.5 km.

Le Condor

14 r. Wateau – ✆ 03 44 27 60 77 – Fax 03 44 27 62 18 – Closed 1st-15 August, 23 February-2 March, Tuesday and Wednesday

Rest – Menu (€19), €24 (weekdays)/37

◆ An elegant inn with a dining room arranged around a small patio, creating areas of privacy. Redecorated interior and traditional cuisine at reasonable prices.

PREIGNAC – 33 Gironde – **335** J7 – see Langon

PRENOIS – 21 Côte-d'Or – **320** J5 – see Dijon

LE PRÉ-ST-GERVAIS – 93 Seine-Saint-Denis – **305** F7 – **101** 16 – see Paris, Area

LA PRESTE – 66 Pyrénées-Orientales – **344** F8 – see Prats-de-Mollo

PRINGY – 74 Haute-Savoie – **328** J5 – see Annecy

PRIVAS P – 07 Ardèche – **331** J5 – pop. 9 170 – alt. 300 m – ✉ 07000
Lyon - Rhone Valley 44 **B3**

Paris 596 – Montélimar 34 – Le Puy-en-Velay 91 – Valence 41

Office de tourisme, 3, place du Général-de-Gaulle ✆ 04 75 64 33 35, Fax 04 75 64 73 95

Site★.

PRIVAS

Bacconnier (R. L.) . . . . B 2
Boeufs (Pl. aux) . . . . A 3
Champ de Mars (Pl. du) . . . . . B 5
Coux (Av. de) . . . . B 7
Durand (R. H.) . . . . B 10
Esplanade (Cours de l') . . . . . . B 9
Faugier (Av. C.) . . . . A 12
Filliat (R. P.) . . . . B 14
Foiral (Pl. du) . . . . A 16
Gaulle (Pl. Ch.-de) . . . . B 17
Hôtel de Ville (Pl. de l') . . . . . . B 18
Mobiles (Bd des) . . . . B 20
Ouvèze (Chemin de la) . . . . . . B 22
Petit Tournon
(Av. du) . . . . B 24
République (R. de la) . . . . B 26
St-Louis (Cours) . . . . A 28
Vanel (Av. du) . . . . B 30

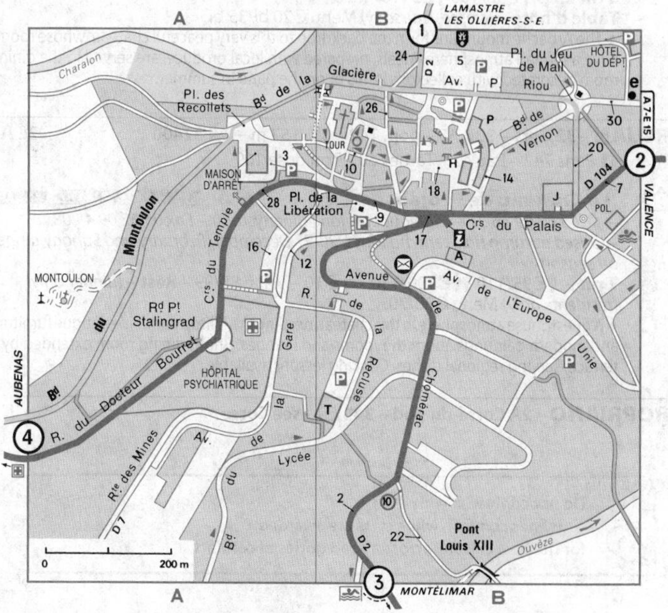

La Chaumette

av. Vanel – ✆ 04 75 64 30 66 – hotelchaumette@wanadoo.fr – Fax 04 75 64 88 25 – Closed 28 October-11 November and 2-15 January B e

36 rm – †€ 52/74 ††€ 57/91, ☕ € 11,50 – ½ P € 63/70 – **Rest** – *(closed Sunday except dinner from June to mid October and Saturday lunch)* Menu € 19 (weekday lunch), € 30/50 – Carte € 40/52

♦ A welcoming hotel with a southern French feel opposite the Conseil Général building. Public areas decorated in ochre tones, with bedrooms that are being renovated in stages. Modern cuisine served in a contemporary, southern French-style dining room or on the terrace overlooking the swimming pool.

Les Châtaigniers

Plaine du Lac – ✆ 04 75 66 39 60 – hotel.chataigniers@free.fr – Fax 04 75 64 68 76

82 rm – †€ 46/51 ††€ 49/54, ☕ € 7 – ½ P € 48/53 – **Rest** – Menu € 17 (weekday lunch), € 19/32 – Carte € 20/34

♦ With its functional, air-conditioned rooms, this hotel is an ideal stopover on the way to the Coiron massif. Breakfast is served in the bar or on the terrace. A menu offering traditional recipes is offered in the light dining room.

in Lyas 7 km by ① and D 2 – **pop. 517 – alt. 350 m –** ✉ **07000**

Château de Liviers

Cheylard road, D2 – ✆ 04 75 64 64 00 – chateau.liviers@wanadoo.fr – Fax 04 75 64 38 00 – Closed January except week-ends

5 rm ☕ – †€ 62/67 ††€ 62/67 – ½ P € 52/55 – **Table d'hôte** – Menu € 21 bi

♦ This former stronghold of Maltese knights stands on a rocky outcrop, at the heart of a forest, facing Privas. The simple rooms are very peaceful, as is the library that contains about 3,000 books and comic strips. The table d'hôte serves good local dishes.

in Rochessauve 11 km by ③, D 2 and D 999 – pop. 300 – alt. 300 m – ✉ 07210

Château de Rochessauve ≤ The Vercors and the Alps,
– ☎ 04 75 65 07 06 – vialley@wanadoo.fr – Closed 1st January to Easter
5 rm – €90/100 €110
Table d'hôte – *(closed Thursday)* Menu €20 bi/35 bi
◆ The Ardèche mountains form the backdrop to this very peaceful château, whose rooms have a refined atmosphere. Meals, prepared with local produce, are served in the dining room decorated with collector's items or on the patio in summer.

PROJAN – 32 Gers – **336** A8 – **pop. 142 – alt. 157 m** – ✉ **32400** 28 **A2**

Paris 742 – Pau 42 – Tarbes 60 – Toulouse 169

Le Château de Projan
– ☎ 05 62 09 46 21 – chateaudeprojan@libertysurf.fr – Fax 05 62 09 44 08 – Closed autumn half-term holidays, 20-27 December, February and Sunday dinner off season
7 rm – €95/110 €100/150, €10 – ½ P €85/99 – **Rest** – *(dinner only) (residents only)* Menu €30/70
◆ A guesthouse atmosphere in this château nestling in a hilltop park. Fine antique furniture and modern paintings adorn the rooms and lounges. Bright dining room extended by a terrace, serving regional dishes. Cooking lessons available.

PROPRIANO – 2A Corse-du-Sud – **345** C9 – **see Corse**

Do not confuse X with ✿!
X defines comfort, while stars are awarded for the best cuisine, across all categories of comfort.

PROVINS – 77 Seine-et-Marne – **312** I4 – **pop. 11 667 – alt. 91 m** – ✉ **77160**
Northern France and the Paris Region 19 **D2**

Paris 88 – Châlons-en-Champagne 98 – Fontainebleau 55 – Sens 47

Office de tourisme, chemin de Villecran ☎ 01 64 60 26 26, Fax 01 64 60 11 97

High town★★ AV: ramparts★★ AY, Caesar tower ★★: ≤★, Grange aux Dîmes★ AV **E** - Place du Chatel★ - Central portal ★ and group of statues★★ in St-Ayoul church BV - Choir ★ of St-Quiriace collegiate church AV - Musée de Povins et du Provinois: collections of sculptures and pottery★ **M.**

St-Loup-de-Naud: portal★★ of church★ 7 km by ④.

Plan on next page

Aux Vieux Remparts
3 r. Couverte - Ville Haute – ☎ 01 64 08 94 00 – vieux-remparts@wanadoo.fr – Fax 01 60 67 77 22 – Closed 21 December-3 January AV **b**
32 rm – €75/260 €88/270, €16 – ½ P €112/189 – **Rest** – Menu €27 (weekdays)/90 – Carte €64/96
◆ This hotel, located in the heart of the upper town, offers guests functional rooms that have been recently renovated. The rooms in the old house have more character. Two dining rooms: One inspired by the Middle Ages; the other, modest and rustic.

Ibis rm,
77 av. du Gén. de Gaulle – ☎ 01 60 67 66 67 – h0856@accor.com – Fax 01 60 67 86 67 AX **d**
51 rm – €59/72 €59/72, €7,50 – **Rest** – Menu €18 – Carte approx. €20
◆ In a quiet area, with architecture reminiscent of the medieval style of the upper town. The rooms are gradually being renovated in a trendy Ibis style. Restaurant with neo-rustic decor and traditional cuisine, fully in keeping with chain standards.

PROVINS

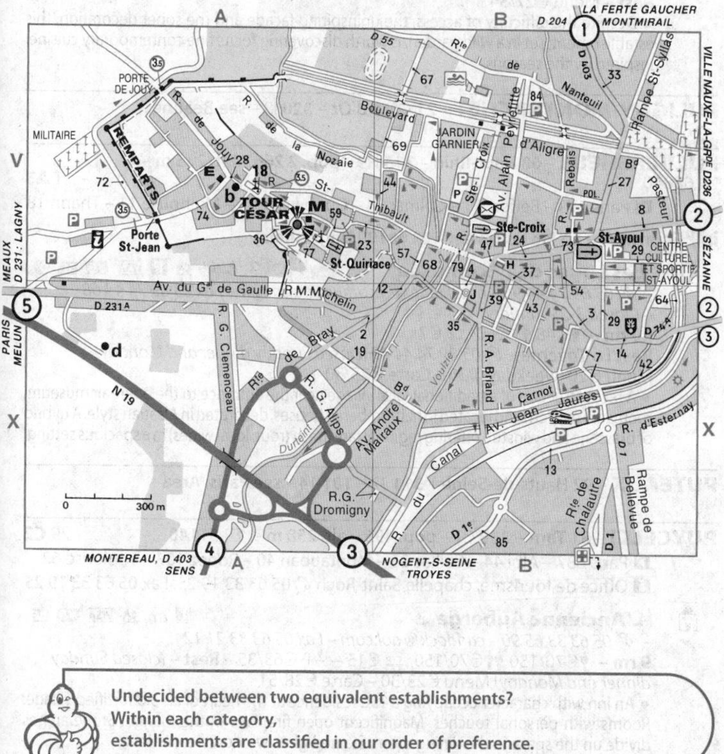

Undecided between two equivalent establishments?
Within each category,
establishments are classified in our order of preference.

PRUNETE – 2B Haute-Corse – **345** F6 – see Corse (Cervione)

PUGIEU – 01 Ain – **328** G6 – see Belley

PUJAUDRAN – 32 Gers – **336** I8 – see l'Isle-Jourdain

PUJOLS – 47 Lot-et-Garonne – **336** G3 – see Villeneuve-sur-Lot

PUJOLS – 33 Gironde – **335** K6 – **pop. 604** – **alt. 60 m** – ✉ **33350** 4 **C2**

Paris 560 – Bordeaux 51 – Mérignac 68 – Pessac 63

Les Gués Rivières rest,

5 pl. du Gén. de Gaulle – ✆ 05 57 40 74 73 – margotte.olivier@wanadoo.fr – Fax 05 57 40 73 26

4 rm – €65 €65 – **Table d'hôte** – Menu (€ 18), € 23

◆ This house, lining the main village square, offers colourful and tastefully-furnished rooms. Gargantuan breakfasts and regional dishes are served on the magnificent terrace facing the vineyards and St Émilion, weather permitting.

La Poudette P VISA

La Rivière, (on D17) – ✆ 05 57 40 71 52 – la-poudette@wanadoo.fr – Closed March, Sunday dinner and Tuesday except July-August and Monday

Rest – Menu € 27/34

◆ Despite the difficulty of access, the uninspiring façade and the sober decoration, this establishment, set in a wild garden, is worth discovering for its fine contemporary cuisine, inspired by the seasons.

PULIGNY-MONTRACHET – 21 Côte-d'Or – **320** I8 – **see Beaune**

PULVERSHEIM – 68 Haut-Rhin – **315** H9 – **pop. 2 266** – **alt. 235 m** – ✉ **68840** 1 **A3**

Paris 473 – Belfort 51 – Colmar 34 – Guebwiller 13 – Mulhouse 11 – Thann 18

in l'Écomusée 2,5 km Northwest – ✉ **68190 Ungersheim**

Les Loges de l'Écomusée P VISA AE

– ✆ 03 89 74 44 95 – hotel.loges@ecomusee-alsace.fr – Fax 03 89 74 44 68 – Closed 3-25 January

40 rm – €48 €60, €7

Rest *La Taverne* – *✆ 03 89 74 44 49 (closed Sunday dinner and Monday)* Menu € 20 (weekdays)/35 – Carte € 25/30

◆ A reconstruction of a traditional local village near the entrance to the open-air museum: rooms are modern and located in half-timbered houses, decorated in Alsatian style. A hybrid of brasserie and winstub offering regional fare (fresh trout, local wines) in a spacious setting.

PUTEAUX – 92 Hauts-de-Seine – **311** J2 – **101** 14 – **see Paris, Area**

PUYCELCI – 81 Tarn – **338** C7 – **pop. 495** – **alt. 258 m** – ✉ **81140** 29 **C2**

Paris 637 – Albi 44 – Gaillac 25 – Montauban 40 – Rodez 107 – Toulouse 62

Office de tourisme, chapelle Saint-Roch ✆ 05 63 33 19 25, Fax 05 63 33 19 25

L'Ancienne Auberge rm, VISA AE

– ✆ 05 63 33 65 90 – caddack@aol.com – Fax 05 63 33 21 12

9 rm – €70/150 €70/150, € 15 – ½ P € 63/85 – **Rest** – *(closed Sunday dinner and Monday)* Menu € 23/30 – Carte € 28/51

◆ An inn with character occupying a 13C residence at the heart of an old fortified village. Rooms with personal touches. Magnificent open fireplace in the lounge. Stone arches divide up the space in the dining room. Stained-glass window decoration.

LE PUY-DE-DÔME – 63 Puy-de-Dôme – **326** E8 – **see Clermont-Ferrand**

LE PUY-EN-VELAY P – 43 Haute-Loire – **331** F3 – **pop. 20 490** – **alt. 629 m** – ✉ **43000** Lyon - Rhone Valley 6 **C3**

Paris 539 – Clermont-Ferrand 129 – Mende 87 – St-Étienne 76

Office de tourisme, 2, place du Clauzel ✆ 04 71 09 38 41, Fax 04 71 05 22 62

du Puy-en-Velay Ceyssac Sénilhac, West: 7 km by D 590, ✆ 04 71 09 17 77.

Site ★★★ - L'île au trésors ★★★ BY : Notre-Dame cathedral ★★★, cloister ★★ - Religious art treasure-house ★★ in the États du Velay - St-Michel d'Aiguilhe AY - Liberal arts painting of the Reliques chapel ★★ - Old town ★ - Rocher Corneille ≤★ - Musée Crozatier: collection of lapidary ★, lace ★.

Polignac★: ✻★ 5 km by ③.

LE PUY-EN-VELAY

Rue	Carré	N°
Aiguières (R. Porte)	AZ	2
Becdelièvre (R.)	AY	3
Bouillon (R. du)	BY	5
Card.-de-Polignac (R.)	BY	8
Chamarlenc (R. du)	AY	10
Charbonnier (Av. C.)	AZ	12
Chaussade (R.)	BZ	
Chênebouterie (R.)	AY	13
Clair (Bd A.)	AZ	14
Collège (R. du)	BZ	17
Consulat (R. du)	AY	19
Courrerie (R.)	AZ	20
Crozatier (R.)	BZ	23
Dr-Chantemesse (Bd)	AY	24
Fayolle (Bd Mar.)	BZ	
Foch (Av. Mar.)	BZ	
For (Pl. du)	BY	27
Gambetta (Bd)	AY	29
Gaulle (Av. Gén.-de)	ABZ	30
Gouteyron (R.)	AY	31
Grangevieille (R.)	AY	32
Martouret (Pl. du)	ABZ	34
Monteil (R. A.-de)	AY	35
Pannessac (R.)	AY	
Philibert (R.)	AY	36
Pierret (R.)	BZ	37
Plot (Pl. du)	AZ	38
Raphaël (R.)	AY	39
République (Bd de la)	BY	40
Roche-Taillade (R.)	AY	42
Saint-François-Régis (R.)	BY	43
Saint-Georges (R.)	BY	45
Saint-Gilles (R.)	AZ	
Saint-Jean (R. du Fg)	BY	46
Saint-Louis (Bd)	AZ	
Saint-Maurice (Pl.)	AY	47
Séguret (R.)	AY	48
Tables (Pl. des)	AY	49
Tables (R. des)	AY	52
Vallès (R. J.)	BY	54
Vaneau (R.)	AY	55
Verdun (R.)	BY	58

Du Parc rest, rest, VISA AE

4 av. C. Charbonnier – 04 71 02 40 40 – francoisgagnaire@wanadoo.fr – Fax 04 71 02 18 72 AZ **s**

18 rm – €70/130 €70/130, €10

Rest ***François Gagnaire*** – see restaurant listing

◆ This hotel, near the Vinay garden, offers well-equipped comfortable rooms, a cosy lounge with bar and a selection of cigars. Reasonably priced.

Regina rm, rest, VISA AE

34 bd Mar. Fayolle – 04 71 09 14 71 – contact@hotelrestregina.com – Fax 04 71 09 18 57 BZ **d**

25 rm – €50/53 €59/60, €10 – 3 suites – ½ P €62

Rest – *(closed Sunday dinner 15 November-15 March)* Menu (€17), €22 (weekdays)/40 – Carte €36/54

◆ This 1905 building is now a hotel that is being gradually renovated. The pleasant rooms, painted in bright colours, are all different and often spacious (some have a Jacuzzi). A cheerful, colourful and comfortable dining room. Traditional cuisine.

Le Brivas rm, P VISA AE

2 av. Charles Massot, at Vals-près-le-Puy 43750 – 04 71 05 68 66 – brivas@wanadoo.fr – Fax 04 71 05 65 88 – Closed 16 December-15 January, Friday dinner, Sunday dinner from 15 October to 15 April and Saturday lunch

48 rm – €56/80 €56/80, €8 – ½ P €53/65 – **Rest** – *(closed Fri evening, Sun evening from 15 Oct - 15 Apr and Sat lunchtime)* Menu €15 (lunch), €19/40 – Carte €25/42

◆ A modern hotel offering functional comfort in a residential district to the south of Le Puy. Pleasant riverside terrace-garden. Fitness area. Traditional cuisine based on local produce, served in a contemporary setting.

Le Val Vert rm, P VISA AE

6 av. Baptiste Marcet, Mende road by ②: 1.5 km by N 88 – 04 71 09 09 30 – info@hotelvalvert.com – Fax 04 71 09 36 49 – Closed 25 December-9 January

23 rm – €53/58 €53/58, €10 – ½ P €55 – **Rest** – *(closed Sat. lunch from Oct. to May)* Menu (€15 bi), €18/40 – Carte €38/48

◆ The busy Mende road passes through verdant country. Partially refurbished colourful rooms, some decorated in an Italian style. Well soundproofed. Large picture windows overlooking the village bring light to the attractive dining room.

Dyke Hôtel without rest VISA

37 bd Mar. Fayolle – 04 71 09 05 30 – dyke.hotel@wanadoo.fr – Fax 04 71 02 58 66 – Closed 25 December-1st January BZ **r**

15 rm – €36/49 €40/55, €6,50

◆ The town is protected by its famous basalt dykes. Simple soundproofed rooms; choose one overlooking the lane. Cordial welcome.

François Gagnaire – Hôtel Du Parc VISA AE

4 av. C. Charbonnier – 04 71 02 75 55 – francoisgagnaire@wanadoo.fr – Fax 04 71 02 18 72 – Closed 23 June-10 July, 3-14 November, 2-19 January, Sunday except lunch from September to June, Tuesday lunch and Monday AZ **a**

Rest – Menu (€27), €33 (weekdays)/90 – Carte €63/83

Spec. Gaspacho de lentilles vertes du Puy, coquillages et condiments (summer). Souris d'agneau confite aux écorces d'orange (autumn-winter). Marrons confits, crème glacée au lait de topinambour. **Wines** Boudes.

◆ The modern elegant restaurant, decorated with Raoul Dufy lithographs, serves delightful, personalised cuisine, made with local and more exotic produce.

Tournayre VISA AE

12 r. Chênebouterie – 04 71 09 58 94 – info@restaurant-tournayre.com – Fax 04 71 02 68 38 – Closed 1st-7 September, 2-31 January, Wednesday dinner, Sunday dinner and Monday

Rest – Menu €23/70 – Carte €52/72

◆ Ribbed vaulted ceilings, exposed stone, woodwork and frescoes make up the decor of this 16C former chapel. Generous Auvergne fare.

XX **L'Olympe** ♿ VISA MC

8 r. Collège – ☎ 04 71 05 90 59 – Fax 04 71 05 90 59 – Closed 16 February-31 March, Saturday lunch except July-August, Sunday dinner and Monday

Rest – Menu (€ 15), € 19/55 – Carte € 44/66 BZ **x**

◆ A stylish restaurant in a steep cobbled lane typical of the picturesque old town. Two dining rooms, one on the first floor, both light and comfortable. Traditional fare.

X **Le Poivrier** ♿ AC VISA MC

69 r. Pannessac – ☎ 04 71 02 41 30 – lepoivrier@orange.fr – Fax 04 71 02 59 25 – Closed Sunday except August AY **v**

Rest – Menu € 15 (weekday lunch), € 20/35 – Carte € 31/40

◆ This restaurant has been redesigned in elegant, contemporary style without losing its warm, relaxed feel. Photography exhibition. Salers and Charolais meat specialities.

X **Lapierre** VISA MC

6 r. Capucins – ☎ 04 71 09 08 44 – Open March-November

Rest – *(closed Sunday except dinner from July to September) (number of covers limited, pre-book)* Menu € 25/32 – Carte € 32/44

◆ A decor composed of bistro furniture, painted panelling and fabrics in shades of grey and food based on organic products and the inevitable Puy lentils. A popular gourmet venue.

X **Bambou et Basilic** VISA MC AE

18 r. Grangevieille – ☎ 04 71 09 25 59 – delphineabrial@hotmail.com – Fax 04 71 09 25 59 – Closed 24 August-1st September, Sunday and Monday

Rest – Menu € 23/45 AY **b**

◆ The young chef draws inspiration from all four corners of the world to create a personal inventive cuisine that can surprise at times. An establishment on the way up.

in Espaly-St-Marcel 3 km by ③ – **pop. 3 552** – **alt. 650 m** – ✉ **43000**

L'Ermitage without rest ♿ P VISA MC

73 av. Ermitage, Clermont-Ferrand road – ☎ 04 71 07 05 05 – hotelermitage@free.fr – Fax 04 71 07 05 00 – Closed January and February

20 rm – €47/75 €47/75, ☕ € 9

◆ The terrace of this fully renovated hotel commands a panoramic view of the Puy. Practical quiet rooms; those facing south overlook the countryside.

XX **L'Ermitage** ♿ P VISA MC AE

73 av. de l'Ermitage, Clermont-Ferrand road – ☎ 04 71 04 08 99 – bruno.chartier@wanadoo.fr – Fax 04 71 04 25 72 – Closed 20-26 October, 14 January-11 February, Sunday dinner and Monday

Rest – Menu (€ 17), € 21 (weekdays)/47 – Carte € 34/56

◆ This attractively restored farmhouse has retained its rustic character and cosy feel. Meals served by the open fire in winter. Good traditional fare.

PUY-GUILLAUME – 63 Puy-de-Dôme – 326 H7 – pop. 2 624 – alt. 285 m – ✉ 63290

6 **C2**

Paris 374 – Clermont-Ferrand 53 – Lezoux 27 – Riom 35 – Thiers 15 – Vichy 21

Relais Hôtel de Marie ♿ rm, P VISA MC

av. E. Vaillant – ☎ 04 73 94 18 88 – hotel.marie@wanadoo.fr – Fax 04 73 94 73 98 – Closed 2-8 September, autumn half-term holidays, Sunday dinner and Monday

15 rm – €35/49 €35/49, ☕ € 6 – ½ P € 50/55 – **Rest** – Menu € 19 (weekdays)/35 – Carte € 22/39

◆ Convenient for an overnight stay. The hotel has been restored and modernised with small, modern, functional rooms, quieter on the car park side. Fresh, simple restaurant where traditional and regional dishes are served.

PUY-L'ÉVÊQUE – 46 Lot – 337 C4 – pop. 2 159 – alt. 130 m – ✉ 46700

Dordogne-Berry-Limousin 28 **B1**

Paris 601 – Agen 71 – Cahors 31 – Gourdon 41 – Sarlat-la-Canéda 52 – Villeneuve-sur-Lot 43

Syndicat d'initiative, place de la Truffière ☎ 05 65 21 37 63, Fax 05 65 21 37 63

Bellevue ← Lot valley, rm, VISA

pl. Truffière – 05 65 36 06 60 – hotelbellevue.puyleveque@wanadoo.fr – Fax 05 65 36 06 61 – Closed 18 November-3 December and 8 January-6 February
11 rm – €65/90 €65/90, €10 – ½ P €62/76
Rest *Côté Lot* – *(closed Tuesday except October-June, Sunday except July-September and Monday)* Menu €28 (lunch)/65
Rest *L'Aganit* – brasserie *(closed Tuesday except October-June, Sunday except July-September and Monday)* Menu €13,50 (weekday lunch), €20/30 – Carte €23/35
◆ The hotel, situated on a spur overlooking the Lot, lives up to its name. Rooms are spacious, contemporary and personalised. Inventive cuisine at the Côté Lot restaurant and a generous view of the valley. On a veranda, local – and brasserie style – disches served at L'Aganit.

in Touzac **8 km West by D 8 – pop. 341 – alt. 75 m – ✉ 46700**
Château de Bonaguil★★ North: 10,5 km.

De la Source Bleue rm, VISA

– 05 65 36 52 01 – sourcebleue@wanadoo.fr – Fax 05 65 24 65 69 – Open 18 April-11 November
12 rm – €79/89 €79/125, €10 – 1 suite – ½ P €75/85
Rest – *(closed Tuesday lunch, Thursday lunch and Wednesday)* Menu (€17), €29 – Carte €32/45
◆ Several 14C mills in a pretty bamboo grove on the banks of the Lot have been converted into a hotel with elegant, minimalist and peaceful rooms. This restaurant occupies a 17C outbuilding with fine beams and stone walls. Contemporary cuisine.

in Mauroux **12 km Southwest by D 8 and D 5 – pop. 417 – alt. 213 m – ✉ 46700**
Syndicat d'initiative, le Bourg 05 65 30 66 70, Fax 05 65 36 49 64

Hostellerie le Vert ← rm, rm, VISA

Lieu dit "Le Vert" – 05 65 36 51 36 – hotellevert@aol.com – Fax 05 65 36 56 84 – Open 1st April-30 October
7 rm – €85/130 €85/130, €9 – ½ P €83/105 – **Rest** – *(closed Thursday dinner) (dinner only)* Menu €38/45 – Carte €34/49
◆ Enjoy warm hospitality at this 14C Quercy farm in the middle of the countryside. Personalised rooms with a mix of period and rustic furniture. Traditional cuisine with a modern twist is on offer beneath the dining room's rustic beams.

in Anglars-Juillac **8 km East by D 811 and D 67 – pop. 331 – alt. 98 m – ✉ 46140**

XX **Clau del Loup** with rm VISA

Métairie Haute, D 8 – 05 65 36 76 20 – Fax 05 65 36 76 29 – Closed 27 October-21 November
5 rm – €90/105 €90/105, €10 – ½ P €90/110 – **Rest** – *(closed Tuesday dinner and Wednesday dinner)* Menu €16 (weekday lunch), €25/65
◆ A lovely residence (1818) in a shady and flowered garden. Modern food served in a wonderful dining room or on the terrace, under old plane trees. Comfortable rooms. Attractive rooms, furnished in varying styles.

PUYMIROL – 47 Lot-et-Garonne – 336 G4 – pop. 864 – alt. 153 m – ✉ 47270

Atlantic Coast 4 **C2**

Paris 649 – Agen 17 – Moissac 35 – Villeneuve-sur-Lot 30
Syndicat d'initiative, 7, place Maréchal Leclerc 05 53 67 80 40, Fax 05 53 95 32 38

Michel Trama rest, VISA

✿✿✿ *52 r. Royale – 05 53 95 31 46 – trama@aubergade.com – Fax 05 53 95 33 80 – Closed 15-30 November, Sunday dinner off season, Monday except dinner in season and Tuesday lunch*
9 rm – €270/470 €270/470, €30 – 1 suite
Rest – Menu €76 (weekdays)/215 – Carte €117/206
Spec. Sucette de foie gras aux noisettes torréfiées. Hamburger de foie gras chaud aux cèpes. Assiette des cinq sens (dessert). **Wines** Côtes de Duras, Buzet.
◆ Luxuriously renovated 13C (former residence of the counts of Toulouse) and 17C houses. Lavish bedrooms designed by Garcia. An unusual 'wall of flavours', an exuberant Baroque dining room, cloister-terrace, well-stocked wine cellar and delightfully inventive and classical cuisine.

PUYRAVAULT – 17 Charente-Maritime – 324 F3 – see Surgères

PUY-ST-PIERRE – 05 Hautes-Alpes – 334 H3 – see Briançon

PUY-ST-VINCENT – 05 Hautes-Alpes – 334 G4 – pop. 267 – alt. 1 325 m – Winter sports : 1 400/2 700 m 16 – ✉ 05290 French Alps 41 C1

Paris 700 – L'Argentière-la-Bessée 10 – Briançon 21 – Gap 83 – Guillestre 30

Office de tourisme, les Alberts ✆ 04 92 23 58 42

Les Prés ★ Southeast: 2 km - ★ Vallouise church North: 4 km.

La Pendine

aux Prés, East : 1 km via D 404 – ✆ 04 92 23 32 62 – contact@lapendine.com – Fax 04 92 23 46 63 – Open 20 June-31 August and 15 December-10 April

25 rm – €45/62 €52/91, €8,50 – ½ P €55/66 – **Rest** – Menu €20 (weekday lunch), €26/36 – Carte €25/49

◆ This hotel perched on the village heights has been attractively renovated: facade lined with wood and rooms simply decorated in a mountain style (some have a balcony). Enjoy traditional and Alpine specialities in the restaurant or on the summer terrace.

Saint-Roch valley and mountains, VISA

aux Prés, East : 1 km via D 404 – ✆ 04 92 23 32 79 – info@hotel-st-roch.com – Fax 04 92 23 45 11 – Open 20 June-31 August and 20 December-5 April

15 rm – €84/86 €84/86, €10 – ½ P €75/90 – **Rest** – self-service in winter Menu €26/45 – Carte €37/64

◆ A 1970s building, ideally situated at the foot of the slopes in this Vallouise resort. The large rooms are simply-furnished and some have a south-facing terrace. Beautiful panoramic view from the restaurant and the terrace; self-service set menu at lunchtime in winter.

PYLA-SUR-MER – 33 Gironde – 335 D7 – ✉ 33115 Atlantic Coast 3 B2

Paris 648 – Arcachon 8 – Biscarrosse 34 – Bordeaux 66

Syndicat d'initiative, 2 , avenue Ermitage ✆ 05 56 54 02 22, Fax 05 56 22 58 84

Dune du Pilat★★.

See plan of Arcachon urban area.

Maminotte without rest VISA

av. Acacias – ✆ 05 57 72 05 05 – hotel-maminotte@wanadoo.fr – Fax 05 57 72 06 06 – Closed 1st January-5 February AY **n**

12 rm – €55/95 €80/105, €9

◆ Villa in a residential area near the beach with rustic rooms, many of them updated. Some with balcony overlooking the pine trees.

XX **L'Authentic d'Éric Thore** VISA

35 bd de l'Océan – ✆ 05 56 54 07 94 – Closed 15 November-15 December, 2 January-10 February, Tuesday and Wednesday except school holidays AY **e**

Rest – Menu €20 (weekday lunch)/30 – Carte €50/85

◆ Renovated in a charming holiday spirit, inspired by the wood cabins of the Arcachon region. Pergola for dining in fine weather. Creative cuisine from the chef-patron.

QUARRÉ-LES-TOMBES – 89 Yonne – 319 G7 – pop. 723 – alt. 457 m – ✉ 89630 Burgundy-Jura 7 B2

Paris 233 – Auxerre 73 – Avallon 18 – Château-Chinon 49 – Clamecy 49 – Dijon 118

Syndicat d'initiative, rue des Ecoles ✆ 03 86 32 22 20

Du Nord rest, VISA

25 pl. de l'Église – ✆ 03 86 32 29 30 – Fax 03 86 32 29 31 – Closed 5 November-14 February, Wednesday dinner and Thursday

8 rm – €45/55 €60/75, €8,50 – 2 suites – ½ P €55/68

Rest – Menu €22 (weekdays)/38 – Carte €31/37

◆ This old hotel opposite the well-known church was saved by a local charitable association. Small, functional, redecorated rooms. The Saint Georges has a bistro style, retro atmosphere and appropriate, traditional food.

Le Morvan with rm — rm, VISA

6 r. des Ecoles – ✆ 03 86 32 29 29 – etiennelemorvan@wanadoo.fr – Fax 03 86 32 29 28 – Closed 6-16 October, 22 December-27 February, Monday and Tuesday

8 rm – †€ 47 ††€ 53/73, ☕ € 10 – ½ P € 58/65

Rest – *(closed Wednesday November- February, Monday and Tuesday)* Menu € 22/49 – Carte € 37/60

◆ Warm welcome at this lovely hotel where you can savour carefully prepared modern dishes in a pleasant dining room with exposed beams. Comfortable rooms.

in Lavaults 5 km Southeast by D 10 – ✉ **89630 Quarré-les-Tombes**

Auberge de l'Âtre with rm — VISA

– ✆ 03 86 32 20 79 – laubergedelatr@free.fr – Fax 03 86 32 28 25 – Closed 15 June-1st July, 11 February-15 March, Tuesday and Wednesday

7 rm – †€ 60/72 ††€ 75/95, ☕ € 9,50 – **Rest** – *(pre-book)* Menu € 32 (weekday lunch), € 49/59 – Carte € 45/72

◆ A Morvan-style farmhouse in the middle of the countryside. Choose a table near the fireplace in a pretty, rustic setting or on the veranda terrace overlooking the flower garden. Tasty regional fare.

QUATRE-ROUTES-D'ALBUSSAC – 19 Corrèze – 329 L5 – alt. 600 m – ✉ 19380 Albussac — 25 C3

▶ Paris 492 – Aurillac 72 – Brive-la-Gaillarde 27 – Mauriac 67 – St-Céré 36 – Tulle 18

◘ Roche de Vic ✲★ South: 2 km then 15 mn, ▮ Dordogne-Berry-Limousin

Roche de Vic — VISA

– ✆ 05 55 28 15 87 – rochevic@orange.fr – Fax 05 55 28 01 09 – Closed 1st-8 October, 1st January-15 March and Monday except July-August

11 rm – †€ 45 ††€ 50/60, ☕ € 7 – ½ P € 50/52 – **Rest** – *(closed Sunday dinner October-March and Monday except July-August)* Menu (€ 13), € 17 (weekday lunch), € 22/40 – Carte € 28/54

◆ A 1950s country house. Neat, discreetly furnished rooms in the style of the period; those overlooking the garden are more attractive. Children's play area. Regional recipes to be sampled before or after you admire the panorama at Roche de Vic.

LES QUATRE-ROUTES-DU-LOT – 46 Lot – 337 F2 – pop. 580 – alt. 127 m – ✉ 46110 — 29 C1

▶ Paris 508 – Brive-la-Gaillarde 24 – Cahors 86 – Figeac 67 – Sarlat-la-Canéda 52

Au Vieux Four with rm — rm, VISA

av. Agustin Farcia – ✆ 05 65 32 01 98 – stephanie.teillard@wanadoo.fr – Closed one week in June, one week in September, Sunday dinner and Monday

5 rm – †€ 49 ††€ 49, ☕ € 6,50 – **Rest** – Menu € 25/34 – Carte € 31/44

◆ The brick oven of this former bakery which now houses a restaurant adorns one of the two rustic, floral dining rooms. Tasty, modern food.

QUÉDILLAC – 35 Ille-et-Vilaine – 309 J5 – pop. 966 – alt. 85 m – ✉ 35290 — 10 C2

▶ Paris 389 – Dinan 30 – Lamballe 45 – Loudéac 57 – Ploërmel 46 – Rennes 39

Le Relais de la Rance with rm — VISA

6 r. de Rennes – ✆ 02 99 06 20 20 – relaisdelarance@21s.fr – Fax 02 99 06 24 01 – Closed 20 December-20 January, Friday evening and Sunday evening

13 rm – †€ 53/70 ††€ 53/70, ☕ € 9,50

Rest – Menu (€ 17), € 21/70 – Carte € 42/59

◆ Granite village house offering an elegant restaurant with frescoes, period furniture and carefully set tables. Traditional cuisine and menu based on local produce.

LES QUELLES – 67 Bas-Rhin – 315 G6 – see Schirmeck

QUELVEN – 56 Morbihan – 308 M6 – see Pontivy

QUEND – 80 Somme – 301 C6 – pop. 1 378 – alt. 5 m – ✉ 80120 36 **A1**

Paris 209 – Amiens 91 – Boulogne-sur-Mer 58 – Abbeville 35 – Outreau 60

Office de tourisme, 8, avenue Vasseur ☏ 03 22 23 32 04, Fax 03 22 23 62 65

Les Augustines without rest

– *☏ 03 22 23 54 26 – hoteldesaugustines@wanadoo.fr – Fax 03 22 24 10 53*

15 rm – €65/75 €65/75, ☕ €9

◆ This hotel offers small ground floor rooms identically decorated in light colours. A friendly establishment ideal for a visit to this lovely region.

QUENZA – 2A Corse-du-Sud – 345 D9 – see Corse

QUESTEMBERT – 56 Morbihan – 308 Q9 – pop. 5 727 – alt. 100 m – ✉ 56230

Brittany 10 **C3**

Paris 445 – Ploërmel 32 – Redon 34 – Rennes 96 – La Roche-Bernard 23 – Vannes 29

Office de tourisme, 15, rue des Halles ☏ 02 97 26 56 00, Fax 02 97 26 54 55

Le Bretagne et sa Résidence (Alain Orillac) with rm

r. St-Michel – ☏ 02 97 26 11 12 – lebretagne@wanadoo.fr – Fax 02 97 26 12 37 – Closed 12-31 January rm, VISA MC AE

9 rm – €70/90 €90/150, ☕ €15 – ½ P €125/145

Rest – *(closed Sunday dinner and Tuesday lunch October-April and Monday) (pre-book)* Menu (€28), €34 (weekdays), €50/100 – Carte €59/179

Spec. Coffre d'araignée, infusion à la criste marine (June-July). Filet de bar rôti, crème de riz soufflé. Selle d'agneau en crumble, millefeuille pomme et navet. **Wines** Muscadet.

◆ A restaurant with an elegant wood-panelled dining room and winter garden. Inventive cuisine. Comfortable guestrooms in the annexe.

QUETTEHOU – 50 Manche – 303 E2 – pop. 1 475 – alt. 14 m – ✉ 50630

Normandy 32 **A1**

Paris 345 – Barfleur 10 – Cherbourg 29 – St-Lô 66 – Valognes 16

Office de tourisme, place de la Mairie ☏ 02 33 43 63 21, Fax 02 33 43 63 21

Demeure du Perron without rest

– *☏ 02 33 54 56 09 – hotel@demeureduperron.com – Fax 02 33 43 69 28 – Closed Sunday from 15 November to 31 March*

20 rm – €52/72 €52/72, ☕ €6

◆ A number of pavilions dotted around an attractive garden where breakfast is served in summer. Well-cared for rooms of varying styles and sizes (recent or more rustic).

Auberge de Ket Hou VISA MC AE

17 r. de Gaulle – ☏ 02 33 54 40 23 – aubergedekethou@wanadoo.fr – Fax 02 33 54 02 11 – Closed Sunday dinner except August and Monday

Rest – Menu €15 (weekday lunch), €19/39 – Carte €28/49

◆ This roadside country inn offers traditional cuisine in a countrified interior of old stone and wood.

LA QUEUE-EN-BRIE – 94 Val-de-Marne – 312 E3 – 101 29 – see Paris, Area

QUÉVEN – 56 Morbihan – 308 K8 – pop. 8 753 – alt. 50 m – ✉ 56530 9 **B2**

Paris 505 – Rennes 154 – Vannes 61 – Lorient 9 – Lanester 9

Manoir de Kerlebert

r. de Kerlebert – ☏ 02 97 80 22 37 – manoirkerlebert@wanadoo.fr – Fax 02 97 80 20 83 – Closed 20 December-5 January

4 rm ☕ – €50 €60/80 – **Table d'hôte** – *(closed Wednesday and Sunday)* Menu €20 bi

◆ Set in parkland, fine 17C long house, renovated in the 1950s, with a plush interior (lounge, billiards, library). Romantic or marine-themed guestrooms. Seafood on the menu in the evening (residents only).

QUEYRIÈRES – 43 Haute-Loire – 331 G3 – pop. 285 – alt. 1 110 m – ✉ 43260

Paris 563 – Clermont-Ferrand 149 – Le Puy-en-Velay 22 – Saint-Étienne 67 – Firminy 51 6 **C3**

La Boria delh Castel

Le bourg – ✆ 04 71 57 70 81 – contact@laboria-queyrieres.com – Fax 04 71 57 70 81 – Open 2 April-30 October

4 rm – €45 €52 – ½ P €63 – **Table d'hôte** – Menu €18 bi

◆ A restored stone farmhouse at the foot of the basalt rock. Attractive bedrooms, a small craft museum and a table d'hôte offering rustic cuisine based on organic produce.

QUIBERON – 56 Morbihan – 308 M10 – pop. 5 073 – alt. 10 m – Casino – ✉ 56170

Brittany 9 **B3**

Paris 505 – Auray 28 – Concarneau 98 – Lorient 47 – Vannes 47

Office de tourisme, 14, rue de Verdun ✆ 08 25 13 56 00, Fax 02 97 30 58 22

Côte sauvage★★ Northwest: 2.5 km.

Sofitel Thalassa

pointe de Goulvars – ✆ 02 97 50 20 00 – h0557@accor.com – Fax 02 97 50 46 32 – Closed 2-26 January B **a**

133 rm – €140/319 €150/419, €22 – 17 suites – ½ P €139/267

Rest – Menu €50 – Carte €57/95

◆ For a breath of sea air, a pleasantly situated hotel complex facing the beach and with direct access to the Thalassotherapy centre. Rooms on the sea side are more spacious. Traditional dishes and choices for healthy eating, seafood selections top the list.

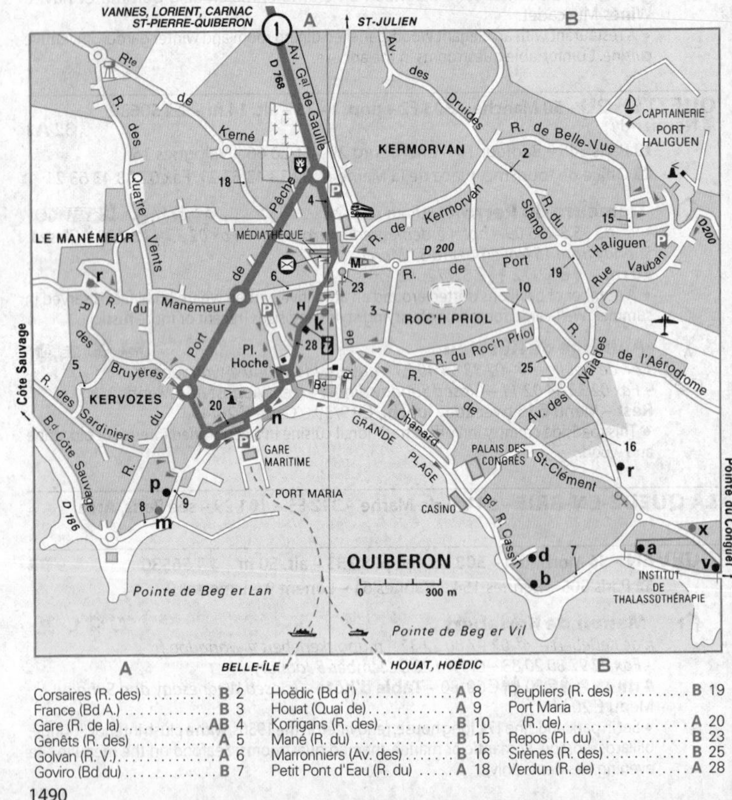

Corsaires (R. des)	B	2	Hoëdic (Bd d')	A	8	Peupliers (R. des)	B	19
France (Bd A.)	B	3	Houat (Quai de)	A	9	Port Maria (R. de)	A	20
Gare (R. de la)	AB	4	Korrigans (R. des)	B	10	Repos (Pl. du)	B	23
Genêts (R. des)	A	5	Mané (R. du)	B	15	Sirènes (R. des)	B	25
Golvan (R. V.)	A	6	Marronniers (Av. des)	B	16	Verdun (R. de)	A	28
Goviro (Bd du)	B	7	Petit Pont d'Eau (R. du)	A	18			

Sofitel Diététique sea and rocks, rm,
pointe de Goulvars – 02 97 50 20 00
– h0562@accor.com – Fax 02 97 30 47 63 – Closed 5-26 January B **v**
74 rm (full-board only in peak season) – 2 suites – ½ P € 259
Rest – rest. diététique Menu € 52
♦ This hotel is particularly popular with guests from the adjoining thalassotherapy institute (direct access). Every room has a balcony facing the sea. Health-focused menus.

Bellevue rest, VISA
r. Tiviec – 02 97 50 16 28 – bienvenue@bellevuequiberon.com
– Fax 02 97 30 44 34 – Open April-September B **d**
38 rm – € 55/102 € 61/119, € 9,50 – ½ P € 62/90 – **Rest** – Menu € 24/30 – Carte € 26/36
♦ Ordinary architecture but a spring-like interior: a wide palette of colours in the rooms which have terraces, some with a sea view. Daily menu and small, traditional à la carte menu served in a bright dining room.

La Petite Sirène without rest VISA
15 bd R. Cassin – 02 97 50 17 34
– info@hotel-lapetitesirene.fr – Fax 02 97 50 03 73
– Open 21 March-6 October and 24 October-6 November B **b**
14 rm – € 62/80 € 62/80, € 10,50
♦ This hotel, on the headland of Beg er Vil, has well-equipped rooms with renovated bathrooms and loggias facing the sea.

Ibis VISA
av. Marronniers, (Pointe de Goulvars) – 02 97 30 47 72 – h0909@accor-hotels.com – Fax 02 97 30 55 78 B **r**
95 rm – € 68/118 € 68/149, € 10 – ½ P € 62/87
Rest – *(closed 5-24 January)* Menu (€ 18), € 23 – Carte € 32/37
♦ Located just a stone's throw from the sea, the Ibis offers simply furnished bedrooms, some of which are split-level. Contemporary-style lounge-bar. Traditional and (upon request) more health-conscious dishes on offer in the wood-panelled dining room.

Le Neptune VISA
4 quai de Houat, at Port Maria – 02 97 50 09 62
– neptune.quiberon@wanadoo.fr – Fax 02 97 50 41 44
– Closed 8 January-15 February A **p**
21 rm – € 51/63 € 60/80, € 8 – ½ P € 62/66 – **Rest** – *(open 1st April-5 November and closed Wednesday)* Menu € 19/32 – Carte € 24/45
♦ Family hotel situated opposite the market. Rooms are furnished in rustic style and often redecorated. Those on the port side have a balcony, with quieter rooms at the rear. Pleasant, colourful dining room paying tribute to Neptune. Regional cuisine.

Villa Margot VISA
7 r. Port-Maria – 02 97 50 33 89 – reservation@villamargot.fr
– Fax 02 97 50 34 79 – Closed 4 January-12 February, Tuesday and Wednesday except July-August and school holidays A **n**
Rest – Menu € 19 (weekdays)/42 – Carte € 33/67
♦ Completely restored villa in light stone. Seafood dishes served on the terrace facing the beach, or in one of the contemporary dining rooms.

Le Verger de la Mer VISA
bd Goulvars – 02 97 50 29 12 – vergerdelamer@wanadoo.fr
– Fax 02 97 50 29 06 – Closed January, February, Sunday dinner off season, Tuesday except lunch off season and Wednesday B **x**
Rest – Menu € 24/38 – Carte € 29/56
♦ The discreet facade of this restaurant close to the thalassotherapy centre hides a colourful, wood panelled decor. Traditional menu made with fresh produce.

La Chaumine VISA
36 pl. Manémeur – 02 97 50 17 67 – Fax 02 97 50 17 67 – Open 13 March-9 November and closed Sunday dinner except July-August and Monday
Rest – Menu € 17 (weekday lunch), € 27/49 – Carte € 27/50
♦ Regional-style building in a former fishing area, serving local cuisine with fresh market produce.

in St-Pierre-Quiberon 5 km North by D 768 – pop. 2 165 – alt. 12 m – ✉ 56510

Pointe du Percho ≤ ★ Northwest: 2,5 km.

De la Plage ≤ rest, VISA

quai d'Orange – ☎ 02 97 30 92 10 – bienvenue@hotel-la-plage.com – Fax 02 97 30 99 61 – Open early April-end-September

39 rm – €50/117 €50/117, ☕ €11 – 2 suites – ½ P €56/89 – **Rest** – *(closed lunch except Saturday and Sunday)* Menu €24 – Carte €35/50

◆ Family-run hotel located on the beach. Recently-renovated rooms, some with a balcony on the bay side. Restaurant offering a traditional menu with a seafood focus and a lovely view of the Atlantic.

in Portivy 6 km north by D 768 and secondary road – ✉56150 St-Pierre-Quiberon

Le Petit Hôtel du Grand Large with rm ≤ rest, VISA

11 quai St-Ivy – ☎ 02 97 30 91 61 – rvbourdon@yahoo.fr – Fax 02 97 30 72 52 – Closed 15 November-8 February

6 rm – €80/100 €100/120, ☕ €9 – **Rest** – *(closed Tuesday and Wednesday except dinner in season)* Menu €37

◆ Fresh produce, particularly non-farmed fish and seafood, is favoured by the proprietor-chef of this maritime-influenced bistro. All the bedrooms in this charming family-run inn have been refurbished by an interior designer, affording views of the sea and this small port on the Côte Sauvage.

QUIÉVRECHAIN – 59 Nord – 302 K5 – see Valenciennes

QUILINEN – 29 Finistère – 308 G6 – see Quimper

QUILLAN – 11 Aude – 344 E5 – pop. 3 542 – alt. 291 m – ✉ 11500

Languedoc-Roussillon-Tarn Gorges 22 **A3**

Paris 797 – Andorra la Vella 113 – Carcassonne 52 – Foix 64 – Limoux 28 – Perpignan 76

Office de tourisme, square André Tricoire ☎ 04 68 20 07 78, Fax 04 68 20 04 91

Défilé de Pierre Lys★ South: 5 km.

Cartier rest, VISA

31 bd Ch. de Gaulle – ☎ 04 68 20 05 14 – contact@hotelcartier.com – Fax 04 68 20 22 57 – Closed 15 January-28 February

28 rm – €36 €47/65, ☕ €8,50 – ½ P €55 – **Rest** – *(closed 15 December-20 March and Saturday lunch October-April)* Menu €19/29 – Carte €21/38

◆ An early 20C building situated on a busy boulevard. A family hotel with simple, but well-kept and soundproofed rooms. A rustic-style dining room with an open fireplace. Aude specialities: rabbit with garlic, cassoulet and rouzolle (sausage meat soup).

Canal with rm VISA

36 bd Ch. de Gaulle – ☎ 04 68 20 08 62 – hotel-canal@wanadoo.fr – Fax 04 68 20 27 96 – Closed 2-31 January, Sunday dinner and Monday except July-August

13 rm – €32/35 €38/42, ☕ €7 – ½ P €43/46 – **Rest** – *(closed Sunday dinner and Monday)* Menu €13 (weekdays)/32 – Carte €22/41

◆ A regional house on the town's main street that invites you to try its traditional and local cuisine in an informal atmosphere. Modest accommodation.

QUIMPER Ⓟ – 29 Finistère – 308 G7 – pop. 63 238 – Built-up area 120 441 – alt. 41 m – ✉ 29000 Brittany 9 **B2**

Paris 564 – Brest 73 – Lorient 67 – Rennes 215 – St-Brieuc 130

Quimper-Cornouaille: ☎ 02 98 94 30 30, by ⑥: 8 km AX.

Office de tourisme, place de la Résistance ☎ 02 98 53 04 05, Fax 02 98 53 31 33

St-Corentin cathedral★★ - Old Quimper★: Rue Kéréon★ ABY - Jardin de l'Évêché ≤★ BZ **K** - Mont-Frugy ≤★ ABZ - Musée des Beaux-Arts★★ BY **M**[1] - Musée départemental breton★ BZ **M**[2] - Musée de la faïence★ AX **M**[3] - Boat trip along the Odet★★ 1 h 30 - Festival de Cornouaille★ (end of July).

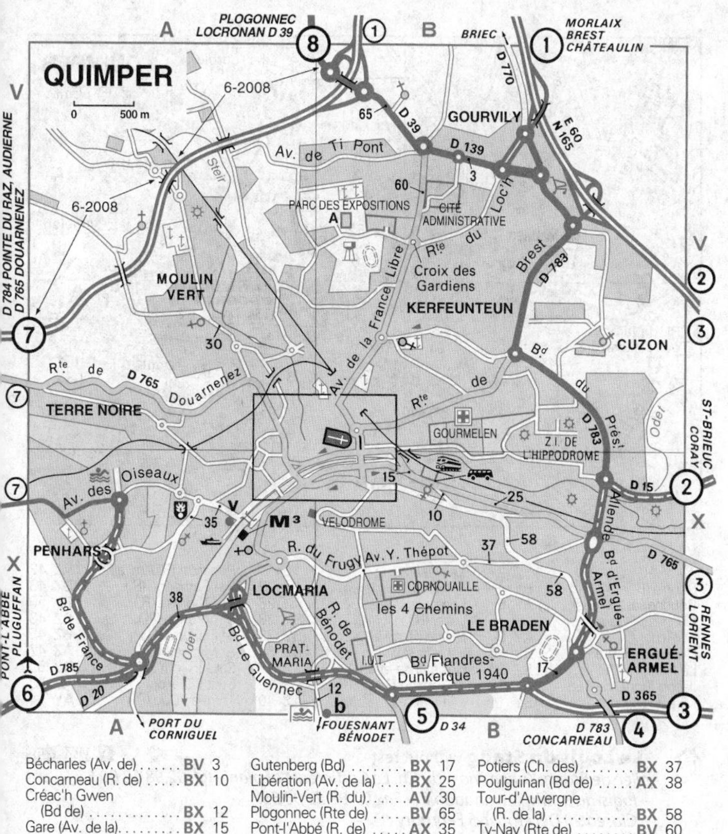

Bécharles (Av. de)	BV 3	Gutenberg (Bd)	BX 17	Potiers (Ch. des)	BX 37
Concarneau (R. de)	BX 10	Libération (Av. de la)	BX 25	Poulguinan (Bd de)	AX 38
Créac'h Gwen (Bd de)	BX 12	Moulin-Vert (R. du)	AV 30	Tour-d'Auvergne (R. de la)	BX 58
Gare (Av. de la)	BX 15	Plogonnec (Rte de)	BV 65	Ty-Nay (Rte de)	BV 60
		Pont-l'Abbé (R. de)	AX 35		

Océania

17 r. Poher, Kerdrézec complex via the Bénodet road – ☎ 02 98 90 46 26 – oceania.quimper@oceaniahotels.com – Fax 02 98 53 01 96

92 rm – 🛉€ 95/125 🛉🛉€ 95/165, ☕ € 12 – **Rest** – Menu (€ 17), € 20/25 – Carte € 19/32

◆ Chain hotel in a commercial district pleasantly surrounded by greenery. Large revamped rooms which are well designed and equipped. Contemporary dining room with slightly cramped tables. Poolside terrace.

Kregenn without rest

13 r. des Réguaires – ☎ 02 98 95 08 70 – information@kregenn.fr – Fax 02 98 53 85 12 BZ **t**

30 rm – 🛉€ 65/200 🛉🛉€ 80/200, ☕ € 13 – 2 suites

◆ Recently renovated, this friendly hotel on a quiet street in the town centre has simply decorated, modern rooms, some of which have Jacuzzis.

Gradlon without rest

30 r. Brest – ☎ 02 98 95 04 39 – contact@hotel-gradlon.com – Fax 02 98 95 61 25 – Closed 13 December-12 January BY **a**

22 rm – 🛉€ 82/160 🛉🛉€ 82/160, ☕ € 12

◆ Pleasant guestrooms with individual touches, most of which overlook a pretty flower-decked courtyard, as does the veranda on which breakfast is served. Attentive service.

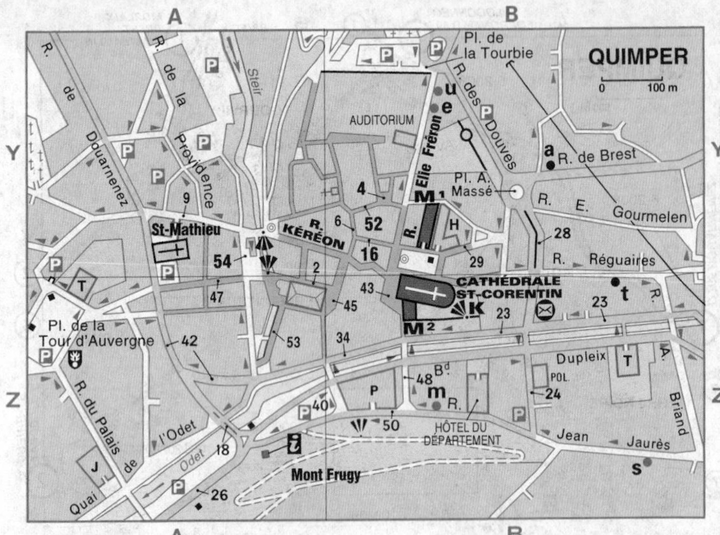

Astor (R.) . . . . **AYZ** 2	Kerguélen (Bd Amiral de) . . . . **BZ** 23	Ronarc'h (R. Amiral) . . . . **AZ** 42
Beurre (Pl. au) . . . . **BY** 4	Locmaria (Allées). . . . . . . **AZ** 26	Ste-Catherine (R.) . . . . . . **BZ** 48
Boucheries (R. des) . . . . **BY** 6	Luzel (R.) . . . . **BY** 28	Ste-Thérèse (R.) . . . . **BZ** 50
Chapeau-Rouge (R. du). . . . . **AY** 9	Mairie (R. de la) . . . . **BY** 29	St-Corentin (Pl.) . . . . **BZ** 43
Guéodet (R. du). . . . . **BY** 16	Parc (R. du) . . . . **ABZ** 34	St-François (R.) . . . . **BZ** 45
Le Hars (R. Th.) . . . . **BZ** 24	Résistance-et-du-Gén.-de-Gaulle (Pl. de la) . . . . **AZ** 40	St-Mathieu (R.) . . . . **AZ** 47
Jacob (Pont Max) . . . . . . **AZ** 18		Sallé (R. du) . . . . **BY** 52
Kéréon (R.) . . . . **ABY**		Steir (Quai du) . . . . **AZ** 53
		Terre-au-Duc (Pl.). . . . . . . **AY** 54

Le Logis du Stang without rest

allée de Stang-Youen, via r. du Ch. Le Goffic, east of plan – 02 98 52 00 55 – logis-du-stang@wanadoo.fr – Fax 02 98 52 00 55 – Closed 20 December-5 February

3 rm – €49/60 €65/80

◆ This 19C manor house, surrounded by a charming enclosed garden, has been tastefully renovated. Three delightful bedrooms, two of which occupy the old barn. Good attention to detail.

Les Acacias

85 bd Creac'h Gwen – 02 98 52 15 20 – acacias-qper@wanadoo.fr – Fax 02 98 10 11 48 – Closed 18 August-8 September, Sunday dinner and Saturday BX **b**

Rest – Menu €19 (weekday lunch)/48 – Carte €43/55

◆ This restaurant occupies a charming modern house with an attractive flower garden. Classic cuisine is served in a bright, contemporary-style dining room.

L'Ambroisie

49 r. Elie Fréron – 02 98 95 00 02 – gilbert.guyon@wanadoo.fr – Fax 02 98 95 00 02 – Closed Sunday dinner except from 14 July to 25 August and Monday BY **u**

Rest – Menu €25 (weekday lunch)/75 – Carte €62/67

◆ A small modern dining room hung with original paintings on wood. Traditional, regional cuisine with the emphasis on local products.

Fleur de Sel

1 quai Neuf – 02 98 55 04 71 – Fax 02 98 55 04 71 – Closed 24 December-2 January, Saturday lunch and Sunday AX **v**

Rest – Menu €22 (weekdays), €26/37 – Carte €26/49

◆ This non-smoking restaurant located in a picturesque part of town serves traditional cuisine in a dining room overlooking the River Odet.

X **Ailleurs** VISA MC

43 r. Elie Fréron – ✆ 02 98 95 56 32 – contact@restaurant-ailleurs.com – Fax 02 98 95 56 32 – Closed 26 August-3 September and 23-29 December, Saturday lunch, Sunday and Monday BY **e**

Rest – Menu (€ 15) – Carte € 39/51

♦ Inspired by a love of travel, the chef here produces seasonal international dishes, with a strong Asian influence. Good selection of wines from around the world to accompany your meal.

X **L'Assiette** VISA MC

5 bis r. J. Jaurès – ✆ 02 98 53 03 65 – Closed 11-31 August, and Sunday BZ **s**

Rest – Menu (€ 13,50), € 18 (lunch)/23 – Carte € 27/33

♦ A pleasant family restaurant situated between the station and the town centre. Bistro-cum-brasserie decor and attractively laid tables. Simple, freshly cooked traditional dishes.

X **La VIIe Vague** VISA MC

72 r. J. Jaurès – ✆ 02 98 53 33 10 – Fax 02 98 52 23 85 – Closed 1st-15 August, Saturday and Sunday BZ **m**

Rest – Menu (€ 15), € 19 (weekday lunch), € 25/30 – Carte € 26/47

♦ This popular restaurant has a simple, restful and trendy decor, a relaxing terrace and delicious regional cuisine (themed menu based on the number 7 in the evening).

in Ty-Sanquer **7 km North by D 770 – ✉ 29000 Quimper**

XX **Auberge de Ti-Coz** P VISA MC

– ✆ 02 98 94 50 02 – restaurant-ty-coz@wanadoo.fr – Fax 02 98 94 56 37 – Closed 15 September-5 October, Tuesday dinner and Wednesday dinner from September to June, Sunday dinner and Monday except public holidays

Rest – Menu € 20 (weekday lunch), € 25/47 – Carte € 31/50

♦ A delightful local inn with a contemporary decor, where the chef prepares traditional dishes with a modern twist (spices, produce from the south, old vegetable varieties etc). Selection of estate-bottled wines.

in Quilinen **11 km by ① and D 770 – ✉ 29510 Landrevarzec**

X **Auberge de Quilinen** VISA MC

– ✆ 02 98 57 93 63 – aubergedequilinen@wanadoo.fr – Fax 02 98 57 94 49 – Closed 4-24 August, Tuesday dinner, Wednesday dinner, Sunday dinner and Monday

Rest – Menu € 19 (weekday lunch), € 26/40 – Carte € 29/42

♦ This attractive building is situated in a hamlet famous for its 15C chapel. The bright, rustic dining room features exposed stone walls and country-style furnishings. Good local cuisine.

Southeast **5 km by boulevard Poulguinan - AX - and D 20 – ✉ 29700 Pluguffan**

XXX **La Roseraie de Bel Air** (Lionel Hénaff) P VISA MC AE

r. Boissière – ✆ 02 98 53 50 80 – roseraie-de-bel-air@wanadoo.fr – Fax 02 98 53 50 80 – Closed 4-14 May, 6 September-2 October, Sunday and Monday

Rest – Menu € 25 (weekday lunch), € 48/85 – Carte € 53/72

Spec. Poissons de petits bateaux. Agneau de l'anse de Pouldon (April to September). Petits ormeaux de l'île Vierge.

♦ Fine 19C Brittany residence. A warmly attractive ambience pervades the long dining hall with its two high granite fireplaces. Reinterpreted regional cuisine.

QUIMPERLÉ – 29 Finistère – 308 J7 – pop. 10 850 – alt. 30 m – ✉ 29300

Brittany 9 **B2**

Paris 517 – Carhaix-Plouguer 57 – Concarneau 32 – Pontivy 76 – Quimper 49 – Rennes 169

Office de tourisme, 45, place Saint-Michel ✆ 02 98 96 04 32, Fax 02 98 96 16 12

Ste-Croix church★★ - Rue Dom-Morice★.

Le Vintage without rest
20 r. Bremond d'Ars – ✆ 02 98 35 09 10 – hotelvintage@wanadoo.fr – Fax 02 98 35 09 29
10 rm – €60 €85, €11
◆ This contemporary hotel devoted to wine has a beautiful 19C facade. Rooms with personal touches, including unique murals and contemporary furniture.

Le Bistro de la Tour
2 r. Dom Morice – ✆ 02 98 39 29 58 – bistrodelatour@wanadoo.fr – Fax 02 98 39 21 77 – Closed Sunday lunch in July-August, Sunday dinner off season, Monday except dinners in July-August and Saturday lunch
Rest – Menu (€21), €30/56 bi – Carte €38/53
◆ This cosy old-fashioned bistro (ornaments, paintings, bottles) serves generous portions of food ranging from traditional to regional. Fine wine list. Gourmet grocers next-door.

La Cigale Egarée
Villeneuve-Braouic on Lorient road – ✆ 02 98 39 15 53 – lacigale29@yahoo.fr – Closed November school holidays, Sunday and Monday
Rest – *(number of covers limited, pre-book)* Menu €21 (weekday lunch), €32/65 – Carte €43/58
◆ The "Lost Cricket" is an atypical restaurant in an ochre-coloured house with a garden. Avant-garde cuisine served to an attractive neo-Provençal backdrop.

Northeast 6 km by Arzano road and D 22 – ✉ 29300 Arzano

Château de Kerlarec rest,
– ✆ 02 98 71 75 06 – chateau-de-kerlarec@wanadoo.fr – Fax 02 98 71 74 55 – Closed 23-27 December
6 rm – €115 €125/150 – ½ P €86/103 – **Table d'hôte** – Menu €30/50
◆ The landlords of this château, dating from the French Second Empire, are enthusiasts of antique goods and have attractively furnished every room with their findings from various periods and of varied styles. The table d'hôte (by request only) offers pancakes, plates of seafood and local dishes.

QUINCIÉ-EN-BEAUJOLAIS – 69 Rhône – 327 G3 – pop. 1 121 – alt. 325 m – ✉ 69430

43 **E1**

Paris 428 – Beaujeu 6 – Bourg-en-Bresse 55 – Lyon 57 – Mâcon 33 – Roanne 66

Le Mont-Brouilly rm, rest,
Le Pont des Samsons, 2,5 km east on D 37 – ✆ 04 74 04 33 73 – contact@hotelbrouilly.com – Fax 04 74 04 30 10 – Closed 22-29 December, 27 January-24 February, Sunday dinner and Monday October-May
29 rm – €60/70 €65/70, €8,50 – ½ P €60/70
Rest – *(closed Sunday dinner October-May and Monday)* Menu €18 (weekday lunch), €23/48 – Carte €34/54
◆ This 1980s hotel stands at the foot of Mont Brouilly in the midst of vineyards. Practical, identically decorated rooms. The vast dining room has a pleasant view of the garden; traditional food served.

QUINÉVILLE – 50 Manche – 303 E2 – pop. 292 – alt. 29 m – ✉ 50310

Normandy

32 **A1**

Paris 338 – Barfleur 21 – Carentan 31 – Cherbourg 37 – St-Lô 59
Office de tourisme, 17, avenue de la Plage ✆ 02 33 21 40 29

Château de Quinéville rm, rest,
– ✆ 02 33 21 42 67 – chateau.quineville@wanadoo.com – Fax 02 33 21 05 79 – Closed 1st January-31 March
30 rm – €65/125 €65/125, €11 – ½ P €77/105
Rest – *(open 23 March-2 November) (dinner only)* Menu €31 – Carte €29/45
◆ The rooms, relatively plain for the most part, are larger and more recent in the former stables than in the 18C château. The park has Roman remains, a 14C tower, greenhouses and a lake. A dining room of character overlooking a lovely green setting. Traditional cuisine.

QUINGEY – 25 Doubs – 321 F4 – pop. 1 049 – alt. 275 m – ✉ 25440 16 B2

Paris 397 – Besançon 23 – Dijon 84 – Dole 36 – Gray 54

La Truite de la Loue

2 rte de Lyon – ✆ 03 81 63 60 14 – latruitedelaloue@wanadoo.fr – Fax 03 81 63 84 77 – Closed January, 17-27 February, Tuesday dinner and Wednesday November-May

10 rm – 🛉€ 38/45 🛉🛉€ 45/51, ☕ € 7 – ½ P € 46 – **Rest** – Menu € 18 (weekdays)/39 – Carte € 20/54

◆ Family guesthouse on the banks of the Loue offering functional rooms of various sizes. A small country dining room with windows overlooking the river. Regional cuisine and specialities based on trout from the tank on the premises.

QUINSON – 04 Alpes-de-Haute-Provence – 334 E10 – pop. 350 – alt. 370 m – ✉ 04500 French Alps 41 C2

Paris 804 – Aix-en-Provence 76 – Brignoles 44 – Castellane 72 – Digne-les-Bains 62

Syndicat d'initiative, rue Saint-Esprit ✆ 04 92 74 01 12, Fax 04 92 74 01 12

Relais Notre-Dame

– ✆ 04 92 74 40 01 – relaisnotredame@orange.fr – Fax 04 92 74 02 10 – Hotel: open 16 March-14 November and closed Monday and Tuesday; restaurant: closed 15 December-15 February, Monday dinner and Tuesday

13 rm – 🛉€ 45/50 🛉🛉€ 55/60, ☕ € 9 – ½ P € 55/60

Rest – Menu € 12 (weekday lunch), € 20/39

◆ On the road to the Verdon gorges, a family-run hotel next to the Prehistory Museum. Pretty garden. Rooms in a rustic Provençal style (no TV), two have been redone. Countrified dining room and peaceful, green terrace. Regional cuisine, truffles in season.

QUINTIN – 22 Côtes-d'Armor – 309 E4 – pop. 2 611 – alt. 180 m – ✉ 22800 Brittany 10 C2

Paris 463 – Lamballe 35 – Loudéac 31 – St-Brieuc 18

Office de tourisme, 6, place 1830 ✆ 02 96 74 01 51, Fax 02 96 74 06 82

Du Commerce

2 r. Rochonen – ✆ 02 96 74 94 67 – hotelducommerce@cegetel.net – Fax 02 96 74 00 94 – Closed 14-27 April, 23 August-1st September and 21 December-5 January

11 rm – 🛉€ 52/62 🛉🛉€ 64/80, ☕ € 9 – ½ P € 53/60 – **Rest** – *(closed Friday lunch 14 July-18 August, Friday dinner 19 August-13 July, Sunday dinner and Monday)* Menu € 15 (weekdays except in season)/45 – Carte € 42/58

◆ 18C house in the middle of the medieval quarter, covered with Virginia creeper. Carefully renovated, non-smoking rooms with modern furniture, pastel tones and new bathrooms. Rustic, non-smoking dining room whose fireplace is adorned with the arms of the Dukes of Brittany.

RABAT-LES-TROIS-SEIGNEURS – 09 Ariège – 343 H7 – see Tarascon-sur-Ariège

RAGUENÈS-PLAGE – 29 Finistère – 308 I8 – ✉ 29920 Nevez Brittany 9 B2

Paris 545 – Carhaix-Plouguer 73 – Concarneau 17 – Pont-Aven 12 – Quimper 38

RAISMES – 59 Nord – 302 I5 – see Valenciennes

RAMATUELLE – 83 Var – 340 O6 – pop. 2 131 – alt. 136 m – ✉ 83350 French Riviera 41 C3

Paris 873 – Fréjus 35 – Le Lavandou 34 – St-Tropez 10 – Ste-Maxime 15 – Toulon 70

Office de tourisme, place de l'Ormeau ✆ 04 98 12 64 00, Fax 04 94 79 12 66

Col de Collebasse ≤★ South: 4 km.

Le Baou ⋖ village, rm, rest,
av. Gustave Etienne – ✆ 04 98 12 94 20 – hostellerie.lebaou@wanadoo.fr – Fax 04 98 12 94 21 – Open beg. May-end September
39 rm – †€ 195/360 ††€ 195/360, ☐ € 20 – 2 suites
Rest *La Terrasse* – *(dinner only)* Menu € 58/74 – Carte € 69/86
◆ Le Baou (the summit in Provençal dialect) suits its name. It dominates the Pampelonne cove. Spacious, contemporary rooms all with a balcony and fine view. An elegant dining room and panoramic terrace overlooking the village and the sea.

La Vigne de Ramatuelle without rest
rte de La Croix-Valmer, at 3 km – ✆ 04 94 79 12 50 – contact@hotel-vignederamatuelle.com – Fax 04 94 79 13 20 – Open 1st April-15 October
14 rm – †€ 125/295 ††€ 125/395, ☐ € 15
◆ Amid the vineyards stands an ochre-walled villa combining charm with tranquillity and creating an atmosphere of a private house. Furniture, fabrics, decorative objects and old books personalise the rooms.

XX **La Forge**
r. Victor Léon – ✆ 04 94 79 25 56 – laforge-ramatuelle@wanadoo.fr – Fax 04 94 79 29 54 – Open 1st April-15 October and closed lunch July-August and Wednesday
Rest – Menu € 38 – Carte € 49/62
◆ The former forge (complete with bellows and anvil) now houses a restaurant dining room with a neat Southern French setting. Friendly atmosphere and roadside teak terrace.

X **L'Ecurie du Castellas et H. Lou Castellas** with rm
rte Moulins de Paillas – ⋖ Ramatuelle countryside,
✆ 04 94 79 11 59 – lecurieducastellas@wanadoo.fr – Fax 04 94 79 21 04
16 rm – †€ 76/95 ††€ 120/160, ☐ € 8 – **Rest** – Menu € 36/48 – Carte € 52/76
◆ Feast your eyes on the charming Provençal dining room, the wide view of countryside and sea, and the appetising regional cuisine!

via St-Tropez road 4 km – ✉ 83350 Ramatuelle

Villa Marie ⋖ rm,
chemin Val Rian – ✆ 04 94 97 40 22 – contact@villamarie.fr – Fax 04 94 97 37 55 – Open 25 April-5 October
43 rm – †€ 280/480 ††€ 450/680, ☐ € 29 – **Rest** – Carte € 68/147
◆ A refined, luxury, charming and enchanting villa nestling in a pine forest overlooking Pampelonne Bay. Appealing restaurant in tones of beige, with original furniture, a shaded terrace, a sea view and sunny cuisine.

in la Bonne Terrasse 5 km East by D 93 and Camarat road – ✉ 83350 Ramatuelle

X **Chez Camille** ⋖
quartier de Bonne Terrasse – ✆ 04 98 12 68 98 – Open 19 April to mid October and closed Friday lunch and Tuesday
Rest – *(pre-book in high season and Sat - Sun)* Menu € 40/70
◆ Father and sons have succeeded one another in the kitchens of this waterside restaurant since 1913. Popular for its bouillabaisse (spicy fish stew) and grilled fish.

RAMBERVILLERS – 88 Vosges – 314 H2 – pop. 5 999 – alt. 287 m – ✉ 88700

27 **C3**

Paris 407 – Epinal 27 – Lunéville 36 – Nancy 68 – St-Dié-des-Vosges 29

Syndicat d'initiative, 2, place du 30 Septembre ✆ 03 29 65 49 10, Fax 03 29 65 25 20

XX **Mirabelle**
6 r. de l'Église – ✆ 03 29 65 37 37 – Closed 16 August-16 September, 10 January-10 February, Wednesday and dinner except Friday and Saturday
Rest – Menu € 19 bi (weekday lunch), € 38 € bi/56 bi – Carte € 28/61
◆ A warm informal welcome in this tiny restaurant decorated in the colours of Lorraine. Culinary classics on the menu such as calf's head, the chef's speciality.

RAMBOUILLET ⊛ – 78 Yvelines – 311 G4 – pop. 24 758 – alt. 160 m – ✉ 78120

Northern France and the Paris Region 18 **A2**

- Paris 53 – Chartres 42 – Mantes-la-Jolie 50 – Orléans 93 – Versailles 35
- Office de tourisme, place de la Libération ✆ 01 34 83 21 21, Fax 01 34 83 21 31
- de Forges-les-Bains Forges-les-Bains Route du Général Leclerc, East: 22 km by D 906 and D 24, ✆ 01 64 91 48 18.
- Château ★ panelling - Park★★: laiterie de la Reine (Queen's dairy)★ Z **B** - chaumière aux coquillages★ Z **E** - Bergerie nationale★ Z - Rambouillet forest★.

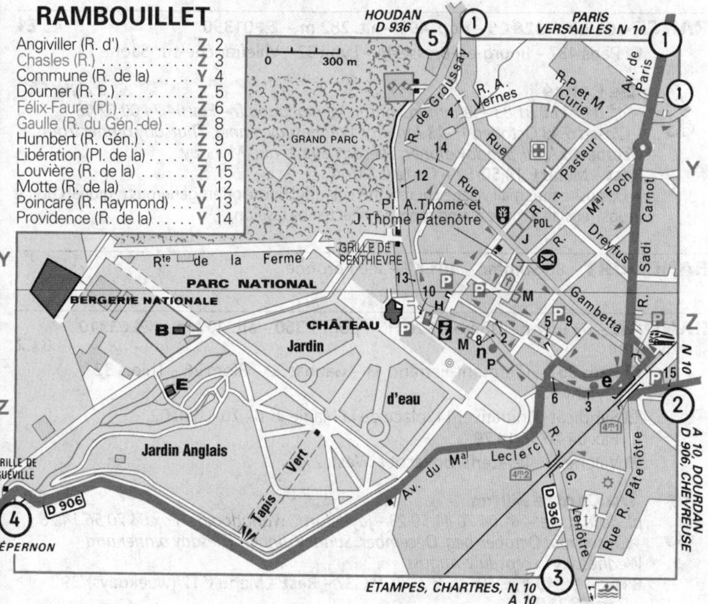

Mercure Relays du Château without rest

1 pl. de la Libération – ✆ 01 34 57 30 00
– relays@mercure-rambouillet.com – Fax 01 30 46 23 91 Z

83 rm – †€ 120 ††€ 130/165, ☕ € 13

◆ A superbly renovated 16C coaching inn, situated opposite the château. The interior decor mixes old and new, while the bedrooms are comfortable and well-equipped.

Cheval Rouge

78 r. Gén. de Gaulle – ✆ 01 30 88 80 61 – cpommier@aol.com
– Fax 01 34 83 91 60 – Closed Tuesday dinner and Wednesday Z **n**

Rest – Menu € 26/32 – Carte € 33/62

◆ The restaurant is widely appreciated for its Provençal decor and traditional cuisine. At midday on week days, the veranda-dining room offers a brasserie-type set menu.

L'Huître sur le Zinc

15 r. Chasles – ✆ 01 30 46 22 58
– lhuitresurlezinc@wanadoo.fr
– Closed 2-11 March, 3-27 August, 21 December-7 January, Sunday and Monday Z **e**

Rest – Menu € 37 (weekday lunch) – Carte € 45/76

◆ This restaurant exclusively offers seafood and fish from the adjacent fishmonger's, run by the chef-landlord's brother. Pleasant sea-themed decoration and fine garden-terrace.

in Gazeran 5 km by ④ – **pop. 1 156 – alt. 162 m –** ✉ **78125**

XXX **Villa Marinette**

20 av. Gén. de Gaulle – ☎ 01 34 83 19 01 – villamarinette@wanadoo.fr – Fax 01 30 88 83 65 – Closed Sunday dinner, Tuesday lunch and Monday

Rest – Menu € 27 (weekday lunch)/60 – Carte € 49/58

◆ The warm, well-kept dining room and terrace in a delightful walled garden offer tasty dishes prepared by the chef. Cosy rooms.

RAMONVILLE-ST-AGNE – **31 Haute-Garonne – 343** G3 – **see Toulouse**

RANCÉ – **01 Ain – 328** C5 – **pop. 498 – alt. 282 m –** ✉ **01390** 43 **E1**

Paris 437 – Bourg-en-Bresse 44 – Lyon 32 – Villefranche-sur-Saône 13

X **De Rancé**

– ☎ 04 74 00 81 83 – jeanmarc.martin3@wanadoo.fr – Fax 04 74 00 87 08 – Closed 6-13 October, 1st-13 January, Wednesday dinner, Thursday dinner from October to April, Sunday dinner, Tuesday dinner and Monday

Rest – Menu € 14,50/52 – Carte € 24/64

◆ Opposite the small village church, this colourful house offers generous regional cuisine (frogs' legs) in a rustic dining room, unaffected by fashion.

RANCOURT – **80 Somme – 301** K7 – **see Péronne**

RANDAN – **63 Puy-de-Dôme – 326** H6 – **pop. 1 360 – alt. 407 m –** ✉ **63310**
Auvergne 6 **C2**

Paris 367 – Clermont-Ferrand 41 – Gannat 22 – Riom 26 – Thiers 32 – Vichy 15

Syndicat d'initiative, 11, place de la Mairie ☎ 04 70 41 50 02, Fax 04 70 56 14 79

Villeneuve-les-Cerfs: dovecot★ West: 2 km.

XX **Du Centre** with rm

pl. de la Halle – ☎ 04 70 41 50 23 – jay-lefort@wanadoo.fr – Fax 04 70 56 14 78 – Closed mid October-beg. December, Sunday dinner, Tuesday dinner and Wednesday except July-August

8 rm – €40 €40, ☐ €7 – ½ P €37 – **Rest** – Menu € 12 (weekdays)/39 – Carte € 21/35

◆ Attractive brick facade and two rustic dining rooms: beams, fireplace and attractive parquet floor in the one and a less countrified atmosphere in the other. Modern rooms.

RÂNES – **61 Orne – 310** H3 – **pop. 964 – alt. 237 m –** ✉ **61150**
Normandy 32 **B3**

Paris 212 – Alençon 40 – Argentan 20 – Bagnoles-de-l'Orne 20 – Falaise 34

Syndicat d'initiative, Mairie ☎ 02 33 39 73 87, Fax 02 33 39 79 77

St-Pierre 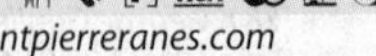

6 r. de la Libération – ☎ 02 33 39 75 14 – info@hotelsaintpierreranes.com – Fax 02 33 35 49 23

12 rm – €52 €58, ☐ €8,50 – ½ P €62 – **Rest** – *(closed Friday dinner)* Menu (€ 16 bi), € 25/45

◆ Fine regional-style house whose small, well-cared for rustic rooms have individual touches and are decorated in warm colours. The cuisine, inspired by local produce, has tripe and frogs' legs in pride of place on the menu. Warm welcome.

"Rest" appears in red for establishments with a ✿ (star) or ☺ (Bib Gourmand).

RAON-L'ÉTAPE – 88 Vosges – 314 J2 – pop. 6 749 – alt. 284 m – ✉ 88110

27 **C2**

Paris 380 – Épinal 45 – Nancy 70 – Neufchâteau 115 – St-Dié 19 – Sarrebourg 59

Office de tourisme, rue Jules Ferry ✆ 03 29 41 28 65, Fax 03 29 41 28 66

Relais Lorraine Alsace

31 r. J. Ferry – ✆ 03 29 41 61 93 – relaislorrainealsace@wanadoo.fr – Fax 03 29 41 93 09 – Closed 23 October-30 November

10 rm – †€ 58/64 ††€ 58/64, ☕ € 6,50 – ½ P € 51 – **Rest** – *(Closed Monday)* Menu € 17 (weekdays)/32 – Carte € 18/51

◆ A nautical inspired brasserie room and a more stylish dining room decorated in orange and ochre. Serves traditional fare. Comfortable, well-kept rooms.

RASTEAU – 84 Vaucluse – 332 C8 – see Vaison-la-Romaine

RAULHAC – 15 Cantal – 330 D5 – pop. 348 – alt. 740 m – ✉ 15800

5 **B3**

Paris 571 – Clermont-Ferrand 157 – Aurillac 31 – Saint-Flour 71 – Arpajon-sur-Cère 26

Château de Courbelimagne

4 km south on Mur-de-Barrez road (D 600) – ✆ 04 71 49 58 25 – jean-louis.welsch@wanadoo.fr – Fax 04 71 49 58 25

5 rm ☕ – †€ 75 ††€ 75/105 – **Table d'hôte** – Menu € 27

◆ In romantic parkland, 16C-19C manor house with period furnishings, collection of rare dried flowers (1850), personalised guestrooms. Naturotherapy sessions. At dinner (residents only), inventive, locally-inspired cuisine featuring organic produce.

LE RAULY – 24 Dordogne – 329 D7 – see Bergerac

LE RAYOL-CANADEL-SUR-MER – 83 Var – 340 N7 – pop. 700 – alt. 100 m – ✉ 83820

41 **C3**

Paris 886 – Fréjus 49 – Hyères 35 – Le Lavandou 13 – St-Tropez 27

Office de tourisme, place Michel Goy ✆ 04 94 05 65 69, Fax 04 94 05 51 80

Rayol Estate Mediterranean Garden★★

Le Bailli de Suffren

< Iles d'Hyères,

Le Rayol – ✆ 04 98 04 47 00 – infos@lebaillidesuffren.com – Fax 04 98 04 47 99 – Open 12 April-12 October

54 rm – †€ 189/443 ††€ 189/443, ☕ € 22

Rest *Praya* – Menu € 60/80 – Carte € 73/83

Rest *L'Escale* – *(open 15 May-30 September) (lunch only except from mid June to end August)* Carte € 44/55

◆ Superb view over the Hyères islands from this attractive hotel looking onto its own private beach. Spacious and refined rooms with a balcony or terrace. A quiet dining room and panoramic terrace are to be found at La Praya. Lunch by the sea at l'Escale.

RÉ (ÎLE) – 17 Charente-Maritime – 324 B2 – see Île de Ré

RÉALMONT – 81 Tarn – 338 F8 – pop. 2 850 – alt. 212 m – ✉ 81120

29 **C2**

Paris 704 – Albi 21 – Castres 24 – Graulhet 18 – Lacaune 57 – St-Affrique 84 – Toulouse 78

Office de tourisme, 8, place de la République ✆ 05 63 79 05 45, Fax 05 63 79 05 36

Les Secrets Gourmands

72 av. Gén. de Gaulle, (D 612) – ✆ 05 63 79 07 67 – les-secrets-gourmands@wanadoo.fr – Fax 05 63 79 07 69 – Closed 25-31 August, 5-25 January, Sunday dinner and Tuesday

Rest – Menu € 20 (weekdays)/50 – Carte € 35/49

◆ Three refined little dining rooms enlivened with modern paintings and opening onto a pleasant summer terrace. Tasty modern cuisine and a menu offering local dishes.

REDON – 35 Ille-et-Vilaine – 309 J9 – pop. 9 499 – alt. 10 m – ✉ 35600
Brittany 10 **C3**

Paris 410 – Nantes 78 – Rennes 65 – St-Nazaire 53 – Vannes 59

Office de tourisme, place de la République ✆ 02 99 71 06 04, Fax 02 99 71 01 59

Tower★ of St-Sauveur church.

XX **La Bogue** VISA

3 r. Etats – ✆ 02 99 71 12 95 – labogue@wanadoo.fr – Fax 02 99 71 12 95 – Closed 1st-10 July, Sunday dinner and Monday

Rest – Menu € 21/60 – Carte € 34/42

◆ The somewhat unfashionable decor of moulded wood panelling and Louis XIII chairs is quickly forgotten in favour of the simple, light traditional fare.

La Gacilly road 3 km by ① and D 873 – ✉ 35600 Redon

XX **Moulin de Via** P VISA

– ✆ 02 99 71 05 16 – Fax 02 99 71 08 36 – Closed 31 March-4 April, 1st-15 September, Thursday dinner and Wednesday from October to June, Sunday dinner, Tuesday dinner and Monday

Rest – Menu € 21/65 – Carte approx. € 40

◆ Country furniture, beams and a fireplace contribute to the rural charm of this old watermill in a green setting. A shady terrace opening onto the garden.

REICHSTETT – 67 Bas-Rhin – 315 K5 – see Strasbourg

REILHAC – 43 Haute-Loire – 331 C3 – see Langeac

REIMS – 51 Marne – 306 G7 – pop. 187 206 – Built-up area 215 581 – alt. 85 m – ✉ 51100 Northern France and the Paris Region 13 **B2**

Paris 144 – Bruxelles 218 – Châlons-en-Champagne 48 – Lille 208

Reims-Champagne: ✆ 03 26 07 15 15, D 74: 6 km U.

Office de tourisme, 2, rue Guillaume de Machault ✆ 03 26 77 45 00, Fax 03 26 77 45 19

de Reims-Champagne Gueux Château des Dames de France, by Paris road: 9 km, ✆ 03 26 05 46 10.

Notre-Dame cathedral ★★★ - St-Rémi basilica ★★: interior★★★ - Palais du Tau★★ BY **V** - Caves de Champagne (cellars)★★ BCX, CZ - Place Royale★ - Porte Mars★ - Hôtel de la Salle★ BY **R** - Foujita chapel ★ - Library★ of the former Collège des Jésuites BZ **C** - Musée St-Rémi★★ CZ **M**[4] - Musée-hôtel Le Vergeur★ BX **M**[3] - Musée des Beaux-Arts★ BY **M**[2].

Fort de la Pompelle (German helmets★) 9 km by ③.

Plans on following pages

Château les Crayères P VISA

64 bd Henry Vasnier – ✆ 03 26 82 80 80 – crayeres@relaischateaux.com – Fax 03 26 82 65 52 – Closed 1st-29 January CZ **a**

17 rm – †€ 300/575 ††€ 300/575, ☕ € 28 – 3 suites

Rest – *(number of covers limited, pre-book)* Menu € 70 (weekday lunch), € 155/225 – Carte € 122/170

Spec. Langoustines en chaud-froid, velouté de cresson. Menu "Autour du champagne". Tarte flambée et ris de veau de lait, coriandre, oignons au goût de lard fumé. **Wines** Champagne, Coteaux Champenois.

◆ A charming patrician residence in a landscaped park, near the Gallo-Roman tunnels used as cellars by the prestigious champagne houses. Luxurious rooms. Sumptuous decor in the dining room, terrace in the main courtyard and up-to-date cuisine.

REIMS

Berthelot (Bd M.) .... U 5
Brébant (Av.) .... U 8
Brimontel (R. de) .... U 10
Carré (R. du Gén.) .... UV 20
Champagne (Av. de) .... V 22
Cognacq-Jay (R.) .... V 25
Danton (R.) .... U 30
Dr-Lemoine (R.) .... U 35
Europe (Av. de l') .... V 42
Farman (Av. Henri) .... V 43
Maison-Blanche (R.) .... V 64
Paris (Av. de) .... V 69
Pompidou (Av. G.) .... V 71
Robespierre (Bd) .... U 74
Tinqueux (R. de) .... V 87
Vaillant-Couturier (Av.) ..... V 89
Witry (Rte de) .... U 91
Zola (R. Émile) .... U 92

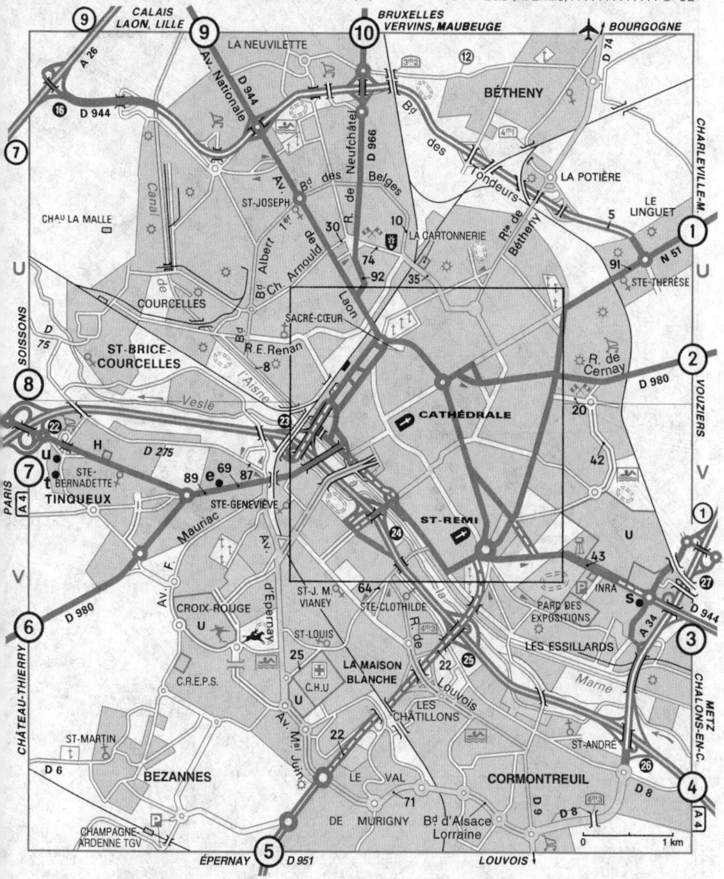

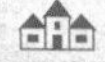

L'Assiette Champenoise (Arnaud Lallement)

rm, rest, rest, VISA

à Tinqueux, 40 av. Paul Vaillant-Couturier ✉ *51430*
– ✆ 03 26 84 64 64 – assiette.champenoise@wanadoo.fr – Fax 03 26 04 15 69

40 rm – €144/194 €144/194, €14 – 15 suites V **e**

Rest – *(closed 22 February-11 March, Wednesday lunch and Tuesday)*
Menu €65 (weekday lunch), €130/150 – Carte €116/136

Spec. Déclinaison de goûts et textures sur langoustines. Turbot breton au vin jaune. Cochon noir de Gascogne à la broche.

Wines Champagne, Bouzy.

◆ This elegant mansion and recently added wing, situated in a floral park, has pleasant, renovated rooms; some with a lounge. Elegant dining room (pastel tones), pleasant terrace and delicious, modern food.

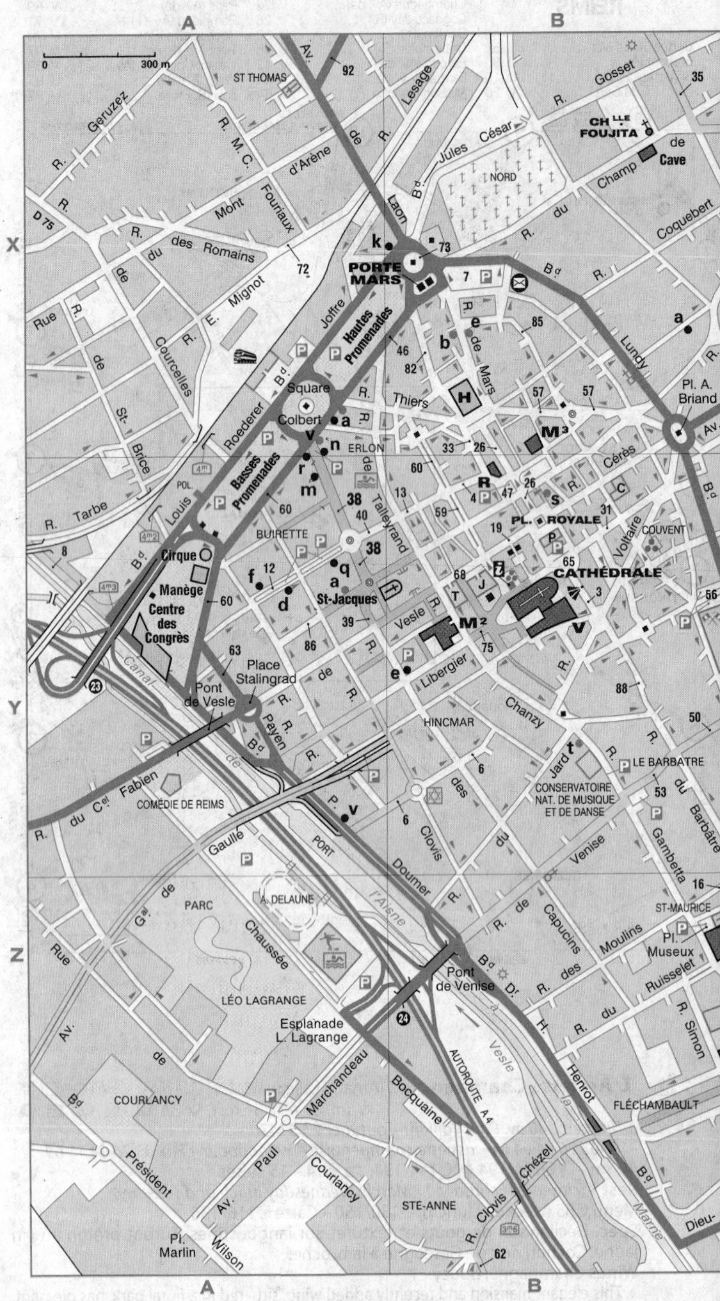
A
B
0
300 m
ST THOMAS
Av.
92
R. Lesage
de Laon
R. Gosset
35
R. Geruzez
R. M. C. Fouriaux
d'Arène
Bd Jules César
CHLLE FOUJITA
de Cave
Champ
NORD
R. du Mont
R. Coquebert
D 75
R. des Romains
X
72
k
73
PORTE MARS
7
Bd
R.
Mignot
R. E.
Joffre
Hautes Promenades
85
a
R. de Mars
e
b
Lundy
46
82
Rue de Courcelles
R. de St-Brice
Bd Roederer
Square Colbert
R. Thiers
H
57
57
Pl. A. Briand
Av.
a
v
n
ERLON
33
26
M3
Cérès
Bd
r
m
de Talleyrand
60
R
47
26
R.
s
C
Basses Promenades
POL.
R. Tarbe
Louis
38
40
13
4
59
PL. ROYALE
31
Voltaire
COUVENT
60
BUIRETTE
19
P
8
Bd
Cirque
38
q
65
CATHÉDRALE
Manège
f
12
d
a
St-Jacques
68
J
T
3
56
Centre des Congrès
60
39
Vesle
R.
M2
V
86
75
63
Place Stalingrad
R. de
e
Libergier
R.
88
Canal
Pont de Vesle
R.
R. Payen
Chanzy
50
Y
HINCMAR
R.
Bd
R.
Jard
t
R.
LE BARBATRE
de
6
CONSERVATOIRE NAT. DE MUSIQUE ET DE DANSE
53
R. du Barbâtre
du Cel Fabien
COMÉDIE DE REIMS
P.
v
6
des
R.
Gaulle
PORT
Clovis
du
Venise
Gambetta
Doumer
A. DELAUNE
l'Aisne
16
de
PARC
R.
R. de Capucins
ST-MAURICE
Ga de
Chaussée
Moulins
Pl. Museux
Z
Rue
Bd Dr.
R. des
Ruisselet
Pont de Venise
LÉO LAGRANGE
R. du
R. Simon
Esplanade L. Lagrange
H.
24
Av.
AUTOROUTE A4
Vesle
de
la
Henrot
Marchandeau
Bocquaine
Bd
COURLANCY
FLÉCHAMBAULT
Président
Paul
Courlancy
Chézel
Bd
Av.
STE-ANNE
Clovis
Marne
Dieu-
Pl. Marlin
Wilson
R.
62
A
B

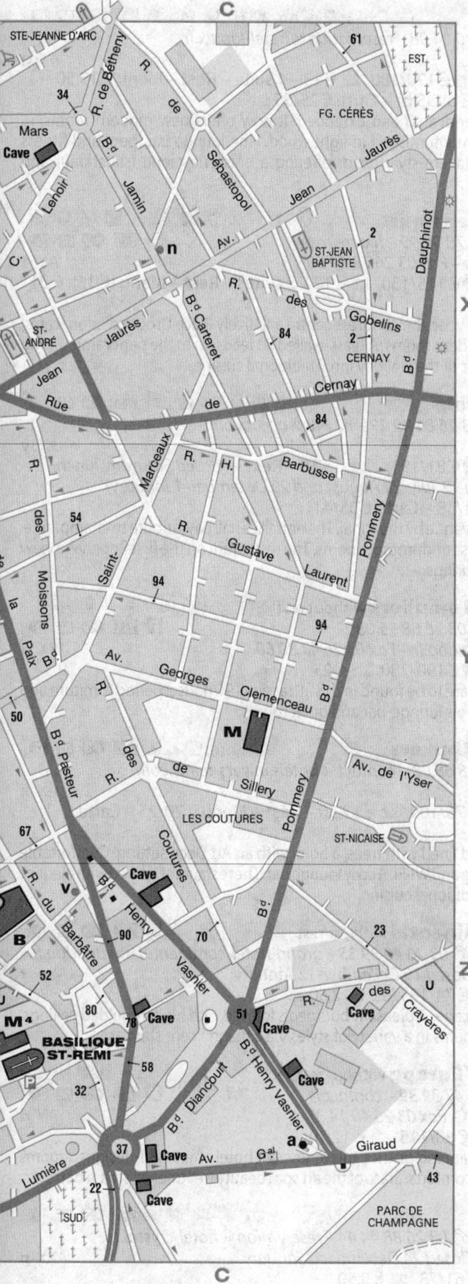

REIMS

Alsace-Lorraine (R. d')	CX	2
Anatole-France (Cours)	BY	3
Arbalète (R. de l')	BY	4
Boulard (R.)	BY	6
Boulingrin (Pl. du)	BX	7
Brébant (Av.)	AY	8
Buirette (R.)	AY	12
Cadran St-Pierre (R.)	BY	13
Carmes (R. des)	BZ	16
Carnégie (Pl.)	BY	17
Carnot (R.)	BY	19
Champagne (Av. de)	CZ	22
Chemin Vert (R. du)	CZ	23
Colbert (R.)	BXY	26
Desteuque (R. E.)	BY	31
Dieu-Lumière (R.)	CZ	32
Dr-Jacquin (R.)	BXY	33
Dr-Knoéri (Pl. du)	CX	34
Dr-Lemoine (R.)	BX	35
Droits-de-l'Homme (Pl. des)	CZ	37
Drouet d'Erlon (Pl.)	AY	38
Dubois (R. Th.)	AY	39
Étape (R. de l')	AY	40
Farman (Av. H.)	CZ	43
Foch (Bd)	ABX	46
Forum (Pl.)	BY	47
Gerbert (R.)	BCY	50
Gouraud (Pl. Gén.)	CZ	51
Grand-Cerf (R. du)	CZ	52
Herduin (R. Lt)	BY	53
Houzeau-Muiron (R.)	CY	54
Jamot (R. Paul)	BY	56
Jean-Jaurès (Av.)	BCX	
J.-J.-Rousseau (R.)	BX	57
Lambert (Bd Victor)	CZ	58
Langlet (Crs J.-B.)	BY	59
Laon (Av. de)	ABX	
Leclerc (Bd Général)	AX	60
Lefèbvre (R. E.)	CX	61
Louvois (R. de)	BZ	62
Magdeleine (R.)	AY	63
Martyrs-de-la-Résistance (Pl. des)	BY	65
Montlaurent (R.)	CY	67
Myron-Herrick (Pl.)	BY	68
Philipe (R. Gérard)	CZ	70
Prés.-F.-Roosevelt (R.)	AX	72
République (Pl. de la)	BX	73
Rockefeller (R.)	BY	75
St-Nicaise (Pl.)	CZ	78
Salines (R. des)	CZ	80
Sarrail (R. Gén.)	BX	82
Strasbourg (R. de)	CX	84
Talleyrand (R. de)	ABY	
Temple (R. du)	BX	85
Thillois (R. de)	AY	86
Université (R. de l')	BY	88
Vesle (R. de)	ABY	
Victor-Hugo (Bd)	CZ	90
Zola (R. Émile)	AX	92
16e-et-22e-Dragons (R. des)	CY	94

De la Paix
9 r. Buirette – ✆ 03 26 40 04 08 – reservation@hotel-lapaix.fr – Fax 03 26 47 75 04 AY **q**

169 rm – €120/180 €120/180, €13 – 1 suite – **Rest** – Menu €13,50 (weekday lunch), €18 € bi/35 bi – Carte €25/55

◆ This hotel has been renovated and extended. It now offers new modern rooms, in addition to those pleasantly furnished in light wood. Fine lounge bar, pool and fitness centre. Restaurant with tavern-style decor offering a brasserie menu (sauerkraut and seafood).

Holiday Inn Garden Court
rm, VISA
46 r. Buirette – ✆ 03 26 78 99 99 – higcreims@alliance-hospitality.com – Fax 03 26 78 99 90 AY **f**

80 rm – €115/130 €115/130, €12 – 2 suites – **Rest** – Menu (€16), €21 – Carte €30/43

◆ A practical location between the congress centre and lively Place Drouet d'Erlon (cafés, restaurants, cinemas). Modern rooms. A glass-walled lift leads up to the panoramic dining room on the seventh floor of the Holiday Inn. Traditional cuisine.

Mercure-Cathédrale
31 bd P. Doumer – ✆ 03 26 84 49 49 – h1248@accor.com – Fax 03 26 84 49 84 AY **v**

131 rm – €76/149 €81/191, €13,50 – **Rest** – *(closed Saturday lunch, Sunday lunch and lunch 12 July-24 August and 20 December-4 January)* Menu €28 (lunch), €31/38 – Carte €35/41

◆ A large building on an avenue by the canal. The entrance hall pays tribute to champagne. Spacious, well-equipped, soundproofed rooms. The restaurant on the first floor has a view of the barges at their moorings.

Grand Hôtel des Templiers without rest
22 r. des Templiers – ✆ 03 26 88 55 08 – hotel.templiers@wanadoo.fr – Fax 03 26 47 80 60 BX **a**

18 rm – €190/280 €190/280, €25

◆ Luxury and refinement are to be found in this attractive 19C house: period furniture and opulent fabrics. A bourgeois lounge-bar and quiet rooms.

Grand Hôtel de l'Univers
rest,
41 bd Foch – ✆ 03 26 88 68 08 – contact@hotel-univers-reims.com – Fax 03 26 40 95 61 AX **a**

42 rm – €68/99 €75/109, €12,50 – **Rest** – Menu €20/25 – Carte €24/35

◆ Situated on a boulevard lined with trees, a hotel with an Art Deco setting. Comfortable rooms with double glazing and Wi-Fi. A cosy lounge bar. The restaurant is lined with elegant dark wood panelling. Traditional cuisine.

Grand Hôtel Continental without rest
93 pl. Drouet-d'Erlon – ✆ 03 26 40 39 35 – grand-hotel-continental@wanadoo.fr – Fax 03 26 47 51 12 – Closed 19 December-12 January AXY **r**

50 rm – €61/185 €74/185, €12,50

◆ An elegant, late-19C façade. A pleasant bourgeois lounge with high, moulded ceilings. Access to the well-kept rooms in a variety of styles via a magnificent staircase.

Grand Hôtel de L'Europe without rest
29 r. Buirette – ✆ 03 26 47 39 39 – contact@hotel-europe-reims.com – Fax 03 26 40 14 37 AY **d**

54 rm – €72/100 €80/115, €12,50

◆ In the heart of a fast-changing district, this renovated hotel offers well-designed rooms equipped with the latest comforts. State of the art spa : beauty treatments, steam bath, etc.

Crystal without rest
86 pl. Drouet-d'Erlon – ✆ 03 26 88 44 44 – reservation@hotel-crystal.fr – Fax 03 26 47 49 28 – Closed 24 December-3 January AXY **n**

31 rm – €54/61 €61/73, €9,50

◆ An attractive restaurant tucked away in a flower garden where one can breakfast once spring arrives. The renovated rooms are small and well-kept.

Porte Mars without rest
2 pl. de la République – ✆ 03 26 40 28 35 – hotel.porte-mars@wanadoo.fr – Fax 03 26 88 92 12 AX **k**
24 rm – †€ 72/88 ††€ 80/130, ☐ € 11
◆ The wood-panelled rooms are perfectly soundproofed and air-conditioned. A snug lounge with a fire burning in the hearth. Gourmet breakfast served in a conservatory.

Grand Hôtel du Nord without rest
75 pl. Drouet-d'Erlon – ✆ 03 26 47 39 03 – grandhoteldunord-reims@wanadoo.fr – Fax 03 26 40 92 26 AY **m**
50 rm – †€ 55/64 ††€ 63/76, ☐ € 8,50
◆ A hotel with a proud façade fronting a lively square. Most of the guestrooms have been renovated (rustic furniture). The lobby and breakfast room have been refurbished in contemporary style.

De la Cathédrale without rest
20 r. Libergier – ✆ 03 26 47 28 46 – hoteldelacathedrale@wanadoo.fr – Fax 03 26 88 65 81 BY **e**
17 rm – †€ 54/62 ††€ 62/68, ☐ € 7
◆ A corner building with rooms of modest dimensions but comfortable and faultlessly kept. Notre Dame Cathedral stands majestically at the other end of the street.

Foch (Jacky Louazé)
37 bd Foch – ✆ 03 26 47 48 22 – mjackylouaze@aol.com – Fax 03 26 88 78 22 – Closed 21 July-18 August, 11-25 February, Saturday lunch, Sunday dinner and Monday AX **a**
Rest – Menu € 33 (weekdays)/75 – Carte € 65/93
Spec. Huîtres Marennes-Oléron au caviar d'Aquitaine, granité de concombre (October to March). Bocal "parfait" de homard bleu aux truffes et topinambours (December to February.). Bar cuit entier en terre d'argile de Vallauris. **Wines** Champagne.
◆ The restaurant borders the Promenades (shaded 18C courtyards). Welcoming, wainscoted dining hall and a cosy lounge. Up-to-date, gourmet cuisine.

Le Millénaire (Laurent Laplaige)
4 r. Bertin – ✆ 03 26 08 26 62 – contact@lemillenaire.com – Fax 03 26 84 24 13 – Closed Saturday lunchtime and Sunday BY **s**
Rest – Menu € 31 (weekdays)/76 – Carte € 69/99
Spec. Langoustines rôties, melon, menthe. Turbot grillé au Champagne. Côte de veau cuite au four, mousseline d'aghatta au beurre salé. **Wines** Champagne.
◆ This restaurant, near the Place Royale, offers a modern setting with painting exhibitions. Tasty, up-to-the-minute cuisine.

Continental
95 pl. Drouet d'Erlon – ✆ 03 26 47 01 47 – lecontinental-restaurant@wanadoo.fr – Fax 03 26 40 95 60 AXY **r**
Rest – Menu € 14 (weekdays)/55 – Carte € 35/63
◆ Bordering a long pedestrianised square, this restaurant has been modernised in keeping with the style of the region. A monumental gilded vine adorns the dining room. Champagne bar and courtyard terrace.

La Vigneraie
14 r. Thillois – ✆ 03 26 88 67 27 – lavigneraie@wanadoo.fr – Fax 03 26 40 26 67 – Closed 29 July-18 August, 24 February-9 March, Sunday dinner, Wednesday lunch and Monday AY **a**
Rest – *(number of covers limited, pre-book)* Menu (€ 17), € 24 (weekday lunch), € 32/64 – Carte € 55/75
◆ A restaurant with a glass façade and a stylish, contemporary dining room, decorated in sunny colours. Cuisine in keeping with current taste. Good wine list.

Flo
96 pl. Drouet d'Erlon – ✆ 03 26 91 40 50 – ljugand@groupeflo.fr – Fax 03 26 91 40 54 AX **v**
Rest – brasserie Menu € 30 – Carte € 30/60
◆ Large, Art Deco-inspired brasserie (and former army club) with many intimate nooks, and a rotunda terrace for fine weather dining.

Au Petit Comptoir
17 r. de Mars – ✆ 03 26 40 58 58 – au.petit.comptoir@wanadoo.fr – Fax 03 26 47 26 19 – Closed in August, Christmas holidays, Sunday and Monday BX **b**
Rest – Menu € 16, € 29/37 – Carte approx. € 46
♦ This restaurant, decorated in a champagne theme, has a simple modern interior. Generous, updated bistro cuisine. Local wines and also from around the world.

Brasserie Le Boulingrin
48 r. Mars – ✆ 03 26 40 96 22 – boulingrin@wanadoo.fr – Fax 03 26 40 03 92 – Closed Sun BX **e**
Rest – Menu € 18 bi (weekdays)/25 – Carte € 24/44
♦ This 1925 brasserie has preserved its pleasant Art Deco setting, the attractive Bacchic murals in particular. It is popular with local people.

Le Jamin
18 bd Jamin – ✆ 03 26 07 37 30 – eurl-jamin@wanadoo.fr – Fax 03 26 02 09 64 – Closed 11-26 August, 19 January-2 February, Sunday dinner and Monday
Rest – Menu (€ 13 bi), € 20 bi/31 – Carte € 27/39 CX **n**
♦ A small local restaurant for meals in a discreet, modern setting. Daily specials are chalked up on a blackboard; traditional cuisine.

Les Charmes
11 r. Brûlart – ✆ 03 26 85 37 63 – jgoyeux@club-internet.fr – Fax 03 26 36 21 00 – Closed 10-20 April, 24 July-24 August, 1st-6 January, Monday dinner, Saturday lunch and Sunday CZ **v**
Rest – Menu € 14,50 (weekday lunch), € 30/37
♦ A pleasant family-run restaurant adorned with painted wood panels near the cellars of the city's main champagne houses and the St-Remi basilica. Good choice of whiskies.

La Table Anna
6 r. Gambetta – ✆ 03 26 89 12 12 – latableanna@wanadoo.fr – Fax 03 26 89 12 12 – Closed spring school holidays, 20 July-15 August, 23 December-2 January, Sunday dinner and Monday BY **t**
Rest – Menu (€ 13 bi), € 20/38 – Carte € 31/37
♦ The "chef-artist-window-dresser" has some of his own paintings on the walls and dresses his own windows. Simple comfort and family atmosphere. Attractive menus.

Châlons-en-Champagne road 3 km to ③ – ✉ 51100 Reims

Mercure-Parc des Expositions rm,
– ✆ 03 26 05 00 08 – h0363@accor.com – Fax 03 26 85 64 72
100 rm – †€ 69/139 ††€ 79/149, ☕ € 13,50 – **Rest** – *(closed Saturday lunch, Sunday lunch and holidays lunch)* Menu € 33/43 – Carte € 24/43 V **s**
♦ A 1970s building with renovated rooms of two different types; either modern or simpler and functional. Restaurant, extended by a veranda, adorned with a mural of a Champagne vineyard.

in Sillery 11 km by ③ and D 8E – pop. 1 655 – alt. 90 m – ✉ 51500

Le Relais de Sillery
– ✆ 03 26 49 10 11 – Fax 03 26 49 12 07 – Closed 12 August-2 September, 1st-8 January, 9-22 February, Tuesday dinner, Sunday dinner and Monday
Rest – Menu € 21 (weekdays)/72 – Carte € 44/59
♦ The dining room has an elegant setting, while the pleasant summer terrace offers a view of the Vesle and fine landscape garden. Appetising classic dishes.

in Montchenot 11 km by ⑤ – ✉ 51500 Villers-Allerand

Grand Cerf (Dominique Giraudeau et Pascal Champion)
50 rte Nationale – ✆ 03 26 97 60 07 – Fax 03 26 97 64 24 – Closed 10-31 August, February school holidays, Sunday dinner, Tuesday dinner and Wednesday
Rest – Menu € 35 (weekday lunch), € 65/92 – Carte € 69/104
Spec. Homard-melon (May to September) ou homard-poire (October to April). Saint-Pierre sauce verjutée. Pied de cochon farci au ris de veau sauce truffe. **Wines** Champagne.
♦ This inn at the foot of the Montagne de Reims has two elegant, wood-panelled dining rooms, one on a veranda giving onto the garden. Fine classic cuisine.

via ⑦ 6 km, A 4 motorway, Tinqueux exit – ✉ 51430 Tinqueux

Novotel rm, VISA
– ✆ *03 26 08 11 61 – h0428@accor.com – Fax 03 26 08 72 05* V **u**
127 rm – €110/130 €110/130, € 14 – **Rest** – Carte € 22/38
◆ A 1970s hotel, close to the motorway interchange, offering rooms that have been pleasantly renovated in a modern spirit. The pleasant restaurant terrace overlooking the swimming pool is very popular.

Tip Top without rest VISA
1 av. d'A.F.N. – ✆ 03 26 83 84 85 – info@tiptop-hotel.com – Fax 03 26 49 58 25
66 rm – €60 €65/129, €7,50 V **t**
◆ A brand new hotel near the motorway. A functional but welcoming concept using high quality materials for travellers looking for a "tip-top" overnight stay.

REIPERTSWILLER – 67 Bas-Rhin – 315 I3 – pop. 933 – alt. 230 m – ✉ 67340
Alsace-Lorraine 1 **A1**

Paris 450 – Bitche 19 – Haguenau 33 – Sarreguemines 48 – Saverne 32 – Strasbourg 54

La Couronne rest, VISA
13 r. Wimmenau – ✆ 03 88 89 96 21 – sb.kuhm@wanadoo.fr – Fax 03 88 89 98 22 – Closed 16-26 June, 12-27 November, 2-12 February
16 rm – €48/52 €51/60, € 10 – ½ P € 55/60 – **Rest** – *(closed Wednesday dinner except June-September, Sunday dinner October- February, Wednesday, Thursday and dinner January- February, Monday and Tuesday)* Menu € 19 (weekday lunch), € 25/49 – Carte € 32/61
◆ The façade of this regional style house sports an unusual wrought iron sculpture. Tasteful rooms and a stunning view of the countryside from the rear. Classic cuisine served in a sumptuous decor of Art Nouveau inspired walnut panelling.

LA REMIGEASSE – 17 Charente-Maritime – 324 C4 – see île d'Oléron

---

REMIREMONT – 88 Vosges – 314 H4 – pop. 8 538 – alt. 400 m – ✉ 88200
Alsace-Lorraine 27 **C3**

Paris 413 – Belfort 70 – Colmar 80 – Épinal 28 – Mulhouse 81 – Vesoul 66
Office de tourisme, 2, rue Charles-de-Gaulle ✆ 03 29 62 23 70, Fax 03 29 23 96 79
Rue Ch.-de-Gaulle★ - Crypt★ of St-Pierre abbey church.

Plan on next page

Du Cheval de Bronze without rest VISA
59 r. Ch. de Gaulle – ✆ 03 29 62 52 24 – hotel-du-cheval-de-bronze@wanadoo.fr – Fax 03 29 62 34 90 – Closed November B **s**
35 rm – €24 €44/56, €7
◆ A hotel in an old post house under the picturesque town centre arcades. Modest, well kept, rustic style rooms. Excellent value for money.

Le Clos Heurtebise VISA
13 chemin des Capucins, via r. Capit. Flayelle B – ✆ 03 29 62 08 04 – Fax 03 29 62 38 80 – Closed 31 August-16 September, 4-20 January, Sunday dinner and Monday
Rest – Menu € 18 (weekdays)/60 – Carte € 43/52
◆ This south-facing establishment in the upper part of the town serves unfussy, classic cuisine embellished with local and Mediterranean influences. Pleasant terrace.

in St-Étienne-lès-Remiremont 2 km by ① – pop. 4 057 – alt. 400 m – ✉ 88200

Le Chalet Blanc with rm rm, VISA
34 r. des Pêcheurs, (opposite the shopping centre) – ✆ 03 29 26 11 80 – lechaletblanc@hotmail.com – Fax 03 29 26 11 81 – Closed 10-25 August and Sunday dinner
7 rm – €54/68 €66/75, € 8 – ½ P € 61/67 – **Rest** – *(Closed Saturday lunch, Sunday dinner and Monday)* Menu (€ 17 bi), € 29/51 – Carte € 54/59
◆ A warm welcome, pleasant panelled dining room and trendy cuisine: this villa in a shopping area is worth the detour. Modern, chalet style rooms.

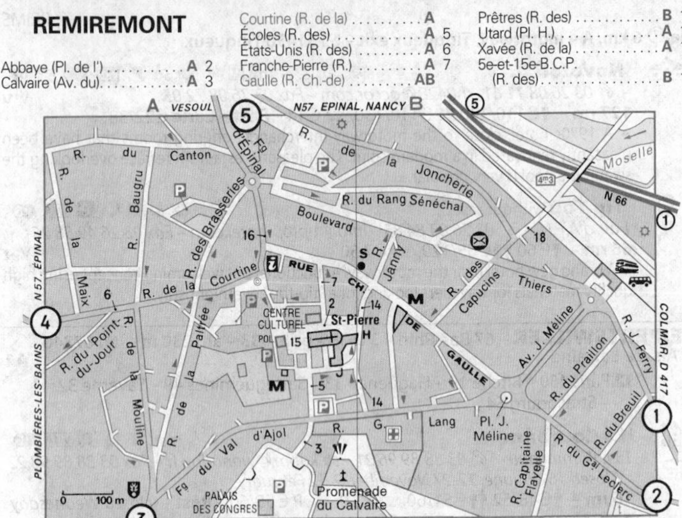

in Girmont-Val-d'Ajol 7 km southeast by D 23, D 57 and secondary road – pop. 273 – alt. 650 m – ✉ 88340

Auberge de la Vigotte
– ✆ 03 29 61 06 32 – courrier@lavigotte.com – Fax 03 29 61 07 88
– Closed 15 October-20 December
16 rm – †€ 55/60 ††€ 55/100, ☕ € 8 – ½ P € 55/58
Rest – *(closed Tues. and Wed.) (dinner only except Sunday) (pre-book)*
Menu (€ 18), € 25/38
◆ Old Vosges farmhouse set amidst forest and ponds. Tasteful rooms decorated with sponge painted walls, attractive furniture and paintings. The dining room has a strong country feel. Modern, international food.

REMOULINS – 30 Gard – 339 M5 – pop. 1 996 – alt. 27 m – ✉ 30210

Provence — 23 **D2**

Paris 685 – Alès 50 – Arles 37 – Avignon 23 – Nîmes 23 – Orange 34 – Pont-St-Esprit 40

Office de tourisme, place des Grands Jours ✆ 04 66 37 22 34, Fax 04 66 37 22 34

in St-Hilaire-d'Ozilhan 4.5 km Northeast by D792 – pop. 640 – alt. 55 m – ✉ 30210

L'Arceau
1 r. Arceau – ✆ 04 66 37 34 45 – contact@hotel-arceau.com – Fax 04 66 37 33 90 – Closed 1st December-14 February, Sunday dinner, Tuesday lunch and Monday from 1st October to 16 March
23 rm ☕ – †€ 78/83 ††€ 78/83 – ½ P € 60 – **Rest** – Menu € 25/60 – Carte € 38/65
◆ 18C residence with a fine stone façade in a village set amongst vineyards and scrubland. Well-kept, simply furnished and quite spacious rooms. Part-traditional, part-regional cuisine served in a Provençal coloured, neo-rustic dining room or on a shaded terrace.

RENAISON – 42 Loire – 327 C3 – pop. 2 653 – alt. 387 m – ✉ 42370

Lyon - Rhone Valley — 44 **A1**

Paris 385 – Chauffailles 43 – Lapalisse 39 – Roanne 11 – St-Étienne 90 – Thiers 74 – Vichy 56

Syndicat d'initiative, 50, route de Roanne ✆ 04 77 62 17 07

Town★ of St-Haon-le-Châtel North: 2 km - Barrage de la Tache: rocher-belvédère★ West: 5 km.

Central
8 r. du 10 Août 1944 – ✆ 04 77 64 25 39 – Fax 04 77 62 13 09 – Closed February
9 rm – †€ 40 ††€ 40, ☐ € 6 – ½ P € 52
Rest – *(closed Wednesday)* Menu € 11 bi (weekday lunch), € 18/32 – Carte € 22/33
◆ This family hotel situated on the village square, houses small, unpretentious rooms with good bedding and modern bathrooms. Tasty regional fare served on a terrace in fine weather.

La Ferme d'Irène without rest
– ✆ 04 77 64 29 12 – contact@platelin.com – Fax 04 77 62 14 79
4 rm ☐ – †€ 65 ††€ 70/85
◆ Delightful, peacefully located 19C farmhouse in the countryside. Snug sitting room (grand piano, earthenware stove). Stylish rooms located in the converted cowshed and hen house.

Jacques Coeur
15 r. Roanne – ✆ 04 77 64 25 34 – restaurant.jacques.coeur@orange.fr – Fax 04 77 64 43 88 – Closed 10-25 March, Tuesday except July-August, Sunday dinner and Monday
Rest – Menu € 21 bi (weekdays), € 39/52 – Carte € 37/46
◆ "Nothing is impossible if you set your mind to it": this restaurant illustrates the motto of Charles VII's famous Treasurer, with its 1946 murals and modern-style decor. Pretty terrace.

St-Haon-le-Vieux 3 km North by D 8 – pop. 810 – alt. 424 m – ✉ 42370

Auberge du Bon Accueil
– ✆ 04 77 64 40 72 – auberge-bon-accueil2@wanadoo.fr – Fax 04 77 64 40 72 – Closed 16-27 April, 25 August-3 September, autumn half-term holidays, 5-11 January and Wednesday
Rest – Menu (€ 14), € 20/52 – Carte € 33/50
◆ This inn set by the side of the main road has a small garden in front of it. Sober, rustic dining room and traditional, well-presented food.

RENNES 🅿 – 35 Ille-et-Vilaine – 309 L6 – pop. 206 229 – Built-up area 272 263 – alt. 40 m – ✉ 35000 Brittany
10 **D2**

Paris 349 – Angers 129 – Brest 246 – Caen 185 – Le Mans 155 – Nantes 108

Rennes-St-Jacques: ✆ 02 99 29 60 00, by ⑦: 7 km.

Office de tourisme, 11, rue Saint-Yves ✆ 02 99 67 11 11, Fax 02 99 67 11 00

de la Freslonnière Le Rheuby Ploërmel road: 7 km, ✆ 02 99 14 84 09 ;

de Cicé Blossac Bruz Domaine de Cicé-Blossac, by Redon road: 10 km, ✆ 02 99 52 79 79 ;

de Cesson-Sévigné Cesson-Sévigné Ile de Tizé, East: 11 km by D 96, ✆ 02 99 83 26 74 ;

de Rennes Saint-Jacques Saint-Jacques-de-la-Lande Le Temple du Cerisier, by Redon road: 11 km, ✆ 02 99 30 18 18.

Old Rennes★★ - Jardin du Thabor★★ - Palais de justice (law courts)★★ - Altar-piece★★ inside★ St-Pierre cathedral AY - Museums: de Bretagne★, des Beaux-Arts★ BY **M.**

Mercure Colombier rm,
1 r. Cap. Maignan – ✆ 02 99 29 73 73 – h1249@accor.com – Fax 02 99 29 54 00
ABZ **m**
142 rm – †€ 50/250 ††€ 62/350, ☐ € 14,50 – **Rest** – *(dinner only)* Carte € 18/24
◆ This Mercure has undergone a large-scale refurbishment. Rooms are partly done up. The décor in the lobby and wine bar (informal dining) evokes the Brocéliande forest.

Le Coq-Gadby rm,
156 r. Antrain – ✆ 02 99 38 05 55 – lecoq-gadby@wanadoo.fr – Fax 02 99 38 53 40
11 rm – †€ 123/170 ††€ 150/187, ☐ € 18 – 1 suite
DU **x**
Rest ***La Coquerie*** – *(closed 1st-10 March, 17 July-19 August, 30 December-6 January, 17-24 February, Sunday and Monday)* Menu (€ 25), € 33 (weekday lunch), € 46/60 – Carte € 58/97
Spec. Foie gras de canard cuit au sautoir, kumquats confits. Turbot sauvage au four, assaisonnement doux et épicé au kari-gosse. Tartelette tiède au chocolat, glace caramel-cannelle.
◆ Charming group of buildings, the oldest dating from the 17C. The refined ambiance continues in the rooms (antiques). Modern, comprehensive spa. Cooking and flower arranging classes. Dining room opening onto the garden with pictures and cockerel trinkets. Classical cuisine.

RENNES

Bourgeois (Bd L.) . . . . DV 3
Canada (Av. du) . . . . CV 6
Churchill (Av. Sir W.) . . . . CU 13
Combes (Bd E.) . . . . DV 14
Duchesse-Anne (Bd de la) . DU 15
Guilloux (R. L.) . . . . CU 23
Laennec (Bd) . . . . DU 31
Leroux (Bd Oscar) . . . . DV 36
Lorient (R. de) . . . . CU 38
Maginot (Av. du Sergent) . . DU 39
Pompidou (Bd G.) . . . . CV 55
St-Brieuc (R. du) . . . . CU 64
St-Jean-Baptiste de la Salle (Bd) . . . . CU 70
Strasbourg (Bd de) . . . . DU 83
Ukraine (Allée d') . . . . CV 84
Vitré (Bd de) . . . . DU 87
Yser (Bd de l') . . . . CV 88
3-Croix (Bd des) . . . . CU 89

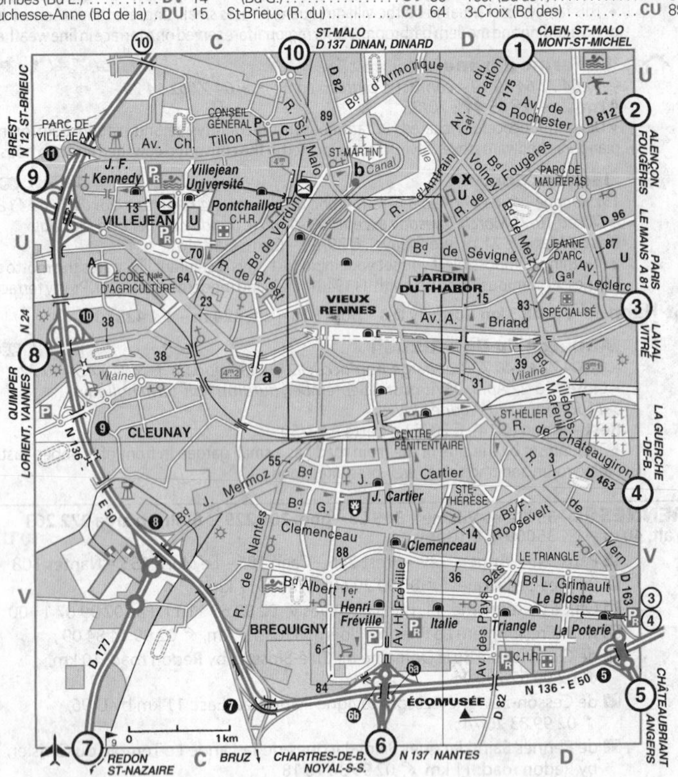

Anne de Bretagne without rest VISA

12 r. Tronjolly – ☎ 02 99 31 49 49 – hotelannedebretagne@wanadoo.fr – Fax 02 99 30 53 48 – Closed 22 December-5 January AZ **q**

42 rm – €85 €96/98, €11

◆ Hotel dating from the 1970s close to the historic town centre. Modern lobby, pleasant bar and spacious, well-equipped bedrooms (six with Jacuzzis).

Mercure Place de Bretagne without rest VISA

6 r. Lanjuinais – ☎ 02 99 79 12 36 – h2027@accor.com – Fax 02 99 79 65 76 AY **n**

48 rm – €55/128 €72/148, €13

◆ Behind its 19C façade lays a modern town centre hotel. Functional rooms with light wood and warm coloured soft furnishings, some overlooking the Vilaine.

Mercure Pré Botté without rest VISA

r. Paul Louis Courier – ☎ 02 99 78 82 20 – h1056@accor.com – Fax 02 99 78 82 21 – Closed 19 December-2 January BZ **t**

104 rm – €80/210 €92/222, €14,50

◆ This building was once where the Ouest France newspaper was printed. Today it offers refurbished spacious rooms and a Breton style breakfast (crepes).

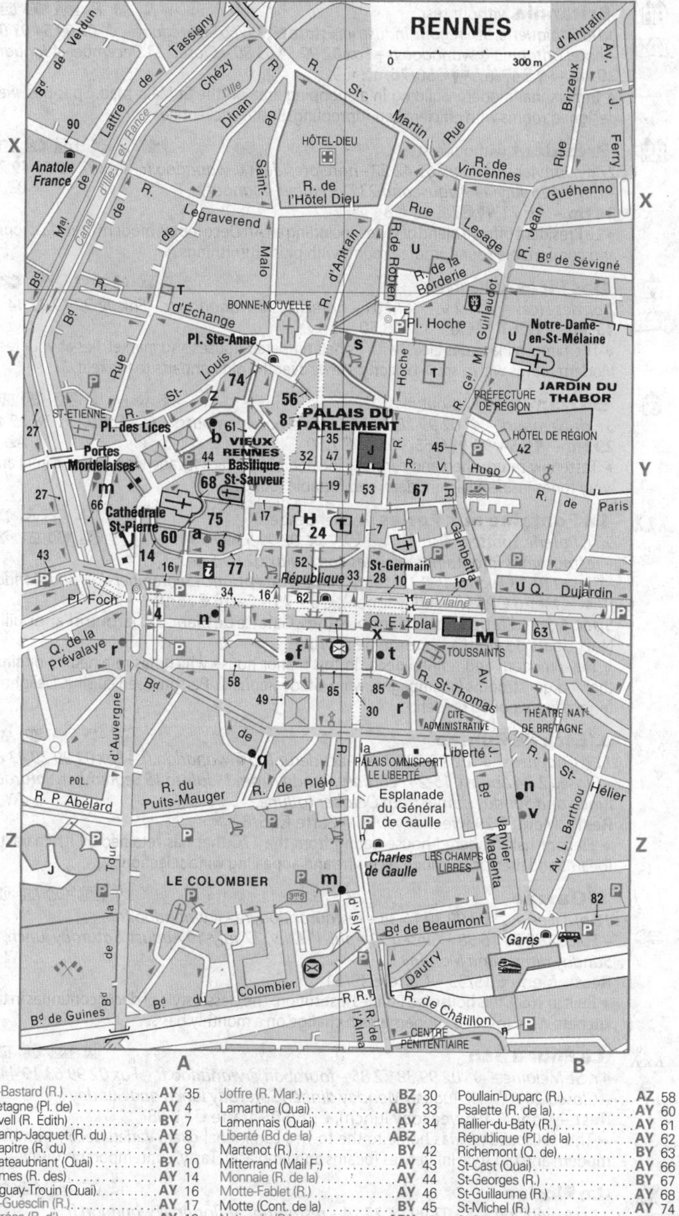

Le-Bastard (R.) .... AY 35
Bretagne (Pl. de) .... AY 4
Cavell (R. Édith) .... BY 7
Champ-Jacquet (R. du) .... AY 8
Chapitre (R. du) .... AY 9
Chateaubriant (Quai) .... BY 10
Dames (R. des) .... AY 14
Duguay-Trouin (Quai) .... AY 16
Du-Guesclin (R.) .... AY 17
Estrées (R. d') .... AY 19
La-Fayette (R.) .... AY 32
Hôtel-de-Ville (Pl. de l') .... AY 24
Ille-et-Rance (Quai) .... AY 27
Jean-Jaurès (R.) .... BY 28
Joffre (R. Mar.) .... BZ 30
Lamartine (Quai) .... ABY 33
Lamennais (Quai) .... AY 34
Liberté (Bd de la) .... ABZ
Martenot (R.) .... BY 42
Mitterrand (Mail F.) .... AY 43
Monnaie (R. de la) .... AY 44
Motte-Fablet (R.) .... AY 46
Motte (Cont. de la) .... BY 45
Nationale (R.) .... ABY 47
Nemours (R. de) .... AZ 49
Orléans (R. d') .... AY 52
Palais (Pl. du) .... BY 53
Pont-aux-Foulons (R. du) .... AY 56
Poullain-Duparc (R.) .... AZ 58
Psalette (R. de la) .... AY 60
Rallier-du-Baty (R.) .... AY 61
République (Pl. de la) .... AY 62
Richemont (Q. de) .... BY 63
St-Cast (Quai) .... AY 66
St-Georges (R.) .... BY 67
St-Guillaume (R.) .... AY 68
St-Michel (R.) .... AY 74
St-Sauveur (R.) .... AY 75
St-Yves (R.) .... AY 77
Solférino (Bd) .... BZ 82
Vasselot (R.) .... AZ 85
41e-d'Infanterie (R.) .... AX 90

Britannia without rest
bd la Robiquette, St Grégoire Industrial Estate ✉ 35760 St-Grégoire – ☎ 02 99 54 03 03 – hotel.britannia@wanadoo.fr – Fax 02 99 54 03 80 – Closed 23 December-4 January
29 rm – €47/67 €50/76, €9
◆ Impersonal modern building in a shopping area on the St Malo road. Spacious, well designed rooms with efficient soundproofing. Business clientele.

Président without rest
27 av. Janvier – ☎ 02 99 65 42 22 – hotelpresident@wanadoo.fr – Fax 02 99 65 49 77 – Closed 25 July-11 August and 23 December-4 January BZ **n**
34 rm – €71 €74, €8
◆ Le Président offers a blend of styles, including an Art Deco lobby, modern breakfast room and comfortable soundproofed rooms with plush furnishings.

Des Lices without rest
7 pl. des Lices – ☎ 02 99 79 14 81 – hotel.lices@wanadoo.fr – Fax 02 99 79 35 44
45 rm – €61 €65, €8,50 AY
◆ The famous Place des Lices, with its half timbered houses and market, lies at your feet. Modern rooms with a small balcony. Views over the old ramparts to the rear.

De Nemours without rest
5 r. de Nemours – ☎ 02 99 78 26 26 – resa@hotelnemours.com – Fax 02 99 78 25 40
29 rm – €54/90 €65/90, €7,50 AZ **f**
◆ Tastefully refurbished and centrally located hotel. Black facade with taupe, camel and ivory tones inside. Plain, modern, comfortable rooms.

La Fontaine aux Perles (Rachel Gesbert)
96 r. Poterie, (pottery district), via ④ – ☎ 02 99 53 90 90 – restaurant@lafontaineauxperles.com – Fax 02 99 53 47 77 – Closed 10-18 August, 1st-12 January, Sunday except lunch September-July and Monday
Rest – Menu €25 (weekday lunch), €35/75 – Carte €75/95
Spec. Cœur d'artichaut aux langoustines. Galette de blanc de barbue à l'andouille. Noix de ris de veau à la crème de morilles.
◆ New, modern and refined decor in this manor house which has retained its original, themed guestrooms (champagne, wine, Stade Rennais). Personalised cuisine. Delightful terrace in a wooded garden.

L'Escu de Runfao
11 r. Chapître – ☎ 02 99 79 13 10 – ecuderunfao@wanadoo.fr – Fax 02 99 79 43 80 – Closed 2-24 August, 15-24 February, Sunday from 1st July to 15 September, Saturday lunch and Sunday dinner from October to June AY **a**
Rest – Menu €29 (weekdays)/56 – Carte €65/82
◆ Elegant half timbered house dating from the 17C that has retained all its character (beams and fireplaces). Modern cuisine and appealing wine selection.

L'Ouvrée
18 pl. Lices – ☎ 02 99 30 16 38 – restaurantlouvree@wanadoo.fr – Fax 02 99 30 16 38 – Closed 21 April-1st May, 27 July-19 August, Saturday lunch, Sunday dinner and Monday AY **z**
Rest – Menu €15/33 – Carte €39/51
◆ Built in 1659, this house is a Rennes institution. The classic style of decor continues in the kitchen. Wine inspired suppers which change on a monthly basis.

Le Four à Ban
4 r. St-Mélaine – ☎ 02 99 38 72 85 – fouraban@wanadoo.fr – Fax 02 99 63 19 44 – Closed 26 July-17 August, Monday dinner, Saturday lunch and Sunday
Rest – Menu €19 (weekday lunch), €26/50 – Carte €41/58
◆ This 17C building was home to the town's communal oven. Varied decor, with both modern and old style influences (beams and fireplace). Tasty, contemporary cuisine.

Le Florian
11 r. A. Rébillon – ☎ 02 99 14 25 14 – restaurant.le-florian@wanadoo.fr – Fax 02 99 14 26 00 – Closed 10-24 August, 24 December-5 January, Saturday lunch, Monday dinner and Sunday CU **b**
Rest – Menu €20 bi (weekday lunch), €24/52 – Carte €37/61
◆ A modern building with bay windows overlooking the banks of the Ille canal and the Rance. Pleasant waterside terrace. Food in keeping with current tastes and Brittany dishes.

XX **Le Guehennec**

33 r. Nantaise – ✆ 02 99 65 51 30 – Fax 02 99 65 68 26 – Closed 2 weeks in August, Saturday lunch, Monday dinner and Sunday AY **m**

Rest – Menu € 19 (lunch), € 30/60

◆ A fine combination of light wooden panelling and modern furniture in chocolate shades help to make this restaurant most appealing. Modern cuisine with market produce.

XX **Le Galopin**

21 av. Janvier – ✆ 02 99 31 55 96 – legalopin@club-internet.fr – Fax 02 99 31 08 95 BZ **v**

Rest – *(closed Saturday lunch and Sunday)* Menu (€ 13), € 17 (weekdays)/45 – Carte € 30/62

◆ Old fashioned wooden frontage contrasts with the dynamic atmosphere inside: modern decor and young staff serving brasserie cuisine and surf and turf (lobster).

X **Le Quatre B**

4 pl. Bretagne – ✆ 02 99 30 42 01 – quatreb@wanadoo.fr – Fax 02 99 30 42 01 – Closed Monday lunch, Saturday lunch and Sunday AYZ **z**

Rest – Menu (€ 13 bi), € 20/27 – Carte € 31/44

◆ Refined dining room with red banquettes, modern chairs and large, floral themed canvasses. Pleasant terrace. The modern style successfully extends to the cuisine.

X **Léon le Cochon**

1 r. Mar. Joffre – ✆ 02 99 79 37 54 – Fax 02 99 79 07 35 – Closed Sunday in July-August BY **x**

Rest – Menu (€ 12,50 bi), € 25 (Sunday) – Carte € 25/43

◆ If you're in the mood for pork, try Léon's excellent dishes, served in a relaxed modern décor (floodlit trees, apple green timbers). Grilled pork and fish.

X **Le Petit Sabayon**

16 r. Trente – ✆ 02 99 35 02 04 – lepetitsabayon@free.fr – Closed 25 August-7 September, 23 February-8 March, Saturday lunch, Sunday dinner and Monday CU **a**

Rest – *(number of covers limited, pre-book)* Menu € 16 (weekday lunch), € 24/32 – Carte € 29/39

◆ Discretely tucked away restaurant in a quiet area of town. The locals come to enjoy the appetising cuisine made using market produce served in the pleasant dining room.

X **Les Carmes**

2 r Carmes – ✆ 02 99 79 28 95 – rome.michel@free.fr – Fax 02 99 79 28 95 – Closed Sunday dinner and Monday BZ **r**

Rest – Menu (€ 14), € 27/60 – Carte € 31/42

◆ This restaurant with a chocolate coloured facade comes highly recommended. The young chef prepares modern cuisine served in a contemporary setting.

in St-Grégoire 3 km North by D82 – pop. 7 644 – alt. 45 m – ✉ 35760

XXX **Le Saison** (David Etcheverry)

1 imp. Vieux Bourg, (near the church) – ✆ 02 99 68 79 35 – contact@le-saison.com – Fax 02 99 68 92 71 – Closed 4-25 August, Sunday dinner and Monday

Rest – Menu € 25 (weekday lunch), € 36/65 – Carte € 60/80

Spec. Bar de ligne et boudin de légumes au laurier. Pied de cochon croquant et bigorneaux, confiture de carotte jaune au cumin. Dacquoise à la rhubarbe.

◆ Large, rebuilt long house surrounded by a garden. Tasty modern cuisine in a contemporary dining room (beige and cocoa shades); pleasant terrace.

in Cesson-Sévigné 6 km by ③ – pop. 14 344 – alt. 28 m – ✉ 35510

Germinal — rest,

9 cours Vilaine, in the village – ✆ 02 99 83 11 01 – le-germinal@wanadoo.fr – Fax 02 99 83 45 16 – Closed 23 December-3 January

20 rm – †€ 75/100 ††€ 85/150, ☕ € 14 – **Rest** – *(closed Sunday)* Menu (€ 18), € 21 (weekday lunch), € 29/50 – Carte € 38/67

◆ This family hotel occupying a former mill is set son a stretch of the Vilaine reached via a bridge. Renovated rooms and communal areas. Lovely dining room/veranda decorated in a contemporary style and a superb modern terrace facing the river. Traditional menu.

L'Adresse
32 cours Vilaine – ✆ 02 99 83 82 06 – Closed 2-24 August, 9-15 February, Monday dinner, Saturday lunch and Sunday
Rest – Menu (€ 13 bi), € 16 bi (weekday lunch)/32 – Carte € 25/36
◆ Small, old style café with waterside terrace shaded by wisteria. A bistro style repertoire is served with Brittany specialities to the fore.

in Noyal-sur-Vilaine 12 km by ③ – pop. 4 698 – alt. 75 m – ✉ 35530

Auberge du Pont d'Acigné (Sylvain Guillemot)
rte d'Acigné: 3 km – ✆ 02 99 62 52 55 – pont.d.acigne@wanadoo.fr – Fax 02 99 62 21 70 – Closed 28 July-20 August, 2-9 September, Saturday lunch, Sunday dinner and Monday
Rest – Menu € 26 (weekday lunch), € 37/55 – Carte € 68/102
Spec. Craquant tomates et télines, sorbet paella (summer). Saint-Pierre à la rhubarbe (summer). Feuille à feuille de fraises, sorbet endive (spring).
◆ Good regional cuisine served in a lovely dining area or on the terrace overlooking the Vilaine. Views of the village. Excellent range of wines by the glass.

Hostellerie Les Forges with rm
22 av. du Gén. de Gaulle – ✆ 02 99 00 51 08 – sarl-lesforges@orange.fr – Fax 02 99 00 62 02 – Closed 8 August-1st September, 15-23 February, Friday dinner, Sunday dinner and dinners holidays
12 rm – € 40/45 € 45/75, € 6,50 – ½ P € 66/70
Rest – Menu € 14,50 (weekday lunch), € 19/35 – Carte € 36/41
◆ This captivating roadside hotel has two dining rooms, one with a rustic decor and attractive fireplace. Simple, modern and comfortable bedrooms.

St-Nazaire road 8 km by ⑦ – ✉35170 Bruz

Kerlann
– ✆ 02 99 05 95 80 – contact@kerlann.fr – Fax 02 99 05 94 10 – Closed 28 July-17 August and 29 December-4 January
52 rm – € 68/88 € 78/110, € 10,50 – 3 suites – ½ P € 98/110
Rest – *(closed Saturday and Sunday)* Menu (€ 19), € 26/32 – Carte € 27/36
◆ Modern building located between the airport and Cicé golf course. The rooms, laid out around a patio, are comfortable and colourful. Asian inspired suites. Brasserie style snacks in a setting with Chinese touches.

Le Rheu 8 km by ⑧ and D 224 – pop. 5 733 – alt. 30 m – ✉ 35650

Le Relais Fleuri
Les Landes d'Apigné – ✆ 02 99 14 60 14 – hotel.lerelaisfleuri@wanadoo.fr – Fax 02 99 14 60 03 – Closed 18-31 August
24 rm – € 35/48 € 40/56, € 7 – ½ P € 50/66 – **Rest** – Menu (€ 11), € 17/24 – Carte € 24/36
◆ Seated at a wooden table in this fresh setting, you'll appreciate the fine choice of home cooking. Simpler dishes available at the bar. Rooms plainly furnished.

Lorient road 6 km by ⑧, N 24 – ✉ 35650 Le Rheu

Manoir du Plessis with rm
– ✆ 02 99 14 79 79 – info@manoirduplessis.fr – Fax 02 99 14 69 60 – Closed 11-18 August, 29 December-5 January and 9-23 February
5 rm – € 90 € 95, € 9 – **Rest** – *(closed Sat. lunchtime, Sun. evening and Mon.)* Menu € 17 (weekday lunch), € 23/38 – Carte € 42/49
◆ A family mansion set in a park. Parquet floors, wood panelling, fireplaces, Louis XVI-style chairs and an attractive terrace create an ideal setting to enjoy your meal.

LA RÉOLE – 33 Gironde – 335 K7 – pop. 4 187 – alt. 44 m – ✉ 33190 4 **C2**

Paris 649 – Bordeaux 74 – Casteljaloux 42 – Duras 25 – Libourne 45 – Marmande 33

Office de tourisme, 18, rue Peysseguin ✆ 05 56 61 13 55, Fax 05 56 71 25 40

Aux Fontaines
8 r. de Verdun La Réole – ☎ 05 56 61 15 25 – Fax 05 56 61 15 25 – Closed 15 November-1st December, 16-22 February, Sunday dinner, Wednesday dinner and Monday
Rest – *(number of covers limited, pre-book)* Menu € 17/48
◆ Restaurant in a large town centre building constructed against a hill. In summer meals are served on the attractive garden terrace. Traditional cuisine.

LA RÉPARA-AURIPLES – 26 Drôme – **332** D6 – see Crest

RESTIGNÉ – 37 Indre-et-Loire – **317** K5 – see Bourgueil

RESTONICA (GORGES) – 2B Haute-Corse – **345** D6 – see Corse (Corte)

RETHONDES – 60 Oise – **305** I4 – see Compiègne

REUGNY – 03 Allier – **326** C4 – **pop. 272** – **alt. 204 m** – ✉ 03190 5 **B1**

Paris 312 – Bourbon-l'Archambault 43 – Montluçon 15 – Montmarault 45 – Moulins 64

Table de Reugny
– ☎ 04 70 06 70 06 – info@restaurant-reugny.com – Fax 04 70 06 77 52 – Closed 24 August-6 September, 2-9 January, Sunday dinner, Monday and Tuesday
Rest – Menu (€ 16), € 21 (weekdays)/47 – Carte approx. € 36
◆ Behind the imposing façade of this roadside restaurant is a welcoming dining room decorated in red, and a terrace overlooking the garden. Enticing contemporary cuisine.

REUILLY-SAUVIGNY – 02 Aisne – **306** D8 – **pop. 213** – **alt. 78 m** – ✉ 02850

Paris 109 – Épernay 34 – Château-Thierry 16 – Reims 50 – Soissons 46 – Troyes 116 37 **C3**

Auberge Le Relais (Martial Berthuit) with rm
2 r. de Paris – ☎ 03 23 70 35 36 – auberge.relais.de.reuilly@wanadoo.fr – Fax 03 23 70 27 76 – Closed 17 August-4 September, 2 February-5 March, Tuesday and Wednesday
7 rm – €71 €94, € 13,50
Rest – Menu € 31 (weekdays)/79 – Carte € 78/98
Spec. Tartelette de légumes à la grecque. Coquille Saint-Jacques (October to March). Noix de ris de veau, queue de gambas, risotto aux câpres et citron. **Wines** Coteaux champenois rouge, Champagne.
◆ Elegant new interior, attractive veranda surrounded by greenery and a delicate cuisine that subtly blends tradition and modernity: a smart inn with boundless appeal.

REVEL – 31 Haute-Garonne – **343** K4 – **pop. 7 985** – **alt. 210 m** – ✉ 31250
Languedoc-Roussillon-Tarn Gorges 29 **C2**

Paris 727 – Carcassonne 46 – Castelnaudary 21 – Castres 28 – Gaillac 62 – Toulouse 54

Office de tourisme, place Philippe VI de Valois ☎ 05 34 66 67 68, Fax 05 34 66 67 67

Du Midi
34 bd Gambetta – ☎ 05 61 83 50 50 – contact@hotelrestaurantdumidi.com – Fax 05 61 83 34 74 – Closed 12-19 November
17 rm – €49 €54/70, € 7 – ½ P € 50
Rest – *(closed 12 November-7 December, Sunday dinner and Monday lunch October-May except holidays)* Menu € 23 (weekdays)/45 – Carte € 31/47
◆ Situated on a busy boulevard, this 19C post house offers a variety of rooms. Those at the rear are quieter. Bright dining room serving a combination of local produce with traditional cuisine.

in St-Ferréol 3 km Southeast by D 629 – ✉ 31250

Bassin de St-Ferréol★.

La Comtadine rm, P VISA MC

– ✆ 05 61 81 73 03 – contact@lacomtadine.com – Fax 05 34 66 53 28

9 rm – †€ 72/84 ††€ 72/84, ☕ € 9 – ½ P € 67/73

Rest – *(dinner only) (resident only)* Menu € 25 bi

◆ A restored peaceful little hotel, just a stone's throw from the lake. Bright modern rooms, enhanced with antique furniture. Non-smoking. Cuisine with a distinctly regional accent.

REVENTIN-VAUGRIS – 38 Isère – 333 C5 – see Vienne

RÉVILLE – 50 Manche – 303 E2 – pop. 1 168 – alt. 12 m – ✉ 50760 32 **A1**

Paris 351 – Carentan 44 – Cherbourg 30 – St-Lô 72 – Valognes 22

La Pernelle ✻★★ of the blockhouse West: 3 km - Pointe de Saire: blockhouse ≤★ Southeast: 2,5 km, **Normandy**

La Villa Gervaiserie without rest P VISA MC AE

17 rte des Monts – ✆ 02 33 54 54 64 – la.gervaiserie@wanadoo.fr – Fax 02 33 54 73 00 – Open March-mid November

10 rm – †€ 85 ††€ 85/112, ☕ € 8

◆ Facing the beach, all this hotel's rooms have a balcony or terrace with a view of the sea or Tatihou Island. Pleasant modern decoration and considerate welcome. Fine wooded garden.

Au Moyne de Saire with rm P VISA MC AE

15 r. Général de Gaulle – ✆ 02 33 54 46 06 – au.moyne.de.saire@wanadoo.fr – Fax 02 33 54 14 99 – Closed 26 October-9 November and Wednesday October-March

12 rm – †€ 49 ††€ 49/62, ☕ € 9 – ½ P € 47/55

Rest – Menu € 17/41 – Carte € 24/53

◆ A family inn that extends a warm welcome to guests. Tasteful refined interior, traditional and Norman cuisine. Small, well-kept rooms.

REY – 30 Gard – 339 G4 – see le Vigan

REZÉ – 44 Loire-Atlantique – 316 G4 – see Nantes

LE RHEU – 35 Ille-et-Vilaine – 309 L6 – see Rennes

LE RHIEN – 70 Haute-Saône – 314 H6 – see Ronchamp

RHINAU – 67 Bas-Rhin – 315 K7 – pop. 2 348 – alt. 158 m – ✉ 67860 1 **B2**

Paris 525 – Marckolsheim 26 – Molsheim 38 – Obernai 28 – Sélestat 28 – Strasbourg 39

Office de tourisme, 35, rue du Rhin ✆ 03 88 74 68 96, Fax 03 88 74 83 28

Au Vieux Couvent (Alexis Albrecht) VISA MC AE

– ✆ 03 88 74 61 15 – restaurant@vieuxcouvent.fr – Fax 03 88 74 89 19 – Closed 30 June-18 July, 20-24 October, 16 February-6 March, Monday dinner, Tuesday and Wednesday

Rest – Menu € 35 (weekdays)/88 – Carte € 71/90

Spec. Anguille du Rhin, salade de quinoa au persil plat. Eclaté d'oie, purée de courge du jardin (November to January). Baba au kirsch et crèmes chantilly. **Wines** Riesling, Pinot noir.

◆ This restaurant, 'The Old Convent', provides a warm atmosphere, with personalised cuisine using home-grown vegetables and herbs.

RIANS – 83 Var – 340 J4 – pop. 3 628 – alt. 406 m – ✉ 83560 40 **B3**

Paris 770 – Aix-en-Provence 40 – Avignon 100 – Manosque 33 – Marseille 69 – Toulon 77

Office de tourisme, place du Posteuil ✆ 04 94 80 33 37, Fax 04 94 80 33 37

La Roquette

1 km par rte de Manosque – ✆ 04 94 80 32 58 – Fax 04 94 80 32 58 – Closed 25 June-2 July, 17-24 November, 2-14 January, Sunday dinner, Wednesday and dinner in winter except Friday and Saturday

Rest – Menu € 26/47 – Carte € 29/47

◆ A family residence converted into a restaurant. Three, discreetly Provençal dining rooms, one after the other. A traditional menu, which changes with the seasons.

RIANTEC – 56 Morbihan – 308 L8 – pop. 4 910 – alt. 4 m – ✉ 56670 9 **B2**

Paris 503 – Rennes 152 – Vannes 59 – Lorient 16 – Lanester 14

La Chaumière de Kervassal without rest

3 km north of Kervassal – ✆ 02 97 33 58 66 – gonzague.watine@wanadoo.fr – Fax 02 97 33 58 66 – Open April-mid October

3 rm – 🛉€ 69 🛉🛉€ 69/100

◆ This former home of the vassal, after whom Kervassal is named, welcomes guests to its cosy sitting room and classic or more modern rooms. Pretty garden.

RIBEAUVILLÉ – 68 Haut-Rhin – 315 H7 – pop. 4 929 – alt. 240 m – Casino – ✉ 68150 Alsace-Lorraine 2 **C2**

Paris 439 – Colmar 16 – Mulhouse 60 – St-Dié 42 – Sélestat 14

Grand'Rue★★: tour des Bouchers★.

Riquewihr★★★ - Château du Haut-Ribeaupierre: ✳★★ - Château de St-Ullrich★: ✳★★.

RIBEAUVILLÉ

Abbé-Kemp (R. de l') . . . . A 2
Château (R. du) . . . . A 3
Flesch (R.) . . . . B 5
Fontaine (R. de la) . . . . A 6
Frères-Mertian (R. des) . . . . A 7
Gaulle (Av. du Gén.-de) . . . . B 9
Gouraud (Pl.) . . . . B 10
Grand'Rue . . . . AB
Grand'Rue de l' Eglise . . . . A 21
Halles-aux-Blés (R.) . . . . B 12
Hôtel de Ville (Pl. de l') . . . . A 13
Ortlieb (R.) . . . . B 14
Ste-Marie-aux-Mines (Rte) . . . . A 15
Sinne (Pl. de la) . . . . A 16
Synagogue (R. de la) . . . . B 17
Tanneurs (R. des) . . . . B 18

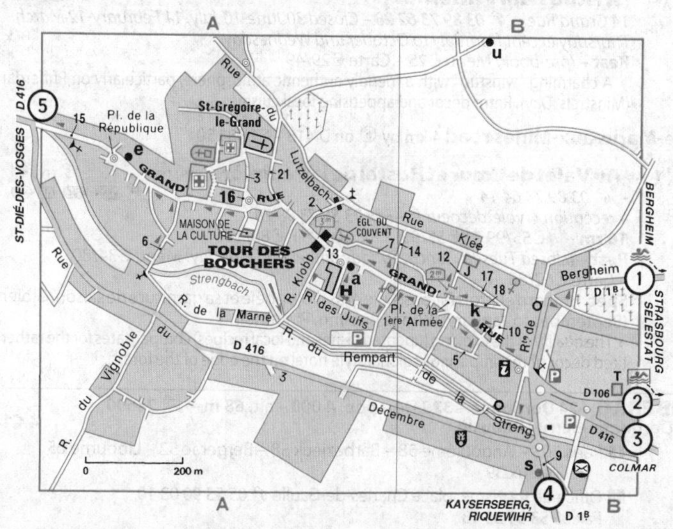

Le Clos St-Vincent ⪡ the plain of Alsace, rm,
rte de Bergheim, 1.5 km north-east by secondary road VISA AE
– ✆ 03 89 73 67 65 – reception.leclos@wanadoo.fr – Fax 03 89 73 32 20
– Open 15 March-15 December B **u**
20 rm – €115/210 €130/240, €15 – 4 suites
Rest – *(closed Tuesday) (dinner only)* Menu €50
◆ Admire the superb view over the Alsace plain from this peaceful 1960s construction among the vineyards. Vast, comfortable rooms, four of which have been recently renovated. Dining room and terrace with splendid panoramic views. Traditional cuisine.

Le Ménestrel without rest VISA AE
27 av. Gén. de Gaulle, via ④ – ✆ 03 89 73 80 52 – menestrel2@wanadoo.fr
– Fax 03 89 73 32 39
29 rm – €65/73 €73/99, €15
◆ Pleasantly-upgraded rooms in a modern style (king-size beds). The owner, a pastry chef, prepares the breakfast pastries and jams himself.

La Tour without rest VISA AE
1 r. de la Mairie – ✆ 03 89 73 72 73 – info@hotel-la-tour.com – Fax 03 89 73 38 74
– Closed 1st January-15 March A **a**
31 rm – €65/89 €71/97, €9
◆ An old winery offering bright, practical rooms. The most recent have been treated to a contemporary Vosgian makeover; those overlooking the attractive courtyard are very quiet.

Cheval Blanc VISA
122 Grand'Rue – ✆ 03 89 73 61 38 – cheval-blanc-ribeauville@wanadoo.fr
– Fax 03 89 73 37 03 – Closed 12-24 November and 19 January-5 March
23 rm – €49 €56, €8 – ½ P €55 – **Rest** – *(closed Tuesday lunchtime and Wednesday)* Menu €18 (weekdays)/43 – Carte €26/47 A **e**
◆ The façade of this Alsace building is decked with flowers in the summer. Rustic interior; modest rooms, those at the rear are quieter; a lounge with fireplace. Slightly extravagant Alsace atmosphere in this restaurant serving traditional cuisine.

Au Relais des Ménétriers VISA
10 av. Gén. de Gaulle – ✆ 03 89 73 64 52 – Fax 03 89 73 69 94 – Closed 14-29 July, Thursday dinner, Sunday dinner and Monday B **s**
Rest – Menu €11,50 (weekday lunch), €23/35 – Carte €38/47
◆ Pride of place to regional specialities using locally grown vegetables and traditional Alsace crockery (authentic *baeckoeffe* dishes). Pleasant rustic décor.

Wistub Zum Pfifferhüs VISA
14 Grand'Rue – ✆ 03 89 73 62 28 – Closed 30 June-10 July, 11 February-12 March, Thursday except from July to October and Wednesday B **k**
Rest – *(pre-book)* Menu €25 – Carte €29/49
◆ A charming "winstub" with a friendly authentic atmosphere, particularly on Pfifferdaj (Minstrels' Day). Retro decor and appetising local cuisine.

Ste-Marie-aux-Mines road 4 km by ⑤ on D 416 – ✉ 68150

Au Valet de Cœur et Hostel de la Pépinière with rm rm, VISA AE
– ✆ 03 89 73 64 14
– reception@valetdecoeur.fr – Fax 03 89 73 88 78
16 rm – €55/99 €55/99, €10 – ½ P €85/105
Rest – *(closed Tuesday lunch, Sunday dinner and Monday)* Menu €34/80
– Carte €62/85
Spec. Homard en trois façons. Foie gras d'oie poêlé et sa garniture de saison. Gibier (September to January). **Wines** Riesling, Pinot noir.
◆ The quality of the cooking (updated dishes and local recipes) compensates for the rather tired decor of this imposing regional style hotel on the edge of the forest.

RIBÉRAC – 24 Dordogne – 329 D4 – pop. 4 000 – alt. 68 m – ✉ 24600
Dordogne-Berry-Limousin 4 **C1**

Paris 505 – Angoulême 58 – Barbezieux 58 – Bergerac 52 – Libourne 65 – Périgueux 39

Office de tourisme, place Charles-de-Gaulle ✆ 05 53 90 03 10, Fax 05 53 91 35 13

Rêv'Hôtel without rest
rte de Périgueux, 1.5 km – ✆ 05 53 91 62 62 – contact@rev-hotel.fr – Fax 05 53 91 48 96
29 rm – †€ 40/60 ††€ 45/65, ☕ € 6
◆ A recent building in a small mixed housing development. Rooms are functional, well-kept and are all on the ground floor.

LES RICEYS – **10 Aube** – **313** G6 – **pop. 1 376** – **alt. 180 m** – ✉ **10340**
Northern France and the Paris Region 13 **B3**

Paris 210 – Bar-sur-Aube 48 – St-Florentin 58 – Tonnerre 37 – Troyes 46

Office de tourisme, 14, place des Héros de la Résistance ✆ 03 25 29 15 38, Fax 03 25 29 15 38

Le Magny with rm
rte de Tonnerre, (D 452) – ✆ 03 25 29 38 39 – lemagny@wanadoo.fr – Fax 03 25 29 11 72 – Closed 24-29 August, 18 January-28 February, Tuesday except from May to September and Wednesday
12 rm – †€ 63/75 ††€ 63/75, ☕ € 9 – ½ P € 64/70 – **Rest** – Menu € 15/36 – Carte € 28/43
◆ In the fief of the famous Rosé wine, this country-style restaurant is in a carefully-restored stone residence. The welcome is warm, menus traditional and rooms comfortable.

RICHELIEU – **37 Indre-et-Loire** – **317** K6 – **pop. 2 165** – **alt. 40 m** – ✉ **37120**
Châteaux of the Loire 11 **A3**

Paris 299 – Joué-lès-Tours 60 – Orléans 175 – Poitiers 66

Office de tourisme, 7, Place Louis XIII ✆ 02 47 58 13 62, Fax 02 47 58 29 86

La Maison without rest
6 r. Henri Proust – ✆ 02 47 58 29 40 – lamaisondemichele@yahoo.com – Fax 02 47 58 29 40 – Open 15 April-30 September
4 rm ☕ – †€ 85 ††€ 100
◆ A fine well-bred house, offering spacious rooms with antique furniture, striped wallpaper and large beds. Pretty garden adorned with a bamboo patch.

RIEC-SUR-BELON – **29 Finistère** – **308** I7 – **pop. 4 008** – **alt. 65 m** – ✉ **29340**

Paris 529 – Carhaix-Plouguer 61 – Concarneau 20 – Quimper 43 – Quimperlé 13

Office de tourisme, 2, rue des Gentilshommes ✆ 02 98 06 97 65, Fax 02 98 06 93 73 9 **B2**

at Port de Belon **4 km south by C 3 and C 5** – ✉ **29340 Riec-sur-Belon**

Chez Jacky
– ✆ 02 98 06 90 32 – chez.jacky@wanadoo.fr – Fax 02 98 06 49 72 – Open 22 March-5 October and closed Sunday dinner and Monday
Rest – *(pre-book in high season)* Menu € 18/80 – Carte € 20/93
◆ An attractive oyster farmer's house on the banks of the Belon. Rustic dining room with a menu focused entirely on fish and seafood. Terrace with pleasant views. The property has its own oyster basin.

RIEDISHEIM – **68 Haut-Rhin** – **315** I10 – **see Mulhouse**

RIEUMES – **31 Haute-Garonne** – **343** E4 – **pop. 2 601** – **alt. 270 m** – ✉ **31370**

Paris 712 – Toulouse 39 – Auch 56 – Foix 75 28 **B2**

Auberge les Palmiers
13 pl. du Foirail – ✆ 05 61 91 81 01 – auberge_lespalmiers@yahoo.fr – Fax 05 61 91 56 36 – Closed 17 August-1st September, 27 October-2 November and 22 December-4 January
12 rm – †€ 58 ††€ 62/78, ☕ € 8 – ½ P € 62/70 – **Rest** – *(closed Sunday dinner and Monday)* Menu (€ 12), € 15, € 23/32 – Carte € 27/51
◆ This welcoming 19C house (non-smoking) sports a happy blend of rustic furniture and contemporary details. Superb junior suite with its own private sauna. Spruce interior. Traditional menu enriched with regional dishes.

RIEUPEYROUX – 12 Aveyron – 338 F5 – pop. 2 157 – alt. 750 m – ✉ 12240 29 **C1**

Paris 632 – Albi 54 – Carmaux 38 – Millau 94 – Rodez 36 – Villefranche-de-Rouergue 24

Office de tourisme, 28, rue de l'Hom ✆ 05 65 65 60 00

Du Commerce VISA AE

60 r. l'Hom – ✆ 05 65 65 53 06 – hotel.j.b.delmas@wanadoo.fr – Fax 05 65 81 43 72 – Closed 1st-10 October, 30 December-1st February, Friday dinner (except hotel), Sunday dinner and Monday except 15 June-15 September

22 rm – €44 €53, €7 – ½ P €50 – **Rest** – Menu €13 (weekday lunch), €18/32 – Carte €25/44

◆ A family-run hotel with well-kept rooms which are constantly being upgraded. Those looking on to the garden and pool are quieter. Try Tripoux du Ségala, Aveyron veau de lait (veal) and duck preserve with tripade in the restaurant.

RIGNY – 70 Haute-Saône – 314 B8 – see Gray

RILLIEUX-LA-PAPE – 69 Rhône – 327 I5 – see Lyon

RIMBACH-PRÈS-GUEBWILLER – 68 Haut-Rhin – 315 G9 – see Guebwiller

RIMONT – 09 Ariège – 343 F7 – pop. 501 – alt. 525 m – ✉ 09420 28 **B3**

Paris 765 – Auch 136 – Foix 32 – St-Gaudens 56 – St-Girons 14 – Toulouse 92

Domaine de Terrac

4 km east on D 117 and secondary road – ✆ 05 61 96 39 60 – domainedeterrac@wanadoo.fr – Closed 15 January-15 February

5 rm – €75 €80/90 – **Table d'hôte** – Menu €20 bi/28 bi

◆ This magnificently restored former farmhouse cannot fail to appeal. It offers charming and peaceful rooms; two of them have a terrace overlooking the valley. Regional cuisine, augmented by vegetarian and Indian dishes.

De la Poste VISA AE

pl. 8-Mai – ✆ 05 61 96 33 23 – restaurantdelaposte@orange.fr – Fax 05 61 96 33 23 – Closed 27 August-1st September, 1st-22 February, Monday dinner, Tuesday dinner and Wednesday dinner except July-August

Rest – Menu €12/32 – Carte €32/47

◆ Retro façade behind which is a bright rustic restaurant with a warm ambiance. Simple, unfussy traditional cuisine.

RIOM – 63 Puy-de-Dôme – 326 F7 – pop. 18 548 – alt. 363 m – ✉ 63200 Auvergne 5 **B2**

Paris 407 – Clermont-Ferrand 15 – Montluçon 102 – Thiers 45 – Vichy 39

Office de tourisme, 27 place de la Fédération ✆ 04 73 38 59 45, Fax 04 73 38 25 15

N.-D.-du-Marthuret church★ : Virgin with bird ★★★ - Maison des Consuls★ **K** - Courtyard ★ of the hôtel Guimeneau **B** - Ste-Chapelle★ of the palais de justice(law courts) **N** - Courtyard ★ of the town hall **H** - Tour de l'Horloge★ **R** - Museums: Régional d'Auvergne★ **M**[1], Mandet★ **M**[2].

Mozac: capitals★★, church★★ treasure-house★ 2 km by ④ - Marsat: Black Virgin★★ in church S-W: 3 km by D 83.

Le Moulin de Villeroze VISA

144 rte Marsat, south-west of Le Plan on the D 83 – ✆ 04 73 38 62 23 – Fax 04 73 38 62 23 – Closed 18 August-4 September, Wednesday dinner, Sunday dinner and Monday

Rest – Menu €21/48 – Carte €43/65

◆ This mill built at the end of the 19C houses two welcoming, contemporary dining rooms with exposed beams. Shady terrace; modern menu.

RIOM

Bade (Fg de la) 2
Chabrol (R.) 3
Châtelguyon (Av. de) 4
Commerce (R. du) ....
Croisier (R.) 6
Daurat (R.) 7
Delille (R.) 8
Fédération (Pl. de la) 9
Hellénie (R.) 10
Horloge (R. de l') ....
Hôtel des Monnaies (R. de l') 12
Hôtel de Ville (R. de l') 13
Laurent (Pl. J.-B.) 14
Layat (Fg) 15
Libération (Av. de la) 16
Madeline (Av. du Cdt) 17
Marthuret (R. du) 18
Martyrs de la Résistance (Pl. des) 19
Menut (Pl. Marinette) 20
Pré Madame (Promenade du) 21
République (Bd de la) 22
Reynouard (Av. J.) 23
Romme (R. G.) 26
St-Amable (R.) 27
St-Louis (R.) 29
Soanen (Pl. Jean) 32
Soubrany (R.) 34
Taules (Coin des) 36

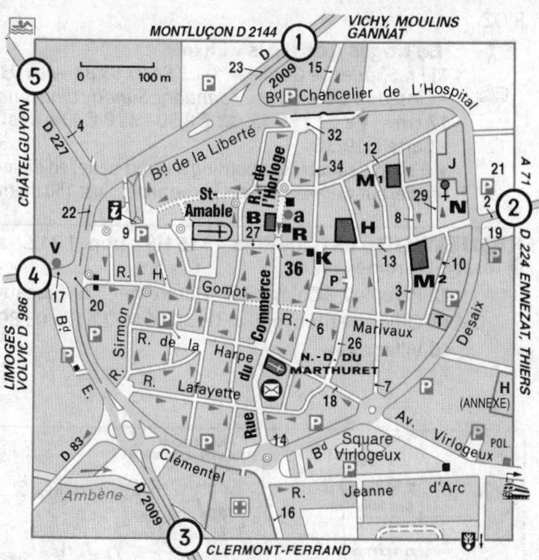

Le Flamboyant

21 bis r. Horloge – ✆ 04 73 63 07 97 – restaurant.leflamboyant@wanadoo.fr – Fax 04 73 64 17 36 – Closed 4-24 August, 26 December-7 January, Sunday dinner and Monday **a**

Rest – Menu € 22 bi (weekdays), € 26/55 bi – Carte approx. € 44

◆ Admire the inner courtyards of the townhouses lining the street before entering the colourful restaurant with its low-key modern decor. Up-to-date cuisine.

Le Magnolia

11 av. Cdt Madeline – ✆ 04 73 38 08 25 – magnolia-gastronomie@wanadoo.fr – Fax 04 73 38 09 29 – Closed 25 February-9 March and 27 July-18 August, Sunday dinner, Saturday lunch Monday **v**

Rest – Menu (€ 18 bi), € 24 (weekdays)/42 – Carte approx. € 40

◆ This restaurant sports a distinctive modern style, featuring brushed cement, exotic wood, burgundy walls and an original layout. Modern cuisine.

RIOM-ÈS-MONTAGNES – 15 Cantal – 330 D3 – pop. 2 842 – alt. 840 m – ✉ 15400

5 **B3**

Paris 506 – Aurillac 80 – Clermont-Ferrand 91 – Ussel 46

Office de tourisme, 1, avenue Fernand Brun ✆ 04 71 78 07 37, Fax 04 71 78 16 87

St-Georges

rm, VISA

5 r. Cap. Chevalier – ✆ 04 71 78 00 15 – hotel.saint-georges@wanadoo.fr – Fax 04 71 78 24 37 – Closed 15-30 January

14 rm – †€ 30/33 ††€ 44/52, ☕ € 8 – ½ P € 38/43

Rest – *(closed Sunday dinner and Monday 15 September-30 June)* Menu (€ 10), € 13,50 (weekdays)/25 – Carte € 23/32

◆ This late-19C stone house in the village centre has small, refurbished, well-equipped rooms, all very well kept. Guests are assured of a courteous welcome. A rustic-bourgeois setting and a menu that gives pride of place to Cantal dishes.

RIORGES – 42 Loire – 327 D3 – see Roanne

RIOZ – 70 Haute-Saône – 314 E8 – pop. 1 134 – alt. 267 m – ✉ 70190

16 **B2**

Paris 386 – Besançon 24 – Gray 48 – Vesoul 24

Syndicat d'initiative, place du Souvenir Français ✆ 03 84 91 84 98, Fax 03 84 91 88 34

Le Logis Comtois with rm

111 r. Charles de Gaulle – ✆ 03 84 91 83 83 – Fax 03 84 91 83 83
– Closed 15 December-27 January, Sunday dinner and Monday lunch

17 rm – †€ 42 ††€ 45, ☕ € 8,50 – ½ P € 43 – **Rest** – Menu € 13 (weekdays)/29 – Carte € 19/36

◆ A simple country inn housing a wood-panelled dining room. Traditional dishes. Small, simple, but well-kept rooms in the annex, just 150 metres away.

RIQUEWIHR – 68 Haut-Rhin – 315 H8 – pop. 1 212 – alt. 300 m – ✉ 68340

Alsace-Lorraine 2 **C2**

Paris 442 – Colmar 15 – Gérardmer 52 – Ribeauvillé 5 – St-Dié 46 – Sélestat 19

Office de tourisme, ✆ 08 20 36 09 22, Fax 03 89 49 08 49

Village★★★.

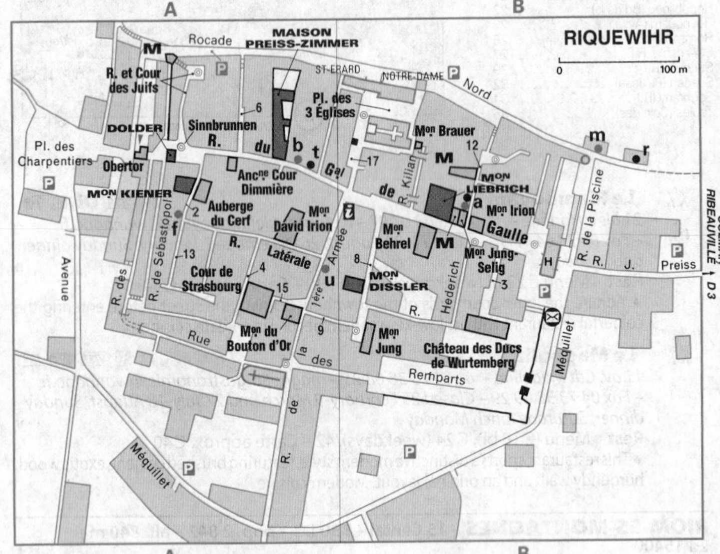

Le Schoenenbourg without rest

r. Schoenenbourg – ✆ 03 89 49 01 11
– schoenenbourg@calixo.net – Fax 03 89 47 95 88 – Closed 5-30 January B **r**

58 rm – †€ 77/123 ††€ 79/226, ☕ € 12

◆ Built in the 1980s, backing onto a vineyard, the hotel offers comfortable, simply decorated rooms. Large heated pool and a peaceful environment.

Riquewihr without rest

rte Ribeauvillé – ✆ 03 89 86 03 00 – reservation@hotel-riquewihr.fr
– Fax 03 89 47 99 76 – Closed 24 December 2008-27 December 2008, 1 January 2009-Mi February 2009 B

50 rm – †€ 60/105 ††€ 60/115, ☕ € 10 – 6 suites

◆ A large, neo-Alsatian style building on a road winding through the vineyards. Rooms are comfortable and well kept, mini fitness centre and generous breakfast buffet.

À l'Oriel without rest
3 r. des Ecuries Seigneuriales – ☎ 00 33 3 89 49 03 13 – info@hotel-oriel.com – Fax 00 33 3 89 47 92 87 B a
22 rm – †€ 69 ††€ 69/155, ☕ € 11,50
◆ In a quiet little street, this 16C hotel has an attractive façade with an oriel window. Rustic personalised rooms, some with boat beds, and cosier to the rear. Bar in the converted cellar.

Le B. Espace Suites without rest
48 r. Gén. de Gaulle – ☎ 03 89 86 54 55 – suites@jlbrendel.com – Fax 03 89 47 87 30 – Closed 12-25 January A t
4 rm – †€ 115/150 ††€ 120/230, ☕ € 15
◆ Four rooms in a former vintner's house with attractive wine-coloured façade. The decor cleverly incorporates the ancient walls, designer furniture, luxury and refinement.

Table du Gourmet (Jean-Luc Brendel)
5 r. 1ère Armée – ☎ 03 89 49 09 09 – table@jlbrendel.com – Fax 03 89 49 04 56 – Closed 2 January-13 February, Wednesday except dinners from April to mid November, Thursday lunch and Tuesday A u
Rest – Menu € 48/90 – Carte € 54/90
Spec. Omble chevalier qui fume à table (autumn, winter). Saint-Pierre cuit en croûte de sel. Pigeon à l'alsacienne (spring). **Wines** Muscat, Riesling.
◆ A contemporary red and black decor sets the scene for the delightfully amusing cuisine, made from only the finest, albeit sometimes very unusual, produce.

Auberge du Schoenenbourg
r. de la Piscine – ☎ 03 89 47 92 28 – auberge-schoenenbourg@wanadoo.fr – Fax 03 89 47 89 84 – Closed 4-30 January, lunch except Sunday, Monday and Wednesday dinner B m
Rest – Menu € 29/81 – Carte € 40/70
◆ A welcoming family home and terrace extension facing the vineyard and ramparts. Succulent cuisine using home-grown produce and herbs from the garden.

Le Sarment d'Or with rm
rm,
4 r. Cerf – ☎ 03 89 86 02 86 – info@riquewihr-sarment-dor.com – Fax 03 89 47 99 23 – Closed 17-24 November and 12 January-10 February
9 rm – †€ 70/80 ††€ 70/80, ☕ € 8 – ½ P € 72/78 – **Rest** – *(closed 30 June-8 July, 17-24 November, 12 January-10 February, Tuesday lunch, Sunday dinner and Monday)* Menu (€ 15), € 20 (weekdays)/48 – Carte € 33/56 A f
◆ Light-coloured wood, exposed beams, fireplace and antiques set the scene for this 17C establishment's carefully prepared traditional cuisine. Cosy bedrooms.

La Grappe d'Or
1 r. Ecuries Seigneuriales – ☎ 03 89 47 89 52 – rest.grappe.or@wanadoo.fr – Fax 03 89 47 85 91 – Closed 25 June-10 July, January, Wednesday from February to March and Thursday B a
Rest – Menu € 20/35 – Carte € 24/43
◆ This welcoming house from 1554 has two dining rooms with well-worn walls, one adorned with rustic tools and the other with a pretty earthenware stove. Locally sourced menu.

d'Brendelstub
48 r. Gén. de Gaulle – ☎ 03 89 86 54 54 – stub@jlbrendel.com – Fax 03 89 47 87 30 – Closed 12-29 January A b
Rest – Menu € 16 (weekday lunch)/30 – Carte € 30/52
◆ Local specialities, roast meats and good Alsatian wines by the glass in a pleasant contemporary winstub ambiance; themed musical evenings.

in Zellenberg **1 km East by D 3 – pop. 391 – alt. 300 m – ✉ 68340**

Maximilien (Jean-Michel Eblin)
19a rte Ostheim – ☎ 03 89 47 99 69 – Fax 03 89 47 99 85 – Closed 25 August-8 September, 23 February-9 March, Friday lunch, Sunday dinner and Monday
Rest – Menu € 31, € 44/80 – Carte € 61/85
Spec. Foie gras d'oie poêlé, mirabelles confites, fraises en aigre-doux (August-September). Goujonnettes de grenouilles en tempura, fricassée de cèpes et escargots au pesto. Poitrine de pigeon rôtie et homard. **Wines** Riesling, Pinot noir.
◆ An Alsatian-style hillside restaurant. The elegant dining room offers attractive views of the vineyards, succulent dishes and a fine choice of wines.

Auberge du Froehn
5 rte Ostheim – 03 89 47 81 57 – Fax 03 89 47 80 28 – Closed 2-18 March, 23 June-3 July, 17-26 November, Tuesday and Wednesday
Rest – Menu € 11,50 (weekday lunch), € 20/37 – Carte € 27/40
◆ This inn, typical of the region, pays homage to the vineyard (and vintage of the same name) that dominates the village. Rustic cellar decor, friendly atmosphere and regional cuisine.

RISCLE – **32 Gers** – **336** B8 – **pop. 1 675** – **alt. 105 m** – ✉ **32400** 28 **A2**

Paris 739 – Aire-sur-l'Adour 17 – Auch 71 – Mont-de-Marsan 49 – Pau 59 – Tarbes 55

Syndicat d'initiative, 6, place du foirail 05 62 69 74 01, Fax 05 62 69 86 07

Le Pigeonneau
36 av. Adour – 05 62 69 85 64 – Fax 05 62 69 85 64 – Closed 1st-15 July, 27 October-5 November, 20-31, Sunday dinner, Monday and Tuesday
Rest – Menu (€ 15) – Carte € 33/43
◆ Old floor tiles and ochre shades emphasise the warmth of this restaurant in the Adour valley. Contemporary cuisine, including pigeon-based dishes.

RISOUL – **05 Hautes-Alpes** – **334** H5 – **pop. 622** – **alt. 1 117 m** – ✉ **05600**

Paris 716 – Briançon 37 – Gap 61 – Guillestre 4 – St-Véran 35 41 **C1**

Office de tourisme, Risoul 1850 04 92 46 02 60, Fax 04 92 46 01 23

Belvédère de l'Homme de Pierre ✳★★ South: 15 km **French Alps**

La Bonne Auberge rest, rest,
in the village – 04 92 45 02 40 – bonneauberge@yahoo.fr – Fax 04 92 45 13 12 – Open 1st June-15 September, 27 December-31 March and closed Wednesday from 1st June to 15 September
25 rm – €55 €55/60, € 7,50 – ½ P € 50/54 – **Rest** – *(dinner only in winter)* Menu € 15 (weekdays)/25
◆ A large chalet set just outside the village. Rooms with a pretty view of the Mont Dauphin fort, built by Vauban. A fairly discreet decor and family guesthouse atmosphere in the restaurant with a panoramic view of the Guillestrois.

RIVA-BELLA – **14 Calvados** – **303** K4 – **see Ouistreham-Riva-Bella**

RIVE-DE-GIER – **42 Loire** – **327** G6 – **pop. 14 383** – **alt. 225 m** – ✉ **42800**
Lyon - Rhone Valley 44 **B2**

Paris 494 – Lyon 38 – Montbrison 65 – Roanne 105 – St-Étienne 23 – Thiers 128 – Vienne 27

Hostellerie La Renaissance with rm
41 r. A. Marrel – 04 77 75 04 31 – restaurant.larenaissance@wanadoo.fr – Fax 04 77 83 68 58 – Closed 11-25 August, 2-7 January, Sunday dinner, Wednesday dinner and Monday
5 rm – €50 €50/60, € 12 – **Rest** – Menu € 30/80 – Carte € 47/85
◆ Rustic furniture, contemporary objects and colourful paintings provide the decor in this dining room overlooking the garden-terrace. Contemporary cuisine.

in Ste-Croix-en-Jarez 10 km Southeast by D 30 – pop. 351 – alt. 450 m – ✉ 42800

Le Prieuré with rm rest,
– 04 77 20 20 09 – prieure.bl@orange.fr – Fax 04 77 20 20 80 – Closed 2 January-13 February
4 rm – €54 €62, € 9,50 – ½ P € 66 – **Rest** – *(closed Monday)* Menu € 18/46 – Carte € 23/50
◆ A restaurant in a converted charterhouse on the edge of an unusual village. A countrified dining room; regional cuisine and home-made sausage and cooked meats.

RIVEDOUX-PLAGE – **17 Charente-Maritime** – **324** C3 – **see Île de Ré**

LA RIVIÈRE – **33 Gironde** – **335** J5 – **see Libourne**

LA RIVIÈRE-ST-SAUVEUR – **14 Calvados** – **303** N3 – **see Honfleur**

LA RIVIÈRE-THIBOUVILLE – 27 Eure – 304 E7 – alt. 72 m – ✉ 27550 Nassandres
33 **C2**

Paris 140 – Bernay 15 – Évreux 34 – Lisieux 39 – Pont-Audemer 34 – Rouen 51

Le Soleil d'Or

– *02 32 45 00 08 – domainedusoleildor@hotmail.com – Fax 02 32 46 89 68 – Closed 5-22 December, Monday lunch and Sunday*

13 rm – €54 €54, €10 – 1 suite – ½ P €52/78 – **Rest** – Menu €19 – Carte €17/32

♦ A big house, with climbing Virginia creeper, entwined by the peaceful waters of the Risle. Spacious modern rooms and magnificent, trendy lounge. The bistro food is suited to the resolutely modern-style dining room.

Le Manoir du Soleil d'Or

23 Côte de Paris – 02 32 44 90 31 – Fax 02 32 44 90 31 – Closed Sunday dinner and Monday

Rest – Menu (€20 bi), €24/51 – Carte €36/48

♦ Norman mansion offering a clear view of the Risle Valley from its terrace and elegant dining room. Modern cuisine.

L'Auberge de la Vallée

7 rte Brionne-Nassandres – 02 32 44 21 73 – Fax 02 32 44 21 73 – Closed August, 24 December-1st January, February holidays, Sunday dinner, Tuesday dinner, Wednesday dinner and Monday

Rest – Menu €13/24 – Carte approx. €24

♦ This restaurant, occupying a fine half-timbered building, houses two country dining rooms, adorned with a collection of wicker baskets. Up-to-date cuisine.

RIXHEIM – 68 Haut-Rhin – 315 I10 – see Mulhouse

ROAIX – 84 Vaucluse – 332 D8 – see Vaison-la-Romaine

ROANNE – 42 Loire – 327 D3 – pop. 38 896 – Built-up area 104 892 – alt. 265 m – ✉ 42300 Lyon - Rhone Valley
44 **A1**

Paris 395 – Clermont-Ferrand 115 – Lyon 84 – St-Étienne 85

Roanne-Renaison: 04 77 66 83 55, by D 9 AV : 5 km.

Office de tourisme, 8, place de Lattre de Tassigny 04 77 71 51 77, Fax 04 77 71 07 11

du Roannais Villerestby Thiers road: 7 km, 04 77 69 70 60.

Musée Joseph-Déchelette: Revolutionary earthenware ★.

Belvédère de Commelle-Vernay ≤★: 7 km South via quai Sémard BV.

Plan on next page

Troisgros (Michel Troisgros)

pl. de la Gare – 04 77 71 66 97 – info@troisgros.com – Fax 04 77 70 39 77 – Closed 4-17 August, February school holidays, Monday lunch October-February, Tuesday and Wednesday CX **r**

11 rm – €185/335 €185/335, €28 – 5 suites

Rest – *(number of covers limited, pre-book)* Menu €95 (weekday lunch), €150/190 – Carte €165/215

Spec. Dentelles de Saint-Pierre et de cèpe frais. Ecrevisses "pattes rouges", concassé d'olives violettes et lard de parme. Tranches de foie de veau à la tomate ratatinée, perce-pierres. **Wines** Condrieu, Beaune.

♦ Superb trendy rooms, a gourmet library, collections of contemporary paintings? A station hotel 21st century style! The Troisgros restaurant, with a three-star rating since 1968, offers excellent, subtly reinterpreted cuisine and a splendid wine list.

Le Grand Hôtel without rest

18 cours de la République, (opposite the station) – 04 77 71 48 82 – granotel@wanadoo.fr – Fax 04 77 70 42 40 – Closed 30 July-20 August and 22 December-7 January CX **f**

31 rm – €60/76 €70/89, €11

♦ An early-20C building offering well-maintained guestrooms with diverse decor (modern furnishings, wrought iron, wicker and bright colours). Comfortable lounge-bar.

ROANNE

Alsace-Lor. (R.) . . . . CY 2
Anatole-France (R.) . . . . CY 3
Benoît (Bd C.) . . . . AV 5
Cadore (R. de) . . . . CX 7
Carnot (R.) . . . . BV 8
Clemenceau (Pl. G.) . . . . DX 10
Clermont (R. de) . . . . CY 12
Dourdein (R. A.) . . . . AV 14
Edgar-Quinet (Bd) . . . . BV 15
Foch (R. Mar.) . . . . CDY
Gaulle (Av. Ch.-de) . . . . AV 16
Gaulle (Bd Ch.-de) . . . . BV 17
Gaulle (R. Ch.-de) . . . . CY 18
Hoche (R.) . . . . AV 19
Hôtel de Ville (Pl.) . . . . DY 20
Jean-Jaurès (R.) . . . . CDY
Joffre (Bd Mar.) . . . . BV 21
Lattre-de-T. (Pl. de) . . . . CX 22
Libération (Av. de la) . . . . DY 23
Loire (Levée de la) . . . . DY 24
Marne (Av. de la) . . . . BV 26
Renaison (Levée du) . . . . DY 28
République (Cours de la) . . . . CXY 32
Roche (R. A.) . . . . DX 34
Semard (Q. P.) . . . . BV 35
Thiers (Bd de) . . . . AV 36
Thomas (Bd A.) . . . . AV 38
Vachet (R. J.) . . . . AV 40
Villemontais (R. de) . . . . AV 42

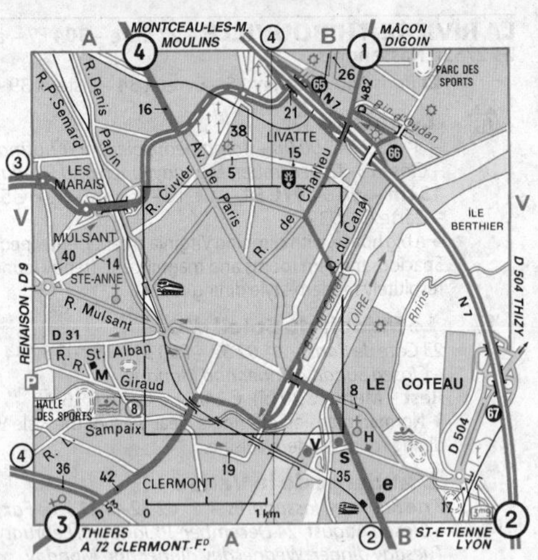

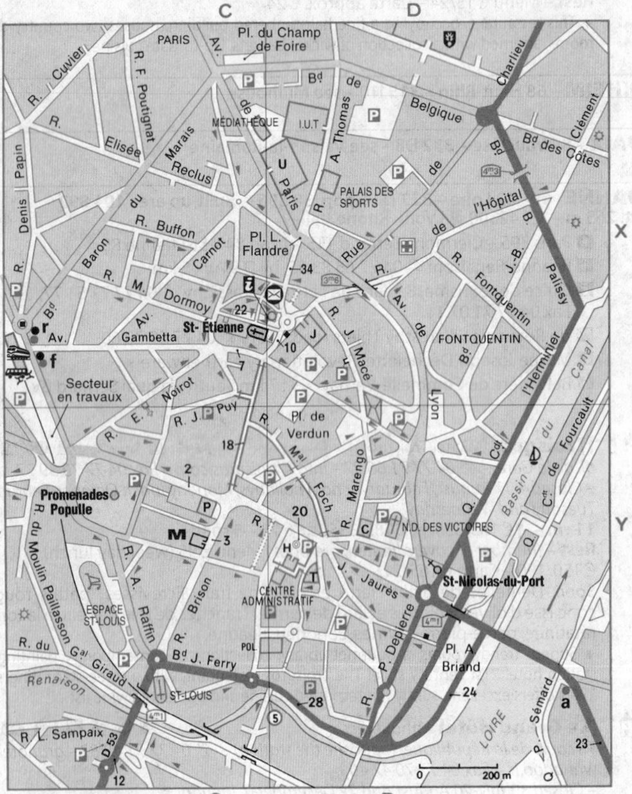

XXX **L'Astrée**

17 bis cours République, (opposite the station) – ✆ 04 77 72 74 22 – simonfalcoz@yahoo.fr – Fax 04 77 72 72 23 – Closed 26 July-17 August, 7-22 February, Saturday and Sunday CX **f**

Rest – Menu € 29/70 – Carte € 42/76

◆ A comfortable, pleasant contemporary decor with wood panelling and paintings by local artists. Personalised cuisine – in homage to the lovers, Astrée and Céladon!

XX **Le Relais Fleuri**

allée Claude Barge – ✆ 04 77 67 18 52 – relaisfleuri@wanadoo.fr – Closed Sunday dinner, Tuesday dinner and Wednesday BV **v**

Rest – Menu € 20 (weekdays)/46 – Carte € 31/43

◆ One of the dining rooms of this former café (1900) boasts a glass dome roof. Attractive shaded garden for the summer months. Up-to-date cuisine.

X **Le Central**

20 cours République, (opposite the station) – ✆ 04 77 67 72 72 – restaurant.lecentral@wanadoo.fr – Fax 04 77 72 57 67 – Closed 10-31 August, 23 December-1st January, Sunday and Monday CX **r**

Rest – bistrot *(pre-book)* Menu (€ 20), € 25 (weekday lunch)/28 – Carte € 37/45

◆ Shelves of gourmet products provide the original decor for this bistro-cum-delicatessen serving simple, tasty cuisine. A friendly atmosphere guaranteed!

in Coteau (right bank of the Loire) – **pop. 7 375 – alt. 350 m – ✉ 42120**

Des Lys

133 av. de la Libération – ✆ 04 77 68 46 44 – hotel.deslys@orange.fr – Fax 04 77 72 23 50 – Closed 2-25 August, 20 December-5 January and Sunday

18 rm – †€ 65 ††€ 95, ☕ € 9 – ½ P € 80

Rest – Menu € 12 (weekday lunch), € 15/25 – Carte € 28/36 BV **e**

◆ Hotel run by the same family for three generations. The well-kept rooms have modern decor or are furnished in 1980s style. Traditional cuisine served in a contemporary dining room decorated with paintings.

Ibis

rm,

53 bd Ch. de Gaulle, (Le coteau – BV industrial estate) – ✆ 04 77 68 36 22 – h0708@accor.com – Fax 04 77 71 24 99

74 rm – †€ 54/69 ††€ 54/69, ☕ € 8 – **Rest** – Menu (€ 10) – Carte € 20/32

◆ Practical hotel with rooms in keeping with the chain's standards (the latest are somewhat more spacious). Modern restaurant decorated in bright colours, plus a terrace overlooking the swimming pool.

XXX **L'Auberge Costelloise** (Christophe Souchon)

2 av. de la Libération – ✆ 04 77 68 12 71 – auberge-costelloise@wanadoo.fr – Fax 04 77 72 26 78 – Closed 27 April-5 May, 9 August-2 September, 26 December-8 January, Sunday and Monday DY **a**

Rest – Menu € 25/66 – Carte € 49/73

Spec. Foie gras poêlé à la vinaigrette de pomme et fruits secs. Saint-Jacques rôties à la patate douce, jus de viande à l'huile d'argan. Carré et filet d'agneau aux herbes et vinaigre de vin vieux. **Wines** Côte Roannaise.

◆ Elegant contemporary-style restaurant with a mini-veranda on the banks of the Loire. Regularly changing classical menu. Artwork on display.

X **Ma Chaumière**

3 r. St-Marc – ✆ 04 77 67 25 93 – ma-chaumiere@wanadoo.fr – Fax 04 77 23 35 94 – Closed 1st-19 August, Sunday dinner and Monday

Rest – Menu (€ 10 bi), € 17/46 – Carte € 26/47 BV **s**

◆ A very simple restaurant well worth a detour for its pleasant atmosphere, hospitality and skilfully prepared traditional dishes.

in Commelle-Vernay 6 km south by D 43 – **pop. 2 792 – alt. 340 m – ✉ 42120**

Château de Bachelard without rest

– ✆ 04 77 71 93 67 – dhnoirard@chateaubachelard.com

5 rm ☕ – †€ 91/98 ††€ 98

◆ A magnificent manor house within an 18-ha estate with a fishing pond, where guests are made to feel at home straight away. Rooms with personal touches and very friendly welcome.

in Riorges 3 km West by D 31 - AV – **pop. 10 074 – alt. 295 m** – ✉ **42153**

XXX **Le Marcassin** with rm
rte de St-Alban-les-Eaux – ✆ 04 77 71 30 18 – lemarcassin@wanadoo.fr – Fax 04 77 23 11 22 – Closed 17-31 August, February school holidays, Sunday dinner and Saturday
9 rm – †€ 51 ††€ 51/59, ☕ € 8 – ½ P € 69 – **Rest** – Menu € 23 (weekdays)/58 – Carte € 34/55
◆ Traditional cuisine served in a vast dining room with round tables, white tablecloths and ceruse furniture. Shaded summer terrace.

in Villerest 6 km by ③ – **pop. 4 243 – alt. 363 m** – ✉ **42300**

Office de tourisme, plage du Plan d'Eau ✆ 04 77 69 67 21

Domaine de Champlong without rest
– ✆ 04 77 69 78 78 – hotel.champlong@wanadoo.fr – Fax 04 77 69 35 45 – Closed 22 December-5 January, 1st-28 February and Sunday from October to December
23 rm – †€ 67/87 ††€ 67/87, ☕ € 9
◆ Recent building with the calm of the country, a step away from a golf course. The spacious and contemporary rooms have balconies or private terraces.

XXX **Château de Champlong**
100 chemin de la Chapelle, (near the golf club) – ✆ 04 77 69 69 69 – chateauchamplong@wanadoo.fr – Fax 04 77 69 71 08 – Closed 17-30 November, February, Sunday dinner, Monday and Tuesday
Rest – Menu € 25/62 – Carte € 52/68
◆ A handsome 18C residence in attractive grounds. The "painting room" is worth a look with its old canvases, parquet floor and imposing fireplace. Elegant lounges. Original cuisine.

ROBION – **84 Vaucluse** – **332** D10 – **pop. 3 844 – alt. 140 m** – ✉ **84440** 42 **E1**

Paris 713 – Aix-en-Provence 69 – Avignon 31 – Marseille 82

Office de tourisme, Place Clément Gros ✆ 04 90 05 84 31, Fax 04 90 06 08 79

Mas la Fausseranne
chemin des mulets, 4 km northeast via D31 and minor road – ✆ 04 90 20 93 48 – fausseranne@wanadoo.fr – Fax 04 90 20 93 48 – Open end February-mid November
3 rm ☕ – †€ 75 ††€ 85/95 – **Table d'hôte** – Menu € 30 bi
◆ This former silkworm farm nestles under the shade of plane trees. An old stone staircase leads to spacious and comfortable rooms that all overlook the Luberon. Meals served under the bower in bloom or in the warm rustic dining room.

X **L'Escanson**
450 av. Aristide Briand – ✆ 04 90 76 59 61 – info@lescanson.fr – Closed 2-28 January, lunch in July, Wednesday lunch and Tuesday
Rest – Menu € 16 (except August), € 24/35 – Carte € 32/41
◆ Pastel tones and wrought iron lend a Provençal ambiance to the brightly lit restaurant. Simple, traditional cuisine. Pleasant shaded terrace.

ROCAMADOUR – **46 Lot** – **337** F3 – **pop. 614 – alt. 279 m** – ✉ **46500**
Dordogne-Berry-Limousin 29 **C1**

Paris 531 – Brive-la-Gaillarde 54 – Cahors 60 – Figeac 47 – St-Céré 31

Office de tourisme, L'Hospitalet ✆ 05 65 33 22 00, Fax 05 65 33 22 01

Site★★★ - Ramparts ✻★★★ - Tapestries★ in the town hall - Black Virgin★ in Notre-Dame chapel - Musée d'Art sacré★ **M**[1] - Musée du Jouet ancien automobile: pedal cars - L'Hospitalet ✻★★: Féerie du rail: model★ by ②.

au château

Château

rte du château – ✆ 05 65 33 62 22
– hotelchateaurocamadour@wanadoo.fr
– Fax 05 65 33 69 00 – Open 21 March-11 November AZ **r**
58 rm – €65/97 €65/97, ☕ €9,50 – ½ P €69/85
Rest – Menu €15 (weekday lunch), €32/44 – Carte €23/63

◆ Away from tourist hustle and bustle, a contemporary hotel with spacious, functional rooms. The peaceful atmosphere, swimming pool, tennis court and garden are much appreciated. 50 m from the hotel, the restaurant serves regional cuisine; modern decor and a terrace in the shade of truffle oaks.

Relais Amadourien

– Open 1st April-3 November AZ **r**
19 rm – €45/48 €48/49, ☕ €7,50 – ½ P €56/58

◆ The motel-style annex of the Château has a sloping roof. It mainly caters for groups in high season. The rooms are simple and well kept.

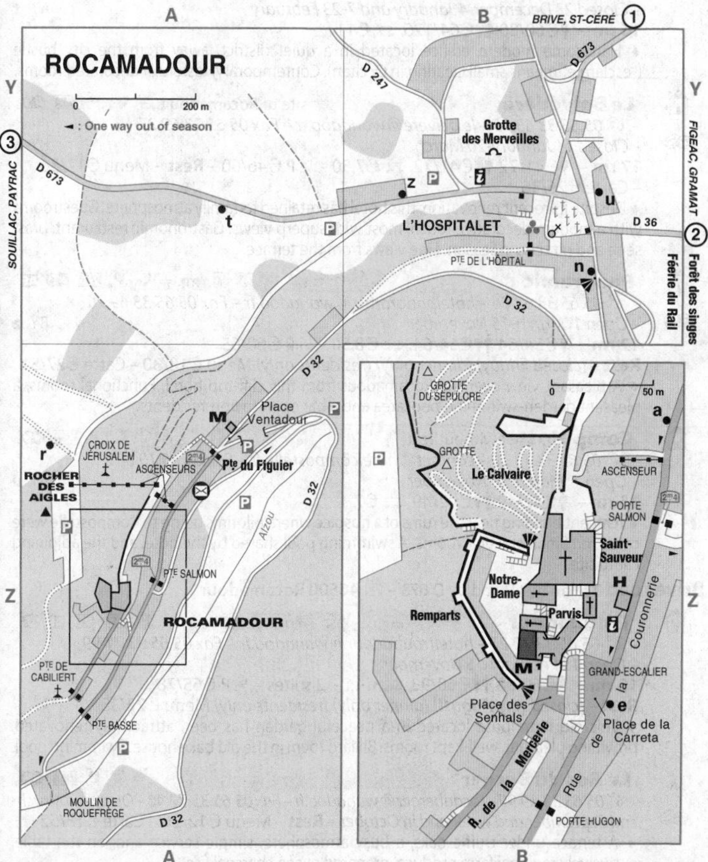

In the Cité

Beau Site

– 05 65 33 63 08 – *info@bestwestern-beausite.com* – *Fax 05 65 33 65 23*
– *Open 9 February-11 November* BZ **a**

38 rm – €42/95 €52/140, €12 – ½ P €69/80

Rest ***Jehan de Valon*** – Menu €19 (lunch), €25/55 – Carte €32/62

◆ In the heart of the town, a 15C house with an attractive, medieval-style lobby and rooms of character. A more modern decor in the annex. Traditional dishes and wines from southwest France and the rest of the world; fine view of the Alzou Valley.

Le Terminus des Pélerins

– 05 65 33 62 14 – *hotelterm.pelerinsroc@wanadoo.fr* – *Fax 05 65 33 72 10*
– *Open 22 March-5 November* BZ **e**

12 rm – €44/55 €49/67, €7 – ½ P €61/69 – **Rest** – *(closed Thursday dinner and Friday except from July to September)* Menu €16/30 – Carte €37/65

◆ At the foot of the steep cliff, a small family hotel with a warm welcome. Neat, well-equipped rooms. Enjoy the view of the valley from the terrace. Airy dining room serving substantial dishes made with local produce.

in l'Hospitalet

Les Esclargies without rest

Payrac road – 05 65 38 73 23 – *infos@esclargies.com* – *Fax 05 65 39 71 07*
– *Closed 23 December-4 January and 7-23 February* AY **t**

16 rm – €60/80 €64/126, €11

◆ Handsome modern edifice located in a quiet district, away from the city bustle ("esclargie" means small clearing in Occitan). Contemporary, tastefully decorated rooms.

Le Belvédère site of Rocamadour,

– 05 65 33 63 25 – *le.belvere@wanadoo.fr* – *Fax 05 65 33 69 25*
– *Closed 1st January-20 March* BY **n**

17 rm – €41/72 €41/72, €7,50 – ½ P €46/60 – **Rest** – Menu €17/36 – Carte €26/36

◆ Despite its recent renovation, this hotel has retained its family atmosphere. Guestrooms with a modern decorative touch, most with superb views. Gastronomic restaurant; brasserie and pizzeria in season. Fine views from the terrace.

Panoramic rm,

– 05 65 33 63 06 – *hotelpanoramic@wanadoo.fr* – *Fax 05 65 33 69 26*
– *Open 1st March-15 November* BY **z**

12 rm – €54/64 €54/64, €8,50 – ½ P €60/65

Rest – *(closed Friday) (dinner only) (residents only)* Menu €18/30 – Carte €27/51

◆ A pleasant view over the Rocamadour from this cliff-top hotel. Functional rooms, a pleasant garden-swimming pool area and a bar open to non-residents.

Comp'Hostel without rest

– 05 65 33 73 50 – *contact@hotelcompostelle.fr* – *Fax 05 65 10 68 21*
– *Open 1st March-30 November* BY **u**

15 rm – €42/49 €42/49, €7

◆ A recent building near the ruins of a hospice where pilgrims going to Compostelle were cared for. Small practical rooms. A swimming pool shared by the hotel and the adjoining camp site.

Brive road 2.5 km by ① and by D 673 – ✉ 46500 Rocamadour

Troubadour rest,

– 05 65 33 70 27 – *hoteltroubadour@wanadoo.fr* – *Fax 05 65 33 71 99*
– *Open 15 February-15 November*

10 rm – €60/98 €60/98, €11 – 2 suites – ½ P €65/78

Rest – *(closed July-August) (dinner only) (residents only)* Menu €27/38

◆ This old farmhouse located in a peaceful garden has been attractively renovated, providing pleasant, well-kept rooms. Billiard room in the old bake house. Swimming pool.

Le Roc du Berger

– 05 65 33 19 99 – *rocduberger@wanadoo.fr* – *Fax 05 65 33 72 46* – *Open end March-end September and week-end in October* – **Rest** – Menu €12/26 – Carte €18/52

◆ A terrace under truffle oaks, a busy atmosphere, simple service and, on the table, exclusively regional farm produce, prepared over a charcoal fire.

in la Rhue 6 km by ① Brive road by D 673, D 840 and secondary road – ✉ 46500 Rocamadour

Domaine de la Rhue without rest
– ✆ 05 65 33 71 50 – *domainedelarhue@wanadoo.fr* – *Fax 05 65 33 72 48*
– *Open 20 March-20 October*
14 rm – €75/78 €75/145, €9
◆ Large, personalised rooms in elegantly-restored 19C stables. Superb rustic lounge with fireplace. Summertime breakfast dining on the terrace. Swimming pool.

Payrac road 4 km by ③, D 673 and secondary road – ✉ **46500 Rocamadour**

Les Vieilles Tours
– ✆ 05 65 33 68 01 – *les.vieillestours@wanadoo.fr* – *Fax 05 65 33 68 59*
– *Open 29 March-11 November*
17 rm – €68/73 € 101/106, € 12 – **Rest** – *(dinner only)* Menu € 39
– Carte € 34/66
◆ In the heart of the countryside, a renovated farmhouse with the most attractive guest room located in the 13C falcon-house. A country-style interior and garden with a view over the valley. Two dining rooms, one more rustic; modern cuisine.

LA ROCHE-BERNARD – 56 Morbihan – 308 R9 – pop. 796 – alt. 38 m –
✉ 56130 Brittany 10 **C3**

Paris 444 – Nantes 70 – Ploërmel 55 – Redon 28 – St-Nazaire 37 – Vannes 42

Office de tourisme, 14, rue du Docteur Cornudet ✆ 02 99 90 67 98, Fax 02 99 90 67 99

de la Bretesche Missillac Domaine de la Bretesche, Southeast: 11 km, ✆ 02 51 76 86 86.

Pont du Morbihan★.

Le Manoir du Rodoir rest,
rte de Nantes – ✆ 02 99 90 82 68 – *lemanoirdurodoir@wanadoo.fr*
– *Fax 02 99 90 76 22* – *Closed 15 December-1st February*
24 rm – €75/120 €75/120, € 12 – ½ P € 71/95 – **Rest** – *(closed lunch July-August, Saturday lunch, Monday lunch and Sunday)* Menu (€ 20) – Carte € 22/39
◆ A 2 ha park surrounds this former foundry, now a hotel offering comfortable, spacious guestrooms, attic-style on the 2nd floor. A concise menu offering a fusion of ingredients and dishes from France, Asia, Mediterranean Europe and South America. Rustic decor.

L'Auberge Bretonne (Jacques Thorel) with rm
2 pl. Duguesclin – ✆ 02 99 90 60 28
– *aubbretonne@relaischateaux.com* – *Fax 02 99 90 85 00*
– *Closed 15 November-15 January except hotel and except public holidays*
11 rm – € 100/280 € 130/280, € 17 – ½ P € 190/275
Rest – *(closed Monday lunchtime, Tuesday lunchtime, Friday lunchtime and Thursday)* Menu € 35 (weekday lunch), € 105/137
Spec. Solette de la baie aux noisettes et au romarin. Léger bouillon d'asperges et truffes de Saint-Jacques en surprise (November to February). Homard rôti au citron et aux pommes. November to February
◆ Elegant restaurant occupying three flower-decked Breton houses. Galleried dining room surrounding a vegetable garden. "Surf'n Turf" menu plus an astonishing wine list.

ROCHECHOUART – 87 Haute-Vienne – 325 B6 – pop. 3 808 – alt. 260 m –
✉ 87600 Dordogne-Berry-Limousin 24 **A2**

Paris 433 – Limoges 43 – Saint-Junien 12 – Panazol 50 – Isle 44

Office de tourisme, 6, rue Victor Hugo ✆ 05 55 03 72 73

De France rm,
7 pl. O-Marquet – ✆ 05 55 03 77 40 – *Fax 05 55 03 03 87*
– *Closed 1st-7 January and Sunday dinner*
14 rm – € 45 € 45, € 7 – ½ P € 55 – **Rest** – Menu (€ 11), € 13/34
– Carte € 24/41
◆ This family-run town centre inn has been treated to a makeover and offers simple, clean and practical rooms decorated in a modern spirit. The chef-patron rustles up regional inspired recipes served in a neo-rustic dining room.

ROCHECORBON – 37 Indre-et-Loire – 317 N4 – see Tours

ROCHEFORT – 17 Charente-Maritime – 324 E4 – pop. 25 797 – alt. 12 m – Spa : mid March-early Dec. – ✉ 17300 Atlantic Coast 38 **B2**

Paris 475 – Limoges 221 – Niort 62 – La Rochelle 38 – Royan 40 – Saintes 44

Access Pont de Matrou: no toll.

Office de tourisme, avenue Sadi-Carnot ✆ 05 46 99 08 60, Fax 05 46 99 52 64

du pays Rochefortais Saint-Laurent-de-la-Prée 1608 route Impériale, Northwest: 7 km by D 137, ✆ 05 46 84 56 36.

Quartier de l'Arsenal★ - Corderie royale (royal rope factory)★★ - Pierre Loti House★ AZ - Musée d'Art et d'Histoire★ AZ **M²** - Les Métiers de Mercure★ (museum) BZ **D**.

Plan on next page

La Corderie Royale

r. Audebert, (near the Corderie Royale) – ✆ 05 46 99 35 35 – corderie.royale@wanadoo.fr – Fax 05 46 99 78 72 – Closed 22-29 January, 1st February-4 March, Saturday lunch, Sunday dinner and Monday from 2 November to 31 March BY **h**

42 rm – €75/165 €75/165, €10 – 3 suites – ½ P €74/152

Rest – Menu €36/96 – Carte €47/75

◆ An overnight hotel, steeped in history, within the walls of the old royal gunnery on the banks of the Charente and the port. Spacious rooms with a good level of comfort. Up-to-the-minute cuisine served on a veranda/dining room with views over the river.

Les Remparts rest,

43 av. C. Pelletan, (at the Thermal Baths) – ✆ 05 46 87 12 44 – hotel.remparts.rochefort@eurothermes.com – Fax 05 46 83 92 62 BY **s**

73 rm – €52/65 €54/67, €8 – ½ P €51/58

Rest – Menu (€15), €21 – Carte €22/39

◆ This 1980s building is regularly renovated and has direct access to the thermal baths and Emperor's spring. Large, functional rooms. A vast, tastefully decorated dining room, and classic fare.

Roca Fortis without rest

14 r. de la République – ✆ 05 46 99 26 32 – hotel-rocafortis@wanadoo.fr – Fax 05 46 99 26 62 – Closed January BY **t**

16 rm – €49/65 €49/65, €6

◆ Two regional houses set around a courtyard where breakfast is served in summer. Attractively-renovated interior (antique furniture, modern tones); very quiet back bedrooms.

Palmier sur Cour without rest

55 r. de la République – ✆ 05 46 99 55 54 – palmiersurcour@wanadoo.fr – Open 10 February-8 November BY **u**

3 rm – €53/58 €58/64

◆ This 19C town house has a clientele of regulars that appreciate its peaceful and refined rooms, tasty breakfasts and attentive service.

Le Tourne-Broche

56 av. Ch. de Gaulle – ✆ 05 46 87 14 32 – letournebroche@free.fr – Closed 15 December-6 January, Sunday dinner, Monday and Tuesday

Rest – Menu €28/42 – Carte €42/59 AZ **e**

◆ In a house built for Colbert's officers, a restaurant that has turned its authentic setting to good account: a fireplace, spit and prettily-laid tables.

via ② 3 km Royan road before Martrou Bridge – ✉ 17300 Rochefort

La Belle Poule

102 av. du 11 nov. 1918 – ✆ 05 46 99 71 87 – belle-poule@wanadoo.fr – Fax 05 46 83 99 77 – Closed 3-24 November, 1st-7 January

20 rm – €54/67 €58/70, €8,50 – ½ P €51/58 – **Rest** – *(closed Friday except dinner in July-August and Sunday dinner)* Menu €25/42 – Carte €41/61

◆ A 1980s hotel surrounded by garden near the Martrou transporter bridge. Comfortable, well-kept rooms. Handsome model boats highlight the countrified decor of this restaurant and are in keeping with the fish menu.

ROCHEFORT

Street	Grid	No.
Audry-de-Puyravault (R.)	ABZ	
Combes (R. Emile)	ABZ	5
Courbet (R. Amiral)	BZ	2
La-Fayette (Av.)	ABZ	
Fosse-aux-Mâts (Av. de la)	BZ	8
Galliéni (R.)	BY	9
Gaulle (Av. Ch.-de)	ABZ	
Grimaux (R. Édouard)	ABZ	10
Laborit (R. Henri)	AY	15
Lesson (R.)	BZ	18
République (R. de la)	ABZ	
Résistance (Bd de la)	AZ	
Rochambeau (Av.)	AZ	23
11-Novembre-1918 (Av. du)	BZ	28
14-Juillet (R. du)	AZ	29

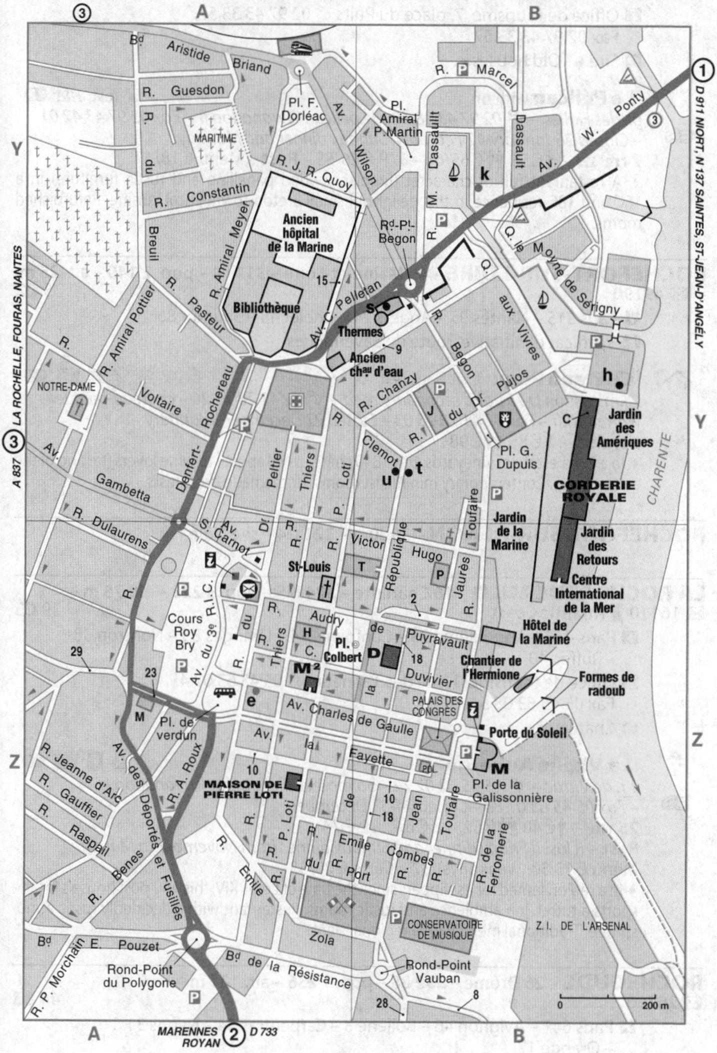

Luxury pad or humble abode?
and denote categories of comfort.

ROCHEFORT-EN-TERRE – 56 Morbihan – 308 Q8 – pop. 693 – alt. 40 m – ✉ 56220 Brittany
10 **C2**

- Paris 431 – Ploërmel 34 – Redon 26 – Rennes 82 – La Roche-Bernard 27 – Vannes 36
- Office de tourisme, 7, place du Puits ✆ 02 97 43 33 57, Fax 02 97 43 33 57
- Site★ - Old houses★.

Le Pélican with rm — rest, VISA MC

pl. des Halles – ✆ 02 97 43 38 48 – le.pelican@wanadoo.fr – Fax 02 97 43 42 01 – Closed 26 January-17 February, Sunday dinner and Monday

7 rm – €58 €65/68 – ½ P €46/55 – **Rest** – Menu €18/47

◆ A restaurant full of character (fireplace, wood panelling and rustic furniture) in a 16C and 18C residence in this delightful small Breton town. Local cuisine. Refurbished rooms.

ROCHEFORT-SUR-LOIRE – 49 Maine-et-Loire – 317 F4 – pop. 2 140 – alt. 25 m – ✉ 49190
35 **C2**

- Paris 315 – Nantes 95 – Angers 24 – Cholet 48 – Saumur 86
- Syndicat d'initiative, route de Savennières

Château Pieguë without rest — P VISA MC

2 km east on D 751 and secondary road – ✆ 02 41 78 71 26 – chateau-piegue@wanadoo.fr – Fax 02 41 78 75 03 – Closed 22 December-4 January

5 rm – €88 €98

◆ In a 27ha estate of vineyards, this 1840 château will appeal to wine lovers (tasting of the estate wine). Contemporary minimalist rooms. Homemade breakfasts.

ROCHEFORT-SUR-NENON – 39 Jura – 321 D4 – see Dôle

LA ROCHEFOUCAULD – 16 Charente – 324 M5 – pop. 3 228 – alt. 75 m – ✉ 16110 Atlantic Coast
39 **C3**

- Paris 446 – Angoulême 23 – Confolens 44 – Limoges 83 – Nontron 38 – Ruffec 40
- Office de tourisme, 1, rue des Tanneurs ✆ 05 45 63 07 45, Fax 05 45 63 08 54
- Château★★.

La Vieille Auberge — P VISA MC

1 r. de Vitrac – ✆ 05 45 62 02 72 – balmorevieilleauberge@wanadoo.fr – Fax 05 45 63 01 88 – Closed 24-31 December

25 rm – €40 €52, €6 – ½ P €74

Rest – *(closed Friday dinner and Sunday dinner from November to March)* Menu €13,50 (weekdays)/37 – Carte €20/53

◆ In a region famed for its slippers since the time of Louis XIV, this 16C post house's façade sports a turret. Inn ambience and rustic rooms. Restaurant with a decidedly rustic atmosphere. Traditional menu with a regional slant.

ROCHEGUDE – 26 Drôme – 332 B8 – pop. 1 236 – alt. 121 m – ✉ 26790
44 **B3**

- Paris 641 – Avignon 46 – Bollène 8 – Carpentras 34 – Nyons 31 – Orange 17

Château de Rochegude — A/C P VISA MC AE

– ✆ 04 75 97 21 10 – chateauderochegude@wanadoo.fr – Fax 04 75 04 89 87 – Closed in November

24 rm – €136/430 €136/430, €20 – 1 suite – ½ P €138/285

Rest – *(closed Monday off season)* Menu €31 bi (weekday lunch), €35/115 – Carte €60/83

◆ An 11C fortress, altered in the 18C, dominates the Côtes du Rhône vineyards. Elegant, personalised rooms (period furniture and Provençal fabrics) and park. Sunny tones in the pleasant dining room. Attractive terrace and fine wine list.

LA ROCHE-L'ABEILLE – 87 Haute-Vienne – 325 E7 – pop. 591 – alt. 400 m – ✉ 87800

Paris 422 – Limoges 34 – Saint-Junien 63 – Panazol 33 – Isle 34

Le Moulin de la Gorce (Pierre Bertranet) with rm
– ✆ 05 55 00 70 66
– *moulingorce@relaischateaux.fr – Fax 05 55 00 76 57*
– *Open 7 February-11 November and closed Monday lunch and Tuesday lunch*
10 rm – €90/170 €90/170, €18 – 1 suite
Rest – Menu €50/95
Spec. Œufs brouillés aux truffes. Lièvre à la royale (October-November). Crêpes roulées, beurre vanillé aux écorces de citron. **Wines** Bergerac, Pécharmant.
◆ A fine 16C mill with outbuildings located on the edge of a pond in a pleasant country park; the interior has character and the cuisine is traditional. Rooms are individually styled.

ROCHE-LEZ-BEAUPRÉ – 25 Doubs – 321 G3 – see Besançon

LA ROCHELLE Ⓟ – 17 Charente-Maritime – 324 D3 – pop. 76 584 – Built-up area 116 157 – alt. 1 m – Casino AX – ✉ 17000 Atlantic Coast 38 A2

Paris 472 – Angoulême 150 – Bordeaux 183 – Nantes 141 – Niort 65

Access to Île de Ré via ③. **toll** bridge in 2006: car(return) 16.50 (in season) 9.00 (off season), car and caravan 27.00 (in season), 15.00 (off season), lorry 18.00 to 45.00, motorcycle 2.00, free for pedestrians and bicycles.
Information from Régie d'Exploitation des Ponts : ✆ 05 46 00 51 10, Fax 05 46 43 04 71.

la Rochelle-Île-de-Ré: ✆ 05 46 42 30 26, Northwest: 4,5 km AV.

Office de tourisme, Le Gabut ✆ 05 46 41 14 68, Fax 05 46 41 99 85

de La Prée La Rochelle MarsillyNorth: 11 km by D 105, ✆ 05 46 01 24 42.

Old harbour ★★: tour St-Nicolas★, ★★ of the tour de la Lanterne★ - Old quarter ★★: Town hall★ Z **H**, Hôtel de la Bourse★ Z **C**, Porte de la Grosse Horloge★ Z **N**, Grande-rue des Merciers★ - Maison Henry II★, arcades★ de la rue du Minage, rue Chaudrier★, rue du Palais★, rue de l'Escale★ - Aquarium★★ CDZ - Museums: Nouveau Monde★ CDY**M**[7], Beaux-Arts★ CDY **M**[2] - d'Orbigny-Bernon★ (history of La Rochelle and ceramics) Y **M**[8], Automates★ (place de Montmartre★★) Z **M**[1], maritime★: Neptunéa C **M**[5] - Muséum d'Histoire naturelle★★ Y.

Plans on following pages

Champlain-France Angleterre without rest
30 r. Rambaud – ✆ 05 46 41 23 99
– larochelle@hotelchamplain.com – Fax 05 46 41 15 19 CY **b**
36 rm – €90/115 €110/140, €12 – 4 suites
◆ Once a private residence, the hotel has a pleasant, romantic garden. A fine central staircase leads to spacious, superbly-furnished rooms.

Résidence de France
43 r. Minage – ✆ 05 46 28 06 00 – info@hotel-larochelle.com
– Fax 05 46 28 06 03 DY **x**
5 rm – €110/170 €110/170, €15 – 11 suites – €150/400
– ½ P €87/117
Rest – *(closed Sunday dinner and Monday)* Menu (€19), €25 – Carte €28/32
◆ A fine 16C abode houses this establishment (part of a hotel residence). Well thought out decor, spacious and serene. Exhibitions of local artists' work. Furniture inspired by the 18C in the dining room, which opens onto a patio-terrace.

Masqhôtel without rest
17 r. Ouvrage, at Cornes – ✆ 05 46 41 83 83 – info@masqhotel.com
– Fax 05 46 07 04 43 DZ **t**
76 rm – €95/170 €95/270, €12
◆ Contemporary Indonesian art adorns the walls of this new hotel in a quiet side street near the station. Designer furniture, chic minimalist and hi-tech ambiance.

LA ROCHELLE

Briand (Av. Aristide) . . . . **AV** 13
Cognehors (Bd de) . . . . **BV** 23
Coligny (Av.) . . . . **AVX** 25
Crépeau (Av. Michel) . . . . . **ABX** 29
Denfert-Rochereau (Av.) . . . **AV** 33
Fétilly (Av. de) . . . . **BV** 47
Joffre (Bd du Mar.) . . . . **BV** 61
Juin (Av. Mar.) . . . . **AV** 62
Lysiack (Av. Cdt.) . . . . **BX** 63
Mail (Allées du) . . . . **AX** 64
Marillac (Av.) . . . . **AX** 65
Moulin (Av. Jean) . . . . **BX** 74
République (Bd de la) . . . . . **BX** 90
Robinet (Av. L.) . . . . **BV** 92
Saintonge (R. A.-de) . . . . **AV** 103
Salengro (Av. Roger) . . . . . . **BX** 106
Sartre (Av. Jean-Paul) . . . . . . **BX** 109
8-Mai-1945 (Av. du) . . . . **BV** 118
11-Novembre-1918 (Av. du) . . . . **BV** 121

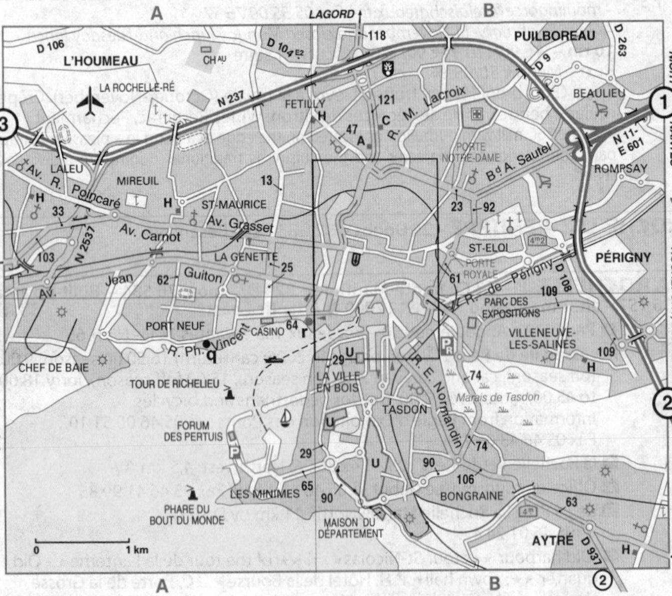

Novotel

rm,

av. Porte Neuve – ✆ 05 46 34 24 24 – h0965@accor.com – Fax 05 46 34 58 32 CY **t**

94 rm – €110/145 €130/165, €13,50

Rest – *(closed Saturday and Sunday off season)* Menu (€19) – Carte €28/43

◆ Renovated from top to toe, this glass building surrounded by a park offers contemporary and minimalist rooms equipped with state-of-the-art fittings. Restaurant opening onto the swimming pool; traditional dishes, and snacks at the bar.

De la Monnaie without rest

3 r. Monnaie – ✆ 05 46 50 65 65 – info@hotel-monnaie.com – Fax 05 46 50 63 19 CZ **z**

31 rm – €82/95 €105/120, €13 – 4 suites

◆ Near the Lantern Tower, a 17C mansion. Spacious rooms facing an attractive inner, cobbled courtyard where breakfast is served in fine weather.

Les Brises without rest

< the islands,

r. P. Vincent, (Chemin de la digue Richelieu) – ✆ 05 46 43 89 37 – infos@hotellesbrises.com – Fax 05 46 43 27 97 AX **q**

48 rm – €122 €122, €11 – 2 suites

◆ The seaside terrace (where breakfast is served in summer) and the view of the harbour alone make a visit worthwhile. Some of the progressively renovated rooms have balconies.

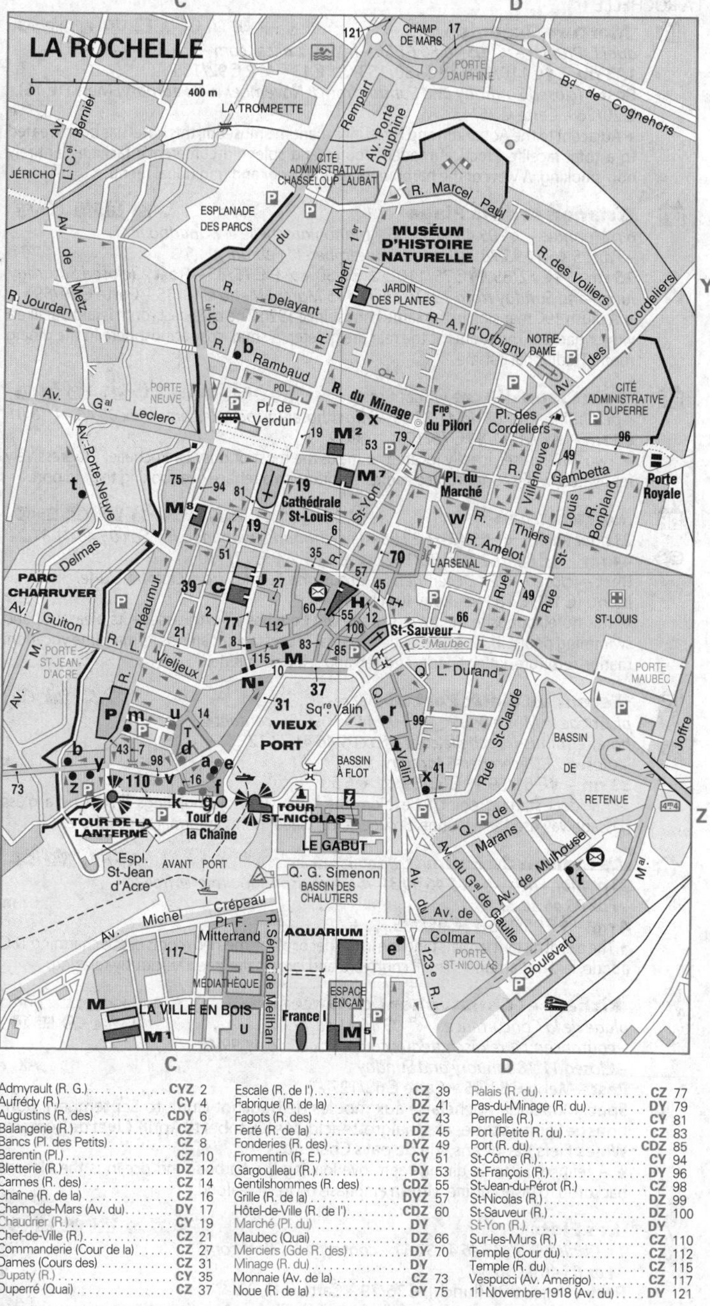

Admyrault (R. G.) . . . . **CYZ** 2
Aufrédy (R.) . . . . **CY** 4
Augustins (R. des) . . . . **CDY** 6
Balangerie (R.) . . . . **CZ** 7
Bancs (Pl. des Petits) . . . . **CZ** 8
Barentin (Pl.) . . . . **CZ** 10
Bletterie (R.) . . . . **DZ** 12
Carmes (R. des) . . . . **CZ** 14
Chaîne (R. de la) . . . . **CZ** 16
Champ-de-Mars (Av. du) . . . . **DY** 17
Chaudrier (R.) . . . . **CY** 19
Chef-de-Ville (R.) . . . . **CZ** 21
Commanderie (Cour de la) . . . . . . **CZ** 27
Dames (Cours des) . . . . **CZ** 31
Dupaty (R.) . . . . **CY** 35
Duperré (Quai) . . . . **CZ** 37
Escale (R. de l') . . . . **CZ** 39
Fabrique (R. de la) . . . . **DZ** 41
Fagots (R. des) . . . . **CZ** 43
Ferté (R. de la) . . . . **DZ** 45
Fonderies (R. des) . . . . **DYZ** 49
Fromentin (R. E.) . . . . **CY** 51
Gargoulleau (R.) . . . . **DY** 53
Gentilshommes (R. des) . . . . **CDZ** 55
Grille (R. de la) . . . . **DYZ** 57
Hôtel-de-Ville (R. de l') . . . . **CDZ** 60
Marché (Pl. du) . . . . **DY**
Maubec (Quai) . . . . **DZ** 66
Merciers (Gde R. des) . . . . **DY** 70
Minage (R. du) . . . . **DY**
Monnaie (Av. de la) . . . . **CZ** 73
Noue (R. de la) . . . . **CY** 75
Palais (R. du) . . . . **CZ** 77
Pas-du-Minage (R. du) . . . . **DY** 79
Pernelle (R.) . . . . **CY** 81
Port (Petite R. du) . . . . **CZ** 83
Port (R. du) . . . . **CDZ** 85
St-Côme (R.) . . . . **CY** 94
St-François (R.) . . . . **DY** 96
St-Jean-du-Pérot (R.) . . . . **CZ** 98
St-Nicolas (R.) . . . . **DZ** 99
St-Sauveur (R.) . . . . **DZ** 100
St-Yon (R.) . . . . **DY**
Sur-les-Murs (R.) . . . . **CZ** 110
Temple (Cour du) . . . . **CZ** 112
Temple (R. du) . . . . **CZ** 115
Vespucci (Av. Amerigo) . . . . **CZ** 117
11-Novembre-1918 (Av. du) . . . . . **DY** 121

Mercure Océanide rm, VISA AE

quai L. Prunier – 05 46 50 61 50 – h0569@accor.com – Fax 05 46 41 24 31
123 rm – €110/138 €130/153, €13 – ½ P €92/105
Rest – *(closed Saturday and Sunday from 8 November to 8 February)* Menu (€16), €20/26 – Carte €25/45 DZ **e**

♦ Adjacent to the Aquarium and Neptunea maritime museum, this hotel has been treated to a total facelift. Practical modern rooms and splendid conference facilities. Entirely non-smoking. A view of the harbour, brasserie decor and traditional menu.

Trianon et de la Plage VISA AE

6 r. Monnaie – 05 46 41 21 35 – trianonlarochelle@wanadoo.fr – Fax 05 46 41 95 78 – Closed 18 December-1st February CZ **b**
25 rm – €72/85 €75/110, €8,50 – ½ P €75/85 – **Rest** – *(closed Saturday lunch and Sunday from 15 October to 15 March)* Menu €19/35 – Carte €19/59

♦ A plush 19C mansion in the same hands since 1920. The breakfast room is laid out like a winter garden. The rooms at the rear are quieter. A snug, cosy atmosphere in the dining room. Traditional cuisine.

Saint Jean d'Acre without rest VISA AE

4 pl. Chaine – 05 46 41 73 33 – info@hotel-la-rochelle.com – Fax 05 46 41 10 01
60 rm – €61/71 €76/199, €12 CZ **a**

♦ Two 18C houses ideally located to make the most of busy La Rochelle. Progressively renovated, well-soundproofed rooms. A suite with a terrace overlooking the old port.

Le Yachtman rm, VISA AE

23 quai Valin – 05 46 41 20 68 – leyachtman@wanadoo.fr – Fax 05 46 41 81 24
44 rm – €86/162 €96/162, €12 – ½ P €77/110
Rest – *(closed 1st-28 December, Saturday and Sunday from October-June)* Menu (€14), €18 (weekday lunch)/30 DZ **r**

♦ This hotel, opposite the towers of the Old Port, has an extra asset – its pleasant patio swimming pool. Simple and practical rooms. The restaurant affirms its maritime vocation: marine furniture, knick-knacks and fish and seafood cuisine.

Terminus Vieux Port without rest VISA

pl. Cdt de la Motte Rouge – 05 46 50 69 69 – contact@hotelterminus-larochelle.com – Fax 05 46 41 73 12 – Closed 21 December-6 January DZ **x**
33 rm – €61/69 €61/69, €6,50

♦ An ideal starting point to explore the town. Two old buildings linked by a glass passageway used as a lounge. Spruce, refurbished rooms. Informal atmosphere.

La Maison du Palmier without rest VISA

23 pl. Mar. Foch – 05 46 50 31 96 – lamaisondupalmier@free.fr – Fax 05 46 50 31 96 CZ **m**
4 rm – €95/135 €95/135, €10

♦ The call of distant lands is tangible in the decor of the themed rooms of this charming 18C abode, laid out around a small courtyard and large palm tree. Deliciously relaxing.

Richard et Christopher Coutanceau entrance to the port, VISA AE

plage de la Concurrence – 05 46 41 48 19 – coutanceau@relaischateaux.com – Fax 05 46 41 99 45 – Closed 11-18 January and Sunday AX **r**
Rest – Menu €52/95 – Carte €68/127

Spec. Mouclade Rochelaise aux moules de bouchot (June to September). Bonbons de Saint-Jacques en vinaigrette acidulée (October to April). Civet de homard.
Wines Fiefs Vendéens, Vin de pays Charentais.

♦ A refined, rotunda dining room overlooking the harbour and ocean is the elegant backdrop to tasty cuisine with an emphasis on fresh seafood.

Les Flots VISA AE

1 r. Chaîne – 05 46 41 32 51 – contact@les-flots.com – Fax 05 46 41 90 80 CZ **g**
Rest – Menu €26 (lunch), €36/79 – Carte €47/82

♦ An 18C tavern, at the foot of the Tour de la Chaîne. A rustic setting, modernised in a nautical style. Seafood with an inventive slant and magnificent wine list (900 choices).

XX **Le Comptoir du Sud**
4 pl. Chaîne – ✆ 05 46 41 06 08 – lcomptoirdusud@orange.fr – Fax 05 46 41 79 77 CZ **e**
Rest – Menu € 19/30 – Carte € 33/52
◆ A slight southern touch in the decor and menu of this restaurant opposite the Chain Tower. Interesting selection of wines from the Mediterranean basin.

XX **Le Comptoir des Voyages**
22 r. St-Jean-du-Pérot – ✆ 05 46 50 62 60 – contact@lecomptoirdesvoyages.com – Fax 05 46 41 90 80 CZ **d**
Rest – Menu € 30
◆ Take a gourmet voyage without moving from the warm, contemporary decor of the "Comptoir" serving dishes prepared with spices from distant lands; selection of world wines.

X **Les Orchidées**
24 r. Thiers – ✆ 05 46 41 07 63 – s.hottlet@wanadoo.fr – Fax 05 46 50 05 16 DY **w**
Rest – Menu (€ 21), € 25/39 – Carte € 55/87
◆ A family bistro near the market and off the main tourist track. The chef prepares traditional dishes; the orchids on show in the dining room are his other passion.

X **André**
pl. Chaîne – ✆ 05 46 41 28 24 – Fax 05 46 41 64 22 CZ **f**
Rest – Menu € 31/37 – Carte € 25/42
◆ Change of owneship at this local institution renowned for its seafood. Ten dining rooms with a pronounced nautical decor and unusual objects.

X **Le Champêtre**
22 r. Verdière – ✆ 05 46 41 12 17 – Closed 2-10 November, 10-25 February, Monday off season and Sunday CZ **u**
Rest – Menu € 31/41 – Carte € 45/50
◆ Near the harbour but off the tourist trail, small restaurant with two dining rooms, one rustic, the other, upstairs, more contemporary and colourful. Well-prepared modern cuisine.

X **L'Entracte**
35 r. St-Jean-du-Pérot – ✆ 05 46 52 26 69 – contact@lentracte.net – Fax 05 46 41 90 80 CZ **v**
Rest – Menu (€ 21 bi), € 30 – Carte € 37/72
◆ Coutanceau-owned bistro with a retro décor (panelling, brass and vintage posters). Up-to-date cuisine.

in Aytré **5 km by ② – pop. 7 725 – ✉ 17440**

XXX **La Maison des Mouettes**
1 r. Claires, (1st floor) – ✆ 05 46 44 29 12 – la-maison-des-mouettes@wanadoo.fr – Fax 05 46 34 66 01
Rest – Menu € 36/75 – Carte € 52/68
Rest *Version Original* – Menu € 22 – Carte € 25/40
◆ This large seaside villa has comfortable, modern dining room with a superb panoramic view on the 1st floor. Modern cuisine served. Trendy lounge ambiance and decor and a simple, appetising menu.

LA ROCHE-POSAY – 86 Vienne – 322 K4 – pop. 1 445 – alt. 112 m – Spa : late Jan.-mid Dec. – Casino – ✉ 86270 Atlantic Coast 39 **D1**

Paris 325 – Le Blanc 29 – Châteauroux 76 – Loches 49 – Poitiers 61 – Tours 92
Office de tourisme, 14, boulevard Victor Hugo ✆ 05 49 19 13 00, Fax 05 49 86 27 94
du Connetable Parc Thermal, South: 2 km by D 3, ✆ 05 49 86 25 10.

Les Loges du Parc without rest
10 pl. de la République – ✆ 05 49 19 40 50 – loges@la-roche-posay.info – Fax 05 49 19 40 51 – Open 31 March-21 October
42 rm – †€ 82/103 ††€ 99/123, ☕ € 10,50 – 2 suites
◆ This huge Belle Epoque structure offers classic hotel accommodation suitable for short breaks or longer stays. Jazz and Egypt are the themes of two superb suites; countless leisure activities.

St-Roch rm, rm, VISA

4 cours Pasteur – 05 49 19 49 00 – contact@la-roche-posay.info – Fax 05 49 19 49 40 – Closed 15 December-25 January

37 rm – †€ 49/77 ††€ 67/104, ☕ € 8 – ½ P € 60/74 – **Rest** – Menu (€ 20), € 24

◆ Those come to take the waters appreciate this centrally-located hotel's direct access to Saint-Roch thermal baths. Practical rooms, some of which overlook the garden. Traditional cuisine in a fresh and bright dining room, which also offers a children's play area.

LE ROCHER – **07 Ardèche** – **331** H6 – **see Largentière**

ROCHESERVIÈRE – **85 Vendée** – **316** G6 – **pop. 2 241** – **alt. 58 m** – ✉ **85620** 34 **B3**

Paris 415 – La Roche-sur-Yon 34 – Nantes 34 – Saint-Herblain 42

Office de tourisme, 1, rue Malcoute 02 51 94 94 05, Fax 02 51 94 94 05

Le Château du Pavillon without rest

r. Gué-Baron – 02 51 06 55 99 – ggilann@aol.com – Fax 02 51 06 55 99 – Open 29 April-13 October

4 rm – †€ 80/120 ††€ 110/190, ☕ € 8,50

◆ This château from 1885, set inside a park with a pond, combines charm, elegance and comfort. Truly romantic rooms and nursery for children under ten.

ROCHESSAUVE – **07 Ardèche** – **331** J5 – **see Privas**

LA ROCHE-SUR-FORON – **74 Haute-Savoie** – **328** K4 – **pop. 8 538** – **alt. 548 m** – ✉ **74800** **French Alps** 46 **F1**

Paris 553 – Annecy 34 – Bonneville 8 – Genève 26 – Thonon-les-Bains 42

Office de tourisme, place Andrevetan 04 50 03 36 68, Fax 04 50 03 31 38

Old town ★★.

Le Foron without rest VISA

imp. de l'Étang, (Le Dragiez Industrial Estate), D 1203 – 04 50 25 82 76 – lf7405@inter-hotel.com – Fax 04 50 25 81 54 – Closed 22 December-4 January and Sunday

26 rm – †€ 55/57 ††€ 63/65, ☕ € 7,50

◆ A practical spot, this small hotel in the Roche-sur Foron industrial area has functional, soundproofed, well-kept rooms.

Le Marie-Jean VISA

590 r. Plaine, at 2 km on Bonneville road – 04 50 03 33 30 – contact@restaurant-lemariejean.com – Fax 04 50 25 99 98 – Closed 2-8 January, Sunday dinner, Monday and Tuesday

Rest – Menu (€ 23), € 36/56 – Carte € 65/75

◆ An elegant house dating from 1890 with a smart period dining room (fine coffered ceiling, pictures, elegant stone floor) plus a small lounge. Modern cuisine.

LA ROCHE-SUR-YON P – **85 Vendée** – **316** H7 – **pop. 49 262** – **alt. 75 m** – ✉ **85000** **Atlantic Coast** 34 **B3**

Paris 418 – Cholet 69 – Nantes 68 – Niort 91 – La Rochelle 77

Office de tourisme, rue Clemenceau 02 51 36 00 85, Fax 02 51 36 90 27

de La Domangère Nesmy La Roche sur Yon, South: 8 km by D 746 and D 85, 02 51 07 65 90.

Plan on next page

Mercure rm, VISA

117 bd A. Briand – 02 51 46 28 00 – h1552@accor.com – Fax 02 51 46 28 98 AZ **u**

67 rm – †€ 92 ††€ 102/112, ☕ € 11 – **Rest** – Menu € 19/26 bi – Carte € 26/39

◆ Midway between the station and Place Napoléon, this recent hotel has spacious, practical and well-soundproofed rooms. A glass roofed breakfast room. Simple dishes in a traditional vein served in a restaurant or terrace, beneath boat sails.

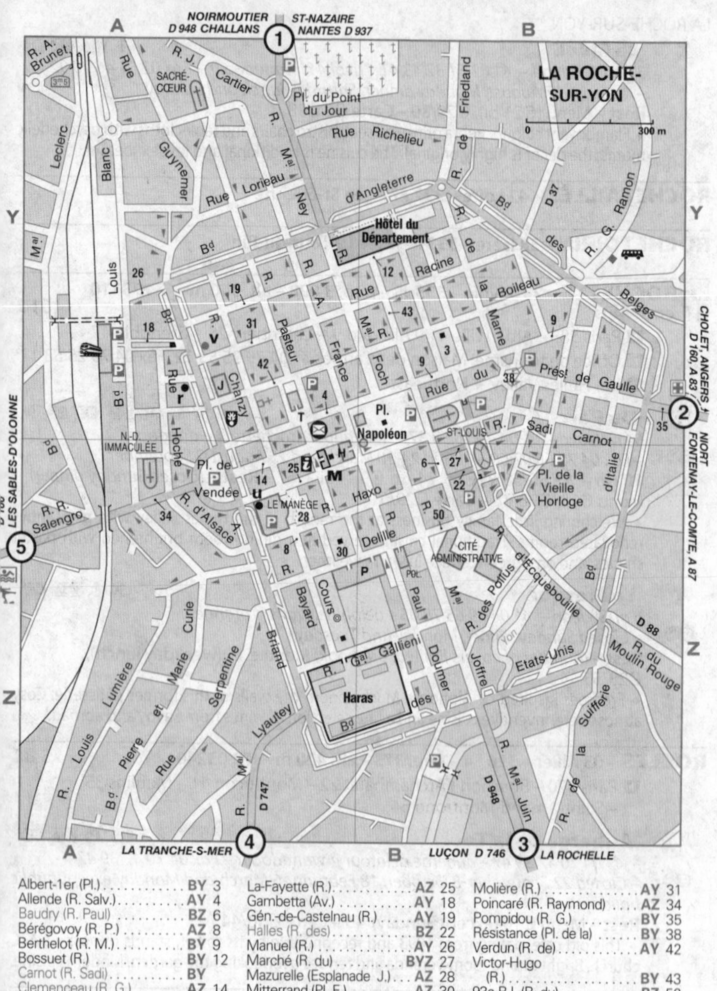

Albert-1er (Pl.) . . . . BY 3
Allende (R. Salv.) . . . . AY 4
Baudry (R. Paul) . . . . BZ 6
Bérégovoy (R. P.) . . . . AZ 8
Berthelot (R. M.) . . . . BY 9
Bossuet (R.) . . . . BY 12
Carnot (R. Sadi) . . . . BY
Clemenceau (R. G.) . . . . AZ 14
La-Fayette (R.) . . . . AZ 25
Gambetta (Av.) . . . . AY 18
Gén.-de-Castelnau (R.) . . . . . AY 19
Halles (R. des) . . . . BZ 22
Manuel (R.) . . . . AY 26
Marché (R. du) . . . . BYZ 27
Mazurelle (Esplanade J.) . . . AZ 28
Mitterrand (Pl. F.) . . . . AZ 30
Molière (R.) . . . . AY 31
Poincaré (R. Raymond) . . . . AZ 34
Pompidou (R. G.) . . . . BY 35
Résistance (Pl. de la) . . . . . . BY 38
Verdun (R. de) . . . . AY 42
Victor-Hugo (R.) . . . . BY 43
93e-R.I. (R. du) . . . . BZ 50

Napoléon without rest
50 bd A. Briand – ✆ 02 51 05 33 56 – hotel-nap@wanadoo.fr – Fax 02 51 62 01 69 – Closed 23 December-1st January AY **r**
29 rm – 🚹€ 61/72 🚹🚹€ 71/88, ☕ € 8,50
◆ Despite the hotel's proximity to a busy boulevard, its spacious, well-kept rooms are surprisingly quiet. Copious breakfasts served in a room decorated in Empire style.

Logis de la Couperie without rest
5 km east on ②, Niort road and D 80 – ✆ 02 51 24 10 18 – Fax 02 51 46 05 59
4 rm ☕ – 🚹€ 80 🚹🚹€ 84/110
◆ With its attractive library, lounges, vegetable garden, park and pond, this charming old hotel is not lacking in areas in which to relax. Personalised bedrooms with old antiques.

Le Rivoli

31 bd A. Briand – 02 51 37 43 41 – rivoli4@wanadoo.fr – Fax 02 51 46 20 92 – Closed 4-17 August, Monday dinner, Saturday lunch and Sunday AY **v**

Rest – Menu (€ 21 bi), € 29/39 – Carte € 31/38

◆ Flamboyant colours, zebra print wall seat, bistro chairs and tablecloths with psychedelic motifs: the decor is highly original. The cuisine is traditional and less exuberant.

ROCHETAILLÉE – **42 Loire** – **327** F7 – **see St-Étienne**

ROCHETOIRIN – **38 Isère** – **333** F4 – **see La Tour-du-Pin**

LA ROCHETTE – **73 Savoie** – **333** J5 – **pop. 3 098** – **alt. 360 m** – ✉ **73110**
French Alps 46 **F2**

Paris 588 – Albertville 41 – Allevard 9 – Chambéry 28 – Grenoble 47

Office de tourisme, Maison des Carmes 04 79 25 53 12, Fax 04 79 25 53 12

Les Huiles Valley ★ Northeast.

Du Parc

64 r. Neuve – 04 79 25 53 37 – hotelduparc.rochette@wanadoo.fr – Fax 04 79 65 07 60 – Closed 24-30 March and 25 August-2 September

10 rm – €56/58 €65/74, €9 – ½ P €67 – **Rest** – *(closed Sunday dinner)* Menu € 18, € 28/38 – Carte € 29/51

◆ Welcoming little family business at the mouth of the Huiles valley with pleasantly-renovated rooms. Traditional cuisine served in a dining room brightened with pastel shades, and on a green terrace in warm weather.

La Fresque

6 pl. St-Jean – 04 79 65 78 05 – delphine.evans@orange.fr – Closed Sunday dinner, Monday and Tuesday

Rest – *(number of covers limited, pre-book)* Menu € 15 (weekday lunch), € 28/55

◆ Frescoes inspired by Alphonse Mucha adorn the walls of this former pâtisserie. Cosy atmosphere, inventive cuisine and a fine selection of wines from Savoy and abroad.

ROCLES – **03 Allier** – **326** F4 – **pop. 373** – **alt. 420 m** – ✉ **03240** 5 **B1**

Paris 320 – Bourbon-l'Archambault 22 – Montluçon 41 – Moulins 35 – Saint-Amand-Montrond 64

Auberge de la Tour

– 04 70 47 39 47 – auberge.delatour@wanadoo.fr – Fax 04 70 47 39 47 – Closed 22 September-8 October, 18 February-6 March and Monday except public holidays

Rest – Menu € 16 (except Sunday)/40 – Carte € 30/44

◆ This old cafe, dating from 1893 and recognisable by its tower, stands opposite a 12C church. Bright dining room-veranda and terrace overlooking the garden. Modern cuisine.

RODEZ P – **12 Aveyron** – **338** H4 – **pop. 23 707** – **alt. 635 m** – ✉ **12000**
Languedoc-Roussillon-Tarn Gorges 29 **C1**

Paris 623 – Albi 76 – Aurillac 87 – Clermont-Ferrand 213

Rodez-Marcillac: 05 65 76 02 00, by ③: 12 km.

Office de tourisme, place Foch 05 65 75 76 77, Fax 05 65 68 78 15

du Grand Rodez Onet-le-Château Route de Marcillac, North: 4 km by D 901, 05 65 78 38 00.

Steeple★★★ of N.-Dame cathedral ★★ - Musée Fenaille★★ BZ M[1] - Wooden galleries★ of the Jesuits chapel.

Plan on next page

La Ferme de Bourran without rest

r. Berlin, in Bourran 1.5 km via ③ – 05 65 73 62 62 – contact@fermedebourran.com – Fax 05 65 73 14 15

7 rm – €90/150 €120/180, €15

◆ Seven rooms are available in this old farmstead perched on a green hillside. Contemporary decoration, comfort, calm and state-of-the-art fittings. Table d'hôte breakfast.

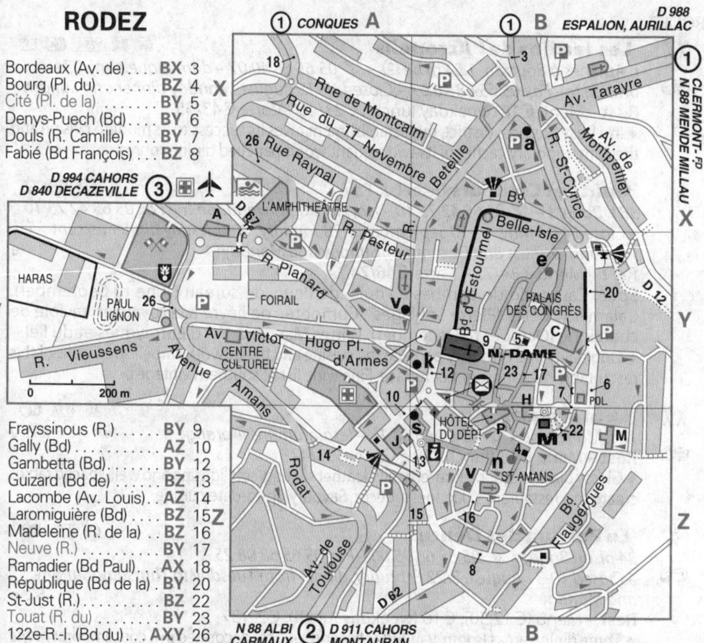

Biney without rest
r. Victoire-Massol – ✆ *05 65 68 01 24* – *hotel.biney@wanadoo.fr* – *Fax 05 65 75 22 98*
26 rm – †€ 71 ††€ 80/140, ☕ € 15 – 2 suites BY **k**
♦ Although some rooms are slightly small, all are individual and rather charming with painted wooden furniture, attractive coloured fabrics and comfortable bedding. Hammam and sauna.

La Tour Maje without rest
bd Gally – ✆ *05 65 68 34 68* – *tourmaje@orange.fr* – *Fax 05 65 68 27 56*
– *Closed 15 December-15 January* BZ **s**
40 rm – †€ 55/65 ††€ 60/72, ☕ € 9,50 – 3 suites
♦ A 1970s hotel backing onto a 14C tower where the rustic-style suites are located (with exposed stone walls). Simple rooms, Provençal in style on the 5th floor.

Ibis without rest
46 r. St-Cyrice – ✆ *05 65 76 10 30* – *h2748-gm@accor.com* – *Fax 05 65 76 10 33*
45 rm – †€ 64/74 ††€ 64/74, ☕ € 7,50 BX **a**
♦ In the heart of a totally renovated district, this chain hotel has small, functional rooms, some with balcony. Meeting rooms and lounge-bar.

Du Midi
rest,
1 r. Béteille – ✆ *05 65 68 02 07* – *hotel.du.midi@wanadoo.fr* – *Fax 05 65 68 66 93*
– *Closed Christmas holidays* ABY **v**
34 rm – †€ 50 ††€ 56, ☕ € 7,50 – ½ P € 52
Rest – *(closed Sunday)* Menu (€ 11), € 16/27 – Carte € 23/40
♦ The hotel's location close to the cathedral is ideal for sightseeing on foot. Simple, functional rooms which are quiet on the courtyard side and soundproofed at the front. Restaurant serving traditional dishes, salads, grills and the inevitable aligot.

Deltour without rest
6 r. Bruxelles, in Bourran, 1,5 km via ③ – ✆ *05 65 73 03 03* – *hoteldeltourrodezb@wanadoo.fr* – *Fax 05 65 73 03 05* – *Closed 21 December-7 January*
39 rm – †€ 35/50 ††€ 35/50, ☕ € 5,50 – 3 suites
♦ This new hotel caters for a business clientele, with bright, functional rooms which are comfortable, well sound-proofed and simply decorated.

Les Jardins de l'Acropolis

r. Athènes à Bourran, 1.5 km by ③ – 05 65 68 40 07 – dominique.panis234@orange.fr – Fax 05 65 68 40 67 – Closed 1st-15 August, Monday dinner and Sunday

Rest – Menu € 18 (weekday lunch), € 23/46 – Carte € 43/55

◆ In a busy business district, this establishment owes its success to its modern cuisine and the contemporary cachet of its two elegant wood-panelled dining rooms.

Goûts et Couleurs (Jean-Luc Fau)

38 r. Bonald – 05 65 42 75 10 – jean-luc.fau@wanadoo.fr – Fax 05 65 42 75 10 – Closed 4-14 May, 1st-10 September, 4-28 January, Wednesday dinner (except June-July-August and December), Sunday and Monday BY **e**

Rest – Menu € 34/75 – Carte € 46/74

Spec. Carpaccio de gambas à l'huile de fleurs de sureau (June to September). Calamars poêlés "Pierre Soulages". Compotée de lièvre à la royale en raviole de châtaigne (October to December). **Wines** Marcillac, Vin d'Entraygues et du Fel.

◆ Originality and creativity pervade the cuisine and the artwork embellished walls of this restaurant. Pleasant summer terrace. Fine wine list of southern vintages.

Le St-Amans

12 r. Madeleine – 05 65 68 03 18 – lesaintamans@orange.fr BZ **v**

Rest – Menu € 18 (lunch)/28 – Carte € 33/47

◆ Glossy black lacquer, mirrored walls, leather seating, soft lighting and well-spaced tables create this restaurant's 'Japanese' decor. Savoury up-to-date cuisine.

Le Parfum des Délices

24 pl. du Bourg – 05 65 68 95 00 – Fax 05 65 68 08 25 – Closed 10-31 August, 8-22 February, dinner from Tuesday to Thursday, Sunday and Monday BZ **n**

Rest – Menu (€ 12,50), € 16 (weekday lunch), € 22/37

◆ Three dining areas (room, vaulted cellar and terrace) decorated in a contemporary style with aubergine walls and dark wood. Spices and herbs feature prominently in the food. Tea room.

Espalion road by ① and D 988

Causse Comtal

12 km – 05 65 74 90 98 – contact@caussecomtal.com – Fax 05 65 46 92 69 – Closed Saturday and Sunday off season

120 rm – € 72/82 € 86/96, € 12 – 2 suites – ½ P € 75/85

Rest – Menu € 18/36 – Carte approx. € 32

◆ This modern building, isolated in the middle of the causse (limestone plateau), has a large stone tower. It has extensive leisure facilities. Practical, colourful rooms. A fresh, cheerful restaurant, with small summer terrace and traditional dishes.

in Olemps 3 km West by ② – pop. 3 020 – alt. 580 m – 12510

Les Peyrières

22 r. Peyrières – 05 65 68 20 52 – hotel-les-peyrieres@wanadoo.fr – Fax 05 65 68 47 88 – Closed 29 December-2 January

51 rm – € 60 € 90, € 10 – ½ P € 55/75 – **Rest** – *(closed Sunday dinner and Monday lunch)* Menu (€ 15), € 22/45 – Carte € 39/49

◆ This long contemporary villa in the residential suburb of Rodez has simple, well-kept rooms. Pleasant welcome. Three dining rooms serving traditional dishes. Terrace overlooking the pool.

Conques road North AX D 901

Hostellerie de Fontanges

at 4 km – 05 65 77 76 00 – fontanges.hotel@wanadoo.fr – Fax 05 65 42 82 29

43 rm – € 56/72 € 79/85, € 9,50 – 5 suites – ½ P € 76/79

Rest – *(closed Saturday lunch and Sunday from November to Easter)* Menu (€ 20), € 24/45 – Carte € 44/53

◆ Large, attractive 16C-17C residence surrounded by parkland and a golf course. Subdued decor in the renovated rooms; suites personalised with period furniture. French manor house-style dining room with veranda extension. Regional cuisine and extensive wine list.

Château de Labro without rest
Onet Village, 7 km on by D 901 and D 586 – 05 65 67 90 62 – chateau.labro@wanadoo.fr – Fax 05 65 67 45 79
14 rm – €80/130 €150/200
♦ This chateau and park are simply divine: romantic rooms with beautiful old furniture and modern bathrooms, and a swimming pool in the old orchard. Breakfast served among the antiques.

ROEUX – 59 Nord – 301 K6 – see Arras

ROISSY-EN-FRANCE – 95 Val-d'Oise – 305 G6 – 101 – see Paris, Area

ROLLEBOISE – 78 Yvelines – 311 F1 – pop. 401 – alt. 20 m – 78270 18 A1

Paris 65 – Dreux 45 – Mantes-la-Jolie 9 – Rouen 72 – Vernon 15 – Versailles 56

La Corniche de Rolleboise < Seine valley,
5 rte de la Corniche – 01 30 93 20 00 – corniche@wanadoo.fr – Fax 01 30 42 27 44
34 rm – €85/280 €85/280, €14 – 2 suites – ½ P €86/183
Rest – Menu €31/55 – Carte €46/80
♦ This "folly", built by Leopold II of Belgium for his last love, dominates the meanders of the Seine. Don't hesitate to ask for the renovated bedrooms. Panoramic summer pool. The low-key contemporary dining room and terrace offer a pretty view of the river.

ROMAGNIEU – 38 Isère – 333 G4 – pop. 1 235 – alt. 298 m – 38480 45 C2

Paris 539 – Grenoble 57 – Chambéry 35 – Lyon 109

Auberge les Forges de la Massotte rm,
West 2 km,exit ⑩ on A 43 – 04 76 31 53 00 – lesforgesdelamassotte@wanadoo.fr – Fax 04 76 31 53 02 – Closed autumn half-term holidays
5 rm – €55/60 €65/70, €9 – ½ P €63
Rest – *(dinner only) (residents only)* Menu €29
♦ The walls of this former forge now house pretty rooms furnished in a solid wood Savoyard or Dauphine style. Peace and quiet, faultless service and hearty breakfasts. Half-regional, half-traditional set menu served in a countrified dining room.

ROMANÈCHE-THORINS – 71 Saône-et-Loire – 320 I12 – pop. 1 717 – alt. 187 m – 71570 Lyon - Rhone Valley 8 C3

Paris 406 – Chauffailles 46 – Lyon 55 – Mâcon 17 – Villefranche-sur-Saône 24
"Le Hameau du vin" ★★ Touroparc Zoo and Amusement Park★.

Les Maritonnes rm,
rte Fleurie – 03 85 35 51 70 – contact@maritonnes.com – Fax 03 85 35 58 14
25 rm – €90/160 €90/160, €13 – **Rest** – *(closed Wednesday and Tuesday off season) (dinner only except Saturday and Sunday)* Menu €35/70 – Carte €40/66
♦ A large, Virginia creeper-clad hotel, next to a wine-growing museum and nestled in its park, full of flowers. Traditional meals enjoyed with the famous local Moulin-à-Vent vintage wine.

ROMANS-SUR-ISÈRE – 26 Drôme – 332 D3 – pop. 32 667 – alt. 162 m – 26100 Lyon - Rhone Valley 43 E2

Paris 558 – Die 78 – Grenoble 81 – St-Étienne 121 – Valence 20 – Vienne 73
Office de tourisme, place Jean Jaurès 04 75 02 28 72, Fax 04 75 05 91 62
de Valence Saint-Didier Saint-Didier-de-Charpeyby Crest road: 15 km, 04 75 59 67 01.
Hangings★★ of St-Barnard collegiate church - Shoe collection of ★ the musée international de la chaussure (international shoe museum) - Musée diocésain d'Art sacré★ to Mours-St-Eusèbe, 4 km by ①.

ROMANS-SUR-ISÈRE

Clercs (R. des) . . . . CY 4
Cordeliers (Côtes des) . . . . . CY
Écosserie (R. de l') . . . . BY 8
Faure (Pl. M.) . . . . BY
Fontaine des Cordeliers (R.) CY 10
Gailly (Pl. E.) . . . . BY
Guilhaume (R.) . . . . AZ 12
Herbes (Pl. aux) . . . . BY 14
Jacquemart (Côte) . . . . BY 15
Jacquemart (R.) . . . . AZ 16
Massenet (Pl.) . . . . CY 17
Mathieu-de-la-Drôme (R.) . . CY 18
Merlin (R.) . . . . CY 20
Mouton (R. du) . . . . BY 22
Palestro (R.) . . . . AZ 24
Perrot-de-Verdun (Pl.) . . . . . BY 26
Sabaton (R.) . . . . CY 28
Ste-Marie (R.) . . . . CY 29
Semard (Av. P.) . . . . AZ 30
Trois Carreaux (R.) . . . . CY 32
Victor-Hugo (Av.) . . . . AZ 34

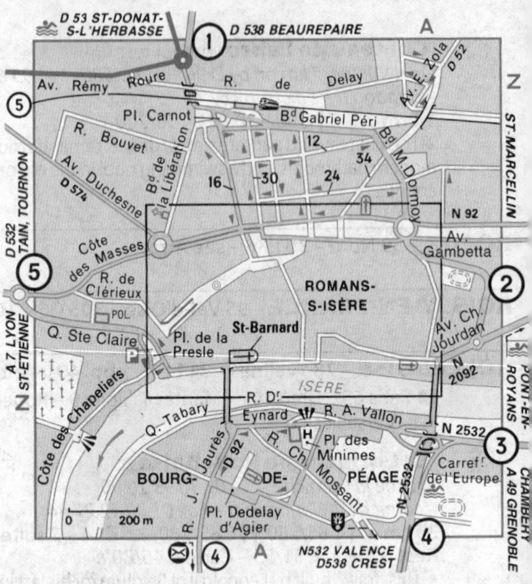

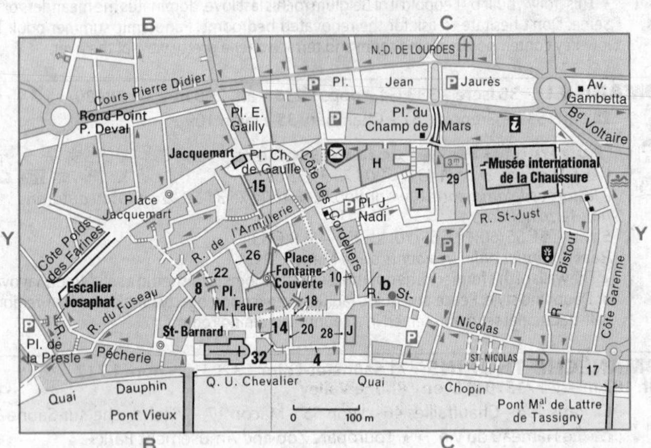

L'Orée du Parc without rest

6 av. Gambetta, via ② – ✆ 04 75 70 26 12 – hotoree-parc@wanadoo.fr – Fax 04 75 05 08 23 – Closed 12-19 October, 28 December-4 January and 6-22 February

10 rm – †€ 80/111 ††€ 83/115, ☕ € 10

◆ This fine, well-bred 1920s house offers pretty rooms named after flowers and with modern personal touches. Good breakfasts served on the veranda or garden (pool). Entirely non-smoking.

Mandrin

70 r. St-Nicolas – ✆ 04 75 02 93 55 – emmanuel.destrait@wanadoo.fr – Fax 04 75 02 93 55 – Closed 3-25 August, 15-23 February, Sunday and Monday

Rest – Menu € 19/36 – Carte € 24/32 CY **b**

◆ Mandrin, a famous French smuggler, is said to have found refuge in this house dating from 1754. The terracotta floor, exposed beams, half-timbering and rolled pebbles give the restaurant dining room a medieval feel. Traditional menu and paella upon request.

in l'Est **4 km by ② and D 92N – ✉ 26750 St-Paul-lès-Romans**

Karene

– ✆ *04 75 05 12 50 – contact@hotelkarene.com – Fax 04 75 05 25 17*
– Closed 22 December-1st January
23 rm – 🚹€ 58/60 🚹🚹€ 67/72, ☕ € 9,50 – ½ P € 65 – **Rest** – *(closed Friday, Saturday, Sunday and public holidays) (dinner only) (residents only)* Menu € 17/29
◆ This former company head office converted into a hotel, is set away from the road and offers functional rooms. Some have air-conditioning. Friendly welcome and traditional dishes served in a dining room adorned with copies of Van Gogh paintings.

in Châtillon-St-Jean **11 km by ② – pop. 888 – alt. 198 m – ✉ 26750**

Maison Forte de Clérivaux without rest

– ✆ *04 75 45 32 53 – contact@clerivaux.fr – Fax 04 75 71 45 43*
– Closed 3 January-3 March
5 rm ☕ – 🚹€ 55 🚹🚹€ 60
◆ These harmoniously renovated 16C and 17C buildings situated in a rustic location have retained much of their old style. Terraces and lovely garden where breakfast is served under the arbour in summer.

in Granges-lès-Beaumont **6 km by ⑤ – pop. 948 – alt. 155 m – ✉ 26600**

Les Cèdres (Jacques Bertrand)

– ✆ *04 75 71 50 67 – Fax 04 75 71 64 39*
– Closed 14-23 April, 18 August-2 September, 22 December-6 January, Sunday dinner, Monday and Tuesday
Rest – *(number of covers limited, pre-book)* Menu € 40, € 57/110
Spec. Raviole de foie gras de canard, girolles et crème d'ail doux (spring). Fraîcheur de homard au vinaigre de Xérès et huile d'olive de Nyons (summer). Trilogie de chasse. **Wines** Crozes-Hermitage, Hermitage.
◆ Welcoming village house offering delicious contemporary cuisine in an elegant dining room. Good choice of Côtes-du-Rhône wines. Lounge with a fireplace. Well-kept garden.

in St-Paul-lès-Romans **8 km by ② – pop. 1 502 – alt. 171 m – ✉ 26750**

La Malle Poste

– ✆ *04 75 45 35 43 – lamalle.poste@wanadoo.fr – Fax 04 75 71 40 48*
– Closed 4-16 August, 1st-14 January, Sunday dinner and Monday
Rest – Menu € 30/56
◆ Here, products are regularly purchased from the Lyon wholesale food market, resulting in original up-to-date cuisine, washed down by wine chosen from a list of more than 350 labels. Fully non-smoking restaurant.

ROMILLY-SUR-SEINE – 10 Aube – 313 C2 – pop. 14 616 – alt. 76 m – ✉ 10100

13 **B2**

Paris 124 – Châlons-en-Champagne 76 – Nogent-sur-Seine 18 – Sens 65 – Troyes 39

Office de tourisme, 27, rue Saint-Laurent ✆ 03 25 24 87 80

Auberge de Nicey

24 r. Carnot – ✆ *03 25 24 10 07 – contact@denicey.com – Fax 03 25 24 47 01*
– Closed 22 December-4 January
23 rm – 🚹€ 79 🚹🚹€ 112, ☕ € 12,50 – ½ P € 89 – **Rest** – *(closed Sunday except dinner in August, Monday lunch and Saturday lunch)* Menu € 22/45 – Carte € 39/54
◆ This comfortable hotel, with functional and well-soundproofed rooms, is located near the railway station. Annex bedrooms are bigger. Two elegant dining rooms, adorned with colourful artwork. Traditional culinary register.

Hotels and restaurants change every year, so change your Michelin guide every year!

ROMORANTIN-LANTHENAY – 41 Loir-et-Cher – **318** H7 – **pop. 18 350** – **alt. 93 m** – ✉ **41200** Châteaux of the Loire 12 **C2**

Paris 202 – Blois 42 – Bourges 74 – Orléans 67 – Tours 95 – Vierzon 38

Office de tourisme, place de la Paix ✆ 02 54 76 43 89, Fax 02 54 76 96 24

Old houses★ **B** - View of bridges★ - Musée de Sologne★ **M²**.

ROMORANTIN-LANTHENAY

Brault (R. Porte) 2
Capucins (R. des) 4
Clemenceau (R. Georges) 6
Four-à-Chaux (R. du) 8
Gaulle (Pl. Gén.-de) 10
Hôtel Dieu (Mail de l') 18
Ile-Marin (Quai de l') 13
Jouanettes (R. des) 14
Lattre-de-Tassigny
(Av. du Mar. de) 15
Limousins (R. des) 17
Milieu (R. du) 20
Orléans (Fg d') 22
Paix (Pl. de la) 23
Pierre (R. de la) 24
Prés.-Wilson (R. du) 26
Résistance (R. de la) 28
St-Roch (Fg) 30
Sirène (R. de la) 33
Tour (R. de la) 34
Trois-Rois (R. des) 36
Verdun (R. de) 37

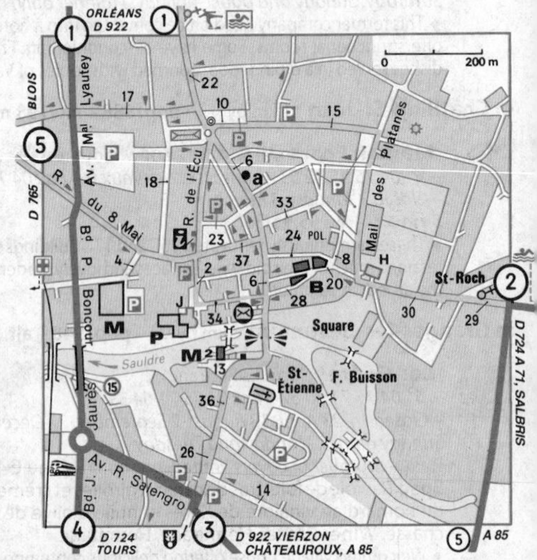

Grand Hôtel du Lion d'Or (Didier Clément) rm, rm, VISA
69 r. Clemenceau – ✆ 02 54 94 15 15
– liondor@relaischateaux.com – Fax 02 54 88 24 87
– Closed 17-28 November and 16 February-27 March **a**
13 rm – €170 €170/400, €24 – 3 suites
Rest – *(closed Tuesday lunch) (number of covers limited, pre-book)* Menu €98/155 – Carte €110/166
Spec. Cuisses de grenouilles à la rocambole. Pigeon farci entre chair et peau, façon babylonienne. Brioche caramélisée, melon candi et sorbet d'angélique. **Wines** Cour-Cheverny, Bourgueil.

◆ This establishment founded in 1774 sports one Renaissance and one Napoleon III façade. Period fixtures (wainscoting and balconies) are combined with modern furniture in the rooms. Updated cuisine and a good choice of Loire wines served in three rooms or on the summer terrace.

Pyramide rm, VISA
r. Pyramide, by ① – ✆ 02 54 76 26 34 – lapyramide@wanadoo.fr
– Fax 02 54 76 22 28
66 rm – €47/72 €56/72, €10 – **Rest** – *(closed 20 December-8 January and Friday lunch)* Menu €17/29 – Carte €28/31

◆ Modern building near a cultural complex. Functional rooms which are all identical, in a modern style. Traditional meals are served in the simple dining room or on the terrace behind the restaurant.

Auberge le Lanthenay with rm rest, VISA
9 r. Notre Dame du Lieu, 2.5 km by ① and D 922 – ✆ 02 54 76 09 19
– lelanthenay@wanadoo.fr – Fax 02 54 76 72 91
– Closed 22 December-6 January, Sunday dinner and Monday
10 rm – €50/55 €50/55, €8 – ½ P €55/58 – **Rest** – *(number of covers limited, pre-book)* Menu €22 (weekdays)/52 – Carte €48/57

◆ Pleasant place to spend the night in a picturesque hamlet, where you'll taste good cuisine combined with quiet surroundings. The dining room is more intimate than the veranda.

RONCE-LES-BAINS – 17 Charente-Maritime – 324 D5 – ✉ 17390 La Tremblade

Atlantic Coast 38 **A2**

Paris 505 – Marennes 9 – Rochefort 31 – La Rochelle 68 – Royan 27

Office de tourisme, place Brochard ✆ 05 46 36 06 02, Fax 05 46 36 38 17

Le Grand Chalet

île d'Oléron, P VISA MC AE

2 av. La Cèpe – ✆ 05 46 36 06 41 – frederic.moinardeau@wanadoo.fr – Fax 05 46 36 38 87 – Closed 4 November-10 February

26 rm – €45/82 €45/82, ☐ €10 – ½ P €53/72 – **Rest** – *(closed Sunday evening in low season, Monday except evenings in high season and Tuesday)* Menu €26/46

♦ A hotel from 1850 overlooking the sea with direct access to the beach. Some of the simple rooms have a fine view of the Ile d'Oléron, others face the hotel garden. In the restaurant some tables have a pleasant view of the ocean. Traditional cuisine.

RONCHAMP – 70 Haute-Saône – 314 H6 – pop. 2 965 – alt. 380 m – ✉ 70250

Burgundy-Jura 17 **C1**

Paris 399 – Belfort 22 – Besançon 88 – Lure 12 – Luxeuil-les-Bains 31 – Vesoul 42

Office de tourisme, 14, place du 14 Juillet ✆ 03 84 63 50 82, Fax 03 84 63 50 82

Notre-Dame-du-Haut Chapel★★.

in Rhien 3 km North – ✉ 70250 Ronchamp

Rhien Carrer

rm, rm, P VISA MC

14 r. d'Orière – ✆ 03 84 20 62 32 – carrer@ronchamp.com – Fax 03 84 63 57 08

19 rm – €40 €48, ☐ €7,50 – ½ P €42 – **Rest** – *(closed Sunday dinner from October to March)* Menu €12 (weekdays)/42 – Carte €26/55

♦ Family-run hotel in a hamlet near the Chapelle Notre Dame du Haut, a masterpiece by Le Corbusier. Comfortable, non-smoking rooms that have been recently renovated. The restaurant menu pays tribute to the region through an interesting choice of local specialities. Summer terrace.

in Champagney 4.5 km East by D 4 – pop. 3 310 – alt. 370 m – ✉ 70290

Le Pré Serroux

P VISA MC AE

4 av. Gén. Brosset – ✆ 03 84 23 13 24 – lepreserroux@wanadoo.fr – Fax 03 84 23 24 33 – Closed 22 December-12 January and lunch in August

25 rm – €65 €70, ☐ €15 – ½ P €54 – **Rest** – Menu €15 (weekday lunch), €20/40 – Carte €28/39

♦ The fully refurbished hotel is next to the Maison de la Négritude (Museum of Slavery and Racial Oppression). Relax in the comfortable rooms, garden, fitness centre or pool. The dining room has retained a slight pre-1940s atmosphere. Summer terrace. Traditional menu.

RONCQ – 59 Nord – 302 G3 – see Lille

LE ROND-D'ORLÉANS – 02 Aisne – 306 B5 – see Chauny

ROOST-WARENDIN – 59 Nord – 302 G5 – see Douai

ROPPENHEIM – 67 Bas-Rhin – 315 M3 – pop. 942 – alt. 117 m – ✉ 67480

1 **B1**

Paris 503 – Haguenau 25 – Karlsruhe 41 – Strasbourg 48 – Wissembourg 35

A l'Agneau

VISA MC

11 r. Principale – ✆ 03 88 86 40 08 – Fax 03 88 86 40 57 – Closed 1st-5 May, 20 July-18 August, 21 December-5 January, Sunday, Monday and lunch except Saturday

Rest – Menu €14 (lunch), €24/53 – Carte €22/56

♦ A typical Alsace-style house, popular for its generous meals (traditional cooking and grills) and very cheerful atmosphere. Showcase for regional products.

ROQUEBILLIÈRE – 06 Alpes-Maritimes – 341 E3 – pop. 1 467 – alt. 650 m – ✉ 06450

41 **D2**

Paris 889 – Marseille 245 – Nice 58 – Cuneo 132 – San Remo 106

Le Provençal

VISA MC AE

5 r. des Héros-de-14-18, (opposite the church) – ☎ 04 93 05 13 13 – jeromecornillon@hotmail.fr – Closed 17 November-10 December, Monday and Tuesday except July-August

Rest – Menu € 13 (weekday lunch)/20 – Carte € 27/37

◆ Decorated in Provençal style, this restaurant serves traditional French cuisine with an emphasis on seasonal garden and market produce.

ROQUEBRUNE-CAP-MARTIN – 06 Alpes-Maritimes – 341 F5 – pop. 11 692 – alt. 70 m – ✉ 06190 French Riviera

42 **E2**

Paris 953 – Menton 3 – Monaco 9 – Monte-Carlo 7 – Nice 26

Office de tourisme, 218, avenue Aristide Briand ☎ 04 93 35 62 87, Fax 04 93 28 57 00

Perched village★★: rue Moncollet★, ✻★★ from the keep★ - Cap Martin ≤★★ X - ≤★★ from the belvédère du Vistaëro (viewpoint) Southwest: 4 km.

Site★ of Gorbio North: 8 km by D 50.

Plans: see Menton.

Vista Palace

≤ Monaco and the coast, rm, AC, rest, P P VISA MC AE

Grande Corniche, 4 km by ③ La Turbie road D 2564 – ☎ 04 92 10 40 00 – info@vistapalace.com – Fax 04 93 35 18 94

64 rm – €185/330 €250/400, ☕ €25 – 4 suites

Rest *Le Vistaero* – *☎ 04 92 10 40 20 (dinner only)* Menu € 55/75 – Carte € 62/84

Rest *La Corniche* – *(lunch only)* Menu € 32 (weekdays), € 48 € (weekdays) – Carte € 52/60

◆ This ultra-modern hotel, with its daring architecture and luxurious decorations, overlooks the Riviera. A beauty salon, panoramic swimming pool and terraced botanical garden. Modern cuisine and a view that will take your breath away. Specialities from the south of France. Southern-inspired recipes at La Corniche.

Victoria without rest

≤ AC VISA MC AE

7 promenade Cap-Martin – ☎ 04 93 35 65 90 – Fax 04 93 28 27 02 – Closed 8 January-8 February

AV **k**

32 rm – €79/114 €79/114, ☕ €10

◆ A hotel in a residential building. Rooms have mainly rattan and bamboo furniture and balconies on the seafront side. Lounge-bar decorated in colonial style. Charming reception.

Alexandra without rest

≤ AC P VISA MC AE

93 av. W. Churchill – ☎ 04 93 35 65 45 – info@alexandrahotel.fr – Fax 04 93 57 96 51

AV **a**

40 rm – €49/92 €60/136, ☕ €10

◆ In this typical 1960s/1970s balconied seaside building, ask for a room with a sea view (top floors); rooms being gradually refurbished.

Le Roquebrune without rest

≤ AC P VISA MC AE

100 av. J. Jaurès, via ③ and Monaco road (D6098) via low road – ☎ 04 93 35 00 16 – info@le-roquebrune.com – Fax 04 93 28 98 36

5 rm ☕ – €100/125 €155/195

◆ Guests are welcomed as friends in this charming house on the water. The brand new rooms are refined and restful (some have garden-terraces).

Les Deux Frères with rm

≤ AC rm, VISA MC AE

pl. des Deux Frères, In the village, 3.5 km via ③ – ☎ 04 93 28 99 00 – info@lesdeuxfreres.com – Fax 04 93 28 99 10

12 rm – €75 €100/250, ☕ €9 – ½ P €98 – **Rest** – *(closed 15 November-15 December, 24-30 March, Sunday dinner, Tuesday lunch and Monday)* Menu € 28 bi/48 – Carte € 54/60

◆ A former local school, on the little square with its sea view, has been turned into a restaurant. Contemporary dishes. Pretty themed rooms ("Africa", "Wedding", etc.).

XX **L'Hippocampe** ← bay and the coast, VISA MC AE

44 av. W. Churchill – ☎ 04 93 35 81 91 – contact@hippocampe-restaurant.com – Fax 04 93 35 81 91 – Closed 3 November-27 December, dinner November-May, Sunday dinner and Monday AV **h**

Rest – *(pre-book)* Menu € 34/50 – Carte € 32/70

◆ This family-run waterfront restaurant reserves one of its terraces for bathers at lunchtime. Fillet of sole is the speciality (Bouillabaisse and coq au vin by request).

LA ROQUEBRUSSANNE – 83 Var – 340 K5 – pop. 1 672 – alt. 365 m – ✉ 83136

41 **C3**

Paris 810 – Aix-en-Provence 61 – Aubagne 48 – Brignoles 15 – Toulon 35

Office de tourisme, 15, rue Georges Clemenceau ☎ 04 94 86 82 11

Auberge de la Loube VISA MC

pl. de l'Église – ☎ 04 94 86 81 36 – Fax 04 94 86 86 79

8 rm – †€ 70/80 ††€ 70/80, ☐ € 8 – ½ P € 75 – **Rest** – Menu € 26/53 – Carte € 58/67

◆ This old, brightly-coloured building, in front of the church, is arranged in Provençal style. Rooms are being gradually renovated. Pleasant dining room, adorned with painted wooden furniture, paintings and antique objects. Shaded terrace. Traditional cuisine.

LA ROQUE-D'ANTHÉRON – 13 Bouches-du-Rhône – 340 G3 – pop. 4 446 – alt. 183 m – ✉ 13640 Provence

42 **E1**

Paris 726 – Aix-en-Provence 29 – Cavaillon 34 – Manosque 60 – Marseille 58

Office de tourisme, 3, cours Foch ☎ 04 42 50 70 74, Fax 04 42 50 70 76

Silvacane abbey ★★ East: 2 km.

Mas de Jossyl rm, AC P VISA MC AE

– ☎ 04 42 50 71 00 – jossyl.mas@wanadoo.fr – Fax 04 42 50 75 94 – Closed 23 August-4 September and 16-23 February

28 rm – †€ 65/117 ††€ 67/131, ☐ € 12 – ½ P € 56/95 – **Rest** – *(closed Sunday dinner, Monday lunch and Tuesday lunch off season)* Menu € 14 (weekday lunch), € 20/36 – Carte € 29/40

◆ In front of the 17C Château de Florans, this recent hotel in regional style has spacious, functional, soundproofed rooms. Recent modern wing and leisure centre. Bright, refurbished dining room and tree-lined terrace. Traditional menu.

ROQUEFORT – 40 Landes – 335 J10 – pop. 1 903 – alt. 69 m – ✉ 40120 Atlantic Coast

3 **B2**

Paris 667 – Bordeaux 107 – Mont-de-Marsan 23 – Saint-Pierre-du-Mont 31 – Aire-sur-l'Adour 40

Syndicat d'initiative, place du Soleil d'Or ☎ 05 58 45 50 46, Fax 05 58 45 53 63

Le Logis de St-Vincent rest, VISA MC

76 r. Laubaner – ☎ 05 58 45 75 36 – contact@logis-saint-vincent.com – Fax 05 58 45 73 59 – Closed 21-25 April, 7-11 July, 4-8 August, 27-October, 9-13 February and Sunday

7 rm – †€ 65/95 ††€ 65/110, ☐ € 17 – 2 suites – ½ P € 72/94 – **Rest** – Menu € 28/43

◆ Lovingly restored 19C manor house. Original parquet, stone walls, soothing tones and period furniture characterise the interior. Cosy dining room, courtyard garden with exotic varieties and regional menu.

ROQUEFORT-LES-PINS – 06 Alpes-Maritimes – 341 D6 – pop. 5 239 – alt. 184 m – ✉ 06330

42 **E2**

Paris 912 – Cannes 18 – Grasse 14 – Nice 25

Syndicat d'initiative, Centre Culturel R D 2085 ☎ 04 93 09 67 54

Auberge du Colombier P VISA MC AE

in Colombier, Nice road, via D2085 – ☎ 04 92 60 33 00 – info@auberge-du-colombier.com – Fax 04 93 77 07 03 – Closed 10 January-15 February

20 rm – †€ 60/90 ††€ 110/130, ☐ € 8 – 2 suites – **Rest** – *(closed Tuesday)* Menu € 23/39 – Carte € 39/68

◆ A house tucked away in a leafy park dominating the valley. The rooms, which are being progressively refurbished, have well-worn wooden furniture. The rustic dining room and pleasant terrace facing the garden are the backdrop to traditional cuisine.

XX **Auberge du Clos des Pins**

35 rte Notre Dame – ✆ 04 93 77 00 23 – Fax 04 93 77 00 23 – Closed Saturday lunch, Monday lunch and Wednesday
Rest – Menu (€ 28 bi), € 34 – Carte € 38/61
◆ Charming auberge facing a roundabout adorned with fountains. Lounge with fireplace, Provençal-style dining room, attractive terrace and contemporary menu created by two chefs, one from Australia and the other from the Vosges.

LA ROQUE-GAGEAC – 24 Dordogne – 329 I7 – pop. 449 – alt. 85 m – ✉ 24250

Dordogne-Berry-Limousin 4 **D3**

Paris 535 – Brive-la-Gaillarde 71 – Cahors 53 – Périgueux 71 – Sarlat-la-Canéda 9

Office de tourisme, le Bourg ✆ 05 53 29 17 01, Fax 05 53 31 24 48

Site★★.

XX **La Belle Étoile** with rm

rest,

– ✆ 05 53 29 51 44 – hotel.belle-etoile@wanadoo.fr – Fax 05 53 29 45 63 – Open 1st April-1st November
15 rm – €50 €50/80, ☕ €9 – ½ P €78 – **Rest** – *(closed Wednesday lunchtime and Monday)* Menu € 26/41
◆ Traditional dishes and modern food to enjoy in the lovely dining rooms or under the arbour of the terrace overlooking the Dordogne. Comfortable rooms.

XX **Auberge La Plume d'Oie** with rm

– ✆ 05 53 29 57 05 – walker.marc@wanadoo.fr – Fax 05 53 31 04 81 – Closed 15 November-20 December, 10 January to beg. March, Tuesday lunch off season and Monday except dinner in July-August
4 rm – €80/90 €80/90, ☕ €14 – **Rest** – *(number of covers limited, pre-book)* Menu € 28 (weekday lunch), € 45/65 – Carte € 64/75
◆ Pleasantly restored old residence with a rustic yet stylish restaurant (exposed stone and beams, view of passing barge traffic). Modern cuisine. Small but comfortable guestrooms.

Vitrac road Southeast by D 703 – ✉ 24250 La-Roque-Gageac

Le Périgord

rest,

3 km – ✆ 05 53 28 36 55 – bienvenue@hotelleperigord.eu – Fax 05 53 28 38 73 – Closed 2 January-28 February
39 rm – €55/65 €55/65, ☕ €8 – ½ P €57/62 – **Rest** – *(closed Monday and Tuesday except May-15 October)* Menu (€ 18), € 22/98 – Carte € 37/43
◆ This regional country home, surrounded by a big garden, stands at the foot of the walled town of Domme. Rustic-inspired, simple rooms, faultless upkeep. Updated cuisine based on Périgord specialities (as you would expect from the name of the restaurant!) Dining room-veranda and summer terrace.

XX **Les Prés Gaillardou**

– ✆ 05 53 59 67 89 – restau.presgaillardou@wanadoo.fr – Fax 05 53 31 07 37 – Closed Wednesday
Rest – Menu (€ 16), € 26/36 – Carte € 31/53
◆ Farm converted into a restaurant. Its three small dining rooms have stone walls and beams and there is an enclosed garden with a pleasant terrace. Local cuisine served.

ROQUEMAURE – 30 Gard – 339 N4 – pop. 4 848 – alt. 19 m – ✉ 30150

Provence 23 **D2**

Paris 665 – Alès 76 – Avignon 18 – Nîmes 47 – Orange 12 – Pont-St-Esprit 32

Office de tourisme, 1, cours Bridaine ✆ 04 66 90 21 01, Fax 04 66 90 21 01

Le Clément V

6 r. P. Semard, Nîmes road – ✆ 04 66 82 67 58 – hotel.clementv@wanadoo.fr – Fax 04 66 82 84 66 – Closed 22 December-28 January
21 rm – €62/72 €67/77, ☕ €8 – ½ P €50/55 – **Rest** – *(dinner only)* Menu € 19/25
◆ The Château of Roquemaure was Pope Clement V's last residence. Its hotel is a colourful 1970s building. At the rear, bedrooms are spacious but lack balconies.

LA ROQUE-SUR-PERNES – 84 Vaucluse – 332 D10 – pop. 447 – alt. 250 m – ✉ 84210 42 E1

Paris 697 – Avignon 34 – Marseille 99 – Salon-de-Provence 49

Château la Roque ≤ village and valley,
– ✆ 04 90 61 68 77 – chateaularoque@wanadoo.fr – Fax 04 90 61 68 78 – Closed 12-20 November

5 rm – €100/240 €100/240, ☐ €18 – ½ P €100/170 – **Rest** – *(closed Sun) (dinner only) (residents only)* Menu €40/60

◆ This medieval château (11C) has been successfully restored, thus magnificently preserving its authenticity. Spacious rooms. Tiered terraces and heated pool overlooking the valley. The landlord is also the chef. Meals served in the Templar Room or garden.

ROQUETTE-SUR-SIAGNE – 06 Alpes-Maritimes – 341 C6 – pop. 4 445 – alt. 12 m – ✉ 06550 42 E2

Paris 912 – Marseille 165 – Nice 44 – Antibes 20 – Cannes 12

La Terrasse VISA AE
484 av. de la République, (Saint Jean district) – ✆ 04 92 19 04 88 – resterrasse.roq@wanadoo.fr – Closed 28 July-3 August, 24-31 December, Saturday lunch and Sunday

Rest – Menu (€ 19 bi), € 24 bi (weekday lunch), € 29/50 – Carte € 44/60

◆ Moderately priced, creative cuisine served in a bright, Mediterranean-inspired dining room (exotic wood, plants, palm trees).

ROSAY – 78 Yvelines – 311 G2 – see Mantes-la-Jolie

ROSBRUCK – 57 Moselle – 307 M4 – see Forbach

ROSCOFF – 29 Finistère – 308 H2 – pop. 3 550 – alt. 7 m – Casino – ✉ 29680 Brittany 9 B1

Paris 563 – Brest 66 – Landivisiau 27 – Morlaix 27 – Quimper 100

Office de tourisme, 46, rue Gambetta ✆ 02 98 61 12 13, Fax 02 98 69 75 75

N.-D.-de-Croaz-Batz church ★ - Exotic garden★.

Plan on next page

Le Brittany ≤ rm, rest, VISA AE
bd Ste Barbe – ✆ 02 98 69 70 78 – hotel.brittany@wanadoo.fr – Fax 02 98 61 13 29 – Open 24 March-11 November Z a

24 rm – €115/145 €135/255, ☐ €19 – 2 suites – ½ P €135/210

Rest *Le Yachtman* – *(closed Monday) (dinner only) (number of covers limited, pre-book)* Menu € 59/106 – Carte € 73/98

Spec. Fraîcheur de homard bleu (May to October). Petite pêche du jour. Dessert autour de l'artichaut "prince de Bretagne" (May to September).

◆ Fine 17C manor house which was entirely dismantled and reconstructed on Roscoff harbour. Very pretty rooms (antique or contemporary furnishings) and attentive service. View over the Ile de Batz and fine seafood cuisine in the elegant dining room.

Talabardon ≤ VISA AE
27 pl. Lacaze Duthiers, (near the church) – ✆ 02 98 61 24 95 – hotel.talabardon@wanadoo.fr – Fax 02 98 61 10 54 – Open beg. March-beg. November Y b

37 rm – €65/143 €77/163, ☐ €13 – ½ P €68/110 – **Rest** – *(closed Sunday dinner and Thursday)* Menu (€ 20), € 26/47 – Carte € 33/55

◆ The most popular rooms in this family hotel overlook the harbour. All the guestrooms have been refurbished in a sober contemporary style. Fish and seafood served in the restaurant, with views over the sea.

Thalasstonic ≤ rm, rest, VISA AE
r. V. Hugo, (Y) – ✆ 02 98 29 20 20 – thalasstonic.roscoff@thalasso.com – Fax 02 98 29 20 19 – Closed 30 November-24 December

74 rm – €69/140 €72/140, ☐ €11 – ½ P €72/106 – **Rest** – Menu €25 – Carte €17/35

◆ This establishment has direct access to the thalassotherapy centre, a wealth of services and practical rooms (the most spacious have a south-facing balcony). Admire the sun setting over the Ile de Batz from the restaurant: guest house and diet menus.

Street	Grid	No.
Auxerre (Quai d')	Z	2
Capucins (R. des)	Z	3
Gambetta (R.)	Y	6
Gaulle (Q. Ch.-de)	Y	7
Johnies (R. des)	Y	8
Jules-Ferry (R.)	Z	9
Keranveyer (R. de)	Z	10
Kléber (R.)	Z	12
Lacaze-Duthiers (Pl.)	Y	13
Lannurien (R. G.-de)	Z	14
Pasteur (R. L.)	Y	15
Pen al Leur (Pl. de)	Z	17
République (Pl. de la)	Z	19
Reveillère (R. Amiral)	Y	20
Ste-Barbe (Bd)	Z	22
Tessier (Pl. G.)	Y	23
Victor-Hugo (R.)	Y	26

La Résidence without rest

14 r. Johnnies – 02 98 69 74 85 – hotel.laresidence.roscoff@orange.fr – Fax 02 98 69 78 63 – Open 1st April-15 November Y **f**

31 rm – €38/58 €45/78, €7

♦ Traditional building between the harbour and the church and separated from the road by a flower garden. Well-presented bedrooms with south-facing balconies. Non-smoking.

Armen Le Triton without rest

r. du Dr. Bagot – 02 98 61 24 44 – resa@hotel-letriton.com – Fax 02 98 69 77 97 – Closed 15 January-15 February Z **u**

44 rm – €45/55 €55/72, €8

♦ This establishment offers a peaceful stay and proximity to the spa centre; rooms are more spacious on the tennis court side. A breakfast room looking onto the garden.

Aux Tamaris without rest

49 r. É. Corbière – 02 98 61 22 99 – contact@hotel-aux-tamaris.com – Fax 02 98 69 74 36 – Open 15 February-15 November Y **d**

26 rm – €49/77 €54/77, €8

♦ This Breton-style house, from 1935, offers sea or countryside-themed rooms, some with sea view. Panoramic breakfast room.

Du Centre

le Port – 02 98 61 24 25 – contact@chezjanie.com – Fax 02 98 61 15 43 – Closed mid November-mid February Y **a**

16 rm – €59/118 €69/118, €8,50 – **Rest** – *(closed Sunday dinner and Tuesday except July-August)* Carte €26/37

♦ This hotel near the post office is down by the port. Tastefully appointed rooms: uncluttered decor, sober furniture and grey walls adorned with poem extracts. Seafood, grilled meats and salads make up the menu of this bar-restaurant facing the Channel.

Ibis without rest

17 pl. Lacaze Duthiers, (pl. de l'église) – 02 98 61 22 61 – h1109@accor.com – Fax 02 98 61 11 94 Y **e**

40 rm – €58/82 €58/82, €7,50

♦ In the centre of Roscoff. Small rooms which conform to the chain's standards, some with views of the Channel. Not a great deal of charm, but well-kept and reasonably priced.

Bellevue without rest VISA

r. Jeanne d'Arc – ✆ 02 98 61 23 38 – hotelbellevue.roscoff@wanadoo.fr – Fax 02 98 61 11 80 – Open from mid March-mid November Z **h**

18 rm – †€ 60/67 ††€ 60/76, ☐ € 8

◆ Vista of the sea from the breakfast room and from most of the slightly cramped and simple yet well-kept rooms. The others look out over a flower patio. Adjoining pub-bar.

Le Temps de Vivre (Jean-Yves Crenn) rm, VISA AE

pl. de l'Église – ✆ 02 98 61 27 28 – contact@letempsdevivre.net – Fax 02 98 61 19 46 – Closed 24 March-10 April, 28 September-17 October, 4-14 January, Sunday dinner except August, Tuesday except dinner from April to December and Monday

Rest – Menu € 39/100 – Carte € 61/96 Y **e**

Spec. Pinces de tourteau rôties. Langoustines poêlées, galette d'artichaut (May to November). Pigeon rôti, chou vert, far noir au lard grillé.

◆ The Channel backdrop makes an elegant setting for enjoying the inventive cuisine based on local fish accompanied by a fine wine list. Recipe for success!

Le Temps de Vivre VISA AE

pl. de l'Église – ✆ 02 98 19 33 19 – contact@letempsdevivre.net – Fax 02 98 19 33 00 – Closed 1st-15 October and 4-14 January

15 rm – †€ 80/140 ††€ 80/268, ☐ € 14

◆ Spacious rooms in a very refined style (with stone, wenge and oak), in privateer houses around a flower-clad patio. Some overlook the sea.

L'Écume des Jours VISA

quai d'Auxerre – ✆ 02 98 61 22 83 – michel.quere2@wanadoo.fr – Fax 02 98 61 22 83 – Closed December, January, Wednesday dinner and Tuesday except from 14 July to 20 August and Wednesday lunch Z **x**

Rest – Menu (€ 20), € 29/49 – Carte € 37/55

◆ The main room of this 16C ship owner's house has retained its period charm and two old fireplaces. Terrace overlooking the harbour and fine regional cuisine.

ROSENAU – 68 Haut-Rhin – 315 J11 – pop. 1 840 – alt. 230 m – ✉ 68128 1 **B3**

Paris 492 – Altkirch 25 – Basel 15 – Belfort 70 – Colmar 59 – Mulhouse 24

Au Lion d'Or AC P VISA

5 r. Village Neuf – ✆ 03 89 68 21 97 – baumlin@auliondor-rosenau.com – Fax 03 89 70 68 05 – Closed 16-28 June, 13-30 October, Tuesday except April-mid June and Monday

Rest – Menu € 13 (weekday lunch), € 23/35 – Carte € 24/37

◆ A welcoming interior (pale woods) and attractive terrace can be found in this pleasant inn, run by the same family since 1928. Fine selection of wines by the glass.

ROSHEIM – 67 Bas-Rhin – 315 I6 – pop. 4 548 – alt. 190 m – ✉ 67560 Alsace-Lorraine

Paris 485 – Erstein 20 – Molsheim 9 – Obernai 6 – Sélestat 33 – Strasbourg 31

Office de tourisme, 94, rue du Général-de-Gaulle ✆ 03 88 50 75 38, Fax 03 88 50 45 49 1 **A2**

St-Pierre and St-Paul church ★.

Hostellerie du Rosenmeer (Hubert Maetz) AC rest, P VISA AE

45 av. de la Gare, 2 km northeast on D 35 – ✆ 03 88 50 43 29 – info@le-rosenmeer.com – Fax 03 88 49 20 57 – Closed from end July to beg. August and 15 February-11 March

20 rm – †€ 40/50 ††€ 61/98, ☐ € 10 – ½ P € 76/85

Rest – *(closed Sunday dinner, Monday and Wednesday)* Menu € 34 bi (weekday lunch), € 47/115 bi – Carte € 38/67

Rest *Winstub d'Rosemer* – *(closed Sunday and Monday)* Menu € 9,50 (weekday lunch), € 25/36 bi – Carte € 21/42

Spec. Pavé de thon rôti à la sauge-ananas. Omble chevalier des Vosges à la purée de persil (spring-summer). Colvert en salmis, champignons des bois (autumn). **Wines** Sylvaner, Riesling.

◆ Alsatian-style, recently-built hotel, on the banks of a stream that has given the building its name. Pleasant rooms on the second floor. Welcoming dining room (wide bay windows and wood panelling) and tasty, inventive food inspired by local produce; gourmets should keep this address in mind!

Auberge du Cerf VISA

120 r. Gén. de Gaulle – ✆ 03 88 50 40 14 – Fax 03 88 50 40 14
– Closed 20 January-2 February, Sunday dinner and Monday
Rest – Menu € 12 (weekday lunch), € 16/25 – Carte € 26/49
◆ In the centre of a wine-growing village, this inn decked out with flowers has two small dining areas serving classic and regional cuisine.

La Petite Auberge with rm rest, P VISA

41 r. Gén. de Gaulle – ✆ 03 88 50 40 60
– restaurant.petite.auberge@wanadoo.fr – Fax 03 88 48 00 90
– Closed 20 June-10 July, February school holidays, Wednesday and Thursday
7 rm – €45 €45, ☕ €7 – ½ P €68
Rest – Menu € 20/46 – Carte € 25/47
◆ This small Alsatian-style building on the main thoroughfare is home to a rustic-style restaurant. The hotel Lys offers rooms equipped with kitchenettes, 50m away.

LA ROSIÈRE – **14 Calvados** – **303** I4 – **see Arromanches-les-Bains**

LA ROSIÈRE 1850 – **73 Savoie** – **333** O4 – **alt. 1 850 m** – **Winter sports : 1 100/2 600 m** 20 – ✉ **73700 Montvalezan** **French Alps** 45 **D2**

Paris 657 – Albertville 76 – Bourg-St-Maurice 22 – Chambéry 125

Relais du Petit St-Bernard mountains, VISA

– ✆ 04 79 06 80 48 – info@petit-saint-bernard.com – Fax 04 79 06 83 40
– Open 29 June-5 September and 14 December-24 April
20 rm – €37/41 €45/51, ☕ €7 – ½ P €49/65
Rest – Menu € 16/20 – Carte € 18/55
◆ Located at the foot of ski runs, this big chalet is a guesthouse, inn-restaurant and souvenir shop rolled into one. Simple, rustic rooms. Some have balconies with panoramic views. A restaurant serving brasserie-type food, with a wood-panelled decor and snow-covered peaks in the background.

Look out for red symbols, indicating particularly pleasant establishments.

LES ROSIERS-SUR-LOIRE – **49 Maine-et-Loire** – **317** H4 – **pop. 2 242** – **alt. 22 m** – ✉ **49350** **Châteaux of the Loire** 35 **C2**

Paris 304 – Angers 32 – Baugé 27 – Bressuire 66 – Cholet 80 – La Flèche 45 – Saumur 18

Syndicat d'initiative, place du Mail ✆ 02 41 51 90 22, Fax 02 41 51 90 22

La Toque Blanche P VISA

rte d'Angers – ✆ 02 41 51 80 75 – Fax 02 41 38 06 38
– Closed 15-30 November, 10-31 January, Tuesday and Wednesday
Rest – Menu € 25 bi/51
◆ A classically decorated dining room with large windows overlooking the river. Traditional cuisine, regional specialities and a choice of Loire Valley wines.

Au Val de Loire VISA

pl. de l'Église – ✆ 02 41 51 80 30 – Fax 02 41 51 95 00
– Closed 15 February-15 March, Thursday dinner, Sunday dinner and Monday except July-August
Rest – Menu € 13/40 – Carte € 41/48
◆ Herbs and flowers provide a fresh touch to the traditional cuisine served in this family-run hotel and restaurant. Redecorated dining rooms and simple rooms available.

ROSNY-SOUS-BOIS – **93 Seine-Saint-Denis** – **305** F7 – **101** 17 – **see Paris, Area**

ROSPEZ – **22 Côtes-d'Armor** – **309** B2 – **see Lannion**

ROSTRENEN – 22 Côtes-d'Armor – 309 C5 – pop. 3 616 – alt. 216 m – ✉ 22110 9 B2

Paris 485 – Quimper 71 – St-Brieuc 58 – Carhaix-Plouguer 22 – Pontivy 38

Office de tourisme, 6, rue Gilbert ✆ 02 96 29 02 72, Fax 02 96 29 02 72

XX L'Eventail des Saveurs

3 pl. Bourg Coz – ✆ 02 96 29 10 71 – leventail-des-saveurs@wanadoo.fr – Fax 02 96 29 34 75 – Closed Tuesday dinner from September to May, Sunday dinner, Wednesday dinner and Monday

Rest – Menu (€ 14,50), € 28/48 – Carte € 39/48

◆ An impressive selection of regional recipes with a modern twist, served in a brightly coloured setting.

Good food and accommodation at moderate prices? Look for the Bib symbols: red Bib Gourmand for food, blue Bib Hotel for hotels.

ROUBAIX – 59 Nord – 302 H3 – pop. 96 984 – alt. 27 m – ✉ 59100

Northern France and the Paris Region 31 C2

Paris 232 – Kortrijk 23 – Lille 15 – Tournai 20

Office de tourisme, 12, place de la Liberté ✆ 03 20 65 31 90, Fax 03 20 65 31 83

du Sart Villeneuve-d'Ascq 5 rue Jean Jaurès, South: 5 km, ✆ 03 20 72 02 51 ;

de Brigode Villeneuve-d'Ascq 36 avenue du Golf, South: 6 km, ✆ 03 20 91 17 86 ;

de Bondues Bondues Château de la Vigne, by D 9: 8 km, ✆ 03 20 23 20 62.

Centre des archives du monde du travail (Labour-related Archive Centre) BX **M**[1] - La Piscine (Swimming pool)★★, Musée d'Art et d'Industrie (Museum of Art and Industry)★ - Chapelle d'Hem (Chapel of Hem)★ (walls-stained glass windows★★ by Manessier) 5 km, see map of Lille JS **B**.

Access and exits: See plan of Lille

Le Grand Hôtel

rest,

22 av. J. Lebas – ✆ 03 20 73 40 00 – grand.hotel.roubaix@wanadoo.fr – Fax 03 20 73 22 42 BX **r**

93 rm – †€ 75/100 ††€ 75/110, ☕ € 14 – **Rest** – *(closed August, Friday and Saturday) (dinner only)* Menu € 21

◆ An huge reception lobby and tasteful decorations (mouldings and columns) make for a smart interior to match the fine architecture of this 19C hotel on a busy street. This Belle Epoque dining room is lit by a big glass roof. Traditional cooking.

XX Le Beau Jardin "saveurs"

av. Le Nôtre, (The Parc Barbieux) – ✆ 03 20 20 61 85 – restaurant@lebeaujardin.fr – Fax 03 20 45 10 65 AY **e**

Rest – Menu € 20/40 bi – Carte € 39/48

◆ This restaurant is matchlessly located at the heart of the park of Barbieux. Attractive contemporary dining room facing a lake and a festival of herbs and spices in the cuisine.

in Lys-lez-Lannoy 5 km southeast by D 206 – alt. 28 m – ✉ 59390

Syndicat d'initiative, 130, rue Jules Guesde ✆ 03 20 82 30 90

XX Auberge de la Marmotte

5 r. J.-B. Lebas – ✆ 03 20 75 30 95 – Fax 03 20 81 16 34 – Closed 28 April-4 May, August, Monday and dinner except Friday and Saturday *Map of Lille* JS **f**

Rest – Menu (€ 14,50 bi), € 29/69 bi – Carte € 25/53

◆ Brick regional-style building housing two dining rooms, one rustic, one more modern and a small, intimate lounge. Traditional cuisine.

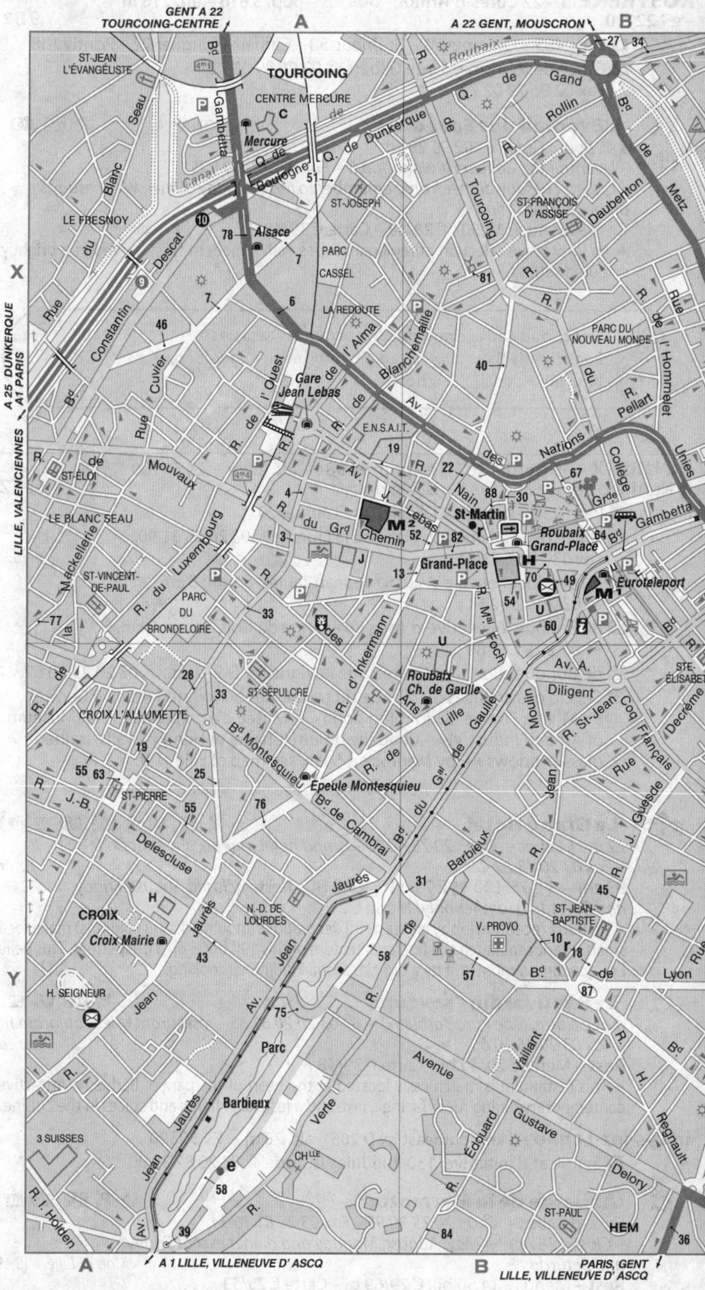
GENT A 22
TOURCOING-CENTRE
A
A 22 GENT, MOUSCRON
B
27
34
ST-JEAN
L'ÉVANGÉLISTE
TOURCOING
CENTRE MERCURE
C
Mercure
Bd Gambetta
Seau
Roubaix
R. de Tourcoing
Q. de Gand
Rollin
Bd de Metz
Q. de Dunkerque
Q. de Boulogne
Canal
51
Blanc
LE FRESNOY
10
78
Alsace
ST-JOSEPH
ST-FRANÇOIS
D' ASSISE
Daubenton
du
Descat
7
PARC
CASSEL
X
9
81
R.
Rue
Constantin
7
46
6
LA REDOUTE
R. de l'Hommelet
PARC DU
NOUVEAU MONDE
A 25 DUNKERQUE
A1 PARIS
Cuvier
R. de l' Alma
Blanchemaille
40
Gare
Jean Lebas
R. de l' Ouest
R. Pellart
Bd
Rue
Av.
E.N.S.A.I.T.
Av. des Nations Unies
R. de Mouvaux
ST-ÉLOI
19
R.
22
67
Collège
Grde
88
30
Nain
4
Av.
Gambetta
LILLE, VALENCIENNES
LE BLANC SEAU
R. du Grd Chemin
M2
Lebas
St-Martin
r
52
82
Roubaix
Grand-Place
64
Bd
Mackellerie
R. du Luxembourg
3
J
Grand-Place
H
Euroteleport
M1
13
70
49
ST-VINCENT-
DE-PAUL
P
54
U
R. Mal Foch
PARC
DU
BRONDELOIRE
33
des
60
77
la
U
Bd
R.
R. de
R. d' Inkermann
Av. A.
Diligent
STE-
ÉLISABET
28
33
ST-SÉPULCRE
Arts
Roubaix
Ch. de Gaulle
Moulin
Coq Français
Decrême
CROIX L'ALLUMETTE
R. de Lille
R. St-Jean
19
Bd Montesquieu
Bd du Gal de Gaulle
Rue
55
63
25
Epeule Montesquieu
Jean
R.
ST-PIERRE
J.-B.
55
76
Bd de Cambrai
R. J. Guesde
Delescluse
Barbieux
R.
31
Jaurès
45
H
CROIX
N.-D. DE
LOURDES
ST-JEAN-
BAPTISTE
Croix Mairie
Jaurès
V. PROVO
10
r
18
43
Jean
58
57
Y
Bd de Lyon
Rue
87
H. SEIGNEUR
Jean
R.
75
Av.
Vaillant
R. H. Regnault
Bd
Parc
Avenue Gustave Delory
R.
Barbieux
Verte
Jaurès
3 SUISSES
Édouard
CHlle
Jean
e
58
R.
R. I. Holden
R.
ST-PAUL
HEM
Av.
39
84
36
A
A 1 LILLE, VILLENEUVE D' ASCQ
B
PARIS, GENT
LILLE, VILLENEUVE D' ASCQ

ROUBAIX

CROIX

Street	Grid	No.
Cheuvreuil (R.)	AY	19
Gaulle (Av. du Gén.-de)	AY	43
Kléber (R.)	AY	55
Liberté (Pl. de la)	AY	63
Raspail (R.)	AX	77

HEM

Street	Grid	No.
Europe (Av. de l')	BY	36
Schuman (R. Robert)	BY	84

LYS-LEZ-LANNOY

Street	Grid	No.
Guesde (R. Jules)	CY	48

ROUBAIX

Street	Grid	No.
Abreuvoir (Pl. de l')	AX	3
Alouette (R. de l')	AX	4
Alsace (Av. d')	AX	6
Armentières (Bd d')	AX	7
Avelghem (R. d')	CX	9
Beaumont (R. de)	BY	10
Beaurepaire (Bd du)	CX	12
Bois (R. du)	BX	13
Braille (R. Louis)	CY	15
Cateau (Bd du)	BY	18
Champier (R. Louise et Victor)	AX	19
Colmar (Bd de)	CX	21
Communauté-Urbaine (R.)	BX	22
Constantine (R. de)	BX	24
Courbet (R. Amiral)	AY	25
Couteaux (Bd des)	BX	27
Cugnot (R.)	AY	28
Curé (R. du)	BX	30
Douai (Bd de)	ABY	31
Epeule (R. de l')	AXY	33
Faidherbe (Pl. du Gén.)	CX	37
Fer-à-Cheval (Carr. du)	AY	39
Fosse-aux-Chênes (R.)	BX	40
Fraternité (Pl. de la)	CY	42
Goujon (R. Jean)	BY	45
Gounod (R. Ch.)	AX	46
Grande-Rue	BCX	
Grand-Place	BX	
Halle (R. de la)	BX	49
Halluin (Bd d')	AX	51
Hospice (R. de l')	BX	52
Hôtel-de-Ville (R. de l')	BX	54
Lacordaire (Bd)	BY	57
Laine (Bd de la)	BX	34
Lannoy (R. de)	BCY	
Lebas (Av. J.)	ABX	
Leclerc (Bd Gén.)	BX	60
Leconte-Baillon (R.)	CY	61
Leers (R. de)	CX	62
Liberté (Pl. de la)	BX	64
Molière (R.)	CX	66
Monnet (R. J.)	BX	67
Motte (R. Pierre)	BX	70
Nadaud (R.)	CX	72
Le Nôtre (Av.)	AY	58
Nyckès (Pont)	CX	73
Peuple-Belge (Av. du)	AY	75
Prof.-Langevin (R. du)	AY	76
République (Bd de la)	AX	78
Rousseau (R. J.-J.)	CY	79
St-Maurice (R.)	BX	81
Sarrail (R. du Gén.)	BX	82
Sévigné (R. de)	CX	85
Travail (Pl. du)	BY	87
Vieil-Abreuvoir (R. du)	BX	88

WATTRELOS

Street	Grid	No.
Briffaut (R. Henri)	CX	16
Monge (R.)	CX	69

ROUDOUALLEC – 56 Morbihan – 308 I6 – pop. 700 – alt. 167 m – ✉ 56110

9 **B2**

Paris 520 – Carhaix-Plouguer 29 – Concarneau 38 – Lorient 64 – Quimper 35 – Vannes 113

Bienvenue

– ✆ 02 97 34 50 01 – lebienvenue@wanadoo.fr – Fax 02 97 34 50 01 – *Closed 5-15 January, 2-14 February, Tuesday dinner and Wednesday except July –August*

Rest – Menu € 17 (weekdays)/58

♦ Banks of hydrangeas and rhododendrons flourish around this restaurant, set on a road running through a village in the Montagnes Noires. Generous portions of local specialities on the menu.

The ✿ award is the crème de la crème.
This is awarded to restaurants which are really worth travelling miles for!

ROUEN Ⓟ – 76 Seine-Maritime – 304 G5 – pop. 106 592 – Built-up area 389 862 – alt. 12 m – ✉ 76000 Normandy

33 **D2**

Paris 134 – Amiens 122 – Caen 124 – Le Havre 87 – Le Mans 204

Ferry : from Dieppedalle ✆ 02 35 36 20 81; from Petit-Couronne ✆ 02 35 32 40 21.

Rouen-Vallée de Seine: ✆ 02 35 79 41 00, by ③: 10 km.

Office de tourisme, 25, place de la Cathédrale ✆ 02 32 08 32 40, Fax 02 32 08 32 44

de Rouen Mont-St-Aignan Mont-Saint-Aignan Rue Francis Poulenc, ✆ 02 35 76 38 65 ;

De Léry Poses Poses Base de Loisirs & de Plein Air, ✆ 02 32 59 47 42 ;

de la Forêt-Verte Bosc-Guérard-Saint-AdrienNorth: 15 km by D 121 and D 3, ✆ 02 35 33 62 94.

★★ Notre-Dame cathedral ★★★ - Old Rouen★★★: St-Ouen church ★★, St-Maclou church ★★Aître St-Maclou★★, palais de justice (law courts)★★, rue du Gros-Horloge★★, rue St-Romain★★ BZ, place du Vieux-Marché★ AY, - Window★★ of Ste-Jeanne-d'Arc churchAY **D**, rue Ganterie★, rue Damiette★ CZ - 35, rue Martainville★ CZ - St-Godard church ★ BY - Residence★ (musée national de l'Éducation) CZ **M¹5** - Stained-glass windows★ of St-Patrice church - Museums: Beaux-Arts★★★, Le Secq des Tournelles★★ BY **M¹3**, Ceramics★★ BY **M³**, départemental des Antiquités de la Seine-Maritime★★ CY **M¹** - Musée national de l'Éducation★ - Jardin des Plantes★ EX - Corniche (cliff road)★★★ de la Côte Ste-Catherine★★★ - Bonsecours★★ FX, 3 km - Centre Universitaire (university) ✻★★ EV.

St-Martin de Boscherville: former abbey church of St-Georges★★, 11 km by ⑦.

Plans on following pages

Mercure Centre without rest

7 r. de la Croix de Fer – ✆ 02 35 52 69 52 – h1301@accor.com – Fax 02 35 89 41 46

BZ **f**

125 rm – †€ 99/170 ††€ 109/180, ☕ € 14 – 4 suites

♦ This hotel's main asset is its ideal location at the heart of old Rouen. Renovated, literature-themed rooms. Some enjoying a view of the cathedral.

Mercure Champ de Mars

12 av. A. Briand – ✆ 02 35 52 42 32 – h1273@accor.com – Fax 02 35 08 15 06

CZ **j**

139 rm – †€ 110/150 ††€ 135/175, ☕ € 13 – **Rest** – *(closed lunch 14 July-25 August, Sunday lunch and Saturday)* Menu € 18/28 – Carte € 30/41

♦ This hotel lines a busy boulevard along the Seine. It offers, mostly to business clients, renovated and very comfortable rooms. Modern restaurant, facing the Champ-de-Mars esplanade. Traditional cooking. Jazz at the bar on some Friday evenings.

Suitehotel without rest
10 quai de Boisguibert – ☎ 02 32 10 58 68 – H6342@accor.com – Fax 02 32 10 58 69 EV **t**
80 rm – †€ 85/103 ††€ 85/103, ☐ € 12
◆ This recent hotel is home to contemporary style rooms that are spacious and light. Equally well suited to business travellers and families (kitchenettes).

Dandy without rest
93 bis r. Cauchoise – ☎ 02 35 07 32 00 – contact@hotels-rouen.net – Fax 02 35 15 48 82 AY **p**
18 rm – †€ 68/95 ††€ 80/125, ☐ € 10
◆ This hotel, located in a pedestrian street leading to the Place du Vieux-Marché, has cosy rooms with Louis XV-style furniture. Those at the rear are quieter. Comfortable bar with Norman decoration.

Du Vieux Marché without rest
15 r. Pie – ☎ 02 35 71 00 88 – hotelduvieuxmarche@wanadoo.fr – Fax 02 35 70 75 94
48 rm – †€ 107/130 ††€ 120/165, ☐ € 14 AY **h**
◆ Beautifully restored in 2001, this fully-equipped group of buildings is set back from the street, for a quiet night in rooms with a cozy atmosphere.

De Dieppe rest,
pl. B. Tissot, (opposite the SNCF station) – ☎ 02 35 71 96 00 – hotel.dieppe@hoteldedieppe.fr – Fax 02 35 89 65 21 BY **z**
41 rm – †€ 87/150 ††€ 97/150, ☐ € 11 – ½ P € 69/109
Rest *Le Quatre Saisons* – *(closed 21 July-10 August and Saturday lunch)*
Menu (€ 15), € 23/58 – Carte € 46/67
◆ This hotel has been run by the same family since 1880. It offers guests neat bedrooms, with customized decoration. Rouen duck is this restaurant's speciality, so duck drawings and objects enhance the dining room's elegant decor.

De l'Europe
87 r. aux Ours – ☎ 02 32 76 17 76 – europe-hotel@wanadoo.fr – Fax 02 32 76 17 77 – Closed 22 December-4 January AZ **e**
26 rm – †€ 70/95 ††€ 70/95, ☐ € 10 – ½ P € 55/65 – **Rest** – *(closed 18 July-23 August, Saturday and Sunday)* Menu (€ 12), € 25 – Carte € 19/28
◆ Modern building splendidly located in the historic quarter. Modern, functional rooms; some have a view of the cathedral towers. Friendly atmosphere and a colourful decor in this restaurant offering traditional cuisine.

De la Cathédrale without rest
12 r. St-Romain – ☎ 02 35 71 57 95 – contact@hotel-de-la-cathedrale.fr – Fax 02 35 70 15 54 BZ **m**
26 rm – †€ 56/76 ††€ 66/95, ☐ € 7,50
◆ This pretty 17C house, with a peaceful patio decked with flowers or comfortable rooms helped Pierre Corneille and Jean-Paul Sartre to find inspiration. Could it do the same for you?

Le Vieux Carré without rest
34 r. Ganterie – ☎ 02 35 71 67 70 – vieux-carre@mcom.fr – Fax 02 35 71 19 17
13 rm – †€ 58 ††€ 62, ☐ € 7 BY **t**
◆ Delightful guesthouse atmosphere in this half-timbered residence (1715) located in the heart of the old town. Cosy lounge, tea room, and small stylish rooms.

Le Cardinal without rest
1 pl. Cathédrale – ☎ 02 35 70 24 42 – hotelcardinal.rouen@wanadoo.fr – Fax 02 35 89 75 14 – Closed 25 December-15 January and holidays BZ **r**
18 rm – †€ 52/66 ††€ 62/86, ☐ € 7,50
◆ Located next to Notre Dame Cathedral, the Gothic masterpiece. All the small rooms in this family-run hotel have been renovated. Breakfast on the terrace in summer.

Le Clos Jouvenet without rest
42 r. Hyacinthe Langlois – ☎ 02 35 89 80 66 – cdewitte@club-internet.fr – Fax 02 35 98 37 65 – Closed 15 December-15 January EV **a**
4 rm ☐ – †€ 80/98 ††€ 80/103
◆ Delightful 19C mansion located above the town in a large, peaceful garden. Cosy, impeccably maintained guestrooms with views of the orchard or church spires.

ROUEN

Alliés (Av. des) .... DX 4
Ango (R. Jean) .... EV 7
Béthencourt (Quai de) .... EV 14
Bicheray (Av. du Cdt) .... DV 15
Boisguilbert (Quai de) .... EV 18
Bois-des-Dames (Av. du) .... EV 17
Bonsecours (Rte de) .... EV 21
Briand (R. Aristide) .... DX 33
Brossolette (Bd) .... DX 34
Bruyères (Rond-Point des) .... EX 36
Caen (Av. de) .... EV 37
Canteleu (Rte de) .... DV 39
Carnot (Av.) .... DV 40
Chasselièvre (R.) .... EV 52
Clères (Chemin de) .... EV 54
Coquelicots (R. des) .... EX 55
Corneille (R. Pierre) .... EX 58
Corniche (Rte de la) .... FV 60
Darnétal (Rte de) .... FV 64
Duclair (R. de) .... DV 69
Elbeuf (R. d') .... EX 75
Europe (Av. de l') .... EV 78
Europe (Bd de l') .... EVX 79
La-Fayette (R.) .... EV 103
Felling (Av. de) .... EX 82
Flaubert (Pt) .... EV 83
Fond-du-Val (Allée du) .... EV 85
France (Quai de) .... DV 87
Gaulle (Bd Charles-de) .... DX 88
Grand'Mare (Av. de la) .... FV 92
Grand-Cours (Av. du) .... EX 91
Jean-Jaurès (Av.) .... DX 97
Jean-Jaurès (Bd) .... DV 99
Leclerc-de-Hauteclocque (Av. du Gén.) .... DX 106
Leclerc (Av. Général) .... DV 105
Lesseps (Bd Ferdinand-de) .... EV 107
Maréchal-Juin (Av. du) .... FV 109
Martyrs-de-la-Résistance (R. des) .... DV 110
Mont-Riboudet (Av. du) .... EV 112
Nansen (R.) .... DV 114
Paris (Rte de) .... FX 158
Pène (R. Annie-de) .... FV 118
Quatre-Mares (Grande R. de) .... EX 122
Renard (R. du) .... EV 125
République (R. de la) .... FV 126
République (R. de la BONSECOURS) .... EX 160
Rondeaux (Av. Jean) .... EV 131
Roosevelt (Bd Franklin) .... DX 132
Ste-Lucie (Rond-Point) .... DX 135
Siegfried (Bd André) .... EV 142
Sotteville (R. de) .... EX 145
Verdun (Bd de) .... EV 150
Verdun (Bd de GRAND-QUEVILLY) .... DX 165
11-Novembre (Bd du) .... EX 157

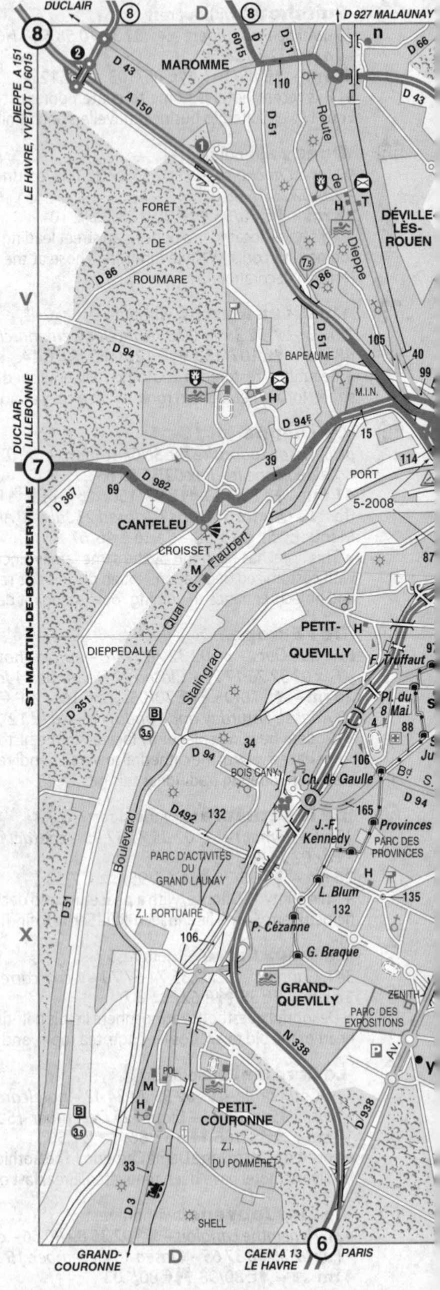

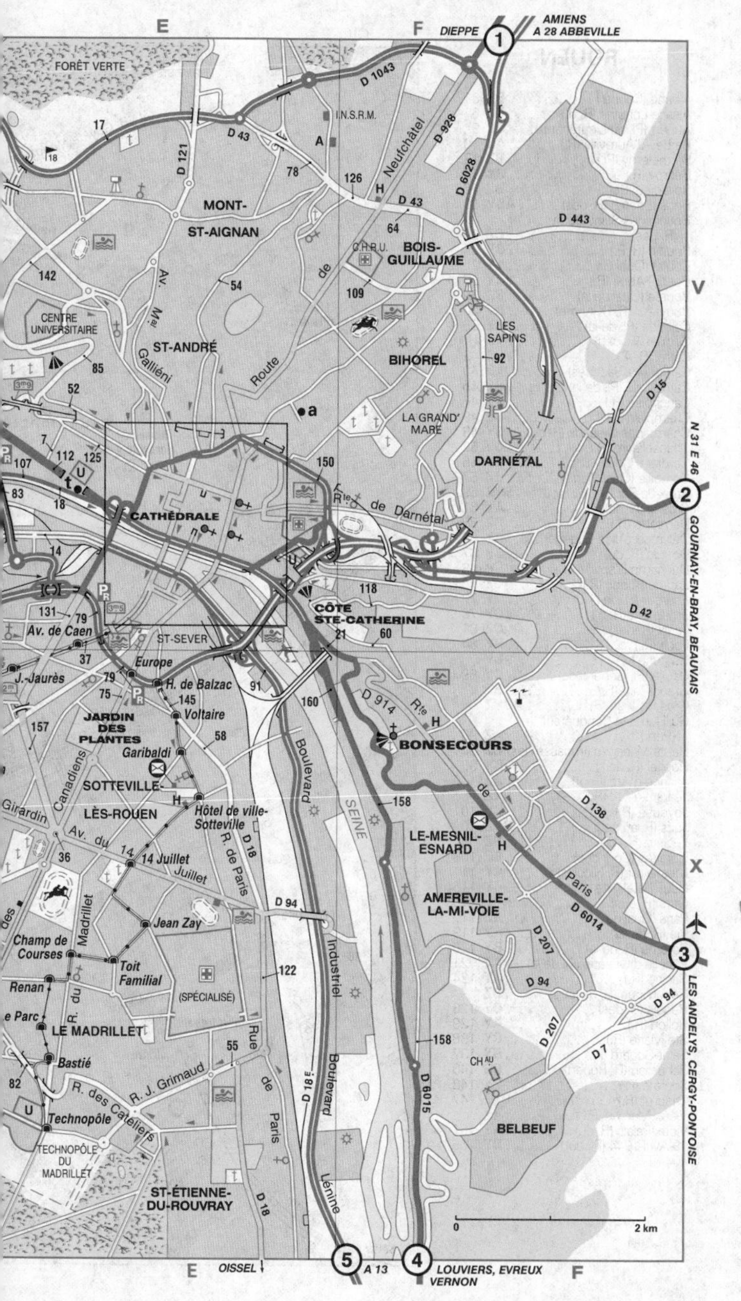

E
F
DIEPPE
AMIENS
A 28 ABBEVILLE
FORÊT VERTE
D 1043
I.N.S.R.M.
D 43
D 121
MONT-
ST-AIGNAN
Neufchâtel
D 928
D 6028
D 443
C.H.R.U.
BOIS-
GUILLAUME
CENTRE
UNIVERSITAIRE
ST-ANDRÉ
Route
de
BIHOREL
LES
SAPINS
LA GRAND' MARE
DARNÉTAL
CATHÉDRALE
Rte de Darnétal
CÔTE
STE-CATHERINE
ST-SEVER
D 42
D 914
BONSECOURS
JARDIN
DES
PLANTES
SOTTEVILLE-
LÈS-ROUEN
Hôtel de ville-
Sotteville
SEINE
LE-MESNIL-
ESNARD
AMFREVILLE-
LA-MI-VOIE
D 6014
D 138
D 15
N 31 E 46
GOURNAY-EN-BRAY, BEAUVAIS
LES ANDELYS, CERGY-PONTOISE
Europe
H. de Balzac
Voltaire
Garibaldi
14 Juillet
Jean Zay
Champ de Courses
Toit Familial
Renan
Bastié
Technopôle
TECHNOPÔLE
DU
MADRILLET
LE MADRILLET
(SPÉCIALISÉ)
R. des Cateliers
R. J. Grimaud
ST-ÉTIENNE-
DU-ROUVRAY
Boulevard Industriel
Boulevard Lénine
D 6015
D 207
D 94
D 7
BELBEUF
0
2 km
OISSEL
A 13
LOUVIERS, EVREUX
VERNON
V
X

ROUEN

Albane (Cour d') BZ 3
Alsace-Lorraine (R. d') CZ 6
Aubert (Pl. du Lieutenant) CZ 9
Barbey-d'Aurevilly (R.) AZ 10
Barthélemy (Pl.) BZ 12
Belfroy (R.) BY 13
Boieldieu (Pont) BZ 16
Bons-Enfants (R. des) ABY 19
Boucheries-Saint-Ouen (R. des) CZ 22
Boudin (R. E.) BY 24
Boulet (Quai G.) AY 25
Bourg-l'Abbé (R.) CY 27
Bourse (Quai de la) BZ 28
Bouvreuil (R. St-André) BY 30
Calende (Pl. de la) BZ 35
Carmes (R. des) BYZ
Carrel (R. A.) CZ 42
Cartier (Av. Jacques) AZ 43
Cathédrale (Pl. de la) BZ 45
Cauchoise (R.) AY 46
Champlain (Av.) BZ 49
Champ-des-Oiseaux (R. du) BY 48
Chasselièvre (R.) AY 52
Cordier (R. du) BY 56
Corneille (Quai Pierre) BZ 57
Croix-de-Fer (R.) BYZ 59
Crosne (R. de) AY 61
Damiette (R.) CZ 63
Delacroix (Allée Eugène) BY 66
Donjon (R. du) BY 67
Duchamp (Espl. M.) BY 68
Eau-de-Robec (R.) CZ 70
Écureuil (R. de l') BY 72
Ernemont (R. d') CY 76
Faulx (R. des) CZ 81
Foch (Pl.) BY 84
Ganterie (R.) BY
Gaulle (Pl. Général-de) CY 89
Grand-Pont (R.) BZ
Gros-Horloge (R. du) ABYZ
Guillaume-le-Conquérant (Pont) AZ 93
Hauts-Mariages (Impasse des) CZ 94
Hôpital (R. de l') BY 96
Jeanne-d'Arc (Pont) AZ 100
Jeanne-d'Arc (R.) BYZ
Joyeuse (R.) CY 101
Juifs (R. aux) BYZ 102
Leclerc (R. du Gén.) BZ
Libraires (Cour des) BZ 108
Mesnager (R. Nicolas) AY 111
Neufchatel (Rte de) CY 115
Ours (R. aux) ABZ 116
Paris (Quai de) BZ 117
Pie (R. de la) AY 119
Poterne (R. de la) BY 120
Pucelle-d'Orléans (Pl. de la) AZ 121
Racine (R.) AY 124
République (R. de la) BZ
Requis (R. des) CY 128
Rollon (R.) AY 129
Ste-Marie (R.) CY 138
Saint-Godard (Pl.) BY 137
Schuman (R. Robert) CS 140
Socrate (R.) BY 143
Thouret (R.) BYZ 147
Vieux-Marché (Pl. du) AY
Vieux-Palais (R. du) AY 152
19-Avril-1944 (Pl. du) BY 155

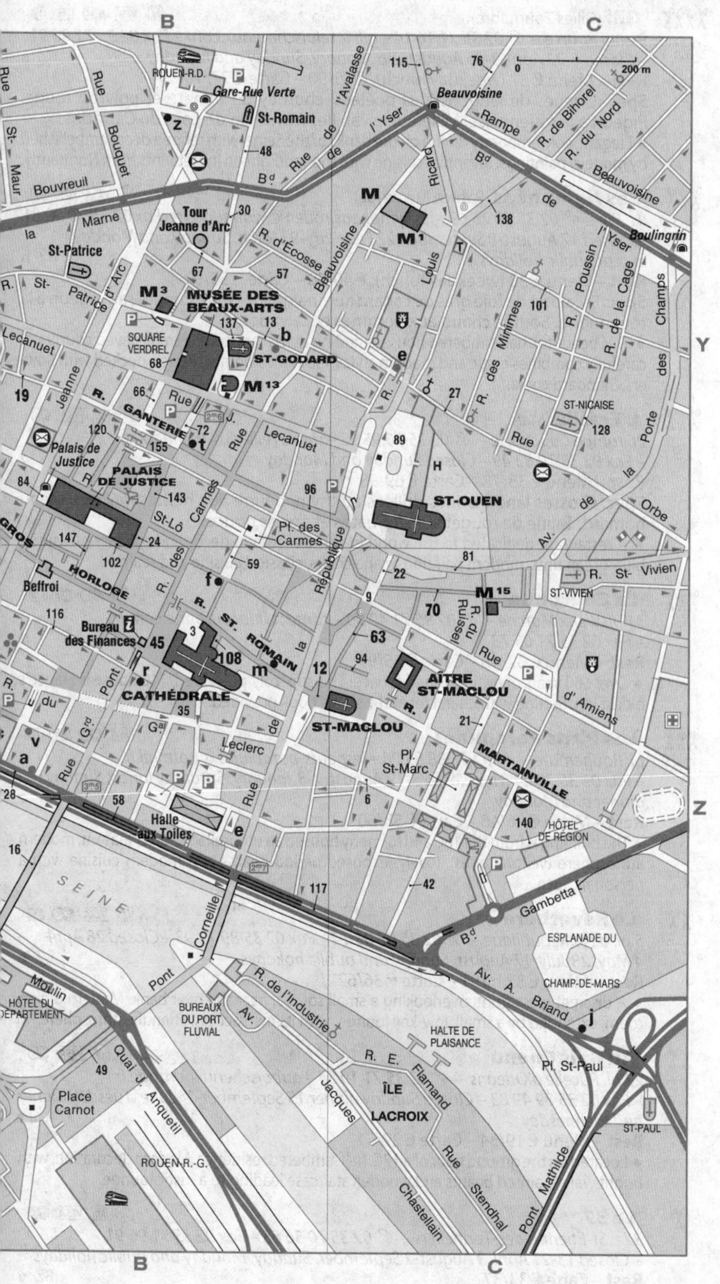
B
C
Y
Z
0
200 m
ROUEN-R.D.
Gare-Rue Verte
St-Romain
Beauvoisine
Rampe
R. de Bihorel
R. du Nord
Beauvoisine
Boulingrin
Rue Bouquet
Rue St-Maur
Bouvreuil
Marne
Rue de l'Avalasse
l'Yser
Bd de l'Yser
Tour Jeanne d'Arc
R. d'Écosse
Beauvoisine
Ricard
Louis
M
M1
St-Patrice
R. St-Patrice
d'Arc
M3
MUSÉE DES BEAUX-ARTS
SQUARE VERDREL
ST-GODARD
M13
Lecanuet
Jeanne
R. GANTERIE
Rue Lecanuet
Palais de Justice
PALAIS DE JUSTICE
R. St-Lô
Rue des Carmes
Pl. des Carmes
République
ST-OUEN
H
R. des Minimes
R. Poussin
R. de la Cage
Champs
Rue des Champs
ST-NICAISE
Rue de la Porte
Av. de la Orbe
R. St-Vivien
ST-VIVIEN
M15
R. du Ruissel
GROS HORLOGE
Beffroi
Bureau des Finances
R. ST-ROMAIN
CATHÉDRALE
AÎTRE ST-MACLOU
ST-MACLOU
Rue d'Amiens
R. MARTAINVILLE
Pl. St-Marc
Rue de la
Rue Gal Leclerc
Rue Grd Pont
R. du
Halle aux Toiles
HÔTEL DE RÉGION
SEINE
Pont Corneille
Gambetta
Bd
ESPLANADE DU CHAMP-DE-MARS
Av. A. Briand
Moulin
HÔTEL DU DÉPARTEMENT
BUREAUX DU PORT FLUVIAL
R. de l'Industrie
Av.
HALTE DE PLAISANCE
R. E. Flamand
ÎLE LACROIX
Pl. St-Paul
ST-PAUL
Place Carnot
Quai J. Anquetil
Jacques
ROUEN-R.-G.
Rue Stendhal
Chastellain
Pont Mathilde
115
76
48
30
138
67
57
101
137
13
b
68
19
66
72
120
155
t
e
27
89
128
84
143
96
147
24
102
59
22
81
f
9
70
116
3
45
108
r
m
12
63
94
21
35
v
a
28
58
6
140
e
16
117
42
49
j
z

Gill (Gilles Tournadre)
9 quai Bourse – ☎ 02 35 71 16 14 – gill@relaischateaux.com – Fax 02 35 71 96 91 – Closed 6-22 April, 3-26 August, 2-6 January, Sunday and Monday BZ **a**
Rest – Menu € 37 (weekday lunch), € 65/90 – Carte € 77/107
Spec. Queues de langoustines poêlées, chutney de tomate et poivron rouge. Pigeon à la rouennaise. Millefeuille vanille. **Wines** Vin de pays du Calvados.
◆ Elegant, contemporary dining on the banks of the Seine, with refined decor embellished by modern paintings. Inventive cuisine with the spotlight on ingredients from Normandy.

Les Nymphéas (Patrice Kukurudz)
9 r. Pie – ☎ 02 35 89 26 69 – lesnympheas.rouen@wanadoo.fr – Fax 02 35 70 98 81 – Closed 17 August-8 September, 22 February-9 March, Sunday and Monday except public holidays AY **h**
Rest – Menu € 30 (weekday lunch), € 40/50 – Carte € 55/91
Spec. Escalope de foie gras de canard au vinaigre de cidre. Canard sauvageon à la rouennaise. Soufflé chaud aux pommes et calvados.
◆ This beautiful, half-timbered house, standing at the far end of a small paved courtyard, carefully combines rustic and modern styles. Pleasant summer terrace, decked with flowers. Standard cooking.

L'Écaille (Marc Tellier)
26 rampe Cauchoise – ☎ 02 35 70 95 52 – marc.Tellier3@wanadoo.fr – Fax 02 35 70 83 49 – Closed Sunday and Monday AY **g**
Rest – Menu € 33/78 – Carte € 69/98
Spec. Grosses langoustines grillées au thym, beurre aux herbes fraîches. Menu homard. Tajine de rouget aux aromates et épices douces.
◆ A restaurant dedicated to the world of the sea both in decor and culinary pleasures; blue-green tints, modern paintings, cane chairs, classical cuisine and seafood.

La Couronne
31 pl. Vieux Marché – ☎ 02 35 71 40 90 – contact@lacouronne.com.fr – Fax 02 35 71 05 78 AY **d**
Rest – Menu € 32/48 – Carte € 55/93
◆ Over 660 years of distinguished service! This superbly-preserved, 14C house is France's oldest inn. Setting with character and visitor's book provided.

Les P'tits Parapluies
pl. Rougemare – ☎ 02 35 88 55 26 – lespetits-parapluies@hotmail.fr – Fax 02 35 70 24 31 – Closed 3-19 August, 2-8 January, Saturday lunch, Sunday dinner and Monday CY **e**
Rest – Menu € 26/46 – Carte € 53/60
◆ The building is from the 16C and formerly housed an umbrella factory. Pleasant, modern atmosphere (yellow tones), lovely, exposed period beams and modern cuisine with a personal touch.

Le Reverbère
5 pl. de la République – ☎ 02 35 07 03 14 – Fax 02 35 89 77 93 – Closed 28 April-4 May, 28 July-17 August, Sunday and public holidays BZ **e**
Rest – Menu € 37 bi/51 – Carte € 36/62
◆ A discreet glass front, overlooking a small square, near the river bank. Modern dining room, extended by a small, low-key lounge, with its own access. Friendly atmosphere.

Au Bois Chenu
23 pl. Pucelle d'Orléans – ☎ 02 35 71 19 54 – auboischenu@orange.fr – Fax 02 35 89 49 83 – Closed Sunday dinner 15 September-1st June, Tuesday dinner and Wednesday AY **r**
Rest – Menu € 19/34 – Carte € 27/51
◆ Located on the ground floor of a 17C, half-timbered residence. Modern decoration, with bright walls, painted beams and wooden staircase leading to a rustic lounge.

Le 37
37 r. St-Étienne-des-Tonneliers – ☎ 02 35 70 56 65 – Fax 02 35 71 96 91 – Closed 13-21 April, 3 August-2 September, Sunday, Monday and public holidays
Rest – Carte € 33/37 BZ **v**
◆ Modern style, Japanese-style decor and a relaxed atmosphere under the auspices of a chef who successfully conjures up the latest dishes. So maybe 37 is a lucky number!

in Franqueville-St-Pierre 9 km southeast by ③ and D 6014 – pop. 5 099 – alt. 140 m – ✉ 76520

Le Vert Bocage
rte de Paris – ✆ 02 35 80 14 74 – vert.bocage@wanadoo.fr – Fax 02 35 80 55 73 – Closed 11-25 August and 2-16 January
19 rm – €47/50 €51/54, €6 – ½ P €50/54 – **Rest** – *(closed Sunday evening and Monday)* Menu (€12,50), €20/40 – Carte €26/42
◆ In a convient location off the main road and close to Boos Airport, offering spacious, bright, soundproofed rooms. This restaurant's name evokes the Norman countryside, but the menu is inspired by the sea. Choose something from the grill or a traditional French dish.

at Parc des Expositions (exhibition park) 6 km south by N 138 – ✉ 76800 St-Étienne-du-Rouvray

Novotel
r. Mare aux Sangsues – ✆ 02 32 91 76 76 – h0432@accor.com – Fax 02 32 91 76 86 DX **y**
134 rm – €104/115 €117/127, €13 – **Rest** – Carte €23/38
◆ Comfortable hotel, pleasantly located on the edge of a forest. Rooms are being gradually renovated. Efficient double-glazing. Spacious and bright dining room. Tables set around the pool in summer.

in Petit Quevilly 3 km southwest – pop. 22 332 – alt. 5 m – ✉ 76140

Les Capucines
16 r. J. Macé – ✆ 02 35 72 62 34 – capucines@cegetel.net – Fax 02 35 03 23 84 – Closed 3 weeks in August, Saturday lunch, Sunday dinner and Monday DX **s**
Rest – Menu €27/52 – Carte €41/62
◆ There is a big, colourful and well-kept restaurant dining room, adorned with paintings, behind the spick-and-span façade. The four, small lounges are reserved for business meals only.

in Montigny 10 km by ⑦, D 94E and D 86 – pop. 1 114 – alt. 110 m – ✉ 76380

Le Relais de Montigny
r. Lieutenant Aubert – ✆ 02 35 36 05 97 – info@le-relais-de-montigny.com – Fax 02 35 36 19 60 – Closed 19 December-5 January
21 rm – €55 €80/86, €10 – ½ P €69/73
Rest – *(closed Friday dinner, Sunday dinner from 20 October to 15 March and Wednesday lunch)* Menu €22 (weekdays)/37 – Carte €31/40
◆ A 1960s building high above town. Choose the rooms overlooking the garden full of flowers (large, peaceful and with balconies). Stop for a meal in this bright restaurant dining room, extended by a green terrace. Traditional menu.

in Notre-Dame-de-Bondeville 8 km northwest – pop. 7 652 – alt. 25 m – ✉ 76960

Les Elfes
303 r. Longs Vallons – ✆ 02 35 74 36 21 – elfes2@wanadoo.fr – Fax 02 35 75 27 09 – Closed 22 July-18 August, Sunday dinner and Wednesday DV **n**
Rest – Menu (€16), €20/40 – Carte €29/61
◆ This regional-style inn is located below a railway line. Its neo-country setting is adorned with coloured tiles. Traditional cuisine.

ROUFFACH – 68 Haut-Rhin – 315 H9 – pop. 4 187 – alt. 204 m – ✉ 68250

Alsace-Lorraine 1 **A3**

Paris 479 – Basel 61 – Belfort 57 – Colmar 16 – Guebwiller 10 – Mulhouse 28 – Thann 26

Office de tourisme, place de la République ✆ 03 89 78 53 15, Fax 03 89 49 75 30

Alsace Golf Club Moulin de Biltzheim, East: 2 km by D 8, ✆ 03 89 78 52 12.

Château d'Isenbourg rest,
– 03 89 78 58 50
– isenbourg@grandesetapes.fr – Fax 03 89 78 53 70
40 rm – €125/440 €125/440, €23 – 1 suite – ½ P €148/305
Rest – Menu €45 bi/86 – Carte €49/86
◆ This 18C château overlooking the old town is surrounded by vineyards. Large, slightly antiquated, plush bedrooms. Sports facilities (fitness centre, tennis court) and a recently opened spa. The château offers two dining options: a 14C vaulted cellar or classic dining room.

A la Ville de Lyon without rest
r. Poincaré – 03 89 49 65 51 – villedelyon@villes-et-vignoble.com
– Fax 03 89 49 76 67
48 rm – €48/59 €55/135, €8,50
◆ An attractive façade refurbished in Renaissance style. The newly renovated rooms have a cosy, contemporary and country-style appearance; the older rooms are more functional. Mosaic swimming pool.

Philippe Bohrer
r. Poincaré – 03 89 49 62 49 – villedelyon@villes-et-vignoble.com
– Fax 03 89 49 76 67 – Closed 3-16 March and 21 July-3 August
Rest – *(closed Monday lunch, Wednesday lunch and Sunday)* Menu €27/80
– Carte €57/64
Rest *Brasserie Chez Julien* – 03 89 49 69 80 – Menu €10/30 – Carte €23/51
Spec. Escalope de foie de canard, streussel à l'amande. Aile et cuisse de pigeon sur crème de petits pois. Déclinaison de rhubarbe à la fraise (season). **Wines** Riesling, Pinot noir.
◆ Sample a personalised, inventive cuisine accompanied by a well-stocked wine cellar (fine selection of Alsace vintages) in a country-chic interior of pinewood. An elegant, friendly brasserie atmosphere in what used to be a cinema.

in Bollenberg 6 km southwest by D 83 and secondary road – ✉ 68250 Westhalten

Auberge au Vieux Pressoir
– 03 89 49 60 04 – info@bollenberg.com – Fax 03 89 49 76 16
– Closed 24-27 December
Rest – Menu €26/73 bi – Carte €28/89
◆ The Alsace setting of this winegrower's house is dominated by fine cupboards and a collection of antique arms. Well-prepared regional dishes and tasting of the local vintages.

ROUFFIAC-TOLOSAN – 31 Haute-Garonne – 343 H3 – see Toulouse

LE ROUGET – 15 Cantal – 330 B5 – pop. 901 – alt. 614 m – ✉ 15290 5 A3

Paris 549 – Aurillac 25 – Figeac 41 – Laroquebrou 15 – St-Céré 37 – Tulle 74

Des Voyageurs
– 04 71 46 10 14 – info@hotel-des-voyageurs.com – Fax 04 71 46 93 89
– Closed 23-27 February
24 rm – €54/57 €54/57, €7,50 – ½ P €54/57 – **Rest** – *(closed Sunday dinner from 15 September to 1st May)* Menu €13 (weekdays)/31 – Carte €23/42
◆ Lively stone building in a small Cantal village. The view from the bedrooms, currently being refurbished, will delight nature lovers. The chef prepares dishes that are both regional and traditional in inspiration. Lovely summer terrace.

ROULLET – 16 Charente – 324 K6 – see Angoulême

LE ROURET – 06 Alpes-Maritimes – 341 D5 – pop. 3 428 – alt. 350 m – ✉ 06650

Paris 913 – Cannes 19 – Grasse 10 – Nice 28 – Toulon, 136 42 E2

Du Clos without rest
3 chemin des Ecoles – 04 93 77 39 18
11 rm – €120/150 €220/250, €15
◆ In a tranquil setting (garden) in the upper village, this elegant mansion with a converted barn offers Provençal-style guestrooms, decorated with individual touches.

XX **Le Clos St-Pierre** (Daniel Ettlinger)
pl. de l'Église – ✆ 04 93 77 39 18 – ettlingercath@aol.com – Fax 04 93 77 39 90 – Closed 23-31 December, 23 February-9 march, Tuesday and Wednesday
Rest – *(number of covers limited, pre-book) (set menu only)* Menu € 31 (weekday lunch), € 45/54
Spec. Saint-Jacques en coquille, crumble aux aromates (mid September to end March). Risotto aux girolles, fines tranches de jambon Iberico. Soupe de châtaignes, escalope de foie gras poêlé, rouelles d'oignon (October to February.).
Wines Côtes de Provence.
◆ On the church square, this welcoming inn serves delicious Mediterranean-inspired food (single set menu that changes daily). Tasteful Provençal interior and pretty terrace.

Good food without spending a fortune?
Look out for the Bib Gourmand

LES ROUSSES – 39 Jura – 321 G8 – pop. 2 927 – alt. 1 110 m – Winter sports : 1 100/1 680 m 40 – ✉ 39220 Burgundy-Jura 16 **B3**

Paris 461 – Genève 45 – Gex 29 – Lons-le-Saunier 64 – Nyon 25 – St-Claude 31
Office de tourisme, Fort des Rousses ✆ 03 84 60 02 55, Fax 03 84 60 52 03
des Rousses Route du Noirmont, East: 1 km by D 29, ✆ 03 84 60 06 25 ;
du Mont Saint-JeanEast: 1 km by D 29, ✆ 03 84 60 09 71.
Gorges de la Bienne ★ West: 3 km.

Chamois
230 montée du Noirmont – ✆ 03 84 60 01 48 – lechamois@wanadoo.fr – Fax 03 84 60 39 38 – Closed 7-21 April
13 rm – †€ 61 ††€ 61/98, ☕ € 10 – ½ P € 55 – **Rest** – Menu (€ 15), € 23 (dinner), € 36/49 – Carte € 33/47
◆ An isolated (non-smoking) chalet above the Rousses ski resort. A warm, contemporary interior in which wood prevails. Peaceful rooms, equipped with a DVD player. A view of the countryside, attractive table settings and creative cuisine.

Redoute
357 rte Blanche – ✆ 03 84 60 00 40 – info@hotellaredoute.com – Fax 03 84 60 04 59 – Closed 7 April-3 May and 13 October-6 December
25 rm – †€ 49/68 ††€ 49/68, ☕ € 8 – ½ P € 55/65 – **Rest** – Menu € 16/27 – Carte € 20/44
◆ This family-run hotel enjoys a good location, despite being near the road. Clean, light and well-soundproofed guestrooms with no frills. A large dining room with exposed beams and wrought-iron chandeliers. Local cuisine.

Du Village without rest
344 r. Pasteur – ✆ 03 84 34 12 75 – auloupblanc@free.fr – Fax 03 84 34 12 76
10 rm – †€ 44/52 ††€ 48/60, ☕ € 8
◆ A small, functional hotel with a central location and fresh, brightly coloured bedrooms. The breakfast room is also used as a lounge. Reception closed between noon and 5pm.

in la Cure 2.5 km southeast by N 5, Geneva road– ✉ 39220 Les Rousses – alt. 1 155 m

XX **Arbez Franco-Suisse** with rm
– ✆ 03 84 60 02 20 – hotel.arbez@netgdi.com – Fax 03 84 60 08 59
10 rm – †€ 49 ††€ 59, ☕ € 7
Rest – *(closed 1st-7 April, November, Sunday dinner and Monday dinner off season)* Menu € 28/36 – Carte € 37/51
Rest *Brasserie* – *(closed 1st-7 April, November, Sunday dinner and Monday dinner off season)* Menu (€ 13) – Carte € 16/33
◆ A border inn serving regional fare in a (non-smoking) dining room that sports a somewhat antiquated but endearing ambience. Simply furnished, wood-panelled guestrooms on the Franco-Swiss border. Cheese recipes in the Brasserie.

by D 25 5 km southwest – ✉ 39200 Prémanon

Darbella

551 rte Darbella – ✆ 03 84 60 78 30 – hotelladarbella@wanadoo.fr – Fax 03 84 60 76 01 – Open 1st June-1st October and 1st December -30 April

16 rm – €39/65 €52/75, €6 – ½ P €45/62 – **Rest** – *(closed Monday and Tuesday off season)* Menu (€11,50), €20/30 – Carte €20/44

♦ Skiers and walkers appreciate this hotel near a ski lift leading to the Rousses domain. Refurbished and well cared for rooms; some designed for families. A small, rustic style dining room serving appetising regional and cheese dishes.

ROUSSILLON – 84 Vaucluse – 332 E10 – pop. 1 161 – alt. 360 m – ✉ 84220

Provence 42 **E1**

Paris 720 – Apt 11 – Avignon 46 – Bonnieux 12 – Carpentras 41 – Cavaillon 25 – Sault 31

Office de tourisme, place de la poste ✆ 04 90 05 60 25, Fax 04 90 05 63 31

Site★★.

Les Sables d'Ocre without rest

rte d'Apt – ✆ 04 90 05 55 55 – sablesdocre@free.fr – Fax 04 90 05 55 50 – Open April-October

22 rm – €65/78 €65/125, €10

♦ This recently-built and inviting farmhouse, set in the heart of Ochre Country, combines modern comfort and Provençal decoration. Cheerful painted metal furniture throughout.

David et Hôtel le Clos de la Glycine with rm ≤ cliffs and valley,

pl. de la Poste – ✆ 04 90 05 60 13 rm,

– le.clos.de.la.glycine@wanadoo.fr – Fax 04 90 05 75 80 – Closed mid January-mid February, Sunday dinner and Wednesday except May-15 October

9 rm – €100/150 €100/170, €13 – 1 suite – ½ P €108/143

Rest – *(pre-book Sat - Sun)* Menu €32/47 – Carte €57/62

♦ Village perched above the Chausée des Géants. Attractively-redecorated dining area and pleasant terrace. Southern style cuisine served. Individually-furnished rooms available.

Le Piquebaure-Côté Soleil

quartier les Estrayas, rte Gordes – ✆ 04 90 05 79 65 – Closed 15 November-15 December, January, Tuesday off season and Monday

Rest – *(dinner only except Sunday)* Menu €32/59 – Carte €40/58

♦ This restaurant takes its name from one of the rocks marking the Ocre circuit. Exposed beams, whitewashed walls hung with paintings. Market fresh cuisine.

ROUSSILLON – 38 Isère – 333 B5 – pop. 7 437 – alt. 200 m – ✉ 38150 44 B2

Paris 505 – Annonay 24 – Grenoble 92 – St-Étienne 68 – Tournon-sur-Rhône 44 – Vienne 19

Office de tourisme, place de l'Edit ✆ 04 74 86 72 07, Fax 04 74 29 74 76

Médicis without rest

r. Fernand Léger – ✆ 04 74 86 22 47 – info@hotelmedicis.fr – Fax 04 74 86 48 05

15 rm – €51 €60, €9

♦ Modern hotel in a quiet residential district with spacious, functional rooms; tiled floors but good soundproofing. Lounge with a large-screen TV.

ROUTOT – 27 Eure – 304 E5 – pop. 1 115 – alt. 140 m – ✉ 27350 Normandy

Paris 148 – Bernay 45 – Évreux 68 – Le Havre 57 – Pont-Audemer 19 – Rouen 36 33 **C2**

La Haye-de-Routot: thousand-year-old yew trees★ North: 4 km.

L'Écurie

pl. Mairie – ✆ 02 32 57 30 30 – patrick.bourgeois1@club.fr – Fax 02 32 57 30 30 – Closed 4-13 August, Tuesday dinner 15 October-31 March, Wednesday dinner, Sunday dinner and Monday

Rest – Menu €15 (weekday lunch), €28/38

♦ This post house near the covered market has a lounge with an attractive stone fireplace and rustic dining room. Traditional cuisine served.

ROUVRES-EN-XAINTOIS – 88 Vosges – 314 E3 – pop. 299 – alt. 330 m – ✉ 88500

26 **B3**

Paris 357 – Épinal 42 – Lunéville 58 – Mirecourt 9 – Nancy 51 – Neufchâteau 34 – Vittel 19

Burnel rm, VISA

– *03 29 65 64 10 – hotelburnel@burnel.fr – Fax 03 29 65 68 88*
– Closed 15-31 December and Sunday dinner off season
21 rm – €50 €62/79, €11 – 2 suites – ½ P €45/50
Rest – *(closed Sunday dinner except 13 July-21 September, Saturday lunch and Monday lunch)* Menu €15 (weekdays)/32 – Carte €33/61

◆ Spacious, very comfortable, countrified rooms. Some overlook the small flower-decked garden. Attractive dining area serving classic cuisine based on market produce.

ROUVROIS-SUR-OTHAIN – 55 Meuse – 307 E2 – see Longuyon (M.-et-M.)

ROYAN – 17 Charente-Maritime – 324 D6 – pop. 17 102 – alt. 20 m – Casino : Royan Pontaillac A – ✉ 17200 Atlantic Coast

38 **A3**

Paris 504 – Bordeaux 121 – Périgueux 183 – Rochefort 40 – Saintes 38

Office de tourisme, rond-point de la Poste 05 46 05 04 71, Fax 05 46 06 67 76

de Royan Saint-Palais-sur-Mer Maine Gaudin, by St-Palais-sur-Mer road: 7 km, 05 46 23 16 24.

Seafront ★ - Notre-Dame church /I★ **E** - Corniche★ and Conche★ de Pontaillac.

Plans on following pages

Novotel sea, rm, rest, VISA AE

6 Allée des Rochers, (Conche du chay) –
05 46 39 46 39 – H1173@accor.com – Fax 05 46 39 46 46 A **b**
83 rm – €122/186 €148/186, €15 – ½ P €118/137
Rest – Menu (€21), €26/31 – Carte €29/60

◆ A well located establishment overlooking the beach; thalassotherapy centre and pleasant rooms done in a contemporary style (balconies). Excellent traditional menu and splendid sea view in this Novotel restaurant.

Family Golf Hôtel without rest VISA AE

28 bd Garnier – 05 46 05 14 66 – family-golf-hotel@wanadoo.fr
– Fax 05 46 06 52 56 – Open 16 March-29 November C **m**
30 rm – €65/87 €71/107, €10

◆ This seafront establishment is regularly spruced up. Half of its rather spacious bedrooms have a sea view. Breakfast served on the terrace in summer.

Les Bleuets without rest VISA AE

21 façade de Foncillon – 05 46 38 51 79 – info@hotel-les-bleuets.com
– Fax 05 46 23 82 00 – Closed 19 December-4 January B **d**
16 rm – €50/88 €50/88, €7,50

◆ Subdued nautical-inspired decor, well-renovated rooms, view of the sea (balconies) or the garden: a pleasant establishment between the harbour and the town centre.

Rêve de Sable without rest VISA AE

10 pl. Foch – 05 46 06 52 25 – revedesable@wanadoo.fr
– Fax 05 46 06 49 87 C **z**
11 rm – €50/80 €50/120, €7

◆ The beach and centre of Royan are a stone's throw from this small family hotel. Light, well-equipped rooms, quieter and cooler to the rear (the others overlook the sea).

Les Filets Bleus VISA

14 r. Notre-Dame – 05 46 05 74 00 – Closed 29 June-6 July, 27 October-4 November, 2-10 January, Saturday lunch and Monday in July-August, Monday lunch and Sunday from September to June B **s**
Rest – Menu (€14), €17 (weekday lunch), €24/58 – Carte €39/60

◆ Restaurant dedicated to seafood and decorated to resemble a boat: blue and white colour scheme, wood, portholes, storm lamps. Special lobster menu in season.

ROYAN

Alsace-Lorraine (R.) . . . . B 3
Briand (Bd A.). . . . . B 5
Conche-du-Chay (Av. de la). A 6
Desplats (R. du Colonel) . . . B 7
Dr-Audouin (Bd du) . . . . B 8
Dr-Gantier (Pl. du) . . . . C 9
Dugua (R. P.) . . . . B 10
Europe (Cours de l') C
Façade de Foncillon . . . . . . B 12
Foch (Pl. Mar.) . . . . C 15
Foncillon (R. de) . . . . B 16
Font-de-Cherves (R.) . . . . . . B 17
Gambetta (R.) . . . . B
Gaulle (Pl. Ch.-de) . . . . B 19
Germaine-de-la-Falaise
(Bd) . . . . AB 20
Grandière (Bd de la) . . . . C 21
Leclerc (Av. Mar.) . . . . C 26
Libération (Av. de la) . . . . . . C 28
Loti (R. Pierre) . . . . B
Notre-Dame (R.) . . . . B 32
Parc (Av. du) . . . . C 35
République (Bd de la) . . . . . . B 40
Rochefort (Av. de) . . . . B 42
Schuman (Pl. R.) . . . . B 45
Semis (Av. des) . . . . C 46
Thibeaudeau (Rd-Pt du Cdt.) B 48
5-Janvier-1945 (Bd du) . . . . . B 52

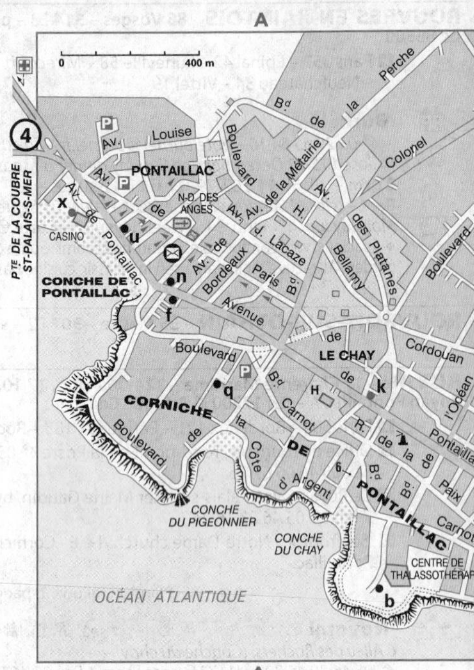

Le Relais de la Mairie

1 r. du Chay – ✆ 05 46 39 03 15
– Alain.gedoux@wanadoo.fr
– Fax 05 46 39 03 15
– Closed 17 November-7 December, Thursday dinner, Sunday dinner and Monday A **k**
Rest – Menu (€ 13), € 17 (weekdays)/34 – Carte € 30/51
◆ Restrained light interior, pleasantly set tables, traditional menu and family service: this little-known establishment is popular with the locals.

in Pontaillac – ✉ 17640

Pavillon Bleu et Résidence de Saintonge

12 allée des Algues – ✆ *05 46 39 00 00* rest, VISA
– le.pavillon.bleu@wanadoo.fr – Fax 05 46 39 07 00
– Open 12 April-20 September A **q**
37 rm (½ board only from 21 June to 6 September) – †€ 36/44 ††€ 46/64, ☕ € 7 – 5 suites – ½ P € 57
Rest – *(open 21 June-6 September) (dinner only) (residents only)*
◆ A substantial renovation programme is underway to breathe new life into this family establishment. The rooms already reveamped are contemporary and pleasant. Traditional cuisine with a marine flavour and a fine selection of Bordeaux wines.

Miramar without rest

VISA
173 av. Pontaillac – ✆ *05 46 39 03 64*
– miramaroyan@wanadoo.fr
– Fax 05 46 39 23 75 A **n**
27 rm – †€ 57/154 ††€ 57/154, ☕ € 10
◆ This well-maintained 1950s building is just across the road from Royan's most fashionable beach. Rather spacious rooms, choose one facing the sea.

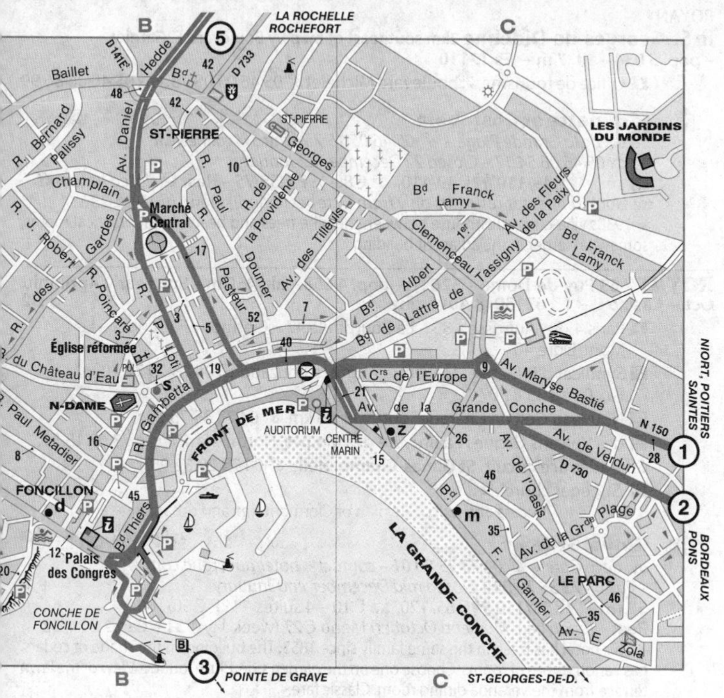

Grand Hôtel de Pontaillac without rest

195 av. Pontaillac – ✆ 05 46 39 00 44 – resa-royan@monalisahotels.com – Fax 05 46 39 04 05 – Open 22 March-31 December A **u**

40 rm – 🛉€ 85/150 🛉🛉€ 85/150, ☕ € 11

◆ This hotel undergoing renovation overlooks Pontaillac Beach. The breakfast room and about half the bedrooms command a fine view of the Atlantic.

Belle-Vue without rest

122 av. Pontaillac – ✆ 05 46 39 06 75 – belle-vueroyan@wanadoo.fr – Fax 05 46 39 44 92 – Open from March to October A **f**

22 rm – 🛉€ 48/78 🛉🛉€ 48/78, ☕ € 7

◆ Situated on an avenue, a vast modernised 1950s villa. The average-sized rooms are prudently rustic and well-kept; ask for one overlooking the sea. Family ambiance.

La Jabotière

Conche de Pontaillac, VISA MC AE

espl. Pontaillac – ✆ 05 46 39 91 29 – Fax 05 46 38 39 93 – Closed 12-18 October, 20-27 December, January, Wednesday dinner, Sunday dinner and Monday A **x**

Rest – Menu € 16 (lunch)/78 – Carte € 50/73

◆ A plush yet rustic beachside restaurant overlooking the Atlantic. Traditional menu and fish; bistro-style lunches.

St-Palais road 3.5 km by ④ – ✉ 17640 Vaux-sur-Mer

Résidence de Rohan without rest

Conche de Nauzan – ✆ 05 46 39 00 75 – info@residence-rohan.com – Fax 05 46 38 29 99 – Open 26 March-10 November

44 rm – 🛉€ 75/132 🛉🛉€ 75/132, ☕ € 11

◆ This handsome 19C residence once housed the Duchess of Rohan's literary salon. It is augmented by a villa in a park overlooking the beach. Romantic rooms, lovely period furniture.

in St-Georges-de-Didonne **2km southeast of map by Boulevard F. Garnier – pop. 5 034 – alt. 7 m – ✉ 17110**

Office de tourisme, 7, boulevard Michelet ✆ 05 46 05 09 73, Fax 05 46 06 36 99

Colinette et Costabela

16 av. de la Grande Plage – ✆ 05 46 05 15 75 – infos@colinette.fr – Fax 05 46 06 54 17 – Closed 22 December-22 January

21 rm – €49/110 €49/110, €8 – ½ P €55/75 – **Rest** – *(closed lunch off season) (dinner for residents only from October to April)* Menu (€19), €23

◆ 1930s villa-cum-guesthouse between the pine trees and beach. Light practical rooms, somewhat larger in the adjacent building.

ROYAT – **63 Puy-de-Dôme – 326** F8 – **pop. 4 658 – alt. 450 m – Spa : early April-mid Oct. – Casino** B – **✉ 63130** **Auvergne** 5 **B2**

Paris 423 – Aubusson 89 – La Bourboule 47 – Clermont-Ferrand 5 – Le Mont-Dore 40

Syndicat d'initiative, 1, avenue Auguste Rouzaud ✆ 04 73 29 74 70, Fax 04 73 35 81 07

Nouveau Golf de CharadeSouthwest: 6 km, ✆ 04 73 35 73 09 ;

des Volcans Orcines La Bruyère des Moines, North: 9 km, ✆ 04 73 62 15 51.

Charade race circuit, St Genès-Champanelle ✆ 04 73 29 52 95.

St-Léger church ★.

Access and exits: See plan of Clermont-Ferrand urban area.

Royal St-Mart

av. de la Gare – ✆ 04 73 35 80 01 – contact@hotel-auvergne.com – Fax 04 73 35 75 92 – Closed mid December-end January B **n**

55 rm – €55/110 €65/120, €10 – 4 suites – ½ P €50/100

Rest – *(open beg. May-end October)* Menu €27 (weekdays)/31 – Carte €24/52

◆ This hotel has been in the same family since 1853. The building, in the shade of cedars, has various types of rooms. Choose one on the garden side. Plush lounge. View of the lawn terrace from the veranda dining room. Classic fare.

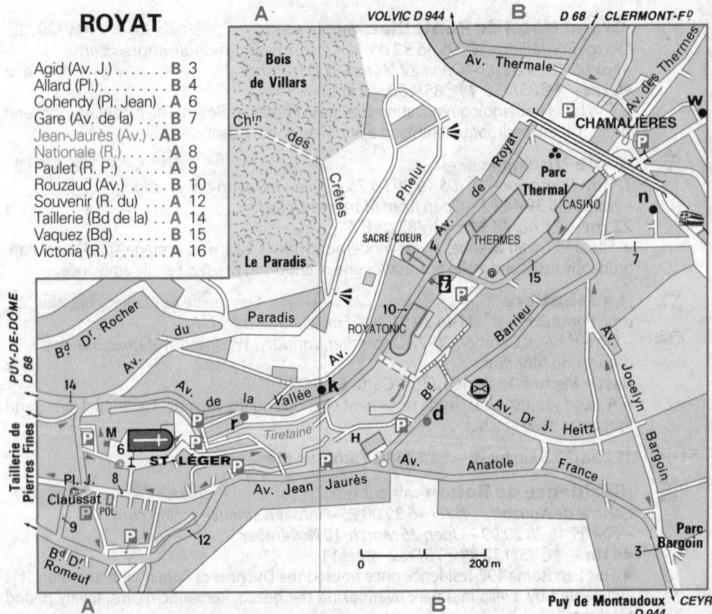

Le Chatel rest, VISA

20 av. Vallée – ✆ 04 73 29 53 00 – info@hotel-le-chatel.com – Fax 04 73 29 53 29 – Closed 15 December-15 January, Friday, Saturday and Sunday from November to March B **k**

26 rm – †€ 55/58 ††€ 61/64, ☕ € 8,50 – 4 suites – ½ P € 51/53

Rest – Menu (€ 13), € 16/43 – Carte € 29/44

♦ An old building with well-kept rooms opposite a park on the banks of the Tiretaine. The largest rooms occupy a neighbouring house. Renovated suites. Pleasant dining room. Traditional and regional cooking, as well as slimline set menus.

Château de Charade without rest

5 km south-west on D 941 and D 5 – ✆ 04 73 35 91 67 – chateau-de-charade@orange.fr – Fax 04 73 29 92 09 – Open 31 March-7 November

5 rm – †€ 68/76 ††€ 68/76, ☕ € 6

♦ Château, dating from the 17C and 19C, on the edge of the Royat golf course. The rooms, all of which overlook the park, are decorated with antique furniture. Attractive lounge and billiard table.

La Belle Meunière with rm VISA

25 av. Vallée – ✆ 04 73 35 80 17 – info@la-belle-meuniere.com – Fax 04 73 35 67 85 – Closed 8-16 March, 11-31 August, Saturday lunch, Sunday dinner and Monday A **r**

6 rm – †€ 48/80 ††€ 55/135, ☕ € 10 – ½ P € 72/95 – **Rest** – Menu € 17 (weekday lunch), € 28/70 – Carte € 42/75

♦ Situated on the banks of the Tiretaine, this restaurant serves innovative cuisine influenced by Asia and the Auvergne. Napoleon III decor, with Art Nouveau stained glass and chinoiseries. The romantic liaison between La Belle Meunière and General Boulanger has inspired the 19C decor of the hotel's bedrooms.

La Pépinière with rm rest, VISA

11 av. Pasteur, (Puy-de-Dôme road) – ✆ 04 73 35 81 19 – info@hotel-la-pepiniere.com – Fax 04 73 35 99 58 – Closed 11-31 August, 2-6 January, Sunday dinner and Monday

4 rm – †€ 45 ††€ 47, ☕ € 6,50 – **Rest** – Menu € 14,50 (weekday lunch)/60 – Carte € 53/61

♦ This rustic dining room above the spa resort, enlivened by contemporary pictures, serves modern cuisine and regional dishes. Renovated rooms.

L'Hostalet VISA

47 bd Barrieu – ✆ 04 73 35 82 67 – Closed 4 January-12 March, Sunday except public holidays and Monday B **d**

Rest – Menu € 16 (weekday lunch), € 23 € bi/34 – Carte € 23/36

♦ The timeless traditional dishes and an extensive wine list are appreciated by the regulars of this family restaurant with a slightly antiquated decor.

ROYE – 80 Somme – 301 J9 – pop. 6 529 – alt. 88 m – ✉ 80700

Northern France and the Paris Region 36 **B2**

Paris 113 – Compiègne 42 – Amiens 44 – Arras 75 – St-Quentin 61

La Flamiche (Marie-Christine Borck-Klopp) VISA

20 pl. Hôtel de Ville – ✆ 03 22 87 00 56 – restaurantlaflamiche@wanadoo.fr – Fax 03 22 78 46 77 – Closed 4-26 August, 2-12 January, Sunday dinner, Tuesday lunch and Monday

Rest – Menu € 32 (weekdays)/178 bi – Carte € 76/109

Spec. Flamiche aux poireaux (October to end April). Turbot côtier à la plancha. Caneton croisé aux baies et vinaigre de sureau.

♦ Artwork on display in the pleasant dining areas in Picardy style. Modern cuisine with regional touches.

Le Florentin Hôtel Central with rm rest, rm, VISA

36 r. Amiens – ✆ 03 22 87 11 05 – Fax 03 22 87 42 74 – Closed 11-25 August, Sunday dinner and Monday

8 rm – †€ 45 ††€ 48, ☕ € 6 – **Rest** – Menu € 16/42 – Carte € 31/52

♦ Restaurant with a red brick façade and Italian-inspired decor including columns, mouldings, marble and frescoes. Traditional cuisine. Functional rooms.

Le Roye Gourmet
1 pl. de la République – ✆ 03 22 87 10 87 – leroye.gourmet@orange.fr – Closed 11-23 August, 2-10 January, Sunday dinner and Monday
Rest – Menu € 16 (weekdays)/45 – Carte € 33/64
◆ Situated on a pretty square, this restaurant specialises in regionally-inspired classical cuisine. One dining room is furnished in contemporary style; the other is adorned with paintings.

Hostellerie La Croix d'Or
123 r. St-Gilles – ✆ 03 22 87 11 57 – Fax 03 22 87 09 81 – Closed Saturday lunch and dinner except Friday and Saturday
Rest – Menu (€ 12), € 17 (weekdays)/35 – Carte € 39/70
◆ A pleasant country atmosphere reigns within the walls of this inn, at the town entrance. Tasty classic cuisine.

ROYE – 70 Haute-Saône – 314 H6 – see Lure

LE ROZIER – 48 Lozère – 330 H9 – pop. 153 – alt. 400 m – ✉ 48150

Languedoc-Roussillon-Tarn Gorges — 22 **B1**

Paris 632 – Florac 57 – Mende 63 – Millau 23 – Sévérac-le-Château 23 – Le Vigan 72

Office de tourisme, route de Meyrueis ✆ 05 65 62 60 89, Fax 05 65 62 60 27

Terrasses du Truel ≤★ East: 3,5 km - Gorges du Tarn★★★.

Chaos de Montpellier-le-Vieux★★★ South: 11,5 km - Corniche du Causse Noir ≤★★ Southeast: 13 km then 15 mn.

Grand Hôtel de la Muse et du Rozier
rest, VISA
in La Muse (D 907), right bank of the Tarn ✉ 12720 Peyreleau (Aveyron) – ✆ 05 65 62 60 01 – info@hotel-delamuse.fr – Fax 05 65 62 63 88 – Open 21 March-12 November
38 rm – €65/80 €85/160, €13
Rest – *(dinner only)* Menu € 33/65 – Carte € 55/70
◆ A private beach on the banks of the Tarn in the garden of this venerable grand hotel. Contemporary minimalist interior that enhances the magnificent surrounding scenery. A creative menu focusing on local produce; riverside terrace.

Doussière without rest VISA
– ✆ 05 65 62 60 25 – galtier.christine@libertysurf.fr – Fax 05 65 62 65 48 – Open Easter-10 November
20 rm – €37/60 €37/60, €8
◆ Two village buildings standing on either side of the Jonte with the older bedrooms situated in the wing. Pleasant view from the breakfast room. Fitness centre.

RUE – 80 Somme – 301 D6 – pop. 3 075 – alt. 9 m – ✉ 80120

Northern France and the Paris Region — 36 **A1**

Paris 212 – Abbeville 28 – Amiens 77 – Berck-Plage 22 – Le Crotoy 8

Office de tourisme, 10, place Anatole Gosselin ✆ 03 22 25 69 94, Fax 03 22 25 76 26

St-Esprit chapel ★: interior★★.

in St-Firmin 3 km west by D 4 – ✉ 80550 Le Crotoy

Auberge de la Dune
rm, rm, VISA
1352 r. Dune – ✆ 03 22 25 01 88 – contact@auberge-de-la-dune.com – Fax 03 22 25 66 74 – Closed December
11 rm – €62/72 €62/72, € 10 – ½ P € 57/63 – **Rest** – Menu (€ 13), € 17 (weekdays)/33 – Carte € 21/41
◆ Isolated in the fields, this small inn is not far from the ornithological park. Rooms are sober, modern and practical; extremely well kept. Country-style dining room serving traditional cuisine and some local specialities.

RUEIL-MALMAISON – 92 Hauts-de-Seine – 311 J2 – 101 14 – see Paris, Area

RUILLÉ-FROID-FONDS – 53 Mayenne – 310 F7 – see Château-Gontier

RULLY – 71 Saône-et-Loire – 320 I8 – pop. 1 463 – alt. 220 m – ✉ 71150 8 C3

Paris 332 – Autun 43 – Beaune 20 – Chalon-sur-Saône 16 – Le Creusot 32

XX **Le Vendangerot** with rm

6 pl. Ste-Marie – ✆ 03 85 87 20 09 – Fax 03 85 91 27 18 – Closed 1st February-15 March, Tuesday and Wednesday

14 rm – †€ 51 ††€ 51, ☕ € 7 – **Rest** – Menu € 18 (weekdays)/45 – Carte € 45/52

◆ A village inn with a flower-decked façade facing a public garden. Dining room decorated with old photos relating to wine-growing. Regional specialities. Bedrooms with traditional charm.

RUMILLY – 74 Haute-Savoie – 328 I5 – pop. 11 230 – alt. 334 m – ✉ 74150

French Alps 45 C1

Paris 530 – Aix-les-Bains 21 – Annecy 19 – Bellegarde-sur-Valserine 37 – Genève 64

Office de tourisme, 4, place de l'Hôtel de Ville ✆ 04 50 64 58 32, Fax 04 50 01 03 53

X **Boîte à Sel**

27 r. Pont-Neuf – ✆ 04 50 01 02 52 – Fax 04 50 01 42 11 – Closed 1st-15 August, Sunday dinner and Monday dinner

Rest – Menu € 22/29 – Carte € 25/37

◆ Modest restaurant in a busy street serving bistro-style cuisine. Friendly welcome and landscape garden trompe-l'œil decor.

RUNGIS – 94 Val-de-Marne – 312 D3 – 101 26 – see Paris, Area

RUOMS – Ardèche – 331 I7 – pop. 2 132 – alt. 121 m – ✉ 07120

Lyon - Rhone Valley 44 A3

Paris 651 – Alès 54 – Aubenas 24 – Pont-St-Esprit 49

Syndicat d'initiative, rue Alphonse Daudet ✆ 04 75 93 91 90

Labeaume★ West: 4 km - Défilé de Ruoms★.

X **Le Savel** with rm

rte des Brasseries – ✆ 04 75 39 60 02 – hotel-le-savel@wanadoo.fr – Fax 04 75 39 76 02 – Rest closed 14-30 September, Monday from May to September, Saturday from October to April and Sunday

14 rm – †€ 54/68 ††€ 54/68, ☕ € 7 – ½ P € 53/60 – **Rest** – *(dinner only) (number of covers limited, pre-book)* Menu € 19/24 – Carte € 27/34

◆ The new owners, who are passionate about local produce, are gradually upgrading this impressive house and grounds dating from 1890. Neat bedrooms and 1940s style decor in the dining room.

RUPT-SUR-MOSELLE – 88 Vosges – 314 H5 – pop. 3 637 – alt. 424 m – ✉ 88360 27 C3

Paris 423 – Belfort 58 – Colmar 80 – Épinal 38 – Mulhouse 68 – St-Dié 63 – Vesoul 61

Centre rest,

r. de l'Église – ✆ 03 29 24 34 73 – hotelcentreperry@wanadoo.fr – Fax 03 29 24 45 26 – Closed 1st-8 May, 2-9 June, 6-13 October, Christmas holidays, Saturday lunch, Sunday evening and Monday

8 rm – †€ 46 ††€ 56, ☕ € 7,50 – ½ P € 50 – **Rest** – Menu € 13,50 (weekday lunch), € 25/48 – Carte € 36/51

◆ A Moselle style house near the church. Clean, comfortable and recently refurbished bedrooms. Informal atmosphere. The roasting spit in the dining room is now purely decorative. Traditional cooking.

Relais Benelux-Bâle

69 r. Lorraine – ✆ 03 29 24 35 40 – contact@benelux-bale.com – Fax 03 29 24 40 47 – Closed 27 July-5 August, 20 December-5 January and Sunday evening

10 rm – †€ 40/52 ††€ 45/62, ☕ € 8 – ½ P € 40/45 – **Rest** – Menu (€ 10), € 12,50 (weekdays)/33 – Carte € 23/47

◆ Rather inviting fully soundproofed roadside chalet. Light, simple and well-equipped bedrooms. The restaurant has been run by the same family since 1921 and offers traditional and regional cooking. Pleasant terrace.

RUSTREL – 84 Vaucluse – 332 F10 – pop. 614 – alt. 400 m – ✉ 84400

Provence 40 **B2**

Paris 747 – Aix-en-Provence 66 – Marseille 94 – Salon-de-Provence 70

La Forge without rest

Notre-Dame-des-Anges, 2 km via rte d'Apt and minor road – ✆ 04 90 04 92 22 – laforge@laforge.com.fr – Fax 04 88 10 05 76 – Open 1st March-15 November

5 rm ☕ – †€ 86/94 ††€ 91/99

◆ A former foundry, partly converted into a welcoming guesthouse, in the depths of what is nicknamed the Provençal Colorado. Large rooms with original and colourful decoration. Garden with an abundance of flowers and fine pool.

LES SABLES-D'OLONNE – 85 Vendée – 316 F8 – pop. 15 532 – alt. 4 m – Casinos : des Pins CY, des Atlantes AZ – ✉ 85100 Atlantic Coast 34 **A3**

Paris 456 – Cholet 107 – Nantes 102 – Niort 115 – La Roche-sur-Yon 36

Office de tourisme, 1, promenade Joffre ✆ 02 51 96 85 85, Fax 02 51 96 85 71

des Olonnes Olonne-sur-Merby La Roche-sur-Yon road: 6 km, ✆ 02 51 33 16 16 ;

de Port-Bourgenay Talmont-Saint-HilaireSouth: 17 km, ✆ 02 51 23 35 45.

Le Remblai★.

Plans on following pages

Mercure rest,

on Tanchet Lake, 2.5 km via coast road – ✆ 02 51 21 77 77 – H1078@accor.com – Fax 02 51 21 77 80 – Closed 6-27 January CY **f**

100 rm – †€ 96/151 ††€ 110/151, ☕ € 13 – ½ P € 89/110 – **Rest** – Menu (€ 26), € 30 – Carte € 31/39

◆ A modern building located within the thalassotherapy centre. Renovated modern bedrooms, decorated in the colours of the Vendée Globe race (overlooking the lake or pine forest). Panoramic restaurant and terrace; traditional and diet menus.

Atlantic Hôtel

5 prom. Godet – ✆ 02 51 95 37 71 – info@atlantichotel.fr – Fax 02 51 95 37 30

30 rm – †€ 61/88 ††€ 78/160, ☕ € 13 – ½ P € 65/106 BY **e**

Rest *Le Sloop* – *(closed 20 December-4 January, Friday and Sunday October-April) (dinner only)* Menu (€ 23), € 33/36 – Carte € 31/67

◆ A 1970s hotel with practical very well-kept bedrooms, some with sea view. The lounge, arranged around the indoor swimming pool, is topped by partially sliding glass roof. Beautiful ocean vista from the restaurant, decorated to look like a ship's cabin.

Arundel without rest

8 bd F. Roosevelt – ✆ 02 51 32 03 77 – arundelhotel@wanadoo.fr – Fax 02 51 32 86 28 – Closed 20 December-4 January AZ **k**

42 rm – †€ 65/150 ††€ 65/150, ☕ € 12

◆ This hotel, well-located opposite the casino, takes its name from a keep that became a lighthouse. Practical comfortable rooms, with balconies on the sea side.

Les Roches Noires without rest

12 promenade G. Clemenceau – ✆ 02 51 32 01 71 – info@bw-lesrochesnoires.com – Fax 02 51 21 61 00 BY **s**

37 rm – †€ 59/125 ††€ 59/125, ☕ € 10

◆ Hotel standing at the end of the beach, near the coast road. It offers practical, bright well soundproofed bedrooms (a few balconies). The breakfast room offers a pretty sea view.

LES SABLES D'OLONNE

Arago (Bd) . . . . BY 4
Baudry (R. P.). . . . . BY 5
Beauséjour (R.) . . . . BY 7
Briand (Av. A.) . . . . CY 9
Castelnau (Bd de) . . . . BY 12
Château-d'Olonne (Rte de) . . CY 13
Dr-Canteleau (R. du) . . . . AY 19
Dr-Schweitzer (R. du) . . . . CY 22
Doumer (Av. P.). . . . . CY 23
Estienne-d'Orves (Rd-Pt H. d') AY 25
Fricaud (R. D.) . . . . BY 26
Gabaret (Av. A.). . . . . BY 27
Godet (Prom. G.) . . . . BY 29
Ile Vertine (Bd de l'). . . . . AY 32
Nouch (Corniche du). . . . . AY 43
Nouettes (R. des) . . . . CY 44
Président-Kennedy (Prom.). . . . . CY 48
Rhin-et-Danube (Av.) . . . . CY 50
St-Nicolas (R.) . . . . AY 55
Sauniers (R. des). . . . . AY 57
Souvenir Français (Bd du) . . . AY 58

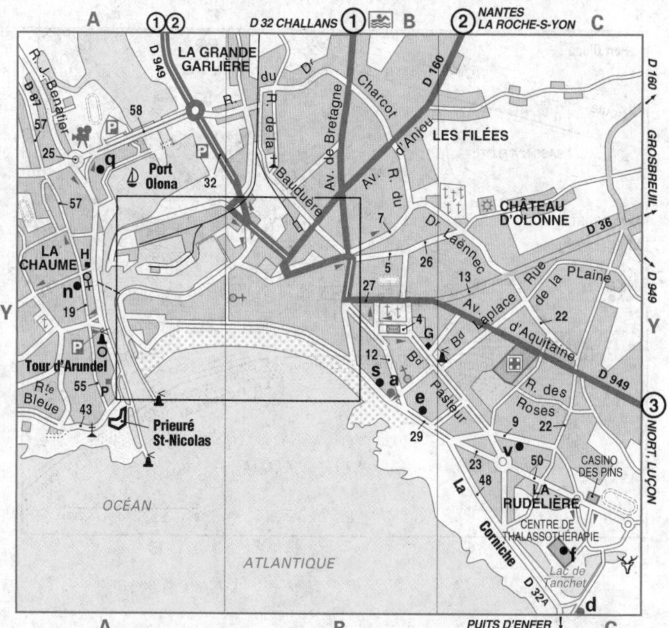

Admiral's without rest
pl. Jean-David Nau, at Port Olona – 02 51 21 41 41 – hotel.admiral@wanadoo.fr – Fax 02 51 32 71 23 AY **q**
33 rm – †€ 61/90 ††€ 61/90, ☕ € 9
◆ A recent building near the salt marshes. Spacious, quiet rooms with loggias; some have a view over the marina, the starting line for the famous Vendée Globe race.

Le Calme des Pins without rest
43 av. A. Briand – 02 51 21 03 18 – calmedespins@wanadoo.fr – Fax 02 51 21 59 85 – Closed 10 November-5 February CY **v**
45 rm – †€ 58/68 ††€ 62/88, ☕ € 9
◆ In a residential district, two modern buildings flank an attractive 1900 villa, which are home to renovated rooms (the others are older but equally well kept).

Antoine
60 r. Napoléon – 02 51 95 08 36 – antoinehotel@club-internet.fr – Fax 02 51 23 92 78 – Open from mid March to mid October AZ **a**
20 rm – †€ 52/65 ††€ 52/65, ☕ € 8 – ½ P € 50/55 – **Rest** – *(dinner only) (residents only)* Menu € 23
◆ This former property (18C) of a ship builder stands half way between the port and the beach. Simple, well proportioned rooms overlooking a small patio. Informal ambience.

Les Embruns without rest
33 r. Lt Anger – 02 51 95 25 99 – info@hotel-lesembruns.com – Fax 02 51 95 84 48 – Closed 11 November-18 January AY **n**
21 rm – †€ 44/54 ††€ 44/60, ☕ € 7,50
◆ This little-known hotel is located in the picturesque La Chaume district. A very warm welcome; small yet smart and well-kept bedrooms.

LES SABLES D'OLONNE

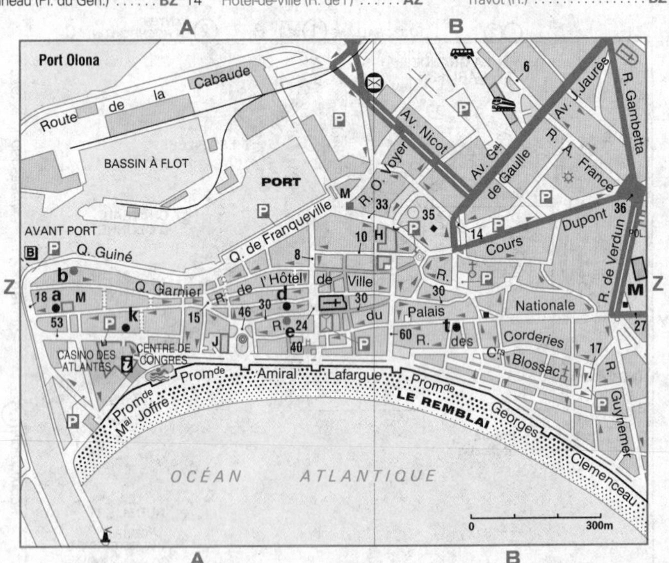

Arc en Ciel without rest
13 r. Chanzy – 02 51 96 92 50
– info@arcencielhotel.com – Fax 02 51 96 94 87
– Open April-October BZ **t**
37 rm – €61/89 €61/89, €9,50
◆ Two minutes from the beach, this hotel offers practical rooms in pastel shades. Breakfast served in a well restored Belle Epoque room. Sitting room with internet access.

Maison Richet without rest
25 r. de la Patrie – 02 51 32 04 12 – infos@maison-richet.fr
– Fax 02 51 23 72 63 – Closed 1st December-31 January AZ **d**
17 rm – €58/68 €58/68, €8,50
◆ Agreeable family establishment with a guesthouse atmosphere. Snug relaxing rooms, pretty patio and cosy sitting room with a collection of guides and globes.

Beau Rivage < Ocean and les Sables, VISA
1 bd de Lattre de Tassigny, near Lake Tanchet (via the coastal road)
– 02 51 32 03 01 – b.rivage@wanadoo.fr
– Fax 02 51 32 46 48
– Closed 29 September-16 October and 5-29 January, Monday lunch in July-August, Sunday dinner and Monday from September to June except public holidays CY **d**
Rest – Menu €43 (weekday lunch), €70/95 – Carte €83/133
Rest *Bistrot "la Mytiliade"* – 02 51 95 47 47 – Menu €23 (weekdays)/38 – Carte €34/45
◆ A panoramic restaurant commanding superb ocean views from its large windows. Fish and seafood predominate. Chic and modern decor at the Bistrot (ground floor) with appetising seafood recipes on offer.

XX **Loulou Côte Sauvage**

19 rte Bleue, at La Chaume AY – ✆ 02 51 21 32 32
– loulou.cotesauvage@orange.fr
– Fax 02 51 23 97 86
– Closed 13 November-12 December, February school holidays, Sunday dinner, Monday and Wednesday

Rest – Menu € 25 (weekdays)/56 – Carte € 37/77

♦ These former fish tanks set in the rock now house a restaurant. The dining room overlooks the sea and wild coastline. Generous portions of seafood.

XX **Le Puits d'Enfer**

56 bd de Lattre de Tassigny, via the cliff road
– ✆ 02 51 21 52 77 – puits.enfer@wanadoo.fr
– Fax 02 51 21 52 77 – Closed 1st-8 December, 12-19 January, 2-25 February, Sunday dinner and Wednesday dinner except July-August and Monday

Rest – Menu (€ 17), € 20 (weekday lunch), € 28/40 – Carte € 49/56

♦ Restaurant facing the sea, decorated in modern minimalist style (wood, slate and designer furniture). Modern cuisine with a focus on spices and market produce.

XX **Le Clipper**

19bis quai Guiné – ✆ 02 51 32 03 61
– leclipper@alicepro.fr
– Fax 02 51 95 21 28
– Closed 9-18 March, 17 November-17 December, 11-28 January, Wednesday except in season, Thursday lunch from 15 June to 15 September and Tuesday AZ **b**

Rest – Menu € 20/35 – Carte € 39/57

♦ This restaurant stands out from the many others on the harbour-side by its decor of mahogany-coloured parquet floor and Louis XVI chairs. Traditional and seafood dishes.

X **La Pilotine**

7 et 8 promenade Clemenceau – ✆ 02 51 22 25 25
– pvp.pilotine@tele2.fr – Fax 02 51 96 96 10
– Closed Sunday except July-August and Monday BY **a**

Rest – Menu € 16 (weekdays except July-August), € 24/47 – Carte € 44/76

♦ A seafront restaurant serving reasonably priced fish and seafood. New, colourful decor and charming service.

X **La Flambée**

81 r. des Halles – ✆ 02 51 96 92 35 – thiburce@wanadoo.fr
– Fax 02 51 96 92 35 – Closed Saturday lunch, Sunday dinner and Monday AZ **e**

Rest – Menu € 25/35 – Carte € 30/52

♦ In the market district a little out of town, this establishment takes special care of its guests: delicious seasonal cuisine using local produce, attentive, friendly welcome.

in l'anse de Cayola 7 km southeast by la Corniche – ✉ 85180 Château-d'Olonne

XXX **Cayola** sea,

76 promenade Cayola – ✆ 02 51 22 01 01 – Fax 02 51 22 08 28
– Closed 2-28 January, Sunday dinner and Monday except public holidays

Rest – Menu € 35/89 – Carte € 60/99

Spec. Foie de canard cuit au torchon, truffe d'été, tiramisu de coco Vendéen (June to August). Homard bleu fumé minute (May to October). Filet de bœuf "Limousin", crème brûlée aux morilles (March to August). **Wines** Fiefs Vendéens.

♦ Behind the shelter of large bay windows, admire the sea as you sample updated cooking. Veranda facing an overflow pool.

SABLES-D'OR-LES-PINS – 22 Côtes-d'Armor – 309 H3 – ✉ 22240 Fréhel

Brittany 10 **C1**

Paris 437 – Dinan 42 – Dol-de-Bretagne 60 – Lamballe 26 – St-Brieuc 39 – St-Malo 40

des Sables-d'Or Fréhel Sables d'Or les Pins, South: 1 km, ✆ 02 96 41 42 57.

La Voile d'Or - La Lagune (Maximin Hellio)
– ☎ 02 96 41 42 49 – la-voile-dor@wanadoo.fr
– Fax 02 96 41 55 45 – Closed end-November-mid February
22 rm – ♦€ 77/92 ♦♦€ 77/225, ☕ € 14 – ½ P € 105/115
Rest – *(closed Tuesday lunch, Wednesday lunch and Monday)* Menu € 36 (weekday lunch), € 50/95 – Carte € 66/84
Spec. Saint-Jacques d'Erquy au cerfeuil tubéreux (October to April). Homard de nos côtes au parfum de vadouvan (June to September). Sablé breton au caramel et beurre salé.
♦ At the entrance to the resort, rooms discreetly decorated or refurbished in a pleasant contemporary style, some facing the River Aber. Designer-style dining room facing the lagoon on one side with a view of the kitchens on the other. Creative regional cuisine with an emphasis on local produce.

Le Manoir St-Michel without rest
1.5 km east via D 34 – ☎ 02 96 41 48 87 – manoir-st-michel@fournel.de
– Fax 02 96 41 41 55 – Open 30 March-5 November
20 rm – ♦€ 47/118 ♦♦€ 47/118, ☕ € 6
♦ Fine 16C manor, overlooking the beach, surrounded by a vast park with an ornamental lake (fishing allowed). The spacious and cosy bedrooms have retained their charm of yesteryear.

Diane
– ☎ 02 96 41 42 07 – hoteldiane@wanadoo.fr – Fax 02 96 41 42 67
– Open 19 March-4 November
47 rm – ♦€ 76/98 ♦♦€ 76/170, ☕ € 10 – ½ P € 76/98 – **Rest** – Menu (€ 18), € 23/45 – Carte € 32/58
♦ Big local-style building, along the main street and a stone's throw from the sea. Functional rooms. Rustic dining room and veranda serving up-to-date dishes, flavoured with home-grown herbs.

Manoir de la Salle without rest
r. du Lac, 1 km southwest by D 34 – ☎ 02 96 72 38 29 – christianlabruyere@hotmail.com – Fax 02 96 72 00 57 – Open May-September
14 rm – ♦€ 38/60 ♦♦€ 70/120, ☕ € 8,50
♦ This noble 16C residence and its small outbuildings are set away from the road. Plain, modern bedrooms. Breakfast room with character.

SABLÉ-SUR-SARTHE – 72 Sarthe – 310 G7 – pop. 12 716 – alt. 29 m – ✉ 72300

Châteaux of the Loire 35 **C1**

Paris 252 – Angers 64 – La Flèche 27 – Laval 44 – Le Mans 61 – Mayenne 60

Office de tourisme, place Raphaël-Elizé ☎ 02 43 95 00 60, Fax 02 43 92 60 77

de Sablé Solesmes Domaine de l'Outinière, South: 6 km by D 159, ☎ 02 43 95 28 78.

in Solesmes 3 km northeast by D 22 – pop. 1 384 – alt. 28 m – ✉ 72300

Statues of the "Saints of Solesmes"★★ in the abbey church★ (Gregorian chant) - Bridge ≤★.

Le Grand Hôtel rest,
16 pl. Dom Guéranger – ☎ 02 43 95 45 10 – solesmes@grandhotelsolesmes.com
– Fax 02 43 95 22 26 – Closed 26 December-2 January
30 rm – ♦€ 85/90 ♦♦€ 106/135, ☕ € 12 – 2 suites – ½ P € 93/105
Rest – *(closed Saturday lunch and Sunday dinner from November to March)* Menu (€ 21), € 26 (weekdays)/66 – Carte € 46/81
♦ A comfortable hotel, facing St. Pierre Abbey, where you can hear Gregorian chants. Spacious and colourful bedrooms, sometimes equipped with a balcony. Modern decor, modernised classic fare, and mouth-watering desserts in the restaurant.

SABLET – 84 Vaucluse – 332 D8 – pop. 1 282 – alt. 147 m – ✉ 84110 40 A2

Paris 670 – Avignon 41 – Marseille 127 – Montélimar 67

Syndicat d'initiative, 8, rue du Levant ☎ 04 90 46 82 46, Fax 04 90 46 82 46

Les Abeilles

4 rte de Vaison – ✆ 04 90 12 38 96
– js@abeilles-sablet.com – Fax 04 90 12 12 70
– Closed 15 November-27 December, 15-25 February, Sunday except lunch from April to September and Monday
Rest – Menu € 30 (weekday lunch)/55 – Carte approx. € 70
◆ This former café, converted into a warm restaurant, offers traditional cuisine with regional touches. Fine modern dining room and charming terrace.

SABRES – 40 Landes – 335 G10 – pop. 1 107 – alt. 78 m – ✉ 40630

Atlantic Coast 3 **B2**

Paris 676 – Arcachon 92 – Bayonne 111 – Bordeaux 94 – Mimizan 41 – Mont-de-Marsan 36

Ecomusée★ de la grande Lande Northwest: 4 km.

Auberge des Pins

rm, VISA AE

– ✆ 05 58 08 30 00 – aubergedespins@wanadoo.fr
– Fax 05 58 07 56 74
– Closed 1st-7 December, January, Monday except dinner July-August and Sunday evening except July-August
25 rm – €60/62 €62/140, € 13 – ½ P € 68/100
Rest – Menu € 18 (weekday lunch), € 25/65
– Carte € 44/69
◆ A large half-timbered Landes house in an attractive wooded park. Attractive, renovated, personalised rooms; those in the annex are simpler. A cosy lounge. Wood panelling and regional antique furniture make this restaurant special. Local cuisine.

SACHÉ – 37 Indre-et-Loire – 317 M5 – see Azay-le-Rideau

SACLAY – 91 Essonne – 312 C3 – 101 24 – see Paris, Area

SAGELAT – 24 Dordogne – 329 H7 – see Belves

SAIGNON – 84 Vaucluse – 332 F10 – see Apt

SAILLAGOUSE – 66 Pyrénées-Orientales – 344 D8 – pop. 820 – alt. 1 309 m – ✉ 66800

Languedoc-Roussillon-Tarn Gorges 22 **A3**

Paris 855 – Bourg-Madame 10 – Font-Romeu-Odeillo-Via 12 – Mont-Louis 12 – Perpignan 93

Office de tourisme, Mairie ✆ 04 68 04 15 47, Fax 04 68 04 19 58

Gorges du Sègre★ East: 2 km.

Planes (La Vieille Maison Cerdane)

VISA AE

6 pl. Cerdagne – ✆ 04 68 04 72 08
– hotelplanes@wanadoo.fr – Fax 04 68 04 75 93
– Closed 5-20 March and 5 November-20 December
19 rm – €46/52 €52/61, € 7 – ½ P € 55/62 – **Rest** – *(closed Sunday dinner and Monday off season)* Menu € 22/49
◆ This former post house in the heart of the village is now a veritable institution. Gradually renovated rooms. Generous local cooking served in a welcoming regional setting. Brasserie-bar serving dishes at the counter and house specialities.

Planotel

VISA AE

5 r. Torrent – Open June-September and school holidays
20 rm – €50/60 €60/70, € 8 – ½ P € 58/68
◆ This 1970s building is ideal if you want to relax in quiet surroundings. Recently refurbished bedrooms with balconies (except two). Swimming pool with sliding roof.

in Llo **3 km east by D 33 – pop. 133 – alt. 1 424 m – ✉ 66800**

Site★.

L'Atalaya

< rest, P VISA MC

– ✆ 04 68 04 70 04 – *atalaya66@orange.fr* – *Fax 04 68 04 01 29* – *Open Easter-14 October and 21 December-14 January*

13 rm – †€ 98/118 ††€ 128/160, ☕ € 12,50 – ½ P € 120 – **Rest** – *(open Easter-14 October) (dinner only except Saturday and Sunday)* Menu € 35 – Carte € 59/67

◆ A pretty inn perched on the Cerdan mountainside. Endearing personalised guesthouse atmosphere. Panoramic pool. Classic country fare, romantic atmosphere (Catalan furniture, piano, bottled fruit) and magnificent view as far as Spain.

ST-ADJUTORY – 16 Charente – 324 M5 – pop. 314 – alt. 192 m – ✉ 16310

39 **C3**

Paris 472 – Poitiers 134 – Angoulême 33 – Saint-Junien 48 – Soyaux 36

Château du Mesnieux

P

Le Mesnieux – ✆ *05 45 70 40 18* – *contact@chateaudumesnieux.com*

4 rm ☕ – †€ 70/85 ††€ 80/95 – **Table d'hôte** – Menu € 25 bi

◆ This small château is set in hilly grounds, ideal for long walks. Fine country-style sitting room and spacious bedrooms furnished with antiques. Meals are served at the family dining table in front of a huge fireplace.

ST-AFFRIQUE – 12 Aveyron – 338 J7 – pop. 7 507 – alt. 325 m – ✉ 12400

Languedoc-Roussillon-Tarn Gorges

29 **D2**

Paris 662 – Albi 81 – Castres 92 – Lodève 66 – Millau 25 – Rodez 80

Office de tourisme, boulevard de Verdun ✆ 05 65 98 12 40, Fax 05 65 98 12 41

Roquefort-sur-Soulzon: Roquefort cellars★, rocher St-Pierre <★.

Le Moderne

VISA MC

54 av. A. Pezet – ✆ *05 65 49 20 44* – *hotel-restaurant-le-moderne@wanadoo.fr* – *Fax 05 65 49 36 55* – *Closed 13-19 October and 20 December-18 January*

Rest – Menu € 19/57 – Carte € 28/55

◆ Cheese lovers will adore this house whose cheese board features no less than 12 different Roquefort cheeses. Regionally sourced menu.

ST-AFFRIQUE-LES-MONTAGNES – 81 Tarn – 338 F9 – pop. 600 – alt. 244 m – ✉ 81290

29 **C2**

Paris 741 – Albi 55 – Carcassonne 53 – Castres 12 – Toulouse 75

Domaine de Rasigous

rm, P VISA MC AE

2 km south on D 85 – ✆ *05 63 73 30 50* – *info@domainederasigous.com* – *Fax 05 63 73 30 51* – *Open 10 March-20 November*

6 rm – †€ 70/90 ††€ 90/130, ☕ € 12 – 2 suites – **Rest** – *(Closed Wednesday) (dinner only) (residents only)* Menu € 30

◆ This 19C residence is a peaceful haven, due to its isolated, green surroundings and limited number of rooms. Carefully decorated interior and guesthouse atmosphere.

ST-AGNAN – 58 Nièvre – 319 H8 – pop. 163 – alt. 525 m – ✉ 58230

7 **B2**

Paris 242 – Autun 53 – Avallon 33 – Clamecy 63 – Nevers 98 – Saulieu 15

La Vieille Auberge

rm, P VISA MC AE

– ✆ *03 86 78 71 36* – *lvasaintagnan@aol.com* – *Fax 03 86 78 71 57* – *Open 14 February-11 November*

8 rm – †€ 45 ††€ 45/60, ☕ € 8,50 – ½ P € 50/60 – **Rest** – *(closed Monday and Tuesday)* Menu € 20 (weekdays)/40 – Carte € 22/39

◆ Former café and grocer's shop in a hamlet near a lake, converted into a family-run inn. Attractive, colourful rooms with recently redone bathrooms. Rustic dining room with a stone fireplace. Attentive service and authentic regional cooking.

ST-AGRÈVE – 07 Ardèche – 331 I3 – pop. 2 688 – alt. 1 050 m – ✉ 07320

Lyon - Rhone Valley 44 **A2**

Paris 582 – Aubenas 68 – Lamastre 21 – Privas 64 – Le Puy-en-Velay 51 – St-Étienne 69

Office de tourisme, Grand'Rue ✆ 04 75 30 15 06, Fax 04 75 30 60 93

Mont Chiniac ≤★★.

XX **Domaine de Rilhac** with rm

2 km southeast by D 120, D 21 and secondary road – ✆ 04 75 30 20 20 – hotel_rilhac@yahoo.fr – Fax 04 75 30 20 00 – Closed 20 December-mid-March, Tuesday evening, Thursday lunchtime and Wednesday

7 rm – †€ 84/114 ††€ 84/114, ☕ € 14 – ½ P € 99/120

Rest – Menu € 23 (weekday lunch), € 38/70 – Carte € 54/65

◆ You're sure to find rest in this former farmhouse, lost in the Ardèche countryside and converted into a hotel. Stylish Provençal bedrooms. Cooking suited to current tastes to be savoured facing the Gerbier-de-Jonc.

X **Faurie** (Philippe Bouissou) with rm

36 av. des Cévennes – ✆ 04 75 30 11 45 – philippebouissou@hotelfaurie.fr – Fax 04 75 29 23 88

3 rm – †€ 120/180 ††€ 120/180, ☕ € 15

Rest – *(number of covers limited, pre-book)* Menu € 35/75

Spec. Vol au vent revu au goût du jour. Pigeon de pays. Millefeuille vertical.

◆ A small restaurant where you're advised to book ahead. The chef takes inspiration from his kitchen garden when creating his daily menus. Pleasant retro setting with terrace.

X **Les Cévennes** with rm rest, VISA

10 pl. de la République – ✆ 04 75 30 10 22 – Fax 07 75 30 10 22 – Closed 16-23 September, 12-26 November and Tuesday except July-August

6 rm – †€ 49 ††€ 53, ☕ € 9 – ½ P € 56/64 – **Rest** – Menu (€ 12), € 14 (weekday lunch), € 18/36 – Carte € 30/38

◆ Modest but well-kept family hotel serving regional dishes in a wooden dining area, with simple quick meals served in the café. Modern rooms available.

ST-AIGNAN – 41 Loir-et-Cher – 318 F8 – pop. 3 542 – alt. 115 m – ✉ 41110

Châteaux of the Loire 11 **A2**

Paris 221 – Blois 41 – Châteauroux 65 – Romorantin-Lanthenay 36 – Tours 62 – Vierzon 70

Office de tourisme, 60, rue Constant Ragot ✆ 02 54 75 22 85, Fax 02 54 75 50 26

Crypt★★ in the church★ - Zoo Parc de Beauval★ South: 4 km.

Hostellerie Le Clos du Cher

✉ 41140 Noyers sur Cher – ✆ 02 54 75 00 03 – accueil@closducher.com – Fax 02 54 75 03 79 – Closed Sunday evening October-March

10 rm – †€ 63 ††€ 92, ☕ € 10 – ½ P € 64/78 – **Rest** – *(closed 13-30 November, 1st-18 January, Friday October-March, Sunday dinner and Monday lunch)* Menu € 16, € 25/35

◆ A mansion dating from the 19C in a quiet wooded park with classic rooms and offering themed weekends (wine, Valentine's Day, etc). Family atmosphere and traditional cuisine in the restaurant decorated in sunny colours.

ST-ALBAN-DE-MONTBEL – 73 Savoie – 333 H4 – see Aiguebelette-le-Lac

ST-ALBAN-LES-EAUX – 42 Loire – 327 C3 – pop. 953 – alt. 410 m – ✉ 42370

Paris 390 – Lapalisse 45 – Montbrison 56 – Roanne 12 – St-Étienne 86 – Thiers 56 – Vichy 61 44 **A1**

XX **Le Petit Prince**

Le bourg – ✆ 04 77 65 87 13 – lp-prince@orange.fr – Fax 04 77 65 96 88 – Closed 18 August-2 September, 27 October-4 November, 5-20 January, Sunday dinner, Monday and Tuesday

Rest – Menu € 22 (weekdays)/54 – Carte € 29/53

◆ The great great aunts of the current owner created this delightful restaurant in 1805. Entrance through a terrace shaded by lime trees. Impeccable updated cuisine.

ST-ALBAN-LEYSSE – 73 Savoie – 333 I4 – see Chambéry

ST-ALBAN-SUR-LIMAGNOLE – 48 Lozère – 330 I6 – pop. 1 598 – alt. 950 m – ✉ 48120
23 **C1**

Paris 552 – Espalion 72 – Mende 40 – Le Puy-en-Velay 75 – St-Chély-d'Apcher 12

Syndicat d'initiative, route de l'hôpital ✆ 04 66 31 57 01, Fax 04 66 31 58 70

Relais St-Roch

Chemin du Carreirou – ✆ 04 66 31 55 48 – rsr@relais-saint-roch.fr – Fax 04 66 31 53 26 – Open 14 April-2 November

9 rm – €98/198 €98/198, € 14 – ½ P €108/168

Rest ***La Petite Maison*** – see restaurant listing

◆ This 19C, pink granite manor house has delightful, well-appointed bedrooms decorated with personal touches. Comfortable lounge. Attractive heated swimming pool in the garden.

La Petite Maison

av. Mende – ✆ 04 66 31 56 00 – rsr@relais-saint-roch.fr – Fax 04 66 31 53 26 – Open 14 April-2 November, Monday except dinner July-August, Tuesday lunch and Wednesday lunch

Rest – Menu (€ 22), € 28/69 – Carte € 44/79

◆ Regional fare served in a warm, romantic decor. Bison and trout specialities, fine whisky selection collected by the owner.

ST-AMAND-MONTROND – 18 Cher – 323 L6 – pop. 11 447 – alt. 160 m – ✉ 18200 Dordogne-Berry-Limousin
12 **C3**

Paris 282 – Bourges 52 – Châteauroux 65 – Montluçon 56 – Nevers 70

Office de tourisme, place de la République ✆ 02 48 96 16 86, Fax 02 48 96 46 64

Noirlac abbey ★★ 4 km by ⑥.

Château de Meillant★★ 8 km by ①.

Plan on next page

Mercure L'Amandois

rm, rest,

7 r. H. Barbusse – ✆ 02 48 63 72 00 – h1890@accor.com – Fax 02 48 96 77 11
B **r**

43 rm – €51/68 €61/78, € 8 – **Rest** – Menu (€ 11,50), € 17 (weekdays)/30 – Carte € 21/38

◆ A chain hotel with a family atmosphere and 16 recent, well-equipped rooms. The guestrooms in the older building have enjoyed a recent facelift. Modern dining room with the standard Mercure menu options.

in Noirlac 4 km by ⑥ and D 35 – ✉ 18200 Bruère-Allichamps

Auberge de l'Abbaye de Noirlac

– ✆ 02 48 96 22 58 – aubergeabbayenoirlac@free.fr – Fax 02 48 96 86 63 – Open 20 February-17 November and closed Tuesday dinner and Wednesday except July-August

Rest – Menu € 21 (weekdays)/33 – Carte € 36/53

◆ A 12C travellers' chapel, converted into a small inn. Dining room with beams and floor-tiles. Terrace facing the Cistercian abbey. Country cooking.

in Bruère-Allichamps 8.5 km by ⑥ – pop. 573 – alt. 170 m – ✉ 18200

Les Tilleuls

rte de Noirlac – ✆ 02 48 61 02 75 – eric.brendel18@orange.fr – Fax 02 48 61 08 41 – Closed 18-25 September, 19-27 October, 21-29 December, 23 February-2 March, Friday evening and Sunday evening mid September-mid June and Monday

11 rm – €52/54 €52/54, € 9 – ½ P € 53/55 – **Rest** – Menu € 20 bi (weekday lunch), € 24/70 bi – Carte € 47/87

◆ This peacefully-situated hotel on the tourist trail along the Cher river, provides small well-kept rooms overlooking the countryside. Take a seat at a table in the Tilleuls and settle in to enjoy a delightful meal at a very reasonable price. Garden terrace.

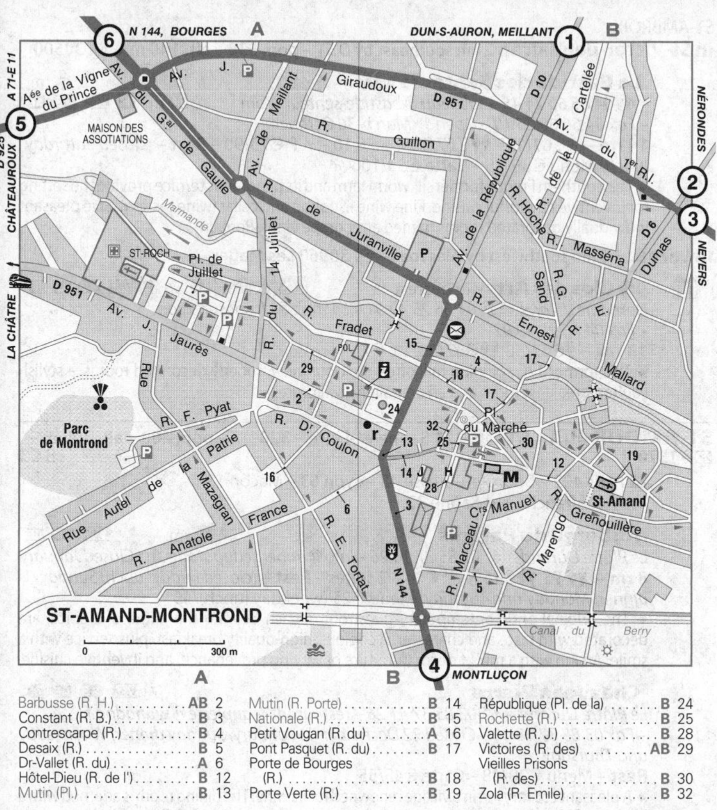

ST-AMARIN – 68 Haut-Rhin – 315 G9 – pop. 2 440 – alt. 410 m – ✉ 68550 — 1 A3

Paris 461 – Belfort 52 – Colmar 53 – Épinal 76 – Gérardmer 40 – Mulhouse 30

Office de tourisme, 81, rue Charles-de-Gaulle ✆ 03 89 82 13 90, Fax 03 89 82 76 44

Auberge du Mehrbächel ≤ Rossberg massif, rest,
4 km east on Mehrbächel road – ✆ 03 89 82 60 68
– kornacker@wanadoo.fr – Fax 03 89 82 66 05 – Closed 25 October-6 November
23 rm – †€ 42 ††€ 62, ☕ € 9 – ½ P € 55 – **Rest** – *(closed Monday evening, Thursday evening and Friday)* Menu € 18 (weekdays), € 22/40 – Carte € 18/43
◆ This former farmhouse, run by the same family since 1886, is conveniently located near a major public footpath. Rustic interior with modern comfort. The restaurant offers Alsatian specialities in a hiker-friendly environment.

ST-AMBROIX – 30 Gard – 339 K3 – pop. 3 365 – alt. 142 m – ✉ 30500 — 23 C1

Paris 686 – Alès 20 – Aubenas 56 – Mende 111

Office de tourisme, place de l'Ancien Temple ✆ 04 66 24 33 36, Fax 04 66 24 05 83

in St-Victor-de-Malcap **2 km southeast by D 51 – pop. 538 – alt. 140 m – ✉ 30500**

XX **La Bastide des Senteurs** with rm rm, rm,
– ✆ *04 66 60 24 45 – subileau@bastide-senteurs.com – Fax 04 66 60 26 10 – Open 1st March-30 October*
14 rm – €67/135 €67/135, € 10 – ½ P € 70/90 – **Rest** – *(closed Saturday lunch)* Menu € 39/75 – Carte € 53/106
◆ This southern French former silkworm farm and its panoramic terrace provide the setting for inventive flavourful cuisine. Fine wine list, shop and cellar (wine tasting). Five pleasant individually decorated rooms named after grape vines. Pool.

in Larnac **3.5 km southwest by Alès road – ✉ 30960 Les Mages**

Le Clos des Arts without rest
Domaine Villaret – ✆ 04 66 25 40 91 – contact@closdesarts.com – Fax 04 66 25 40 92
13 rm – €52/58 €52/58, € 7
◆ This former 17C spinning mill offers spacious, new, soberly decorated rooms, a stylish vaulted breakfast room and an art gallery (sculptures).

ST-AMOUR-BELLEVUE – 71 Saône-et-Loire – 320 I12 – pop. 460 – alt. 306 m – ✉ 71570

8 **C3**

Paris 402 – Bourg-en-Bresse 48 – Lyon 63 – Mâcon 13 – Villefranche-sur-Saône 32

Auberge du Paradis rm,
Le Plâtre Durand – ✆ 03 85 37 10 26 – info@aubergeduparadis.fr – Closed January
8 rm – € 95 € 155, € 14 – 2 suites – **Rest** – *(closed Friday lunch, Sunday dinner, Monday and Tuesday)* Menu € 25 (weekday lunch)/45
◆ The original and contemporary guestrooms, each bearing the name of a spice, are decorated with taste and character. A copious, high-quality breakfast, plus service with a smile. An inn with a mix of decor (furniture of varying provenance) and inventive cuisine.

XX **Chez Jean Pierre**
Le Plâtre Durand – ✆ 03 85 37 41 26 – restaurant-jeanpierre@wanadoo.fr – Fax 03 85 37 18 40 – Closed 22 December-11 January, Sunday dinner, Wednesday and Thursday
Rest – Menu € 20/48 – Carte € 45/55
◆ A pleasant country inn in a village renowned for its wine. The dining room is adorned with a blue glazed fireplace, large butcher's block, and a lobster tank. Shaded, flower-decked terrace.

ST-ANDIOL – 13 Bouches-du-Rhône – 340 E3 – pop. 2 605 – alt. 55 m – ✉ 13670

Paris 692 – Avignon 19 – Aix-en-Provence 63 – Arles 36 – Marseille 80

Syndicat d'initiative, avenue Alphonse Daudet ✆ 04 90 95 48 95, Fax 04 32 61 08 79

42 **E1**

Le Berger des Abeilles
– ✆ 04 90 95 01 91 – abeilles13@aol.com – Fax 04 90 95 48 26 – Open 15 March-15 November
8 rm – € 65/108 € 80/118, € 5 – ½ P € 70/88 – **Rest** – *(closed Thursday lunch, Monday, Tuesday and Wednesday)* Menu € 29/59 – Carte € 48/59
◆ This remote, little country Provençal farmhouse offers rustic, well-kept rooms. Three ground-floor rooms open onto the peaceful garden. Dining room in sunny tones and terrace shaded by a majestic plane tree. Regional cuisine.

ST-ANDRÉ-DE-ROQUELONGUE – 11 Aude – 344 I4 – pop. 828 – alt. 72 m – ✉ 11200

22 **B3**

Paris 821 – Béziers 53 – Montpellier 112 – Perpignan 71

Demeure de Roquelongue
53 av. de Narbonne – ✆ 04 68 45 63 57 – demeure-de-roquelongue@wanadoo.fr – Fax 04 68 45 63 57 – Open 1st April-14 November
5 rm – € 90/130 € 90/130 – **Table d'hôte** – Menu € 30 bi
◆ This elegant, former wine growers' house (1885) boasts an exquisite lush green patio. Tastefully decorated rooms with antique furniture and old-fashioned bathrooms. Cosy sitting room.

ST-ANDRÉ-DE-VALBORGNE – Gard – 339 H4 – pop. 368 – alt. 450 m – ✉ 30940 23 C1

Paris 653 – Alès 53 – Mende 69 – Millau 81

Office de tourisme, les Quais ✆ 04 66 60 32 11

Bourgade with rm VISA MC

place de l'Eglise – ✆ 04 66 56 69 32 – info@restaurant-bourgade.com – Fax 04 66 25 81 92 – Closed 2 January-1st March, Tuesday, Wednesday, Thursday from mid October to end December, Sunday dinner March-June and September-mid October and Monday except July-August

10 rm – €45/50 €50/55, €8 – ½ P €55/60 – **Rest** – Menu €17/80 bi – Carte €29/57

◆ This welcoming 17C-coaching inn has a terrace scented with wisteria. Market fresh cuisine is offered and suited to current tastes. A few small practical rooms.

ST-ANDRÉ-LES-VERGERS – 10 Aube – 313 E4 – see Troyes

ST-ANDRÉ-LEZ-LILLE – 59 Nord – 302 G4 – see Lille

ST-ANTHÈME – 63 Puy-de-Dôme – 326 K9 – pop. 809 – alt. 950 m – ✉ 63660 6 C2

Paris 461 – Ambert 23 – Clermont-Ferrand 100 – Feurs 50 – Montbrison 24 – St-Étienne 57

Office de tourisme, place de l'Aubépin ✆ 04 73 95 47 06, Fax 04 73 95 41 06

in Raffiny 5 km south by D 261 – ✉ 63660 St-Romain

Au Pont de Raffiny P VISA MC

– ✆ 04 73 95 49 10 – hotel.pont.raffiny@wanadoo.fr – Fax 04 73 95 80 21 – Closed 1st January to end March, Sunday dinner and Monday except July-August

11 rm – €33/34 €44/46, €7 – ½ P €45/47 – **Rest** – Menu (€12), €17 (weekdays)/33 – Carte €26/35

◆ This country inn, occupying a stone building on the road through the hamlet, offers cosy rooms with wood panelling. Two chalets, 50 m away, with private gardens. Pool and fitness area. Spacious, rustic restaurant (beams, fireplace and fountain); regional recipes.

ST-ANTOINE-L'ABBAYE – 38 Isère – 333 E6 – pop. 910 – alt. 339 m – ✉ 38160 Lyon - Rhone Valley 43 E2

Paris 553 – Grenoble 66 – Romans-sur-Isère 26 – St-Marcellin 12 – Valence 49

Office de tourisme, place Ferdinand Gilibert ✆ 04 76 36 44 46, Fax 04 76 36 40 49

Abbey church ★.

Auberge de l'Abbaye A/C VISA MC

Mail de l'Abbaye – ✆ 04 76 36 42 83 – leydierl@wanadoo.fr – Fax 04 76 36 46 13 – Closed 5 January-5 February, Monday and Tuesday except lunch 1st July-19 September and Sunday dinner

Rest – Menu €20/50 – Carte €30/64

◆ Pretty house (14C), at the centre of a Medieval village. Warm, Louis XIII-style interior and terrace overlooking the abbey-church, where you can savour standard cooking.

ST-ARCONS-D'ALLIER – 43 Haute-Loire – 331 D3 – pop. 164 – alt. 560 m – ✉ 43300 6 C3

Paris 515 – Brioude 37 – Mende 87 – Le Puy-en-Velay 34 – St-Flour 60

Les Deux Abbesses rm, P VISA MC AE

– ✆ 04 71 74 03 08 – abbesses@relaischateaux.com – Fax 04 71 74 05 30 – Open 21 March-2 November

6 rm (½ board only) – 6 suites – ½ P €220/320 – **Rest** – *(dinner only) (number of covers limited, pre-book)* Menu €60

◆ A delightful hotel with rooms spread around several houses in this magnificent hilltop village. A romantic atmosphere, well-kept garden, massage room and swimming pool. A seasonal menu is served every evening in the château. Classic cuisine given a contemporary or exotic twist.

ST-AUBIN-DE-LANQUAIS – 24 Dordogne – 329 E7 – pop. 256 – alt. 110 m – ✉ 24560

4 C1

Paris 548 – Bergerac 13 – Bordeaux 101 – Périgueux 56

L'Agrybella without rest

pl. de l'Église – ✆ 05 53 58 10 76 – legall.ma@wanadoo.fr – Open 15 February-30 October

5 rm – €85 €85

♦ This appealing 18C residence, next to the church, houses unusual themed rooms named: Coloniale, Rétro, Marine, Périgourdine and Surprise (suite devoted to the circus). A real success.

ST-AUBIN-DE-MÉDOC – 33 Gironde – 335 G5 – pop. 4 990 – alt. 29 m – ✉ 33160

3 B1

Paris 592 – Angoulème 132 – Bayonne 193 – Bordeaux 19 – Toulouse 261

Le Pavillon de St-Aubin

rte de Lacanau – ✆ 05 56 95 98 68 – pavillon.saintaubin@wanadoo.fr – Fax 05 56 05 96 65 – Closed Sunday evening

12 rm – €70/80 €70/80, €9 – **Rest** – *(closed 18-31 August, 2-7 January, Saturday lunch, Sunday dinner and Monday)* Menu (€24), €35/50

♦ This colonial-inspired modern hotel is a nice stop on an itinerary through upper Médoc. Basic rooms, prettily coloured. Pleasant restaurant with sunny colours, fireplace, knick-knacks, carefully prepared tables. Traditional cuisine.

ST-AUBIN-DE-SCELLON – 27 Eure – 304 C6 – pop. 314 – alt. 172 m – ✉ 27230

33 C2

Paris 152 – Le Havre 64 – Lisieux 21 – Rouen 70

Les Clématites without rest

1 km south-east on D 41 – ✆ 02 32 45 46 52 – la.charterie@wanadoo.fr

4 rm – €55 €60

♦ Dashing rooms with Jouy print-inspired decorative patterns, arranged in a former stately house, surrounded by outbuildings with character and a landscape garden.

ST-AUBIN-SUR-MER – 14 Calvados – 303 J4 – pop. 1 810 – Casino – ✉ 14750

Normandy

32 B2

Paris 252 – Arromanches-les-Bains 19 – Bayeux 29 – Cabourg 32 – Caen 20

Office de tourisme, digue Favreau ✆ 02 31 97 30 41, Fax 02 31 96 18 92

Le Clos Normand

Digue Guynemer – ✆ 02 31 97 30 47 – clos-normand@wanadoo.fr – Fax 02 31 96 46 23 – Closed 6 January-8 March

31 rm – €60/90 €60/159, €10 – ½ P €62/99 – **Rest** – Menu €24/64 – Carte €36/59

♦ Large building, well situated facing the English Channel. Most of the rooms have a sea view and marine-style decor. Rustic-style dining room and pleasant, sheltered terrace overlooking the beach. Fish and seafood specialities.

ST-AVÉ – 56 Morbihan – 308 O8 – see Vannes

ST-AVIT-DE-TARDES – 23 Creuse – pop. 194 – alt. 560 m – ✉ 23200

25 C2

Paris 415 – Limoges 151 – Guéret 55 – Ussel 67 – Aubusson 16

Le Moulin de Teiteix

– ✆ 05 55 67 34 18 – yvette.louisbrun@wanadoo.fr

5 rm – €55 €75 – 1 suite – **Table d'hôte** – Menu €22 bi

♦ On the banks of a stream full of fish, this peaceful 19C mill extends a rustic welcome to guests. Spacious rooms decorated individually. The traditional cuisine served at the table d'hôte is made with regional produce.

ST-AVOLD – 57 Moselle – 307 L4 – pop. 16 922 – alt. 260 m – ✉ 57500

Alsace-Lorraine 27 **C1**

Paris 372 – Metz 46 – Saarbrücken 33 – Sarreguemines 29 – Strasbourg 127

Office de tourisme, 28, rue des Américains ☎ 03 87 91 30 19, Fax 03 87 92 98 02

de Faulquemont Faulquemont Avenue Jean Monnet, Southwest: 16 km by D 20, ☎ 03 87 81 30 52.

Carved group★ in St-Nabor church.

Mine-image★ of Freyming-Merlebach Northeast: 10 km.

Domaine du Moulin without rest

13 r. de la vallée, at Dourd'hal, 2 km west on D 633 and D103p – ☎ 03 87 92 55 15 – domaine.du.moulin@free.fr – Fax 03 87 92 55 15

5 rm – †€ 60 ††€ 70

◆ This former mill once belonged to Longeville Abbey. It has been carefully restored with high-quality materials and contains stylish and rustic rooms. Friendly welcome.

Europe

7 r. Altmayer – ☎ 03 87 92 00 33 – sodextel@wanadoo.fr – Fax 03 87 92 01 23

Rest – *(Closed Saturday lunch, Sunday dinner and Monday)*

Menu € 25 (weekdays)/60 – Carte € 40/71

◆ Large and warm dining room in yellow and orange tones, serving traditional market fresh dishes. Good choice of wines.

North : 2.5 km on D 633 (near A 4 junction) – ✉ 57500 St-Avold

Novotel

rm,

– ☎ 03 87 92 25 93 – h0433@accor.com – Fax 03 87 92 02 47

61 rm – †€ 58/115 ††€ 58/115, € 12,50 – **Rest** – Menu (€ 15), € 19 – Carte € 22/38

◆ This Novotel on the edge of the forest offers spacious and regularly redecorated bedrooms; the best and quietest ones overlook the swimming pool. Fitness course. A meal without surprises at this restaurant. Summer terrace overlooking the trees.

ST-AY – 45 Loiret – 318 H4 – pop. 2 966 – alt. 100 m – ✉ 45130 12 **C2**

Paris 140 – Orléans 13 – Blois 48 – Châteaudun 52 – Pithiviers 55 – Vendôme 63

Syndicat d'initiative, Mairie ☎ 02 38 88 44 44, Fax 02 38 88 82 14

La Grande Tour

21 rte Nationale – ☎ 02 38 88 83 70 – contact@lagrandetour.com – Fax 02 38 80 68 05 – Closed 11-25 August, Wednesday dinner, Sunday dinner and Monday

Rest – Menu € 24/44 – Carte € 41/66

◆ The Marquise de Pompadour used to stay in this former post-house which has retained all its character. Terrace opening onto a garden with a fountain. Contemporary-style cuisine.

ST-AYGULF – 83 Var – 340 P5 – ✉ 83370 French Riviera 41 **C3**

Paris 872 – Brignoles 69 – Draguignan 35 – Fréjus 6 – St-Raphaël 9 – Ste-Maxime 14

Office de tourisme, place de la Poste ☎ 04 94 81 22 09, Fax 04 94 81 23 04

Catalogne without rest

290 av. Corniche d'Azur – ☎ 04 94 81 01 44 – hotel.catalogne@wanadoo.fr – Fax 04 94 81 32 42 – Open 1st April-20 October

32 rm – †€ 86/118 ††€ 86/118, € 10

◆ This hotel, built in 1969, stands 100m away from the Corailleurs rocky inlet. It offers rather spacious and comfortable bedrooms, some with a terrace overlooking the garden.

Red = Pleasant. Look for the red and symbols.

ST-BARD – 23 Creuse – 325 L5 – pop. 101 – alt. 640 m – ✉ 23260 25 D2

Paris 423 – Limoges 158 – Guéret 63 – Ussel 54 – Aubusson 23

Château de Chazelpaud

D 941 – ☎ 05 55 67 33 03 – albrightpatrick@aol.com – Fax 05 55 67 30 25 – Open April-September

5 rm – €65/70 €70/85 – **Table d'hôte** – Menu €25 bi

◆ A delightful neo-Renaissance folly with Italian mosaics, high ceilings and large personalised bedrooms with frescoes in the bathrooms. Panelled dining room embellished with a magnificent sculpted fireplace.

ST-BAZILE-DE-MEYSSAC – 19 Corrèze – 329 L5 – pop. 152 – alt. 230 m – ✉ 19500 25 C3

Paris 514 – Limoges 125 – Tulle 37 – Brive-la-Gaillarde 28 – Sarlat-la-Canéda 80

Le Manoir de la Brunie without rest

– ☎ 05 55 84 23 07 – appierre@wanadoo.fr

3 rm – €80/100 €80/100

◆ The garden of this 18C manor is perfect for relaxing. The lobby-sitting room with fireplace and breakfast room is adorned with period furniture. The bedrooms are in the same style.

ST-BEAUZEIL – 82 Tarn-et-Garonne – 337 B5 – pop. 132 – alt. 181 m – ✉ 82150 28 B1

Paris 631 – Agen 32 – Cahors 55 – Montauban 64 – Villeneuve-sur-Lot 23

Château de l'Hoste rm, rm, VISA AE

rte d'Agen, (D 656) – ☎ 05 63 95 25 61 – mail@chateaudelhoste.com – Fax 05 63 95 25 50

26 rm – €75/140 €75/140, €14 – ½ P €80/117 – **Rest** – *(closed Sunday dinner, Monday lunch and Thursday lunch mid October-end March)* Menu (€24), €30 (weekday lunch), €34/50 – Carte €36/46

◆ Pretty 17C manor surrounded by a wooded park, in the heart of the Quercy countryside. Pleasant and comfortable non-smoking rooms. The dining room combines both a country and aristocratic atmosphere. Terrace in the park.

ST-BÉNIGNE – 01 Ain – 328 C2 – see Pont-de-Vaux

ST-BENOÎT-SUR-LOIRE – 45 Loiret – 318 K5 – pop. 1 876 – alt. 126 m – ✉ 45730 Châteaux of the Loire 12 C2

Paris 166 – Bourges 92 – Châteauneuf-sur-Loire 10 – Gien 32 – Montargis 43 – Orléans 42

Office de tourisme, 44, rue Orléanaise ☎ 02 38 35 79 00, Fax 02 38 35 10 45

Basilica★★.

Germigny-des-Prés: church ★★ mosaic ★ Northwest: 6 km.

Labrador without rest VISA AE

7 pl. de l'Abbaye – ☎ 02 38 35 74 38 – hoteldulabrador@wanadoo.fr – Fax 02 38 35 72 99 – Closed 26 December-8 January

40 rm – €57 €64, €7,50

◆ Hotel opposite the Romanesque basilica made up of several regional-style buildings. The rooms in the most recent wing have the advantage of the peaceful garden. Tearoom.

Grand St-Benoît A/C VISA AE

7 pl. St-André – ☎ 02 38 35 11 92 – hoteldulabrador@wanadoo.fr – Fax 02 38 35 13 79 – Closed 19 August-2 September, 21 December-6 January, Saturday lunch, Sunday dinner and Monday

Rest – *(number of covers limited, pre-book)* Menu (€18), €25/47 – Carte €46/59

◆ A dining room with exposed beams and contemporary furniture and a terrace on the pedestrian square of the village where the poet, Max Jacob is buried. Carefully prepared trendy cuisine.

ST-BERNARD – 01 Ain – 328 B5 – pop. 1 282 – alt. 250 m – ✉ 01600 43 E1

Paris 443 – Lyon 29 – Bourg-en-Bresse 57 – Villeurbanne 37 – Lyon 03 30

Le Clos du Chêne rm,

370 chemin du Carré – ☎ 04 74 00 45 39 – leclosduchene@orange.fr – Fax 04 74 08 03 51 – Closed 15 February-1st March

5 rm – †€ 112/133 ††€ 112/133 – ½ P € 86/97

Table d'hôte – *(closed Saturday and Tuesday)* Menu € 30 bi

◆ On the banks of the Saône, this establishment has cosy, romantic rooms that combine the appeal of a country home with modern fixtures and fittings. The decor has an equestrian theme.

ST-BERTRAND-DE-COMMINGES – 31 Haute-Garonne – 343 B6 – pop. 237 – alt. 581 m – ✉ 31510 Languedoc-Roussillon-Tarn Gorges 28 B3

Paris 783 – Bagnères-de-Luchon 33 – Lannemezan 23 – St-Gaudens 17 – Tarbes 68

du Comminges Montréjeau Capélé, North: 9 km by N125, ☎ 05 61 95 90 20.

Site★★ - Ste-Marie-de-Comminges cathedral ★: cloister★★, panelling★★ and treasure-house★ - Saint-Just ★ de Valcabrère basilica (apse★) Northeast: 2 km.

in Valcabrère 2 km east by D 26 – pop. 139 – alt. 460 m – ✉ 31510

Le Lugdunum

1 km south on N 125 – ☎ 05 61 94 52 05 – Fax 05 61 94 52 06 – Closed 15 December-31 January

Rest – *(closed from Monday to Thursday and Sunday dinner during term time and closed Sunday dinner and Monday during school holidays) (pre-book)* Menu € 39 – Carte € 62/77

◆ In partnership with the National Research Centre, the chef has brought the recipes of Ancient Rome back to life. Explanations galore and a decor to match.

ST-BOIL – 71 Saône-et-Loire – 320 I10 – pop. 406 – alt. 240 m – ✉ 71390 8 C3

Paris 357 – Chalon-sur-Saône 23 – Cluny 27 – Montceau-les-Mines 37 – Mâcon 50

Auberge du Cheval Blanc with rm rm,

– ☎ 03 85 44 03 16 – Fax 03 85 44 07 25 – Closed 2 February-15 March and Wednesday

11 rm – †€ 71 ††€ 74/120, € 12 – ½ P € 79 – **Rest** – *(dinner only)* Menu € 40

◆ Two buildings, separated by a road. A fine residence (1870) with refreshing rooms on one side, and a family inn, serving copious regional cooking, on the other.

ST-BÔMER-LES-FORGES – 61 Orne – 310 F3 – pop. 954 – alt. 250 m – ✉ 61700

Paris 261 – Caen 88 – Alençon 73 – Flers 16 – Argentan 58 32 B3

Château de la Maigraire without rest

2 km east on D 260 – ☎ 02 33 38 09 52 – la.maigraire@wanadoo.fr – Fax 02 33 38 09 52

3 rm – †€ 85 ††€ 95/115

◆ The owners of this handsome country château (1860) enjoy sharing their lovingly decorated sitting rooms and theme guestrooms (Marie Antoinette, Blue Bird, etc.) furnished in period style.

ST-BONNET-EN-CHAMPSAUR – 05 Hautes-Alpes – 334 E4 – pop. 1 466 – alt. 1 025 m – ✉ 05500 French Alps 41 C1

Paris 652 – Gap 16 – Grenoble 90 – La Mure 50

Office de tourisme, place Grenette ☎ 04 92 50 02 57, Fax 04 92 50 02 57

la Crémaillère

4 rte de la Motte – ☎ 04 92 50 00 60 – alacremaillere@wanadoo.fr – Fax 04 92 50 01 57 – Open 25 January-25 October

21 rm – †€ 58 ††€ 63, € 9 – ½ P € 60 – **Rest** – *(closed Monday lunch, Tuesday lunch and Wednesday lunch)* Menu € 18/30 – Carte € 26/42

◆ Large, peaceful chalet, surrounded by a fine garden, on the edge of the Écrins National Park. Attractive rooms, often south-facing, with the Massif du Champsaur and Pic de l'Aiguille in the distance. Local dishes to be enjoyed in a large and bright dining room or on the terrace.

ST-BONNET-LE-CHÂTEAU – 42 Loire – 327 D7 – pop. 1 562 – alt. 870 m – ✉ 42380 Lyon - Rhone Valley 44 A2

Paris 484 – Ambert 48 – Montbrison 31 – Le Puy-en-Velay 66 – St-Étienne 34

Syndicat d'initiative, 7, place de la République ✆ 04 77 50 52 48, Fax 04 77 50 13 46

Collegiate church apse ≤★ - Chemin des Murailles★.

Le Béfranc

7 rte d'Augel – ✆ 04 77 50 54 54 – info@hotel-lebefranc.com – Fax 04 77 50 73 17 – Closed 20-27 October, 2 February-2 March, Sunday evening and Monday except July-August

17 rm – †€ 40 ††€ 46, ☐ € 7 – ½ P € 45/53 – **Rest** – Menu € 13 bi (weekday lunch), € 18/36 – Carte € 20/33

◆ On the outskirts of a locality known as "La perle du Forez", this former gendarmerie today houses a fine and...honest hotel! The rooms are well-kept. Choice of traditional dishes served at mealtimes.

La Calèche

2 pl. Cdt Marey – ✆ 04 77 50 15 58 – Fax 04 77 50 15 58 – Closed 2-16 January, 10-25 February, Monday dinner October-March, Sunday dinner, Tuesday dinner and Wednesday

Rest – Menu € 21 (weekdays)/54 – Carte € 32/54

◆ Restaurant in a protected 17C building spread over three dining rooms with colourful decor. Contemporary cuisine to which the chef adds his personal touch.

ST-BONNET-LE-FROID – 43 Haute-Loire – 331 I3 – pop. 194 – alt. 1 126 m – ✉ 43290 6 D3

Paris 555 – Annonay 27 – Le Puy-en-Velay 58 – St-Étienne 51 – Valence 68 – Yssingeaux 31

Office de tourisme, place de la Mairie ✆ 04 71 65 64 41, Fax 04 71 65 64 41

Le Clos des Cimes

the village – ✆ 04 71 65 63 62 – contact@regismarcon.fr – Fax 04 71 59 93 40 – Closed January, 1st-23 March, Sunday evening from November to June, Monday and Tuesday

12 rm – †€ 180/240 ††€ 180/240, ☐ € 20

Rest *Régis et Jacques Marcon* – see restaurant listing

Rest *Bistrot la Coulemelle* – Menu € 25/40

◆ Le Clos has lovely rooms, as elegant as they are cosy, overlooking the countryside. Delicious regional dishes (the formula features a selection of starters and trilogy of desserts) served in the country chic decor of the Bistrot.

Le Fort du Pré

– ✆ 04 71 59 91 83 – info@le-fort-du-pre.fr – Fax 04 71 59 91 84 – Closed 31 August-4 September, 20 December-5 March, Sunday evening and Monday except July-August

34 rm – †€ 68/90 ††€ 68/90, ☐ € 9,50 – ½ P € 65/89

Rest – Menu € 20 (weekdays)/68 – Carte € 37/55

◆ Restored farmhouse much frequented for its leisure activities (covered pool, fitness centre, games room). Simple, colourful and practical rooms. Veranda-dining room which opens onto the countryside. Rural produce served.

Régis et Jacques Marcon

≤ Ardèche landscape, (dinner)

Larsiallas, in the upper reaches of the village: (rooms due to open) – ✆ 04 71 59 93 72 – contact@regismarcon.fr – Fax 04 71 59 93 40 – Open 22 March-21 December and closed Monday dinner from November to May, Monday lunch in June-July, Tuesday and Wednesday

Rest – *(pre-book)* Menu € 115/170 – Carte € 154/202

Spec. Homard bleu aux lentilles vertes du Puy, façon cassoulet. Omble chevalier poêlé "amandes artichauts". Le menu "champignons" (spring et autumn). **Wines** Viognier, Vin de pays des Côtes de l'Ardèche.

◆ This restaurant, wonderfully combining stone, wood and glass, overlooks the surrounding hills, which is the ideal setting for a captivating cuisine inspired by local produce (mushrooms) from the Auvergne.

André Chatelard

pl. aux Champignons – ✆ 04 71 59 96 09 – restaurant-chatelard@wanadoo.fr – Fax 04 71 59 98 75 – Closed 4 January-5 March, Tuesday except in August, Sunday dinner and Monday

Rest – Menu € 19 (weekdays)/72 – Carte € 31/56

♦ The rustic restaurant is in a delightful village between Velay and Vivarais, where guests enjoy tasty and savoury regional cuisine. Crèche for the very young.

ST-BONNET-TRONÇAIS – 03 Allier – 326 D3 – pop. 789 – alt. 224 m – ✉ 03360 Auvergne 5 **B1**

Paris 313 – Clermont-Ferrand 137 – Moulins 60 – Montluçon 44 – Saint-Amand-Montrond 26

in Tronçais 2 km southeast by D 250 – ✉ 03360

Le Tronçais

on D 978 – ✆ 04 70 06 11 95 – contact@letroncais.com – Fax 04 70 06 16 15 – Open 10 March-16 November and closed Sunday evening, Tuesday lunch and Monday in March -April

12 rm – †€ 43/73 ††€ 48/73, ☕ € 8 – ½ P € 53/62 – **Rest** – Menu (€ 17 bi), € 24/37 – Carte € 28/53

♦ With park, lake and the Tronçais forest nearby, this hotel offers a peaceful retreat. Guestrooms of varying size in the main building and annexe. Large, attractive dining room where the focus is on traditional dishes.

ST-BRANCHS – 37 Indre-et-Loire – 317 N5 – pop. 2 211 – alt. 97 m – ✉ 37320 11 **B2**

Paris 259 – Orléans 135 – Tours 24 – Joué-lès-Tours 19 – Saint-Cyr-sur-Loire 29

Le Diable des Plaisirs

2 av. des Marronniers – ✆ 02 47 26 33 44 – lediabledesplaisirs@club-internet.fr – Closed Sunday dinner and Wednesday

Rest – Menu (€ 16), € 20/35 – Carte € 39/44

♦ Enjoy the colourful, playful and nostalgic ambiance of this restaurant set in an old classroom outside the village centre. Friendly welcome; modern cuisine.

ST-BRÈS – 30 Gard – 339 K3 – see St-Ambroix

ST-BREVIN-LES-PINS – 44 Loire-Atlantique – 316 C4 – pop. 9 594 – alt. 9 m – Casino – ✉ 44250 Atlantic Coast 34 **A2**

Paris 442 – Nantes 57 – Saint-Herblain 62 – Saint-Nazaire 15

Office de tourisme, 10, rue de l'Église ✆ 02 40 27 24 32, Fax 02 40 39 10 34

Du Beryl

55 bd de l'Océan – ✆ 02 28 53 20 00 – resa.stbrevin@hotelduberyl.com – Fax 02 28 53 20 20

34 rm – †€ 89/120 ††€ 89/250, ☕ € 15 – **Rest** – Menu € 19 (weekday lunch), € 25/39 – Carte € 27/37

♦ Modern seafront hotel, built where the casino once stood. The spacious and well-soundproofed rooms are adorned with light wood furniture and good bedding. A minimalist, fashionable decor and an ocean view form the backdrop to classic dishes.

ST-BRIAC-SUR-MER – 35 Ille-et-Vilaine – 309 J3 – pop. 2 054 – alt. 30 m – ✉ 35800 10 **C1**

Paris 411 – Dinan 24 – Dol-de-Bretagne 34 – Lamballe 41 – St-Brieuc 62 – St-Malo 13

Office de tourisme, 49, Grande Rue ✆ 02 99 88 32 47, Fax 02 99 88 32 47

in Lancieux (22 Côtes-d'Armor) 2 km Southwest by D 786 – pop. 1 220 – alt. 24 m – ✉ 22770

Office de tourisme, square Jean Conan ✆ 02 96 86 25 37

Des Bains without rest

20 r. Poncel – ✆ 02 96 86 31 33 – bertrand.mehouas@wanadoo.fr – Fax 02 96 86 22 85 – Closed Sunday from December to March

12 rm – €58/98 €65/98, €8

◆ A family run hotel near the shore founded in 1894. Functional rooms, some with kitchenettes. Breakfast served on the veranda.

ST-BRICE-EN-COGLÈS – 35 Ille-et-Vilaine – 309 N4 – pop. 2 395 – alt. 105 m – ✉ 35460 10 D2

Paris 343 – Avranches 34 – Fougères 17 – Rennes 57 – St-Malo 65

Office de tourisme, 7, place Charles-de-Gaulle ✆ 02 99 97 85 44

Le Lion d'Or rm, rest,

r. Chateaubriant – ✆ 02 99 98 61 44 – le-lion-dor3@wanadoo.fr – Fax 02 99 97 85 66

36 rm – €59/68 €59/68, €8,50 – **Rest** – *(closed Sunday dinner except 15 July-25 August)* Menu €16 (weekdays)/42 – Carte €26/50

◆ This old, granite fronted coach house is home to simple rooms that are however regularly refurbished. Comfortable restaurant with a veranda serving traditional and local dishes. Brasserie section at lunchtime.

Look out for red symbols, indicating particularly pleasant establishments.

ST-BRIEUC P – 22 Côtes-d'Armor – 309 F3 – pop. 46 087 – Built-up area 121 237 – alt. 78 m – ✉ 22000 Brittany 10 C2

Paris 451 – Brest 144 – Quimper 127 – Rennes 101 – St-Malo 71

St-Brieuc-Armor: ✆ 02 96 94 95 00, 10 km by ①.

Office de tourisme, 7, rue Saint-Gouéno ✆ 08 25 00 22 22, Fax 02 96 61 42 16

Club la Crinière Lamballe Manoir de la Ville Gourio, by Lamballe road and D 786: 15 km, ✆ 02 96 32 72 60.

St-Étienne cathedral ★ - Tertre Aubé (mound) ≤★ BV.

Plan on next page

De Clisson without rest

36 r. Gouët – ✆ 02 96 62 19 29 – contact@hoteldeclisson.com – Fax 02 96 61 06 95 AY e

25 rm – €58/88 €72/120, €9,50

◆ This white building, away from the town centre, offers a charming welcome. Rooms with various styles of furniture: those equipped with hydromassage baths are larger. Pretty garden.

Ker Izel without rest

20 r. Gouët – ✆ 02 96 33 46 29 – bienvenue@hotel-kerizel.com – Fax 02 96 61 86 12 – Closed 28 October-9 November and 28 December-4 January AY a

22 rm – €44/46 €54/56, €6,50

◆ This Breton house, believed to be the oldest hotel in St-Brieuc, has been updated: modernised rooms, a new swimming pool, and a peaceful garden. Warm welcome guaranteed.

Champ de Mars without rest

13 r. Gén. Leclerc – ✆ 02 96 33 60 99 – hoteldemars@wanadoo.fr – Fax 02 96 33 60 05 – Closed 12 December-4 January BZ s

21 rm – €44/50 €51/57, €8

◆ This town-centre hotel is conveniently located near a large public car park. The identical rooms are simple and functional.

ST-BRIEUC

Abbé-Garnier (R.) . . . . **AX** 2
Armor (Av. d') . . . . **BZ** 3
Chapitre (R. du) . . . . **AZ** 4
Charbonnerie (R.) . . . . **AY** 5
Corderie (R. de la) . . . . **AX** 13
Ferry (R. Jules) . . . . **AX** 16
Gambetta (Bd) . . . . **AV** 17
Gaulle (Pl. Gén.-de) . . . . **AY** 18
Glais-Bizoin (R.) . . . . **ABY** 20
Le Gorrec (R. P.) . . . . **AZ** 28
Hérault (Bd) . . . . **AV** 23
Jouallan (R.) . . . . **AY** 26
Libération (Av. de la) . . . . **BZ** 29
Lycéens-Martyrs (R.) . . . . **AZ** 32
Martray (Pl. du) . . . . **AY** 33
Quinquaine (R.) . . . . **AY** 38
Résistance (Pl. de la) . . . . **AY** 39
Rohan (R. de) . . . . **AYZ** 40
St-Gilles (R.) . . . . **AY** 43
St-Gouéno (R.) . . . . **AY** 44
St-Guillaume (R.) . . . . **BZ** 46
Victor-Hugo (R.) . . . . **BX** 50
3-Frères-Le-Goff (R.) . . . . **AY** 52
3-Frères-Merlin (R.) . . . . **AY** 53

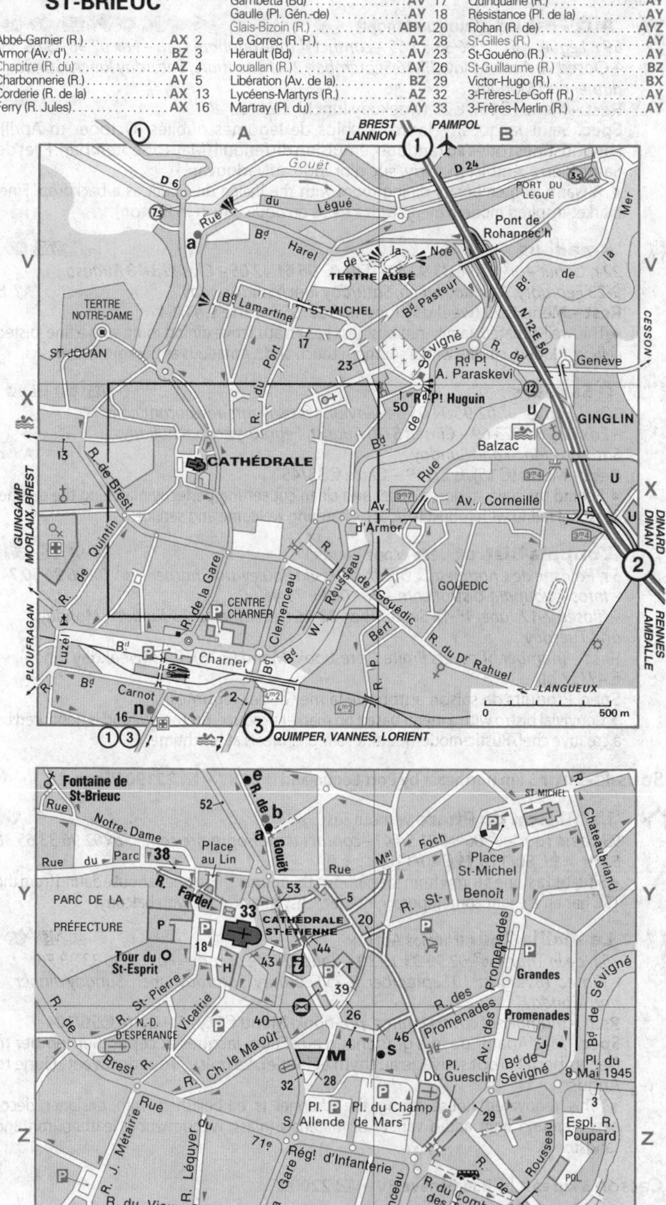

Aux Pesked (Mathieu Aumont)
59 r. Légué – ☎ 02 96 33 34 65 – contact@maisonphare.com – Fax 02 96 33 65 38 – Closed 28 April-4 May, 1st-15 September, 2 – 13 January, Saturday lunch, Sunday dinner and Monday AV **a**
Rest – Menu (€ 19), € 23 (weekday lunch), € 38/63
Spec. Saint-Jacques, velouté et chips de légumes oubliés (October to April). Langoustines rôties au tandoori, émulsion de fenouil (May to September). Filet de Saint-Pierre, émulsion curry, suc d'orange au vadouvan.
◆ A warm, contemporary dining room with the Vallée du Gouët as a backdrop. Fine, market-inspired modern menu with a focus on *pesked* (fish in Breton).

Amadeus
22 r. Gouët – ☎ 02 96 33 92 44 – Fax 02 96 61 42 05 – Closed 3-18 August, 9-23 February, Monday lunch, Saturday lunch and Sunday AY **b**
Rest – Menu € 20 (weekday lunch), € 33/65 – Carte € 41/54
◆ This well-situated, family-run business has an attractive dining room with a fine joisted ceiling. Modern cuisine with a southern touch and... Amadeus as background music!

Ô Saveurs
10 r. J. Ferry – ☎ 02 96 94 05 34 – lavigne@osaveurs-restaurant.com – Fax 02 96 7523 69 – Closed 5-20 August, February school holidays, Saturday lunch and Sunday AX **n**
Rest – Menu (€ 15), € 27/49 – Carte € 33/45
◆ Behind the train station, a sober and clean cut setting perfectly matching the cuisine. Seasonal menu with robust flavours. Charming welcome and service.

Youpala Bistrot (Jean-Marie Baudic)
5 r. Palasne de Champeaux, South-west via Boulevard Charner – ☎ 02 96 94 50 74 – infos@youpala-bistrot.com – Fax 02 96 75 46 50 – Closed 2-17 June, 1st-16 September, 22-25 December, 2-13 January, Monday and Tuesday
Rest – *(number of covers limited, pre-book)* Menu (€ 18), € 23 (weekday lunch), € 47/57 bi
Spec. Produits de saison autour de la mer et des légumes.
◆ Convivial bistro with a menu based on market produce. Breton seafood is honoured by a creative chef. Rustic-modern setting. Simpler meals at lunchtime.

in Sous-la-Tour 3 km northeast by Port Légué and D 24 BV – ✉ **22190 Plérin**

La Maison du Phare without rest
93 r. de la Tour – ☎ 06 84 81 54 41 – contact@maisonphare.com – Fax 02 96 33 65 38
5 rm – †€ 80/110 ††€ 80/110, ☕ € 8
◆ Situated a stone's throw from the harbour, this former shipowner's house dating from the 19C has an elegant contemporary interior. Cosy guestrooms with balcony.

La Vieille Tour (Nicolas Adam)
75 r. de la Tour – ☎ 02 96 33 10 30 – ugho777@aol.com – Fax 02 96 33 38 76 – Closed 18 August-10 September, 9-25 February, Saturday lunch, Sunday dinner and Monday
Rest – *(number of covers limited, pre-book)* Menu € 26/75 – Carte € 56/104
Spec. "Mac'Adam" de foie gras chaud aux Saint-Jacques et cèpes (September to December). Turbot sauvage au thym et laurier. La fraise "Tout de Sweet" (June to August)
◆ This renovated house facing the channel is embellished with designer decor based around light and a variety of materials (glass, wenge wood, leather, iron and sandstone).

in Cesson 3 km east by Rue Genève BV – ✉ **22000**

La Croix Blanche
61 r. de Genève – ☎ 02 96 33 16 97 – Fax 02 96 62 03 50 – Closed 1st-20 August, February school holidays, Sunday dinner and Monday
Rest – Menu € 22/85 – Carte € 47/51
◆ This restaurant, located in a residential area, includes several comfortable, individually-decorated dining rooms overlooking the garden. Delicious modern cuisine.

Manoir le Quatre Saisons

61 chemin Courses – 02 96 33 20 38 – manoirlequatresaisons@hotmail.com – Fax 02 96 33 77 38 – Closed 3-17 March, 13-27 October, Sunday dinner and Monday
Rest – Menu € 18 (weekdays), € 29/73
◆ Country inn, nestling in a small valley that leads to the sea. Traditional cuisine served in two spruce dining rooms with pretty Art Nouveau details.

ST-CALAIS – 72 Sarthe – 310 N7 – pop. 3 785 – alt. 155 m – ✉ 72120

Châteaux of the Loire 35 **D1**

Paris 188 – La Ferté-Bernard 33 – Le Mans 47 – Tours 66 – Vendôme 32

Office de tourisme, pl. de l'Hôtel de ville 02 43 35 82 95, Fax 02 43 35 15 13

Front★ of Notre-Dame church.

À St-Antoine

pl. St-Antoine – 02 43 35 01 56 – asaintantoine@club-internet.fr – Fax 02 43 35 01 56 – Closed 1st-15 March, 25 July-7 August, Sunday dinner and Wednesday
Rest – Menu (€ 11,50), € 13/32 – Carte € 20/39
◆ Small dining room, simply redecorated and furnished in a bistro style, occupying the former village café, close to the church. Traditional cuisine.

la Ferté-Bernard road 3 km North by D 1

Château de la Barre

– 02 43 35 00 17 – info@chateaudelabarre.com – Fax 02 43 35 00 17 – Closed 10 January-10 February
5 rm – €130 €150/390, €15 – **Table d'hôte** – *(closed Sunday dinner, Monday dinner, Wednesday dinner and Friday dinner)* Menu € 65 bi
◆ This fine château, surrounded by a 40-ha park, has belonged to the same family since the 15C. The refined rooms, with individual touches, boast authentic antique furniture. Fine cuisine served in a dining room adorned with a magnificent dresser.

ST-CANNAT – 13 Bouches-du-Rhône – 340 G4 – pop. 4 634 – alt. 216 m – ✉ 13760

Provence 40 **B3**

Paris 731 – Aix-en-Provence 17 – Cavaillon 39 – Manosque 65 – Marseille 46

Syndicat d'initiative, avenue Pasteur 04 42 57 34 65, Fax 04 42 50 82 01

South 2 km by Éguilles road and secondary road – ✉ 13760 St-Cannat

Mas de Fauchon

rm, rm, VISA

1666 chemin de Berre – 04 42 50 61 77 – contact@masdefauchon.fr – Fax 04 42 57 22 56
14 rm – €110/240 €110/240, €15 – 2 suites – **Rest** – Menu € 30 (weekday lunch), € 38/60 – Carte € 48/69
◆ Surrounded by a pine forest, this 17C sheepfold oozes with charm: extremely comfortable, plush Provençal inspired rooms with terraces. Peace and quiet guaranteed. Appealing rustic dining room serving traditional cuisine.

ST-CAPRAISE-DE-LALINDE – 24 Dordogne – 329 E6 – see Lalinde

ST-CAST-LE-GUILDO – 22 Côtes-d'Armor – 309 I3 – pop. 3 187 – alt. 52 m – ✉ 22380

Brittany 10 **C1**

Paris 427 – Avranches 91 – Dinan 32 – St-Brieuc 50 – St-Malo 31

Office de tourisme, place Charles-de-Gaulle 02 96 41 81 52, Fax 02 96 41 76 19

de Saint-Cast Pen-Guen Chemin du Golf, South: 4 km, 02 96 41 91 20.

Pointe de St-Cast ★★ - Pointe de la Garde ★★ - Pointe de Bay ★ South: 5 km.

Ker Flore

in the village, near the church – 02 96 81 03 79 – ker.flore@wanadoo.fr – Closed 15 September-6 October, 22 December-1st February, Sunday dinner, Tuesday dinner, Wednesday dinner and Monday
Rest – Menu (€ 13), € 20/26 – Carte € 23/37
◆ Restaurant in a country setting with brightly coloured walls and objets d'art. Traditional dishes inspired by the market.

ST-CÉRÉ – 46 Lot – 337 H2 – pop. 3 515 – alt. 152 m – ✉ 46400

Dordogne-Berry-Limousin 29 **C1**

Paris 531 – Aurillac 62 – Brive-la-Gaillarde 51 – Cahors 80 – Figeac 44 – Tulle 54

Office de tourisme, 13, avenue Francois de Maynard ✆ 05 65 38 11 85, Fax 05 65 38 38 71

de Montal Saint-Jean-LespinasseWest: 3 km by D 807, ✆ 05 65 10 83 09.

Site★ - Jean Lurçat tapestries ★ in the casino - Jean Lurçat workshop-museum ★ - Château de Montal★★ West: 3 km.

Cirque d'Autoire★: ≤★★ via Autoire (site★) West: 8 km.

Les Trois Soleils de Montal (Frédérik Bizat)

rte de Gramat, 2 km via D 673 – ✆ 05 65 10 16 16 – lestroissoleils@wanadoo.fr – Fax 05 65 38 30 66 – Closed 1st December-31 January

26 rm – €65/95 €80/119, €14 – 4 suites – ½ P €90/117

Rest – *(closed Sunday dinner, Tuesday lunch and Monday October-March, Monday lunch April-September)* Menu €29 (weekday lunch), €39/69 – Carte €54/67

Spec. Escargots de bourgogne à la crème d'oseille. Pigeonneau de grain rôti. Crumble glacé thym-chocolat. **Wines** Cahors, Côtes du Marmandais.

♦ This large house near the Château de Montal enjoys a peaceful location within a park in the middle of the country. Spacious, modern guestrooms. Delicious contemporary cuisine served in an elegant dining room embellished with 19C paintings.

De France

rte d'Aurillac – ✆ 05 65 38 02 16 – lefrance-hotel@wanadoo.fr – Fax 05 65 38 02 98 – Closed 20 December-25 January and Friday evening from 15 October to 8 February

18 rm – €43/48 €54, €7 – ½ P €51/54 – **Rest** – *(dinner only except Sunday)* Menu €23/38 – Carte €33/54

♦ Simple, rustic rooms (choose one overlooking the garden) near the Casino art gallery (works by J. Lurçat). Comfortable, rustic-style restaurant with a shaded terrace. Traditional dishes with a focus on the cuisine of Quercy.

Villa Ric ≤ Quercy plateau,

rte Leyme, 2.5 km on D 48 – ✆ 05 65 38 04 08 – hotel.jpric@libertysurf.fr – Fax 05 65 38 00 14 – Open 6 April-11 November

5 rm – €75 €75/105, €10 – ½ P €75/105 – **Rest** – *(dinner only) (number of covers limited, pre-book)* Menu €34/58

♦ A house nestled against the side of a hill with cosy bedrooms decorated in pastel tones. A restful setting and a guesthouse ambience. Modern cuisine served in a bright dining room. Terrace with panoramic views of the valley.

ST-CERGUES – 74 Haute-Savoie – 328 K3 – pop. 2 513 – alt. 615 m – ✉ 74140

Paris 547 – Annecy 54 – Annemasse 9 – Bonneville 25 – Genève 19 – Thonon-les-Bains 21 46 **F1**

De France with rm

1044 r. Allobroges – ✆ 04 50 43 50 32 – hoteldefrance74@wanadoo.fr – Fax 04 50 94 66 45 – Closed 21 April-9 May, 18 August-4 September, Sunday dinner, Wednesday lunch and Monday

18 rm – €52/62 €55/65, €9 – ½ P €58/63 – **Rest** – Menu (€13), €16/50 – Carte €39/66

♦ Run by four generations of the same family, this hotel is rightly proud of its decor, welcome and cuisine. Elegant restaurant, pleasant garden-terrace and modern rooms.

ST-CERNIN-DE-LARCHE – 19 Corrèze – 329 J5 – pop. 456 – alt. 300 m – ✉ 19600

24 **B3**

Paris 492 – Limoges 104 – Tulle 48 – Brive-la-Gaillarde 17 – Sarlat-la-Canéda 54

Le Moulin de Laroche rm,

La Roche Ouest, 1,5 km par D 59 – ✆ 05 55 85 40 92 – Fax 05 55 85 34 66 – Open 15 March-15 November

6 rm – €57/70 €60/75 – **Table d'hôte** – Menu €22 bi

♦ In a park on a hill, this 1693 farm with a water mill offers the perfect peaceful hideaway. Antiques and period furniture. Regional cuisine served in a conservatory.

ST-CHAMAS – 13 Bouches-du-Rhône – 340 F4 – pop. 6 595 – alt. 15 m –
✉ 13250 Provence 40 **A3**

Paris 738 – Arles 43 – Marseille 50 – Martigues 26 – Salon-de-Provence 16

Office de tourisme, Place Saint Pierre ✆ 04 90 50 90 54, Fax 04 90 50 90 10

Embarden without rest

rte de Grans – ✆ 06 84 95 57 16 – claude.dunan@9online.fr

6 rm – €50 €100

◆ This manor house, set in grounds home to grazing sheep and a water feature, offers characterful, delightfully 1940s rooms. Cottage garden, orchard and pool. Country life at its best!

Le Rabelais VISA AE

8 r. A. Fabre, (town centre) – ✆ 04 90 50 84 40 – le.rabelais@wanadoo.fr – Fax 04 90 50 84 40 – Closed 25-31 August, Sunday dinner except July-August and Monday

Rest – Menu € 26 (weekday lunch), € 37/60 – Carte € 28/45

◆ This restaurant, near the former powder factory, is housed in the attractive 17C corn mill with a vaulted ceiling. Pleasant terrace decked with flowers. Inventive cuisine.

ST-CHAMOND – 42 Loire – 327 G7 – pop. 37 378 – alt. 388 m – ✉ 42400
Lyon - Rhone Valley 44 **B2**

Paris 505 – Feurs 55 – Lyon 50 – Montbrison 53 – St-Étienne 11 – Vienne 38

Office de tourisme, 23, avenue de la Libération ✆ 04 77 31 04 41, Fax 04 77 22 04 34

Les Ambassadeurs rest, VISA AE

28 av. de la Libération – ✆ 04 77 22 85 80 – pierrelecroisey@aol.com – Fax 04 77 31 96 95 – Closed 1st-10 May and 1st-13 August BZ **a**

16 rm – €54 €68, € 8,50 – ½ P € 54 – **Rest** – *(closed 26 July-13 August, Friday dinner, Sunday dinner and Saturday)* Menu (€ 17 bi), € 21 (weekdays)/72 – Carte € 34/88

◆ A. Pinay and A. Prost are among the town's most illustrious "ambassadors". Most of the rooms of this hotel, housed in a 1970s building, have been modernized. The updated dining room decor is discreet and pleasant; classical cuisine.

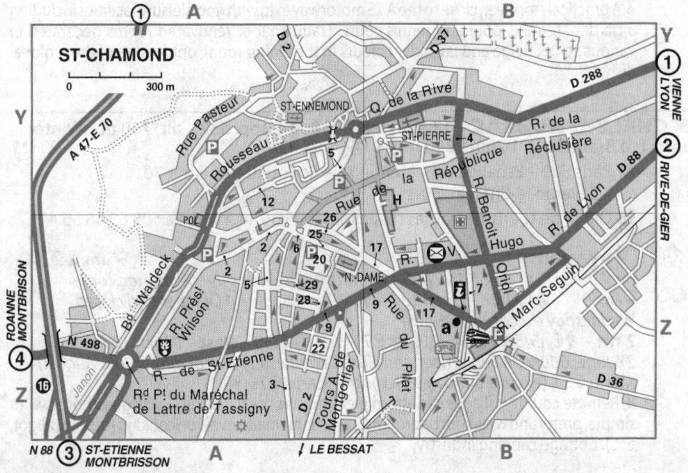

ST-CHARTIER – 36 Indre – 323 H7 – see La Châtre

ST-CHÉLY-D'APCHER – 48 Lozère – 330 H6 – pop. 4 316 – alt. 1 000 m – ✉ 48200

22 **B1**

Paris 540 – Aurillac 106 – Mende 45 – Le Puy-en-Velay 85 – Rodez 114 – St-Flour 36

Office de tourisme, place du 19 mars 1962 ☎ 04 66 31 03 67, Fax 04 66 31 30 30

Les Portes d'Apcher

rte de St Flour, 1.5 km north on D 809 – ☎ 04 66 31 00 46 – Fax 04 66 31 28 85 – Closed 21 December-25 January and Friday evening October-April

16 rm – €54 €54, ☕ €7,50 – ½ P €50

Rest – Menu €19/57 – Carte €20/52

♦ There are at least two good reasons for stopping at this simple and modern hotel: a nearby motorway access and a fine view of the Aubrac and Margeride. A rotunda dining hall with timbered ceiling - an ideal setting to enjoy some delightful local specialities.

in La Garde 9 km north by D 809 – ✉ 48200 Albaret-Ste-Marie

Château d'Orfeuillette

rm, VISA

at Exit 32 of the A 75, on the D809, towards La Garde – ☎ 04 66 42 65 65 – orfeuillette48@aol.com – Fax 04 66 42 65 66 – Closed 20-27 December

23 rm – €85/180 €85/180, ☕ €16 – ½ P €92/115 – **Rest** – *(closed Thursday lunch, Sunday off season, Monday lunch and Saturday lunch)*
Menu €29 (weekday lunch), €32/42 – Carte €23/41

♦ This château, built on 16C foundations and completed in the late 1800s, is surrounded by extensive gardens. The attractive bedrooms in the main building are full of character, while those in the orangery are simpler in style. The restaurant has ancient walls and a fireplace but a modern decor, suited to its updated cuisine.

Le Rocher Blanc

rest, VISA

– ☎ 04 66 31 90 09 – hotel@lerocherblanc.com – Fax 04 66 31 93 67 – Open Easter-5 January

19 rm – €51/55 €51/79, ☕ €8 – ½ P €74/97

Rest – Menu €13 (weekday lunch), €21/60 bi – Carte €18/41

♦ A practical stopover, close to the A 75 motorway exit, with good leisure facilities including a garden, terrace, pool and tennis court. Traditional or renovated rooms decorated in various styles. Beige and lavender colours in the dining room; opt for one of the regional dishes.

ST-CHÉLY-D'AUBRAC – 12 Aveyron – 338 J3 – pop. 532 – alt. 700 m – Winter sports : to Brameloup 1 200/1 390 m 9 – ✉ 12470

29 **D1**

Paris 589 – Espalion 20 – Mende 74 – Rodez 50 – St-Flour 70 – Sévérac-le-Château 60

Office de tourisme, route d'Espalion ☎ 05 65 44 21 15, Fax 05 65 48 55 41

Voyageurs

rm, VISA

av. Aubrac – ☎ 05 65 44 27 05 – contact@hotel-conserverie-aubrac.com – Fax 05 65 44 21 67 – Open 12 April-27 June, 6 July-14 October and closed Wednesday except July-August

7 rm – €45/50 €45/50, ☕ €7 – ½ P €47/50 – **Rest** – *(Open 12 April-27 June, 6 July-30 September and closed Wednesday except dinner July-August)*
Menu €17 (except Sunday lunch)/24 – Carte €26/39

♦ Remote country villages can afford pleasant surprises! A small family guesthouse, with simple, pretty and well-kept bedrooms. Tasty homemade Aveyron cooking (tripoux, aligot, etc.). Cottage canning industry.

A good night's sleep without spending a fortune?
Look for a Bib Hôtel.

ST-CHÉRON – 91 Essonne – 312 B4 – pop. 4 444 – alt. 100 m – ✉ 91530

▶ Paris 42 – Chartres 54 – Dourdan 10 – Étampes 21 – Fontainebleau 58 – Orléans 91 18 **B2**

in St-Évroult 1.5 km south by V 6 – ✉ 91530 St-Chéron

XX **Auberge de la Cressonnière** VISA MC AE

– *01 64 56 60 55 – la.cressonniere@wanadoo.fr – Fax 01 64 56 56 37 – Closed 20 August-10 September, Thursday dinner, Sunday dinner and Monday*

Rest – Menu € 21 (weekday lunch), € 27/45 – Carte € 37/53

◆ An inn with a rustic setting located on the banks of the Orge serving tasty Aveyron-inspired dishes. A superb steam engine sits imposingly in the flower garden.

ST-CHRISTOL – 84 Vaucluse – 332 F9 – alt. 856 m – ✉ 84390 40 B2

▶ Paris 737 – Carpentras 53 – Cavaillon 63 – Marseille 113

Le Lavandin P VISA MC AE

Apt, road, 3 km south-west – 04 90 75 09 18 – le-lavandin2@wanadoo.fr – Fax 04 90 75 09 17 – Closed January and February

32 rm – †€ 55 ††€ 60/140, ☕ € 9 – **Rest** – *(Closed Monday and Tuesday)* Menu (€ 15), € 20/32

◆ Modern hotel on the Plateau d'Albion, set between fields of lavender and an oak-tree forest, offering clean and functional rooms. Some have a private terrace, while others can accommodate families. Restaurant offering both traditional and regional cuisine.

Your opinions are important to us: please write and let us know about your discoveries and experiences – good and bad!

ST-CHRISTOPHE-LA-GROTTE – 73 Savoie – 333 H5 – see les Échelles

ST-CIERS-DE-CANESSE – 33 Gironde – 335 H4 – pop. 718 – alt. 40 m – ✉ 33710

▶ Paris 548 – Blaye 10 – Bordeaux 45 – Jonzac 54 – Libourne 41 3 **B1**

Citadelle de Blaye★ Northwest: 8 km, **Pyrenees Aquitaine.**

La Closerie des Vignes rm, P VISA MC

village Arnauds, 2 km north by D 250 and D 135 – 05 57 64 81 90 – la-closerie-des-vignes@wanadoo.fr – Fax 05 57 64 94 44 – Open 1st April-31 October

9 rm – †€ 78/94 ††€ 83/94, ☕ € 10 – ½ P € 77/81 – **Rest** – *(closed Tuesday) (dinner only)* Menu (€ 25,50), € 33/36 – Carte € 33/40

◆ Modern house, surrounded by Blaye vineyards. Spacious and quiet bedrooms, equipped with simple, modern furniture. Panelled dining room with views over the vine stock and garden. Simple, traditional cuisine.

ST-CIRQ-LAPOPIE – 46 Lot – 337 G5 – pop. 207 – alt. 320 m – ✉ 46330

Dordogne-Berry-Limousin 29 **C1**

▶ Paris 574 – Cahors 26 – Figeac 44 – Villefranche-de-Rouergue 37

Office de tourisme, place du Sombral 05 65 31 29 06, Fax 05 65 31 29 06

Site★★ - Remains of the former château ≤★★ - Le Bancourel ≤★ - Bouziès: chemin de halage du Lot(towpath)★ Northwest: 6,5 km.

Auberge du Sombral "Les Bonnes Choses" VISA MC AE

– *05 65 31 26 08 – Fax 05 65 30 26 37 – Open 2 April-14 November and closed Thursday except July-August*

8 rm – †€ 50 ††€ 70/78, ☕ € 8 – **Rest** – *(closed Thursday except July-August and dinner except Friday and Saturday)* Menu (€ 15), € 19 (lunch)/27 – Carte € 25/36

◆ A family inn in the heart of a picturesque, medieval hillside village. Small simple rooms. The breakfast room sports a countrified decor of old tiles and a fireplace. An attractively-restored old house on a small busy square in this charming medieval village overlooking the River Lot. Rooms are rather small but pleasant.

Le Gourmet Quercynois
– ✆ *05 65 31 21 20 – Fax 05 65 31 36 78 – Closed mid-November to mid-December and January*
Rest – Menu (€ 14,50), € 20/36 – Carte € 31/47
◆ This cosy restaurant in a 17C house offers local cuisine focusing on duck. There is a small wine museum and a shop selling regional products.

in Tour-de-Faure **2 km east by D 8 – pop. 350 – alt. 137 m –** ✉ **46330**

Les Gabarres without rest
– ✆ *05 65 30 24 57 – Fax 05 65 30 25 85 – Open Easter-15 October*
28 rm – €54 €54, €8
◆ Modern hotel located on the banks of the Lot, at the foot of a picturesque hilltop village. Practical rooms and a swimming pool.

Maison Redon without rest
– ✆ *05 65 30 24 13 – patrice@maisonredon.com – Fax 05 65 30 24 13*
5 rm – €59/69 €59/69
◆ At the foot of a beautiful listed village, this 18C ivy clad manor house welcomes guests into a warm interior. Recent rooms furnished with antiques. Pool.

The red symbol?
This denotes the very essence of peace –
only the sound of birdsong first thing in the morning…

ST-CLAIR – **83 Var** – **340** N7 – **see le Lavandou**

ST-CLAR – **32 Gers** – **336** G6 – **pop. 868** – **alt. 150 m** – ✉ **32380**
Languedoc-Roussillon-Tarn Gorges 28 **B2**

Paris 706 – Agen 49 – Auch 37 – Toulouse 79
Office de tourisme, 2, place de la Mairie ✆ 05 62 66 34 45, Fax 05 62 66 31 69

La Garlande without rest
pl. de la Mairie – ✆ 05 62 66 47 31 – nicole.cournot@wanadoo.fr
– Fax 05 62 66 47 70 – Open 21 March-2 November
3 rm – €49 €68
◆ This residence, opposite the 13C covered market, offers attractive and peaceful rooms (antique furniture, tapestries, red floor tiles, parquet flooring, etc...). Reading room and delightful, well-kept garden with an abundance of flowers.

ST-CLAUDE – **39 Jura** – **321** F8 – **pop. 12 303** – **alt. 450 m** – ✉ **39200**
Burgundy-Jura 16 **B3**

Paris 465 – Annecy 88 – Genève 60 – Lons-le-Saunier 59
Office de tourisme, 1, avenue de Belfort ✆ 03 84 45 34 24, Fax 03 84 41 02 72
de la Valserine Mijoux La Pellagrue, by Genève road: 24 km, ✆ 04 50 41 31 56.
Site★★ - St-Pierre cathedral★: stalls★★ Z - Exhibittion of pipes, diamonds and fine stone Z **E.**
Georges du Flumen★ by ② - Morez Road ≤★★ 7 km by ①.

Plan on next page

Jura rest,
40 av. de la Gare – ✆ 03 84 45 24 04 – jura.hotel@wanadoo.fr
– Fax 03 84 45 58 10 Z **a**
35 rm – €47/57 €50/60, €7,50 – ½ P €47/57
Rest – *(closed 24 December-5 January and Sunday dinner)* Menu € 14 (weekday lunch), € 17/28 – Carte € 35/42
◆ Practical, unpretentious hotel dominating the river opposite the station. Small rooms (half are for non smokers); some have a small terrace. The restaurant commands a fine view of the town and the River Bienne.

ST-CLAUDE

Abbaye (Pl. de l') . . . . . . Z 2
Belfort (Av. de) . . . . Y 3
Christin (Pl.) . . . . Y 5
Gambetta (R.) . . . . Z 6
Janvier (R. A.) . . . . Z 7
Lamartine (R.) . . . . Y 9
Louis-XI (Pl.) . . . . Z 12
Marché (R. du) . . . . Z 20
Pré (R. du) . . . . YZ
République (Bd de la) . . Y 23
Rosset (R.) . . . . Z 24
Victor-Hugo (R.) . . . . Y 25
Voltaire (Pl.) . . . . Y 26
9-Avril-1944 (Pl. du) . . . . Y 27

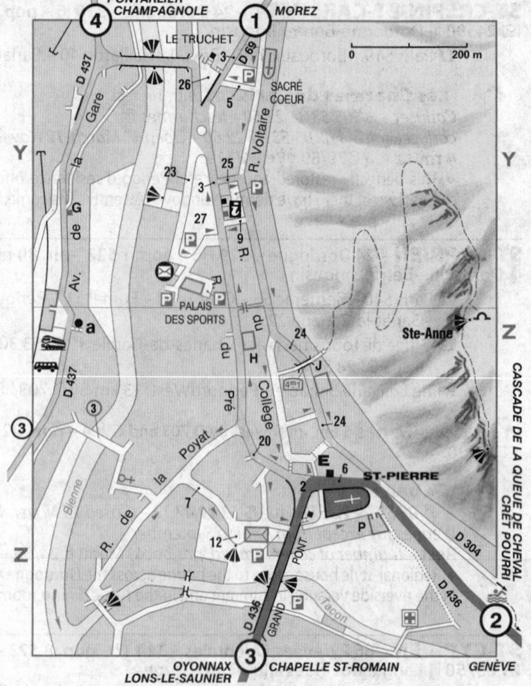

ST-CLÉMENT-DES-BALEINES – 17 Charente-Maritime – **324** A2 – **see Île de Ré**

ST-CLÉMENT-LES-PLACES – 69 Rhône – **327** F5 – **pop. 536** – **alt. 625 m** – ✉ **69930** 44 **A1**

▶ Paris 458 – Lyon 54 – Saint-Étienne 69 – Villeurbanne 63 – Lyon 03 56

XX **L'Auberge de Saint-Clément**

Le bourg – *✆ 04 74 26 03 83 – Closed dinner except Friday, Saturday and Wednesday*

Rest – Menu € 16 (weekday lunch)/20

◆ Situated in a village in the Monts du Lyonnais, this peaceful auberge boasts views of the surrounding countryside (attractive terrace). Delicious bistro-style cuisine made with local ingredients.

ST-CLOUD – 92 Hauts-de-Seine – **311** J2 – **101** 14 – **see Paris, Area**

ST-CONSTANT – 15 Cantal – **330** B6 – **pop. 553** – **alt. 260 m** – ✉ **15600** 5 **A3**

▶ Paris 573 – Aurillac 48 – Decazeville 17 – Figeac 23 – Rodez 55 – Tulle 98

Maurs church: statues★ and reliquary bust★ Northwest: 4.5 km, **Auvergne-Rhone Valley**

X **Auberge des Feuillardiers**

– ✆ 04 71 49 10 06 – lesfeuillardiers@wanadoo.fr – Closed 24 August-8 September, 16-28 February and Wednesday except July-August

Rest – *(number of covers limited, pre-book)* Menu € 15/42 – Carte € 18/38

◆ This country-style restaurant away from the noise of the main road is an appreciated feature of this hamlet. The chef breathes a lease of new life into regional recipes.

ST-CRÉPIN-ET-CARLUCET – 24 Dordogne – 329 I6 – pop. 407 – alt. 262 m – ✉ 24590 Dordogne-Berry-Limousin 4 D3

Paris 519 – Bordeaux 196 – Brive-la-Gaillarde 40 – Sarlat-la-Canéda 12

Les Charmes de Carlucet without rest

Carlucet – ✆ 05 53 31 22 60 – lescharmes@carlucet.com – Fax 05 53 31 22 60 – Open 1st March-12 November

4 rm – €79/89 €84/119

◆ This perfectly restored and peaceful Périgord residence offers simple and spacious rooms. Two of them have dormer windows. Attentive welcome.

ST-CYPRIEN – 24 Dordogne – 329 H6 – pop. 1 522 – alt. 80 m – ✉ 24220 Dordogne-Berry-Limousin 4 D3

Paris 540 – Bergerac 53 – Cahors 68 – Fumel 51 – Périgueux 57 – Sarlat-la-Canéda 22

Office de tourisme, place Charles-de-Gaulle ✆ 05 53 30 36 09, Fax 05 53 28 55 05

de Lolivarie Siorac-en-PérigordWest: 13 km by D 703, ✆ 05 53 30 22 69.

in Allas-les-Mines 5 km southwest by D 703 and C 204 – pop. 224 – alt. 85 m – ✉ 24220

Gabarrier

– ✆ 05 53 29 22 51 – Fax 05 53 29 47 12 – Closed 15 November-beg. February and Wednesday except from April to September

Rest – *(number of covers limited, pre-book)* Menu € 24/55 – Carte € 46/65

◆ Regional-style house, close to the bridge across the Dordogne. Country cooking, served in the riverside veranda in summer and in the rustic dining room in winter.

ST-CYPRIEN – 66 Pyrénées-Orientales – 344 J7 – pop. 8 573 – alt. 5 m – Casino – ✉ 66750 Languedoc-Roussillon-Tarn Gorges 22 B3

Paris 859 – Céret 31 – Perpignan 17 – Port-Vendres 20

Office de tourisme, quai A. Rimbaud ✆ 04 68 21 01 33, Fax 04 68 21 98 33

de Saint-Cyprien Saint-Cyprien-Plage Mas d'Huston, North: 1 km, ✆ 04 68 37 63 63.

in St-Cyprien-Plage 3 km northeast by D 22 – ✉ 66750 St-Cyprien

Mas d'Huston rm, rest,

at the golf course – ✆ 04 68 37 63 63 – contact@golf-st-cyprien.com – Fax 04 68 37 64 64 – Closed 8 November-13 December and 6 January-11 February

50 rm – €100/160 €100/160, € 14 – ½ P € 85/115

Rest *Le Mas* – *(dinner only)* Menu € 32 bi/48 bi – Carte € 47/57

Rest *L'Eagle* – brasserie *(lunch only)* Menu (€ 15 bi), € 20 bi

◆ Henri Quinta has renovated this hotel and furnished the modern rooms (with balcony or terrace) in his trademark brightly coloured striped linen. Classic menu and a trendy decor at the Mas. Simple cuisine and designer setting at the Eagle.

in St-Cyprien-Sud 3 km – ✉ 66750 St-Cyprien

L'Ile de la Lagune rm,

bd de l'Almandin – ✆ 04 68 21 01 02 – contact@hotel-ile-lagune.com – Fax 04 68 21 06 28

18 rm – €130/185 €155/220, € 18 – 4 suites – ½ P € 136/168

Rest *L'Almandin* – *(closed Monday and Tuesday October-April)* Menu € 30 bi (weekday lunch), € 49/105 – Carte € 72/87

Spec. Escabèche de rouget, gambas et pistes aux artichauts violets. Pièce de filet de veau "Vedell Catlan" rôtie. Macaron pistache, crème chiboust et framboises tièdes. **Wines** Collioure blanc, Côtes du Roussillon.

◆ Recently-built, Spanish and Moorish-style hotel, on a small marina island. Functional rooms with balconies. Free launch to the beach in season. Tasty seasonal cuisine, based on reinterpreted local specialities. Terrace veranda.

La Lagune ← rm, rm, VISA AE
– ✆ 04 68 21 24 24 – contact@hotel-lalagune.com – Fax 04 68 37 00 00
– Open 22 March-11 November
49 rm – †€ 85/140 ††€ 85/168, ☕ € 12 – ½ P € 77/105 – **Rest** – Menu (€ 14), € 26/33
◆ A hotel on the beach, part of a residential complex that was designed for a "club" clientèle. Practical rooms overlooking the pool or the lagoon. Billiards room. Musical events and meals served on the terrace in summer. Simple cuisine.

ST-CYR-AU-MONT-D'OR – 69 Rhône – 327 I5 – see Lyon

ST-CYR-EN-TALMONDAIS – 85 Vendée – 316 H9 – pop. 301 – alt. 31 m – ✉ 85540

34 **B3**

Paris 444 – La Rochelle 57 – Luçon 14 – La Roche-sur-Yon 30 – Les Sables-d'Olonne 38

Syndicat d'initiative, Mairie ✆ 02 51 30 82 82, Fax 02 51 30 88 29

Auberge de la Court d'Aron VISA
– ✆ 02 51 30 81 80 – d.orizet@wanadoo.fr – Closed 24 November-7 December, 26 January-8 February, Monday lunch in July-August, Sunday dinner and Wednesday off season
Rest – Menu (€ 13,50), € 23/46 – Carte € 26/43
◆ This auberge occupies the stables of the château of the same name. Welcoming rustic interior, covered terrace, and garden.

ST-CYR-SUR-MER – 83 Var – 340 J6 – pop. 8 898 – alt. 10 m – ✉ 83270

French Riviera

40 **B3**

Paris 810 – Bandol 8 – Le Beausset 10 – Brignoles 70 – Marseille 40 – Toulon 23

Office de tourisme, place de l'Appel du 18 Juin, les Lecques ✆ 04 94 26 73 73, Fax 04 94 26 73 74

18 de Frégate Route de Bandol, South: 3 km by D 559, ✆ 04 94 29 38 00.

Les Lecques – ✉ 83270 St-Cyr-sur-Mer

Grand Hôtel des Lecques ← AC VISA AE
24 av. du Port – ✆ 04 94 26 23 01
– info@lecques-hotel.com – Fax 04 94 26 10 22 – Open 1st March-8 December
60 rm – †€ 90/188 ††€ 99/209, ☕ € 14 – ½ P € 92/147
Rest – Menu € 19 (weekday lunch), € 33/51 – Carte € 34/54
◆ An elegant Belle Époque residence in the middle of a park full of flowers. Bedrooms with bright decor on the upper floors; those on the front are preferable. Enjoy traditional cuisine in the winter garden or on the attractive terrace.

Bandol road 4 km by D 559 – ✉ 83270 St-Cyr-sur-Mer

Dolce Frégate ← the coast, 27 rm, AC
– ✆ 04 94 29 39 39 VISA AE
– reservation-fregate@dolce.com – Fax 04 94 29 39 40
100 rm – †€ 239/499 ††€ 239/499, ☕ € 25 – 33 suites
Rest *Le Mas des Vignes* – *✆ 04 94 29 39 47 (closed Tuesday and Wednesday except July-August) (dinner only)* Menu € 55/75 – Carte € 58/64
Rest *Restanque* – *✆ 04 94 29 38 18 (lunch only except July-August)* Menu € 31/35
◆ This estate in the middle of the vineyards includes a hotel, 27-hole golf course, leisure complex and conference centre. A quiet atmosphere with Provençal decor throughout. Sunny colours and panoramic terrace at the Mas de Vignes. Relaxed dining at the Restanque.

ST-DALMAS-DE-TENDE – 06 Alpes-Maritimes – 341 G3 – see Tende

ST-DALMAS-VALDEBLORE – 06 Alpes-Maritimes – 341 E3 – see Valdeblore

ST-DENIS-DE-L'HOTEL – 45 Loiret – 318 J4 – pop. 2 621 – alt. 115 m – ✉ 45550 12 C2

Paris 153 – Orléans 19 – Gien 48 – Montargis 52 – Pithiviers 37

Le Dauphin without rest

3 av. des Fontaines – ✆ 02 38 46 29 29 – hotel.le.dauphin@wanadoo.fr – Fax 02 38 59 07 63 – Closed 2 weeks in August and 26 December-3 January

21 rm – †€ 47 ††€ 54, ☕ € 7

♦ On the road to the Loire castles, this pleasant family hotel offers welcoming and well-kept rooms equipped with practical furniture.

ST-DENIS-LE-FERMENT – 27 Eure – 304 K6 – see Gisors

ST-DENIS-LÈS-REBAIS – 77 Seine-et-Marne – 312 I2 – pop. 780 – alt. 149 m – ✉ 77510 19 D2

Paris 72 – Chelles 58 – Meaux 35 – Noisy-le-Grand 57

Brie Champagne without rest

22 Chantareine – ✆ 01 64 65 46 45 – contact@chambres-brie-champagne.com

4 rm ☕ – †€ 55 ††€ 65

♦ A former farmhouse, from 1750, with a wisteria and Virginia creeper-clad façade. Local Brie-style rooms. Breakfast by the fireplace or under the bower.

ST-DENIS-SUR-LOIRE – 41 Loir-et-Cher – 318 F6 – see Blois

ST-DÉSIRAT – 07 Ardèche – 331 K2 – pop. 707 – alt. 130 m – ✉ 07340 43 E2

Paris 533 – Lyon 71 – Privas 83 – Saint-Étienne 53 – Valence 44

La Désirade

– ✆ 04 75 34 21 88 – contact@desirade-fr.com – Closed December and January

6 rm ☕ – †€ 40 ††€ 53 – ½ P € 45 – **Table d'hôte** – *(closed Sunday and Wednesday) (pre-book)* Menu € 18

♦ This hotel, a stone's throw from the Musée de l'Alambic, occupies a family house dating from 1860. Stylish bedrooms, each named after a flower. A well-maintained hotel with a friendly welcome and attractive, shaded garden-terrace. The cuisine prepared by the owner of this property has a strong focus on local products.

ST-DIDIER – 35 Ille-et-Vilaine – 309 N6 – see Châteaubourg

ST-DIDIER – 84 Vaucluse – 332 D9 – see Carpentras

ST-DIDIER-DE-LA-TOUR – 38 Isère – 333 F4 – see La Tour-du-Pin

ST-DIDIER-EN-VELAY – 43 Haute-Loire – 331 H2 – pop. 2 891 – alt. 830 m – ✉ 43140 6 D3

Paris 538 – Le Puy-en-Velay 55 – St-Étienne 25 – St-Agrève 45

Office de tourisme, 11, rue de l'ancien Hôtel de Ville ✆ 04 71 66 25 72, Fax 04 71 61 25 83

Auberge du Velay

Grand'place – ✆ 04 71 61 01 54 – Fax 04 71 61 15 80 – Closed 1st-5 September, 5-9 January, Sunday dinner and Monday

Rest – Menu € 18 bi (weekday lunch), € 25/45

♦ This appealing inn, where local dishes have been served for three centuries, was taken over in 2005 by a creative young chef. Unusual table settings (pewter).

ST-DIÉ-DES-VOSGES – 88 Vosges – 314 J3 – pop. 22 569 – alt. 350 m – 88100 Alsace-Lorraine

27 **C3**

Paris 397 – Colmar 53 – Épinal 53 – Mulhouse 108 – Strasbourg 97

Office de tourisme, 8, quai du Mal de L. de Tassigny ✆ 03 29 42 22 22, Fax 03 29 42 22 23

St-Dié cathedral ★ - Gothic cloister★.

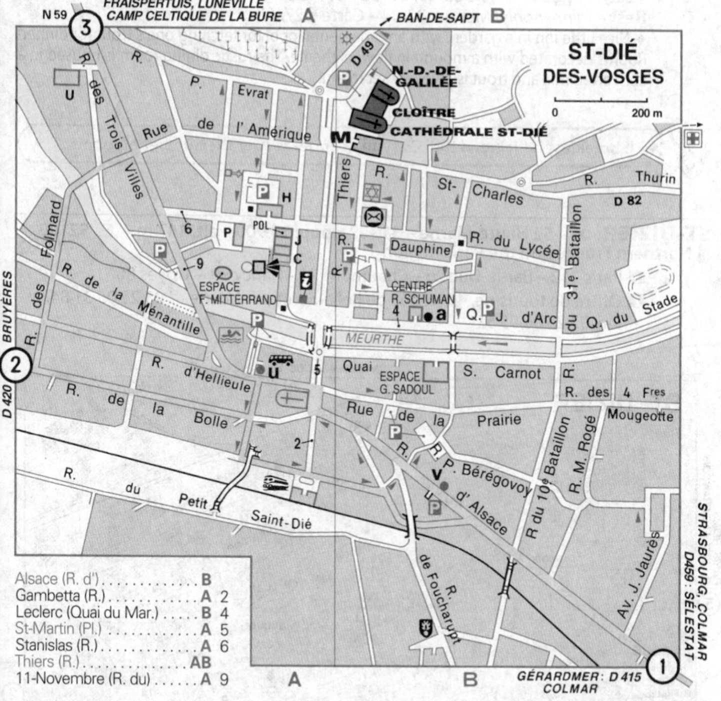

Ibis

rm, rm, rest, VISA

5 quai Jeanne d'Arc – ✆ 03 29 42 24 22 – h1102@accor.com – Fax 03 29 55 49 15

58 rm – 🚹€ 54/68 🚹🚹€ 54/68, ☕ € 7,50 – **Rest** – Menu (€ 12,50), € 16 – Carte approx. € 20 B **a**

◆ Chain hotel on the banks of the Meurthe whose rooms, although a little cramped, have been refurbished in a contemporary style. Opt for one overlooking the river. Restaurant with bistro atmosphere (wood decor and beer bar look); concise, improvised menu.

Voyageurs

VISA

22 r. Hellieule – ✆ 03 29 56 21 56 – lesvoyageurs88@wanadoo.fr – Closed Sunday dinner and Monday A **u**

Rest – Menu (€ 16), € 19/30 – Carte € 31/41

◆ In a bright, yellow coloured decor, this establishment serves traditional cuisine based on market fresh produce. Homemade desserts. Concise list of mainly Alsace wines.

La Table de Manaïs with rm

P VISA

64 r. d'Alsace – ✆ 03 29 56 11 71 – Fax 03 29 56 45 06 – Closed Sunday

10 rm – 🚹€ 45 🚹🚹€ 47, ☕ € 8,50 – ½ P € 58 B **v**

Rest – Menu (€ 15), € 21/28 – Carte € 32/47

◆ This restaurant is located on a shopping street. Relaxed decor, light colours and tasty, classic menu that varies with the seasons. Small rooms.

ST-DISDIER – 05 Hautes-Alpes – 334 D4 – pop. 141 – alt. 1 024 m – ✉ 05250

French Alps — 40 **B1**

Paris 643 – Gap 46 – Grenoble 81 – La Mure 41

La Souloise defile ★ N.

La Neyrette

– ✆ 04 92 58 81 17 – info@la-neyrette.com – Fax 04 92 58 89 95
– *Open 2 February-14 April and 1st May-10 October*

12 rm – †€ 56/68 ††€ 68/80, ☕ € 8 – ½ P € 61/67

Rest – *(dinner only)* Menu € 22/34 – Carte € 27/41

◆ Nice little inn in a garden, with an ornamental pool for fetching one's trout for dinner! Rooms decorated with a mountain flowers theme. The rustic dining room is housed in a converted mill and trout is on every set menu.

If breakfast is included the ☕ symbol appears after the number of rooms.

ST-DIZIER – 52 Haute-Marne – 313 J2 – pop. 30 900 – alt. 147 m – ✉ 52100

Northern France and the Paris Region — 14 **C2**

Paris 212 – Bar-le-Duc 26 – Chaumont 74 – Nancy 99 – Troyes 86

Office de tourisme, 4, avenue de Belle-Forêt-sur-Marne ✆ 03 25 05 31 84, Fax 03 25 06 95 51

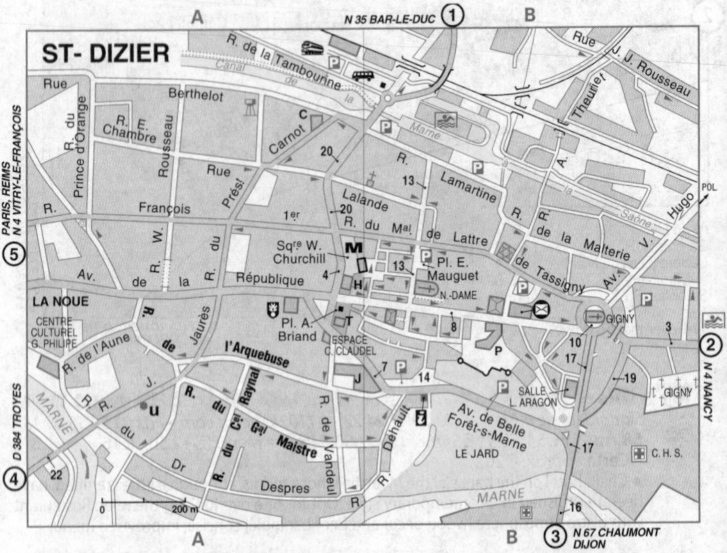

ST- DIZIER

Alsace-Lorraine (Av. d') . . . . . . B 3
Cartier (Av. M.) . . . . . . A 4
Commune de Paris (R. de la) . . . . . . AB 7
Gambetta (R.) . . . . . . B 8
Gaulle (Pl. du Gén.-de) . . . . . . B 10
Giros (R. E.) . . . . . . B 13
Liberté (Pl. de la) . . . . . . B 14
Pasteur (Av.) . . . . . . B 17
Paul Bert (R.) . . . . . . B 16
République (Av. de la) . . . . . . A
Tanneurs (R. des) . . . . . . B 19
Verdun (Av. de) . . . . . . A 20
Vergy (R. de) . . . . . . A 22

La Gentilhommière

29 r. J. Jaurès – ✆ 03 25 56 32 97 – Fax 03 25 06 32 66 – Closed 1st-22 August, 17-25 February, Saturday lunch, Sunday and Monday — A **u**

Rest – Menu € 24/30 – Carte € 39/49

◆ House behind a low boxwood hedge with warm, elegant dining room in beige and yellow tones. Bright veranda. Well-prepared market cuisine.

in Chamouilley 8 km by ②, D 8A and D 172 – pop. 883 – alt. 161 m – ✉ 52410

Le Moulin
– ✆ 03 25 55 81 93 – lemoulinchamouilley@wanadoo.fr – Fax 03 25 55 81 93
– Closed 29 December-4 January
5 rm – €49 €70 – **Table d'hôte** – Menu €29 bi
♦ This restored, former mill's assets are the pleasant welcome, tastefully decorated, comfortable rooms and tranquillity of the neighbouring park. Table d'hôte (reservations only).

ST-DONAT-SUR-L'HERBASSE – 26 Drôme – 332 C3 – pop. 3 132 – alt. 202 m – ✉ 26260 Lyon - Rhone Valley 43 E2

Paris 545 – Grenoble 92 – Hauterives 20 – Romans-sur-Isère 13 – Valence 27

Office de tourisme, 32, avenue Georges Bert ✆ 04 75 45 15 32, Fax 04 75 45 20 42

Chartron with rm
av. Gambetta – ✆ 04 75 45 11 82 – info@restaurant-chartron.com – Fax 04 75 45 01 36 – Closed 28 April-8 May, 1st-24 September, 2-8 January, Wednesday except dinner in July-August and Tuesday
7 rm – €60 €70, €9,50 – ½ P €75/90 – **Rest** – Menu €26/80
♦ Big stone building, enlarged by a glass rotunda. Large modern dining room, serving up-to-date cuisine and dishes with truffles, in season. Rooms with modern decor.

La Mousse de Brochet
pl. de la Marne – ✆ 04 75 45 10 47 – Fax 04 75 45 10 47 – Closed 25 June-16 July, 21 January-12 February, weekday dinner September-May, Sunday dinner and Monday
Rest – Menu €17 (weekdays)/56
♦ After admiring the collegiate's organ, take a break in this former café, with a slightly bijou-type decor, to enjoy a Mousse de Brochet, the speciality of the house.

ST-DOULCHARD – 18 Cher – 323 K4 – see Bourges

ST-DYÉ-SUR-LOIRE – 41 Loir-et-Cher – 318 F6 – pop. 945 – alt. 96 m – ✉ 41500 Châteaux of the Loire 11 B2

Paris 173 – Beaugency 21 – Blois 17 – Orléans 52 – Romorantin-Lanthenay 45

Office de tourisme, 73, rue Nationale ✆ 02 54 81 65 45, Fax 02 54 81 65 45

Manoir Bel Air rm, rest, VISA
1 rte d'Orléans – ✆ 02 54 81 60 10 – manoirbelair@free.fr – Fax 02 54 81 65 34 – Closed end January to beg. March
42 rm – €40/60 €75/200, €7 – ½ P €68/75 – **Rest** – Menu €28 (weekdays)/54 – Carte €38/76
♦ This 17C mansion was the property of a wine trader then a Guadeloupe governor. Large rooms and gardens overlooking the Loire. Pleasant panoramic dining room overlooking the river. Traditional dishes and vintage wines in the cellar.

SAINTE voir après la nomenclature des Saints

ST-ÉMILION – 33 Gironde – 335 K5 – pop. 2 345 – alt. 30 m – ✉ 33330 Atlantic Coast 4 C1

Paris 584 – Bergerac 58 – Bordeaux 40 – Langon 49 – Libourne 9 – Marmande 59

Office de tourisme, place des Créneaux ✆ 05 57 55 28 28, Fax 05 57 55 28 29

Site★★ - Monolithic church★ - Cloître des Cordeliers (cloister) ★ - ≤★ from the château du Roi tower.

Hostellerie de Plaisance

5 pl. du Clocher – ✆ 05 57 55 07 55 – contact@hostelleriedeplaisance.com – Fax 05 57 74 41 11 – Closed 14 December-10 February

21 rm – 🚹€ 330/620 🚹🚹€ 330/620, ☕ € 26 – 4 suites

Rest – *(closed Wednesday lunch, Thursday lunch, Sunday and Monday)* Menu € 55/120 – Carte € 90/120

Spec. Lasagne de foie gras de canard et champignons des bois à l'émulsion de truffe. Enrubannée de langoustines au wok et feuille de blette. Viennoise de ris de veau grenobloise. **Wines** Côtes de Castillon, Bordeaux blanc.

◆ A comfortable and well-kept 14C residence in the heart the city. Built in pale stone and boasting cosy rooms with personal touches. Fine, flavourful cuisine and an impressive Saint-Emilion wine list at the restaurant.

Palais Cardinal

pl. 11-novembre-1918 – ✆ 05 57 24 72 39 – hotel@palais-cardinal.com – Fax 05 57 74 47 54 – Open April-November

27 rm – 🚹€ 67 🚹🚹€ 80/154, ☕ € 14 – ½ P € 76/140 – **Rest** – *(closed Tuesday lunch, Thursday lunch and Wednesday)* Menu € 25/40

◆ The hotel occupies part of the residence once occupied by a cardinal in the 14C. The rooms in the recent wing are large and refined. Pretty little garden and pleasant swimming pool. A stylishly furnished restaurant serving traditional dishes and Saint-Emilion from the family estate.

Au Logis des Remparts without rest

18 r. Guadet – ✆ 05 57 24 70 43 – contact@logisdesremparts.com – Fax 05 57 74 47 44 – Closed 15 December-31 January

16 rm – 🚹€ 78/165 🚹🚹€ 78/165, ☕ € 13 – 1 suite

◆ Two houses (14C and 17C) with modern rooms furnished with a personal touch. Breakfast veranda, terrace, and an attractive pool in the garden on the edge of the vineyards.

Auberge de la Commanderie without rest

r. des Cordeliers – ✆ 05 57 24 70 19 – contact@aubergedelacommanderie.com – Fax 05 57 74 44 53 – Closed 20 December-20 February

17 rm – 🚹€ 70/100 🚹🚹€ 70/100, ☕ € 11

◆ This former 17C commandery is now home to a hotel with compact yet smart bedrooms refurbished in contemporary style. Those in the annexe are larger and more suited to families.

Le Tertre

r. Tertre de la Tente – ✆ 05 57 74 46 33 – Fax 05 57 74 49 87 – Closed 11 November-7 February, Thursday in February-March and Wednesday

Rest – Menu € 20 (weekday lunch), € 28/65 – Carte € 45/84

◆ Next to the church, this countrified restaurant features a shellfish tank at the back, and a little wine cellar carved into the rock. Traditional fare and Bordeaux wines.

Le Clos du Roy

– ✆ 05 57 74 41 55 – Fax 05 57 74 41 55

Rest – Menu (€ 20), € 28/46 – Carte € 50/62

◆ A pale stone establishment off the tourist circuit. Dining rooms combining the rustic-styled and the contemporary. Carefully done up-to-date cuisine.

Libourne road 4 km by D 243 – ✉ 33330 St-Émilion

Château Grand Barrail

– ✆ 05 57 55 37 00 – welcome@grand-barrail.com – Fax 05 57 55 37 49

rm, rest,

37 rm – 🚹€ 185/480 🚹🚹€ 185/480, ☕ € 23 – 5 suites – ½ P € 130/190

Rest – *(closed Sunday evening, Tuesday lunchtime and Monday from November to March)* Menu € 52/65 – Carte € 52/64

◆ A tastefully restored 19C château in grounds (with a lake) hidden amid the vines. Refined bedrooms, beautiful spa, fitness centre and swimming pool for the summer months. One of the three magnificent dining rooms boasts a Moorish decor. Modern cuisine and a splendid wine list.

ST-ESTÈPHE – 33 Gironde – 335 G3 – pop. 1 683 – alt. 15 m – ✉ 33180 3 B1

Paris 619 – Bordeaux 61 – Mérignac 57 – Saint-Médard-en-Jalles 55 – Le Bouscat 57

XX **Château Pomys** with rm rest, VISA

rte de Poumeys, (in Leyssac) – ✆ 05 56 59 73 44 – chateau-pomys@orange.fr – Fax 05 56 59 30 25 – Open 2 March-9 November and closed Sunday dinner and Monday (except hotel)

10 rm – €77 €87, €8 – **Rest** – Menu (€ 18), € 27 (weekdays), € 35/75 – Carte approx. € 42

◆ Château surrounded by a pleasant tree-lined park. Classically decorated dining-room and peaceful terrace at the rear. Contemporary dishes. Small, well-kept rooms.

ST-ÉTIENNE P – 42 Loire – 327 F7 – pop. 180 210 – Built-up area 291 960 – alt. 520 m – ✉ 42000 Lyon - Rhone Valley 44 A2

Paris 517 – Clermont-Ferrand 147 – Grenoble 154 – Lyon 61 – Valence 122

St-Étienne-Bouthéon: ✆ 04 77 55 71 71, by ⑤: 15 km.

Office de tourisme, 16, avenue de la Libération ✆ 08 92 70 05 42, Fax 04 77 49 39 03

de St-Étienne 62 rue Saint Simon, by Annonay road and D 501: 18 km, ✆ 04 77 32 14 63.

Old St-Etienne★ - Musée d'Art moderne★★ T M² - Puits Couriot (coal mine), musée de la mine★ AY - Musée d'Art et d'Industrie★★ - Site of the "Manufacture des Armes et Cycles de St-Étienne": planetarium★.

Plans on following pages

Mercure Parc de l'Europe rest, VISA AE

r. Wuppertal, south - east of plan, via cours Fauriel – ✆ 04 77 42 81 81 – h1252@accor.com – Fax 04 77 42 81 89 V a

120 rm – €99/129 €109/139, €13,50

Rest *La Ribandière* – *(closed 26 July-24 August, 20 December-4 January, Saturday, Sunday and public holidays)* Menu (€ 22), € 28 – Carte € 26/49

◆ This hotel has been given a new lease of life: decor based on a theatrical theme, individually furnished rooms, new bathrooms and pleasant lounge and bar. This contemporary restaurant shows off produce from the Forez region and Côtes-du-Rhône wines.

Du Golf rm, VISA AE

opposite the golf course by r. Revollier – ✆ 04 77 41 41 00 – resa@hoteldugolf42.com – Fax 04 77 38 28 16

48 rm – €115 €135, €13,50 – 5 suites – **Rest** – Menu (€ 16), € 22/36 – Carte € 31/53

◆ Recently built hotel, nicely located on a hill facing the town golf course and the Forez plain. Cane furniture and floral curtains in the rooms. Bar facing the pool. Modern rotunda-style dining room overlooking the golf course. Traditional cuisine.

Du Midi without rest VISA AE

19 bd. Pasteur – ✆ 04 77 57 32 55 – contact@hotelmidi.fr – Fax 04 77 57 28 00 – Closed 26 July-27 August and 26 December-8 January V e

33 rm – €58/79 €68/100, €9

◆ Two buildings linked by a pleasant lounge adorned with an unusual fireplace. Smallish but practical, soundproofed and well-kept rooms.

XXX **Nouvelle** (Stéphane Laurier) VISA AE

30 r. St-Jean – ✆ 04 77 32 32 60 – Fax 04 77 41 77 00 – Closed 11-25 August, Sunday and Monday BY v

Rest – Menu € 30 (weekday lunch), € 54/90

Spec. Endive et jambon, foie gras de canard et truffe noire. Thon rouge mi-cuit, nage réglissée à l'agastache et aubergine, crème brûlée à l'ail. Velouté de topinambour à la bière blanche, Saint-Jacques et huile de truffe noire. **Wines** Vin de Pays d'Urfé, Côtes du Forez.

◆ Modern furniture, a grey and brown colour scheme, a conservatory and old paintings - a setting that is both minimalist and relaxing; inventive tasty dishes.

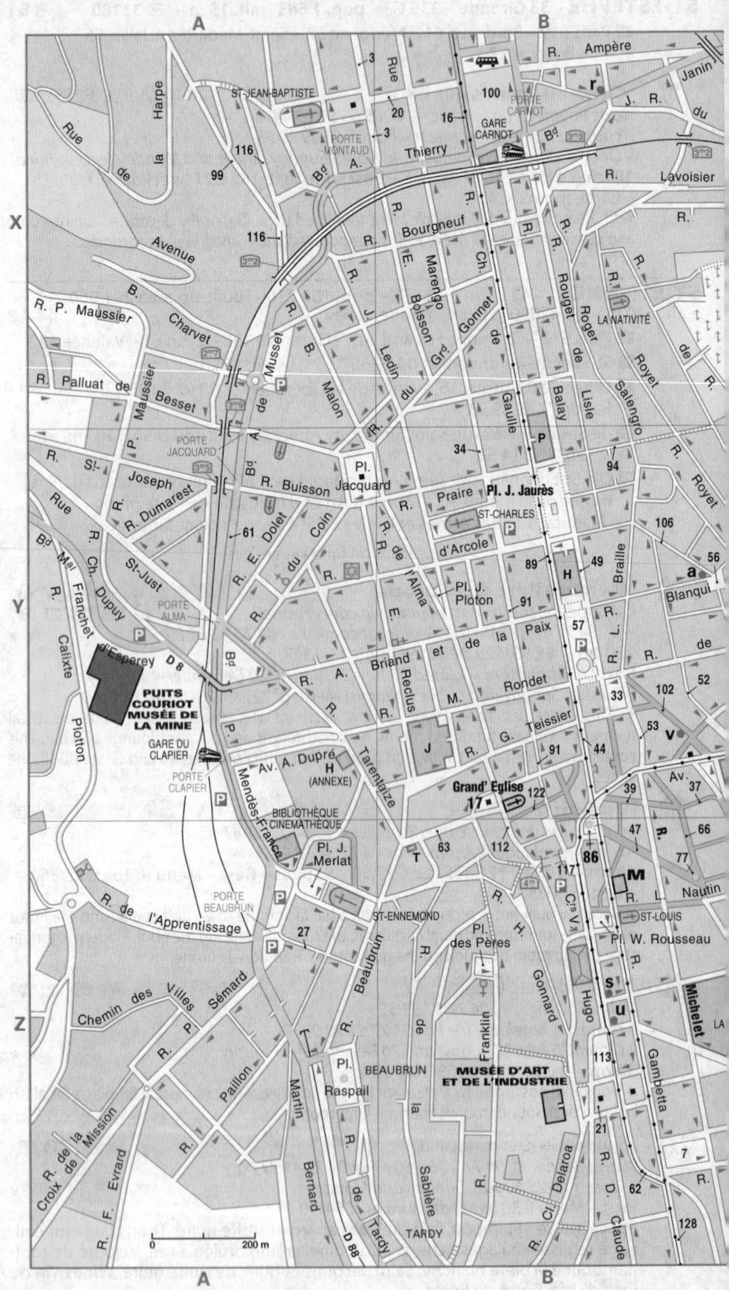

A
B
X
Y
Z
R. Ampère
Janin
J. R.
du
100
PORTE CARNOT
GARE CARNOT
16
Bd
R. Lavoisier
R.
ST-JEAN-BAPTISTE
3
Rue
20
PORTE MONTAUD
Thierry
Bd A.
116
99
Rue de la Harpe
Avenue
B. Charvet
R. P. Maussier
R. Bourgneuf
R. J.
R. E. Marengo
R. Boisson
Ch. de Gaulle
R. Rouget de Lisle
R. Roger Salengro
LA NATIVITÉ
R. Royet
R. de
R. Palluat de Besset
P. Maussier
R. Musset
R. B. Malon
Ledin
du Grd Gonnet
Balay
PORTE JACQUARD
R. St-Joseph
R. Dumarest
Rue St-Just
Bd A. de
R. Buisson
Pl. Jacquard
34
94
R. Royet
Prairie
Pl. J. Jaurès
ST-CHARLES
d'Arcole
106
56
a
61
R. E. Dolet
R. du Coin
R. R. de l'Alma
Pl. J. Ploton
89
49
H
R. Braille
Blanqui
Bd Mal Franchet d'Esperey
R. Ch. Dupuy
PORTE ALMA
R. E. Reclus
91
R. de la Paix
57
R. L.
R. de
Calixte Plotton
D 8
R. A. Briand et
R. M. Rondet
33
102
52
PUITS COURIOT MUSÉE DE LA MINE
GARE DU CLAPIER
PORTE CLAPIER
P.
R.
J
R. G. Teissier
91
44
53
v
Av. A. Dupré
H (ANNEXE)
Tarentaize
Grand' Eglise
17
122
39
Av.
37
BIBLIOTHÈQUE CINÉMATHÈQUE
Mendès-France
Pl. J. Merlat
63
T
112
47
R.
66
86
117
77
M
R. L. Nautin
ST-LOUIS
R. de l'Apprentissage
PORTE BEAUBRUN
ST-ENNEMOND
27
R. Beaubrun
R.
Pl. des Pères
R. H. Gonnard
Crs V. Hugo
Pl. W. Rousseau
R.
s
u
Michelet
Chemin des Villes
R. P. Sémard
R.
R. Paillon
R. de la Sablière
Franklin
113
R. Gambetta
Pl. Raspail
BEAUBRUN
MUSÉE D'ART ET DE L'INDUSTRIE
21
R. de la Croix de Mission
R. F. Evrard
R.
Martin Bernard
R. de Tardy
D 88
TARDY
R.
Cl. Delaroa
R. D. Claude
62
7
R.
128
0
200 m

ST-ÉTIENNE

Street	Grid	No.
Albert-1er (Bd)	ABX	3
Anatole-France (Pl.)	BZ	7
Badouillère (R. de la)	CZ	9
Barbusse (R. H.)	CZ	12
Bérard (R. P.)	BCY	14
Bergson (R.)	BX	16
Boivin (Pl.)	BY	17
Chavanelle (Pl.)	CZ	18
Clovis-Hugues (R.)	BX	20
Comte (Pl. Louis)	BZ	21
Denfert-Rochereau (Av.)	CY	26
Descours (R.)	AZ	27
Dorian (Pl.)	BY	33
Dormoy (R. M.)	BXY	34
Dupré (R. G.)	BY	37
Durafour (R. A.)	CZ	38
Escoffier (R. D.)	BY	39
Fougerolle (R.)	CZ	41
Fourneyron (Pl.)	CY	42
Foy (R. Gén.)	BY	44
Frappa (R. J.)	BZ	47
Gambetta (R.)	BZ	
Gaulle (R. Ch.-de)	BXY	
Gérentet (R.)	BY	49
Gervais (R. E.)	CY	50
Gillet (R. F.)	BY	52
Grand Moulin (R. du)	BY	53
Guesde (Pl. J.)	BY	56
Hôtel-de-Ville (Pl. de l')	BY	57
Jacob (R.)	CX	58
Krumnow (Bd F.)	AY	61
Leclerc (R. du Gén.)	BZ	62
Libération (Av. de la)	BCY	
Loubet (Av. du Président E.)	BZ	63
Martyrs-de-Vingré (R. des)	BYZ	66
Michelet (R.)	BYZ	
Moine (Pl. Antonin)	CYZ	68
Moulin (Pl. J.)	CY	72
Mulatière (R. de la)	CZ	75
Neuve (Pl.)	BZ	77
Peuple (Pl. du)	BZ	86
Pointe-Cadet (R.)	BCZ	87
Président-Wilson (R.)	BY	89
République (R. de la)	BCY	
Résistance (R. de la)	BY	91
Rivière (R. du Sergent)	CX	93
Robert (R.)	BY	94
Ruel (R. A.)	AX	99
Sadi-Carnot (Pl.)	BX	100
St-Jean (R.)	BY	102
Sauzéa (Cours H.)	CY	103
Servet (R. M.)	BY	106
Stalingrad (Square de)	CY	109
Théâtre (R. du)	BYZ	112
Thomas (Pl. A.)	BZ	113
Tilleuls (R. des)	AX	116
Ursules (Pl. des)	BZ	117
Valbenoite (Bd)	CZ	119
Villeboeuf (Pl.)	CZ	123
Ville (R. de la)	BY	122
11-Novembre (R. du)	BZ	128

ST-ÉTIENNE

Aciéries (R. des) . . . . T 2
Barrouin (R.) . . . . T 13
Crozet-Boussingault (R.) . . . . . V 22
Daguerre (Bd) . . . . UV 24
Déchaud (R. H.) . . . . V 25
Dr-F.-Merlin (R. du) . . . . T 30
Drs-Charcot (R. des) . . . . V 31
Drs-H.-et-B.-Muller (R. des) . . . T 32
Dunkerque (R. de) . . . . V 36
Fraissinette (Bd A.-de) . . . . . . V 45
Franchet-d'Esperey (Bd Mar.) U 46
Gauthier-Dumont (R.) . . . . U 48
Grignard (R. V.) . . . . T 55
Marx (Bd Karl) . . . . UV 67
Oddé (R. C.) . . . . T 78
Ogier (R. J.-B.) . . . . U 79
Paré (R. A.) . . . . V 131
Passementiers (R. des) . . . . . V 82
Pasteur (Bd) . . . . V 83
Péri (R. G.) . . . . V 84
Pompidou (Bd G.) . . . . T 88
Revollier (R. J.-F.) . . . . T 92
Robespierre (R.) . . . . V 95
Rochetaillée (Av. de) . . . . V 98
Scheurer-Kestner (R.) . . . . T 104
Terrenoire (R. de) . . . . U 110
Valbenoite (Bd) . . . . UV 119
Verdun (Av. de) . . . . T 120
Vivaraize (R. de la) . . . . V 125
8-Mai-1945 (Bd du) . . . . T 127
11-Novembre (R. du) . . . . V 128
38e-R.-I. (Bd du) . . . . U 130

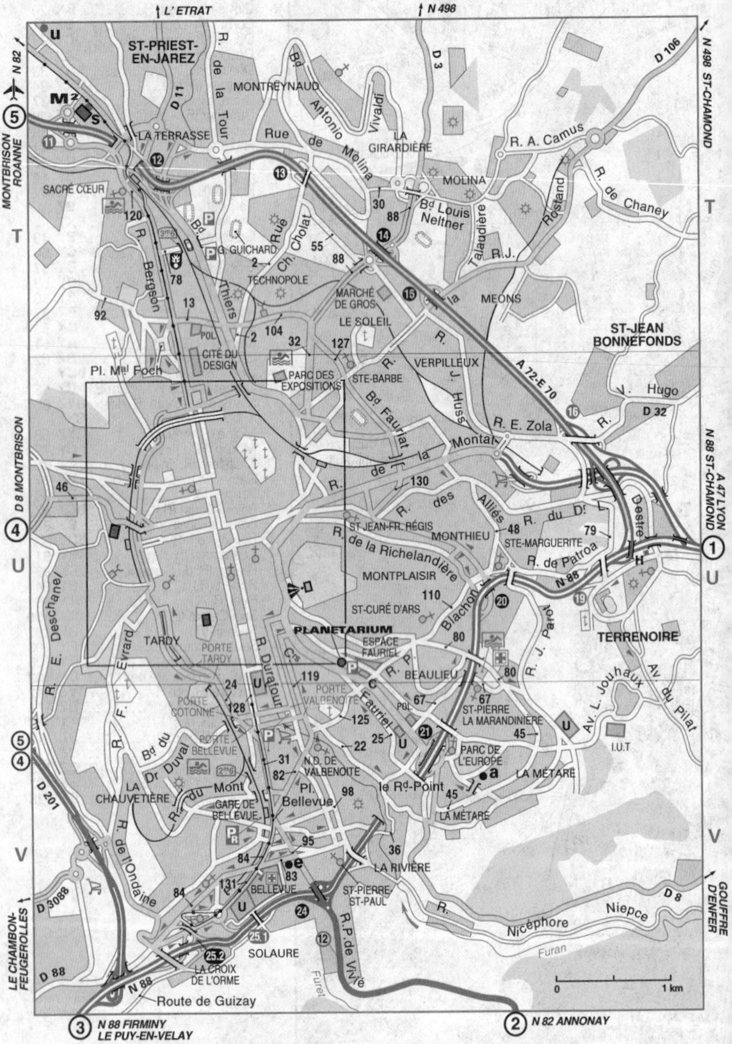

XXX **André Barcet** A/C VISA MC AE

19bis cours V. Hugo – ✆ 04 77 32 43 63 – restaurantbarcet@wanadoo.fr – Fax 04 77 32 23 93 – Closed 14 July-3 August, Sunday dinner and Wednesday

Rest – Menu € 35 (weekday lunch)/67 – Carte € 57/75 BZ **u**

◆ Elegant facade near the covered market. A comfortable English-style lounge precedes a refined dining room, enhanced by flowers, where one can enjoy a classic menu.

XX **Evohé** VISA MC AE

10 pl. Villeboeuf – ✆ 04 77 32 70 22 – Fax 04 77 32 91 52 – Closed 31 July-25 August, Monday dinner, Saturday lunch and Sunday

Rest – Menu (€ 20), € 35 bi (weekdays)/45 CZ **n**

◆ Restaurant overlooking a garden and near the Cultural Centre. The coloured walls are hung with paintings for sale, and the dining area has an intimate feel.

XX **Le Chantecler** A/C VISA MC AE

5 cours Fauriel – ✆ 04 77 25 48 55 – lechantecler42@hotmail.fr – Fax 04 77 37 62 75 – Closed 1st-13 August and Sunday dinner CZ **q**

Rest – Menu € 25/45 – Carte € 27/49

◆ This restaurant facing the Massenet conservatory named after the composer born in Saint-Étienne, has a classic culinary repertory and a bourgeois décor of murals and red walls.

XX **Régency** A/C VISA MC AE

17 bd J. Janin – ✆ 04 77 74 27 06 – alexis.bessette@laposte.net – Fax 04 77 74 98 24 – Closed August, 1st-9 January, Saturday and Sunday

Rest – Menu € 30/47 – Carte € 33/47 BX **r**

◆ Cheery facade, colourful dining room in sharp yellow and orange tones, beautiful red-brick vaulting. The market and the season influence the menu.

X **Corne d'Aurochs** VISA MC

18 r. Michel Servet – ✆ 04 77 32 27 27 – bruno.billamboz@wanadoo.fr – Fax 04 77 32 72 56 – Closed 1st-12 May, 27 July-31 August, Monday lunch, Saturday lunch and Sunday BY **a**

Rest – Menu € 18 (weekday lunch), € 21/40 – Carte € 24/47

◆ This wood-fronted bistro has a unique interior with a collection of pastrymaking whisks and book-festival lithographs. Lyon-style cuisine.

X **L'Escargot d'Or** VISA MC AE

5 cours V. Hugo – ✆ 04 77 41 24 04 – Fax 04 77 37 27 79 – Closed 5-11 May, 28 July-19 August, 23 February-4 March, Sunday dinner and Monday BZ **s**

Rest – Menu € 16 (weekdays), € 23/35 – Carte € 29/47

◆ Small restaurant on the first floor of a bar, with a tasteful and simple modern decor. Attractively presented traditional cuisine.

in l'Étrat **5 km north by D 11 – alt. 460 m – ✉ 42580**

XX **Yves Pouchain** P VISA MC

rte St-Héand – ✆ 04 77 93 46 31 – Fax 04 77 93 90 71 – Closed 18-31 August, 19-31 January, Wednesday dinner, Sunday dinner and Monday

Rest – Menu € 21/53 – Carte € 39/51

◆ In this farm dating from 1879, an antique doll collection, old stoves, a mural, wood chandeliers, stone and beams make up a decor with character.

in Sorbiers **10 km north by D 106, N 82 and D 3 – pop. 7 399 – alt. 560 m – ✉ 42290**

ℹ Office de tourisme, 2, avenue Charles-de-Gaulle ✆ 04 77 01 11 42, Fax 04 77 53 07 27

X **Le Valjoly** P VISA MC

9 r. de l'Onzon – ✆ 04 77 53 60 35 – levaljoly@free.fr – Closed 28 April-2 May, 28 July-25 August, Sunday dinner, Wednesday dinner and Monday

Rest – Menu (€ 13,50), € 17/48 – Carte € 21/50

◆ A welcome with a smile, pretty floral decoration and colourful touches make up for the passing traffic noise and simple setting in this inn, which offers a traditional cuisine.

in Rochetaillée **8 km southeast by D 8 – ✉ 42100**

XX **Yves Genaille**
3 r. du Parc – ✆ 04 77 32 88 48 – restaurant.genaille@wanadoo.fr – Fax 04 77 46 06 41 – Closed 19-27 April, August, dinner off season, Saturday lunch, Sunday dinner, Tuesday dinner and Monday
Rest – rôtisserie *(pre-book)* Menu € 24 (weekday lunch), € 30/60 – Carte € 47/58
◆ One wall of the panoramic dining room in this restaurant located in the centre of the village is emblazoned with culinary awards. Contemporary cuisine and rotisserie dishes.

in St-Victor-sur-Loire **10 km west by ④ and D 25 (to Firminy) – ✉ 42230**

XX **Auberge La Grange d'Ant'**
lieu-dit Bécizieux – ✆ 04 77 90 45 36 – Fax 04 77 90 45 36 – Closed 2 January-7 February
Rest – *(number of covers limited, pre-book)* Menu € 18/55 – Carte € 40/78
◆ 15min from the town centre, this restored old barn has retained its pleasant rustic-style quality (stone, beams and fireplace). Cuisine with personal touches; lots of menu choices.

in St-Priest-en-Jarez **4 km northwest -T – pop. 5 812 – alt. 605 m – ✉ 42270**

XXX **Clos Fleuri**
76 av. A. Raimond – ✆ 04 77 74 63 24 – f.deville@closfleuri.fr – Fax 04 77 79 06 70 – Closed 11-18 August, 2-7 January, Wednesday dinner, Sunday dinner and Monday T **u**
Rest – Menu € 20 (weekday lunch), € 27/70 – Carte € 52/62
◆ A large flower-decked villa with an elegant dining room with cane furniture and shaded terraces. Contemporary cuisine.

X **Du Musée**
Musée d'Art Moderne-la Terrasse – ✆ 04 77 79 24 52 – Fax 04 77 79 92 07 – Closed 10-25 August, Wednesday dinner, Sunday dinner and Monday T **s**
Rest – Menu (€ 19), € 26/36 – Carte € 33/50
◆ Food for the mind, then food for the tummy...or vice versa, depending on your appetite! The Museum of Modern Art's bistro serves its menu based on market produce in a determinedly contemporary décor.

in La Fouillouse **8.5 km northwest by N 82 – pop. 4 234 – alt. 438 m – ✉ 42480**

X **La Route Bleue**
Le Vernay – ✆ 04 77 30 12 09 – Fax 04 77 30 27 16 – Closed 14 July-20 August, February half term holidays and Saturday
Rest – *(lunch only)* Menu € 17/35 – Carte € 26/51
◆ Creeper-covered family restaurant, frequented by regular customers. Traditional cuisine served in a simple setting.

ST-ÉTIENNE-DE-BAÏGORRY – 64 Pyrénées-Atlantiques – 342 D5 – pop. 1 525 – alt. 163 m – ✉ 64430 Atlantic Coast

3 **A3**

Paris 813 – Biarritz 51 – Cambo-les-Bains 31 – Pau 116 – St-Jean-Pied-de-Port 11

Office de tourisme, place de l'Église ✆ 05 59 37 47 28, Fax 05 59 37 49 58

St-Etienne church ★.

Arcé
col d'Ispéguy road – ✆ 05 59 37 40 14 – reservations@hotel-arce.com – Fax 05 59 37 40 27 – Open mid March-mid November
20 rm – €70/75 €125/145, € 10 – 3 suites – ½ P € 100/105
Rest – *(closed Wednesday lunch and Monday lunch 15 September-15 July except public holidays) (pre-book Sat - Sun)* Menu € 27/40 – Carte approx. € 42
◆ Situated on the banks of the River Nivelle, this attractive auberge was formerly a café where pelota was played. Lovely garden and pool on the opposite bank. Large, well-maintained guestrooms. The restaurant occupies a converted *trinquet* (pelota hall). Terrace shaded by plane trees. Regional dishes and wines from Irrouléguy.

ST-ÉTIENNE-DE-FURSAC – 23 Creuse – 325 G4 – see La Souterraine

ST-ÉTIENNE-LA-THILLAYE – 14 Calvados – 303 M4 – pop. 437 – alt. 20 m – ✉ 14950

32 **A3**

Paris 198 – Caen 45 – Le Havre 47 – Lisieux 28 – Hérouville-Saint-Clair 48

La Maison de Sophie

– ✆ 02 31 65 69 97 – *sophie@lamaisondesophie.fr* – *Fax 02 31 65 69 98* – *Closed January, Sunday and Monday except school holidays*

5 rm – €150/170 €150/170 – **Table d'hôte** – *(open Friday dinner and Saturday dinner)* Menu €60 bi

◆ Former presbytery (1789) sympathetically restored with park and gardens. Carefully chosen décor, with exotic rooms decorated on musical and aromatic themes. Contemporary recipes and cooking classes by TV cook Sophie!

ST-ÉTIENNE-LÈS-REMIREMONT – 88 Vosges – 314 H4 – see Remiremont

ST-EUTROPE-DE-BORN – 47 Lot-et-Garonne – 336 G2 – see Cancon

ST-EVROULT-NOTRE-DAME-DU-BOIS – 61 Orne – 310 L2 – pop. 430 – alt. 355 m – ✉ 61550 Normandy

33 **C2**

Paris 155 – Argentan 42 – Caen 91 – Lisieux 52

Le Relais de l'Abbaye

rm, VISA

r. principale – ✆ *02 33 84 19 00* – *le.relais.de.labbaye@wanadoo.fr* – *Fax 02 33 84 19 04*

11 rm – €34/40 €43/50, €7 – **Rest** – *(closed Sunday dinner and Friday)* Menu €10,50, €22/38

◆ Fully renovated hotel in the main street of a village known for its old Norman abbey. Functional and well-soundproofed rooms. Restaurant set under an original pyramid-shaped glass roof. Traditional cuisine.

ST-FARGEAU – 89 Yonne – 319 B6 – pop. 1 814 – alt. 175 m – ✉ 89170 Burgundy-Jura

7 **A2**

Paris 180 – Auxerre 45 – Clamecy 48 – Gien 41

Office de tourisme, 3, pl. de la République ✆ 03 86 74 10 07, Fax 03 86 74 10 07

Château★.

Les Grands Chênes without rest

VISA

Les Berthes-Bailly, 4.5 km south by D 18 – ✆ *03 86 74 04 05* – *contact@hotel-de-puisaye.com* – *Fax 03 86 74 11 41* – *Closed 24 August-1st September, 21 December-4 January and 22 February to 8 March*

12 rm – €69/72 €69/72, €7

◆ Halfway between a guesthouse and a country residence, a charming bourgeois manor with colourful rooms, near the Guédelon medieval château site.

ST-FÉLIX-LAURAGAIS – 31 Haute-Garonne – 343 J4 – pop. 1 301 – alt. 332 m – ✉ 31540 Languedoc-Roussillon-Tarn Gorges

29 **C2**

Paris 716 – Auterive 46 – Carcassonne 58 – Castres 38 – Gaillac 71 – Toulouse 43

Syndicat d'initiative, place Guillaume de Nogaret ✆ 05 62 18 96 99

Site★.

Auberge du Poids Public (Claude Taffarello) with rm

– ✆ *05 62 18 85 00* – *poidspublic@wanadoo.fr* – *Fax 05 62 18 85 05* – *Closed January and autumn half-term holidays*

AC VISA

11 rm – €62/65 €70/102, €11,50 – 1 suite – ½ P €70/89

Rest – *(closed Sunday dinner except July-August)* Menu €30 (except public holidays)/70 – Carte €55/90

Spec. Thon blanc cuit à la plancha. Pigeonneau du Lauragais rôti. Macaron fruits rouges, crème chocolat-caramel. **Wines** Pic-Saint-Loup, Vin de pays des Côtes du Tarn.

◆ An agreeable semi-rustic, semi-modern decor with a collection of old tools and a panoramic view of the countryside at this delightful inn. Excellent up-to-date menu with a regional slant. Ask for a room with a view of the Lauragais plain.

ST-FERRÉOL – 31 Haute-Garonne – 343 K4 – see Revel

ST-FIRMIN – 80 Somme – 301 C6 – see Rue

ST-FLORENT – 2B Haute-Corse – 345 E3 – see Corse

ST-FLORENTIN – 89 Yonne – 319 F3 – pop. 5 748 – alt. 120 m – ✉ 89600

Burgundy-Jura 7 **B1**

Paris 169 – Auxerre 32 – Chaumont 145 – Dijon 172 – Sens 45 – Troyes 51

Syndicat d'initiative, 8, rue de la Terrasse ☎ 03 86 35 11 86, Fax 03 86 35 11 86

Church★ stained-glass windows **E**.

Les Tilleuls

rm, VISA MC AE

3 r. Decourtive – ☎ 03 86 35 09 09 – lestilleuls.stflorentin@wanadoo.fr – Fax 03 86 35 36 90 – Closed 17-24 November, 24 December-6 January, 16 February-16 March, Sunday dinner from mid September to mid June and Monday

9 rm – †€ 44/48 ††€ 51/62, ☕ € 9,50 – **Rest** – Menu € 16 (weekday lunch), € 26/40

♦ A family hotel converted from a Capuchin monastery dating back to 1635. Some of the comfortable rooms overlook a shady garden with lime trees. A pleasant restaurant enhanced by coloured beams; greenery predominates on the terrace and the cuisine is traditional.

XXX La Grande Chaumière with rm

P VISA MC AE

3 r. des Capucins – ☎ 03 86 35 15 12 – lagrandechaumiere@wanadoo.fr – Fax 03 86 35 33 14 – Closed 31 August-15 September (except hotel), 20 December-20 January, Wednesday and Thursday

10 rm – †€ 69/75 ††€ 75/130, ☕ € 12 – ½ P € 90 – **Rest** – Menu € 29 (weekday lunch), € 41/59 – Carte € 62/78

♦ Elegant regional establishment whose decor is a tasteful combination of modern ideas and old materials (superb tiled floor). Comfortable rooms. Beautiful terrace facing the garden.

Red = Pleasant. Look for the red X and 🏠 symbols.

ST-FLOUR – 15 Cantal – 330 G4 – pop. 6 625 – alt. 783 m – ✉ 15100

Auvergne 5 **B3**

Paris 513 – Aurillac 70 – Issoire 67 – Le Puy-en-Velay 94 – Rodez 111

Office de tourisme, 17 bis, place d'Armes ☎ 04 71 60 22 50, Fax 04 71 60 05 14

Site★★ - Cathedral ★ - Brassard★ in the musée de la Haute Auvergne **H**.

Plan on next page

Lower town

Grand Hôtel de l'Étape

VISA MC AE

18 av. de la République, via ② – ☎ 04 71 60 13 03 – info@hotel-etape.com – Fax 04 71 60 48 05 – Closed Sunday evening except July-August

23 rm – †€ 56 ††€ 77, ☕ € 9 – ½ P € 62/64

Rest – *(closed Sunday dinner and Monday except July-August)* Menu (€ 15 bi), € 22/48 – Carte € 29/45

♦ A family-run, 1970s establishment. Spacious and practical rooms; choose one with a mountain view. There is a Seventies feel to the restaurant serving authentic regional cuisine. Most of the vegetables come from the establishment's cottage garden.

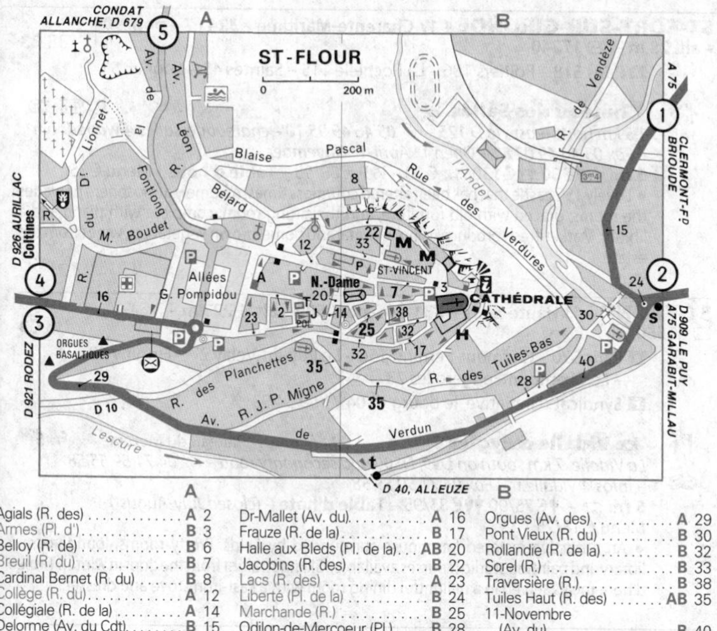

Agials (R. des)	A	2	Dr-Mallet (Av. du)	A	16	Orgues (Av. des)	A	29
Armes (Pl. d')	B	3	Frauze (R. de la)	B	17	Pont Vieux (R. du)	B	30
Belloy (R. de)	B	6	Halle aux Bleds (Pl. de la)	AB	20	Rollandie (R. de la)	B	32
Breuil (R. du)	B	7	Jacobins (R. des)	B	22	Sorel (R.)	B	33
Cardinal Bernet (R. du)	B	8	Lacs (R. des)	A	23	Traversière (R.)	B	38
Collège (R. du)	A	12	Liberté (Pl. de la)	B	24	Tuiles Haut (R. des)	AB	35
Collégiale (R. de la)	A	14	Marchande (R.)	B	25	11-Novembre (Av. du)	B	40
Delorme (Av. du Cdt)	B	15	Odilon-de-Mercoeur (Pl.)	B	28			

Auberge de La Providence

rm, P, VISA, MC, AE

1 r. Château d'Alleuze, via D 40 (south of plan) – ☎ 04 71 60 12 05 – info@auberge-providence.com – Fax 04 71 60 33 94 – Closed 15 November-5 January

12 rm – †€ 56/70 ††€ 56/70, ☕ € 8,50 – ½ P € 48/50 B **t**

Rest – *(closed Friday and Saturday in winter and Sunday) (dinner only)*
Menu (€ 20), € 28/35 – Carte € 30/36

♦ Slightly out of the centre, this welcoming family inn has modest, but well-kept, soundproofed rooms (two with terrace). The large sideboard, its wood worn smooth with age, gives character to the country restaurant; simple recipes with a regional flavour.

St-Jacques

AC rest, VISA, MC, AE

8 pl. de la Liberté – ☎ 04 71 60 09 20 – info@hotelsaintjacques.com – Fax 04 71 60 33 81 – Closed 9 November-3 January and Friday dinner from January to Easter B **s**

28 rm – †€ 45 ††€ 53, ☕ € 7

Rest – *(closed Saturday lunch, Sunday dinner and Monday)*
Menu € 14 – Carte € 21/36

Rest Grill – *(closed Friday dinner and Saturday lunch)* Carte € 21/36

♦ This establishment, on a small square, used to be a stop on the route to Compostella. A few family rooms and an attractive view of the upper town from the swimming pool. A colourful restaurant offering dishes from the Indian Ocean area. Bistro style and traditional dishes at the Grill.

in St-Georges by ②, D 909 and secondary road: 5 km – pop. 939 – alt. 860 m – ✉ 15100

Le Château de Varillettes

rest, P, VISA, MC, AE

– ☎ 04 71 60 45 05 – varillettes@leshotelsparticuliers.com – Fax 04 71 60 34 27 – Open May to September

12 rm – †€ 117/147 ††€ 117/252, ☕ € 15 – ½ P € 106/121

Rest – Menu € 32/45 – Carte € 39/58

♦ Treat yourself to the charm of yesteryear and the comfort of today in this 15C château, a summer residence of the bishops of St-Flour. Ask for a room with a view over the medieval garden. The vaulted restaurant dining room with its old fireplace is full of character.

ST-FORT-SUR-GIRONDE – 17 Charente-Maritime – 324 F7 – pop. 904 – alt. 28 m – ✉ 17240

38 **B3**

Paris 518 – Poitiers 186 – La Rochelle 115 – Saintes 45 – Cognac 51

Château des Salles

1.5 km north-east via D 125 – ✆ 05 46 49 95 10 – chateaudessalles@wanadoo.fr – Fax 05 46 49 02 81 – Open 1st April-1st November

5 rm – †€ 80 ††€ 130, ☐ € 10 – ½ P € 85/95 – **Table d'hôte** – Menu € 35

◆ Lovely 15C castle that has been altered countless times. A homely atmosphere pervades the rooms, graced with old furniture, and the sitting room, complete with piano and a library. Market-fresh produce using regional and home-grown vegetables, wines from the estate.

ST-FRONT – 43 Haute-Loire – 331 G4 – pop. 509 – alt. 1 223 m – ✉ 43550

6 **C3**

Paris 570 – Clermont-Ferrand 156 – Le Puy-en-Velay 27 – Firminy 69 – Le Chambon-Feugerolles 73

Syndicat d'initiative, le bourg ✆ 04 71 59 54 93

La Vidalle d'Eyglet

Plateau du Mezenc,

La Vidalle, 7 km south on D39, D500 and secondary road – ✆ 04 71 59 55 58 – infos@vidalle.fr – Fax 04 71 59 55 58

5 rm ☐ – †€ 75/90 ††€ 85/95 – **Table d'hôte** – *(closed July-August)* Menu € 18/25

◆ An attractive restored farmhouse surrounded by fields. Pretty rooms, lounge-cum-library and painting studio (courses available). Skiing straight from the door in winter. Table d'hôte meals served in a delightful dining room with a cast-iron stove and dresser.

ST-GALMIER – 42 Loire – 327 E6 – pop. 5 293 – alt. 400 m – Casino – ✉ 42330

Lyon - Rhone Valley

44 **A2**

Paris 457 – Lyon 82 – Montbrison 25 – Montrond-les-Bains 11 – Roanne 68 – St-Étienne 24

Office de tourisme, Le Cloître, 3, boulevard Cousin ✆ 04 77 54 06 08, Fax 04 77 54 06 07

Vierge du Pilier★ and triptych★ in the church.

La Charpinière

rm, rest,

– ✆ 04 77 52 75 00 – charpiniere.hot.rest@wanadoo.fr – Fax 04 77 54 18 79

49 rm – †€ 77/117 ††€ 77/117, ☐ € 12 – ½ P € 65/85

Rest ***La Closerie de la Tour*** – *(closed Sunday dinner from November to March)* Menu € 24/49 – Carte € 25/52

◆ A vast walled park surrounds this small ivy-clad manor house, making it a haven of peace and quiet. Countless leisure activities. The rooms are above all practical. Winter garden-style restaurant serving up-to-date recipes and a menu that varies with the seasons.

Hostellerie du Forez

6 r. Didier Guetton – ✆ 04 77 54 00 23 – contact@hostelleriedouforez.com – Fax 04 77 54 07 49

16 rm – †€ 48/56 ††€ 56/65, ☐ € 9,50 – ½ P € 67 – **Rest** – *(closed 5-25 August, 26 December-5 January, Sunday dinner and Monday lunch)* Menu (€ 15 bi), € 17/33 – Carte € 24/39

◆ Now an inn, this abode, which is in perfect condition, used to be a post house in the 19C. Well kept functional rooms, currently in the process of renovation. Updated menu served in a rustic dining room.

Le Bougainvillier

Pré Château – ✆ 04 77 54 03 31 – bougain@wanadoo.fr – Fax 04 77 94 95 93 – Closed 28 July-25 August, 9-23 February, Wednesday dinner, Sunday dinner and Monday

Rest – *(pre-book)* Menu € 29/62 – Carte € 46/67

◆ Treat yourself to a gourmet stay in this impressive 19C house. The restaurant is made up of three rooms, one of which leads into the garden. Appealing contemporary cuisine.

ST-GATIEN-DES-BOIS – 14 Calvados – 303 N3 – pop. 1 163 – alt. 149 m – ✉ 14130
32 **A3**

▶ Paris 195 – Caen 58 – Le Havre 36 – Deauville 10 – Honfleur 13 – Lisieux 27

Le Clos Deauville St-Gatien

4 r. Brioleurs – ☎ 02 31 65 16 08 – hotel@clos-st-gatien.fr – Fax 02 31 65 10 27

58 rm – †€ 78/185 ††€ 78/185, ☕ € 13 – ½ P € 81/134

Rest *Le Michels* – Menu (€ 21), € 31/75 – Carte € 37/82

◆ An old farm and outbuildings set in a tree lined garden. A variety of leisure and seminar facilities enable guests to combine business with pleasure. Original beams and half-timbering constitute the charm of this restaurant.

ST-GAUDENS – 31 Haute-Garonne – 343 C6 – pop. 10 845 – alt. 405 m – ✉ 31800 Languedoc-Roussillon-Tarn Gorges
28 **B3**

▶ Paris 766 – Bagnères-de-Luchon 48 – Tarbes 68 – Toulouse 94

ℹ Office de tourisme, 2, rue Thiers ☎ 05 61 94 77 61, Fax 05 61 94 77 50

◉ Boulevards des Pyrénées ≤★ - Viewpoints★.

Du Commerce

rm, rm,

av. de Boulogne – ☎ 05 62 00 97 00 – hotel.commerce@wanadoo.fr – Fax 05 62 00 97 01 – Closed 19 December-12 January Y e

48 rm – †€ 55/70 ††€ 55/73, ☕ € 8,50 – ½ P € 51/61 – **Rest** – Menu € 20/36 – Carte € 26/52

◆ A modern hotel located a stone's throw from the town centre. Functional rooms in a variety of styles, all with air-conditioning. Sunny colours, a happy blend of old and new, and cuisine where cassoulet takes pride of place.

ST-GENIEZ-D'OLT – 12 Aveyron – 338 J4 – pop. 1 841 – alt. 410 m – ✉ 12130 Languedoc-Roussillon-Tarn Gorges
29 **D1**

▶ Paris 612 – Espalion 28 – Florac 80 – Mende 68 – Rodez 46 – Sévérac-le-Château 25

ℹ Office de tourisme, Le Cloître ☎ 05 65 70 43 42, Fax 05 65 70 47 05

Hostellerie de la Poste

3 pl. Gén de Gaulle – ☎ 05 65 47 43 30 – hotel@hoteldelaposte12.com – Fax 05 65 47 42 75 – Open 16 March-9 November

50 rm – †€ 55/62 ††€ 55/62, ☕ € 8 – ½ P € 60

Rest *Le Rive Gauche* – Menu € 28 – Carte € 36/81

◆ Different types of rooms of varying size and comfort in this centrally-located hotel, which occupies a number of separate buildings, surrounded by greenery. Popular with groups. The Rive Gauche's regional menu can be enjoyed in its dining rooms or on the terrace by the swimming pool.

ST-GENIS-POUILLY – 01 Ain – 328 J3 – pop. 6 383 – alt. 445 m – ✉ 01630
46 **F1**

▶ Paris 524 – Bellegarde-sur-Valserine 28 – Bourg-en-Bresse 100 – Genève 12 – Gex 10

ℹ Office de tourisme, 11 rue de Gex ☎ 04 50 42 29 37, Fax 04 50 28 32 94

⛳ des Serves Route de Meyrin, East: 2 km by D 984, ☎ 04 50 42 16 48.

L'Amphitryon

– ☎ 04 50 20 64 64 – lafay.claudie@hotmail.fr – Fax 04 50 42 06 98 – Closed 30 July-20 August, 30 December-20 January, Tuesday dinner, Sunday dinner and Monday

Rest – Menu € 17 (weekday lunch), € 34 € bi/50 – Carte € 39/59

◆ The unassuming facade of this modern pavilion hides the impressive dining area with frescos, vaulted ceiling and small antique-style statues. Classic cuisine and good selection of wines.

ST-GENIX-SUR-GUIERS – 73 Savoie – 333 G4 – pop. 1 817 – alt. 235 m – ✉ 73240
45 **C2**

▶ Paris 513 – Belley 22 – Chambéry 34 – Grenoble 58 – Lyon 74

ℹ Office de tourisme, rue du faubourg ☎ 04 76 31 63 16, Fax 04 76 31 71 30

in Champagneux 4 km northwest by D 1516 – pop. 379 – alt. 214 m – ✉ 73240

Bergeronnettes rm,
near the church – ✆ 04 76 31 50 30 – gourjux@aol.com – Fax 04 76 31 61 29 – Closed 26 December-1st January
18 rm – €60 €60/125, €10 – ½ P €62 – **Rest** – *(closed Sunday dinner)* Menu €13,50/36 – Carte €26/35
◆ A country hotel nestling in a verdant setting; the recently constructed wing has large bedrooms. Buffet-style breakfasts. Modern restaurant serving simply prepared regional cuisine. Terrace under a marquee.

ST-GEORGES – 15 Cantal – 330 G4 – see St-Flour

ST-GEORGES-DE-DIDONNE – 17 Charente-Maritime – 324 D6 – see Royan

---

ST-GEORGES-D'ESPÉRANCHE – 38 Isère – 333 D4 – pop. 2 840 – alt. 400 m – ✉ 38790

44 **B2**

Paris 496 – Bourgoin-Jallieu 25 – Grenoble 92 – Lyon 40 – Vienne 22

Castel d'Espéranche rm,
14 rte Lafayette – ✆ 04 74 59 18 45 – info@castel-esperanche.com – Fax 04 74 59 04 40 – Closed 27 October-8 November, 9-27 February, Monday, Tuesday and Wednesday
Rest – Menu (€18), €25/55 – Carte €45/58
◆ Restaurant partly in the 13C guard tower, with a few of its vestiges embellishing the dining rooms. Regional cuisine and "medieval" menu.

ST-GEORGES-DES-SEPT-VOIES – 49 Maine-et-Loire – 317 H4 – pop. 570 – alt. 83 m – ✉ 49350

35 **C2**

Paris 314 – Nantes 127 – Angers 30 – Saumur 27 – La Flèche 71

Auberge de la Sansonnière with rm rest, rest,
(near the Town Hall) – ✆ 02 41 57 57 70 – contact@auberge-sansonniere.com – Fax 02 41 57 51 38 – Closed 3-20 March, 12 November-5 December, Sunday dinner and Monday
7 rm – €55/70 €55/70, €8 – ½ P €50/57 – **Rest** – Menu (€11,50 bi), €17/35 – Carte €34/46
◆ A jewel of an inn, this former priory has been beautifully restored in a modern bistro style with beams, stone and bright colours. Appealing, revisited traditional cuisine. Charming and welcoming, albeit small, bedrooms.

ST-GEORGES-SUR-CHER – 41 Loir-et-Cher – 318 D8 – pop. 2 155 – alt. 70 m – ✉ 41400

11 **A1**

Paris 225 – Blois 40 – Orléans 102 – Tours 40

Prieuré de la Chaise without rest
8 r. Prieuré – ✆ 02 54 32 59 77 – prieuredelachaise@yahoo.fr – Fax 02 54 32 69 49
5 rm – €60 €120
◆ Charming 16C château, surrounded by a park. Rooms with red floor tiles and antique furniture. Dining room with pleasant log fire in winter.

ST-GERMAIN-DE-JOUX – 01 Ain – 328 H3 – pop. 476 – alt. 507 m – ✉ 01130

45 **C1**

Paris 487 – Bellegarde-sur-Valserine 13 – Belley 61 – Bourg-en-Bresse 63 – Nantua 13

Reygrobellet with rm
D 1084 – ✆ 04 50 59 81 13 – reygrobellet@orange.fr – Fax 04 50 59 83 74 – Closed 17-25 February, 29 June-17 July, 22 October-10 November, Wednesday dinner, Sunday dinner and Monday
10 rm – €50/55 €60/65, €8,50 – ½ P €60/65 – **Rest** – Menu €22/55
◆ In addition to its comfortable, countrified interior, this house is popular for its generous portions of classic dishes and lovely desserts. Partially refurbished simple rooms.

ST-GERMAIN-DES-VAUX – 50 Manche – 303 A1 – pop. 457 – alt. 59 m – ✉ 50440
32 **A1**

Paris 383 – Barneville-Carteret 48 – Cherbourg 28 – Nez de Jobourg 7 – St-Lô 104

Baie d'Ecalgrain★★ South: 3 km - Port de Goury★ Northwest: 2 km.

Nez de Jobourg★★ South: 7.5 km then 30 mn - ≤★★ on Vauville cove Southeast: 9.5 km by Herqueville, **Normandy**

Le Moulin à Vent

(Hamlet of Danneville), 1.5 km east via D 45 – ☎ 02 33 52 75 20 – contact@le-moulin-a-vent.fr – Fax 02 33 52 22 57 – Closed 3-27 December and Wednesday October-June

Rest – *(pre-book)* Menu € 26/37 – Carte € 28/42

◆ This inn enjoys an attractive and remote location at the tip of the Cotentin peninsula. Modern cuisine served in a contemporary dining room with superb views.

ST-GERMAIN-DU-BOIS – 71 Saône-et-Loire – 320 L9 – pop. 1 765 – alt. 210 m – ✉ 71330 Burgundy-Jura
8 **D3**

Paris 367 – Chalon-sur-Saône 33 – Dole 58 – Lons-le-Saunier 29 – Mâcon 75 – Tournus 40

Hostellerie Bressane with rm

2 rte de Sens – ☎ 03 85 72 04 69 – la.terrinee4@wanadoo.fr – Fax 03 85 72 07 75 – Closed 1st-8 September, February school holidays, Sunday dinner except July-August and Monday

9 rm – †€ 48 ††€ 52, ☕ € 5,50 – ½ P € 54 – **Rest** – Menu € 13 (weekday lunch), € 20/37 – Carte € 32/42

◆ An 18C town house with a picturesque regional-style interior. Fine frescoes dating from 1900 can be seen in one of the rooms. Carefully prepared regional cuisine with original touches. Renovated guestrooms.

ST-GERMAIN-EN-LAYE – 78 Yvelines – 311 I2 – 101 13 – see Paris, Area

ST-GERMAIN-LÈS-ARLAY – 39 Jura – 321 D6 – pop. 503 – alt. 255 m – ✉ 39210
16 **B3**

Paris 398 – Besançon 74 – Chalon-sur-Saône 58 – Dole 46 – Lons-le-Saunier 11

Hostellerie St-Germain with rm

– ☎ 03 84 44 60 91 – hoststgermain@wanadoo.fr – Fax 03 84 44 63 64 – Closed 10-30 November, Tuesday except dinner in July August and Monday

7 rm – †€ 52/72 ††€ 52/72, ☕ € 7 – ½ P € 61 – **Rest** – Menu € 17 (weekday lunch), € 22/59 – Carte € 39/60

◆ Worth a detour for its regional cuisine, matched by a fine selection of Jura wines. Elegantly rustic ambiance; well-presented rooms (quieter on the terrace side).

ST-GERMER-DE-FLY – 60 Oise – 305 B4 – pop. 1 761 – alt. 105 m – ✉ 60850 Northern France and the Paris Region
36 **A2**

Paris 92 – Les Andelys 40 – Beauvais 26 – Gisors 21 – Gournay-en-Bray 8 – Rouen 58

Syndicat d'initiative, 11, place de Verdun ☎ 03 44 82 62 74, Fax 03 44 82 23 56

Church ★ - ≤★ of the D 129 Southeast: 4 km.

Auberge de l'Abbaye

5 pl. de L' Abbaye – ☎ 03 44 82 50 73 – Fax 03 44 82 64 54 – Closed Sunday evening, Tuesday evening and Wednesday

Rest – Menu € 14,50 bi/31

◆ The ivy-covered facade of this restaurant facing the abbey conceals a large dining room with exposed beams. Traditional and regional cuisine. Tearoom.

ST-GERVAIS – 33 Gironde – 335 I4 – pop. 1 219 – alt. 39 m – ✉ 33240 3 B1

Paris 543 – Bordeaux 29 – Mérignac 38 – Pessac 44

Au Sarment

50 r. la Lande – ☎ 05 57 43 44 73 – ausarment33@free.fr – Fax 05 57 43 90 28 – Closed 22 February-1 0 March, 18 August-1st September, Saturday lunch, Sunday dinner and Monday

Rest – Menu € 39/59 – Carte € 51/68

◆ A fine country house, plain and bright décor, now a restaurant whose landlord and chef, of Caribbean origin, prepares up-to-date dishes with Creole touches. Terrace.

ST-GERVAIS-D'AUVERGNE – 63 Puy-de-Dôme – 326 D6 – pop. 1 272 – alt. 725 m – ✉ 63390 Auvergne 5 B2

Paris 377 – Aubusson 72 – Clermont-Ferrand 55 – Gannat 41 – Montluçon 47 – Riom 39

Office de tourisme, rue du Général Desaix ☎ 04 73 85 80 94

Castel Hôtel 1904

– ☎ 04 73 85 70 42 – castel.hotel.1904@orange.fr – Fax 04 73 85 84 39 – Open Easter-11 November

15 rm – €59 €65/79, €9,50 – ½ P €55 – **Rest** – Menu € 17/60 – Carte €24/37

◆ This enchanting 17C residence offers recently refurbished rooms decorated with period furnishings. Warm welcome from the family that has been at the helm since 1904. Dining room with a delightful olde world charm, serving classic dishes.

Le Relais d'Auvergne

rte de Châteauneuf – ☎ 04 73 85 70 10 – relais.auvergne.hotel@wanadoo.fr – Fax 04 73 85 85 66 – Open from March to November and closed Sunday evening and Monday in October, November and March

12 rm – €52 €52/62, €7 – ½ P €50

Rest – Menu € 13 (weekday lunch), € 18/35 – Carte € 24/41

◆ The profusion of old furniture and knick-knacks from the region (shop) depicts the old-fashioned atmosphere. Rooms personalised with antique and period furniture. Handsome countrified dining room. Traditional dishes and local specialities.

ST-GERVAIS-EN-VALLIÈRE – 71 Saône-et-Loire – 320 J8 – pop. 305 – alt. 203 m – ✉ 71350 7 A3

Paris 324 – Beaune 16 – Chalon-sur-Saône 24 – Dijon 57 – Mâcon 84 – Nevers 164

in Chaublanc 3 km Northeast by D 94 and D 183 – ✉ 71350 St-Gervais-en-Vallière

Le Moulin d'Hauterive rm, rest, rest,

– ☎ 03 85 91 55 56 – info@moulinhauterive.com – Fax 03 85 91 89 65 – Closed 1st December-12 February, Sunday evening except July-August and Monday

10 rm – €70/119 €109/139, €15 – 10 suites – ½ P €107/142

Rest – *(closed Sunday dinner November-May, Monday except dinner July-August, Tuesday lunch, Wednesday lunch and Thursday lunch)* Menu € 25 (weekday lunch), €40/62 – Carte € 53/73

◆ Located in the heart of the countryside, this old flour mill on the banks of the Dheune was built in the 12C by the monks of Cîteaux Abbey. Rooms with a personal touch, fine antique furniture. Two plush dining rooms and a pretty riverside terrace; wine shop.

ST-GERVAIS-LES-BAINS – 74 Haute-Savoie – 328 N5 – pop. 5 276 – alt. 820 m – Winter sports : 1 400/2 000 m 2 25 – Spa : all year – Casino – ✉ 74170 French Alps 46 F1

Paris 597 – Annecy 84 – Bonneville 42 – Chamonix-Mont-Blanc 25 – Megève 12

☎ 3635 (0,34 €/mn)

Office de tourisme, 43, rue du Mont-Blanc ☎ 04 50 47 76 08, Fax 04 50 47 75 69

Route du Bettex★★★ 8 km by ③ then D 43.

ST-GERVAIS-LES-BAINS LE FAYET

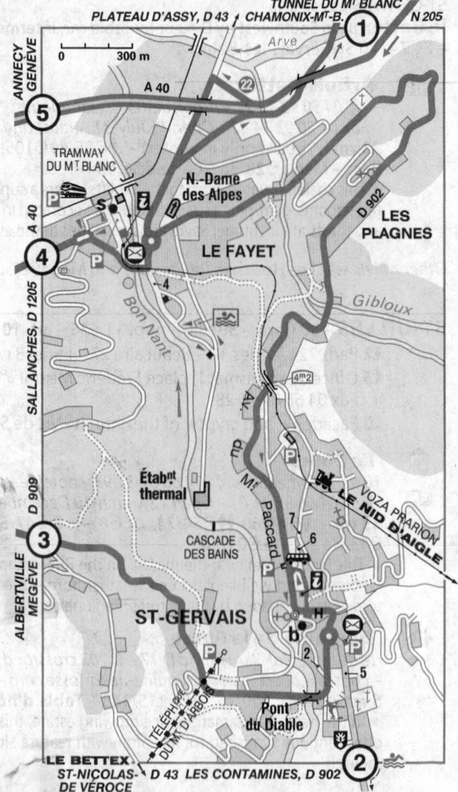

Val d'Este — VISA

pl. de l'Église – ✆ 04 50 93 65 91 – hotelvaldeste@voila.fr – Fax 04 50 47 76 29 – Closed 12 November-15 December b

14 rm – †€ 52/88 ††€ 52/88, ☐ € 8 – ½ P € 56/88

Rest ***Le Sérac*** – see restaurant listing

◆ This hotel in the centre of the resort has well-soundproofed guestrooms which are gradually being renovated. Those with a view of the mountains have a bathtub.

Le Sérac — VISA

– ✆ 04 50 93 80 50 – Fax 04 50 93 86 31 – Closed 9 November-4 December, Thursday lunch and Wednesday except 16 July-20 August and 24 December-18 March

Rest – Menu € 18 (weekday lunch), € 24/62 – Carte € 46/62 b

◆ With the mountains as a backdrop, this restaurant combines regional specialities with Mediterranean cuisine. Chocolate lovers won't be able to resist the dessert menu!

in Fayet **4 km northwest by D 902 – ✉ 74190**

Office de tourisme, 104, avenue de la gare ✆ 04 50 93 64 64

Deux Gares — P VISA

(near the station) – ✆ 04 50 78 24 75 – hotel.2gares@wanadoo.fr – Fax 04 50 78 15 47 – Closed 27 April-4 May, 28 September-5 October and 1st November-15 December s

28 rm – †€ 42/45 ††€ 52/54, ☐ € 8 – 2 suites – ½ P € 42/44

Rest – *(dinner only) (residents only)* Menu € 14

◆ The hotel faces the famous Mont Blanc tramway station. Small, simply furnished guestrooms which are being renovated in stages - ask for one of the most recent. Attractive indoor swimming pool.

in Bettex **8 km Southwest by D 43 or by cable car, intermediate station – ✉ 74170 St-Gervais-les-Bains**

Arbois-Bettex ◇ Mont - Blanc Massif,
– ✆ *04 50 93 12 22 – arboisbettex@wanadoo.fr* rest, **P** VISA
– Fax 04 50 93 14 42 – Open 1st July-31 August and 22 December-20 April
33 rm (½ board only in winter) – †€ 85 ††€ 105, ☐ € 12 – ½ P € 105/180 –
Rest – Menu € 28/38 – Carte € 36/54
◆ This chalet, situated close to the ski-lifts, offers a superb view of Mont Blanc. Functional guestrooms, gym, plus a spacious lounge decorated in Austrian style. Salads, buffets, grills and roasts at lunchtime; Savoyard specialities in the evening. South-facing terrace.

Other hotels see : **Les Houches** *(at Prarion) and* **Megève** *(summit of Mont d'Arbois)*

ST-GILLES – 30 Gard – 339 L6 – pop. 11 626 – alt. 10 m – ✉ 30800 Provence

Paris 724 – Arles 18 – Beaucaire 27 – Lunel 31 – Montpellier 64 – Nîmes 20

Office de tourisme, 1, place Frédéric Mistral ✆ 04 66 87 33 75, Fax 04 66 87 16 28 23 **D2**

Façade★★ and crypt★ of the church - Vis de St-Gilles★.

Le Cours VISA
10 av. F. Griffeuille – ✆ 04 66 87 31 93 – hotel-le-cours@wanadoo.fr
– Fax 04 66 87 31 83 – Open 12 March-10 December
33 rm – †€ 44/60 ††€ 54/74, ☐ € 8 – ½ P € 47/59 – **Rest** – Menu (€ 11,50), € 13/34 – Carte € 21/40
◆ This family hotel near the marina on the Rhône canal offers small, practical rooms, all renovated and well kept. In fine weather, forget the dining room-veranda and sit at a terrace table, shaded by plane trees. Regional fare.

Domaine de la Fosse rm, rest, **P** VISA
rte de Sylvéréal, 7km on via D 179, D 202 crossroads – ✆ 04 66 87 05 05
– christine.abeccassis@domaine-de-la-fosse.com – Fax 04 66 87 40 90
5 rm ☐ – †€ 100/120 ††€ 115/145 – **Table d'hôte** – Menu € 35 bi
◆ In the heart of a Camargue rice growing estate, this former Templar stronghold (17C) offers antique furnished rooms, often with feature sloping ceilings. Sauna, steam bath, Jacuzzi.

ST-GILLES-CROIX-DE-VIE – 85 Vendée – 316 E7 – pop. 6 797 – alt. 12 m – Casino : Le Royal Concorde – ✉ 85800 Atlantic Coast 34 **A3**

Paris 462 – Cholet 112 – Nantes 79 – La Roche-sur-Yon 44 – Les Sables-d'Olonne 29

Office de tourisme, boulevard de l'Égalité ✆ 02 51 55 03 66, Fax 02 51 55 69 60

des Fontenelles L'Aiguillon-sur-Vie Route de Coëx, East: 11 km by D 6, ✆ 02 51 54 13 94.

Le Casier VISA
pl. du Vieux Port – ✆ 02 51 55 01 08 – restaurantlecasier@orange.fr
– Closed 20 December-6 March, Sunday dinner, Wednesday, Tuesday from November to March and Monday
Rest – Menu (€ 19 bi) – Carte € 19/39
◆ Friendly nautical-inspired bistro decor, simple well-prepared seafood; the chef of this former pork butcher's shop near the quays has successfully swapped his apron for a chef's hat.

in Coex **14 km East by D 6 – ✉ 85220**

Syndicat d'initiative, place de l'Église ✆ 02 51 54 28 80, Fax 02 51 55 54 10

Carpe Diem VISA
Golf des Fontenelles, 2 km west via D 6 – ✆ 02 51 49 13 98 – carpediemvendee@aol.com – Closed Monday and Tuesday
Rest – Menu € 21/41 – Carte € 33/55
◆ This restaurant enjoys a splendid view of the golf course (the terrace looks onto the ninth hole). Contemporary decor and seasonal cuisine flavoured with spices.

in Sion-sur-l'Océan **5 km west by the Corniche Vendéenne – ✉ 85270**

Frédéric without rest
25 r. des Estivants – ✆ 02 51 54 30 20 – hotelfrederic@wanadoo.fr – Fax 02 51 54 11 68
13 rm – †€ 62 ††€ 62/118, ☕ € 12
◆ This attractive 1930s villa has been modernised without losing any of its former character. Ask for one of the rooms with a sea view. Delightfully old-fashioned oyster bar.

ST-GINGOLPH – 74 Haute-Savoie – 328 N2 – pop. 565 – alt. 385 m – ✉ 74500

French Alps 46 **F1**

Paris 560 – Annecy 102 – Évian-les-Bains 19 – Montreux 21 – Thonon-les-Bains 28

Aux Ducs de Savoie
r. 23 Juillet 44 – ✆ 04 50 76 73 09 – ducsdesavoie@orange.fr – Fax 04 50 76 74 31 – Closed 9-24 February, Monday and Tuesday except public holidays
Rest – Menu (€ 17), € 21 (weekday lunch), € 40/65 – Carte € 35/64
◆ Just below the village, this chalet is surrounded by plane trees. Shaded terrace facing the lake, traditional cuisine prepared with skill.

ST-GIRONS – 09 Ariège – 343 E7 – pop. 6 254 – alt. 398 m – ✉ 09200

Languedoc-Roussillon-Tarn Gorges 28 **B3**

Paris 774 – Auch 123 – Foix 45 – St-Gaudens 43 – Toulouse 101
Office de tourisme, place Alphonse Sentein ✆ 05 61 96 26 69

Eychenne AC rest,
8 av. P. Laffont – ✆ 05 61 04 04 50 – hotel-eychenne@wanadoo.fr – Fax 05 61 96 07 20 – Closed December, January, Sunday dinner and Monday except public holidays, from November to end March
42 rm – †€ 52/57 ††€ 175/200, ☕ € 10,50 – ½ P € 70/135
Rest – Menu € 28/57 – Carte € 35/66
◆ A converted post house with a pleasant, bourgeois atmosphere. Careful interior decor and antique furniture in the rooms. Some have a view of the Pyrenees. Personalised welcome. Traditional fare and fine terrace in the midst of a lovely garden.

Château de Beauregard rest, AC rest,
av. de la Résistance – ✆ 05 61 66 66 64 – contact@chateaubeauregard.net – Fax 05 34 14 07 93
10 rm – †€ 60/80 ††€ 60/80, ☕ € 10 – 6 suites – ½ P € 70/80
Rest *Auberge d'Antan* – *(closed 10 March-2 April, 10 November-4 December and Monday except in summer) (dinner only except weekends)* Menu € 29/34
◆ This small 19C château and its hunting lodge are surrounded by a peaceful, pleasant park and rose garden. Charming retro-style rooms (period furniture). Rustic decor and traditional fare cooked on a wood fire at the Auberge d'Antan.

La Clairière
av. de la Résistance – ✆ 05 61 66 66 66 – reservation@hotel-clairiere.com – Fax 05 34 14 30 30
19 rm – †€ 58/68 ††€ 58/68, ☕ € 10 – ½ P € 63/66 – **Rest** – Menu (€ 21), € 28/64 bi
◆ Set in a park, this unusual modern construction with a shingle roof reaching to the ground offers small yet comfortably renovated rooms. Restaurant offering modern cuisine and good selection of Languedoc-Roussillon wines.

ST-GRÉGOIRE – 35 Ille-et-Vilaine – 309 L6 – see Rennes

ST-GUÉNOLÉ – 29 Finistère – 308 E8 – ✉ 29760 Penmarch Brittany 9 **A2**

Paris 587 – Douarnenez 47 – Guilvinec 8 – Pont-l'Abbé 14 – Quimper 34
Office de tourisme, Pl. du Mar. Davout ✆ 02 98 58 81 44, Fax 02 98 58 86 62
Musée préhistorique★ - ≤★★ of Eckmühl lighthouse★ South: 2.5 km - Penmarch ★ church Southeast: 3 km - Pointe de la Torche ≤★ Northeast: 4 km.

Sterenn ≤ pointe de PenMar., rest, VISA MC
plage de la Joie – ✆ 02 98 58 60 36 – contactsterenn@free.fr – Fax 02 98 58 71 28 – Open 7 June-28 September
16 rm – †€ 50/98 ††€ 50/98, ☕ € 11 – ½ P € 72/98 – **Rest** – *(dinner only) (residents only)* Menu € 18/62 – Carte € 26/56
◆ Large building (1978) facing the beach, with a slate roof. Simple, tidy rooms and the Côte Sauvage nature reserve for a backdrop.

Les Ondines VISA MC AE
r. Pasteur, le phare d'Eckmühl road – ✆ 02 98 58 74 95 – hotel@lesondines.com – Fax 02 98 58 73 99 – Open 8 April-16 November and closed Tuesday except July-August
14 rm – †€ 50/65 ††€ 50/65, ☕ € 8 – ½ P € 50/60 – **Rest** – Menu € 15/37 – Carte € 24/59
◆ No through road leads to this Breton establishment a step away from the sea, at the far tip of the Bigouden region. Pleasant rooms with marine-style decor. Dining room-veranda where the sea reigns over everything, even the sauerkraut!

La Mer with rm rest, VISA MC
184 r. F. Péron – ✆ 02 98 58 62 22 – Fax 02 98 58 53 86 – Closed 11-30 November, 20 January-10 February
10 rm – †€ 49/65 ††€ 49/65, ☕ € 8,50 – ½ P € 70/78 – **Rest** – *(closed Sunday dinner, Tuesday dinner off season and Monday except dinner in season)*
Menu € 21/45 – Carte € 51/63
◆ This restaurant, situated on the first floor of a country house, offers a lovely view over the bay. Regional recipes honour the local fishermen.

ST-GUILHEM-LE-DESERT – 34 Hérault – 339 G6 – pop. 245 – alt. 89 m – ✉ 34150 23 C2

Paris 726 – Montpellier 41 – Lodève 31 – Millau 90
Office de tourisme, 2, rue de la Font du Portal ✆ 04 67 57 44 33

Le Guilhaume d'Orange rm, rm, VISA MC
2 av. Guillaume d'Orange – ✆ 04 67 57 24 53 – contact@guilhaumedorange.com – Fax 04 67 60 38 56 – Closed 22-28 December and Wednesday (except lunch) October-April
10 rm – †€ 66 ††€ 86, ☕ € 7 – ½ P € 56/71 – **Rest** – Menu € 19/27
◆ This building has been carefully restored, thus retaining its original character. Pretty rooms simply decorated in traditional style, yet offering modern comforts. The friendly dining room is extended by a pleasant summer terrace with a panoramic view. Simple family cooking.

ST-GUIRAUD – 34 Hérault – 339 F6 – see Clermont-l'Hérault

ST-HAON – 43 Haute-Loire – 331 E4 – pop. 370 – alt. 1 000 m – ✉ 43340 6 C3

Auvergne

Paris 559 – Langogne 25 – Mende 68 – Le Puy-en-Velay 29

Auberge de la Vallée with rm ≤ VISA MC
– ✆ 04 71 08 20 73 – aubergevallee43@wanadoo.fr – Fax 04 71 08 29 21 – Closed 1st January-20 March, Sunday dinner and Monday from October to April
10 rm – †€ 36/39 ††€ 41/47, ☕ € 8 – ½ P € 45
Rest – Menu € 17/37 – Carte € 22/44
◆ Unassuming family-run inn in an alpine village. Large, plainly decorated restaurant serving regionally inspire cuisine. Neat rooms.

ST-HAON-LE-VIEUX – 42 Loire – 327 C3 – see Renaison

ST-HERBLAIN – 44 Loire-Atlantique – 316 G4 – see Nantes

ST-HILAIRE-DE-BRETHMAS – 30 Gard – 339 J4 – see Alès

ST-HILAIRE-DES-LOGES – 85 Vendée – 316 L9 – pop. 1 840 – alt. 48 m – ✉ 85240
35 **C3**

▶ Paris 444 – Nantes 130 – La Roche-sur-Yon 77 – Niort 34 – Bressuire 53

Le Pantagruelion

9 r. Octroi – ✆ 02 51 00 59 19 – lepantagruelion@wanadoo.fr – Fax 02 51 51 29 55 – Closed 2-9 January, Saturday lunch, Sunday dinner and Wednesday

Rest – Menu € 21/35 – Carte € 34/49

◆ A beamed ceiling, stone walls and floor matting add to the pleasant rustic feel of this restaurant serving appetising traditional cuisine based on ingredients sourced from local producers.

ST-HILAIRE-D'OZILHAN – 30 Gard – 339 M5 – see Remoulins

ST-HILAIRE-DU-HARCOUËT – 50 Manche – 303 F8 – pop. 4 368 – alt. 70 m – ✉ 50600 Normandy
32 **A3**

▶ Paris 339 – Alençon 100 – Avranches 27 – Caen 102 – Fougères 29 – Laval 66 – St-Lô 69

Office de tourisme, place du Bassin ✆ 02 33 79 38 88, Fax 02 33 79 38 89

Centre d'Art Sacré★.

Le Cygne et Résidence

rm, rest,

Fougères road – ✆ 02 33 49 11 84 – contact@hotel-le-cygne.fr – Fax 02 33 49 53 70 – Closed Friday dinner and Sunday dinner from October to Easter

VISA AE

30 rm – €46/53 €58/70, € 8 – ½ P € 59/78 – **Rest** – Menu € 17/75 bi – Carte € 35/58

◆ Family style accommodation in a pleasant, middle-class residence of recent construction. Soberly furnished rooms; quieter to the rear. Seafood and Normandy dishes on the menu. Good wine list. Terrace on the garden side.

ST-HILAIRE-LE-CHÂTEAU – 23 Creuse – 325 I5 – pop. 276 – alt. 453 m – ✉ 23250
25 **C1**

▶ Paris 385 – Guéret 27 – Le Palais-sur-Vienne 56 – Limoges 64

East 3 km by D 941 (Aubenas road), D10 and secondary road
✉ 23250 St-Hilaire-le-Château

Château de la Chassagne

La Chassagne – ✆ 05 55 64 55 75 – m.fanton@tiscali.fr – Fax 05 55 64 55 75

4 rm – €95/120 €95/120 – **Table d'hôte** – Menu € 30 bi

◆ Fine 15C and 17C château, nestling in a park with grazing horses. A spiral staircase serves the refined rooms, including one with magnificent exposed timberwork.

ST-HILAIRE-ST-FLORENT – 49 Maine-et-Loire – 317 I5 – see Saumur

ST-HIPPOLYTE – 25 Doubs – 321 K3 – pop. 1 045 – alt. 380 m – ✉ 25190 Burgundy-Jura
17 **C2**

▶ Paris 490 – Basel 93 – Belfort 48 – Besançon 89 – Montbéliard 32 – Pontarlier 71

Office de tourisme, place de l'Hôtel de Ville ✆ 03 81 96 58 00

Site★ - Le Dessoubre Valley ★ S.

Le Bellevue

VISA

rte de Maîche – ✆ 03 81 96 51 53 – hotel.bellevue@free.fr – Fax 03 81 96 52 40 – Closed 2-16 January, Sunday dinner and Friday dinner from September to April

16 rm – €53/55 €55/62, € 10 – ½ P € 58/60

Rest – *(closed Monday lunch)* Menu € 25/42 – Carte € 35/65

◆ Former hostelry on the banks of the Dessoubre. Most of the renovated rooms offer a glimpse of the mountain and forest. Enjoy river fish or game depending on the season in the charming dining room or on the panoramic terrace.

ST-HIPPOLYTE – 68 Haut-Rhin – 315 I7 – pop. 1 060 – alt. 234 m – ✉ 68590 2 **C1**
Alsace-Lorraine

Paris 439 – Colmar 21 – Ribeauvillé 8 – St-Dié 42 – Sélestat 10 – Villé 18

Château du Haut-Koenigsbourg★★: ❄★★ Northwest: 8 km.

Le Parc rm, rest, VISA

6 r. du Parc – 03 89 73 00 06 – hotel-le-parc@wanadoo.fr – Fax 03 89 73 04 30 – Closed 30 June-10 July and 11 January-5 February
26 rm – €75/85 €85/145, €12 – 5 suites – ½ P €86/120
Rest – *(closed Sunday dinner, Monday and Tuesday)* Menu (€36), €45/70
Rest ***Winstub Rabseppi-Stebel*** – *(closed Mon. lunch and Tues. lunch)*
Menu €20/27 – Carte €29/43
◆ A riot of colour inside and outside this hotel, located opposite a park. Gradually renovated elegant rooms and extensive leisure facilities. Updated cuisine in the restaurant. Alsatian specialities and wines are served in the Winstub.

Hostellerie Munsch Aux Ducs de Lorraine rm, rest, VISA

– 03 89 73 00 09 – hotel.munsch@wanadoo.fr – Fax 03 89 73 05 46 – Closed 15-30 November and mid January-mid February
40 rm – €52/70 €79/180, €11,50 – ½ P €82/102 – **Rest** – *(closed 29 June-10 July, 15-30 November, mid January-mid February, Tuesday dinner and Wednesday)* Menu €16 (weekday lunch), €23/55 – Carte €23/56
◆ Striking Alsatian-style inn. Individual rooms some with a balcony, overlooking the Haut-Koenigsbourg Castle or the vineyards. Sculpted wood and a flower-decked terrace. Traditional cuisine and house wines.

ST-HUBERT – 57 Moselle – 307 I3 – pop. 197 – alt. 220 m – ✉ 57640 27 **C1**

Paris 336 – Luxembourg 63 – Metz 21 – Saarbrücken 69

La Ferme de Godchure without rest

r. Principale – 03 87 77 03 96 – godchure@wanadoo.fr
4 rm – €70/90 €70/90
◆ A former Cistercian farm, on the edge of a country village, with a barn converted into a charming guesthouse. Rooms with personal touches, friendly welcome and attentive service.

ST-ISIDORE – 06 Alpes-Maritimes – 341 E5 – see Nice

ST-JACQUES-DES-BLATS – 15 Cantal – 330 E4 – pop. 325 – alt. 990 m – ✉ 15800 5 **B3**

Paris 536 – Aurillac 32 – Brioude 76 – Issoire 91 – St-Flour 39

L'Escoundillou rm, VISA

Route de la Gare – 04 71 47 06 42 – hotel.escoundillou@cantal.com – Fax 04 71 47 00 97 – Closed 17 November-25 December, Friday dinner and Saturday from 10 October to 17 November
12 rm – €41/44 €41/58, €7 – ½ P €44/47
Rest – Menu €13,50/22
◆ A little hiding-place ("escoundillou" in the local dialect) on a picturesque country road, ideal for nature-lovers. Bright, clean rooms. Bright, airy, modern dining room serving locally sourced produce.

Le Brunet rest, VISA

– 04 71 47 05 86 – hotel.brunet@wanadoo.fr – Fax 04 71 47 04 27 – Closed 1st October-20 December
15 rm – €47 €47, €7 – ½ P €44/48
Rest – Menu €16/28 – Carte €20/25
◆ Recent buildings in the local style below the village. Well thought-out rooms, often with balconies facing the Cère valley. Auvergne specialities served in a sober decor or on the terrace overlooking the meadows in summer.

Le Griou

– ✆ *04 71 47 06 25 – hotel.griou@wanadoo.fr – Fax 04 71 47 00 16 – Closed 15 October-20 December*
16 rm – †€ 43/53 ††€ 43/53, ☕ € 7 – ½ P € 44/48 – **Rest** – Menu € 15/30 – Carte € 23/29
◆ A pretty guesthouse where the garden, overlooking the river, blends into the surrounding natural setting. Some rooms have a fine view of the Cantal summits. Dining room overlooking the countryside. Auvergne stews and pountis take pride of place on the menu.

ST-JAMES – 50 Manche – 303 E8 – pop. 2 917 – alt. 100 m – ✉ 50240

Normandy 32 **A3**

Paris 357 – Avranches 21 – Fougères 29 – Rennes 69 – St-Lô 78 – St-Malo 61
Office de tourisme, 21, rue de la Libération ✆ 02 33 89 62 12
American cemetery

Normandie

2 pl. Bagot – ✆ 02 33 48 31 45 – Fax 02 33 48 31 37 – Closed 20 December-5 January and Sunday dinner except public holidays
10 rm – †€ 45/50 ††€ 45/50, ☕ € 6,50 – ½ P € 49/53 – **Rest** – Menu (€ 9), € 12,50 (weekday lunch), € 16/24 – Carte € 20/38
◆ Village inn on the borders of Brittany and Normandy. The discreetly furnished rooms are larger on the first floor. A restaurant with a rustic setting and predominantly seafood menu. Daily lunchtime specials served at the busy counter.

ST-JEAN – 06 Alpes-Maritimes – 341 C6 – see Pégomas

ST-JEAN-AUX-AMOGNES – 58 Nièvre – 319 D9 – pop. 466 – alt. 230 m – ✉ 58270

7 **B2**

Paris 252 – Bourges 81 – Château-Chinon 51 – Clamecy 61 – Nevers 16

Le Relais de Bourgogne

– ✆ *03 86 58 61 44 – Fax 03 86 58 61 44 – Closed 1st-15 January, Sunday dinner and Wednesday except public holidays*
Rest – Menu € 22/40 – Carte € 33/46
◆ The recently-renovated facade of this village building conceals a warm country-style interior, with a veranda overlooking the pleasant garden terrace. Traditional meals served.

ST-JEAN-AUX-BOIS – 60 Oise – 305 I4 – see Pierrefonds

ST-JEAN-CAP-FERRAT – 06 Alpes-Maritimes – 341 E5 – pop. 1 895 – alt. 12 m – ✉ 06230

French Riviera 42 **E2**

Paris 935 – Menton 25 – Nice 8
Office de tourisme, 59, avenue Denis Semeria ✆ 04 93 76 08 90, Fax 04 93 76 16 67
Site of the Villa Ephrussi-de-Rothschild★★ **M** : Musée Île de France (Ile de France Museum)★★, gardens★★ - Phare ✳★★ - Pointe de St-Hospice : ≤★ of the chapel, footpath★ - Promenade Maurice-Rouvier★.

Plan on following page

Grand Hôtel du Cap Ferrat ≤ sea, rm, VISA MC AE

71 bd Gén.de Gaulle, at Cap-Ferrat – ✆ 04 93 76 50 50 – reserv@grand-hotel-cap-ferrat.com – Fax 04 93 76 04 52 – Open 1st May-30 September **a**
44 rm – †€ 550/1550 ††€ 550/1550, ☕ € 45 – 9 suites
Rest – Menu € 135 – Carte € 136/191
Rest *Club Dauphin* – pool restaurant – ✆ *04 93 76 50 21 (lunch only)* Carte € 80/116
Spec. Risotto carnaroli de langoustines au parmesan reggiano. Saint-Pierre rôti à l'arête, artichaut et citron confit. Croustillant de fraises et rhubarbe à la réglisse.
◆ A private (air-conditioned) funicular transports guests across a superb park to the infinity pool of this luxury hotel (1908) on a remarkable site overlooking the Mediterranean. Luxurious restaurant, magnificent terrace and classic cuisine.

ST-JEAN-CAP-FERRAT

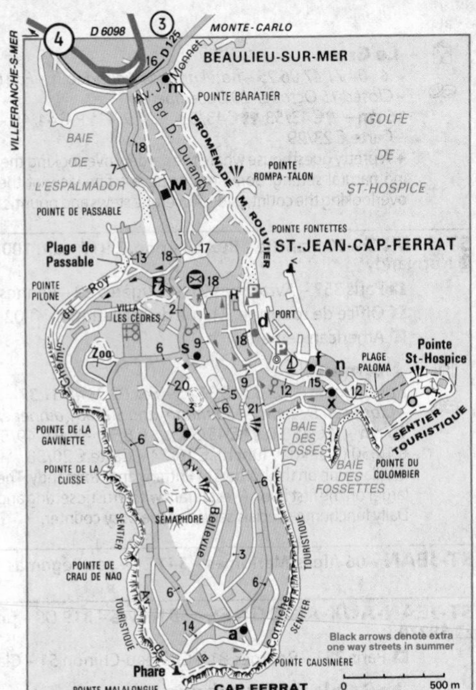

Royal Riviera
3 av. J. Monnet – ☎ 04 93 76 31 00
– resa@royal-riviera.com – Fax 04 93 01 23 07
– Closed 25 November-13 January **m**
94 rm – €240/1350 €240/1350, €35 – 2 suites – ½ P €291/1401
Rest *Le Panorama* – *(dinner only in July-August)* Menu €51 – Carte €73/120
Rest *La Pergola* – pool restaurant – *(open Easter-15 October) (lunch only)*
Carte €47/77
◆ Early 20C luxury hotel with a handsome waterside garden. Elegant rooms, most overlooking the sea (contemporary Provençal décor in the Orangerie). Elegant, quiet dining rooms are to be found at the Panorama. A buffet and grilled meats at Le Pergola, brunch on Sundays.

Voile d'Or port and gulf,
At the port – ☎ 04 93 01 13 13
– reservation@lavoiledor.fr – Fax 04 93 76 11 17
– Open beg. April-beg. October **f**
45 rm – €169/785 €236/889, €32 – **Rest** – *(dinner only in July-August)*
Menu €48 bi (weekday lunch), €68/95 – Carte €96/142
◆ Ideal location opposite the marina, seafront swimming pools and a studied decor mean that a pleasant stay is guaranteed. Panoramic dining room, lovely summer terrace and classic menu. Snacks served on the beach.

Brise Marine without rest Cape and gulf,
av. J. Mermoz – ☎ 04 93 76 04 36
– info@hotel-brisemarine.com – Fax 04 93 76 11 49
– Open from February to October **x**
16 rm – €145/172 €145/172, €13
◆ An 1878 Italian-style villa overlooking a quiet street. Elegant rooms; in summer breakfast is served on the terrace overlooking the garden of ornamental fruit trees.

Le Panoramic without rest — Cape and gulf,
3 av. Albert 1er – ☎ 04 93 76 00 37 – info@hotel-lepanoramic.com – Fax 04 93 76 15 78 – Closed 15 November-25 December s
20 rm – €140/170 €140/170, €12
◆ The name of this 1950s family hotel says it all: exceptional view of the gulf, the headland and the town. Simple, somewhat old-fashioned but well-kept rooms with balcony.

Clair Logis without rest
12 av. Centrale – ☎ 04 93 76 51 81 – hotelclairlogis@orange.fr – Fax 04 93 76 51 82 – Closed 10 November-20 December and 10 January-6 March b
18 rm – €80 €170, €12
◆ General de Gaulle was one of the famous guests at this Provençal villa tucked away in a pretty park. Characterful rooms, simpler comforts in the annexe.

La Table du Cap
2 av. Denis-Séméria – ☎ 04 93 76 03 97 – latableducap@laurentpoulet.com – Fax 04 93 76 05 39 d
Rest – Menu (€37), €56/80 – Carte €70/102
◆ Attractive restaurant that hosts contemporary art and sculpture exhibitions. Shaded terrace. Updated, inventive look at Provençal culinary classics.

Capitaine Cook
11 av. J. Mermoz – ☎ 04 93 76 02 66 – Fax 04 93 76 02 66 – Closed 3 November-26 December, Thursday lunch and Wednesday n
Rest – Menu €26/31 – Carte €33/54
◆ A spruce restaurant tucked away on the headland with tightly packed tables in the rustic dining room or small terrace. Traditional cuisine with a seafood bias.

ST-JEAN D'ALCAS – 12 Aveyron – 338 K7 – ✉ 12250
Languedoc-Roussillon-Tarn Gorges 29 **D2**

Paris 677 – Toulouse 170 – Rodez 118 – Millau 35 – Saint-Affrique 14

Le Moulin de Gauty without rest
– ☎ 05 65 97 51 90 – contact@moulindegauty.com
3 rm – €65/110 €75/120
◆ This former mill in a rural setting is the perfect place to recharge your batteries. Stylish modern bedrooms plus an attractive riverside garden. Pool and mountain bikes available.

ST-JEAN-D'ANGÉLY – 17 Charente-Maritime – 324 G4 – pop. 7 681 – alt. 25 m – ✉ 17400 Atlantic Coast
38 **B2**

Paris 444 – La Rochelle 72 – Niort 48 – Royan 69 – Saintes 36

Office de tourisme, 8, rue Grosse Horloge ☎ 05 46 32 04 72, Fax 05 46 32 20 80

Plan on following page

De la Place rm,
pl. Hôtel de Ville – ☎ 05 46 32 69 11 – infobox@hoteldelaplace.net – Fax 05 46 32 08 44 – Closed autumn half-term holidays and 1st-21 January
10 rm – €48/54 €55/64, €6,50 – ½ P €64/70 B a
Rest – Menu €18/46 – Carte €32/49
◆ In the heart of the town and near the historic centre, this family-run hotel offers simple, well-soundproofed rooms. Renovation underway. Cuisine with a contemporary touch served in a bistro style dining room.

Le Scorlion
5 r. Abbaye – ☎ 05 46 32 52 61 – robertcr@hotmail.com – Fax 05 46 59 99 90 – Closed 14-20 April, 28 October-12 November, 23 February-8 March, Wednesday dinner from October to May, Sunday dinner and Monday A e
Rest – Menu €17/36
◆ This pleasant, comfortable restaurant inside a former royal abbey successfully mixes old and new. Culinary register in keeping with current taste.

ST-JEAN-D'ANGÉLY

Abbaye (R. de l') . . . . **A** 2
Aguesseau (R. d') . . . . **A** 3
Bancs (R. des) . . . . **A** 4
Bourcy (R. Pascal) . . . . **B** 6
Cumont (Bd P.-de). . . . . **B** 8
Dubreuil (R. L. A.) . . . . **A** 10
Gambetta (R.) . . . . **A**
Grosse Horloge (R.) . . . . **B** 12
Gymnase (R. du) . . . . **B** 13
Hôtel de Ville (Pl. de l') . . . . . **B** 14
Jacobins (R. des) . . . . **B** 16
Libération (Square de la) . . . . . **B** 17
Maréchal-Leclerc (Av. du) . . . . **B** 19
Maréchaux (R. des) . . . . **AB** 20
Porte de Niort (R. de la) . . . . . **B** 24
Port Mahon (Av. du) . . . . **AB** 25
Regnaud (R.) . . . . **A** 27
Remparts (R. des) . . . . **B** 28
Rose (R.) . . . . **B** 29
Taillebourg (Fg) . . . . **A**
Texier (R. Michel) . . . . **A** 31
Tourneur (R. L.) . . . . **B** 32
Tour Ronde (R.) . . . . **B** 33
Verdun (R. de) . . . . **A** 35
3-Frères-Gautreau (R. des) . . . **A** 37
4-Septembre (R. du) . . . . **B** 39
11-Novembre (R. du) . . . . . . **AB** 40

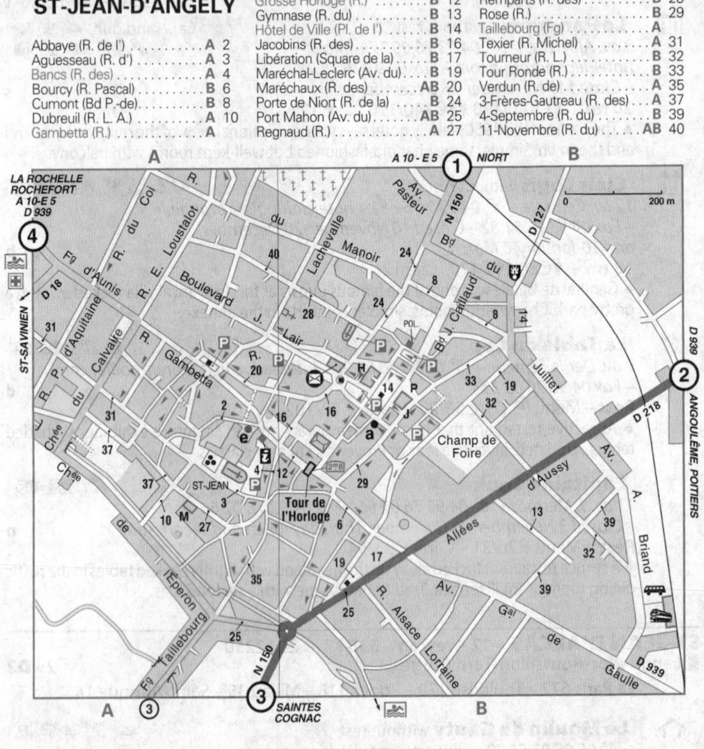

ST-JEAN-DE-BLAIGNAC – 33 Gironde – 335 K6 – pop. 401 – alt. 50 m – ✉ 33420 4 C1

Paris 592 – Bergerac 56 – Bordeaux 40 – Libourne 17 – La Réole 29

XX **Auberge St-Jean** AC VISA MC AE

– *✆ 05 57 74 95 50 – Fax 05 57 84 51 57 – Closed 11-25 November, Wednesday dinner and Thursday*

Rest – Menu € 45/90 – Carte € 65/73

◆ Former post house facing the Dordogne. A plush sitting room adorned with copperware leads into two tasteful dining rooms that include a covered terrace. Modern-classic menu.

ST-JEAN-DE-BRAYE – 45 Loiret – 318 I4 – see Orléans

ST-JEAN-DE-LUZ – 64 Pyrénées-Atlantiques – 342 C4 – pop. 13 247 – alt. 3 m – Casino ABY – ✉ 64500 Atlantic Coast 3 A3

Paris 785 – Bayonne 24 – Biarritz 18 – Pau 129 – San Sebastián 31

Office de tourisme, place du Maréchal Foch ✆ 05 59 26 03 16, Fax 05 59 26 21 47

de Chantaco Route d'Ascain, by Ascain road: 2 km, ✆ 05 59 26 14 22 ;

de la Nivelle Ciboure Place William Sharp, South: 3 km by D 704, ✆ 05 59 47 18 99.

Harbour★ – St-Jean-Baptiste church ★★ – Maison Louis-XIV★ **N** – Corniche basque (cliff road)★★ by ④ – Sémaphore de Socoa ≤★★ 5 km by ④.

Parc Victoria

5 r. Cépé by bd Thiers and rte Quartier du Lac – ☎ 05 59 26 78 78 – parcvictoria@relaischateaux.com – Fax 05 59 26 78 08 – Open 15 March-14 November and 19 December-4 January

13 rm – †€ 135/310 ††€ 165/350, ☕ € 20 – 5 suites – ½ P € 136/227

Rest *Les Lierres* – *(closed lunch except weekend and public holidays)* Menu € 39/80 – Carte € 63/83

◆ Beautiful late-19C villa and outhouses nestling in a flower-decked park (pool and Jacuzzi). Plush Art Deco interior. Suites with a small private garden. A villa in a verdant setting with two small veranda-dining rooms (conservatory or 1930s style).

Grand Hôtel

✿ *43 bd Thiers – ☎ 05 59 26 35 36 – direction@luzgrandhotel.fr – Fax 05 59 51 99 84 – Closed 4-31 January* BY **d**

45 rm – †€ 165/490 ††€ 165/490, ☕ € 29 – 4 suites

Rest *Le Rosewood* – *(closed Monday, Tuesday and lunch)* Menu € 70/95 – Carte € 78/107

Rest *La Rôtisserie* – *(closed dinners from Wednesday to Sunday)* Menu € 50/70

Spec. Gros chipiron au jambon pata negra, comme un rôti. Saveur de langoustines royales (June to October). Découpe de cochon noir du Pays Basque. **Wines** Jurançon, Irouléguy.

◆ This grand seaside hotel dates from the early 1900s. Its elegant furnishings, modern comforts and refined rooms are most appreciated. Luxurious spa. Trendy cuisine is the focus of the dinner menu at the Rosewood. Rotisserie open at lunchtime.

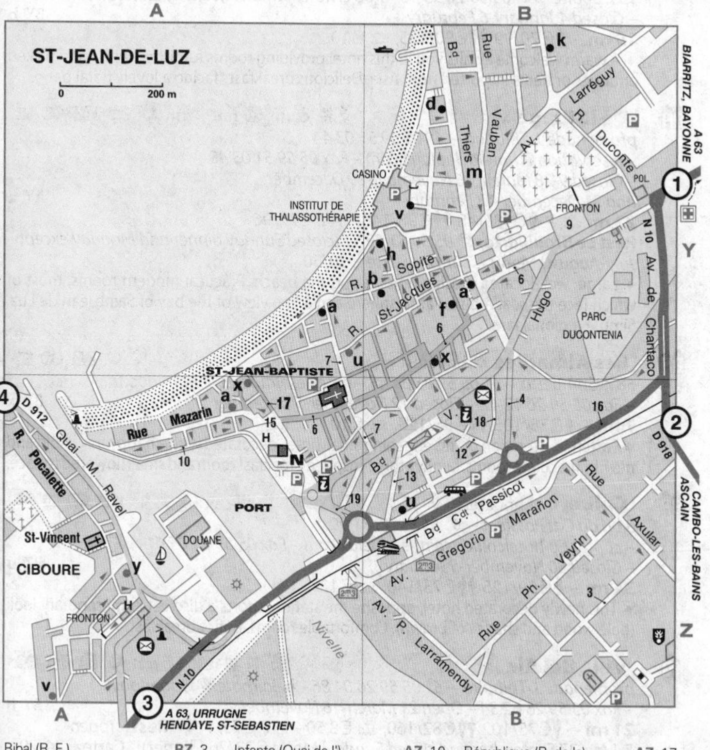

ST-JEAN-DE-LUZ

Bibal (R. F.) . . . . **BZ** 3
Chauvin-Dragon (R.) . . . . . . **BZ** 4
Elizaga (Sq.) . . . . **BY** 9
Gambetta (R.) . . . . **AZ, BY** 6
Garat (R.) . . . . **AYZ** 7
Infante (Quai de l') . . . . **AZ** 10
Jaurréguiberry (Av.) . . . . **BZ** 12
Labrouche (Av.) . . . . **BZ** 13
Louis-XIV (Pl.) . . . . **AZ** 15
Pyrénées (Av. des) . . . . **BZ** 16
République (R. de la) . . . . . . **AZ** 17
Salagoity (R. de) . . . . **BZ** 18
Verdun (Av. de) . . . . **AZ** 19
Victor-Hugo (Bd) . . . . **BYZ**

Zazpi Hôtel without rest
21 bd Thiers – ✆ 05 59 26 07 77 – info@zazpihotel.com – Fax 05 59 26 27 77 BY **a**
6 rm – €160/280 €160/280, €15 – 1 suite
◆ Townhouse dating from 1900 with seven (zazpi is Basque for seven) high tech, designer guestrooms named after the seven Basque provinces. Tiny pool and sun deck on the rooftop.

Hélianthal rm, rm, rest,
pl. M. Ravel – ✆ 05 59 51 51 08 – helianthal@helianthal.fr – Fax 05 59 51 51 10 – Closed 24 November-22 December BY **v**
100 rm – €94/178 €104/188, €15 – **Rest** – Menu €40/44
◆ Hotel linked to a splendid spa (residents only). A 1930s style in the guest rooms, all of which are practical and identical. An ocean liner theme (fresco) depicts this bright, colourful restaurant. Large terrace overlooking the bay.

La Devinière without rest
5 r. Loquin – ✆ 05 59 26 05 51 – la.deviniere.64@wanadoo.fr – Fax 05 59 51 26 38 BY **f**
10 rm – €120/165 €120/165, €12
◆ Paintings, knick-knacks, photos and old books help create the charm of this Basque house. Attractive rooms with balconies on the garden side. Rustic tearoom.

La Marisa without rest
16 r. Sopite – ✆ 05 59 26 95 46 – info@hotel-lamarisa.com – Fax 05 59 51 17 06 – Closed 4 January-6 February BY **b**
15 rm – €70/99 €90/155, €10
◆ A warm welcome awaits you in this hotel providing rooms furnished with hand picked antiques or items imported from Asia. Delicious breakfasts facing a lovely floral patio.

De la Plage rm, rm, rm,
promenade J. Thibaud – ✆ 05 59 51 03 44 – reservation@hoteldelaplage.com – Fax 05 59 51 03 48 – Closed 9-28 March, 16 November-19 December and 31 December-12 February AY **a**
22 rm – €98/148 €98/148 – ½ P €72/96
Rest *Le Brouillarta*, *✆ 05 59 51 29 51 (closed Sunday dinner and Monday except July-August)* Menu €30/52 – Carte €30/50
◆ Large, well-located seaside hotel facing the beach. Practical modern rooms, most of which face the sea. A bistro atmosphere and a fine view of the bay of Saint Jean de Luz. Simple regional fare.

Les Almadies without rest
58 r. Gambetta – ✆ 05 59 85 34 48 – hotel.lesalmadies@wanadoo.fr – Fax 05 59 26 12 42 – Closed 12 November-5 December BY **x**
7 rm – €75/105 €95/125, €10
◆ Tasteful restoration of this engaging small hotel, decorated with a happy mix of old and new. Immaculate rooms, faintly ethnic-inspired breakfast room and small flowered terrace.

Colbert without rest
3 bd du Cdt Passicot – ✆ 05 59 26 31 99 – contact@hotelcolbertsaintjeandeluz.com – Fax 05 59 51 05 61 – Closed 30 November-5 January BZ **u**
34 rm – €69/125 €73/140, €12
◆ This newly decorated hotel, opposite the station, sports a discreet contemporary look (pale wood and shades of brown). Comfortable rooms. Buffet breakfast.

Villa Bel Air rest, rest,
promenade J. Thibaud – ✆ 05 59 26 04 86 – belairhotel@wanadoo.fr – Fax 05 59 26 62 34 – Open 21 March-16 November BY **h**
21 rm – €75/102 €82/160, €8,50 – ½ P €75/114 – **Rest** – *(open 3 June-27 September and closed Sunday)* Menu €23/26 (dinner) – Carte €24/29
◆ A slight boarding house feel to this large Basque seaside villa built in 1850. Cosy lounge and well-kept rooms, most overlooking the beach. The bay windows of the dining room offer a view of the seafront promenade.

Les Goëlands rest, VISA AE
4 av. Etcheverry – 05 59 26 10 05 – reception@hotel-lesgoelands.com – Fax 05 59 51 04 02 BY **k**
35 rm – €50/80 €57/125, €8 – ½ P €60/95
Rest – *(open 20 March-3 November) (residents only)* Menu €22
◆ Calm, family guesthouse atmosphere in a residential area. These two charming Basque villas dating from 1902 have been well renovated. Antiques and charming interior.

Villa Argi-Eder without rest P
av. Napoléon III, 3 km on ①, D 810 and secondary road – 05 59 54 81 65 – villa-argi-eder.@wanadoo.fr – Fax 05 59 51 26 51
4 rm – €50/55 €50/55, €5,50
◆ A peaceful and friendly hotel, a stone's throw from the beach. Quiet, spacious ground floor rooms opening onto private terraces, where breakfast is served.

Le Kaïku VISA
17 r. République – 05 59 26 13 20 – Fax 05 59 51 07 47 – Closed 15-30 November, 15-30 January, Tuesday and Wednesday except July August AZ **x**
Rest – Menu €20 (weekday lunch), €30/50 – Carte €35/58
◆ This restaurant, situated partly in the basement of the oldest house in Saint Jean de Luz (16C) has an excellent reputation locally. Seafood and contemporary fare.

Zoko Moko VISA
6 r. Mazarin – 05 59 08 01 23 – zokomoko@hotmail.com – Fax 05 59 51 01 77 – Closed 12 November-10 December, lunch except week-ends from 10 July to 4 September and Monday AZ **a**
Rest – Menu (€18), €24 (weekday lunch), €40/48 – Carte €44/46
◆ Elegant, contemporary decor and Mediterranean food peppered with exotic flavours are the features of this 'quiet spot' (zoko moko in Basque) set in an 18C house.

Petit Grill Basque "Chez Maya" VISA AE
2 r. St-Jacques – 05 59 26 80 76 – Fax 05 59 26 80 76 – Closed 20 December-20 January, Thursday lunch off-season and Wednesday AY **u**
Rest – Menu €20/40 – Carte €22/43
◆ Authentic Basque inn with Louis Floutier frescoes and plates, copperware and an amusing manual ventilation system. Timeless regional cuisine.

Olatua VISA AE
30 bd Thiers – 05 59 51 05 22 – olatua@wanadoo.fr – Fax 05 59 51 32 99 BY **m**
Rest – Menu (€29), 33
◆ Large well-known brasserie decorated in bright colours with indoor plants. Updated Basque cuisine. Enjoy a meal outside in the small garden in fine weather.

in Urrugne 4 km by ③ – pop. 7 043 – alt. 34 m – ✉ 64122

Office de tourisme, place René Soubelet 05 59 54 60 80, Fax 05 59 54 63 49

Château d'Urtubie without rest P VISA AE
– 05 59 54 31 15 – chateaudurtubie@wanadoo.fr – Fax 05 59 54 62 51 – Open April-October
10 rm – €75/150 €85/160, €11
◆ On the road to Spain, a 14C fortress, modified through the ages. Now a museum and country inn, it has rooms of character with period furniture.

Auberge Chez Maïté with rm rest, VISA AE
pl. de la Mairie – 05 59 26 14 62 – aubergechezmaite@orange.fr – Fax 05 59 26 64 20 – Closed 10 November-14 December and 5 January-15 February
6 rm – €80/110 €110/145, €12 – 1 suite – ½ P €85/115
Rest – *(closed Sunday dinner and Monday)* Menu €29 – Carte €43/52
◆ On the town hall square, a small dining room decorated in the Basque style, where you will sample some traditional cooking from the Southwest shoulder to shoulder. On the town hall square, a small dining room decorated in the Basque style, where you will sample some traditional cooking from the Southwest shoulder to shoulder.

in Ciboure 1 km by ④ – pop. 6 282 – alt. 3 m – ✉ 64500

Office de tourisme, 27, quai Maurice Ravel ✆ 05 59 47 64 56, Fax 05 59 47 64 55

N.-D. de Socorri chapel: site★ 5 km by ③.

see plan of St-Jean-de-Luz

Chez Dominique

15 quai M. Ravel – ✆ 05 59 47 29 16 – Fax 05 59 47 29 16 – Closed 15 February-15 March, Sunday dinner, Monday in winter and Tuesday except August

Rest – Menu € 29 – Carte € 46/50 AZ **y**

◆ On the quayside stand the birthplace of Maurice Ravel (at no. 27) and this welcoming restaurant with its pleasant marine decor lit by fishermen's lights. Seafood and regional wines.

Chez Mattin

63 r. E. Baignol – ✆ 05 59 47 19 52 – Fax 05 59 47 05 57 – Closed 20 January-10 March, Sunday dinner off season and Monday

Rest – Carte € 30/41 AZ **v**

◆ This rustic restaurant set in an old country house is marked by a family ambience. Choice of fish dishes depending on the day's catch; typically local cuisine.

in Socoa 3 km by ④ – ✉ 64122

Iguski-Begui without rest

8 chemin d'Atalaya – ✆ 06 63 08 03 93 – info@iguski-begui.com – Fax 05 59 47 21 19

4 rm – €65 €65, € 7,50

◆ This attractive house, overlooking the Rhune and the bay of St Jean de Luz, offers rooms with individual touches. Choose Sémaphore for a view of the Socoa lighthouse.

Pantxua

at port de Soccoa – ✆ 05 59 47 13 73 – Fax 05 59 47 01 54 – Closed January

Rest – Carte € 25/48

◆ Numerous canvases by Basque painters hang on the dining room walls. The popular veranda and terrace open onto the bay. Fresh fish takes pride of place at the table.

ST-JEAN-DE-MAURIENNE – 73 Savoie – 333 L6 – pop. 8 902 – alt. 556 m – ✉ 73300 French Alps 46 **F2**

Paris 635 – Albertville 62 – Chambéry 75 – Grenoble 105

Office de tourisme, place de la Cathédrale ✆ 04 79 83 51 51, Fax 04 79 83 42 10

Ciborium★ and stalls★★ of St-Jean-Baptiste cathedral.

Nord rest,

pl. Champ de Foire – ✆ 04 79 64 02 08 – info@hoteldunord.net – Fax 04 79 59 91 31 – Closed 12-27 April, 25 October-9 November, Sunday dinner except July-August and Monday lunch

19 rm – €45 €56, € 8,50 – ½ P € 48 – **Rest** – Menu € 17/52 – Carte € 33/56

◆ A former coaching inn near the Cathédrale St Jean Baptiste and the Musée Opinel. All the spacious rooms have been renovated. Restaurant set under the stone vaults of an old stable, serving modern and traditional cuisine prepared with local produce. Good wine list.

St-Georges without rest

334 r. de la République – ✆ 04 79 64 01 06 – info@hotel-saintgeorges.com – Fax 04 79 59 84 84

22 rm – €46/50 €60/64, € 9

◆ This venerable hotel (1866) near the town centre has been fully renovated by its owners. Practical rooms; those at the rear are quieter.

Dorhotel without rest

r. L. Sibué – ✆ 04 79 83 23 83 – info@dorhotel.com – Fax 04 79 83 23 00

41 rm – €40/47 €49, € 8

◆ A practical hotel with functional rooms, 500 m from the station. Buffet menu for breakfast, served in a large modern dining room.

ST-JEAN-DE-MONTS – 85 Vendée – 316 D7 – pop. 6 886 – alt. 16 m – Casino : La Pastourelle – ✉ 85160 Atlantic Coast 34 A3

Paris 451 – Cholet 123 – Nantes 73 – La Roche-sur-Yon 61 – Les Sables-d'Olonne 47

Office de tourisme, 67, esplanade de la Mer ☎ 08 26 88 78 87, Fax 02 51 59 87 87

de Saint-Jean-de-Monts Avenue des Pays de la Loire, West: 2 km, ☎ 02 51 58 82 73.

Mercure

16 av. Pays de Monts – ☎ 02 51 59 15 15 – hotelmercurestjean@wanadoo.fr – Fax 02 51 59 91 03 – Closed 3 January-1st February

44 rm – €87/151 €94/458, € 14 – ½ P €85/117 – **Rest** – *(closed Sunday lunch from 5 October to 20 December)* Menu (€20), €25/35 – Carte €32/52

♦ Well located near the beach, golf course and thalassotherapy spa resort. Comfortable rooms, all with balconies. Choose from the classic or diet menu. Fine view over the pine forest.

De la Forêt without rest

13 r. Pouvreau – ☎ 02 51 58 00 36 – hotel.foret@gmail.com – Closed beg. January-end February

16 rm – €61/99 €61/99, € 10

♦ This hotel, near the forest, has just been fully renovated. The colourful and well-soundproofed rooms occupy several houses around a small pool.

L'Espadon

8 av. de la forêt – ☎ 02 51 58 03 18 – info@hotel-espadon.com – Fax 02 51 59 16 11

27 rm – €51/75 €51/75, € 8 – ½ P €52/63 – **Rest** – *(closed mid November-beg. February, Sunday dinner, Tuesday lunch and Monday except June-September)* Menu €19/39 – Carte €26/43

♦ Located on the wide avenue down to the beach, this 1970s building has small but well-kept rooms (most with a balcony). Two pleasantly bright dining rooms serving seafood cuisine.

Le Robinson

28 bd Gén. Leclerc – ☎ 02 51 59 20 20 – infos@hotel-lerobinson.com – Fax 02 51 58 88 03 – Closed December and January

74 rm – €45/69 €45/74, € 9 – ½ P €50/65 – **Rest** – Menu (€12), €16/44 – Carte €25/46

♦ Occupying several buildings centred around a patio, the rooms vary in comfort. Fine indoor pool and small weights room. Three welcoming dining rooms serving seafood.

La Cloche d'Or

26 av. des Tilleuls – ☎ 02 51 58 00 58 – carole-meulle@voila.fr – Fax 02 51 58 82 85 – Closed 21 December-7 February

21 rm – €40/75 €40/75, € 8 – ½ P €43/64 – **Rest** – Menu (€9,50), €14 (weekdays)/32 – Carte €25/41

♦ Half way between the centre of town and the beach, this quiet establishment is ideally located for walking. The well-kept rooms are a little narrow yet practical. Simply furnished in a rustic style. Classic cuisine.

Le Petit St-Jean

128 rte Notre-Dame de Monts – ☎ 02 51 59 78 50 – Closed Sunday dinner and Monday

Rest – Menu €25/29 – Carte €30/37

♦ Stone, beams, ornaments, copperware and old furniture decorate this inn where you are served local dishes featuring seafood.

La Quich'Notte

200 rte Notre-Dame-de-Monts – ☎ 02 51 58 62 64 – ferdi.quichnotte@hotmail.fr – Open 21 March-15 September and closed Tuesday lunch, Monday except July-August and Saturday lunch

Rest – Menu €19/35 – Carte €24/46

♦ Local dishes (frogs' legs and eel) served in a cosy setting in a Vendée "bourrine" dating back to the 19C. The glass rotunda is used on crowded days.

in Orouet 7 km southeast on D 38 – ✉ 85160

La Chaumière rest, **P** VISA MC AE

103 av. Orouët – ✆ 02 51 58 67 44 – hotelchaumiere@wanadoo.fr – Fax 02 51 58 98 12 – Closed 12 November-3 February

32 rm – †€ 47/82 ††€ 47/82, ☕ € 9,50 – ½ P € 93/101 – **Rest** – *(closed Sunday dinner and Monday from October to March)* Menu (€ 11,50), € 14,50 (weekday lunch), € 17/32 – Carte € 18/40

◆ Long building with a thatched roof, set in a large garden with indoor-outdoor swimming pool. The rooms are small, but neat and well-kept (a few have a balcony). The neo-rustic dining areas feature exposed beams. Traditional menu.

ST-JEAN-DE-SIXT – 74 Haute-Savoie – 328 L5 – pop. 1 005 – alt. 963 m – ✉ 74450 French Alps 46 F1

Paris 561 – Annecy 28 – Bonneville 22 – Chamonix-Mont-Blanc 76 – La Clusaz 4 – Genève 48

Office de tourisme, ✆ 04 50 02 70 14, Fax 04 50 02 78 78

Défilé des Étroits★ Northwest: 3 km.

Beau Site rest, **P** VISA MC

La Ruaz – ✆ 04 50 02 24 04 – hotelbeausite@hotmail.com – Fax 04 50 02 35 82 – Open 10 June-10 September and 22 December-2 April

15 rm – †€ 40/55 ††€ 55/80, ☕ € 7 – ½ P € 43/60 – **Rest** – Menu (€ 14), € 16 (weekdays), € 18/22 – Carte € 21/26

◆ This hotel has two types of room - Savoyard, with panelling and warm furnishings, or modern and functional. In any case, peace and quiet assured. The bay windows of the restaurant command a pretty view of the village. Family cooking.

ST-JEAN-DU-BRUEL – 12 Aveyron – 338 M6 – pop. 642 – alt. 520 m – ✉ 12230 Languedoc-Roussillon-Tarn Gorges 29 D2

Paris 676 – Lodève 43 – Millau 40 – Montpellier 97 – Rodez 108 – Le Vigan 36

Office de tourisme, 32, Grand'Rue ✆ 05 65 62 23 64, Fax 05 65 62 12 82

Gorges de la Dourbie★★ Northeast: 10 km.

Du Midi-Papillon **P** VISA MC

– ✆ 05 65 62 26 04 – Fax 05 65 62 12 97 – Open 22 March-11 November

18 rm – †€ 35/62 ††€ 35/62, ☕ € 5,50 – ½ P € 40/55

Rest – Menu € 14 (weekdays), € 22/39 – Carte € 21/42

◆ This cosy, romantic establishment along the Dourbie combines a faultless welcome with individually decorated, comfortable rooms. The appetising local fare will delight the taste buds, and for the eye, a splendid view over the river and medieval bridge.

ST-JEAN-EN-ROYANS – 26 Drôme – 332 E3 – pop. 2 895 – alt. 250 m – ✉ 26190 French Alps 43 E2

Paris 584 – Die 62 – Romans-sur-Isère 28 – Grenoble 71 – St-Marcellin 20 – Valence 44

Office de tourisme, 13, place de l'Église ✆ 04 75 48 61 39, Fax 04 75 47 54 44

at col de la Machine 11 km southeast by D 76 – alt. 1 011 m – ✉ 26190

Combe Laval★★★.

Du Col de la Machine rest, rest, **P** VISA MC AE

– ✆ 04 75 48 26 36 – Jfaravello@aol.com – Fax 04 75 48 29 12 – Closed 9-21 March, 23 November-26 December, Tuesday evening and Wednesday except July-August and school holidays

12 rm – †€ 49/53 ††€ 55/58, ☕ € 9 – ½ P € 59/62 – **Rest** – *(closed Wednesday lunch in July-August)* Menu € 18/42 – Carte € 20/49

◆ At the start of the rigorous Combe Laval trek, a great regional building run by the same family since 1848 set in a garden at the edge of the forest. Modern rooms. Dining room attractively redecorated in a chalet style. Friendly welcome and attentive service.

ST-JEAN-LE-THOMAS – 50 Manche – 303 C7 – pop. 395 – alt. 20 m – ✉ 50530

Paris 350 – Avranches 16 – Granville 18 – St-Lô 71 – St-Malo 82 – Villedieu-les-Poêles 37 32 **A2**

Syndicat d'initiative, 21, place Pierre le Jaudet ✆ 02 33 70 90 71, Fax 02 33 70 90 71

Des Bains

– ✆ 02 33 48 84 20 – hdbains@orange.fr – Fax 02 33 48 66 42
– Open 21 March-2 November and closed Wednesday in October

30 rm – †€ 47/75 ††€ 54/75, ☕ € 7,50 – ½ P € 54/65

Rest – *(closed Monday lunch, Wednesday lunch and Thursday lunch except in August and Wednesday in October)* Menu (€ 12), € 18/35 – Carte € 22/44

◆ The same family has greeted guests here since 1912 in this group of village houses. Old-fashioned rooms, simply furnished. Garden with swimming pool. An immense flower-decked rustic dining room with a pretty bar. 'Surf n'turf' cuisine.

ST-JEAN-PIED-DE-PORT – 64 Pyrénées-Atlantiques – 342 E6 – pop. 1 417 – alt. 159 m – ✉ 64220 Atlantic Coast 3 **B3**

Paris 817 – Bayonne 54 – Biarritz 55 – Pau 106 – San Sebastián 96

Office de tourisme, 14, place Charles-de-Gaulle ✆ 05 59 37 03 57, Fax 05 59 37 34 91

Route of the pilgrims ★ of Santiago de Compostella.

Plan on next page

Les Pyrénées (Philippe et Firmin Arrambide)

pl. Ch. de Gaulle – ✆ 05 59 37 01 01
– pyrenees@relaischateaux.com – Fax 05 59 37 18 97
– Closed 20 November-22 December, 5-28 January, Monday evening from November to March and Tuesday from 20 September to 30 June except public holidays **a**

16 rm – †€ 100/110 ††€ 170/200, ☕ € 16 – 4 suites – ½ P € 140/210

Rest – *(pre-book in high season and Sat - Sun)* Menu € 42/88 – Carte € 58/108

Spec. Assiette de langoustines "en quatre façons". Saumon frais de l'Adour grillé béarnaise (March to July). Lasagne au foie gras et aux truffes. **Wines** Jurançon sec, Irouléguy.

◆ A former coaching inn with spacious, elegant rooms (beautiful bathrooms). Swimming pool in luxuriant verdant surroundings. Fine Basque cuisine from a father and son team served in the contemporary dining room or on the veranda.

Central

pl. Ch. de Gaulle – ✆ 05 59 37 00 22 – Fax 05 59 37 27 79
– Open 11 March-30 November and closed Tuesday from March to June **s**

12 rm – †€ 56/72 ††€ 60/75, ☕ € 8 – ½ P € 58/68

Rest – Menu € 20/45 – Carte € 30/58

◆ As its name suggests, this hotel is located a stone's throw from the citadel. A two-century-old polished staircase leads to the spacious traditional guestrooms. Enjoy local cuisine in the dining room-veranda or on the tiny terrace on the banks of the Nive.

Etche Ona

15 pl. Floquet – ✆ 05 59 37 01 14 – Fax 05 59 37 35 69 – Closed 14 November-4 December, 18 February-5 March, Wednesday dinner and Thursday **v**

Rest – Menu € 29

◆ The younger generation has taken over this family-run restaurant at the entrance to the old town. Rustic decor, elegantly laid tables, a small terrace and regional dishes chalked on a blackboard.

in Esterençuby 8 km south by D 301 – pop. 382 – alt. 229 m – ✉ 64220

Artzain Etchea

rte d'Iraty, 1km – ✆ 05 59 37 11 55 – info@artzain-etchea.fr – Fax 05 59 37 20 16
– Open 2 March-19 November and closed Tuesday and Wednesday except in season

11 rm – †€ 50 ††€ 50, ☕ € 6,50 – ½ P € 47 – **Rest** – Menu € 25/29

◆ This large white building, built on the mountainside, overlooks the Nive. Simple, well-kept rooms; some with balconies. Hunting and fishing packages. Dining room with exposed beams and pastoral photos. Basque cuisine.

ST-JEAN-PIED-DE-PORT

Çaro (Rte de) 2
Çitadelle (R. de la) 4
Église (R. de l') 6
Espagne (R. d') 10
France (R.) 12
Fronton (Av. du) 15
Gaulle (Pl. Ch.-de) 16
Liberté (R. de la) 17
St-Jacques (Ch. de) 18
St-Michel (Rte de) 21
Trinquet (Pl. du) 24
Uhart (R. d') 27
Zuharpeta (R.) 30

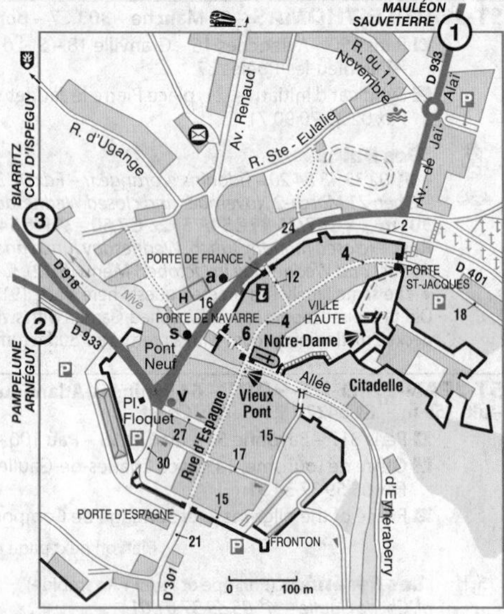

Les Sources de la Nive
at Béherobie – ✆ 05 59 37 10 57 – source.nive@wanadoo.fr – Fax 05 59 37 39 06
– Closed January and Tuesday off season
26 rm – †€ 45 ††€ 45, ☐ € 8 – ½ P € 44 – **Rest** – Menu € 14/30 – Carte € 18/46
♦ This small hotel on the banks of the Nive is the perfect base for nature-lovers. Simply furnished but well-maintained guestrooms, renovated gradually. Dining room decorated in Basque style, plus a veranda overlooking the river. Regional cuisine.

in Aincille by ① and D 18: 7 km – pop. 103 – alt. 253 m – ✉ 64220

Pecoïtz with rm
rte d'Iraty – ✆ 05 59 37 11 88 – pecoitz@wanadoo.fr – Fax 05 59 37 35 42
– Open 1st April-1st January and closed Wednesday dinner and Thursday except school holidays
14 rm – †€ 45/48 ††€ 45/48, ☐ € 5 – ½ P € 45 – **Rest** – Menu € 15 (weekdays), € 23/35 – Carte € 26/35
♦ Copious home cooking with a regional flavour served in a colourful setting (one dining room with a view over the countryside). Simple bedrooms.

ST-JEAN-ST-MAURICE-SUR-LOIRE – 42 Loire – 327 D4 – ✉ 42155

Lyon - Rhone Valley 44 **A1**

Paris 406 – Lyon 95 – Roanne 15 – Vichy 79

L'Échauguette
– ✆ 04 77 63 15 89 – contact@echauguette-alex.com
4 rm ☐ – †€ 57/67 ††€ 67/77 – **Table d'hôte** – Menu € 27 bi
♦ These three maisonnettes open onto the calm waters of the Villerest Lake. The rooms are tastefully decorated in various styles and benefit from a separate entrance. Meals served in an open kitchen or on the terrace, weather permitting.

ST-JEAN-SAVERNE – 67 Bas-Rhin – 315 I4 – see Saverne

ST-JEAN-SUR-VEYLE – 01 Ain – 328 C3 – pop. 958 – alt. 200 m – ✉ 01290

44 **B1**

Paris 402 – Bourg-en-Bresse 32 – Mâcon 12 – Villefranche-sur-Saône 45

La Petite Auberge

Le bourg – 03 85 31 53 92 – lapetiteaubergeperonnet@wanadoo.fr – Closed 1st-15 September, 31 December-19 January, Tuesday dinner, Sunday dinner and Monday

Rest – Menu (€ 12 bi), € 22/41 – Carte € 40/50

◆ The inviting dining room of this half-timbered building (red brick, beams and art by local artists) forms the backdrop to regional specialities.

ST-JOACHIM – 44 Loire-Atlantique – 316 C3 – pop. 3 772 – alt. 5 m – ✉ 44720

Brittany 34 **A2**

Paris 435 – Nantes 61 – Redon 40 – St-Nazaire 14 – Vannes 64

Tour of Fédrun island ★ West: 4.5 km - Barge trip★★.

La Mare aux Oiseaux with rm

Ile de Fedrun – 02 40 88 53 01 – courriel@mareauxoiseaux.fr – Fax 02 40 91 67 44 – Closed 6 January-13 February and Monday lunch

10 rm – € 120/185 € 120/185, € 16 – ½ P € 168/204

Rest – Menu € 38/80 – Carte € 74

◆ Lovely cottage surrounded by the Brière marshland, ideal for bird watchers and food lovers. Inventive cuisine. Pleasant, quite spacious, uncluttered rooms.

ST-JOSSE – 62 Pas-de-Calais – 301 C5 – pop. 1 052 – alt. 35 m – ✉ 62170

Northern France and the Paris Region 30 **A2**

Paris 223 – Lille 144 – Arras 94 – Boulogne-sur-Mer 39 – Abbeville 49

Le Relais de St Josse

17 pl. de L' Eglise – 03 21 94 61 75 – pascalou.loumi@orange.fr – Fax 03 21 84 88 72 – Closed 7 January-8 February, Wednesday dinner and Sunday dinner off season and Thursday except public holidays

Rest – Menu € 28/36 – Carte € 29/45

◆ With its colourful façade and London taxi cab parked outside, this auberge definitely catches the eye. Fine contemporary cuisine served in an attractive dining room with parquet flooring and library.

in Moulinel 2 km northeast by D 145 – ✉ 62170 St-Josse

Auberge du Moulinel

116 chaussée de l'Avant Pays – 03 21 94 79 03 – Fax 03 21 09 37 14 – Closed 5-25 January, Sunday dinner, Monday and Tuesday except July-August

Rest – Menu € 28/48 – Carte € 62/69

◆ This inn, set away from busy roads, offers three pleasant dining rooms, serving up-to-date cuisine with market produce.

ST-JOUIN-BRUNEVAL – 76 Seine-Maritime – 304 A4 – pop. 1 576 – alt. 110 m – ✉ 76280

33 **C1**

Paris 202 – Fécamp 25 – Le Havre 20 – Rouen 92

Le Belvédère sea,

– 02 35 20 13 76 – Closed 5 January-5 February, Sunday dinner, Wednesday dinner and Thursday

Rest – Menu € 21/40 – Carte € 39/58

◆ You can enjoy an impressive panoramic view of the cliffs and the sea, while savouring traditional dishes as well as fish and seafood specialities. Neat contemporary decor.

ST-JULIEN-AUX-BOIS – 19 Corrèze – 329 N5 – pop. 501 – alt. 594 m – ✉ 19220

Paris 524 – Aurillac 53 – Brive-la-Gaillarde 66 – Mauriac 29 – St-Céré 60 – Tulle 50 – Ussel 63 25 **C3**

Auberge de St-Julien-aux-Bois with rm

– 05 55 28 41 94 – auberge_st_julien@hotmail.com – Fax 05 55 28 37 85 – Closed February school holidays and Sunday from September to June

6 rm – € 41 € 48/55, € 7 – ½ P € 46/50 – **Rest** – *(closed Sunday dinner and Wednesday dinner except July-August, Wednesday lunch)* Menu (€ 13), € 15/46 – Carte € 24/37

◆ This village house makes a point of serving healthy organic produce; the desserts are German in style. Country setting; the pretty rooms are graced with fresh flowers.

ST-JULIEN-CHAPTEUIL – 43 Haute-Loire – 331 G3 – pop. 1 804 – alt. 815 m – ✉ 43260 Lyon - Rhone Valley 6 C3

Paris 559 – Lamastre 52 – Privas 88 – Le Puy-en-Velay 20 – St-Agrève 32 – Yssingeaux 17

Office de tourisme, place Saint-Robert ✆ 04 71 08 77 70, Fax 04 71 08 42 20

Site★ - Montagne du Meygal★: Grand Testavoyre ✱★★ Northeast: 14 km then 30 mn.

Vidal

VISA MC AE

18 pl. du Marché – ✆ 04 71 08 70 50 – info@restaurant-vidal.com – Fax 04 71 08 40 14 – Closed 27-30 June, 1st-4 September and 13 January-21 February

Rest – *(closed Tuesday dinner off season, Thursday dinner and Monday)* Menu € 27/75 – Carte € 50/75

Rest *Bistrot de Justin* – bistrot *(closed Sunday and Monday) (lunch only)* Menu (€ 14 bi), € 19 bi – Carte approx. € 21

◆ Murals depicting the region, lace table mats, light wooden furniture and old doors embellish the decor of this rustic restaurant in the Velay region.

ST-JULIEN-DE-CREMPSE – 24 Dordogne – 329 E6 – see Bergerac

ST-JULIEN-D'EMPARE – 12 Aveyron – 338 E3 – see Capdenac-Gare

ST-JULIEN-DU-SAULT – 89 Yonne – 319 C3 – pop. 2 380 – alt. 82 m – ✉ 89330 Bourgogne

Paris 137 – Dijon 189 – Auxerre 42 – Melun 98 – Troyes 93

Les Bons Enfants

VISA MC

4 pl. de la Mairie – ✆ 03 86 91 17 38 – bonsenfants@orange.fr – Fax 03 86 91 14 19 – Closed 18-31 August, Sunday dinner and Tuesday

Rest – Menu (€ 28), € 32/60

◆ Imposing house in the centre of the village. Creative menu with vegetables to the fore; more traditional dishes at the bistro.

ST-JULIEN-EN-CHAMPSAUR – 05 Hautes-Alpes – 334 E5 – pop. 275 – alt. 1 050 m – ✉ 05500 41 C1

Paris 658 – Gap 17 – Grenoble 95 – La Mure 55 – Orcières 21

Les Chenets with rm

AC rest, VISA MC AE

– ✆ 04 92 50 03 15 – les-chenets@wanadoo.fr – Fax 04 92 50 73 06 – Closed April, 11 November-27 December, Sunday dinner and Wednesday off season

18 rm – †€ 25/29 ††€ 38/43, ☐ € 6,50 – ½ P € 42/45 – **Rest** – Menu € 20/36 – Carte € 32/51

◆ This convivial restaurant in the heart of the green Champsaur area features a neat decor pleasantly combining wood, stone and glass. Appetising traditional cuisine. A few rooms available.

ST-JULIEN-EN-GENEVOIS – 74 Haute-Savoie – 328 J4 – pop. 9 140 – alt. 460 m – Casino – ✉ 74160 46 F1

Paris 525 – Annecy 35 – Bonneville 36 – Genève 11 – Nantua 56 – Thonon-les-Bains 47

Office de tourisme, 2, place du Crêt ✆ 04 50 04 71 63, Fax 04 50 04 89 76

in Archamps 5 km east by A40, 13.1 exit – pop. 1 235 – alt. 535 m – ✉ 74160

Porte Sud de Genève

P VISA MC AE

parc d'affaire international, (Site d'Archamps) – ✆ 04 50 31 16 06 – hotel-portesudgva@site-archamps.com – Fax 04 50 31 29 71

90 rm – †€ 78/196 ††€ 89/216, ☐ € 13 – **Rest** – *(closed lunch on public holidays, Saturday and Sunday)* Menu (€ 19), € 24 – Carte € 31/49

◆ A modern hotel set in the heart of the Franco-Swiss technology belt. The contemporary rooms are both relaxing and well thought out for business guests. A bright dining room, a terrace facing the garden and traditional recipes.

in Bossey 7 km east by D 1206 – pop. 545 – alt. 438 m – ✉ 74160

XXX **La Ferme de l'Hospital** (Jean-Jacques Noguier)
✿ *– ✆ 04 50 43 61 43 – jjnoguier@wanadoo.fr – Fax 04 50 95 31 53*
– Closed 30 July-18 August, February school holidays, Sunday and Monday
Rest – *(pre-book)* Menu € 38 (weekday lunch), € 48/70 – Carte € 64/83
Spec. Ravioli de caille, morilles et foie gras à l'émulsion des bois. Meunière de féra du lac, girolles du pays, émulsion au parmesan. Râble de lapereau cuit à basse température, jus à la sariette. **Wines** Chignin-Bergeron, Mondeuse d'Arbin.
◆ This 17C farmhouse was once the property of the Geneva hospital. Interiors have a lot of character. Pleasant terrace, up-to-date cuisine and carefully selected wines.

Annecy road 9.5 km south by N 201 – ✉ 74350 Cruseilles

Rey without rest
on the Mont Sion pass – ✆ 04 50 44 13 29 – resa@hotelrey.com
– Fax 04 50 44 05 48 – Closed 21 December-6 January
29 rm – †€ 56/69 ††€ 59/76, ☕ € 7,50 – 1 suite
◆ Hidden from the road by a swathe of greenery, this hotel offers practical, cheerful rooms, quieter to the rear. Breakfast served on the veranda overlooking the garden.

ST-JULIEN-LE-FAUCON – 14 Calvados – 303 M5 – pop. 582 – alt. 40 m – ✉ 14140

33 **C2**

▶ Paris 192 – Caen 41 – Falaise 32 – Lisieux 14

X **Auberge de la Levrette**
48 r. Lisieux – ✆ 02 31 63 81 20 – Fax 02 31 63 97 05 – Closed 16-24 June, 22 December-13 January, Monday and Tuesday except public holidays
Rest – Menu € 27/40 – Carte € 36/57
◆ Formerly an important coaching inn, this half-timbered house in typical Pays d'Auge style was built in 1550. The fireplace in the dining room dates from the same period. Traditional, seasonal cuisine.

ST-JULIEN-MOLIN-MOLETTE – 42 Loire – 327 G8 – see Annonay

ST-JULIEN-SUR-CHER – 41 Loir-et-Cher – 318 H8 – pop. 663 – alt. 110 m – ✉ 41320

12 **C2**

▶ Paris 227 – Blois 51 – Bourges 66 – Châteauroux 62 – Vierzon 25

X **Les Deux Pierrots**
9 r. Nationale – ✆ 02 54 96 40 07 – Closed August, Monday and Tuesday
Rest – Menu € 25/38 – Carte approx. € 37
◆ This village inn has a rustic style dining area with exposed beams, opening onto the vegetable garden in summer. Simple and traditional cuisine.

ST-JULIEN-VOCANCE – 07 Ardèche – pop. 241 – alt. 680 m – ✉ 07690

44 **B2**

▶ Paris 553 – Saint-Étienne 56 – Valence 68 – Annonay 18

XX **Julliat**
Le Marthouret – ✆ 04 75 34 71 61 – contact@restaurant-julliat.com
– Fax 04 75 34 79 19 – Closed 2-7 January, 16-28 February, Wednesday except July-August and Tuesday dinner
Rest – Menu € 18/75 – Carte € 38/55
◆ This old, prettily restored house is a happy blend of contemporary decoration and old stone work where you are served appetising, modern food.

ST-JUNIEN – 87 Haute-Vienne – 325 C5 – pop. 10 666 – alt. 240 m – ✉ 87200

Dordogne-Berry-Limousin

24 **A2**

▶ Paris 416 – Angoulême 73 – Bellac 34 – Confolens 27 – Limoges 32

Office de tourisme, place du Champ de Foire ✆ 05 55 02 17 93, Fax 05 55 02 94 31

de Saint-Junien Les Jouberties, West: 4 km, ✆ 05 55 02 96 96.

Collegiate church ★ B.

Le Relais de Comodoliac

22 av. Sadi-Carnot – ✆ 05 55 02 27 26 – comodoliac@wanadoo.fr – Fax 05 55 02 68 79 – Closed 21 February-1st March

29 rm – †€ 54 ††€ 70, ☕ € 9 – ½ P € 60

Rest – *(closed Sunday dinner October-Easter)* Menu € 16/38 – Carte € 30/48

◆ This horizontal building at the western entrance of the town dates back to the 1970s. It is separated from the road by a pretty garden. Functional rooms. A veranda dining room opening onto a delightful terrace. Classic menu.

South : 2 km by Rochechouart road, D 675 and secondary road – ✉ 87200 St-Junien

Lauryvan

– ✆ 05 55 02 26 04 – lauryvan@nomade.fr – Fax 05 55 02 25 29 – Closed 2-7 January, Sunday dinner, Monday and dinner on public holidays

Rest – Menu € 33/74 bi – Carte € 25/49

◆ Pavilion in an area of thick vegetation, near a pond. The dining room serves low priced regional dishes and classic fare. Garden terrace.

ST-JUST-ET-VACQUIERES – 30 Gard – 339 K4 – pop. 260 – alt. 190 m – ✉ 30580

23 **C1**

Paris 699 – Montpellier 104 – Nîmes 54 – Alès 18 – Orange 75

Mas Vacquières without rest

Hameau de Vaquières – ✆ 04 66 83 70 75 – info@masvac.com

6 rm ☕ – †€ 65/110 ††€ 75/125

◆ This typical house, tucked away in a lane of the hamlet, is set in a delightfully peaceful garden. Spotless, pleasant rooms and generous breakfasts (terrace).

ST-JUSTIN – 40 Landes – 335 J11 – pop. 888 – alt. 90 m – ✉ 40240

3 **B2**

Paris 694 – Aire-sur-l'Adour 38 – Casteljaloux 49 – Dax 84 – Mont-de-Marsan 25 – Pau 89

Office de tourisme, place des Tilleuls ✆ 05 58 44 86 06, Fax 05 58 44 86 06

France with rm

pl. des Tilleuls – ✆ 05 58 44 83 61 – Fax 05 58 44 83 89 – Closed 15 November-2 December, Sunday and Monday

8 rm – †€ 39/48 ††€ 39/48, ☕ € 6,50

Rest – Menu € 27/33 – Carte € 38/48

Rest *Bistrot* – *(closed Saturday dinner, Sunday, Monday and public holidays)* Menu € 13,50

◆ The building is under the arcades of the medieval square where, in season, a terrace operates. Copious and traditional cuisine. Home-made jams at breakfast. Village café atmosphere and blackboard menu at the Bistrot.

ST-JUST-ST-RAMBERT – 42 Loire – 327 E7 – pop. 13 192 – alt. 380 m – ✉ 42170

44 **A2**

Paris 542 – St Etienne 17 – Lyon 81 – Montbrison 18 – Roanne 74

Office de tourisme, place de la Paix ✆ 04 77 52 05 14, Fax 04 77 52 15 91

Le Neuvième Art (Christophe Roure)

pl. 19 Mars 1962 – ✆ 04 77 55 87 15 – le.neuvieme.art@wanadoo.fr – Fax 04 77 55 80 77 – Closed 8-31 August, 21-26 December, 8-22 February, Sunday and Monday

Rest – *(number of covers limited, pre-book)* Menu € 56/95 – Carte € 73/80

Spec. Brochette de grosses langoustines en kadaïf. Barrette de foie gras (winter). Verrines superposées d'un chocolat intense, gelée passion (autumn-winter).

Wines Vin de pays d'Urfé, Côtes du Forez.

◆ The hall of this former train station is full of surprises: creative, flavourful cuisine, a lovely, almost minimalist, designer decor and impeccable service.

ST-LARY – 09 Ariège – **343** D7 – **pop. 136** – **alt. 692 m** – ✉ **09800** 28 **B3**

Paris 786 – Bagnères-de-Luchon 48 – St-Gaudens 36 – St-Girons 24 – Salies-du-Salat 197

Auberge de l'Isard
– ✆ 05 61 96 72 83 – aubergeisard@aol.com – Fax 05 61 96 73 71
– Closed 7 January-3 February and Monday off season
8 rm – €38/40 €40/42, €6 – ½ P €45
Rest – *(open beg. March-beg. December and closed Monday off season)*
Menu €18/29 – Carte €22/42
◆ Pleasant well-maintained hotel which also houses the village bar and a shop selling regional produce. Rustic decor in the well-equipped rooms. Separated by a stream from the hotel, the restaurant serves traditional fare.

ST-LARY-SOULAN – 65 Hautes-Pyrénées – **342** N8 – **pop. 1 024** – **alt. 820 m** – **Winter sports : 1 680/2 450 m** 2 30 – **Spa : early April-late Oct.** – ✉ **65170**
Languedoc-Roussillon-Tarn Gorges 28 **A3**

Paris 830 – Arreau 12 – Auch 103 – Bagnères-de-Luchon 44 – St-Gaudens 66 – Tarbes 74

Office de tourisme, 37, rue Vincent Mir ✆ 05 62 39 50 81, Fax 05 62 39 50 06

La Pergola
25 r. Vincent Mir – ✆ 05 62 39 40 46 – jean-pierre.mir@wanadoo.fr
– Fax 05 62 40 06 55 – Closed November
20 rm – €61/75 €67/109, €10 – 2 suites – ½ P €62/89
Rest ***L'Enclos des Saveurs*** – *(closed Monday lunch and Tuesday lunch in winter)*
Menu €18 (weekday lunch), €29/50 – Carte €46/54
◆ A peaceful house set in a well-kept garden. Large rooms with elegant personal touches. Seven of them have a terrace or balcony with a view of the mountain peaks. Attentive service. Up-to-date menu and local dishes available at the Enclos des Saveurs.

Les Arches without rest
15 av. des Thermes – ✆ 05 62 49 10 10 – contact@hotel-les-arches.com
– Fax 05 62 49 10 15 – Closed 2-16 November
30 rm – €50/64 €50/64, €7,50
◆ This new hotel has simple, functional, but well-kept rooms. Welcoming breakfast room and pleasant lounge where log fires are lit on chilly days.

Aurélia
at Vielle-Aure – ✆ 05 62 39 56 90 – hotel-aurelia@wanadoo.fr
– Fax 05 62 39 43 75 – Closed 27 September-14 December
20 rm – €40/44 €48/55, €7,50 – ½ P €47/53 – **Rest** – *(residents only)*
◆ Hotel with a family atmosphere and good leisure facilities, just 600m from the fitness centre. Well-kept rooms, with roof windows on the third floor; two duplex rooms also available.

De la Neste
– ✆ 05 62 39 42 79 – hoteldelaneste@wanadoo.fr – Fax 05 62 39 58 77
– Closed November
17 rm – €48/57 €48/57, €7,80 – 3 suites – ½ P €49/58
Rest – *(dinner only) (residents only)*
◆ This hotel for non-smokers only, renovated in 2004, is pleasantly set alongside a river, next to a thermal and leisure centre and not far from the cable car or village. Rooms brightened by mountain photos. Six have dormer windows.

Pons "Le Dahu"
4 r. Coudères – ✆ 05 62 39 43 66 – contact@hotelpons.com – Fax 05 62 40 00 86
– Closed 20 April-8 May
39 rm – €60 €70, €8 – ½ P €56 – **Rest** – Menu (€13), €16/30 – Carte €17/34
◆ These 1950s buildings are set in a residential area near the cable car and town centre. The largest rooms are in the annexe and all have balconies. Tasty and copious traditional dishes can be enjoyed in a guesthouse atmosphere.

XX **La Grange**
– ✆ 05 62 40 07 14 – contact@angleterre-arreau.com – Fax 05 62 98 69 60
– Closed 21 April-10 May, 16 November-15 December, Tuesday and Wednesday except dinner in season
Rest – Menu (€ 15), € 19/42 – Carte € 36/52
◆ This old barn was converted into a comfortable and pretty restaurant with a warm wooden decor. In winter, attractive flames in the fireplace. Regional menus.

ST-LATTIER – 38 Isère – 333 E7 – pop. 1 031 – alt. 170 m – ✉ 38840 43 E2

Paris 571 – Grenoble 67 – Romans-sur-Isère 13 – St-Marcellin 15 – Valence 34

Le Lièvre Amoureux
La Gare – ✆ *04 76 64 50 67 – lelievreamoureux@wanadoo.fr*
– Closed 10-24 August and 9-22 February
7 rm – †€ 65 ††€ 80/130, ☕ € 9,50 – ½ P € 115
Table d'hôte – *(closed Sunday)* Menu € 40/65
◆ This former hunting lodge was successfully renovated to provide three fine, spacious rooms with personal touches, as well as two duplexes. This dining room has a large fireplace and offers tasty local Dauphinois dishes.

X **Auberge du Viaduc** with rm
D1092 (hamlet of La Rivière) – ✆ *04 76 64 51 65*
– auberge.du.viaduc@wanadoo.fr – Fax 04 76 64 30 93
– Closed 28 November-15 January, Sunday dinner December-April, Tuesday (except hotel), Wednesday lunch June-September and Monday
6 rm – †€ 82 ††€ 82, ☕ € 10 – 1 suite – ½ P € 85 – **Rest** – *(number of covers limited, pre-book)* Menu € 28/54 – Carte € 40/56
◆ Long-standing family residence, opening onto a pleasant garden. Intimate dining rooms, with a veranda and a log fire in winter. Pretty regional furniture in the rooms.

X **Brun** with rm
Les Fauries, D 1092 – ✆ *04 76 64 54 08 – contact@hotel-brun.com*
– Fax 04 76 64 31 78 – Closed 13-29 October, 18 January-5 March and Sunday dinner
10 rm – †€ 45 ††€ 55, ☕ € 7 – ½ P € 46 – **Rest** – Menu € 13,50 (weekday lunch), € 18/50 – Carte € 30/38
◆ A country restaurant extended by a fine terrace shaded by linden trees on the banks of the Isère. Accommodation in a building 400 m away.

ST-LAURENT-DE-CERDANS – 66 Pyrénées-Orientales – 344 G8 – pop. 1 218 – alt. 675 m – ✉ 66260 Languedoc-Roussillon-Tarn Gorges 22 B3

Paris 901 – Céret 28 – Perpignan 60

Syndicat d'initiative, 7, rue Joseph Nivet ✆ 04 68 39 55 75, Fax 04 68 39 59 59

Southwest 6.5 km by D 3 and secondary road – ✉ 66260 St-Laurent-de-Cerdans

Domaine de Falgos
– ✆ *04 68 39 51 42 – contact@falgos.com*
– Fax 04 68 39 52 30 – Open 15 March-11 November
25 rm – †€ 96/143 ††€ 140/233, ☕ € 18 – 7 suites – **Rest** – Menu € 27 bi (lunch), € 37/47 (dinner) – Carte € 29/45
◆ Situated in an isolated spot on the Spanish border, this old mountain farmhouse has been redeveloped into a hotel complex with a golf course and fitness centre. Cosy, spacious and well-appointed guestrooms. Brasserie-style menu at lunchtime and traditional cuisine in the evening. Summer terrace overlooking the golf course.

ST-LAURENT-DE-LA-SALANQUE – 66 Pyrénées-Orientales – 344 I6 – pop. 7 932 – alt. 2 m – ✉ 66250 22 B3

Paris 845 – Elne 26 – Narbonne 62 – Perpignan 19 – Quillan 80 – Rivesaltes 12

Syndicat d'initiative, place Gambetta ✆ 04 68 28 31 03

Fort de Salses★★ Northwest: 9 km, Languedoc-Roussillon-Tarn Gorges

Le Commerce with rm — rest,
2 bd de la Révolution – ✆ 04 68 28 02 21 – contact@lecommerce66.com – Fax 04 68 28 39 86 – Closed 27 October-25 November, Sunday dinner except July-August and Monday except dinner July-August
11 rm – †€ 51 ††€ 55, ☕ € 8,50 – ½ P € 53
Rest – Menu € 19/39 – Carte € 39/61
◆ At the centre of the village, regional fare served in a rustic dining room painted in bright yellow colours. Small rooms with Catalan furniture.

ST-LAURENT-DE-MURE – 69 Rhône – 327 J5 – pop. 4 694 – alt. 252 m – ✉ 69720

43 **E1**

Paris 478 – Lyon 19 – Pont-de-Chéruy 16 – La Tour-du-Pin 38 – Vienne 38

Hostellerie Le St-Laurent — rm,
8 r. Croix Blanche – ✆ 04 78 40 91 44 – le.st.laurent@wanadoo.fr – Fax 04 78 40 45 41 – Closed 1st-4 May, 8-11 May, 2-24 August, 26 December-4 January, Friday dinner, Saturday, Sunday and dinner on public holidays
30 rm – †€ 68/120 ††€ 68/120, ☕ € 9
Rest – Menu € 25 (weekdays), € 38/62 – Carte € 45/61
◆ A fine 18C Dauphiné abode nestling in wooded parkland. The simple rooms vary in size, but those in the annexe are smaller. In summer, meals are served on the terrace under a 300 year-old lime tree.

ST-LAURENT-DES-ARBRES 30 Gard – 339N4 – pop. 1 743 – alt. 60 m – ✉ 30126

Paris 673 – Alès 70 – Avignon 20 – Nîmes 47 – Orange 22 — 23 **D2**

Office de tourisme, Tour de Ribas ✆ 04 66 50 10 10, Fax 04 66 50 10 10

Le Saint-Laurent without rest
pl. de l'Arbre – ✆ 04 66 50 14 14 – info@lesaintlaurent.biz – Fax 04 66 50 46 30 – Closed 12 November-8 December
9 rm – †€ 75/95 ††€ 75/165, ☕ € 15 – 1 suite
◆ This former wine-grower's house, nestling in the village, is full of character and carefully decorated. Antique furniture, cosy rooms and a pretty inner courtyard. A real little treasure.

Felisa without rest
6 r. Barris – ✆ 04 66 39 99 84 – information@maison-felisa.com – Open 3 April-3 January
5 rm ☕ – †€ 100/130 ††€ 120/150
◆ A zen spirit reigns over this stone abode (1830) that offers massages, yoga and a pool. Minimalist rooms (on the theme of fragrances) and a trendy, youthful ambience.

ST-LAURENT-DU-PONT – 38 Isère – 333 H5 – pop. 4 222 – alt. 410 m – ✉ 38380 French Alps

45 **C2**

Paris 560 – Chambéry 29 – Grenoble 34 – La Tour-du-Pin 42 – Voiron 15

Office de tourisme, place de la Mairie ✆ 04 76 06 22 55, Fax 04 76 06 21 21

Gorges du Guiers Mort★★ Southeast: 2 km - Site★ of the Chartreuse de Curière Southeast: 4 km.

La Blache
av. de la Gare – ✆ 04 76 55 29 57 – Closed 28 April-13 May, 1st-16 September, 5-20 January, Sunday dinner, Monday and Tuesday
Rest – Menu € 30/58 – Carte € 33/63
◆ Unusual wooden armchairs adorn this tasteful establishment in a former train station near the Guiers Mort gorge. The market fresh menu changes with the seasons.

ST-LAURENT-DU-VAR – 06 Alpes-Maritimes – 341 E5 – pop. 27 141 – alt. 18 m – ✉ 06700 French Riviera

42 **E2**

Paris 919 – Antibes 16 – Cagnes-sur-Mer 5 – Cannes 26 – Grasse 31 – Nice 10 – Vence 16

Syndicat d'initiative, 18-19, route du Bord de Mer ✆ 04 93 31 31 21, Fax 04 93 14 92 83

Corniche du Var★ North.

See plan of NICE urban area

in Cap 3000

Novotel rm, VISA

40 av. de Verdun – ✆ 04 93 19 55 55 – h0414@accor.com – Fax 04 93 19 55 59

103 rm – €90/145 €90/145, €14 – ½ P €88 – **Rest** – Carte €25/43

◆ A recently renovated modern hotel in a suburban shopping area near Nice-Côte-d'Azur Airport. Choose between an outside table in a haven of greenery, or the cool air-conditioned dining room much appreciated when it is scorching hot.

in Port St-Laurent

Holiday Inn Resort rm, VISA

promenade Flots Bleus – ✆ 04 93 14 80 00 – resort@wanadoo.fr – Fax 04 93 07 21 24

124 rm – €180/280 €200/300, €20 – ½ P €130/180

Rest *Chez Panisse* – Menu (€20 bi), €24/29 bi – Carte €28/51

◆ A prestigious international hotel right on the beach, with a carefully kept modern look. The spacious and well-equipped rooms have a view of the sea or of the countryside. Seaside resort ambiance, traditional cuisine and spit-roasted meats.

La Mousson VISA

promenade Flots Bleus – ✆ 04 93 31 13 30 – barthelemi.eric@wanadoo.fr – Closed 1 week in November, Christmas holidays, Monday October-May and Sunday

Rest – Menu (€24), €29/41 – Carte €34/50

◆ Thai savours and exotic spices transport you to the kingdom of Siam during your meal, while you are pleasantly seated in this seafront restaurant.

ST-LAURENT-DU-VERDON – 04 Alpes-de-Haute-Provence – 334 E10 – pop. 74 – alt. 468 m – ✉ 04500 41 C2

Paris 806 – Brignoles 49 – Castellane 70 – Digne-les-Bains 59 – Manosque 37

Le Moulin du Château rm, rest, VISA

– ✆ 04 92 74 02 47 – info@moulin-du-chateau.com – Fax 04 92 74 02 97 – Open 8 March-3 November

10 rm – €76/99 €79/105, €9 – 1 suite

Rest – *(closed Mon and Thu) (dinner only) (residents only)* Menu €30 (dinner)

◆ To the rear of the château is this 17C mill, now a hotel. Dining room with millstone feature. Spacious contemporary rooms. Convivial ambiance.

ST-LAURENT-LA-GÂTINE – 28 Eure-et-Loir – 311 F3 – pop. 401 – alt. 134 m – ✉ 28210 11 B1

Paris 77 – Évreux 66 – Orléans 121 – Versailles 57

Clos St-Laurent without rest

6 r. de l'Église – ✆ 02 37 38 24 02 – james@clos-saint-laurent.com – Closed 22 December-5 January

4 rm – €65 €70

◆ The former farm building houses three large rooms, tastefully decorated in a smart rustic style. Charming breakfast room and garden-terrace.

ST-LAURENT-NOUAN – 41 Loir-et-Cher – 318 G5 – pop. 3 686 – alt. 84 m – ✉ 41220 12 C2

Paris 161 – Beaugency 9 – Blois 28 – Orléans 40 – Romorantin-Lanthenay 44

Office de tourisme, 58, route Nationale ✆ 02 54 87 01 31, Fax 02 54 87 01 31

Les Bordes rm, rest, VISA

6 km north-east on D925 and secondary road – ✆ 02 54 87 72 13 – golf.les.bordes@wanadoo.fr – Fax 02 54 87 78 61 – Closed 23 December-18 January

41 rm – €150/190 €170/210, €15 – **Rest** – Menu €25 (lunch), €45/85 – Carte €50/87

◆ Golfers prize this property owing to its idyllic location in the middle of 600ha of woods and ponds. Lovely, simple, rustic rooms, shared out over nine cottages. Meals served beneath fine timberwork or, in summer, on the verdant terrace.

ST-LAURENT-SUR-SAÔNE – 01 Ain – 328 C3 – see Mâcon

ST-LÉON – 47 Lot-et-Garonne – 336 D4 – pop. 258 – alt. 80 m – ✉ 47160 4 C2

Paris 667 – Bordeaux 107 – Agen 43 – Villeneuve-sur-Lot 44 – Marmande 35

Le Hameau des Coquelicots without rest

2 km south on D 285 – ✆ 05 53 84 06 13 – contact@lehameaudescoquelicots.com – Fax 05 53 84 06 13

5 rm – €85/100 €90/105

◆ Three houses in the middle of the countryside offering tranquillity, a warm welcome and a sober décor featuring natural materials and artworks. Kitchen garden and "natural" swimming pool.

ST-LÉONARD-DE-NOBLAT – 87 Haute-Vienne – 325 F5 – pop. 4 764 – alt. 347 m – ✉ 87400 Dordogne-Berry-Limousin 24 B2

Paris 407 – Aubusson 68 – Brive-la-Gaillarde 99 – Guéret 62 – Limoges 21

Office de tourisme, place du Champ de Mars ✆ 05 55 56 25 06, Fax 05 55 56 36 97

Church ★: steeple★★.

Relais St-Jacques

6 bd A. Pressemane – ✆ 05 55 56 00 25 – le.relais.st.jacques@orange.fr – Fax 05 55 56 19 87 – Closed 16 February-8 March, Sunday dinner and Monday lunch October-May

7 rm – €46/49 €46/49, €7 – ½ P €48/51 – **Rest** – Menu €15/35

◆ Traditional building in an avenue skirting the town centre. Small fresh rooms, simply furnished and well-maintained. Simply decorated dining room serving traditional cooking and country dishes. Hospitable welcome.

Le Grand St-Léonard with rm

23 av. Champs de Mars – ✆ 05 55 56 18 18 – grandsaintleonard@wanadoo.fr – Fax 05 55 56 98 32 – Closed 20 December-20 January, Monday except dinner from 15 June to 15 September and Tuesday lunch

14 rm – €56 €60, €11 – ½ P €78

Rest – Menu (€15 bi), €26 (except Sunday lunch)/60 – Carte €56/64

◆ This former post house is defiantly proud of its provincial atmosphere. Classic dishes offered in a rustic setting; collection of cake moulds and Limoges chinaware. Prettily provincial, sometimes antiquated, rooms.

ST-LIGUAIRE – 79 Deux-Sèvres – 322 C7 – see Niort

ST-LÔ P – 50 Manche – 303 F5 – pop. 20 090 – alt. 20 m – ✉ 50000 Normandy 32 A2

Paris 296 – Caen 62 – Cherbourg 80 – Laval 154 – Rennes 141

Office de tourisme, place Général-de-Gaulle ✆ 02 33 77 60 35, Fax 02 33 77 60 36

Centre Manche Saint-Martin-d'Aubigny Le Haut Boscq, by D900: 20 km, ✆ 02 33 45 24 52.

Haras national★ - Hanging of the Love of Gombaut and Macée in the musée des Beaux-Arts.

Plan on next page

Mercure

rest,

1 av. Briovère – ✆ 02 33 05 10 84 – H1072@accor.com – Fax 02 33 56 46 92

67 rm – €79/88 €90/98, €12 – **Rest** – *(Closed Saturday lunch and Sunday dinner)* Menu €21/45 – Carte €39/55 A **v**

◆ Two hotels have been joined together to create this relatively contemporary establishement facing the ramparts. New or recently redone rooms with a good level of comfort. Traditional cuisine with regional touches.

Gonivière

rd-pt du 6 Juin, (1st floor) – ✆ 02 33 05 15 36 – Fax 02 33 05 01 72 – Closed 29 December-2 January, Saturday lunch and Sunday dinner A **r**

Rest – Menu €20 (weekday lunch), €27/53 – Carte €30/54

◆ Pastel colours, stained wooden furniture and modern art set the scene for this welcoming restaurant above a brasserie-bar. Traditional cuisine.

Le Péché Mignon

84 r. Mar. Juin – ✆ 02 33 72 23 77 – restaurant-le-peche-mignon@wanadoo.fr – Fax 02 33 72 27 58 – Closed 14 July-1st August, 16-22 February and Monday B e

Rest – Menu (€ 11), € 17/50 – Carte € 30/56

◆ This restaurant offers two small, simple but comfortable dining rooms in a building near the national stud farm. Traditional meals with a touch of modernity.

in Calvaire 7 km by ② and D 972 – ✉ **50810 St-Pierre-de-Semilly**

La Fleur de Thym

– ✆ 02 33 05 02 40 – lafleurdethym@west-telecom.com – Fax 02 33 56 29 32 – Closed 10-29 August, 1st-19 January, Saturday lunch, Sunday and Monday

Rest – Menu € 21 (weekdays)/60 – Carte € 45/98

◆ This old farmstead has a shaded summer terrace that is well protected from the traffic noise of the nearby road. Classic repertoire enhanced by southern flavours.

ST-LOUBÈS – 33 Gironde – 335 I5 – pop. 7 090 – alt. 28 m – ✉ 33450 3 B1

Paris 568 – Bordeaux 18 – Créon 20 – Libourne 18 – St-André-de-Cubzac 15

Le Coq Sauvage with rm

AC rest, VISA

71, av. du Port-Cavernes, in Cavernes, north-west : 4 km – ✆ 05 56 20 41 04 – coq.sauvage@wanadoo.fr – Fax 05 56 20 44 76 – Closed 9-24 August and 24 December-11 January

6 rm – 🛉€ 55 🛉🛉€ 55, ☕ € 6,50 – ½ P € 95 – **Rest** – *(closed Saturday and Sunday)* Menu € 17 bi (week)/39 bi (weekend) – Carte € 32/44

◆ Charming rustic house on the marina, with the Dordogne beyond. Regional dishes served on the pleasant patio in summer. Quiet rooms.

ST-LOUIS – 68 Haut-Rhin – 315 J11 – pop. 19 961 – alt. 250 m – ✉ 68300 1 B3

Paris 498 – Altkirch 29 – Basel 5 – Belfort 76 – Colmar 65 – Ferrette 24 – Mulhouse 30

Hôtellerie La Cour du Roy
10 av. de Bâle – ✆ 03 89 70 33 33 – contact@hotelfp-saintlouis.com – Fax 03 89 70 33 30 – Closed 24-30 December
30 rm – 🛉€ 54/114 🛉🛉€ 54/114, ☕ € 11 – **Rest** – Menu € 29/39 – Carte € 36/49
◆ The Maison Katz, a former beer depot built in 1906 in neo-Renaissance style, now houses rooms with a distinctive contemporary look. The atmosphere in this restaurant is both modern and opulent. Pleasant, wood-ceilinged bar, plus a terrace-courtyard during the summer months.

Ibis
17 r. Gén. de Gaulle – ✆ 03 89 69 06 58 – h5612@accor.com – Fax 03 89 69 45 03
65 rm – 🛉€ 60/68 🛉🛉€ 60/68, ☕ € 7 – **Rest** – *(closed Sun)* Menu € 13 bi
◆ The red-brick façade of this recent hotel stands just a few minutes from the cinemas and Coupole theatre. Practical, generously proportioned and well-kept rooms. Fast food establishment where you select your menu on a touch screen.

Berlioz without rest
r. Henner, (near the station) – ✆ 03 89 69 74 44 – info@hotelberlioz.com – Fax 03 89 70 19 17 – Closed 22 December-3 January
20 rm – 🛉€ 55/65 🛉🛉€ 65, ☕ € 7
◆ This small 1930s building has practical, well-equipped and immaculately kept rooms. Copious buffet breakfast served in a pleasant sitting room.

Le Trianon
46 r. du Mulhouse – ✆ 03 89 67 03 03 – raphael@le-trianon.fr – Closed 21 July-19 August, Sunday dinner, Monday dinner and Wednesday dinner
Rest – Menu € 21, € 28/62 – Carte € 38/53
◆ This former taxation office facing a tiny square is now a restaurant. Well laid tables, classic cuisine and fine wine list.

in Huningue **2 km east by D 469 – pop. 6 097 – alt. 245 m – ✉ 68330**

Tivoli
15 av. de Bâle – ✆ 03 89 69 73 05 – info@tivoli.fr – Fax 03 89 67 82 44
41 rm – 🛉€ 58/80 🛉🛉€ 63/95, ☕ € 10 – ½ P € 63/86
Rest *Philippe Schneider* – *(closed 23 July-15 August, 22 December-7 January, Saturday and Sunday)* Menu € 24/47 – Carte € 37/64
◆ A stone's throw from the Swiss and German borders. The renovated rooms sport a modern decor. The others are far from outdated and well kept. A relatively plush restaurant serving updated cuisine and a trendier room with a blackboard menu.

in Village-Neuf **3 km northeast by D 66 and D 21 – pop. 3 108 – alt. 240 m – ✉ 68128**
Office de tourisme, 81, rue Vauban ✆ 03 89 70 04 49, Fax 03 89 67 30 80

Au Cerf
72 r. Gén. de Gaulle – ✆ 03 89 67 12 89 – Lorpasc.martin@wanadoo.fr – Fax 03 89 69 85 57 – Closed 14 July-10 August, 24 December-1st January, Thursday dinner, Sunday dinner and Monday
Rest – Menu € 9,50 (weekday lunch), € 18/41 – Carte € 24/49
◆ Near the Alsatian Petite Camargue – see above, a family inn of rustic inspiration adorned with hunting trophies. Traditional cuisine and asparagus and game specialities in season.

in Hésingue **4 km west by D 419 – pop. 1 921 – alt. 290 m – ✉ 68220**

Au Bœuf Noir
– ✆ 03 89 69 76 40 – j.giuggiola@tiscali.fr – Fax 03 89 67 77 29 – Closed 18-25 March, 18-31 August, Saturday lunch, Sunday and Monday
Rest – Menu € 36 (weekday lunch), € 45/60 – Carte € 55/72
◆ Near a busy junction, pleasant restaurant with modern paintings by the artist owner. Carefully prepared modern dishes.

ST-LOUP-DE-VARENNES – **71 Saône-et-Loire** – **320** J9 – **see Chalon-sur-Saône**

ST-LUNAIRE – **35 Ille-et-Vilaine** – **309** J3 – **see Dinard**

ST-LYPHARD – 44 Loire-Atlantique – 316 C3 – pop. 3 178 – alt. 12 m – ✉ 44410
Brittany 34 **A2**

Paris 447 – La Baule 17 – Nantes 73 – Redon 43 – St-Nazaire 22

Office de tourisme, place de l'Eglise ✆ 02 40 91 41 34, Fax 02 40 91 34 96

Church steeple ✳★★.

Les Chaumières du Lac et Auberge Les Typhas

rte Herbignac – ✆ 02 40 91 32 32 – jclogodin@leschaumieresdulac.com – Fax 02 40 91 30 33 – Closed 20 December-14 February, Wednesday lunch and Tuesday except dinner in season

20 rm – †€ 64/74 ††€ 64/110, ☕ € 10 – ½ P € 70/80

Rest – Menu (€ 15), € 20 (weekday lunch), € 22/42 – Carte € 49/61

◆ Hamlet of thatch roofed cottages in the Brière Regional Nature Park. Vast rooms, some refurbished. Excellent breakfasts featuring farm produce. Pleasant, renovated dining room leading onto a terrace. Modern-style cuisine.

St-Nazaire road 3 km south by D 47 – ✉ 44410 St-Lyphard

Auberge le Nézil

– ✆ 02 40 91 41 41 – aubergelenezil@wanadoo.fr – Fax 02 40 91 45 39 – Closed 29 September-7 October, 12 November-10 December, Wednesday dinner October-May, Sunday dinner and Monday

Rest – Menu (€ 20), € 27/50 – Carte € 36/61

◆ Charming cottage on the edge of the Grande Brière marshland. Recently renovated rustic interior. Tasty classic cuisine served outdoors in summer.

in Bréca 6 km south by D 47 and secondary road – ✉ 44410 St-Lyphard

Auberge de Bréca

– ✆ 02 40 91 41 42 – aubergedebreca@wanadoo.fr – Fax 02 40 91 37 41 – Closed January, Wednesday dinner from November to March, Sunday dinner and Thursday except July-August

Rest – Menu (€ 19,50), € 28/55

◆ This Brière cottage (1903) is today a warm regional restaurant with a lovely veranda. Garden and terrace overlooking the marshland in fine weather.

in Kerbourg 6 km southwest by D 51 (Guérande road) – ✉ 44410 St-Lyphard

Auberge de Kerbourg (Bernard Jeanson)

– ✆ 02 40 61 95 15 – Fax 02 40 61 95 36 – Closed 17 December-14 February, Tuesday lunch, Sunday dinner and Monday

Rest – *(pre-book in season)* Menu € 40/70 – Carte € 57/75

Spec. Alose de Loire (spring). Lièvre à la royale (autumn-winter). Canard du marais breton au "cuir de Russie". **Wines** Muscadet de Sèvre et Maine sur lie, Chinon.

◆ Fine residence dating back to 1753 with a thatched roof, flowering in season. Warm welcome. Interiors are in country style and the cuisine is up-to-date and inviting.

ST-MACAIRE – 33 Gironde – 335 J7 – see Langon

ST-MACLOU – 27 Eure – 304 C5 – pop. 463 – alt. 114 m – ✉ 27210 32 **A3**

Paris 179 – Le Grand-Quevilly 67 – Le Havre 35 – Rouen 73

La Crémaillère with rm

– ✆ 02 32 41 17 75 – Fax 02 32 42 50 90 – Closed 2-11 July, 12-21 November, 24 February-6 March, Tuesday dinner and Wednesday; hotel open 15 April-15 November

5 rm – †€ 30 ††€ 46, ☕ € 6,50 – ½ P € 41

Rest – Menu € 12,50 (weekday lunch), € 20/37 – Carte € 30/51

◆ Charming, flower-decked little inn in the heart of the village. Pleasant brightly coloured and wood-panelled dining room that opens onto a summer terrace. Creative regional cuisine.

ST-MAIXENT-L'ÉCOLE – 79 Deux-Sèvres – 322 E6 – pop. 6 602 – alt. 85 m –
✉ 79400 Atlantic Coast 38 **B2**

Paris 383 – Angoulême 106 – Niort 24 – Parthenay 30 – Poitiers 52

Syndicat d'initiative, porte Châlon ✆ 05 49 05 54 05, Fax 05 49 05 76 25

du Petit Chêne Mazières-en-GâtineWest: 20 km by D 6, ✆ 05 49 63 20 95.

Abbey church ★ - Musée du sous-officier (collection of uniforms★).

Le Logis St-Martin

chemin Pissot – 05 49 05 58 68 – contact@logis-saint-martin.com – Fax 05 49 76 19 93

12 rm – €110/120 €150/165, €16 – 1 suite – ½ P €115/135

Rest – *(closed Monday except dinner for residents and in season, Saturday lunch and Tuesday lunch)* Menu €48/78 – Carte €61/109

◆ This 17C stately home, which has been tastefully restored, nestles in a park by the River Sèvre. Individually decorated rooms. Classic dishes prepared in front of guests and served in the refined and cosy setting of the dining room. Good choice of wines, even by the glass.

ST-MAIXME-HAUTERIVE – 28 Eure-et-Loir – 311 D4 – pop. 349 – alt. 194 m – ✉ 28170

11 **B1**

Paris 105 – Chartres 31 – Évreux 61 – Orléans 112

La Rondellière

11 r. de la Mairie – 02 37 51 68 26 – jeanpaul.langlois@wanadoo.fr – Fax 02 37 51 08 53

4 rm – €33 €42 – **Table d'hôte** – Menu €15 bi

◆ The spacious and well-arranged rooms occupy the former haylofts of this farm that is still in the cereal business. Guaranteed peace and quiet and friendly welcome. Table d'hôte serving dishes prepared with home-grown vegetable-garden produce (booking essential).

ST-MALO – 35 Ille-et-Vilaine – 309 J3 – pop. 50 675 – alt. 5 m – Casino AXY – ✉ 35400 Brittany

10 **D1**

Paris 404 – Avranches 68 – Dinan 32 – Rennes 70 – St-Brieuc 71

Dinard-Pleurtuit-St-Malo: 02 99 46 18 46, by ③: 14 km.

Office de tourisme, esplanade Saint-Vincent 08 25 13 52 00, Fax 02 99 56 67 00

Ramparts★★★ - Château★★: musée d'Histoire de la ville et d'Ethnographie du pays malouin★ M², Quic-en-Groigne tower ★ DZ **E** - Fort national★: ≤★★ 15 mn - Stained-glass windows★ of St-Vincent cathedral - Mystères de la mer (Mysteries of the sea) ★★ (aquarium) via ③ - Rothéneuf: musée-manoir Jacques-Cartier★, 3 km by ① - St Servan sur Mer: corniche d'Aleth (cliff road) ≤★, tour Solidor★,views of the parc des Corbières★, belvédère du Rosais (Viewpoint)★.

Plans on following pages

Intra muros

Central

6 Gde-rue – 02 99 40 87 70 – centralbw@wanadoo.fr – Fax 02 99 40 47 57

50 rm – €60/108 €80/130, €11 – 3 suites – **Rest** – Menu €18/30 – Carte €32/53 DZ **n**

◆ Right at the heart of the privateer town and with renovated functional rooms, the Central is the ideal base from which to discover St Malo's charms. Restaurant serving seafood with fishing tackle decorating the walls.

Ajoncs d'Or without rest

10 r. Forgeurs – 02 99 40 85 03 – hotel-ajoncs-dor@wanadoo.fr – Fax 02 99 40 80 70 – Closed December and January DZ **a**

22 rm – €70/97 €89/145, €13

◆ In a quiet street in the old town, rooms with individual touches (nautical pictures). Wood panelled breakfast and dining rooms decorated with prints.

Hôtel du Louvre without rest

2 r. Marins – 02 99 40 86 62 – contact@hoteldulouvre-saintmalo.com – Fax 02 99 40 86 93 DZ **b**

50 rm – €70/125 €70/139, €14

◆ Plain, modern decor in this hotel renovated from top to bottom. Dark wood, paintings, pastel coloured walls and warm feature colours in the rooms and breakfast room.

La Cité without rest

26 r. Ste-Barbe – 02 99 40 55 40 – hotelcite-stmalo@wanadoo.fr – Fax 02 99 40 10 04 DZ **v**

41 rm – €51/83 €65/220, €13

◆ Building in the old town with functional, well-sized rooms. Enjoy breakfast served under the exposed beams with views over the ramparts.

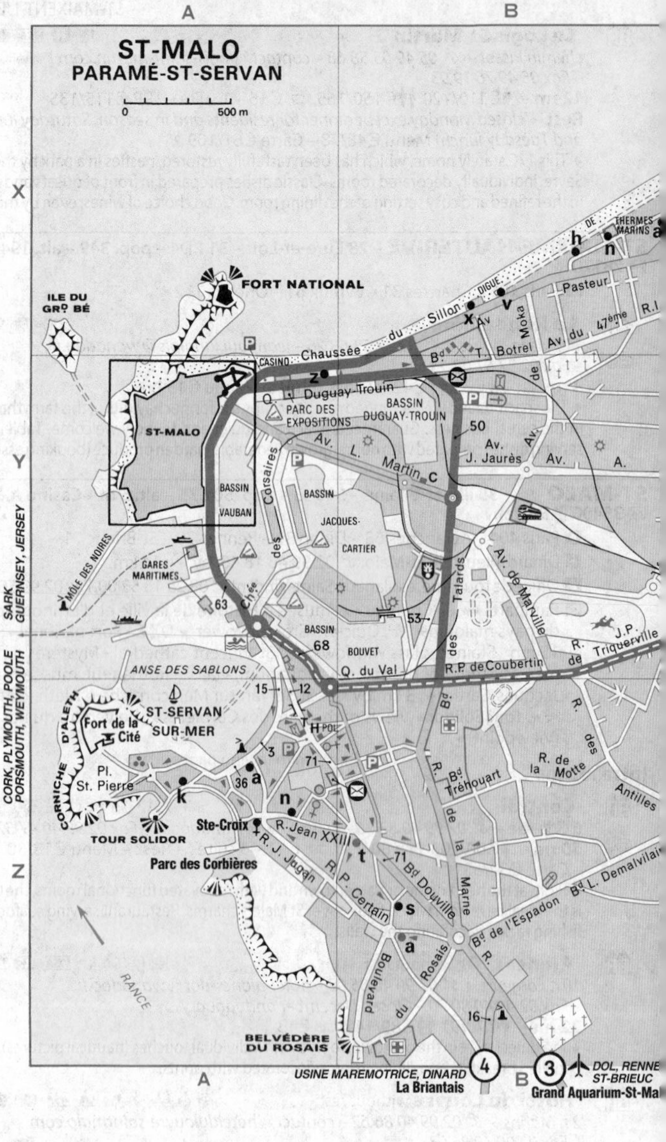

ST-MALO
PARAMÉ-ST-SERVAN

0 — 500 m

San Pedro without rest

1 r. Ste-Anne – ✆ 02 99 40 88 57

– hotelsanpedro@wanadoo.fr

– Fax 02 99 40 46 25

– Open 1st March-15 November DZ **f**

12 rm – 🚹€ 46/50 🚹🚹€ 55/70, ☕ € 7,50

◆ This small hotel is a stone's throw from Bon Secours beach. Wonderful warm welcome. Tiny but perfectly well-kept rooms. Impeccable breakfast.

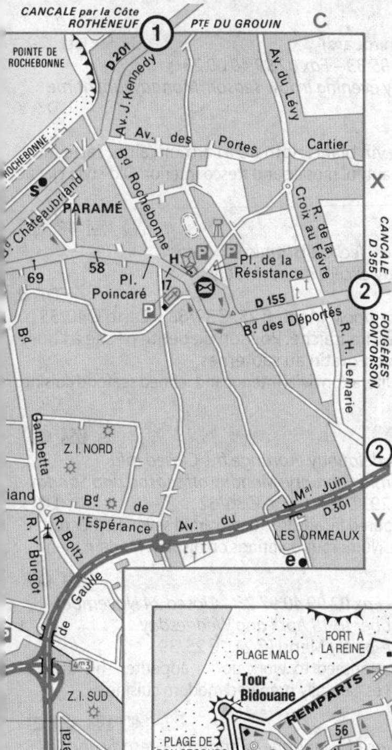

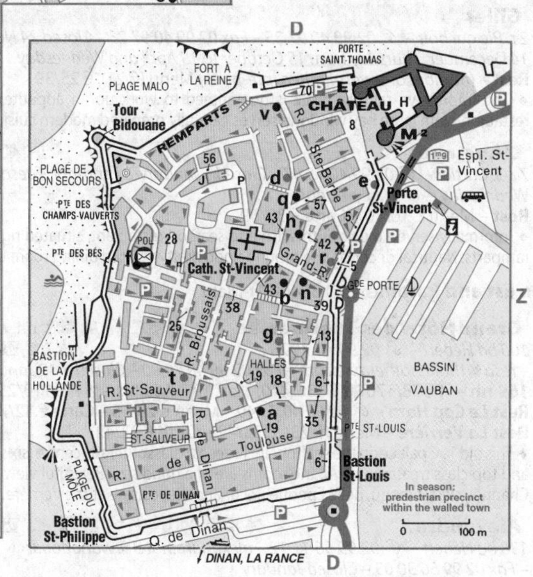

Bardelière (R. M. de la) . . . . . CZ 2
Bas-Sablons (R. des) . . . . . . AZ 3
Broussais (R.) . . . . DZ
Cartier (R. J.) . . . . DZ 5
Chartres (R. de) . . . . DZ 6
Chateaubriand (Pl.) . . . . DZ 8
Clemenceau (R. Georges) . . AZ 12
Cordiers (R. des) . . . . DZ 13
Dauphine (R.) . . . . AZ 15
Dinan (R. de) . . . . DZ
Doutreleau (R.) . . . . BZ 16
Flaubert (R. G.) . . . . CX 17
Forgeurs (R. du) . . . . DZ 18
Fosse (R. de la) . . . . DZ 19
Herbes (Pl. aux) . . . . DZ 25
Lamennais (Pl. Fr.) . . . . DZ 28
Mettrie (R. de la) . . . . DZ 35
Mgr-Duchesne (Pl.) . . . . AZ 36
Pilori (Pl. du) . . . . DZ 38
Poids-du-Rois (Pl. du) . . . . . DZ 39
Poissonnerie (Pl. de la) . . . . . DZ 42
Porcon-de-la-Barbinais (R.) . . DZ 43
République (Bd de la) . . . . . BY 50
Roosevelt (Av. F.) . . . . BY 53
St-Benoist (R.) . . . . DZ 56
St-Vincent (R.) . . . . DZ 57
Schuman
(R. du Président-Robert) . CX 58
Tabarly (Chaussée Eric) . . . . AY 63
Trichet (Q. de) . . . . AY 68
Umbricht (R. du R. P.) . . . . . CX 69
Vauban (Pl.) . . . . DZ 70
Ville-Pépin (R.) . . . . ABZ 71

Le Croiseur without rest
2 pl. de la Poissonnerie – ✆ 02 99 40 80 40
– hotel.le.croiseur@free.fr – Fax 02 99 56 83 76
– Closed 11 November-1st January DZ **h**
14 rm – †€ 55/69 ††€ 59/69, ☕ € 6,50
◆ Brown leather and wenge furniture endow this hotel with a contemporary minimalist look. In summer, breakfast is served on a pretty cobbled square complete with fishmonger.

A la Duchesse Anne (Serge Thirouard)
5 pl. Guy La Chambre – 02 99 40 85 33 – Fax 02 99 40 00 28 – Closed December, January, Sunday evening in low season, Monday lunchtime and Wednesday DZ **e**
Rest – Menu € 74 – Carte € 33/70
Spec. Filets de maquereaux frais au vin blanc. Homard à l'armoricaine. Tarte tatin.
◆ A St Malo institution (1945) with beautiful mosaic and fresco interior. Old style classic cuisine.

Le Chalut (Jean-Philippe Foucat)
8 r. Corne de Cerf – 02 99 56 71 58 – lechalutstmalo@aol.com – Fax 02 99 56 71 58 – Closed Tuesday except dinner in July-August and Monday DZ **d**
Rest – *(number of covers limited, pre-book)* Menu € 25, € 39/68 – Carte € 40/55
Spec. Filet de Saint-Pierre à la coriandre fraîche. Poisson de petite pêche à l'huile d'orange et safran. Fruits de saison en gratin au sauternes.
◆ Beautiful facade recalling the sailors' life, a convivial interior and refined seafood cuisine: three good reasons to stop by!

Delaunay
6 r. Ste-Barbe – 02 99 40 92 46 – bdelaunay@orange.fr – Closed mid November-mid December, January-mid February, Monday off season and Sunday
Rest – *(dinner only)* Menu (€ 26), € 29, € 48 – Carte € 36/62 DZ **x**
◆ This small dining area with wine coloured facade is situated amid several other restaurants, and has been newly refurbished. Numerous paintings on display. Modern menu.

Gilles
2 r. Pie qui boit – 02 99 40 97 25 – Fax 02 99 40 97 25 – Closed 24 November-14 December, Thursday from 15 October to 15 April and Wednesday DZ **t**
Rest – *(number of covers limited, pre-book)* Menu (€ 21), € 25/39
◆ The impressive rampart walk is guaranteed to work up an appetite. This discreet restaurant with large bay windows serves carefully prepared modern cuisine.

L'Ancrage
7 r. J. Cartier – 02 99 40 15 97 – Closed 5 January-8 February, Tuesday and Wednesday except July-August DZ **r**
Rest – Menu € 16/36 – Carte € 35/59
◆ Informally served meals at this fish and seafood restaurant, situated right against the ramparts. Nautical decor on the ground floor, pretty vaulted dining room upstairs.

St-Malo Est and Paramé – ✉ 35400 St-Malo

Grand Hôtel des Thermes rm, rest,
100 bd Hébert – 02 99 40 75 75 – resa@thalassotherapie.com – Fax 02 99 40 76 00 – Closed 6-19 January
169 rm – €78/170 €136/410, € 19 – 7 suites – ½ P € 110/255 BX **n**
Rest *Le Cap Horn* – 02 99 40 75 40 – Menu € 28/55 – Carte € 42/73
Rest *La Verrière* – Menu (€ 23), € 33/42 – Carte € 32/42
◆ This old 19C palace on the seafront includes a thalassotherapy centre (six seawater pools and top class treatments). All the rooms are of a good size. Beautiful view of the English Channel; classic menu. Belle Epoque decor and diet cuisine at the Verrière.

Alexandra
138 bd Hébert – 02 99 56 11 12 – alexandra.hotel@wanadoo.fr – Fax 02 99 56 30 03 – Closed January BX **h**
31 rm – €70/130 €95/180, € 14 – ½ P € 86/130 – **Rest** – Menu € 28/72 – Carte € 40/57
◆ The rooms of this building offer a fine view of the bay or of the city's rooftops. Simple, functional decor, new bathrooms. A brasserie style restaurant offering a traditional menu inspired by the sea.

La Villefromoy without rest
7 bd Hébert – 02 99 40 92 20 – villefromoy.hotel@wanadoo.fr – Fax 02 99 56 79 49 – Closed 17 November-18 December and 5 January-5 February CX **s**
21 rm – €85/165 €85/165, € 12 – 2 suites
◆ A charming welcome awaits at these two villas in a residential district. Tranquil atmosphere in the lounge (in the French Second Empire villa). Mahogany furniture in the rooms.

Grand Hôtel Courtoisville rest, rm, rest, rest,
69 bd Hébert – ✆ 02 99 40 83 83
– hotel@courtoisville.com – Fax 02 99 40 57 83
– Closed 1st-19 December and 5 January-5 February BX **a**
44 rm – †€ 75/149 ††€ 75/149, ☕ € 13 – ½ P € 66/103 – **Rest** – Menu € 24/30
– Carte € 26/50
◆ Early 20C family-run guesthouse not far from the seawater baths, surrounded by a garden. Spacious and quiet rooms, most with relaxation beds. Plush dining room where you can enjoy traditional dishes and seafood.

Mercure without rest
36 chaussée Sillon – ✆ 02 23 18 47 47 – h3225@accor.com – Fax 02 23 18 47 48
51 rm – †€ 71/140 ††€ 79/145, ☕ € 13 AY **z**
◆ A Mercure hotel ideally placed on the Sillon, facing the sea. Basic layout and up-to-date decor. Buffet breakfast also available as room service.

Alba without rest
17 r. des Dunes – ✆ 02 99 40 37 18 – info@hotelalba.com – Fax 02 99 40 96 40
22 rm – †€ 60/125 ††€ 75/171, ☕ € 12 BX **v**
◆ This villa is well situated facing the beach. All the rooms are elegant and contemporary in style; half of them offer views of the sea.

Beaufort without rest
25 chaussée Sillon – ✆ 02 99 40 99 99 – contact@hotel-beaufort.com
– Fax 02 99 40 99 62 BX **x**
22 rm – †€ 77/207 ††€ 77/207, ☕ € 12
◆ Colonial-style rooms in this imposing regional abode with a distinctive mustard coloured façade. Those facing onto rue du Sillon are not as peaceful.

Aubade without rest
8 pl. Duguesclin – ✆ 02 99 40 47 11 – contact@aubade-hotel.com
– Fax 02 99 56 10 49 – Closed 17 January-3 February
20 rm – †€ 74/110 ††€ 79/136, ☕ € 11
◆ Warm modern decor at this hotel with reception-cum-library, orange and cocoa coloured bar, designer furniture and a different colour for each floor (good linen).

Brocéliande without rest
43 chaussée Sillon – ✆ 02 99 20 62 62 – logis.broceliande@wanadoo.fr
– Fax 02 99 40 42 47 – Open March-mid November BX **v**
9 rm – †€ 90/142 ††€ 100/164, ☕ € 12
◆ This large 19C residence now offers B&B style-accommodation. Each room is decorated with Laura Ashley fabrics and bears the name of a Broceliande hero. A hospitable welcome awaits you.

La Malouinière du Mont Fleury without rest
2 r. Montfleury – ✆ 02 23 52 28 85 – bob.haby@
wanadoo.fr – Fax 02 23 52 28 85 CY **e**
4 rm ☕ – †€ 75/105 ††€ 75/105
◆ Beautiful St Malo house dating from the 18C set in a peaceful garden. Quiet rooms (two of them duplex) decorated with various themes – the sea, the Orient, China and America.

in St-Servan-sur-Mer – ✉ **35400 St Malo**

Valmarin without rest
7 r. Jean XXIII – ✆ 02 99 81 94 76 – levalmarin@wanadoo.fr – Fax 02 99 81 30 03
– Closed January AZ **n**
12 rm – †€ 95/135 ††€ 95/135, ☕ € 10
◆ Elegant residence providing individually decorated rooms, named after famous local people. The most attractive rooms afford views of the peaceful wooded park.

Manoir du Cunningham without rest
9 pl. Mgr Duchesne – ✆ 02 99 21 33 33
– cunningham@wanadoo.fr – Fax 02 99 21 33 34
– Open mid March-mid November AZ **a**
13 rm – †€ 90/190 ††€ 90/190, ☕ € 10
◆ Appealing manor-like building facing the Sablons cove. The rooms, named after islands, are pleasant and well furnished; most command sea views.

L'Ascott without rest

35 r. Chapitre – ✆ 02 99 81 89 93 – informations@ascotthotel.com – Fax 02 99 81 77 40 BZ **s**

10 rm – €85/95 €100/155, €12

◆ A pleasant blend of contemporary decor (designer furniture) and antique features (chandeliers and paintings) in this charming bourgeois house in a residential district.

La Rance without rest

15 quai Sébastopol, (Solidor port) – ✆ 02 99 81 78 63 – hotel-la-rance@wanadoo.fr – Fax 02 99 81 44 80 – Open beg. February-mid November AZ **k**

11 rm – €55/85 €55/85, €8

◆ Hotel located in the Solidor district, with small, old-fashioned bedrooms (redecoration planned) with sloping ceilings on the top floor. You will be received as if by friends.

Le St-Placide (Luc Mobihan)

6 pl. Poncel – ✆ 02 99 81 70 73 – imobihan@wanadoo.fr – Closed 29 June-11 July, 10-21 November, 15-26 February, Wednesday except dinner 14 July-15 August and Tuesday BZ **a**

Rest – Menu (€20), €26 (weekday lunch), €45/75 – Carte €56/82

Spec. Croustillant langoustine, parmesan et basilic. Bar de ligne, émulsion pomme de terre et truffe (winter). Panna-cotta framboises, balsamique (summer).

◆ Traditional house (1907) flanked by a modern veranda. The curvy contemporary dining room invites you to try out the tasty modern cuisine.

Les Corbières

6 pl. Mgr Juhel – ✆ 02 99 82 07 46 – jullianpekle@yahoo.fr – Closed 18-30 June, 5-30 November, 15-28 February, Tuesday except dinner in July-August and Monday BZ **t**

Rest – Menu €23 (weekdays)/52 – Carte €41/56

◆ A discreet brown facade hides this restaurant with a modern feel (Murano lighting) in the heart of the Corbières district. Aesthetically pleasing and inventive cuisine.

Rennes road 3 km by ③ and Ave Gén. de Gaulle – ✉ 35400 St-Malo

La Grassinais rm, rest, rm,

12 allée Grassinais – ✆ 02 99 81 33 00 – manoirdelagrassinais@wanadoo.fr – Fax 02 99 81 60 90 – Closed 20 December-31 January

29 rm – €52/80 €58/80, €8 – ½ P €61/72

Rest – *(closed Tuesday lunch in August, Saturday lunch, Monday and Sunday dinner from September to July)* Menu (€19), €24/46

◆ Just outside St-Malo, this former farm has been prettily restored. Modern, comfortable, refurbished rooms. Warm, panelled dining room and traditional gourmet recipes prepared with great care.

ST-MANDÉ – 94 Val-de-Marne – 312 D2 – 101 27 – see Paris, Area

---

ST-MARC-A-LOUBAUD – 23 Creuse – 325 I5 – pop. 122 – alt. 705 m – ✉ 23460 25 **C2**

Paris 411 – Aubusson 24 – Guéret 54 – Limoges 78 – Tulle 87 – Ussel 57

Les Mille Sources

– ✆ 05 55 66 03 69 – Fax 05 55 66 03 69 – Open 21 March-6 November and closed Sunday dinner and Monday except school holidays

Rest – *(pre-book)* Menu €32/48 – Carte €40/54

◆ A pleasantly converted farm where you will be welcomed as long-lost friends. Ducks from Challans and legs of lamb are roasted in the period fireplace in the attractive rustic dining room.

ST-MARCEL – 36 Indre – 323 F7 – see Argenton-sur-Creuse

ST-MARCEL – 71 Saône-et-Loire – 320 J9 – see Chalon-sur-Saône

ST-MARCEL-DU-PÉRIGORD – 24 Dordogne – 329 F6 – pop. 140 – alt. 160 m – ✉ 24510 4 C1

Paris 538 – Bordeaux 144 – Périgueux 58 – Bergerac 26 – Sarlat-la-Canéda 55

Auberge Lou Peyrol
au bourg – ✆ 05 53 24 09 71 – fiona.wavrin@wanadoo.fr
– Closed 31 March-9 April, 24 November-10 December, 12 January-13 February, Wednesday from 7 October to 19 March and Tuesday
Rest – Menu € 26/33 – Carte € 29/50
◆ The English owner upped sticks for the rustic charm of this Perigord inn. Terrace shaded by a lime tree, and regional, seasonally-inspired cuisine.

ST-MARCEL-EN-DOMBES – 01 Ain – 328 C5 – pop. 1 059 – alt. 265 m – ✉ 01390

Paris 440 – Bourg-en-Bresse 36 – Lyon 30 – Meximieux 21 – Villefranche-sur-Saône 26 43 E1

La Colonne
– ✆ 04 72 26 11 06 – Fax 04 72 08 59 24 – Closed 23 December-16 January, Monday dinner and Tuesday
Rest – Menu € 16 (weekday lunch), € 20/38 – Carte € 22/39
◆ The name of this hotel refers to the 16C stone column standing in the middle of the dining room (oak wood panelling and French-style ceiling). Regional cuisine. Garden-terrace.

ST-MARCEL-LÈS-SAUZET – 26 Drôme – 332 B6 – see Montélimar

ST-MARCELLIN – 38 Isère – 333 E7 – pop. 6 955 – alt. 282 m – ✉ 38160
Lyon - Rhone Valley 43 E2

Paris 570 – Die 76 – Grenoble 55 – Valence 46 – Vienne 71 – Voiron 47
Office de tourisme, 2, avenue du Collège ✆ 04 76 38 53 85, Fax 04 76 38 17 32

La Tivollière
Château du Mollard – ✆ 04 76 38 21 17 – Fax 04 76 38 94 51
– Closed 1st-7 August, 1st-21 January, Thursday dinner, Sunday dinner and Monday
Rest – Menu € 20/43
◆ A restaurant with a rather unexpected modern decor in a 15C castle overlooking the town. The shaded terrace offers a glimpse of the Vercors.

ST-MARTIAL-DE-NABIRAT – 24 Dordogne – 329 I7 – pop. 513 – alt. 175 m – ✉ 24250 4 D2

Paris 556 – Bordeaux 213 – Périgueux 82 – Cahors 43 – Sarlat-la-Canéda 20

Le Saint-Martial
au bourg – ✆ 05 53 29 18 34 – le-saint-martial@tiscali.fr – Fax 005 53 29 73 45
– Closed Tuesday and Wednesday except dinner from 15 July to 31 August
Rest – Menu (€ 23), € 32/44 – Carte € 42/63
◆ The wrought iron furniture on the village-square terrace invites you to take your seat. Inside, the small dining room is particularly convivial. Up-to-date dishes.

ST-MARTIN-AUX-CHARTRAINS – 14 Calvados – 303 N4 – see Pont-L'Évêque

ST-MARTIN-DE-BELLEVILLE – 73 Savoie – 333 M5 – pop. 2 532 – alt. 1 450 m – Winter sports : 1 450/2 850 m 9 37 – ✉ 73440 French Alps 46 F2

Paris 624 – Albertville 44 – Chambéry 93 – Moûtiers 20
Office de tourisme, immeuble L'Épervière ✆ 04 79 00 20 00, Fax 04 79 08 91 71

St-Martin
rm, rm, rest,
– ✆ 04 79 00 88 00 – hotelsaintmartin@wanadoo.fr – Fax 04 79 00 88 39
– Open 16 December-19 April
27 rm – € 138/200 € 196/404, € 17 – 5 suites – ½ P € 98/202
Rest *Le Grenier* – Menu € 30/50 – Carte € 35/82
◆ This pretty chalet with a stone-slab roof is tastefully decorated. Warm wood decor and modern facilities in the rooms, all of which have balconies. Local dishes and daily specials announced on large blackboards. Savoyard atmosphere.

L'Edelweiss

r. Saint-François – ✆ 04 79 08 96 67 – hoteledelweiss@wanadoo.fr – Fax 04 79 08 90 40 – Open 10 July-31 August and 20 December-26 April

16 rm – 🚹€ 85/105 🚹🚹€ 115/145, ☕ € 12 – ½ P € 90/105 – **Rest** – Menu € 28/33 – Carte € 37/57

◆ The mountain spirit flourishes at the Edelweiss. All the rooms are well kept, and some have been renovated. Sauna much appreciated by skiers. A traditional restaurant open during the summer season.

La Bouitte (René et Maxime Meilleur) with rm

at St-Marcel 2 km south-east – ✆ 04 79 08 96 77 – info@la-bouitte.com – Fax 04 79 08 96 03 – Open 1st July-3 September and 2 December-30 April

6 rm ☕ – 🚹€ 165/200 🚹🚹€ 245/258 – 2 suites

Rest – *(closed Monday in summer)* Menu € 48/165 – Carte € 85/135

Spec. Demi-lobe de foie gras grillé à sec, rouleau de pomme, herbes fraîches. Omble chevalier, tartare de légumes, coulis de tapenade (summer). Langoustines royales à l'unilatéral, perles d'agrumes (winter). **Wines** Chignin-Bergeron, Vin de Savoie passerillé.

◆ With its pretty, old chalet-style decor, creative, sweet and savoury cooking using mountain herbs and faultless hospitality, La Bouitte is a real Savoyard delight. Stunning Alpine inspired rooms.

Étoile des Neiges

r. Saint-Martin – ✆ 04 79 08 92 80 – hoteledelweiss@wanadoo.fr – Fax 04 79 08 90 40 – Open 10 July-30 August, and 20 December-25 April

Rest – Menu € 30 (dinner)/45 (dinner) – Carte € 45/79

◆ Traditional restaurant and summer terrace. Dining rooms with a mountain setting warmed by a central fireplace. Upstairs mezzanine.

Le Montagnard

– ✆ 04 79 01 08 40 – info@le-montagnard.com – Open 1st July-31 August and 15 December-1st May

Rest – Carte € 28/58

◆ This pleasant and lively restaurant, on the village heights, has a warm mountain decor of rough woodwork, limewashed walls, solid furniture and old tools. Local dishes.

ST-MARTIN-DE-LONDRES – 34 Hérault – 339 H6 – pop. 1 894 – alt. 194 m – ✉ 34380 Languedoc-Roussillon-Tarn Gorges 23 C2

Paris 744 – Montpellier 25 – Le Vigan 37

Office de tourisme, Maison de Pays ✆ 04 67 55 09 59, Fax 04 67 55 70 91

Les Muscardins

19 rte des Cévennes – ✆ 04 67 55 75 90 – trousset@les-muscardins.fr – Fax 04 67 55 70 28 – Closed 18 February-10 March, Monday and Tuesday except public holidays

Rest – Menu (€ 29), € 44/74

◆ The dining room and side lounge have been entirely redecorated in warm tones. Colourful paintings on the walls. Cuisine in keeping with modern taste. Catering service.

South 12 km by D 32, D 127 and D 127E6 – ✉ **34380 Argelliers**

Auberge de Saugras with rm

– ✆ 04 67 55 08 71 – auberge.saugras@wanadoo.fr – Fax 04 67 55 04 65 – Closed 11-27 August, 22 December-14 January, Monday lunch July-August, Tuesday except dinner July-August and Wednesday

7 rm – 🚹€ 42/83 🚹🚹€ 42/83, ☕ € 8 – ½ P € 55/76

Rest – *(pre-book)* Menu (€ 16), € 19 (weekdays)/50 – Carte € 30/108

◆ This 12C, rough, stone-built farmhouse is difficult to reach since it stands alone in the midst of nature; generous local cuisine, terrace and renovated rooms.

ST-MARTIN-D'ENTRAUNES – 06 Alpes-Maritimes – 341 B3 – pop. 88 – alt. 1 050 m – ✉ 06470 41 C2

Paris 778 – Barcelonnette 50 – Castellane 66 – Digne-les-Bains 104 – Nice 108

Hostellerie de la Vallière

– ✆ 04 93 05 59 59 – info@hotel-lavalliere.com – Fax 04 93 05 59 60 – Open 15 April-15 October

10 rm – †€ 44 ††€ 44/55, ☕ € 7 – ½ P € 46 – **Rest** – Menu € 20

♦ Hikers and weary urbanites appreciate this colourful inn that faces the Mercantour massif. Countrified decor and unpretentious comfort (no TV) in the rooms. Classic menu (no fish) in a dining room extended by a small terrace.

ST-MARTIN-DE-LA-PLACE – 49 Maine-et-Loire – **317** I5 – **pop. 1 130** – **alt. 80 m** – ✉ **49160** 35 **C2**

Paris 314 – Nantes 147 – Angers 60 – Saumur 11 – La Flèche 70

Syndicat d'initiative, Mairie ✆ 02 41 38 43 06, Fax 02 41 38 09 93

Domaine de la Blairie

rm, rest,

5 r. de la Mairie – ✆ 02 41 38 42 98 – contact@hotel-blairie.com – Fax 02 41 38 41 20 – Closed 15 December-31 January and Sunday evening from 15 November to 15 March

44 rm – †€ 56/65 ††€ 66/75, ☕ € 8,50 – ½ P € 59/65 – **Rest** – *(closed Sunday dinner 15 November-15 March, Wednesday and Thursday)* Menu (€ 13), € 17 (weekday lunch), € 25/42 – Carte € 32/45

♦ This tufa stone construction offers practical, well-kept rooms spread over three buildings. Both the nearby Saumur village and the large garden with pool are refreshingly peaceful. Attractively priced traditional cuisine served in a warm setting.

ST-MARTIN-DE-RÉ – 17 Charente-Maritime – **324** B2 – see Île de Ré

ST-MARTIN-DU-FAULT – 87 Haute-Vienne – **325** E5 – see Limoges

---

ST-MARTIN-DU-TOUCH – 31 Haute-Garonne – **343** G3 – see Toulouse

---

ST-MARTIN-DU-VAR – 06 Alpes-Maritimes – **341** E5 – **pop. 2 197** – **alt. 110 m** – ✉ **06670** 41 **D2**

Paris 938 – Antibes 34 – Cannes 44 – Nice 28 – Puget-Théniers 40 – Vence 22

Jean-François Issautier

3 km Nice road (D 6202) – ✆ 04 93 08 10 65 – jf.issautier@wanadoo.fr – Fax 04 93 29 19 73 – Closed 27 October-5 November, beg. January-beg. February, Sunday dinner, Monday and Tuesday

Rest – Menu € 43/115 – Carte € 79/108

Spec. Pied de cochon cuit croustillant. "Cul" d'agneau rôti sur purée de pommes de terre aux olives noires de Nice. Soupe aux fraises de Carros, glace à l'huile d'olive (spring-summer). **Wines** Bellet, Côtes de Provence.

♦ A conifer hedge separates this discreet restaurant from the road. Classic and regional repertoire served in an elegant high-ceilinged dining room.

ST-MARTIN-EN-BRESSE – 71 Saône-et-Loire – **320** K9 – **pop. 1 639** – **alt. 192 m** – ✉ **71620** 8 **C3**

Paris 353 – Beaune 48 – Chalon-sur-Saône 18 – Dijon 86 – Dôle 56 – Lons-le-Saunier 48

Au Puits Enchanté

1 pl. René Cassin – ✆ 03 85 47 71 96 – Chateau.Jacky@wanadoo.fr – Fax 03 85 47 74 58 – Closed 10-16 March, 29 September-5 October, 1st-10 January, Monday except from March to October, Sunday evening and Tuesday

13 rm – †€ 47 ††€ 47, ☕ € 8,50 – ½ P € 50/55 – **Rest** – *(closed Sunday dinner, Monday and Tuesday)* Menu € 20/45 – Carte € 28/46

♦ This family hotel stands in the centre of a Bresse town. Rooms, although on the small side, are well kept. Breakfast is served on the veranda. The wines and cuisine of the region inspire the chef.

ST-MARTIN-LA-MÉANNE – 19 Corrèze – 329 M4 – pop. 365 – alt. 500 m – ✉ 19320 25 C3

Paris 510 – Aurillac 67 – Brive-la-Gaillarde 54 – Mauriac 48 – St-Céré 53 – Tulle 32 – Ussel 65

Barrage du Chastang★ Southeast: 5 km, Dordogne-Berry-Limousin

Des Voyageurs with rm VISA AE

pl. Mairie – ☎ 05 55 29 11 53 – info@hotellesvoyageurs.com – Fax 05 55 29 27 70 – Open 14 March-5 November and closed Sunday dinner and Monday except from May to September

8 rm – †€ 43/46 ††€ 43/54, ☕ € 7 – ½ P € 44/50 – **Rest** – Menu (€ 17), € 23/37 – Carte € 37/47

◆ Time stands still in this charming stone inn that serves earthy food in an authentic country setting, or in summer, in the garden stretching out to a pond (fishing).

ST-MARTIN-LE-BEAU – 37 Indre-et-Loire – 317 O4 – pop. 2 481 – alt. 55 m – ✉ 37270 Châteaux of the Loire 11 B2

Paris 231 – Amboise 9 – Blois 45 – Loches 34 – Tours 20

Auberge de la Treille with rm A/C VISA

2 r. d'Amboise – ☎ 02 47 50 67 17 – auberge-de-la-treille@wanadoo.fr – Fax 02 47 50 20 14 – Closed 7-13 April, 17-23 November, Sunday dinner and Monday

8 rm – †€ 50 ††€ 50/60, ☕ € 7,50 – ½ P € 52

Rest – Menu € 13 (weekday lunch), € 20/39

◆ A stone's throw from the Touraine Aquarium. Modern menu served in the two rustic, half-timbered dining rooms. Simple bedrooms, which are bright and colourful.

ST-MARTIN-LE-GAILLARD – 76 Seine-Maritime – 304 I2 – pop. 315 – alt. 60 m – ✉ 76260 Normandy 33 D1

Paris 168 – Amiens 99 – Dieppe 27 – Eu 12 – Neufchâtel-en-Bray 34 – Rouen 87

Moulin du Becquerel VISA

Northwest : 1.5 km on D 16 – ☎ 02 35 86 74 94 – moulindubecquerel@free.fr – Fax 02 35 86 99 78 – Closed 20 January-6 March, Sunday dinner, Monday, Tuesday and Wednesday except July-August and public holidays

Rest – Menu € 20/28 – Carte € 27/49

◆ An appealing riverside Norman house. Rustic interior and pleasant terrace overlooking the countryside. Traditional cuisine based on seasonal market produce.

ST-MARTIN-VÉSUBIE – 06 Alpes-Maritimes – 341 E3 – pop. 1 098 – alt. 1 000 m – ✉ 06450 French Riviera 41 D2

Paris 845 – Antibes 73 – Barcelonnette 111 – Cannes 83 – Menton 88 – Nice 66

Office de tourisme, place Félix Faure ☎ 04 93 03 21 28, Fax 04 93 03 21 44

Venanson : ≤★, Frescoes ★ of St-Sébastien chapel South: 4,5 km.

Le Boréon★★ (waterfall★) North : 8 km - Cirque★★ du vallon de la Madone de Fenestre Northeast : 12 km.

Gelas without rest VISA AE

27 r. Dr Cagnoli – ☎ 04 93 03 21 81 – contact@hotel-gelas.com – Fax 04 93 03 24 87 – Closed November

10 rm – †€ 66 ††€ 66, ☕ € 8

◆ Charming welcome in this family establishment renovated by a skiing enthusiast. Panelled rooms and breakfast in a winter sports setting or on the terrace.

La Trappa VISA

7 pl. du Marché – ☎ 04 93 03 29 23 – Closed 20 October-18 November, Wednesday in July-August, Sunday dinner and Monday

Rest – Menu € 20/26 – Carte € 24/39

◆ This typical Niçois restaurant stands on the main pedestrian street, where tables are laid in summer. Rustic-style dining room. Compagnon du Tour de France chef.

ST-MATHIEU-DE-TRÉVIERS – 34 Hérault – 339 I6 – pop. 3 713 – alt. 81 m – ✉ 34270 23 C2

Paris 761 – Marseille 176 – Montpellier 22 – Nice 334 – Nîmes 53 – Toulouse 261

Lennys

266 av. Louis Cancel, D 17 – ✆ 04 67 55 37 97 – restaurant.lennys@wanadoo.fr – Fax 04 67 54 71 82 – Closed 6-30 September, 10-19 January, Saturday lunch, Sunday dinner and Monday

Rest – Menu (€ 29), € 42/82 – Carte € 66/74

◆ Pleasant inn near the St Loup Peak, after which the local wine is named. Mediterranean setting, shaded terrace and appetising up-to-date cuisine.

ST-MATHURIN – 85 Vendée – 316 F8 – pop. 1 256 – alt. 30 m – ✉ 85150 34 A3

Paris 451 – Nantes 95 – La Roche-sur-Yon 29 – Challans 66 – Les Sables-d'Olonne 10

Le Château de la Millière without rest

La Millière – ✆ 02 51 22 73 29 – chateaudelamiliere@club-internet.fr – Fax 02 51 22 73 29 – Open 1st May-30 September

5 rm – € 85 € 85/100, € 7,50

◆ This romantic 19C château has extensive grounds with a swimming pool, ponds, bridle paths and barbecue. The building has retained its original character, while still providing modern levels of comfort.

ST-MAUR-DES-FOSSÉS – 94 Val-de-Marne – 312 D3 – 101 27 – see Paris, Area

ST-MAXIMIN-LA-STE-BAUME – 83 Var – 340 K5 – pop. 12 402 – alt. 289 m – ✉ 83470 Provence 40 B3

Paris 793 – Aix-en-Provence 44 – Marseille 51 – Toulon 55

Office de tourisme, Hôtel de Ville ✆ 04 94 59 84 59, Fax 04 94 59 82 92

Couvent Royal

pl. Jean Salusse – ✆ 04 94 86 55 66 – contact@hotelfp-saintmaximin.com – Fax 04 94 59 82 82 – Closed Feb., Sun. evening and Mon.

67 rm – € 85/153 € 85/153, € 12 – ½ P € 95/98

Rest – *(closed Monday from November to April)* Menu (€ 26), € 35/45 – Carte € 43/52

◆ An unusual hotel adjoining a 13C basilica. The monks' cells have been converted into snug rooms. Panoramic pool, spa and fitness centre. Classic fare served in the lovely chapter house or in the pretty cloister.

ST-MÉDARD – 46 Lot – 337 D4 – pop. 153 – alt. 170 m – ✉ 46150 28 B1

Paris 571 – Cahors 17 – Gourdon 34 – Villeneuve-sur-Lot 59

Gindreau (Alexis Pélissou)

– ✆ 05 65 36 22 27 – le.gindreau@wanadoo.fr – Fax 05 65 36 24 54 – Closed 3-20 March, 20 October-14 November, Monday and Tuesday

Rest – *(pre-book Sat - Sun)* Menu € 38 (weekdays)/105 – Carte € 55/81

Spec. Truffes fraîches (December to March). Agneau fermier du Quercy. Soufflé à la truffe flambé au marasquin (November to June). **Wines** Cahors, Vins de Pays du Lot.

◆ Old village school elegantly turned into two pastel coloured dining rooms. Chestnuts shade the terrace. Tasty contemporary menu with a strong regional influence.

ST-MÉDARD-EN-JALLES – 33 Gironde – 335 G5 – pop. 25 566 – alt. 22 m – ✉ 33160

3 **B1**

Paris 591 – Blaye 62 – Bordeaux 18 – Jonzac 97 – Libourne 48 – Saintes 129

Tournebride

at Hastignan – ✆ 05 56 05 09 08 – Fax 05 56 05 09 08 – Closed Wednesday dinner, Sunday dinner and Monday

Rest – Menu € 13 (weekday lunch), € 18/36 – Carte € 25/36

◆ Refurbished dining room, prettily decorated with a fresco of the Arcachon Bay. The other dining room has a wine and vine theme. Regional specialities.

ST-MICHEL-EN-L'HERM – 85 Vendée – 316 I9 – pop. 1 931 – alt. 9 m – ✉ 85580

34 **B3**

Paris 453 – La Rochelle 46 – Luçon 15 – La Roche sur Yon 47 – Les Sables-d'Olonne 54

Syndicat d'initiative, 5, place de l'Abbaye ✆ 02 51 30 21 89, Fax 02 51 30 21 89

La Rose Trémière

4 r. de l'Église – ✆ 02 51 30 25 69 – rose.tremiere@wanadoo.fr – Fax 02 51 97 63 25 – Closed 6-22 October, 16 February-5 March, Monday dinner and Tuesday except July-August, Sunday dinner and Wednesday

Rest – Menu € 12 (weekday lunch), € 17/45 – Carte € 30/47

◆ An old house with a pleasant dining room decorated in a tastefully rustic style, with tables laid out around the central fireplace. Traditional cuisine.

ST-MICHEL-ESCALUS – 40 Landes – 335 D11 – pop. 231 – alt. 23 m – ✉ 40550

3 **B2**

Paris 721 – Bayonne 67 – Bordeaux 135 – Dax 30

La Bergerie-St-Michel without rest

St-Michel, on the D 142, rte de Castets – ✆ 05 58 48 74 04 – bergerie-saintmichel@wanadoo.fr – Fax 05 58 48 74 04 – Open 1st June-30 September

3 rm – €85/120 €95/130

◆ The Landes Forest surrounds this magnificently restored former farmhouse. Very comfortable rooms, decorated with contemporary paintings. Copious breakfasts.

ST-MICHEL-MONT-MERCURE – 85 Vendée – 316 K7 – pop. 1 729 – alt. 284 m – ✉ 85700 Atlantic Coast

34 **B3**

Paris 383 – Bressuire 36 – Cholet 35 – Nantes 85 – Pouzauges 7 – La Roche-sur-Yon 52

✳★★ from the church steeple.

Château de la Flocellière

La Flocellière, 2 km east – ✆ 02 51 57 22 03 – flocelliere.chateau@wanadoo.fr – Fax 02 51 57 75 21

5 rm – €125/205 €155/205, € 12

Table d'hôte – Menu € 54 bi/61 bi

◆ This building full of history was an important Lower Poitou fortress during the Middle Ages. It now houses spacious and peaceful rooms, overlooking the park. Those inside the keep are magnificent. Medieval or Renaissance-themed evening meals in a breathtaking 16C dining room.

Auberge du Mont Mercure

8 r. l'Orbrie, (near the church) – ✆ 02 51 57 20 26 – contact@aubergemontmercure.com – Fax 02 51 57 78 67 – Closed autumn and Easter school holidays, Monday dinner from September to June, Tuesday dinner and Wednesday

Rest – Menu € 14 (weekdays)/33 – Carte € 20/39

◆ Perched on top of the hill, this inn benefits from a large panoramic view over the Vendée. Children's play area. Ideal for families.

ST-MIHIEL – 55 Meuse – 307 E5 – pop. 5 260 – alt. 228 m – ✉ 55300
Alsace-Lorraine 26 **B2**

Paris 287 – Metz 63 – Nancy 66 – Bar-le-Duc 35 – Toul 52 – Verdun 36

Office de tourisme, rue du Palais de Justice ✆ 03 29 89 06 47, Fax 03 29 89 06 47

de Madine Nonsard Base de Loisirs, Northeast: 25 km by D 901 and D 179, ✆ 03 29 89 56 00.

Sepulchre★★ in St-Étienne church - Swoon of the Virgin★ in St-Michel church.

in Heudicourt-sous-les-Côtes 15 km northeast by D 901 and D 133 – pop. 188 – alt. 240 m – ✉ 55210

Butte de Montsec: ❋★★, monument★ South: 13 km.

Lac de Madine

– ✆ 03 29 89 34 80 – hotel-lac-madine@wanadoo.fr – Fax 03 29 89 39 20 – Closed 20-28 December, 2 January-13 February

44 rm – †€ 55/95 ††€ 55/95, ☕ € 9,50 – ½ P € 60

Rest – *(closed Mon. lunchtime)* Menu € 23/60 – Carte € 38/60

◆ Old, renovated house near a lake offering neat modern rooms. Ten of them have a Jacuzzi tub, and the ground floor rooms in the wing enjoy the use of a garden. A neo-rustic restaurant whose fine timberwork provides a shaft of light. Shaded terrace.

ST-NAZAIRE – 44 Loire-Atlantique – 316 C4 – pop. 65 874 – Built-up area 136 886 – alt. 4 m – ✉ 44600 Brittany
34 **A2**

Paris 435 – La Baule 19 – Nantes 61 – Vannes 79

Access Pont de Saint-Nazaire: no toll.

Office de tourisme, boulevard de la Légion d'Honneur ✆ 02 40 22 40 65, Fax 02 40 22 19 80

de Savenay Savenay Le Chambeau, by Nantes road: 27km, ✆ 02 40 56 88 05 ;

de Guérande Guérande Ville Blanche, by Guérande road: 22 km, ✆ 02 40 60 24 97.

Submarine base ★ - Dry dock "Louis-Joubert"★ - Terrace with a panoramic view★ **B** - St-Nazaire-St-Brévin road bridge ★ by ①.

Plan on next page

Le Berry

1 pl. Pierre Semard – ✆ 02 40 22 42 61 – berry.hotel@wanadoo.fr – Fax 02 40 22 45 34 – Closed 23 December-4 January AY **r**

27 rm – †€ 75/130 ††€ 82/140, ☕ € 10

Rest – *(closed Sunday lunch and Saturday)* Menu € 20/30 – Carte € 31/73

Rest *Brasserie* – brasserie *(closed Sunday lunch and Saturday)* Menu € 16 – Carte € 24/48

◆ This post-war hotel standing opposite the station, offers cheerful, well-soundproofed rooms. Light, pleasant restaurant serving traditional cuisine; lobster tank. The Brasserie serves daily set dishes, chalked up on a slate, and jugs of Loire wines.

Au Bon Accueil

39 r. Marceau – ✆ 02 40 22 07 05 – au-bon-accueil44@wanadoo.fr – Fax 02 40 19 01 58 – Closed 18-24 February and 14 July-3 August AZ **n**

17 rm – †€ 82 ††€ 82/180, ☕ € 10 – ½ P € 73 – **Rest** – *(closed Sunday evening)* Menu (€ 17), € 21/55 – Carte € 40/60

◆ This building that escaped the Second World War is home to simple, well-kept rooms. Modern rooms and duplexes in a more recent construction. Traditional food served in a spruce dining room with prettily laid tables.

De Touraine without rest

4 av. de la République – ✆ 02 40 22 47 56 – hoteltouraine@free.fr – Fax 02 40 22 55 05 – Closed 21 December-2 January AZ **a**

18 rm – †€ 33/43 ††€ 33/43, ☕ € 7,50

◆ Right in the town centre, simply furnished neat rooms; quieter to the rear and double-glazing on the street side. In summer, breakfast in the garden. Very hospitable.

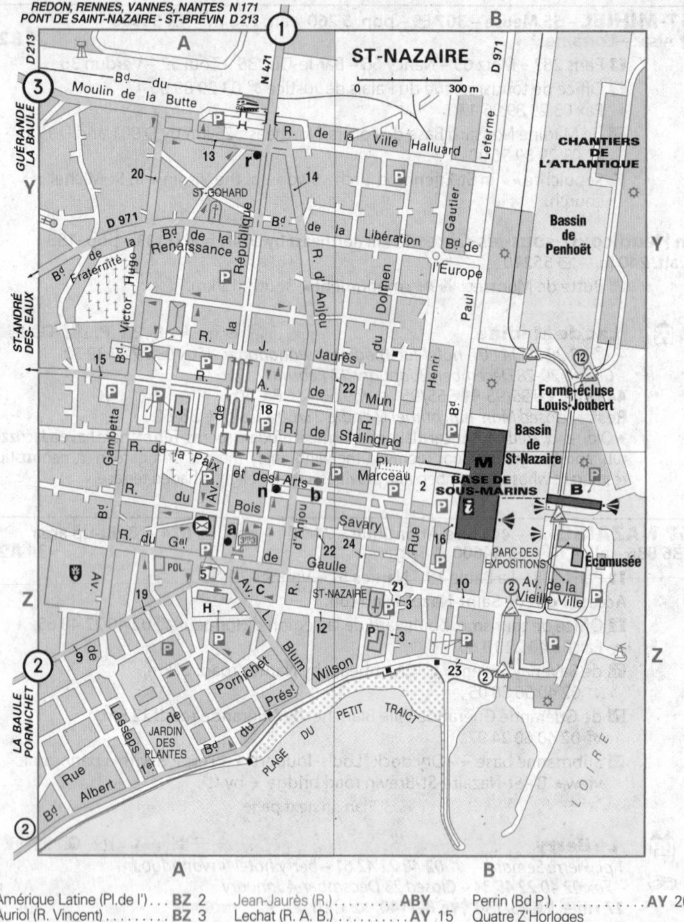

Amérique Latine (Pl.de l') . . . **BZ** 2	Jean-Jaurès (R.) . . . . **ABY**		Perrin (Bd P.) . . . . **AY** 20		
Auriol (R. Vincent) . . . . **BZ** 3	Lechat (R. A. B.) . . . . **AY** 15		Quatre Z'Horloges (Pl. des) . . . . **BZ** 21		
Blancho (Pl. F.) . . . . **AZ** 5	Légion-d'Honneur (Bd de la) . . . . **BZ** 16		République (Av. de la) . . **AYZ**		
Chêneveaux (R.) . . . . **AZ** 9	Martyrs-de-la-Résistance (Pl. des) . . . . **AY** 18		Salengro (R. R.) . . . . **AYZ** 22		
Coty (Bd René) . . . . **BZ** 10	Mendès-France (R.) . . . . . **AZ** 19		Verdun (Bd de) . . . . **BZ** 23		
Croisic (R. du) . . . . **AZ** 12	Paix et des Arts (R. de la) . . **AYZ**		28-Février-1943 (R. du) . . . . **BZ** 24		
Herminier (Av. Cdt-l') . . . . . . **AY** 13					
Ile-de-France (R. de l') . . . . **AY** 14					

Le Sabayon

VISA MC

7 r. de la Paix – ✆ 02 40 01 88 21 – Fax 02 40 22 04 77 – Closed 13-21 April, August, Sunday and Monday AZ **b**

Rest – Menu € 17/49 – Carte € 36/50

◆ Behind its nautical inspired façade this 1880 house specialises in fish but also meat dishes (game in season). Classic repertory made with fresh produce.

ST-NAZAIRE-EN-ROYANS – 26 Drôme – 332 E3 – pop. 498 – alt. 172 m –

✉ 26190 French Alps 43 **E2**

▶ Paris 576 – Grenoble 69 – Pont-en-Royans 9 – Romans-sur-Isère 19 – Valence 35

Rome rest, VISA MC AE

– *04 75 48 40 69 – hotel.rome@orange.fr – Fax 04 75 48 31 17*
– *Closed 12-30 November, Sunday dinner except July-August and Monday*
10 rm – €47 €55, €7 – **Rest** – Menu €17 (weekdays)/39
– Carte €26/43

◆ Large house offering refreshing soundproofed rooms; some overlook the imposing aqueduct and water reservoir. The famous ravioli so appreciated by gourmets is among this little Drôme restaurant's specialities, devoted as it is to regional cuisine.

Muraz "du Royans" AC VISA MC

– *04 75 48 40 84 – restaurant@muraz.com – Fax 04 75 48 47 06*
– *Closed 2-10 June, 29 September-29 October, Monday dinner except July-August and Tuesday*
Rest – Menu €18 bi (weekdays)/45 – Carte €27/43

◆ This small family-run restaurant has a brightly coloured dining room enhanced by paintings. Traditional and regional cuisine prepared with fresh produce.

ST-NECTAIRE – 63 Puy-de-Dôme – 326 E9 – pop. 675 – alt. 700 m – Spa – Casino – 63710 Auvergne 5 B2

Paris 453 – Clermont-Ferrand 43 – Issoire 27 – Le Mont-Dore 24

Office de tourisme, les Grands Thermes 04 73 88 50 86, Fax 04 73 88 40 48

Church★★: treasure-house★★ - Puy de Mazeyres ★ East: 3 km then 30 mn.

Mercure rm, VISA MC AE

Les Bains Romains – 04 73 88 57 00 – h1814-gm@accor.com
– Fax 04 73 88 57 02
71 rm – €80/100 €80/100, €12 – ½ P €75/80
Rest – *(closed 12 November-20 December)* Carte €25/39

◆ Old thermal baths and wooded grounds provide a nostalgic backdrop to this enchanting hotel. The comfortable rooms have been or are being refurbished. The pastel coloured dining room sports a refined low-key atmosphere. Meals served around the pool in summer.

ST-NEXANS – 24 Dordogne – 329 E7 – see Bergerac

ST-NICOLAS-LA-CHAPELLE – 73 Savoie – 333 L3 – see Flumet

ST-NIZIER-LE-BOUCHOUX – 01 Ain – 328 D2 – pop. 713 – alt. 216 m – 01560 44 B1

Paris 394 – Lyon 126 – Bourg-en-Bresse 43 – Chalon-sur-Saône 55 – Mâcon 40

La Closerie P

Jassans, (1.5 km south by D 97 and secondary road) – 04 74 52 96 67
– francois-bongard@wanadoo.fr – Fax 04 74 52 96 67
5 rm – €48 €54 – **Table d'hôte** – Menu €18 bi

◆ In the Bresse countryside, charming farm (1830) with its original timbering and idyllic rustic setting. Brightly decorated rooms, named after flowers.

ST-OMER – 62 Pas-de-Calais – 301 G3 – pop. 15 747 – alt. 23 m – 62500 Northern France and the Paris Region 30 B2

Paris 257 – Arras 77 – Boulogne-sur-Mer 52 – Calais 43 – Ieper 57 – Lille 65

Office de tourisme, 4, rue du Lion d'Or 03 21 98 08 51, Fax 03 21 98 08 07

Saint-Omer Golf Club Acquin Chemin des Bois, by Boulogne-sur-Mer road: 15 km, 03 21 38 59 90.

Cathedral district★★ : cathédrale Notre-Dame (Notre-Dame Cathedral)★★ - Hôtel Sandelin and museum★ AZ - Anc. Chapelle des Jésuites (Former Jesuit chapel)★ AZ **B** - Jardin public (Public garden)★ AZ.

Boat lift of Les Fontinettes★ Southeast: 5,5 km - Coupole d'Helfaut-Wizernes★★, South: 5 km.

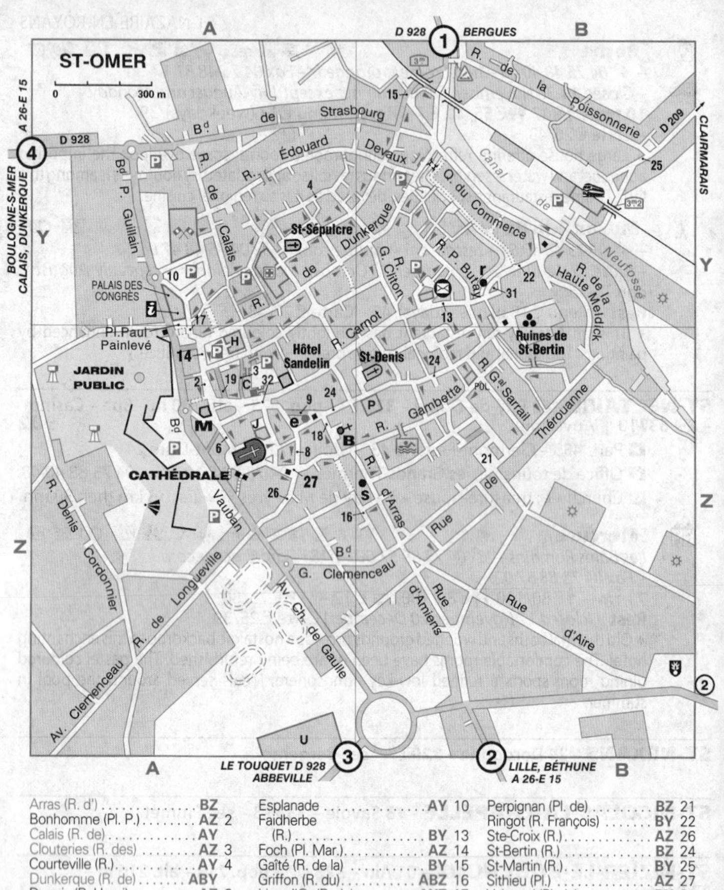

Arras (R. d') . . . BZ	Esplanade . . . AY 10	Perpignan (Pl. de) . . . BZ 21
Bonhomme (Pl. P.) . . . AZ 2	Faidherbe (R.) . . . BY 13	Ringot (R. François) . . . BY 22
Calais (R. de) . . . AY	Foch (Pl. Mar.) . . . AZ 14	Ste-Croix (R.) . . . AZ 26
Clouteries (R. des) . . . AZ 3	Gaîté (R. de la) . . . BY 15	St-Bertin (R.) . . . BZ 24
Courteville (R.) . . . AY 4	Griffon (R. du) . . . ABZ 16	St-Martin (R.) . . . BY 25
Dunkerque (R. de) . . . ABY	Lion-d'Or (R. du) . . . AYZ 17	Sithieu (Pl.) . . . AZ 27
Dupuis (R. Henri) . . . AZ 6	Lycée (R. du) . . . AZ 18	Vainquai (Pl. du) . . . BY 31
Écusserie (R. de l') . . . AZ 8	Martel (R. Louis) . . . AZ 19	Victor-Hugo (Pl.) . . . AZ 32
Epeers (R. des) . . . AZ 9		

St-Louis

rest, rest, VISA

25 r. d'Arras – ☎ 03 21 38 35 21 – contact@hotel-saintlouis.com – Fax 03 21 38 57 26 – Closed 18 December-5 January BZ **s**

30 rm – †€ 59 ††€ 72, ☕ € 8 – ½ P € 59 – **Rest** – *(closed lunch 14 July-19 August, Saturday lunch and Sunday lunch)* Menu € 15 (weekdays)/26 – Carte € 21/33

♦ This pleasant arcaded hotel, formerly a post house, is close to the cathedral district. Warm, practical rooms; those in the annexe have been recently renovated. Dining room furnished in modern brasserie style. Traditional menu.

Le Bretagne

VISA

2 pl. Vainquai – ☎ 03 21 38 25 78 – accueil@hotellebretagne.com – Fax 03 21 93 51 22

75 rm – †€ 60 ††€ 70/85, ☕ € 9

Rest – *(closed 1st-15 January, lunch from 4-17 August, Saturday lunch, Sunday dinner and dinner on public holidays)* Menu € 15 (weekdays)/30 bi – Carte € 22/54 BY **r**

♦ This imposing modern building, pleasantly situated in the town centre, houses extremely well-kept rooms. Red velvet benches, mirrors and wall lights bring a Parisian brasserie style to this restaurant; traditional food.

XXX **Le Cygne**

8 r. Caventou – ✆ 03 21 98 20 52 – Fax 03 21 95 57 12 – Closed 27 July-19 August, February school holidays, Sunday dinner and Monday except public holidays AZ **e**

Rest – Menu € 14/48 – Carte € 36/55

◆ The bright, stylish dining room, preceded by a reception area with a fireplace, leads onto a terrace. Well-prepared traditional dishes.

in Blendecques **4 km by ② and D 211 – pop. 5 186 – alt. 25 m – ✉ 62575**

X **Le Saint Sébastien**

2 Grand-Place – ✆ 03 21 38 13 05 – saint-sebastien@wanadoo.fr – Fax 03 21 39 77 85 – Closed 22-30 December, Sunday dinner, Monday and dinners on public holidays

Rest – Menu (€ 14,50), € 17/37 – Carte € 37/47

◆ A good address to be found in a small suburb of the Audomarois agglomeration: friendly welcome, rustic well-kept decor and good, traditional recipes.

in Tilques **6 km by ④, D 943 and secondary road – pop. 947 – alt. 27 m – ✉ 62500**

Château Tilques

– ✆ 03 21 88 99 99 – chateau-tilques.hotel@najeti.com – Fax 03 21 38 34 23

53 rm – †€ 145/165 ††€ 145/195, ☕ € 19 – 1 suite – ½ P € 121/136

Rest – Menu € 28 (lunch), € 38/88 – Carte € 63/76

◆ The park is planted with trees and has a pond with swans and peacocks that run free at this brick-built château from 1891. Period furniture in the rooms, more modern in the annexe. The old castle stables house the restaurant in a smart setting. Classic cuisine.

ST-OUEN – 41 Loir-et-Cher – **318** D5 – see Vendôme

ST-OUEN – 93 Seine-Saint-Denis – **305** F7 – **101** 16 – see Paris, Area

---

ST-OUEN-LES-VIGNES – 37 Indre-et-Loire – **317** O4 – see Amboise

---

ST-OUTRILLE – 18 Cher – **323** H4 – **pop. 203 – alt. 108 m – ✉ 18310** 12 **C3**

Paris 233 – Blois 71 – Bourges 46 – Châteaudun 39 – Romorantin-Lanthenay 30

X **La Grange aux Dîmes**

2 pl. de l'église – ✆ 02 48 51 12 13 – Fax 02 48 51 12 13 – Closed 2-25 March, 1st-15 October, Sunday dinner and Monday

Rest – Menu (€ 15), € 20/60 bi – Carte € 32/47

◆ Pleasant family restaurant housed in a former barn on the collegiate church square, tastefully decorated and furnished in rustic style. Traditional menu.

ST-PAIR-SUR-MER – 50 Manche – **303** C7 – see Granville

ST-PALAIS – 64 Pyrénées-Atlantiques – **342** F5 – **pop. 1 701 – alt. 50 m – ✉ 64120** Atlantic Coast 3 **B3**

Paris 788 – Bayonne 52 – Biarritz 63 – Dax 60 – Pau 74 – St-Jean-Pied-de-Port 32

Office de tourisme, place Charles-de-Gaulle ✆ 05 59 65 71 78, Fax 05 59 65 69 15

La Maison d'Arthezenea

42 r. du Palais de Justice – ✆ 05 59 65 85 96 – francois.barthaburu@wanadoo.fr – Fax 05 59 65 85 96 – Open April-December

4 rm ☕ – †€ 63/68 ††€ 68/73 – **Table d'hôte** – Menu € 25 bi

◆ Fine stone-built residence in a pretty garden, where you will be made to feel at home. The rooms, adorned with antique furniture, have different colour schemes and names. The table d'hôte serves tasty specialities (home-made foie gras, lamb sweetbread and flambéd woodpigeon in season).

XX **Trinquet** with rm — rest, VISA MC

– ✆ 05 59 65 73 13 – hoteltrinquet.saintpalais@wanadoo.fr – Fax 05 59 65 83 84 – *Closed 21 April-12 May, 22 September-13 October, Monday except hotel in season and Sunday dinner*

9 rm – †€ 55 ††€ 55/65, ☕ € 7 – ½ P € 55/65

Rest – Menu (€ 12) – Carte € 26/43

◆ Charming retro establishment on the main square, with a foremast dating from 1891. Appetising regional cuisine served in redecorated rooms. All the rooms have been renovated.

ST-PALAIS-SUR-MER – 17 Charente-Maritime – 324 D6 – pop. 3 343 – alt. 5 m – ✉ 17420 Atlantic Coast

38 **A3**

Paris 512 – La Rochelle 82 – Royan 6

Office de tourisme, 1, avenue de la République ✆ 05 46 23 22 58, Fax 05 46 23 36 73

La Grande Côte★★ Northwest: 3 km - Zoo de la Palmyre★★ Northwest: 10 km.

Primavera — rm, P VISA MC AE

12 r. Brick, via av. Gde Côte – ✆ 05 46 23 20 35 – contact@hotel-primavera.com – Fax 05 46 23 28 78 – Closed 15 November-15 December

40 rm – †€ 75/135 ††€ 75/135, ☕ € 14 – 2 suites – **Rest** – *(closed Tuesday lunch, Wednesday lunch and Monday)* Menu € 24/45 – Carte € 36/86

◆ An elegant 1900 "folly" of medieval inspiration and two superbly situated annexes in a peaceful park overlooking the sea. Comfortable rooms. Refined partly panoramic restaurant. Traditional sea-inspired cuisine.

Ma Maison de Mer — P VISA MC

21 av. du Platin – ✆ 05 46 23 64 86 – reservations@mamaisondemer.com – Fax 05 46 23 64 86

5 rm ☕ – †€ 75/115 ††€ 75/155 – **Table d'hôte** – *(closed Tuesday, Thursday and week-ends)* Menu € 29 bi

◆ Surrounded by a garden and pine forest and only 300 m from the beach. An English family now runs this plush establishment, whose lovely sea-theme decor is enchanting. Breakfast is prepared with fresh market produce.

XX **Les Agapes** — VISA MC

8 r. M. Vallet – ✆ 05 46 23 10 23 – patrick.morin25@wanadoo.fr – Fax 05 46 23 09 23 – Closed autumn half-term holidays, January, Sunday dinner April-June and September-October, Wednesday lunch and Tuesday November-April and Monday

Rest – Menu € 25/48 – Carte € 52/57

◆ Modern interior and pleasant terrace at this restaurant near the market. In the kitchens, the chef concocts refined traditional recipes, some creatively reinterpreted.

X **Le Flandre** — P VISA MC

av. Tamaris, rte de la Palmyre – ✆ 05 46 23 36 16 – yves.minot@wanadoo.fr – Fax 05 46 23 48 95 – Closed 19 November-31 January, Tuesday October-May and Wednesday except July-August

Rest – Menu (€ 17), € 21/39 – Carte € 27/61

◆ This restaurant, nestling in the Palmyre forest, asserts its nautical roots with an upturned ship's hull ceiling, lobster aquarium and seafood on the menu.

ST-PAL-DE-MONS – 43 Haute-Loire – 331 H2 – pop. 1 748 – alt. 840 m – ✉ 43620

Paris 516 – Clermont-Ferrand 177 – Le Puy-en-Velay 57 – Saint-Étienne 35 – Saint-Chamond 43

6 **D3**

Les Feuillantines — rest, VISA MC AE

La Vialatte – ✆ 04 71 75 63 25 – contact@lesfeuillantines.com – Fax 04 71 75 63 24 – Closed 28 April-5 May, 4-25 August, 26 December-5 January and Sunday

12 rm – †€ 58/63 ††€ 58/63, ☕ € 8 – ½ P € 57/62 – **Rest** – *(closed Sunday dinner and Friday)* Menu (€ 16), € 19 (weekdays)/46 – Carte € 29/47

◆ Opened in 2006, most of this hotel's rooms overlook the valley and peaks. Spacious and practical comfort (some with balcony). Fine bucolic views from the restaurant's large bay windows.

ST-PARDOUX-LA-CROISILLE – 19 Corrèze – 329 M4 – pop. 157 – alt. 410 m – ✉ 19320

25 **C3**

Paris 497 – Aurillac 79 – Brive-la-Gaillarde 49 – Mauriac 47 – St-Céré 65 – Tulle 23 – Ussel 56

Beau Site rest, VISA

– ☎ 05 55 27 79 44 – contact@hotel-lebeausite-correze.com – Fax 05 55 27 69 52 – *Open 1st May-1st October and closed Monday dinner except July-August*

28 rm – €60 €70/75, €8,50 – ½ P €56/72

Rest – *(closed Tuesday lunch and Wednesday lunch)* Menu (€15), €20 (weekdays), €29/41 – Carte €31/47

♦ A 1935 building facing the forest. Its grounds with pond are well-equipped for leisure activities. Room decor is either modern and colourful or more modest. Dining rooms overlooking the countryside. Tasty traditional cuisine featuring country produce.

ST-PATRICE – 37 Indre-et-Loire – 317 K5 – see Langeais

ST-PAUL – 06 Alpes-Maritimes – 341 D5 – pop. 2 847 – alt. 125 m – ✉ 06570

French Riviera

42 **E2**

Paris 922 – Antibes 18 – Cagnes-sur-Mer 7 – Cannes 28 – Grasse 22 – Nice 21 – Vence 4

Office de tourisme, 2, rue Grande ☎ 04 93 32 86 95, Fax 04 93 32 60 27

Site★ - Ramparts★ - Maeght Foundation ★★.

Le Saint-Paul rest, VISA

86 r. Grande, (in the village) – ☎ *04 93 32 65 25* – *stpaul@relaischateaux.com* – *Fax 04 93 32 52 94* – *Closed January*

16 rm – €220/340 €220/340, €28 – 2 suites

Rest – *(closed Wednesday lunch and Tuesday from November to March)* Menu €48 (lunch), €70/100 – Carte €92/107

Spec. Paupiette d'aubergine et cabillaud à l'émietté d'araignée de mer. Lasagne de homard et pousses de salade poêlées. Surprise chocolatée. **Wines** Bellet, Côtes de Provence.

♦ High in a medieval village; beautiful stonework, frescoes, a fountain and colourful furniture make for a refined ambiance in this 16C abode. Flavoursome cuisine that follows the seasons; elegant vaulted dining room and verdant terrace.

La Colombe d'Or rm, VISA

pl. Ch. de Gaulle – ☎ *04 93 32 80 02* – *contact@la-colombe-dor.com* – *Fax 04 93 32 77 78* – *Closed 22 October-20 December and 10-20 January*

15 rm – €200/280 €220/280, €15 – 11 suites – ½ P €155/245

Rest – Carte €32/90

♦ This hotel-museum, appreciated by both artists and celebrities, has a superb collection of modern paintings and sculptures. "Old Provence" setting and rooms with personal touches. A deliciously shady outdoor terrace and a comfortable dining room decorated with faultless taste.

Le Mas de Pierre rest, VISA

2320 rte des Serres, 2 km southward – ☎ *04 93 59 00 10* – *info@lemasdepierre.com* – *Fax 04 93 59 00 59*

46 rm – €230/700 €230/700, €29 – 2 suites

Rest – Menu (€42), €50 (weekday lunch) – Carte €79/102

♦ The elegant rooms are located in five bastides set around a splendid pool in the heart of a lush green garden. Luxury, comfort and well being (spa). Two smart dining rooms or outdoor dining. Traditional fare in the evening and spit roast meat at lunchtime.

La Toile Blanche with rm VISA

826 chemin Pounchounière – ☎ *04 93 32 74 21* – *info@toileblanche.com* – *Fax 04 93 32 87 43*

6 rm – €155/185 €160/250, €15 – **Rest** – *(open 15 June-15 September) (dinner only) (number of covers limited, pre-book)* Menu €50

♦ Appetising fixed menu (evenings only) with an emphasis on inventive, contemporary cuisine. Outdoor dining in the summer months. Pleasant guestrooms with contemporary furnishings and a backdrop of grey and Provençal tones. Garden with swimming pool.

via La Colle-sur-Loup road – ✉ **06570 St-Paul**

Mas d'Artigny – rm,
3 km Hauts de St-Paul road – *✆ 04 93 32 84 54 – mas@grandesetapes.fr – Fax 04 93 32 95 36*
55 rm – €159/539 €159/539, ☕ €25 – 30 suites – ½ P €169/359
Rest – Menu €35 (weekday lunch), €43/95 – Carte €32/68
◆ Audacious hotel complex in a park enjoying a view extending as far as the Baie des Anges. Apartments with private pools, an immense lavish spa and sculpture park. Panoramic dining room and terrace; culinary repertoire dominated by seafood.

La Grande Bastide without rest
1350 rte de la Colle – ✆ 04 93 32 50 30 – stpaullgb@wanadoo.fr – Fax 04 93 32 50 59 – Closed 26 November-20 December and 15 January-15 February
14 rm – €130/190 €150/305, ☕ €17
◆ This well-restored 18C mas extends a friendly welcome to guests. Pretty Provençal-style rooms with a balcony, view of the pool or greenery; generous breakfasts.

Les Vergers de St Paul without rest
940 Route de la Colle – ✆ 04 93 32 94 24 – h.vergers@wanadoo.fr – Fax 04 93 32 91 07
17 rm – €125/150 €135/245, ☕ €16
◆ A hotel nestling in a garden offering a view over St Paul. The tasteful rooms, with a terrace or a balcony, overlook the pool and sport white walls, striped fabrics and parquet floors.

Le Hameau without rest
at 500 m. – ✆ 04 93 32 80 24 – lehameau@wanadoo.fr – Fax 04 93 32 55 75 – Open 20 February-16 November
15 rm – €105/190 €120/190, ☕ €15 – 2 suites
◆ Rustic-styled setting, terraced gardens and small tastefully furnished rooms make up this former Provençal farm's charm. Surrounded by pretty little white cottages. Hamman, Jacuzzi.

Hostellerie des Messugues without rest
500m, Gardettes district by Route de la Fondation Maeght – ✆ 04 93 32 53 32 – info@messugues.com – Fax 04 93 32 94 15 – Open 15 March-31 October
15 rm – €85/140 €85/140, ☕ €10
◆ A well-restored Mediterranean villa and original swimming pool in a quiet pine grove. A striking effect in the corridors: the doors of the rooms come from a 19C prison!

South 4 km by D 2 and secondary road - ✉ **06570 St-Paul**

Les Bastides de St-Paul without rest
880 Chemin Blaquières (D 336 – Cagnes-Vence trunk road) – ✆ 04 92 02 08 07 – bastides@tiscali.fr – Fax 04 93 20 50 41
20 rm – €80/140 €85/140, ☕ €11
◆ Set back a little from a busy road, a colourful establishment with spacious, functional rooms with good soundproofing. A trefoil-shaped pool.

ST-PAUL-DES-LANDES – 15 Cantal – 330 B5 – pop. 1 100 – alt. 554 m – ✉ 15250

Paris 544 – Aurillac 13 – Figeac 59 – St-Céré 49 **5 A3**

Voyageurs
– ✆ 04 71 46 38 43 – lesvoyageurs15@ifrance.com – Fax 04 71 46 38 08 – Closed 22 December-5 January, Saturday from September to May and Monday dinner
Rest – Menu €17/27 – Carte €19/29
◆ This hotel looks onto the town's main street; the atmosphere is warm and friendly. The cooking is 100% home-made to match the rustic decor of the dining hall. Summer terrace.

ST-PAUL-DOUEIL – 31 Haute-Garonne – 343 B8 – see Bagnères-de-Luchon

ST-PAUL-LÈS-DAX – 40 Landes – 335 E12 – see Dax

ST-PAUL-LÈS-ROMANS – 26 Drôme – 332 D3 – see Romans-sur-Isère

ST-PAUL-TROIS-CHÂTEAUX – 26 Drôme – 332 B7 – pop. 7 277 – alt. 90 m – ✉ 26130 Lyon - Rhone Valley 44 B3

Paris 628 – Montélimar 28 – Nyons 39 – Orange 33 – Vaison-la-Romaine 34 – Valence 73

Office de tourisme, place Chausy ✆ 04 75 96 59 60, Fax 04 75 96 90 20

St-Paul cathedral ★ - Barry ≤★★ South: 8 km.

Villa Augusta
rm, VISA

14 r. Serre Blanc – ✆ 04 75 97 29 29 – contact@villaaugusta.fr – Fax 04 75 97 29 27 – Closed January

23 rm – €110/130 €130/200, € 18 – 1 suite – ½ P € 128/163

Rest *David Mollicone* – *(closed Sunday dinner and Monday except July-August)* Menu € 28 (weekday lunch), € 45/75 – Carte € 60/75

◆ Lovely, 19C residence in a superb, leafy garden. The decoration artfully combines bright colours and old and new styles; non-smoking rooms. Elegant, modern dining room, charming terrace and modern cuisine.

L'Esplan
rest, VISA

pl. l'Esplan – ✆ 04 75 96 64 64 – saintpaul@esplan-provence.com – Fax 04 75 04 92 36 – Closed 19 December-11 January

36 rm – €67/96 €67/114, € 10 – ½ P € 75/88

Rest – *(closed Sunday from October to April) (dinner only)* Menu € 25/52 – Carte € 41/62

◆ This 16C mansion in the heart of the town has a beautiful contemporary interior and well cared for rooms decorated in warm colours. Restaurant brightened up by pastel hues. Original recipes focusing on herbs, flowers and home-grown plants.

Vieille France-Jardin des Saveurs
VISA

1.2 km La Garde Adhémar road – ✆ 04 75 96 70 47 – vieillefrance.jardindessaveurs@wanadoo.fr – Fax 04 75 96 70 47 – Closed 29 April-13 May, 12 November-3 December, lunch except Sunday in July-August, Tuesday from September to June and Monday

Rest – *(number of covers limited, pre-book)* Menu (€ 25), € 32 (weekday lunch), € 47/55

◆ Provençal farmhouse in the countryside. Warm contemporary decor, pleasant shady terrace, tasty Mediterranean cuisine and fine Côtes-du-Rhône wine list. Seasonal menu with truffles.

L et Lui
VISA

2 r. Charles-Chaussy – ✆ 04 75 46 61 14 – caputicik@wanadoo.fr – Closed 25-31 August, 25 December-1st January, lunch in July-August, Tuesday and Sunday from September to June

Rest – Menu € 27 (lunch), € 32/49 – Carte € 27/47

◆ At this charming address, Cédric concocts creative dishes using produce cultivated by Cathy in the kitchen garden, while every month, a different winemaker is given pride of place. Vivid décor in the dining room.

ST-PÉ-DE-BIGORRE – 65 Hautes-Pyrénées – 342 L4 – pop. 1 257 – alt. 330 m – ✉ 65270 Languedoc-Roussillon-Tarn Gorges 28 A3

Paris 859 – Pau 33 – Tarbes 32 – Toulouse 184

Office de tourisme, place des Arcades ✆ 05 62 41 88 10, Fax 05 62 41 87 70

Le Grand Cèdre

6 r. du Barry – ✆ 05 62 41 82 04 – chp@legrandcedre.fr

5 rm – €65 €72/80 – **Table d'hôte** – Menu € 27 bi

◆ This 17C house, guarded by a 300 year-old cedar tree, offers rooms individually decorated with fine antique furniture. Park and rose bower. Enjoy tasty home-made dishes in a rustic dining room (booking essential).

ST-PÉE-SUR-NIVELLE – 64 Pyrénées-Atlantiques – 342 C4 – pop. 4 331 – alt. 30 m – ✉ 64310 3 A3

Paris 785 – Bayonne 22 – Biarritz 17 – Cambo-les-Bains 17 – Pau 129 – St-Jean-de-Luz 14

Office de tourisme, place du Fronton ✆ 05 59 54 11 69, Fax 05 59 85 86 38

XX **L'Auberge Basque** with rm

Quartier Helbarron, D307 (old St-Pée road to St-Jean-de-Luz) – ☎ 05 59 51 70 00 – contact@aubergebasque.com – Fax 05 59 51 70 17 – Closed 10-23 November, 19 January-18 February

9 rm – †€ 90/160 ††€ 90/160, ☕ € 15 – 2 suites

Rest – *(closed Tuesday lunch and Monday)* Menu € 43/48 – Carte € 57/69

◆ Contemporary auberge with a bright dining room and large terrace, both of which make the most of the surrounding scenery. Updated regional cuisine. New guestrooms, which are both spacious and cosy.

XX **Le Fronton**

St-Jean-de-Luz road – ☎ 05 59 54 10 12 – jeanbaptiste.daguerre@wanadoo.fr – Fax 05 59 54 18 09 – Closed 11 February-14 March, Tuesday from October to April, Sunday dinner and Monday

Rest – Menu € 37 – Carte approx. € 45

◆ Traditional cuisine with an emphasis on market produce and fresh fish is served in the comfortable, conservatory-style formal dining room. Terrace.

ST-PÉRAY – 07 Ardèche – 331 L4 – pop. 6 502 – alt. 124 m – ✉ 07130 43 E2

Paris 562 – Lamastre 35 – Privas 39 – Tournon-sur-Rhône 15 – Valence 4

Office de tourisme, 45, rue la République ☎ 04 75 40 46 75, Fax 04 75 40 55 72

Ruins of château de Crussol: site★★★ and ≤★★ Southeast: 2 km.

Saint-Romain-de-Lerps ※★★★ Northwest: 9,5 km by D 287,

Auvergne-Rhone Valley

in Soyons 7 km south by D 86 – pop. 1 721 – alt. 106 m – ✉ 07130

Domaine de Soyons rm, rest,

D 86, 670 Nîmes road – ☎ 04 75 60 83 55 – info@ledomainedesoyons.fr – Fax 04 75 60 85 21 – Closed 1st-10 October, 1st-10 January

28 rm – †€ 89/149 ††€ 119/169, ☕ € 18 – **Rest** – Menu (€ 20), € 25 (lunch), € 33/39 – Carte € 41/73

◆ A warm friendly atmosphere pervades this beautiful 19C dwelling surrounded by a verdant park (300-year-old cedar tree). Empire-style furniture in the rooms. Tasty, modern recipes served in a pleasant dining room with a veranda.

ST-PÈRE – 89 Yonne – 319 F7 – see Vézelay

ST-PHILBERT-DE-GRAND-LIEU – 44 Loire-Atlantique – 316 G5 – pop. 6 253 – alt. 10 m – ✉ 44310 Atlantic Coast 34 B2

Paris 405 – Nantes 27 – Niort 150 – Rennes 138 – La Roche-sur-Yon 50 – Tours 218

Office de tourisme, place de l'Abbatiale ☎ 02 40 78 73 88, Fax 02 40 78 83 42

La Bosselle rest, rm,

– ☎ 02 40 78 73 47 – Fax 02 40 78 01 85

14 rm – †€ 54/58 ††€ 54/58, ☕ € 8 – ½ P € 63 – **Rest** – Menu € 12 (weekday lunch), € 23/36 – Carte € 24/40

◆ Family-run hotel near the abbey church. Recently built, well laid out rooms with simple furnishings. Fully refurbished restaurant with food grilled in the fireplace, local produce and freshwater fish specialities from the lake.

ST-PHILBERT-DES-CHAMPS – 14 Calvados – 303 N4 – see Breuil-en-Auge

ST-PHILIBERT – 56 Morbihan – 308 N9 – pop. 1 258 – alt. 15 m – ✉ 56470

Paris 489 – Rennes 137 – Vannes 29 – Lorient 50 – Lanester 45 9 A3

Le Galet rest,

rte de la Trinité-sur-Mer, 1.2 km north by D 28 and D 781 – ☎ 02 97 55 00 56 – contact@legalet.fr – Fax 02 97 55 19 77

21 rm – †€ 67/125 ††€ 67/125, ☕ € 12 – 2 suites – ½ P € 67/96

Rest – *(dinner only)* Menu € 21

◆ A quiet night's sleep is guaranteed in this hotel surrounded by a garden just two minutes from La Trinité sur Mer. Tastefully redecorated hotel; modern bedrooms.

ST-PIERRE-D' ALBIGNY – 73 Savoie – 333 J4 – pop. 3 583 – alt. 410 m – ✉ 73250 46 F2

▶ Paris 596 – Lyon 137 – Chambéry 29 – Annecy 77 – Aix-les-Bains 45

ℹ Office de tourisme, place de l'Europe ✆ 04 79 71 44 07, Fax 04 79 71 44 55

Château des Allues

Les Allues – ✆ 06 75 38 61 56 – info@chateaudesallues.com – Closed beg. November-mid December

5 rm – €90/120 €100/130 – ½ P €75/95 – **Table d'hôte** – *(closed Monday)* Menu €40 bi

◆ Tastefully-renovated old manor house with views of the mountains. Spacious rooms in traditional or contemporary style. Dishes using vegetables from the garden served at the large dining table.

ST-PIERRE-DE-CHARTREUSE – 38 Isère – 333 H5 – pop. 770 – alt. 885 m – Winter sports : 900/1 800 m 1 13 – ✉ 38380 French Alps 46 F2

▶ Paris 571 – Belley 62 – Chambéry 39 – Grenoble 28 – La Tour-du-Pin 52 – Voiron 25

ℹ Office de tourisme, place de la Mairie ✆ 04 76 88 62 08, Fax 04 76 88 68 78

◉ Town hall terrace ≤★ - Prairie de Valombré ≤★ West: 4 km - Site★ of Perquelin East: 3 km - La Correrie: musée Cartusien★ of the Grande Chartreuse convent Northwest: 3,5 km - Decoration★ of St-Hugues-de-Chartreuse church South: 4 km.

Beau Site

rest, VISA

– ✆ 04 76 88 61 34 – hotel.beausite@libertysurf.fr – Fax 04 76 88 64 69 – Closed 2 April-2 May and 15 October-26 December

26 rm – €58/65 €61/75, €10 – ½ P €61/72

Rest – *(closed 8 January-11 February, Tuesday lunch, Sunday dinner and Monday)* Menu €16/36 – Carte €21/43

◆ This century-old hotel boasts a collection of paintings by local painter Arcabas. Simple but comfortable rooms, all renovated. Swimming pool with a view of the valley. Spacious dining room, panoramic terrace and traditional dishes.

ST-PIERRE-DE-JARDS – 36 Indre – 323 H4 – pop. 137 – alt. 148 m – ✉ 36260 12 C3

▶ Paris 232 – Bourges 35 – Issoudun 22 – Romorantin-Lanthenay 40 – Vierzon 21

Les Saisons Gourmandes

VISA

pl. des Tilleuls – ✆ 02 54 49 37 67 – Fax 02 54 49 37 67 – Closed 20 October-5 November, 5-28 January, Tuesday dinner and Wednesday except July-August and Monday dinner

Rest – Menu €21/39 – Carte €28/44

◆ Early-20C local-style house converted into a restaurant. Here you are served classic dishes on the terrace or under the original, Berry blue-painted beams.

ST-PIERRE-DE-MANNEVILLE – 76 Seine-Maritime – 304 F5 – pop. 774 – alt. 6 m – ✉ 76113 Normandy 33 C2

▶ Paris 150 – Évreux 72 – Rouen 18 – Sotteville-lès-Rouen 20

Manoir de Villers without rest

30 rte de Sahurs – ✆ 02 35 32 07 02 – contact@manoirdevillers.com – Fax 02 35 32 07 02 – Closed 15 December-15 January

3 rm – €130/140 €140/160, €9

◆ This fabulous 19C manor house has the air of a museum. Period decor in the public areas; rooms with parquet flooring and fine antique furniture.

ST-PIERRE-D'ENTREMONT – 73 Savoie – 333 I5 – pop. 372 – alt. 640 m – ✉ 73670 French Alps 46 F2

▶ Paris 564 – Belley 63 – Chambéry 26 – Les Echelles 12 – Grenoble 38 – Lyon 104

ℹ Office de tourisme, Maison Intercommunale ✆ 04 79 65 81 90, Fax 04 79 65 88 78

◉ Cirque de St-Même★★ Southeast: 4,5 km - Gorges du Guiers Vif★★ and Pas du Frou★★ West: 5 km - Château du Gouvernement★: ≤★ Southwest: 3 km.

Château de Montbel

– ✆ 04 79 65 81 65 – *hotel-chateau-montbel@club-internet.com* – *Fax 04 79 65 89 49 – Closed 13-26 April, 27 October-7 December, Sunday dinner and Monday off season*

12 rm (½ board only) – 🚹€ 36/40 🚹🚹€ 43/48 – ½ P € 46/50 – **Rest** – *(dinner only) (residents only)*

◆ Hotel with a warm atmosphere in a small mountain village on the borders of the Dauphiné and the Savoie. Simple, well-kept rooms. Rustic furniture, panelled room and open fire: a pleasant place to enjoy traditional cuisine.

ST-PIERRE-DES-CHAMPS – 11 Aude – 344 G4 – pop. 127 – alt. 146 m – ✉ 11220

Paris 808 – Perpignan 84 – Carcassonne 41 – Narbonne 41 22 **B3**

La Fargo

rm, rm, VISA

– ✆ 04 68 43 12 78 – *contact@lafargo.fr – Fax 04 68 43 29 20* – *Open 16 March-14 November*

6 rm – 🚹€ 68/160 🚹🚹€ 68/160, ☕ € 7 – **Rest** – *(closed Tuesday lunch and Monday) (dinner only except July-August and weekends)* Carte € 32/51

◆ This old forge hidden in the Corbières is ideal for a relaxing healthy stay (non-smoking). Rooms are tastefully furnished, with Indonesian details. Pleasant, shady terrace and rustic-style dining room.

ST-PIERRE-D'OLÉRON – 17 Charente-Maritime – 324 C4 – see île d'Oléron

ST-PIERRE-DU-MONT – 14 Calvados – 303 G3 – pop. 85 – alt. 25 m – ✉ 14450

Paris 291 – Caen 58 – Saint-Lô 58 – Bayeux 29 – Valognes 58 32 **B2**

Le Château Saint Pierre without rest

1 km à l'Ouest sur D 514 – ✆ *02 31 22 63 79 – chateaustpierre@orange.fr*

4 rm – 🚹€ 50 🚹🚹€ 65, ☕

◆ An ideal base for visiting the Normandy landing beaches. Surrounded by a garden, this 1600 château is decorated in a country style with comfortable rooms.

ST-PIERRE-DU-PERRAY – 91 Essonne – 312 D4 – 101 38 – see Paris, Area (Sénart)

ST-PIERRE-LA-NOAILLE – 42 Loire – 327 D2 – see Charlieu

ST-PIERRE-LÈS-AUBAGNE – 13 Bouches-du-Rhône – 340 I6 – see Aubagne

ST-PIERREMONT – 88 Vosges – 314 H2 – pop. 162 – alt. 251 m – ✉ 88700 27 C2

Paris 366 – Lunéville 24 – Nancy 56 – St-Dié 43

Le Relais Vosgien

rest, VISA

– ✆ 03 29 65 02 46 – *relais.vosgien@wanadoo.fr – Fax 03 29 65 02 83* – *Closed 10-22 January*

20 rm – 🚹€ 62/75 🚹🚹€ 75/99, ☕ € 11 – 6 suites – ½ P € 68/100

Rest – *(closed Sunday dinner)* Menu € 28/61 – Carte € 41/66

◆ In the country, close to a pond, this old restored farmhouse with its family atmosphere is also a service-station and bar-tabac. The garden facing rooms are the most modern. Traditional dishes served in a rustic dining room or out on the terrace.

ST-PIERRE-QUIBERON – 56 Morbihan – 308 M9 – see Quiberon

ST-PIERRE-SUR-DIVES – 14 Calvados – 303 L5 – pop. 3 977 – alt. 30 m – ✉ 14170 Normandy 33 C2

Paris 194 – Caen 35 – Hérouville-Saint-Clair 34 – Lisieux 27

Syndicat d'initiative, 23, rue Saint-Benoist ✆ 02 31 20 97 90, Fax 02 31 20 36 02

Auberge de la Dives with rm rm, VISA

27 bd Collas – ✆ 02 31 20 50 50 – auberge-de-la-dives@wanadoo.fr – Fax 02 31 20 50 50 – Closed 17 November-7 December, 26 January-8 February, Sunday dinner from 17 November to 31 March, Monday dinner and Tuesday

5 rm – €35 €39, €6 – ½ P €54

Rest – Menu (€14), €19/37 – Carte €30/48

◆ This stylish inn is worth a detour, with its pleasant country-style dining room, small riverside terrace and carefully prepared traditional cuisine. Clean, cheerful rooms.

ST-POL-DE-LÉON – 29 Finistère – 308 H2 – pop. 7 121 – alt. 60 m – ✉ 29250

Brittany 9 **B1**

Paris 557 – Brest 62 – Brignogan-Plages 31 – Morlaix 21 – Roscoff 6

Office de tourisme, Pavillon du Tourisme ✆ 02 98 69 05 69, Fax 02 98 69 01 20

de Carantec Carantec Rue de Kergrist, South: 10 km by D 58, ✆ 02 98 67 09 14.

Steeple★★ of Kreisker chapel ★: ★★ from the tower - of the former cathedral★ - Rocher Ste-Anne: ★ downhill.

France without rest VISA AE

29 r. des Minimes – ✆ 02 98 29 14 14 – hotel.de.france.finistere@wanadoo.fr – Fax 02 98 29 10 57

22 rm – €35/55 €50/65, €6,50

◆ A quiet side street is the setting for this elegant regional abode dating from the 1930s. Well-kept practical rooms; ask for one giving onto the garden.

Auberge La Pomme d'Api VISA AE

49 r. Verderel – ✆ 02 98 69 04 36 – yannick.lebeaudour@free.fr – Fax 02 98 29 06 53 – Closed 12-30 November, Sunday dinner and Monday except July-August

Rest – Menu (€17 bi), €23 bi (weekday lunch), €35/70 bi – Carte €55/86

◆ Beams, stone and a huge fireplace make up this 16C Breton lodging's rustic-styled setting. "Surf and turf" cuisine, mixing seafood, spices and exotic flavours.

ST-PONS – 04 Alpes-de-Haute-Provence – 334 H6 – see Barcelonnette

ST-PONS – 07 Ardèche – 331 J6 – pop. 203 – alt. 350 m – ✉ 07580 44 **B3**

Paris 621 – Aubenas 24 – Montélimar 21 – Privas 24 – Valence 66

Hostellerie Gourmande "Mère Biquette" VISA AE

4 km north on secondary road – ✆ 04 75 36 72 61 – info@merebiquette.fr – Fax 04 75 36 76 25 – Closed 12 November-10 February, Sunday dinner October-March, Monday lunch and Wednesday lunch

15 rm – €61/108 €61/108, €9,50 – ½ P €57/86 – **Rest** – Menu €21/45 – Carte €28/46

◆ Nature and quiet lovers will appreciate this Ardèche farm nestled between the vines and chestnut trees. Spacious countrified rooms. Regional dishes served in the dining room/veranda with views over the valley.

ST-PONS-DE-THOMIÈRES – 34 Hérault – 339 B8 – pop. 2 287 – alt. 301 m – ✉ 34220

Languedoc-Roussillon-Tarn Gorges 22 **B2**

Paris 750 – Béziers 54 – Carcassonne 64 – Castres 54 – Lodève 73 – Narbonne 53

Office de tourisme, place du Foirail ✆ 04 67 97 06 65, Fax 04 67 97 95 07

Grotte de la Devèze★ Southwest: 5 km.

Les Bergeries de Pondérach VISA AE

1 km via rte de Narbonne – ✆ 04 67 97 02 57 – bergeriesponderach@wanadoo.fr – Fax 04 67 97 29 75 – Open 15 March-5 November

7 rm – €75/89 €75/105, €12 – ½ P €85/92 – **Rest** – *(closed lunch except Sunday and public holidays)* Menu €29/42 – Carte €35/44

◆ A 17C sheepcote - one of the manor house outbuildings - with rooms overlooking the countryside. Pleasant, rustic restaurant. Terrace in the inner courtyard.

ST-PORCHAIRE – 17 Charente-Maritime – 324 E5 – pop. 1 335 – alt. 16 m – ✉ 17250 38 **B2**

Paris 474 – La Rochelle 56 – Niort 77 – Rochefort 27 – Royan 36 – Saintes 16

Le Bruant with rm — rest, rm, VISA

76 r. Nationale – ☎ 05 46 94 65 36 – lebruantotel@aol.com – Fax 05 46 94 71 00 – Closed 4-25 November, Sunday dinner and Monday

4 rm – †€ 45 ††€ 55, ☕ € 8 – **Rest** – Menu (€ 14), € 19/40 – Carte € 25/40

◆ This house, built in typical Charente style, is resolutely modern in feel, with its chic, country-style decor and wonderful attention to detail. Attractive, flower-decked terrace. The modern decor in the rooms is made up of bright colours, animal sculptures and flowers.

ST-PORQUIER – 82 Tarn-et-Garonne – 337 D7 – pop. 1 023 – alt. 95 m – ✉ 82700

Paris 651 – Colomiers 60 – Montauban 18 – Toulouse 55 28 **B2**

Les Hortensias without rest — P

– ☎ 05 63 31 85 57 – bernard-barthe075@orange.fr

3 rm ☕ – †€ 60 ††€ 60

◆ This pink-brick house offers colourful rooms. You will also appreciate the former wine store where breakfast is now served, as well as the pleasant flower garden.

ST-PÔTAN – 22 Côtes-d'Armor – 309 I3 – pop. 735 – alt. 55 m – ✉ 22550

Paris 429 – Rennes 79 – Saint-Brieuc 46 – Saint-Malo 35 10 **C1**

Auberge du Manoir — VISA AE

31 r. du 19 mars 1962 – ☎ 02 96 83 72 58 – Closed 10-30 November, 14-26 February, Tuesday and Wednesday

Rest – Menu € 12 (weekday lunch), € 31/50 – Carte € 34/69

◆ A pleasant gourmet stop-over in this welcoming house, located in the village. Appealing lunchtime daily specials and a longer traditional menu to be discovered in the neo-rustic dining room.

ST-POURÇAIN-SUR-SIOULE – 03 Allier – 326 G5 – pop. 5 266 – alt. 234 m – ✉ 03500 Auvergne 5 **B1**

Paris 325 – Montluçon 66 – Moulins 33 – Riom 61 – Roanne 79 – Vichy 28

Office de tourisme, 29, rue Marcellin Berthelot ☎ 04 70 45 32 73, Fax 04 70 45 60 27

de Briailles 15 rue de Metz, East: 3 km, ☎ 04 70 45 49 49.

Ste-Croix church ★ - Musée de la Vigne et du Vin★.

Le Chêne Vert — P VISA AE

bd Ledru-Rollin – ☎ 04 70 47 77 00 – hotel.chenevert@wanadoo.fr – Fax 04 70 47 77 39 – Closed 6-20 January and Sunday off season

29 rm – †€ 45/55 ††€ 53/65, ☕ € 7,50 – **Rest** – *(closed 6-28 January, Sunday dinner off season and Monday except dinner in season)* Menu € 18/38 – Carte € 26/47

◆ Two types of rooms: contemporary and less so - 1970s style - while awaiting an upcoming renovation. A little gallery exhibits regional products. Smart dining room and pleasant terrace. Traditional cuisine complemented by local wines.

ST-PRIEST-BRAMEFANT – 63 Puy-de-Dôme – 326 H6 – pop. 647 – alt. 290 m – ✉ 63310 6 **C2**

Paris 365 – Clermont-Ferrand 49 – Riom 34 – Thiers 26 – Vichy 13

Château de Maulmont — rest, P VISA AE

1.5 km south on D 59 – ☎ 04 70 59 03 45 – info@chateau-maulmont.com – Fax 04 70 59 11 88 – Open 16 March-1st November

19 rm – †€ 80/185 ††€ 80/185, ☕ € 16 – 3 suites – ½ P € 74/144

Rest – *(closed Tuesday lunch, Sunday dinner and Monday)* Menu € 38/85 bi – Carte € 57/65

Rest *Taverne des Templiers* – *(closed Sunday lunch and public holidays)* Menu € 25/30 – Carte € 27/30

Spec. Gigolettes de grenouilles, compotée de pomme. Ris de veau meunière, poêlée de girolles (mid June-end October). Compotée de figues, sablé breton (mid July-end September). **Wines** Saint-Pourçain blanc et rouge.

◆ A pretty château, altered in the 19C by Adélaïde, the sister of Louis-Philippe. It has everything from period furniture and carved wood panelling to a classical formal garden! Tasty, modern food, oak panelled dining room and panoramic terrace.

ST-PRIEST-EN-JAREZ – 42 Loire – 327 F7 – see St-Étienne

ST-PRIEST-TAURION – 87 Haute-Vienne – 325 F5 – pop. 2 613 – alt. 255 m – ✉ 87480 Dordogne-Berry-Limousin 24 B2

Paris 387 – Bellac 47 – Bourganeuf 33 – Limoges 15 – La Souterraine 53

- ≤★ of Montméry Park North: 9 km by D 44.

Relais du Taurion with rm

– ✆ *05 55 39 70 14 – Fax 05 55 39 67 63 – Closed 15 December-15 January, Sunday dinner and Monday*

8 rm – €52/58 €52/58, €9 – ½ P €58/63 – **Rest** – Menu €21/40 – Carte €39/50

◆ A bourgeois home surrounded by a large garden. Traditional fare served on the terrace or in a spruce dining room adorned with fresh flowers and paintings. Small rustic rooms. Non-smokers only.

ST-PRIVAT-DES-VIEUX – 30 Gard – 339 J4 – see Alès

ST-PRIX – 71 Saône-et-Loire – 320 E8 – pop. 225 – alt. 464 m – ✉ 71990 7 B2

Paris 308 – Dijon 107 – Le Creusot 41 – Montceau-les-Mines 54

Chez Franck et Francine

Le bourg – ✆ 03 85 82 45 12 – chez-franck-et-francine@wanadoo.fr – Closed January, Sunday dinner and Monday

Rest – *(number of covers limited, pre-book)* Menu €36/55

◆ Village restaurant with a family atmosphere. Simply-decorated dining room arranged around a fireplace. Up-to-date cuisine with personal touches.

ST-PRIX – 95 Val-d'Oise – 305 E6 – 101 5 – see Paris, Area

ST-PUY – 32 Gers – 336 E6 – pop. 603 – alt. 171 m – ✉ 32310 28 A2

Paris 731 – Agen 52 – Auch 32 – Toulouse 107

La Lumiane

Grande rue – ✆ 05 62 28 95 95 – info@lalumiane.com – Fax 05 62 28 59 67

5 rm – €41/57 €49/65 – **Table d'hôte** – Menu €21 bi

◆ This 17C dignitary's house, next to the 12C church, offers fine stylishly rustic rooms, a peaceful reading room and pleasant flower garden. The table d'hôte menu is dominated by local dishes.

ST-QUAY-PORTRIEUX – 22 Côtes-d'Armor – 309 F3 – pop. 3 114 – alt. 25 m – Casino – ✉ 22410 Brittany 10 C1

Paris 470 – Étables-sur-Mer 3 – Guingamp 29 – Lannion 54 – Paimpol 26 – St-Brieuc 22

Office de tourisme, 17 bis, rue Jeanne d'Arc ✆ 02 96 70 40 64, Fax 02 96 70 39 99

des Ajoncs d'Or, West: 7 km, ✆ 02 96 71 90 74.

Ker Moor without rest ≤ coast and sea,

13 r. Prés. Le Sénécal – ✆ 02 96 70 52 22 – hotelkermoor@orange.fr – Fax 02 96 70 50 49 – Open mid March-mid December

27 rm – €104/159 €104/159, €12

◆ This century-old villa with a Moorish touch is perched on top of a low cliff. Rooms have balconies and offer a fine view of the sea.

Gerbot d'Avoine rest,

bd Littoral – ✆ 02 96 70 40 09 – gerbotdavoine@wanadoo.fr – Fax 02 96 70 34 06 – Closed 15 November-15 December, 5 January-5 February and Monday from February to Easter

20 rm – €46 €50, €9,50 – ½ P €60/75 – **Rest** – *(closed Monday and Tuesday except July-August)* Menu €22 (weekdays)/42 – Carte €34/58

◆ A Breton house in a seaside resort. Some of the rooms overlook the English Channel. Two dining rooms, one facing the sea - from which the chef draws his inspiration.

Le Saint-Quay with rm
72 bd. Foch – 02 96 70 40 99 – lestquayhotel@orange.fr – Fax 02 96 70 34 04 – Closed 10-14 May, 17-27 November, 12-20 January and Tuesday in season
7 rm – €45 €52, €7,50 – **Rest** – Menu €22/48 – Carte €35/72
◆ Small family-run restaurant with a simple neo-rustic setting. Savour traditional cuisine listed on a blackboard. Simple refurbished rooms.

ST-QUENTIN – 02 Aisne – 306 B3 – pop. 59 066 – Built-up area 103 781 – alt. 74 m – ✉ 02100 Northern France and the Paris Region 37 C2

Paris 165 – Amiens 81 – Charleroi 161 – Lille 113 – Reims 99

Office de tourisme, espace Victor Basch 03 23 67 05 00, Fax 03 23 67 78 71

de Saint-Quentin-Mesnil Mesnil-Saint-Laurent Rue de Chêne de Cambrie, Southeast: 10 km by D 12, 03 23 68 19 48.

Basilica★ - Town hall ★ - Collection of portraits by Maurice Quentin de La Tour★★ at the musée Antoine-Lécuyer.

Plan on next page

Le Grand Hôtel without rest
6 r. Dachery – 03 23 62 69 77 – grand-hotel2@wanadoo.fr – Fax 03 23 62 53 52
24 rm – €72 €90, €9 BZ **n**
◆ This large building at the foot of the hill has spacious, functional rooms reached by a panoramic lift.

Des Canonniers without rest
15 r. Canonniers – 03 23 62 87 87 – info@hotel-canonniers.com – Fax 03 23 62 87 86 – Closed 4-17 August and Sunday dinner AZ**m**
7 rm – €52/91 €60/119, €12
◆ The entrance to this stately home is via a pretty cobbled courtyard. Quiet rooms with personal touches (kitchenette). Lovely wainscoted salons facing the park.

Ibis without rest
14 pl. Basilique – 03 23 67 40 40 – H1641@accor.com – Fax 03 23 67 84 90
76 rm – €51/68 €51/68, €7,50 ABZ **r**
◆ Ideally located in the heart of town and a step away from the tourist sights. Behind its elegant red brick façade are rooms that are large for a chain hotel.

Mémorial without rest
8 r. Comédie – 03 23 67 90 09 – contact@hotel-memorial.com – Fax 03 23 62 34 96 AZ **b**
18 rm – €55/86 €55/94, €8,50
◆ This old townhouse boasts a large tree-lined inner courtyard. Each of the rooms (renovation underway) is individually decorated (double glazing on the street side).

Villa d'Isle
111-113 r.d'Isle – 03 23 67 08 09 – contact@villadisle.fr – Fax 03 23 67 06 07 – Closed 1st-15 August, Saturday lunch, Sunday dinner and Monday BZ **h**
Rest – Menu (€16 bi), €23 bi (weekdays)/30 – Carte €28/49
◆ This lovely old house has been cleverly renovated and the remains of the past mingle with modern touches. Appetising bistro fare: ox tail, black pudding, calf's head, etc.

Auberge de l'Ermitage
331 rte de Paris, 3 km by ⑤ – 03 23 62 42 80 – auberge.ermitage@wanadoo.fr – Fax 03 23 64 29 28 – Closed 4-21 August, 2-8 March, Saturday lunch, Sunday dinner and Wednesday
Rest – Menu €26/52 – Carte €47/60
◆ An inn whose façade, terrace and freshly painted exterior cannot fail but catch the eye. Tasty traditional dishes served in a pleasantly neat, rustic décor.

Le Rouget Noir
19 r. Victor-Basch – 03 23 62 44 44 – lerougenoir@wanadoo.fr – Fax 03 23 07 87 98 – Closed 2-8 January, Saturday lunch, Sunday dinner and Wednesday AYZ **a**
Rest – Menu (€16 bi), €35/45 – Carte €37/59
◆ This handsome contemporary establishment is unsurprisingly done up in red and black and adorned with original works by an artist friend of the chef. Flavoursome cuisine.

ST-QUENTIN

Aumale (R. d') . . . . AZ 2
Basch (R. Victor) . . . . AYZ 3
Basilique (Pl. de la) . . . . ABY 4
Campions (Pl. des) . . . . AZ 5
Croix-Belle-Porte (R.) . . . . AY 6
Dufour-Denelle (Pl.) . . . . AZ 7
États-Généraux (R. des) . . . . AY 8
Foy (R. du Gén.) . . . . AZ 10
Gaulle (Av. du Gén.-de) . . . . . BZ 13
Gouvernement (R. du) . . . . . BY 15
Héros-du-2-Septembre-1945 (Pl. des) . . . . BZ 16
Herriot (R. Édouard) . . . . BZ 17
Hôtel-de-Ville (Pl. de l') . . . . . AZ 18
Isle (R. d') . . . . BZ
Leclerc (R. Gén.) . . . . BZ 21
Lyon (R. de) . . . . BZ 24
Mulhouse (Pl.) . . . . BY 25
Ovres (R. E.) . . . . BY 26
Paringault (R.) . . . . ABY 27
Pompidou (R. G.) . . . . AY 28
Prés.-J.-F.-Kennedy (R. du) . . AY 29
Raspail (R.) . . . . AY
Rémicourt (Av. de) . . . . BY 31
St-André (R.) . . . . AY 32
Sellerie (R. de la) . . . . BZ 33
Le Sérurier (R.) . . . . AY 23
Sous-Préfecture (R. de la) . . BZ 34
Thomas (R. A.) . . . . AY 36
Toiles (R. des) . . . . BZ 37
Verdun (Bd) . . . . AZ 38
Zola (R. Émile) . . . . AZ
8-Octobre (Pl. du) . . . . BZ 41

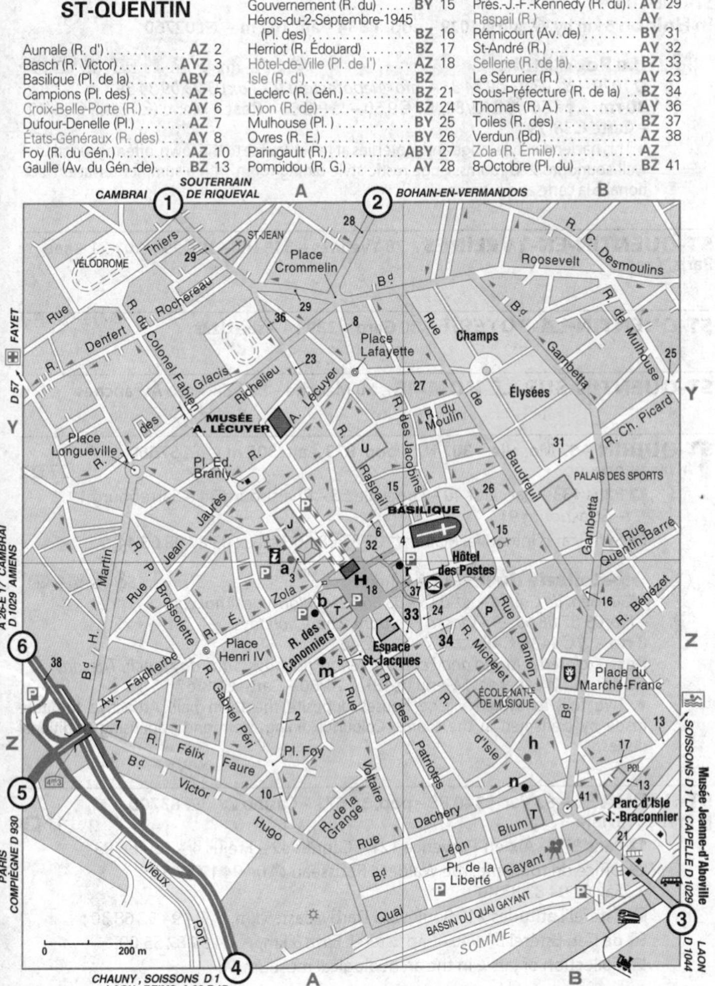

in Neuville-St-Amand 3 km by ③ and D 12 – pop. 908 – alt. 82 m – ✉ 02100

Château rm, rm, VISA AE
– ✆ 03 23 68 41 82 – *chateaudeneuville.st.amand@wanadoo.fr*
– *Fax 03 23 68 46 02 – Closed 4-25 August, 22 December-5 January, Saturday lunch, Sunday dinner and Monday*
15 rm – €67 €78, €11 – **Rest** – Menu €28 (weekdays)/65
– Carte €32/64
◆ A well-tended park surrounds this restored manor house and gives it a welcome peaceful atmosphere. Personalised bedrooms with spacious bathrooms. At meal times, the chef concocts traditional fare from fresh, good quality produce.

in Holnon 6 km by ⑥ and D 1029 – pop. 1 334 – alt. 102 m – ✉ 02760

Le Pot d'Étain rm, VISA MC AE

D 1029 – ☎ 03 23 09 34 35 – info@lepotdetain.fr – Fax 03 23 09 34 39

30 rm – €56 €62/88, ☕ €9,50 – ½ P €68 – **Rest** – Menu (€18 bi), €28/42 – Carte €38/79

◆ This hacienda-style lodge and motel lies at the entrance to the town, offering functional, well-soundproofed rooms. Huge rustic-style dining room with a summer terrace. Traditional à la carte and set menus.

ST-QUENTIN-EN-YVELINES – 78 Yvelines – 311 H3 – 106 29 – 101 21 – see Paris, Area

---

ST-QUENTIN-LA-POTERIE – 30 Gard – 339 L4 – see Uzès

ST-QUENTIN-SUR-LE-HOMME – 50 Manche – 303 E8 – see Avranches

ST-QUIRIN – 57 Moselle – 307 N7 – pop. 873 – alt. 305 m – ✉ 57560

Alsace-Lorraine 27 **D2**

Paris 433 – Baccarat 40 – Lunéville 56 – Phalsbourg 34 – Sarrebourg 19 – Strasbourg 91

Syndicat d'initiative, Mairie ☎ 03 87 08 60 34, Fax 03 87 08 66 44

Hostellerie du Prieuré with rm rm, VISA MC

163 r. Gén. de Gaulle – ☎ 03 87 08 66 52 – tbllorraine@aol.com – Fax 03 87 08 66 49 – Closed February school holidays

8 rm – €44 €48, ☕ €7 – ½ P €46

Rest – *(closed autumn and February school holidays, Saturday lunch, Tuesday dinner and Wednesday)* Menu (€18), €24/60 – Carte €28/67

◆ Two fully-renovated village houses opposite the town hall. Attractive furniture made by craftsmen in the rooms. Colourful dining room and appetising traditional dishes.

ST-RAPHAËL – 83 Var – 340 P5 – pop. 30 671 – Casino Z – ✉ 83700

French Riviera 41 **C3**

Paris 870 – Aix-en-Provence 121 – Cannes 42 – Fréjus 4 – Toulon 93

Office de tourisme, rue Waldeck Rousseau ☎ 04 94 19 52 52, Fax 04 94 83 85 40

Esterel Latitudes 745 Boulevard Darby, East: 5 km, ☎ 04 94 52 68 30 ;

de Cap Estérel BP 940 - Cap Esterel, East: 3 km, ☎ 04 94 82 55 00.

Collection of jars★ in the archeological museum **M.**

Access and exits: See plan of Fréjus.

Continental without rest AC VISA MC AE

100 promenade René Coty – ☎ 04 94 83 87 87 – info@hotels-continental.com – Fax 04 94 19 20 24 – Open March-beg. November and 17 December-2 January Z **e**

44 rm – €75/118 €75/229, ☕ €13

◆ Opposite the beach, in the lively part of town, this hotel occupies the first floor of a huge white neo-Classical building. Comfortable bright rooms, the best ones face the sea.

La Marina AC VISA MC AE

port Santa-Lucia, via ① – ☎ 04 94 95 31 31 – hotel@bestwestern-lamarina.com – Fax 04 94 82 21 46

100 rm – €96/178 €96/178, ☕ €12 – **Rest** – Menu €24 – Carte €31/43

◆ Hotel just outside town, built around a pool with a view of the marina. Practical rooms of various sizes, mainly decorated in blue or red and often with a balcony. Restaurant with a terrace on the quayside. Traditional menu.

ST-RAPHAËL

Aicard (R. J.) . . . Z 2	Baux (R. Amiral) . . . Y 9	Libération (Bd de la) . . . Z 22
Albert-1er (Quai) . . . Z 3	Carnot (Pl.) . . . Y 10	Liberté (R. de la) . . . Y 23
Allongue (R. Marius) . . . Y 5	Coty (Promenade René) . . . Z 13	Martin (Bd Félix) . . . YZ 24
Barbier (R. J.) . . . Z 6	Doumer (Av. Paul) . . . Z 14	Péri (Pl. Gabriel) . . . Y 26
Basso (R. Léon) . . . Y 7	Gambetta (R.) . . . Y 15	Remparts (R. des) . . . Y 28
	Gounod (R. Ch.) . . . Z 17	Rousseau (R. W.) . . . Y 30
	Guilbaud (Cours Cdt) . . . Y 18	Vadon (R. H.) . . . Z 31
	Karr (R. A.) . . . Y 21	

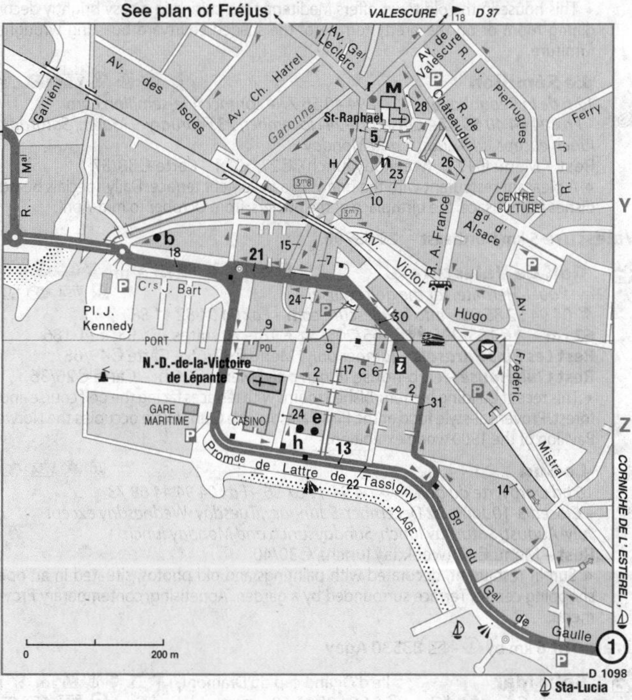

Excelsior

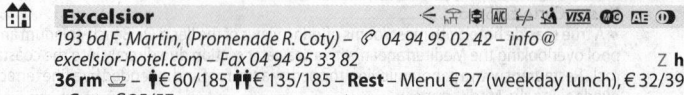

193 bd F. Martin, (Promenade R. Coty) – ✆ 04 94 95 02 42 – info@excelsior-hotel.com – Fax 04 94 95 33 82 Z **h**

36 rm – €60/185 €135/185 – **Rest** – Menu €27 (weekday lunch), €32/39 – Carte €35/57

◆ Fine early 20C hotel complex on the seafront, near the grand casino, with renovated rooms that either overlook the pool or harbour. Regional cuisine served in two dining rooms with a modern setting or on the terrace facing the Mediterranean.

Santa Lucia without rest

418 Corniche D'Or, via ① – ✆ 04 94 95 23 00 – contact@hotelsantalucia.fr – Fax 04 94 19 49 79 – Closed 21 December-31 January

12 rm – €64/134 €79/149

◆ Family-run hotel with nautical decor and individualised rooms, each of which is designed in the style of a different country (Morocco, Italy, Japan etc). Ask for one of the rooms with a sea view at the back of the hotel.

Provençal without rest

195 r. Garonne – ✆ 04 98 11 80 00 – reception@hotel-provencal.com – Fax 04 98 11 80 13 Y **b**

24 rm – €55/80 €55/80, €8

◆ slightly away from the busy port, an entirely renovated building containing modern functional rooms with good soundproofing.

XXX **L'Arbousier**
6 av. Valescure – ✆ 04 94 95 25 00 – arbousier.restaurant@wanadoo.fr – Fax 04 94 83 81 04 – Closed 22 December-7 January, Tuesday except dinner in season and Monday Y **r**
Rest – Menu € 28 (lunch), € 36/59 – Carte € 65/78
◆ This house in the old town offers Mediterranean cuisine in a cosy brightly decorated dining room or on the pretty terrace of the shaded courtyard boasting wrought-iron furniture.

X **Le Sémillon**
12 r. de la République – ✆ 04 94 40 56 77 – contact@le-semillon.com – Fax 04 94 40 56 77 – Closed 10-24 November, 23 February-9 March, Saturday lunch except July-August and Monday Y **n**
Rest – Menu € 17 bi (weekday lunch), € 27/50 bi – Carte € 38/57
◆ A pleasant restaurant with the bonus of a pavement terrace. Daily specials board plus dishes from Alsace, the birthplace of the owners, from October to mid-April.

in Valescure 5 km Northeast – ✉ 83700

Golf de Valescure rm, rest,
av. Paul L'Hermite, (at the golf course) – ✆ 04 94 52 85 00 – info@valescure.com – Fax 04 94 82 41 88
62 rm – €165/205 €165/205, € 18 – 20 suites – ½ P € 124/186
Rest *Les Pins Parasols* – *(dinner only)* Menu € 37/65 – Carte € 49/68
Rest *Club House* – club-house *(lunch only)* Menu € 26 bi – Carte € 26/36
◆ This recent building has refurbished rooms with terraces facing the golf course and pine forest. Provençal-style food at the Pins Parasols. The Club House occupies the Norwegian Pavilion of the 1900 world exhibition.

X **Le Sud**
16 bd Darby, rte du golf – ✆ 04 94 44 67 86 – Fax 04 94 44 68 73 – Closed 3-10 June, 22 December-5 January, Tuesday, Wednesday except July-August, Saturday lunch, Sunday lunch and Monday lunch
Rest – Menu € 17 (weekday lunch), € 30/40
◆ Sun-lit restaurant, decorated with paintings and old photos, situated in an open-air shopping centre. Terrace surrounded by a garden. Appetising, contemporary Provençal menu.

in Dramont 6 km by ① – ✉ 83530 Agay

Sol e Mar Ile d'Or and cap du Dramont, rm, rest,
rte de la Corniche d'Or – ✆ 04 94 95 25 60 – resa-agay@monalisahotels.com – Fax 04 94 83 83 61 – Open 15 March-11 November
45 rm – €70/163 €70/163, € 11 – 5 suites – ½ P € 74/117
Rest – Carte € 35/46
◆ A true seaside hotel with most rooms offering views of the Iles d'Or. Beach-solarium and pool overlooking the Mediterranean with a seawater section dug directly into the coastal rock. Restaurant with a panoramic view topped by a sun roof and extended by a fine terrace overlooking the Mediterranean.

ST-RÉMY – 71 Saône-et-Loire – 320 J9 – see Chalon-sur-Saône

ST-RÉMY-DE-CHARGNAT – 63 Puy-de-Dôme – 326 G9 – see Issoire

ST-RÉMY-DE-PROVENCE – 13 Bouches-du-Rhône – 340 D3 – pop. 9 806 – alt. 59 m – ✉ 13210 Provence

42 **E1**

Paris 702 – Arles 25 – Avignon 20 – Marseille 89 – Nîmes 45

Office de tourisme, place Jean Jaurès ✆ 04 90 92 05 22, Fax 04 90 92 38 52

de Servanes Mouriès Domaine de Servanes, Southeast: 17 km, ✆ 04 90 47 59 95.

Le plateau des Antiques★★: Mausoleum★★, Arc municipal★, Glanum★ 1km by ③ - Cloister★ of the former St-Paul-de-Mausole monastery by ③ - Hôtel de Sade: lapidary deposit★ **L** - Donation Mario Prassinos★ **S.**

✳★★ of La Caume 7 km by ③.

ST-RÉMY-DE-PROVENCE

Commune (R.) . . . . Z 2
Estrine (R.) . . . . YZ 3
La-Fayette (R.) . . . . Z 6
Hoche (R.) . . . . Z 4
Libération (Av. de la) . . . . . . Y 7
Mauron (Av. Ch.) . . . . Y 8
Mirabeau (Bd) . . . . YZ 9
Nostradamus (R.) . . . . Y 10
Parage (R.) . . . . Y 12
Pelletan (R. C.) . . . . YZ 14
Résistance (Av.) . . . . Z 15
Roux (R.) . . . . Z 16
Salengro (R. R.) . . . . Y 18
8 Mai 1945 (R. du) . . . . Z 20

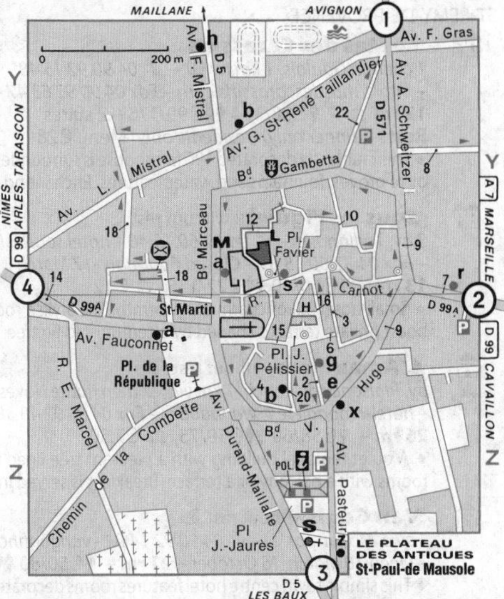

Hostellerie du Vallon de Valrugues

chemin Canto Cigalo, 1 km by ② – ✆ 04 90 92 04 40 – resa@vallondevalrugues.com – Fax 04 90 92 44 01 – Open 1st March-3 November

VISA MC AE

53 rm – †€ 190/310 ††€ 190/310, ☕ € 23 – 7 suites

Rest – *(number of covers limited, pre-book)* Menu € 55/98 – Carte € 79/90

◆ Large villa in a residential area, surrounded by a beautiful tree-shaded garden. Luxurious decor, rooms brightened with Provençal colours, and a full range of leisure facilities. Pierre Reboul is responsible for the deliciously creative cooking. Served in an elegant, low key dining room, opening onto a delightful flower-decked shaded terrace.

Le Château des Alpilles

rm, rm, rest,

2 km west by D 31 – ✆ 04 90 92 03 33 – chateau.alpilles@wanadoo.fr – Fax 04 90 92 45 17 – Open 13 March-4 January

VISA MC AE

15 rm – †€ 180/198 ††€ 200/339, ☕ € 19 – 3 suites

Rest – *(closed Thursday lunch and Wednesday off season)* Menu € 19/40 – Carte € 40/61

◆ Splendid 19C abode surrounded by grounds planted with three century-old plane trees. Attractively decorated rooms, ranging from classical in the main wing to modern in the outbuildings. Happily poised between plush opulence and the 1970s, the restaurant serves regional food.

Les Ateliers de l'Image

36 bd V. Hugo – ✆ 04 90 92 51 50 – info@hotelphoto.com – Fax 04 90 92 43 52 – Closed from mid December to end of February

VISA MC AE

Z x

28 rm – †€ 165/380 ††€ 165/380, ☕ € 19 – 4 suites

Rest – *(closed lunch except public holidays)* Menu € 44/59 – Carte € 47/65

◆ A park in the town centre provides the backdrop to this 'hotel workshop' devoted to photography (exhibitions, gallery, photo lab). Stylish, minimalist rooms (half boast a terrace) and unique tree cabin suite. The restaurant has a choice of sushi or a Provence style menu.

Gounod without rest

VISA MC AE

18 pl. de la République – ✆ 04 90 92 06 14 – contact@hotel-gounod.com – Fax 04 90 92 56 54 – Closed 22 December-5 January and 18 February-17 March

30 rm ☕ – †€ 99/130 ††€ 110/220

Z a

◆ Charles Gounod stayed here in 1863 to compose his Mireille opera. A relaxed atmosphere, pretty, well-renovated, Baroque-inspired decor, as well as a garden, pool and cosy tearoom.

Le Mas des Carassins rm, rest,
1 chemin Gaulois, 1 km by ③ – 04 90 92 15 48 VISA
– info@masdescarassins.com – Fax 04 90 92 63 47 – Closed 5 January-12 March
12 rm – €88/164 €99/175 – 2 suites
Rest – *(dinner only) (residents only)* Menu €28
◆ This faultlessly decorated 19C farmhouse is surrounded by lavender, thyme, lemon trees, olive groves, fountains and water features. Enchanting Provençal style rooms.

Sous les Figuiers without rest VISA
3 av. Taillandier – 04 32 60 15 40 – hotel.souslesfiguiers@wanadoo.fr
– Fax 04 32 60 15 39 – Closed 6 January-17 March Y **b**
13 rm – €60/80 €72/135, €12
◆ Small hotel full of charm and warmth. The stylish rooms (quilts and antique furniture) boast private terraces shaded by a century-old fig tree. Painting workshop.

L'Amandière without rest VISA
av. Plaisance du Touch, 1 km via ① then Route Noves – 04 90 92 41 00
– hotel-amandiere@wanadoo.fr – Fax 04 90 92 48 38
26 rm – €58/60 €58/75, €7,50
◆ A quiet regional building with a pleasant tree-lined flower garden. Peaceful, practical rooms with a balcony or a terrace. Breakfast is served in the winter garden.

Van Gogh without rest VISA
1 av. J. Moulin par ② – 04 90 92 14 02 – vangoghhot@aol.com – Fax 04 90 92 09 05
– Open 10 March-15 October – **21 rm** – €50/80 €50/80, €7,50
◆ This simple town centre hotel features rooms decorated with a Provençal note. Those on the first floor have dormer windows. Attractive poolside terrace.

Du Soleil without rest VISA
35 av. Pasteur – 04 90 92 00 63 – info@hotelsoleil.com – Fax 04 90 92 61 07
– Open 10 March-5 November – **21 rm** – €56/74 €56/85, €7 Z **z**
◆ Buildings over a century old (converted factory), around a vast enclosed courtyard (terrace, fountain, garden, pool). Peaceful, unostentatious rooms.

Le Chalet Fleuri without rest VISA
15 av. Frédéric Mistral – 04 90 92 03 62 – le.chalet.fleuri@orange.fr
– Fax 04 90 92 60 28 – Closed January Y **h**
12 rm – €64/74 €64/74, €7,50
◆ A friendly establishment two minutes from the town centre. Cheerful, practical rooms. In summertime, breakfast in the garden (chestnut, pine, lime and palm trees).

La Maison du Village without rest VISA
10 r. du 8 mai 1945 – 04 32 60 68 20 – contact@lamaisonduvillage.com
– Fax 04 32 60 68 21 – **5 rm** – €150/210 €150/210, €12 Z **b**
◆ This 18C house in the heart of the historic centre is delightfully decorated. The rooms are superb and the courtyard-terrace enchanting.

Mas de Figues rm, rm, VISA
Vieux chemin d'Arles, 3 km via chemin de la Combette – 04 32 60 00 98
– info@masdesfigues.com – Fax 04 32 60 00 95 – Open March to November
3 rm – €100/140 €120/200, €20 – 2 suites – ½ P €95/140
Table d'hôte – *(pre-book)* Menu €28/33
◆ Old Provençal farmhouse surrounded by lavender and olive trees. Rooms with four-poster beds named after Alphonse Daudet's characters. Southern French cuisine made from farm grown produce. Stylish setting (large table, timber structure).

La Maison Jaune (François Perraud) VISA
15 r. Carnot – 04 90 92 56 14 – lamaisonjaune@wanadoo.fr – Fax 04 90 92 56 32
– Closed 2 January-2 March, Sunday dinner in winter, Tuesday lunch from June to September and Monday Y **s**
Rest – *(number of covers limited, pre-book)* Menu €36/66 – Carte €48/81
Spec. Asperges vertes de Provence, poutargue, herbes en vinaigrette (April). Filets d'anchois frais marinés, cocos et cébettes (July). Petits encornets de Méditerranée, légumes crus au vinaigre (August). **Wines** Vin de pays des Bouches du Rhône, Coteaux d'Aix-en-Provence-les-Baux.
◆ Overlooking the old town, this beautiful abode has a large shaded upstairs terrace with teak furniture and a roof of local tiles. Delicious modern Provençal cuisine.

XX **Alain Assaud**

13 bd Marceau – ✆ 04 90 92 37 11 – Open 15 March-15 November and closed Thursday lunch, Saturday lunch and Wednesday Y **a**

Rest – Menu € 28/44 – Carte € 48/69

◆ Pleasant rustic style restaurant (exposed stone and beams, paintings, old clock) with a country buffet and traditional food menu with a southern French touch.

X **Le Bistrot Découverte**

19 bd Victor Hugo – ✆ 04 90 92 34 49 – Fax 04 90 92 34 49 – Closed 25-31 August, 1st February-8 March, Sunday dinner except July-August and Monday Z **e**

Rest – Menu (€ 15), € 30 – Carte € 29/43

◆ The characterful bistro and veranda-terrace serve traditional Provençal dishes. Splendid stone vaulted cellar with a fine wine list to be sampled on the spot or taken home.

X **L'Aile ou la Cuisse**

5 r. Commune – ✆ 04 32 62 00 25 – laileoulacuisse@orange.fr – Closed 15 December-28 February, Sunday October-June and Monday Z **g**

Rest – *(dinner only)* Menu € 35 – Carte € 42/51

◆ Set in the refectory of a former convent, this restaurant has a lot of appeal: simple, chic and understated interior, superb patio terrace and tasty bistro cuisine.

at Domaine de Bournissac 11 km by ②, D 30 and D 29 – ✉ 13550 Paluds-des-Noves

La Maison de Bournissac (Christian Peyre)

– ✆ 04 90 90 25 25 – bournissac@wanadoo.fr – Fax 04 90 90 25 26 – Closed 3 January-10 February

13 rm – †€ 130/230 ††€ 130/230, ☕ € 15 – 3 suites – ½ P € 120/170

Rest – *(closed Monday and Tuesday from October to April)* Menu € 45/120 – Carte € 62/92

Spec. Escargots "petits gris" en déclinaison. Langoustine en deux façons (spring-summer). Pigeon fermier rôti sur coffre. **Wines** Cairanne, Côtes de Luberon.

◆ This old farmhouse, standing on a hillside amid vineyards and olive groves, overlooks the Lubéron, Alpilles and Ventoux. Snug sitting rooms and romantic bedrooms. Regional gourmet fare, warm dining room and terraces (one on a patio shaded by fig trees).

in Verquières 11 km by ②, D 30 and D 29 – pop. 801 – alt. 48 m – ✉ 13670

XX **Le Croque Chou**

pl. de l'Église – ✆ 04 90 95 18 55 – folzfamily@le-croque-chou.fr – Fax 04 32 61 15 05 – Closed 29 September-4 October, 5-10 January, 23 February-7 March, Tuesday lunch mid June-mid September, Sunday dinner and Wednesday dinner mid September-mid June and Monday

Rest – *(pre-book)* Menu (€ 22), € 48/124 bi – Carte € 51/70

◆ Old ivy clad sheepcote serving inventive, sun drenched dishes made from high quality produce. Countrified interior and tree-lined terrace.

via ④ 4,5 km and Les Baux road D 27 – ✉ 13210 St-Rémy-de-Provence

Domaine de Valmouriane

– ✆ 04 90 92 44 62 – info@valmouriane.com – Fax 04 90 92 37 32 – Closed 18 November-7 December and 15-26 January

12 rm – †€ 130/305 ††€ 130/335, ☕ € 16 – 1 suite – ½ P € 140/190

Rest – Menu € 28/75 – Carte € 45/67

◆ This comfortable farmhouse amid pine trees lies at the foot of the Alpilles. Bar with piano and fireplace, spacious, period furnished rooms. Wellness centre (open-air massages). Vaulted, colourful dining room serving up-to-date and theme cuisine.

in Maillane 7 km Northwest by D 5 – pop. 1 880 – alt. 14 m – ✉ 13910

XX **L'Oustalet Maïanen**

– ✆ 04 90 95 74 60 – contact@oustaletmaianen.com – Fax 04 90 95 76 17 – Closed 23 June-2 July, November-January, Tuesday lunch July-August, Saturday lunch April-October, Sunday dinner except July-August, Tuesday and Wednesday February-March and Monday

Rest – Menu (€ 18), € 25/40 – Carte € 38/57

◆ A pleasant restaurant opposite the former home of the poet Mistral. Provençal dining room, arboured terrace and tasty regional cuisine.

ST-RÉMY-DU-PLAIN – 35 Ille-et-Vilaine – 309 M4 – pop. 698 – alt. 108 m – ✉ 35560 10 D2

Paris 383 – Rennes 38 – Saint-Malo 58 – Fougères 40 – Vitré 44

La Haye d'Irée

1.5 km south on D 90 and D 12 – ✆ 02 99 73 62 07 – m.deprevoisin@orange.fr – Open April-October

4 rm – €65 €85/115 – **Table d'hôte** – Menu €25

◆ This granite house set in a large garden (lake, pool and rose garden) has an old fashioned atmosphere: lounge with fireplace, stonework, beams and antique filled rooms. Traditional meals (reservation required) served in a rustic dining room.

ST-RIQUIER – 80 Somme – 301 E7 – see Abbeville

ST-ROMAIN-LE-PUY – 42 Loire – 327 D6 – see Montbrison

ST-ROME-DE-TARN – 12 Aveyron – 338 J6 – pop. 715 – alt. 360 m 29 D2

Paris 660 – Millau 21 – Rodez 68 – Toulouse 170

Syndicat d'initiative, place du Terral ✆ 05 65 62 50 89, Fax 05 65 58 44 00

Les Raspes

rm, VISA AE

– ✆ 05 65 58 11 44 – lesraspes@wanadoo.fr – Fax 05 65 58 11 45 – Closed 25 October-10 November

15 rm – €45/65 €65/85, €8,50 – ½ P €70

Rest – *(closed 8-17 February, Sunday dinner, Monday lunch, Wednesday lunch and Saturday lunch from 24 October to 2 May)* Menu €18/60 – Carte €28/63

◆ This traditional stone house in the high-perched village was originally a convent. Today its cells are cosy, well-cared for elegant rooms. Attractive dining room and terrace, where guests enjoy local dishes with a southern accent.

ST-SATUR – 18 Cher – 323 N2 – see Sancerre

ST-SATURNIN – 63 Puy-de-Dôme – 326 F9 – pop. 1 115 – alt. 520 m – ✉ 63450 Auvergne 5 B2

Paris 438 – Clermont-Ferrand 24 – Cournon-d'Auvergne 18 – Riom 37 – Chamalières 25

Château de Saint-Saturnin

VISA

– ✆ 04 73 39 39 64 – chateaudesaintsaturnin@yahoo.fr – Fax 04 73 39 30 86 – Open 20 March-3 November

5 rm – €140/190 €140/190, €10 – **Table d'hôte** – Menu €28 bi/45 bi

◆ Step back in time to the Middle Ages in this authentic 13C château dominating the village. Generously proportioned rooms and suites furnished with antiques. Regionally-inspired bourgeois cooking served to guests in the evenings in a vaulted dining room.

ST-SATURNIN – 72 Sarthe – 310 J6 – see Le Mans

ST-SATURNIN-DE-LUCIAN – 34 Hérault – 339 F6 – see Clermont-l'Hérault

ST-SATURNIN-LÈS-APT – 84 Vaucluse – 332 F10 – pop. 2 341 – alt. 420 m – ✉ 84490 Provence 42 E1

Paris 728 – Apt 9 – Avignon 55 – Carpentras 44 – Manosque 50

Domaine des Andéols with rm

P VISA AE

D2 – ✆ 04 90 75 50 63 – info@domaine-des-andeols.fr – Fax 04 90 75 43 22 – Open 28 February-30 November

10 suites – €250/1140, €22 – **Rest** – *(closed Tuesday lunch, Wednesday lunch and Monday except from June to September)* Menu €42 (weekday lunch), €68/90 – Carte €64/97

◆ A truly magical place in the heart of the Luberon; this inventive hotel-restaurant offers an ultra-designer setting, with open kitchens, carefully-personalised apartments and an indoor pool with hammam.

ST-SAUD-LACOUSSIÈRE – 24 Dordogne – 329 F2 – pop. 868 – alt. 370 m – ✉ 24470
4 **C1**

Paris 443 – Brive-la-Gaillarde 105 – Châlus 23 – Limoges 57 – Nontron 16 – Périgueux 62

Hostellerie St-Jacques
– *05 53 56 97 21 – hostellerie.st.jacques@wanadoo.fr – Fax 05 53 56 91 33 – Open 2 March-30 November and closed Monday lunch, Tuesday lunch, Wednesday lunch from 16 June to 14 September, Sunday dinner, Monday and Tuesday from 15 September to 15 June*
12 rm – €70/200 €70/200, € 12 – 2 suites – ½ P €82/147
Rest – Menu €25 bi (weekday lunch), €37/69 – Carte €49/80
◆ Once a stopover on the old pilgrimage route to Santiago de Compostela, this hotel surrounded by greenery has delightful, individually furnished bedrooms, a swimming pool and a flower garden. Dining room and shaded terrace. Traditional cuisine and good wine list.

ST-SAUVANT – 17 Charente-Maritime – 324 G5 – see Saintes

ST-SAUVES-D'AUVERGNE – 63 Puy-de-Dôme – 326 D9 – see La Bourboule

ST-SAUVEUR-D'AUNIS – 17 Charente-Maritime – 324 E2 – pop. 1 069 – alt. 19 m – ✉ 17540
38 **B2**

Paris 451 – La Rochelle 25 – Niort 43 – Poitiers 117

Le Logis de l'Aunis without rest
8 r. de Ligoure – 05 46 09 02 14 – jocelyne.ecarot@wanadoo.fr
3 rm – €73/87 €73/87
◆ The lady of the house has tastefully and originally decorated the rooms as well as the veranda with its Ile de Ré hues. Flower and vegetable garden and swimming pool.

ST-SAUVEUR-DE-MONTAGUT – 07 Ardèche – 331 J5 – pop. 1 248 – alt. 218 m – ✉ 07190
44 **B3**

Paris 597 – Le Cheylard 24 – Lamastre 29 – Privas 24 – Valence 38
Syndicat d'initiative, quartier de la Tour 04 75 65 43 13, Fax 04 75 65 43 13

Le Montagut with rm
pl. de l'Église – 04 75 65 40 31 – lemontagut@aol.com – Closed 16-30 June, Tuesday dinner and Monday except from June to September
4 rm – €40/45 €40/45, €6 – **Rest** – *(closed Tuesday dinner, Wednesday dinner and Monday except July-August)* Menu €16 bi (weekday lunch), €20/40 – Carte €32/40
◆ Regional flavours on the menu at this family-run inn in an Ardèche village. Simply decorated dining room and a large terrace under a canopy. Small, functional rooms.

ST-SAVIN – 65 Hautes-Pyrénées – 342 L7 – see Argelès-Gazost

ST-SAVIN – 86 Vienne – 322 L5 – pop. 1 009 – alt. 76 m – ✉ 86310
Atlantic Coast
39 **D1**

Paris 344 – Poitiers 44 – Belac 62 – Châtellerault 48 – Montmorillon 19
Wall paintings ★★★ of the Abbey★★.

De France rm, rest,
38 pl. de la République – 05 49 48 19 03 – hotel-saint-savin@wanadoo.fr – Fax 05 49 48 97 07 – Closed 22 December-6 January
11 rm – €48 €48, €6,50 – **Rest** – *(closed Monday lunch, Saturday lunch and Sunday)* Menu €11/21
◆ This hotel is set in a country house on the village square. Practical, often spacious rooms, decorated with taste. Warm tones brighten this restaurant serving traditional and regional fare.

XX **Christophe Cadieu**

15 r. de l'Abbaye – ✆ 05 49 48 17 69 – Fax 05 49 48 17 69 – Closed 23 June-2 July, 22 September-8 October, 5-21 January, Wednesday except lunch from April to October, Sunday dinner and Monday

Rest – Menu € 40/70

Spec. Timbale croustillante aux cèpes, mousseline de pomme de terre ratte (autumn). Lièvre à la royale du Sénateur Couteau (season). Palet de chocolat noir praliné. **Wines** Vin de pays de la Vienne, Montlouis.

◆ This converted barn near the abbey is now a comfortable restaurant with a pleasant rustic atmosphere, pretty tables and appetising modern cuisine.

ST-SEINE-L'ABBAYE – 21 Côte-d'Or – 320 I5 – pop. 355 – alt. 451 m – ✉ 21440

Burgundy-Jura 8 **C2**

Paris 289 – Autun 78 – Dijon 28 – Châtillon-sur-Seine 57 – Montbard 48

Office de tourisme, place de l'Église ✆ 03 80 35 07 63, Fax 03 80 35 07 63

Dolce Chantilly Salives Larçon, North: 32 km by D 16, ✆ 03 80 75 68 54.

La Poste

17 r. Carnot – ✆ 03 80 35 00 35 – contact@postesoleildor.fr – Fax 03 80 35 07 64 – Closed 23 December-6 January, February and Sunday

15 rm – †€ 52/58 ††€ 63/70, ☐ € 10 – ½ P € 63/67 – **Rest** – *(closed Saturday and Sunday) (dinner only)* Menu € 25/35 – Carte € 27/53

◆ Louis XIV is said to have stayed in this former post-house, appreciated for its peaceful shaded garden. Good-sized and well-kept rooms. The restaurant, adorned with a fine fireplace, has retained all its rustic character. Traditional and regional cuisine.

ST-SERNIN-SUR-RANCE – 12 Aveyron – 338 H7 – pop. 530 – alt. 300 m – ✉ 12380

Languedoc-Roussillon-Tarn Gorges 29 **D2**

Paris 694 – Albi 50 – Castres 69 – Lacaune 29 – Rodez 83 – St-Affrique 32

Syndicat d'initiative, avenue d'Albi ✆ 05 65 99 29 13, Fax 05 65 97 60 77

Carayon

– ✆ 05 65 98 19 19 – contact@hotel-carayon.fr – Fax 05 65 99 69 26 – Closed Tuesday lunch, Sunday dinner, Monday except July-August and public holidays

74 rm – †€ 38/50 ††€ 38/75, ☐ € 8 – ½ P € 47/77 – **Rest** – Menu € 15/54 – Carte € 28/39

◆ Several types of room are available in this hotel offering numerous leisure activities. 55 rooms are in the main building, with 19 in the outbuildings within the grounds (dovecote, fisherman's house, chalet and pavilion). Copious local cuisine is served in the two bright and spacious dining rooms or on the terrace.

ST-SERVAN-SUR-MER – 35 Ille-et-Vilaine – 309 K3 – see St-Malo

---

ST-SEURIN-D'UZET – 17 Charente-Maritime – 324 F6 – pop. 572 – alt. 47 m – ✉ 17120

38 **B3**

Paris 516 – Poitiers 183 – La Rochelle 113 – Rochefort 67 – Saintes 49

Blue Sturgeon

3 r. de la Cave – ✆ 05 46 74 17 18 – reservations@bluesturgeon.com – Open from March to October

5 rm – †€ 120 ††€ 120, ☐ € 15 – **Table d'hôte** – Menu € 35/40

◆ The English owner, an interior decorator, has skilfully restored this 17C wine-grower's barn. A happy blend of old and new including a number of "home-made" paintings, garden and small lake. Splendid high ceilings and painted beams set the scene in the dining room.

ST-SIFFRET – 30 Gard – 339 L4 – see Uzès

ST-SILVAIN-BELLEGARDE – 23 Creuse – 325 K5 – pop. 216 – alt. 535 m – ✉ 23190 25 **D1**

Paris 413 – Limoges 148 – Guéret 53 – Montluçon 75 – Ussel 66

Les Trois Ponts

rm,

– ✆ 05 55 67 12 14 – info@lestroisponts.nl – Fax 05 55 67 12 14
– Open from March to November
5 rm – €50 €75 – ½ P €188 – **Table d'hôte** – Menu €25 bi

◆ A Dutch couple have renovated this old mill on the banks of the Tardes, preserving its authenticity. Cosy bedrooms with a Provençal feel. Good choice of leisure facilities. A warm friendly atmosphere is assured in the superb setting of the table d'hôte.

ST-SORLIN-D'ARVES – 73 Savoie – 333 K6 – pop. 325 – alt. 1 550 m – ✉ 73530

French Alps 45 **C2**

Paris 657 – Albertville 84 – Le Bourg-d'Oisans 50 – Chambéry 97 – St-Jean-de-Maurienne 22

Office de tourisme, Champ Rond ✆ 04 79 59 71 77, Fax 04 79 59 75 50

Site★ of St-Jean-d'Arves church Southeast: 2.5 km.

Col de la Croix de Fer ✻★★ West: 7.5 km then 15 mn - Col du Glandon ≤★ then Combe d'Olle★★ West: 10 km.

Beausoleil

rest,

Le Pré – ✆ 04 79 59 71 42 – info@hotel-beausoleil.com – Fax 04 79 59 75 25
– Open 1st July-31 August and 10 December-24 April
21 rm – €44/54 €55/65, €10 – ½ P €55/77 – **Rest** – Menu (€13), €18/25 – Carte €22/36

◆ This truly peaceful chalet stands at the foot of the ski runs, in the upper part of town. Refreshing, functional rooms. Dining room with a modern setting, panoramic terrace and Savoyard cuisine.

ST-SORNIN – 17 Charente-Maritime – 324 E5 – pop. 328 – alt. 16 m – ✉ 17600

Atlantic Coast 38 **B2**

Paris 500 – La Rochelle 56 – Poitiers 167 – Rochefort 26

La Caussolière

10 r. du Petit Moulin – ✆ 05 46 85 44 62 – reservations@caussoliere.com
– Fax 05 46 85 44 62 – Open from March to October
4 rm – €57/73 €68/88 – **Table d'hôte** – *(open from May to September)* Menu €24 bi

◆ This 19C farmhouse opens onto a magnificent garden with a pond. All the cosy rooms have a separate entrance. Friendly welcome. Market and local produce (seafood in season) take pride of place on the menu.

ST-SULIAC – 35 Ille-et-Vilaine – 309 K3 – pop. 853 – alt. 30 m – ✉ 35430

Brittany 10 **D1**

Paris 396 – Rennes 62 – Saint-Malo 14 – Granville 87 – Dinan 26

La Ferme du Boucanier

2 r. de l'Hôpital – ✆ 02 23 15 06 35 – simonpitou@wanadoo.fr
– Fax 02 99 19 51 32 – Closed 8-20 December, Wednesday except dinner May-September, Thursday lunch off season and Tuesday
Rest – Menu (€15), €19 (weekday lunch), €28/35

◆ Two restaurants in one: in summer, a retro room serving updated dishes full of spices; in winter, a regional decor with fireplace for spit roasts and rustic cuisine. A gourmet delight!

ST-SULPICE – 81 Tarn – 338 C8 – pop. 4 801 – alt. 112 m – ✉ 81370 29 **C2**

Paris 666 – Albi 46 – Castres 54 – Montauban 44 – Toulouse 32

Office de tourisme, parc Georges Spenale ✆ 05 63 41 89 50, Fax 05 63 40 23 30

de Palmola Buzet-sur-Tarn Route d'Albi, West: 9km by N 88, ✆ 05 61 84 20 50.

XX **Auberge de la Pointe**

D 988 – ✆ 05 63 41 80 14 – chabbert.patrick@wanadoo.fr – Fax 05 63 41 90 24 – Closed 23 September-16 October, 6-22 January, Thursday except dinner July-August, Tuesday except July-August and Wednesday
Rest – Menu (€ 12), € 20/42 – Carte € 31/43
◆ Old coaching inn with a pink façade and fine rustic interior. Inviting, shady terrace overlooking the Tarn. Traditional cuisine.

ST-SULPICE-LE-VERDON – 85 Vendée – 316 H6 – pop. 609 – alt. 65 m – ✉ 85260 Atlantic Coast 34 B3

Paris 430 – Nantes 45 – Angers 130 – Cholet 51 – La Roche-sur-Yon 31
Office de tourisme, Logis de la Chabotterie ✆ 02 51 43 48 18

XXX ✿ **Thierry Drapeau Logis de la Chabotterie**

– ✆ 02 51 09 59 31 – contact@restaurant-thierrydrapeau.com – Fax 02 51 09 59 27 – Closed 30 June-13 July, 27 October-9 November, 26-30 December, Sunday dinner, Tuesday dinner and Monday
Rest – Menu € 35 bi (weekday lunch), € 55/100 bi – Carte € 63/84
Spec. L'artichaut macau en fine tartelette flammeküche. Lièvre à la royale (October to February.). Pamplemousse rose, macaron de pamplemousse et de fraise parfumé à la rose. **Wines** Fiefs Vendéens.
◆ Restaurant occupying a residence-museum close to the historical site where the Vendée War ended. Tasty modern cuisine served in the rustic, timber-framed dining room.

ST-SULPICE-SUR-LÈZE – 31 Haute-Garonne – 343 F5 – pop. 1 639 – alt. 200 m – ✉ 31410 28 B2

Paris 709 – Auterive 14 – Foix 53 – St-Gaudens 66 – Toulouse 36

XX **La Commanderie**

pl. Hôtel de Ville – ✆ 05 61 97 33 61 – la-commanderie2@wanadoo.fr – Fax 05 61 97 32 60 – Closed 22 October-7 November, 23-30 December, February school holidays, Tuesday and Wednesday
Rest – Menu € 21 (weekday lunch), € 35/60
◆ Fine decor mixing ancient and modern, friendly service and a subtle combination of flavours on the menu, in a former 13C Templar building.

ST-SYLVESTRE-CAPPEL – 59 Nord – 302 C3 – see Cassel

ST-SYLVESTRE-SUR-LOT – 47 Lot-et-Garonne – 336 G3 – see Villeneuve-sur-Lot

ST-SYMPHORIEN – 72 Sarthe – 310 I6 – pop. 500 – alt. 135 m – ✉ 72240 35 C1

Paris 231 – Laval 65 – Le Mans 28 – Nantes 201

X **Relais de la Charnie** with rm

4 pl. Louis des Cars – ✆ 02 43 20 72 06 – relais.charnie@wanadoo.fr – Fax 02 43 20 70 59 – Closed 25 July-11 August, 8-23 February, Sunday dinner and Monday
6 rm – †€ 45 ††€ 45/58, ☕ € 6,50 – ½ P € 56 – **Rest** – Menu € 16/53 – Carte € 30/56
◆ The dining room of this former post-house has a slightly old-world atmosphere and is graced by a big fireplace. You can enjoy traditional, inventive cuisine here. Simple and perfectly well-kept rooms.

ST-THÉGONNEC – 29 Finistère – 308 H3 – pop. 2 267 – alt. 83 m – ✉ 29410 Brittany 9 B1

Paris 549 – Brest 50 – Châteaulin 50 – Morlaix 13 – Quimper 70 – St-Pol-de-Léon 28
Parish enclosure★★ - Guimiliau: Parish enclosure ★★ , Southwest: 7,5 km.

Auberge St-Thégonnec

6 pl. de la Mairie – ✆ 02 98 79 61 18 – auberge@wanadoo.fr – Fax 02 98 62 71 10 – Closed 20 December-15 January and Sunday

19 rm – €75/90 €85/110, €10 – **Rest** – *(closed 20 December-31 January and Sunday) (dinner only)* Menu €24 (weekdays), €26/44 – Carte €51/60

◆ A Breton establishment facing the church and its famous enclosure. Modern rooms, most overlooking the garden. Carefully prepared traditional dishes and a regionally inspired decor of furniture and paintings at the restaurant.

Ar Presbital Koz

18 r. Lividic – ✆ 02 98 79 45 62 – ar.presbital.koz@orange.fr – Fax 02 98 79 48 47

5 rm – €44 €50 – ½ P €44 – **Table d'hôte** – *(closed 10 July-20 August, Sunday and public holidays)* Menu €20 bi

◆ This former presbytery (1750) is certainly peaceful. The cosy good-sized rooms have been carefully decorated by the landlord. Traditional cuisine with a subtly spicy twist. Table d'hôte menu.

ST-THIBAULT – 18 Cher – 323 N2 – see Sancerre

ST-THIERRY – 51 Marne – 306 F7 – pop. 572 – alt. 140 m – ✉ 51220 13 B2

Paris 149 – Châlons-en-Champagne 64 – Reims 18 – Soissons 66 – Laon 43

Le Clos du Mont d'Hor without rest

8 r. du Mont-d'Hor – ✆ 03 26 03 12 42 – info@mhchampagne.com – Fax 03 26 03 02 80

6 rm – €83 €83, €7

◆ Discover the secrets of champagne in this beautiful restored farmhouse surrounded by vineyards. Comfortable (split level) rooms decorated on a travel theme.

ST-THOMÉ – 07 Ardèche – 331 J6 – pop. 358 – alt. 140 m – ✉ 07220 44 B3

Paris 628 – Lyon 165 – Privas 46 – Montélimar 19 – Orange 59

La Bastide Bernard without rest

at Chasser, 1.5 km south-east on D 107 – ✆ 04 75 96 39 72 – bastide@bastidebernard.com – Fax 04 75 96 45 34

4 rm – €49/70 €80

◆ This hillside house commands a fine view over Saint Thomé. Uncluttered, spacious, light rooms. Pleasant breakfast terrace and pool with sun loungers.

ST-TROJAN-LES-BAINS – 17 Charente-Maritime – 324 C4 – see île d'Oléron

ST-TROPEZ – 83 Var – 340 O6 – pop. 5 444 – alt. 4 m – ✉ 83990 French Riviera

Paris 872 – Aix-en-Provence 123 – Cannes 73 – Draguignan 47 – Fréjus 34 – Toulon 69 41 C3

Office de tourisme, 40, rue Gambetta ✆ 08 92 68 48 28, Fax 04 94 55 98 59

de Sainte-Maxime Sainte-Maxime Route du Débarquement, by Ste-Maxime road: 16 km, ✆ 04 94 55 02 02 ;

Gassin Golf Country Club Gassin Route de Ramatuelle, South: 9 km by D 93, ✆ 04 94 55 13 44.

Harbour★★ - Musée de l'Annonciade★★ - Môle Jean Réveille ≤★ - Citadel★: ≤★ of the ramparts, ★★ of the musée de la Citadelle - Ste-Anne chapel ≤★ South: 1 km via av. P. Roussel.

Plan on following page

Byblos rest,

av. P. Signac – ✆ 04 94 56 68 00 – saint-tropez@byblos.com – Fax 04 94 56 68 01 – Open 17 April-5 October Z d

52 rm – €315/490 €410/850, €35 – 44 suites

Rest *Bayader* – *✆ 04 94 56 68 19 (closed Sunday and Monday except July-August) (dinner only)* Menu €52 – Carte €53/82

Rest *Spoon Byblos* – *✆ 04 94 56 68 20 (closed Tuesday and Wednesday off season) (dinner only)* Menu €69 – Carte €56/104

◆ A hamlet of richly tinted houses separated by gardens and patios, this luxurious Provençal residence is among the exclusive places of St-Tropez. Colourful cocktails and southern flavours. Creative food, world wines and a design ambiance.

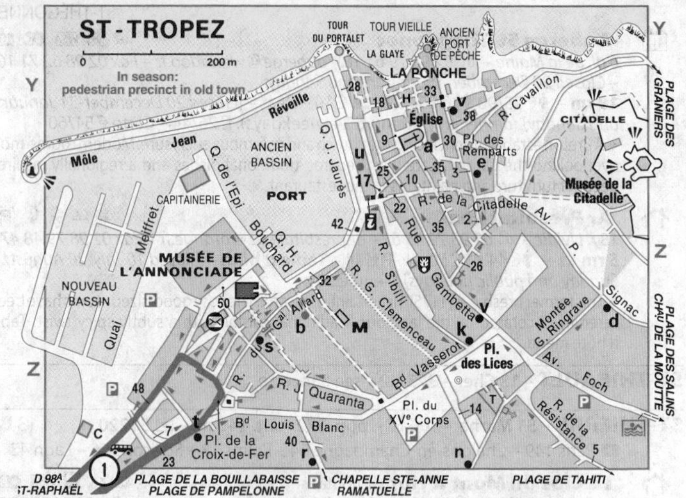

Street			Street			Street		
Aire du Chemin (R.)	Y	2	Herbes (Pl. aux)	Y	17	Péri (Quai Gabriel)	Z	32
Aumale (Bd d')	Y	3	Hôtel de ville (Pl. de l')	Y	18	Ponche (R. de la)	Y	33
Belle Isnarde (Rte de la)	Z	5	Laugier (R. V.)	Y	22	Portail Neuf (R. du)	YZ	35
Blanqui (Pl. Auguste)	Z	7	Leclerc (Av. Général)	Z	23	Remparts (R. des)	Y	38
Clocher (R. du)	Y	9	Marché (R. du)	Y	25	Roussel (Av. Paul)	Z	40
Commerçants (R. des)	Y	10	Miséricorde (R.)	Z	26	Suffren (Quai)	Y	42
Grangeon (Av.)	Z	14	Mistral (Quai Frédéric)	Y	28	8-Mai-1945 (Av. du)	Z	48
Guichard (R. du Cdt)	Y	15	Ormeau (Pl. de l')	Y	30	11-Novembre (Av. du)	Z	50

Résidence de la Pinède
1 km via ①, at Bouillabaisse beach – gulf of St - Tropez, rm, VISA
– *℘ 04 94 55 91 00 – reservation@residencepinede.com – Fax 04 94 97 73 64*
– Open 1st May-7 October

35 rm – †€ 380/395 ††€ 465/945, ☕ € 29 – 4 suites

Rest – *(dinner only)* Menu € 95/170 – Carte € 135/207

Spec. Cannelloni de homard au curry. Suprême de volaillle de Bresse cuit en vessie, macaroni truffés. Millefeuille aux framboises, chiboust à la rose. **Wines** Cassis, Côtes de Provence.

◆ This elegant house by the sea combines luxury and well-being. Cosy individually decorated rooms. Private beach and jetty. Refined dining room, with wood panelling and pleasant terrace under the pine trees with views of the Mediterranean.

La Bastide de St-Tropez
rm, VISA
Carles road: 1 km on av. P. Roussel -Z –
℘ 04 94 55 82 55 – contact@bastidesaint-tropez.com – Fax 04 94 97 21 71
– Closed 1st January-7 February

18 rm – †€ 235/620 ††€ 235/620, ☕ € 25 – 8 suites

Rest – Menu € 65 – Carte € 52/88

◆ Fine interior decoration, large bedrooms with terraces or balconies and swimming pool surrounded by a luxuriant garden contribute to the charm of these five Provence houses. Small dining room and veranda, prettily decorated. Open terrace facing a lush garden.

Domaine de l'Astragale
rm, rm, rest, VISA
1,5 km by ①, chemin de la Gassine
✉ 83580 Gassin – *℘ 04 94 97 48 98 – message@lastragale.com*
– Fax 04 94 97 16 01 – Open beg. May-end September

34 rm – †€ 300/440 ††€ 300/440, ☕ € 20 – 16 suites – **Rest** – Menu € 55 – Carte € 66/86

◆ Villa with colourful extensions set around the swimming pool. Spacious bedrooms with balcony or terrace. Meals are served in winter in a small bourgeois dining room and in summer in an open-air pavilion.

Pan Deï Palais

52 r. Gambetta – ✆ 04 94 17 71 71 – saint-tropez@pandei.com – Fax 04 94 17 72 Z **v**

11 rm – €195/480 €195/970, ☕ €30 – 1 suite

Rest – *(closed Monday from January to March)* Carte €59/94

♦ A peaceful atmosphere reigns in this mansion built for an Indian princess in 1835. Sheltered garden and swimming pool, peaceful exotic interior and hammam. Innovative cuisine served in an intimate dining room. A lighter menu is available at lunchtime.

Le Yaca

1 bd Aumale – ✆ 04 94 55 81 00 – hotel-le-yaca@wanadoo.fr – Fax 04 94 97 58 50 – Open Easter-30 October Y **e**

25 rm – €270/350 €320/600, ☕ €25 – 3 suites

Rest – *(closed Monday except July-August) (dinner only)* Carte €55/83

♦ Three beautiful ivy-clad adjoining houses (18C) popular with De Funès, well-known St Tropez actor. Luxurious rooms with antique furniture. Enjoy inventive Italian cuisine on the intimate poolside terrace.

La Mandarine — rm, rest,

rte de Tahiti, 0.5 km south by Ave P. Roussel – ✆ 04 94 79 06 66 – message@hotellamandarine.com – Fax 04 94 97 33 67 – Open beg. May-mid October

44 rm – €245/420 €245/620, ☕ €20

Rest – *(dinner only)* Menu €55 – Carte €48/84

♦ Original design for this hotel made up of several maisonettes surrounding a venerable olive tree. Ask for a refurbished room. Pleasant piano-bar. Small dining room-veranda brightened up by a fresco. Simplified set menus at lunchtime, à la carte menu in the evening.

La Ponche

pl. Révelin – ✆ 04 94 97 02 53 – hotel@laponche.com – Fax 04 94 97 78 61 – Open 15 February-1st November Y **v**

17 rm – €150/260 €190/305, ☕ €19 – 1 suite

Rest – Menu €25 (lunch)/38 – Carte €41/86

♦ Romy Schneider and many other celebrities stayed in this charming hotel made up of colourful old fishermen's houses in the picturesque Ponche district. The Provençal spirit can be felt in the decor and dishes of this restaurant.

Y without rest

av. Paul Signac – ✆ 04 94 55 55 15 – hotel-le-y@wanadoo.fr – Fax 04 94 55 55 19 – Closed 26 March-20 May and 30 October-27 December Z **d**

11 rm – €295/525 €295/525, ☕ €25 – 2 suites

♦ This Provençal building at the foot of the citadel houses very comfortable rooms with modern facilities (plasma screen and perfect soundproofing).

La Mistralée

1 av. Gén. Leclerc – ✆ 04 98 12 91 12 – contact@hotel-mistralee.fr – Fax 04 94 43 48 43 Z **t**

8 rm – €190/460 €190/460, ☕ €20 – 2 suites

Rest – *(closed 10 October-30 April except week-ends)* Carte €50/80

♦ Former pied-à-terre of Alexandre de Paris, this villa (1870) surrounded by a garden retains the decorative baroque style which the hairdresser of the stars liked. Individually styled rooms. Restaurant serving Mediterranean and Oriental cuisine.

La Maison Blanche without rest

pl. des Lices – ✆ 04 94 97 52 66 – hotellamaisonblanche@wanadoo.fr – Fax 04 94 97 89 23 – Closed February Z **k**

9 rm – €180/390 €180/780, ☕ €30

♦ This fine residence was once owned by a St. Tropez doctor. An immaculate design decor, a champagne bar and a delightful terrace: the house is starting its second life.

Pastis without rest

61 av. Gén. Leclerc, via ① – ✆ 04 98 12 56 50 – reception@pastis-st-tropez.com – Fax 04 94 96 99 82

9 rm – €200/600 €200/600, ☕ €30

♦ Antique, provençal, oriental and contemporary furnishings and objets d'art: each room of this magnificent hotel is unique. The rooms overlooking the pool and garden are quieter.

Des Lices without rest
av. Augustin Grangeon – ✆ 04 94 97 28 28 – contact@hoteldeslices.com – Fax 04 94 97 59 52 – Open 21 March-12 November and 26 December-7 January
42 rm – €85/190 €130/300, €15 Z **n**
◆ Near the famous Place des Lices, a 1970s building. There is a spacious reception lounge and neat rooms with functional furnishings.

Villa les Chamerops without rest
South by Route Belle Isnarde, towards Tahiti beach – ✆ 04 94 97 57 18 – info@villa-chamerops.com – Fax 04 94 97 58 30 – Open from mid March to mid October
10 rm – €150/305 €150/458, €13
◆ This recent hotel gets its name from a species of dwarf palm tree. Spacious rooms, discreetly decorated in modern style; most are on the ground floor and all face the swimming pool.

Mouillage without rest
port du Pilon, via ① – ✆ 04 94 97 53 19 – contact@hotelmouillage.fr – Fax 04 94 97 50 31 – Closed mid November-mid December
12 rm – €100/240 €100/240, €15
◆ Drop anchor just a cable's length from Pilon harbour in this hotel decorated in glistening Provençal colours. Rooms furnished in Moroccan and Asian styles.

Playa without rest
57 r. Allard – ✆ 04 98 12 94 44 – playahotel@aol.com – Fax 04 98 12 94 45 – Open from March to October Z **s**
16 rm – €90/235 €90/247, €12
◆ At the foot of the establishment, a plethora of shops and restaurants! The decoration of the rooms is tastefully simple. Breakfast on the patio with a glass roof.

Lou Cagnard without rest
av. P. Roussel – ✆ 04 94 97 04 24 – Fax 04 94 97 09 44 – Closed 1st November-27 December Z **r**
19 rm – €52/64 €62/122, €9
◆ This old St Tropez house is gradually renovating its rooms, which are simply furnished. In summer, breakfast is served in the shade of the mulberry trees. Families welcome.

Le Banh Hoï
12 r. Petit St-Jean – ✆ 04 94 97 36 29 – banh-hoi@wanadoo.fr – Fax 04 98 12 91 47 – Open 4 April-11 October Y **a**
Rest – *(dinner only)* Carte €50/58
◆ Dimmed lighting, walls and ceiling painted with black lacquer, and Asian decorative objects make up the setting of this house where you will be offered Vietnamese and Thai cuisine.

Le Petit Charron
6 r. Charrons – ✆ 04 94 97 73 78 – c-benoit@wanadoo.fr – Fax 04 94 56 55 78 – Open 16 March-30 October and closed 1st-15 August and Sunday Z **b**
Rest – *(dinner only) (number of covers limited, pre-book)* Menu €49/51 – Carte €49/57
◆ Simplicity is the key to this small family-run restaurant with its bistro-style decor, *La Nioulargue* pennants and posters on the walls, and tasty regional cuisine (dinner only).

South-East by Avenue Foch - Z – ✉ **83990 St-Tropez**

Benkiraï
11 chemin du Pinet, at 3 km – ✆ 04 94 97 04 37 – info@hotel-benkirai.com – Fax 04 94 97 04 98 – Open beg. April-mid October
39 rm – €240/1150 €240/1150, €24 – **Rest** – Menu €70 – Carte €52/66
◆ The minimalist look of the rooms in this brand new hotel is the work of designer Patrick Jouin. Almost all of them have a balcony or terrace overlooking the pool and bar. Distinctive contemporary dining room serving subtle Thai cuisine.

La Bastide des Salins without rest
4 km – ✆ 04 94 97 24 57 – info@labastidedessalins.com – Fax 04 94 54 89 03 – Open from March to October
14 rm – €200/550 €200/550, €27
◆ Former country house alone in a large and impeccably well-kept garden of trees and flowers. Spacious rooms, pleasantly simple. Salon with plenty of character. Beautiful swimming pool.

Le Levant without rest
2.5 km – 04 94 97 33 33 – lelevant@hotelleriedusoleil.com – Fax 04 94 97 76 13 – Open 18 April-18 October
28 rm – €85/150 €85/230, €15
◆ The well-kept rooms, occupying several bungalows, are all on a level with the lush garden or pool. Stylish lounge.

South-East by Avenue Paul Roussel and Tahiti road

Château de la Messardière rm, rest,
2 km on ✉ 83990 – 04 94 56 76 00 – hotel@messardiere.com – Fax 04 94 56 76 01 – Open 21 March-3 November
75 rm – €300/800 €300/800, €28 – 40 suites
Rest – *(closed Monday dinner except from June to August)* Menu €50 (lunch), €68 € (dinner)/112 – Carte €85/104
◆ In a 10ha pinewood overlooking the bay, this 19C castle and luxurious villas surround a patio. A festival of ochre colours and oriental touches. Elegant Provencal dining room and flower-decked terrace with magnificent views of the sea.

Ferme d'Augustin without rest
4 km ✉ 83350 – 04 94 55 97 00 – info@fermeaugustin.com – Fax 04 94 97 59 76 – Open April-October
46 rm – €110/625 €155/625, €14
◆ 100m from Tahiti beach, buildings surrounded by greenery and flowers. Choose the pretty refurbished rooms. Lounge decorated with ornaments. Attentive family welcome.

St-Vincent rm, rm,
4 km ✉ 83350 – 04 94 97 36 90 – hotelsaintvincent@wanadoo.fr – Fax 04 94 54 80 37 – Open 20 March-12 October
20 rm – €110/250 €110/250, €15 – **Rest** – pool restaurant *(open 1st May-14 September and closed Monday)* Carte €32/40
◆ In the peaceful setting of a vineyard, four Provençal houses decorated with oleanders. Spacious rooms some with terrace. Beautiful garden. Sun-flavoured recipes, grilled food and salads to enjoy by the pool.

Mas Bellevue rm, rest,
2 km ✉ 83990 – 04 94 97 07 21 – masbellevue@wanadoo.fr – Fax 04 94 97 61 07 – Open 23 April-3 November
46 rm – €95/285 €95/285 – ½ P €78/173 – **Rest** – pool restaurant Carte €39/69
◆ Accessible by a path, a Provence house surrounded by bungalows nestling in a lovely park. Spacious rooms with balconies. Panoramic swimming pools. Rustic dining room and terrace where a small menu is served at lunchtime and a more substantial choice is on offer for dinner.

La Figuière rm, rm,
4 km ✉ 83350 – 04 94 97 18 21 – la.figuiere@wanadoo.fr – Fax 04 94 97 68 48 – Open 20 March-6 October
41 rm – €100/145 €125/250, €13
Rest – rest. de piscine Carte €33/57
◆ Set amid vineyards, a restored farm with rooms that are simply but individually decorated and contain antique furniture. The duplex rooms are the most recent. Beside the swimming pool, a terrace set in the shade of the mulberry trees with kitchen and grill visible to all.

Ramatuelle road by ① and D 93le – ✉ 83350 Ramatuelle

La Romarine rm, rm,
quartier des Marres, (Beach road), 3 km on via secondary road – 04 94 97 32 26 – hromarine@aol.com – Fax 04 94 97 44 45 – Open 4 April-12 October
18 rm – €160/235 €160/235, €12 – 9 suites
Rest *La Romarine* – pool restaurant *(open July-August)* Carte €25/38
◆ In a park designed for relaxation and leisure, this village-hotel contains spacious rooms and villas which are particularly well-equipped for families. Simple meals served under the terrace parasols, facing the pool.

Les Bouis — sea, rm, rm, VISA MC AE

on secondary road – 04 94 79 87 61 – hotellesbouis@aol.com – Fax 04 94 79 85 20 – Open 25 March-15 October

23 rm – €170/218 €218/240, €14 – **Rest** – pool restaurant *(open 15 April-30 September) (lunch only) (residents only)* Menu €25 bi/35 bi

◆ Fine location on the heights surrounding St Tropez for this hotel surrounded by stone pines. Neat refreshing rooms. Pleasant patio. Family style dishes and grills served on the poolside terrace.

Deï Marres without rest — VISA MC AE

at 3 km on secondary road – 04 94 97 26 68 – hoteldeimarres@wanadoo.fr – Fax 04 94 97 62 76 – Open 15 March-10 October

24 rm – €84/135 €99/190, €10

◆ Note for tennis lovers: this family hotel in a green setting has four tennis courts. If you want more space and comfort, book a room in the annexe.

Auberge de l'Oumède with rm — rm, rm, VISA MC AE

at 7 km on secondary road – 04 94 44 11 11 – contact@aubergedeloumede.com – Fax 04 94 79 93 63 – Open Easter-30 November and 25 December-5 January

7 rm – €150/370 €150/370, €20 – **Rest** – *(closed Wednesday April-June) (dinner only in July-August)* Carte €69/102

◆ On a road surrounded by vineyards, this welcoming dining room is extended by a small corner lounge, bistro and a terrace under mulberry trees. Up-to-date menu. Three attractive Provençal-style rooms arranged around the heated pool.

via ① and secondary road – 83580 Gassin

Villa Belrose — gulf of St - Tropez, rm, rest, VISA MC AE

bd des Crêtes, 3 km – 04 94 55 97 97 – info@villabelrose.com – Fax 04 94 55 97 98 – Open 25 March-26 October

40 rm – €220/500 €280/830, €30 – 3 suites

Rest – *(closed lunch July-August)* Menu €55 (lunch), €90/175 bi – Carte €87/150

Spec. Langoustines royales crues et cuites, citrons de Menton, légumes et herbes (July-August). Grosse pièce de bar confite à l'huile de Ligurie (July-August). Pigeon de Racan comme un coq au vin (July-August). **Wines** Côtes de Provence.

◆ Ideal location for this villa-hotel with three terraces facing the sea. Opulent interior and very comfortable rooms. Elegant restaurant decorated in the Florentine style with a pleasant terrace offering pretty views of the gulf.

ST-VAAST-LA-HOUGUE – 50 Manche – 303 E2 – pop. 2 097 – alt. 4 m – 50550 Normandy

32 **A1**

Paris 347 – Carentan 41 – Cherbourg 31 – St-Lô 68 – Valognes 19

Office de tourisme, 1, place Général de Gaulle 02 33 23 19 32, Fax 02 33 54 41 37

La Granitière without rest — VISA MC AE

74 r. Mar. Foch – 02 33 54 58 99 – contact@hotel-la-granitiere.com – Fax 02 33 20 34 91

10 rm – €55/80 €55/106, €9

◆ A resort and a fishing village, "St-Va" is home to this fine old house of grey granite where you will really feel at home. Individually styled rooms and cosy lounge.

France et Fuchsias — rest, VISA MC AE

20 r. Mar. Foch – 02 33 54 40 41 – reception@france-fuchsias.com – Fax 02 33 43 46 79 – Closed 1st-10 December, 4 January-20 February, Tuesday lunch and Monday except July-August and Tuesday dinner from November to March

35 rm – €48/132 €48/132, €10,50 – ½ P €59/99

Rest – Menu (€21), €28/62 – Carte €48/99

◆ Pleasant family hotel where fuchsias abound in an elegant garden of palm trees, mimosas and eucalypti. Simple rooms; larger and more recent in the annexe. Dining room-veranda, attractive terrace and good traditional cuisine enhanced by local specialities.

Le Chasse Marée

8 pl. Gén. de Gaulle – ☎ 02 33 23 14 08 – Closed from mid December to January, Monday and Tuesday except from July to September
Rest – Menu € 16 (weekday lunch), € 21/30 – Carte € 24/66
◆ Photos of boats and pennants left by sailing guests decorate this pleasant little restaurant and terrace on the port. Locally fished produce served.

ST-VALERY-EN-CAUX – 76 Seine-Maritime – 304 E2 – pop. 4 782 – alt. 5 m – Casino – ✉ 76460 Normandy 33 C1

Paris 190 – Bolbec 46 – Dieppe 35 – Fécamp 33 – Le Havre 80 – Rouen 59 – Yvetot 31
Office de tourisme, Maison Henri IV ☎ 02 35 97 00 63, Fax 02 35 97 32 65
Falaise d'Aval ≤★ West: 15 mn.

Du Casino

VISA MC AE

14 av. Clemenceau – ☎ 02 35 57 88 00 – contact@hotel-casino-saintvalery.com – Fax 02 35 57 88 88
76 rm – †€ 75/94 ††€ 81/100, ☕ € 11 – ½ P € 71/78 – **Rest** – Menu (€ 18), € 22/40 – Carte € 26/42
◆ This fully-renovated hotel has spacious rooms with simple and restful contemporary decoration. Half the rooms overlook the harbour. Restaurant with a modern setting, simply-laid tables and up-to-date cuisine.

Les Remparts without rest

VISA MC

4 r. des Bains – ☎ 02 35 97 16 13 – Fax 02 35 97 19 89 – Closed 1st-7 January
15 rm – †€ 40 ††€ 46/56, ☕ € 7
◆ Small, pleasant hotel, near the sea and cliffs. Perfectly well-kept rooms, adorned with antique furniture (1930s style). Very friendly welcome.

La Maison des Galets without rest

VISA MC

22 cour Le Perrey – ☎ 02 35 97 11 22 – contact@lamaisondesgalets.fr – Fax 02 35 97 05 83 – Closed 12-25 January
14 rm – †€ 39/43 ††€ 60/79, ☕ € 9
◆ Hotel and bedrooms renovated in a minimalist style, some facing the sea. Continental or regional breakfasts served in a panoramic breakfast room.

Du Port

≤ VISA MC

quai d'Amont – ☎ 02 35 97 08 93 – Fax 02 35 97 28 32 – Closed Sunday dinner, Thursday dinner and Monday
Rest – Menu € 23/41 – Carte € 40/77
◆ Tucked behind the appealing façade are two small restaurants with views of the boats entering the harbour. Fish and seafood specialities.

Southeast 7 km by D 20 and D 70 - ✉ 76740 Ermenouville

Château du Mesnil Geoffroy without rest

≤ P VISA MC

– ☎ 02 35 57 12 77 – contact@chateau-mesnil-geoffroy.com – Fax 02 35 57 10 24
5 rm – †€ 80/85 ††€ 80/140, ☕ € 10
◆ A château set in a park with a rose garden. Louis XV style rooms, an 18C period breakfast room, and a table d'hôte offering 18C inspired dishes on Saturday evenings.

Fécamp road 3 km to Le Bourg-Ingouville by D 925 and D 68 – ✉ 76460 Ingouville-sur-Mer

Les Hêtres with rm

P VISA MC

24 r. des Fleurs – ☎ 02 35 57 09 30 – leshetres@wanadoo.fr – Fax 02 35 57 09 31 – Closed 12 January-12 February, Tuesday lunch Easter-September, Wednesday lunch and Tuesday October-March and Monday
5 rm – †€ 90/160 ††€ 90/160, ☕ € 17
Rest – Menu € 40/85 – Carte € 80/108
◆ Attractive 17C longhouse surrounded by a well-kept garden. Antique furniture, exposed beams and a superb stone fireplace provide a refined dining room setting. Inventive cuisine.

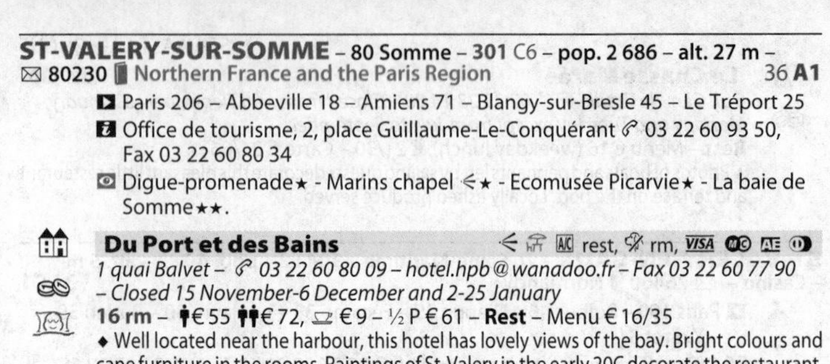

ST-VALERY-SUR-SOMME – 80 Somme – 301 C6 – pop. 2 686 – alt. 27 m – ✉ 80230 Northern France and the Paris Region 36 A1

Paris 206 – Abbeville 18 – Amiens 71 – Blangy-sur-Bresle 45 – Le Tréport 25

Office de tourisme, 2, place Guillaume-Le-Conquérant ✆ 03 22 60 93 50, Fax 03 22 60 80 34

Digue-promenade★ - Marins chapel ≤★ - Ecomusée Picarvie★ - La baie de Somme★★.

Du Port et des Bains
≤ rest, rm, VISA AE

1 quai Balvet – ✆ 03 22 60 80 09 – hotel.hpb@wanadoo.fr – Fax 03 22 60 77 90 – Closed 15 November-6 December and 2-25 January

16 rm – †€ 55 ††€ 72, ☕ € 9 – ½ P € 61 – **Rest** – Menu € 16/35

◆ Well located near the harbour, this hotel has lovely views of the bay. Bright colours and cane furniture in the rooms. Paintings of St-Valery in the early 20C decorate the restaurant. Traditional dishes and seafood.

Picardia without rest
P VISA AE

41 quai Romerel – ✆ 03 22 60 32 30 – contact@picardia.fr – Fax 03 22 60 76 69 – Closed 7-26 January

26 rm – †€ 80 ††€ 80/140, ☕ € 11

◆ This welcoming country house stands next to the small medieval quarter. Bright and spacious guestrooms - those with a mezzanine are perfect for families.

Le Relais Guillaume de Normandy
≤ rest, rest, P VISA AE

46 quai Romerel – ✆ 03 22 60 82 36 – relaisguillaumedenormandy@akeonet.com – Fax 03 22 60 81 82 – Closed 21 December-11 January and Tuesday except from 15 July to 19 August

14 rm – †€ 53 ††€ 62/80, ☕ € 9 – ½ P € 62/72

Rest – Menu € 18/42 – Carte € 26/59

◆ Guillaume (William) left Saint-Valéry to conquer England. This pretty brick manor facing the bay of the Somme houses a few practical rooms, some of which have been renovated. The panoramic dining room offers a pleasant view of the sea; summer terrace and classic menu.

Le Nicol's
VISA AE

15 r. La Ferté – ✆ 03 22 26 82 96 – nicols@wanadoo.fr – Fax 03 22 60 97 46 – Closed Wednesday dinner, Monday, Thursday October-March, Monday dinner and Wednesday May-June

Rest – Menu € 15/32 – Carte € 21/52

◆ This restaurant in a central shopping street has a lovely regional facade and a warm, rustic dining area serving traditional meals with an emphasis on produce from the sea.

in Noyelles-sur-Mer – pop. 742 – alt. 7 m – ✉ 80860

Auberge du Château de Nolette
P VISA AE

4 rte Ponthoile – ✆ 03 22 23 24 15 – hotel.hpb@wanadoo.fr – Fax 03 22 23 21 81 – Open 16 March-14 November and closed Monday from 15 March to 30 April

10 rm – †€ 55 ††€ 72, ☕ € 9 – ½ P € 61 – **Rest** – Menu € 15 (weekdays)/35

◆ Ideally situated for discovering the bay of the Somme, this 17C castle-farm with a garden welcomes you in renovated and individually styled rooms. Pleasant dining room-veranda; traditional cuisine.

ST-VALLIER – 26 Drôme – 332 B2 – pop. 4 154 – alt. 135 m – ✉ 26240 Lyon - Rhone Valley 43 E2

Paris 526 – Annonay 21 – St-Étienne 61 – Tournon-sur-Rhône 16 – Valence 35 – Vienne 41

Office de tourisme, avenue Désiré Valette ✆ 04 75 23 45 33, Fax 04 75 23 44 19

d'Albon Saint-Rambert-d'Albon Château de Senaud, North: 9 km by N 7 and D 122, ✆ 04 75 03 03 90.

Le Bistrot d'Albert et Hôtel Terminus with rm
P VISA AE

116 av. J. Jaurès, (Lyon road) – ✆ 04 75 23 01 12 – bistrot.albert@wanadoo.fr – Fax 04 75 23 38 82 – Closed 17-28 August and February school holidays

10 rm – †€ 54 ††€ 58, ☕ € 7 – **Rest** – Menu € 15/29 – Carte € 24/34

◆ High ceilings, a luminous veranda and tasty market-based cuisine: friendly atmosphere guaranteed in this bistro near the station. Small, practical rooms.

Northeast 8 km by N 7, D 122 and D 132 – ✉ 26140 Albon

Domaine des Buis

rte de St-Martin-des-Rosiers – ✆ 04 75 03 14 14 – info@domaine-des-buis.com – Fax 04 75 03 14 14 – Open beg. March-end November
7 rm – †€ 95/120 ††€ 95/120, ☕ € 12 – 1 suite
Rest – *(dinner only) (residents only)* Menu € 30
♦ An 18C residence, in a park surrounded by hills with the fragrance of cedar and magnolia. Spacious rooms, with English furniture. "Guest house" atmosphere. Dinner prepared by the *patronne* and served in a most refined dining room.

ST-VALLIER – 71 Saône-et-Loire – 320 G10 – see Montceau-les-Mines

---

ST-VALLIER-DE-THIEY – 06 Alpes-Maritimes – 341 C5 – pop. 2 261 – alt. 730 m – ✉ 06460 French Riviera

42 **E2**

Paris 907 – Cannes 29 – Castellane 52 – Draguignan 57 – Grasse 12 – Nice 47
Syndicat d'initiative, 10, place du Tour ✆ 04 93 42 78 00, Fax 04 93 42 78 00
Pas de la Faye ≤★★ Northwest: 5 km - Grotte de Beaume Obscure★ South: 2 km - Col de la Lèque ≤★ Southwest: 5 km.

Le Relais Impérial

(2 and 4 pl. Cavalier Fabre), Napoléon road – ✆ 04 92 60 36 36 – info@relaisimperial.com – Fax 04 92 60 36 39
28 rm – †€ 40/55 ††€ 50/75, ☕ € 10 – ½ P € 50/63
Rest – Menu (€ 14), € 19 (weekday lunch), € 26/41 – Carte € 28/44
Rest *Le Grill du Relais* – pizzeria – *✆ 04 92 60 36 30* – Menu (€ 13), € 19 – Carte € 25/40
♦ This former coaching inn along the Route Napoléon (the Emperor stopped here on 2 March, 1815) has small, partly-renovated, rustic rooms. Traditional cuisine served in a Louis XIII style dining room or on the veranda. Pizzas and simple dishes at the Grill.

ST-VÉRAN – 05 Hautes-Alpes – 334 J4 – pop. 267 – alt. 2 042 m – the highest commune in Europe – Winter sports : 1 750/3 000 m 15 – ✉ 05350 French Alps

41 **C1**

Paris 729 – Briançon 49 – Guillestre 32
Office de tourisme, la ville ✆ 04 92 45 82 21, Fax 04 92 45 84 52
Old village★★ - Musée du Soum★.

L'Astragale

– ✆ 04 92 45 87 00 – astragale@queyras.com – Fax 04 92 45 87 10 – Open 13 June-30 August and 19 December-30 March
21 rm – †€ 86/165 ††€ 100/244, ☕ € 14,50 – ½ P € 72/144
Rest – *(dinner only)* Menu € 24/26
♦ This modern and regularly revamped chalet has considerable charm, with its mountain-style setting, large comfortable rooms (all with a video player) and view of the mountain peaks:. A welcoming dining room with fireplace. Tea room.

ST-VÉRAND – 71 Saône-et-Loire – 320 I12 – pop. 182 – alt. 300 m – ✉ 71570

8 **C3**

Paris 401 – Bourg-en-Bresse 49 – Lyon 66 – Mâcon 14 – Villefranche-sur-Saône 35

Auberge du St-Véran

– ✆ 03 85 23 90 90 – direction@auberge-saint-veran.com – Fax 03 85 23 90 91 – Closed 6-29 January, Monday and Tuesday off season
11 rm – †€ 48 ††€ 68, ☕ € 10 – ½ P € 70/73 – **Rest** – Menu € 20 (weekday lunch)/52 – Carte € 31/49
♦ Old water mill with real country charm in the heart of the vineyards. The comfortable bedrooms have all been named after local vintages. Regional cuisine served in a rustic-style restaurant, with a terrace overlooking the swimming pool. Traditional cuisine and good choice of Mâcon and Beaujolais wines.

ST VIANCE – 19 Corrèze – 329 J4 – pop. 1 413 – alt. 119 m – ✉ 19240
Dordogne-Berry-Limousin 24 **B3**

Paris 479 – Limoges 90 – Tulle 45 – Brive-la-Gaillarde 12 – Sarlat-la-Canéda 67

Auberge sur Vézère rest, VISA
Le bourg – ✆ 05 55 84 28 23 – aubergesurvezere@wanadoo.fr – Fax 05 55 84 42 47 – Closed 20 December-30 January and Sunday except July-August
10 rm – €57/60 €62/65, €8 – ½ P €55/80 – **Rest** – *(closed Saturday lunch, Sunday dinner and Monday) (pre-book)* Menu €20 (weekday lunch), €25/37
♦ This small country inn at the entrance to the village is run by a friendly Franco-British couple. Functional but well-appointed guestrooms. The menu served in the Provençal-style dining room or under the trees on the terrace is resolutely contemporary.

ST-VIATRE – 41 Loir-et-Cher – 318 I6 – pop. 1 188 – alt. 107 m – ✉ 41210 12 **C2**

Paris 179 – Orléans 53 – Blois 106 – Vierzon 53 – Fleury-les-Aubrais 60

Villepalay without rest
2 km on Nouan le Fuzelier road – ✆ 02 54 88 22 35 – navucet@wanadoo.fr – Closed March
3 rm – €53/65 €58/70
♦ A warm welcome at this old Sologne farm with bucolic charm. Well turned out bedrooms and organic breakfast.

ST-VICTOR – 03 Allier – 326 C4 – see Montluçon

ST-VICTOR-DE-MALCAP – 30 Gard – 339 K3 – see St-Ambroix

ST-VICTOR-DES-OULES – 30 Gard – 339 L4 – pop. 219 – alt. 168 m – ✉ 30700 23 **D2**

Paris 686 – Montpellier 101 – Nîmes 56 – Avignon 45 – Arles 82

Villa Saint Victor rest, VISA
pl. du Château – ✆ 04 66 81 90 47 – info@villasaintvictor.com – Fax 04 66 81 93 30 – Closed 24 November-15 December and 5 January-28 February
19 rm – €70/140 €90/230, €15 – ½ P €110/140
Rest – *(closed Sunday dinner and Monday)* Menu €18 (weekday lunch)/39
♦ An informal ambience reigns throughout this small 19C castle set in wooded parkland. Personalised interior of antiques, 1940s or boudoir style; Jouy wall hangings. Two separate pavilions. Meals (evenings by reservation) feature market fresh, regionally inspired cuisine.

ST-VICTOR-SUR-LOIRE – 42 Loire – 327 E7 – see St-Étienne

ST-VINCENT – 43 Haute-Loire – 331 F3 – pop. 831 – alt. 605 m – ✉ 43800 6 **C3**

Paris 543 – La Chaise-Dieu 37 – Le Puy-en-Velay 18 – St-Étienne 76

La Renouée VISA
at Cheyrac, 2 km northward along the D 103 – ✆ 04 71 08 55 94 – auberge.larenouee@laposte.net – Fax 04 71 08 15 89 – Closed autumn half-term holidays, 5 January-5 March, Tuesday dinner, Wednesday dinner and Thursday dinner from 29 October to 31 March, Sunday dinner and Monday
Rest – Menu €19/43 – Carte €21/36
♦ A hundred year-old establishment with a little garden in front. A huge stone hearth and a lovely cherry wood dresser adorn the main dining room. Creative regional fare.

ST-VINCENT-DE-TYROSSE – 40 Landes – 335 D13 – pop. 5 360 – alt. 24 m – ✉ 40230 3 B3

▶ Paris 743 – Anglet 32 – Bayonne 29 – Bordeaux 157

ℹ Office de tourisme, placette du Midi ✆ 05 58 77 12 00, Fax 05 58 77 12 00

Le Hittau

1 r. du Nouaou – ✆ 05 58 77 11 85 – hittau@orange.fr – Closed 1st-9 July, 21 October-5 November, 19 February-12 March, Tuesday except 14 July-30 August and Wednesday

Rest – Menu € 34/70 – Carte approx. € 46

◆ This former sheepcote has a certain charm, with its exposed timberwork and monumental fireplace. Pleasant garden terrace. Up-to-date cuisine using regional produce.

ST-VINCENT-SUR-JARD – 85 Vendée – 316 G9 – pop. 871 – alt. 10 m – ✉ 85520 Atlantic Coast 34 B3

▶ Paris 454 – Luçon 34 – La Rochelle 70 – La Roche-sur-Yon 35 – Les Sables-d'Olonne 23

ℹ Syndicat d'initiative, place de l'Eglise ✆ 02 51 33 62 06, Fax 02 51 33 01 23

L'Océan

rm, rest,

1 km south: (near Clemenceau's house) – ✆ 02 51 33 40 45 – hotel.locean@wanadoo.fr – Fax 02 51 33 98 15 – Closed 18 November-23 February and Wednesday October-March

37 rm – †€ 51/85 ††€ 51/85, ☕ € 7 – ½ P € 52/72 – **Rest** – Menu € 21/60 – Carte € 26/45

◆ Not far from the beach, the impressive seaside villa has been run by the same family for three generations. Simple rooms, garden shaded by pine trees and veranda for breakfasts. The restaurant serves a classic repertoire emphasising seafood.

Le Chalet St-Hubert

rte de Jard – ✆ 02 51 33 40 33 – lechaletsthubert@orange.fr – Fax 02 51 33 41 94 – Closed 1st-15 October, 23 February-8 March, Sunday dinner and Monday off season

Rest – Menu € 16/32 – Carte € 25/45

◆ An old house with a wood-panelled dining room serving traditional cuisine with the emphasis on fish and seafood.

ST-YBARD – 19 Corrèze – 329 K3 – see Uzerche

ST-YORRE – 03 Allier – 326 H6 – see Vichy

ST-ZACHARIE – 83 Var – 340 J5 – pop. 4 184 – alt. 265 m – ✉ 83640 40 B3

▶ Paris 786 – Aix-en-Provence 37 – Brignoles 31 – Marseille 34 – Rians 40 – Toulon 63

ℹ Office de tourisme, square Reda Caire ✆ 04 42 32 63 28, Fax 04 42 32 63 28

Urbain Dubois

rte St-Maximin, on D 560: 1 km – ✆ 04 42 72 94 28 – urbain-dubois@wanadoo.fr – Fax 04 42 72 94 28 – Closed Sunday evening, Tuesday lunchtime, Wednesday lunchtime and Monday except public holidays

Rest – Menu € 22 (weekday lunch), € 42/72 – Carte € 55/65

◆ This former ceramic works has been turned into a charming rustic restaurant with a lovely terrace displaying a village fresco. Inventive recipes on offer.

STE-ANNE-D'AURAY – 56 Morbihan – 308 N8 – pop. 1 844 – alt. 42 m – ✉ 56400 Brittany 9 A3

▶ Paris 475 – Auray 7 – Hennebont 33 – Locminé 27 – Lorient 44 – Quimperlé 58 – Vannes 16

ℹ Office de tourisme, 26, rue de Vannes ✆ 02 97 57 69 16, Fax 02 97 57 79 22

◉ Treasure-house★ of the basilica - Pardon (26 July).

L'Auberge
56 r. de Vannes – ✆ 02 97 57 61 55 – auberge-jl-larvoir@wanadoo.fr – Fax 02 97 57 69 10 – Closed January, Tuesday lunch and Wednesday lunch from 1st November to 23 March
16 rm – €50/80 €60/90, € 12 – 2 suites – ½ P €65/80
Rest – Menu €25/75 – Carte €43/68
◆ Two types of decor and two distinct atmospheres. A focus on Art Deco in the hotel, with its rosewood and burr elm, Mucha and Lempicka reproductions, and Lalique wall lamps. The regional style auberge is decorated with attractive Breton furniture. South facing terrace in the garden. New guestrooms (two suites) with modern comforts. Contemporary cuisine.

Myriam without rest
35 bis r. Parc – ✆ 02 97 57 70 44 – contact@hotellemyriam.com – Fax 02 97 57 67 49 – Open 15 February-15 November
30 rm – €48/58 €48/58, € 7,50
◆ This 1970s hotel in a pleasant residential area provides simple updated rooms and a breakfast area with marine decor.

STE-ANNE-DU-CASTELLET – 83 Var – 340 J6 – see le Castellet

STE-ANNE-LA-PALUD (Chapel) – 29 Finistère – 308 F6 – alt. 65 m – ✉ 29550 Brittany 9 A2

Paris 584 – Brest 68 – Châteaulin 20 – Crozon 27 – Douarnenez 12 – Quimper 24
Pardon (enf of August).

De La Plage
at the beach – ✆ 02 98 92 50 12 – laplage@relaischateaux.com – Fax 02 98 92 56 54 – Open 22 March-2 November
28 rm – €180/323 €180/323, € 19 – 4 suites – ½ P €163/234
Rest – *(dinner only except Thursday and weekends)* Menu €52/93 – Carte €76/110
◆ In an isolated shorefront location with views of the Douarnenez bay. Old-fashioned or contemporary furnishings in the rooms; good for beach walks. Seafood cuisine; both simple dining rooms have coastal views.

STE-CÉCILE – 71 Saône-et-Loire – 320 H11 – pop. 251 – alt. 250 m – ✉ 71250 8 C3

Paris 391 – Charolles 35 – Cluny 8 – Mâcon 22 – Roanne 73

L'Embellie
– ✆ 03 85 50 81 81 – sarl.delagrange@wanadoo.fr – Fax 03 85 50 81 81 – Closed 23 June-11 July, 27 October-21 November, Sunday dinner except July-August, Tuesday except lunch September-June and Wednesday
Rest – Carte €24/47
◆ A restaurant occupying former stone stables that have retained all their rustic character, with exposed beams, ashwood furniture and warm winter fireplace. Pleasant shaded summer terrace with a view of the Carmel (convent). Classic cuisine.

STE-CÉCILE-LES-VIGNES – 84 Vaucluse – 332 C8 – pop. 2 100 – alt. 108 m – ✉ 84290 40 A2

Paris 646 – Avignon 47 – Bollène 13 – Nyons 26 – Orange 17 – Vaison-la-Romaine 19

La Farigoule
26 cours M. Trintignant – ✆ 04 90 30 89 89 – farigoule.raphael@wanadoo.fr – Fax 04 90 30 78 00 – Closed 24 November-8 December and 18 February-17 March
9 rm – €47 €59, € 7 – ½ P €63 – **Rest** – *(closed Sunday evening and Monday except July-August)* Menu €18 (weekdays)/39 – Carte €39/51
◆ Attractive, recently refurbished inn situated in the centre of this village surrounded by the Côtes du Rhône vineyards. Small, functional bedrooms. Light dining room, wrought iron arbour, and terrace sheltered by lush vegetation. Regional dishes.

Campagne, Vignes et Gourmandises

rte de Suze-la-Rousse – ☎ 04 90 63 40 11 – sylfernandes@wanadoo.fr – Fax 04 90 63 40 25 – Closed 30 December-20 January, Tuesday off season and Monday

Rest – *(number of covers limited, pre-book)* Menu € 21/51 – Carte € 48/58

♦ In a peaceful residential neighbourhood, small farmhouse set amidst the vines. Country-style dining room and attractive terrace. Up-to-date cuisine with a southern accent.

STE-COLOMBE – **84 Vaucluse** – **332** E9 – **see Bédoin**

STE-CROIX – **01 Ain** – **328** D5 – **see Montluel**

STE-CROIX-DE-VERDON – **04 Alpes-de-Haute-Provence** – **334** E10 – **pop. 102** – **alt. 530 m** – ✉ **04500** French Alps 41 **C2**

Paris 780 – Brignoles 59 – Castellane 59 – Digne-les-Bains 51 – Manosque 44 – Salernes 35

L'Olivier lake,

– ☎ *04 92 77 87 95 – Fax 04 92 77 87 95 – Open from mid February to mid November and closed Monday and Tuesday except July-August*

Rest – Menu € 28/38

♦ This restaurant, in a village clinging to the cliff, invites travellers to sit down at a terrace-veranda table and admire a splendid plunging view of Lake Sainte Croix.

STE-CROIX-EN-JAREZ – **42 Loire** – **327** G7 – **see Rive-de-Gier**

STE-CROIX-EN-PLAINE – **68 Haut-Rhin** – **315** I8 – **see Colmar**

STE-ÉNIMIE – **48 Lozère** – **330** I8 – **pop. 509** – **alt. 470 m** – ✉ **48210** Languedoc-Roussillon-Tarn Gorges 23 **C1**

Paris 612 – Florac 27 – Mende 28 – Meyrueis 30 – Millau 57 – Sévérac-le-Château 49

Office de tourisme, village ☎ 04 66 48 53 44, Fax 04 66 48 47 70

★★ on the canyon du Tarn South: 6,5 km by D 986.

Auberge du Moulin rm,

r. Combe – ☎ 04 66 48 53 08 – Fax 04 66 48 58 16 – Open end March-mid November and closed Sunday evening except July-August and public holidays

10 rm – € 55/65 € 55/65, € 7,60 – ½ P € 55/60

Rest – *(closed Monday except July-August and public holidays)* Menu (€ 13,50), € 18/36 – Carte € 19/31

♦ Beautiful stone building in a village popular with tourists in an extraordinary site. Half of the spruce bedrooms face the Tarn. Opt for a quiet outdoor table overlooking the river rather than the huge dining room.

STE-EULALIE – **07 Ardèche** – **331** H5 – **pop. 253** – **alt. 1 233 m** – ✉ **07510** 44 **A3**

Paris 587 – Aubenas 47 – Langogne 47 – Privas 51 – Le Puy-en-Velay 48 – Thueyts 36

Syndicat d'initiative, Mairie ☎ 04 75 38 89 78, Fax 04 75 38 87 37

Du Nord rest,

– ☎ *04 75 38 80 09 – hotelnord.mouyon@wanadoo.fr – Fax 04 75 38 85 50 – Open 8 March-11 November and closed Tuesday dinner and Wednesday except 14 July-15 August*

15 rm – € 50/53 € 50/53, € 7,50 – ½ P € 51/54

Rest – Menu € 20/38 – Carte € 26/34

♦ Pleasant family inn popular with those who fish in the nearby River Loire. Comfortable, regularly renovated rooms. Local cuisine, a family atmosphere and a neo-rustic setting characterise this restaurant.

STE-EULALIE-D'OLT – 12 Aveyron – 338 J4 – pop. 327 – alt. 425 m – ✉ 12130

Paris 615 – Espalion 25 – Rodez 45 – Sévérac-le-Château 28 29 **D1**

Office de tourisme, rue Fon Sainte-Anne ✆ 05 65 47 82 68

Au Moulin d'Alexandre with rm

– ✆ 05 65 47 45 85 – Fax 05 65 52 73 78 – *Closed dinner from 1st November to Easter*

9 rm – €48/55 €48/55, €9 – ½ P €51 – **Rest** – *(closed Sunday dinner from November - 20 March)* Menu €13 (weekday lunch), €24/29 – Carte €37/44

♦ This 16C mill helps to liven up this charming Aveyron village: bar and newsagents, hotel and restaurant. The dining room has retained a pleasant rustic atmosphere (fireplace, exposed beams and stonework). The rooms offer rather basic comfort.

STE-EUPHÉMIE – 01 Ain – 328 B5 – pop. 1 118 – alt. 247 m – ✉ 01600 43 E1

Paris 435 – Bourg-en-Bresse 49 – Dijon 168 – Lyon 36

Au Petit Moulin

VISA

– ✆ 04 74 00 60 10 – Fax 04 74 00 60 10 – *Closed 1st February-6 March, Monday, Tuesday and Wednesday*

Rest – Menu €23 (weekdays)/30 – Carte €29/39

♦ On the menu in this modest country inn near the Dombes region: frogs, freshwater fish and poultry, carefully cooked and copiously served.

STE-FEYRE – 23 Creuse – 325 I4 – see Guéret

STE-FLORINE – 43 Haute-Loire – 331 B1 – pop. 3 002 – alt. 440 m – ✉ 43250

Paris 465 – Brioude 16 – Clermont-Fd 55 – Issoire 19 – Murat 60 – Le Puy-en-Velay 77 6 **C2**

Le Florina with rm

rm, VISA AE

pl. Hôtel de Ville – ✆ *04 73 54 04 45* – *info@hotel-leflorina.com* – *Fax 04 73 54 02 62* – *Closed 21 December-14 January*

14 rm – €35 €40/58, €6,50 – ½ P €40/50

Rest – *(closed Sunday evening)* Menu (€9,50), €15/25 – Carte €19/38

♦ This recent building houses a restaurant that offers regional specialities. Rooms are functional or, if booked ahead, more colourful and personalised.

STE-FOY-LA-GRANDE – 33 Gironde – 335 M5 – pop. 2 788 – alt. 10 m – ✉ 33220 Atlantic Coast 4 **C1**

Paris 555 – Bordeaux 71 – Langon 59 – Marmande 44 – Périgueux 67

Office de tourisme, 102, rue de la République ✆ 05 57 46 03 00, Fax 05 57 46 16 62

Chateau des Vigiers Golf Club MonestierSoutheast: 9 km by D 18, ✆ 05 53 61 50 33.

Plan on next page

Au Fil de l'Eau

VISA AE

at Port-Ste-Foy – ✆ *05 53 24 72 60* – *Fax 05 53 24 94 97* – *Closed 5-18 March, 27 October-5 November, 4 January-3 February, Wednesday dinner in winter, Sunday dinner except July-August and Monday* s

Rest – Menu €14 (weekday lunch), €21/53 – Carte €40/72

♦ The establishment might seem commonplace but it pays, especially in summertime, to seek a table on the pretty terrace overlooking the Dordogne. Regional updated cuisine.

Southeast : 8 km on D 18 – ✉ 24240 Monestier

Château des Vigiers

rm, rm, VISA AE

at the Les Vigiers Golf Course – ✆ *05 53 61 50 00* – *reception@vigiers.fr* – *Fax 05 53 61 50 20* – *Closed 16 December-26 January*

87 rm – €165/330 €165/330, €26 – ½ P €120/195

Rest ***Les Fresques*** – ✆ *05 53 61 50 39 (open 1st May-30 September and closed Tuesday and Wednesday) (dinner only)* Menu €45/70 – Carte €53/65

Rest ***Brasserie Le Chai*** – ✆ *05 53 61 50 39* – Menu (€19), €20 (weekday lunch), €35/40 – Carte €26/36

♦ This 16C chateau and its outbuildings are located in a park converted into a golf course. Rooms are spacious and personalised. Elegant decor, contemporary cuisine and wines from the estate set the scene. This brasserie is delightfully located in a former wine cellar.

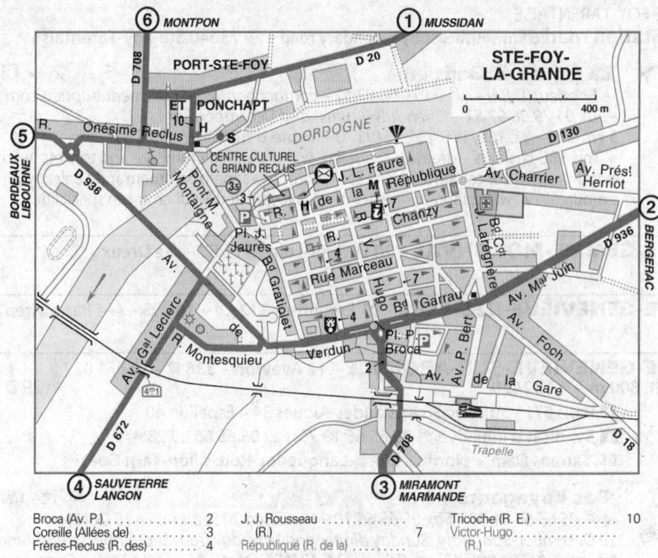

via ⑤ and secondary road – ✉ 33220 Port-Ste-Foy

L'Escapade

La Grâce – ✆ 05 53 24 22 79 – info@escapade-dordogne.com – Fax 05 53 57 45 05 – Open 2 February-14 October and closed Friday and Sunday dinner in February-March

12 rm – 🛉€ 48/52 🛉🛉€ 52, ☕ € 7 – ½ P € 55 – **Rest** – *(dinner only) (pre-book)* Menu € 20/30 – Carte € 36/84

◆ A 17C tobacco farm next to a horse riding centre on the Compostelle pilgrim route. Rustic styled rooms, sauna, summer pool, and the peace and quiet of the countryside. A countrified dining room and a terrace serving regional specialities.

STE-FOY-L'ARGENTIÈRE – 69 Rhône – 327 F5 – pop. 1 167 – alt. 430 m – ✉ 69610

Paris 487 – Lyon 49 – Saint-Étienne 52 – Villeurbanne 52 44 **A2**

Manoir de Tourville

8 km north on D 483 and secondary road – ✆ 04 74 26 66 57 – tourville@manoirdetourville.com – Fax 04 74 26 66 57

6 rm ☕ – 🛉€ 60/80 🛉🛉€ 60/120 – **Table d'hôte** – Menu € 24 bi/45 bi

◆ This 15C manor house is pleasantly located on the edge of meadows with horses and ponds. Delightful rooms with personal touches; suite in tower. Attractive wood-panelled dining room and classic cuisine.

STE-FOY-TARENTAISE – 73 Savoie – 333 O4 – pop. 681 – alt. 1 050 m – ✉ 73640 French Alps

45 **D2**

Paris 647 – Albertville 66 – Chambéry 116 – Moûtiers 40 – Val-d'Isère 20

Office de tourisme, station ✆ 04 79 06 95 19, Fax 04 79 06 95 09

Le Monal rest,

– ✆ 04 79 06 90 07 – le.monal@wanadoo.fr – Fax 04 79 06 94 72 – Closed Sat - Sun from 10 Oct to early Nov

20 rm – 🛉€ 60/75 🛉🛉€ 70/90, ☕ € 10 – ½ P € 65/80 – **Rest** – *(closed from 10 Oct. - 15 Nov.)* Menu € 16 (weekday lunch), € 25/35 – Carte € 35/55

◆ The same family has been running this hotel since1935. Rooms in the main wing are awaiting renovation and a new extension should soon be opened. The first floor panoramic dining room serves daily specials and a choice of regional and brasserie dishes. View of Mont Pourri.

la Station road 6 km southeast by secondary road – ✉ 73640 Ste-Foy-Tarentaise

La Ferme du Baptieu

Le Baptieu, (D 84) – ☎ 04 79 06 97 52 – contact.baptieu@lafermedubaptieu.com – Fax 04 79 06 97 52 – Open July-August and December-April

5 rm – €150/170 €150/170 – **Table d'hôte** – Menu €37

◆ This 18C chalet is extremely charming, with its antique furniture and trinkets, warm wood-panelling or colourful fabrics. Each room has a superb bathroom and a balcony with a mountain view. Restaurant offering tasty Savoyard and Mediterranean specialities.

STE-GEMME-MORONVAL – 28 Eure-et-Loir – 311 E3 – see Dreux

STE-GENEVIÈVE-DES-BOIS – 91 Essonne – 312 C4 – 101 35 – see Paris, Area

---

STE-GENEVIÈVE-SUR-ARGENCE – 12 Aveyron – 338 I2 – pop. 1 027 – alt. 800 m – ✉ 12420 29 **D1**

Paris 571 – Aurillac 56 – Chaudes-Aigues 34 – Espalion 40

Syndicat d'initiative ☎ 05 65 66 19 75, Fax 05 65 66 29 28

Sarrans Dam ★ North: 8 km, Languedoc-Roussillon-Tarn Gorges

Des Voyageurs with rm

– ☎ 05 65 66 41 03 – Fax 05 65 66 10 94 – Closed 20 September-10 October, 20 December-5 January, Sunday dinner and Saturday from September to end June

14 rm – €42 €42, €6 – ½ P €42/45 – **Rest** – Menu €11/31 – Carte €18/33

◆ This former coaching house has been welcoming travellers since 1872. Countrified setting in the restaurant overlooking a garden; regional traditionally prepared dishes. Simple and practical rooms.

STE-HERMINE – 85 Vendée – 316 J8 – pop. 2 256 – alt. 28 m – ✉ 85210 34 **B3**

Paris 433 – Nantes 93 – La Roche-sur-Yon 35 – La Rochelle 59 – Les Herbiers 44

Office de tourisme, la Gare ☎ 02 51 27 39 32, Fax 02 51 27 39 32

Clem'otel

parc Atlantique Vendée, 2 km south on D 137 – ☎ 02 51 28 46 94 – clem.otel@wanadoo.fr – Fax 02 51 28 46 81 – Closed 24 December-5 January

49 rm – €52/54 €62/64, €7 – ½ P €51 – **Rest** – *(closed Sunday from November to end March)* Menu (€11,50), €16/24 – Carte €18/24

◆ This new hotel has light, well-soundproofed guestrooms. Palm trees and sunflowers add an exotic touch to the central patio. Enjoy grilled dishes (prepared in front of you) or traditional cuisine in a rustic, yet contemporary decor.

STE-LUCIE-DE-PORTO-VECCHIO – 2A Corse-du-Sud – 345 F9 – see Corse

---

STE-LUCIE-DE-TALLANO – 2A Corse-du-Sud – 345 D9 – see Corse

STE-MAGNANCE – 89 Yonne – 319 H7 – pop. 353 – alt. 310 m – ✉ 89420
Burgundy-Jura 7 **B2**

Paris 224 – Avallon 15 – Auxerre 65 – Dijon 68 – Saulieu 24

Tomb★ in the church.

Auberge des Cordois

D 606 – ☎ 03 86 33 11 79 – Closed 23 June-2 July, 12-19 November, 2-25 January, Monday, Tuesday and Wednesday

Rest – Menu €27/38 – Carte €34/48

◆ This two hundred-year-old building near the road has a yellow façade. Bistro set menu or regional cuisine served in a dining room with an ochre and violet decor.

STE-MARGUERITE (ÎLE) – 06 Alpes-Maritimes – **341** D6 – see Île Sainte-Marguerite

STE-MARIE – 44 Loire-Atlantique – **316** D5 – see Pornic

STE-MARIE-AUX-MINES – 68 Haut-Rhin – **315** H7 – **pop. 5 816 – alt. 350 m** – ✉ 68160 Alsace-Lorraine 1 **A2**

Paris 422 – Colmar 43 – St-Dié 25 – Sélestat 23

Ste-Marie-aux-Mines Tunnel : closed for repairs until late 2008- Info : www.bison-fute.equipement.gouv.fr.

Office de tourisme, 86, rue Wilson ✆ 03 89 58 80 50, Fax 03 89 58 67 92

Aux Mines d'Argent with rm

8 r. Dr Weisgerber, (near the town hall) – ✆ 03 89 58 55 75 – wistubwillmann@orange.fr – Fax 03 89 58 65 49

9 rm – €45 €45/55, €10 – ½ P €45/55 – **Rest** – Menu €10 (weekday lunch), €14/32 – Carte €18/40

◆ Wood-panelling, Alsatian furniture, wood-carvings (mining scenes) - an authentic winstub in a 16C residence. An attractive terrace skirted by a stream. Regional menu.

STE-MARIE-DE-RÉ – 17 Charente-Maritime – **324** C3 – see Île de Ré

STE-MARIE-DE-VARS – 05 Hautes-Alpes – **334** I5 – see Vars

STES-MARIES-DE-LA-MER – See after Saintes

STE-MARIE-SICCHÉ – 2A Corse-du-Sud – **345** C8 – see Corse

STE-MARINE – 29 Finistère – **308** G7 – see Bénodet

STE-MAURE – 10 Aube – **313** E3 – see Troyes

STE-MAURE-DE-TOURAINE – 37 Indre-et-Loire – **317** M6 – **pop. 3 909 – alt. 85 m** – ✉ 37800 Châteaux of the Loire 11 **B3**

Paris 273 – Le Blanc 71 – Châtellerault 39 – Chinon 32 – Loches 31 – Thouars 73 – Tours 40

Office de tourisme, rue du Château ✆ 02 47 65 66 20, Fax 02 47 34 04 28

Hostellerie des Hauts de Ste-Maure rm,

av. Gén. de Gaulle – ✆ 02 47 65 50 65 – hauts-de-ste-maure@wanadoo.fr – Fax 02 47 65 60 24 – Closed January, Monday (except hotel) and Sunday October-May

20 rm – €119/135 €119/240, €14 – 1 suite – ½ P €119/135

Rest *La Poste* – *✆ 02 47 65 51 18 (closed Monday lunch and Sunday from October to May)* Menu €48/86 – Carte €57/70

◆ This former post house provides modern rooms with personal touches in the adjacent building (rooms in the main building are being renovated). Spa pool, garden and vegetable plot. Classic cuisine, good wine list and elegant rustic setting.

Le Grand Menasson without rest

2 km by old Loches road and secondary road – ✆ 06 11 08 51 80 – ghislaine@augrandmenasson.fr – Fax 02 47 65 21 24

3 rm – €62 €70/75

◆ Guests can be certain of a warm welcome at this quiet old Virginia creeper clad farm. Extensive grounds with pond, rooms decorated in a country style or with antiques.

in Pouzay 8 km southwest – pop. 755 – alt. 51 m – ✉ 37800

Au Gardon Frit VISA

– ✆ 02 47 65 21 81 – Fax 02 47 65 21 81 – Closed 15-23 April, 16 September-2 October, 13-28 January, Tuesday and Wednesday except public holidays

Rest – Menu € 13 (weekday lunch), € 23/38 – Carte € 21/55

◆ This seafood restaurant also has a bar selling tobacco. The dining area has a marine-style decor and a lovely courtyard terrace.

Chinon road 2.5 km west: by D 760 – ✉ 37800 Noyant-de-Touraine

La Ciboulette P VISA

78 rte de Chinon, (opposite A10 junction, exit 25) – ✆ 02 47 65 84 64 – laciboulette@wanadoo.fr – Fax 02 47 65 89 29 – Closed Sunday dinner, Monday dinner, Tuesday dinner and Wednesday dinner from October to March except school holidays and public holidays

Rest – Menu (€ 19), € 23/41 – Carte € 30/54

◆ An attractive menu of classic dishes served in a large ivy clad house. Tastefully decorated dining room and summer terrace.

in Noyant-de-Touraine 5 km west – pop. 646 – alt. 92 m – ✉ 37800

Château de Brou rest, P VISA AE

2 km north on secondary road – ✆ 02 47 65 80 80 – info@chateau-de-brou.fr – Fax 02 47 65 82 92 – Closed 14-25 December, 4 January-5 February, Sunday and Monday October-March

10 rm – †€ 115/170 ††€ 115/170, ☕ € 15 – 2 suites – ½ P € 123/235

Rest – Menu € 35/65 – Carte € 46/70

◆ A beautiful 15C château lost in a huge park. Remarkable historic decor adapted for the comfort of guests. Attic room converted into a suite and 19C chapel. Elegant, small dining room embellished with a pretty fireplace; traditional menu.

STE-MAXIME – 83 Var – 340 O6 – pop. 11 785 – alt. 10 m – Casino – ✉ 83120

French Riviera 41 **C3**

Paris 872 – Cannes 59 – Draguignan 34 – Fréjus 20 – Toulon 72

Office de tourisme, 1, promenade Simon-Loriere ✆ 04 94 55 75 55, Fax 04 94 55 75 56

de Sainte-Maxime Route du Débarquement, North: 2 km, ✆ 04 94 55 02 02 ;

de Beauvallon Boulevard des Collines, by Toulon road: 4 km, ✆ 04 94 96 16 98.

Plan on next page

Le Beauvallon gulf of St-Tropez, rest, P VISA AE

5 km by St-Tropez road – ✆ 04 94 55 78 88 – reservation@lebeauvallon.com – Fax 04 94 55 78 78 – Open 18 April-12 October

65 rm – †€ 210/900 ††€ 210/900, ☕ € 27 – 5 suites – **Rest *Les Colonnades*** – *(closed Monday) (dinner only)* Menu € 80/95 – Carte € 74/115

Rest *Beauvallon Beach* – *(lunch only except July-August)* Carte € 56/87

◆ A luxurious 1913 hotel in the middle of a 4 ha park (pine trees and palms) overlooking the shore. Elegant and spacious rooms. Art Deco style, beautiful terrace and classic cuisine at the Colonnades. Pretty coastal view over Beauvallon Beach.

Hostellerie la Belle Aurore gulf of St-Tropez, P VISA AE

5 bd Jean Moulin, via ③ – ✆ 04 94 96 02 45 – info@belleaurore.com – Fax 04 94 96 63 87 – Open beg. April-mid October

16 rm – †€ 145/325 ††€ 145/325, ☕ € 19 – 1 suite – ½ P € 131/221

Rest – *(closed Wed. except July - Aug.)* Menu € 39/85 – Carte € 80/95

◆ A waterside stone building looking like a Provence country house with rooms that have been prettily refurbished, all with terrace or balcony. This rotunda-shaped restaurant, towering over the sea, offers lovely views of the gulf of St Tropez.

Villa les Rosiers without rest P VISA AE

4 chemin de Guerrevieille Beauvallon-Grimaud, 5 km via ③ – ✆ 04 94 55 55 20 – info@villa-les-rosiers.com – Fax 04 94 55 55 33 – Open 16 March-31 October and 23 December-9 January

12 rm – †€ 140/440 ††€ 140/440, ☕ € 22

◆ This recent villa has original contemporary paintings and sculptures, as well as a sea view. Rooms decorated with elegance and sobriety; some have a terrace.

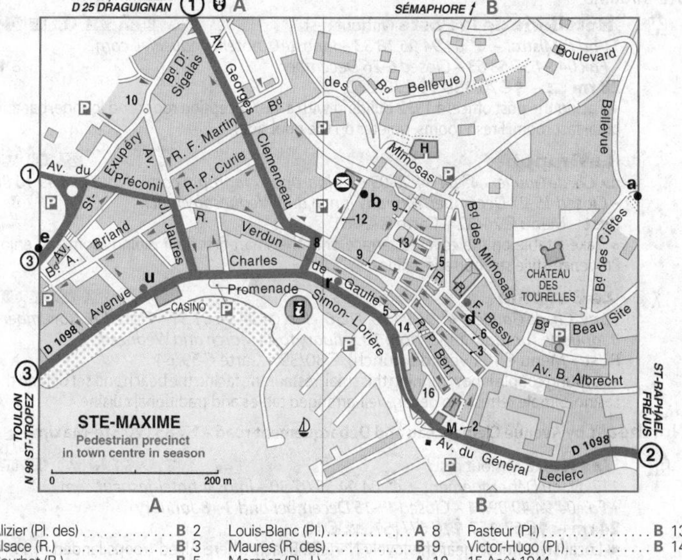

A   B

Alizier (Pl. des)	B 2	Louis-Blanc (Pl.)	A 8	Pasteur (Pl.)	B 13
Alsace (R.)	B 3	Maures (R. des)	B 9	Victor-Hugo (Pl.)	B 14
Courbet (R.)	B 5	Mermoz (Pl. J.)	A 10	15-Août-1944 (Pl. du)	B 16
Hoche (R.)	B 6	Mistral (Bd F.)	B 12		

Les Santolines without rest

La Croisette via ③ – 04 94 96 31 34 – hotel.les.santolines@wanadoo.fr – Fax 04 94 49 22 12

14 rm – €55/145 €75/330, €11

◆ Santolinas perfume this pleasant hotel surrounded by a flower garden and facing the Mediterranean. Its stylish modern rooms are well soundproofed.

Montfleuri rm,

3 av. Montfleuri, via ② – 04 94 55 75 10 – hotelmontfleuri@wanadoo.fr – Fax 04 94 49 25 07 – Closed 10 November-23 December and 2 January-1st March

30 rm – €45/85 €45/195, €10 – **Rest** – *(dinner only)* Menu €28 – Carte €27/50

◆ This establishment in a residential area houses refreshing colourful rooms. Some have balconies with sea views. Attractive Mediterranean garden. Contemporary dining room and traditional cuisine.

Le Mas des Oliviers without rest

quartier de la Croisette, 1 km on ③ – 04 94 96 13 31 – masdesoliviers@9business.fr – Fax 04 94 49 01 46 – Closed December-January

20 rm – €57/155 €57/155, €12

◆ On the hillside, in a cul de sac, a modern building with a Mediterranean colour scheme. Spacious rooms with loggias overlooking the Gulf or the garden.

Le Petit Prince without rest

11 av. St-Exupéry – 04 94 96 44 47 – lepetit.prince@wanadoo.fr – Fax 04 94 49 03 38 A e

31 rm – €55/75 €75/110, €10

◆ Modern and well-soundproofed rooms, some with balcony, situated on a busy avenue close to the beach. Solariums and terrace for breakfast.

Croisette without rest

2 bd Romarins, via ③ – 04 94 96 17 75 – hotel.la.croisette@wanadoo.fr – Fax 04 94 96 52 40 – Open mid March-mid October

18 rm – €65/170 €65/170, €11

◆ Oleanders, palm and fig trees surround this villa situated in a residential area. Some of the rooms command a view of the sea.

Hôtellerie de la Poste without rest
11 bd F. Mistral – 04 94 96 18 33 – laposte@hotelleriedusoleil.com – Fax 04 94 55 58 63 – Closed 6-26 December B **b**
28 rm – €70/130 €70/220
◆ Facing the post office, a 1932 building with a vast reception room and lounge, bar and breakfast room. Fresh rooms, quieter on the pool side.

La Gruppi
av. Ch. de Gaulle – 04 94 96 03 61 – lagruppi@lagruppi.com – Fax 04 94 49 16 86 – Closed 15-27 December, Monday lunch and Wednesday lunch B **r**
Rest – Menu € 24/32 – Carte € 43/61
◆ Take a table on the covered terrace or in the smart first floor dining room and enjoy Provence-style seafood specialities.

Le Dauphin
16 av. Ch. de Gaulle – 04 94 96 31 56 – Fax 04 94 96 81 31 – Closed 26 November-8 January, Tuesday dinner from 10 January to 24 March and Wednesday
Rest – Menu € 19 (weekday lunch), € 30/39 – Carte € 39/64 A **u**
◆ A young couple is now running this small restaurant, facing the beach and set behind the casino. Simple refreshing decor, well-arranged tables and traditional cuisine.

Northeast by Avenue Clemenceau and Débarquement road – ✉ 83120 Ste-Maxime

Jas Neuf without rest
112 av. du Débarquement – 04 94 55 07 30 – infos@hotel-jasneuf.com – Fax 04 94 49 09 71 – Closed 1st-15 December and 3-18 January
24 rm – €67/157 €67/157, € 10
◆ Local style house near the lovely Nartelle Beach where Allied troops landed in 1944. Pretty rooms, most with terraces.

in La Nartelle 4 km by ② – ✉ 83120 Ste-Maxime

Hostellerie de la Nartelle without rest
48 av. Gén. Touzet du Vigier – 04 94 96 73 10 – hostel.nartelle@wanadoo.fr – Fax 04 94 96 64 79 – Open end March-beg. November
18 rm – €65/137 €65/137, €9,50
◆ If possible choose the rooms on the first floor to benefit from the best views of the beach from the large balconies. The hotel is soberly decorated.

in Val d'Esquières 6 km northwest by Les Issambres road – ✉ 83520 Roquebrune-sur-Argens

La Villa
122 av. Croiseur Léger Le Malin, (D 559), at La Garonnette – 04 94 49 40 90 – contact@hotellavilla.fr – Fax 04 94 49 40 85 – Closed 1st December-6 February
8 rm – €65/130 €65/130, € 7 – 4 suites – **Rest** – *(dinner only)* Menu € 19
◆ This renovated hotel near the beaches has small, refreshing and well-kept rooms with personal touches. Some have a sea view. Warm shades and cane armchairs form the pleasant setting of this restaurant. Provencal dishes are prepared with care.

STE-MENÉHOULD – 51 Marne – 306 L8 – pop. 4 979 – alt. 137 m – ✉ 51800

Northern France and the Paris Region 14 **C2**

Paris 221 – Bar-le-Duc 50 – Châlons-en-Champagne 48 – Reims 80 – Verdun 48
Syndicat d'initiative, 5, place du Général Leclerc 03 26 60 85 83, Fax 03 26 60 27 22
≤★ from the hillock called "The château" - Château of Braux-Ste-Cohière★ West: 5.5 km.

Le Cheval Rouge
1 r. Chanzy – 03 26 60 81 04 – rouge.cheval@wanadoo.fr – Fax 03 26 60 93 11 – Closed 22 December-11 January
24 rm – €45 €45, € 7,50 – ½ P € 50
Rest – *(closed Sunday dinner and Monday)* Menu € 18/60 – Carte € 50/69
Rest *La Brasserie* – Menu € 12 (weekdays) – Carte € 19/30
◆ A building from 1873, near the town hall, offering peaceful nights in its perfectly well-kept rooms. Dining room adorned with an imposing fireplace, serving classic cuisine. La Brasserie offers a bistro-type decor and tasty traditional dishes.

in Futeau 13 km east by D 603 and D 2 – pop. 154 – alt. 190 m – ✉ 55120

XXX **L'Orée du Bois** with rm
1 km south – ☎ 03 29 88 28 41 – oreedubois@free.fr – Fax 03 29 88 24 52 – Closed 24 November-24 January, Monday and Tuesday except dinner Easter-end September and Sunday dinner off season
14 rm – €70/80 €85/150, €13 – ½ P €95/135 – **Rest** – Menu €26/67 – Carte €52/71
◆ On the edge of the Argonne forest, an attractive inn with two dining rooms facing the countryside. Spacious, comfortable rooms (reserve a more modern one).

STE-MÈRE-ÉGLISE – 50 Manche – 303 E3 – pop. 1 585 – alt. 28 m – ✉ 50480

Paris 321 – Bayeux 57 – Cherbourg 39 – St-Lô 42 32 **A2**

Office de tourisme, 6, rue Eisenhower ☎ 02 33 21 00 33, Fax 02 33 21 53 91

Southwest 6 km by D 67 and D 70 - ✉ 50360 Picauville

Château de L'Isle Marie without rest
– ☎ 02 33 21 37 25 – info@islemarie.com – Fax 02 33 21 42 22 – Open 2 March-9 November – **5 rm** – €145/155 €145/155, €10 – 2 suites
◆ This lavish medieval castle set in an immense estate has belonged to the same family for centuries. A unique mix of comfort, romance and authenticity.

STE-NATHALENE – 24 Dordogne – 329 I6 – pop. 495 – alt. 145 m – ✉ 24200

Paris 538 – Périgueux 74 – Brive-la-Gaillarde 63 – Sarlat-la-Canéda 9 4 **D3**

La Roche d'Esteil
La Croix d'Esteil – ☎ 05 53 29 14 42 – contact@larochedesteil.com – Open 15 March-15 November – **5 rm** – €60/98 €60/98, €6 – **Table d'hôte** – Menu €24 bi
◆ Domaine restored with taste in traditional Perigord fashion. Fine guestrooms with independent access, situated in the former barns. In the evening, table d'hôte in a convivial, modern setting.

STE-PREUVE – 02 Aisne – 306 F5 – pop. 85 – alt. 115 m – ✉ 02350 37 D2

Paris 188 – Saint-Quentin 69 – Laon 29 – Reims 49 – Soissons 62

Domaine du Château de Barive rest,
3.2 km southwest – ☎ 03 23 22 15 15 – contact@lesepicuriens.com – Fax 03 23 22 08 39
18 rm – €120/230 €120/230, €18 – 4 suites
Rest *Les Epicuriens* – Menu €36/90 – Carte €63/92
◆ This beautiful 19C building nestled in a vast park offers the tranquillity of the Picardy countryside. Cosy rooms; those on the second floor are beneath the eaves. New suites. Personal service. Revamped dining room and veranda in a conservatory style. Updated classical food.

SAINTES – 17 Charente-Maritime – 324 G5 – pop. 25 595 – alt. 15 m – ✉ 17100 Atlantic Coast 38 B3

Paris 469 – Bordeaux 117 – Poitiers 138 – Rochefort 42 – Royan 38

Office de tourisme, 62, cours National ☎ 05 46 74 23 82, Fax 05 46 92 17 01

de Saintonge Fontcouverte, by Niort road: 5 km, ☎ 05 46 74 27 61.

Abbaye aux Dames: abbey church★ - Old town★ - Arc of Germanicus★ **B** - St-Eutrope church: lower church★ **E** - Gallo-Roman amphitheatre★ - Musée des Beaux-Arts★: Musée du Présidial **M**[5] - Musée Archéologique: parade carriage★.

Plan on next page

Relais du Bois St-Georges rm,
r. de Royan, (D 137) – ☎ 05 46 93 50 99 – info@relaisdubois.com – Fax 05 46 93 34 93 Y **d**
30 rm – €80/85 €230/345, €21 – **Rest** – Menu €40/140 bi – Carte €55/83 – **Rest *La Table du Bois*** – Menu (€24 bi), €29 bi
◆ This hotel, built on the site of an old wine cellar, has rooms with individual touches that are sometimes very original: Captain Nemo, Timbuktu, Monte Cristo, etc. Park with pond. The rustic dining room opens onto the surrounding greenery. A bistro atmosphere and cosy ambiance at the Table du Bois.

SAINTES

Allende (Av. Salvador) . . . . Y 2
Alsace-Lorraine (R.) . . . . AZ 3
Arc-de-Triomphe (R.) . . . . BZ 4
Bassompierre (Pl.) . . . . BZ 5
Berthonnière (R.) . . . . AZ 7
Blair (Pl.) . . . . AZ 9
Bois d'Amour (R.) . . . . AZ 10
Bourignon (R.) . . . . Y 12
Brunaud (R. A.) . . . . AZ 13
Clemenceau (R.) . . . . AZ 15
Denfert-Rochereau (R.) . . . . . BZ 16
Dufaure (Av. J.) . . . . Y 18
Foch (Pl. Mar.) . . . . AZ 20
Gambetta (Av.) . . . . BZ
Jacobins (R. des) . . . . AZ 25
Jean (R. du Dr) . . . . Y 27
Kennedy (Av. J.-F.) . . . . Y 31
Lacurie (R.) . . . . Y 33
Leclerc (Crs Mar.) . . . . Y 34
Lemercier (Cours) . . . . AZ 35
Marne (Av. de la) . . . . BZ 37
Mestreau (R. F.) . . . . BZ 38
Monconseil (R.) . . . . AZ 39
National (Cours) . . . . AZ
République (Quai) . . . . AZ 41
St-Eutrope (R.) . . . . AZ 42
St-François (R.) . . . . AZ 43
St-Macoult (R.) . . . . AZ 45
St-Pierre (R.) . . . . AZ 46
St-Vivien (Pl.) . . . . AZ 47
Victor-Hugo (R.) . . . . AZ 49

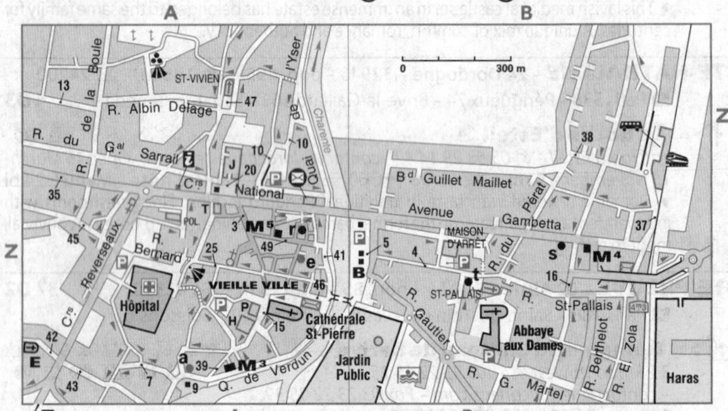

Des Messageries without rest

r. des Messageries – ✆ 05 46 93 64 99 – info@hotel-des-messageries.com – Fax 05 46 92 14 34 AZ **r**

34 rm – €57/78 €62/130, €8

◆ This former coaching inn dating from 1792 is near the historic quarter. Some of the rooms have been renovated. Local produce at breakfast. Delightful welcome.

L'Avenue without rest

114 av. Gambetta – ✆ 05 46 74 05 91 – contact@hoteldelavenue.com – Fax 05 46 74 32 16 – Closed 24 December-4 January BZ **s**

15 rm – €39 €57/58, €7,50

◆ A warm welcome awaits you in this 1970s hotel close to the main road. The personalised, cosy rooms face the rear and are quiet and peaceful.

Le Saintonge

complexe Saintes-Végas, (Royan road) – ✆ 05 46 97 00 00 – sasercol@wanadoo.fr – Fax 05 46 97 21 46 – Closed Sunday dinner and Monday dinner Y **f**

Rest – Menu (€ 20), € 25/45 – Carte € 58/68

◆ A rotunda-restaurant, well-lit with a rather elegant setting, in the "Saintes-Vegas" complex (concert venue, lounges and discotheque). Classic cuisine.

Le Bistrot Galant

28 r. St-Michel – 05 46 93 08 51 – bistrot.galant@club-internet.fr – Fax 05 46 90 95 58 – Closed 17-23 March, 6-19 October, Sunday and Monday

Rest – Menu (€ 13), € 16/36 – Carte € 35/41 AZ **e**

♦ This glass-fronted restaurant lies in a quiet street. Two brightly coloured dining areas; modern cuisine served.

La Table de Marion

10 pl. Blair – 05 46 74 16 38 – latabledemarion@orange.fr – Closed 1st-15 January, Sunday and Monday AZ **a**

Rest – *(number of covers limited, pre-book)* Menu € 29 (lunch)/47

♦ On a small square overlooking the Charente, this modern restaurant with stone walls serves light meals at lunchtime and inventive cuisine in the evening. Organic wines.

Saveurs de l'Abbaye with rm

1 pl. St Palais – 05 46 94 17 91 – info@saveurs-abbaye.com – Fax 05 46 94 47 54 – Closed 22 September-5 October, February school holidays BZ **t**

8 rm – †€ 45 ††€ 48, ☕ € 6 – ½ P € 59/80 – **Rest** – *(closed Sunday and Monday)* Menu € 21/31 – Carte € 27/37

♦ An inviting family home, two minutes from the Abbaye aux Dames. Contemporary bistro-style interior and inventive cuisine focused on regional produce, herbs and spices. Modern bedrooms with personalised touches that reflect the names (Asian colours, Seaside, etc.).

in St-Sauvant 13 km east by ② and N 141 – pop. 508 – alt. 18 m – ✉ 17610

Design Hôtel des Francs Garçons

1 r. des Francs-Garçons – 05 46 90 33 93 – contact@francsgarcons.com

5 rm – †€ 80/95 ††€ 80/105, ☕ € 10 – 2 suites – **Rest** – *(dinner only) (residents only)* Menu € 23/35 – Carte € 33/43

♦ In a medieval village, architect-renovated construction on several floors. Modern décor, old stone, designer furniture and mood lighting. Swimming pool opposite the church.

in Thénac 10 km south by ③ and D 6 – pop. 1 214 – alt. 62 m – ✉ 17460

L'Atelier Gourmand de Jean-Yves

41 r. de la République – 05 46 97 84 26 – agjy@orange.fr – Closed Sunday dinner and Monday

Rest – Menu (€ 20 bi), € 24 (weekday lunch), € 27/55 – Carte € 39/48

♦ Convivial restaurant set in the former stables of a wine warehouse. Attractive rustic dining room with a view of the kitchens. Terrace opposite the park.

STE-SABINE – 21 Côte-d'Or – 320 H6 – see Pouilly-en-Auxois

STE-SABINE – 24 Dordogne – 329 F7 – pop. 375 – alt. 133 m – ✉ 24440 4 C2

Paris 565 – Bordeaux 130 – Périgueux 79 – Bergerac 32 – Villeneuve-sur-Lot 38

La Gentilhommière

– 05 53 74 08 79 – anvi.lucas@wanadoo.fr

4 rm ☕ – †€ 80/95 ††€ 80/95 – **Table d'hôte** – Menu € 30

♦ Convivial old Perigord house set in a large garden with majestic trees. Personalised rooms with themed décor (romantic, oriental, alpine...).

STE-SAVINE – 10 Aube – 313 E4 – see Troyes

STES-MARIES-DE-LA-MER – 13 Bouches-du-Rhône – 340 B5 – pop. 2 478 – alt. 1 m Provence 40 A3

Paris 778 – Marseille 129 – Nîmes 67 – Arles 39 – Istres 84

Office de tourisme, 5, avenue Van Gogh 04 90 97 82 55, Fax 04 90 97 71 15

STES-MARIES -DE-LA-MER

Aubanel (R. Théodore) . . . . . . A 2
Bizet (R. Georges) . . . . A 6
Carrière (R. Marcel) . . . . B 8
Châteaubriand (R.) . . . . A 10
Château d'eau (R. du) . . . . A 12
Crin Blanc (R.) . . . . A 15
Eglise (Pl. de l') . . . . A 17
Espelly (R.) . . . . A 18
Etang (R. de l') . . . . A 20
Ferrade (R. de la) . . . . B 22
Fouque (R. du Capitaine) . . . . A 23
Gambetta (Av. Léon) . . . . . . AB 25
Lamartine (Pl.) . . . . A 27
Marquis-de-Baroncelli (Pl.) . . . . A 28
Médina (R. François) . . . . B 29
Pénitents Blancs (R. des) . . . . A 30
Portalet (Pl.) . . . . A 32
Razeteurs (R. des) . . . . A 34

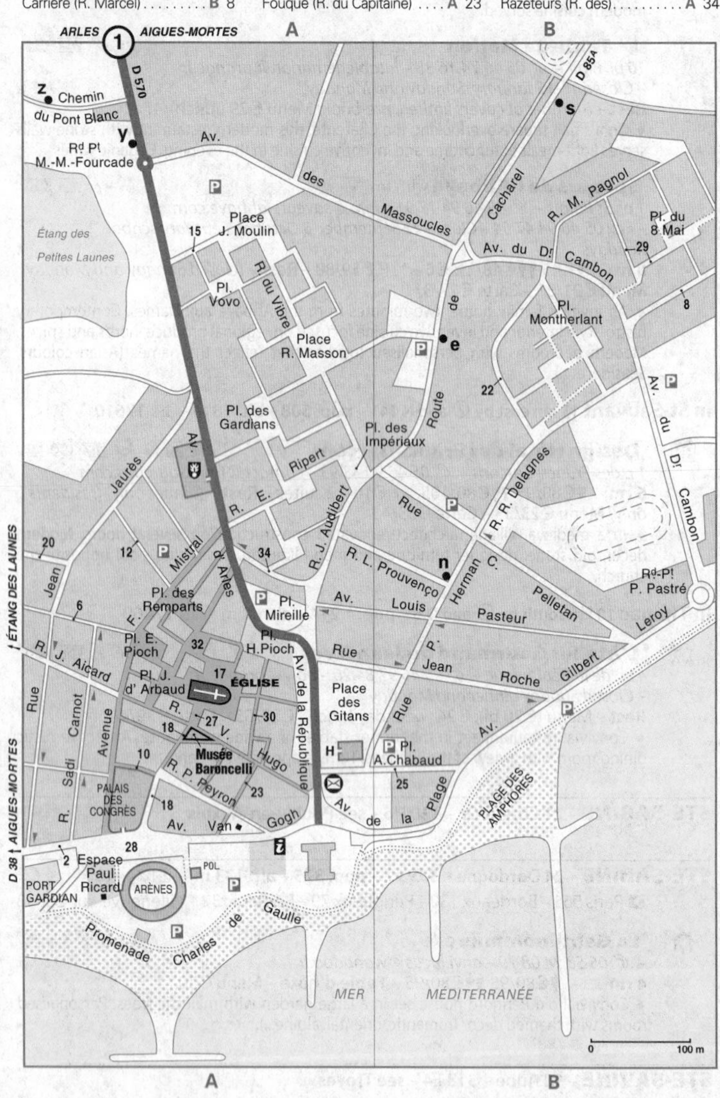

Le Galoubet without rest

rte de Cacharel – 𝒞 04 90 97 82 17 – info@hotelgaloubet.com – Fax 04 90 97 71 20 – Closed 7-26 December and 4 January-13 February B s

20 rm – †€ 50/55 ††€ 65/72, ☕ € 6

◆ This nice family hotel has rustic-style Provençal rooms; on the first floor, four of them have a balcony with a wide view of the Impériaux Nature Reserve. Meticulously well maintained.

Pont Blanc without rest

chemin du Pont Blanc, via Arles road – 04 90 97 89 11 – hotel.du.pont.blanc@wanadoo.fr – Fax 04 90 97 87 00 – Closed 25 November-27 December A **z**

15 rm – €48/58 €48/66, €6

◆ The rooms of this small white, flower-decked farmhouse surround a pool and boast terraces overlooking the countryside. Two duplex rooms in a caretaker's lodge.

Le Mas des Salicornes

rte d'Arles – 04 90 97 83 41 – info@hotel-salicornes.com – Fax 04 90 97 85 70 – Closed January- February A **y**

22 rm – €61/71 €69/79, €8 – ½ P €54/95

Rest – *(closed 15 November-31 March) (dinner only)* Menu €25

◆ Construction all on one level in in keeping with local tradition. Some rooms have been renovated; six formof them are housed in the recently-built wing and all have private terraces. This restaurant has a rustic-Provençal setting and offers a regional, set daily menu.

Le Fangassier without rest

rte de Cacharel – 04 90 97 85 02 – fangassier@camargue.fr – Fax 04 90 97 76 05 – Closed 15 November-21 December and 6 January-8 February B **e**

23 rm – €40/56 €40/56, €6

◆ This traditional blue shuttered house sports a sober, rustic interior. The ground floor rooms to the rear boast a small terrace; those on the second floor have sloping ceilings.

Les Arcades without rest

r. P. Herman – 04 90 97 73 10 – contact@lesarcades.camargue.fr – Fax 04 90 97 75 23 – Open 1st March-11 November B **n**

17 rm – €40/57 €43/57, €6

◆ New hotel on a street corner, a step away from the town centre. Colourful, well looked after and regularly revamped rooms. Those upstairs are larger. Very reasonable prices.

Bac du Sauvage road 4 km northwest by D 38 – 13460 Les Stes-Maries-de-la-Mer

Le Mas de la Fouque

rm,

– 04 90 97 81 02 – info@masdelafouque.com – Fax 04 90 97 96 84 – Open 26 March-14 November

17 rm – €220/340 €270/420, €20 – 6 suites

Rest – Menu €60 – Carte €49/57

◆ This southern-style farmhouse surrounded by ponds enjoys a quiet, idyllic setting in the Camargue. Spacious, elegant rooms. Heliport. Refined spa. Smart exotic interior overlooking the park. Regional cuisine with a focus on natural, organic produce. Terrace under a Balinese style gazebo.

L'Estelle

rm, rest,

rte Petit-Rhône, (D 38) – 04 90 97 89 01 – reception@hotelestelle.com – Fax 04 90 97 80 36 – Open 15 March-23 November and 20 December-4 January

19 rm – €175/230 €190/390 – 1 suite – ½ P €135/235

Rest – *(closed Mon. lunch and Tues. lunch)* Menu €40/85 – Carte €57/98

◆ Delightful garden and comfortable Provençal rooms overlooking the infinity pool or lakes. A charming establishment on the banks of the Petit-Rhône. Up-to-the-minute cuisine served in the plush restaurant or on the pretty terrace. Bistro area.

Arles road Northwest by D 570 – 13460 Les Stes-Maries-de-la-Mer

Le Pont des Bannes

rm,

1 km – 04 90 97 81 09 – contact@pontdesbannes.net – Fax 04 90 97 89 28 – Closed 13 November-4 December and 9 February-8 March

27 rm – €130/166 €130/166 – **Rest** – Menu (€32) – Carte approx. €40

◆ Establishment with character; rustic or contemporary rooms housed in herdsman-style cabins in the heart of the marshland. Horse-riding centre. Traditional red tiling, beams, a fireplace and wide bay windows overlooking the swimming pool form the setting of this restaurant.

Mas Ste-Hélène

small lake,

at 800 m. – 04 90 97 83 29 – Fax 04 90 97 89 28

13 rm – €130/166 €130/166

◆ The Ste-Hélène farmhouse, located on a peninsula jutting out into the Launes lake, has rooms with a terrace ideal for admiring the flora and fauna. Reception at Pont des Bannes.

Les Rizières without rest
at 2.5 km – 04 90 97 91 91 – contact@lesrizieres-camargue.com – Fax 04 90 97 70 77 – Closed December and January
27 rm – €66/105 €66/105, €8
◆ Rooms arranged around the patio. The lobby and breakfast room have already been renovated and the rest is underway.Modern or rustic inspired interior.

Hostellerie du Pont de Gau with rm
5 km – 04 90 97 81 53 – hotellerie-du-pont-de-gau@wanadoo.fr – Fax 04 90 97 98 54 – Closed Wednesday from 15 November to Easter except school holidays
9 rm – €53 €53, €8,50 – ½ P €68 – **Rest** – Menu €22/55 – Carte €48/63
◆ Located near the Bird Sanctuary, this restaurant boasts exposed beams, a fireplace and trompe l'œil. Pleasant blue and white veranda. Tasty local dishes.

LES SAISIES – 73 Savoie – 333 M3 – Winter sports : 1 600/1 870 m 24 – 73620

Paris 597 – Albertville 29 – Annecy 61 – Bourg-St-Maurice 53 – Chamonix-Mont-Blanc 55 – Megève 23 — 45 **D1**

Office de tourisme, avenue des Jeux Olympiques 04 79 38 90 30, Fax 04 79 38 96 29

Le Calgary
– 04 79 38 98 38 – contact@hotelcalgary.com – Fax 04 79 38 98 00 – Open 21 June-6 September and 13 December-26 April
39 rm – €55/95 €75/185, €11 – 1 suite – ½ P €67/127 – **Rest** – *(closed lunch except January, March and April)* Menu €26 – Carte €26/47
◆ The sign of this Tyrolian-style chalet pays tribute to the victories of native son, Franck Piccard, during the 1988 Olympic Games. Spacious and comfortable rooms. Classic dishes enriched with Savoy specialities, served in a sober setting.

SALBRIS – 41 Loir-et-Cher – 318 J7 – pop. 6 029 – alt. 104 m – 41300

Châteaux of the Loire — 12 **C2**

Paris 187 – Blois 65 – Bourges 62 – Montargis 102 – Orléans 64 – Vierzon 24

Office de tourisme, 1, rue du Général Girault 02 54 97 22 27, Fax 02 54 97 22 27

de Nançay at Domaine de Samord, Southeast: 15 km, 02 48 51 86 55.

Domaine de Valaudran
South West : 1.5 km via rte Romorantin – 02 54 97 20 00 – info@hotelvalaudran.com – Fax 02 54 97 12 22 – Closed 20 December-7 January, mid January-mid March and Sunday September-May
32 rm – €69/106 €92/106, €12 – ½ P €50/80 – **Rest** – *(closed Monday lunch and Sunday from September to May and Saturday lunch)* Menu (€27), €32 (weekdays)/55
◆ It is difficult to resist the charm of this 19C manor house whose parkland and pool are an invitation to relax. Spruce modern rooms; some have dormer windows. Cottage garden vegetables and regional specialities take pride of place in the restaurant.

Le Parc
8 av. d'Orléans – 02 54 97 18 53 – reservation@leparcsalbris.com – Fax 02 54 97 24 34 – Closed 19 December-4 January
23 rm – €44/71 €55/97, €9,50 – ½ P €55/72 – **Rest** – *(closed Sunday dinner, Tuesday lunch and Monday from December to March) (pre-book)* Menu €24/50 – Carte €29/54
◆ Large bourgeois abode set in wooded parkland. The tastefully decorated rooms are regularly refurbished. Pleasant sitting rooms. Homemade dishes that are a masterful blend of tradition and seasonal produce.Rustic interior; terrace.

SALERS – 15 Cantal – 330 C4 – pop. 401 – alt. 950 m – 15140 Auvergne

Paris 509 – Aurillac 43 – Brive-la-Gaillarde 100 – Mauriac 20 – Murat 43

Office de tourisme, place Tyssandier d'Escous 04 71 40 70 68, Fax 04 71 40 70 94 — 5 **B3**

Grande-Place ★★ - Church ★ - Esplanade de Barrouze ≤★.

Le Bailliage

r. Notre-Dame – ✆ 04 71 40 71 95 – info@salers-hotel-bailliage.com – Fax 04 71 40 74 90 – Closed 15 November-6 February
24 rm – €60/95 €60/95, ☕ €10 – 3 suites – ½ P €61/110
Rest – *(closed Monday lunch October-April)* Menu €15/45
◆ This regional-style house offers spacious, personalized and tastefully renovated rooms, overlooking either the garden or the countryside. Welcoming dining room and attractive terrace; appetising Auvergne cuisine.

Demeure de Jarriges

at 300 m – Closed 30 November-13 February
5 rm – €78/100 €78/100, ☕ €10
◆ Snug rooms, a house in the country atmosphere and a lush green garden, ideal for catnaps.

Le Gerfaut without rest

rte de Puy Mary, 1 km north-east on t D 680 – ✆ 04 71 40 75 75 – info@salers-hotel-gerfaut.com – Fax 04 71 40 73 45 – Open from March to October
25 rm – €48/77 €48/77, ☕ €8,50
◆ Modern functional building on the little market town's heights, where you will sleep well. The refurbished rooms, with balconies or terraces, face the valley.

Saluces without rest

r. Martille – ✆ 04 71 40 70 82 – contact@hotel-salers.fr – Fax 04 71 40 71 70 – Closed 11 November-11 December
8 rm – €50/60 €50/90, ☕ €9
◆ Simple, elegant rooms, antiques, breakfast under the chestnut tree or facing the lovely fireplace in the sitting room: nothing lacks in the former home of the Marquis de Lur Saluces.

in Fontanges 5 km south by D 35 – pop. 241 – alt. 692 m – ✉ 15140

Auberge de l'Aspre

– ✆ 04 71 40 75 76 – auberge-aspre@wanadoo.fr – Fax 04 71 40 75 27 – Closed 15 November-15 March, Sunday dinner, Wednesday dinner, Monday October-May, Monday lunch and Friday lunch June-September
8 rm – €54 €54, ☕ €9 – ½ P €58 – **Rest** – Menu €18/26 – Carte €25/45
◆ This old farm in the heart of the country has colourful up-to-date rooms with original bathrooms on a mezzanine. A rustic dining hall with a veranda opening onto a garden and a tree-shaded terrace; the appetising menus are regional.

in Theil 6 km southwest by D 35 and D 37 – ✉ 15140 St-Martin-Valmeroux

Hostellerie de la Maronne — rest, rest,

– ✆ 04 71 69 20 33 – maronne@maronne.com – Fax 04 71 69 28 22 – Open 12 April-12 November
17 rm – €100/150 €100/160, ☕ €12 – 4 suites
Rest – *(dinner only)* Menu €30/45
◆ Late 19C Auvergne establishment in the heart of the country. Spacious refreshing rooms, library-lounge and a flower garden. The restaurant has a bucolic view of the meadows and surrounding hills. A discreetly elegant decor.

SALIES-DE-BÉARN – 64 Pyrénées-Atlantiques – 342 G4 – pop. 4 759 – alt. 50 m – Spa : early March-mid Dec. – Casino – ✉ 64270 Atlantic Coast 3 B3

Paris 762 – Bayonne 60 – Dax 36 – Orthez 17 – Pau 64 – Peyrehorade 26
Office de tourisme, rue des Bains ✆ 05 59 38 00 33, Fax 05 59 38 02 95
Sauveterre-de-Béarn: site★, ≤★★ of the old bridge, South: 10 km.

Maison Léchémia

quartier du Bois, 3 km north-west via rte de Caresse and minor road – ✆ 05 59 38 08 55 – Fax 05 59 38 08 55
3 rm ☕ – €40 €53/55 – **Table d'hôte** – Menu €23 bi
◆ This old remote country farmhouse is both welcoming and comfortable. Small, but tastefully decorated rooms. The one with a mezzanine is popular with families. Restaurant offering garden produce, served on the terrace or in front of the fireplace.

La Demeure de la Presqu'île rest,

22 av. des Docteurs-Foix – ✆ 05 59 38 06 22 – info@demeurepresquile.com – Fax 05 59 38 06 22

5 rm – €60 €70 – ½ P €95 – **Table d'hôte** – Menu €28

♦ This fine residence surrounded by a park, close to the town centre, offers spacious rooms, adorned with antique furniture, as well as family suites. At this table d'hôte, meals are prepared by a former pastry cook and served, weather permitting, beneath a magnificent magnolia tree.

in Castagnède 8 km southwest by D 17, D 27 and D 384 – pop. 211 – alt. 38 m – ✉ 64270

La Belle Auberge with rm VISA

– ✆ 05 59 38 15 28 – Fax 05 59 65 03 57 – Closed 1st-15 June and from mid December to end January

14 rm – €41/45 €45/48, €7 – ½ P €44 – **Rest** – *(closed Sunday dinner and Monday dinner except July-August)* Menu €12/22 – Carte €18/32

♦ This peaceful small Béarn village boasts a pleasant inn in a rustic setting serving carefully prepared regional cooking. Simple bedrooms. Beautiful swimming pool and flower garden.

SALIES-DU-SALAT – 31 Haute-Garonne – 343 D6 – pop. 1 943 – alt. 300 m – Spa : early April-late Oct. – Casino – ✉ 31260 Languedoc-Roussillon-Tarn Gorges

Paris 751 – Bagnères-de-Luchon 73 – St-Gaudens 27 – Toulouse 79 28 **B3**

Office de tourisme, boulevard Jean Jaurès ✆ 05 61 90 53 93, Fax 05 61 90 49 39

Du Parc without rest VISA AE

6 r. d'Austerlitz – ✆ 05 61 90 51 99 – philippe.robic1@orange.fr – Fax 05 61 90 43 07

22 rm – €41 €48, €6,50

♦ A well-maintained 1920s hotel in the casino park. Practical rooms with good sound-proofing. Breakfast buffets, served on the terrace in summer.

SALIGNAC-EYVIGUES – 24 Dordogne – 329 I6 – pop. 1 008 – alt. 297 m – ✉ 24590 Dordogne-Berry-Limousin 4 **D1**

Paris 509 – Brive-la-Gaillarde 34 – Cahors 84 – Périgueux 70 – Sarlat-la-Canéda 18

Syndicat d'initiative, pl. du 19 Mars 1962 ✆ 05 53 28 81 93, Fax 05 53 28 85 26

Northwest 3 km by D 62B and secondary road – ✉ 24590 Salignac-Eyvigues

La Meynardie VISA

– ✆ 05 53 28 85 98 – lameynardie24@wanadoo.fr – Fax 05 53 28 82 79 – Open April-October and closed Tuesday off season and Wednesday

Rest – Menu €13 (weekday lunch), €22/42 – Carte €34/59

♦ Beams, stones, pebbled flooring and a fireplace dating from 1603 make up the original rustic setting of this Périgord farm lost in the countryside. Trellis-shaded terrace.

SALINS-LES-BAINS – 39 Jura – 321 F5 – pop. 3 333 – alt. 340 m – Spa : late Feb.-early Dec. – Casino – ✉ 39110 Burgundy-Jura 16 **B2**

Paris 419 – Besançon 41 – Dole 43 – Lons-le-Saunier 52 – Poligny 24 – Pontarlier 46

Office de tourisme, place des Salines ✆ 03 84 73 01 34, Fax 03 84 37 92 85

Site★ - Fort Belin★.

Grand Hôtel des Bains VISA

pl. des Alliés – ✆ 03 84 37 90 50 – hotel.bains@wanadoo.fr – Fax 03 84 37 96 80

31 rm – €63/85 €63/85, €9,50 – ½ P €57/68 – **Rest** – Menu (€13), €20/30 – Carte €32/44

♦ A contemporary makeover for this 1860 building with a superb listed sitting room. Functional rooms, thermal pool and independent fitness centre. Restaurant in a pleasant rustic setting. Classic cuisine with regional influences. Separate brasserie serving simpler meals.

Charles Sander without rest VISA

26 r. de la République – ✆ 03 84 73 36 40 – residencesander@wanadoo.fr – Fax 03 84 73 36 46 – **14 rm** – €59/89 €59/95, €8

♦ Attractive old house with new, welcoming rooms (only one without a kitchenette). Wine buffs will want to spend time in the delicatessen on the ground floor.

Champagnole road 5 km south by D 467 – ✉ 39110 Salins-les-Bains

Le Relais de Pont d'Héry

– ✆ *03 84 73 06 54 – claude-troussard@wanadoo.fr – Fax 03 84 73 19 00 – Closed 29 October-9 November, 23 February-8 March, Tuesday from September to June and Monday*

Rest – Menu € 19 (weekday lunch), € 35/75 bi – Carte € 35/60

◆ This restaurant is renowned for its modern, regional cuisine and its excellent selection of wines from Burgundy and the Jura. The wine is chosen by the owner's son, the best sommelier in the region.

SALLANCHES – 74 Haute-Savoie – 328 M5 – pop. 14 383 – alt. 550 m – ✉ 74700

French Alps 46 **F1**

Paris 585 – Annecy 72 – Bonneville 29 – Chamonix-Mont-Blanc 28 – Megève 14

Office de tourisme, 32, quai de l'Hôtel de Ville ✆ 04 50 58 04 25, Fax 04 50 58 38 47

✱★★ of Mt-Blanc - Médonnet chapel: ✱★★ - Cascade d'Arpenaz★ North: 5 km.

Hostellerie des Prés du Rosay

rm, rest, VISA AE

285 rte de Rosay – ✆ *04 50 58 06 15 – contact@hotellerie-pres-du-rosay.com – Fax 04 50 58 48 70*

15 rm – †€ 66/73 ††€ 79/86, ☕ € 9 – ½ P € 74/77

Rest – *(closed 5-15 May, 5-30 July, 1st-7 January, Saturday and Sunday)* Menu € 16 (lunch), € 25/34 – Carte € 33/41

◆ Modern chalet in a residential area. The simple functional rooms (new bedding and Wi-Fi system) overlook the alpine countryside. The restaurant has smart decor, a lovely view of the meadows and traditional food.

Auberge de l'Orangerie

VISA

carrefour de la Charlotte, 2.5 km on Passy road(D 13) – ✆ *04 50 58 49 16 – orangerie74@orange.fr – Fax 04 50 58 54 63 – Closed June*

18 rm – †€ 50/60 ††€ 56/68, ☕ € 9 – **Rest** – *(closed June, January, Sunday dinner, Tuesday lunch, Wednesday lunch, Thursday lunch and Monday)* Carte € 35/54

◆ Charming welcome, comfortable mountain-style rooms (good beds with duvets). Some have a balcony. Traditional cuisine and local specialities on offer in a friendly (non-smoking) setting.

Le St-Julien

VISA

53 r. Chenal – ✆ *04 50 58 02 24 – Closed 23 June-8 July, 7-20 January, Sunday dinner, Monday and Wednesday*

Rest – Menu € 22/38 – Carte € 31/38

◆ A welcoming flower-decked façade in summer. A wood-panelled dining room serving dishes that change with the seasons and a few regional specialities.

Au Fil des Saisons

VISA

131 r. Pellissier – ✆ *04 50 90 59 80 – Fax 04 50 90 59 80 – Closed 29 June-17 July, 16-26 November, Sunday dinner, Tuesday dinner and Wednesday*

Rest – *(number of covers limited, pre-book)* Menu € 21/32

◆ Simple but delicious regional cuisine, pleasant Alpine decor and faultless service are the keys to the success of this tiny restaurant.

SALLES-LA-SOURCE – 12 Aveyron – 338 H4 – pop. 1 800 – alt. 450 m –

✉ 12330 Languedoc-Roussillon-Tarn Gorges 29 **C1**

Paris 670 – Toulouse 160 – Rodez 13 – Villefranche-de-Rouergue 71 – Onet-le-Château 11

Gîtes de Cougousse

in Cougousse 4 km North-west via D 901 – ✆ *05 65 71 85 52 – gites.de.cougousse@wanadoo.fr – Open 1st April-15 October*

4 rm ☕ – †€ 45 ††€ 52 – **Table d'hôte** – *(closed Saturday dinner in July-August and Monday)* Menu € 20 bi

◆ Large, handsome 15C (non-smoking) abode in a riverside garden with vegetable plot. Personalised, quiet rooms and an inviting rustic lounge in the former kitchen. Gîtes available.

LES SALLES-SUR-VERDON – 83 Var – 340 M3 – pop. 186 – alt. 440 m – ✉ 83630 ▌French Alps 41 **C2**

▶ Paris 790 – Brignoles 57 – Draguignan 49 – Digne-les-Bains 60 – Manosque 62

ℹ Office de tourisme, place Font Freye ✆ 04 94 70 21 84, Fax 04 94 84 22 57

◉ Ste-Croix lake ★★.

Auberge des Salles without rest

18 r. Ste-Catherine – ✆ 04 94 70 20 04 – auberge.des.salles@wanadoo.fr – Fax 04 94 70 21 78 – Open 16 April-30 September and closed Tuesday except 15 June-15 September

30 rm – †€ 55/75 ††€ 55/75, ☕ € 7

♦ Watersports enthusiasts will enjoy this hotel on the banks of the Lac de Ste-Croix. Rustic furniture in the rooms.

SALON-DE-PROVENCE – 13 Bouches-du-Rhône – 340 F4 – pop. 37 129 – alt. 80 m – ✉ 13300 ▌Provence 40 **B3**

▶ Paris 720 – Aix-en-Provence 37 – Arles 46 – Avignon 50 – Marseille 54

ℹ Office de tourisme, 56, cours Gimon ✆ 04 90 56 27 60, Fax 04 90 56 77 09

⛳ de Miramas Miramas Mas de Combe, Southwest: 10 km, ✆ 04 90 58 56 55 ;

⛳ Pont Royal Country Club Mallemort Domaine de Pont Royal, Northeast: 16 km by D 538 and D 17, ✆ 04 90 57 40 79.

◉ Musée de l'Empéri★★.

SALON-DE-PROVENCE

Ancienne Halle (Pl.) .... BY 2
Capucins (Bd des) .... BZ 3
Carnot (Cours) .... AY 4
Centuries (Pl. des) .... BY 6
Clemenceau (Bd Georges) .... AY 7
Coren (Bd Léopold) .... AY 8
Craponne (Allées de) .... BZ 10
Crousillat (Pl.) .... BY 12
Farreyroux (Pl.) .... BZ 13
Ferrage (Pl.) .... BZ 14
Fileuses de Soie (R. des) .... AY 15
Frères J. et R.-Kennedy (R. des) .... AY
Gambetta (Pl.) .... BZ 18
Gimon (Cours) .... BZ
Horloge (R. de l') .... BY 20
Ledru-Rollin (Bd) .... AY 22
Massenet (R.) .... AY 23
Médicis (Pl. C. de) .... BZ 24
Mistral (Bd Frédéric) .... BY 26
Moulin d'Isnard (R.) .... BY 27
Nostradamus (Bd) .... AY 28
Pasquet (Bd) .... BZ 30
Pelletan (Cours Camille) .... AY 32
Raynaud-d'Ursule (R.) .... BZ 34
République (Bd de la) .... AY 33
St-Laurent (Square) .... BY 35
Victor-Hugo (Cours) .... BY 38

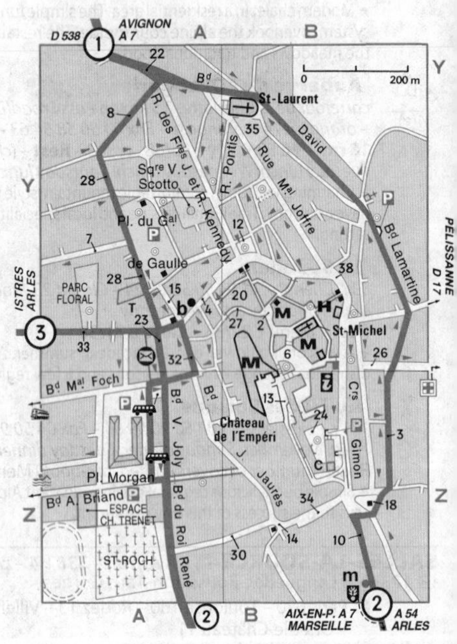

Angleterre without rest

98 cours Carnot – ✆ 04 90 56 01 10 – hoteldangleterre@wanadoo.fr – Fax 04 90 56 71 75 – Closed 20 December-6 January AY **b**

26 rm – †€ 44/48 ††€ 48/56, ☕ € 6,50

♦ This hotel near the museums is very conveniently located. Renovated rooms; some are air-conditioned. Breakfast buffet under a glass cupola.

XXX **Le Mas du Soleil** with rm

38 chemin St-Côme, (east on D 17 -BY) – 04 90 56 06 53 – mas.du.soleil.@wanadoo.fr – Fax 04 90 56 21 52

10 rm – €110/120 €140/285, €13 – ½ P €105/195

Rest – *(Closed Sunday dinner and Monday except public holidays)* Menu €43/87 – Carte €55/90

♦ French Riviera villa serving tasty southern dishes in a bright modern decor overlooking the garden. Some of the comfortable rooms open onto the garden.

XX **Le Craponne**

146 allées Craponne – 04 90 53 23 92 – Fax 04 90 53 23 86 – Closed 12 August-3 September, 23 December-3 January, Sunday dinner, Wednesday dinner and Monday

Rest – Menu €24/37 – Carte €32/56 BZ **m**

♦ The name of this restaurant refers to a local benefactor. Dark wood panelling, yellow walls and rustic furniture. In fine weather, meals served in a small flower-decked courtyard. Family welcome.

Northeast 5 km by D 17 BY then D 16 – ✉ 13300 Salon-de-Provence

Abbaye de Sainte-Croix

– 04 90 56 24 55 – saintecroix@relaischateaux.com – Fax 04 90 56 31 12 – Closed mid December-mid January, mid February-mid March and Sunday-Friday from November to March

21 rm – €138/262 €138/349, €23 – 4 suites – ½ P €173/323

Rest – *(closed Monday-Friday October and April and open only Saturday dinner November-March)* Menu €46 (weekday lunch), €71/109 – Carte €74/129

♦ A 12C abbey overlooking Salon, in the heart of an isolated garrigue park. Up-to-date rooms or rustic former monks' cells. Provençal dining hall and shaded, panoramic terrace. Modern cuisine in the evening; more limited choice at lunchtime.

in la Barben 8 km Southeast by ②, D 572 and D 22^E – pop. 555 – alt. 105 m – ✉ 13330

XX **La Touloubre** with rm

29 chemin Salatier – 04 90 55 16 85 – latouloubre@wanadoo.fr – Fax 04 90 55 17 99

12 rm – €55/85 €55/115, €8 – ½ P €56/71 – **Rest** – Menu €19/40 – Carte €33/57

♦ The new owners have adorned their property in sunny southern shades to enhance the enchanting Provençal setting. Inviting terrace shaded by plane trees and generous regional cooking. Tastefully redone rooms with personalised touches.

South 5 km by ②, N 538, N 113 and D 19 (direction Grans) – ✉ 13250 Cornillon-Confoux

Devem de Mirapier without rest

rte de Grans – 04 90 55 99 22 – contact@mirapier.com – Fax 04 90 55 86 14 – Closed 15 December-15 January, Saturday and Sunday from 15 October to 15 March

15 rm – €80/95 €100/165, €10 – 2 suites

♦ Peacefully located amid scrubland and pine trees. The pretty rooms have been spruced up. Pleasant poolside terrace and sitting room with billiards table.

SALT-EN-DONZY – 42 Loire – 327 E5 – see FEURS

SALVAGNAC – 81 Tarn – 338 C7 – pop. 927 – alt. 231 m 29 C2

Paris 657 – Albi 44 – Montauban 33 – Toulouse 49

Office de tourisme, les Sourigous 05 63 33 57 84, Fax 05 63 33 58 78

Le Relais des Deux Vallées

Grand'rue – 05 63 33 61 90 – relais-2-vallees@wanadoo.fr – Fax 05 63 33 61 91 – Closed 25-31 August, 2-7 January

10 rm – €42 €46, €7 – ½ P €50 – **Rest** – *(closed Mon.)* Menu €11 bi (weekday lunch), €18/35 – Carte €21/57

♦ Small family-run hotel on the village square. Charming little rooms with wooden or wrought iron furniture. Some have a terrace. The bay windows of the dining room overlook the countryside. Simple and tasty traditional cuisine.

SAMATAN – 32 Gers – 336 H9 – pop. 1 832 – alt. 170 m – ✉ 32130 28 B2

Paris 703 – Auch 37 – Gimont 18 – L'Isle-Jourdain 21 – Rieusmes 206

Office de tourisme, 3, rue du chamoine Dieuzaide ✆ 05 62 62 55 40, Fax 05 62 62 50 26

du Château de Barbet Lombez Route de Boulogne, Southwest: 5 km, ✆ 05 62 62 08 54.

Les Logis du Canard without rest

La Rente, D 632 – ✆ 05 62 62 49 81 – contact@aucanardgourmand.com

5 rm – €65/85 €75/95

◆ A profusion of colours, bric-a-brac and paintings and a mixture of old and new... Whether decorated in contemporary or ethnic style, the rooms are all refined and cosy. Charming welcome.

Au Canard Gourmand

La Rente, on D 632 – ✆ 05 62 62 49 81 – contact@aucanardgourmand.com – Closed Monday dinner and Tuesday

Rest – *(number of covers limited, pre-book)* Menu € 12 bi (weekday lunch), € 24/35 bi – Carte € 33/43

◆ Duck-inspired restaurant name and bric-a-brac. This original, winter-garden-style restaurant pays tribute to our web-footed friends. Modern cuisine. Bar with tapas in summer.

LE SAMBUC – 13 Bouches-du-Rhône – 340 D4 – ✉ 13200 40 A3

Paris 742 – Arles 25 – Marseille 117 – Stes-Marie-de-la-Mer 50 – Salon-de-Provence 68

Le Mas de Peint

2.5 km via rte Salins – ✆ 04 90 97 20 62 – hotel@masdepeint.net – Fax 04 90 97 22 20 – Open 15 March-12 November and 19 December-10 January

11 rm – € 205 € 205/395, € 22 – **Rest** – *(closed Tuesday lunchtime, Thursday lunchtime and Wednesday) (number of covers limited, pre-book)* Menu € 57 – Carte € 37/66

◆ This stunning 17C farmhouse and vast grounds continue to uphold Camargue traditions. Cosy rooms, garden with pool, equestrian centre with riding arena. Admire the kitchen's "vintage" decor as you watch the chef prepare appetising regional dishes.

SAMER – 62 Pas-de-Calais – 301 D4 – pop. 3 377 – alt. 70 m – ✉ 62830 30 A2

Paris 244 – Lille 132 – Arras 112 – Calais 50 – Boulogne-sur-Mer 17

Office de tourisme, rue de Desvres ✆ 03 21 87 10 42

Le Clos des Trois Tonneaux

73 r. de Montreuil – ✆ 03 21 92 33 33 – Fax 03 21 30 50 94 – Closed 4-26 January, Sunday dinner and Monday

Rest – Menu € 22 (weekday lunch), € 29/55 – Carte € 39/64

◆ This former distillery on three floors has been successfully modernised. Comfortable lounge in the vaulted cellar. Up-to-date cuisine and good wines.

SAMOËNS – 74 Haute-Savoie – 328 N4 – pop. 2 323 – alt. 710 m – Winter sports : 720/2 480 m 8 70 – ✉ 74340 French Alps 46 F1

Paris 581 – Annecy 75 – Chamonix-Mont-Blanc 60 – Genève 53 – Thonon-les-Bains 56

Office de tourisme, gare routière ✆ 04 50 34 40 28, Fax 04 50 34 95 82

Place du Gros Tilleul★ - Ja sinia Alpine garden ★.

La Rosière ≤★★ North: 6 km - Cascade du Rouget★★ South: 10 km - Cirque du Fer à Cheval★★ East: 13 km.

Neige et Roc rest,

– ✆ 04 50 34 40 72 – resa@neigeetroc.com – Fax 04 50 34 14 48 – Open 8 June-19 September and 21 December-11 April

50 rm – € 80/160 € 80/160, € 12 – ½ P € 72/135

Rest – Menu € 22 (weekday lunch), € 35/50 – Carte € 40/50

◆ A large chalet housing cosy rooms with balconies. Another building offers lovely studio flats with kitchenettes. Winter and summer swimming pools and spa. Large, rustic veranda/dining room (beams, light wood and stonework). Regional menu.

Les Glaciers

– ✆ 04 50 34 40 06 – contact@hotel-les-glaciers.com – Fax 04 50 34 16 75 – Open 16 June-8 September and 21 December-14 April

42 rm – 🚹€ 70/105 🚹🚹€ 100/130, ☕ € 15 – ½ P € 95/120

Rest – *(dinner only in winter)* Menu € 25

◆ Large building in the centre of the resort. Rooms with light wood panelling and pine furniture. Full leisure facilities including a private lake 6km away for fishing and jet skiing. Large restaurant with family guesthouse ambiance. Regionally inspired cuisine.

Edelweiss

mountains, VISA MC AE

La Piaz, 1.5 km north-west on Plampraz road – ✆ 04 50 34 41 32 – *hotel-edelweiss@wanadoo.fr* – *Fax 04 50 34 18 75* – *Closed 19 April-7 May and 25 October-10 November*

20 rm – 🚹€ 58/70 🚹🚹€ 68/80, ☕ € 8,50 – ½ P € 56/66

Rest – *(closed 19 April-31 May and 21 September-21 December) (dinner only)* Menu € 20/38 – Carte € 34/44

◆ The edelweiss is one of the 5,000 species growing in the Alpine garden created by Madame Cognacq-Jay near this simple, comfortable chalet-hotel. Panoramic view of the village and valley. South facing dining room, extending onto a terrace. Traditional cuisine.

Gai Soleil

rest, VISA MC

– ✆ 04 50 34 40 74 – hotel.gai-soleil@wanadoo.fr – Fax 04 50 34 10 78 – Open 2 June-12 September and 21 December-18 April

22 rm – 🚹€ 61/85 🚹🚹€ 67/95, ☕ € 9,50 – ½ P € 63/81

Rest – *(dinner only) (residents only)* Menu € 20/27 – Carte € 22/38

◆ On the outskirts of the village, this chalet-type building has simple guestrooms with wide balconies. Savoyard style in some of the rooms.

Le Monde à L'Envers

VISA MC

pl. Criou – ✆ *04 50 34 19 36 – Closed 1st June-2 July and 28 October-12 December, Wednesday lunch and Tuesday off season*

Rest – Menu (€ 17 bi) – Carte € 37/44

◆ Both the decor and the cuisine in this restaurant have an international feel. The dining room is decorated with objects from around the world, while the dishes are a happy combination of the exotic and the traditional.

in Morillon **4.5 km west – pop. 498 – alt. 687 m – Winter sports : 700/2 200 m 5 74 – ✉ 74440**

Office de tourisme, Chef-lieu ✆ 04 50 90 15 76

Morillon

rest, VISA MC

– ✆ 04 50 90 10 32 – infos@hotellemorillon.com – Fax 04 50 90 70 08 – Open 2 June-19 September and 16 December-14 April

22 rm – 🚹€ 65/130 🚹🚹€ 65/130, ☕ € 10 – ½ P € 60/105 – **Rest** – *(dinner only)* Menu € 25/35 – Carte € 33/43

◆ Sculpted wood, local furniture and fireside armchairs add to the Alpine feel of this pleasant chalet. Small rooms, most of which have wide balconies. Alpine specialities served in a pleasantly relaxed atmosphere.

SAMOUSSY – 02 Aisne – 306 E5 – see Laon

SAMPANS – 39 Jura – 321 C4 – see Dole

Undecided between two equivalent establishments?
Within each category,
establishments are classified in our order of preference.

SANARY-SUR-MER – 83 Var – 340 J7 – pop. 16 995 – alt. 1 m – ✉ 83110

French Riviera 40 **B3**

Paris 824 – Aix-en-Provence 75 – La Ciotat 23 – Marseille 55 – Toulon 13

N.-D.-de-Pitié chapel ≤★.

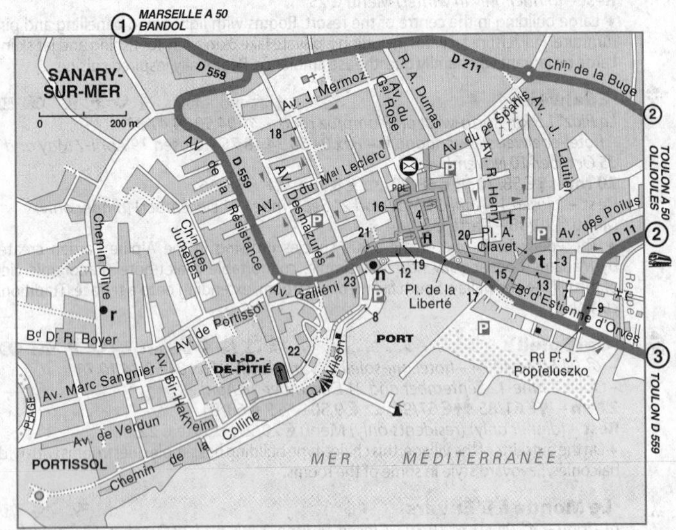

Avenir (Bd de l')	3	Giboin (R.)	13	Pacha (Pl. Michel)	19
Blanc (R. Louis)	4	Granet (R.)	15	Péri (R. Gabriel)	20
Clemenceau (Av. G.)	7	Gueirard (R. L.)	16	Prudhomie (R. de la)	21
Esménard (Quai M.)	8	Jean-Jaurès (Av.)	17	Sœur-Vincent (Montée)	22
Europe-Unie (Av. de l')	9	Lyautey (Av. Mar.)	18	Tour (Pl. de la)	23
Gaulle (Quai Charles-de)	12				

Soleil et Jardin Le Parc without rest

445 av. Europe Unie, via ② – ✆ 04 94 25 80 08
– hotelsanarysoleiljardin@wanadoo.fr – Fax 04 94 26 63 90
27 rm – †€ 130/190 ††€ 165/230, ☕ € 15

◆ This attractive regional-style building, near the beach, houses new, well-equipped and stylishly arranged rooms. Excellent soundproofing. Friendly welcome.

La Tour

quai Gén. de Gaulle – ✆ 04 94 74 10 10 – la.tour.sanary@wanadoo.fr
– Fax 04 94 74 69 49 **n**
24 rm – †€ 58/84 ††€ 65/110, ☕ € 8 – ½ P € 70/94 – **Rest** – *(closed 1st December-15 January, Tuesday except July-August and Wednesday)* Menu € 33/48 – Carte € 37/59

◆ Adjoining an 11C watchtower, this old building has most of its rooms overlooking the harbour. Eat in the classic-style dining room or on the terrace, where you can watch the fishermen returning. Choice of seafood and fish.

Synaya without rest

92 chemin Olive – ✆ 04 94 74 10 50 – hotelsynaya@wanadoo.fr
– Fax 04 94 34 70 30 – Open 21 March-6 November **r**
11 rm – †€ 65/140 ††€ 65/140, ☕ € 9,50

◆ Far from the summer turmoil of the town centre, this little family hotel is adorned with a garden of palms and lemon trees. Fully renovated simple rooms.

San Lazzaro

10 pl. Albert Cavet – ✆ 04 94 88 41 60 – Fax 04 94 74 07 84 – Closed lunch except Sunday from September to June and Monday **t**
Rest – Menu € 29/55 – Carte approx. € 49

◆ A pleasant small family restaurant set on a charming village square. Bright red contemporary decor and menus with a decidedly Italian and Provençal flavour.

SANCERRE – 18 Cher – 323 M3 – pop. 1 799 – alt. 342 m – ✉ 18300
Dordogne-Berry-Limousin 12 **D2**

- Paris 198 – Bourges 46 – La Charité-sur-Loire 30 – Salbris 69 – Vierzon 68
- Office de tourisme, rue de la croix de bois ✆ 02 48 54 08 21, Fax 02 48 78 03 58
- du Sancerrois: 6 km by D 9 and D4, ✆ 02 48 54 11 22.
- Esplanade of Caesar's gate ⩽★★ - D 923 and D 7 intersection ⩽★★ West: 4 km by D955.

SANCERRE

Abreuvoirs (Remp. des)	2	Paix (R. de la)	8	Puits-des-Fins (R. du)	16
Marché-aux-Porcs (R. du)	5	Panneterie (R. de la)	9	St-André (R.)	18
Nouvelle Place	6	Pavé-Noir (R. du)	12	St-Jean (R.)	20
		Porte-César (R.)	13	St-Père (R.)	22
		Porte-Serrure (R.)	15	Trois-Piliers (R. des)	23

 **Panoramic** ⩽ VISA AE

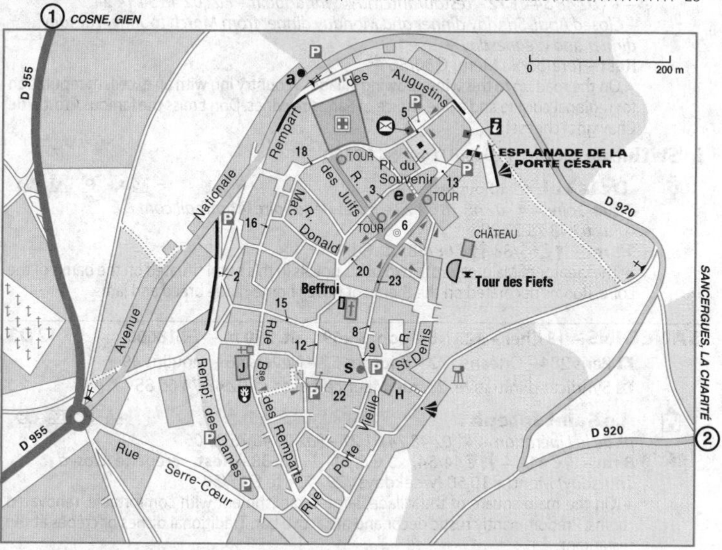

rempart des Augustins – ✆ 02 48 54 22 44 – panoramicotel@wanadoo.fr – Fax 02 48 54 39 55 **a**

57 rm – €54/98 €54/98, ☕ €12,50 – 2 suites – ½ P €75

Rest *Les Augustins* – *✆ 02 48 54 01 44 (closed 5-20 January and Monday lunch)* Menu (€18), €24/45 – Carte €26/59

◆ This aptly named hotel has magnificent views of the surrounding vineyards. Recently renovated, the hotel offers cosy, comfortable guestrooms, plus a lounge and wine shop. Hushed atmosphere and muted colours in the restaurant; good traditional cuisine.

XXX **La Tour** VISA AE

Nouvelle Place – ✆ 02 48 54 00 81 – info@la-tour-sancerre.fr – Fax 02 48 78 01 54

Rest – Menu €27/80 bi – Carte €49/69 **e**

◆ Restaurant topped by a 14C tower. Two dining rooms, one in elegant rustic-style, the other (upstairs) with a modern decor and a view of the vineyards. Good selection of Sancerre wines.

X **La Pomme d'Or** VISA

pl. de la Mairie – ✆ 02 48 54 13 30 – Fax 02 48 54 19 22 – Closed autumn half-term holidays, Sunday dinner November-March, Tuesday dinner and Wednesday April-October **s**

Rest – *(number of covers limited, pre-book)* Menu €19 (weekdays)/46

◆ This popular restaurant a stone's throw from the town hall serves delicious traditional cuisine. The small dining room is brightened by an attractive fresco depicting the Sancerre hills.

in St-Satur 3 km by ① and D 955 – pop. 1 731 – alt. 155 m – ✉ 18300

Office de tourisme, 25, rue du Commerce ✆ 02 48 54 01 30, Fax 02 48 54 01 30

La Chancelière without rest

5 r. Hilaire-Amagat – ✆ 02 48 54 01 57 – jaudibert@wanadoo.fr

5 rm – €105 €130

◆ The terrace of this 18C town house offers a fine view of Sancerre and its vineyards. Tiled floor, exposed beams and antique furniture add a touch of character to the rooms.

in Chavignol 4 km by ① and D 183 – ✉ 18300

La Côte des Monts Damnés

– ✆ 02 48 54 01 72 – restaurantcmd@wanadoo.fr – Fax 02 48 54 14 24 – Closed April, Sunday dinner and Monday dinner from March to June, Tuesday dinner and Wednesday

Rest – *(pre-book)* Menu € 30/56

◆ On the road up to this wine-growing village, a country inn with an excellent reputation for regional cuisine and a fine choice of Sancerre wines. Don't miss the famous Crottin de Chavignol cheese!

in St-Thibault 4 km by ① and D 4 – ✉ 18300

De la Loire without rest

2 quai Loire – ✆ 02 48 78 22 22 – hotel-de-la-loire@hotmail.com – Fax 02 48 78 22 29

11 rm – €65/88 €68/88, € 14

◆ The creator of Maigret wrote two of his novels in this hotel situated on the banks of the Loire. Rooms decorated on the theme of travel; home-made bread and jams.

SANCOINS – 18 Cher – 323 N6 – pop. 3 269 – alt. 210 m – ✉ 18600 12 D3

Paris 284 – Orléans 172 – Bourges 51 – Nevers 46 – Moulins 49

Syndicat d'initiative, 23, rue Maurice-Lucas ✆ 02 48 74 65 85

Le Saint Joseph

pl. de la Libération – ✆ 02 48 74 61 21 – Fax 02 48 76 88 06

8 rm – €44/54 €44/54, € 6,50 – ½ P € 38 – **Rest** – crêperie *(closed Thursday)* Menu € 10,50 (weekdays)/29 – Carte € 17/39

◆ On the main square of the village, large establishment with comfortable, renovated rooms. Predominantly rustic decor and attractive bar. Traditional dishes or crêpes at the restaurant.

SANCY – 77 Seine-et-Marne – 312 G2 – pop. 306 – alt. 142 m – ✉ 77580 19 C2

Paris 55 – Château-Thierry 48 – Coulommiers 14 – Meaux 13 – Melun 50

Château de Sancy

1 pl. de l'Église – ✆ 01 60 25 77 77 – infos@chateaudesancy.com – Fax 01 60 25 60 55

21 rm – €127/175 €127/244, € 14 – ½ P € 145/165

Rest – Menu € 30 (weekdays)/60

◆ The wide variety of leisure equipment on offer on the estate of this 18C manor house invites guests to relax. Cosy rooms, those in the pavilion are more functional. A well-appointed, intimate dining room serving dishes that change according to the seasons.

SAND – 67 Bas-Rhin – 315 J6 – pop. 1 073 – alt. 159 m – ✉ 67230 1 B2

Paris 501 – Barr 15 – Erstein 7 – Molsheim 26 – Obernai 16 – Sélestat 22 – Strasbourg 34

Hostellerie la Charrue

rest,

4 r. 1er décembre – ✆ 03 88 74 42 66 – info@lacharrue.com – Fax 03 88 74 12 02 – Closed 30 June-7 July, 29 December-12 January

23 rm – €50/55 €60/65, € 8 – ½ P € 50/55 – **Rest** – *(closed Monday and lunch except Sunday and public holidays)* Menu € 22/35 – Carte € 24/42

◆ Former carters' hostel with refreshing, well-fitted rooms, some of them redecorated in Alsatian style. Pleasant living room under the eaves. Wood panelling and bright colours make up the warm decor of the dining room.

SANDARVILLE – 28 Eure-et-Loir – 311 E5 – pop. 342 – alt. 171 m – ✉ 28120 11 B1

Paris 105 – Brou 23 – Chartres 16 – Châteaudun 36 – Le Mans 109 – Nogent-le-Rotrou 47

XX **Auberge de Sandarville** VISA MC

14 r. Sente aux Prêtres, (near the church) – ☎ 02 37 25 33 18 – Fax 02 37 25 40 34 – Closed 18 August-1st September, 8-22 January, 22 February -2 March, Tuesday dinner in winter, Sunday dinner and Monday

Rest – Menu (€ 25), € 31/41 – Carte € 49/63

♦ Three charming country-style dining rooms in a Beauce farm dating from 1850, with beams, fireplace, red floor tiles, furniture and knickknacks from here and there. Pretty terrace in the flower garden.

SANDILLON – 45 Loiret – 318 J4 – pop. 3 405 – alt. 101 m – ✉ 45640 12 C2

Paris 148 – Orléans 13 – Châteaudun 65 – Châteauneuf-sur-Loire 16 – Montargis 60

XX **Rest. Saisons d'Ailleurs et H. un Toit pour Toi** with rm P VISA MC AE

2 r. Villette – ☎ 02 38 41 00 22 – 1toitpourtoi@wanadoo.fr – Fax 02 38 41 07 74 – Closed 24-30 December

12 rm – †€ 48 ††€ 64, ☕ € 8 – ½ P € 52 – **Rest** – *(closed 4-19 August, Sunday dinner and Monday)* Menu € 26 (weekday lunch), € 42/65 – Carte € 49/113

♦ Wonderful, inventive cuisine is served in this pleasant, family-run auberge situated on the edge of the Sologne. Simpler fare is available in the bistro (brasserie-style menu). The guestrooms have been partly furnished in contemporary style.

SANILHAC – 07 Ardèche – 331 H6 – see Largentière

SAN-MARTINO-DI-LOTA – 2B – 345 F3 – see Corse (Bastia)

SAN-PEIRE-SUR-MER – 83 Var – 340 P5 – see les Issambres

SANTA-GIULIA (GOLFE) – 2A Corse-du-Sud – 345 E10 – see Corse (Porto-Vecchio)

SANT'ANTONINO – 2B Haute-Corse – 345 C4 – see Corse

SANTENAY – 21 Côte-d'Or – 320 I8 – pop. 904 – alt. 225 m – Casino – ✉ 21590

Burgundy-Jura 7 A3

Paris 330 – Autun 39 – Beaune 18 – Chalon-sur-Saône 25 – Le Creusot 29 – Dijon 63

Office de tourisme, gare SNCF ☎ 03 80 20 63 15, Fax 03 80 20 69 15

XX **Le Terroir** AC VISA MC

pl. Jet d'Eau – ☎ 03 80 20 63 47 – Restaurant.le.Terroir@wanadoo.fr – Fax 03 80 20 66 45 – Closed 4 December-11 January, Wednesday dinner from November to March, Sunday dinner and Thursday

Rest – Menu € 21/48 – Carte € 32/49

♦ This restaurant in the centre of the village offers tasty local dishes in a pleasant blend of rustic and modern decor. Vaulted 15C cellar full of regional wines.

LE SAPPEY-EN-CHARTREUSE – 38 Isère – 333 H6 – pop. 942 – alt. 1 014 m – Winter sports : to Sappey and to Col de Porte 1 000/1 700 m 11 – ✉ 38700

French Alps 45 C2

Paris 577 – Chambéry 61 – Grenoble 14 – St-Pierre-de-Chartreuse 14 – Voiron 37

Syndicat d'initiative, Le Bourg ☎ 04 76 88 84 05

Charmant Som ★★★ Northwest: 9 km then 1 h.

Les Skieurs with rm

– ✆ 04 76 88 82 76 – hotelskieurs@wanadoo.fr – Fax 04 76 88 85 76 – Closed Easter and Christmas holidays and Sunday

11 rm – †€ 89 ††€ 89, ☐ € 12 – ½ P € 83

Rest – *(closed Tuesday lunch, Sunday dinner and Monday)* Menu € 28 (weekdays), € 32/42 – Carte € 54/60

◆ Charming chalet-style wood-panelled dining room with fireplace and rustic furniture. Copious, regional cuisine. Attractive terrace. Delightful interior with wood everywhere, small practical rooms (some with a balcony), attentive welcome and a calm setting... This hotel oozes with charm.

Le Dagobert

pl. de l'Église – ✆ 04 76 88 80 26 – Fax 04 76 88 80 26 – Closed Wednesday

Rest – Menu € 16/29 – Carte € 29/46

◆ Rustic dining room fronted by a small wine bar and adorned with a fireplace. Pleasant shaded summer terrace. Traditional cuisine.

SARE – **64 Pyrénées-Atlantiques** – **342** C5 – **pop. 2 184** – **alt. 70 m** – ✉ **64310**

Atlantic Coast 3 **A3**

Paris 794 – Biarritz 26 – Cambo-les-Bains 19 – Pau 138 – St-Jean-de-Luz 14

Office de tourisme, Herriko Etxea ✆ 05 59 54 20 14, Fax 05 59 54 29 15

Arraya rm, VISA AE

– ✆ 05 59 54 20 46 – hotel@arraya.com – Fax 05 59 54 27 04 – Open 28 March-5 November

20 rm – †€ 84/130 ††€ 84/130, ☐ € 10 – ½ P € 77/100 – **Rest** – *(closed Monday lunch, Thursday lunch and Sunday dinner except st July-14 September)* Menu € 22/32 – Carte € 40/49

◆ Former post-house in typical regional architecture, set on the village square on the Compostela route. Lovely rustic interior and Basque-style rooms. Delightful garden. The decor of the restaurant has character; a shady terrace, regional cuisine and a shop selling local produce.

Pikassaria rm, rest, VISA

– ✆ 05 59 54 21 51 – hotelpikassaria@orange.fr – Fax 05 59 54 27 40 – Open 15 March-11 November

18 rm – †€ 55 ††€ 58, ☐ € 7 – ½ P € 49/51

Rest – *(open 15 March-11 November, 26 December-6 January and closed Tuesday lunch, Wednesday lunch and Monday)* Menu (€ 16), € 21/28 – Carte € 25/39

◆ Local-style building in a pleasant rural setting, at the foot of the St Ignace pass. Rooms of varying sizes, some with a mountain view. The Table du Pikassaria lives up to its name with flavours from Basque cooking.

Baratxartea rm, rest, VISA AE

quartier Ihalar, 2 km east – ✆ 05 59 54 20 48 – contact@hotel-baratxartea.com – Fax 05 59 47 50 84 – Open 15 March-11 November and closed Monday lunch, Tuesday except 1st July-15 September

22 rm – †€ 40/54 ††€ 42/60, ☐ € 8 – ½ P € 41/53

Rest – Menu € 17/23 – Carte € 19/28

◆ Family house set away from the town whose Basque name means 'between gardens'. The rooms are small and simple, but well kept. The most modern are to be found in the annexe. A country-style restaurant extended by a bright veranda (no-smoking area); regional cuisine.

Olhabidea with rm rest, VISA

quartier Sainte-Catherine, St-Pée road – ✆ 05 59 54 21 85 – Closed December, January and Monday

3 rm ☐ – †€ 75 ††€ 82 – **Rest** – *(closed 15 November-13 February, lunch except Sunday, Tuesday except July-August, Sunday dinner and Monday) (number of covers limited, pre-book) (set menu only)* Menu € 35

◆ An extremely charming former farmhouse, nestling in the greenery. The menu, prepared with local produce, changes every day. Upstairs, a wooden balcony gives access to the large and cosy rooms decorated with works by local artists.

SARLAT-LA-CANÉDA – 24 Dordogne – 329 I6 – pop. 9 707 – alt. 145 m – ✉ 24200 Dordogne-Berry-Limousin 4 D3

Paris 526 – Bergerac 74 – Brive-la-Gaillarde 52 – Cahors 60 – Périgueux 77

Office de tourisme, rue Tourny ☎ 05 53 31 45 45, Fax 05 53 59 19 44

du Domaine de Rochebois Route de Montfort, South: 8 km by D 46, ☎ 05 53 31 52 52.

Old Sarlat★★★: place du marché aux trois Oies★ Y, hôtel Plamon★ Y, hôtel de Maleville★ Y - La Boétie House ★ Z - West district ★.

Decoration★ and furniture★ of the château de Puymartin Northwest: 7 km by ④.

Plan on next page

Clos La Boëtie without rest

97 av. Selves – ☎ 05 53 29 44 18 – hotel@closlaboetie-sarlat.com – Fax 05 53 28 61 40 – Open 15 March-15 November V **b**

11 rm – €190/320 €190/320, €20 – 3 suites

◆ This fully-renovated residence has a beautifully-arranged interior combining old and new. Very comfortable rooms with a romantic and refined atmosphere.

De Selves without rest

93 av. de Selves – ☎ 05 53 31 50 00 – hotel@selves-sarlat.com – Fax 05 53 31 23 52 – Closed 4 January-12 February V **v**

40 rm – €65/100 €75/125, €12

◆ A modern construction with up-to-date functional rooms; some have loggias with bay windows opening onto the garden. Indoor pool becomes outdoor pool in summer. Sauna.

La Madeleine

1 pl. Petite Rigaudie – ☎ 05 53 59 10 41 – hotel.madeleine@wanadoo.fr – Fax 05 53 31 03 62 – Closed 1st January-15 February Y **e**

39 rm – €61/91 €68/105, €9,50 – ½ P €67/91

Rest – *(open 15 March-15 Nov. and closed Monday lunchtime and Tuesday lunchtime except July-August)* Menu €28/47 – Carte €39/140

◆ This beautiful 19C abode at the edge of the old town is one of Sarlat's top establishments. Spruce, well-equipped rooms. This recently refurbished restaurant is comfortable and airy. Regional cooking.

Le Renoir without rest

2 r. Abbé-Surgier – ☎ 05 53 59 35 98 – info@hotel-renoir-sarlat.com – Fax 05 53 31 22 32 – Closed 10 December-15 January X **u**

35 rm – €65/95 €70/135, €12,50 – 1 suite

◆ This inviting establishment boasts a swimming pool in the main courtyard. The medium sized rooms are well cared for and prettily decorated with period furniture.

Compostelle without rest

66 av. de Selves – ☎ 05 53 59 08 53 – info@hotel-compostelle-sarlat.com – Fax 05 53 30 31 65 – Open 1st February-15 November V **r**

23 rm – €65/84 €65/148, €8,50

◆ A welcoming hotel just 400m from the historic centre with guestrooms that are being gradually renovated. Choose the more modern rooms, with their contemporary feel.

Le Mas del Pechs without rest

1.5 km east, via Chemin des Monges -VX- – ☎ 05 53 31 12 11 – contact@sarlat-hotel.com – Fax 05 53 31 16 99 – Open 14 March-12 November

18 rm – €48/61 €51/64, €7

◆ A quiet country residence in the hills above Sarlat. Opt for the more stylish, more recent guestrooms, all of which are on garden level.

La Maison des Peyrat

Le Lac de la Plane, to the east via Chemin des Monges -VX- – ☎ 05 53 59 00 32 – hoteldecharme@maisondespeyrat.com – Fax 05 53 28 56 56 – Open 1st April-15 November

10 rm – €53/95 €53/95, €8,50 – ½ P €57/78

Rest – *(closed Wednesday and Sunday)* Menu €22

◆ Attractive establishment hidden amidst the greenery including a restful garden and a salt-water swimming pool. Country-style guestrooms (stone, beams, wood). Attentive service. Local dishes, rustic decor and bistro furniture in the restaurant. Terrace.

SARLAT-LA-CANÉDA

Albusse (R. d') . . . . YZ 2
Allende (Pl. Salvador) . . . . Y 3
Arlet (Bd Henri) . . . . YZ
La Boétie (R. de) . . . . Z 21
Bouquerie (Pl. de la) . . . . Y
Breuil (R. du) X
Brossard (Av.) . . . . V 4
Cahors (R. de) X
Cahuet (R. Alberic) . . . . YZ
Chanoines (Cour des) . . . . Z 6
Consuls (R. des) . . . . Y 7
Cordil (R. du) . . . . Z 8
Delpeyrat (R. J.-Baptiste) . . . . X 10
Desmouret (Chemin de) V
Escande (R. J.-Joseph) . . . . . . Z
Faure (R. Émile) . . . . X, Z 12
Fénelon (R.) . . . . Y
Fontaines (Cour des) . . . . Z 13
Frères Chambon (R. des) . . . . Z 16
Gabin (R. Jean) . . . . V 17
Gallière (R.) X
Gambetta (Av.) . . . . V 18
Gaubert (R.) V
Gaulle (Av. du Gén.-de) . . . . . . Y 20
Grande Rigaudie (Pl. de la) . . . Z
Jean-Jaurès (R.) V
J.-J.-Rousseau (R.) . . . . Y
Lakanal (R.) . . . . Z 22
Landry (R.) . . . . Y 25
Leclerc (Av. du Gén.) . . . . . X, Z 26
Leroy (Bd Eugène) . . . . Y
Libération (Pl. de la) X
Liberté (Pl. de la) . . . . Y 27
Liberté (R. de la) . . . . YZ 30
Marché aux Oies (Pl. du) . . . . . Y
Monges (Chemin des) V
Montaigne (R.) . . . . Z
Montfort (R. Sylvia) . . . . V 31
Moulin (R. Jean) . . . . V 32
Nessmann (Bd Victor) . . . . Y
Papucie (R.) . . . . Y 34
Pasteur (Pl.) X
Peyrou (Pl. du) . . . . Z 35
Plantier (Chemin du) X
Présidial (R. du) . . . . Y 36
République (R. de la) . . . . . . YZ
Rossignol (R. Pierre) . . . . X 38
Rousset (R.) . . . . Z 39
Salamandre (R. de la) . . . . Y 40
Ségogne (Pass. Henri-de) . . . . Z 42
Selves (Av. de) . . . . V 43
Siège (R. du) . . . . Z
Thiers (Av.) X
Tourny (R.) . . . . Z 44
Trappe (R. de la) . . . . X 46
Trois Conils (R. des) . . . . Z 47
Troubadour Cayrels (R. du) . . . V 48
Tunnel (R. du) . . . . X 50
Turenne (R. de) . . . . Z 51
Victor-Hugo (R.) . . . . Y 52
Voltaire (Bd) . . . . X, Z
8-Mai-1945 (Square du) . . . . . Y
11-Novembre (Pl. du) . . . . Y
14-Juillet (Pl. du) . . . . Z
19-Mars-1962 (Pl. du) . . . . . . V 54
26-Juin-1944 (R. du) . . . . V 55

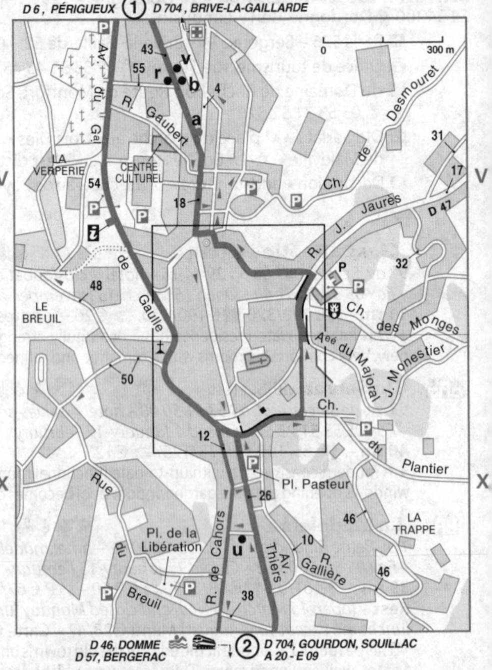

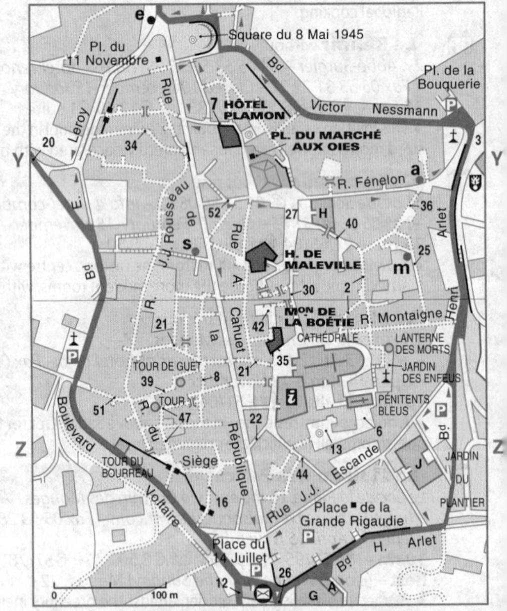

Les Peyrouses without rest
at Les Peyrouses, 2 km west – 05 53 28 89 25 – lespeyrouses24@wanadoo.fr – Fax 05 53 28 89 25
5 rm – €50/69 €50/69, €7
◆ A quiet establishment, a stone's throw from the centre of Sarlat. Modern sitting room with fireplace; spacious rooms, prettily furnished in a rustic vein.

XX **Le Présidial** VISA
6 r. Landry – 05 53 28 92 47 – Fax 05 53 59 43 84 – Open 1st April-11 November and closed Monday lunch and Sunday Y **m**
Rest – Menu €26/42 – Carte €43/64
◆ A charming flower garden is laid out in front of this 17C building, the former seat of the tenant-farming appeal court. It offers stately decor, a shaded terrace and regional cuisine.

XX **Le Grand Bleu** (Maxime Lebrun) VISA
43 av. de la Gare, by ② – 05 53 31 08 48 – contact@legrandbleu.eu – Fax 05 53 31 08 48 – Closed Tuesday lunch, Wednesday lunch, Sunday dinner and Monday
Rest – Menu €29/39
Spec. Foie gras cuit au torchon, granité au vin de noix. Poisson façon rossini. Orange rôtie au romarin.
◆ Delicious, seasonally-inspired up-to-date cuisine served in a dining room which combines spaciousness with sobriety (stone walls, pale wood).

XX **Le Quatre Saisons** VISA AE
2 Côte Toulouse – 05 53 29 48 59 – Fax 05 53 59 53 74 – Closed 23-29 June, Tuesday and Wednesday except July-August Y **s**
Rest – Menu (€19), €27/32
◆ An old country house near the 16C Hôtel de Maleville. Regional cuisine served in a contemporary dining room. Impressive spiral staircase, plus a terrace framed by ancient walls.

X **Rossignol** VISA
15 r. Fénelon – 05 53 31 02 30 – Fax 05 53 31 02 30 – Closed Monday
Rest – Menu €17/60 – Carte €33/53 Y **a**
◆ Although recently renovated, the dining room has kept its pleasant rustic atmosphere with wooden furniture and copper utensils on the walls. Family-style regional menus.

X **Le Bistro de L' Octroi** VISA
111 av. de Selves – 05 53 30 83 40 – bistrodeloctroi@orange.fr V **a**
Rest – Menu €15 bi (weekday lunch), €18/26 – Carte €18/26
◆ Bistro serving regional cuisine in an ancient tollhouse. Two dining rooms, one rustic (stone, bricks), the other traditional. Large and popular terrace.

via ②, 5 km Gourdon road then La Canéda road and secondary road – ✉ 24200 Sarlat-la-Canéda

Le Mas de Castel without rest
Le Sudalissant – 05 53 59 02 59 – info@hotel-lemasdecastel.com – Fax 05 53 28 25 62 – Open 31 March-11 November
13 rm – €46/60 €48/80, €7,50
◆ Out in the country, an old farm building has been turned into a pleasant inn. It offers peaceful nights in well-kept, comfortable rustic rooms, six of which open onto the garden.

via ②, 3 km Bergerac road and secondary road – ✉24200 Sarlat-la-Canéda

Relais de Moussidière without rest
Moussidière Basse – 05 53 28 28 74 – contact@moussidiere.com – Fax 05 53 28 25 11 – Open April-October
35 rm – €85/100 €90/140, €10
◆ Enjoy complete peace and quiet in this house full of character, built into the rock, with terraced grounds descending to the lake. Comfortable, personalised guestrooms.

par ②, Souillac road – ✉ 24200 Sarlat-la-Canéda

Abbys without rest
ZA E. Vialard – 05 53 30 85 50 – contact@abbys-hotel.com – Fax 05 53 30 85 51
30 rm – €34/39 €34/39, €5
◆ This recent establishment will suit those looking for a hotel that is essentially practical and not too expensive. Modern, well-equipped and simply decorated ground-floor rooms.

SARLIAC-SUR-L'ISLE – 24 Dordogne – 329 G4 – pop. 885 – alt. 102 m – ✉ 24420 4 C1

Paris 473 – Brive-la-Gaillarde 65 – Limoges 86 – Périgueux 15

Chabrol with rm VISA MC

3 r. de l'Eglise – ✆ 05 53 07 83 39 – Fax 05 53 07 86 53 – Closed 1st September-7 October, Sunday dinner and Monday

10 rm – †€ 38/40 ††€ 38/80, ☕ € 5 – **Rest** – Menu € 15/50 – Carte € 25/48

◆ Unassuming family run inn in two old buildings. Regional cuisine prepared by the lady of the house, served in a rustic dining room. Modest family inn made up of two old buildings. Simple meticulously kept rooms; ask for one of the renovated ones in the annexe. Bar with a local ambiance.

SARPOIL – 63 Puy-de-Dôme – 326 H10 – see Issoire

SARRAS – 07 Ardèche – 331 K2 – pop. 1 829 – alt. 133 m – ✉ 07370 43 E2

Paris 527 – Annonay 20 – Lyon 72 – St-Étienne 60 – Tournon-sur-Rhône 18 – Valence 36

from D 506 view★★ of the St-Vallier defile★ South: 5 km,

Auvergne-Rhone Valley

Le Vivarais with rm AC rest, P VISA MC AE

– ✆ 04 75 23 01 88 – levivarais@wanadoo.fr – Fax 04 75 23 49 73 – Closed 1st-23 August, 16 February-4 March, Sunday dinner, Monday dinner and Tuesday

6 rm – †€ 45 ††€ 50, ☕ € 7 – **Rest** – Menu € 18/54 – Carte € 36/54

◆ Family inn serving classic cuisine in an elegant dining room decorated in lively colours. Rooms are practical for a stop on the 'route du soleil'.

SARREBOURG – 57 Moselle – 307 N6 – pop. 13 330 – alt. 282 m – ✉ 57400 Alsace-Lorraine 27 D2

Paris 426 – Épinal 86 – Lunéville 59 – Metz 95 – St-Dié 72 – Strasbourg 73

Office de tourisme, place des Cordeliers ✆ 03 87 03 11 82, Fax 03 87 07 13 93

du Pays de Sarrebourg Route de Winkelhof, West: 2 km, ✆ 03 87 23 01 02.

Stained-glass window★ in the Cordeliers chapel **B**.

Plan on next page

Les Cèdres VISA MC AE

3 km, leisure zone via ③ and Chemin d'Imling – ✆ 03 87 03 55 55 – info@hotel-lescedres.fr – Fax 03 87 03 66 33 – Closed 21 December-2 January

44 rm – †€ 57/64 ††€ 63/70, ☕ € 8 – ½ P € 74

Rest – *(closed Saturday lunchtime and Sunday evening)* Menu € 14 (weekday lunch), € 22/50 – Carte € 30/57

◆ Quiet stop in the heart of a leisure area, near a forest and pond, in this modern hotel with bright and functional rooms. Modern, spacious dining room, opening onto the surrounding countryside, serving regional cuisine.

Mathis (Ernest Mathis) AC VISA MC AE

7 r. Gambetta – ✆ 03 87 03 21 67 – Fax 03 87 23 00 64 – Closed 27 July-8 August, 8-15 September, 3-8 November, 2-12 January, Sunday dinner, Tuesday dinner and Monday s

Rest – Menu € 30/75 – Carte € 48/71

Spec. Poêlée de grosses langoustines "meunière aux épices" (May to September). Grillade de foie de canard mulard "fleur de sel et poivre" (September to February). Pigeon fermier légèrement fumé rôti aux copeaux de truffe de Bourgogne (September-October). **Wines** Pinot blanc, Muscat.

◆ Carefully thought-out table decoration, as one would expect in the land of crystal and ceramics. Warm welcome and inventive food in this restaurant with many assets.

SARREBOURG

Berrichons et Nivernais (R. des) 2
Bossuet (R.) 3
Cordeliers (Pl. des) 5
Erckmann-Chatrian (R.) 7
Fayolle (Av. Gén.) 8
Foch (R. Mar.) 10
France (Av. de) 12
Gare (R. de la) 13
Grand'Rue
Jardins (R. des) 15
Jean-XXIII (Quai) 16
Lebrun (Quai) 18
Marché (Pl. du) 19
Napoléon (R.) 20
Poincaré (Av.) 21
Président-Schuman (R.) 22
St-Pierre (R.) 24

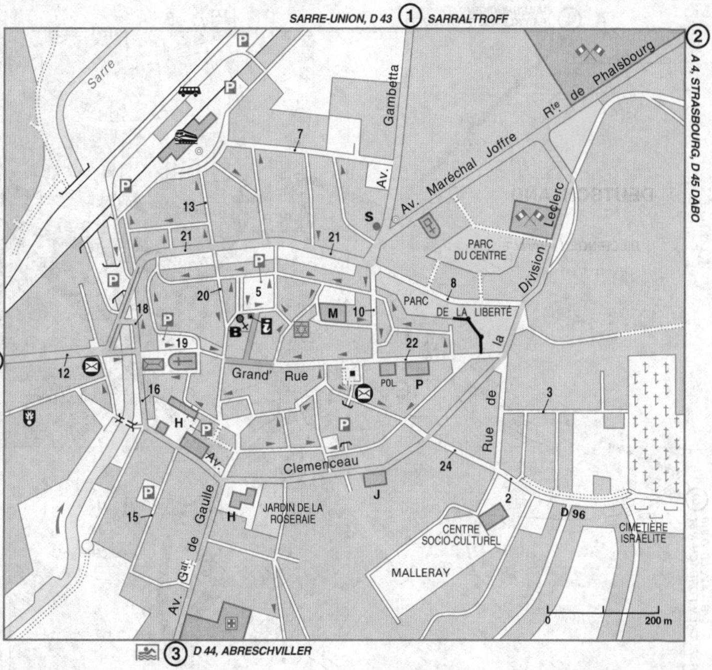

SARREGUEMINES – 57 Moselle – 307 N4 – pop. 23 202 – alt. 210 m – ✉ 57200 Alsace-Lorraine 27 D1

Paris 396 – Metz 70 – Nancy 96 – Saarbrücken 18 – Strasbourg 106

Office de tourisme, 11, rue rue du Maire Massing ☎ 03 87 98 80 81, Fax 03 87 98 25 77

de Sarreguemines Chemin Départemental n 81 A, West: 3 km by D 81, ☎ 03 87 27 22 60.

Museum: Winter garden★★, collection of ceramics★ BZ **M.**

Bliesbruck-Reinheim European Archeological Park: spa★, 9.5 km by ①.

Plan on next page

Auberge St-Walfrid (Stéphan Schneider) rm, rest, rm, P VISA
2 km by ③ and Grosbliederstroff road –
☎ 03 87 98 43 75 – stwalfrid@free.fr – Fax 03 87 95 76 75
– Closed 27 July-11 August and 8-23 February
11 rm – €95/158 €95/158, €15 – **Rest** – *(closed Saturday lunchtime, Monday lunchtime and Sunday)* Menu €25/72 – Carte €51/78
Spec. Escalope de foie gras de canard poêlée (spring-summer). Sole de petit bâteau meunière. Escalope de chevreuil poêlée, blettes au massalé (May to January). **Wines** Vin de Moselle.
◆ Fine stone house where five generations of the same family have played hosts. The decor attractively combines rustic and modern features. Well-kept rooms. Dining room adorned with colourful paintings and ceramic objects. Tasty regional cuisine.

SARREGUEMINES

Chamborand (R. du Marquis-de) . . . . . . **BZ** 2
Chapelle (R. de la) . . . . **BZ** 3
Cremer (R. des Généraux) **ABZ** 6
Faïenceries (Bd des) . . . . **BZ** 7
France (R. de) . . . . **AZ** 8
Gare (Av. de la) . . . . **BZ** 12
Louvain (Chaussée de) . . . **BYZ** 15
Marché (Pl. du) . . . . **AZ** 17
Nationale (R.) . . . . **ABZ** 20
Or (R. de l') . . . . **AZ** 22
Paix (R. de la) . . . . **AY** 23
Pasteur (R. L.) . . . . **BZ** 24
Ste-Croix (R.) . . . . **BZ** 27
St-Nicolas (R.) . . . . **AZ** 26
Sibille (Pl. du Gén.) . . . . **BZ** 28
Utzschneider (R.) . . . . **BZ** 30
Verdun (R. de) . . . . **AZ** 33

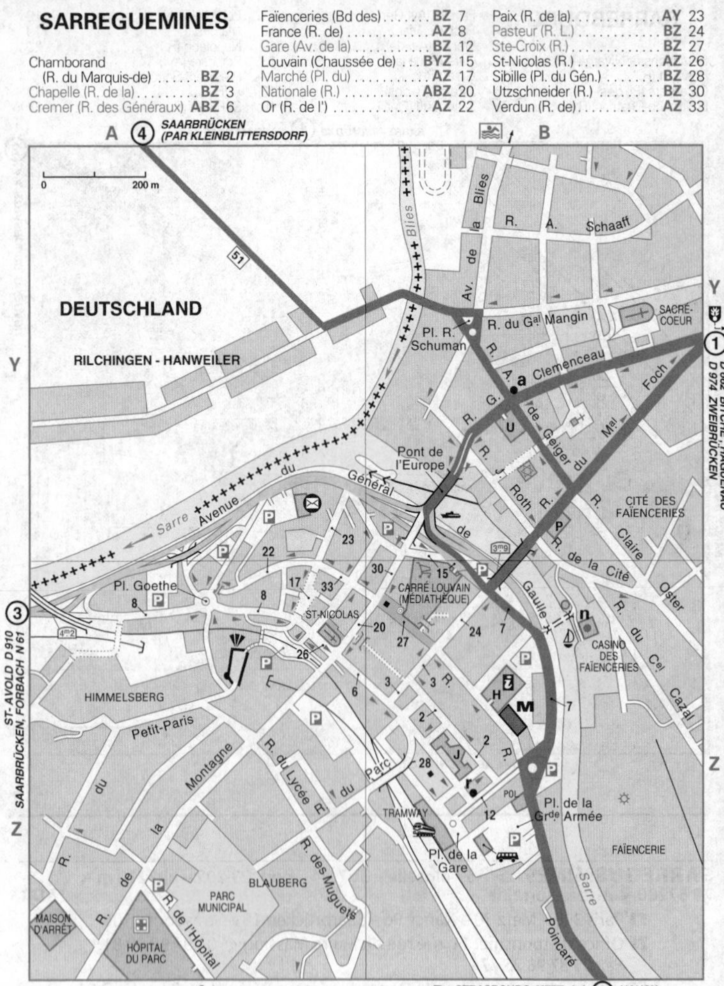

Amadeus without rest

7 av. de la Gare – ✆ 03 87 98 55 46 – amadeushotel@aol.com – Fax 03 87 98 66 92

39 rm – €52/56 €59/60, €7,50 BZ **r**

◆ A successful facelift for this 1930s building next to the station. Rooms of varying sizes rearranged in a colourful modern style.

Union rest,

28 r. Geiger – ✆ 03 87 95 28 42 – union.hotel@wanadoo.fr – Fax 03 87 98 25 21 BY **a**

27 rm – €47/59 €54/64, €6,50 – ½ P €40/44 – **Rest** – *(closed 23 December-1st January, Saturday and Sunday)* Menu €16/20 – Carte €24/42

◆ Union - a precursory name in this border town. Simple and functional rooms, some with furniture designed by an Alsatian cabinet maker. The restaurant's dining room is adorned with wood panelling and Sarreguemines earthenware. Regional cuisine.

Thierry Breininger - Le Vieux Moulin
135 r. France, 1.5 km by ③ – ✆ 03 87 98 22 59 – Fax 03 87 28 12 63 – Closed 15-30 August, 1st-10 January and Thursday
Rest – Menu € 45 bi/70 – Carte € 59/67
Spec. Effeuillé de foie gras et artichauts aux kumquats. Saint-Jacques au bouillon de céleri-branche (October to March). Pastilla de pigeonneau, jus à la cannelle.
◆ Discreet inn housing a spacious stylish dining room, enhanced by wood panelling and exposed beams. Seasonal inventive cuisine and fine selection of wines.

Bitche road 11 km by ① on D 662 – ✉ 57200 Sarreguemines

Pascal Dimofski
– ✆ 03 87 02 38 21 – pascal.dimofski@gmail.com – Fax 03 87 02 21 36 – Closed 18 August-9 September, 16 February-3 March, Monday and Tuesday
Rest – Menu € 25/72 – Carte € 48/84
◆ A country inn in the woods where beams, a fireplace and smart leather armchairs create a unique feel. Personalised cuisine and fine wine list.

SARRE-UNION – 67 Bas-Rhin – 315 G3 – pop. 3 356 – alt. 240 m – ✉ 67260

Paris 407 – Metz 81 – Nancy 84 – St-Avold 37 – Sarreguemines 24 – Strasbourg 83 1 **A1**

Strasbourg road 10 km southeast by N 61 – ✉ 67260 Burbach

Windhof
(Lieu dit Windhof) – ✆ 03 88 01 72 35 – bernard.kehne@wanadoo.fr – Fax 03 88 01 72 71 – Closed 4-21 August, 1st-16 January, Sunday dinner, Tuesday dinner and Monday
Rest – Menu € 12 (weekday lunch), € 28/65 – Carte € 35/57
◆ This restaurant, just off the motorway, is housed in an opulent building. Dining area with wood panelling, serving classic and traditional meals.

SARS-POTERIES – 59 Nord – 302 M6 – pop. 1 541 – alt. 181 m – ✉ 59216

Northern France and the Paris Region 31 **D3**

Paris 258 – Avesnes-sur-Helpe 12 – Charleroi 46 – Lille 107 – Maubeuge 15 – St-Quentin 77

Office de tourisme, 20, rue du Gal-de-Gaulle ✆ 03 27 59 35 49, Fax 03 27 59 36 23

Musée du Verre★.

Marquais without rest
– ✆ 03 27 61 62 72 – hoteldumarquais@aol.com – Fax 03 27 57 47 35 – Closed 1st-15 January

11 rm – €50 €60, €8
◆ Two sparkling twin sisters – around 70 years old! – run this small hotel to perfection. Antique furniture and candybox colours in the rooms. No television. Rest and relaxation guaranteed.

L'Auberge Fleurie with rm
67 r. Gén. de Gaulle, (D 962) – ✆ 03 27 61 62 48 – fauberge@wanadoo.fr – Fax 03 27 61 56 66 – Closed 18 August-2 September, 2-16 January, Sunday dinner and Monday lunch
8 rm – €65 €85/95, € 12 – ½ P € 70/125
Rest – Menu € 28/62 – Carte € 39/60
◆ Enjoy good service in this rustic, smart-looking restaurant serving traditional cuisine. Spacious, personalised guest rooms in light colours.

SARTÈNE – 2A Corse-du-Sud – 345 C10 – see Corse

SARZEAU – 56 Morbihan – 308 O9 – pop. 6 143 – alt. 30 m – ✉ 56370 Brittany

Paris 478 – Nantes 111 – Redon 62 – Vannes 23 9 **A3**

Office de tourisme, rue du Père Coudrin ✆ 02 97 41 82 37, Fax 02 97 41 74 95

de Rhuys Saint-Gildas-de-Rhuys, West by D 780: 7 km, ✆ 02 97 45 30 09.

Ruins★ of the château de Suscinio Southeast: 3.5 km - Presqu'île de Rhuys★.

in Penvins 7 km southeast by D 198 – ✉ 56370 Sarzeau

XX **Mur du Roy** with rm ← rest, P VISA MC
– ✆ 02 97 67 34 08 – contact@lemurduroy.com – Fax 02 97 67 36 23 – Closed 15 December-15 January, Monday and Tuesday September-June except hotel
10 rm – €52/86 €52/86, ☕ €10 – ½ P €66/83 – **Rest** – Menu €19 (weekday lunch), €32/48 – Carte €37/60
◆ Seafood served on two verandas brightened with nautical decor and pleasantly overlooking the terrace, the garden and the ocean. Small, very quiet rooms.

SASSENAY – 71 Saône-et-Loire – 320 J9 – see Chalon-sur-Saône

SASSETOT-LE-MAUCONDUIT – 76 Seine-Maritime – 304 D3 – pop. 957 – alt. 89 m – ✉ 76540 33 C1

Paris 198 – Bolbec 29 – Fécamp 16 – Le Havre 55 – Rouen 65 – Yvetot 30

Office de tourisme, 4, rue des Fusillés ✆ 02 35 29 79 88

XX **Le Relais des Dalles** with rm VISA MC AE
6 r. Elizabeth d'Autriche, near the château – ✆ 02 35 27 41 83
– le-relais-des-dalles@wanadoo.fr – Fax 02 35 27 13 91
– Closed 22 December-8 January, February holidays, Monday and Tuesday except dinner from 14 July to 24 August
4 rm – €72/140 €72/140, ☕ €12 – ½ P €72/105
Rest – *(pre-book Sat - Sun)* Menu €24/55 – Carte €32/59
◆ A friendly inn, near the castle. The carefully prepared traditional dishes are served either in the rustic Norman-style interior or on the terrace among greenery, depending on the season. Cosy rooms.

SAUBUSSE – 40 Landes – 335 D13 – pop. 742 – alt. 10 m – Spa : early March-late Nov. – ✉ 40180 3 B3

Paris 736 – Bayonne 43 – Biarritz 50 – Dax 19 – Mont-de-Marsan 72

Syndicat d'initiative, rue Vieille ✆ 05 58 57 76 68, Fax 05 58 57 37 37

XX **Villa Stings** (Francis Gabarrus) ← AC VISA MC AE
– ✆ 05 58 57 70 18 – villa-stings@wanadoo.fr – Fax 05 58 57 71 86
– Closed 9-16 June, 10-17 November, February, Sunday dinner from 21 September to 13 July, Wednesday dinner from 17 September to 30 April, Tuesday lunch from 15 July to 9 September, Saturday lunch and Monday
Rest – Menu €35/80
Spec. Escalope de foie gras au gingembre. Pigeonneau poêlé au parfum de cacao (summer). Crème chiboust aux olives noires et citron vert (summer). **Wines** Jurançon, Madiran.
◆ Large 19C stone building on the banks of the Adour. Elegant dining room serving up-to-date cuisine prepared with high-quality produce.

SAUGUES – 43 Haute-Loire – 331 D4 – pop. 2 013 – alt. 960 m – ✉ 43170
Auvergne 6 C3

Paris 529 – Brioude 51 – Mende 72 – Le Puy-en-Velay 43 – St-Flour 52

Office de tourisme, cours Dr Gervais ✆ 04 71 77 71 38, Fax 04 71 77 71 38

La Terrasse AC rest, VISA MC AE
cours Dr Gervais – ✆ 04 71 77 83 10 – laterrasse-saugues@wanadoo.fr
– Fax 04 71 77 63 79 – Closed December, January, Sunday evening and Monday except from May to September
10 rm – €55 €65/85, ☕ €9 – ½ P €55
Rest – *(closed Sunday dinner, Tuesday lunch and Monday except July-August)* Menu €18 (weekdays)/49
◆ In the village centre dominated by the Tour des Anglais, this former residence of a notary has been in the same family since 1795. Freshly redecorated rooms. Rustic dining room with fireplace and stylish table settings. Traditional cuisine.

SAUJON – 17 Charente-Maritime – **324** E5 – **pop. 5 392 – alt. 7 m** – ✉ **17600**
Saujon 38 **B3**

▶ Paris 499 – Poitiers 165 – La Rochelle 71 – Saintes 28 – Rochefort 34

ℹ Syndicat d'initiative, 22, place du Général-de-Gaulle ✆ 05 46 02 83 77

Le Richelieu
rm, AC rm, VISA MC

pl. Richelieu – ✆ 05 46 02 82 43 – richelieu.saujon@wanadoo.fr – Fax 05 46 02 82 43

20 rm – €52/72 €52/77, € 8,50 – 2 suites – ½ P € 51/64

Rest *Le Ménestrel* – *✆ 05 46 06 92 35 (closed Sunday and Monday)*
Menu € 23/46

◆ A wind of change at this Saintonge hotel which boasts functional, contemporary-style rooms in an ancient construction (18C) and its recent extension. In the restaurant, the décor is in keeping with the chef-patron's up-to-date cooking.

SAULES – 25 Doubs – **321** G4 – see Ornans

SAULGES – 53 Mayenne – **310** G7 – **pop. 334 – alt. 97 m** – ✉ **53340** Normandy

▶ Paris 249 – Château-Gontier 37 – La Flèche 48 – Laval 33 – Le Mans 55 – Mayenne 41 35 **C1**

ℹ Syndicat d'initiative, 4, place Jacques Favrot ✆ 02 43 90 49 81, Fax 02 43 90 55 44

L'Ermitage
rm, P VISA MC

3 pl. St-Pierre – ✆ 02 43 64 66 00 – info@hotel-ermitage.fr – Fax 02 43 64 66 20 – Closed 21 December-25 January

35 rm – €72/122 €72/122, € 9,50 – ½ P € 76/101 – **Rest** – *(closed Friday dinner and Sunday dinner from October to March)* Menu € 23/59 – Carte € 38/48

◆ An old house with pretty rooms facing the countryside or the village. Those in the "Relais" have been well renovated and are more modern. Pool, crazy golf, garden. Revamped restaurant under a glass canopy overlooking a lush green terrace. Classic fare.

SAULIEU – 21 Côte-d'Or – **320** F6 – **pop. 2 837 – alt. 535 m** – ✉ **21210**
Burgundy-Jura 8 **C2**

▶ Paris 248 – Autun 40 – Avallon 39 – Beaune 65 – Clamecy 78 – Dijon 73

ℹ Syndicat d'initiative, 24, rue d'Argentine ✆ 03 80 64 00 21, Fax 03 80 64 00 21

◎ St-Andoche basilica ★: capitals★★ - Le Taureau★ (sculpture) by Pompon.

Plan on next page

Le Relais Bernard Loiseau
✿✿✿

rm, VISA MC AE

2 r. Argentine – ✆ 03 80 90 53 53 – loiseau@relaischateaux.com – Fax 03 80 64 08 92 – Closed 5 January-5 February, and Tuesday from 6 February to 14 April and from 18 November to 20 December e

23 rm – €145/195 €145/345, € 30 – 9 suites

Rest – *(closed Tuesday lunch and Wednesday lunch 14 October-18 November and 6 February-15 May, Tuesday dinner 18 November-20 December and 6 February-31 March)* Menu € 98 bi (weekday lunch), € 120/185 – Carte € 132/179

Spec. Turbot rôti en croûte de pomme de terre à l'andouille de Guéméné, jus au chablis. Filet de charolais cuit au foin en croûte d'argile, toast de moelle glacé au vin. Les "Grands Classiques" de Bernard Loiseau . **Wines** Puligny-Montrachet, Chambolle-Musigny.

◆ This luxurious 18C hostelry is the essence of this stopover-town that has for centuries paid homage to Burgundy's tradition of hospitality. Elegant rooms open onto the English-style garden; inspired recipes by Patrick Bertron pay homage to the master of Saulieu.

Hostellerie la Tour d'Auxois
AC VISA MC AE

sq. Alexandre Dumaine – ✆ 03 80 64 36 19 – info@tourdauxois.com – Fax 03 80 64 93 10 – Closed February r

29 rm – €107/127 €107/127, € 13 – 6 suites – **Rest** – *(closed Tuesday lunch October-May, Sunday dinner and Monday)* Menu € 29/62 – Carte € 58/64

◆ This lovely hotel in a former convent has been treated to a new lease of life. Cosily inviting rooms, landscaped garden and generous breakfasts. Contemporary gastronomy in a warm and elegant traditional setting.

SAULIEU

Argentine (R. d') 3
Bertin (R. J.) 4
Collège (R. du) 6
Courtépée (R.) 7
Foire (R. de la) 8
Fours (R. des) 9
Gambetta (R.) 10
Gare (Av. de la) 12
Gaulle (Pl. Ch.-de) 14
Grillot (R.) 15
Marché (R. du) 17
Parc des Sports (R. du) 18
Sallier (R.) 19
Tanneries (R. des) 20
Vauban (R.) 21

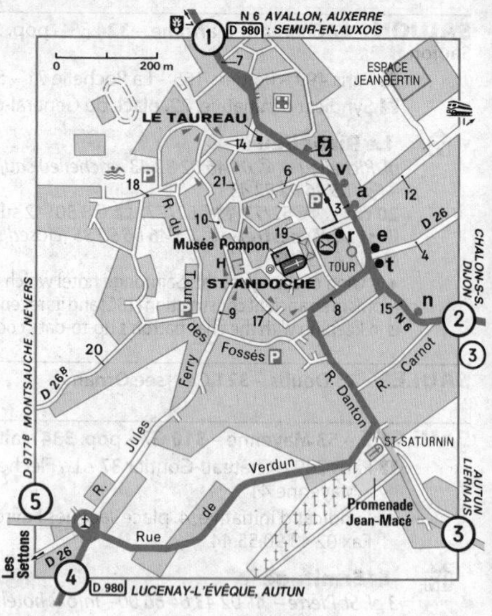

De la Poste
rest, P VISA

1 r. Grillot – 03 80 64 05 67 – lestlaurent@orange.fr – Fax 03 80 64 10 82 t

40 rm – €60 €75, €8 – ½ P €70

Rest – *(closed Wednesday)* Menu €24/49

◆ The four buildings making up this former17C coaching inn, on the great old Paris-to-Lyon road, are organised around a square courtyard. Classically arranged rooms. Traditional restaurant combining rustic and Belle Epoque styles. Appealing old-world atmosphere.

La Borne Impériale with rm
P VISA

16 r. Argentine – 03 80 64 19 76 – Fax 03 80 64 30 63 – Closed 10 January-10 February, Monday dinner and Tuesday except July-August v

7 rm – €40 €55, €9,50 – **Rest** – Menu €23/56 – Carte €46/74

◆ A traditional inn, serving tasty regional cuisine in a well-kept dining room or on the inviting terrace, overlooking a fine garden. Functional rooms upstairs.

Auberge du Relais with rm
rm, P VISA AE

8 r. Argentine – 03 80 64 13 16 – taverna.serge@wanadoo.fr – Fax 03 80 64 08 33 a

5 rm – €49 €56, €8,50 – ½ P €52/59

Rest – Menu (€17), €20/38 – Carte €29/47

◆ Inn highlighting regional dishes. Low-key rustic interior and peaceful terrace. Small, renovated rooms upstairs.

La Vieille Auberge with rm
rm, P VISA

15 r. Grillot – 03 80 64 13 74 – lavieilleauberge3@wanadoo.fr – Fax 03 80 64 13 74 – Closed 30 June-10 July, 12-30 January, 27 February-11 March, Tuesday dinner and Wednesday from 1st September to 13 July n

5 rm – €35 €35/42, €6 – ½ P €47/57

Rest – Menu €13/35 – Carte €23/39

◆ A small, family-run inn near the town centre serving local specialities in a dining room redecorated in yellow and orange tones. Courtyard terrace. Clean and comfortable rooms on the first floor.

SAULON-LA-RUE – 21 Côte-d'Or – 320 K6 – pop. 526 – alt. 215 m – ✉ 21910

Paris 324 – Dijon 12 – Beaune 43 – Gevrey-Chambertin 9 – Seurre 30 8 **D1**

Château de Saulon

rte de Seurre – ☎ 03 80 79 25 25 – info@chateau-saulon.com – Fax 03 80 79 25 26 – Closed 8-29 February – **30 rm** – €70/123 €87/135, €13 – ½ P €78/102

Rest – *(closed Sunday dinner October-May and Monday lunch)* Menu €20 (weekday lunch), €31/57 – Carte €40/60

◆ A pretty 17C château in a wooded park with an attractive swimming pool and small private lake. All the rooms have been renovated. Pleasant dining room in an outbuilding, serving up-to-date cuisine. Wine shop and tasting.

SAULT – 84 Vaucluse – 332 F9 – pop. 1 171 – alt. 765 m – ✉ 84390 French Alps

Paris 718 – Aix-en-Provence 86 – Apt 31 – Avignon 69 – Carpentras 42 – Digne-les-Bains 96 42 **E1**

Office de tourisme, avenue de la Promenade ☎ 04 90 64 01 21, Fax 04 90 64 15 03

Gorges de la Nesque★★: viewpoint★★ Southwest: 11 km by D 942 - Mont Ventoux ✻★★★ Northwest: 26 km.

Hostellerie du Val de Sault < mont - Ventoux,

2 km, St-Trinit road and secondary road – ☎ 04 90 64 01 41 – valdesault@aol.com – Fax 04 90 64 12 74 – Open from beg. April to 3 November

15 rm – €124/169 €124/169, €12 – 5 suites – ½ P €120/139

Rest – *(closed lunch April-June and15 September-3 November, except weekends)* Menu €39, €45/92

◆ Lavender fragrance, enchanting view, rooms with a lounge and small terrace or duplexes with an Asian décor account for the irresistible appeal of this establishment. Dashing, mixed-style dining room and pretty terrace, serving a regional cuisine, highlighted by truffles.

SAULXURES – 67 Bas-Rhin – 315 G6 – pop. 457 – alt. 535 m – ✉ 67420 1 **A2**

Paris 407 – Épinal 71 – Strasbourg 67 – Lunéville 65 – Saint-Dié 30

La Belle Vue rm,

36 r. Principale – ☎ 03 88 97 60 23 – labellevue@wanadoo.fr – Fax 03 88 47 23 71 – Closed 12-26 November

11 rm – €86/115 €86/126, €11 – ½ P €74/94 – **Rest** – *(closed Tuesday and Wednesday)* Menu €20/58

◆ The same family has been running this inn for four generations. Tastefully decorated suites, duplexes and rooms (exposed timbers, modern art). The up-to-date cuisine is served in the attractive setting of a glassed-in dining room overlooking the garden and a mezzanine.

SAUMUR – 49 Maine-et-Loire – 317 I5 – pop. 29 857 – alt. 30 m – ✉ 49400
Châteaux of the Loire 35 **C2**

Paris 300 – Angers 67 – Le Mans 124 – Poitiers 97 – Tours 64

Office de tourisme, place de la Bilange ☎ 02 41 40 20 60, Fax 02 41 40 20 69

de Saumur Saint-Hilaire, West: 5 km by D 751 and D 161, ☎ 02 41 50 87 00.

Château★★: musée d'Arts décoratifs★★, musée du Cheval★, tour du Guet ✻★ - N.-D.-de-Nantilly church ★: tapestries★★ - Old quarter★ BY : Town hall★ **H** ,tapestries★ of St-Pierre church - Musée de l'école de Cavalerie★ **M**[1] - Musée des Blindés★★ in the South.

Plan on next page

Château de Verrières without rest

53 r. d'Alsace – ☎ 02 41 38 05 15 – contact@chateau-verrieres.com – Fax 02 41 38 18 18 AY **v**

9 rm – €120/245 €120/245, €14

◆ You are welcomed as if you were a friend of the family in this lovely 18C castle set in the heart of a 2ha park. Luxuriously elegant interior (Napoleon III sitting rooms and period furniture).

St-Pierre without rest

8 r. Haute-St-Pierre – ☎ 02 41 50 33 00 – contact@saintpierresaumur.com – Fax 02 41 50 38 68 BY **b**

16 rm – €85/150 €100/190, €14

◆ Establishment located in well-restored 17C houses. Massive beams, half-timbered façade, spiral staircase and period furniture set the scene for this charming hotel.

SAUMUR

Anjou (R. d') .... BZ 2
Beaurepaire (R.) .... AY 3
Bilange (Pl. de la) .... BY 4
Cadets (Ponts des) .... BX 5
Dr-Bouchard (R. du) .... AZ 6
Dupetit-Thouars (Pl.) .... BZ 7
Fardeau (R.) .... AZ 9
Gaulle (Av. Général-de) .... BX
Leclerc (R. du Mar.) .... AZ
Nantilly (R. de) .... BZ 10
Orléans (R. d') .... ABY
Poitiers (R. de) .... AZ 12
Portail-Louis (R. du) .... BY 13
République (Pl. de la) .... BY 15
Roosevelt (R. Fr.) .... BY 16
St-Jean (R.) .... BY 18
St-Pierre (Pl.) .... BY 19
Tonnelle (R. de la) .... BY 20
Vieux-Pont (R. du) .... BY 22

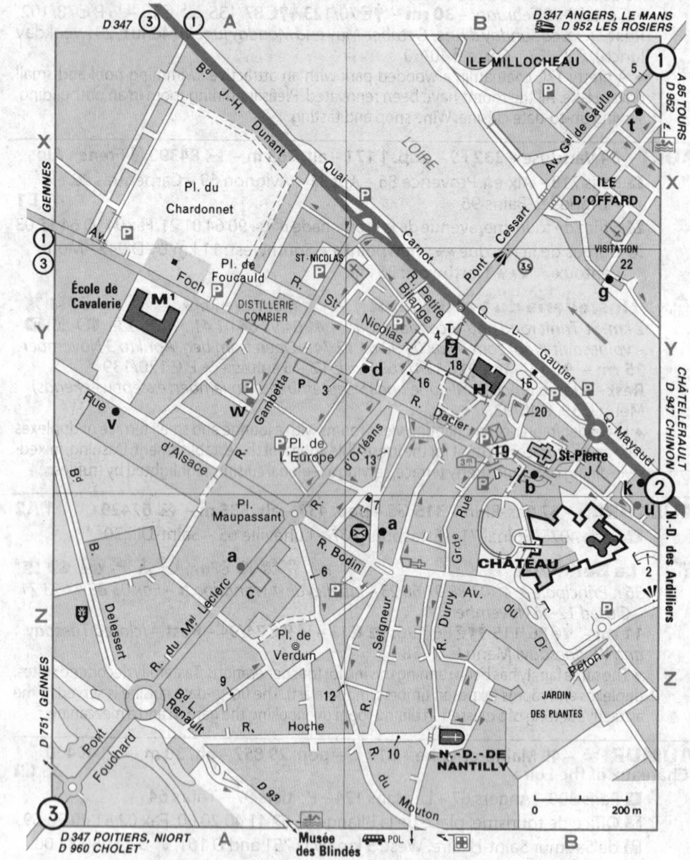

Anne d'Anjou without rest

32 quai Mayaud – ✆ 02 41 67 30 30 – contact@hotel-anneanjou.com – Fax 02 41 67 51 00 BY **k**

45 rm – €79/125 €97/195, €13

♦ Fine 18C manor with Empire-style or modern rooms facing the river or castle. In summer, breakfast is served in the lovely inner courtyard.

Adagio without rest

94 av. du Gén. de Gaulle – ✆ 02 41 67 45 30 – contact@hoteladagio.com – Fax 02 41 67 74 59 – Closed 23-26 December BX **t**

36 rm – €67/75 €81/99, €12 – 2 suites

♦ Five hundred metres from the station, this inviting establishment offers a choice of five categories of rooms, all prettily decorated in a modern, colourful style. Some overlook the Loire.

Mercure bord de Loire
r. du vieux Pont – ☎ 02 41 67 22 42 – loire-hotel@saumur.net – Fax 02 41 67 88 80 BY **g**
45 rm – €49/140 €72/155, ☕ €12 – 1 suite
Rest – Menu (€14,50), €19 (weekdays)/40 – Carte €23/45
◆ This modern hotel on the Ile d'Offard provides renovated, functional rooms, some with a fine view of the château and the Loire The restaurant has a new look but its view of the river and Saumur is timeless.

Kyriad without rest
23 r. Daillé – ☎ 02 41 51 05 78 – kyriad.saumur@multi-micro.com – Fax 02 41 67 82 35 BY **d**
29 rm – €60/79 €65/120, ☕ €8
◆ In the town centre but nevertheless quiet, this particularly hospitable hotel offers tastefully decorated rooms, two of which are very spacious and brand new.

Le Volney without rest
1 r. Volney – ☎ 02 41 51 25 41 – contact@levolney.com – Fax 02 41 38 11 04 BZ **a**
14 rm – €35 €35/55, ☕ €7
◆ Opposite the post office, simple, well kept and regularly revamped rooms. An affordable place to stay and discover the delights of the Anjou region.

Les Ménestrels
11 r. Raspail – ☎ 02 41 67 71 10 – menestrel@wanadoo.fr – Fax 02 41 50 89 64 – Closed 21-28 December, Monday except dinner April-October and Sunday BZ **u**
Rest – Menu €31/68 – Carte €55/74
◆ A fine selection of Loire wines accompanies the updated cuisine, which is served in two dining rooms, one in a former 14C chapel. Unexpected Moroccan menu.

Gambetta
12 r. Gambetta – ☎ 02 41 67 66 66 – legambetta@neuf.fr – Fax 02 41 50 83 23 – Closed 28 July-21 August, 2-17 January, Wednesday dinner, Sunday dinner and Monday AY **w**
Rest – Menu €19 (weekday lunch), €26/74 bi – Carte €50/72
◆ This country mansion near the Ecole de Cavalerie has two, simply furnished dining rooms. Summer terrace in the courtyard. Tasty seasonal dishes.

in St-Hilaire-St-Florent **3 km by Ave Foch** AXY **and D 751 – ✉ 49400 Saumur**
École nationale d'Équitation (National Horse-Riding School) ★.

Les Terrasses de Saumur
≤ Saumur,
chemin de l'Alat – ☎ 02 41 67 28 48 – contact@lesterrassesdesaumur.fr – Fax 02 41 67 13 71 – Closed 21 December-19 January
22 rm – €45/170 €65/170, ☕ €12 – ½ P €73/125
Rest – *(closed Monday lunch and Tuesday lunch)* Menu €31/65 – Carte €37/70
◆ This hotel overlooking Saumur and the castle is enjoying a new lease of life: attractively refurbished rooms (bright colours and good quality fittings), some with terrace. Classic cuisine served in a rotunda dining room overlooking the town or by the pool.

in Chênehutte-les-Tuffeaux **8 km by Ave Foch** AXY **and D 751 – pop. 1 102 – alt. 29 m – ✉ 49350**

Le Prieuré
≤ la Loire, rest,
– ☎ 02 41 67 90 14 – prieure@grandesetapes.fr – Fax 02 41 67 92 24
21 rm – €143/328 €143/328, ☕ €22 – 1 suite – **Rest** – Menu (€23), €29 (weekday lunch), €32/100 bi – Carte €32/76
◆ Well-located 12-16C priory overlooking the Loire. Tasteful, period furnished rooms, all of which command a fine view. The plush restaurant commands an unforgettable view of the valley. Local vegetables, fish and wines on the menu.

Les Résidences du Prieuré
– prieure@grandesetapes.fr
15 rm – €128 €128, ☕ €22
◆ In six bungalows, rooms with terrace and private garden are spread around the large wooded park.

SAUSHEIM – 68 Haut-Rhin – 315 I10 – see Mulhouse

LA SAUSSAYE – 27 Eure – 304 F6 – pop. 1 954 – alt. 137 m – ✉ 27370 33 D2

Paris 130 – Évreux 40 – Louviers 20 – Pont-Audemer 49 – Rouen 25

Manoir des Saules (Jean-Paul Monnaie) rm,
2 pl. St Martin – ✆ 02 35 87 25 65
– manoirdessaules@wanadoo.fr – Fax 02 35 87 49 39
– Closed 10 November-3 December, 23 February-6 March, Sunday dinner from September to April, Monday and Tuesday
9 rm – €165 €195/265, €20
Rest – *(number of covers limited, pre-book)* Menu €60/120 – Carte €65/107
Spec. Foie gras de canard au torchon. Poissons sauvages (depending on catch). Soufflé chaud au Grand Marnier.

◆ Half-timbering and turrets decorate the facade of this Norman manor with a garden. Beautiful antique furniture and original decoration in the rooms. Elegant dining rooms serving well-prepared, tasty, modern cuisine. Extensive wine list.

SAUSSET-LES-PINS – 13 Bouches-du-Rhône – 340 F6 – pop. 7 233 – alt. 15 m – ✉ 13960 Provence 40 B3

Paris 768 – Aix-en-Provence 41 – Marseille 37 – Martigues 13 – Salon-de-Provence 48

Syndicat d'initiative, 16, avenue du Port ✆ 04 42 45 60 65, Fax 04 42 45 60 68

Paradou-Méditerranée rest,
– ✆ 04 42 44 76 76 – hotel.paradou@wanadoo.fr
– Fax 04 42 44 78 48
41 rm – €87/112 €97/119, €10 – ½ P €67/78
Rest – *(closed 20 December-4 January)* Menu €34/50 – Carte €24/47

◆ A perfect location facing the sea with the additional benefits of a swimming pool and garden. Refurbished colourful rooms with balconies and sea views. Provençal-inspired dining room serving dishes full of the rich flavours of the Mediterranean.

Les Girelles
r. Frédéric Mistral – ✆ 04 42 45 26 16 – restaurant-les-girelles@wanadoo.fr
– Fax 04 42 45 49 65 – Closed 2-31 January, Tuesday lunch, Wednesday lunch in July-August, Sunday dinner from September to June and Monday
Rest – Menu €29/40 – Carte €42/84

◆ A comfortable veranda (round tables and medallion chairs) and terrace overlooking the sea. Provençal interior. Up-to-date cuisine with a seafood focus.

SAUTERNES – 33 Gironde – 335 I7 – pop. 586 – alt. 50 m – ✉ 33210 Atlantic Coast 3 B2

Paris 624 – Bazas 24 – Bordeaux 49 – Langon 11

Office de tourisme, 11, rue Principale ✆ 05 56 76 69 13, Fax 05 57 31 00 67

Relais du Château d'Arche without rest vineyard,
0.5 km north, Bommes road – ✆ 05 56 76 67 67
– chateaudarche@wanadoo.fr – Fax 05 56 76 69 76
9 rm – €120/160 €120/160, €10

◆ A fine, 17C charterhouse on the wine estate of Château d'Arches. Sample the grands crus after a visit. Cosy, personalised rooms. Reception room.

Saprien
14 r. Principale – ✆ 05 56 76 60 87 – saprien@tiscali.fr – Fax 05 56 76 68 92
– Closed 1st-8 March, 22 December-12 January, 16-22 February, Sunday dinner, Wednesday dinner, Monday and dinner in winter except Friday and Saturday
Rest – Menu (€17), €25/37 – Carte €42/58

◆ Typical winegrower's house with a charming rustic interior with fireplace and terrace giving directly onto the vines. Good selection of Sauternes by the glass.

SAUVE – 30 Gard – 339 I5 – pop. 1 690 – alt. 103 m – ✉ 30610 23 C2

Paris 747 – Montpellier 48 – Alès 28 – Nîmes 40 – Le Vigan 38

Office de tourisme, place René Isouard ✆ 04 66 77 57 51, Fax 04 66 77 05 99

La Magnanerie with rm
rte de Nîmes – 04 66 77 57 44 – la.magnanerie@wanadoo.fr – Fax 04 66 77 02 31
8 rm – €49/57 €56/115, €7 – ½ P €53/61
Rest – *(closed 15-30 November, Wednesday dinner except July-August, Tuesday lunch and Monday)* Menu (€14 bi), €26/36 – Carte €46/50
♦ This peaceful riverside 17C house is surrounded by a garden, in which the remains of an aqueduct can be seen. Practical rooms. Tasty, updated culinary repertory.

SAUVETERRE – 30 Gard – 339 N4 – pop. 1 696 – alt. 23 m – ✉ 30150 23 D2

Paris 669 – Alès 77 – Avignon 15 – Nîmes 49 – Orange 15 – Pont-St-Esprit 36

Château de Varenne without rest
pl. Saint-Jean – 04 66 82 59 45 – info@chateaudevarenne.com – Fax 04 66 82 84 83 – Closed 6 January-18 February
13 rm – €98/148 €98/380, €18
♦ A French-style park adds to the charm of this elegant 18th-century residence. Fine rooms, with individual furnishings enhanced by rich fabrics and antiques.

SAUVETERRE-DE-BEARN – 64 Pyrénées-Atlantiques – 342 G2 – pop. 1 304 – alt. 69 m – ✉ 64390 Atlantic Coast 3 B3

Paris 777 – Pau 64 – Bayonne 60 – Orthez 22 – Peyrehorade 25 – Saint-Jean-Pied-de-Port 44

Office de tourisme, place Royale 05 59 38 32 86

La Maison de Navarre
– 05 59 38 55 28 – infos@lamaisondenavarre.com – Fax 05 59 38 55 71 – Closed 27 August-3 September, November, 16 February-1st March
7 rm – €53/63 €58/74, €7,50 – ½ P €79/89 – **Rest** – *(closed Sunday dinner except July-August and Wednesday)* Menu €19 bi (weekdays) – Carte €30/44
♦ A charming residence set in a garden offering a fine view of the Pyrenees. Patiently collected antique furniture, parquet flooring and bright colours enhance the rooms. Restaurant with cosy setting, lovely terrace and half-Béarnaise, half-Provençal cuisine.

Domaine de Betouzet
Andrein, 3 km east on the D 27 – 05 59 38 91 40 – book@betouzet.com – Fax 05 59 38 91 51 – Open 20 March-30 November
5 rm – €150/200 €150/200, €12
Table d'hôte – Menu €24 bi (weekday lunch), €30 € bi/45 bi
♦ Hundred-year-old trees and immaculate box hedges adorn the grounds of this attractive manor house. Quiet, comfortable guestrooms, a boudoir and a wellness centre. Informal suppers of traditional dishes. Cookery courses are also on offer here.

SAUVETERRE-DE-COMMINGES – 31 Haute-Garonne – 343 C6 – pop. 720 – alt. 480 m – ✉ 31510 28 B3

Paris 777 – Bagnères-de-Luchon 36 – Lannemezan 31 – Tarbes 71 – Toulouse 104

Les 7 Molles
at Gesset – 05 61 88 30 87 – contact@hotel7molles.com – Fax 05 61 88 36 42 – Closed 15 February-15 March, Tuesday and Wednesday off season
18 rm – €79/83 €83/195, €12 – ½ P €92/127
Rest – *(closed lunch weekdays)* Menu €30/47 – Carte €43/60
♦ The rooms with balcony overlook the pretty flower garden adorned with seven locally sourced millstones (Molles). Somewhat old-fashioned but definitely comfortable. Local ceramic tableware adorns the handsome dining room. Traditional cuisine.

SAUVETERRE-DE-ROUERGUE – 12 Aveyron – 338 F5 – pop. 832 – alt. 460 m – ✉ 12800 Languedoc-Roussillon-Tarn Gorges 29 C1

Paris 652 – Albi 52 – Millau 88 – Rodez 30 – St-Affrique 78 – Villefranche-de-Rouergue 44

Office de tourisme, place des Arcades 05 65 72 02 52, Fax 05 65 72 02 85

Place centrale★.

Le Sénéchal (Michel Truchon) VISA

– *05 65 71 29 00 – info@hotel-senechal.fr – Fax 05 65 71 29 09*
– Closed 1st January-15 March, Tuesday lunch and Thursday lunch except July-August and Monday
8 rm – €105 €105, €16 – 3 suites – ½ P €120/150
Rest – *(number of covers limited, pre-book)* Menu €26/125 – Carte €45/85
Spec. Foies gras de canard chauds et froids. Viandes et volailles de pays. Desserts aux fruits de saison. **Wines** Marcillac, Vin de pays de l'Aveyron.

◆ This charming inn occupies a royal bastide dating from the 13C. Completely rebuilt in local style, the interior decor is a mix of old and new. Contemporary dishes and an unusual decor: a goldfish bowl on every table, contemporary iron artwork and designer sitting room.

SAUVIAT-SUR-VIGE – 87 Haute-Vienne – 325 G5 – pop. 1 044 – alt. 450 m – ✉ 87400

24 **B2**

Paris 404 – Limoges 34 – Guéret 49 – Panazol 30 – Isle 38

Auberge de la Poste VISA

141 r. Emile Dourdet – 05 55 75 30 12 – aubergedelaposte@wanadoo.fr – Fax 05 55 75 33 60 – Closed 23 December-3 January
10 rm – €40 €50, €6,50 – ½ P €48 – **Rest** – *(closed Sunday dinner and Monday)* Menu €17 (weekdays)/38 – Carte €24/47

◆ Family-run inn on the village high street. The functional, rustic inspired rooms are housed in a building sheltered from the noise of the street. Classic dishes served in an attractive country setting with bare beams, stonework and parquet floors.

SAUVIGNY-LES-BOIS – 58 Nièvre – 319 C10 – see Nevers

SAUXILLANGES – 63 Puy-de-Dôme – 326 H9 – pop. 1 082 – alt. 460 m – ✉ 63490 Auvergne

6 **C2**

Paris 455 – Ambert 46 – Clermont-Ferrand 45 – Issoire 14 – Thiers 45 – Vic-le-Comte 20

Syndicat d'initiative, place de l'Ancienne Poste 04 73 96 37 63, Fax 04 73 96 87 24

Pic d'Usson ✻★ Southwest: 4 km.

Restaurant de la Mairie VISA

11-17 pl. St-Martin – 04 73 96 80 32 – contact@fontbonne.fr – Fax 04 73 96 89 92 – Closed 26 June-4 July, 22 September-3 October, 5-23 January, Tuesday dinner and Wednesday dinner from 1st November to Easter, Sunday dinner and Monday
Rest – Menu €20 (weekdays)/50 – Carte €29/52

◆ Opposite the town hall, this village house dates back to 1811. Pleasantly renovated contemporary dining room and lounge with a fireplace. Mix of traditional and regional cuisine.

LE SAUZE – 04 Alpes-de-Haute-Provence – 334 I6 – see Barcelonnette

SAUZON – 56 Morbihan – 308 L10 – see Belle-Ile-en-Mer

SAVERNE – 67 Bas-Rhin – 315 I4 – pop. 11 201 – alt. 200 m – ✉ 67700 Alsace-Lorraine

1 **A1**

Paris 450 – Lunéville 88 – St-Avold 89 – Sarreguemines 65 – Strasbourg 39

Office de tourisme, 37, Grand'Rue 03 88 91 80 47, Fax 03 88 71 02 90

Château★: façade★★ - Old half-timbered houses★ **N.**

Plan on next page

Europe without rest VISA

7 r. de la Gare – 03 88 71 12 07 – info@hotel-europe-fr.com – Fax 03 88 71 11 43 – Closed 21 December-6 January
28 rm – €63/68 €67/125, €9,50

A **e**

◆ This hotel sports a European inspired decor. Spacious, functional rooms with modern bathrooms. Faultless upkeep. Stylish lounge and cosy bar overlooking the street.

SAVERNE

Bouxwiller (R. de) .... B 2
Clés (R. des) .... B 3
Côte (R. de la) .... B 5
Dettwiller (R. de) .... B 6
Églises (R. des) .... B 8
Foch (R. Mar.) .... A 12
Gare (R. de la) .... A 13
Gaulle (Pl. Gén.-de) .... B 14
Grand'Rue .... AB
Joffre (R. Mar.) .... B 15
Murs (R. des) .... AB 16
Pères (R. des) .... B 17
Poincaré (R.) .... A 20
Poste (R. de la) .... B 22
Tribunal (R. du) .... B 24
19-Novembre (R. du) .... A 26

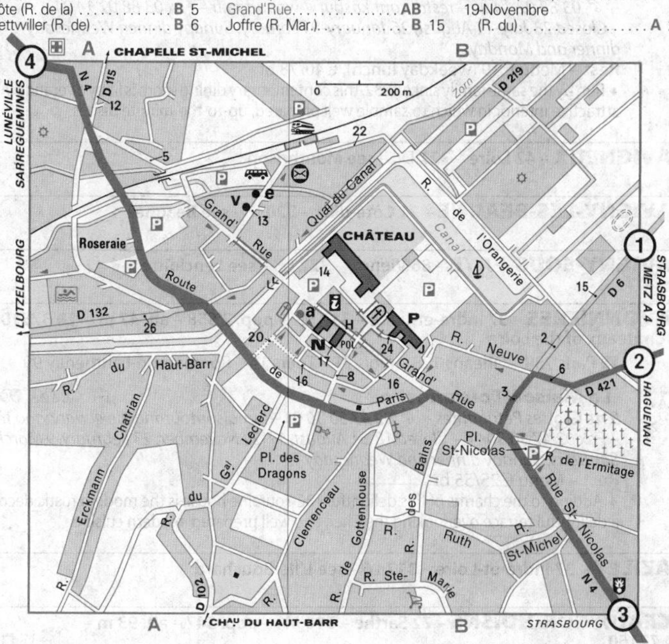

Chez Jean

3 r. de la Gare – ☎ 03 88 91 10 19 – chez.jean@wanadoo.fr – Fax 03 88 91 27 45 – Closed 2-11 January A **v**

25 rm – €63/66 €79/84, ☕ €9,50 – ½ P €68/74

Rest – *(closed 22 December-12 January, Sunday dinner and Monday)* Menu €15 (weekday lunch), €29/42 – Carte €32/55

Rest *Winstub s'Rosestiebel* – *(closed 22 December-12 January, Sunday dinner and Monday)* Menu €15 (weekday lunch), €29/42 – Carte €32/55

◆ Two steps from the pedestrian centre, this house offers light, well-equipped rooms in an Alsace style: wainscoting, duvets and pretty bed linen. Regional cuisine served in a wood-panelled dining room. Pleasant meals in the convivial atmosphere of the Winstub s'Rosestiebel.

Zum Staeffele

1 r. Poincaré – ☎ 03 88 91 63 94 – michel.jaeckel@wanadoo.fr – Fax 03 88 91 63 94 – Closed 21 July-8 August, 22 December-5 January, Sunday dinner, Wednesday and Thursday B **a**

Rest – Menu €22 (weekday lunch), €38/55 – Carte €46/52

◆ Stone house dating from the 18C and 19C, situated opposite Rohan castle. Tasteful interior adorned with paintings. Up-to-date cuisine made with good quality produce.

Le Clos de la Garenne with rm

1,5 km via rte de Haut Barr – ☎ 03 88 71 20 41 – clos-garenne@wanadoo.fr – Fax 03 88 02 08 86

15 rm – €35/50 €50/95, ☕ €10 – ½ P €62/80

Rest – *(closed Saturday lunch, Tuesday dinner and Wednesday)* Menu €18 (weekday lunch), €40/80 – Carte €56/75

◆ A cuisine with fresh produce and updated details served in a light, rustic interior. The rooms invite you to cocoon amid old wainscoting and chequered fabric.

via ② 3 km on D 421 – ✉ 67700 Monswiller

XX **Kasbür**

– ✆ *03 88 02 14 20 – restaurant.kasbur@wanadoo.fr – Fax 03 88 02 14 21 – Closed 28 July-11 August, 26 January-9 February, Sunday dinner, Wednesday dinner and Monday*

Rest – Menu € 19 (weekday lunch), € 40/78 bi

◆ Run by the same family since 1932, this contemporary dining room is lit by a veranda. An attractive interior in which to sample well prepared, up-to-the-minute dishes.

SAVIGNEUX – 42 Loire – 327 D6 – see Montbrison

SAVIGNY-LÈS-BEAUNE – 21 Côte-d'Or – 320 I7 – see Beaune

SAVIGNY-SOUS-FAYE – 86 Vienne – 322 H3 – see Lencloitre

SAVONNIÈRES – 37 Indre-et-Loire – 317 M4 – pop. 2 558 – alt. 47 m – ✉ 37510

Châteaux of the Loire

Paris 238 – Orléans 128 – Blois 71 – Tours 14 – Romorantin-Lanthenay 99

XX **La Maison Tourangelle**

9 rte Grottes Pétrifiantes – ✆ 02 47 50 30 05 – lamaisontourangelle@wanadoo.fr – Fax 02 47 50 30 94 – Closed 18-31 August, 17-24 November, 23 February-9 March, Saturday, Sunday dinner and Wednesday

Rest – Menu € 25/55 bi

◆ Adding to the charms of this delightful 18C Touraine house is the modern rustic decor, a delightful terrace overlooking the Cher, and well prepared, modern cuisine.

SAZILLY – 37 Indre-et-Loire – 317 L6 – see L'Île-Bouchard

SCEAUX-SUR-HUISNE – 72 Sarthe – 310 M6 – pop. 547 – alt. 93 m – ✉ 72160

35 **D1**

Paris 173 – Châteaudun 75 – La Ferté-Bernard 12 – Mamers 41 – Le Mans 35 – Nogent-le-Rotrou 34

XX **Le Panier Fleuri**

1 av. Bretagne – ✆ 02 43 93 40 08 – Fax 02 43 93 43 86 – Closed 14-30 July, 1st-14 January, Sunday dinner, Tuesday dinner and Wednesday

Rest – Menu € 20/30 – Carte € 22/50

◆ A 19C house in the centre of the village. Refurbished dining room with exposed beams and rustic furniture; cellar and cosy lounge.

SCHERWILLER – 67 Bas-Rhin – 315 I7 – pop. 2 614 – alt. 185 m – ✉ 67750

Paris 439 – Barr 21 – Colmar 27 – St-Dié 42 – Sélestat 5 2 **C1**

Office de tourisme, 30, rue de la Mairie ✆ 03 88 92 25 62

Auberge Ramstein rm,

1 r. Riesling – ✆ 03 88 82 17 00 – hotel.ramstein@wanadoo.fr – Fax 03 88 82 17 02 – Closed 23 December-10 January and February school holidays

15 rm – †€ 48 ††€ 60, ☕ € 8 – ½ P € 58/61 – **Rest** – *(closed Sunday, Wednesday and lunch from 15 July to 15 August)* Menu € 24/43 – Carte € 30/41

◆ Pleasant local house overlooking the Alsatian vineyards on all sides. Spacious and well-equipped rooms. Breakfast served in the salon. Welcoming restaurant where you can enjoy modern cuisine accompanied by a fine selection of wines.

SCHIRMECK – 67 Bas-Rhin – 315 H6 – pop. 2 177 – alt. 315 m – ✉ 67130

Alsace-Lorraine 1 **A2**

Paris 412 – Nancy 101 – St-Dié 41 – Saverne 48 – Sélestat 59 – Strasbourg 53

Office de tourisme, 114, Grand'Rue ✆ 03 88 47 18 51, Fax 03 88 97 09 59

La Bruche Valley ★ North and South.

in Quelles 7.5 km southwest by D 1420, D 261 and forest road – ✉ 67130 La Broque

Neuhauser ◇ rm, rest, VISA MC AE

– ✆ *03 88 97 06 81 – hotelneuhauser@wanadoo.fr – Fax 03 88 97 14 29*
– Closed 17-30 November and 20 February-10 March
20 rm – †€ 68 ††€ 85/132, ☕ € 12 – ½ P € 72/110 – **Rest** – Menu € 22/50
– Carte € 27/56

◆ Peace and quiet are guaranteed in this country inn nestling in the middle of the forest. Rustic style rooms and chalets, indoor pool and sauna. Tasty, regional fare, and after the meal, the brandy from the family distillery is a must!

LA SCHLUCHT (COL) – 88 Vosges – 314 K4 – see Col de la Schlucht

---

SECLIN – 59 Nord – 302 G4 – pop. 12 089 – alt. 30 m – ✉ 59113

Northern France and the Paris Region 31 **C2**

Paris 212 – Lens 26 – Lille 17 – Tournai 33 – Valenciennes 47

Office de tourisme, 70, rue Roger Bouvry ✆ 03 20 90 12 12, Fax 03 20 90 12 00

Hospital★ courtyard.

Auberge du Forgeron with rm VISA MC AE

17 r. Roger Bouvry – ✆ 03 20 90 09 52 – contact@aubergeduforgeron.com
– Fax 03 20 32 70 87 – Closed 26 July-18 August and 24-30 December
16 rm – †€ 55/72 ††€ 72/89, ☕ € 10 – 1 suite – **Rest** – *(Closed Saturday lunch and Sunday)* Menu € 38/91 bi – Carte € 55/84

◆ Old red-brick house. The fireplace and spit roast create a warm atmosphere in the dining room-veranda. Contemporary repertoire and fine wine list. Comfortable modern rooms.

SEDAN – 08 Ardennes – 306 L4 – pop. 20 548 – alt. 154 m – ✉ 08200

Northern France and the Paris Region 14 **C1**

Paris 246 – Charleville-Mézières 25 – Metz 134 – Reims 101

Office de tourisme, place du Château Fort ✆ 03 24 27 73 73, Fax 03 24 29 03 28

Fortified castle ★★.

Plan on next page

Hôtellerie le Château Fort VISA MC AE

in the fortified castle: access via Porte des Princes – ✆ 03 24 26 11 00
– contact@hotelfp-sedan.com – Fax 03 24 27 19 00 BY **a**
52 rm – †€ 69/129 ††€ 69/129, ☕ € 12 – 1 suite – **Rest** – *(closed Sunday dinner and Monday lunch)* Menu (€ 22), € 28/55 – Carte € 46/57

◆ The hotel occupies the former gunpowder room of the 15C castle. Modern and comfortable decor. Appealing rooms, adorned with medieval-themed paintings. The restaurant serves an up-to-date cuisine in a simple, modern decor.

Au Bon Vieux Temps A/C VISA MC AE

3 pl. de la Halle – ✆ 03 24 29 03 70 – restaurant.au.bon.vieux.temps@wanadoo.fr
– Fax 03 24 29 20 27 – Closed 25 August-1st September, 26-31 December, 16 February-9 March, Sunday dinner, Wednesday dinner and Monday BYZ **r**
Rest – Menu (€ 19), € 25/48 – Carte € 36/74
Rest *Marmiton* – *(Closed Sunday and Monday) (lunch only)* Menu € 13/18
– Carte € 15/20

◆ Lovely naive murals (views of Sedan and Ardennes landscapes) decorate this comfortable restaurant near the château. Classic menu available downstairs. The Marmiton offers a simple menu and lunchtime daily specials in a bistro atmosphere above the Bon Vieux Temps.

in Bazeilles 3 km by ① – pop. 1 879 – alt. 161 m – ✉ 08140

Château de Bazeilles rm, VISA MC AE

– ✆ *03 24 27 09 68 – contact@chateau-bazeilles.com – Fax 03 24 27 64 20*
20 rm – †€ 74 ††€ 92, ☕ € 9 – ½ P € 83/102
Rest *L'Orangerie* – *(closed 24-30 December, Sunday dinner from 15 November to 15 March and Saturday lunch)* Menu € 22 (weekdays)/50 – Carte € 34/64

◆ A hotel occupying the outbuildings and caretaker's lodge of an 18C château, where Sedan's bourgeoisie used to meet. Cool, spacious rooms. L'Orangerie offers inventive cuisine, by an open fire, under an unusual upturned ship's hull, or on the summer terrace facing the gardens.

SEDAN

Alsace-Lorraine (Pl. d') . . . . BZ 2
Armes (Pl. d') . . . . BY 3
Bayle (R. de) . . . . BY 4
Berchet (R.) . . . . BY 5
Blanpain (R.) . . . . BY 6
Capucins (Rampe) . . . . BY 7
Carnot (R.) . . . . BY 8
Crussy (Pl.) . . . . BY 9
Fleuranges (R. de) . . . . AY 10
Francs-Bourgeois (R. des) . . . . BY 12
Gambetta (R.) . . . . BY 13
Goulden (Pl.) . . . . BY 14
Halle (Pl. de la) . . . . BY 15
Horloge (R. de l') . . . . BY 17
Jardin (Bd du Gd) . . . . BY 18
Lattre-de-Tassigny (Bd Mar.-de) . . . . AZ 21
Leclerc (Av. du Mar.) . . . . BY 24
Margueritte (Av. du G.) . . . . . ABY 26
Martyrs-de-la-Résistance (Av. des) . . . . AY 27
Mesnil (R. du) . . . . BY
Nassau (Pl.) . . . . BZ 31
Promenoir-des-Prêtres . . . . BY 33
Rivage (R. du) . . . . BY 34
La Rochefoucauld (R. de) . . . . BY 20
Rochette (Bd de la) . . . . BY 35
Rovigo (R.) . . . . BY 36
Strasbourg (R. de) . . . . BZ 39
Turenne (Pl.) . . . . BY 41
Vesseron-Lejay (R.) . . . . AY 42
Wuildet-Bizot (R.) . . . . BZ 44

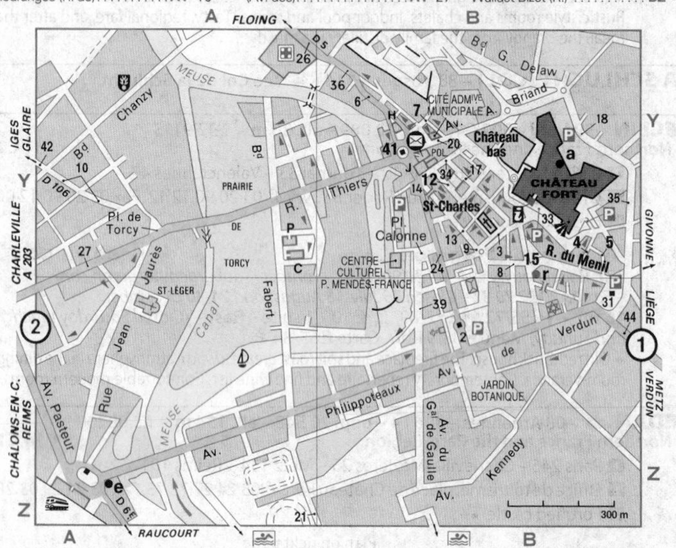

Auberge du Port

south: 1 km via rte Remilly-Aillicourt – ☎ 03 24 27 13 89 – auberge-du-port@wanadoo.fr – Fax 03 24 29 35 58 – Closed 1st-25 August, 19 December-5 January
20 rm – †€ 55 ††€ 65/70, ☕ € 8 – ½ P € 55 – **Rest** – *(closed Friday except dinner 1st April-30 October, Saturday lunch and Sunday dinner)* Menu € 18 (weekday lunch), € 24/53

◆ This peaceful country inn, enclosed by a garden on the banks of the Meuse, offers an excellent choice of wines (wine for sale, plus tastings available). Simple rooms, many of which have been renovated. Pleasant restaurant-veranda, extended by a terrace surrounded by greenery. Classic cuisine and good vintage wines.

SÉES – 61 Orne – 310 K3 – pop. 4 504 – alt. 186 m – ✉ 61500 Normandy

33 C3

Paris 183 – L'Aigle 42 – Alençon 22 – Argentan 24 – Domfront 66 – Mortagne-au-Perche 33

Office de tourisme, place du Général-de-Gaulle ☎ 02 33 28 74 79, Fax 02 33 28 18 13

Notre-Dame cathedral ★: choir and transept ★★ - Ecouves forest ★★ Southwest: 5 km.

in Macé 5,5 km by Argentan road, D 303 and D 747 – pop. 476 – alt. 173 m – ✉ 61500

Château d'O ★ Northwest: 5 km.

Ile de Sées rest,

– ☎ 02 33 27 98 65 – ile-sees@ile-sees.fr – Fax 02 33 28 41 22
– Open 1st March-30 November and closed Sunday evening
16 rm – †€ 55 ††€ 65, ☕ € 8 – ½ P € 60 – **Rest** – *(closed Sunday dinner, Monday lunch, Tuesday lunch and Wednesday lunch)* Menu € 18 (weekdays)/35 – Carte € 21/42

◆ Hotel with extensive grounds in the middle of the Normandy countryside. Pleasant guestrooms (stained wood furniture, pastel shades). Copious buffet breakfast. A welcoming, rustic yet stylish dining room, serving traditional cuisine.

SEGONZAC – 19 Corrèze – 329 I4 – pop. 239 – alt. 345 m – ✉ 19310

Dordogne-Berry-Limousin 24 **B3**

Paris 506 – Limoges 117 – Tulle 58 – Brive-la-Gaillarde 31 – Périgueux 69

Pré Laminon

– ✆ 05 55 84 17 39 – *prelaminon@wanadoo.fr – Open 1st April-30 September*

3 rm – 🚹€ 40/50 🚹🚹€ 52/60 – **Table d'hôte** – Menu € 18 bi

◆ An old Corrèze-style barn in hilly surroundings. The interior is as welcoming as an Alpine chalet, with its rustic wood decor, cosy bedrooms etc. Swimming pool.

SÉGOS – 32 Gers – 336 A8 – see Aire-sur-l'Adour

SÉGURET – 84 Vaucluse – 332 D8 – see Vaison-la-Romaine

SEIGNOSSE – 40 Landes – 335 C12 – pop. 2 427 – alt. 15 m – ✉ 40510 3 **A3**

Paris 747 – Biarritz 36 – Dax 32 – Mont-de-Marsan 85 – Soustons 11

Office de tourisme, avenue des Lacs ✆ 05 58 43 32 15, Fax 05 58 43 32 66

de Seignosse Avenue du Belvédère, West: 4 km by D 86, ✆ 05 58 41 68 30.

Golf Hôtel

rm, VISA MC AE

av. du Belvédère, at the golf club, 4 km west via D86 – ✆ 05 58 41 68 40 – Fax 05 58 41 68 41 – Closed 15 December-18 February

45 rm – 🚹€ 74/95 🚹🚹€ 100/142, € 12 – **Rest** – *(dinner only)* Menu € 28/36 – Carte € 31/55

◆ A colourful Louisiana-style wood construction, in a pine grove, part of a fine golf course. Immense reception hall lit by a glass roof. Some rooms have balconies. Traditional cuisine served in the restaurant in the evening and lunchtime set menu at the club-house.

Villa de l'Etang Blanc

rm, VISA MC AE

2265, rte Etang Blanc, 2.5 Km north by D 185 and D 432 – ✆ 05 58 72 80 15 – lavilladeetangblanc@wanadoo.fr – Fax 05 58 72 83 67 – Open from March to October

10 rm – 🚹€ 65/110 🚹🚹€ 65/155, € 15 – ½ P € 80/125

Rest – *(open 15 March-15 October and closed Tuesday lunch, Sunday dinner and Monday off season, lunch except weekends and public holidays from 1st July-15 September)* Menu € 25/45 – Carte € 34/56

◆ A retro ambience with the occasional exotic touch pervades this charming house with an attractive garden. Elegant guestrooms and junior suites. Glass-enclosed dining room, overlooking the pond after which the villa is named, and delightful terrace facing the canal, where fishing boats are moored.

SEILH – 31 Haute-Garonne – 343 G2 – see Toulouse

SEILHAC – 19 Corrèze – 329 L3 – pop. 1 635 – alt. 500 m – ✉ 19700 25 **C3**

Paris 461 – Aubusson 97 – Brive-la-Gaillarde 33 – Limoges 73 – Tulle 15 – Uzerche 16

Office de tourisme, place de l'Horloge ✆ 05 55 27 97 62

Au Relais des Monédières

VISA MC AE

1 km Tulle road – ✆ 05 55 27 04 74 – Fax 05 55 27 90 03 – Closed 29 March-5 April, 30 June-6 July, 23 December-15 January, Friday dinner, Saturday lunch and Sunday dinner off season and public holidays

16 rm – 🚹€ 48/51 🚹🚹€ 48/60, € 7 – ½ P € 49/52 – **Rest** – Menu € 14/34 – Carte € 20/36

◆ Set in a pretty park with pond, this family hotel facing the Monédières mountains will appeal to anglers. Modest but impeccably kept rooms. Rustic restaurant and green terrace covered by a canopy. Traditional and regional dishes.

SEILLANS – 83 Var – 340 O4 – pop. 2 115 – alt. 350 m – ✉ 83440 41 **C3**

Paris 890 – Marseille 142 – Toulon 106 – Antibes 54 – Cannes 43

Syndicat d'initiative, 1, rue du Valat ✆ 04 94 76 85 91, Fax 04 94 39 13 53

Des Deux Rocs
1 pl. Font.d' Amont – ✆ 04 94 76 87 32 – hoteldeuxrocs@wanadoo.fr – Fax 04 94 76 88 68 – Closed 17-23 November and 4 January-14 February
14 rm – †€ 65/135 ††€ 65/135, ☕ € 12 – **Rest** – *(closed Sunday dinner and Tuesday lunch except from June to September and Monday)*
Menu (€ 30), € 37 – Carte € 42/52
◆ Hostelry of character in a fine 18C country house set above the village. Pretty, individualised rooms, furnished with old family pieces and antiques. Meals served around the fireplace or in the shade of plane trees on the village square.

Le Relais d'Oléa
1 pl. Thouron – ✆ 04 94 60 18 65 – contact@lerelaisdolea.com – Fax 04 94 60 10 92 – Closed 8 November-10 December, Wednesday except in summer and Tuesday
Rest – Menu € 28/43 – Carte € 32/46
◆ In a former coaching inn, this restaurant in the upper part of the village has a contemporary décor. Modern menu based on quality produce. Terrace shaded by plane trees.

SEILLONNAZ – 01 Ain – 328 F6 – pop. 123 – alt. 530 m – ✉ 01470 45 C1

Paris 498 – Lyon 87 – Bourg-en-Bresse 66 – Villeurbanne 75 – Chambéry 73

La Cigale d'Or
au village – ✆ 04 74 36 13 61 – cigaledor@wanadoo.fr – Fax 04 74 36 15 64 – Closed 3-9 November, 22-28 December, Sunday dinner, Tuesday dinner and Wednesday
Rest – Menu € 25/39 – Carte € 29/51
◆ Don't miss this village restaurant, renowned for its delicious contemporary cuisine, served in a comfortable, vaulted dining room. Terrace overlooking the valley.

SEIN (ÎLE) – 29 Finistère – 308 B6 – see Île de Sein

SÉLESTAT – 67 Bas-Rhin – 315 I7 – pop. 17 179 – alt. 170 m – ✉ 67600

Alsace-Lorraine 2 C1

Paris 441 – Colmar 24 – Gérardmer 65 – St-Dié 44 – Strasbourg 55
Office de tourisme, boulevard Leclerc ✆ 03 88 58 87 20, Fax 03 88 92 88 63
Old town★: Ste-Foy church★, St-Georges church★, Bibliothèque humaniste★ M.
Ebermunster: interior★★ of abbey church★, 9 km by ①.

Plan on next page

Hostellerie de l'Abbaye la Pommeraie
8 av. Mar. Foch – ✆ 03 88 92 07 84 – pommeraie@relaischateaux.com – Fax 03 88 92 08 71 BY a
12 rm – †€ 142 ††€ 158/248, ☕ € 16 – 2 suites
Rest *Le Prieuré* – *(closed Sunday dinner and Monday lunch)* Menu € 28 (weekday lunch), € 51 € bi/91 – Carte € 69/108
Rest *S'Apfelstuebel* – Menu € 28 (weekday lunch)/51 bi – Carte € 38/56
Spec. Foie gras d'oie poêlé, chutney de coing. Saint-Pierre cuit au plat, canneloni de verdures. Filet de chevreuil, compotée d'oignons et chou rouge au cumin.
Wines Pinot blanc, Alsace.
◆ In the old town, a noble 17C house, formerly an outbuilding of the Baumgarten Abbey. Pleasant rooms furnished with pretty, period-style furniture. At the Prieuré, you will find an elegant setting and classic, well-prepared food. Local decor and dishes at the S'Apfelstuebel winstub.

Vaillant
rest,
7 r. Ignace Spiess – ✆ 03 88 92 09 46 – hotel-vaillant@wanadoo.fr – Fax 03 88 82 95 01
47 rm – †€ 58/77 ††€ 68/98, ☕ € 9 – ½ P € 53/74 AZ e
Rest – *(closed 22 December-2 January, Saturday lunch and Sunday dinner off season)* Menu € 15/29 – Carte € 29/45
◆ Many works by local artists are displayed in this modern hotel flanked by a floral park, near the town centre. Bright rooms with individual touches. Restaurant with carefully thought-out decor offering traditional dishes and regional specialities.

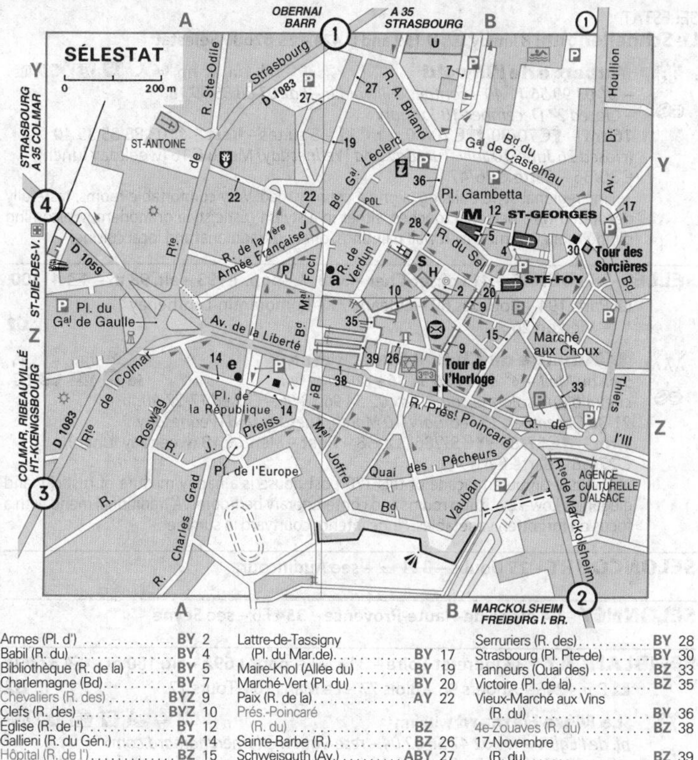

Armes (Pl. d') . . . . BY 2	Lattre-de-Tassigny (Pl. du Mar.de) . . . . BY 17	Serruriers (R. des) . . . . BY 28
Babil (R. du) . . . . BY 4	Maire-Knol (Allée du) . . . . BY 19	Strasbourg (Pl. Pte-de) . . . . BY 30
Bibliothèque (R. de la) . . . . BY 5	Marché-Vert (Pl. du) . . . . BY 20	Tanneurs (Quai des) . . . . BZ 33
Charlemagne (Bd) . . . . BY 7	Paix (R. de la) . . . . AY 22	Victoire (Pl. de la) . . . . BZ 35
Chevaliers (R. des) . . . . BYZ 9	Prés.-Poincaré (R. du) . . . . BZ	Vieux-Marché aux Vins (R. du) . . . . BY 36
Clefs (R. des) . . . . BYZ 10	Sainte-Barbe (R.) . . . . BZ 26	4e-Zouaves (R. du) . . . . BZ 38
Église (R. de l') . . . . BY 12	Schweisguth (Av.) . . . . ABY 27	17-Novembre (R. du) . . . . BZ 39
Gallieni (R. du Gén.) . . . . AZ 14		
Hôpital (R. de l') . . . . BZ 15		

X **La Vieille Tour**

8 r. Jauge – ✆ 03 88 92 15 02 – vieille.tour@wanadoo.fr – Fax 03 88 92 19 42 – Closed 22 July-4 August, 17 February-3 March and Monday BY **s**

Rest – Menu € 11,50 (weekday lunch), € 26/55 bi – Carte € 31/46

◆ A pretty Alsace style house flanked by an old tower. Refreshingly rustic dining rooms and fine regional cooking (using local produce). Reasonably priced wines.

in Rathsamhausen **5 km East by D 21 and D 209 – ✉ 67600 Baldenheim**

Les Prés d'Ondine rm, rest,

5 rte Baldenheim – ✆ 03 88 58 04 60 – message@presdondine.com – Fax 03 88 58 04 61

12 rm – †€ 60/132 ††€ 70/132, ☕ € 12 – ½ P € 79/110 – **Rest** – table d'hôte *(closed 1st-15 March, Sunday dinner and Wednesday) (pre-book)* Menu € 22 bi (weekday lunch)/32 bi

◆ This pleasant, early 20C forester's house provides a homely atmosphere. Cosy lounge, library and rooms with poetry-inspired decor. Regional dishes and a view of the Ill are the main assets of the elegant restaurant.

in Baldenheim **8,5 km by ①, D 21 and D 209 – pop. 924 – alt. 170 m – ✉ 67600**

XX **Couronne**

r. Sélestat – ✆ 03 88 85 32 22 – la-couronne-baldenheim@wanadoo.fr – Fax 03 88 85 36 27 – Closed 29 July-12 August, 5-12 January, Thursday dinner, Sunday dinner and Monday

Rest – Menu € 32/70 – Carte € 48/70

◆ A village inn with a muted atmosphere, beautiful wood panelling, attentive service, a well-stocked cellar and, most importantly – carefully prepared cuisine.

Le Schnellenbuhl 8 km by ②, D 159 and D 424 – ✉ 67600 Sélestat

Auberge de l'Illwald rm, rm, VISA AE
– ✆ *03 90 56 11 40 – contact@illwald.fr – Fax 03 88 85 39 18*
– Closed 24 December-10 January
16 rm – †€ 70/80 ††€ 70/80, ☕ € 11 – 5 suites – **Rest** – ✆ 03 88 85 35 40
(closed 26 June-10 July, Tuesday and Wednesday) Menu € 16 (weekday lunch), € 30/36 – Carte € 26/47
♦ Fine regional-style building, along a country road. Very comfortable rooms, tastefully decorated with personal touches, either in a stylish rustic style or modern. Welcoming dining room, adorned with wall paintings, offering traditional and local cuisine.

SELLES-ST-DENIS – **41 Loir-et-Cher** – **318** I7 – **pop. 1 193** – **alt. 98 m** – ✉ **41300**

Paris 194 – Bourges 69 – Orléans 71 – Romorantin-Lanthenay 16 – Vierzon 26 12 **C2**

L'Auberge du Cheval Blanc with rm rm, rest, VISA AE
5 pl. du Mail – ✆ 02 54 96 36 36 – auberge@chevalblanc-sologne.com – Fax 02 54 96 13 96 – Closed 17-27 August, 21-30 December, 15 February-10 March, Tuesday and Wednesday
7 rm – †€ 57/86 ††€ 57/86, ☕ € 8 – **Rest** – Menu € 18 (weekday lunch), € 27/56 – Carte € 41/77
♦ The half-timbered façade of this 17C post house is a happy mixture of rusticity and elegance. Low-key sitting rooms and contemporary bedrooms. A traditional menu with a focus on forgotten vegetables. Huge interior courtyard in summer.

SELONCOURT – **25 Doubs** – **321** L2 – **see Audincourt**

SELONNET – **04 Alpes-de-Haute-Provence** – **334** F6 – **see Seyne**

SEMBLANÇAY – **37 Indre-et-Loire** – **317** M4 – **pop. 1 692** – **alt. 100 m** – ✉ **37360**

Paris 248 – Angers 96 – Blois 77 – Le Mans 70 – Tours 17 11 **B2**

La Mère Hamard with rm VISA AE
pl. de l'Église – ✆ 02 47 56 62 04 – reservation@lamerehamard.com – Fax 02 47 56 53 61 – Closed 5-12 January, 15 February-15 March, Sunday dinner, Tuesday lunch and Monday
11 rm – †€ 67 ††€ 70/92, ☕ € 12 – ½ P € 75/85
Rest – Menu € 21 (weekdays)/55 – Carte € 50/64
♦ Regional style houses separated by the road – comfortable rooms on one side and an elegant restaurant on the other. Classical cuisine and fine selection of Loire wines.

SEMÈNE – **43 Haute-Loire** – **331** H1 – **see Aurec-sur-Loire**

SEMNOZ (MONTAGNE) – **74 Haute-Savoie** – **328** J6 – **See Montagne du Semnoz**

SEMUR-EN-AUXOIS – **21 Côte-d'Or** – **320** G5 – **pop. 4 453** – **alt. 286 m** – ✉ **21140** Burgundy-Jura 8 **C2**

Paris 246 – Auxerre 87 – Avallon 42 – Beaune 78 – Dijon 82 – Montbard 20

Office de tourisme, 2, place Gaveau ✆ 03 80 97 05 96

du Pré-Lamy Précy-sous-Thil Le Brouillard, South: 18 km by D980, ✆ 03 80 64 46 83.

N.-Dame church ★ - Pont Joly ≤★.

Plan on next page

Hostellerie d'Aussois ≤ rm, rest, VISA AE
rte de Saulieu – ✆ 03 80 97 28 28 – info@hostellerie.fr – Fax 03 80 97 34 56 **s**
42 rm – †€ 68/80 ††€ 78/90, ☕ € 12 – ½ P € 66/71 – **Rest** – Menu € 24/46 – Carte € 38/44
♦ A 1980s establishment with functional rooms that are being gradually renovated, either overlooking the town or the countryside. Restaurant with a modern setting and pool-side terrace, with Semur's ramparts in the background. Good up-to-date dishes.

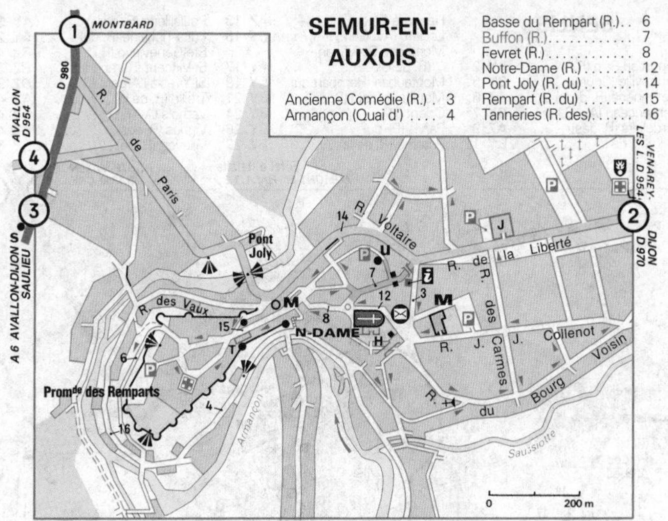

Les Cymaises without rest

7 r. Renaudot – ✆ 03 80 97 21 44 – hotel.cymaises@libertysurf.fr – Fax 03 80 97 18 23 – Closed 3 November-7 December and 5 February-3 March u

18 rm – †€ 55 ††€ 65, ☕ € 7

◆ Old and elegant looking building (18C-19C) at the heart of the medieval town. Classically arranged, quiet rooms. Breakfast served on the veranda. Restful courtyard and garden.

at Lac de Pont 3 km east by D 103B – ✉ **21140 Pont-et-Massène**

Lac

– ✆ 03 80 97 11 11 – hoteldulacdepont@wanadoo.fr – Fax 03 80 97 29 25 – Closed 30 March-7 April, 30 November-31 December, Sunday and Monday from October to June

20 rm – †€ 41/47 ††€ 49/60, ☕ € 8,50 – ½ P € 53/58 – **Rest** – *(closed Sunday dinner September-June, Monday except dinner July-August and Tuesday lunch)* Menu € 16/34

◆ A large white building, near the lake, surrounded by greenery and housing purely functional rooms or more traditional ones, adorned with period or painted-wood furniture. A country-style dining room and pretty, teak-furnished summer terrace shaded by a vine arbour.

SÉNART – 312 E4 – 101 39 – see Paris, Area

SENLIS – 60 Oise – 305 G5 – pop. 16 327 – alt. 76 m – ✉ 60300

Northern France and the Paris Region 36 **B3**

- Paris 52 – Amiens 102 – Beauvais 56 – Compiègne 33 – Meaux 40
- Office de tourisme, place du Parvis Notre Dame ✆ 03 44 53 06 40, Fax 03 44 53 29 80
- d'Apremont Apremont CD 606, Northwest: 5 km by D 1330, ✆ 03 44 25 61 11 ;
- Dolce Chantilly Vineuil-Saint-Firmin Route d'Apremont, by Chantilly road: 8 km, ✆ 03 44 58 47 74 ;
- Château Raray Paris Golf Club Raray Domaine de Raray, by Compiègne road: 26 km, ✆ 03 44 54 70 61.
- N.-Dame cathedral ★★ - Old streets ★ ABY - Place du Parvis★ BY - Royal St-Frambourg chapel ★ B - Jardin du Roy ≤★ - Musée d'Art et d'Archéologie★.
- Parc Astérix★★ South: 12 km by A1 motorway.

SENLIS

Apport-au-Pain (R.) . . . . AY 2
Boutteville (Cours) . . . . BY 5
Bretonnerie (R. de la) . . . . . . AZ 6
Clemenceau (Av. G.). . . . . . . BY 7
Cordeliers (R. des) . . . . AZ 9
Halle (Pl. de la) . . . . BY 12
Heaume (R. du) . . . . AZ 13
Leclerc (Av. Gén.) . . . . BY 15
Montagne St-Aignan (R. de la). . . . . AY 17
Montauban (Rempart du). . . AY 19
Moulin St-Rieul (R. du) . . . . . BY 21
Odent (R.) . . . . BY 24
Parvis (Pl. du) . . . . BY 26
Poterne (R. de la) . . . . BZ 29
Poulaillerie (R. de la) . . . . AY 31
Puits-Tiphaine (R. du) . . . . . . AY 27
Ste-Geneviève (R.) . . . . BZ 40
St-Vincent (Rempart) . . . . BZ 36
St-Yves-à-l'Argent (R.). . . . . . BZ 38
Treille (R. de la) . . . . AY 42
Vernois (Av. F.). . . . . AY 47
Vignes (R. des) . . . . BZ 49
Villevert (R. de) . . . . BY 52

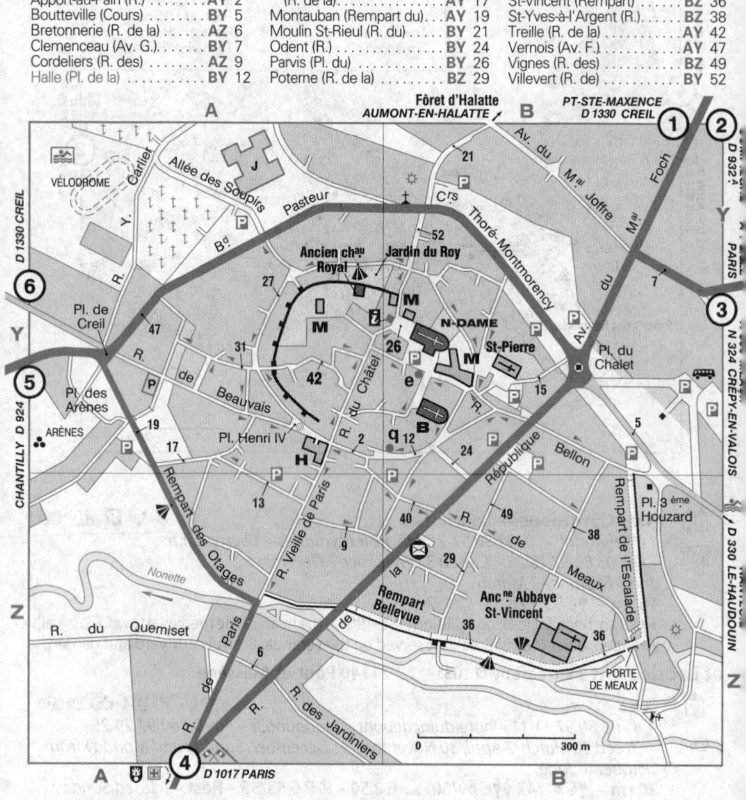

Ibis

2 km via ③ on D 1324 – ✆ 03 44 53 70 50 – Fax 03 44 53 51 93

92 rm – †€ 55/75 ††€ 55/75, ☕ € 7,50

Rest – Menu (€ 14), € 17 – Carte € 24/34

◆ Practical hotel just off the motorway. All the rooms in the main building and extension have been renovated in keeping with the chain's latest concept. Country-style decor (exposed beams, fireplace); grilled meats the speciality.

Le Scaramouche

4 pl. Notre-Dame – ✆ 03 44 53 01 26 – info@le-scaramouche.fr – Fax 03 44 53 46 14 – Closed 11-23 August, Tuesday and Wednesday BY **e**

Rest – Menu € 29/70 – Carte € 44/80

◆ Warm house with pretty painted wood exterior. Pleasant interior with paintings and tapestries; the attractive terrace overlooks the cathedral of Notre-Dame (12C).

Le Bourgeois Gentilhomme

3 pl. de la Halle – ✆ 03 44 53 13 22 – Fax 03 44 53 15 11 – Closed 3-25 August, Saturday lunch, Sunday and Monday BY **q**

Rest – Menu (€ 25), € 39 – Carte € 47/75

◆ Molière inspired the name and decor of this restaurant in a busy shopping street in the old town. Intimate dining room. Wine-tasting in the 12C vaulted cellar.

SENNECÉ-LÈS-MÂCON – 71 Saône-et-Loire – 320 J11 – see Mâcon

SENNECEY-LE-GRAND – 71 Saône-et-Loire – 320 J10 – pop. 2 962 – alt. 200 m – ✉ 71240 Burgundy-Jura 8 C3

Paris 359 – Dijon 89 – Mâcon 42 – Chalon-sur-Saône 18 – Le Creusot 53

Office de tourisme, place de l'hôtel de ville ✆ 03 85 44 82 54, Fax 03 85 44 86 19

L'Amaryllis (Cédric Burtin) VISA

78 av. du 4 Septembre – ✆ 03 85 44 86 34 – Fax 03 85 44 96 92 – Closed January, Sunday dinner except July-August and Wednesday

Rest – Menu € 18 (weekday lunch), € 27/60 – Carte € 42/53

Spec. Grenouilles en trois façons. Selle d'agneau aux olives noires et basilic. Soufflé chaud aux noix de pécan et son cœur au caramel liquide.

◆ A modern, welcoming restaurant opposite the Hôtel-Dieu. Generous and inventive cuisine prepared by a chef who makes a point of working with local producers.

SENONCHES – 28 Eure-et-Loir – 311 C4 – pop. 3 143 – alt. 223 m – ✉ 28250

Paris 115 – Chartres 38 – Dreux 38 – Mortagne-au-Perche 42 – Nogent-le-Rotrou 34 11 B1

Syndicat d'initiative, 2, rue Louis Peuret ✆ 02 37 37 80 11, Fax 02 37 37 80 11

La Pomme de Pin with rm P VISA

r. M. Cauty – ✆ 02 37 37 76 62 – restaurantlapommedepin@wanadoo.fr – Fax 02 37 37 86 61 – Closed 20-26 October, 2-27 January, Friday dinner from October to April, Tuesday lunch from June to September, Sunday dinner and Monday

10 rm – € 42/48 € 55/68, € 7,50 – ½ P € 60/68 – **Rest** – Menu € 24/45 – Carte € 38/71

◆ A former post-house with a fine half-timbered facade, offering a pleasant dining room with a terrace and a lounge featuring a fireplace. Small simple rooms.

SENONES – 88 Vosges – 314 J2 – pop. 2 906 – alt. 340 m – ✉ 88210 Alsace-Lorraine 27 C2

Paris 392 – Épinal 57 – Lunéville 50 – St-Dié 23 – Strasbourg 80

Office de tourisme, 18, place Dom Calmet ✆ 03 29 57 91 03, Fax 03 29 57 83 95

Senones road to col du Donon (Donon Pass)★ Northeast: 20 km.

Au Bon Gîte with rm P VISA AE

3 pl. Vaultrin – ✆ 03 29 57 92 46 – Fax 03 29 57 93 92 – Closed 1st-20 March, 6-29 September, Sunday dinner and Monday

7 rm – € 45/55 € 45/55, € 7 – ½ P € 60/68

Rest – Menu (€ 15), € 20/35 – Carte € 30/46

◆ Smart house in the centre of the former capital of the Salm principality. Tasty modern cuisine served in a contemporary setting, dotted with photographs and knick knacks of all sorts.

SENS – 89 Yonne – 319 C2 – pop. 26 904 – alt. 70 m – ✉ 89100 Burgundy-Jura 7 B1

Paris 116 – Auxerre 59 – Fontainebleau 54 – Montargis 50 – Troyes 71

Office de tourisme, place Jean Jaurès ✆ 03 86 65 19 49, Fax 03 86 64 24 18

du Senonais Lixy Les Ursules, West: 22 km by D 26, ✆ 03 86 66 58 46.

St-Étienne cathedral ★ - Treasure-house★★ - Musée et palais synodal★ M[1].

Plan on next page

Paris et Poste rm, rest, VISA AE

97 r. de la République – ✆ 03 86 65 17 43 – hotelparisposte@orange.fr – Fax 03 86 64 48 45 a

26 rm – € 75/160 € 75/160, € 14 – 4 suites – ½ P € 90/180

Rest – *(closed Friday dinner, Sunday dinner and Monday)* Menu (€ 25), € 36/74

◆ A traditional inn with a provincial atmosphere. Rooms of varying sizes, the most spacious and modern rooms open onto an elegant patio. Reinterpreted classic cuisine served in an inviting dining room or pleasant veranda.

SENS

Alsace-Lorraine (R. d') 2
Beaurepaire (R.) 3
Chambonas (Cours) 8
Cornet (Av. Lucien) 9
Cousin (Square J.) 10
Déportés-et-de-la-Résistance (R. des)
Foch (Bd Mar.) 12
Garibaldi (Bd des) 13
Gateau (R. A.) 15
Grande-R. 16
Leclerc (R. du Gén.) 19
Maupéou (Bd de) 21
Moulin (Quai J.) 23
République (Pl. de la) 27
République (R. de la) 28

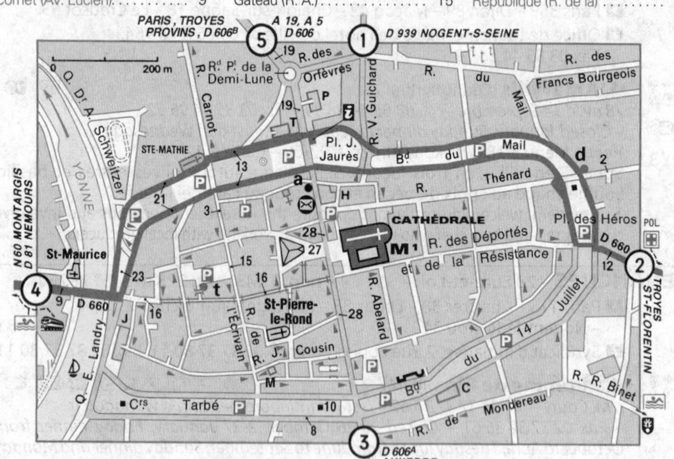

XXX **La Madeleine** (Patrick Gauthier)

✿✿ *1 r. Alsace-Lorraine, (1st floor) – ✆ 03 86 65 09 31 – Fax 03 86 95 37 41 – Closed 1st-16 June, 9-26 August, 20 December-6 January, Tuesday lunch, Sunday, Monday and public holidays* **d**

Rest – *(number of covers limited, pre-book)* Menu € 50 (weekday lunch), € 60/110 – Carte € 102/120

Spec. Foie gras chaud au cassis, pomme safran. Tourteau de Roscoff, tomates confites, cœur de fenouil et sauce corail. Quasi d'agneau du Quercy, jus au naturel et petits légumes. **Wines** Côtes d'Auxerre, Epineuil.

◆ Smart restaurant in pastel tones, serving contemporary gourmet cuisine. The hall sports a kitchen stove and shelves filled with groceries.

XX **Le Clos des Jacobins**

49 Gde-Rue – ✆ 03 86 95 29 70 – lesjacobins@wanadoo.fr – Fax 03 86 64 22 98 – Closed 29 April-6 May, 13-27 July, 23 December-6 January, Sunday dinner, Tuesday dinner and Wednesday **t**

Rest – Menu € 29/52 – Carte € 37/70

◆ Comfortable lounge bar and plush brightly painted dining room with black leather chairs and attractively laid tables. Serves modern cuisine.

XX **La Potinière**

51 r. Cécile de Marsangy, via ④ – ✆ 03 86 65 31 08 – la.potiniere@abs.m.com – Fax 03 86 64 60 19 – Closed 20 August-4 September, February school holidays, Sunday dinner, Monday dinner and Tuesday

Rest – *(pre-book in high season)* Menu € 29/65 – Carte € 52/74

◆ Former open air dancing venue with shaded terrace by the Yonne. Popular with river cruising tourists (landing stage). Bright, trendy dining room; modern cuisine.

X **Au Crieur de Vin**

1 r. Alsace-Lorraine – ✆ 03 86 65 92 80 – Fax 03 86 95 37 41 – Closed 1st-16 June, 9-25 August, 20 December-6 January, Tuesday lunch, Sunday, Monday and public holidays **d**

Rest – Menu € 25/52 – Carte € 48/79

◆ Top marks for this restaurant: a pleasant bistro atmosphere, classic dishes, spit roast meat and selected vintages.

in Subligny 7 km by ④ and D 660 – pop. 478 – alt. 150 m – ✉ 89100

La Haie Fleurie
30 rte de Coutenay, South West : 2 km – ✆ 03 86 88 84 44 – Fax 03 86 88 86 67 – Closed 28 July-10 August, 29 December-4 January, Sunday dinner, Wednesday dinner and Thursday
Rest – Menu € 27/49 – Carte € 36/58
♦ Situated along the road going through a village, this inn has a small lounge reception area leading to a pleasant dining room in modern-rustic style. Flower-decked terrace. Traditional cuisine.

in Villeroy 7 km by ④ and D 81 – pop. 254 – alt. 184 m – ✉ 89100

Relais de Villeroy with rm
rte de Nemours – ✆ 03 86 88 81 77 – reservation@relais-de-villeroy.com – Fax 03 86 88 84 04 – Closed 30 June-11 July, 20 December-8 January and Sunday dinner
8 rm – †€ 50/60 ††€ 50/60, ☕ € 8
Rest – *(closed 15 February-1st March, Wednesday lunch, Thursday lunch, Monday and Tuesday)* Menu € 32/60 – Carte € 29/68
Rest ***Bistro Chez Clément*** – *✆ 03 86 88 86 73 (closed Wednesday dinner, Thursday dinner, Friday dinner, Saturday and Sunday)* Menu € 18/25
♦ This smart regional house is home to small comfortable bedrooms. Traditional recipes are served in the veranda with a view of the delightful flower-filled garden. At Chez Clément you will find bistro cooking, rustic decor and a friendly welcome.

SEPT-SAULX – 51 Marne – 306 H8 – pop. 510 – alt. 96 m – ✉ 51400 13 B2

Paris 167 – Châlons-en-Champagne 29 – Épernay 29 – Reims 26 – Rethel 51 – Vouziers 58

Le Cheval Blanc
– ✆ 03 26 03 90 27 – cheval.blanc-sept-saulx@wanadoo.fr – Fax 03 26 03 97 09 – Closed February, Wednesday lunchtime and Tuesday from October to March
21 rm – †€ 63/73 ††€ 69/134, ☕ € 11 – 3 suites – ½ P € 93/138
Rest – Menu € 25 (weekday lunch), € 30/88 bi – Carte € 56/68
♦ Three buildings, including a former post-house, in the heart of the prestigious Champagne vineyards. The rooms open onto a large and peaceful riverside garden. The plush restaurant of the Cheval Blanc overlooks a flower-decked courtyard which doubles as a terrace in summer.

SÉREILHAC – 87 Haute-Vienne – 325 D6 – pop. 1 595 – alt. 322 m – ✉ 87620

Paris 405 – Confolens 50 – Limoges 19 – Périgueux 77 – St-Yrieix-la-Perche 37 24 B2

Le Relais des Tuileries
aux Betoulles, 2 km north-eastward on the N 21 – ✆ 05 55 39 10 27 – contact@relais-tuileries.fr – Fax 05 55 36 09 21 – Closed 12-26 November, 12 January-3 February, Sunday dinner and Monday except July-August
10 rm – †€ 55/57 ††€ 55/62, ☕ € 9 – ½ P € 56/58 – **Rest** – Menu € 16/46 – Carte € 27/48
♦ Old tile factory flanked by two pavilions, set in a hamlet. All the rooms have been renovated, and open out onto the garden. Local set menus offered in a rustic dining room embellished by exposed beams and an open fireplace.

SÉRIGNAN – 34 Hérault – 339 E9 – pop. 6 134 – alt. 7 m – ✉ 34410 23 C2

Paris 770 – Montpellier 70 – Béziers 12 – Narbonne 39

Office de tourisme, place de la Libération ✆ 04 67 32 42 21, Fax 04 67 32 37 97

L'Harmonie
chemin de la Barque – ✆ 04 67 32 39 30 – lharmonie@wanadoo.fr – Fax 04 67 32 39 30 – Closed 14-27 April, 27 October-9 November, Tuesday dinner from September to June, Thursday lunch in July-August, Saturday lunch and Wednesday
Rest – Menu € 22/52 – Carte € 38/70
♦ This restaurant, next to the Cigalière, looks like a large theatre. Modern decor with wrought iron furniture, a terrace by the Orb and attractively prepared, up-to-date cuisine.

SÉRIGNAN-DU-COMTAT – 84 Vaucluse – 332 C8 – see Orange

SERMAIZE-DU-BAS – 71 Saône-et-Loire – 320 F11 – see Paray-le-Monial

SERMERSHEIM – 67 Bas-Rhin – 315 J6 – pop. 829 – alt. 160 m – ✉ 67230

2 **C1**

Paris 506 – Lahr/Schwarzwald 41 – Obernai 21 – Sélestat 14 – Strasbourg 40

Au Relais de l'Ill without rest
r. du Rempart – ☎ 03 88 74 31 28 – relais-de-lill@wanadoo.fr – Fax 03 88 74 17 51 – Closed 20 December-10 January
23 rm – †€ 50/58 ††€ 65/75, ☕ € 7
◆ Recent family hotel unaffected by the noise of the nearby expressway. A warm reception awaits you, with spacious, well-kept rooms on offer. Flower-decked surroundings

SERRE-CHEVALIER – 05 Hautes-Alpes – 334 H3 – alt. 2 483 m – Winter sports : 1 200/2 800 m 9 67 – ✉ 05330 French Alps

41 **C1**

Paris 678 – Briançon 7 – Gap 95 – Grenoble 110 – Col du Lautaret 21

Office de tourisme, Chantemerle ☎ 04 92 24 98 98, Fax 04 92 24 98 84

✳★★.

in Chantemerle – alt. 1 350 m – ✉ 05330 St-Chaffrey

Col de Granon ✳★★ North: 12 km.

Plein Sud
– ☎ 04 92 24 17 01 – lynne@hotelpleinsud.com – Fax 04 92 24 10 21 – Closed 16 April-15 May and 15 October-5 December
41 rm – †€ 78/118 ††€ 110/175, ☕ € 10 – **Rest** – *(dinner only in December and in April)* Menu € 16/35 – Carte € 30/41
◆ Centrally located hotel. Choose a room facing south, they are larger and have loggias overlooking the larch forest. Internet access and fine attractive pool with opening roof. Restaurant serving traditional cuisine and set buffets. Snack menu in the pub.

Les Marmottes
22 r. du Centre – ☎ 04 92 24 11 17 – lucas.marmottes@wanadoo.fr – Fax 04 92 24 11 17
5 rm ☕ – †€ 57/95 ††€ 76/127 – ½ P € 60/86 – **Table d'hôte** – Menu € 22 bi
◆ Former barn carefully converted into a comfortable guesthouse (non-smokers only). Attractive fireside lounge and rooms with personal touches with views of the surrounding peaks. Restaurant offering well-prepared family cooking (single menu modified every day).

in Villeneuve-la-Salle – ✉ 05240 La-Salle-Les-Alpes

St-Marcellin church ★ of La-Salle-les-Alpes.

Le Mont Thabor without rest
1 bis chemin Envers – ☎ 04 92 24 74 41 – hotelmonthabor@wanadoo.fr – Fax 04 92 24 99 50 – Closed 19 April-15 June and 1st September-1st December
27 rm – †€ 85/130 ††€ 95/175, ☕ € 8 – ½ P € 63/88
◆ This brand new hotel (non-smokers only) has a mountain decor with Provençal touches. Comfortable and very well-equipped rooms, sauna, jacuzzi...

Christiania rest,
– ☎ 04 92 24 76 33 – le.christiania@wanadoo.fr – Fax 04 92 24 83 82 – Open 14 June-15 September and 13 December-13 April
26 rm – †€ 95/105 ††€ 95/105, ☕ € 9 – ½ P € 76/85 – **Rest** – *(open 28 June-7 September and 19 December-5 April) (dinner only)* Menu € 23/27 – Carte € 28/38
◆ A family welcome, a rustic bar-lounge warmed by a fireplace, and rooms judiciously decorated in mountain style, characterise this hotel on the banks of the Guisane. Restaurant with an Alpine setting enhanced by antique objects. Garden terrace next to a fast flowing stream.

in Monêtier-les-Bains – **pop. 1 009** – **alt. 1 480 m** – ✉ **05220**

L'Auberge du Choucas
17 r. de la Fruitière – ✆ 04 92 24 42 73 – auberge.du.choucas@wanadoo.fr – Fax 04 92 24 51 60 – Closed 14 April-30 May and 3 November-6 December
16 rm – €80/180 €100/300, €17 – ½ P €90/240
Rest – *(closed 14 April-30 May, 13 October-14 December, and lunch Monday-Thursday in April, June, September and October)* Menu €29/79 – Carte €51/70
◆ A charming inn (non-smokers only) near the 15C church. Rooms and duplexes with a regional decor. Small, simple studio flats in the annexe. A vaulted dining room, adorned with an attractive collection of copperware; up-to-date cuisine.

L'Alliey rest, VISA
– ✆ 04 92 24 40 02 – hotel@alliey.com – Fax 04 92 24 40 60
– Open 1st July-1st September and 15 December-25 April
22 rm – €79/99 €89/129, €13 – 2 suites – ½ P €82/119 – **Rest** – *(dinner only)* Menu €32/45
◆ This village residence provides a charming and warm atmosphere due to its attractive wooden setting. Cosy mountain-style rooms and fine balneotherapy area. The young, but experienced couple that has taken over this restaurant prepares fine inventive cuisine with the best mountain flavours.

Le Chazal VISA
Les Guibertes, 2.5 km south-east on Briançon road – ✆ 04 92 24 45 54 – Closed 22 June-3 July, 1st-10 October, 23 November-12 December and Monday
Rest – *(dinner only except Sunday)* Menu €27/52 bi – Carte €35/55
◆ This former sheep barn now houses two vaulted dining rooms with a rustic ambience. Modern, award-winning cuisine with a personal touch. "Discovery" menu with a judicious choice of accompanying wines.

SERRIÈRES – **07 Ardèche** – **331** K2 – **pop. 1 078** – **alt. 140 m** – ✉ **07340**
Lyon - Rhone Valley 43 **E2**

Paris 514 – Annonay 16 – Privas 91 – St-Étienne 55 – Vienne 29

Syndicat d'initiative, quai Jule Roche ✆ 04 75 34 06 01, Fax 04 75 34 06 01

Schaeffer with rm rm, VISA
D 86 – ✆ 04 75 34 00 07 – mathe@hotel-schaeffer.com – Fax 04 75 34 08 79 – Closed 4-18 August, 24 October-4 November, 2-17 January, Sunday dinner and Monday
15 rm – €48/56 €64/88, €8 – **Rest** – *(closed Saturday lunch, Sunday dinner and Monday)* Menu (€23), €35/110 – Carte €59/88
◆ Opulent restaurant with a veranda that overlooks the suspension bridge spanning the Rhône. Classic cuisine served with local Côtes-du-Rhône wines. Functional rooms.

SERRIS – **77 Seine-et-Marne** – **312** F2 – **see Paris, Area (Marne-la-Vallée)**

SERVIERS-ET-LABAUME – **30 Gard** – **339** L4 – **see Uzès**

SERVON – **50 Manche** – **303** D8 – **pop. 251** – **alt. 25 m** – ✉ **50170** 32 **A3**

Paris 352 – Avranches 15 – Dol-de-Bretagne 30 – St-Lô 72 – St-Malo 55

Auberge du Terroir with rm rm, VISA
– ✆ 02 33 60 17 92 – aubergeduterroir@wanadoo.fr – Fax 02 33 60 35 26 – Closed 15 November-10 December, February school holidays, Thursday lunch, Saturday lunch and Wednesday
6 rm – €50/56 €56/78, €10 – ½ P €60/75
Rest – *(pre-book)* Menu €19/45 – Carte €30/55
◆ Set in a former girls' school and an old presbytery, a country inn serving good traditional fare. Attractive rooms.

SERVOZ – **74 Haute-Savoie** – **328** N5 – **pop. 818** – **alt. 816 m** – ✉ **74310**
French Alps 46 **F1**

Paris 598 – Annecy 85 – Bonneville 43 – Chamonix-Mont-Blanc 14 – Megève 22

Office de tourisme, ✆ 04 50 47 21 68, Fax 04 50 47 27 06

Les Gorges de la Diosaz with rm

– *04 50 47 20 97 – infos@hoteldesgorges.com – Fax 04 50 47 21 08*
– Closed 15-30 May and 4-30 November
6 rm – €60/70 €60/70, €7,50 – **Rest** – *(closed Sunday dinner and Monday)* Menu (€15 bi), €24/42 – Carte €32/46
♦ Chalet-style property in a village along the Route des Gorges. Typical mountain decor in the reception and dining room. Updated regional cuisine. Terrace with panoramic views.

SESSENHEIM – 67 Bas-Rhin – 315 L4 – pop. 1 783 – alt. 120 m – 67770

Alsace-Lorraine — 1 **B1**

Paris 497 – Haguenau 18 – Strasbourg 39 – Wissembourg 44

Au Bœuf

1 r. Église – 03 88 86 97 14 – contact@auberge-au-boeuf.com
– Fax 03 88 86 04 62 – Closed Monday and Tuesday
Rest – Menu €28/58 – Carte €38/60
♦ 18C church stalls decorate one of the dining rooms of this Alsatian building, which boasts a lovely terrace, a small Goethe museum and a boutique selling regional products.

SÈTE – 34 Hérault – 339 H8 – pop. 39 542 – alt. 4 m – Casino – 34200

Languedoc-Roussillon-Tarn Gorges — 23 **C2**

Paris 787 – Béziers 48 – Lodève 63 – Montpellier 35

Office de tourisme, 60, rue Mario Roustan 04 67 74 71 71, Fax 04 67 46 17 54

Mont St-Clair★: terrace of N.-D. de la Salette chapel's presbytery ✻★★ AZ - Le Vieux Port★ - marine cemetery ★.

Plan on next page

Le Grand Hôtel

17 quai Mar. de Lattre de Tassigny – 04 67 74 71 77
– info@legrandhotelsete.com – Fax 04 67 74 29 27
– Closed 24 December-4 January — AY **t**
43 rm – €75/135 €75/135, €10 – 1 suite – ½ P €64/94
Rest *Quai 17* – *04 67 74 71 91 (closed 29 June-4 August, 2-12 January, Saturday lunch and Sunday)* Menu (€19), €26/45 – Carte €30/54
♦ Near the birthplace of Georges Brassens, an elegant hotel (1882) by the canal. Refined rooms, fine period furniture and a pleasant glass patio. High ceilings, mouldings and pretty murals recalling Sète's maritime history adorn the dining room. Regional cuisine.

Port Marine

Môle St-Louis – 04 67 74 92 34 – contact@hotel-port-marine.com
– Fax 04 67 74 92 33 — AZ **d**
46 rm – €70/80 €77/110, €10 – 6 suites – ½ P €69/86
Rest – Menu €26 – Carte €32/48
♦ Modern architecture facing the St Louis pier from which the Exodus set sail in 1947. The simple décor of the rooms recalls the inside of a ship's cabin. Rooftop sunlounge. The restaurant offers traditional cuisine; brasserie-style at lunchtime and buffet at weekends.

Paris Méditerranée

47 r. Pierre Semard – 04 67 74 97 73 – Closed 1st-15 July, 1 week in February, Saturday lunch, Sunday and Monday — BY **p**
Rest – Menu (€22), €28
♦ The landlady's original decoration is perfectly in keeping with the inventive and tasty dishes that you can savour in this slightly unusual but truly appealing restaurant.

On the Corniche 2 km south of map by D 2 – 34200 Sète

Les Tritons without rest

bd Joliot-Curie – 04 67 53 03 98 – info@hotellestritons.com
– Fax 04 67 53 38 31
55 rm – €39/75 €45/110, €7
♦ Functional and colourful rooms. Those at the front have air conditioning and a sea view, while those at the back are refreshing and peaceful. Marine decor in the hall.

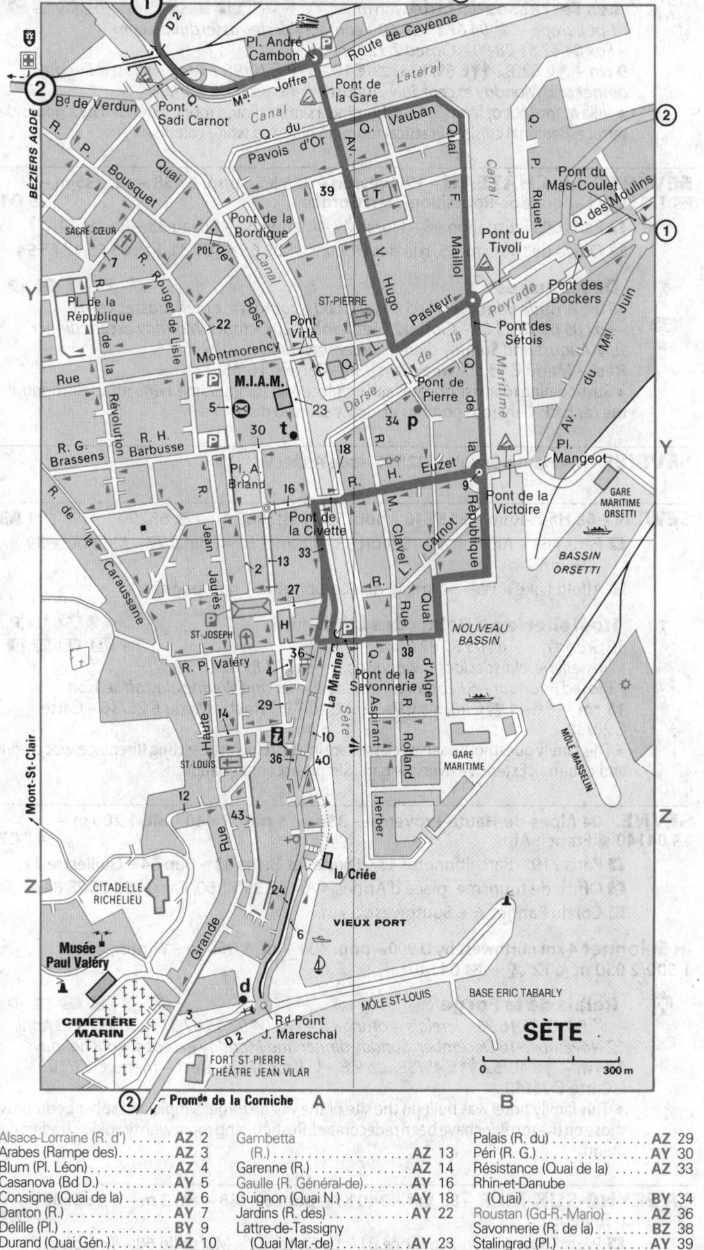

Alsace-Lorraine (R. d') . . . . AZ 2
Arabes (Rampe des) . . . . AZ 3
Blum (Pl. Léon) . . . . AZ 4
Casanova (Bd D.) . . . . AY 5
Consigne (Quai de la) . . . . AZ 6
Danton (R.) . . . . AY 7
Delille (Pl.) . . . . BY 9
Durand (Quai Gén.) . . . . AZ 10
Euzet (R. H.) . . . . BY
Franklin (R.) . . . . AZ 12

Gambetta (R.) . . . . AZ 13
Garenne (R.) . . . . AZ 14
Gaulle (R. Général-de) . . . . AY 16
Guignon (Quai N.) . . . . AY 18
Jardins (R. des) . . . . AY 22
Lattre-de-Tassigny (Quai Mar.-de) . . . . AY 23
Marty (Prom. J.-B.) . . . . AZ 24
Mistral (R. F.) . . . . AZ 27

Palais (R. du) . . . . AZ 29
Péri (R. G.) . . . . AY 30
Résistance (Quai de la) . . . . AZ 33
Rhin-et-Danube (Quai) . . . . BY 34
Roustan (Gd-R.-Mario) . . . . AZ 36
Savonnerie (R. de la) . . . . BZ 38
Stalingrad (Pl.) . . . . AY 39
Valéry (Rampe P.) . . . . AZ 40
Villaret-Joyeuse (R.) . . . . AZ 43

XX **Les Terrasses du Lido** with rm

rd-pt Europe – ✆ 04 67 51 39 60 – contact@lesterrassesdulido.com – Fax 04 67 51 28 90 – Closed 2-12 January

9 rm – €62/82 €69/125, €10 – ½ P €70/95 – **Rest** – *(closed Sunday dinner and Monday except July-August)* Menu (€27), €32/48

◆ Villa at the foot of Mont St Clair, housing a simple dining room, extended by a pool-side terrace. Regional cuisine. Practical rooms in blue and white colours.

SÉVÉRAC-LE-CHÂTEAU – **12 Aveyron** – **338** K5 – **pop. 2 458** – **alt. 735 m** – ✉ **12150** Languedoc-Roussillon-Tarn Gorges 29 **D1**

Paris 605 – Espalion 46 – Florac 74 – Mende 64 – Millau 33 – Rodez 51

Office de tourisme, 5, rue des Douves ✆ 05 65 47 67 31, Fax 05 65 47 65 94

X **Des Causses**

38 av. Aristide Briand – ✆ 05 65 70 23 00 – contact@hotel-causses.com – Fax 05 65 70 23 04 – Closed 23 September-20 October, Monday except dinner July-August and Sunday dinner September-June

Rest – Menu €13,50 (weekdays)/36 – Carte €16/45

◆ Rustic dining room with beams and fireplace or in summertime, beneath an elm opposite the car park. Generous portions of locally sourced dishes.

SÉVRIER – **74 Haute-Savoie** – **328** J5 – **see Annecy**

SEWEN – **68 Haut-Rhin** – **315** F10 – **pop. 530** – **alt. 500 m** – ✉ **68290** 1 **A3**

Paris 462 – Altkirch 41 – Belfort 33 – Colmar 66 – Épinal 77 – Mulhouse 39 – Thann 24

Alfeld Lake★ West: 4 km, Alsace-Lorraine-Champagne

X **Hostellerie au Relais des Lacs** with rm

30 Grand'rue – ✆ 03 89 82 01 42 – hostellerierelaisdeslacs@wanadoo.fr – Fax 03 89 82 09 29 – Closed 6 January-6 February, Tuesday dinner and Wednesday off season

13 rm – €44 €46, €7 – ½ P €46/49 – **Rest** – Menu €25/36 – Carte €20/38

◆ This family guesthouse serves classic fare in a tasteful rustic setting (fireplace, woodwork and country). Extensive riverside park. Simple accommodation.

SEYNE – **04 Alpes-de-Haute-Provence** – **334** G6 – **pop. 1 440** – **alt. 1 200 m** – ✉ **04140** French Alps 41 **C2**

Paris 719 – Barcelonnette 43 – Digne-les-Bains 43 – Gap 54 – Guillestre 71

Office de tourisme, place d'Armes ✆ 04 92 35 11 00, Fax 04 92 35 28 84

Col du Fanget ≤★ Southwest: 5 km.

in Selonnet **4 km northwest by D 900** – **pop. 404** – **alt. 1 060 m** – **Winter sports : 1 500/2 050 m** 12 – ✉ **04140**

Relais de la Forge

– ✆ 04 92 35 16 98 – lerelais@orange.fr – Fax 04 92 35 07 37 – Closed 5-13 April, 12 November-16 December, Sunday dinner and Monday except school holidays

14 rm – €40/52 €45/58, €8 – ½ P €43/52 – **Rest** – Menu €15/30 – Carte €26/40

◆ This family hotel was built on the site of the village forge. Simple and sober bedrooms; those on the top floor have been redecorated. Rustic dining room with fireplace; traditional menu.

LA SEYNE-SUR-MER – **83 Var** – **340** K7 – **pop. 60 188** – **alt. 3 m** – ✉ **83500** French Riviera 40 **B3**

Paris 830 – Aix-en-Provence 81 – La Ciotat 32 – Marseille 60 – Toulon 8

Office de tourisme, corniche Georges Pompidou ✆ 04 98 00 25 70, Fax 04 98 00 25 71

≤★ of the Balaguier fort terrace East: 3 km.

in Fabrégas 4 km south by St-Mandrier road and secondary road – ✉ 83500 La Seyne-sur-Mer

XX **Chez Daniel et Julia "rest. du Rivage"**
– ✆ 04 94 94 85 13 – Fax 04 94 87 25 25 – Closed November, Sunday dinner and Monday
Rest – Menu € 38/90 – Carte € 50/65
◆ Welcoming, family-run restaurant nestling in a pretty creek. Dining room in rustic-Provençal style, with a collection of old tools. A focus on fish and seafood. Terrace overlooking the water.

in Sablettes 4 km southeast – ✉ 83500 La Seyne-sur-Mer

XX **La Parenthèse**
espl. Henry Boeuf – ✆ 04 94 94 92 34 – fageslaffontpartners@orange.fr – Fax 04 94 87 60 45 – Closed 19 January-8 February, Sunday dinner and Monday September-June and lunch Monday-Wednesday in July-August
Rest – Menu € 32 (weekdays)/75 – Carte € 42/71
◆ Contemporary cuisine served in a modern dining room decorated in shades of red, white and brown. In summer, dine on the shady terrace, furnished with wrought-iron tables and enclosed by wood panels.

SÉZANNE – 51 Marne – 306 E10 – pop. 5 585 – alt. 137 m – ✉ 51120

Northern France and the Paris Region 13 **B2**

Paris 116 – Châlons-en-Champagne 59 – Meaux 78 – Melun 89 – Sens 83 – Troyes 62

Office de tourisme, place de la République ✆ 03 26 80 51 43, Fax 03 26 80 54 13

De la Croix d'Or rest,
53 r. Notre-Dame – ✆ 03 26 80 61 10 – contact@hotel-lacroixdor.fr – Fax 03 26 80 65 20 – Closed 2-15 January, Sunday evening and Wednesday
13 rm – €45 €60, €8 – ½ P €45/54
Rest – Menu € 15/31 – Carte € 27/45
◆ Country house with a pleasantly provincial feel. The rooms, of various sizes, have been refurbished. Pleasant breakfast room. The restaurant decor has been carefully rejuvenated and the food is traditional.

Le Relais Champenois rm, rest,
157 r. Notre-Dame – ✆ 03 26 80 58 03 – relaischamp@infonie.fr – Fax 03 26 81 35 32 – Closed 20-27 August, 25 December-3 January and Sunday evening
19 rm – €36/65 €46/78, €9,50
Rest – Menu (€ 16), € 21/48 – Carte € 31/47
◆ Renovated Champagne-style façade, attractively decorated with flowers. Fresh and well-furnished rooms that are quieter in the annexe (two have air-conditioning). Country-style dining rooms, with woodwork and exposed beams. Great choice of traditional menus.

in Mondement-Montgivroux – pop. 48 – alt. 188 m – ✉ 51120

Domaine de Montgivroux without rest
rte d' Epernay, 12 km on D 951 and D 439 – ✆ 03 26 42 06 93 – domainedemontgivroux@wanadoo.fr – Fax 03 26 42 06 94
20 rm – €70 €210, €15 – 1 suite
◆ Set in an immense estate, this superbly restored 17C Champagne-region farmhouse boasts spacious, thoughtfully-decorated rooms.

SIERCK-LES-BAINS – 57 Moselle – 307 J2 – pop. 1 872 – alt. 147 m – ✉ 57480

Alsace-Lorraine 27 **C1**

Paris 355 – Luxembourg 40 – Metz 46 – Thionville 17 – Trier 52

Office de tourisme, rue du Château ✆ 03 82 83 74 14, Fax 03 82 83 22 10

≤★ of the fortified castle.

in Montenach 3.5 km southeast on D 956 – **pop. 410 – alt. 200 m** – ✉ **57480**

Auberge de la Klauss

1 rte de Kirschnaumen – ✆ 03 82 83 72 38 – la-klauss@wanadoo.fr – Fax 03 82 83 73 00 – Closed 24 December-7 January and Monday

Rest – Menu € 16/52 – Carte € 31/64

♦ Free range ducks and pigs are raised on this farm built in 1869. The inn has a pretty rustic setting. Home-made produce (including delicious foie gras) and fine wine list. Fresh produce for sale.

in Manderen 7 km east by D 654 and D 64 – **pop. 383 – alt. 290 m** – ✉ **57480**

Relais du Château Mensberg rm,

15 r. du Château – ✆ 03 82 83 73 16 – aurelaismensberg@aol.com – Fax 03 82 83 23 37 – Closed 26 December-25 January, Monday lunch and Tuesday

13 rm – €36/48 €45/60, € 9,50 – ½ P € 48/55 – **Rest** – Menu (€ 13), € 18/50 – Carte € 16/60

♦ This old farmhouse standing guard at the foot of Malbrouck castle (15C) offers small, simple, and functional rooms. Traditional dishes served in three rustic dining rooms, including two on mezzanines. Trout from the fishpond.

SIERENTZ – **68 Haut-Rhin** – **315** I11 – **pop. 2 442** – **alt. 270 m** – ✉ **68510** 1 **A3**

Paris 487 – Altkirch 19 – Basel 18 – Belfort 65 – Colmar 54 – Mulhouse 16

Syndicat d'initiative, 57, rue Rogg-Haas ✆ 03 89 81 68 58, Fax 03 89 81 60 49

Auberge St-Laurent (Marco Arbeit) with rm

1 r. Fontaine – ✆ 03 89 81 52 81 – marco.arbeit@wanadoo.fr – Fax 03 89 81 67 08 – Closed 14-22 April, Monday and Tuesday

10 rm – €80 €100, € 13 – ½ P € 91

Rest – Menu (€ 19 bi), € 28/65 bi – Carte € 61/85

Spec. Foie gras de canard et confit de choucroute. Croustillant de bar à l'unilatéral, purée de pomme de terre au caviar d'Aquitaine. Carré d'agneau simplement rôti au four. **Wines** Riesling, Sylvaner.

♦ This former post house has a semi-rustic, semi-bourgeois feel; delicate classic cuisine with well-balanced flavours. Enjoyable terrace. Delightful personalised rooms.

SIGNY-L'ABBAYE – **08 Ardennes** – **306** I4 – **pop. 1 340** – **alt. 240 m** – ✉ **08460**

Northern France and the Paris Region 13 **B1**

Paris 208 – Charleville-Mézières 31 – Hirson 41 – Laon 74 – Rethel 23 – Rocroi 30 – Sedan 52

Syndicat d'initiative, cour Rogelet ✆ 03 24 53 10 10, Fax 03 24 53 10 10

Auberge de l'Abbaye with rm

2 pl. A. Briand – ✆ 03 24 52 81 27 – aubergeabbaye@wanadoo.fr – Fax 03 24 53 71 72 – Closed 12 January-8 March

7 rm – €39/55 €55/58, € 7 – ½ P € 39/48 – **Rest** – *(closed Tuesday dinner and Wednesday)* Menu € 15/37 – Carte € 24/52

♦ A former 17C post-house run by the same family since1803. Rustic dining rooms with fireplace, classic local dishes (home-produced beef and mutton) and rooms with rustic touches.

SIGNY-LE-PETIT – **08 Ardennes** – **306** H3 – **pop. 1 314** – **alt. 238 m** – ✉ **08380**

Paris 228 – Charleville-Mézières 37 – Hirson 15 – Chimay 959 13 **B1**

Syndicat d'initiative, place de l'Église ✆ 03 24 53 55 44, Fax 03 24 53 51 32

Au Lion d'Or rm,

pl. de l'Église – ✆ 03 24 53 51 76 – blandine-bertrand@wanadoo.fr – Fax 03 24 53 36 96 – Closed 27 June-10 July, 19 December-11 January and Sunday

12 rm – €64 €64, € 9 – 2 suites – ½ P € 59 – **Rest** – *(closed Sunday except lunch October-March, Tuesday lunch, Wednesday lunch and Saturday lunch) (pre-book Sunday)* Menu € 20/59 bi

♦ Hotel-restaurant for non-smokers set in a local-style house, near a fortified church. Rooms in a variety of styles. Lounge set aside for inveterate smokers. La Hulotte restaurant is named for a night owl, and revellers will enjoy the contemporary cuisine.

SILLÉ-LE-GUILLAUME – 72 Sarthe – 310 I5 – pop. 2 585 – alt. 161 m – ✉ 72140 Normandy 35 C1

Paris 230 – Alençon 39 – Laval 55 – Le Mans 35 – Mayenne 40

Office de tourisme, place de la Résistance ✆ 02 43 20 10 32, Fax 02 43 20 01 23

XX **Le Bretagne** with rm — rest, P VISA MC

pl. Croix d'Or – ✆ 02 43 20 10 10 – hotelrestaurantlebretagne@wanadoo.fr – Fax 02 43 20 03 96 – Closed 24 July-12 August, 23 December-2 January, Saturday lunch October-March, Friday dinner and Sunday dinner

15 rm – †€ 44/69 ††€ 60/76, ☕ € 7,50 – ½ P € 58/68

Rest – Menu € 17 (weekdays)/50 – Carte € 51/55

◆ Former coaching inn (1850) on the edge of the Normandie-Maine Regional Park. Carefully prepared traditional cuisine served in a sober dining room. Pleasant rooms.

SILLERY – 51 Marne – 306 G7 – see Reims

SION-SUR-L'OCÉAN – 85 Vendée – 316 E7 – see St-Gilles-Croix-de-Vie

SIORAC-EN-PÉRIGORD – 24 Dordogne – 329 G7 – pop. 893 – alt. 77 m – ✉ 24170 Dordogne-Berry-Limousin 4 C3

Paris 548 – Sarlat-la-Canéda 29 – Bergerac 45 – Brive-la-Gaillarde 73 – Périgueux 60

Syndicat d'initiative, place de Siorac ✆ 05 53 31 63 51

de LolivarieSouth: 5 km by D 51, ✆ 05 53 30 22 69.

Relais du Périgord Noir — rm, AC rm, rest, VISA MC

– ✆ 05 53 31 60 02 – hotel@relais-perigord-noir.fr – Fax 05 53 31 61 05 – Open 15 April-30 September

44 rm – †€ 65/98 ††€ 65/98, ☕ € 9 – ½ P € 60/65 – **Rest** – *(dinner only) (residents only)* Menu € 30/45 – Carte € 46/61

◆ Fully renovated 1870s house, well suited to disabled guests. Practical guestrooms. Choice of two sitting rooms, one adorned with prehistoric artefacts, the other with a snooker table. Sample traditional dishes in the dining room decorated with frescos or on the veranda.

SISTERON – 04 Alpes-de-Haute-Provence – 334 D7 – pop. 6 964 – alt. 490 m – ✉ 04200 French Alps 40 B2

Paris 704 – Barcelonnette 100 – Digne-les-Bains 40 – Gap 52

Office de tourisme, 1, place de la République ✆ 04 92 61 12 03, Fax 04 92 61 19 57

Old Sisteron★ - Site★★ - Citadel★: ≤★ - Notre-Dame-des-Pommiers cathedral ★.

Plan on next page

Grand Hôtel du Cours — rm, AC rest, VISA MC AE

pl. de l'Église – ✆ 04 92 61 04 51 – hotelducours@wanadoo.fr – Fax 04 92 61 41 73 – Open 1st March-5 November Z r

45 rm – †€ 60/70 ††€ 70/88, ☕ € 10 – 5 suites – ½ P € 65/75

Rest – *(open 1st March-10 December)* Menu € 24/29 – Carte € 30/45

◆ Hotel in the historic centre, a step away from the 14C fortifications. Rooms at the rear are quieter and more spacious. A pleasant Provençal-style restaurant, luminous veranda and shady terrace overlooking the square.

XX **Les Becs Fins** — AC VISA MC AE

16 r. Saunerie – ✆ 04 92 61 12 04 – becsfins@aol.com – Fax 04 92 61 28 33 – Closed 10-20 June, 25 November-15 December, Sunday dinner and Monday except July-August Y a

Rest – Menu (€ 19), € 25/57 – Carte € 31/75

◆ A pleasant town centre restaurant with a shady terrace on a pedestrian street. Modern, refurbished decor, lively, relaxed atmosphere and traditional cuisine.

SISTERON

Arène (Av. Paul). . . . . YZ 3
Basse des Remparts (R.) . . . . Y 4
Combes (R. des) . . . . Z 6
Cordeliers (R. des). . . . . Z 8
Deleuze (R.). . . . . YZ 9
Dr-Robert (Pl. du). . . . . Y 10
Droite (R.). . . . . Y
Font-Chaude (R.) . . . . Y 12
Gaulle (Pl. Gén.-de) . . . . Z 13
Glissoir (R. du) . . . . Y 14
Grande École (Pl. de la). . . . . . Z 15
Horloge (Pl. de l'). . . . . Y 16
Libération (Av. de la) . . . . Z 17
Longue-Andrône (R.). . . . . Y 18
Melchior-Donnet (Cours) . . . . Y 20
Mercerie (R.) . . . . Y 22
Moulin (Av. Jean). . . . . Z 23
Porte-Sauve (R.). . . . . Z 24
Poterie (R.). . . . . Y 25
Provence (R. de) . . . . Z 26
République (Pl. de la). . . . . Z 28
Ste-Ursule (R.) . . . . Z 29
Saunerie (R.) . . . . Y
Tivoli (Pl. du). . . . . Y 30
Verdun (Allée de). . . . . Z 32

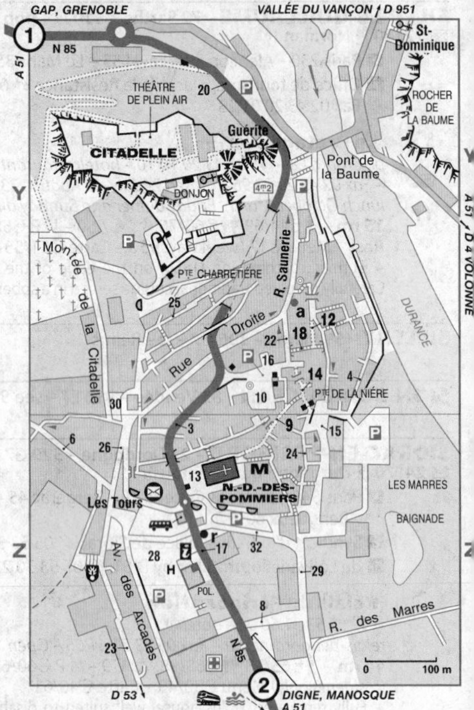

Northwest by ① and D 4085 – ✉ 04200 Sisteron

Les Chênes
300 rte de Gap, 2 km on – ✆ 04 92 61 13 67 – leschenes.hotel@wanadoo.fr – Fax 04 92 61 16 92 – Closed 20 December-31 January, Saturday except from April to September and Sunday except from June to September
23 rm – 🚹€ 53/55 🚹🚹€ 55/71, ☕ € 8 – ½ P € 51/59 – **Rest** – *(closed Saturday and Sunday)* Menu (€ 17), € 19/34 – Carte € 29/44
◆ Practical establishment not far from the Durance. The small, functional rooms are soundproofed. Swimming pool and garden with oak trees to the rear. Traditional recipes served in a simple dining room or on the shady terrace.

SIX-FOURS-LES-PLAGES – 83 Var – 340 K7 – pop. 32 742 – alt. 20 m – ✉ 83140 French Riviera
40 **B3**

Paris 830 – Aix-en-Provence 81 – La Ciotat 33 – Marseille 61 – Toulon 12

Office de tourisme, promenade Charles-de-Gaulle ✆ 04 94 07 02 21, Fax 04 94 25 13 36

Six-Fours Fort ✻★ North: 2 km - Presqu'île de St-Mandrier★: ✻★★ East: 5 km - ✻★★ St Mandrier-sur-Mer cemetery East: 4 km.

Chapelle N.-D.-du-Mai ✻★★ South: 6 km.

Le Clos des Pins
101 bis r. de la République – ✆ 04 94 25 43 68 – cavagnac.dominique@wanadoo.fr – Fax 04 94 07 63 07
25 rm – 🚹€ 54/78 🚹🚹€ 60/91, ☕ € 10 – ½ P € 79/112 – **Rest** – *(dinner only)* Menu € 18/26
◆ A well-soundproofed hotel standing amid pine trees along a busy road. Practical rooms that are being gradually renovated. Pretty terrace with wrought-iron furniture. The restaurant offers family cooking.

in Brusc 4 km south – ✉ 83140 Six-Fours-les-Plages

XX **Le St-Pierre - Chez Marcel**

– ✆ *04 94 34 02 52 – contact@lesaintpierre.fr – Fax 04 94 34 18 01 – Closed January, Sunday dinner, Tuesday dinner from September to June and Monday*
Rest – Menu € 19/36 – Carte € 29/61
◆ A former fisherman's house near the harbour. Its bright, air-conditioned dining room offers fish dishes with regional flavours.

SIZUN – 29 Finistère – **308** G4 – **pop. 1 850** – **alt. 112 m** – ✉ **29450**
Brittany 9 **B2**

Paris 572 – Brest 37 – Châteaulin 36 – Landerneau 16 – Morlaix 36 – Quimper 59
Office de tourisme, 3, rue de l'Argoat ✆ 02 98 68 88 40
Parish enclosure★ - Bannières★ in Locmélar church North: 5 km.

Les Voyageurs rm, **P**

2 r. Argoat – ✆ 02 98 68 80 35 – hotelvoyag@aol.com – Fax 02 98 24 11 49 – Closed 15 September-6 October, Sunday evening and Saturday October-June
22 rm – €51 €51, ☕ €7 – ½ P €47 – **Rest** – *(closed Friday dinner, Sunday dinner and Saturday)* Menu (€11), €14 (weekdays), €26/35
◆ At the centre of Sizun, this family establishment stands close to the church walls. The simple and well-kept rooms are larger in the main building. Traditional menus at reasonable prices served next to the fireplace in a country-style dining room.

SOCHAUX – 25 Doubs – **321** L1 – **pop. 4 491** – **alt. 310 m** – ✉ **25600**
Burgundy-Jura 17 **C1**

Paris 478 – Audincourt 5 – Belfort 18 – Besançon 77 – Montbéliard 5 – Mulhouse 56
Musée de l'Aventure Peugeot★★ AX.

See plan of Montbéliard urban area.

Arianis rest, **P**

11 av. Gén. Leclerc – ✆ 03 81 32 17 17 – arianis@wanadoo.fr – Fax 03 81 32 00 90
65 rm – €70 €75/93, ☕ €7 – ½ P €60 X **u**
Rest – *(closed Friday dinner, Sunday dinner and Saturday)* Menu €14/42 – Carte €34/52
Rest *Brasserie de l'Arianis* – *(closed Friday dinner, Sunday dinner and Saturday)* Menu €13/16 – Carte €23/37
◆ Various models of Peugeot cars are displayed in the reception lobby of this recent hotel. Rooms are well equipped and soberly decorated. The restaurant offers traditional set menus in a modern setting. Dining room, veranda and eclectic menu at La Brasserie.

in Étupes 3 km by ③ and D 463 – **pop. 3 543** – **alt. 337 m** – ✉ **25460**

XX **Au Fil des Saisons**

3 r. de la Libération – ✆ 03 81 94 17 12 – aufildessaisons@clubinternet.fr – Fax 03 81 32 36 04 – Closed 4-24 August, 22 December-4 January, Saturday lunch, Sunday and Monday
Rest – Menu €22/29 – Carte €31/53
◆ This restaurant keeps pace with the seasons, as its name suggests. A good choice of fish on the family-style menu. Attractively redecorated dining area.

SOCOA – 64 Pyrénées-Atlantiques – **342** B2 – see St-Jean-de-Luz

---

SOCX – 59 Nord – **302** C2 – **pop. 980** – **alt. 24 m** – ✉ **59380** 30 **B1**

Paris 287 – Lille 64 – Calais 52 – Dunkerque 20 – Roeselare 68

X **Au Steger**

27 rte de St-Omer – ✆ 03 28 68 20 49 – restaurant.steger@wanadoo.fr – Fax 03 28 68 27 83 – Closed 1st-20 August and Saturday lunch
Rest – *(lunch only except Saturday)* Menu €12 (weekday lunch), €17/30 – Carte €21/42
◆ This family grocers has been converted into a tavern-style restaurant; delicious traditional recipes and Flemish dishes.

SOISSONS ⟨SP⟩ – 02 Aisne – 306 B6 – pop. 29 453 – alt. 47 m – ✉ 02200

Northern France and the Paris Region 37 **C2**

- ▶ Paris 102 – Compiègne 39 – Laon 37 – Reims 59 – St-Quentin 61
- ℹ Office de tourisme, 16, place Fernand Marquigny ✆ 03 23 53 17 37, Fax 03 23 59 67 72
- ◉ Former St-Jean-des-Vignes abbey★★ - St-Gervais and St-Protais cathedral★★.

SOISSONS

Street	Square	No.
Arquebuse (R. de l')	**BZ**	2
Château-Thierry (Av.)	**BZ**	4
Collège (R. du)	**AY**	5
Commerce (R. du)	**BY**	6
Compiègne (Av.)	**AY**	8
Desmoulins (Bd C.)	**ABZ**	12
Gambetta (Bd L.)	**BY**	14
Intendance (R. de l')	**BY**	15
Leclerc (Av. Gén.)	**BZ**	22
Marquigny (Pl. F.)	**BY**	23
Paix (R. de la)	**BY**	24
Panleu (R. de)	**AY**	25
Prés.-Kennedy (Av.)	**AZ**	26
Quinquet (R.)	**ABY**	28
Racine (R.)	**BZ**	29
République (Pl. de la)	**BZ**	30
St-Antoine (R.)	**BY**	31
St-Christophe (Pl.)	**AY**	32
St-Christophe (R.)	**AY**	33
St-Jean (R.)	**AZ**	34
St-Martin (R.)	**BY**	35
St-Quentin (R.)	**BY**	36
St-Rémy (R.)	**AY**	37
Strasbourg (Bd de)	**BY**	38
Villeneuve (R. de)	**BZ**	39

L'Assiette Gourmande
16 av. de Coucy – 03 23 93 47 78 – Fax 03 23 93 47 78 – Closed 23-30 March, August, Saturday lunch, Sunday dinner, dinner on public holidays and Monday BY **e**
Rest – Menu € 15 (weekday lunch), € 29/50 – Carte € 36/56
◆ This restaurant has conquered the heart of locals thanks to its elegant décor, cosy ambiance and flavourful, updated traditional dishes.

Chez Raphaël
7 r. St Quentin – 03 23 93 51 79 – chez.raphael@wanadoo.fr – Fax 03 23 93 26 50 – Closed 18-31 August, 1st-8 January, 23-28 February, Saturday lunch, Sunday dinner and Monday BY **a**
Rest – Menu € 20 (weekday lunch), € 25/42 – Carte € 37/51
◆ Pleasant establishment located in a shopping street. Welcoming dining room in bistro style where tasty local dishes are on offer.

in Belleu **3 km south by D 1 and D 690 – pop. 4 031 – alt. 55 m – ✉ 02200**

Le Grenadin
19 rte de Fère-en-Tardenois – 03 23 73 20 57 – restaurantlegrenadin@free.fr – Fax 03 23 73 11 61 – Closed 15-31 January, Sunday dinner, Monday and public holidays BZ **f**
Rest – Menu (€ 17), € 23/45 – Carte € 28/49
◆ A cherub watches over the façade of this sympathetic house serving carefully prepared traditional cuisine. Rustic, country-style dining room and garden terrace during summer.

SOLAIZE – 69 Rhône – 327 I6 – pop. 2 256 – alt. 232 m – ✉ 69360 44 B2

Paris 472 – Lyon 17 – Rive-de-Gier 25 – La Tour-du-Pin 58 – Vienne 17

Soleil et Jardin
44 r. de la République – 04 78 02 44 90 – soleiletjardin@wanadoo.fr – Fax 04 78 02 09 26 – Closed 1st-17 August
22 rm – €110/150 €120/190, € 10 – **Rest** – *(closed Saturday and Sunday)* Menu € 34 – Carte € 36/53
◆ On the village square, hotel with bright functional rooms; three of which have a terrace. Sunshine and laughter flood the dining room extended by a flower-decked terrace. Well-planned classic menu.

SOLENZARA – 2A Corse-du-Sud – 345 F8 – see Corse

SOLESMES – 72 Sarthe – 310 H7 – see Sablé-sur-Sarthe

SOLIGNAC – 87 Haute-Vienne – 325 E6 – pop. 1 367 – alt. 251 m – ✉ 87110

Paris 400 – Bourganeuf 55 – Limoges 10 – Nontron 70 – Périgueux 90 – Uzerche 52 24 B2

Office de tourisme, place Georges Dubreuil 05 55 00 42 31, Fax 05 55 00 56 44

St-Éloi
66 av. St-Éloi – 05 55 00 44 52 – lesaint.eloi@wanadoo.fr – Fax 05 55 00 55 56 – Closed 2-9 June, 17-30 September, 3-26 January, Saturday lunch, Sunday dinner and Monday
15 rm – €55/60 €60/65, € 10 – ½ P € 65/80
Rest – Menu € 20 (weekday lunch), € 25/45 – Carte € 36/50
◆ Beyond the stone and half-timbered façade, lies an interior full of character in which you will find bright, modern bedrooms and a designer lounge. Stylish cuisine served in a light non-smoking room adorned with an immense fireplace. Picturesque terrace.

For a pleasant stay in a charming hotel, look for the red ... symbols.

SOMMIÈRES – 30 Gard – 339 J6 – pop. 3 677 – alt. 34 m – ✉ 30250 23 C2

Paris 734 – Montpellier 35 – Nîmes 29

Office de tourisme, 5, quai Frédéric Gaussorgues ✆ 04 66 80 99 30, Fax 04 66 80 06 95

Auberge du Pont Romain rest, VISA AE
2 r. Emile Jamais – ✆ 04 66 80 00 58 – aubergedupontromain@wanadoo.fr – Fax 04 66 80 31 52 – Closed November, 15 January-15 March and Monday lunch
19 rm – †€ 74/110 ††€ 74/110, ☐ € 13 – ½ P € 85/145
Rest – Menu (€ 25), € 35/60 – Carte € 55/65
◆ This beautiful, imposing house built in local Gard stone was a woollen sheet factory back in the 19C. Large well-bred rustic-style rooms, quieter on the garden side. Country chic dining room serving updated tasty fare.

De l'Estelou without rest VISA AE
at 200m on Aubais road – ✆ 04 66 77 71 08 – hoteldelestelou@free.fr – Fax 04 66 77 08 88 – Closed 25 December-14 January
24 rm – †€ 42/68 ††€ 52/72, ☐ € 8
◆ This hotel located in the former Sommières train station (1870) has character: modern rooms tastefully decorated, a pretty veranda for breakfast and a quiet garden with swimming pool.

in Boisseron 3 Km south by D 610 – pop. 1 151 – alt. 32 m – ✉ 34160

XX **La Rose Blanche** A/C VISA AE
51 r. Maurice Chauvet – ✆ 04 67 86 60 76 – restoroseblanche@yahoo.fr – Fax 04 67 86 60 76 – Closed 12-22 October, 5-22 January, Sunday dinner October-March, Tuesday lunch and Monday
Rest – Menu (€ 19), € 27/55 – Carte € 51/56
◆ In the former guardroom of the castle, modern furniture, fabrics and art mix easily with 12C vaulted ceilings and exposed stone walls. Modern cuisine.

SONDERNACH – 68 Haut-Rhin – 315 G9 – pop. 614 – alt. 540 m – ✉ 68380 1 A2

Paris 466 – Colmar 27 – Gérardmer 41 – Guebwiller 39 – Thann 42

X **À l'Orée du Bois** with rm P VISA
4 rte du Schnepfenried – ✆ 03 89 77 70 21 – contact@oredubois.com – Fax 03 89 77 77 58 – Closed 23-30 June and 5 January-5 February
7 rm – †€ 43 ††€ 51, ☐ € 4 – ½ P € 45 – **Rest** – *(closed Wednesday lunchtime and Tuesday)* Menu € 14/32 – Carte € 23/40
◆ Welcoming countrified dining room (woodwork, earthenware stove), regional menu of tartes flambées and fondues, mountain-inspired rooms: the essence of Alsatian hospitality.

SONNAC-SUR-L'HERS – 11 Aude – 344 C4 – pop. 128 – alt. 362 m – ✉ 11230 22 A3

Paris 784 – Montpellier 218 – Carcassonne 52 – Pamiers 41 – Castelnaudary 56

Le Trésor VISA
– ✆ 04 68 69 37 94 – contact@le-tresor.com – Fax 04 68 69 37 94 – Closed January
4 rm ☐ – †€ 80/100 ††€ 80/100 – **Table d'hôte** – Menu € 25 bi/35 bi
◆ An English couple has bought this house opposite the church. Neat and tidy bedrooms with good-quality bedding. Breakfast on the terrace; other meals served in the garden. Le Trésor's hallmarks are its intimate setting, attention to detail, local products (single menu) and wines from the region.

SONNAZ – 73 Savoie – 333 I4 – see Chambéry

SOPHIA-ANTIPOLIS – 06 Alpes-Maritimes – 341 D6 – see Valbonne

SORBIERS – 42 Loire – 327 F7 – see St-Étienne

SORÈZE – 81 Tarn – 338 E10 – pop. 2 164 – alt. 272 m – ✉ 81540

Languedoc-Roussillon-Tarn Gorges 29 **C2**

Paris 732 – Toulouse 59 – Carcassonne 44 – Castelnaudary 26 – Castres 27 – Gaillac 64

Office de tourisme, rue Saint-Martin ✆ 05 63 74 16 28, Fax 05 63 50 86 61

Hôtel Abbaye Ecole Le Logis des Pères

rm, VISA AE

r. Lacordaire – ✆ 05 63 74 44 80 – reception@hotelfp.soreze.com – Fax 05 63 74 44 89

52 rm – €95/150 €95/150, € 12 – ½ P € 81/108 – **Rest** – *(closed Sunday dinner)* Menu € 21/50 – Carte € 29/46

◆ A hotel in a wing of the famous Benedictine abbey-school (17C) founded in 754 by Pepin the Short. Attractively decorated rooms and a 6-ha wooded park. Traditional cuisine served in the old refectory or under the shade of the plane trees.

Le Pavillon des Hôtes

VISA AE

20 rm – €55/65 €55/65, € 12 – ½ P € 61/66

◆ This annexe is in another part of the Abbey. Simple, tastefully decorated rooms are arranged around an interior courtyard and the prices are reasonable.

SORGES – 24 Dordogne – 329 G4 – pop. 1 123 – alt. 178 m – ✉ 24420

Dordogne-Berry-Limousin 4 **C1**

Paris 463 – Brantôme 24 – Limoges 77 – Nontron 36 – Périgueux 20 – Thiviers 15

Syndicat d'initiative, écomusée de la Truffe ✆ 05 53 46 71 43, Fax 05 53 46 71 43

Auberge de la Truffe

AC rest, VISA AE

sur N 21 – ✆ 05 53 05 02 05 – contact@auberge-de-la-truffe.com – Fax 05 53 05 39 27

19 rm – €48/55 €52/65, € 10 – 4 suites – ½ P € 58/85

Rest – *(closed Sunday dinner and Monday lunch 12 November-15 March)* Menu (€ 12 bi), € 18 (weekdays), € 24/100 – Carte € 28/87

◆ A welcoming village inn near the Maison de la Truffe with spacious, well-furnished rooms, some at garden level. A spruce dining room and cuisine based on local produce with truffles (the black diamond) and foie gras in pride of place.

SOSPEL – 06 Alpes-Maritimes – 341 F4 – pop. 2 885 – alt. 360 m – ✉ 06380

French Riviera 41 **D2**

Paris 967 – Menton 19 – Nice 41 – Tende 38 – Ventimiglia 28

Office de tourisme, 19, avenue Jean Médecin ✆ 04 93 04 15 80, Fax 04 93 04 19 96

Old village★: Old bridge★, Immaculate Virgin ★ in St-Michel church - St-Roch Fort ★ South: 1 km by D 2204.

Des Étrangers

rm, VISA

7 bd Verdun – ✆ 04 93 04 00 09 – sospel@sospel.net – Fax 04 93 04 12 31 – Open March-November

27 rm – €65/71 €72/90, € 8 – ½ P € 70/89 – **Rest** – *(closed Wednesday lunch and Tuesday)* Menu € 24/35 – Carte € 31/46

◆ This hotel, run by the same family since 1883, greets guests warmly. The rooms sport a fresh Provençal style (wrought iron, patinated walls and pastel shades). Jacuzzi in the basement. Regional and tasty cuisine, prepared with garden and market produce.

SOUILLAC – 46 Lot – 337 E2 – pop. 3 671 – alt. 104 m – ✉ 46200

Dordogne-Berry-Limousin 28 **B1**

Paris 516 – Brive-la-Gaillarde 39 – Cahors 68 – Figeac 74 – Sarlat-la-Canéda 29

Office de tourisme, boulevard Louis-Jean Malvy ✆ 05 65 37 81 56, Fax 05 65 27 11 45

Souillac Country Club Lachapelle-Auzac, North: 8 km by D 15, ✆ 05 65 27 56 00.

Former abbey church: low-relief "Isaïe"★★, back of the portal★ - Musée national de l'Automate et de la Robotique★.

SOUILLAC

Abbaye (Pl. de l') .... Z 2
Barebaste (R.) .... Z 4
Barnicou (Pl.) .... Z 5
Bénétou (R.) .... Y 7
Betz (Pl. Pierre) ..... Z
La Borie (Pl. de) ..... Y 20
La Borie (R. de) ..... Y
Bouchier (Pl. J.-B.) ... Z 8
Doussot (Pl.) .... Z 9
Figuier (Pl. du) .... Y 12
Forail Marsalès (Pl. du) .... YZ
Frégière (R. de la) .... Z
Gambetta (Av.) ...... Y 14
Gaulle (Av. du Gén.-de) ... Y 15
Gourgue (R. de) ...... Z 16
Granges (R. des) ..... Z
Grozel (R. de) .... Y
Halle (R. de la) .... Y 17
Juillet (R. de) .... Y
Louqsor (R.) .... Z 21
Malvarès (R.) .... Y 22
Malvy (Av. Martin) .... Y
Malvy (Bd Louis-Jean) .. YZ
Morlet (R.) .... Z 24
Pons (Pl. de l'Abbé) .. Y 25
Pont (R. du) .... Z 26
Puits (Pl. du) .... Y 28
Rajol (Pl. du) .... Y 29
Recège (R. de la) ...... Y
St-Martin (R.) .... Z 32
Sarlat (Av. de) .... Z
Verlhac (Av. P.) .... Y

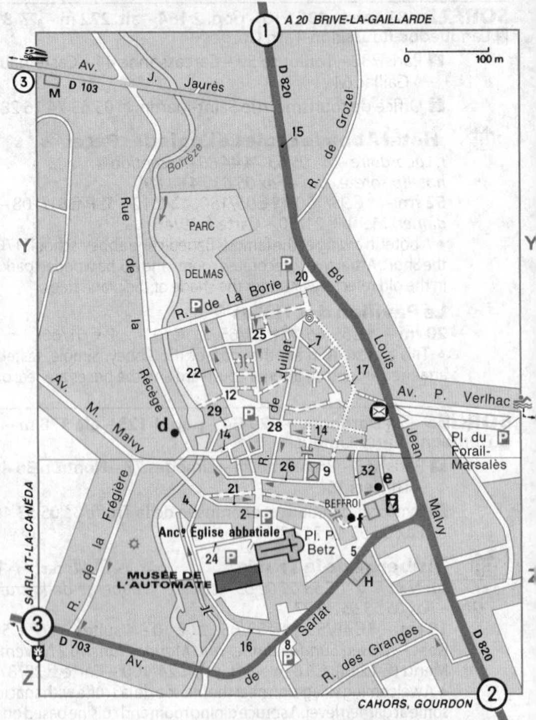

Grand Hôtel

1 allée Verninac – ✆ 05 65 32 78 30 – grandhotel-souillac@wanadoo.fr – Fax 05 65 32 66 34 – Open from 17 March-8 December Z **e**

30 rm – €49 €58, €7 – ½ P €58 – **Rest** – Menu €11,50 (weekday lunch), €19/28 – Carte €24/42

◆ This hundred-year-old building offers guests a choice of modern, individually furnished rooms. A pleasant patio provides welcome light to the breakfast room. Traditional cuisine served in modern surroundings. In summer, choose between the veranda with its sliding roof or the plane tree-shaded terrace.

Le Pavillon St-Martin without rest

5 pl. St-Martin – ✆ 05 65 32 63 45 – contact@hotel-saint-martin-souillac.com – Fax 05 65 32 75 37 Z **f**

11 rm – €48/73 €48/73, €8

◆ Opposite the church tower, this distinctive 16C villa offers personalised rooms that marry classic and contemporary details. Pleasant vaulted breakfast room.

Le Quercy without rest

1 r. Récège – ✆ 05 65 37 83 56 – reservation@le-quercy.fr – Fax 05 65 37 07 22 – Open 20 March-15 December Y **d**

25 rm – €35/50 €55/60, €8

◆ A comfortable family-run hotel away from the busy centre. Well-maintained guestrooms, most of which have a balcony overlooking the flower-decked terrace or swimming pool.

Belle Vue without rest

68 av. J. Jaurès, (in the station) – ✆ 05 65 32 78 23 – hotelbellevue.souillac@wanadoo.fr – Fax 05 65 37 03 89

26 rm – €40/42 €48/50, €6,50

◆ Large 1960s building near the train station. Simple but clean rooms. Sports installations on the garden side (pool, tennis) and a small boutique of regional products.

Le Redouillé

28 av. de Toulouse, via ② – ✆ 05 65 37 87 25 – leredouille.souillac@wanadoo.fr – Closed 11-31 March, 12 January-2 February, Monday and Tuesday
Rest – Menu € 17/45 – Carte € 36/72
◆ Two dining rooms - one bright and sunny, inspired by the colours of Provence - separated by a sitting room. Traditional cuisine with the occasional modern touch. Summer terrace.

SOULAC-SUR-MER – **33 Gironde** – **335** E1 – **pop. 2 720** – **alt. 7 m** – **Casino : de la Plage** – ✉ **33780** Atlantic Coast 3 **B1**

Paris 515 – Bordeaux 99 – Lesparre-Médoc 31 – Royan 12

Office de tourisme, 68, rue de la plage ✆ 05 56 09 86 61, Fax 05 56 73 63 76

in l'Amélie-sur-Mer **5 km southwest by D 101^E** – ✉ **33780 Soulac-sur-Mer**

Des Pins rest, rm,

– ✆ 05 56 73 27 27 – info@hotel-des-pins.com – Fax 05 56 73 60 39 – Open 15 March-4 January and closed Saturday lunch, Sunday dinner and Monday off season
31 rm – †€ 45/90 ††€ 60/98, ☕ € 9,50 – ½ P € 45/78
Rest – Menu (€ 17), € 20 (weekday lunch), € 26/40 – Carte € 27/64
◆ A renovated late 19C building on the edge of the pines 100m from the beach – fine sand as far as the eye can see. Two annexes. Rooms variously furnished. Bright restaurant serving fish and regional cuisine.

SOULAINES-DHUYS – **10 Aube** – **313** I3 – **pop. 267** – **alt. 153 m** – ✉ **10200** 14 **C3**

Paris 228 – Bar-sur-Aube 18 – Chaumont 48 – Troyes 58

La Venise Verte

r. Plessis – ✆ 03 25 92 76 10 – accueil@logis-venise-verte.com – Fax 03 25 92 73 97 – Closed 24-30 December
12 rm – †€ 65 ††€ 65, ☕ € 9 – ½ P € 68 – **Rest** – *(closed Sunday dinner 21 September-16 March)* Menu € 16 (weekdays)/59 bi – Carte € 30/50
◆ This welcoming hotel next to the road has good soundproofing. The small rooms are fresh and practical. An ideal base for visiting the village and its half-timbered houses. Sunny dining room, summer terrace in the inner courtyard and traditional dishes.

LA SOURCE – **45 Loiret** – **318** I5 – **see Orléans**

SOURDEVAL – **50 Manche** – **303** G7 – **pop. 3 038** – **alt. 217 m** – ✉ **50150** 32 **B2**

Paris 310 – Avranches 36 – Domfront 30 – Flers 31 – Mayenne 64 – St-Lô 53 – Vire 14

Office de tourisme, jardin de l'Europe ✆ 02 33 79 35 61, Fax 02 33 79 35 59

Sée Valley ★ O, Normandy

Le Temps de Vivre

12 r. St-Martin – ✆ 02 33 59 60 41 – le-temps-de-vivre@wanadoo.fr – Fax 02 33 59 88 34 – Closed 22-29 September, 4-18 February, Sunday dinner and Monday except August
10 rm – †€ 33 ††€ 39/48, ☕ € 5,50 – ½ P € 36 – **Rest** – Menu (€ 9,50), € 16/29 – Carte € 15/32
◆ Hotel on the village square, by the cinema, with a granite façade brightened by flower boxes. Small rooms that are recent and well kept. Pleasant restaurant, ideal for taking it easy while enjoying simple dishes at reasonable prices.

SOURZAC – **24 Dordogne** – **329** D5 – **see Mussidan**

SOUSCEYRAC – 46 Lot – 337 I2 – pop. 988 – alt. 559 m – ✉ 46190 29 C1

Paris 548 – Aurillac 47 – Cahors 96 – Figeac 41 – Mauriac 69 – St-Céré 17

Office de tourisme, place de l'Église ☎ 05 65 33 02 20, Fax 05 65 11 66 19

Au Déjeuner de Sousceyrac (Patrick Lagnès) with rm

– ☎ 05 65 33 00 56 – Fax 05 65 33 04 37

– Closed January, Sunday dinner and Monday except from July to September

10 rm – €45 €45, €8 – ½ P €60

Rest – *(number of covers limited, pre-book)* Menu €15/45 – Carte €34/48

Spec. Hamburger de foie gras aux truffes. Ris de veau, gratin de macaroni au cantal. Paris-Brest.

◆ A warm welcome, brightly coloured, renovated rustic-style décor and fine regional cuisine, are the highlights of this pretty house on the village square. The rooms have been entirely redone.

SOUS-LA-TOUR – 22 Côtes-d'Armor – 309 F3 – see St-Brieuc

SOUSTONS – 40 Landes – 335 D12 – pop. 5 743 – alt. 9 m – ✉ 40140

Atlantic Coast 3 B2

Paris 736 – Anglet 51 – Bayonne 47 – Bordeaux 150

Office de tourisme, grange de Labouyrie ☎ 05 58 41 52 62, Fax 05 58 41 30 63

Domaine de Bellegarde

23 av. Ch. de Gaulle, dir. N 10 – ☎ 05 58 41 24 06 – info@qsun.co.uk

– Fax 05 58 41 24 06 – Open April-October

5 rm – €100/200 €120/270 – ½ P €154/176

Table d'hôte – *(pre-book)* Menu €40 bi (weekday lunch)/45 bi

◆ Set in a park, a fine house with features from the Landes region and Basque country, offering rooms and suites that are all furnished in the same style (coconut flooring, wrought-iron bed, etc...). One has a terrace, while another has a private sauna. Family fare varying according to market availability.

LA SOUTERRAINE – 23 Creuse – 325 F3 – pop. 5 320 – alt. 390 m – ✉ 23300

Dordogne-Berry-Limousin 24 B1

Paris 344 – Bellac 41 – Châteauroux 79 – Guéret 35 – Limoges 58

Office de tourisme, place de la Gare ☎ 05 55 63 10 06

Church★.

in l'Est : 7 km by N 145, D 74 and secondary road – ✉ 23300 La Souterraine

Château de la Cazine rm, rest,

Domaine de la Fôt – ☎ 05 55 89 60 00

– chateau-de-la-cazine@wanadoo.fr – Fax 05 55 63 71 85

– Closed 23 December-13 January

20 rm – €60/100 €60/100, €12 – 2 suites – ½ P €63/80

Rest – Menu €22 (weekday lunch), €33/60 – Carte €67/74

Spec. Terrine de foie gras, figues pochées au porto. Médaillon de filet de bœuf du Limousin. Moelleux au chocolat araguani.

◆ A quiet, enjoyable stay is guaranteed at this small and charming 19C château set in extensive grounds. Three dining rooms, a terrace facing the surrounding countryside, and classic cuisine endowed with great finesse.

in St-Étienne-de-Fursac 11 km south by Fursac road (D 1) – pop. 816 – alt. 322 m – ✉ 23290

Nougier with rm

2 pl. de l'Église – ☎ 05 55 63 60 56 – Fax 05 55 63 65 47 – Open from mid March-end November and closed Monday except dinner July-August, Sunday dinner from September to June and Tuesday lunch

12 rm – €48 €60/68, €10 – ½ P €60/67 – **Rest** – Menu (€13), €20/42 – Carte €33/47

◆ Fifty years and three generations later, the same family continues to receive guests in the attractive, country-style dining room. Sophisticated gourmet cuisine. Rustic bedrooms and a charming garden and pool.

SOUVIGNY – 03 Allier – 326 G3 – pop. 1 952 – alt. 242 m – ✉ 03210
Auvergne 5 **B1**

Paris 301 – Bourbon-l'Archambault 16 – Montluçon 70 – Moulins 13

Prieuré St-Pierre★★ - Calendar★★ in St-Marc church-museum.

Auberge des Tilleuls
pl. St-Éloi – 04 70 43 60 70 – Fax 04 70 43 60 70 – Closed 25 August-2 September, 29 December-5 January, February school holidays, Tuesday dinner except July-August, Wednesday dinner November-March, Sunday dinner and Monday

Rest – Menu € 12 (weekday lunch), € 19/43 – Carte € 26/48

◆ This smart inn welcomes you in two carefully rustic-style dining rooms, one with trompe l'oeil half-timbering. Narrow, shaded terrace at the back.

SOUVIGNY-EN-SOLOGNE – 41 Loir-et-Cher – 318 J6 – pop. 410 – alt. 210 m – ✉ 41600
12 **C2**

Paris 171 – Gien 43 – Lamotte-Beuvron 15 – Montargis 63 – Orléans 39

Auberge de la Grange aux Oies
2 r. du Gâtinais – 02 54 88 40 08 – Fax 02 54 88 40 08 – Closed Sunday dinner, Tuesday dinner and Wednesday

Rest – Menu € 27 (weekday lunch), € 40/51 – Carte € 30/49

◆ Beams and floor tiles create a pleasant country atmosphere in this pretty, half-timbered 17C and 18C house. Traditional dishes typical of the Sologne region with game in season.

SOYAUX – 16 Charente – 324 L6 – see Angoulême

SOYONS – 07 Ardèche – 331 L4 – see St-Péray

STEENVOORDE – 59 Nord – 302 D3 – pop. 4 024 – alt. 50 m – ✉ 59114
30 **B1**

Paris 259 – Calais 73 – Dunkerque 33 – Hazebrouck 12 – Lille 45 – St-Omer 28

Syndicat d'initiative, place Jean-Marie Ryckewaert 03 28 42 97 98

Auprès de Mon Arbre
932 rte d'Eecke – 03 28 49 79 49 – aupres.de.mon.arbre457@orange.fr – Fax 03 28 49 72 29 – Closed dinner except Friday and Saturday

Rest – Menu € 18 (weekday lunch), € 29/42

◆ This renovated farm has a fireplace and Godin stove that guests don't want to leave, except perhaps in summer to sit in the lovely garden. Carefully prepared authentic dishes.

STELLA-PLAGE – 62 Pas-de-Calais – 301 C5 – see le Touquet

STENAY – 55 Meuse – 307 C2 – pop. 2 952 – alt. 182 m – ✉ 55700 26 **A1**

Paris 251 – Carignan 20 – Charleville-Mézières 58 – Longwy 51 – Sedan 34 – Verdun 46

Office de tourisme, 5, place R. Poincaré 03 29 80 64 22, Fax 03 29 80 62 59

Du Commerce
16 r. A. Briand – 03 29 80 30 62 – Fax 03 29 80 61 77 – Closed 23 December-15 January, Monday lunch, Friday dinner, Saturday lunch and Sunday dinner

16 rm – †€ 55 ††€ 55, € 8,50 – ½ P € 63 – **Rest** – Menu (€ 13), € 19/35 – Carte € 27/47

◆ Near the European Beer Museum, a flower-decked country inn. Well-equipped rooms, some in bright colours. Two rustic-style dining rooms, one with a large fireplace. Traditional cuisine and speciality recipes cooked in beer.

STIRING-WENDEL – 57 Moselle – 307 M3 – see Forbach

Guittot/Diaf/PHOTONONSTOP

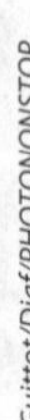

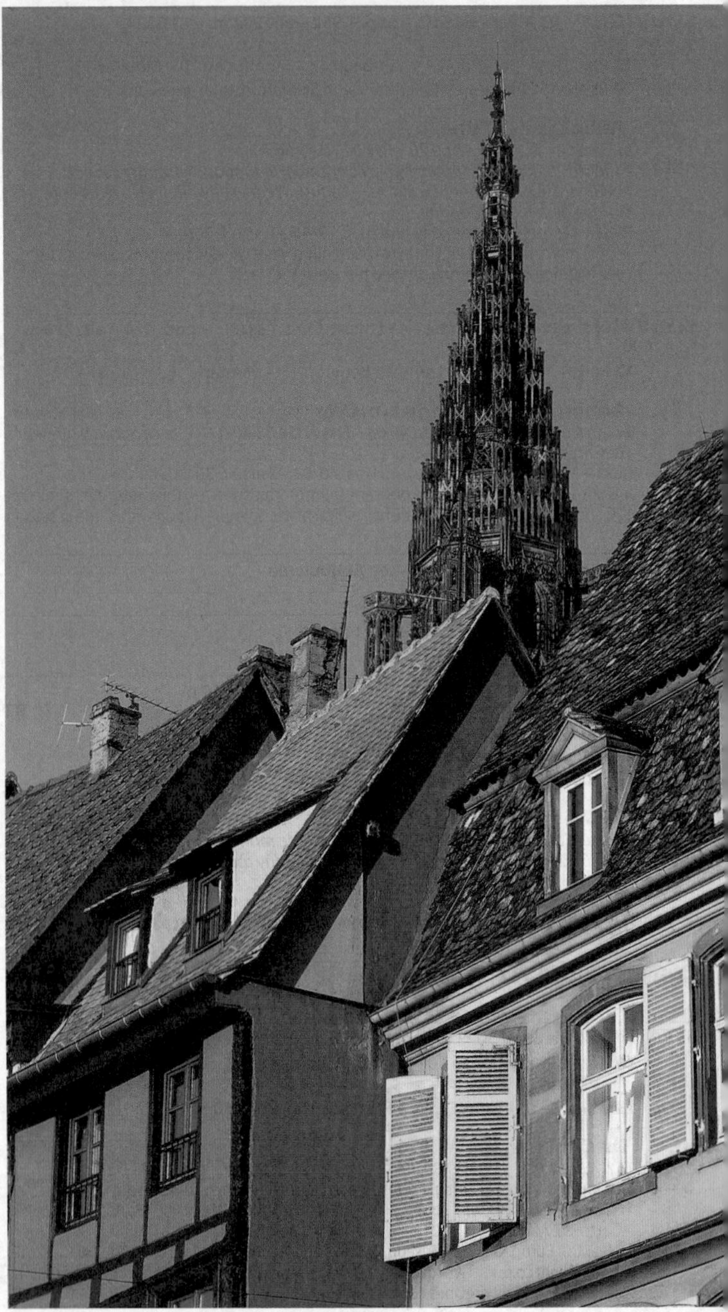

Old Strasbourg and the spire of Notre-Dame Cathedral

STRASBOURG

🅿 **Department:** 67 Bas-Rhin
Michelin LOCAL map: n° **315** K5
▶ Paris 489 – Basel 141 – Karlsruhe 81 – Stuttgart 149

Population: 264 115 1 **B1**
Pop. built-up area: 427 245
Altitude: 143 m – **Postal Code:** ✉ 67000
▮ **Alsace-Lorraine**

USEFUL INFORMATION

TOURIST OFFICES

17 place de la Cathédrale ✆ 03 88 52 28 28, Fax 03 88 52 28 29
place de la Gare ✆ 03 88 32 51 49

TRANSPORT

Auto-train ✆ 3635 et tapez 42 (0,34€/mn)

AIRPORT

Strasbourg-International ✆ 03 88 64 67 67 **AT**

A FEW GOLF COURSES

La Wantzenau C.D. 302, ✆ 03 88 96 37 73 ;
Le Kempferhof Golf Club Plobsheim 351 rue du Moulin, South: 15 km by D 468, ✆ 03 88 98 72 72.

TO BE SEEN

CATHEDRAL DISTRICT

Notre-Dame Cathedral ★★★ : astronomical clock★ ⋞ ★of the spire - Place de la cathédrale ★: maison Kammerzell ★ KZ Musée★★ du palais Rohan★- Musée alsacien★★ KZ M[1] Musée de l'Oeuvre Notre-Dame★★ KZ M[6] - Musée historique★ KZ M[5]

PETITE FRANCE

Rue du Bains-aux-Plantes★★ HJZ - covered bridges★ HZ - Barrage Vauban ✳★★ HZ - Mausoleum of the Marshal de Saxe★★ in St-Thomas church JZ - Musée d'Art moderne et contemporain★★ HZ **M**[3] - Boat trip on the River Ill

AROUND PLACE KLÉBER AND PLACE BROGLIE

Place Kléber★, the most famous square in Strasbourg, flanked by the Aubette in the North JY Place Broglie : Town hall ★KY H

EUROPE IN STRASBOURG

Palais de l'Europe★ FGU - Nouveau palais des Droits de l'Homme (new human rights centre) GU - Orangerie★ FGU

Régent Petite France rm, VISA
5 r. Moulins – 03 88 76 43 43
– rpf@regent-hotels.com – Fax 03 88 76 43 76 p. 8 JZ **f**
60 rm – †€ 255/380 ††€ 276/401, € 21 – 6 suites
Rest – *(closed Sunday, Monday and lunch October-May)* Menu (€ 32), € 41/71 bi
◆ A contemporary hotel occupying an old ice factory on the banks of the Ill. Spacious, comfortable guestrooms with high-tech equipment, a terrace-solarium and sauna. Modern menu in keeping with the trendy feel of the restaurant, with bar-lounge and views of the river.

Sofitel VISA
pl. St-Pierre-le-Jeune – 03 88 15 49 00 – h0568@accor.com
– Fax 03 88 15 49 99 p. 8 JY **s**
153 rm – †€ 135/380 ††€ 155/400, € 23 – 2 suites
Rest – *(closed Saturday lunch, Sunday and public holidays)* Carte € 43/61
◆ Two types of room – classic and those designed on a European political theme on offer at this Sofitel. A full range of modern facilities, plus patio and fitness centre. Modern, Japanese-inspired design and luxury brasserie-style service at the restaurant.

Hilton rm, VISA
av. Herrenschmidt – 03 88 37 10 10 – info@hilton-strasbourg.com
– Fax 03 88 36 83 27 p. 6 EU **e**
238 rm – †€ 152/345 ††€ 152/345, € 27 – 5 suites
Rest *La Table du Chef* – *03 88 37 41 42 (closed July-August, Saturday and Sunday) (lunch only)* Menu (€ 29), € 35
Rest *Le Jardin du Tivoli* – *03 88 35 72 61* – Menu € 30 – Carte € 34/46
◆ This glass and steel hotel provides standardised comfort in its spacious guestrooms. Lobby with shops, a multimedia centre and bars. Traditional lunches and a British feel at La Table du Chef; wine bar in the evening. Buffet dining at the Jardin du Tivoli.

Régent Contades without rest VISA
8 av. de la Liberté – 03 88 15 05 05 – rc@regent-hotels.com
– Fax 03 88 15 05 15 p. 9 LY **f**
47 rm – †€ 190/255 ††€ 210/480, € 18,50
◆ A 19C hotel with an opulent and refined decor of wood panelling, numerous paintings and a Belle-Époque breakfast room. Spacious, frequently refurbished guestrooms.

Beaucour without rest VISA
5 r. Bouchers – 03 88 76 72 00 – info@hotel-beaucour.com – Fax 03 88 76 72 60
49 rm – †€ 70/101 ††€ 124/191, € 12 p. 9 KZ **k**
◆ These two elegant 18C Alsatian buildings are linked by a flower-decked patio. The most pleasant guestrooms are decorated in local rustic style with wood panelling and exposed beams.

Maison Rouge without rest VISA
4 r. des Francs-Bourgeois – 03 88 32 08 60 – info@maison-rouge.com
– Fax 03 88 22 43 73 p. 8 JZ **g**
140 rm – †€ 85 ††€ 100/330, € 14 – 2 suites
◆ Behind the red stone façade is an elegant hotel with a cosy atmosphere. Well-designed bedrooms with a personal touch, and an attractively decorated lounge on each floor.

Monopole-Métropole without rest VISA
16 r. Kuhn – 03 88 14 39 14
– info@bestwestern-monopole.com – Fax 03 88 32 82 55 p. 8 HY **p**
86 rm – †€ 75/185 ††€ 85/185
◆ Near the station, hotel split into two wings (one old and rustic, the other far more contemporary, featuring works by local artists). Lounges decorated with handicrafts.

Novotel Centre Halles rm, VISA
4 quai Kléber – 03 88 21 50 50 – h0439@accor.com
– Fax 03 88 21 50 51 p. 8 JY **k**
96 rm – †€ 79/197 ††€ 79/207, € 13,50
Rest – Menu € 20/75 bi – Carte € 20/39
◆ Refurbished rooms in a pleasant, contemporary style at this hotel in the Les Halles shopping centre. Gym on the 8th floor with a view of the cathedral. A modern look in the bar and restaurant; simplified and practical menu.

BISCHHEIM

Marais (R. du) .... CS 121
Périgueux (Av. de) .... BS 159
Robertsau (R. de la) .... BS 179
Triage (R. du) .... BS 219

ECKBOLSHEIM

Gaulle (Av. du Gén.-de) .... BS 67
Wasselonne (Rte de) .... BS 237

HŒNHEIM

Fontaine (R. de la) .... BR 55
République (R. de la) .... BR 174

ILLKIRCH-GRAFFENSTADEN

Bürkell (Rte) .... BT 24
Ceinture (R. de la) .... BT 27
Faisanderie (R. de la) .... BT 48
Industrie (R. de l') .... BT 97
Kastler (R. Alfred) .... BT 99
Lixenbühl (R.) .... BT 115
Messmer (Av.) .... BT 138
Neuhof (Rte de) .... BT 144
Strasbourg (Rte de) .... BT 207
Vignes (R. des) .... BT 233

LINGOLSHEIM

Eckbolsheim (R. d') .... BS 44
Ostwald (R. d') .... BT 152
Près (R. des) .... BS 168

OBERHAUSBERGEN

Mittelhausbergen (Rte de) .... BS 139
Oberhausbergen (Rte de) .... BS 149

OSTWALD

Foch (R. du Maréchal) .... BT 50
Gelspolsheim (R. de) .... BT 73
Leclerc (R. du Gén.) .... BT 112
Vosges (R. des) .... BT 232
23-Novembre (R. du) .... BT 246

SCHILTIGHEIM

Bischwiller (Rte de) .... BS 18
Gaulle (Rte du Gén.-de) .... BS 70
Hausbergen (Rte de) .... BS 81
Mendès-France (Av. P.) .... BS 132
Pompiers (R. des) .... BS 164

STRASBOURG

Atenheim (Rte d') .... CT 8
Austerlitz (Pont d') .... BS 9
Bauerngrund (R. de) .... CT 15
Ganzau (R. de la) .... BT 66
Holtzheim (R. de) .... AS 88
Ill (R. de l') .... CS 96
Neuhof (Rte de) .... CT 144
Plaine des Bouchers (R. de la) .... BS 163
Polygone (Rte du) .... BS 165
Pont (R. du) .... BT 166
Ribeauvillé (R. de) .... CS 177
Romains (Rte des) .... BS 180
Schirmeck (Rte de) .... BS 198

WOLFISHEIM

Oberhausbergen (R. d') .... AS 148
Seigneurs (R. des) .... AS 204

STRASBOURG AGGLOMÉRATION

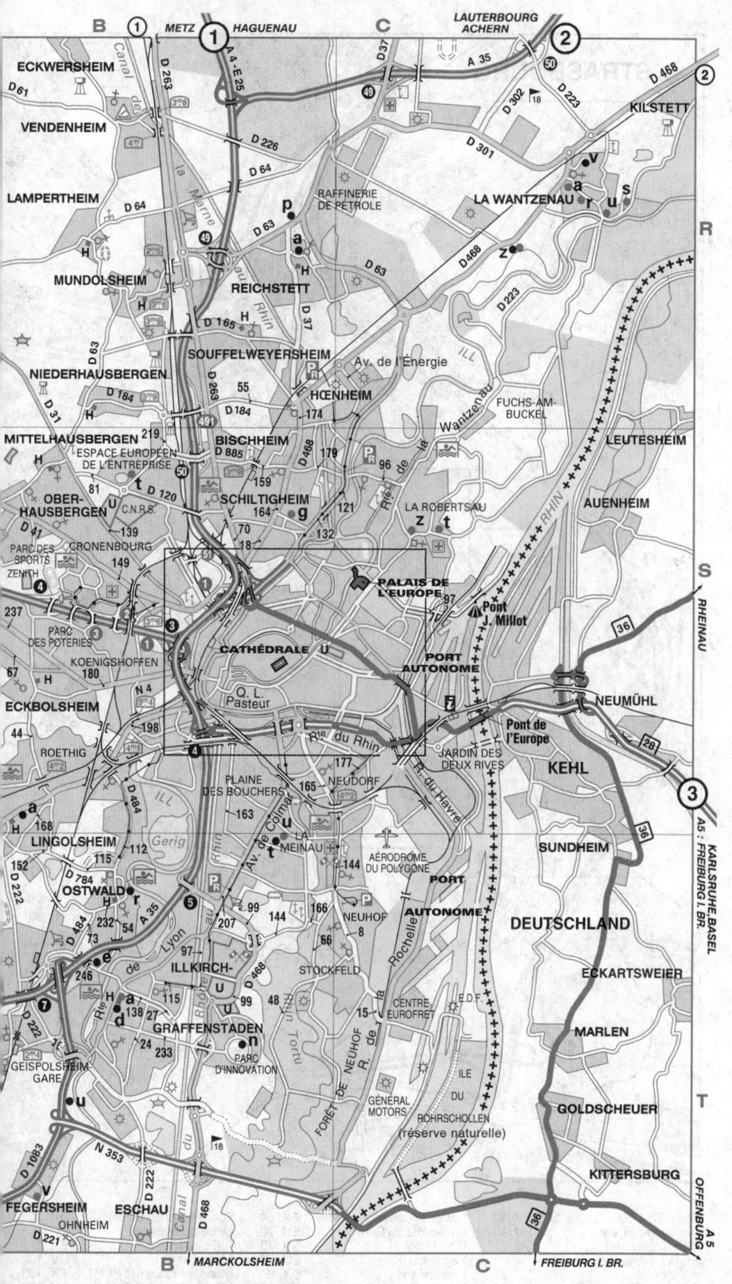
METZ
HAGUENAU
LAUTERBOURG
ACHERN
ECKWERSHEIM
VENDENHEIM
LAMPERTHEIM
MUNDOLSHEIM
REICHSTETT
RAFFINERIE DE PÉTROLE
LA WANTZENAU
KILSTETT
SOUFFELWEYERSHEIM
NIEDERHAUSBERGEN
HŒNHEIM
Av. de l'Énergie
FUCHS-AM-BUCKEL
MITTELHAUSBERGEN
ESPACE EUROPEEN DE L'ENTREPRISE
BISCHHEIM
SCHILTIGHEIM
LEUTESHEIM
OBER-HAUSBERGEN
C.N.R.S.
LA ROBERTSAU
AUENHEIM
CRONENBOURG
PARC DES SPORTS ZENITH
PALAIS DE L'EUROPE
Pont J. Millot
PARC DES POTERIES
CATHÉDRALE
KOENIGSHOFFEN
PORT AUTONOME
Q. L. Pasteur
NEUMÜHL
ECKBOLSHEIM
Rte du Rhin
Pont de l'Europe
ROETHIG
JARDIN DES DEUX RIVES
KEHL
PLAINE DES BOUCHERS
NEUDORF
R. du Havre
Av. de Colmar
LA MEINAU
LINGOLSHEIM
Gerig
AÉRODROME DU POLYGONE
SUNDHEIM
OSTWALD
NEUHOF
PORT AUTONOME
DEUTSCHLAND
STOCKFELD
R. de la Rochelle
ILLKIRCH-GRAFFENSTADEN
ECKARTSWEIER
CENTRE EUROFRET
E.D.F.
PARC D'INNOVATION
MARLEN
GEISPOLSHEIM-GARE
Rhin Tortu
FORÊT DE NEUHOF
ILE DU ROHRSCHOLLEN (réserve naturelle)
GÉNÉRAL MOTORS
GOLDSCHEUER
KITTERSBURG
FEGERSHEIM
ESCHAU
OHNHEIM
Canal du Rhône au Rhin
MARCKOLSHEIM
FREIBURG I. BR.
OFFENBURG
A 5 : FREIBURG I. BR.
KARLSRUHE, BASEL
RHEINAU
RHIN
ILL
la Marne
Canal de
Rte de Lyon
Rte de la Wantzenau

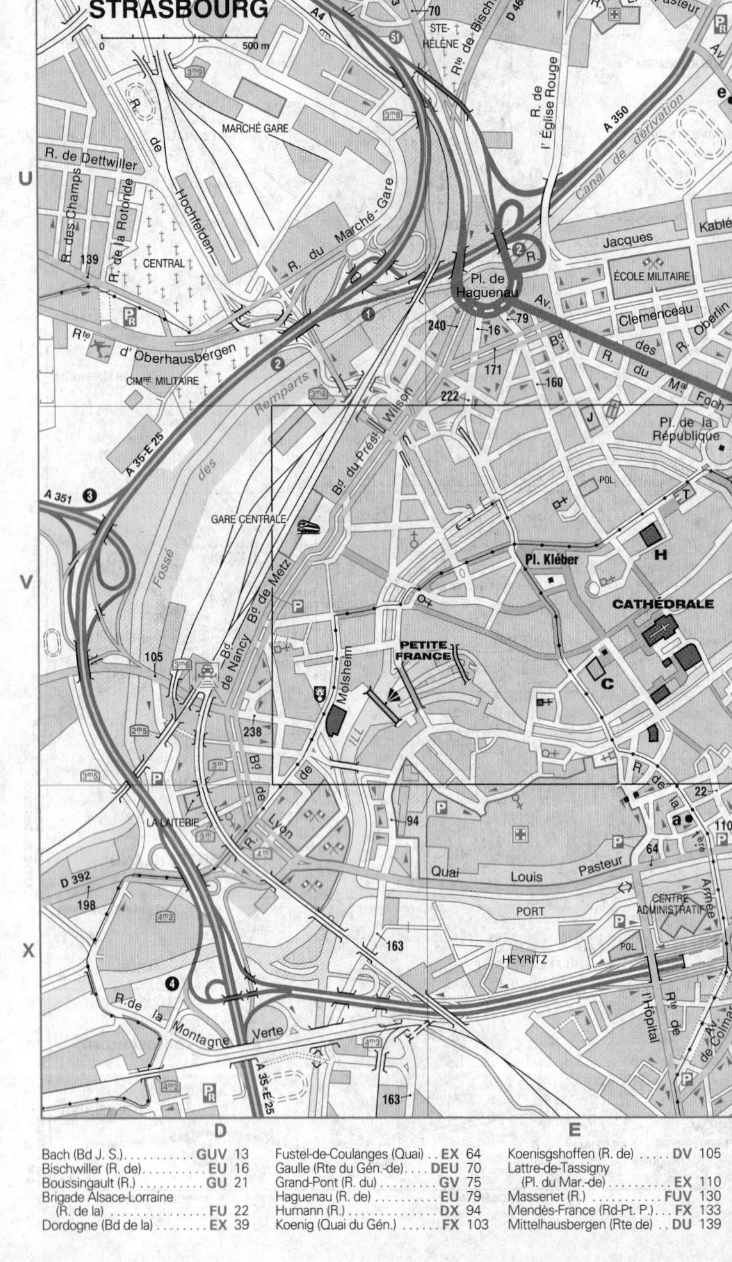
STRASBOURG
MARCHÉ GARE
CENTRAL
GARE CENTRALE
PETITE FRANCE
CATHÉDRALE
Pl. Kléber
Pl. de Haguenau
Pl. de la République
ÉCOLE MILITAIRE
LA LAITERIE
PORT
HEYRITZ
CENTRE ADMINISTRATIF
Quai Louis Pasteur

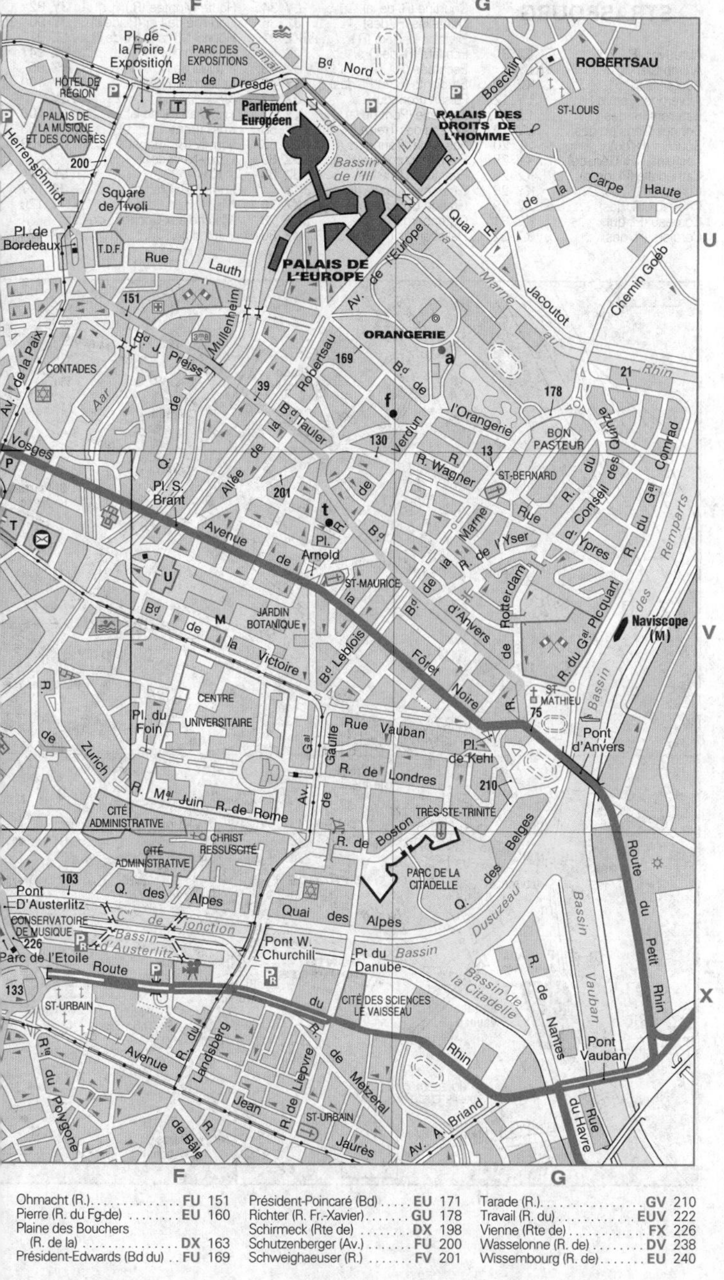

Ohmacht (R.) FU 151
Pierre (R. du Fg-de) EU 160
Plaine des Bouchers (R. de la) DX 163
Président-Edwards (Bd du) FU 169
Président-Poincaré (Bd) EU 171
Richter (R. Fr.-Xavier) GU 178
Schirmeck (Rte de) DX 198
Schutzenberger (Av.) FU 200
Schweighaeuser (R.) FV 201
Tarade (R.) GV 210
Travail (R. du) EUV 222
Vienne (Rte de) FX 226
Wasselonne (R. de) DV 238
Wissembourg (R. de) EU 240

STRASBOURG

Abreuvoir (R. de l') . . . . **LZ** 3
Arc-en-Ciel (R. de l') . . . . . **KLY** 7
Austerlitz (R. d') . . . . **KZ** 10
Auvergne (Pont d') . . . . **LY** 12
Bateliers (R. des) . . . . **LZ** 14
Bonnes-Gens (R. des) . . . . . **JY** 19
Bouclier (R. du) . . . . **JZ** 20
Castelnau (R. Gén.-de) . . . . **KY** 25
Cathédrale (Pl. de la) . . . . . . **KZ** 26
Chaudron (R. du) . . . . **KY** 28
Cheveux (R. des) . . . . **JZ** 29
Corbeau (Pl. du) . . . . **KZ** 31
Cordiers (R. des) . . . . **KZ** 32
Courtine (R. de la) . . . . **LY** 34
Dentelles (R. des) . . . . **JZ** 36
Division-Leclerc (R.) . . . . . **JKZ**
Écarlate (R. de l') . . . . **JZ** 43
Escarpée (R.) . . . . **JZ** 45
Étudiants (R. et Pl. des) . . . **KY** 46
Faisan (Pont du) . . . . **JZ** 47
Fonderie (Pont de la) . . . . . **KY** 52
Fossés-des-Treize (R. du) . . **KY** 58
Fossé-des-Tanneurs (R. du) **JZ** 57
Francs-Bourgeois (R. des) . **JZ** 60
Frey (Quai Charles) . . . . **JZ** 63
Grandes-Arcades (R. des) **JKY**
Grande-Boucherie (Pl. de la) **KZ** 76
Gutenberg (R.) . . . . **JKZ** 78
Hallebardes (R. des) . . . . . . **KZ** 80
Haute-Montée (R.) . . . . **JY** 82
Homme de Fer (Pl. de l') . . **JY** 90
Hôpital-Militaire (R. de l') . . . **LZ** 91
Humann (R.) . . . . **HZ** 94
Ill (Quai de l') . . . . **HZ** 95
Kellermann (Quai) . . . . **JY** 100
Kléber (Pl.) . . . . **JY**
Krutenau (R. de la) . . . . **LZ** 106
Kuss (Pont) . . . . **HY** 108
Lamey (R. Auguste) . . . . . . **LY** 109
Lezay-Marnésia (Quai) . . . . **LY** 114
Luther (R. Martin) . . . . **JZ** 117
Maire Kuss (R. du) . . . . **HY** 120
Marché-aux-Cochons-de-Lait (Pl. du) . . . . **KZ** 124

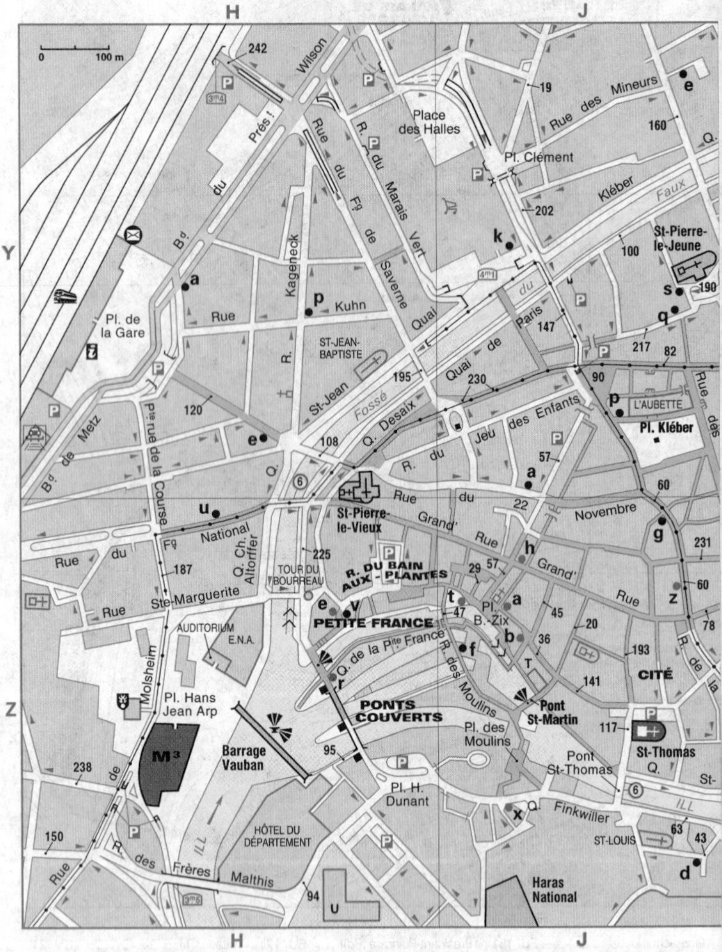

H J

Y Z

Marché-aux-Poissons (Pl. du) .... **KZ** 125
Marché-Gayot (Pl. du) ... **KYZ** 126
Marché-Neuf (Pl. du) .... **KYZ** 127
Maroquin (R. du) .... **KZ** 129
Mercière (R.) .... **KZ** 135
Mésange (R. de la) ...... **JKY** 136
Monnaie (R. de la) .... **JZ** 141
Munch (R. Ernest) .... **LZ** 142
Noyer (R. du) .... **JY** 147
Nuée-Bleue (R. de la) ..... **KY**
Obernai (R. d') .... **HZ** 150
Outre (R. de l') .... **KY** 153
Paix (Av. de la) .... **KLY** 154
Parchemin (R. du) .... **KY** 156
Pierre (R. du Fg-de) .... **JY** 160
Pontonniers (R. des) ...... **LY** 167
Récollets (R. des) .... **KLY** 172
Ste-Madeleine (Pont et R.) **KLZ** 192
St-Étienne (Quai) .... **LY** 183
St-Michel (R.) .... **HZ** 187
St-Nicolas (Pont) .... **KZ** 189
St-Pierre-le-Jeune (Pl.) ... **JKY** 190
Salzmann (R.) .... **JZ** 193
Sanglier (R. du) .... **KY** 194
Saverne (Pont de) .... **HY** 195
Schoelcher (Av. Victor) .... **LY** 199
Sébastopol (R. de) .... **JY** 202
Serruriers (R. des) .... **JKZ** 205
Temple-Neuf (Pl. du) ...... **KY** 213
Temple-Neuf (R. du) ...... **KY** 214
Théâtre (Pont du) .... **KY** 216
Thomann (R. des) .... **JY** 217
Tonneliers (R. des) .... **KZ** 220
Turckheim (Quai) .... **HZ** 225
Vieil-Hôpital (R. du) ...... **KZ** 228
Vieux-Marché-aux-Poissons (R. du) .... **KZ** 229
Vieux-Marché-aux-Vins (R. et Pl. du) .... **JY** 230
Vieux-Seigle (R. du) .... **JZ** 231
Wasselonne (R.) .... **HZ** 238
Wodli (R. Georges) .... **HY** 242
22-Novembre (R. du) .... **HJYZ**

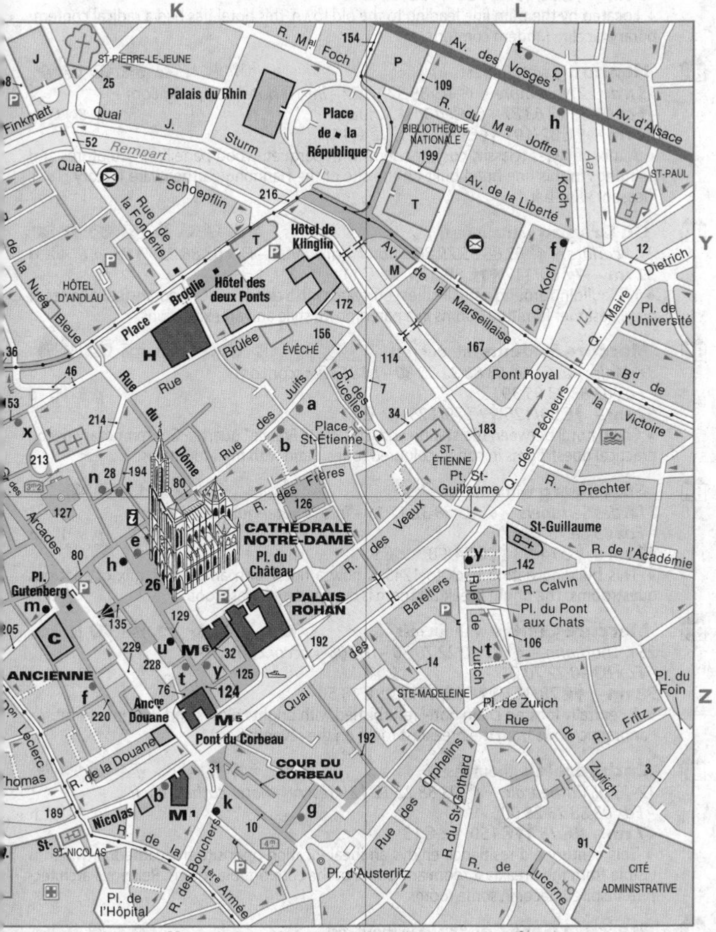

Chut - Au Bain aux Plantes rm, rm, VISA

4 r. Bain-aux-Plantes – ☎ 03 88 32 05 06 – contact@hote-strasbourg.fr – Fax 03 88 32 05 50 *p. 9* KZ **u**

8 rm – €80/90 €90/160, €8 – 1 suite – **Rest** – *(closed 25-31 March, 12-22 August, 3-20 January, Sunday and Monday)* Carte €22/45

◆ Designer or antique materials and furniture, spacious guestrooms and a relaxing, minimalist feel are the hallmarks of this stylish hotel-cum-guesthouse. The varied menu, featuring the subtle use of myriad spices, changes daily. Charming courtyard terrace.

Diana-Dauphine without rest VISA AE

30 r. de la 1ère Armée – ☎ 03 88 36 26 61 – info@hotel-diana-dauphine.com – Fax 03 88 35 50 07 – Closed 22 December-2 January *p. 6* EX **a**

45 rm – €90/135 €90/135, €11

◆ Located by the tram line leading to the old town, this hotel has had a radical contemporary facelift. Modern comforts.

Hannong without rest VISA AE

15 r. du 22 Novembre – ☎ 03 88 32 16 22 – info@hotel-hannong.com – Fax 03 88 22 63 87 – Closed 1st-4 January *p. 8* JY **a**

72 rm – €82/191 €104/191, €14

◆ A mix of styles (classic, cosy, modern) with parquet, wood panelling, sculptures and paintings in this fine hotel built on the site of the Hannong earthenware factory (18C). Pleasant wine bar.

Du Dragon without rest VISA AE

2 r. Écarlate – ☎ 03 88 35 79 80 – hotel@dragon.fr – Fax 03 88 25 78 95 *p. 8* JZ **d**

32 rm – €69/112 €89/124, €11

◆ 17C building around a small quiet courtyard with a clearly contemporary feel. Shades of grey, designer furniture, rooms in a pared-down style and art exhibitions.

Mercure St-Jean without rest VISA AE

3 r. Maire Kuss – ☎ 03 88 32 80 80 – h1813@accor.com – Fax 03 88 23 05 39 *p. 8* HY **e**

52 rm – €59/125 €79/125, €13

◆ Chain hotel between the station and the "Petite France" quarter. Contemporary decor; practical guestrooms in coffee-coloured tones. Patio with mini-fountains.

Gutenberg without rest VISA AE

31 r. des Serruriers – ☎ 03 88 32 17 15 – info@hotel-gutenberg.com – Fax 03 88 75 76 67 *p. 9* KZ **m**

42 rm – €74/98 €74/98, €9

◆ This building dating back to 1745 is now a hotel with an eclectic mix of spacious guestrooms. The bright breakfast room is crowned by a glass roof.

Mercure Centre without rest VISA AE

25 r. Thomann – ☎ 03 90 22 70 70 – h1106@accor.com – Fax 03 90 22 70 71 *p. 8* JY **q**

98 rm – €78/161 €88/177, €13,50

◆ A centrally located chain hotel refurbished with bright colours and designer furniture. Panoramic views from the breakfast room on the seventh floor.

Cathédrale without rest VISA AE

12-13 pl. Cathédrale – ☎ 03 88 22 12 12 – reserv@hotel-cathedrale.fr – Fax 03 88 23 28 00 *p. 9* KZ **h**

47 rm – €75 €150, €13

◆ This century-old residence enjoys an ideal location opposite the cathedral, which is visible from the breakfast room and some of the comfortable rooms. Religious architecture-inspired decor in some rooms.

Mercure Gare Centrale without rest VISA AE

14 pl. de la Gare – ☎ 03 88 15 78 15 – h2149@accor.com – Fax 03 88 15 78 16 *p. 8* HY **a**

70 rm – €69/129 €79/149, €13,50

◆ Contemporary interior behind a plain façade opposite the railway station. Glass-roofed lobby and lounge; functional bedrooms decorated in warm tones. Wine bar.

Cardinal de Rohan without rest VISA

17 r. Maroquin – ☎ 03 88 32 85 11 – info@hotel-rohan.com – Fax 03 88 75 65 37 p. 9 KZ **u**

36 rm – €65/139 €69/149, ☐ €13

◆ Located near the cathedral in the pedestrianised part of town, this hotel offers guestrooms furnished in different styles (Louis XV, Louis XVI and rustic). Quality breakfast.

Des Princes without rest VISA

33 r. Geiler – ☎ 03 88 61 55 19 – hoteldesprinces@aol.com – Fax 03 88 41 10 92 – Closed 25 July-22 August and 2 January-10 January p. 7 FV **t**

43 rm – €105 €118/130, ☐ €12,50

◆ A welcoming hotel in a quiet residential neighbourhood. Guestrooms with classic furnishings and large bathrooms. Breakfast served to a backdrop of bucolic frescoes.

Le Kléber without rest VISA

29 pl. Kléber – ☎ 03 88 32 09 53 – hotel-kleber-strasbourg@wanadoo.fr – Fax 03 88 32 50 41 p. 8 JY **p**

30 rm – €55/72 €62/80, ☐ €8

◆ "Meringue", "Strawberry" and "Cinnamon" are just a few of the names of the rooms in this comfortable hotel. Contemporary, colourful decor with a sweet-and-savoury theme.

Couvent du Franciscain without rest P VISA

18 r. du Fg de Pierre – ☎ 03 88 32 93 93 – info@hotel-franciscain.com – Fax 03 88 75 68 46 – Closed 24 December-4 January p. 8 JY **e**

43 rm – €39/40 €66/72, ☐ €9

◆ A simple yet comfortable hotel at the end of a cul-de-sac. Pleasant lounge; breakfast in a "winstub-style" basement (amusing mural).

Aux Trois Roses without rest VISA

7 r. Zürich – ☎ 03 88 36 56 95 – hotel3roses@aol.com – Fax 03 88 35 06 14 p. 9 LZ **y**

32 rm – €49/79 €65/79, ☐ €7

◆ Cosy duvets and pine furniture add to the welcoming feel of the quiet guestrooms in this elegant building on the banks of the Ill. Fitness area with sauna and Jacuzzi.

Pax without rest rest, VISA

24 r. Fg National – ☎ 03 88 32 14 54 – info@paxhotel.com – Fax 03 88 32 01 16 – Closed 2-11 January p. 8 HYZ **u**

106 rm – €55/60 €73, ☐ €8,50

◆ This hotel is on a street accessible only to tramway traffic. Simply furnished but immaculate guestrooms.

La Belle Strasbourgeoise without rest VISA

13 r. Gén.-Offenstein – ☎ 03 88 39 68 15 – contact@la.belle.strasbourgeoise.fr p. 5 BST **t**

3 rm ☐ – €80 €90

◆ Cosy guesthouse hotel with a charming garden just a stone's throw from the centre. Tastefully decorated rooms with all the creature comforts. Copious breakfast on the terrace.

La Villa Novarina without rest P VISA

11 r. Westercamp – ☎ 03 90 41 18 28 – clauschristine@wanadoo.fr – Fax 03 90 41 49 91 p. 7 FGU **f**

6 rm – €75/150 €95/170, ☐ €15

◆ Attractive villa in modern style near the Parc de l'Orangerie. Interior decorated with family paintings and furniture. Peaceful garden, pool and courteous welcome.

Au Crocodile (Émile Jung) VISA

10 r. Outre – ☎ 03 88 32 13 02 – info@au-crocodile.com – Fax 03 88 75 72 01 – Closed 15 July-5 August, 24 December-6 January, Sunday and Monday p. 9 KY **x**

Rest – Menu €60 (weekday lunch), €88/130 – Carte €75/151

Spec. Sandre et laitance de carpe au mille-choux. Lièvre à la royale (season). Meringue glacée à l'extrême aux fruits chauds, sorbet aux lychees. **Wines** Riesling, Pinot gris.

◆ Splendid wood panelling, paintings and the famous crocodile brought back from the Egyptian campaign by an Alsatian captain adorn this restaurant. Refined classical cuisine.

XXX **Buerehiesel** (Éric Westermann)
✿ *dans le parc de l'Orangerie – ✆ 03 88 45 56 65 – contact@buerehiesel.fr – Fax 03 88 61 32 00 – Closed 1st-21 August, 31 December-21 January, Sunday and Monday* *p. 7* GU **a**
Rest – Menu € 35 (weekday lunch), € 65/108 – Carte € 48/84
Spec. Pâté en croûte de veau et cochon au foie de canard. Brochet d'Alsace rôti, jus de volaille à la coriandre. Brioche à la bière, caramélisée à la bière, glace à la bière et poire rôtie.
◆ An attractive half-timbered house with a modern conservatory surrounded by trees in the Parc de l'Orangerie. Eric Westermann has replaced his father Antoine as chef.

XXX **Maison Kammerzell et Hôtel Baumann** with rm
16 pl. de la Cathédrale – ✆ 03 88 32 42 14 – info@maison-kammerzell.com – Fax 03 88 23 03 92 – Closed 3 weeks in February *p. 9* KZ **e**
9 rm – †€ 75 ††€ 108/121, ☐ € 10 – **Rest** – Menu € 30/45 – Carte € 29/57
◆ With its stained-glass windows, paintings, wood carvings and Gothic vaulting, this 16C construction retains the feel of the Middle Ages. Sober guestrooms. An excellent brasserie menu based around traditional local cuisine. Choucroute a speciality.

XXX **Maison des Tanneurs dite "Gerwerstub"**
42 r. Bain aux Plantes – ✆ 03 88 32 79 70 – maison.des.tanneurs@wanadoo.fr – Fax 03 88 22 17 26 – Closed 27 July-11 August, 29 December-23 January, Sunday and Monday *p. 8* JZ **t**
Rest – Menu € 25 (weekday lunch)/30 (lunch) – Carte € 41/62
◆ Ideally located by the Ill, this typical Alsatian house in La Petite France district is the place to go to if you love sauerkraut.

XX **L'Atable 77**
77 Grand'Rue – ✆ 03 88 32 23 37 – latable77@free.fr – Fax 03 88 32 50 24 – Closed 4-12 May, 13 July-4 August, 11-26 January, Sunday, Monday and lunch on public holidays
Rest – Menu (€ 24), € 30/75 bi *p. 8* JZ **h**
◆ A trendy restaurant with a resolutely contemporary feel throughout, from the paintings on the walls to the designer tableware and appetising creative cuisine.

XX **La Cambuse**
1 r. des Dentelles – ✆ 03 88 22 10 22 – Fax 03 88 23 24 99 – Closed 6-21 April, 27 July-18 August, 21 December-5 January, Sunday and Monday *p. 8* JZ **a**
Rest – *(number of covers limited, pre-book)* Carte € 45/53
◆ Intimate dining room decorated in the style of a boat cabin. Fish and seafood are the specialities here, prepared in a blend of French and Asian styles (herbs, spices etc).

XX **Le Violon d'Ingres**
1 r. Chevalier Robert, at La Robertsau – ✆ 03 88 31 39 50 – Fax 03 88 31 39 50 – Closed 4-25 August, Saturday lunch, Sunday dinner and Monday *p. 5* CS **z**
Rest – Menu € 30/65 – Carte € 49/61
◆ Traditional Alsatian building in the residential district of Robertsau. Elegant dining area and shaded terrace; contemporary cuisine with a focus on fish.

XX **La Casserole** (Éric Girardin)
✿ *24 r. des Juifs – ✆ 03 88 36 49 68 – Fax 03 88 24 25 12 – Closed 21 March-1st April, 3-25 August, Christmas holidays, Saturday lunch, Sunday and Monday* *p. 9* KY **b**
Rest – *(pre-book)* Menu (€ 33), € 38/58
Spec. Œuf à la coque, meurette de betterave, jeunes pousses de red chard. Carré d'agneau rôti, endive confite, jus de viande. Mousse soufflée chaude de chocolat, crème glacée au Grand Marnier.
◆ Carefully-chosen wines at reasonable prices at this restaurant, run by two sommeliers. Contemporary cuisine, in tune with the original designer decor.

XX **Serge and Co** (Serge Burckel)
✿ *14 r. Pompiers ✉ 67300 Schiltigheim – ✆ 03 88 18 96 19 – serge.burckel@wanadoo.fr – Fax 03 88 83 41 99 – Closed Saturday lunch, Sunday dinner and Monday*
Rest – Menu € 28 (weekday lunch), € 49/88 – Carte € 60/88 *p. 5* BS **g**
Spec. Thon rouge mariné. Grenouilles "clin d'œil aux escargots". "Cigare" au chocolat. **Wines** Muscat, Pinot gris.
◆ After a long trip through Asia and America, chef Serge is back home serving appetising cuisine inspired by his travels. Contemporary decor with a slightly exotic feel.

XX **La Vieille Tour** AC VISA MC

1 r. A. Seyboth – ✆ 03 88 32 54 30 – lercher@hotmail.fr – Closed Sunday except lunch in December and Monday *p. 8* HZ **e**

Rest – Menu € 25 (weekday lunch)/39

◆ The decor of this spruce, small dining room includes a Southern French colour scheme, floral displays, whole hams and fruit jars. Market menu presented on the blackboard.

XX **Côté Lac** AC P VISA MC

2 pl. Paris, Espace Européen de l'Entreprise ✉ 67300 Schiltigheim – ✆ 03 88 83 82 81 – info@cote-lac.com – Fax 03 88 83 82 83 – Closed 22 December-2 January, Saturday lunch, Monday dinner, Sunday and public holidays

Rest – Menu (€ 20), € 25 (weekday lunch), € 36/53 *p. 5* BS **t**

◆ The large windows of this modern building open onto a small lake. Original, chic, neo-industrial decor, waterside terrace and contemporary cuisine.

XX **Gavroche** AC VISA MC AE

4 r. Klein – ✆ 03 88 36 82 89 – restaurant.gavroche@free.fr – Closed 5-11 March, 30 July-19 August, 24 December-1st January, Saturday and Sunday *p. 9* KZ **g**

Rest – Menu (€ 26), € 35 – Carte € 43/52

◆ Adorned with window-boxes, the red façade of the Gavroche conceals a cosy dining room (straw tones, wooden banquettes) serving delicious, market-inspired contemporary cuisine.

XX **Umami** AC MC AE

8 r. des Dentelles – ✆ 03 88 32 80 53 – contact@restaurant-umami.com – Closed 1st-12 January, Sunday and Monday *p. 8* JZ **b**

Rest – Menu € 18 (weekday lunch), € 50/70 – Carte € 48/54

◆ A bright, modern restaurant in the heart of historic *Petite-France*. The talented Alsatian chef returned from Asia with not only a name for his restaurant (the fifth basic taste) but also with marked spice and plant influences for his contemporary cuisine.

XX **Le Pont aux Chats** VISA MC AE

42 r. de la Krutenau – ✆ 03 88 24 08 77 – le-pont-aux-chats.restaurant@orange.fr – Fax 03 88 24 08 77 – Closed 2 weeks in August, February school holidays, Saturday lunch, Tuesday and Wednesday *p. 9* ZL **t**

Rest – Menu (€ 19) – Carte € 42/63

◆ A charming interior featuring a successful fusion of ancient timbers and contemporary furniture, with an adorable courtyard terrace. Modern menu based around seasonal produce.

XX **Pont des Vosges** VISA MC AE

15 quai Koch – ✆ 03 88 36 47 75 – pontdesvosges@noos.fr – Fax 03 88 25 16 85 – Closed Sunday *p. 9* LY **h**

Rest – Carte € 32/60

◆ Located on the corner of a stone building, this brasserie is renowned for its copious traditional cuisine. Antique advertising posters and mirrors decorate the dining room.

XX **L'Alsace à Table** AC VISA MC AE

8 r. Francs-Bourgeois – ✆ 03 88 32 50 62 – info@alsace-a-table.fr – Fax 03 88 22 44 11

Rest – Menu (€ 22), € 27 *p. 8* JZ **z**

◆ Welcoming brasserie specialising in fish and seafood with a charming Belle-Époque decor (frescoes, wood panelling, stained glass). Oyster counter, lobster tank and traditional service.

XX **L'Écrin des Saveurs** AC VISA MC

5 r. Leitersperger ✉ 67100 – ✆ 03 88 39 21 20 – Fax 03 88 39 16 05 – Closed 1st-8 May, 21 July-12 August, 22 December-7 January, Monday dinner, Saturday lunch and Sunday *p. 5* BTS **u**

Rest – Menu € 24/38 – Carte € 33

◆ Close to Meinau football stadium, this restaurant stands out from the crowd. The modern cuisine contrasts slightly with the old-fashioned yet cosy dining room. Cheerful service.

X **L'Atelier du Goût** AC VISA MC

17 r. des Tonneliers – ✆ 03 88 21 01 01 – ateliergout.morabito@free.fr – Fax 03 88 23 64 36 – Closed February school holidays, 28 July-10 August, Saturday except dinner in December, Sunday and public holidays *p. 9* KZ **d**

Rest – Menu (€ 21 bi) – Carte € 35/48

◆ Colourful, designer decor provides the backdrop for this former winstub, transformed into a laid-back restaurant. Appetising dishes feature high-quality organic and seasonal produce.

L'Amuse Bouche
3a r. Turenne – ✆ 03 88 35 72 82 – lamuse-bouche@wanadoo.fr – Fax 03 88 36 75 30 – Closed in March, 18-31 August, Saturday lunch, Monday dinner and Sunday
Rest – Menu € 36/50 – Carte € 34/52 p. 9 LY **t**
♦ A sober décor (white walls, mirrors) is the setting for delicious contemporary cuisine.

La Vignette
29 r. Mélanie, at La Robertsau – ✆ 03 88 31 38 10 – lavignetterobertsau@cegetel.net – Fax 03 88 45 48 66 – Closed 15-25 August, 23 December-3 January, Saturday, Sunday and public holidays p. 5 CS **t**
Rest – Carte € 31/43
♦ An earthenware stove and old photos of the neighbourhood adorn the dining room of this café-style restaurant. Appetising, market-inspired cuisine.

La Table de Christophe
28 r. des Juifs – ✆ 03 88 24 63 27 – Fax 03 88 24 64 37 – Closed 28 July-18 August, Monday dinner and Sunday p. 9 KY **a**
Rest – *(pre-book)* Menu (€ 11,50) – Carte € 31/36
♦ A small neighbourhood restaurant with a rustic, welcoming feel. The chef blends local and modern culinary influences, with a respect for seasonality.

WINSTUBS: *regional food and wines in a typical Alsatian ambiance.*

L'Ami Schutz
1 Ponts Couverts – ✆ 03 88 32 76 98 – info@ami-schutz.com – Fax 03 88 32 38 40 – Closed Christmas holidays p. 8 HZ **r**
Rest – Menu (€ 20 bi), € 24/48 bi – Carte € 32/55
♦ Between the meanders of the Ill, typical "winstub" with wood panelling and cosy banquettes (the smaller dining room has greater charm). Terrace beneath the lime trees.

S'Burjerstuewel - Chez Yvonne
10 r. Sanglier – ✆ 03 88 32 84 15 – info@chez-yvonne.net – Fax 03 88 23 00 18 – Closed Christmas holidays p. 9 KYZ **r**
Rest – *(pre-book)* Carte € 24/53
♦ This winstub has become one of the city's institutions, witnessed by the photos and dedications of its famous guests. Regional cuisine with a modern twist.

Le Clou
3 r. Chaudron – ✆ 03 88 32 11 67 – winstuble.clou@wanadoo.fr – Fax 03 88 21 06 43 – Closed Wednesday lunchtime, Sunday and public holidays
Rest – Carte € 25/53 p. 9 KY **n**
♦ Traditional decor (a doll's house feel upstairs) and a friendly atmosphere characterise this well-known winstub situated near the cathedral. Generous portions.

Au Bon Vivant
7 r. Maroquin – ✆ 03 88 32 77 81 – Fax 03 88 32 95 12 – Closed Thursday and Friday from November to Easter p. 9 KZ **t**
Rest – Menu € 16/30 – Carte € 26/44
♦ Customers flock here to enjoy the fine food! The modernised decor is not what you'll find in a typical winstub, though the menu remains faithful to tradition.

Fink'Stuebel with rm
26 r. Finkwiller – ✆ 03 88 25 07 57 – finkstuebel@orange.fr – Fax 03 88 36 48 82 – Closed 2-7 March, 4-26 August, Sunday and Monday p. 8 JZ **x**
4 rm – †€ 66 ††€ 66, ☕ € 9 – **Rest** – Menu (€ 25 bi) – Carte € 29/60
♦ A half-timbered construction with bare floorboards, regional furniture and floral tablecloths, the Fink'Stuebel is the epitome of a traditional winstub. Local cuisine; foie gras to the fore. Recently refurbished and well-appointed guestrooms decorated in Alsatian style.

Au Pont du Corbeau
21 quai St-Nicolas – ✆ 03 88 35 60 68 – corbeau@reperes.com – Fax 03 88 25 72 45 – Closed 28 July-26 August, February half-term holidays, Sunday lunch and Saturday except in December p. 9 KZ **b**
Rest – Menu (€ 11) – Carte € 24/38
♦ Renowned restaurant on the banks of the Ill, next to the Alsatian Folk Art Museum. Regionally inspired Renaissance decor, and a menu that focuses on local specialities.

S'Muensterstuewel
8 pl. Marché aux Cochons de Lait – ☎ 03 88 32 17 63 – munsterstuewel@wanadoo.fr – Fax 03 88 21 96 02 – Closed 29 April-13 May, 25 August-2 September, 27 October-4 November, 1st-7 January, Saturday and Sunday p. 9 KZ **y**
Rest – Menu € 30/45 bi – Carte € 35/55
◆ Former butcher's shop transformed into a traditional winstub. Terrace overlooking the picturesque Place du Marché aux Cochons de Lait. Home-produced salted and cured meats.

Surrounding area

in Reichstett 7 km north by D 468 and D 37 or by A 4 and D 63 – pop. 4 882 – alt. 141 m – ✉ 67116

L'Aigle d'Or without rest
(near the church) – ☎ 03 88 20 07 87 – info@aigledor.com – Fax 03 88 81 83 75 – Closed 8-24 August and 26 December-4 January p. 5 BR **a**
17 rm – †€ 59/99 ††€ 59/99, ☕ € 10
◆ Attractive half-timbered façade in the heart of a picturesque village. Small yet charming rooms decorated in warm tones. Smart breakfast room.

in La Wantzenau 12 km northeast by D 468 – pop. 5 462 – alt. 130 m – ✉ 67610

Hôtel Au Moulin
South : 1.5 km via D 468 – ☎ 03 88 59 22 22 – moulin-wantzenau@wanadoo.fr – Fax 03 88 59 22 00 – Closed 24 December-5 January p. 5 CR **z**
20 rm – †€ 70/87 ††€ 72/110, ☕ € 11 – ½ P € 73/86
Rest *Au Moulin* – see restaurant listing
◆ A tranquil country setting, pleasant lounge, exquisitely decorated guestrooms, display of artwork and a splendid breakfast are the main selling-points of this former mill on the banks of the Ill.

Relais de la Poste (Jérôme Daull) with rm rest,
21 r. Gén. de Gaulle – ☎ 03 88 59 24 80 – info@relais-poste.com – Fax 03 88 59 24 89 – Closed 21 July-3 August, 2-15 January and 16-22 February p. 5 CR **a**
18 rm – †€ 80/90 ††€ 80/130, ☕ € 13 – ½ P € 130 – **Rest** – *(closed Saturday lunch, Sunday dinner and Monday)* Menu € 42 bi (weekday lunch), € 48/165 bi – Carte € 63/93
Spec. Émincé de homard au pamplemousse rose. Bar grillé aux herbes de provence. Caille farcie, sauce morilles. **Wines** Riesling, Pinot noir.
◆ Typical Alsatian house with an elegant decor of panelling, frescoes, coffered ceiling and veranda overlooking the garden. Updated traditional cuisine and impressive wine list. Guestrooms gradually renovated in contemporary style.

Zimmer
23 r. Héros – ☎ 03 88 96 62 08 – zimmer-nadeau@club-internet.fr – Fax 03 88 96 37 40 – Closed 4-10 August, 27 October-10 November, Sunday dinner and Monday except public holidays p. 5 CR **r**
Rest – Menu (€ 21), € 32 (weekdays), € 36 € bi/59 bi – Carte € 50/63
◆ A good choice of contemporary dishes served in three small and tastefully decorated dining rooms.

Les Semailles
10 r. Petit-Magmod – ☎ 03 88 96 38 38 – info@semailles.fr – Fax 03 88 68 09 06 – Closed 11-31 August, 15 February-2 March, Sunday dinner, Wednesday and Thursday p. 5 CR **s**
Rest – Menu (€ 21), € 27 (weekday lunch), € 40/46
◆ This 19C house has benefited from a recent facelift, both inside and out. Attractive veranda and shaded terrace perfect for summer dining. Up-to-date menu.

Rest. Au Moulin – Hôtel Au Moulin
South: 1.5 km via D 468 – ☎ 03 88 96 20 01 – philippe.clauss@wanadoo.fr – Fax 03 88 68 07 97 – Closed 8-28 July, 26 December-7 January, 16-24 February, Sunday dinner and dinner on public holidays p. 5 CR **z**
Rest – Menu (€ 20), € 25 (weekdays)/60 – Carte € 38/64
◆ Elegant modernised dining rooms occupying the outbuildings of a former mill. Contemporary cuisine with an emphasis on local produce and regional specialities.

Le Jardin Secret
32 r. de la Gare – ✆ 03 88 96 63 44 – Fax 03 88 96 64 95
– Closed 1 - 20 August *p. 5* CR **v**
Rest – Menu € 31/33 – Carte € 34/37
♦ Welcoming restaurant offering up-to-date cuisine. Minimalist interior embellished by displays of artwork.

Au Pont de l'Ill
2 r. Gén. Leclerc – ✆ 03 88 96 29 44 – aupontdelill@wanadoo.fr
– Fax 03 88 96 21 18 – Closed 8-31 August and Saturday lunch *p. 5* CR **u**
Rest – Menu (€ 15), € 22/37 – Carte € 25/52
♦ Seafood and fish recipes are given pride of place in this brasserie spread over five rooms in different styles: marine style, Art Nouveau, etc. Shaded terrace.

in Illkirch-Graffenstaden 5 km by Colmar road BST **or by A 35 (exit 7) – pop. 23 815 – alt. 140 m – ✉ 67400**

D'Alsace
187 rte Lyon – ✆ 03 90 40 35 00 – contact@hotelalsace.com – Fax 03 90 40 35 01
– Closed 31 December-4 January *p. 5* BT **d**
40 rm – †€ 58/70 ††€ 58/70, ☐ € 9 – ½ P € 46/52
Rest – *(closed 20 December-4 January, Saturday, Sunday and public holidays)*
Menu € 11,50/25 – Carte € 21/34
♦ Overlooking the main square, this hotel has bright, functional and spacious guestrooms. Those at the back are quieter. A few Alsace-themed frescoes add a cheery atmosphere to the rustic dining room. Traditional menu.

À l'Agneau
185 rte de Lyon – ✆ 03 88 66 06 58 – guillaume.kern@neuf.fr – Fax 03 88 67 05 84
– Closed 4 August-2 September, 31 December-13 January, Sunday dinner, Monday and Tuesday *p.5* BT **a**
Rest – Menu (€ 14), € 33 (weekdays)/63 bi – Carte € 42/52
♦ Behind the façade and fresco are two attractive dining rooms extended by a sitting room decorated with paintings on wood. Up to the minute recipes of Alsatian inspiration.

direction ④ 11 km on D 1083 – ✉ 67400 Illkirch-Graffenstaden

Novotel Strasbourg-Sud
Exit 7, Z. A. de l'Ill ✉ 67118 Geispolsheim –
✆ 03 88 66 21 56 – h0441@accor.com – Fax 03 88 67 21 63 *p. 5* BT **u**
76 rm – †€ 69/135 ††€ 69/145, ☐ € 12,50 – **Rest** – Carte € 23/39
♦ Chain hotel, near main roads, offering spacious rooms renovated according to the new Novotel standards. Mini golf. Restaurant with contemporary setting and automobile-theme bar. Small flower garden and vegetable garden.

in Fegersheim 14 km to ④ by A 35 (exit 7), N 283 and D 1083 – pop. 4 533 – alt. 145 m – ✉ 67640

Auberge du Bruchrhein
24 r. de Lyon – ✆ 03 88 64 17 77 – Fax 03 88 64 17 77 – Closed Sunday dinner, Monday dinner and Thursday dinner *p.4* AT **x**
Rest – Menu (€ 12,50), € 17 (weekday lunch), € 23/28
– Carte € 28/43
♦ Modern, unpretentious cuisine, based around high-quality produce and with a regional bias. Simple interior, small terrace, and the bonus of a warm and welcoming atmosphere.

in Lipsheim to ④ by A 35, D 1083 and D 221 – pop. 2 268 – alt. 146 m – ✉ 67640

Alizés without rest
– ✆ 03 88 59 02 00 – hotellesalizes@wanadoo.fr – Fax 03 88 64 21 61
– Closed 23 December-1st January *p. 4* AT **e**
49 rm – †€ 61 ††€ 68, ☐ € 10
♦ A property built in local style, whose primary asset is its quiet rural location. Bright, functional guestrooms, plus a swimming pool which overlooks the forest.

in Blaesheim 19 km by A 35 (exit 9), D 1422 and D 84 – pop. 1 369 – alt. 150 m – ✉ 67113

Au Bœuf rm, rest, VISA
– ✆ 03 88 68 68 99 – auboeuf.resa@wanadoo.fr – Fax 03 88 68 60 07
– Closed 23 July-5 August and 3-17 January p. 4 AT **q**
22 rm – †€ 57 ††€ 72, ☕ € 11 – 2 suites – ½ P € 60 – **Rest** – *(closed Friday lunch and Saturday lunch)* Menu (€ 8,50), € 15/27 – Carte € 20/43
◆ A village inn with identical guestrooms that are large, comfortable and well-maintained. Regional dishes served in a veranda dining room with a mix of contemporary and rustic decor (earthenware plates, stove and wood panelling).

Schadt VISA
8 pl. de l'Église – ✆ 03 88 68 86 00 – Schadt@wanadoo.fr – Fax 03 88 68 89 83
– Closed August, Sunday dinner and Monday p. 4 AT **v**
Rest – Menu (€ 12), € 25/39 – Carte € 30/63
◆ A former bakery converted into two dining rooms with an out-of-the-ordinary decoration: murals, ornaments, paintings and...saucy humour upstairs (behind the curtain!). Alsatian cuisine.

in Entzheim 12 km by A 35 (exit 8), D 400 and D 392 – pop. 1 855 – alt. 150 m – ✉ 67960

Père Benoît rm, rest, VISA
34 rte de Strasbourg – ✆ 03 88 68 98 00 – hotel.perebenoit@wanadoo.fr
– Fax 03 88 68 64 56 – Closed 28 July-18 August and 22 December-4 January
60 rm – †€ 59 ††€ 65, ☕ € 8,50 p. 4 AT **h**
Rest *Steinkeller* – *(closed Saturday lunch, Monday lunch and Sunday)* Menu € 19 (lunch)/24 – Carte € 22/46
◆ A delightful, Alsace-style half-timbered farmhouse dating from the 18C. Large flower-decked courtyard. Traditional food and cosy atmosphere. Attractive rustic dining crowned by a vaulted ceiling, with more of a winstub style on the first floor. Regional menu, including wood-baked "flammekueches" (Alsatian pizza).

in Ostwald 7 km by Schirmeck road D 392 and D 484 orby A35 (exit 7) and D 484 – pop. 10 761 – alt. 140 m – ✉ 67540

Château de l'Île l'Ill, VISA
4 quai Heydt – ✆ 03 88 66 85 00
– ile@grandesetapes.fr – Fax 03 88 66 85 49 p. 5 BT **r**
60 rm – †€ 195/610 ††€ 195/610, ☕ € 22 – 2 suites
Rest – Menu € 50/92 – Carte € 37/60
Rest *Winstub* – tavern Menu € 25/37 – Carte € 28/44
◆ 19C manor house surrounded by recent, half-timbered homes in a wooded, 4-ha park bordering the Ill. Well-kept rooms with period-style furniture. Refined dining room where the emphasis is on classical cuisine. Attractive riverside terrace. This elegant winstub in a verdant setting offers a sophisticated take on traditional cuisine.

in Lingolsheim 5 km by Schirmeck road (D 392) – pop. 16 860 – alt. 140 m – ✉ 67380

Kyriad without rest VISA
59 r. Mar. Foch – ✆ 03 88 76 11 00 – hotelkyriad@evc.net – Fax 03 88 77 39 31
37 rm – †€ 55/74 ††€ 55/81, ☕ € 8,50 p. 5 BS **a**
◆ The Kyriad is part of a residential and shopping centre near the airport. Comfortable, functional and well-appointed guestrooms, plus a pleasant modern lounge-bar.

in Mittelhausbergen 5 km northwest by D 31 – pop. 1 680 – alt. 155 m – ✉ 67206

Tilleul with rm VISA
5 rte de Strasbourg – ✆ 03 88 56 18 31 – info@autilleul.fr – Fax 03 88 56 07 23
– Closed 1st-17 August, 23 February-7 March, Tuesday dinner and Wednesday except hotel p. 5 BS **v**
12 rm – †€ 60/65 ††€ 65/70, ☕ € 12 – ½ P € 72/78
Rest – Menu € 34/39 – Carte € 40/50
Rest *La Stub 1888* – Menu € 17 (weekday lunch)/23 – Carte € 23/39
◆ This traditional auberge dating back to 1888 is undergoing major renovation in contemporary style. Modern cuisine in an elegant setting at the restaurant. Neo-rustic feel and local dishes at La Stub.

in Pfulgriesheim 10 km northwest by D 31 – pop. 1 171 – alt. 135 m – ✉ 67370

Bürestubel

8 r. Lampertheim – ✆ 03 88 20 01 92 – rest.burestubel@orange.fr – Fax 03 88 20 48 97 – Closed 28 July-13 August, 23 February-8 March, Tuesday from February to October, Sunday from November to January and Monday

Rest – Menu € 17/27 – Carte € 21/48 *p. 4* AR **a**

◆ Pretty half-timbered farmhouse home to a vast "winstub". Rustic or stately rooms, with colourful ceilings. Flambéed tarts and other regional specialities.

in Plobsheim 17 km by A35 (exit 7) N 283, N 353 and D 468 – pop. 3 634 – alt. 150 m – ✉ 67115

Le Kempferhof

au golf – ✆ 03 88 98 72 72 – info@golf-kempferhof.com – Fax 03 88 98 74 76 – Closed 20 December-28 February

25 rm – †€ 120/150 ††€ 150/330, ☕ € 18 – 4 suites – ½ P € 120/210

Rest – *(closed Sunday dinner)* Menu (€ 16), € 20 (weekday lunch), € 38/45 – Carte € 25/47

◆ Attractive 19C property on a wooded 85-hectare estate with 18-hole golf course. Individually furnished rooms, those in the outbuildings decorated in contemporary style. Bright dining room-veranda and terrace overlooking the green. International menu with a good choice of wines.

STURZELBRONN – 57 Moselle – 307 Q4 – pop. 189 – alt. 250 m – ✉ 57230 27 D1

Paris 449 – Strasbourg 68 – Bitche 13 – Haguenau 39 – Wissembourg 34

Au Relais des Bois

13 r. Principale – ✆ 03 87 06 20 30 – denis.hoff@wanadoo.fr – Fax 03 87 06 21 22 – Closed Monday and Tuesday

Rest – Menu (€ 19 bi), € 25/27 – Carte € 25/39

◆ Small family-run establishment in the heart of a village of the Vosges du Nord regional park. Rustic setting, local cuisine, terrace and garden.

SUBLIGNY – 89 Yonne – 319 C2 – see Sens

SUCY-EN-BRIE – 94 Val-de-Marne – 312 E3 – 101 28 – see Paris, Area

SULLY-SUR-LOIRE – 45 Loiret – 318 L5 – pop. 5 907 – alt. 115 m – ✉ 45600 12 C2

Châteaux of the Loire

Paris 149 – Bourges 84 – Gien 25 – Montargis 40 – Orléans 51 – Vierzon 84

Office de tourisme, place de Gaulle ✆ 02 38 36 23 70, Fax 02 38 36 32 21

de Sully-sur-Loire Domaine de l'Ousseau, by Bourges road: 4 km, ✆ 02 38 36 52 08.

Château★: framework★★.

SULLY-SUR-LOIRE

Abreuvoir (R. de l') 2
Béthune (Av. de) 3
Champ-de-Foire (Bd du) 4
Chemin-de-Fer (Av. du) 5
Grand-Sully (R. du) 6
Jeanne-d'Arc (Bd) 7
Marronniers (R. des) 9
Porte-Berry (R.) 10
Porte-de-Sologne (R.) 12
St-François (R. du Fg) 15
St-Germain (R. du Fg) 16
Venerie (Av. de la) 20

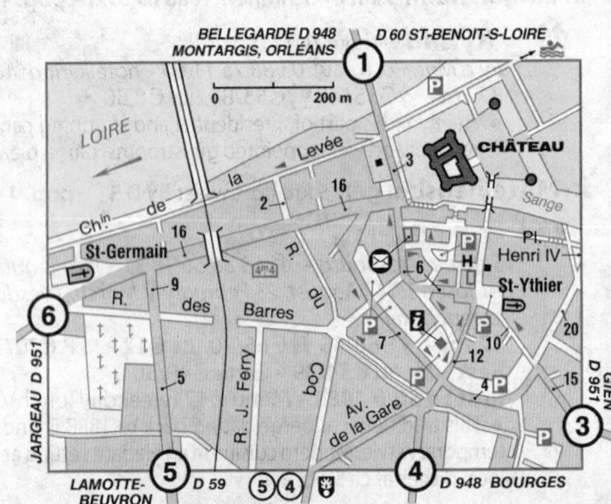

Hostellerie du Château

4 rte Paris à St-Père-sur-Loire, 1 km by ① – ✆ 02 38 36 24 44 – resasylvie@wanadoo.fr – Fax 02 38 36 62 40

42 rm – †€ 46/68 ††€ 46/68, ☕ € 9 – ½ P € 62 – **Rest** – Menu (€ 25), € 28/46 – Carte € 45/74

♦ This recently built hotel provides very well-kept, functional and pleasant rooms. Half of them offer a view of Sully château. Slightly British atmosphere in the comfortable dining room decorated with wood panelling. Traditional menu.

aux Bordes **6 km by ①, D 948 and D 961 – pop. 1 445 – alt. 132 m – ✉ 45460**

La Bonne Étoile

D 952 – ✆ 02 38 35 52 15 – Fax 02 38 35 52 15
– Closed 10-23 March, 1st-14 September, Sunday dinner and Monday

Rest – Menu € 16 (weekdays)/36 – Carte € 18/33

♦ Small and attractive country inn along a busy road. The dining room has recently been given a facelift, with new decor, chairs and tableware. Traditional cuisine.

SUPERDÉVOLUY – **05 Hautes-Alpes** – **334** D4 – **Winter sports : 1500/2500m** 1 28 – ✉ **05250** **French Alps** 40 **B1**

Paris 654 – Gap 36 – Grenoble 92 – La Mure 52

Les Chardonnelles

– ✆ 04 92 58 86 90 – info@hotel-chardonnelles.com – Fax 04 92 58 87 76
– Open 13 June-7 September and 22 December-22 April

40 rm – †€ 60/82 ††€ 80/120, ☕ € 9 – ½ P € 65/82 – **Rest** – Menu € 15 (weekday lunch), € 18/25 – Carte € 27/33

♦ This large chalet just outside the resort is the starting point of a number of rambling itineraries. Warm Alpine-style rooms with a balcony and mountain view. Restaurant offering Alpine cuisine with a choice of tartiflettes, fondues and raclettes.

LE SUQUET – **06 Alpes-Maritimes** – **341** E4 – **alt. 400 m** – ✉ **06450**
LANTOSQUE 41 **D2**

Paris 878 – Levens 19 – Nice 46 – Puget-Théniers 48 – St-Martin-Vésubie 21

Auberge du Bon Puits

– ✆ 04 93 03 17 65 – lebonpuits@wanadoo.fr – Fax 04 93 03 10 48
– Open 20 April-1st December and closed Tuesday except 10 July-30 August

8 rm – †€ 62/65 ††€ 63/68, ☕ € 15 – ½ P € 65/70 – **Rest** – Menu € 25/35 – Carte € 32/34

♦ The road separates this solid house from a small animal park with children's area on the banks of the Vésubie. Renovated and soundproofed rooms. Beams and a monumental stone fireplace decorate the dining room. Regional cuisine.

SURESNES – **92 Hauts-de-Seine** – **311** J2 – **101** 14 – **see Paris, Area**

SURGÈRES – **17 Charente-Maritime** – **324** F3 – **pop. 6 051** – **alt. 16 m** – ✉ **17700**
Atlantic Coast 38 **B2**

Paris 442 – Niort 35 – Rochefort 27 – La Rochelle 38 – St-Jean-d'Angély 30 – Saintes 55

Office de tourisme, 5, rue Bersot ✆ 05 46 07 20 02, Fax 05 46 07 20 30

Notre-Dame church ★.

Le Vieux Puits

6 r. P. Bert, (near the castle) – ✆ 05 46 07 50 83
– gireaudrestauration@wanadoo.fr
– Closed 28 September-14 October, 17-28 February, Sunday dinner and Thursday

Rest – Menu € 17/36

♦ The restaurant stands unobtrusively at the back of a paved courtyard (summer terrace). Rustic interior with open fireplace in the welcoming dining room. Seasonal menu.

in Puyravault 6 km Northwest by D 115 and D 205 – ✉ 17700

Le Clos de la Garenne rm, VISA

9 r. Garenne – ✆ 05 46 35 47 71 – info@closdelagarenne.com – Fax 05 46 35 47 91 – Closed Christmas holidays

4 rm ☕ – 🚹€ 60 🚹🚹€ 67/77 – **Table d'hôte** – *(closed Wednesday, Saturday and Sunday)* Menu € 25 bi

◆ Each of the rooms in this authentic Charentes-style residence evokes a different period: Belle Epoque room, large 18C lounge, 17C dining room, etc. The 4-ha park is home to donkeys, sheep and hens. Family cooking varying with the seasons and market availability.

SURVILLIERS – 95 Val-d'Oise – 305 G6 – pop. 3 654 – alt. 110 m – ✉ 95470

19 **C1**

Paris 37 – Chantilly 14 – Compiègne 48 – Meaux 39 – Pontoise 45 – Senlis 14

Novotel rm, rest, VISA

D 16, via Survilliers interchange of A1 – ✆ 01 34 68 69 80 – h0459@accor.com – Fax 01 34 68 64 94

79 rm – 🚹€ 70/250 🚹🚹€ 70/250, ☕ € 14 – **Rest** – Carte € 20/40

◆ Functional and soundproofed bedrooms. There is a volleyball court, children's play area and a boules pitch. Traditional menu served in a dining room extended by a veranda or on a poolside summer terrace.

SUZE-LA-ROUSSE – 26 Drôme – 332 C8 – pop. 1 564 – alt. 92 m – ✉ 26790

Provence

44 **B3**

Paris 641 – Avignon 59 – Bollène 7 – Nyons 28 – Orange 23 – Valence 85

Office de tourisme, le village ✆ 04 75 04 81 41

Les Aiguières

r. Fontaine-d'Argent – ✆ 04 75 98 40 80 – brigitte@les-aiguieres.com – Closed 22 December-5 January

5 rm – 🚹€ 72 🚹🚹€ 82, ☕ € 5 – **Table d'hôte** – Menu € 25 bi

◆ Provençal inspired rooms in this 18C house with large sitting room (open fire in winter), garden and pool, two minutes from the château and its university of wine. Wholesome home cooking, special "wine and food pairing" menu by reservation.

TAILLECOURT – 25 Doubs – 321 L2 – see Audincourt

TAIN-L'HERMITAGE – 26 Drôme – 332 C3 – pop. 5 503 – alt. 124 m – ✉ 26600

43 **E2**

Paris 545 – Grenoble 97 – Le Puy-en-Velay 105 – St-Étienne 76 – Valence 18 – Vienne 59

Office de tourisme, place du 8 mai 1945 ✆ 04 75 08 06 81, Fax 04 75 08 34 59

Belvédère de Pierre-Aiguille (Viewpoint) ★ North: 4 km by D 241.

Plan on next page

Le Pavillon de l'Ermitage rm, VISA

1 av. P. Durand – ✆ 04 75 08 65 00 – pavillon.26@wanadoo.fr – Fax 04 75 08 66 05 C **e**

44 rm – 🚹€ 75/80 🚹🚹€ 86/91, ☕ € 11 – **Rest** – *(closed 25 December-2 January, Saturday and Sunday from November to March)* Menu € 23

◆ A large building with recently renovated rooms; ask for one on the swimming pool side, with a balcony overlooking the Hermitage vineyard and the Tournon heights. Traditional dishes on the terrace or in the dining room depending on the weather.

Les 2 Coteaux without rest VISA

18 r. J. Péala – ✆ 04 75 08 33 01 – hotel2coteaux@wanadoo.fr – Fax 04 75 08 44 20 B **a**

18 rm – 🚹€ 52 🚹🚹€ 57, ☕ € 9

◆ This family-run hotel is in a quiet location opposite the old bridge spanning the Rhone. Bright and airy guestrooms, some with a balcony.

TAIN-L'HERMITAGE		
Batie (Quai de la)	C	3
Defer (Pl. H.)	C	8
Église (Pl. de l')	C	12
Gaulle (Q. Gén.-de)	C	14
Grande-Rue	B	16
Jean-Jaurès (Av.)	BC	
Michel (R. F.)	C	21
Peala (R. J.)	B	24
Prés.-Roosevelt (Av.)	C	29
Rostaing (Q. A.)	C	30
Seguin (Q. M.)	B	32
Souvenir-Français (Av. du)	C	33
Taurobole (Pl. du)	BC	
8-Mai-1945 (Pl. du)	BC	39

TOURNON-SUR-RHÔNE		
Dumaine (R. A.)	B	9
Faure (R. G.)	B	13
Grande-Rue	B	
Juventon (Av. M.)	B	19
Thiers (R.)	B	35

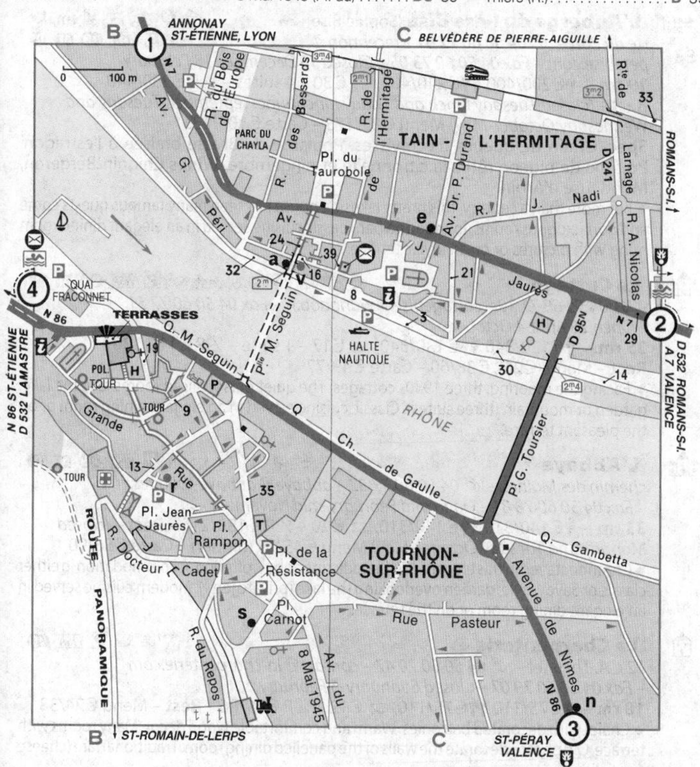

Le Quai

17 r. J.-Péala – ✆ 04 75 07 05 90 – chabran@michelchabran.fr – Fax 04 75 06 55 55 B v

Rest – Menu € 31 – Carte € 36/53

◆ The Rhône flows past this restaurant, with views of the vineyards in the distance. Updated dining room with a minimalist feel (wenge furniture, old photos); pleasant terrace.

Romans road 4 km by ② – ✉ 26600 Tain-l'Hermitage

L'Abricotine

rest, VISA MC AE

rte de Romans – ✆ 04 75 07 44 60 – hotel.abricotine@wanadoo.fr – Fax 04 75 07 47 97 – Closed 24 December-3 January

11 rm – †€ 53/65 ††€ 53/65, ☕ € 7 – ½ P € 52 – **Rest** – *(dinner only) (residents only)* Menu (€ 18), € 23 – Carte approx. € 27

◆ Drôme orchards surround this modern building. Stylish rooms with personal touches, some with a terrace or balcony. This soberly furnished, family style restaurant offers two traditional menus.

TALANT – 21 Côte-d'Or – 320 J5 – see Dijon

TALLOIRES – 74 Haute-Savoie – 328 K5 – pop. 1 448 – alt. 470 m – ✉ 74290

French Alps 46 **F1**

Paris 551 – Albertville 34 – Annecy 13 – Megève 49

Office de tourisme, rue A. Theuriet ✆ 04 50 60 70 64, Fax 04 50 60 76 59

Site★★ - Site★★ of the St-Germain hermitage ★ East: 4 km.

L'Auberge du Père Bise (Sophie Bise) rm,

rte du Port – ✆ 04 50 60 72 01 – reception@perebise.com – Fax 04 50 60 73 05 – Closed 15 December-13 February

19 rm – †€ 200/400 ††€ 240/400, ☕ € 30 – 4 suites – ½ P € 250/440

Rest – *(closed Tuesday lunch and Friday lunch June-September, Tuesday and Wednesday October-May)* Menu € 82/175 – Carte € 104/133

Spec. Gratin de queues d'écrevisses. Poularde de Bresse braisée à l'estragon. Poitrine de pigeon rôti à la citronnelle et gingembre. **Wines** Chignin-Bergeron, Mondeuse d'Arbin.

◆ For more than a century, this pretty lakeside house has seen many famous guests come and go. Luxurious rooms, lounge and bar. Classic cuisine served in an elegant dining room hung with pictures or on an idyllic terrace.

Le Cottage rest,

– ✆ 04 50 60 71 10 – cottagebise@wanadoo.fr – Fax 04 50 60 77 51 – Open 28 April-4 October

35 rm – †€ 130/340 ††€ 130/340, ☕ € 17 – 1 suite – ½ P € 110/230

Rest – Menu (€ 26), € 38/60 – Carte € 49/77

◆ Facing the mooring, three 1930s cottages. The quiet personalised rooms face the lake, garden or mountain (three suites). Classic cuisine served in an elegant dining room or on the pleasant terrace.

L'Abbaye

chemin des Moines – ✆ 04 50 60 77 33 – abbaye@abbaye-talloires.com – Fax 04 50 60 78 81 – Open mid February-mid November

33 rm – †€ 140/310 ††€ 140/310, ☕ € 20 – ½ P € 130/215 – **Rest** – *(closed Monday and Tuesday October-May)* Menu € 45/75 (dinner) – Carte € 58/90

◆ Cézanne stayed in this elegant 17C Benedictine abbey, offering accommodation in either classic or Savoy style; garden overlooking the lake (private jetty). Modern cuisine served in an elegant dining room or on the terrace.

La Charpenterie

72 r. A. Theuriet – ✆ 04 50 60 70 47 – contact@la-charpenterie.com – Fax 04 50 60 79 07 – Closed 6 January-6 February

18 rm – †€ 75/110 ††€ 75/110, ☕ € 12 – ½ P € 69/86 – **Rest** – Menu € 24/38

◆ Chalet with decorated balconies. Warm and comfortable wood decor. Many rooms with terrace. Old photos decorate the walls of the panelled dining room. Traditional fare (cheese specialities).

Villa des Fleurs with rm

rte du Port – ✆ 04 50 60 71 14 – lavilladesfleurs@wanadoo.fr – Fax 04 50 60 74 06 – Closed 25 November-10 February, Sunday dinner and Monday

8 rm – †€ 86 ††€ 96/132, ☕ € 12,50 – ½ P € 98/109

Rest – Menu (€ 20), € 32/60 – Carte € 40/72

◆ In the village, a comfortable Savoy villa surrounded by greenery. Local cuisine and fish from Lake Annecy; peaceful little rooms.

in Angon 2 km south by D 909a – ✉ 74290 Veyrier-du-Lac

Les Grillons rest,

– ✆ 04 50 60 70 31 – accueil@hotel-grillons.com – Fax 04 50 60 72 19

30 rm – †€ 55/120 ††€ 60/120, ☕ € 11 – ½ P € 55/79

Rest – *(open 24 April-15 October)* Menu € 25/49 – Carte € 21/53

◆ Guesthouse-style hotel with well-maintained rooms, most with views of the lake. The large swimming pool is very pleasant in summer. The dining room has a new contemporary look with exposed beams, plants and a red and white colour scheme.

Look out for red symbols, indicating particularly pleasant establishments.

TALMONT-SUR-GIRONDE – 17 Charente-Maritime – 324 E6 – pop. 83 – alt. 20 m – ✉ 17120 Atlantic Coast
38 **B3**

Paris 503 – Blaye 72 – La Rochelle 93 – Royan 18 – Saintes 36

Site★ of Ste-Radegonde church ★.

L'Estuaire with rm — rest, rm, VISA

au Caillaud, 1 av. Estuaire – ✆ 05 46 90 43 85 – Fax 05 46 90 43 88 – Hotel: open April-September and closed Monday, Tuesday except July-August and Wednesday

7 rm – €49 €49, €7,50 – ½ P €50 – **Rest** – *(closed 1st- 15 October, 15 January-15 February, Monday dinner, Tuesday except July-August and Wednesday)* Menu €20/40 – Carte €22/60

◆ Rustic restaurant in pastel tones superbly situated overlooking the Gironde. Regional dishes and local fish on the menu. Quiet, spacious and well-kept rooms.

TAMNIÈS – 24 Dordogne – 329 H6 – pop. 317 – alt. 200 m – ✉ 24620
4 **D3**

Paris 522 – Brive-la-Gaillarde 47 – Périgueux 60 – Sarlat-la-Canéda 14

Laborderie — rest, VISA

– ✆ 05 53 29 68 59 – hotel.laborderie@worldonline.fr – Fax 05 53 29 65 31 – Open 5 April-2 November

45 rm – €32/80 €36/88, €8,50 – ½ P €43/72

Rest – *(closed Wednesday lunch and Monday)* Menu €21/43 – Carte €23/60

◆ Périgord establishment, its three annexes and vast park overlooking the valley, offering quiet rooms, some rustic, some modern. Fine, regional cuisine served in a country-style dining room or on the terrace in season.

TANCARVILLE – 76 Seine-Maritime – 304 C5 – pop. 1 234 – alt. 10 m – ✉ 76430 Normandy
33 **C2**

Paris 175 – Caen 86 – Le Havre 32 – Pont-Audemer 24 – Rouen 64

Access Tancarville Bridge. toll in 2006 : car 2.30, car and caravan 2.90, lorries and coaches 3.50 to 6.10, free for motorcycles ✆ 02 35 39 65 60.

★ sur estuaire.

La Marine with rm — suspension bridge and the Seine, VISA AE

10 rte du Havre, at the end of the bridge (D 982) – ✆ 02 35 39 77 15 – hoteldelamarine2@wanadoo.fr – Fax 02 35 38 03 30 – Closed 20 July-20 August and Sunday dinner

9 rm – €65/75 €65/85, €9 – ½ P €75/90

Rest – *(closed Saturday lunch and Monday)* Menu €27 (weekdays)/60 – Carte €60/91

Rest *Le Bistrot* – *(closed Monday from Easter to September, Saturday and Sunday) (lunch only)* Menu €13/20

◆ Hotel on the banks of the Seine, at the foot of the famous Tancarville bridge. Traditional seasonal cuisine based on fresh market produce and fish. Recently renovated bedrooms. Bistro with a wooden decor.

LA TANIA – 73 Savoie – 333 M5 – see Courchevel

TANINGES – 74 Haute-Savoie – 328 M4 – pop. 3 140 – alt. 640 m – ✉ 74440 French Alps
46 **F1**

Paris 570 – Annecy 68 – Chamonix-Mont-Blanc 51 – Genève 42 – Thonon-les-Bains 46

Office de tourisme, avenue des Thézières ✆ 04 50 34 25 05, Fax 04 50 34 83 96

La Crémaillère — VISA

at lac de Flérier, 1 km south-west – ✆ 04 50 34 21 98 – Fax 04 50 34 34 88 – Closed 23 June-4 July, 5 January-5 February, Monday dinner and Wednesday except July-August and Sunday dinner

Rest – *(number of covers limited, pre-book)* Menu €25/45 – Carte €42/61

◆ Fine lakeside position. Sit near the bay window or on the panoramic terrace in fine weather. Quintessentially traditional cuisine.

TANNERON – 83 Var – 340 Q4 – pop. 1 307 – alt. 376 m – ✉ 83440
French Riviera 42 **E2**

Paris 903 – Cannes 20 – Draguignan 53 – Grasse 20 – Nice 49 – Saint-Raphaël 37

Syndicat d'initiative, place de la Mairie ☎ 04 93 60 71 73

XX **Le Champfagou** with rm — VISA MC AE

pl. du Village – ☎ 04 93 60 68 30 – Fax 04 93 60 70 60 – Closed in November, dinner in January and February, Monday July-August, Sunday dinner, Tuesday dinner and Wednesday

9 rm – †€ 50 ††€ 50, ☕ € 8 – ½ P € 60 – **Rest** – Menu € 30/55

◆ A discreetly Provençal dining room and pleasant flower-decked terrace in a peaceful village, renowned for its mimosas. Provençal cuisine with personal touches. Small simple rooms.

TANTONVILLE – 54 Meurthe-et-Moselle – 307 H8 – pop. 600 – alt. 300 m – ✉ 54116
26 **B2**

Paris 327 – Épinal 48 – Lunéville 35 – Nancy 29 – Toul 37 – Vittel 44

XX **La Commanderie** — VISA MC

1 r. Pasteur – ☎ 03 83 52 49 83 – contact@restaurant-la-commanderie.com – Fax 03 83 52 49 83 – Closed 24 August-10 September, 2-10 January, Tuesday dinner, Wednesday dinner, Sunday dinner and Monday

Rest – Menu € 13,50 (weekday lunch), € 24/45 – Carte € 26/56

◆ This early 20C house, formerly the headquarters of the Tourtel brothers, is now an elegant restaurant in Provençal style. Beautiful terrace with fountain.

TANUS – 81 Tarn – 338 F6 – pop. 436 – alt. 439 m – ✉ 81190
29 **C2**

Paris 668 – Albi 33 – Rodez 46 – St-Affrique 62

Syndicat d'initiative, Mairie ☎ 05 63 76 36 71, Fax 05 63 76 36 10

Viaduc du Viaur★ Northeast: 7 km,.

Des Voyageurs — AC rest, VISA MC

11 av. Paul Bodin – ☎ 05 63 76 30 06 – ddelpous@wanadoo.fr – Fax 05 63 76 37 94 – Closed Sun. evening and Mon. except July - Aug.

15 rm – †€ 43/55 ††€ 43/65, ☕ € 7 – ½ P € 58 – **Rest** – Menu € 15 (weekdays)/30 – Carte € 17/47

◆ Near the church, a simple hotel with a small garden in the shade of a weeping willow. Rooms with country furnishings, the quieter ones being at the back. Traditional cuisine and small selection of wines served in a comfortable dining room.

TARARE – 69 Rhône – 327 F4 – pop. 10 420 – alt. 383 m – ✉ 69170
Lyon - Rhone Valley 44 **A1**

Paris 463 – Lyon 45 – Montbrison 60 – Roanne 40 – Villefranche-sur-Saône 33

Office de tourisme, place Madeleine ☎ 04 74 63 06 65, Fax 04 74 63 52 69

Burnichon — VISA MC AE

1.5 km east via D 307 – ☎ 04 74 63 44 01 – hotelburnichon@wanadoo.fr – Fax 04 74 05 08 52 – Closed 22-28 December

34 rm – †€ 39/46 ††€ 46/53, ☕ € 9 – ½ P € 45 – **Rest** – *(closed Saturday dinner and Sunday)* Menu € 14 (weekdays), € 25/35 – Carte € 22/35

◆ 1980s hotel with functional rooms which have retained their original furniture. Swimming pool surrounded by greenery just 50 metres away. Veranda-dining room, with a buffet of first courses and a straightforward traditional menu. Summer terrace.

XXX **Jean Brouilly** — VISA MC AE

3ter r. de Paris – ☎ 04 74 63 24 56 – contact@restaurant-brouilly.com – Fax 04 74 05 05 48 – Closed 4-11 August, 12-26 January, Sunday dinner and Monday

Rest – Menu € 35/72 – Carte € 45/69

◆ A charming property in extensive grounds with a gastronomic reputation centred on classical cuisine. Elegant dining room and a wine list with a strong Burgundian influence.

TARASCON – 13 Bouches-du-Rhône – 340 C3 – pop. 12 668 – alt. 8 m – ✉ 13150
Provence 42 **E1**

Paris 702 – Arles 20 – Avignon 24 – Marseille 102 – Nîmes 27

Office de tourisme, 59, rue des Halles ✆ 04 90 91 03 52, Fax 04 90 91 22 96

Château of the roi René★★: ※★★ - Ste-Marthe church ★ - Musée Charles-Deméry★ (Souleïado) **M.**

Les Échevins

26 bd Itam – ✆ 04 90 91 01 70 – contact@hotel-echevins.com – Fax 04 90 43 50 44 – Open Easter-1st November Y **a**

40 rm – †€ 57 ††€ 63/72, ☕ € 10 – ½ P € 58

Rest *Le Mistral* – *✆ 04 90 91 27 62 (closed Saturday lunchtime and Wednesday)* Menu € 16/23 – Carte approx. € 27

◆ Guests will enjoy this 17C dwelling with family atmosphere. Modest but well maintained rooms. Beautiful staircase with wrought iron railing. Colourful veranda-restaurant and traditional cuisine blown in with the Mistral.

North-West **3 km by D 35 and D 970 - ✉ 13150 Tarascon**

Le Mas des Comtes de Provence

petite rte d'Arles – ✆ 04 90 91 00 13 – valo@mas-provence.com – Fax 04 90 91 02 85

9 rm – †€ 140/180 ††€ 140/380, ☕ € 12,50 – ½ P € 125/155

Table d'hôte – Menu € 20 (lunch)/40

◆ This 15C local-style farmhouse is simply superb! Magnificent antique furniture, worthy of a museum. Gorgeous rooms, park and large pool in keeping with the rest.

TARASCON-SUR-ARIÈGE – 09 Ariège – 343 H7 – pop. 3 446 – alt. 474 m – ✉ 09400
Languedoc-Roussillon-Tarn Gorges 29 **C3**

Paris 777 – Ax-les-Thermes 27 – Foix 18 – Lavelanet 30

Office de tourisme, avenue Paul Joucla ✆ 05 61 05 94 94, Fax 05 61 05 57 79

Parc pyrénéen de l'art préhistorique★★ West: 3 km - Grotte de Niaux★★ (prehistoric drawings) Southwest: 4 km - Grotte de Lombrives★ South: 3 km by N 20.

Domaine Fournié

2.5 km north-west on D 618 Col de Port road – ✆ 05 61 05 54 52 – contact@domaine-fournie.com – Fax 05 61 02 73 63 – Closed 23 December-2 January

5 rm ☕ – †€ 45/50 ††€ 54/58 – ½ P € 90/95 – **Table d'hôte** – *(closed Thursday and weekdays except school holidays)* Menu € 20 bi

◆ The rooms of this 17C house boast a cinema-theme decor. Some are adorned with antique furniture. Breakfast room with a fireplace.

in Rabat-les-Trois-Seigneurs 5.5 km northwest by D 618 and D 223 – ✉ 09400

La Table de la Ramade

r. des Écoles – ✆ 05 61 64 94 32 – latabledelaramade@orange.fr – Fax 05 61 64 94 32 – Closed Monday

Rest – Menu € 17/33 – Carte € 24/52

◆ Former forge in a narrow alley at the top of the village. Charming little first floor rustic restaurant and roof terrace. Appealing modern cuisine.

TARBES P – 65 Hautes-Pyrénées – 342 M5 – pop. 46 275 – Built-up area 109 892 – alt. 320 m – ✉ 65000
Languedoc-Roussillon-Tarn Gorges 28 **A3**

Paris 831 – Bordeaux 218 – Lourdes 19 – Pau 44 – Toulouse 158

Tarbes-Lourdes-Pyrénées: ✆ 05 62 32 92 22, by ④: 9 km.

✆ 3635 (0,34 €/mn)

Office de tourisme, 3, cours Gambetta ✆ 05 62 51 30 31, Fax 05 62 44 17 63

de Tarbes les Tumulus Laloubère 1 rue du Bois, by Bagnères-de-Bigorre road: 2 km, ✆ 05 62 45 14 50 ;

Hippodrome de La Loubère Laloubère Rue de la Châtaigneraie, by Bagnères-de-Bigorre road: 3 km, ✆ 05 62 45 07 10.

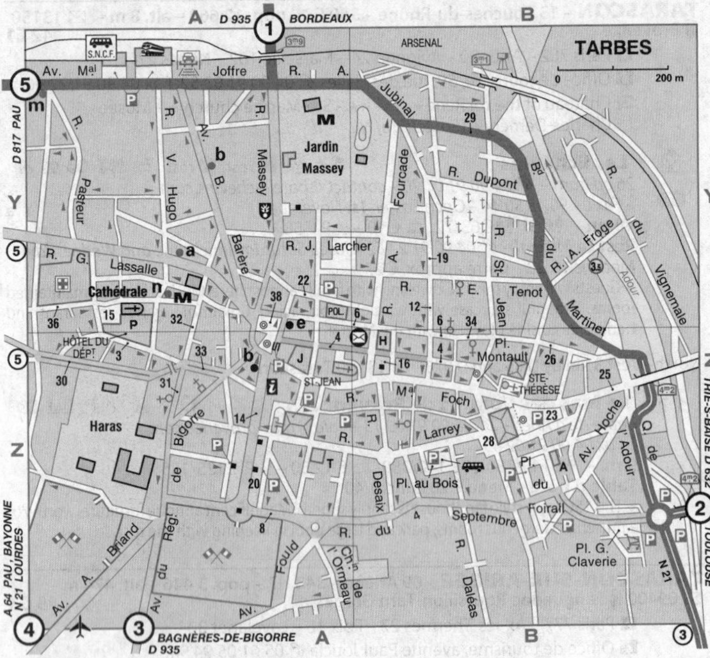

TARBES

Street	Grid	No.
Bigorre (R. de la)	AZ	3
Brauhauban (R.)	ABZ	4
Clemenceau (R. G.)	ABY	6
Cronstadt (R. de)	AZ	8
Deville (R.)	BY	12
Foch (R. Maréchal)	ABZ	
Fourcade (R. A.)	BY	
Gambetta (Cours)	AZ	14
Gaulle (Pl. Gén.-de)	AY	15
Jean-Jaurès (Pl.)	BZ	16
Laporte (R. H.)	BY	19
Larcher (R. J.)	ABY	
Leclerc (Allées Gén.)	AZ	20
Magnoac (R. G.)	AY	22
Marcadieu (Pl.)	BZ	23
Marne (Av. de la)	BZ	25
Michelet (R.)	BZ	26
Parmentier (Pl.)	BZ	28
Péreire (R.)	BY	29
Pradeau (Prom. du)	AZ	30
Pyrénées (R. des)	AZ	31
Ramond (R.)	AYZ	32
Reffye (Cours)	AZ	33
St-Frai (R. Marie)	BYZ	34
Sède (R. de la)	AY	36
Verdun (Pl. de)	AYZ	38

Le Rex Hotel

8 cours Gambetta – ✆ 05 62 54 44 44 – reception@lerexhotel.com – Fax 05 62 54 45 45

86 rm – †€ 110/180 ††€ 110/180, ☕ € 15 – ½ P € 75/88 AZ **b**

Rest – *(closed Sunday)* Menu (€ 16), € 27/39

◆ The façade of this striking glass and aluminium building is enlivened at night by special lighting effects. Ultra-modern public areas and guestrooms designed by Starck and Panton. Lounge-bar and restaurant with designer decor. Contemporary-style cuisine. Musical entertainment.

Foch without rest

18 pl. Verdun – ✆ 05 62 93 71 58 – hotelfoch@wanadoo.fr – Fax 05 62 93 34 59

30 rm – †€ 52 ††€ 57, ☕ € 7,50 AYZ **e**

◆ This establishment alongside a lively square place is well soundproofed. The spacious and comfortable rooms on the top two floors open onto pleasant balconies.

L'Ambroisie (Daniel Labarrère)

48 r. Abbé Torné – ✆ 05 62 93 09 34 – lambroisie@wanadoo.fr – Fax 05 62 93 09 24 – Closed 1st-11 May, 1st-7 September, 22-30 December, 2-11 January, Sunday and Monday AY **n**

Rest – Menu € 25 (weekday lunch), € 34/80 – Carte € 76/83

Spec. Pavé de cabillaud au chorizo, Ossau Iraty et haricots tarbais. Grosse côte de veau rôtie, petits légumes au beurre. Mi-cuit au chocolat noir. **Wines** Madiran, Jurançon.

◆ Exquisite food to be savoured in a former presbytery. The house, dating back to 1882, offers a fine comfortable dining room, extended by a summer terrace in the pretty garden.

Le Petit Gourmand

62 av. B. Barère – ✆ 05 62 34 26 86 – Fax 05 62 34 26 86 – Closed mid August-beg. September, 2-10 January, Saturday lunch, Sunday dinner and Monday AY **b**

Rest – Menu € 18 – Carte approx. € 29

◆ Gourmands will appreciate this brasserie-style venue decorated with old advertisements, the modern cuisine and Languedoc-Roussillon wines.

Le Fil à la Patte

30 r. G. Lassalle – ✆ 05 62 93 39 23 – lefilalapatte@cegetel.net – Fax 05 62 93 39 23 – Closed 11-25 August, Saturday lunch, Sunday and Monday AY **a**

Rest – Menu € 15 (weekday lunch), € 20/25 – Carte approx. € 28

◆ Regional and market cuisine can be enjoyed in an open, friendly atmosphere: this small restaurant in sunny colours has already attracted a good number of regular clients.

L'Isard

70 av. Mar.-Joffre – ✆ 05 62 93 06 69 – Fax 05 62 93 06 69 – Closed Saturday lunch, Sunday dinner and Wednesday AY **m**

Rest – Menu € 19 (weekdays)/26 – Carte € 33/42

◆ A simple décor and pleasant shaded terrace with views of the vegetable garden at this traditional table serving *Gascogne* specialities.

Lourdes by Juillan road 4 km by ④ on D 921^{A} – ✉ 65290 Juillan

L'Aragon with rm

rest, rest, VISA

2 ter rte de Lourdes – ✆ 05 62 32 07 07 – hotel-restaurant.laragon@wanadoo.fr – Fax 05 62 32 92 50 – Closed 4-19 August, 15-29 January and Sunday dinner

12 rm – 🚹€ 49 🚹🚹€ 58, ☕ € 7,50 – ½ P € 53

Rest – *(closed Saturday lunch and Monday)* Menu € 35/58 – Carte € 53/69

Rest *Bistrot* – *(closed Saturday lunch)* Menu (€ 14,50 bi), € 19 bi – Carte € 24/46

◆ Up-to-date dishes served in an elegant, rustic dining room or on the shaded terrace. Each room offers a different theme (rugby, golf, sea, wine, etc.). The Bistrot offers a contemporary setting, simply laid tables and regional dishes.

Pau road 6 km by ⑤ – ✉ 65420 Ibos

La Chaumière du Bois

rm, VISA

D 817 – ✆ 05 62 90 03 51 – hotel@chaumieredubois.com – Fax 05 62 90 05 33

22 rm – 🚹€ 58/66 🚹🚹€ 68/76, ☕ € 8 – ½ P € 66

Rest – *(closed 27 April-5 May, 31 August-9 September, 21 December-15 January, Sunday dinner except 14 July-15 August and Monday)* Menu € 18/28 – Carte € 32/45

◆ A country atmosphere in this motel-style accommodation with thatched roofs. The functional rooms overlook a pleasant garden planted with palm and umbrella pine trees. A rotunda-shaped dining room with a high roof structure and tree-shaded terrace.

TARNAC – 19 Corrèze – 329 M1 – pop. 356 – alt. 700 m – ✉ 19170

Dordogne-Berry-Limousin 25 **C2**

Paris 434 – Aubusson 47 – Bourganeuf 44 – Limoges 68 – Tulle 62 – Ussel 45

Des Voyageurs

rest, rest, VISA

– ✆ 05 55 95 53 12 – voyageurstarnac@voila.fr – Fax 05 55 95 40 07 – Closed 23-30 June, 20 December-22 January, 24 February-10 March, Sunday dinner and Monday (except hotel July-August)

15 rm – 🚹€ 45 🚹🚹€ 48, ☕ € 8,50 – ½ P € 55

Rest – Menu € 16 (weekdays)/30 – Carte € 25/39

◆ Simply furnished but refreshing rooms await guests in this pleasant village hotel bordering the Millevaches plateau. Breakfasts are particularly appetising. Delicious local specialities amply compensate for the simplicity of the dining hall's decor.

TASSIN-LA-DEMI-LUNE – 69 Rhône – 327 H5 – see Lyon

TAVEL – 30 Gard – 339 N4 – pop. 1 529 – alt. 100 m – ✉ 30126 23 D2

Paris 673 – Avignon 15 – Alès 68 – Nîmes 41 – Orange 22

Le Pont du Roy

rest, VISA

3 km south-east on D 4 and D 976 – ✆ 04 66 50 22 03 – contact@hotelpontduroy.fr – Fax 04 66 50 10 14 – Open 21 March-30 September

14 rm – †€ 63/95 ††€ 63/95, ☐ € 8 – ½ P € 67/74 – **Rest** – *(dinner only) (residents only)* Menu € 27/50 – Carte € 42/57

◆ A fully renovated local farmhouse-style building in the heart of the famous wine-producing area. Rooms in pastel shades with rustic or Provençal-style furniture. Pretty garden.

Les Chambres de Vincent

r. Grillons – ✆ 04 66 50 94 76 – nancy@chambres-de-vincent.com – Open 8 February-8 November

5 rm ☐ – †€ 55/60 ††€ 65/75 – ½ P € 55 – **Table d'hôte** – *(Closed Tuesday)* Menu € 20/30

◆ A distinctive country house offering small, practical and colourful bedrooms. Mediterranean species in the garden. Wisteria and vine shaded terrace. Home cooking (bouillabaisse to order) prepared by the owner, who hails from Avignon.

Auberge de Tavel with rm

rest, VISA AE

Voie Romaine – ✆ 04 66 50 03 41 – info@auberge-de-tavel.com – Fax 04 66 50 24 44 – Closed 15 February-15 March

11 rm – †€ 60/105 ††€ 75/160, ☐ € 12 – ½ P € 75/131

Rest – *(Closed Wednesday)* Menu (€ 22), € 27/72 – Carte € 39/56

◆ Under the beams of the pleasant, rustic dining room or on the terrace, you can discover a modern cuisine that explores local Provençal products with wonderful results. Unpretentious rooms adorned with country furniture. Those at the rear are quieter.

TAVERS – 45 Loiret – 318 G5 – see Beaugency

TEILHÈDE – 63 Puy-de-Dôme – 326 F7 – pop. 374 – alt. 500 m – ✉ 63460 5 B2

Paris 401 – Clermont-Ferrand 31 – Cournon-d'Auvergne 32 – Vichy 45

Château des Raynauds

VISA

2 km west on the D 17 – ✆ 04 73 64 30 12 – info@chateau-raynauds.com – Fax 04 73 64 30 12

4 rm ☐ – †€ 63 ††€ 81 – **Table d'hôte** – Menu € 29 bi

◆ An 11C-12C castle, converted into a hunting lodge in the late 16C: spiral staircase, fireplace, antiques and rooms with king size beds. This Louis XIII style table d'hôte serves classic fare.

TENCE – 43 Haute-Loire – 331 H3 – pop. 2 890 – alt. 840 m – ✉ 43190

Lyon - Rhone Valley 6 D3

Paris 564 – Lamastre 38 – Le Puy-en-Velay 46 – St-Étienne 52 – Yssingeaux 19

Office de tourisme, place du Chatiague ✆ 04 71 59 81 99, Fax 04 71 59 83 50

Hostellerie Placide

rest, VISA

av. de la Gare, rte d'Annonay – ✆ 04 71 59 82 76 – placide@hostellerie-placide.fr – Fax 04 71 65 44 46 – Closed January-mid March, Monday lunch and Tuesday lunch July-August, Sunday dinner, Monday and Tuesday September-June

12 rm – †€ 72/100 ††€ 72/100, ☐ € 10 – ½ P € 66/86

Rest – Menu € 13 (weekday lunch), € 32/63 – Carte € 45/54

◆ A former coaching inn (1902) with a distinctive plant covered façade. Cosy, personalised rooms (warm tones, period or modern furniture). Plush interior and up-to-the-minute classical menu. Drinks in the garden in summer.

Les Prairies without rest

1 r. du Prè-Long – ✆ 04 71 56 35 80 – thomas.bourgeois@freesbee.fr – Open 15 April-1st November

5 rm ☐ – †€ 63 ††€ 71

◆ A stone residence, from 1850, houses this bed and breakfast, nestling in a wooded park. Simple and tasteful decor. Pleasant winter evenings around the warm fireplace.

TENCIN – 38 Isère – 333 I6 – pop. 897 – alt. 257 m – ✉ 38570 46 F2

Paris 604 – Chambéry 38 – Grenoble 25 – Lyon 137

Syndicat d'initiative, route du Lac - Grangeneuve ✆ 04 76 13 00 00, Fax 04 76 45 71 92

XX **La Tour des Sens** VISA

La Tour, 1 km Theys road – ✆ 04 76 04 79 67 – contact@latourdessens.fr – Fax 04 76 04 79 67 – Closed 13-21 April, 27 July-20 August, 26 October-3 November, 21-30 December, Saturday lunch, Monday lunch, Sunday and holidays

Rest – Menu € 21 (weekday lunch), € 34/71 bi – Carte € 40/73

◆ The restaurant offers a view of the Massif de la Chartreuse. The warm shades of its interior brighten the modern, dark-wood furniture. Inventive cuisine.

TENDE – 06 Alpes-Maritimes – 341 G3 – pop. 1 844 – alt. 815 m – ✉ 06430

French Riviera 41 D2

Paris 888 – Cuneo 47 – Menton 56 – Nice 78 – Sospel 38

Office de tourisme, avenue du 16 septembre 1947 ✆ 04 93 04 73 71, Fax 04 93 04 68 77

de Vievola Hameau de Vievola, North: 5 km by D 6204, ✆ 04 93 04 88 91.

Site★ - Old town★ - Frescoes★★★ of Notre-Dame des fontaines chapel ★★ Southeast: 11 km.

X **L'Auberge Tendasque** VISA

65 av. 16-Septembre-1947 – ✆ 04 93 04 62 26 – Fax 04 93 04 68 34

Rest – *(lunch only)* Menu (€ 13,50), € 16/24 – Carte € 24/43

◆ This tall house stands at the foot of a medieval village. Regional cuisine in rustic surroundings. Fine painted ceiling and watercolours by a local artist.

in St-Dalmas-de-Tende 4 km south by D 6204 – ✉ 06430

Le Prieuré rest, VISA

r. J. Medecin – ✆ 04 93 04 75 70 – contact@leprieure.org – Fax 04 93 04 71 58 – Closed 25 December-1st January

24 rm – †€ 43/59 ††€ 49/64, ☕ € 10 – ½ P € 46/56 – **Rest** – Menu (€ 11,50), € 19/26 – Carte € 20/52

◆ This former priory is home to simple, rustic rooms. The hamlet is also the site of an amazing monumental train station built on Mussolini's orders. Traditional dishes served in a vaulted dining room or on a shaded terrace.

in la Brigue 6.5 km southeast by D 6204 and D 43 – pop. 595 – alt. 810 m – ✉ 06430

Office de tourisme, 26, avenue du Général de Gaulle ✆ 04 93 79 09 34

St-Martin collegiate church ★.

Mirval VISA

– ✆ 04 93 04 63 71 – lemirval@club-internet.fr – Fax 04 93 04 79 81 – Open 1st April-2 November

18 rm – †€ 45/48 ††€ 52/70, ☕ € 8 – ½ P € 45/60 – **Rest** – *(closed Friday lunch)* Menu (€ 17), € 20 (weekday lunch)/24 – Carte approx. € 26

◆ A pretty stone bridge straddles a fish-filled river and leads to this attractive 19C mountain inn. Practical, tidy rooms. The owner is also a hiker. Contemporary dining room and veranda with view of the peaks; simple regional fare.

TERGNIER – 02 Aisne – 306 B5 – pop. 15 069 – alt. 55 m – ✉ 02700 37 C2

Paris 136 – Compiègne 54 – Saint-Quentin 27 – Amiens 99 – Laon 29 – Soissons 37

X **La Mandoline** VISA

45 pl. Herment – ✆ 03 23 57 08 71 – Fax 03 23 57 08 71 – Closed Sunday dinner and Monday

Rest – Menu € 23/45 – Carte € 37/61

◆ In good weather, the flower-decked front makes it easy to find this restaurant near the town centre. Traditional recipes served.

TERMES – 48 Lozère – **330** H6 – **pop. 202** – **alt. 1 120 m** – ✉ **48310** 22 **B1**

Paris 545 – Aurillac 112 – Chaudes-Aigues 19 – Mende 56 – St-Flour 41

Auberge du Verdy

– *04 66 31 60 97 – Open 2 April-19 December*

10 rm – €38/45 €38/45, €6 – ½ P €38 – **Rest** – Menu €11 bi (weekdays), €13/23 – Carte €17/33

◆ Large country house dating from the 1990s, situated at the foot of the village. Basic, fairly spacious rooms. Children's play area. Meat grilled "à la pierrade" and local specialities on the menu in this restaurant with a regional-style fireplace that roars away in winter.

TERRASSON-LAVILLEDIEU – 24 Dordogne – **329** I5 – **pop. 6 180** – **alt. 90 m** – ✉ **24120** Dordogne-Berry-Limousin 4 **D1**

Paris 497 – Brive-la-Gaillarde 22 – Lanouaille 44 – Périgueux 53 – Sarlat-la-Canéda 32

Office de tourisme, place du Foirail 05 53 50 86 82, Fax 05 53 50 55 61

Les jardins de l'imaginaire★.

L'Imaginaire (Éric Samson) with rm

pl. Foirail, (direction St-Sour church) – 05 53 51 37 27 – limaginaire@club-internet.fr – Fax 05 53 51 60 37 – Closed 3-11 March, 10 November-4 December, 5-16 January, Tuesday lunch and Sunday dinner from September to April and Monday

7 rm – €85/115 €85/115, €12 – ½ P €97/129

Rest – Menu €27 (weekday lunch), €43/92 bi

Spec. Grillade de foie gras au caramel de fruit de la passion (spring-summer). Dos d'esturgeon laqué au vin de noix (September to May). Feuille à feuille de crêpes dentelles, crémeux citron vert, quelques framboises (May to October). **Wines** Côtes de Bergerac, Pécharmant.

◆ Treat your eyes and palate to painstakingly prepared modern cuisine in the elegant setting of this vaulted dining room in a former 17C hospice. Comfortable guestrooms decorated in relaxing cream and beige tones.

TERTENOZ – 74 Haute-Savoie – **328** K6 – **see Faverges**

TÉTEGHEM – 59 Nord – **302** C1 – **see Dunkerque**

TEYSSODE – 81 Tarn – **338** D9 – **pop. 338** – **alt. 270 m** – ✉ **81220** 29 **C2**

Paris 699 – Albi 54 – Castres 27 – Toulouse 51

Domaine d'En Naudet without rest

D 43 – 05 63 70 50 59 – contact@domainenaudet.com

5 rm – €75/86 €83/98

◆ This very peaceful residence with character, perched on a hill, overlooks the countryside. Fine, stylish, rustic bedrooms, sports room, pretty garden, etc. Charming welcome.

THANN – 68 Haut-Rhin – **315** G10 – **pop. 8 033** – **alt. 343 m** – ✉ **68800** Alsace-Lorraine 1 **A3**

Paris 464 – Belfort 42 – Colmar 44 – Épinal 87 – Guebwiller 22 – Mulhouse 21

Office de tourisme, 7, rue de la 1ère Armée 03 89 37 96 20, Fax 03 89 37 04 58

St-Thiébaut collegiate church ★★ - Grand Ballon ★★★ North: 19 km.

Le Parc

23 r. Kléber – 03 89 37 37 47 – reception@alsacehotel.com – Fax 03 89 37 56 23

21 rm – €69/190 €79/190, €16 – ½ P €79/140

Rest – *(closed 5-25 January, Monday lunch, Tuesday lunch and Wednesday lunch)* Menu €25 (lunch)/39 – Carte €49/60

◆ Set in wooded grounds, this fine early 20C house has palatial features; elegantly refined lounge and modern accommodation with baroque touches. Swimming pool. Luminous dining room, peaceful summer terrace and traditional cuisine.

Le Moschenross

42 r. Gén. de Gaulle – ✆ 03 89 37 00 86 – info@le-moschenross.com – Fax 03 89 37 52 81

23 rm – †€ 35/48 ††€ 40/58, ☕ € 7 – ½ P € 37/46 – **Rest** – *(Closed Saturday lunch and Sunday dinner)* Menu (€ 9), € 11 (weekday lunch), € 17/48 – Carte € 30/54

◆ Dominated by the famous Rangen vineyard, this central hotel with colourful brick-red façade has modern rooms (quieter at the back). Bright, spacious and pleasant dining room. Unpretentious modern cuisine.

Aux Sapins

3 r. Jeanne d'Arc – ✆ 03 89 37 10 96 – aux.sapins.hotel@free.fr – Fax 03 89 37 23 83 – Closed 24 December-4 January

17 rm – †€ 42 ††€ 52, ☕ € 7 – ½ P € 48 – **Rest** – *(closed 3-17 August, 24 December-4 January and Saturday)* Menu € 17/35 – Carte € 25/36

◆ A few pine trees shade this 1980s building a little out of town. Attentive service and personalised rooms in pastel shades. Contemporary dining room and smart winstub style bistro; traditional cuisine.

THANNENKIRCH – 68 Haut-Rhin – 315 H7 – pop. 446 – alt. 520 m – ✉ 68590

Alsace-Lorraine 2 **C2**

Paris 436 – Colmar 25 – St-Dié 40 – Sélestat 17

Schaentzel ★ road (D 48[1]) North: 3 km.

Auberge La Meunière

30 r. Ste Anne – ✆ 03 89 73 10 47 – info@aubergelameuniere.com – Fax 03 89 73 12 31 – Open 11 March-22 December

25 rm – †€ 58 ††€ 60/98, ☕ € 8 – ½ P € 47/73 – **Rest** – Menu (€ 13), € 17 (except Sunday lunch)/35 – Carte € 27/48

◆ This elegant inn sports a happy mix of rustic and contemporary styles. The spacious rooms, many with balconies, command fine views of the countryside. Welcoming dining room, panoramic terrace and regionally inspired, seasonal menu.

Touring-Hôtel

2 rte du Haut Koenigsbourg – ✆ 03 89 73 10 01 – touringhotel@free.fr – Fax 03 89 73 11 79 – Closed 7 January-9 March

45 rm – †€ 49/59 ††€ 49/129, ☕ € 10 – ½ P € 54/99

Rest – Menu (€ 18), € 25/35 – Carte € 20/47

◆ Large family hotel in the village, at the foot of the Taennchel mountain range. Smart Alsatian-style rooms. Wellness centre. Country buffet for breakfast. Regional dishes and wines take pride of place in this dining room.

THARON-PLAGE – 44 Loire-Atlantique – 316 C5 – ✉ 44730 34 **A2**

Paris 437 – Challans 53 – Nantes 57 – St-Nazaire 24

Le Belem

56 av. Convention – ✆ 02 40 64 90 06 – loirat-thierry@wanadoo.fr – Fax 02 40 39 43 14 – Closed 2 January-6 February, Sunday dinner off season and Monday

Rest – Menu (€ 17 bi), € 23/45 – Carte € 39/45

◆ A stone's throw from the beach, this 1980s decorated restaurant sports plants and a mural of the Belem tall ship. Up-to-the-minute menu.

THÉDIRAC – 46 Lot – 337 D4 – pop. 275 – alt. 270 m – ✉ 46150 28 **B1**

Paris 588 – Toulouse 151 – Cahors 25 – Sarlat-la-Canéda 41 – Fumel 44

Le Manoir de Surges

à Surges , 1.5 km north – ✆ 05 65 21 22 45 – manoirdesurges@orange.fr – Closed Christmas holidays

3 rm ☕ – †€ 61/76 ††€ 61/76 – **Table d'hôte** – *(closed July-August, Wednesday and Sunday)* Menu € 22 bi/34 bi

◆ 17C manor set in a vast garden. Bedrooms with antique furniture. *Table d'hôte* serving local duck specialities such as *foie-gras* and *confit*.

LE THEIL – 15 Cantal – 330 C4 – see Salers

LE THEIL – 03 Allier – 326 F4 – pop. 413 – alt. 450 m – ✉ 03240 5 B1

Paris 343 – Clermont-Ferrand 92 – Montluçon 46 – Vichy 43

Château du Max

2 km north-west on the D235 – ☎ 04 70 42 35 23 – chateaudumax@club-internet.fr – Fax 04 70 42 34 90

4 rm – †€ 60 ††€ 70/80 – ½ P € – **Table d'hôte** – Menu € 25 bi

◆ Château from the 13C and 15C, surrounded by a moat. Rooms and suites have been tastefully decorated by the landlady who was a former theatre designer. Restaurant serving local dishes in a magnificent medieval setting.

THÉNAC – 17 Charente-Maritime – 329 D7 – see Saintes

THENAY – 36 Indre – 323 E7 – pop. 827 – alt. 120 m – ✉ 36800 11 B3

Paris 299 – Châteauroux 33 – Limoges 104 – Le Blanc 30 – La Châtre 49

Auberge de Thenay VISA

– ☎ 02 54 47 99 00 – orain.pascal@wanadoo.fr – Closed 1st-9 September, 19-31 January, Sunday dinner and Monday

Rest – *(number of covers limited, pre-book)* Menu € 12 bi (weekday lunch), € 23/33

◆ A jovial ambience reigns in this little shop and inn. The daily set menu is based on spit-roasted meat. Wonderful selection of whiskies and wines from around the world.

THÉOULE-SUR-MER – 06 Alpes-Maritimes – 341 C6 – pop. 1 296 – ✉ 06590 42 E2

French Riviera

Paris 895 – Cannes 11 – Draguignan 58 – Nice 42 – St-Raphaël 30

Office de tourisme, 1, corniche d'Or ☎ 04 93 49 28 28, Fax 04 93 49 00 04

Massif de l'Estérel★★★.

in Miramar 5 km by D 6098 - St-Raphaël road – ✉ 06590 Théoule-sur-Mer

French Riviera

Pointe de l'Esquilon ≤★★ Northeast: 1 km then 15 mn.

Miramar Beach ≤ sea, rm, VISA

47 av. Miramar – ☎ 04 93 75 05 05 – reservation@mbhotel.com – Fax 04 93 75 44 83

56 rm – †€ 140/370 ††€ 140/370, € 19 – 1 suite – ½ P € 127/242

Rest *L'Étoile des Mers* – Menu € 38 (lunch), € 45/90 bi – Carte € 68/87

◆ The charm of this establishment is derived from its location in a deep narrow crevice of red rock. Elegant Provençal-style rooms and sumptuous Oriental inspired spa. Panoramic restaurant and summer terrace.

at port de la Rague

Riviera Beach hôtel without rest ≤ port and sea, VISA

La Rague port – ☎ 04 92 97 11 99 – beachaffaires@orange.fr – Fax 04 92 97 12 10 – Closed 1st December-2 January

9 rm – †€ 128/228 ††€ 138/260

◆ Smart guestrooms with a nautical flavour and south-facing balconies from which to enjoy the sea views. Swimming pool and jacuzzi on the roof, a designer-style bar, and a location on the port, a stone's throw from the beach.

THÉRONDELS – 12 Aveyron – 338 I1 – pop. 478 – alt. 965 m – ✉ 12600 29 D1

Paris 561 – Aurillac 44 – Chaudes-Aigues 48 – Murat 43 – Rodez 88 – St-Flour 49

Miquel rm, VISA

– ☎ 05 65 66 02 72 – hotel-miquel@wanadoo.fr – Fax 05 65 66 19 84 – Open 16 March-14 December

20 rm – †€ 50/60 ††€ 50/80, € 8 – ½ P € 44/52

Rest – *(closed Sunday dinner and Monday)* Menu € 11 bi (weekdays)/32

◆ An early 20C building in the same family for three generations. The simple, well-kept rooms either overlook the garden or village square. Dining room opening onto a small terrace and Aveyron-inspired cuisine.

THIAIS – 94 Val-de-Marne – **312** D3 – **101** 26 – see Paris, Area

THIERS – 63 Puy-de-Dôme – 326 I7 – pop. 13 338 – alt. 420 m – ✉ 63300

Auvergne 6 **C2**

- Paris 388 – Clermont-Ferrand 43 – Lyon 133 – St-Étienne 108 – Vichy 36
- Office de tourisme, maison du Pirou ☎ 04 73 80 65 65, Fax 04 73 80 01 32
- Site★★ - Old Thiers★: Maison du Pirou★ **N** - Rampart terrace ★ - Rocher de Borbes ≤★ South: 3.5 km by D 102.

L'Aigle d'Or

rm, VISA

8 r. de Lyon – ☎ 04 73 80 00 50 – aigle.dor@wanadoo.fr – Fax 04 73 80 17 00 – Closed 18-31 March, 25 October-17 November, Monday lunch and Sunday Y **a**

18 rm – €45 €57, €7 – ½ P €48

Rest – Menu €12 (weekday lunch), €16/25 – Carte approx. €35

◆ This establishment, founded in 1836, houses a comfortable sitting room and well-soundproofed rooms. A 19C setting and rustic furniture make up the dining room decor where traditional food is served.

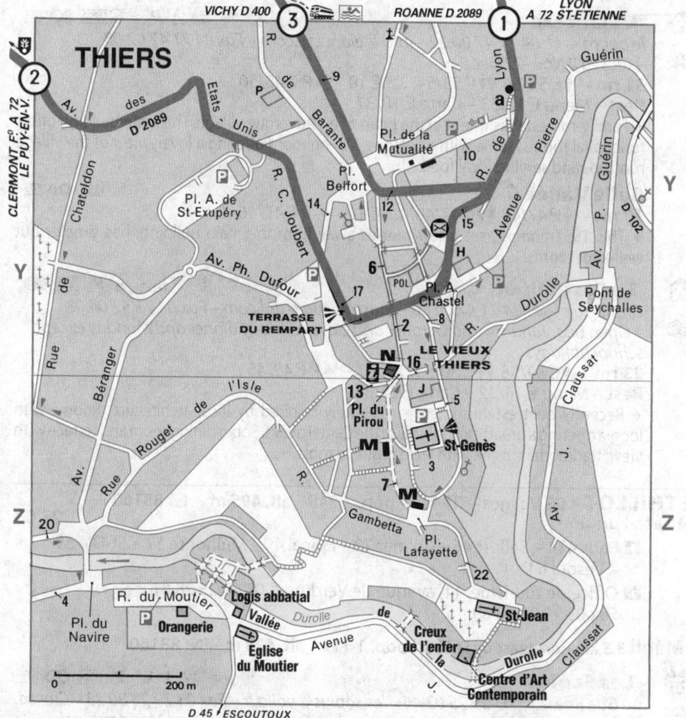

Bourg (R. du) . . . . . Y 2	Dr-Dumas (R. des) . . . . . Y 9	Mitterrand (R. F.) . . . . . Y 15
Brugière (Imp. Jean) . . . . . Z 3	Duchasseint (Pl.) . . . . . Y 10	Pirou (R. du) . . . . . Y 16
Chabot (R. M.) . . . . . Z 5	Dumas (R. Alexandre) . . . . . Y 8	Terrasse (R.) . . . . . Y 17
Clermont (R. de) . . . . . Z 4	Grammonts (R. des) . . . . . Y 12	Voltaire (Av.) . . . . . Z 20
Conchette (R.) . . . . . Y 6	Grenette (R.) . . . . . Z 13	4-Septembre
Coutellerie (R. de la) . . . . . Z 7	Marilhat (R. Prosper) . . . . . Y 14	(R. du) . . . . . Z 22

in Pont-de-Dore 6 km by ② by D 2089 – ✉ 63920 Peschadoires

Eliotel

rte de Maringues – ✆ 04 73 80 10 14 – direliotel@wanadoo.fr – Fax 04 73 80 51 02 – Closed 4-15 August and 21 December-11 January

12 rm – €52/73 €52/73, €7,50 – ½ P €52/61

Rest – Menu €18 bi/51 – Carte €31/52

◆ Pleasant establishment run by an enthusiast of Thiers' knives (display case). Well proportioned rooms; ask for one of the more recent ones. The chef, who is from Armorique, proposes Auvergne dishes and Breton specialities.

"Rest" appears in red for establishments with a ✿ (star) or ☺ (Bib Gourmand).

THIÉZAC – 15 Cantal – **330** E4 – pop. 614 – alt. 805 m – ✉ 15800

Auvergne 5 **B3**

Paris 542 – Aurillac 26 – Murat 23 – Vic-sur-Cère 7

Office de tourisme, le Bourg ✆ 04 71 47 03 50, Fax 04 71 47 03 83

Pas de Compaing★ Northeast: 3 km.

L'Elancèze

le bourg – ✆ 04 71 47 00 22 – info@elanceze.com – Fax 04 71 47 02 08 – Closed 2 Nov.-22 Dec.

31 rm – €53/54 €53/54, €10 – ½ P €48/50

Rest – Menu €17/33 – Carte €18/37

◆ Family-run establishment in the heart of an Auvergne village. The main building offers functional rooms, some with a balcony. Dining room offering a lovely view of the village rooftops and serving local food.

Belle Vallée

10 rm – €47/48 €47/48, €10 – ½ P €45/46

◆ This 1957 annexe, set a few metres away from the main building, has simpler but well-kept rooms.

Le Casteltinet rest,

Grand-rue – ✆ 04 71 47 00 60 – faustmacua@aol.com – Fax 04 71 47 04 08 – Open beg. January-end October and closed Sunday dinner and Monday except school holidays

23 rm – €39/58 €39/58, €7 – ½ P €42/45

Rest – Menu €14/32 – Carte €27/36

◆ Recently built establishment successfully inspired by local architecure. Rooms with loggia offering a breathtaking view of the Cantal peaks. Sober dining room and terrace with view; traditional cuisine with solid regional roots.

LE THILLOT – 88 Vosges – **314** I5 – pop. 3 945 – alt. 495 m – ✉ 88160

Alsace-Lorraine 27 **C3**

Paris 434 – Belfort 46 – Colmar 72 – Épinal 49 – Mulhouse 57 – St-Dié 59 – Vesoul 64

Office de tourisme, 11, avenue de Verdun ✆ 03 29 25 28 61, Fax 03 29 25 38 39

in Ménil 3.5 km northeast by D 486 – pop. 1 117 – alt. 524 m – ✉ 88160

Les Sapins

60 Gde Rue – ✆ 03 29 25 02 46 – les.sapins@voila.fr – Fax 03 29 25 80 23 – Closed 23 June-6 July, 21 November-17 December, Sunday dinner and Monday lunch

22 rm – €45 €52, €9 – ½ P €50/62

Rest – Menu €22/45 – Carte €28/47

◆ Unusual architecture designed according to feng shui principles, individually decorated rooms and a faultless welcome. Homemade jams. Up-to-the-minute cuisine served to a background of contemporary art.

THIONVILLE – 57 Moselle – 307 I2 – pop. 40 907 – Built-up area 130 480 – alt. 155 m – ✉ 57100 Alsace-Lorraine

26 **B1**

Paris 339 – Luxembourg 32 – Metz 30 – Nancy 84 – Trier 77 – Verdun 88

Office de tourisme, 16, rue du vieux collège ✆ 03 82 53 33 18, Fax 03 82 53 15 55

Château de la Grange★.

THIONVILLE

Afrique (Chaussée d') . . . . **AV** 3
Amérique (Chaussée d') . . . . . **BV** 4
Asie (Chaussée d') . . . . **AV** 6
Bel Air (Allée) . . . . **AV** 7
Comte-de-Bertier (Av.) . . . . **BV** 10
Europe (Chaussée d') . . . . **AV** 13
Guentrange (Rte de) . . . . **AV** 15
Longwy (R. de) . . . . **AV** 18
Océanie (Chaussée d') . . . . **BV** 25
Paul-Albert (R.) . . . . **AV** 28
Pyramides (R. des) . . . . **BV** 29
Romains (R. des) . . . . **AX** 31
Terrasse (Allée de la) . . . . **AV** 34
14-Juillet (Av. du) . . . . **AV** 37

 **Saint-Hubert** without rest

2 r. G. Ditsch – ✆ 03 82 51 84 22
– hotel@bestwestern-sainthubert.com
– Fax 03 82 53 99 61 DZ **s**

44 rm – €70/78 €74/82, €9

◆ Modern-looking hotel between the Mairie and St Maximin church, offering comfortable rooms, a low-key bar and a bright breakfast room with a view of the town.

 **Des Oliviers** without rest

1 r. Four Banal – ✆ 03 82 53 70 27
– contact@hoteldesoliviers.com – Fax 03 82 53 23 34
– Closed 25 December-1st January DY **n**

26 rm – €52 €54, €7

◆ Old house set in a pedestrian street of the town centre. Colourful hall, practical rooms, modern breakfast area and small summer terrace. Wifi equipment.

THIONVILLE

Berthe-au-Grand-Pied (R.) . . **DY** 8
Ditsch (R. G.) . . . . **DZ** 12
Hoche (R. Lazare) . . . . **DY** 16
Luxembourg (R. du) . . . . **DY** 19
Marchal (Quai P.) . . . . **DY** 21
Marché (Pl. du) . . . . **DY** 22
Marie-Louise (Pl.) . . . . **CZ** 24
Paris (R. de) . . . . **DZ** 27
République (Pl.) . . . . **CZ** 30
St-Pierre (R. de) . . . . **CZ** 33

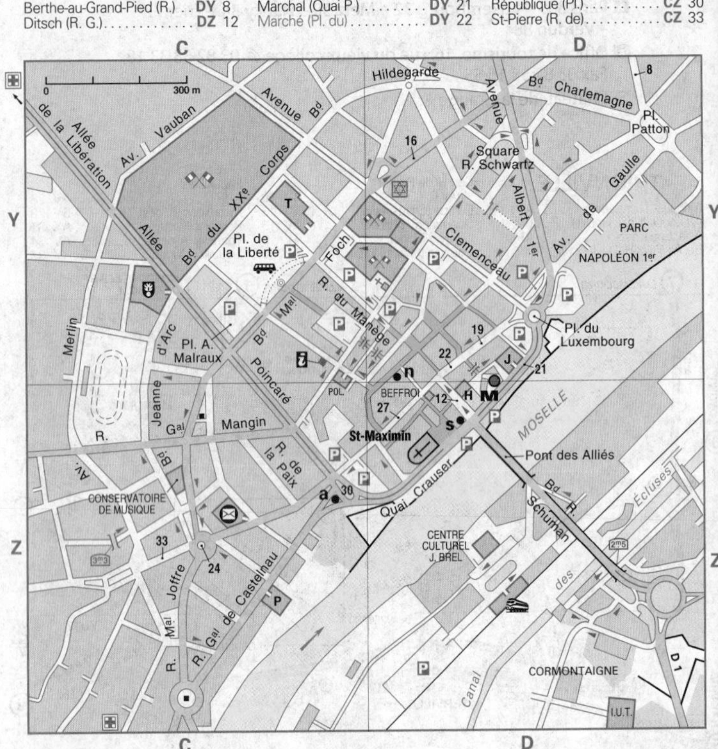

Du Parc without rest

10 pl. de la République – ✆ 03 82 82 80 80 – contact@hoteldu-parc.com – Fax 03 82 82 71 82 CZ **a**

41 rm – 🛉€ 62/69 🛉🛉€ 62/69, ☕ € 8,50

◆ Early 20C building just off the town centre, facing a small public park. The rooms, spread over six floors, are functional and all similar.

Aux Poulbots Gourmets

9 pl. aux Fleurs – ✆ 03 82 88 10 91 – ardizzoia@club-internet.fr – Fax 03 82 88 42 76 – Closed 23 July-16 August, 2-20 January, Saturday lunch, Sunday dinner, Wednesday dinner and Monday AV **p**

Rest – Menu € 36/60 – Carte € 40/65

◆ This restaurant with a good local reputation offers classic-traditional cuisine in a both bright and low-key dining room, with a friendly atmosphere.

in Yutz 3 km by ③ – **pop. 14 687 – alt. 155 m – ✉ 57970**

Les Alérions

102 r. Nationale – ✆ 03 82 56 26 63 – Fax 03 82 56 26 65 – Closed 14-20 April, 18 August-2 September, Sunday dinner, Tuesday dinner and Monday BV **t**

Rest – Menu € 16 (weekday lunch), € 22/48 – Carte € 26/55

◆ The name refers to the coat of arms of Lorraine (three small eagles without beaks or feet). The interior has a fireplace, whitened wood panelling, red walls and period seats. Traditional dishes.

in Crève-Cœur – ✉ 57100 Thionville

L'Horizon rest, VISA

– ☎ *03 82 88 53 65 – hotel@lhorizon.fr – Fax 03 82 34 55 84 – Closed 20 December-20 January and Sunday dinner from November to March* AV **e**

13 rm – †€ 90/110 ††€ 120/160, ☕ € 14 – ½ P € 140/170

Rest – *(closed Sunday dinner from November to March, Monday lunch, Tuesday lunch, Friday lunch and Saturday lunch)* Menu € 40/60 – Carte € 49/63

♦ An old house covered with Virginia creeper and surrounded by flower-filled gardens. Low-key atmosphere, elegant rooms, stylish lounges and a bar with a panoramic view. Restaurant with classic cuisine and decor, including an Aubusson tapestry in the dining room. Good views of the town.

Auberge du Crève-Coeur VISA

9 Le Crève-Coeur – ☎ 03 82 88 50 52 – aubergeducrevecoeur@wanadoo.fr – Fax 03 82 34 89 06 – Closed Sunday dinner, Monday dinner and Wednesday AV **b**

Rest – Menu € 32/48 – Carte € 45/69

♦ Inn run by the same family since 1899. Wine-themed décor with tapestries, casks and giant 18C press. Generous local cuisine and terrace overlooking Thionville.

THIRON-GARDAIS – 28 Eure-et-Loir – 311 C6 – pop. 1 121 – alt. 237 m – ✉ 28480

11 **B1**

Paris 148 – Chartres 48 – Lucé 46 – Orléans 95

Syndicat d'initiative, 11, rue du Commerce ☎ 02 37 49 49 01, Fax 02 37 49 49 07

La Forge VISA

1 r. Alfred Chasseriaud – ☎ 02 37 49 42 30 – Closed Monday and dinner except Friday and Saturday

Rest – Menu € 13 bi (weekdays), € 31 € (weekend)/50 (weekend)

♦ The artist-chef displays his works in the restaurant that occupies the former forge of a 16C abbey. Up-to-date cuisine and good wine selection.

THIVIERS – 24 Dordogne – 329 G3 – pop. 3 261 – alt. 273 m – ✉ 24800

Dordogne-Berry-Limousin 4 **C1**

Paris 449 – Brive-la-Gaillarde 81 – Limoges 62 – Périgueux 34 – St-Yrieix-la-Perche 32

Office de tourisme, place du Marechal Foch ☎ 05 53 55 12 50, Fax 05 53 55 12 50

De France et de Russie without rest VISA

51 r. Gén. Lamy – ☎ 05 53 55 17 80 – info@thiviers-hotel.com – Fax 05 53 55 01 42

10 rm – †€ 50/60 ††€ 60/70, ☕ € 7

♦ The name of this 18C residence recalls Thiviers' love of Russia, and the famous foie gras that was so appreciated by the tsar's court. Simply furbished rooms.

THIZY – 69 Rhône – 327 E3 – pop. 2 483 – alt. 553 m – ✉ 69240

44 **A1**

Paris 414 – Lyon 65 – Montbrison 74 – Roanne 22

Office de tourisme, rue Eugène Dechavanne ☎ 04 74 64 35 23

La Terrasse rm, VISA

Le bourg Marnand, 2 km north-east on D 94 – ☎ 04 74 64 19 22 – francis.arnette@wanadoo.fr – Fax 04 74 64 25 95 – Closed autumn half-term holidays, February school holidays and Sunday dinner except in summer

10 rm – †€ 40 ††€ 46, ☕ € 6 – ½ P € 41 – **Rest** – *(closed Sunday dinner and Monday except in summer)* Menu € 15 (weekdays)/42 – Carte € 37/63

♦ An old textile factory converted into a hotel. The pretty rooms opening onto the garden are named after herbs and are decorated, even fragranced, according to this theme. Modern dining room and lovely terrace facing the Lyon mountains.

THOIRY – 01 Ain – **328** I3 – **pop. 4 063** – **alt. 500 m** – ✉ **01710** 45 **C1**

Paris 523 – Bellegarde-sur-Valserine 27 – Bourg-en-Bresse 99 – Gex 13

Holiday Inn

av. Mont-Blanc – ✆ 04 50 99 19 99 – hi.geneve@wanadoo.fr – Fax 04 50 42 27 40
95 rm – †€ 80/300 ††€ 90/320, ☕ € 14 – **Rest** – *(closed Sat. lunchtime and Sun. lunchtime)* Menu € 19/29 – Carte € 29/39
◆ This hotel, next to the Swiss border and Geneva airport, is somewhat outdated but well maintained. An ideal stopover for international business travellers. Comfortable, light-wood dining room, quick set menus, buffets and theme weeks.

Les Cépages (Jean-Pierre Delesderrier)

– ✆ 04 50 20 83 85 – Fax 04 50 41 24 58
– Closed in March, in October, Sunday dinner, Monday and Tuesday
Rest – *(pre-book)* Menu € 30 (weekday lunch), € 48/146 bi – Carte € 60/87
Spec. Raviole de foie gras de canard. Nage de homard juste saisi, sauce aux arômes d'Asie. Pigeonneau de l'Ain rôti, laqué au banyuls. **Wines** Pinot gris du Bugey, Manicle.
◆ Classic cuisine prepared with care and served in the elegant contemporary dining room or on the terrace overlooking the flower garden. Good choice of vintage wines.

THOLLON-LES-MÉMISES – 74 Haute-Savoie – **328** N2 – **pop. 593** – **alt. 920 m** – **Winter sports : 1 000/2 000 m** 1 18 – ✉ **74500** French Alps 46 **F1**

Paris 588 – Annecy 95 – Évian-les-Bains 11 – Thonon-les-Bains 21
Office de tourisme, station ✆ 04 50 70 90 01, Fax 04 50 70 92 80
Pic de Mémise ✳★★ 30 mn.

Bellevue

– ✆ 04 50 70 92 79 – hotelbellevuethollon@wanadoo.fr – Fax 04 50 70 97 63
– Open 1st May-mid October and mid December-30 March
35 rm – †€ 46/59 ††€ 52/100, ☕ € 8,50 – ½ P € 50/55
Rest – *(closed Thursday off season)* Menu € 17/31 – Carte € 27/50
◆ Large chalet on the hillside of the "Balcon du Léman". Functional and well-kept rooms, some for families. Sauna and jacuzzi. The terrace of this Savoyard restaurant commands a fine view of the village; traditional dishes.

THONES – 74 Haute-Savoie – **328** K5 – **pop. 5 212** – **alt. 650 m** – ✉ **74230** French Alps 46 **F1**

Paris 560 – Lyon 171 – Annecy 21 – Genève 59 – Chambéry 73
Office de tourisme, place Avet ✆ 04 50 02 00 26, Fax 04 50 02 11 87

Le Clos Zénon

rte de Bellossier – ✆ 04 50 02 10 86 – hotel@thones-chalet-hotel.com
– Fax 04 50 02 10 86 – Open 1st April-18 December
6 rm ☕ – †€ 50/55 ††€ 62/82 – ½ P € 55/67 – **Table d'hôte** – Menu € 30
◆ A good address for nature lovers. A recently built chalet in a mountain setting with pool, pleasant welcome and snug rooms. Savoie inspired meals served in a warm dining room with fine fireplace.

in La Balme-de-Thuy 2,5 km Southwest by D 909 and secondary road – **pop. 360** – **alt. 623 m** – ✉ **74230**

Le Paddock des Aravis without rest

Les Chenalettes, towards Sappey – ✆ 04 50 02 98 28 – nathalie@le-paddock-des-aravis.com – Fax 04 50 02 94 52
5 rm ☕ – †€ 80/105 ††€ 85/110
◆ Beautiful view of the Tournette from this farm's isolated vantage point. The light-wood interior, neutral tones and the comfortable rooms are all refined but cosy.

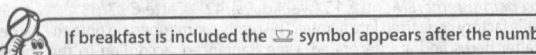

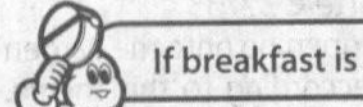
If breakfast is included the ☕ symbol appears after the number of rooms.

THONON-LES-BAINS – 74 Haute-Savoie – 328 L2 – pop. 28 927 – alt. 431 m – Spa : early April-early Dec. – ✉ 74200 French Alps 46 F1

- Paris 568 – Annecy 75 – Chamonix-Mont-Blanc 99 – Genève 34
- Office de tourisme, place du Marché ✆ 04 50 71 55 55, Fax 04 50 26 68 33
- Évian Masters Golf Club Évian-les-Bains Rive Sud du Lac de Genève, by Évian road: 8 km, ✆ 04 50 75 46 66.
- Viewpoints on Lake Geneva★★ ABY - Vaults★ of St-Hippolyte church - Domaine de Ripaille★ North: 2 km.

Arc en Ciel without rest

18 pl. Crête – ✆ 04 50 71 90 63 – info@hotel-arcenciel.com – Fax 04 50 26 27 47 – Closed 25 April-6 May and 19 December-6 January BZ **k**

40 rm – †€ 54/69 ††€ 62/79, ☕ € 7,50

◆ Near the town centre, a modern hotel with a garden and pool. Spacious and well-equipped rooms with balcony or terrace; some have a small kitchen.

THONON-LES-BAINS

Allobroges (Av. des) . . . . BZ 2
Arts (R. des) . . . . BZ 3
Bordeaux (Pl. Henry) . . . . . AY 4
Grande-Rue . . . . AYZ
Granges (R. des) . . . . BY 5
Léman (Av. du) . . . . BY 6
Michaud (R.) . . . . AY 10
Moulin (Pl. Jean) . . . . AY 12
Ratte (Ch.de la) . . . . BZ 13
Trolliettes (Bd des) . . . . AZ 15
Ursules (R. des) . . . . BY 16
Vallées (Av. des) . . . . BZ 18

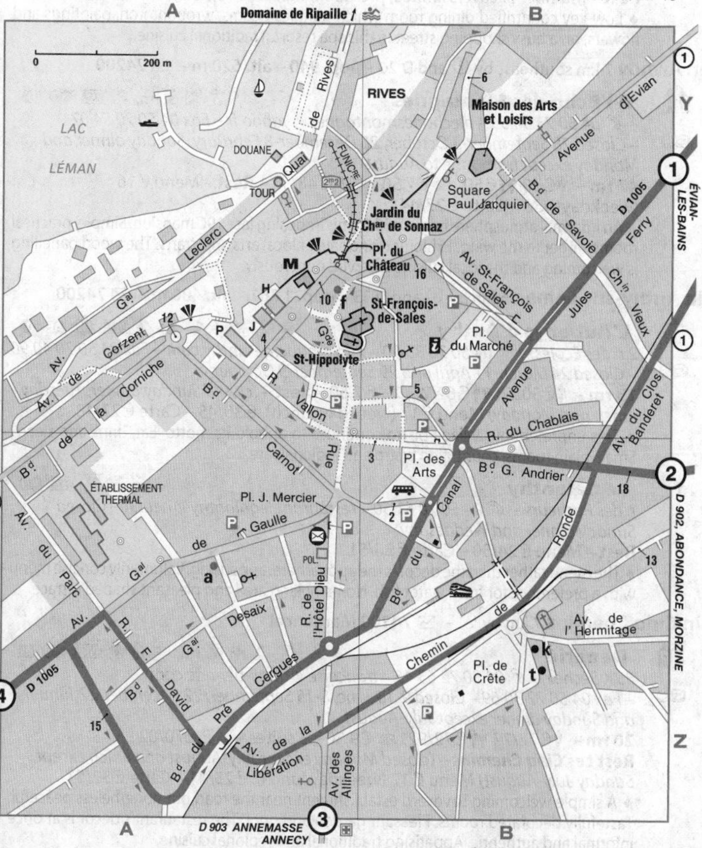

À l'Ombre des Marronniers VISA AE
17 pl. Crête – ✆ 04 50 71 26 18 – info@hotel-marroniers.com – Fax 04 50 26 27 47 – Closed 25 April-6 May and 20 December-5 January BZ **t**
17 rm – €45/54 €50/62, €6,50 – ½ P €45/52
Rest – *(closed 25 April-6 May, 20 December-17 January, Sunday dinner and Monday 15 November-21 May)* Menu €13 (weekdays)/32 – Carte €25/49
◆ The rooms in this hotel-chalet may be a little antiquated but are nonetheless practical. Dining room-veranda and terrace shaded by chestnut trees; traditional and regional food.

Le Prieuré (Charles Plumex) VISA AE
68 Gde rue – ✆ 04 50 71 31 89 – plumex-prieuré@wanadoo.fr – Fax 04 50 71 31 09 – Closed 3-18 March, 10-25 November, Sunday dinner, Monday and Tuesday AY **f**
Rest – Menu €38/80 – Carte €69/105
Spec. Grosses langoustines en croustillant de tartiffle. Filets de perche à la manière des "Gens-d'en-Haut", rôtis au jus de viande. Ris de veau caramélisé, jus de veau réduit. **Wines** Ripaille, Chignin-Bergeron.
◆ Standing at the entrance to an old mansion, a vaulted restaurant with woodwork and modern paintings. Carefully prepared and generously served inventive cuisine.

Les Alpes VISA AE
3 bis r. des Italiens – ✆ 04 50 26 51 24 – restaurant.lesalpes@club-internet.fr – Fax 04 50 26 51 24 – Closed 15 July-13 August, Sunday dinner and Wednesday AZ **a**
Rest – *(number of covers limited, pre-book)* Menu (€18), €23/55 – Carte €41/52
◆ Low-key countrified dining room which mingles beams, wrought iron, paintings and flowers, on a busy shopping street in this spa resort. Traditional cuisine.

in Armoy 7 km southeast by ② and D 26 – pop. 940 – alt. 620 m – ✉ 74200

À l'Écho des Montagnes rm, P VISA
– ✆ 04 50 73 94 55 – alechodesmontagnes@yahoo.fr – Fax 04 50 70 54 07 – Closed 28 September-3 October, 20 December-8 February, Sunday dinner and Monday except from June to August
47 rm – €30 €50, €7,50 – ½ P €48/52 – **Rest** – Menu €16 (weekdays)/38 – Carte €27/44
◆ An informal atmosphere reigns within this imposing late 19C mansion. Simple, practical rooms, larger in the wing. Exhibition and sale of local arts and crafts. The wood panelling is welcoming and the local cuisine is served generously.

in Anthy-sur-Léman 6 km by ④ and D 33 – pop. 1 767 – alt. 400 m – ✉ 74200

L'Auberge d'Anthy VISA AE
2 r. des Écoles – ✆ 04 50 70 35 00 – info@auberge-anthy.com – Fax 04 50 70 40 90 – Closed 24 March-11 April and 29 September-9 October
13 rm – €50/64 €62/75, €7,50 – **Rest** – *(closed Sunday dinner, Tuesday lunch and Monday)* Menu €17 (weekday lunch), €30/45 – Carte €27/48
◆ This unpretentious village bistro continues to uphold its motto 'Eat, drink and sleep'. Small, plain rooms, countrified bistro and regional fare.

Le Galanthy P VISA
r. des Pêcheurs – ✆ 04 50 70 61 50 – restaurant.legalanthy@neuf.fr – Closed Sunday dinner and Wednesday
Rest – Menu €24/50 – Carte €36/51
◆ The menu rather than the decor is the appeal here: appetising, voluntarily concise menu with a preference for fresh water fish. Non-smoking area and pleasant shaded terrace.

in Cinq Chemins 7 km by ④ – ✉ 74200 Margencel

Denarié AC rm, P VISA AE
25 r. Séchex – ✆ 04 50 72 63 45 – francoise@hotel-denarie.com – Fax 04 50 72 30 69 – Closed 9-16 June, 8-15 September, 22 December-22 January and Sunday dinner except July-August
20 rm – €72/77 €72/92, €9,50 – 3 suites – ½ P €70/82
Rest *Les Cinq Chemins* – *(closed Monday except July-August and lunch except Sunday July-August)* Menu €17 (weekday lunch), €25/41 – Carte €32/51
◆ A simple welcoming Savoyard establishment near the road but nonetheless peaceful. Tastefully decorated rooms. Pleasant garden and pool. The restaurant's decor is at once informal and authentic. Appetising traditional and regional cuisine.

in Port-de-Séchex 7 km by ④ – ✉ 74200

Le Clos du Lac
Port de Séchex – ✆ 04 50 72 48 81 – le-clos-du-lac@wanadoo.fr – Fax 04 50 72 48 81 – Closed 1st-10 July, 1st-10 October, 5-29 January, Sunday dinner and Monday
Rest – Menu (€ 20), € 27/58 – Carte € 44/63
♦ In this restored farmhouse, the old stone mangers happily rub shoulders with contemporary decor and artwork. Faultlessly prepared menu designed to suit current tastes.

in Bonnatrait 9 km by ④ – ✉ **74140 Sciez**

Hôtellerie Château de Coudrée
– ✆ 04 50 72 62 33 – chcoudree@coudree.com – Fax 04 50 72 57 28 – Closed 28 October-3 December
19 rm – €138/346 €138/346, € 18 – **Rest** – *(closed lunch weekdays December-April, Tuesday and Wednesday except July-August)*
Menu € 41 (weekday lunch), € 60/80 – Carte € 77/89
♦ This château on the edge of the lake is an imposing reminder of the Middle Ages. Rooms, individually furnished with old-style decor, include an unusual one in the dungeon. Dignified dining room (wainscoting, tapestries, fireplace) and contemporary menu.

THORÉ-LA-ROCHETTE – 41 Loir-et-Cher – 318 C5 – pop. 883 – alt. 75 m – ✉ 41100

11 **B2**

Paris 176 – Blois 42 – La Flèche 94 – Le Mans 72 – Vendôme 9

Du Pont
15 r. du Mar. de Rochambeau – ✆ 02 54 72 80 62 – Fax 02 54 72 70 95 – Closed 16 August-5 September, 19 January-11 February, Tuesday dinner and Monday
Rest – Menu € 20/48 – Carte € 34/51
♦ Regional wines and cuisine are served in this simple little restaurant close to where the Loir-Valley tourist train stops.

THORENC – 06 Alpes-Maritimes – 341 B5 – alt. 1 250 m – ✉ 06750 Andon

41 **C2**

Paris 832 – Castellane 35 – Draguignan 64 – Grasse 40 – Nice 58 – Vence 41

Col de Bleine ≤★★ Nprth: 4 km, **French Alps**

Auberge Les Merisiers with rm
24 av. Belvédère – ✆ 04 93 60 00 23 – info@aubergelesmerisiers.com – Fax 04 93 60 02 17 – Closed 10 March-4 April, Monday dinner and Tuesday except school holidays
12 rm – €45 €45, € 10 – ½ P € 48 – **Rest** – Menu (€ 20), € 25/32 – Carte € 25/40
♦ Practical for a stop on the way up through the Bleine Pass, this little mountain inn serves regional cuisine in a simple rustic interior. Well-kept small rooms.

LE THORONET – 83 Var – 340 M5 – pop. 1 533 – alt. 120 m – ✉ 83340

41 **C3**

Paris 831 – Brignoles 24 – Draguignan 21 – St-Raphaël 51 – Toulon 62

Office de tourisme, boulevard du 17 août 1944 ✆ 04 94 60 10 94

Thoronet abbey★★ West: 4.5 km, **French Riviera**

Hostellerie de l'Abbaye rm, rm,
chemin du Château – ✆ 04 94 73 88 81 – info@hotelthoronet.fr – Fax 04 94 73 89 24 – Closed 15 December-3 February
23 rm – €56/73 €56/73, € 8 – ½ P € 55/64 – **Rest** – *(closed Sunday dinner and Monday from November to March)* Menu € 21 (weekdays)/39 – Carte € 33/52
♦ Close to the oldest Cistercian abbey in Provence, a modern building around a pool. Practical rooms. Brightly coloured restaurant and covered terrace. Wine list favouring local vintages.

THOUARCÉ – 49 Maine-et-Loire – 317 G5 – pop. 1 682 – alt. 35 m – ✉ 49380

35 **C2**

Paris 318 – Angers 29 – Cholet 43 – Saumur 38

Syndicat d'initiative, Mairie ✆ 02 41 54 14 36, Fax 02 41 54 09 11

★★ de Brissac-Quincé, Northeast: 12 km, Châteaux of the Loire

XX **Le Relais de Bonnezeaux** VISA AE

1 km Angers road – ✆ 02 41 54 08 33 – relais.bonnezeaux@wanadoo.fr – Fax 02 41 54 00 63 – Closed 26 December-20 January, Tuesday dinner, Sunday dinner and Monday

Rest – Menu € 26 (weekdays)/56 bi – Carte € 28/47

◆ Restaurant along the Wine Route, situated in a former country station. The tables on the veranda have views of the vineyards. Traditional cuisine and local wines served.

THOUARS – 79 Deux-Sèvres – 322 E3 – pop. 10 656 – alt. 102 m – ✉ 79100

Atlantic Coast

38 **B1**

Paris 336 – Angers 71 – Bressuire 31 – Châtellerault 72 – Cholet 56

Office de tourisme, 3 bis, boulevard Pierre Curie ✆ 05 49 66 17 65, Fax 05 49 67 87 58

Façade★★ of St-Médard church ★ - Site★ - Old houses★.

Hôtellerie St-Jean rest, VISA AE

25 rte de Parthenay – ✆ 05 49 96 12 60 – hotellerie-st-jean@wanadoo.fr – Fax 05 49 96 34 02 – Closed February school holidays and Sunday dinner

18 rm – €40 €40/45, € 6 – ½ P € 40/43

Rest – Menu € 16 (weekdays)/46 – Carte € 41/59

◆ A 1970s building overlooking the old town. Well-kept rooms with a refreshing decor in yellow and orange shades. Those at the back are quieter. A simple but cheerful dining room serving classic cuisine.

Du Relais without rest VISA AE

3 km north on Saumur road – ✆ 05 49 66 29 45 – Fax 05 49 66 29 33

15 rm – €37 €37, € 5

◆ In the industrial area, a large villa with comfortable inviting rooms on three floors. Pleasant veranda serving breakfasts on the mezzanine.

THOURON – 87 Haute-Vienne – 325 E5 – pop. 427 – alt. 374 m – ✉ 87140

24 **B1**

Paris 380 – Bellac 23 – Guéret 79 – Limoges 28

La Pomme de Pin rest, rm, VISA

étang de Tricherie, 2,5 km north-eastward along the D 225 – ✆ 05 55 53 43 43 – Fax 05 55 53 35 33 – Closed 1st-30 September, 26 January-12 February, Tuesday lunch and Monday

7 rm – €60 €70, € 7 – ½ P € 55

Rest – Menu € 19/28 – Carte € 33/53

◆ Comfortable guestrooms occupy some of the stone buildings of this attractive complex, which is also home to a watermill fed by a small stream and a shady garden. Rustic dining room lit by a hearth where the chef grills Limousin beef over a wood fire.

THURET – 63 Puy-de-Dôme – 326 G7 – pop. 703 – alt. 330 m – ✉ 63260

5 **B2**

Paris 379 – Clermont-Ferrand 32 – Vichy 24 – Cournon-d'Auvergne 35 – Riom 16

Château de la Canière rest, VISA AE

2 km au Nord par D 212 et D 12 – ✆ 04 73 97 98 44 – info@caniere.com – Fax 04 73 97 98 42

45 rm – €125/139 €145/325, € 14,50 – 2 suites

Rest *Lavoisier* – Menu € 28/85 – Carte € 63/90

◆ An intelligently renovated 19C castle, most of whose rooms sport an Empire style. Pool, wooded park and formal gardens: a haven of peace and quiet. Creativity meets science in the restaurant devoted to Lavoisier, an 18C scientist.

THURY – 21 Côte-d'Or – **320** H7 – **pop. 297** – **alt. 382 m** – ✉ **21340** 8 **C2**

▶ Paris 303 – Beaune 33 – Autun 25 – Avallon 80 – Dijon 71

Manoir Bonpassage VISA

1 km south on D 36 and secondary road – ✆ 03 80 20 26 16 – bonpassage@wanadoo.fr – Fax 03 80 20 26 17 – Open 1st April-31 October
9 rm – €59/80 €59/80, ☕ €8,50 – **Rest** – *(closed Sunday, Tuesday and Thursday) (dinner only) (residents only)* Menu €23
◆ Former farmhouse offering simple rooms, some overlooking the countryside (one is more recent and comfortable). Swimming pool in summer, peace and quiet, guesthouse ambiance.

THURY-HARCOURT – 14 Calvados – **303** J6 – **pop. 1 825** – **alt. 45 m** – ✉ **14220**
Normandy 32 **B2**

▶ Paris 257 – Caen 28 – Condé-sur-Noireau 20 – Falaise 27 – Flers 32 – St-Lô 68 – Vire 41

Office de tourisme, 2, place Saint-Sauveur ✆ 02 31 79 70 45, Fax 02 31 79 15 42

Château park and gardens★ - Boucle du Hom★ Northwest: 3 km.

Le Relais de la Poste with rm VISA AE

7 r. de Caen – ✆ 02 31 79 72 12 – relaisdelaposte@ohotellerie.com – Fax 02 31 39 53 55 – Closed March and 20-31 December
10 rm – €64 €64, ☕ €11 – ½ P €67/105
Rest – *(closed Saturday lunch October-May and Friday except lunch May-October)* Menu €22 (weekday lunch), €27/47 – Carte €44/58
◆ A former coaching inn facing a courtyard and garden filled with flowers in spring and summer. Traditional cuisine, good wine list and small, renovated guestrooms.

We try to be as accurate as possible when giving room rates. But prices are open to change, so please check rates when booking.

TIERCÉ – 49 Maine-et-Loire – **317** G3 – **pop. 3 605** – **alt. 30 m** – ✉ **49125** 35 **C2**

▶ Paris 278 – Angers 22 – Château-Gontier 34 – La Flèche 34

Syndicat d'initiative, Mairie ✆ 02 41 31 14 41, Fax 02 41 34 14 41

La Table d'Anjou VISA AE

16 r. Anjou – ✆ 02 41 42 14 42 – latabledanjou@club-internet.fr – Fax 02 41 42 64 80 – Closed 21 July-13 August, 5-15 January, Tuesday dinner off season, Wednesday dinner, Sunday dinner and Monday
Rest – Menu €19 (weekday lunch), €25/72 – Carte €40/79
◆ Friendly restaurant in the centre of the village with two bright neo-rustic dining rooms and a small flower-decked terrace at the back. Pleasant service.

TIFFAUGES – 85 Vendée – **316** J5 – **pop. 1 328** – **alt. 77 m** – ✉ **85130**
Atlantic Coast 34 **B3**

▶ Paris 374 – Angers 85 – Cholet 20 – Clisson 19 – La Roche-sur-Yon 56 – Nantes 53

Manoir de la Barbacane without rest VISA AE

pl. de l'Église – ✆ 02 51 65 75 59 – manoir@hotel-barbacane.com – Fax 02 51 65 71 91
16 rm – €62/95 €65/105, ☕ €11 – 3 suites
◆ A 19C manor house near the Château de Barbe-Bleu. Ask for one of the more spacious rooms on the first floor, or one of the new rooms decorated in contemporary style. Attractive winter garden.

TIGNES – 73 Savoie – 333 O5 – pop. 2 220 – alt. 2 100 m – Winter sports : 1 550/3 450 m 4 44 – ✉ 73320 French Alps 45 **D2**

Paris 665 – Albertville 85 – Bourg-St-Maurice 31 – Chambéry 134 – Val-d'Isère 14

Office de tourisme, Tignes Accueil ✆ 04 79 40 04 40, Fax 04 79 40 03 15

du Lac de Tignes Le Val Claret, South: 2 km, ✆ 04 79 06 37 42.

Site★★ - Dam★★ Northeast: 5 km - Panorama of la Grande Motte★★ Southwest.

Les Suites du Montana

rm, rest, VISA MC AE D

Les Almes – ✆ 04 79 40 01 44 – contact@vmontana.com – Fax 04 79 40 04 03 – Open December-end April

19 rm – †€ 105/203 ††€ 160/306, ☕ € 12 – 9 suites – ½ P € 195/265

Rest – *(dinner only)* Menu € 47/59

♦ A "hamlet" of chalets with spacious and refined suites, decorated in Savoyard, Austrian or Provençal style, equipped with balconies facing directly south and private saunas. Spit roasting before your eyes at the 'all-wood' rotisserie with view of the slopes.

Les Campanules

rest, VISA MC AE

– ✆ 04 79 06 34 36 – campanules@wanadoo.fr – Fax 04 79 06 35 78 – Open 8 July-26 August and 11 November-2 May

31 rm – †€ 100/190 ††€ 120/220, ☕ € 18 – 16 suites – ½ P € 110/165

Rest – Menu € 27 (lunch), € 38/50 – Carte € 50/65

♦ In the centre of the resort, a pretty chalet with spacious and comfortable rooms, duplex apartments on top floor. Panoramic gym. The fresco decorating the walls of the restaurant recalls the old village that was sunk with the construction of the Tignes Dam in 1952.

Village Montana

rest, VISA MC AE D

Les Almes – ✆ 04 79 40 01 44 – contact@vmontana.com – Fax 04 79 40 04 03 – Open end June-mid September and beg. November-beg. May

78 rm – †€ 105/203 ††€ 160/306, ☕ € 12 – 4 suites – ½ P € 97/170

Rest – Menu € 25 – Carte € 23/35

Rest *La Chaumière* – *(open beg. December-beg. May)* Menu € 19 (lunch)/35 – Carte € 19/34

♦ These splendid chalets combine tradition, modern comforts and peace and quiet in spacious family rooms facing the ski area. A mountain atmosphere, panoramic terrace and regional specialities: the Chaumière truly honours the Savoy region.

Le Lévanna

rm, VISA MC AE

– ✆ 04 79 06 32 94 – info@levanna.com – Fax 04 79 06 33 18 – Open 2 October-9 May

40 rm – †€ 90/153 ††€ 160/294, ☕ € 18 – ½ P € 125/162

Rest – Menu € 35/105 – Carte € 36/55

♦ This large, new chalet situated in the heart of the resort has rooms with wood panelling and balconies with a view. Jacuzzi, sauna, hammam. Stop for a meal in this mountain-style dining room or on the terrace that enables you to watch the skiers' ballet.

Le Refuge without rest

VISA MC AE D

– ✆ 04 79 06 36 64 – info@hotel-refuge-tignes.com – Fax 04 79 06 33 78 – Closed 8 May-1st July and 8 September-18 October

33 rm ☕ – †€ 61/112 ††€ 95/171

♦ Attractive, renovated chalet only 50 metres from the ski lifts and overlooking the lake. Rooms with south-facing balconies. Top floor lounge with billiards. Fitness area, terrace.

L'Arbina

VISA MC AE

– ✆ 04 79 06 34 78 – hotelarbina@aol.com – Fax 04 79 06 32 99 – Open 8 July-4 September and 16 October-9 May

22 rm – †€ 42/57 ††€ 72/120, ☕ € 12 – ½ P € 76/98

Rest – *(open 16 November-9 May)* Menu € 27 (weekdays)/80 – Carte € 35/63

♦ This family-run hotel located at the bottom of the slopes has rooms decorated in a contemporary mountain style. Terraces face the Grande Motte glacier. Restaurant on the first floor with a hint of Provence offering a traditional menu.

Gentiana rest, VISA AE
– 04 79 06 52 46 – serge.revial@wanadoo.fr – Fax 04 79 06 35 61
– *Open 1st July-25 August and 1st December-4 May*
40 rm – €73/93 €112/172, €16 – ½ P €78/120
Rest – *(dinner only)* Menu €28/45
◆ This family hotel has been renovated with wood and well-chosen fabrics in the rooms some of which have balconies. Cosy lounge and bar. Classic cuisine and Savoyard dishes served in an interior of wood and warm colours.

Le Paquis VISA
Le Rosset – 04 79 06 37 33 – info@hotel-lepaquis.fr – Fax 04 79 06 36 59

– *Closed May* – **36 rm** (½ board only) – ½ P €66/110
Rest – *(open October-April)* Menu €14 (lunch), €20/58 – Carte €37/48
◆ On the heights overlooking Tignes, a robust 1960s building offering functional rooms. Choose one of the more recent, renovated in a chalet style. Taste traditional Savoyard cuisine in the alpine setting of the dining room.

La Ferme des 3 Capucines P VISA
Le Lavachet – 04 79 06 35 10 – Fax 04 79 06 35 10 – *Open 8 July-28 August and 8 December-5 May*
Rest – *(pre-book)* Menu €23 (lunch)/29 – Carte €23/36
◆ This friendly Savoyard dairy farm happily combines a fireplace, beams and old objects with tasty regional specialities prepared with home produce.

in Val Claret **2 km southwest – alt. 2 100 m – ✉ 73320 Tignes**

Le Ski d'Or P VISA AE
– 04 79 06 51 60 – pbg@hotel-skidor.com – Fax 04 79 06 45 49
– *Open 1st December-2 May*
27 rm – €117/182 €180/280, €20 – ½ P €115/215
Rest – *(dinner only)* Menu €39 – Carte €41/57
◆ A 1960s building near the funicular. The comfortable contemporary rooms have all been renovated and command fine views of the slopes. Refined modern cuisine and a direct view of the kitchens from the pleasant dining room.

TILQUES – 62 Pas-de-Calais – 301 G3 – see St-Omer

LES TINES – 74 Haute-Savoie – 328 O5 – see Chamonix-Mont-Blanc

TONNEINS – 47 Lot-et-Garonne – 336 D3 – pop. 9 041 – alt. 26 m – ✉ 47400

Paris 683 – Agen 44 – Nérac 38 – Villeneuve-sur-Lot 37 4 **C2**
Office de tourisme, 3, avenue Charles-de-Gaulle 05 53 79 22 79, Fax 05 53 79 39 94
de Barthe Tombebœuf Route de Villeneuve, Northeast: 20 km by D 120, 05 53 88 83 31.

Des Fleurs without rest P VISA
rte de Marmande – 05 53 79 10 47 – hoteldesfleurs@wanadoo.fr
– Fax 05 53 79 46 37 – *Closed 23-31 December, 25 February-4 March*
26 rm – €37/57 €37/60, €7
◆ An establishment on the town's main street. The rooms are rather small but practical, colourful, well-equipped, set back from the street and are gradually being renovated.

TONNERRE – 89 Yonne – 319 G4 – pop. 5 979 – alt. 156 m – ✉ 89700
Burgundy-Jura 7 **B1**

Paris 199 – Auxerre 38 – Châtillon-sur-Seine 49 – Montbard 45 – Troyes 60
Office de tourisme, place Marguerite de Bourgogne 03 86 55 14 48, Fax 03 86 54 41 82
de Tanlay Tanlay Parc du Château, by Châtillon-s-Seine road: 9 km, 03 86 75 72 92.
Fosse Dionne★ - Interior★ of the former hospital: burial★ - Château de Tanlay★★ 9 km by ①.

L'Auberge de Bourgogne
2 km on D 944 and Dijon road – ✆ 03 86 54 41 41
– auberge.bourgogne@wanadoo.fr – Fax 03 86 54 48 28
– Closed 15 December-15 January
39 rm – †€ 54/58 ††€ 58, ☕ € 8 – ½ P € 52
Rest – *(closed Saturday lunch and Sunday)* Menu € 17/24 – Carte € 29/34
◆ A modern building bordering the Epineuil vineyards. Rooms are soberly functional and those at the rear offer a fine view of the countryside. Boeuf Bourguignon takes pride of place on the menu. Bright and spacious restaurant.

TORCY – 71 Saône-et-Loire – **320** G9 – see le Creusot

TORNAC – 30 Gard – **339** I4 – see Anduze

TÔTES – 76 Seine-Maritime – **304** G3 – **pop. 1 084** – **alt. 150 m** – ✉ **76890** 33 **D1**

Paris 168 – Dieppe 34 – Fécamp 60 – Le Havre 80 – Rouen 37

Auberge du Cygne
5 r. G. de Maupassant – ✆ 02 35 32 92 03 – Fax 02 35 32 92 03
– Closed Sunday dinner, Monday dinner and Thursday 16 September-14 February
Rest – Menu € 28/44 – Carte € 39/60
◆ This post-house, founded in 1611, houses a very fine, typical country-style dining room, with its original, exposed beams, monumental fireplace and collection of earthenware.

TOUL – 54 Meurthe-et-Moselle – **307** G6 – **pop. 16 945** – **alt. 209 m** – ✉ **54200** 26 **B2**
Alsace-Lorraine

Paris 291 – Bar-le-Duc 62 – Metz 75 – Nancy 23 – St-Dizier 78 – Verdun 80

Office de tourisme, parvis de la Cathédrale ✆ 03 83 64 11 69, Fax 03 83 63 24 37

St-Étienne cathedral ★★ and cloister★ - St-Gengoult church: cloister★★ - Façade★ of the former bishop's palace **H** - Musée municipal★: salle des malades (patients hall)★ **M.**

Plan on next page

L'Europe without rest
373 av. V. Hugo, (near the station) – ✆ 03 83 43 00 10
– hoteldeleurope.toul@wanadoo.fr – Fax 03 83 63 27 67
– Closed 10-24 August AY **s**
21 rm – †€ 47/50 ††€ 47/58, ☕ € 12
◆ A convenient hotel when travelling by train. The ground floor still has a retro atmosphere. The well-kept rooms have all been renovated. Family hospitality.

La Villa Lorraine without rest
15 r. Gambetta – ✆ 03 83 43 08 95
– hotel.villalorraine@wanadoo.fr – Fax 03 83 64 63 64
– Closed autumn half-term holidays AZ **a**
21 rm – †€ 42 ††€ 47, ☕ € 6,50
◆ Small family-run hotel in the heart of the fortified town. Rooms are furnished in a rustic style and well soundproofed. Attractively laid out breakfast room.

in Lucey 5 km by ⑤ and D 908 – **pop. 579** – **alt. 260 m** – ✉ **54200**

Auberge du Pressoir
7 pl. des Pachenottes – ✆ 03 83 63 81 91 – Fax 03 83 63 81 38
– Closed 16 August-3 September, 9-25 December, 22-28 February, Sunday dinner, Wednesday dinner and Monday
Rest – Menu € 13 (weekdays)/30
◆ The old village station has become a restaurant with a renovated simple decor. Some regional country ornaments decorate the walls. Sunny terrace.

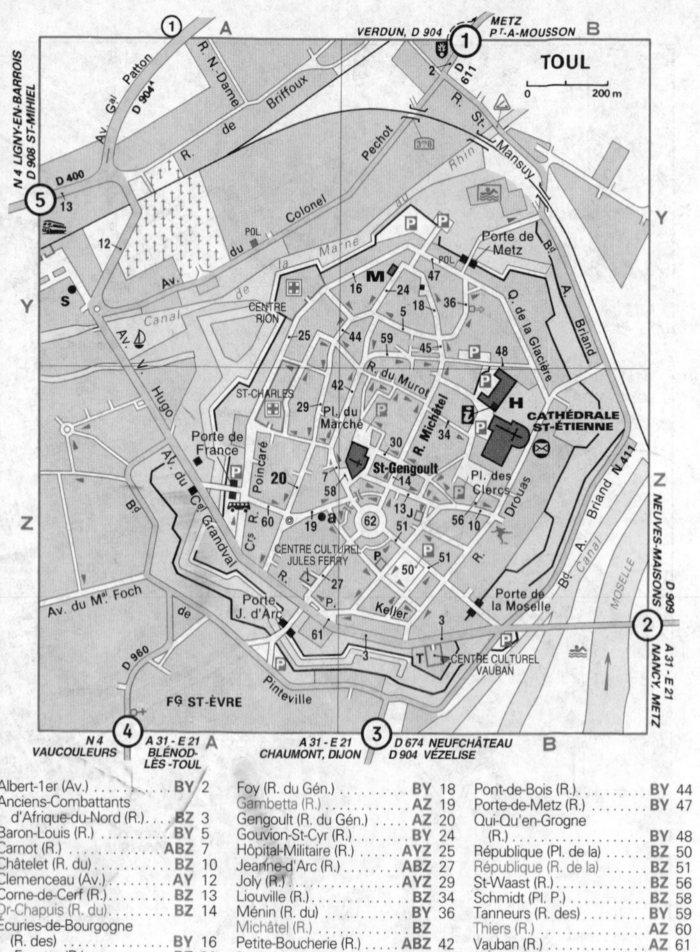

Albert-1er (Av.) .... BY 2	Foy (R. du Gén.) .... BY 18	Pont-de-Bois (R.) .... BY 44
Anciens-Combattants d'Afrique-du-Nord (R.) .... BZ 3	Gambetta (R.) .... AZ 19	Porte-de-Metz (R.) .... BY 47
Baron-Louis (R.) .... BY 5	Gengoult (R. du Gén.) ..... AZ 20	Qui-Qu'en-Grogne (R.) .... BY 48
Carnot (R.) .... ABZ 7	Gouvion-St-Cyr (R.) .... BY 24	République (Pl. de la) ...... BZ 50
Châtelet (R. du) .... BZ 10	Hôpital-Militaire (R.) ...... AYZ 25	République (R. de la) ...... BZ 51
Clemenceau (Av.) .... AY 12	Jeanne-d'Arc (R.) .... ABZ 27	St-Waast (R.) .... BZ 56
Corne-de-Cerf (R.) .... BZ 13	Joly (R.) .... AYZ 29	Schmidt (Pl. P.) .... BZ 58
Dr-Chapuis (R. du) .... BZ 14	Liouville (R.) .... BZ 34	Tanneurs (R. des) .... BY 59
Écuries-de-Bourgogne (R. des) .... BY 16	Ménin (R. du) .... BY 36	Thiers (R.) .... AZ 60
La-Fayette (R.) .... BZ 30	Michâtel (R.) .... BZ	Vauban (R.) .... AZ 61
	Petite-Boucherie (R.) ..... ABZ 42	3-Évêchés (Pl. des) .... BZ 62
	Pont-des-Cordeliers (R.) .... BY 45	

TOULON Ⓟ – **83 Var** – **340** K7 – **pop. 160 639** – **Built-up area 519 640** – **alt. 10 m** – ✉ **83000** French Riviera 41 **C3**

- Paris 835 – Aix-en-Provence 86 – Marseille 66
- Toulon-Hyères: ✆ 0 825 01 83 87, by ①: 21 km.
- ✆ 3635 (0,34 €/mn)
- For Corsica: SNCM (April-October) 49 av. Infanterie de Marine ✆ 3260 say "SNCM" (0.15 €/mn).
- Office de tourisme, place Raimu ✆ 04 94 18 53 00, Fax 04 94 18 53 09
- de Valgarde La Garde Chemin de Rabasson, East: 10 km by D 29, ✆ 04 94 14 01 05.
- Harbour★★ - Port★ - Old town★ GYZ: Atlantes statues★ of the mairie d'honneur **F**, Musée de la marine★ - Porte★ de la Corderie.
- Corniche du Mont Facon ⋞★ of the cable car - Memorial museum of the Provence Landing★ and ⋞★★★ North.

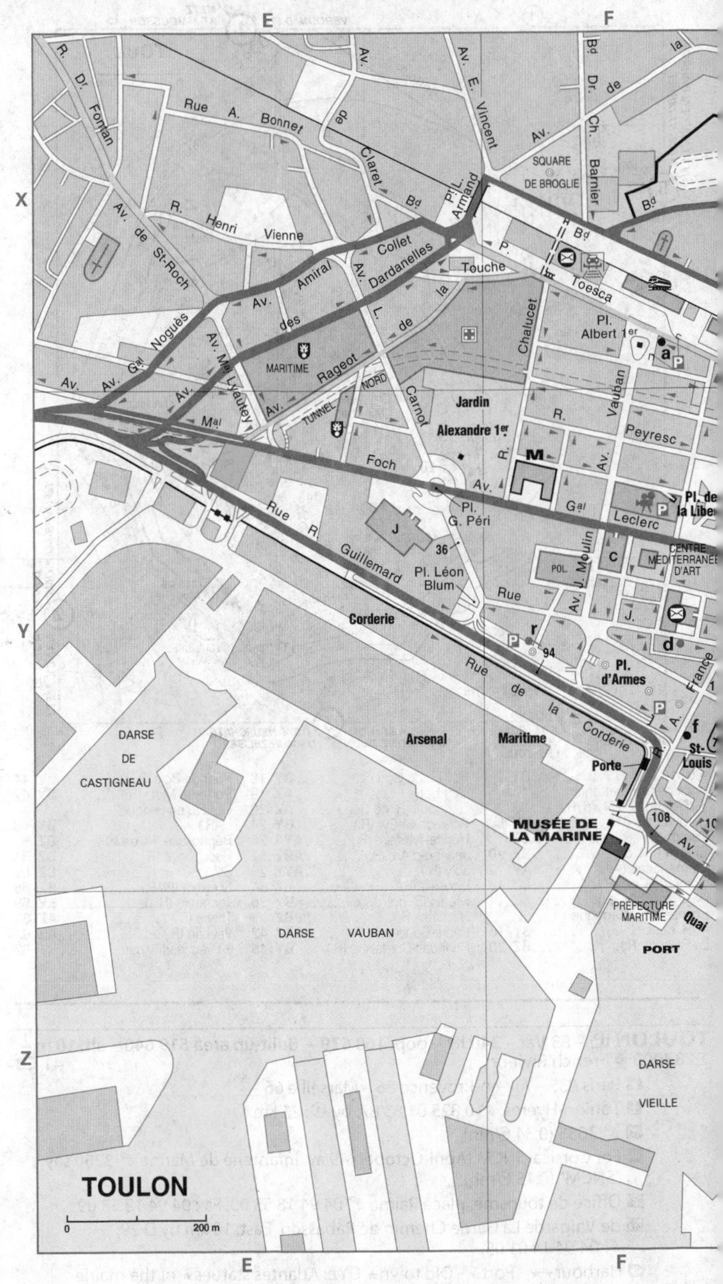

TOULON
0
200 m
E
F
X
Y
Z
DARSE DE CASTIGNEAU
DARSE VAUBAN
DARSE VIEILLE
Arsenal
Maritime
Corderie
Jardin Alexandre 1er
MUSÉE DE LA MARINE
PRÉFECTURE MARITIME
PORT
SQUARE DE BROGLIE
CENTRE MÉDITERRANÉEN D'ART
Pl. G. Péri
Pl. Léon Blum
Pl. d'Armes
Pl. Albert 1er
Porte
St-Louis

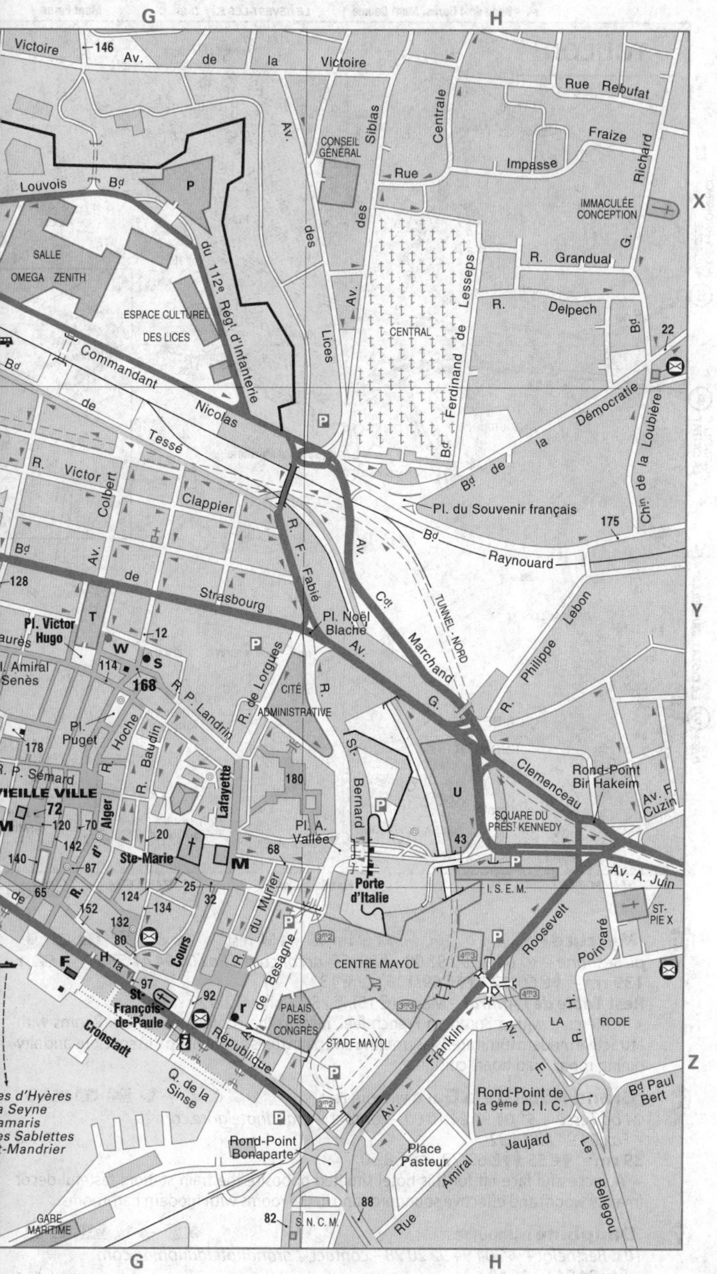
G
H
X
Y
Z
Victoire
146
Av. de la Victoire
Rue Rebufat
Av. des Siblas
Centrale
CONSEIL GÉNÉRAL
Fraize
Impasse
Richard
Rue
Louvois
Bd
P
IMMACULÉE CONCEPTION
Bd du 112e. Régt d'Infanterie
des
R. Grandual
G.
SALLE OMEGA ZENITH
Av. des Lices
R. Delpech
ESPACE CULTUREL DES LICES
CENTRAL
Ferdinand de Lesseps
Bd
22
Commandant Nicolas
Bd de Tessé
Bd de la Démocratie
Chin de la Loubière
R. Victor Clappier
Colbert
Pl. du Souvenir français
175
Bd Raynouard
Bd
Av. de Strasbourg
R. F. Fabié
Av. Cdt Marchand
TUNNEL - NORD
128
T
Pl. Victor Hugo
12
Pl. Noël Blache
Av. G. Clemenceau
R. Philippe Lebon
W
S
114
168
Amiral Senès
R. P. Landrin
R. de Lorgues
CITÉ ADMINISTRATIVE
R. St-Bernard
Pl. Puget
R. Hoche
R. Baudin
178
R. P. Sémard
VIEILLE VILLE
Lafayette
180
U
Rond-Point Bir Hakeim
Av. F. Cuzin
72
120
70
R. d'Alger
SQUARE DU PRÉST KENNEDY
142
140
87
20
Ste-Marie
68
Pl. A. Vallée
43
Av. A. Juin
M
Porte d'Italie
I. S. E. M.
65
124
25
32
134
152
132
R. du Murier
ST-PIE X
80
Cours Lafayette
R. de Besagne
CENTRE MAYOL
Roosevelt
Poincaré
F
H
97
St-François-de-Paule
92
r
PALAIS DES CONGRÈS
STADE MAYOL
Av. Franklin
Av. E.
R. H.
LA RODE
Cronstadt
Av. de la République
Q. de la Sinse
Rond-Point de la 9ème D. I. C.
Bd Paul Bert
es d'Hyères
a Seyne
amaris
es Sablettes
-Mandrier
Rond-Point Bonaparte
Place Pasteur
Rue Amiral Jaujard
Le Bellegou
88
82
S. N. C. M.
GARE MARITIME

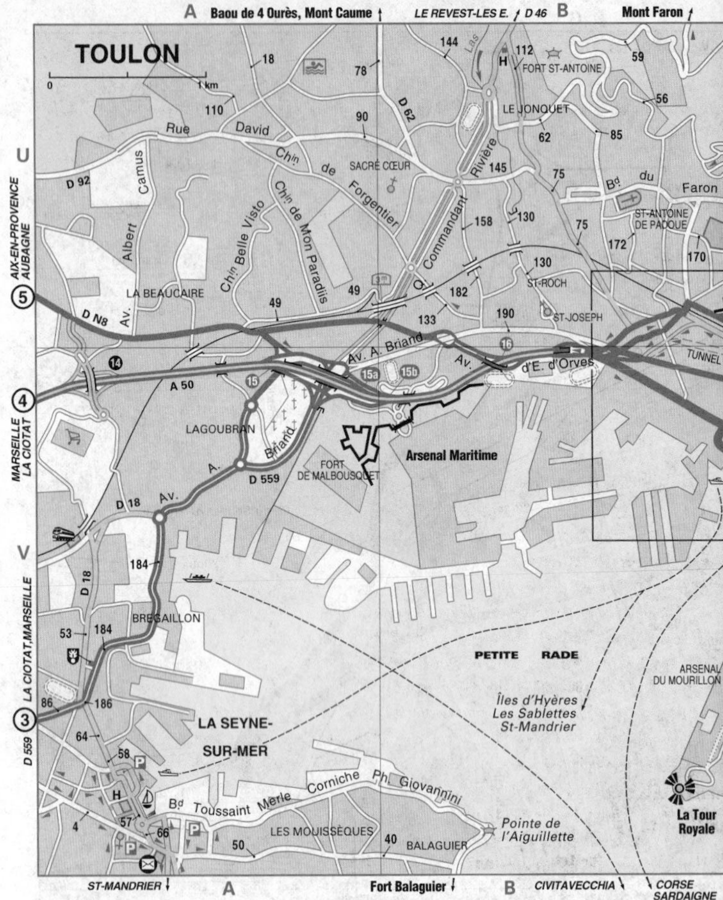

Mercure

pl. Besagne – ✆ 04 98 00 81 00 – h2095@accor.com – Fax 04 94 41 57 51 GZ **r**
139 rm – †€ 60/127 ††€ 69/136, ☕ € 13
Rest *Table de l'Amiral* – Menu (€ 15), € 25 – Carte € 22/29
◆ A Mercure with a Southern French feel, next to the conference centre. Rooms with attractive modern furniture. Glass roofing and palm trees brighten up this spacious and airy dining room. Traditional cuisine.

Grand Hôtel de la Gare without rest

14 bd Tessé – ✆ 04 94 24 10 00 – contact@grandhotelgare.com – Fax 04 94 22 34 82 FX **a**
39 rm – †€ 55 ††€ 62/72, ☕ € 8,50
◆ A successful face-lift for this hotel situated opposite the train station: tasteful decor (mainly wood) and effective soundproofing in the rooms with modern bathrooms.

Dauphiné without rest

10 r. Berthelot – ✆ 04 94 92 20 28 – contact@grandhoteldauphine.com – Fax 04 94 62 16 69 GY **s**
55 rm – †€ 49/54 ††€ 60/64, ☕ € 8,50
◆ Well-placed for exploring the network of narrow streets of the old town. The well-kept rooms are being gradually renovated.

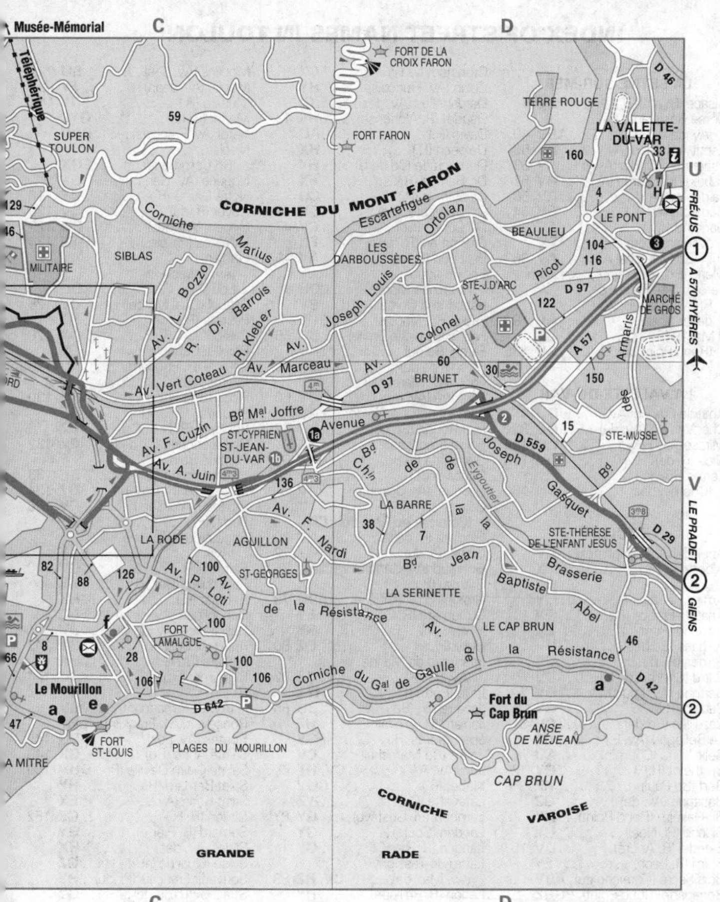

Bonaparte without rest

16 r. Anatole-France – ✆ 04 94 93 07 51 – reservation@hotel-bonaparte.com – Fax 04 94 93 24 55 FY **f**

22 rm – €50/52 €55/57, ☕ €8 – 3 suites

◆ Town centre building with warm Provençal decor. The bedrooms to the rear are quieter and cooler (good news in summer). Table d'hôte-style breakfast.

Le Jardin du Sommelier

20 allée Amiral Courbet – ✆ 04 94 62 03 27 – scalisi@le-jardin-du-sommelier.com – Fax 04 94 09 01 49 – Closed Saturday lunch and Sunday FY **r**

Rest – Menu (€27), €34/39

◆ Red and grey are the dominant colours in this comfortable restaurant serving appetising cuisine accompanied by an interesting wine list.

Blanc le Bistro

290 r. Jean Jaurès – ✆ 04 94 10 20 40 – blanc.lebistro@wanadoo.fr – Fax 04 94 10 20 39 – Closed 25 July-10 August, 2-10 January, Monday dinner, Saturday lunch and Sunday FY **d**

Rest – Menu (€18 bi), €29/35 – Carte €40/53

◆ This contemporary bistro used to be a cinema. The chef now expresses his culinary vein through different media: quality ingredients and generous flavours.

INDEX OF STREET NAMES IN TOULON

Au Sourd

10 r. Molière – ✆ 04 94 92 28 52 – Fax 04 94 91 59 92 – Closed Sunday and Monday
Rest – Menu € 28 – Carte € 42/143 GY **w**

◆ This restaurant was established by one of Napoleon III's artillerymen... who came home deaf! Located in the old town, it is famous for its fish specialities.

in Mourillon – ✉ **83100 Toulon**

Tour royale ⁕★.

La Corniche without rest

17 littoral F. Mistral – ✆ 04 94 41 35 12 – info@cornichehotel.com – Fax 04 94 41 24 58 CV **a**
25 rm – €95/130 €105/150, ☕ €14 – 4 suites

◆ 1960s building overlooking the bay of Toulon, a stone's throw from the lovely Mourillon beaches. Rooms facing the sea or overlooking a fragrant garden.

Le Gros Ventre

279 littoral F. Mistral – ✆ 04 94 42 15 42 – Fax 04 94 31 40 32 – Closed Saturday lunch, Thursday and Friday CV **e**
Rest – *(dinner only in July-August except Tuesday)* Menu € 28/48 – Carte € 38/91

◆ Opposite Fort St-Louis, on the ground floor of a modern building of the "Corniche Varoise". Fish and beef specialities for small and large appetites.

in Cap Brun – ✉ **83100 Toulon**

Les Pins Penchés

3182 av. de la Résistance – ✆ 04 94 27 98 98 – infos@restaurant-pins-penches.com – Fax 04 94 27 98 27 – Closed Sunday dinner, Tuesday lunch and Monday DV **a**
Rest – Menu € 58/68

◆ A superb situation for this 19C villa overlooking the bay. Elegant dining rooms and terraces with a view over the park (listed trees) and of the Mediterranean beyond.

in Camp-Laurent 7.5 km by ④ **A 50 motorway, Ollioules exit – ✉ 83500 La Seyne-sur-Mer**

Novotel

Z.A. Capellane – ✆ 04 94 63 09 50 – info@novoteltoulon.com – Fax 04 94 63 03 76
86 rm – €102/120 €117/120, ☕ €12,50 – **Rest** – Menu (€ 24), € 29 bi – Carte € 27/51

◆ This Novotel with its adequately sized rooms is a useful stopover in the Var region. Swimming pool and games area. Whether you dine by the pool in summer or in the comfortable dining room, there is the standard range of dishes to choose from and a children's menu.

TOULON-LA-MONTAGNE – 51 Marne – 306 F9 – ✉ 51130 13 B2

Paris 128 – Châlons-en-Champagne 40 – Épernay 29 – Reims 58

Les Corettes

chemin du Pâti – ✆ 03 26 59 06 92 – Fax 03 26 59 06 92 – Closed 1st December-1st March
5 rm ☕ – €52 €60 – **Table d'hôte** – Menu € 38 bi

◆ Appealing residence overlooking the wine-growing village. Rooms with personal touches, billiard lounge and flower garden. Rustic dining room serving traditional cuisine and good wine from the family cellar.

Good food and accommodation at moderate prices?
Look for the Bib symbols: red Bib Gourmand for food,
blue Bib Hotel for hotels.

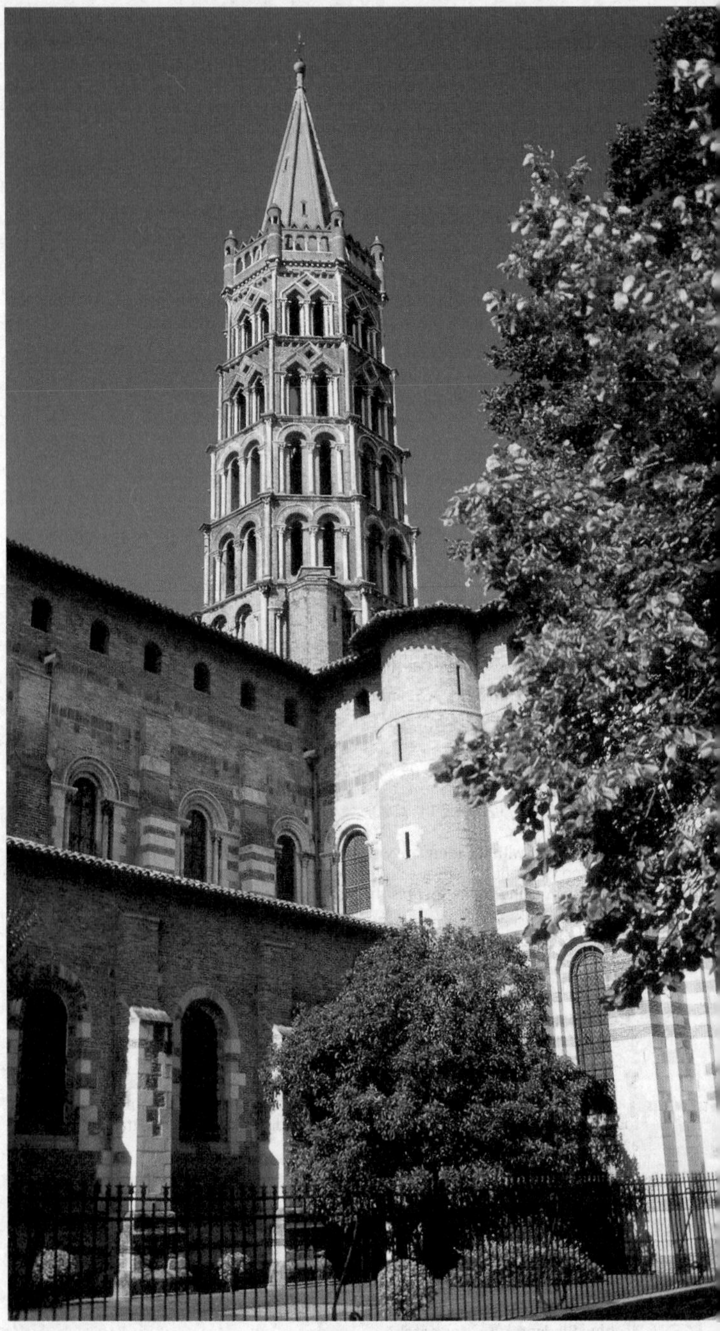
J.-P. Garcin/PHOTONONSTOP

Saint Sernin Basilica

TOULOUSE

P **Department:** 31 Haute-Garonne
Michelin LOCAL map: n° **343** G3
Paris 677 – Barcelona 320 – Bordeaux 244 – Lyon 535 – Marseille 405

Population: 390 350 28 **B2**
Pop. built-up area: 761 090
Altitude: 146 m – **Postal Code:** ✉ 31000
Languedoc-Roussillon-Tarn Gorges

USEFUL INFORMATION

TOURIST OFFICE

donjon du Capitole ✆ 05 61 11 02 22, Fax 05 61 23 74 97

TRANSPORT

Auto-train ✆ 3635 (0,34 €/mn)

AIRPORT

Toulouse-Blagnac ✆ 0 825 380 000 (0,15€/mn) AS

A FEW GOLF COURSES

- 18 de Toulouse La Ramée Tournefeuille Ferme du Cousturier ✆ 05 61 07 09 09 ;
- 18 de Toulouse Vieille-Toulouse South: 9 km by D 4, ✆ 05 61 73 45 48 ;
- 9 Saint-Gabriel Montrabé "Lieu dit Castié", by Lavaur road: 10 km, ✆ 05 61 84 16 65 ;
- 36 Seilh Toulouse Seilh Route de Grenade, by Seilh road: 12 km, ✆ 05 62 13 14 14 ;
- 9 de Borde-Haute Drémil-Lafage Borde-Haute, by Castres road (N126): 15 km, ✆ 05 62 18 84 00 ;
- 18 de Teoula Plaisance-du-Touch 71, avenue des Landes, Southwest: 20 km by D 632, ✆ 05 61 91 98 80 ;
- 18 de Palmola Buzet-sur-Tarn Route d'Albi, Northeast: 22 km by A 68, exot 4, ✆ 05 61 84 20 50.

CASINO

Hippodrome de la Cépière, 1 Chemin des Courses ✆ 05 34 39 01 45

TO BE SEEN

TOULOUSE AND AERONAUTICS

Clément-Ader factory at Colomiers in the western suburbs by ⑦

ST-SERNIN BASILICA AND CAPITOLE DISTRICTS

- St-Sernin basilica★★★ - Musée St-Raymond★★ - Les Jacobins church ★★ (church nave★★) - Capitole★ - Staircase tower★ of the Hôtel de Bernuy EY

FROM PLACE DE LA DAURADE TO CATHEDRAL

- Hôtel d'Assézat and Bemberg Foundation ★★ EY - St-Étienne cathedral ★ - Musée des Augustins★★ (sculptures★★★) FY

OTHER SIGHTS

Muséum d'histoire naturelle★★ FZ - Musée Paul-Dupuy★ FZ - Musée Georges-Labit★DV M[2]

INDEX OF STREET NAMES IN TOULOUSE

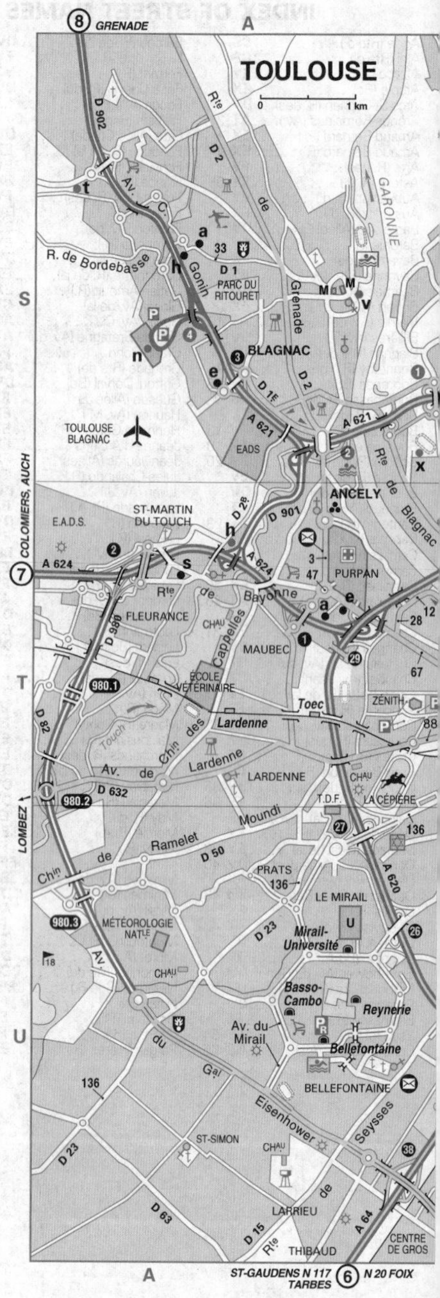
TOULOUSE
GRENADE
A
S
T
U
BLAGNAC
TOULOUSE BLAGNAC
PARC DU RITOURET
R. de Bordebasse
GARONNE
EADS
E.A.D.S.
ANCELY
ST-MARTIN DU TOUCH
COLOMIERS, AUCH
PURPAN
FLEURANCE
MAUBEC
ÉCOLE VÉTÉRINAIRE
ZÉNITH
Lardenne
LARDENNE
LA CÉPIÈRE
T.D.F.
LOMBEZ
PRATS
LE MIRAIL
Mirail-Université
MÉTÉOROLOGIE NAT^LE
Basso-Cambo
Reynerie
Av. du Mirail
Bellefontaine
BELLEFONTAINE
ST-SIMON
LARRIEU
THIBAUD
CENTRE DE GROS
ST-GAUDENS N 117 TARBES
N 20 FOIX

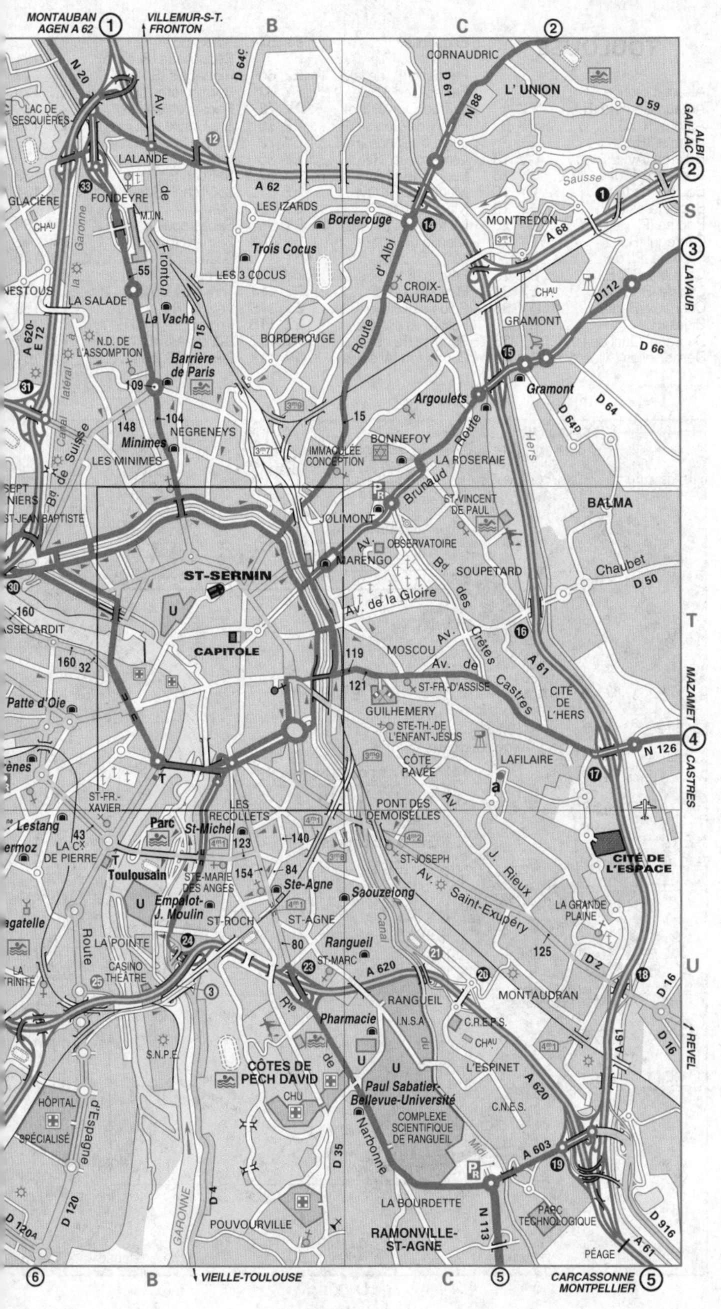
MONTAUBAN AGEN A 62
VILLEMUR-S-T. FRONTON
L' UNION
CORNAUDRIC
ALBI GAILLAC
LAVAUR
LALANDE
A 62
LES IZARDS
Borderouge
Trois Cocus
LES 3 COCUS
MONTREDON
A 68
CROIX-DAURADE
GRAMONT
BORDEROUGE
Barrière de Paris
Argoulets
Gramont
NEGRENEYS
Minimes
LES MINIMES
BONNEFOY
IMMACULÉE CONCEPTION
LA ROSERAIE
ST-VINCENT DE PAUL
BALMA
JOLIMONT
OBSERVATOIRE
MARENGO
SOUPETARD
ST-SERNIN
CAPITOLE
Av. de la Gloire
MOSCOU
Av. de Castres
ST-FR.-D'ASSISE
CITÉ DE L'HERS
GUILHEMERY
STE-TH.-DE L'ENFANT-JÉSUS
MAZAMET
CASTRES
N 126
LAFILAIRE
CÔTE PAVÉE
Patte d'Oie
PONT DES DEMOISELLES
ST-FR.-XAVIER
LES RECOLLETS
Parc
St-Michel
Lestang
LA CX DE PIERRE
Toulousain
CITÉ DE L'ESPACE
ST-JOSEPH
STE-MARIE DES ANGES
Ste-Agne
Saouzelong
Av. Saint-Exupéry
J. Rieux
LA GRANDE PLAINE
Empalot-J. Moulin
ST-ROCH
ST-AGNE
LA POINTE
Rangueil
ST-MARC
A 620
CASINO THÉATRE
RANGUEIL
MONTAUDRAN
Pharmacie
I.N.S.A
C.R.E.P.S.
REVEL
S.N.P.E.
CÔTES DE PECH DAVID
L'ESPINET
Paul Sabatier-Bellevue-Université
C.N.E.S.
HÔPITAL SPÉCIALISÉ
COMPLEXE SCIENTIFIQUE DE RANGUEIL
A 603
LA BOURDETTE
PARC TECHNOLOGIQUE
POUVOURVILLE
RAMONVILLE-ST-AGNE
PÉAGE
VIEILLE-TOULOUSE
CARCASSONNE MONTPELLIER

TOULOUSE

Alsace-Lorraine (R. d') . **EXY**
Arnaud-Bernard (R.) . . . . **EX** 4
Astorg (R. d') . . . . **FY** 5
Baronie (R.) . . . . **EY** 9
Billières (Av. E.). . . . . **DV** 13
Bonrepos (Bd) . . . . **DV** 16
Boulbonne (R.) . . . . **FY** 18
Bouquières (R.) . . . . **FZ** 19
Bourse (Pl. de la). . . . . . . **EY** 20
Cantegril (R.) . . . . **FY** 23
Capitole (Pl. du). . . . . **EY**
Cartailhac (R. E.) . . . . **EX** 26
Chaîne (R. de la) . . . . **EX** 31
Cugnaux (R. de) . . . . **DV** 35
Cujas (R.). . . . . **EY** 36
Daurade (Quai de la). . . . **EY** 38
Demoiselles (Allée des). **DV** 40

Esquirol (Pl.) . . . . **EY** 54
La-Fayette (R.) . . . . **EY**
Fonderie (R. de la). . . . . . **EZ** 60
Frères-Lion (R. des) . . . . **FY** 62
Griffoul-Dorval (Bd) . . . . **DV** 72
Henry-de-Gorsse (R.) . . . **EZ** 76
Jules-Chalande (R.). . . . . **EY** 79
Lapeyrouse (R.). . . . . **FY** 85
Leclerc (Bd Mar.) . . . . . . **DV** 87
Magre (R. Genty) . . . . . . **EY** 91
Malcousinat (R.) . . . . **EY** 92
Marchands (R. des) . . . . **EY** 95
Mercié (R. A.) . . . . **EY** 103
Metz (R. de) . . . . **EFY**
Peyras (R.). . . . . **EY** 113
Pleau (R. de la) . . . . **FZ** 114
Poids-de-l'Huile (R.) . . . . **EY** 115
Polinaires (R. des) . . . . . . **EZ** 116
Pomme (R. de la) . . . . . **EFY** 117
Pompidou (Allée) . . . . . . **DV** 118

Rémusat (R. de) . . . . **EX**
République (R. de la) . . . **DV** 124
Riguepels (R.) . . . . **FY** 127
Romiguières (R.). . . . . . . **EY** 129
Roosevelt (Allées) . . . . **FXY** 130
Ste-Ursule (R.). . . . . **EY** 137
St-Antoine-du-T. (R.) . . . . **FY**
St-Etienne (Port). . . . . . . **DV** 133
St-Michel (Gde-R.) . . . . . **DV** 134
St-Rome (R.). . . . . **EY**
Sébastopol (R. de) . . . . . **DV** 139
Semard (Bd P.). . . . . **DV** 142
Suau (R. J.) . . . . **EY** 146
Temponières (R.) . . . . . . **EY** 147
Trinité (R. de la). . . . . **EY** 149
Vélane (R.). . . . . **FZ** 158
Wilson (Pl. Prés.). . . . . . . **FY**
3-Journées (R. des) . . . . **FY** 162
3-Piliers (R. des) . . . . **EX** 164

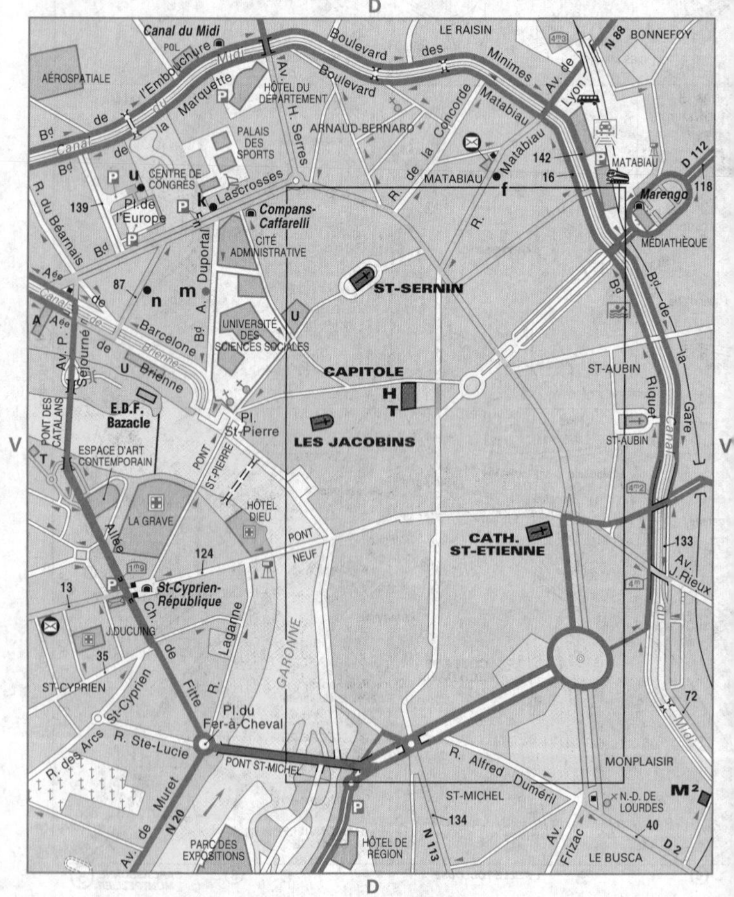

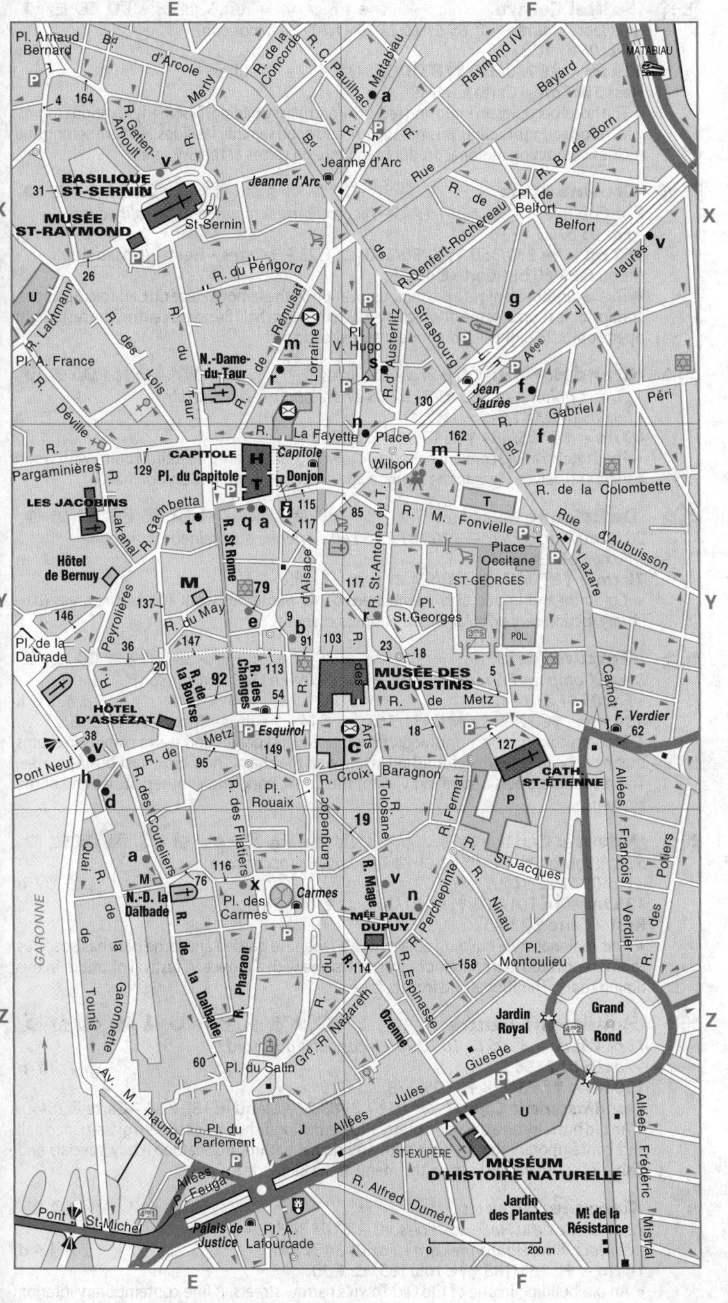
E
F
X
Y
Z
BASILIQUE ST-SERNIN
MUSÉE ST-RAYMOND
N.-Dame-du-Taur
CAPITOLE
Pl. du Capitole
Capitole
Donjon
LES JACOBINS
Hôtel de Bernuy
MUSÉE DES AUGUSTINS
HÔTEL D'ASSÉZAT
CATH. ST-ÉTIENNE
N.-D. la Dalbade
Mée PAUL DUPUY
Grand Rond
Jardin Royal
MUSÉUM D'HISTOIRE NATURELLE
Jardin des Plantes
Mt de la Résistance
Palais de Justice
Pl. A. Lafourcade
Pl. du Parlement
Pl. du Salin
Pl. des Carmes
Carmes
Esquirol
Jeanne d'Arc
Jean Jaurès
F. Verdier
Place Wilson
Place Occitane
ST-GEORGES
Pl. St.Georges
Pl. Jeanne d'Arc
Pl. V. Hugo
Pl. St-Sernin
Pl. Arnaud Bernard
Pl. A. France
Pl. de la Daurade
Pl. Rouaix
Pl. Montoulieu
Pl. de Belfort
MATABIAU
GARONNE
Pont Neuf
Pont St-Michel
ST-EXUPÉRY
0
200 m

Sofitel Centre rm, rest,
84 allées J. Jaurès – ✆ 05 61 10 23 10 – h1091@accor.com
– Fax 05 61 10 23 20 *p. 7* FX **v**
119 rm – €280/320 €310/350, €22 – 14 suites
Rest *SW Café* – Carte €34/59
◆ The hotel occupies an imposing red-brick and glass building. Discreetly luxurious rooms, with good soundproofing. Business centre and good seminar facilities. Modern setting and recipes combining regional products and foreign spices at the SW café.

Crowne Plaza rm,
7 pl. Capitole – ✆ 05 61 61 19 19 – hicptoulouse@alliance-hospitality.com
– Fax 05 61 23 79 96 *p. 7* EY **t**
162 rm – €280/350 €280/350, €23 – 3 suites – **Rest** – *(closed Aug.)*
Menu €29/60 bi – Carte €46/69
◆ This luxury hotel enjoys a prestigious location on the famous Place du Capitole. Spacious, comfortable rooms, some of which overlook the town hall. Business centre. The restaurant opens onto a delightful Florentine-inspired patio.

Grand Hôtel de l'Opéra without rest
1 pl. du Capitole – ✆ 05 61 21 82 66 – hotelopera@guichard.fr
– Fax 05 61 23 41 04 *p. 7* EY **a**
49 rm – €185/484 €185/484, €22
◆ This hotel in a 17C convent has an air of serenity and charm. Beautiful rooms with wood panels and velvet. Pleasant bar lounge and attractive vaulted reception hall.

De Brienne without rest
20 bd du Mar. Leclerc – ✆ 05 61 23 60 60 – brienne@hoteldebrienne.com
– Fax 05 61 23 18 94 *p. 6* DV **n**
70 rm – €70/93 €70/93, €10 – 1 suite
◆ Colourful and impeccably maintained rooms, numerous work and leisure areas (bar-library, patio): very popular with a business clientele.

Mercure Atria
8 espl. Compans Caffarelli – ✆ 05 61 11 09 09 – h1585@accor.com
– Fax 05 61 23 14 12 *p. 6* DV **k**
134 rm – €121/153 €131/163, €14 – 2 suites – **Rest** – Carte €16/27
◆ Modern comfortable furnishings, decorative wood panels and warm colours in rooms that have been recently refurbished in line with the chain's new look. Vast business area. The restaurant offers a soothing view of the public park, and another, busier one of the kitchen.

Novotel Centre rm,
5 pl. A. Jourdain – ✆ 05 61 21 74 74 – h0906@accor.com
– Fax 05 61 22 81 22 *p. 6* DV **u**
135 rm – €101/165 €101/165, €14 – 2 suites
Rest – Carte €22/40
◆ This regional-style building adjacent to a Japanese garden and large park has spacious rooms renovated in a contemporary spirit, some with a terrace. A festival of colour in this dining room. Traditional and local cuisine.

Holiday Inn Centre rm,
13 pl. Wilson – ✆ 05 61 10 70 70 – hicapoul@guichard.fr
– Fax 05 61 21 96 70 *p. 7* FY **n**
130 rm – €95/178 €95/178, €16
Rest *Brasserie le Capoul* – *✆ 05 61 21 08 27* – Menu (€18), €24 – Carte €28/40
◆ An old hostelry on a busy and pretty square, distinguished by its superb glass-paned hall and contemporary rooms, each with an original bathroom. Seafood, daily specials and dishes of southwest France on the menu at the Brasserie le Capoul.

Garonne without rest
22 descente de la Halle aux Poissons – ✆ 05 34 31 94 80
– contact@hotelgaronne.com – Fax 05 34 31 94 81 *p. 7* EY **d**
14 rm – €165/185 €165/185, €20
◆ An old building in one of the Old Town's narrow streets. A fine contemporary interior: stained-oak parquet flooring, design furniture, silk draperies and the odd Japanese touch.

Des Beaux Arts without rest

1 pl. du Pont-Neuf – ☎ 05 34 45 42 42 – contact@hoteldesbeauxarts.com – Fax 05 34 45 42 43 p. 7 EY **v**

20 rm – †€ 108 ††€ 178/230, ☐ € 16

◆ Tastefully done 18C establishment with cosy refined rooms, most with a view of the Garonne. Number 42 enjoys the additional benefit of a mini-terrace.

Les Capitouls without rest

29 allées J. Jaurès – ☎ 05 34 41 31 21 – reservation@hotel-capitouls.com – Fax 05 61 63 15 17 p. 7 FX **g**

55 rm – †€ 130/181 ††€ 130/181, ☐ € 13,50 – 2 suites

◆ Right by the Jean Jaurès metro station, this old town house has a distinctive foyer with pink brick vaulting. The rooms have Wifi access.

Mermoz without rest

50 r. Matabiau – ☎ 05 61 63 04 04 – reservation@hotel-mermoz.com – Fax 05 61 63 15 64 p. 7 DV **f**

52 rm – †€ 125 ††€ 125, ☐ € 12

◆ This hotel's spare decor recalls the Aeropostale's heroic pilots. Bright, candy-coloured rooms. Flower-decked glassed-in area or tree-shaded outside tables for breakfast.

Mercure Wilson without rest

7 r. Labéda – ☎ 05 34 45 40 60 – h1260@accor.com – Fax 05 34 45 40 61 p. 7 FY **m**

95 rm – †€ 98/153 ††€ 108/198, ☐ € 14

◆ Comfortable well-equipped and cheerful rooms await behind a characteristic Toulouse façade. Breakfasts served on the terrace in summer. Practical garage.

Athénée without rest

13 bis r. Matabiau – ☎ 05 61 63 10 63 – hotel-athenee@wanadoo.fr – Fax 05 61 63 87 80 p. 7 FX **a**

35 rm – †€ 74/137 ††€ 84/157, ☐ € 10,50

◆ A discreet building 500m from St-Sernin basilica. Functional guestrooms decorated in bright colours. Exposed stone and brickwork in the lounge.

Albert 1er without rest

8 r. Rivals – ☎ 05 61 21 17 91 – toulouse@hotel-albert1.com – Fax 05 61 21 09 64 p. 7 EX **r**

47 rm – †€ 55/98 ††€ 65/98, ☐ € 10

◆ A very practical base for discovering the "pink city" by foot. Ask for one of the refurbished rooms, or one at the rear for peace and quiet.

Ours Blanc-Centre without rest

2 r. Porte Sardane – ☎ 05 61 21 25 97 – centre@hotel-oursblanc.com – Fax 05 61 23 96 27 p. 7 FX **s**

44 rm – †€ 75 ††€ 81, ☐ € 7

◆ The hotel is pleasantly located near the town's main attractions. Small, well-equipped rooms with air-conditioning which are regularly maintained. Double-glazing.

Castellane without rest

17 r. Castellane – ☎ 05 61 62 18 82 – castellanehotel@wanadoo.fr – Fax 05 61 62 58 04 p. 7 FX **f**

53 rm – †€ 72 ††€ 72/94, ☐ € 8

◆ A nice welcome at this hotel set around a patio. Simple, redecorated rooms, some with terraces. Some are particularly suited to families.

Les Jardins de l'Opéra

1 pl. Capitole – ☎ 05 61 23 07 76 – contact@lesjardinsdelopera.com – Fax 05 61 23 63 00 – Closed 4-25 August, 1st-7 January, Sunday and Monday p. 7 EY **q**

Rest – Menu (€ 35 bi), € 42 bi (lunch), € 70/100 – Carte approx. € 92

◆ The elegant dining rooms under a glass roof and separated by a fountain dedicated to Neptune. Unusually, the menu offers dishes in "trilogy": three dishes on the same plate.

XXX ✿✿ **Michel Sarran**

21 bd A. Duportal – ✆ 05 61 12 32 32 – restaurant@michel-sarran.com – Fax 05 61 12 32 33 – Closed 2 August-1st September, 20-28 December, Wednesday lunch, Saturday and Sunday *p. 6* DV **m**

Rest – *(pre-book)* Menu € 48 bi (lunch), € 98/165 bi – Carte € 88/126

Spec. Soupe tiède de foie gras à l'huître Belon. Turbot, jus mousseux au combawa. L'œuf et la poule au caviar d'Aquitaine.

♦ This delightful 19C abode, whose friendly atmosphere immediately makes one feel at home, has been decorated in a purposely minimalist style to better set off the chef's inventive cuisine.

XX ✿ **En Marge** (Frank Renimel)

8 r. Mage – ✆ 05 61 53 07 24 – contact@restaurantenmarge.com – Closed 10 August-9 September and 21 December-6 January *p. 7* ZF **v**

Rest – *(number of covers limited, pre-book)* Menu € 30 (lunch), € 50 € (dinner)/75

Spec. Crevettes pimentées en gaspacho. Noix de veau et pata negra. Soufflé rhum et caramel.

♦ A new restaurant with a homely atmosphere, friendly service and delicious, innovative cuisine. Limited number of tables in a modern decor with a hint of Baroque.

XX ✿ **Metropolitan**

2 pl. Auguste-Albert – ✆ 05 61 34 63 11 – Fax 05 61 52 88 91 – Closed 1st-21 August, 25-30 December, Saturday lunch, Sunday and Monday *p. 5* CT **a**

Rest – Menu € 26 (weekday lunch), € 39/53 – Carte € 48/72

Spec. Déclinaison autour de la tomate. Filet de canette rôti. Barre fondante au chocolat amer et praliné.

♦ A modern restaurant which gets full marks for its delicious, contemporary cuisine, designer-style dining room (with bar), small interior terrace adorned with vines, and efficient, friendly service.

XX **Valentin**

21 r. Perchepinte – ✆ 05 61 53 11 15 – Closed Saturday lunch, Sunday and Monday *p. 7* ZF **n**

Rest – Menu € 13,50 (lunch), € 33/54 bi – Carte € 45/61

♦ A glass door crowned with an arch leads to this attractive restaurant, whose young chef specialises in inventive cuisine. Elegant decor with period furniture, vaulted cellar and brick walls.

XX **7 Place St-Sernin**

7 pl. St-Sernin – ✆ 05 62 30 05 30 – restaurant@7placesaintsernin.com – Fax 05 62 30 04 06 – Closed Saturday and Sunday *p. 7* EX **v**

Rest – Menu (€ 18 bi), € 24 bi (weekday lunch), € 34/60 bi – Carte € 48/66

♦ This restaurant set in a typical Toulouse house boasts flamboyant colours and is elegantly arranged and brightened with contemporary paintings. Modern dishes.

XX **La Corde**

4 r. Chalande – ✆ 05 61 29 09 43 – Fax 05 61 29 09 43 *p. 7* EY **e**

Rest – Menu € 20 (weekday lunch), € 32/100 – Carte € 51/105

♦ This impressive 15C tower, all that remains of a mansion that used to belong to prominent families of Toulouse, is home to the city's oldest restaurant (1881). Updated regional dishes.

XX **Brasserie Flo "Les Beaux Arts"**

1 quai Daurade – ✆ 05 61 21 12 12 – Fax 05 61 21 14 80 *p. 7* EY **v**

Rest – Menu € 30 – Carte € 28/68

♦ Popular with locals, this brasserie on the banks of the Garonne was once frequented by Ingres, Matisse and Bourdelle. Retro decor and a varied menu.

XX **Le 19**

19 descente de la Halle aux Poissons – ✆ 05 34 31 94 84 – contact@restaurantle19.com – Fax 05 34 31 94 85 – Closed 1st-12 May, 11-17 August, 22 December-6 January, Monday lunch, Saturday lunch and Sunday *p. 7* EY **h**

Rest – Menu (€ 20 bi), € 25 bi (lunch), € 40/60 – Carte € 47/70

♦ Welcoming, contemporary-style dining rooms (one with a superb 16C rib-vaulted ceiling), plus an open-view wine cellar. Hearty local cuisine.

XX **Chez Laurent Orsi "Bouchon Lyonnais"**

13 r. de l'Industrie – ✆ 05 61 62 97 43 – orsi.le-bouchon-lyonnais@wanadoo.fr – Fax 05 61 63 00 71 – Closed Saturday lunch and Sunday except public holidays

Rest – Menu € 20 (lunch)/33 – Carte € 33/58 *p. 7* FY **f**

◆ A large bistro whose leather banquettes, closely-packed tables and mirrors are reminiscent of the brasseries of the 1930s. Dishes from the southwest and Lyon, as well as fish and seafood.

XX **Émile**

13 pl. St-Georges – ✆ 05 61 21 05 56 – restaurant-emile@wanadoo.fr – Fax 05 61 21 42 26 – Closed 21 December-5 January, Monday except dinner May-September and Sunday *p. 7* FY **r**

Rest – Menu € 19 (lunch), € 35/50 – Carte € 37/60

◆ A restaurant with a popular terrace and a menu focused on local dishes and fish (cassoulet is the house speciality). Fine wine list.

XX **Brasserie de l'Opéra**

1 pl. Capitole – ✆ 05 61 21 37 03 – infojpgroupe@gmail.com – Fax 05 62 27 16 49 – Closed Sunday and Monday *p. 7* EY **a**

Rest – Menu € 18 (lunch), € 25/32 – Carte € 26/50

◆ Chic 1930s style brasserie where you meet everyone in Toulouse, along with stars who leave their photo to mark a visit. Typical, seasonally influenced brasserie cuisine.

X **L'Adresse**

4 r. Baronie – ✆ 05 61 22 55 48 – Fax 05 61 22 55 48 – Closed 3-24 August, 8-16 February, Tuesday dinner, Sunday and Monday *p. 7* EY **b**

Rest – Menu € 18 (weekday lunch), € 25/35 – Carte € 39/52

◆ Contemporary furniture, mirrors, bookshelves, bottles and dishes of the day on a blackboard form the backdrop of this fashionable establishment serving tasty up-to-date cuisine.

X **L'Empereur de Huê**

17 r. Couteliers – ✆ 05 61 53 55 72 – Closed Sunday and Monday *p. 7* EZ **a**

Rest – *(dinner only) (pre-book)* Menu € 36 – Carte € 43/51

◆ If the decor of this family restaurant is contemporary, the cooking retains its Vietnamese roots.

X **Michel, Marcel, Pierre et les Autres**

35 r. Rémusat – ✆ 05 61 22 47 05 – bistrot@michelmarcelpierre.com – Fax 05 61 22 47 05 – Closed 10-18 August, Sunday and Monday *p. 7* EX **m**

Rest – Menu € 16 (lunch)/22 (lunch) – Carte € 33/39

◆ A warm welcome is guaranteed in this bistro named after a film by Claude Sautet. Rugby matches on the TVs and sports shirts on the walls. Seasonal food.

X **Brasserie du Stade**

114 r. Troënes ✉ 31200 – ✆ 05 34 42 24 20 – Fax 05 34 42 24 21 – Closed 18 July-26 August, 20 December-1st January, Monday dinner, Tuesday dinner, Saturday and Sunday – **Rest** – Carte € 32/42 *p. 4* AS **x**

◆ This large restaurant is located inside Toulouse's rugby stadium. Amongst photos and trophies, guests are served carefully prepared brasserie-style dishes.

X **Rôtisserie des Carmes**

38 r. Polinaires – ✆ 05 61 53 34 88 – rotisserie@wanadoo.fr – Closed 28 July-25 August, 24 December-2 January, Saturday, Sunday and public holidays *p. 7* EZ **x**

Rest – Menu (€ 17), € 22 (lunch), € 28 € bi/32 bi – Carte € 32/71

◆ Proximity to the Carmes market means that the small menu and the dishes of the day depend on the latest catch. The colourful owner supervises in the open kitchen.

in Gratentour **15 km North by D 4 and D 14 – pop. 3 035 – alt. 174 m – ✉ 31150**

Le Barry

47 r. Barry – ✆ 05 61 82 22 10 – le-barry@wanadoo.fr – Fax 05 61 82 22 38 – Closed 20 December-4 January, Friday, Saturday and Sunday except 1st April-30 September

22 rm – †€ 52 ††€ 64, ☕ € 8 – ½ P € 60 – **Rest** – *(closed 1st-24 August, Friday dinner, Saturday dinner October-March, Saturday lunch and Sunday)* Menu € 14,50 (weekday lunch), € 22/29 – Carte € 19/41

◆ This attractive pink-brick farmhouse in a tranquil setting has been transformed into a simple but welcoming hotel. Garden, swimming pool and the Frontonnais vineyards nearby. Warm, refined dining room. Traditional culinary repertoire.

in l'Union 7 km Northeast – pop. 12 141 – alt. 146 m – ✉ 31240

XX **La Bonne Auberge**

2 bis r. Autan-Blanc, (N 88) – ✆ 05 61 09 32 26 – bonne.auberge.la@wanadoo.fr – Fax 05 61 09 97 53 – Closed 10 August-1st September, 21 December-5 January, Sunday and Monday

Rest – Menu € 18 (weekday lunch), € 25/46 – Carte € 36/49

◆ Occupying a restored barn, this restaurant on the village's main road has rustic furniture, beams and brick fireplace. Modern menu.

in Rouffiac-Tolosan 12 km by ② – pop. 1 404 – alt. 210 m – ✉ 31180

XXX **Ô Saveurs** (Daniel Gonzalez et David Biasibetti)

8 pl. Ormeaux, (au Village) – ✆ 05 34 27 10 11 – o.saveurs@free.fr – Fax 05 62 79 33 84 – Closed 27 April-5 May, 17 August-8 September, Saturday lunch, Sunday dinner and Monday

Rest – Menu € 25 (weekday lunch), € 42/85 – Carte € 73/105

Spec. Fricassée de langoustines et foie frais de canard aux pleurotes et coulis de corail. Pavé de bar poêlé, espuma de fenouil et tartare de langoustine aux agrumes (April to July). Pigeon rôti et ses cuisses braisées au vin rouge (April to September).
Wines Fronton, Bergerac.

◆ A charming cottage and terrace set up on the paved square of this picturesque village. Traditional menu spiced up with a zest of creativity. Delicious!

XX **Le Clos du Loup** with rm

N 88 – ✆ 05 61 09 28 39 – hotel-leclosduloup@orange.fr – Fax 05 61 35 13 97 – Closed 26 December-2 January and Sunday evening

18 rm – †€ 62 ††€ 62/110, ☐ € 8 – ½ P € 74 – **Rest** – *(closed August, Saturday lunch, Sunday dinner and Friday)* Menu € 22/30 – Carte € 34/50

◆ Don't be nervous...the Big Bad Wolf is no more! Shimmering colours and beams in the bright rustic dining room. Simple, traditional cuisine and spick-and-span rooms.

in Labège 6 km southeast by D 2 and D 16, towards SNCF station – ✉ 31670

XXX **L'Orangerie de Labège-L'Arôme et le Grain**

4 r. Isatis – ✆ 05 62 47 54 53 – orangeriedelabege@wanadoo.fr – Fax 05 62 47 54 51 – Closed 3-27 August, 21-29 December, Saturday lunch, Sunday and Monday

Rest – Menu € 26 (weekday lunch), € 52/95 – Carte € 57/65

◆ This 17C farmhouse has a hushed ambience, with cosy lounges, pink brickwork and designer furniture. Sophisticated contemporary cuisine. Pretty patio-terrace.

in Ramonville-St-Agne 6 km southeast by D 113 – pop. 11 696 – alt. 162 m – ✉ 31520

Péniche Soleïado

Pont de Mange-Pomme, near the Pont-Sud, along the D 113, towards the Ferme de Cinquante – ✆ 06 86 27 83 19 – peniche.soleiado@cegetel.net – Fax 05 62 19 07 71 – **5 rm** ☐ – †€ 80 ††€ 80 – **Table d'hôte** – Menu € 30 bi

◆ This barge moored in the Canal du Midi has a warm interior, offering three small, yet really delightful rooms.

in Castanet-Tolosan 8 km by ⑤ and N 113 – pop. 10 250 – alt. 164 m – ✉ 31320

X **La Table des Merville**

3 pl. Richard – ✆ 05 62 71 24 25 – contact@table-des-merville.fr – Fax 05 34 66 18 56 – Closed 13-21 April, 27 July-18 August, 26 October-3 November, 21 December-1st January, Sunday and Monday

Rest – Menu (€ 14), € 25/37 – Carte € 36/56

◆ This family restaurant serves appetising cuisine based on daily market produce prepared in front of your eyes. The modern paintings on display are for sale. A charming setting!

in Lacroix-Falgarde 13 km South by D 4 – pop. 1 485 – alt. 154 m – ✉ 31120

XX **Le Bellevue**

1 av. Pyrénées – ✆ 05 61 76 94 97 – Fax 05 62 20 96 57 – Closed 15 October-16 November, Wednesday from September to April and Tuesday

Rest – Menu € 19 (weekday lunch), € 27/39 – Carte € 38/58

◆ This former open-air dance hall, surrounded by greenery, is along the Ariège. In fine weather the outdoor riverside tables are popular. Traditional dishes and southwest French specialities.

in Tournefeuille 10 km West by D 632 AT – **pop. 22 758 – alt. 155 m – ✉ 31170**

XX **L'Art de Vivre**
279 chemin Ramelet-Moundi – ☎ 05 61 07 52 52 – contact@lartdevivre.fr – Fax 05 61 06 41 94 – Closed Easter holidays, 10-31 August, 20-31 December, Sunday dinner, Monday dinner, Tuesday dinner and Wednesday
Rest – Menu € 23 (weekday lunch), € 34/54 – Carte € 49/81
♦ On fine days, this house near the golf course is extended by a charming outside dining area in the middle of a brookside garden. Up-to-date cuisine.

in Purpan 6 km west by N 124 - ✉ **31300 Toulouse**

Palladia
271 av. Grande Bretagne – ☎ 05 62 12 01 20 – info@hotelpalladia.com – Fax 05 62 12 01 21 *p. 4* AT **e**
90 rm – †€ 102/195 ††€ 102/195, ☕ € 18 – 3 suites – **Rest** – *(closed Sunday and public holidays)* Menu (€ 25 bi), € 35/59 bi – Carte € 41/69
♦ An imposing building between the airport and city centre. Particularly well thought-out layout. The spacious and comfortable rooms are being progressively updated. Bright, modern dining room. Summer terrace shaded by parasols.

Novotel Aéroport
23 impasse Maubec – ☎ 05 61 15 00 00 – h0445@accor.com – Fax 05 61 15 88 44 *p. 4* AT **a**
123 rm – †€ 80/155 ††€ 80/155, ☕ € 14 – **Rest** – Carte € 18/38
♦ The rooms of this chain hotel are fully soundproofed. Children's amusements, free shuttle to the airport, Wi-fi and plenty of green space. The restaurant and pleasant terrace offer a view of the pool. Updated menu, specials and diet meals.

in St-Martin-du-Touch to ⑦ – ✉ **31300 Toulouse**

Airport Hôtel without rest
176 rte de Bayonne – ☎ 05 61 49 68 78 – airporthotel@wanadoo.fr – Fax 05 61 49 73 66 *p. 4* AT **s**
45 rm – †€ 68 ††€ 86, ☕ € 9 – 3 suites
♦ 1980s building in red brick near the airport. The simple rooms are well protected against noise and are quite comfortable.

XX **Le Cantou**
98 r. Velasquez, (D 2B) – ☎ 05 61 49 20 21 – le.cantou@wanadoo.fr – Fax 05 61 31 01 17 – Closed 9 August-1st September, 21 December-4 January, Saturday and Sunday *p. 4* AT **h**
Rest – Menu € 30/56 – Carte € 43/57
♦ A haven of greenery shelters this pretty old farmhouse. Terrace set around a pretty well. Tasty, updated menu and remarkable wine list (1 300 vintages).

in Colomiers 10 km by ⑦, **exit n° 3 then direction Cornebarrieu by D 63 – pop. 28 538 – alt. 182 m – ✉ 31770**

XXX **L'Amphitryon** (Yannick Delpech)
✿✿ *chemin de Gramont – ☎ 05 61 15 55 55 – contact@lamphitryon.com – Fax 05 61 15 42 30*
Rest – Menu € 32 (weekday lunch), € 58/105 – Carte € 87/114
Spec. Sardine fraîche taillée au couteau, crème de morue et caviar de hareng. Thon rouge mariné puis juste saisi. Canette du Lauragais en croûte de poivre noir, coriandre et cumin. **Wines** Gaillac, Côtes du Frontonnais.
♦ A welcoming, modern dining room-veranda overlooking the surrounding countryside. Brilliantly inventive cuisine takes local produce to new heights.

in Pibrac 12 km by ⑦, **exit n° 6 – pop. 7 440 – alt. 157 m – ✉ 31820**

X **Le Pavillon Saint Jean**
1 chemin Beauregard – ☎ 05 61 06 71 71 – pierre-jean.darroze@orange.fr – Fax 05 61 86 35 63 – Closed 4-31 August, Saturday lunch, Sunday dinner and Monday
Rest – Menu € 18 (weekday lunch), € 26/46 – Carte € 42/59
♦ This peaceful provincial house, slightly out of the centre, serves good classic cooking in a restrained modern dining room, or on the terrace when the weather permits.

in Blagnac 7 km Northwest – pop. 20 586 – alt. 135 m – ✉ 31700

Pullman rm, VISA

2 av. Didier Daurat, dir. airport (exit n° 3) – ✆ 05 34 56 11 11 – h0565@accor.com – Fax 05 61 30 02 43 p. 4 AS **e**

100 rm – €175/290 €175/290, €22 – **Rest *Le Caouec*** – *(closed 2-17 August, Saturday, Sunday and public holidays)* Carte €31/63

◆ 1970s hotel being treated to a complete facelift. Contemporary style public areas, with some guestrooms updated in a similar vein. Free shuttle to the airport. Tapas-type snacks served at the bar and more traditional menu in the dining room.

Holiday Inn Airport rm, VISA

pl. Révolution – ✆ 05 34 36 00 20 – tlsap@ichotelsgroup.com – Fax 05 34 36 00 30 p. 4 AS **h**

149 rm – €105/240 €105/255, €21 – **Rest** – *(closed Saturday and Sunday)* Menu €22/35 – Carte €22/46

◆ Both peaceful and warm shades adorn the rooms decorated with modern furniture. A well-appointed seminar area. A shuttle links the hotel to the airport. A pleasant brasserie-style restaurant decorated with frescoes depicting olive trees.

Le Cercle d'Oc VISA

6 pl. M. Dassault – ✆ 05 62 74 71 71 – cercledoc@wanadoo.fr – Fax 05 62 74 71 72 – Closed 3-24 August, 25 December-1st January, Saturday and Sunday

Rest – Menu €34 bi (lunch), €43/55 p. 4 AS **t**

◆ This pretty 18C farm is an island of greenery in the middle of a shopping area. English club atmosphere in the elegant dining rooms, billiards room and pleasant terrace.

Le Pré Carré VISA

aéroport Toulouse-Blagnac, (2nd Floor) – ✆ 05 61 16 70 40 – Fax 05 61 16 70 51 – Closed beg. May-end August, Saturday and Sunday p. 4 AS **n**

Rest – *(lunch only)* Menu (€35), €42/45

◆ Pleasant airport restaurant overlooking the runways, in a brasserie setting. Design decor in red tones and wood furnishings. Modern menu.

in Seilh 15 km by ⑧ – pop. 2 086 – alt. 133 m – ✉ 31840

Latitudes Golf de Seilh rm, VISA

rte Grenade – ✆ 05 62 13 14 15 – toh@latitudeshotels.com – Fax 05 61 59 77 97

172 rm – €85/140 €85/140, €13 – 2 suites – **Rest** – Menu (€15), €18

◆ This vast hotel complex opens onto two golf courses and welcomes a great many seminars and sports stays. Studio flats and apartments are also available for rental. Decoration inspired by the early airmail service; cuisine with southwestern bias.

TOUQUES – 14 Calvados – 303 M3 – see Deauville

LE TOUQUET-PARIS-PLAGE – 62 Pas-de-Calais – 301 C4 – pop. 5 299 – alt. 5 m – Casino : du Palais BZ, the 4 Saisons AYZ – ✉ 62520

Northern France and the Paris Region 30 **A2**

Paris 242 – Abbeville 58 – Arras 99 – Boulogne-sur-Mer 30 – Calais 68

Office de tourisme, place de l'Hermitage ✆ 03 21 06 72 00, Fax 03 21 06 72 01

du Touquet Avenue du Golf, South: 2 km, ✆ 03 21 06 28 00.

Plan on next page

Westminster rest, rest, VISA

av. Verger – ✆ 03 21 05 48 48 – reception@westminster.fr – Fax 03 21 05 45 45

115 rm – €80/270 €116/300, €20 – 1 suite BZ **a**

Rest *Le Pavillon* – *(closed 2 January-9 April and Tuesday except July-August) (dinner only)* Menu €55/135 – Carte €80/120

Rest *Les Cimaises* – ✆ *03 21 06 74 95* – Menu (€32 bi), €37 – Carte €50/76

Spec. Langoustines, niçoise de légumes, glace roquette (1st June-15 September). Turbot, huître et concombre en transparence. Côte de veau de lait, jambon cru en émulsion.

◆ Attractive Anglo-Norman style hotel (1925-1928) built between the sea and pine forest. Superb elevators in the lobby; Art-Deco or retro-style guestrooms. Popular terrace in summer. The Pavillon offers classic cuisine with personal touches and an outstanding wine list. Les Cimaises offers buffets and brasserie dishes.

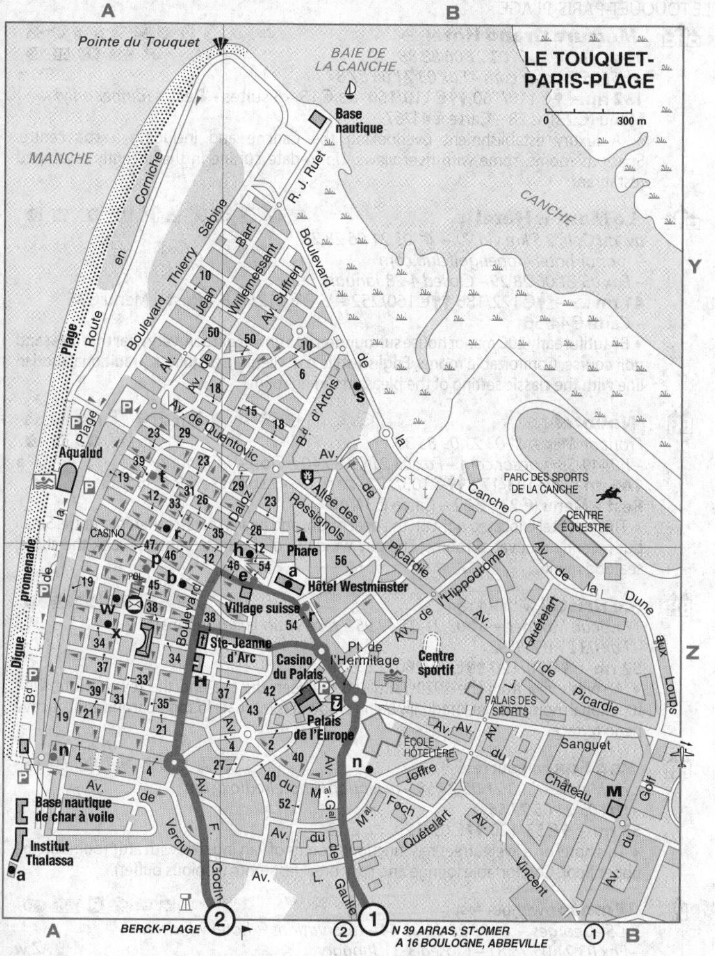

Aboudaram (Av. L.) . . . . BZ 2	Garet (Av. et R. L.) . . . . ABY 26	Pins (Av. des) . . . . BZ 40
Atlantique (Av. de l') . . . . . . ABZ 4	Genets (Av. des) . . . . ABZ 27	Recoussine (Av. F.) . . . . BZ 42
Bardol (R. E.) . . . . BY 6	Hubert (Av. L.) . . . . ABY 29	Reine-May (Av. de la) . . . . . ABZ 43
Bourdonnais (Av. de la) . . . ABY 10	Londres (R. de) . . . . AYZ 31	St-Amand (R.) . . . . AZ 45
Bruxelles (R. de) . . . . AYZ 12	Metz (R. de) . . . . AYZ 33	St-Jean (Av. et R.) . . . . ABZ 46
Calais (R. de) . . . . BY 15	Monnet (R. J.) . . . . AZ 34	St-Louis (R.) . . . . AZ 47
Desvres (R. de) . . . . ABY 18	Moscou (R. de) . . . . AYZ 35	Tourville (Av. de l'Amiral) . . ABY 50
Docteur-J.-Pouget (Bd du) . . . . AYZ 19	Oyats (Av. et R. des) . . . . . ABZ 37	Troènes (Av. des) . . . . BZ 52
Dorothée (R.) . . . . AZ 21	Paix (Av. et R. de la) . . . . . . ABZ 38	Verger (Av. du) . . . . BZ 54
Duboc (Av. et R. J.) . . . . . . ABY 23	Paris (R. de) . . . . AYZ 39	Whitley (Av. J.) . . . . BZ 56

Holiday Inn 🐎 rm, rest,

av. Mar. Foch – ✆ 03 21 06 85 85 – *hotel@holidayinnletouquet.com* – *Fax 03 21 06 85 00* P VISA MC AE D BZ **n**

86 rm – 🚹€ 125/175 🚹🚹€ 125/175, ☕ € 16 – 2 suites – ½ P € 101/126

Rest ***Le Picardy*** – Menu (€ 20), € 36

◆ Modern hotel on the edge of the forest, with functional rooms accessed via a flower-decked gallery. The "privilege" category rooms have been recently renovated. A parquet floor and plants add a touch of originality to the rotunda dining room. Classic menu.

Mercure Grand Hôtel rest, VISA AE BY **s**
4 bd Canche – 03 21 06 88 88 – H5605@accor.com – Fax 03 21 06 87 87
132 rm – €110/160 €110/160, €15 – 5 suites – **Rest** – *(dinner only)* Menu (€23), €28 – Carte €41/67
◆ A luxury establishment overlooking the Canche and including a spa centre. Spacious rooms, some with river views. Up-to-date cuisine in this recently revamped restaurant.

Le Manoir Hôtel VISA AE
av. du Golf, 2.5 km via ② – 03 21 06 28 28 – manoirhotel@opengolfclub.com – Fax 03 21 06 28 29 – Closed 4-28 January
41 rm – €122/186 €160/252 – ½ P €112/158 – **Rest** – Menu €35 – Carte €44/56
◆ Beautiful early 20C manor house surrounded by a flower garden, very near the forest and golf course. Comfortable rooms, English-style bar, clientele of golfers. Traditional food in line with the classic setting of the pleasant dining room.

Novotel rest, rest, VISA AE AZ **a**
Front de Mer – 03 21 09 85 30 – h0449-SB@accor.com – Fax 03 21 09 85 40 – Closed in January
146 rm – €103/172 €103/172, €15 – 3 suites – ½ P €88/123
Rest – Menu (€23), €32 – Carte €34/48
◆ This Novotel is located right on the beachfront and near a thalassotherapy centre. Small but recently renovated rooms. The bay windows of the restaurant overlook the shore; seafood menu.

Le Bristol without rest VISA AE AZ **x**
17 r. Jean Monnet – 03 21 05 49 95 – reservations@hotelbristol.fr – Fax 03 21 05 90 93
52 rm – €70/120 €80/280, €10
◆ A stylish villa from the 1920s, situated between the sea and the town centre, with functional rooms that are gradually being renovated. Intimate lounge-bar and an attractive patio terrace.

Red Fox without rest VISA AE AY **r**
r. de Metz – 03 21 05 27 58 – reception@hotelredfox.com – Fax 03 21 05 27 56
53 rm – €53/120 €65/120, €13
◆ This hotel on a lively street has functional rooms of varying size, with attic rooms on the upper floor. Comfortable lounge and cosy breakfast room (copious buffet).

Windsor without rest VISA AZ **w**
7 r. St-Georges – 03 21 05 05 44 – reservations@hotel-windsor.fr – Fax 03 21 05 75 81 – Closed 3-31 January
28 rm – €50/60 €60/70, €8
◆ This hotel near the beach offers comfortable accommodation with the choice ranging from single to four-bedded rooms. Pleasant lounge. Breakfast room with a painted stucco ceiling.

La Forêt without rest VISA AE AZ **b**
73 r. de Moscou – 03 21 05 09 88 – Fax 03 21 05 59 40 – Closed 15 December-15 January
10 rm – €45 €53/59, €7
◆ A family hotel, ideally located in the town centre, offering functional, quiet, and well-maintained bedrooms. Attractive breakfast room.

Villa Fierval without rest VISA AE BY **h**
6 av. Léon-Garet – 06 08 33 20 07 – fierval@wanadoo.fr – Fax 03 21 05 91 55 – Closed 10 January-5 February
4 rm – €47/69 €69/95
◆ Serge Gainsbourg is just one famous guest to have stayed in this family-run establishment. An elegant façade conceals a spacious interior with comfortable, well-equipped rooms.

Flavio

av. Verger – ✆ 03 21 05 10 22 – flavio@flavio.fr – Fax 03 21 05 91 55 – Closed 10 January-10 February, Sunday dinner October-December, Monday except July-August and 15-30 November BZ **r**

Rest – Menu (€ 20 bi), € 60/148 – Carte € 58/97

◆ This elegant restaurant serves a range of tempting fish and seafood dishes, with a focus on top-quality produce. A piano, chandeliers and period furniture add to the ambience.

Le Village Suisse

52 av. St-Jean – ✆ 03 21 05 69 93 – contact@levillagesuisse.fr – Fax 03 21 05 66 97 – Closed 24 November-8 December, Sunday dinner October-April, Tuesday lunch and Monday September-June BZ **e**

Rest – Menu € 26/80 – Carte € 44/72

◆ This villa was built in 1905 for the daughter of a wealthy Swiss citizen. It now houses a restaurant with a beautiful terrace above antique shops.

Le Paris

88 r. de Metz – ✆ 03 21 05 79 33 – Closed 23 June-2 July, 17-28 November, Sunday dinner off season, Tuesday dinner and Wednesday AZ **p**

Rest – Menu € 18 (weekdays)/38 – Carte € 37/50

◆ Very central restaurant with contemporary decor pleasantly combining red and chocolate tones, where you can enjoy modern-style recipes.

Côté Sud

187 bd du Dr Pouget – ✆ 03 21 05 41 24 – cotesud62@orange.fr – Fax 03 21 86 54 48 – Closed 16-25 June, 24 November-10 December, Sunday dinner off season, Monday lunch and Wednesday AZ **n**

Rest – Menu (€ 15), € 19/31 – Carte € 41/53

◆ Situated on Le Touquet's seafront, this restaurant is decorated in minimalist style with elegant white furnishings. The contemporary cuisine focuses mainly on fish dishes.

Ricochet

49 r. de Paris – ✆ 03 21 06 41 36 – contact@ricochet-letouquet.com – Fax 03 21 06 50 90 – Closed January, Tuesday and Wednesday AY **t**

Rest – Menu € 14 (weekday lunch)/31 – Carte € 27/44

◆ A trendy restaurant in the centre of the resort with a designer decor, interior garden and young staff. Good variety of unfussy dishes listed on the blackboard.

in Stella-Plage 7 km by ② – ✉ **62780 Cucq**

Office de tourisme, Place Jean Sapin ✆ 03 21 09 04 32, Fax 03 21 84 49 88

Des Pelouses

bd E. Labrasse – ✆ 03 21 94 60 86 – hotel.des.pelouses@wanadoo.fr – Fax 03 21 94 10 11 – Closed 20 December-2 February, Sunday dinner and Monday October-Easter

27 rm – †€ 49/52 ††€ 60/70, ☕ € 9 – ½ P € 60/70 – **Rest** – Carte € 21/36

◆ This square-shaped building situated 1,800m from the beach has undergone many renovations. Neat rooms, more spacious at the back. Regional recipes take pride of place in the appetising menu served in the simply decorated dining room.

Good food and accommodation at moderate prices? Look for the Bib symbols: red Bib Gourmand for food, blue Bib Hotel for hotels.

TOURCOING – 59 Nord – 302 G3 – pop. 93 540 – alt. 37 m – ✉ 59200

Northern France and the Paris Region 31 **C2**

Paris 234 – Kortrijk 19 – Gent 61 – Lille 17 – Oostende 81 – Roubaix 5

Office de tourisme, 9, rue de Tournai ✆ 03 20 26 89 03, Fax 03 20 24 79 80

des Flandres Marcq-en-Barœul 159 boulevard Clémenceau, by D 670: 9 km, ✆ 03 20 72 20 74.

Access and exits: See plan of Lille

TOURCOING

Allende (Bd Salvador)	BY	2
Anges (R. des)	BYZ	3
Austerlitz (R. d')	ABZ	4
Bienfaisance (R. de la)	BY	6
Brun Pain (R. du)	AY	
Buisson (R. Ferdinand)	BZ	7
Chateaubriand (R.)	CZ	8
Cherbourg (Quai de)	BZ	9
Clavell (Pl. Miss)	BY	10
Cloche (R. de la)	BY	12
Condorcet (R.)	BY	13
Courbet (R. de l'Amiral)	BY	15
Croix Blanche (R. de la)	CX	16
Croix Rouge (R. de la)	CXY	
Delobel (R.)	BY	18
Doumer (R. Paul)	BY	19
Dron (Av. Gustave)	BZ	
Duguay-Trouin (R.)	CY	21
Faidherbe (R.)	BZ	22
Famelart (R.)	BZ	24
La-Fayette (Av.)	BZ	33
Froissart (R. Jean)	AY	25
Gambetta (Bd)	BZ	27
Gand (R. de)	BXY	
Grand'Place	BY	28
Hassebroucq (Pl. V.)	BY	30
Hénaux (R. Marcel)	BXY	31
Leclerc (R. du Gén.)	BY	36
Lefrançois (Av. Alfred)	CZ	37
Marne (Av. de la)	BZ	39
Marseille (Quai de)	BZ	40
Menin (R. de)	BXY	
Millet (Av. Jean)	AY	42
Moulin Fagot (R. du)	BY	43
Nationale (R.)	ABY	
Péri (R. Gabriel)	BY	45
Petit Village (R. du)	AY	46
Pompidou (Av. G.)	BZ	48
Pont de Neuville (R. du)	CX	49
République (Pl. de la)	BY	51
Résistance (Pl. de la)	BY	52
Ribot (R. Alexandre)	BY	54
Roosevelt (R. F.)	BY	55
Roussel (Pl. Ch.-et-A.)	BY	57
St-Jacques (R.)	BY	58
Sasselange (R. Ed.)	BZ	60
Testelin (R. A.)	CX	61
Thiers (R.)	BZ	63
Tournai (R. de)	BY	64
Turenne (R.)	BZ	66
Ursulines (R. des)	BYZ	68
Victoire (Pl. de la)	BZ	69
Wailly (R. de)	BY	70
Wattine (R. Ch.)	BZ	72

WATTRELOS

Vaneslander (R. M.)	CZ	67

Altia rm,

r. Vertuquet, to the North near Neuville-en -Ferrain interchange (exit 18)
✉ 59535 Neuville-en-Ferrain
– ☎ 03 20 28 88 00
– reservation@altia-hotel.com
– Fax 03 20 28 88 10

Map of Lille HR **e**

108 rm – †€ 55/105 ††€ 55/115, ☐ € 13
Rest – Menu € 35 bi/45 bi – Carte € 20/37

◆ 300 m from the Belgian border, this hotel is gradually being brought up to the chain's latest standards. Ask for one of the renovated, more modern and comfortable rooms. The kitchens can be seen from the dining room, facing a terrace and the pool.

Ibis

r. Carnot – ✆ 03 20 24 84 58 – h0642@accor.com – Fax 03 20 26 29 58 BZ **s**

102 rm – 🛉€ 69 🛉🛉€ 69, ☕ € 7,50 – **Rest** – Menu € 21/27 – Carte € 19/27

◆ This building benefits from a central location which is handy for those who want to make the most of the town. Choose the renovated rooms. The restaurant menu offers traditional French recipes and a few slightly more exotic dishes.

La Baratte

395 r. Clinquet – ✆ 03 20 94 45 63 – la.baratte@wanadoo.fr – Fax 03 20 03 41 84 – Closed 4-25 August, Saturday lunch, Sunday dinner and Monday

Rest – Menu € 21 (weekdays), € 27/80 bi – Carte € 45/55 *plan de Lille*

◆ An inviting rustic-style dining room, partly overlooking the garden. Generous tasty cuisine. Full marks for this former family butchers!

LA TOUR-D'AIGUES – 84 Vaucluse – 332 G11 – pop. 3 860 – alt. 250 m – ✉ 84240 Provence

40 **B2**

Paris 752 – Aix-en-Provence 29 – Apt 35 – Avignon 81 – Digne-les-Bains 92

Office de tourisme, le Château ✆ 04 90 07 50 29, Fax 04 90 07 35 91

Le Petit Mas de Marie

rm, VISA MC AE

quartier Revol, 1 km, Pertuis road: – ✆ 04 90 07 48 22 – lepetitmasdemarie@wanadoo.fr – Fax 04 90 07 34 26 – Closed autumn and February school holidays

15 rm – †€ 44/69 ††€ 50/73, ☐ € 10 – ½ P € 60/71 – **Rest** – *(closed Saturday lunch, Sunday dinner and Monday October-March)* Menu € 13,50 (weekday lunch), € 25/34 – Carte € 35/53

◆ This welcoming country house in Aigues is surrounded by a peaceful garden. Impeccably kept Provencal rooms. Spacious, bright dining room with a terrace overlooking the greenery and filled with the chirping of crickets.

Auberge de la Tour

AC VISA MC AE

51 r. A. de Tres – ✆ 04 90 07 34 64 – Fax 04 90 07 34 64 – Closed 27 October-4 November, 2-10 January, Saturday lunch, Sunday dinner and Monday

Rest – Menu € 12 bi (weekday lunch), € 17/25 – Carte € 22/28

◆ At this very simple restaurant, near the village church, typically Provencal dishes are lovingly prepared and served in a rustic and relaxed atmosphere.

TOUR-DE-FAURE – 46 Lot – 337 G5 – see St-Cirq-Lapopie

LA TOUR-DU-PIN – 38 Isère – 333 F4 – pop. 6 553 – alt. 350 m – ✉ 38110 Lyon - Rhone Valley

45 **C2**

Paris 516 – Aix-les-Bains 57 – Chambéry 51 – Grenoble 67 – Lyon 55 – Vienne 57

Office de tourisme, rue de Châbons ✆ 04 74 97 14 87, Fax 04 74 83 34 74

du Château de Faverges Faverges-de-la-TourEast: 9 km by D 1516, ✆ 04 74 88 89 51.

Mercure

VISA MC

439 av. Gén. de Gaulle, opposite the nautical centre – ✆ 04 74 83 31 31 – relais.latour@wanadoo.fr – Fax 04 74 97 87 01

60 rm – †€ 70 ††€ 84, ☐ € 12 – ½ P € 69 – **Rest** – *(Closed Saturday lunch and Sunday dinner)* Menu (€ 15), € 18/30 – Carte € 25/48

◆ This large 1970s building dominates the town. Modern, comfortable rooms, peaceful garden and outdoor swimming pool. Fitness facilities. Restaurant with a trendy decor (dark-wood panelling, design furniture). Up-to-date menu.

Le Bec Fin

VISA MC

pl. Champs-de-Mars – ✆ 04 74 97 58 79 – Closed 4-27 August, Sunday dinner and Monday

Rest – Menu € 17 (weekday lunch), € 24/43

◆ The former home of a wine merchant is now a restaurant run by a friendly young couple. Generous regional dishes in the form of menus, served in two yellow and green dining rooms.

in St-Didier-de-la-Tour 3 km east by N 6 – pop. 1 419 – alt. 380 m – ✉ 38110

Ambroisie

AC VISA MC

beside the lake – ✆ 04 74 97 25 53 – ambroisie2@wanadoo.fr – Fax 04 74 97 01 93 – Closed Wednesday

Rest – Menu € 16 (weekday lunch), € 37/57

◆ A lakeside country lodge with plush dining room/veranda and delightful terrace beneath plane trees, serving contemporary cuisine with Provençal influences.

in Rochetoirin 4 km northwest by N 6 and D 92 – pop. 980 – alt. 449 m – ✉ 38110

Le Rochetoirin

VISA MC

au village – ✆ 04 74 97 60 38 – lerochetoirin@wanadoo.fr – Closed 25 August-7 September, 23 December-15 January, Tuesday dinner and Wednesday dinner from October to April, Sunday dinner and Monday

Rest – Menu € 18 (weekday lunch), € 20/42 – Carte € 26/44

◆ This restaurant offers two culinary styles, either traditional or creative, renewed every season. Three seating options: one small informal dining room, a second rather smart and cosy, and a terrace.

TOURNEFEUILLE – 31 Haute-Garonne – 343 G3 – see Toulouse

TOURNON-SUR-RHÔNE – 07 Ardèche – 332 B3 – pop. 9 946 – alt. 125 m – ✉ 07300 Lyon - Rhone Valley 43 E2

Paris 545 – Grenoble 98 – Le Puy-en-Velay 104 – St-Étienne 77 – Valence 18 – Vienne 60

Office de tourisme, 2, place Saint-Julien ✆ 04 75 08 10 23

Château ★ terraces B - Panoramic road★★★ B.

Plan: see Tain-l'Hermitage

Les Amandiers without rest

13 av. de Nîmes – ✆ 04 75 07 24 10 – hotel@hotel-amandiers.com – Fax 04 75 07 06 30 – Closed 19 December-4 January C **n**

25 rm – †€ 54/59 ††€ 59/69, ☕ € 8

♦ Modern hotel popular with business people during the week. Renovated, air-conditioned rooms with good soundproofing and large bathrooms.

Azalées rm,

6 av. Gare – ✆ 04 75 08 05 23 – contact@hotel-azalees.com – Fax 04 75 08 18 27 – Closed 27 October-2 November and 22 December-4 January B **s**

37 rm – †€ 52 ††€ 52/70, ☕ € 8 – ½ P € 48

Rest – *(closed Sunday evening from 15 October to 15 March)* Menu € 18/32 – Carte € 19/28

♦ Between the railway station and the town centre, the rooms of this hotel are in two buildings on either side of an inner courtyard. Choose one of the more recent rooms. A gratin of ravioli, Picodon cheese, the scent of thyme: the cuisine has a definite bias for local produce. Small terrace.

Tournesol

44 av. Mar. Foch – ✆ 04 75 07 08 26 – contact@letournesol.net – Closed 1st-24 August, autumn and February school holidays, Sunday dinner, Tuesday dinner and Wednesday B **v**

Rest – Menu € 17 (weekdays)/33 – Carte € 30/42

♦ In this contemporary restaurant, enjoy up-to-date cuisine prepared with fresh ingredients and a good selection of Côtes du Rhône (on display in a glass-fronted cellar). Terrace.

Le Chaudron

7 r. St-Antoine – ✆ 04 75 08 17 90 – Fax 04 75 08 06 61 – Closed 2 -24 August, 23 December-6 January, Tuesday dinner, Thursday dinner and Sunday B **r**

Rest – Menu € 26/35 – Carte € 30/52

♦ Dark-wood panelling, green leatherette bench seats and an attractive terrace are the setting for this pleasant bistro. Tasty local cuisine and lengthy Côtes-du-Rhone wine list.

TOURNUS – 71 Saône-et-Loire – 320 J10 – pop. 6 231 – alt. 193 m – ✉ 71700 Burgundy-Jura 8 C3

Paris 360 – Bourg-en-Bresse 70 – Chalon-sur-Saône 28 – Mâcon 37

Office de tourisme, 2, place de l'abbaye ✆ 03 85 27 00 20, Fax 03 85 27 00 21

Abbey★★.

Plan on next page

Hôtel de Greuze without rest

5 pl. Abbaye – ✆ 03 85 51 77 77 – hoteldegreuze@free.fr – Fax 03 85 51 77 23 **e**

19 rm – †€ 115/290 ††€ 145/320, ☕ € 16 – 2 suites

♦ The St Philibert bell tower overlooks this fine, renovated Bresse-style house. Refined decoration in the rooms that have each been given a different style: Louis XVI, Directoire, French Empire, etc. Some offer a view of the abbey. A most distinguished residence.

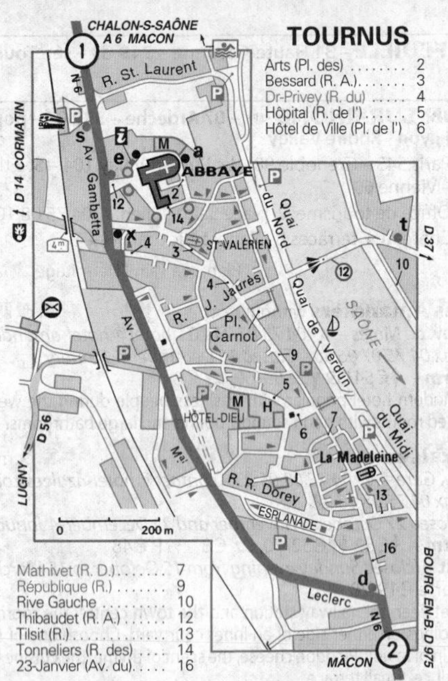

Le Rempart

2 av. Gambetta – ✆ 03 85 51 10 56 – lerempart@wanadoo.fr – Fax 03 85 51 77 22

23 rm – †€ 95/145 ††€ 115/165, ☕ € 16 – 11 suites – ½ P € 98/158 **x**

Rest – *(closed Wednesday and Thursday from 15 October to 15 April except school holidays)* Menu € 33/77 – Carte € 59/76

Rest *Le Bistrot* – Menu € 19/26 – Carte € 26/38

◆ A 15C house built on the old ramparts of Tournus. Almost all the rooms have been treated to a contemporary makeover with high quality materials, fixtures and fittings. A plush restaurant serving updated et cuisine. Romanesque remains. Regional menu at the Bistrot.

La Tour du Trésorier without rest

9 pl. Abbaye – ✆ 03 85 27 00 47 – michel.vialle@worldonline.fr – Fax 03 85 27 00 48 – Closed 4 January-8 February – **5 rm** ☕ – †€ 120/170 ††€ 130/180 **a**

◆ An impressive house of medieval origin flanked by an imposing tower, located opposite the abbey and alongside the Musée Bourguignon. A warm welcome, cosy lounge and guestrooms full of charm.

Rest. Greuze (Laurent Couturier)

1 r. A. Thibaudet – ✆ 03 85 51 13 52 – greuze@wanadoo.fr – Fax 03 85 51 75 42 – Closed 11 November-11 December **e**

Rest – Menu € 50 (weekdays)/105 – Carte € 81/126

Spec. Foie gras de canard à la croque de caramel. Langoustines en trois préparations. Collection de desserts. **Wines** Mâcon Uchizy, Rully.

◆ The owner chef of this venerable house in the centre of town happily reinterprets classic recipes, adding his own inimitable touch to traditional French recipes.

Aux Terrasses (Jean-Michel Carrette) with rm

18 av. 23-Janvier – ✆ 03 85 51 01 74 – courrier@aux-terrasses.com – Fax 03 85 51 09 99 – Closed 1st-12 June, 16-27 November, 4-26 January, Sunday dinner, Tuesday lunch and Monday **d**

18 rm – †€ 62/75 ††€ 62/75, ☕ € 11 – **Rest** – Menu € 26 (weekday lunch), € 32/80 – Carte € 44/77

Spec. Minute d'escargots de Bourgogne en raviole ouverte. Sandre bardé au jambon du Morvan (October to April). Filet de bœuf charolais à la plancha, sauce béarnaise. **Wines** Mâcon Viré-Clessé, Givry.

◆ This charming hotel has soundproofed guestrooms and an attractive restaurant, furnished in classical, Baroque and modern styles. Regional cuisine.

Le Terminus with rm
21 av. Gambetta – ✆ 03 85 51 05 54 – reservation@hotel-terminus-tournus.com – Fax 03 85 51 79 11 – Closed Wednesday s
13 rm – †€ 48 ††€ 67, ☕ € 9 – ½ P € 75
Rest – Menu € 18 (weekdays)/45 – Carte € 40/59
◆ Early-20C house near the railway station where guests can enjoy modern cuisine in a contemporary setting. Original, "100% Charolais" menu. All rooms are non-smoking.

Meulien
1 bis av. Alpes – ✆ 03 85 51 20 86 – vmeulien@wanadoo.fr – Fax 03 85 51 20 86 – Closed 24 November-7 December, Sunday dinner, Tuesday lunch and Monday
Rest – Menu € 15 (weekday lunch), € 20/54 – Carte € 30/76 t
◆ This left-bank restaurant boasts a contemporary decor in shades of cream and chocolate. Warm family atmosphere and carefully prepared up-to-date cuisine.

in Villars 4 km South by N 6 and D 210 – pop. 235 – alt. 184 m

L'Auberge des Gourmets
pl. de l'Église – ✆ 03 85 32 58 80 – laubergedesgourmets@orange.fr – Fax 03 85 51 08 32 – Closed 4-11 June, 29 October-7 November, 24-27 December, 5-29 January, Sunday dinner, Tuesday dinner and Wednesday except public holidays
Rest – Menu € 20 (weekdays)/46 – Carte € 35/53
◆ Small inn, with a yellow façade. It offers traditional meals with personal touches, under the painted beams of a dining room whose fine exposed stonework is brightened by temporary art exhibitions. Friendly welcome and service.

in Brancion 14 km west by D 14 - ✉ 71700 Martailly-les-Brancion

Château keep ≤★.

La Montagne de Brancion ≤ mounts of Mâconnais, rest,
on the Briancon pass – ✆ 03 85 51 12 40 – lamontagnedebrancion@wanadoo.fr – Fax 03 85 51 18 64 – Closed 1st-20 December and 5 January-10 March
19 rm – †€ 80/106 ††€ 100/170, ☕ € 18 – ½ P € 106/161
Rest – *(closed Tuesday lunch, Wednesday lunch and Thursday lunch)* Menu € 28 (weekday lunch), € 48/78 – Carte € 46/98
◆ This charming residence on a hillside in the middle of the vineyard has a pleasant view of the Mâcon hills. The prettily decorated rooms are quiet and well kept. Tasty modern cuisine generously served in the restaurant with fine views.

TOURRETTES – 83 Var – 340 P4 – pop. 2 180 – alt. 350 m – ✉ 83440

French Riviera 41 **C3**

Paris 884 – Castellane 56 – Draguignan 31 – Fréjus 35 – Grasse 26

Auberge des Pins rm, rest, rest,
Domaine Le Chevalier, 2 km south on D 19 – ✆ 04 94 76 06 36 – auberge.des.pins@wanadoo.fr – Fax 04 94 76 27 50
16 rm – †€ 54/120 ††€ 54/120, ☕ € 7 – **Rest** – Menu € 22/50
◆ In an estate of many leisure facilities, modern rooms and duplex studio flats spread across three pavilions. The dining room decor is a permanent reminder of the surrounding countryside. Local cuisine and grills on an open wood fire (in the evening only).

South 6 km on D 56 – ✉ 83440 Tourrettes

Four Seasons Resort Provence at Terre Blanche rest, rest,
Domaine de Terre Blanche – ✆ 04 94 39 90 00 – reservations.provence@fourseasons.com – Fax 04 94 39 90 01
114 suites ☕ – ††€ 395/925
Rest *Faventia* – see restaurant listing
Rest *Gaudina* – Menu € 48 – Carte € 62/92
Rest *Tousco Grill* – grill *(open 1st June-30 September and closed Tuesday and Wednesday) (lunch only 1st-15 June and 1st-15 September)* Carte € 40/53
◆ Magnificent hotel complex on an estate including two 18-hole golf courses, a large Provençal residence and 45 villas housing vast, superbly decorated suites. Southern flavours at Gaudina. The Tousco Grill offers grilled meat and buffets by the pool.

Faventia – Hôtel Four Seasons Resort Provence at Terre Blanche
– ☎ 04 94 39 90 00
– reservations.provence@fourseasons.com – Fax 04 94 39 90 01
– Closed 2 November-22 December, 4 January-6 April, Sunday and Monday
Rest – *(dinner only)* Menu € 68/120 – Carte € 83/124
Spec. Foie gras de canard du Gers autour de deux idées. Tronçon de turbot cuit en cocotte aux feuilles de figuier. Barre de chocolat aux éclats de fruits croustillants, glace pistache. **Wines** Côtes de Provence.
♦ Attractive, contemporary dining room and pleasant terrace overlooking the valley offering clear views of the nearby hilltop villages. Modern Southern food.

TOURRETTES-SUR-LOUP – 06 Alpes-Maritimes – 341 D5 – pop. 3 870 – alt. 400 m – ✉ 06140 French Riviera

42 **E2**

Paris 929 – Grasse 18 – Nice 29 – Vence 6

Office de tourisme, 2, place de la Libération ☎ 04 93 24 18 93, Fax 04 93 59 24 40

Old village★ - ≤★ of the village on Les Quenières road.

Résidence des Chevaliers without rest ≤ village and coast,
Caire road – ☎ 04 93 59 31 97
– hoteldeschevaliers06@wanadoo.fr – Fax 04 93 59 27 97 – Open 1st April-1st Oct.
12 rm – ♦€ 90 ♦♦€ 120/200, ☕ € 14
♦ This attractive flower-decked stone establishment overlooks a medieval village and the coast. Rustic-style rooms. Breakfast served on a lovely terrace.

La Demeure de Jeanne without rest
907 rte Vence – ☎ 04 93 59 37 24 – yolande6@libertysurf.fr – Fax 04 93 24 39 95
– Open 15 March-15 October
4 rm ☕ – ♦€ 100/150 ♦♦€ 100/150
♦ Typical villa with personalised rooms. Olive trees in the garden, sea views, cosy lounge and breakfast served alongside the pool in summer.

Histoires de Bastide without rest
chemin du Moulin à Farine – ☎ 04 93 58 96 49 – histoiresdebastide@wanadoo.fr
– Fax 04 93 59 08 46
4 rm – ♦€ 130/190 ♦♦€ 130/190, ☕ € 15
♦ This charming bastide has an elegant Provençal ambience. Delightful guestrooms named after the works of Marcel Pagnol. Terrace, lovely swimming pool and old olive trees in the garden.

Les Bacchanales (Christophe Dufau)
21 Grand-Rue – ☎ 04 93 24 19 19 – lesbacchanales06@orange.fr
– Fax 04 93 24 12 17
– Closed 23-30 June, 1st November-15 December, Tuesday and Wednesday
Rest – *(number of covers limited, pre-book)* Menu € 28 (weekday lunch), € 40/52
Spec. Consommé de crabes verts, ravioles de tourteau, yaourt et fruits de la passion. Colinot de Méditerranée vapeur, brocoletti à la poutargue et olives de Nice. Mûres et mûres sauvages marinées à l'huile d'olive douce, mayonnaise vanille, sorbet cacao.
♦ Small gourmet bistro with an ambitious and creative repertoire on its blackboard menu. Modern yet rustic decor enlivened by the proprietress's contemporary artwork.

Médiéval
6 Grand-Rue – ☎ 04 93 59 31 63 – Closed 15 December-15 January, Wednesday and Thursday
Rest – Menu € 20/30 – Carte € 39/51
♦ Family-run restaurant in a narrow street of this delightful old village with its many artists and craftsmen. A long narrow rustic dining room where a rich traditional cuisine is served.

The sun's out – let's eat alfresco!
Look for a terrace:

TOURS Ⓟ – 37 Indre-et-Loire – **317** N4 – **pop. 132 820** – **Built-up area 297 631** – **alt. 60 m** – ✉ **37000** Châteaux of the Loire 11 **B2**

Paris 237 – Angers 124 – Bordeaux 346 – Le Mans 84 – Orléans 117

Tours-Val de Loire ✆ 02 47 49 37 00, Northeast: 7 km U.

Office de tourisme, 78-82, rue Bernard Palissy ✆ 02 47 70 37 37, Fax 02 47 61 14 22

de Touraine Ballan-Miré Château de la Touche, Southwest: 10 km by D 751, ✆ 02 47 53 20 28 ;

d'Ardrée Saint-Antoine-du-RocherNorth: 12 km by D 2, ✆ 02 47 56 77 38.

Cathedral district★★: St-Gatien cathedral ★★, musée des Beaux-Arts★★ - La Psalette (St-Gratien cloister)★, Place Grégoire-de-Tours★ - Old Tours★★★: place Plumereau★ , hôtel Gouin★, rue Briçonnet★ - Quartier de St-Julien★: musée du Compagnonnage★★, Jardin de Beaune-Semblançay★ BY **K** - Musée des Équipages militaires et du Train★ V **M**5 - St-Cosme priory ★ West: 3 km V.

Plans on following pages

De l'Univers rm, VISA MC AE

5 bd Heurteloup – ✆ 02 47 05 37 12 – contact@hotel-univers.fr – Fax 02 47 61 51 80 CZ **u**

85 rm – €198/270 €198/270, ☕ €18 – 2 suites

Rest ***La Touraine*** – *(closed lunch 14 July-24 August and Sunday except dinner November-March)* Menu (€22), €28/41 – Carte €35/59

◆ The superb murals representing famous hotel guests from 1846 onwards is the establishment's pride and joy. Plush rooms and luxurious suites complete the opulent picture. Traditional food served in a bright and comfortable dining room; low-key bar.

Central Hôtel without rest VISA MC AE

21 r. Berthelot – ✆ 02 47 05 46 44 – bestwestern.centralhotel@wanadoo.fr – Fax 02 47 66 10 26 – Closed 23 December-1st January CY **r**

37 rm – €99/120 €120/139, ☕ €13 – 2 suites

◆ Among the many assets of this establishment are the garage, regularly spruced up rooms (some overlooking an inner garden), splendid bathrooms, and summer terrace.

Mercure Centre without rest VISA MC AE

29 r. E. Vaillant – ✆ 02 47 60 40 60 – h3475@accor.com – Fax 02 47 64 74 81 DZ **f**

92 rm – €80/130 €100/150, ☕ €13

◆ A convenient location two minutes from the train station. Functional rooms painted in soft colours, overlooking either the street or the railway lines (well soundproofed). Full breakfast.

Kyriad without rest VISA MC AE

65 av. Grammont – ✆ 02 47 64 71 78 – contact@kyriadtours.com – Fax 02 47 05 84 62 V **s**

50 rm – €78/80 €88/90, ☕ €8,50

◆ Stylish modern fixtures and fittings depict the rooms of this impeccably refurbished hotel. Elegant sitting room (fireplace and wainscoting) and winter garden-style breakfast room.

L'Adresse without rest VISA MC AE

12 r. de la Rôtisserie – ✆ 02 47 20 85 76 – contactladresse@aol.com – Fax 02 47 05 74 87 AY **u**

17 rm – €50 €70/90, ☕ €8

◆ The small cosy rooms are a happy blend of old (beams) and new, making this 18C abode in the historic district a delightful destination.

Turone rm, VISA MC AE

4 pl. de la Liberté – ✆ 02 47 05 50 05 – contact@hotelturone.com – Fax 02 47 20 22 07 V **z**

120 rm – €92/150 €92/150, ☕ €12 – **Rest** – Menu (€15), €20/29 – Carte €30/39

◆ A popular hotel due to its practical location, spacious garage and pleasant, modern rooms (including seven more comfortable rooms under the eaves). Extremely quiet courtyard. Brasserie style dining room and traditional menu.

TOURS

Amandiers (R. des) . . . . **CY** 4
Berthelot (R.) . . . . **BCY** 7
Bons Enfants (R. des) . . . . **BY** 8
Bordeaux (R. de) . . . . **CZ**
Boyer (R. Léon) . . . . **AZ** 10
Briçonnet (R.) . . . . **AY** 13
Carmes (Pl. des) . . . . **BY** 16
Châteauneuf (Pl. de) . . . . . . **BY** 17
Châteaunuef (R. de) . . . . . . **AY** 18
Coeur-Navré (Passage du) . **CY** 21
Commerce (R. du) . . . . **BY**
Constantine (R. de) . . . . . . **BY** 24
Corneille (R.) . . . . **CY** 25
Courier (R. Paul-Louis) . . . . **BY** 27
Courteline (R. G.) . . . . **AY** 28
Cygne (R. du) . . . . **CY** 29
Descartes (R.) . . . . **BZ** 33
Dolve (R. de la) . . . . **BZ** 35
Favre (R. Jules) . . . . **BY** 38
Fusillés (R. des) . . . . **BY** 41
Gambetta (R.) . . . . **BZ** 43
Giraudeau (R.) . . . . **AZ** 46
Grammont (Av. de) . . . . **CZ**
Grand-Marché (Pl. du) . . . . **AY** 49

Le Grand Hôtel without rest

9 pl. du Gén. Leclerc – ✆ 02 47 05 35 31 – contact@legrandhoteltours.com – Fax 02 47 64 10 77 – Closed 18 December-7 January CZ **z**

107 rm – †€ 72/93 ††€ 82/113, ☕ € 12

◆ Initially designed in 1927 by architect Pierre Chareau, the new owner has set about restoring this hotel to its former glory. Ask for one of the renovated rooms.

Grand Passage . . . . **CZ** 50
Grégoire-de-Tours (Pl.) . . . . **DY** 52
Grosse-Tour (R. de la) . . . . . **AY** 55
Halles (Pl. des) . . . . **AZ**
Halles (R. des) . . . . **BY**
Herbes (Carroi aux) . . . . **AY** 56
Lavoisier (R.) . . . . **CY** 60
Manceau (R.) . . . . **DY** 61
Marceau (R.) . . . . **BYZ**
Merville (R. du Prés.) . . . . . **BY** 65
Meusnier (R. Gén.) . . . . **DY** 66
Monnaie (R. de la) . . . . **BY** 68
Mûrier (R. du) . . . . **AY** 71
Nationale (R.) . . . . **BYZ**
Paix (R. de la) . . . . **BY** 73
Petites-Boucheries (Pl. des) . . . . **DY** 80
Petit-Cupidon (R. du) . . . . . **DY** 77
Petit-St-Martin (R. du) . . . . . **AY** 78
Racine (R.) . . . . **DY** 84
Rapin (R.) . . . . **AZ** 85
St-Pierre-le-Puellier (Pl.) . . . . **ABY** 93
Scellerie (R. de la) . . . . . . **BCY**
Sully (R. de) . . . . **BZ** 96
Victoire (Pl. de la) . . . . **AY** 103
Vinci (R. Léonard de) . . . . . . **BZ** 104

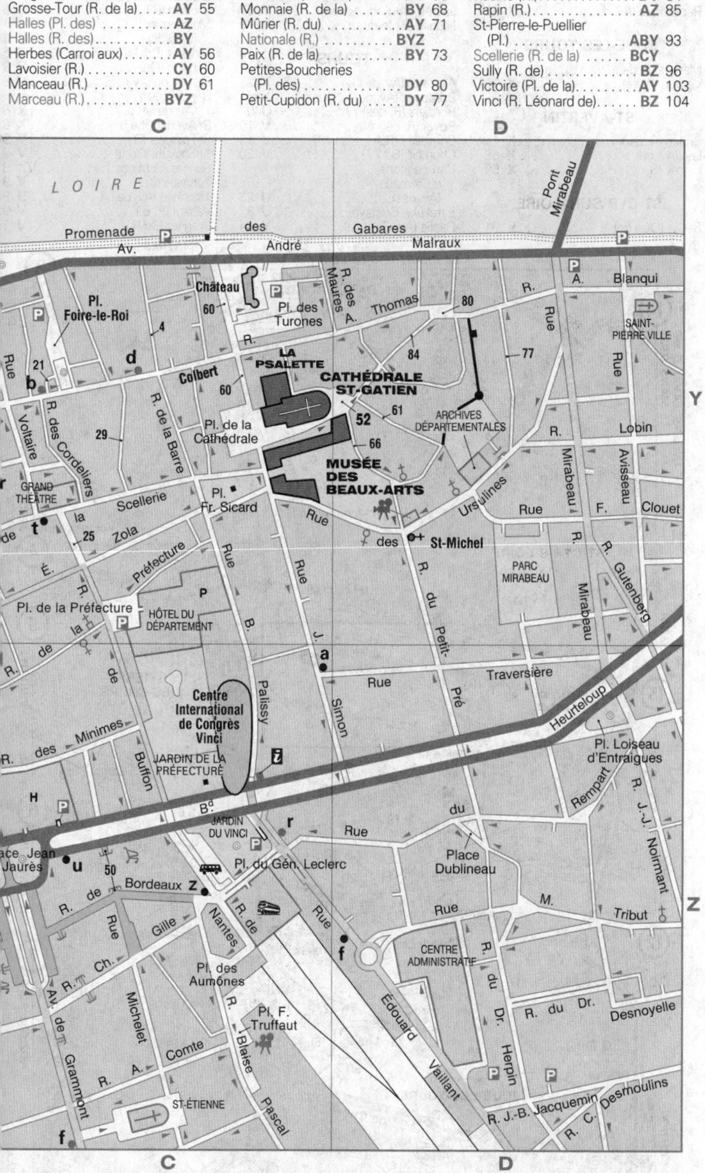

Du Manoir without rest

2 r. Traversière – ✆ 02 47 05 37 37 – manoir37@wanadoo.fr – Fax 02 47 05 16 00
19 rm – €49/56 €56/62, €8 CZ **a**

♦ This 19C town house has well-kept classical rooms, furnished with antiques and a few canopied bedsteads. Homemade produce adorns the breakfast table, served in a pretty, vaulted room.

CHAMBRAY-LÈS-TOURS

République (Av. de la) . . . . **X** 88

JOUÉ-LÈS-TOURS

Martyrs (R. des) . . . . **X** 64
Verdun (R. de) . . . . **X** 102

ST-AVERTIN

Brulon (R. Léon) . . . . **X** 14
Lac (Av. du) . . . . **X** 58
Larçay (R. de) . . . . **X** 59

ST-CYR-SUR -LOIRE

St-Cyr (Quai de) . . . . **V** 91

ST-PIERRE-DES-CORPS

Jaurès (Boulevard Jean) . . . . **V** 57
Moulin (R. Jean) . . . . **V** 70

TOURS

Alouette (Av. de l') . . . . **X** 2
Bordeaux (Av. de) . . . . **X** 51
Bordiers (R. des) . . . . **U** 9
Boyer (R. Léon) . . . . **V** 10
Chevallier (R.A.) . . . . **V** 19
Churchill (Bd W.) . . . . **V** 20
Compagnons
d'Emmaüs
(Av. des) . . . . **U** 23
Eiffel (Av. Gustave) . . . . **U** 37
Gaulle (Av. Gén.-de) . . . . **V** 44
Giraudeau (R.) . . . . **V** 4
Grammont (Av. de) . . . . **V** 47
Groison (R.) . . . . **U** 5
Marmoutier
(Quai de) . . . . **U** 6
Monnet (Bd J.) . . . . **V** 6
Portillon (Quai de) . . . . **U** 8
Proud'hon (Av.) . . . . **V** 82
République
(Av. de la) . . . . **X** 8
St-Avertin (Rte de) . . . . **X** 8
St-François (R.) . . . . **V** 9
St-Sauveur (Pont) . . . . **V** 9
Sanitas (Pont du) . . . . **VX** 9
Tonnellé (Bd) . . . . **V** 9
Tranchée (Av. de la) . . . . **U** 9
Vaillant (R. E.) . . . . **V** 9
Wagner (Bd R.) . . . . **V** 1

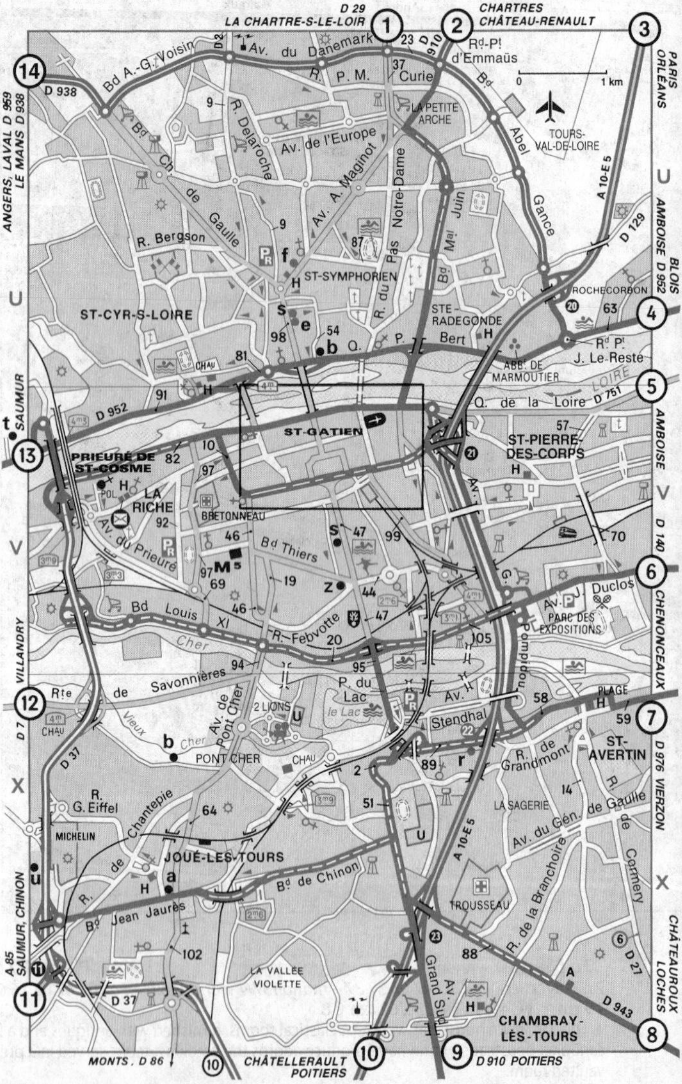

Mondial without rest
3 pl. de la Résistance – 02 47 05 62 68 – info@hotelmondialtours.com – Fax 02 47 61 85 31 – Closed 24 December-7 January, 8-17 February, Friday and Saturday from November to January BY **g**
21 rm – €52 €56, €8
◆ Standing on a town centre square, this hotel is as popular for its location as for its pleasantly updated modern interior. Find a grey and pastel colour scheme and impeccable rooms.

Du Théâtre without rest
57 r. Scellerie – 02 47 05 31 29 – hoteldutheatre.tours@wanadoo.fr – Fax 02 47 61 20 78 CY **t**
14 rm – €50 €56, €8,50
◆ The interior of this 15C house is almost intimate in feel: small, welcoming, well kept rooms with exposed timberwork. Rooms on the courtyard side are quieter.

Châteaux de la Loire without rest
12 r. Gambetta – 02 47 05 10 05 – contact@hoteldeschateaux.fr – Fax 02 47 20 20 14 – Open 9 March-20 December BZ **x**
30 rm – €45/54,50 €45/64, €7
◆ To make the most of this hotel, which is gradually being renovated (double glazing and an overall makeover), ask for one of the renovated rooms to the rear.

Castel Fleuri without rest
10-12 r. Groison – 02 47 54 50 99 – hotelcastelfleuri@wanadoo.fr – Fax 02 47 54 86 59 – Closed 25 July-7 August, 28 December-2 January and Sunday U **b**
15 rm – €43/51 €53/65, €8
◆ This unpretentious family hotel in a residential neighbourhood is quiet and convenient. There is a car park, small tasteful rooms (ask for a renovated one), and sensible prices.

La Roche Le Roy (Alain Couturier)
55 rte St-Avertin – 02 47 27 22 00 – laroche.leroy@wanadoo.fr – Fax 02 47 28 08 39 – Closed 1st-26 August, 21 February-9 March, Sunday and Monday X **r**
Rest – Menu €36 (weekday lunch), €56/72 – Carte €58/76
Spec. Dos de sandre en croûte de pain d'épice. Matelote d'anguille "dite blanche" au Vouvray. Poitrine de pigeonneau de Racan "Apicius". **Wines** Montlouis, Bourgueil.
◆ This charming small manor, characteristic of the Tours region, invites you to taste seasonal culinary specialities in an intimate atmosphere. Pleasant terrace.

Charles Barrier (Hervé Lussault)
101 av. Tranchée – 02 47 54 20 39 – charles_barrier@yahoo.fr – Fax 02 47 41 80 95 – Closed Saturday lunch and Sunday except public holidays U **e**
Rest – Menu €29 (weekdays)/89 – Carte €69/125
Spec. Grosses langoustines croustillantes au curry de Madras. Suprême de géline de Touraine au gingembre rose. Pigeonneau du pays de Racan rôti, jus au foie gras. **Wines** Vouvray, Chinon.
◆ The personal recipes of the young chef have restored this handsome bourgeois home to its illustrious gastronomic past. Pleasant veranda and peaceful flower garden terrace.

La Chope
25 bis r. Grammont – 02 47 20 15 15 – Fax 02 47 05 70 51 – Closed 28 July-11 August CZ **f**
Rest – Menu (€17), €19/24 – Carte €30/49
◆ A chic brasserie decorated in the Belle Époque style with red velvet bench seats, mirrors and tulip lamps. The menu offers a wide choice of fish and seafood and several exceptional clarets.

La Deuvalière
18 r. de la Monnaie – 02 47 64 01 57 – ladeuvaliere@wanadoo.fr – Fax 02 47 64 01 57 – Closed Saturday lunch, Sunday and Monday BY **e**
Rest – Menu (€13), €28/32
◆ A good combination of old stonework from a characteristic 15C house mingled with modern details (dark wood, orange hues). Tasty, updated traditional dishes.

L'Odéon

10 pl. Gén. Leclerc – ✆ 02 47 20 12 65 – l.odeon@orange.fr
– Fax 02 47 20 47 58
– Closed 4-17 August and Sunday CZ **r**

Rest – Menu € 24/36 – Carte € 33/53

◆ The same chef has been at the helm of this restaurant for over twenty years. It was originally opened in 1893 and is one of the oldest in Tours. Tasteful Art Deco, brasserie style decoration. Traditional menu.

La Trattoria des Halles

31 pl. G.-Pailhou – ✆ 02 47 64 26 64 – latratteria-tours@wanadoo.fr
– Fax 02 47 20 14 65 – Closed August, Sunday and Monday AZ **b**

Rest – Menu € 15/35 – Carte € 26/45

◆ A smart yet informal atmosphere reigns in this contemporary bistro opposite the Halles. The chef, of Russian origin, rustles up tasty meals with an Italian flavour.

Les Linottes Gourmandes

22 r. Georges Courteline – ✆ 02 47 38 34 82
– leslinottesgourmandes@hotmail.fr
– Closed 7-13 April, 28 July-18 August, Sunday and Monday AY **b**

Rest – *(number of covers limited, pre-book)*
Menu € 18 (weekday lunch), € 25/35

◆ An old half-timbered house is the rustic setting for the warm restrained decor (beams, fireplace) of this restaurant, whose bistro cuisine is as tasty as it is attractive.

Cap Sud

88 r. Colbert – ✆ 02 47 05 24 81 – Fax 02 45 05 01 26
– Closed 20 July-4 August, Sunday and Monday CY **d**

Rest – Menu (€ 19), € 21/32 – Carte € 35/46

◆ This little restaurant has a Mediterranean atmosphere, both in its warm decor with sunny colours and up-to-date cuisine. Short but well selected wine list.

L'Atelier Gourmand

37 r. Étienne Marcel – ✆ 02 47 38 59 87 – mail@lateliergourmand.fr
– Fax 02 47 50 14 23 – Closed 20 December-15 January, Saturday lunch,
Sunday and Monday AY **z**

Rest – Menu € 10 (weekday lunch)/20 – Carte € 28/34

◆ This 15C residence is in the historic district of Tours. It houses a charming little restaurant with a colourful rustic dining room, and a pleasant terrace in the inner courtyard.

Le Bistrot de la Tranchée

103 av. Tranchée – ✆ 02 47 41 09 08 – charles_barrier@yahoo.fr
– Fax 02 47 41 80 95
– Closed 15-31 August, Sunday and Monday U **s**

Rest – Menu (€ 9), € 12 (weekday lunch), € 17/25 – Carte € 26/38

◆ Attractive wood facade, simple but charming decor, view of the kitchen, traditional cuisine and dishes of the day chalked up on the blackboard mean that this pleasant bistro is often crowded.

Le Rif

12 av. Maginot – ✆ 02 47 51 12 44 – Fax 02 47 51 14 50
– Closed 21 July-21 August, Wednesday dinner from September to June,
Sunday except lunch in July-August and Monday U **f**

Rest – Menu (€ 26 bi) – Carte € 20/35

◆ North African cuisine and a matching tasteful decor adorned with Moroccan ornaments and pottery lamps. Friendly welcome.

Le Petit Patrimoine

58 r. Colbert – ✆ 02 47 66 05 81 – Closed 15-31 July, Christmas holidays,
Sunday and Monday CY **b**

Rest – Menu € 16/25 – Carte € 24/34

◆ The rustic interior of this elongated structure, the wholesome country dishes from a past era, and the pleasant service make this establishment a must.

via ② 9 km

Mercure

r. Aviation, (Milletière industrial estate) ✉ 37100 Tours – ✆ 02 47 49 55 00 – h1572@accor.com – Fax 02 47 49 55 25

93 rm – €90/110 €110/130, ☕ €12 – ½ P €92/102

Rest – Menu (€18), €23/30 bi – Carte €23/40

◆ A modern building near the motorway slip road, with simple, spacious, functional rooms. Popular with business travellers. Bright restaurant overlooking the summer terrace, traditional fare and regional wines.

L'Arche de Meslay

14 r. Ailes ✉ 37210 Parçay-Meslay – ✆ 02 47 29 00 07 – Fax 02 47 29 04 04 – Closed 3-25 August, Sunday and Monday except public holidays

Rest – Menu €16 (weekdays)/44 – Carte €43/62

◆ The colonnade standing in the centre of the dining room, large mirrors and kitchens in full view of the customers, all make a wonderful setting. Regional and seasonal menus.

in Rochecorbon 6 km by ④ – **pop. 2 982 – alt. 58 m – ✉ 37210**

Office de tourisme, place du Croissant ✆ 02 47 52 80 22

Les Hautes Roches

86 quai Loire – ✆ 02 47 52 88 88 – hautes.roches@wanadoo.fr – Fax 02 47 52 81 30 – Closed 25 January-27 March

15 rm – €145/280 €145/280, ☕ €19 – ½ P €165/220

Rest – *(closed Sunday dinner, Tuesday lunch and Monday)* Menu €54/65 – Carte €51/78

Spec. Foie gras de canard à la façon d'un nougat. Poissons au beurre blanc nantais ou béarnaise. Tarte fine aux pommes caramélisées. **Wines** Vouvray, Bourgueil.

◆ This unusual 18C manor house overlooking the River Loire was once a monastery (the bar was the old summer kitchen). Attractive rooms, some cut into the rock. An elegant dining room and delightful panoramic terrace facing the river.

in Chambray-lès-Tours 6.5 km South, by Poitiers road - X – **pop. 10 275 – alt. 90 m – ✉ 37170**

Novotel

Z.A.C. La Vrillonnerie, (D 910) – ✆ 02 47 80 18 10 – h0453@accor.com – Fax 02 47 80 18 18

127 rm – €95/115 €95/115, ☕ €12,50

Rest – Carte €22/40

◆ A busy shopping district surrounds this functional hotel; ask for one of the quieter rooms overlooking the garden. 24hr service at the Novotel Café. Modern restaurant has a view of the kitchen and overlooks the pool. Traditional well thought out menu.

in Joué-lès-Tours 5 km Southwest, by Chinon road – pop. 36 517 – alt. 65 m – ✉ 37300

Office de tourisme, 39, avenue de la République ✆ 02 47 80 05 97

Château de Beaulieu

67 r. Beaulieu – ✆ 02 47 53 20 26 – chateaudebeaulieu@wanadoo.fr – Fax 02 47 53 84 20 X **b**

19 rm – €70/120 €90/155, ☕ €12 – ½ P €85/120

Rest – Menu €29 (weekday lunch), €40/75 – Carte €54/68

◆ A landscaped park surrounds this 18C manor house whose view extends as far as Tours. Period furniture in the spacious rooms (10 in a separate pavilion). An elegant setting in the dining room. Classic culinary repertoire and good wine list.

Mercure

rest,

parc des Bretonnières – ✆ 02 47 53 16 16 – h1788@accor.com – Fax 02 47 53 14 00 X **u**

75 rm – €75/115 €85/135, ☕ €12,50

Rest – Menu €18/24 – Carte €27/34

◆ This hotel, part of the Malraux Congress Centre, offers well-soundproofed, contemporary rooms decorated in a restful colour scheme. Excellent fitness facilities. A dining room extending onto a garden terrace and traditional cuisine with regional touches.

Chéops rm, rest, VISA AE

75 bd J. Jaurès – ✆ 02 47 67 72 72 – hotel.cheops@wanadoo.fr – Fax 02 47 67 85 38 X a

58 rm – †€ 50/72 ††€ 58/72, ☕ € 7 – ½ P € 49/52

Rest – *(closed 19 December-1st January, Friday, Saturday and Sunday October-April) (dinner only)* Menu (€ 13,50), € 17 – Carte € 20/29

◆ A recent hotel that is part of a residential and shopping centre in the heart of Joué. Bright colours and wrought iron give the small rooms, half of which are air-conditioned, a Provençal style. Pleasant, sunny dining room decorated with modern furniture.

in La Guignière 4 km by ⑬, Langeais road - ✉37230 Fondettes

Manoir without rest VISA

10 r. de Beaumanoir, D 952 – ✆ 02 47 42 04 02 – chantelard.patrick@wanadoo.fr – Fax 02 47 49 79 29 V t

16 rm – †€ 38 ††€ 48, ☕ € 7

◆ A 1970s villa in a quiet residential neighbourhood. Some of the rooms, adorned with pretty wall fabrics, command fine views of the Loire.

in Vallières 8 km by ⑬, Langeais road - ✉37230 Fondettes

Auberge de Port Vallières VISA

D 952 – ✆ 02 47 42 24 04 – Fax 02 47 49 98 83 – Closed 18 August-1st September, 23 February-9 March, Tuesday dinner off season, Sunday dinner, Wednesday dinner and Monday

Rest – Menu € 18 (weekday lunch), € 27/45 – Carte € 42/55

◆ Touraine inspired cuisine awaits you in this former open-air café, converted into an inn many years ago. Decor of antique bric-a-brac. Table d'hôte available.

TOURS-SUR-MARNE – 51 Marne – 306 G8 – pop. 1 207 – alt. 79 m – ✉ 51150

13 **B2**

Paris 156 – Châlons-en-Champagne 25 – Épernay 14 – Reims 29

Touraine Champenoise with rm VISA AE

r. Magasin – ✆ 03 26 58 91 93 – touraine-champenoise@wanadoo.fr – Fax 03 26 58 95 47 – Closed 1st-15 January and Thursday

7 rm ☕ – †€ 68/72 ††€ 80/84 – ½ P € 72 – **Rest** – Menu € 30/50 – Carte € 28/46

◆ By the canal, a traditional house that has been run by the same family since 1907. Local cuisine served in an attractively rustic dining room. Simple, country-style rooms.

TOURTOUR – 83 Var – 340 M4 – pop. 472 – alt. 652 m – ✉ 83690

French Riviera

41 **C3**

Paris 827 – Aups 10 – Draguignan 17 – Salernes 11

Syndicat d'initiative, Château communal ✆ 04 94 70 59 47, Fax 04 94 70 59 47

Church ❊★.

La Bastide de Tourtour ← Massif des Maures, rm, rm, VISA AE

rte de Flayosc – ✆ 04 98 10 54 20 – bastide@bastidedetourtour.com – Fax 04 94 70 54 90

25 rm – †€ 110/140 ††€ 150/350, ☕ € 23

Rest – *(closed Monday, Tuesday, Wednesday, Thursday and Friday lunch 15 September-22 December and 3 January-15 June)* Menu € 30/75 – Carte € 53/81

◆ Provençal house on a hillside in the middle of pine and oak trees. Some of the individualised rooms have their own loggia. Attractive vaulted dining room and idyllic shaded terrace. Classical dishes.

La Petite Auberge ← Massif des Maures, VISA AE

rte de Flayosc, 1.5 km by D 77 – ✆ 04 98 10 26 16 – aubergetourtour@orange.fr – Fax 04 98 10 26 50 – Open 15 March-15 October

11 rm – †€ 55/170 ††€ 55/250, ☕ € 12 – 1 suite – ½ P € 65/165

Rest – *(closed Monday) (dinner only)* Menu € 30 (weekdays)/45

◆ Farmhouse surrounded by lush vegetation. Spacious rooms, including four recent and attractive ones next to the pool. Beautiful, elegant dining room with stone fireplace and terrace facing the Maures mountain range.

Auberge St-Pierre

3 km east by D 51 and secondary road – 04 94 50 00 50 – aubergestpierre@wanadoo.fr – Fax 04 94 70 59 04 – Open 11 April-19 October
16 rm – €80 €80/103, €12 – ½ P €85/89 – **Rest** – *(dinner only except Saturday, Sunday and public holidays)* Menu €26/41
◆ A 16C inn, in the heart of a large farming estate, set near the former sheepcote. Rooms with loggias overlooking the countryside. Pool and small fitness room. Rustic dining room extended by a fine terrace overlooking the countryside. Traditional cuisine with local touches.

Le Mas des Collines Massif des Maures, rm,

chemin des collines, 2.5 km by Villecroze road (D 51) and secondary road – 04 94 70 59 30 – lemasdescollines@wanadoo.fr – Fax 04 94 70 57 62 – Open mid April to beg. November
7 rm – €75/90 €80/90, €5 – ½ P €74 – **Rest** – *(dinner only)* Menu €25/35
◆ As the name suggests, a hotel lost in the middle of the countryside. The functional rooms have balconies and there is a pool where you can enjoy the splendid views.

Les Chênes Verts (Paul Bajade) with rm rest,

rte de Villecroze, 2 km by D 51 – 04 94 70 55 06 – Fax 04 94 70 59 35 – Closed 1st June-20 July, Tuesday and Wednesday
3 rm – €100 €110, €20
Rest – *(number of covers limited, pre-book)* Menu €53/135 – Carte €80/174
Spec. Truffes noires du pays. Écrevisses sautées aux herbes. Agneau de pays.
Wines Côtes de Provence.
◆ Provence-style house away from it all in a pretty forest setting. Regional cuisine with lots of character (truffle specialities) to be savoured in two fine dining rooms or on the terrace.

LA TOUSSUIRE – 73 Savoie – 333 K6 – alt. 1 690 m – Winter sports : 1 800/2 400 m 19 – ✉ 73300 French Alps 46 F2

Paris 651 – Albertville 78 – Chambéry 91 – St-Jean-de-Maurienne 16

Les Soldanelles rest,

r. des Chasseurs Alpins – 04 79 56 75 29 – infos@hotelsoldanelles.com – Fax 04 79 56 71 56 – Open 28 June-31 August and 21 December-19 April
38 rm – €44/64 €65/120, €10 – ½ P €93/106 – **Rest** – Menu €33/50 – Carte €32/56
◆ On the slopes of the resort, a family hotel with spacious rooms that are well laid out; ask to be on the south side for the view and the sun. Elegant restaurant offering a panoramic view and traditional cuisine with a taste of the sea.

Les Airelles

– 04 79 56 75 88 – info@hotel-les-airelles.com – Fax 04 79 83 03 48 – Open July-August and 15 December-20 April
31 rm – €65/70 €72/82, €10,50 – ½ P €76/87 – **Rest** – Menu €20 (weekdays)/28 – Carte €26/31
◆ The many renovations undertaken in this large mountain building, situated at the foot of the ski lifts, have included the refreshing comfortable rooms. The bay windows of the restaurant offer perfect views of the skiers.

TOUZAC – 46 Lot – 337 C5 – see Puy-l'Évêque

TRACY-SUR-MER – 14 Calvados – 303 I3 – see Arromanches-les-Bains

---

TRAENHEIM – 67 Bas-Rhin – 315 I5 – pop. 556 – alt. 200 m – ✉ 67310 1 A1

Paris 471 – Haguenau 54 – Molsheim 8 – Saverne 22 – Strasbourg 25

Zum Loejelgucker

17 r. Principale – 03 88 50 38 19 – loejelgucker@traenheim.net – Fax 03 88 50 36 31 – Closed 30 December-5 January, 23 February-8 March, Monday dinner and Tuesday
Rest – Menu (€7,50), €11 (weekday lunch), €17/44 – Carte €24/45
◆ An 18C Alsatian farmhouse in a village at the foot of the Vosges. Dark woodwork, frescoes and flower-filled courtyard in summer. Regional dishes.

LA TRANCHE-SUR-MER – 85 Vendée – 316 H9 – pop. 2 510 – alt. 4 m – ✉ 85360 Atlantic Coast 34 B3

Paris 459 – La Rochelle 64 – La Roche-sur-Yon 40 – Les Sables-d'Olonne 39

Office de tourisme, place de la Liberté ☎ 02 51 30 33 96, Fax 02 51 27 78 71

Parc de Californie★ (ornithological park) East: 9 km.

Les Dunes

68 av. M. Samson – ☎ 02 51 30 32 27 – info@hotel-les-dunes.com – Fax 02 51 27 78 30 – Open 22 March-30 September

45 rm – †€ 39/56 ††€ 57/104, ☕ € 8,50 – ½ P € 53/81 – **Rest** – Menu (€ 13), € 18/33 – Carte € 20/48

◆ Hotel popular for its quiet location, faultless upkeep and superb pool with a glass roof, facing the sea. Some rooms have balconies and benefit from a sea view. The menu lists fish and seafood, including fresh crayfish and lobster.

in la Grière 2 km east by D 46 - ✉85360 La-Tranche-sur-Mer

Les Cols Verts

48 r. de Verdun – ☎ 02 51 27 49 30 – info@hotelcolsverts.com – Fax 02 51 30 11 42 – Open 5 April-30 September

32 rm – †€ 49/68 ††€ 61/94, ☕ € 9 – ½ P € 59/79 – **Rest** – Menu € 20/38 – Carte € 38/48

◆ A 1970s building 150m from the beach. Well-maintained rooms; quieter and smaller in the annexe on the other side of the garden. Swimming pool in an adjacent building. Pleasant terrace and traditional dishes with a clear preference for sea produce.

TRAVEXIN – 88 Vosges – 314 I5 – see Ventron

TRÈBES – 11 Aude – 344 F3 – see Carcassonne

TRÉBEURDEN – 22 Côtes-d'Armor – 309 A2 – pop. 3 451 – alt. 81 m – ✉ 22560 Brittany 9 B1

Paris 525 – Lannion 10 – Perros-Guirec 14 – St-Brieuc 74

Office de tourisme, place de Crec'h Héry ☎ 02 96 23 51 64, Fax 02 96 15 44 87

Le Castel ≤★ 30 mn - Pointe de Bihit ≤★ Southwest: 2 km - Pleumeur-Bodou: Radôme and musée des Télécommunications★, Planétarium du Trégor★, Northeast: 5.5 km.

Manoir de Lan-Kerellec

≤ the coast, rest,

– ☎ 02 96 15 00 00 – lankerellec@relaischateaux.com – Fax 02 96 23 66 88 – Open beginning March-15 November

19 rm – †€ 105/180 ††€ 155/435, ☕ € 20 – ½ P € 155/295

Rest – *(closed lunch Monday-Thursday)* Menu € 49/70 – Carte € 59/106

Spec. Araignée de mer décortiquée, foie gras et pomme granny (March to mid June). Homard bleu au beurre salé. Bar de ligne en filet poêlé, mousseline d'artichaut.

◆ A noble 19C Breton manor facing the islands and providing rooms with personal touches. With its ship's hull roof structure, model clippers, view of the Pink Granite Coast and up-to-date fish and seafood cuisine, the restaurant offers Brittany in a seashell!

Ti al Lannec

≤ the coast, rest,

14 allée de Mezo Guen – ☎ 02 96 15 01 01 – resa@tiallannec.com – Fax 02 96 23 62 14 – Open from beg. March-mid November

32 rm – †€ 88/113 ††€ 162/255, ☕ € 17 – 1 suite – ½ P € 140/236

Rest – Menu (€ 25), € 27 bi (weekday lunch), € 38/78 – Carte € 60/152

◆ "Heathland house" perched on a hill, in the middle of a wooded park reaching down to the beach. Well-kept rooms. Balneotherapy centre. A seascape that has to be seen ... and fish and seafood worthy of a healthy appetite !

Toëno without rest

1.5 km on régastel road – ☎ 02 96 23 68 78 – toeno@wanadoo.fr – Fax 02 96 15 42 54 – Closed 5 January-2 February

17 rm – †€ 52/87 ††€ 57/97, ☕ € 9

◆ Recently built hotel. Functional, simply decorated, light rooms, all with balconies or terraces; some of them have a view of the English Channel.

Le Quellen with rm VISA MC
18 corniche Goas Treiz – ✆ 02 96 15 43 18 – lequellen@wanadoo.fr – Fax 02 96 23 64 43 – Closed 26 March-16 April, 29 September-5 October, 5-19 November, Sunday dinner off season, Monday and Tuesday
6 rm – †€ 41/65 ††€ 41/65, ☕ € 6,50 – ½ P € 44/52 – **Rest** – Menu € 25/65 – Carte € 33/59
◆ Restaurant on the main road through Trébeurden, serving traditional cuisine in a bright neo-rustic setting. Dining room displaying a coffee mill collection. Functional rooms.

TRÉBOUL – 29 Finistère – 308 E6 – see Douarnenez

TREFFORT – 38 Isère – 333 G8 – pop. 129 – alt. 618 m – ✉ 38650 45 C2

Paris 598 – Grenoble 36 – Monestier-de-Clermont 9 – La Mure 43

at the lakeside 3 km south by D 110E – ✉ 38650 Treffort

Le Château d'Herbelon rm, P VISA MC
– ✆ 04 76 34 02 03 – chateaudherbelon@wanadoo.fr – Fax 04 76 34 05 44 – Open 1st March-15 November and closed Monday and Tuesday except July- August
10 rm – †€ 65/95 ††€ 65/95, ☕ € 9 – ½ P € 69/84 – **Rest** – Menu € 23/46 – Carte € 27/43
◆ A 17C building covered with Virginia creeper and climbing roses, next to Lake Monteynard. Spacious rooms. In winter, an imposing fireplace warms the rustic dining room. A few outdoor tables on the lawn in summer.

TREFFORT – 01 Ain – 328 F3 – pop. 1 910 – alt. 280 m – ✉ 01370 44 B1

Paris 436 – Bourg-en-Bresse 18 – Lons-le-Saunier 57 – Mâcon 51 – Oyonnax 42

L'Embellie rest, P VISA MC
pl. Champ de Foire – ✆ 04 74 42 35 64 – embellietreffort@aol.com – Fax 04 74 51 25 81 – Closed 1st-11 January
8 rm – †€ 38/39 ††€ 45/47, ☕ € 5 – ½ P € 48/50
Rest – *(closed Sunday dinner off season)* Menu € 12 (weekday lunch), € 19/33
◆ This inviting stone house on the village square offers small, simple rooms, currently being redecorated. Traditional food and Bresse dishes served in a modern setting or on the pleasant terrace.

TRÉGASTEL – 22 Côtes-d'Armor – 309 B2 – pop. 2 234 – alt. 58 m – ✉ 22730

Brittany 9 B1

Paris 526 – Lannion 11 – Perros-Guirec 9 – St-Brieuc 75 – Trébeurden 11 – Tréguier 26

Office de tourisme, place Sainte-Anne ✆ 02 96 15 38 38, Fax 02 96 23 85 97

de Saint-Samson Pleumeur-Bodou Avenue Jacques Ferronière, South: 3 km, ✆ 02 96 23 87 34.

Rocks★★ - Ile Renote★★ NE - Viewpoint indicator ≤★.

Park Hotel Bellevue P VISA MC AE
20 r. Calculots – ✆ 02 96 23 88 18 – bellevue.tregastel@wanadoo.fr – Fax 02 96 23 89 91 – Open 17 March-11 November
31 rm – †€ 55/85 ††€ 57/140, ☕ € 11 – ½ P € 107
Rest – *(open 1st May-30 September and closed Sunday May-June) (dinner only)* Menu (€ 22), € 26/59 – Carte € 34/113
◆ A refurbished 1930s establishment with garden. Rooms of varying sizes (one third enjoy a sea view), lounge/bar and billiards room. A spacious modern dining room with colourful tablecloths and exotic-looking chairs. Sea-facing terrace.

Beau Séjour
5 plage du Coz-Pors – ✆ 02 96 23 88 02 – daniellaveant@wanadoo.fr – Fax 02 96 23 49 73 – Closed 11 November-15 December and 10 January-10 February
16 rm – €50/77 €60/77, €10 – **Rest** – *(closed 1st- 25 October, 5 November-30 March and Monday) (dinner only)* Menu €37 – Carte €33/81
◆ Ideally located near the Forum and beach, a wide choice of rooms with sea views and a copious breakfast buffet: all the ingredients for a "beau séjour", as they say in French! With the Côte de Granit rose (trompe-l'oeil painting) as a backdrop, this restaurant focuses on contemporary-style cuisine.

De la Mer et de la Plage without rest
Coz-Pors beach – ✆ 02 96 15 60 00 – hoteldelamer.tregastel@laposte.net – Fax 02 96 15 31 11 – Open 1st April-15 November
20 rm – €42/95 €42/95, €8,50
◆ This regional-style house stands on the beach, next to the Forum. Light walls and bluish fabrics give a nautical feel to the decor of the neat, functional rooms.

Auberge Vieille Église
at Trégastel-Bourg, 2.5 km south (Lannion road) – ✆ 02 96 23 88 31 – bruno.le-fessant@wanadoo.fr – Fax 02 96 15 33 75 – Closed March, Sunday dinner, Tuesday dinner except July-August and Monday
Rest – Menu €16 (weekdays)/36 – Carte €36/48
◆ This Breton inn, covered with flowers in summer, is close to a lovely pink granite church. Exposed beams and stonework in the back room, mini-terrace and provincial atmosphere.

in la plage de Landrellec **3 km south by D 788 and secondary road – ✉22560 Pleumeur-Bodou**

Le Macareux
21 r. des Plages – ✆ 02 96 23 87 62 – infos@lemacareux.com – Fax 02 96 15 94 97 – Closed 1st January-13 February, Sunday dinner, Tuesday lunch except July and Monday
Rest – Menu €24/53 – Carte €29/80
◆ This pleasant Breton-style house, facing the foreshore, offers lobster specialities in a well-kept interior with rustic touches or on its summer terrace.

TRÉGUIER – 22 Côtes-d'Armor – 309 C2 – pop. 2 679 – alt. 40 m – ✉ 22220 Brittany

Paris 509 – Guingamp 28 – Lannion 19 – Paimpol 15 – St-Brieuc 61 9 **B1**
Office de tourisme, 67, rue Ernest Renan ✆ 02 96 92 22 33
St-Tugdual cathedral ★★: cloister★.

In the harbour – ✉22220 Tréguier

Aigue Marine rm, rest, rest
5 r. M. Berthelot – ✆ 02 96 92 97 00 – aiguemarine@aiguemarine.fr – Fax 02 96 92 44 48 – Closed 21-25 December, 4 January-24 February and Sunday from November to March
33 rm – €74/99 €74/99, €14 – 15 suites – ½ P €79/91
Rest – *(closed Saturday lunch, Sunday dinner and Monday off season and lunch except Sunday from June to September)* Menu €33/51 – Carte €48/64
◆ A hotel where relaxation is the byword. The functional rooms overlook the harbour or the pool and garden. Some have balconies, others welcome families. Well-prepared breakfast buffet. Restaurant serving up-to-date cuisine in a bright, modern setting. Fresh flowers in the dining room.

Lannion road **2 km southwest by D 786 and secondary road – ✉22220 Tréguier**

Kastell Dinec'h rest
– ✆ 02 96 92 49 39 – kastell@club-internet.fr – Fax 02 96 92 34 03 – Open 25 March-5 October and 26 October-31 December and closed Tuesday dinner and Wednesday off season
15 rm – €79/80 €90/92, €13,50 – ½ P €79/109 – **Rest** – *(dinner only) (residents only)* Menu €32/53
◆ A former fortified farmhouse benefiting from the peaceful surrounding countryside, a well-kept garden and small, cosy rooms set in the main building and outbuildings. Traditional meals served in a rustic setting warmed by an old fireplace.

TRÉGUNC – 29 Finistère – 308 H7 – pop. 6 354 – alt. 45 m – ✉ 29910 9 B2

▶ Paris 543 – Concarneau 7 – Pont-Aven 9 – Quimper 29 – Quimperlé 27

ℹ Office de tourisme, Kérambourg ✆ 02 98 50 22 05, Fax 02 98 50 18 48

Auberge Les Grandes Roches

r. Grandes Roches, 0.6 km northeast by secondary road – ✆ 02 98 97 62 97 – hrlesgrandesroches@club-internet.fr – Fax 02 98 50 29 19 – Closed 22 December-1st February

17 rm – 🚹€ 80/130 🚹🚹€ 80/130, ☕ € 12 – 1 suite – ½ P € 75/105

Rest – *(closed Tuesday and Wednesday)* Menu € 45 – Carte € 55/59

◆ This superb hamlet of farms, turned into a hotel and located in a park of dolmens and standing stones, has a pleasant rustic character. Cosy rooms in the best imaginable taste. Delightful inviting restaurant in which stone and wood prevail. Up-to-date cooking.

TREIGNAC – 19 Corrèze – 329 L2 – alt. 500 m – ✉ 19260 25 C2

▶ Paris 490 – Limoges 77 – Tulle 40 – Brive-la-Gaillarde 76 – Ussel 62

Maison Grandchamp

9 pl. des Pénitents – ✆ 05 55 98 10 69 – teyssier.marielle@wanadoo.fr – Open April-December

3 rm ☕ – 🚹€ 65/70 🚹🚹€ 75/80 – **Table d'hôte** – Menu € 20 bi/25 bi

◆ 16C family house, decorated with antiques and ancestral portraits. Attractive guestrooms. Table d'hôte in the large dining room or in the garden, weather permitting.

TRÉLAZÉ – 49 Maine-et-Loire – 317 G4 – see Angers

TRÉLON – 59 Nord – 302 M7 – pop. 2 828 – alt. 188 m – ✉ 59132

Northern France and the Paris Region 31 D3

▶ Paris 218 – Avesnes-sur-Helpe 15 – Charleroi 53 – Lille 115 – St-Quentin 68 – Vervins 35

ℹ Office de tourisme, 3, rue Clavon Collignon ✆ 03 27 57 08 18, Fax 03 27 57 06 80

Le Framboisier

rte Val Joly – ✆ 03 27 59 73 34 – Fax 03 27 57 07 47 – Closed 19 February-5 March, 18 August-10 September, Sunday dinner, Tuesday dinner and Monday

Rest – Menu € 15 (weekday lunch), € 26/42 – Carte € 31/54

◆ Old farmhouse along a busy road. Welcoming façade, and intimate dining rooms in the rustic style. Cuisine changes with the seasons.

TREMBLAY-EN-FRANCE – 93 Seine-Saint-Denis – 305 G7 – 101 18 – see Paris, Area

LE TREMBLAY-SUR-MAULDRE – 78 Yvelines – 311 H3 – pop. 813 – alt. 132 m – ✉ 78490 18 A2

▶ Paris 42 – Houdan 24 – Mantes-la-Jolie 32 – Rambouillet 18 – Versailles 24

⛳ du Domaine du Tremblay Place de l'Eglise, South: by D 34, ✆ 01 34 94 25 70.

Laurent Trochain

3 r. Gén. de Gaulle – ✆ 01 34 87 80 96 – trochain.laurent@wanadoo.fr – Fax 0134 87 91 52 – Closed Easter holidays, 15-30 August, 1st-15 January, Monday and Tuesday

Rest – Menu (€ 35 bi), € 42 bi (weekday lunch)/48 – Carte approx. € 48

Spec. L'esprit d'un lièvre à la royale (in season). Fromages marinés dans différentes huiles. Déclinaison d'une salade de fruits et sorbets (summer).

◆ This village inn (former manor house) is run by a new team. Half-rustic, half-elegant, decor and fine, modern cuisine with the chef's personal touch.

The ✿ award is the crème de la crème.
This is awarded to restaurants which are really worth travelling miles for!

TRÉMEUR – 22 Côtes-d'Armor – 309 I4 – pop. 627 – alt. 62 m – ✉ 22250 10 C2

Paris 407 – Dinan 26 – Loudéac 54 – Rennes 57 – St-Brieuc 46 – St-Malo 56

Les Dineux rest, VISA MC AE

voie express N 12, Z.A. Les Dineux – ✆ 02 96 84 65 80 – les-dineux.hotel-village@wanadoo.fr – Fax 02 96 84 76 35 – Closed 20 December-4 January and 7-23 February

12 rm – €48/52 €53/60, €10 – ½ P €55/59 – **Rest** – *(closed Saturday and Sunday except July-August)* Menu €17/28 – Carte €18/26

◆ All the rooms in this motel-style establishment, most of them duplexes, have a small terrace with a view of the countryside. Wood panelling, green plants, timberwork and bay windows add style to this restaurant; traditional fare.

TRÉMOLAT – 24 Dordogne – 329 F6 – pop. 571 – alt. 53 m – ✉ 24510 Dordogne-Berry-Limousin 4 C3

Paris 532 – Bergerac 34 – Brive-la-Gaillarde 87 – Périgueux 46 – Sarlat-la-Canéda 50

Syndicat d'initiative, ilot Saint-Nicolas ✆ 05 53 22 89 33, Fax 05 53 22 69 20

Belvédère de Racamadou (viewpoint) ★★ North: 2 km.

Le Vieux Logis rm, VISA MC AE

– ✆ 05 53 22 80 06 – vieuxlogis@relaischateaux.com – Fax 05 53 22 84 89

26 rm – €158/330 €158/355, €18 – ½ P €159/258

Rest – Menu €36 (weekday lunch), €39/89 – Carte €63/113

Spec. Asperges blanches du pays en vinaigrette (spring). Foie gras poêlé, pomme Berthane et artichaut. Pêches jaunes rôties entières en cocotte lutée (summer).

Wines Bergerac blanc et rouge.

◆ A former 16-17C priory, this house tells the story of the 450 year-old family of the present owners. Cosy rooms, comfortable sitting rooms and a superb garden. Unusually located in a former tobacco drying building. Terrace, and a tempting, classic menu.

Bistrot d'en Face VISA MC

– ✆ 05 53 22 80 69 – vieuxlogis@relaischateaux.com – Fax 05 53 22 84 89

Rest – Menu €13,50 (weekday lunch), €23/26 – Carte €24/36

◆ In the heart of the village where Chabrol filmed Le Boucher (1970). Old stonework, beams and tasty country cuisine including andouillette and confit de canard.

TRÉMONT-SUR-SAULX – 55 Meuse – 307 B6 – see Bar-le-Duc

TRÉPIED – 62 Pas-de-Calais – 301 C5 – see le Touquet-Paris-Plage

LE TRÉPORT – 76 Seine-Maritime – 304 I1 – pop. 5 900 – alt. 12 m – Casino – ✉ 76470 Normandy 33 D1

Paris 180 – Abbeville 37 – Amiens 92 – Blangy-sur-Bresle 26 – Dieppe 30 – Rouen 95

Office de tourisme, quai Sadi Carnot ✆ 02 35 86 05 69, Fax 02 35 86 73 96

Calvaire des Terrasses (calvary) ★.

Golf Hôtel without rest VISA MC

102 rte de Dieppe, (D 940) – ✆ 02 27 28 01 52 – evergreen2@wanadoo.fr – Fax 02 27 28 01 51 – Closed 21-27 December

10 rm – €42/48 €45/75, €7,50

◆ A tree-lined alleyway leads to this Norman-style residence surrounded by a park. Well-kept rooms, furnished in an English spirit. Charming rustic breakfast room.

Le St-Louis VISA MC AE

43 quai François 1er – ✆ 02 35 86 20 70 – Fax 02 35 50 67 10 – Closed 16 November-19 December

Rest – Menu €18 (weekdays)/60 – Carte €31/56

◆ Large bay window overlooking the docks in this friendly brasserie-style restaurant. Seafood cuisine.

TRÉVOU-TRÉGUIGNEC – 22 Côtes-d'Armor – 309 B2 – pop. 1 144 – alt. 56 m – ✉ 22660 9 B1

Paris 524 – Guingamp 36 – Lannion 14 – Paimpol 27 – Perros-Guirec 11 – St-Brieuc 72

Syndicat d'initiative, 28, rue de Trestel ✆ 02 96 23 74 05, Fax 02 96 91 73 82

Kerbugalic ← Trestel bay, P VISA MC AE

1 Vieille Côte de Trestel – ✆ 02 96 23 72 15 – kerbugalic@voila.fr – Fax 02 96 23 74 71 – Closed 10 January-15 February

18 rm – €55/90 €55/90, €10 – **Rest** – *(closed lunch except Friday, Saturday and Sunday)* Menu €25/38 – Carte €32/56

♦ A Breton-style house facing the foreshore, surrounded by a flower garden. The rooms in the main building have been renovated, while some of those in the annexe have a private terrace-veranda. Restaurant with a colourful, modern decor, facing the sea. Modern menu focused on seafood.

TRIEL-SUR-SEINE – 78 Yvelines – 311 I2 – 101 10 – see Paris, Area

TRIGANCE – 83 Var – 340 N3 – pop. 150 – alt. 800 m – ✉ 83840 41 C2

Paris 817 – Castellane 20 – Digne-les-Bains 74 – Draguignan 43 – Grasse 70

Office de tourisme, RD 955 - ferme de la Sagne ✆ 04 94 85 68 40, Fax 04 94 85 68 40

Château de Trigance ← valley and mountains, P VISA MC AE

access via private road – ✆ 04 94 76 91 18 – chateautrigance@wanadoo.fr – Fax 04 94 85 68 99 – Open 22 March-31 October

10 rm – €115/125 €125/195, €14,50 – ½ P €115/140

Rest – *(closed Wed. lunch out of season)* Menu €28 (weekday lunch), €38/48 – Carte €50/66

♦ Perched on a rocky outcrop, a hotel with plenty of character housed inside a castle. Individually furnished rooms with four-poster beds. The restaurant is located in what was once the armoury and is hewn from the rock. A medieval setting but modern cuisine.

Le Vieil Amandier rm, P VISA MC AE

Montée de St-Roch – ✆ 04 94 76 92 92 – levieilamandier@free.fr – Fax 04 94 85 68 65 – Open 16 April-2 November

12 rm – €45/55 €64/88, €9 – ½ P €67/77 – **Rest** – *(dinner only) (residents only)*

♦ At the foot of the village, a modern building surrounded by a Mediterranean garden. All the rooms have been renovated. A handsome raftered ceiling adorns this dining room; traditional cuisine with a taste of the south of France.

TRILBARDOU – 77 Seine-et-Marne – 312 F2 – see Meaux

LA TRINITÉ-SUR-MER – 56 Morbihan – 308 M9 – pop. 1 530 – alt. 20 m – Casino – ✉ 56470 Brittany 9 B3

Paris 488 – Auray 13 – Carnac 4 – Lorient 52 – Quiberon 23 – Quimperlé 66 – Vannes 31

Office de tourisme, 30, cours des Quais ✆ 02 97 55 72 21, Fax 02 97 55 78 07

Kerisper bridge ←★.

Le Lodge Kerisper without rest P VISA MC

4 r. Latz – ✆ 02 97 52 88 56 – contact@lodgekerisper.com – Fax 02 97 52 76 39

17 rm – €95/255 €95/255, €18 – 3 suites

♦ This hotel arranged in two low-lying 19C cottages, has a warm, refined interior, harmoniously combining antique furniture and carefully selected fabrics. Several rooms have a terrace.

Petit Hôtel des Hortensias rest, VISA

4 pl. de la Mairie – 02 97 30 10 30 – leshortensias@aol.com – Fax 02 97 30 14 54 – Closed January

6 rm – €99/155 €99/155, €11,50

Rest *L'Arrosoir* – *02 97 30 13 58 (open end- February to end-November and closed Tuesday lunch, Wednesday lunch and Monday)* Carte €30/47

◆ The Scandinavian outline of this charming villa (1880) overlooks the harbour. Elegant nautical interior, antique furniture and ornaments, guesthouse ambiance. A rare jewel! Ravishing naval bistro decor, splendid panoramic terrace and tasty seafood.

L'Azimut VISA AE

1 r. Men-Dû – 02 97 55 71 88 – azimut56@orange.fr – Fax 02 97 55 80 15 – Closed 24 November-5 December, 7-11 January, 16-27 February, Tuesday and Wednesday except July-August

Rest – Menu (€20), €25 (weekday lunch), €35/60 – Carte €43/60

◆ The dining room is distinctly nautical and the terrace overlooks the port. Updated menu of seafood inspiration.

TRIZAY – 17 Charente-Maritime – 324 E4 – pop. 1 122 – alt. 20 m – ✉ 17250

38 **B2**

Paris 475 – Rochefort 13 – La Rochelle 52 – Royan 36 – Saintes 27

Syndicat d'initiative, 48, rue de la République 05 46 82 34 25, Fax 05 46 82 19 64

at Bois Fleuri Lake 2.5 km west by D 238, D 123 and secondary road – ✉ 17250 Trizay

Les Jardins du Lac with rm rm, rest, VISA AE

– 05 46 82 03 56 – hotel@jardins-du-lac.com – Fax 05 46 82 03 55 – Closed February school holidays, Sunday dinner, Monday and Tuesday from November to March

8 rm – €83/89 €83/89, €13 – **Rest** – Menu (€31), €35/50 – Carte €50/73

◆ These two recent pavilions in a park above a lake are connected by a glass roofed footbridge straddling a stream. Lake view from the restaurant and rooms (with terrace or balcony).

LES TROIS-ÉPIS – 68 Haut-Rhin – 315 H8 – alt. 658 m – ✉ 68410

Alsace-Lorraine

2 **C2**

Paris 445 – Colmar 11 – Gérardmer 51 – Munster 18 – Orbey 12

Office de tourisme, 2, Impasse Poincaré 03 89 49 80 56, Fax 03 89 49 80 68

Villa Rosa rest, VISA

4 r. Thierry Schoeré – 03 89 49 81 19 – contact@villarosa.fr – Fax 03 89 78 90 45 – Closed January, February-mid March, November and Thursday dinner

8 rm – €58/60 €60/65, €8 – ½ P €60/65 – **Rest** – table d'hôte *(dinner for residents only)* Menu €20/25

◆ Charming rooms named after roses. Themed stays. A guesthouse feel to this 1900s construction, surrounded by a flower garden. In the restaurant, Anne-Rose prepares regional dishes using organic and home-grown produce.

TRONÇAIS – 03 Allier – 326 D3 – see St-Bonnet-Tronçais

LE TRONCHET – 35 Ille-et-Vilaine – 309 K4 – pop. 845 – alt. 65 m – ✉ 35540

Brittany

10 **D2**

Paris 391 – Saint-Malo 27 – Dinan 19 – Fougères 56 – Rennes 57 – Saint-Brieuc 82

Golf & Country Club rm, VISA

– 02 99 58 98 99 – saintmalogolf@st-malo.com – Fax 02 99 58 10 39 – Closed 20 November-1st March

29 rm – €75/135 €75/135, €10 – ½ P €75/105

Rest – Menu €17 (weekday lunch), €20/30 – Carte €23/40

◆ This 19C former priory is set on a golf course. It houses good-sized rooms decorated in light colours and pretty fabrics with either a patio or a small terrace. The restaurant commands a view of the pond and greens. Traditional cuisine.

Le Mesnil des Bois without rest

2 km south-west on D9 and D3 – 02 99 58 97 12 – villette@le-mesnil-des-bois.com – Closed mid November-end February

5 rm – €90/120 €90/120

◆ This handsome 16C manor farm in an isolated rural location on the edge of a forest once belonged to the family of the pirate Surcouf. Pretty bedrooms adorned with antiques.

TRONGET – 03 Allier – 326 F4 – pop. 928 – alt. 460 m – 03240 5 B1

Paris 317 – Bourbon-l'Archambault 24 – Montluçon 53 – Moulins 30

Du Commerce rm, VISA

16 rte départementale 945 – 04 70 47 12 95 – Fax 04 70 47 32 53

11 rm – €40 €48, €7 – ½ P €53 – **Rest** – Menu €16/36 – Carte €30/52

◆ This establishment in the heart of the little town comprises two buildings. The main building is home to the café-restaurant, while the recently built annexe houses functional and well-kept rooms. Classic rustic-styled restaurant offering a traditional repertoire of dishes.

TROUVILLE-SUR-MER – 14 Calvados – 303 M3 – pop. 5 411 – alt. 2 m – Casino AY – 14360 Normandy 32 A3

Paris 201 – Caen 51 – Le Havre 43 – Lisieux 30 – Pont-l'Évêque 13

Deauville-St-Gatien: 02 31 65 65 65, by ②: 7 km BZ.

Office de tourisme, 32, boulevard Fernand-Moureaux 02 31 14 60 70, Fax 02 31 14 60 71

de l'Amirauté Tourgéville Route Départementale 278, by Pont-L'Évêque road and D 278: 5 km, 02 31 14 42 00.

Cliff road ≤★.

Plan on next page

Hostellerie du Vallon without rest VISA AE

12 r. Sylvestre Lasserre – 02 31 98 35 00 – resahduvallon@wanadoo.fr – Fax 02 31 98 35 10 BZ **v**

62 rm – €105/180 €110/180, €14,50 – 1 suite

◆ This Norman-style inn offers a pretty panoramic view of the town's heights. Spacious rooms with balconies. Several lounges and a billiards room.

Mercure rm, VISA AE

pl. Foch – 02 31 87 38 38 – h1048@accor.com – Fax 02 31 87 35 41

80 rm – €86/153 €86/153, €13 – **Rest** – Menu (€17), €21 (weekdays)/40 – Carte €17/30 AY **k**

◆ The rooms are being gradually renovated in a simple, modern style (Bordeaux shades, refined furniture); those awaiting renovation remain functional and well-kept. Traditional cuisine and regional dishes served in the interior courtyard in summer.

St-James without rest VISA

16 r. de la Plage – 02 31 88 05 23 – Fax 02 31 87 98 45 – Closed January

11 rm – €90/100 €100/120, €14 AY **e**

◆ This small family establishment near the beach has rooms with charming personal touches. In winter, a low-key atmosphere in the lounge invites you to stay by the fireside.

Le Flaubert without rest ≤ VISA

2 r. Gustave Flaubert – 02 31 88 37 23 – hotel@flaubert.fr – Fax 02 31 88 21 56 – Open mid February-mid November AY **t**

33 rm – €64/125 €64/200, €9

◆ Romantic feel guaranteed if you choose a room with a sea view in this Thirties building, ideally situated at the foot of the Trouville boardwalks. A "retro" decor.

Le Fer à Cheval without rest VISA

11 r. V. Hugo – 02 31 98 30 20 – info@hotel-trouville.com – Fax 02 31 98 04 00 AY **u**

34 rm – €50/80 €73/85, €10

◆ In the centre of the resort, two adjoining houses with functional rooms and cosy family suites. Home-baked pastries for breakfast and tearoom in the afternoon.

TROUVILLE-SUR-MER

Street	Square	No.
Bains (R. des)	**AY**	3
Carnot (R.)	**AY**	5
Chalet-Cordier (R.)	**BY**	6
Chapelle (R. de la)	**AY**	7
Foch (Pl. Mar.)	**AY**	9
Gaulle (R. Gén.-de)	**BZ**	10
Lattre-de-Tassigny (Pl. Mar.-de)	**AY**	12
Maigret (R. A.-de)	**AY**	20
Moureaux (Bd F.)	**BZ**	
Moureaux (Pl. F.)	**BZ**	22
Notre-Dame (R.)	**BY**	23
Plage (R. de la)	**AY**	26
Verdun (R. de)	**BY**	29
Victor-Hugo (R.)	**AY**	31

A B
0 200 m
MANCHE
RTE DE LA CORNICHE
D 513
1 HONFLEUR
"Les Planches"
R. Gal Leclerc
Musée Villa Montebello
Boulevard A. Briand
Pl. Thénard
Savignac
R. Pasteur
Promenade
N.-D. DE BONSECOURS
R. d'Orléans
Aquarium
R. de Paris
R. de la Cavée
Bd d'Hautpoul
CASINO
Q. Albert 1er
N.-D. DES VICTOIRES
Bd Fernand Moureaux
Touques
Rue Gambetta
Q. de la Marine
Quai de la Touques
DEAUVILLE
Rue Mirabeau
Pl. Morny
POL
P. des Belges
R. d'Aguesseau
D 535
Pt DE NORMANDIE HONFLEUR
D 677 Pt-L'ÉVÊQUE A 13 ROUEN, CAEN
X Y Z

Le Central
5 et 7 r. des Bains – 02 31 88 80 84 – central-hotel@wanadoo.fr – Fax 02 31 88 42 22 AY **n**
21 rm – €84/117 €84/128, €8,50 – ½ P €69/75
Rest ***Brasserie*** – *02 31 88 13 68* – Menu €20/29 – Carte €28/39
◆ A harbour hotel with a reception area on the first floor and tastefully renovated, well-soundproofed rooms occupying two buildings. A very lively brasserie with a Thirties-style decor and vast terrace, heated in winter.

Les Sablettes without rest
15 r. P.-Besson – 02 31 88 10 66 – info@trouville-hotel.com – Fax 02 31 88 59 06 – Closed January AY **r**
18 rm – €40/45 €52/65, €6,50
◆ One of the assets of this pleasant little hotel is its rather quiet yet central location. Simple, clean rooms, brightened up by light colours.

La Petite Auberge
7 r. Carnot – 02 31 88 11 07 – lapetiteauberge@wanadoo.fr – Fax 02 31 88 96 39 – Closed Tuesday except July-August and Wednesday
Rest – *(pre-book)* Menu €31/49 AY **f**
◆ Decorated in sea-blue colours, with wooden tables and decorative plates on the walls, this inn is located away from the tourist bustle. Menu offering both traditional and regional dishes.

Les Mouettes
11 r. Bains – 02 31 98 06 97 – central-hotel@wanadoo.fr AY **d**
Rest – Menu €13,50/27
◆ Friendly atmosphere, typical bistro decoration, pretty painted trompe-l'œil ceiling and menu offering ordinary and simply prepared dishes, such as tripe, mackerel, mussels, etc.

Casa Cubaine
1 r. Paul Besson – 02 31 88 18 10 – Closed Wednesday AY **a**
Rest – *(dinner only)* Menu €17/22 – Carte €31/58
◆ Bar-lounge, opposite the casino, with a colourful veranda evoking a Caribbean atmosphere. Lobster is the star of the refreshing and original Franco-Cuban menu.

TROYES P – **10 Aube** – **313** E4 – **pop. 60 958** – **Built-up area 128 945** – **alt. 113 m** – ✉ **10000** Northern France and the Paris Region 13 **B3**

Paris 170 – Dijon 185 – Nancy 186

Troyes-Barberey 03 25 71 79 00, Northwest: 5 km AV

Office de tourisme, 16, boulevard Carnot 03 25 82 62 70, Fax 03 25 73 06 81

de la Forêt d'Orient Rouilly-Sacey Route de Geraudot, by Nancy road: 11 km, 03 25 43 80 80 ;

de Troyes Chaource Château de la Cordelière, by Tonnerre road (D 444): 31 km, 03 25 40 18 76.

Old Troyes★★ BZ: Ruelle des Chats★ - St-Pierre and St-Paul cathedral ★★ - Rood-screen ★★ of Ste-Madeleine church ★ - St-Urbain basilica ★ BCY **B** - St-Pantaléon church ★ - Apothicary's★ of the Hôtel-Dieu CY **M**[4] - Musée d'Art Moderne★★ CY **M**[3] - Maison de l'Outil et de la Pensée ouvrière (House of Workers' tools and thinking) ★★ in the Hôtel de Mauroy★★ BZ **M**[2] - Musée historique de Troyes et de Champagne★ and musée de la Bonneterie in the Hôtel de Vauluisant★ BZ **M**[1] - Musée des Beaux-Arts et d'Archéologie★ in St-Loup abbey.

Plans on following pages

La Maison de Rhodes
18 r. Linard Gonthier – 03 25 43 11 11 – message@maisonderhodes.com – Fax 03 25 43 10 43 CY **e**
8 rm – €143/198 €143/198, €17 – 3 suites – **Rest** – *(closed January and February) (dinner only)* Menu €54/62 – Carte approx. €56
◆ Beautiful 17C residence nestling in a small paved backstreet. Beams, stonework, daub, floor tiles, old and modern furniture combine with elegance at this lovely hotel. Charming rustic dining room overlooking a miniscule garden. Traditional menu.

TROYES

Anatole-France (Av.) . . . . AX 2
Brossolette (Av. Pierre) . . . . AX 6
Buffard (Av. M.) . . . . AV 8
Chanteloup (R. de) . . . . AX 9
Clemenceau (R. G.) . . . . AV 12
Croix-Blanche (R. de la) . . . . AX 13
Croncels (R. du Faubourg) . . AX 14
Jean-Jaurès (Av.) . . . . AV 18
Lattre-de-Tassigny (Av. Mar.-de) . . . . AV 21
Leclerc (Av. Gén.) . . . . AV 22
Marots (R. des) . . . . AV 24
Noës (R. des) . . . . AX 26
Notre-Dame-des-Prés (R.) . . . . AX 27
Pasteur (R.) . . . . AV 32
Salengro (Av. Roger) . . . . AV 36
Salengro (R. Roger) . . . . AV 37
Schuman (Av. Robert) . . . . . AV 38
Vouldy (Chaussée du) . . . . . AX 42
1er Mai (Av. du) . . . . AV 48

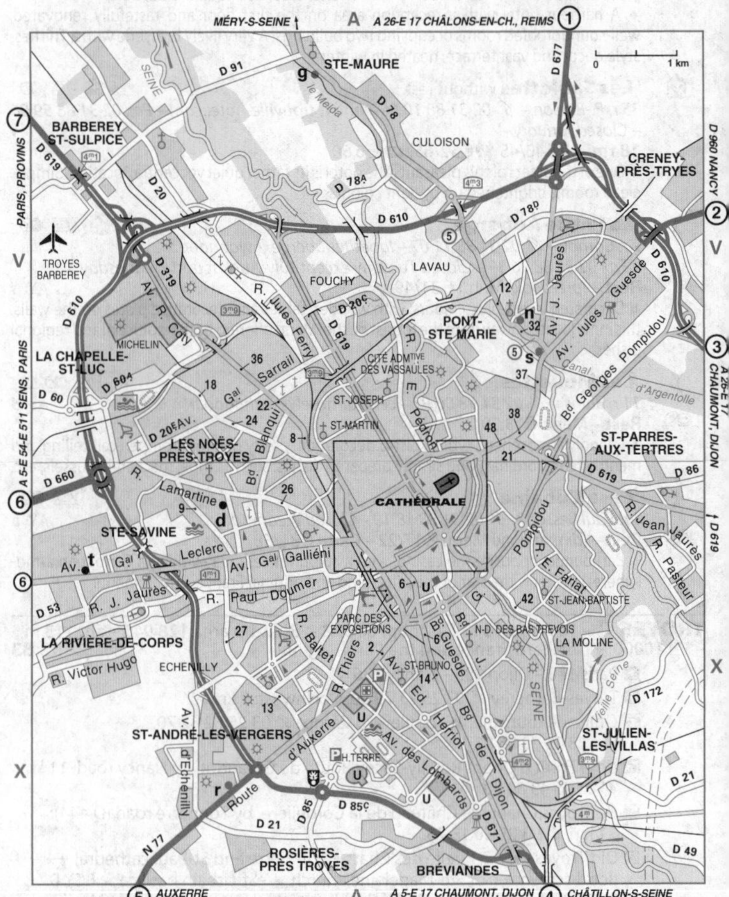

Le Champ des Oiseaux without rest

20 r. Linard Gonthier – ✆ 03 25 80 58 50 – message@champdesoiseaux.com – Fax 03 25 80 98 34 CY **e**

12 rm – †€ 130 ††€ 130, ☕ € 17 – 1 suite

◆ Attractive, cosy rooms in three venerable 15 and 16C corbelled houses. Charm, peace and quiet and attentive service.

Mercure without rest

11 r. Bas-Trévois – ✆ 03 25 46 28 28 – h3168@accor.com – Fax 03 25 46 28 27 CZ **h**

70 rm – †€ 99/115 ††€ 109/185, ☕ € 13

◆ The decoration of the spacious and restful rooms and the 19C loom standing in pride of place in the hall bring to mind the origin of this hotel, once a hosiery factory.

TROYES

Boucherat (R.) .... CY 4
Champeaux (R.) .... BZ 12
Charbonnet (R.) .... BZ 13
Clemenceau (R. G.) .... BCY 15
Comtes-de-Champagne (Q. des) .... CY 16
Dampierre (Quai) .... BCY 17
Delestraint (Bd Gén.-Ch.) ... BZ 18
Driant (R. COl.) .... BZ 20
Girardon (R.) .... CY 22
Hennequin (R.) .... CY 23
Huez (R. Claude) .... BYZ 27
Israël (Pl. Alexandre) .... BZ 28
Jaillant-Deschaînets (R.) .... BZ 29
Jean-Jaurès (Pl.) .... BZ 31
Joffre (Av. Mar.) .... BZ 33
Langevin (Pl. du Prof.) ...... BZ 35
Libération (Pl. de la) .... CZ 49
Marché aux Noix (R. du) .... BZ 36
Michelet (R.) .... CY 39
Molé (R.) .... BZ 44
Monnaie (R. de la) .... BZ 45
Paillot-de-Montabert (R.) ... BZ 47
Palais-de-Justice (R.) .... BZ 48
République (R. de la) .... BZ 51
St-Pierre (Pl.) .... CY 52
St-Rémy (Pl.) .... BY 53
Siret (R. Nicolas) .... CZ 79
Synagogue (R. de la) .... BZ 54
Tour-Boileau (R. de la) ...... BZ 59
Trinité (R. de la) .... BZ 60
Turenne (R. de) .... BZ 61
Voltaire (R.) .... BZ 64
Zola (R. Émile) .... BCZ
1er-R.A.M. (Bd du) .... BZ 69

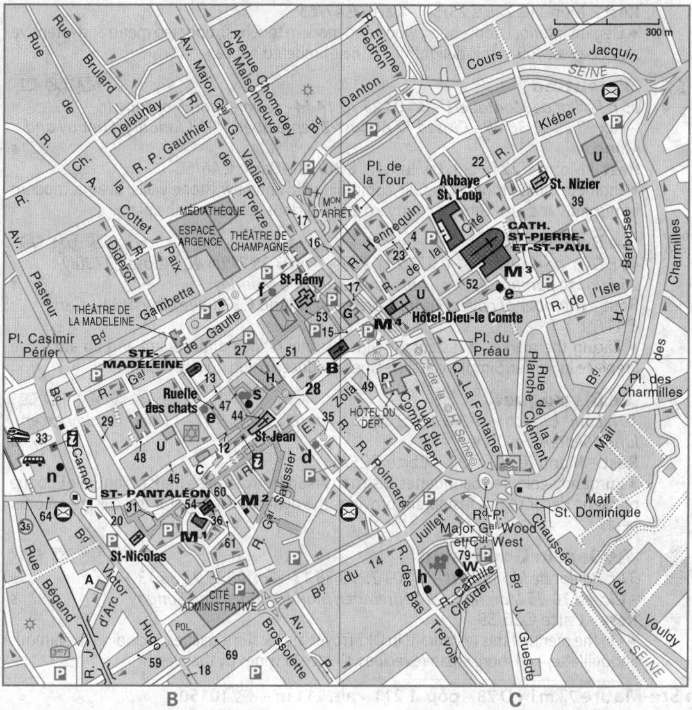

Le Relais St-Jean without rest — VISA MO AE

51 r. Paillot de Montabert – ☎ 03 25 73 89 90 – infos@relais-st-jean.com – Fax 03 25 73 88 60 — BZ **s**

25 rm – †€ 90/135 ††€ 95/140, ☕ € 15

◆ Charming half-timbered house on a pedestrian street. Contemporary rooms, those on the 4th floor have attractive original beams. Lounge bar with a billiard table.

Royal Hôtel — rm, VISA MO AE

22 bd Carnot – ☎ 03 25 73 19 99 – reservation@royal-hotel-troyes.com – Fax 03 25 73 47 85 – Closed 19 December-12 January — BZ **n**

40 rm – †€ 65/75 ††€ 78/90, ☕ € 10 – ½ P € 69/75

Rest – *(closed Saturday lunch, Monday lunch and Sunday)* Menu € 25/30 – Carte € 46/64

◆ A building on a busy boulevard with simple, functional and well-kept rooms. Pleasant, refined lounge-bar and elegant modern dining room furnished with a Flemish Renaissance-style mirror and dresser.

Ibis without rest
r. Camille Claudel – ☎ 03 25 75 99 99 – H5546@accor.com – Fax 03 25 75 90 69 CZ **w**
77 rm – †€ 59/67 ††€ 59/67, ☕ € 8
◆ A new hotel with all the latest Ibis comfort: air-conditioned rooms, new-look bathrooms, pleasant breakfast room, etc.

La Mignardise
1 ruelle des Chats – ☎ 03 25 73 15 30 – Fax 03 25 73 15 30 – Closed Sunday dinner and Monday BZ **e**
Rest – Menu (€ 22), € 25/50 – Carte € 47/65
◆ Elegant interior (stone, brick, wood and modern touches), updated menu and attentive service await you in this delightful 16C half-timbered house.

Valentino
35 r. Paillot de Montabert – ☎ 03 25 73 14 14 – le.valentino@orange.fr – Fax 03 25 41 36 75 – Closed 17 August-2 September, 1st-13 January, Sunday and Monday BZ **s**
Rest – Menu € 22 (weekday lunch), € 30/50 – Carte € 46/66
◆ Intimate dining room tastefully combining old and new (stone walls, beams, modern furnishings and art). Terrace-courtyard and delicious flavours on the plate.

Le Bourgogne
40 r. Gén. de Gaulle – ☎ 03 25 73 02 67 – Fax 03 25 71 06 40 – Closed 27 July-26 August, Sunday dinner, Thursday dinner and Monday BY **f**
Rest – *(number of covers limited, pre-book)* Menu € 33 (weekdays)/54 – Carte € 41/71
◆ Facing the market, a restaurant with a subtly refined atmosphere and an attractive fireplace in winter. Simple, classic recipes produced using quality products.

Le Bistroquet
10 r. Louis Ulbach – ☎ 03 25 73 65 65 – Fax 03 25 73 55 91 – Closed Sunday except lunch September-June BZ **d**
Rest – Menu (€ 20), € 32 – Carte € 25/46
◆ Burgundy-coloured banquettes, bistro chairs and retro lamps – the Parisian Belle Époque brasserie decor of this restaurant provides the perfect backdrop for the cuisine on offer here.

Au Jardin Gourmand
31 r. Paillot de Montabert – ☎ 03 25 73 36 13 – Fax 03 25 73 36 13 – Closed 10-25 March, 1st-21 September, Monday lunch and Sunday BZ **s**
Rest – Carte € 26/59
◆ On the menu of this restaurant in Old Troyes are local specialities, including the famous andouillette, and more creative recipes. Choice of wines by the glass.

in Ste-Maure 7 km by D 78 – pop. 1 211 – alt. 111 m – ✉ 10150

Auberge de Ste-Maure
99 rte Mery – ☎ 03 25 76 90 41 – auberge.saintemaure@wanadoo.fr – Fax 03 25 80 01 55 – Closed 22 December-26 January, Sunday dinner and Monday AV **g**
Rest – Menu € 26/50 – Carte € 44/74
◆ Elegant dining room with fine rafters and pleasant summer terrace on the banks of the Melda. Up-to-date cuisine and excellent regional wines.

in Pont-Ste-Marie 3 km by D 77 – pop. 4 936 – alt. 110 m – ✉ 10150

Hostellerie de Pont-Ste-Marie (Christian Chavanon)
34 r. Pasteur, (near the church) – ☎ 03 25 83 28 61 – chavanon3@wanadoo.fr – Fax 03 25 81 67 85 – Closed 1st-24 August, 2-12 January, Sunday dinner, Tuesday dinner and Wednesday AV **n**
Rest – Menu € 43/119 bi – Carte € 58/84
Spec. Homard au piment d'Espelette, croustillant à l'anis vert. Le cochon en folie. Pain perdu aux souvenirs d'antan, aux saveurs de maintenant. **Wines** Rosé des Riceys, Champagne.
◆ A restaurant located in two cottages near the fine 16C church. An inviting dining room decorated in a mixture of old and new and appetising contemporary menu.

Bistrot DuPont

5 pl. Ch. de Gaulle – ✆ 03 25 80 90 99 – Closed 7-13 April, 14 July-3 August, 27 December-3 January, Thursday dinner, Sunday dinner and Monday AV **s**

Rest – *(pre-book)* Menu € 19/29 – Carte € 27/56

◆ Near the Seine, this nice bistro-style establishment offers generous and well-prepared cuisine. Don't miss the andouillette, a house speciality.

in Moussey 10 km by ④, D 671 and D 444 – pop. 399 – alt. 131 m – ✉ 10800

Domaine de la Creuse without rest

– ✆ 03 25 41 74 01 – contact@domainedelacreuse.com – Closed 20 December-5 January

4 rm – €95 €100/115

◆ This traditional (18C) Champagne-style residence is set around a central courtyard garden. Large, delightful ground-floor rooms.

in St-André-les-Vergers 5 km – pop. 11 125 – alt. 112 m – ✉ 10120

Syndicat d'initiative, 21, avenue Maréchal Leclerc ✆ 03 25 71 91 11, Fax 03 25 49 67 71

La Gentilhommière

180 rte Auxerre – ✆ 03 25 49 35 64 – gentilhommiere@wanadoo.fr – Fax 03 25 75 13 55 – Closed Tuesday dinner and Wednesday AX **r**

Rest – Menu € 19/53 – Carte € 39/56

◆ This restaurant in a modern villa is comfortable and refined with period furnishings, old paintings and toile de Jouy. Two summer terraces and modern cuisine.

in Ste-Savine 3 km – pop. 10 125 – alt. 116 m – ✉ 10300

Chantereigne without rest

128 av. Gén. Leclerc – ✆ 03 25 74 89 35 – contact@hotel-chantereigne.com – Fax 03 25 74 47 78 – Closed 23 December-2 January AX **t**

30 rm – €54/65 €58/65, € 8

◆ A U-shaped building with slightly cramped but functional rooms facing the rear. Breakfast buffet.

Motel Savinien

87 r. Fontaine – ✆ 03 25 79 24 90 – motel.savinien@orange.fr – Fax 03 25 78 04 61 AX **d**

49 rm – €48/60 €54/68, € 8 – ½ P € 50/55 – **Rest** – *(closed Sunday dinner and Monday)* Menu (€ 13), € 23/31 – Carte € 24/39

◆ Large, quiet well-maintained 1970s building. Rooms are practical, regularly updated and some have been renovated. Sauna, jacuzzi and small gym. Traditional cuisine served on the terrace, weather permitting.

TRUN – 61 Orne – 310 J1 – pop. 1 307 – alt. 90 m – ✉ 61160 33 C2

Paris 198 – Caen 63 – Alençon 60 – Lisieux 47 – Flers 59

Syndicat d'initiative, place Charles-de-Gaulle ✆ 02 33 36 93 55

La Villageoise

66 r. de la République – ✆ 08 71 38 56 87 – lavillageoise@orange.fr – Fax 02 33 39 13 07

5 rm – €55 €60, € 12 – **Table d'hôte** – Menu € 25 bi

◆ This establishment sports an attractive living-room which opens onto a courtyard garden, around which most of the ornament-filled rooms are scattered. Charming welcome and regional specialities served in a rustic setting.

TULETTE – 26 Drôme – 332 C8 – pop. 1 714 – alt. 147 m – ✉ 26790 44 B3

Paris 657 – Lyon 195 – Valence 95 – Avignon 56 – Montélimar 50

Syndicat d'initiative, place des Tisserands ✆ 04 75 98 34 53, Fax 04 75 98 36 16

K-Za

rte du Moulin – ✆ 04 75 98 34 88 – k-za@wanadoo.fr – Fax 04 7 97 49 70

5 rm – €130 €130/230 – **Table d'hôte** – Menu € 30 bi/50 bi

◆ Elizabeth, the owner of this "bella casa" is Italian. The 17C house made out of Rhône pebbles sports an attractive designer interior and is a masterpiece of contemporary sophistication. Mediterranean inspired cuisine and local wines served at the table d'hôte.

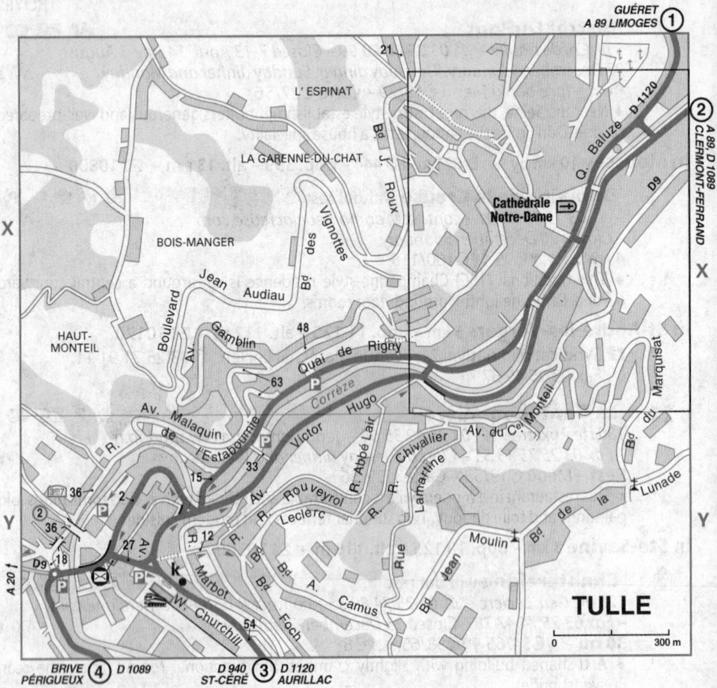

GUÉRET A 89 LIMOGES ①
A 89, D 1089 CLERMONT-FERRAND ②
L' ESPINAT
LA GARENNE-DU-CHAT
BOIS-MANGER
HAUT-MONTEIL
Cathédrale Notre-Dame
Bd J. Roux
Bd des Vignottes
Boulevard Jean Audiau
Av. Gamblin
Quai de Rigny
Q. Baluze
D 1120
D9
Corrèze
Av. Victor Hugo
Av. Malaquin
R. de l'Estabournie
R. Abbé Lair
R. Chivallier
R. Lamartine
Av. du Cel Monteil
Bd du Marquisat
Bd de la Lunade
Av. Rouveyrol
R. Leclerc
Rue Jean Moulin
Bd A. Camus
Bd Foch
R. Marbot
Av. W. Churchill
A 20
D9
TULLE
0 300 m
BRIVE PÉRIGUEUX ④ D 1089
D 940 ST-CÉRÉ ③ D 1120 AURILLAC

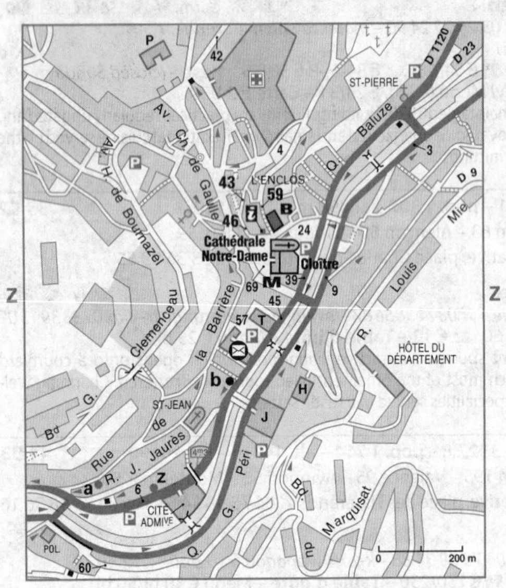

Alsace-Lorraine (Av.)	Y	2
Baluze (Quai)	Z	
Briand (Quai A.)	Z	3
Bride (Pl. de la)	Z	4
Brigouleix (Pl. Martial)	Z	6
Chammard (Quai A.-de)	Z	9
Condamines (R. des)	Y	12
Dunant (R. Henri)	Y	15
Faucher (Pl. Albert)	Y	18
Faugeras (Bd J.-F.)	X	21
Gambetta (Pl.)	Z	24
Gaulle (Av. Ch.-de)	Z	
Jean-Jaurès (R.)	Z	
Lovy (R. Sergent)	Y	27
Mermoz (R.)	Y	33
Pauphile (R.)	Y	36
Perrier (Quai Edmond)	Z	39
Poincaré (Av.)	Z	42
Portes-Chanac (R. des)	Z	43
République (Quai de la)	Z	45
Riche (R.)	Z	46
Roche-Bailly (Bd de la)	X	48
Sampeix (R. Lucien)	Y	54
Tavé (Pl. Jean)	Z	57
Tour-de-Maïsse (R. de la)	Z	59
Vialle (R. Anne)	Z	60
Victor-Hugo (Av.)	XY	
Vidalie (Av.)	X	63
Zola (Pl. Émile)	Z	69

TULLE 🅿 – 19 Corrèze – 329 L4 – pop. 15 553 – alt. 210 m – ✉ 19000
Dordogne-Berry-Limousin 25 **C3**

Paris 475 – Aurillac 83 – Brive-la-Gaillarde 27 – Clermont-Ferrand 141

Office de tourisme, 2, place Emile Zola ✆ 05 55 26 59 61, Fax 05 55 20 72 93

Maison de Loyac★ Z **B** - Steeple★ of Notre-Dame cathedral.

Plan on next page

Mercure without rest

16 quai de la République – ✆ 05 55 26 42 00 – h5065@accor.com – Fax 05 55 20 31 17 Z **b**

48 rm – €64 €74/78, ☕ €8,50 – 1 suite

◆ This impeccable town-centre hotel has a spacious hall, a comfortable bar and new rooms, which are welcoming and soundproofed, they are more spacious on the quay side.

De la Gare

25 av. W. Churchill – ✆ 05 55 20 04 04 – hotel.de.la.gare@wanadoo.fr – Fax 05 55 20 15 87 – Closed 20 August-3 September and February half-term holidays Y **k**

11 rm – €51 €51, ☕ €7 – ½ P €51 – **Rest** – *(closed Sunday evening in winter)* Menu €15/24

◆ Attractive little hotel opposite the train station. The well-proportioned practical rooms are arranged around a patio (overlooked by the 1st floor rooms). This restaurant is rustic in style, the menu traditional and the bill delightfully reasonable.

Le Central

12 r. Barrière – ✆ 05 55 26 24 46 – r-poumier@internet19.fr – Fax 05 55 26 53 16 – Closed 28 July-10 August, Sunday dinner and Saturday Z **a**

Rest – Menu €25/60 – Carte €46/61

◆ Stonework, beams and period dressers make up the cosy decor of this restaurant with a half-timbered façade (18C). Charming welcome, traditional dishes. Ground floor brasserie.

La Toque Blanche

pl. M. Brigouleix – ✆ 05 55 26 75 41 – toque.blanche@orange.fr – Fax 05 55 20 93 95 – Closed one week in July, 15-26 February, Sunday dinner and Monday Z **z**

Rest – Menu €24/29 – Carte €45/61

◆ An elegant and rustic dining room with exposed beams where one can enjoy traditional cuisine based on local produce.

TUNNEL DU MONT-BLANC H.-Savoie – 74 H.-Savoie – 328 O5 – see Chamonix-Mont-Blanc

TUNNEL SOUS LA MANCHE voir à Calais.

LA TURBALLE – 44 Loire-Atlantique – 316 A3 – pop. 4 042 – alt. 6 m – ✉ 44420
Brittany 34 **A2**

Paris 457 – La Baule 13 – Guérande 7 – Nantes 84 – La Roche-Bernard 31 – St-Nazaire 27

Office de tourisme, place du Général-de-Gaulle ✆ 02 40 23 39 87, Fax 02 40 23 32 01

Les Chants d'Ailes without rest

11 bd Bellanger – ✆ 02 40 23 47 28 – hotel.chantsdailes@wanadoo.fr – Fax 02 40 62 86 43 – Closed 17 November-17 December and 19 January-6 February

19 rm – €38/48 €46/67, ☕ €7

◆ Set on the extended beachfront, functional rooms being gradually renovated. Those located at the front have ocean views. A bright breakfast room.

Le Manoir des Quatre Saisons without rest

744 bd de Lauvergnac – ✆ 02 40 11 76 16 – jean-philippe.meyran@club-internet.fr – Fax 02 40 11 76 16

5 rm ☕ – €60/70 €85/89

◆ This is a successfully reconstructed long cottage. Its colourful rooms often have a small lounge. Gigantic breakfast served in front of the fireplace in winter.

Le Terminus
18 quai St-Paul – ✆ 02 40 23 30 29 – terminus44420@aol.com
– Closed 1 week in October, February school holidays, Sunday dinner, Tuesday dinner and Wednesday except in season and during school holidays
Rest – Menu (€ 16), € 22/47 – Carte € 21/73
◆ New contemporary style decor in this restaurant specialising in seafood dishes. All the tables overlook La Turballe port.

in Pen-Bron 3 km south by D 92 – ✉ 44420 La Turballe

Pen Bron
– ✆ 02 28 56 77 99 – hotelpenbron@wanadoo.fr – Fax 02 28 56 77 77
– Closed 2 weeks in November
45 rm – €55/95 €55/95, € 10 – **Rest** – *(closed Monday and Tuesday in winter)* Menu € 30 – Carte € 31/47
◆ A Breton house remarkably located at the end of the peninsula opposite Croisic. Specially designed facilities for disabled guests. Traditional food served in a pleasant restaurant facing the waves.

LA TURBIE – 06 Alpes-Maritimes – 341 F5 – pop. 3 021 – alt. 495 m – ✉ 06320

42 **E2**

Paris 943 – Monaco 8 – Menton 13 – Nice 16

Hostellerie Jérôme (Bruno Cirino) with rm
20 r. Comte de Cessole – ✆ 04 92 41 51 51 – hostellerie.jerome@wanadoo.fr
– Fax 04 92 41 51 50 – Closed 6 November-10 February, Monday and Tuesday except dinner July-August and except public holidays
5 rm – €95/150 €95/150, € 15 – **Rest** – Menu € 50 (weekday lunch), € 65/120 – Carte € 98/140
Spec. Dégustation de légumes du potager. Composition de homard aux truffes, petits pois et macaroni (spring and winter). Agneau de Sisteron croustillé aux fleurs et herbes de la garrigue, petits farcis niçois. **Wines** Bellet, Côtes de Provence.
◆ The restaurant was once the refectory of Cistercian monks who lived here in the 13C. Delicious Mediterranean-influenced cuisine and attractive, personalised guestrooms.

Café de la Fontaine
4 av. Gén. de Gaulle – ✆ 04 93 28 52 79 – Fax 04 92 41 51 51 – Closed Monday from November to March
Rest – Menu € 23/28 – Carte € 23/28
◆ This lively village café is always crowded. Hardly surprising... as it offers tasty local dishes made with fresh market produce!

TURCKHEIM – 68 Haut-Rhin – 315 H8 – pop. 3 594 – alt. 225 m – ✉ 68230

Alsace-Lorraine

2 **C2**

Paris 471 – Colmar 7 – Gérardmer 47 – Munster 14 – St-Dié 51 – le Thillot 66

Office de tourisme, Corps de Garde ✆ 03 89 27 38 44, Fax 03 89 80 83 22

Le Berceau du Vigneron without rest
10 pl. Turenne – ✆ 03 89 27 23 55 – hotel-berceau-du-vigneron@wanadoo.fr
– Fax 03 89 30 01 33 – Closed 8-21 January
16 rm – €43/57 €43/72, € 9
◆ Half-timbered house partly built on the ramparts of the old town. Refreshing rooms, quieter at the back. In summer, breakfast is served in the interior courtyard.

Les Portes de la Vallée
rest,
29 r. Romaine – ✆ 03 89 27 95 50 – mail@hotelturckheim.com
– Fax 03 89 27 40 71 – Closed 4 - 20 Mar.
14 rm – €38/57 €45/74, € 8 – ½ P € 40/63 – **Rest** – *(closed Sunday) (dinner only) (residents only)* Menu € 18
◆ The hotel's two buildings are linked by a leafy arbour. A quiet setting, with the bright rooms in the modern wing perhaps preferable. Alsace dishes are served in the winstub-style dining room.

À l'Homme Sauvage

19 Grand'Rue – ✆ 03 89 27 56 15 – homme.sauvage.sarl@wanadoo.fr – Fax 03 89 80 82 03 – Closed 25 October-8 November, 17-27 February, Tuesday dinner from November to April, Sunday dinner and Wednesday

Rest – Menu (€ 13), € 18/36

◆ This inn has been welcoming satisfied diners since 1609. Modern cuisine served in a half-rustic, half-contemporary setting, with dining in the shaded paved courtyard in summer.

TURENNE – 19 Corrèze – 329 K5 – pop. 742 – alt. 350 m – ✉ 19500

Dordogne-Berry-Limousin — 24 **B3**

Paris 496 – Brive-la-Gaillarde 15 – Cahors 91 – Figeac 76

Office de tourisme, place du Belvédère ✆ 05 55 24 08 80, Fax 05 55 24 58 24

Site★ of the château and ✳★★ Caesar Tower.

Collonges-la-Rouge: village★★ East: 10 km.

Clos Marnis — rm,

pl. de la Halle – ✆ 05 55 22 05 28 – keny.sourzat@wanadoo.fr – Closed 15 November-15 December

6 rm – €57 €78 – ½ P €51/61 – **Table d'hôte** – Menu € 22 bi

◆ Handsome 18C residence built by a religious fraternity. Characterful rooms, furnished with period or modern pieces and a fine view of the castle from the pleasant garden. Buffet service; regional produce takes pride of place (by reservation only).

Maison des Chanoines with rm — rest, rm, VISA

– ✆ 05 55 85 93 43 – maisondeschanoines@wanadoo.fr – Fax 05 55 85 93 43 – Open 12 April-15 October

7 rm – €55 €65/95, €9 – ½ P €66/80 – **Rest** – *(closed Wednesday dinner in June and lunch except Sunday and public holidays) (number of covers limited, pre-book)* Menu € 32/40

◆ An enchanting 16C house: carved entrance door, spiral staircase, vaulted dining room (furnished in a Majorelle style), smart rooms. Cuisine combining tradition and creativity.

TURQUANT – 49 Maine-et-Loire – 317 J5 – pop. 448 – alt. 68 m – ✉ 49730

35 **C2**

Paris 294 – Angers 76 – Châtellerault 68 – Chinon 21 – Saumur 10 – Tours 58

Demeure de la Vignole — VISA AE

imp. Marguerite d'Anjou – ✆ 02 41 53 67 00 – demeure@demeure-vignole.com – Fax 02 41 53 67 09 – Open 15 March-15 Nov.

8 rm – €80 €89, €9 – 3 suites – ½ P €73/93 – **Rest** – *(closed Sunday and Monday) (dinner only)* Menu € 28

◆ Guesthouse atmosphere in this elegant tufa residence built on a hillside. Tastefully decorated rooms and troglodytic suite (and pool). Terrace overlooking the vineyards.

TUSSON – 16 Charente – 324 K4 – pop. 317 – alt. 125 m – ✉ 16140

39 **C2**

Paris 421 – Angoulême 41 – Cognac 49 – Poitiers 83

Office de tourisme, le bourg ✆ 05 45 21 26 70

Le Compostelle — VISA

– ✆ 05 45 31 15 90 – le-compostelle@wanadoo.fr – Fax 05 45 31 15 90 – Closed 29 September-13 October, 2-26 January, Sunday dinner, Monday except dinner in August and Thursday

Rest – Menu € 14 bi (weekday lunch), € 25/38 – Carte € 42/53

◆ A pleasant rustic restaurant situated in the heart of the village on the old pilgrims' way. Varied regional menu.

TY-SANQUER – 29 Finistère – 308 G6 – see Quimper

UBERACH – 67 Bas-Rhin – **315** J3 – **pop. 1 091** – **alt. 175 m** – ✉ **67350** 1 **B1**

Paris 473 – Baden-Baden 59 – Offenburg 64 – Strasbourg 38

De la Forêt

94 Grande Rue – ✆ 03 88 07 73 17 – bernardohl@wanadoo.fr – Fax 03 88 72 50 33 – Closed 28 July-16 August, 29 December-3 January, 23 February-7 March, Monday dinner, Tuesday dinner and Wednesday

Rest – Menu (€ 8,50), € 15 (weekday lunch), € 25/60 bi – Carte € 32/54

◆ A former brasserie converted into a stylish restaurant. Well-kept interior and warm atmosphere. Traditional, authentic fare prepared with vegetables from the garden.

UCHAUX – 84 Vaucluse – **332** B8 – **pop. 1 465** – **alt. 80 m** – ✉ **84100** 40 **A2**

Paris 645 – Avignon 40 – Montélimar 45 – Nyons 37 – Orange 11

Château de Massillan rm, rm, VISA MC AE

3 km north by D 11 and secondary road – ✆ 04 90 40 64 51 – chateau-de-massillan@wanadoo.fr – Fax 04 90 40 63 85 – Open 1st April-30 October

13 rm – €150/450 €185/450, € 16 – 1 suite – ½ P € 140/280

Rest – Menu € 30 (weekdays), € 48/110 bi

◆ A fine 16C château in the heart of a magnificent park surrounded by vineyards. Appealing modern decoration, combined with period stonework and beams. Inventive cuisine served in a very pretty setting: ultramodern furniture, white walls and pendant lights.

Côté Sud VISA MC

rte d'Orange – ✆ 04 90 40 66 08 – restaurantcotesud@wanadoo.fr – Fax 04 90 40 64 77 – Closed 27 October-3 November, 22 December-7 January, Monday dinner and Tuesday except July-August and Wednesday

Rest – *(number of covers limited, pre-book)* Menu € 24/47 – Carte € 41/51

◆ Scrubland and hills...the cuisine pays tribute to Provence. The delightful stone house has a chic interior. Enchanting garden.

Le Temps de Vivre VISA

Les Farjons – ✆ 04 90 40 66 00 – cuisine.passion904@orange.fr – Closed 22 December-21 January, Thursday lunch from September to April and Wednesday

Rest – Menu € 18 (weekday lunch), € 28/35 – Carte € 41/53

◆ The sound of crickets in the background, the *garrigue* and vineyards all around... This large 18C stone house with country ambiance and a terrace offers contemporary cooking with market fresh produce.

UGINE – 73 Savoie – **333** L3 – **pop. 6 963** – **alt. 484 m** – ✉ **73400** 45 **C1**

Paris 581 – Annecy 37 – Chambéry 63 – Lyon 162

Office de tourisme, 15, place du Val d'Arly ✆ 04 79 37 56 33, Fax 04 79 89 01 69

La Châtelle VISA MC AE

3 r. Paul Proust – ✆ 04 79 37 30 02 – lachatelle@yahoo.fr – Fax 04 79 37 30 02 – Closed 13-27 August, 1st-14 January, Saturday lunch, Sunday dinner and Monday

Rest – Menu € 19 (weekday lunch), € 24/67 – Carte € 30/61

◆ A vaulted dining room adorned with antique furniture and a terrace with a panoramic view of the mountains. This unusual 13C fortified house is also worth a detour for its very tasty creative cuisine.

L'UNION – 31 Haute-Garonne – **343** G3 – see Toulouse

UNTERMUHLTHAL – 57 Moselle – **307** Q5 – see Baerenthal

URÇAY – 03 Allier – **326** C3 – **pop. 298** – **alt. 169 m** – ✉ **03360** 5 **B1**

Paris 297 – La Châtre 55 – Montluçon 34 – Moulins 66 – St-Amand-Montrond 15

L'Étoile d'Urçay with rm rm, VISA MC

42 rte Nationale – ✆ 04 70 06 92 66 – letoiledurcay@orange.fr – Closed 24 November-3 December, 16 February-11 March, Tuesday October-June, Sunday dinner and Monday

5 rm €35 €35, € 5,50 – ½ P € 41 – **Rest** – Menu € 14,50 bi/30 – Carte € 41/48

◆ This pleasant rustic-style restaurant, on the road through this little market town, offers traditional cuisine. Simple and convivial eating near the Tronçais forest.

URDOS – 64 Pyrénées-Atlantiques – 342 I7 – pop. 108 – alt. 780 m – ✉ 64490 3 **B3**

Paris 850 – Jaca 38 – Oloron-Ste-Marie 41 – Pau 75

Col du Somport★★ Southeast: 14 km, **Atlantic Coast**

Voyageurs-Somport

– ✆ 05 59 34 88 05 – hotel.voyageurs.urdos@wanadoo.fr – Fax 05 59 34 86 74 – Closed 20 October-2 December, Sunday dinner and Monday except school holidays

28 rm – †€ 32/35 ††€ 35/45, ☕ € 5,50 – ½ P € 35/42 – **Rest** – Menu € 13/29 – Carte € 19/38

◆ A former coaching house on the Santiago de Compostela route in the valley of Aspe. As well as warm hospitality, it offers rustic rooms, which are quieter at the back. Country-style dining room where traditional, unpretentious food is served.

URIAGE-LES-BAINS – 38 Isère – 333 H7 – alt. 414 m – Spa : late Jan.-early Dec. – Casino : Palais de la Source – ✉ 38410 **French Alps** 45 **C2**

Paris 576 – Grenoble 11 – Vizille 11

Office de tourisme, 5, avenue des Thermes ✆ 04 76 89 10 27, Fax 04 76 89 26 68

Uriage Vaulnaveys-le-Haut Les Alberges, South, ✆ 04 76 89 03 47.

Prémol forest★ Southeast: 5 km by D 111.

Grand Hôtel

– ✆ 04 76 89 10 80 – grandhotel.fr@wanadoo.fr – Fax 04 76 89 04 62 – Closed 21 December-5 January

39 rm – †€ 100/173 ††€ 125/198, ☕ € 20 – 3 suites

Rest *Les Terrasses* – *(closed 18 August-1st September, 21 December-21 January, Sunday except July-August, Tuesday except dinner September-June, Friday lunch July-August, Wednesday lunch, Thursday lunch and Monday)* Menu € 55 (weekday lunch), € 85/145 – Carte € 115/120

Spec. Truite pochée au bleu du Vercors. Foie gras "confit-poêlé". Pintade "rôtie-confite". **Wines** Roussette, Mondeuse.

◆ This handsome Napoleon III hostelry, once frequented by Coco Chanel and Sacha Guitry and linked to the central spa, offers a choice of elegant, spacious personalised rooms. An elegant restaurant and a delightful terrace - two settings in which to enjoy an inspired cuisine.

Les Mésanges

1.5 km St-Martin-d'Uriage road and Bouloud road – ✆ 04 76 89 70 69 – prince@hotel-les-mesanges.com – Fax 04 76 89 56 97 – Open 1st February-20 October

33 rm – †€ 67/80 ††€ 67/80, ☕ € 9 – **Rest** – *(closed Sunday dinner, Monday and Tuesday)* Menu (€ 18), € 26/58 – Carte € 41/62

◆ A number of buildings overlooking the valley and resort offer practical, well-kept rooms, some with a balcony or terrace. In summer, a charming terrace in the shade of plane trees and in winter, a bright dining room.

Le Manoir

62 rte Prémol – ✆ 04 76 89 10 88 – contact@hotel-manoir.fr – Fax 04 76 89 20 63 – Open 16 February-14 November

15 rm – †€ 35 ††€ 41/63, ☕ € 7,50 – ½ P € 40/84 – **Rest** – *(closed lunch weekdays except 29 March-21 October and Sunday dinner)* Menu (€ 14), € 19/34 – Carte € 36/51

◆ This 1900 establishment at the entrance to the resort sports an attractive colourful facade. Large first floor rooms; smaller but renovated in a modern style on the second floor. Inviting dining rooms, cosy sitting room and veranda opening onto a pleasant terrace. Traditional dishes.

South 2 km by D 524 - ✉ 38410 Uriage-les-Bains

Le Manoir des Alberges

251 chemin des Alberges – ✆ 04 76 51 92 11 – contact@lemanoirdesalberges.com

5 rm ☕ – †€ 105 ††€ 120 – **Table d'hôte** – Menu € 25 bi

◆ This house, the central section of which dates from the 1930s, overlooks a golf course. Five guestrooms, each with their own individual style: Bavarian, Indian, ethnic, Art Deco etc. Inventive cuisine concocted by the *patronne*, served on the terrace during the summer months.

URMATT – 67 Bas-Rhin – 315 H5 – pop. 1 357 – alt. 240 m – ✉ 67280 1 A2

Paris 487 – Molsheim 15 – Saverne 37 – Sélestat 49 – Strasbourg 44 – Wasselonne 23

Church ★ of Niederhaslach Northeast: 3 km,

Alsace-Lorraine-Champagne

Clos du Hahnenberg rm, VISA AE

65 r. du G. de Gaulle – ✆ 03 88 97 41 35 – clos.hahnenberg@wanadoo.fr – Fax 03 88 47 36 51 – Closed 11-24 February and Friday evening

43 rm – €40/65 €45/65, €9,50 – ½ P €45/55

Rest *Chez Jacques* – Menu €14 (weekday lunch), €20/29 – Carte €28/46

◆ On the main village street, this hotel takes special care of its rooms which are more spacious, bright and soundproofed in the modern part. Jacques' place has a rustic interior and traditional cooking with a few Alsatian specialities.

La Poste rest, rm, VISA AE

– ✆ 03 88 97 40 55 – hotelrestlaposte@multimania.com – Fax 03 88 47 38 32 – Closed 16-30 July and 24 December-5 January

14 rm – €41 €59, €7,50 – ½ P €58 – **Rest** – *(closed Sunday dinner and Monday)* Menu (€8,50), €18/51 – Carte €22/49

◆ Family atmosphere guaranteed in this 100-year-old village inn located opposite the town hall. The rooms are comfortable and well-maintained; some have been carefully renovated. Stained-glass windows and wood panelling heighten the decor of the dining rooms. Regional cuisine.

URRUGNE – 64 Pyrénées-Atlantiques – 342 B4 – see St-Jean-de-Luz

URT – 64 Pyrénées-Atlantiques – 342 E4 – pop. 1 702 – alt. 41 m – ✉ 64240 3 B3

Paris 757 – Bayonne 17 – Biarritz 24 – Cambo-les-Bains 28 – Pau 97 – Peyrehorade 19

Office de tourisme, Mairie ✆ 05 59 56 20 33

Auberge de la Galupe (Stéphane Rouville) VISA AE

au port de l'Adour – ✆ 05 59 56 21 84 – galupe@wanadoo.fr – Fax 05 59 56 28 66 – Closed 1st-13 March, 23 June-2 July, 24 November-December, 16-28 February, Wednesday lunch and Saturday lunch except August, Sunday dinner and Monday

Rest – *(pre-book Sat - Sun)* Menu €35 (weekday lunch), €70/82 – Carte €61/92

Spec. Alose de l'Adour aux pruneaux (April to June). Palombe en deux cuissons, rôtie et salmis (October to November). Tarte soufflée aux pruneaux, glace au vieil armagnac. **Wines** Irouléguy, Jurançon.

◆ Exposed beams, old flagstones and modern furniture are the attractions of this old mariner's inn on the banks of the Adour. Delicious regional cuisine with an emphasis on local fish.

USCLADES-ET-RIEUTORD – 07 Ardèche – 331 G5 – pop. 102 – alt. 1 270 m – ✉ 07510 44 A3

Paris 590 – Aubenas 45 – Langogne 41 – Privas 59 – Le Puy-en-Velay 51 – Thueyts 98

in Rieutord - ✉ 07510 Usclades-et-Rieutord

Ferme de la Besse

– ✆ 04 75 38 80 64 – Fax 04 75 38 80 64 – Closed 22 December-31 January and weekdays from 15 October to 30 April

Rest – *(pre-book)* Menu €27/35

◆ An authentic 15C farm with a beautiful slab-stone roof. Superbly well-preserved rustic interior, with stonework, beams and fireplace. Earthy cuisine with local products.

USSAT – 09 Ariège – 343 H8 – see Tarascon-sur-Ariège

USSEAU – 86 Vienne – 322 J3 – see Châtellerault

USSEL – 19 Corrèze – 329 O2 – pop. 10 753 – alt. 631 m – ✉ 19200
Dordogne-Berry-Limousin 25 **D2**

Paris 444 – Aurillac 99 – Clermont-Ferrand 83 – Guéret 101 – Tulle 63
Office de tourisme, place Voltaire ✆ 05 55 72 11 50, Fax 05 55 72 54 44

de Neuvic Neuvic Legta Henri Queuille, South: 14 km, ✆ 05 55 95 98 89 ;
du Chammet Peyrelevade Geneyte, Northwest: 42 km, ✆ 05 55 94 77 54.

Auberge de l'Empereur
La Goudouneche, (l'Empereur business park), 5 km south-west on D 1089 – ✆ 05 55 46 04 30 – xavierconcept@wanadoo.fr – Fax 05 55 72 29 05 – Closed 2-11 February, Sunday dinner and Monday
Rest – *(pre-book)* Menu € 20 (weekday lunch), € 26/50 – Carte € 31/56
◆ This former barn with high ceilings, beams, panelling and an eccentric décor enjoys a peaceful setting. Contemporary cuisine.

USSON-EN-FOREZ – 42 Loire – 327 C7 – pop. 1 232 – alt. 925 m – ✉ 42550

Paris 472 – Issoire 86 – Montbrison 41 – Le Puy-en-Velay 52 – St-Étienne 48
Office de tourisme, place de la Vialle ✆ 04 77 50 66 15, Fax 04 77 50 66 15 44 **A2**

Rival with rm
– ✆ 04 77 50 63 65 – hotelrival@msn.com – Fax 04 77 50 67 62 – Closed 15 June-1st July, 12 November-1st December and Monday except July-August
11 rm – †€ 42 ††€ 42/68, ☕ € 6,50 – ½ P € 41 – **Rest** – Menu € 13 (except Sunday)/40 – Carte € 22/40
◆ This simple family enterprise is near the town's Eco Museum on the Compostelle route. Regional dishes served in a rustic dining room. Refurbished rooms. Discounts for pilgrims.

UTELLE – 06 Alpes-Maritimes – 341 E4 – pop. 488 – alt. 800 m – ✉ 06450
French Riviera 41 **D2**

Paris 883 – Levens 24 – Nice 51 – Puget-Théniers 53 – St-Martin-Vésubie 34
Alatr-piece★ in St-Véran church - Madonna of Utelle ✳★★★ Southwest: 6 km.

Bellevue
rte de la Madone – ✆ 04 93 03 17 19 – Fax 04 93 03 19 17 – Closed 8 January-8 February and Wednesday except July-August
Rest – *(lunch only)* Menu € 14/30 – Carte € 18/39
◆ Hidden away in the mountains, this house sports a rustic decor with open hearth and alpine view. Regional cuisine using home-grown produce. Terrace shaded by plane trees.

UZER – 07 Ardèche – 331 H6 – pop. 385 – alt. 165 m – ✉ 07110 44 **A3**

Paris 663 – Lyon 196 – Privas 44 – Alès 63 – Montélimar 50

Château d'Uzer
– ✆ 04 75 36 89 21 – chateau-uzer@wanadoo.fr – Fax 04 75 36 02 59 – Closed 20 December-4 February
5 rm ☕ – †€ 90/120 ††€ 100/130 – **Table d'hôte** – *(closed Wednesday and Sunday)* Menu € 32 bi
◆ This medieval chateau has it all: welcoming proprietors with a sense of decorative style mixing old and new elements, the semi-wild garden, a swimming pool, and home-made breakfast. Regional dishes, served on the terrace in good weather.

UZERCHE – 19 Corrèze – 329 K3 – pop. 3 062 – alt. 380 m – ✉ 19140
Dordogne-Berry-Limousin 24 **B3**

Paris 444 – Brive-la-Gaillarde 38 – Limoges 57 – Périgueux 106 – Tulle 30
Office de tourisme, place de la Libération ✆ 05 55 73 15 71, Fax 05 55 73 88 36
Ste-Eulalie ≤★ East: 1 km.

Teyssier
r. Pont Turgot – ✆ 05 55 73 10 05 – reservation@hotel-teyssier.com – Fax 05 55 98 43 31 – Closed 13 December-5 January and 21 February-9 March
14 rm – †€ 54 ††€ 66, ☕ € 8 – ½ P € 54/60 – **Rest** – Menu € 19/40 – Carte € 31/78
◆ This 18C inn near the banks of the Vézère has been fully renovated (air-conditioning throughout) and now offers extremely comfortable rooms. A modern panoramic dining room that contrasts with an older more rustic room. Simple dishes with a southern flavour.

Ambroise
av. Ch. de Gaulle – ✆ 05 55 73 28 60 – hotelambroise@orange.fr – Fax 05 55 98 45 73 – Closed 4 November-4 December, Sunday evening except July-August and Monday except hotel
14 rm – †€ 41 ††€ 44, ☕ € 8 – ½ P € 41 – **Rest** – Menu € 15 (weekdays)/33 – Carte € 25/59
◆ The simple rooms of this family hotel all overlook the river and greenery. Attractive rustic-styled dining room and, in summer, a terrace-balcony overlooking the garden allowing diners to enjoy the sun as they savour the delicious food.

in St-Ybard 6 km Northwest by D 920 and D 54 – pop. 593 – alt. 320 m – ✉ 19140

Auberge St-Roch
2 r. du Château – ✆ 05 55 73 09 71 – contact@auberge-saint-roch.fr – Fax 05 55 98 41 63 – Closed 20 June-8 July, 20 December-20 January, dinner from 4 November to 1st April, Sunday dinner and Monday
Rest – Menu € 13 (weekdays)/38 – Carte € 20/55
◆ Country inn located in the centre of a village with two handsome dining rooms and a bar popular with the locals. Pleasant shaded terrace overlooking the church. Regional fare.

UZÈS – 30 Gard – 339 L4 – pop. 8 007 – alt. 138 m – ✉ 30700

Provence 23 **D2**

Paris 682 – Montpellier 83 – Alès 34 – Arles 52 – Avignon 38 – Nîmes 25

Office de tourisme, place Albert 1er ✆ 04 66 22 68 88, Fax 04 66 22 95 19

d'Uzès Mas de la Place, by Avignon road: 5 km, ✆ 04 66 22 40 03.

Old town★★ - Duchy ★: ✳★★ from Bermonde tower - Fenestrelle tower ★★ - Place aux Herbes★ - Organs★ of St-Théodorit cathedral V.

Plan on next page

Hostellerie Provençale
1-3 r. Grande-Bourgade – ✆ 04 66 22 11 06 – contact@hostellerieprovencale.com – Fax 04 66 75 01 03 A **a**
9 rm – †€ 75/88 ††€ 85/135, ☕ € 20 – **Rest** – *(closed 15 November-15 December, Monday and Tuesday)* Menu € 34 – Carte approx. € 39
◆ A prettily renovated old house near the Place aux Herbes where exposed stonework, red floor tiles and antique furniture create a warm atmosphere. Several Jacuzzi tubs. Market-based menu served in a pleasant, colourful dining room.

Mercure rest,
rte de Nîmes, via ②: 0.5 km – ✆ 04 66 03 32 22 – mercure.relaisuzes@wanadoo.fr – Fax 04 66 03 32 10
65 rm – †€ 68/78 ††€ 68/78, ☕ € 10 – **Rest** – *(dinner only)* Menu (€ 16), € 25
◆ A group of buildings around a pool and a shaded terrace make up this hotel on the doorstep of Uzès. Spruce rooms. An informal guesthouse rather than a chain atmosphere. Provençal coloured dining room or a pretty terrace in summertime.

Le Patio de Violette
chemin Trinquelaïgues, (lieu dit la Perrine) – ✆ 04 66 01 09 83 – contact@patiodeviolette.com – Fax 04 66 59 33 61
25 rm – †€ 60/75 ††€ 60/75, ☕ € 8 – ½ P € 55/63 – **Rest** – *(dinner only) (residents only)* Menu € 21/23 – Carte € 20/32
◆ A modern patio and pleasant terrace are the heart of this recent, contemporary construction. Minimalist decor. Up-to-date restaurant offering simple dishes chalked up on a slate and local wines.

UZÈS

Street	Square	No.
Alliés (Bd des)	A	2
Boucairie (R.)	B	4
Collège (R. du)	B	6
Dampmartin (Pl.)	A	7
Dr-Blanchard (R.)	B	8
Duché (Pl. du)	A	9
Entre les Tours (R.)	A	10
Évêché (R. de l')	B	12
Foch (Av. Mar.)	A	13
Foussat (R. Paul)	A	14
Gambetta (Bd)	A	
Gide (Bd Ch.)	AB	
Marronniers (Prom. des)	B	16
Pascal (Av. M.)	B	17
Pelisserie (R.)	A	18
Plan de l'Oume (R.)	B	19
Port Royal (R.)	B	20
Raffin (R.)	B	21
République (R.)	A	23
St-Étienne (R.)	A	25
St-Théodorit (R.)	B	27
Uzès (R. J.-d')	A	29
Victor-Hugo (Boulevard)	A	32
Vincent (Av. Gén.)	A	
4-Septembre (R.)	A	35

Le 80 Jours

2 pl. Albert-1er – ✆ 04 66 22 09 89
– Closed Wednesday except July-August and Sunday A **b**
Rest – Menu € 19 (weekday lunch), € 26/34
– Carte € 30/39

◆ The vaulted ceilings, old stones, ethnic decor and pretty shaded patio are an invitation to take a seat in this modern brasserie whose name is inspired by Jules Verne and the owner's voyages.

Les Trois Salons

18 r. Dr Blanchard – ✆ 04 66 22 57 34
– les3salons@orange.fr – Fax 04 66 72 71 42
– Closed Monday and Tuesday B **d**
Rest – Menu € 22 (weekday lunch), € 39/57
– Carte € 43/49

◆ The sign outside this house built in 1699 near Duché doesn't lie: the tables are set in three pretty but uncluttered sitting rooms. Modern menu with a regional twist.

in Arpaillargues-et-Aureillac 4.5 km by ③ – pop. 785 – alt. 107 m – ✉ 30700

Château d'Arpaillargues

r. Château – ✆ 04 66 22 14 48
– arpaillargues@wanadoo.fr – Fax 04 66 22 56 10
– Open 2 April-14 October
29 rm – †€ 80/270 ††€ 80/270, ☕ € 14
Rest – Menu € 26/48 – Carte € 31/53

◆ A lovely 18C château (once home to Franz Liszt's companion) and a former silkworm farm where the rooms are individually furnished and offer a view of the park or the village. Contemporary menu, inviting setting and pleasant terrace.

in St-Quentin-la-Poterie 5 km by ① and D 5 – pop. 2 731 – alt. 113 m – ✉ 30700

Clos de Pradines

pl. Pigeonnier – ✆ 04 66 20 04 89 – contact@clos-de-pradines.com – Fax 04 66 57 19 53 – Closed 17-30 November, 12 January-1st February

18 rm – €68/112 €68/162, €12 – ½ P €71/93 – **Rest** – *(closed Tuesday lunch, Wednesday lunch, Thursday lunch, Friday lunch from November to March, Sunday dinner and Monday except July-August)* Menu €29/38 – Carte €34/44

◆ This new hotel on the village heights offers delightful neo-Provençal style rooms with small south facing terraces or balconies. This restaurant offers a lovely terrace overlooking the valley, a modern dining room and traditional food.

in St-Siffret 5 km by ① and D982 – pop. 792 – alt. 140 m – ✉ 30700

L'Authentic

– ✆ 04 66 22 60 09 – lauthenticrestaurant@wanadoo.fr – Fax 04 66 22 60 09 – Closed 15 November-1st December, 15 February-1st March, Monday from December to mid April, Tuesday and Wednesday

Rest – *(number of covers limited, pre-book)* Menu €20 (weekday lunch), €28/38

◆ Southern inspired cuisine (market fresh produce) and a wine list chalked up on a slate, served in a former classroom of the old school, now a delightful inn!

in Serviers et Labaume 6 km by ④ and D 981 – pop. 355 – alt. 114 m – ✉ 30700

L'Olivier with rm

Le village – ✆ 04 66 22 56 01 – info@l-olivier.fr – Fax 04 66 22 54 49 – Closed 10-17 November, 1st January-28 February and Monday

5 rm – €70 €70 – **Rest** – *(number of covers limited, pre-book)* Menu €22 (lunch), €43/65 – Carte €48/53

◆ This old village café is now a charming restaurant: sunny decor, wrought iron furniture and flower-decked patio. Fine, modern cuisine and local wines. New rooms.

in Montaren-et-St-Médiers 6 km by ④ and D 337 – pop. 1 328 – alt. 115 m – ✉ 30700

Clos du Léthé without rest

Hameau de St-Médiers – ✆ 04 66 74 58 37 – info@closdulethe.com – Open mid March-mid November

5 rm – €170/270 €170/270

◆ Intimacy, luxurious comfort, designer interior, delightful service, peace and quiet, overflow pool, steam bath and cookery courses. A stone built home (former priory) of great appeal!

VAAS – 72 Sarthe – 310 K8 – pop. 1 540 – alt. 41 m – ✉ 72500

Châteaux of the Loire 35 **D2**

Paris 237 – Angers 77 – Château-du-Loir 8 – Château-la-Vallière 15 – Le Mans 42

Le Vedaquais with rm

pl. Liberté – ✆ 02 43 46 01 41 – levedaquais@orange.fr – Fax 02 43 46 37 60 – Closed November, Christmas and February school holidays, Friday dinner, Sunday dinner and Monday

12 rm – €50/65 €50/65, €8 – ½ P €50/65 – **Rest** – Menu €17/33 bi – Carte €36/50

◆ The former school and village town hall now houses guest rooms, a tastefully decorated restaurant, an Internet area and shop. Spicy up-to-date cuisine.

LA VACHETTE – 05 Hautes-Alpes – 334 I3 – see Briançon

Good food and accommodation at moderate prices? Look for the Bib symbols: red Bib Gourmand for food, blue Bib Hotel for hotels.

VACQUEYRAS – 84 Vaucluse – 332 C9 – pop. 1 061 – alt. 117 m – ✉ 84190

42 **E1**

Paris 662 – Avignon 35 – Nyons 34 – Orange 19 – Vaison-la-Romaine 18

Syndicat d'initiative, place de la Mairie ✆ 04 90 12 39 02, Fax 04 90 63 83 28

Le Pradet without rest

– ✆ 04 90 65 81 00 – hotellepradet@wanadoo.fr – Fax 04 90 65 80 27

32 rm – †€ 52 ††€ 61, ☕ € 9

◆ This recent building at the entrance to the village houses functional and soundproofed rooms. Some have a small terrace or balcony. Games room and fitness area.

in Montmirail 2 km East by secondary road – ✉ 84190

Montmirail rm,

– ✆ 04 90 65 84 01 – hotel-montmirail@wanadoo.fr – Fax 04 90 65 81 50 – Open 26 March-14 October

39 rm – †€ 58/69 ††€ 80/115, ☕ € 12 – ½ P € 82/100

Rest – *(closed Thursday lunch and Saturday lunch)* Menu (€ 24), € 34 (weekday lunch), € 36/40 – Carte € 41/46

◆ This 19C residence with character stands in a pleasant garden planted with trees, at the foot of the famous Dentelles de Montmirail. Well maintained rooms. Rustic dining room enlivened by Provençal fabrics and appealing terrace shaded by tall plane trees.

VACQUIERS – 31 Haute-Garonne – 343 G2 – pop. 1 032 – alt. 200 m – ✉ 31340

28 **B2**

Paris 658 – Albi 71 – Castres 80 – Montauban 35 – Toulouse 31

La Villa les Pins

2 km west via D 30 – ✆ 05 61 84 96 04 – Fax 05 61 84 28 54

15 rm – †€ 57 ††€ 67, ☕ € 9 – ½ P € 58 – **Rest** – *(closed Saturday and Sunday) (dinner only) (residents only)* Menu € 17

◆ Large villa built in the heart of wooded parkland. A marble staircase leads up to comfortable recently refurbished rooms, albeit with somewhat old-fashioned fittings. Elegant dining rooms and a terrace overlooking the estate; simple traditional fare.

VAGNAS – 07 Ardèche – 331 I7 – pop. 430 – alt. 200 m – ✉ 07150

44 **A3**

Paris 678 – Alès 38 – Aubenas 37 – Mende 112 – Orange 57

La Bastide d'Iris without rest

D 579 – ✆ 04 75 88 44 77 – labastidediris@wanadoo.fr – Fax 04 75 38 61 29 – Closed January

12 rm – †€ 68/89 ††€ 73/113, ☕ € 10

◆ This charming brand-new country house has rooms with attractively coloured walls, assorted fabrics, customized furniture and cheerful bathrooms. Pleasant garden.

VAIGES – 53 Mayenne – 310 G6 – pop. 1 071 – alt. 90 m – ✉ 53480

35 **C1**

Paris 255 – Château-Gontier 35 – Laval 24 – Le Mans 61 – Mayenne 32

Commerce rm, rest,

– ✆ 02 43 90 50 07 – oger-samuel.hotel-du-commerce@wanadoo.fr – Fax 02 43 90 57 40 – Closed 24 December-18 January, Sunday evening and Friday evening from October to 1st May

32 rm – †€ 66/90 ††€ 70/110, ☕ € 10 – ½ P € 68/90

Rest – Menu € 23/50 – Carte € 35/59

◆ In a village of the Mayenne countryside, this hotel, run by the same family since 1883, offers well-equipped rooms. Billiard table and sauna. Beneath a lovely ceiling of timber rafters, rustic dining rooms and open fires. Conservatory.

VAILLY-SUR-SAULDRE – 18 Cher – 323 L2 – pop. 806 – alt. 205 m – ✉ 18260

Dordogne-Berry-Limousin

12 **C2**

Paris 182 – Aubigny-sur-Nère 17 – Bourges 55 – Cosne-sur-Loire 25 – Gien 36 – Sancerre 23

Office de tourisme, 5 bis, place du 8 mai 1945 ✆ 02 48 73 87 57, Fax 02 48 73 87 57

Le Lièvre Gourmand (William Page) A/C VISA MC

14 r. Grande Rue – ✆ 02 48 73 80 23
– contact@lelievregourmand.com – Fax 02 48 73 86 13
– Closed 31 March-8 April, 23 June-1st July, 1st-9 September, 5-30 January, Sunday dinner, Monday and Tuesday

Rest – *(number of covers limited, pre-book)* Menu € 39/59

Spec. Homard en cappuccino et parmentier. Filets de grondins frits, petites rattes fumées. Chocolat blanc, confiture d'endives, biscotti. **Wines** Sancerre, Reuilly.

◆ These old village houses offer an elegant, rustic restaurant (non-smoking) and a cosy lounge. Fine inventive cuisine and wines from Australia and the region.

VAISON-LA-ROMAINE – 84 Vaucluse – 332 D8 – pop. 5 904 – alt. 193 m –

✉ 84110 Provence 40 **B2**

Paris 664 – Avignon 51 – Carpentras 27 – Montélimar 64 – Pont-St-Esprit 41

Office de tourisme, place du Chanoine-Sautel ✆ 04 90 36 02 11, Fax 04 90 28 76 04

Gallo-Roman remains★★ : théatre antique (ancient theatre)★ , musée archéologique Théo-Desplans (Théo-Desplans Archaeological Museum)★ M - Haute Ville (Upper Town)★ - cloître (cloister)★ B.

VAISON-LA-ROMAINE

Street	Grid	No.
Aubanel (Pl.)	Z	2
Bon Ange (Chemin du)	Y	3
Brusquet (Chemin du)	Y	4
Burrus (R.)	Y	5
Cathédrale (Pl. de la)	Y	6
Chanoine-Sautel (Pl.)	Y	7
Coudray (Av.)	Y	8
Daudet (R. A.)	Y	9
Église (R. de l')	Z	10
Évêché (R. de l')	Z	12
Fabre (Cours H.)	Y	13
Foch (Quai Maréchal)	Z	14
Géoffray (Av. C.)	Z	15
Gontard (Quai P.)	Z	17
Grande-Rue	Y	18
Jean-Jaurès (R.)	Y	22
Mazen (Av. J.)	Y	23
Mistral (R. Frédéric)	Y	24
Montée du Château	Z	25
Montfort (Pl.)	Y	26
Noël (R. B.)	Y	27
Poids (Pl. du)	Z	29
République (R.)	Y	32
St-Quenin (Av.)	Y	33
Sus Auze (Pl.)	Y	34
Taulignan (Crs)	Y	35
Victor-Hugo (Av.)	Y	36
Vieux Marché (Pl. du)	Z	38
11 Novembre (Pl. du)	Y	40

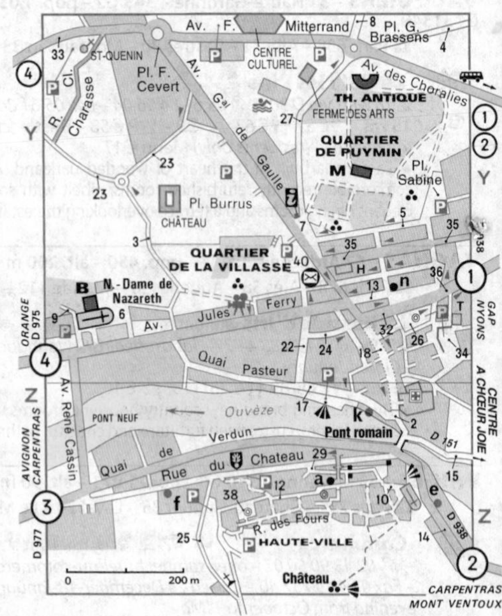

Hostellerie le Beffroi rest, VISA MC AE

Haute Ville – ✆ 04 90 36 04 71 – lebeffroi@wanadoo.fr
– Fax 04 90 36 24 78 – Closed 20 January to end March and 21-26 December Z **a**

22 rm – €70/90 €70/140, € 12 – ½ P € 106

Rest – *(open 16 March-end October and closed Tuesday and lunch weekdays)*
Menu € 29/46 – Carte € 32/53

◆ At the foot of the castle, dominating the town, two houses from the 16C and 17C that have retained their charm. Rooms are tastefully decorated. Beautiful terraced garden. Tables are set out in a rustic dining room or in the pretty courtyard. Classic menus, salad bar and tea room.

Burrhus without rest
2 pl. Monfort – ✆ 04 90 36 00 11 – info@burrhus.com – Fax 04 90 36 39 05 – Closed 15 December-19 January Y **n**
39 rm – †€ 46/82 ††€ 46/115, ☕ € 8
◆ A house with ochre shades, brightened by painting and sculpture displays. Fourteen of the rooms are trendy, while the others are either modern or Provencal in style.

Le Moulin à Huile (Robert Bardot) with rm
quai Mar. Foch – ✆ 04 90 36 20 67 – info@moulin-huile.com – Fax 04 90 36 20 20 – Closed Sunday evening and Monday Z **e**
3 rm – †€ 120 ††€ 120/150, ☕ € 30
Rest – *(pre-book)* Menu (€ 28), € 40 (weekday lunch), € 60/75 – Carte € 78/88
Spec. Boudin de homard sur mousse de lait coco (June to October). Saint-Jacques aux copeaux de truffe (January to March). Millefeuille à la crème vanillée. **Wines** Châteauneuf du Pape blanc, Côtes du Luberon.
◆ It is difficult to resist the charm of this former oil mill on the banks of the Ouvèze. Appealing up-to-date cuisine either served in the veranda that opens onto a pretty terrace or in the vaulted cellar, according to the season. Cosy and tastefully decorated rooms.

Le Bistro du O
– ✆ 04 90 41 72 90 – info@legrandpre.com – Closed mid November-mid December, Monday lunch and Sunday Z **f**
Rest – *(number of covers limited, pre-book)* Menu (€ 19), € 26/32 bi
◆ An elegant and refined bistro setting with vaulting, stone, and a mix of old and contemporary furniture. A single menu which changes daily. Carefully chosen, reasonably priced wine list.

Le Bateleur
1 pl. Théodore Aubanel – ✆ 04 90 36 28 04 – Fax 04 90 36 05 71 – Closed 23 June-3 July, 24 November-8 December, Sunday November-April, Monday October-June, Saturday lunch May-October, Thursday dinner May-June and October, Monday lunch and Thursday lunch mid July-end August Z **k**
Rest – Menu (€ 16), € 20 (weekday lunch), € 28/44 – Carte € 43/54
◆ This pleasant establishment in old Vaison offers simple, up-to-date dishes. Some tables overlook the Ouvèze.

in Crestet 5 km by ②, D 938 and D 76 – **pop. 432 – alt. 310 m** – ✉ **84110**

Mas de Magali ← Mont - Ventoux,
– ✆ 04 90 36 39 91 – masmagali@wanadoo.fr – Fax 04 90 28 73 40 – Open 22 March-13 October
11 rm – †€ 85/95 ††€ 85/95, ☕ € 9 – ½ P € 71/75 – **Rest** – *(Closed Wednesday) (dinner only)* Menu € 29
◆ Surrounded by countryside, this colourful building stands in a garden perfumed with the scents of Southern France. Attractive Provençal decor. Most of the rooms have a terrace. Swimming pool.

in Entrechaux 7 km by ②, D 938 and D 54 – **pop. 869 – alt. 280 m** – ✉ **84340**
French Alps

St-Hubert
– ✆ 04 90 46 00 05 – Fax 04 90 46 00 06 – Closed 6-17 October, 26 January-8 March, Tuesday and Wednesday
Rest – Menu € 16 (weekday lunch), € 26/50 – Carte € 28/51
◆ Since 1929, the same family has been welcoming guests to the two rustic-style dining rooms. In summer, dine under the wisteria-clad terrace. Game in season.

in Séguret 10 km by ③, D 977 and D 88 – **pop. 892 – alt. 250 m** – ✉ **84110**

Domaine de Cabasse rm,
rte Sablet – ✆ 04 90 46 91 12 – info@cabasse.fr – Fax 04 90 46 94 01 – Open 20 March-16 November
13 rm – †€ 73/87 ††€ 101/150, ☕ € 12,50 – ½ P € 91/110 – **Rest** – Menu € 29
◆ At the foot of the Montmirail Dentelles, this hotel forms part of a wine producing estate (tour, tastings). The simple, neat rooms benefit from the peace and quiet of the vineyards. At midday there is a small simple menu; in the evening you can enjoy the menu of the day. Wines from the estate.

XXX **La Table du Comtat** with rm

< plain and Dentelles de Montmirail, rest, P VISA AE
– *04 90 46 91 49 – table.comtat@wanadoo.fr – Fax 04 90 46 94 27*
– Closed 18 November-8 December, February, Sunday dinner, Tuesday dinner and Wednesday except July-August
8 rm – €80/110 €80/110, €14 – ½ P €95/100
Rest – Menu €20 (weekday lunch), €35/49 – Carte €30/50
◆ The main attraction of this stone house situated high up in the village is the superb panoramic view of the plain and the Montmirail Dentelles. Beautiful shaded terrace.

X **Le Mesclun** VISA AE

r. Poternes, (pedestrian access) – 04 90 46 93 43 – mesclunseguret@aol.com
– Fax 04 90 46 93 48 – Closed January, Tuesday except July-August and Monday
Rest – Menu (€19), €25 (lunch), €32/43 – Carte €42/54
◆ A pleasant restaurant in a charming village built on a hillside. Small dining rooms in shades of yellow, nice shaded terrace and Mediterranean cuisine with personal touches.

in Rasteau 9 km by ④, D 975 and D 69 – pop. 674 – alt. 200 m – ✉ 84110

Syndicat d'initiative, place Laparent 04 90 46 18 73

Bellerive < vineyards and Dentelles de Montmirail,

rte Violès – 04 90 46 10 20 rm, P VISA AE
– hotel-bellerive@wanadoo.fr – Fax 04 90 46 14 96 – Open mid April-mid October
20 rm – €75/170 €75/170, €15 – ½ P €94/140 – **Rest** – *(closed Monday lunch, Friday lunch and Tuesday)* Menu €27/50 – Carte €45/72
◆ Large villa surrounded by vines with swimming pool. Rooms endowed with pleasant loggias opening onto the Ouvèze valley. You will enjoy tasting the Rasteau wine whether you sit in the Provençal dining room or on the terrace.

in Roaix 5 km by ④ and D 975 – pop. 587 – alt. 168 m – ✉ 84110

XX **Le Grand Pré** (Raoul Reichrath) P VISA AE

rte de Vaison-la-Romaine – 04 90 46 18 12 – info@legrandpre.com
– Fax 04 90 46 17 84 – Open from mid February to mid November and closed Saturday lunch and Tuesday
Rest – *(pre-book)* Menu €32 bi (weekday lunch), €52/110 bi – Carte €66/90
Spec. Menu "figues" (September-October). Pigeonneau rôti au four, jus de café-turc.Vichyssoise de tomates, glaçon de truffe d'été (June to August). **Wines** Côtes du Rhône, Côtes du Rhône-Villages.
◆ Cuisine based on southern flavours and a wonderful selection of Côtes du Rhône wines, served in the elegant old farmhouse with its white interior. Terrace overlooks a herb garden.

VAÏSSAC – 82 Tarn-et-Garonne – **337** F7 – **pop. 599 – alt. 134 m** – ✉ 82800 29 **C2**

Paris 620 – Albi 60 – Montauban 23 – Toulouse 76 – Villefranche-de-Rouergue 66

Terrassier P VISA AE

– *05 63 30 94 60 – hotel-rest.terrassier@wanadoo.fr – Fax 05 63 30 87 40*
– Closed 19 to 25 November, 1st to 15 January, Friday evening and Sunday evening
18 rm – €45/85 €45/85, €7 – ½ P €45/60 – **Rest** – Menu €12,50 (weekday lunch), €21/42 – Carte €29/48
◆ This family-run inn is an ideal base for exploring the Quercy and Albigeois. Well-maintained rooms, with those in the recent annexe the pick of the bunch. Bright, modern dining room decorated in yellow tones. Regional cuisine.

Undecided between two equivalent establishments?
Within each category,
establishments are classified in our order of preference.

LE VAL – 83 Var – **340** L5 – **pop. 3 363** – **alt. 242 m** – ✉ **83143** 41 **C3**

▶ Paris 818 – La Seyne-sur-Mer 63 – Marseille 70 – Toulon 55

ℹ Office de tourisme, place de la Mairie ✆ 04 94 37 02 21, Fax 04 94 37 31 96

La Crémaillère AC VISA MC

23 r. Nationale – ✆ 04 94 86 40 00 – lacremaillere83@wanadoo.fr – Fax 04 94 86 40 00 – Closed 24-30 November, 22-28 February, Sunday dinner December-February, Wednesday except dinner in season and Monday except dinner July-August

Rest – Menu (€ 20 bi), € 24/32 – Carte € 26/34

◆ A welcoming family-run restaurant in the centre of this pretty village, with a Provencal decor and cuisine. Shaded terrace.

VALADY – 12 Aveyron – **338** G4 – **pop. 1 133** – **alt. 350 m** – ✉ **12330** 29 **C1**

▶ Paris 625 – Decazeville 20 – Rodez 20

Auberge de l'Ady VISA MC

1 av. du Pont-de-Malakoff, (near the church) – ✆ 05 65 72 70 24 – auberge.ady@orange.fr – Fax 05 65 72 68 15 – Closed 2 January-10 February, Sunday dinner, Tuesday dinner and Monday

Rest – Menu € 16 (weekday lunch), € 27/64 bi – Carte € 39/65

◆ The owner has returned to his roots at this informal inn-turned-contemporary-table in the heart of a rural *Aveyron* village. Up-to-date cuisine.

LE VAL-ANDRÉ – 22 Côtes-d'Armor – **309** G3 – see Pléneuf-Val-André

VALAURIE – 26 Drôme – **332** B7 – **pop. 508** – **alt. 162 m** – ✉ **26230** 44 **B3**

▶ Paris 622 – Montélimar 21 – Nyons 33 – Pierrelatte 14

Le Moulin de Valaurie rm, P VISA MC AE

Le Foulon – ✆ 04 75 97 21 90 – info@lemoulindevalaurie.com – Fax 04 75 98 63 72 – Closed 25 October-11 November, February and Sunday from October to March

16 rm – € 110/215 € 110/215, € 12 – **Rest** – *(closed Sunday dinner off season, Wednesday lunch in July-August, Tuesday lunch and Monday)* Menu € 36/42

◆ A path surrounded by vines leads to this 19C mill which is now a hotel full of character. Spacious Provençal rooms, antique ornaments and furniture, a lovely park; very quiet. An elegant dining room and wrought-iron terrace; traditional and regional food.

Domaine Les Mejeonnes rm, P VISA MC AE

2 km Montélimar road – ✆ 04 75 98 60 60 – contact@mejeonnes.com – Fax 04 75 98 63 44

10 rm – € 70/76 € 70/76, € 8 – ½ P € 60/63 – **Rest** – Menu (€ 18), € 23/28 – Carte € 26/35

◆ A charming stone farm on a hillside, bordered with a lavender- and rosemary-scented garden. Beautiful rustic interior. Small rooms brightened with Provençal fabrics. Decor and recipes with a local influence. Pleasant terrace in summer.

VALBERG – 06 Alpes-Maritimes – **341** C3 – **alt. 1 669 m** – **Winter sports : 1 430/2 100 m** 26 – ✉ **06470 Péone** French Alps 41 **D2**

▶ Paris 803 – Barcelonnette 75 – Castellane 67 – Nice 84 – St-Martin-Vésubie 57

ℹ Office de tourisme, Centre Administratif ✆ 04 93 23 24 25, Fax 04 93 02 52 27

Interior★ of N.-D.-des-Neiges chapel.

Le Chalet Suisse without rest VISA MC

– ✆ 04 93 03 62 62 – info@chalet-suisse.com – Fax 04 93 03 62 64 – Open mid June-September and mid December-March

23 rm – € 68/85 € 86/117, € 10

◆ Recently renovated, this Swiss-style chalet is situated in the centre of the resort. Comfort and relaxation are the main features of this hotel, with its attractive guestrooms, sauna and hammam.

L'Adrech de Lagas

63 av. Valberg – ✆ 04 93 02 51 64 – adrech-hotel@wanadoo.fr – Fax 04 93 02 52 33 – Open from June to September and from December to March
20 rm – †€ 60/108 ††€ 65/114, ☕ € 10 – ½ P € 67/91 – **Rest** – Menu € 19/24 – Carte € 19/40
◆ The name of this new chalet at the foot of the ski runs recalls the Catalan origins of the area's inhabitants. Colourful rooms, some of which have been renovated, with south-facing loggias. Good portions of traditional cuisine are on offer in the bright dining room of this restaurant.

Blanche Neige

10 av. Valberg – ✆ 04 93 02 50 04 – contact@hotelblancheneige.fr – Fax 04 93 02 61 90 – Closed November, April, Monday evening and Tuesday
17 rm – †€ 79/90 ††€ 79/90, ☕ € 10 – ½ P € 130 – **Rest** – *(open end December-mid March, July-August and closed Monday and Tuesday) (dinner only) (residents only)*
◆ Charming, recently redecorated chalet, the image of the Seven dwarves' cottage with its cosy little rooms and pretty chintzes. Diners enjoy regional cooking by the fire in winter or on the terrace in summer.

Côté Jardin

1 pl. Cluot de la Mule – ✆ 04 93 02 64 70 – aupaysdecocagne@hotmail.com – Fax 04 93 02 64 70 – Closed Sunday dinner and Wednesday October-November and April-June
Rest – Menu € 16 (lunch), € 19/29 – Carte € 29/45
◆ This restaurant has a cosy atmosphere, which becomes more festive during themed evenings. Provençal cuisine on the menu, as well as specialities such as home-made foie gras.

VALBONNE – 06 Alpes-Maritimes – 341 D6 – pop. 10 746 – alt. 250 m – ✉ 06560

French Riviera 42 **E2**

Paris 907 – Antibes 14 – Cannes 13 – Grasse 11 – Mougins 7 – Nice 32 – Vence 21

Office de tourisme, 1, place de l'Hôtel de Ville ✆ 04 93 12 34 50, Fax 04 93 12 34 57

Victoria Golf Club Chemin du Val Martin, South: 4 km, ✆ 04 93 12 23 26 ;

Opio Valbonne Opio Route de Roquefort les Pins, North: 1 km, ✆ 04 93 12 00 08.

La Bastide de Valbonne without rest

107 rte Cannes – ✆ 04 93 12 33 40 – bastide-de-valbonne@wanadoo.fr – Fax 04 93 12 33 41 – Closed 25 October-10 November
34 rm – †€ 95/120 ††€ 95/250, ☕ € 15
◆ New establishment with a cheerful yellow facade brightened with blue shutters. The rooms in the rear are quiet and have a view of the pool. Pleasant Provençal setting.

Les Armoiries without rest

pl. des Arcades – ✆ 04 93 12 90 90 – valbonne@hotellesarmoiries.com – Fax 04 93 12 90 91
16 rm – †€ 94/142 ††€ 94/163, ☕ € 12
◆ This beautifully decorated 17C building stands in the pedestrian area of this picturesque village. Rooms with personal touches and antique furniture.

Lou Cigalon (Alain Parodi)

4 bd Carnot – ✆ 04 93 12 27 07 – Fax 04 93 12 09 96 – Closed Sunday and Monday
Rest – *(number of covers limited, pre-book)* Menu € 29 (weekday lunch), € 49/100 – Carte € 50/92
Spec. Encornets et poulpes sur une gelée de tomate, chorizo. Pigeonneau rôti aux épices. Calisson glacé, soufflé aux agrumes. **Wines** Bellet, Côtes de Provence.
◆ A discreet house with two pleasant dining rooms featuring rough stone walls and exposed rafters. Produce from the sun-drenched markets is used in the kitchen. Wines from southeast France.

L'Auberge Fleurie

rte de Cannes, (D 3): 1.5 km – ✆ 04 93 12 02 80 – Fax 04 93 12 22 27 – Closed 1st December-5 January, Monday and Tuesday

Rest – Menu € 27/33 – Carte € 38/56

◆ Attractive establishment surrounded by a flower garden. Provençal-style dining room and a small terrace where generous portions of traditional food are served.

Le Bistro de Valbonne

11 r. Fontaine – ✆ 04 93 12 05 59 – lebistrotdevalbonne@cegetel.net – Fax 04 93 12 05 59 – Closed 24-30 November, 5-17 January, Monday lunch, Thursday lunch and Sunday off season and lunch July-August

Rest – *(number of covers limited, pre-book)* Menu (€ 18), € 33 – Carte € 38/54

◆ Mirrors, banquettes, subdued lighting, paintings, and old photos all create a warm, cosy atmosphere in this attractive vaulted dining room. Copious, traditional cuisine.

at golf d'Opio-Valbonne Northeast: 2 km by Biot road (D 4 and D 204) – ✉ 06650 Opio

Château de la Bégude rm,

rte de Roquefort les Pins – ✆ 04 93 12 37 00 – begude@opengolfclub.com – Fax 04 93 12 37 13 – Closed 16 November-27 December

31 rm – €78/200 €96/240, € 19 – 4 suites – **Rest** – *(closed dinner 16 November-27 December and Sunday dinner from 1st October to 31 March)* Menu € 38 (weekday lunch), € 48/62 – Carte € 43/71

◆ Edged by a line of cork oaks, on one of the region's best known golf courses, a charming 16C farm and sheep barn. Cosy, renovated guestrooms. Dining room-veranda and pleasant terrace overlooking the ninth hole of the golf course.

Antibes road South by D 3 – ✉ 06560 Valbonne

Castel Provence without rest

30 chemin Pinchinade, at 2.5 km – ✆ 04 93 12 11 92 – reservation@hotelcastelprovence.com – Fax 04 93 12 90 01

36 rm – €85/130 €98/160, € 15

◆ This recent regional-style construction is home to spacious and well-decorated rooms; some command a view of the pool and garden.

Daniel Desavie

1360 rte d'Antibes – ✆ 04 93 12 29 68 – desavie@wanadoo.fr – Fax 04 93 12 18 85 – Closed 30 June-14 July, 9-24 November, 22 February-9 March, Sunday and Monday

Rest – Menu € 31 (weekday lunch), € 41/65 – Carte € 49/78

◆ Modern cuisine making the most of local produce to be savoured in the contemporary dining room or under the arches of a gallery facing the flower garden.

in Sophia-Antipolis 7 km southeast by D 3 and D 103 - ✉ 06560 Valbonne

Sophia Country Club Grand Mercure rest,

Les Lucioles 2 - 3550 rte Dolines – ✆ 04 92 96 68 78 – H1279@accor.com – Fax 04 92 96 68 96 – Closed 23 December-6 January

155 rm – €155/185 €175/280, € 17

Rest *Le Club* – ✆ 04 92 96 68 98 – Menu (€ 20), € 26 (lunch)/42 – Carte € 33/58

◆ Hotel complex with a very complete sports centre: tennis club, driving range, fitness area, pools. Try to get one of the new rooms, which are spacious and carefully decorated. Restaurant-brasserie and terrace overlooking the pool. Modern cuisine.

Novotel

Les Lucioles 1, 290 r. Dostoievski – ✆ 04 92 38 72 38 – h0398@accor.com – Fax 04 93 95 80 12

97 rm – €101/137 €101/137, € 13,50 – **Rest** – Menu € 24 – Carte € 19/39

◆ This hotel in the heart of Sophia-Antipolis stands in the grounds of a pleasant garden. Quiet, comfortable and well-equipped rooms. Swimming pool and tennis court surrounded by trees. This restaurant with terrace serves Provençal cuisine in a restful, green setting.

Mercure

Les Lucioles 2, r. A. Caquot – 04 92 96 04 04 – h1122@accor.com – Fax 04 92 96 05 05

104 rm – €115/145 €125/150, €14

Rest – Menu (€23), €30 – Carte €29/44

♦ Modern building in Provençal colours situated on the vast wooded plateau of Sophia-Antipolis. Rooms gradually being renovated. Swimming pool and Mediterranean plants in the garden. Menu based on market offerings with regional touches and refreshing summer salads.

Relais Omega

Les Lucioles 1, 49 r. L. Van Beethoven – 04 92 96 07 07 – reservation@hotelomega.com – Fax 04 92 38 98 08 – Closed 17 December-2 January

60 rm – €99/109 €109/119, €12 – 4 suites – **Rest** – Menu €25/35 – Carte €30/50

♦ A sophisticated Provençal decoration and faultless facilities (air-conditioning, wifi, seminar room) await you in this fully refurbished comfortable hotel. In the restaurant you can expect traditional simple fare full of the flavour of southern France.

VALCABRÈRE – 31 Haute-Garonne – 343 B6 – see St-Bertrand-de-Comminges

VALCEBOLLÈRE – 66 Pyrénées-Orientales – 344 D8 – pop. 49 – alt. 1 470 m – ✉ 66340

22 **A3**

Paris 856 – Bourg-Madame 9 – Font-Romeu-Odeillo-Via 27 – Perpignan 107 – Prades 62

Auberge Les Ecureuils

– 04 68 04 52 03 – auberge-ecureuils@wanadoo.fr – Fax 04 68 04 52 34 – Closed 5 November-5 December

16 rm – €70/98 €70/98, €11 – ½ P €66/78 – **Rest** – Menu €25/52 – Carte €26/48

♦ An old sheep barn converted into a charming rustic inn. Pleasant rooms with a personal touch. Garden by a mountain stream. Outings organised; skis and rackets for hire. Distinguished dining room; classic cuisine and Catalan specialities. Pancakes too.

VAL-CLARET – 73 Savoie – 333 O5 – see Tignes

VALDAHON – 25 Doubs – 321 I4 – pop. 4 027 – alt. 645 m – ✉ 25800

17 **C2**

Paris 436 – Besançon 33 – Morteau 33 – Pontarlier 32

Relais de Franche Comté

1 r. Charles Schmitt – 03 81 56 23 18 – relais.de.franche.comte@wanadoo.fr – Fax 03 81 56 44 38 – Closed 1st-6 May, 25-30 August, 19 December – 11 January, Friday dinner, Saturday lunch except July-August, and Sunday dinner from September to June

20 rm – €43/45 €52/56, €7,50 – ½ P €52/56

Rest – Menu €13,50/49 – Carte €22/45

♦ This imposing hotel near the road has been recently renovated. Modern, practical rooms decorated with brightly-coloured fabrics. A bright restaurant serving traditional, seasonal cuisine, including game during the hunting season.

LE VAL-D'AJOL – 88 Vosges – 314 G5 – pop. 4 452 – alt. 380 m – ✉ 88340

Alsace-Lorraine

27 **C3**

Paris 382 – Épinal 41 – Luxeuil-les-Bains 18 – Plombières-les-Bains 10 – Remiremont 16

Office de tourisme, 17, rue de Plombières 03 29 30 61 55, Fax 03 29 30 56 78

La Résidence rm, VISA AE

5 r. des Mousses, by Hamanxard road – 03 29 30 68 52 – contact@la-residence.com – Fax 03 29 66 53 00 – Closed 26 November-26 December

49 rm – €46/58 €65/90, €10 – ½ P €66/78

Rest – *(closed Sunday dinner from November to April except school holidays and public holidays)* Menu (€13), €19 (weekday lunch), €25/44 – Carte €30/56

◆ In the heart of wooded parkland, a beautiful mid-19C bourgeois residence with two wings. The bedrooms are attractive if a little antiquated. The chef's unusual, regional menu varies from classic to innovative.

VALDEBLORE (Commune) – 06 Alpes-Maritimes – 341 E3 – pop. 686 – alt. 1 050 m – Winter sports : to la Colmiane 1 400/1 800 m 7 – ✉ 06420 French Riviera

Paris 841 – Cannes 89 – Nice 72 – St-Étienne-de-Tinée 46 – St-Martin-Vésubie 11

Syndicat d'initiative, la Roche 04 93 23 25 90 41 **D2**

in St-Dalmas-Valdeblore – ✉ 06420 Valdelblore

Pic de Colmiane ★★ East 4.5 km access by chairlift.

Auberge des Murès VISA

rte du col St-Martin – 04 93 23 24 60 – aubergesdesmures@wanadoo.fr – Fax 04 93 23 24 67 – Closed 15 November-15 December, Monday, Tuesday and Wednesday except school holidays

7 rm – €48/61 €48/61, €8,50 – ½ P €51/58 – **Rest** – Menu €25

◆ Small family inn recalling a chalet, offering a pretty view of the mountain from the balconies of the rooms. Feels just like home. In winter, a restaurant with exposed stones and beams; in summer, a lovely terrace facing the peaks.

VAL-DE-MERCY – 89 Yonne – 319 E5 – see Coulanges-la-Vineuse

VAL-D'ESQUIÈRES – 83 Var – 340 P5 – see Ste-Maxime

VAL-D'ISÈRE – 73 Savoie – 333 O5 – pop. 1 632 – alt. 1 850 m – Winter sports : 1 850/2 560 m 6 45 – ✉ 73150 French Alps 45 **D2**

Paris 667 – Albertville 86 – Chambéry 135

Office de tourisme, 04 79 06 06 60, Fax 04 79 06 04 56

du Lac de Tignes Tignes Le Val Claret, by Bourg-St-Maurice road: 14km, 04 79 06 37 42.

Bellevarde Rock ★★★ by cable car - Iseran road ★★★.

Plan on next page

Les Barmes de l'Ours rest, rest, VISA AE

chemin des Carats – 04 79 41 37 00 – welcome@hotel-les-barmes.com – Fax 04 79 41 37 01 – Open 6 December-26 April A **b**

55 rm – €410/1170 €440/1200, €30 – 21 suites – ½ P €270/1925

Rest *La Table de l'Ours* – *(open 6 December-19 April and closed Sunday) (dinner only)* Menu €75/135 – Carte €91/104

Rest *Le Pas de l'Ours* – Menu €65

Spec. Pressé d'omble chevalier ou de féra. Barbue en gros dominos colorés, canneloni de chou vert au reblochon. Suprême de volaille de Bresse, jus perlé au safran et citron. **Wines** Mondeuse, Vin de pays d'Allobrogie.

◆ This superb chalet is extremely refined. Choice of four styles of rooms: Scandinavian, Far North, Savoyard and modern. Lounge bar, spa. La Table de l'Ours serves tasty modern cuisine. Le Pas de l'Ours offers a rotisserie.

Christiania rm, VISA AE

– 04 79 06 08 25 – welcome@hotel-christiania.com – Fax 04 79 41 11 10 – Open mid December to mid April A **a**

68 rm – €278/510 €292/524 – 1 suite – **Rest** – Menu €36 (lunch), €48/60 – Carte €55/125

◆ Splendid chalet with a fine view of the ski runs, luxurious rooms and a comprehensive fitness centre. This restaurant is well-known in the Val: warm wood panelling, elegant draperies, plush lounge and panoramic terrace.

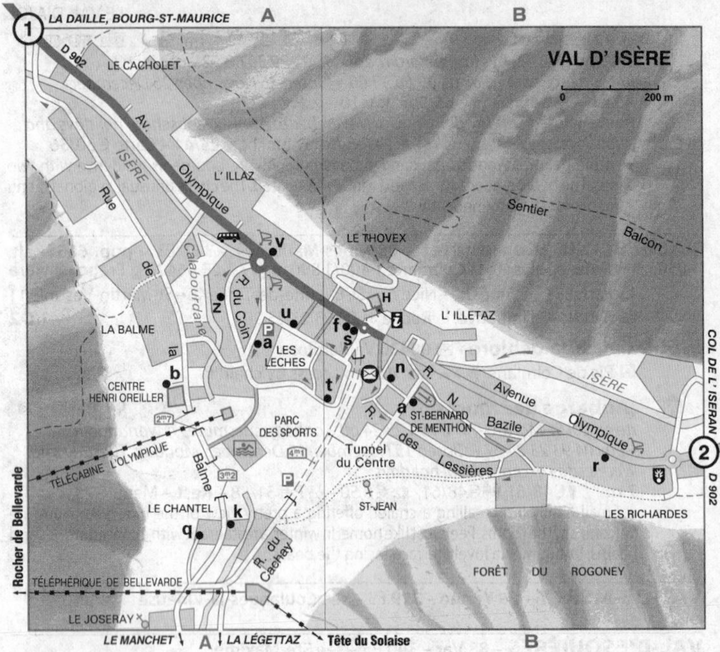

LA DAILLE, BOURG-ST-MAURICE A B

VAL D' ISÈRE

0 200 m

D 902 – LE CACHOLET – Av. Olympique – ISÈRE – Rue de la Balme – L' ILLAZ – Calabourdane – R. du Coin – LE THOVEX – Sentier Balcon – L' ILLETAZ – LA BALME – LES LECHES – CENTRE HENRI OREILLER – PARC DES SPORTS – Tunnel du Centre – ST-BERNARD DE MENTHON – R. N. Bazile – R. des Lessières – Avenue Olympique – TÉLÉCABINE L'OLYMPIQUE – Balme – ST-JEAN – LE CHANTEL – R. du Cachay – LES RICHARDES – FORÊT DU ROGONEY – TÉLÉPHÉRIQUE DE BELLEVARDE – LE JOSERAY – Rocher de Bellevarde – COL DE L' ISERAN – D 902

LE MANCHET A LA LÉGETTAZ Tête du Solaise B

Le Blizzard

VISA

– ✆ *04 79 06 02 07 – information@hotelblizzard.com*
– Fax 04 79 06 04 94
– Open 10 December-4 May B **f**
79 rm – €274/902 €274/902, ☕ €15 – ½ P €181/495
Rest – *(open 15 December-3 May)* Menu €52
– Carte €53/73

◆ Wood structure, exposed beams, parquet floors and wood panelling: Wood eigns supreme in this elegant interior. Charming rooms, some with fireplaces. Pleasant restaurant sheltered from the blizzard in winter and offering a poolside terrace in summer.

La Savoyarde

VISA

r. Noël Machet – ✆ *04 79 06 01 55*
– hotel@la-savoyarde.com
– Fax 04 79 41 11 29 – Open 2 December-8 May A **u**
50 rm – €165/224 €246/331, ☕ €16 – ½ P €164/294
Rest – Menu €36/43 (dinner) – Carte €47/62

◆ Chalet with decorative balconies in the centre of the resort. A fitness area and cosy lounges await you on the way back from the Espace Killy (300 km of slopes). A warm dining room panelled with carved light wood. Up-to-date cuisine.

Le Tsanteleina

VISA

av. Olympique – ✆ *04 79 06 12 13*
– info@tsanteleina.com – Fax 04 79 41 14 16
– Open 5 July-24 August and 6 December-4 May B **s**
59 rm – €100/275 €100/385, ☕ €15 – 12 suites – ½ P €91/240
Rest – Menu (€22), €29 (lunch), €36/60
– Carte €34/70

◆ The name is taken from one of the summits overlooking the resort. Spacious rooms boasting different styles (simple or warm); those facing south have a balcony. Dining room all in white with bay windows opening onto the terrace.

Grand Paradis rest, VISA MC AE

– 04 79 06 11 73 – grandparadis@wanadoo.fr – Fax 04 79 41 11 13
Open beg. December-beg. May B t
40 rm (½ board only) – ½ P € 145/300
Rest – Menu € 22 (lunch)/56 – Carte € 40/50

♦ This Grand Paradise.of skiers is a hotel set next to the spectacular Face de Bellevarde. Rooms have either an Austrian or Savoyard decor, according to the floor. Pleasant restaurant with bay windows facing the snowfields and a lunchtime brasserie.

Kandahar rm, VISA MC

av. Olympique – 04 79 06 02 39 – hotel.kandahar@wanadoo.fr
– *Fax 04 79 41 15 54 – Open 1st December-4 May* A v
41 rm – € 133/285 € 160/390 – ½ P € 115/220
Rest – *(dinner only)* Carte € 23/59

♦ The name suggests the Far East or a prestigious Austrian ski competition. The spruce, warm rooms are undeniably Savoyard. Alsace takes pride of place on the menu of this "all-wood" bar.

Les Lauzes without rest VISA MC

pl. de l'Église – 04 79 06 04 20 – lauzes@club-internet.fr – Fax 04 79 41 96 84
– *Open 28 November-4 May* B a
23 rm – € 100/159 € 110/220, € 9

♦ Pleasant mountain-style rooms near the Baroque church; those on the last floor offer a view over the village rooftops. Cosy lounge with a fireplace.

Altitude rm, rest, VISA MC AE

– 04 79 06 12 55 – booking@hotelaltitude.com – Fax 04 79 41 11 09
– *Open 30 June-23 August and 2 December-26 April* A k
40 rm – € 114/195 € 148/290, € 12 – ½ P € 104/175
Rest – Menu € 28/32 (dinner)

♦ A restful stay in this hotel at the bottom of the ski lifts. All rooms have balconies and are being gradually renovated. Some of the more spacious are suitable for families. The Savoyard setting of this restaurant combines stone and wood. Terrace overlooking the pool.

La Becca rm, VISA MC AE

Le Laisinant, rte de l'Iseran, 0,8 km via ② – 04 79 06 09 48 – info@labecca-val.com – *Fax 04 79 41 12 03 – Open July-August and December to May*
11 rm – € 185/235 € 185/235, € 17 – ½ P € 126/186
Rest – *(open December to May)* Menu € 32 (lunch)/58 – Carte € 57/83

♦ A pleasant chalet nestling in the heart of a quiet hamlet. The "all-wood" rooms have pretty personal touches such as murals and painted furniture. Alpine-style restaurant around a stone fireplace. Savoyard specialities and modern dishes.

Bellier VISA MC

– 04 79 06 03 77 – info@hotelbellier.com – Fax 04 79 41 14 11
– *Open 1st December-2May* A z
22 rm (½ board only) – ½ P € 100/200 – **Rest** – Menu € 30

♦ A 1950s building near the centre but in a quiet area. Rooms being gradually renovated (most with a balcony); lounge with fireplace and sauna. Simple guesthouse-style restaurant. The south-facing terrace looks out onto the garden.

La Galise without rest VISA MC

r. de la Poste – 04 79 06 05 04 – lagalise@wanadoo.fr – Fax 04 79 41 16 16
– *Open 15 December-22 April* B n
30 rm – € 68/105 € 120/190

♦ In the busy centre of the Olympic resort, well-kept rooms with wood-panelling and rendering on the walls. Relaxation area with billiards table to recover from a hard day on the slopes.

L'Avancher without rest VISA MC

– 04 79 06 02 00 – hotel@avancher.com – Fax 04 79 41 16 07
– *Open 6 December-1st May* B r
17 rm – € 57/68 € 90/134, € 15

♦ This typical alpine building offers the chance of a rest away from the centre of the busy ski resort. Wood furnished bedrooms.

in la Daille 2 km by ① - ✉ 73150 Val-d'Isère

Le Samovar
– *☎ 04 79 06 13 51 – samovar@wanadoo.fr – Fax 04 79 41 11 08*
– Open 2 December-19 April
18 rm – †€ 125/195 ††€ 135/290, ☕ € 17
Rest – Menu € 14 (weekdays), € 20/45
◆ This large chalet near the foot of the funicular ("Funival") that climbs the Bellevarde rock, offers spacious and cosy rooms. The Hotel Samovar's brasserie-pizzeria offers unpretentious service and fare.

VALENÇAY – 36 Indre – 323 F4 – pop. 2 736 – alt. 140 m – ✉ 36600

Châteaux of the Loire 11 **B3**

Paris 233 – Blois 59 – Bourges 73 – Châteauroux 42 – Loches 50 – Vierzon 51
Office de tourisme, 2, avenue de la Résistance ☎ 02 54 00 04 42, Fax 02 54 00 27 67
Castle★★★.

Relais du Moulin rm,
94 r. Nationale – ☎ 02 54 00 38 00 – valencay@valvvf.fr – Fax 02 54 00 38 79
– Open 6 April-6 November
54 rm – †€ 57/59 ††€ 63/65, ☕ € 7 – ½ P € 56/59
Rest – Menu € 18 (weekday lunch), € 23/27 – Carte € 24/34
◆ Recent hotel complex against a former spinning-mill from Talleyrand's time. Basic rooms with good soundproofing. The modern dining room and terrace overlook a garden with the Nahon flowing alongside. Traditional cuisine.

in Veuil 6 km South by D 15 and secondary road – pop. 364 – alt. 140 m – ✉ 36600

Auberge St-Fiacre
5 r. de la fontaine – ☎ 02 54 40 32 78 – Fax 02 54 40 35 66 – Closed 1st-22 September, January, Tuesday from November to March, Sunday dinner and Monday
Rest – Menu € 21/44 – Carte € 31/47
◆ Located a charming village, a 17C house with outside tables under the chestnut trees lulled by the murmur of a brook. Beautiful rustic interior and up-to-date cuisine.

VALENCE Ⓟ – 26 Drôme – 332 C4 – pop. 64 260 – Built-up area 117 448 – alt. 126 m – ✉ 26000 Lyon - Rhone Valley

43 **E2**

Paris 558 – Avignon 126 – Grenoble 96 – St-Étienne 121
Valence-Chabeuil: ☎ 04 75 85 26 26, by ③: 5 km AX.
Office de tourisme, 11, boulevard Bancel ☎ 08 92 70 70 99, Fax 04 75 44 90 41
des Chanalets Bourg-lès-Valence Route de Châteauneuf sur Isère, by Lyon road: 6 km, ☎ 04 75 83 16 23 ;
New Golf du Bourget MontmeyranSouth: 17 km by D 538, ☎ 04 75 59 48 18.
Maison des Têtes★ CY - interior★ of St-Apollinaire cathedral BZ - Champ de Mars ←★ BZ - Red chalk drawings by Hubert Robert★★ in the musée des Beaux-Arts (Fine arts museum) BZ.
Site★★★ of Cruzol 5 km O.

Plans on following pages

Pic (Anne-Sophie Pic) rm,
285 av. V. Hugo – ☎ 04 75 44 15 32 – contact@pic-valence.com
– Fax 04 75 40 96 03 – Closed 2-26 January AX **f**
12 rm – †€ 200/450 ††€ 200/450, ☕ € 28 – 3 suites
Rest *Le 7* – see restaurant listing
Rest – *(closed Sunday and Monday) (pre-book Sat - Sun)* Menu € 110/195 – Carte € 148/235
Spec. Soufflé au gouda millésimé V.S.O.P, cœur coulant à la truffe noire (winter). Bar de ligne meunière, oignons doux des Cévennes confits, coulant de caramel aux noix de pays, vin jaune (autumn). Ris de veau, pomme rôtie au sautoir, transparence et fondant de carotte à la lavande (spring). **Wines** Saint-Péray, Hermitage.
◆ This fine family-run residence with modernised decor is an institution in Valence. Stylish rooms. Following in the footsteps of her grandfather and father, the chef has also reached star-studded renown thanks to her deliciously inventive cuisine. Fine wine list.

VALENCE

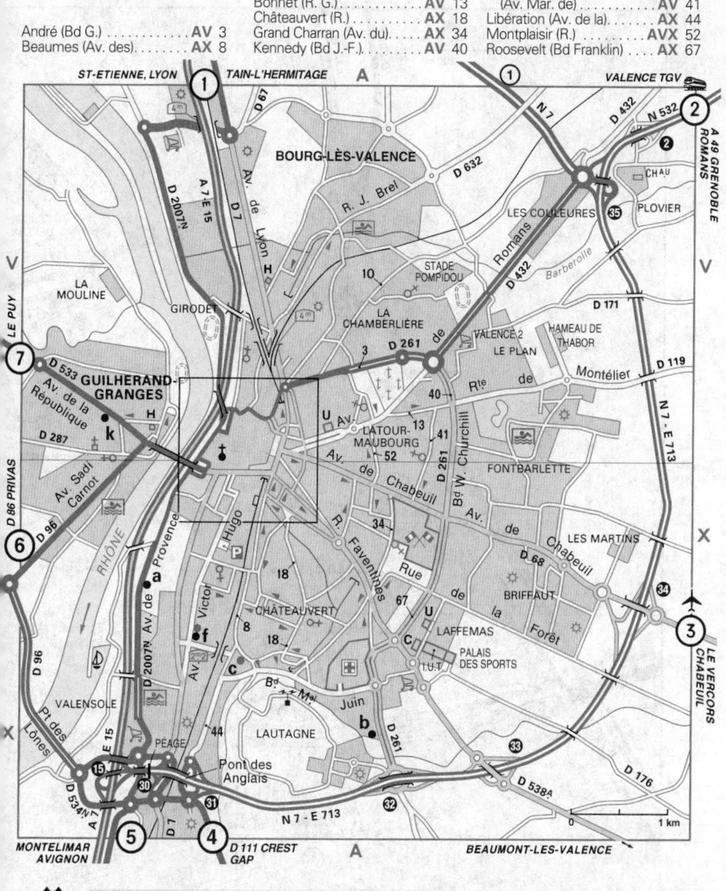

Clos Syrah
rm,

Quartier Maninet, rte Montéléger – ☎ 04 75 55 52 52 – info@clos-syrah.com – Fax 04 75 42 27 37 AX **b**

36 rm – †€ 60/90 ††€ 60/90, ☕ € 12 – **Rest** – *(closed 25 December-1st January, Sunday from September to May and Saturday except dinner from June to August)* Menu € 20/28 – Carte € 27/74

◆ A 1980s building near the hospital. Rooms with light-wood furniture and electric roller shutters, as well as terrace or balcony overlooking the pool and park. Traditional meals are served in a comfortable dining room.

De France without rest

16 bd du Gén. de Gaulle – ☎ 04 75 43 00 87 – info@hotel-valence.com – Fax 04 75 55 90 51 CZ **w**

34 rm – †€ 51/82 ††€ 66/82, ☕ € 9

◆ Hotel with a well-renovated façade, lounges and well-soundproofed rooms. It is ideally located for exploring the old town on foot.

Atrium without rest
rest,

20 r. J.-L. Barrault – ☎ 04 75 55 53 62 – info@atrium-hotel.fr – Fax 04 75 55 53 68

69 rm – †€ 58 ††€ 66/73, ☕ € 7 DY **c**

◆ A modern-looking hotel, ideal for a long stay as each room has a kitchenette. The top floor offers duplexes overlooking the Vercors or the Ardèche.

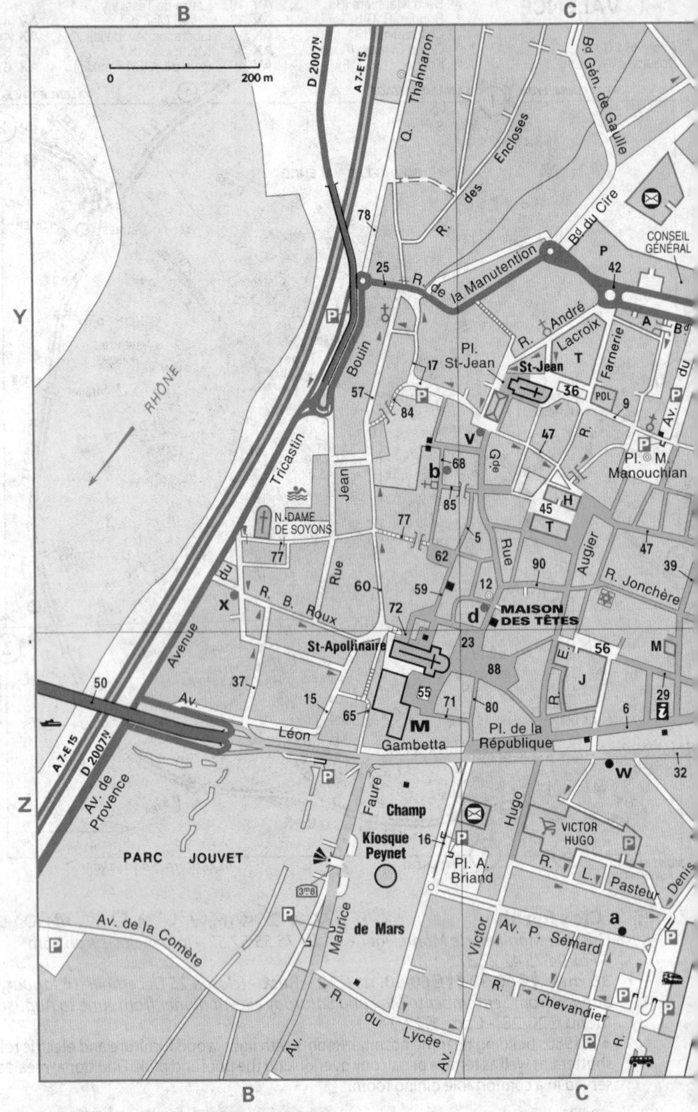

De l'Europe without rest

15 av. Félix Faure – ✆ 04 75 82 62 65
– hoteleurope.valence@wanadoo.fr
– Fax 04 75 82 62 66
– Closed 20-27 December

DY **f**

26 rm – €42/48 €46/52, ☕ €6,50

◆ This hotel, situated on a busy avenue, has had a face-lift: colourful rooms, period furniture and double-glazing ensuring soundproofing.

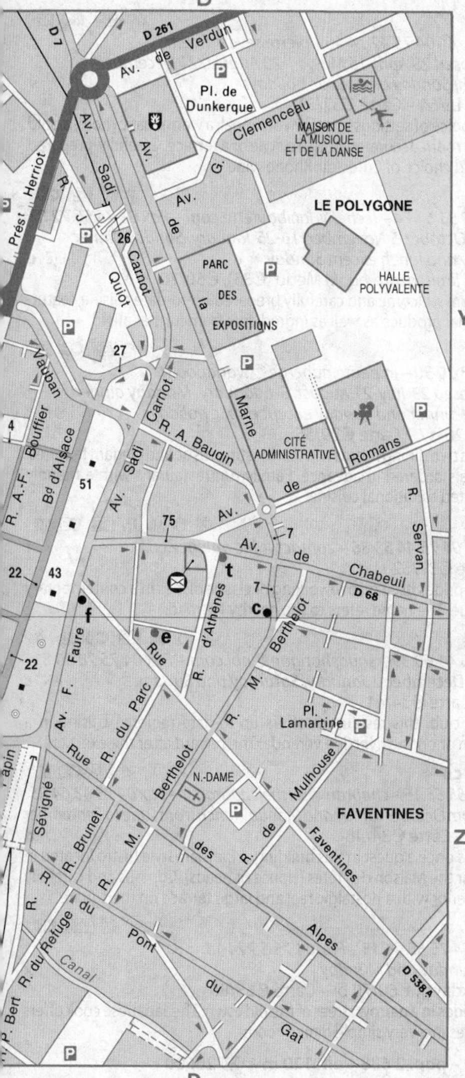

VALENCE

Alsace (Bd d') . . . . **DY**
Arménie (R. d') . . . . **DY** 4
Augier (R. Émile) . . . . **CYZ**
Balais (R. des) . . . . **BCY** 5
Bancel (Bd) . . . . **CY** 6
Barrault (R. J.-L.) . . . . . . **DY** 7
Belle Image (R.) . . . . **CY** 9
Bonaparte (R. du Lieutenant) . . **BCY** 12
Chambaud (R. Mirabel) **BZ** 15
Championnet (Pl.) . . . . . **BCZ** 16
Chapeliers (Côte des) . . **BY** 17
Clercs (Pl. des) . . . . . . **BCZ** 23
Clerc (Bd M.) . . . . **CYZ** 22
Docteur-Schweitzer (R. du) . . **BY** 25
Dragonne (Pl. de la) . . . **DY** 26
Dupré-de-Loire (Av.) . . . **DY** 27
Farre (R. du Gén.) . . . . . **CZ** 29
Félix-Faure (Av.) . . . . **DZ**
Gaulle (Bd du Gén.-de) . **CZ** 32
Huguenel (Pl. Ch.) . . . . . **CY** 36
Jacquet (R. V.) . . . . **BZ** 37
Jeu-de-Paume (R. du) **CYZ** 39
Lecardonnel (Pl. L.) . . . . **CY** 42
Leclerc (Pl. Gén.) . . . . . **DY** 43
Liberté (Pl. de la) . . . . . **CY** 45
Madier-de-Montjau (R.) **CY** 47
Mistral (Pont Frédéric) . **BZ** 50
Montalivet (Pl. de) . . . . . **DY** 51
Ormeaux (Pl. des) . . . . . **BZ** 55
Palais (Pl. du) . . . . **CZ** 56
Paré (R. Ambroise) . . . . **BY** 57
Pérollerie (R.) . . . . **BY** 59
Petit Paradis (R.) . . . . . . **BY** 60
Pierre (Pl. de la) . . . . **BY** 62
Repenties (R. des) . . . . . **BZ** 65
République (Pl. de la) . . **CZ**
Sabaterie (R.) . . . . **BY** 68
St-Didier (R.) . . . . **BCZ** 71
St-Estève (Côte) . . . . . . **BY** 72
St-Jacques (Faubourg) . **DY** 75
St-Martin (Côte et R.) . . **BY** 77
St-Nicolas (Q.) . . . . **BY** 78
Saunière (R.) . . . . **CZ** 80
Semard (Av.) . . . . **CZ**
Sylvante (Côte) . . . . **BY** 84
Temple (R. du) . . . . . . **BCY** 85
Université (Pl. de l') . . . . **CZ** 88
Vernoux (R.) . . . . **CY** 90
Victor-Hugo (Av.) . . . . . . **CZ**

Les Négociants — rest, VISA AE

27 av. Pierre-Sémard – ✆ 04 75 44 01 86 – hotel.les-negociants@wanadoo.fr – Fax 04 75 44 77 57 CZ **a**

37 rm – 🚹€ 40/49 🚹🚹€ 40/56, ☕ € 6 – ½ P € 54/75 – **Rest** – *(closed 11-17 August, Saturday and Sunday)* Menu € 13/19 – Carte € 25/40

◆ Sober, contemporary-style hotel just a stone's throw from the station. Guestrooms in varying shades of brown, some with air-conditioning. Substantial breakfast. Simple family cooking is the order of the day in this contemporary-style restaurant.

XX **L'Épicerie**

18 pl. St-Jean, (ex Belat) – ☎ 04 75 42 74 46 – pierre.seve@free.fr – Fax 04 75 42 10 87 – Closed 28 April-15 May, 1st-20 August, 21 December-3 January, Saturday lunch, Sunday and public holidays CY **v**

Rest – Menu (€ 18), € 25 bi/64 – Carte € 37/51

◆ A 16C house offering a choice of settings to enjoy your meal: a warm rustic room, a bold design dining room, a third room decorated in bistro style or a terrace. Carefully-prepared traditional cuisine and good choice of Côtes-du-Rhône wine.

XX **La Ciboulette**

6 r. Commerce – ☎ 04 75 55 67 74 – lechef@laciboulette.com – Fax 04 75 56 72 83 – Closed 4-11 August, 25 October-5 November, 16-25 January, Sunday dinner, Thursday dinner, Monday and lunch except Sunday DZ **e**

Rest – *(number of covers limited, pre-book)* Menu (€ 35), € 50/70

◆ Restaurant offering a warm welcome and carefully prepared up-to-date cuisine, featuring a subtle blend of regional produce as well as ingredients from further afield.

XX **La Petite Auberge**

1 r. Athènes – ☎ 04 75 43 20 30 – la.petite.auberge@wanadoo.fr – Fax 04 75 42 67 79 – Closed 23 July-21 August, 3-6 January, Monday dinner June-August, Wednesday dinner and Sunday except public holidays DY **t**

Rest – Menu (€ 18 bi), € 26/47 – Carte € 29/55

◆ The ordinary facade hides two dining rooms with contrasting rustic and elegant features. The smaller one is for meals ordered in advance. Family-run restaurant with a friendly atmosphere, cleverly updated traditional cuisine.

X **Le 7** – Hôtel Pic

285 av. Victor-Hugo – ☎ 04 75 44 53 86 – contact@pic-valence.com AX **f**

Rest – Menu € 28 – Carte € 37/52

◆ Anne-Sophie Pic's bistro prides itself on a reworking of classic dishes in a contemporary decor with a hint of Baroque. The name refers to the nearby N7 road.

X **L'Origan**

58 av. Baumes – ☎ 04 75 41 60 39 – squashorigan@aol.com – Fax 04 75 78 30 81 – Closed 4-27 August, 24 December-2 January, Saturday and Sunday AX **c**

Rest – Menu € 18/37 – Carte € 34/41

◆ Next-door to a squash club, this restaurant offers up-to-date regional cuisine in a contemporary dining room or on the riverside veranda. The reward after the exertion!

X **Le Bistrot des Clercs**

48 Grande rue – ☎ 04 75 55 55 15 – chabran@michelchabran.fr – Fax 04 75 43 64 85 – Closed Sunday dinner from October to May and Monday lunch from June to September

Rest – Menu € 22/31 bi – Carte € 34/48 CY **d**

◆ Napoleon Bonaparte was once a guest in this building, a Parisian-style bistro located in the pedestrian district, near the Maison des têtes (House of heads). Copious and carefully prepared bistro dishes, interior with a nostalgic feel and large terrace on the square.

X **La Cachette**

16 r. des Cévennes – ☎ 04 75 55 24 13 – Fax 04 75 55 24 13 – Closed 2-20 January, Sunday and Monday BY **x**

Rest – Menu € 25 (weekdays), € 60/70 bi – Carte € 55/80

◆ This pocket restaurant hides in a narrow street of the old town. The Japanese cook offers appealing up-to-date dishes in a very simple dining room.

in Pont de l'Isère 9 km by ① – pop. 2 688 – alt. 120 m – ✉ 26600

XXX **Michel Chabran** with rm

N 7 – ☎ 04 75 84 60 09 – chabran@michelchabran.fr – Fax 04 75 84 59 65 – Closed Monday lunch in July-August, Wednesday dinner and Sunday dinner from October to March, Wednesday lunch and Thursday lunch

11 rm – €115/165 €150/185, € 23 – ½ P € 185/290

Rest – Menu € 42 (weekday lunch), € 59/102 – Carte € 92/161

Spec. Menu "Autour de la truffe" (November to March). Ravioles de la région de Romans au rythme des saisons. Dos d'agneau de Sisteron cuit sur l'os, jus aux senteurs provençales. **Wines** Crozes-Hermitage, Hermitage.

◆ Elegant restaurant serving up-to-date cuisine and a fine selection of northern Côtes-du-Rhône wine. Wide choice of menus. House with a Rhône-pebble façade, offering comfortable, discreetly decorated rooms, overlooking either the garden or the road.

XXX **Auberge Chalaye**

17 r. 16-août-1944 – ✆ 04 75 84 59 40 – Fax 04 75 58 27 06 – Closed 9-15 June, 1st-7 September, Sunday dinner, Monday, Tuesday and Wednesday

Rest – Menu € 33/60

◆ Discreet inn nestling in greenery in a residential area. Classic cuisine served in three small rustic-style dining rooms or on the pleasant garden terrace, in fine weather.

in Guilherand-Granges (07 Ardèche) – **pop. 10 707 – alt. 130 m** – ✉ **07500**

Alpes-Cévennes without rest

641 av. de la République – ✆ 04 75 44 61 34 – alpescevennes@aol.com – Fax 04 75 41 12 41 AV **k**

26 rm – †€ 33/36 ††€ 40/46, ☕ € 5

◆ On the right bank of the Rhône, this Ardèche hotel provides spacious rooms containing mass-produced furniture, that are gradually being renovated. Efficient soundproofing. Friendly service.

VALENCE-SUR-BAÏSE – 32 Gers – 336 E6 – pop. 1 151 – alt. 117 m – ✉ 32310

28 **A2**

▶ Paris 734 – Agen 50 – Auch 36 – Condom 9

ℹ Syndicat d'initiative, rue Jules Ferry ✆ 05 62 28 59 19, Fax 05 62 28 97 66

◉ Flaran abbey★ Northwest: 2 km, ▮ **Languedoc-Roussillon-Tarn Gorges**

La Ferme de Flaran rm,

rte de Condom – ✆ 05 62 28 58 22 – hotel-flaran@wanadoo.fr – Fax 05 62 28 56 89 – Closed 20 December-31 January, Sunday from September to June and Monday from October to March

15 rm – †€ 49/59 ††€ 55/65, ☕ € 8 – ½ P € 56/61

Rest – *(closed Tuesday lunch from October-May, Sunday dinner and Monday except from 13 July-25 August)* Menu (€ 16), € 20/38 – Carte € 37/52

◆ This Gascon farmhouse, once an outbuilding of the nearby Cistercian abbey, has retained its rustic atmosphere. The country-style rooms are quieter on the swimming pool side. An authentic, rustic dining room with a pleasant, terrace serving carefully-prepared dishes with a Gers flavour.

VALENCIENNES – 59 Nord – 302 J5 – pop. 41 278 – Built-up area 357 395 – alt. 22 m – ✉ 59300 ▮ Northern France and the Paris Region

31 **C2**

▶ Paris 208 – Arras 68 – Bruxelles 105 – Lille 54 – St-Quentin 80

ℹ Office de tourisme, 1, rue Askièvre ✆ 03 27 28 89 10, Fax 03 27 28 89 11

18 de Mormal Preux-au-Sart Bois Saint Pierre, by Maubeuge road: 13 km, ✆ 03 27 63 07 00 ;

9 de Valenciennes Marly Rue du Chemin Vert, East: 1 km, ✆ 03 27 46 30 10.

◉ Musée des Beaux-Arts★ BY **M** - Bibliothèque des Jésuites★.

Plan on next page

Le Grand Hôtel

8 pl. de la Gare – ✆ 03 27 46 32 01 – grandhotel.val@wanadoo.fr – Fax 03 27 29 65 57 AX **d**

86 rm – †€ 74/82 ††€ 83/91, ☕ € 10 – ½ P € 102

Rest – Menu € 30 (weekdays), € 39/50 – Carte € 36/63

Rest *Brasserie Hans* – Menu € 15 – Carte € 24/35

◆ The same family has been welcoming guests to this fine early 20C building for several generations. Comfortable rooms with a classic touch. Traditional restaurant specialising in spit-roast meat and flambéed dishes. The Alsatian spirit pervades throughout the Brasserie Hans.

Auberge du Bon Fermier

64 r. Famars – ✆ 03 27 46 68 25 – beinethierry@hotmail.com – Fax 03 27 33 75 01

16 rm – †€ 85 ††€ 105, ☕ € 9,50 AY **n**

Rest – Menu € 26/49 – Carte € 31/55

◆ This authentic 17C post house has kept its charm - old brick and stone façade, characterful rooms with lovely furniture and a pretty interior courtyard. The stables of this inn now house a restaurant-grill. A terrace and game in season.

VALENCIENNES

Street	Grid	No.
Albert-1er (Av.)	BY	2
Amsterdam (Av. d')	BY	5
Armes (Pl. d')	AY	6
Barbusse (R. H.)	CV	8
Bourgeois (Ch. des)	BV	9
Cairns (Av. Serg.)	ABZ	13
Capucins (R. des)	BY	15
Cardon (Pl.)	BZ	16
Charles-Quint (R.)	CV	17
Clemenceau (Av. G.)	AX	18
Desandrouin (Av.)	BV	20
Digue (R. de la)	AZ	22
Duchesnois (Av.)	CV	23
Dunkerque (Av. de)	AX	25
Faidherbe (Av.)	BV	26
Famars (R. de)	AYZ	
Ferrand (R.)	AY	33
Fg de Cambrai (R.)	BV	29
Fg de Paris (R. du)	BV	30
Foch (Av. Mar.)	AX	34
Froissart (Pl. J.)	BY	35
Gaulle (Pl. Gén.-de)	BY	36
Glacis (R. des)	CV	37
Jacob (Pont)	AX	38
Jean-Jaurès (R.)	BV	39
Juin (Av. du Mar.)	AX	40
Lattre-de-Tassigny (Av. Mar.-de)	AX	42
Leclerc (Av. Mar.)	AX	43
Liège (Av. de)	BX	44
Lille (R. de)	AX	46
Marquis (R. du)	CV	48
Paix (R. de la)	BY	50
Paris (R. de)	AY	52
Perdrix (R. J.)	CV	53
Pompidou (Av. G.)	AZ	54
Reims (Av. de)	BZ	56
St-Amand (Av. de)	BV	58
St-Géry (R.)	BY	59
Sénateur-Girard (Av.)	AX	63
Tholozé (R.)	AX	65
Vaillant-Couturier (R. Paul)	BV	67
Vauban (Av.)	BV	68
Verdun (Av. de)	BZ	69
Vieille-Poissonnerie (R.)	AY	73
Villars (Av.)	AY	74
Watteau (Square)	AY	76

Le Chat Botté without rest VISA
25 r. Tholozé – ☎ 03 27 14 58 59 – hotel.lechatbotte@wanadoo.fr – Fax 03 27 14 58 60 AX **p**
33 rm – €67/76 €67/85, €9
◆ Wrought iron, wood, contemporary furniture and bright colours set the amusing scene in this pleasant welcoming house; peaceful cosy bedrooms.

Baudouin without rest VISA
90 r. Baudouin l'Édifieur – ☎ 03 27 22 80 80 – hotel-baudouin@wanadoo.fr – Fax 03 27 22 80 81 BZ **k**
69 rm – €58 €58, €8
◆ A hotel near the Nungesser football stadium. Practical well-soundproofed rooms. Secure car park, garage and several small kitchens.

Notre Dame without rest VISA
1 pl. Abbé Thellier de Poncheville – ☎ 03 27 42 30 00 – hotel.notredame@wanadoo.fr – Fax 03 27 45 12 68 – Closed 20 December-4 January BY **s**
35 rm – €50/63 €58/65, €8
◆ Two buildings facing a 15C church. Bourgeois rooms in the old part, more functional in the other and quiet all around for those facing the garden.

Le Grand Duc VISA
104 av. de Condé – ☎ 03 27 46 40 30 – contact@legrandduc.fr – Fax 03 27 46 40 30 – Closed August BV **e**
5 rm – €85 €85, €9 – ½ P €122/133 – **Table d'hôte** – *(Closed Saturday lunch and Sunday dinner)* Menu €28/39
◆ This bourgeois abode has been brought back to life since its artist owner renovated it in a contemporary style that enhances the original structure. Table d'hôte by reservation in a dining room overlooking a walled English-style garden.

Le Musigny VISA
90 av. de Liège – ☎ 03 27 41 49 30 – Fax 03 27 47 91 19 – Closed 5-11 January, Sunday dinner, Monday and dinner on public holidays except Saturday
Rest – Menu €35/90 bi – Carte €63/101 CV **v**
◆ Restaurant with a discreet façade hiding a intimate comfortable dining room. Classic cuisine in which fish takes pride of place.

L'Endroit VISA
69 r. du Quesnoy – ☎ 03 27 42 99 23 – lionel.coint@nordnet.fr – Fax 03 27 42 99 23 – Closed Sunday dinner and Monday BY **f**
Rest – Menu €25/55 – Carte €39/57
◆ A TV screen crowns the dining room, broadcasting the bustle of the kitchen live. Elegant contemporary setting, fashionable atmosphere, market-fresh menu.

Les Salons Brabant VISA
68 r. de Paris – ☎ 03 27 26 04 03 – lessalonsbrabant@aol.com – Fax 03 27 26 04 03 – Closed Sunday dinner and Monday AY **e**
Rest – Menu €35/48 – Carte €31/51
Rest *La Véranda* – *(closed Sunday and Monday)* Menu €17 bi/25 – Carte €20/25
◆ Napoleon III style decor, (mouldings, stucco, paintings, etc.) and contemporary furniture provide an original setting for this lovely glass-roofed dining room. Traditional fare. A bistro-style setting and simple assorted dishes of the day at the Véranda.

Brasserie Arthur A/C VISA
46 bis r. Famars – ☎ 03 27 46 14 15 – jletouze@nordnet.fr – Fax 03 27 41 62 96 – Closed Sunday dinner and Monday AY **u**
Rest – Carte €22/34
◆ A simple brasserie with benches, high ceilings, glass canopy and ad hoc cuisine. The countless paintings on the walls reflect the artistic allure of the "Athens of the North".

in Quiévrechain 12 km northeast by D 630 – pop. 6 069 – alt. 32 m – ✉ 59920

Le Manoir de Tombelle P VISA
135 av. J. Jaurès – ☎ 03 27 35 12 30 – Fax 03 27 26 27 61 – Closed 1st-15 August, 26 December-2 January and dinner except Saturday
Rest – Menu (€20 bi), €25 (weekday lunch), €27/49
◆ Bourgeois 1920s villa in a large garden with a pond. Comfortably furnished dining rooms with fireplace and arbour. Traditional cuisine.

in Artres 11 km by ④, D 958 and D 400 – pop. 1 071 – alt. 65 m – ✉ 59269

La Gentilhommière VISA AE
(opposite the church) – ☎ 03 27 28 18 80 – la.gentilhommiere@wanadoo.fr – Fax 03 27 28 18 81 – Closed 4-25 August, 26-30 December and Sunday dinner
10 rm – †€ 85 ††€ 85/110, ☐ € 13 – ½ P € 130
Rest – Menu € 35/64 – Carte € 39/62
◆ This 18C farm set in two hectares of greenery has been well renovated. The spacious quiet rooms overlook an interior garden. Vaults and red-brick walls form the backdrop to the generous helpings of modern food.

Z. I. de Prouvy-Rouvignies 5 km by ⑤ and D 630 – ✉ 59300 Valenciennes

Novotel rm, VISA AE
– ☎ 03 27 21 12 12 – h0456@accor.com – Fax 03 27 21 06 02
80 rm – †€ 59/129 ††€ 59/129, ☐ € 12,50 – **Rest** – Menu € 20/45 (weekend) – Carte € 23/37
◆ By the motorway from Paris to Brussels and 15 mins from the centre, this hotel has recently been renovated to the chain's new standards (pleasant contemporary interior). A convenient lunch stop or place for an evening meal at this Novotel restaurant.

in Raismes 5 km northwest by D 169 – pop. 13 699 – alt. 23 m – ✉ 59590

La Grignotière VISA AE
6 r. J. Jaurès – ☎ 03 27 36 91 99 – lagrignotiere@free.fr – Fax 03 27 36 74 29 – Closed Tuesday dinner, Wednesday dinner, Sunday dinner and Monday
Rest – Menu (€ 19), € 25 (weekdays), € 31 € bi/34 – Carte € 37/75
◆ This former posthouse next-door to the church is home to a prettily decorated cosy dining room and a pleasant garden terrace. Traditional fare with a creative flair.

VALESCURE – 83 Var – 340 P5 – see St-Raphaël

VALGORGE – 07 Ardèche – 331 G6 – pop. 450 – alt. 560 m – ✉ 07110

Lyon - Rhone Valley 44 **A3**

Paris 614 – Alès 76 – Aubenas 37 – Langogne 46 – Privas 69 – Le Puy-en-Velay 83

Le Tanargue VISA AE
– ☎ 04 75 88 98 98 – hoteltanargue@wanadoo.fr – Fax 04 75 88 96 09 – Open 14 March-28 November and closed Sunday dinner and Monday except 16 March-29 September and autumn half-term holidays
22 rm – †€ 37/51 ††€ 44/58, ☐ € 7,50 – ½ P € 44/55 – **Rest** – Menu (€ 11), € 16/32 – Carte € 31/48
◆ Family-run inn at the foot of the Tanargue range. Some of the comfortable, immaculately kept rooms boast a balcony overlooking the park or the valley. A rustic-style dining room decorated with old objects and furnishings. Local gastronomic products are on sale here.

VALIGNAT – 03 Allier – 326 F5 – see Charroux

VALLAURIS – 06 Alpes-Maritimes – 341 D6 – see Golfe-Juan

VALLERAUGUE – 30 Gard – 339 G4 – pop. 1 009 – alt. 346 m – ✉ 30570

Languedoc-Roussillon-Tarn Gorges 23 **C2**

Paris 684 – Mende 100 – Millau 75 – Nîmes 86 – Le Vigan 22

Office de tourisme, quartier des Horts ☎ 04 67 82 25 10, Fax 04 67 64 82 15

Hostellerie Les Bruyères VISA
– ☎ 04 67 82 20 06 – Fax 04 67 82 20 06 – Open 1st May-30 September
20 rm – †€ 47 ††€ 47/60, ☐ € 7 – ½ P € 47/54
Rest – Menu € 15/37 – Carte € 24/41
◆ Former post-house in the heart of this picturesque Cévennes village. A fine staircase leads to the simple, neat rooms equipped with comfortable beds. The countrified dining room leads onto a charming riverside terrace in summer.

Mont-Aigoual road 4 km on D 986 – ✉ 30570

Auberge Cévenole
La Pénarié – ✆ 04 67 82 25 17 – auberge.cevenole@wanadoo.fr – Fax 04 67 82 26 26 – Closed 17 November-19 December, Monday dinner and Tuesday except July-August
6 rm – €42 €42, ☕ €7 – ½ P €47 – **Rest** – Menu €16/27 – Carte €20/43
◆ The Hérault idles at the foot of this pleasant Cévennes inn on the Mt Aigoual road. Small renovated rooms with regional furniture. Attractive dining room (beams, fireplace, rural objects) and terrace overlooking the river.

VALLET – 44 Loire-Atlantique – 316 I5 – pop. 6 807 – alt. 54 m – ✉ 44330 34 B2

Paris 375 – Ancenis 27 – Cholet 36 – Clisson 10 – Nantes 27

Syndicat d'initiative, 1, place Charles-de-Gaulle ✆ 02 40 36 35 87, Fax 02 40 36 29 13

Château d'Yseron without rest
4 km north-east on D 116 – ✆ 02 51 71 70 40 – ostalbin@wanadoo.fr – Fax 02 51 71 70 11
4 rm ☕ – €80/120 €80/120
◆ Charming residence dating from 1830 set in the middle of the vineyards. Furniture from the 18C and 19C in the bedrooms. Collection of beautiful paintings and Muscadet produced on site.

Don Quichotte with rm rest, VISA
35 rte de Clisson – ✆ 02 40 33 99 67 – donquichottevallet@wanadoo.fr – Fax 02 40 33 99 72 – Closed 23 December-8 January
12 rm – €55 €59, ☕ €9 – ½ P €58
Rest – *(closed 15-28 July, Monday lunch, Friday dinner and Sunday dinner)* Menu (€16), €19/29 – Carte approx. €30
◆ Large murals decorate the walls of this former mill situated among the vineyards. Traditional dishes according to seasonal market produce (preferably organic) served in dining room/veranda.

VALLIÈRES – 37 Indre-et-Loire – 317 M4 – see Tours

VALLOIRE – 73 Savoie – 333 L7 – pop. 1 243 – alt. 1 430 m – Winter sports : 1 430/2 600 m 2 31 – ✉ 73450 French Alps 45 D2

Paris 664 – Albertville 91 – Briançon 52 – Chambéry 104 – Lanslebourg-Mont-Cenis 57

Office de tourisme, rue des Grandes Alpes ✆ 04 79 59 03 96, Fax 04 79 59 09 66

Col du Télégraphe ≤★ North: 5 km.

Grand Hôtel de Valloire et du Galibier VISA
r. des Grandes Alpes – ✆ 04 79 59 00 95 – info@grand-hotel-valloire.com – Fax 04 79 59 09 41 – Open 15 June-12 September and 21 December-11 April
44 rm – €70/90 €70/100, ☕ €13,50 – ½ P €72/103
Rest *L'Escarnavé* – Menu €22/55 – Carte €41/66
◆ An imposing hotel, facing the slopes, with spacious and renovated rooms. Reserve those facing south and east. Fine dining room in a rotunda set around a copper fireplace where bonfires ("escarnavé", in the local dialect) are lit; classic cuisine.

Christiania rest, VISA
r. Tigny – ✆ 04 79 59 00 57 – info@christiania-hotel.com – Fax 04 79 59 00 06 – Open 15 June-15 September and 10 December-20 April
24 rm – €52/65 €55/70, ☕ €10 – 1 suite – ½ P €57/77
Rest – Menu (€16), €20/35 – Carte €25/49
◆ Chalet decked with flowers, on the avenue where an unusual snow-sculpture competition takes place. Well-kept rooms, renovated in an alpine spirit. One can be sure of a warm welcome in this country style restaurant. The bar is a meeting place for the resort's ski instructors.

in Verneys 2 km south – ✉ 73450 Valloire

Relais du Galibier
– ✆ *04 79 59 00 45 – info@relais-galibier.com – Fax 04 79 83 31 89*
– Open 11 June-9 September and 21 December-9 April
26 rm – 🛉€ 51/55 🛉🛉€ 56/63, ☕ € 9,50 – ½ P € 56/77
Rest – Menu € 17/33 – Carte € 25/35
♦ Welcoming hotel in the peace and quiet of pastures in summer and 100 metres from the slopes in winter. Some rooms with views of the Grand Galibier. A restaurant lit by large picture windows, serving a copious cuisine based on regional products.

Le Crêt Rond
– ✆ *04 79 59 01 64 – info.@hotel-cret-rond.com – Fax 04 79 83 33 24*
– Open 15 June-20 September and 20 December-5 April
16 rm – 🛉€ 49 🛉🛉€ 64, ☕ € 8 – ½ P € 52/61
Rest – Menu € 14/26 – Carte € 13/32
♦ The establishment is on the Galibier route, well-known to Tour de France superstars. All rooms overlook the mountain and often have a balcony. Rustic dining room with a convivial guesthouse atmosphere.

VALLON-PONT-D'ARC – **07 Ardèche** – **331** I7 – **pop. 2 027** – **alt. 117 m** – ✉ **07150** Lyon - Rhone Valley 44 **A3**

Paris 658 – Alès 47 – Aubenas 32 – Avignon 81 – Carpentras 95 – Montélimar 59

Office de tourisme, 1, place de l'ancienne gare ✆ 04 75 88 04 01, Fax 04 75 88 41 09

Gorges de l'Ardèche★★★ Southeast - Arche★★ de Pont d'Arc Southeast: 5 km.

Le Clos des Bruyères rm, rest, rm,
rte des Gorges – ✆ *04 75 37 18 85*
– clos.des.bruyeres@online.fr – Fax 04 75 37 14 89 – Open April-end September
32 rm – 🛉€ 56/72 🛉🛉€ 59/72, ☕ € 8 – ½ P € 58/62
Rest – ✆ 04 75 88 14 84 *(closed Wednesday except July-August and dinner September)* Menu € 22/30 – Carte € 20/35
♦ A newly established hotel situated 100m from the River Ardèche (canoe hire). Spacious, discreetly decorated rooms, with balconies or opening onto the garden. Beneath the timber ceiling of the dining room you will taste traditional fare with a regional slant.

Le Manoir du Raveyron rm,
r. Henri Barbusse – ✆ *04 75 88 03 59 – le.manoir.du.raveyron@wanadoo.fr*
– Fax 04 75 37 11 12 – Open mid March-20 October
8 rm ☕ – 🛉€ 55/60 🛉🛉€ 66/86 – ½ P € 58/63
Rest – *(dinner only except Thursday and Sunday)* Menu € 25/42 – Carte € 31/49
♦ This 16C residence situated in a quiet street has small, attractive and personalised rooms. Pleasant, shady and flower-decked courtyard. Pleasant, vaulted dining room where you can enjoy modern dishes prepared with local produce.

VALLORCINE – **74 Haute-Savoie** – **328** O4 – **pop. 390** – **alt. 1 260 m** – **Winter sports : 1 260/1 400 m** 2 – ✉ **74660** French Alps 45 **D1**

Paris 628 – Annecy 115 – Chamonix-Mont-Blanc 19 – Thonon-les-Bains 96

Office de tourisme, Maison du Betté ✆ 04 50 54 60 71, Fax 04 50 54 61 73

L'Ermitage without rest
at Buet, 2 km south-west on D 1506 and secondary road – ✆ *04 50 54 60 09*
– hotel-ermitage@wanadoo.fr – Fax 04 50 54 64 38 – Open 7 February-4 May, 7 June-21 September and 26 December-4 January
15 rm – 🛉€ 40/70 🛉🛉€ 68/78, ☕ € 11
♦ A charming chalet with a warm atmosphere, overlooking the village, just 400 m from the railway station. Simple, differently furnished rooms. Small pleasantly shaded garden.

VALLOUX – **89 Yonne** – **319** G6 – **see Avallon**

VALMONT – 76 Seine-Maritime – 304 D3 – pop. 1 010 – alt. 60 m – ✉ 76540
Normandy 33 **C1**

Paris 193 – Bolbec 22 – Dieppe 58 – Fécamp 11 – Le Havre 48 – Rouen 67 – Yvetot 28

Syndicat d'initiative, Mairie ✆ 02 35 10 08 12, Fax 02 35 10 08 12

Abbey★.

XX **Le Bec au Cauchois** with rm

22 r. A.-Fiquet, 1.5 km west by Fécamp road – ✆ 02 35 29 77 56 – lebecaucauchois@orange.fr – Fax 02 35 29 77 52 – Closed 3-12 March, 7-22 October and 5-21 January

5 rm – †€ 70/75 ††€ 70/75, ☕ € 10 – ½ P € 70 – **Rest** – *(closed Wednesday except dinner May-September and Tuesday)* Menu (€ 17), € 26/56 – Carte € 40/61

◆ Enjoy a gastronomic break in this country inn with its rustic decor of exposed beams and large fireplace. Modern menu featuring local produce. Bright, simple ground floor rooms with balcony overlooking a pond.

VALOJOULX – 24 Dordogne – 329 H5 – pop. 236 – alt. 75 m – ✉ 24290 4 **D1**

Paris 523 – Bordeaux 195 – Périgueux 65 – Brive-la-Gaillarde 53 – Sarlat-la-Canéda 25

La Licorne

– ✆ 05 53 50 77 77 – licornelascaux@free.fr – Fax 05 53 50 77 77 – Open from April to October

5 rm ☕ – †€ 58 ††€ 65/85 – **Table d'hôte** – *(closed Sunday dinner)* Menu € 21

◆ Looking for a peaceful, friendly hideaway to discover *Périgord* specialities? This is the place, with smartly rustic bedrooms and a vast garden. The *table d'hôte* is set under a magnificent wooden ceiling.

VALRAS-PLAGE – 34 Hérault – 339 E9 – pop. 3 625 – alt. 1 m – Casino – ✉ 34350
Languedoc-Roussillon-Tarn Gorges 23 **C2**

Paris 767 – Agde 25 – Béziers 16 – Montpellier 76

Office de tourisme, place René Cassin ✆ 04 67 32 36 04, Fax 04 67 32 33 41

Mira-Mar rm, rm, VISA

bd Front de Mer – ✆ 04 67 32 00 31 – info@hotel-miramar.org – Fax 04 67 32 51 21 – Open March-end October

27 rm – †€ 56/98 ††€ 56/98, ☕ € 8 – 3 suites – ½ P € 53/79 – **Rest** – *(closed Sunday dinner and Wednesday except July-August)* Menu € 15/33 – Carte € 26/57

◆ It's true! Most rooms look out to sea - "mira el mar" as they say in Spanish. Bright, practical rooms. Four spacious apartments. Ice-cream bar. Low-key dining room, terrace overlooking the Mediterranean and traditional menu.

Albizzia without rest VISA

bd Chemin Creux – ✆ 04 67 37 48 48 – hotelalbizziavalras@wanadoo.fr – Fax 04 67 37 58 10 – Closed January

27 rm – †€ 48/63 ††€ 51/74, ☕ € 7

◆ This newly established hotel 200m from the beach extends a friendly welcome. Basic rooms; those overlooking the pool have a loggia. Delightful little Mediterranean garden.

XX **Le Delphinium** VISA

av. Élysées, (opposite the casino) – ✆ 04 67 32 73 10 – ledelphinium@wanadoo.fr – Fax 04 67 32 73 10 – Closed autumn half-term holidays, 16-26 February, Saturday lunch, Sunday dinner and Monday

Rest – Menu (€ 19 bi), € 26/45 – Carte € 52/79

◆ Discreet facade near the casino, housing a pleasant modern dining room with wrought-iron furniture. Summer terrace and sunny up-to-date cuisine.

XX **La Méditerranée** VISA

32 r. Ch. Thomas – ✆ 04 67 32 38 60 – mediterranee32@wanadoo.fr – Fax 04 67 32 30 91 – Closed 12-30 November, 5-23 January, Tuesday except dinner in season and Monday

Rest – Menu € 16/39 – Carte € 22/63

◆ Small family-run restaurant in a pedestrian street, near the mouth of the River Orb. Traditional cuisine served in a rustic setting.

VALRÉAS – 84 Vaucluse – 332 C7 – pop. 9 425 – alt. 250 m – ✉ 84600 ▮ Provence

▶ Paris 639 – Avignon 67 – Crest 51 – Montélimar 38 – Nyons 14 – Orange 37

ℹ Office de tourisme, avenue Maréchal Leclerc ✆ 04 90 35 04 71, Fax 04 90 35 03 60 40 **A2**

XX **Au Délice de Provence** VISA MC

6 La Placette, (town centre) – ✆ 04 90 28 16 91 – Fax 04 90 37 42 49 – Closed Tuesday and Wednesday

Rest – Menu (€ 15), € 20/46 – Carte € 46/64

◆ This large, sunlit dining room, divided into two by attractive arches, occupies an old synagogue. Appetising contemporary cuisine.

VALS-LES-BAINS – 07 Ardèche – 331 I6 – pop. 3 536 – alt. 210 m – Spa : late Feb.-early Dec. – Casino – ✉ 07600 ▮ Lyon - Rhone Valley 44 **A3**

▶ Paris 629 – Aubenas 6 – Langogne 58 – Privas 33 – Le Puy-en-Velay 87

ℹ Office de tourisme, 116 bis, avenue Jean Jaurès ✆ 04 75 89 02 03, Fax 04 75 89 02 04

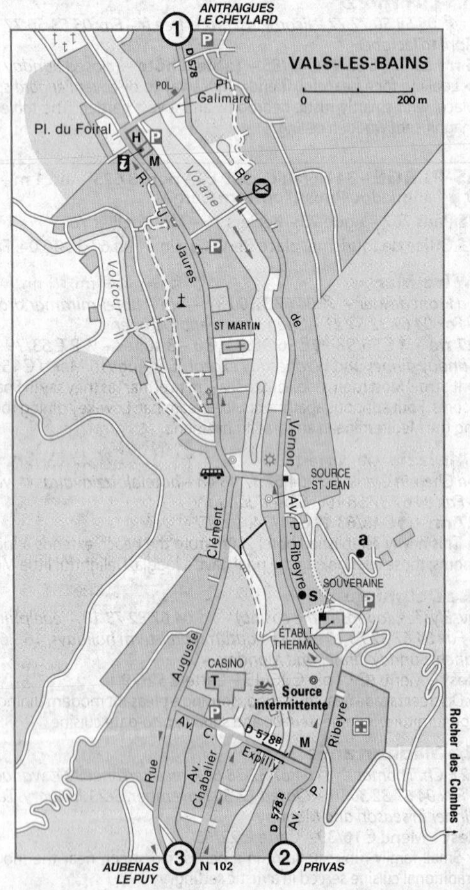

Grand Hôtel de Lyon rm, VISA MC

av. P. Ribeyre – ✆ 04 75 37 43 70 – info@grandhoteldelyon.fr – Fax 04 75 37 59 11 – Open 13 April-4 October s

34 rm – †€ 60/72 ††€ 66/92, ☕ € 9 – ½ P € 55/68 – **Rest** – Menu (€ 15), € 20/42 – Carte € 26/46

◆ This very centrally located hotel is just 100m from the park of the intermittent spring. Spacious renovated and well-kept rooms. Indoor/outdoor pool. This comfortable restaurant with an unusual mural has large bay windows that fill the room with light.

Château Clément P VISA MC

La Châtaigneraie – ✆ 04 75 87 40 13 – contact@chateauclement.com – Closed January- February a

5 rm ☕ – †€ 120/170 ††€ 125/220 – **Table d'hôte** – *(closed Tuesday, Wednesday and Sunday)* Menu € 50 bi/60 bi

◆ This 19C property, surrounded by a park planted with exotic plant species, overlooks the town. Admire the elegant sitting rooms and superb, tastefully decorated bedrooms and suite. Traditional menu made with organic and regional produce at the table d'hôte.

VAL-THORENS – **73 Savoie** – **333** M6 – **alt. 2 300 m** – **Winter sports : 2 300/ 3 200 m** 4 25 – ✉ **73440 St-Martin-de-Belleville** ▌**French Alps** 46 **F2**

Paris 640 – Albertville 60 – Chambéry 109 – Moûtiers 36

Office de tourisme, immeuble Eskival ✆ 04 79 00 08 08, Fax 04 79 00 00 04

Cime de Caron ★★★ (access by cable car from Caron).

Fitz Roy rm, rest, VISA MC AE

– ✆ 04 79 00 04 78 – welcome@hotelfitzroy.com – Fax 04 79 00 06 11 – Open 6 December-30 April

60 rm – †€ 180/390 ††€ 560/680, ☕ € 30 – 4 suites – **Rest** – Menu € 60/90 – Carte € 70/142

◆ Luxurious rooms (partly refurbished), many with balconies providing splendid mountain views. Open fire in the sitting room, indoor pool and a health and beauty centre. At lunchtime, a buffet is served on the panoramic terrace of this plush, inviting restaurant.

Le Val Thorens rm, VISA MC AE

– ✆ 04 79 00 04 33 – contact@levalthorens.com – Fax 04 79 00 09 40 – Open 6 December-26 April

80 rm – †€ 111/210 ††€ 182/412, ☕ € 12 – ½ P € 91/170

Rest *Le Bellevillois* – *(open 7 December-19 April) (dinner only)*
Menu € 22/45 – Carte € 42/63

Rest *La Fondue* – *(open 22 December-14 April) (dinner only)*
Menu € 22 – Carte € 42/62

◆ A modern building in the centre of the resort with large rooms with balconies. Piano bar, sauna and solarium. Restaurant offering traditional and brasserie dishes. Le Bellevillois offers classic cuisine. Alpine ambience and recipes at La Fondue.

Mercure rest, VISA MC AE

– ✆ 04 79 00 04 04 – h0457@accor.com – Fax 04 79 00 05 93 – Open 2 December-26 April

104 rm – †€ 110/173 ††€ 160/230, ☕ € 10 – ½ P € 128/153

Rest – Menu € 23 (lunch), € 30/40 – Carte € 33/48

◆ A comfortable hotel at the foot of the slopes, with rooms offering fine views of the glaciers. Lively bar and shop selling skiing equipment.

Le Sherpa VISA MC

– ✆ 04 79 00 00 70 – info@lesherpa.com – Fax 04 79 00 08 03 – Open 29 November-4 May

52 rm – †€ 77/135 ††€ 135/260, ☕ € 12 – 4 suites – ½ P € 77/175

Rest – Menu (€ 20), € 28/32 – Carte € 23/44

◆ Modern chalet a stone's throw from the ski slopes. Renovated rooms and duplex apartments: wood panelling, white walls and pine furniture. Sitting-room bar with fireplace; internet access. The restaurant has a warm Savoyard chalet atmosphere and offers traditional dishes.

Les Trois Vallées rest, VISA

Grande Rue – 04 79 00 01 86 – reservation@hotel3vallees.com – Fax 04 79 00 04 08 – Open 24 November-5 May

29 rm – €79/160 €108/220, €12 – 3 suites – ½ P €79/135

Rest – *(dinner only)* Menu €25/29 – Carte €28/57

◆ The largest ski area in the Alps lends its name to this modern building. Functional rooms, including seven for families. Fine view of the peaks from the lounge-bar. Dining room decorated in Alpine style. Traditional menu.

L'Oxalys (Jean Sulpice) VISA AE

– 04 79 00 12 00 – jean-sulpice@loxalys.com – Fax 04 79 00 24 10 – Open 1st December-24 April

Rest – Menu €48/105 – Carte €80/106

Spec. Variation de légumes d'hiver sur fine pâte de polenta. Châtaigne de l'Ardèche en soupe, chaud-froid de parmesan et râpé de truffes. Fruits exotiques en brunoise et sorbets. **Wines** Roussette de Savoie, Mondeuse d'Arbin.

◆ A hotel designed in the form of a hamlet houses this restaurant. Attractive contemporary decor, a superb terrace opposite the slopes and inventive good food.

LE VALTIN – 88 Vosges – 314 K4 – pop. 98 – alt. 751 m – ✉ 88230 27 D3

Paris 440 – Colmar 46 – Épinal 55 – Guebwiller 55 – St-Dié 27 – Col de la Schlucht 10

Auberge du Val Joli with rm VISA AE

– 03 29 60 91 37 – contact@levaljoli.com – Fax 03 29 60 81 73 – Closed 17 November-12 December, Sunday dinner, Monday dinner, Tuesday lunch except school holidays and Monday lunch except public holidays

7 rm – €80 €85, €12 – 3 suites – ½ P €73 – **Rest** – Menu €22/70 – Carte €42/67

◆ Two dining areas, one rustic, the other with a conservatory leading onto the terrace facing the countryside. Regional dishes with modern touches. Renovated rooms.

LA VANCELLE – 67 Bas-Rhin – 315 H7 – see Lièpvre

VANDŒUVRE-LÈS-NANCY – 54 Meurthe-et-Moselle – 307 H7 – see Nancy

VANNES P – 56 Morbihan – 308 O9 – pop. 51 759 – Built-up area 118 029 – alt. 20 m – ✉ 56000 Brittany 9 A3

Paris 459 – Quimper 122 – Rennes 110 – St-Brieuc 107 – St-Nazaire 86

Office de tourisme, 1, rue Thiers 08 25 13 56 10, Fax 02 97 47 29 49

de Baden Baden Kernic, by Auray road and D 101: 14 km, 02 97 57 18 96.

Old town ★★ AZ : Place Henri-IV★ AZ 10, St-Pierre cathedral ★ B, Ramparts★, Promenade de la Garenne ★★ - La Cohue★ (former covered market) - Musée archéologique★ - Aquarium océanographique et tropical★ - Golfe du Morbihan ★★ by boat.

Plan on next page

Mercure VISA AE

The Gulf park, 2 km south Conleau road – 02 97 40 44 52 – h2182-gm@accor-hotels.com – Fax 02 97 63 03 20

89 rm – €79/142 €87/152, €13

Rest *Brasserie Edgar* – 02 97 40 68 08 – Carte €20/45

◆ Near the Aquarium, a modern hotel providing spacious and soundproofed rooms with views of the Morbihan gulf. The bay windows of the dining room open onto the terrace facing a little corner of greenery.

Villa Kerasy without rest VISA AE

20 av. Favrel et Lincy – 0 297 683 683 – info@villakerasy.com – Fax 0 297 683 684 – Open from March to October BY **r**

12 rm – €97/160 €125/190, €13

◆ Each room is unusually decorated on the theme of the East India Company's ports of call. Charming, attentive service. Delicious breakfasts. Japanese garden.

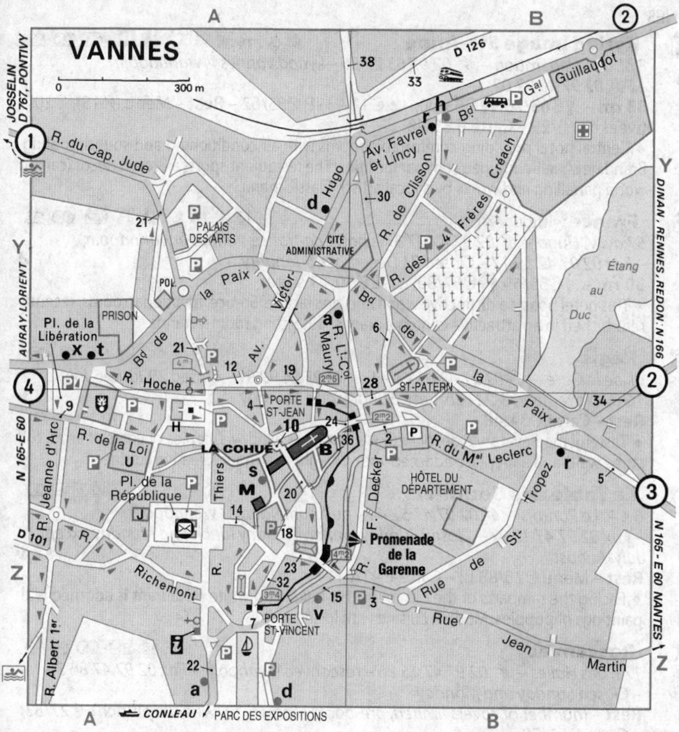

VANNES

Best Western Vannes Centre

6 pl. de la Libération – ☎ 02 97 63 20 20 – info@bestwestern-vannescentre.com – Fax 02 97 63 80 22 — AY **t**

58 rm – †€ 69/115 ††€ 69/120, ☕ € 11 – **Rest** – Menu (€ 13,50) – Carte € 23/34

◆ Recent construction close to the historic and shopping centres. Uncluttered, contemporary décor in the rooms. Meeting facilities for the business clientele; fitness. Traditional dishes in a similarly modern setting at the restaurant.

Marébaudière without rest

4 r. A. Briand – ☎ 02 97 47 34 29 – marebaudiere@wanadoo.fr – Fax 02 97 54 14 11 — BZ **r**

41 rm – †€ 67/106 ††€ 74/106, ☕ € 9

◆ A regional, slate roofed building, five minutes from the ramparts. Home to colourful (blue, yellow and rust), highly practical and well-equipped rooms. Immaculate upkeep.

Manche-Océan without rest

31 r. Lt-Col. Maury – ☎ 02 97 47 26 46 – info@manche-ocean.com – Fax 02 97 47 30 86 – Closed 20 December-4 January — AY **a**

41 rm – †€ 51/75 ††€ 65/95, ☕ € 8

◆ Recently renovated hotel: spacious well-equipped rooms (king size beds, functionally furnishings), excellent soundproofing and seminar facilities.

Kyriad Image Ste-Anne rm, VISA AE
8 pl. de la Libération – 02 97 63 27 36 – kyriad.vannes@wanadoo.fr – Fax 02 97 40 97 02 AY **x**
33 rm – €63/70 €63/80, €11 – ½ P €55/62 – **Rest** – Menu (€15), €20 (weekdays)/29 – Carte €35/48
◆ Central hotel providing comfortable rooms with air conditioning and soundproofing. Brand new well-equipped seminar facilities. The restaurant sports a Breton decor (carved wood panelling and works by a local artist). Classic menu.

France without rest VISA AE
57 av. V. Hugo – 02 97 47 27 57 – hotel-de-france-vannes@wanadoo.fr – Fax 02 97 42 59 17 – Closed 21 December-5 January AY **d**
30 rm – €55/65 €57/80, €8,50 – 1 suite
◆ This hotel boasts a distinctive wood and zinc façade. Spruce, functional rooms, recently refurbished in an attractive contemporary spirit. Sitting room-veranda.

Régis VISA
pl. de la Gare – 02 97 42 61 41 – Fax 02 97 54 99 01 – Closed 29 June-6 July, 16-30 November, 8-22 February, Sunday and Monday BY **h**
Rest – Carte €34/48
◆ Tasteful medieval style decor with stained glass windows, copies of coats of arms, tuff stone walls and a fireplace adorned with a knight in armour. Creative cuisine.

La Table des Gourmets VISA
6 r. A. Le Pontois – 02 97 47 52 44 – guillaumelaura@wanadoo.fr – Fax 02 97 47 15 87 – Closed Sunday dinner, Tuesday lunch and Monday except July-August AZ **v**
Rest – Menu €26/88 bi – Carte €41/61
◆ Facing the ramparts of the old town, this beige and white restaurant is adorned with paintings of poppies. Modern cuisine with local touches.

Roscanvec VISA AE
17 r. des Halles – 02 97 47 15 96 – roscanvec@yahoo.fr – Fax 02 97 47 86 39 – Closed Sunday and Monday AZ **s**
Rest – *(number of covers limited, pre-book)* Menu €20 (weekday lunch), €27/53 – Carte €51/58
◆ Half-timbered house in a picturesque pedestrian street. Tables on the ground floor with views of the kitchen. Main room upstairs. Inventive menu.

Le Carré Blanc VISA AE
28 r. du Port – 02 97 47 48 34 – lionelcolson@.fr – Fax 02 97 47 48 34 – Closed 1st January-8 February, Saturday lunch, Sunday dinner and Monday AZ **a**
Rest – Menu €14,50 (lunch)/25
◆ Le Carré Blanc is utterly inviting hidden away in a timber-framed house where contemporary paintings and furniture decorate a spotless interior. Modern, well presented food.

La Table Alsacienne VISA
23 r. Ferdinand Le Dressay – 02 97 01 34 53 – Fax 02 97 01 34 53 – Closed 15-24 April, August, Sunday except lunch October-March and Monday
Rest – Menu (€12), €22 – Carte €25/37 AZ **d**
◆ This restaurant on the first floor of a house facing the marina is decorated in a winstub style. Here the Bretons enjoy copious servings of Alsatian specialities.

in St-Avé by ① and D 767, North: 6 km (near "centre hospitalier spécialisé" (specialised hospital)) – pop. 8 303 – alt. 50 m – ✉ 56890

Le Pressoir (Bernard Rambaud) VISA AE
rte de Plescop, (near the hospital), at 1.5 km – 02 97 60 87 63 – le.pressoir.st-ave@wanadoo.fr – Fax 02 97 44 59 15 – Closed 3-18 March, 1st-8 July, 1st-21 October, Sunday dinner, Monday and Tuesday
Rest – Menu €35 (weekday lunch), €55/95 – Carte €63/130
Spec. Langoustines crues à la crème acidulée au caviar d'Aquitaine. Galette de rouget aux pommes de terre et au romarin. Queue de homard breton à peine cuite aux épices et xérès "Amontillado". **Wines** Muscadet sur lie.
◆ A hotel much appreciated for its inventive cuisine paying tribute to the Armor. It also has a fine wine cellar and a new contemporary interior dotted with floral arrangements.

in Conleau southwest: 4.5 km – ✉ 56000 Vannes

Presqu'île de Conleau ★ 30 mn.

Le Roof VISA AE

– ✆ 02 97 63 47 47 – *leroof@club-internet.fr* – *Fax 02 97 63 48 10*

40 rm – €82/119 €104/144, € 12,50 – ½ P € 87/107

Rest – Menu € 28/55 – Carte € 40/80

Rest *Café de Conleau* – Menu (€ 14,50) – Carte € 23/40

♦ This hotel enjoys a privileged location on a peninsula facing a lovely cove where sailboats drop anchor. The rooms are functional and some command a sea view. Extensive views of the Morbihan Gulf from the restaurant. A bistro atmosphere pervades the Café de Conleau.

Arradon road by ④ and D 101: 5 km – ✉ 56610 Arradon

L'Arlequin

parc d'activités de Botquelen, (3 allée D.-Papin) – ✆ *02 97 40 41 41* – *arlequin.caradec@wanadoo.fr* – *Fax 02 97 40 52 93* – *Closed 8-16 March, 31 August-15 September, Saturday lunch, Sunday dinner and Wednesday*

Rest – Menu € 17 (weekday lunch), € 22/40 – Carte € 34/50

♦ This pleasant, rotunda dining room boasts a timber ceiling and a view of the countryside. Updated menu that mixes tradition and fusion cuisine. Be sure to book!

in Arradon by ④, D 101, D 101^{A} and D 127: 7 km – **pop. 4 719** – **alt. 40 m** – ✉ **56610**

Syndicat d'initiative, 2, place de l'église ✆ 02 97 44 77 44

★.

Le Logis de Parc er Gréo without rest VISA AE

au Gréo, 2 km west (towards le Moustoir) – ✆ *02 97 44 73 03* – *contact@parcergreo.com* – *Fax 02 97 44 80 48* – *Open 13 March-11 November*

14 rm – €75/138 €75/138, € 14 – 1 suite

♦ House surrounded by greenery with a fine interior. Prettily furnished lounge decorated with model boats and fine watercolours. Cosy, individually furnished rooms. Heated pool.

Les Vénètes gulf and islands, VISA AE

à la pointe, 2 km – ✆ *02 97 44 85 85* – *contact@lesvenetes.com* – *Fax 02 97 44 78 60* – *Closed 6-18 January*

10 rm – €90/190 €90/220, € 10 – ½ P € 100/140

Rest – *(Closed Sunday dinner)* Menu € 28 (weekday lunch)/58 – Carte € 53/74

♦ At the water's edge, prettily arranged rooms with exceptional views of the gulf. Those on the first floor have balconies. A pleasant dining room with a marine decor, superbly situated on the shores of the "mor bihan" (Breton for little sea).

Le Médaillon VISA AE

10 r. Bouruet Aubertot – ✆ *02 97 44 77 28* – *Fax 02 97 44 79 08* – *Closed 22-28 December, Sunday dinner, Tuesday dinner and Wednesday except 14 July-31 August*

Rest – Menu € 15/35 – Carte € 34/51

♦ On the village outskirts, a former bar converted into a restaurant. Exposed beams and stone work adorn the unassuming dining room. Summer arboured terrace and children's games.

LES VANS – 07 Ardèche – 331 G7 – pop. 2 664 – alt. 170 m – ✉ 07140

Lyon - Rhone Valley 44 **A3**

Paris 663 – Alès 44 – Aubenas 37 – Pont-St-Esprit 66 – Privas 68 – Villefort 24

Office de tourisme, place Ollier ✆ 04 75 37 24 48, Fax 04 75 37 27 46

Le Carmel rm, VISA AE

montée du Carmel – ✆ *04 75 94 99 60* – *contact@le-carmel.com* – *Fax 04 75 94 34 29* – *Open 15 March-1st November*

26 rm – €45/55 €65/75, € 9 – ½ P € 60/75 – **Rest** – Menu € 28/42 – Carte € 36/57

♦ The rooms in this former Carmelite convent, overlooking the medieval town, have been renovated - Provençal fabrics, ochre walls, wrought-iron furniture and new bathrooms. Attractive garden. Dining room with sunny colours and a shaded terrace. Dishes of the day.

South 6 km by D 901 – ✉ 07140 Les Vans

Mas de l'Espaïre VISA AE
Combe de Mège – ✆ 04 75 94 95 01 – espaire@wanadoo.fr – Fax 04 75 37 21 00 – Open Easter-11 November
30 rm – †€ 37/87 ††€ 57/87, ☕ € 8 – ½ P € 62/77 – **Rest** – *(closed Sunday and Monday except May to September) (dinner only) (residents only)*
◆ At the edge of the Païolive wood, a former silkworm farm lulled by the crickets' song. The walls of the large rooms show traces of the original stone. King size beds.

VANVES – 92 Hauts-de-Seine – **311** J3 – **101** 25 – **see Paris, Area**

VARADES – 44 Loire-Atlantique – **316** J3 – **pop. 3 190** – **alt. 13 m** – ✉ 44370 34 **B2**

Paris 333 – Angers 40 – Cholet 42 – Laval 95 – Nantes 54
Syndicat d'initiative, place Jeanne d'Arc ✆ 02 40 83 41 88

La Closerie des Roses la Loire, VISA AE
La Meilleraie, 1.5 km south by Cholet road – ✆ 02 40 98 33 30 – Fax 02 40 09 74 23 – Closed 6-22 October, 12 January-4 February, Sunday dinner, Monday dinner, Tuesday dinner and Wednesday
Rest – Menu € 17 (weekday lunch), € 26/56 – Carte € 44/53
◆ This restaurant, established in 1938, faces the River Loire and St Florent-le-Vieil Abbey. The chef buys his freshwater fish from local anglers; regional menu.

VARENGEVILLE-SUR-MER – 76 Seine-Maritime – **304** F2 – **pop. 1 179** – **alt. 80 m** – ✉ 76119 Normandy 33 **D1**

Paris 199 – Dieppe 10 – Fécamp 57 – Fontaine-le-Dun 18 – Rouen 68
Site★ of the church - Parc des Moustiers★ - Colombier★ of Ango manor, South: 1 km - Ste-Marguerite: church ★ arcades West: 4.5 km - Ailly lighthouse ★ Northwest: 4 km.

in Vasterival 3 km northwest by D 75 and secondary road – ✉ 76119 Varengeville-sur-Mer

De la Terrasse rest, VISA AE
– ✆ 02 35 85 12 54 – francois.delafontaine@wanadoo.fr – Fax 02 35 85 11 70 – Open 16 March-11 October
22 rm – †€ 52/62 ††€ 52/62, ☕ € 8 – ½ P € 52/58
Rest – Menu € 17 (weekday lunch), € 22/35 – Carte € 27/38
◆ At the end of a pine-lined road, a fine house (1902) surrounded by a large shaded garden. Half the rooms enjoy a view of the sea. Sitting room with board games. The new minimalist decor in the restaurant sets off the splendid view of the Channel.

LA VARENNE-ST-HILAIRE – 94 Val-de-Marne – **312** E3 – **101** 28 – **see Paris, Area**

VARENNES-SUR-ALLIER – 03 Allier – **326** H5 – **pop. 4 072** – **alt. 245 m** – ✉ 03150 6 **C1**

Paris 327 – Digoin 59 – Lapalisse 20 – Moulins 31 – St-Pourçain-sur-Sioule 11 – Vichy 26
Office de tourisme, place de l'Hôtel de Ville ✆ 04 70 47 45 86, Fax 04 70 47 45 86

in Boucé 8 km East by N 7 and D 23 – **pop. 512** – **alt. 310 m** – ✉ 03150

Auberge de Boucé VISA
1 rte de Cindré – ✆ 04 70 43 70 59 – auberge-de-bouce@orange.fr – Fax 04 70 43 70 87 – Closed Tuesday dinner, Sunday dinner and Monday
Rest – Menu € 14 (weekdays)/34 – Carte € 22/36
◆ Village inn with a warm country ambience. Pleasant terrace and sunny dining room decorated with paintings by the owner. Traditional cuisine served.

in la Ferté-Hauterive **8 km North by N 7 and D 32 – pop. 285 – alt. 230 m – ✉ 03340**

Demeure d'Hauterive
– ✆ 04 70 43 04 85 – *j.lefebvre@demeure-hauterive.com – Fax 04 70 43 04 85*
5 rm – €65 €80 – **Table d'hôte** – Menu €22 bi/30 bi
◆ The owners of this house, dating from 1860, enjoy painting and hunting for antiques. Therefore, the tasteful decoration of the spacious rooms and reception areas with paintings and furniture from various periods comes as no surprise. Restaurant serving regional cuisine.

VARENNES-SUR-USSON – 63 Puy-de-Dôme – 326 G9 – see Issoire

VARETZ – 19 Corrèze – 329 J4 – see Brive-la-Gaillarde

VARS – 05 Hautes-Alpes – 334 I5 – pop. 637 – alt. 1 650 m – ✉ 05560

French Alps 41 **C1**

Paris 726 – Barcelonnette 41 – Briançon 46 – Digne-les-Bains 126 – Gap 71
Office de tourisme, cours Fontanarosa ✆ 04 92 46 51 31

in Ste-Marie-de-Vars – ✉ **05560 Vars**

L'Alpage
– ✆ *04 92 46 50 52 – info@hotel-alpage.com – Fax 04 92 46 64 23*
– Open 15 June-1st September and 15 December-15 April
17 rm – €56/124 €72/124, €9 – ½ P €48/87 – **Rest** – Menu €20/29 – Carte €23/28
◆ In the centre of Vars, a family chalet, recently enlarged by a new wing. Well-kept rooms, all renovated in regional style. Billiard table and fitness room. The restaurant occupies an attractive vaulted building which was once a cowshed. Traditional cuisine.

Le Vallon rest,
– ✆ *04 92 46 54 72 – info@hotelvallon.com – Fax 04 92 46 61 62*
– Open 1st July-31 August and 19 December-19 April
34 rm – €38/65 €57/98, €7,50 – ½ P €47/70 – **Rest** – Menu (€13,50), €18/21 – Carte €18/26
◆ A large building at the foot of the ski slopes, with a mountain atmosphere and decor. Renovated rooms (all overlooking a natural landscape). Billiards and table tennis. A guest-house-type dining room decorated with photographs of alpine landscapes.

in Claux – ✉ **05560 Vars – Winter sports : 1 650/2 750 m 2 56**

L'Écureuil without rest
– ✆ *04 92 46 50 72 – hotel.ecureuil@wanadoo.fr – Fax 04 92 46 62 51*
– Open 23 June-6 September and 6 December-24 April
21 rm – €65/90 €80/160, €7,50
◆ Savoy-style chalet 150m from the cable-car. Comfortable and warm-feeling interior where wood is predominant. Nice rooms, most with a balcony. Sauna.

Les Escondus
– ✆ *04 92 46 67 00 – hotel.les.escondus@wanadoo.fr – Fax 04 92 46 50 47*
– Open 1st July-31 August and 1st December-30 April
22 rm – €37/56 €94/140, €8 – ½ P €65/96 – **Rest** – Menu €19/25 – Carte €23/38
◆ Easy access to the ski slopes, simple and practical rooms, some with balconies, a relaxation room and very lively piano bar are the assets of this establishment built in the local style. Dining room panelled in light wood and terrace facing the forest.

Chez Plumot
– ✆ *04 92 46 52 12 – Open July-August and December- April*
Rest – Menu €18/29 – Carte €30/60
◆ A family-run restaurant in the centre of the resort. Simple traditional dishes... and from South-West France. Shorter lunchtime menu in winter (snacks and a few house specialities).

VASSIVIÈRE (LAC) – **23 Creuse** – **326** i6 – **see Peyrat-le-Château (87 H.-Vienne)**

VASTERIVAL – **76 Seine-Maritime** – **304** F2 – **see Varengeville-sur-Mer**

VAUCHOUX – **70 Haute-Saône** – **314** E7 – **see Port-sur-Saône**

VAUCHRÉTIEN – **49 Maine-et-Loire** – **317** G5 – **pop. 1 509** – **alt. 67 m** – ✉ **49320** 35 **C2**

Paris 313 – Nantes 119 – Angers 22 – Cholet 66 – Saumur 45

Syndicat d'initiative, Mairie ✆ 02 41 91 24 18, Fax 02 41 91 20 06

Le Moulin de Clabeau without rest

5 km north on D 55 and D 123 – ✆ 02 41 91 22 09 – moulin-clabeau@gite-brissac.com – Closed 24-31 August

3 rm – €60/65 €60/65, – 1 suite

◆ This 1320 mill on the banks of the Aubance offers rooms with exposed beams and stonework. Homemade jams and cakes at breakfast. Exhibitions and sale of local produce.

VAUCRESSON – **92 Hauts-de-Seine** – **311** I2 – **101** 23 – **see Paris, Area**

VAUDEVANT – **07 Ardèche** – **331** J3 – **pop. 197** – **alt. 600 m** – ✉ **07410** 44 **B2**

Paris 558 – Lyon 96 – Privas 89 – Saint-Étienne 67 – Valence 50

La Récré

– ✆ 04 75 06 08 99 – restaurant-la-recre@wanadoo.fr – Fax 04 75 06 08 99 – Closed 14 December-20 January, Tuesday except lunch July-August, Sunday dinner September-June and Monday

Rest – *(number of covers limited, pre-book)* Menu € 12 (weekday lunch), € 19/44 – Carte € 32/42

◆ This restaurant was once the village school, which explains the name and decor (blackboard, photos of schoolchildren, wall maps etc). Modern, refined dining in a convivial atmosphere.

VAUGINES – **84 Vaucluse** – **332** F11 – **pop. 466** – **alt. 375 m** – ✉ **84160** 42 **E1**

Paris 736 – Digne-les-Bains 112 – Apt 23 – Cavaillon 36 – Salon-de-Provence 37

L'Hostellerie du Luberon

cours St-Louis – ✆ 04 90 77 27 19 – hostellerieduluberon@hostellerieduluberon.com – Fax 04 90 77 13 08 – Open 10 March-10 November

16 rm – €80/83 €80/99, € 10 – ½ P € 70 – **Rest** – *(closed Wednesday lunch)* Menu (€ 21), € 32/41

◆ Facing the Durance plain, a family hotel with simple, refurbished rooms. The swimming pool is set in a pleasant garden. A spruce, light dining room with a terrace at the end, practically in the water.

VAULT-DE-LUGNY – **89 Yonne** – **319** G7 – **see Avallon**

VAUX-EN-BEAUJOLAIS – **69 Rhône** – **327** G3 – **pop. 946** – **alt. 360 m** – ✉ **69460** 43 **E1**

Paris 443 – Lyon 49 – Villeurbanne 58 – Lyon 03 51 – Lyon 08 51

Auberge de Clochemerle with rm

r. Gabriel-Chevallier – ✆ 04 74 03 20 16 – contact@aubergedeclochemerle.fr – Fax 04 74 03 20 74 – Closed Tuesday and Wednesday except July-August

7 rm – €60 €65, € 8 – ½ P € 95 – **Rest** – Menu € 28/65 – Carte € 52/60

◆ An auberge in a village made famous by Gabriel Chevallier's novel, "Clochemerle". Creative, contemporary cuisine and good wine list. Pleasant neo-rustic decor. Bright guestrooms embellished with homely furniture.

VAUX-LE-PÉNIL – 77 Seine-et-Marne – 312 F4 – see Melun

VAUX-SOUS-AUBIGNY – 52 Haute-Marne – 313 L8 – pop. 705 – alt. 275 m – ✉ 52190 14 C3

Paris 304 – Dijon 44 – Gray 43 – Langres 25

Auberge des Trois Provinces

r. de Verdun – ✆ 03 25 88 31 98 – Fax 03 25 84 25 61 – Closed 17-23 November, 5-25 January, Sunday dinner and Monday

Rest – *(pre-book)* Menu € 19/29 – Carte € 39/51

◆ Frescoes, painted beams and handsome floors make up the pleasant decor of this family restaurant in an old stone house. Fine modern cuisine.

Hôtel Le Vauxois

r. de Verdun – ✆ 03 25 84 36 74 – Fax 03 25 84 25 61 – Closed 17-23 November, 5-25 January, Sunday dinner and Monday

9 rm – †€ 48 ††€ 55, ☕ € 6,50

◆ The new, functional and colourful rooms are situated 50m from the Auberge des Trois Provinces and a stone's throw from the church. Bright breakfast area.

VÉLIZY-VILLACOUBLAY – 78 Yvelines – 311 J3 – 101 24 – see Paris, Area

VELLÈCHES – 86 Vienne – 322 J3 – pop. 371 – alt. 69 m – ✉ 86230 39 C1

Paris 302 – Poitiers 58 – Joué-lès-Tours 60 – Châtellerault 21 – Chambray-lès-Tours 60

La Table des Écoliers

1 bis r. de l'Étang – ✆ 05 49 93 35 51 – christelle.vaneroux@wanadoo.fr

Rest – *(closed Tuesday and Wednesday)* Menu € 29/42

◆ Journey back to childhood for an interesting lesson in taste in this former classroom, complete with school desks and coat-hangers. Charming welcome and contemporary cooking.

VELLUIRE – 85 Vendée – 316 K9 – see Fontenay-le-Comte

VENAREY-LES-LAUMES – 21 Côte-d'Or – 320 G4 – pop. 3 274 – alt. 235 m – ✉ 21150 Burgundy-Jura 8 C2

Paris 259 – Avallon 54 – Dijon 66 – Montbard 15 – Saulieu 42 – Semur-en-Auxois 13

Office de tourisme, place Bingerbrück ✆ 03 80 96 89 13, Fax 03 80 96 13 22

in Alise-Ste-Reine 2 km east – pop. 674 – alt. 415 m – ✉ 21150

Mont Auxois★: ❋★ - Château of Bussy-Rabutin★.

Cheval Blanc

r. du Miroir – ✆ 03 80 96 01 55 – regisbolatre@free.fr – Closed 1st-9 September, 2 January-6 February, Sunday dinner except July-August, Monday and Tuesday except public holidays

Rest – Menu € 19 (weekdays)/43 – Carte € 41/49

◆ A stone building near the town hall. Rustic dining room serving tasty Burgundy cuisine, with a pleasant log fire burning on chilly days.

VENASQUE – 84 Vaucluse – 332 D10 – pop. 966 – alt. 310 m – ✉ 84210 Provence 42 E1

Paris 690 – Apt 32 – Avignon 33 – Carpentras 13 – Cavaillon 30 – Orange 36

Office de tourisme, Grand 'Rue ✆ 04 90 66 11 66, Fax 04 90 66 11 66

Baptistry★ - Gorges★ East: 5 km by D 4.

Auberge La Fontaine

– ✆ 04 90 66 02 96 – fontvenasq@aol.com – Fax 04 90 66 13 14 – Closed January

5 suites – ††€ 125, ☕ € 10 – **Rest** – *(closed Wed.) (dinner only) (number of covers limited, pre-book)* Menu € 20/38

◆ Old building with guesthouse feel facing the town fountain. The skilfully arranged split-level rooms overlook the patio or rooftops. Dining room decorated with old furniture and ornaments; dinner-concerts.

La Garrigue rest, VISA AE

rte de l'Appié – ☎ 04 90 66 03 40 – hotel-lagarrigue@club-internet.fr – Fax 04 90 66 61 43 – Open 15 March-15 October
15 rm – €47 €58, €8 – ½ P €54/64 – **Rest** – *(closed Saturday and Sunday) (dinner only) (residents only)* Menu €20/23
◆ At the entrance to a hilltop village, this fully renovated family establishment has well-maintained rooms, some with air conditioning. Provencal style breakfast room.

VENCE – 06 Alpes-Maritimes – 341 D5 – pop. 16 982 – alt. 325 m – ✉ 06140

French Riviera 42 **E2**

- Paris 923 – Antibes 20 – Cannes 30 – Grasse 24 – Nice 23
- Office de tourisme, 8, place du Grand Jardin ☎ 04 93 58 06 38, Fax 04 93 58 91 81
- Rosaire chapel★ (Matisse chapel) - Place du Peyra★ B **13** - Stalls★ of the cathedral B **E** - ≤★ from the château terrace N. D. des Fleurs Northwest: 2.5 km km by D 2210.
- Col de Vence ✵★★ Nortwest: 10 km by D 2 - St-Jeannet: site★, ≤★ 8 km by ③.

Alsace Lorr. (R.)	B	3
Évêché (R. de l')	B	5
Hôtel de Ville (R.)	B	6
Leclerc (Av. Gén.)	A	9
Marché (R. du)	B	10
Meyère (Av. Col.)	B	12
Peyra (Pl. du)	B	13
Place Vieille (R. de la)	B	14
Poilus (Av. des)	A	15
Portail Levis (R. du)	B	16
Résistance (Av. de la)	A, B	17
Rhin et Danube (Av.)	A	18
St-Lambert (R.)	B	19
Tuby (Av.)	A	21

Château du Domaine St-Martin ≤ Vence and the coast, rm, VISA AE

2.5 km Coursegoules road on D 2 – ☎ 04 93 58 02 02 – stmartin@relaischateaux.com – Fax 04 93 24 08 91 – Open 8 March-14 November
34 rm – €400/800 €400/800, €34 – 6 suites
Rest – *(closed lunch Monday-Thursday 15 June-31 August)* Menu €46 (lunch), €75/105 – Carte €89/161
Rest *L'Oliveraie* – grill *(open 1st June-30 September) (lunch only)* Carte €47/95
◆ A superb Provençal luxury hotel in a park planted with olive groves and with a view that extends as far as the sea. Peace, comfort and charm. Up-to-date dishes, a lovely viewpoint terrace and a seaside panorama. In summertime, enjoy lunch outdoors at L'Oliveraie.

Cantemerle rm, VISA AE

258 chemin Cantemerle, via Ave Col. Meyère B – ☎ 04 93 58 08 18 – info@hotelcantemerle.com – Fax 04 93 58 32 89 – Open end March-mid October
9 rm – €190/210 €190/235, €15 – 18 suites – €215/500
Rest – *(open May-September and closed Monday)* Carte €47/63
◆ This Riviera-style villa is laid out around a pool and shaded garden. Impeccable Art Deco-inspired interior. Spacious, elegant rooms; the duplex rooms have a terrace. Restaurant surrounded by greenery; traditional cuisine.

Diana without rest
av. des Poilus – ✆ 04 93 58 28 56 – info@hotel-diana-vence.com – Fax 04 93 24 64 06 A **a**
27 rm – †€ 100/130 ††€ 110/140, ☕ € 13
◆ Centrally located hotel with bright, comfortable bedrooms; those facing the garden are quieter. Breakfast is served on the attractive veranda. Solarium and jacuzzi on the roof terrace. Gym.

Floréal
440 av. Rhin et Danube, via ② – ✆ 04 93 58 64 40 – hotel.floreal@wanadoo.fr – Fax 04 93 58 79 69 – Closed 1st-26 December
41 rm – †€ 60/170 ††€ 78/190, ☕ € 12 – ½ P € 62/98 – **Rest** – *(closed Sunday off season) (dinner only)* Menu € 25/32 – Carte € 23/43
◆ A garden of Mediterranean trees and shrubs surrounds this 1970s establishment just outside Vence. Redecorated rooms with balconies. Unassuming dining room and terrace overlooking the pool surrounded by greenery.

Mas de Vence rest,
539 av. E. Hugues – ✆ 04 93 58 06 16 – mas@azurline.com – Fax 04 93 24 04 21 A **r**
41 rm – †€ 69/84 ††€ 89/104, ☕ € 9 – ½ P € 74/84
Rest – Menu (€ 16 bi), € 29/35 – Carte € 29/38
◆ This recent ochre-toned construction overlooks a busy road. Rooms with good soundproofing, impeccably kept, often with a loggia. Hall with glass roof. Large dining room and arcaded terrace next to the hotel pool. Traditional and Mediterranean fare.

Miramar without rest
167 av. Bougearel, (Plateau St-Michel), via av. Col. Meyère B – ✆ 04 93 58 01 32 – contact@hotel-miramar-vence.com – Fax 04 93 58 20 22 – Closed 17 November-12 December
18 rm – †€ 68/88 ††€ 78/155, ☕ € 12
◆ This attractive 1920s building overlooks the mountains and valley. Public areas adorned with wall paintings, lovely guestrooms with individual touches, and a charming terrace.

Villa Roseraie without rest
128 av. Henri Giraud – ✆ 04 93 58 02 20 – accueil@villaroseraie.com – Fax 04 93 58 99 31 – Closed 5 November-14 December and 5 January-15 February A **x**
14 rm – †€ 85/145 ††€ 85/145, ☕ € 13
◆ Pleasant 1900 villa in the middle of a garden-cum-oasis. Small rooms delightfully decorated with Souleiado fabrics, decorative beds and dried flowers.

La Colline de Vence without rest ≤ Baou des Blancs and Coast,
806 chemin des Salles, 1.5 km on Plampraz road – ✆ 04 93 24 03 66 – contact@colline-vence.com – Fax 04 93 24 03 66 –
4 rm ☕ – †€ 74/135 ††€ 74/135
◆ The well-restored outbuildings of the château contain pretty rooms with personal touches. All overlook the mountains and Mediterranean. Flower garden and pool.

La Bastide aux Oliviers without rest
3 km via ② 1260 Chemin de la Sine – ✆ 04 93 24 20 33 – frenchclaude@wanadoo.fr – Fax 04 93 58 55 78
4 rm ☕ – †€ 90/120 ††€ 100/175
◆ This attractive country house, built in local stone, is surrounded by a large garden, with a swimming pool and tennis court. Provençal-style rooms. Breakfast served on the terrace.

Auberge Les Templiers
39 av. Joffre – ✆ 04 93 58 06 05 – lestempliers3@wanadoo.fr – Fax 04 93 58 92 68 – Closed 17 November-7 December, 19 January-2 February, lunch Monday-Thursday in July-August, Monday and Wednesday September-June A **k**
Rest – Menu € 39/63 – Carte € 52/70
◆ There is an attractive shaded terrace is front of this old inn. A renovated and refreshing setting in Provençal style.

Le Vieux Couvent

37 av. Alphonse Toreille – ✆ 04 93 58 78 58 – levieuxcouventvence@tiscali.fr – Fax 04 93 58 78 58 – Closed 15 January-15 February, Thursday lunch and Wednesday B **f**

Rest – *(number of covers limited, pre-book)* Menu € 27/37 – Carte € 42/56

◆ Exposed stonewalls, pillars and ribbed vaulting make up the decor of this restaurant housed in a 17C seminary chapel. Regional dishes.

Auberge des Seigneurs with rm

1, r. du Dr Binet – ✆ 04 93 58 04 24 – sandrine.rodi@wanadoo.fr – Fax 04 93 24 08 01 – Open March-October B **s**

6 rm – 🚹€ 60 🚹🚹€ 95, ☕ € 9 – ½ P € 95 – **Rest** – *(closed mid December-end January, Sunday and Monday)* Menu € 32/42 – Carte € 44/55

◆ Francis I, Renoir, Modigliani, etc. This historic inn in a wing of Villeneuve château has had many famous guests. Provençal dishes, spit-roasted lamb.

L'Armoise

9 pl. du Peyra – ✆ 04 93 58 19 29 – Closed 23-30 June, 3-20 November, 18-25 February, lunch in July-August, Sunday dinner, Tuesday lunch and Monday B **a**

Rest – *(number of covers limited, pre-book)* Menu € 36 – Carte € 40/50

◆ Specialising in fish and seafood, this restaurant occupies an old fishmonger's on the pretty Place du Peyra. Traditional favourites (bouillabaisse) and house specialities on the menu.

La Litote

5 r. Evéché – ✆ 04 93 24 27 82 – stephanefurlan@wanadoo.fr – Closed 12 November-16 December, 14 January-5 February, Tuesday from October to May, Saturday lunch, Wednesday and Thursday from June to September, Sunday dinner and Monday B **e**

Rest – Menu € 18 (weekday lunch), € 28/38 – Carte € 33/39

◆ A small restaurant opening onto a little square in the pedestrianised old quarter of Vence. Friendly welcome, attentive service, modern, Provençal-influenced menu, and a terrace in the shade of a linden tree.

VENDÔME – 41 Loir-et-Cher – 318 D5 – pop. 17 707 – alt. 82 m – ✉ 41100

Châteaux of the Loire 11 **B2**

Paris 169 – Blois 34 – Le Mans 78 – Orléans 91 – Tours 56

Office de tourisme, parc Ronsard ✆ 02 54 77 05 07, Fax 02 54 73 20 81

de La Bosse Oucques La Guignardière, by Beaugency road: 20 km, ✆ 02 54 23 02 60.

Former Trinité abbey★: abbey church★★, museum★ BZ **M** - Château: terraces ≤★.

Plan on next page

Le St-Georges

14 r. Poterie – ✆ 02 54 67 42 10 – contact@hotel-saint-georges-vendome.com – Fax 02 54 67 42 20 AZ **t**

28 rm – 🚹€ 65 🚹🚹€ 65/100, ☕ € 8 – ½ P € 90 – **Rest** – *(closed Sunday dinner)* Menu (€ 17 bi), € 27/39 – Carte € 30/42

◆ This street corner building in the town centre is home to a distinctly modern hotel. Practical rooms decorated in a modern style, some with spa tubs. The menu features cooking and flavours from four continents served in an ethnic setting. African style lounge bar.

Mercator

rte de Blois, 2 km via ③ – ✆ 02 54 89 08 08 – hotelmercator.vendome@wanadoo.fr – Fax 02 54 89 09 17

53 rm – 🚹€ 54 🚹🚹€ 54, ☕ € 7,50 – ½ P € 42 – **Rest** – *(closed Christmas holidays, lunch in August, Saturday and Sunday)* Menu (€ 15), € 18

◆ Although close to a roundabout, this hotel is surrounded by greenery. Compact yet comfortable modern bedrooms and attentive service. Restaurant with minimalist, contemporary decor and traditional recipes.

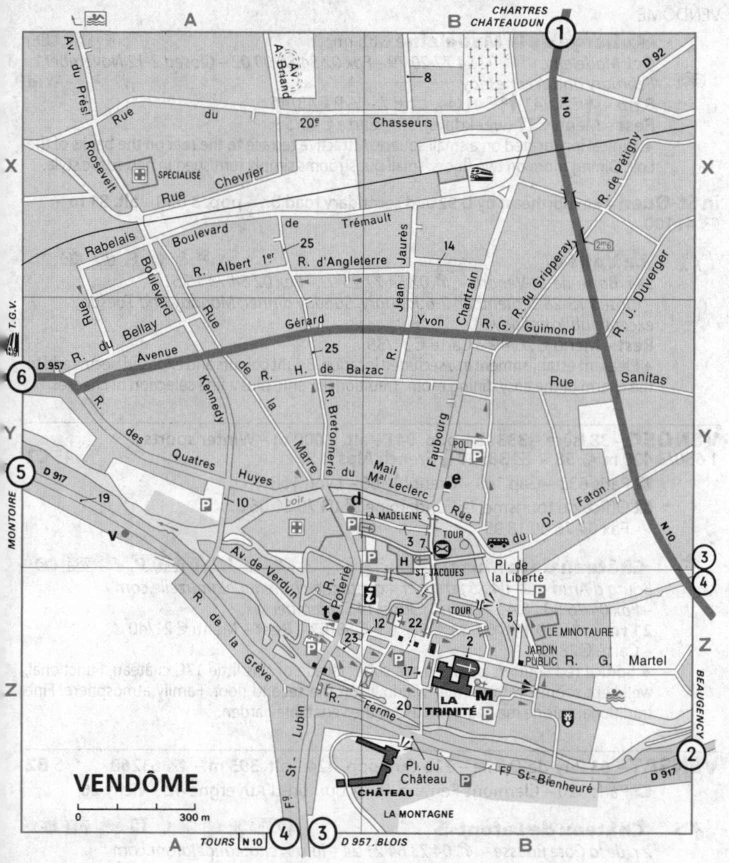

Abbaye (R. de l') .... BZ 2
Béguines (R. des) .... BY 3
Bourbon (R. A) .... BZ 5
Change (R. du) .... BY 7
Clemenceau (Av. G.) .... BX 8
États-Unis (R. des) .... AY 10
Gaulle (R. Gén.-de) .... BZ 12
Italie (R. d') .... BX 14
Poterie (R.) .... AZ
République (Pl. de la) .... BZ 17
Rochambeau (R. Mar.) .... AY 19
St-Bié (R.) .... BZ 20
St-Martin (Pl.) .... BZ 22
Saulnerie (R.) .... AZ 23
Verrier (R. Cdt) .... AXY 25

Le Vendôme without rest VISA AE

15 fg Chartrain – ✆ 02 54 77 02 88
– info@hotelvendomefrance.com
– Fax 02 54 73 90 71 Y **e**

35 rm – †€ 59/65 ††€ 68/85, ☕ € 10

◆ Family-run hotel in the town centre. A white façade conceals plainly decorated, functional bedrooms. Extensive buffet breakfast.

Le Terre à TR VISA AE

14 r. du Mar.-de-Rochambeau
– ✆ 02 54 89 09 09
– leterreatr@orange.fr
– Fax 02 54 89 09 09 AY **v**

Rest – Menu (€ 17 bi), € 26/30

◆ The unusual feature of this restaurant in the town's suburbs is its setting in a troglodyte cave. Up-to-date cuisine and summer terrace.

Auberge de la Madeleine with rm

6 pl. Madeleine – ✆ 02 54 77 20 79 – Fax 02 54 80 00 02 – Closed 2-12 November, February and Wednesday AY **d**

8 rm – €37/41 €41/44, €7 – ½ P €43/46

Rest – Menu €17 (weekdays)/38 – Carte €40/53

◆ Typical inn located on a small square. Attractive terrace to the rear on the banks of the Loir. Dining room on two floors; small guestrooms simply furnished in neo-rustic style.

in St-Ouen **4 km northeast by D 92 and secondary road** BX **– pop. 3 050 – alt. 81 m – ✉ 41100**

La Vallée

34 r. Barré-de-St-Venant – ✆ 02 54 77 29 93 – Fax 02 54 73 15 51 – Closed 15-28 September, 2-6 January, Sunday dinner, Monday and Tuesday except public holidays

Rest – Menu €26/49 – Carte €31/39

◆ Pleasant establishment in a secluded location. Bright colours and exposed beams add to the charm of the cosy dining room. Traditional menu, plus a fine selection of cheeses.

VENOSC – **38 Isère** – **333** J8 – **pop. 941** – **alt. 1 000 m** – **Winter sports : 1 650/3 420 m** **58** – ✉ **38520** **French Alps** 45 **C2**

Paris 633 – Gap 105 – Grenoble 66 – Lyon 166

Office de tourisme, la Condamine ✆ 04 76 80 06 82, Fax 04 76 80 18 95

Château de la Muzelle rest,

Bourg d'Arud – ✆ 04 76 80 06 71 – contact@chateaudelamuzelle.com – Fax 04 76 80 20 44 – Open 1st June-14 September

21 rm – €60 €60, €9 – ½ P €58/62 – **Rest** – Menu €21/40 – Carte €28/51

◆ Spruce red shutters brighten the sober façade of this little 17C château. Functional, well-kept rooms, with dormer windows on the second floor. Family atmosphere. Fine traditional cuisine making good use of the vegetable garden.

VENSAT – **63 Puy-de-Dôme** – **326** G6 – **pop. 424** – **alt. 395 m** – ✉ **63260** 5 **B2**

Paris 370 – Clermont-Ferrand 40 – Cournon-d'Auvergne 42 – Vichy 26

Château de Lafont

2 r. de la Côte Rousse – ✆ 04 73 64 21 24 – info@chateaudelafont.com – Fax 04 73 64 50 83

4 rm – €40/105 €45/110 – ½ P €65 – **Table d'hôte** – Menu €25 bi

◆ This family-run estate includes a château, a working farm and pretty parkland. Comfortable and peaceful rooms within 15C walls. Breakfast and meals served in a wood-panelled dining room.

VENTABREN – **13 Bouches-du-Rhône** – **340** G4 – **pop. 4 552** – **alt. 210 m** – ✉ **13122** **Provence** 40 **B3**

Paris 746 – Aix-en-Provence 14 – Marseille 33 – Salon-de-Provence 27

Syndicat d'initiative, 11, boulevard de Provence ✆ 04 42 28 76 47, Fax 04 42 28 96 92

★ Château ruins.

La Table de Ventabren

r. F. Mistral – ✆ 04 42 28 79 33 – contact@latabledeventabren.com – Fax 04 42 28 83 15 – Closed 24 December-31 January, Wednesday dinner, Sunday from 1st October to 31 March, Sunday dinner in April and Monday

Rest – *(pre-book in high season and Sat - Sun)* Menu €27 (weekday lunch), €39/47 – Carte €37/57

◆ Restaurant in the heart of the picturesque perched village. Enjoy its friendly atmosphere in the pretty vaulted dining rooms or on the terrace overlooking the valley. Up-to-date cuisine.

VENTRON – 88 Vosges – **314** J5 – **pop. 979** – **alt. 630 m** – **Winter sports : 850/1 110 m** 8 – ✉ 88310 27 **C3**

Paris 441 – Épinal 56 – Gérardmer 25 – Mulhouse 51 – Remiremont 30 – Thann 31

Office de tourisme, 4, place de la Mairie ✆ 03 29 24 07 02, Fax 03 29 24 23 16

Grand Ventron ★★ Northeast: 7 km, Alsace-Lorraine-Champagne

in l'Ermitage-du-Frère-Joseph 5 km south by D 43 and D 43E- ✉ 88310 Ventron – Winter sports : 850/1 110 m 8

Les Buttes rm, VISA AE

– ✆ 03 29 24 18 09 – info@frerejo.com – Fax 03 29 24 21 96
– Closed 11 November-20 December
26 rm – €99/188 €99/188, € 14 – 1 suite – ½ P € 99/169
Rest – *(closed lunch except Sunday and public holidays)* Menu (€ 23), € 31
♦ This charming chalet-hotel, decorated with chic mountain decor and pictures of Épinal, has snug bedrooms (some with jacuzzis) and a cosy lounge. Light-wood panelling and southern tones create a warm setting; traditional menu.

in Travexin ***3 km west*** - ✉ **88310 Cornimont**

Le Géhan VISA AE

9 rte de Travexin – ✆ 03 29 24 10 71 – le.gehan@online.fr – Fax 03 29 24 10 70
– Closed 28 July-12 August
11 rm – €48 €48, € 8 – ½ P € 53 – **Rest** – *(closed Sunday dinner, Wednesday lunch and Monday)* Menu (€ 12), € 27/39 – Carte € 25/41
♦ Yellow and blue shades enliven the functional, well soundproofed bedrooms of this establishment, situated at a junction. Exemplary upkeep and attentive welcome. A bright renovated dining room; traditional fare and a few regional dishes.

VERBERIE – 60 Oise – **305** H5 – **pop. 3 283** – **alt. 33 m** – ✉ **60410** 36 **B3**

Paris 70 – Beauvais 56 – Clermont 31 – Compiègne 16 – Senlis 18 – Villers-Cotterêts 31

XX **Auberge de Normandie** with rm VISA AE

26 r. Pêcherie – ✆ 03 44 40 92 33 – christiane.maletras@wanadoo.fr
– Fax 03 44 40 50 62
3 rm – €52 €52, € 6,50 – ½ P € 55 – **Rest** – *(Closed Sunday dinner)*
Menu (€ 17), € 22/42 – Carte approx. € 35
♦ Country inn around a courtyard with exposed beams, woodwork and fireplace. Ask for a table near the garden.

VERDUN – 55 Meuse – **307** D4 – **pop. 19 624** – **alt. 198 m** – ✉ **55100**
Alsace-Lorraine 26 **A1**

Paris 263 – Metz 78 – Bar-le-Duc 56 – Châlons-en-Champagne 89 – Nancy 95

Office de tourisme, place de la Nation ✆ 03 29 86 14 18, Fax 03 29 84 22 42

High town★: Notre-Dame cathedral ★, BYZ Palais épiscopal★ (World Peace Centre) BZ - Underground citadel★: circuit★★ BZ - Battlefields★★★: Mémorial de Verdun, Fort et Ossuaire de Douaumont, Tranchée des Baïonnettes, le Mort-Homme, la Cote 304.

Plan on next page

Hostellerie du Coq Hardi rm, VISA AE

8 av. Victoire – ✆ 03 29 86 36 36 – coq.hardi@wanadoo.fr – Fax 03 29 86 09 21
33 rm – €74/120 €98/150, € 16 – 2 suites – ½ P € 100/130 CY **v**
Rest – *(closed mid February to mid March, Sunday dinner and Friday)*
Menu € 45/96 – Carte € 61/92
Rest ***Le Bistrot*** – *(Closed Sunday evening and Friday from October to April)*
Menu € 20 (weekdays)/35 bi – Carte € 28/53
♦ This traditional house (1827), on the banks of the Meuse, has a charming interior: lounge with fireplace, furniture from Lorraine and a few rooms with superb four-poster beds. Very stylish restaurant dining room offering classic cuisine and a good wine list. Simple, quick meals at the Bistrot. Summer terrace.

Montaulbain without rest — VISA MC

4 r. Vieille-Prison
– ✆ 03 29 86 00 47
– Fax 03 29 84 75 70 — BCY **e**

10 rm – 🚹€ 30/38 🚹🚹€ 35/40, ☕ € 5,50

◆ Hotel in a pedestrian street, with small renovated rooms that are extremely well kept. The reception hall is also the breakfast room. The cellar was used as the town jail in the 14C.

L'Atelier — VISA MC

33 r. des Gros-Degrés
– ✆ 03 29 84 45 29
– atelier_d@hotmail.fr
– Closed 24 August-2 September, Sunday dinner and Monday — BZ **d**

Rest – Menu (€ 10,50), € 13,50 (weekday lunch), € 29/45
– Carte € 26/38

◆ Brick coloured walls, polished wood tables and wrought iron bistro chairs set the scene at this pleasant restaurant. Up-to-the-minute seasonal menu.

VERDUN

Street	Grid	No.
Alsace-Lorraine (Av.)	CZ	2
Beaurepaire (R.)	CZ	3
Belle-Vierge (R. de la)	BY	4
Chevert (Pl.)	CZ	5
Douaumont (Av. de)	CY	6
Foch (Pl. Mar.)	CY	7
Fort de Vaux (R. du)	CZ	8
Frères-Boulhaut (R. des)	CY	9
Lattre-de-Tassigny (Av. Mar.-de)	CY	10
Mautroté (R.)	BY	13
Mazel (R.)	CY	14
Prés.-Poincaré (R.)	CZ	17
République (Quai de la)	CY	18
Rû (R. de)	BZ	19
St-Paul (R.)	CY	20
St-Pierre (R.)	BY	21
Soupirs (Allée des)	BY	24

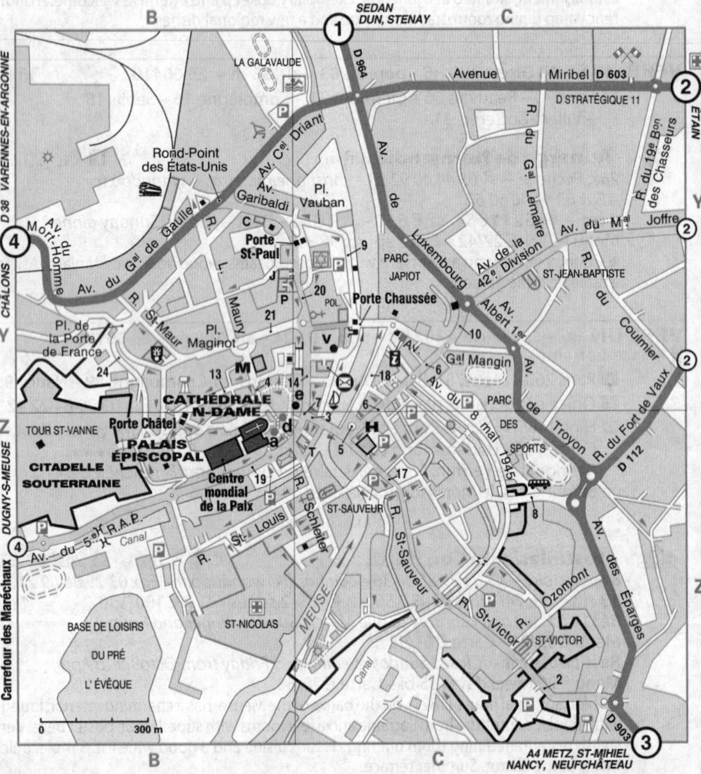

in Monthairons 13 km by ④ and D 34 – **pop. 388 – alt. 200 m** – ✉ **55320**

Hostellerie du Château des Monthairons
– ✆ *03 29 87 78 55*
– accueil@chateaudesmonthairons.fr – Fax 03 29 87 73 49
– Closed 1st January-10 February, Sunday and Monday from 15 November to 31 December and from 10 February to 31 March
23 rm – €75/160 €90/190, ☕ €15 – 2 suites – ½ P €120/195
Rest – *(closed Sunday dinner 15 November-31 December and 10 February-31 March, Monday except dinner from 1st August to 15 November and Tuesday lunch and public holidays)* Menu €37/85 – Carte €56/69
◆ Fine 19C château in parkland on the banks of the prettily meandering Meuse. Elegant rooms and suites, plus modern duplex accommodation, hammam, sauna, Jacuzzi and private beach. Contemporary cuisine served in the refined surroundings of an elegant interior or on the terrace.

in Charny-sur-Meuse 8 km North by D 38 – **pop. 466 – alt. 197 m** – ✉ **55100**

Syndicat d'initiative, 4, place de la Mairie ✆ 03 29 84 33 44, Fax 03 29 84 85 84

Les Charmilles without rest
12 r. de la Gare – ✆ 03 29 86 93 49 – valerie@les-charmilles.com
– Fax 03 29 84 65 30 – Closed January
3 rm ☕ – €45 €55
◆ Once a café, this early 20C building is now a hotel offering pretty rooms with both old and new features.

VERDUN-SUR-LE-DOUBS – 71 Saône-et-Loire – 320 K8 – pop. 1 199 – alt. 180 m – ✉ 71350 Burgundy-Jura — 7 B3

Paris 332 – Beaune 24 – Chalon-sur-Saône 24 – Dijon 65 – Dole 49 – Lons-le-Saunier 56

Office de tourisme, 3, place Charvot ✆ 03 85 91 87 52

Hostellerie Bourguignonne with rm
rte Ciel – ✆ 03 85 91 51 45
– hostelleriebourguignonne@hotmail.com – Fax 03 85 91 53 81
– Closed 27 October-2 November, 23 February-8 March, Sunday dinner off season, Tuesday except dinner May-September and Wednesday lunch
9 rm – €90 €90/120, ☕ €13 – ½ P €85/130 – **Rest** – Menu €22 (weekday lunch), €38/80 – Carte €58/82
◆ Charming and pleasant inn serving traditional local dishes, including the famous pôchouse, a house speciality. Superb Burgundy wine selection. Refined country decor in the large dining room. Fine terrace and individually furnished rooms.

VERGÈZE – 30 Gard – 339 K6 – pop. 3 643 – alt. 30 m – ✉ 30310 — 23 C2

Paris 724 – Montpellier 43 – Nîmes 20

Office de tourisme, 4, rue Basse ✆ 04 66 35 45 92, Fax 04 66 35 45 92

La Passiflore without rest
– ✆ 04 66 35 00 00 – hotel.lapassiflore@orange.fr – Fax 04 66 35 09 21
11 rm – €46/67 €46/67, ☕ €7,50
◆ Former 18C farmhouse with an attractive facade, offering small, simple rooms overlooking a pretty courtyard.

VERGONCEY – 50 Manche – 303 D8 – pop. 209 – alt. 70 m – ✉ 50240 — 32 A3

Paris 352 – Caen 120 – Saint-Lô 86 – Saint-Malo 60 – Fougères 37

Château de Boucéel without rest
4 km eastward along the D 108, D 40 and D 308 – ✆ 02 33 48 34 61
– chateaudebouceel@wanadoo.fr – Fax 02 33 48 16 26 – Closed January
5 rm ☕ – €140/165 €140/165
◆ Surrounded by landscaped gardens and pools, this family château dating from 1763 is adorned with period furniture, parquet floors and ancestral portraits. Guestrooms with individual touches.

LA VERNAREDE – 30 Gard – 339 J3 – pop. 389 – alt. 345 m – ✉ 30530 23 C1

Paris 708 – Montpellier 124 – Nîmes 74 – Alès 29 – Aubenas 79

Lou Cante Perdrix with rm rest, rest, VISA

Le Château – ✆ 04 66 61 50 30 – lou.cante.perdrix@wanadoo.fr – Fax 04 66 61 43 21 – Closed 2 January-15 February

12 rm – €52/58 €52/70, €9 – ½ P €52/55 – **Rest** – *(closed Sunday dinner, Monday and Tuesday except 16 June-20 September)* Menu €18 (weekday lunch), €28/55 – Carte €51/60

◆ Tucked away in a pine forest, this impressive stone house (1860) is home to a smart dining room (fireplace, plants, paintings) serving traditional fare.

VERNET-LES-BAINS – 66 Pyrénées-Orientales – 344 F7 – pop. 1 440 – alt. 650 m – Spa : mid March-late Nov. – Casino – ✉ 66820

Languedoc-Roussillon-Tarn Gorges 22 B3

Paris 904 – Mont-Louis 36 – Perpignan 57 – Prades 11

Office de tourisme, 2, rue de la chapelle ✆ 04 68 05 55 35, Fax 04 68 05 60 33

Site★ - Saint-Martin-du-Canigou abbey 2.5 km South★★.

Princess rest, rm, VISA

r. des Lavandières – ✆ 04 68 05 56 22 – contact@hotel-princess.fr – Fax 04 68 05 62 45 – Open 15 March-23 November

40 rm – €45/52 €54/94, €8 – ½ P €49/69 – **Rest** – Menu €17/33 – Carte €26/39

◆ At the foot of old Vernet. Most of the rooms have been renovated in a modern spirit; some enjoy a balcony with a view of the mountains, others overlook the village rooftops. Immense non-smoking dining room and terrace. Several menus including a regional one.

Mas Fleuri without rest VISA

bd Clemenceau – ✆ 04 68 05 51 94 – hotel.masfleuri@wanadoo.fr – Fax 04 68 05 50 77 – Open 15 April-15 October

30 rm – €69/110 €69/110, €11

◆ In this 1970s hotel, all the renovated rooms with balcony command a view of the parkland. Large swimming pool. Buffet breakfast in an adjoining house.

VERNEUIL-SUR-AVRE – 27 Eure – 304 F9 – pop. 6 619 – alt. 155 m – ✉ 27130

Normandy 33 C3

Paris 114 – Alençon 77 – Argentan 77 – Chartres 57 – Dreux 37 – Évreux 43

Syndicat d'initiative, 129, place de la Madeleine ✆ 02 32 32 17 17, Fax 02 32 32 17 17

de Center Parcs Center Parcs, by Mortagne road: 9 km, ✆ 02 32 60 50 02.

La Madeleine church ★ - Statues★ of Notre-Dame church.

Plan on next page

Hostellerie Le Clos rm, VISA

98 r. Ferté-Vidame – ✆ 02 32 32 21 81 – leclos@relaischateaux.com – Fax 02 32 32 21 36 – Closed 21-28 December and 4 January-6 February

4 rm – €180/225 €180/225, €21 – 6 suites – €225/295 n

– ½ P €190/210 – **Rest** – *(closed Tuesday lunch and Monday)* Menu €60/85 – Carte €54/78

◆ This red brick Norman château with a slate roof has a wealth of detail: waxed parquet floors and period furniture create a setting of great elegance. The dining rooms are as refined as those of fine ancestral homes. Charming terrace; good choice of Bordeaux wines.

Du Saumon VISA

89 pl. Madeleine – ✆ 02 32 32 02 36 – hotel.saumon@wanadoo.fr – Fax 02 32 37 55 80 – Closed 19 December-10 January and Sunday dinner from November to March a

29 rm – €48/58 €48/65, €7,50 – **Rest** – Menu €16/51 – Carte €31/49

◆ A late 18C post-house facing an inner courtyard. Rooms in the main building are larger and have antique furniture. Be it raw, smoked, marinated, fried, grilled or on a skewer; salmon (the name of the restaurant) takes pride of place here.

VERNEUIL-SUR-AVRE

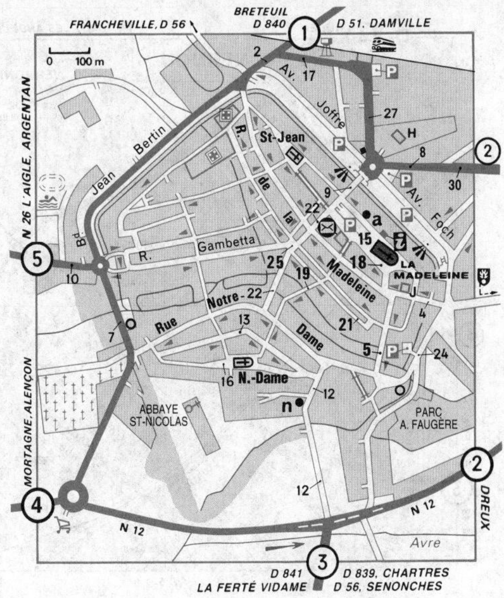

in Barils 7 km by ⑤, D 926 and D 166 – pop. 164 – alt. 201 m – ✉ 27130

Auberge des Barils

2 r. Verneuil – ✆ 02 32 60 05 88 – Fax 02 32 60 05 88 – Closed 8-14 September, 2-16 January, Tuesday from September to April and Wednesday

Rest – Menu € 19/57 – Carte € 28/59

◆ This charming house, opposite the village church, offers two low-key dining rooms and a terrace. Traditional, Norman-based cuisine.

VERNON – 27 Eure – 304 I7 – pop. 24 056 – alt. 32 m – ✉ 27200

Normandy 33 **D2**

Paris 77 – Beauvais 66 – Évreux 34 – Mantes-la-Jolie 25 – Rouen 62

Office de tourisme, 36, rue Carnot ✆ 02 32 51 39 60, Fax 02 32 51 86 55

Notre-Dame church ★ - Château of Bizy★ 2 km by ③ - Giverny★ 3 km.

Plan on next page

D'Évreux

11 pl. d'Évreux – ✆ 02 32 21 16 12 – contact@hoteldevreux.fr – Fax 02 32 21 32 73 BY **x**

12 rm – †€ 38/61 ††€ 38/61, ☕ € 6 – ½ P € 75/82

Rest – *(closed Sun)* Menu € 22/28 – Carte € 38/69

◆ A 17C half-timbered house was once the residence of the Count of Evreux and later a post-house. Rooms with rustic-style furniture and an old-world feel. Pleasant Norman dining room with exposed beams and an attractive fireplace.

Normandy

1 av. P.-Mendès-France – ✆ 02 32 51 97 97 – normandye.hotel@wanadoo.fr – Fax 02 32 21 01 66 BY **t**

50 rm – †€ 77 ††€ 77, ☕ € 10 – ½ P € 72 – **Rest** – *(closed Monday lunch and Sunday)* Menu (€ 17), € 25/31 – Carte € 20/40

◆ This hotel, located in the town centre, offers renovated rooms featuring functional furniture. Lounge and bar with a cosy atmosphere. The restaurant offers traditional cuisine to be savoured in a pleasant brasserie-pub-style setting.

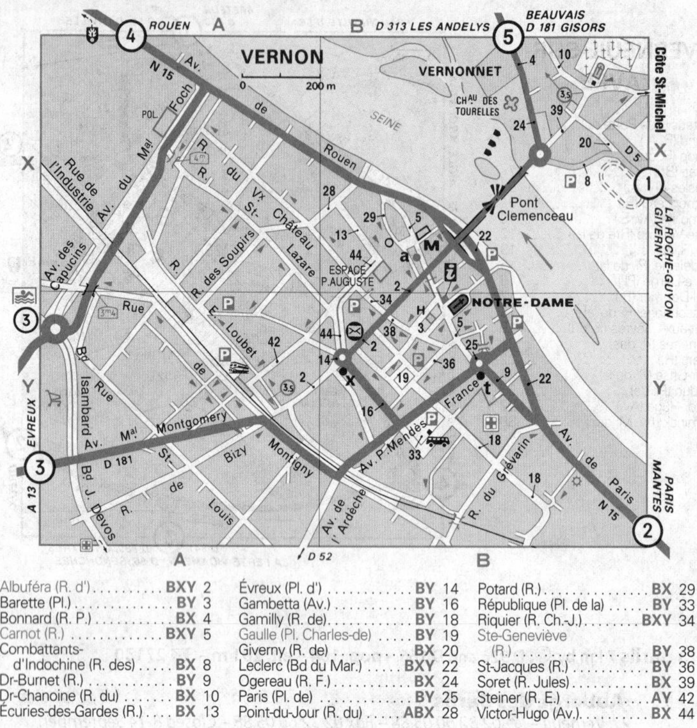

Albuféra (R. d') . . . . **BXY** 2
Barette (Pl.) . . . . **BY** 3
Bonnard (R. P.) . . . . **BX** 4
Carnot (R.) . . . . **BXY** 5
Combattants-d'Indochine (R. des) . . . . . **BX** 8
Dr-Burnet (R.) . . . . **BY** 9
Dr-Chanoine (R. du) . . . . **BX** 10
Écuries-des-Gardes (R.) . . . . **BX** 13
Évreux (Pl. d') . . . . **BY** 14
Gambetta (Av.) . . . . **BY** 16
Gamilly (R. de) . . . . **BY** 18
Gaulle (Pl. Charles-de) . . . . . **BY** 19
Giverny (R. de) . . . . **BX** 20
Leclerc (Bd du Mar.) . . . . . **BXY** 22
Ogereau (R. F.) . . . . **BX** 24
Paris (Pl. de) . . . . **BY** 25
Point-du-Jour (R. du) . . . . . . **ABX** 28
Potard (R.) . . . . **BX** 29
République (Pl. de la) . . . . . . **BY** 33
Riquier (R. Ch.-J.) . . . . **BXY** 34
Ste-Geneviève (R.) . . . . **BY** 38
St-Jacques (R.) . . . . **BY** 36
Soret (R. Jules) . . . . **BX** 39
Steiner (R. E.) . . . . **AY** 42
Victor-Hugo (Av.) . . . . **BX** 44

Les Fleurs
VISA MC AE

71 r. Carnot – ✆ 02 32 51 16 80
– lesfleurs@tele2.fr – Fax 02 32 21 30 51
– Closed Sunday dinner from September to April and Monday BX **a**
Rest – *(number of covers limited, pre-book)* Menu (€ 20 bi), € 26/53
– Carte € 38/71
◆ A venerable old house with a fine half-timbered rear part, in a narrow street of the town centre. Pleasant modern dining room with a relaxed atmosphere. Traditional menu.

Le Bistro
VISA MC

73 r. Carnot – ✆ 02 32 21 29 19 – Fax 02 32 21 29 19
– Closed 1st-25 August, Sunday and Monday BX **a**
Rest – Menu € 17 bi – Carte € 21/34
◆ This former bar has retained its counter for serving customers who are in a hurry. Decor of old posters. Traditional dishes of the day chalked up on the blackboard.

in Douains 8 km by ③, D 181 and D 75 – pop. 465 – alt. 128 m – ✉ 27120

Château de Brécourt
rest, P VISA MC AE

– ✆ 02 32 52 40 50
– brecourt@leshotelsparticuliers.com – Fax 02 32 52 69 65
26 rm – †€ 105/220 ††€ 105/220, ☕ € 15 – 4 suites – ½ P € 109/166
Rest – Menu € 32 (weekday lunch), € 48/78 – Carte € 45/77
◆ 17C château in the heart of the Norman countryside, surrounded by moats and a vast park. Grand Siècle decor with beams, antique floor tiles and fireplaces. Individually furnishes rooms. A bar housed in the converted guard house and a restaurant with a noble atmosphere.

VERNOUILLET – 28 Eure-et-Loir – **311** E3 – see Dreux

VERQUIÈRES – 13 Bouches-du-Rhône – **340** E2 – see St-Rémy-de-Provence

VERRIÈRES – 86 Vienne – **322** J6 – pop. 799 – alt. 115 m – ✉ 86410 39 **C2**

Paris 368 – Poitiers 31 – Châtellerault 68 – Buxerolles 33 – Chauvigny 26

Les Deux Porches without rest VISA MC AE

pl. de la Mairie – ✆ 05 49 42 83 85 – hddp@wanadoo.fr – Fax 05 49 42 83 79

16 rm – †€ 43 ††€ 45, ☕ € 9

◆ The central location and functional bedrooms decorated in a modern style make this hotel a popular and practical choice. Friendly welcome and limited dining facilities.

VERSAILLES – 78 Yvelines – **311** I3 – **101** 23 – see Paris, Area

VERT-EN-DROUAIS – 28 Eure-et-Loir – **311** D3 – see Dreux

Red = Pleasant. Look for the red ✗ and 🏠 symbols.

VERTEUIL-SUR-CHARENTE – 16 Charente – **324** L4 – pop. 718 – alt. 100 m – ✉ 16510 Poitou Charentes Vendée 39 **C2**

Paris 414 – Poitiers 78 – Angoulême 42 – Soyaux 44 – Ruelle-sur-Touvre 41

Le Couvent des Cordeliers VISA MC

– ✆ 05 45 31 01 19 – barbou@lecouventdescordeliers.com – Closed January

6 rm ☕ – †€ 85 ††€ 95 – **Table d'hôte** – Menu € 28 bi

◆ An establishment of character located in a 16C convent with a past rich in history. Sophisticated inviting rooms. Exhibitions and concerts in the former chapel. The lady of the house introduces guests to the region of Charentes at her table d'hôte.

VERTOU – 44 Loire-Atlantique – **316** H4 – see Nantes

VERTUS – 51 Marne – **306** G9 – pop. 2 513 – alt. 85 m – ✉ 51130
Northern France and the Paris Region 13 **B2**

Paris 139 – Châlons-en-Champagne 30 – Épernay 21 – Montmirail 39 – Reims 48

in Bergères-les-Vertus 3.5 km south by D 9 – pop. 540 – alt. 108 m – ✉ 51130

Hostellerie du Mont-Aimé VISA MC AE

4-6 r. Vertus – ✆ 03 26 52 21 31 – mont.aime@wanadoo.fr – Fax 03 26 52 21 39 – Closed 24 December-1st January and Sunday dinner

46 rm – †€ 65/90 ††€ 80/130, ☕ € 12 – ½ P € 90 – **Rest** – Menu € 25 (weekdays)/75 – Carte € 59/92

◆ Near Mont Aimé, a former village café that is now a comfortable hotel with modern decor. Renovated rooms; many open onto the garden. Take a seat in this comfortable dining room to sample its traditional cuisine and fine wine list.

LES VERTUS – 76 Seine-Maritime – **304** G2 – see Dieppe

VERVINS – 02 Aisne – **306** F3 – pop. 2 653 – alt. 147 m – ✉ 02140
Northern France and the Paris Region 37 **D2**

Paris 187 – Charleville-Mézières 70 – Laon 36 – Reims 89 – St-Quentin 52 – Valenciennes 76

Office de tourisme, place de l'Hôtel de ville ✆ 03 23 98 11 98, Fax 03 23 98 02 47

Tour du Roy & rm, AC, P, VISA, MC, AE
45 r. Gén. Leclerc – ✆ 03 23 98 00 11 – latourduroy@wanadoo.fr – Fax 03 23 98 00 72 – Closed 5-25 January, Tuesday lunch and Monday
22 rm – †€ 75 ††€ 110, ☕ € 15 – ½ P € 105/175 – **Rest** – Menu € 40/70 – Carte € 65/70
◆ This aristocratic manor with a prestigious past, flanked with three towers, overlooks the town. The elegant individually furnished rooms bear evocative names. "Divine" duplexes. Anne of Brittany, Henry IV, Charles de Gaulle and François Mitterrand have all dined at the restaurant.

VERZY – 51 Marne – 306 G8 – pop. 1 058 – alt. 210 m – ✉ 51380
Northern France and the Paris Region 13 **B2**

Paris 163 – Châlons-en-Champagne 32 – Épernay 23 – Reims 22 – Rethel 52 – Vouziers 56

Syndicat d'initiative, place de l'Hôtel de Ville ✆ 03 26 97 93 65, Fax 03 26 97 95 74

Faux de Verzy★ South: 2 km.

XX **Au Chant des Galipes** VISA, MC
2 r. Chanzy – ✆ 03 26 97 91 40 – chantdesgalipes@wanadoo.fr – Fax 03 26 97 91 44 – Closed 17 August-3 September, 21 December-21 January, Monday dinner from October to April, Sunday dinner, Tuesday dinner and Wednesday
Rest – Menu € 19 (weekday lunch)/38 – Carte € 39/53
◆ Located in the centre of a wine-growing town, not far from the forest of twisted beech trees, this establishment boasts modern dining rooms, a private lounge and a small courtyard terrace serving up-to-date cuisine,.

VESCOUS – 06 Alpes-Maritimes – 341 D4 – see Gilette

LE VÉSINET – 78 Yvelines – 311 I2 – 101 13 – see Paris, Area

VESOUL P – 70 Haute-Saône – 314 E7 – pop. 17 168 – alt. 221 m – ✉ 70000
Burgundy-Jura 16 **B1**

Paris 360 – Belfort 68 – Besançon 47 – Épinal 91 – Langres 76 – Vittel 86

Office de tourisme, 2,rue Gevrey ✆ 03 84 97 10 85, Fax 03 84 97 10 84

Plan on next page

Du Lion without rest P, VISA, MC, AE
4 pl. de la République – ✆ 03 84 76 54 44 – hoteldulion@wanadoo.fr – Fax 03 84 75 23 31 – Closed 3-17 August and 26 December-4 January a
18 rm – †€ 46 ††€ 46/52, ☕ € 6,50
◆ Rooms with simple modern decor near the shopping streets of this town after which a song by Jacques Brel was named. In summer, breakfast is served on the terrace.

X **Le Caveau du Grand Puits** VISA, MC, AE
r. Mailly – ✆ 03 84 76 66 12 – Fax 03 84 76 66 12 – Closed 5-15 May, 11 August-4 September, 23 December-3 January, Wednesday dinner, Saturday lunch, Sunday and public holidays u
Rest – Menu € 17/37 – Carte € 25/58
◆ In a small street in the old town, vaulted cellar with stone walls and a second dining room with mezzanine. Inner courtyard where meals are served on fine days.

in Épenoux 5 km by ①, St-Loup-sur-Semouse road and D10 – 479 h. alt. 240 – ✉ 70000 Pusy-et-Épenoux

Château d'Épenoux rm, P, VISA, MC
5 r. Ruffier d'Épenoux – ✆ 03 84 75 19 60 – chateau.epenoux@orange.fr – Fax 03 84 76 45 05
5 rm ☕ – †€ 85 ††€ 100 – **Table d'hôte** – Menu € 24
◆ A small 18C château hidden inside its park, planted with hundred-year-old trees. Antique furniture and chandeliers give a personal touch to the spacious rooms. Large, low-key lounge. Enjoy your meals in an elegant yellow dining room. Refined cuisine.

VESOUL

Aigle-Noir (R. de l') 2
Alsace-Lorraine (R. d') 3
Annonciades (R. des) 4
Bains (R. des) 6
Banque (R. de la) 7
Châtelet (R. du) 8
Faure (R. Edgar) 10
Fleurier (R. de) 12
Gare (Av. de la) 13
Gaulle (Bd Ch.-de) 14
Genoux (R. Georges) 15
Gevrey (R.) 16
Girardot (R. du Cdt) 20
Grandes-Faulx (R. des) 22
Grand-Puits (Pl. du) 21
Ilottes (R. des) 23
Kennedy (Bd) 24
Leblond (R.) 25
Maginot (R. A.) 26
Moilly (R. de) 36
Morel (R. Paul) 27
Moulin-des-Prés (Pl. du) 28
République (Pl. de la) 29
St-Georges (R.) 30
Salengro (R. Roger) 31
Tanneurs (R. des) 32
Vendémiaire (R.) 33
Verlaine (R.) 35

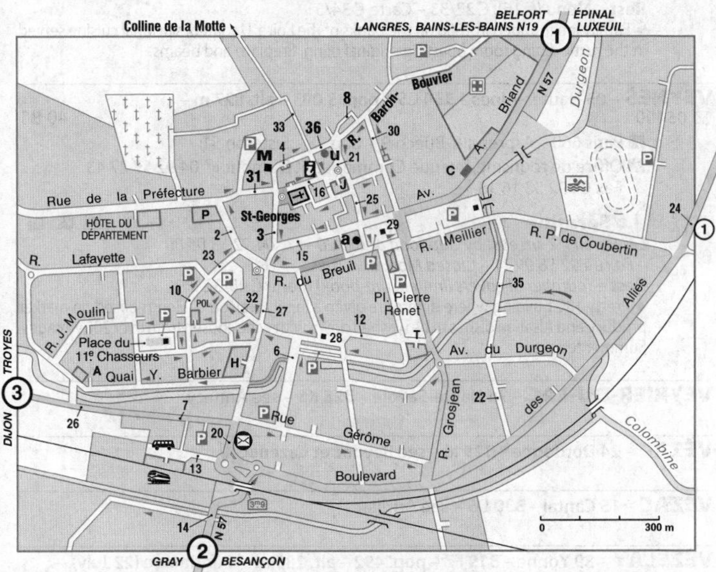

VEUIL – 36 Indre – 323 F4 – see Valençay

VEULES-LES-ROSES – 76 Seine-Maritime – 304 E2 – pop. 676 – alt. 15 m – ✉ 76980 Normandy 33 C1

Paris 188 – Dieppe 27 – Fontaine-le-Dun 8 – Rouen 57 – St-Valery-en-Caux 8
Office de tourisme, 27, rue Victor-Hugo ✆ 02 35 97 63 05, Fax 02 35 57 24 51

XXX **Les Galets** VISA MC
at the beach – ✆ 02 35 97 61 33 – plaisance-les-galets@wanadoo.fr – Fax 02 35 57 06 23 – Closed 1st January-8 February, Tuesday and Wednesday
Rest – Menu € 36/76 – Carte € 47/69
◆ Brick house close to a shingle beach typical of the Alabaster Coast. Comfortable dining rooms-veranda, nice table settings and modern cuisine.

LE VEURDRE – 03 Allier – 326 F2 – pop. 578 – alt. 190 m – ✉ 03320 Auvergne

Paris 272 – Bourges 66 – Montluçon 73 – Moulins 36 – Nevers 34 – St-Amand-Montrond 48 5 B1

Le Pont Neuf rm, P VISA MC AE
– ✆ 04 70 66 40 12 – hotel.le.pontneuf@wanadoo.fr – Fax 04 70 66 44 15 – Closed mid November-mid February and Sunday dinner 15 October-31 March
46 rm – †€ 45/50 ††€ 55/105, ☕ € 9 – ½ P € 52/85
Rest – Menu € 18 (weekdays)/40 – Carte € 24/57
◆ Modernised traditional hotel, appreciated for its sports installations. The rooms at the back face the peaceful park; the more recent ones are in the annexe. Country-style restaurant where seasonal suggestions enhance the à la carte menu and traditional set menus.

VEUVES – 41 Loir-et-Cher – 318 D7 – pop. 216 – alt. 62 m – ✉ 41150 11 A1

Paris 205 – Bourges 135 – Orléans 84 – Poitiers 137 – Tours 38

X **L'Auberge de la Croix Blanche**

2 av. de la Loire – ✆ 02 54 70 23 80 – jean.claude.sichi@orange.fr – Fax 02 54 70 21 47 – Closed February school holidays, Wednesday lunch Easter-October, Wednesday dinner November-Easter, Tuesday dinner 15 January-Easter, Monday except dinner July-August and Sunday dinner

Rest – Menu (€ 16), € 22/33 – Carte € 34/51

◆ Family inn founded in 1888 on the banks of the Loire. Updated, seasonal cuisine served in the rustic dining room boasting original tiling, fireplace and beams.

VEYNES – 05 Hautes-Alpes – 334 C5 – pop. 3 093 – alt. 827 m – ✉ 05400 40 B1

Paris 660 – Aspres-sur-Buëch 9 – Gap 25 – Sisteron 51

Office de tourisme, avenue Commandant Dumont ✆ 04 92 57 27 43, Fax 04 92 58 16 18

XX **La Sérafine**

Les Paroirs, 2 km east by Gap road and D 20 – ✆ 04 92 58 06 00 – Fax 04 92 58 09 11 – Closed Mon. and Tues.

Rest – *(number of covers limited, pre-book)* Menu € 25/32

◆ Pretty 18C building where diners are given a family welcome. Menus based on market produce and Alsatian dishes to be washed down with wine chosen from over 200 vintages. Summer terrace.

VEYRIER-DU-LAC – 74 Haute-Savoie – 328 K5 – see Annecy

VÉZAC – 24 Dordogne – 329 I6 – see Beynac et Cazenac

VÉZAC – 15 Cantal – 330 D5 – see Aurillac

VÉZELAY – 89 Yonne – 319 F7 – pop. 492 – alt. 285 m – Pilgrimage (22 July). – ✉ 89450 Burgundy-Jura 7 B2

Paris 221 – Auxerre 52 – Avallon 16 – Château-Chinon 58 – Clamecy 23

Office de tourisme, 12, rue Saint-Etienne ✆ 03 86 33 23 69, Fax 03 86 33 34 00

Ste-Madeleine basilica ★★★: tympanum of the central portal★★★, capitals★★★.

Poste et Lion d'Or

– ✆ 03 86 33 21 23 – lion.dor.vezelay@wanadoo.fr – Fax 03 86 32 30 92 – Closed January and February

38 rm – †€ 65/83 ††€ 69/104, ☕ € 11 – ½ P € 63/80

Rest – *(closed Monday October-May, Tuesday November-March, Tuesday lunch April-May and October)* Menu € 18 (weekday lunch), € 24/37 – Carte € 33/52

◆ This smart former coaching inn has been welcoming guests for over 200 years! Comfortable classic-style rooms. Those overlooking the countryside are very popular. Restaurant offering a new take on local country dishes. Local produce on sale in the shop.

Compostelle without rest

– ✆ 03 86 33 28 63 – le.compostelle@wanadoo.fr – Fax 03 86 33 34 34 – Closed 1st-27 December and 3 January-15 February

18 rm – †€ 49/61 ††€ 49/61, ☕ € 9

◆ A small family hotel with functional rooms, some of which at ground level or with a balcony, overlooking the valley. Panoramic breakfast room.

XX **Le St-Étienne**

39 r. St-Étienne – ✆ 03 86 33 27 34 – lesaintetienne@aol.com – Fax 03 86 33 34 79 – Closed mid January-end February, Wednesday and Thursday

Rest – Menu (€ 18), € 27/57 – Carte € 40/91

◆ This 18C building lines the main street leading to the basilica. Cosy rustic interior with lovely painted beams; up-to-date cuisine.

Le Bougainville VISA MC

28 r. St-Etienne – ✆ 03 86 33 27 57 – Fax 03 86 33 35 12 – Closed mid November-mid February, Tuesday and Wednesday
Rest – Menu € 20/27 – Carte € 24/35

◆ A family restaurant with retro character in an old house on the road to the Basilica. Local cuisine washed down with regional wines.

in St-Père **3 km southeast by D 957 – pop. 385 – alt. 148 m – ✉ 89450**

N.-Dame church ★.

L'Espérance (Marc Meneau) rest, P VISA MC AE

– ✆ 03 86 33 39 10 – marc.meneau@wanadoo.fr – Fax 03 86 33 26 15 – Closed 15 January-1st March, Monday lunch, Wednesday lunch and Tuesday except public holidays
20 rm – €100/150 €250/300, ☕ €30 – 7 suites
Rest – *(pre-book)* Menu € 90 bi (weekday lunch), € 160/200 – Carte € 136/181
Spec. Galets de pomme de terre, caviar, sardine, navet. Turbot cuit en pâte de sel au beurre de homard. Le dessert de Marie-Antoinette. **Wines** Bourgogne-Vézelay, Chablis.

◆ Guests have a choice of rooms: elegant in the handsome manor house, modern and deluxe at the Pré des Marguerites and rustic at the Moulin. Glass-roofed restaurant which looks out onto a delightful garden. Creative, classical cuisine and a superb selection of burgundies.

Renommée without rest P VISA MC

19 et 20 rte de Vézelay – ✆ 03 86 33 21 34 – la.renommee89@wanadoo.fr – Fax 03 86 33 34 17 – Open 1st March-15 December and closed Sunday dinner except from May to August
18 rm – €34 €49/62, ☕ €7

◆ This hotel in the village centre is also a bar, tobacconist and newsagents. Ask for one of the rooms in the wing opposite, they are more recent and comfortable.

in Fontette **5 km east by D 957 – ✉ 89450 Vézelay – ✉ 89450**

Crispol hill of Vézelay, rm, P VISA MC

rte d'Avallon – ✆ 03 86 33 26 25 – crispol@wanadoo.fr – Fax 03 86 33 33 10 – Closed January, February and Monday from November to April
12 rm – €74 €74, ☕ €9 – ½ P €74 – **Rest** – *(closed Tuesday lunch and Monday)* Menu € 23/54 – Carte € 32/49

◆ Stone house on the doorstep of the village, with the hill in the background. The wing is home to spacious rooms decorated with works by the artist/owner. Bright dining room whose bay windows command a fine view of the basilica.

in Pierre-Perthuis **6 km southeast by D 957 and D 958 – pop. 104 – alt. 220 m – ✉ 89450**

Les Deux Ponts rm, P VISA MC

– ✆ 03 86 32 31 31 – lesdeuxponts@gmail.com – Fax 03 86 32 35 80 – Open March-November and closed Wednesday except from June to September and Tuesday
7 rm – €50 €55, ☕ €7 – ½ P €57 – **Rest** – *(number of covers limited, pre-book)* Menu € 23 – Carte € 31/47

◆ A welcoming, flower-decked house on a country lane. Simple rooms (no television) with good bedding and well-equipped bathrooms. An original dining room with a refined setting, brightened up by amusing Dutch glass lights.

VIA – 66 Pyrénées-Orientales – 344 D8 – see Font-Romeu

GARABIT VIADUCT ★★ – 15 Cantal – 330 H5 – ✉ 15100 Auvergne 5 **B3**

Paris 520 – Aurillac 84 – Mende 74 – Le Puy-en-Velay 90 – St-Flour 14

Maison du paysan (Farmer's House)★ à Loubaresse South: 7 km - Belvédère de Mallet ≤★★ Southwest: 13 km then 10 mn.

Beau Site

≤ viaduct and lake, rest,

N 9 – ✆ 04 71 23 41 46 – info@beau-site-hotel.com – Fax 04 71 23 46 34 – Open 3 April-3 November

VISA AE

17 rm – †€ 34/53 ††€ 48/63, ☕ € 10 – 3 suites – ½ P € 51/64

Rest – Menu (€ 13,50), € 19/40 – Carte € 26/46

◆ Viaduct, lake or garden view? A difficult choice among the fresh, neat rooms (most of which have a flat-screen TV)! Tennis court, swimming pool and children's play area. The restaurant affords a view of Gustave Eiffel's famous viaduct, attractively illuminated at night.

Anglards-de-St-Flour 3 km north – pop. 283 – alt. 840 m – ✉ 15100

La Méridienne

VISA

– ✆ 04 71 23 40 53 – info@hoteldelameridienne.com – Fax 04 71 23 91 05 – Closed 15 December-1st February

16 rm – †€ 41/55 ††€ 41/55, ☕ € 7,50 – ½ P € 48 – **Rest** – Menu € 15/49 – Carte € 28/67

◆ Guests receive a warm welcome to this new establishment. Practical, unpretentious but very well-kept rooms; some overlook the large garden (children's play area). The menu features regional dishes; seafood platters and zarzuela by request.

VIBRAC – 16 Charente – 324 J6 – see Jarnac

VIC-EN-BIGORRE – 65 Hautes-Pyrénées – 342 M4 – pop. 4 788 – alt. 216 m – ✉ 65500 28 **A2**

Paris 775 – Pau 47 – Aire sur l'Adour 53 – Auch 62 – Mirande 37 – Tarbes 19

Le Tivoli

rest, VISA AE

pl. Gambetta – ✆ 05 62 96 70 39 – hotel.tivoli@wanadoo.fr – Fax 05 62 96 29 74

24 rm – †€ 43/50 ††€ 46/52, ☕ € 10 – ½ P € 40/47 – **Rest** – *(closed Sunday dinner and Monday lunch)* Menu € 12,50/36 – Carte € 19/48

◆ A practical hotel for an overnight stay in the Adour area, located on the main square in Vic. It has simple, well-kept rooms, most of which have been renovated. Two dining rooms, including an Eiffel-style veranda. In fine weather, tables are laid in a courtyard planted with trees. Traditional cuisine.

VICHY – 03 Allier – 326 H6 – pop. 26 528 – alt. 340 m – Spa : 1er March-late Nov. – Casinos : Le Grand Café BZ, Elysée Palace – ✉ 03200 Auvergne 6 **C1**

Paris 353 – Clermont-Ferrand 55 – Montluçon 99 – Moulins 57 – Roanne 74

Office de tourisme, 19, rue du Parc ✆ 04 70 98 71 94, Fax 04 70 31 06 00

du Sporting Club de Vichy Bellerive-sur-Allier Allée Georges Baugnies, ✆ 04 70 32 39 11 ;

la Forêt de Montpensier Bellerive-sur-Allier Domaine du château de Rilhat, by Clermont-Ferrand road: 8 km, ✆ 04 70 56 58 39.

Parc des Sources★ - Allier parks ★ - Chalets★ (boulevard des États-Unis) BYZ - The thermal district★ - Grand casino-theatre★.

Plan on next page

Sofitel Les Célestins

rest,

111 bd États-Unis – ✆ 04 70 30 82 00 – h3241@accor.com – Fax 04 70 30 82 01 – Closed December

VISA AE

BY **e**

131 rm – †€ 180/240 ††€ 220/280, ☕ € 20 – 5 suites

Rest *N 3* – Menu € 42/140 bi – Carte € 48/84

Rest *Le Bistrot des Célestins* – *(closed Sunday dinner except public holidays)* Menu € 26 – Carte € 26/40

◆ This modern hotel is next to the famous chalets where Napoleon III stayed. Modern rooms. Fitness centre and superb panoramic swimming pool. Inventive cuisine, contemporary decor and handsome summer terrace. At Le Bistrot enjoy traditional fare and grilled meats.

BELLERIVE-SUR-ALLIER

VICHY

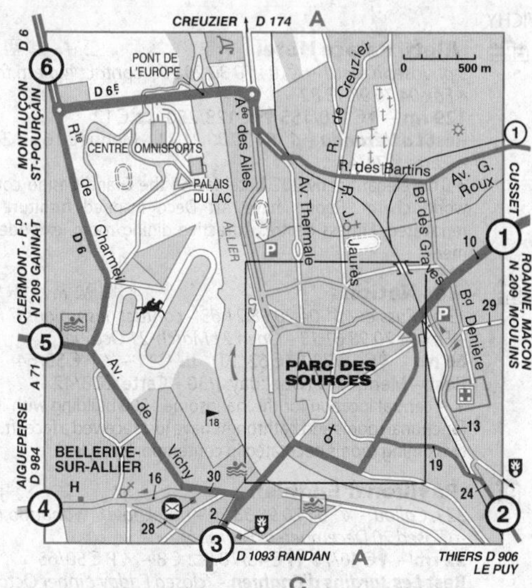

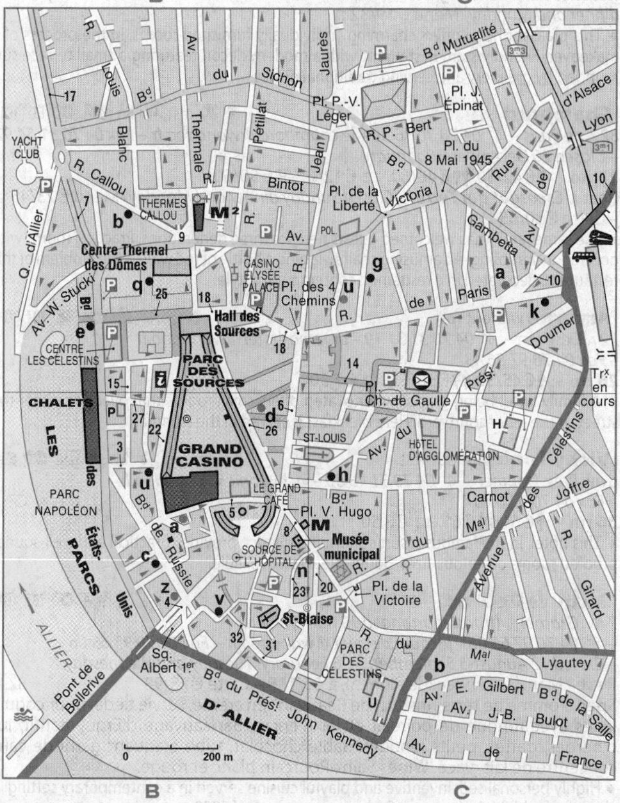

Aletti Palace Hôtel

3 pl. Joseph Aletti – 04 70 30 20 20 – contact@aletti.fr – Fax 04 70 98 13 82 BZ **u**

129 rm – €110/155 €128/250, €12

Rest *La Véranda* – *04 70 30 21 21* – Menu (€16), €21 (weekdays)/55 – Carte €24/41

◆ This elegant early 20C hotel facing the Grand Casino combines modernity and old-world charm. Rooms have Art Deco inspired furniture and are gradually being renovated. Fitness centre. Attractive dining room, extended by a veranda; traditional menu.

Les Nations

rest, rest,

13 bd Russie – 04 70 98 21 63 – contact_lesnations@lesnations.com – Fax 04 70 98 61 13 – Open 21 March-21 October BZ **c**

66 rm – €55/73 €62/101, €11 – ½ P €55/64

Rest – Menu €19 (weekdays)/30 – Carte €28/42

◆ A central location for this handsome 1900 building with its finely worked façade. The functional rooms and bathrooms have just received a facelift. Traditional cuisine served in two dining rooms decorated in contemporary style.

Pavillon d'Enghien

32 r. Callou – 04 70 98 33 30 – hotel.pavi@wanadoo.fr – Fax 04 70 31 67 82 – Closed 20 December-1st February BY **b**

22 rm – €46/78 €46/78, €8 – ½ P €50/65

Rest *Les Jardins d'Enghien* – *(closed Friday dinner October-March, Sunday dinner and Monday)* Menu €19/32

◆ This pleasant hotel offers charming, individually furnished rooms, in the process of a makeover. Friendly staff. Restaurant with a modern décor, featuring a small terrace surrounded by greenery and serving traditional dishes.

Chambord

rest,

82 r. de Paris – 04 70 30 16 30 – le.chambord@wanadoo.fr – Fax 04 70 31 54 92 – Closed 20 December-30 January CY **k**

27 rm – €42/50 €48/60, €12 – ½ P €50/60

Rest *L'Escargot qui Tette* – *(Closed Sunday dinner and Monday)* Menu €23/45 – Carte €30/55

◆ The same family has welcomed guests here for three generations. Practical rooms with good soundproofing. An amusing snail swigging a bottle of red wine is the emblem of this restaurant, decorated in a restrained contemporary style.

Arverna without rest

12 r. Desbrest – 04 70 31 31 19 – arverna-hotel@wanadoo.fr – Fax 04 70 97 86 43 CY **g**

26 rm – €45/50 €50/65, €7,50

◆ A family hotel being gradually renovated offers small rooms that overlook either the street or the inner courtyard. Here breakfast is served in the summer.

Vichy Tonic without rest

6 av. Prés. Doumer – 04 70 31 45 00 – vichy.tonic@wanadoo.fr – Fax 04 70 97 67 37 CZ **h**

36 rm – €61 €61, €8,50

◆ This hotel, in the famous resort's shopping district, provides practical and well-soundproofed rooms of various sizes. Buffet-breakfast available.

Jacques Decoret

7 av. Gramont, (transfer arranged 10 Rue Prunelle) – 04 70 97 65 06 – jacques.decoret@wanadoo.fr – Fax 04 70 97 65 06 – Closed 12 August-5 September, 5-26 February, Tuesday and Wednesday

Rest – Menu €45 (weekday lunch), €65/115 – Carte €78/98 BZ **b**

Spec. Pomme de terre "institut de Beauvais" en crème, servie tiède, pour coquillages avec fondue de poireau et jet d'encre. Bar sauvage d'Erquy confit, jus d'herbes, dattes, petits fenouils. Sablé chocolat, tube craquant garni de café, concentré de lait glacé. **Wines** Saint-Pourçain blanc et rouge.

◆ Highly personalised, inventive and playful cuisine served in a contemporary setting. A change of address is on the cards during the course of 2008.

L'Alambic

8 r. N.-Larbaud – ✆ 04 70 59 12 71 – alambic.vichy@orange.fr – Fax 04 70 97 98 88 – Closed 10 August-3 September, 8 February-25 March, Sunday dinner, Monday and Tuesday CY **u**

Rest – *(number of covers limited, pre-book)* Menu € 26/45

◆ A modern menu, attentive service, and an intimate ambience await in this tiny restaurant near the shops. Simply decorated in grey and green.

La Table d'Antoine

8 r. Burnol – ✆ 04 70 98 99 71 – Fax 04 70 98 99 71 – Closed 24-29 June, 2-7 November, 3-23 February, Thursday dinner November-March, Sunday dinner and Monday except public holidays

Rest – Menu € 22 (weekday lunch), € 28/59 – Carte € 44/74 BZ **d**

◆ Up-to-date cuisine served amid a refreshingly modernised, Baltard-inspired decor of glass and cast iron. Fine Auvergne cheese platter. Terrace on a pedestrian street.

L'Aromate

9 r. Besse – ✆ 04 70 32 13 22 – Fax 04 70 32 13 22 – Closed 20 July-12 August, 2-15 January, Sunday dinner, Tuesday dinner and Wednesday CZ **n**

Rest – *(pre-book)* Menu (€ 15), € 20/42 – Carte € 34/39

◆ A high-ceilinged dining room with Napoleon III mirrors and paintings, in the street where Albert Londres was born. Herbs and spices add personal touches to the cuisine.

L'Envolée

44 av. E. Gilbert – ✆ 04 70 32 85 15 – lenvolee@dbmail.com – Fax 04 70 32 85 15 – Closed 15 July-6 August, 18 February-5 March, Tuesday and Wednesday

Rest – Menu € 19 (weekday lunch), € 25/40 – Carte € 34/45 CZ **b**

◆ In a quiet street, behind a glass facade, this bright modern restaurant decorated with paintings serves fine traditional fare.

Brasserie du Casino

4 r. du Casino – ✆ 04 70 98 23 06 – bdcvichy@wanadoo.fr – Fax 04 70 98 53 17 – Closed 20 October-19 November, 22 February-5 March, Tuesday and Wednesday BZ **a**

Rest – Menu (€ 16), € 26 – Carte € 33/47

◆ Authentic 1920s setting for this brasserie, its walls adorned with photos of singers who performed at the nearby opera. Pavement terrace.

L'Hippocampe

3 bd de Russie – ✆ 04 70 97 68 37 – Fax 04 70 97 68 37 – Closed 2-23 June, 17 November-8 December, Tuesday lunch, Sunday dinner and Monday BZ **z**

Rest – Menu (€ 17 bi), € 26/55 – Carte € 29/48

◆ Sumptuous and unusual villas all along this boulevard. Simple setting and kitchens visible from the dining room. Seafood has pride of place on the menu.

in Abrest 4 km by ② – pop. 2 428 – alt. 290 m – ✉ 03200

La Colombière with rm

< Allier valley, rest,

136 av. de Thiers, on D 906 – ✆ 04 70 98 69 15 – lacolombiere@wanadoo.fr – Fax 04 70 31 50 89 – Closed 1st-15 October, mid January-mid February, Sunday dinner and Monday

4 rm – †€ 39/42 ††€ 56/65, ☕ € 8,50 – ½ P € 58

Rest – Menu € 20 (weekdays)/46 – Carte € 37/46

◆ Charming 1950s hillside villa, with a dovecote and a terraced garden that extends down to the Allier. Stunning panoramic view of the valley; traditional fare. Personalised, impeccably looked after rooms; friendly welcome.

in St-Yorre 8 km by ② – pop. 2 840 – alt. 275 m – ✉ 03270

L'Auberge Bourbonnaise

rm,

2 av. Vichy – ✆ 04 70 59 41 79 – aubergebourbonnaise@wanadoo.fr – Fax 04 70 59 24 94 – Closed 1st February-17 March, Saturday lunch, Sunday dinner and Monday except July-August

21 rm – †€ 52 ††€ 52, ☕ € 9 – ½ P € 50/54 – **Rest** – Menu (€ 10), € 17 (weekdays)/45 – Carte € 25/46

◆ Despite their nearness to the road the rooms are quiet owing to the good soundproofing. The annexe offers spacious duplexes with a refreshing tasteful decor. Rustic dining room-veranda and terrace; good choice of traditional set menus.

XX **Piquenchagne**
Les Jarraux, south: 2 km via rte Thiers
– ✆ 04 70 59 23 77 – Fax 04 70 59 23 77
– Closed 23 June-4 July, 5-16 January and Monday
Rest – Menu € 20/42 – Carte € 29/50
◆ This restored old farmhouse has two simple, welcoming dining rooms. A terrace faces the English-style garden. Reasonably priced regional dishes.

VIC-LE-COMTE – 63 Puy-de-Dôme – 326 G9 – pop. 4 404 – alt. 472 m – ✉ 63270

Auvergne 5 **B2**

Paris 433 – Ambert 56 – Clermont-Ferrand 23 – Issoire 16 – Thiers 40

Ste-Chapelle★ - Château of Busséol★ North: 6,5 km.

in Longues 4 km northwest by D 225 - ✉ 63270 Vic-le-Comte

XX **Le Comté**
186 bd. du Gén. de Gaulle – ✆ 04 73 39 90 31 – Fax 04 73 39 24 58
– Closed 15-30 July, Wednesday dinner, Sunday dinner and Monday
Rest – Menu € 20/50 – Carte € 28/49
◆ Regional early-20C house next to the Bank of France. Classic interior. Understandably, it is a favourite with many of the local bigwigs.

VIC-SUR-CÈRE – 15 Cantal – 330 D5 – pop. 1 890 – alt. 678 m – ✉ 15800

Auvergne 5 **B3**

Paris 549 – Aurillac 19 – Murat 29

Office de tourisme, avenue André Mercier ✆ 04 71 47 50 68,
Fax 04 71 47 58 56

Family Hôtel rm, rest,
av. E. Duclaux – ✆ 04 71 47 50 49 – francois.courbebaisse@wanadoo.fr
– Fax 04 71 47 51 31 – Closed 1 - 17 Dec.
55 rm – †€ 44/66 ††€ 55/76, ☕ € 7 – 16 suites – ½ P € 46/57
Rest – *(closed 15 November-15 December)* Menu € 15/32 – Carte € 16/27
◆ A simple restaurant with view of the valley and traditional cuisine.

Bel Horizon
– ✆ 04 71 47 50 06 – bouyssou@wanadoo.fr – Fax 04 71 49 63 81
– Closed November and 3-26 January
24 rm – †€ 40/50 ††€ 43/54, ☕ € 8 – ½ P € 48/56
Rest – Menu € 18 (weekdays)/42 – Carte € 21/52
◆ Traditional building near the railway station. The scenic view of the Carladès relief explains the hotel's name. Fully renovated small rooms. A dining room with large bay windows overlooking the surrounding plateaux.

at Col de Curebourse 6 km southeast by D 54 – alt. 994 m – ✉15800 St-Clément

Hostellerie St-Clément mountain and valley,
– ✆ 04 71 47 51 71 – hostelleriesaintclement@wanadoo.fr – Fax 04 71 49 63 02 – Closed 13 January-2 February, Sunday dinner and Monday except July-August
23 rm – †€ 46/55 ††€ 46/64, ☕ € 8,50 – ½ P € 46/70
Rest – Menu € 25/61 – Carte € 50/71
◆ A long façade overlooking the valley at an altitude of 1000m. The rooms, most of which have been refurbished, give onto the park. Non-smoking establishment. The restaurant offers a panoramic view of the Carladès plateau and ravines, and serves tasty traditional food.

VIDAUBAN – 83 Var – 340 N5 – pop. 7 311 – alt. 60 m – ✉ 83550 41 C3

Paris 841 – Cannes 63 – Draguignan 19 – Fréjus 29 – Toulon 61

Office de tourisme, 56, avenue du Président Wilson ✆ 04 94 73 10 28,
Fax 04 94 73 07 82

La Fontaine rest,

60 rte Départementale 84, Thoronet road: 1.5 km – ☎ 04 94 99 91 91 – hotel.la.fontaine.vidauban@wanadoo.fr – Fax 04 94 73 16 49

13 rm – €59 €59/65, €8 – ½ P €59 – **Rest** – *(dinner only)* Menu €19/26 – Carte €26/33

◆ Standing on a junction, a modern hotel with a colourful façade with rereshing simple rooms that are impeccably well kept. The dining room and the traditional cuisine are unpretentious and perfectly matched.

La Bastide des Magnans with rm rm,

20 av. de la Résistance, rte La Garde-Freinet – ☎ 04 94 99 43 91 – magnans83@orange.fr – Fax 04 94 99 44 35 – Closed 25 June-4 July, 24-31 December, Sunday and Wednesday off season

5 rm – €75/85 €85/95, €8 – **Rest** – *(closed Sunday dinner, Wednesday dinner and Monday off season)* Menu (€18), €28/72 – Carte €61/106

◆ This former silkworm nursery is home to two bright dining rooms redecorated in chic country style. This bastide has five new, charming rooms, each of which is decorated according to a different theme.

Concorde

pl. G. Clemenceau – ☎ 04 94 73 01 19 – alainboeuf@provencariviera.com – Fax 04 94 73 01 19 – Closed Tuesday dinner and Wednesday

Rest – Menu (€19), €29 (weekdays)/60 – Carte €36/70

◆ This restaurant on the main square has increased its capacity with the addition of the covered terrace. The menu includes seasonal game and mushroom specialities.

VIEILLEVIE – 15 Cantal – 330 C7 – pop. 114 – alt. 220 m – ✉ 15120 5 B3

Paris 600 – Aurillac 45 – Entraygues-sur-Truyère 15 – Figeac 44 – Montsalvy 14 – Rodez 50

La Terrasse

– ☎ 04 71 49 94 00 – hotel-de-la-terrasse@wanadoo.fr – Fax 04 71 49 92 23 – Open 16 March-5 November

26 rm – €49/64 €49/64, €9,50 – ½ P €52/60 – **Rest** – *(closed Sunday dinner and Monday except July-August, and Monday lunch in July)* Menu €23 (weekdays)/42 – Carte €32/43

◆ This hotel, managed by the same family since 1870, stands on the banks of the Lot. There are good leisure facilities, country-style rooms and a bar with a local clientele. A wisteria perfumes and shades the terrace of this village restaurant, overlooking the pool. Regional fare.

VIENNE – 38 Isère – 333 C4 – pop. 29 975 – alt. 160 m – ✉ 38200

Lyon - Rhone Valley 44 B2

Paris 486 – Grenoble 89 – Lyon 31 – St-Étienne 49 – Valence 73

Office de tourisme, cours Brillier ☎ 04 74 53 80 30, Fax 04 74 53 80 31

St-Maurice cathedral ★★ - Temple of Augustus and Livia ★★ **R** - Théâtre romain★ - Church★ and cloister★ of St-André-le-Bas - Esplanade du Mont Pipet ≤★ - Former St-Pierre church ★ - Carved group★ of Ste-Colombe church AY - Gallo-Roman town of St-Romain-en-Gal★★ (museum★, site★).

Plans on following pages

La Pyramide (Patrick Henriroux) rm,

14 bd F. Point, Cours de Verdun, south of the map – ☎ 04 74 53 01 96 – pyramide@relaischateaux.com – Fax 04 74 85 69 73 – Closed 12-20 August and 12 February-6 March

21 rm – €195 €255, €20 – 4 suites

Rest – *(closed Tuesday and Wednesday)* Menu €58 bi (weekday lunch), €98/158 – Carte €103/172

Spec. Crème soufflée de crabe dormeur au caviar osciètre. Cul de veau de lait cuit au sautoir, jus à l'ancienne. Piano au chocolat praliné, amandes, noisettes, sauce café. **Wines** Condrieu, Côte-Rôtie.

◆ Attractive regional construction with vast and elegant Provence-inspired guestrooms and a pleasant garden. Fine cuisine with up-to-date flavours, plus a superb cellar boasting some rare vintages. Very reasonably priced, midweek lunchtime "menu du marché".

STE-COLOMBE

Briand (Pl. A.) . . . . AY
Çochard (R.) . . . . AY
Égalité (Pl. de l') . . . . AY
Garon (R.) . . . . AY
Herbouville (Q. d') . . . . AY
Joubert (Av.) . . . . AY
Nationale (R.) . . . . AY
Petits Jardins (R. des) . . . . AY

VIENNE

Allmer (R.) . . . . BZ 2
Allobroges (Pl. des) . . . . AZ
Anatole-France (Quai) . . . . . . BCY
Aqueducs (Ch. des) . . . . CY
Asiaticus (Bd) . . . . AZ
Beaumur (Montée) . . . . BCZ
Boson (R.) . . . . AZ
Bourgogne (R. de) . . . . BY
Brenier (R. J.) . . . . BY
Briand (Pl. A.) . . . . BY 3
Brillier (Cours) . . . . ABZ
Capucins (Pl. des) . . . . BCY
Célestes (R. des) . . . . CY 4
Chantelouve (R.) . . . . BY 5
Charité (R. de la) . . . . BCY 6
Cirque (R. du) . . . . CY 7
Clémentine (R.) . . . . BY 8
Clercs (R. des) . . . . BY 9
Collège (R. du) . . . . BY 10
Coupe-Jarret (Montée) . . . . BZ
Éperon (R. de l') . . . . BY 12
Gère (R. de) . . . . CY
Jacquier (R. H.) . . . . BY
Jean-Jaurès (Q.) . . . . AYZ
Jeu-de-Paume (Pl. du) . . . . BY 15
Jouffray (Pl. C.) . . . . AZ
Juiverie (R. de la) . . . . BZ 16
Lattre-de-Tassigny (Pont de) . ABY
Laurent (R. Florentin) . . . . AZ
Marchande (R.) . . . . BY
Miremont (Pl. de) . . . . BY 18
Mitterrand (Pl. F.) . . . . BY 19
Orfèvres (R. des) . . . . BY 20
Pajot (Quai) . . . . BY 22
Palais (Pl. du) . . . . BY 23
Peyron (R.) . . . . BZ 24
Pilori (Pl. du) . . . . BY 25
Pipet (R.) . . . . CY
Pompidou (Bd Georges) . . . . AZ
Ponsard (R.) . . . . BY 28
République (Bd et Pl.) . . . . . . ABZ 29
Riondet (Quai) . . . . AZ
Rivoire (Pl. A.) . . . . CY
Romanet (R. E.) . . . . ABZ
Romestang (Cours) . . . . BZ
St-André-le-Haut (R.) . . . . CY 34
St-Louis (Pl.) . . . . BY
St-Marcel (Montée) . . . . CYZ
St-Maurice (Pl.) . . . . AY
St-Paul (Pl.) . . . . BY
St-Pierre (Pl.) . . . . AZ
Schneider (R.) . . . . CY 37
Sémard (Pl. P.) . . . . BZ
Table-Ronde (R. de la) . . . . BY 38
Thomas (R. A.) . . . . CY
Tupinières (Montée des) . . . . CZ
Ursulines (R. des) . . . . CY 39
Verdun (Cours de) . . . . AZ
Victor-Hugo (R.) . . . . BCYZ
11-Novembre (R. du) . . . . AZ 43

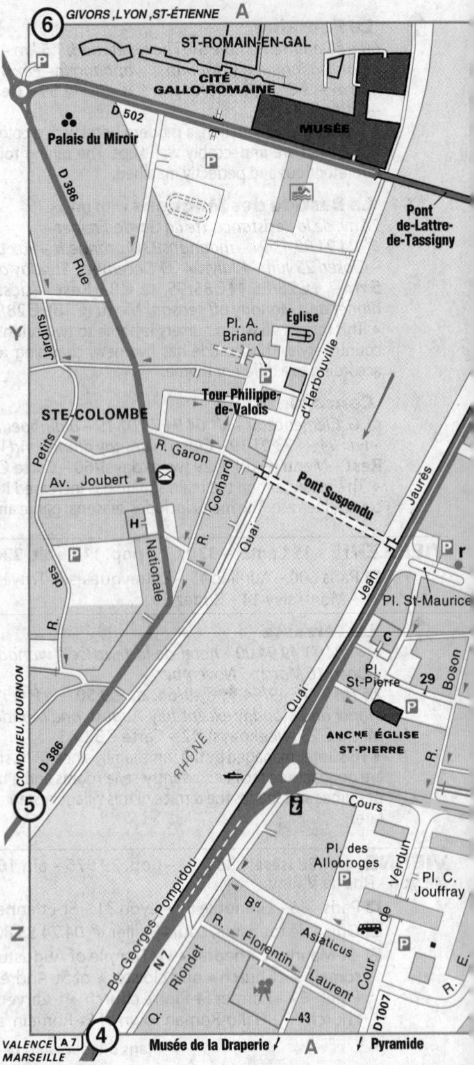

XX **Le Bec Fin**

7 pl. St-Maurice
– ✆ 04 74 85 76 72
– Fax 04 74 85 15 30
– Closed 30 June-8 July, Christmas holidays, Wednesday dinner, Sunday dinner and Monday AY **r**

Rest – Menu € 21 (weekdays)/58 – Carte € 35/64

♦ The traditional-regional cuisine of this restaurant has character, just like its owner. Simple decor; outside dining on the square in summer.

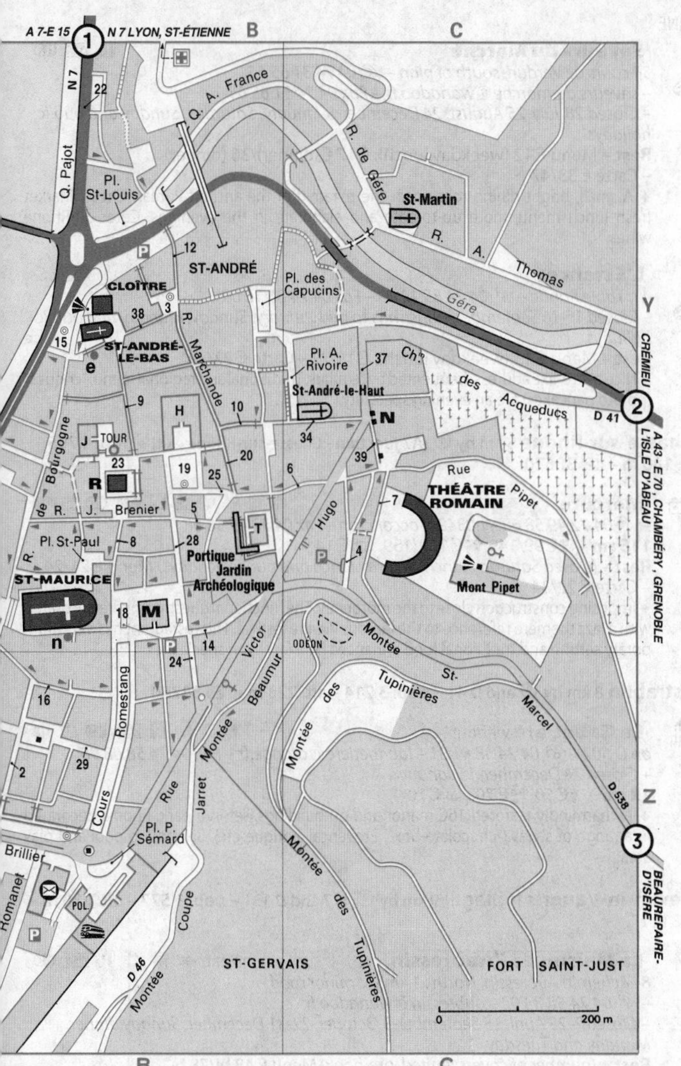

Le Cloître

2 r. Cloîtres – ✆ 04 74 31 93 57

– cloitre@netgdi.com

– Fax 04 74 85 03 51 BY **n**

Rest – *(closed Saturday and Sunday)* Menu (€ 16), € 24/41

– Carte € 40/55

◆ Pleasant establishment at the foot of the St Maurice cathedral. Stained-glass windows, stone and wooden beams provide the backdrop for contemporary cuisine and a good wine list.

Saveurs du Marché A/C VISA MC

34 cours de Verdun, south of plan – ✆ 04 74 31 65 65
– saveurs.du.marche@wanadoo.fr – Fax 04 74 31 65 65
– Closed 28 July-25 August, 24 December-5 January, Saturday, Sunday and public holidays
Rest – Menu € 12 (weekday lunch), € 17 € (dinner)/36 (dinner)
– Carte € 33/47

◆ A small, bright dining room near the pyramid of the ancient Roman Circus. Market fresh lunch menu, more up-to-date and elaborate in the evenings. Côtes-du-Rhône wines.

L'Estancot VISA MC

4 r. Table Ronde – ✆ 04 74 85 12 09 – Fax 04 74 85 12 09
– Closed 1st-16 September, Christmas to mid January, Sunday, Monday and public holidays BY **e**
Rest – Menu € 13 (weekday lunch), € 19/27 – Carte € 22/39

◆ Nice bistro-like address, frequented by regulars. Traditional and regional menu; "criques" (potato pancakes) are an evening speciality.

in Chasse-sur-Rhône 8 km by ① (A7 junction - Chasse-sur-Rhône exit) – pop. 4 795 – alt. 180 m – ✉ 38670

Mercure A/C P VISA MC AE

– ✆ 04 72 49 58 68 – h0349@accor.com – Fax 04 72 49 58 88
115 rm – €99/149 €109/159, ☕ € 14
Rest – *(closed Saturday lunch, Sunday lunch and public holidays)* Menu € 21/24
– Carte € 22/34

◆ Imposing construction close to the motorway. The functional guestrooms are decorated with a jazz theme, a reference to the famous Vienne festival. This restaurant has a contemporary setting and traditional food enhanced by a few Lyon specialities.

in Estrablin 8 km by ② and D 41 – pop. 3 214 – alt. 223 m – ✉ 38780

La Gabetière without rest P VISA MC AE

on D 502 – ✆ 04 74 58 01 31 – lagabetiere@orange.fr – Fax 04 74 58 08 98
– Closed 24 December-15 January
12 rm – €50 €70, ☕ € 10

◆ A charmingly restored 16C manor and outbuildings, set in a park. Rooms decorated in a range of styles ("chocolate-box", Provençal, antique etc). Swimming pool and play area.

in Reventin-Vaugris (village) 9 km by ④, N 7 and D 131 – pop. 1 577 – alt. 230 m – ✉ 38121

La Maison de l'Aubressin < Pilat, P VISA MC

847 chemin Aubressin, North : 1 km via minor road
– ✆ 04 74 58 83 02 – aubressin@wanadoo.fr
– Closed 7-25 April, 15 September-3 October, 22-31 December, Sunday dinner, Monday and Tuesday
Rest – *(number of covers limited, pre-book)* Menu € 48 bi/78 bi
– Carte € 27/65

◆ Ivy-clad establishment perched on a hill with views of Mont Pilat. Traditional cuisine served amidst reproductions of tapestries from the Cluny Museum, or on the terrace.

in Chonas-l'Amballan 9 km south by ④ and N 7 – pop. 1 219 – alt. 250 m – ✉ 38121

Hostellerie Le Marais St-Jean without rest P VISA MC AE

chemin Marais – ✆ 04 74 58 83 28
– contact@domaine-de-clairefontaine.fr – Fax 04 74 58 80 93
– Closed 18-26 August and 20 December-15 January
10 rm – €82/90 €82/90, ☕ € 17

◆ A restored old farm building with a tasteful, sober interior. The south-facing terrace is the perfect spot for breakfast in summer. Herb garden.

Domaine de Clairefontaine (Philippe Girardon) with rm
chemin Fontanettes – rm, rest, VISA
04 74 58 81 52 – contact@domaine-de-clairefontaine.fr – Fax 04 74 58 80 93 – Closed 18-26 August, 20 December-15 January, Monday and Tuesday
9 rm – €45/85 €45/85, €17 – ½ P €88/108
Rest – Menu €38 bi (weekday lunch), €65/115 – Carte €76/111
Spec. Dos de bar de ligne et langoustine royale truffée. Pigeon des terres froides de l'Isère et foie gras de canard, jus de truffe. Stradivarius au chocolat "pur caraïbes" et lait de poule aux noix torréfiées. **Wines** Saint-Joseph, Vin de pays des Collines Rhodaniennes.
♦ Once a retreat for Lyon bishops, this elegant residence nestling in a 3ha park is now a gourmet destination: studied and contemporary cuisine.

Les Jardins de Clairefontaine
18 rm – €125 €125, €17 – ½ P €128 VISA
♦ A blend of peace and quiet, space and greenery. Guestrooms with a balcony or terrace. Reception in the main building.

South At Mas de Gerbey, 10 km by ④ and D 4 - ✉ 38121 Chonas-l'Amballan

L'Atelier d'Antoine VISA
2176 Mas de Gerbey – 04 74 56 41 21 – latelierdantoine@orange.fr – Closed Tuesday and Wednesday
Rest – Menu €15 (weekday lunch), €27/35
♦ A modern take on traditional cuisine with the occasional exotic touch is the order of the day here. Classic decor with a screen displaying action live from the kitchen. Terrace.

VIENNE-EN-VAL – 45 Loiret – 318 J5 – pop. 1 549 – alt. 112 m – ✉ 45510 12 C2

Paris 157 – La Ferté-St-Aubin 22 – Montargis 57 – Orléans 23 – Sully-sur-Loire 20

Auberge de Vienne VISA
– 02 38 58 85 47 – Fax 02 38 58 63 29 – Closed 1st-16 September, 19 January-3 February, Sunday dinner, Monday and Tuesday except public holidays
Rest – Menu €22 (weekday lunch), €33/57 – Carte €55/63
♦ Old village establishment on the border of Sologne. Pleasant rustic dining room featuring half-timbering and a lovely fireplace. Traditional cuisine.

VIENNE-LE-CHÂTEAU – 51 Marne – 306 L7 – pop. 625 – alt. 129 m – ✉ 51800 14 C2

Paris 236 – Châlons-en-Champagne 52 – Saint-Memmie 50 – Verdun 49

Binarville road 1 km north by D 63 – ✉ 51800 Vienne-le-Château

Le Tulipier rest, VISA
r. St-Jacques – 03 26 60 69 90 – tulipier.le@wanadoo.fr – Fax 03 26 60 69 91
38 rm – €55/71 €66/80, €8,50 – **Rest** – Menu €22/55 – Carte €34/49
♦ This modern hotel, nestling in the Argonne Forest, is ideal for guests looking for peace and quiet in a country setting. Functional rooms, indoor pool and fitness room. Pleasant modern dining room with a design fireplace as its focal point. Up-to-date cuisine.

VIERZON – 18 Cher – 323 I3 – pop. 29 719 – alt. 122 m – ✉ 18100 Dordogne-Berry-Limousin 12 C2

Paris 207 – Bourges 39 – Châteauroux 58 – Orléans 84 – Tours 120

Office de tourisme, 11, rue de la Société Française 02 48 53 06 14, Fax 02 48 53 09 30

de la Picardière Chemin de la Picardière, by Gien road: 8 km, 02 48 75 21 43 ;

de Nançay Nançay Domaine de Samord, Northeast: 18 km by D 926 and D 944, 02 48 51 86 55.

Plan on next page

Continental VISA
104 bis av. Ed. Vaillant, via ①: 1.5 km – 02 48 75 35 22 – hotel.continental18@orange.fr – Fax 02 48 71 10 39
37 rm – €45 €57, €7 – **Rest** – *(dinner only) (residents only)* Carte €20/27
♦ A good base for exploring Vierzon, this comfortable hotel has guestrooms which are regularly refurbished. Restaurant serving simple dishes.

VIERZON

Baron (R. Bl.) . . . . A 2
Briand (Pl. Aristide) . . . . B 3
Brunet (R. A.) . . . . B
Dr-P.-Roux (R. du) . . . . B 6
Foch (Pl. du Mar.) . . . . B 7
Gaucherie (R. de la) . . . . A 8
Gaulle (R. Gén.-de) . . . . A 9
Joffre (R. du Mar.) . . . . B 12
Larchevêque (R. M.) . . . . A 13
Nation (Bd de la) . . . . A 14
Péri (Pl. Gabriel) . . . . A
Ponts (R. des) . . . . B
République (Av. de la) . . . . . . A 16
Roosevelt (R. Th.) . . . . B 18
Voltaire (R.) . . . . B 20
11-Novembre-1918 (R. du) . . . . A 22

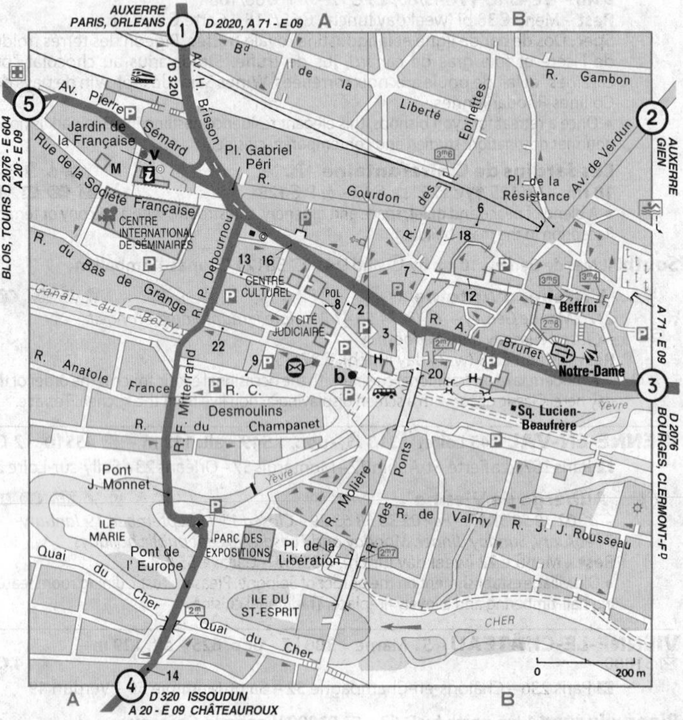

Arche Hôtel

13 r. du 11 Novembre 1918 – ✆ 02 48 71 93 10 – laurent.brechemier@free.fr – Fax 02 48 71 83 63 A **b**

40 rm – †€45 ††€54, ☕ €8 – ½ P €49/59

Rest – snack *(closed Sunday) (dinner only)* Menu €20 – Carte €20/31

◆ Located close to the arches of the old bridge spanning the Yèvre, this hotel has a modern glass facade and interior decor influenced by American pop culture. Well-appointed, functional guestrooms. An unpretentious place to break for salads and grilled foods in an up-to-date setting.

La Maison de Célestin (Pascal Chaupitre)

20 av. P. Sémard – ✆ 02 48 83 01 63
– lamaisondecelestin@wanadoo.fr
– Fax 02 48 71 63 41
– Closed 11-31 August, 1st-15 January, Saturday lunch, Sunday dinner and Monday A **v**

Rest – Menu (€20), €25 (weekday lunch), €35/65

Spec. Gâteau de saumon fumé, pistou noisette-céleri, crème glacée au chavignol. Côte de veau au poêlon, feuille de vigne farcie aux champignons des bois, "bernache" de quincy réduite. Les petits pots de crème brûlée.

◆ This 19C town house has an elegant and contemporary loft-style interior and a veranda and terrace overlooking a public park. Refined contemporary cuisine.

Tours road 2.5 km by ⑤ – ✉ 18100 Vierzon

Le Champêtre
89 rte de Tours – ✆ 02 48 75 87 18 – Fax 02 48 71 67 04
– Closed 25 July-15 August, Monday dinner, Wednesday dinner, Sunday dinner and Tuesday
Rest – Menu € 18 (weekdays)/39 – Carte € 27/43
◆ Attractive small restaurant with a rustic-style dining room. Tempting menu featuring delicious classical and regional dishes.

VIEUX-BOUCAU-LES-BAINS – 40 Landes – 335 C12 – pop. 1 379 – alt. 5 m – ✉ 40480 Atlantic Coast 3 A2

Paris 740 – Bayonne 41 – Biarritz 48 – Castets 28 – Dax 37 – Mont-de-Marsan 90

Office de tourisme, Le Mail ✆ 05 58 48 13 47, Fax 05 58 48 15 37

de Pinsolle Soustons Port d'Albret Sud, South: 9 km by D 4, ✆ 05 58 48 03 92.

Marinero with rm
15 Grande Rue – ✆ 05 58 48 14 15 – marinero2@wanadoo.fr – Fax 05 58 48 38 18
– Open from end March to end September
19 rm – €32/43 €35/61, € 7 – **Rest** – *(closed Tuesday off season and Monday except dinners in July-August)* Menu € 18/31 – Carte € 26/37
◆ Blue and white shades, mahogany furniture, sea-themed paintings and knick-knacks all give this restaurant a marine bistro atmosphere. Spanish-Landes fish and seafood cuisine.

VIEUX-MOULIN – 60 Oise – 305 I4 – see Compiègne

VIEUX-VILLEZ – 27 Eure – 304 H6 – see Gaillon

LE VIGAN – 30 Gard – 339 G5 – pop. 4 429 – alt. 221 m – ✉ 30120 Languedoc-Roussillon-Tarn Gorges 23 C2

Paris 707 – Alès 66 – Lodève 50 – Mende 108 – Millau 72 – Montpellier 61 – Nîmes 77

Office de tourisme, place du Marché ✆ 04 67 81 01 72, Fax 04 67 81 86 79

Musée Cévenol ★.

in Rey 5 km east by D 999 – ✉ 30570 St-André-de-Majencoules

Château du Rey
– ✆ 04 67 82 40 06 – contact@chateaudurey.fr – Fax 04 67 82 47 79 – Open from April to October
13 rm – €75/98 €75/148, € 8 – ½ P € 68/104
Rest – *(closed Sunday dinner and Monday)* Menu € 22/43 – Carte € 28/48
◆ Viollet-le-Duc restored this medieval castle, set in the heart of a riverside park (fishing available). Individually styled rooms adorned with antique furniture. The vaulted dining room is in the castle's 13C former sheepcote; pleasant terrace.

in Pont d'Hérault 6 km east by D 999 – ✉ 30570 Valleraugue

Maurice rest,
– ✆ 04 67 82 40 02 – hotelmaurice@aol.com – Fax 04 67 82 46 12
– Closed January
14 rm – €65 €65/95, € 8 – ½ P € 65/85
Rest – *(dinner for residents only)* Menu € 38/62 – Carte approx. € 55
◆ Traditional inn run by the same family for three generations, located on a pretty country road along the Hérault. Comfortable rooms, quieter on the riverside. Colourful dining room and pleasant terrace overlooking the pool and the valley.

LE VIGAN – 46 Lot – 337 E3 – see Gourdon

VIGNOUX-SUR-BARANGEON – 18 Cher – 323 J3 – pop. 1 885 – alt. 157 m – ✉ 18500 12 C3

Paris 215 – Bourges 26 – Cosne-sur-Loire 69 – Gien 70 – Issoudun 37 – Vierzon 9

Office de tourisme, 23, rue de la République ✆ 02 48 51 11 41, Fax 02 48 51 11 46

Le Prieuré with rm rm, rm, VISA

r. Jean Graczyk – ✆ 02 48 51 58 80 – prieurehotel@wanadoo.fr – Fax 02 48 51 56 01 – Closed autumn and February school holidays, Tuesday and Wednesday

6 rm – €57/76 €57/76, €7 – ½ P €68/76

Rest – Menu (€21), €28 (weekday lunch), €36/68 – Carte €54/58

◆ This moderatly contemporary restaurant is housed in a 19C presbytery. Pleasant poolside terrace. Up-to-date cuisine. Simple rooms.

VILLAGE-NEUF – 68 Haut-Rhin – 315 J11 – see St-Louis

VILLAINES-LA-JUHEL – 53 Mayenne – 310 H4 – pop. 3 179 – alt. 185 m – ✉ 53700 35 C1

Paris 222 – Alençon 32 – Bagnoles-de-l'Orne 31 – Le Mans 58 – Mayenne 28

Syndicat d'initiative, boulevard du Général-de-Gaulle ✆ 02 43 03 78 88, Fax 02 43 03 77 92

Oasis without rest VISA

1 km on Javron road – ✆ 02 43 03 28 67 – oasis@oasis.fr – Fax 02 43 03 35 30

14 rm – €42 €50/59, €9

◆ An old farm with a restored interior that still has a rural flavour. Beams and brick walls in all the rooms. Small park with a pool and crazy golf.

VILLARD-DE-LANS – 38 Isère – 333 G7 – pop. 3 798 – alt. 1 040 m – Winter sports : 1 160/2 170 m 2 27 – Casino – ✉ 38250 French Alps 45 C2

Paris 584 – Die 67 – Grenoble 34 – Lyon 123 – Valence 67 – Voiron 44

Office de tourisme, 101, place Mure Ravaud ✆ 08 11 46 00 15, Fax 04 76 95 98 39

de Corrençon-en-VercorsSouth: 6 km by D 215, ✆ 04 76 95 80 42.

Gorges de la Bourne★★★ – Valchevrière road ★ West by D 215ᶜ.

VILLARD-DE-LANS

Adret (R. de l') 2
Chabert (Pl. P.) 4
Chapelle-en-Vercors (R. de la) 5
Croix Margot (Chemin de la) 27
Dr-Lefrançois (R. du) 6
Francs-Tireurs (Av. des) 8
Galizon (Chemin de) 9
Gambetta (R.) 10
Gaulle (Av. Gén.-de) 12
Libération (Pl. de la) 13
Lycée Polonais (R. du) 14
Martyrs (Pl. des) 15
Moulin (R. Jean) 16
Mure-Ravaud (Pl. R.) 17
Pouteil-Noble (R. P.) 19
Professeur Nobecourt (Av.) 20
République (R. de la) 22
Roux-Fouillet (R. A.) 23
Victor-Hugo (R.) 26

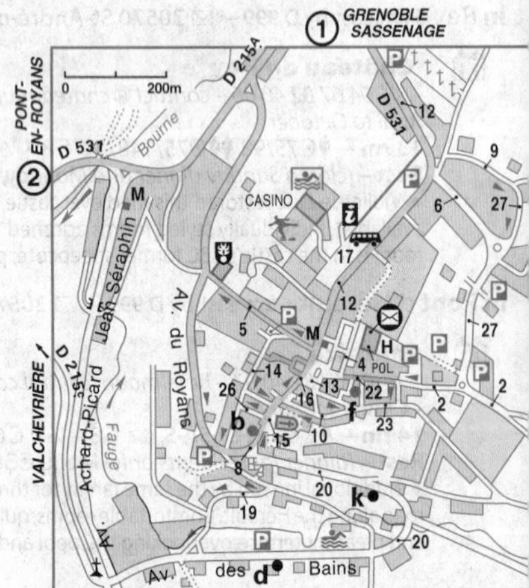

Le Christiania rest, VISA MC AE
av. Prof. Nobecourt – ✆ 04 76 95 12 51 – info@hotel-le-christiania.fr – Fax 04 76 95 00 75 – Open 20 May-30 September and 21 December-mid April **k**
23 rm – †€ 67/97 ††€ 85/188, ☕ € 10 – ½ P € 82/120
Rest ***Le Tétras*** – *(open 21 May-31 August and 20 December-31 March)* Menu € 17 (weekday lunch), € 25/50 – Carte € 38/70
◆ A chalet hotel offering individually styled spacious rooms, some of them wood panelled in the Savoy fashion. Almost all have a balcony and a view of the mountain. Indoor pool. Restaurant decorated with knick knacks and hunting trophies; regional food.

Les Trente Pas VISA MC
16 r. Francs-Tireurs – ✆ 04 76 94 06 75 – Fax 04 76 95 80 69 – Closed April and mid November-mid December, Monday and Tuesday except public holidays **b**
Rest – Menu € 14,50 (weekday lunch), € 27/49 bi – Carte € 35/41
◆ Small restaurant serving generous portions of traditional cuisine, a few steps from the village church. A local artist's work is on display in the dining area.

Southwest **By Col du Liorin road – ✉38250 Villard-de-Lans**

Auberge des Montauds rest, P VISA MC
aux Montauds: 4 km – ✆ 04 76 95 17 25 – aubergedesmontauds@wanadoo.fr – Fax 04 76 95 17 69 – Closed 14 April-1st May and 4 November-18 December
11 rm – †€ 45/50 ††€ 50/77, ☕ € 6,50 – ½ P € 52/55
Rest – *(closed Monday and Tuesday except July-August)* Menu € 19/29 – Carte € 24/36
◆ This picturesque old farm stands on the outskirts of a mountain hamlet. Warm, welcoming, chalet-style rooms. Traditional dishes and regional specialities. Raclettes and fondues served in the dining room with fireplace or on the terrace.

La Ferme du Bois Barbu with rm P VISA MC
at Bois- Barbu: 3 km – ✆ 04 76 95 13 09 – contact@fermeboisbarbu.com – Closed 7-13 April, 6-10 October, 12 November-5 December
8 rm – †€ 48 ††€ 56, ☕ € 9 – ½ P € 54 – **Rest** – *(closed Sunday dinner and Wednesday)* Menu (€ 19), € 23/55
◆ Not far from the cross-country skiing tracks. A pleasant dining area (wood panelling, fireplace, etc.). Classic, regionally inspired menu. Alpine style rooms.

in Balcon de Villard **Côte 2000 road, 4 km southeast by D 215 and D 215B – ✉ 38250 Villard-de-Lans**

Les Playes P VISA MC
– ✆ 04 76 95 14 42 – contact@hotel-playes.com – Fax 04 76 95 58 38 – Open 1st June-20 September and 21 December-15 April
23 rm – †€ 50/55 ††€ 70/82, ☕ € 10 – ½ P € 65/74 – **Rest** – *(open 15 June-15 September and 21 December-15 April) (dinner only in winter)* Menu € 26/35 – Carte € 35/43
◆ This sturdy chalet offers rooms, gradually renovated in an updated alpine spirit. Some have balconies overlooking the Grande Moucherolle mountains. Restaurant and terrace with a lovely view of the peaks; regional fare in winter, classic in summer.

in Corrençon-en-Vercors **6 km south by D 215 – pop. 322 – alt. 1 105 m – ✉ 38250**
i Office de tourisme, place du Village ✆ 04 76 95 81 75

du Golf P VISA MC AE
Les Ritons – ✆ 04 76 95 84 84 – hotel-du-golf@wanadoo.fr – Fax 04 76 95 82 85 – Open 2 May-14 October and 16 December-29 March
22 rm – †€ 70/95 ††€ 100/190, ☕ € 12 – 6 suites – ½ P € 92/135
Rest – *(closed lunch except Sunday and public holidays)* Menu € 30/60 – Carte € 34/45
Spec. Lapin de La Narce, pressé de foie gras et pommes au gamay du Diois. Pigeon en cocotte lutée en fumée de pousses de sapin. Raviole transparente de vin de Maury, mousse chocolat blanc, griottes amarena.
◆ Delightful rooms, superb, all-wood extension, cosy bar, brand new sauna and Jacuzzi, generous breakfasts: nothing is lacking in this family run hotel! Subtly inventive recipes (regional produce) served by the fire or on the pretty terrace.

VILLARD-RECULAS – 38 Isère – 333 J7 – pop. 57 – alt. 1 450 m – ✉ 38114

Bonsoir Clara — La Muzelle and Le Taillefert, VISA

23 rte des Alpages – ✆ 04 76 80 37 20 – il-fera-beau-demain@wanadoo.fr – Fax 04 76 80 37 20 – Open 16 June-30 September and 16 December-30 April
Rest – *(pre-book the weekend)* Menu € 30/35 – Carte € 31/53
◆ Find up-to-date recipes featuring regional produce and oriental spices at Clara's delightful chalet overlooking the village. Fine wine list.

LE VILLARS – 71 Saône-et-Loire – 320 J10 – see Tournus

VILLARS-LES-DOMBES – 01 Ain – 328 D4 – pop. 4 190 – alt. 281 m – ✉ 01330

Lyon - Rhone Valley 43 **E1**

Paris 433 – Bourg-en-Bresse 29 – Lyon 37 – Villefranche-sur-Saône 29

Office de tourisme, 3, place de l'Hôtel de Ville ✆ 04 74 98 06 29, Fax 04 74 98 29 13

du Clou RN 83, South: 3 km by D 1083, ✆ 04 74 98 19 65 ;

du Gouverneur Monthieux Château du Breuil, Southwest: 8 km by D 904 and D 6, ✆ 04 72 26 40 34.

Parc ornithologique (Ornithological park)★★ South: 1 km.

Ribotel — rm, VISA

rte de Lyon – ✆ 04 74 98 08 03 – ribotel@wanadoo.fr – Fax 04 74 98 29 55 – Closed 23 December-7 January
45 rm – †€ 50 ††€ 58, ☕ € 8,50 – ½ P € 59
Rest *La Villardière* – *(closed 23 December-15 January, Sunday dinner and Monday)* Menu € 19 (weekday lunch), € 23/35 – Carte € 30/44
◆ This recent construction is on the doorstep of a bird sanctuary. Most of its rooms have been freshened up and have a small sitting room (club armchairs, flat screen). La Villardière's rotunda dining room serves a traditional menu.

in Bouligneux 4 km northwest by D 2 – pop. 290 – alt. 282 m – ✉ 01330

Auberge des Chasseurs — VISA

– ✆ 04 74 98 10 02 – Fax 04 74 98 28 87 – Closed 1st-10 September, 20 December-20 January, Monday dinner 15 November-15 March, Tuesday and Wednesday
Rest – Menu € 30 (weekdays)/65 – Carte € 44/68
◆ This restaurant near the church provides friendly hospitality to hunters and other guests. Regional cuisine served in a country-style dining room, and in the garden in summer.

Hostellerie des Dombes

– ✆ 04 74 98 08 40 – Fax 04 74 98 16 63 – Closed end August, February school holidays, Wednesday and Thursday
Rest – Menu € 22 (weekdays)/49 – Carte € 33/52
◆ In the town centre, a traditional house home to a countrified dining room and pleasant terrace. Serves fine regional cuisine including frogs' legs and game in season.

Le Thou — AC VISA

au village – ✆ 04 74 98 15 25 – lethou@orange.fr – Fax 04 74 98 13 57 – Closed February school holidays, Sunday dinner, Monday and Tuesday
Rest – Menu € 29/56 – Carte € 32/57
◆ A light, conservatory style lobby in this former village inn smothered in flowers. The menu pays homage to the regions of Bresse and Dombes (frogs' legs in season).

VILLARS-SOUS-DAMPJOUX – 25 Doubs – 321 K2 – pop. 403 – alt. 362 m – ✉ 25190

17 **C2**

Paris 482 – Baume-les-Dames 50 – Besançon 81 – Montbéliard 24 – Morteau 49

in Bief 3 km south – pop. 123 – alt. 362 m – ✉ 25190

L'Auberge Fleurie — VISA

– ✆ 03 81 96 53 01 – Fax 03 81 96 55 64 – Closed 23 January-7 March, Monday and Tuesday
Rest – Menu € 10,50 (weekday lunch), € 19/32 – Carte € 22/36
◆ This simple little village inn faces a chapel and overlooks the Doubs. Traditional regional cuisine served in an attractive colourful dining room.

VILLÉ – 67 Bas-Rhin – 315 H6 – pop. 1 743 – alt. 260 m – ✉ 67220
Alsace-Lorraine 2 C1

Paris 445 – Lunéville 82 – St-Dié 48 – Ste-Marie-aux-Mines 27 – Sélestat 16 – Strasbourg 56

Office de tourisme, place du Marché ☎ 03 88 57 11 69, Fax 03 88 57 24 87

La Bonne Franquette VISA MC

6 pl. Marché – ☎ 03 88 57 14 25 – bonne-franquette@wanadoo.fr – Fax 03 88 57 08 15 – Closed 3-10 July, 26 October-9 November and 23 February-10 March

10 rm – †€ 36/47 ††€ 40/55, ☐ € 7 – ½ P € 43/55 – **Rest** – *(Closed Saturday lunch, Sunday dinner and Monday)* Menu € 20/39 – Carte € 27/51

♦ Located on a small square in the town centre, this attractive, family-run inn is flower-decked in season. Well-kept rooms with rustic furniture. The restaurant attracts a local clientele with its tasty traditional dishes, served informally.

LA VILLE-AUX-CLERCS – 41 Loir-et-Cher – 318 D4 – pop. 1 197 – alt. 143 m – ✉ 41160 11 B2

Paris 159 – Brou 41 – Châteaudun 29 – Le Mans 74 – Orléans 73 – Vendôme 18

Syndicat d'initiative, Mairie ☎ 02 54 80 62 35, Fax 02 54 80 30 08

Manoir de la Forêt P VISA MC AE

at Fort-Girard, east: 1.5 km on secondary road – ☎ 02 54 80 62 83 – manoirdelaforet@wanadoo.fr – Fax 02 54 80 66 03 – Closed 7-13 January, Sunday dinner and Monday October-April

18 rm – †€ 51 ††€ 58/80, ☐ € 12,50 – ½ P € 75/81 – **Rest** – Menu (€ 18), € 27/51 – Carte € 48/65

♦ A 19C isolated hunting lodge, surrounded by a park. The rooms adorned with period furniture and the lounge with its fireplace make up a stylish setting. Classic cuisine served in a comfortable and low-key dining room.

LA VILLE-BLANCHE – 22 Côtes-d'Armor – 309 B2 – see Lannion

VILLECOMTAL-SUR-ARROS – 32 Gers – 336 D9 – pop. 743 – alt. 177 m – ✉ 32730 28 A2

Paris 760 – Pau 70 – Aire-sur-l'Adour 67 – Auch 48 – Tarbes 26

Rive Droite VISA MC

– ☎ 05 62 64 83 08 – rive-droite2@wanadoo.fr – Fax 05 62 64 84 02 – Closed Monday, Tuesday and Wednesday except 14 July-17 August

Rest – Carte approx. € 35

♦ George Sand is said to have been a guest in this former 18C riverside charterhouse. The decor successfully combines old and new. Fine updated local cuisine.

VILLECROZE – 83 Var – 340 M4 – pop. 1 087 – alt. 300 m – ✉ 83690
French Riviera 41 C3

Paris 835 – Aups 8 – Brignoles 38 – Draguignan 21

Office de tourisme, rue Amboise Croizat ☎ 04 94 67 50 00, Fax 04 94 67 50 00

Viewpoint★: ★ North: 1 km.

Le Colombier with rm rm, rm, rm, P VISA MC

rte de Draguignan – ☎ 04 94 70 63 23 – hotel-restaurant@lecolombier-var.com – Fax 04 94 70 63 23 – Closed 20 November-12 December

6 rm – †€ 65/80 ††€ 80/100, ☐ € 9 – ½ P € 70/80 – **Rest** – *(closed Sunday dinner and Monday except public holidays)* Menu (€ 20), € 28/55 – Carte € 42/82

♦ This regional-style building (non-smokers only) offers an appealing traditional menu, served in a pleasant Provençal setting in winter, and under the veranda in summer. Attractive rooms with balconies.

VILLECROZE

Southeast 3 km by Draguignan road and secondary road – ✉ 83690 Salernes

Au Bien Être with rm – VISA MC AE

– ✆ 04 94 70 67 57 – aubienetre@libertysurf.fr – Fax 04 94 70 67 57 – Closed 1st-15 November, 10 January-10 February, Monday lunch, Tuesday lunch and Wednesday lunch

8 rm – †€ 50/69 ††€ 50/69, ☕ € 8 – **Rest** – Menu (€ 19), € 26/68 – Carte € 36/51

◆ Restaurant at the heart of an attractive park. Relaxed setting, new-look red and white décor and pleasant shaded terrace overlooking the garden. Locally inspired dishes.

VILLE-D'AVRAY – 92 Hauts-de-Seine – 311 J3 – see Paris, Area

VILLEDIEU-LES-POÊLES – 50 Manche – 303 E6 – pop. 4 102 – alt. 105 m – ✉ 50800 Normandy

32 **A2**

Paris 314 – Alençon 122 – Avranches 26 – Caen 82 – Flers 59 – St-Lô 35

Office de tourisme, place des Costils ✆ 02 33 61 05 69, Fax 02 33 91 71 79

Bell foundry★.

Le Fruitier – rm, rest, VISA MC AE

pl. Costils – ✆ 02 33 90 51 00 – hotel@lefruitier.com – Fax 02 33 90 51 01

48 rm – †€ 48/60 ††€ 48/89, ☕ € 8 – ½ P € 52/66

Rest – *(closed 24 December-2 January)* Menu € 14 (weekdays)/40 – Carte € 16/50

◆ Near the tourist office, a welcoming family hotel with functional, well-kept rooms and duplexes. Conference room. The restaurant has a colourful painted ceiling and murals with a fruit theme. Classic seafood cuisine.

Ferme de Malte – VISA MC

11 r. Jules Tétrel – ✆ 02 33 91 35 91 – contact@lafermedemalte.fr – Fax 02 33 91 35 90 – Closed 24 December-28 January, Sunday dinner and Monday

Rest – Menu € 24 (weekday lunch), € 26/40 – Carte € 49/74

◆ Former farm of the Order of Malta turned into a restaurant. Welcoming dining room (stonework, beams, woodwork and trinkets) partially overlooking the garden. Regional cuisine.

Manoir de l'Acherie with rm – rm, VISA MC AE

at l'Acherie, 3.5 km east by D 975 and D 554 (A 84 motorway, exit 38) – ✆ 02 33 51 13 87 – manoir@manoir-acherie.fr – Fax 02 33 51 33 69 – Closed 17 November-4 December, 9-26 February, Sunday dinner from 15 September to 16 March and Monday except from 14 July to 31 August

19 rm – †€ 55 ††€ 55/105, ☕ € 9 – ½ P € 70/95 – **Rest** – Menu (€ 13,50), € 17/37 – Carte € 25/51

◆ This 17C manor and small chapel are set around a flower garden in the heart of the Norman countryside. Pleasant rustic interior, local dishes and charcoal-braised meats.

VILLEFARGEAU – 89 Yonne – 319 E5 – see Auxerre

VILLEFORT – 48 Lozère – 330 L8 – pop. 620 – alt. 600 m – ✉ 48800 Languedoc-Roussillon-Tarn Gorges

23 **C1**

Paris 616 – Alès 52 – Aubenas 61 – Florac 63 – Mende 58 – Pont-St-Esprit 90

Office de tourisme, rue de l'Église ✆ 04 66 46 87 30, Fax 04 66 46 85 33

Balme – VISA MC

pl. Portalet – ✆ 04 66 46 80 14 – hotelbalme@free.fr – Fax 04 66 46 85 26 – Closed 15-20 October, 15 November-15 February, Sunday dinner and Monday except July-August

16 rm – †€ 47 ††€ 52/54, ☕ € 7,50 – ½ P € 58 – **Rest** – Menu € 21/36

◆ In the centre of a peaceful village which is one of the gateways to the Parc National des Cévennes, an old traditional house with rooms of varying sizes and levels of comfort. Local cuisine and concoctions with a personal touch.

VILLEFRANCHE-DE-CONFLENT – 66 Pyrénées-Orientales – **344** F7 – **pop.** 225 – **alt.** 435 m – ✉ 66500 Languedoc-Roussillon-Tarn Gorges 22 **B3**

- Paris 898 – Mont-Louis 31 – Olette 11 – Perpignan 51 – Prades 6 – Vernet-les-Bains 6
- Office de tourisme, place de l'Église ✆ 04 68 96 22 96, Fax 04 68 96 07 66
- Ville forte★ - Fort Liberia: ≤★★.

Auberge Saint-Paul VISA

7 pl. de l'Église – ✆ 04 68 96 30 95 – auberge-st-paul@wanadoo.fr – Fax 04 68 05 60 30 – Closed 23 June-1st July, 24 November-4 December, 5-29 January, Tuesday off season, Sunday dinner and Monday

Rest – Menu € 20 bi/110 bi – Carte € 52/73

◆ This 13C chapel today houses a rustic-style restaurant. The up-to-date cuisine evolves with the seasons. Fine choice of Burgundy and Roussillon wines. Shaded terrace.

VILLEFRANCHE-DE-ROUERGUE – 12 Aveyron – **338** E4 – **pop.** 11 919 – **alt.** 230 m – ✉ 12200 Languedoc-Roussillon-Tarn Gorges 29 **C1**

- Paris 614 – Albi 68 – Cahors 61 – Montauban 80 – Rodez 60
- Office de tourisme, promenade du Guiraudet ✆ 05 65 45 13 18, Fax 05 65 45 55 58
- La Bastide★: place Notre-Dame★, Notre-Dame church ★ - Former St-Sauveur charterhouse ★ by ③.

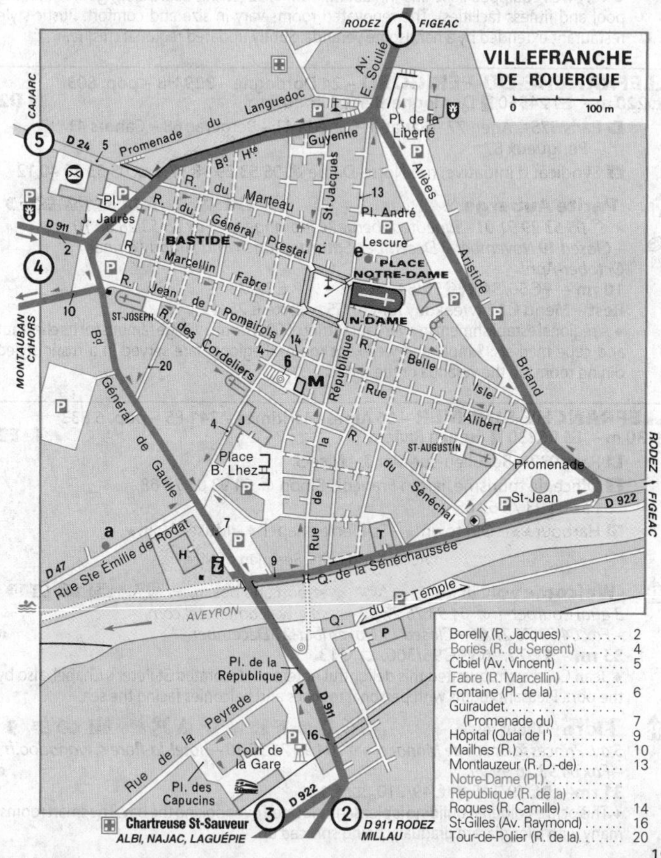

Borelly (R. Jacques)	2
Bories (R. du Sergent)	4
Cibiel (Av. Vincent)	5
Fabre (R. Marcellin)	
Fontaine (Pl. de la)	6
Guiraudet (Promenade du)	7
Hôpital (Quai de l')	9
Mailhes (R.)	10
Montlauzeur (R. D.-de)	13
Notre-Dame (Pl.)	
République (R. de la)	
Roques (R. Camille)	14
St-Gilles (Av. Raymond)	16
Tour-de-Polier (R. de la)	20

L'Épicurien
8bis av. R.-St-Gilles – ✆ 05 65 45 01 12 – Fax 05 65 45 01 12 – Closed 30 April-6 May, 17 November-2 December, Sunday dinner and Tuesday from 15 September to 15 June and Monday
Rest – Menu € 14,50 bi (weekday lunch), € 24/40 – Carte € 29/51
◆ Warm atmosphere in this former hardware shop with a terrace which is very pleasant in the evening. Tasty cuisine, based on fish and local produce.

L'Assiette Gourmande
pl. A. Lescure – ✆ 05 65 45 25 95 – Closed 19 March-3 April, 11-18 June, 10-17 September, 17 December-4 January, Sunday except lunch September-June, Tuesday dinner and Wednesday except July-August e
Rest – Menu € 15 (weekdays)/34 – Carte € 31/47
◆ A 13C building splendidly located in the heart of the old town, renovated in a semi-modern, semi-rustic style. Grilled dishes and regional recipes.

in Farrou 4 km by ① – ✉ **12200 Villefranche-de-Rouergue**

Relais de Farrou rm,
– ✆ 05 65 45 18 11 – le.relais.de.farrou@wanadoo.fr – Fax 05 65 45 32 59 – Closed 1st-11 March, 24 October-6 November, 22-29 December and 16-28 February
25 rm – €48/70 €65/86, ☕ € 8,50 – ½ P € 59/74 – **Rest** – *(closed Sat. lunch, Sun. evening and Mon. out of season)* Menu € 21/44 – Carte € 43/55
◆ Very well equipped coaching inn dating from 1792 (tennis court, crazy golf, swimming pool and fitness facilities). The renovated rooms vary in size and comfort. Rustic-style restaurant extended by a handsome veranda. Subtly updated regional cuisine.

VILLEFRANCHE-DU-PÉRIGORD – 24 Dordogne – 329 H8 – pop. 803 – alt. 220 m – ✉ 24550 Dordogne-Berry-Limousin 4 D2

Paris 575 – Agen 77 – Sarlat-la-Canéda 41 – Bergerac 68 – Cahors 41 – Périgueux 87

Syndicat d'initiative, rue Notre-Dame ✆ 05 53 29 98 37, Fax 05 53 30 40 12

Petite Auberge
– ✆ 05 53 29 91 01 – lapetiteauberge24@orange.fr – Fax 05 53 28 88 10 – Closed 19 November-3 December, Saturday lunch and Sunday dinner October-April
10 rm – €50/54 €50/54, ☕ € 7 – ½ P € 72/75
Rest – Menu € 12 (weekday lunch)/55 – Carte € 25/49
◆ A regional establishment in a verdant setting, 500m from a village famous for its chestnut and cepe markets. Simple and well-kept rooms. Regional fare served in a rustic styled dining room, on the veranda or the terrace.

VILLEFRANCHE-SUR-MER – 06 Alpes-Maritimes – 341 E5 – pop. 6 833 – alt. 30 m – ✉ 06230 French Riviera 42 E2

Paris 932 – Beaulieu-sur-Mer 3 – Nice 5

Office de tourisme, jardin François Binon ✆ 04 93 01 73 68, Fax 04 93 76 63 65

Harbour★★ - Old town ★ - St-Pierre chapel ★ - Musée Volti★.

Access and exits: See plan of Nice

Welcome without rest ← port and beach,
3 quai Courbet – ✆ 04 93 76 27 62 – resa@welcomehotel.com – Fax 04 93 76 27 66 – Closed 11 November-21 December n
35 rm – €72/96 €96/366, ☕ € 13
◆ Jean Cocteau frequented this delightful hotel and decorated St Peter's Chapel, also by the port. Pleasant rooms with personal touches and balconies facing the sea.

Flore without rest ←
5 av. Princesse Grace de Monaco – ✆ 04 93 76 30 30 – hotel-la-flore@wanadoo.fr – Fax 04 93 76 99 99 e
31 rm – €49/145 €49/210, ☕ € 12
◆ This ochre-coloured building is pleasantly located overlooking the bay. The smart rooms, many with a loggia, are gradually being spruced up.

VILLEFRANCHE-SUR-MER

Cauvin (Av. V.) 2
Corderie (Quai de la) 3
Corne d'Or (Bd de la) 5
Courbet (Quai Amiral) 6
Église (R. de l') 7
Foch (Av. du Maréchal) 8
Gallieni (Av. Général) 9
Gaulle (Av. Général-de) 10
Grande-Bretagne (Av. de) 12
Joffre (Av. Maréchal) 14
Leclerc (Av. Général) 15
Marinières (Promenade des) . . . 16
May (R. de) 18
Obscure (R.) 19
Paix (Pl. de la) 20
Poilu (R. du) 22
Pollonais (Pl. A.) 24
Ponchardier (Quai Amiral) 25
Poullan (Pl. F.) 26
Sadi-Carnot (Av.) 28
Settimelli-Lazare (Bd) 30
Soleil d'Or (Av. du) 31
Verdun (Av. de) 32
Victoire (R. de la) 34
Wilson (Pl.) 35

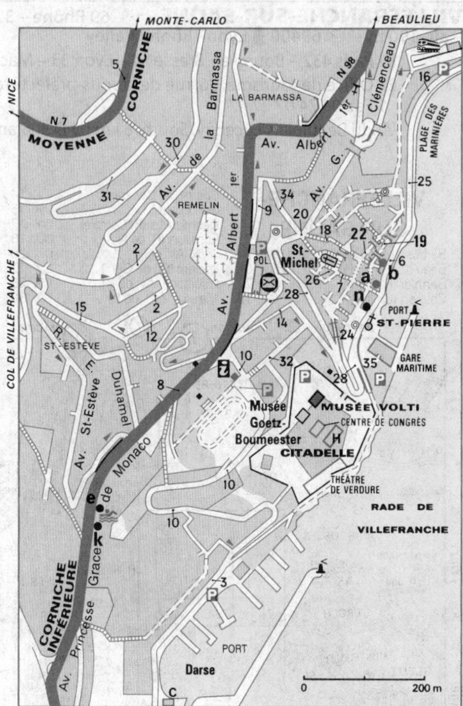

Versailles

roads, rest, rm, VISA

7 bd Princesse Grace de Monaco – ✆ 04 93 76 52 52 – contact@hotelversailles.com – Fax 04 93 01 97 48 – Open 15 March-mid October **k**

46 rm – €120/150 €140/280, €16

Rest – *(closed Tuesday off season and Monday)* Menu €38/40

◆ All the rooms of this family establishment overlooking the bay command an unforgettable panoramic view. Those with a shower have been renovated. Modern dining room and large terrace offering a superb view; regional menu.

L'Oursin Bleu

VISA

11 quai Courbet – ✆ 04 93 01 90 12 – oursinbleu@club-internet.fr – Fax 04 93 01 80 45 – Closed 10 January-10 February and Tuesday from 1st November to 30 March **b**

Rest – Carte €47/83

◆ A fish tank, portholes, fountains, frescoes and a lovely quayside terrace facing the harbour. A tribute to the sea in the decor and the updated gourmet menu.

La Mère Germaine

VISA

9 quai Courbet – ✆ 04 93 01 71 39 – contact@meregermaine.com – Fax 04 93 01 96 44 – Closed 12 November-24 December **a**

Rest – Menu €41 – Carte €52/88

◆ A beautiful location on the fishing port for this fish and seafood restaurant. Two rustic-styled dining rooms and a terrace overlooking the trawlers. Tender for yachties.

VILLEFRANCHE-SUR-SAÔNE – 69 Rhône – 327 H4 – pop. 30 647 – alt. 190 m – ✉ 69400 Lyon - Rhone Valley

43 **E1**

Paris 432 – Bourg-en-Bresse 54 – Lyon 33 – Mâcon 47 – Roanne 73

Office de tourisme, 96, rue de la sous-préfecture ✆ 04 74 07 27 40, Fax 04 74 07 27 47

du Beaujolais Lucenay, South: 8 km by D 306 and D 30, ✆ 04 74 67 04 44.

VILLEFRANCHE-SUR-SAÔNE

Street		
Barbusse (Bd Henri)	CX	2
Beaujolais (Av. du)	CX	3
Berthier (R. Pierre)	DX	7
Chabert (Ch. du)	CX	12
Charmilles (Av. des)	CX	14
Condorcet (R.)	DX	15
Desmoulins (R. Camille)	DX	17
Écossais (R. de l')	DX	18
Joux (Av. de)	DX	25
Leclerc (Bd du Gén.)	CX	27
Libération (Av. de la)	CX	28
Maladière (R. de la)	CX	30
Nizerand (R. du)	CX	35
Paradis (R. du)	CX	37
Pasquier (Bd Pierre)	DX	39
Plage (Av. de la)	DX	40
St-Roch (Montée)	CX	43
Salengro (Bd Roger)	CX	46
Savoye (R. C.)	DX	48
Tarare (R. de)	CX	54

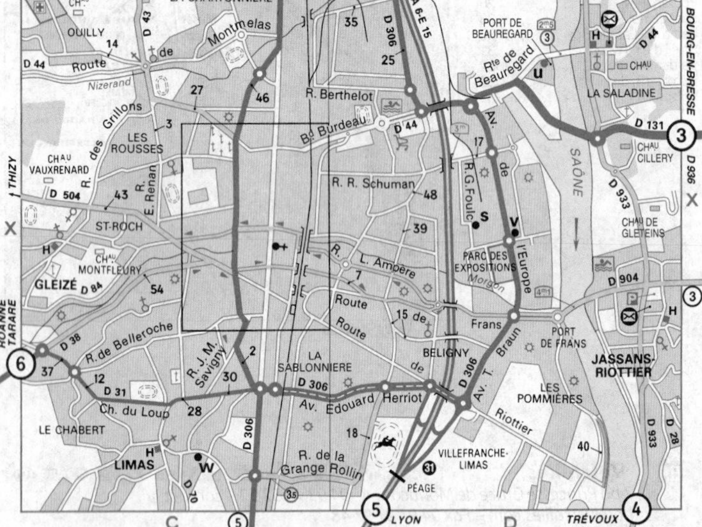

La Ferme du Poulet

rm, VISA

180 r. Mangin, (Northeast Industrial Area) – ✆ 04 74 62 19 07 – la.ferme.du.poulet@wanadoo.fr – Fax 04 74 09 01 89 – Closed 23 December-2 January, Sunday evening and Monday DX **s**

10 rm – €105 €110, €14

Rest – Menu €38/62 – Carte €42/108

◆ This sturdy 17C farmhouse has been attractively renovated to create a rustic, yet contemporary feel. Light and spacious guestrooms. Elegant restaurant with a French-style ceiling.

Plaisance

rest, VISA

96 av. de la Libération – ✆ 04 74 65 33 52 – hotel.plaisance@wanadoo.fr – Fax 04 74 62 02 89 – Closed 23 December-2 January AZ **n**

73 rm – €62/85 €95, €10

Rest – *(closed 1st-21 August, 23 December-6 January, Saturday from November to March and Sunday) (dinner only)* Menu (€16), €20/25 – Carte €25/31

◆ 1970s building in the heart of the Beaujolais capital. The well-equipped rooms are gradually being modernised. Parking and garage available. Dining room decorated with frescos; traditional food.

VILLEFRANCHE-SUR-SAÔNE

Belleville (R. de)	BY	5
Carnot (Pl.)	BZ	9
Faucon (R. du)	BY	19
Fayettes (R. des)	BZ	20
Grange-Blazet (R.)	BZ	23
Marais (Pl. des)	BZ	32
Nationale (R.)	BYZ	
République (R. de la)	AZ	41
Salengro (Bd Roger)	AY	46
Savigny (R. J.-M.)	AZ	47
Sous-Préfecture (Pl.)	AZ	49
Sous-Préfecture (R.)	AZ	50
Stalingrad (R. de)	BZ	52

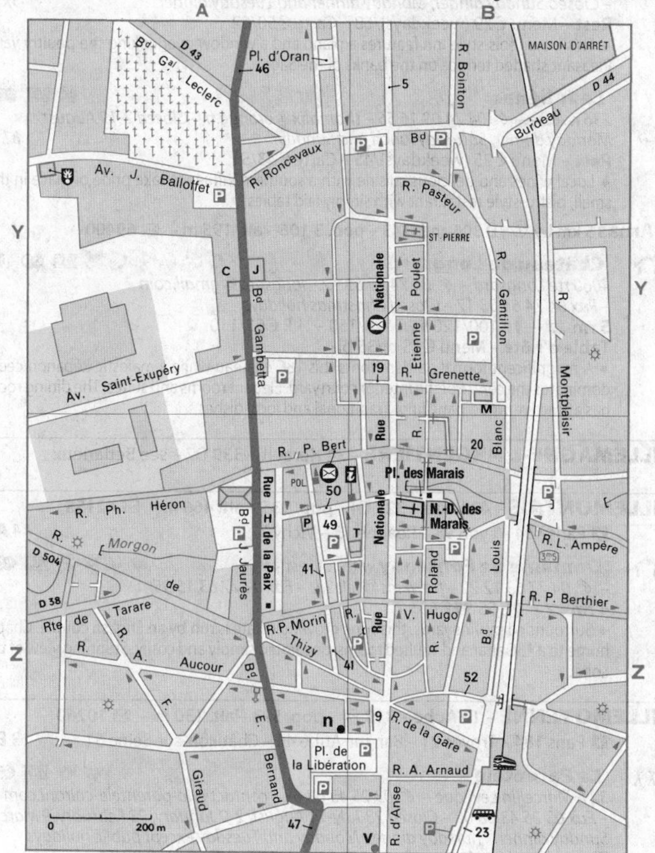

Newport

610 av. de l'Europe, (Northeast Industrial Area) – ✆ 04 74 68 75 59 – newport.mdb@orange.fr – Fax 04 74 09 08 89 – Closed 24 December-4 January

48 rm – †€ 58 ††€ 69, ☕ € 7 – ½ P € 54 – **Rest** – *(Closed Sat lunchtime, Sun and public holidays)* Menu € 15 (weekdays)/42 – Carte € 21/48 DX **v**

◆ The rooms in this large pavilion near the road and by the exhibition centre have good soundproofing. Modern rooms in warm colours in the recent wing. Restaurant decorated with enamelled plaques. Traditional dishes, regional recipes and wines.

Le Clos de la Barre without rest

14 r. Barre, 2 km south to Limas – ✆ 04 74 65 97 85 – ajoffard@wanadoo.fr – Fax 04 74 09 13 28 – Open 1st May-31 August CX **w**

6 rm ☕ – †€ 85 ††€ 85/110

◆ Water features, copious irises and hundred-year-old trees create a decorative backdrop to this 1830 house. The rooms and suites are prettily decorated and all have a small lounge.

Le Faisan Doré

Beauregard bridge, 2.5 km northeast – ✆ 04 74 65 01 66 – auberge.lefaisandore@wanadoo.fr – Fax 04 74 09 00 81 – Closed Sunday dinner, Monday dinner and Tuesday dinner DX **u**

Rest – Menu € 29 (weekdays)/68 – Carte € 50/62

◆ This bourgeois-style inn features a piano and a window overlooking the poultry yard. Pleasant shaded terrace on the banks of the Saône.

Le Juliénas

236 r. Anse – ✆ 04 74 09 16 55 – thomalix@orange.fr – Closed 2-19 August, Monday dinner, Saturday lunch and Sunday BZ **v**

Rest – Menu € 25 (weekdays)/45 – Carte € 43/51

◆ Local wines and delicious cuisine with a southern influence take pride of place in this small, bistro-style restaurant with simply laid tables.

in Arnas 5 km by ⑦, D 306 and D 43 – pop. 3 106 – alt. 195 m – ✉ 69400

Château de Longsard

4060 rte Longsard – ✆ 04 74 65 55 12 – longsard@gmail.com – Fax 04 74 65 03 17 – Closed Christmas holidays

5 rm – †€ 100/120 ††€ 120/150 – ½ P € 95/110

Table d'hôte – Menu € 25 bi/35 bi

◆ A magnificent formal garden fronts this 18C chateau while a majestic Lebanon cedar dominates the centre of the interior courtyard. Elegant rooms and suites. The dining room has attractive wood panelling. Traditional and local dishes.

VILLEMAGNE-L'ARGENTIÈRE – 34 Hérault – 339 D7 – see Bédarieux

VILLEMONTAIS – 42 Loire – 327 C4 – pop. 935 – alt. 466 m – ✉ 42155

Paris 404 – Lyon 95 – Roanne 13 – Vichy 77 44 **A1**

Domaine de Fontenay without rest

– ✆ 04 77 63 12 22 – hawkins@tele2.fr – Fax 04 77 63 15 95

4 rm – †€ 55 ††€ 65

◆ Surrounded by vineyards, this wine growing estate is run by an English couple. Chapel home to a 15C altar and vaulted rooms, decorated simply and cosily. Stunning view of the Loire.

VILLEMOYENNE – 10 Aube – 313 F4 – pop. 523 – alt. 130 m – ✉ 10260

Paris 184 – Troyes 21 – Bar-sur-Aube 46 – Châtillon-sur-Seine 51 13 **B3**

La Parentèle

32 r. Marcellin Lévêque – ✆ 03 25 43 68 68 – contact@la-parentele-caironi.com – Fax 03 25 43 68 69 – Closed 28 July-11 August, 2-9 January, 23 February-9 March, Sunday dinner, Thursday dinner, Monday and Tuesday except public holidays

Rest – *(number of covers limited, pre-book)* Menu (€ 19 bi), € 29/66 – Carte € 42/63

◆ Enjoy modern cuisine either in the contemporary-style dining room or on the terrace overlooking the village square. Expert wine advice.

VILLEMUR-SUR-TARN – 31 Haute-Garonne – 343 H1 – pop. 4 929 – alt. 108 m – ✉ 31340 Languedoc-Roussillon-Tarn Gorges 28 **B2**

Paris 646 – Albi 63 – Castres 73 – Montauban 24 – Toulouse 39

Office de tourisme, 1, rue de la République ✆ 05 34 27 97 40, Fax 05 61 35 78 34

South 5 km by D 14, D 630 and secondary road – ✉ 31340 Villemur-sur-Tarn

Auberge du Flambadou with rm

– ✆ 05 61 09 40 72 – bienvenue@aubergeduflambadou.com – Fax 05 61 09 29 66

9 rm – †€ 75 ††€ 75, € 9 – ½ P € 65 – **Rest** – *(closed Sunday dinner and Monday)* Menu (€ 12 bi), € 15 bi (weekday lunch), € 22/52 – Carte € 41/67

◆ A manger converted into a wine cellar, exotic fish and exhibition-sale of artwork: this rustic restaurant is far from conventional. Traditional unfussy dishes.

VILLENEUVE D'ASCQ – 59 Nord – 302 G4 – see Lille

VILLENEUVE-DE-BERG – 07 Ardèche – 331 J6 – pop. 2 429 – alt. 320 m – ✉ 07170 Lyon - Rhone Valley 44 B3

Paris 628 – Aubenas 16 – Largentière 27 – Montélimar 27 – Privas 30 – Valence 73

Syndicat d'initiative, Grande Rue ✆ 04 75 94 89 28, Fax 04 75 94 89 28

XX **La Table de Léa**

Le Petit Tournon, 1.5 km south-west on D 558 – ✆ 04 75 94 70 36 – Fax 04 75 94 26 91 – Closed November, 9-15 February, Wednesday and lunch Monday-Thursday

Rest – *(number of covers limited, pre-book)* Menu € 26/50 – Carte € 42/46

◆ This modernised barn has an attractive terrace beneath the chestnut trees. Regional cuisine based on local seasonal produce.

VILLENEUVE-DE-MARSAN – 40 Landes – 335 J11 – pop. 2 112 – alt. 80 m – ✉ 40190 3 B2

Paris 701 – Auch 88 – Langon 81 – Marmande 86 – Mont-de-Marsan 17 – Pau 73

Syndicat d'initiative, 181, Grand'Rue ✆ 05 58 45 80 90, Fax 05 58 45 88 38

Hervé Garrapit rest, VISA

21 av. Armagnac – ✆ 05 58 45 20 08 – hotelrestauranthervegarrapit@wanadoo.fr – Fax 05 58 45 34 14

8 rm – †€ 95/216 ††€ 95/216, ☕ € 18 – ½ P € 108/168 – **Rest** – Menu € 35/85 – Carte € 61/89

◆ A former post-house with a pleasant garden that has been in the family for several generations. Fine, refurbished rooms, all with a balcony overlooking the courtyard. Lovely, Louis XVI-style dining room facing a pretty square with century-old trees.

VILLENEUVE-LA-GARENNE – 92 Hauts-de-Seine – 311 J2 – 101 15 – see Paris, Area

VILLENEUVE-L'ARCHEVÊQUE – 89 Yonne – 319 E2 – pop. 1 203 – alt. 111 m – ✉ 89190 Burgundy-Jura 7 B1

Paris 135 – Troyes 44 – Auxerre 58 – Sens 24

Syndicat d'initiative, 38, rue de la République ✆ 03 86 86 74 58, Fax 03 86 86 76 88

XX **Auberge des Vieux Moulins Banaux** with rm

1 km south on D 84 – ✆ 03 86 86 72 55 – contact@bourgognehotels.fr – Fax 03 86 86 78 94 – Closed 26 May-1st June, 27 October-7 November, 24-28 December and 2-24 January

14 rm – †€ 42/51 ††€ 42/51, ☕ € 8,50 – ½ P € 54/62

Rest – *(closed Mon. lunchtime)* Menu € 26/29

◆ A 16C mill in a park across which the Vanne flows (fish farming). Preserved machinery, beams and stonework form the charming décor of this restaurant. Simple but pretty rooms.

VILLENEUVE-LA-SALLE – 05 Hautes-Alpes – 334 H3 – see Serre-Chevalier

VILLENEUVE-LE-COMTE – 77 Seine-et-Marne – 312 F3 – pop. 1 683 – alt. 126 m – ✉ 77174 19 C2

Paris 40 – Lagny-sur-Marne 13 – Meaux 19 – Melun 38

XXX **A la Bonne Marmite**

15 r. Gén. de Gaulle – ✆ 01 60 43 00 10 – labonnemarmite@wanadoo.fr – Fax 01 60 43 11 01 – Closed 10-28 August, 23-28 November, 25 January-12 February, Sunday dinner, Monday and Tuesday

Rest – Menu € 32 (weekdays)/68 – Carte € 50/72

◆ Two elegant and carefully decorated dining rooms in a fine Briard-style house. The largest opens onto a terrace shaded by trellis. Up-to-date cuisine.

VILLENEUVE-LE-ROI – 94 Val-de-Marne – 312 D3 – 101 26 – see Paris, Area

VILLENEUVE-LÈS-AVIGNON – 30 Gard – 339 N5 – pop. 11 791 – alt. 23 m – ✉ 30400 Provence 23 D2

Paris 678 – Avignon 8 – Nîmes 46 – Orange 28 – Pont-St-Esprit 42

Office de tourisme, 1, place Charles David ✆ 04 90 25 61 33, Fax 04 90 25 91 55

St-André fort and abbey ★: ≤★★ AV - Tour Philippe-le-Bel ≤★★ AV - Virgin★★ in the musée municipal Pierre de Luxembourg★ AV **M** - Chartreuse du Val-de-Bénédiction★ AV.

Plan: see Avignon

Le Prieuré

7 pl. Chapître – ✆ 04 90 15 90 15 – leprieure@relaischateaux.com – Fax 04 90 25 45 39 – Closed January AV **t**

26 rm – €140 €200/320, €19 – 7 suites

Rest – *(closed Monday except July-August)* Menu €40 bi (weekday lunch), €72/92 – Carte €84/90

◆ This former priory has recently been treated to a makeover and its rooms now sport a distinctly contemporary look. A magical site in the heart of a magnificent park. Immaculate white setting for updated gourmet cuisine with southern accents.

La Magnaneraie

37 r. Camp de Bataille – ✆ 04 90 25 11 11 – magnaneraie.hotel@najeti.com – Fax 04 90 25 46 37 – Closed 2 January-5 February AV **b**

29 rm – €125/245 €125/245, €20 – 3 suites

Rest – *(closed Sunday dinner, Wednesday from 1st March to 30 April and Saturday lunch)* Menu (€26 bi), €33/80 – Carte €60/72

◆ Elegant 15C residence enjoying a new lease of life thanks to refurbishment: refined rooms (romantic, colonial...), cosy sitting-room/bar, pretty garden. Dining room enhanced by frescoes and pillars; lush green terrace.

L'Atelier without rest

5 r. Foire – ✆ 04 90 25 01 84 – hotel-latelier@libertysurf.fr – Fax 04 90 25 80 06 – Closed 2-30 January AV **e**

23 rm – €56/95 €56/102, €10,50

◆ This charming 16C house features a lovely staircase, antique furniture, exposed beams and objets d'art. Shaded patio ideal for breakfast in summertime.

La Banaste

28 r. de la République – ✆ 04 90 25 64 20 – restaurant@la-banaste.com – Closed Thursday except from 1st July to 15 August AV

Rest – *(dinner only) (number of covers limited, pre-book)* Menu €28/46 – Carte €40/63

◆ The welcome matches the décor in this warm restaurant, named after a wicker basket. Traditional cuisine served.

in Angles AV – **pop. 7 578** – **alt. 66 m** – ✉ 30133

Roques without rest

30 av. Verdun, via ⑤ – ✆ 04 90 25 41 02 – reservation@hotel-roques.com – Fax 04 32 70 22 93

16 rm – €65/75 €75/95, €10

◆ Traditional house offering rooms (most of which have been renovated) decorated in bright colours and matching fabrics. Those to the rear are quietest. Attractive pool.

Fabrice Martin

22 bd Victor-Hugo – ✆ 04 90 84 09 02 – laubrice@neuf.fr – Fax 04 90 84 09 02 – Closed 25 August-7 September, 27 October-5 November, 9-23 February, Monday except July-August, Saturday lunch and Sunday dinner

Rest – *(number of covers limited, pre-book)* Menu (€18), €26 (weekday lunch), €40/60 – Carte €53/70

◆ A modern gourmet menu that changes with the seasons is served in this colourful villa with a contemporary interior and pleasantly shaded terrace.

VILLENEUVE-LÈS-BÉZIERS – 34 Hérault – 339 E9 – see Béziers

VILLENEUVE-LOUBET – 06 Alpes-Maritimes – 341 D6 – pop. 12 935 – alt. 10 m – ✉ 06270 French Riviera 42 E2

Paris 915 – Antibes 12 – Cannes 22 – Grasse 24 – Nice 15

Office de tourisme, 16, avenue de la Mer ✆ 04 92 02 66 16, Fax 04 92 02 66 19

de Villeneuve-Loubet Route de Grasse, by D 2085: 4 km, ✆ 04 93 22 52 25.

Musée de l'Art culinaire★ AX **M²**.

See plan of Cagnes-sur-Mer-Villeneuve-Loubet Haut-de-Cagnes.

XX **L'Auberge Fleurie**

au village, 13 r. Mesures – ✆ 04 93 73 90 92 – Fax 04 93 73 90 92 – Closed from mid November to 10 December, Thursday except dinner in July-August and Wednesday AX **u**

Rest – *(pre-book)* Menu € 22 (weekdays)/69 – Carte € 36/58

◆ Pleasant inn offering country dishes in the village where the famous chef Auguste Escoffier was born. Beams, stonework and modern pictures; summer terrace.

in Villeneuve-Loubet-Plage – ✉ 06270

Galoubet without rest

174 av. Castel – ✆ 04 92 13 59 00 – hotel.galoubet@wanadoo.fr – Fax 04 92 13 59 29

22 rm – †€ 59/78 ††€ 59/78, ☕ € 9 AY **s**

◆ Despite the name, the sound of the galoubet (a wind instrument) will not trouble guests staying in the up-to-date rooms furnished in cane.

XX **Daniel**

marina Baie des Anges – ✆ 04 93 73 41 66 – laurent.barrazza@orange.fr – Closed mid November-end January, Tuesday and Wednesday

Rest – Menu € 35 – Carte € 39/64

◆ Chic, bistro-style establishment with flowered terrace overlooking the marina. The regionally inspired menu focuses on fish. Good service.

VILLENEUVE-SUR-LOT – 47 Lot-et-Garonne – 336 G3 – pop. 22 782 – alt. 51 m – ✉ 47300 Atlantic Coast 4 C2

Paris 622 – Agen 29 – Bergerac 60 – Bordeaux 146 – Cahors 70

Office de tourisme, 3, place de la Libération ✆ 05 53 36 17 30, Fax 05 53 49 42 98

de Villeneuve-sur-Lot Castelnaud-de-Gratecambeby Bergerac road: 12 km, ✆ 05 53 01 60 19.

La Résidence without rest

17 av. L. Carnot – ✆ 05 53 40 17 03 – contact@hotellaresidence47.com – Fax 05 53 01 57 34 – Closed 27 December-5 January BZ **s**

18 rm – †€ 29/54 ††€ 29/60, ☕ € 6,50

◆ At the entrance to the medieval bastide, hotel offering simple accommodation in a convivial atmosphere. The brighter, quieter rooms on the courtyard side enjoy views of the surrounding gardens.

in Pujols 4 km southwest by D 118 – pop. 3 546 – alt. 180 m – ✉ 47300

Office de tourisme, place Saint Nicolas ✆ 05 53 36 78 69, Fax 05 53 36 78 70

<★.

Des Chênes without rest

– ✆ 05 53 49 04 55 – hotel.des.chenes@wanadoo.fr – Fax 05 53 49 22 74 – Closed 19 December-11 January and Sunday from November to April

21 rm – †€ 51/72 ††€ 66/87, ☕ € 10,50

◆ Located facing the hilltop village of Pujols, a typical example of the architecture of the region. Quiet, well-kept rooms with a fresh feel. Swimming pool and terrace.

XXX **La Toque Blanche**

– ✆ 05 53 49 00 30 – latoque.blanche@wanadoo.fr – Fax 05 53 70 49 79 – Closed 23 June-8 July, 17-25 November, 19-27 January, Tuesday lunch, Sunday dinner and Monday

Rest – Menu € 25 (weekdays)/85 – Carte € 61/107

◆ Hillside lodge facing the little market town. Service in a veranda-winter garden with a panoramic view at lunchtime, in an elegant dining room in the evenings. Traditional cuisine.

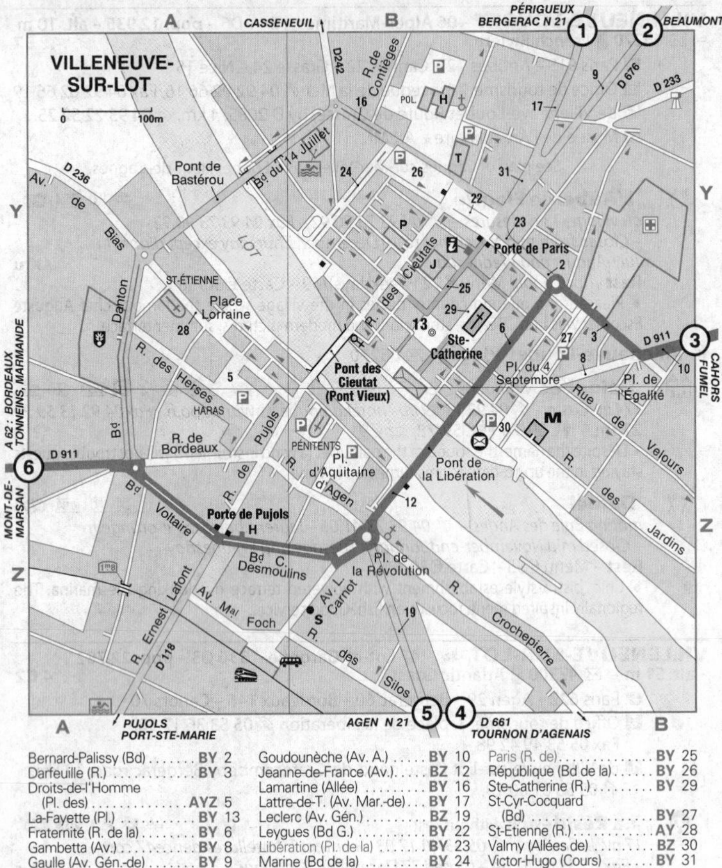

Bernard-Palissy (Bd) . . . . BY 2
Darfeuille (R.) . . . . BY 3
Droits-de-l'Homme (Pl. des) . . . . AYZ 5
La-Fayette (Pl.) . . . . BY 13
Fraternité (R. de la) . . . . BY 6
Gambetta (Av.) . . . . BY 8
Gaulle (Av. Gén.-de) . . . . BY 9
Goudounèche (Av. A.) . . . . . BY 10
Jeanne-de-France (Av.) . . . . . BZ 12
Lamartine (Allée) . . . . BY 16
Lattre-de-T. (Av. Mar.-de) . . . BY 17
Leclerc (Av. Gén.) . . . . BZ 19
Leygues (Bd G.) . . . . BY 22
Libération (Pl. de la) . . . . BY 23
Marine (Bd de la) . . . . BY 24
Paris (R. de) . . . . BY 25
République (Bd de la) . . . . . . BY 26
Ste-Catherine (R.) . . . . BY 29
St-Cyr-Cocquard (Bd) . . . . BY 27
St-Etienne (R.) . . . . AY 28
Valmy (Allées de) . . . . BZ 30
Victor-Hugo (Cours) . . . . BY 31

Lou Calel

Villeneuve, VISA

Le bourg – ☎ 05 53 70 46 14 – restaurantloucal@orange.fr – Fax 05 53 70 46 14 – Closed 28 May-4 June, 8-22 October, 6-22 January, Tuesday dinner, Thursday lunch and Wednesday

Rest – Menu € 18 bi (weekday lunch), € 22/38 – Carte € 34/60

♦ This village auberge has two rustic dining rooms (one with a panoramic view) and a terrace overlooking the Lot Valley. Delicious local cuisine.

in St-Sylvestre-sur-Lot 8 km by ③ **and D 911 – ✉ 47140 – pop. 2 060 – alt. 65 m**

Château Lalande

rm, rest, VISA AE

– ☎ 05 53 36 15 15

– chateau.lalande@wanadoo.fr – Fax 05 53 36 15 16

18 rm – €95/215 €95/215, ☕ €18 – ½ P €131/252

Rest – *(closed 5-20 November, 5-20 January, Wednesday lunch and Tuesday)*
Menu € 29 (weekday lunch), € 39/74 – Carte € 50/67

♦ Sympathetically restored château (13C and 18C) set in extensive grounds. Impressive classical decor and facilities, including swimming pools in the courtyard and a heliport. Refurbished dining room, veranda and summer terrace. Contemporary cuisine.

VILLENEUVE-SUR-TARN – 81 Tarn – 338 G7 – alt. 272 m
– ⊠ 81250 Curvalle 29 **C2**

Paris 714 – Albi 33 – Castres 67 – Lacaune 44 – Rodez 64 – St-Affrique 50

Hostellerie des Lauriers
rm, VISA

– ✆ 05 63 55 84 23 – sudreetregnier@wanadoo.fr – Fax 05 63 55 94 85 – Open mid March-mid October

9 rm – †€ 42/54 ††€ 52/62, ☐ € 8,50 – ½ P € 51/56

Rest – *(closed Sunday dinner and Monday off season) (dinner only)* Menu € 16 (weekdays)/32

♦ House built of local stone in a park on the banks of the Tarn, ideal for a "country" holiday: functional rooms, covered swimming pool, jacuzzi and organised walks. Simple dining room with a terrace; traditional cuisine and local dishes.

VILLENEUVE-SUR-YONNE – 89 Yonne – 319 C3 – pop. 5 404 – alt. 74 m –
⊠ 89500 Burgundy-Jura 7 **B1**

Paris 132 – Auxerre 46 – Joigny 19 – Montargis 45 – Nemours 59 – Sens 14 – Troyes 77

Syndicat d'initiative, quai Roland-Bonnion ✆ 03 86 87 12 52, Fax 03 86 87 12 01

Porte de Joigny★.

La Lucarne aux Chouettes
VISA

quai Bretoche – ✆ 03 86 87 18 26 – lesliecaron-auberge@wanadoo.fr – Fax 03 86 87 22 63 – Closed January, Monday except July-August and Sunday dinner

Rest – *(closed mid Nov. to mid Dec.)* Menu € 25 (weekday lunch)/46 – Carte € 48/59

♦ On the banks of the River Yonne, these four 17C former warehouses have been renovated with style and elegance. Superb dining room with exposed roof beams. Contemporary cuisine.

VILLEPARISIS – 77 Seine-et-Marne – 312 E2 – 101 19 – see Paris, Area

VILLEREST – 42 Loire – 327 D4 – see Roanne

VILLEROY – 89 Yonne – 319 C2 – see Sens

VILLERS-BOCAGE – 14 Calvados – 303 I5 – pop. 2 904 – alt. 140 m – ⊠ 14310
Normandy 32 **B2**

Paris 262 – Argentan 83 – Avranches 77 – Bayeux 26 – Caen 30 – Flers 44 – St-Lô 47 – Vire 35

Syndicat d'initiative, place du Général de Gaulle ✆ 02 31 77 16 14, Fax 02 31 77 65 46

Des Trois Rois with rm
VISA

2 pl. Jeanne d'Arc – ✆ 02 31 77 00 32 – les3rois@orange.fr – Fax 02 31 77 93 25 – Closed 5-15 January and Sunday evening from October to May

11 rm – †€ 60/95 ††€ 65/80, ☐ € 15 – ½ P € 85/90

Rest – *(closed Sunday dinner and Monday)* Menu € 24 (weekdays)/70 – Carte € 44/86

♦ A stone building surrounded by a vegetable garden. Recently taken over by a family team, it has a spacious, refurbished dining room, and two generations of bedrooms.

in Longvillers 4 km by D6 and secondary road – ⊠ 14310

Manoir de Mathan without rest

lieu dit Mathan – ✆ 02 31 77 10 37 – mathan.normandie@caramail.com – Open 13 April-11 November

4 rm ☐ – †€ 35 ††€ 50

♦ Picturesque 15C manor, flanked by a farmhouse. A superb spiral staircase leads to spacious and good-quality rooms (no TV). Breakfast served in the family kitchen.

VILLERS-COTTERÊTS – 02 Aisne – 306 A7 – pop. 9 839 – alt. 126 m – ✉ 02600

Northern France and the Paris Region 37 **C3**

- Paris 81 – Compiègne 32 – Laon 61 – Meaux 41 – Senlis 41 – Soissons 23
- Office de tourisme, 6, place Aristide Briand ✆ 03 23 96 55 10, Fax 03 23 96 49 13
- Château of François 1er: grand staircase★.
- Forêt de Retz★.

Le Régent without rest

26 r. Gén. Mangin – ✆ 03 23 96 01 46 – info@hotel-leregent.com – Fax 03 23 96 37 57 – Closed 25-30 December

30 rm – †€ 57/67 ††€ 72/80, ☕ € 8

◆ 18C post-house set around a paved courtyard with original drinking trough. Old-world rooms (antique furniture), gradually being redone in modern style.

VILLERSEXEL – 70 Haute-Saône – 314 G7 – pop. 1 444 – alt. 287 m – ✉ 70110

Burgundy-Jura 17 **C1**

- Paris 386 – Belfort 41 – Besançon 59 – Lure 18 – Montbéliard 34 – Vesoul 27
- Office de tourisme, 33, rue des Cités ✆ 03 84 20 59 59, Fax 03 84 20 59 59

La Terrasse

rte de Lure – ✆ 03 84 20 52 11 – laterrassevillersexel@wanadoo.fr – Fax 03 84 20 56 90 – Closed 20 December-7 January, Friday dinner and Sunday dinner October-March

13 rm – †€ 45 ††€ 52/54, ☕ € 7 – ½ P € 49 – **Rest** – Menu (€ 11,50), € 15/30 – Carte € 25/49

◆ Fishermen will enjoy this inn by a river where fish abound. Renovated rooms, some of which overlook the garden. Neo-rustic restaurant, roadside shaded terrace and unpretentious traditional cuisine.

Du Commerce

1 r. 13 septembre 1944 – ✆ 03 84 20 50 50 – commviller@aol.com – Fax 03 84 20 59 57 – Closed 24 December-8 January and Sunday dinner

24 rm – †€ 45 ††€ 45, ☕ € 7 – ½ P € 59 – **Rest** – Menu € 23/30 – Carte € 23/51

◆ A set of two houses as you enter the little town. Simple and well-kept rooms. A large fireplace adorns the rustic dining room, brightened by colourful tablecloths. Traditional cuisine, fresh frogs and game in season.

VILLERS-LE-LAC – 25 Doubs – 321 K4 – pop. 4 196 – alt. 730 m – ✉ 25130

Burgundy-Jura 17 **C2**

- Paris 471 – Basel 116 – Besançon 68 – La Chaux-de-Fonds 18 – Morteau 7 – Pontarlier 38
- Office de tourisme, rue Pierre Berçot ✆ 03 81 68 00 98, Fax 03 81 68 00 98
- Saut du Doubs★★★ Northeast: 5 km - Chaillexon Lake ★ Northeast: 2 km - Musée de la montre★.

Le France (Hugues Droz)

8 pl. Cupillard – ✆ 03 81 68 00 06 – info@hotel-restaurant-lefrance.com – Fax 03 81 68 09 22 – Closed 5-16 November and 5 January-5 February

12 rm – †€ 55/65 ††€ 55/65, ☕ € 9 – ½ P € 55/70

Rest – *(closed Tuesday lunch October-March, Sunday dinner and Monday)* Menu € 20 (lunch)/68 – Carte € 38/68

Spec. Duo de foie gras aux morilles. Filet de charolais à la réduction de trousseau. Pyramide de chocolat guanaja, moelleux aux épices. **Wines** Côtes du Jura, Arbois.

◆ Since 1900, a tradition of hospitality has been maintained by four generations of the same family at this hotel. Modern decor in the rooms. Beautiful dining room with panelling and a collection of kitchen utensils. Modern dishes and Arbois wines.

VILLERS-SUR-MER – 14 Calvados – 303 L4 – pop. 2 318 – alt. 10 m – Casino

Normandy 32 **A3**

- Paris 208 – Caen 35 – Le Havre 52 – Deauville 8 – Lisieux 31 – Pont-l'Évêque 21
- Office de tourisme, place Jean Mermoz ✆ 02 31 87 01 18, Fax 02 31 87 46 20

Domaine de Villers

chemin Belvédère – 02 31 81 80 80 – info@domainedevillers.com – Fax 02 31 81 80 70

17 rm – €120/165 €120/165, €13 – ½ P €97/160

Rest – *(closed Wednesday and lunch from Monday to Thursday)* Menu €32/44 – Carte €49/60

◆ A peaceful park surrounds this fine Norman manor house overlooking the sea. The spacious and luxurious rooms are either modern, nautical, Art Déco or Directoire. Appealing up-to-date menu served by the fireplace in a comfortable dining room.

VILLERVILLE – 14 Calvados – 303 M3 – see Honfleur

VILLEURBANNE – 69 Rhône – 327 I5 – see Lyon

VILLIÉ-MORGON – 69 Rhône – 327 H3 – pop. 1 614 – alt. 262 m – 69910

Lyon - Rhone Valley 43 **E1**

Paris 412 – Lyon 54 – Mâcon 23 – Villefranche-sur-Saône 22

La Terrasse ★★ near Fût d'Avenas pass Northwest: 7 km

Le Villon

bd du Parc – 04 74 69 16 16 – hotel_restaurant.le_villon@libertysurf.fr – Fax 04 74 69 16 81 – Closed 21 December-19 January, Sunday dinner and Monday mid October-end April

45 rm – €53/59 €63/69, €8,50 – ½ P €54

Rest – Menu €23/55 – Carte €23/44

◆ A building overlooking the village, with rooms (five of them with their own terrace) that are simple and practical and have views over the Morgon vineyard. Neo-rustic dining room decor and terrace with views of the hillside vineyards. Traditional cuisine.

in Morgon 2 km south by D 68 – 69910

Le Morgon

– 04 74 69 16 03 – Fax 04 74 69 16 03 – Closed 15 December-1st February, dinner on public holidays, Tuesday dinner from February to March, Sunday dinner and Wednesday

Rest – Menu €14 (weekdays), €19/40 – Carte €21/40

◆ This village hotel counts among its outstanding features a rustic setting (lovely open fires in winter), a pleasant terrace, warm welcome and fine local cuisine.

VILLIERS-LE-MAHIEU – 78 Yvelines – 311 G2 – pop. 615 – alt. 127 m – 78770

18 **A2**

Paris 53 – Dreux 37 – Évreux 63 – Mantes-la-Jolie 18 – Rambouillet 33 – Versailles 36

Château de Villiers le Mahieu without rest

– 01 34 87 44 25 – accueil@chateauvilliers.com – Fax 01 34 87 44 40 – Closed 23 December-1st January

95 rm – €203 €203, €18

◆ This 13C fortress was once the residence of Bernard Buffet. Extensive park and very pleasant rooms, those in the new wing sport a colonial style.

VILLIERS-SOUS-GREZ – 77 Seine-et-Marne – 312 E6 – pop. 764 – alt. 86 m – 77760

19 **C3**

Paris 75 – Corbeil-Essonnes 42 – Évry 43 – Savigny-sur-Orge 52

La Cerisaie without rest

10 r. Larchant – 01 64 24 23 71 – andre.chastel@free.fr – Fax 01 64 24 23 71

4 rm – €65 €70

◆ You will soon be charmed by this outstandingly well-restored 19C farmhouse. Its individually styled rooms have evocative names: Photographe, Orientale, Musicale and Voyageur. Warm welcome.

VILLIERS-SUR-MARNE – **52 Haute-Marne** – **313** K4 – ✉ **52320** 14 **C3**

Paris 282 – Bar-sur-Aube 41 – Chaumont 31 – Neufchâteau 52 – Saint-Dizier 46

XX **La Source Bleue**

– ✆ 03 25 94 70 35 – Fax 03 25 05 02 09 – *Closed 22 December-21 January, Sunday dinner, Monday and Tuesday*

Rest – Menu € 18 (weekday lunch), € 28/55 – Carte € 50/56

◆ An 18C mill surrounded by a large park running along the river where you can pick water cress. Simple, pleasant interior, waterside terrace and tasty, modern cuisine.

VINAY – **51 Marne** – **306** F8 – **see Épernay**

VINCELOTTES – **89 Yonne** – **319** E5 – **see Auxerre**

VINCENNES – **94 Val-de-Marne** – **312** D2 – **101** 17 – **see Paris, Area**

VINCEY – **88 Vosges** – **314** F2 – **see Charmes**

VINON-SUR-VERDON – **83 Var** – **340** J3 – **pop. 2 992** – **alt. 280 m** – ✉ **83560** 40 **B2**

Paris 775 – Aix-en-Provence 47 – Brignoles 52 – Digne-les-Bains 70 – Manosque 16

Syndicat d'initiative, rue Saint-André ✆ 04 92 78 84 45, Fax 04 92 78 83 74

X **Relais des Gorges** with rm

230 av. de la République – ✆ 04 92 78 80 24 – bertet.relais@wanadoo.fr – Fax 04 92 78 96 47 – Closed 26 October-9 November, 19-29 December and Sunday dinner October-March

9 rm – €40 €50, ☕ €6,50 – ½ P €48 – **Rest** – Menu € 19 (weekdays)/37 – Carte € 41/59

◆ In the centre of the village, this guesthouse provides tasty traditional cuisine. A restorative stop downriver from the spectacular Verdon gorge.

VIOLÈS – **84 Vaucluse** – **332** C9 – **pop. 1 536** – **alt. 94 m** – ✉ **84150** 42 **E1**

Paris 659 – Avignon 34 – Carpentras 21 – Nyons 33 – Orange 14 – Vaison-la-Romaine 17

Mas de Bouvau

2 km Cairanne road – ✆ 04 90 70 94 08 – henri.hertzog@wanadoo.fr – Fax 04 90 70 95 99 – Closed 1st-9 June, 18-25 October, 20-30 December, 2 January-6 February, lunch 15 June-15 September, dinner November-February, Tuesday lunch, Sunday dinner and Monday

6 rm – €62 €62/73, ☕ €9 – ½ P €65 – **Rest** – *(number of covers limited, pre-book)* Menu € 26/36 – Carte € 28/42

◆ Isolated in the middle of the vineyards, this authentic Provence farmhouse offers a warm welcome. Traditional cuisine served in a conventional Provencal setting.

VIRE – **14 Calvados** – **303** G6 – **pop. 12 815** – **alt. 275 m** – ✉ **14500**
Normandy 32 **B2**

Paris 296 – Caen 64 – Flers 31 – Laval 103 – Rennes 135 – St-Lô 39

Office de tourisme, square de la Résistance ✆ 02 31 66 28 50, Fax 02 31 66 28 55

de Vire la Dathée Saint-Manvieu-Bocage La Basse Haie, Southeast: 8 km by D 150, ✆ 02 31 67 71 01.

Flers road 2.5 km via D 524 – ✉ **14500 Vire**

XXX **Manoir de la Pommeraie**

– ✆ 02 31 68 07 71 – Fax 02 31 67 54 21 – Closed 4-20 August, Sunday dinner and Monday

Rest – Menu € 23 (weekday lunch), € 34/65 – Carte € 47/66

◆ Far from the noise of the town, a little 18C manor with two dining rooms opening onto a pleasant park with hundred-year-old trees. Classic menu.

VIRÉ – 71 Saône-et-Loire – **320** J11 – **pop. 954 – alt. 225 m** – ✉ **71260** 8 **C3**

Paris 378 – Mâcon 20 – Cluny 23 – Tournus 19

XX **Relais de Montmartre**

pl. A. Lagrange – ☎ 03 85 33 10 72 – relais-de-montmartre@wanadoo.fr – Fax 03 85 33 98 49 – Closed 1st-7 July, 6-13 October, 19 January-9 February, Saturday lunch, Sunday dinner and Monday

Rest – Menu € 22 (weekday lunch), € 30/68 – Carte € 40/59

◆ This former village café in the Mâcon area delights guests with its customized traditional cuisine. Elegant dining room (draperies, Murano glass chandeliers, etc.).

VIRIVILLE – Isère – **333** E6 – **pop. 1 281 – alt. 380 m** – ✉ **38980** 43 **E2**

Paris 549 – Lyon 92 – Grenoble 62 – Saint-Priest 73 – Saint-Martin-d'Hères 64

Hostellerie de Chambaran

185 Grande Rue Jeanne-Sappey – ☎ 04 74 54 02 18 – hostelleriedechambaran@wanadoo.fr – Fax 04 74 54 11 83

19 rm – †€ 50/70 ††€ 65/90, ☕ € 10 – ½ P € 62/75 – **Rest** – *(closed Saturday lunch, Sunday dinner and Monday)* Menu € 23/55 – Carte € 22/46

◆ In the heart of a picturesque village of cobblestone houses, a family affair whose unpretentious but spruced up rooms overlook a large garden with pool. Welcoming dining room, shaded terrace, and traditional fare on the table.

VIRONVAY – 27 Eure – **304** H6 – **see Louviers**

VIRY-CHÂTILLON – 91 Essonne – **312** D3 – **101** 36 – **see Paris, Area**

VISCOS – 65 Hautes-Pyrénées – **342** L7 – **pop. 41 – alt. 800 m** – ✉ **65120** 28 **A3**

Paris 880 – Pau 75 – Tarbes 50 – Argelès-Gazost 17 – Cauterets 23 – Lourdes 30

La Grange aux Marmottes ← mountains,

au village – ☎ 05 62 92 88 88 – hotel@grangeauxmarmottes.com – Fax 05 62 92 93 75 – Closed 11 November-15 December

6 rm – †€ 71/92 ††€ 71/92, ☕ € 10 – ½ P € 65/73 – **Rest** – Menu € 20/42 – Carte € 27/54

◆ Those looking for total peace and quiet will find this converted stone barn, situated at the gates of the Pyrenees National Park, quite attractive. Spacious and comfortable rooms. A country atmosphere reigns in the dining room where you are served regional food.

Les Campanules without rest

– ☎ 05 62 92 88 88 – hotel@grangeauxmarmottes.com – Fax 05 62 92 93 75 – Closed 11 November-15 December

8 rm – †€ 60/76 ††€ 60/76, ☕ € 10

◆ This former sheepcote with its fine slate roof and pretty flowers houses a few simply decorated rooms. Some of them, along with the perched outdoor pool, enjoy a mountain view.

VITERBE – 81 Tarn – **338** D8 – **pop. 254 – alt. 141 m** – ✉ **81220** 29 **C2**

Paris 693 – Albi 62 – Castelnaudary 52 – Castres 31 – Montauban 69 – Toulouse 55

XX **Les Marronniers**

– ☎ 05 63 70 64 96 – viala.marronniers@wanadoo.fr – Fax 05 63 70 60 96 – Closed 3-23 November, 23-28 February, Monday dinner November-March, Tuesday dinner and Wednesday

Rest – Menu (€ 11,50), € 19 (weekdays)/40 bi – Carte € 27/45

◆ A collection of naïve or modern paintings adorn the walls of the pleasant modern dining room. Fine terrace overlooking the garden. Traditional cuisine.

VITRAC – 24 Dordogne – 329 I7 – pop. 767 – alt. 150 m – ✉ 24200 4 D3

Paris 541 – Brive-la-Gaillarde 64 – Cahors 54 – Périgueux 85 – Sarlat-la-Canéda 8

Office de tourisme, lieu-dit le bourg ✆ 05 53 28 57 80

du Domaine de Rochebois Sarlat-la-Canéda Route de Montfort, Southeast: 2 km, ✆ 05 53 31 52 52.

Château of Montfort★ Northeast: 2 km - Cingle de Montfort★ Northeast: 3.5 km, **Dordogne-Berry-Limousin**

Domaine de Rochebois
rm, rest,

2 km east by D 703 – ✆ 05 53 31 52 52 – info@rochebois.com – Fax 05 53 29 36 88 – Open beg. May to end October

40 rm – €145/350 €145/350, €18 – ½ P €127/264

Rest – *(dinner only)* Menu €42

◆ Located in a large park with a 9-hole golf course, terraced garden, good swimming pool and fine interior decor, this 19C house is a slice of paradise in the heart of Périgord Noir. Modern food served in the opulent dining room or on the pleasant terrace.

Plaisance
rm,

au port – ✆ 05 53 31 39 39 – plaisance@wanadoo.fr – Fax 05 53 31 39 38 – Open 2 March-11 November

48 rm – €54 €61/100, €9 – ½ P €61/77 – **Rest** – *(closed Sunday dinner and Friday October-April, Friday lunch and Saturday lunch May-September)* Menu €15 (weekday lunch), €24/45 – Carte €31/68

◆ Regional establishment built in 1808 on a rocky slope. Well-kept rooms. Garden bordering the Dordogne on the other side of the road. Tastefully decorated dining room and terrace shaded by lime trees. Regional cuisine.

Le Clos Roussillon without rest

1 km west along the D 703 and secondary road – ✆ 05 53 28 13 00 – hotel@closroussillon-perigord.com – Fax 05 53 59 40 25 – Open 21 March-3 November

31 rm – €50/65 €50/75, €10

◆ 1980s hotel which has been totally renovated. Modern comfortable rooms, some with balcony and kitchenettes. Pleasant, peaceful wooded grounds.

La Treille with rm

Le Port – ✆ 05 53 28 33 19 – hotel@latreille-perigord.com – Fax 05 53 30 38 54 – Closed 15 November-15 December, 15 February-5 March, Tuesday except dinner 15 June-15 October and Monday

10 rm – €50/52 €51/85, €7,50 – ½ P €65

Rest – Menu €18 (weekday lunch), €25/38 – Carte €36/74

◆ This virginia-creeper-clad establishment has been run by the Latreille family since 1866. Simple dining room and veranda. Outside tables shaded by a trellis. Périgord cuisine.

VITRAC – 15 Cantal – 330 B6 – pop. 277 – alt. 490 m – ✉ 15220 5 A3

Paris 561 – Aurillac 26 – Figeac 44 – Rodez 77

Auberge de la Tomette
rm, rest,

– ✆ 04 71 64 70 94 – latomette@wanadoo.fr – Fax 04 71 64 77 11 – Open Easter-12 November

16 rm – €74/91 €74/91, €10 – ½ P €66/78 – **Rest** – *(dinner only)* Menu €28/69 – Carte €37/40

◆ Small, well-kept rooms undergoing renovation, pleasant flower garden, indoor/outdoor swimming pool, relaxation centre with sauna and hammam. An inn with much appeal. A restaurant with wood panelling, tiled floor, antique furniture; a terrace with pergola.

VITRÉ – 35 Ille-et-Vilaine – 309 O6 – pop. 15 313 – alt. 106 m – ✉ 35500 Brittany

Paris 310 – Châteaubriant 52 – Fougères 30 – Laval 38 – Rennes 38

Office de tourisme, place Gal-de-Gaulle ✆ 02 99 75 04 46, Fax 02 99 74 02 01

des Rochers Sévigné Château des Rochers, by Argentré road: 6 km, ✆ 02 99 96 52 52. 10 D2

Château★★: tour de Montalifant ≤★, tryptich★ - The town★: rue Baudrairie★★ A 5, ramparts★, Notre-Dame church ★ B - Tertres noirs ≤★★ via ④ - Park gardens★ by ③ - ≤★★ D178 B and D857 A - Champeaux: place★, church stalls ★ and stained-glass windows★ 9 km by ④.

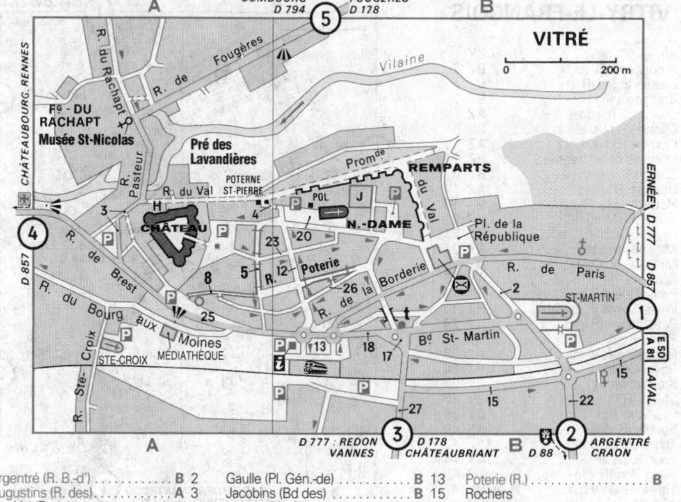

Argentré (R. B.-d') . . . . B 2	Gaulle (Pl. Gén.-de) . . . . B 13	Poterie (R.) . . . . B
Augustins (R. des) . . . . A 3	Jacobins (Bd des) . . . . B 15	Rochers (Bd des) . . . . B 22
Bas-Val (R. du) . . . . A 4	Leclerc (Pl. Gén.) . . . . B 17	St-Louis (R.) . . . . AB 23
Baudrairie (R. de la) . . . . A 5	Liberté (R. de la) . . . . B 18	St-Yves (Pl.) . . . . A 25
Borderie (R. de la) . . . . B	Notre-Dame (Pl. et R.) . . . . B 20	Sévigné (R.) . . . . B 26
En-Bas (R. d') . . . . A 8	Paris (R. de) . . . . B	70e-R.I. (R. du) . . . . B 27
Garengeot (R.) . . . . B 12	Pasteur (R.) . . . . A	

Ibis without rest — VISA MC AE

1 bd Chateaubriant, via ③ – ✆ 02 99 75 51 70 – H6233@accor.com – Fax 02 99 75 51 71

50 rm – †€ 49/66 ††€ 49/66, ☕ € 7,50

◆ This new Ibis hotel near the medieval centre offers practically furnished rooms with a small dressing room. Those overlooking the park to the rear are quietest.

Le Pichet — VISA MC AE

17 bd Laval, via ① – ✆ 02 99 75 24 09 – restaurant@lepichet.fr – Closed Wednesday dinner, Thursday dinner and Sunday

Rest – *(number of covers limited, pre-book)* Menu € 18 (weekday lunch), € 26/50 – Carte € 34/50

◆ This regional-style building features a lovely garden planted with trees where outside tables are laid out in summer (barbecue). Bright comfortable dining room-veranda.

Le Potager — VISA MC AE

5 pl. Gén. Leclerc – ✆ 02 99 74 68 88 – restaurant_lepotager@wanadoo.fr – Fax 02 99 75 38 13 – Closed 11-24 August, Sunday dinner and Monday

Rest – Menu € 17 (weekdays)/32 – Carte € 27/42 B **t**

◆ This charming bistro area and pleasant modern dining room have an attractive decor in rich warm shades of aubergine, orange and green. Updated cuisine; set lunchtime menu.

VITRY-LE-FRANÇOIS – 51 Marne – 306 J10 – pop. 16 737 – alt. 105 m – ✉ 51300 Northern France and the Paris Region 13 **B2**

Paris 181 – Bar-le-Duc 55 – Châlons-en-Champagne 33 – Verdun 96

Office de tourisme, place Giraud ✆ 03 26 74 45 30, Fax 03 26 74 84 74

La Poste — VISA MC AE

pl. Royer-Collard – ✆ 03 26 74 02 65 – hoteldelaposte.vitry@wanadoo.fr – Fax 03 26 74 54 71 – Closed 3-24 August, 23 December-6 January and Sunday BZ **a**

29 rm – †€ 49/57 ††€ 65/95, ☕ € 8 – **Rest** – Menu € 24/75 – Carte € 46/69

◆ Ideally situated for discovering the town rebuilt by Francis I, with well renovated bright and practical rooms. An elegant neo-classical dining room serving updated cuisine.

VITRY-LE-FRANÇOIS

Armes (Pl. d') .... ABY
Arquebuse (R. de l') .... BZ 2
Beaux-Anges (R. des) .... BZ 4
Bourgeois (Fg Léon) .... BZ 7
Briand (R. Aristide) .... AZ
Chêne-Vert (R. du) .... BY 9
Dominé (Bd du Col.) .... AZ 10
Domyné-de-Verzet (R.) .... BZ 13
Grande-Rue-de-Vaux .... BY
Guesde (R. Jules) .... AZ 14
Hôtel-de-Ville (R. de l') .... BZ 19
Joffre (Pl. Mar.) .... BZ 21
Leclerc (Pl. Mar.) .... BY 23
Minimes (R. des) .... AY 24
Moll (Av. du Col.) .... AZ 25
Paris (Av. de) .... AY 26
Petite-Rue-de-Vaux .... BY 29
Petite-Sainte (R. de la) .... BZ 30
Petit-Denier (R. du) .... AY 28
Pont (R. du) .... AY
République (Av. de la) .... BZ 33
Royer-Collard (Pl.) .... BZ 34
Ste-Memje (R.) .... BY 37
St-Éloi (R.) .... BY 35
St-Michel (R.) .... ABY 36
Soeurs (R. des) .... AY 40
Tanneurs (R. des) .... AYZ 42
Tour (R. de la) .... AY 44
Vieux-Port (R. du) .... BZ 46
Vitry-le-Brûlé (Fg de) .... BY 47
106e-R.-I. (Av. du) .... BZ 49

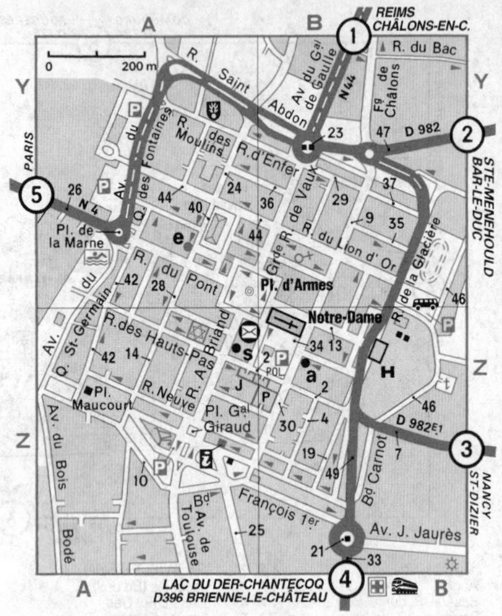

De la Cloche

34 r. A. Briand – ☎ 03 26 74 03 84 – chef.sautetepicerie@wanadoo.fr – Fax 03 26 74 15 52 – Closed 23 December-3 January and Sunday dinner 1st October-31 May — AZ s

22 rm – †€ 52 ††€ 57, ☕ € 9 – ½ P € 62
Rest *Jacques Sautet* – Menu € 27/60 – Carte € 45/88
Rest *Vieux Briscard* – brasserie Menu (€ 12), € 17/25

◆ Centrally located hotel with a few renovated, attractively decorated rooms as well as simpler rooms. A pleasant restaurant offering a fine choice of tasty house specialities. The former bar is home to the Vieux Briscard. Brasserie menu.

Gourmet des Halles

11 r. Soeurs – ☎ 03 26 74 48 88 – Fax 03 26 72 54 28 – Closed Tues. evening — AY e

Rest – Menu (€ 7,50), € 11 (weekdays)/23 – Carte € 17/39

◆ Pleasant stop just by the Halles. A pretty fresco enhances one of the three dining rooms. In summer, you can enjoy your meal on the pavement terrace.

VITTEAUX – 21 Côte-d'Or – 320 H5 – pop. 1 114 – alt. 320 m – ✉ 21350

Burgundy-Jura — 8 **C2**

Paris 259 – Auxerre 100 – Avallon 55 – Beaune 64 – Dijon 47 – Montbard 34 – Saulieu 34

Office de tourisme, 16, rue Hubert Languet ☎ 03 80 33 90 14, Fax 03 80 33 90 14

Vieille Auberge

19 r. Verdun – ☎ 03 80 49 60 88 – Fax 03 80 49 68 14 – Closed 16-30 June, 7-27 October, 6-16 January, Sunday dinner, Thursday dinner from November to March, Tuesday dinner, Wednesday dinner and Monday

Rest – Menu (€ 10), € 14 (weekdays)/26 – Carte € 18/36

◆ Family-run village inn whose bar, with a country atmosphere, serves two rustic and renovated dining rooms. Small terrace and garden. Area for playing boules. Traditional dishes.

VITTEL – 88 Vosges – **314** D3 – **pop. 6 117 – alt. 347 m – Spa : early April-mid Dec. – Casino** AY – ✉ **88800** ▮ **Alsace-Lorraine** 26 **B3**

- Paris 342 – Belfort 129 – Chaumont 84 – Épinal 43 – Langres 80 – Nancy 85
- Office de tourisme, place de la Marne ✆ 03 29 08 08 88, Fax 03 29 08 37 99
- de Vittel Ermittage Hotel Ermitage, ✆ 03 29 08 81 53 ;
- du Bois de Hazeau Centre Préparation Olympique, Southwest: 1 km, ✆ 03 29 08 20 85.
- Park★.

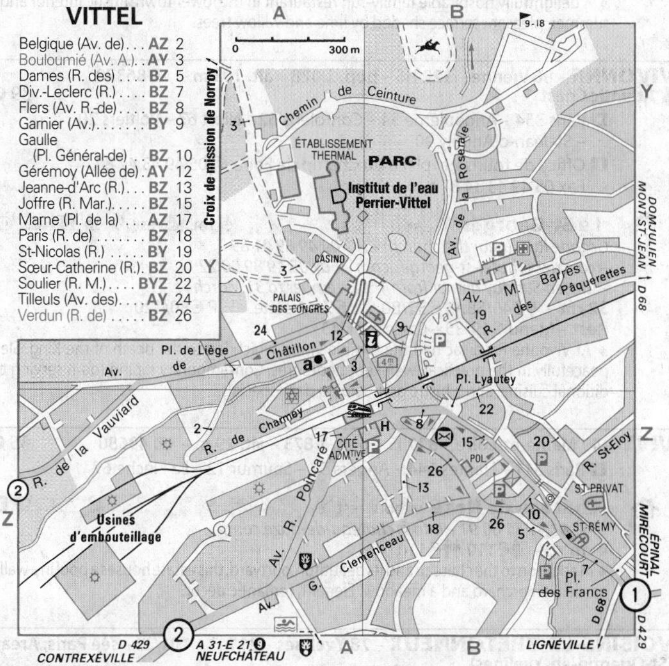

Providence

125 av. Châtillon – ✆ 03 29 08 08 27 – providence.vittel@wanadoo.fr – Fax 03 29 08 62 60 – 1 Apr - 31 Dec AY **a**

38 rm – 🚹€ 55/75 🚹🚹€ 65/85, ☕ € 10

◆ This Vittel establishment has been renovated. Attractive, small rooms in warm colours, and larger, well-equipped junior suites (big bathtubs).

West 3 km by La Vauviard road AZ – ✉ **88800 Vittel**

L'Orée du Bois

– ✆ 03 29 08 88 88 – info@loreeduboisvittel.fr – Fax 03 29 08 01 61

39 rm – 🚹€ 50/86 🚹🚹€ 60/86, ☕ € 9 – ½ P € 59/71

Rest – Menu € 17/34 – Carte € 27/49

◆ Opposite the golf course, this modern hotel provides a wide range of leisure activities: spa, massage, sauna, steam bath. Stylish rooms (try one of the 'chambres biologiques'). Classic menu whose flair for modernity does not spurn its regional roots. Garden terrace.

VIVÈS – 66 Pyrénées-Orientales – **344** H7 – **see le Boulou**

VIVIERS – 07 Ardèche – **331** K7 – **pop. 3 413 – alt. 65 m** – ✉ **07220** 44 **B3**

Paris 618 – Lyon 163 – Marseille 167 – Montpellier 158 – Valence 63

Office de tourisme, 5, place Riquet ☎ 04 75 52 77 00, Fax 04 75 52 81 63

Le Relais du Vivarais with rm — rm, P VISA MC

31 rte Nationale 86 – ☎ 04 75 52 60 41 – relais.viviers@wanadoo.fr
– Closed 1st-21 March
5 rm – €70/72 €70/72, €9
Rest – *(closed 1st-21 March, 22 December-3 January and Sunday dinner except residents)* Menu €25/46

◆ A delightfully hospitable family-run restaurant in the lower town. Rustic interior and in summer, pleasant terrace shaded by lime and willow trees.

VIVONNE – 86 Vienne – **322** H6 – **pop. 3 028 – alt. 103 m** – ✉ **86370**
Atlantic Coast 39 **C2**

Paris 354 – Angoulême 94 – Confolens 62 – Niort 67 – Poitiers 20 – St-Jean-d'Angély 90

Office de tourisme, place du Champ de Foire ☎ 05 49 43 47 88, Fax 05 49 43 34 87

Le St-Georges — rm, rest, VISA MC

Grande Rue, (near the church) – ☎ 05 49 89 01 89
– courrier@hotel-st-georges.com – Fax 05 49 89 00 22
– Closed Sunday dinner from 1st November to 31 March
32 rm – €46/58 €52/80, €7 – 1 suite – ½ P €80/120
Rest – Menu €19/35 – Carte €31/43

◆ At Vivonne Ravaillac had the terrible vision which led to the death of the King. Sleep peacefully in the practical, well-kept bedrooms. Contemporary dining room serving traditional cuisine, and a bistro area serving daily specials.

VIVY – 49 Maine-et-Loire – **317** I5 – **pop. 1 873 – alt. 29 m** – ✉ **49680** 35 **C2**

Paris 311 – Nantes 144 – Angers 57 – Saumur 12 – La Flèche 67

Château de Nazé without rest — P

– ☎ 02 41 51 80 91 – info@chateau-de-naze.com
4 rm – €110 €110

◆ In addition to the château and its beautiful courtyard, this estate houses a pool in a walled garden, an orchard and a meadow. Elegant, romantic décor.

VOISINS-LE-BRETONNEUX – 78 Yvelines – **311** I3 – **101** 22 – **see Paris, Area (St-Quentin-en-Yvelines)**

VOITEUR – 39 Jura – **321** D6 – **pop. 718 – alt. 260 m** – ✉ **39210** 16 **B3**

Paris 409 – Besançon 79 – Dole 51 – Lons-le-Saunier 12

Office de tourisme, 1 place de la Mairie ☎ 03 84 44 62 47, Fax 03 84 44 64 86

Château St-Martin without rest — P

– ☎ 03 84 44 91 87 – kellerbr@wanadoo.fr – Fax 03 84 44 91 87
– Closed December and January
4 rm – €90 €100

◆ This listed château offers an aperitif to its guests on arrival. Some of its differently-styled rooms overlook the park and 14C chapel. Piano available.

VOLLORE-VILLE – 63 Puy-de-Dôme – **326** I8 – **pop. 684 – alt. 540 m** – ✉ **63120**

Paris 408 – Clermont-Ferrand 58 – Roanne 63 – Vichy 52 6 **C2**

Château de Vollore without rest — P VISA MC

– ☎ 04 73 53 71 06 – chateau.vollore@wanadoo.fr – Fax 04 73 53 72 44
5 rm – €110/160 €130/230

◆ A castle 'with a view' belonging to the La Fayette family. The great grandson of the historic character is married to the owners' daughter. Period furnished rooms and suites.

VOLNAY – 21 Côte-d'Or – 320 I7 – see Beaune

VONNAS – 01 Ain – 328 C3 – pop. 2 422 – alt. 200 m – ✉ 01540 Burgundy-Jura

Paris 409 – Bourg-en-Bresse 23 – Lyon 69 – Mâcon 21 – Villefranche-sur-Saône 41 43 **E1**

Syndicat d'initiative, rue du Moulin ✆ 04 74 50 04 47, Fax 04 74 50 09 74

Georges Blanc

pl. du Marché – ✆ 04 74 50 90 90 – blanc@relaischateaux.com – Fax 04 74 50 08 80 – Closed January

35 rm – €180/450 €180/450, €28 – 6 suites

Rest – *(closed Wednesday lunch, Monday and Tuesday) (number of covers limited, pre-book)* Menu €120/230 – Carte €123/185

Spec. Sot-l'y-laisse et huître creuse. Duo de ris de veau, légumes du marché, jus noisette. Palet de chocolat "pur caraïbes" au vieux Maury. **Wines** Mâcon-Azé, Moulin-à-Vent.

◆ Hidden away in a flower garden on the banks of the Veyle, this half-timbered and red brick hotel provides plush, spacious rooms. The delicious Bresse cuisine make this one of France's finest restaurants. Superb wine cellar.

Résidence des Saules without rest

– ✆ 04 74 50 90 51 – blanc@relaischateaux.com – Fax 04 74 50 08 80 – Closed January

6 rm – €150 €150, €28 – 4 suites

◆ This smart, geranium-decked house is practically the annexe of the Georges Blanc hotel on the other side of the square. The comfortable rooms are located above the shop.

L'Ancienne Auberge

– ✆ 04 74 50 90 50 – auberge1900@georgesblanc.com – Fax 04 74 50 08 80 – Closed January

Rest – Menu €25 (weekday lunch), €30/49 – Carte €36/66

◆ In a former lemonade factory. The idealised 1940s bistro decor pays tribute to the inn opened by the Blanc family in the late 19C (old photos and posters). Regional cuisine.

VOSNE-ROMANÉE – 21 Côte-d'Or – 320 J7 – pop. 460 – alt. 242 m – ✉ 21700

Paris 330 – Chalon-sur-Saône 49 – Dijon 21 – Dole 71 8 **D1**

Le Richebourg without rest

ruelle du Pont – ✆ 03 80 61 59 59 – hotel@lerichebourg.com – Fax 03 80 61 59 50 – Closed 23-27 December

24 rm – €95/185 €95/185, €15 – 2 suites

◆ Hotel in a tiny wine-growing village offering modern-style rooms with functional furniture and two suites with all mod cons. Fitness area with sauna, hammam and jacuzzi.

VOUGEOT – 21 Côte-d'Or – 320 J6 – pop. 187 – alt. 239 m – ✉ 21640 Burgundy-Jura

Paris 325 – Beaune 27 – Dijon 17 8 **D1**

Château du Clos de Vougeot★ O.

Clos de la Vouge

1 r. Moulin – ✆ 03 80 62 89 65 – closdelavouge@wanadoo.fr – Fax 03 80 62 83 14 – Closed 24 December-31 January

10 rm – €50/69 €90/125, €10 – **Rest** – *(closed Monday and Tuesday 1st November-31 March)* Menu €24/36 – Carte €27/61

◆ This restored regional-style building is close to the renowned Château du Clos de Vougeot. Spacious, comfortable, soundproofed rooms.

in Gilly-lès-Cîteaux 2 km east by D 251 – pop. 567 – alt. 227 m – ✉ 21640

Château de Gilly

– ✆ 03 80 62 89 98 – gilly@grandesetapes.fr – Fax 03 80 62 82 34

37 rm – €160/312 €160/312, €22 – 11 suites – ½ P €80

Rest *Clos Prieur* – *(closed lunch except Sunday)* Menu €42/65 – Carte €48/224

Rest *Côté Terroirs* – *(closed dinner and Sunday)* Menu €20/25

◆ Calm and refinement characterise this former Cistercian abbot's residence; spacious personalised rooms. Pleasant formal French gardens. This restaurant is located in a superb 14C rib-vaulted cellar. Bistro ambiance at Côté Terroirs.

L'Orée des Vignes without rest
6 rte d'Épernay – ✆ 03 80 62 49 77 – info@oreedesvignes.com – Fax 03 80 62 49 76 – Closed 21 December-4 January
26 rm – †€ 64/124 ††€ 64/124, ☐ € 9
◆ Former 16C farm buildings housing rather spacious rooms with functional furniture. Breakfast area and two pleasant meeting rooms.

in Flagey-Échezeaux 3 km southeast by D 971 and D 109 – pop. 494 – alt. 227 m – ✉ 21640

Losset without rest
10 pl. de l'Église – ✆ 03 80 62 46 00 – hotel.losset@wanadoo.fr – Fax 03 80 62 46 08
7 rm – †€ 85/130 ††€ 85/130, ☐ € 8
◆ A new hotel with rather large, comfortable rooms (with beams) adorned with rustic or modern furniture. Small lounge with fireplace.

Petit Paris without rest
6 r. du Petit-Paris – ✆ 03 80 62 84 09 – petitparis.bourgogne@free.fr – Fax 03 80 62 83 88
4 rm ☐ – †€ 85 ††€ 85
◆ Warm welcome and personalised rooms in this 17C house set in parkland. Painting courses for adults and children.

Simon
12 pl. de l'Église – ✆ 03 80 62 88 10 – famille.simon7@wanadoo.fr – Fax 03 80 62 88 10 – Closed 1st-13 August, 22-26 December, 18 February – 15 March, Sunday dinner and Wednesday
Rest – Menu (€ 20), € 30 bi/80 – Carte € 35/71
◆ This restaurant, in the centre of a wine-growing village, has a country setting and a new dining room serving appetising traditional cuisine.

VOUGY – 74 Haute-Savoie – 328 L4 – see Bonneville

VOUILLÉ – 86 Vienne – 322 G5 – pop. 2 774 – alt. 118 m – ✉ 86190 39 C1

Paris 345 – Châtellerault 46 – Parthenay 34 – Poitiers 18 – Saumur 89 – Thouars 55

Office de tourisme, 10, place de l'Eglise ✆ 05 49 51 06 69, Fax 05 49 50 87 48

Cheval Blanc with rm
3 r. Barre – ✆ 05 49 51 81 46 – lechevalblanc.clovis@wanadoo.fr – Fax 05 49 51 96 31 – Closed February half-term holidays
14 rm – †€ 49 ††€ 49/53, ☐ € 6 – ½ P € 46 – **Rest** – Menu € 18/45
◆ In the centre of the small town, this establishment has modern dining rooms, (one with a beautiful fireplace) overlooking the river, as does the summer terrace. Practical bedrooms.

Clovis
– Closed February half-term holidays
30 rm – †€ 49 ††€ 49/53, ☐ € 6 – ½ P € 46
◆ A new building 100m from the main house offers functional well-kept rooms. Breakfast buffet.

VOUTENAY-SUR-CURE – 89 Yonne – 319 F6 – pop. 189 – alt. 130 m – ✉ 89270 7 B2

Paris 206 – Auxerre 37 – Avallon 15 – Vézelay 15

Auberge Le Voutenay with rm
– ✆ 03 86 33 51 92 – auberge.voutenay@wanadoo.fr – Fax 03 86 33 51 91 – Closed 16-24 June, 1st-21 January, Sunday dinner, Monday and Tuesday
7 rm – †€ 40 ††€ 55/65, ☐ € 8 – ½ P € 65
Rest – *(number of covers limited, pre-book)* Menu € 25/55
◆ This 18C abode beside the N 6 overlooks pleasant tree-lined grounds. Rustic yet elegant dining room and a small shop selling regional produce. 1940s style in the rooms.

VOUVRAY – 37 Indre-et-Loire – 317 N4 – pop. 3 046 – alt. 55 m – ✉ 37210
Châteaux of the Loire 11 **B2**

Paris 240 – Amboise 18 – Blois 51 – Château-Renault 25 – Tours 10

Office de tourisme, 12, rue Rabelais ✆ 02 47 52 68 73, Fax 02 47 52 70 88

Domaine des Bidaudières without rest

r. Peu Morier, Vernou-sur-Brenne on D 46 – ✆ 02 47 52 66 85 – contact@bidaudieres.com – Fax 02 47 52 62 17

7 rm – €95/105 €105/160

♦ This 18C building has peaceful rooms, decorated with Jouy prints and antique furniture. Views of the magnificent park.

Le Grand Vatel

8 av. Brûlé – ✆ 02 47 52 70 32 – legrandvatel@orange.fr – Fax 02 47 52 74 52 – Closed 5-15 March, 20-28 December, Sunday dinner and Monday

Rest – Menu € 20/72 – Carte € 47/59

♦ This regional-style stone residence has two dining rooms, one of which is decorated in 1920s style. Classical cuisine. Vouvray takes pride of place on the wine list.

VOVES – 28 Eure-et-Loir – 311 F6 – pop. 2 928 – alt. 146 m – ✉ 28150 12 **C1**

Paris 99 – Ablis 36 – Bonneval 23 – Chartres 25 – Châteaudun 38 – Étampes 51 – Orléans 61

Le Quai Fleuri

15 r. Texier Gallas – ✆ 02 37 99 15 15 – quaifleuri@wanadoo.fr – Fax 02 37 99 11 20

21 rm – €58 €64, € 9 – 4 suites – ½ P € 82

Rest – *(closed Sunday dinner)* Menu € 15 (weekdays)/44 – Carte € 43/65

♦ This recently-established hotel, flanked by a reconstructed mill, has a few small rooms with personal touches. Those in the annexe are larger and on a level with the park. Restaurant with a bright modern decor, serving traditional cuisine.

VRON – 80 Somme – 301 D6 – pop. 721 – alt. 15 m – ✉ 80120 36 **A1**

Paris 211 – Abbeville 27 – Amiens 76 – Berck-sur-Mer 17 – Calais 89 – Hesdin 24

L'Hostellerie du Clos du Moulin

1 r. Maréchal Leclerc – ✆ 03 22 23 74 75 – contact@leclosdumoulin.fr – Fax 03 22 23 74 76

15 rm – €95/125 €110/145, € 10 – ½ P € 80/98 – **Rest** – Menu (€ 30), € 37/47 – Carte approx. € 54

♦ Surrounded by a pretty garden, the former stables of this estate are home to cosy personalised guestrooms, some with lounge. Traditional decor and modern facilities. The dining rooms located in the 16C stables are full of character.

WAHLBACH – 68 Haut-Rhin – 315 I11 – see Altkirch

LA WANTZENAU – 67 Bas-Rhin – 315 K5 – see Strasbourg

WASSELONNE – 67 Bas-Rhin – 315 I5 – pop. 5 542 – alt. 220 m – ✉ 67310
Alsace-Lorraine 1 **A1**

Paris 464 – Haguenau 42 – Molsheim 15 – Saverne 15 – Sélestat 51 – Strasbourg 27

Syndicat d'initiative, 22, place du Général Leclerc ✆ 03 88 59 12 00, Fax 03 88 04 23 57

Au Saumon with rm

rm, VISA

r. Gén. de Gaulle – ✆ 03 88 87 01 83 – weltythierry@neuf.fr – Fax 03 88 87 46 69 – Closed 1st-15 July, Sunday dinner, Tuesday dinner and Wednesday

5 rm – €45 €45, € 6 – ½ P € 50

Rest – Menu (€ 9,50), € 11,50 (weekday lunch), € 18/41 – Carte € 34/54

♦ After a recent makeover, this house now offers contemporary style rooms and a veranda flooded with light. Classic bourgeois menu.

WATTIGNIES – 59 Nord – 302 G4 – see Lille

WENGELSBACH – 67 Bas-Rhin – 315 K2 – see Niedersteinbach

WESTHALTEN – 68 Haut-Rhin – 315 H9 – pop. 816 – alt. 240 m – ✉ 68250
Alsace-Lorraine 1 **A3**

Paris 480 – Colmar 22 – Guebwiller 11 – Mulhouse 28 – Thann 27

Auberge du Cheval Blanc (Gilbert Koehler) with rm
20 r. Rouffach – ☎ 03 89 47 01 16 rm, VISA
– chevalblanc.west@wanadoo.fr – Fax 03 89 47 64 40
– Closed 14 June-1st July, 12 January-5 February, Tuesday lunch, Sunday dinner and Monday
12 rm – €60/75 €68/85, €12 – ½ P €80/92
Rest – Menu €36/87 – Carte €54/84
Spec. Dégustation de nos foies gras d'oie en trois services. Noisettes de chevreuil à l'alsacienne (season). Canette de la Dombes rôtie aux épices tandoori (season).
Wines Sylvaner, Riesling.

◆ Elegant house owned by the same family of wine-growers since 1785. Classic, creative cuisine and fine selection of Alsatian wines including those from the estate. The recently redone rooms are spacious, comfortable and modern.

WETTOLSHEIM – 68 Haut-Rhin – 315 H8 – see Colmar

WEYERSHEIM – 67 Bas-Rhin – 315 K4 – pop. 2 993 – alt. 140 m – ✉ 67720
1 **B1**

Paris 486 – Haguenau 18 – Saverne 49 – Strasbourg 21 – Wissembourg 50

Auberge du Pont de la Zorn VISA
2 r. République – ☎ 03 88 51 36 87 – debeer.m@wanadoo.fr – Fax 03 88 51 36 87
– Closed 20 August-4 September, 9-22 February, Saturday lunch, Wednesday and Thursday
Rest – Menu (€11,50), €16 (weekdays)/35 – Carte €23/39

◆ Reproductions of drawings by Hansi, exposed beams and regional pottery: Alsace in a nutshell! Bucolic terrace by the Zorn river. Flambé tarts served in the evening.

WIERRE-EFFROY – 62 Pas-de-Calais – 301 D3 – pop. 747 – alt. 28 m – ✉ 62720
30 **A2**

Paris 262 – Calais 29 – Abbeville 88 – Boulogne-sur-Mer 14 – Saint-Omer 47

La Ferme du Vert rest, VISA
r. du Vert – ☎ 03 21 87 67 00 – ferme.du.vert@wanadoo.fr – Fax 03 21 83 22 62
– Closed 14 December-20 January and Sunday October-March
16 rm – €57/89 €62/123, €11 – 2 suites – ½ P €65/95
Rest – *(closed Saturday lunch October-April, Monday lunch and Sunday)*
Menu €28/45 – Carte €30/50

◆ Rural tranquillity reigns at this old Boulogne region farmhouse. Rooms of various sizes are decorated with taste and simplicity. Tasting and sale of homemade cheese. In the restaurant, you can enjoy tasty traditional dishes concocted with local produce.

WIMEREUX – 62 Pas-de-Calais – 301 C3 – pop. 7 493 – alt. 7 m – ✉ 62930
Northern France and the Paris Region 30 **A2**

Paris 269 – Arras 125 – Boulogne-sur-Mer 7 – Calais 33 – Marquise 13

Office de tourisme, quai Alfred Giard ☎ 03 21 83 27 17, Fax 03 21 32 76 91

Du Centre rest, VISA
78 r. Carnot – ☎ 03 21 32 41 08 – hotel.du.centre@wanadoo.fr
– Fax 03 21 33 82 48 – Closed 21 December-30 January
23 rm – €58/82 €58/82, €8,50 – **Rest** – *(closed Mon.)* Menu (€18), €21/31 – Carte €23/44

◆ An old building situated on the main street of a seaside resort on the Opal Coast. The rooms have been renovated and some have a mezzanine. The dining room sports a pleasant bistro look. Traditional dishes and seafood.

Liégeoise et Atlantic Hôtel with rm — the sea, rm, rest,
digue de mer – 03 21 32 41 01 – Alain.delpierre@wanadoo.fr – Fax 03 21 87 46 17
18 rm – €76/90 €90/123, €10 – **Rest** – Menu €35/61 – Carte €59/75
◆ Well situated on the dyke-promenade, facing the Channel. Beautiful panoramic dining room nicely furnished in the Louis XVI style. Choose one of the new rooms overlooking the sea.

Épicure (Philippe Carrée)
1 r. Pompidou – 03 21 83 21 83 – Fax 03 21 33 53 20 – Closed 20 August-5 September, 20 December-6 January, Wednesday dinner and Sunday
Rest – *(number of covers limited, pre-book)* Menu €24/39 (dinner) – Carte €38/56
Spec. Huîtres spéciales, purée de pois chiches, gelée de queue de bœuf (October to March). Homard côtier, ravioles d'aubergine et tomate (October to March). Pomme de ris de veau au four, jus au thé fumé (September to May).
◆ In the town centre, behind a discreet façade, a very small dining room with an intimate hushed setting. Attractive modern cooking focusing on seafood.

WINKEL – 68 Haut-Rhin – 315 H12 – pop. 334 – alt. 575 m – 68480 1 A3

Paris 466 – Altkirch 23 – Basel 35 – Belfort 50 – Colmar 92 – Montbéliard 46 – Mulhouse 42

Au Cerf with rm
76 r. Principale – 03 89 40 85 05 – g.koller@tiscali.fr – Fax 03 89 08 11 10 – Closed 22-30 September, 2-24 February
6 rm – €43/49 €47/60, €6,50 – ½ P €49
Rest – *(closed Monday and Thursday)* Menu (€10), €25/50 – Carte €25/50
◆ Close to the source of the Ill, this friendly inn with a red façade has several dining rooms including one in winstub style. Pleasant rooms under the eaves.

WISEMBACH – 88 Vosges – 314 K3 – pop. 428 – alt. 500 m – 88520 27 D3

Paris 413 – Colmar 54 – Épinal 69 – St-Dié 16 – Ste-Marie-aux-Mines 11 – Sélestat 34

Blanc Ru with rm
19 r. du 8 mai 45 – 03 29 51 78 51 – Fax 03 29 51 70 67 – Closed 23 September-8 October, 3 February-4 March, Tuesday dinner, Sunday dinner and Monday
7 rm – €48 €48/59, €8 – ½ P €48/58
Rest – Menu €23/42 – Carte €33/58
◆ Take a seat either in the pretty winter garden or in the spacious, countrified dining room. Classic repertory (frogs' legs are the speciality of the house). Neat rooms.

WISSEMBOURG – 67 Bas-Rhin – 315 L2 – pop. 8 170 – alt. 157 m – 67160

Alsace-Lorraine 1 B1

Paris 512 – Haguenau 33 – Karlsruhe 42 – Sarreguemines 80 – Strasbourg 67

Office de tourisme, 9, place de la République 03 88 94 10 11, Fax 03 88 94 18 82

Old town ★: St-Pierre and St-Paul church ★.

Village★★ of Hunspach 11 km by ②.

Au Moulin de la Walk — rm, rm,
2 r. Walk – 03 88 94 06 44 – info@moulin-walk.com – Fax 03 88 54 38 03 – Closed 9-31 January A s
25 rm – €55/70 €55/70, €8 – ½ P €70 – **Rest** – *(closed 20 June-4 July, 9-31 January, Friday lunch, Sunday dinner and Monday)* Menu €34/44 – Carte €39/53
◆ On the banks of a river, three buildings grafted onto the remains of a former mill whose wheel is still turning. Well-renovated rooms enhanced by modern wood panelling. The restaurant has a flowered setting and tile stove. Pretty summer terrace.

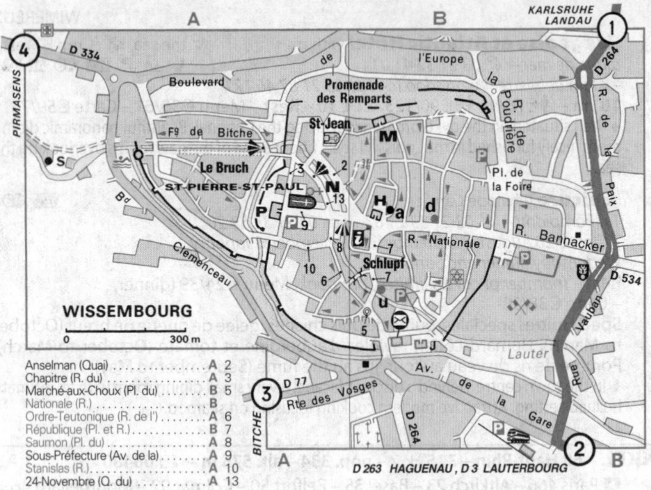

XX **Hostellerie du Cygne** with rm — AC rest, rm, VISA MC AE

3 r. Sel – ✆ 03 88 94 00 16 – hostellerie-cygne@wanadoo.fr – Fax 03 88 54 38 28 – Closed 7-20 July, 10-23 November, 16 February-2 March and Wednesday
16 rm – †€ 50/65 ††€ 50/75, ☐ € 9 – ½ P € 52/70
Rest – *(closed Thursday lunch, Sunday dinner and Wednesday)*
Menu € 30/65 B **a**

◆ Two adjacent houses, one dating back to the end of the 14th century, the other already listed as an inn in 1535. Dining room brightened by a beautiful marquetry ceiling. Renovated rooms.

XX **L'Ange** — VISA MC AE

2 r. de la République – ✆ 03 88 94 12 11 – pierrel4@wanadoo.fr – Fax 03 88 94 12 11 – Closed 16-26 June, 10-18 November, 23 February-10 March, Sunday dinner in winter, Monday and Tuesday B **u**
Rest – Menu € 29/38 – Carte € 39/48

◆ This former post-house is reached through a small paved courtyard-terrace which is very pleasant in summer. Two rooms in succession one of which is more rustic. Cuisine adapted to modern trends.

XX **Le Carrousel Bleu** — AC VISA MC

17 r. Nationale – ✆ 03 88 54 33 10 – le.carroussel-bleu@orange.fr – Closed 19 July-5 August, 26 December-3 January, Sunday dinner, Monday and Wednesday B **d**
Rest – Menu € 22 (weekday lunch), € 28/50

◆ This pleasant restaurant, situated on the main road, offers original and unusual recipes that will transport you thousands of miles from 'Little Venice'.

in Altenstadt 2 km by ② - ✉67160

XX **Rôtisserie Belle Vue** — AC P VISA MC

1 r. Principale – ✆ 03 88 94 02 30 – Fax 03 88 54 80 14 – Closed 1st-6 March, 4-28 August, Sunday dinner, Monday and Tuesday
Rest – Menu € 25, € 53 – Carte € 29/55

◆ This large family restaurant serves traditional cuisine in two plush dining rooms, providing attractive views of the garden. Daily specials served at the bar.

XONRUPT-LONGEMER – **88 Vosges** – **314** J4 – **see Gérardmer**

YERRES – 91 Essonne – 312 D3 – pop. 27 455 – alt. 45 m – ✉ 91330 21 D3

Paris 28 – Évry 20 – Boulogne-Billancourt 36 – Montreuil 29 – Argenteuil 52

Château du Maréchal de Saxe

rm, rest,

av. Grange, 2 km by D 94 towards Créteil –

01 69 48 78 53 – saxe@leshotelsparticuliers.com – Fax 01 69 83 84 91

25 rm – €105 €250, €16 – 2 suites – ½ P €109/181

Rest – Menu €32 (weekday lunch), €48/78 – Carte €45/77

♦ This red-brick château was a folly of Maréchal de Saxe. Elegant decor in the main bedrooms; a more contemporary feel to those in the annexe. Huge park. Two classical dining rooms adorned with allegorical frescoes, old crockery etc. Traditional cuisine.

YERVILLE – 76 Seine-Maritime – 304 F4 – pop. 2 170 – alt. 156 m – ✉ 76760

Paris 164 – Dieppe 44 – Fécamp 48 – Le Havre 69 – Rouen 33 33 C1

de Yerville 367 rue des Acacias, Northwest: 0.5 km, 02 32 70 15 49.

Hostellerie des Voyageurs

3 r. Jacques Ferny – 02 35 96 82 55 – andre.jumel@hostellerie-voyageurs.com – Fax 02 35 96 16 86 – Closed Sunday evening and Monday

Rest – Menu €18 (weekday lunch), €27/48 – Carte €51/58

♦ Local-style former post-house (1875) with a partly rustic, partly classic interior. Garden terrace serving aperitifs and coffee. Menus based on market produce.

YEU (ÎLE) – 85 Vendée – 361 BC7 – see Île d 'Yeu

YGRANDE – 03 Allier – 326 E3 – pop. 753 – alt. 333 m – ✉ 03160

Paris 304 – Clermont-Ferrand 110 – Moulins 34 – Bourges 100 – Nevers 71

Château d'Ygrande

countryside,

Le Mont, 4 km east by D 192 and secondary road –

04 70 66 33 11 – reservation@chateauygrande.fr – Fax 04 70 66 33 63 – Closed 1st January-28 February, Sunday and Monday October-April

17 rm – €116/210 €116/210, €18 – ½ P €117/164

Rest – *(closed Sunday evening and Monday except July-August)* Menu €27/64 – Carte approx. €50

♦ An attractive, 19C château with romantic charm. Its 40-ha park blends into the peaceful Bourbonnais landscape. Inside, elegance and good taste reign. A Directoire style dining room and modern menu using ingredients from the vegetable garden.

YSSINGEAUX – 43 Haute-Loire – 331 G3 – pop. 6 492 – alt. 829 m – ✉ 43200

Lyon - Rhone Valley 6 C3

Paris 565 – Ambert 73 – Privas 98 – Le Puy-en-Velay 27 – St-Étienne 52 – Valence 93

Office de tourisme, 16, place Foch 04 71 59 10 76, Fax 04 71 56 03 12

Le Bourbon

rest,

5 pl. Victoire – 04 71 59 06 54 – le.bourbon.hotel@wanadoo.fr – Fax 04 71 59 00 70 – Closed 19 June-2 July, 9-22 October, 21 December-23 January, Sunday dinner, Tuesday lunch and Monday

11 rm – €65/75 €65/75, €12 – ½ P €60 – **Rest** – Menu €21/45

♦ A small, welcoming inn on a revamped square. Neat, functional rooms with attractive modern bathrooms. A colourful restaurant reputed for its tasty regional menu made with produce from local growers.

YUTZ – 57 Moselle – 307 I2 – see Thionville

YVETOT – 76 Seine-Maritime – 304 E4 – pop. 10 770 – alt. 147 m – ✉ 76190

Normandy 33 C1

Paris 171 – Dieppe 57 – Fécamp 35 – Le Havre 58 – Lisieux 85 – Rouen 36

Office de tourisme, 8, place Maréchal Joffre 02 35 95 08 40, Fax 02 35 95 08 40

de Yerville Yerville 367 rue des Acacias, Northeast: 13 km, 02 32 70 15 49.

Windows★★ of St-Pierre church **E**.

Du Havre
pl. des Belges – ✆ 02 35 95 16 77 – hotel-du-havre@tiscali.fr – Fax 02 35 95 21 18
23 rm – †€ 52/66 ††€ 54/68, ☐ € 9 – ½ P € 50/56
Rest – *(closed Sunday except holidays)* Menu (€ 21), € 25 – Carte € 32/41
♦ An ordinary-looking building, opposite the post office, offering small and simple but individually styled rooms. Traditional cuisine in a dining room whose decoration varies according to the season and the news, in particular sports news.

Le Manoir aux Vaches
2 r. Guy de Maupassant – ✆ 02 35 95 65 65 – hotel-du-havre@tiscali.fr – Fax 02 35 95 21 18
9 rm ☐ – †€ 86/106 ††€ 96/136 – ½ P € 69
♦ A new hotel honouring cattle via its bovine collection.

Southeast 5 km on D 5 – ✉ 76190 Yvetot

Auberge du Val au Cesne with rm
rte Duclair – ✆ 02 35 56 63 06 – valaucesne@hotmail.com – Fax 02 35 56 92 78 – Closed 25 August-7 September, and 19 January-10 February
5 rm – †€ 90 ††€ 90, ☐ € 9 – ½ P € 82
Rest – *(closed Mon. and Tues.)* Menu € 28/60 bi – Carte € 31/60
♦ Delightful half-timbered farmhouse (17C), lost in the countryside. Several very stylish rustic dining rooms with well chosen bric-a-brac, wooden beams and fine fireplaces. Slightly bijou-type rooms. Dense garden adorned with a summer terrace and aviary.

in Motteville 9 km east by D 929 and D 20 – pop. 730 – alt. 160 m – ✉ 76970

Auberge du Bois St-Jacques
à la gare – ✆ 02 35 96 83 11 – bsj.nicolas@wanadoo.fr – Fax 02 35 96 23 18 – Closed August, 23 February-1st March, Sunday dinner, Monday dinner and Tuesday
Rest – Menu € 20 (weekdays)/41 – Carte approx. € 42
♦ The former station buffet has two dining rooms, one rustic (exposed beams, copperware) and the other modern in shades of red and rotunda-shaped. Traditional cuisine and fine wine selection, notably by the glass.

YVOIRE – 74 Haute-Savoie – 328 K2 – pop. 639 – alt. 380 m – ✉ 74140

French Alps — 46 **F1**

Paris 563 – Annecy 71 – Bonneville 41 – Genève 26 – Thonon-les-Bains 16
Office de tourisme, place de la mairie ✆ 04 50 72 80 21, Fax 04 50 72 84 21
Medieval village ★★: jardin des Cinq Sens★.

Les Flots Bleus — lake, rm
– ✆ 04 50 72 80 08 – contact@flotsbleus-yvoire.com – Fax 04 50 72 84 28 – Open 1st April-30 October
17 rm – †€ 120/180 ††€ 120/195, ☐ € 11 – ½ P € 93/130
Rest – Menu € 22 (weekdays)/88 – Carte € 33/64
♦ The attractive guestrooms in this hotel have stunning views of the lake. Rooms with either a terrace or balcony, modern comforts and top-of-the-range facilities. Contemporary or traditional Alpine furnishings. New modern dining room (there are plans to renovate the old one). Traditional cuisine.

Le Pré de la Cure — rest,
pl. de la Mairie – ✆ 04 50 72 83 58 – lepredelacure@wanadoo.fr – Fax 04 50 72 91 15 – Open 1st March-11 November
25 rm – †€ 72/82 ††€ 72/96, ☐ € 10 – ½ P € 80/85
Rest – Menu € 21 (weekdays)/47 – Carte € 35/50
♦ At the entrance to this picturesque medieval village. Large functional rooms command views of the lake or the quiet garden. Attentive staff. Regional cuisine served in the veranda/dining room or on the riverside terrace.

Vieille Porte
– ✆ 04 50 72 80 14 – info@la-vieille-porte.com – Fax 04 50 72 92 04 – Closed 16 November-12 February and Monday except July-August
Rest – Menu € 25/40 – Carte € 47/53
♦ 14C house that has belonged to the same family since 1587! Elegant interior with beams, terracotta and old stone. Terrace shaded by the ramparts.

XX **Du Port** with rm ≤ lake, 🏠 ◻ AC rm, ✂ rm, 📞 VISA MC AE
r. du Port – ✆ 04 50 72 80 17 – hoteldupport.yvoire@wanadoo.fr – Fax 04 50 72 90 71 – Open 1st March-5 November
7 rm – †€ 110/130 ††€ 110/210, ☕ € 12 – ½ P € 150/250
Rest – *(closed Wednesday except from May to September)* Menu € 30 (weekdays)/50 – Carte € 41/65
♦ Terrace by the lake and pretty, flower-covered façade for this house with its ideal location on the harbour. Fish specialities. Pretty rooms with lakeside decor.

YVOY-LE-MARRON – 41 Loir-et-Cher – 318 I6 – pop. 538 – alt. 129 m – ✉ 41600 12 C2

▶ Paris 163 – Orléans 35 – Blois 45 – La Ferté-St-Aubin 13 – Lamotte-Beuvron 15 – Romorantin-Lanthenay 34

ℹ Syndicat d'initiative, route de Chaumont ✆ 02 54 88 07 14, Fax 02 54 88 07 14

🏠 **Auberge du Cheval Blanc** 🏠 ♿ rm, P VISA MC
1 pl. Cheval Blanc – ✆ 02 54 94 00 00 – auberge.cheval.blanc@wanadoo.fr – Fax 02 54 94 00 01
15 rm – †€ 68 ††€ 86, ☕ € 10 – ½ P € 83
Rest – *(closed Tuesday lunch and Monday except July-August)* Menu € 20 (weekdays)/38
♦ This welcoming Sologne building in the centre of the small village offers warm, refined, good quality rooms in shades of ochre, red and yellow. Carefully preserved half-timbering and floor tiles give character to this dining room. Modern menu.

YZEURES-SUR-CREUSE – 37 Indre-et-Loire – 317 O8 – pop. 1 476 – alt. 74 m – ✉ 37290 11 B3

▶ Paris 318 – Châteauroux 72 – Châtellerault 28 – Poitiers 65 – Tours 85

🏠 **La Promenade** VISA MC
– ✆ 02 47 91 49 00 – Fax 02 47 94 46 12 – Closed 20 December-31 January, Monday and Tuesday
15 rm – †€ 53 ††€ 56/61, ☕ € 13 – ½ P € 53 – **Rest** – Menu € 20 (weekdays)/37 – Carte € 30/54
♦ Former post-house dating from 1780, near the village church, offering rooms with a carefully chosen decor. Rustic-styled restaurant with exposed beams, stone and an imposing fireplace. Traditional cuisine.

ZELLENBERG – 68 Haut-Rhin – 315 H7 – see Riquewihr

ZIMMERSHEIM – 68 Haut-Rhin – 315 I10 – see Mulhouse

ZONZA – 2A Corse-du-Sud – 345 E9 – see Corse

ZOUFFTGEN – 57 Moselle – 307 H2 – pop. 608 – alt. 250 m – ✉ 57330 26 B1

▶ Paris 341 – Luxembourg 20 – Metz 48 – Thionville 18

XXX ✿ **La Lorraine** (Marcel Keff) with rm 🌳 🏠 AC rest, 📞 P VISA MC
80 r. Principale – ✆ 03 82 83 40 46 – info@la-lorraine.fr – Fax 03 82 83 48 26 – Closed 18 August-2 September, 22 December-6 January, Monday and Tuesday
3 rm – †€ 120 ††€ 150, ☕ € 15
Rest – Menu € 40/70 – Carte € 72/99 🍇
Spec. Fricassée d'escargots au coulis de persil. Cochon de lait rôti, tarte de pomme de terre au lard. Œufs tièdes au chocolat noir. **Wines** Vins de Moselle.
♦ Border establishment popular for its well-prepared, modern cuisine. The floor provides views into the well-stocked wine cellar. Modern dining room with extensions in the greenhouse and garden terrace. Large, richly decorated rooms in the Lorraine style. Gourmet breakfast.

R. Gold AGE/Hoaqui

Andorran landscape

PRINCIPALITY OF ANDORRA

Michelin LOCAL map: n° **343** H9
Population: 72 320
Altitude: 2 946 m
Languedoc-Roussillon-Tarn Gorges

USEFUL INFORMATION

TOURIST OFFICE

rue du Dr-Vilanova, Andorre-la- Vieille ✆ (00-376) 82 02 14, Fax (00-376) 82 58 23
The Principality of Andorra, covering an area of 464 km², is set in the heart of the Pyrenees, between France and Spain. Since 1993, the Principality is a sovereign state, member of the U.N. The official language is Catalan but most of the people also speak French and Spanish.
The local currency is the euro.
To enter Andorra, European Union citizens require a valid passport or identity card.
Access from France: N 22 trunk road via Envalira Tunnel.

TRANSPORT

Coach links: from Toulouse-Blagnac Airport via Cie Novatel, information (00-376) 803 789 and Cie Nadal (00-376) 805 151.From SNCF railway stations of l'Hospitalet and Latour-de-Carol via Cie Hispano-Andorranne, information (00-376) 807 000.

ANDORRA-LA-VELLA Capitale de la Principauté – 343 H9 – alt. 1 029 m

28 **B3**

Paris 861 – Carcassonne 165 – Foix 102 – Perpignan 170

Vallée du Valira del Nord (Valira del Nord valley) ★ N.

Plaza — rest, VISA MC AE

r. Maria Pla 19 – (00-376) 87 94 44 – hotelplaza@hotels.andorra.com – Fax (00-376) 87 94 45 C **a**

92 rm – €59/269 €73/336, €14 – 8 suites

Rest – Menu €19

◆ Two elevators offering panoramic views serve the six floors of this luxury hotel laid out around a lush patio. Superb rooms with views of the Andorra summits.

Carlton Plaza — rest, VISA MC AE

av. Meritxell 23-25 – (00-376) 87 29 99 – carltonplaza@hotels.andorra.com – Fax (00-376) 87 29 98 B **m**

66 suites – €73/336, €14 – **Rest** – Menu €18

◆ The hotel franchise's latest arrival, the Plaza, offers its customers spacious suites with a living room, decorated in a very modern style.

Arthotel — VISA MC AE

r. Prat de la Creu 15-25 – (00-376)76 03 03 – arthotel@andorra.ad – Fax (00-376)76 03 04

125 rm – €100/128 €133/168

Rest – Menu €27

◆ Big modern building opened in 2002. Comfortable, large and well-equipped rooms. Some have whirlpool baths. Two restaurants. The one on the fifth floor enjoys a panoramic view. A more simple one on the ground floor.

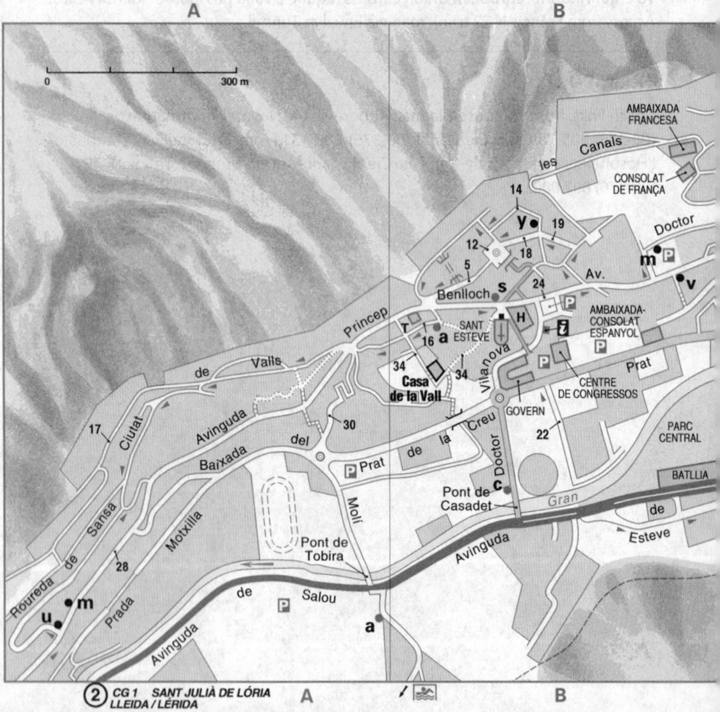

Mercure

rest, VISA AE

r. de la Roda – (00-376) 87 36 02 – mercureandorra@riberpuig.ad – Fax (00-376) 87 36 52 C **f**

164 rm – †€ 126/177 ††€ 186/262, ☕ € 12 – 9 suites

Rest – buffet Menu € 30

◆ The most pleasant of the chain's three hotels. Spacious public areas and countless leisure activities (indoor pool on the seventh floor). Buffet restaurant and English-style cafeteria.

Cèntric H.

VISA AE

av. Meritxell 87-89 – (00-376) 87 75 00 – husacentric@andornet.ad – Fax (00-376) 87 75 01 C **h**

74 rm ☕ – †€ 91/126 ††€ 132/192 – 6 suites

Rest – Menu € 22

◆ A modern hotel located in the middle of a shopping centre. Spacious rooms, some with a terrace. Pleasant bathrooms with separate shower. The well-lit dining room overlooks a busy street and is completed by a lounge with a fireplace.

President

rest, VISA

av. Santa Coloma 44 – (00-376) 87 72 77 – janhotels@andornet.ad – Fax (00-376) 87 62 22 A **m**

109 rm – †€ 60/320 ††€ 80/427, ☕ € 7,50 – 2 suites

Rest – Menu € 19

◆ This attractive hotel complex offers modern, comfortable rooms. Indoor pool and sundeck on the seventh floor. This modern, minimalist restaurant offers a fine view of Andorra's mountains.

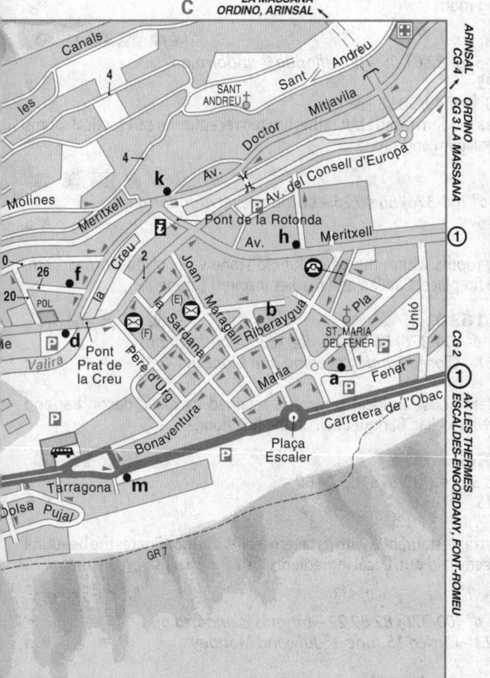

ANDORRA LA VELLA

Baixada del Molí	A	
Bonaventura Armengol	C	2
Bonaventura Riberaygua	C	
Canals	BC	
Casadet (Pont de)	B	
Ciutat de Valls	A	
Consell d'Europa (Av. del)	C	
Creu Grossa	C	4
Doctor Mitjavila (Av.)	C	
Doctor Molines	BC	
Doctor Néqui	B	5
Doctor Vilanova	B	
Escaler (Pl.)	C	
Esteve Dolça Pujal	BC	
Fener	C	
Fiter i Rossell	C	10
Guillemó (Pl.)	B	12
Joan Maragall	C	
Llacuna	B	14
Major (Antic Carrer)	B	16
Maria Pla	C	
Meritxell (Av.)	C	
Mestre Xavier Plana	A	17
Mossèn Cinto Verdaguer	B	18
Mossèn Tremosa	B	19
Obac	C	
Pere d'Urg	C	
Pompeu Fabra	C	20
Prada Casadet	B	22
Prada de la Creu	BC	
Prada Motxilla	A	
Prat de la Creu (Pont)	C	
Príncep Benlloch (Av. de)	AB	
Rebés (Pl.)	B	24
Roda	C	26
Rotonda (Pont de la)	C	
Roureda de Sansa	A	
Salou (Av.)	A	
Santa Coloma (Av. de)	A	28
Sant Andreu	C	
Sardana	C	
Tarragona (Av. de)	BC	
Toriba	A	30
Toriba (Pont de)	A	
Unió	C	
Vall	B	34

Hesperia Andorra la Vella without rest
av. Doctor Mitjavila 1 – (00-376) 88 08 80
– hotel@hesperia-andorralavella.com – Fax (00-376) 88 08 81 C **k**
59 rm – €50/60 €65/90, €10 – 1 suite
◆ This hotel has been fully renovated. The communal areas are a little small, but the large and well-equipped rooms offer full modern comforts.

Diplomatic (heated) rest, VISA
av. Tarragona – (00-376) 80 27 80 – hoteldiplomatic@andorra.ad
– Fax (00-376) 80 27 90 C**m**
81 rm – €63/98 €89/139 – 2 suites – **Rest** – Menu €18
◆ This recent cubic construction, some distance from the town centre, houses practical rooms attractive to both tourists and business people. International, unpretentious food served in a discreet contemporary setting.

Cérvol rest, VISA
av. Santa Coloma 46 – (00-376) 80 31 11 – hc@hotelcervol.com
– Fax (00-376) 80 31 22 A **u**
99 rm – €59/112 €67/168 – **Rest** – Menu €16
◆ The hotel is centrally located and offers well-equipped rooms. Half the rooms have water massage showers. Choice of buffet menu in the restaurant or cafeteria that gives directly onto the street.

De l'Isard rest, VISA
av. Meritxell 36 – (00-376) 87 68 00 – direccioisard@andorra.ad
– Fax (00-376) 87 68 01 B **v**
61 rm – €59/95 €67/138 – **Rest** – *(closed Sunday dinner and Monday in spring)* Menu €17
◆ A fully renovated interior lies behind the typical, regional style façade of this unpretentious hotel. The rooms are not huge but well equipped. Traditional recipes served in a pleasantly well-lit dining room.

Florida without rest VISA
r. Llacuna 15 – (00-376) 82 01 05 – hotelflorida@andorra.ad
– Fax (00-376) 86 19 25 B **y**
48 rm – €37/63 €49/90
◆ Family-run hotel with a modern façade but rather limited reception area. Practical rooms with parquet floors. Small gym and sauna.

XX **Borda Estevet** VISA
rte de La Comella 2 – (00-376) 86 40 26 – bordaestevet@andorra.ad
– Fax (00-376) 86 40 26 A **a**
Rest – Carte €33/48
◆ Several rustic dining rooms within the beautiful old stone walls of this former barn. Andorran furniture and fireplace. Catalan and market-inspired cuisine.

XX **La Borda Pairal 1630** VISA
r. Doctor Vilanova 7 – (00-376) 86 99 99 – lbp1630@andorra.ad
– Fax (00-376) 86 66 61 – Closed Sunday evening and Monday B **c**
Rest – Carte €24/37
◆ This old Andorran farmhouse in local stone has retained its rustic decor. Bar and restaurant with visible wine cellar. Banquet hall on the first floor.

XX **Taberna Ángel Belmonte** VISA
r. Ciutat de Consuegra 3 – (00-376) 82 24 60
– Fax (00-376) 82 35 15 C **b**
Rest – Carte €46/66
◆ What a pleasant place this restaurant is with its tavern feel! Wood dominates the beautiful decor, where all is perfectly laid out. Local ingredients, fish and shellfish on the menu.

XX **Can Benet** VISA
antic carrer Major 9 – (00-376) 82 89 22 – bruguis@andorra.ad
– Fax (00-376) 82 89 22 – Closed 15 June-1st July and Monday B **a**
Rest – Carte €25/34
◆ Small ground floor lobby and bar. The upstairs dining room has a typically Andorran decor of stone walls and wooden ceiling.

ANSALONGA – see Ordino

ARINSAL – **343** G9 – **alt. 1 145 m** – **Winter sports : 1 550/2 560 m** **3**
30 28 **B3**

Andorra la Vella 11

Xalet Verdú rest, VISA AE
– (00-376) 73 71 40 – *xaletverdu@andornet.ad* – *Fax (00-376) 73 71 41*
– Closed May and November
52 rm – €51/97 €72/124
Rest – *(dinner only)* Menu €24
◆ A large, newly-built, regional-style edifice popular with skiers as it is close to the cable car. Numerous rooms overlooking the peaks. International cuisine and a short wine list to recover one's strength between downhill runs.

CANILLO – **343** H9 – **alt. 1 531 m** 29 **C3**

Andorra la Vella 12

Crucifixion★ in Sant Joan de Caselles church Northeast: 1 km – Sanctuaire de Meritxell★ Southeast: 3 km.

Ski Plaza rest, rest, VISA AE
rte General – (00-376) 73 94 44 – *skiplaza@hotels.andorra.com*
– Fax (00-376) 73 94 45
115 rm – €59/269 €73/336, €14
Rest – Menu €23
◆ This particularly well-equipped establishment, at an altitude of 1600m, offers very comfortable, mountain-style rooms. Some have jacuzzis and a few are intended for children. For meals, gourmet restaurant or brasserie with internet access.

Roc del Castell without rest VISA
rte General – (00-376) 85 18 25 – *hotelroccastell@andorra.ad*
– Fax (00-376) 85 17 07
44 rm – €40/71 €51/101
◆ Beautiful stone building along the road, with comfortable and well soundproofed rooms. Minimal decor in the lounge and breakfast room.

ENCAMP – **343** H9 – **alt. 1 313 m** 29 **C3**

Andorra la Vella 8

Coray rest, VISA
r. Caballers 38 – (00-376) 83 15 13 – *Fax (00-376) 83 18 06*
– Closed November
85 rm – €30/36 €55/62
Rest – buffet Menu €10,50
◆ Great location overlooking the locality. Modern communal areas and functional bedrooms, most of them looking out onto the surrounding fields. A large, well-lit dining room offering mainly buffet service.

Univers VISA
r. René Baulard 13 – (00-376) 73 11 05 – *hotelunivers@andorra.ad*
– Fax (00-376) 83 19 70 – Closed November
31 rm – €37/40 €62/72
Rest – Menu €13,50
◆ This pleasant family hotel lies on the banks of the Valira d'Orient. Modern, comfortable rooms. The small, well-arranged dining room serves traditional cuisine. Select menu.

El Cyrano VISA
av. Caprinces Episcopal 32 – (00-376) 83 19 13 – *reserves@elcyrano.com*
– Closed 1st-15 May, 20 August-11 September, Sunday dinner and Tuesday
Rest – Carte €56/67
◆ The modern, cosy dining room is decorated in a personal style. The chef-patron, attentive to every little detail, prepares fusion cuisine made with first rate produce.

ESCALDES-ENGORDANY – 343 H9 – alt. 1 105 m 28 **B3**

Andorra-la-Vella 2

Office de tourisme, place dels Co-Princeps ☎ (00-376) 82 09 63, Fax (00-376) 82 66 97

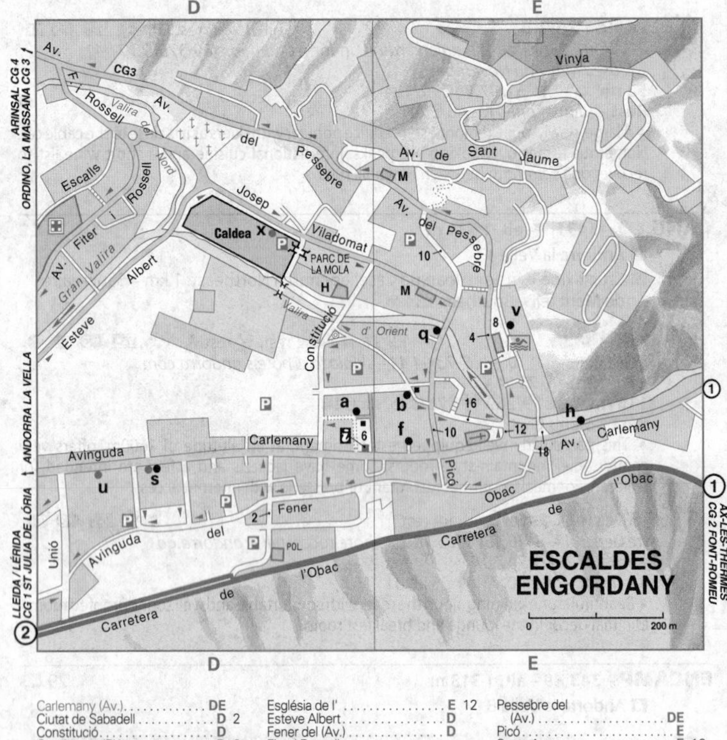

Roc de Caldes

rest, rest, VISA

rte d'Engolasters, via ① rte de l'Obac – ☎ (00-376) 87 45 55 – rocdecaldes@andorra.ad – Fax (00-376) 86 33 25

45 rm – †€ 110/240 ††€ 110/240, ☕ € 16 – **Rest** – Menu € 30

◆ A luxury mountainside hotel whose contemporary architecture blends with the natural surroundings. The tastefully decorated rooms enjoy a superb view. Restaurant with an elegant setting, lovely panoramic view and international cuisine.

Roc Blanc

VISA

pl. dels Co-Princeps 5 – ☎ (00-376) 87 14 00 – hotelrocblanc@rocblanchotels.com – Fax (00-376) 87 14 44 D **a**

170 rm ☕ – †€ 89/219 ††€ 135/337– **Rest *L'Entrecôte*** – Carte € 25/51
Rest *El Pí* – Carte approx. € 50

◆ This modern hotel, located in the town centre yet protected from the urban bustle, is appreciated for its numerous services. Elegant interior decoration. Rooms are being gradually renovated. International cuisine is available at the Brasserie L'Entrecôte. Welcoming, rustic dining room at the El Pí.

Fènix
av. Prat Gran 3-5 – ✆ (00-376) 76 07 60 – info@andorrafenixhotel.com – Fax (00-376) 76 08 00 E **b**
120 rm – €79/132 €90/159 – **Rest** – Menu €25
◆ This modern hotel boasts spacious public areas and a heated pool on the top floor. Comfortable rooms with parquet floors. The restaurant, brightly lit and functional, offers appetising cuisine.

Carlemany
av. Carlemany 4 – ✆ (00-376) 87 00 50 – carlemany@hotelcarlemany.ad – Fax (00-376) 87 00 90 – Closed May E **h**
33 rm – €56/181 €84/250, €12 – **Rest** – Menu €18
◆ This elegant hotel boasts an attractive interior and very well equipped rooms; some are split level.Spa centre fed with water from the springs. Traditional, balanced cuisine served in a prettily arranged dining room.

Casa Canut
av. Carlemany 107 – ✆ (00-376) 73 99 00 – hotelcanut@andorra.ad – Fax (00-376) 82 19 37 D **s**
33 rm – €120/250 €120/250, €15
Rest *Casa Canut* – see restaurant listing
◆ Although the façade is rather plain, once inside, the refined character of this hotel will charm you. Very comfortable rooms in up-to-date style.

Eureka rest,
av. Carlemany 36 – ✆ (00-376) 88 06 66 – hoteleureka@andorra.ad – Fax (00-376) 86 68 00 E **f**
75 rm – €42/76 €63/121 – **Rest** – Menu €13
◆ This comfortable hotel located in the heart of the spa is based on a decidedly modern concept. Elegant, well-maintained setting. Sample market-inspired recipes in the dining room adorned with attractive ceramic paintings.

Metropolis without rest
av. de les Escoles 25 – ✆ (00-376) 80 83 63 – info@hotel-metropolis.com – Fax (00-376) 86 37 10 E **q**
68 rm – €56/132 €70/150 – 1 suite
◆ This establishment with its simple and very classy decoration enjoys a privileged location halfway between Caldea and the duty-free shops. Functional rooms.

Ibis
av. Miquel Mateu 25, 1 km northeast by ① – ✆ (00-376) 87 23 00 – ibisandorra@riberpuig.com – Fax (00-376) 87 23 50
166 rm – €94/131 €138/194, €12 – **Rest** – buffet *(dinner only)* Menu €26
◆ A modern building with rooms in accordance with the chain's standards. Some of the largest rooms can accommodate families. Panoramic pool. Bright restaurant on the seventh floor offering a pretty view and buffet options.

Espel
pl. Creu Blanca 1 – ✆ (00-376) 82 08 55 – hotelespel@andorra.ad – Fax (00-376) 82 80 56 – Closed 4 May-4 June E **v**
85 rm – €45/68 €60/96 – **Rest** – *(set menu only)* Menu €15
◆ Hot water drawn from Andorra's underground lakes supplies the bathrooms in this establishment, which is gradually being renovated. Nice local ambience. Simple food to escape the bustle of "Carlemany" Avenue.

Aquarius (Christian Zanchetta)
Parc de La Mola 10, (Caldea) – ✆ (00-376) 80 09 80 – acuarius@caldea.ad – Fax (00-376) 86 96 93 – Closed 2-13 June, 10-14 November and Tuesday
Rest – Carte €57/76 D **x**
Spec. Ravioli de cacao au foie gras, sauté de langoustines aux pistaches. Selle d'agneau des Pyrénées au sirop de sapin, gratin de mimolette vieille. Gâteau "chocoloco", granité au champagne rosé, émulsion au chocolat blanc.
◆ A very pleasant restaurant with a panoramic view and a modern decor, inside the spa centre, offering an exceptional view of the baths. Creative cuisine including a special tasting menu.

XXX **Casa Canut** – Hôtel Casa Canut

av. Carlemany 107 – ✆ (00-376) 73 99 00 – hotelcanut@andorra.ad – Fax (00-376) 82 19 37 D **x**

Rest – Carte € 55/68

◆ This elegant town-centre restaurant has several rooms, one with a view of the kitchen. Traditional cuisine, fresh market produce, fish and seafood.

XXX **San Marco**

av. Carlemany 115, (5th floor - C.C. Júlia) – ✆ (00-376) 86 09 99 – sari@andorra.ad – Fax (00-376) 80 41 75 – Closed Sunday dinner and Monday D **u**

Rest – Carte approx. € 55

◆ Dining room with a panoramic view on the fifth floor of the Julia Centre, reached via a bubble-lift. Very tasteful decor, pretty view of the town and the mountains.

LA MASSANA – 343 H9 – alt. 1 241 m 28 B3

Andorra la Vella 7

Office de tourisme, avenue Sant-Antoni ✆ (00-376) 82 56 93, Fax (00-376) 82 86 93

Rutllan (heated) rest,

av. del Ravell 3 – ✆ (00-376) 83 50 00 – info@hotelrutllan.com – Fax (00-376) 83 51 80

96 rm – € 49/90 € 85/150 – **Rest** – Menu € 28

◆ A large family-run chalet with a predominantly wood decor. The comfortable rooms all have balconies, adorned with flowers in season. Copper and ceramic vases provide the decor in this classically styled restaurant serving traditional dishes.

Abba Suite H. rest,

rte de Sispony, 1.7 km south – ✆ (00-376) 73 73 00 – suite@abbahoteles.com – Fax (00-376) 73 73 01

36 suites – € 80/172, € 9 – **Rest** – Menu € 20

◆ Attractive mountainside hotel. All the rooms are suites with a sitting room and two bathrooms. This contemporary restaurant serves international cuisine in a relaxing atmosphere.

XXX **El Rusc**

1,5 km par rte d'Arinsal – ✆ (00-376) 83 82 00 – info@elrusc.com – Fax (00-376) 83 51 80 – Closed 15 June-15 July, Sunday dinner and Monday

Rest – Carte € 40/62

◆ An attractive regional house is home to a fine rustic dining room decorated with wood and stone. Traditional dishes, Basque specialities and a fine wine selection.

MERITXELL – 343 H9 28 B3

Andorra la Vella 10 – Canillo 4 – La Seu d'Urgell 31 – Foix 91 – Puigcerdà 50

L'Ermita

Meritxell – ✆ (00-376) 75 10 50 – info@hotelermita.com – Fax (00-376) 85 25 10 – Closed 4 June-11 July and 21 October-27 November

27 rm – € 33/50 € 55/90 – **Rest** – Menu € 13

◆ Unpretentious family-run hotel in the heart of the mountains near the sanctuary of the Virgin of Meritxell. Practical, well-kept and partially wood-panelled rooms. Extensive regional menu, country style decor and view of the peaks.

ORDINO – 343 H9 – alt. 1 304 m – Winter sports : 1940/2 640 m 14 28 B3

Andorra la Vella 9

Coma rest,

– ✆ (00-376) 73 61 00 – hotelcoma@hotelcoma.com – Fax (00-376) 73 61 01

48 rm – € 37/95 € 74/130 – **Rest** – *(closed November)* Menu € 18

◆ Since 1932 the same family has been welcoming travellers in this well equipped hotel. The rooms, many of which have a terrace, feature design furniture and baths with hydromassage equipment. This restaurant serves tasty traditional cuisine.

in Ansalonga

Sant Miquel ≤ rest, P VISA MC
rte d'el Serrat, 1.8 km northwest - ✉ Ordino – ✆ (00-376) 74 90 00 – hotel@santmiquel.com – Fax (00-376) 85 05 71 – Closed May
20 rm – €38/52 €52/72 – **Rest** – Menu €12
◆ This small hotel offers modern, pine furnished rooms. They all have a balcony overlooking the river and the picturesque village houses. A friendly welcome and healthy home cooking await you in this bright dining room.

via Canillo road **West: 2.3 km**

Babot ≤ valley and mountains, rest, P VISA MC
✉ Ordino – ✆ (00-376) 74 70 47 – hotelbabot@andorra.ad – Fax (00-376) 83 55 48 – Closed 5 November-4 December
55 rm – €41/83 €70/116 – **Rest** – Menu €12
◆ This high altitude, mountainside hotel, surrounded by a huge park, offers a magnificent view of the valley and peaks. Attractive, comfortable rooms. A restaurant with a panoramic view from its large windows.

PAS-DE-LA-CASA – 343 I9 – alt. 2 085 m – Winter sports : 2050/2640 m 1 26 29 C3

Andorra-la-Vella 29
Site★
Col d'Envalira★★

Reial Pirineus VISA MC
r. de la Solana 64 – ✆ (00-376) 85 58 55 – reialpirineus@andorra.ad – Fax (00-376) 85 58 45 – Closed 2-16 June
39 rm – €51/150 €72/240 – **Rest** – buffet *(open in winter) (dinner only)* Menu €30
◆ This mountainside building is located above the Pas de la Case and is therefore right next to the snowfields. Rooms with a zen-type decor. Piano-bar in the high season. This restaurant serves buffet dinners only in winter.

Soldeu road **Southeast: 10 km**

Grau Roig ≤ rest, P VISA MC AE
Grau Roig, ✉ Pas de la Casa – ✆ (00-376) 75 55 56 – hotelgrauroig@andorra.ad – Fax (00-376) 75 55 57 – Open from December to end April and from mid June to mid September
42 rm – €100/270 €150/360 – 1 suite – **Rest** – Carte approx. €40
◆ A typical mountain-style building with the Pessons Cirque as its setting. Charming well-equipped rooms. A fine setting, with coffered ceiling, wood panelling, stonework and antiques.

SANT-JULIÀ-DE-LÒRIA – 343 G10 – alt. 909 m 28 B3

Andorra-la-Vella 7

Imperial without rest AC P VISA MC
av. Rocafort 27 – ✆ (00-376) 84 34 78 – imperial@andornet.ad – Fax (00-376) 84 34 79
44 rm – €46/74 €64/107
◆ On the Gran Valira's left bank, a modern edifice with a very nicely finished interior. Warm and welcoming rooms, including one with hydromassage equipment in the shower. Friendly welcome.

Southeast : **7 km**

Coma Bella ≤ rest, P VISA MC
forêt de La Rabassa, alt. 1 300, ✉ Sant Julià de Lória – ✆ (00-376) 84 12 20 – comabella@myp.ad – Fax (00-376) 84 14 60 – Closed 6-23 April and 3-26 November
30 rm – €35/55 €53/92 – **Rest** – Menu €12
◆ This peaceful hotel enjoys a beautiful location in the Forêt de la Rabassa. Some of the rooms have a jacuzzi. The restaurant offers a fine view of the surrounding peaks.

SANTA-COLOMA – 343 G10 – alt. 970 m 28 B3

Andorra-la-Vella 3

Borda can Travi

av. Verge del Renei 9 – (00-376) 72 44 44 – bordacantravi@gruptravi.com – Fax (00-376) 72 23 28

Rest – Carte € 32/56

◆ This mountain restaurant boasts a pretty garden at the front. Country-style dining room with fireplace; updated cuisine with regional influences.

SOLDEU – 343 H9 – alt. 1 826 m – Winter sports : 1710/2560 m 3 21 29 C3

Andorra la Vella 20

Sport H. Hermitage

ski slopes and mountain,

rte de Soldeu – (00-376) 87 06 70 – hotel.hermitage@sporthotels.ad – Fax (00-376) 87 06 71

114 rm – €155/260 €310/520 – 6 suites – **Rest** – Carte € 44/59

◆ Handsome interior design at this luxury hotel. Relatively spacious rooms, in minimalist and contemporary styles (wood to the fore), overlooking the slopes. Full spa facilities. Choice of Mediterranean and Asian specialities.

Xalet Montana

rte General – (00-376) 73 93 33 – hotelnaudi@andornet.ad – Fax (00-376) 73 93 31 – Open from December to March

40 rm – €85/108 €114/144 – **Rest** – *(residents only)* Menu € 20

◆ Carefully decorated hotel whose rooms all overlook a snowbound landscape. Pleasant Nordic setting in the lounge. Inviting relaxation area.

in El Tarter West: 3 km

Nordic

rest,

Canillo – (00-376) 73 95 00 – hotelnordic@grupnordic.ad – Fax (00-376) 73 95 01 – Closed November

120 rm – €60/190 €80/250 – **Rest** – buffet *(dinner only)* Menu € 18

◆ This large hotel has a vast hall adorned with vintage motorbikes. Carefully arranged rooms and private terraces. Simple buffet meals available.

Del Tarter

Canillo – (00-376) 80 20 80 – heltarter@andornet.ad – Fax (00-376) 80 20 81 – Closed from May to end June

37 rm – €37/84 €49/111 – **Rest** – *(closed Wednesday)* Menu € 18

◆ Small hotel with an attractive stone façade and a traditional, predominantly wood, mountain-style interior. Comfortable rooms, sauna. Restaurant providing considerate service and cuisine with a French flavour.

Del Clos

Canillo – (00-376) 75 35 00 – hoteldelclos@grupnordic.ad – Fax (00-376) 85 15 54 – Open from December to end April

54 rm – €58/122 €80/250 – **Rest** – buffet *(dinner only)* Menu € 18

◆ This beautiful dwelling with views of the mountains is surrounded by typical Andorran farms. Spacious bedrooms, some with a balcony, furnished in regional style. Stone, wooden beams and carved wood combine to give this restaurant a mountain feel.

EL TARTER – see Soldeu

The casino of Monte-Carlo
2004

PRINCIPALITY OF MONACO

Michelin LOCAL map: n° **341** F5 **115**]27]28
Population: 31 800
Altitude: 140 m
French Riviera

USEFUL INFORMATION

TOURIST OFFICE

2a boulevard des Moulins Monte Carlo ✆ (00-377)92166116,
Fax (00-377) 92 16 60 00

Sovereign state, enclosed within the French Alpes-Maritimes department along the Mediterranean Sea. It has an area of 1.5 km^2 which includes: Monaco Rock (old town) and Monte-Carlo (new town) joined together by La Condamine (harbour), Fontvieille in the West (industry) and Le Larvotto in the East (beach). In 1993, the Principality became a member of the U.N. There are daily links with Nice-Côte d'Azur Airport from the Monaco-Fontvieille heliport. Information: Héli Air Monaco
✆ (00-377) 92 05 00 50

GOLF

18 Monte-Carlo , par rte d'Èze : 11 km, ✆ (00-377) 93 41 09 11.

URBAN MOTOR-RACING CIRCUIT

✆ (00-377) 93 15 26 00, Fax (00-377) 93 25 80 08

MONACO **Capitale de la Principauté – MCO MCO - Monaco –** ✉ **98000** 42 **E2**

▶ Paris 949 – Menton 11 – Nice 23 – San Remo 41

ℹ Office de tourisme, 2, boulevard des Moulins, Monte Carlo
✆ (00-377) 92 16 61 16, Fax (00-377) 92 16 60 00

Urban race circuit.

👁 Exotic garden★★ CZ: ⩽★ - Grotte de l'Observatoire★ CZ **D** - Jardins St-Martin★ DZ - Set of Niçois primitives★★ in the cathedral DZ - Recumbent Christ ★ in the la Miséricorde chapel D **B** - Place du Palais★ CZ - Palais du Prince★: musée napoléonien et des Archives du palais★ CZ - Museums: océanographique★★ DZ (aquarium★★, ⩽★★ of the terrace), d'anthropologie préhistorique★ CZ **M³**, - Collection of vintage cars★ CZ **M¹**.

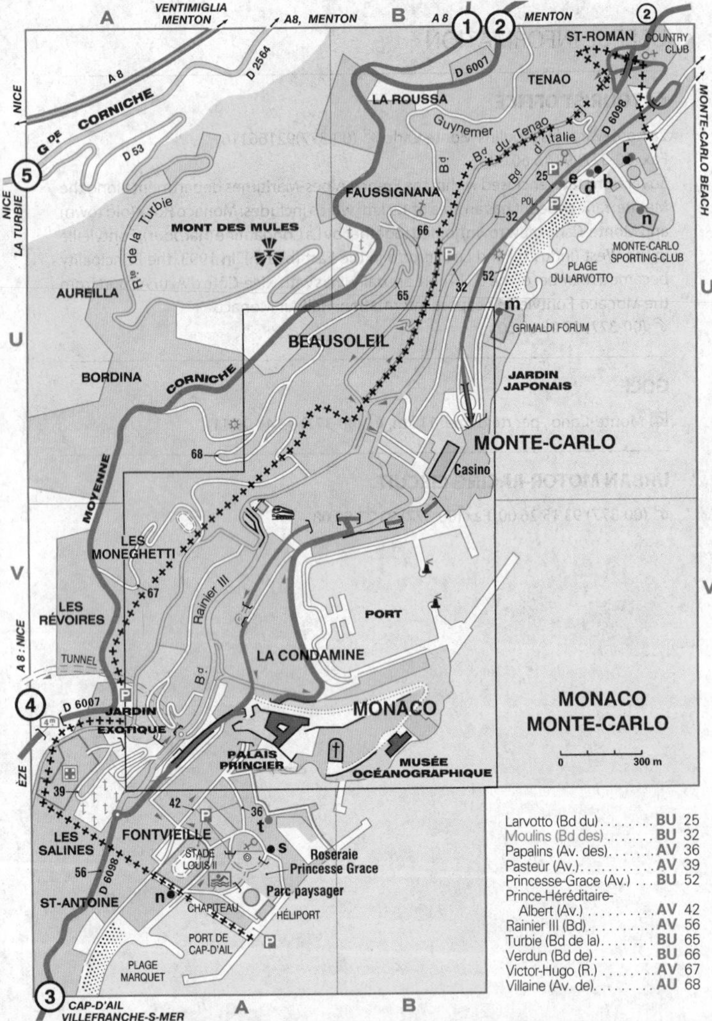

XX **Castelroc**

pl. du Palais – ✆ (00-377) 93 30 36 68 – castelroc@libello.com – Fax (00-377) 93 30 59 88 – Closed 1st December-1st February, Sunday dinner and Monday dinner May-September, Saturday and dinner October-April CZ **p**

Rest – Menu € 22 (lunch)/44 – Carte € 34/78

◆ A lovely bright mural-adorned dining room and an elegant shaded terrace from where guests can study the Palace at leisure. Regional cuisine.

in Fontvieille

Columbus

23 av. Papalins – ✆ (00-377) 92 05 90 00 – info@columbushotels.com – Fax (00-377) 92 05 91 67 AV **s**

170 rm – †€ 280/480 ††€ 280/610, ☕ € 25 – 11 suites

Rest – Carte € 44/59

◆ This hotel, lying between the harbour and the Princess Grace rose garden, offers plush rooms with refined modern furniture. Most have balconies. Fine amphitheatre. Stylish, brasserie-style restaurant extending onto a pleasant terrace.

XX **Amici Miei**

16 quai J.-C. Rey – ✆ (00-377) 92 05 92 14 – amici-miei@monte-carlo.mc – Fax (00-377) 92 05 31 74 AV **t**

Rest – Menu € 28 – Carte € 33/53

◆ This restaurant with its naive-style paintings will delight Italian food lovers. In summer, head for the terrace overlooking Fontvieille port.

MONTE-CARLO **Centre Mondain de la Principauté – MCO MCO - Monaco – Casinos : Grand Casino DY, Monte-Carlo Sporting Club BU, Sun Casino DX** 42 **E2**

Paris 947 – Menton 9 – Monaco 2 – Nice 20 – San Remo 40

Terrace★★ of the Grand casino DXY - Musée de poupées et automates★ DX **M**[5] - Japanese garden ★ U.

Plan on following page

Paris

pl. du Casino – ✆ (00-377) 98 06 30 00 – hp@sbm.mc – Fax (00-377) 98 06 59 13 DY **y**

143 rm – †€ 410/1480 ††€ 410/1480, ☕ € 38 – 44 suites

Rest ***Le Louis XV-Alain Ducasse et Grill*** – see restaurant listing

Rest ***Salle Empire*** – *✆ (00-377) 98 06 89 89 (open July - Aug.) (dinner only)* Carte € 57/188

Rest ***Côté Jardin*** – *✆ (00-377) 98 06 39 39 (lunch only)* Menu € 50 – Carte € 70/103

◆ Idyllic location, sumptuous setting, a rich past and famous guests; live the legend of Monaco's most prestigious palace hotel, inaugurated in 1864. A majestic Empire room complete with gold, stucco and crystal. Terrace commanding a view of the Rocher.

Métropole

4 av. Madone – ✆ (00-377) 93 15 15 15 – metropole@metropole.com – Fax (00-377) 93 25 24 44 DX **z**

126 rm – †€ 400/590 ††€ 650/1000, ☕ € 37 – 15 suites

Rest ***Joël Robuchon Monte-Carlo*** – see restaurant listing

◆ Luxury hotel (1886) treated to a masterful facelift by Jacques Garcia in 2004. Attractive pool and Italian-style courtyard-garden, conference facilities and lavish spa.

Hermitage

square Beaumarchais – ✆ (00-377) 98 06 40 00 – hh@sbm.mc – Fax (00-377) 98 06 59 70 DY **r**

252 rm – †€ 370/940 ††€ 370/940, ☕ € 35 – 28 suites

Rest ***Vistamar*** – see restaurant listing

Rest ***Limun Bar*** – *✆ (00-377) 98 06 48 48* – Menu (€ 29 bi) – Carte € 34/48

◆ Italian-styled murals and loggias adorn this splendid façade facing the port. A cast-iron-and-glass cupola by Eiffel; luxurious rooms. The Limùn Bar offers simple dishes and changes into a tea room in the afternoon.

MONACO MONTE-CARLO

Méridien Beach Plaza

22 av. Princesse Grace, at the Larvotto beach – ✆ (00-377) 93 30 98 80 – reservations.montecarlo@lemeridien.com – Fax (00-377) 93 50 23 14

403 rm – €230/770 €230/770, €31 – 12 suites BU **b**

Rest *L'Intempo* – *✆ (00-377) 93 15 78 88* – Menu €50/85 – Carte €60/135

Rest *Bar and Lunch* – *(open end May-end September) (lunch only)* Carte €30/77

♦ Partially renovated contemporary hotel. Rooms in two glass towers with panoramic sea views. Sumptuous suites, luxurious conference centre, private beach. L'Intempo (open 24 hours a day) offers Mediterranean cuisine. The Bar and Lunch has a seaside atmosphere.

Monte Carlo Bay Hôtel and Resort < Sea and Coast,
– *(00-377) 98 06 02 00* VISA MC AE
– info@montecarlobay.mc – Fax (00-377) 98 06 00 03 BU **r**
323 rm – €315/770 €315/770, €30 – 10 suites – ½ P €1152/2085
Rest *Le Blue Bay* – *(00-377) 98 06 03 60 (dinner only from May to September)* Menu (€28), €40 bi (weekday lunch), €75/85 – Carte €52/127
Rest *L'Orange Verte* – *(00-377) 98 06 03 63* – Carte €37/66
Rest *Las Brisas* – *(00-377) 98 06 03 63 (open from May to September) (lunch only)* Carte €44/185

◆ This Monaco luxury hotel covers 4ha along the seafront. Extremely modern rooms, suites and duplexes. Lagoon pool. The Blue Bay offers a cuisine rich in spices. L'Orange Verte offers tartares and carpaccios. Las Brisas offers an up-to-date menu.

Port Palace < Port and Rock, rm,
7 av. J. F. Kennedy – (00-377) 97 97 90 00 VISA MC AE
– reservation@portpalace.com – Fax (00-377) 97 97 90 08 DY **t**
50 rm – €295/680 €295/1765, €29
Rest *Mandarine* – *(closed Sunday dinner, Monday dinner, Tuesday dinner and Wednesday dinner from November to January)* Menu €35 (weekday lunch), €75/150
– Carte €62/86

◆ This modern harbour luxury hotel offers superbly equipped rooms facing the Rock. Top-floor restaurant with a panoramic view. Modern decor and up-to-date menu with some classic dishes.

Fairmont-Monte-Carlo < rm, rest,
12 av. Spélugues – (00-377) 93 50 65 00 VISA MC AE
– montecarlo@fairmont.com – Fax (00-377) 93 30 01 57 DX **e**
589 rm – €279/1700 €279/1700 – 30 suites
Rest *Pistou* – *(open April-September)* Carte €44/82
Rest *L'Argentin* – *(closed lunch November-March)* Menu €35 – Carte €60/111

◆ Vast hotel complex built on piles. Functional rooms, magnificent seafront views. Shopping arcade, conference centre.

Novotel VISA MC AE
16 bd. Princesse-Charlotte – (00-377)99 99 83 00 – h5275@accor.com – Fax (00-377)99 99 83 10 CY **j**
201 rm – €99/450 €99/450, €15 – 17 suites
Rest *Les Grandes Ondes* – Menu €40 bi/60 – Carte approx. €80
Rest *Novotel Café* – Carte approx. €25

◆ This new hotel situated in the upper section of the principality is built in contemporary style, making the most of the natural light of its surroundings. Huge functional rooms, many with a loggia. At Les Grandes Ondes, Provençal cuisine in a bright, simply decorated setting.

Le Louis XV-Alain Ducasse – Hôtel de Paris
pl. du Casino – (00-377) 98 06 88 64 VISA MC AE
– lelouisxv@alain-ducasse.com – Fax (00-377) 98 06 59 07
– Closed 1st-30 December, 24 February-11 March, Wednesday except dinner 18 June-20 August and Tuesday DY **y**
Rest – Menu €130 bi (weekday lunch), €190/250
Spec. Légumes des jardins de Provence à la truffe noire. Poissons de la pêche locale du jour. "Louis XV" au croustillant de pralin.
Wines Bandol, Côtes de Provence.

◆ The Louis XV has fine Mediterranean dishes, a sumptuous classic decor, a terrace overlooking the casino and exceptional wines. An outstanding experience.

Grill de l'Hôtel de Paris < the Principality,
pl. du Casino – (00-377) 98 06 88 88 – legrill@sbm.mc – Fax (00-377) 98 06 59 03 – VISA MC AE
Closed January and lunch in July-August DY **y**
Rest – Menu €68 bi (weekday lunch) – Carte €75/240
Spec. King crab, condiment fenouil et citrons de Menton en marmelade. Carré d'agneau en croûte de pignons. Soufflé "Tradition".
Wines Bellet, Vin de pays des Bouches du Rhône.

◆ Enjoy a fine view of the Principality from the eighth floor of this hotel, with the sea in the background. Sliding roof under blue skies.

Joël Robuchon Monte-Carlo – Hôtel Métropole
4 av. Madone – ☎ (00-377)93 15 15 10 – restaurant@metropole.com – Fax (00-377)93 25 24 44 DX **z**
Rest – *(dinner only from 14 July to 24 August)* Menu € 70 bi (lunch)/170 (dinner) – Carte € 56/365
Spec. Foie gras de canard chaud, "hummu" et menthe fraîche. King crab, tomate farcie de légumes acidulés. Saint-Pierre aux saveurs méridionales. **Wines** Côtes de Provence, Vin de pays du Var.
◆ The colonnaded dining room commands a fine view of the magnificent kitchens where creative cuisine is prepared. Pleasant terrace with a view of Monaco.

Vistamar – Hôtel Hermitage ← Port and Principality,
pl. Beaumarchais – ☎ (00-377) 98 06 98 98 – hh@sbm.mc – Fax (00-377) 98 06 59 70 – Closed lunch in July-August
Rest – Menu € 45 bi (weekday lunch), € 72/89 – Carte € 72/124 DY **r**
Spec. Soupe de poissons des pêcheurs "Rinaldi". La bouillabaisse en deux services. Loup au four sur un lit de pommes de terre, tomate et olivettes noires. **Wines** Bellet, Côtes de Provence.
◆ Breathtaking panoramic sea view from the terrace and bay windows in the dining room; the menu offers classic dishes and seafood cuisine.

Bar Boeuf & Co
av. Princesse Grace, (at Sporting-Monte-Carlo) – ☎ (00-377) 98 06 71 71 – b.b@sbm.mc – Fax (00-377) 98 06 57 85 – Open May-September BU **n**
Rest – *(dinner only)* Carte € 71/109
Spec. Épais morceau de bar doré aux herbes fraîches, artichauts fondants. Filet de boeuf façon "Rossini", royale champi-truffes, melba au foie gras. Turron noir aux pignons, sorbet chocolat fort. **Wines** Côtes de Provence.
◆ A place popular with night owls and gourmets, with a modern-style decor by Philippe Starck, a bass 'n' beef menu and wine from around the world.

Le Saint Benoit ← the port and the Rock,
10 ter av. Costa – ☎ (00-377) 93 25 02 34 – lesaintbenoit@montecarlo.mc – Fax (00-377) 93 30 52 64 – Closed 21 December-7 January, Sunday dinner and Monday DY **b**
Rest – Menu € 28/39 – Carte € 34/100
◆ Finding this restaurant is not so easy, but the panoramic view from the terrace is worth the trouble. Spacious modern dining room.

Café de Paris
pl. Casino – ☎ (00-377) 98 06 76 23 – brasseriecp@sbm.mc – Fax (00-377) 98 06 59 30 DY **n**
Rest – Carte € 40/76
◆ In 1897 Edouard Michelin made a famous arrival here...at the wheel of his car! Belle Epoque brasserie decor. Popular terrace in season.

Maya Bay
24 av. Princesse Grace – ☎ (00-377) 97 70 74 67 – mayabay@mayabay.mc – Fax (00-377) 97 77 58 10 – Closed November, Sunday and Monday BU **d**
Rest – Menu (€ 20 bi), € 69 – Carte € 49/76
◆ Buddha watches over the bar of this Japan-influenced restaurant. Lounge decorated with kimonos opening onto a bonsai-adorned terrace. Personalised cuisine.

Zébra Square
10 av. Princesse Grace, (Grimaldi Forum: 2e floor, by lift) – ☎ (00-377) 99 99 25 50 – monaco@zebrasquare.com – Fax (00-377) 99 99 25 60 BU **m**
Rest – Carte € 58/82
◆ Same zebra decor, same "trendy" ambience, same up-to-date cuisine as in the Parisian establishment, but with a little extra: the beautiful terrace with a view of the sea.

La Maison du Caviar
1 av. St-Charles – ☎ (00-377) 93 30 80 06 – lamaisonducaviar@monaco377.com – Fax (00-377) 93 30 23 90 – Closed in July, Saturday lunch and Sunday DX **r**
Rest – Menu € 27/59 – Carte € 32/94
◆ Considered a local treasure, this family restaurant has offered classic cuisine since 1954 in a setting that combines wrought iron, wine-bottle cases and rustic furniture.

Chez Gianni
39 av. Princesse Grace – ✆ (00-377) 93 30 46 33 – Fax (00-377) 93 30 54 86 – Closed Saturday lunchtime and Sunday lunchtime BU **e**
Rest – Menu (€ 38), € 50/60 – Carte € 48/70
◆ This little restaurant offers a foretaste of nearby Italy's cuisine. Transalpine inspiration in both decor and cuisine. Convivial ambience in the evening.

Loga
25 bd des Moulins – ✆ (00-377) 93 30 87 72 – kettyvigon@hotmail.com – Fax (00-377) 93 25 06 41 – Closed 10-26 August, dinner and Sunday DX **v**
Rest – Menu € 37/41 – Carte € 32/53
◆ Pleasant little family restaurant offering regional cuisine and daily specials, displayed on a blackboard that are very popular with regulars. Light-wood interior decor and pavement terrace.

Polpetta
2 r. Paradis – ✆ (00-377) 93 50 67 84 – Fax (00-377) 93 50 67 84 – Closed 10-30 June and Tuesday CY **f**
Rest – Menu € 23 – Carte € 24/48
◆ Three different settings in this little Italian restaurant: the veranda on the street side; the rustic dining room; and finally a cosier and more intimate area at the back.

in Monte-Carlo-Beach (France Alpes-Mar.) 2.5 km northeast BU – ✉ **06190 Roquebrune-Cap-Martin**

Monte-Carlo Beach Hôtel < sea and Monaco, rm, rest,
av. Princesse Grace – ✆ 04 93 28 66 66 – bh@sbm.mc – Fax 04 93 78 14 18 – Open 8 March-30 September
44 rm – €265/815 €265/815, € 33 – 3 suites
Rest *La Salle à Manger* – *✆ 04 93 28 66 72* – Carte € 51/115
Rest *Le Deck* – *✆ 04 93 28 66 42 (open 19 April-19 October) (lunch only)* Carte € 38/96
Rest *La Vigie* – *✆ 04 93 28 66 44 (open 27 June-31 August and closed Monday)* Menu € 44 (lunch)/59
Rest *Le Sea Lounge* – *✆ 04 93 28 66 43 (open 10 May-31 August) (dinner only)* Carte € 32/79
◆ This Florentine-villa-style hotel, founded in 1929, welcomed Nijinski, Cocteau, Morand, etc. Superb seaside complex. La Salle à Manger (Dining Room) offers classic Mediterranean dishes. The Deck features a brasserie. La Vigie offers grilled fish. The Sea Lounge offers tapas.

see also hotels at **Beausoleil** *and* **Cap d'Ail**

Place with at least

- a hotel or a restaurant
- a starred establishment
- a restaurant « Bib Gourmand »
- a hotel « Bib Hôtel »
- a particularly pleasant restaurant
- a particularly pleasant guesthouse
- a particularly pleasant hotel
- a particularly quiet hotel

Localité possédant au moins

- un hôtel ou un restaurant
- une table étoilée
- un restaurant « Bib Gourmand »
- un hôtel « Bib Hôtel »
- un restaurant agréable
- une maison d'hôte agréable
- un hôtel agréable
- un hôtel très tranquille

La località possiede come minimo

- un albergo o un ristorante
- una delle migliori tavole dell'anno
- un ristorante « Bib Gourmand »
- un albergo « Bib Hotel »
- un ristorante molto piacevole
- un piacevole agriturismo
- un albergo molto piacevole
- un esercizio molto tranquillo

Ort mit mindestens

- einem Hotel oder Restaurant
- einem der besten Restaurants des Jahres
- einem Restaurant « Bib Gourmand »
- einem Hotel « Bib Hotel »
- einem sehr angenehmen Restaurant
- ein angenehmes Gästehaus
- einem sehr angenehmen Hotel
- einem sehr ruhigen Haus

Localidad que posee com mínimo

- un hotel o un restaurante
- una de los mejores mesas del año
- un restaurante « Bib Gourmand »
- un hotel « Bib Hotel »
- un restaurante muy agradable
- una casa rural agradable
- un hotel muy agradable
- un hotel muy tranquilo

Maps

Regional maps of listed towns

Cartes

Cartes régionales des localités citées

Carta

Carta regionale delle località citate

Regionalkarten

Regionalkarten der erwähnten Orte

Mapas

Mapas de las localidades citadas, por regiones

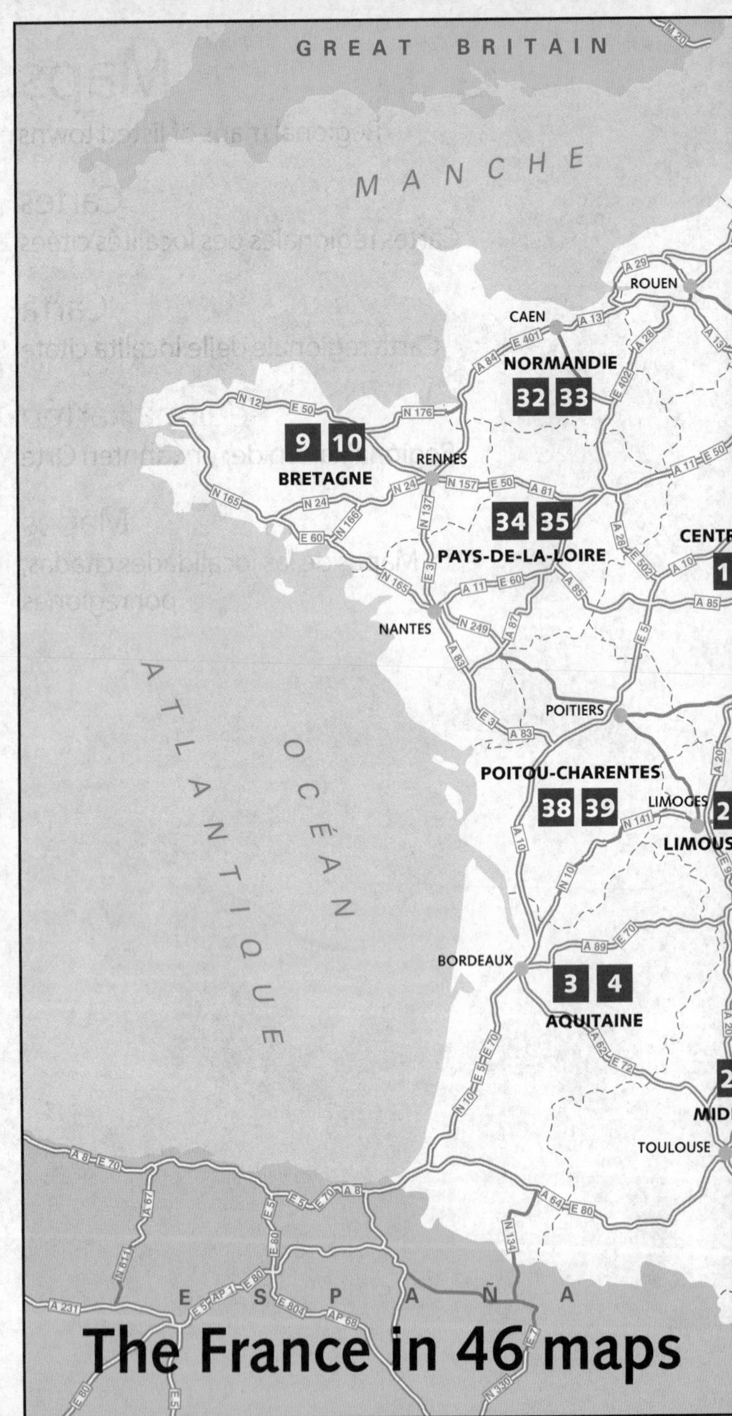

The France in 46 maps

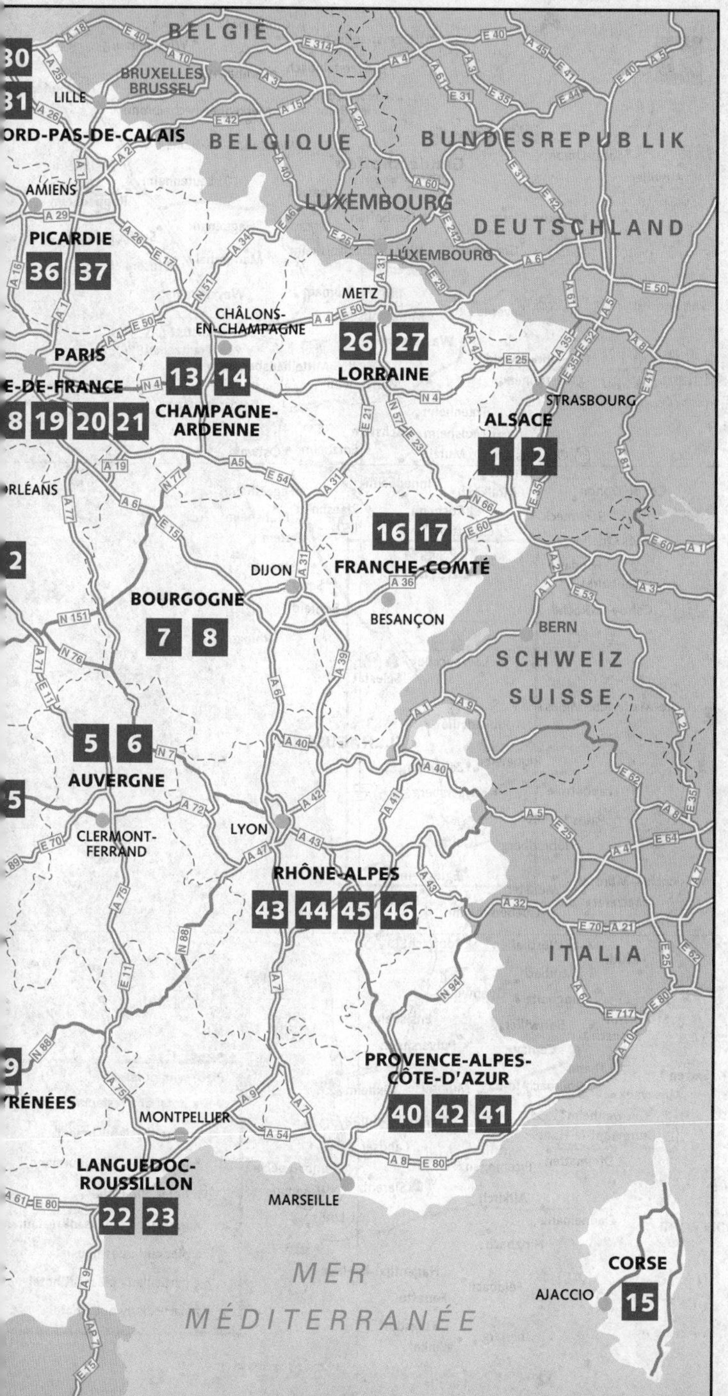
BELGIË
BRUXELLES
BRUSSEL
LILLE
ORD-PAS-DE-CALAIS
BELGIQUE
BUNDESREPUBLIK
DEUTSCHLAND
LUXEMBOURG
AMIENS
PICARDIE
36
37
30
31
METZ
CHÂLONS-
EN-CHAMPAGNE
26
27
LORRAINE
PARIS
E-DE-FRANCE
13
14
CHAMPAGNE-
ARDENNE
8
19
20
21
STRASBOURG
ALSACE
1
2
ORLÉANS
16
17
FRANCHE-COMTÉ
DIJON
BESANÇON
BOURGOGNE
7
8
BERN
SCHWEIZ
SUISSE
5
6
AUVERGNE
CLERMONT-
FERRAND
LYON
RHÔNE-ALPES
43
44
45
46
ITALIA
PROVENCE-ALPES-
CÔTE-D'AZUR
40
42
41
YRÉNÉES
MONTPELLIER
LANGUEDOC-
ROUSSILLON
22
23
MARSEILLE
CORSE
AJACCIO
15
MER
MÉDITERRANÉE

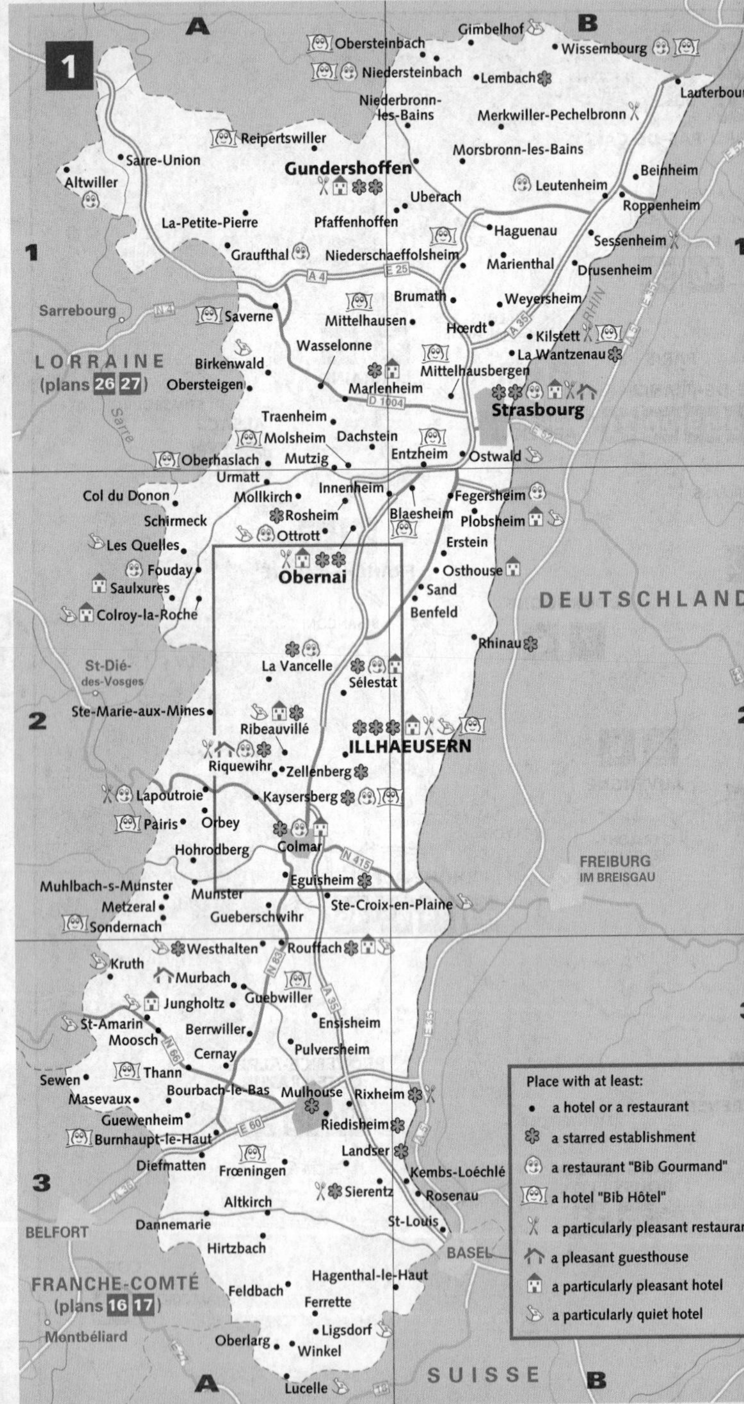
1
A
B
Obersteinbach
Niedersteinbach
Gimbelhof
Wissembourg
Lembach
Lauterbourg
Niederbronn-les-Bains
Merkwiller-Pechelbronn
Reipertswiller
Morsbronn-les-Bains
Sarre-Union
Altwiller
Gundershoffen
Beinheim
Leutenheim
Uberach
Roppenheim
La-Petite-Pierre
Pfaffenhoffen
Haguenau
Sessenheim
Graufthal
Niederschaeffolsheim
Marienthal
Drusenheim
Brumath
Weyersheim
Sarrebourg
Saverne
Mittelhausen
Hoerdt
Kilstett
La Wantzenau
LORRAINE
(plans 26 27)
Birkenwald
Wasselonne
Mittelhausbergen
Obersteigen
Marlenheim
Strasbourg
Traenheim
Molsheim
Dachstein
Entzheim
Ostwald
Oberhaslach
Mutzig
Urmatt
Col du Donon
Mollkirch
Innenheim
Fegersheim
Schirmeck
Rosheim
Blaesheim
Plobsheim
Les Quelles
Ottrott
Erstein
Fouday
Obernai
Osthouse
Saulxures
Sand
Colroy-la-Roche
Benfeld
DEUTSCHLAND
Rhinau
St-Dié-des-Vosges
La Vancelle
Sélestat
Ste-Marie-aux-Mines
2
Ribeauvillé
ILLHAEUSERN
Riquewihr
Zellenberg
Lapoutroie
Kaysersberg
Pairis
Orbey
Hohrodberg
Colmar
FREIBURG
IM BREISGAU
Muhlbach-s-Munster
Eguisheim
Munster
Metzeral
Ste-Croix-en-Plaine
Gueberschwihr
Sondernach
Westhalten
Rouffach
Kruth
Murbach
Guebwiller
Jungholtz
St-Amarin
Ensisheim
Moosch
Berrwiller
Pulversheim
Cernay
Thann
Sewen
Bourbach-le-Bas
Mulhouse
Rixheim
Masevaux
Riedisheim
Guewenheim
Burnhaupt-le-Haut
Landser
Diefmatten
Frœningen
Kembs-Loéchlé
3
Sierentz
Rosenau
Altkirch
BELFORT
Dannemarie
St-Louis
Hirtzbach
BASEL
FRANCHE-COMTÉ
(plans 16 17)
Feldbach
Hagenthal-le-Haut
Ferrette
Montbéliard
Ligsdorf
Oberlarg
Winkel
SUISSE
Lucelle
Place with at least:
a hotel or a restaurant
a starred establishment
a restaurant "Bib Gourmand"
a hotel "Bib Hôtel"
a particularly pleasant restaurant
a pleasant guesthouse
a particularly pleasant hotel
a particularly quiet hotel

Alsace 2

C

1 1

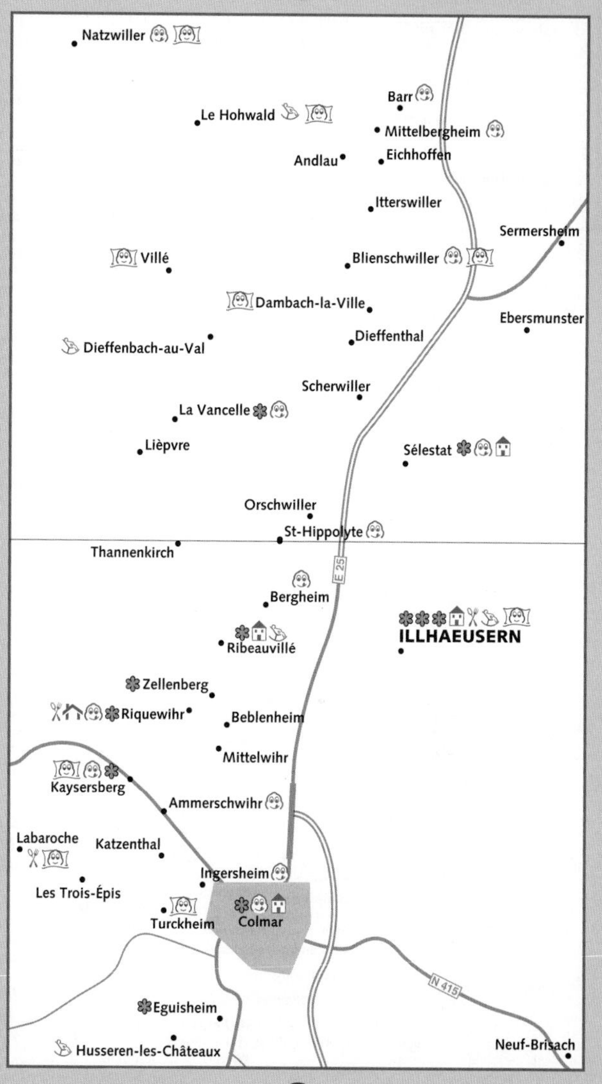
Natzwiller
Barr
Le Hohwald
Mittelbergheim
Andlau
Eichhoffen
Itterswiller
Sermersheim
Villé
Blienschwiller
Dambach-la-Ville
Ebersmunster
Dieffenbach-au-Val
Dieffenthal
Scherwiller
La Vancelle
Lièpvre
Sélestat
Orschwiller
St-Hippolyte
Thannenkirch
E 25
Bergheim
ILLHAEUSERN
Ribeauvillé
Zellenberg
Riquewihr
Beblenheim
Mittelwihr
Kaysersberg
Ammerschwihr
Labaroche
Katzenthal
Ingersheim
Les Trois-Épis
Turckheim
Colmar
N 415
Eguisheim
Husseren-les-Châteaux
Neuf-Brisach

2 2

C

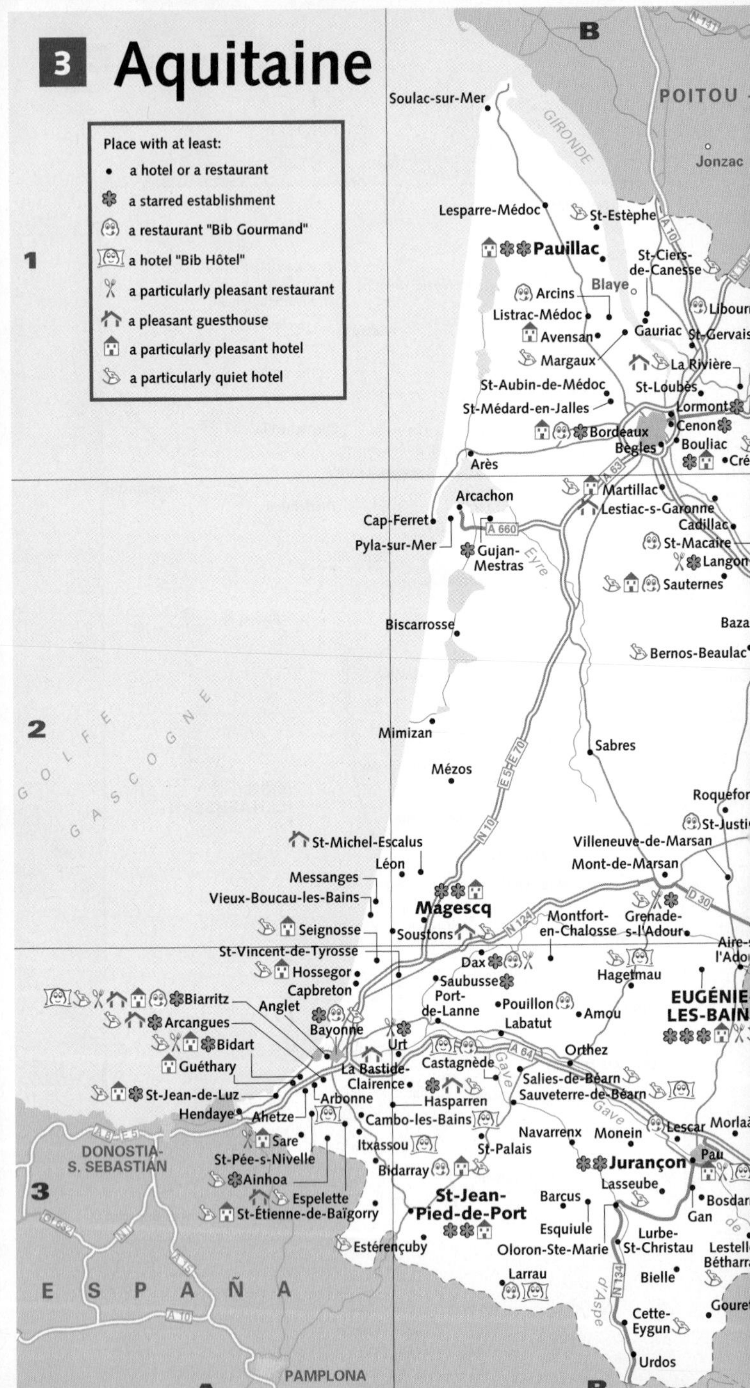
3
Aquitaine
Place with at least:
a hotel or a restaurant
a starred establishment
a restaurant "Bib Gourmand"
a hotel "Bib Hôtel"
a particularly pleasant restaurant
a pleasant guesthouse
a particularly pleasant hotel
a particularly quiet hotel
A
B
1
2
3
POITOU
Jonzac
GIRONDE
Soulac-sur-Mer
Lesparre-Médoc
St-Estèphe
Pauillac
St-Ciers-de-Canesse
Blaye
Arcins
Listrac-Médoc
Avensan
Gauriac
St-Gervais
Libourne
Margaux
La Rivière
St-Aubin-de-Médoc
St-Loubès
St-Médard-en-Jalles
Lormont
Cenon
Bordeaux
Bègles
Bouliac
Arès
Martillac
Arcachon
Lestiac-s-Garonne
Cap-Ferret
Cadillac
Pyla-sur-Mer
Gujan-Mestras
Eyre
St-Macaire
Langon
Sauternes
Biscarrosse
Baza
Bernos-Beaulac
GOLFE DE GASCOGNE
Mimizan
Sabres
Mézos
Roquefort
St-Justin
St-Michel-Escalus
Villeneuve-de-Marsan
Léon
Mont-de-Marsan
Messanges
Vieux-Boucau-les-Bains
Magescq
Montfort-en-Chalosse
Grenade-s-l'Adour
Seignosse
Soustons
Aire-s-l'Adour
St-Vincent-de-Tyrosse
Dax
Hossegor
Hagetmau
Capbreton
Saubusse
Biarritz
Anglet
Port-de-Lanne
Pouillon
Amou
EUGÉNIE-LES-BAINS
Arcangues
Bayonne
Labatut
Bidart
Urt
Orthez
Guéthary
La Bastide-Clairence
Castagnède
Salies-de-Béarn
St-Jean-de-Luz
Arbonne
Hasparren
Sauveterre-de-Béarn
Hendaye
Ahetze
Cambo-les-Bains
Lescar
Morlaàs
Sare
Itxassou
Navarrenx
Monein
DONOSTIA-S. SEBASTIÁN
St-Pée-s-Nivelle
St-Palais
Jurançon
Pau
Ainhoa
Bidarray
Lasseube
Espelette
St-Jean-Pied-de-Port
Barcus
Bosdarros
St-Étienne-de-Baïgorry
Gan
Esquiule
Estérençuby
Oloron-Ste-Marie
Lurbe-St-Christau
Lestelle-Bétharram
Larrau
Bielle
ESPAÑA
Cette-Eygun
Gourette
Urdos
PAMPLONA
A 10
N 10
E 5-E 70
A 63
A 660
N 124
D 30
A 64
N 134
A 8-E 5
A 15
N 141
Gave
d'Aspe

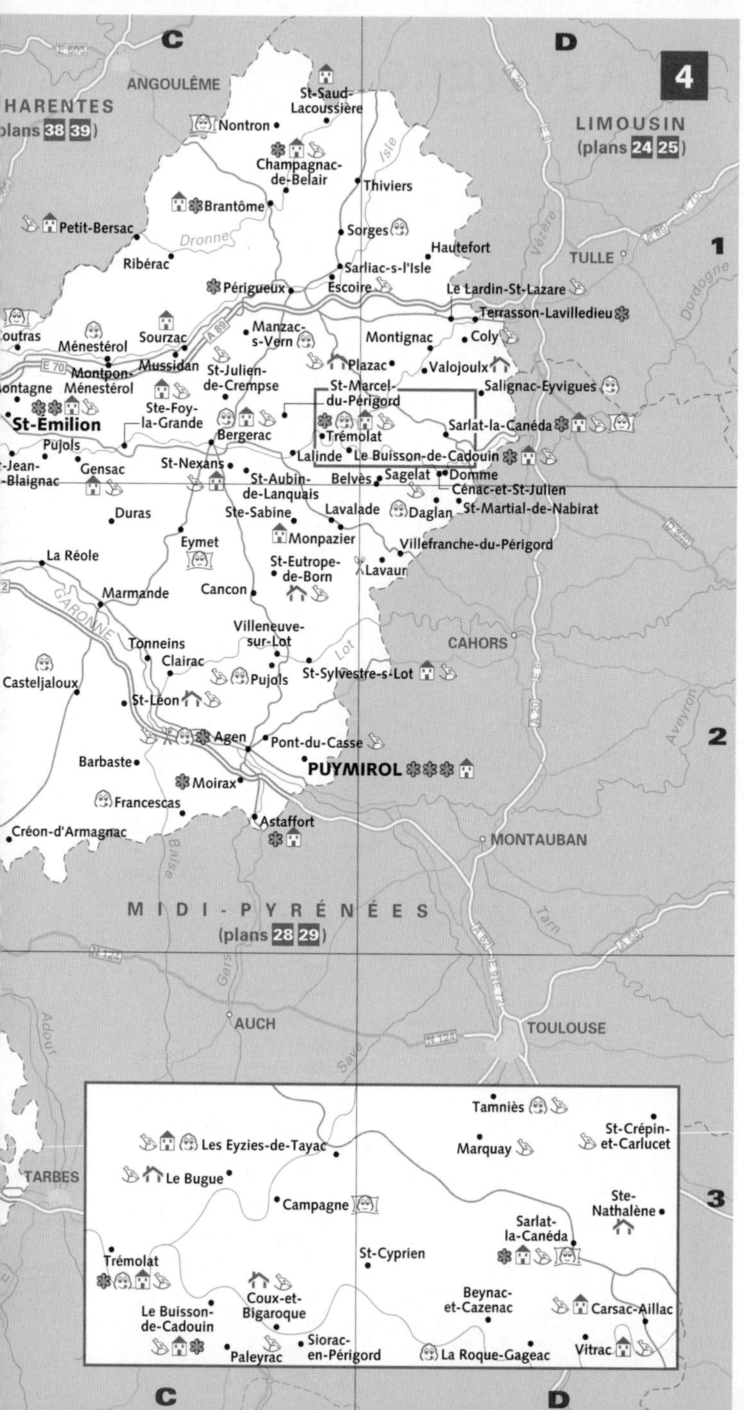
4
C
D
ANGOULÊME
HARENTES
plans 38 39)
LIMOUSIN
(plans 24 25)
St-Saud-Lacoussière
Nontron
Champagnac-de-Belair
Thiviers
Brantôme
Petit-Bersac
Sorges
Hautefort
Ribérac
Dronne
Isle
Sarliac-s-l'Isle
TULLE
1
Périgueux
Escoire
Le Lardin-St-Lazare
Terrasson-Lavilledieu
Coutras
Ménestérol
Sourzac
Manzac-s-Vern
Montignac
Coly
Montpon-Ménestérol
Mussidan
St-Julien-de-Crempse
Plazac
Valojoulx
Montagne
St-Marcel-du-Périgord
Salignac-Eyvigues
St-Émilion
Ste-Foy-la-Grande
Bergerac
Sarlat-la-Canéda
Trémolat
Pujols
Lalinde
Le Buisson-de-Cadouin
St-Jean-de-Blaignac
Gensac
St-Nexans
St-Aubin-de-Lanquais
Belvès
Sagelat
Domme
Cénac-et-St-Julien
Duras
Ste-Sabine
Lavalade
Daglan
St-Martial-de-Nabirat
Eymet
Monpazier
Villefranche-du-Périgord
La Réole
St-Eutrope-de-Born
Lavaur
Marmande
Cancon
GARONNE
Villeneuve-sur-Lot
CAHORS
Tonneins
Clairac
Lot
Casteljaloux
Pujols
St-Sylvestre-s-Lot
St-Léon
Agen
Pont-du-Casse
2
Barbaste
PUYMIROL
Moirax
Francescas
Astaffort
Créon-d'Armagnac
MONTAUBAN
Baïse
MIDI-PYRÉNÉES
(plans 28 29)
Tarn
Gers
AUCH
TOULOUSE
Save
Adour
TARBES
Tamniès
St-Crépin-et-Carlucet
Les Eyzies-de-Tayac
Marquay
Le Bugue
Ste-Nathalène
3
Campagne
Sarlat-la-Canéda
Trémolat
St-Cyprien
Coux-et-Bigaroque
Beynac-et-Cazenac
Le Buisson-de-Cadouin
Carsac-Aillac
Siorac-en-Périgord
Paleyrac
La Roque-Gageac
Vitrac
C
D

5 Auvergne

Place with at least:
a hotel or a restaurant
a starred establishment
a restaurant "Bib Gourmand"
a hotel "Bib Hôtel"
a particularly pleasant restaurant
a pleasant guesthouse
a particularly pleasant hotel
a particularly quiet hotel
CENTRE (plans 11 12)
LIMOUSIN (plans 24 25)
MIDI-PYRÉNÉES (plans 28 29)
A
B
1
2
3
St-Amand-Montrond
Le Veurdre
St-Bonnet-Tronçais
Tronçais
Urçay
Meaulne
Cérilly
Bourbon-l'Archambault
Coulandon
Ygrande
Souvigny
Reugny
Estivareilles
Rocles
Tronget
Montluçon
Le Theil
Montmarault
St-Pourçain-s-Sioule
Néris-les-Bains
Chantelle
Charroux
Gannat
GUÉRET
Vensat
St-Gervais-d'Auvergne
Pont-du-Bouchet
Teilhède
Thuret
Davayat
Châtelguyon
Riom
Aubusson
Pontaumur
Clermont-Ferrand
Pont-du-Château
Pontgibaud
Mazaye
Orcines
Puy de Dôme
Royat
Lempdes
Pérignat-lès-Sarliève
Orcival
Laqueuille
St-Saturnin
Vic-le-Comte
Vienne
Lac Chambon
La Bourboule
Champeix
Le Mont-Dore
St-Nectaire
Montaigut-le-Blanc
Ussel
Issoire
Bagnols
Besse-et-St-Anastaise
Boudes
Champs-s-Tarentaine
Blesle
Riom-Ès-Montagnes
TULLE
Massiac
Mauriac
Dordogne
Ally
Salers
Dienne
Brive-la-Gaillarde
Le Falgoux
Le Theil
Murat
Lascelle
St-Jacques-des-Blats
St-Flour
Marmanhac
Thiézac
St-Georges
St-Paul-des-Landes
Polminhac
Vic-s-Cère
Pailherols
Viaduc-de-Garabit
Lacapelle-Viescamp
Aurillac
Pierrefort
Neuvéglise
Le Rouget
Vézac
Raulhac
Chaudes-Aigues
Vitrac
Boisset
Truyère
Calvinet
Montsalvy
St-Constant
Vieillevie
Figeac
Cher
A 71
N 145
D 2371
N 79
D 2009
D 941
D 2089
A 89
A 75
D 840

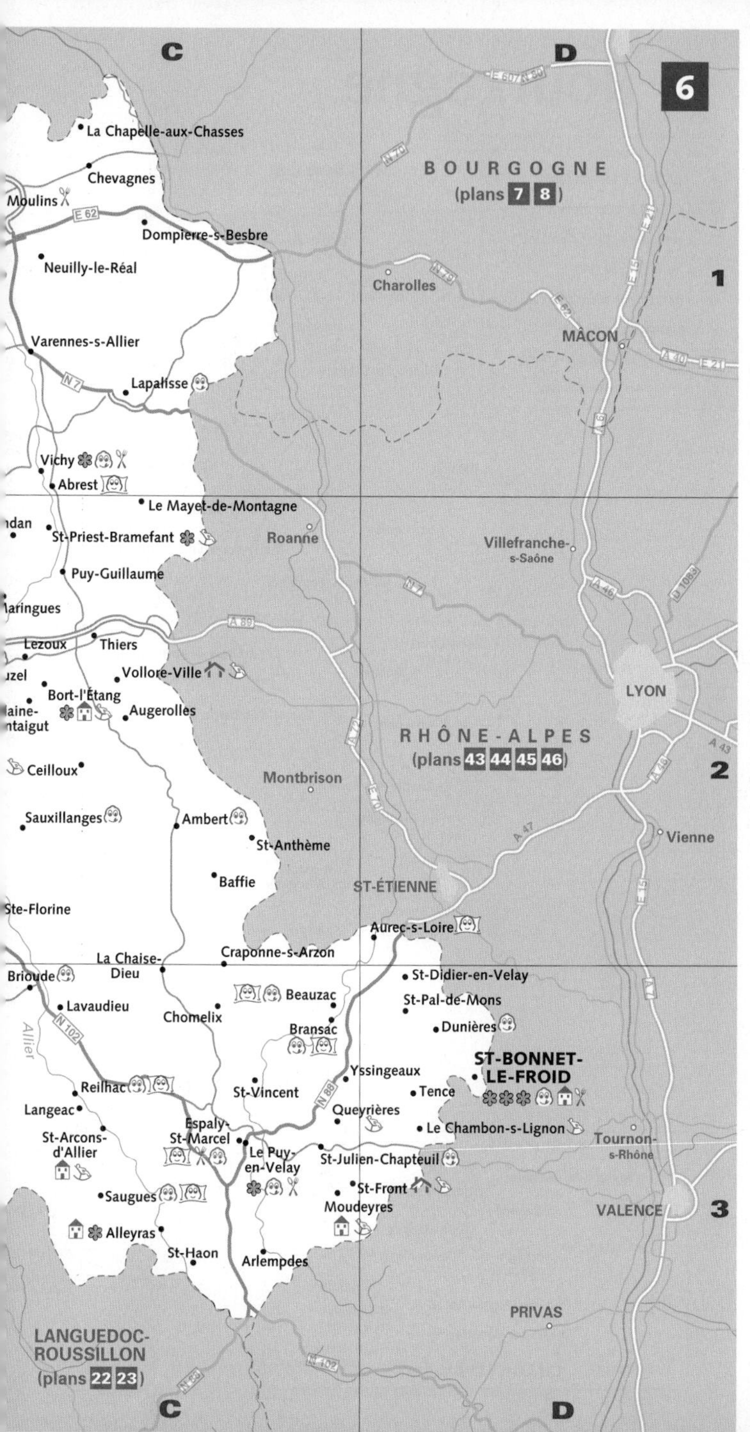
6
C
D
1
2
3
BOURGOGNE
(plans 7 8)
RHÔNE-ALPES
(plans 43 44 45 46)
LANGUEDOC-ROUSSILLON
(plans 22 23)
La Chapelle-aux-Chasses
Chevagnes
Moulins
Dompierre-s-Besbre
Neuilly-le-Réal
Varennes-s-Allier
Lapalisse
Vichy
Abrest
Le Mayet-de-Montagne
St-Priest-Bramefant
Puy-Guillaume
Lezoux
Thiers
Vollore-Ville
Bort-l'Étang
Augerolles
Ceilloux
Sauxillanges
Ambert
St-Anthème
Baffie
Ste-Florine
La Chaise-Dieu
Craponne-s-Arzon
Brioude
Lavaudieu
Chomelix
Beauzac
Bransac
Reilhac
Langeac
St-Arcons-d'Allier
St-Vincent
Espaly-St-Marcel
Le Puy-en-Velay
Saugues
Alleyras
St-Haon
Arlempdes
Yssingeaux
Queyrières
St-Julien-Chapteuil
St-Front
Moudeyres
Aurec-s-Loire
St-Didier-en-Velay
St-Pal-de-Mons
Dunières
ST-BONNET-LE-FROID
Tence
Le Chambon-s-Lignon
Charolles
MÂCON
Roanne
Villefranche-s-Saône
LYON
Montbrison
ST-ÉTIENNE
Vienne
Tournon-s-Rhône
VALENCE
PRIVAS
Allier
E 62
N 7
N 70
N 79
E 607 N 80
E 21
E 15
A 40
A 6
A 46
A 89
A 72
E 70
A 47
A 43
A 7
N 102
N 88
N 88
D 1083

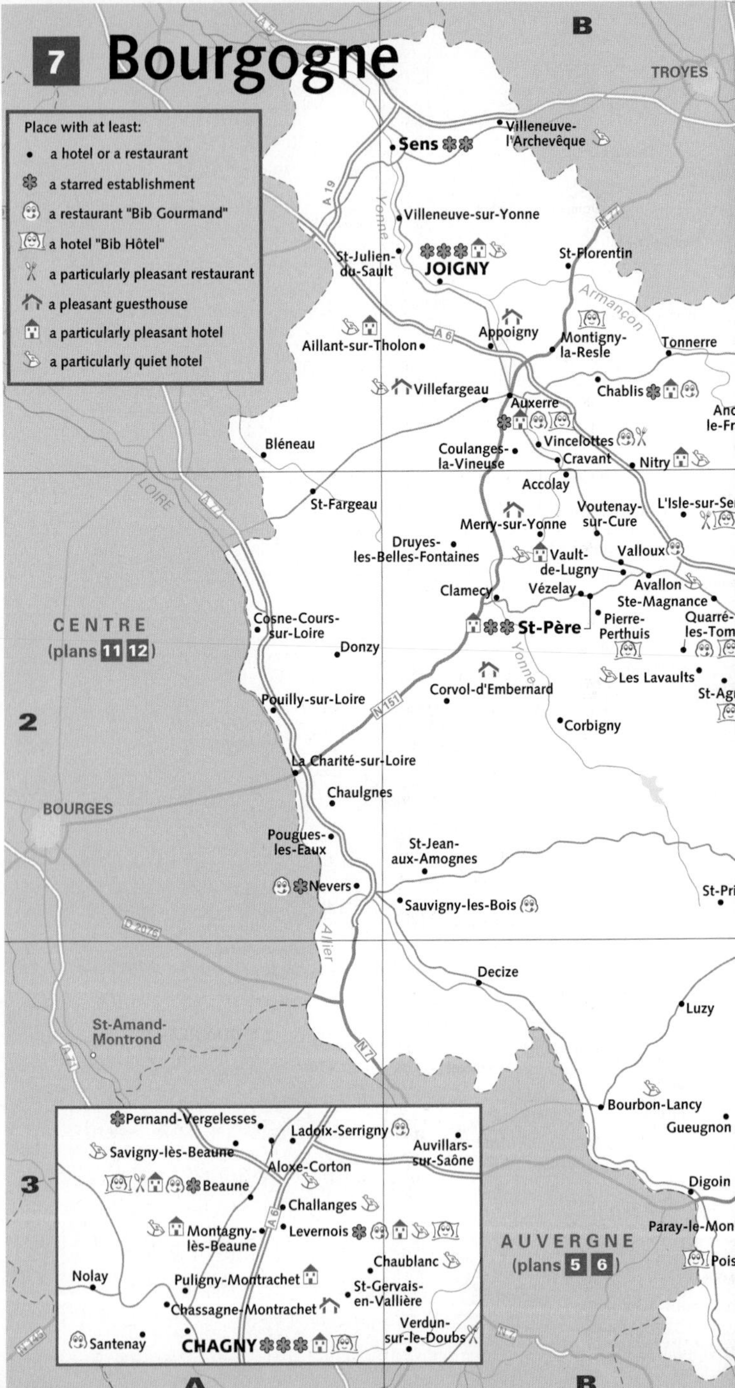
7 Bourgogne
Place with at least:
a hotel or a restaurant
a starred establishment
a restaurant "Bib Gourmand"
a hotel "Bib Hôtel"
a particularly pleasant restaurant
a pleasant guesthouse
a particularly pleasant hotel
a particularly quiet hotel
B
TROYES
Villeneuve-l'Archevêque
Sens
Villeneuve-sur-Yonne
St-Julien-du-Sault
JOIGNY
St-Florentin
Aillant-sur-Tholon
Appoigny
Montigny-la-Resle
Tonnerre
Villefargeau
Auxerre
Chablis
Bléneau
Coulanges-la-Vineuse
Vincelottes
Cravant
Nitry
Accolay
St-Fargeau
Voutenay-sur-Cure
L'Isle-sur-Ser
Merry-sur-Yonne
Druyes-les-Belles-Fontaines
Vault-de-Lugny
Valloux
Clamecy
Vézelay
Avallon
Ste-Magnance
Cosne-Cours-sur-Loire
St-Père
Pierre-Perthuis
Quarré-les-Tomb
CENTRE
(plans 11 12)
Donzy
Les Lavaults
Corvol-d'Embernard
Pouilly-sur-Loire
2
Corbigny
La Charité-sur-Loire
Chaulgnes
BOURGES
Pougues-les-Eaux
St-Jean-aux-Amognes
Nevers
Sauvigny-les-Bois
St-Prix
Decize
Luzy
St-Amand-Montrond
Bourbon-Lancy
Gueugnon
Pernand-Vergelesses
Ladoix-Serrigny
Auvillars-sur-Saône
Savigny-lès-Beaune
Aloxe-Corton
3
Beaune
Challanges
Montagny-lès-Beaune
Levernois
Digoin
Paray-le-Moni
AUVERGNE
(plans 5 6)
Chaublanc
Nolay
Puligny-Montrachet
St-Gervais-en-Vallière
Chassagne-Montrachet
Verdun-sur-le-Doubs
Santenay
CHAGNY
A
B

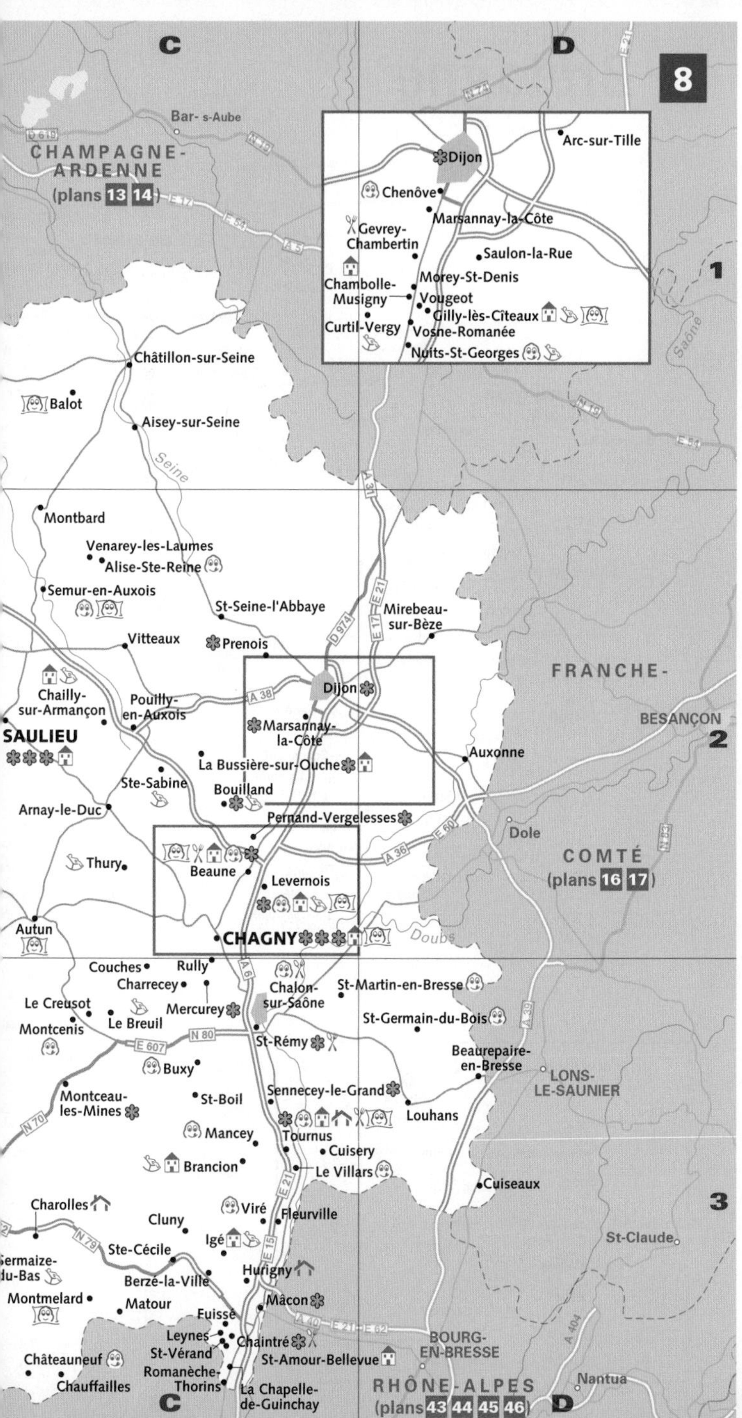
8
C
D
1
2
3
Bar-s-Aube
CHAMPAGNE-ARDENNE
(plans 13 14)
Dijon
Arc-sur-Tille
Chenôve
Marsannay-la-Côte
Gevrey-Chambertin
Saulon-la-Rue
Chambolle-Musigny
Morey-St-Denis
Vougeot
Gilly-lès-Cîteaux
Curtil-Vergy
Vosne-Romanée
Nuits-St-Georges
Saône
Châtillon-sur-Seine
Balot
Aisey-sur-Seine
Seine
Montbard
Venarey-les-Laumes
Alise-Ste-Reine
Semur-en-Auxois
St-Seine-l'Abbaye
Mirebeau-sur-Bèze
Vitteaux
Prenois
Chailly-sur-Armançon
Pouilly-en-Auxois
Dijon
Marsannay-la-Côte
FRANCHE-
BESANÇON
SAULIEU
Auxonne
La Bussière-sur-Ouche
Ste-Sabine
Bouilland
Arnay-le-Duc
Pernand-Vergelesses
Dole
Thury
Beaune
Levernois
COMTÉ
(plans 16 17)
Autun
CHAGNY
Doubs
Couches
Rully
Charrecey
Chalon-sur-Saône
St-Martin-en-Bresse
Le Creusot
Le Breuil
Mercurey
Montcenis
St-Germain-du-Bois
St-Rémy
Buxy
Beaurepaire-en-Bresse
LONS-LE-SAUNIER
Montceau-les-Mines
St-Boil
Sennecey-le-Grand
Louhans
Mancey
Tournus
Cuisery
Brancion
Le Villars
Cuiseaux
Charolles
Viré
Fleurville
Cluny
St-Claude
Igé
Ste-Cécile
Sermaize-du-Bas
Hurigny
Berzé-la-Ville
Montmelard
Matour
Mâcon
Fuissé
Leynes
Chaintré
St-Vérand
BOURG-EN-BRESSE
Châteauneuf
St-Amour-Bellevue
Romanèche-Thorins
Nantua
Chauffailles
La Chapelle-de-Guinchay
RHÔNE-ALPES
(plans 43 44 45 46)

9 Bretagne

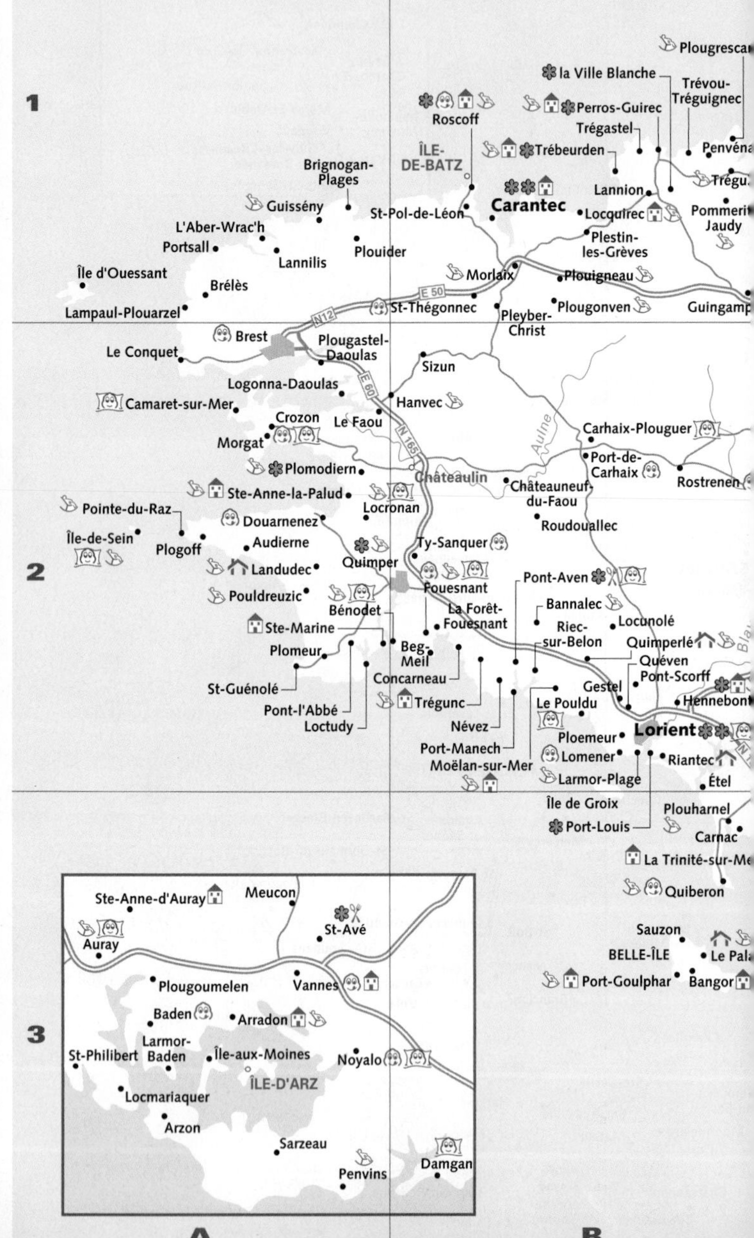

B
1
2
3
A
B
Plougrescant
la Ville Blanche
Trévou-Tréguignec
Roscoff
Perros-Guirec
Trégastel
ÎLE-DE-BATZ
Trébeurden
Penvénan
Brignogan-Plages
Lannion
Tréguier
Carantec
Guissény
St-Pol-de-Léon
Locquirec
Pommerit-Jaudy
L'Aber-Wrac'h
Plestin-les-Grèves
Portsall
Plouider
Lannilis
Île d'Ouessant
Morlaix
Plouigneau
Brélès
E 50
St-Thégonnec
Plougonven
Guingamp
Lampaul-Plouarzel
N12
Pleyber-Christ
Brest
Plougastel-Daoulas
Le Conquet
Sizun
Logonna-Daoulas
E 60
Hanvec
Camaret-sur-Mer
Crozon
Le Faou
Aulne
Carhaix-Plouguer
Morgat
N 165
Port-de-Carhaix
Plomodiern
Châteaulin
Rostrenen
Ste-Anne-la-Palud
Châteauneuf-du-Faou
Locronan
Pointe-du-Raz
Douarnenez
Roudouallec
Île-de-Sein
Audierne
Plogoff
Ty-Sanquer
Quimper
Landudec
Fouesnant
Pont-Aven
Pouldreuzic
Bannalec
Bénodet
La Forêt-Fouesnant
Locunolé
Ste-Marine
Riec-sur-Belon
Quimperlé
Plomeur
Beg-Meil
Quéven
Concarneau
Pont-Scorff
St-Guénolé
Gestel
Le Pouldu
Hennebont
Pont-l'Abbé
Trégunc
Loctudy
Névez
Lorient
Ploemeur
Port-Manech
Lomener
Riantec
Moëlan-sur-Mer
Larmor-Plage
Étel
Île de Groix
Plouharnel
Port-Louis
Carnac
La Trinité-sur-Mer
Quiberon
Sauzon
BELLE-ÎLE
Le Palais
Port-Goulphar
Bangor
Ste-Anne-d'Auray
Meucon
St-Avé
Auray
Plougoumelen
Vannes
Baden
Arradon
Larmor-Baden
St-Philibert
Île-aux-Moines
Noyalo
ÎLE-D'ARZ
Locmariaquer
Arzon
Sarzeau
Penvins
Damgan

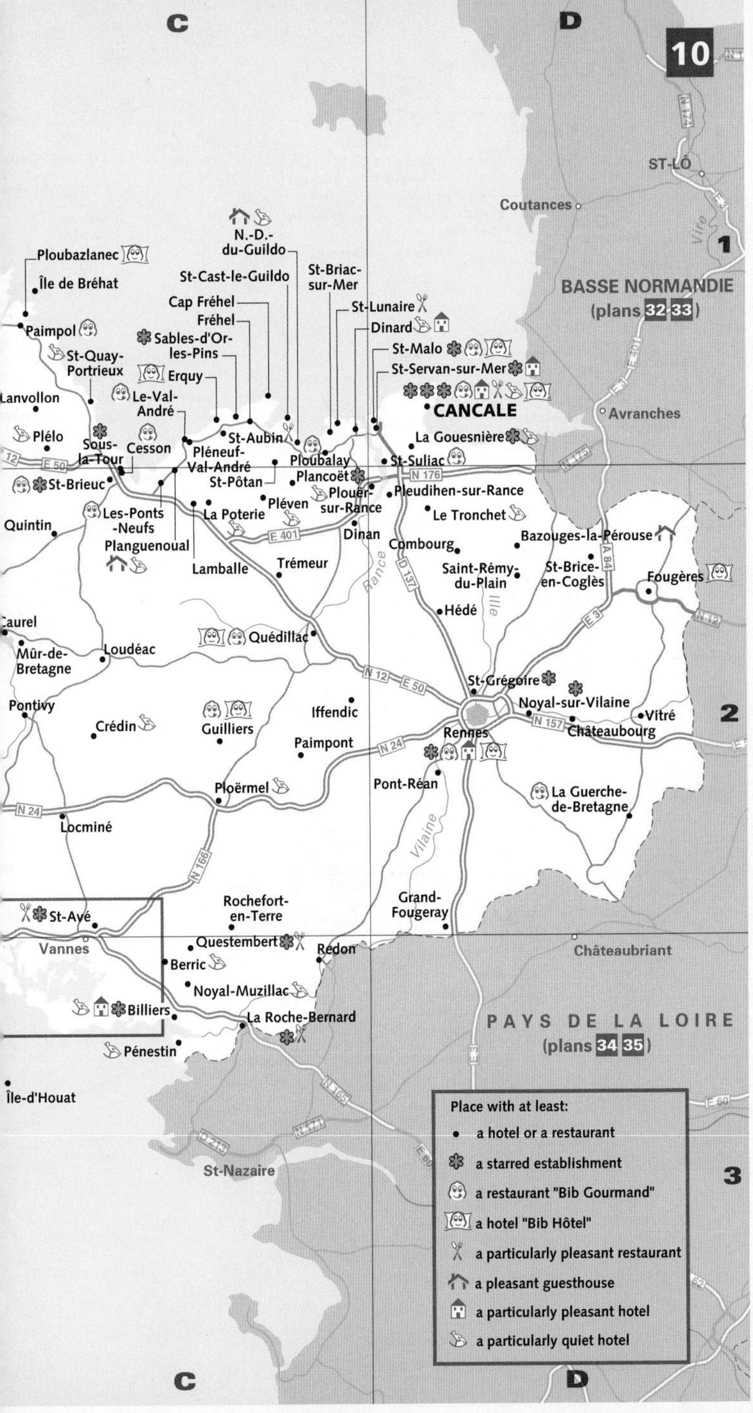
C
D
10
1
2
3
ST-LÔ
Coutances
Vire
BASSE NORMANDIE
(plans 32 33)
Avranches
N.-D.-
du-Guildo
Ploubazlanec
Île de Bréhat
St-Cast-le-Guildo
St-Briac-
sur-Mer
Cap Fréhel
Fréhel
St-Lunaire
Dinard
Paimpol
Sables-d'Or-
les-Pins
St-Malo
St-Servan-sur-Mer
St-Quay-
Portrieux
Erquy
CANCALE
Lanvollon
Le-Val-
André
Plélo
Sous-
la-Tour
Cesson
St-Aubin
Pléneuf-
Val-André
Ploubalay
La Gouesnière
St-Suliac
St-Brieuc
St-Pôtan
Plancoët
Plouër-
sur-Rance
Pleudihen-sur-Rance
Quintin
Les-Ponts
-Neufs
La Poterie
Pléven
Le Tronchet
Dinan
Planguenoual
Combourg
Bazouges-la-Pérouse
Lamballe
Trémeur
Saint-Rémy-
du-Plain
St-Brice-
en-Coglès
Fougères
Rance
Hédé
Ille
Caurel
Mûr-de-
Bretagne
Loudéac
Quédillac
St-Grégoire
Noyal-sur-Vilaine
Vitré
Pontivy
Crédin
Guilliers
Iffendic
Rennes
Châteaubourg
Paimpont
Ploërmel
Pont-Réan
La Guerche-
de-Bretagne
Locminé
Vilaine
Rochefort-
en-Terre
Grand-
Fougeray
St-Avé
Vannes
Questembert
Redon
Châteaubriant
Berric
Noyal-Muzillac
Billiers
La Roche-Bernard
PAYS DE LA LOIRE
(plans 34 35)
Pénestin
Île-d'Houat
St-Nazaire
N 176
E 401
D 137
A 84
E 3
N 12
E 50
N 157
N 24
N 166
N 165
N 171
D 213
E 60
N 175
N 174
Place with at least:
a hotel or a restaurant
a starred establishment
a restaurant "Bib Gourmand"
a hotel "Bib Hôtel"
a particularly pleasant restaurant
a pleasant guesthouse
a particularly pleasant hotel
a particularly quiet hotel

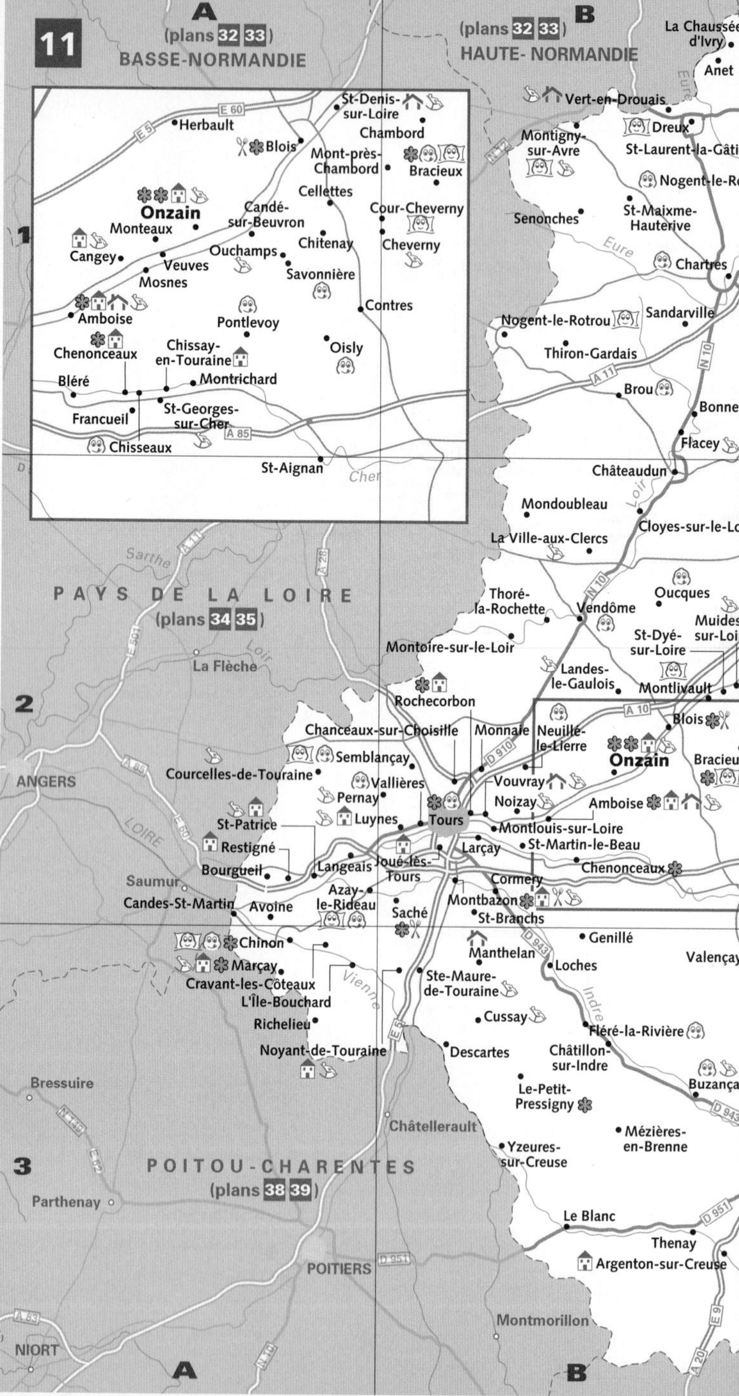

11
A
(plans 32 33)
BASSE-NORMANDIE
B
(plans 32 33)
HAUTE-NORMANDIE
Herbault
Blois
St-Denis-sur-Loire
Chambord
Mont-près-Chambord
Bracieux
Onzain
Cellettes
Candé-sur-Beuvron
Cour-Cheverny
Monteaux
Cheverny
Chitenay
Cangey
Ouchamps
Veuves
Savonnière
Mosnes
Contres
Amboise
Pontlevoy
Chenonceaux
Chissay-en-Touraine
Oisly
Bléré
Montrichard
St-Georges-sur-Cher
Francueil
Chisseaux
St-Aignan
La Chaussée-d'Ivry
Anet
Vert-en-Drouais
Dreux
Montigny-sur-Avre
St-Laurent-la-Gâtine
Nogent-le-Roi
Senonches
St-Maixme-Hauterive
Chartres
Sandarville
Nogent-le-Rotrou
Thiron-Gardais
Brou
Bonneval
Flacey
Châteaudun
Mondoubleau
Cloyes-sur-le-Loir
La Ville-aux-Clercs
PAYS DE LA LOIRE
(plans 34 35)
Thoré-la-Rochette
Vendôme
Oucques
Muides-sur-Loire
St-Dyé-sur-Loire
Montoire-sur-le-Loir
La Flèche
Landes-le-Gaulois
Montlivault
2
Rochecorbon
Blois
Chanceaux-sur-Choisille
Monnaie
Neuillé-le-Lierre
Onzain
Bracieux
Semblançay
ANGERS
Courcelles-de-Touraine
Vallières
Vouvray
Pernay
Noizay
Amboise
Luynes
Tours
St-Patrice
Montlouis-sur-Loire
Restigné
Larçay
St-Martin-le-Beau
Bourgueil
Langeais
Joué-lès-Tours
Chenonceaux
Saumur
Azay-le-Rideau
Cormery
Candes-St-Martin
Avoine
Saché
Montbazon
St-Branchs
Chinon
Genillé
Marçay
Manthelan
Loches
Valençay
Cravant-les-Côteaux
Ste-Maure-de-Touraine
L'Île-Bouchard
Richelieu
Cussay
Fléré-la-Rivière
Noyant-de-Touraine
Descartes
Châtillon-sur-Indre
Bressuire
Buzançais
Le-Petit-Pressigny
Châtellerault
Mézières-en-Brenne
3
POITOU-CHARENTES
(plans 38 39)
Yzeures-sur-Creuse
Parthenay
Le Blanc
Thenay
POITIERS
Argenton-sur-Creuse
Montmorillon
NIORT
A
B

Centre 12

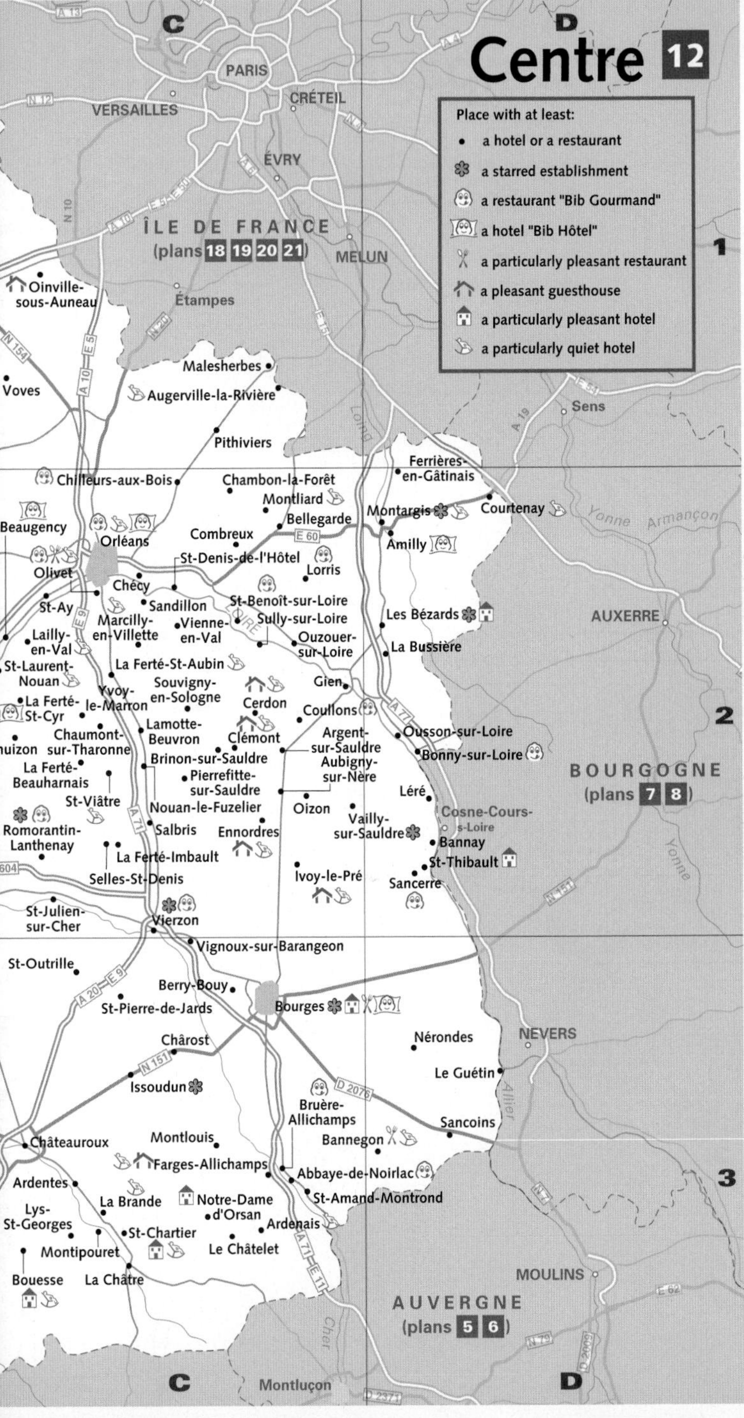

Place with at least:
a hotel or a restaurant
a starred establishment
a restaurant "Bib Gourmand"
a hotel "Bib Hôtel"
a particularly pleasant restaurant
a pleasant guesthouse
a particularly pleasant hotel
a particularly quiet hotel
PARIS
VERSAILLES
CRÉTEIL
ÉVRY
ÎLE DE FRANCE
(plans 18 19 20 21)
MELUN
Oinville-sous-Auneau
Étampes
Malesherbes
Voves
Augerville-la-Rivière
Pithiviers
Sens
Ferrières-en-Gâtinais
Chilleurs-aux-Bois
Chambon-la-Forêt
Montliard
Courtenay
Montargis
Bellegarde
Beaugency
Orléans
Combreux
Amilly
St-Denis-de-l'Hôtel
Olivet
Lorris
Chécy
St-Benoît-sur-Loire
St-Ay
Sandillon
Les Bézards
AUXERRE
Marcilly-en-Villette
Vienne-en-Val
Sully-sur-Loire
Lailly-en-Val
Ouzouer-sur-Loire
La Bussière
St-Laurent-Nouan
La Ferté-St-Aubin
Gien
Yvoy-le-Marron
Souvigny-en-Sologne
Cerdon
La Ferté-St-Cyr
Coullons
Lamotte-Beuvron
Chaumont-sur-Tharonne
Clémont
Argent-sur-Sauldre
Ousson-sur-Loire
Bonny-sur-Loire
Brinon-sur-Sauldre
Aubigny-sur-Nère
BOURGOGNE
(plans 7 8)
La Ferté-Beauharnais
Pierrefitte-sur-Sauldre
Léré
St-Viâtre
Nouan-le-Fuzelier
Oizon
Cosne-Cours-s-Loire
Vailly-sur-Sauldre
Romorantin-Lanthenay
Salbris
Ennordres
Bannay
La Ferté-Imbault
St-Thibault
Selles-St-Denis
Ivoy-le-Pré
Sancerre
St-Julien-sur-Cher
Vierzon
Vignoux-sur-Barangeon
St-Outrille
Berry-Bouy
St-Pierre-de-Jards
Bourges
Nérondes
NEVERS
Chârost
Le Guétin
Issoudun
Bruère-Allichamps
Sancoins
Châteauroux
Montlouis
Bannegon
Farges-Allichamps
Abbaye-de-Noirlac
Ardentes
St-Amand-Montrond
La Brande
Notre-Dame d'Orsan
Lys-St-Georges
Ardenais
St-Chartier
Le Châtelet
Montipouret
MOULINS
Bouesse
La Châtre
AUVERGNE
(plans 5 6)
Montluçon

13 Champagne Ardenne

Place with at least:
- a hotel or a restaurant
- a starred establishment
- a restaurant "Bib Gourmand"
- a hotel "Bib Hôtel"
- a particularly pleasant restaurant
- a pleasant guesthouse
- a particularly pleasant hotel
- a particularly quiet hotel

PICARDIE (plans 36 37)

ÎLE DE FRANCE (plans 18 19 20 21)

BOURGOGNE (plans 7 8)

Signy-le-Petit, Vervins, Charleville-Mézières, Fagnon, Signy-l'Abbaye, LAON, Rethel, Compiègne, Soissons, St-Thierry, Lavannes, Fismes, Crugny, Reims, Senlis, Montchenot, Sept-Saulx, Ludes, Verzy, Champillon, Bouzy, Château-Thierry, Dormans, Ambonnay, Épernay, Tours-sur-Marne, Vinay, Ay, Mutigny, L'Épine, Meaux, Le Mesnil-sur-Oger, Châlons-en-Champagne, Vertus, Toulon-la-Montagne, Mondement-Montgivroux, CRÉTEIL, Sézanne, Vitry-le-François, Provins, Romilly-sur-Seine, MELUN, Nogent-sur-Seine, Fontainebleau, Piney, Brévonnes, Pont-Ste-Marie, Troyes, Estissac, Mesnil-St-Père, Dolancourt, Sens, Moussey, Villemoyenne, Eaux-Puiseaux, Fouchères, Bar-sur-Seine, Chaource, Gyé-sur-Seine, Les Riceys, Montargis, AUXERRE, Montbard

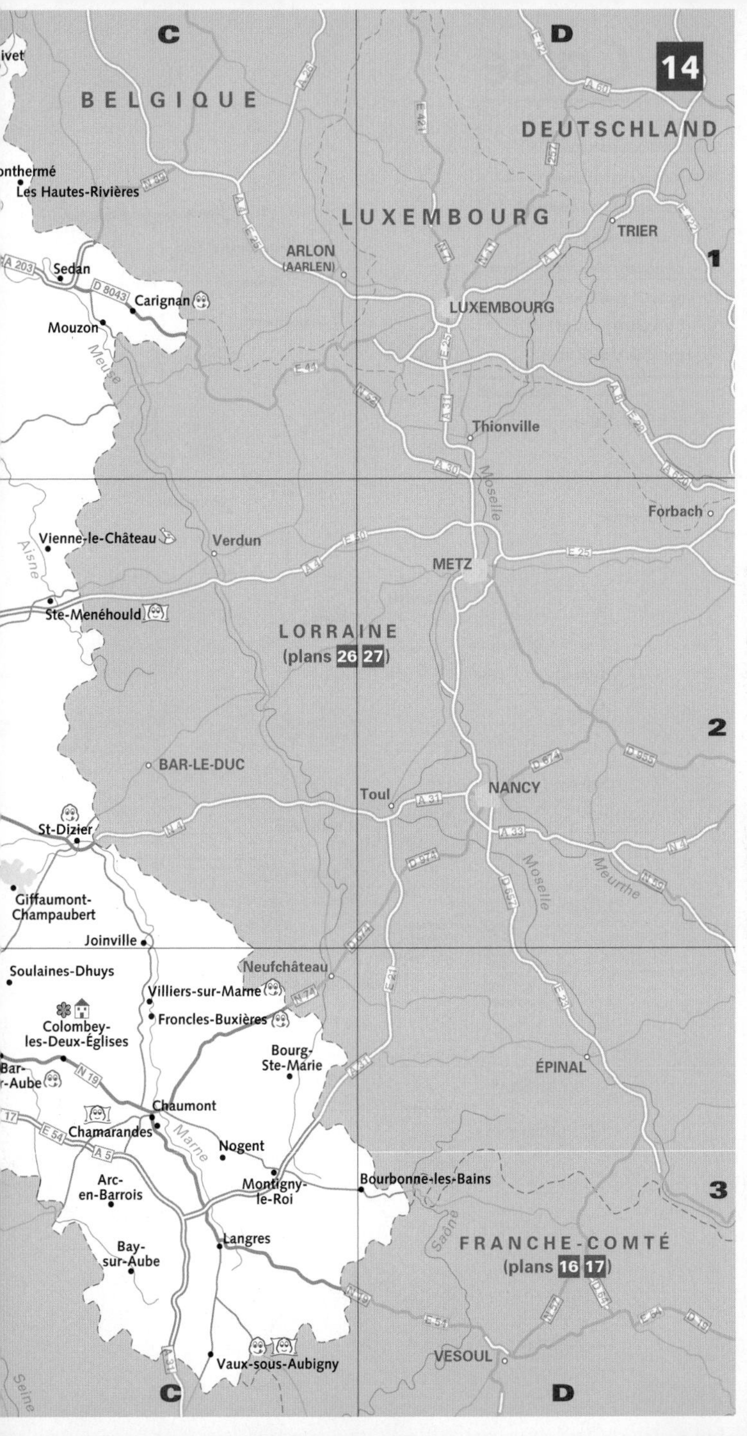
C
D
14
BELGIQUE
DEUTSCHLAND
LUXEMBOURG
Les Hautes-Rivières
ARLON
(AARLEN)
TRIER
1
Sedan
Carignan
Mouzon
Meuse
LUXEMBOURG
Thionville
Moselle
Forbach
Vienne-le-Château
Verdun
Aisne
METZ
Ste-Menéhould
LORRAINE
(plans 26 27)
2
BAR-LE-DUC
Toul
NANCY
St-Dizier
Moselle
Meurthe
Giffaumont-
Champaubert
Joinville
Soulaines-Dhuys
Neufchâteau
Villiers-sur-Marne
Froncles-Buxières
Colombey-
les-Deux-Églises
Bourg-
Ste-Marie
ÉPINAL
Chaumont
Chamarandes
Marne
Nogent
Arc-
en-Barrois
Montigny-
le-Roi
Bourbonne-les-Bains
3
Langres
Saône
FRANCHE-COMTÉ
(plans 16 17)
Bay-
sur-Aube
VESOUL
Vaux-sous-Aubigny
Seine
C
D

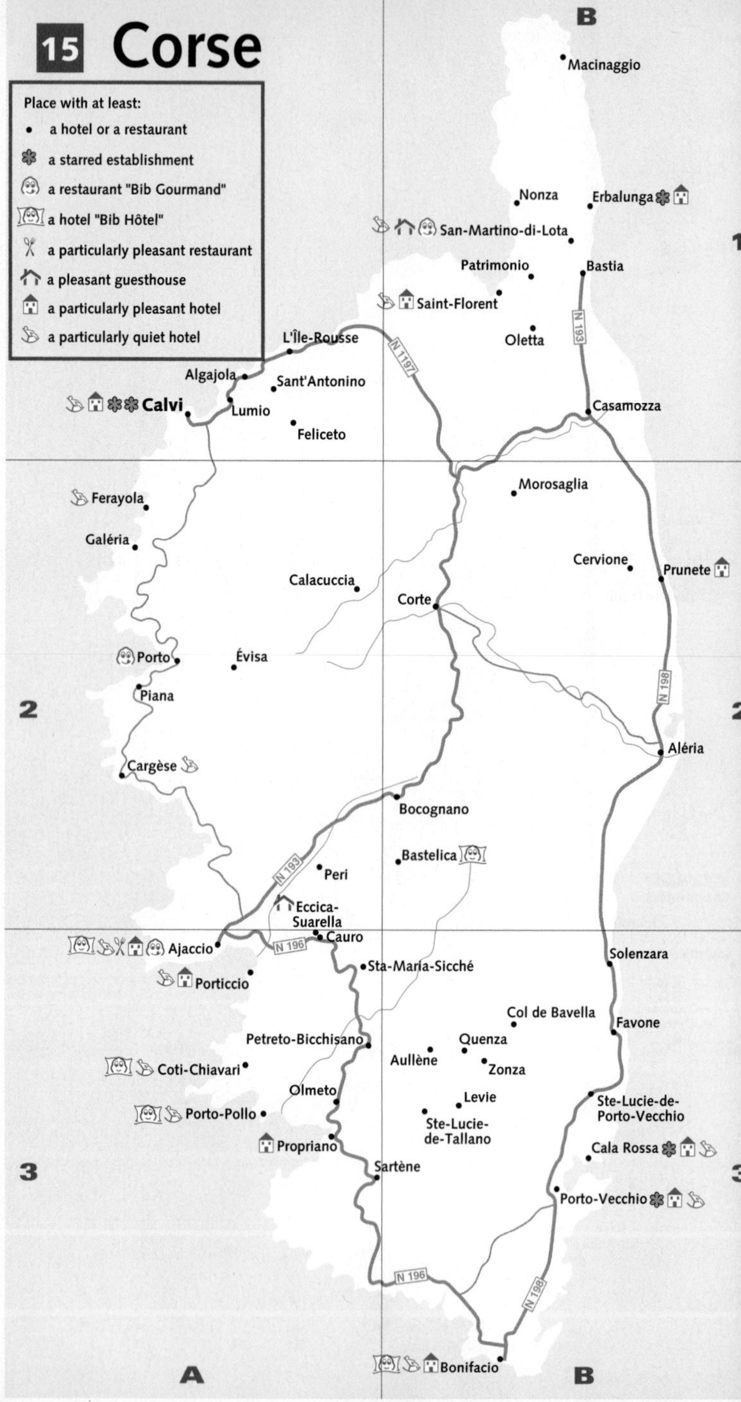
15 Corse
Place with at least:
a hotel or a restaurant
a starred establishment
a restaurant "Bib Gourmand"
a hotel "Bib Hôtel"
a particularly pleasant restaurant
a pleasant guesthouse
a particularly pleasant hotel
a particularly quiet hotel
A
B
1
2
3
Macinaggio
Nonza
Erbalunga
San-Martino-di-Lota
Patrimonio
Bastia
Saint-Florent
Oletta
L'Île-Rousse
Algajola
Sant'Antonino
Calvi
Lumio
Feliceto
Casamozza
N 193
N 1197
Morosaglia
Ferayola
Galéria
Cervione
Prunete
Calacuccia
Corte
Porto
Évisa
Piana
N 198
Aléria
Cargèse
Bocognano
Bastelica
Peri
N 193
Eccica-Suarella
Cauro
N 196
Ajaccio
Sta-Maria-Sicché
Porticcio
Solenzara
Col de Bavella
Favone
Petreto-Bicchisano
Quenza
Aullène
Zonza
Coti-Chiavari
Olmeto
Levie
Ste-Lucie-de-Porto-Vecchio
Porto-Pollo
Ste-Lucie-de-Tallano
Propriano
Cala Rossa
Sartène
Porto-Vecchio
N 196
N 198
Bonifacio

The MICHELIN Guide

A collection to savor!

Belgique & Luxembourg
Deutschland
España & Portugal
France
Great Britain & Ireland
Italia
Nederland
Österreich
Portugal
Suisse-Schweiz-Svizzera
Main Cities of Europe

Also:

Las Vegas
London
Los Angeles
New York City
Paris
San Francisco
Tokyo

16 Franche-Comté

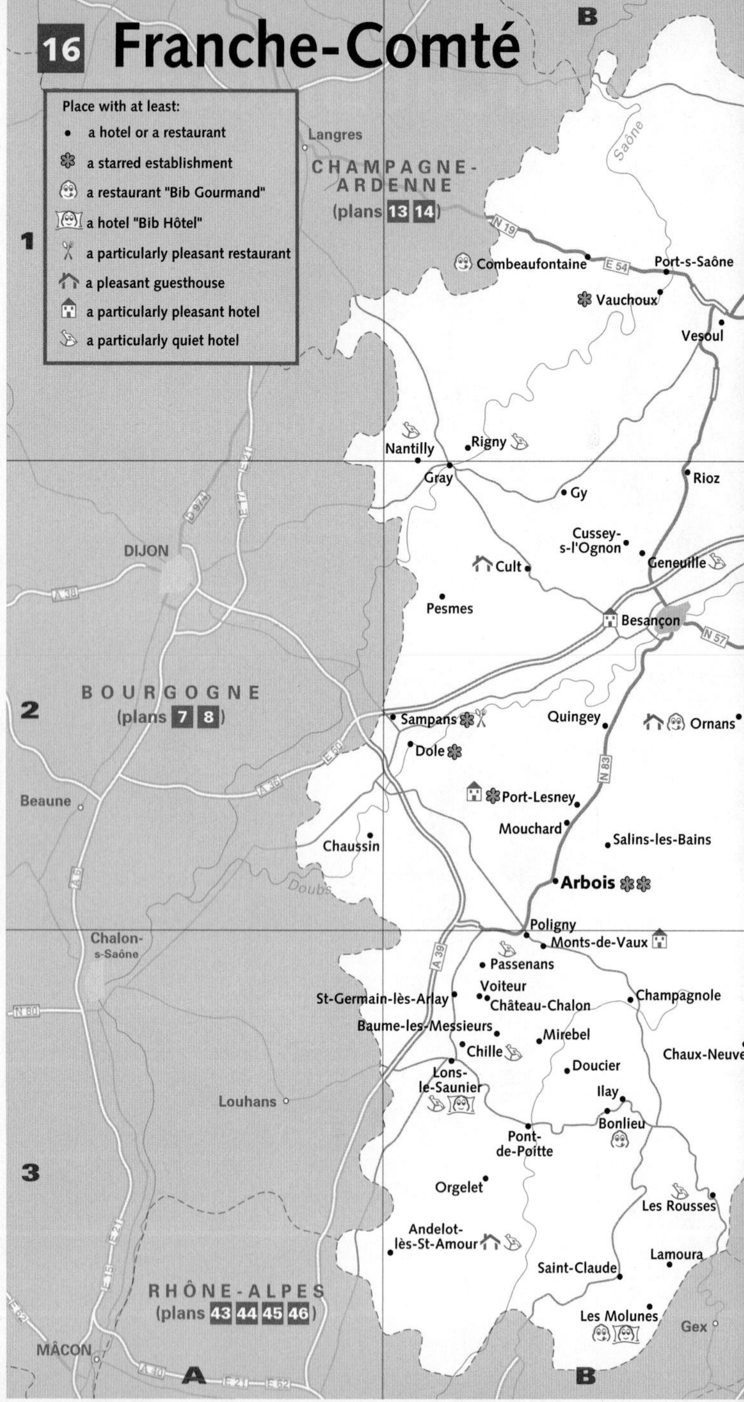

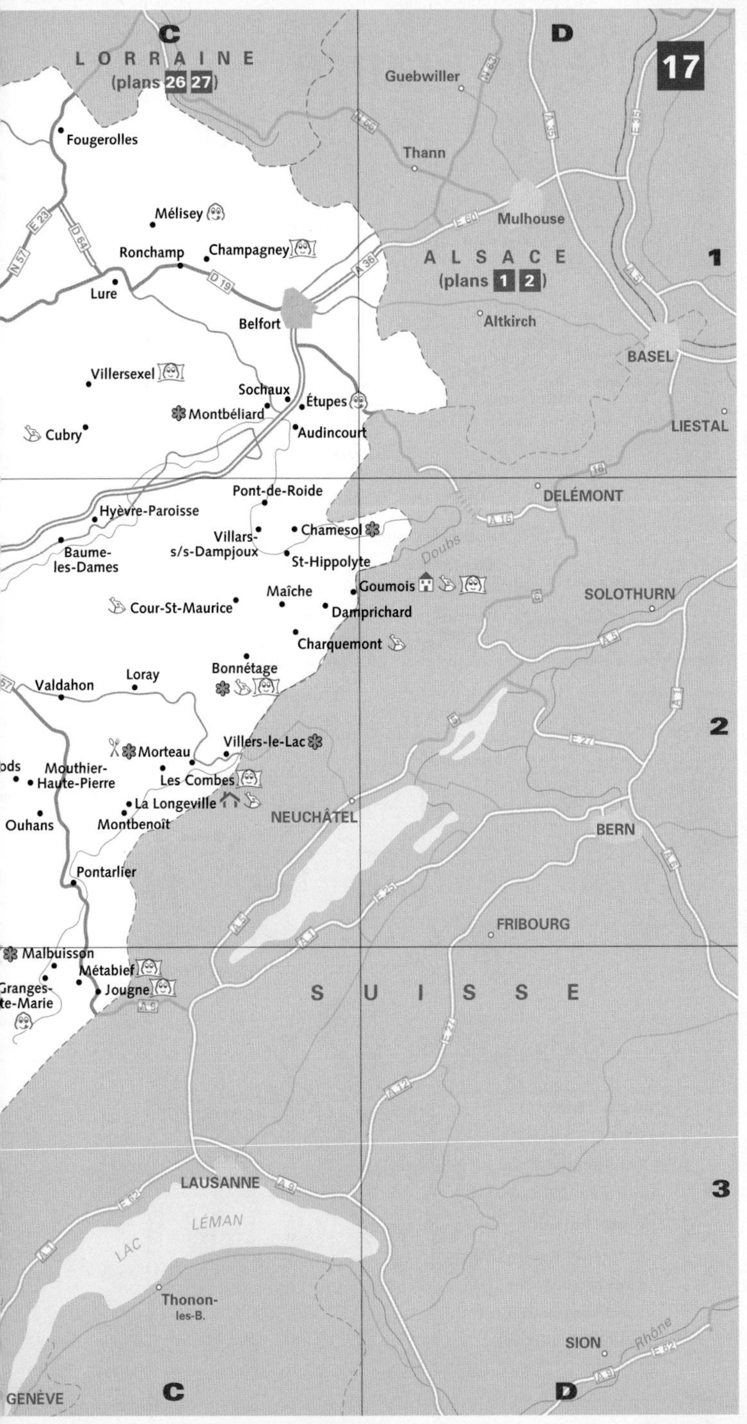

C
D
17
LORRAINE
(plans 26 27)
Guebwiller
Thann
Mulhouse
Fougerolles
Mélisey
Ronchamp
Champagney
Lure
Belfort
ALSACE
(plans 1 2)
Altkirch
BASEL
LIESTAL
1
Villersexel
Sochaux
Étupes
Montbéliard
Audincourt
Cubry
Pont-de-Roide
DELÉMONT
Hyèvre-Paroisse
Villars-s/s-Dampjoux
Chamesol
Baume-les-Dames
St-Hippolyte
Doubs
Goumois
Maîche
SOLOTHURN
Cour-St-Maurice
Damprichard
Charquemont
Bonnétage
Loray
Valdahon
2
Villers-le-Lac
Morteau
Mouthier-Haute-Pierre
Les Combes
La Longeville
Ouhans
Montbenoît
NEUCHÂTEL
BERN
Pontarlier
FRIBOURG
Malbuisson
Métabief
Jougne
Granges-Ste-Marie
SUISSE
LAUSANNE
3
LAC LÉMAN
Thonon-les-B.
SION
Rhône
GENÈVE
C
D

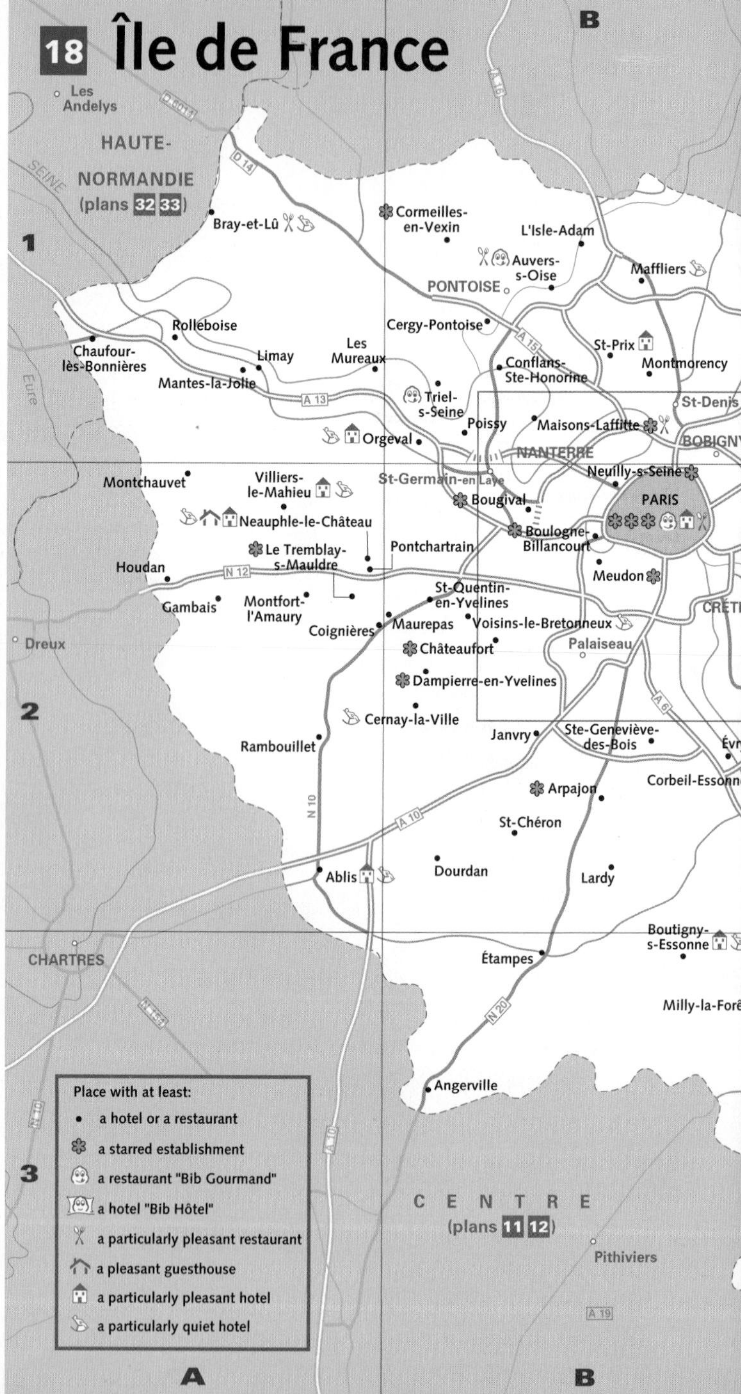
18 Île de France
B
Les Andelys
HAUTE-NORMANDIE
(plans 32 33)
SEINE
1
Bray-et-Lû
Cormeilles-en-Vexin
L'Isle-Adam
Auvers-s-Oise
Maffliers
PONTOISE
Rolleboise
Chaufour-lès-Bonnières
Limay
Les Mureaux
Cergy-Pontoise
St-Prix
Montmorency
Mantes-la-Jolie
Conflans-Ste-Honorine
Eure
A 13
Triel-s-Seine
St-Denis
Poissy
Maisons-Laffitte
Orgeval
NANTERRE
BOBIGNY
Montchauvet
Villiers-le-Mahieu
St-Germain-en Laye
Neuilly-s-Seine
Bougival
PARIS
Neauphle-le-Château
Boulogne-Billancourt
Le Tremblay-s-Mauldre
Pontchartrain
Houdan
N 12
Meudon
St-Quentin-en-Yvelines
Gambais
Montfort-l'Amaury
Coignières
Maurepas
Voisins-le-Bretonneux
Dreux
Châteaufort
Palaiseau
Dampierre-en-Yvelines
2
Cernay-la-Ville
Janvry
Ste-Geneviève-des-Bois
Rambouillet
Corbeil-Essonne
Arpajon
N 10
A 10
St-Chéron
Ablis
Dourdan
Lardy
Boutigny-s-Essonne
CHARTRES
Étampes
N 154
Milly-la-Forê
N 20
Angerville
Place with at least:
a hotel or a restaurant
a starred establishment
a restaurant "Bib Gourmand"
a hotel "Bib Hôtel"
a particularly pleasant restaurant
a pleasant guesthouse
a particularly pleasant hotel
a particularly quiet hotel
3
CENTRE
(plans 11 12)
Pithiviers
A 19
A
B

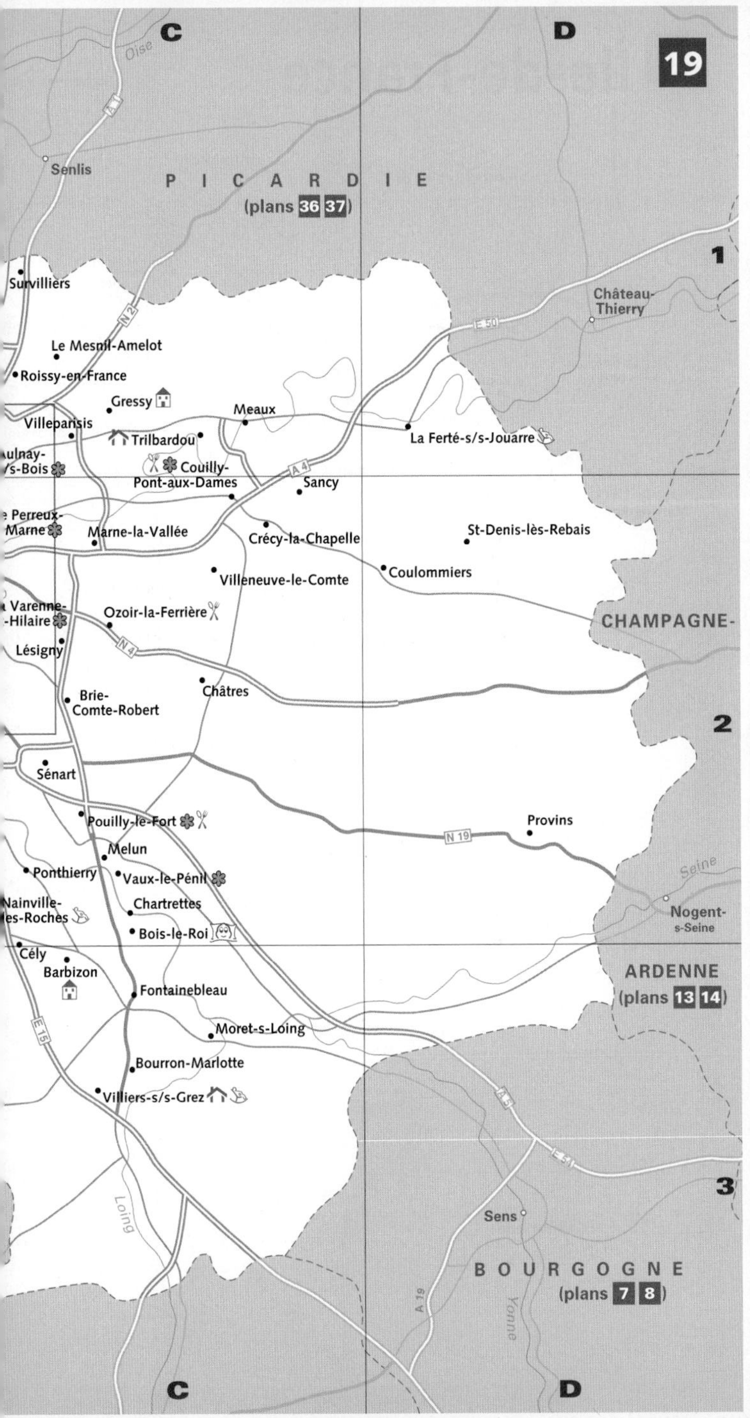
19
C
D
Oise
A 1
Senlis
PICARDIE
(plans 36 37)
1
Survilliers
N 2
Château-Thierry
E 50
Le Mesnil-Amelot
Roissy-en-France
Gressy
Meaux
Villeparisis
Trilbardou
La Ferté-s/s-Jouarre
Aulnay-s/s-Bois
Couilly-Pont-aux-Dames
A 4
Sancy
Le Perreux-Marne
Marne-la-Vallée
Crécy-la-Chapelle
St-Denis-lès-Rebais
Coulommiers
Villeneuve-le-Comte
La Varenne-St-Hilaire
Ozoir-la-Ferrière
CHAMPAGNE-
Lésigny
N 4
Châtres
Brie-Comte-Robert
2
Sénart
Pouilly-le-Fort
Provins
N 19
Melun
Ponthierry
Vaux-le-Pénil
Seine
Nainville-les-Roches
Chartrettes
Nogent-s-Seine
Bois-le-Roi
Cély
Barbizon
ARDENNE
(plans 13 14)
Fontainebleau
E 15
Moret-s-Loing
Bourron-Marlotte
A 5
Villiers-s/s-Grez
E 51
3
Loing
Sens
BOURGOGNE
(plans 7 8)
A 19
Yonne
C
D

20 Île-de-France

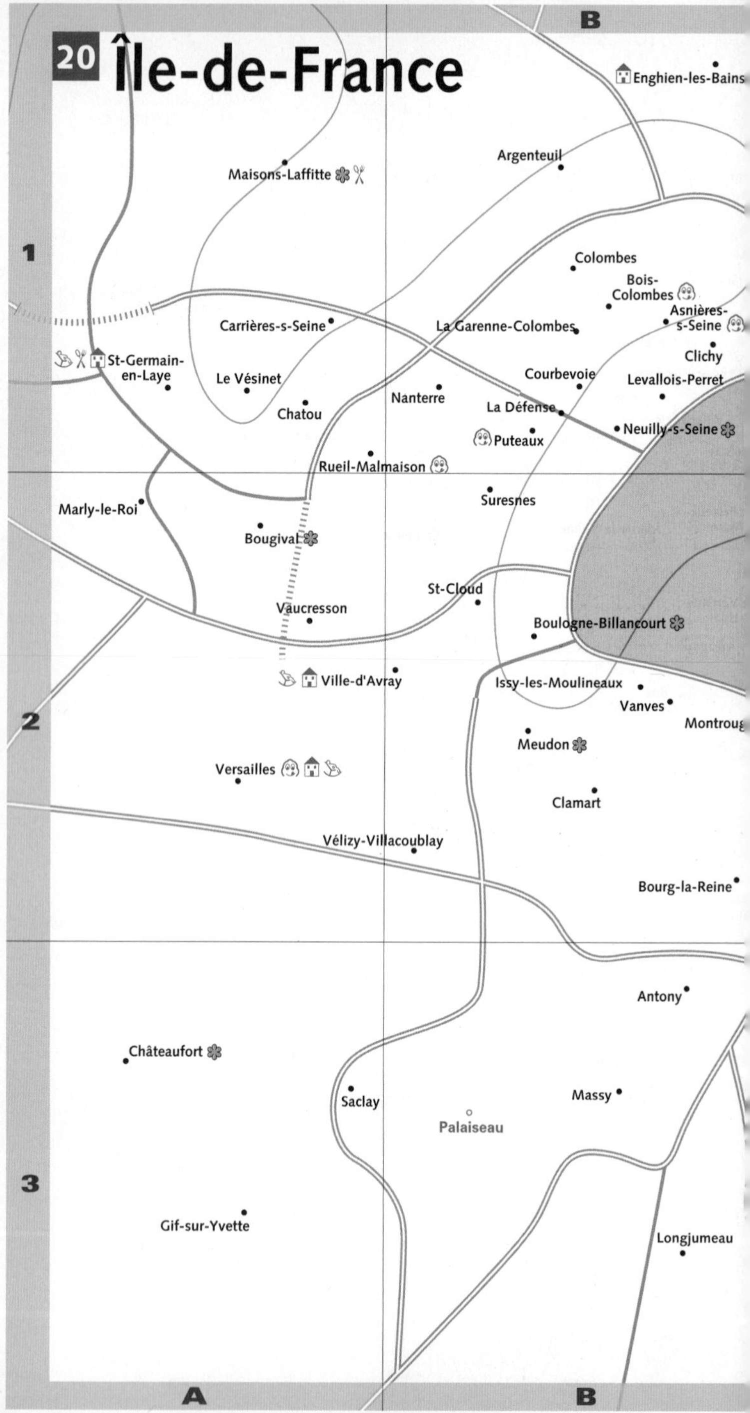

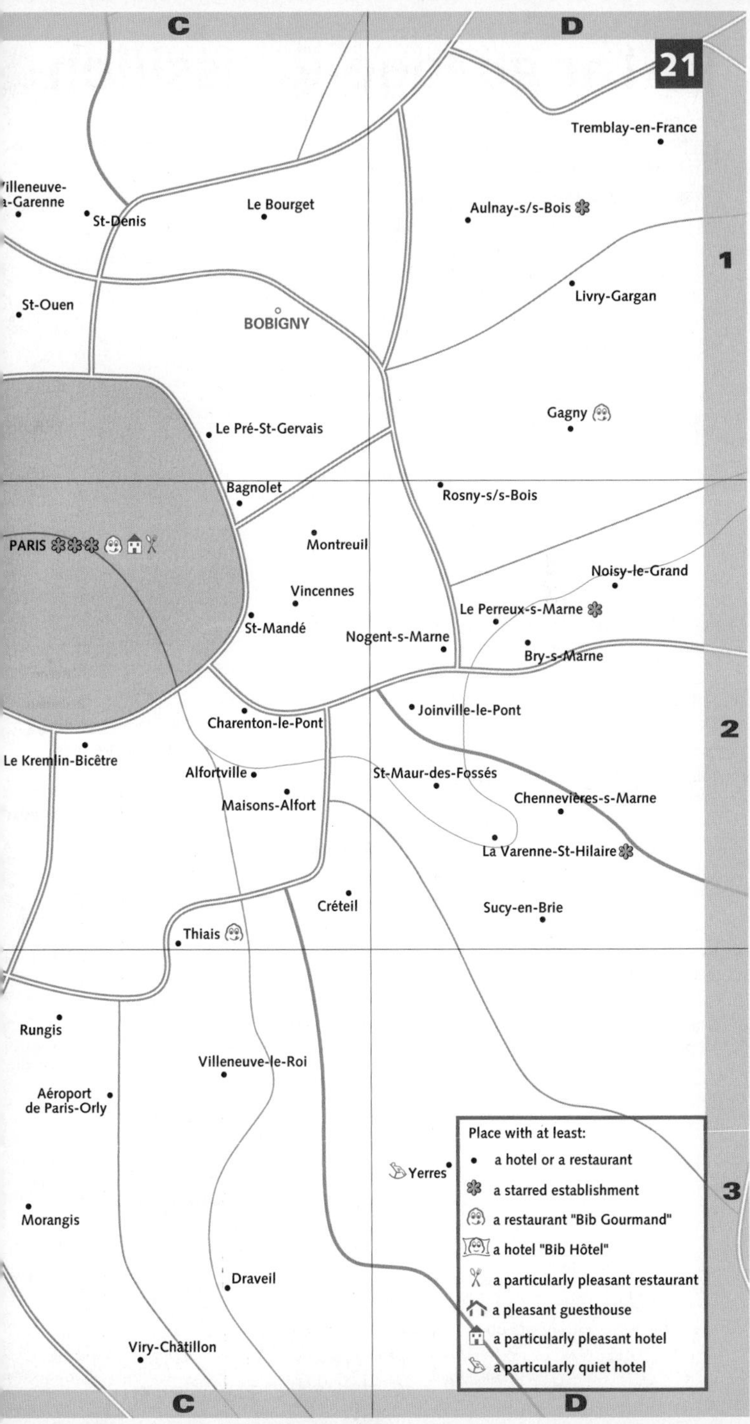

C
D
21
Tremblay-en-France
Villeneuve-la-Garenne
St-Denis
Le Bourget
Aulnay-s/s-Bois
1
Livry-Gargan
St-Ouen
BOBIGNY
Gagny
Le Pré-St-Gervais
Bagnolet
Rosny-s/s-Bois
PARIS
Montreuil
Noisy-le-Grand
Vincennes
Le Perreux-s-Marne
St-Mandé
Nogent-s-Marne
Bry-s-Marne
Joinville-le-Pont
Charenton-le-Pont
2
Le Kremlin-Bicêtre
Alfortville
St-Maur-des-Fossés
Maisons-Alfort
Chennevières-s-Marne
La Varenne-St-Hilaire
Créteil
Sucy-en-Brie
Thiais
Rungis
Villeneuve-le-Roi
Aéroport de Paris-Orly
Place with at least:
a hotel or a restaurant
a starred establishment
a restaurant "Bib Gourmand"
a hotel "Bib Hôtel"
a particularly pleasant restaurant
a pleasant guesthouse
a particularly pleasant hotel
a particularly quiet hotel
Yerres
3
Morangis
Draveil
Viry-Châtillon
C
D

22 Languedoc-Roussillon

Place with at least:
- a hotel or a restaurant
- a starred establishment
- a restaurant "Bib Gourmand"
- a hotel "Bib Hôtel"
- a particularly pleasant restaurant
- a pleasant guesthouse
- a particularly pleasant hotel
- a particularly quiet hotel

A B

1 2 3

La Garde
Termes
St-Chély-d'Apcher
Truyère
Nasbinals
Figeac
Lot
D 840
Les Hermaux
Banassac
Villefranche-de-Rouergue
RODEZ
N 88
Aveyron
Le Rozier
Millau
Tarn
MONTAUBAN
ALBI
Tarn
A 62
A 68
MIDI-PYRÉNÉES
(plans 28 29)
Avène
Bédarieux
Agout
TOULOUSE
N 124
Villemagne-l'Argentière
Castres
Lamalou-les-Bains
St-Pons-de-Thomières
Magalas
Muret
Ariège
La Pomarède
Bize-Minervois
Lastours
Minerve
Béziers
Castelnaudary
A 61
Colombiers
Conques-sur-Orbiel
Lézignan-Corbières
Nissan-Lez-Enserune
A 66
Bram
Lespignan
Montredon
Conilhac-Corbières
Ornaisons
Carcassonne
Narbonne
Cavanac
Gasparets
Bages
Pamiers
Aude
Lagrasse
Gruissan
St-Pierre-des-Champs
St-André-de-Roquelongue
Portel-des-Corbières
Limoux
Fontjoncouse
Port-la-Nouvelle
Sonnac-sur-l'Hers
FOIX
Cascastel-des-Corbières
Couiza
Fitou
Leucate
A 9
Quillan
Cucugnan
Belcaire
Maury
St-Laurent-de-la-Salanque
Gincla
Montner
N 20
Canet-en-Roussillon
Pézilla-la-Rivière
Perpignan
Molitg-les-Bains
N 116
Laroque-des-Albères
St-Cyprien
Villefranche-de-Conflent
Prades
Brouilla
Argelès-s-Mer
PRICIPAUTÉ-D'ANDORRE
Font-Romeu-Odeillo-Via
Mont-Louis
Le Boulou
Vernet-les-Bains
Céret
Collioure
Dorres
Latour-de-Carol
Llo
Amélie-les-Bains-Palalda
Maureillas-las-Illas
Saillagouse
Las Illas
Port-Vendres
ESPAÑA
La Preste
Banyuls-s-Mer
Valcebollère
Prats-de-Mollo-la-Preste
St-Laurent-de-Cerdans
A B

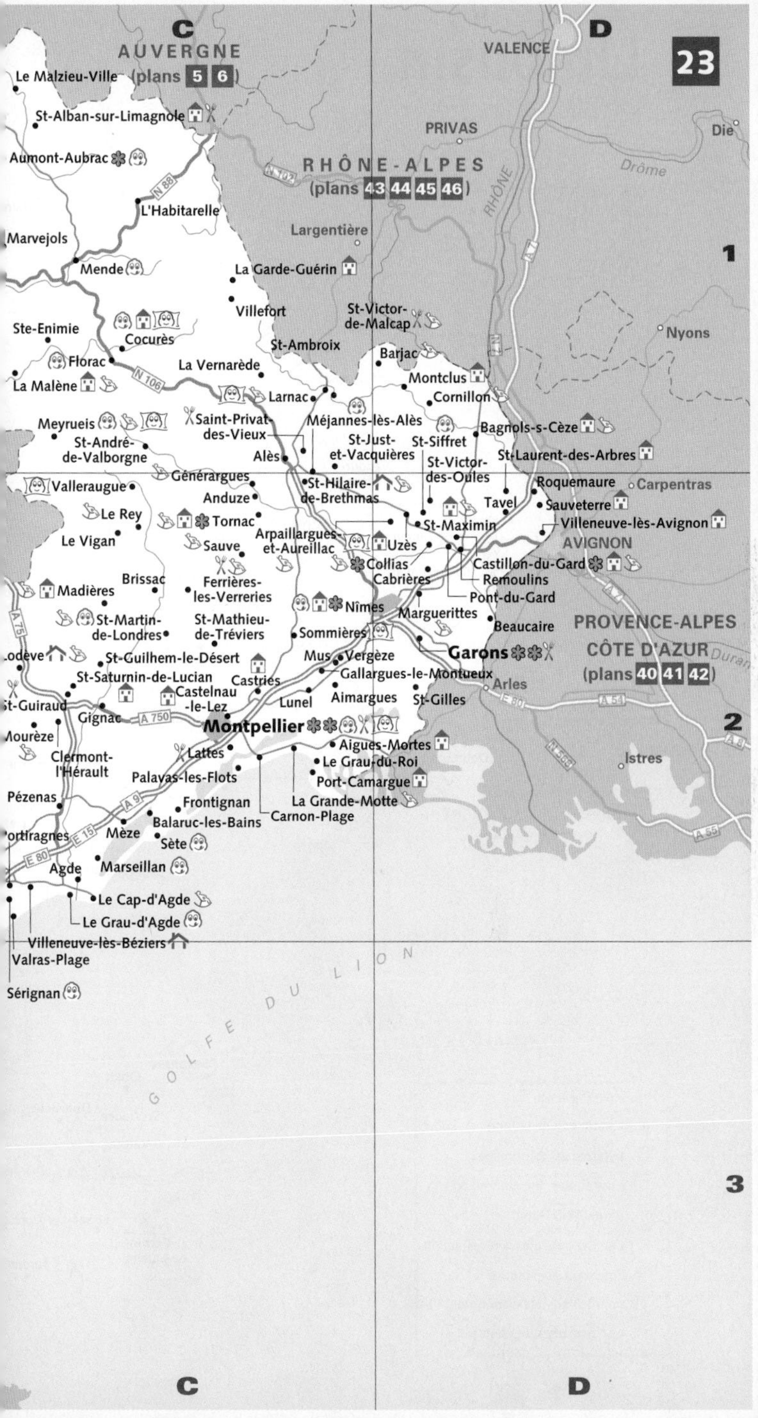
C
D
23
AUVERGNE
(plans 5 6)
VALENCE
Le Malzieu-Ville
St-Alban-sur-Limagnole
PRIVAS
Die
Aumont-Aubrac
RHÔNE-ALPES
(plans 43 44 45 46)
Drôme
RHÔNE
N 102
N 88
L'Habitarelle
Largentière
Marvejols
1
Mende
La Garde-Guérin
Villefort
St-Victor-de-Malcap
Ste-Enimie
Cocurès
St-Ambroix
Nyons
Florac
Barjac
La Vernarède
La Malène
N 106
Montclus
Larnac
Cornillon
Meyrueis
Saint-Privat-des-Vieux
Méjannes-lès-Alès
Bagnols-s-Cèze
St-André-de-Valborgne
St-Just-et-Vacquières
St-Siffret
Alès
St-Laurent-des-Arbres
St-Victor-des-Oules
Générargues
Valleraugue
St-Hilaire-de-Brethmas
Roquemaure
Carpentras
Anduze
Tavel
Sauveterre
Le Rey
Tornac
St-Maximin
Villeneuve-lès-Avignon
Le Vigan
Arpaillargues-et-Aureillac
Uzès
AVIGNON
Sauve
Collias
Castillon-du-Gard
Brissac
Ferrières-les-Verreries
Cabrières
Remoulins
Madières
Pont-du-Gard
Nîmes
Marguerittes
St-Martin-de-Londres
St-Mathieu-de-Tréviers
Beaucaire
PROVENCE-ALPES
A 75
Sommières
CÔTE D'AZUR
Lodève
St-Guilhem-le-Désert
Mus
Vergèze
Garons
Durance
St-Saturnin-de-Lucian
Gallargues-le-Montueux
(plans 40 41 42)
Castries
Castelnau-le-Lez
Arles
St-Guiraud
Lunel
Aimargues
St-Gilles
E 80
A 54
Gignac
A 750
Montpellier
2
Mourèze
Aigues-Mortes
A 8
Clermont-l'Hérault
Lattes
N 568
Istres
Le Grau-du-Roi
Palavas-les-Flots
Port-Camargue
Pézenas
Frontignan
La Grande-Motte
A 9
Balaruc-les-Bains
Carnon-Plage
Portiragnes
Mèze
E 15
A 55
Sète
E 80
Marseillan
Agde
Le Cap-d'Agde
Le Grau-d'Agde
Villeneuve-lès-Béziers
Valras-Plage
GOLFE DU LION
Sérignan
3
C
D

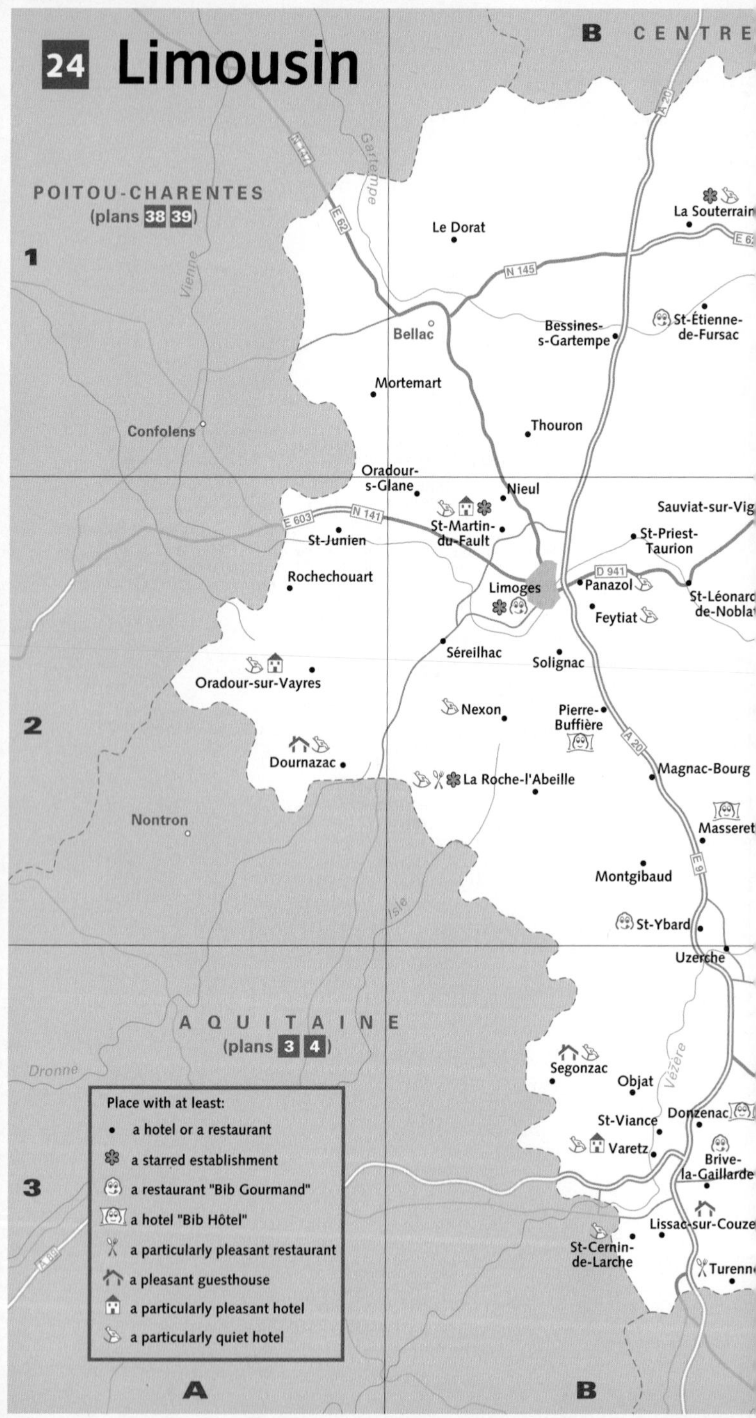

24 Limousin
B CENTRE
POITOU-CHARENTES
(plans 38 39)
1
2
3
A
B
AQUITAINE
(plans 3 4)
Gartempe
Vienne
Isle
Vézère
Dronne
N 147
E 62
N 145
N 141
E 603
D 941
A 20
E 9
A 89
La Souterrain
Le Dorat
Bellac
Bessines-s-Gartempe
St-Étienne-de-Fursac
Mortemart
Thouron
Confolens
Oradour-s-Glane
Nieul
St-Martin-du-Fault
Sauviat-sur-Vig
St-Priest-Taurion
St-Junien
Rochechouart
Limoges
Panazol
St-Léonard-de-Noblat
Feytiat
Séreilhac
Solignac
Oradour-sur-Vayres
Nexon
Pierre-Buffière
Dournazac
La Roche-l'Abeille
Magnac-Bourg
Nontron
Masseret
Montgibaud
St-Ybard
Uzerche
Segonzac
Objat
St-Viance
Donzenac
Varetz
Brive-la-Gaillarde
Lissac-sur-Couze
St-Cernin-de-Larche
Turenne
Place with at least:
a hotel or a restaurant
a starred establishment
a restaurant "Bib Gourmand"
a hotel "Bib Hôtel"
a particularly pleasant restaurant
a pleasant guesthouse
a particularly pleasant hotel
a particularly quiet hotel

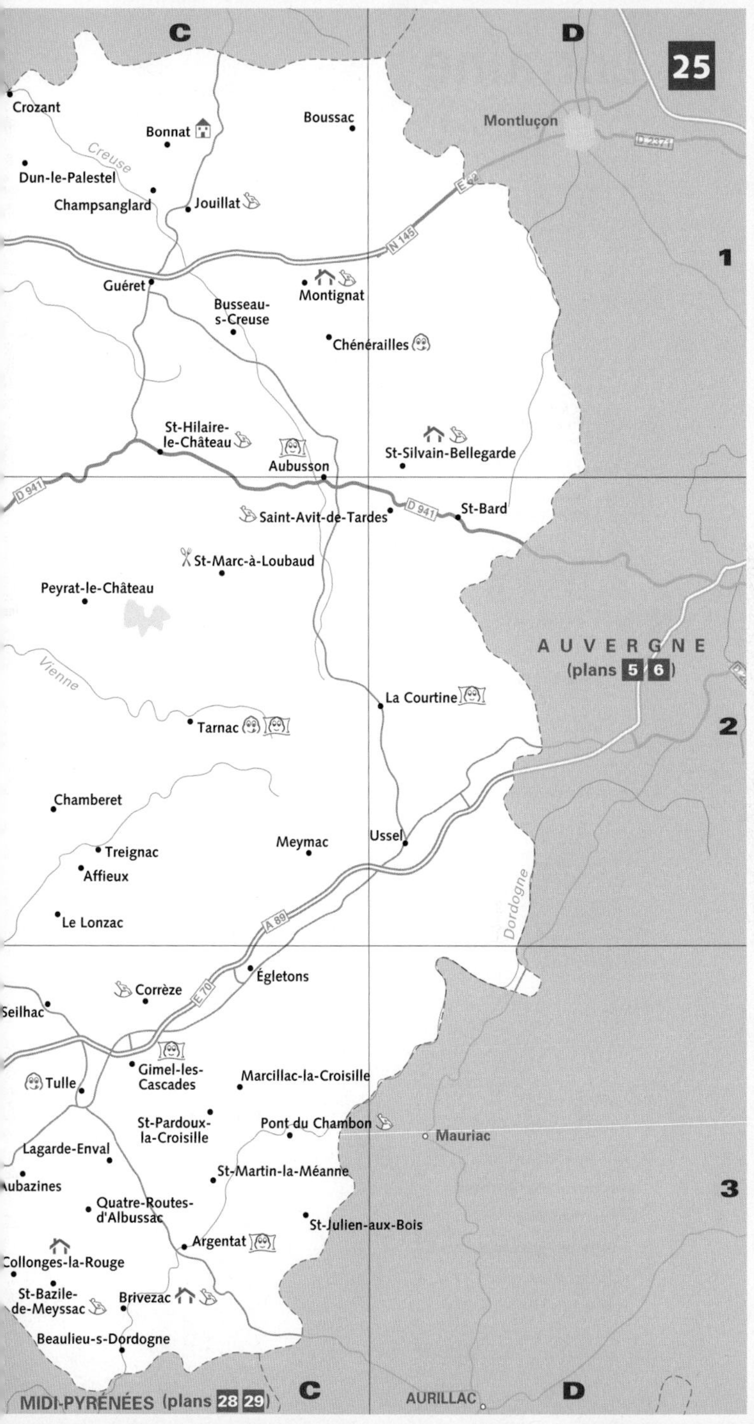

C
D
25
Crozant
Bonnat
Boussac
Montluçon
D 2371
Creuse
Dun-le-Palestel
Champsanglard
Jouillat
E 62
N 145
1
Guéret
Montignat
Busseau-
s-Creuse
Chénérailles
St-Hilaire-
le-Château
Aubusson
St-Silvain-Bellegarde
D 941
Saint-Avit-de-Tardes
D 941
St-Bard
St-Marc-à-Loubaud
Peyrat-le-Château
AUVERGNE
(plans 5 6)
Vienne
La Courtine
Tarnac
2
Chamberet
Ussel
Meymac
Treignac
Affieux
Le Lonzac
Dordogne
A 89
Égletons
Corrèze
E 70
Seilhac
Gimel-les-
Cascades
Tulle
Marcillac-la-Croisille
St-Pardoux-
la-Croisille
Pont du Chambon
Mauriac
Lagarde-Enval
Aubazines
St-Martin-la-Méanne
3
Quatre-Routes-
d'Albussac
St-Julien-aux-Bois
Argentat
Collonges-la-Rouge
St-Bazile-
de-Meyssac
Brivezac
Beaulieu-s-Dordogne
MIDI-PYRÉNÉES (plans 28 29)
C
AURILLAC
D

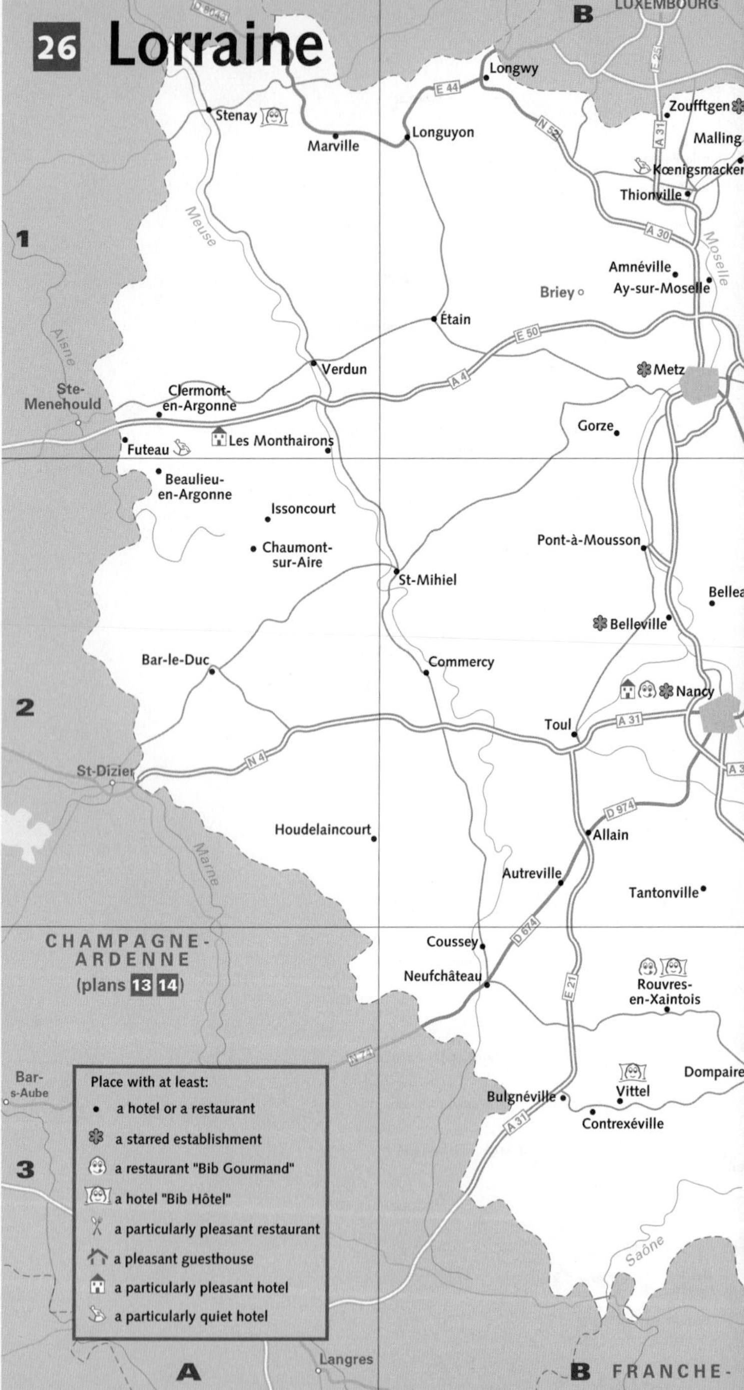

26 Lorraine
B
LUXEMBOURG
D 8043
E 25
Longwy
E 44
Zoufftgen
Malling
Stenay
Marville
Longuyon
N 52
A 31
Kœnigsmacker
Thionville
Meuse
A 30
Moselle
1
Amnéville
Ay-sur-Moselle
Briey
Étain
E 50
Aisne
Verdun
A 4
Metz
Ste-Menehould
Clermont-en-Argonne
Futeau
Les Monthairons
Gorze
Beaulieu-en-Argonne
Issoncourt
Chaumont-sur-Aire
Pont-à-Mousson
St-Mihiel
Bellea
Belleville
Bar-le-Duc
Commercy
Nancy
2
Toul
A 31
N 4
St-Dizier
A 3
D 974
Houdelaincourt
Allain
Marne
Autreville
Tantonville
CHAMPAGNE-ARDENNE
(plans 13 14)
Coussey
D 674
Neufchâteau
Rouvres-en-Xaintois
E 21
N 74
Bar-s-Aube
Dompaire
Vittel
Bulgnéville
Contrexéville
A 31
3
Place with at least:
a hotel or a restaurant
a starred establishment
a restaurant "Bib Gourmand"
a hotel "Bib Hôtel"
a particularly pleasant restaurant
a pleasant guesthouse
a particularly pleasant hotel
a particularly quiet hotel
Saône
A
Langres
B
FRANCHE-

C
D
DEUTSCHLAND
Sierck-les-Bains
SAARBRÜCKEN
1
St-Hubert
Creutzwald
Boulay-Moselle
Stiring-Wendel
Forbach
Condé-Northen
Sarreguemines
Landonvillers
St-Avold
Hambach
Bitche
Sturzelbronn
Faulquemont
Baerenthal
Philippsbourg
Meisenthal
Hinsingen
UNTERMUHLTHAL
Delme
Château-Salins
Phalsbourg
Saverne
Languimberg
Sarrebourg
Lutzelbourg
Champenoux
La Hoube
2
Abreschviller
Lunéville
St-Quirin
STRASBOURG
Molsheim
Sarre
Moselle
Meurthe
ALSACE
(plans 1 2)
Baccarat
St-Pierremont
Raon-l'Étape
Senones
Charmes
Rambervillers
St-Dié-des-Vosges
Sélestat
Wisembach
Ban-de-Laveline
Grandvillers
Ribeauvillé
Épinal
Xonrupt-Longemer
Le-Valtin
Gérardmer
COLMAR
Col de la Schlucht
3
Bas-Rupts
Remiremont
La Bresse
Plombières-les-Bains
Girmont-Val-d'Ajol
Ventron
Ermitage-du-Frère-Joseph
Guebwiller
Rupt-sur-Moselle
Le-Val-d'Ajol
Le Ménil
Le Thillot
Thann
COMTÉ (plans 16 17)
C
D
A 8
E 29
A 620
A 6
A 62
E 25
A 4
N 4
D 674
D 955
D 1004
N 59
D 1083
E 23
E 25
N 415
N 83
N 66
A 35
E 35

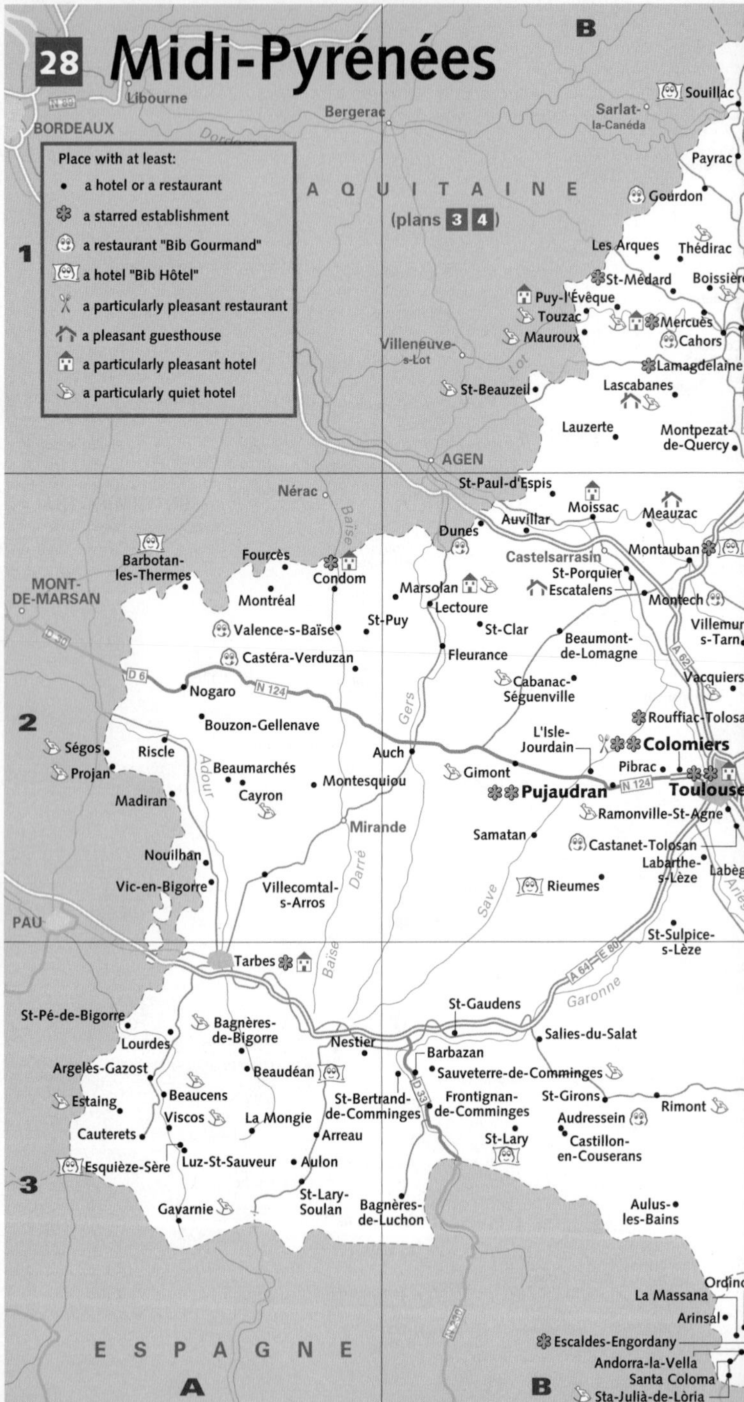
28
Midi-Pyrénées
Place with at least:
a hotel or a restaurant
a starred establishment
a restaurant "Bib Gourmand"
a hotel "Bib Hôtel"
a particularly pleasant restaurant
a pleasant guesthouse
a particularly pleasant hotel
a particularly quiet hotel
AQUITAINE
(plans 3 4)
ESPAGNE
A
B
1
2
3
Libourne
BORDEAUX
Bergerac
Sarlat-la-Canéda
Souillac
Payrac
Gourdon
Les Arques
Thédirac
St-Médard
Boissière
Puy-l'Évêque
Touzac
Mercuès
Mauroux
Cahors
Villeneuve-s-Lot
Lamagdelaine
St-Beauzeil
Lascabanes
Lauzerte
Montpezat-de-Quercy
AGEN
Nérac
St-Paul-d'Espis
Moissac
Meauzac
Auvillar
Dunes
Castelsarrasin
Montauban
Barbotan-les-Thermes
Fourcès
Condom
St-Porquier
MONT-DE-MARSAN
Montréal
Marsolan
Escatalens
Montech
Lectoure
St-Puy
St-Clar
Villemur-s-Tarn
Valence-s-Baïse
Beaumont-de-Lomagne
Castéra-Verduzan
Fleurance
Vacquiers
Nogaro
Cabanac-Séguenville
Bouzon-Gellenave
Rouffiac-Tolosan
L'Isle-Jourdain
Colomiers
Ségos
Riscle
Auch
Pibrac
Projan
Beaumarchés
Gimont
Montesquiou
Pujaudran
Toulouse
Madiran
Cayron
Ramonville-St-Agne
Mirande
Samatan
Castanet-Tolosan
Nouilhan
Labarthe-s-Lèze
Labège
Vic-en-Bigorre
Villecomtal-s-Arros
Rieumes
PAU
St-Sulpice-s-Lèze
Tarbes
St-Gaudens
St-Pé-de-Bigorre
Bagnères-de-Bigorre
Salies-du-Salat
Lourdes
Nestier
Barbazan
Argelès-Gazost
Beaudéan
Sauveterre-de-Comminges
Beaucens
St-Bertrand-de-Comminges
Frontignan-de-Comminges
St-Girons
Estaing
Rimont
Viscos
La Mongie
Audressein
Cauterets
Arreau
St-Lary
Castillon-en-Couserans
Esquièze-Sère
Luz-St-Sauveur
Aulon
St-Lary-Soulan
Gavarnie
Bagnères-de-Luchon
Aulus-les-Bains
Ordino
La Massana
Arinsal
Escaldes-Engordany
Andorra-la-Vella
Santa Coloma
Sta-Julià-de-Lòria
N 89
D 30
D 6
N 124
A 62
A 64
E 80
D 33
N 230
Dordogne
Lot
Baïse
Gers
Adour
Arros
Save
Ariège
Garonne

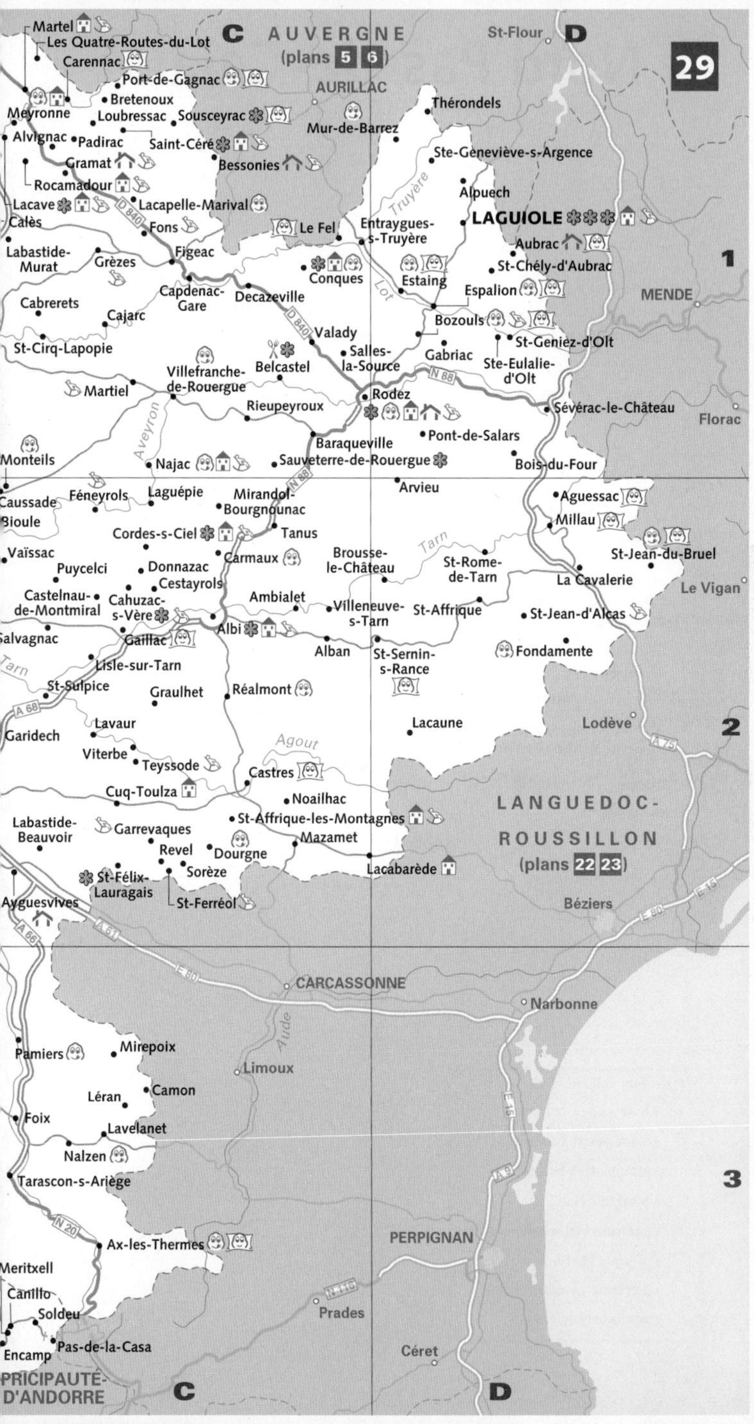
C
AUVERGNE
(plans 5 6)
D
AURILLAC
St-Flour
Martel
Les Quatre-Routes-du-Lot
Carennac
Port-de-Gagnac
Bretenoux
Meyronne
Loubressac
Sousceyrac
Mur-de-Barrez
Thérondels
Alvignac
Padirac
Saint-Céré
Gramat
Bessonies
Ste-Geneviève-s-Argence
Rocamadour
Alpuech
Lacave
Lacapelle-Marival
LAGUIOLE
Calès
Fons
Le Fel
Entraygues-s-Truyère
Aubrac
Labastide-Murat
Grèzes
Figeac
Conques
Estaing
St-Chély-d'Aubrac
Capdenac-Gare
Decazeville
Espalion
MENDE
Cabrerets
Cajarc
Bozouls
Valady
St-Geniez-d'Olt
St-Cirq-Lapopie
Salles-la-Source
Gabriac
Ste-Eulalie-d'Olt
Villefranche-de-Rouergue
Belcastel
Martiel
Rodez
Sévérac-le-Château
Rieupeyroux
Florac
Baraqueville
Pont-de-Salars
Monteils
Najac
Sauveterre-de-Rouergue
Bois-du-Four
Arvieu
Caussade
Féneyrols
Laguépie
Mirandol-Bourgnounac
Aguessac
Bioule
Millau
Cordes-s-Ciel
Tanus
Vaïssac
Carmaux
Brousse-le-Château
St-Rome-de-Tarn
St-Jean-du-Bruel
Puycelci
Donnazac
Cestayrols
La Cavalerie
Le Vigan
Castelnau-de-Montmiral
Cahuzac-s-Vère
Ambialet
Villeneuve-s-Tarn
St-Affrique
St-Jean-d'Alcas
Salvagnac
Albi
Gaillac
Alban
St-Sernin-s-Rance
Fondamente
Lisle-sur-Tarn
St-Sulpice
Graulhet
Réalmont
Lacaune
Lodève
Garidech
Lavaur
Viterbe
Teyssode
Castres
Cuq-Toulza
Noailhac
LANGUEDOC-ROUSSILLON
(plans 22 23)
Labastide-Beauvoir
Garrevaques
St-Affrique-les-Montagnes
Mazamet
Revel
Dourgne
Sorèze
Lacabarède
St-Félix-Lauragais
St-Ferréol
Ayguesvives
Béziers
CARCASSONNE
Narbonne
Pamiers
Mirepoix
Limoux
Léran
Camon
Foix
Lavelanet
Nalzen
Tarascon-s-Ariège
Ax-les-Thermes
PERPIGNAN
Meritxell
Canillo
Soldeu
Prades
Encamp
Pas-de-la-Casa
Céret
PRICIPAUTÉ-D'ANDORRE
C
D
1
2
3

30 Nord Pas-de-Calais

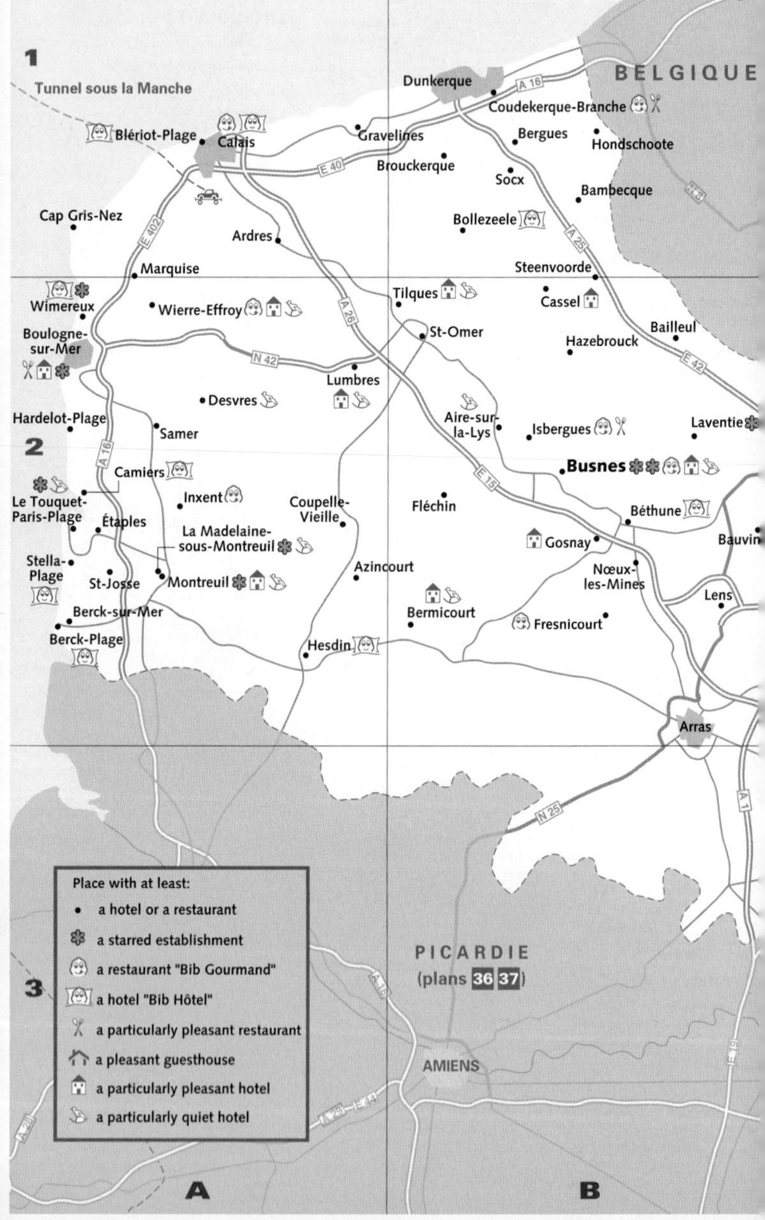

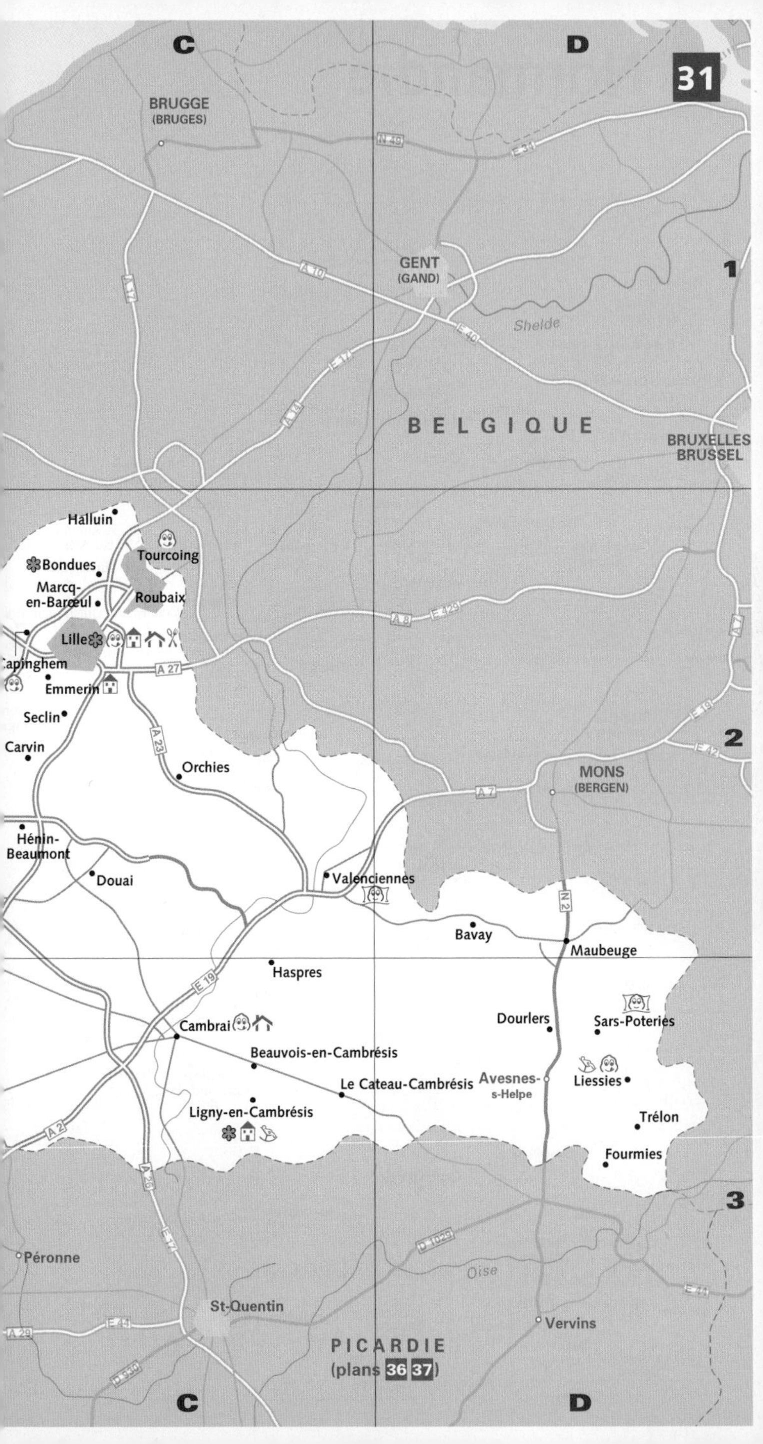

C
D
31
BRUGGE
(BRUGES)
N 49
E 34
GENT
(GAND)
A 10
A 17
Sheide
E 40
E 17
A 14
1
BELGIQUE
BRUXELLES
BRUSSEL
Halluin
Tourcoing
Bondues
Marcq-
en-Barœul
Roubaix
A 8
E 429
A 7
Lille
Capinghem
A 27
Emmerin
Seclin
A 23
E 19
2
Carvin
E 42
Orchies
MONS
(BERGEN)
A 7
Hénin-
Beaumont
Douai
Valenciennes
N 2
Bavay
Maubeuge
Haspres
E 19
Cambrai
Dourlers
Sars-Poteries
Beauvois-en-Cambrésis
Avesnes-
s-Helpe
Liessies
Le Cateau-Cambrésis
Ligny-en-Cambrésis
Trélon
A 2
Fourmies
A 26
3
E 17
D 1029
Péronne
Oise
E 44
St-Quentin
Vervins
A 29
E 44
D 930
PICARDIE
(plans 36 37)
C
D

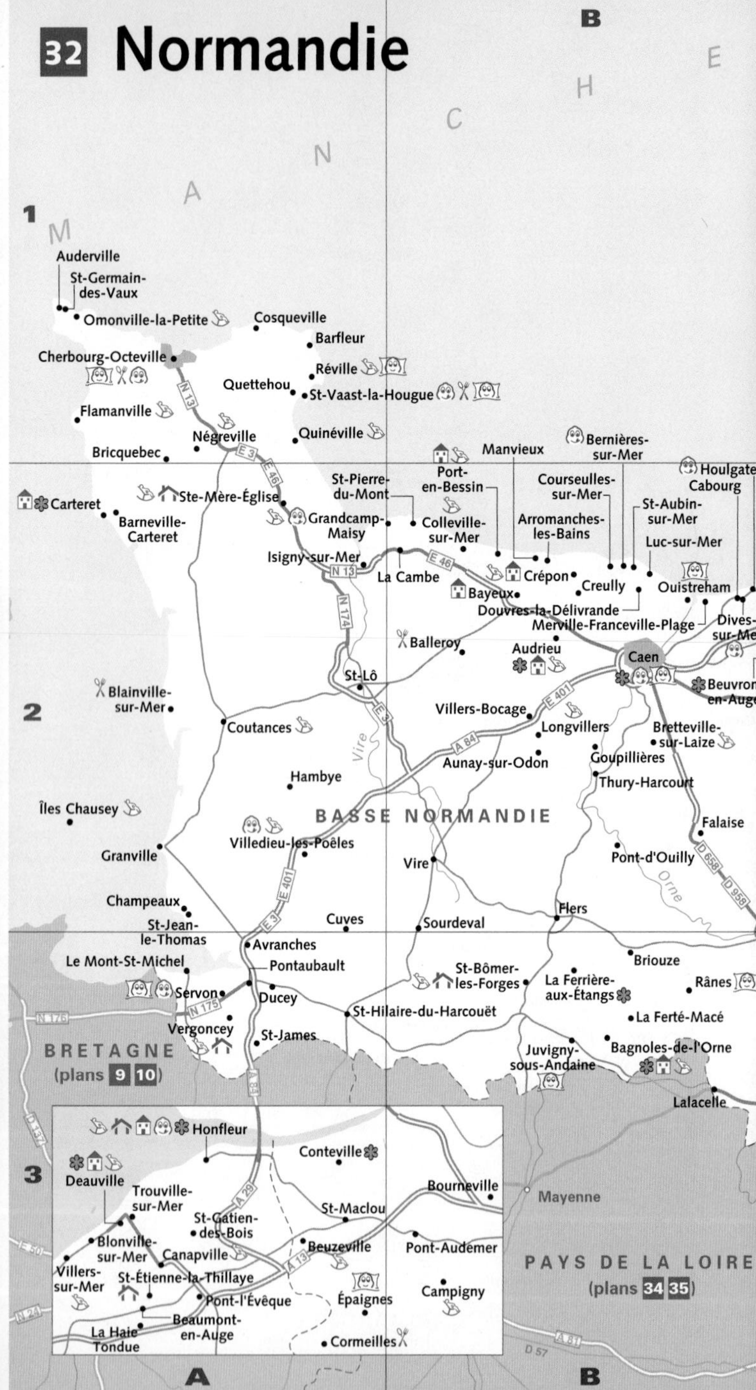
32 Normandie
M A N C H E
A
B
1
2
3
Auderville
St-Germain-des-Vaux
Omonville-la-Petite
Cosqueville
Barfleur
Cherbourg-Octeville
Réville
Quettehou
St-Vaast-la-Hougue
Flamanville
Négreville
Quinéville
Bricquebec
Manvieux
Bernières-sur-Mer
Houlgate
Cabourg
Port-en-Bessin
St-Pierre-du-Mont
Courseulles-sur-Mer
St-Aubin-sur-Mer
Carteret
Ste-Mère-Église
Barneville-Carteret
Grandcamp-Maisy
Colleville-sur-Mer
Arromanches-les-Bains
Luc-sur-Mer
Isigny-sur-Mer
La Cambe
Crépon
Creully
Ouistreham
Bayeux
Douvres-la-Délivrande
Merville-Franceville-Plage
Dives-sur-Mer
Balleroy
Audrieu
Caen
Beuvron-en-Auge
St-Lô
Blainville-sur-Mer
Villers-Bocage
Longvillers
Coutances
Bretteville-sur-Laize
Goupillières
Aunay-sur-Odon
Hambye
Thury-Harcourt
Îles Chausey
BASSE NORMANDIE
Falaise
Villedieu-les-Poêles
Pont-d'Ouilly
Granville
Vire
Champeaux
Flers
Cuves
Sourdeval
St-Jean-le-Thomas
Avranches
Le Mont-St-Michel
Pontaubault
Briouze
St-Bômer-les-Forges
La Ferrière-aux-Étangs
Rânes
Servon
Ducey
St-Hilaire-du-Harcouët
La Ferté-Macé
Vergoncey
St-James
Juvigny-sous-Andaine
Bagnoles-de-l'Orne
BRETAGNE
(plans 9 10)
Lalacelle
Honfleur
Conteville
Deauville
Trouville-sur-Mer
Bourneville
Mayenne
St-Gatien-des-Bois
St-Maclou
Blonville-sur-Mer
Beuzeville
Pont-Audemer
Canapville
Villers-sur-Mer
St-Étienne-la-Thillaye
Épaignes
Campigny
PAYS DE LA LOIRE
(plans 34 35)
Pont-l'Évêque
Beaumont-en-Auge
La Haie Tondue
Cormeilles
Vire
Orne
N 13
E 3
E 46
N 174
E 401
A 84
D 658
D 958
N 175
N 176
A 84
A 29
A 13
E 50
N 24
D 137
A 81
D 57

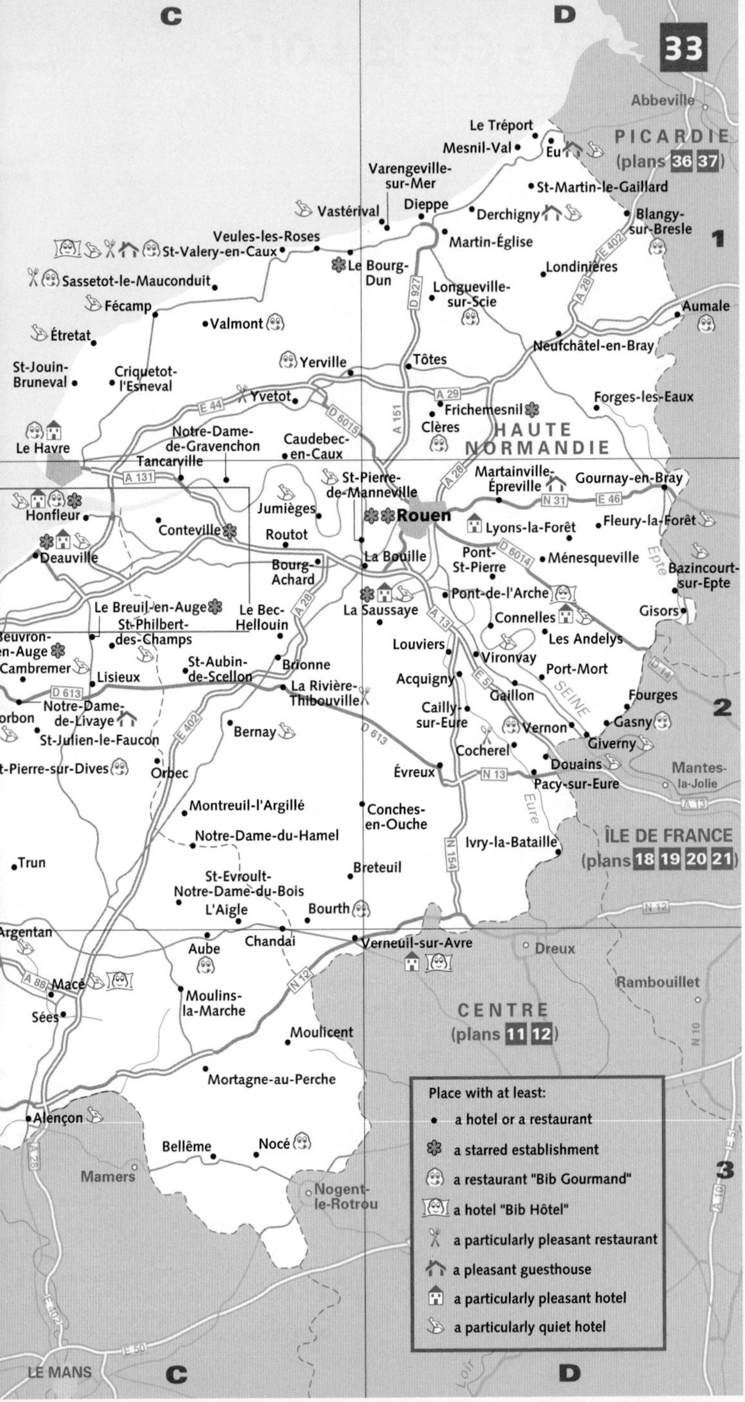
C
D
PICARDIE (plans 36 37)
HAUTE NORMANDIE
ÎLE DE FRANCE (plans 18 19 20 21)
CENTRE (plans 11 12)
1
2
3
Abbeville
Le Tréport
Mesnil-Val
Eu
St-Martin-le-Gaillard
Varengeville-sur-Mer
Dieppe
Derchigny
Blangy-sur-Bresle
Vastérival
Veules-les-Roses
St-Valery-en-Caux
Martin-Église
Le Bourg-Dun
Londinières
Sassetot-le-Mauconduit
Longueville-sur-Scie
Fécamp
Valmont
Aumale
Étretat
Neufchâtel-en-Bray
Yerville
Tôtes
St-Jouin-Bruneval
Criquetot-l'Esneval
Yvetot
Frichemesnil
Forges-les-Eaux
Clères
Le Havre
Notre-Dame-de-Gravenchon
Caudebec-en-Caux
Tancarville
St-Pierre-de-Manneville
Martainville-Épreville
Gournay-en-Bray
Honfleur
Jumièges
Rouen
Conteville
Lyons-la-Forêt
Fleury-la-Forêt
Routot
Deauville
Bourg-Achard
La Bouille
Pont-St-Pierre
Ménesqueville
Bazincourt-sur-Epte
Pont-de-l'Arche
Le Breuil-en-Auge
Le Bec-Hellouin
La Saussaye
Connelles
Gisors
St-Philbert-des-Champs
Beuvron-en-Auge
Les Andelys
Louviers
Vironvay
Cambremer
St-Aubin-de-Scellon
Brionne
Lisieux
Acquigny
Port-Mort
La Rivière-Thibouville
Gaillon
Fourges
Notre-Dame-de-Livaye
Corbon
Cailly-sur-Eure
Gasny
Bernay
Vernon
St-Julien-le-Faucon
Giverny
Cocherel
St-Pierre-sur-Dives
Orbec
Évreux
Douains
Mantes-la-Jolie
Pacy-sur-Eure
Montreuil-l'Argillé
Conches-en-Ouche
Notre-Dame-du-Hamel
Ivry-la-Bataille
Trun
Breteuil
St-Evroult-Notre-Dame-du-Bois
L'Aigle
Bourth
Argentan
Chandai
Verneuil-sur-Avre
Dreux
Aube
Macé
Rambouillet
Sées
Moulins-la-Marche
Moulicent
Mortagne-au-Perche
Alençon
Bellême
Nocé
Mamers
Nogent-le-Rotrou
LE MANS
Epte
SEINE
Eure
Loir
A 28
A 29
A 151
A 131
A 13
A 88
A 10
D 927
D 6015
D 6014
D 613
D 14
E 44
E 46
E 5
E 402
E 50
N 31
N 13
N 154
N 12
N 10
Place with at least:
a hotel or a restaurant
a starred establishment
a restaurant "Bib Gourmand"
a hotel "Bib Hôtel"
a particularly pleasant restaurant
a pleasant guesthouse
a particularly pleasant hotel
a particularly quiet hotel

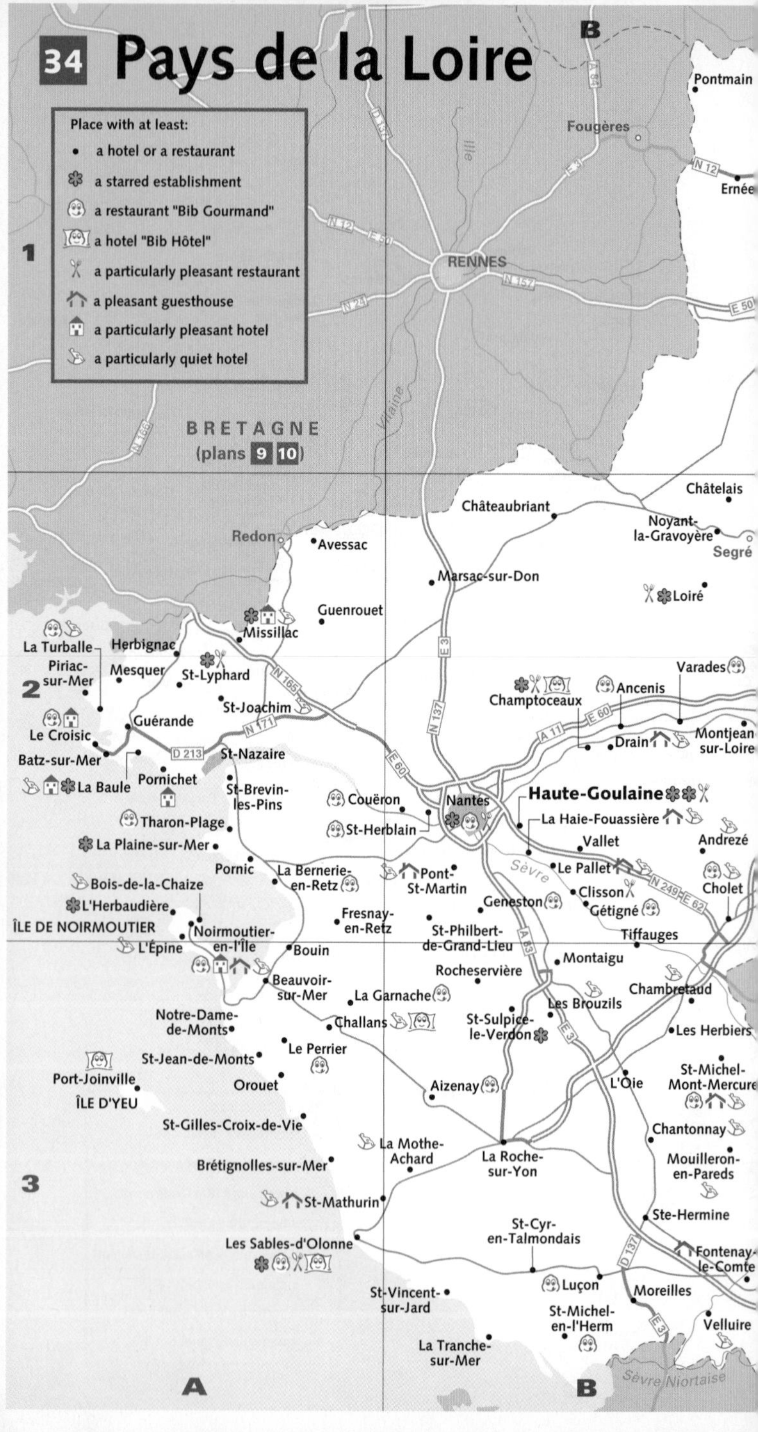

34 Pays de la Loire
Place with at least:
a hotel or a restaurant
a starred establishment
a restaurant "Bib Gourmand"
a hotel "Bib Hôtel"
a particularly pleasant restaurant
a pleasant guesthouse
a particularly pleasant hotel
a particularly quiet hotel
BRETAGNE
(plans 9 10)
A
B
1
2
3
Pontmain
Fougères
Ernée
RENNES
Vilaine
Ille
Châtelais
Châteaubriant
Noyant-la-Gravoyère
Segré
Redon
Avessac
Marsac-sur-Don
Loiré
Guenrouet
Missillac
La Turballe
Herbignac
Piriac-sur-Mer
Mesquer
St-Lyphard
St-Joachim
Varades
Ancenis
Champtoceaux
Montjean-sur-Loire
Drain
Guérande
Le Croisic
Batz-sur-Mer
La Baule
Pornichet
St-Nazaire
St-Brevin-les-Pins
Couëron
St-Herblain
Nantes
Haute-Goulaine
La Haie-Fouassière
Vallet
Andrezé
Tharon-Plage
La Plaine-sur-Mer
Pornic
La Bernerie-en-Retz
Pont-St-Martin
Le Pallet
Cholet
Bois-de-la-Chaize
L'Herbaudière
Fresnay-en-Retz
Geneston
Clisson
Gétigné
Sèvre
ÎLE DE NOIRMOUTIER
Noirmoutier-en-l'Île
L'Épine
Bouin
St-Philbert-de-Grand-Lieu
Tiffauges
Montaigu
Rocheservière
Beauvoir-sur-Mer
La Garnache
Chambretaud
Les Brouzils
Notre-Dame-de-Monts
Challans
St-Sulpice-le-Verdon
Les Herbiers
Le Perrier
St-Jean-de-Monts
Port-Joinville
ÎLE D'YEU
Orouet
Aizenay
L'Oie
St-Michel-Mont-Mercure
St-Gilles-Croix-de-Vie
Chantonnay
La Mothe-Achard
La Roche-sur-Yon
Brétignolles-sur-Mer
Mouilleron-en-Pareds
St-Mathurin
Ste-Hermine
St-Cyr-en-Talmondais
Les Sables-d'Olonne
Fontenay-le-Comte
Luçon
Moreilles
St-Vincent-sur-Jard
St-Michel-en-l'Herm
Velluire
La Tranche-sur-Mer
Sèvre Niortaise
A 84
D 155
E 3
N 12
E 50
N 157
N 24
N 166
N 165
N 171
D 213
E 60
N 137
A 11
N 249
E 62
A 83
D 137

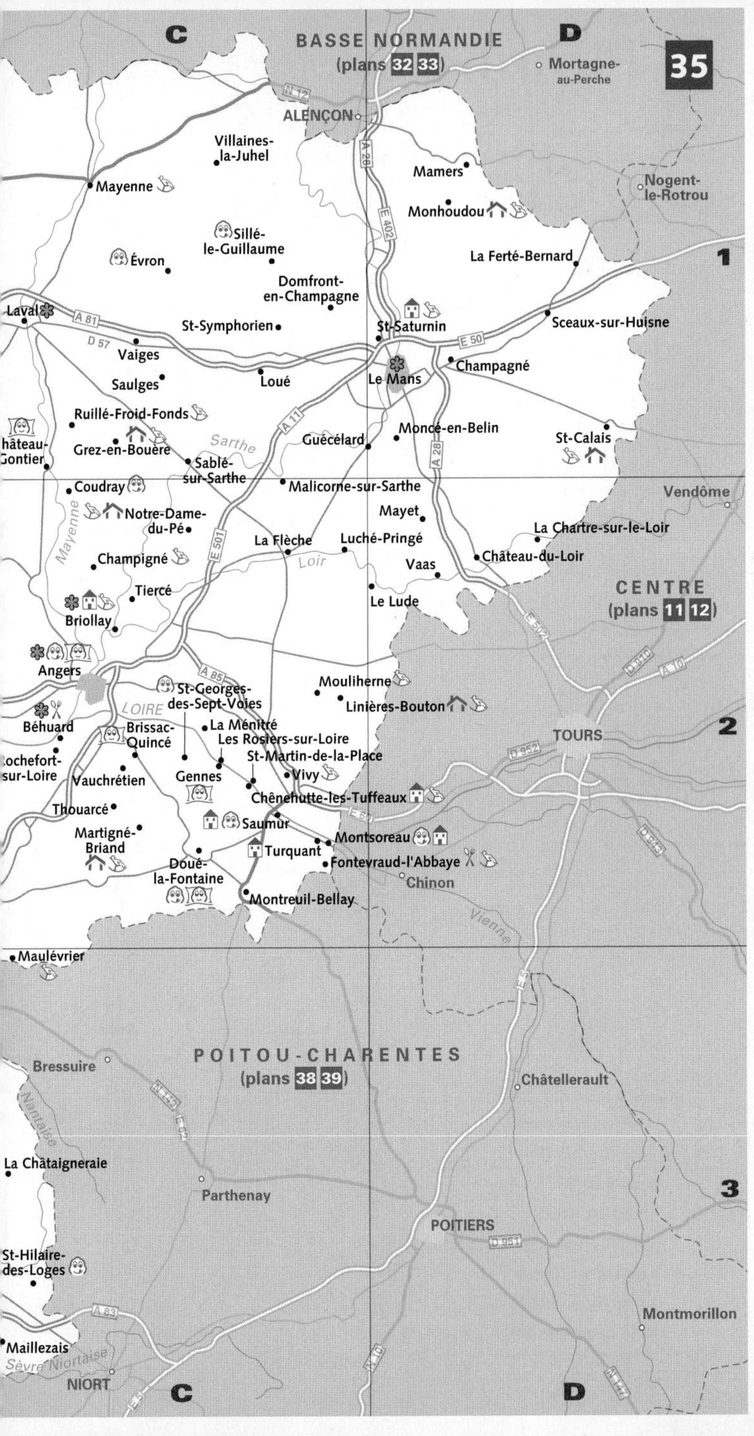

C
D
BASSE NORMANDIE
(plans 32 33)
Mortagne-au-Perche
ALENÇON
Villaines-la-Juhel
Mayenne
Mamers
Nogent-le-Rotrou
Monhoudou
Sillé-le-Guillaume
Évron
La Ferté-Bernard
1
Domfront-en-Champagne
Laval
St-Symphorien
St-Saturnin
Sceaux-sur-Huisne
Vaiges
Saulges
Loué
Le Mans
Champagné
Ruillé-Froid-Fonds
Grez-en-Bouère
Château-Gontier
Sarthe
Guécélard
Moncé-en-Belin
St-Calais
Sablé-sur-Sarthe
Coudray
Malicorne-sur-Sarthe
Vendôme
Notre-Dame-du-Pé
Mayet
La Chartre-sur-le-Loir
Mayenne
La Flèche
Luché-Pringé
Champigné
Loir
Château-du-Loir
Vaas
Tiercé
Le Lude
CENTRE
(plans 11 12)
Briollay
Angers
Mouliherne
St-Georges-des-Sept-Voies
Linières-Bouton
LOIRE
Béhuard
Brissac-Quincé
La Ménitré
Les Rosiers-sur-Loire
TOURS
2
Rochefort-sur-Loire
St-Martin-de-la-Place
Gennes
Vivy
Vauchrétien
Chênehutte-les-Tuffeaux
Thouarcé
Saumur
Martigné-Briand
Montsoreau
Turquant
Fontevraud-l'Abbaye
Chinon
Doué-la-Fontaine
Montreuil-Bellay
Vienne
Maulévrier
POITOU-CHARENTES
(plans 38 39)
Bressuire
Châtellerault
Nantaise
La Châtaigneraie
Parthenay
3
POITIERS
St-Hilaire-des-Loges
Montmorillon
Maillezais
Sèvre Niortaise
NIORT
C
D

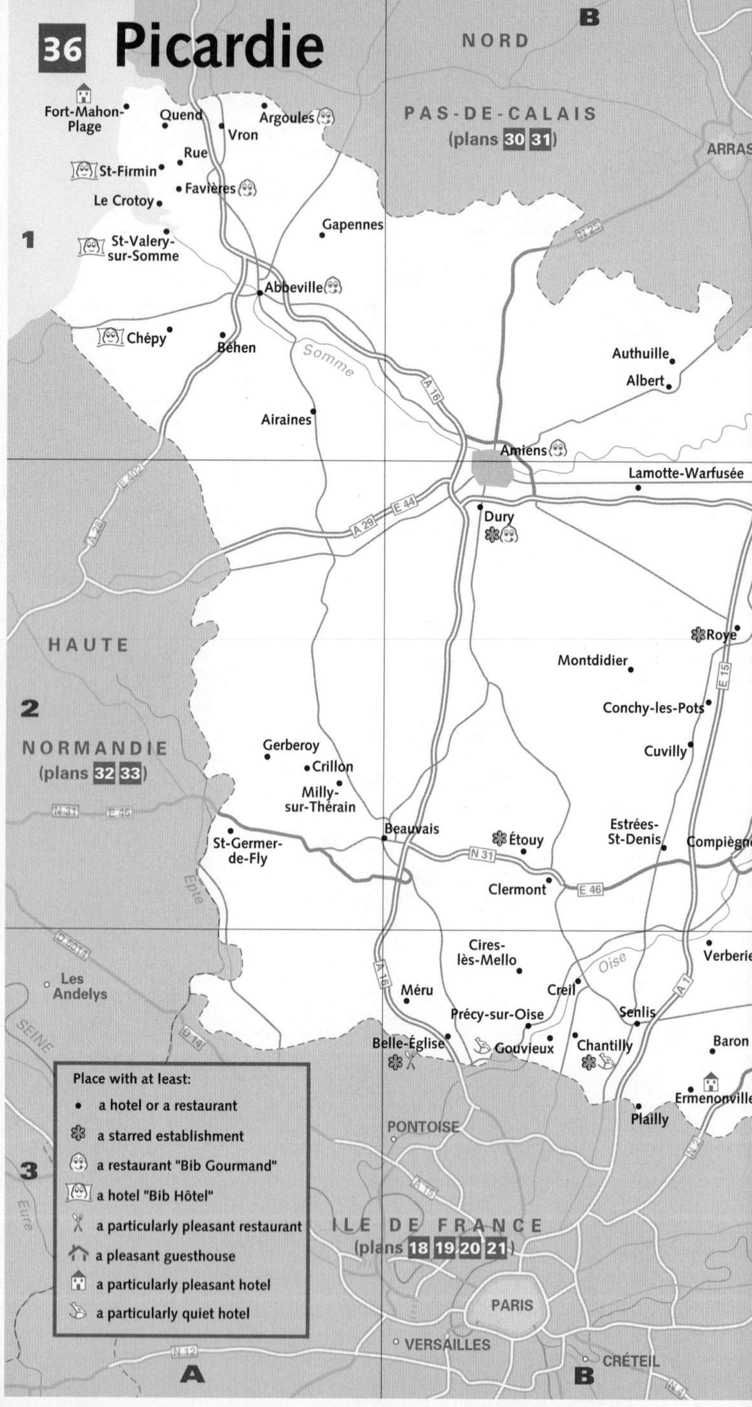
36 Picardie
NORD
PAS-DE-CALAIS
(plans 30 31)
ARRAS
Fort-Mahon-Plage
Quend
Argoules
Vron
Rue
St-Firmin
Favières
Le Crotoy
Gapennes
St-Valery-sur-Somme
Abbeville
Chépy
Béhen
Somme
Authuille
Albert
Airaines
Amiens
Lamotte-Warfusée
Dury
HAUTE
NORMANDIE
(plans 32 33)
Roye
Montdidier
Conchy-les-Pots
Cuvilly
Gerberoy
Crillon
Milly-sur-Thérain
Beauvais
St-Germer-de-Fly
Étouy
Estrées-St-Denis
Compiègne
Clermont
Epte
Les Andelys
SEINE
Cires-lès-Mello
Oise
Verberie
Méru
Creil
Senlis
Précy-sur-Oise
Belle-Église
Gouvieux
Chantilly
Baron
Ermenonville
Plailly
PONTOISE
ILE DE FRANCE
(plans 18 19 20 21)
PARIS
VERSAILLES
CRÉTEIL
Eure
A 16
A 29
E 44
E 402
A 28
N 25
E 15
A 1
N 31
E 46
D 6014
D 14
A 15
N 2
N 12
N 4
1
2
3
A
B
Place with at least:
• a hotel or a restaurant
a starred establishment
a restaurant "Bib Gourmand"
a hotel "Bib Hôtel"
a particularly pleasant restaurant
a pleasant guesthouse
a particularly pleasant hotel
a particularly quiet hotel

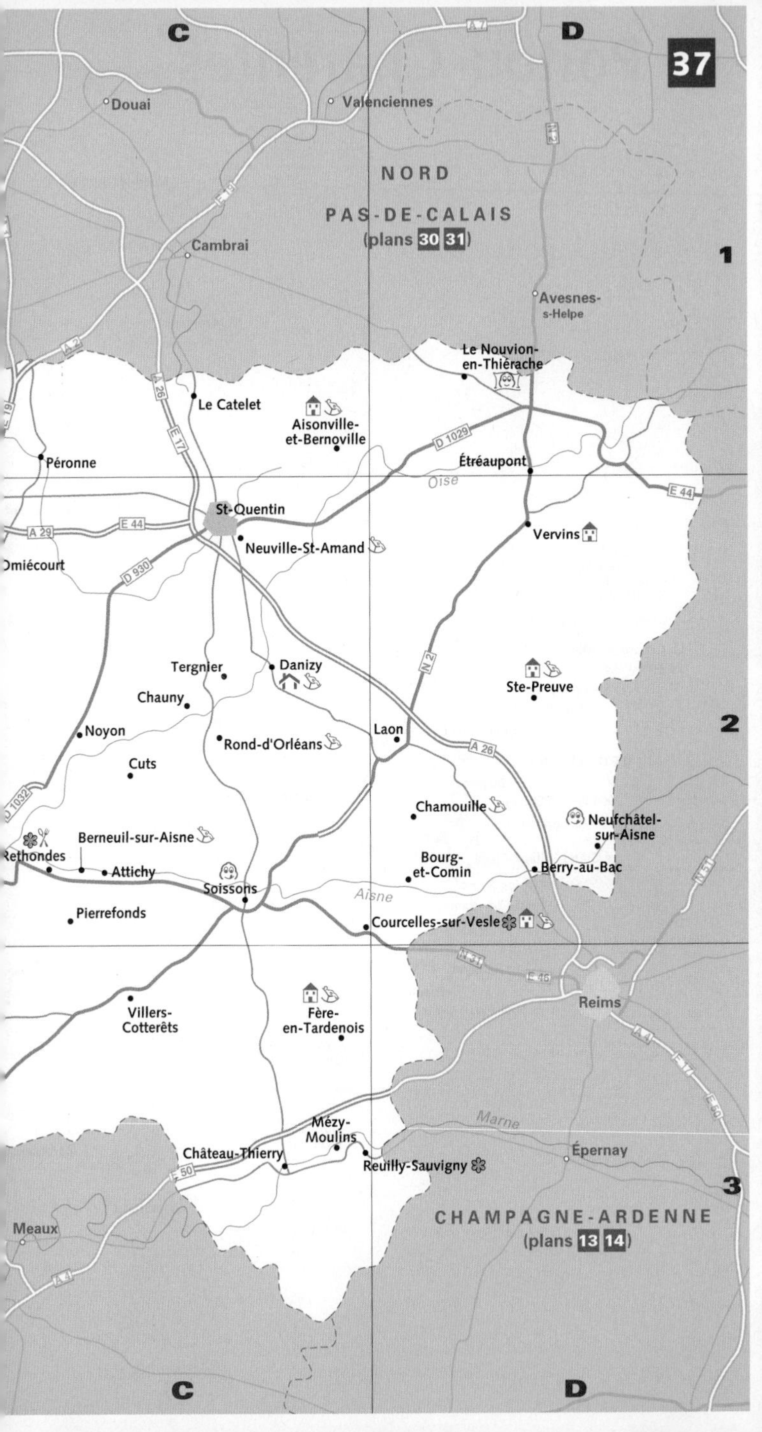
C
D
37
Douai
Valenciennes
NORD
PAS-DE-CALAIS
(plans 30 31)
1
Cambrai
Avesnes-
s-Helpe
Le Nouvion-
en-Thiérache
Le Catelet
Aisonville-
et-Bernoville
Péronne
Étréaupont
Oise
St-Quentin
Neuville-St-Amand
Vervins
Omiécourt
Tergnier
Danizy
Chauny
Ste-Preuve
Noyon
Rond-d'Orléans
Laon
2
Cuts
Chamouille
Neufchâtel-
sur-Aisne
Berneuil-sur-Aisne
Rethondes
Attichy
Soissons
Bourg-
et-Comin
Berry-au-Bac
Aisne
Pierrefonds
Courcelles-sur-Vesle
Reims
Villers-
Cotterêts
Fère-
en-Tardenois
Marne
Mézy-
Moulins
Château-Thierry
Reuilly-Sauvigny
Épernay
3
CHAMPAGNE-ARDENNE
(plans 13 14)
Meaux
C
D

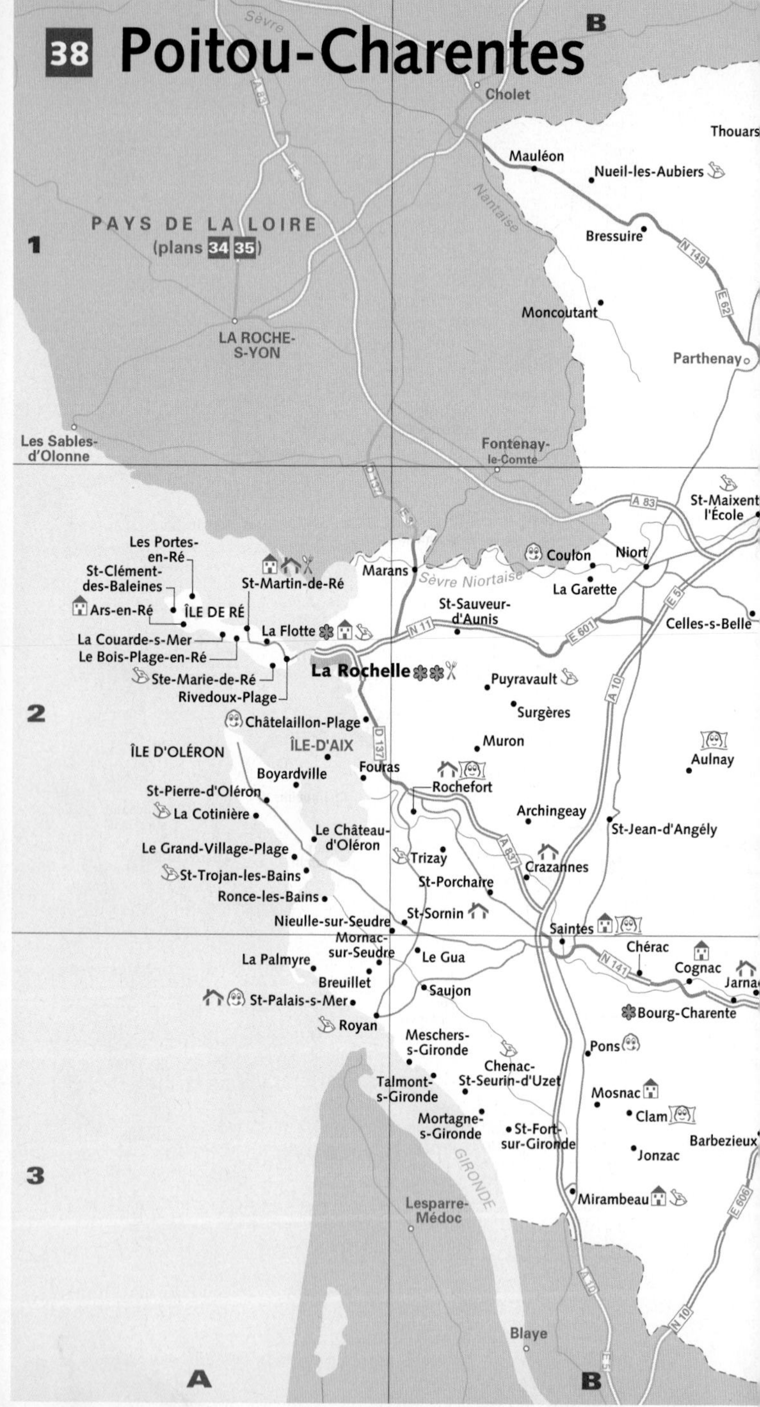

38 Poitou-Charentes
PAYS DE LA LOIRE
(plans 34 35)
LA ROCHE-S-YON
Les Sables-d'Olonne
Cholet
Thouars
Mauléon
Nueil-les-Aubiers
Bressuire
Moncoutant
Parthenay
Fontenay-le-Comte
St-Maixent-l'École
Niort
Coulon
La Garette
Marans
Sèvre Niortaise
Les Portes-en-Ré
St-Clément-des-Baleines
Ars-en-Ré
ÎLE DE RÉ
St-Martin-de-Ré
La Couarde-s-Mer
Le Bois-Plage-en-Ré
La Flotte
Ste-Marie-de-Ré
Rivedoux-Plage
La Rochelle
St-Sauveur-d'Aunis
Celles-s-Belle
Puyravault
Surgères
Châtelaillon-Plage
ÎLE D'OLÉRON
ÎLE-D'AIX
Muron
Aulnay
Boyardville
Fouras
Rochefort
St-Pierre-d'Oléron
La Cotinière
Archingeay
St-Jean-d'Angély
Le Château-d'Oléron
Le Grand-Village-Plage
Trizay
Crazannes
St-Trojan-les-Bains
St-Porchaire
Ronce-les-Bains
St-Sornin
Nieulle-sur-Seudre
Saintes
Mornac-sur-Seudre
Chérac
La Palmyre
Le Gua
Cognac
Jarna
Breuillet
Saujon
St-Palais-s-Mer
Bourg-Charente
Royan
Meschers-s-Gironde
Pons
Chenac-St-Seurin-d'Uzet
Talmont-s-Gironde
Mosnac
Clam
Mortagne-s-Gironde
St-Fort-sur-Gironde
Barbezieux
Jonzac
GIRONDE
Mirambeau
Lesparre-Médoc
Blaye
A
B
1
2
3

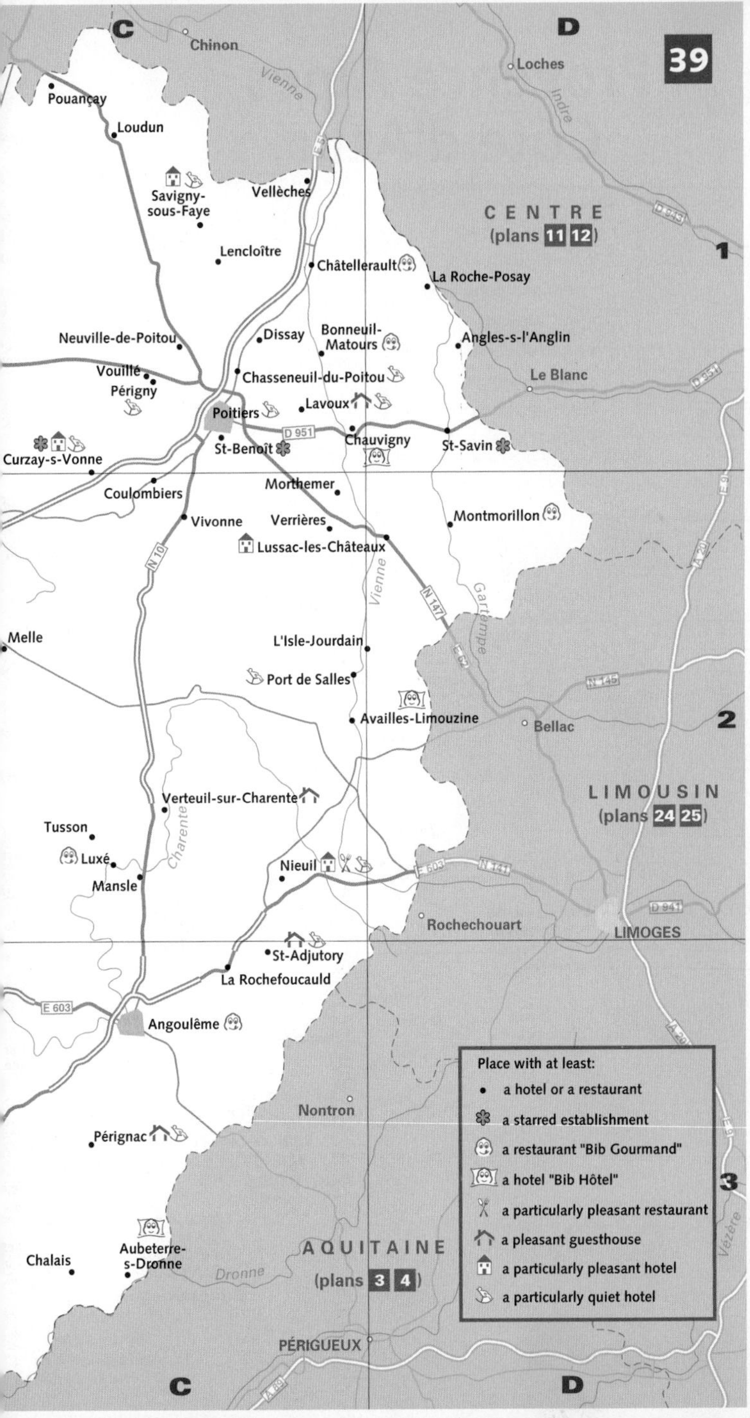

C
D
39
Chinon
Loches
Vienne
Indre
Pouançay
Loudun
Savigny-sous-Faye
Vellèches
CENTRE
(plans 11 12)
1
Lencloître
Châtellerault
La Roche-Posay
Neuville-de-Poitou
Dissay
Bonneuil-Matours
Angles-s-l'Anglin
Vouillé
Périgny
Chasseneuil-du-Poitou
Le Blanc
Poitiers
Lavoux
D 951
Chauvigny
St-Savin
Curzay-s-Vonne
St-Benoît
Coulombiers
Morthemer
Vivonne
Verrières
Montmorillon
Lussac-les-Châteaux
N 10
N 147
Gartempe
Melle
L'Isle-Jourdain
Port de Salles
N 145
Availles-Limouzine
Bellac
2
LIMOUSIN
(plans 24 25)
Verteuil-sur-Charente
Charente
Tusson
Luxé
Mansle
Nieuil
E 603
N 141
Rochechouart
LIMOGES
D 941
St-Adjutory
La Rochefoucauld
E 603
Angoulême
Nontron
Pérignac
3
AQUITAINE
(plans 3 4)
Chalais
Aubeterre-s-Dronne
Dronne
Vézère
PÉRIGUEUX
C
D
Place with at least:
a hotel or a restaurant
a starred establishment
a restaurant "Bib Gourmand"
a hotel "Bib Hôtel"
a particularly pleasant restaurant
a pleasant guesthouse
a particularly pleasant hotel
a particularly quiet hotel

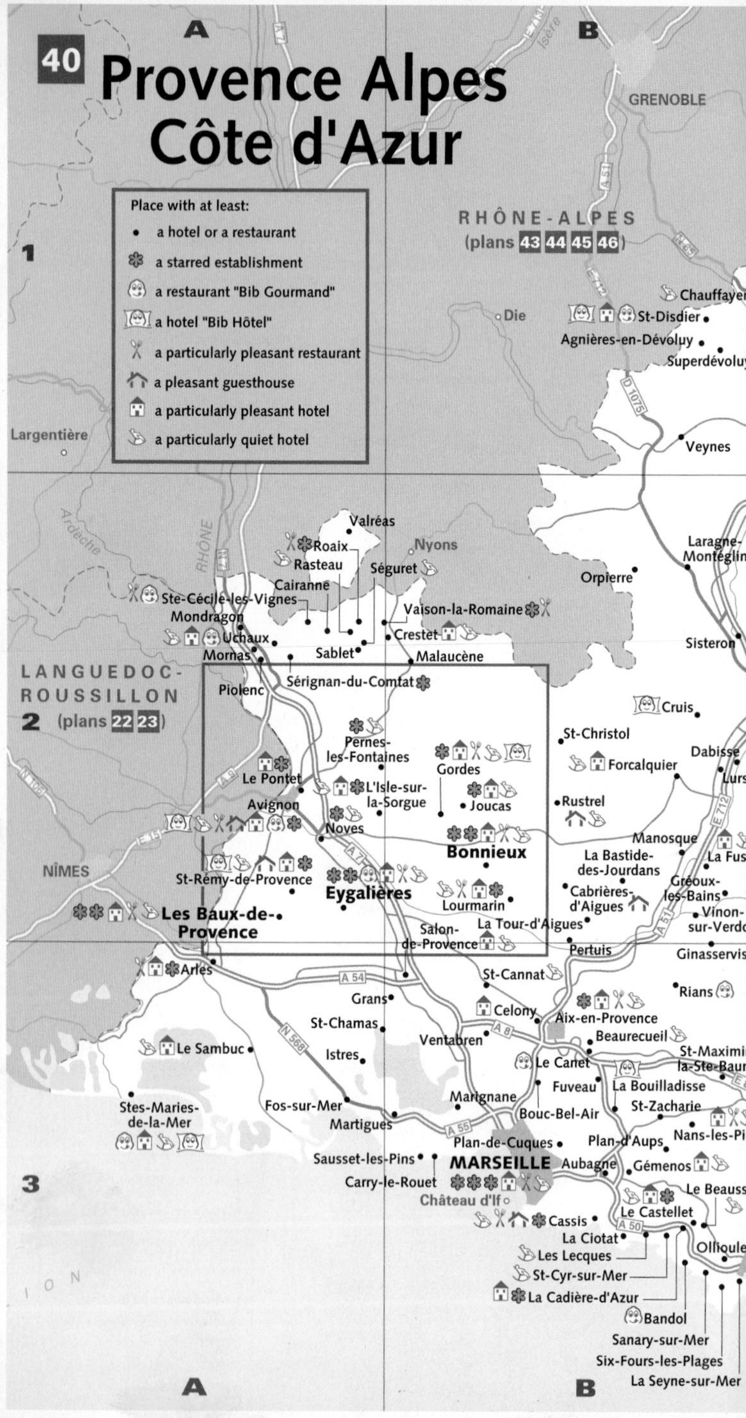

40
Provence Alpes Côte d'Azur
A
B
Place with at least:
a hotel or a restaurant
a starred establishment
a restaurant "Bib Gourmand"
a hotel "Bib Hôtel"
a particularly pleasant restaurant
a pleasant guesthouse
a particularly pleasant hotel
a particularly quiet hotel
GRENOBLE
RHÔNE-ALPES
(plans 43 44 45 46)
1
2
3
LANGUEDOC-ROUSSILLON
(plans 22 23)
Chauffayer
Die
St-Disdier
Agnières-en-Dévoluy
Superdévoluy
Largentière
Veynes
Valréas
Roaix
Nyons
Rasteau
Séguret
Laragne-Montéglin
Orpierre
Cairanne
Ste-Cécile-les-Vignes
Mondragon
Vaison-la-Romaine
Uchaux
Crestet
Sisteron
Mornas
Sablet
Malaucène
Sérignan-du-Comtat
Piolenc
Cruis
St-Christol
Pernes-les-Fontaines
Dabisse
Gordes
Forcalquier
Lurs
Le Pontet
L'Isle-sur-la-Sorgue
Avignon
Joucas
Rustrel
Noves
Manosque
Bonnieux
La Bastide-des-Jourdans
La Fust
NÎMES
St-Rémy-de-Provence
Eygalières
Gréoux-les-Bains
Cabrières-d'Aigues
Lourmarin
Les Baux-de-Provence
Vinon-sur-Verdo
La Tour-d'Aigues
Salon-de-Provence
Pertuis
Ginasservis
Arles
St-Cannat
Rians
Grans
Celony
St-Chamas
Aix-en-Provence
Ventabren
Beaurecueil
Le Sambuc
Istres
Le Canet
St-Maximin-la-Ste-Baum
Fuveau
La Bouilladisse
Marignane
St-Zacharie
Stes-Maries-de-la-Mer
Fos-sur-Mer
Bouc-Bel-Air
Martigues
Plan-de-Cuques
Plan-d'Aups
Nans-les-Pin
Sausset-les-Pins
MARSEILLE
Aubagne
Gémenos
Carry-le-Rouet
Le Beauss
Château d'If
Le Castellet
Cassis
La Ciotat
Ollioules
Les Lecques
St-Cyr-sur-Mer
La Cadière-d'Azur
Bandol
Sanary-sur-Mer
Six-Fours-les-Plages
La Seyne-sur-Mer
RHÔNE
Isère
Ardèche
A 7
A 51
A 9
A 54
A 8
A 55
A 50
E 712
N 568
D 1075

C
D
TORINO
La Grave
Col du Lautaret
Névache
Le Monêtier-les-Bains
Serre-Chevalier
Briançon
Pelvoux
La Chapelle-en-Valgaudémar
Puy-St-Vincent
Arvieux
Molines-en-Queyras
St-Véran
Orcières
Guillestre
Ceillac
St-Julien-en-Champsaur
Risoul
Vars
Col Bayard
Embrun
La Bâtie-Neuve
Gap
Baratier
ITALIA
Jausiers
St-Pons
Barcelonnette
CUNEO
Seyne
Allos
Auron
St-Martin-d'Entraunes
Tende
Beuil
Valberg
Digne-les-Bains
Valdeblore
St-Martin-Vésubie
Roquebillière
Bairols
Lantosque
Plan-du-Var
Annot
Utelle
Le Suquet
Gilette
Sospel
Castellane
Vescous
Levens
La Palud-sur-Verdon
La Garde
Moustiers-Ste-Marie
Point Sublime
Thorenc
St-Martin-du-Var
Contes
La Turbie
Les Salles-sur-Verdon
La Martre
Peillon
Menton
MONTE-CARLO
St-Paul
Trigance
La Bastide
Grasse
Nice
Èze
Le Rouret
Quinson
Comps-sur-Artuby
Fayence
Beaulieu-sur-Mer
Seillans
Tourrettes
Biot
Aups
Ampus
Mougins
Valbonne
Cagnes-sur-Mer
Tourtour
Callas
Villecroze
Châteaudouble
Montauroux
Cannes
Cap d'Antibes
Cotignac
Draguignan
Lorgues
Flayosc
La Motte
La Napoule
Le Thoronet
Les Arcs
Fréjus
St-Raphaël
Le Val
Le Luc
Vidauban
St-Aygulf
La Celle
Le Cannet-des-Maures
Plan-de-la-Tour
Les Issambres
La Roquebrussanne
Courruero
Ste-Maxime
Carnoules
Port-Grimaud
Grimaud
Belgentier
Saint-Tropez
Cogolin
Cuers
La Croix-Valmer
Gassin
Bormes-les-Mimosas
Ramatuelle
Gigaro
Cavalaire-sur-Mer
Hyères
Rayol-Canadel-sur-Mer
Carqueiranne
Cavalière
Le Pradet
Cabasson
Aiguebelle
Giens
Le Lavandou
Île de Port-Cros
Île de Porquerolles
1
2
3
A 32
A 21
E 70
N 94
N 85
D 6204
D 6085
A 8
A 57
E 74
Drac
Verdon
Stura

Provence Alpes Côte d'Azur

E

E

Rhône-Alpes

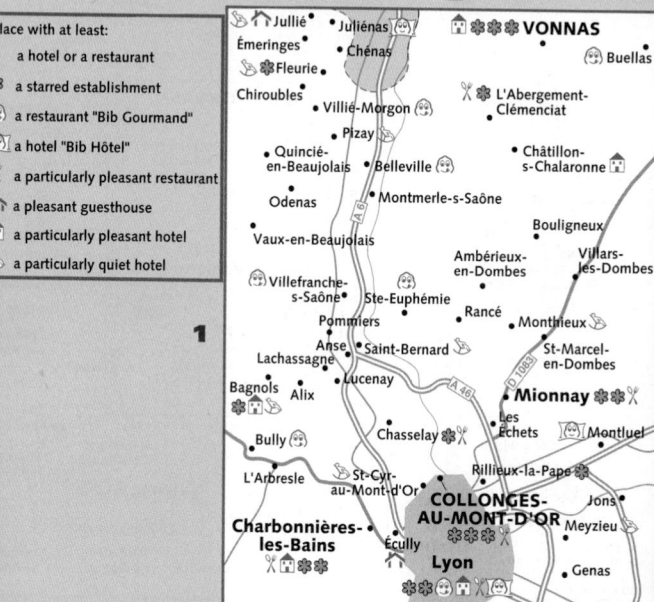

Place with at least:

- a hotel or a restaurant
- a starred establishment
- a restaurant "Bib Gourmand"
- a hotel "Bib Hôtel"
- a particularly pleasant restaurant
- a pleasant guesthouse
- a particularly pleasant hotel
- a particularly quiet hotel

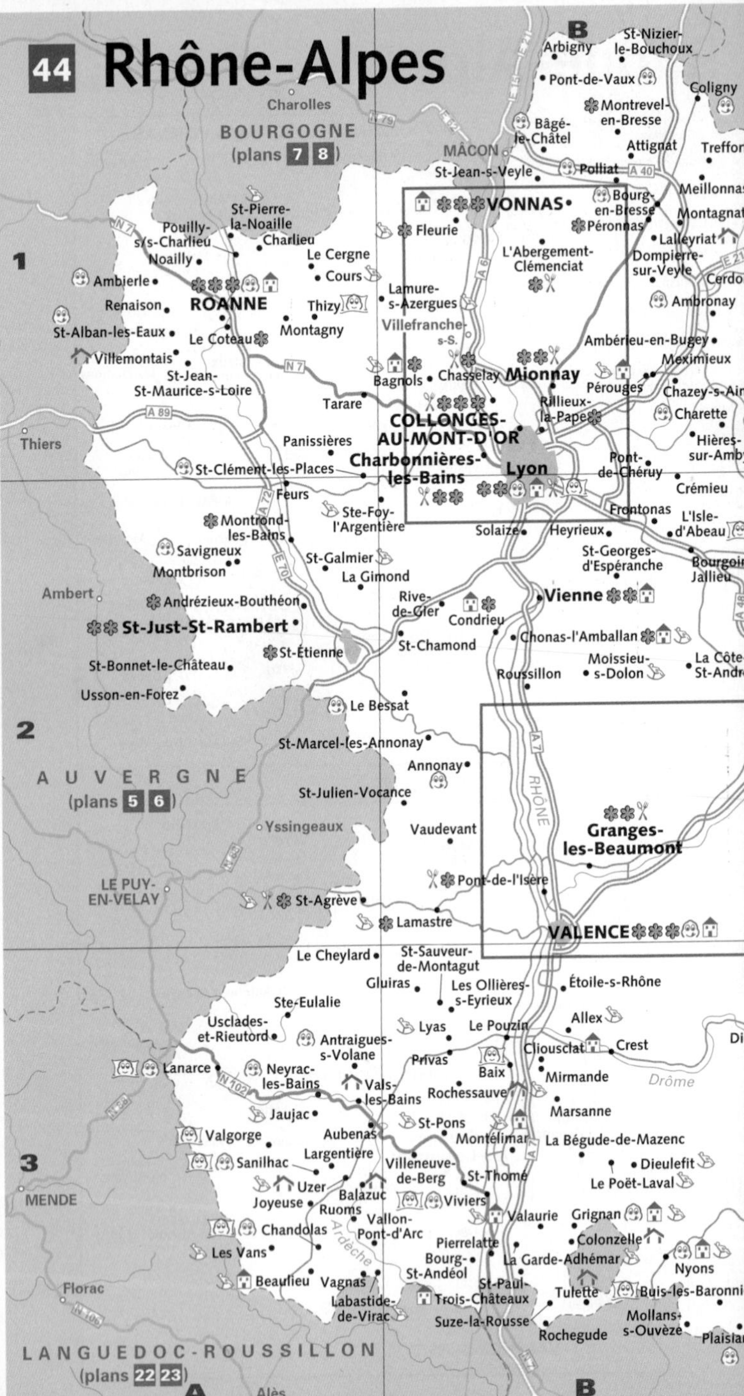

44 Rhône-Alpes
BOURGOGNE
(plans 7 8)
Charolles
MÂCON
AUVERGNE
(plans 5 6)
LANGUEDOC-ROUSSILLON
(plans 22 23)
A
B
1
2
3
Arbigny
St-Nizier-le-Bouchoux
Pont-de-Vaux
Coligny
Montrevel-en-Bresse
Bâgé-le-Châtel
Attignat
Treffort
St-Jean-s-Veyle
Polliat
Meillonnas
VONNAS
Bourg-en-Bresse
Montagnat
Fleurie
Péronnas
Lalleyriat
L'Abergement-Clémenciat
Dompierre-sur-Veyle
Cerdon
Ambronay
St-Pierre-la-Noaille
Pouilly-s/s-Charlieu
Charlieu
Noailly
Le Cergne
Cours
Ambierle
ROANNE
Lamure-s-Azergues
Renaison
Thizy
St-Alban-les-Eaux
Le Coteau
Montagny
Villefranche-s-S.
Ambérieu-en-Bugey
Villemontais
Meximieux
St-Jean-St-Maurice-s-Loire
Bagnols
Chasselay
Mionnay
Pérouges
Chazey-s-Ain
Tarare
Rillieux-la-Pape
Charette
Thiers
COLLONGES-AU-MONT-D'OR
Hières-sur-Amby
Panissières
Charbonnières-les-Bains
Lyon
Pont-de-Chéruy
St-Clément-les-Places
Crémieu
Feurs
Frontonas
L'Isle-d'Abeau
Ste-Foy-l'Argentière
Montrond-les-Bains
Solaize
Heyrieux
Savigneux
St-Georges-d'Espéranche
Bourgoin-Jallieu
Montbrison
St-Galmier
La Gimond
Ambert
Rive-de-Gier
Vienne
Andrézieux-Bouthéon
Condrieu
St-Just-St-Rambert
Chonas-l'Amballan
St-Chamond
St-Étienne
Moissieu-s-Dolon
La Côte-St-André
St-Bonnet-le-Château
Roussillon
Usson-en-Forez
Le Bessat
St-Marcel-les-Annonay
Annonay
St-Julien-Vocance
Yssingeaux
Vaudevant
Granges-les-Beaumont
RHÔNE
LE PUY-EN-VELAY
Pont-de-l'Isère
St-Agrève
Lamastre
VALENCE
Le Cheylard
St-Sauveur-de-Montagut
Gluiras
Les Ollières-s-Eyrieux
Étoile-s-Rhône
Ste-Eulalie
Usclades-et-Rieutord
Lyas
Le Pouzin
Allex
Antraigues-s-Volane
Cliousclat
Crest
Die
Privas
Lanarce
Neyrac-les-Bains
Baix
Mirmande
Drôme
Vals-les-Bains
Rochessauve
Jaujac
Marsanne
St-Pons
Valgorge
Aubenas
Montélimar
La Bégude-de-Mazenc
Largentière
Sanilhac
Villeneuve-de-Berg
Dieulefit
St-Thomé
Le Poët-Laval
MENDE
Uzer
Balazuc
Joyeuse
Viviers
Ruoms
Valaurie
Grignan
Vallon-Pont-d'Arc
Chandolas
Colonzelle
Pierrelatte
Ardèche
Les Vans
Bourg-St-Andéol
La Garde-Adhémar
Nyons
Beaulieu
Vagnas
St-Paul-Trois-Châteaux
Tulette
Buis-les-Baronnies
Florac
Labastide-de-Virac
Suze-la-Rousse
Mollans-s-Ouvèze
Rochegude
Plaisians
Alès
N 7
A 89
A 72
E 70
A 6
A 40
E 21
A 7
N 102
N 88
N 106
A 48
N 79
E 62
N 88

45
C
D
FRANCHE-COMTÉ
(plans 16 17)
LÉMAN
LAC
Thonon-les-Bains
Douvaine
SION
SUISSE
Oyonnax
Chézery-Forens
Thoiry
GENÈVE
Péron
Challex
Nantua
St-Germain-de-Joux
Bossey
Bellegarde-s-Valserine
Éloise
Vallorcine
1
Argentière
Les Praz-de-Chamonix
Le Lavancher
Cordon
Chamonix-Mont-Blanc
Évosges
Annecy
VEYRIER-DU-LAC
Megève
Rumilly
Chindrieux
Talloires
AOSTA/AOSTE
Les Saisies
Belley
Jongieux
Faverges
Ugine
Hauteluce
Tertenoz
Arèches
Beaufort
Champagneux
St-Genix-s-Guiers
Novalaise
Le-Bourget-du-Lac
La Rosière-1850
Bourg-St-Maurice
Ste-Foy-Tarentaise
Aoste
Romagnieu
Chambéry-le-Vieux
Aime
Les Arcs
Peisey-Nancroix
Lépin-le-Lac
Champagny-en-Vanoise
Tignes
La Bâtie-Divisin
Val-d'Isère
La Tania
St-Christophe-la-Grotte
Les Échelles
Courchevel 1850
St-Martin-de-Belleville
Pralognan-la-Vanoise
Bonneval-s-Arc
St-Laurent-du-Pont
Bessans
Lanslevillard
Val-Thorens
Lanslebourg-Mont-Cenis
Le Sappey-en-Chartreuse
Aussois
2
Meylan
St-Sorlin-d'Arves
Autrans
Grenoble
Valloire
Uriage-les-Bains
Alpe-d'Huez
Villard-de-Lans
Villard-Reculas
Mizoën
ITALIA
Corrençon-en-Vercors
Le Freney-d'Oisans
Venosc
Les Deux-Alpes
Treffort
Briançon
Monestier-de-Clermont
Corps
Clelles
PROVENCE-ALPES-CÔTE D'AZUR
(plans 40 41 42)
GAP
Place with at least:
a hotel or a restaurant
a starred establishment
a restaurant "Bib Gourmand"
a hotel "Bib Hôtel"
a particularly pleasant restaurant
a pleasant guesthouse
a particularly pleasant hotel
a particularly quiet hotel
3
Montauban-s-l'Ouvèze
Durance
C
D

F

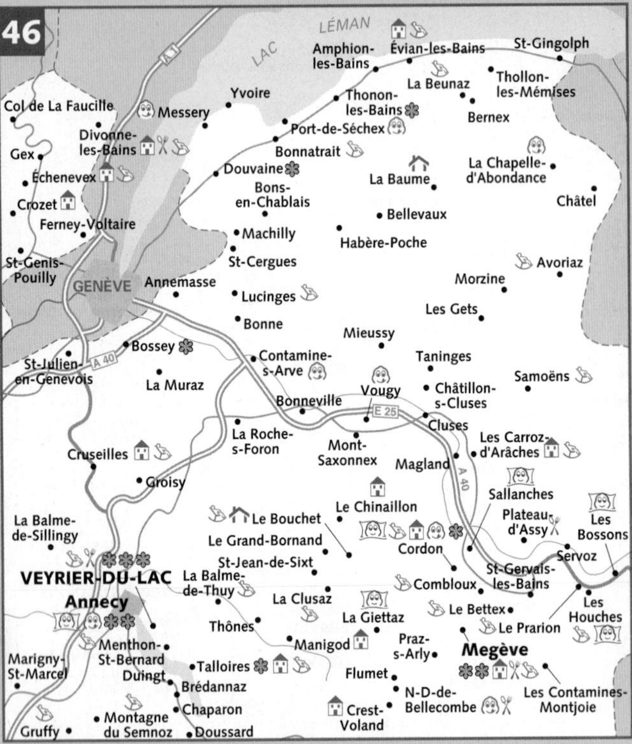

46
LÉMAN
LAC
Amphion-les-Bains
Évian-les-Bains
St-Gingolph
La Beunaz
Thollon-les-Mémises
Bernex
Yvoire
Thonon-les-Bains
Col de La Faucille
Messery
Port-de-Séchex
Divonne-les-Bains
Bonnatrait
La Chapelle-d'Abondance
Gex
Douvaine
La Baume
Échenevex
Châtel
Bons-en-Chablais
Crozet
Bellevaux
Ferney-Voltaire
Machilly
Habère-Poche
St-Cergues
Avoriaz
St-Genis-Pouilly
GENÈVE
Annemasse
Morzine
Lucinges
Les Gets
Bonne
Mieussy
Bossey
Contamine-s-Arve
Taninges
St-Julien-en-Genevois
A 40
Samoëns
La Muraz
Vougy
Châtillon-s-Cluses
Bonneville
E 25
Cluses
La Roche-s-Foron
Mont-Saxonnex
Les Carroz-d'Arâches
Cruseilles
Magland
A 40
Groisy
Sallanches
Le Chinaillon
Plateau-d'Assy
Les Bossons
La Balme-de-Sillingy
Le Bouchet
Le Grand-Bornand
Cordon
Servoz
St-Jean-de-Sixt
St-Gervais-les-Bains
VEYRIER-DU-LAC
La Balme-de-Thuy
Combloux
Annecy
La Clusaz
Les Houches
Le Bettex
La Giettaz
Thônes
Le Prarion
Praz-s-Arly
Manigod
Megève
Menthon-St-Bernard
Marigny-St-Marcel
Talloires
Duingt
Flumet
Brédannaz
Les Contamines-Montjoie
N-D-de-Bellecombe
Chaparon
Crest-Voland
Montagne du Semnoz
Gruffy
Doussard

1 1

F

Aix-les-Bains
Albertville
Les Catons
Le-Bourget-du-Lac
Cevins
Chambéry-le-Vieux
Grésy-s-Isère
St-Pierre-d'Albigny
Isère
Feissons-s-Isère
Aiton
Chambéry
Chamousset
D 1090
La Léchère
Coise
Aiguebelette-le-Lac
A 43
Moûtiers
Apremont
Montmélian
Brides-les-Bains
La Rochette
La Tania
St-Pierre-d'Entremont
Méribel
Allevard
St-Martin-de-Belleville
St-Pierre-de-Chartreuse
Les Menuires
Val-Thorens
Tencin
A 41
St-Jean-de-Maurienne
La Toussuire

2

F

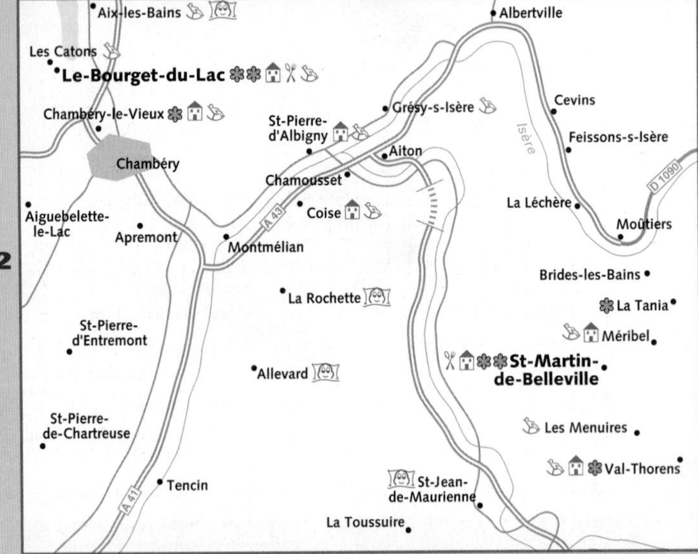